FOR SUSAN—
HOPING NOW AS
ALWAYS THAT THESE
BRING YOU ALL
THE GOOD LUCK
THAT YOU DESERVE!

Love,
[illegible]

Civil War EXTRA

A Newspaper History of the Civil War from Nat Turner to 1863

VOLUME I

From the Collection of Eric C. Caren
Introduction by Brian C. Pohanka

CASTLE BOOKS

ACKNOWLEDGEMENTS

I would like to dedicate *Civil War Extra, Volume 1 & 2,* to Dr. Stephen A. Goldman—friend, partner, and Civil War newspaper guru! Additionally, I extend my gratitude to Dr. Goldman for the use of the following newspapers for this set: Albany Evening Journal (11/7/1860), Jacksonville Republican (1/17/1861), Charleston Mercury Extra (4/13/1861), The White Man (11/21/1861), Richmond Enquirer (6/29/1862), Unconditional US Grant (10/24/1863), Columbia Phoenix (3/21/1865), Richmond Whig + map (4/11/1865).

Eric C. Caren

The following have been reprinted with permission from *The Plain Dealer*: April 15, 1861 © 1861, October 20, 1864 © 1864. All rights reserved.

The New York Times kindly grants the use of the following: April 10, 1865, April 15, 1865, 2 am edition, April 15, 1865, 11:15 am edition. Copyright © 1865 by The New York Times. Reprinted by permission.

We offer special thanks to the *Philadelphia Inquirer* for their permission to the use of the following: May 19, 1860, June 28, 1860, January 26, 1861, April 16, 1861, July 6, 1861, July 13, 1861, July 22, 1861, September 21, 1861, November 2, 1861, November 23, 1861, January 18, 1862, January 28, 1862, February 19, 1862, March 1, 1862, March 10, 1862, March 15, 1862, March 29, 1862, April 11, 1862, April 17, 1862, May 30, 1862, June 2, 1862, August 2, 1862, January 27, 1863, February 15, 1865, February 20, 1865, April 4, 1865, April 8, 1865, April 10, 1865, April 15, 1865, April 17, 1865, April 20, 1865, April 25, 1865, April 26, 1865, April 28, 1865, May 5, 1865, May 10, 1865, May 16, 1865, May 18, 1865, May 19, 1865, May 20, 1865, May 22, 1865, May 31, 1865, June 14, 1865.

Published by Castle Books,
a division of Book Sales, Inc.
114 Northfield Avenue
Edison, NJ 08837, USA

Compiled by Eric C. Caren

ISBN 0-7858-1137-0
Printed in the United States of America

INTRODUCTION

The Civil War—that fiery crucible that forged a nation at a cost of more than 600,000 lives—was a defining watershed in the history of American journalism, as it was for the country as a whole. Editors whose papers had fueled the divisive passions that led to war found themselves caught up in a bloodletting of epic proportions. As contending armies numbering in the hundreds of thousands waged simultaneous campaigns in multiple theaters of operations, the press dispatched scores of reporters to the front. Adventuresome, fiercely competitive and frequently daring in their quest for a scoop, these self-styled "Bohemians" were a link between the soldiers and their families behind the lines.

No more powerfully illustrated was that connection between reporter and reader than in the journals' almost daily publication of casualty lists. Those grim enumerations in columns that bore the stark heading "Wounded and Killed" became painfully commonplace; but, as the editor of the Charlotte, North Carolina *Daily Bulletin* reminded his patrons, "Some eye reads the name to whom it is dear as life, and some heart is struck or broken with the blow made by that name among the list. . . . Every name in that list is a lightning stroke to some heart, and breaks like thunder over some house, and falls like a long black shadow upon some hearthstone."

That poignant observation is but one insight to America's Tragic Era that appears in these fascinating volumes, selected from among the thousands of Civil War newspapers in the Eric C. Caren Collection. Spanning the history of journalism from the sixteenth century to the present day, the Caren Collection comprises the most important assemblage of newspapers in private hands and includes numerous rare and one of a kind editions. Many of the pages reproduced here are not to be found in archival institutions, while others are unique in having survived the ravages of time and the devastation wrought by war. The significant number of Confederate newspapers in the Caren Collection is especially noteworthy, and the samples included here offer a telling view of the plight of the beleaguered Southern states. Reflecting the vast scope of Civil War journalism—from the roots of the conflict to the ultimate reconciliation—*Civil War Extra* provides a veritable window on the past, enabling us to read the news of the day as it was presented to mid-nineteenth century Americans, whose lives were forever altered by those stirring and catastrophic events.

If the folks at home were eager for reports of their loved ones at the front, the soldiers themselves had an insatiable desire for news—not only of their families and communities, but of military actions beyond the limited scope of their own company or regiment. Writing to his hometown paper in Poughkeepsie, New York in December 1861, Sergeant Stephen Bogardus expressed the well-nigh universal complaint of the fighting men when he lamented, "We are as much out of the way of news as if we were confined in a convent." One of the Sergeant's comrades in the 5th New York Infantry Regiment, William McIlvaine grumbled, "For all the war news we hear we might as well be a thousand miles off." Confederate soldiers generally felt even more isolated from the outer world, as lines of supply and communication were increasingly disrupted by marauding Federal armies.

The soldiers coveted journals of any kind, and that craving provided a substantial economic incentive for newspaper vendors to market their wares at the front. In his 1866 memoir, war correspondent George Alfred Townsend recalled one enterprising fourteen-year-old newsboy who regularly purchased several hundred papers for one and a half cents apiece in Washington and sold them in the military camps for ten cents each. The youth's daily earnings were rarely less than thirty-five dollars—nearly three times the monthly salary of a private soldier—and Townsend fully expected the boy to have his own "army express and general agency" by the war's end.

Newspapers were something of a luxury to soldiers in the field, awaited with anticipation and eagerly devoured by private and general alike. The great Confederate commander Thomas J. "Stonewall" Jackson was in the habit of asking one of his staff officers to read the pertinent news aloud. A satirical biography of Jackson that appeared in the New York *Mercury*—one of many Northern papers that fell into Confederate hands during Jackson's victorious Shenandoah Valley campaign—brought a smile to the face of the habitually reserved and serious Southern commander. When regular delivery of papers was possible, it lent an air of domesticity to an otherwise austere and frequently uncomfortable existence. "We have made arrangements with the mail agent to supply us with newspapers so that the *Herald* is in my tent every day when I return from dinner," Union Colonel Charles Wainwright noted in his diary. Wainwright, a New York patrician whose political leanings tended to the Democratic Party, thought the *Herald* "the best paper," even if "half of what it publishes is not true."

Fraternization between the opposing forces was not uncommon in a war that pitted American against American. When the white flags went up signifying a temporary truce, and the burial parties in blue and gray set about the grim task of evacuating the mangled wounded and interring fallen comrades, Union and Confederate officers would meet between the lines with an amicability that belied their deadly business. Often the handshakes and banter were accompanied by an exchange of newspapers—ragged about the edges perhaps, and weeks old, but providing a broader perspective of the contending armies and of the world beyond the battlefield. Though the concept of military intelligence was in its infancy, officers nonetheless recognized that in an era when press censorship was spotty at best, their enemy's hometown papers contained information of potential value to the generals in command. And once the journals made the round of the camp, they generally found their way to headquarters.

Preoccupied with creature comforts, meager though they may be, the typical enlisted man rarely bothered about matters of military security, and was even less concerned with grand strategy. But newspapers did provide temporary relief from the boredom and routine of soldier life, and Yank and Reb regularly included papers with their most popular items of exchange—Northern coffee for Southern tobacco. Officers tended to frown upon this trade unless it occurred during an official truce. But the men in the ranks were not so particular, and when their commanders weren't looking, found all manner of ingenious ways to barter with their counterparts.

The penchant for fraternization became particularly marked during the long winter hiatus from active campaigning, when the armies settled into sprawling encampments of log huts equipped with hearths and chimneys that provided a comfort bordering on the luxurious, by soldiers' standards. During the winter of 1862-1863, when General Joseph Hooker's Army of the Potomac and General Robert E. Lee's Army of Northern Virginia were encamped on opposite sides of the Rappahannock River, the opposing pickets maintained a flourishing trade through the use of miniature boats. Pouches of coffee beans or tobacco were placed in a hollowed-out log, often equipped with a mast constructed of intertwined sticks, with a newspaper like the *New York Herald* or *Richmond Examiner* furnishing the sail.

"The exchange of coffee and tobacco was a comparatively harmless matter," recalled Lieutenant Frederick Hitchcock of the 132nd Pennsylvania, "but the sending of Northern papers into their line, containing news of every movement of our forces, was a thing that must be prohibited. . . . The tobacco our men were allowed to take, but the boat and all rebel newspapers had to be sent to army headquarters." The lieutenant admitted that it was "a traffic very difficult to suppress, for our men wanted the tobacco and were unwilling to take that without sending back the proper *quid pro quo*."

In large volunteer armies comprised of men from all walks of life, it was not uncommon for a given regiment to have in its ranks a number of soldiers whose prewar occupations of type-setter or printer enabled them to produce their own unit newspaper. These volumes include an exceptional sampling of those army journals. *The Vidette,* a broadside "printed and published semi-occasionally" by members of Colonel John Hunt Morgan's swashbuckling Confederate cavalry brigade, disseminated official orders and denounced Yankee "outrages" and "atrocities" against Southern civilians. A Union soldier paper, the *Camp Journal* of the hard-fighting First Division in the Army of the Potomac's Second Corps, reflected similar partisan chauvinism in its motto, "No Peace While Traitors are in Arms."

An extremely rare variation of this unofficial military press appears in the pages of the Berryville, Virginia *Conservator* for March 11 and 12, 1862. Abandoned when Federal troops closed in on the town, the *Conservator's* office was occupied by members of the 1st Minnesota Infantry—a unit whose compliment included some two dozen former newspapermen who styled themselves "The Printer's Fraternity." The Union soldiers displayed their technical and editorial skills by using the captured presses to produce a satirical edition of the Berryville paper, mocking the departed editor and his staff. In July of 1864, publication of the *Lynchburg Virginian* ceased when General David Hunter's Union army launched an attack on the city's defenses. The *Virginian's* editor later apologized to his readers, noting, "Every man connected with the office, including an old man 70 years of age, deaf as a post, and blind in one eye, shouldered arms and went to the field."

While publication of the *Berryville Conservator* and *Lynchburg Virginian* were only temporarily disrupted—in both cases the Yankees soon retreated north down the Shenandoah Valley—many Rebel papers were confiscated, suppressed or taken over as the Federal forces increasingly tightened their hold on Confederate territory. Some papers, like Alabama's *Daily Huntsville Confederate*, literally packed up the presses and moved out with the evacuating Southern troops. But if journals in occupied Southern communities wished to continue publication, they did so under the relentless scrutiny of their Northern garrison, who habitually used the papers to disseminate pronouncements to the conquered citizens.

Such was the case when New Orleans fell under the draconian rule of Union General Benjamin Butler, who compelled *The Daily Delta* to print his notorious General Order of May 5, 1862. The directive stipulated that any woman who should "insult or show contempt" to Union officers or soldiers would be "regarded and held liable to be treated as a woman of the town [i.e. a prostitute] plying her avocation." The *Delta's* editor did "not feel at liberty to decline the publication of said order," but exacted some measure of revenge by publishing a humorous satire titled "The Shunamitish Woman." Couched in Biblical language, it parodied the misadventures of a drunken Yankee officer whose pocket was picked by one of New Orleans' soiled doves.

Editors in Confederate communities that escaped Northern subjugation were confronted with an ever-growing shortage of the ink and paper stock necessary to maintain publication. But Southern publishers met the challenge in a number of ingenious ways, and the Caren Collection includes numerous rare editions of so-called "necessity papers." Heralding an erroneous report that Stonewall Jackson's troops had captured Washington, D.C., the September 20, 1862 edition of *The Confederate States* of New Iberia, Louisiana was printed on wallpaper. Tongue in cheek, the editor confessed that "the existing times have 'driven us to the wall' to procure our supply of paper for printing purposes." Another unusual necessity paper, *The Houston Daily Telegraph* of March 19, 1864, was printed on cornhusks.

That press freedom was severely tried by the hatreds engendered by the Civil War is also evident in the case of Union and Confederate journals whose political stance was not in keeping with the majority opinion of their respective communities. Those editors who dared to publish views that went against the popular grain risked having their offices sacked by angry mobs. Such was the fate of *The Crisis*—a pro-Southern or "Copperhead" paper in Columbus, Ohio—and of the Troy, New York *Weekly Times*, whose attackers disapproved of the draft as a means of prosecuting the Union war effort. One need only consider the disparate views of Abraham Lincoln reflected in this volume to realize that the Nation's divisions were not always clearly defined by the Mason-Dixon Line. It is but one of many fascinating aspects of that epic and terrible conflict that readers will find in the pages of *Civil War Extra*.

Brian C. Pohanka
Alexandria, Virginia

TABLE OF CONTENTS, Volume I

Editor's note to the Table of Contents– Terms used below to describe the issues included in this book :

Broadsheet–A single sheet newspaper with printing on both sides.

Broadside–A single sheet newspaper with printing on one side only and a blank reverse. Commonly used for posting.

Copperhead–Term used for newspapers from Northern cities that were pro-South in sentiment.

Necessity paper–When usual paper supplies ran out (mainly in the South), editors had to resort to using various alternate paper such as wrapping paper, wall paper, and cornhusk. Also, different colored papers were used including blue, yellow, green, brown, and pink.

Occupation paper–When a Southern town fell to Union troops, a new paper would usually be started, turning their point of view from Confederate to Northern.

Troop/Regimental newspaper–Both Union and Confederate forces sometimes carried portable presses into the field and would print up newspapers to inform and entertain the soldiers in camp.

Extra–A special edition outside the normal press sequence (i.e. daily, weekly, etc.). Usually occasioned by late news of importance which was too late for the previous scheduled edition.

Supplement–An addition to the regular edition added at the last moment before going to press.

Publications are presented chronologically except where adjustments have been made to accommodate spreads.

71-73	Apr. 20, 1861	CHARLESTON MERCURY (SC)	Additional particulars of the bombardment of Fort Sumter. "The War Declared" by President Jefferson Davis and the Confederacy. Very polite correspondence from General Beauregard to General Anderson warning of the impending bombing of Fort Sumter if they do not vacate, and Anderson's polite reply.
74	Apr. 20, 1861	NY ILLUSTRATED NEWS EXTRA	"Opening of the War" with feature on Major Anderson.
75-78	Apr. 20, 1861	GAZETTE AND SENTINEL (Plaquemine, LA)	Regular issue plus broadside extra of this rare small-town Louisiana Confederate newspaper. "War Begun"
79	Apr. 23, 1861	LYNCHBURG DAILY VIRGINIAN	Captain Robert E. Lee proudly profiled in his native state's newspaper.
80-81	Apr. 26, 1861	DAILY DISPATCH (Richmond, VA)	Virginia secession reported in this Richmond, VA newspaper.
82	Apr. 27, 1861	ANGLO-AFRICAN EXTRA (NY)	Very rare broadside extra issued, according to the prospectus in last column, "to afford a medium of communication whereby we, the people of color, might become better known to each other and to the community at large."
83	Apr. 28, 1861	NY HERALD	Front page war map shows seat of war just weeks after fighting had begun.
84-86	May 1861	HARDEE'S TACTICS (Supplement to the Philadelphia Inquirer)	"Hardee's Tactics", special military supplement
87	May 2+3, 1861	DAILY TELEGRAPH (Painesville, OH)	Tiny paper that promoted in the name it chose, the latest and quickest mode of transporting news.
88-89	May 9, 1861	TRI-WEEKLY MERCURY (SC)	"War Declared"
90	May 11, 1861	ILLUSTRATED LONDON NEWS	Beautifully detailed portrait of "Major Anderson, late Commandant of Fort Sumter, by Thomas Nast.
91	May 15, 1861	DAILY DELTA (New Orleans, LA)	"Lincoln's Blockade"
92-93	May 28, 1861	NY SEMI-WEEKLY TRIBUNE	Murder of Col. Elmer Ellsworth
94	June 1, 1861	GAZETTE AND SENTINEL (Plaquemine, LA)	Robert E Lee described.
95	June 15, 1861	HARPER'S WEEKLY (NY)	Woodcut illustration, "The Murder of Colonel Ellsworth" who attempted to remove a Confederate flag from a house in Alexandria, Virginia.
96	June 15, 1861	GAZETTE AND SENTINEL (Plaquemine, LA)	The Battle of Bethel
97	June 19, 1861	SUPPLEMENTARY SHEET (Plaquemine, LA)	Confederate broadside extra on "The War in Missouri", headed by a roaring cannon.
98	June 22, 1861	GAZETTE AND SENTINEL (Plaquemine, LA)	The Battle of Bethel
99	June 30, 1861	THE GOLDEN ERA (San Francisco, CA)	Red, white, and blue flag overprint is some of the earliest use of color illustration to appear in a newspaper. In this case, it is employed to leave no doubt as to the loyalty of California to the Union.
100	July 6, 1861	PHILADELPHIA INQUIRER	"Pennsylvania Avenue, Washington–The Grand Parade of the U.S. Army"
101	July 4, 1861	THE NATIONAL GUARD (Camp Pennsylvania-Baltimore, MD)	Special "4th of July Extra- Pictorial Edition" of this very scarce newspaper printed at Camp Pennsylvania in Baltimore, MD. It is filled with lighthearted cartoons to, no doubt, lift the spirits of the resident soldiers.
102-103	July 13, 1861	PHILADELPHIA INQUIRER	Battle of Rich Mountain, VA plus an unusually large full page map of the seat of war.
104	July 18, 1861	DAILY DELTA (New Orleans, LA)	The Rich Mountain affair.
105	July 20, 1861	GAZETTE AND SENTINEL (Plaquemine, LA)	"A Great Victory–Battle of Bull's Run", "Battle of Springfield, MO", "Skirmish at Newport News"
106	July 22, 1861	DAILY DISPATCH (Richmond, VA)	Almost local coverage of the Battle of Bull Run. Several reports grace this page.
107-108	July 22, 1861	PHILADELPHIA INQUIRER	Front page illustration of troop positions with an account of the Battle of Bull Run.
109-110	July 22, 1861	THE WORLD (NY)	The Battle of Bull Run
111	July 22, 1861	NY HERALD	The Battle of Bull Run
112-113	July 22, 1861	NY ILLUSTRATED NEWS	Double page woodcut engraving of the "Battle of Carthage, Missouri"
114	July 23, 1861	DAILY DISPATCH - EXTRA (Richmond, VA)	The Battle of Bull Run is reported in this rare extra Confederate broadside. "We have met the Enemy and They are Ours"
115-117	July 24, 1861	THE SOUTH (Baltimore, MD)	As the title suggests, this border state newspaper allied its sympathies with the Confederacy. Accounts of the Battle of Bull Run.
118	July 26, 1861	DAILY DELTA (New Orleans, LA)	The Battle of Bull Run
119-121	July 27, 1861	GAZETTE AND SENTINEL (Plaquemine, LA)	Confederate accounts of Bull Run and front page anecdote, "One of the Horrors of Battle".
122-123	July 30, 1861	DAILY DELTA (New Orleans, LA)	The Battle of Bull Run
124	c. July 1861	THE LONDON AMERICAN (London, England)	"Map of the Seat of War" Broadside map published in England soon after the first Battle of Bull Run, presumably for Americans living in England.
125	Aug. 3, 1861	DAILY ALTA CALIFORNIA (San Francisco, CA)	News of Bull Run reaches California. "Arrival of the Pony" The Pony Express would only be used in the first months of the war before being replaced by the Overland Telegraph–see issue dated Nov. 6, 1861.
126	Aug. 3, 1861	FRANK LESLIE'S ILLUSTRATED NEWSPAPER (New York)	Hand-to-hand combat as NY Fire Zouaves assault a "Rebel Battery" at the Battle of Bull Run.
127	Aug. 12, 1861	NY ILLUSTRATED NEWS	A front page look at "Major-General McClellen (sic), Commanding the Troops now on the Potomac".
128-129	Aug. 17, 1861	HARPER'S WEEKLY (NY)	Illustrated center-fold depicts "Uniforms of the Confederate Army".
130-132	Aug. 25, 1861	NASHVILLE PATRIOT (TN)	Front page map of "The Battle of Manassas Plain" (Bull Run). Illustrations in Confederate newspapers are highly unusual. Also, front page printing of the "Constitution of the Confederate States of America".
133	Aug. 26, 1861	NY ILLUSTRATED NEWS	This political cartoon takes a poke at England and her lending policies. Note also the smaller engraving of "Ben McCulloch, the rebel General commanding traitors in Southern Missouri".
134	Sept. 1, 1861	SUNDAY DELTA (New Orleans, LA)	"Bull Run" Russell's account of the Battle of Manassas.
135	Sept. 12, 1861	NY HERALD	Full page war map headed, "The National Battle Ground", and showing parts of Maryland and Virginia with Union troop positions. It is said that Confederates would use these Union war map newspapers to find the enemy.
136	Sept. 14, 1861	ILLUSTRATED LONDON NEWS	Federalist Texas Rangers "Reconnoiting Between Alexandria and Fairfax, VA". Makes for a dramatic illustrated cover in the British equivalent of *Harper's Weekly*.
137	Sept. 14, 1861	NY HERALD	"The National Popular Loan" showing " A Facsimile of a Hundred Dollar Treasury note with coupon attached".
138	Sept. 21, 1861	DAILY DELTA (New Orleans, LA)	The Fighting in Kentucky and promotion of Braxton Bragg.
139-140	Sept. 21, 1861	PHILADELPHIA INQUIRER	Extraordinary full page illustration of Maj.-Gen. George J. McClellan. Plus a front page story, "President Lincoln a Good Shot", Lincoln practices with the sharpshooters.
141	Sept. 22, 1861	DAILY LOUISVILLE DEMOCRAT (Louisville, KY)	Robert Anderson takes command in Kentucky and urges his countrymen "To Arms!, To Arms!" , in order to fight off the Confederate invaders of the state.
142-144	Sept. 25, 1861	SOUTH BRANCH INTELLIGENCER (Romney, VA)	A Union soldier takes a confederate newspaper right off the printing press and sends it home as a war souvenir. Note the handwritten penciled letter on the blank back.
145	Sept. 28, 1861	DAILY LYNCHBURG VIRGINIAN	Fighting in West Virginia
146	Oct. 12, 1861	ILLUSTRATED LONDON NEWS (London, England)	A fine and romantic engraved view of a young pony express rider. The west coast would receive their news via this method in the early months of the war.
147	Oct. 26, 1861	DAILY LYNCHBERG VIRGINIAN	Col. 3–"The Battle of Leesburg", Col. 4–"Further From the Fight at Leesburg"
148-150	Nov. 1861	BRITISH WORKMAN (London, England)	A Slave Auction.
151	Nov. 4, 1861	NY ILLUSTRATED NEWS	Beautiful woodcut representation of "D'Epineuil Zouaves" showing costumes of officer and private.
152	Nov. 2, 1861	PHILADELPHIA INQUIRER	"The Great Naval Expedition–From Fortress Monroe, Oct. 29."
153	Nov. 6, 1861	DAILY ALTA CALIFORNIA (San Francisco, CA)	Civil War news now reaches California. "By Overland Telegraph" replacing the old Pony Express system–see issue dated August 3, 1861.
154-157	Nov. 8, 1861	THE DAILY SUN (Columbus, GA)	Front page letter from General Beauregard relating to Bull Run. Back page printing of Georgia State Constitution. Note all of the war-related ads.
158	Nov. 16, 1861	HARPER'S WEEKLY	"Brilliant Charge of General Fremont's Body Guard Through the Town of Springfield, Missouri."
159	Nov. 23, 1861	PHILADELPHIA INQUIRER	A front page look at "Major-General H.W. Halleck, U.S.A."

160-161	Nov. 21, 1861	THE WHITE MAN (Weatherford, TX)	Southern re-wording of the “Star Spangled Banner” The publication’s title leaves no doubts as to it’s sentiments.
162	Nov. 25, 1861	THE SUN (NY)	A front page look at “Commodore Samuel F. Dupont, of the Great Naval Expedition”. Dupont was a commander at the capture of Port Royal.
163-166	Nov. 26, 1861	LOUISVILLE DAILY COURIER (Bowling Green, KY)	A provisional Confederate government is organized in this Kentucky city and all the news is obviously from a Confederate standpoint. The headquarters of this paper had been seized in September by the Federals.
167-168	Dec. 13, 1861	THE FIRST DIVISION PROCLAMATION (Otterville, MO)	“Published weekly in the camp of the First Division–Department of the West” Otterville, MO
169	Dec. 14, 1861	ILLUSTRATED LONDON NEWS (London, England)	The Trent Affair–Engraved portraits of the Union Captain Wilks and his captives, the two confederate commissioners James M. Mason and John Sidell who would be imprisoned at Fort Warren. This incident almost led to war between the Union and Great Britain.
170	Dec. 21, 1861	FORNEY’S WAR PRESS (Philadelphia, PA)	Portrait of Parson Brownlow, editor of *Brownlow’s Knoxville Whig and Rebel Ventilator,* (see Nov. 16, 1864).
171	Jan. 1862	FRANK LESLIE’S WAR MAPS (NY)	Special Edition put out as a compilation of war maps.
172	Jan. 1, 1862	N Y HERALD NEWSMEN’S NEW YEARS ADDRESS	Patriotic Union Broadside–Carriers address is surrounded by portraits of Lincoln, his cabinet and generals. Broadsides such as this were gifts for subscribers to solicit holiday tips for the news carriers.
173	Jan. 11, 1862	FORNEY’S WAR PRESS (Philadelphia, PA)	A front page look at General Buell surrounded by Burnside, Franklin, and others.
174-175	Jan. 11, 1862	THE WEEKLY DELTA (New Orleans, LA)	The Trent Affair
176	Jan. 17, 1862	ST. JOHN’S MIRROR EXTRA (Jacksonville, FL)	Extremely rare Florida Confederate Extra broadside.
177	Jan. 18, 1862	PHILADELPHIA INQUIRER	A front page look at “General Don Carlos Buell”.
178	Jan. 20, 1862	THE “ELEVENTH OHIO” (Point Pleasant, VA)	Volume I, # I issue of this regimental.
179	Jan 22, 1862	THE WEEKLY CASKET (NY)	“Indians and their Influence on our Present War”
180	Jan. 28, 1862	PHILADELPHIA INQUIRER	Portrait and articles on Secretary of War Edwin M. Stanton.
181	Feb. 1, 1862	LOUISVILLE DAILY DEMOCRAT (Louisville, KY)	Unusually large (for the period) illustrated gun advertisement employs testimonials from Union officers.
182-184	Feb. 1, 1862	FORNEY’S WAR PRESS (Philadelphia, PA)	Illustrations of Major-General Halleck and two other Union generals. Plus illustrations of the building of a “new iron-plated Steamship”. P. 2 –”The Victory at Mill Springs” P. 6 -” Battle Between Union Indian Troops and Texas Rangers”
185-186	Feb. 3, 1862	DAILY DISPATCH (Richmond, VA)	Front page printing of General Beauregard’s official report on the Battle of Bull Run.
187-188	Feb. 4, 1862	TRI-WEEKLY SOUTH CAROLINIAN	Note front page advertisement for “Guano” for cotton plantations. “The Burnside Expedition”
189	Feb. 8, 1862	N Y HERALD	“The Important Victory in Tennessee”, war map shows “The Capture of Fort Henry”
190	Feb. 13, 1862	N Y HERALD	War map headed, “Brilliant Operations at Roanoke Island”
191-192	Feb. 19, 1862	PHILADELPHIA INQUIRER	Grant’s Victory at Fort Donelson near Nashville, TN with portraits of two of his leading Generals in the battle. Plus a list of the new Confederate Congress is called “A Rebel Blacklist”.
193	Feb. 22, 1862	RICHMOND ENQUIRER	Very rare local broadside extra printing of “President Jefferson Davis’ Inaugural Address”.
194	Feb. 23, 1862	SUNDAY DELTA (New Orleans, LA)	Jefferson Davis’ Inaugural Address and the formation of “Sharp Shooter”–see first column
195-196	Mar. 1, 1862	HARPER’S WEEKLY (NY)	“The Surrender of Fort Donelson” plus, “Gallant Charge of Hawkins’ Zouaves Upon the Rebel Batteries on Roanoke Island”
197	Mar. 1, 1862	PHILADELPHIA INQUIRER	Front page portraits of Major-General U.S. Grant and Captain W.D. Porter
198	Mar. 5, 1862	TRI-WEEKLY TELEGRAPH (Houston, TX)	“Jefferson Davis Inaugurated President of the C.S.A.
199	Mar. 5, 1862	N Y HERALD	“The Present Area of the Rebellion” is illustrated using a shaded map of the divided United States.
200	Mar. 7, 1862	TRI-WEEKLY TELEGRAPH (Houston, TX)	“The Battles at Fort Donelson!”, “General Pillow’s Report”
201-204	Mar. 7, 1862	CAMDEN CONFEDERATE (Camden, SC)	Front page, last column has a short but dramatic report of how Confederate Gen. Johnson was dealing harshly with cowardly conduct in the ranks. P. 2–The Federals occupy Nashville, TN p. 3-4–Interesting advertisements
205-206	Mar. 8, 1862	ANDERSON ZOUAVE (Tenlytown, DC)	First issue of an actual Zouave regimental newspaper.
207	Mar. 10, 1862	PHILADELPHIA INQUIRER	Front page map showing the area of conflict between the Monitor and the Merrimac.
208-211	Mar. 11+12, 1862	BERRYVILLE CONSERVATOR AND FIRST MINNESOTA (Berryville, VA)	One of the most unusual newspapers published in the war. This has two front pages. The first printed by the Confederates and the second by the troops of the “First Minnesota” regiment when they took the town of Berryville. It is no surprise that the latter page is full of boastful mockery of the former editor and the Confederates who had held charge of this VA town. Note articles, “To Our Friends”, “Run away Editor”, “The Stars and Stripes in Berryville Again”, “Too bad”.
212-215	Mar. 15, 1862	THE NEW SOUTH (Port Royal, SC)	Volume I, # I issue of this Union Occupation newspaper.
216	Mar. 15, 1862	PHILADELPHIA INQUIRER	Front page illustrations of “The New Iron Clad War Steamer” and “Captain John Lorimer Worden” of the Monitor
217	Mar. 22, 1862	FORNEY’S WAR PRESS (Philadelphia, PA)	Illustration–”The Naval Battle in Hampton Roads Between the Monitor and the Merrimac”.
218	Mar. 27, 1862	DAILY LYNCHBURG VIRGINIAN	“Battle Near Winchester”, “ General (Stonewall) Jackson Repulsed”
219	Mar. 29, 1862	HARPER’S WEEKLY (NY)	“The Battle of Pea Ridge, Arkansas–The Final Advance of Our Troops”
220	Mar. 29, 1862	DAILY LYNCHBURG VIRGINIAN	“The Fight Near Winchester”
221	Mar. 29, 1862	PHILADELPHIA INQUIRER	A front page look at “General Nathaniel P. Banks”
222	Apr. 8, 1862	THE WEEKLY COURIER (Natchez, MS)	Yellow necessity paper issue with Confederate account of the Battle of Shiloh.
223-224	Apr. 8, 1862	THE DAILY DELTA (New Orleans, LA)	Confederate account of the Battle of Shiloh.
225	Apr. 10, 1862	N Y HERALD	Front page map showing scene of the Battle of Shiloh
226	Apr. 10, 1862	THE DAILY DELTA (New Orleans, LA)	Confederate account of the Battle of Shiloh
227	Apr. 11, 1862	PHILADELPHIA INQUIRER	The Battle of Shiloh and front page portraits of “The Heroes of the Recent Glorious Union Victory at Pittsburg Landing” Grant and Buell.
228	Apr. 11, 1862	N Y HERALD	“The Great Victories”, The Battle of Shiloh (or Pittsburg Landing)
229	Apr. 15, 1862	N Y HERALD	The Union takes island Number 10.
230	Apr. 16, 1862	NY DAILY TRIBUNE	Front page war map showing “The Fall of Fort Pulaski - Approaches to Savannah”
231	Apr. 17, 1862	PHILADELPHIA INQUIRER	The Battle of Shiloh and “Slavery Abolished in the Capital”
232	Apr. 19, 1862	NY WEEKLY CAUCASIAN	Anti-Black and anti-war rhetoric employed by this Copperhead NY newspaper.
233	Apr. 19, 1862	DAILY DELTA (New Orleans, LA)	Lengthy account of the Battle of Shiloh
234-235	Apr. 22, 1862	TRI-WEEKLY MERCURY (Charleston, SC)	Rare front page illustration in a Confederate newspaper, plus the Battle of Shiloh.
236	Apr. 23, 1862	DE LA RENAISSANCE LOUISIANAISE (New Orleans, LA)	This French language extra broadside was printed just two days before the city fell to Admiral David Farragut’s fleet. Also, a letter reporting incidents of the Battle of Shiloh is presented.
237-238	Apr. 24, 1862	EVENING DELTA (New Orleans, LA)	Extra broadsheet Confederate newspaper, “Union Gunboats Pass the Forts on the Way to Taking of New Orleans”.
239	Apr. 25, 1862	TRI-WEEKLY TELEGRAPH (Houston, TX)	“The Battle of Shiloh”
240	Apr. 26, 1862	FORNEY’S WAR PRESS (Philadelphia, PA)	Front page engravings of “Yorktown” and the Union gunboats there. “Fort Pulaski After it was Captured By the Union Troops”
241	Apr. 28, 1862	NY DAILY TRIBUNE	“New Orleans Captured” is accompanied by a “Map of New Orleans and the Mississippi Delta”
242-243	Apr. 28, 1862	NEWBERN DAILY PROGRESS (Newbern, NC)	This Union occupation paper decides to reprint the Declaration of Independence on its front page. Plus, note ads on page 3. Many are geared to the soldiers stationed there, such as “Smith’s Bullet Proof Vest”.
244	Apr. 29, 1862	TRI-WEEKLY MERCURY (Charleston, SC)	In a front page story headed, “The Fall of New Orleans”, the editor blames things on “the military policy and administration of Mr. Jefferson Davis.” Plus, new Lincoln message abolishing slavery in District of Columbia.

245-246	Apr. 30, 1862	DAILY TRUE DELTA (New Orleans, LA)	The fall of New Orleans, "The Latest Agony" plus messages from the mayor of New Orleans as well as Admiral Farragut. Back page, "The Great Agony Over"
247	May 1. 1862	THE DAILY DELTA (New Orleans, LA)	The surrender of the forts protecting New Orleans plus front page article on "The City of New Orleans".
248-251	May 2, 1862	SEVENTH BRIGADE JOURNAL (Columbia, TN)	Rare regimental newspaper published by members of the 7th Brigade stationed in Tennessee after the Battle of Shiloh.
252	May 2, 1862	THE DAILY DELTA (New Orleans, LA)	Profile of "The U.S. Military Commander" B.F.Butler and "Correspondence Between the Mayor and Capt. Farragut". Also, "Landing of U.S. Troops", who played *Yankee Doodle* as they marched through New Orleans.
253	May 6, 1862	THE DAILY DELTA (New Orleans, LA)	An extraordinary transitional paper still published by the Confederate editor but note his 2nd column explanation of being forced by General Butler to print "his advertisements and orders" or face suspension of the paper and seizure of his offices. Also, "Our First Sunday Under United States Domination".
254	May 15, 1862	THE CAMP KETTLE (Beaufort, SC)	Tiny paper "Published every opportunity by the 100th Penn'a (Roundhead) Regt.–Col. Leasure, Commanding"
255-257	May 16, 1862	THE PEOPLE'S PRESS (Salem, NC)	Front page "The Fall of New Orleans" P. 2–"The Battles in Virginia" P. 3–"The Evacuation of Norfolk"
258	May 16, 1862	THE DAILY DELTA (New Orleans, LA)	Occupied New Orleans residents read the infamous General Order #28 in the first column and the editor makes a comment on it in the second. Shortly thereafter Major-General Butler was given the nickname, "The Beast".
259-261	May 17, 1862	FRANK LESLIE'S ILLUSTRATED NEWS WAR SUPPLEMENT (NY)	Illustrations of the Battle of Shiloh (Pittsburg Landing)
262-263	May 21, 1862	THE COURIER (Natchez, MS)	Confederate Newspaper printed on green colored necessity paper. Also contains the Battle of Glorietta.
264-266	May 24, 1862	FRANK LESLIE'S ILLUSTRATED NEWS WAR SUPPLEMENT (NY)	Battle of Williamsburg, VA and "Farragut's Fleet Taking New Orleans".
267-268	May 27, 1862	DAILY LYNCHBURG VIRGINIAN	Stonewall Jackson's victories at Front Royal and Winchester, VA
269	May 27, 1862	TRUE DEMOCRAT BULLETIN (Little Rock, AK)	An extremely rare Arkansas Confederate extra broadside bringing the news of Stonewall Jackson's victories.
270-271	May 28, 1862	THE WEEKLY COURIER (Natchez, MS)	Major-General Butler's Gag Laws" and "Battle of Shiloh–Gen. Beauregard's Official Report"
272-273	May 28, 1862	DAILY LYNCHBURG VIRGINIAN	More on Stonewall Jackson's recent victories.
274	May 30, 1862	PHILADELPHIA INQUIRER	Window display poster (broadside) to promote sales of the newspaper that day Headlines include "The Battle of Shiloh - Beauregard's Report - Rebel Loss 10,699".
275	May 31, 1862	FORNEY'S WAR PRESS (Philadelphia, PA)	Front page view of "Richmond - The Capital of Rebeldom"
276	June 3, 1862	PHILADELPHIA INQUIRER	Window display poster–"Battle of Seven Pines"
277	June 4, 1862	NATCHEZ WEEKLY COURIER (Natchez, MS)	Rare cartoon, "The Anaconda" as well as interesting pieces on Jackson's victories at Front Royal and Winchester. Also, "Col. Morgan in Tennessee–His Narrow Escape from Capture".
278	June 5, 1862	NY DAILY TRIBUNE	Front page war map accompanying account of the Battle of Seven Pines in VA
279	June 5, 1862	DAILY MISSISSIPPIAN (Jackson, MS)	All about "Beast" Butler and General Order # 28.
280-281	June 7, 1862	NY DAILY TRIBUNE	Unusually detailed front page street map of Memphis. Also, "The Rebel General Johnson (was) Mortally Wounded"
282	June 11, 1862	DAILY LYNCHBURG VIRGINIAN	"More Glorious News from (Stonewall) Jackson" and "Shields Routed with Immense Loss"
283-284	June 11, 1862	CHRISTIAN BANNER (Fredericksburg, VA)	Printed on necessity wrapping paper. An early Union occupation paper.
285-287	June 14, 1862	PENNSYLVANIA RESERVE (Camp near Fredericksburg, VA)	First issue of a Union Army Camp newspaper to be "Published Semi-Occasionally"
288-289	June 14, 1862	HARPER'S WEEKLY (NY)	Winslow Homer, perhaps the finest artist working in illustrated journalism at the time, rendered this centerfold. It demonstrates how crucial news and newspapers were to soldiers, officers, and most importantly, to loved ones on the home front.
290	June 14, 1862	FORNEY'S WAR PRESS (Philadelphia, PA)	"Desperate Bayonet Charge of the Twenty-third Pennsylvanians, at the Battle of Fair Oaks"
291	June 29, 1862	RICHMOND ENQUIRER (VA)	Rare local broadside reporting the Seven Days Battle for Richmond.
292-293	July 1, 1862	DAILY LYNCHBURG VIRGINIAN	"The Seven Days Battle for Richmond"
294-295	July 3, 1862	DAILY LYNCHBURG VIRGINIAN	More on the Seven Days Battle for Richmond. Also note, "Old Abe Makes a Speech", in which General Scott is referred to as "the hoary old Virginia traitor".
296-297	July 5, 1862	HARPER'S WEEKLY (NY)	"Cavalry Charge," as depicted by Winslow Homer.
298	July 16, 1862	N Y HERALD	Full page war map showing the "Scene of the Seven Days Battles"
299	July 26, 1862	TRI-WEEKLY COURIER (Charleston, SC)	General Johnston's official report of the Battle of Seven Pines.
300-301	Aug. 2, 1862	FORNEYS WAR PRESS (Philadelphia, PA)	Illustrated biography of "Morgan, the Guerrilla Leader".
302	Aug. 2, 1862	PHILADELPHIA INQUIRER	Front page portrait of Union General H. Halleck who was named General-in-Chief July 11, 1862.
303	Aug. 8, 1862	WEEKLY PIONEER AND DEMOCRAT (St. Paul, MN)	The Battle of Malvern Hill "Rebel Account"
304	Aug. 13, 1862	N Y HERALD	The Battle of Cedar Mountain described along with accompanying battle map.
305	Aug. 18, 1862	TELEGRAPHIC (Great Salt Lake City, UT)	Residents in Territorial Utah receive war reports in this extremely rare broadside thanks to the completion of the Overland Telegraph in late October, 1861.
306	Aug. 19 1862	N Y HERALD	The Battle of Baton Rouge described along with accompanying battle map.
307	Aug. 19, 1862	VIDETTE EXTRA (From the field, Huntsville, TN)	Extraordinary autographed broadside extra issued by Confederates in "Morgan's Brigade" also known popularly as Morgan's Raiders. It contains a printed proclamation by John H. Morgan warning that he will retaliate for Northern outrages by employing equally tough tactics. This copy is pencil signed in upper left, "Respects General John H. Morgan"
308-311	Aug. 22, 1862	WEEKLY PIONEER AND DEMOCRAT (St. Paul, MN)	Front page "The Battle of Culpepper", P. 3 "The Battle of Cedar Mountain", P. 4 "Sioux Uprising Begins" P. 8, Col. 1, The patriotism exhibited by local printers as well as a local woman.
312-314	Aug. 29, 1862	WEEKLY PIONEER AND DEMOCRAT (St. Paul, MN)	Front page printing of Lincoln's famous response to Greeley's "Prayer of the 20 Millions" in which he says, "If I could save the Union without freeing any slaves, I would do it...' Plus, more on the Sioux uprising.
315	Aug. 30, 1862	CHARLESTON TRI-WEEKLY COURIER (Charleston, SC)	Major-General Jeb Stuart and one of his successful cavalry raids in the Second Bull Run Campaign.
316-318	Sept. 2, 1862	LYNCHBURG VIRGINIAN	This issue is chock full of interesting articles. P. 2–"Another Great Victory" regarding 2nd Bull Run, "Blockade Prices", "Perfidy of the Enemy" about Union advertisement offering forged "Confederate Treasury Notes", "Col. John H. Morgan's Proclamation" refers to the Aug. 19, 1862 issue of *THE VIDETTE* (see p. 307). ""Brutalities of Pope's Army" Note ad in last column, "Blockade Run" P. 3 "The Great Battle of Manassas"
319-320	Sept. 2, 1862	TRI-WEEKLY MERCURY (Charleston, SC)	The Second Battle of Bull Run and "Exploits of Morgan"
321-322	Sept. 6, 1862	THE NEW ERA (Key West, FL)	Occupation newspaper printed on cornhusk. "2nd Battle of Bull Run" plus, Florida responds to Lincoln's order to "employ Negroes and utilize them in military and naval efforts"-see Col. 1 & 2.
323	Sept. 8, 1862	THE SUN (NY)	A front page look at "A Noted Rebel General–Stonewall Jackson" and "Maryland Invaded"
324	Sept. 8, 1862	THE DAILY MISSISSIPPIAN (Jackson, MS)	"Bull Run No.Two!"
325	Sept. 18, 1862	THE SUN (NY)	"The Seat of War in Maryland and Pennsylvania" This map includes area where Battle of Antietam took place.
326	Sept. 18, 1862	DAILY LYNCHBURG VIRGINIAN	The Battle of Harpers Ferry

327-328	Sept. 20, 1862	THE CONFEDERATE STATES (New Iberia, LA)	Extremely rare Confederate newspaper printed on wall paper. Note the false front page report of the taking of the Capitol by the Confederacy. The editor's spirit is exhibited in this back page explanation of his use of wallpaper.
329	Sept. 20, 1862	N Y HERALD	The Bloodiest Battle of the War– The Battle of Antietam, with a map of the scene of battle.
330-331	Sept. 22, 1862	DAILY MISSISSIPPIAN (Jackson, MS)	"The Battles of Harpers Ferry and Antietam" and, "The Beast Once More" is taken from a British newspaper and relates to "his brutal order respecting the women of New Orleans."
332-333	Sept. 23, 1862	N Y HERALD	Front page printing of Lincoln's preliminary Emancipation Proclamation which would go into effect the following New Year's Day.
334	Sept. 23, 1862	DAILY LYNCHBURG VIRGINIAN	The Battles of Antietam and Harpers Ferry
335-336	Sept. 23, 1862	TRI-WEEKLY MERCURY (Charleston, SC)	The Battle of Antietam
337-338	Sept. 23, 1862	NATIONAL INTELLIGENCER (Washington, DC))	First printing of Lincoln's Emancipation Proclamation.
339-341	Sept. 26, 1862	DAILY MISSISSIPPIAN (Jackson, MS	Battles in Maryland and Harpers Ferry Page 2 "The Confederate Senate and the Press" bemoans that the Confederacy is not allowing exemptions for army service for members of the press. "The Battle of Antietam (Sharpsburg)". Note also the highly racist article in the last column, "The Elephant Becoming Troublesome" (from a Northern Newspaper). Page 3 Sentimental piece headed "An Incident"
342	Sept. 27, 1862	NATIONAL ANTI-SLAVERY STANDARD (NY)	This organ of the American Anti-Slavery Society happily prints Lincoln's Emancipation Proclamation.
343-345	Sept. 27, 1862	THE CAMP GAZETTE (Camp Joe Hooker, Lakeville, MA)	"We believe this is the first camp in the state that has a newspaper connected with it." News and ads of interest to the Union men stationed here.
346	Sept. 27, 1862	SOUTHERN ILLUSTRATED NEWS (Richmond, VA)	A front page look at General J.E.B. Stuart
347-348	Oct. 1, 1862	N Y TRIBUNE	McClellan's official report on the Battles of Antietam and South Mountain. Plus an editorial titled, "If This is Going To Be an Abolition War I Shall Resign!"
349	Oct. 1, 1862	THE SUN (NY)	A look at Rebel Commander-In-Chief Robert E. Lee –"Very good looking but he can't come in."
350	Oct. 18, 1862	SOUTHERN ILLUSTRATED NEWS (Richmond, VA)	The famed illustrated Confederate weekly offers its readers an illustrated biography of "Miss Belle Boyd"–The Rebel Spy"
351	Nov. 1, 1862	SOUTHERN ILLUSTRATED NEWS (Richmond, VA)	A front page look at General Joseph E. Johnston
352-355	Nov. 1, 1862	THE NEW SOUTH (Port Royal, SC)	Contains a black-bordered announcement of the "Death of General Mitchel" who had been "commanding this department".
356	Nov. 10, 1862	THE SUN (NY)	A look at "Our New Commander Brave Gen. Burnside"
357-358	Nov. 14, 1862	RICHMOND WHIG AND PUBLIC ADVERTISER	The capital of the Confederacy, Richmond, learns that McClellan has been relieved of command as head of the Army of the Potomac.
359-361	Nov. 17, 1862	THE COUNTRYMAN (Turnwald, Putnam County, GA)	Unusual Confederate newspaper. Published on the editor's plantation.
362-363	Nov. 21, 1862	THE CAMDEN CONFEDERATE (Camden, SC)	Black-bordered for the local funeral of General J. B. Villepigue. Plus, declaration by the Governor of South Carolina.
364	Nov. 22, 1862	SOUTHERN ILLUSTRATED NEWS (Richmond, VA)	A front page look at Major-General Ambrose P. Hill
365-366	Dec. 6, 1862	THE VOLUNTEER (Nicholasville, KY)	"Devoted to the Interest of the Union. Published Frequently–Once in a While–If Not Oftener" Troop paper printed by the 3rd Division on a single sheet of paper. Crude illustration of "Bragg's Retreat From Perryville"
367	Dec. 12, 1862	THE SUN (NY)	"Great Victory in Virginia–Capture of Fredericksburg" Includes war map.
368	Dec. 16, 1862	NY HERALD	Front page war map showing "The Battle at Fredericksburg"
369	Dec. 18, 1862	DAILY MISSISSIPPIAN (Jackson, MS)	"Particulars of the Battle near Fredericksburg" Plus, an amusing offer from three young ladies.
370	Dec. 20, 1862	SOUTHERN ILLUSTRATED NEWS (Richmond, VA)	A break from their usual tradition of simple front page portraits is this lively view of "Morgan's Raiders" on their mounts.
371	Dec. 23, 1862	TRI-WEEKLY MERCURY (Charleston, SC)	Front page coverage of "The Battle of Fredericksburg"

NATIONAL GAZETTE AND LITERARY REGISTER.

PRINCIPLES *AND* MEN.

Vol. XII. PHILADELPHIA, TUESDAY, AUGUST 30, 1831. No. 1637.

PRINTED AND PUBLISHED ON TUESDAYS, THURSDAYS, & SATURDAYS, *BY WILLIAM FRY,* *No. 72, South Second Street,* PHILADELPHIA.

TERMS: One Year, Five Dollars—Six Months, Three Dollars—Three Months, Two Dollars. To be paid in advance.

THE NATIONAL GAZETTE.

PHILADELPHIA:
MONDAY, AUGUST 29, 1831.

INSURRECTION IN VIRGINIA.

Extract of a letter from a gentleman to his friend in Baltimore, dated *Richmond, August* 23.

An express reached the governor this morning, informing him that an insurrection had broken out in Southampton, and that, by the last accounts, there were seventy whites massacred, and the militia retreating. Another express to Petersburg says that the blacks were continuing their destruction; that three hundred militia were retreating in a body, before six or eight hundred blacks. A shower of rain coming up as the militia were making an attack, wet the powder so much that they were compelled to retreat, being armed only with shot-guns. The negroes are armed with muskets, scythes, axes, &c. &c. Our volunteers are marching to the scene of action. A troop of cavalry left at four o'clock P.M. The artillery, with four field pieces, start in the steam boat Norfolk, at 6 o'clock, to land at Smithfield. Southampton county lies 80 miles south of us, below Petersburg.

[From the Richmond Whig of Tuesday.]

Disagreeable rumors having reached this city of an insurrection of the slaves in Southampton county, with loss of life, in order to correct exaggeration, and at the same time to induce all salutary caution, we state the following particulars:

An express from the Hon. James Trezvant states that an insurrection had broken out, that several families had been murdered, and that the negroes were embodied, requiring a considerable military force to reduce them.

The names and precise numbers of the families are not mentioned. A letter to the Post Master corroborates the intelligence. Prompt and efficient measures are being taken by the Governor, to call out a sufficient force to put down the insurrection, and place lower Virginia on its guard.

Serious danger of course there is none. The deluded wretches have rushed on assured destruction.

The Fayette Artillery and the Light Dragoons will leave here this evening for Southampton; the artillery go in a steamboat, and the troop by land.

We are indebted to the kindness of our friend Lyford for the following extract of a letter from the editors of the Norfolk Herald, containing the particulars of a most murderous insurrection among the blacks of Southampton County,* Virginia.

NORFOLK, 24th Aug., 1831.

I have a horrible, a heart rending tale to relate, and least even its worst features might be distorted by rumour and exaggeration, I have thought it proper to give you all and the worst information, that has as yet reached us through the best sources of intelligence which the nature of the case will admit.

A gentleman arrived here yesterday express from Suffolk, with intelligence from the upper part of Southampton county, stating that a band of insurgent slaves (some of them believed to be runaways from the neighbouring swamps,) had turned out on Sunday night last, and murdered several whole families, amounting to forty or fifty individuals. Some of the families were named, and among them was that of Mrs. Catherine Whitehead, sister of our worthy townsman, Dr. N. C. Whitehead,—who with her son and five daughters, fell a sacrifice to the savage ferocity of these demons in human shape.

The insurrection was represented as one of the most alarming character, though it is believed to have originated only in a design to plunder, and not a view to a more important object—as Mrs. Whitehead being a wealthy lady, was supposed to have had a large sum of money in her house. Unfortunately a large number of effective male population was absent at Camp Meeting, in Gates county, some miles off; a circumstance which gave a temporary security to the brigands in the perpetration of their butcheries; and the panic which they struck at the moment prevented the assembling of a force sufficient to check their career.

As soon as this intelligence was received, our authorities met, and decided on making an immediate application to Col. House, commanding at Fortress Monroe, who at 6 o'clock this morning embarked on board the Steamboat Hampton, with three companies and a piece of artillery for Suffolk. These troops were re-inforced in the roads by detachments from the U. S. ships Warren and Natchez, the whole amounting to nearly 300 men.

To-day another express arrived from Suffolk, confirming the disastrous news of the preceding one, adding still more to the number of slain. The insurgents are believed to have from 100 to 150 mounted men, and about the same number on foot. They are armed with fowling pieces, clubs, &c. and have had a rencounter with a small number of the militia, who killsd six and took eight of them prisoners.—They are said to be on their way to South Quay, probably making their way to the Dismal Swamp, in which they will be able to remain for a short time in security. For my part, I have no fears of their doing much further mischief.

There is very little disaffection* in the slaves generally, and they cannot muster a force sufficient to effect any object of importance. The few who have thus rushed headlong into the arena, will be shot down like crows, or captured and made examples of. The militia are collecting in all the neighbouring counties, and the utmost vigilance prevails.—I subjoin a list of the victims of their savage vengeance:

Mrs. Waters and family, 14; Mrs. Whitehead, 7; Mrs. Vaughan, 5, Jacob Williams, 5; Mr. Travis, 5, Wm. Reese, 4; Mr. Williams, 3; Mr. Baines, 2; Mrs. Turner, 3; Unknown, 10—Total, 58.

Besides these, a private letter adds the families of Mr. Barrow, and Henry Bryant; numbers not mentioned.

Muskets, pistols, swords, and amumnition, have been forwarded to Suffolk to-day, by Com. Warrington, at the request of our civil authorities and a number of our citizens have accoutred and formed themselves as a troop of cavalry, and set off to assist their fellow citizens in Southampton. I trust the next news you hear will be that all is quiet again.

In haste, yours.

Extract from another letter to the same gentleman, dated at Norfolk, 5 o'clock P. M.—"It is now 5 o'clock—Thompson's stage has just arrived----the above statement is confirmed; and in addition it is stated that 300 negroes, well mounted and armed, and headed by one or two white men, is the amount of the insurgent force.

[* Southampton is bounded by the counties of Isle of Wight on the North, and Northampton, in North Carolina, on the South.]

It will be seen by the communication of our correspondent G. that the New Orleans operatic *troupe* may be expected to arrive here in a few days. Their advent will doubtless be hailed with the pleasure with which their previous visits have been welcomed, as, according to all the accounts we have heard, they comprise as much capability of affording delight as ever.

COMMUNICATION.

OPERA FRANCAIS.

Les acteurs Français de la Nouvelle Orléans ont enfin quitté New-York pour revenir parmi nous, recueillir les palmes que le bon gôut et la politesse des Philadelphiens leur ont toujours si généreusement accordés. Aussi le directeur de cette compagnie s'efforce-t-il toujours de nous donner des nouveautés choisies, et d'enroler sous sa bannière des acteurs digne de les répresenter. *Napoléon & Schœnnbrun, Le Comte Ory, Guillaume Tell, &c.* paraîtront successivement devant nous, et ne manqueront pas d'attirer bon nombre d'auditeurs. *Napoléon* est un drame qui ne peut qu'intéresser vivement un auditoire Français, et même Américain. Là, cet homme étonnant est fidèlement représenté d'abord à Vienne, dans tout l'éclat de sa gloire militaire, faisant trembler des rois d'origine antique, et dictant ses lois à l'Europe: mais, là, aussi, nous le voyons dans les fers. Là, Hudson Lowe, vil instrument de la haine et de la vengeance, se montre sous une forme trop hideuse pour ne pas inspirer le dégôut. Il nous semble que le bût d'une pièce de théatre ne devrait point être d'exciter la haine d'une nation contre une autre, et cependent tel doit infailliblement être l'effet de celle-ci. Ce seroit être bien injuste que de rendre la nation Anglaise entière responsable de la conduite vile et lâche de quelques-uns de ses ministres.

Letellier a cessé de faire partie de cette compagnie, et M. St. Aubin le remplace. Nous regrettons qu'une indisposition l'ait empêché de jouer pendant notre séjour à New-York, mais nous avons appris qu'il était en tout digne de son prédécesseur. Quoiqu'il en soit, il porte un nom célèbre dans les annales de l'Opéra-comique, et nous espérons qu'il lui fera honneur.

Mde. St. Clair que nous avons entendu avec tant de plaisir l'année dernière nous promet aussi quelques heures de plaisir. Elle est sans contredit audessus de celles qui l'ont précédé dans son emploi. G.

The Augusta Courier of the 15th instant, says---"We are almost glad Mr. Calhoun is a *Nullifier*: It has made Georgia the most thorough-going State against *Nullification* in the whole Union.

19,469 bbls whale oil, 1901 sperm do., and 150,799 lbs whalebone, have arrived at Sag Harbor (N. Y.) this season.

Rhode Island.---The National Republican Convention at Providence, 22d inst., unanimously nominuated Messrs. Pearce and Burges for re-election as members of Congress: election to take place 30th inst.

The Montreal Emigrant Society have forwarded, this season, above twenty-five hundred emigrants to different parts of the country: principally to Upper Canada.

Yale College.---The annual commencement of this College takes place on the 14th of September. Among other interesting exercises, an oration will be delivered before the Phi Beta Kappa Society, by Chancellor Kent.

The U. S. ship Natchez, bearing the broad pendant of Jesse D. Elliot, Esq. commander-in-chief of the West India fleet, arrived in Hampton Roads on Monday last, from Pensacola: officers and crew all well.

The Louisville Focus of the 17th instant says—"It is believed that Mr. A. G. Hawes is elected to Congress in the eleventh district, by a majority of 13 votes over Mr. Chilton."

A letter from Carlisle, Indiana, states that Judge Law, a Clay man, has been elected to represent that district in Congress, in the place of R. Boon, a Jacksonite.

NEW ORLEANS, Aug. 13.

By the schooner Cometa, arrived this morning from Tampico, we have letters from that place to the 3d instant, and papers from the city of Mexico to the 19th ultimo. By the English packet ship Shyr, which was to sail in a day or two from Tampico, was shipped to London $10,500 for paying the dividend on the foreign loan. Nothing of moment has transpired of late in the republic. The most perfect tranquillity continues to exist throughout the country.

ONE DAY LATER FROM EUROPE.

The ship Hercules arrived at Boston from Liverpool, has brought London evening papers of the 13th July. The following are extracts:

GREAT BRITAIN.

In the House of Commons on the 12th, Lord John Russell moved that the House should go into committee on the Reform bill. After a long debate, the question was taken and carried without a division, at half past seven in the morning. During the night's session there were seven divisions on various questions. The first was on a motion for receiving a petition that counsel might be heard at the bar against the disfranchisement of Appleby. The motion was negatived by a majority of 97 votes, viz: for it, 187, against it, 284.

The number of members of the House of Commons, who voted on the second reading of the Reform bill was 621, viz: 378 for the bill, and 243 against it, majority 135. There were 12 vacancies in the representation, and 24 members absent. These numbers, with one for the Speaker, made the whole number of members composing the House 658.

From the votes taken on the following questions in succession, it appears that at every struggle the majority of the Reformers was increased.

"In the course of the succeeding debate there were not less than seven divisions on successive motions of adjournment. On Captain Gordon's motion (for immediate adjournment) there were for ministers, 328; against the bill, 102; majority, 226 On the question that the speaker do leave the chair, for ministers, 286; against the bill, 90; majority. 196. Sir Charles Wetherell's motion for an adjournment to Thursday, for ministers, 235; against the bill, 63; majority, 172. On Lord Stormount's adjournment till five this day, for ministers, 214; against the bill, 44; majority, 170. Another motion of Sir C. Wetherell's for adjournment, for ministers, 203; against the bill, 37; majority 166. On Mr. Praed's motion of adjournment to Friday, for ministers, 187; against the bill, 25; majority, 162. Another m[illegible]n was made for adjournment, on which the numbers were, for ministers, 187; against the bill, 24; majority, 163."

It will be seen, from the successive decrease in the number of opponents of the bill on each division, that the more sensible, or prudent, or honest of the party, got ashamed of the factious opposition; but we should put it---and strongly to the supporters of the bill---that the greatest danger the measure now runs, is from their absenting themselves without the pairing off with an opponent. We repeat, in the words of the morning papers---"No friend of the Bill should leave the House without a pair." The names of such as do should be published, that their constituents may know who have discharged and who have neglected their duty.---*Globe.*

In the House of Lords, July 11, it was arranged that the production of the evidence and documents relative to the massacre at Newtownbarry, Ireland, should take place the 13th. Lord Farnham desired the production of these, not only that they might have correct information, but that the public mind might be disabused.

The London Herald states that in the House of Lords, night of 12th, on the occasion of the third reading of Lord Melbourne's bill, to extend to Ireland the benefit of lords-lieutenant for counties, the Marquis of Londonderry availed himself to defend himself against attacks, which he stated had been heretofore made upon him by various lords, and afterwards to attack the provisions of the bill as giving powers exceeding those of any previous enactment regarding Ireland. Lord Farnham, however, defended the bill—after Lord Plunkett had vindicated the conduct of the government respecting the measure.

The House on the 8th refused, 117 to 96, to issue a writ for another election in Liverpool, Mr. Dennison, chosen for that place and Nottinghamshire both, having declared in favour of the latter, and left Liverpool unrepresented: it appears, therefore, that she will remain so, unless on a fourth effort a writ is granted.

It is said that Lord Brougham has abandoned his Bankrupt Court Bill for the present session, owing to the absence of professional members on the Circuit.

Lord John Russell has been honored with the freedom of the City of London. After the ceremony was concluded, a most sumptuous banquet was served, at which a long list of distinguished personages were present.

The Morning Herald of the 11th has the following paragraph from the Edinburgh Evening Post. "We have just heard from good authority that Sir Walter Scott is very ill, and in great danger."

Mr. Simond, the Traveller in England and Italy, died lately at Geneva, of apoplexy. Mr. Simond was a resident for many years in this country.

The British Funds, July 12, had risen slightly in consequence it was supposed of the settlement of the Belgian question; and the favorable result of the French elections. Three per cent. Red. $83\frac{1}{4}$, Cons. 83; do. for the opening, July 30, $84\frac{1}{4}$ a $\frac{1}{2}$. French 3 percents. 61fr.; 5 per cents. 61fr., 5 per cents, 89,50. Scrip 5 a $5\frac{1}{2}$ per cent. premium. Exchange, 25fr. 30c.

The Liverpool Courier of the 12th July says—"We are happy to notice that the export trade, the chief vent for which is Liverpool, has been particularly brisk during the past month. Cotton manufactures to the value of upwards of £1,100,000, were exported, and woollen manufactures, which were thought some time ago to be decaying, to the value of nearly £600,000, and the infant manufacture of silks has exceeded the amount of £18,000 for the month only.

The Railway.—Since the opening of the branch of the Liverpool and Manchester Railway from Bolton, there have been conveyed 1515 passengers. The average receipts for fares and carriage of merchandise is at the rate of £10,000 per annum, and the effect has been to drive every stage coach from off the road between Bolton and Liverpool.

FRANCE.

The latest papers received at London state that the Electoral returns were pouring in from the departments, and that the ministerial preponderance was rather acquiring than losing weight. It is stated authoritatively, that the king's opening speech to the Chambers will disclose new and more worthy views with respect to Poland.

The Paris Messager of the 11th July says, up to the present moment the elections of 354 Deputies have been announced;—of these, the Minister may reckon as his supporters 248.

It is asserted in the Gazette de France to be the intention of the French Ministry in the Royal Message at the opening of the Chambers to declare in favor of the cause of Poland.

The French ministry has renounced the maintenance of the hereditary Peerage, and they are about framing a system exclusive or restrictive of the rights of birth.

Paris letters dwell upon the intensity of the heat and upon the gratifying prospects of the most superb harvest and vintage known for many years.

A proclamation has been circulated in France by the agents of the Duchess of Berri, from Charles X. in which the French are called on to rally around the standard of Henry V. and the Duchess of Berri is declared to be Regent of the Kingdom. The Carlists were making active efforts to rally a party in France, and to concentrate them in La Vendee. It was reported in Paris that the Police had arrested 160 Carlists.

Great numbers of French people of rank have lately gone to England; in consequence of which the government enforces the strictest search at the ports. £500,000 in silver coins of Henry V. have been struck in England, and circulated in La Vendee. Many arrests have taken place at Paris, and a member of the late corps of Swiss guards had received passports for the Province of Morbikan in the west, and their pay in advance.

We are assured by respectable private correspondents from France, that M. Casimir Perier's administration will derive much strength from the elections. Of the good understanding which exists between our Government and that of France, now that the Belgian affair is adjusted to the satisfaction of both parties, there can be no question; neither can there be any doubt of their common desire to maintain the peace of Europe. Two objects are, we have reason to believe, in the constant view of our Ministers, to which they, in conjunction with the French Ministers, will, we believe, *now* apply their energies. So long as the affairs of Belgium were uncertain in their issue, there could be no conjoint efforts made to effect objects highly important to both and to the cause of humanity. The two Governments may now, we hope, successfully endeavour to assist the Poles, at least by mediation; and if that should fail, by all other means than those which might have the effect of plunging the whole of Europe into another long and expensive war.

A second and most important object to which the governments of France and England will undoubtedly apply themselves, is the slave trade, which, for want of a hearty co-operation on the part of the French people, is now carried on to an extent and with a cruelty which was never exceeded, perhaps never equalled in the worst of times. The Americans should be called on to unite with England and France in some great and well sustained effort to put an end forever to this horrid traffic: a traffic which, so long as one nation is allowed to carry it on and acquires riches by it, will defeat all the efforts of humane and enlightened persons to destroy domestic slavery in particular islands. Let a mutual right of search be agreed to, and all men engaged in the traffic be treated as pirates; and a supply of new slaves being thus rendered impossible, it may not be difficult to persuade all parties concerned in slave property to seek their common and true interest, by making friends of those who are by the present unnatural arrangements compelled to feel themselves ill-treated and oppressed by those who ought to protect and raise them from a condition in which they were originally placed by fraud, force, and folly, but from which they can only be relieved through the influence of justice and wisdom.—*London Globe, July* 13.

SPAIN.

A Spanish army of 20,000 men has been ordered to the frontiers of Portugal.

BELGIC AFFAIRS.

The Belgian deputation, charged with the definitive offer of the crown to Prince Leopold, had arrived at the Brunswick Hotel, in Jermyn street, London. They were received in the different towns of Flanders through which they passed with the greatest enthusiasm, and during the changing of horses immense crowds of citizens surrounded the carriages, crying "*Vive le Roi!*" "*Vive Lebeau!*" "*Vive notre patriotique Ministre!*" On the evening of the 12th, the deputies waited on the Prince, and were received with the most marked cordiality. They remained with his royal highness till eleven o'clock. It was arranged during the interview that, the Prince shall be called "Leopold, Premier Roi des Belges." It was also settled that the Prince should leave London on Saturday the 16th of July, and proceed to Brussels by way of Calais, where he will sleep; he will then proceed to Ostend, leave again on Monday morning for Bruges, Ghent, and Alost, and make his public entry into the metropolis on Tuesday, at 12 o'clock. The deputation were to dine with the Duchess of Kent on the 14th; Prince Leopold, the cabinet Mintsters, the Foreign Ambassadors, and Lord Ponsonby were also invited. The King of Holland has signified his intention of acceding to the preliminaries. It is M. De Muelinacre, Governor of West Flanders, who makes the fifth Belgian Deputy. The acceptance on the part of the Belgians of the preliminaries of peace was received by Lord Palmerston on Monday the 11th of July. It was signed by M. Lebeau as Minister for Foreign Affiars.

[Besides his pension of fifty thousand pounds a year from England, Prince Leopold, as well as being a Field Marshal, has enjoyed all the emoluments of a colonelcy of cavalry for fifteen years, his Royal Highness having been appointed Colonel of the 5th Dragoon Guards, in 1816. This Colonelcy, of course becomes vacant by his acceptance of the crown of Belgium.]

RUSSIA AND POLAND.

The Cholera had appeared at Twer, Jaroslaw, Nesburey, Novogorod, and in the government of Witepsh. In the government of Minsk, from March 31 to June 1, 2268 persons had been attacked, of whom 1246 had died, and 926 had recovered. The disease was making frightful ravages in Moldavia. The number of persons who died of it in Jassy on the 10th was 95, on the 11th 125, and on the 12th 145. Letters from Jassy of the 17th say that the disorder was increasing, and the deaths were 300 daily. The government of Jassy advised the inhabitants to retire into the country, and they were flying in all directions.

Brussels papers of July 9th contain some official notices by the Polish General and Government of the recent movements of their troops, in which they do not affect to conceal the reverses reported of them by the Russian accounts.

Warsaw, June 27.—Since the action of Rudiger, hostilities have at last been suspended in the kingdom of Poland; for Lithuania and the other revolted provinces are still in flames. For some days peace was spoken of as near at hand. Almost all the troops were assembled about Warsaw. Skrzynecki, it was said, depending on the intervention of foreign powers, kept the army inactive, in order to prevent useless bloodshed; but it now appears these reports were false. War is again talked of; the troops are to be put in motion again in a few days, and renew the contest. The treachery of Janikowski is almost the only subject of conversation. Every body is incensed, the soldiers are ferocious, and if he had shewn himself to them after the battle, his life might have paid the forfeit of his conduct. Skrzynecki was so certain of the destruction of Rudiger, that he had given orders to General Rubinski to occupy Brzesc Litewski. Thus all the communications with Russia would have been turned and intercepted, and they would only have that with Prussia open, if it is true, as reported, that the seaport of Polugese is in the hands of the insurgents. Already on the day after Jankowski set out, it was said that Rudiger was defeated, 20,000 men made prisoners, &c. Russian spies must have been made acquainted with the plans of the Commander-in-Chief. Meantime our hopes have been disappointed in one point, the situation of the Russians is not the more brilliant on that account. They do not venture to pass the Vistula, The war is protracted because no decisive blow is struck, but we hope it will this time be struck by Skrzynecki.

London, July 12.—The death of Constantine is considered a fortunate event for Poland. Arbitrary and unrelenting to a degree of atrocity, and uncontrolled in his tyrannical career by the ministry of his imperial brother, the brave Poles suffered long and severely beneath the iron rule of his despotism, but futher endurance at length appeared as a national disgrace, and the eventful struggle commenced; he was constantly with the Russian army, and is said to have been the merciless author of the barbarities perpetrated upon the patriotic prisoners.

RICHMOND ENQUIRER

BY RITCHIE & COOK. RICHMOND, VIRGINIA, FRIDAY, NOVEMBER 4, 1831. VOL. XXVII.---NO. 51.

☞The ENQUIRER is published twice a week generally and three times a week during the session of the State Legislature, price, the same as heretofore, Five Dollars per annum, payable in advance. Notes of chartered, specie-paying banks, (only) will be received in payment. The Editors will gurantee the safety of remitting them by mail; the postage of all letters being paid by the writers.

☞No paper will be discontinued (but at the discretion of the Editors) until all arrearages have been paid up.

☞Whoever will guarantee the payment of nine papers shall have the tenth GRATIS.

TERMS OF ADVERTISING.

☞One square, OR LESS—First insertion 75 cents—each continuance, 50 cents.

*₊*No advertisement inserted, until it has either been paid for, or assumed by some person in this city, or its environs.

POLITICAL.

From the New York Evening Post.

CONSTITUTIONALITY OF THE TARIFF—AND NULLIFCATION.

Who shall set bounds to human ignorance?

It is gravely insisted, even in the Tariff Convention where there are so many respectable men, that the constitutionality of the tariff laws, if disputed, ought to be brought before the proper tribunal, that is the Supreme Court of the United States.

Let the friends of high preaches have the law amended so that the question *can be tried*, and then we will resort to the proper tribunal. Let them pass a law in which it shall be distinctly declared that it is expedient to lessen the importation of foreign goods, for the encouragement of domestic manufacture—that is all we ask. But for Heaven's sake, let us not be taunted with the complaint that we will not go to the proper tribunal, when we cannot get there. Do the gentlemen of the Convention know that the Act of 1789, which contained the Preamble "whereas it is necessary for the support of Government—for the discharge of the debts of the United States, and *the encouragement and protection of Domestic Manufactures that duties be laid*" was *repealed* in 1790 by an act with a similar preamble, except that *it left out that part as to the encouragement of manufactures*.

So that the laws since 1790 have been clear of all legal objection. I stay not to explain why the above preamble, if it had been retained, would have been insufficient to test the question. It is enough that the Act of '89 was repealed.

One word as to a gross blunder which is constantly harped on in sundry papers sound in empty professions, but in their general course of remarks unsound, i. e. hollow. There has been an attempt to impute the doctrines of nullification to the free trade convention. This is a gross libel.

To assert the unconstitutionality of a law is one thing—to attempt to resist the law by means unknown to the Constitution, is another. The right freely to discuss the constitutionality of a law was never denied by any but partisans of a system which is designed to oppress the many, and especially the poor, for the benefit of a few, and those principally the rich.

A FRIEND OF THE PEOPLE.

To the Editors of the Evening Post.

Constitutionality of the Tariff.—The power to protect manufactures not being expressly granted to Congress, nor impliedly as necessary and proper for the execution of other powers; but having been positively withheld, is it expedient? In a free country and enlightened age, perhaps it ought to be; for it is not the business of Government to do more than protect from foreign ... to that system, to the extent carried by Congress in 1820—Mr. Webster, in his celebrated anti-tariff speech in the House of Representatives, at the period just mentioned, held this language:—

He certainly thought it might be doubted whether Congress would not be acting somewhat against the spirit and intention of the Constitution, in exercising a power to control essentially the pursuits and occupations of individuals in their private concerns—a power to force great and sudden changes, both of occupation and property, upon individuals, not as incidental to the exercise of any other power, but as substantial and direct power. If such changes were wrought incidentally only, and were the necessary consequence of such imposts as Congress, for the leading purpose of revenue, should enact, then they could not be complained of. But he doubted whether Congress fairly possessed the power of turning the incident into the principal; and instead of leaving manufactures to the protection of such laws as should be passed with a primary regard to revenue, of enacting laws, with the avowed object of giving a preference to particular manufactures, with an entire disregard to all the considerations of revenue, and instead of laying such imposts as would best answer the purpose of raising revenue, with the least burden on the public, carrying the impost on certain articles to a burdensome excess, with a full knowledge that the increase of duty will diminish the amount of revenue raised.

When the bill denounced by Mr. Webster had passed the House, it was sent to the Senate, where the Hon. H. G. Otis pronounced it "a manifesto of the disposition of a committee, and of one branch of the Legislature, to listen to the claim of the manufacturers for a bounty of five millions of dollars in the outset," &c. Is not such a "bounty" as that spoken of by Mr. Otis "against the spirit and intention of the Constitution"?—Will any one deny the proposition? We think no.

It has often been asserted—and never denied, to our knowledge—that the memorial presented to Congress in 1820 by the citizens of Salem was drawn up by Judge Story. The following short extract from that masterly document will show what the opinion entertained by the Judge—of duties for the protection of manufactures—at the time referred to—

Upon the whole, the memorialists would respectfully state their unequivocal opinion that all the measures to which they have alluded, are calculated to impair our naval strength and glory, to injure our most profitable commerce, to diminish in an alarming degree the public revenue, to promote unjustifiable speculation, to enhance the prices of manufactures, to throw the great business and trade of the nation into the hands of a few ... industrious and enterprising ... general distress ... agriculturists, to agitate classes of the ... undue appetite, to *destroy many* ... institution *of the* ... and adopted ... the memorialists ... *the great objects* ... *ly from* ... *and* ...

Judge Story upon the protective system, as expressed in the Salem memorial, from his pen, have often been quoted in the columns of this paper; and we are satisfied that he, as well as Mr. Webster, Mr. Otis, and other distinguished lawyers and statesmen, once held ...

RICHMOND (VA.) FRIDAY, NOV 4.

LATEST NEWS.—Warsaw has fallen.—And great excitement prevails in Paris.

Gen. Nat. Turner apprehended!—There is no doubt that Nat Turner is caught at last—on the very scene of his atrocities. Rumor says that he displayed no sort of enterprize in the attempt to escape, nor any degree of courage in resisting the person who captured him. Private letters informed, that he had been taken, and committed to the jail of Southampton.—The Official account confirms the intelligence. We are indebted to the Governor for a copy of the following letter:

"SUSSEX, 31st October, 1831.

"SIR: Perhaps this will reach you before any other intelligence of the capture of Gen. NAT. TURNER; and as you have had so many accounts of his being taken in different places, you may yet be disposed to doubt. Nevertheless, he was taken yesterday by Benjamin Phipps, in the county of Southampton in a Cave, within a few miles of where the principal part of the depredations were committed, and was this day seen by Mr. Littleton Barker, in confinement, and in the presence, as Barker supposed, of nearly one hundred persons, who had collected for the purpose of gratifying their curiosity. I forbear to say more, as the whole of the particulars will reach you in a few days.

"I am, Sir, respectfully, yours, &c.

"Gen. JOHN FLOYD, Governor, Richmond, Va."

We shall attempt to obtain as accurate an account as possible, of the conduct of this murderous Bandit. We shall place it upon record—in order, that if any future historian should hereafter paint him incorrectly, as the Albany Fabulist has done the Insurgent Gabriel, the facts may be ready to refute his falsehoods.

EMANCIPATOR EXTRA.

THE JUDGMENT OF FREEDOM AGAINST THE MASSACRE, NOVEMBER 7, 1837, AT ALTON, ILL.

LIBERTY'S MARTYR.

Rev. Elijah Parish Lovejoy.

As this paper is designed to exhibit the views and feelings of the American people with reference to the late horrible massacre at Alton, it is proper to begin with the following historical account of the victim, taken from the Cincinnati Journal, for which paper it was prepared by a friend.

Rev. Elijah Parish Lovejoy was a native of Albion, in Maine, and was the son of Rev. Daniel Lovejoy, a Congregational minister. He was born November 9th, 1802, and would have been 35 years' old the morning that he was buried. He graduated with honor at Waterville College, and soon after emigrated to Missouri, where for several years he taught a school. He then became editor of the St. Louis Times, a political paper, advocating the election of Henry Clay to the Presidency, in which he showed talents of the first order. His mental powers were superior, especially in the study of the languages, in the acquisition of which he had a remarkable facility, which, if he had devoted himself to this department of learning, would have made him one of the first linguists of the country.

During the first few years of his residence at St. Louis, he was destitute of vital piety, though not a confirmed infidel.

During a revival of religion in that place in 1832, he was converted, and soon abandoning his profession, he studied divinity at Princeton, where he was licensed to preach. Being earnestly invited by some friends of religion in St. Louis, to edit the "St. Louis Observer," he consented, and arrived Nov. 11th, 1833, and soon commenced its publication. His course as an editor was marked with great boldness and a firm adherence to what he considered the course of duty. He soon became interested in developing the character of Romanism, and so fearlessly disclosed its abominations, as to excite the hatred of many of the Catholics in that city. Especially after the consecration of their cathedral, in which the troops and the flag of the United States were engaged, his bold rebukes excited the bitter hostility of the Catholic populace. He was denounced as an abolitionist, and his office was entered and his types destroyed. His powerful and patriotic appeal to the public produced a reaction in his favor. He was at this time a colonizationist, and strongly opposed to the abolition societies and presses, and rebuked them with great plainness. But when the murder of McIntosh, a colored man, who was burned to death by the mob, took place, and the charge of Judge Lawless was published, the severity of his rebuke so exasperated the mob, that they attacked and destroyed his office. He then removed his paper to Alton. Previous, however, to his going there, he had a meeting with a number of citizens, in which he explained his course to them. When questioned as to his course in reference to slavery, he said that in his opinion it was a subject that ought faithfully to be discussed in our religious and political journals, and as an editor he should never relinquish his right to discuss that or any other subject as he might think it his duty to do so. "I do not know," said he, "that I shall feel it my duty to discuss it here as fully as at St. Louis. There, where its enormities were constantly before me, I felt bound to lift up my voice against it. This I claim as my constitutional right—a right which I shall never relinquish to any man or body of men. To discuss the subject of slavery is not the object of my paper, except as a great moral subject in connection with others. My object is to publish a religious journal, which shall be instructive and profitable to my fellow citizens. As to the subjects I shall discuss and the manner of doing them, I shall ever claim the right of determining for myself, always accepting counsel from others with thankfulness."

The night after the press was landed, it was destroyed, having been left on the bank of the river during the night. A public meeting of the citizens was then called to express their sentiments on this outrage, at which they took a noble stand that raised the reputation of Alton abroad as a law abiding city. At this meeting Mr. Lovejoy reiterated in substance the remarks just quoted. He said he did not come there for the purpose of publishing an abolition paper, but one strictly religious, in which he claimed the right to discuss any subject, always holding himself responsible to the laws of his country. He did not ask the citizens of Alton to grant him the right to publish such a paper or any other. He claimed this as the right of an American citizen. It has been stated by some of the abettors of the mob, that Lovejoy violated a pledge made to the citizens, by becoming avowedly the supporter of abolition doctrines, though he was not an abolitionist when he commenced publishing at Alton, yet he never pledged himself not to discuss the subject of slavery, but avowed his right and intention to do it. The statement that he pledged himself not to do so is extremely improbable in itself considered, as well as contrary to the recollection of many who heard him. Lovejoy was not a man to promise that he would not discuss any subject, and especially a subject whose evils he had so long seen, and for speaking of which, he had been driven by violence from his former home. The paper was immediately published, the title being changed from St Louis to Alton Observer. The progressing interest felt by Lovejoy in the subject of slavery, although he had not yet united himself as a member with any anti-slavery or abolition society, yet was so strongly expressed in his paper as to lead to its destruction by a mob on the 22d of August, 1837. Soon after this he openly avowed his adherence to the cause of immediate abolition, and issued a call for a convention for the organization of a state anti-slavery society.

On the 26th of October, the convention assembled at Upper Alton. A large number of persons not friendly to the object of the call, came in, professing to adopt the sentiments of the call, and enrolled themselves as members, and succeeded in passing resolutions in opposition to the intentions of those who called the meeting. At this meeting, U. F. Linder, Esq., and Rev. John Hogan, a Methodist minister, took very prominent parts, and succeeded in their underhanded and dishonorable designs. The next day, however, the friends of the abolition cause met at the house of Rev. T. B. Hurlbut, and about sixty delegates being present, they organized a state society, and elected their officers.

On the following Sabbath, President Beecher preached in both towns with great plainness and effect on the subject of slavery. On Monday, 30th, several members of the convention, and some of the principal citizens of Alton, met in the store of Alexander & Co., to consult on the expediency of establishing the press again in Alton, and defending it. After much deliberation, it was advised that Mr. Lovejoy go on and re-establish the press, and that it was the duty of the friends of free discussion to stand to the last in his defence. This was the uniform counsel of the friends of order to the last.

In addition to the above, it is proper to mention that it was the 20th of *July*, that he published in the Observer a Declaration of his Sentiments on the subject of slavery, and issued the call for a Convention, *before* the riot of 22d August.

From the first commencement of the paper at Alton, he had freely discussed the subject of slavery, and the *very first* number published there contains a bold avowal of his fixed determination to discuss it as he judged proper.

Prior to the meeting of the Convention, and during the intensity of the excitement, a meeting was called, which was at first intended to be for the particular object of removing the Observer; but at length it was deemed expedient to change it to a colonization meeting. The speeches of that meeting, by Messrs. Edwards, Parker, of New Orleans, and Peck, were admirably suited to fan the fury into an out-breaking flame.

Mr. Lovejoy was highly esteemed and exceedingly popular, as an editor, *before* he began to discuss the subject of slavery; his popularity waned as he verged towards abolitionism, and upon his adopting the doctrine of immediate emancipation and renouncing colonization, like all other men who have had reputation to lose with the advocates and apologists of slavery, he lost the whole.

The popularity with which his Alton Observer commenced, as the *religious* paper of Illinois, presented him the opportunity as well as a strong temptation to retrieve his unpopular steps at St Louis. Under these circumstances did Mr. Lovejoy arrive at his *immediate abolitionism*. What but the resistless power of truth upon the conscience could have carried him directly against such a tremendous head wind of interest, expediency, and danger? His opinions, therefore, were not only sealed by his death, but every step of the reasoning by which he arrived at them, was taken at his peril.

Mr. Lovejoy was always calm, considerate, and kind in his discussion of slavery, while his sentiments were ever warm with the life of liberty. The following extracts from his principles will show *why he died*.

ANTI-SLAVERY PRINCIPLES,

Published in the Alton Observer, July 27, 1837.

FIRST PRINCIPLES.

1. Abolitionists hold that "all men are born free and equal, endowed by their Creator with certain inalienable rights, among which are life, LIBERTY, and the pursuit of happiness." They do not believe that these rights are abrogated, or at all modified by the color of the skin, but that they extend alike to every individual of the human family.

2. As the above-mentioned rights are in their nature inalienable, it is not possible that one man can convert another into a piece of property, thus at once annihilating all his personal rights, without the most flagrant injustice and usurpation. But American slavery does this—it declares a slave to be a "THING," a "CHATTEL," an article of personal "PROPERTY," a piece of "MERCHANDISE," and now actually holds TWO AND A HALF MILLIONS of our fellow-men in this precise condition.

3. Abolitionists, therefore, hold American Slavery to be a *wrong*, a legalized system of inconceivable injustice, and a SIN. That it is a sin against God, whose prerogative as the rightful owner of all human beings is usurped, and against the slave himself, who is deprived of the power to dispose of his services as conscience may dictate, or his Maker requires. And as whatever is morally wrong can never be politically right, and as the Bible teaches, and as abolitionists believe, that "righteousness exalteth a nation, while sin is a reproach to any people," they also hold that slavery is a political evil of unspeakable magnitude, and one which, if not removed, will speedily work the downfall of our free institutions, both civil and religious.

4. As the Bible inculcates upon man but one duty in respect to sin, and that is, immediate repentance, abolitionists believe that all who hold slaves, or who approve the practice in others, should *immediately* cease to do so.

5. Lastly. Abolitionists believe, that as all men are *born free*, so all who are now held as slaves in this country were BORN FREE, and that they are slaves now is the sin, not of those who introduced the race into this country, but of those, and those alone, who now hold them, and have held them in slavery from their birth. Let it be admitted, for argument's sake, that A. or B. has justly forfeited his title to freedom, and that he is now the rightful slave of C., bought with his money, how does this give C. a claim to the posterity of A. down to the latest generation? And does not the guilt of enslaving the successive generations of A.'s posterity belong to their respective masters, whoever they be? No where are the true principles of freedom and personal rights better understood than at the South, though their practice corresponds so wretchedly with their theory. Abolitionists adopt, as their own, the following sentiments expressed by Mr. Calhoun in a speech on the tariff question, delivered in the Senate of the United States, in 1833: "He who *earns* the money—*who digs it out of the earth* with the sweat of his brow, has a *just title* to it against the Universe. *No* one has a right to touch it, *without his consent*, except his government, and *it only* to the extent of its legitimate wants: to take more is *robbery*" Now, this is precisely what slaveholders do, and abolitionists do but echo back their own language when they pronounce it "*robbery*."

EMANCIPATION—WHAT IS MEANT BY IT?

Simply, that the slaves shall cease to be held as *property*, and shall henceforth be held and treated as human beings. Simply, that we should take our feet from off their necks. Perhaps we cannot express ourselves better than to quote the language of another southerner. In reply to the question, what is meant by emancipation, the answer is—

"1. It is to reject with indignation the wild and guilty phantasy, that man can hold *property* in man. 2. To pay the laborer his hire, for he is worthy of it. 3. No longer to deny him the right of marriage, but to 'let every man have his own wife,' as saith the apostle. 4 To let parents have their own children, for they are the gift of the Lord *to them*, and no one else has any right to them. 5. No longer to withhold the advantages of education and the privilege of reading the Bible. 6. To put the slave under the protection of law, instead of throwing him beyond its salutary influence."

Now, who is there that is opposed to slavery at all, and believes it to be wrong and a sin, but will agree to all this?

HOW AND BY WHOM IS EMANCIPATION TO BE EFFECTED?

To this question the answer is, by the *masters themselves*, and by no others. No others can effect it, nor is it desirable that they should, even if they could. Emancipation, to be of any value to the slave, must be the free, voluntary act of the master, performed from a conviction of its propriety. This avowal may sound very strange to those who have been in the habit of taking the principles of the abolitionists from the misrepresentations of their opponents. Yet this is, and always has been, the cardinal principle of abolitionists. If it be asked, then, why they intermeddle in a matter where they can confessedly do nothing themselves, in achieving the desired result, their reply is, that this is the very reason why they do and ought to intermeddle. It is because they cannot emancipate the slaves, that they call upon those who can to do it. Could they themselves do it, there would be no need of discussion—instead of discussing they would act, and with their present views the work would soon be accomplished.

EXTRACTS FROM MR. LOVEJOY'S LETTERS.

On the 8th of September, not long after the then recent outrages upon his press, Mr. Lovejoy wrote as follows to the Executive Committee of the American Anti-Slavery Society:

"Satan triumphs now, though I trust and believe his triumphing is short. For myself, I am not discouraged; but the rather feel, that all these commotions are only a part of the overturning and overturning, which is to precede the coming of Him whose right it is to reign. The Lord reigneth, let the earth rejoice. * * * We have, on the whole, come to the conclusion, that duty requires the press to be re-established here, without delay. Some think it will be mobbed again, as soon as it arrives. In my own opinion, it will not be; but I anticipate that violence will be committed on my person. I do not, however, think it will amount to more than tar and feathers, and perhaps riding on a rail; and these I disregard as I do all other consequences personal to myself. But in regard to the re-establishment of the press, supposing there is a certainty that it will be mobbed down again, what is your advice on the whole? Ought we to persevere, at whatever risk, whether of property or life? Is this the best way to expend property in the cause of truth? For one, I trust and think I am willing to do whatever duty requires. I never can expend my energies in a better cause; and had I a thousand lives, I would give them freely."

October 19th, he wrote:

"Your letter, accompanying a commission from your society as local agent, was duly received. I cheerfully accept the commission, and will do all I can to further the Society's views and plans; though I cannot promise that just now I can do much. I feel that my great business just now, is to re-establish my press, and maintain it in the face of all opposition. This opposition is dreadful, both from the mob, and from many professed Christians in this place and elsewhere. Even our friends here do not realize their responsibilities. Nevertheless, the cause is undoubtedly advancing in this state, and that very rapidly too. Complete victory is just ahead; I can already 'seize it with my mind's eye.' From this time forth, slavery will be the all-absorbing topic of discussion in Illinois, until the public sentiment shall have been completely revolutionized."

In closing his letter after the murderous attack at St Charles, Oct. 3, he writes:

And now, my dear brother, if you ask what are my own feelings at a time like this, I answer, perfectly calm, perfectly resigned.—Though in the midst of danger, I have a constant sense of security that keeps me alike from fear or anxiety. "Thou wilt keep him in perfect peace, whose mind is stayed on thee, because he trusteth in thee." This promise I feel has been literally fulfilled unto me. I read the promises of the Bible, and especially the Psalms, with a delight, a refreshing of soul, I never knew before. Some persons here call me courageous, and others pronounce me stubborn; but I feel and know that I am neither one nor the other. That I am enabled to continue firm in the midst of my trials, is all of God. Let no one give me any credit for it. I disclaim it. I should feel that I were robbing Him, if even in thought, should claim the least share to myself. He has said, "As thy day is so shall thy strength be," and he has made his promise good. To Him be all the praise. Pray for me.

We have a few excellent brethren here in Alton. They are sincerely desirous to know their duty in this crisis, and to do it. But as yet they cannot see that duty requires them to maintain their cause here at all hazards. Our convention meets the last Thursday of this month. And of this be assured, the cause of truth still lives in Illinois, and will not want defenders. Whether our paper starts again will depend on our friends, East, West, North and South. So far as depends on me it shall go. By the blessing of God, I will never abandon the enterprise so long as I live, and until success has crowned it. And there are those in Illinois who join me in this sentiment. And if I am to die it cannot be in a better cause.

Yours in the cause of truth and holiness,

ELIJAH P. LOVEJOY.

PARTICULARS OF THE MASSACRE.

The following account, it is presumed, is the most candid and important that is within our reach. It is from the Peoria, Illinois, Register, of Dec. 16th. The editor of that paper is a slaveholder, but he does not forget that he is also a citizen. Having visited Alton the week after the massacre, he published on his return an extract from a communication in the Cincinnati Journal, which he says he had ascertained to be generally authentic and trustworthy.

"On Monday night, (Nov. 6th,) the obnoxious press, so long looked for, arrived. Its friends had taken the precaution to have it landed late in the night, when it was supposed a mob would hardly be raised. They took the further precaution to have about fifty armed men secreted in the ware-room, ready for the service of the Mayor at any moment. While the press was landing, the spies o the enemy were seen lurking about, and the sound of their horn was raised shrill and long. But whether the enemies of peace and order were buried too deep in the arms of Bacchus and sleep, or whether they feared the formidable preparations that were made to receive them, I know not. There was no further molestation than the throwing of a stone or two, while the press was removed into the ware-room of Messrs. Godfrey, Gilman & Co.

"Things remained quiet on Tuesday, saving the threats and imprecations that were heard along the streets, against Mr. Lovejoy and the press. Mr. L.'s life was threatened openly and repeatedly. The Attorney General was heard to say, emphatically and significantly, that 'Mr. L. would be killed within two weeks.' Soon after dark, there were unwonted gatherings in certain coffee-houses. Here the spirit of vengeance which had been rankling in their breasts, was excited to desperation by spirit behind the counter. By about ten o'clock they were prepared for the work. Accordingly they repaired to the ware-house of Messrs. Godfrey, Gilman & Co. They commenced the attack by hurling volleys of stones through the windows and doors. Mr. W. S. Gilman appeared in the door of the second story, and addressed the mob in his peculiarly kind and impressive manner. He earnestly and affectionately advised them to desist from violence; told them that the property was left with him on storage; that he was bound to protect it; assured them that nobody in the building had any ill will against any of them, and that they should all deprecate doing any of them any injury. At the same time he assured them that the press would not be delivered up, but that he and his associates would defend it at the risk and sacrifice of their lives. He was answered by a fresh volley of stones. Those inside then disposed of themselves at the different doors and windows, and prepared to defend it to the last. They all agreed that no gun should be fired till the doors were burst open, or till there was some firing from without. Volley after volley of stones were hurled into the windows and against the doors, then a gun was fired into the window from the mob. Presently a second gun was fired. The balls were heard to whistle through the window, but neither of them did any injury. At this juncture, one of the party within, with the consent and by the advice of the rest, levelled his gun upon the mob. One man fell mortally wounded. His associates took him up and carried him away to a physician, and the mob dispersed. The young man died in about half an hour.

"In about half an hour after the mob had had time to *revive their spirits*, and recruit their courage in the aforesaid *coffee-houses*, they returned with increased numbers, armed with guns, muskets, &c. &c., and recommenced the attack with renewed violence. They formed on the east side of the store, where there are no doors or windows, and occasionally a fire was given from each party. Whiskey was brought and distributed profusely among them, and all were exhorted to be 'good men and true.' Occasionally one of the mob was heard to sing out, 'If any more guns and whiskey are wanted, away to the French coffee-house.' Baffled in their attempt to gain admittance into the store by the doors and windows, they resolved unanimously, with a shout which cleft the air, to fire the building, and 'shoot every damned abolitionist in it, as they should attempt to escape.' Accordingly a ladder was made, and combustibles prepared, and a man ascended to the roof. Presently it was in a blaze. Meantime the company within sent out a detachment of four or five of their number to prevent it. Mr. Lovejoy was of the number. The man on the ladder was fired at and wounded. Just about this time, Mr. Lovejoy, who stood near the ladder, was deliberately aimed at by a man who stood a few yards from him, and shot down. He jumped up after he was shot, went into the counting room, exclaiming, 'I am shot, I am a dead man,' and fell down and expired in a few minutes."

Remarks by the Editor of the Register.

We have remarked that this statement was vouched to us in Alton as being in the main strictly correct. There is one fact, however, of much importance, which is not adverted to. The defenders of the press had frequent conversations with the Mayor on Tuesday, to know how far they might rely on the civil authorities, and how far they might themselves proceed in defending it. He assured them that they had a perfect right to take fire-arms into the building, and use them if they were attacked. Indeed, no plan of defence was determined on until the Mayor had been first informed thereof, and his acquiescence gained. That he could not sustain the defenders of the house afterwards, was not his fault. He endeavored to do so, whereby he exposed himself to great peril, but without success.

The narrative does not detail all the circumstances immediately connected with the death of Mr. Lovejoy. The mob were chiefly collected in front of the north end of the building, which has a vacant lot on each side of it, and extends from Second-street to the bank of the river. The ladder was fixed to the east side, on which there are no windows. To defend that side, Mr. Lovejoy, Mr. Weller, and two or three others, went resolutely out of the south door, and fired at such of the mob as they could see in Second-street and elsewhere, and dispersed them. They then returned into the house without sustaining any injury, and remained perhaps half an hour, when they were informed that the roof was on fire. Mr. Lovejoy and Mr. Weller again went out at the south door, where they saw no one, and both stepped to the end of the building. Mr. L. then saw a man on the ladder, fired at him and stepped behind the corner, his face fronting the east. At the same instant he received the contents of a musket, containing four balls, in his breast, fired from behind a pile of boards, 30 yards distant. Mr. Weller was at his side, and received a wound in his leg, below the knee, while another bullet passed through his hat. He thinks he heard three guns fired.

During all this time the bells were ringing, and the party in the house were not without hope that the citizens would come to their rescue. Mr. Lovejoy was killed, Mr. Weller lay wounded by his side, and the roof over their heads was on fire. There was no way of attacking the mob without being instantly sacrificed. If a door or window were opened, a shower of bullets would be instantly discharged into the room.

STATE OF THINGS AT ALTON.

The editor of the Peoria Register also says:—

"Business calling us to St. Louis the next week following, we stopped at Alton. On entering the Piazza house, a gentleman observed to us that he was about forwarding to us a letter containing the names of several new subscribers, who were disposed in that way to show their approbation of our remarks,—above given. We said, 'Let there be no mistake, sir: I am not an abolitionist, but am opposed to them.' He replied, 'Neither am I an abolitionist; yet I was one of the defenders of the press in the riot, and am an advocate for its freedom. I am opposed to mobs, and so are you. Not a newspaper has been received here, except yours, that has spoken in condemnation of them. Our's are silent, and dare not speak out, however they may think. Imagine then whether we were not gratified at finding that there was at least one press in Illinois that agreed with us, and had the courage to proclaim its sentiments.' This was a few days after the enactment of the tragedy in which Mr. Lovejoy was foully murdered, and before a response could have been had from the press generally. That response came immediately afterwards. It continues to come, borne on every breeze, from one end of our land to the other, and speaks in accents,

"trumpet-tongued, against
The deep damnation of his taking off."

It is all that the gallant defenders of liberty could desire. It indicates the healthfulness of the public mind, and encourages the hope that the murderers of Mr. Lovejoy will one day receive their deserts upon the gallows. They are safe in Alton. But let them not go beyond that hiding place. The mark of Cain is upon them, and if they venture forth, justice will arrest them and demand the forfeiture of their lives. We repeat they are safe in Alton. With the right of challenging jurors, which the law allows every felon, they may laugh at a criminal presentment; but out of that place, a jury of independent men will be found who will render strict and impartial justice."

THE VOICE OF THE MUSE.

Poetry is free by nature, and a favorite minister of freedom; and so terrible an outrage upon liberty as that which took place at Alton, could not pass unheeded by the muse.

From the New Hampshire Herald of Freedom.

TO THE MEMORY OF REV. E. P. LOVEJOY.

We mourn for thee, O brother,
Not as the mother may,
When the children of her bosom
By the sword are swept away,—
Not as a nation mourneth
When her strong and mighty die,
And her banners torn and trodden
On the field of battle lie.

O we mourn as when the altar
Hath cast down its holy light,
And the angel's wings are spreading
For his departing flight.
We mourn as when the freedom
Of a WORLD has been betrayed,
And at the feet of Violence
A PEOPLE'S RIGHTS are laid.

Fallen! a thousand voices
From thy blood shall cry to Heaven,
And in judgment and in terror
Shall an answer back be given.
The right arm of JEHOVAH
Shall be stretched abroad in wrath,
And hail stones and coals of fire
Smite and burn along His path.

Through the deep glades of the forest,
Where the woodsman's axe is heard,
Where the thick grass of the prairie
By a human foot is stirred,—
From the valleys to the hill-tops,
Shall a thrilling cry go out,
And a thousand torrent waters
Swell and render back the shout.

From the free land of the Pilgrims,
Sea crag and mountain glen,—
From the mighty nation risen
Round thy sepulchre, O Penn,—
From the ocean lakes rock-girded,
As when a storm is nigh,
And the deep roar of its waters
Is gathered in the sky:—

Swift from the Western Highlands
Which the red sun sinks behind,—
A strong sound, like the rushing
Of a great and mighty wind,
O'er the Alleghanys sweeping
Down the Mississippi's wave,
Shall be heard through all the regions
Where MAN is held a SLAVE!

A stern rebuke shall thunder
As if the heavens spake—
The voice which FREEDOM utters,
In her indignation wake,
For Truth and Right the PULPIT
Shall raise its trumpet plea,
And, blood-besprinkled Brother,
The PRESS shall still be free!

On the fresh mound heaped above thee,
Laying brow and bosom bare,
Solemnly, in consecration,
Kneeling unto God in prayer,—
In renewedness of purpose,
In the strength of Love and Faith,
We will bind ourselves together
Unto triumph or to death.

The spirit of our fathers
Is in our bosoms yet,
Our hearts are as unshrinking,
And our nerves as firmly set,
We will speak as we have spoken,
With our words unmeted still,
With the INTELLECT forever
FREE FROM THE DESPOT'S WILL!

J. H. K.

HYMN,

Written by Miss P. P. Morse, and sung at a meeting in Lowell, to commemorate the death of E. P. Lovejoy.

Now "rouse ye"—for "the storm hath come,"
The wise have presaged long;
Ye men of iron hearts and nerves
Be firm for truth, and strong.
The banner's folds are stained with gore,
The stars are drenched in blood,
The eagle's crest is covered with
The crimson of that flood.

And must the stern New Englander,
Upon his sterile sod,
Bow with his forehead to the South,
In worship to his God?
And must he speak no more for truth,
And stand no more for right—
But when the storm of malice comes,
A refuge seek in flight?

Never—'tis written on the earth
His feet have always trod,
And deeply on his inmost soul
'Tis graven by his God.
Never—there's life within the land;
The forest oak shall bow
Beneath the summer breeze as soon
As thou, New England, thou.

From the N. Y. Evangelist.

Awake! ye warriors of the Truth! wake all,
Who for eternal right with God's own sword
Stand in your hearts committed; nor recall
One step already taken, nor one word
True to that cause which hath been once averred.
Let not your brother's fate your souls appal!
Not thus were ancient martyrs e'er deterred
From their own purpose. Hark! on you they call—
"Prepare! to fill the posts of those that earliest fall."

The suffering of the faithful and the just,
Beneath Oppression's hand, and for the oppressed,
Shall never be in vain! Their holy TRUST
In God's own undeceiving word once placed,
Firm as the house which Wisdom builds, shall rest
On the deep rock unshaken! It shall stand,
Pouring forth blessings while itself is blessed,
Growing more strong, more visible, more grand,
Until, a glorious orb, it shines o'er every land!

From the National Enquirer.

Oh, nobly hast thou fallen, in the fight
Of holy Freedom, and thy name shall be
Henceforth the watchword of the good and free,
Whose hearts are nerved to battle for the *Right!*
In the dark days before us—'mid the night
Of a stern tyranny, we'll think of thee,
Martyr of God! and strike for Liberty
With an unwavering faith and arm of might!
Not unavenged, Oh brother! shall thy blood
Sink in the ground! its voice shall upward ring,
A fearful cry to wake the slumbering,
Reaching the ear of an avenging God!
And millions, roused, shall swear upon thy grave,
Death to oppression! Freedom to the slave!

Weep—for a brother fallen!—weep for him
Who first hath found a glorious martyrdom!
Weep for the broken Heart!—the desolate home
Whose light of gladness is forever dim!
Who of us, next, on Slavery's bloody altar
Shall meet his doom? Thou only knowest, God!
Yet will we tread the path our brother trod,
Trusting in thee! Our spirits shall not falter
Amidst the darkness of the coming strife,
Though drunk with agony the soul should reel!
Here, *Lovejoy!* on thy bloody grave we kneel,
And pledge anew our fortune—honor—life—
All—for the slave!
Farewell!—thy rest is won!
One tear for thee!—then, strengthened, press we on!

Philadelphia, Nov. 28, 1837. W. H. B.

From the Philanthropist.

"THE VOICE OF BLOOD."

I'M THE VOICE OF BLOOD! and I will wail along
As the wind sweeps sullenly by,
All choked and still is its wonted song,
As soft, or solemn, or brisk, or strong,
It sung to the answering sky.
One breath, one shuddering breath—a moan
Like the flap of a pall on a coffin of stone,
Or a dead man's last long sigh!—

It comes to thee, ALTON; by day or by night
Where Freedom's champion stood;
And the child, when he hears it, shall cry for light!
Tho' the sun is high and the day is bright;
And the mother, in frantic mood,
Shall shriek as it mutters, the cradle near,
In a whisper so loud that the dead might hear;
"I AM BLOOD!—THE VOICE OF BLOOD!"

Wake, wake ILLINOIS! for through prairie and glen,
There is blood! there's the voice of blood!
It bids thee arouse; or the rust on their chain,
Shall scar the fair necks of your daughters—a stain
Bleached alone by your hearts' hot flood:
Your sons low in manacles crouch at your feet,
Where the prairie-fowl starts as the young lambkins bleat,
In the fields where your free dwellings stood.
Rouse, rouse thee!—or purchase for Freedom a shroud,
And bury your hopes in her grave:
Then hush'd be the glee of your laborers proud,
As, driven with the mule and the ass, in a crowd
They slink to the task of the slave;—
With a curse on their lip and a scowl in their eye
As they mope by your tomb-stones and tauntingly cry,
"Ho! here go the sons of the brave!"

From the Christian Mirror.

THE MARTYRED LOVEJOY.

The Patriot for his country falls—
The Hero dies where honor calls—
Lovejoy! for nobler ends thou'st bled—
For the whole race thy blood is shed!

Father in Heaven! to Thee we turn!
In hopeless grief we would not mourn—
In Thee we trust! Oh, wilt thou bless
This cause of Truth and Righteousness!

Be Freedom's champions all inspired
With such a zeal as Lovejoy fired!
Rejoice for Truth to give up all,
And even *die*, if duty call!

Prepared to be sung at the Solemn Commemoration Meeting in Concord, N. H.

Thou'rt fallen, our first martyr!
In thine early grave thou'rt lying,
Defender of our charter
For freedom nobly dying—
Thy blood's first sacrifice
To Slavery's demon given,
But still from earth it cries
In thunder tones to Heaven!

Thou'rt fallen—though we're weeping,
We cannot now deplore thee:
The tempest still is sweeping,
But the turf lies lightly o'er thee:
While evil men are scorning,
Triumphant o'er thy breast,
Thou'rt waking to the morning
Of Heaven's soft Sabbath rest!

Happy art thou, our brother!
In this dark and evil time,
When clouds arounds us gather
To have fallen in thy prime;
From the sorrow and the wasting,
The hope deferred and lone,
From the grief that we are tasting,
O, happy to have gone!

Yet, we shrink not from the trial—
Nor to die as thou hast died—
Till, by the seven-fold vial,
The land be sanctified;
And thy spirit shall be leading,
Unseen, but not in vain,
Our holy warfare speeding,
Till the land hath burst its chain!

M.

SELECT STANZAS.

He is dead! but his spirit lives on
In the quenchless devotion we feel;
And think not, ye despots, we'll turn at your frown,
Or quail at your fagot and steel.
Ye thought to extinguish his name,
When you doomed him to death and despair,
When ye laughed as he writhed in the conquering flame,
And ye drowned with your curses his prayer.
But he's gone as a glorious conqueror home,
And his name shall be hallowed through ages to come.

Will Freemen fear the ruffian band
Who struck the dauntless Martyr low?
Will Freemen tremble when the land
Is trodden by the deadly foe?
No! by the Eternal Heavens! No;
Let this our glorious motto be—
"Even though the storm may fiercer grow,
We live or die for liberty."
We bear the flag our fathers bore,
When Princes bade them kneel;
We swear the oath our fathers swore—
Their hopes, and all their valor feel.

Lamented Lovejoy! cold in death thy form—
No demon's shout disturbs thy silent rest;
Thou hearest not the raging of the storm,
That now is rolling through the mighty West;
For the cold clod is lying on thy breast.
The flag of freedom o'er thy dust shall wave,
And round thy mouldering bones shall tread the ransomed slave.

EFFECT ON THE PUBLIC MIND.

The news of the massacre of Mr. Lovejoy produced a thrill of horror throughout the free states, such as has not been elicited in a long time.

AMERICAN ANTI-SLAVERY SOCIETY.

The Executive Committee of the American Anti-Slavery Society immediately held a meeting, and adopted the following resolutions:—

Whereas, intelligence has been received by this Committee, that the Rev. Elijah P. Lovejoy, while defending his press, on the night of the 7th instant, was by lawless men deliberately murdered, for his constancy in maintaining the right of freedom of discussion, and his devoted zeal in the cause of universal liberty—

Resolved, That in view of a transaction so bloody, so open, and tending so much to disgrace us as a people, it becomes the inhabitants of this land, everywhere, to hold solemn convocations before God; that, while they render thanks for his mercies, and make confession of their sins, they may supplicate him, that he will not yet turn away from a nation whose criminal indifference to the oppression of the slave has, at length, emboldened the lawless to the murder of the free.

That public religious services be held in commemoration of this event, on Tuesday next, in the Broadway Tabernacle in this city—and that a public collection be there taken up for the benefit of the widow and orphans of our deceased fellow citizen and brother, who are left dependent on others by the murder of the husband and the father.

That we recommend a similar course to our fellow-citizens everywhere throughout the land.

That while we mourn for our departed brother, as the first martyr in the holy cause of abolition in this nation, we praise God for the noble sentiments which he avowed, and the devotedness with which he offered himself on the altar of human rights.

That we deem it due to the memory of the deceased to state, that he was slain, so far as we have knowledge of the facts, whilst engaged in defending his property and his rights in a manner justified by the laws of his and of all other civilized countries.

That we deeply sympathise with the friends of human rights in Illinois, who have labored and suffered with the martyred Lovejoy, and ardently hope they may persevere with redoubled diligence in all Christian efforts to maintain the freedom of speech and the press, against the violence of American oppressors.

That a copy of these resolutions be transmitted, by the Secretary, to Mrs. Lovejoy, together with a deep expression of our condolence with her and her bereaved little one in this affliction.

Numerous public meetings were held, in pursuance of the above recommendation. Many sermons were preached by clergymen of different denominations, some of which have been published. Perhaps the most impressive religious meeting was that held in the Broadway Tabernacle.

VOICE FROM THE CRADLE OF LIBERTY.

So great is the subserviency of leading influences in our commercial cities, to the dictation of slavery, that the Mayor and Aldermen at first rejected a request of a large number of citizens, headed by the distinguished Unitarian divine, Dr. Wm. E. Channing, for the use of Faneuil Hall, to send forth from the old Cradle of Liberty, a voice against the despotism of mobs, and the destruction of Freedom's chosen engine, the press. But so loud a vote of remonstrance was raised by *the people*, that the vote was soon re-considered, and the meeting was held, December 7th, and attended by an immense crowd of citizens.

[*From the Boston Daily Advertiser.*]

MEETING AT FANEUIL HALL.—Agreeably to previous notice, a meeting was held on Friday morning, in Faneuil Hall, for the purpose of expressing the opinions of this community on the "freedom of speech, the liberty of the press, and the importance of maintaining the supremacy of the laws." The meeting was called to order by Mr. Abner Phelps. Hon. Jona. Phillips was chosen moderator. Mr. Phillips read the petition for the use of the Hall, and briefly stated the purposes of the meeting. G. W. Phillips and John A. Bolles were chosen secretaries. Prayer was offered by Rev. E. M. P. Wells, of the Episcopal church. The Rev. Dr. Channing then arose and addressed the meeting, explaining his motives in wishing to call a meeting of the citizens, and the manner in which he became identified with the call—it having originated with himself. Benj. F. Hallet, Esq., presented the following resolutions, prepared, as he stated, by the Rev. Dr. Channing:

Resolved, That our civil and religious liberties which have come down to us from our fathers sealed with their blood, are a most precious bequest, and that when liberty is invaded, this consecrated Hall is the chosen spot where its friends should meet together to pledge themselves to its support.

That we are assembled here to assume the badge of no party, to narrow ourselves to no local or temporary interests, but to maintain the supremacy of the laws, and to give expression and support to those universal principles of justice and freedom, on which popular institutions and the hopes of philanthropy rest.

That it has pleased God to commit to this people, above all others, the cause of human freedom; that we are called to the high office of manifesting the power of free institutions to enable and bless a people; and that in proving false to this trust, we shall not only cast away our own happiness, but shall betray the interests of the human race, and shall deserve the condemning sentence of all nations and of future times.

That to offer violence to the rights of the citizens in a free country, where these rights are understood and recognized and taken under protection of the laws, is a more heinous crime and of more fatal influence, than the oppressions of absolute hereditary power.

That by the ordination of Providence we are passing through a stage of society, in which principles and institutions are subjected to the severest scrutiny: and that, in such a period, earnest conflicts of opinion can not be escaped, and ought to be cheerfully endured, as inseparable from the exercise of a privilege which is essential to the progress and best interests of the human race.

That it is the fundamental idea of the freedom of speech and the press, that the citizen shall be protected from violence, in uttering opinions opposed to those which prevail around him;—that if by such freedom nothing more were intended than the liberty of publishing what none would deny, then absolute governments might boast of it as loudly as republics; so that, to put the citizen in peril, on the ground that he presumptuously persevere in uttering what is unpopular, or what the majority do not approve, is to assail this freedom in its very foundation, and to destroy its very life.

That in a free country, the laws, enacted according to the prescriptions of the Constitution are the voice of the people—are the only forms by which the sovereignty of the people is exercised and expressed, and that, of consequence, a mob, or its combination of citizens for the purpose of suspending by force the administration of the laws, or of taking away the rights which these have guarantied, is treason against the people, a contempt of their sovereignty, and deserves to be visited with exemplary punishment.

Resolved, That the spirit of mobs is a spirit of indiscriminate destruction; that when the press shall have become its prey, its next victim will be property; that there is no power so terrible as human passion, unbridled by principle and law, and inflamed to madness by the sympathies of a crowd; and that if we silently and passively abandon any portion of our fellow-citizens to this power, we shall have no right to complain, when our own turn shall have come to feel its rapaciousness and fury.

That in this country, the mightiest influence is public opinion; that mobs can not prevail without a criminal apathy in the public mind; that one of the darkest omens of our times, is the indifference with which the nation has looked on the triumphs of lawless force, and that the time is now come for this people to shake of their lethargy, to vindicate the insulted majesty of the laws, and pronounce a sentence on unprincipled violence, which the reckless and turbulent will be unable to withstand.

That when a fellow-citizen has been destroyed in defending property and the press, it is alike weak and criminal to reproach him as responsible for the deed, because he refused to surrender his undoubted rights at the command of his murderers; that with equal justice the highwayman may throw the blame of his crime on the slaughtered traveler, or who refuses when summoned to surrender his purse; and even if our fellow-citizens, who recently fell in defence of the freedom of the press, was driven by the violence which assailed him into rash and injudicious deeds, we are bound so to express our grief as in no degree to screen his lawless assailants from the reprobation which is their due:

That the Christian is not authorised by his religion to look with indifference on public affairs, and that he ought particularly to be roused by acts of cruelty and violence which degrade our country to the level of heathenism.

That we deem this occasion too solemn for the language of passion; that we have come to this place to establish and diffuse the principles of order and peace; that we acknowledge our obligation to cherish in the community a spirit of mutual forbearance and good will; and that we earnestly desire, whilst we vindicate the rights of speech and the press; that these may be most conscientiously exercised in obedience to the dictates of justice and philanthropy.

That our affection for our country is undiminished by the public crimes by which it is dishonored; that we implore for it the blessing of Almighty God; and that we pledge ourselves according to our power, to sustain its laws, to give stability to its union, and to transmit its free institutions unimpaired to posterity.

The meeting was eloquently addressed by G. T. Hillard, Esq., Wendell Phillips Esq., and George Bond, in favor of the resolutions, and by the *Attorney General*, Austin, in opposition, after which the resolutions were adopted by an overwhelming majority.

At one of the preliminary meetings, to procure the use of the Hall, held pursuant to *public* notice, in the Old Supreme Court Room, the following were unanimously adopted;

Whereas, in times when any constitutional right, affecting life, liberty and property, is denied or called in question by our rulers, it is peculiarly befitting a free people to assemble together to consult on the common good. And Whereas, FANEUIL HALL, belonging to us all, and 'consecrated' to liberty and free discussion, has been denied to a portion of the citizens who petitioned for leave to meet there for the purpose of 'noticing in a suitable manner the recent murder, in the city of Alton, of a native of New England, a citizen of the free state of Illinois, *who fell in defence of the freedom of the press.*'

Resolved, That the citizens here assembled, appealing to the searcher of hearts for the rectitude of their intentions, will discard all party considerations, all topics about which there can be a division among the friends of liberty, and confine themselves to the single question now at issue between the people and their rulers in this city, viz: the right to hold a public meeting to give utterance to their deep abhorrence of the spirit of mobs, and their solemn reprobation of the violence which has been offered to the freedom of speech and the press, by the murder of a citizen while engaged in maintaining that sacred right.

That when a citizen of these United States has fallen by lawless violence in defence of the liberty of the press; the question should never be asked by Freemen what doctrine did he support, or to what party or sect did he belong; but was he standing under the broad shield of the Constitution of the Union and

PHILADELPHIA SATURDAY COURIER.

☞ THIS PAPER CIRCULATES EACH PUBLICATION OVER 33,000 COPIES IN ALL PARTS OF THE UNITED STATES. ☞ TERMS—$2 PER ANNUM IN ADVANCE.

PRINTED AND PUBLISHED BY
A. M'MAKIN & E. HOLDEN,
At No. 72 Dock Street, corner of Walnut.

Philadelphia, Sept. 7, 1839.

TERMS.

Of Subscription—$3 per annum: $2 if paid in advance $1,25 in advance for six months.

Of Advertising—$1 per square for each insertion. No yearly advertising admitted. These terms have been adopted both because the number of subscribers are so much larger than all the daily papers united, as to make them actually cheaper, and because a repetition of old advertisements affords no interest to the readers.

☞ Papers discontinued only at the option of the publishers, while arrearages are due.

☞ Any person forwarding $10 will be entitled to six copies.

☞ When a single paper is ordered by an agent, and postage accrues, it is invariably charged to the subscriber.

☞ All remittances of money by mail are acknowledged in the "*Receipts by Mail.*"

☞ POSTAGE on letters must invariably be paid.

☞ TRAVELLING AGENTS will much oblige by sending the *numbers* and *time paid for*, as well as invariably the names paid.

☞ Directions must always be accompanied with the name of the subscriber, and the Post Office at which a paper is discontinued or paid for, and in case of removal, the office from, as well as to, which the paper is to be changed.

☞ When individuals wish to subscribe to the Courier, a sure way is to enclose the money in a letter, and direct it to us. Or, if they choose, their Postmasters will attend to it for them. Postmasters are always our agents.

☞ Small notes on all solvent Banks are received at par in payment of subscriptions.

☞ Moneys collected by travelling and local agents should be forwarded to us by mail as soon as received.

☞ Any subscriber may remit to us direct by mail, suitable sums. The mails are always safe.

☞ Any of our country brethren who insert our advertisement, will receive the Courier regularly, and the Views of Fairmount and Girard College, if they desire them.

☞ We sometimes find that subscribers, who have heretofore paid in advance, think strange because we have not sent them the two Views. It should be observed that we promise them to all who may *hereafter* pay up arrearages and a year in advance. The object is a trifling return of our good wishes to those who promptly pay for their Courier.

Interesting to Subscribers.

The following is an extract of a letter which the Postmaster General lately addressed to the Postmaster at Newport, R. I.: "Postmasters may enclose the money in a letter to the publisher of a newspaper, to pay the subscription of a third person, and frank the letter."

To Readers and Correspondents.

"Autumn," a prose sketch by our correspondent, R. D., (who has occasionally favoured our readers with very creditable poetical productions,) will come in season next week.

The author of "THE STORY OF AMERICAN LIFE."—A week or two since we intimated that the author of "The Father" was probably the writer of the first named tale. She informs us that she was not, and we are gratified to say so, in the pleasant opportunity of making the acquaintance of the latter, as we should be equally happy to make that of the former. They are both fair correspondents, from whose pens productions will be ever welcome.

"The Dying Student," and the "Temperance Ode" shall appear.

"L. S.'s friends of his childhood," (if they are sensible people) would not thank him if we should print the lines he has addressed to them. But we shan't.

"W. N." is declined.

"P. P." will have an opportunity to sing to our readers, when the proper season shall have arrived.

"Improvisator, by Paul Sobolewski," will be printed.

"D." will appear.

The remarks of "W." on the Cotton Trade, will be inserted in our next.

"A Subscriber" is informed that we cannot furnish him with complete volumes of any of the former years' Saturday Courier. Perhaps some of our subscribers can? If so, and they will inform us of the particular volumes for sale, with the price, we will announce it.

☞ In our slight notice of Judge Hopkinson, last week, some way another we were made to say that the Judge had delivered some of the best practical lectures before the "Franklin Institute," [illegible] into the little paragraph, except it be that our compositors (good fellows) are such profound admirers of the practical philosophy of [illegible] that they like to [illegible] occasions.

The Silk Business in our Country.

That we have taken proper interest in the Silk Culture, we think our readers will bear us testimony. We have faithfully and diligently presented them all new facts that were pertinent and available. But we have not chosen to keep our columns crammed, week after week, with Munchausen stories, far more likely to disgust, than to persuade, the good, common sense, practical farmers of our land, into this branch of national industry.

The present aspect of the business, however, we regard as peculiarly justifying a candid statement of facts, which may be relied upon.

1st. As it is always with all business that is comparatively new, and making its way in our country, there will be many men who will rush into it without the least calculation or the least knowledge. So has it been, to some extent, in the silk business. Men, who did not first inform themselves, as to the proper mode of taking care of and cultivating the trees, have purchased those which had been sold and re sold at auction, until all their vitality was destroyed, and when they were planted, they were about as good as so many dead trees. Great losses by the inexperienced have been submitted to the present season, in this way.

2d. But that constitutes no objection to prudent, practical, intelligent men (and every body may easily render themselves so,) going successfully, profitably, and permanently forward with the Silk culture. So far as the coming season is concerned, it is an argument in favour of increased efforts by the prudent, because it is indisputably true that the loss of a considerable portion of last season's crop of trees, by the speculating mania, and the bandying of stock, by the uninformed, will go far to diminish the amount of trees which will be this fall brought into the market for sale, and materially contribute to render prices high.

3d. This has proved to be the case, from all the sales that have been thus far made, this season. For instance, in June, July and August, the contracts, in some parts of Connecticut, for

Morus Multicaulis Trees, amounted to 112,000, at an average of 30 cts. per tree.

In Pennsylvania, New Jersey and Maryland, within two weeks, we notice sales of

210 Multicaulis Trees, at an average of 37½ cents, different lots and at different prices, from 25 to 50 cents per tree.

Within the last week, sales are observed, the totals of which are

243,000 Multicaulis Trees, the average of which is 40 cts per tree.

These prices are considerably higher than they were last year, at corresponding periods, and appear to justify the position we assumed. But the loss of a portion of last year's crop, through the miserable management of speculators, will go far to make prices uniformly high the present season.

4th. It is now established beyond a doubt that our soil and climate are peculiarly favourable to the Silk culture. The judicious farmers are seeing this, and taking hold of it. They see that it is a culture which can be added to their present farming operations, with little or no augmentation of labour, because their children, or perhaps aged persons, dependent upon them for a livelihood, may perform the labour of the Silk culture, and thus, instead of remaining *dependent*, they may become *independent* members of their household.

5th. The fluctuations in the price of the Cotton crops, are beginning to convince many of the most intelligent of the Southern Planters, that a safer plan would be to devote a portion of their plantations to the Silk Culture. They see that we may and shall ultimately, become exporters of Raw Silk to England, as we now do Cotton, and more profitably, and far less likely to fluctuation in price. At all events, they see plain enough that, so long as we have to send twenty or twenty-five millions of dollars out of the country, every year, to pay foreign nations for our silk importions, there is a certainty that for years and years onward, the farmers who go permanently into the Silk culture, will always find a cash market at home, for all the raw Silk that can possibly be produced.

But so much has already been said on this subject, many will be disposed to enquire if any thing has yet been accomplished toward the actual produce of silk itself. We have made some enquiry in reference to this matter, and learn that the experiments in feeding the worm, in this neighborhood, have been very successful as well as extensive. The Mondendron Company have fed, we are told, about two millions of worms. The Messrs. Cheyneys nearly as many, and with unusual success. James Swaim, Esq., of this city, advertised to purchase 10,000 pounds of the Morus Multicaulis leaves, he having a cocoonery near Bristol eighty feet long by twenty-eight in width, capable of feeding one million of worms. He intends exporting a considerable portion of his reeled silk to France. Some beautiful specimens of silk manufactured into ribbons, vesting, plush, &c., were recently exhibited at the Agricultural Society in this city by Dr. Meigs. This was cultivated at Harmony, the well known establishment of Mr. Rapp. Mr. Raymond, hatter, Chesnut street, has for sale already very superior sewing silk, silk braid, guard chains, cord, ribbon, &c., manufactured of American silk, from worms fed this season [illegible] Morus Multicaulis. Competent judges [illegible] it equal to any and superior to m[illegible] the sewing silk especially is [illegible] quality, strong, fine, glossy, and perfect[illegible]. The cocoonery of P. Physick, Esq., son of the distinguished and truly eminent Dr. Physick, has attracted great attention, being, it is said, the largest in the world. It is one hundred and twenty feet long, thirty-five feet wide, and three stories high. Not having had leisure yet to accept the invitation to visit this establishment, we avail ourselves of a portion of the notice made by our neighbour of the United States Gazette. He says:

"We saw a small room in which the eggs of the silk worm are hatched, and learned that in a single morning no less than thirty-five thousand were hatched in it.

"The *feeding* room, which is also the place where the *spinning* is done, is an immense hall, supplied with rows of shelves, in which were hurdles for the worms, many thousands of which, of different sizes, were eating as heartily as if they were dining out; arrangements were made immediately above the hurdles for spinning, or formation of the cocoons. The galleries between these ranges of shelves were laid with railways, and *locomotive* steps for reaching the different hurdles, were placed on the rails, so that the persons thus employed could move along with entire ease."

The produce of silk from this extensive establishment, is already before the public, and in reference to its excellent quality, some of our Market street silk merchants, as well as Mr. Wiltbank, have certified. The certificate of this latter gentleman is the more valuable from the fact of his being largely engaged in the manufacture of silk, importing himself the raw material to supply his spindles.

Mr. Maupay has converted his green houses into cocooneries, feeding a million of worms.—Messrs. L. & S. L. Bailey fed 100,000. Mr. Hazlehurst, on the other side of the river, fed 100,000. Joseph White, 40,000. At Camden, cocooneries have been made by Mr. Ellis, the Messrs. Hatch, Mr. A. Browning, and others. The beautiful pocket handkerchiefs, sewing silk, and other articles, made from silk raised by Messrs. Carson at Lancaster, have been much admired, as have also been the Westchester Silk Company. Mr. Esher, at Germantown, fed 100,000. Mr. S. C. Humes, 400,000, and has arrangements for 100,000,000 worms. Mr. Pierce, in the neighborhood of this city, 500,000. Mr. Physick 200,000. Mr. Church, at Bethlehem, produced a large amount of raw silk. Mr. Atwood manufactured 30,000 skeins silk twist. Mr. Newkirk, opposite this city, fed 50,000 worms. I. W. Cooper, 30,000. The Messrs. Bradshaw, 50,000. All these have been eminently successful. A number of villages, both in this and the adjoining States, have entered with spirit into the silk business. For instance, at the little village of Haddonfield, in New Jersey, W. [illegible]; S. M. Reeves & Co. one million; the Rev. E. Lippincott, 250,000; Mr. Thornton, 200,000; Miss Handry 200,000; Miss Clement 200,000; [illegible] 20,000 to 100,000. These are all feeding on the genuine morus multicaulis. This is but a beginning to what is intended next year. Several companies are forming to go into it extensively.

In several of the Southern States, and in Ohio, a number of persons have commenced in earnest the feeding of worms, while in most of the New England States an amount of silk will be produced this year, which will surprise those who have entertained doubts on this subject.

But it will too far extend this article should we proceed to enumerate all the cocooneries and manufactures of American Silk which have come to our knowledge. They are numerous and on the increase. We shall content ourselves with remarking that the quantity, and more especially the quality of silk produced this season, are both amply sufficient—or ought to be—to satisfy the most incredulous. We therefore conclude by subjoining the following evidence of the interest which our New York neighbours are beginning to take in the matter.

Exhibition of Silk.

The Fair of the American Institute will be held at New York on the 17th of October next. A formal resolution of a large meeting, consisting of most of the distinguished members of the legislature, and others, held at the capitol in Albany, was unanimously adopted, requesting the American Institute to call a convention of silk culturists, and those friendly to their interests, during the ensuing fair. In consequence the managers say:

"Arrangements are making for a full display of American Silk in all forms, from the cocoon to the finished fabric. Much good, we think, will result to the country from the preparations for the raising of silk. Our climate is peculiarly congenial to the insect that produces it. The women, children, and infirm persons scattered among our population, from whose labours little or nothing is now realized, are competent to supply twenty millions of dollars value in silk, per annum, instead of which we have imported in one year nearly double of that amount. A sum double the value of the whole exported products of the United States, for the same period, from all our boasted fisheries, with all the exports from our forests, of skins, furs, timber, masts, and all our manufactures of wood; our naval stores, tar, pitch, turpentine, pot and pearl ashes, &c., and also from our almost innumerable farms: all our exported beef, tallow, hides and cattle, butter, cheese, pork, bacon, horses, mules, &c., with our entire exports of wheat, corn and flour, superadded. The whole catalogue of this formidable portion of a nation's hard earnings for foreign exportation did not, in 1836, equal twelve millions of dollars, while the imports of silk the same year exceeded twenty millions of dollars; and by including silk and worsted goods, of which silk constituted an important part, amounted to over twenty-three millions five hundred thousand dollars. This alarming statement the report from the treasury department will fully verify. Is it not high time that silk should command our attention?"

"The Mammoth Scheme" again.

We have done justice to the public in regard to the great imposition, attempted to be played upon the community, under the stolen name of "Sylvester & Co. of New York." The Governor of Florida has—honorably to himself and the cause of morality and truth—put an injunction upon the pretended lottery. This stops the designs of the swindlers who were at the bottom of it. Many of the best Southern papers denounce the whole concern in no measured terms. The editor of the Mobile Chronicle says he has made a closer calculation than we did, in regard to the cost of advertising, and taking the terms in his own paper as a basis, for *all* the papers of the Union, the single item of advertising from May to January, would amount to $649,000, to say nothing of the papers of the West Indies and the British Provinces. Will any body tell who were the swinders at the bottom of this "Mammoth Scheme" to cheat the public? They should be holden up to the contempt and scorn of the whole country.—But it is gratifying that the press has succeeded in arousing the action of proper authority, to prevent the furtherance of this grand scheme of swindling and mischief.

Sentence of Dr. Dyott.

An immense throng assembled on Saturday, to learn the sentence of the "Manual Labor Banker." Judge Todd pronounced it. The sentence was "*three years solitary confinement in the cells of the Eastern Penitentiary at hard labor.*" Judge Bouvier remarked that he was in favor of dealing a sentence of at least *five years*, that the magnitude of the prisoners frauds, and the number of sufferers, who were his dupes, demanded a heavy sentence.

The prisoner was then conducted to a carriage, and started off on his way to Francisville Penitentiary. The crowd in front of the Court House manifested their approbation of the sentence by shouts.

Previous, however, to Dr. Dyott's leaving the Court for the last time, he put in an affidavit, asseverating that he had no property concealed, and that he was pennyless. He is 70 years old. Let young men, commencing trade, take a lesson from so lamentable a case and so fearful a result.

Suits are still pending against Mr. Ridgway for the deposites.

Dr. Hines in Limbo.

This notorious swindler has been caught at last. He was arrested in Cincinnati at the instance of a gentleman whom he robbed last year of his pocket book, while in a steamboat near Memphis, Tennessee, which contained $360. Hines made a speech, and told Judge Doty that he was not answerable except to the laws of Tennessee; but the Judge thought differently, and sent him to prison, till he can be demanded by the authorities of that State. He ought to send his likeness to all the landlords of the country, for they stand a slim chance of getting any thing else for their "feed and fixings" for the Doctor. "Our Landlord" (him of "The Merchants") took his pay in discounting notes from his diary, certainly for the edification of our readers, if not for his own amusement.

Crim. Con.—Flounders vs. Fuller.

On a former occasion, we mentioned that Mr. Flounders, a book, chart and map agent, had commenced a suit against Rev. Zelotes Fuller, for an alledged assault and battery on his wife, while the husband was absent from the city. It will be pertinent here to observe that Mr. Fuller is not now, nor has he been for several years, the pastor of any church.

The charge of Mr. Flounders—as we learn it—is this. That Mr. Fuller frequently called at his house, while he was absent, on the pretence of wishing to hear from Mr. Flounders, who was then travelling on his agency business in New York. On one occasion, Mr. Flounders alledges that Mr. Fuller went or followed Mrs. Flounders up stairs into her bed-chamber, on the avowed business of desiring her to read to him a letter, which she said she had received from her husband—Mr. Fuller declaring that he wished to procure her husband's agency to sell copies of an engraved likeness of himself which had been recently published. Mr. Fuller had married Mr. Flounders to Eliza a few months previously, and was therefore acquainted with the wife. Mr. Flounders avers that the assault and battery took place at this interview, viz: that Mr Fuller attempted to kiss Eliza, the recently made wife of Mr. Flounders, and, consequently he brought a suit to recover damages therefor.

Mr. Fuller, on his part, avers this is all a get-up to extort money; and forthwith brought a suit against Mr. Flounders, for a libel upon his character. He gravely asseverates, that instead of his having forgot himself so much as to attempt to kiss Eliza, it was all the other way, and that Eliza, *sans ceremonie*, actually did kiss him. He says that while she was sitting upon the couch beside him, she looked him smilingly in the face, and observed—

"Why, Mr. Fuler, what beautiful white teeth you've got; I've a good mind to kiss you."

"And," continued Mr. Fuller, "before I knew what she was going to do, she leaned over and *did* kiss me upon the face. I then said, well, Eliza, as I did not pay you the usual compliment when I married you, perhaps I had better do so now, and so I arose and kissed Eliza upon the forehead, and then left the room."

[illegible] and Messrs. J. Brewster and Allison for the defence. The court room is exceedingly full with the curious.

A small portion of the testimony is appended. When the trial closes, we shall give the pith of both sides.

Mrs. Elizabeth Flounders.—A few days after my husband went away he called first; he said he called to hear from my husband, and when he was coming back; he spoke about my husband and did'nt stay long. I had lost a child about that time. When he was there on the last time he came in without knocking, and asked me why I did'nt say "come in." I said he did not knock. He asked me if I was'nt lonesome, and said it was too bad for me to be staying alone; he said he wanted a kiss very bad, and had'nt had a kiss since he had kissed his sister; he said he wished he had got aquainted with me before William did, that he loved me and wished I was his wife. He then took hold of me violently, and in an indelicate manner, and kissed me by force. He said he'd go down then, and went to the door. He hadn't hold of me a minute. He pushed me back against the bed, and that's all. After I was away from him, he said he was sorry for what he had done, and didn't want me to tell William. I said if he would go right out of the room, I would not tell William; he said he would go, but was afraid I would tell William. I told him that I would not tell, and then he said I must keep my promise; he went out of the room then.

Wisconsin—Climate, Soil, Extent, Productions.

The other week, we bestowed some attention upon the sister Territory of Iowa, and to-day we will take a hasty glance at Wisconsin.

This territory is becoming interesting to every portion of the country, from many causes. It is fast filling with enterprising individuals from other and distant parts of the country, and they uniformly give so favorable an account of its advantages, that others are looking thither for the home of their future days.

Wisconsin is situated between the latitudes of 41 deg. 40 min. and 49 deg. north, and is bounded on the east by Lake Michigan and on the west by the Mississippi river. The whole territory contains more than 8,000 square miles, and has now about 30,000 inhabitants. It is well watered in the interior by the numerous springs, and by large rivers, which are navigable; and is most eligibly situated for commerce. It has a variety of soils, all of which are warm and fertile; and in every part of the country limestone is abundant. It possesses a salubrity of climate which is unequalled in the West.

The general face of the country is undulating without mountains, and is covered with grass. For the purpose of grazing, it is not surpassed. The farmers raise wheat, rye, oats, barley, corn and potatoes. Thirty bushels of wheat to the acre, and forty bushels of corn, with common cultivation, are not unusual crops. The potatoes are superior to any in the United States.

An intelligent correspondent of the New Orleans Bulletin, after a residence of 18 years, speaks in the highest terms of its resources, climate and natural advantages.

Roads are being constructed in various directions through the country, at the expense of the United States, and, it is understood, they are about to open a free steamboat navigation from Green Bay to the Mississippi, by the Fox and Wisconsin rivers. For these works of internal improvement, the people pay no taxes; and they are only taxed about one mill on the dollar for all the expenses of their government. In this respect, the people of Wisconsin are differently situated from those of other western States.

It may also be important to foreigners to know that, by the laws of Wisconsin, *aliens* can hold and convey real estate, the same as native born citizens, which cannot be done in most of the States.

In Wisconsin timber and prairie are interspersed so that farms can be obtained with a due proportion of each. There are now more than one hundred townships of six miles square, or 2,304,000 acres, in the Green Bay land district, which are offered for sale by Government at one dollar and twenty-five cents the acre, no part of which has been purchased by individuals. This is a good opportunity for farmers and mechanics to make a selection, who wish to obtain cheap and comfortable homes, without competition in price; and almost every part of this tract is accessible to boats by Green Bay and the Fox river.

We look upon it as important at times, to make known, to men of enterprise and industry, the opportunities which various portions of the West present, and with this view we have glanced at Wisconsin.

We think it worthy high consideration of the thousands in our overrun cities, many of whom never expect, by remaining in them, to advance themselves by a life of toil an inch beyond living from day to day, from hand to mouth. Every portion of the overteeming West presents rare lands, that with ordinary industry and prudence, will, in a few years advance them to plenty, independence and happiness, for no men are so well off and independent, as the frugal owners and cultivators of their own vineyards.

Decision of the Court on board the Washington in relation to the Mutineers.

The court held the best portion of two days, and resulted in the following decisions—

That Joseph Cinquez, the leader, and 38 others, as named in the indictment, stand committed for trial before the next Circuit Court at Hartford, to be holden on the 17th day of September, inst.

The three girls, and Antonio, the cabin boy, are ordered to give bonds in the sum of $100 each, to appear before the said court, and give evidence in the aforesaid case, and for want of such bonds to be committed to the county jail in the city of New Haven. These persons were not indicted.

Lieut. R. W. Meade, Don Jose Ruiz, and Don Pedro Montez, are ordered to recognise in the sum of $100 each, to appear and give evidence in said case, before the aforesaid court.

The court then finally adjourned, having given an order to the U. S. Marshal to transport them to New Haven.

Senor Ruiz states that many of the slaves were attached to him, and that they did not intend to kill him, but to take him with them to Africa, and then let him find his way back as best he might.—Senor Montez, however, would have been killed beyond a doubt.

Look Out for Thieves.

The season is now at hand, when the idle and dissolute, who have been living upon the refuse of the markets and fruit stalls, and sleeping in the open air, must "make a raise" for cold weather, off of some unwary housekeeper, whose spare plate, or portable furniture, is left within grabbing distance. That family is lucky who buys vigilance for the winter at the cost of but a slight experimental inroad upon the chattles. Those who do not wish to wait for such warning, will do well to take it from this paragraph.

A Sword of Honor.

Messrs. Bailey & Kitchen of Chesnut st., have just finished a most splendid tribute of respect, voted by the State of Delaware to her gallant citizen, COL. S. B. DAVIS.—It is gold mounted straight sword, with a very richly wrought guard and handle, with a helmet surrounded by the American Eagle, holding in his beak a rich chain attached to the guard. The blade is beautifully etched with a view of the battle of Lewistown on one side and the arms of the State of Delaware on the other. The scabbard is ornamented with rich chasing, and bears the following inscription:

Presented by the State of Delaware to COL. S. B. DAVIS, for his gallant conduct in defence of Lewistown on the 6th and 7th of April, 1813.

The arms of the State are engraved in a shield on the guard, and on the opposite side the family crest and motto, *Tout ou rien*.

The Woodlands.

This lovely place, belonging to the estate of the late William Hamilton, Esq., situated on the west bank of the Schuylkill a few rods above Grey's Ferry, has been taken by those gentlemen of untiring enterprise, Messrs. Hirst & Dreer, seedsmen, of 95 Chesnut street, who are now busied in carrying out the extensive plans of [illegible] ful and liberal minded projector, intending to do [illegible] an ornament to the neighborhood.

Twenty Arrested—Eight Shot.

The troops which were sent last week to quell the disturbance on the canal in Allegheny county, Md., have adopted very decisive measures with all who resisted their authority. About twenty of the ringleaders have been made prisoners, eight or ten have been shot and several wounded, one of whom is not expected to recover. Several shantees were burnt down and others torn up, by the troops, whose owners had refused admittance when demanded; and all the fire arms found in the possession of the canal hands were seized and destroyed on the spot. Their severe treatment it is said, was no worse than exigency required.

United States and Texas.

The Hon. John Forsyth, on the part of the United States Government, and Gen. Memucan Hunt on the part of the Texan Government, have been appointed commissioners to run and mark the boundary line between the two countries, as established by the treaty of 1828, between the United States and Mexico. The ratifications of the convention to this effect have been exchanged, and the Commissioners must enter upon their duties on or before the 12th of October next.

RECORD OF POLITICS.

APPOINTMENT BY THE GOVERNOR.—Samuel Humes to be inspector of tobacco for the Port of Philadelphia, in the room of John Humes, deceased.

SOUTH CAROLINA.—The Hon. F. H. Elmore, member of Congress elect from Barnwell district, South Carolina, has resigned his seat.

WISCONSIN.—Judge Doty (Whig) has been re-elected to Congress, by a majority over both his competitors.

RHODE ISLAND ELECTION.—The Providence Journal gives complete returns from every town in the State. The following is the result:

Average Whig majority	381
Tillinghast over Dorr	405
Cranston over Thurston	357
Tillinghast over all	367
Cranston over all	257
Tillinghast over Thurston	467

NEW INVENTIONS & DISCOVERIES.

NEW METHOD OF RAISING VESSELS.—The Bostonians have invented a method of raising vessels in the water, by which they can be enabled to cross bars, though of large draught and deeply laden. This is accomplished by cylindrical bags, made air tight by a composition of India rubber, placed under the vessel's bottom, and afterwards filled with atmospheric air, by means of a forcing pump.

IMPORTANT DISCOVERY.—It is stated in a late French paper that an experiment has been tried by some medical gentlemen in Paris of inflating the lungs of a still-born infant, when in a few moments the blood began to circulate, and the child was returned to its parents alive. It is now five months old and doing well.

LITHOGRAPHIC PAINTINGS.—M. Sege, of Bordeaux, has lately applied, with complete success, the lithographic art to pottery. A patent has been granted for this invention, which, while it will greatly facilitate the ornamental work on the various wares, will enable the inventor to apply drawings and subjects from the best masters.—[Colman's Miscellany.

NEW MODE OF PRINTING CALICOES, &C.—A late invention has been made in printing calicoes, or other fabrics, by enclosing them in a chamber, case or compartment, filled with an artificial atmosphere, devoid of its free oxygen; and then printing the said fabrics with a solution of deoxydized indigo, when required to produce a blue color, or the same, with other materials, when other colors are desired; after which, the goods are exposed to the action of the atmosphere, in order to imbibe the necessary oxygen to fix the colors.—Colman's Miscellany.

PUBLICATIONS.

Memoir of the Life and Writings of Mrs. Hemans. By her Sister. Philad. Lea & Blanchard.

A biography of one sister by another, can be little less than a eulogy, especially when the subject of the Memoir is Felicia Dorothea Hemans. We have read the biography with unusual interest, and have been both gratified and pained.—Gratified to know more closely in her habits and thoughts such a poetess, and pained to find that the days of marriage were not all of bliss, and that disease and want visited not too kindly the home of the minstrel. We have no analysis of the work to make, for its facts were pretty generally known before, and criticism is disarmed, when it enters on the labours of love bestowed on the memory of the dead, by the living sister.

We closed the work with a sigh, and feel much disposed to doubt, from reading the lives of eminent women, if great fame be not to them a bitterness; and if the warmth of their public performances, do not scorch up and wither their domestic comforts. Miss Jewsbury—alluded to in the volume before us—seemed to think so when she broke forth, "Ah, what is genius to a woman but a splendid misfortune. What is fame to a woman but a dazzling degradation!" . . . "She is a reed shaken by the wind, an exotic nurtured for display. She is the Hebrew whose songs are demanded in a strange land; Ruth standing amid the alien corn; her affections are the dew that society exhales, but gives not back to her in rain. She is a jewelled captive; bright, desolate and sad." Mournful as these sentiments may seem, they came from one competent to judge and write; and enforce us to the conviction, that females seldom rise to eminence, without being compelled by the very demands of their greatness to yield up their domestic indulgencies, and to forego the cultivation of those "home feelings" which so often nearly ally women to the angels.

Murray's Travels in North America. New York: Harper & Brothers.

This is a candid and a good book—one of the best that has been produced upon North America—and, besides, it is an instructive and entertaining one. Mr. Murray, an English gentleman of good standing, expended the years 1834-5 & '6 in various portions of North America, studying and understanding what he saw and attempts to describe. He passed a summer with the Pawnee tribe of Indians, in the remote prairies of the Missouri; and he also paid a visit to Cuba and the Azore Islands. The information relating to these regions is peculiarly interesting.

John Harris tied to a tree by the Indians. J. T. Bowen, Walnut st.

One of the finest specimens of the Lithographic Art we have ever seen, is a very large engraving coming out this week, from a celebrated painting of "Harris tied up by the Savages to be burnt."

This picture is descriptive of a scene in the life of John Harris. He was a native of Yorkshire, in England, and is supposed to have settled at the present site of Harrisburg, about the year 1725. At this place was born in the year 1726, his son John Harris, the proprietor of Harrisburg, *who was the first white child born in Pennsylvania, west of the Conewago Hills.* The elder John Harris engaged in agriculture on the present site of Harrisburg, and *first introduced the plough on the banks of the Susquehanna.* He also engaged in an extensive trafic with the Indians; carrying the skins, obtained from them, on pack horses to Philadelphia—on one occasion a band of Indians came to his house and demanded rum, being refused, they became exasperated and tied him to a tree for burning—whilst they were engaged with the necessary preparations, the alarm was given in some way not now certainly known, and the neighboring Indians coming generally from their towns across the river, arrived in time to release him.

In pursuance of his own directions, he was, at his death, which happened many years afterwards, buried under the tree to which he had been fastened.

Religious Offering for 1840. Philad. Marshall & Co.

This is one of the Annuals for the coming season. It purports to be edited by Miss Catharine H. Waterman. The literary contents are mostly from well known writers, viz: Ellen Rand, [illegible], John A. Clark, Miss Lynch, William Howett, Professor Wines, &c. Many of the productions are of a finished character, and some of them, to which the names of the writers are not appended, would credit the writers if they had given their names in full. There are some articles which we think unworthy the place they fill.

Of the engravings, we suppose the publishers have used those which were last year inserted in more expensive Annuals, for the purpose of making a cheaper work for 1840, as all or nearly all of them belong to last year's annuals. This, we take it, is all fair enough, provided the buyer is first made to understand that the engravings are not sent out as original ones. That was probably the intention of the publishers, although we do not see it stated in the preface to the work.

The same publishers have nearly ready for publication, The Annual Christian Keepsake, edited by the Rev. John A. Clarke, and embellished with nine appropriate engravings. We have been favored with a glance at a specimen copy, beautifully bound in embossed morocco. Its literary contents are from the best pens of the day. The Gem of the book, in the way of engravings, is we think "Reading the Scriptures," painted by Kyle, and engraved by Neagle. The embellisment least worthy of special commendation, is also painted by Kyle, the subject, Washington praying in the forest. Its fault is a marked one. A more extended notice will be given hereafter. We may treat our readers to a taste of its literary qualities at an early day.

Catholic Family Library, No. 1 Philad: Carey & Hart.

Our neighbors have set up a new idea, viz: a "Catholic Library." The first number (we have only time this week to say) is before us. It is the Life of Sir Thomas More and The Times, in which he acted. It is a close imitation of Harper's Family Library. The memoir is by W. Joseph Walter, Late of St. Edmund's College, a gentleman of well known abilities; and when we have read his work, we will endeavor to do him justice.

The Ladies' Companion: New York: Wm. W. Snowden, Fulton st.

This magazine, the neatest in the style of its typography of the many now issued, and flourishing from the American press, is punctually on our table for the month of September. It displays a rich table of contents, and embraces some excellent articles from able pens. To the prose articles, we give the decided preference; and among the poetical pieces entitled "Old Trinity," and "To a Mountain Streamlet," are the best. Mr. Neale's article on "The Sea" is racy, speculative, and instructive. The publisher does not permit his exertions to relax to make his magazine a good one. Orrin Rogers, 67 South Second st. is the agent for this city.

Burton's Gentleman's Magazine, and American Monthly Review, for September.

The number for this month is before us, enriched with good articles and a well-written biography of Richard Penn Smith, Esq., introduced by a mezzotinto likeness of that gentleman, by Sartain, from an excellent portrait by Williams. The editors are abroad among their correspondents, and have furnished, the one a good story and the other, a reminiscent extract of antique and goodly import. The "Log Book of Old Ironsides" is again unfolded, and a few pages of her adventurous "march upon the mountain waves" transcribed with the usual skill of the narrator. In "Gymnastics and Gymnasia," Mr. Barrett's institution in Walnut st., and the gymnatory amusements therein held, are promised to be discoursed upon at large in the next number, in that portion devoted to "Field Sports and Manly Pastimes." The review department is well sustained.

The Lady's Book, for this month, has two sheets of fashions—one coloured, and one uncoloured. It has also a charming steel engraving on "Rustic Life." The music is the "Pennsylvania Waltz," quite seasonable. The tales are mostly from good writers. John Neal has "The Runaway," which no reader of the book will runaway from perusing. R. P. Smith has an unique Eastern Fable. Prof. Ingrahame has wooed the muses on the theme of "The Birth and Nestling of Love." Mrs. Loud has a sweet gem to "Flowers." Mr. Wilmer and many other writers have also contributed. The fact is, neighbour Godey is not to be outdone, and it must be gratifying that his book maintains the place of "the favourite of the ladies."

Colman's Monthly Miscellany for September, 1839.

The work opens with a full-length portrait of George Combe, the philosopher and phrenologist. —The contents for the present month are as follows:—Our Colleges, Academies, and Common Schools, by L. D. Chapin; The Last Days of Timotheus Tuttle, by N. Deering; Song, by I Graham; Ballad, by J. F. Otis; The Hermit of Cetara, by I. Graham; The School Boy's Laurel, by Calvin Peters; On seeing a Picture of Theodosia Burr, by the same; Old Times and Modern Times, by Prentiss Mellen; The French Revolution, by E. Holden; True Love and False, by G. Mellen; The Great Rivers of America, by J. Borron; Greek Statues, by Mrs. Borron; Definitions, by W. Cutter; Wild Flowers from New England, by B. B. Thatcher; The Unknown Clime, by D. C. Colesworthy; Wallace on the Eye, by L. D. Chapin; Lyric Poetry, by W. Cutter; The Good Match, by the same; Popular Science and the Arts; Hyperion; Silhouettes.

The Casket for September presents a rich mezzotint engraving of the "Mammoth Cave in Kentucky." The Stanzas by "Childers," one of the editors, are very creditable, and we give them place:

Oh! tell me not of brighter lands, or sunny climes away,
Where moving winds breathe low salutes, and zephyrs ever play,
And streamlets murmur pleasantly, and all is gay and fair;
Oh! tell me not of brighter lands—I care not to be there.

They sing of homes in verdant isles upon a tranquil sea,
Where sylph-like forms at even dance beneath the citron tree,
And dark eyed beauties whisper love, and sooth the brow of care,
And life is like a marriage feast—I care not to be there.

Oh! tell me not of eastern climes where rich acacias blow,
And perfume floats on every breeze, and fountains tinkle low,
The bulbul warbles to its mate beside the star lit streams,
And love smiles on us all the day, and whispers in our dreams.

Oh! tell me not of brighter lands, though Houris from the skies
Should charm us there to soft repose beneath their love-lit eyes,
Or woo us in their Eden bowers to linger by their side,
Breathing their vows like fairy songs upon a moonlit tide.

Oh! tell me not of other lands, I have one brighter still;
And dear to me is every wood, and stream, and vale, and hill;
But dearer far the smiling home where still I love to be,
For one low voice, and dark, deep eye, are all the world to me.

The Forget-Me-Not of Miss Waterman is feeling. Story of "The Murder Trial" well drawn. The music is "Come, the Moon Plays on the Rose."

We give from the last Southern Literary Messenger, a sweet and simple poetical gem.

Love Unchanging.

And is it just, or kind, my mother,
To break my heart to soothe your own?
And would you give me to another
Than him I love and love alone?
Shall I be false to every feeling,
To every plighted vow untrue—
And with poor smiles my thoughts concealing,
Bestow this wedded heart anew?

I never loved but once—no, never!
And when a heart like mine is given—
It fondly loves and loves forever,
Unchanging as the truth of Heaven.
Before the sacred marriage-altar,
With him alone, hand linked in hand,
Sustained by trust that cannot falter,
Dear mother, will your daughter stand!

Then deem not that such love will perish,
By any change, or time or chance,
Or I can ever cease to cherish
The thoughts you vainly call "romance."
Undimmed will glow my true devotion,
Now rendered to its dearest name;
Unfaded bloom each sweet emotion,
Throughlife, throughlife—the same, the same!

PARK BENJAMIN.

The Harpers are about to publish a volume of Poems by Park Benjamin.

Lady Blessington has a new novel in press, called "The Governess."

Willis has a new work in the press called "Two ways of getting a Husband." It is said he is going to make a tour in Ireland, and publish it.

We learn that Mrs. Smith's excellent little book, "Riches without Wings," has passed through two editions, and that the third is now published. She's the lady of "The Original Jack Downing."

Stocks.

United States Bank Stock, in New York, on Wednesday, sold at 104½; Bank of Kentucky, 78¾; Illinois Bank, 73½; and Stonington Rail Road 32½, buyer 30. Exchange on London 8½ @ 9 per cent. prem.

Coiners Arrested.

Two brothers, Ebenezer and Eli Kain, were last week arrested at Yonkers, N. Y., charged with coining spurious half dollars.

Distressing.

Miss Hannah Eno, of Paquonock, was crushed to death in the machinery of a factory last week. The machinery was set in motion by the foreman, without knowing she was in danger.

Sudden Death.

Mr. Thos. Magnier, tavern keeper, in Washington city, died very suddenly in his bed last week.

Liberal Support of the Press.

The London Coffee and Eating Houses expend $2,000 annually on newspapers and periodicals, for the use of their customers.

GLORIOUS CROPS IN MAINE.—The crops of all kinds are said to be most abundant in this State. In the article of potatoes alone, it is said they have raised enough this season to serve as a supply for the whole of the States. Send us ten barrels of *good* ones.

DEATH OF BISHOP BOWEN.—The Right Rev. Nathaniel Bowen, D. D., Bishop of the Protestant Episcopal Church, in the Diocese of South Carolina, died at Charleston on the 25th inst.

DELICATE INSINUATION.—A Western editor calls one of his contemporaries, a brandy cask.

Butter at Lebanon, Pa., is now selling at 12½ cents per pound.—Baltimore Sun.

Citizens of Lebanon, is that a fact? If so here's our order for a lot of prime, say 200 weight.

The deaths in the city of Baltimore, for the week ending the 3d of September, were 48.

A fine new steamer of 500 tons, called the North America, has just been launched at St. John's New Brunswick, to run from thence to Boston. She supplies the place of the Royal Tar, burnt some years since. Her captain is a Yankee.

Edward T. McManus, a native of Pennsylvania, who was boarding at the house of Hugh Mulligan in Lexington st., opposite the Market, Baltimore, committed suicide by cutting his throat with a razor.

Mr. Snow of Worcester county, Md., says he has only 100 subscribers to his weekly Banner. He must have a potatoe patch to live on then.

The Cincinnati Post (a Harrison paper) is for sale. So is the Lynn Freeman, (Whig.)

There are over 1500 newspapers in the United States.

Daniel Bitner, a lad aged 16, while driving a wagon in Bloomfield, Pa., was thrown out, and falling beneath the wheel, his head was crushed to atoms!

The Harrisburg rioters (as they have been called) have all been discharged.

It appears to be regarded as a matter of course, that France is to acknowledge the independence of Texas.

The Texan papers ridicule all idea of an invasion of that country by Mexico.

A colored woman recently died in New Orleans, at the advanced age of 107.

THE "LONG, LOW, BLACK, RAKISH-LOOKING SCHOONER."

Full and accurate Particulars relative to the Spanish Schooner L'Amistad, Her sailing from Havana—The Massacre on board of her Narrative of her Voyage—Perilous Situation of the Survivors—Death of ten of the Negroes. Her capture by the United States Brig Washington. Taken into New Haven—Judicial Examination—Commitment of the Mutineers. Together with a Likeness of Joseph Cinquez, the Leader of the Negroes.

In our last, we presented a brief account of the capture of the Spanish schooner L'Amistad—but as we feel sure every particular will be perused with great interest, we shall to-day furnish an extended narrative of all particulars, availing ourselves of our own sources of information—of the extra of our friends of the New York Sun, and of the slips from the Newport offices so kindly addressed us.

In June, Don Jose Ruiz, a wealthy Spaniard, left his estate at Principe for Havana, to buy slaves. At Havana, he purchased 49 from a cargo which had just arrived from the coast of Africa.—He chartered the schooner L'Amistad, Ramon Ferres master and sole owner. With his slaves he shipped a number of packages, partly his own and partly on freight, viz: some crockery, some copper, and many dry goods, besides fancy articles for amusement or luxury. He had but little money on board, although the captain was supposed to have specie to the amount of $8000 in doubloons. Besides this cargo, the L'Amistad received on board Don Pedro Montez and four slaves as passengers. The slaves of Senor Montez were from the same cargo as those of Ruiz, and were all children between the ages of 7 and 12. Three of the four were females, and one a male. The crew of the schooner consisted of the captain, his two slaves, and two white men. The slaves of Ruiz and Montez were all Congolese negroes, only one of whom, at least, had been spent on the passage.—One of the captain's slaves was a mulatto, and employed as cook; the other a black boy, named Antonio, who is yet on board the schooner.

The schooner is of Baltimore clipper build, 170 tons burthen, 6 years old, and was called the Friendship, while being Hispaniolised, means L'Amistad. She was insured at Havana to her full value. Senor Ruiz is insured $20,000, and it is supposed the rest of the shippers also were.

The L'Amistad sailed from Havana 25th June, for Guanja, 300 miles distant. All went well on board until the fourth night, when the captain while asleep on a mattrass on deck, with his mulatto slave by his side, he was attacked by Joseph Cinquez, with a sugar knife.

Joseph was one of the slaves purchased by Ruiz, and was the son of an African chief. Possessing far more sagacity and courage than his race generally do, he had been accustomed to command. His countenance, when in repose, looks heavy, but under excitement it assumes an expression of great intelligence. In height he is just 5 feet 7½ inches, has a full chest, large joints and muscles, and is built for strength and agility. His personal appearance is altogether remarkable, his demeanor noble and dignified; and he was the master spirit of his band. We present here an accurate likeness of him, taken from life, by an excellent artist.

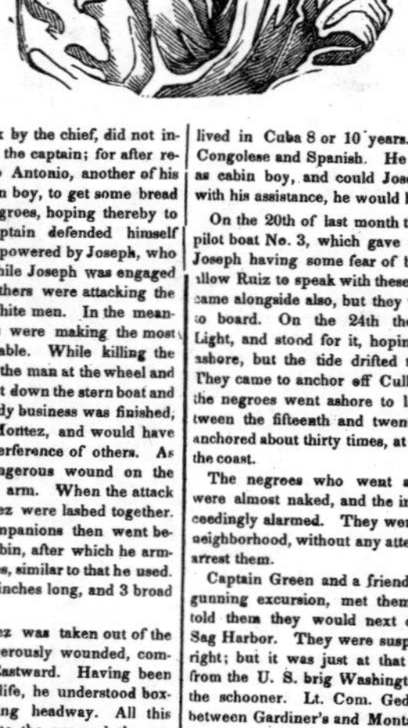

The first blow struck by the chief, did not inflict great injury upon the captain; for after receiving it, he called to Antonio, another of his own slaves, and a cabin boy, to get some bread and throw among the negroes, hoping thereby to pacify them. The captain defended himself bravely, but he was overpowered by Joseph, who split his head open. While Joseph was engaged with the captain, three others were attacking the mulatto slave and the white men. In the meantime the other negroes were making the most dreadful noises imaginable. While killing the captain and the mulatto, the man at the wheel and another Spanish sailor, let down the stern boat and escaped. After the bloody business was finished, Joseph attacked Senor Montez, and would have killed him, but for the interference of others. As it was, he received a dangerous wound on the head, and another on the arm. When the attack ceased, Ruiz and Montez were lashed together. Joseph and his three companions then went below and ransacked the cabin, after which he armed them with sugar knives, similar to that he used. This weapon is about 28 inches long, and 3 broad at the end.

Next morning, Montez was taken out of the cabin, and although dangerously wounded, compelled to steer to the Eastward. Having been master of a ship in early life, he understood boxing about without making headway. All this time the negroes pointed to the sun and then to their knives, and if for a moment the vessel veered perceptibly, they brandished their knives over the head of Montez in a most horrible manner.—The poor wretches knew that they had come from where the sun appeared to rise, but they understood nothing of navigation, and were easily deluded.

About two days after the rising, they had a heavy gale, which drifted them into the Bahama Channel. Here they boxed about again, but saw no vessels. At last, being out of water, the negroes ordered Montez to make the nearest land, which proved to be the Island of St. Andrews. Here the negroes met no one. After this, Montez steered for New Providence, but the negroes were not disposed to land. By this time, Joseph had learned to steer, and he took the helm in the day, leaving one of the white men to steer at night. Every night Joseph slept near the helm, and had two of the most trusty negroes by his side watching, and ready to awake him on the least alarm.

During this interval, the negroes broke open the hatches and pillaged the cargo. Among it they found wine, raisins, and a great quantity of medicines; all these they ate indiscriminately. Ten died in a short time, and others would have done so, had not Joseph forbidden the rest to touch any thing but what he gave them. Any infraction of this wholesome regulation brought down on the head of the offender a severe personal chastisement from the hands of the chief. Joseph lived abstemiously during the whole voyage, and insisted on the most perfect obedience to his orders. The only food eaten was portioned out by his hand, and not a box of the cargo opened but under his direction. He divided the spoil, taking the smallest portion for himself. During all this time, the whites were in a most wretched condition, and their hope of escape very small. In the night they steered to the west, and succeeded in persuading Joseph to keep to the north of east in the day.

About the fifteenth of last month, as the Spaniards suppose, for they had lost knowledge of dates and days, they came in sight of Long Island. In the interval they had been boarded by several vessels, one of which supplied them with a demijohn of water. They had seen many vessels and signalized them, but were unable to call their attention. When any vessel came alongside, Joseph would stand by Ruiz, the only man on board who spoke English, and watch him with fearful intensity.

The organ of communication between Senor Ruiz and the Congolese, was Antonio, the captain's slave. He is by birth an African, but has lived in Cuba 8 or 10 years. He speaks both Congolese and Spanish. He had been employed as cabin boy, and could Joseph have dispensed with his assistance, he would have been killed.

On the 20th of last month they were hailed by pilot boat No. 3, which gave them some apples. Joseph having some fear of betrayal, would not allow Ruiz to speak with these. Pilot boat No. 4 came alongside also, but they were not permitted to board. On the 24th they made Montauk Light, and stood for it, hoping to run the vessel ashore, but the tide drifted them up the bay.—They came to anchor off Culloden Point, where the negroes went ashore to lay in water. Between the fifteenth and twenty-fourth, they had anchored about thirty times, at different places on the coast.

The negroes who went ashore at Culloden were almost naked, and the inhabitants were exceedingly alarmed. They were two days in the neighborhood, without any attempt being made to arrest them.

Captain Green and a friend, who were on a gunning excursion, met them at Culloden, and told them they would next day pilot them into Sag Harbor. They were suspicious all was not right; but it was just at that time that the boat from the U. S. brig Washington went alongside the schooner. Lt. Com. Gedney was cruising between Gardiner's and Montauk Point (having heard nothing of the schooner being off the coast) when he saw the suspicious-looking vessel, and at once bore down for her.

Immediately on arriving alongside, two white men claimed protection. They were Pedro Montez, passenger, and John Ruiz, owner of the slaves and part of the cargo. When Mr. Porter, the prize-master, assured Pedro Montez of his safety, he threw his arms around his neck, while gushing tears, coursing down his furrowed cheeks, bespoke the overflowing transport of his soul. Every now and then he clasped his hands, and with uplifted eyes give thanks to "the Holy Virgin" who had led him out of all his troubles.

Lieuts. Porter and Meade took possession, disarmed the negroes, and took the schooner in tow. Joseph (the master spirit) on seeing this, went below, and tieing some gold about his person, he leaped out of the main hatch, and at one bound was over the side. While under the water, he disengaged the gold, and came up about 100 yards from the vessel, having been under water at least 5 minutes, when he was taken. He begged to be permitted to return to the schooner. From humanity he was so, when he made a speech to his comrades in Congolese, telling them that there was only one way of ending their career, and that was to murder the whites, and then the whites would kill them. This speech was interpreted by Antonio, the slave of the murdered captain, whom we have named before. The negro chieftain was then manacled and reconveyed to the Washington, Antonio thus reports his speech to his comrades (for one of the editors of the New York Sun, while he was at New Haven:)

"Friends and Brothers—We would have returned, but the sun was against us. I would not see you serve the white man, so I induced you to help me kill the captain. I thought I should be killed—I expected it. It would have been better. You had better be killed, than live many moons in misery. I shall be hanged, I think, every day. But this does not pain me. I could die happy, if by dying I could save so many of my brothers from the bondage of the white man."

The Washington proceeded at once to New Haven with the schooner, when Lt. Gedney despatched information to the U. S. Marshal and Judge Judson of the U. S. District Court. On Thursday morning, both of these gentlemen went on board the Washington and held a court.—This judicial examination resulted in a confirmation of the narrative of facts, as they are detailed above. Senor Don Pedro Montez, Senor Don Jose Ruiz, and Antonio, the murdered captain's slave, were the witnesses examined. Lieutenant Meade, of the Washington, who speaks the Spanish, acted as interpreter. [See another column.]

THE COLORED AMERICAN.

VOL. III.—NO. 29 | CHARLES B. RAY & CO.,—PROPRIETORS. | WHOLE NO. 126.

TWO DOLLARS | NEW-YORK SATURDAY, OCTOBER 5, 1839. | PER ANNUM.

THE COLORED AMERICAN,
Printed and published EVERY SATURDAY, *by the Proprietors,*
No. 161 DUANE-STREET, N. Y.

TERMS OF THE PAPER.

☞ *Two Dollars per annum, in advance.* ☜

Agents' Fees.—Travelling Agents allowed one third deduction; Local Agents, one fourth.

All Letters &c. must be directed to Messrs. C. B. RAY & co. 161 Duane street, N. York. Postage must be paid on all letters, unless containing $5, or upwards.

Communications intended for the paper must be directed (post paid) as above.

A PROCLAMATION.

C. Campbell. *By His Excellency Lieutenant-General Sir Colin Campbell, K. C. B. Lieutenant Governor and Commander in Chief in and over Her Majesty's Province of Nova-Scotia, &c. &c. &c.*

WHEREAS, the Government of Her Majesty's Island of Trinidad having passed a Law for the encouragement of Labouring Persons, of African Descent, who may desire to remove to that Island, I have thought fit, by means of this my Proclamation, to make known, for the benefit of such as it may concern, the following information, which, by desire of the Government of that Island, has been conveyed to me as the Lieutenant-Governor of this Province, on the subject, that is to say:—

First.—The Government of Trinidad, by a Law lately enacted there, has engaged to pay the sum of *Twenty-five dollars* for the passage from this and the neighbouring Provinces, of each Labouring Person, whether male or female, of African descent—the same sum for the passage of two Children, between fourteen and seven years of age—and the same sum for the passage of three Children, between seven years and one year old. This money will be paid as a free gift, and no claim will exist for its repayment in any shape; and strict provision is also made for ensuring good Vessels and convenient accommodation for the passage of such Persons as may choose to remove to that Island.

Secondly.—According to the rate of Wages given on the Island, a Labourer, whether male or female, may easily earn daily, between sunrise and sunset, Wages equal to Four Shillings and Five Shillings Nova Scotia Currency, together with an allowance of One Pound Dry Cod Fish; and such Labourers as do not choose to work steadily the whole day are at liberty to perform as much work during the day as will entitle them to half those allowances. In addition to which each family engaged at work is allowed the use of a good Cottage and half an acre of productive ground free from rent or any other charge.

Thirdly.—The soil is of great fertility, and, from the want of Population, Land is easily procured at a cheap rate.—Lands in the most settled Districts are sold by private individuals at from Four to Sixteen Dollars for an acre, and Crown Lands, which are only disposed of by Auction, averaged at the last Sales Two Dollars an acre.

The Wages given for the Labour of a few days are therefore sufficient for the purchase of Land which, if cultivated with common industry and care, will fully supply the wants of a family in that fine climate; and an active Labourer, with prudence, may in a little time become owner of a productive Farm.

Fourthly.—Religious Sects are equally protected and assisted by the Government—the Ministers of every Church receive moderate annual allowances from the Colonial Treasury; and it has been the constant habit to encourage the building of Churches and Chapels by giving the same amount of public money as the people may at any time raise among themselves for that purpose. Public Schools also are supported, where Children, whose Parents cannot afford to pay, are taught without charge. Of these Schools there are 76 at present, besides many private Schools. Great exertions have been lately made to give instruction to the whole Labouring People, and the number of Schools is fast increasing.

Fifthly.—The Parliament of Great Britain having abolished Slavery, persons of color, of African race or descent, are as free in Trinidad as any other whatever of the subjects of our Gracious Queen. And Her Majesty, who has always shown the most benevolent and earnest desire to promote the happiness of this class of Her Subjects, has appointed in each District in Trinidad a Stipendiary Magistrate, who is paid by the Crown, to see justice done between the Labourers, and those they work for. As respects, therefore, there perfect freedom and just privileges, Colored Persons, who may desire to remove to Trinidad, need have no fear; more especially as that Island is a Colony entirely under the control of our Gracious Queen Victoria, whose desire to make free and happy the African Race throughout all her Territories has been so strongly shown. At the present time several large Sugar Estates, besides others producing Cocoa and Coffee, are owned by Colored Proprietors, among whom some have risen to offices of honor and emolument under Her Majesty's Government; and there are now in Trinidad many Colored Persons who went thither from this Province several years ago, and who remain contented and pleased with their circumstances, supporting themselves and those naturally dependent on them both aged and young, easily and comfortably, without the aid of public or private charity.

And lastly.—I do hereby make known that a copy of the Law of the Government of Trinidad before referred to, and the other papers which have been laid before me, containing more at large the information hereby made public, are lodged in the office of the Secretary of the Province, at Halifax, for the benefit of all persons who may feel interested on the subject; where also, the names of those persons or families who desire to take advantage of the favorable opportunity now offered for settling in Trinidad should be given in before the fifteenth day of October next.

Given under my Hand and Seal at Arms at Halifax, this eighth day of August, in the third year of Her Majesty's Reign, and in the Year of our Lord 1839.

By His Excellency's Command,
RUPERT D. GEORGE.

GOD SAVE THE QUEEN.

From the Note book of a Colonist.

CAPTAIN JACK.

In the year 1823 I was employed as overseer on a sugar plantation on the east coast of the river Demerara, in South America. Early in that year an insurrection broke out amongst the negroes, and the white servants on the estates were assembled at Stabroek, the capital of the colony, embodied into a corps of riflemen, and brigaded in different parts of the country with the regular troops.

It so happened that I was stationed with a party of the —th regiment, commanded by Colonel ——, close to the property on which I had for several years resided. I was thereby enabled to be of considerable use to the military authorities on several occasions, from my intimate knowledge of the localities of the neighborhood, and of the character of the people by whom we were surrounded.

The communications between the plantations on the coast and the town of Stabroek, is kept up by means of small schooners, which carry thither weekly the produce ready for shipping on board the merchantmen in the river, and return laden with coals, provisions, and other necessary supplies. These droghers, as they are called, are manned and commanded by negroes: to be a boat captain is a situation of great trust and emolument, which is always filled with the best man on each estate. The boat-captains contrive to pick up a good deal of money by carrying letters and passengers, the profit arising from which is their perquisite,

Whenever I had occasion to go town, I generally gave the preference to a schooner belonging to Plantation Eugenia; she was the fastest boat on the coast, and her commander, Captain Jack, was a smart active, well-behaved fellow, whose popularity with white and black, stood him in good stead; for, whenever it was known that the Eugenia schooner was to sail, the other droghers had but small chance of passengers.

On one unlucky evening, soon after the insurrection broke out, Captain Jack returned from Stabroek with his boat full of strange negroes, who were cordially welcomed in the slave yard of the Eugenia. That very night the dwelling-house of Mr. Forester, the proprietor of the estate, was attacked, and burnt to the ground, and he himself only escaped at the time, to die shortly afterwards of a fever brought on by the hardships he had been forced to undergo in concealing himself from his quick-sighted enemies. For two days he lay without food or shelter in the cane pieces exposed to a scorching sun and heavy dews of a tropical climate, and at night waded along the sea-shore, up to his neck in mud and water, until he reached the house of a friend near town, where he expired in a few days. Colonel —— wished to send notice of this outrage to the officer commanding at Stabroek: and, as Captain Jack's character was above suspicion, he selected him to convey the express to town, and sent a sergeant on horseback to direct him to prepare to weigh immediately.

The man rode to the the Eugenia, and went on board the schooner; which was lying high and dry on the sand. There was nobody on board of her; her sails and rigging were cut to pieces, her rudder burnt, her anchor and chain gone. Captain Jack was nowhere to be found. The sergeant returned to Mahaica post, and made his report. Colonel —— sent for me. He told me that he was aware I was well acquainted with Jack; and that he was informed a sort of friendship existed between us—if, indeed, in those days, a friendship could be said to exist between a negro and a white man; that I knew his haunts and connections; and that, if any body could find him, I could. He said that he was now convinced that Jack was implicated in the crime committed on Plantation Eugenia, and that he would give me fifty joes to secure him, dead or alive before night.

At this period the very existence of the colony was in a most critical position; the numerical odds against the whites was as a hundred to one; the negroes equaled us in courage, and surpassed us in animal strength and endurance; on the other hand we were better armed, and possessed that confidence in each other, so essential in the hour of danger. We had also in the coly the regiment which Colonel —— commanded, and a small detachment of artillery.

From circumstances which had occurred during my residence on the east coast, I had acquired such a regard for my friend Jack, that I declare I would sooner have been instrumental in arresting any white man in the colony, with the conviction which I had in this case, that his death would be the inevitable consequence of his apprehension. Still, this was no time for a man to swerve from his duty, however painful it might be; horrible atrocities had been committed by the insurgents, and signal must be the punishment inflicted on the perpetrators, whenever they could be discovered. I therefore shouldered my rifle, and sallied forth, determined to do my best to apprehend Jack; not without a hope, however, that his well known sagacity and activity might render my exertions fruitless.

I had hardly walked half a mile, when, at an angle of the road, I came full on the very man of whom I had been sent in quest. I at once sprang forward, and seized him by the throat. His astonishment at this unfriendly greeting from me was so great, that he made no resistance whatever. My uniform showed that I was on duty, and his conscience probably apprized him of the cause of this hostile proceeding on my part.

"Colonel —— has sent for you, Jack," said I. "I trust you will be able to account for the state in which your boat was found, when he wished you take his despatches to town."

Jack made no reply, but shook his head mournfully. I motioned to him to walk on before me toward the military post. He did so. Presently he stopped, and turned round. Seeing that I unslung and cocked my rifle, he said,

"Massa Edward, suppose Jack run away, you no shoot him?"

"That I most certainly will, Jack. I have been ordered to convey you dead or alive to Mahaica; and dead or alive you shall go thither. I am sorry for you, from the bottom of my heart, for I am sure you have been unwillingly compelled to join in the destruction of Mr. Forester's property."

We soon reached the post, where I delivered over my prisoner to the guard. He was instantly taken before Colonel —— and several officers, and I lingered in the guard-room, ostensibly for the purpose of reposing myself, but really to see how my poor friend Jack would fare. After some time had elapsed, I grew tired of waiting, and shouldering my rifle, was walking out of the gate, when Colonel —— advanced to the front of the gallery before the officers' apartments, and exclaimed in an angry tone,

"Where the hell are you going to, sir? How dare you leave your prisoners without orders?"

"I thought, Colonel, that my duty had been ended when I delivered my prisoner to the guard."

"Did you, sir? Remain where you are, and I'll soon convince you of the contrary."

He then returned into the house for a moment, and reappeared followed by the other officers, and by Jack, who walked slowly down the steps towards me, while the Colonel and his friends remained leaning over the front of the gallery.

"Now, Sergeant," continued Colonel ——, "place your prisoner on his knees, with his face towards you."

Jack knelt down—not a muscle of his countenance quivered—he was entirely naked, and was a remarkably muscular and well made man. He looked like a fine bronze statue. Both he and I knew perfectly well that his life was forfeited, and that he was about to die; but neither of us was prepared for what followed.

"Fall back ten paces," roared Colonel ——, I obeyed.

"*Now shoot your prisoner through the heart.*"

I was horror-stricken, Well aware that poor Jack's hours were numbered, I had never contemplated the possibility of being compelled myself to become his executioner in cold blood. I knew, moreover, that Colonel —— had no right to make me carry the sentence of the drum-head court-martial into effect. I was a civilian, a volunteer, and a non-commissioned officer; and, from the various services which my local knowledge had enabled me to render him, I had no reason to expect such brutal treatment at his hands.

As soon as I could recover from my astonment and horror, I advanced toward the gallery in order to remonstrate with the Colonel. He turned away from me, and called to the officer of the guard to send two men forward. The men stepped out, and at his command, cocked their pieces, and levelled them at me. Colonel —— then said to them.

"I am going to give my orders to that d——d mutineer. If he does not obey them instantly, shoot him. Now, Sergeant, make ready—present—fire!"

Jack sprang to his feet, and fell dead on his face. My bullet pierced his brain.

Colonel —— tossed the purse containing the reward offered for Jack's apprehension on the ground, close by his dead body, and walked coolly into the house, observing, that until the Volunteers and Bucks formed some idea of military discipline from experience, they would give more trouble than assistance to the regulars.

He lived to see the day when he gladly would have exchanged his whole regiment for a score of our good rifles; yet he lived not long—for three days after the tragedy which I have here related, he attempted, against the advice of the colonists, to pursue a body of negroes into the bush, with the whole force at Mahaica, unaccompanied either by Volunteers or Indians. His men, incumbered by their heavy clothing and accoutrements exhausted by the heat, and bewildered by the tremendous torrents of rain which flooded the savannahs, fell an easy prey to their naked enemies. Not more than a dozen escaped to tell the tale of their defeat. Colonel K—— received a musket shot which broke his thigh. He fell alive into the hands of his enemies. They had been Captain Jack's comrades and friends, and horribly they avenged his death.

SPANISH SLAVE TRADE.

The Spanish slave trade was to have finally ceased, according to the stipulations in the Treaty between Spain and England, of the 5th of July and 28th of August, 1814, in 1820. But within these two years, and perhaps at this very moment, slave ships have been publicly fitted out from Cuba, and immense numbers of slaves have been imported into that island, *with the open connivance of the authorities.* A mixed commissioners, has been established at Havana, for the condemnation of vessels proved to have been engaged in the slave trace. But we are officially informed by Mr. Macleary, one of the Commissioners, that since the establishment of the court, no seizure of a slave vessel has ever taken place but on the interference and denunciation of the British Commissioners: and *even then, such seizure has only been made to be instantly followed, by a perfect acquittal, in the Spanish tribunals!*—[McCulloch's Dictionary of Commerce,

---

CARNIVOROUS BIRDS.

Carnivorous birds, by many striking traits evince the destiny for which they had been created; they are provided with wings of great length, supported by powerful muscles, which enable them to fly with energy, and soar with ease at the loftiest elevations in which they are visible. They are armed with strong and hooked bills; and with the sharp and formidable claws of the tiger; they are also further distinguished by their large heads, short necks, strong muscular thighs in aid of their retractile talons, and a sight so piercing as to enable them, while soaring at the greatest height, to perceive their prey, upon which they sometimes descend, like an arrow, with undeviating aim. In these birds the stomach is smaller than in the graniverous kinds, and their intestines are shorter. Like beasts of prey, they are of an unsociable nature; and so far from herding together like the inoffensive tribes, they drive even their offspring from the eyry, and seek habitually the shelter of desert rocks, neglected ruins, or the solitude of the darkest forest, from whence they utter loud, terrific, or piercing cries in accordance with the gloomy rage and inquietude of their insatiable desires.

Besides these grand divisions of the winged nations, there are others, which in their habits and manners, might be compared to the amphibious animals, as they live chiefly on the water and feed on its productions. To enable them to swim and dive in quest of their aquatic food, their toes are connected by broad membranes or webs, with which, like oars, they strike the water and are impelled with force. In this way even the seas, lakes, and rivers abounding with fish, insects, and seeds, swarm with birds of various kinds, which all obtain an abundant supply. There are other aquatic birds, frequenting marshes and the margins of lakes, rivers and the sea, which seem to partake of an intermediate nature between the land and water tribes. Some of these feed on fishes and reptiles; others, with long and sensible bills and extended necks, seek their food in wet and muddy marshes. These birds are not made for swimming; but, familiar with water, they wade, and many follow the edge of the retiring waves of the sea, gleaning their insect prey at the recession of the tides; for this kind of life nature has provided them with long legs, bare of feathers even above the knees; their toes unconnected by webs, are only partially furnished with membranous appendages, just sufficient to support them on the soft and boggy grounds they frequent. To this tribe belong the Cranes, Snipes, Sandpipers, Woodcocks, and many others.

POPULAR ORATORS.

It may be remarked generally, that a speaker who thinks to lower his composition in order to accommodate himself to the habits and taste of his audience, when addressing the multitude, will find that he commits a grievous mistake. All the highest powers of eloquence consist in producing passages which may at once affect even the most promiscuous assembly; but even the graces of composition are not thrown away upon such auditors. Clear, strong, terse, yet natural and not strained expressions; happy antitheses; apt comparisons; forms of speech that are natural without being obvious; harmonious periods, yet various, spirited, and never monotonous or too regularly balanced; these are what will be always sure to captivate every audience, and yet in these mainly consists finished, and elaborate, and felicitous diction. "Mirabile est," says Cicero, "cum plurinum in faciendo intersit inter doctum et rudem, quam non multum differat in judicando." The best speakers of all times have never failed to find that they could not speak too well and too carefully to a popular assembly; that if they spoke their best, the best they could address to the most learned and critical assembiy, they were sure to succeed; although it may be very true that the converse of the proposition is not equally well founded; for bad diction and false taste will not be so sure to obtain their merited reprobation from a promiscuous auditory.

SICILIAN FACTS.

The Devil's Bridge.—The bridge over the Cantara, the Onobola of the Greeks, is called the Devil's Bridge. It derived this name, according to the peasants, from the following circumstance, which they relate with great gravity, and firmly believe. The stream, so runs the tale, was so impetuous, that no architect could throw a bridge over it, the torrent invariably carrying it away before it could be completed. In this perplexity resource was had to the devil, who is accounted an excellent workman; an angel acquainted him that if he would undertake to build one, the first that passed over it should become his prey. Ever on the watch to lay his claws on us poor mortals, the infernal mason soon terminated his task, and sharpening his talons, sat down in expectation of his victim, when a dog crossed it. Enraged at being thus outwitted and disappointed, his Satannic Majesty, stamping with his foot, struck out a stone; for a long time it was impossible to find another to fill up the gap, and the bridge consequently continued useless, untill Saint Somebody, I have forgot his name, gave it his benediction, when the defect was immediately remedied, and the bridge rendered fit for its purper use.

INDESTRUCTIBILITY OF MATTER.

The destruction produced by fire is most striking. In many cases, as in the burning of a piece of charcoal or a taper, there is no smoke, nothing visible dissipated and carried away; the burning body wastes and disappears, while nothing seems to be produced but warmth and light, which we are not in the habit of considering as substances; and when all has disappeared, except, perhaps some trifling ashes, we naturally suppose it is gone, lost, destroyed. But, when the question is examined more exactly, we detect in the invisible stream of heated air which ascends from the glowing coal or flaming wax, the whole ponderable matter, only united in a new combination with the heated air, and dissolved in it. So far from being thereby destroyed, it is only become again what it was before it existed in the form of charcoal or wax, an active agent in the business of the world, and the main support of vegetable and animal life, and is still susceptible of running again the same round, as circumstances may determine; so that, for aught we can see to the contrary, the same identical atom may be concealed for thousands of centuries in a limestone rock, may at length be quarried, set free in the limekiln, mix with the air, be absorbed from it by plants, and, in succession, become a part of the frames of living beings, till some concurrence of events consigns it once more to long repose, which, however, no way unfits it from again resuming its former activity.

From the British Emancipator.

"RUIN AND STARVATION.

Every fact which presents itself in relation to the great experiment of negro liberty goes to contradict and stultify the passionate denunciations of the planters. Five months of the year 1838 were passed in freedom; and we have heard nothing but loud and incessant outcries of deficient labor, neglected cultivation, ruinate estates, and beggared proprietors. "The official returns will show," said these angry gentlemen, "the justice of our complaints." Very well. The official returns for 1838 are made out, and we find in the Colonial Gazette the following abstract of them, so far as relates to the staple imports from the West India and Mauritius in 1838, as compared with the two proceeding years:

	1836	1837	1838
Sugar cwts	4,099,093	3,843,806	4 124,862
Molasses "	526,535	576,097	637,407
Rum galls.	4,870,473	4,412,971	4,642,203
Coffee lbs.	18 922,611	15,577,956	17,639,280
Cotton "	1,734,337	1,640,227	1,528,296
Cocoa "	1,612,104	1,847,145	2 149,637

The quantity of sugar included in the above figures, imported from each of the principal colonies was—

	1836	1837	1838
Barbadoes	273,428	445,713	473 587
Jamaica	1,054 042	903 933	1 053,181
Trinidad	312,141	295,367	286,247
Guiaha	1,077,848	943,388	835,300
Mauritius	497,302	537,455	606,019

Our contemporary observes very justly, that "there is nothing of these quantities that would indicate the progress of a great social change affecting the relative condition of employers and laborers." On the contrary, from all that appears here, it might be supposed that the negroes were still apprentices or even slaves. But most especially is it to be observed that, in the funny island of Jamaica, the cultivators of which seem to go by the rule contrary, and to bellow out their complaints just in proportion to their good fortune, the sugar exported in 1838, exceeds, by nearly 150,000 cwt., the export of 1837!—What a volume of commendation is this for the system of free labor, and the character of the emancipated peasantry!

THE BOY AND MAN.

From "The School Boy," a work by the Rev. John S. C. Abbot just published.

A few years ago, there was in the city of Boston, a portrait painter, whose name was Mr. Copley. He did not succeed very well in his business, and concluded to go to England, to try his fortunes there. He had a little son, whom he took with him, whose name was John Singleton Copley.

John was a very studious boy, and made such rapid progress in his studies, that his father sent him to college.—There he applied himself so closely to his books, and became so distinguished a scholar, that his instructors predicted that he would make a very eminent man.

After he graduated he studied law.—And when he entered upon the practice of his profession; his mind was so richly stored with information, and so highly disciplined by his previous diligence, that he almost immediately obtained celebrity. One or two causes of very great importance being intrusted to him, he managed them with so much wisdom and skill, as to attract the admiration of the whole British nation.

The king and his cabinet, seeing what a learned man he was and how much influence he had acquired, felt it to be important to secure his service for the government. They therefore raised him from one post of honor to another till he was created Lord High Chancellor of England—the very highest post of honor to which any subject can attain; so that John Singleton Copley is now Lord Lyndhurst, Lord High Chancellor of England. About sixty years ago, he was a little boy in Boston. His father was a poor portrait painter, hardly able to get his daily bread. Now,

THE FUGITIVE SLAVE LAW!

America's Bill of Abominations!!

A BILL TO AMEND THE ACT ENTITLED, 'AN ACT RESPECTING FUGITIVES FROM JUSTICE, AND PERSONS ESCAPING FROM THE SERVICE OF THEIR MASTERS."

Be it enacted by the Senate and House of Representatives of the United States in Congress assembled,—That the persons who have been, or may hereafter be, appointed *Commissioners*, in virtue of any act of Congress, by the Circuit Courts of the United States, and who, in consequence of such appointments, are authorized to exercise the powers that any Justice of the Peace or other Magistrate of any of the United States may exercise in respect to offenders for any crime or offence [illegible] prisoning, or bailing the same under and by virtue of the thirty-third section of the Act of the twenty-fourth of September, seventeen hundred and eighty-nine, entitled "An Act to establish the Judicial Courts of the United States," shall be, and are hereby authorized and required to exercise and discharge all the powers and duties conferred by this Act.

SECT. 2. *And be it further enacted*,—That *the Superior Court of each organized Territory of the United States* shall have the same power *to appoint Commissioners* to take acknowledgments of bail and affidavit, and to take depositions of witnesses in civil causes, which is *now possessed by the Circuit Courts of the United States*; and *all Commissioners* who shall hereafter be appointed for such purposes by the Superior Court of any organized Territory of the United States shall possess all the powers and exercise all the duties conferred by law upon the Commissioners appointed by the Circuit Courts of the United States for similar purposes, and *shall moreover exercise and discharge all the powers and duties conferred by this Act*.

SECT. 3. *And be it further enacted*,—That the Circuit Courts of the United States and the Superior Courts of each organized Territory of the United States, shall from time to time enlarge the number of Commissioners, *with a view to afford reasonable facilities to reclaim fugitives from labor*, and to the prompt discharge of the duties imposed by this Act.

SECT. 4. *And be it further enacted*,—That *the Commissioners* above named *shall have concurrent jurisdiction with the judges of the Circuit and District Courts of the United States*, in their respective Circuits and Districts within the several States, and the Judges of the Superior Courts of the Territories severally and collectively, in term time and vacation; and *shall grant certificates to such claimants*, upon satisfactory proof being made, *with authority to take and remove such fugitives from service or labor*, under the restrictions herein contained, to the State or Territory from which such persons may have escaped or fled.

SECT. 5. *And be it further enacted*, That it shall be the duty of all *Marshals* and *Deputy Marshals* to obey and execute all warrants and precepts issued under the provisions of this Act, when to them directed, and *should any Marshal or Deputy Marshal refuse* to receive such warrant or other process, when tendered, or to use all proper means diligently to execute the same, HE SHALL, on conviction thereof, BE FINED IN THE SUM OF ONE THOUSAND DOLLARS to the use of such claimant, on the motion of such claimant, by the Circuit or District Court for the District of such Marshal; and *after arrest of such Fugitive* by the Marshal or his Deputy, or whilst at any time in his custody, under the provisions of this Act, *should such Fugitive escape*, WHETHER WITH OR WITHOUT THE ASSENT OF SUCH MARSHAL or his Deputy, SUCH MARSHAL SHALL BE LIABLE, on his official bond, TO BE PROSECUTED, for the benefit of such claimant, FOR THE FULL VALUE OF THE SERVICE OR LABOR OF SAID FUGITIVE, in the State, Territory or District whence he escaped; and the better to enable *the said Commis*[illegible] duties faithfully and efficiently, in conformity to the requirements of the Constitution of the United States and this Act, they *are hereby authorized and empowered*, within their counties respectively, *to appoint in writing under their hands, any one or more suitable persons*, from time to time, *to execute all such warrants and other process as may be issued* by them in the lawful performance of their respective duties; *with an authority to such Commissioners*, or the persons to be appointed by them, *to execute process as aforesaid*, to *summon and call to their aid* THE BY STANDERS or *posse comitatus* of the proper County, when necessary to insure a faithful observance of the clause of the Constitution referred to, in conformity with the provisions of this Act; and ALL GOOD CITIZENS ARE HEREBY COMMANDED TO AID AND ASSIST IN THE PROMPT AND EFFICIENT EXECUTION OF THIS LAW, whenever their services may be required, as aforesaid, for that purpose; and said warrants shall run and be executed by said officers anywhere in the State within which they were issued.

SECT. 6. *And be it further enacted*,—That when a person held to service or labor in any State or Territory of the United States, has heretofore, or shall hereafter escape into another State or Territory of the United States, the person or persons to whom such service or labor may be due, or his, her, or their Agent or Attorney, duly authorized by power of attorney, in writing, acknowledged and certified under the seal of some legal office or court of the State or Territory in which the same may be executed, may pursue and reclaim such Fugitive person, either by procuring a warrant from some one of the Courts, Judges, or Commissioners aforesaid, of the proper Circuit, District, or County, for the apprehension of such Fugitive from service or labor, or by *seizing and arresting such Fugitive where the same can be done* WITHOUT PROCESS; and by taking or causing such persons to be taken, forthwith before such Court, Judge, or Commissioner, whose duty it shall be to hear and determine the case of such claimant IN A SUMMARY MANNER; and upon satisfactory proof being made by deposition or affidavit, in writing, to be taken and certified by such Court, Judge, or Commissioner, or by *other satisfactory testimony*, duly taken and certified by some Court, Magistrate, Justice of the Peace, or other legal officer authorized to administer an oath and take depositions under the laws of the State or Territory from which such person owing service or labor may have escaped, with a certificate of such Magistrate or other authority, as aforesaid, with the seal of the proper Court or officer thereto attached, *which seal shall be sufficient to establish competency of the proof*, and with proof, also by affidavit, of the identity of the person whose service or labor is claimed to be due as aforesaid, that the person so arrested does in fact owe service or labor to the person or persons claiming him or her, in the State or Territory from which such Fugitive may have escaped as aforesaid, and that said person escaped, *to make out and deliver to such claimant*, his or her *Agent or Attorney*, *a cer*[illegible] *substantial facts* as to the service or labor due from such Fugitive to the claimant, and of his or her escape from the State or Territory in which such service or labor was due to the State or Territory in which he or she was arrested, *with authority to such claimant*, or his or her Agent or Attorney, TO USE SUCH REASONABLE FORCE AND RESTRAINT as may be necessary, under the circumstances of the case, TO TAKE and REMOVE SUCH FUGITIVE PERSON BACK to the State or Territory from whence he or she may have escaped as aforesaid. IN NO TRIAL OR HEARING under this Act SHALL THE TESTIMONY OF SUCH ALLEGED FUGITIVE BE ADMITTED IN EVIDENCE; and the *certificates* in this and the first section mentioned, SHALL BE CONCLUSIVE of the right of the person or persons in whose favor granted to remove such Fugitive to the State or Territory from which he escaped, AND SHALL PREVENT ALL MOLESTATION OF SAID PERSON OR PERSONS BY ANY PROCESS ISSUED BY ANY COURT, JUDGE, MAGISTRATE, OR OTHER PERSON WHOSOEVER.

SECT. 7. *And be it further enacted*,—That *any person who shall* knowingly and willingly *obstruct, hinder or prevent such claimant*, his Agent or Attorney, or any person or persons lawfully assisting him, her, or them, *from arresting such a Fugitive* from service or labor, *either with or without process* as aforesaid; or shall *rescue, or attempt to rescue, such Fugitive* from service or labor from the custody of such claimant, his or her Agent or Attorney or other person or persons lawfully assisting as aforesaid, when so arrested, pursuant to the authority herein given and declared; or *shall aid, abet, or assist* such person, so owing service or labor, as aforesaid, directly or indirectly, *to escape* from such claimant, his Agent or Attorney, or other person or persons legally authorized as aforesaid; or *shall harbor or conceal such Fugitive*, so as to prevent the discovery and arrest of such person, after notice or knowledge of the fact that such person was a Fugitive from service or labor as aforesaid, SHALL FOR EITHER OF SAID OFFENCES, be subject to a FINE not exceeding ONE THOUSAND DOLLARS, and IMPRISONMENT not exceeding SIX MONTHS, by indictment and conviction before the District Court of the United States for the District in which such offence may have been committed, or before the proper court of criminal jurisdiction, if committed within any one of the organized Territories of the United States; AND SHALL moreover FORFEIT AND PAY, by way of civil damages to the party injured by such illegal conduct, THE SUM OF ONE THOUSAND DOLLARS FOR EACH FUGITIVE SO LOST as aforesaid, to be recovered by action of debt in any of the District or Territorial Courts aforesaid, within whose jurisdiction the said offence may have been committed.

SECT. 8. *And be it further enacted*,—That the *Marshals*, their *Deputies*, and the *Clerks* of the said Districts and Territorial Courts, *shall be paid* for their services *the like fees* as may be allowed to them *for similar services in other cases*; and where such services are rendered exclusively in the arrest, custody, and delivery of the Fugitive to the claimant, his or her Agent or Attorney, or where such supposed Fugitive may be discharged out of custody from the want of sufficient proof as aforesaid, then such fees are to be paid in the whole by such complainant his Agent or Attorney; and *in all cases where the proceedings are before a Commissioner*, HE SHALL BE ENTITLED TO A FEE OF TEN DOLLARS in full for his services IN EACH CASE, UPON THE DELIVERY OF THE SAID CERTIFICATE TO THE CLAIMANT, his or her Agent or Attorney; OR A FEE OF FIVE DOLLARS *in cases where proof* SHALL NOT, *in the opinion of such Commissioner*, WARRANT SUCH CERTIFICATE AND DELIVERY, inclusive of all services incident to such arrest and examination, to be paid, in either case, by the claimant, his or her Agent or Attorney. The *person or persons authorized to execute the process to be issued by such Commissioners* for the arrest and detention of Fugitives from service or labor as aforesaid, SHALL ALSO BE ENTITLED TO A FEE OF FIVE DOLLARS EACH FOR EACH PERSON he or they may arrest and take before any such Commissioner as aforesaid, at the instance and request of such claimant, *with such other fees as may be deemed reasonable* by such *Commissioner* for such other additional services as may be necessarily performed by him or them: such as attending to the examinations, keeping the Fugitive in custody and providing him with food and lodgings during his detention, and until the final determination of such Commissioner; and in general for performing such other duties as may be required by such claimant, his or her Attorney or Agent or Commissioner in the premises; such fees to be made up in conformity with the fees usually charged by the officers of the Courts of Justice within the proper District or County, as near as may be practicable, and paid by such claimants, their Agents or Attorneys, whether such supposed Fugitive from service or labor be ordered to be delivered to such claimants by the final determination of such Commissioners or not.

SECT. 9. *And be it further enacted*, That *upon affidavit made by the claimant of such Fugitive* his Agent or Attorney, after such certificate has been issued, *that he has reason to apprehend that such Fugitive will be rescued* by force from his or their possession before he can be taken beyond the limits of the State in which the arrest is made, *it shall be the duty of the officer making the arrest to retain such Fugitive in his custody, and to remove him to the State whence he fled*, and there to deliver him to the said claimant, his Agent or Attorney. And *to this end* the officer aforesaid is hereby AUTHORIZED AND REQUIRED TO EMPLOY SO MANY PERSONS AS HE MAY DEEM NECESSARY to overcome such force, and to retain them in his service so long as circumstances may require; THE SAID OFFICER AND HIS ASSISTANTS, while so employed, *to receive the same compensation*, and *to be allowed the same expenses as are now allowed by law for the transportation of criminals*, to be certified by the Judge of the District within which the arrest is made, and PAID OUT OF THE TREASURY OF THE UNITED STATES.

SECT. 10. *And be it further enacted*, That when any person held to service or labor in any State or Territory, or in the District of Columbia shall escape therefrom, the party to whom such service or labor shall be due, his heirs, or their Agent or Attorney, may apply to any Court of record therein, or Judge thereof in vacation, and make such satisfactory proof to such Court or Judge thereof in vacation, of the escape aforesaid and that the person escaping owed service or labor to such party. Whereupon *the Court shall cause* A RECORD TO BE MADE OF THE MATTERS SO PROVED, and also a general description of the person so escaping, with such convenient certainty as may be; and A TRANSCRIPT OF SUCH RECORD, authenticated by the attestation of the Clerk, and of the seal of the said Court being produced in any other State, Territory, or District in which the person so escaping may be found, and being exhibited to any Judge, Commissioner, or other officer authorized by the law of the United States to cause persons escaping from service or labor to be delivered up, SHALL BE HELD AND TAKEN TO BE FULL AND CONCLUSIVE EVIDENCE OF THE FACT OF ESCAPE, AND THAT THE SERVICE OR LABOR OF THE PERSON ESCAPING IS DUE TO THE PARTY *in such record mentioned*. And upon the production by the said party *of other* and further *evidence, if necessary*, either oral or by affidavit, *in addition to what is contained in said record* of the identity of the person escaping, *he or she shall be delivered up* to the claimant. And said court, Commissioner, Judge, or other person authorized by this Act to grant certificates to claimants of Fugitives, *shall upon the production of the record*, and other evidences aforesaid, *grant to such claimant a certificate of his right to take any such person*, identified and proved to be owing service or labor as aforesaid, *which certificate shall authorize such claimant to seize, or arrest, and transport such person to the State or Territory from which he escaped*: *Provided*, that nothing herein contained shall be construed *as requiring the production of a transcript of such record as evidence* as aforesaid, but IN ITS ABSENCE, the *claim shall be heard and determined* upon OTHER satisfactory PROOFS competent in law.

IN SENATE, August 23 1850,
Passed. WILLIAM R. KING,
President.

IN HOUSE OF REPS., Sept. 12, 1850.
Passed. HOWELL COBB,
Speaker.

APPROVED, September 18, 1850.
MILLARD FILLMORE.

To the People of the United States!----The Issue before the Nation!

We present you this Document for the Campaign in order that its doctrines may be scanned before the minds of men become steeled against the power of just reasoning, by the intense zeal and party prejudice of an exciting election. It is a simple and earnest appeal to the reason, adapted to the calmer mood, and wishing to have naught to do with the passionate and fiery declamations of a later day.

The whole subject of the coming political struggle cannot be presented in the brief space to which I am limited. For this reason my argument is based upon the assumption that the readers of this paper acknowledge the American system of slavery to be an unmitigable evil, the continuance and perpetuity of which were a social and national crime. To the honest *thinking men* of all parties, creeds and divisions, the reasoning and sentiments of this missive are respectfully, earnestly, and with confidence commended.

The three principal political parties have marshalled their forces, promulgated their principles and measures, and have chosen their leaders. The Democrats are led by Franklin Pierce; the Whigs by Winfield Scott, and the Free Democracy by John P. Hale. Each party, at its national convention, builded a platform, which was designed and is received as the basis of its political effort in the coming contest, and of the policy of the government in the event of success. Each candidate is possessed of talent, energy and worth; the names of all have been connected with the history of the country, and each has done his native land some service.

Thus much we must know of the banner bearers, to ensure confidence in their honor and abilities. Knowing this, we have little else to do with the candidates, except to ascertain whether or not they will carry into practice the principles of the parties with which they are severally connected. There are few exceptions to the rule which supposes that the successful aspirant for so high an office will favor the measures and develope the principles upon which his election was secured. Policy and honor both require it, and that is a singular man who is heedless of the requisitions of either and both these influences! The defection of John Tyler is scarcely in point, as an offset here, for that gentleman was elected as a mere appendage to the chief "embodiment;" and as the peculiar mortality of Whig Presidents was then unknown, he could not have foreseen the emergency which uncovered his singularities! Each of the nominees is fully committed to a hearty support of the platform of his party. Franklin Pierce adopts the resolutions of the convention "because the principles they embrace command the approbation of my judgment." Winfield Scott accepts "the nomination with the resolutions annexed." John P. Hale has signified his acceptance of the nomination, and will unquestionably endorse and seek to carry out the principles embraced in the resolutions of the Pittsburg Convention.

To whatever quibbling the objectors may resort, it is clear that the nominees designed to convey the assurance that, in the event of success, the policy of the administration would correspond in tone and substance with the platform of the party. If they are honorable men they will fulfil that assurance.

If the foregoing observations are correct, we may let the candidates alone, and in this discussion refer only to the measures and principles of the several parties, as laid down and promulgated by authority at the Baltimore and Pittsburg Conventions. No personal predilection for a nomination will justify a vote in favor of disastrous, unjust, or injurious measures! No amount of past public service entitles an individual to a position of power, when that power will be used against the governmental application of just principles! Is the presidential chair a reward for services already requited, or a position of responsibility, of arduous labor and stern duty?

We will proceed to examine those platforms.

The Democratic party will favor the national appropriation of the proceeds of public lands, the principles laid down in the Kentucky and Virginia Resolutions of 1792—1798, and in the report of Mr. Madison to the Virginia Legislature in 1799.

And the party will oppose the exercise of doubtful constitutional powers, a general system of internal improvements, the assumption of local State debts fostering of one branch of industry to the detriment of any other, the repeal or modification of the COMPROMISE ACTS, including the FUGITIVE SLAVE LAW, the agitation of the slavery question, monopolies and exclusive legislation, the taking from the Presidents the qualified veto power.

And the party declares that the war with Mexico was a just and necessary war on our part, and congratulates the American people on the results of that war.

The Whig party will favor the reserved rights of the State, the constitutional powers of the General Government—obedience to the Constitution, laws and treaties—a discriminating tariff for revenue—such internal improvements as are national and constitutional.

And the party will oppose the exercise of other than constitutional powers, intervention, the repeal or modification of the COMPROMISE ACTS, including the FUGITIVE SLAVE LAW—all efforts to continue the agitation of the slavery question.

And the party declares the Federal and State government, are parts of one system, alike necessary to the common prosperity, peace and security.

The Free Democracy will favor the early policy of the country, to limit, localize and discourage slavery—the separation of the national funds from banking institutions, cheap postage, a moderate revenue—the election of civil officers by the people—such internal improvements as are national and constitutional—the cordial reception of emigrants and exiles from the old world—the grant of the Public Lands free of cost, to landless settlers—the immediate repeal of the Fugitive Slave Law—the recognition of the independence of Hayti—an arrangement in future treaties for a resort to decisive arbitration.

And the party will oppose the exercise of doubtful constitutional powers—the demand for more slave States, new slave territories, and the nationalization of slavery—foreign interference with the right of a nation to govern itself.

And the party declares none can be deprived of life, liberty, and the pursuit of happiness, by valid legislation, except for crime—the fundamental principle of equal rights, strict justice, and economical administration, should be applied to public affairs—the Government should relieve itself, by all constitutional means, from the responsibility of slavery—the Compromise Acts are unjust, and a settlement, no law nor usage can sanction or mitigate the crime of slavery—no human law is a *finality*—the General Government should protect all persons visiting the United States, from any infringement of their rights—the laws for the imprisonment of colored seamen are unconstitutional and iniquitous—the purpose of the Free Democracy is the possession of the Federal Government, and to administer it for the better protection of the rights and interests of the whole country.

No person can study the platforms of the two old parties without being struck with their general correspondence. Nor will a careful and minute examination of their several points develop any important antagonism. There is a difference without a contrast. On several subjects there is a positive and unshrinking agreement. On no one point is there a clear and decided contrariety.

On the 5th June, the Democratic party laid down, with great care, the Declaration, of which the sketch that we have given is a just synopsis. Those resolutions were designed to embrace and exhibit the distinctive features of the Democratic creed—the main and momentous principles and measures upon which that party bases its demand of support from the American people.

On the 8th June, the Whig party, after thirteen days of criticism and deliberation, presented its own Platform, upon which it claims the preference of the country. This declaration, like that of the Democratic party, is understood to embody the prominent principles and measures which characterize and distinguish the powerful organization by which it is adopted. It were rational to expect that a rival demand of the suffrages of the American people would be based upon a policy quite distinct from, and really adverse to, that of its eminent antagonist. But such is not the case. In this campaign the great competitors have joined issue upon neither a principle nor a question of governmental polity. The impetuous battle is to be fought upon a question of personal ascendency, upon the spur of ambition, and through the incentives of individual fancy and dislike.

The two sets of resolutions of which we are writing, are so entirely void of contrast, that the one might be appended to the other, and together they would form an entirely harmonious platform, with one slight impropriety—an occasional repetition of the same principle. The several propositions may be classified in the following order: 1. Those upon which there is a clearly expressed agreement. 2. Those upon which there is an agreement in substance, obscured by a difference of expression. 3. Those to which no reference is made by the counter organization. Under the first class we find the 1st, 7th and 8th propositions in our synopsis of the Democratic Platform, corresponding with the 5th, 7th and 8th of the Whig synopsis. Under the second class we find the resolves which refer to internal improvements. The Democratic policy is opposed to "*a general system*" of internal improvements. The Whig policy favors only such as are "*national and general in their character.*" A distinction without a difference; or, at most, a difference without a contrast. The third class embraces the remaining items of party policy. The former party expresses its sentiments upon the Public Lands, State debts, monopolies, the veto power, the Mexican war. The latter declines a reference to those subjects, and thus tacitly assents to their justness, or asserts their insignificance. The Whig Convention indicated its policy with reference to State Rights, obedience to Laws, &c., Tariff, Intervention, the relations of the Federal and State Governments. To none of these had the former Convention alluded; nor have we reason to believe that the policy of a Democratic administration would differ materially from that suggested above.

Those of my readers who have attentively considered the foregoing observations, will not fail to acknowledge that the two principal parties are preparing for a battle, the result of which is of little consequence to any but office-holders and office-seekers. Important principles and measures are left out of the contest. A change in the administration will not, so far as may be seen now, produce an essential change in the policy of the Government. The great rivals have descended from the dignity of champions of a principle, and are squabbling in the petty business of personal ascendency. Why join in the fiery turmoil of such a canvass? Why urge a partizan warfare on a basis so unworthy the greatness of the acting? Let the unprincipled and prejudiced run the race of meanness, if they will; but let the honest, the high-minded, the untrammelled, stand aloof or oppose.

I have dwelt so minutely upon the want of contrast and the direct resemblance in the creeds of the two prominent parties, in order to silence those Whigs who refuse to vote with the Free Democracy, lest an evil befall the country, in the election of Franklin Pierce over Winfield Scott; and those Democrats who pursue an opposite course for the contrary reason. Occupying synonymous positions, the triumph or defeat of either must be a matter of indifference to all; saving and excepting the expectants of public emoluments and public honors. If it be contended that the past history of either party entitles it to credit for the possession of any prominent virtue, we reply that the continual changes in the aspect of affairs destroys the binding force of party positions; and further, that each party has clearly defined its *present* attitude upon the questions of the day, and demands our support, on the ground of expediency, and the justice of the posture.

The intrepid Free Democracy have sought the arena of political strife, with a determination to oppose each of these powerful clock-work organizations. They publish a platform which presents a point-blank contrast to either and both the others. They claim the support of the people, because their policy is founded in Right and Justice; and because the application of that policy to governmental affairs, cannot be secured by the triumph of any other party. The general character and tone of the Free Democratic basis is eminently popular. In the strict synopsis which has been given, not an item can be found which does not lean clearly and unequivocally on the side of the people. Of the twenty-three points thus presented, four correspond with the expressed or supposed sentiments of the opposite parties. Of the remaining nineteen, eight are supposed to be antagonistic, because contrary to the practice; and eleven are diametrically opposed to their last explicit declarations. The limits of this paper forbid a notice of the second class of items, further than a mere statement of the subjects. Cheap postage; election of officers by the people; reception of emigrants and exiles; Haytien independence; decisive arbitration; just administration; imprisonment of colored seamen; protection to sojourners. Few, beside aristocrats and oppressors, will deny that, on these subjects, the position of the Free Democracy is tenable and true. We turn next to the third class.

A protest against, and a proper opposition to, foreign interference, with the right of a nation to govern itself.

This does not imply a rash and indiscriminate participation in continental quarrels! It suggests a cool and dignified attitude of opposition to such encroachments, more or less decided and prominent, as circumstances shall justify. Surely the cause of constitutional freedom requires thus much!

The remaining articles take the ground of opposition to slavery in all its various political phases.

While the attitude of the Free Democracy is that of a general championship of the rights of the humbler classes, being thus distinguished from both the others, its position upon the slavery question affords the *great* contrast, and entitles it to the support of the lovers of Freedom and Right. Whigs and Democrats assure us that, in the event of success, the policy of the government shall be to extend, nationalize, and encourage slavery. The Free Democracy take up the gauntlet, and call upon the people to sustain them in the effort to carry the country back to the policy of the fathers. The former parties stand ready to receive with fraternal welcome and kind caresses, those stained and feculent States, on whose forehead is written a deeper and blacker sign than the mark of Cain. The Free Democracy demand that none shall be admitted to this republican brotherhood who shall bring with them a taint and a snare. The old organism would fasten upon the general government the responsibility of a crime which knows no mitigation or excuse. The Free Democracy would hurl back this responsibility upon the perpetrators of the deed. Whigs and Democrats would sanction slavery by law. The Free Democracy forbid the high-handed endeavor. The former pronounce the compromise acts of the 31st Congress, including the Fugitive Law, to be a final settlement, in principle and substance, of the questions they embrace. The Free Democracy brand the same as unjust and incompatible with the principles of a popular government; and, denying the binding force of the Fugitive Slave Law, demand its immediate repeal. The ancient organizations pledge themselves to resist the discussion of the slavery question, whenever, wherever, and however such discussion shall be attempted. The Free Democracy defy their pledge and their power, and proclaim afar the determination to examine and discuss all questions, and especially that of slavery, till the spell shall be broken, and the nation relieved from the responsibility of this crime.

That the principal questions now before the country are those arising from the relations of the General Government to the system of slavery, is so surely a fact as to require no demonstration here. That the two great political parties are not opposed on any considerable point of governmental policy, and that the same are united in feeling and action upon the slavery side of the great question of the day, has been shown in the course of these remarks. That the principles and measures of the Free Democracy form a clear and open contrast to the basis established by the older parties, is a fact too palpable to receive contradiction. It follows that a vote for either of the former candidates, is as truly a vote in favor of the sustenance, defence and encouragement of American slavery in all its hideousness, as a vote for the devil were a vote in favor of sin. And it follows, also, that a ballot cast in behalf of the Free Democratic organization tells directly in favor of the just policy of the fathers "to limit, localize and discourage slavery." All this being true, it is quite impossible that a real friend of liberty can support either Pierce or Scott without doing violence to his own good sense, integrity or conscience.

Thus much for the national view of the subject. It is true of political parties that the State divisions receive their impression and hue from the character of the complete national organization. So that, however much local questions may divert attention from the general tendency of the brotherhood, it is fair to presume that the real character of the lesser department does not differ materially from that of the whole. It is also true, and to this point we call attention, as one especially germane to the topic in hand, that the duty of supporting a given national party, also involves the obligation to seek the supremacy of that party in the State, county and town. It were idle to attempt a general triumph, if the local victories are regarded as unimportant. The discipline which augurs success, demands as strict a fulfilment of the tactics of companies and battalions as of those of brigades and armies.

The true conception of the responsibility of the ballot is that which embraces an enlarged and beneficent view, and reckons upon the future as well as the present. Immediate effect should never be the acme of endeavor. The consequences of political effort reach forward and spread, so that certain defeat in the proximate future may be the attitude to which we are driven by duty, and the harbinger of the happiest ultimate results. The effort to prove that a ballot is thrown away when cast in the ranks of a party having little prospect of present success, is an endeavor to establish a sheer and palpable fallacy. The duty to build up a new party on a basis of justice, may be as clear and decided as the obligation to support an organism already perfected

One of the most cowardly charges against the Free Democracy is that of an endeavor to disorganize the American Union. They have no such design or desire. They are acting in the legitimate and proper sphere of good citizens, in an effort to purify the government of this great confederacy from the contamination of a horrid crime. It happens that a few of the criminals threaten a disruption of the Union in the event of a fair and honorable success. Supposing it all happens, who are the real disunionists? Those who act under the constitution, or those who rend and trample it in the dust?

This communication were quite incomplete did it fail to refer to the attitude of the party in Massachusetts, in regard to its connection with the Democratic organization. No room is left for the discussion of the expediency of the arrangement; but upon the propriety thereof we have the following observations to make. The fundamental principles of the Democratic party of the Commonwealth are of a popular character, opposed to a dry conservatism and a favored monopoly. Such are those of the Free Democracy. Only on the subject of slavery are the two bodies antagonistic. Now a vote in favor of a combination, is a positive vote in behalf of popular measures, and a neutral vote on the subject of slavery. To cast such a ballot is no desertion of principle, or dereliction of duty.

In dismissing this paper and its subject for the present, the writer has to regret that the narrowness of his limits has compelled a minuteness which may be tedious to the reader, and a conciseness which may have destroyed any attraction that the missive would otherwise have possessed. But perhaps the earnest seeker after truth and the pathway of political duty, will be thankful the necessity has prevented the hard kernel of thought from being covered and hidden beneath the almost impenetrable bar of rhetorical embellishment.

Respectfully submitted by
Your friend and fellow citizen,
ALEXANDER.

National Anti-Slavery Standard.

VOL. XVII. NO. 43. NEW YORK, SATURDAY, MARCH 14, 1857. WHOLE NO. 875.

National Anti-Slavery Standard.
PUBLISHED WEEKLY, ON SATURDAY,
AT TWO DOLLARS PER ANNUM,
BY THE
AMERICAN ANTI-SLAVERY SOCIETY,
At its Office, 138 Nassau St., New York,
AND AT THE OFFICE OF THE
PENNSYLVANIA ANTI-SLAVERY SOCIETY,
31 *North Fifth St., Philadelphia.*

NORRIS & JOHNSTON, PRINTERS.

Pro-Slavery.

THE DRED SCOTT CASE.

JUDGMENT OF THE U. S. SUPREME COURT.

Abstract, by the National Intelligencer.

Negroes not Citizens—Prohibition of Slavery in the Territories Unconstitutional.

WASHINGTON, Friday, March 6, 1857.

CHIEF Justice Taney, in delivering the opinion of the Court, said that this case, after argument at the last Term, was directed to be reargued at the present Term, owing to difference of opinion existing among members of the Court, and in order to give the subject [illegible] deliberation.

There were two leading questions: first, had the Circuit Court of the United States for the District of Missouri jurisdiction in the case? and if it had jurisdiction, was its decision erroneous or not?

The defendant denied, by plea in abatement, the jurisdiction of the Circuit Court of the United States on the ground that the plaintiff "is a negro of African descent, his ancestors were of pure African blood, and were brought into this country and sold as slaves," and therefore the plaintiff "is not a citizen of the State of Missouri." To this plea the plaintiff demurred, and the Court sustained the demurrer. Thereupon the defendant pleaded over, and justified the trespass on the ground that the plaintiff and his family were his negro slaves; and a statement of facts, agreed to by both parties, was read in evidence.

The Chief Justice, having stated the facts in the case, proceeded (in a tone of voice almost inaudible) to say, in substance, that the question first to be decided was whether the plaintiff was entitled to sue in a Court of the United States. This was a peculiar question, and for the first time brought before the Court under such circumstances; but it had been brought here, and it was the duty of the Court to meet and to decide it. The question was simply this, can a negro, whose ancestors were imported and sold as slaves, become a member of the political community formed and brought into existence by the Constitution of the United States, and, as such, become entitled to all the rights and immunities of a citizen, one of which rights is suing in the Courts of the United States in cases therein specified? In discussing this question we must not confound the rights of a citizen which a State may confer within its own limits with the rights of a citizen within the limits of the United States. No one can be a citizen of the United States unless under the provisions of the Constitution; but it does not follow that a man, being a citizen of one State, must be recognised as such by every State in the Union. He may be a citizen in one State and not recognised as such in another. Previous to the adoption of the Constitution, every State might confer the character of a citizen, and endow a man with all the rights pertaining to it. This was confined to the boundaries of a State, and gave him no rights beyond its limits. Nor have the several States surrendered this power by the adoption of the Constitution. Every State may confer the right upon an alien or on any other class or description of persons, who would, to all intents and purposes, be a citizen of the State, but not a citizen in the sense used in the Constitution of the United States. He would not thereby become a citizen of the United States, and, therefore, could not sue in any Court in the United States, nor could he enjoy the immunities of a citizen in the other States. His rights would be confined strictly to his own State. The Constitution gives Congress the power to establish "a uniform rule of naturalization"; consequently, no State, by naturalizing an alien, could confer upon him the rights and immunities of all the States under the General Government. It is very clear, therefore, that no State can, by any act, introduce a new member into the political Union created by the Constitution. The question then arises, whether the provisions of the Constitution of the United States in relation to personal rights to which a citizen of a State is entitled embraced negroes of the African race, at that time in the country, or afterwards imported, or made free from any State; and whether it is in the power of any State to make such a one a citizen of the State, and endow him with full citizenship in any other States without their consent. Does the Constitution of the United States act upon him, and clothe him with all the rights of a citizen? The Court think the affirmative cannot be maintained; and, if not, the plaintiff could not be a citizen of Missouri within the meaning of the Constitution, nor a citizen of the United States, and, consequently, not entitled to sue in its Courts.

It is true that every person, and every class and description of persons, at the time of the adoption of the Constitution, regarded as citizens of the several States, became citizens of this new political body, and none other. It was formed for them and their posterity, and for nobody else; and all the rights and immunities were intended to embrace only those of State communities, or those who became members according to the principles on which the Constitution was adopted. It was a union of those who were members of the political communities, whose power, for certain specified purposes, extended over the whole Territories of the United States, and gave each citizen rights outside his State which he did not before possess, and placed all rights of persons and property on an equality.

It becomes necessary, therefore, to determine who were citizens of the several States when the Constitution was adopted. In order to do this we must recur to the Colonies when they separated from Great Britain, formed new communities, and took their place among the family of nations. They who were recognised as citizens of the States declared their independence of Great Britain, and defended it by force of arms. Another class of persons, who had been imported as slaves, or their descendants, were not recognised or intended to be included in that memorable instrument, the Declaration of Independence. It is difficult at this day to realize the state of public opinion respecting that unfortunate class, with the civilized and enlightened portion of the world, at the time of the Declaration of Independence and the adoption of the Constitution; but history shows they have for more than a century been regarded as beings of an inferior order, and unfit associates for the white race, either socially or politically, and had no rights which white men were bound to respect; and the black man might be reduced to slavery, bought and sold, and treated as an ordinary article of merchandise. This opinion, at that time, was fixed and universal with the civilized portion of the white race. It was regarded as an axiom in morals, which no one thought of disputing, and every one habitually acted upon it, without doubting for a moment the correctness of the opinion. And in no nation was this opinion more fixed and generally acted upon than in England, the subjects of which Government not only seized them on the Coast of Africa, but took them, as ordinary merchandise, to where they could make a profit on them. The opinion thus entertained was universally impressed on the Colonists this side of the Atlantic; accordingly, negroes of the African race were regarded by them as property, and held and bought, and sold, as such in every one of the thirteen Colonies which united in the Declaration of Independence, and afterward formed the Constitution. The doctrine of which we have spoken was strikingly enforced by the Declaration of Independence. It begins thus: "When, in the course of human events, it becomes necessary for one people to dissolve the political bonds which have connected them with another, and to assume among the powers of the earth the separate and equal station to which the laws of nature and of nature's God entitle them, a decent respect to the opinions of mankind requires that they should declare the causes which impel them to the separation"; and then proceeds: "We hold these truths to be self-evident: that all men are created equal; that they are endowed by their Creator with certain inalienable rights; that among these are life, liberty and the pursuit of happiness; that to secure these rights, Governments are instituted among men, deriving their just powers from the consent of the governed," &c. The words before quoted would seem to embrace the whole human family; and if used in a similar instrument at this day would be so understood. But it is too clear for dispute that the enslaved African race was not intended to be included, for, in that case, the distinguished men who framed the Declaration of Independence would be flagrantly against the principles which they asserted. They who framed the Declaration of Independence were men of too much honour, education and intelligence, to say what they did not believe; and they knew that in no part of the civilized world were the negro race, by common consent, admitted to the rights of freemen. They spoke and acted according to the practices, doctrines and usages of the day. That unfortunate race was supposed to be separate from the whites, and was never thought or spoken of except as property. These opinions underwent no change when the Constitution was adopted. The preamble sets forth for what purpose and for whose benefit it was formed. It was formed by the people—such as had been members of the original States—and the great object was to "secure the blessings of liberty to ourselves and our posterity." It speaks in general terms of citizens and people of the United States when providing for the powers granted, without defining what description of person should be included, or who should be regarded as citizens. But two clauses of the Constitution point to the negro race as separate, and not regarded as citizens, for whom the Constitution was adopted. One clause reserves the right to import slaves until 1808, and in the second the States pledge themselves, one to another, to preserve the rights of the master, and to deliver up slaves escaping to their respective Territories. By the first clause the right to purchase and hold this property is directly sanctioned and authorized by the persons who framed the Constitution, for twenty years; and the States pledged themselves to uphold the right of the master as long as the Government then formed should endure. And this shows conclusively that another description of persons were embraced in the other provisions of the Constitution. These two clauses were not intended to confer upon them or their posterity the blessings of liberty so carefully conferred upon the whites. None of this class ever emigrated to the United States voluntarily. They were all articles of merchandise. The number emancipated was few as compared with those who were held in slavery, and not sufficiently numerous to attract public attention as a separate class, and were regarded as a part of the slave population, rather than free.

It cannot be supposed that the States conferred citizenship upon them; for all those States at that time established police regulations for the security of themselves and families, as well as of property. In some minor cases there were different modes of trial, and it could not be supposed that those States would have formed or consented to a government which abolished this right and took from them the safeguards essential to their own protection. They have not the right to bear arms and appear at public meetings to discuss political questions or urge measures of reform which they might deem advisable. They cannot vote at elections, nor serve as jurors, nor appear as witnesses where whites are concerned. These rights are secured in every State to white men. It is impossible to believe that the men of the slaveholding States, who took so large a share in the formation of the Constitution, could be so regardless of themselves and the safety of those who trusted and confided in them.

Every law of naturalization confines citizenship to *white* persons. This is a marked separation from the blacks. Under the Confederation every State had a right to decide for itself, and the term "free inhabitant," the generality of form, certainly excluded the African race. Laws were framed for the latter especially. Under the Constitution the word "citizen" is substituted for "free inhabitant." After further elaboration on this point, the Chief Justice said, from the best consideration, we have come to the conclusion that the African race who came to this country, whether free or slave, were not intended to be included in the Constitution for the enjoyment of any personal rights or benefits; and the two provisions which point to them treat them as property, and make it the duty of the Government to protect them as such. Hence the Court is of opinion, from the facts stated in the plea in abatement, that Dred Scott is not a citizen of Missouri, and is not, therefore, entitled to sue in the United States Courts. The following facts appear on the record:

"In the year 1834, the plaintiff was a negro slave belonging to Dr. Emerson, who was a surgeon in the army of the United States. In that year (1834) said Dr. Emerson took the plaintiff from the State of Missouri to the military post at Rock Island, in the State of Illinois, and held him there as a slave until the month of April, 1836. At the time last mentioned, said Dr. Emerson removed the plaintiff from said military post at Rock Island to the military post at Fort Snelling, situated on the west bank of the Mississippi river, in the Territory known as Upper Louisiana, acquired by the United States from France, and situated north of the latitude of 36 deg. 30 min. north, and north of the State of Missouri. Said Dr. Emerson held the plaintiff in slavery at said Fort Snelling until the year 1838.

"In the year 1835, Harriet (who is named in the second count of the plaintiff's declaration) was the slave of Major Taliaferro, who belonged to the army of the United States. In that year (1835) said Major Taliaferro took said Harriet to said Fort Snelling, a military post situated as hereinbefore stated, and kept her there as a slave until the year 1836, and then sold and delivered her as a slave at Fort Snelling unto said Dr. Emerson, hereinbefore named; and said Dr. Emerson held said Harriet in slavery at said Fort Snelling until the year 1838.

"In the year 1836, the plaintiff and said Harriet, at said Fort Snelling, with the consent of said Dr. Emerson, who then claimed to be their master and owner, intermarried and took each other for husband and wife. Eliza and Lizzie, named in the third count of the plaintiff's declaration, are the fruit of that marriage. Eliza is about 14 years old, and was born on board the steamboat Gipsey, north of the north line of the State of Missouri, and upon the Mississippi river; Lizzie is about seven years old, and was born in the State of Missouri, at the military post called Jefferson Barracks.

"In the year 1838, said Dr. Emerson removed plaintiff and said Harriet, and their said daughter Eliza, from said Fort Snelling to the State of Missouri, where they have ever since resided.

"Before the commencement of this suit, said Dr. Emerson sold and conveyed the plaintiff, said Harriet, Eliza and Lizzie, to the defendant as slaves, and the defendant claimed to hold each of them as slaves.

"At the times mentioned in the plaintiff's declaration, the defendant, claiming to be owner as aforesaid, laid his hands upon said plaintiff, Harriet, Eliza and Lizzie, and imprisoned them; doing in this respect, however, no more than what he might lawfully do if they were of right his slaves at such times."

The Chief Justice proceeded to examine the statement, assuming that this part of the controversy presented two questions.

Firstly: Was he (Scott) and all his family free in Missouri; and,

Secondly: If not, were they free by reason of their removal to Rock Island, Illinois.

The act of Congress on which the plaintiff relies contains the clause that slavery and involuntary servitude, except for crime, shall be forever prohibited in that part of the Territory acquired by treaty from Louisiana, and not included within the limits of the State of Louisiana. The difficulty which meets us at the threshold is, whether Congress is not authorized to pass such a law under the powers granted to it by the Constitution? The plaintiff dwells much on the clause which gives Congress power "to make all needful rules and regulations respecting the Territory or other property of the United States!" But this provision has no bearing on the present controversy. The power there given is confined to the Territory which then belonged to the United States, and can have no influence on Territory which was acquired from foreign Governments. The Justice then referred to the cessions of land by Virginia and other States, saying the only object was to put an end to existing controversies, and to enable Congress to dispose of the lands for the common benefit. Undoubtedly the power of sovereignty and eminent domain was ceded in the act. This was proper to make it essential. There was then no Government in existence with enumerated powers. What were called the States were thirteen independent Colonies, which entered into confederation for mutual protection. It was little more than a Congress of Embassadors, in which all had a common concern. It was this Congress which accepted the cession from Virginia. They had no right to do so under the articles of the Confederation, but they had a right, as independent powers, to accept the land for the common benefit; but it is clear, having no superior to control them, they had a right to exercise absolute dominion, subject only to the restrictions which Virginia imposed. The ordinance of 1787 was adopted, by which the Territory should be governed, and among other provisions was one that slavery or involuntary servitude should be prohibited, except for crime.

This was the state of things when the Constitution was formed. The territory ceded by Virginia belonged to the several confederate States as common property. The States were about to dissolve the Confederation, and surrender a portion of their power for the formation of a new government, and the language used limited and specified the objects to be accomplished. It was obvious that some provision was now necessary to give the new government the power to carry into effect every object for which the territory was ceded. It was necessary that the lands should be sold to pay the war debt, and that power should be given to protect the citizens who might emigrate, with their rights of property, arms, military stores (as well as ships of war), which were the "common property of the States existing in their independent character, and they had a right to take their property to the territory, without the authority of the States." The object was to place these things under the guardianship of a new Government, which gives Congress the power "to make all needful rules and regulations respecting the territory or other property of the United States." It applied only to property held in common at the time, and not with reference to any property which the sovereignty might subsequently acquire. It applied to the territory then in existence and known as the territory of the United States—then in the minds of the framers of the Constitution. It refers to the sale or raising of money. This is different from the power to legislate over the territories. With the words "to make all needful rules and regulations respecting the territory" are coupled the words "*and other property* of the United States." And the concluding words render this construction irresistible: "And nothing in this Constitution shall be so construed as to prejudice any claims of the United States *or of any particular State.*"

It is obvious that the Congress, under the new Government, regarded the above clause as necessary to carry into effect the principles and provisions of the Ordinance of 1787, which they regarded as an act of the States in the exercise of their political power at the time; and these representatives of the same States under the new Government did not think proper to depart from any essential principle, and did not attempt to undo anything that was done.

As to territory acquired without the limits of the United States, it remains territory until admitted into the Union. No power is given in the Constitution to acquire territory to be held and governed in that character; and, consequently, there cannot be found in the Constitution a[illegible] definition of power which Congress may lawfully exercise before it becomes a State. The power to acquire territory until it is in a condition to become a State on an equal footing with the other States must necessarily [illegible] on sound discretion, and it becomes the duty of the Government to administer the laws of the United States for the protection of personal rights and property therein.

Whatever territory is acquired is for the common [illegible] of the people of the United States, which is but a [illegible]. At the time that territory was obtained from F[illegible] contained no population to be admitted as a State. It therefore became necessary to hold possession of [illegible] settled and inhabited by a civilized community, [illegible] self-government and for admission into the Union. [illegible] as we before said, it was acquired by the Federal Government as the representative and trustee of the people of the United States, and must be held for their common and equal benefit; for it was the acquisition of the people of the United States, acting through their agents, and Government held it for the common benefit until it should become associated as a member of the Union. Until that time arrived it was undoubtedly necessary that some government be established to protect the inhabitants in their persons and property. The power to acquire carries with it the power to preserve. The form of government necessarily rests on the discretion of Congress. It is their duty to establish the best suited for the United States, and that must depend on the number of its inhabitants, and the character and situation of the territory. What government is the best must depend on the condition of the territory at the time, to be continued until it shall become a State. But there can never be a mere discretionary power over persons and property. These are plainly defined by the Constitution. The Constitution provides that "Congress shall make no law respecting an establishment of religion, or prohibiting the free exercise thereof; or abriding the freedom of speech, or of the press; or the right of the people peaceably to assemble, and to petition the Government for a redress of grievances," &c. Thus the rights of property are united with the personal rights, and this extends to the Territories as well as to the States. Congress cannot authorize the territories to do what it cannot do itself; it cannot confer on the territories power to violate the provisions of the Constitution.

It seems, however, that there is supposed to be a difference between slaves and other property. The people, in the formation of the Constitution, delegated to the General Government certain enumerated powers, and forbade the exercise of others. It has no powers over persons and property of citizens except those enumerated in the Constitution. If the Constitution recognises the right of master and slave, and makes no difference between slaves and other property, no tribunal acting under the authority of the United States can draw such a distinction and deny the provisions and guarantees secured against the encroachment of the Government. As we have already said, the right of property in a slave is expressly conferred in the Constitution, and guaranteed to every State. This is in language too plain to be misunderstood; and no words can be found in the Constitution giving Congress greater power over slaves than over any other description of property.

It is, therefore, the opinion of this Court that the Act of Congress which prohibits citizens from holding property of this character north of a certain line is not warranted by the Constitution, and is therefore void; and neither Dred Scott nor any one of his family were made free by their residence in Illinois. The plaintiff was not a citizen of Missouri, but was still a slave, and therefore had no right to sue in a Court of the United States.

THE INAUGURAL ADDRESS.

FELLOW-CITIZENS: I appear before you this day to take the solemn oath that I will faithfully execute the office of President of the United States, and will, to the best of my ability, preserve, protect and defend the Constitution of the United States. In entering upon this great office, I must humbly invoke the God of our fathers for wisdom and firmness to execute its high and responsible duties in such a manner as to restore harmony and the ancient friendship among the people of the several States, and to preserve our free institutions throughout many generations. Convinced that I owe my election to the inherent love for the Constitution and the Union which still animates the heart of the American people, let me earnestly ask their powerful support in sustaining all just measures calculated to perpetuate these, the richest political blessings which Heaven has ever bestowed upon any nation. Having determined not to become a candidate for reëlection, I shall have no motive to influence my conduct in administering the Government except the desire ably and faithfully to serve my country and to live in the grateful memory of my countrymen.

We have recently passed through a Presidential contest in which the passions of our fellow-citizens were excited to the highest degree by questions of deep and vital importance; but when the people proclaimed their will, the tempest at once subsided, and all was calm. The voice of the majority, speaking in the manner prescribed by the Constitution, was heard, and instant submission followed. Our own country could alone have exhibited so grand and striking a spectacle of the capacity of man for self-government. What a happy conception, then, was it for Congress to apply this simple rule, that the will of the majority shall govern to the settlement of the question of domestic slavery in the Territories! Congress is neither to legislate slavery into any Territory or State nor to exclude it therefrom; but to leave the people thereof perfectly free to form and regulate their domestic institutions in their own way, subject only to the Constitution of the United States. As a natural consequence, Congress has also prescribed that when the Territory of Kansas shall be admitted as a State, it shall be received into the Union with or without slavery, as their Constitution may prescribe at the time of their admission. A difference of opinion has arisen in regard to the time when the people of a Territory shall decide this question for themselves. This is happily a matter of but little practical importance, and, beside, it is a judicial question, which legitimately belongs to the Supreme Court of the United States, before whom it is now pending, and will, it is understood, be speedily and finally settled. To their decision, in common with all good citizens, I shall cheerfully submit, whatever this may be, though it has been my individual opinion that, under the Nebraska-Kansas act, the appropriate period will be when the number of actual residents in the Territories shall justify the formation of a Constitution with a view to its admission as a State into the Union. But, be this as it may, it is the imperative and indispensable duty of the Government of the United States to secure to every resident inhabitant the free and independent expression of his opinion by his vote. This sacred right of each individual must be preserved. This being accomplished, nothing can be fairer than to leave the people of a Territory free from all foreign interference to decide their own destiny for themselves, subject only to the Constitution of the United States. The whole territorial question being thus settled upon the principle of popular sovereignty—a principle as ancient as free government itself—everything of a practical nature has been decided, and no other question remains for adjustment, because all agree that, under the Constitution, slavery in the States is beyond the reach of any human power, except that of the respective States themselves wherein it exists. May we not then hope that the long agitation on this subject is approaching its end, and that the geographical parties to which it has given birth, so much dreaded by the Father of his Country, will speedily become extinct. Most happy will it be for the country when the public mind shall be diverted from this question to others of more pressing and practical importance. Throughout the whole progress of this agitation, which has scarcely known any intermission for more than twenty years, while it has been productive of no positive good to any human being, it has been the prolific source of great evils to the master, to the slave and to the whole country; it has alienated and estranged the people of the sister States from each other, and has even seriously endangered the very existence of the Union. Nor has the danger yet entirely ceased. Under our system there is a remedy for all mere political evils in the sound sense and sober judgment of the people. Time is a great corrective. The political subjects which but a few years ago exasperated the public mind have passed away and are now nearly forgotten; but this question of domestic slavery is of far greater importance than any mere political question, because, should the agitation continue, it may eventually endanger the personal safety of a large portion of our countrymen where the institution exists. In that [illegible], no form of government, however productive of [illegible] benefits, can compensate for the loss of peace [illegible] domestic security around the family altar. Let every [illegible] loving man, therefore, exert his best influence to [illegible] this agitation, which, since the recent legislation [illegible] Congress, is without any legitimate object. It is an [illegible] of the times that men have undertaken to calculate the mere material value of the Union.

Reasoned estimates have been presented of the pecuniary profits and local advantages which would result to different States and sections from its dissolution, and of the comparative injuries which such an event would inflict [illegible] other States and sections. Even descending to this [illegible] and narrow view of the mighty question, all such calculations are at fault. The bare reference to a single consideration will be conclusive on this point.

We at present enjoy a free trade throughout our extensive and expansive country, such as the world never [illegible]. This trade is conducted on railroads and [illegible], on noble rivers and arms of the sea, which bind [illegible] the North and the South, the East and the West [illegible] Confederacy. Annihilate this trade, arrest its free [illegible] by the geographical lines of jealous and hostile [illegible], and you destroy the prosperity and onward march [illegible] whole and every part, and involve all in one com[illegible].

[illegible] such considerations, important as they are in them[illegible] into insignificance when we reflect on the ter[illegible] which would result from disunion to every por[illegible] Confederacy, to the North not more than to [illegible], to the East not more than to the West. These I shall not attempt to portray, because I feel an humble confidence that the kind Providence which inspired our fathers with wisdom to frame the most perfect form of government and union ever devised by man will not suffer it to perish until it shall have been peacefully instrumental, by its example, in the extension of civil and religious liberty throughout the world.

* * * * * * *

It may be right that, on this occasion, I should make some brief remarks as to our rights and duties as a member of the great Family of Nations. In our intercourse with them, there are some plain principles, approved by our own experience, from which we should never depart. We ought to cultivate peace, commerce and friendship with all nations, and this not merely as the best means of promoting our own national interest, but in a spirit of Christian benevolence toward fellow-men, wherever their lot may be cast. Our diplomacy should be direct and frank, neither seeking to obtain more nor accepting less than is our due. We ought to cherish a sacred regard for the independence of all nations, and never attempt to interfere in the domestic concerns of any, unless this shall be imperatively required by the great law of self-preservation. To avoid entangling alliances has been a maxim of our policy ever since the days of Washington, and its wisdom no one will attempt to dispute. In short, we ought to do justice, in a kindly spirit, to all nations, and require justice from them in return. It is our glory that while other nations have extended their dominions by the sword, we have never acquired any territory except by fair purchase, or, as in the case of Texas, by the voluntary determination of a brave, kindred and independent people to blend their destinies with our own. Even our acquisitions from Mexico form no exception. Unwilling to take advantage of the fortune of war against a sister Republic, we purchased these possessions, under the treaty of peace, for a sum which was considered at the time a fair equivalent. Our past history forbids that we shall in the future acquire territory unless this be sanctioned by the laws of justice and honour. Acting on this principle, no nation will have a right to interfere or to complain if, in the progress of events, we shall still further extend our possessions. Hitherto, in all our acquisitions, the people under the protection of the American flag have enjoyed civil and religious liberty, as well as equal and just laws, and have been contented, prosperous and happy. Their trade with the rest of the world has rapidly increased, and thus every commercial nation has shared largely in their successful progress. I shall now proceed to take the oath prescribed by the Constitution, while humbly invoking the blessing of Divine Providence on this great people.

JAMES BUCHANAN.

Selections.

[illegible]NE AND INHUMAN LEGISLATION IN PENNSYLVANIA.

From The Bucks County Intelligencer.

SOME laws are to be found on our Statute Books which we shall ever contemplate with mingled emotions of pride and admiration. Such are those enactments designed to protect the poor and friendless, whose position in life has, in a particular manner, exposed them to the grinding evils of poverty, oppression and wrong. The negro race of this country are prominent among this class; and it is to the glory of this State, that she has been among the first of the Confederacy to extend the shield of protection over this unfortunate portion of her children.

The Emancipation Act of 1780 is a memorable specimen of *humane* legislation; and the preamble setting forth the motives for its passage is couched in a strain of eloquent pathos that has rarely found a place in legal authorities: "When we contemplate our abhorrence of that condition to which the arms and tyranny of Great Britain were exerted to reduce us, when we look back on the variety of dangers to which we have been exposed, and how miraculously our wants in many instances have been supplied, and our deliverance wrought, when even hope and human fortitude have become unequal to the conflict, we are unavoidably led to a serious and grateful sense of the manifold blessings which we have undeservedly received from the hand of that Being from whom every good and perfect gift cometh. Impressed with these ideas, we conceive it to be our duty, and we rejoice that it is in our power, to extend a portion of that freedom to others, which has been extended to us, and release from that state of thraldom to which we, ourselves, were tyrannically doomed, and from which we have now every prospect of being delivered. It is not for us to inquire why, in the creation of mankind, the inhabitants of the several parts of the earth were distinguished by a difference in feature or complexion—it is sufficient to know that all are the work of an Almighty hand. We find, in the distribution of the human species, that the most fertile as well as the most barren parts of the earth are inhabited by men of complexions different from ours, and from each other; from whence we may reasonably as well as religiously infer that He who placed them in their various situations hath extended equally His care and protection to all, and it becometh not us to counteract His mercies. We esteem it a peculiar blessing granted to us that we are enabled this day to add one more step to universal civilization, by removing as much as possible the sorrows of those who have lived in undeserved bondage, and from which, by the assumed authority of the kings of Great Britain, no effectual, legal relief could be obtained. [illegible], by a long course of experience, from those narrow prejudices and partialities we had imbibed, we find our hearts enlarged with kindness and benevolence towards men of all conditions and nations; and we conceive ourselves at this particular period extraordinarily called upon, by the blessings which we have received, to manifest the sincerity of our profession, and to give a substantial proof of our gratitude."

An attempt is now about to be made to introduce into this State a very different species of legislation from that contemplated in the above preamble. It is now proposed by legal authority to exclude from our State that very class of wretched outcasts whom the Legislators of our State, *more than three-quarters of a century since, commiserated as unfortunate, persecuted friends and brethren!* It seems that the petitioners for this inhuman enactment are from the Counties of Philadelphia and Bucks, and that Senator Ely, of Bucks County, has been selected as the appropriate instrument to advocate their wishes. I will not object to the propriety of the *agency*—but, as a citizen of Bucks, I could wish the disgrace of originating such a scheme of persecution might be traced to its true source—the *Slavocracy*—who are ever casting about for the aid of Northern doughfaces to perform their selfish and heartless deeds! And what is the pretext for legislative action in the premises? The petitioners complain, "that they are subject to trouble and expense, in consequence of an influx of fugitives and manumitted blacks," &c. Truly, this must be a serious calamity to the petitioners? "Trouble and expense," forsooth! Have their feelings ever suggested to them the *trouble* of the flying bondmen pursued by their tormentors? or compared the trifling pittance of expense which they themselves have endured with the trials and perils suffered by the fugitive as, in his desperate struggle for liberty, he leaves his friends, frequently at a most inclement season, and wends his way towards the goal of his hopes, houseless and friendless, and in constant fear of detection?

[illegible]t the feelings of the said petitioners are *very acute!* and here is an additional aggravation: The fugitives are "pursued into this State, and their reclamation is attended by mobs and excitement, &c."! And because this terrible wrong is inflicted upon them, they must be cut off from their last refuge, and be denied even the solace of a temporary home and the means to support a life by asking "leave to toil"! If there should be in every part of this Union a guarantee for the enjoyment of "life, liberty and the unobstructed pursuit of happiness," it would not be lo[illegible] before the "mobs and excitement" incident to their "reclamation" would teach the pursuers a lesson dictated no less by feelings of humanity than by the principles of Eternal Justice! Such a public sentiment would create an arm of protection that would shield the fugitive, and not only make his reclamation impossible, but place his pursuers on the same footing of *respectability* with the thief that seeks the cover of the night to commit his depredations!

But the question naturally occurs: by whom is the redress of these grievances asked? Does it come from a band of avowed *aristocrats*, who disclaim all sympathy for the poor suffering millions who are doomed to incessant toil? Were such the fact, I could more readily excuse the deed—but it owes its paternity to a class who are loud in their professions of their equal distribution of the principles of liberty and equality to all. The Democracy of our County claim the honour of this movement! And the Legislator who is put forward in the work will be entitled to a large share of the reputation of the body of which he is a member should such an iniquitous law as the one asked for ever be found on our Statute Books.

But I will not even anticipate the possibility of such a result. I believe in a better state of public sentiment among Pennsylvania Legislators than would tolerate such an inhuman law. I further believe that the principles of a spurious Democracy are fast yielding to those of a more enlightened and liberal cast. Democracy (as it should be) lies at the foundation of the great principles of human rights—moral, religious and political—and its great and noble aim is to establish the platform of human brotherhood throughout the earth.

Through all disguise, power, place and name,
Even in the flaunting robes of sin,
Through poverty's disgusting home,
Thou lookest at the MAN WITHIN.
Beneath thy broad, impartial eye
How fade the lines of caste and birth!
How equal in their sufferings lie
The groaning multitudes of earth!

HUMANITAS.

New Hope, Second mo. 14th, 1857.

A PRECIOUS DOCUMENT—THE BUCKS COUNTY DEMOCRACY IN THE FIELD!—We published last week in our Legislative news a report of the discussion in the Senate on the reception of a petition purporting to come from citizens of Bucks and Philadelphia Counties, praying for a law to prevent negroes from other States acquiring a residence in Pennsylvania. In the course of the debate the unterrified Democracy were effectually cornered, and a number of them took the opportunity to disavow any sympathy whatever with the views of the petitioners, whose cause could not find a single apologist. We are now enabled to present the petition itself—a specimen of composition eminently worthy its origin—with some of the names that were appended to it.

To the Honourable the Senate and House of Representatives:

We, the undersigned, "*Males and Females*," of Bucks and Philadelphia Counties, respectfully represent: That they are subjected to trouble, inconvenience and expense, on account of runaway *niggers* from other States. We further represent and claim to be *white folks*, and wish to remain so—*Black Republicanism* to the contrary notwithstanding: therefore, we ask your honourable body to take the matter into consideration, and pass a general law prohibiting negroes from coming into or acquiring a residence in the State. There is, beyond doubt, a necessity for some such law, as too many worthless blacks already are in our midst and rapidly on the increase. We are neither Abolitionists nor amalgamationists, and conceive, as citizens, to be entitled to protection, at your hands, from negro violence, impudence and insults, hence the necessity for said law.

W. Jasper Alburger, David Garner, Patrick Kessler, George Miller, Charles W. Stark, Henry A. Stark, Samuel Stark, Christian Stark, Edward P. Knight, T. Jefferson Myers, A. Willet Myers, Francis Mahan, Elizabeth P. Knight, Eliza M. Alburger, Sallie W. Barnes, Emma V. Alburger, Jane Levins, Sarah Ellen Levins, E. Virginia Alburger, Mary Connelly, Ann Connelly, Franklin Seckel, and 98 others.

In contrast with the above, we append a remonstrance, from the Society of Progressive Friends, presented at the same time by Senator Lewis, which was ordered to be printed.

To the Senate and House of Representatives of the Commonwealth of Pennsylvania.

The memorial of Kennett Quarterly Meeting of the religious society of Progressive Friends, held at Longwood, Chester Co., respectfully represents:

That we have learned with surprise and regret that a petition has been presented to your body, signed by one hundred and eight citizens of Philadelphia and Bucks Counties, praying for the passage of a law prohibiting negroes and mulattoes from coming into the State with a view of acquiring a residence.

It is with feelings of no ordinary character that we attempt to address our remonstrance against any movement on the part of our beloved Commonwealth, to throw any additional obstacle in the way of this already cruelly wronged and outraged class of our fellow-men. Surely it is enough that nearly four millions of these people, in the country of Washington, Jefferson, Franklin and Penn, are already SLAVES, driven to unpaid toil, and subjected to all the horrors of our American slave system; and the Federal Constitution is believed to require the prompt return of the fugitive, whenever he may chance to escape from his master; that many of our citizens acknowledge no higher law than constitutional obligations and legal enactments, and hence are ever ready to join with alacrity in the humiliating slave hunt, which often results in consigning its victims to chains and slavery, more to be dreaded than death itself, by as much as liberty is dearer than life. Must the character of our State, the spirit of our free institutions, the claims of humanity, and the principles of the Christian religion, be totally disregarded and set at naught by granting the prayer of these petitioners? We trust not. We will not believe it. We cannot believe that any attempt to procure the passage of a law having the slightest bearing in that direction can receive for one moment your serious consideration.

Thus hoping, and thus confidently trusting, we subscribe ourselves yours, for the cause of humanity and liberty.

On behalf of the meeting,

Mary Pennock, Joseph A. Dugdale, Hannah Cox, William Barnard, Philena Heald, John G. Jackson, Sallie Pusey, Thos. Hambleton, Hannah Heuk, E. P. Wickersham, Lizzie McFarlan, Lewis Marshall, Lea Pusey, Thomas Borton.

PERSONAL LIBERTY LAW OF WISCONSIN.

AN ACT, relating to the Writ of Habeas Corpus to Persons claimed as Fugitive Slaves, the Right of Trial by Jury, and to Prevent Kidnapping in this State.

The People of the State of Wisconsin, represented in the Senate and Assembly, do enact as follows:

SECTION 1. The same power is hereby given to, and the same duties imposed upon, the Judges of the County Courts of the several Counties in this State which are given to and imposed upon the Judges of the Circuit and Supreme Courts by the Constitution and Laws of this State, for the purposes hereinafter provided.

SEC. 2. It shall be the duty of the District-Attorneys, within their respective Counties, whenever any inhabitant of this State is arrested or claimed as a fugitive slave, on being informed thereof, diligently and faithfully to use all lawful means to protect, defend, and procure to be discharged, every such person so arrested or claimed as a fugitive slave.

SEC. 3. The application of any District-Attorney, in writing, or any one of the Judges of the Supreme Court, or any Judge of the County or Circuit Courts, signed by said District-Attorney in his official capacity, stating, in substance, the name of the person, and the name of the person detaining him or her, if known, and that the person arrested, claimed and imprisoned as a fugitive slave, shall be sufficient authority to authorize the issuing of the writ of habeas corpus, as provided in chapter one hundred and twenty-four of the Revised Statutes of Wisconsin, and said writ may be signed by any one of the said Judges, or by the Clerk of the Supreme or Circuit Court; and said writ shall be made returnable before either the Circuit or County Court, when in session, in the County where such application is made, and in vacation said writ may be made returnable forthwith before either of the Judges aforesaid.

SEC. 4. It shall be the duty of all Judicial and Executive officers in this State, in their respective Counties, who shall know, or have good reason to believe, that any inhabitant of this State is about to be arrested or claimed as a fugitive slave, forthwith to give notice thereof to the District-Attorney of the County in which such person resides.

SEC. 5. Whenever the writ of habeas corpus is granted in vacation, as provided in this act, or as provided by existing laws, if, upon the hearing of the same before any one of the Judges aforesaid, the person imprisoned, arrested or claimed as a fugitive slave shall not be discharged, such person shall be entitled to an appeal to the next stated term of the Circuit Court in the County where such hearing was had, on furnishing such bail, and within such time as the Judge granting the writ, on hearing the case, shall adjudge to be reasonable and proper.

SEC. 6. The Court to which such appeal is taken, and any other Court to which a writ of habeas corpus in behalf of any such person claimed or arrested as a fugitive slave is made returnable, may and shall, on the application of either party to such proceedings, allow and direct a trial by jury on all questions of fact in issue between the parties in the matter aforesaid; and the taxable cost of such trial shall be chargeable to the State, whenever the same would be otherwise chargeable to the person arrested or claimed as a fugitive slave.

SEC. 7. Every person who shall falsely and maliciously declare, represent or pretend that any free person within this State is a slave, or owes service or labour to any person or persons, with intent to procure, or to aid, or assist in procuring the forcible removal of such free person from this State as a slave, shall pay a fine of one thousand dollars, and be imprisoned in the State prison not more than five nor less than one year: *Provided*, That nothing in this act shall be construed as applying to any claim of service from an apprentice for a fixed time.

SEC. 8. No declaration, representation or pretence that any person being or having been in this State is or was a slave shall be deemed proved, except by the testimony of at least two credible witnesses, testifying to facts directly tending to establish the truth of such declaration, representation or pretence, or by legal evidence equivalent thereto; and any person who, upon any trial arising under this and the foregoing section, shall falsely and wilfully represent or pretend, with intent to aid any party accused under this act, that any person was or is a slave, or owes or did owe service or labour to any person or persons, shall pay a fine of one thousand dollars, and be imprisoned in the State prison not less than one year.

SEC. 9. On the trial of any prosecution arising under this act, no deposition shall be received as evidence.

SEC. 10. Every person who shall obstruct any officer in the service of any warrant issued in accordance with this act, or who shall aid in the escape of any person accused under sections seven and eight of this act, or who shall aid in the escape of any person accused under said sections seven and eight while pursued by such officer, or in his custody, shall be imprisoned in the State prison not less than one year.

SEC. 11. No judgment recovered against any person or persons for any neglect or refusal to obey, or any violations of the Act of Congress commonly termed the Fugitive Slave Act, approved September 18, 1850, or any of the provisions thereof, shall be a lien on any real estate within this State, nor shall any such judgment be enforceable by sale on execution of any real estate or personal property within this State, but all such sales shall be absolutely void; and in case of seizure or sale of any personal property by virtue of any execution issued on such judgment, the defendant in said execution may maintain an action of replevin, or other action, to recover possession thereof in the manner prescribed by law, and a further statement therein that said execution issued on a judgment rendered under the provisions of the Act of Congress aforesaid; and the provisions of this section shall also apply to judgments heretofore rendered.

SEC. 12. This act shall be considered a public act, and shall be construed favourably by all Courts and in all places, and shall take effect and be in force from and after its passage.

Approved, Feb. 19, 1857.

THE NEW YORK CONVENTIONS.

WE have been absent from our editorial post, for a short time, to attend a series of Anti-Slavery Conventions at Rochester, Syracuse, Utica, and Albany, in company with Wendell Phillips (who was present only at Albany), Parker Pillsbury, Samuel J. May, Charles L. Remond, Stephen S. Foster, Aaron M. Powell, Susan B. Anthony, and Sarah P. Remond.

Prior to the holding of these Conventions, a series of others had been held in various localities in Western New York, during the severest part of the Winter, by Mr. Powell, Mr. Remond, Miss Remond, and Miss Anthony, in one direction, and by S. S. Foster, and Benjamin S. and Jane Elizabeth Jones, in another—with as much success as could be expected, under the circumstances. Wherever these earnest and uncompromising labourers went, they produced a healthy excitement, woke the lethargic from their death-like repose, shocked the conservative, unmasked the hypocritical, convinced the wavering, strengthened the feeble, refreshed the true-hearted, opened the eyes of the blind, and caused the deaf to hear and the lame to walk. It was new ground, to a great extent, and the difficulties encountered were manifold; whatever of real or latent pro-slavery existed was very quickly revealed, especially in the garb of a spurious religion; but the word was spoken "in demonstration of the spirit and with power," and it can never return void. It is only by such self-denying, courageous and persevering labours that the land has been shaken, in regard to its colossal sin and crime, and that the desired revolution in public sentiment can be consummated, to the utter extinction of slavery. Few can realize what faith in principle, what fidelity to the right, what resoluteness of purpose, what courage of heart, what self-abnegation are needed, in carrying on such a moral crusade by those who enter the lecturing field as the agents of the American Anti-Slavery Society. To go from town to town, from village to village, without friends or acquaintance, with the certainty of being fiercely assailed by all the religious influences and basely calumniated by political demagogueism, branded as "infidels" by the pulpit and as "traitors" by a venal press, compelled to speak in some obscure hall or petty schoolhouse, with few to hear and fewer to respond to the noble utterances of the occasion, frequently at considerable pecuniary expense—the elements of nature themselves often conspiring to baffle what otherwise might have been an excellent gathering, the mercury sometimes ranging at zero, and occasionally at thirty degrees below, and appointments to be kept in the face of driving snow-storms and roads almost impassible for either man or beast—all this is a task, which, outside from the godlike object which inspires to effort, might well appal the stoutest heart, and induce the most intrepid to shrink from its prosecution.

There are none who deserve such thanks, such warm appreciation for their labours in the cause, as those faithful men and women who, in imitation of Jesus, making themselves of no reputation for righteousness' sake, go forth to plead the cause of the enslaved millions in our land. It is by their sacrifices and labours that it is made possible for such men as Joshua R. Giddings, Charles Sumner, William H. Seward and John P. Hale to obtain seats in Congress, and deliver such anti-slavery sentiments as fall from their lips. Blessings on those who kindly take these storm-proof champions to their homes, share with them their hospitable board, give them the friendly grasp of the hand, speak an encouraging word, and lend what coöperation is in their power! They have their reward in the gratitude of those who are ready to perish.

Of the various speakers who attended the Conventions alluded to, we may name Miss Anthony, who, by her public labours in the cause of Education and of Woman's Rights, has won for herself the respect and friendship of thousands; whose executive talent and sound judgment, as financial and general agent, were admirably displayed; and whose cogent and impressive manner of address did excellent service.

Miss Sarah P. Remond (a sister of C. L. Remond) made her first efforts at public speaking on this extended tour, and everywhere commanded the respect and secured the attention of her auditors. Her calm, dignified manner, her winning personal appearance, and her earnest appeals to the conscience and heart, produced a most favourable impression. She only needs practice to become a very useful lecturer.

Mr. Remond never failed to arouse and inspire those whom he addressed, by his stirring and eloquent appeals, and obtained the heartiest endorsement of his sentiments. He not only fulfilled every appointment made in the whole series, but spoke on other occasions not laid down in the programme, notwithstanding the severity of the weather and the delicate state of his health.

Mr. Powell, though a young man, and comparatively a new lecturer in the field, is a most valuable acquisition to the cause, and acquitted himself with marked ability. In maturity of mind, in clearness of vision, in solid worth, and in nobleness of aim, he is far beyond his years. Of Quaker origin and education, his spirit spurns all sectarian trammels; his heart is a well-spring of humanity; and his moral nature greatly perfected.

Though the Conventions we addressed were not numerously attended (undoubtedly owing to the general exhaustion which has followed the tremendous excitement arising from the lawless invasion of Kansas, and from the late Presidential Election), those who were present were of the more intelligent and reflective portion; and the truths which were uttered evidently made a deep and powerful impression.—*Liberator.*

THE REPUBLICAN PARTY.

[Extract from a Letter to the Abolitionists of the United States, by GERRIT SMITH.]

AT first, the Abolitionists looked to the Whig party; then to the Free Soil party; then to the Free Democratic party; and now they are bewitched with the insane notion that it is the Republican party which is to do the work of the Abolitionists. That they are to do their own work, instead of depending upon an enemy to do it, would seem to be the very last idea that can be got into their heads. Well do I remember how hard, and yet how vainly, a few of us toiled to convince them that the Whigs were not their brothers, nor cousins, nor friends, but simply their foes; and then how we taxed ourselves with a similar and no less useless labour to disabuse them of their like delusion in regard to the Free Soilers; and afterward to disabuse them of their like delusion in regard to the Free Democrats. And now the springing up of the Republican party has brought another such work upon our hands. Yes, the great majority of the Abolitionists are infatuated with the idea that the Republican party will achieve the abolition of slavery. Hence, they see it to be no desertion of their principles to join it, but to be altogether for the success of those principles to take their place in a great and, as they trust, ere long triumphant party, rather than remain identified with a hopeless handful. The depth of their present delusion is, after all, not surprising. It is the natural result of a succession of delusions, each one of which has prepared the way for a deeper one.

I will do no injustice to the Republican party. Compared with its rival parties, it merits praise only. It is to them "Hyperion to a Satyr." Earnestly does it contend for the freedom of Kansas; and should slavery go into any of the Territories, I trust it will not be with the consent of the Republican party. Not the least of its

Illinois State Journal.

BAILHACHE & BAKER, Proprietors.

SPRINGFIELD:

FRIDAY MORNING, OCT. 1, 1858.

☞See first page for Interesting Matter.

REPUBLICAN STATE TICKET.

For State Treasurer,
COL. JAMES MILLER, of McLean County.

For Superintendent of Public Instruction,
PROF. N. BATEMAN, of Morgan County.

INDEPENDENT CANDIDATE FOR CONGRESS—6TH DISTRICT:
JAMES H. MATHENY, of Sangamon Co.

SANGAMON COUNTY TICKET.

FOR REPRESENTATIVES:
JAMES N. BROWN.
JOHN COOK.

FOR SHERIFF:
JOHN W. SMITH.

FOR CORONER:
WILLIAM PERCE.

MR. LINCOLN'S APPOINTMENTS.

Mr. Lincoln will address the people at the following times and places:

Pittsfield, Pike	do	October	1
Metamora, Woodford	do	"	4
Pekin, Tazewell	do	"	5
Galesburg, Knox	do	"	7
Oquawka, Henderson	do	"	9
Monmouth, Warren	do	"	11
Quincy, Adams	do	"	13
Alton, Madison	do	"	15
Mount Sterling, Brown	do	"	18
Rushville, Schuyler	do	"	20
Carthage, Hancock	do	"	22
Macomb, McDonough	do	"	25
Vermont, Fulton	do	"	27
Petersburg, Menard	do	"	29

JUDGE TRUMBULL'S APPOINTMENTS.

Judge Trumbull will address the people at the following times and places:

Galena, Saturday	October	2
Peoria, Tuesday	"	7
Lacon, Thursday	"	5
Canton, Saturday	"	9
Charleston, Monday	"	18
Paris, Tuesday	"	19
Marshall, Thursday	"	21
Majority Point, Saturday	"	23

Political Discussion.

Mr. Lincoln and Mr. Douglas will address the people, in oint debate, at the following places and times:

Galesburg, Knox county	October 7
Quincy, Adams county	October 13
Alton, Madison county	October 15

Douglas will open the discussion at Ottawa, Jonesboro, Galesburg and Alton, and speak one hour; Lincoln will follow speaking one hour and a half, and Douglas will reply for half an hour. At Freeport, Charleston and Quincy, Lincoln will open the discussion, Douglas reply, and Lincoln rejoin
dawtf

COUNTY MEETINGS.

There will be public speaking at the following places on the days herein specified, at 2 o'clock P. M.

Farmington, Watt's School House	Monday, Oct.	4
Auburn	Wednesday, "	6
Wolf Creek, Constant's School House	Friday, "	8
Laomi, at Lebanon	Monday, "	11
Buffalo Hart, Chapel	Wednesday, "	13
Chatham	Thursday, "	14
Salisbury	Thursday, "	15
Prairie Creek, Gardner's School House	Monday, "	18
Cotton Hill, Brunk's School House	Wednesday, "	20
Richland, at Pleasant Plains	Friday, "	22
Lower Lick Creek, Renshaw's School House,	Monday, "	25
Mechanicsburg	Tuesday, "	26
Rochester	Wednesday, "	27
Williamsville	Thursday, "	28
Berlin	Friday, "	29

Whigs, Americans, Republicans and Democrats, are respectfully invited to attend.

Addresses may be expected from some of the following speakers viz: James H. Matheny, Wm. H. Herndon, James C. Conkling, S. M. Cullom, C. C. Brown, J. D. Bail, C. S Zane, and others.

Lincoln Stands on the Old Whig Platform.

The following are Douglas' Questions and Lincoln's Answers at Freeport:

Question 1. "I desire to know whether Lincoln to-day stands, as he did in 1854, in favor of the unconditional repeal of the fugitive slave law!"

Answer I do not now, nor ever did, stand in favor of the unconditional repeal of the fugitive slave law.

Q. 2 "I desire him to answer whether he stands pledged to-day, as he did in 1854, against the admission of any more slave States into the Union, even if the people want them?"

A. I do not now, nor ever did, stand pledged against the admission of any more slave States into the Union.

Q. 3. "I want to know whether he stands pledged against the admission of a new State into the Union, with such a Constitution as the people of that State may see fit to make."

A. I do not stand pledged against the admission of a new State into the Union, with such a Constitution as the people of that State may see fit to make.

Q. 4. "I want to know whether he stands to-day pledged to the abolition of slavery in the District of Columbia?"

A. I do not stand to-day pledged to the abolition of slavery in the District of Columbia.

Q. 5. "I desire him to answer whether he stands pledged to the prohibition of the slave trade between the different States?"

A. I do not stand pledged to the prohibition of the slave trade betweett the different States.

Q. 6. "I desire to know whether he stands pledged to prohibit slavery in all the Territories of the United States, North as well as South of the Missouri Compromise, line."

A. I am impliedly, if not expressly, pledged to a belief in the right and duty of Congress to prohibit slavery in all the United States Territories.

Q. 7. "I desire him to answer whether he is opposed to the acquisition of any new Territory unless slavery is first prohibited therein."

A. I am not generally opposed to honest acquisition of territory; and, in any given case. I would, or would not, oppose such acquisition. accordingly as I might think such acquisition would or would not agitate the slavery question among ourselves.

Mr. Lincoln stands on the Old Whig Platform, with Clay and Webster.

The Forgery Acknowledged.

Douglas and his sattelites stand convicted of the crime of willful forgery, in quoting a set of resolutions adopted by a "People's" Convention at Aurora, and trying to pass them off as the Republican platform of 1854.

Read the retraction, taken from the Chicago *Times* of August 24th:

"In the speech made by Judge Douglas, at Ottawa, on Saturday, he quoted the resolutions which contained the Republican platform of 1858. *Misled by the paper in which he found the resolutions published, he located their adoption at a Convention held at Springfield.* The particular resolutions WERE NOT THE ONES ADOPTED AT THE SPRINGFIELD CONVENTION."

THE RECORD! THE RECORD!!

Our readers will find in one of the sections of the Toombs bill the following provision:

"That the following proposition be and the same are hereby offered to the convention of the people of Kansas, when formed for their free acceptance of rejection, which if accepted by the convention, *and ratified by the people at the election for the adoption of the Constitution*, shall be obligatory on the United States and upon the said State of Kansas."

In the bill as reported by Douglas, the words in italic were left out, * * Senator Douglas DID strike out the clause.—*Chicago Times, Aug. 13th.* [dawtf

QUESTION for the PEOPLE to ANSWER.

If Thirty-five Thousand People are enough to form a Slave State, why should they not be enough to form a Free State

From the Chicago Press and Tribune.

Poor Little Dug!

Douglas grows fainter and weaker as he progresses. His one act comedy is losing interest with all sorts of hearers. We have printed it so many times since the canvass opened that there is hardly a man in Illinois who is not acquainted with its beginning, middle and end. He does not vary it enough in all his turning and twistings upon the Dred Scott decision to give it the charm of novelty anywhere. His voice is growing hollow and husky, his temper is bad; and his whole appearance jaded and worn, Hence his crowds fall off in number and lack in enthusiasm. His brass cannon dragged in his train by two gunners, wearing cavalry sabres, shooting caps and red shirts, awakens no responsive cheers in the rural districts where its booming is heard. Discharged when he approaches the spot where he is to be delivered, no shouts answers its thunder; discharged half a dozen times during each speech, at the periods where applause ought to come in, no applause is heard. Discharged when he leaves the town wherein he has labored, he is suffered to depart in sullen silence, nevertheless. He carries with him, and leaves behind him a villainous smell of brimstone and bogus Popular Sovereignty—nothing more! We take it that the game is about up—that the Little Giant is nearly played out; a few more spasms and he goes down. Poor Little Dug! Who will fire that gun over the spot to bring you up?

☞The proposition to loan the credit of the city of Rockford to the amount of $50,000 to complete the Rockford and Kenosha road, was decided in the affirmative, last week, by the voters of that city.

The "Mud Sills" of Society.

The "Mud Sill" speech of Senator Hammond of South Carolina, one of the leading Democratic spirits of the United States Senate and a follower of J. C. Calhoun, whose doctrines Douglas now advocates, has heretoforce been published and criticized by us. The following is one of the choice morsels of that Democratic Senator's characteristic Democratic speech:

"In all social systems there must be a class to perform the drudgery of life—that is, a class requiring but *a low order of intellect, and but little skill.* Such a class you must have, or you would not have that other class which leads progress, civilization and refinement. *It constitutes the very mud-sill of society* and of political government; and you might as well attempt to build a house in the air, as to build either one or the other except on this mud sill. THE MAN WHO LIVES BY DAILY LABOR, and hardly lives at that, and who has to put out his labor in the market, and take the best he can get for it; in short, YOUR WHOLE CLASS OF MANUAL LABORERS and operatives, as you call them, ARE ESSENTIALLY SLAVES."

We commend this to the hod carriers, brick layers, carpenters, masons and laborers who train in Democratic ranks and constitute the "mud-sills" of the Democratic party. See what your political masters say of you. "Essentially *slaves*" are you?

But this Democratic idea that the laborers are the "mud-sills" of society is not original with Senator Hammond. Another Senator, equally as Democratic in his politics, a few years ago attempted a similar slur upon the free working men of the north. It was in a debate, which took place in 1850 on the Compromise measures of Mr. Clay. Mr. Downs, of Louisiana, had the impudence to draw a parallel between the slaves of the south and laboring people of the north, giving the preference in all points of condition and happiness to the slaves of the south. He was answered by Mr. Webster.

"Who," said Mr. Webster, "are the laboring people of the north? They are the whole north. They are the people, who till their own farms with their own hands; freeholders, educated men independent men. Let me say, sir, that five sixths of the whole property of the north is in the hands of the laborers of the north; they cultivate their farms, they educate their children, they provide the means of independence. If they are not freeholders they earn wages; these wages accumulate, are turned into capital into new freeholds, and small capitalists are created. Such is the case, and such the course of things, among the industrious and frugal.—And what can these people think when so respectable and worthy a gentleman as the member from Louisiana undertakes to prove, that the absolute ignorance and the abject slavery of the south are more in conformity with the high purposes and destiny of immortal, rational human beings, than the educated, the independent free labor of the north?"

The so called statesmen of the South are grossly ignorant of the laboring millions of the North. They regard the men, who are the solid basis of our free society—who are the source of our strength and prosperity—who build and man our ships and steamboats,—who construct our railroads, build our cities, develop our resources and exalt and give renown to our country—as mere "slaves" and they suppose the laborers to be in favor of an agrarian law!

Yet these "mud sills," these despised laboring men are annually called upon to cast their votes in favor of candidates misnamed "Democratic"—who recognize such slaveholding aristocrats as Hammond, Foote, Jones, Douglas, Stephens and company as leaders of the Democratic party. Senator Hammond says the South controls the North through the Democratic party—and this is true. The South does control the Democracy and those who act with that party, and those who indorse and vote for its candidates should be prepared to recognize and applaud Senator Hammond in his assaults upon their condition. He views laborers as serfs and "slaves;" he calls them "mud sills;" yet he is recognized as a leader of the Democracy. How long will the people of the free, laboring North support a Democracy which affiliates with such men?

Laborers of Illinois, do you mean to indorse a Democracy which heaps such slurs and insults upon you and your families? Is it true as the Southern aristocrats declare that your condition is below that of the negroes of the Southern plantations? Are you for allowing Southern slaves to occupy the Territories and crowd you from your birth-rights? If you think so, you do right to vote with the slave Democracy; if you do not; you should refuse to uphold men for office who flout and scorn you. If you are true men, you will refuse to indorse by your votes the demagogues, who consort with your enemies and violate their pledges at the bidding of pro-slavery leaders.

General Jackson's Method of Interpreting the Constitution.

In General Jackson's celebrated Bank veto message we find the following views of that Democratic statesman, and it is singular that those who now call themselves Democrats condemn all as traitors who hold to the views of the great Jackson:

"If the opinion of the Supreme Court covers the whole ground of this act, it ought not to control the co-ordinate authorities of this government. The Congress, the Executive, and the Court must each for itself be guided by its own opinion of the Constitution. Each public officer who takes an oath to support the Constitution, swears that he will support it as he understands it and not as it is understood by others. It is as much the duty of the House of Representatives, of the Senate, and of the President to decide upon the constitutionality of any bill or resolution, which may be presented to them for passage or approval, as it is of the Supreme Judges when it may be brought before them for Judicial decision. The authority of the Supreme Court must not, therefore, be permitted to control the Congress or the Executive.

The following were the views of Thomas Jefferson, that old Democrat who made the Declaration of Independence, and was the father of the Supreme Judiciary:

"You seem to consider the judges as the ultimate arbiters of all constitutional questions—a very dangerous doctrine indeed, and one which would place us under the despotism of an oligarchy. Our Judges are as honest as other men, and not more so. They have with others the same passions for party, for power, and the privilege of their corps."

"The judiciary of the United States is the subtile corps of sappers and miners constantly working under ground to undermine the foundations of our confederated fabric. They are construing the Constitution from the co-ordination of a general and special government to a general and supreme one alone."

Jefferson uttered more treason, according to present Democratic interpretation in the Dred Scott case, than all the Republicans that ever lived.

WALKING UPON THE WATER.—At Amsterdam there has been a regetta of young men who walk the water in shoes called podoschaphea. One of them, Mr. Gchaner, who gained the prize, accomplished the feat of walking up the Rhine, from Rotterdam to Cologne, where he arrived on the 22d of August, having started from Rotterdam on the 13th.

For the Illinois State Journal.

Springfield Female Seminary.

Springfield is behind the age in educational institutions of the highest grade. The capital of a great, growing and wealthy State, she ought to lead the State in such enterprises, but she has fallen behind By proper effort she might have secured the State Normal School. Bloomington carried off the prize, worth $20,000 a year in the way of direct trade, aside from all other considerations The moneyed men of our city stands in the way of their own greater prosperity by failure to inaugurate a liberal policy in this regard. Educational institutions of the right character will invite to our city a larger class of intelligent men, who having secured wealth, will settle permanently where, other things being equal, their children can receive a thorough education. So far are we from adding such men to our population in large numbers, we do not even retain all of those we have. They stay here to work, and when satisfied with their accumulations they remove to some other place to secure desirable advantages for their children. All the attractions of our city (and they are neither few nor unimportant) cannot counterbalance the want indicated. Probably ten men of wealth and culture settle in Jacksonville where one settles in Springfield; and for no other reason than the superior educational facilities of Jacksonville. We have many noble-hearted, public-spirted men. Will they not turn their attention to the educational wants of this city, and devise liberal things? An opportunity is afforded now by the effort to establish a Female Seminary, under the care of the three Presbyterian churches of the city. They are determined to make it equal to the best, and as it will promote the interests of all, they confidently rely upon the generous aid of all. The grade of study is as high as in the best institutions of the East. The design is to afford a thorough Christian training. No religious and moral sentiments will be taught but those of the Bible. While the three churches will conduct the school upon the most liberal principles, they will hold themselves responsible for the character and management of the school. The Constitution of the Seminary requires that the Principal shall be a Christian scholar, able to interest and guide the pupils in the daily study of the Holy Scriptures as well as in other studies. The Board of Trustees have devised a plan for the establishment of the Institution. It is liberal and feasible. An endowment fund of $20,000, and a building and Apparatus Fund of $30,000—the former to remain with subscribers for ten years if they desire it, they binding themselves to a semi-annual payment of interest at the rate of six *per cent. per annum*, dating from the 1st *proximo*—the latter to be paid in quarterly installments of 25 per cent., beginning March 1st, 1859. The Trustees have resolved that no subscriber to either fund shall be called upon for the payment of a single dollar of his subscription to such fund until the entire fund to which he subscribes is pledged by responsible men. If those who desire to see such an Institution founded in our city will come up nobly to its endowment, it will be put beyond the probability of failure; delay will prove fatal as it is not intended by a few subscriptions to prolong a painful existence from year to year, failing of all right ends contemplated in the founding of the Institution. Subscribers may rest assured that all funds will be preserved inviolate, sacred to the uses named in the subscription.

There is also another way in which our citizens can aid the Institution, and that is by receiving into their families pupils from abroad and boarding them until other and permanent accommodations can be provided in the family of the Principal. It would be injurious to the interests of all concerned to turn away pupils, coming from a distance. Indeed we are persuaded there is too much hospitality in our city for this. Families willing to accommodate pupils will confer a favor by leaving a card at the Seminary, stating name of the family, number of pupils that will be received, and price of board. CIVIS.

From the Chicago Press and Tribune.

Douglas Helpers.

Senator Jones, of Tennessee, whose efforts in this State in behalf of Douglas we have before noticed, has the most unenviable record of any man in the whole south. It is necessary for us to point out but one of his expressions of opinion; from that our readers can judge what manner of man he is and what is his motive in stumping in Illinois.

On the 25th of June, 1855, this man Jones, in reply to Senator Wilson, in his place in the Senate Chamber, said:

The Senator from Massachusetts read with much feeling and indignation a portion of the laws passed by the Legislature of Kansas on the subject of slavery; and I will again read the extract, in order that it may be understood. "I wish to call the attention of the Senate and of the country to some of their laws forced upon the people who were allured to Kansas by the assurance that they were empowered to shape their own institutions.

Here is a precious enactment:

If any person print, write, introduce or publish or circulate or cause to be brought into printed, written, published or circulated, or shall knowingly aid or assist in bringing into, publishing or circulating within the Territory, any book, paper, pamphlet, magazine, handbill or circular, containing any statements, arguments, opinion, sentiment, doctrine, advice or innuendo, calculated to produce a disorderly, dangerous or rebellious disaffection among the slaves in this Territory, or to induce such slaves to escape from their masters, or to resist their authority, shall be guilty of a felony, and be punished by imprisonment, at hard labor, for a term not less than five years.

Sir, I would make the law which the Senator quoted a little different. Instead of making it a penitentiary offense, *I would hang the wretch until he is dead*, DEAD, DEAD."

See App. Con. Globe, 1st Sess. 34th Congress, page 101.

After that extract has been placed in the hands of the voters of this State, Jones, who has been snuffed out in Tennessee, may be safely turned out loose amongst men. He is a marvellously proper supporter of the author of the Kansas-Nebraska bill, and we would be glad to have him speak on every stump in Illinois.

"THE EXILES OF FLORIDA."—Johnson & Bradford have received a supply of Joshua R. Giddings' new book, entitled as above. This work portrays with eminent ability the crimes committed by our government against the Maroons who fled from South Carolina and other slave States, seeking protection under Spanish laws. It shows the bad faith exercised towards the Indians of Florida, and presents a true view of the long-fought Florida war, which was in reality a war for slavery.

The *Atlantic Monthly*, in a lengthy notice, says:

A cruel story this, Mr. Giddings tells us.—Too cruel, but too true. It is full of pathetic and tragic interest, and melts and stirs the heart at once with pity for the sufferers and with anger that sins not, at their mean and ruthless oppressors.

Every American citizen should read it, for it is an indictment which recites crimes which have been committed in his name, perpetrated by troops and officials in his service; and all done at his expense. The whole nation is responsible at the bar of the world, and before the tribunal of posterity for these atrocities, devised by members of its Cabinet and its Congress, directed by its Presidents, and executed by its armies and its courts.

Mr. Giddings has done his task admirably well. It is worthy to be the crowning work of his long life of public service. His style is of that best kind which is never remarked upon, but serves as a clear medium through which the events he portrays are seen without distortion or exageration. He has done his country one more service, in entire consistency with those that have filled up the whole course of his honorable and beneficent life.

☞Judge Kellogg, the Republican candidate for Congress in the Peoria district, is making an active and effective canvass, and is sure of being elected by a largely increased majority. Wherever he has spoken he has been enthusiastically received, and every assurance of hearty support has been given him.

SPECIAL NOTICE.

THE NEXT TERM OF THE SANGAMON County Circuit court will commence on the third Monday 18th day of October instant, at which term all Foreigners, entitled by law to become citizens can procure their final naturalization papers. PRESCO WRIGHT clk.
oct1 3t*

LIST OF LETTERS

REMAINING IN THE POSTOFFICE AT Springfield OCTOBER 1st, which, if not called for in three months, will be forwarded to the Dead Letter Office, at Washington.

Ayers David C 2
Allen C W
Ayers David D 2
Allen H W
Allen John Att'y at Law
Attix John B
Anderson John
Abott John
Allen J W
Archer Mrs Margaret
Andrews L N
Burup Andrew
Briant Aaron C
Bobzin N W
Barnhill A J
Ball Mrs Amanda
Black Mrs Anna C
Burton David
Beecher David S
Bennett Fred C
Bell Miss Eliza A
Biddle Mrs Emma
Burk Miss Ellen
Boon F
Burly Mr E
Busber Mrs Emily
Breadth Geo
Billington John
Boyle James
Balbet John C
Baulas J P
Brodwell Josiah
Baldwin Johnson
Boyd J M
Burns John
Boulburg Mrs Jack
Boyle James 2
Brundage James
Bozarth John W
Brundage John A
Buck James
Barre Mr N
Bingamin Lewis
Bancroft Nelson T
Bradley Ledbetter
Bunce Michael
Brown Miss Mary J
Baldwin Philo 2
Bennett Mrs Mary A
Bull S M
Bodge Mrs Vienna
Bradley Mrs Virginia
Boxley Wm S
Blood Ward
Brookie Wm T
Burgett Wm
Bokan Warden and child
Chaney Abraham
Calahan Mrs Bridget
Conoly Mrs
Croval Mrs Antineta
Clark Thomas
Chase D
Clifford Mrs Chas
Carr Mrs Carrie F
Callahan David
Corderman Mrs Catherine
Cumming D M
Chase Edward
Cowins Mrs C
Campfield Miss Elen
Cook Frank
Cardinal Henry
Cotton Mrs Harriet
Carr Mrs Hariet Jane
Cook Geo W
Carnel John
Coover J P 2
Callaway James
Clark Mr Jos
Crowley John
Cantrell John M
Clay John
Conner John C
Coming Jesse & Son
Calhoun John C
Childs N C 2
Conkle Mike
Clark Mrs Lewis
Christman Mathas
Connell Mrs Marga't
Cloyd Miss Mary A
Conway Pat
Cannon Mrs L
Carpenter Sanford
Connelly R C
Carr Samuel
Compbell Thomas F
Clark Thomas
Cook Wm
Cullimore Wm A
Cantrall W M
Clay Wm
Cott Rev W B M
Dunn B W
Distle Miss Anna
Dorsey Dennis
Douglas Curtis
Daval Crawford
Deger Mrs C
Debusk Isaac
Dade James T
Dunlap James S
Dunie John
Downey John
Dalton Mary
Dillon Samuel
Davis Reese
Dumny Mrs Rebeca 2
Drake Samuel
Dunn Thomas
Demmer F
Doyle Thomas H
Dalloff Wm P
Eckler Mrs Anna
Elliott A H
Earnest Miss Henrietta
Eaton H P
Evans John F
Ellms Joseph J
Everett Joseph T
Everhart Mr Mathias
Eckler Mrs N A
Elmer Rufus
Foster Alex H
Farley Bridget
Fane Chas F
Flynn Miss Catherine
Faubee E
Faith Miss Emma
Flowers Miss Ella
Fitzgerald Mis Ellen
Flowers Mrs Ellen
Fisher H J
Foulk Geo W
Foster Geo S 2
Field John
Finn Michael
Fawsett Miss Martha C
Fortune Lawrence
Fox Thomas
Fitzsimmons Wm 2
Foster W B
Fittssimons Wm 2
Fitzsimons Wm H
Gitlette Dr B
Grehn & Kauser
Gleason Mr
Graham Chas
Gregory Mr C
Graham Elizabus
Greenstreet George
Gray H D
Glynn Miss Helen
Goodwing Hugh
Gray John W
Gaddis J H
Gray Joseph B
Gibson Miss Louisa
Greenawn L
Graham Miss S J
Goff Susan E
Garrett Thomas
Gallaher Wm K
Humphreys Benj
Herrick Andrew J
Hopkins & King
Haldeman & Bro
Hagno Chas
Hinchaw Cyrus
Hrath Enos
Hubbard H
Howard G C
Hough H A
Hathaway G
Howard G L
Hufman Geo
Gairgrove John A
Henderson James
Hill J S
Henderson James H
Howard Miss Kate
Houghs Miss Mary
Halll Miss Mary
Harwood L A
Hays Pat
Hughes Sarah Jane
Hook Sarah C
Howey Robt 2
Haire Thomas J
Hartman F S
Harris Wash'n H
Hazelett Wm P
Hunt Wm
Henry Mary
Johnson James
Jonnings Miss Netie
Jeffres Robt J
Johnson Rob
Judson B W 2
Jackson Rev Wm
Jack Wm
Jacobi Wm
Johnsou Wm S
Kiger Amanda M 2
Keethler Alex
Kinffsley C A
Kneisel Chas
Ling Miss Fanny
Kennie Isaac A
Klein Henry
Keeler Ceo B
Keith James
Kent J
Kelley Lawrence
Kint Richard
Kneff S W
Leach Alex
Ludlom Benj
Looker Albert L
Lane Mrs Aaron
Lanigan Dennis
Lynch Mrs Catherine
Letz Geo W
Lourders Henry
Lightfoot Goodrich
Livery H A
Logan J B
Lyman Dr J
Luck Mrs Jane
Lyday J H & Co
Little Mr O L
Leyrer Raymond
Lewis Richard
Laswell Mrs Virginia B
Lorel Thomas
Leigfried T
Lick Wm
Magill A M
Metcalf Adam 2
Muhl Miss Anna C
Murphy Andrew
Mink Benj
Mayberry A J
Morris Benj
Miller Mrs Agnes
Myers David
Muller Charles
Mastevron Carson
Miller David
Murray Dennis
Meredith Charles
Marteny Delos
Morse C E
Miles Edward J
Montgomery M H
Miller Miss Eliza
Myers Rev Frederic
Muckelston Elizab'h
Morgan Horace
Mester Herman
Marsh Henry
Magary Hugh J
Magill A M
Marragh Jas O
Mathews Jas H
Mahony John
Moore John
Murcheuf J
Marks Jacob
Meyers John
May Jacob
Mather Jas
Manson J H
Maner Justin
marsh John
Muldon John
Masterron John M
Martin Miss Maria
Miller Miss Mary 2
Maisel Miss Lena
Meyer Miss Louisa
Miller Miss Mary
Mischler Martin
Malony Michael
Miller Miss M S
Massam R B 4
Moore Miss Sarah A
Mathews Miss Rose
Mathews Miss S S
Mauphat Thos
Meader Timothy
Mackeroy Wm
Newman Caroline
Norris Miss Emily
Nihoff Joseph 2
Noavalle Mis Mary E
Nester Miss Magaret
Noler Miss Maria
Neu M
O'Donovan John
Ogden J B
O'Crien Margaret
O'Gara Neil
Patterson & Davis
Prettyman B S
Porter C M
Prickett David
Parker Mrs Elmira
Parker Mrs George
Payne Jonathan T 2
Proprietors Ousley's Hotel
P[illegible]pp John
Pynchon Dr John
Pefer L
Power Michael
Preston Mrs Margaret
Palmer S
Pletz Samuel
Parker S G
Pierson Miss S L 2
Proctor Wm F
Quirk D W
Quinlan John
Quinn Jas
Quigley John
McAdams & Scholton
McLain Daniel
McField Miss Clary
McQuithey Horace P
McHenry John R
McCue John 2
McLaud John K
McLenon John
McKay John
McLain John
McCau John
McCoskill John
McCormack Mis Jane
McClure Jacob W
McGee Luther
McGarry Martin
McKamare Mis Susa
Richwood B F
Ross Miss Annie M
Robinson Abraham
Rust Adolph
Robinson Daniel K
Reading E M D
Robinson J
Rodger J
Randolph John C
Robards M N
Robb Miss Lucinda
Robb P W
Rourke Owen 2
Rogan Patrick
Ryan Robert
Russell Miss Saran
Roberson Terrell
Roberson Z D
Rhodes Wm E
Rhobinson W H
Leiment Wm
Silvernail Aaron 2
Sittler B A
Snow Andrew F
Suttle Mrs Anna J
Smith B R
Spaulding Dr
Snow C B 2
Shea Miss Catherine
Swaburgh C
Schwanz Frederick
Stillman E J
Smith Mrs Elizabeth
Shoup Miss Elizzie 2
Spicer Geo W 2
Schinning George
Stewart George
Shoemaker Henry
Sherwood John W 2
Seymour Joseph
Sherwood Jacob
Smith John Moore
Swan John Moore
Sheehan Mrs J E
Sullivan J E
Schneider J
Shaver Jas
Shankland J H
Snelling John
Scanlon John
Short Miss M E
Smallwood N B
Seifert Peter
Selson P D
Spicer T C
Sigfried T F
Snow Mrs T W
Smith Mrs Wm L
Smith Wm
Stewert Wilbert
Steward Wm W
Taylor Dick S 2
Taunhill D S
Tooke Eempster 2
Tempey Miss Eliza
Taylor Elijah
Tipton Geo W
Torrence Geo W
Thrall Joseph
Thorne Joshua
Turner John O
Tierney Miss Mary
Trindall Robert B
Tuttle J E
Thorpe Thos
Veach Mrs Eliza 2
Vaderen John
Vauanker J D 2
Vaupatten John O
Vance Mrs Maria
Verdi M
Vanderen Miss J
Vunce Semuel
Vanderslice Thos
Walker Calvin
Wurst Charles
Wochner G
Waters C
White Craig
White Miss Cardine
Willon Mrs Eliza Jane
Wickhain Mrs E L
Wright Ezra P
Worrell F A
Wood H H
Winchester George
Wyatt J B
Wilbar J S
Wheeler Dr John
Waddell Jas
Willis John M
Wright J C
Watson Jas
Wolf John B
Wood J W
Wimberly Jas
Willis Jacob
Woodruff Hettie
Wall Mrs Mary
Waskins Mrs Nancy
Waters Rev Simeon
Warren Louis
Walker Miss J M
Weast Robert
Walker R S
Williams J A
Wise Richard
Wese Miss Ruth Jane
Walsh Thos
Wickham I B
Woodruff I J
Willcox Wm
Warwick Wm
Watson W W
Wood M C
White Wm
Young David
Young Rev J C
Yates W H
Ziek Wm

JAMES W. KEYES P. M.

NOTICE IS HEREBY GIVEN THAT THE undersigned has lost two promissory notes, one of said notes executed by William Taylor to me for $577,50 dated 10th April 1858 due one day after date, with ten per cent. The other note executed by James L. Beggo to me for $64. said note was dated in May or June 1858 and due one day after date, said note being the only note signed by said parties, or either of them and payable to me. I hereby notify the Public from purchasing or trading for said notes.
sept30-d1tw1m* JOHN H. CROW.

SPECIAL NOTICES.

Lincoln Stands on the Old Whig Platform.

The following are Douglas' Questions and Lincoln's Answers at Freeport:

Question 1. "I desire to know whether Lincoln to-day stands, as he did in 1854, in favor of the unconditional repeal of the fugitive slave law!"

Answer I do not now, nor ever did, stand in favor of the unconditional repeal of the fugitive slave law.

Q. 2 "I desire him to answer whether he stands pledged to-day, as he did in 1854, against the admission of any more slave States into the Union, even if the people want them?"

A. I do not now, nor ever did, stand pledged against the admission of any more slave States into the Union.

Q. 3. "I want to know whether he stands pledged against the admission of a new State into the Union, with such a Constitution as the people of that State may see fit to make."

A. I do not stand pledged against the admission of a new State into the Union, with such a Constitution as the people of that State may see fit to make.

Q, 4. "I want to know whether he stands to-day pledged to the abolition of slavery in the District of Columbia?"

A. I do not stand to-day pledged to the abolition of slavery in the District of Columbia.

Q. 5. "I desire him to answer whether he stands pledged to the prohibition of the slave trade between the different States?"

A. I do not stand pledged to the prohibition of the slave trade betweett the different States.

Q. 6. "I desire to know whether he stands pledged to prohibit slavery in all the Territories of the United States, North as well as South of the Missouri Compromise, line."

A. I am impliedly, if not expressly, pledged to a belief in the right and duty of Congress to prohibit slavery in all the United States Territories.

Q. 7. "I desire him to answer whether he is opposed to the acquisition of any new Territory unless slavery is first prohibited therein."

A. I am not generally opposed to honest acquisition of territory; and, in any given case. I would, or would not, oppose such acquisition. accordingly as I might think such acquisition would or would not agitate the slavery question among ourselves.

Mr. Lincoln stands on the Old Whig Platform, with Clay and Webster.

Lynchburg Daily Virginian.

"THE RIGHTS OF THE STATES, AND THE UNION OF THE STATES."

BY CHARLES W. BUTTON. | LYNCHBURG SATURDAY MORNING, OCTOBER 22, 1859. | VOL. 8---NO 70.

TERMS

The VIRGINIAN is published daily at $6 and Tri-Weekly at $5 per annum in advance, and Weekly at $2, invariably in advance, otherwise, $2,50 will be charged in all cases. No paper will be discontinued except at the option of the Proprietor until all arrearages shall have been paid.

ADVERTISEMENTS are inserted for 50 cents per square of 10 lines, or less for the first insertion, and 37½ cents for each continuance unless ordered inner-form or weekly and then 50 cents per square will be charged for each insertion. If the number of insertions be not marked on the MSS, it will be published till ordered out and charged accordingly.

THE YEARLY RATES ARE:

For one square daily	$35
For two squares, daily	50
For one square tri-weekly	28
For two squares tri-weekly	40

☞ Advertisements intended for both papers subject to special contract.

☞ Annual advertisers will be limited to their immediate business, or the advertisements charged for transient rates.

☞ All new advertisements appear in the daily and tri-weekly papers.

☞ Obituary notices which exceed eight lines are charged rateably for the excess.

Daily Virginian.

Insurrection at Harper's Ferry
FULL PARTICULARS.

The insurrection at Harper's Ferry is over and the mails brings in full particulars of the bloody tragedy.

THE COMMENCEMENT OF THE INSURRECTION.

The first active movement of the insurrectionists was made about half-past ten o'clock on Sunday night. Wm. Williams, watchman on the Harper's Ferry bridge, whilst walking across towards the Maryland side, was seized by a number of men, who said he was their prisoner and must come with them. He recognized Brown and Cook among the men, and knowing them treated the matter as a joke, but enforcing silence they conducted him to the armory which he found already in their possession. He was retained till after daylight and then discharged. The watchman who was to relieve Williams at midnight, found the bridge lights all out, and immediately was seized. Supposing it an attempt at robbery, he broke away and his pursuers stumbling over the track he escaped.

The next appearance of the insurrectionists was at the house of Col. Lewis Washington, a large farmer and slave-holder, living about four miles from the Ferry. A party headed by Cook proceeded there, roused Col. W. and told him he was a prisoner. They also seized all the slaves near the house, took a carriage and horse and a large wagon with two horses. When Col. Washington saw Cook he immediately recognized him as a man who had called upon him some months previous, to whom he had exhibited some valuable arms in his possession, including an antique sword presented by Frederick the Great to General Washington, and a pair or pistols presented by Lafayette to Washington, both heir-looms in the family. Before leaving, Cook invited Col. Washington to a trial of skill at shooting, and exhibited considerable certainty as a markesman. When he made his visit on Sunday night he alluded to his previous visit and the courtesy with which he had been treated, regretting the necessity which made it his duty to arrest Col. W. He, however, took advantage of the knowledge he obtained by the former visit, to carry off all the Colonel's valuable collection of arms, which he did not re-obtain until after the final defeat of the insurrection,

From Col. Washington's they proceedrd with him a prisoner in his carriage, and twelve of his negroes in the wagon, to the house of Mr. Allstadt another large farmer on the same road. Mr. Allstadt, and his son, a lad of sixteen, were taken prisoners, all their negroes within reach forced to join the movement, and they returned to the Armory at the Ferry.—All these movements seem to have been made without exciting the slightest alarm in the town, nor did the detention of Capt. Phelp's train at the upper end of the town attract attention. It was not until the town was thoroughly waked up and found the bridge guarded by armed men, and a guard stationed at all the avenues, that the people found that they were prisoners. A panic appears to have immediately ensued, and the number of the insurrectionists at once magnified from fifty, which was probably their greatest force including the slaves forced to join, to from five or six hundred. In the meantime, a number of workmen knowing nothing of what had occurred, entered the Armory, and were instantly taken prisoners, until at one time they had no less than sixty men confiued. Among those thus entrapped were Armistead Ball, Chief Draughtsman of the Armory, Benjamin Mills, Master of the Armory and J. E. P. Dangerfield, Paymaster's Clerk.—These three gentlemen were imprisoned in the engine house, which afterwards became the chief fortress of the insurgents, and were not released until after the final assault. The workmen were imprisoned in a building farther down the yard, and were rescued by the brilliant Zouave dash made by the railroad company's men who came down from Martinsburg

This was the condition of things at daylight, about which time Captain Cook with two white men, accompanied by thirty slaves, and taking with them Col. Washington's large wagon, went over the bridge and struck up the mountain road toward Pennsylvania. It was then believed that the large wagon was used to convey away the Paymaster's safe, containing $17,000 in government funds, and also that it was filled with Minnie rifles taken out to supply other bands in the mountains who were to come down upon Harper's Ferry in overwhelming force. These suppositions both proved untrue, as neither money nor arms were disturbed.

THE BEGINNING OF THE FIGHT—SHOOTING OF A PRISONER.

As the day advanced, and the news spread around, and the people came into the Ferry, the first demonstrations of resistence were made to the insurrectionists. A guerrilla warfare commenced, chiefly led on by a man named Chambers whose house commanded the Armory yard. The colored man named Hayward, railroad porter, was shot early in the morning for refusing to join the movement. Next man shot was Joseph Burnley, a citizen of Harper's Ferry. He was shot whilst standing in his own door. About this time also, Geo W. Turner Esq., was shot dead. He was coming into town on horseback, carrying a gun, when he was shot from the Armory, receiving a wound of which he died during the day.—He was a graduate of West Point, and greatly respected in the neighborhood for his high character and noble qualities.

The insurrectionists at this time, finding a disposition to resist them, had withdrawn nearly all within the Armory grounds, leaving only a guard on the bridge. About noon, the Charlestown troops, under command of Col. Robert W. Baylor, arrived, crossing the Potomac river some distance up and marching down the Maryland side to the mouth of the bridge. Firing a volley they mada a gallant dash across the bridge, clearing it of the insurrectionists who retreated rapidly down toward the Armory. In this movement one of the insurrectionists, named Wm. Thompson, was taken prisoner. The Shepherdstown troops next arrived, marching down the Shenandoah side and joining the Charlestown forces at the bridge. A desultory exchange of shots followed, one of which struck Mr. Fontaine Beckham, Mayor of the town and agent of the Railroad Company, in the breast passing entirely through his body, the ball was a large elongated slug, making a dreadfnl wound. He died almost immediately. Mr. Beckham was without arms and was exposed only for a moment whilst approaching the water-station. His assailant, one of Brown's sons, was shot almost immediately, but managed to get back to the engine-house, where his dead body was found the next day.

The murder of Mr. Beckham excited the people and the cry was immediately made to bring out the prisoner Thompson. He was brought out on the bridge and shot down; from the bridge he fell into the water, and some appearance of life remaining he was again riddled with balls.

SHARP FIGHTING COMMENCING.

At this time a general charge was made down the street from the bridge towards the Armory gate by the Charlestown and Shepherdstown and the Ferry people. From behind the Armory wall a fusilade was kept up and returned by the insurrectionists from the Armory building.—Whilst this was going on, the Martinsburg levies arrived at the upper end of the town, and entering the Armory grounds by the rear, made an attack from that end. This force was largely composed of the railroad employees gathered from the tonnage trains at Martinsburg, and their attack was generally spoken of as showing the greatest amount of fighting pluck exhibited during the day. Dashing on, firing and cheering, and gallantly led by Captain Alburtis, they carried the building in which the Armory men were imprisoned and released the whole of them. They were, however, but poorly armed, some with pistols and others with shot-guns, and when they came within range of the engine house, where the *elite* of the insurrectionists were gathered, and were exposed or their rapid and dexterous use of Sharp's rifles, they were forced to fall back, suffering pretty severely. Conductor Evan Dorsey, of Baltimore, was mortally wounded, and Conductor George Richardson received a wound from which he died during the day. Several others were wounded, among them a son of Dr. Murphy, of Harper's Ferry.

A guerilla warfare was maintained during the rest of the day, resulting in the killing of three of the insurgents and the wounding of a fourth. One of them crawled out through a culvert leading into the Potomac, and attempted to cross to the Maryland side, whether with a view of escaping or of conveying information to Cook's party, was not known. He was shot whilst crossing the river and fell dead on the rocks. An adventurous lad waded out and secured his Sharps rifle, and the body was afterward stripped of a portion of its clothing. In one of his pockets was found a captain's commission, drawn up in full form, and declaring the bearer, Capt. Lenham, held that command under Maj. General Brown! A light mulatto was also shot just outside the Armory gate. The ball went through and through his throat, tearing away all the arteries, and killing him instantly. His name was not known, but he was one of the free negroes who came with Capt. Brown. His body was left exposed in the street up to noon yesterday; exposed to every indignity that could be heaped upon it by the excited populace. At this time a tall, powerful man, named Aaron Stevens, came out from the Armory conducting some prisoners, it was said, and was shot twice, once in the side of the face, and once in the breast. He was captured and taken into the tavern, and after the insurrection had been quelled, was turned over, in a dying condition, to the United States authorities. Another man was shot in the Arsenal yard.

During the afternoon a sharp littlle affair took place on the Shenandoah side of the town. The insurrectionists had also seized Hall's rifle works, and a party of their assailants found their way in through the mill-race and dislodged them. Intnis rencontre it was said that three of the insurrectionists were killed, but we found but one dead body, that of a negro, on that side of the city. Nigt by this time had come on and active operations ceased. Guards were placed around the Armory and every precaution taken to prevent escapes.

ARRIVAL OF THE BALTIMORE MILITARY.

At 10 o'clock on Monday night the train with the Baltimore military and United States marines arrived at Sandy Hook, where they waited for the arrival of Col. Lee, deputised by the War Department to take command. The reporters pressed on leaving their military allies behind. They found the bridge in possession of the military, and entered the besieged and beleagured town without difficulty, the occasional report of a gun or the singing motion of a Sharpe's rifle ball, warning them that it was advisable to keep out of range of the Armory. Their first visit was to the bedside of Aaron Stevens, the wounded prisoner, They found him a large, exceedingly athletic man, a perfect Sampson in appearance. He was in a small room, filled with excited armed men, who more than once threatened to shoot him where he was, groaning with pain, but answering with composure and apparent willingness every question in relation to the foray in which he was engaged. He said he was a native of Connecticut, but had lately lived in Kansas, where he knew Capt. Brown. He had also served in the United States Army. The sole object of the attempt was to give the negroes freedom, and Captain Brown had represented that as soon as they seized the Armory the negroes would flock to them by thousands, and they would soon have force enough to accomplish their purpose. He believed that the freeing of the negroes was a proper purpose, one for which he would sacrifice his life, but thought that Capt. Brown had been greatly deceived in relation to the movement. He said preparations had been making for some months for this movement, but that the whole force consisted of seventeen white men and five negroes. This statement was repeated without variation by all the prisoners with whom we conversed. They all agreed as to the number in the movement, and as to its objects, which some of them called the work of philanthropy.

Lewis Leary, the negro shot at the rifle mill, stated before he died that he enlisted with Capt. Brown for the insurrection at a Fair held in Lorraine county, Ohio, and received money from him to pay his expenses. They all came down to Chambersburg, Pa., and from there traveled across the country to Brown's farm.

HOW THE NIGHT PASSED.

The night passed without serious alarmes, but not without excitement. The marines were marched over immediately after the arrival of Col. Lee and were stationed within the armory grounds, so as to completely surround the engin-house.—Occasional shots were fired by the county volunteers—what for was not understood; but there was only one return fire from the insurgents.—The broken telegraph was soon repaired through the exertions of Superintendents Westervelt and Talcott, who accompained the expedition, and the announcement that communicated was opened with Baltimore gave the "press representatives" abundant employment.

There was no finding any bed, and daylight was awaited with anxeity. Its earliest glimpses were availed of to view the scene. A visit to the different localities in which the corpses of the insurrectionists were lying stark and bloody, a peep, close or far off, according to the courage of the observer, at the "Malakoff" of the insurgants, was the established order of sight-seeing, varied with a discussion of all sorts of terrible rumors.

FORT OF THE INSURGENTS.

The building in which the insurgents had made their stand was the fire engine house, and no doubt the most defensible building in the armory. It has dead brick walls on three sides, and on the forth large doors, with window-sashes, above, some eight feet from the ground. A dead stillness surrounded the building, and except that now and then a man might be seen peeping from the nearly closed centre door, or a dog's nose slightly protruded, there was no sign of life, much less of hostility, given. Various opinions were given as to the number of persons within, and the amount of resistance they would be able to offer. Cannon could not be used without endangering the safety of Col. Washington, Mr. Dangerfield, Mr. Ball other citizens, who they still held prisoners. The doors and walls of the building had been pierced for rifles, but it was evident that from these holes no range could be had, and that without opening the door they would be shooting in the dark. The murder of the prisoners held was thought by many to be determined upon, and then a fight to the death as an ending of their desperate attempt. Whilst people thus looked and speculated, the door was thrown open and one of the prisoners was sent out with a flag of truce, and delivered what was supposed to be terms of capitulation. The continuance of the preparations for assault showed that they were not accepted.

THE DEMAND FOR SURRENDER—THE ATTACK AND CAPTURE.

Shortly after seven o'clock, Lieut. J. E. B. Stuart, of the 1st Cavalry, who was acting as aid for Col. Lee, advanced to parley with the beseiged, Samuel Strider, Esq., an old and respectable citizen, bearing a flag of truce. They were received at the door by Capt. Cook. Lieut. Stuart demanded an unconditional surrender, only promising them protection from immediate violence and trial by law. Capt. Brown refused all terms but those previously demanded, which were substantially: "That he should be permitted to march out with his men and arms, taking their prisoners with them; that they should proceed unpursued to the second toll-gate, when they would free their prisoners. The soldiers were then at liberty to pursue, and they would fight if they could not escape." Of course this was refused, and Lieut. Stuart pressed upon Brown his desperate position, and urged a surrender. This expostulation, though beyond ear-shot, was evidently very earnest, and the coolness of the Lieutenant and the courage of his aged flag bearer won warm praise.

At this moment the interest of the scene was intense. The volunteers were arranged all around the building, cutting off escape in every direction. The marines, divided in two squads, were ready for a dash at the door. Finally, Lieut. Stuart, having exhausted all argument with the determined Captain Brown, walked slowly from the door. Immediately the signal for attack was given, and the marines, headed by Colonel Harris and Lieutenant Green advanced in two lines on each side of the door. Two powerful fellows sprang between the lines, and with heavy sledge hammers attempted to batter down the door. The door swung and swayed, but appeared to be secured with a rope, the spring of which deadened the effect of the blows. Failing thus to obtain a breach, the marines were ordered to fall back, and twenty of them took hold of a ladder, some forty feet long, and advancing at a run, brought it with tremendous power against the door. At the second blow it gave way, one leaf falling inward in a slanting position. The marines immediately advanced to the breach, Major Russell and Lieutenant Green leading. A marine in the front fell; the firing from the interior is rapid and sharp, they fire with deliberate aim, and for the moment the resistance is serious and desperate enough to excite the spectators to something like a pitch of frenzy. The next moment the marines pour in, the firing ceases, and the work was done, whilst the cheers rang from every side, the general feeling being that the marines had done their part admirably.

When the insurgents were brought out—some dead, others wounded—they were greeted with execrations, and only the precautions that had been taken saved them from immediate execution. The crowd, nearly every man of which had a gun, swayed with tumultuous excitement, and cries of "shoot them," "shoot them," rang from every side. The appearance of the liberated prisoners, all of whom, through the steadiness of the marines, escaped without injury, changed the current of feeling, and prolonged cheers took the place of howls and execrations. In the assault private Ruppert, of the marines, received a ball in the stomach and was believed to be fatally wounded; another received a slight flesh wound in the face.

THE DEAD AND WOUNDED.

The lawn in front of the engine-house, after the assault, presented a dreadful sight. Lying on it were two bodies of men killed the previous day and found inside the house; three wounded men, one just at the gasp of life; two others groaning in pain. One of the dead was Capt. Brown's son Ottowa, the wounded man his son Watson, whilst the father himself laid upon the grass, a gory spectacle, his face and hair clotted with blood and a severe bayonet wound in his side.

A son of the leader, named Brown, was taken out stark and cold, he having been killed the day previous; Stewart Taylor, also killed instantly by a ball through his head and one through his body, and Albert Haslitt, killed instantly. The wounds were shocking to behold. The writer had a conversation with the dying man, Anderson. He said that the elder Brown had been their leader, and that he had always looked up to him as a great man. A letter was found in his pocket from his brother, J. J. Anderson, of Chilicothe, stating that the contents of his last letter upon the subject of slavery were devoured with eagerness."—Upon the body of Haslitt was found a look of his wife's hair and a piece of her dress.

INCIDENTS, &c.

Upon the person of the leader, the notorious "Ossawottamie Brown," of Kansas, was found by one of the volunteer surgeons of the division, Dr. David M'Laughlin, the sum of $305 in gold, which was handed by him over to Major Russell, of the marine corps. In a conversation with the writer as he lay weltering in his blood, he stated that he had figured in Kansas, and was known as "Ossawottomie Brown," or "Old Brown," He had had a son killed in Kansas (as well as two here.) He hated slavery, and he desired to avenge his son's death. His confederates desired to surrender when they were summoned by Col. Lee; but he refused because he did not believe that the general government would slaughter his companions for the sake of killing him. He had always treated his prisoners with courtesy. He hoped that his interrogators would not put words in his mouth, but permit him to make his own declarations. He hoped Major Russell would permit him to die in peace, and would treat him humanely. Major Russell suggested that he had better not make any declarations calculated to compromise him in law, and also requested the gentlemen present to withdraw from the room in order that he might not be disturbed. It has been stated subsequently that his wounds are not mortal, unfortunately perhaps for himself.

The prisoner Edwin Copper, upon being asked what he expected would be his fate, said that he only asked his country to give him a fair trial and he would abide the consequences. He manifested no concern or apprehension with respect to his punishment. The prisoner Brown, son of the leader, was too debilitated from his wounds to realize his situation.

The wounded have been removed to the hospital of the arsenal, including the rioter A. D. Stevens. Such was the excitement on Monday night that Stevens would have been shot in his bed, had it not been for the restraint exercised by others upon those who permitted their passions to become ungovernable. The wretched man stated his willingness to go out in the morning and be shot upon his coffin, but begged them not to shoot him in his bed. He is reported to be mortally wounded; but it is thought by some that his four wounds are not fatal.

About the middle of the stream of the broad Potomac lies the body of one of the insurgents named Wm. H. Leeman, who was shot on Monday, while attempting to make his escape from the town. His black hair may just be seen floating upon the surface of the water and waving with every ripple.

There was taken from the person of Stevens a printed pamphlet of twenty-five pages, containing the constitution, &c., of Mr. Brown's provisional government. The work is in the possession of Col. Lee, and would be treasonable were it not too ridiculous.

EXCITING SCENES.

During the morning armed men continued to pour into Harper's Ferry, in all sorts of costume and with every variety of arms. Over 200 men came on horseback, and probably there were from 1,000 to 1200 men assembled there. The desire to inflict summary vengeance was exhibited in the strongest manner, and the vindictive feeling found one mode of expressure not at all commendable. The body of one of Brown's party shot in the river the previous day, was dislodged from the rock on which it fell and came floating down. As it passed down towards the bridge it was made the target for probably 100 shots, and must have been thoroughly riddled with balls.

HARPER'S WEEKLY.
A JOURNAL OF CIVILIZATION.

Vol. III.—No. 150.] NEW YORK, SATURDAY, NOVEMBER 12, 1859. [Price Five Cents.

A NEW SERIAL.

We shall commence in an early number of *Harper's Weekly* a new Serial Tale by Wilkie Collins, Esq., of which we have purchased the advance proof-sheets from the author. This Tale will be continued through the *Weekly* till it is completed.

In reply to several inquiries, we beg to say that Mr. Dickens's new Serial, "A Tale of Two Cities," was commenced in *Harper's Weekly* on May 7, and Mr. Curtis's delicious Story of American Society, entitled "Trumps," on April 9. We can send back numbers from those dates, or from the beginning of the year, to any person who remits the money.

We print from 80,000 to 93,000 copies per week.

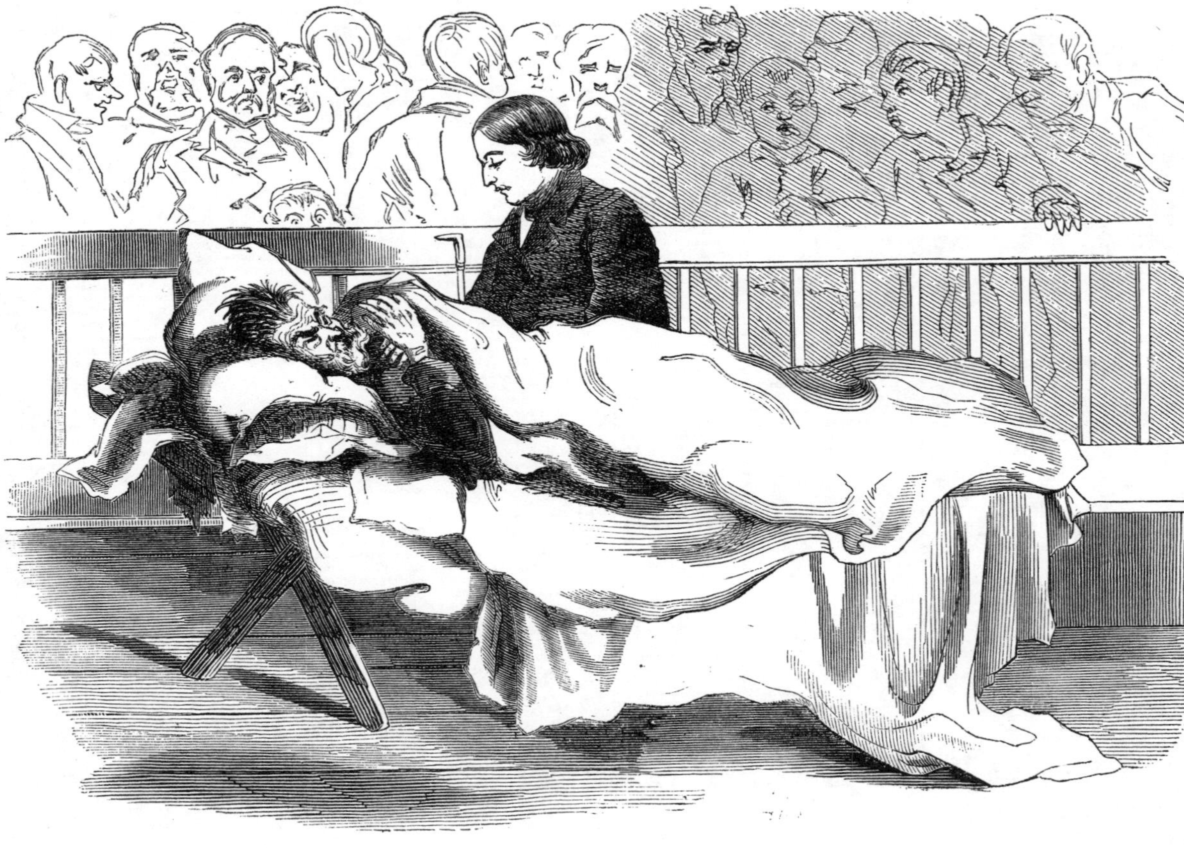

THE PRISONER BROWN AND HIS BOSTON COUNSEL, MR. HOYT.—Drawn by Porte Crayon.—[See Page 729.]

Our Illustrations.

We continue in this number our Illustrations of the Harper's Ferry outbreak, drawn by our special artist, Porte Crayon. We have now published the following Illustrations of this memorable event:

1. Harper's Ferry.
2. Another view of the same, showing the Armory, etc., etc.
3. The attack on the Engine-house by the U. S. Marines.
4. The Guard-room, with the wounded prisoners.
5. Brown, wounded and a prisoner, during his examination by Governor Wise.
6. Body of Brown's son.
7. The trial of Brown at Charlestown.
8. The arraignment.
9. Brown and his counsel, Mr. Hoyt.
10. Portrait of Colonel Washington.
11. Brown's arms—swivel gun and pike.
12. The school-house in the mountain, used by Brown as an arsenal.

THE ARRAIGNMENT.—Drawn by Porte Crayon.—[See Page 729.]

THE POSITION OF THE SOUTH.

THE CHARLESTON CONVENTION.

Election of Delegates in South Carolina.

MEETING OF THE CITIZENS OF CHARLESTON.

THE PLATFORM PUT IN A NUTSHELL,

&c., &c., &c.

[From the Charleston Mercury, Feb. 24.]

A public meeting of the citizens of Charleston in favor of the representation of South Carolina in the approaching Convention of the national democratic party in this city, was held at the Hibernian Hall last evening. The weather was stormy, but the hall was nearly half full, and the meeting entirely respectable.

SAM'L LORD, Jr., Esq., announced the nominations of the Committee on Organization, and moved that Hon. Jas. Simons be called to the chair, which was carried. Gen. Simons took his seat amid the applause of the meeting. Captain Lord then moved that the meeting be further organized by requesting sixty five gentlemen, whose names he read, to act as vice presidents. The vice presidents were invited to take chairs upon the platform by the president. Four secretaries were then selected in the same manner. The organization was concluded and accepted by the meeting as follows:—

Hon. JAMES SIMONS, Chairman.

VICE PRESIDENTS.

Hon. H. D. Lesesne.	W. B Dingle.
Hon. A. P. Hayne.	Chas. T. Lowndes.
Hon. James Rose.	Col. Chas. Kanapaux.
Hon. John Schnierle.	Robert Mure.
Hon. T. L. Hutchinson.	A. McDowall.
E. Geddings, M. D.	Arch. Cameron.
Hugh R. Banks.	Jacob Cohen.
Col. D. L. McKay.	Col. F. Lanneau.
Wm. Bull Pringle.	J. J. McCarter.
W. H. Gilliland.	W. J. Magrath.
W. H. Houston.	Jacob Small.
Col. John Phillips.	Geo. W. Black.
F. Melchers.	F. M. Robertson, M. D.
Alex. H. Brown.	H. W. Conner.
H. F. Strohecker.	Rob't. Caldwell.
William Ravenel.	Wm. B. Smith.
Sam'l. Lord, Sr.	J. H. Steinmeyer.
Richard Yeadon,	Robert M. Welch,
Geo. M. Coffin,	Henry T. Peake,
Nelson Mitchell,	Wm. Kirkwood,
Henry C. King,	Capt. Henry Gerdts,
G. N. Reynolds, Jun.,	M. W. St. Amand,
Wm. M. Martin,	Col. R. W. Seymour,
E. W. Edgerton,	John F. O'Neill,
John S. Riggs,	Geo. C. Wharton,
A. H. Dunkin,	W. S. Hastie,
Charles Alston,	D. F. Fleming,
Dr. J. B. Patrick,	Col. C. B. Sigwald,
C. L. Burckmyer,	Theo. Cordes,
Arthur M. Huger,	A. McKenzie,
Geo. W. Williams,	A. S. Johnston,
Henry Cobia,	Richard M. Butler.
B. C. Pressley,	

SECRETARIES.

Wm. S. Elliott,	Thaddeus Street,
Robert Pringle, Jun.,	C. B. Artope.

Gen. SIMONS then expressed his satisfaction and acknowledgment at the compliment and honor done him, and proceeded to address the meeting. He regarded it as the inauguration of a movement of great importance, and explained the object to be to decide the question whether the parishes of St. Philip and St. Michael should send delegates to the Columbia Convention, which would answer the query whether the citizens desired the State to be represented in the Charleston Convention. He discussed the subject as to whether it was principle or expediency. The principle he considered settled by the action of the Convention at Columbia in 1843, following which Messrs. Elmore and Pickens went to Baltimore, both made speeches and sanctioned the choice of that Convention. As to policy, in 1852 co-operation was established, that South Carolina would not go out of the Union. Gen. Simons declared isolation to be antagonism to the other Southern States, and advised his fellow citizens to strengthen their hands among their enemies. *It would be greatly to the advantage of the country to have the Union preserved. The battle should be fought in the Union.* If there was not faith in the democratic party, where was it? Gen. Simons closed with an allusion to the unfruitfulness of Col. Memminger's mission to Virginia, and declaring that he had not then, never had, and never would have, opinions which he was afraid to exhibit, gracefully declared the meeting open.

Mr. WM. C. CLAYTON rose to address the chair, but was interrupted with cries of "Sit down," "Put him out," &c. He only found an opportunity to say it was a public meeting, and he would not sit down, when an officer of the guard took his arm and very politely, but firmly, carried him from the hall. Mr. Clayton protested in vain.

SAMUEL Y. TUPPER, Esq., then submitted to the consideration of the meeting the prepared preamble and resolutions, on which duty he entered without doubt as to the propriety of the course. He was fully aware that attempts had been made to render the Convention odious, but he claimed to bear as true allegiance to his native State and the South as any. He considered that the honor of South Carolina demanded that she should be represented. The democratic party was the only barrier to fanaticism, and if the South was to maintain her position in the Union, it was best to enter the democratic Convention and defend her rights.

Mr. TUPPER then read the following:—

The period is near at hand when the National Democratic Convention will be assembled, according to appointment, in this city, for the purpose of selecting candidates for the Presidency and the Vice-Presidency of the United States. We have reason to believe that every State in the Union will be here represented through its democratic citizens; and certainly there has been no time since the foundation of the government when questions of greater constitutional value or of more momentous practical consequences were to be discussed and determined. It is enough to say that peace and prosperity on the one hand, and intestine strife and revolution on the other, hang trembling in the scales.

The country is now divided into two great parties, that have utterly absorbed all others. One of these is the republican party; the other the democratic party. The former is confined exclusively to the North, and has no rest for the sole of its foot in any Southern State; the latter, with a larger constitutional embrace, finds a home and a recognition in every State of the Confederacy, North and South. The one wages war against the social system of one of the two great sections of the Union; the other proclaims equality of right to all sections alike. The republican party is animated by the fell spirit of fanaticism, compounded with the lust of exclusive political domination. The democratic party, rebuking the passions and prejudices that seek the elevation of one part of the country in the proscription and degradation of the other, proposes to take its stand on the ground of principle, to make its appeal to the justice and magnanimity of the country, and to stake its political fortunes upon its success or defeat in the great battle about to be fought for the equal rights of the States.

It cannot be denied that the democratic party is now the only national constitutional party in the country. To place it upon the true ground of principle, and then to strengthen its arm for the conflict, would seem to be the duty of every patriot, and this is what we propose to do.

We regard the Convention only as a policy, and as a means and instrumentality whereby the opinion and the principles of the party may be moulded into a fixed and definite form and its choice concentrated upon two individuals as the exponents and representatives of that opinion and those principles. The principles we regard as if infinitely greater importance than the men, and therefore it is that we desire to have a voice in the discussion, and a vote in the settlement of them. If it be true that an effort will be made in the Convention to evade the full and fair recognition of our Territorial rights, it is the stronger reason why the moral and political weight of South Carolina should be there to foil any such attempt; and if there will be represented in the Convention Northern States that cannot give a democratic vote, is not that of itself a cogent argument why every Southern State that can give a democratic vote should be present to designate the conditions on which alone that vote can be had? In the event of a division or a contest, let the States' Rights men and the Southern Rights men, whether of the North or of the South, have all the encouragement and strength that can be brought within support. In fact, nothing is plainer or better understood than that the people of the Southern States constitute, for all practical purposes, the democratic party; and that no constitutional right or principle which they unite in demanding can be ignored or refused. Let them be true to themselves, acting in concert as a people should who have a common interest and a common destiny; demanding nothing but what is right, and submitting to nothing that is wrong; asserting their constitutional right to an equal enjoyment of the Territories as the common property of the people of all the States, and the constitutional duty of the government, in all its departments, to protect them in that as in all their other rights—and we do not yet despair that there is good sense and virtue enough left, both in the party and in the country, to carry through triumphantly a cause that deserves to succeed, because it has its foundation in the plainest principles of justice and of the constitution.

We are not ignorant or unmindful of the great peril that threatens the South, nor do we yield to any in real devotion to her rights and honor. That peril consists in the feelings, principles, and purposes out of which the republican party has sprung; and its consummation will be reached in the accession of that party to the powers and control of the government. *We do not believe in a dissolution of the Union as a thing to be desired for itself, but we do believe that there are greater evils than a dissolution of the Union, and that one of these is unconditional submission to a purely sectional dominion that is politically and socially hostile to us.* Such a dominion is the worst form of despotism; and it is precisely because we do not believe that the people of the South will or ought to submit to a bondage so humiliating, *that we seek to avert the terrible alternative of civil revolution by the discomfiture and utter prostration of the republican party.* Our motto—"is Equality in the Union or safety and independence out of it." So the first, as members of the Union, we shall address our efforts in all good faith and sincerity or purpose. We will not stand by and see that battle fought without taking our part in the heat and burden of the conflict. If there were no other or higher call upon us, we owe this duty to the good and true men of the North who have been stricken down in our cause, or who are still ready manfully to maintain it; and to the good and true men of the South who have an equal stake with ourselves in the issue, and have also equal intelligence to know their rights and equal courage to maintain them. If this resource fail, and the madness of the people shall hurry on to the destruction of a republic for which so much blood has been shed, and in which so many hopes have been centred, we shall still have left to us the last alternative of a people who prefer revolution to dishonor; and in making this final appeal to the principle and the duty of self-preservation, we shall be sustained by the proud consciousness that we have left no effort untried to maintain the integrity of the constitution, without which the Union would not be worth the preserving. Be it, therefore,

Resolved, That in the opinion of this meeting it is right and proper that the State of South Carolina, in common with her sister States of the South, should be represented in the democratic Convention, to meet in this city on the 23d of April next.

Resolved, That the following gentlemen be, and they are hereby appointed, delegates to represent these parishes in the State Convention, to be held at Columbia, for the purpose of selecting suitable delegates to the National Democratic Convention, to wit:—

Col. J. J. Pope,	M. A. Pringle,
Col. T. Y. Simons,	T. G. Barker,
Col. Henry Buist,	Saml. Lord, Jr.,
Col. F. Lanneau,	W. S. Hastie,
David Ramsay,	C. L. Burckmyer,
M. P. O'Connor,	A. McKenzie,
G. N. Reynolds, Jr.,	John S. Riggs,
Samuel D. Stoney,	W. S. Elliott,
A. A. Allemong,	F. Melchers,
Col. J. J. Pettigrew,	W. Y. Leitch.
Edw. Magrath.	

On motion of Col. J. J. Pope, Samuel Y. Tupper, Esq., was added to the delegation, which completed the required number.

Col. T. Y. Simons then proceeded to address the meeting in favor of the passage of the resolutions. Col. Simons' speech was the set speech of the occasion, and we will briefly recapitulate the points he made:—

The President is the representative of the whole country, of this State, as well as of others. He must be elected either by the democratic or the republican party. There was no middle party. The only cohesive element in the republican party was the violation of Southern rights, and the destruction of the constitution. The democratic party alone prevented this party from triumphing. In proof of this, he cited the unanimous support given to Mr. Bocock, during the recent contest for Speaker, quoted from Vallandigham of Ohio, Fernando Wood of New York, and Senator Fitch of Indiana.

The only way to select a President was by a convention. The Democratic National Convention had never nominated an unsound man. South Carolina must stand or fall with the fourteen other slave States, who would have delegates at the Convention. There were as good men in the other Southern States as in South Carolina. South Carolina should go in and help select a good man, and not act the Pharisee, thanking God she was better than others. Mr. Calhoun did not oppose conventions in themselves, but only the mode of electing delegates in some States. The South had a guaranty in the two-third rule. Gentlemen could not desire a Chinese wall about the State, or to degrade her to a mere San Marino republic. Let them attend the Convention, and hail the Northern and great the Southern delegates.

Col. Simons' speech was delivered in an earnest and impassioned style, and he seemed to carry his audience with him.

HENRY C KING, Esq., seconded the resolutions in a short speech, in which he acknowledged he had been an old whig and would speak for that party. It was idle to dispute on policy. Party ties were broken. South Carolina should not know more than her sister States. He urged the taking of counsel with the Southern States. To him Seward's irrepressible conflict doctrine was naught. When it came he would be prepared to meet it. The loudest preacher did not practice the most. He approved of the preamble and resolutions and seconded them, and he trusted that the people of South Carolina would meet the honest men in the Convention face to face, ready to grasp the hand of friendship, or with the sword to repel the very breath of insult.

Col. R. W. Seymour being loudly called for responded. It is but justice to say that he out Seymoured Seymour in this speech. At one time he advocated the issues of the meeting, and at another stormed at its opponents. He ridiculed the idea of dying alone for patriotism; he preferred to live and walk about after such were dead. But stenography, phonography, and all the 'ographies combined would fail to report the Colonel's speech, and we forbear. It was received with much applause, and voted by all a remarkable effort. It was the closing address of the meeting.

Gen. SIMONS then put the resolutions to the vote, and they were carried with but a single dissentient voice; and on motion of Col. POPE the meeting adjourned.

The Convention of Southern States.

LETTER OF THE MISSISSIPPI COMMISSIONER.

Governor Letcher on the 21st instant communicated to the Legislature of Virginia the resolutions of the State of Mississippi, recommending a convention of the slaveholding States, accompanied by the following letter of the Hon. Peter B. Starke, the Commissioner appointed from Mississippi to urge upon Virginia the propriety of joining her sister States in such a convention:—

FEB. 20, 1860.

I herewith present to your Excellency a series of resolutions adopted by the State of Mississippi on a subject of vital interest to the slaveholding States particularly, and of no less importance to the lovers of our constitutional Union in the non-slaveholding States of the Union:—

The Legislature of Mississippi have been so explicit in the declaration of their views on the important questions which now agitate the whole people of these confederated States, disturb their peace and threaten the very existence of the government itself, that but little more remains to be done by her Commissioner than to ask your Excellency to invite the serious attention of the Legislature of the great commonwealth of Virginia to their import.

This is done in the sincere conviction that Virginia will recognise in these resolutions no principle not sanctioned by her great statesmen in times past, and no suggestion not warranted by sovereign States, whose safety, both present and future, is menaced by the seditious teachings and fanatical aggressions of the people of other States.

African slavery has ever been regarded by those amongst whom it exists as a question of domestic policy; a question to be dealt with by the States which have adopted it according to their own views of expediency, and without molestation or interference from other States, or even the general government, except for its protection, as provided for by the constitution of the United States. And this view, so justly maintained by the slaveholding States, was, for the past half century of the existence of our constitutional Union, recognized and acquiesced in by the non-slaveholding States. But these States, or at least very many of their people, in disregard of the obligations of good neighborhood, in contempt of the constitution of the United States, the supreme law of the land, and in obedience to the dictates of what they denominate the "higher law" (which means the madness of unbridled power), have recently denied the rights of individual property, trampled upon the rights of sovereign and independent States, and in their insolence and wickedness havn actually shed slaveholding blood upon slaveholding soil, for the avowed purpose of destroying, without their consent, the relation of master and slave.

Although, sir, it was not Mississippi soil that was thus polluted by the invader's foot, nor Mississippi's jurisdiction that was thus defied and aggressed upon by insolence and wickedness, I beg to assure your Excellency, and, through you, the people of Virginia, that they whose voice I this day speak were not less indignant, nor less willing to avenge the outrage than if it had been perpetrated upon their own territory. But it is consoling to know that the same historic page that records the foul deed will also transmit to posterity the noble manner in which Virginia repelled the insult, avenged the wrong, and vindicated her claim to the motto "*sic semper tyrannus*," which she so proudly and justly wears.

Mississippi, though less exposed to such aggressions and outrages than Virginia and the other border States, feels a common interest in he institution of African slavery, as it exists in the Southern States of this Union, and a common duty to join with them in the adoption of all measures necessary for its protection and perpetuation. Actuated by this sense of her obligation, and deeply sensible of the value of her elder sister (Virginia) in Council, Mississippi unites with South Carolina in earnestly invoking the co-operation of Virginia in the Convention proposed in the third resolution of the series already referred to.

Seeing, as Mississippi does, that the Northern States persist in the denial of our rights in the common Territories of the Union, and continue to repeat their aggressions with more and more aggravation, and, above all, apprehending "the election of a President of the United States by one section of the Union only, on the ground that there exists an irreconcilable conflict between the two sections in reference to their respective systems of labor, and with an avowed purpose of hostility to the institution of slavery as it prevails in the Southern States," she thinks the time has surely come when they shall consult together and recommend what shall be done in an event boding so much mischief and calamity to their rights and interests. She will deplore, as much as any State in the Union, the necessity of dissolving the constitutional ties which bind them into one common government, and she hopes and believes that a timely council with her sister States of the South will devise some remedy consistent with their interest and honor in the Union.

If Mississippi had been influenced by a determination or even a desire to withdraw from this sisterhood of States, I am very sure that she would have selected another agent to plead her cause before the State of Virginia. But if in her sincere desire to be enabled to enjoy all the rights of perfect equality in the Union (as she hopes to do by means of this proposed conference) she shall be disappointed, then I have no hesitation in saying that she will prefer and resort to independence out of it.

This whole question has been recently so ably and so elaborately discussed by the eminent and distinguished gentleman who presented the resolutions of South Carolina, that I feel to say more would be an unnecessary and wanton intrusion.

I will only add that the Legislature of Mississippi, pursuant to the provisions of the third resolution, have elected seven delegates to the proposed Convention, all of whom are amongst the ablest and most faithful of her citizens, and without regard to existing party organizations.

And now, sir, hoping that Virginia, the land of my birth, will yield to the solicitation of Mississippi, the home of my adoption, and send delegates to the proposed convention to be held at Alanta on the first Monday of next June, I have the honor to be, &c. P. B. STARKE.

Coroners' Inquests.

DEATH OF A CHILD FROM BURNS.—Coroner Schirmer held an inquest yesterday, at No. 308 East Twelfth street, on the body of a little girl, four years old, named Ann Muller, who died on Sunday evening, from the effects of burns received on the 17th inst. It seems that she had been playing with the fire while her mother was absent from the room; and, as she was lighting a pine stick, the flames caught her dress, and before they could be subdued, burned her so severely as to cause her death.

ANOTHER CHILD FATALLY BURNED.—An inquest was held by Coroner Schirmer on the body of a little boy aged three years and six months, who was burned to death on Saturday at No. 219 Sullivan street. The boy accidentally set his clothes on fire while playing at the stove with a piece of paper, and rushed to his mother, who threw him into a tub of water to extinguish the flames. The child was so severely burned, however, that it did not recover.

SCALDED TO DEATH.—Coroner Schirmer also held an inquest on the body of James Breer, an infant, ten months old, whose parents reside at 163 East Twenty-sixth street, who was fatally scalded on Saturday afternoon by the by the upsetting of a kettle of boiling water, which was standing on the stove, and which was overturned by the falling of a piece of the stovepipe.

FATAL FALL DOWN AN AREA.—Coroner Schirmer held an inquest upon the body of Wm. Burke, a native of Dublin, Ireland, thirty-five years of age, who was found lying dead in the area of the new building corner of Whitehall and Pearl streets, at an early hour yesterday morning. From the fact that his watch and money were found upon his person, the impression at first that he was the victim of a highway robbery was clearly disproved. A verdict of accidental death was rendered.

STEAMSHIP MOVEMENTS.

Sale of the Steamers Illinois and Moses Taylor—New Lines, &c.

The steamers Illinois and Moses Taylor, belonging to the old United States Mail Steamship Company, recently sold a the Merchants' Exchange at public auction, were re-sold yesterday, and both bid off by Commodore Vanderbilt for $25,000 each.

These ships, with three others, were publicly sold from the same stand by the same parties on the 20th inst., and bid off by B. H. Cheever—the Illinois for $106,000, and the Moses Taylor for $102,000.

The terms of sale, as announced from the stand by the auctioneer, was cash down. The purchaser failing to deposit ten per cent of his bid before two o'clock, the sale was declared null and void, and the ships advertised and re-sold yesterday.

Wm. Chase Barney was present and bid $30,000 on each ship, being $5,000 over Commodore Vanderbilt—these were the only bids offered. Barney was distinctly told by Mr. Roberts, who acted as auctioneer, that no more bogus bids would be accepted—that they had once been sold to a bogus bidder—that if he expected to get the ships the money must be paid down before he left the stand.

A letter was also read by Mr. Roberts from B. H. Cheever, before the sale, protesting against the sale, claiming that he was the lawful owner of the ships, and offering to comply with the terms of his purchase.

After the ships were fairly struck off to Commodore Vanderbilt, Barney protested against the sale, and offered o deposit the money ($50,000) by three o'clock, but the Commodore being present with two certified checks of $100,000 each, was rather too much for his competitor.

W. Chase Barney, it will be recollected, was the especial friend of Commodore Johnson, the great mail contractor, who were jointly bidders for nearly every mail contract between New York, New Orleans, California and Oregon, last fall.

Marshal O. Roberts, President of the company, announced from the stand to the gentlemen present at the first sale (20th instant) that the Philadelphia would be sold subject to the claim of government—owing to which fact it no doubt was that she brought so low a price—only $5,000.

The charge against the Philadelphia is "libel for forfeiture," under third section of act of Congress of 20th April, 1818, same law under which the Pampero, of Lopez notoriety, was seized, forfeited and sold by government.

The Philadelphia, one of the steamers sold, is now, and has been for some four or five months, in the hands of the United States government at New Orleans, charged with being engaged in a filibustering expedition to Nicaragua.

The case is to be tried in the United States District Court for the Eastern District of Louisiana. It has been several times postponed by government, ostensibly for the purpose of obtaining additional proofs of the steamer's guilt, but the real and legitimate cause being no doubt to see if the owners would not reconsider their determination of holding the government responsible for the ship (which they have done) and accept of the steamer and call it square.

This the company will not do—whole hog or nothing—they will either lose, or have full compensation from Uncle Sam for the damage sustained by the loss of their steamer, and the injury done their reputation by being charged with filibustering.

The Nicaragua route will be opened by Commodore Vanderbilt under somewhat different arrangements than it would have been had not the grand consolidation of interests, which has recently taken place, been effected.

The iron steamer for the San Juan river, which has been contracted for with Harlan, Hollingsworth & Co., of Wilmington, Del., will be constructed more with a view of carrying freight, and the traffic in the interior, than for carrying passengers, which she was originally intended for. This route will now be used, when opened, more for trade and traffic along the lakes and rivers of the interior, which it will furnish, more than it did when opened before, which was found to be quite profitable, especially the cattle trade, which frequently yielded to the owners of the boat a net profit of from $500 to $800 each trip on cattle alone.

The steamer contracted for with J. Simonson, will not be built at present, but two smaller boats adapted to the lakes will be built instead—so that the Commodore will not forfeit anything by the change. The water on the bar at the entrance of the harbor at San Juan del Norte is now reported at 13 feet.

What disposition is to be made with the North Atlantic Company's steamers (Collins'), is not known—two of the directors being absent, the subject has not yet been talked over.

It seems to be generally understood that these steamers, in connection with the C. Vanderbilt, will run to Havre and Southampton—forming a weekly line between those ports and New York.

Commodore Vanderbilt has for some time been running a semi-monthly line on this route, composed of the Ocean Queen and C. Vanderbilt, which has proved very successful and profitable.

This line has carried the United States mails, for which Vanderbilt has received as remuneration the sea postage, which sometimes amounts to as high as $13,000 a trip.

Should this line be formed (Collins' ships) the Ocean Queen will be withdrawn and placed on the Aspinwall route, in connection with the North Star and Northern Light, forming a tri-monthly line, leaving this port on the 5th, 20th and 30th of every month.

This schedule of sailing days has already gone into operation.

The Baltic makes her last trip on the 5th of March.

A steamer is already advertised to leave on the 30th of March, which will probably be the Ariel.

The Ocean Queen, Ariel, Illinois, Empire City, Star of the West, Moses Taylor, St. Louis and Daniel Webster will be used for running the line between New York, Havana and Nicaragua, and between New Orleans, Havana, Greytown and Aspinwall, and also for a spare steamer between New York and the last named port.

ACCOUNT BY ANOTHER REPORTER.

Under the following advertisement the steamships *Illinois* and Moses Taylor were yesterday offered for sale at the Merchants' Exchange:—

Notice is hereby given, that in pursuance of the deed of trust executed on the 17th day of August, A. D. 1847, the undersigned trustees will sell at public auction, on Tuesday, the 10th of January next, at 1 o'clock, P. M., in the Rotunda of the Merchants' Exchange, New York city, the following named steamships, together with the tackle, apparel, furniture, and all other appurtenances thereunto belonging, to wit: Illinois, Star of the West, Empire City, Moses Taylor, Philadelphia. Terms of sale, cash. Dated in the city of New York, this 5th day of November, A. D. 1859.

MARSHALL O. ROBERTS,
HORACE F. CLARK,
EDWARD N. DICKERSON, } Trustees.

All the above named steamships having been sold at auction on the 20th day of February, 1860, and the purchaser of two of them, to wit, the Illinois and Moses Taylor, not having complied with the terms of the sale as advertised and announced from the auction stand, notice is hereby given that the said steamers, Illinois and Moses Taylor, will be sold at public auction, at the Merchants' Exchange, on Monday, Feb. 27, 1860, at one o'clock P. M. Terms of sale—cash.

MARSHALL O. ROBERTS,
HORACE F. CLARK,
EDWARD N. DICKERSON, } Trustees.

Dated New York, Feb. 21, 1860.

Precisely at one o'clock, Mr. Narshall O. Roberts and a Mr. Matthews, a regular licensed auctioneer, mounted the stand, and the latter read the above advertisement; thereupon a person presented the following letter to M. O. Roberts, which was read by Mr. Matthews:—

NEW YORK, Feb. 27, 1860.

Notice is hereby given to all whom it may concern, that the steamships Illinois and Moses Taylor were sold to me on the 20th inst., at this place, by Mr. Roberts; that I have offered and am ready to pay the whole amount of my bids upon receiving a proper conveyance of a good title to said ships, and am still ready to pay the amount of my bids and take such conveyance. I claim to be the owner of said ships by virtue of such purchase, if the seller had a right to make the sale, and I shall insist upon my rights as a purchaser. BENJAMIN H. CHEEVER.

Mr. Roberts then announced that the purchaser must pay the purchase money before three o'clock.

He then offered the "Illinois," and said he was authorized to bid $25,000 for her. He continued to cry "25,000," "25,000, once"—"25,000," "25,000, twice"—whereupon Mr. W. C. Barney offered $30,000. This bid appeared to be a bombshell thrown into the crowd. After consultation with Mr. Dickerson, Mr. Roberts announced that he would not receive the bid. Mr. Barney then said that he (Roberts) could not refuse the bid; that it was a public sale at auction, under the laws of the State of New York. After some further parley with Mr. Dickerson and others, Mr. Roberts announced that he should require the purchase money to be paid down. Mr. Barney then claimed that he (Roberts) could not change the terms of sale—having already accepted a bid under his first announcement of "cash before three o'clock." Mr. Roberts, however, refused to accept Mr. Barney's bid, who stated that he was prepared to pay the cash before three o'clock, according to the terms first proposed by Mr. Roberts when he accepted the first bid of $25,000.

Mr. Roberts got no other bid, and the "Illinois" was knocked down for $25,000. Mr. Roberts announced the purchaser to be Cornelius Vanderbilt. The same proceedings took place in regard to the "Moses Taylor," which also was knocked down to Cornelius Vanderbilt for $25,000, although Mr. Barney bid $30,000, and said he was prepared to pay the cash before 3 P. M., according to the first terms of sale proposed.

MRS. BLUNT'S READINGS.—This very talented and estimable lady gives another reading at the Hope Chapel, in Broadway, this evening, and it is to be hoped that her numerous friends from the North and South will support her on this occasion. She is a widow, her husband having died in the service of his country, a lieutenant in our navy; and she gives these readings with the laudable desire of raising sufficient funds to educate her children, without being dependent on friends for their support. She belongs to one of the best families at the South, and her father (Mr. Key) was the author of that beautiful national rallying song, "The Star Spangled Banner," which he wrote while in sight of his native State of Maryland, a prisoner on board of an English man-of-war, in the last struggle with Great Britain. This inspiring piece of poetry, at the request of her friends, Mrs. Blunt will recite on this occasion.

Court Calendar—This day.

SUPREME COURT—Part 2.—484, 510, 550, 490, 280, 399, 153, 317, 413, 952, 369, 144, 293, 311, 405, 403, 555, 508, 375, 219, 121, 414.

A Lemoine Case in this City.

A MOTHER DESTROYS THE BODY OF HER ILLEGITIMATE CHILD BY BURNING IT IN A FURNACE.

About six o'clock on Sunday afternoon the family of the Rev. John Cotton Smith, rector of the Episcopal Church of the Ascension, corner of Fifth avenue and Tenth street, observed a peculiar and mysterious odor pervading the whole premises. A search was immediately instituted to ascertain its cause, and almost every part of the house had been examined before the cellar was finally searched. The large furnace which is there located was examined, and the body of a child, burnt almost to a crisp, was discovered on the coals.

Suspicion at once fell upon a young Irish servant girl, named Grace Heenan, and Capt. Dilks, of the Fifteenth precinct, was sent for. He came, bringing with him Police Surgeon Dr. Jones, who made an examination of the girl's person, and discovered unmistakable evidence of the recent child birth. She finally confessed to having put the body of the child in the furnace, stating that it was still-born, and that she had been seduced by a man living on Long Island. She also said that she was delivered of the child about two o'clock on Sunday morning, and that she thrust it into the furnace to destroy it.

The body of the child was removed to the Fifteenth precinct station house, where Coroner Schirmer held an inquest yesterday afternoon.

Margaret Miller, being duly sworn, said:—I live at the residence of Rev. John Cotton Smith, No. 61 Tenth street, as domestic; Grace Heenan was about two months there; she was the cook; I had suspicion of her condition from appearances; I slept in the same bed with her; she got up about four o'clock on Sunday morning, complaining that she was unwell; she came back into bed without leaving the room; I asked her how she felt, and she said she had a pain in her side; did not see her again until four o'clock in the afternoon; she got up out of bed after I left her; she got some clothes belonging to her, took a pail of water and went up stairs; she remained there about an hour and came down again, with some sheets in her hand; did not see any blood on them; I went up stairs, and I became convinced that a confinement had taken place; I heard a noise as of shovelling coal in the cellar, and also noticed a great stench; went down into the cellar to ascertain the cause; I saw Grace by the furnace; I asked her what she was doing; she said she was fixing the fire; I took a poker and stirring the body in the furnace asked her what it was; she said she did not know; I drew the body out of the fire to the mouth of the furnace; I asked Grace if that was not a baby; she would not answer me, but went up stairs; I followed her, locking the cellar door behind me; I told the lady of the house, Mrs. Smith's sister, of the fact; when I went up stairs Grace had some linen in a tub washing it; during the night I slept with Grace I heard no groan nor cry.

Dr. Alanson S. Jones, Police Surgeon of the Fifteenth precinct, being duly sworn, said:—I live at No. 42 University place; about eight o'clock on Sunday evening I was called to the house No. 61 Tenth street; on proceeding to the cellar, I found the body of a male infant—the one here present—it was in a charred and mutilated condition; I took the body and sent it to the station house; I then proceeded to the kitchen, and there found Grace Heenan, whom I examined, and ascertained that she had recently been delivered; upon charging her with being the mother of the infant found in the cellar, she, after some hesitation, admitted that she was the mother; that it had been born the night previous, saying that it had never cried; she stated that the child lay dead in bed all day Sunday with her; that about two hours previous to our interview she brought the child from the upper part of the house into the cellar and placed it in the furnace; she seemed a rather ignorant girl, and did not seem to appreciate that she had been doing anything wrong; I was present at the post mortem examination; saw the hydrostatic test applied to the lungs; there was no evidence to show that the child ever breathed.

Geo. B. Bouton, M. D., being duly sworn, deposed as follows:—I have made a post-mortem examination of the body of the dead child now lying in this station; I find it to be that of a male child of small size; externally there are indications of extensive burns; the right arm is burned and the right side of the body charred; the right lung was also charred; both lungs, when subjected to the hydrostatic test, did not indicate that respiration had been established.

The evidence here closed, and the case was submitted to the jury, who, after a short deliberation, brought in a verdict of "Stillborn."

Grace Heenan is still lying in a rather precarious condition at the house of her employer. She is a young girl, being only twenty-one years of age, and is devoid of any great personal beauty. When examined by Dr. Jones, she stated, on being closely questioned by him, that while living at service with a farmer on Long Island last summer, her bedroom was entered in the night by a laborer, one of the farm hands, who violated her person, and that an improper intimacy had succeeded, with the result shown above.

City Intelligence.

THE CLEANING OF THE CITY.—According to our announcement in Saturday's paper, the work of cleaning the streets of this city was set about yesterday morning by Mr. Smith, the machine man, and Broadway was swept from Fourteenth street to the Battery. The contractor's first object will be the regulation of the removal of the ashes and garbage, and clearing up the winter accumulations of dirt from the streets. Should the season prove favorable it is hoped that this can be done by the beginning of April, after which he will then clean the streets as often in each week as the Mayor, Comptroller and City Inspector may direct or deem necessary to keep them clean. In the prosecution of this work of sweeping Mr. Smith intends using his new street sweepers the advantages of which over his old ones being, that they are completely covered in, so as to prevent dust from flying; they also gather up the dirt by their sweeping apparatus into a box, thereby obviating the old plan of sweeping into winrows. The force of men employed will average about three hundred, which, with the machines, will make the entire working force on the streets during the spring and summer equal to about one thousand men—a sufficiency to have the streets in good order all the time. Let the contractor have fair play in carrying out this important matter. In taking hold of the job he finds everything in chaos, out of which he has to introduce order and system—no small undertaking in our modern Babel. It appears no formal contract has as yet been entered into with Mr. Smith, the arrangement with the City Inspector being merely conditional, and even without the concurrence of the Mayor and Comptroller.

"WHAT IS IT?"—They have added to the list of curiosities at Barnum's Museum a most extraordinary freak of nature, consisting of a creature supposed to belong to the ouran-outang species, but having all the appearance of a human being. It was said to have been captured in the interior of Africa, on the border of the river Gambia, by a party who were in search of the famous gorilla. It stands about four feet high, and it weighs some fifty pounds; its age cannot be correctly ascertained, but it is supposed to be over twenty years. The formation of its hands, arms and head are those of an ouran-outang, but its movements are those of a human being. Those who are fond of looking at the freaks nature frequently indulges in, should stop in, and form for themselves an opinion as to "What is it?" After viewing the creature above described, about which hangs a cloud of doubt and uncertainty, we turned into the "lecture room," where the "Octoroon" was being performed. This play having had the run of two of our theatres, has been taken up and placed upon the stage at Barnum's, where for the last four weeks it has attracted crowds. It is very well put upon the stage, and the acting is highly creditable to the managers. The novelty of the Museum appears never to wear off, and with its endless variety of strange things—its bears, seals and lecture room—will always draw full houses, despite the hard times and the season of Lent, which affects nearly all places of amusements.

FIRE IN CANAL STREET—NARROW ESCAPE OF THE OCCUPANTS OF THE BUILDING FROM SUFFOCATION.—Between three and four o'clock yesterday morning, a fire broke out in the millinery and children's furnishing goods store of Madam L. Pestioux, No. 336 Canal street. Mrs. Pestioux, her son and servant, slept in the building, and were awoke by the smoke. Finding all exit by the stairs cut off, they were compelled to make their escape through the windows. The girl got out at the rear, and Mrs. P. and her son in front. Mrs. Pestioux became exhausted and fell to the floor; but, regaining her strength, she at last managed to break the glass, when, with the assistance of some persons outside, she was taken to the sidewalk. Her face and hands were cut, but not seriously. The flames extended to the roof of the building, and also to the roofs of Nos. 334 and 338, before the fire was extinguished. The damage done to Mrs Pestioux's stock and furniture will amount to about $1,500. Insured for $2,000 in the North American Insurance Company.

No. 334 is occupied by Mrs. Laycock, as a millinery store and dwelling. The stock and furniture is damaged by fire and water about $500; insured for $800 in the Excelsior Insurance Company. The second floor is occupied by Mrs. Whitney as a dwelling; her furniture is damaged by water about $160; no insurance.

No. 338 is occupied by Madame Demorest Goodall, as a pattern store and dwelling. Her stock is damaged by water about $200; insured for $1,000 in the Pacific Insurance Company.

The building No. 334 is owned by Judge Mitchell; it is damaged about $300, and is insured.

Buildings Nos. 336 and 338 are owned by Mrs. Colt. They are damaged about $700, and are said to be insured. The origin of the fire is unknown at present.

MISSIONARIES SAILED.—Rev. Solomon Carpenter, D. D., and wife, sailed for Shanghae, China, in the ship N. B. Palmer, on the 24th inst., as missionaries of the Seventh Day Baptist church. Che-shang-la, a native teacher, who came to this country with Mr. Carpenter on his return last year, also returned in the N. B. Palmer. Thus the attention of the heathen world is to be held to the consideration of the Sabbath of the seventh day as well as the Sabbath of the first day of the week. The controversy will be represented by the no-Sabbath party, the old and the new Sabbatarians.

STEALING LETTERS FROM THE NEW POST OFFICE BOXES.—A little girl named Jane Ann McGuire, was arrested by officer Jordan, of the Sixth precinct, yesterday, charged with stealing a letter and newspaper from a letter box at the corner of Broadway and White street. She was seen to thrust her hand into the opening and draw forth the letter and newspaper, and the officer was called, who took her into custody.

A TRIBUTE TO THE MEMORY OF DANIEL FANSHAW.—The New York Typographical Society held a meeting on last Saturday evening, when Mr. Charles McDevitt announced Mr. Fanshaw's death, pronouncing an eloquent eulogium on the deceased, and giving a brief sketch of his life. Resolutions of condolence with the family of Mr. F., and also ordering, as a mark of respect to their departed brother, that the rooms of the Society be draped in mourning for the term of thirty days, were unanimously adopted.

LAW LECTURE BY JUDGE CLERKE.—The tenth of a course of exceedingly interesting lectures on law, by Judge Clerke, of the Supreme Court, will be delivered this evening at the Law University, in Chambers street. Subject—"The relation of Guardian and Ward, and Infancy, in which the liability of infants to the civil and criminal law will be especially considered."

THE PRESIDENTIAL CAMPAIGN.

Another Republican Orator on the Stump.

Speech of the Hon. Abraham Lincoln, of Illinois,

&c., &c., &c.

The announcements that the Hon. Abraham Lincoln, of Illinois, would "speak" at the Cooper Institute, drew together a large assemblage at that building last night. The tax of twenty-five cents per capita did not—as it very frequently does—act as a preventative on the visitors, but they continued, on the contrary to pour in in considerable numbers until the large hall was about three-quarters filled. Among the audience there were, as is usual in these republican assemblages, a goodly number of ladies.

At about a quarter to eight o'clock, ex-Governor King made his appearance on the platform, and was greeted with loud applause, which he seemed to enjoy mightily, as with a smile of benevolent gravity he settled himself in a chair.

The arrival of D. Dudley Field, accompanied by William Cullen Bryant and the speaker of the evening, was the signal for the most tumultuous applause.

Mr. FIELD said—Fellow republicans, I beg leave to nominate as chairman of this meeting a republican whom you all know well—William Cullen Bryant. (Applause.) Those of you who are in favor of Mr. Bryant will be pleased to say "Aye." (Loud cries of "Aye.") Those who are opposed will say "No." (No response.) There is no "No." (Laughter.)

Mr. WILLIAM CULLEN BRYANT then came forward amid loud applause. He said—My friends, it is a grateful office that I perform in introducing to you at this time an eminent citizen of the West, whom you know—whom you have known hitherto only by fame, but who has consented to address a New York assembly this evening. The great West, my friends, is a potent auxiliary in the battle we are fighting for freedom against slavery, in behalf of civilization against barbarism, for the occupation of some of the fairest region of our continent, on which settlers are now building their cabins. I see a higher and wiser agency than that of man in the causes that have filled with a hardy population the vast and fertile region which forms the northern part of the valley of the Mississippi—a race of men who are not ashamed to till their acres with their own hands, and who would be ashamed to subsist by the labor of slaves. (Loud applause.) These children of the West, my friends, form a living bulwark against the advances of slavery, and from them is recruited the vanguard of the armies of liberty. (Applause.) One of them will appear before you this evening. I present to you a gallant soldier of the political campaign of 1856, who then rendered good service to the republican cause, and who was since the great champion of that cause in the struggle which took place two years later for the supremacy of the republicans in the Legislature of Illinois—who took the field there against Douglas, and would have won the victory but for the unjust apportionment law of the State, which allowed a minority of the people to elect a majority of the Legislature. (Applause.) I have only, my friends, to pronounce the name of Abraham Lincoln, of Illinois—(loud cheers)—to receive the profoundest attention. (Renewed cheers.)

Mr. Lincoln is a tall, thin man, dark complexioned, and apparently quick in his perceptions. He is rather unsteady in his gait, and there is an involuntary comical awkwardness which marks his movements while speaking. His voice, though sharp and powerful at times, has a frequent tendency to dwindle into a shrill and unpleasant sound. His enunciation is slow and emphatic, and a peculiar characteristic of his delivery was a remarkable mobility of his features, the frequent contortions of which excited the merriment which his words alone could not well have produced.

ADDRESS BY HON. ABRAHAM LINCOLN.

When the applause which greeted Mr. Lincoln had subsided, he said:—

MR. PRESIDENT AND FELLOW CITIZENS OF THE CITY OF NEW YORK—The facts with which I shall deal this evening are mainly old and familiar; nor is there anything new in the general use I shall make of them. If there shall be any novelty, it will be in the mode of presenting the facts, and the inferences and observations following that presentation. In his speech last autumn, at Columbus, Ohio, as reported in the New York *Times*, Senator Douglas said:—

> Our fathers, when they framed the government under which we live, understood this question just as well, and even better, than we do now.

I fully endorse this, and I adopt it as a text for this discourse. (Applause.) I so adopt it because it furnishes a precise and an agreed starting point for a discussion between republicans and that wing of the democracy headed by Senator Douglas. It simply leaves the inquiry, What was the understanding those fathers had of the question mentioned? What is the frame of government under which we live? The answer must be, The constitution of the United States. That constitution consists of the original, framed in 1787 (and under which the present government first went into operation), and twelve subsequently framed amendments, the first ten of which were framed in 1789. Who were our fathers that framed the constitution? I suppose the "thirty-nine" who signed the original instrument may be fairly called our fathers who framed that part of the present government. It is almost exactly true to say they framed it, and it is altogether true to say they fairly represented the opinion and sentiment of the whole nation at that time. Their names, being familiar to nearly all, and accessible to quite all, need not now be repeated. I take these "thirty-nine," for the present, as being "our fathers who framed the government under which we live." What is the question which, according to the text, those fathers understood just as well, and even better than we do now? It is this:—Does the proper division of local from federal authority, or anything in the constitution, forbid our federal government to control as to slavery in our federal Territories? Upon this Douglas holds the affirmative, and republicans the negative. This affirmative and denial form an issue; and this issue, this question, is precisely what the text declares our fathers understood better than we. (Cheers.) Let us now inquire whether the "thirty-nine," or any of them, ever acted upon this question; and if they did, how they acted upon it—how they expressed that better understanding. In 1784, three years before the constitution, the United States then owning the Northwestern territory, and no other, the Congress of the confederation had before them the question of prohibiting slavery in that Territory; and four of the "thirty-nine" who afterwards framed the constitution were in that Congress, and voted on that question. Of these Roger Sherman, Thomas Mifflin and Hugh Williamson voted for the prohibition, thus showing that, in their understanding, no line dividing local from federal authority, nor anything else, properly forbade the federal government to control as to slavery in federal territory. The other of the four, James McHenry, voted against the prohibition, showing that for some cause he thought it improper to vote for it. In 1787, still before the constitution, but while the Convention was in session framing it, and while the Northwestern territory still was the only territory owned by the United States—the same question of prohibiting slavery in the territory again came before the Congress of the confederation; and three more of the "thirty-nine" who afterwards signed the constitution were in that Congress and voted on the question. They were William Blount, William Few and Abraham Baldwin, and they all voted for the prohibition, thus showing that, in their understanding, no line dividing local from federal authority, nor anything else, properly forbade the federal government to control as to slavery in federal territory. This time the prohibition became a law, being a part of what is now well known as the Ordinance of 1787. The question of federal control of slavery in the Territories seems not to have been directly before the Convention which framed the original constitution; and hence it is not recorded that the "thirty-nine," or any of them, while engaged on that instrument, expressed any opinion on that precise question. In 1789, by the first Congress which sat under the constitution, an act was passed to enforce the Ordinance of 1787, including the prohibition of slavery in the Northwestern territory. The bill for this act was reported by one of the "thirty-nine," Thomas Fitzsimmons, then a member of the House of Representatives from Pennsylvania. It went through all its stages without a word of opposition, and finally passed both branches without yeas and nays, which is equivalent to a unanimous passage. (Cheers.) In this Congress there were sixteen of the "thirty-nine" fathers who framed the original constitution They were:—

John Langdon,	Thos. Fitzsimmons,	Richard Bassett,
Nicholas Gilman,	William Few,	George Read,
Wm. S. Johnson,	Abraham Baldwin,	Pierce Butler,
Roger Sherman,	Rufus King,	Daniel Carroll,
Robert Morris,	William Patterson,	James Madison,
George Clymer,		

This shows that, in their understanding, no line dividing local from federal authority, nor anything in the constitution, properly forbade Congress to prohibit slavery in the federal territory; else both their fidelity to correct principle and their oath to support the constitution would have constrained them to oppose the prohibition. Again, George Washington, another of the "thirty-nine," was then President of the United States, and, as such, approved and signed the bill, thus completing its validity as a law, and thus showing that, in his understanding, no line dividing local from federal authority, nor anything in the constitution, forbade the federal government to control as to slavery in federal territory. (Loud applause.) No great while after the adoption of the original constitution, North Carolina ceded to the federal government the country now constituting the State of Tennessee; and a few years later Georgia ceded that which now constitutes the States of Mississippi and Alabama. In both deeds of cession it was made a condition by the ceding States that the federal government should not prohibit slavery in the ceded country. Beside this, slavery was then actually in the ceded country. Under these circumstances Congress, on taking charge of these countries, did not absolutely prohibit slavery within them. But they did interfere with it—take control of it—even there, to a certain extent. In 1798 Congress organized the Territory of Mississippi. In the act of organization they prohibited the bringing of slaves into the Territory, from any place without the United States, by fine, and giving freedom to slaves so brought. This act passed both branches of Congress without yeas and nays. In that Congress were three of the "thirty nine" who framed the original constitution. They were John Langdon, George Read and Abraham Baldwin. They all, probably, voted for it. Certainly they would have placed their opposition to it upon record if, in their understanding, any line dividing local from federal authority, or anything in the constitution properly forbade the federal government to control as to slavery in federal territory. (Applause.) In 1803 the federal government purchased the Louisiana country. Our former territorial acquisitions came from certain of our own States, but this Louisiana country was acquired from a foreign nation. In 1804 Congress gave a Territorial organization to that part of it which now constitutes the State of Louisiana. New Orleans, lying within that part, was an old and comparatively large city. There were other considerable towns and settlements, and slavery was extensively and thoroughly intermingled with the people. Congress did not, in the Territorial act, prohibit slavery; but they did interfere with it—take control of it—in a more marked and extensive way than they did in the case of Mississippi. The substance of the provision therein made in relation to slaves was:—

First, That no slave should be imported into the Territory from foreign parts.

Second, That no slave should be carried into it who had been imported into the United States since the first day of May, 1798.

Third, That no slave should be carried into it, except by the owner, and for his own use as a settler; the penalty in all the cases being a fine upon the violator of the law and freedom to the slave. (Prolonged cheers.)

This act also was passed without yeas and nays. In the Congress which passed it, there were two of the "thirty-nine." They were Abraham Baldwin and Jonathan Dayton. As stated in the case of Mississippi, it is probable they both voted for it. They would not have allowed it to pass without recording their opposition to it, if, in their understanding, it violated either the line properly dividing local from federal authority or any provision of the constitution. In 1819 and 1820 came and passed the Missouri question. Many votes were taken, by yeas and nays, in both branches of Congress, upon the various phases of the general question. Two of the "thirty-nine"—Rufus King and Charles Pinckney—were members of that Congress. Mr. King steadily voted for slavery prohibition and against all compromises, while Mr. Pinckney as steadily voted against slavery prohibition, and against all compromises. (Cheers.) By this Mr. King showed that, in his understanding, no line dividing local from federal authority, nor anything in the constitution, was violated by Congress prohibiting slavery in federal territory; while Mr. Pinckney, by his votes, showed that, in his understanding, there was some sufficient reason for opposing such prohibition in that case. The cases I have mentioned are the only acts of the "thirty-nine," or of any of them, upon the direct issue, which I have been able to discover. To enumerate the persons who thus acted, as being four in 1784, three in 1787, seventeen in 1789, three in 1798, two in 1804, and two in 1819-20—there would be thirty-one of them. But this would be counting John Langdon, Roger Sherman, William Few, Rufus King and George Read, each twice, and Abraham Baldwin four times. (Applause.) He was a Georgian, too. (Renewed applause and laughter.) The true number of those of the "thirty-nine" whom I have shown to have acted upon the question, which, by the text, they understood better than we, is twenty-three, leaving sixteen not shown to have acted upon it in any way. Here, then, we have twenty-three of our "thirty nine" fathers who framed the government under which we live, who have, upon their official responsibility and their corporal oaths, acted upon the very question which the text affirms they "understood just as well, and even better than we do now;" and twenty-one of them—a clear majority of the whole "thirty-nine"—so acting upon it as to make them guilty of gross political impropriety and wilful perjury, if, in their understanding, any proper division between local and federal authority, or anything in the constitution they had made themselves and sworn to support, forbade the federal government to control as to slavery in the federal Territories. (Cheers.) Thus the twenty-one acted; and as actions speak louder than words, so actions under such responsibility speak still louder. Two of the twenty-three voted against Congressional prohibition of slavery in the federal Territories, in the instances in which they acted upon the question. But for what reasons they so voted is not known. They may have done so because they thought a proper division of local from federal authority, or some provision or principle of the constitution, stood in the way; or they may, without any such question, have voted against the prohibition, on what appeared to them to be sufficient grounds of expediency. No one who has sworn to support the constitution can conscientiously vote for what he understands to be an unconstitutional measure, however expedient he may think it; but one may and ought to vote against a measure which he deems constitutional, if, at the same time, he deems it inexpedient. It, therefore, would be unsafe to set down even the two who voted against the prohibition, as having done so because, in their understanding, any proper division of local from federal authority, or anything in the constitution, forbade the federal government to control as to slavery in federal territory. (Laughter and prolonged applause). The remaining sixteen of the "thirty-nine," so far as I have discovered, have left no record of their understanding upon the direct question of federal control of slavery in the federal Territories. But there is much reason to believe that their understanding upon that question would not have appeared different from that of their twenty-three compeers, had it been manifested at all. For the purpose of adhering rigidly to the text, I have purposely omitted whatever understanding may have been manifested, by any person, however distinguished, other than the thirty-nine fathers who framed the original constitution; and, for the same reason, I have also omitted whatever understanding may have been manifested by any of the "thirty-nine" even, on any other phase of the general question of slavery. If we should look into their acts and declarations on those other phases, as the foreign slave trade, and the morality and policy of slavery generally, it would appear to us that on the direct question of federal control of slavery in federal Territories, the sixteen, if they had acted at all, would probably have acted just as the twenty-three did. Among that sixteen were several of the most noted anti-slavery men of those times—as Dr. Franklin (Cheers), Alexander Hamilton, and Gouverneur Morris—while there was not one now known to have been otherwise, unless it may be John Rutledge of South Carolina. (Applause) The sum of the whole is, that of our "thirty-nine" fathers who framed the original constitution, twenty-one—a clear majority of the whole—certainly understood that no proper division of local from federal authority, nor any part of the constitution, forbade the federal government to control slavery in the federal Territories, while all the rest probably had the same understanding. Such, unquestionably, was the understanding of our fathers who framed the original constitution; and the text affirms that they understood the question better than we. (Laughter and cheers.) But, so far I have been considering the understanding of the question manifested by the framers of the original constitution. In and by the original instrument a mode was provided for amending it; and, as I have already stated, the present frame of government under which we live consists of that original, and twelve amendatory articles framed and adopted since. Those who now insist that federal control of slavery in federal Territories violates the constitution, point us to the provisions which they suppose it thus violates; and, as I understand, they all fix upon provisions in these amendatory articles, and not in the original instrument. The Supreme Court, in the Dred Scott case plant themselves upon the fifth amendment, which provides that "no person shall be deprived of property without due process of law;" while Senator Douglas and his peculiar adherents plant themselves upon the tenth amendment, providing that "the powers not granted by the constitution, are reserved to the States respectively, and to the people." Now, it so happens that these amendments were framed by the first Congress which sat under the constitution—the identical Congress which passed the act already mentioned, enforcing the prohibition of slavery in the Northwestern Territory. (Applause.) Not only was it the same Congress, but they were the identical, same individual men who, at the same session, at the same time within the session, had under consideration, and in progress toward maturity, these constitutional amendments and this act prohibiting slavery in all the territory the nation then owned. The constitutional amendments were introduced before and passed after the act of enforcing the ordinance of '87; so that during the whole pendency of the act to enforce the ordinance the constitutional amendments were also pending. That Congress, consisting in all of seventy-six members, including sixteen of the framers of the original constitution, as before stated, were pre-eminently our fathers who framed that part of the government under which we live which is now claimed as forbidding the federal government to control slavery in the federal Territories. Is it not a little presumptuous in any one at this day to affirm that the two things which that Congress deliberately framed, and carried to maturity at the same time, are absolutely inconsistent with each other? And does not such affirmation become impudently absurd when coupled with the other affirmation, from the same mouth, that those who did the two things alleged to be inconsistent understood whether they really were inconsistent better than we—better than he who affirms that they are inconsistent? (Applause and great merriment.) It is surely safe to assume that the "thirty-nine" framers of the original constitution, and the seventy-six members of the Congress which framed the amendments thereto, taken altogether, do certainly include those who may be fairly called "our fathers who framed the government under which we live." And so assuming, I defy any man to show that any one of them ever in his whole life declared that, in his understanding, any proper division of local from federal authority, or any part of the constitution, forbade the federal government to control as to slavery in the federal Territories. (Loud applause.) I go a step further. I defy any one to show that any living man in the whole world ever did, prior to the beginning of the present century, (and I might almost say prior to the beginning of the last half of the present century,) declare that, in his understanding, any proper division of local from federal authority, or any part of the constitution, forbade the federal government to control as to slavery in the federal Territories. To those who now so declare I give, not only "our fathers who framed the government under which we live," but with them all other living men within the century in which it was framed, among whom to search, and they shall not be able to find the evidence of a single man agreeing with them. Now and here, let me guard a little against being misunderstood. I do not mean to say we are bound to follow implicitly in whatever our fathers did. To do so would be to discard all the lights of current experience—to reject all progress—all improvement. What I do say is, that if we would supplant the opinions and policy of our fathers, in any case, we should do so upon evidence so conclusive, and argument so clear, that even their great authority, fairly considered and weighed, cannot stand; and most surely not in a case whereof we ourselves declare they understood the question better than we. (Laughter.) If any man, at this day, sincerely believes that a proper division of local from federal authority, or any part of the constitution, forbids the federal government to control as to slavery in the federal Territories, he is right to say so, and to enforce his position by all truthful evidence and fair argument which he can. But he has no right to mislead others, who have less access to history and less leisure to study it, into the false belief that "our fathers, who framed the government under which we live," were of the same opinion—thus substituting falsehood and deception for truthful evidence and fair argument. (Applause.) If any man at this day sincerely believes "our fathers, who framed the government under which we live," used and applied principles, in other cases, which ought to have led them to understand that a proper division of local from federal authority, or some part of the constitution, forbids the federal government to control as to slavery in the federal Territories, he is right to say so. But he should, at the same time, brave the responsibility of declaring that, in his opinion, he understands their principles better than they did themselves—(great laughter)—and especially should he not shirk that responsibility by asserting that they "understood the question just as well, and even better, than we do now." (Applause.) But enough. Let all who believe that "our fathers, who framed the government under which we live, understood this question just as well, and even better than we do now," speak as they spoke, and act as they acted upon it. This is all republicans ask—all republicans desire—in relation to slavery. As those fathers marked it, so let it be again

HARPER'S WEEKLY
A JOURNAL OF CIVILIZATION

Vol. IV.—No. 173.] NEW YORK, SATURDAY, APRIL 21, 1860. [Price Five Cents.

HON. STEPHEN A. DOUGLAS, UNITED STATES SENATOR FROM ILLINOIS.—From a Photograph by Brady.—[See next Page.]

The Philadelphia Inquirer.

ESTABLISHED 1829. | PHILADELPHIA, SATURDAY, MAY 19, 1860. | PRICE TWO CENTS.

THE PHILADELPHIA INQUIRER,

PUBLISHED EVERY MORNING, BY

WILLIAM W. HARDING.

INQUIRER BUILDING, 121 SOUTH THIRD ST.

TERMS—Cash invariably in advance.

All letters to be addressed to the Publisher.

The daily INQUIRER will be served to subscribers in the City, at the reduced price of TWELVE CENTS a week, payable to the carriers—and mailed to subscribers out of the city at the rate of SIX DOLLARS a year, payable invariably in advance.

☞ Subscribers in the city desirous of paying for the paper by the year in advance can do so at the office.

The tri-weekly INQUIRER will be mailed to subscribers out of the city on the mornings of Tuesday, Thursday, and Saturday of every week, at the rate of FOUR DOLLARS a year, invariably in advance.

LOCAL INTELLIGENCE.

Amusements this Evening.

WALNUT STREET THEATRE.—"The Wife's Secret," "Ella Rosenburg," and "Life in Philadelphia."

ARCH STREET THEATRE.—"The Robbers," and "Don Cæsar De Bazan."

NATIONAL THEATRE.—"The Midnight Assault," "Bianco," and other entertainments.

SOLOMON'S TEMPLE.—Open from 10 A. M. until 10 P. M. at National Hall.

ASSEMBLY BUILDING.—Dolly Dutton's Levees this afternoon and evening at 3 and 8 o'clock.

PENNSYLVANIA ACADEMY OF THE FINE ARTS.—Open every day from 9 A. M. till 10 P. M.

Miscellaneous.

RETAIL MARKETING.—The weather during the greater portion of this week has contributed to accelerate the downward tendency in the prices of several articles of household consumption, especially vegetables and dairy produce. The rise in the price of Beef Cattle at the Drove Yards, and the small stock brought in have had little or no effect upon the retail market. Beef, Mutton and Veal generally are dull. In Fish there there is no change to notice. The following were the current rates yesterday:—

BEEF.—Roasting pieces, ℔ lb, 11@12c.; chuck roast, 10c; round, 9c.; sirloin steaks, 14@15c.; rump do 12@14c.; coarse corned, 8@10c.; dried beef, 15@20c. tripe, 4@5c; liver, 4@5c.; tongue, piece, 44@75c.

MUTTON.—Hind quarters, 8@9c. ℔ lb; fore do. 5@6c.; legs and loins, 9@10c.; chops, 9@10c.

VEAL.—Hind quarters, 9c. ℔ lb; fore do. 7c.; cutlets, 12 @14c.

PORK.—Fresh, 11@12c. ℔ lb.; salted, 10@12c.; lard, 12@14c.; hams, 10@14c; sausage, 11@14c.

POULTRY AND GAME.—Chickens ℔ pair, 75c.@$1·50; squabs, 28@31c; wild duck, 75@87c.; partridges, 37@50c.; pheasants, 50@52c.; snipe, 37@50c.

DAIRY PRODUCE—Is continually falling off. Butter, ℔ lb 25@31c.; Roll Butter, 20@22c.; Cheese, 12@16c.; Pine, Apple Cheese, ℔ lb., 25c.; Eggs, ℔ dozen. 15@16c.; Lard 14c.

FISH.—Lobsters, ℔ lb., 10@12; fresh codfish, 7@8; flounders, 5@8; boiling rock, 12@15; smelts, 12@15; haddock, 6@8; perch 12@—; moccasins, 10@12; black fish, 10@12; catfish, ℔ bunch, 10@11; eels do., 12@14; shad, a piece, 18@31.

VEGETABLES.—Potatoes, ℔ half peck, 8@12c; beets, ℔ bunch, 8@10c.; cabbage, each, 8@9; onions, ℔ bunch, 1@2.; pickles, per hundred, 18@20; radishes, ℔ bunch, 2@3; rhubarb, 3@4.

FRUIT.—Apples, ℔ half peck, 37@50; Dried Apples, ℔ qt., 7@8c.; do. Peaches, 10@16c.; do. Cherries, ℔@10c.; Cranberries, 16@18c.; Currants, 8@10c.; Lemons, ℔ dozen, 12@18c.; Oranges, 13@31c.

NEW CORPORATIONS.—The following charters of Incorporation will be granted by the Court of Common Pleas, on the first Monday in June, unless exceptions are filed thereto:—

1. Mount Airy Fire Company.
2. Howard Building and Saving Fund Association, No. 3.
3. Lafayette Building and Saving Fund Association, No. 2.
4. Washington Building and Saving Fund Association No. 2.
5. The Freeholders Land and Building Association.
6. Continental Saving Fund and Building Association.
7. St. James M. E. Church at Olney.
8. Oxford Provident Building Association of Frankford.
9. Skaters' Club of the City of Philadelphia.
10. The Cottage Home Society—Amendment.
11. The Bishop Neuman Beneficial Society of Philadelphia.
12. St. John's Church of the Evangelical Association of Philadelphia.
13. Humboldt Building and Saving Fund Association.
14. Girard do. do. do. do. No. 2.
15. Centennial Methodist Episcopal Church of Philada.
16. North Kensington Building and Saving Fund Association.
17. The Young Men's Western Home Mission of the Methodist Episcopal Church.
18. The Old Man's Home.
19. The Jefferson Building and Saving Fund Association.
20. The Gustav do. do. do. do.
21. Orphans' Home and Asylum for the Aged and Infirm of the Evangelical Lutheran Church.
22. Irving Literary Institute.
23. Real Estate Saving Fund and Loan Association of Philadelphia.

Application for admission to the Bar, at the next term of Court, will be made by P. ABELL BROWNE, of this city.

PROPOSED ENCAMPMENT.—The Brandywine battle-ground has been offered to the Seventh Regiment, National Guards, New York militia, for the purpose of an encampment the coming summer, and there is said to be some prospect of its being accepted. The Philadelphia and Baltimore Central Railroad passes within a few hundred yards of "Chadd's Ford," where the British crossed the Brandywine in front of the American army. The directors of this railroad and also of the West Chester railroad, with which it connects, have tendered the free use of their road for the transportation of the Seventh Regiment, between Philadelphia and the battle-ground.

ANOTHER MARKET.—The Delaware Avenue Market Company are about to purchase the property bounded by Spruce, Dock and Front streets, and to the Warden's line on the river, for the purpose of erecting a market house. It is to be of sufficient size and capacity, with wharves and docks, to accommodate the fishermen and dealers in produce that arrive at the market by way of the river Delaware.

THE WORKHOUSE FOR PAUPERS.—The structure which is to be used as a work shop for the able-bodied male inmates of the Blockley Almshouse is rapidly approaching completion. It is already roofed in. All the stone and carpenter work upon this building have been done by inmates of the Almshouse.

THE COUNT FOR CONTROLLER.—The examination of the votes cast for City Controller, by the counsel for Messrs. DOWNING and HUFTY, was concluded on Thursday, and the result differed from the official return to the extent of twenty votes.

IN PORT.—The following vessels were in port yesterday afternoon: Steamships 3; ships 8; barques 23; brigs 13; and schooners 65. This is quite an increase over last week. It is seldom that over twenty barques are in port at the same time.

OBITUARY.—THOMAS BROCH, an old and respected citizen of this city, died at the residence of his son, in West Mount Vernon street, on Thursday evening. He had been a resident of Philadelphia for more than fifty years.

GREY EAGLE SHOT.—PHILIP WORRALL, of Springfield, Chester County, the other day, killed a grey eagle on the wing. The bird, when "spread," was six feet two and a half inches between the tips of its wings.

JAPAN.—A lecture on Japan will be delivered, on Monday evening, at Musical Fund Hall, by Lieut. Wm. B. WHITING, who was sent out to Japan by the Government as Hydrographer to the Expedition under Commodore PERRY.

THE BAPTIST WATCHMAN, GEORGE MUNDAY, will hold forth to-morrow afternoon, at 3 o'clock, in the Wharton Market House, Jefferson avenue. The subject will be "Things as they are, not as they seem."

RESIGNED.—Gen. A. L. ROUMFORT has resigned the Superintendency of the Eastern Division of the Pennsylvania Railroad, the duties of which he has discharged several years.

DISMISSED.—ROBERT P. MOORE, telegraph operator, has been discharged by Mayor Henry.

THE JAPANESE COMING TO PHILADELPHIA—HOW WILL THEY BE RECEIVED?—It is represented by the Committee that visited Washington for the purpose of inviting the Japanese to this city, that the Embassy will arrive in Philadelphia by the first of June. Quarters have been secured for them at the Continental hotel. The entire Chesnut street front of the second floor, with a large portion of the Ninth street front of the same floor, will be appropriated to the principal members of the Embassy; while the inferior personages will have quarters assigned them higher up in the building. Care will be taken to keep them excluded from the rest of the house, as has been done at WILLARD's hotel, in Washington, and they will enjoy all the privacy they may desire. The strangers will also visit the principal places of attraction in and about the city. Particular desire is also felt to give them an insight into our extensive manufacturing establishments and the workings of our local police and fire alarm telegraph. It has also been proposed by some members of the committee to invite manufacturers of various kinds of goods to send to the Embassy specimens of their workmanship, bearing the names of their manufacturers, and the locality of their workshops. Those that would not be taken away by the Embassy, would be carefully dissected by the mechanics attached to the legation, and accurate drawings would be taken of the whole, and of their component parts, by the corps of skilful artists who accompany the legation. By this means, better, perhaps, than by any other, a correct idea of the mechanical and artistic resources of Philadelphia will reach Japan. It appears that the Japanese are very eager for the visit to Philadelphia. They will stay here five or six days, and then proceed to New York, and from the latter city to Boston.

FORGERIES UPON THE MECHANICS' BANK.—On Monday last, a stranger called at Messrs. BAKER, STEWART, & Co.'s banking house, on Third street, above Chesnut, and sold to the firm $300 of uncurrent funds, receiving in return a check for the amount. On the following Monday, the genuine check, and a forged one for $1400, were presented at the same time and paid. On Wednesday, another forged check, purporting to be drawn by Messrs. KOONS & Co., was presented and cashed by the paying teller of the same institution. The forgeries are remarkably well executed. The police are investigating the matter.

ROBBERY AND ASSAULT.—Three ruffians went, on Thursday night, into the confectionery store of Mrs. SEIFERT, at the southeast corner of Seventh and Master streets, and plundered the till. Mrs. SEIFERT followed them into the street, and caught one of the thieves by the coat-tail. The fellow struck her on the forehead with a billy, cutting the flesh to the bone, and hurting her seriously. The scoundrels escaped. One of the trio left his cap behind.

OFF THE TRACK.—Freight cars of the Dock street railroad got off the track yesterday afternoon, at Third street, running across the street and obstructing all kinds of travel. As usual, the passenger cars were detained, and a long line were awaiting the opportunity to move.

THE DOG CATCHERS.—Captain JIM FRANCIS is making preparations to commence operations upon the canines. There are several localities up town which need the captain's services.

THE GUARDIANS OF THE POOR will hold their next stated meeting on Monday next, at Blockley Almshouse. Heretofore their meetings have been held at their office, in Seventh street, above Market.

SLIGHT FIRE.—The alarm of fire yesterday morning was caused by the burning of a bed in St. John street, below Buttonwood.

Religious.

HOME MISSIONS.—The Board of Home Missions of the United Presbyterian Church of North America is holding meetings in Rev. Dr. DALE's Church, Race street, near Sixteenth, preparatory to the session of the General Assembly.

UNION PREACHING.—The services usually held on Sunday afternoon, in American Mechanics' Hall, will be transferred to-morrow, to the Fifth Street Methodist Episcopal Church, as the Hall is occupied by a Fair.

Rev. R. A. CARDEN will repeat, by request, a Sermon with the title, "Every Heart Knoweth its Own Bitterness." It will be necessary for all wishing seats to go early.

The Sermon delivered in the Hall, last Sunday afternoon, by Rev. R. H. PATTISON, was an excellent production. The meeting will be continued at the Hall on the following Sunday, when the Rev. J. W. CRACRAFT, of the Church of the Epiphany, will preach.

Cricket.

A MATCH will be played to-day between the Second Eleven of the Young America Club and the Olympian Club, on the grounds of the former, Turnpike Bridge, Germantown.

A cricket match will take place at Camden on the 18th and 19th of May, between the *Philadelphia* and *Germantown* Cricket clubs. A large attendance, and an interesting match, may with confidence be looked for. The following players have been selected:—

GERMANTOWN.—Barclay, Bayard, Cadwalader, Clark, Davis, Fisher, Kephardt, Large, Newhall, J. Wister, F. Wister.

PHILADELPHIA.—Collis, Facon, Howe, Johnson, Knox, Senior, Sharratt, Stevens, Vernon, Waterman, W. Wister.

CRICKET.—A match between two Elevens of the St. George's Club will be played on their grounds, Camac's Woods, on Monday next.—Wickets pitched at 10 o'clock, A. M.

A CONSOLIDATION of the Keystone and Commonwealth Cricket Clubs has taken place, under the name of the former.

Casualties.

SAD DROWNING CASE.—At 8 o'clock last evening, a small boat containing two men was upset on the Schuylkill, above the dam, and one them, named WILLIAM MEANS, residing at No. 1401 Barclay street, was drowned. He leaves a wife and four children. The other one clung to the bottom of the boat, and was rescued by the members of a boat club that happened to be in the vicinity.

DEATH OF MR. FAIRMAN.—We have been shown a telegraphic despatch from Washington, D. C., stating that Mr. GEO. W. FAIRMAN fell dead in the street at that place, on Thursday afternoon last. Mr. FAIRMAN was a resident of this city, and had a large circle of acquaintances. He was engaged at the time in canvassing for the *American Encyclopedia*.

ACCIDENT.—Yesterday a man named JAS. KIRK received a compound facture of his right arm by having it caught in the machinery of Messrs. GARSED & Co.'s woolen and cotton cloth manufactory, near Front street and the Germantown road. He was conveyed to the Pennsylvania Hospital.

FELL FROM A WINDOW.—A lad named JAMES MCNAMEE, aged five years, fell from a window of a house on Hurst street, below Lombard, yesterday morning, and was much injured internally. He was conveyed to the Pennsylvania Hospital.

TELEGRAPHIC NEWS.

FROM CHICAGO.

The Republican National Convention.

Hon. Abram Lincoln, of Illinois, Nominated for President.

Hon. Hannibal Hamlin, of Maine, for Vice President.

CHICAGO, May 18.—The Wigwam was closely packed for a full hour before the Convention assembled this morning.

The interest in the proceedings appeared to be on the increase as the time of balloting approached.

A crowd numbered by thousands has been outside the building since 9 o'clock, anxiously awaiting intelligence from the inside.

Arrangements have been made for passing the result of the ballots up from the platform to the roof of the building and through the skylight, men being stationed above to convey it to the multitude in the streets.

The President, on opening the proceedings, begged the audience to refrain as much as possible from applause, and to preserve the decorum and dignity of the meeting.

The President announced the reception of an invitation for an excursion over the Chicago and Galena Railroad.

Also, a communication from the workingmen of Brooklyn, Williamsburg, and Greensburg, New York, in favor of bestowing the Government lands on actual settlers, and for arresting the further sale of public lands.

Both communications were ordered to be entered on the record.

The President announced the motion pending to be, to take a ballot for candidate for President of the United States.

Mr. BLAIR (Md.) announced that, in consequence of the adoption, by the Convention, of a rule restricting the vote of Maryland to the number of delegates present, that delegation had, last evening, filled up its number, and asked leave to present the credentials of five new delegates, to fill the number from that State.

Mr. SARGENT (Cal.) inquired whether the five additional votes now added would increase the vote to sixteen, or leave it at eleven, which was the number assigned to that State by the report of the Committee of Credentials. If it was designed to increase the vote above eleven he was opposed to it.

Mr. W. T. COLE (Md.) said that Maryland had been entitled to eleven votes only, because the necessary number of delegates for the sixteen votes were not present.

The delegates had power, by action of the State Convention to fill vacancies. They had now done so under that authority, and claimed the right to cast a full vote.

The President said that he understood the rule adopted in the report of the Committee on Credentials to have restricted Maryland to eleven votes. The additional delegates would not entitle them to a greater vote.

Mr. BLAIR (Md.) desired to correct the error of the Chair. As he understood it, the number was only limited because the delegates were not present. The Delegation had a right to fill vacancies and had done so in consequence of the rule adopted yesterday by the Convention.

Mr. ARMOUR (Md.) protested against the reception of the credentials of the new [illegible] from his State. The delegation had met without his knowledge, and without the knowlege of at least more than one delegate, and filled up their numbers with men who lived, God only knows where. A resident of the State had been refused admission to the delegation, and what object his colleagues had in filling the Delegation with non-residents he did not know. He hoped the motion to admit these delegates would be voted down.

The motion to admit the extra delegates was lost, amidst applause.

The Convention then voted to proceed to a ballot for a candidate for President of the United States.

WILLIAM R. EVARTS (N. Y.) did not rise for the purpose of making a speech, but only to ask if, at this time, it is in order to put candidates in nomination.

The President.—The Chair considers it in order to name the candidates without debate.

A delegate from Pennsylvania drew attention to the fact that the delegates' seats were occupied by outsiders.

A Voice.—It is the same here in Ohio.

The President.—This affords an opportunity for the Chair to read a communication just received from the door-keepers.

The communication stated that the delegates, as soon as they got into the Hall, passed their tickets out to friends. The officers, therefore, found it impossible to prevent admission of outsiders, but the fault rested with the delegates.

The President suggested that the only method to pursue would be for each delegate to claim his own seat with vigor.

After some delay, occasioned by the clearing of the platform and distributing ballots, the Convention proceeded to a ballot.

Mr. WM. M. EVARTS rose and said—I beg leave to offer the name of WM. H. SEWARD as a candidate before this Convention for nomination for President of the United States.

This nomination was received with long continued applause.

Mr. JUDD (Ill.) rose and said—Mr. President, I beg leave to offer as a candidate before this Convention for President of the United States, the name of ABRAM LINCOLN, of Illinois.

The crowded audience greeted this nomination with perfectly deafening applause, the shouts swelling into a perfect roar, and being continued for several minutes. The wildest excitement and enthusiasm prevailed.

At the close of the applause some hisses were heard, but the pressure for LINCOLN was tremendous.

Mr. DUDLEY (N. J.) presented the name of WM. L. DAYTON. (Slight applause.)

Governor REEDER (Pa.)—The State of Pennsylvania desires to present as her candidate the name of SIMON CAMERON. (Applause.)

Mr. CARTER (Ohio) put forward the name of SALMON P. CHASE of Ohio. (Loud applause.)

Mr. SMITH (Md.)—I am instructed by the State of Indiana to second the nomination of ABRAM LINCOLN. (Another outburst of enthusiastic applause from the body of the Hall, mingled with hisses.)

FRANCIS P. BLAIR (Mo.) nominated EDWARD BATES, of Missouri. (Applause.)

Mr. BLAIR, (Mich.)—On the part of Michigan, I desire to say that the Republicans of that State second the nomination of WM. H. SEWARD for the Presidency.

Tremendous applause followed this speech; thousands of those present rising and waving their hats and handkerchiefs, and swelling the applause to a thundering roar, lasting through several minutes.

This applause was followed by some hisses and loud applause for LINCOLN when the friends of SEWARD again rallied, determined not to be put down in applause by the friends of LINCOLN.

At this second trial of lungs, however, it was evident that the crowd were more divided than at first appeared, and the LINCOLN men apparently had the majority.

Hon. TOM CORWIN (Ohio,) nominated JOHN MCLEAN, of Ohio, for the Presidency. (Loud applause.)

Mr. CARL SCHURZ, (Wis) on the part of his State, here rose and seconded the nomination of WILLIAM H. SEWARD.

Upon this, another scene of the greatest enthusiasm and tumultuous applause and excitement ensued.

Mr. NORTH (Minn.) seconded, on the part of Minnesota, the nomination of Mr. SEWARD.—(Tremendous applause.)

Mr. WILSON (Kansas)—The delegates and people of Kansas also second the nomination.—(Renewed cheers.)

Mr. DELANO (Ohio)—On the part of a large number of the people of Ohio, I desire to second the nomination of the man who can split rails and maul Democrats, ABRAM LINCOLN. (Rounds of applause by the LINCOLN men.)

A delegate from Iowa also seconded the nomination of Mr. LINCOLN on the part of that State, ami lst renewed applause.

A Voice—ABE LINCOLN has it by sound—now let us ballot. (Cheers and hisses.)

Judge LOGAN (Ill.)—Mr. President—In order or out of order, I propose that this Convention give three cheers for the man who is evidently their nomtnee. (Hisses and cries of No! No! Call the roll!)

The President—If the Convention will get over this irrepressible excitement, the calling of the roll will be commenced.

The Convention then proceeded to a ballot.

Applause at the different announcements was wiih difficulty checked.

When Maryland was called, the Chairman of the delegation cast the vote of the State for Mr. BATES. Fouro f the delegates claimed their right to individual votes.

After some discussion, the Convention rejected the votes as cast by the Chairman, and received the votes of the delegates separately.

The First Ballot.

Resulted as follows:—

FOR MR. SEWARD.

Maine	10	Wisconsin	10
New Hampshire	1	Iowa	2
Massachusetts	21	California	8
New York	70	Minnesota	8
Pennsylvania	1½	Kansas	6
Maryland	3	Nebraska	2
Virginia	8	District Columbia	2
Kentucky	5		
Michigan	12	Total	173½
Texas	4		

FOR MR. LINCOLN.

Maine	6	Ohio	8
New Hampshire	7	Indiana	26
Massachusetts	4	Illinois	22
Connecticut	2	Iowa	2
Pennsylvania	4	Nebraska	1
Virginia	14		
Kentucky	6	Total	108

FOR MR. BATES.

Rhode Island	1	Texas	2
Connecticut	7	Iowa	1
Maryland	8	Oregon	5
Delaware	6		
Missouri	18	Total	48

FOR MR. CHASE.

New Hampshire	1	Ohio	34
Rhode Island	1	Nebraska	2
Connecticut	2		
Kentucky	8	Total	49
Iowa	1		

FOR MR. CAMERON.

Pennsylvania	47½	Nebraska	1
Virginia	1		
Iowa	1	Total	50½

FOR MR. McLEAN.

Rhode Island	5	Iowa	1
Pennsylvania	1		
Kentucky	1	Total	12
Ohio	4		

FOR MR. WADE.

Connecticut	1
Kentucky	2
Total	3

FOR MR. DAYTON.		FOR JUDGE READ.	
New Jersey	14	Rhode Island	1
FOR MR. FREMONT.		FOR MR. COLLAMER.	
New Hampshire	1	Vermont	10

FOR MR. SUMNER.

Kentucky	1

RECAPITULATION.

Whole number of votes	465
Necessary to a choice	233
For W. H. Seward, of New York	173½
For Abram Lincoln, of Illinois	102
For Simon Cameron, of Pennsylvania	50½
For Edward Bates, of Missouri	48
For Salmon P. Chase, of Ohio	48
For John McLean, of Ohio	12
For Mr. Wade, of Ohio	3
For Mr. Dayton, of New Jersey	14
For John C. Fremont, of California	1
For Charles Sumner, of Massachusetts	1
For John M. Read, of Pennsylvania	1
For Jacob Collamer, of Vermont	10

The second ballot was then taken.

Mr. CAMERON's name was withdrawn.

The ballot stood as follows:—

For Abram Lincoln	181
For William H. Seward	184½
For Edward Bates	35
For Judge McLean	8
For Solomon P. Chase	42½
For Simon Cameron	2
For Wm. Dayton	10
For C. M. Clay	2

The following is the vote in detail:—

FOR MR. LINCOLN.		FOR MR. SEWARD.	
Maine	6	Maine	10
New Hampshire	9	New Hampshire	1
Massachusetts	[illegible]		
Connecticut	2	Pennsylvania	2½
Rhode Island	3	Maryland	3
Pennsylvania	48	Virginia	8
Delaware	6	New Jersey	4
Virginia	14	Kentucky	7
Kentucky	9	Michigan	12
Ohio	14	Texas	6
Iowa	5	Wisconsin	10
Indiana	26	Iowa	2
Illinois	22	California	8
Nebraska	1	Minnesota	8
		Kansas	6
Total	181	Nebraska	3
		District of Columbia	2
		Total	184½

The Third Ballot

Was then taken amidst wild excitement and cries for the ballot. The most intense feeling existed during the ballot, each vote being awaited in breathless silence and expectancy.

FOR MR. LINCOLN.

Maine	6	Virginia	14
New Hampshire	9	Kentucky	13
Vermont	10	Ohio	29
Massachusetts	8	Iowa	5
Rhode Island	5	Indiana	26
Connecticut	2	Illinois	22
New Jersey	8	Nebraska	3
Pennsylvania	5	Oregon	4
Delaware	6		
Maryland	[illegible]	Total	231

As each State voted the applause was overpowering. The vote of Oregon gave LINCOLN 230½ votes, or within 1½ of a nomination.

Mr. ANDREWS (Mass.) then rose and corrected the vote of Massachusetts, by changing four votes and giving them to LINCOLN, thus nominating him by 2½ majority.

The Convention immediately became a scene of wild excitement. A large portion of the delegates who had kept the tally, at once said the struggle was decided, and half the Convention rose, cheering, shouting and waving their hats. The audience took up the cheers, and the confusion became deafening.

State after State rose shouting to change their votes to the winning candidate, but the noise and enthusiasm rendered it impossible for the delegates to make themselves heard.

Maine cast her 16 votes for LINCOLN.

Massachusetts changed, giving 18 votes to LINCOLN and 8 to SEWARD.

The intelligence of the nomination, when conveyed to the people outside, caused a scene of the wildest excitement, beggaring description.

Cheer upon cheer rent the air, while the cannon sent forth roar after roar of salutes. At least 30,000 people participated in the excitement.

Missouri changed her 18 votes to LINCOLN.

Iowa, Connecticut and Minnesota also changed their votes.

The result of the third ballot was then announced:—

Whole number of votes	466
Necessary to a choice	234

ABRAM LINCOLN received 350, and was declared duly nominated.

The States that still voted for SEWARD were:—

New York	70	New Jersey	5
Massachusetts	8	Pennsylvania	1½
Maryland	2	Michigan	12
Wisconsin	10	California	3
Total	111½		

The announcement of the result was received with renewed applause.

The Nomination Made Unanimous.

When silence was restored,

Mr. WM. M. EVARTS (N. Y.) spoke as follows:—

Mr. President and Gentlemen of the National Convention:—The State of New York, by a full delegation and with complete unanimity of purpose at home, came to this Convention and presented as its choice one of its citizens who had served the State from boyhood up—had labored for it and loved it. We came here a great State, with, as we thought, a great statesman, and our love of a great Republic from which we are all delegates—the great Republic of the American Union. Our love of the great Republican party of the Union, and our love for our statesman and candidate, made us think that we did our duty to the country, and the whole country, in expressing our preference and love for him.

Gentlemen—It was from Governor SEWARD that most of us learned to love Republican principles and the Republican party. His fidelity to the country, the Constitution and the laws—his fidelity to the party and the principle that majority govern—his interest in the advancement of our party to its victory—that our country may rise to its true glory—induces me to declare that I speak his sentiments, as I do the united opinion of our delegation, when I move you, sir, as I do now, that the nomination of ABRAM LINCOLN, of Illinois, as the Republican candidate for the suffrages of the whole country for the office of Chief Magistrate of the American Union be made unanimous.

Loud applause greeted this speech and three cheers were given for New York.

Eloquent speeches were then made by Messrs. ANDREWS (Mass.), CARL SHURZ (Wis.), BLAIR (Miss.), BROWNING (Ill.), endorsing the nomination of Mr. LINCOLN.

The nomination of Mr. LINCOLN was then made unanimous amid loud cheers.

The Convention adjourned till 5 o'clock, P. M.

Evening Session.

The Convention re-assembled at 5 o'clock P. M.

A large banner was brought on the platform by the Pennsylvania delegates, bearing the inscription—

"*Pennsylvania good for 20,000 majority for the People's candidate—Abe 'Lincoln.'*"

The appearance of the banner was greeted with loud applause.

The Convention then proceeded to ballot for Vice President.

Mr. WILDER (Kansas) nominated JOHN HICKMAN, of Pennsylvania.

Mr. CARTER (O.) named HANNIBAL HAMLIN, of Maine.

Mr. BARTWELL (Mass.) nominated N. P. BANKS, of Massachusetts.

Mr. SMITH (Ind.) nominated CASSIUS M. CLAY, of Kentucky.

Mr. LOWRY (Pa.) named Governor REEDER, of Pennsylvania.

The nominations were severally greeted with applause.

FIRST BALLOT FOR VICE PRESIDENT.

Hannibal Hamlin, of Maine	194
John Hickman, of Pennsylvania	58
N. P. Banks, of Massachusette	38½
Cassius M. Clay, of Kentucky	101
Governor Reeder, of Pennsylvania	51
Henry Winter Davis, of Maryland	8
Sam Houston, of Texas	6
Wm. L. Dayton, of New Jersey	3
John M. Read, of Pennsylvania	1
Whole number of votes	460½
Necessary to a choice	232

On the second ballot, Massachusetts withdrew the name of BANKS, and cast 26 votes for HAMLIN.

Pennsylvania withdrew the name of Governor REEDER, and cast 54 votes for HAMLIN.

New York cast her 70 votes for HAMLIN.

The result of the second ballot was then announced as follows:—

Hamlin	364
Clay	86
Hickman	13

The result was received with tumultous applause, and the nomination was subsequently made unanimous.

After the delivery of congratulatory speeches by a number of delegates, JOSHUA R. GIDDINGS moved the adoption of the following resolution:—

Resolved, That we deeply sympathize with those men who have been driven, some from their native States, and others from the States of their adoption, and who are now exiled from their homes on account of their opinions, and that we hold the Democratic party responsible for the gross violation of that clause of the Constitution which declares that the citizens of each State shall be entitled to all the privileges and immunities of the citizens of the several States.

The resolution was adopted.

Mr. TUCK (N. H.) moved that the President of this Convention and the Chairmen of the several delegations, be appointed a committee to inform Messrs. LINCOLN and HAMLIN of their nomination. Adopted.

Mr. LANE (Ind.) took the floor, and made an eloquent speech in favor of the whole ticket, pledging Indiana for 10,000 majority.

Cries were here made for HORACE GREELEY, which were met with applause and hisses.

Mr. GOODRICH (Minn.) announced that a triumphal procession would parade the streets tonight, and march to the Wigwam, where a grand ratification meeting will be held.

The announcement was greeted with loud cheers.

Mr. GOODRICH moved that the thanks of the Convention be tendered to the ladies and gentlemen of Chicago for the liberality displayed in building and decorating the Wigwam. Carried unanimously.

The Convention accepted the invitation to excursions on the Rock Island and Chicago and Galena Railroads.

Mr. ASHLEY (O.) then moved the following resolution:—[illegible] they hereby are instructed to prescribe uniform rules that shall operate equally in all the States and Territories, whereby, in the future, the wishes and preferences of the electors in the Republican organization, in the choice of President and Vice President, may be fully ascertained; and that the basis of the nominating vote be fixed as near as may be in proportion to the number of Republican electors found to reside, at the last general State election preceding the said nomination, in each Congressional District throughout the Union.

After some skirmishing this resolution was laid on the table.

Mr. WASHBURNE (Me.) moved that the thanks of the Convention be tendered to the President for his ability and courtesy while in the chair. Carried unanimously.

A vote of thanks was also passed to the other officers of the Convention, especially the Recording Secretary, Mr. PRATT, of Indiana.

The National Committee.

The following was announced as the National Committee for the next four years, Pennsylvania alone being unfilled:—

C. J. Gilman, Maine.	Edwin D. Morgan, N. York.
G. G. Fogg, N. Hampshire.	Downing Duer, New Jersey.
L. Brainard, Vermont.	J. T. Wagoner, Maryland.
J. Q. Goodrich, Mass.	U. B. Smithers, Delaware.
T. G. Turner, Rhode Island.	Alfred Caldwell, Virginia.
Gideon Wellers, Conn.	Cassius M. Clay, Kentucky.
Thomas Spooner, Ohio.	Carl Shurz, Wisconsin.
S. Meredith, Indiana.	A. J. Stevens, Iowa.
Asa L. Jones, Missouri.	D. W. Cheesman, California.
Austin Blair, Michigan.	John McKeesick, Minnesota.
U. B. Judd, Illinois.	W. C. Johnson, Oregon.
D. Henderson, Texas.	O. H. Irish, Nebraska.
Wm. A. Phillips, Kansas.	Jos. Gerdart, Dist. of Colum.

The President, Mr. ASHMAN, then, in a few brief remarks, returned his thanks to the Convention for the honor it had conferred on him. He fully endorsed the character and ability of both of the nominees, and expressed the conviction that victory must crown the efforts of the party in November.

The Convention then adjourned *sine die*, with nine hearty cheers for the nominee.

Immediately on the adjournment, a hundred guns were fired from the roof of the Tremont House, in honor of the nominees.

Old School Presbyterian General Assembly.

From Our Special Correspondent.

ROCHESTER, N. Y., May 17, 1860.

The General Assembly of the Presbyterian Church of the United States met this morning, and was opened with a most excellent discourse by Dr. W. A. SCOTT, of California.

After singing by the choir, Dr. SCOTT offered prayer and read a portion of Scripture. The familiar hymn commencing "Jesus shall reign where'er the sun," &c., was then sung by the choir and congregation. The venerable Dr. SPRING, of New York, occupied the pulpit with Dr. SCOTT.

After the reading of another selection from the Scriptures, Dr. SPRING followed in a prayer most humble, grateful and fervent. The hymn, "I love thy Kingdom Lord," was then sung.

Dr. SCOTT announced as the text of his discourse the 2d verse of the 2d chap. of 1st Cor.:—"For I determined to know nothing among you save Jesus Christ and him crucified." Dr. SCOTT was appointed to preach in the absence of Dr. N. S. BRECKINRIDGE, President of Oakland College, Mississippi, who was the last moderator. At the close of the sermon, the hymn—

"How beauteous are their feet
Who stand on Zion's Hill," &c.,

was sung. Benediction by Dr. SCOTT.

After a portion of the audience had retired, the constituting prayer was offered by Dr. SCOTT.

The roll of delegates present was then reported by the permanent clerk.

On motion, Dr. KREBS, Rev. Mr. DELANCEY and Mr. MCCORD were appointed Committee on Elections, to whom defective commissions were reported.

Several new Presbyteries were reported, and on motion duly recognized, when the Assembly took a recess to 3 P. M.

The attendance is full, about 300 members being present.

Dr. JOHN W. YEOMAN, of Danville, Pennsylvania, formerly President of Lafayette College, was elected Moderator, and the Assembly adjourned to give the Moderator time to appoint Committees, &c.

The body is as fine a looking collection of men as the country ever saw. Many men of a national reputation are seen as you look around you. Judge SHARSWOOD and J. ROSS SNOWDEN, with Drs. BOARDMAN and CHEESEMAN, of your city, are well known.

The sermon of Dr. SCOTT was intended to show that the minister should make Christ his model, both as to matter and manner. It was excellent, and will be published. J. H. B.

SCHOOL HOUSE.—A new school house is to be erected adjoining Mr. MALACHI's Church, Frankford. The corner stone will be laid next week. The building will be of brick, four stories high, 90 feet deep, and 20 feet wide.

HON. ABRAM LINCOLN,

REPUBLICAN CANDIDATE FOR PRESIDENT.

THE REPUBLICAN PLATFORM,

AS EXPOUNDED BY

HON. ABRAM LINCOLN.

In a Speech Delivered before the Cooper Institute, February, 1860.

The announcement that the Hon. ABRAM LINCOLN, of Illinois, would "speak" at the Cooper Institute, New York city, drew together a large assemblage at that building on the night of Tuesday, February 28, 1860. The tax of twenty-five cents per capita did not—as it very frequently does—act as a preventative on the visitors, but they continued, on the contrary, to pour in in considerable numbers until the large hall was about three-quarters filled. Among the audience there were, as is usual in these Republican assemblages, a goodly number of ladies.

At about a quarter to eight o'clock, ex-Governor KING made his appearance on the platform, and was greeted with loud applause, which he seemed to enjoy mightily, as with a smile of benevolent gravity he settled himself in a chair.

The arrival of D. DUDLEY FIELD, accompanied by WILLIAM CULLEN BRYANT and the speaker of the evening, was the signal for the most tumultuous applause.

Address by Hon. Abram Lincoln.

When the applause which greeted Mr. LINCOLN had subsided, he said:—

MR. PRESIDENT AND FELLOW-CITIZENS OF THE CITY OF NEW YORK.—The facts with which I shall deal this evening are mainly old and familiar; nor is there anything new in the general use I shall make of them. If there shall be any novelty, it will be in the mode of presenting the facts, and the inferences and observations following that presentation. In his speech, last autumn, at Columbus, Ohio, as reported in the New York *Times*, Senator DOUGLAS said:—

"Our fathers, when they framed the [illegible] which we live, under[illegible]

[illegible] and I adopt it as a text [illegible] because it furnishes a precise and an agreed starting point for a discussion between the Republicans and that wing of the Democracy headed by Senator DOUGLAS. It simply leaves the inquiry—What was the understanding those fathers had of the question mentioned? What is the frame of government under which we live? The answer must be—the Constitution of the United States. That constitution consists of the original, framed in 1787, (and under which the present government first went into operation), and twelve subsequently framed amendments, the first ten of which were framed in 1789.

The Fathers of the Constitution.

Who were our fathers that framed the Constitution? I suppose the "thirty-nine" who signed the original instrument may be fairly called our fathers who framed that part of the present government. It is almost exactly true to say they framed it, and it is altogether true to say they fairly represented the opinion and sentiment of the whole nation at that time. Their names being familiar to nearly all, and accessible to quite all, need not now be repeated. I take these "thirty-nine," for the present, as being "our fathers who framed the government under which we live." What is the question which, according to the text, those fathers understood as well and even better than we do now? It is this:—"Does the proper division of local from federal authority, or anything in the Constitution, forbid our Federal Government to control as to slavery in our Federal Territories?

Douglas and Lincoln.

Upon this DOUGLAS held the affirmative, and Republicans the negative. The affirmative and denial form an issue; and this issue, this question, is precisely what the text declares our fathers understood better than we. (Cheers.) Let us inquire whether the "thirty-nine," or any of [illegible] ever acted upon this question; and if th[illegible] how they acted upon it—how they ex[illegible] better understanding. In 1784, th[illegible] the Constitution, the United St[illegible] the Northwestern territory, an[illegible] gress of the confederation [illegible] question of prohibiting sla[illegible] and four of the "thirty-[illegible] framed the Constitution [illegible] and voted on that que[illegible] SHERMAN, THOMAS MI[illegible] LIAMSON voted for the [illegible] that, in their understand[illegible] cal from federal author[illegible] perly forbade the Fed[illegible] as to slavery in Fede[illegible] The other of the [illegible] against the prohib[illegible] cause he thought it i[illegible] 1787, still before the Con[illegible] Convention was in session fran[illegible] the Northwestern territory still was [illegible] ritory owned by the United States—the same question of prohibiting slavery in the territory again came before the Congress of the Confederation; and three more of the "thirty-nine" who afterwards signed the Constitution were in that Congress and voted on that question. They were WILLIAM BLOUNT, WILLIAM FEW and ABRAHAM BALDWIN, and they all voted for the prohibition, thus showing that, in their understanding, no line dividing local from federal authority, nor anything else, properly forbade the Federal Government to control as to slavery in Federal Territory.

The Ordinance of 1787.

This time the prohibition became a law, being a part of what is now well known as the Ordinance of 1787. The question of Federal control of slavery in the Territories seems not to have been directly before the Convention which framed the original Constitution; and hence it is not recorded that the "thirty-nine," or any of them, while engaged on that instrument, expressed any opinion on that precise question. In 1789, by the first Congress which sat under the Constitution, an act was passed to enforce the ordinance of 1787 including the prohibition of slavery in the Northwestern territory. The bill for this act was reported by one of the "thirty-nine," THOMAS FITZSIMMONS, then a member of the House of Representatives from Pennsylvania. It went through all its stages without a word of opposition, and finally passed both branches without yeas and nays, which is equivalent to a unanimous passage. (Cheers.) In this Congress there were sixteen of the "thirty-nine" fathers who framed the original Constitution. They were:—

John Langdon,	Thos. Fitzsimmons,	Richard Bassett,
Nicholas Gilman,	William Few,	George Read,
Wm. S. Johnson,	Abraham Baldwin,	Pierce Butler,
Roger Sherman,	Rufus King,	Daniel Carroll,
Robert Morris,	William Patterson,	James Madison,
George Clymer.		

This shows that, in their understanding, no line dividing local from federal authority, nor anything in the Constitution, properly forbade Congress to prohibit slavery in the Federal Territory, else both their fidelity to correct principle, and their oath to support the Constitution, would have constrained them to oppose the prohibition.

Opinion of George Washington.

Again, GEORGE WASHINGTON, another of the "thirty-nine," was then President of the United States, and, as such, approved and signed the

HARPER'S WEEKLY.
A JOURNAL OF CIVILIZATION.

Vol. IV.—No. 178.] NEW YORK, SATURDAY, MAY 26, 1860. [Price Five Cents.

HON. ABRAM LINCOLN, OF ILLINOIS.

REPUBLICAN CANDIDATE FOR PRESIDENT.

We engrave herewith the portr ait—from a photograph by Brady—of Hon. Abram Lincoln, of Illinois, the Republican candidate for President. The following sketch of his career is from the *Herald:*

Abram Lincoln, the Republican candidate for the Presidency in the campaign of 1860, is a native of Harden County, Kentucky. He was born February 12, 1809. His parents were born in Virginia, and were of very moderate circumstances. His paternal grandfather, Abram Lincoln, emigrated from Rockingham County, Virginia, to Kentucky about 1781–'82, where, a year or two later, he was killed by Indians. His ancestors, who were respectable members of the Society of Friends, went to Virginia from Berks County, Pennsylvania. Descendants from the same lineage still reside in the eastern part of Pennsylvania.

Abram Lincoln, the subject of this memoir, further removed from Kentucky to Spencer County, in Indiana, in 1816.

Mr. Lincoln received a limited education. In 1830 he removed to Illinois, and passed the first year in Macon County, engaged in agricultural pursuits. He next went to New Salem, at that time in Sagamon County, now Chenard County, where he remained about one year as a clerk in a store. About this time the Florida or Black Hawk War broke out, and on the call from the Federal Government for volunteers, a company was raised in New Salem, and Lincoln was elected captain. He served during this memorable campaign. On his return to Illinois, in 1832, he became a candidate for the State Legislature, but was defeated. The next three succeeding biennial elections he was elected to the Legislature by the Whig party. During his legislative term he studied law, and subsequently engaged practically in the profession at Springfield; but his practice at the bar did not withdraw his attention from politics, and for many years he was one of the leaders of the Whig party in Illinois, and was on the electoral ticket in several presidential campaigns. He was a disciple of Henry Clay, and exerted himself in his behalf in 1844, by making a tour of Illinois and advocating Clay's election to the Presidency. He was elected to Congress in 1846, and served until 1849.

While in Congress the Wilmot Proviso warfare was in progress, and which disturbed the peace and harmony of the country until it shook the foundation of the Union from its centre to its circumference. He voted forty-two times for the Proviso. He was also active, in connection with Seward, Chase, Giddings, and other abolitionists, in the agitation of that subject. He also opposed the Mexican War, and declared it unconstitutional and wrong, and voted against the bill granting 160 acres of land to the volunteers.

In the National Convention of 1848, of which he was a member, he advocated the nomination of General Taylor, and sustained the nomination by a canvass of his own State. In 1852 he was efficient in his efforts for General Scott, and was considered by the Whigs of Illinois and the Northwest as one of their leaders. From 1849 to 1854 Mr. Lincoln was engaged in the practice of his profession.

In 1849 he was a candidate before the Illinois Legislature for United States Senator, prior to which he stumped the State for the Whigs. When the Legislature met, the Democracy was in the majority, and General Shields, the Democratic candidate, was elected. In 1855 he was again the candidate of the Whigs for United States Senator before the Legislature chosen that year; but the Democracy being in the majority, Lincoln was again defeated and Judge Trumbull, the Democratic candidate, elected. In 1856 Mr. Lincoln's name headed the Frémont electoral ticket in Illinois. In 1858 it was the desire of the Illinois Republican State Committee to have Mr. Lincoln succeed Douglas in the United States Senate, and to effect this he stumped the State for the Republicans; and it was during this campaign that Mr. Lincoln made the best political speeches of his life, and from which the people of the Union will at once read his sentiments on the great questions of the day. He is a tariff man, in favor of a protective policy, opposed to the Dred Scott decision, urging as an especial reason for his position that it deprives the negro of the rights of that clause in the Constitution of the United States which guarantees to the citizens of each State all the rights, privileges, and immunities of the several States.

In the campaign in Illinois in 1858, when he stumped the State in opposition to Douglas, he showed himself an adept in political strategy, and suited his speeches to the locality in which he spoke. His partisans claim that he had the advantage of the Illinois Senator as well in eloquence as in tact, and commend very highly the manliness and courage which he displayed on several occasions when they met in debate.

In personal appearance Mr. Lincoln, or, as he is more familiarly termed among those who know him best, "Old Uncle Abe," is long, lean, and wiry. In motion he has a great deal of the elasticity and awkwardness which indicate the rough training of his early life, and his conversation savors strongly of Western idioms and pronunciation. His height is six feet three inches. His complexion is about that of an octoroon; his face, without being by any means beautiful, is genial looking, and good humor seems to lurk in every corner of its innumerable angles. He has dark hair tinged with gray, a good forehead, small eyes, a long penetrating nose, with nostrils such as Napoleon always liked to find in his best generals, because they indicated a long head and clear thoughts; and a mouth which, aside from being of magnificent proportions, is probably the most expressive feature of his face.

As a speaker he is ready, precise, and fluent. His manner before a popular assembly is as he pleases to make it, being either superlatively ludicrous or very impressive. He employs but little gesticulation, but when he desires to make a point produces a shrug of his shoulders, an elevation of his eyebrows, a depression of his mouth, and a general malformation of countenance so comically awkward that it never fails to "bring down the house." His enunciation is slow and emphatic, and his voice, though sharp and powerful, at times has a frequent tendency to dwindle into a shrill and unpleasant sound; but, as before stated, the peculiar characteristic of his delivery is the remarkable mobility of his features, the frequent contortions of which excite a merriment his words could not produce.

Mr. Lincoln is the author of the basis upon which Seward formed his "irrepressible conflict" platform, as will be seen from the subjoined extracts from his speeches. Lincoln's "irrepressible conflict" sentiments were uttered in a speech delivered at Springfield, Illinois, June 17, 1858, and Seward's speech on the same topic in October, 1858. Mr. Lincoln, in his speech at Springfield, Illinois, on the 17th of June, 1858, said:

In my opinion it will not cease [the slavery agitation.—*Ed.*] until a crisis shall have been reached and passed. "A house divided against itself can not stand." I believe this Government can not endure permanently, half slave and half free. I do not expect the Union to be dissolved—I do not expect the house to fall—but I do expect it will cease to be divided. It will become all one thing, or all the other. Either the opponents of slavery will arrest the further spread of it, and place it where the public mind shall rest in the belief that it is in the course of ultimate extinction; or its advocates will push it forward, till it shall become alike lawful in all the States—old as well as new—North as well as South.

In another speech at Chicago, on the 16th of July, 1858, he said:

I have always hated slavery, I think, as much as any Abolitionist. I have been an Old Line Whig. I have always hated it, and I always believed it in course of ultimate extinction. If I were in Congress, and a vote should come up on a question whether slavery should be prohibited in a new Territory, in spite of the Dred Scott decision I would vote that it should.

In another speech at Springfield, Illinois, July 17, 1858, he said:

I nevertheless did not mean to go on the banks of the Ohio and throw missiles into Kentucky, to disturb them in their domestic institutions.

In another speech at Galesburg, October 7, 1858, he said:

I believe that the right of property in a slave is not distinctly and expressly affirmed in the Constitution.

Mr. Lincoln was comparatively unknown to the

HON. ABRAM LINCOLN, OF ILLINOIS, REPUBLICAN CANDIDATE FOR PRESIDENT.

[Photographed by Brady.]

Philadelphia Inquirer—Supplement.

PHILADELPHIA, JUNE 28, 1860.

POLITICAL.

REPUBLICAN PLATFORM, Adopted at Chicago, May, 1860.

Resolved. That we, the delegated representatives of the Republican Electors of the United States, in Convention assembled, in discharge of the duty we owe to our constituents and our country, unite in the following declarations:—

First, That the history of the nation during the last forty years has fully established the propriety and necessity of the organization and perpetuation of the Republican party, and that the causes which called it into existence are permanent in their nature, and now more than ever before demand its peaceful and constitutional triumph.

Second. That we solemnly re-assert the self-evident truths, that all men are endowed by the Creator with certain inalienable rights, among which are those of life, liberty, and the pursuit of happiness; that governments are intended among men to secure the enjoyments of these rights. That the maintenance of the principles promulgated in the Declaration of Independence, and embodied in the Federal Constitution, is essential to the preservation of our Republican institutions, and that the Federal Constitution, the rights of the States, and the Union of the States, must and shall be preserved.

Third. That to the Union of the States this nation owes its unprecedented increase in population; its surprising development of material resources; its rapid augmentation of wealth; its happiness at home and its honor abroad; and we hold in abhorrence all schemes for disunion, come from whatever source they may; and we congratulate the country that no Republican member of Congress has uttered or countenanced a threat of disunion, so often made by Democratic members of Congress without rebuke and with applause from their political associates; and we denounce those threats of disunion, in case of a popular overthrow of their ascendency, as denying the vital principles of a free Government, and as an avowal of contemplated treason, which it is the imperative duty of an indignant people strongly to rebuke and forever silence.

Fourth. That the maintenance inviolate of the rights of the States, and especially the rights of each State, to order and control its own domestic institutions according to its own judgment exclusively, is essential to that balance of power on which the perfection and endurance of our political faith depends, and we denounce the lawless invasion by armed force of any State or Territory, no matter under what pretext, as among the gravest of crimes.

Fifth. That the present Democratic Administration has far exceeded our worst apprehensions in its measureless subserviency to the exactions of a sectional interest, as is especially evident in its desperate exertions to force the infamous Lecompton Constitution upon the protesting people of Kansas—in construing the personal relation between master and servant to involve an unqualified property in persons—in its attempted enforcement everywhere, on land and sea, through the intervention of Congress and the Federal Courts, of the extreme pretensions of a purely local interest, and in its general and unvarying abuse of the power entrusted to it by a confiding people.

Sixth. That the people justly view with alarm the reckless extravagance which pervades every department of the Federal Government; that a return to rigid economy and accountability is indispensable to arrest the system of plunder of the public treasury by favored partisans; while the recent startling developments of fraud and corruption at the Federal metropolis, show that an entire change of administration is imperatively demanded.

Seventh. That the new dogma that the Constitution, [illegible] slavery into any or all the Territories of the United States, is a dangerous political heresy, at variance with the explicit provisions of that instrument itself, with contemporaneous exposition, and with legislative and judicial precedent, is revolutionary in its tendency and subversive of the peace and harmony of the country.

Eighth. That the normal condition of all the territory of the United States is that of Freedom; that as our republican fathers, when they had abolished slavery in all our national territory, ordained that no person should be deprived of life, liberty or property, without due process of law, it becomes our duty, by legislation, whenever such legislation is necessary, to maintain this provision of the Constitution against all attempts to violate it; and we deny the authority of Congress, of a Territorial Legislature, or of any individuals, to give legal existence to slavery in any Territory of the United States.

Ninth. That we brand the recent re-opening of the African slave trade, under the cover of our national flag, aided by perversions of judicial power, as a crime against humanity, a burning shame to our country and age, and we call upon Congress to take prompt and efficient measures for the total and final suppression of that execrable traffic.

Tenth. That in the recent vetoes by their Federal Governors of the acts of the Legislatures of Kansas and Nebraska, prohibiting slavery in those Territories, we find a practical illustration of the boasted Democratic principle of non-intervention and Popular Sovereignty, embodied in the Kansas and Nebraska bill, and a denunciation of the deception and fraud involved therein.

Eleventh. That Kansas should of right be admitted as a State under the Constitution recently formed and adopted by her people, and accepted by the House of Representatives.

Twelfth. That while providing revenue for the support of the General Government by duties upon imposts, sound policy requires such an adjustment of these imposts as to encourage the development of the industrial interest of the whole country, and we commend that policy of national exchanges which secures to the workingmen liberal wages, to agriculture remunerating prices, to mechanics and manufacturers an adequate reward for their skill, labor and enterprise, and to the nation commercial prosperity and independence.

Thirteenth. That we protest against any sale or alienation to others of the public lands held by actual settlers, and against any view of the free Homestead policy which regards the settlers as paupers or supplicants for public bounty, and we demand the passage by Congress of the complete and satisfactory Homestead measure which has already passed the House.

Fourteenth. That the National Republican party is opposed to any change in our Naturalization laws, or any State legislation by which the rights of citizenship hitherto accorded by immigrants from foreign lands shall be abridged or impaired; and in favor of giving a full and efficient protection to the rights of all classes of citizens, whether native or naturalized, both at home or abroad.

Fifteenth. That appropriations by Congress for River and Harbor Improvements of a national character, required for the accommodation and security of an existing Commerce, are authorized by the Constitution and justified by an obligation of the Government to protect the lives and property of its citizens.

Sixteenth. That a railroad to the Pacific Ocean is imperatively demanded by the interests of the whole country; that the Federal Government ought to render immediate and efficient aid in its construction, and that as preliminary thereto a daily overland mail should be promptly established.

Seventeenth. Finally, having thus set forth our distinctive principles and views, we invite the co-operation of all citizens, however differing on other questions, who substantially agree with us in their affirmance and support.

CONSTITUTIONAL UNION PLATFORM, Adopted at Baltimore, May, 1860.

Whereas, Experience has demonstrated that all platforms adopted by political parties have the effect to mislead and cause political divisions, by encouraging geographical and sectional parties; therefore,

Resolved, That both patriotism and duty requires that they should recognize no policy or principles but those resting on the broad foundation of the Constitution of the country, the union of the States, and the enforcement of the laws, (great applause, and six cheers); and that, as representatives of the Constitutional Union party and of the country, they pledge themselves to maintain, protect and defend these principles, thus affording security at home and abroad, and secure the blessings of liberty to themselves and posterity.

Adopted by acclamation.

ABRAHAM LINCOLN.

ABRAHAM LINCOLN, the Republican candidate, is a native of Harden county, Kentucky. He was born February 12, 1809. His parents were born in Virginia, and were of very moderate circumstances. He removed from Kentucky to Spencer county, in Indiana, in 1816. Mr. LINCOLN received a limited education. In 1830 he removed to Illinois, and passed the first year in Macon county, engaged in agricultural pursuits. He next went to New Salem, where he remained about one year as a clerk in a store. About this time the Black Hawk war broke out, and a company was raised in New Salem, and LINCOLN was elected captain. He served during this campaign. On his return to Illinois, in 1832, he became a candidate for the State Legislature, but was defeated. The next three succeeding biennial elections he was elected to the Legislature by the Whig party. During his legislative term he studied law, and subsequently engaged practically in the profession at Springfield. For many years he was one of the leaders of the Whig party in Illinois, and was on the electoral ticket in several Presidential campaigns. He was a disciple of HENRY CLAY, and exerted himself in his behalf in 1844, by making a tour

of Illinois, and advocating CLAY'S election to the Presidency. He was elected to Congress in 1846, and served until 1849. While in Congress he voted forty-two times for the Wilmot Proviso. From 1849 to 1854, Mr. LINCOLN was engaged in the practice of his profession. In 1849 he was a candidate before the Illinois Legislature for United States Senator, prior to which he stumped the State for the Whigs. When the Legislature met the Democracy was in the majority, and General SHIELDS, the Democratic candidate, was elected. In 1855 he was again the candidate of the Whigs for United States Senator before the Legislature chosen that year; but the Democracy being in the majority, LINCOLN was again defeated. In 1856, Mr. LINCOLN'S name headed the FREMONT electoral ticket in Illinois. In 1858, it was the desire of the Illinois State Central Committee to have Mr. LINCOLN succeed DOUGLAS in the United States Senate, and to effect this he stumped the State for the Republicans; and it was during this campaign that Mr. LINCOLN made the political speeches from which the people of the Union will at once read his sentiments on the great questions of the day.

STEPHEN A. DOUGLAS

Was born in the town of Brandon, in the State of Vermont, on the 23d of April, 1813, and is now in the forty-eighth year of his age. His father, whose name he bears, was a native of Rensselaer county, in New York, where he was a practising physician. He died leaving two children, one of them the subject of this notice, who was but two months old at that time. STEPHEN ARNOLD DOUGLAS, at the age of fourteen years, apprenticed himself to learn the trade of a cabinetmaker, at Milbury. At this trade he wrought for two years, and getting wearied of it, he sought the means of procuring an education. He was admitted as a pupil in the Canandaigua Academy, entered upon a course of classical studies, and at the same time studied law with an attorney of that village. In 1833 he moved to Illinois, and for some time taught school in the village of Winchester, in that State. While engaged in teaching school he still continued his legal studies, and was admitted to the bar in 1834. In the following year, at the age of twenty-two years, he was appointed State Attorney, which office he resigned in 1836 to take his seat in the Legislature. He subsequently held, for a short time, the post of Receiver of the Land Office at

Springfield, Illinois. By this time he became a prominent politician, and ran for Congress in 1838, but was beaten by five votes. He stumped the State for VAN BUREN for the Presidency in 1840. In December, 1840, he was elected Secretary of State, and in the following February was elected by the Legislature a Judge of the Supreme Court. He was subsequently twice elected as a member of Congress, but only served one term, when he was elected to the United States Senate, in 1847. In 1858 he was again elected to the Senate, after a most exciting contest with Mr. LINCOLN. His engineering of the Kansas Nebraska Bill, and course on the doctrine of "squatter sovereignty," have made him chiefly remarkable.

HISTORICAL PARALLELS.—"A peerage or Westminster Abbey," exclaimed NELSON, when he came in sight of the French at Aboukir Bay: "the scaffold and imprisonment rather than compliance," saith Archbishop HUGHES, when called on to obey or fork over: "a dozen of silver spoons, or a revolver," is MONTGOMERY'S choice to the assailant of his honor. So we go.

JOHN BELL

Was born near Nashville, Tennessee, February 18, 1797. He was the son of a farmer in moderate circumstances, who was, however, able to give him a good education at Cumberland College, now Nashville University, where he graduated in 1814. He studied law, and was admitted to the bar in 1816, and settled at Franklin, Williamson county, Tennessee, and was elected to the State Senate in 1817. In 1826 he became a candidate for Congress against FELIX GRUNDY, one of the popular men in the State of Tennessee, and was elected. By successive elections he continued a member of the House of Representatives for fourteen years. He entered Congress a warm admirer of Mr. CALHOUN, and strongly opposed to the protective system, against which he made a speech in 1832. Subsequent investigations and reflection induced him to change his opinions on that subject. Mr. BELL opposed the South Carolina doctrine of nullification, and was made Chairman of the Judiciary Committee of the House of Representatives, with special reference to the question at that time. His refusal to vote for a resolution approving of the removal of the deposits, was one of the causes which led to the subsequent breach between himself and President JACKSON and the Democratic party, and finally to his cooperation with the Whigs. This change of

party relations was much accelerated by his election to the Speakership of the House of Representatives in 1834, as he was supported by the Whigs. In 1835, Mr. BELL was re-elected to Congress, and an impulse was given to the political character of Tennessee, which arrayed it in opposition to the Democracy during the four succeeding Presidential elections, 1840–'44–'48–'52. When the reception of petitions for the abolition of slavery in the District of Columbia was agitated in the House of Representatives, in 1836, Mr. BELL alone, of the Tennessee delegation, favored their reception. Subsequently, in 1838, when ATHERTON'S resolutions were introduced, proposing to receive and lay these petitions on the table, he maintained his consistency by voting in the negative. When President HARRISON, in 1841, was forming his Cabinet, Mr. BELL was invited to accept the War Department Secretaryship, to which he readily assented. Mr. BELL remained in retirement until called by the people of his county, in 1847, to represent them in the State Senate, in which year, on the occurrence of a vacancy, he was elected to the United States Senate, to which he was re-elected in 1853. His term of service expired in March, 1859, since which time he has been living in retirement from public life.

JOHN C. BRECKINRIDGE.

Mr. BRECKINRIDGE was born near Lexington, Ky., January 16, 1821; was educated at Centre College, Kentucky; spent a few months at Princeton; studied law at the Transylvania Institute, and was admitted to the bar at Lexington where he practiced his profession with success. During the war with Mexico he served in one of the Kentucky regiments as Major, made many warm friends amongst the officers of the army, and established an honorable reputation as a soldier and a gentleman. After the war he returned to the practice of law in Kentucky, soon becoming distinguished for learning, eloquence and acumen. In 1841 he was elected to the State Legislature, there gaining repute as an orator. His style is compact, severe and logical, whilst his views on public questions are marked by solidity and [illegible] gress in opposition to Gen. LESLIE COOMBS, a strong man—and the result was the election of the Democratic nominee. In 1853 he was re-elected, after one of the hottest canvasses ever known in the State. His opponent was Gen. R. P. LETCHER. During his administration President PIERCE tendered to him the mission to Spain, but domestic affairs forbade its acceptance. Ever ready, however, to do battle for his party, he did not hesitate to accept the nomination for Vice-President on the ticket with JAMES BUCHANAN. He was elected, and entered upon the duties of his

office March, 1857. By virtue of his office he is the President of the United States Senate. As a presiding officer he takes a high rank. He has just been elected to the United States Senate for six years from the 4th of March, 1861, to take the place of Mr. CRITTENDEN, whose term then expires. Mr. BRECKINRIDGE is about thirty-nine years old, and is possessed of a moderate fortune, accumulated by his own efforts.

DEMOCRATIC PLATFORM, Adopted by the Maryland Institute Convention, at Baltimore, June 23d, 1860.

Originally adopted by the Seceders at Charleston, April 30th, 1860.

Resolved, That the platform adopted by the Democratic party at Cincinnati, be affirmed, with the following explanatory resolutions:—

1. That the Government of a Territory organized by an act of Congress is provisional and temporary, and during its existence all citizens of the United States have an equal right to settle with their property, in the Territory, without their rights, either of person or property, being destroyed or injured by Congressional or Territorial legislation.

2. That it is the duty of the Federal Government, in all its departments, to protect the rights of persons and property in the Territories, and wherever else its constitutional authority extends.

3. That when the settlers in a Territory having an adequate population, form a State Constitution, the right of sovereignty commences, and being consummated by their admission into the Union, they stand on an equality with the people of other States, and a State thus organized ought to be admitted into the federal Union, whether the Constitution prohibits or recognizes the institution of slavery.

Resolved, That the Democratic party are in favor of the acquisition of the Island of Cuba, on such terms as shall be honorable to ourselves and just to Spain, at the earliest practicable moment.

Resolved, That the enactment of State Legislatures to defeat the faithful execution of the Fugitive Slave law are hostile in character, subversive of the Constitution, and revolutionary in their effect.

Resolved, That the Democracy of the United States recognize it as the imperative duty of the government to protect the naturalized citizen in all his rights, whether at home or in foreign lands, to the same extent as its native born citizens.

Whereas, One of the greatest necessities of the age, in a political, commercial, postal and military point of view, is a speedy connection between the Pacific and Atlantic Coasts; therefore, be it

Resolved, That the National Democratic party do hereby pledge themselves to use every means in their power to secure the passage of some bill, to the extent of their constitutional authority by Congress, for the construction of a Pacific Railroad from the Mississippi River to the Pacific Ocean, at the earliest practicable moment.

The following is the Cincinnati Platform:—

DEMOCRATIC PLATFORM. Adopted at Cincinnati, June 6, 1856

Resolved, That the American Democracy place their trust in the intelligence, the patriotism, and the discriminating justice of the American people.

Resolved, That we regard this as a distinctive feature of our political creed, which we are proud to maintain before the world as a great moral element in a form of government springing from and upheld by the popular will; and we contrast it with the creed and practice of Federalism, under whatever name or form, which seeks to palsy the will of the constituent, and which conceives no imposture too monstrous for the popular credulity.

Resolved, therefore, That entertaining these views the Democratic party of this Union, through their delegates assembled in general Convention, coming together in a spirit of concord, of devotion to the doctrines and faith of a free representative government, and appealing to their fellow-citizens for the rectitude of their intentions, renew and re-assert before the American people, the declarations of principles avowed by them, when, on former occasions, in general Convention, they have presented their candidates for the popular suffrage.

1. That the Federal Government is one of limited power, derived solely from the Constitution, and the grants of power made therein ought to be strictly construed by all the departments and agents of the Government, and that it is inexpedient and dangerous to exercise doubtful constitutional powers.

2. That the Constitution does not confer upon the General Government the power to commence and carry on a general system of internal improvements.

3. That the Constitution does not confer authority upon the Federal Government, directly or indirectly, to assume the debts of the several States, contracted for local and internal improvements, or other State purposes, nor would such assumption be just or expedient.

4. That justice and sound policy forbid the Federal Government to foster one branch of industry to the detriment of another, or to cherish the interests of one portion of our common country; that every citizen and every section of the country has a right to demand and insist upon an equality of rights and privileges, and a complete and ample protection of persons and property from domestic violence and foreign aggression.

5. That it is the duty of every branch of the Government to enforce and practise the most rigid economy in conducting our public affairs, and that no more revenue ought to be raised than is required to defray the necessary expenses of the Government, and gradual but certain extinction of the public debt.

6. That the proceeds of the public lands ought to be sacredly applied to the national objects specified in the Constitution, and that we are opposed to any law for the distribution of such proceeds among the States, as alike inexpedient in policy, and repugnant to the Constitution.

7. That Congress has no power to charter a National Bank; that we believe such an institution one of deadly hostility to the best interests of this country, dangerous to our republican institutions and the liberties of the people, and calculated to place the business of the country within the control of a concentrated money power and above the laws and will of the people; and the results of the Democratic legislation in this and all other financial measures upon which issues have been made between the two political parties of the country, have demonstrated to candid and practical men of all parties their soundness, safety, and utility in all business pursuits.

8. That the separation of the moneys of the Government from banking institutions is indispensable to the safety of the funds of the Government and the rights of the people.

9. That we are decidedly opposed to taking from the President the qualified veto power, by which he is enabled, under restrictions and responsibilities amply sufficient to guard the public interests, to suspend the passage of a bill whose merits cannot secure the approval of two-thirds until the judgment of the people can be obtained thereon, and which has saved the American people from the corrupt and tyrannical dominion of the Bank of the United States, and from a corrupting system of general internal improvements.

10. That the liberal principles embodied by JEFFERSON in the Declaration of Independence, and sanctioned in the Constitution, which makes ours the land of liberty and the asylum of the oppressed of every nation, have ever been cardinal principles in the Democratic faith; and every attempt to to abridge the principles of becoming citizens and the owners of soil among us ought to be resisted with the same spirit which swept the alien and sedition laws from our statute books.

And whereas, Since the foregoing declaration was uniformly adopted by our predecessors in National Conventions, an adverse political and religious test has been secretly organized by a party claiming to be exclusively Americans, and it is proper that the American Democracy should clearly define its relations thereto; and declare its determined opposition to all secret political societies, by whatever name they may be called.

Resolved, That the foundation of the Union of States having been laid in, and its prosperity, expansion and preëminent example in free government, built upon entire freedom of matters of religious concernment, and no respect of persons in regard to rank, or place of birth, no party can justly be deemed national, constitutional, or in accordance with American principles, which bases its exclusive organization upon religious opinions and accidental birth-place. And hence a political crusade in the ninteenth century, and in the United States of America, against Catholics and foreign-born is neither justified by the past history or future prospects of the country, nor in unison with the spirit of toleration, and enlightened freedom which peculiarly distinguishes the American system of popular government.

Resolved, That we reiterate with renewed energy of purpose the well considered declarations of former conventions upon the sectional issue of domestic slavery, and concerning the reserved rights of the States:—

1. That Congress has no power under the Constitution to interfere with or control the domestic institutions of the several States, and that all such States are the sole and proper judges of everything appertaining to their own affairs not prohibited by the Constitution; that all efforts of the Abolitionists or others made to induce Congress to interfere with questions of slavery, or to take incipient steps in relation thereto, are calculated to lead to the most alarming and dangerous consequences, and that all such efforts have an inevitable tendency to diminish the happiness of the people, and endanger the stability and permanency of the Union, and ought not to be countenanced by any friend of our political institutions.

2. That the foregoing proposition covers and was intended to embrace the whole subject of slavery agitation in Congress, and therefore the Democratic party of the Union, standing on this national platform, will abide by and adhere to a faithful execution of the acts known as the Compromise measures, settled by the Congress of 1850: "the act for reclaiming fugitives from service or labor" included; which act being designed to carry out an express provision on the Constitution, cannot, with fidelity thereto, be repealed, or so changed as to destroy or impair its efficiency.

3. That the Democratic party will resist all attempts at renewing in Congress, or out of it, the agitation of the slavery question, under whatever shape or color the attempt may be made.

4. That the Democratic party will faithfully abide by and uphold the principles laid down in the Kentucky and Virginia resolutions of 1792 and 1798, and in the report of Mr. MADISON to the Virginia Legislature in 1799—that it adopts these principles as constituting one of the main foundations of its political creed, and is resolved to carry them out in their obvious meaning and import.

And that we may more distinctly meet the issue on which a sectional party, subsisting exclusively on slavery agitation, now relies to test the fidelity of the people North and South, to the Constitution and the Union.

1. *Resolved,* That claiming fellowship with and desiring the coöperation of all who regard the preservation of the Union under the Constitution as the paramount issue, and repudiating all sectional parties and platforms concerning domestic slavery, which seek to embroil the States and incite to treason and armed resistance to law in the Territories, and whose avowed purpose, if consummated, must end in civil war and disunion, the American Democracy recognize and adopt the principles contained in the organic laws establishing the Territories of Nebraska and Kansas, as embodying the only sound and safe solution of the slavery question, upon which the great national idea of the people of this whole country can repose in its determined conservation of the Union, and non-interference of Congress with slavery in the Territories or in the District of Columbia.

2. That this was the basis of the compromises of 1850, confirmed by both the Democratic and Whig parties in National Conventions, ratified by the people in the election of 1852, and rightly applied to the organization of the Territories in 1854.

3. That by the uniform application of the Democratic principle to the organization of Territories, and the admission of new States with or without domestic slavery, as they may elect, the equal rights of all the States will be preserved intact, the original compacts of the Constitution maintained inviolate, and the perpetuity and expansion of this Union insured to its utmost capacity of embracing, in peace and harmony, every future American State that may be constituted or annexed with a republican form of government.

Resolved, That we recognize the right of the people of all the Territories, including Kansas and Nebraska, acting through the legally and fairly expressed will of the majority of the actual residents, and whenever the number of their inhabitants justifies it, to form a Constitution, with or without domestic slavery, and be admitted into the Union upon terms of perfect equality with the other States.

Resolved, finally, That in view of the condition of the popular institutions in the Old World (and the dangerous tendencies of sectional agitation, combined with the attempt to enforce civil and religious disabilities against the rights of acquiring and enjoying citizenship in our own land,) a high and sacred duty is involved with increased responsibility upon the Democratic party of this country, as the party of the Union, to uphold and maintain the rights of every State and thereby the union of the States—and to sustain and advance among us constitutional liberty, by continuing to resist all monopolies and exclusive legislation for the benefit of the few at the expense of the many, and by vigilant and constant adherence to those principles and compromises of the Constitution—which are broad enough and strong enough to embrace and uphold the Union as it was, the Union as it is, and the Union as it shall be—in the full expression of the energies and capacity of this great and progressive people.

1. *Resolved,* That there are questions connected with the foreign policy of this country which are inferior to no domestic question whatever. The time has come for the people of the United States to declare themselves in favor of free seas, and progressive free trade throughout the world, and, by solemn manifestations to place their moral influence at the side of their successful example.

2. *Resolved,* That our geographical and political position with reference to the other States of this continent, no less than the interest of our commerce and the development of our growing power

AND POPULAR SOVEREIGNTY ADVOCATE.

Terms, 50 cts., Single Copy. CLEVELAND, OHIO, SATURDAY, JULY 21, 1860. NO. 4.

THE EMPIRE STATE O. K.

Lincoln Laid Out in New York and in the Union.

The Silver Gray, Bell & Everett Party go for Douglas in a body.

Without New York there can be no election of Lincoln by the People.

There can be no election of a Black Republican President by the House of Representatives.

Our "Empire" Cock.

New York State Constitutional Union Convention at Utica.

Speeches of Gen. Prescott, Hon. Washington Hunt and Hon. Jas. Brooks.

The following report of the proceedings of the friends of Bell and Everett at Utica on Wednesday, will be read with interest:

REMARKS OF GEN. A. H. PRESCOTT.

Mr. Prescott, President of the Convention, on taking the Chair, briefly returned thanks for the honor. He need not remind the Convention that this was an important meeting. They had assembled to decide what course as Union-loying men they were to pursue at this election. He had met with them in 1856, and he did not believe one single man present regretted the vote he then cast; nor did he believe any here present were less opposed to the organization they then fought against than they were in 1856.—[Cheers.] That organization had thrown overboard the most prominent and best known statesmen, and taken up one less distinctly recognized as Republican; but their sectional principles remained precisely the same now as in 1856, and the Union men could no more support them now than they could then. [Applause.] He believed the Convention would never desire, directly or indirectly, to put into the Presidential chair the candidate of a sectional party in bitter hostility to one section of the Union. The Democratic Party, which once took the position of a great national party, was now broken in twain, and one half of it was as sectional and as objectionable as the Republican party of the North. The Convention was, he trusted, as much opposed to sectionalism in one division of the Union as in the other. There was, however, a party in the field upon which they could unite—a party that recognized the Constitution and the Union as their platform. He had been in favor of the nomination of Houston by that party—[Applause]—but had cheerfully yielded to the party will of the majority, and was prepared to do whatever would be most likely to secure the success of Bell and Everett in the Union. [Applause.]

SPEECH OF HON. WASHINGTON HUNT.

Hon. Washington Hunt, as a delegate at large to the Baltimore Union Convention, stated that the convention had been called together by an organization, with John J. Crittenden at the head, to once more endeavor to uphold the Constitution and the Union, and defeat the sectional and disunion schemes of those who strove to involve the nation in agitation and sectional strife. A properly constituted authority had called together a convention of union men at Baltimore, and the privilege of attending that convention as a delegate was one of the proudest privileges of his life.

Delegates from all States of the Union, from North and South, were there, and he believed there never assembled a more patriotic and intelligent body of men since the adoption of the Federal Constitution. There were some men there whose names were known throughout the union as able and experienced statesmen. They pledged themselves to stand by the Union and the Constitution. The names presented to the Convention for a choice of candidates were among the ablest known in the history of the country. Among others was that of John J. Crittenden, and a majority of the Convention would have tendered him the nomination had he not refused to allow nis name to be used for such purpose. The convention had finally chosen John Bell, of Tennessee. [Loud applause.] A delegate (Mr. Brooks) who had favored, before the nomination, Mr. Houston, of Texas, had moved that the nomination be unanimous, which was done. The name of Edward Everett was then, by one unanimous vote from one end of the Union to the other, chosen to the second place on the ticket. [Loud applause.] On the matter of platform they had experienced no embarrassment. They discarded all words capable of constructions numerous enough to suit all sections alike, and resolved to march to battle upagainst the party that they ignored the question of slavery; that they failed to express their sentiments on that overshadowing issue. He asked if at the time the Declaration of Independence was signed, or when the Constitution of the United States was adopted, the question of slavery would never have been permitted to disturb the fraternal deliberations of the fathers of the Republic? If so, the Declaration of Independence and Constitution of the United States would never have been adopted. The friends of Bell and Everett were told that it was useless to support those candidates, for they would not be elected, and they ought therefore to go over to one or the other stronger parties.

Now there are four candidates in the field.—It is proper to assume that no sectional party—that is, no party running in only one sections of the Union, like the Republican Party, can secure the election by a majority of the people.—They have their party in one section of the Union only, and in that, if in a majority at all, they have a large minority against them. Neglected, then, their election could only be in the Electoral College, representing a minority of the people of the Union, and only one section of the Union at that. Yet the Republicans talk much about an election by the people. Was this such an election as contemplated by the Constitution? He believed it was an election much to be deplored and likely to prove fatal to the Union.—He was in favor of throwing the election into Congress if no party running in the whole Union could receive a majority of the people of the Union in his favor. It was said that Congress was so constituted that it could not elect a President in accordance with the obligation under the Constitution.

He believed under such a state of affairs, the man most likely to be elected—he almost said that the only man that could be elected—is John Bell of Tennessee. [Applause.] How was it possible to throw the election into Congress, when it was found that no candidate could secure a majority of the people of the whole Union? In his judgement, every lover of the Union should throw aside his prejudices, and unite to secure such a result. If men who never had political sentiment in common can combine and unite to entail agitation and strife upon a nation and create sectional hate between those who are of common lineage, and have a common country to protect, why, in God's name, cannot those who love the Union and revere the Constitution, combine and unite to do a great and good act. [Tremenduous applause.

A Voice—Say that over again. [Laughter and cheers.]

Mr. Hunt—No, no. I have said it once, now let us act upon it. He declared that information from the South gave indication of the success of the Union ticket in a large majority of the States. The people of the South are tired of agitation and the distraction consequent upon a discussion of these abstractions. They desire peace and rest from sectional strife. He believed the day going by when the people of the States of New York and Virginia would longer fight over the abstract question, whether Slavery shall or shall not be allowed in the deserts of Utah or New Mexico. In conclusion, he declared that he should hold himself bound by all the principles of honor and duty to do all in his power to promote the election of Bell and Everett. As to the mode by which they can secure this result, they must be practical men, and do their best to defeat the candidates who represent sectionalism North or South. He was not prepared to say what was the precise way to accomplish the object, but where ther's a will there's a way and if all determine so to do, it can be done.

He believed that this State can now be thrown so as to secure the defeat of the sectional candidate by a minority of the people. This was his platform. [Loud applause.] There might be differences of opinion here as to the best mode to pursue. He should not be willing himself at this early period of the canvass to form an electoral ticket and put it forth to the Union men for support. Come what might, they would stand firmly by the Union, and maintain the principles of Washington and Jefferson in all their purity and not as misinterpreted by sectional parties of the present day. Washington and Jefferson never called upon the North to set itself up as a political section in a geographical South but both warned them of the Union and the Constitution he would stand by the party to the last. [Loud protracted cheers.]

SPEECH OF HON. JAMES BROOKS.

Hon. James Brooks, in appropriate remarks, announced that it was his pleasing duty to move the ratification of the nominations made at Baltimore. He had himself originally been a Houston man, believing that his strong arm, well versed as he was in politics and in war, was necessary to put down the growing and dangerous spirit of aggression. He enlarged upon the evils of sectional parties, and declared that the very evils which Washington foresaw in his Farewell Address, were now upon the country—hence the necessity of this Union Convention; hence this meeting of old gentlemen; hence he and others like him, who had not been in a Convention for eight years, rose and laid aside their mummy clothes, and came forward to support the Union. He admitted that there were many Union-loving men in the Republican party, but they were compelled to follow the lead of men like Sumner, Garrison and others, in the sectional and objectionable principles which they teach. He (Brooks) declared that higher and holier objects than protection for this or that article should now animate all patriotic men, and he for one was willing to join hands with any true Union man, no matter what his former political standing may have been, whether a Douglas man or a Republican, in support of the Union and Constitution. He urged upon the Convention the pactical necessity of using their strength wisely in this State. They were not strong enough to carry the State alone. They had tried it in 1856, and then, while powerless themselves, the vote proved that they really held the power to prevent the election of either of the other parties. Last year they had made a ticket composed in part of the nominations of the Democratic and Republican parties, and had elected it. Here was a clue to their future policy. He agreed with the remarks of the gentleman who had preceded him, that it was unwise now to make an electoral ticket. The future was not yet clear, and he was prepared at a future day to adopt such measures as would best secure the object Union men now had in view. He denied that there was any intention to abandon their principles. He reviewed the actions of the Whigs on the compromise measures of 1850, showing that the policy then adopted by that party was Congressional non-intervention with slavery, and entire freedom of the people of the Territories to decide on their own institutions. The Democratic party under Douglas was not the author of Popular Sovereignty. He was now on Whig ground in that respect, as well as in opposition to the Federal tyranny.

The noblest fight ever fought against Federal interference and tyranny was that fought by Douglas, of Illinois, against the power of the Administration. [Loud cheers.]—He declared that the Union party had already achieved much. It had compelled the Republican Party to throw overboard their leading champion, Wm. H. Seward. The minority did this. It was fear of their power that compelled them to sacrifice Seward. It is fear of the power of the minority that forced from the Republicans false professions of attachment to the Union. It is fear of that power that makes the Republicans tremble when their Sumners and their Phillips speak before the public. He assumed that the object of this minority now is to throw the election into the House. Then Mr. Bell must be elected if any person, and if not then the election must go the Senate when Hamlin and Edward Everett alone will be there for election. [Loud applause.] To accomplish this object, to defeat the election of a candidate by a minority of the people of the Union, and by a section of the Union only, the minority are prepared to vote for the Union ticket, no matter it Douglas or any person else be on it. Was there anything wrong in this? [Cries of "No, no."] Was it not the duty of old gentlemen to rise from their political graves and teach this policy to the people? [Laughter.] In conclusion he urged Union-loving men to rally to this cause and join hands with the conservative men of the South for the preservation of the Constitution and the Union.

There were other considerations to induce a union against the Republicans in the State. One the leaders of the party a set of robbers and thieves, worse than any in Auburn or Sing Sing. They robbed the city of New York out of millions, and stolen water rights of countless value. There are bandits—regularly organized bandits—in Albany, who rob the State in an organized manner; and against these thieves and robbers every honest man should combine. In the last Legislature the ferry rights of the people of Brooklyn were outraged, and to this end $20,000 were placed in Thurlow Weed's hands for days to be used in corruption. He knew that Mr. Weed would abuse him for this, but his case was adamantine and cared nothing for abuse. He called upon all honest men all over the country to rise and to protect the State against the thieves and robbers of the Republican party at Albany, who, under the guise of negro philanthropy, plunder the State wholesale. He offered a resolution endorsing the names of Bell and Everett as the candidates of the Uoion party for the Presidency and Vice-Presidency of the United States. [Cheers.]

The resolution was odopted unonimously.

The Albany *Atlas* comments as follows:—

"The American Movement — Its Significance.—The Convention which has just adjourned at Utica, has determined upon a course of action that exasperates and alarms the partisans of Lincoln, while it leaves to them no opportunity to meet and combat it or by present or direet, action, counteract its purpose.

The Convention was composed of Union men, of Old Whigs, of the Silver Greys, of the Americans who were never tainted with the sectionalism and proscriptiveness which distinguished the men who figured in the earlier days of Know-Nothingism.

The duty of opposing and defeating Lincoln and the partisans of the irrepressible conflict was conceded on all hands; and to that end the purpose of the Convention was directed. Accordingly, a resolution was adopted, placing the subject of the Electoral ticket in hands of a commitee of thirty-two reliable men, four chosen from each Judicial District, and the majority clothed with all the powers of the Convention on that subject.

What this movement means, and what is to be the result of it, is not a subject of much incertitude. It will present the Douglas ticket to the Conservative electors, not only as a political necessity, but as a choice. We do not assume that any consultation of the members of the Committee indicates such a purpose; but such will be the instruction of public opinion and the imperative demand of circumstances.

We do not wonder that through the ranks of the Lincoln Abolitionists there runs a shudder of distrust and a premonitory chill of despair, at this indication of the signs of the times. It is the accession of from 50,000 to 100,000 men to the army of Democracy, on the eve of the battle. It is Blucher marching up with the Prussians, and deciding the field of Waterloo.

We do not intend to overrate the importance of such an accession to the Douglas ranks. The Fillmore electors in 1856 cast 126,600 votes; and if this force has diminished in intervening contests, it must not be forgotten that this has been owing in great part, to the falling off the aggregate vote. The total number cast in '56 was 596,486. The total of last fall was 503,728. Allowing for the new votes, it is clear that over One Hundred Thousand of the electors of the State have not voted since 1856. Most of these are conservative men, who are only drawn into an electoral contest by the great excitements of a Presidential question.

While Mr. Douglas' strength from this and from every source, must increase; that of Lincoln can never reach the point which Fremont attained in 1856. The Fremont vote has continuously fallen off, year after year, in this State, and is destined to more severe losses, by the desertion and apathy of dissatisfied followers.

The Republicans have no hope of New York, except such as they count upon from the divisions in the Democratic ranks. They urge, and will do much and *pay much*, to bring into the field a Breckinridge Electoral ticket, (whether the real friends of Breckinridge want it or not,) and upon this they count to draw off some thousands of votes, and to discourage the Democracy in the very outset of the contest.

They reckon without their host! The proposition put forth by Tucker & Co. has already fied and factious votes, which otherwise would go for Lincoln. Instead of disheartening the Democracy, it has given them encouragemet.

Never have the Democratic ranks in this State been animated by such a general sympathy and such a spirit of hopefulness. They stand shoulder to shoulder, and they see Victory before them. They invite all who believe the people should rule, and who expect in this faith to triumph, to unite under their banner. It is a noble cause and glorious is the promise that already smiles.

BUCHANAN ON THE STUMP!

GREAT SERENADE SPEECH!

At the Yancey, Breckinridge, and Office Holder's fandango in Washington, on Monday night, the President is reported as having delivered the following address:—

"Fellow Office Holders:—I have lived to be nearly seventy years of age. I was admitted into the Democratic party just before I became forty. All my previous life had been spent in trying to destroy it. I hated it with an intensity of a natural aristocrat, and as I mounted to one high position after another by the aid of the votes of that party, I was resolved, if I could ever achieve the Presidency, to give it the final blow. Therefore it is that I cordially greet you to-night. In your standard bearer I recognize a man whom I have always detested, while I supposed him to be my rival, and whom I now only love because he has consented to be my tool in the great work of destroying the only national party. I tell those of you who are listening to me, and who hold office under me, that if you do not assist me in this delightful occupation, you shall be summarily dismissed, and now, my friends and followers, my servants and subordinates, good night. You will proceed hence to be addressed by my Secretary of the Treasury, Howell Cobb, of Georgia, by my beloved friend, Col. Florence, of Pennsylvania, by my Secretary of the Interior, Jacob Thompson, of Mississippi, by my District Attorney, Mr. Black, and by all others who believe that "it will be a great deal better to elect Abraham Lincoln than Stephen A. Douglas." Great sensation!

Seward not to take the Stump for "Old Abe."

The Repnblican newspapers are making a great fuss over a letter Mr. Seward wrote to Michigan which they interpret into a belief that he would take the stump for "Old Abe." This is all a mistake as Mr. Adams, of the Syracuse *Journal*, who went a fishing a few days ago with the Senator, remarks. The *Journal* says:

"We think the papers are saying rather too much when they announce that Gov. Seward will "take the stump" in this campaign. His letter, saying that he will speak to the people of Michigan at their earnest solicitation, should not be interpreted in too broad a sense. We are not aware that there is any occasion for Mr. Seward taking the stump, in the sense of spending his time in making campaign speeches."

Not at all—its all labor lost, and Greeley, and his crew would not thank him for it. Its asking too much of a man after being killed outright politically, to go through the country delivering funeral orations on himself as every speech for "Old Abe" would be. Mr. Seward has too much self-respect.

The People Reporting.

PUBLIC SENTIMENT.

We last week condensed a day's mail to show the public sentiment as it came up from the voters in every direction. We to-day take a hurried glance at a single day's mail to give the latest from the people as the true index:

H. M., of Shelby, O., writes: * * "This makes 56 copies for Shelby, and the Lord knows how many there will be in two weeks more if the Republican Journals keep up their howl for Breckinridge and Lane. You see "things is working" right and so is the PLAIN DEALER, for when it comes it "*charges along the whole line.*" ——C. Y., of Hiram, O., writes: * * * "Douglas is all the rage here, only one Breckinridge man in town."——J. G. G. L., of Milford, Ind., writes: * * "The CAMPAIGNER is the death knell to the small remnant of sectionalisms that exists here. DOUGLAS stock is above par and the Democracy is sure to win the day over all isms here."——H. B. T., of Corunna, Mich. writes: * * "We are going to carry this county this fall if hard work will accomplish anything. We are all DOUGLAS to the back bone, in fact there is not a BRECKINRIDGE man in the county. Give us the documents and we will redeem Shiawassa."——N. S., of Marshallville, O., writes: * * "We have but one administration man here, and he is on the fence."——G. B., of Canal Fulton, O.: * * "Out of 180 Democratic voters in this township there is but one for Breckinridge and Lane, the Stark county *Democrat* notwithstanding. About one-half of the "*Democrat*" papers sent to this office have been sent back and more will be soon."——S. C. B., of Decator Ind.: * * The Little Giant is all the go in this county. The Bolter's ticket will not get five votes in the county."——M. B., of Peninsula, O: * * * "Enclosed find $5 more for CAMPAIGNERS. It takes in Boston. Not a Breckinridge Democrat in this township."——A. A. of Sharon, Pa., * * "Our County Committee met yesterday and endorsed the nomination of Douglas and Johnson without a dissenting voice, and appointed a Committee to prepare an address to voters of the county (Mercer.")——W. J. of Albion, Mich.: * * "You may count Michigan about safe for Douglas and Johnson."——J. L. C., *the P. M. at —— writes: "HOORAH FOR DOUGLAS* and JOHNSON! J. W. GRAY, your excellent Campaign Pictorial paper came to hand all right.—The general opinion is, that the old gentleman who lost his horns in '58, and turned out to be a J—k in '60 has got his foot in it, and no mistake. So also has J. C. B. J. C. B. is as deep in the mud, as J. B. is in the mire." BRECKINRIDE and LANE, Bah! *They are played out.* With Douglas and Johnson, the people's candidates, we can sweep the platter. That's so, and prove that old *honest* Abe's boots are stationary. Mark that. We are all for Douglas in this part of the country. If you doubt it, mark the majority old Franklin county will give this fall for Douglas, Johnson and our ever faithful representative Hon. S. S. Cox."——L. C. B., of East Pembroke, N. Y.: * * "Great enthusiasm prevails amongst us in this vicinity, and Douglas is gaining ground slowly."——A. P. B., of Bloomfield, Iowa: * * "The skies look bright in Iowa. Look out for a Douglas victory here in November." R. M. L., of Tipton, Iowa: * * "There are no disunion seceders in our county. All are for the Little Giant."——Z. R., of Guilford, O.: * * "No Breckinridge men in our conuty." J. E., of Thebes, Ill.: * * "Egypt will give a good account of herself this fall. If she can't do it in one day, she will in *three*. Three cheers for the Little Giant!"——S. J. Mc., of Henry, Ill.: * * We are all for "Little Dugg." except the P. M. God bless the Danites, "their days are few and full of trouble." The "Nationals" in our county are all in for Douglas and Johnson, with the harness buckled on, ready for the work. We don't intend to leave a grease "spot" of old honest Abe in this State. We feel confident that we can whip the Black Republicans and Danites both, as easy as rolling off a log. Pitch the hot shot into *both parties*. We, the people, are with you. The Republicans are all wide asleep in this State. They can get up no excitement here in Lincoln's own State."——J. M. F., of Dallas, Ill.: * * "Everybody and everything in this county is for Douglas and he will carry old Hancock by 1,000 maj., and the State by 20,000."——M. H., of Sandusky, N. Y: * * "Enclosed find funds and 97 names. We will send more and continue to *work* for the LITTLE GIANT."——N. and B., of Somerton, O.: * * Politics high. Douglas gaining. Belmont county good for 800."——J. B. G., of Dayton, Ind.: * * "I have been travelling since last spring in the Northwest, and I find plenty of friends of the Little Giant and the PLAIN DEALER everywhere. The prospects for Douglas in this, Tippecanoe, and adjoining counties are growing bright and beautifully brighter daily, and if I am not much mistaken, Indiana will next fall give the Little giant the largest majority on record for many years. Democrats who thought we yielded too much to the South and left us, see that we are now standing handsomely up and they are flocking back by hundreds."——W. G., of Auburn, Ind.: * * "There were Clubs formed here who sent for the Boston *Post*, before the Convention met at Baltimore, but as it sustains the seceders, it misrepresents this community and we are sending them back. We send you 40 names."——J. W., of Medina: * * Enclosed find additional names making 127 in all, will send another batch soon. (Herald Club amounts to 25). Who Rah for Douglas——J. M. W., of McConnellsville, O.: * * "The getter up of the Club is in the country taking census. Add the following to his list and when he comes in you may expect another batch."——J. C., of Mason, Mich.: * * "If you go Douglas, send 20 Campaigners for the enclosed, if not, return the money."——A. B. E., of Birmingham, O.: * * I think we will poll from 75 to 100 more votes for Douglas than we did for Buchanan."

J. E., a P. M. in Wisconsin writes on a post bill: The State of Wisconsin will go for Douglas as sure as the sun rises and sets——H. S., of Park, Mich.: A peddler that chanced to stop with me threw out an old paper, saying: "I don't know how I came by a damn Democrat paper in my rags." It was a PLAIN DEALER, a copy of which I had never seen before. We are all Douglas here. Enclosed find —.——The P. M. of ——, O: There is not a disunion Breckinridge man in this place or township. There was one, but he is converted and is now as good a Douglas man as need be. Do not publish this letter as you know the guillotine is ready to fall.——The P. M. of ——, N. Y.: Western New York will do the clean thing for Douglas.——J. C. C., of Bellville, O.: There will be a gain of 50 for Douglas in this township. Such a breaking of old rails and scamper of rats as will be in old Richland this fall you never did see.——G. R. M., of Rockport, Ind.: The ball is rolling—Douglas forever.——C. J. B., of New Paris, O.: The Democracy here are a unit for Douglas. No disunion bolters among us, and with Douglas for our standard bearer and our own gallant Vall to lead the van, this third district will roll up a majority that will strike terror to the hearts of the abolitionists and fire eaters, particularly to Flood, Johnson, Hall, Belden & Co.——C. H. L., of Carlisle, Ill.: The work goes bravely on. The Little Giant will carry this State in November.

[Of course it is understood that though Old Buck says Democrats may vote for the regular candidate or the bolter's ticket, yet if an officer votes for the regular ticket, Douglas and Johnson, "off goes his head off." This explains why we dare not give a Post Master's name and address. Isn't this a free country?]

A. C. C., P. M. at ——, Iowa: Inclosed find draft on Park Bank of New York for $25 for CAMPAIGNERS for the following names * * Send 20 extra copies and I will remit next week. Will probably send you another large list in a few days. Douglas is all the go here.——E. L. R., of Leeds Center, Wis.: The joy of the Democrats of Wisconsin at the nomination of Judge Douglas is unbounded. He is emphatically the people's choice, and with him we will redeem the Badger State from Black Republican nullification. The course of the Administration has made him lots of friends. Set it down as a fact that he will carry Wisconsin in November.——A. J. G., of Duck Creek, Ind.: Douglas is all right in our conntry. I don't know of a Breckinridge man. The Republicans say there are some, but I guess they are like milk sickness, 30 miles ahead always. The Democratic party will gain 100 in our county.——J. S. W., of Polk, O.: We have 170 Douglas to 3 J. B. Democrats. The census-taker did not get any of old Flood's papers to come to this office. They charge me with discouraging the paper and I plead guilty, for I don't want Democrats to take a paper that will read themselves out of the party every time they read it.——S. C., of Oakwood, Mich.: You think Douglas cannot carry Massachusetts, Vermont and *Michigan*. You may cut Michigan off of that black list, for no future event is surer than that Michigan goes for Douglas.——D. P. W., of Leon, Iowa: We are going to do something here this year. Mark that.——G. Mc., of Bluffton, Ind.: Douglas stock runs high in our locality. Wells county will increase her Democratic vote. The bolters cannot get 5 votes in the county.

—The Washington correspondent of the Cincinnati *Gazette* says the Breckinridge party "really prefer the election of Lincoln to the success of Douglas."

CHIEF OF THE WIGWAM.

"OLD ABE" IN HIS NEW CHARACTER.

The Republicans are endeavoring to strengthen a weak nomination by some of the stale electioneering tricks borrowed from former campaigns. Every one recollects how, in the time of Harrison, the log cabin and hard cider dodge was worked throughout the country. Large amounts of money were invested in pine logs and apple juice, in order to get up a factitious excitement. There was not a city, town or village in the Unioni wthout its scores of these improvised huts, in which, from early morning to midnight, were to be heard the sounds of tipsey revelry, interspersed with the favorite refrain of "Tippecanoe and Tyler too."

Having cast aside a candidate who, but for treachery, might have been run on his own personal merits, the Republicans have resorted to the device of investing their present choice with imaginary antecedents, which they think have a chance of appealing to the popular heart. With this view they are building wigwams in our large cities, in order to get up an excitement similar to that which was manufactured on the "log cabin and hard cider campaign." The idea, however, does not seem to have elicited much enthusiasm. People can see no sort of connection between a wigwam and "Old Abe Lincoln's" career. The only chance he ever had of seeing "a live fighting Indian," was in the Black Hawk war, and than, as he admits himself, he never came within a mile of one. This dodge, therefore, wont tell, unless it is dressed up after another fashion. To make the wigwams popular they must be rendered amusing. Let some of the harlequins and turncoats of the party paint and dress themselves as Indians, and then they may render the new Republican rendezvous attractive. Paint is cheap, and feathers are to be had for the plucking.

As a model for their new *modus operandi*, we present them a life-like portrait of their own distinguished Chief in his Wigwam [illegible] walk in the leg but tremendous in the head.

Model Constitution for a Douglas Club.

Article 1.—This association shall be called the——

Article 2.—Any Elector of the township of ——in favor of the election of Douglas and Johnson to the offices of President and Vice President of the United States may become a member of this Association by affixing his name to this Constitution.

Article 3.—The officers of the Club shall consist of a President, two Vice Presidents, a Secretary, a Treasurer, and an Executive Committee composed of three persons.

Let every Town and Ward in the United States adopt this model and organize forthwith.

Let her Rip.

LEWISTOWN, Fulton Co., Ill., July 11.

ED. P. D.—DEAR SIR:—We have just received the second number of your paper. It is just the paper for the Democracy. The Democrats of Fulton county are wide awake, and will elect their ticket by the largest majority they have ever done yet. We have just held a meeting at Canton where there was present about 5000 people, all Douglas Democrats. The rail splitter does not take in our county. DEMOCRAT.

Presidential Calculations.

The commercial editor of the Augusta *Constitutionalist*, Mr. Pritchard, after consulting with all the leading men at Baltimore, and visiting Washington and New York for the purpose of obtaining information, thinks the following States can be relied on to give their electoral vote for Douglas and Johnson:

New York	35
Pennsylvania	27
Ohio	23
Indinia	13
Illinois	11
New Jersey	7
Iowa	4
Minnesota	4
Wisconsin	5
Missouri	9
Maryland	8
Louisiana	6
Total, and enough to elect	152

It is also believed by many, Mr. Pritchard says, that the following States will vote for Douglas and Johnson:

Alabama	9
Delaware	3
Arkansas	4
Connecticut	6
New Hampshire	5
California	4
Oregon	3
Michigan	6

Mr. Pritchard made up his calculation very soon after the nominations were announced. We think it safe to say at present that Connecticut is nearly certain for Lincoln and that Maine, New Hampshire, Michigan and Arkansas are certain for Douglas. Our belief is that in the North and West Mr. Lincoln has lost at least five per. cent of his strength since the Baltimore nominations were made; and that the split in the Democratic party, instead of doing us harm, *is actually doing us good* in every one of the free States. The Republican thunder is gone, and Abe Lincoln is scarcely thought of in the fight.

POLITICAL AND MISCELLANEOUS.

—Douglas has lost his fighting-cock. Pryor crows for Breckinridge.—*Louisville Journal.*

He lost his spurs, before Douglas lost him.

—Caleb Cushing is spoken of in relation to the vacancy on the Supreme Bench. A friend can't believe that it is such a hard bench as to need a Cushing on it. What does he mean?

—Don't touch the lute when drums are resounding. A wise man remains silent while fools are speaking.

—Truth is never drowned; in vain you plunge her beneath the water; she always rises to the surface.

—"You seem to walk more erect than usual, my dear sir." "Yes, I have been straitened by circumstances."

—The great leaders of the Breckinridge party are Wm. L. Yancey, who has not voted a Democratic ticket in many years, and Humphrey Mary shall, who never voted one in his life.

DESTRUCTION OF THE WORLD.—The Boston *Courier* is afraid that if the proposed canal is run into Vesuvius, it will generate enough steam to blow the world up. Put on the safety valves.

KENTUCKY.—At the regular Democratic Convention in Campbell county, Kentucky, the nomination of Douglas was endorsed by a vote of nearly seven to one. Whereupon the Breckinridge men, true to their instincts, seceded, and set up for themselves.

—A good constitution is like a money-box: the full value of it is never known until it is broken.

—If a gentlemen should unite in partnership with a blacksmith, would he be legally connected with a forgery.

—Don't have too much commiseration for the accomplished, amiable and charming wife of a defaulter, until you know that she has not, by extravagance and pride, induced him to use money not his own, or to speculate with a view to gratify her wishes.

—The Disunionists of Georgia are burning the Democratic candidate for Vice-President, Herschel V. Johnson, in effigy. If they don't do him any more injury than that, we think he will spite them by occupying the Vice-President's chair in the Senate.—*Cin. Enquirer.*

The Disunionists of the North have done that same to DOUGLAS, and still he lives. "Persecution hallows where it hits."

—The Rome (Ga.,) *Southerner* predicts the election of Douglas, though its own proclivities are anti-Douglas. The Augusta (Ga.,) *Constitutionalist*, one of the ablest papers in the country, supports Douglas. It is expected that nearly all the Democratic papers of Georgia will hoist the Douglas flag before the campaign is over.

—In Mississippi the Hon. Mr. Kinyon is making Douglas speeches, and has had a discussion with a Mr. Mathews, which resulted in a Douglas ratification meeting. The Democratic paper at Corinth hoists the Douglas flag, and a ratification meeting has been held there.

tend to strike for an amendment of the Constitution. They want things fixed so that one man may be at the same time President, Vice President, and Cabinet.

—The President and Vice President of the United States occupy a most self-stultifying position. They repudiate and condemn the platform on which they were elected, and by which they hold their present positions. It is so objectionable in their opinion, that a re-affirmation of it, without anything more on the slavery question, is sufficient cause to break up a Convention of their own party, in order to defeat its candidate.

—Gen. Lane has published a letter accepting his nomination and putting his trust in Divine Providence. The General's faith exceeds that of the old lady when the horse ran away—she trusted in Providence until the breeching broke. The General trusts in Providence, although the Democratic breeching has given out entirely in in Oregon. A new Legislature has been elected which will lay him on the shelf. He had better cling to Providence now, for nothing else can save him.

THE SLEEPING MAID.

BY INA B. CARSLEY.

The gold-fringed curtains looped aside
From round the couch whereon she lies,
The charmed seal of slumber pressed
Upon the waxen lidded eyes;
Awhile the moonlight glimmers through
The leaves that climb the casement o'er,
And fling their quivering shadows forth
Upon the tesselated floor.

She sleeps: the pale light softly falls
Across the maiden's sculptured face,
And o'er her bosom's pearly snow,
Upheaving 'neath the rose of lace;
And dreams: while through the dimpling smiles
That keep the moist, red lips apart,
The white teeth glow—a wedge of pearl
Within a ruby's crimson heart.

How lightly, on the silken couch,
Reclines the full, yet perfect form,
The soft brown tresses nestling close
About the milk white, rounded arm,
That half supports the drooping head,
And glossy weight of truant curls,
Escaping from the poisoning band
Of large, white oriental pearls.

So still she lies, while languidly
The lashes dark, and soft and sleek,
Veiling the lustrous orbs beneath,
Rest on the rose-tinged ivory cheek;
While over lip, and eyes and brow,
The warm enamored moonbeams creep,
Encircling with their light the form
Thus clasped within the arms of sleep.

REMEMBRANCE.

'Tis sweet to be remembered,
When far away I roam,
From those I love so fondly,
In my dear native home.

'Tis sweet to be remembered,
Where'er my steps I wend;
Give me the choicest gem of earth,
A true and constant friend.

'Tis sweet to be remembered,
In youth's resplendent day:
While yet no clouds of sorrow,
Drive happiness away.

'Tis sweet to be remembered,
Poets have sung before;
And sages sigh "remember."
Till Time shall be no more.

'Tis sweet to be remembered,
In pleasure's giddy train,
In hours of sad reflection,
In sorrow and in pain.

'Tis sweet to be remembered,
Whate'er my fate may be—
O! memory and human hope,
A mystery are ye.

'Tis sweet to be remembered,
And sad to be forgot—
Yes, deep indeed the anguish,
To be remembered not.

Hurrah for Lizzie Ficklin!

It is a fact, beyond all question that the women, one and all, are for the Little Giant. It would be a libel on the sex to say that they could for a moment lean towards a man of whom the N. Y. *Times* says "he looks so like the devil," while his opponent is renowned for looks combined with good sense — having evinced the latter and his admiration of female beauty by marrying the belle of Washington society. Out in Illinois every woman—excepting the one who shook her crinoline at the Cleveland *Herald's* correspondent just after Lincoln's nomination—is for Douglas. At Paris, Ill., the Democracy concluded to have a ratification meeting and invited Hon. O. B. Ficklin to deliver the speech of the occasion. Mr. F. was absent from home and his wife answered the Committee's letter in the following style:

CHARLESTON, Ill., June 29, 1860.

GENTLEMEN.—Mr. Ficklin has not returned from Washington, but may get home to-night; if so we shall claim his services in Charleston, as our ratification comes off to-morrow. The candidate for Vice President (Herschel V. Johnson) is one of Georgia's noblest and brightest sons—an able statesman the embodiment of honesty—a man of nerve and deliberation. I have known the Governor for years, only to admire him, and feel I canno say too much in his praise. His voice in Old Georgia, like the bugle blast of Rhoderick Dhu, is equal to a thousand men and ten thousand majority! The Democracy South—Douglas and anti-Douglas, "blue spirits and red" will unite in a mighty effort to save the country from the humiliation and disgrace of electing to the office of President one so unworthy the regards of patriots as Mr. Lincoln. Three cheers for Governor Johnson and three for Old Georgia. From one of Georgia's daughters.

LIZZIE FICKLIN.

Mr. Ficklin did not get home in time to speak, and the above letter, from a proud-spirited and true-hearted woman, was read, and went straight to the hearts of the audience, and met with loud and enthusiastic cheering from all the vast crowd. Three cheers were given with a will for Douglas and Johnson, and then three more for Mrs. LIZZIE FICKLIN.

PICTORIAL PLAIN DEALER

FOR THE

PRESIDENTIAL CAMPAIGN.

THE CAMPAIGN DEALER will be issued every Saturday, and continued until after the Presidential Election, the last number containing the grand result. It will be a

PICTORIAL PAPER,

Devoted to "Plain Dealing," Popular Sovereignty and the Presidency. It will go for

DOUGLAS & JOHNSON,

Popular Sovereignty and the People. It will go against Black Republicanism and Bolters, Higher Lawism and Secessionism, and will oppose every body who does no go against them. We are in the midst of a Revolution, bloodless as yet! Disunion is determined upon by the *politicians* of the South. Their candidates are in the [illegible]. What the result may be, God only knows. He that is wisest [illegible] the future deepest.

Every number of the CAMPAIGN DEALER will contain an

"Original Cut,"

designed and engraved by our own Artists. As this is probably the only

Pictorial Campaigner

That will be published in the United States, and will be gotten up with great care and expense for political use, we hope Democrats everywhere will use extra exertions to give it a National circulation.

TERMS, &c.

One Copy	50 Cents
Five Copies to one Post Office	$2 00
Ten " "	4 00
Twenty " "	5 00

☞ COUNTY COMMITTEES, CLUBS, and other Political Associations furnished in quantites for gratuitous distribution at $1 50 per hundred or $10 per thousand.

☞ Now is the time to get into the hands of the people a cheap, cheerful, spicy and spirited Political Paper, precisely adapted to the wants of the party and the temper of the times. We hope every Democrat will make himself an active Agent for the "CAMPAIGN DEALER," and secure the names of all in his immediate neighborhood forthwith. Address,

J. W GRAY,
CLEVELAND, OHIO.

READ, READ,

READ!

AGENTS, ATTENTION!

We want Agents in every nook and corner of the United States, to sell our Campaign Songsters. From $10 to $50 can be made at ever political meeting, from $5 to $50 can be made in every village, town and city, by selling our Campaign Songsters, Badges, &c.

THE

DEMOCRATIC CAMPAIGN SONGSTER, NO. 1,

Is just issued, containing a choice collection of Democratic Campaign Songs.

Single copies 10 cents postage paid, on receipt of price. To agents we will send 20 copies by mail postage paid for $1. By express we will send 100 copies for $4, the Agent paying freight. Address

AMERICAN PUBLISHING HOUSE,
Cincinnati, Ohio.

N. B.—We will pay $10 for the best, $5 for the second best, $3 each for the next five best, and $1 00 for the next ten best Democratic Campaign Songs, that are sent to us before the 25th of July, 1860

AMERICAN PUBLISHING HOUSE,
Cincinnati, Ohio.

DEMOCRATIC BADGES,

With a Likeness of STEPHEN A. DOUGLAS, the Democratic candidate for President. Printed on Silk Ribbon, 2½ by 6 inches.

Single Badges, 13 cents. To Agents 16 Badges for $1 00; 35 for $2, or 60 or $3. Sent, postage paid, to any person, on receipt of the money. Address

AMERICAN PUBLISHING HOUSE,

1t* CINCINNATI, OHIO.

The Rail  Splitter.

"The People of the United States are the Rightful Masters of both Congress and Courts."—Abraham Lincoln.

VOL. I. CHICAGO, ILL., SATURDAY, AUGUST 11, 1860. NO. 8.

THE UNION NOW!--THE UNION EVER!!!

Who cries dissolve? What traitor hand
Would rend this sacred chain asunder?
Each link a memory of the band
Who forged it 'mid despotic thunder.
Has Wonder lost her stolid gaze?
Is Reason trampled down by Madness?
Shall Freedom's temple be ablaze?
No, patriots, no! Ne'er say dissever!
The Union now—the Union ever!

Stand forth the fiend—for man there's none—
Who shrinks not from the dread ambition
Of clouding Liberty's bright sun,
At cost of more than hell's perdition!
Living, by conscience ever stung—
Dead, a recusant's page in story—
Whose infamy would e'er be sung,
Till Nature yields and Time grows hoary.
Hope, patriots, hope! Ne'er say dissever!
The Union now—the Union ever!

But hark! the North sends forth a voice—
The loyal South returns her greeting—
While the East and West with shouts rejoice,
And hail the glad fraternal meeting.
Their banners to the sky are flung,
While every breeze the folds are kissing;
We gaze the firmament among,
And not a single star is missing.
Cheer, patriots, cheer! Ne'er say dissever!
The Union now—the Union ever!

Mt. Vernon's tomb its gates outspread—
Look where the rev'rent shade is weeping!
While Monticello's sage, though dead,
A fearful ghostful vigil's keeping.
Yet list! another spirit's moan;
"Ye have a boon, nor scarce deserve it!
That lost, earth's hope is ever gone;
By the Eternal, then preserve it!"
Up, patriots, up! Ne'er say dissever!
The Union now—the Union ever!

A Calm Appeal to Conservatives.

We are aware that many of our allies in the old Whig & American ranks still hesitate as to where their path of duty lies in the pending Presidential campaign. To all who now occupy this doubtful position, and are "halting between two opinions," we commend the following earnest appeal from the Buffalo *Commercial Advertiser*, formerly a leading American paper, but now zealously enlisted in the cause of Republicanism:

Whom will you support? What candidate is most in accordance with your principles? And can you, by voting for him, do him or yourself any practical good? Expediency, though often sneered at, is after all, only another name for practicality. Doubtless Bell and Everett are the candidates having the strongest claim upon your sympathies. Their platform is in their political history, and that you approve. If a vote were a mere expression of opinion, a declaration of principle, you could come nearest your private sentiments by voting for them. But a vote is something else. It is not a principle, not necessarily an expression of principle, but an engine of power by which you endeavor to produce certain results in harmony with your principles. In using it you should endeavor to make it practical, to do the most good for the principle, and not to make it a mere empty word of approval, a compliment to men who are not to be benefitted by it. Now, will a vote for Bell and Everett be anything more or less than this? You know that by no possibility can John Bell secure the electoral vote of this State. In voting for him you assume the position of a neutral in the war, and that, too, when your positive action is needed, when a vote for John Bell is half a vote for the Democratic party. Compare your own position with that of the Republicans of Maryland. They will vote for John Bell, not because they prefer him to Lincoln, but because they wish to do some active good in the campaign. And were we in Maryland we should look upon a vote cast for Lincoln there as quite as impolitic as a vote cast for Bell here. It is purely a question of locality. The opposition has three wings the Republican party North, the Union party South, and the People's party in Pennsylvania, New Jersey and Delaware. These three are one in their main purposes. The first and last act together now; the union of the second with them is a dead certainty after the 4th of March next.

We have not alluded as yet to the possibility of your voting for Douglas or Breckinridge. We do not see how you can do so in honor, or with any degree of consistency. In all matters of local or State policy, canals, railroads, the power of corporate monopolies, and the numerous questions which affect your taxation at home, and the development of the resources of the resources of the State, you are diametrically opposed to the Democracy. To you, practically, these questions are far more important than that of slavery. You cannot honorably aid in placing the Democracy in power against the best interests of the State. But on the slavery issue, how near are you to Douglas? You support the compromises of 1850. Ten years have proved their wisdom. Four years after their enactment, Mr. Douglas, actuated by motives purely selfish or purely subservient to Southern aggression, introduced and carried through Congress the Kansas-Nebraska bill, which your leader, Mr. Fillmore, has strongly characterized as the Pandora's box of evil. Under the wise and prudent administration of Mr. Fillmore, aided by the last grand energies of the dying Clay, the slavery question was adjusted on a fair and honorable basis, and accepted by both the Whig and Democratic parties in 1852. Mr. Douglas re-opened the whole issue, spread new dissensions, broke the peace which Mr. Fillmore had ratified, plunged the country into fierce excitement, and reddened the plains of Kansas with blood. Will you now reward him for this? Will you vote to forward a policy which makes this quarrel eternal, takes it out of the hands and power of Congress, and refers it to the fierce passions of a frontier people, without law or authority to guide them, and compels them to resort to civil war as the only practical arbitrament?

As to Breckinridge, there is at least in him a prospect of the settlement of the slavery issue. He wipes it out by the sacrifice of all the rights of the North, by enthroning Southern sectionalism and establishing slavery, with all its vast consequences, social and political, upon the domain we have conquered in the name of liberty.

But Lincoln, you fear, is sectional—supported by a geographical party. Will it be a geographical when he is elected? Must he not then have a party at the South, and is it not ready made to his hand in the Union organization? In a month after his election, when Southern conservatives are in his cabinet, when Southern Whig statesmen in House and Senate support his policy, when Southern men are raised to high offices and are scattered all over the Slave States to defend and support the grand old Union of which he is the representative man, where will your geographical party be then? Cannot you act with some faith in the future, some foresight, some perception of the inevitable course of events? The cry of disunion has already ceased at the South, and the people of that region are avowedly reconciling themselves to Lincoln's election. And why should they not? Lincoln only echoes Henry Clay, when in his noble speech of February 6, 1850, the old Whig champion declared in the United States Senate: "Sir, I have said that I never could vote for it, and I repeat that I never can and never will vote for it; and no earthly power shall ever make me vote to plant slavery where slavery does not exist!" Two weeks later, on the 20th of February, 1850, he said again in the same arena: "From the earliest moment when I could consider the institution of slavery, I have held, and I have said that from that day down to the present again and again, and I shall go to the grave with the opinion, that it is an evil, a social and political evil, and that it is a wrong as it respects those who are subject to the institution of slavery." Friends, what Henry Clay said then, in that most alarming struggle of sections, may be said now. If not, if we are to be choked down by abject fear as not to repeat the words of our gallant old leader, then have we fallen on evil times. Lincoln is the follower of Clay. He sucked in the milk of his political gospel from that most honored statesman, and we at least, and you, we believe, will rally to the support of a man who so nearly represents the author of the American system.

Fred. P. Stanton at St. Louis.

Fred. P. Stanton, late secretary of Gov. Walker, in Kansas, addressed a large Republican meeting in St. Louis, on the evening of July 23. The meeting was held in Carr square, where a platform was erected, decorated with Chinese lanterns, torches, transparencies, &c. The *Democrat* says six thousand persons were present. The arrival of Lincoln and Hamlin clubs, and of "Wide Awakes," was welcomed by enthusiastic cheering. Mr. Stanton was received with cheers. He said he was present at the solicitation of Mr. Blair, that he might aid in returning him to Congress. He referred particularly to his concurrence with Mr. Blair in the policy of sending free blacks to Central or South America, where they shall find a chance to elevate themselves. He himself, while in Congress, as chairman of the Naval committee, reported a bill nicknamed "The ebony line of steamers," which proposed to establish a line of African steamers that should assist the Colonization society in the exportation of negroes. The bill failed to pass and that was the end of it. He indorsed the soundness of Mr. Blair's views of protection, and his courage to meet all issues that are likely to be raised in Congress without any dodging. Mr. Stanton then proceeded to speak of certain events in Kansas, which had fallen under his own observation. He said that for ten years he was a Democratic Congressman from Tennessee, that he was disinclined to become Gov. Walker's secretary, but yielded to the persuasion of the President and the Cabinet. Of the condition of the territory, on his arrival, he said;

"But the singular fact was revealed when we arrived there that the minority was ruling the majority, and imposing on them measures that were hateful and obnoxious to all their sentiments. The great mass of the people derided the territorial government, laughed at it, and would not have anything to do with it. Governor Walker and myself resolved to try to persuade the majority to get things in their own hands by voting. Governor Walker pledged his honor that they should be treated fairly, and have a full opportunity to exhibit their strength, if in a majority; and we endeavored by speeches, and all means in our power, to get them to take the position of the Governor. They said it was idle; that border ruffians had control of everything. Every Magistrate, every Constable, and every Sheriff was appointed simply to defraud Free State men."

He explained how elections were carried, thus:

"One day I was in my office alone, after it was well understood that the Free State men had carried the election by a large majority. A messenger came in with a big roll of paper, which he gave to me as the returns from Oxford. I asked him: 'Are you sure these are the returns from Oxford?' He said yes, and grew serious about it. I broke the seal and unrolled the package, the same as a shopkeeper would a roll of silk, and threw it from me on the floor about fifty feet. It was a list of 1,600 or 1,700 names, purporting to be a list of voters at a small village on the border, not containing probably twenty voters. I expressed surprise and looked at the man again. This time there was a twinkle in his eye, but he insisted that these were the returns. I bowed him out of the office and locked up the papers. A few days after Gov. Walker and myself examined these papers, and decided that they bore on their face the most incontestable evidences of fraud, and that we would reject them. This, however, was not all. Hitching up a vehicle we went a journey of one hundred miles to Oxford, and found it a small place of about sixty houses, two-thirds of them on the Missouri side, and the rest in Kansas. We went there *incog.*, and before they found out whom we were we inquired about the election. Well, they said men came here and voted from all directions, but principally from Missouri. Even at that, they said that there were not over 200 or 300 voted at the outside. It leaked out, however, whom we were, and then they shut down and didn't tell a thing.—We found out, however, that two clerks had hired a house about one mile from town, and had been busy for two days, fitting up this list of voters. We rejected the returns. As soon as it was known in Washington, the tone and policy of the administration became changed, Governor Walker was forced to resign; and as for myself, I was unceremoniously kicked out of my office."

He claimed that he had been a democrat all his life and that he had not materially changed now. He charged that the President and the party in Congress had drifted away from Democratic principles. He referred to the Douglas and the anti-Lecompton Democrats in the following terms:

"You are all aware that in company with Governor Walker and myself there were others who sustained us throughout, and known generally as anti-Lecompton Democrats, led on by Douglas. I haven't an unkind word against him, but I shall not vote for him. I admire him to some extent for the position he occupies. I believe Popular Sovereignty to be correct, but not as embodied in the Kansas-Nebraska bill, because the people of Kansas had no chance to assert their majority. Douglas sustained them for a while; but he has fallen from it. Had he sustained that position I would not now be advocating Lincoln and Hamlin for the Presidency. Douglas has not maintained his position to the end. After the Democratic party had abandoned its principles, he ought not to have gone to Charleston at all. He should have hoisted the standard of true Democracy, and defied the Charleston Democracy; and this, gentlemen, is what I, in my humble way, advised him to do. He thought different, and wished to purify the party. I told him that they would crush him, and they have done it. They decapitated him from the chairmanship of the Committee on Territories, and Senator Green substituted in his place. I thought then he would take my advice, but I was chagrined to find that he didn't meet this outrage as I would have done."

He closed his speech with an earnest exhortation that all voters should strive to return Mr. Blair to Congress, to vindicate the purity of the ballot-box, and contribute to the election of Lincoln and Hamlin.

OUR PORTRAIT GALLERY.--No. 8.

DOUGLAS PULLING CHESTNUTS FROM THE FIRE FOR JO LANE.

For "The Rail Splitter."

RAIL [illegible] —No. 8.

Quoth jocko, as he cocked his tail,
To win the North, I can but fail;
But if the little bustling giant,
Will play into my hands so pliant,
And beard the Lion in his den,
By winning Suckerdom and Penn—
The South is mine, and I shall grace
The crafty *james buchanan's* place.

Gov. Reeder on Douglas.

The distinguished Pennsylvanian, Gov. Reeder, is now on a visit to Kansas, where he seems to be quite popular. He made a speech at Lawrence in which allusion is made to various incidents which occurred while he was Governor of that Territory. And having incidentally to speak of Douglas, he gives the following, which may be regarded as his "private opinion publicly expressed," of that distinguished individual:

The Governor then passed in his remarks to a consideration of national politics. He showed how the Republican party had grown up by a necessity, out of the aggressions of the slave power. He defended it triumphantly against the attacks of its enemies, and showed it to be the guardian of popular rights and the defender of the Constitution and Union. He told how he had been a life-long Democrat, but he had been forced to leave that party by its foul treachery to the rights of the people. He commented in terms of great severity upon the course of Mr. Douglas. He said that, previous to Mr. Douglas' celebrated Kansas report, so full of all manner of slander and falsehood against the people of Kansas, he (Gov. Reeder,) being still connected with the Democratic party, had visited Washington, and, at Mr. Douglas' request had met him, and had several long interviews with him, and fully posted him in regard to the actual facts of the Kansas difficulties. Other gentlemen from Kansas, acquaintances of Mr. Douglas, had done the same, so that he perfectly understood the true state of the case. Under these circumstances Gov. Reeder said he looked with great interest for Mr. Douglas' report, anticipating that he would do justice to the Free State people. Judge, then, of his surprise, when, upon taking it up, he found it filled with the grossest assaults and slanders upon them, the facts of the case entirely suppressed or misrepresented, and the whole report a burden of fallacy and deceit. "I threw it from me in disgust," said the Governor, "and from that day forward, I have had no confidence whatever in the honesty or sincerity of Stephen A. Douglas."

☞ Parson Brownlow is decidedly opposed to any fusion with either Democratic faction. He says:

In this split, we are pleased to see the factions so equally divided, and we hope, in their wrestle, they will make a *dog fall* of it! Let all honest, patriotic Union-loving men stand aloof from both, praying in their family devotion, that God in mercy to the country may politically damn both factions!

What Has he Done?

We will give a "pretty thing" to any rampant Douglas man who will point us to a single act of any consequence performed by Douglas during the session of Congress just closed. Take any question of importance to the people, upon which an issue can be made, and upon which a first-class statesman ought to occupy a firm open, unequivocal stand, and show where Douglas has spoken or voted for or against it. He has kept mum, with an eye single to the Presidency.

When the Senate committees were being re-constructed in such a manner, and for such a purpose, that any Senator with a spark of manliness, independence or dignity would have been there, and made himself heard—in other words, when the Senate was heaping insult and indignity upon Douglas—where was he? He had the *pleurisy!*

When the death of Broderick was announced—the man who had died fighting Douglas' battles—when tributes were to be paid to his memory, and when Douglas, of all living men should have been there, among the foremost in honoring the memory of the martyr—where was he? He had the *diarrhœa*.

When the Homestead Bill was to be voted upon, giving to the poor laboring man a free home, for the use and support of himself and his family—where was Douglas? He had a *sore throat!*

When the bill for the admission of Kansas was up, where was Douglas, the champion of Popular Sovereignty, who had divided the Democratic party upon the Kansas question? He was *paired off!*

So we might go on. Whenever a question was up, on which a Senator might show himself to be a *man*, or upon which an issue might be made before the people, or when his enemies were handling him and his dogmas without mercy, Douglas was invariably absent—cause, pleurisy, diarrhea, &c. No! he opened his mouth on one occasion—that was when he introduced his invasion bill, under the pretense of protecting the Slave State against invasions and insurrections, but in reality to gag free speech in the North, and gain the smiles of the Southern lords, who had been kicking and cuffing him for more than a year. Here Douglas stood up and talked fluently and bombastically, but the effort failed in the effect for which it was intended. We believe he also produced a rehash of his Squatter Sovereignty harangues and Magazine essays, but that likewise fell stillborn to the earth.

Such is Douglas—called, by way of burlesque, a "Statesman," the "Little Giant," and so forth—whom intelligent people are coolly and impudently asked to vote for!—[*Kansas Chief*.

The National Finances.

The posting of the books at Washington on the 30th of June—the close of the fiscal year—shows a balance of only $4,000,000 in the national treasury subject to draft, $10,000,000 less than ought to be there according to the estimates of the Secretary of the Treasury in December last—an error which, remembering its "Democratic" source, ought not to excite surprise. It is now probable that the country is in debt no less than $65,000,000—one of the results of Democratic misrule. When the Democracy took upon themselves the work of reconciling the country to the Dred Scott decision, there was a balance of nearly, if not quite $20,000,000 in the treasury.—They have squandered this sum, spent all of the current receipts and run up the debt to the enormous amount that we have set down above. The purchase of enough "pure patriots" to insure the endorsement of that Dred Scott iniquity by the party has proved to be unexpectedly expensive. But between army, navy, coal, transportation and victualling contracts, the whole has been accomplished; and Dred Scott is endorsed; but the tax-payers will be compelled to foot the bills.—[*Pa. Tel.*

How Slaves Drive Out Free Labor.

The Missouri Republican State Central Committee in its late address says:

There are now in Missouri at least fifty thousand men who cannot get full employment for their energies and enterprise, owing to the depression of the past two years, and there are now in Missouri more than one hundred thousand slaves, occupying and filling the most lucrative agricultural and mechanical positious of the interior. It is the demand of the Republican party that slave labor shall make room for free white labor, and take itself away.

☞ The following good hit is from a speech of Hon. F. P. Blair, Jr., speaking of Mr. Lincoln he says:—"He is called a rail splitter. Well my friends, he has commenced splitting rails again, and he is making the Democratic party into a nice stack of them. He has got them split in half now, and if there is any rail-timber in that party, you will find that "Old Abe" will have enough rails out of it to fence in the whole country. The fact is, that Mr. Douglas is not a very good specimen of rail-timber out in the West; he is rather stumpy, rather short. But my friends, I think "Old Abe" will split him up into staves to make whisky barrels of. We are bound to put him to some use, if any use is to be had out of him, and they do say that he holds whisky amazingly well.

Stephen Arnold Douglas.

Favorable circumstances, rather than moral integrity and statesmanlike qualities, have given this gentleman an enviable notoriety, but now a change of circumstances threaten to bury him in unenviable obscurity. The history of our country affords but one similar instance of an unmerited rise, speedily followed by universal execration.

Less than ten years ago, Mr. Douglas was the leader of the Democratic party. The Senate heard his "stumpish oration," and submitted to his haughty dictation. In the eye of the populace, his fearlessness, energy, and bluff suavity, made him the *beau ideal* of the statesman. But, in an evil hour for his fame and fortunes, he resolved, at all hazards, to win the Presidency. The Northern Democrats had given so many proofs of party fidelity, by submitting to Southern dictation, that he felt sure of their support. He thought he only needed to lay a great sacrifice at the feet of his political masters, and his election would be secure.

His life-long devotion to their interest was not sufficient. They demanded the pound of flesh; and, to gratify an inordinate ambition, he prepared his breast for the knife. Through his instrumentality the 'Missouri Compromise" was repealed. The Southern shylocks were jubilant. The name of Douglas became a household word with the breeders of Virginia and planters of South Carolina.

But mutterings of wrath were heard at the North. Even in the cotton-dyed cities of Philadelphia and New York, the "Little Giant" met with a chilling reception. At Trenton he was saluted with hisses and groans. He went home, but his constituents were not in a pleasant mood. He endeavored to justify himself in their estimation, but the meeting broke up in confusion.

Had it not been for the evil days of Frank Pierce and James Buchanan, Mr. But their deeper degradation, made him appear in a less repulsive guise. They went so far beyond him in their submission to slaveocracy, that his treason to liberty was partly forgotten. With a tact—of which he did not think himself possessed—he endeavored to take advantage of Buchanan's unpopularity to mend his own political future.

He mounted the hobby of Squatter Sovereignty and rode furiously. His hopes were high. His friends prophesied that he would win the race, but what slave can hope for success who dares expostulate with a tyrant? The North heard his professions of repentance with incredulity. He might be on the side of Constitutional freedom *now*, but his activity in repealing the Missouri Compromise was not forgotten. The South turned from him in disgust. The Democrats of the South will rather ruin the party than acknowledge his leadership, and they make their election accordingly.

We bid adieu to S. A. Douglas. He will soon disappear from public view, ruined in health, fortune, and reputation.

Prefers Lincoln to Douglas.

The editor of the Cumberland (Md.) Telegraph, the American organ, referring to a statement that the opposition party of Alabama had, in Convention, repudiated Bell and Everett, and declared their purpose to support Breckinridge and Lane, says:

We prefer Mr. Lincoln before either of the Democratic nominees, and if driven from our support of Mr. Bell by the trickery of our leading men—if our party is to be sold out to either wing of the Democracy—then we are for Lincoln, with tens of thousands of others in good old Maryland.

An Affecting Epitaph.

The following inscription on a monument erected over the political remains of a Western Senator is not very bad:

Here Lyeth ye Remaines of a Lytle Giante, who was kild in ye irrepressibile conflicte for ye Prisidency, at Charles Town May the 2, 1860. Ambitious youth, take warning by his fall, and never stryve to fill ye place for which you are too small.

What Caleb Cushing Says of Lincoln.

In a conversation between Caleb Cushing and Col. Parker, author of Reminiscences of Rufus Choate, Cushing said:—"Abraham Lincoln is a much abler man than is generally supposed, even in his own party. In his canvass with Douglas he beat him in argument, beat him at law, beat him in wit, and the published debates of that canvass will sustain this assertion."

Straws.

The La Crosse (Wis.) *Nord Stern*, heretofore a zealous and influential organ of the Democracy in the German language, hauls down the Douglas flag and runs up the Lincoln.

Judge Grant, of Davenport, declines the honor of being Democratic candidate for Supreme Judge in Iowa, and Le Grand Boyington, Democrat, of being candidate for State Elector.

☞ "Why," said Prince John Van Buren the other day, "Why is President Buchanan like a tallow-chandler?" The Prince said, "Because all his works are *wicked*, and all his wicked works are brought to *light!*" Pretty good, eh?

Recapture of Col. James Buchanan Cross.

From the Philadelphia Bulletin, of Friday.

Col. James Buchanan Cross was last night recaptured at a house in the Twentieth Ward, and restored to his old quarters at Moyamensing prison. The fugitive was traced to his lair after a patient and careful search, and he was finally captured by the exercise of a ruse.

It seems that on Saturday morning, after the escape of Cross from the hands of tipstave Porter, he was rapidly driven down the "Neck" for a short distance, and the wagon was then turned about and driven up town at a moderate pace. By this means the fugitive quietly sought a hiding place in the upper part of the city, while the police, thrown upon a wrong scent, were searching for him down town. Cross went to a house in the neighborhood of Columbia avenue and Broad street, where he remained until Sunday night, when he went to a small dwelling, occupied by a poor woman, in a small clump of houses which stand back from Columbia avenue, between Twelfth and Thirteenth streets. A house had been rented for the Colonel in an out of the way location, and to this he was to have been removed last night.

A party of detectives, under the lead of District Attorney Mann, proceeded to the house at about 11 P. M. disguised as laboring men, and after waiting some time for Cross to make his appearance outside, they stationed a guard about the house, and then rapped for admission. The door was opened by the woman of the house, and at the instant it was opened, Mr. Mann and several other officers rushed in past the woman and up stairs. The house has but one room on a floor. There was no Cross on the first floor, and on the second a man was found lying on a bed. This man was not the object of their search, and continuing on up stairs, the fugitive was found coolly sitting upon a trunk, and in his shirt sleeves. Excepting that he was divested of his coat, he was dressed just as he was when he slipped off on Saturday. He had laid aside his wig and shaved off his moustache and whiskers; but the officers had no difficulty in recognizing him, even without his bland manner and musical voice.

The prisoner was unembarrassed and polite as usual, remarking about the scantiness of the furniture in the room, and expressing regret that he had no chairs to offer his visitors. Mr. Porter, the officer from whom the forger had escaped, became very much excited, and bursting into a hysterical laugh, he seized Cross by the collar, and screamed out :—"Old fellow, it makes me the happiest man in the world to see you. There is nobody I wanted to see worse!"

To this the adept coolly replied that he would be happy to see him (Mr. Porter,) but not under existing circumstances.

Porter remarked that if the prisoner got away from him again he would have to be smarter than ever.

Cross replied that the officers had the advantage of him as they were all strangers to him, intimating that regular officers, in their ordinary dress, would have had some trouble in trapping him.

The recaptured rogue was taken at once to prison in Mr. Mann's wagon, the District-Attorney retaining his laborer's "rig," and driving the horses. So complete was his disguise that the prisoner did not recognise him until they arrived at the prison and Mr. Mann jestingly demanded his fare.

On the road to Moyamensing, the prisoner jested with his captors regarding his escape and recapture. He pretended to sympathize deeply with Mr. Porter, who had fallen into disgrace upon his account, and who had become an object of suspicion. He said he could not help the matter at the time, but he had determined to make Porter a rich man before he died!

Cross was finally lodged in his cell about midnight, and we presume that after the experience of the past, he will have to remain in strong quarters until the law is done with him.

A Thrilling Scene.

FOUR MEXICAN DROVERS AND THEIR CATTLE SURROUNDED BY FIRE—TWO MEN CONSUMED.

Correspondence of the Missouri Democrat.

BARCLAY'S FORT, N. M., July 9, 1860.

A friend, just arrived from Santa Fe, states that four Mexican herders were driving a herd of cattle through the mountains north of that place, a short time since, when the following incident occurred, which I give as I received it :—

The mountains were on fire at the time, but thinking the way clear before them, they proceeded up a valley until they found their way barred by an impenetrable wall of fire; in alarm they hastily retraced their steps, in the vain hope that escape might still be possible. But alas! they were still too late; fire had closed the avenue by which they had entered the valley, and a broad belt of flame encircled them on every side, the area of which was rapidly diminishing every moment. The long drouth had rendered the rubbish and undergrowth below as dry as tinder, and the flames licked them up with fearful rapidity; and springing upward, caught the pine leaves above, glossy with rosin, and then leaping from tree to tree, forming a billow of fire awful to behold. The affrighted herd, bellowing with fear, dashed through the flames, the most of them escaping badly burned, but some perished. Two of the herders attempted to follow them; but who can breathe in such an atmosphere, walk on burning coals, enveloped in flame, and live?

A few steps only were taken, when their nerves became contracted with the intense heat, their limbs refused to perform their office, and they sunk shrieking on a bed of fire, never more to rise. Their comrades heard the dying groans of their companions, the wild bellowing of the herd, as they dashed through the sea of fire; and the roaring and crackling of the flames, as they came surging onward, and maddened by despair, they dashed wildly from side to side, eagerly seeking that which they dare not hope to find, and already suffering in anticipation, the agonies of a death too fearful to think of, when a huge rock barred their way, and they saw with a thrill of joy, that a small spring of water gushed out at its foot. Hope revived within them at the sight, and with an energy such as emergency only could inspire, they improved the few remaining moments ere the flames should reach them, in preparing to resist them. Every thing combustible was removed, until the increasing heat forced them to desist, then inserting some dry branches in the crevices of the rock above the spring, they saturated their blankets with water and spread them out upon them and seating themselves under their shelter, continued to apply the water as fast as the scanty supply permitted.

Ashes, coals and burning branches fell thickly around them, and their hopes fluctuated rapidly between hope and despair, as their chances of escape increased or lessened. Moments seemed lengthened into hours, and doubtless more than the agonies of death were passed by these poor herders, ere hope ripened into certainty, and they knew that they were indeed saved, as "brands from the burning."

Respectfully yours, S. B. WATROUS.

Literary News.

"*A Political Text Book for* 1860, compiled by HORACE GREELEY and JOHN F. CLEVELAND. Price one dollar." Besides a record of the Congressional Caucusses, National Conventions, Platforms, &c., &c., of 1860, with the letters of acceptance of the several candidates, this book contains speeches of Messrs. Lincoln, Douglas, Seward, Breckenridge, Hamlin, H. V. Johnson, Benjamin, &c., with the important letters, propositions, and votes of the foregoing, and of Messrs. Webster, Bell, Cass, Van Buren, Everett, Bates, Jeff. Davis, S. P. Chase, J. L. Pugh, Clayton, Wilmot, Yancey, &c., &c. At the close, is presented at a single view the vote by States and counties throughout the Union of every Presidential Election since (and including) 1840, with the latest votes for Governor and Congress in all the contested or doubtful States.

"*Rosa, or The Parisian Girl,*" is a pleasant little story for the young, giving a truthful picture of domestic life in France. It is translated from the French of Madame de Pressensé by Mrs. J. C. FLETCHER. Published by Harper & Brothers, and for sale here by W. B. Sprague, Jr.

"*Studies in Animal Life,*" by GEORGE HENRY LEWES. A delightful volume, descriptive of observations through the microscope of the habits and structure of some of those forms of vitality which are so minute as almost to escape notice. It is less intended for the instruction of the scientific than for the entertainment of the general reader. Published by Harper & Brothers, and for sale here by W. B. Sprague, Jr.

"*Jack Hopeton, or The Adventures of a Georgian,*" is a lively, spirited story of Southern life, giving a vivid, but hardly exaggerated picture, of scenes and character in that part of the Union. It is by WILLIAM W. TURNER, of Putnam Co., Georgia. Published by Derby & Jackson, and for sale here by W. B. Sprague, Jr.

"*The Queens of Society,*" by GRACE and PHILIP WHARTON, being entertaining biographies of noted women of the last two centuries. Among them are Sarah, Duchess of Marlborough, Madame Roland, Lady Montagu, the Duchess of Devonshire, Miss Landon, Madame De Sévigné, Lady Morgan, the Duchess of Gordan, Madame Recamier, Lady Hervey, Madame De Staël, Mrs. Thrale, Lady Caroline Lamb, Mrs. Damer, the Marquise du Deffand, the Countess of Pembroke, and the Marquise de Mantenon. The life of each of these celebrated personages has all the interest of a romance. The volume is illustrated with engravings. Published by Harper & Brothers, and for sale here by W. B. Sprague, Jr.

STARTLING AND SPLENDID DISCOVERY.—We find this "item" in the N. Y. Express:—It is said that Mayor Tiemann, at his paint factory in Manhattanville, has accidentally made a discovery that threatens to revolutionize horticulture. One of the workmen having thrown some light liquid green paint of a particular kind on a flower-bed occupied by white anemones, the flowers have since made their appearance with petals as green as grass. The paint had in it a peculiar and very penetrating chemical mixture, which Mr. Tiemann has since applied, with other colors, to other plants, annual, biennial, and the shrub kind—the result being invariably that the flowers so watered took the hue of the liquid deposited at their roots.

EVENING JOURNAL.

SATURDAY EVENING, AUGUST 11, 1860.

REPUBLICAN NOMINATIONS.

FOR PRESIDENT,

ABRAHAM LINCOLN.

FOR VICE-PRESIDENT,

HANNIBAL HAMLIN.

REPUBLICAN STATE CONVENTION.

The Republican Electors of the State of New York are requested to choose two delegates from each Assembly District, to meet in State Convention in the City of SYRACUSE, ON WEDNESDAY, THE TWENTY-SECOND DAY OF AUGUST NEXT, at 11 o'clock A. M., for the purpose of presenting candidates to be supported for the offices of Governor, Lieutenant Governor, Canal Commissioner, State Prison Inspector, and Presidential Electors, and for the transaction of such other business as may come before the Convention.

Dated July 19, 1860.

JAMES KELLY,	HENRY FITZHUGH,
B. F. MANIERRE,	S. D. HUNGERFORD,
JAMES W. NYE,	WILLIAM SMYTH,
E. M. MADDEN,	G. J. J. BARBER,
D. STRONG,	H. O. GOODWIN,
CHARLES L. BEALE,	S. C. CUYLER,
C. R. RICHARDS,	R. B. VAN VALKENBURGH
T. R. HORTON,	S. H. WELLS,
EDWARD DODD,	E. R. REYNOLDS,
W. A. DART,	E. G. SPAULDING,
JOHN WILKINSON,	WILLIAM BRISTOL,
	JAMES B. COOPER,

Republican State Committee.

☞ SEE FOURTH PAGE for Miscellany.

Ward Primary Meetings on Monday.

The Republicans of the several Wards should remember that on Monday, from 12 to 1 o'clock, they are to elect Ward Delegates to the District Conventions called to appoint Delegates to the State Convention. The places of meeting are subjoined :—

Republican General Committee Rooms, 356 BROADWAY, AUGUST 3, 1860.—At a meeting of the Republican General Committee, held on Friday evening, 3d inst., the following resolutions were unanimously adopted :—

Resolved, That the several Assembly District Committees (except the Fourth, which has been called for the 6th inst.,) be requested to hold Conventions on THURSDAY THE SIXTEENTH inst., at 12 o'clock, M., for the purpose of choosing two delegates to represent their respective Districts in the Republican State Convention to be held at Syracuse on the 22d inst.

Resolved, That elections by ballot be held in the several Wards of the city on MONDAY THE THIRTEENTH inst., between the hours of 12 M. and 1 P. M., at the places hereinafter designated, for the election of Delegates to said Assembly District Conventions; and that the Republican electors of each Town appoint Delegates in such manner as Town Committees may direct—Delegates to consist of five persons from each Ward and Town.

Resolved, That the polls in the city of Albany be held at the following places, to wit :—

1st Ward—G. Schreiber's, 79 Schuyler street.
2d " —Wide-Awake Club Room, 148 South Pearl.
3d " —Daniel Halpin's, 248 Broadway.
4th " —Justices' Court Room.
5th " —Brooks' Exchange Hotel, 25 Maiden lane.
6th " —Wide-Awake Headquarters, 697 Broadway.
8th " —Wide-Awake Headquarters, 58 Clinton av.
9th " —Republican Headquarters, corner Hawk and Washington avenue.
10th " —John Cooke's, 164 State street.

B. H. MILLS, President.

THOMAS J. COWELL, JAMES O'SULLIVAN, } Secretaries.

From the New York World.

It has been a matter of common talk, for some time past, that the Republicans in this State were not entirely at peace among themselves. As has been stated before, a large portion of the party took umbrage at Mr. GREELEY's opposition to Mr. SEWARD in the Chicago Convention, and measures have been taken to thwart what political plans he might make with reference to the approaching State Convention at Syracuse. As an instance of what is doing, it may be mentioned here that a secret caucus was held at the Everett House, a few evenings since, which was convened by a circular, sent by prominent Republicans in Albany to certain gentlemen of the Eighth ward, in this city. The document contained the request that the persons addressed, together with any others that they might choose to invite, would confer with each other concerning the proper men to be proposed as delegates to Syracuse. It also suggested the names of two gentlemen, both of whom are quite well known in the ward for their strong Republican antecedents.

The caucus met, as stated above, but failed to come to any definite determination as to future action. Most of those present openly expressed their dislike of such dictation, especially as it came from politicians out of the city. Of course, the object sought by those who issued the circular was, that New York city should be represented in the State Convention by delegates opposed to Mr. GREELEY. This fact, together with the efforts that are making for renominating Gov. MORGAN, rendered the primary elections of last evening unusually exciting.

Had such an article appeared in the *Herald*, where such gossip belongs, instead of the *World*, where we look for at least "a *kernel* of wheat in a bushel of chaff," it would have passed without a word of comment.

To the *World*, therefore, we say that its entire article—warp and filling—is fabulous. No such "Circular," nor *any* Circular, has been "sent by prominent Republicans in Albany," to the "eighth," or any other ward in New York. Mr. SEWARD's friends have not dreamed, by "Circular" or otherwise, of interfering with any of "Mr. GREELEY's political plans."

We speak, of course, for ourselves and for such Republicans as act with us, at whom it is evident the *World's* article is aimed. If there was, from any Republicans, such a "Circular," the *World* will see the propriety of relieving us from its imputation of attempted "dictation."

From the Atlas and Argus.

We shall, of course, be very happy to be undeceived in relation to the intention of this resolution and the construction to be put upon it, and to learn that under its authority the State Committee of that Convention are prepared to agree upon a ticket, which the friends of DOUGLAS, BRECKENRIDGE and BELL can in common support, with a view to take the thirty-five votes of New York from LINCOLN and defeat the election of a Black Republican President.

To these "base uses" has the Democracy "come at last." Its central organ openly avows its readiness to support an Electoral Ticket which will vote either for DOUGLAS, BRECKENRIDGE or BELL! It has denounced BELL as a United States Bank man for thirty years, and now denounces BRECKENRIDGE as the Candidate of "Disunionists," and is yet ready to go for either!

This is just where we want to see our antagonists. Let them make this "black-leg," "thimble-rigging" bargain. Let the coalition be open, shameless and profligate—so *open*, shameless and profligate as to sicken and disgust fair-minded, honorable men of all parties.

☞ Col. JEWETT is overboard! His office of Marshal of Northern New York has been taken from him by a *Democratic* President! This is an immolation which we never expected to witness. It is an outrage which Tyranny sometimes perpetrates, but for which the perpetrator ought to be execrated.

We have known Col. JEWETT intimately for thirty-eight years, as an untiring, efficient, hard-working Democrat. If we are entitled to be regarded as a steady, inflexible *opponent* of Democracy, Col. JEWETT is entitled, from his Party, to the credit of being its supporter, for we have all the while been in distinct and diametrical opposition. His never cooling zeal and indomitable energy, always made him a formidable opponent. And he worked, for more than thirty years, without political reward. In his old age and impaired health he was appointed to the office from which he has been ruthlessly deposed! We have had many evidences of the malignity and meanness of BUCHANAN, and we do not generally care how much those who made the old viper President, are punished; but the proscription of a man who has devoted his time and money, and destroyed his health and constitution in the service of his Party, is an act of such wanton and heartless cruelty that it cannot fail to intensify the hatred and contempt that all classes and all parties entertain for a President who will go out of office amid the curses and hissings of those who supported and those who opposed his Election.

From the World.

Quite unexpectedly, Mr. THURLOW WEED appeared in the city yesterday morning, and spent most of the day in conference with the Police Commissioners. This somewhat startled the friends of Mr. GREELEY, but did not prevent the election of the regular ticket in every ward.

A lively imagination only could have mystified an interview of less than ten minutes into "most of the day." And that "*this did not prevent the election of the regular ticket in every ward,*" is not at all *startling*, when it is known that we neither attempted nor desired to "prevent" such results.

☞ The Atlas heads an article from a Michigan correspondent thus :—"*Douglas in the West.*" The correspondent dates his letter "Detroit, Aug. 7. Here, we are in *the Straits.*" We would advise the Atlas to reply, "Here, we are in *the Narrows.*" These two phrases would represent the true condition of the Democratic party *everywhere.*

Delegates to Republican State Convention.

HERKIMER.—1st dist., JAS. H. WEATHERWAX and S. GRAVES.

ULSTER.—1st dist. GEORGE H. SHARP. EGBERT WHITTAKER; 2d, GEO. T. PIERCE, JOHN W. HASBROUCK; 3d, JOHN LYON, HARVEY S. LADEW.

WYOMING COUNTY.—JAMES H. LOOMIS, of Attica, and WILLIAM BRISTOL, of Gainesville. Alternates—JOHN H. BAILEY and D. E. HOLT.

Resolutions were passed in favor of the renomination of Gov. MORGAN and of returning Hon. A. FRANK to Congress.

Relief for the Syrian Christians.

No one can be indifferent to the benevolent enterprise of aiding the bereaved, homeless, and starving Christians of Palestine—our kindred in faith in the land where that faith had its origin, and which is associated in our minds with the great leading events of its history.

But to be effective, relief must be speedy. Those whom we would aid are perishing daily for lack of it. Every dollar given now will do more good than ten can hereafter.

Messrs. ALEXANDER ABCARIUS and B. F. N. SOUSSA, who have just arrived in this country from Beyrout, were sent out on a special mission for this purpose, by the Christians of Syria. Letters from the leading men of the country and from the American Missionaries attest their authority, and warmly appeal to the American public. The long journey thus undertaken to a country of which the Syrians know nothing save by reputation, and which is to them like the other end of the Earth, evinces a touching confidence on their part, in American benevolence and Christian brotherhood. It will not prove to have been erroneous.

Whatever is entrusted to these gentlemen will promptly forwarded and judiciously applied by the most competent hands. Mr. ABCARIUS is at present at the Delavan House in this city. Contributions may be given to him personally during his stay, or if sent to this office, will be acknowledged and transmitted to them with pleasure.

☞ The California Democracy are in a ludicrous state of perplexity. They dare not commit themselves to the support of either Ticket for fear the other may prove the strongest. Remote as they are from the main scene of hostilities, and depending on a tedious mail for information as to how the battle is going, they await every arrival with eagerness, and many of them change their creed every time they get the Eastern newspapers. At first there was a pretty general disposition to go in for DOUGLAS. Then, on learning of the stand taken by the Administration, there was a sudden caving in for BRECKENRIDGE. The San Francisco Herald and other papers that had boldly run up the Douglas flag, hastily ran it down again. Office holders who at first declared for Douglas, with a view to a reappointment under the next Administration, suddenly reversed their opinions in order to save their heads under this one. Those who are not obliged to avow their sentiments maintain an uncomfortable position "on the fence" waiting further advices. Meanwhile the Republicans take heart and hope from the confusion of their enemies. The State has been so long and so completely in the Democratic Slough of Despond, that it has seemed, until now, the work of years to effect a deliverance. But the prospect is now encouraging for a speedy change for the better. Ere long the Republican strength of California will be doubled. The general tone of public sentiment is well and aptly illustrated by the way the news from Baltimore was received at San Francisco. A gun was brought out and a salute fired for Douglas. Then some of those concerned, getting frightened at their own action, proposed to give another salute for Breckenridge. This was done, and was followed by another salute fired by the Republicans, who concluded that, after all, they had the best right of anybody to rejoice over the Democratic Nominations!

☞ Although the whole South has been claimed for BRECKENRIDGE, the recent election in Missouri indicates that one at least of the Slave States will be difficult for him to get. The Douglas men, encouraged by their show of strength at the State election, are making great efforts for the Presidential one. Of the Democratic newspapers in that State, no less than thirty-six have now come out for DOUGLAS, BRECKENRIDGE not having half that number.

☞ The Breckenridge men in this State say they will fuse with the "Softs" if DOUGLAS is withdrawn. These are "Hard" terms; but, hard as they are, if the "Softs" are wise, they will accept them. Such a fusion would not take the State from LINCOLN, but it would preserve DOUGLAS from an exposure of his weakness. Friends who offer to do that should be treated with courtesy.

☞ The New York Express thinks the following State Ticket could be elected :—

For Governor—WILLIAM KELLY, of Dutchess.
For Lieut. Governor—WASHINGTON HUNT, of Niagara.
For Canal Commissioner—MR. JAYCOX, of Onondaga.
For Inspector of State Prisons—WILLIAM C. RHODES, of Chemung.

Here is Succotash for you! But would it be palatable to the Democracy?

☞ The Douglas men are industriously casting about for a candidate for Governor—*to be beaten*. Who is to be the martyr? Rumor points to a gentleman whom the wire-pullers would scarcely think of were they sure of success. Democracy, in the minority, often appears respectable in the personal character of its nominees. It is less particular when strong.

☞ The Argus this morning conceded that DOUGLAS stands no chance of carrying a single Southern State; but claims that he may carry "Pennsylvania and enough other Northern States to prevent the election of LINCOLN!" This confession of weakness will drive thousands into the ranks of Breckenridge.

☞ When the "Dough Faces" united have been unable, through the years which have intervened since the last Presidential election, to reconquer any of the solid phalanx of Republican States, is it not the sheerest nonsense to suppose they can do so in a Presidential contest when they are broken into fragments?

☞ In St. Louis the Americans all voted for BARRETT, but the Democrats wouldn't vote for TODD. They are cheats there as every where. But no one will pity TODD. Americans unprincipled enough to fuse with Democracy deserve to be cheated.

☞ Georgia Breckenridge State Convention was held Thursday and Electors nominated. The Breckenridge men do not expect to carry the State, but are able to throw the election into the Legislature, which chooses Electors in case none receive a majority of the whole popular vote.

☞ The re-election of BLAIR is a significant fact. It places the indelible stamp of Republicanism upon the commercial mart of the great Southwest. And its bright impress will be seen long after Slavery shall be wiped out.

☞ Republicanism has taken no step backward from the first hour of its birth. Every city and county and State once captured is still held. Even from St. Louis the white banner of Freedom still waves in triumph. Long may it wave!

☞ The editorials of the Argus just now are in the tone of "The Beggar's Petition." It is pitiful to see it on its knees to those whom it has been spitting at these three years. It should be more manly and "die game."

☞ Dr. E. W. FRISBIE, a man of large philanthropy and eminent devotion to the principles of liberty, died at his residence in Phelps, Ontario county, a few days since, from injuries received from the kick of a horse.

☞ RUFUS H. KING, Esq., of this city, has been awarded the Buffalo 7 per cent. $100,000 loan, payable in four years. He pays a premium of 1-20th per cent.

☞ It is a significant fact that the New England States send up twelve United States Senators, and there is not a Judas among them.

National Teachers' Association.

Correspondence of the Evening Journal.

BUFFALO, August 8, 1860.

The Association met at 7½ o'clock. After some introductory business Prof. Edward North, of Hamilton College, was introduced and delivered an address on "The Scholarship of Shakspere." It was replete with evidence of patient research, and its rich, terse, classic style, interspersed with broad humor, and an occasional sally of wit, kept the attention of a large audience that hung upon his words.

He defended Shakspere's classic fame against the pretense of those who affect to despise elegant culture, that he was possessed of few literary attainments. But no poor attempt of mine can hint at the richness of his sententious style, the scope of his mind in all that may claim the name of literature, his exhaustive research in all that can give piquancy, grace, strength and beauty.

The meeting, thus far, has not been fruitful in much that may yield a synopsis to the reportorial pencil, yet this may be attributed to the fullness rather than the meagerness of its matter. American Hall is crammed, and every train since the commencement of the meeting has brought in new recruits. The best educational talent of the Union is represented, and it needs no prophet to see that the results of these two Conventions will tell mightily upon the educational interests of the country.

Anson G. Chester, Esq., now of the Buffalo Express, is delivering his new poem on "The Gods." He delivered it first at the recent commencement of Hamilton College. It is full of telling hits, rich similes, satire, fun and humor. Mr. Chester's well-earned fame will not suffer from to-night's efforts. A rich programme is offered for to-morrow.

SECOND DAY.

BUFFALO, August 9, 1860.

The Association convened at 9 A. M., and was called to order by the President and opened with prayer by Rev. Mr. Wilbur. Letters were read from absent members, and also a communication from the Kentucky State Teachers' Association, inviting this body to visit the Mammoth Cave under the auspices of that Association.

A large number of new members were elected.

Delegates from eighteen States are in attendance.

The discussion for the morning is on "Oral Instruction, and the proper use of Text-Books.

The discussion was opened by Mr. Charles Ansorge, of Massachusetts. He contrasted the method of instruction from book, with that of the living teacher. Oral instruction comes first, and is the peculiar province of the primary school. It should look forward to the preparation of the child for self-instruction in the coming years. Our text-books are defective, from the fact that most of them are made by persons not actually engaged in the duties of the School-room.

Mr. Stowits, of Batavia, New York, remarked that text-books are but aids—only by contact with the living soul of the live teacher can the child receive its first and best impulses.

Mr. Sawyer, of South Carolina, took a large and exhaustive view of the subject, holding that the child at first is taught through the senses, and that oral instruction is the law. When a degree of intellectual maturity has prepared the mind for independent investigation, the textbook becomes his monitor; yet the teacher should be, himself, so superior to his subject, that he may aid in clearing up every point of difficulty, encouraging to personal effort, rather than cramming with an intellectual surfeit.

Mr. E. P. Stone, of Massachusetts, illustrated his idea of proper mental culture, by remarking, that when we speak of physical education, we do not mean cramming the body with food; so true education has for its object the cultivation of independent thought.

The discussion was continued by Messrs. Greenleaf, of Brooklyn; Northrop, of Massachusetts, and Marvin of Ohio.

Mr. Webster, of Rochester, gave some happy illustrations of the methods of teaching, by actual experiment, objects, and familiar things.

Mr. McJilton, of Maryland, made some practical and searching remarks.

The discussion was one of the most interesting, if not the very best, to which it has been my happiness to listen, during many years of educational experience. The subject will probably be referred to a committee to report in full at next meeting.

At 11 o'clock, Mr. Richard Edwards, of St. Louis, delivered an address on "Our Progressive Ancestry," tracing in a masterly manner the history, progress and methods of education, from the ancient time, through the seers, prophets, the family, the groves of the academy, and the study of the philosopher.

At its close the Association adjourned to meet at 3 P. M.

At the opening of the afternoon session, several business committees were appointed.

The discussion of the afternoon on the subject of adult education was opened by Mr. W. E. Shelden, of Massachusetts. The effect of this question is, what appliances shall be instituted especially in our large cities and towns for the education of unlettered immigrants, and persons from the less favored portions of our own country, residents therein. Mr. S. regarded lyceums (debating societies) and public lectures as an important means, and that it is the duty of the educator to take such lead in these measures as shall bring this class of people under their influence.

Prof. Thomson, of New York, referred to the success that has attended the establishment of evening schools in that city.

Gen. H. K. Oliver, of Lawrence, Mass., gave some interesting incidents of the progress and means of adult education in the city of his residence. A large number, of from 16 to 60 years of age, have been under instruction in the night schools during the past winter.

The hour for that order having arrived, W. H. Wells, Esq., Superintendent of Schools, Chicago, delivered an eloquent address on the Philosophy of Education.

At the conclusion of the address, Prof. Phelps of New Jersey, presented a series of resolutions on the decease of Paul Farnum, Esq., late of Beverly, N. J., who had donated property and money to the amount of $50,000 to the Normal School of that State.

Pending the adoption of the resolutions, several gentlemen made pertinent remarks; and Mr. Gildersleeve stated that a number of years since a sum of money was bequeathed for the establishment of a Normal School in Buffalo, which now amounts to nearly $20,000,—and "Father Ketchum" has given real estate valued at $30,000.

Prof. Thomson, of New York, offered the following resolutions, as supplementary to the discussion of the afternoon :—

Resolved, That the education of adults, who from any cause have been deprived of its blessings in their earlier days, is a subject worthy the attention and sympathy of all teachers and friends of humanity.

Resolved, That we heartily commend the formation of *adult classes*, in connection with evening schools, to the attention and coöperation of School Committees, Boards of Education, and Philanthropists in all our large towns and cities, where such persons are usually found.

Mr. Sheldon, from the Committee to nominate officers for the ensuing year, reported the following:—

President—John D. Philbrick, Boston, Mass.

Vice-Presidents—Wm. Roberts, Philadelphia, Penn.; Geo. F. Phelps, New Haven, Conn.; Isaac Stone, Ottawa, Ill.; C. S. Pennell, St. Louis, Mo.; C. H. Allen, Madison, Wis.; J. N. M'Jilton, Baltimore, Md.; Wm. F. Phelps, Trenton, N. J.; C. C. Nestlerode, Tipton, Iowa; R. McMillan, Salem, Ohio; James G. Eliott, Faison's, N. C.; Z. Richards, Washington, D. C.; Charles Ansorge, Dorchester, Mass.

Secretary—James Cruikshank, Albany, N. Y.

Treasurer—O. C. Wight, Washington, D. C.

Counsellors—Wm. H. Wells, Chicago, Ill.; Wm. E. Sheldon, West Newton, Mass.; C. H. Gildersleeve, Buffalo, N. Y.; W. D. Henkle, Lebanon, Ohio; Edward J. Brodie, Philadelphia, Penn.; F. A. Sawyer, Charleston, S. C.; David N. Camp, New Britain, Conn.; J. Escobar, Chihuahua, Mexico; Richard Edwards, St. Louis, Mo.; D. McNeil Turner, Tallahassee, Fla.; J. C. Taylor, Wilmington, Del.; J. C. Pelton, San Francisco, Cal.; Sylvester Scott, Alexandria, Va.; D. Franklin Wells, Iowa City, Iowa; S. H. Wiley, Salisbury, N. C.

A ballot was taken, and the ticket unanimously elected.

The Association met this evening in the North Presbyterian Church.

Prof. Phelps presented the subject of heating and ventilation of school buildings, and explained the plan adopted at the Insane Asylum at Utica. Dr. Gray had stated to him that since the adoption of the present plan the ratio of deaths was but one-half of what it has been in former years. Several gentlemen made remarks, when the subject was referred to a committee, consisting of Messrs. Phelps, of New Jersey; Richards, of Washington; Northrop, of Massachusetts; Henkle of Ohio, and Wells of Chicago, to make a full and exhaustive examination of the subject, and report at next meeting.

Prof. E. S. Youmans, of New York, was introduced, and delivered a lecture on "The Study of Nature and the Progress of Man."

The moral of the lecture and that which made it eminently appropriate to the occasion, was couched in the suggestion at its close, that the study of the physical sciences should be made a more prominent feature in the educational system of the day.

The lecture was the gem of the meeting.

THIRD DAY—MORNING SESSION.

Mr. Richards, of Washington, D. C., presented an able paper on the Phonetic Alphabet.

The subject was discussed by Messrs. Grosvenor, of Massachusetts; Stowels, of New York; Griswold, of Illinois; Cruikshank, of New York; Wells, of Illinois; McJilton, of Maryland; Philbrick, of Massachusetts. The debate called out the result of much careful experiment—the results of teaching by the Phonetic Alphabet, and the easy transition to common type.

Mr. John Kneeland, of Massachusetts, was then introduced, and gave a well considered lecture upon "The Teacher and his Work."

Adjourned till afternoon. The session will close to-night. C.

Senator John J. Crittenden's Manly Rebuke of Barnard, Brooks & co.

The following is taken from Senator CRITTENDEN's recent speech at Louisville :—

But it is said Mr. Lincoln's election will consummate the dissolution of the Union—that he will not be permitted to take his seat! How is that? If a man is elected by a majority of the people, in a fair and legal way, though you voted against him, won't you say he is entitled to his seat? Would you not consider the power very arbitrary that would undertake to keep him out of his office? You have a right to elect him or anybody else, and, if a man is constitutionally elected President of the United States, shall a minority of the people start up and say, "We will make a revolution; we will, by force of arms, resist it, and drive him out?" Is not that a destruction of all government? The majority must, of necessity, rule in all republics, and if you do not like the law of the majority, set aside all free government, and *go to some place where you will have no elections, where hereditary rulers shall take the place of your elective government.* Who will say that if Mr. Lincoln or anybody else is constitutionally elected to the Chief Magistracy, he shall not take his seat? Have we come to this? If so, let us change the whole government, and let the minority rule, though even then would not the majority men object to the election of a man by the minority?

What could be more truthful and cutting than the following:—

I know there are those who speculate upon the speedy dissolution of the Union, but they are *self-conceited men*, unfaithful in their natures and unfaithful to the great government of which they ought to be proud.

The "self-conceited men" thus rebuked, destitute of the patriotism which influences JOHN J. CRITTENDEN's war upon Democracy, are hobnobbing with DOUGLAS, as if they coveted nothing so much as to do the dirtiest menial work for those whom Senator CRITTENDEN heartily despises.

The Syrian Massacres.

We are glad to perceive that the appeals of the American Missionaries in Syria are meeting with a response from their respective Churches and Societies. The following Card appears in the New York papers to-day :—

A CARD.—The undersigned, in compliance with the spontaneous desires of many benevolent friends, as well as their own, would respectively invite those gentlemen who feel interested in behalf of the tens of thousands of Christians in Syria who have been made wretched wanderers, shelterless, and ready to perish with famine by a most ruthless and fanatical war, to meet at the American Tract Society's House next Monday, at 3 P. M., to devise measures for having the subject of sending relief to these poor people brought, as soon as possible, before the Churches in an effective and responsible manner. NEW YORK, Aug. 11, 1860.

James Brown,	Wm. C. Alexander,
Fred. S. Winston,	Thos. L. Rushmore,
Shepherd Knapp,	O. E. Wood,
L. Bangs,	J. R. Spaulding,
Gerard Hallock,	W. A. Booth,
Smith Sheldon,	Stewart Brown,
S. E. Morse, Jr. & Co.,	Francis Hall.

The editors of the Journal of Commerce are permitted to publish the following letter from Rev. W. M. Thompson, American missionary in Syria, to Wm. A. Booth, Esq. :—

BEIRUT, Syria, June 27th, 1860.

As there are thousands of widows and orphans, and tens of thousands whose houses are burnt, and their effects plundered, an enormous amount of suffering is inevitable, do what we may. During the warm, dry months, parents and children *can* sleep under the trees, as they are now doing; but the cold, rainy months will be on us, and then the people must have *clothes* and a *shelter* of some sort or other, or *die*. Are there not some of your wealthy friends who will aid us to alleviate this dreadful calamity? Every cent will purchase a little loaf for some one, who otherwise have none. We shall make an appeal to England also, and elsewhere wherever there is benevolence to be reached. As you and your sons and family know something about this country, you will doubtless be happy to act as the channel through which charities can reach this wretched people.

As to the prospects of our mission, it is too early to speak with any confidence. Any interference of France or Russia in the affairs of this country, would probably send us all to the sea for personal safety. We *might* lay off shore in a ship until the fight is over, and then return to our homes. We *may* be driven to Cyprus, Rhodes, Malta, &c., &c. No human sagacity can predict what is to take place *to morrow*. There is but too much reason to apprehend such a foreign interference, and it may come any hour.

Pray for us, and urge all who feel an interest in our mission to unite with you in earnest prayer on our behalf. We are passing through deep waters. We are surrounded with darkness, and involved in perplexities that bewilder. Light and salvation can only come from the Lord. Dr. Van Dyck and wife are in Germany. Mr. Eddy and wife left us yesterday for America. We propose to remain by the stuff, and gather up the fragments of thirty years' labor, so soon as the storm lulls sufficiently to admit of such work. All my family unite in Christian salutation to you and yours. May the blessing of the Lord ever rest upon you all.

Yours, in the best bonds, W. M. THOMSON.

Speculations in Life Policies.

The Rochester Union has an article from which we extract the following. Some of the policies alluded to are known to be in the hands of very shrewd capitalists in Rochester :—

The averment is made that a most unusual and extraordinary amount of insurance has been effected on one or more lives for other than legitimate purposes. One of the parties so alleged to be insured is Robert Spence, who is said to be a pedlar, a poor man, himself unable to raise the large sum required for the first premiums. It is also stated, we know not whether correctly or not, that he has had one or more shocks of paralysis. The amount for which his life has been insured is variously given from $30,000 to $50,000. One insurance man gives it to us at $40,000; another states it positively at $30,000. The policies, we hear, are in sums of $5,000 each and are distributed among a number of companies—none that we hear of having more than one policy.

☞ Col. LEVI LEWIS, late Agent of the Auburn State Prison, and a resident in that city for upwards of sixty years, died yesterday at the residence of his son, Walter Lewis, in Watkins, Schuyler county. Col. Lewis has been gradually failing for the last year. He was an honorable and honest man and an excellent citizen. He was sixty-nine years of age.

☞ When all pulling together, the Democrats were unable to carry a single Northern State. Can they do any better when they are pulling apart?

☞ The Detroit Tribune announces Governor SEWARD to speak at Detroit September 4th; at Lansing Sept. 6th, and at Kalamazoo Sept. 8th.

☞ Several meteors of considerable size are reported to have been seen recently by observers in different parts of the Union.

☞ Gen. CASS has gone to Washington.

Always be quite as careful in your business transactions of taking credit as of giving.

ILLINOIS ALIVE!

COMING TOGETHER OF THE MASSES AT "OLD ABE'S" HOME.

An Immense Turn Out, and a Glorious Time.

From the Chicago Journal, 9th.

The Republicans of Illinois had a glorious time at Springfield yesterday. For its almost unaccountable numbers and its almost frantic enthusiasm, this meeting deserves a large place in the history of this campaign, when it shall be written. It was an extraordinary assemblage. The number present at the meeting is variously estimated. The grounds, the streets, the whole town, swarmed so with the living and moving mass of men, that it was almost impossible to make a guess as to the number. There were probably over **50,000** people there—possibly **100,000.** We never witnessed such an immense throng of human beings in one place and at one time before. The trains from the North, South, East and West came in, long and crowded—crowded with enthusiastic Republicans, who had come to join their brethren in grand council together. And delegations from the towns of Sangamon and the adjacent counties, with banners and music, came in, dozens at a time, and defying all efforts at enumeration. Indeed, there was a literal *out-pouring* of the people of Central Illinois.

There were fifty Wide-Awake clubs (some five thousand men) from various parts of the State in attendance, all dressed in regular uniform, and presenting an imposing appearance. It took the procession of people between two and three hours to pass any given point. It could not have been less than two miles long. The multitudes cheered enthusiastically as they passed Mr. Lincoln's house, and he stood on his porch, good humored and smiling, when they passed by. He received the honors of the occasion with that gentle modesty which characterizes the old leader.

The meeting proper was held at the State Fair grounds, where telling speeches were made by Senator Trumbull, Senator Doolittle, and Messrs. Gillispie, Palmer, Washburne, Oglesby, Browning, Gen. John Wilson, Judd, and several others. Speaking was in progress from six different stands. In the evening speaking was in progress in various parts of the city.

The most striking feature of the day was the visit of Mr. Lincoln to the grounds while the meeting was progressing. He arrived in about the middle of the afternoon, in a carriage, accompanied by a few friends, and no sooner was the fact made known than the multitude of thousands who swarmed around the speakers' stands, rushed almost simultaneously for Lincoln's carriage. They surrounded him with a wall of men that would have proved strong enough to resist and overcome the whole Disunion party of the South and their Northern Doughface allies with them, in open fight. It is such a wall of patriots and determined men that will surround him at Washington, in case of danger to himself, the Union or the laws. They pressed Mr. Lincoln for a speech. He could not well get rid of a response. He was taken from the carriage, and the vociferous cheering having in a degree subsided, he said:

My Fellow Citizens—I appear among you upon this occasion with no intention of making a speech. It is my purpose, since I have been placed in my present position, to make no speeches. This assembly having been drawn together at the place of my residence, it appeared to be the wish of those constituting this vast assemblage to see me, and it certainly is my wish to see all of you. I appear upon the ground here at this time only for the purpose of offering myself the best opportunity of seeing you and enabling you to see me. I confess with gratitude, be it understood, that I did not suppose that my appearance among you would create the tumult which I now witness. I am profoundly grateful for this manifestation of your feelings. I am grateful because it is a tribute such as can be paid to no man as a man. It is the evidence that four years from this time you will give a like manifestation to the new man who is to be the representative of the truth on the questions that now agitate the public mind; and it is because you will then fight for this cause as you do now, or with even greater ardor than now, though I be dead and gone. I most profoundly and sincerely thank you. Having said thus much, allow me now to say that it is my wish that you will hear this public discussion by others of our friends who are present for the purpose of addressing you, and that you will kindly let me be silent.

He modestly retired amid the wild, deafening and general cheering of that vast multitude, who it is very evident, almost adore the plain, honest and noble standard-bearer.

Last night Springfield was in a literal blaze, and in a literal noise. Bonfires were burning on every corner, while a torch-light procession of some five thousand Wide Awakes—an imposing army—paraded the streets. Everybody cheered, everybody felt good, everybody seemed to feel proud that he was a Republican—an Illinois Republican—an Old Abe Republican.

Those who were present at this grand and indescribable demonstration of the friends of an earnest and a right cause, will never forget the day. Such an event is not easily erased from memory, for to witness one such in a life-time falls to the lot of but few men. We have seen many large meetings, but this doubly beats every meeting we have ever before witnessed. It was a *great mass meeting* in the largest sense of the term—and sent conviction to the minds of all, that the men who are enlisted in the Cause that this meeting was called together to promote, are earnest in their professions, intentions and aims.

We are more firm than ever before in the belief that Illinois is all right for Old Abe—that his majority will be *great*, and that Yates and the other candidates for State officers are sure of election. Yes, Illinois is all right for Old Abe, and the whole West is all right for him. Let us continue to work without faltering till the victory is won.

Carl Schurz on the Bell Platform.

The following is an extract from a speech which was delivered at St. Louis :—

"Let us pass in review our political parties, and the remedies they propose.

"Here we encounter the Union party, with Bell and Everett, who tell us the best way to settle the conflict, is to ignore it. [Laughter.]

"Ignore it! Ignore it, when attempts are made to plunge the country into war and disgrace, for the purpose of Slavery extension. Ignore it, when slavery and free labor wage their fierce war about the possession of the national domain! Ignore it, when the liberties of speech and press are attacked! Ignore it, when the actual settler claims the virgin soil, and the slaveholding capitalists claim it also! Ignore it, when the planting interests seeks to establish and maintain its exclusive supremacy in our economical policy! Ignore it, indeed! Ignore the fire that consumes the corner posts of the house! Ignore the storm that breaks the rudder and tears to tatters the sails of your ship! Conjure the revolted elements with a meek Mount Vernon lecture! Pour upon the furious waves the placid oil of a quotation from Washington's Farewell Address. [Cheers and laughter.]

"It is true they tell us they will enforce the laws and the Constitution. Well enough! But what laws? Those that free labor demand, or those that Slavery give us? What Constitution? That of Washington or Madison, or that of Slidell, Douglas and Taney? [Loud and long continued cheering.]

"The conflict stands there with the stubborn, brutal force of reality. However severely it may disturb the nerves of timid gentlemen, there it stands and speaks the hard stern language of fact. I understand well that great problems and responsibilities should be approached with care and caution. But times like these demand the firm action of men who know what they will, *and will it*, not that eunuch policy, which, conscious of its own unproductiveness, invites us blandly to settle down into the imbecile contentment of general impotency. They *cannot* ignore the conflict if they would, but have not nerve enough to decide it if they could."

AFFRAY AT CLEVELAND.—CLEVELAND, Aug. 10—Last night, about 10 o'clock, two negroes entered the saloon of Wm. Pickersgill, on Seneca st., and, becoming troublesome, Pickersgill attempted to eject them, when one of the negroes drew a large knife and made several lunges, which took effect on Wm. Salmon, a white man, who was just then passing out of the door. Salmon ran a little way and fell dead. The negroes fled, but were subsequently arrested.

An Unfounded Imputation.

From the Albany Atlas and Argus, Aug. 8.

On Saturday, a paragraph contained near the close of a letter from Rochester, giving political intelligence, found its way into our paper, which made a gross charge against the editor of the Rochester Democrat of connection with the Legislative lobby. Had the sentence been seen by us it would have been excluded from our columns, for we neither know nor have heard anything which even gives color to such a charge. The editor of the Democrat spent considerable time in Albany as the Clerk of the Senate, and as things go, it is highly to his credit, that, so far as we ever heard, he escaped all suspicion of acting the part of a lobbyman in legislative matters; and sustained in all respects an irreproachable reputation. We should do him injustice, if we allowed the remark of our correspondent, thus inadvertently admitted to our columns, to pass without disavowing it and regretting its publication. We know not how sensitive our professional friend at Rochester may be on the subject, but looking at the history of a few years past, we think any man of fair reputation may well consider the imputation of complicity with the lobby, as a serious aspersion of his good name.

From the Rochester Democrat.

The above is a full and satisfactory retraction of a gross libel upon the editor of this paper, and we can ask no more of the Atlas and Argus, except that the name of our calumniator be furnished to us. To that we are entitled. And if the coward who anonymously attacks us in a paper at Albany can do so, he shall have the opportunity of proving that "the stench of the Albany lobby clings to his (our) garments." We have never, while Clerk of the Senate, or at any other time, been connected, directly or indirectly, with the lobby, and the scoundrel who made and procured the publication of the charge, could have been actuated by no other than malicious motives. We propose to smoke him out and give him the fullest opportunity to sustain his charge, and if he will call as witnesses the members of the Senate, from 1856 to 1860, and any number of others he pleases, we will agree to rest the matter without ourselves calling a witness? Dare he come forth and assume the responsibility of his libels?

Adultery and Murder.

From the Baltimore Sun, of the 9th.

On Monday night last, the vicinity of Curtis' Creek, Anne Arundel county, was the scene of an affair which yesterday resulted in the death of Mrs. Gray, wife of Leonard W. Gray, formerly of this city. Gray, it appears, has been absent for two or three months at Richmond, Va., but returned home on Monday evening in the 7 o'clock Washington train. Thinking to surprise his wife, he went directly to Mrs. Gault's, at whose house, in Holliday street, near Pleasant, she was staying. He did not find her there, but was told she had gone to Samuel Acton's, at Curtis' Creek. Thither Gray went, and was surprised at not finding his wife there, nor had she been there. Gray then proceeded along the lane, in company with Acton and another man. Without stating any peculiar or antecedent fact which led to his making a search, he states that in the road they detected a foot print in the sand, and Gray following it up, traced his wife to an unfinished house not far from the highway. He heard a noise in the house, as of a man and woman in conversation, and attempted to break down the door, but could not. He then got a piece of scantling, and forcibly broke down the back door and rushed up stairs.

As he did so Mrs. Gray came from behind a carpenter's bench, greatly agitated, and divested of nearly all her clothing. Gray said, "Oh, Mary!" and struck her twice with the piece of scantling, once over the head and once above the eye. She fell bleeding at the nose, but Gray says he did not think at the time that he had hurt her much. Becoming alarmed, however, Gray picked his wife up from the floor, and carried her in his arms to Brooklyn city, two miles distant. She never spoke, except when Gray said to her, "Oh, Mary, how could you treat me so!" when she replied, "He forced me to it"—meaning her seducer. On Tuesday, Dr. Brewer, of this city, was sent for, and yesterday morning Mrs. Gray was brought to this city, and taken to the house of Mrs. Townson, in Mosher-street, near Walsh, where she died yesterday afternoon, between one and two o'clock.

Gray immediately went to the office of Justice Reid and surrendered himself to the magistrate, who gave him into the custody of Policeman Clinton, of the Western District. He appeared greatly distressed, and asked to be taken to Annapolis jail at once. He was taken to the office of the Marshal of Police, who sent him to Annapolis, in charge of Policeman Clinton, in the 4:20 train.

Gray is about 30 years of age, and was married to his victim about three years ago. The deceased was about 27 years of age. The man who was heard talking with the woman in the house, it is said, escaped out of the window, and that he was known to Gray.

Town of Salisbury, Md., nearly Destroyed by Fire.

BALTIMORE, August 10.

The town of Salisbury, Somerset county, was nearly consumed by fire on Wednesday, the 8th inst. Over forty dwelling houses, stores, etc., were destroyed. The town is represented as almost in complete ruins. The Episcopal Church, one of the oldest in the State, was destroyed, notwithstanding great efforts were made to save it. The conflagration swept away the stores of Messrs. Reder & Tradwine, Wm. Burkhead, C. F. Dashields, Bush's Hotel. Several other stores and their contents were partially destroyed. A large amount of personal property, goods, &c., were saved, though the aggregate loss is very great. Most of the sufferers are insured in the Mutual Insurance Company of Delaware. The origin of the fire is not known, but it is suspected to have been the work of an incendiary.

A SHOCKING ACCIDENT—A BOY FEARED TO BE FATALLY BURNED.—Last evening about half-past eight o'clock, a small German boy was shockingly burned by the explosion of some high wines. He works for a Mr. Krug, who keeps a saloon and vinegar factory in North street. Mr. Krug sent the lad into the cellar of his building with a large tin measure and a lighted candle, to draw some high wines which he wished to use. The injured boy did as directed and on returning the flame from the candle, communicated to the spirits and an explosion followed. The liquid was scattered all over the person of the boy and in an instant he was a mass of flames. Several men who were in the saloon heard the report and started out into the yard. They threw water on the burning lad and the fire was extinguished. The skin on his breast, face and hands peeled off, and it is feared that he is fatally burned.—[Rochester Union.

MURDER.—BURLINGTON, N. J., August 9.—George Aiken was shot and instantly killed at Red Lion, near Vincentown, Burlington county, N. J., yesterday, by John H. Conover. It was alleged that Aiken had ravished Conover's wife, and was forbidden to come to the house. Conover, in the meanwhile, got out a warrant, and placed it in the hands of a constable. When Aiken heard of it, he threatened to kill him if he did not withdraw the warrant, and went to Conover's house yesterday, when Conover shot him in the neck, killing him instantly. Conover gave himself up to the authorities, and was placed in jail last evening at Mount Holly.

THE CINCINNATI EMBEZZLEMENT CASE.—TORONTO, August 10.—In the Cincinnati embezzlement case to-day, upon the arrival of witnesses from Cincinnati and New York, the magistrate decided that the case did not come under the Ashburton extradition treaty, and discharged Montague. The money amounting to $25,500 was delivered to the Cincinnati detective.

The Frenchman likes to catch his truth in the most summary way, and put it in his game-bag at once. The German, when he has got his truth, by circumventing it, prefers to let it go again, and watch its hare-like doublings, and if he can lose sight of it altogether, for a while, so much the better. There are both sorts of minds in England.

LITERARY PARTNERSHIP.—The members of the Southern Literary Society have, we understand, commenced a joint novel, each member to write one chapter. If the whole work is kept up to the standard of the three chapters already written, it will be a decided success.

[New Orleans Delta.

THE ZOUAVES.—ST. LOUIS, August 10.—The Chicago Zouaves arrived this evening and were received by the National Guards. They will drill in Washington Theatre to-morrow, and leave for Springfield Monday.

Great acquired skill with the weapons of the duel, in the days of Henry IV., was considered such a mark of cowardice and of trying to gain an unfair advantage, that those who practised for the duel did so covertly.

DIED:

On the 11th inst., infant daughter of A. B. and ANTIONETT VAN GAASBECK.

The friends of the family are respectfully invited to attend the funeral to-morrow (Sunday) afternoon at 3 o'clock from No. 4 Hall Place.

Suddenly, on the Friday morning the 10th inst., of disease of the heart, Capt. JAMES BELL, in the 62d year of his age.

The relatives, friends and acquaintances of the family and those of sons, Wm. J. and John H. Bell, are respectfully invited to attend his funeral on Sunday afternoon at 4 o'clock, from St. Paul's Church.

In this city, on the 10th inst., WILLIAM FISK, in the 44th year of his age.

The funeral will take place tomorrow at 4 o'clock, from his late residence, 165 Elm street. Relations and friends are respectfully invited to attend.

COMMERCIAL.

Albany Market, Aug 11.

FLOUR AND MEAL—There is a moderate business doing in fresh ground new wheat Flour but old is very dull and for this description the market is heavy and drooping. Corn Meal is quiet and unchanged in value.

GRAIN—In Wheat nothing worthy of notice has transpired. For Amber State $1 15 is bid and $1 17@1 18 asked. Corn is firmer and less active. Sales 6,400 bu. Western Mixed at 60½. Rye quiet. Oats in limited request with sales 3 600 bu. State at 38.

WHISKEY—A quiet market at 20½ for Prison.

Local and News Items.

Hurrah for Old Abe!

POLE RAISING!

A Republican Pole-raising will be held on SATURDAY of this week at Cleveland's corners, in the north-west part of the township of Marshall. Good speakers will be on hand—PRESTON, RHINES, and others. The latch-string will be out, and DEVILLO HUBBARD will be on hand with that promised barrel of cider. Let there be a general turn-out

☞ The North Carolina *Standard* has learned that HARVEY M. DIXON, PRENT. HEWITT, and CY. LOVELL have gone over to the Democracy; *ergo*, Michigan is safe for Douglas.

☞ We are glad to learn that our young friend PETER JOHNSON, who took Abby Kelly and her colt down to Kalamazoo, drew a premium of $60 on the horse, and $15 on the colt.

REMOVAL.—Miss MCCULLEY will, on the 1st of October next, remove her school to the house formerly occupied by J. P. HUNT, Esq., on Mansion street. This is a fine location, and, situated as it is in a quiet part of the city, will doubtless prove much more eligible for educational purposes than the one she is at present occupying.

☞ The State Fair will be held at Detroit on the 2d, 3d, 4th and 5th days of October. The annual address will be delivered by Hon. CASSIUS M. CLAY, of Kentucky, on the third day of the Fair, at 3 o'clock P. M. Membership tickets are each $1.00, which will entitle the holder to four admission tickets. Admission tickets, 25 cts. All the railroads in the State will carry passengers to and from the Fair at the usual reduced rates.

BLOODY AFFRAY.—Our usually quiet city was honored with a visit from the "Union" Circus on Monday last. On Monday night a horse-doctor from Jackson, whose name, we learn is PETTIS, was assaulted by three members of the organization, for reasons not known, and was struck a number of blows on the head and face, which had the effect of prostating him. He was then struck again and received several severe gashes on the top and side of his head. He lay on the side-walk for some time, and then got up and went into the National, where he is at present. He bled profusely. Medical aid was immediately summoned, and the patient is now in a comfortable condition. He assigns no reasons for the act.

Fairs in the County.

The *County Fair* will take place at the Fair [illegible] Marshall, on the 9th, 10th, and 11th days of October. The annual address will be delivered by L. D. DIBBLE, Esq., of Battle Creek.—The Executive Committee are making every needed preparation for the Fair. A large building is in process of erection, which will protect all articles from the weather.

The *Battle Creek Fair* comes off on the 26th, 27th and 28th days of September. The annual address is to be delivered by AMBROSE STEVENS, Esq., of Batavia, N. Y.

The *Homer Fair* takes place on the 21st and 22d days of September.

We trust these Fairs will be largely attended and liberally patronized.

Senator Chandler's Speech.

Senator WADE, of Ohio, having gone down to address the benighted people of the Key-Stone State, and Senator BINGHAM being out West, filling a list of appointments in Iowa, but one of the celebrated speakers promised us by the State Central Committee was here to address the citizens of this place on the 12th. Senator CHANDLER was in town and made a speech in the evening of that day at the Court House. He was the guest of Col. DICKEY while in town, from whose residence he was escorted to the place of meeting by the Wide-Awakes. The Court House was filled with a large and intelligent audience. Mr. CHANDLER was introduced to the audience by the President of the evening, C. T. GORHAM, Esq., and immediately proceeded to the discussion of the great political questions of the day, laying open, in his peculiar and popular style, the criminality and corruption of the Democratic administration at Washington, and vindicating the character of the Republican State administration at home. He exposed the fallacy of "squatter sovereignty," and effectually disposed of the disunion bug-a-boo. The Senator spoke in his happiest strain, and was frequently loudly applauded by the audience. We noticed a large number of ladies present, at which we were rejoiced; and we hope hereafter to enjoy the sunshine of their presence whenever a meeting of this description is held.

After the meeting was dismissed, the Wide-Awakes formed in line and escorted the Senator back to the residence of Col. DICKEY, where they were addressed by him, and complimented as being the best disciplined company in the State.—Should ever the South attempt to resist the inauguration of Mr. LINCOLN, he would call on the Marshall Wide-Awakes, *and wait till they came.*—He won't have to wait long.

Mr. Dixon's Card--Retrenchment.

We do not depart from our usual rule and custom—to avoid all personalities—when we reply to Mr. Dixon's authoritative announcement, that "if "he shall be elected Sheriff the price of boarding "prisoners in jail will be reduced to eighteen and "three fourth cents a day."

If we are correctly informed by the old supervisors, who have examined and audited Mr. Dixon's bills from 1854 to 1858, Mr. Dixon has charged the county fifty cents per day for the board and care of prisoners in jail, and has either officially certified to the correctness and justice of every charge or has sworn to it, amounting to the same thing in either case.

He now admits, if his announcement is honestly made, and is designed for anything else than Buncombe, that he robbed the county during the time he was Sheriff, of about two-thirds of the amount charged for boarding prisoners, which in 1858, amounted to the sum of $1,800, as we are informed, and this too, in the face of the rule of the board of supervisors, which requires that all claims of officers be either sworn to, or their justness and correctness certified to by the official certificate of the officer who presents the claim.

We are also informed that not only were these items of account thus verified by Mr. Sheriff Dixon, but that the most pressing and urgent representations were made by him to the board, that this sum was not adequate compensation for the responsibilities, risk and trouble incident to the boarding of the prisoners—and that the board reluctantly gave way to these representations, and allowed the claim, although ten cents per day, in their opinion, too high.

Under these circumstances, if we are to understand from Mr. Dixon's card that 18¾ cents per day is a fair price for boarding these men, what are we to considers as the value of those *verifications of his former accounts as a sworn officer of this county?* We suggest that the enquiry is pertinent, and ought to be considered in connection with the present offer, whether made in earnest, or as the mere utterance of that spirit of brag which is so eminently useful to the Douglas Democracy of the day.

If Mr. Dixon's offer is made in earnest, as his estimate of the true value of the board of prisoners—he stands before the public an outrageous extortionist—if in mockery, and for the purpose of clap-trap, we have little doubt his offer will meet the contempt it so richly deserves at the hands of the public.

Mr. Dixon admits that Mr. Crane charged less, voluntarily, by 50 cents a week, than he did, or $3 per week. This, we think, is about the average charged in Kalamazoo, Hillsdale, Branch and Jackson counties, and is only equivalent to the 30 cents or 25 cents per day charged by the old Democratic Sheriff, and allowed by the old Democratic board. Why? the raw material consumed then was full 100 per cent. lower than now—i. e. wheat was from fifty to sixty cents per bushel, potatoes 15 to 20 cents, pork $2 50 to $3 50, and all the necessaries of life at the same or corresponding prices.

As Dixon has voluntarily put himself in this position out of pure bravado, we shall honor him occasionally by noticing him and posting him up in the opinion of the public, out of pure regard for his personal welfare.

☞ MRS. L. WING will please accept our thanks for a pan of excellent grapes.

AN OLD WHIG ON REPUBLICANISM.—Hon. Robert C. Schenck said in a recent speech:—

"I am a Republican because I am a conservative Whig, and always have been. I am for the Constitution and the Union, and who is not? and I hold to the interpretations that seventy years of our history have given to that constitution. And the main purpose of the Republican party is to put an end to this double dealing policy upon the question of slavery—not to dodge it and avoid it, but to meet and settle it by returning to the policy of the early days of the government."

A SOUTHERN LINCOLNITE ON HIS TRAVELS.—The Vicksburg *Sun* of Thursday last, says:

"When last heard of, the Lincolnite who gave his opinions an airing so freely in our city on Monday, and for doing so was sent adrift on the Mississippi river, after being well tarred, was about twenty miles from here, slowly progressing towards New Orleans, in mid river. A stout cord and a strong limb is the only fit punishment for such incendaries of evil."

Sala tells, through an English paper, that once on his travels he had the honor of meeting an American gentleman, who was proceeding to the Amoor river as Consul for the United States, and who had the American flag made up in the form of an umbrella, in order that in the hottest and most tempestuous weather he might still be under the shelter of the stars and stripes.

☞ The Douglasites accuse the Republicans of being a "one-idea party."

Take the "popular sovereignty" humbug from Douglasism, and what "idea" will there be left in it?

☞ Throw a piece of meat among bears and a purse of gold among men, and which will behave most outrageously, the men or the beasts?

HOW THEY DO IT IN VERMONT.—Saxe, the Douglas candidate for Governor of Vermont, gets *four* votes in the three towns of Halifax, Guilford and Vernon.

DIED:

After a painful illness of four weeks, Mr. GEORGE W. NASH, departed this life on the 15th inst., in the 23d year of his age.

His demise has thrown his immediate relations into deep mourning, with whom a large circle of friends and acquaintances very truly sympathise. He was the last remaining son of his aged parents. Their declining years are left without that strong staff upon which they had hoped to lean. Blessed thought it is, that they have a stronger staff, even Jesus Christ.

Mr. NASH was a young man of unusual mildness and amiability of character. He had many friends. It is not known that he had an enemy.

Although always an example of strict morality, he regarded something more necessary in order for preparation for faithful living or peaceful dying. Therefore, some years since, when death seemed to him far in the future, he sought and obtained a hope in Christ. This hope was his stay while traversing the dark valley of the shadow of death.

He felt the cold hand of death upon him without a shudder, and manifested entire resignation to the will of God. The world held out many inducements to him—the future was bright before him—few were better qualified to enjoy life here—his prospects for this world were above the average—there were many strong ties that bound him to earth,—yet when it appeared probable to him that his Master wished to remove him hence, he calmly set his house in order, called his friends around him, said his last words of endearment, bade them farewell, and said, "I am ready."

Who that witnessed his calm and peaceful departure can doubt the necessity and efficacy of a hope in Christ? His life and his death are an exhortation to his young friends to seek first the Kingdom of Heaven.

"How blest the righteous when he dies,—
When sinks a weary soul to rest!
How mildly beam the closing eyes!
How gently heaves th' expiring breast!

"So fades a summer cloud away;
So sinks the gale when storms are o'er;
So gently shuts the eye of day;
So dies a wave along the shore."

Marshall, Sept. 18th, 1860. W.

SPECIAL NOTICES.

CHANCERY SALE.—State of Michigan, the Circuit Court for the County of Calhoun, in Chancery: Martin D. Strong, complainant, vs. Erastus N. Bates and Fanny W. Bates, defendants.

In pursuance and by virtue of the decree in this cause, dated the 5th day of September, A. D., 1860, I, the subscriber, the Circuit Court Commissioner of the County of Calhoun, will sell at public auction or vendue, to the highest bidder, at the East front door of the Court House in the City of Marshall, in said county, on the tenth day of November next, at two o'clock in the afternoon, the lands and tenements contained in the mortgage set forth in the bill of complaint in this cause, and described in said decree as follows: The East half of the North West quarter of section number twenty-six (26) in township one South of range seven West, containing eighty acres of land more or less, lying and being in the township of Penfield in the County of Calhoun and State of Michigan.

Dated Sept., 17, 1860. GEO. WOODRUFF,
Circuit Court Com'r. for Calhoun Co.
HUGHES & WOOLLEY, Sol'rs.

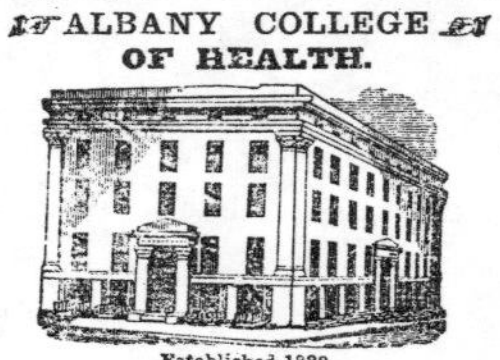

Mich. Central Rail Road—1860.

Summer Arrangement of Trains.

ON and after Monday, June 4, Passenger Trains will run as follows:

TRAINS EASTWARD.

LEAVE	Day Express	Night Express	Marshall Accomoda.
Marshall——Dine—	2.40 p. m.	3 15 a. m.	5.30 a. m.

TRAINS WESTWARD.

LEAVE		
Marshall——Dine—	12.50 p.m.	12 20 a. m

THE RAIL  MAULER

SETH T. HURD, Editor. BROWNSVILLE, PA., FRIDAY, SEPTEMBER 21, 1860. No. 12.

THE RAIL MAULER,

Is published at the Clipper Office, Brownsville, Fayette County, Pa., every FRIDAY, and will be continued until after the Presidential Campaign.

TERMS:—Single copy, 25 cents, in advance.

PRICE TO CLUBS.—Any person forwarding the names and address of four subscribers, accompanied by $1 cash, will be entitled to a fifth copy *gratis*, and in the same proportion for a larger number.

☞ Postage Stamps, where more convenient, as for a single copy, may be remitted in place of cash.

THE RAIL MAULER.

BROWNSVILLE PA.,

FRIDAY, SEPTEMBER 21, 1860.

FOR PRESIDENT,
ABRAHAM LINCOLN,
OF ILLINOIS.

FOR VICE-PRESIDENT,
HANNIBAL HAMLIN,
OF MAINE.

FOR GOVERNOR,
ANDREW G. CURTIN,
OF CENTRE COUNTY.

FOR CONGRESS,
HON. ANDREW STEWART,
OF UNIONTOWN.

COUNTY TICKET

FOR SENATE,
DR. SMITH FULLER,
OF UNIONTOWN.

FOR ASSEMBLY,
JOHN COLLINS,
OF UNIONTOWN.

FOR PROTHONOTARY,
JOHN B. KREPPS,
OF BROWNSVILLE.

FOR REGISTER AND RECORDER,
JOHN G. FARMER,
OF GERMAN TOWNSHIP.

FOR COMMISSIONER,
JOSIAH KING,
OF PERRY TOWNSHIP.

AUDITOR,
JEFFRIES A. HAGUE,
OF SOUTH UNION TOWNSHIP.

POOR HOUSE DIRECTOR,
HENRY B. GOE,
OF JEFFERSON TOWNSHIP.

Mauler Terms Reduced.

The Terms of the MAULER, until after the Presidential returns are all in from the most distant State in the Union, will be only

TWENTY-FIVE CENTS.

payable invariably IN ADVANCE. Any one sending us the names of four subscribers, and One Dollar, cash or postage stamps, will receive a fifth copy gratis, and in the same proportion for a larger number.

We have on hand a few copies of the back numbers, so that any one wishing the whole number, for binding or reference, can be furnished therewith, by applying soon, at the former terms.

There will be no further reduction hereafter in the terms of the "Mauler."

Where is Joshua R. Giddings?—*Review.*

☞ He resides in Warren, Asthabula county, Ohio.

THE IMMACULATE PATRIOT.

Seth T. Hurd, of the Brownsville *Clipper*, calls Mr. Douglas a "two-faced hypocritical demagogue." Well, that fixes the matter for the Little Giant!—doubtless Douglas will hide his head after this.—*Washington Review.*

☞ Yes, that fixes the matter; if it doesn't, just read the following "record" of "the boy who couldn't find his mother." And after a careful perusal, please tell us by what species of political philosophy a man proves that he is *one-faced* and consistent, who says to a household of "squatters"—"My friends, there is a Southern gentleman at the door with half a dozen niggers, which he wishes to take into the house, to live and remain with you as a part and parcel of your household. The Constitution gives you the right to determine whether they shall come in and abide with you or not. There are fifty of you, and we will put the question to vote. As many of the "Squatter Sovereigns" present as are in favor of letting in the gentleman with his six niggers, will raise the right hand. Three hands up. As many as are opposed to letting in the gentleman and his "property," will raise the right hand. Forty seven hands up—44 majority; so gentleman "Squatters," you decide that the gentleman and his niggers *shall not come in*. Now, if you please I will go out and tell the gentleman, that you have constitutionally, and *Squatter-sovereigntly* decided against the admission of his "chattels." He accordingly goes out and says:

"My Christian friend, you are well aware that "Squatter Sovereignty gives to those fifty territorial gentlemen within doors, the constitutional right to say whether you shall come in and with your "stock" or stay out with it. Forty seven to three, have decided by vote, that you shall *stay out; therefore*, you can *go in* with your "property," whenever you please, in spite of their decision; because, my Christian friend, you must also, be aware, that the Supreme Court have decided that your niggers are "property" and that you can take your "property" right straight into that house, if you choose to do so, to live, abide, and be protected among those fifty "*squatters*" who have the right to decide, as they have decided, that you *shan't come in*. That is to say, my Christian friend, Squatter Sovereignty says you *shan't come in*. That's right and constitutional, I go that. But the Supreme Court's decision says, you *shall* go in if you wish, even against the positive and unanimous decision of those in-door gentlemen. That's right and constitutional, I go that; and hence, you perceive, my Christian friend, that I have only *one face*, and that my views upon this question are perfectly harmonious and consistent!"

Now, the man who undertakes to palm off these clearly and palpably antagonistic positions of Douglas, as consistent with each other, is a knave; every time he asserts their consistency he proves himself a liar, and if he hasn't sense enough to discover the discrepancy, he's a fool!

From the New York Tribune.

DOUGLAS SMOKED OUT!

Mr. Douglas on Saturday achieved two important ends—he found his long-sought mother, and he mustered courage to answer the question first asked him by a veteran clergyman at Augusta (Maine) at least a month ago, which he then promised but failed to respond to. He had then his tour in Virginia and North Carolina before him; it is now past, and, though his supporters will bother the Breckinridge men in many if not most of the Slave States, he has no ground of hope of carrying one of them, Missouri excepted. So, being cornered at Clifton Springs, he turns short about, and, to the question

"Have the people of a Territory the right, according to the doctrine of non-intervention, to abolish or exclude Slavery from a Territory, while in a territorial condition?"

responds as follows:

"I have only a word to say in reply. If that gentleman has read any one speech that I have made on the subject in the last five years, he would have found an unequivocal answer to the question. I have made more than fifty speeches this year in which I have answered the question, and yet political opponents insist on putting it to me, for the purpose of creating doubt on the subject. I cannot believe there is a man in America of ordinary intelligence who does not know that I hold that the people of a Territory, while a Territory and during a territorial condition, may introduce, exclude, abolish, or regulate Slavery just as they please. I have said that North and South, and held the same doctrine everywhere. When I have seen newspapers and small politicians renewing that question, it has excited in my bosom no other feeling than that of unmitigated contempt that they should pretend to have doubts on the subject." [Loud applause.]

Mr. Douglas is a miracle of audacity, but it will not serve him here. He knows perfectly—no one better—that he has *not* hitherto taken the bold ground he now takes on this subject, nor anything like it. He did, indeed, at Freeport, Ill., when crowded to the wall by Mr. Lincoln, avow his belief that the people of a Territory might. "by unfriendly legislation," countervail the existence of Slavery therein; but this was very different from his present broad, unqualified assertion that they "may, while a Territory, and during a territorial condition, introduce, exclude, abolish, or regulate Slavery just as they please." Let us call his attention, and that of the public, to a few undeniable facts:

Mr. Douglas, in a speech at New Orleans, on the 6th of December, 1858, (just after his re-election to the Senate,) said:

"I, in common with the Democracy of Illinois, accept the Dred Scott decision of the Supreme Court of the United States, in the Dred Scott case, *as an authoritative exposition of the Constitution.* Whatever limitations the Constitution, as expounded by the courts, impose on the authority of a Territorial Legislature, we cheerfully recognize and respect in conformity with that decision. Slaves are recognized as property, and placed on an equal footing with all other property. Hence, the owner of slaves—the same as the owner of any other species of property—has *a right* to remove to a Territory and carry his property with him."

Now the Dred Scott decision is thus summed up in the syllabus prefixed to it by the official reporter of that decision (Howard's Reports, Vol. 19), and Mr. Benjamin, in his great speech of May 22d last, says that this syllabus was prepared by Chief-Justice Taney himself. Here it is:

"The clause in the Constitution authorizing Congress to make all needful rules and regulations for the government of the Territory and other property of the United States, applies only to territory within the chartered limits of some one of the States when they were Colonies of Great Britain, and which was surrendered by the British Government to the old Confederation of the States, in the treaty of peace. It does not apply to territory acquired by the present Federal Government, by treaty or conquest, from a foreign nation.

"The United States, under the present Constitution, cannot acquire territory to be held as a colony, to be governed at its will and pleasure. But it may acquire territory which, at the time has not a population that fits it to become a State, and may govern it as a Territory until it has a population which, in the judgment of Congress entitles it to be admitted as a State of the Union.

"While it remains a Territory, Congress may legislate over it within the scope of its constitutional powers, in relation to citizens of the United States, and may establish a Territorial Government, and the form of this local government must be regulated by the discretion of Congress, but with powers not exceeding those which Congress itself, by the Constitution, is authorized to exercise over citizens of the United States, in respect to their rights of persons or rights of property.

"The territory thus acquired, is acquired by the people of the United States for their common and equal benefit, through their agent and trustee—the Federal Government. Congress can exercise no power over the rights of persons or property of a citizen in the Territory which is prohibited by the Constitution. The Government and the citizen, whenever the Territory is open to settlement, both enter with their respective rights defined and limited by the Constitution.

"Congress has no right to prohibit the citizens of any particular State or States from taking up their homes there, while it permits citizens of other States to do so. Nor has it a right to give privileges to one class of citizens which it refuses to another. The territory is acquired for their equal and common benefit, and, if open to any, it must be open to all upon equal and the same terms.

"*Every citizen has a right to take with him into the Territories any article of property which the Constitution of the United States recognizes as property.*"

"*The Constitution of the United States recognizes slaves as property and pledges the Federal Government to PROTECT IT.* And Congress cannot exercise any more authority over property of any other kind.

"The act of Congress, therefore, prohibiting a citizen of the United States from taking with him his slaves when he removes to the Territory in question to reside, is an exercise of authority over private property which is not warranted by the Constitution, and the removal of the plaintiff, by his owner, to that Territory, gave him no tide to freedom."

The Court decides, you see, that Congress has no authority to prohibit slaveholding in a Territory—and that a Territorial Legislature, being a creature of Congress, has no power exceeding that of its creator—in other words, no power to abolish Slavery. Mr. Douglas declares, at New Orleans and elsewhere, that he accepts that decision as "an authoritative interpretation of the Constitution," and then tells his Clifton audience that he has always held and often asserted the right of a Territory to prohibit Slavery, and that everybody knows it!

Now see what the Cincinnati Platform —which Mr. Douglas has so often accepted and eulogized as his confession of faith —says touching this point:

Resolved, That we recognize the right of the people of all the Territories, including Kansas and Nebraska, acting through the legally and fairly expressed will of the majority of the actual residents, and *whenever the number of their inhabitants justifies it*, to form a Constitution, with or without domestic Slavery, and be admitted into the Union upon terms of perfect equality with the other States.

"*Whenever the number of their inhabitants justifies it*," you see, they may form a State Constitution, and therein establish or exclude Slavery. But *until* the Territory has reached the point where it ceases to be a Territory and becomes a State, Mr. Douglas's platform has no hint, no suggestion, of a right in the people to exclude Slavery. And when Gov. Chase moved to add to Mr. Douglas's declaration that his bill was intended to "leave the people thereof perfectly free to form and regulate their domestic institutions in their own way, subject only to the Constitution"—the following:

"*Under which the people of the Territory, through their appropriate representatives, may if they see fit, prohibit the existence of slavery therein*"—

it was *voted down*—Yeas 10 (Free-Soilers); Nays 36, including *John Bell* and Stephen A. Douglas!

We might go on, showing how Douglas has at least forty times taken ground utterly inconsistent with that he now assumes; but quote only the last plank in Mr. Douglas's platform—that on which he alone stands as a candidate for President—adopted by *his* Convention at Baltimore last June, after it had been fully considered between himself and Pierre Soule the day before at Washington. This plank was moved by Lieut. Gov. Wickliffe of La., seconded by H. B. Payne of Ohio, and unanimously adopted by the Douglas National Convention. Here it is:

"*Resolved*, That it is in accordance with the interpretation of the Cincinnati Platform, that, during the existence of the Territorial Governments, *the measure of restriction, whatever it may be, imposed by the Federal Constitution on the power of the Territorial Legislatures over the subject of the domestic relations*, as the same has been, or shall hereafter be, finally determined by the Supreme Court of the United States, should be respected by all good citizens and enforced with promptness and fidelity by every branch of the General Government."

Can any man fail to understand this? Is it not directly in the teeth of Mr. Douglas's Clifton position? Was there ever before a candidate for President who, in the desperation of his canvass, publicly repudiated and scouted the very platform on which he was nominated? What but defeat—and not defeat merely, but wreck and utter ruin—can await a party so recklessly led; a candidate so regardless of his own public committals and professions?

THE RAIL MAULER:

FRIDAY, SEPTEMBER 21, 1860.

Hello, the Uniform!

Here it comes—the uniform for the Brownsville Wide Awakes. Republican enthusiasm runs high in this diocese about these days—over two hundred Wide Awakes up to the present writing —hurra for Old Abe. Give us a turn out to-morrow night, Cap'n, do, we can't wait—the boys are afire—put 'em through —don't wait. Two hundred Wide Awakes in Brownsville, and there will be two hundred more! What d'ye think o' that, Master Brooks—four hundred Wide Awakes, under the general guidance of a sprightly young lad of 80, named Miller—Hurrah for Old Abe—don the capes, on with the caps, hoist the torches—music in front—three cheers —Hurrah!

Found his Mother.

Little Dug has found his mother. He has. The poor boy has had a hard time of it. Wherever the roads "forked," he seems most unluckily and unaccountably, to have taken the wrong one, and has thus traveled thousands of miles 'out of his way,' living on clams, crabs, and sour grapes. To the question, "Does your mother know you're out?" he is reported to have nerely given a knowing wink of his left eye, as much as to say, "what the d——l do you suppose I care about findin' mother. I know where she is, and what I'm about" and when the undutiful youngster was informed that his ma was very much *down* about the way he was actin', he is further reported to have said he "didn't care a d—— whether she was "down" or "up."

Negro! Negro! Negro!—One of our citizens informs us that he listened for two hours and a half to the speeches on Friday last, and there *was* not fifteen *minutes* of the time occupied with anything else but negroes. *Is* there no white *men* in this country. Or *is* their *interests* of so little importance as not to deserve notice.—*Wash. Review.*

☞ O yes, there *is* a great many white *men* in this country, and their *interests is* of the greatest importance; so much so indeed, that even though but "fifteen *minutes was* occupied with general subjects," we should have been better pleased to record that *they was* devoted to the "negro" in precisely the same way, and for the same objects that the *two hours and a half*—'bating the 15 minutes—*was* devoted to the "negro." And how was that? Why by arguing against the injustice and inexpediency of the locofoco doctrine which seeks to open the way for the "negro" to occupy every inch of the public territory, which the Republicans are trying to preserve for the "interests" and occupancy of "white men," unsaturated, and untainted with negro slavery.

A Clincher.—The stock in trade of the Republican party—is the danger of the extention of slavery over territories now free. The *humbug* of this, as of most of the arguments upon which *republicans attempts* to establish their claims to public confidence, *meet* with frequent *exposes*.—*Review.*

☞ There is no doubt "the *humbug meet* with frequent *exposes*," especially when "*republicans attempts*" to establish their claims, &c. Well, well.

Chopping Down a Republican Pole!

$100 REWARD!

About four miles below Brownsville, a few rods back from the right bank of the Monongahela, resides an elderly and highly esteemed widow lady, whose political sympathies, as was the case with her late venerable and respected husband, happen to be with the Republican party.

During almost every presidential campaign for a long series of years, the patriotic husband of this estimable lady, has caused to be erected on the bank of the river in front of his residence, a tall pole, from the top of which, floated the stars and stripes, until the close of the then impending contest. The lamented patriot, however, is no more, but the return of the present quardrenial struggle, had revived and rendered so vivid the recollections of the past, that the good lady, partly out of respect to the cause to which she had become so ardently attached, not only for its own sake, but because it was that of her deceased husband, and partly as a token of respect to the memory of one who had so oft gazed from his own door, upon the proud banner of his country, as it fluttered in the breeze, at the towering point of the accustomed spire, expressed a wish to a few gallant and patriotic spirits, that a 'pole' and flag might stand and float in the place of its predecessors, until the close of the present struggle. Her wishes were promptly complied with; a splendid pole, 116 feet high, was raised, and the national flag, a large and beautiful banner, manufactured and presented by the young ladies of the neighborhood, was displayed at its top. A large and orderly concourse of people, including both sexes, assembled on the occasion, when several speeches were delivered, and much enthusiasm manifested, without the aid of artificial stimulants.

At the close of the proceedings the kind and generous widow invited as many of the crowd as chose to remain, without distinction of party, to a sumptious repast, which herself and daughters had prepared for those in attendance, after which they retired to their respective homes.

A night or two thereafter, a number of high minded and patriotic democrats committed an act of noble and unparalleled gallantry, by chopping, or rather *boring* down the magnificent flag-staff, which had been erected by the liberality of the good widow, under the circumstances above detailed, and carrying down over the embankment, the beautiful banner of our common country, which fair hands had wrought and presented to a common object.

Now if any human mind can conceive of a meaner, more dastardly or contemptible act than this, it possesses powers of conception more subtle and refined than any we ever saw exhibited by the most heartless thief or burglar.

Were the case politically reversed, and Republicans had sneakingly, and stealthily bored down a democratic pole, erected at the instance, and by the liberality of a democratic lady, and sent to the river the national banner, the work and free-will offering of democratic maiden hands, we would not, in alluding to such craven-hearted villany, soften the severity of our language in the slightest degree.

The patriotic and noble-hearted lady has resolved that another flag-staff shall be erected in the place of the one despoiled, and a large number of gallant young Republicans in the neighborhood, have agreed to take turns, in watching and defending it *every night* until after the election, rifle in hand, and have sworn a solemn oath, that they will put a bullet through the first lousy, loathsome, God-abandoned miscreant that dares molest it, be the consequences what they may.

We are authorised by a gentleman who feels justly indignant at this mean and cowardly insult to a worthy and estimable lady, to offer a reward of one hundred dollars, for the names of the prowling, midnight scoundrels who perpetrated this wanton and cowardly deed.

Another Pole Up.

Since writing the foregoing article, we observe by the following, from the "Valley Spirit," that the prostration of the beautiful flag staff alluded to, has been followed by the erection of another still larger and higher, and we learn, personally, also, that several respectable democrats who were indignant at the outrage, have since become "Straight out Republicans," and even assisted in raising the latter pole.

The "Spirit" says:—As the publication of our paper has been delayed, we are enabled to announce the erection of another and better pole upon the site of the one which fell at the touch of the foul hands of midnight prowlers. On Tuesday afternoon, a large number of Republicans, including several straight-outs from the disgusted Democracy, assembled upon the ground, and reared a magnificent pole. After sending up the flag again to the breeze, and making the welkin ring with three long and hearty cheers for Lincoln, Hamlin and the cause of truth, the editor of the Valley Spirit was called upon to address the meeting, and in a brief and pointed speech, responded to the call. The meeting adjourned with three hearty cheers.

Wide-Awakes in Brownsville.

One of the most spirited and enthusiastic Republican meetings we have attended this campaign, was held in the Town Hall, in Brownsville, on Monday evening last, for the purpose of forming a regular, uniformed, torch-light, Wide-Awake Club, composed of Republicans of Brownsville, Bridgeport, West Brownsville, and the surrounding neighborhoods.

Oliver C. Cromlow, was appointed President, and John Cunningham, Secretary, whereupon 107 good and true Republicans gave in their names as members of the Wide-Awake Club, among whom was the venerable Israel Miller, an old Henry Clay Whig—now for "Old Abe," and the announcement of whose name was received with cheers.

The meeting adjourned with three cheers for "Old Abe," to meet again on Tuesday (last) evening, for the purpose of choosing officers, and making the necessary arrangements for procuring the "Wide-Awake" uniform, consisting of Cap, Cape, and Torch-light.

We write on Tuesday morning, and will, if we can, without delaying our papaper, give the result of the proceedings to-night in this week's issue. If not, we will give it in the "Mauler" of Friday.

Wednesday Morning, 19th.

Wide-Awake Enthusiasm.

The most stiring and enthusiastic political gathering we have ever witnessed in Brownsville, was the adjourned Wide-Awake Meeting last night at the Town Hall. The room was packed to its utmost capacity, and upwards of 50 names added to the Wide-Awake Club. Arrangements were made for procuring the W. A. uniforms immediately, and the first procession of the Club will probably take place as early as Saturday evening or Monday evening.

The following are the names of the several Officers and Committees:—

President W. A. Club—Israel Miller.
Vice Presidents—S. A. Wood,
S. Bennington,
J. T. Colvin.
Rec. Secretary—Wm. Parkhill, Jr.
Asst. do Ed. Morgan, Jr.
Cor. Secretary—John S. Wilgus.
Treasurer—Jacob McKennan.
Committee on Constitution and By-Laws—Jason Baker,
Freeman Wise,
Seth T. Hurd.
Com. on Uniforms—J. T. Worthington,
A. G. Minehart,
Sam. A. Wood,
S. S. Snowdon,
J. B. McKennan.
Captain—John T. Worthington.
1st Lieutenant—Dunham Williams.
2nd do John B. Patterson.
3rd do William Holmes.

☞ The Wide-Awake Club will meet at the Town Hall, on Monday evening next.

The Curtin Meetings.

Our columns this week are so much crowded with matter, either in type or on hand, previous to the advent among us, of our noble candidate for Governor, Hon. Andrew G. Curtin, accompanied by Hon. Messrs. Grow, McMichael and Jordan, that we find it impossible to give an extended notice of the meetings and their several addresses on the occasion of their visit to this place and to Uniontown. We have only space to say, that the gentlemen above named arrived here from Washington, and each in turn addressed a large and impromptu meeting of our citizens on Saturday morning, from the balcony of Wyatt's Hotel; that they proceeded from thence to Uniontown, where they met and addressed a large concourse of Republicans and others assembled in the Court House; and that Mr. Grow and Mr McMichael returned to Brownsville Saturday evening, where, from the same stand they had occupied in the morning, Mr. Grow enchained, for nearly two hours, a very large and enthusiastic crowd which had assembled in front of the hotel. His speech was exceedingly eloquent, argumentative and convincing, and was frequently interrupted by loud and enthusiastic bursts of applause.

At the conclusion of Mr. Grow's speech, loud calls were made for M'Michael, but that gentleman, being much exhausted from long journeying and much speaking, had retired to rest.

These gentlemen all bring the most cheering tidings from the eastern portion of the State, and express the most entire confidence in the success of the Republican Ticket.

Some of the Whigs who fought under the banner of Henry Clay in 1844, are now in various ways trying to secure the election of Douglas. Have they forgotten that "Harry of the West" was defeated in the contest of '44 by slanders like the following, taken from a speech delivered during the canvass by Stephen A. Douglas?

"I denounced him (CLAY) in the Congress of the United States, and I now denounce him as A TRAITOR—AN OLD BLACK-HEARTED TRAITOR—the first American statesman who ever attempted *to sell his country for British gold.*"

ATTENTION!

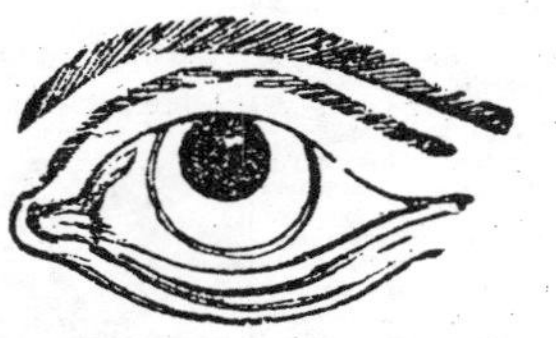

WIDE-AWAKES.

A regular meeting of the Wide Awake Club, will be held in the Town Hall, on Monday evening next, 24th instant.

Meeting at Greenfield.

The Republicans of Washington, Fayette, Greene, and surrounding counties, will hold a Grand Rally, at Greenfield, on to-morrow, (Saturday) Sept. 22d. A number of distinguished speakers will address the meeting. Turn out!

LINCOLN AND HAMLIN!

Curtin and Victory!

Grand Republican Mass Meeting at Pittsburgh,
Thursday, September 27th.

The people of Pennsylvania, who are in favor of protection to American industry; who are in favor of free homesteads to actual settlers; who are in favor of protecting Territories now free from the blight of slavery extension; who are in favor of maintaining our National Union and the supremacy of the laws inviolate, are invited to attend a Grand Mass Meeting, at Pittsburgh, on Thursday, September 27th.

The following distinguished gentlemen are expected to attend and deliver addresses: Hon. Wm. H. Seward, Hon. F. Hassaurek, Hon. Cassius M. Clay, Hon. B. F. Wade, Hon. E. Cowan, Hon. J. P. Campbell, Hon. W. D. Kelly, Hon. Andrew G. Curtin, of Penn'a, People's candidate for Governor; Hon. Carl Schurz, of Wisconsin; Hon. John Sherman, of Wisconsin; Hon. Thos. Corwin, of Ohio; Hon. Simon Cameron, Hon. Morton McMichael, Hon. John Hickman, Hon. James Pollock, Hon. John Covode, of Penn'a.

The Lincoln, Hamlin and Curtin Clubs throughout the State, and especially in all the Western counties, are expected to attend, properly organized.

The Wide Awakes are invited and expected to attend in full force, and a Wide Awake Torchlight Procession will take place on the Evening of the 26th.

Excursion Tickets will be issued on all the Railways, good for the time necessary to go to Pittsburgh, attend the meeting, and return home.

Disappeared.—Hurd of the Brownsville *Clipper* and his opposition to Stewart. He did show his teeth, but a kick from Stewart and a growl from the *Standard* seduced him.—*Wash. Review.*

☞ We had thought that the *purities* of the "Dove's Nest," who do up the *editorials* for the *Review*, had had quite enough to do with "seduction," and other *consequent* matters pertaining to the duties of the private accouchment department of the aforesaid "Dove's Nest;" but it seems they can't write a four-line squib without the use of terms, however forced the application, expressive of the thoughts which still appear to be uppermost in their minds. Nice fellows, those about the "Dove's Nest," for "Sunday-School Teachers!"

What Popular Sovereignty Has Done.

Read! Read!! Read!!!

The following is an extract from Mr. Douglas' last great speech in the Senate, in which he magnifies the triumphs of Popular Sovereignty for the cause of Slavery. This speech was made with a view of coaxing the Southerners into supporting him for President at the then approaching Charleston Convention. While it failed of its object at the South, it has had the effect to open the eyes of Northern Democrats as to the real bearing of "non-intervention" in reference to Slavery. This speech ought to be read by every Free Laborer and every citizen of the Free States:

From Douglas' Speech in the Senate, May 16, 1860.

"But, we are told the necessary result of this doctrine of non-intervention, which gentlemen, by way of throwing ridicule upon, call popular sovereignty, is to deprive the South of all participation in what they call the common Territories of the United States. That was the ground on which the gentleman from Mississippi [Mr. Davis] predicated his opposition to the Compromise Measure of 1850. He regarded a refusal to repeal the Mexican law as equivalent to the Wilmot Proviso; a refusal to deny to a Territorial Legislature the right to exclude slavery as equivalent to an exclusion. He believed at that time that this doctrine did amount to a denial of Southern rights; but they doubted it. Now let me see how far his predictions and suppositions have been verified. I infer that he told the people so, for he makes it a charge in his bill of indictment against me, that I am hostile to Southern rights, because I gave those notes.

Now, what has been the result? My views were incorporated into the Compromise Measure of 1850, and his were rejected. Has the South been excluded from all the Territory acquired from Mexico? What says the bill from the House of Representatives now on your table, repeating the slave code in New Mexico established by the people themselves? It is a part of the history of the country that under this doctrine of non-intervention, this doctrine that you delight to call squatter sovereignty, the people of New Mexico have INTRODUCED and PROTECTED Slavery in the WHOLE OF THAT TERRITORY, more than FIVE TIMES THE SIZE OF THE STATE OF NEW YORK. Under this doctrine, Slavery has been extended from the Rio Grande to the Gulf of California and from the line of the Republic of Mexico, not only up to 36 deg. 30 m., but up to 38 deg., giving you a degree and a half more Slave territory than you ever claimed. In '48 and '49 and 1850 you only asked to have the line of 36 d. 30 m. The Nashville Convention fixed that as its ultimatum. I offered it in the Senate in August, 1848, and it was adopted here but rejected in the House of Representatives. You asked only up to 36 deg. 30 min., and NON-INTERVENTION HAS GIVEN YOU SLAVE TERRITORY UP TO 38 deg., a DEGREE AND A HALF MORE THAN YOU ASKED; and yet you say that this is a sacrifice of Southern rights?

These are the fruits of THIS PRINCIPLE which the Senator from Missippi regards as hostile to the rights of the South. Where did you ever get any other fruits that were more palatable to your tastes or more refreshing to your strength?—WHAT OTHER INCH OF FREE TERRITORY HAS BEEN CONVERTED INTO SLAVE TERRITORY OF THE AMERICAN CONTINENT, SINCE THE REVOLUTION, EXCEPT IN NEW MEXICO AND ARIZONIA, UNDER THE PRINCIPLE OF NON-INTERVENTION affirmed at Charleston. If it be true that this principle of non-intervention has conferred upon you all that immense Territory; PROTECTED SLAVERY in that comparatively Northern and cold region, where you did not expect to go, CANNOT YOU TRUST THE SAME PRINCIPLE FURTHER SOUTH WHEN YOU COME TO ACQUIRE ADDITIONAL TERRITORY FROM MEXICO? If it is true this principle of non-intervention has given to Slavery all New Mexico, which was surrounded on nearly every side by Free Territory, will not the same principle protect you in the Northern States of Mexico when they are acquired, since they are now surrounded by Slave Territory; are several hundred miles further South; have many degrees of greater heat, and have a climate and soil adapted to Southern products? ARE YOU NOT SATISFIED WITH THESE PRACTICAL RESULTS?

GIVES IT UP.

The Baltimore *Patriot*, one of the most enthusiastic Bell and Everett papers in Maryland, says the Pittsburgh *Gazette*, in its issue of Saturday takes down the names of its candidates, and gives the following leader in explanation of its course, and as an indication of its future policy:

"Under the full conviction that the Presidential election is settled, and that nothing which we can do or say can have any influence in changing the inevitable result, now so obvious to every reflecting mind, we shall henceforward turn our especial attention to the promotion of education in Maryland, the forwarding of every feasible scheme for opening the direct trade between Baltimore and Europe, to the improvement of agriculture and its kindred branches of tillage, to the extension of mechanical, manufacturing and manual industry upon the soil of our own State, and to the encouragement of the inventive powers of Maryland minds. In the remaining two months, therefore, of the Presidential campaign, which we regard as virtually ended, we shall content ourselves with merely noting its progress, as a matter of news, for the information and entertainment of our readers; but as we have said, we shall direct our editorial energies to the promotion of the objects enumerated above, and in the pursuit of the labors, we hope to have the aid, assistance, and generous encouragement of all who sympathise with these things."

The natural inquiry is, how does the *Patriot* think the election is going? For Lincoln and Hamlin. In the conclusion of the article above it gives a letter written from New York, from which we make the following extract:

"I see that our Maryland friends are counting largely on New York going against Lincoln. Don't be deceived. There is no possible hope for so desirable an issue. Differing widely from you upon the question of coalitions, deeming them to be legitimate political weapons, whenever they can be used to effect an object that cannot be effected without them, and not considering any moral question to be involved, I went into the plan of uniting the Opposition to Lincoln in this State, heart and soul, but alas! the votes did not and they will not be transferred.—The devil or somebody else, has got into them. Why, what do you think? The Lincoln men have the names of 81,000 of the very men who voted for Fillmore in 1856 inscribed on their poll lists for Lincoln—not put there by guess, but by actual, veritable, personal inquiry of each man as to his course."

The Warrenton (Va.) *Whig* (Bell) notices a meeting in that town at which Extra Billy Smith (of egg-nog memory) and Albert Rust, of Arkansas, were expected to speak. Gov. Smith refused to speak on the same stand with Mr. Rust, and the *Whig* remarks:—"Both being Locofocos, we wanted to see them meet, and choke each other to their heart's content, we occupying all the time the position of the woman, who watched with intense satisfaction the terrible fight, recorded in history, between her beloved spouse and a large specimen of the bear kind."

Charges have been preferred against the Washington City postmaster by Hon. Preston King, for refusing to send thro' the mails documents bearing the frank of Republican members of Congress, and at the same time, sending off Breckinridge documents bearing the franks of gentlemen known to be in Washington. The matter will be laid before Postmaster General Holt.

THE "FUSION."

Its Absurdities and Impossibilities.

Hon. Henry J. Raymond's Speech at Brooklyn exposes truthfully and forcibly the character of the Douglas-Bell-Breckenridge Fusion, and the hopelessness of its prospects. The following are extracts from it:—

We have, it is true, four parties with four candidates and four platforms; but the Republican party is the only one of them all that stands its ground and maintains the honor of its flag. [Applause.] The leaders of all the others are busy in cheating their opponents, or in betraying their followers. [Applause.] The whole aim of the three opposition parties in this State is to form a Coalition,—to *fuse*, in support of one electoral ticket. We hear nothing of their principles,—no vindication of their distinctive opinions and purposes,—nothing but a clamorous cry, the offspring partly of fear and partly of hate—the ignoblest passions of the human heart,—for a union of their forces and their votes. Yet these three parties have each a distinctive platform. One asserts the principle that the Constitution carries Slavery into every Territory, and that when there the Federal Government must protect it. The other denies and denounces this doctrine, and asserts the right of the people of the Territories to admit or exclude it at pleasure. The third asserts the supreme, paramount duty of having no opinion on the subject, and of ignoring utterly every political question important enough to create a difference of opinion among the people [Cheers.] There is not a solitary political principle on which these parties do not hold sentiments utterly hostile to each other. They are not agreed upon a single measure of government or a single feature of public policy. Yet their great endeavor, the sole object of their efforts and their ambition thus far in the canvass has been,—not to convince each other or the country of the truth of their principles, but so to assign the places on the electoral ticket, that each party should be content with its share of the spoils and that all might vote together! Has not this been the burthen of their song? Have not their organs, day after day and week after week, insisted upon this as the great object of of their efforts? ["Yes, yes."] But what do we see now? Does any one of the parties to this Coalition abate anything of its peculiar pretensions? Have they drawn up any programme of principles on which, for the sake of saving the country, they are willing to unite, and by which they have solemnly agreed that the country shall be governed in the event of their success? Nothing of the kind! Not only has nothing of the kind been done, but nothing of the kind has even been attempted! [Cheers.] Retaining each his peculiar views—hating each other with all their ancient cordiality—and watching each other all the time, as gamblers at the card table watch each other for fear of being cheated, these volunteer saviours of the country have simply agreed that one shall have *seven*, another *eighteen*, and the other *ten*, Electors—as the price of their mutual support! They have divided up the vote of the Empire State for the Presidency, precisely as needy adventurers might divide up the chances of a lottery, or as gamblers might share the hazards of a faro-bank. [Applause.]

Here, then, is my first great objection to voting for the Fusion ticket. I do not know *what* or *who* will succeed, if it succeeds. It has no basis in principle. It rests upon no solid foundation of public policy. I do not know in the least what measures it would adopt, or what candidate it would select for the Presidency. I am not willing thus to cast my vote in the dark as to every point on which votes are expected to tell.

If that Fusion ticket should succeed, is the country to be saved by the gospel according to Breckenridge, or Douglas, or Bell? Is the danger which threatens the country to be averted by adopting a Slave code for the Territories and by re-opening the African Slave trade;—or by leaving territorial squatters to regulate their own affairs and ours also;—or by leaving everything at loose ends, having no opinions and no policy on any question, dealing solely in "generalities," so very general that they don't even "glitter," trusting everything to chance, and leaving the ship of State to drift, without helm or compass, over the wide sea of contending interests and howling passions? Each of these policies is represented upon that ticket,—and you ask us to vote for it. Tell us, first, *which* of them we put in the ascendant, if we elect the ticket! Are we to vote for all these principles at once? Must the country go to destruction unless I vote for three candidates who detest each other most cordially, and upon perfectly good and substantial grounds? [Laughter.] Can the Union be saved only by my voting for three platforms, diametrically hostile to each other,—any one of which, if acted on, would ruin the country, unless both the others are utterly and absolutely false?

Every Douglas man, therefore, who votes the Fusion ticket casts *seven* votes for Breckenridge, a Slave Code, the nationalization of Slavery and the reopening of the African Slave Trade,—and *ten* votes for Bell and the rump of the Know Nothing Party. Every Breckenridge man who votes that ticket, casts *eighteen* votes for Douglas, who broke up the Democratic Party at Charleston, and Squatter Sovereignty,—and *ten* votes for Bell and Everett. And every Bell man who votes for Fusion gives *seven* votes for Breckenridge and *eighteen* for Douglas—twenty-five in all, for the men who have waged ceaseless and unrelenting war against every principle the Bell Party has ever professed and every man it has ever put in nomination for any office. [Applause.] What a splendid political position all these men will occupy in the contests may that divide the country hereafter! With what admirable grace they can denounce their opponents for political inconsistency,—and boast of their own steady adherence to one line of political conduct! Most men are satisfied to vote for one candidate and one party;—but they vote for all the parties and all the candidates but one, whom they find in the field! [Applause and laughter.

THE THEORY THAT ELECTORS AND NOT THE PEOPLE ARE TO CHOOSE A PRESIDENT.

But we have a reply to this objection. Gov. Hunt, whom I regard as the author of the Fusion, as he certainly was the earliest and the most zealous laborer for it, has set forth, in speeches and public addresses, the theory on which it rests. He tells us that the Constitution never intended that the People should elect a President. They were only to choose *electors*, who should elect a President for them. The Electoral College was to be a Convention of unpledged, uncommitted, irresponsible delegates;—and they were to choose the President, with whom directly the people had nothing to do. Now if that really is Gov. Hunt's opinion, he has departed very widely from his own theory in having any Presidential candidate at all. What business has he to support Bell and Everett if the people are only to choose unpledged electors, and the electors to choose the President? And if this is the theory of the Fusion movement—if that movement aims only to choose good electors who will exercise their own discretion in the choice of President,—how happens it that every one engaged in it has his own Presidential candidate? Why is every Elector pledged to one man or another? Why all this feverish anxiety to secure a satisfactory division of the ticket among the friends of the three Fusion candidates for the Presidency?

Gov. Hunt has more than once declared that it would be in the highest degree dangerous to have a President elected by less than a majority of all the people. He seems to have forgotten that Mr. Buchanan had 377,000 less than a majority—that Gen. Taylor had 151 000 less—that Mr Polk was in a minority of about 25,000—and that, in fact, very few of our Presidents have had an absolute majority of the popular vote. And he has no objection apparently to having a President elected by seventeen *States*, with less than *one-fifth* of the aggregate population of the United States. [Applause] He has no objection to nullify the three millions of people in New York by the vote of 47,000 in Florida. His respect for majorities does not take that direction.

The object of the coalition is to take away the election of President from the people, and give it to the House of Representatives. ["That's it," and applause.] *This is the issue:*—and in my judgment, it is one of infinitely more importance than any other single issue involved in the present canvass. [Applause.] Its decision touches more nearly the very foundations of our Government, and will affect more profoundly for weal or woe the prosperity of the country, than any other question dependent on the result of this election.

No President will be elected by the people unless it be Abraham Lincoln. [Cheers.] Neither Breckenridge, nor Douglas, nor Bell hope for, or dream of, an election by the popular vote. The object of this fusion movement, therefore, is *to defeat any election of President by the People* The whole movement is based on a profound distrust of the ability of the people to choose their own rulers and make their own laws.

Literary News.

"*A Comprehensive Dictionary of the English Language*," by Joseph E Worcester. This is substantially a combination of the two excellent Dictionaries published by the same author in 1849 and 1855. In addition to the common words of the language, it compises numerous technical terms in the various arts and sciences, local and provincial words, and such words from foreign languages as are often met with in English books. The definitions are concise, but comprehensive and exact. A peculiarly valuable feature is the care and precision with which synonymes are noted. Besides the Dictionary proper, the volume contains remarks on pronunciation and grammar tables of Greek and Latin Scriptural, Geographical and Historical names, with their Pronunciation, Abbreviations, Quotations, &c. The design has been to give the greatest quantity of useful matter in the most condensed form. It has been eminently successful, for although but a small octavo, it contains about all the really useful matter for the general public that is to be found in the large folio dictionaries. Published by Swan, Brewer and Tileston, Boston, and for sale here by S. R. Gray.

EVENING JOURNAL.

WEDNESDAY EVENING OCT. 10, 1860.

REPUBLICAN NOMINATIONS.

FOR PRESIDENT,

ABRAHAM LINCOLN.

FOR VICE-PRESIDENT,

HANNIBAL HAMLIN.

FOR PRESIDENTIAL ELECTORS.

At Large:

WILLIAM C. BRYANT, JAMES O. PUTNAM.

Districts:

1. John A. King.	18. Henry Churchill.
2. Edwards W. Fiske.	19. James R. Allaben.
3. Andrew Carrigan.	20. Benj N. Huntington
4. James Kelly.	21 Sherman D. Phelps.
5. Sigismund Kauffmann.	22. John J Foote.
6. Frederick Kapp.	23. Hiram Dewey.
7. Washington Smith.	24. James L Voorhees.
8. William A Darling.	25. William Van Marter.
9. Wm H Robertson.	26. John E. Seeley.
10. George M Grier.	27. Frank L. Jones.
11. Rufus H King	28. James S. Wadsworth.
12. Jacob B Carpenter.	29. Ezra M. Parsons.
13. John F. Winslow.	30. Charles C. Parker.
14. Jacob H Ten Eyck.	31. Elisha S. Whalen.
15. N Edson Sheldon.	32. John Greiner, Jr.
16. Robert S Hale.	33. James Parker.
17. Abijah Beckwith.	

FOR GOVERNOR,

EDWIN D. MORGAN.

FOR LIEUT. GOVERNOR,

ROBERT CAMPBELL.

FOR CANAL COMMISSIONER,

SAMUEL H. BARNES.

FOR INSPECTOR OF STATE PRISONS,

JAMES K. BATES.

THE ELECTIONS YESTERDAY.

Overshadowing Republican Victories!—Pennsylvania, Ohio and Indiana Sure for Lincoln.

The State Elections yesterday in Pennsylvania, Ohio and Indiana, have virtually decided the result of the Presidential Election. The large Republican gains even in the Democratic strongholds—the increased majorities in every Republican locality, and the success of Republican nominees for Congress and State Offices, indicate clearly and significantly that the "game is up."

It needs very little arithmetic to solve the question that remains. If the Douglas, Bell and Breckenridge men are beaten in these States even now, when they are united, how will it be at the Presidential contest when they are divided?

With these auspicious tidings to cheer our efforts, let the few remaining weeks be devoted to work, to secure the Victory within our grasp.

Seward's Western Speeches.

Weed, Parsons & Co. have in press, and will publish immediately, in one pamphlet, Governor Seward's speeches at Detroit, Lansing, Madison, St. Paul, Dubuque, St. Josephs, Leavenworth, Lawrence, Atchison City, St. Louis, Springfield, Chicago, Cleveland, Buffalo, &c.

Prices—Single copies, 10 cents; per hundred, $7.

Mr. Douglas's "Popular Sovereignty."

Like all other public measures, Mr. Douglas's Popular Sovereignty can best be judged by its fruits. What has it accomplished thus far?

It deprived the people of Kansas of access to the ballot box. It denied them a voice in their own Capitol, excluded them from seats in their own Legislature or on their own Bench. It filled their offices with officials from other States, and their Statute Book with Laws transcribed from those of Missouri for the express purpose of oppressing them. It shed their blood and dug their graves, under pretence of "allowing them to regulate their own affairs," and kept the whole Union six years in turmoil, under pretence of "ending agitation." It has consigned to private life nearly every Northern member of Congress that voted for it, has overthrown two Administrations that supported it, has ruined its author and split his Party!

Such are the achievements of "Squatter Sovereignty" thus far. Its future work will be of the same sort. It will be the political death of the faction who now uphold it.

The Election in the House.

The utmost that any of the three parties opposed to Lincoln hope to effect, is to throw the Election into the House. They give up beforehand all idea of electing any candidate by the popular vote, and rest their hopes on the House of Representatives.

But will their chances be any better in the House, even should the Election go there?

In the House, votes for President are cast by States. Each State has one vote. The majority of the Congressional Delegation from each State of course determine how that vote shall be cast. There are 33 States, and 17 votes are necessary to elect.

Fifteen of the States in the House are certain for Lincoln. Thirteen are for Breckenridge, one for Douglas, and one for Bell. Three, Kentucky, Maryland and North Carolina, are equally divided between Americans and Democrats.

Only three candidates, those who have received the highest number of Electoral votes, can be voted for in the House. This would exclude either Douglas or Bell, more probably Douglas, for Bell may get some Electoral votes, while Douglas is likely to get none.

Lincoln, then, in the House, would lack but two votes of an Election, while Breckenridge would lack four, and Bell would lack sixteen. Even if all the tied States should vote for Breckenridge, it would not elect him, unless he could also get the vote either of Mr. Douglas's State of Illinois, or Mr. Bell's State of Tennessee. Neither of these is probable. A change of a single vote in the Illinois Delegation would suffice to give the vote of that State to Lincoln, who then would lack but one.

The triple-headed Fusionists, therefore, are fighting for a desperate hope. They cannot elect any one of their three candidates on the popular vote, and even if they throw the Election into Congress, they are by no means certain of success.

The Slave Trade.—Hardly a week passes that a Slave Trading vessel is not heard of, either as captured or as escaping to continue the prosecution of her nefarious traffic. The great and increasing activity of the Traffic suggests the inquiry whether some additional legislation by Congress for its suppression might not be useful.

A bill was introduced in the Senate last winter by Mr. Seward for this purpose. Its principal provisions were for hiring ten steamers to be employed in cruising on either coast where needed: authorising any State to pass laws prohibiting the African Slave Trade within its limits: requiring that no ship shall sail for the African coast without a clearance from the U. S. District Attorney: and that the Secretary of the Treasury designate the ports of Africa where American Consuls shall reside, and where only commerce shall be carried on.

While no doubt was expressed as to the efficiency of these provisions, the Act was opposed by the Democrats in Congress as unnecessary. They contended that there was no probability or possibility of the revival of the Slave Trade, and that it was a mere waste of time and trouble to bestow thought upon it.

Present events are proving the fallacy of these views. Had this proposed Law been enacted last winter, and faithfully enforced, the traffic now going on so briskly would have been in a great measure broken up.

☞ We understand that the Hon. James T. Brady regards his nomination for Governor as meaning something; that *his* name was not set up to be taken down; and that *he* will not be found "cuddling" with all sorts of unclean birds "under the same dirty bed-clothes."

The Atlas and Argus on Taxation.

The Atlas, true to its instincts, has again commenced its annual growling about debt and taxation, and assails a Republican Legislature for imposing:—

1st. A tax of one and one-eighth of a mill to pay the salaries of the public officers, and to defray the ordinary expenses of the Government—a tax which has been levied by every Legislature since 1842, though not for the same amount every year. Two-eighths of this tax is fairly chargeable to the late Democratic Canal Board, in reducing the rates of tolls on the Canals so low that the revenues were not sufficient to pay the $350,000 devoted by the Constitution to the interest on the General Fund Debt.

2d. A tax to pay the interest on the new Canal Debt. It is a great crime in a State to provide the means to pay the interest on its public Stock Debt, and yet no press in the country has been more clamorous than the Atlas has been heretofore that this public obligation should be met promptly by direct taxation. The late Democratic Canal Board came into power on the 1st of January, 1858, and held its power two years. One of its first financial acts was to reduce the rates of toll, so that the gross revenues that year were about $2,110,000, instead of $3,000,000, as they should have been, and would have been under any honest Administration. It tried its hand again in 1859 to increase the revenue by a further needless and wicked reduction of the rates on the Canals, and we got about $1,723,000 of gross revenue, and expended $927,879 of it in superintendence, collection and repairs. This was the result of two years Democratic Administration honesty, in which the State may be said to have lost $2,000,000. It was this policy that drove the State to the hard alternative of meeting its obligations by a tax.

When the present Republican State Officers came into power last January, one of their first financial acts was to adjust the rates of toll, in order to obtain a revenue from the Canals, and what has been the result? Already an increase of about $900,000 over 1859, which will exceed a million before the close of navigation, and a gross revenue up to the 1st of October exceeding any year since 1853. This tax is chargeable to the indomitable Democracy.

3d. A half mill tax to complete the public works. This the Atlas pronounces the *most outrageous tax of all*. The Atlas has always been opposed to the completion of the canals. It was so opposed in 1842 and has been ever since. And now, because there are no other means at hand, it objects to a small tax for this object. The friends of the Canals will understand and appreciate this old and ancient hostility. It is an outrage, is it, to raise the means to complete and finish the work almost done, and pay the land holder his damages for lands taken for the public use?

4th. A tax of three-quarters of a mill for school purposes. This is a permanent tax imposed by a law passed in 1856. The last legislature had nothing to do with imposing it. The monies levied are expended in the counties where raised. The people in the counties get back all the money they pay, for school purposes. This is only another mode of obtaining the means to sustain a liberal system of public instruction. It takes the place of the old method of rate bills and local school district taxation, where one-quarter of the sums directed to be raised was eaten up by Collectors' fees, non-resident exemptions, &c.

5th. A tax to pay the interest and redeem the principal of the $2,500,000 floating debt loan. We repeat what we said about this tax the other day. The last Legislature had nothing to do in regard to this loan or the tax to be raised the present year. The law authorising that loan was submitted to and approved by the people at the last general election. The people have sanctioned the law which is now a part of the Constitution, and we shall have no fears that the tax will not be cheerfully paid.

It is easy to call hard names and make blustering pretensions, and the Atlas is perfectly welcome to resort to them, so long and as much as it likes. The first and only Republican State Officers, since the party came into existence, are now in the State Hall, and they will be known by their acts. We have no fears of public disapproval.

Too Late!—While the Sun was setting, gloriously, last evening, upon Republican Triumphs in Pennsylvania, Ohio and Indiana, the Breckenridge State Committee was *ingloriously* withdrawing their Electoral Ticket. This, after inducing Mr. Brady to stand fast, was treating him shabbily. But we do not blame Mr. Green. Buchanan not only deserted, but threatened to remove all who held out.

The odds and ends are all together now. Breckenridge, Bell and Douglas men—Democrats, Whigs and Know Nothings—are all *cuddling together under the same dirty bed-clothes.*" This is just as we desired. Faction, fanaticism and folly are now "fused." This will render our Triumph complete and enduring.

To the Editors of the N. Y. Tribune:

Sir—In the Tribune of the 26th ult. I find the following:—

"A correspondent earnestly inquires our opinion concerning the nomination for members of the Legislature of D. C. Littlejohn at Oswego and Austin Myers at Syracuse. On this subject our opinion has been so often expressed that it cannot be in doubt. Both these persons were prominent in the corrupt legislation of last winter Accordingly, both of them ought now to be defeated. Or, if they must be sent back to pursue their career at Albany, it should not be the work of Republican voters."

As this article, and others which have appear in your columns, assail my official integrity, I cannot longer allow them to pass unnoticed.

If the time which intervenes before the Election at which my constituents will pass judgment upon my public acts was sufficient to insure a decision, I would gladly afford my assailants an opportunity to prove their charges of corruption before a legal tribunal, or compel them to abide the consequences of an unwarranted and libelous attack upon my character.

As it is, I content myself, for the present, by a denial of the charges you have made against me

During the six years in which I have represented my district in the Assembly, I have never received, nor do I expect to receive, any pecuniary or other consideration, directly or indirectly, for my support of any bill or measures whatever, not excepting the bills which you allege were passed over the Governor by corrupt appliances

I shall, at a proper time, give to the public the reasons which influenced my votes on these bills, confident that they will so far commend themselves that all fair minded persons will concede there was room for an honest difference of opinion between the Governor and myself as to their merits, and the general interests to be promoted by their passage.

By giving this communication the same publicity already given in your columns to the article quoted above, your will oblige,

Yours, &c., D. C. LITTLEJOHN.

Oswego, Oct. 1, 1860.

Mr. Littlejohn has been for six years a Member of the Assembly, and for four years its Presiding Officer. He has discharged his duties acceptably to his immediate constituents, with fidelity to his party, and in reference to all general interests, with zeal and ability. Nor, until a general warfare is being waged against Republican Members of the Legislature, was his integrity ever impugned. That it is now unjustly impugned we do not entertain a doubt. Nor do we doubt that the constituents whom he has served so long and so beneficially, will manifest their sense of his worth in his triumphant re-election.

Panic-Makers.—The twins (Bennett and Brooks) of the Herald and Express tried the effect of Panic-Making upon Pennsylvania. But it was an abortive effort. The People would be Republicans. Fools sold Stocks and sensible men bought, as they will again, to-day. Lincoln's Election is now assured; and while here and there an Incendiary Press and Fire-eating Politician will threaten to Dissolve the Union, all men of sense and honesty, North and South, will enjoy, in an eminent degree, the bounties and blessings which, under a good Providence, will flow from an enlightened, patriotic Administration.

Correspondence of the Evening Journal.

Washington, Oct. 8, 1860.

The Administration, in urging the withdrawal of the Breckenridge Electoral Ticket in New York, avows that their object is to "leave Douglas out in the cold." If by fusing in New York Lincoln is defeated there, the question will go to the House of Representatives, to be decided between Lincoln, Breckenridge and Bell—Douglas being "no where." Yours, H.

The attempt thus to cheat Douglas will prove abortive, for in spite of all their "fusions," Lincoln will be elected by the People. His friends—spare us from *such* friendship—are a party to this swindle. They are in a scheme which ends his last chance! So he is spending his time, strength and money for nought!

COHOES A-BLAZE!

Immense Mass Gathering of Working Men:

2,000 WIDE-AWAKES IN LINE!

The very pleasantest meeting of the campaign was held at Cohoes last evening. It was unparalleled in numbers and in enthusiasm. The workmen of that bee-hive of American Labor made the occasion a Jubilee; and the large army of young women operatives of the Factories seemed inspired with the spirit and joyousness of the occasion.

Hon. Charles L. Beale, of Columbia, made the principal speech of the evening; and it was an eloquent exposé of the principles at issue. The constant applause which accompanied its delivery showed that the speaker was at once master of his great theme and of the hearts of his audience. Its impressive truths and glowing eloquence will be remembered at the polls.

Soon after 9 o'clock, the Wide-Awakes from Troy, Lansingburgh, Waterford, West Troy, Crescent and Albany began to arrive. Seven hundred and fifty-six went up from here; large delegations from Troy, and full Clubs from the other localities. Their brethren of Cohoes received them gladly, and commenced the line of march promptly. Over two thousand were in the procession; the beautiful village was gorgeously illuminated; the masses cheered lustily; the ladies indicated, in their own pleasant way, the deep interest which they felt in the campaign; and everybody was generally, specially and specifically happy.

Without an incident to mar the pleasure of the occasion; with the remembrance of nothing but kindly greetings from even political opponents; and with new hopes and increased zeal for the good cause, the Wide Awakes exchanged greetings with each other, gave renewed pledges of hard work to secure victory; and returned home—all wide-awake, and ready to respond to every new call to duty.

AN IMPROMPTU JUBILEE!

The Wide-Awakes Making Merry at Midnight!

CALL UPON WM. M. EVERTS, AND A GOOD TIME GENERALLY OVER PENNSYLVANIA!

Soon after 10 o'clock last night, reliable news began to be received from Pennsylvania. At 11 o'clock, it was pretty certainly known that all was well; and by half-past 11, Indiana and Ohio began to assume pleasant proportions along side of Pennsylvania.

The 750 Wide-Awakes who had gone up to Cohoes were expected back at 12 o'clock. The proposition to "go down and tell the boys" was favorably received; and, on their arrived at half-past 12, they were made exceedingly jubilant by the intelligence that Pennsylvania had given at least 15,000 majority in the right direction.

Although the Colonel had issued his order, before getting home, that each Club should, on its arrival, retire directly to its quarters, a simple request to "vacate the order" was promptly complied with, and the whole line marched for the telegraph office. There a halt was ordered, the details of the news announced, its purport passed along the line, extending from State street to the Delavan House, and such cheers sent up as we have not heard these twenty years. It was a grand, exciting and glorious scene—not the least extraordinary being that, amid all the excitement, not a Wide-Awake left his place in the ranks.

Having thus entered upon their impromptu jubilee, the Battallion, hearing that William W. Evarts, the Chairman of the New York delegation in the Chicago Convention, was at Congress Hall, demanded the order to visit him. It was given, of course, and on arriving there, the several Clubs were compacted on the east front of the Hall, Schreiber's Band performed an appropriate piece of music, calls were made for Mr. Evarts, (who arose from his bed to respond) tumultuous cheers were given him on his appearance, and he responded briefly, but in a tone and spirit which harmonized with the joyous occasion.

Other short speeches were made by Messrs. Benedict and Dawson, several rounds of cheers given for Pennsylvania, "Old Abe," "Evarts," "Morgan," and "Our Friends everywhere," when the Clubs retired (cheering Gov. Morgan on passing his residence) to their rooms, quite content with the "signs of the times." and with only kindly feelings for the "Quakers" of Pennsylvania.

The Lincoln and Hamlin Pyramid—Fall Fashions!

MAINE!
OHIO!!
VERMONT!!
INDIANA!!!!
CONNECTICUT!!!!!
PENNSYLVANIA!!!!!!

Earnings of the Auburn Prison.

We adverted yesterday, to the gratifying increase in the earnings of the Auburn Prison, which, together with the reduction of expenses under the vigilant supervision of Agent and Warden Kirkpatrick, has changed the Prison from an unproductive into a paying piece of property for the State. We have, to-day, the precise figures. They are as follows:—

Total earnings and expenditures of Auburn Prison for the month of September, 1860.

Total contract earnings	$7,438 11
Miscellaneous do.	8 441 37
Total earnings	$15 879 48
Total expenses for ordinary support..	5,449 81
Earnings over expenditures	$10,429 67
Total receipts for the year ending September 30, 1860, is	$100,345 74
Total ordinary expenses during same time	75,191 89
Profits over exp'tures for the year	$25,153 85

Gov. Seward at Le Roy.

Correspondence of the Evening Journal.

Le Roy, October 8th.

The reception of Gov. Seward at Le Roy on Saturday last was most enthusiastic. He arrived there with his party, consisting of Gen. Nye, Mr. Adams, grandson of John Quincy Adams, C. S. Wilson, Editor Chicago Journal, Hon. Trumbull Cary, of Batavia, and several ladies, about one o'clock. From the Depot the party was conveyed in carriages provided by Hon. A. S. Upham, to his residence, where the citizens of the place and surrounding county, without distinction of party, called to pay their respects. The whole party were entertained at dinner by Mr. and Mrs. Upham. Mrs. Upham had but an hour's notice of the arrival of the party, but notwithstanding the short notice a most sumptuous dinner was spread before her guests at 3 o'clock, which they enjoyed exceedingly. They proceeded to the Depot and took the evening train, Gov. Seward intending to reach home that night. At the Depot an immense concourse of people had assembled, and the excitement was at the highest pitch, all anxious to do honor to the great statesman. Gov. Seward and his party took seats in a special car provided for the purpose, but was not allowed to depart without addressing the people. After repeated calls of a character which demonstrated that the people would not submit to a refusal, Gov. Seward came forward and spoke in an eloquent and exceedingly appropriate manner. The crowd then successively called for Gen. Nye and Mr. Adams, and they also responded, after which the train was allowed to proceed with tumultuous and enthusiastic cheers for Gov. Seward, Gen. Nye, Mr. Adams, and three times three for Lincoln and Hamlin.

Republican Local Nominations.

Kings County.—
Assembly, 2d dist.—Marcus D. Moore.

Queens County.—
County Treasurer—Robert Cornwell.
Sup't County Poor—Stephen R. Hicks.
Coroner—Obadiah J. Downing.
Justice Sessions—John I. Rurroughs.
Assembly, 1st dist.—John Ordronaux.
School Commissioner—Joseph S. Morrell.
Assembly, 2d dist.—Edwin Mills.
School Com'r—Edward H. Seaman.

Fire—Republican Nomination—New York, Oct. 10.—The splendid residence of E. C. Litchfield, on Prospect Hill, Brooklyn, was burnt this morning.

Hon. Luther C. Carter was yesterday re-nominated for Congress by the Republicans of the 1st District.

Why should egotists be regarded superstitiously? Because they are possessed of the evil eye (I).

Central Campaign Club.—James O'Sullivan and F. Mather, Esq., of Connecticut, speak to-morrow evening in the Central Club room.

☞ Garibaldi's disagreement with the Sardinian Government excites great uneasiness among the Italian Liberals. His Sicilian Ministry declared they will be under the necessity of resigning if the difficulty continues. Kossuth has written him a letter of remonstrance, and Victor Emanuel is said to be going to try the effect of a personal visit to dissuade him.

It is not to be wondered at, however, that Garibaldi finds it impossible to look upon Louis Napoleon with as favorable eyes as the Sardinians. To the latter Napoleon has been a powerful friend, to Garibaldi he has been the reverse. Garibaldi was leading a successful Revolution in Rome eleven years ago, when Napoleon's Troops marched thither, put it down, and drove him into exile. Garibaldi was born in Nice, and within a year he has seen his home and birthplace severed from Italy and sold to France, to satisfy Napoleon's demands. Embittered personal recollections incline him to distrust the Emperor in whom Cavour and the King confide.

Old Dutchess Awake—First Fruits of Fusion.

Correspondence of the Evening Journal.

Rhinebeck, Oct. 6th, 1860.

Perhaps it may not be uninteresting to know what is going on in Old Dutchess. I can assure you we are wide-awake, and having two prominent candidates from our own town, one for Governor and one for Congress, it increases the interest of the campaign. We turn out from 80 to 90 torches in our club, interchange visits with our neighboring clubs in Ulster, and keep the fires warmly burning. Last evening we had a large and very enthusiastic meeting in our Wigwam, which was addressed in an able manner by Mr. Bisbee, of New York; and a very interesting circumstance transpired at the same meeting, showing the first fruits of Fusion. A young and active Democrat from Milan took the stand and openly renounced all connection with the Democratic party,—declaring his belief that "the only *real* Democratic party is the Republican," and attributing the change in his views to the miserable conglomeration called "Fusion." It was a stunning blow to the Democrats, for he has been called in times past "a Democratic wheel-horse."

We expect soon to have a mass meeting here, with some prominent speakers to address us, and shall show our opponents a crowd that will astonish them.

You may rest assured we shall do our best, notwithstanding all we have to contend with.

Yours, truly, K.

Address to the Mechanics and Laborers of the State of New York.

PROTECTION TO THE WORKING MAN.

The time has come when it behooves every mechanic and laborer to act energetically not only on the defensive, but the offensive. The fatal results to their prosperity which has flowed and still flows from the past and present policy of Government not only in the injudicious management of prisons in permitting capitalists to purchase convict labor for less than one-quarter of its actual value, thus enabling them to throw in every mart and avenue of trade, the cheap products of their labor, which bids defiance to competition on the part of the orderly and industrious mechanic; but also in permitting our prisons to be turned into vast work shops for manufacturing purposes, thus filching from honest labor the very means of its subsistence, and thus creating necessity and want, the mother of crime, and inflicting the innocent with the punishment of the guilty, and creating vice with the same weapon with which it seeks to extinguish it under the false garb of economy and reform, must be thwarted. It is the innocent that demand protection, not the visitation of calamity and affliction, while you punish the guilty.

Among the many evils that now prevail growing out of the present system of States Prison discipline is the fact:—

1st. That the innocent mechanic and not the capitalist is compelled, indirectly, to maintain our convicts, because the former cannot obtain fair and remunerative prices for their labor, and while the capitalist profits by it, the free laborer sustains an irreparable injury.

2d. Convict apprentices and fellons are forced into an already overdone mechanical profession, contrary to their natural inclinations, contrary to the policy of Government and the well being of society.

3d. It brings woe and want to the families of many innocent mechanics, adds to the lists of the alms and charnel houses under the guise of economy and reform.

There are sufficient laborers outside of our Prisons to do all our mechanical labor, and whose necessities peremptorily demand it, and they should not be deprived of it under any pretense whatever. There are about 14,000 convicts now in our Prisons and Penitentiaries in this State. The mechanical labor now performed by them at proper remunerative prices, would make 14,000 orderly mechanics and their families prosperous and happy. Over 43,000 mechanics have been turned out of our Prisons during the last thirty years, a host larger than the Colonial army in the Revolutionary war.

Our Government, be it said to our reproach, is different in this respect from all other Governments of the civilized world. England has never permitted and will not now permit any mechanical labor to be performed in her prisons, and she is to-day one of the most enlightened nations on the face of the globe. It is true, her convict laborers are employed on the public works when there is a necessity for it, and when not, they are made to go through some manual exercise, such as treading a huge water-wheel or the like. When a culprit is sent to our prisons it is not regarded with the proper terror and dismay as a punishment, but it has become a matter of derision among the masses and persons of doubtful reputation; and even among our courts, and on enquiry in reference to the absent delinquent, we are often met with the disrespectful expression, "O, he has gone to learn a trade."

While our Government takes into consideration the questions of economy and reform, it overlooks the interests and prosperity of the orderly mechanic. It overlooks the fact that the want of prosperity among our mechanics deleteriously affects every branch and avenue of trade; and while it overlooks this, it forgets that hundreds and thousands of dollars are annually thrown away upon some corrupt politicians or other worthless objects.

There is another great evil, the defect in our insolvent laws, which we desire to remedy. The great and sudden changes in the commercial world; frequently brought about by a variety of causes and unforseen events and improvident or corrupt capitalists, render it necessary for the enactment of a law that will protect and secure to the mechanic and laborer his hard earnings; making a provision peremptorily requiring that the laborer shall receive his wages upon which his and that of his family subsistence solely depends, in preference to any other creditor.

We invoke every orderly mechanic and laborer and good citizen in every section of this State to join us in this our glorious cause; to organize societies to reform these gigantic evils, that are not only undermining the prosperity of the mechanic and laborer, but sending a blighting curse through every branch and avenue of commerce, to the great detriment of the commonwealth. The policy of our Government requires that its concerns should be so conducted that all may prosper and receive its blessings. Our motto is free labor, free speech, free territory, and Protection to Home Industry in our free land. No slaves in our territories, nor prison convicts in our State, nor underpaid and undefied workmen in other countries, are in any manner entitled to be brought in competition with us to retard the prosperity of the laborer, and thus to deprive him of the means of earning an honest livelihood.

Let our territories be consecrated to free homes for the laborer to the exclusion of land monopolists and speculators, and the sale of labor, black, copper-colored, red or pale faced.

We invoke all mechanics and laborers abroad to co-operate with us, and to see to it that the candidates for the Legislature from their respective localities are favorable to our cause, and to use all their energies to the end that none other be elected, and we must and will succeed.

We will be happy to correspond with any body that may be organised abroad in this noble work. Our headquarters are at 856 Broadway, Albany, and we invite all mechanics, laborers and citizens of Albany, favorable to our cause, to meet with us on Monday night, at 7½ o'clock, at our Club Rooms.

Papers in this City and State favorable to us please copy.

Whatever opinion may be held of the efficacy of a "stitch in time," it is vastly preferable to a stitch in the side.

At most hotels, the term waiters should be transferred from table servants to the guests on whom they attend.

Every profligate youth must have the satisfaction, on his death-bed, of having led a well-spent life.

The charity that begins at home is of a very domestic character. It rarely goes out visiting.

The poetic youth, who stole a joy from fate, has been arrested for robbing anger of her frown.

Can any one inform us of the rate of the "rent the envious Casca made?"

FALL FASHIONS FOR '60!

Heavy Blows from the Rail Splitter!

Fusion Badly Squelched!

THREE STATES IN LINE.

OLD ABE TAKING BREATH!

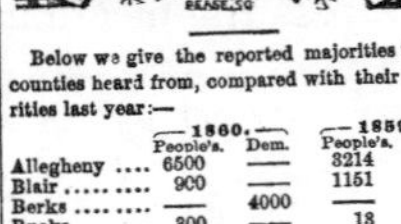

Below we give the reported majorities in the counties heard from, compared with their majorities last year:—

	1860. People's.	1860. Dem.	1859. People's.	1859. Dem.
Allegheny	6500	—	3214	—
Blair	900	—	1151	—
Berks	—	4000	—	1193
Bucks	300	—	13	—
Carbon	—	400	—	149
Cambria	—	600	—	275
Chester......	1200	—	1022	—
Dauphin	1000	—	1114	—
Erie	2300	—	1206	—
Huntington ...	700	—	480	—
Lancaster	4500	—	4169	—
Lycoming.....	150	—	—	359
Lehigh	—	500	—	243
Monroe	—	1300	—	1368
Montgomery ..	—	1650	—	521
Mifflin......	227	—	—	67
Northampton..	—	1600	—	1280
Philadelphia ..	—	2043	3159	—
Susquehanna..	1000	—	716	—
Union	300	—	523	—
York	—	1300	—	220
	19,077	13,398	16,767	5,675

Last year the People's Party carried the State by a majority of 17,291.

Philadelphia, Oct. 9, 1860—5 P. M.

T. Weed, Esq.—I think Foster will have four thousand majority in this city. Lancaster city will give a majority for Foster on account of the Bell men going for him. After that we have nothing to fear. The State is all right.

R. VAN VALKENBURGH.

Philadelphia, Oct 9, 1860.

T. Weed—"All goes merry as a marriage bell." The State is ours handsomely—not less probably than twenty thousand. Twenty Republican Congressmen. C. C.

LATEST RETURNS.

[*By Telegraph this Morning.*]

Philadelphia City Vote.—8th ward—Curtin 1,198, Foster 1,622; 22d ward—Curtin 1,746, Foster 1,286; 20th ward—Curtin 2,496; Foster 2,868; 18th ward—Curtin 1,974, Foster 1,262; 17th ward—Curtin 1,102, Foster 1,925; 19th ward—Curtin 2,361, Foster 2,516. 15th and 21st yet to be heord from.

Chester County.—Curtin, 1,650 majority. Democratic loss 628. Hickman is elected by 1,400 majority. Scattering returns from a few towns in Berks county show Democratic gains of 600.

Montgomery County.—Foster, 1650 majority Democratic gain, 1,100. The majority for Davis in the 5th Congressional District is estimated at 916.

Philadelphia, Oct. 10—3:30 A. M.

Later returns show that the People's Philadelphia County Ticket is elected—the Bell and Everett men having run a separate ticket.

Further returns from Berks county give Foster 4,000 majority—a Democratic gain of 2,807. Democratic County Ticket is elected by a small majority. The Republicans are now in great glee about the result in this State.

A despatch to the World says that there is probably not less than 25,000 majority for Curtin. The Republicans will probably have twenty Congressmen, and a large majority in the Legislature.

A despatch to the Times says the returns for Governor received, would indicate the certain re-election of the following Republicans:—6th District, Hickman; 9th, Stevens; 11th, Kellinger; 12th, Scranton; 14th, Grow; 18th, Blair; 21st, Mooreland; 22d, McKnight. Also, the election of the following Anti-Republicans, to take the place of the two present Anti-Republican members, who were not candidates for re-election:—1st District, Lehman, in place of Florence; 18th, Johnson, in place of Dimmick.

STILL LATER AND VERY GOOD.

Philadelphia, Oct. 10.—Foster's majority in the city is 2,043, a Democratic gain of 2,965 over Mayor Henry's vote in the Spring.

The full People's Ticket is elected, the highest majority being 1,798 and the lowest 326.

The Bell-Everett Congressional tickets received a united vote in the city of nearly 6 500.

Nichols, Republican, is elected State Senator over Andrews, Democrat.

The members of the Lower House stand—7 People's and 6 Democrats, with four districts to hear from.

Indiana county gives Curtin a majority of 1800, a Democratic loss of 705.

John Covode, Republican, is elected in the 19th district by 1700 majority, a gain of 200 over his vote of two years ago.

Blair county gives Curtain 832 majority, a Democratic gain of 319.

Blair, Republican, for Congress, in the 18th district, is elected by between 500 and 600 maj.

Susquehanna Co. gives Curtin 1550 maj.

Wyoming Co. gives Foster 150 maj.

Philadelphia, Oct. 10.—In the 7th Congressional District, Cooper (Dem) is elected. In the 13th Congressional District, Johnson (Dem.) is elected. In the 17th District, comprising Fulton and Adams counties, Schell (Dem.) has 75 maj. Franklin, Bedford and Juniata are yet to be heard from.

It is reported that Allegany Co. gives Curtin 7,000, and that Lancaster gives him 6,000 maj.

The 1st Congressional District is in doubt. Lehman (Douglas Dem.) claims about 30 maj. The Republicans await the official canvass.

In the 5th Congressional District, with Pottstown to hear from, Davis (Rep.) has over 100 maj. There is little doubt of his election.

OHIO! ALL HAIL!

20,000 OR 30,000 MAJORITY.

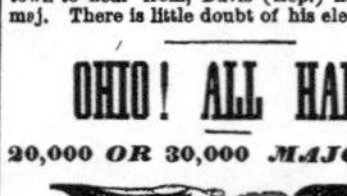

The reported majorities in the Counties heard from compare with those of last year as follows:

	1860 Rep.	1860 Dem.	1859 Rep.	1859 Dem.
Cuyahoga.....	3000	—	1719	—
Huron........	1400	—	1356	—
Lorain	2000	—	1702	—
Summit	1200	—	826	—
	7 600	—	5,603	—
	5 603			
Rep. gain.	1,997			

The Republican majority last year in the State was 13,236.

LATEST—2 o'clock.

MORE AND GOOD ENOUGH!

It is thought a Republican majority on the State ticket in Ohio will reach 20,000. Pendleton, Dem., is elected from the 1st District, Vallandigham in the 3d, and Cox, in the 12th, are reëlected.

It is reported that Warren B. Noble, Dem., is elected from the 9th District. This is a Democratic gain.

INDIANA REDEEMED!

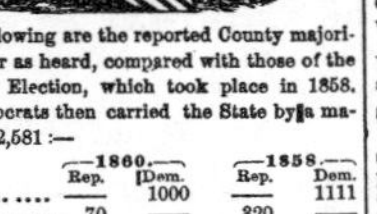

The following are the reported County majorities, so far as heard, compared with those of the last State Election, which took place in 1858. The Democrats then carried the State by a majority of 2,581:—

	1860. Rep.	1860. Dem.	1858. Rep.	1858. Dem.
Allen.........	—	1000	—	1111
Elkhart	70	—	320	—
Laporte	1000	—	464	—
Noble	260	—	70	—
St. Joseph....	700	—	393	—
Wayne	2000	—	1254	—
	4,030	1,000	2 501	1,111
	1,000		1,111	
	3 030		1,390	
	1,390			
Rep. gain.	1640			

LATER—FIVE OR TEN THOUSAND!

From Indianapolis To-Day!

The Democrats of Indianapolis concede the election of the Republican State Ticket by 5,000 to 10,000, and 8 Republican Congressmen.

The Legislature is probably Republican.

CONGRESSMEN ELECTED.

The following are reported as probably elected:

Pennsylvania.

1st District—W. E. Lehman, Democrat.
2d " J. Broadhead, Democrat.
3d " John P. Verree, Republican.
4th " W. D. Kelly, Republican.
5th " H. Ingersoll, Democrat.
6th " John Hickman, Republican.
7th " Thomas B. Cooper, Dem.
8th " H. E Ancony, Democrat.
9th " Thaddeus Stevens, Rep.
10th " John W. Kellinger, Rep.
11th " James H Campbell, Rep.
12th " George W. Scranton, Rep.
13th " Philip Johnson, Democrat.
14th " Galusha A. Grow, Republican.
15th " James T Hale, Republican.
16th " Joseph Bailey, Democrat.
17th " Edward McPherson, Rep.
18th " Samuel S. Blair, Republican.
19th " John Covode, Republican.
20th " Andrew Stewart, Democrat.
21st " James K. Moorhead, Rep.
22d " Robert M. Knight, Rep.
23d " J. W. Wallace, Republican.
24th " John Patten, Republican.
25th " Elijah Babbitt, Republican.
Republicans, 17; Democrats, 8.

Ohio.

1st District—George H. Pendleton, Dem.
2d " John A. Gurley, Republican.
3d " C. L. Vallandigham, Democrat.
4th " J. H. Hart, Republican.
5th " James M. Ashley, Republican.
6th " Chilton A. White, Democrat.
7th " Thomas Corwin, Republican.
8th " S. Shellabarger, Republican.
9th " John Carey, Republican.
10th " Carey A. Trimble, Rep.
11th " C. D. Martin, Democrat.
12th " Samuel S. Cox, Democrat.
13th " John Sherman, Republican.
14th " Hamson G. Blake, Republican.
15th " William Helmick, Republican.
16th " W. P. Cutter, Republican.
17th " Thomas C. Theaker, Rep.
18th " Sidney Egerton, Republican.
19th " A. G. Riddle, Republican.
20th " John Hutchins, Republican.
21st " John A. Bingham, Republican.
Republicans, 16; Democrats, 5.

Indiana.

1st District—John Lord, Democrat.
2d " J. A. Craven, Democrat.
3d " Wm. M. Dunn, Republican.
4th " Wm. S. Holman, Democrat.
5th " George W. Julian, Republican.
6th " Albert G. Porter, Republican.
7th " T. H. Nelson, Republican.
8th " Albert S. White, Republican.
9th " Schuyler Colfax, Republican.
10th " William Mitchell, Republican.
11th " J. P. C. Shanks, Republican.
Republicans, 8; Democrats, 3.

THE LOSS OF THE CONNAUGHT.

GALLANT RESCUE OF PASSENGERS AND CREW.

STATEMENT OF THE DISASTER BY A PASSENGER.

New York, October 9—P. M.

The brig Minnie Scheffer arrived at 1 o'clock. She is about 300 tons burthen, and the standing room on her was completely covered by the rescued passengers of the Connaught. Mr. H. Whittell, of New York, a passenger on the Connaught, furnishes the following statement as to the loss of that fine steamship. Passing over the circumstances of the voyage from Galway, which port we left at 5 P. M. of the 25th, until about 8 P. M. of Saturday the 6th inst., he says:—

"While heading westward, the wind blowing a northerly gale, the ship began to roll to the larboard with singular motion, going far down and keeping that way a long time, which caused some alarm; meantime the Captain was heard giving orders about steering, manning the pumps, &c. The firemen below the lee of the paddle-box were observed whispering, and there were other manifestations that something was not right; considerable water was observed through the gratings; the engine soon after stopped for awhile; after strenuous exertions by Captain Leitch and crew the ship righted and the wheels continued turning, when the passengers became more composed; the sea was rough, the wind blowing what sailors call an ordinary full gale; most of the passengers turned in, but passed a restless night.

"Sunday, 8 A. M.—The ship began to roll again with that shaking motion similar to the evening previous; the captain and crew could neither tack nor wear the ship; soon after the engine stopped, and steam could not be raised in the boilers; the ship rolled frightfully to the larboard, and the pumps were manned, and gangs of men commenced bailing with buckets; at 10 it was reported that the water was not gaining, but on the contrary the pumps and boilers were gaining on the leak, and if the wind would stiffen would reach Boston that night; but these hopes were soon changed to extreme terror, when the words passed around in low tones, 'The ship is on fire!' accompanied by the smell of burning wood; the fire appeared between the decks; gangs were immediately formed with pumps and buckets to extinguish the flames, taking water from the sea and passing it in buckets; as the fire gained the boilers began to slacken work, and all eyes staring around the horizon in hopes to see some means of safety; several false reports of a vessel in sight were made, but at last we discovered a sail to the northward, and soon after another to the westward, both very low down, when it became plain at 1 o'clock that the vessel steering north had three masts and the one west only two.

We soon found out that the larger was passing while the other still neared, without showing any signals that she noticed us, which kept us in extreme anxiety and doubt until she bore directly for us, evidently showing that she observed the steamer's flag of distress which had been hoisted since mid-day. We then commenced to steer away and launch boats, which was a very difficult job, the ship lying almost on her side in a rough sea. By this time the fire had cut off all communication with the saloon. The first quarter boat lowered was struck by the counter and lost, which caused hesitation about launching the others; but the worst of our fears was, that the boats could ride the sea, which then showed signs of moderating, and that we could safely launch and fill them with passengers. There was no chance of remaining but a short time on board—the fire making such progress. The flames were momentarily expected to burst out and sweep the deck; the fire gangs having giving up all hopes of extinguishing it, but continuing to apply wet blankets, &c. The sides of the ship was then so hot that when she rolled it would hiss and make steam of the sea water.

"The gallant little Yankee brig sailed alongside and hove to, seeing our deplorable condition and showing every sign of anxiety for us, but we began to think it would be impossible to store all our number on board, she looked so small. We have since ascertained that she was only 198 tons burthen. Capt. Leitch made all haste to get us into the boats, which was extremely difficult, being lowered one by one with ropes—commencing with women and children. Capt. Leitch stood by all the time, but with all the exertions that could be made when the sun went down only 200 had been got on board the brig.

"Capt. Wilson, of the brig, said: 'This is a horrible affair, to see the sun going down and so many people yet on board the wreck, settling down and burning up. I will do all in my power to save them.' Several of the boat's crew, on reaching the brig, refused to return, when Capt. Wilson said: 'I will go almost alongside and take a hawser from on board, and then you will be in little or no danger. I must get every one from the wreck.' This he tried, which had the effect of giving confidence, and by great exertion all were got on board the brig by 11 o'clock P. M.

"Capt. Leitch and his first officer remained on board until almost surrounded with flames, and until every soul was saved, Capt. Wilson then went alongside to beg him to come away. The flames were shooting up the mast, throwing a strange and melancholy light over the sea. Capt. Leitch reached the brig just at midnight. Scarcely a parcel of baggage was saved, the trunks and even the money of the cabin passengers being left below during the confusion and alarm which called them on deck in the morning, after which communication was cut off by the water and the flames."

Mr. Whittell speaks in the highest terms, as do all the passengers, of the kindness and energy of Captain John Wilson, of the brig Minnie Scheffer. He was from Malaga for Boston with a cargo of fruit.

The Connaught had £10,000 in gold on board, Government money taken at St. Johns, which was lost with the ship.

Three hundred of the passengers went to New York by the Fall river route. The remainder are taken care of here by their friends.

STATEMENT OF CAPTAIN ROBERT LEITCH.

Captain Robert Leitch, the commander of the steamer Connaught, accompanied by Mr. Cox, a passenger, who was on board the ill-fated ship, arrived in this city this forenoon, from Scituate, where they landed from the brig Minnie Schiffer. Our reporter had an interview with Capt. Leitch immediately upon his arrival, and obtained the following particulars of the disasters:—

The steamer sailed from Galway at 3 o'clock P. M., on the 25th of September, and arrived at St. Johns on the morning of Wednesday, the 3d inst. After repairing the paddle floats, which were damaged on the passage, the steamer left St. Johns for Boston.

She had on board when she left Galway 467 passengers, of whom 48 were cabin passengers. At St. Johns eight passengers were landed and ten taken on board.

The steamer experienced heavy weather after leaving St. Johns, but nothing of a serious nature occurred until 8 o'clock P. M. on Saturday last, when the steamer, at that time about 150 miles east of Boston, sprung aleak in the engine room. The water was gaining fast, when discovered, and all hands were immediately called to free the vessel. The engine pumps were set to work, and the force pumps from on deck were taken below and manned. The crew and passengers, with buckets, were busily employed, in the vain attempt to keep the water from rising. These efforts continued unabated until 8 o'clock Sunday morning, the water gaining steadily all the time.

At about a quarter past 9 a new danger was discovered, which added horror to the situation of the already imperiled passengers and crew. Smoke was discovered issuing from the engine room, and shortly after a fire broke out over the after boiler.

The pumps were immediately got on deck, the hose connected, and set to work to extinguish the flames. The buckets, which had before been used to throw water overboard, were now turned upon a new enemy, and employed in unavailing efforts to quench the fire.

The passengers quitted the saloons and steerage, leaving their baggage and everything except the clothes they had on. The crew, firemen and officers of the vessel left the hold, and all came on deck. No one went below after half-past 10 o'clock, the flames having made such progress as to render hazardous all attempts to go below.

Every precaution was now taken by Capt. Leitch to exclude the air from the interior of the vessel. The entrances to the saloons, engine room and steerage were closed and covered with wet blankets. Every possible precaution of this nature was made, the passengers and crew continuing their efforts the while to subdue the flames by pouring water into the vessel. At 11 o'clock A. M. on Sunday, two hours after the fire was discovered, the water had risen so high as to extinguish the fires in the boilers, and the ship, having lost headway, was tossed about in a heavy sea.

At this time all hope of saving the steamer was given up, and a number of hands were set to work to get out the boats, eight in number. A rough sea was running, and in attempting to lower the first boat it was swamped and sunk by a heavy wave.

The fire still increasing, all hands directed their efforts towards getting the boats over the sides as quickly as possible.

At 12 o'clock, Sunday, made out a barque to the windward. She was close hauled, and kept on her course. Shortly after a brigantine was discovered, which bore down upon the steamer. The brig proved to be the Minnie Shiffer, Capt. Wilson, from Malaga, bound for Boston. Capt. Wilson proffered his assistance, which was gladly accepted.

In the meantime every possible preparation had been made to disembark the passengers from the steamer. The seven remaining boats were all safely launched, and the passengers lowered on board, to be in readiness when the brig hove to. It was with the greatest difficulty that the boats made the passage between the steamer and the brig, and not until a warp was got out, was the thing safely accomplished. The passengers and crew were all safely on board the Minnie Shiffer at 2 o'clock, no accident having occurred in the transportation.

Capt. Leitch, who was the last to leave the steamer, succeeded in getting out seven or eight bags of bread, a plenty of beef, pork, sugar, tea and coffee, which were safely conveyed to the brig.

He left the steamer at 10½ o'clock Sunday night. at which time the flames enveloped the hull aft of the wheels. About 3 o'clock Monday morning the steamer was last seen enveloped in flames fore and aft, and the supposition is that she has gone down.

Meeting of the Breckinridge State Committee.

A meeting of the National Democratic State Committee, and of the candidates for Presidential Electors, was held at the Astor House.

The Hon. Gideon J. Tucker offered the following resolution:—

Resolved, That in order to unite the Anti-Republican voters of this State upon a single electoral ticket, and thereby, if possible, to defeat the election of Lincoln and Hamlin by the people, and throw the choice of President and Vice-President upon Congress, we deem it advisable to decline nominations tendered us for the office of Presidential Electors, by the National Democratic State Convention held at Syracuse on the 7th day of August last, and that a communication to that effect be made by the Chairman and Secretary of this meeting to the State Committee.

Which, after debate was agreed to.

The State Committee having reconvened, the communication of the electoral candidates was received, and their resignations were accepted by a unanimous vote.

Mr. Maltby offered the following resolution, which was agreed to:—

Resolved, That it is recommended by the State Committee, that the National Democracy of the State of New York, representing the friends of Breckinridge and Lane, meet together in their several Assembly, County, and Congressional Districts throughout the State, and perfect their several local organizations, and place in nomination their separate and independent candidates for local offices at as early a day as possible.

Republican Delegate Elections.

The following were to-day elected Delegates to the Republican County Convention and the Assembly District Conventions:—

First Ward.—*County Convention*—John Grady, P. H. Daily, Thomas Braidwood, Charles Scheferdecker, James Smith.

Assembly—John Desch, Jr., John Burns, Fred. Clare, Augustus Tolle, John Himler.

Inspectors of Election—Richard Rock, Chas. T. Murky, Thomas Braidwood.

Second Ward.—*County Convention*—Thomas Hillson, Patrick Murphy, Charles Wooster, George Lilly, Lawrence Sammons.

Assembly—John P. Goewey, Thomas Patterson, Edward Stevens, John Dobbs, Philip Mork.

Third Ward.—*County Convention*—B. H. Mills, I. N. Keeler, George Kirk, M. W. Bender, Hiram Livingston.

Assembly—Justus Haswell, T. V. Van Heusen, Gaylor Sheldon, John Marks, David Thomas.

Inspectors of Election—David Winne, Henry B. Haswell, James McEntee.

Fourth Ward.—*County Convention*—C. Van Allen, J. Fredenrich, N. Thauer, J. Vandermark, Benj. W. Southwick.

Assembly—E. Bent, L. L. Derby, J. Koonz, George Degener, Philip George.

Fifth Ward.—*County Convention*—J. P. White, J. Lawless, A. Van Santvoord, Henry Reiler, J. Weldon.

Assembly—P. Carmichael, G. Harris, P. H. Brooks, M. Clarke, W. H. Haskell.

Inspectors of Election—N. S. Dean, P. H. Brooks, E. A. Veazie.

Sixth Ward.—*County*—A. H. Hoff, H. S. Hulbert, William Headlam, Jr., James H. Carroll, A. T. Foster.

Assembly—John Rogers, Otis Allen, Amos C James, A. S. Van Santford, Alex. A. Edmondson.

Seventh Ward.—*County Convention*—M. L. Norton, John R. Green, Jas. Ward, Cornelius Seaman, Jas. Murray.

Assembly—John Chrisler, Teunis Visscher, John Scott, B. B. Dunham, Wm. Thornton, Jos. Stott, Wm. Murray.

Eighth Ward.—*County*—Thos. Cowell, Geo. W. Hogaboom, Francis M. Stone, William Bruce, E. Van Valkenburgh.

Assembly—J. W. Coates, Edwin Day, Andrew Keefe, William Coulter, Samuel Gross.

Ninth Ward.—*County*—L. Benedict, Jr., John Desch, James Kinnear, George N. Geary, Casper Wheeler.

Assembly—Philip Shafer, W. L. Warren, Geo. Mink, M. L. Schemerhorn, Louis Schmidt, G. W. Warren.

Tenth Ward.—*County*—Charles D. Rathbone, John G. Treadwell, James Coates, J. H. Chase, Frederick Hinkel.

Assembly—Philip Fredenrich, Henry A. Clement, James Milwain, Frederick Piepenbrink, Wm. A. Jackson.

Bethlehem.—*County*—W. E. Haswell, C. V. Baker, David Jones, A. C. L. Van Cott, George Krank.

Assembly—Jacob J. Soop, A. W. Becker, Cor. Niver, David Couse, R. B. Hagadorn.

The Way to Work.—Fourteen meetings are called in Wayne county for next week. Systematic work is most effective.

THE MERCHANTS OF NEW YORK IN COUNCIL.

Treason Rebuked where it was Hatched.

From the N. Y. Evening Post.

The merchants of New York, without distinction of party, who believe "that the election of Lincoln is the only means of preventing the transference of the present contest for the Presidency to the halls of Congress, where it would be certain to renew in an intensified form the disgraceful and threatening scenes of last winter, and thus subject our Government to more fearful peril than any it has hitherto encountered, and believing that the unscrupulous efforts now making by leading partizans of the Administration and their organs to affect the popular vote by threats and other appliances calculated to destroy confidence, paralyze business and depreciate the value of property, deserve the indignant rebuke of every good citizen, were called together to-day at 3 o'clock. It was a large gathering, and among those present were the most prominent business men in the city. It was organized by the appointment of the following officers:—

For President—JAMES GALLATIN.

FOR VICE-PRESIDENTS.

Pelatiah Perit,	Jonathan Sturges,
John Jacob Astor,	Wm. A. Booth,
A. A. Low,	John C. Green,
Morris Ketchum,	George Opdyke,
Chas. H. Marshall,	Wm. E. Dodge,
Moses H. Grinnell,	Shepherd Knapp,
Geo. Griswold, Jr.,	James G. King,
Robt. H. McCurdy,	Samuel Hotaling,
James Harper,	Charles E. Beebe,
Wm. T. Brady,	Henry A. Hurlbut,
Wm. M. Vermilye,	D. Randolph Martin,
Timothy G. Churchill,	S. S. Wyckoff,

Isaac Seymour.

FOR SECRETARIES.

George W. Farlee,	Edw'd A. Stansbury,
Henry A. Oakley,	John B. Durbrow.

The following resolutions were read by John Jacob Astor, Esq., and adopted:—

RESOLUTIONS.

Whereas, it is now conceded on all sides that to-morrow's election must inevitably result either in the success of Lincoln or in the failure to choose a President by the people, in which event the choice will devolve on the House of Representatives; and whereas, persistent efforts are making to stifle a free expression of the public will by threats of Disunion, seconded by concerted movements to create a panic deeply injurious to commerce and other industrial interests of the country; and whereas, in a conjuncture like this, it is the duty of every citizen to exert his influence in behalf of the right, by a frank declaration of his sentiments and convictions: therefore,

Resolved, That as citizens and merchants deeply interested in the honor and welfare of our country, we cannot contemplate without painful anxiety the grave perils of transferring the Presidential contest to the House of Representatives; that events in our own experience, as well as all political history, warn us of the hazard of entrusting such an election to the legislative body, where the sure results are scenes of intrigue, corruption and violence, embittered by intense sectional animosity; and that neither the composition nor the temper of the present Congress as illustrated in the struggle for its organization, dispose us to trust the peace of the country in its hands, when the prize at stake is the Presidency of the United States, with a patronage of three hundred and fifty millions of dollars.

Resolved, That we have witnessed with surprise and regret the renewed efforts of ultra Southern politicians and presses, by menaces of secession in the case of Lincoln's election, to deter the people of the North from an independent exercise of the elective franchise.

Resolved, That while we will yield to none in our devotion to the Union and fidelity to the Constitution, nor in our determination to uphold the constitutional rights of every section of the country, we must yet say to our Southern brethren, in all frankness, that we are determined to maintain with equal firmness our own right to exercise all the privileges of citizenship that we accord to them; and that we should regard it as a derogation from our manhood and forfeiture of self-respect to yield to arguments which have been lately addressed not to our reason but to our fears.

Resolved, That the base attempts of the unscrupulous partisans to influence the election by setting on foot a panic designed to injure the business interests of our country, deserves and should receive the stern condemnation of the whole community; and that it is high time a party using such means to coerce public opinion and court votes, should be expelled from power.

Resolved, That relying on the good sense of the body of our people, we believe that they entertain neither the seditious sentiments charged upon the South, nor the desire to infringe on constitutional privileges ascribed to the North.

Resolved, That in our opinion the time has come when every one who believes in the fundamental principle of our institutions, namely, that the will of the majority is the law of the land within constitutional limits, shall manfully rally to the support of the party proclaiming this principle, and frown down all seditious attempts to break up the Union by threats of secession from any quarter.

Resolved, That we recommend our fellow-citizens to vote for Mr. Lincoln, the Republican candidate.

The Temper of Northern Mercantile Correspondence.

The following letter from a New York commercial firm is addressed to one of its southern customers. It is of even tenor, if not date, with many others that are following the birds about these days towards the equator. We suspect the South will get enough of disunion to satisfy them, before it comes; if so, so much the better:

"NEW YORK, October 24, 1860.

"GENTLEMEN:—Yours of the 19th inst. is received. We notice your order and especially your remarks in relation to the Presidential election. We regret extremely the tone of our recent southern correspondence, and the threatened consequences in case Mr. Lincoln should be the choice of a majority of the people of the United States, which now seems hardly doubtful. This state of feeling in your section is unfortunate, not only from patriotic and fraternal considerations, but from commercial ones as well. We must of course decline to fill your order, and indeed, to sell to your section, except for cash, even to customers with whom we have long done business with the greatest confidence and pleasure, as well as profit. The condition of revolution and war does not permit the citizen to act his own pleasure, and we cannot now say how soon your circumstances may make it impossible to reach you through our usual traveling agents, or even by the post office or express, nor how long the most solvent and trustworthy of you will be able to meet your engagements. The numerous drafts upon your population to fill the ranks of a hostile army, and the heavy taxes which will be necessary to provide and maintain an army and a navy, and to keep up all the complicated and extensive arrangements, at home and abroad, of a new general government, in the midst of unfriendly and dangerous influences, and surrounded by a frontier of vast extent, excited, alarmed and undefended, can hardly fail to be fatal for a considerable period, to the productiveness of your plantations, to the value of your property, and to the business resources of your customers. We are, therefore, compelled to give more attention to extending our trade westward and northward, where the avenues of trade will be safer and its rewards surer than where the result of an election is considered a cause of war.

"With repeated thanks for the favors of past years, with unabated friendly feelings, and the hope that the evils which your politicians threaten may be avoided, we remain still,

"Very truly yours, ———."

Good-Bye.

The reporter of the Boston *Herald* wafts the following touching "good-bye" to the Prince as the last sail of the royal fleet went down beneath the horizon, homeward bound from Portland:

Good-bye, Wales; give our love to your mother. Good-bye; be virtuous, and you will be happy! You have seen some very sensible men in this country, Albert Edward, and you must remember them; you have seen nearly all of our snobs and lickspittles, and you will not remember them. You have heard the tune—"God Save the Queen," a great many times Renfrew, but you have persistently whistled "Dixie's Land." You have been very much squeezed, Albert Edward, and it will be good for you. You have been rubbed against, and it will make you bright. A great many stories have been told about you, Mr. Wales, some of which are true, and some false. You have worn very good clothes, but not a handsome hat. You have ridden about with some very good horses, and you have received some of our choicest variety of mud turtles to take home. You have visited institutions which you didn't care a snap about, and you have danced with some of the best dressed old ladies to be found in America. You like to dance, but you don't dance the Lancers very well.—Still you are a pretty clever fellow. If you lived in this country, you would stand a chance to be ruined, Albert Edward. You would certainly join a fire company and then you might be elected to Congress, and then you would lose all your self-respect, and you would be done. Reporters have bothered you very much, you say, Albert Edward. They have bribed your chambermaids and bought up men of your suite. You have been a god-send in the way of "items," Albert Edward, and in behalf of the reporters of Boston, I bid you an affectionate farewell. "Ich Dien" is played out on this side, Albert Edward, and you have taken home something of "E. Pluribus Unum." One thing to your credit, Albert Edward, you have paid your bills with remarkable promptness, and you have done your tour in good shape. You seemed to have any quantity of money, and you put it out freely. You have been going it, and now you are gone! Good-bye.

REGISTRY OF NEW YORK.—New York, Nov. 5. The number of registered votes in this city is 116,891.

REPUBLICAN NOMINATIONS.

Election, Tuesday, Nov. 6, 1860.

FOR PRESIDENT,

ABRAHAM LINCOLN

FOR VICE-PRESIDENT,

HANNIBAL HAMLIN.

FOR PRESIDENTIAL ELECTORS,

AT LARGE:

WILLIAM C. BRYANT. JAMES O. PUTNAM.

DISTRICTS:

1. JOHN A. KING.	18. HENRY CHURCHILL.
2. EDWARDS W. FISKE.	19. JAMES R. ALLABEN.
3. ANDREW CARRIGAN.	20. BENJAMIN N. HUNTINGTON.
4. JAMES KELLY.	21. SHERMAN D. PHELPS.
5. SIGISMUND KAUFMANN.	22. JOHN J. FOOTE.
6. FREDERICK KAPP.	23. HIRAM DEWEY.
7. WASHINGTON SMITH.	24. JAMES L. VOORHEES.
8. WILLIAM A. DARLING.	25. WILLIAM VAN MARTER.
9. WM. H. ROBERTSON.	26. JOHN E. SEELEY.
10. GEORGE M. GRIER.	27. FRANK L. JONES.
11. RUFUS H. KING.	28. JAMES S. WADSWORTH.
12. JACOB B. CARPENTER.	29. EZRA M. PARSONS.
13. JOHN F. WINSLOW.	30. CHARLES C. PARKER.
14. JACOB H. TEN EYCK.	31. ELISHA S. WHALEN.
15. N. EDSON SHELDON.	32. JOHN GREINER, Jr.
16. ROBERT S. HALE.	33. JAMES PARKER.
17. ABIJAH BECKWITH.	

FOR GOVERNOR,

EDWIN D. MORGAN.

FOR LIEUTENANT-GOVERNOR,

ROBERT CAMPBELL.

For Canal Commissioner,

SAMUEL H. BARNES.

For Inspector of State Prisons,

JAMES K. BATES.

For Representative in Congress---14th District,

THOMAS W. OLCOTT.

For County Treasurer,

ROBERT TAYLOR.

For Sessions,

CHRISTOPHER WHITE.

For Coroners,

DANIEL WASSERBACH. WILLIAM B. WINNE.

For Members of Assembly,

First District, - - JOHN I. SLINGERLAND.
Second District, - - LEWIS BENEDICT, Jr.
Third District, - - ROBERT H. PRUYN.
Fourth District, - - ALBERT G. SAGE.

For School Commissioners,

FIRST DISTRICT.	*SECOND DISTRICT.*	*THIRD DISTRICT.*
L. CARTER TUTTLE.	**GEORGE L. BOUTON.**	**THOMAS HELME.**

Further Foreign News by the Steamer Adriatic.

A despatch from Ancona says voting on the annexation is decreed for the 4th and 5th of November.

The English Squadron left Syria for the Adriatic. Two French vessels remained at Beirut.

It was reported that agitation prevailed in Damascus and threats were made against the Christians in consequence of the war tax. Fuad Pacha had returned there.

The new charter by the Emperor of Austria accords a Court of Chancery to Hungary, and the Chancellor is to be a member of the Ministry. The number of members of the Reichsrath is to be increased 100 by the Councellors elected by the Provisional diets.

LATEST.—A Warsaw despatch says the principle of an European Congress is adopted.

Advices from Constantinople say that the Grand Vizier is favorable to a forced loan. Ali Pacha was named as foreign minister. The withdrawal of Riza Pacha from the Ministry was expected.

A great fight occurred at the election of the Greek Patriarch.

The British Government have proposed to the Porte a modification of the treaty of 1830.

It is confirmed that Austria has 100,000 men in Verona alone. Mantua and Peschiera are likewise strongly garrisoned.

The Pope has assured the representatives of France at Rome that he has no intention of leaving.

Commercial Intelligence.

LONDON, Oct. 27.—Baring reports Wheat firm. White 64s.@68s., red 63s @64s.

MONEY.—Consols closed on Friday at 92⅞@92 for money and account. Market generally unchanged, but there is less demand for discount.

The weekly returns of the Bank of England shows a decrease in bullion of £ 49,000.

AMERICAN SECURITIES.—The latest sales of Ill. Cen. R 21½@21 discount; Erie 39½@40; N. Y. Cen. 84.

COTTON.—LIVERPOOL, Sunday, Oct. 28.—Sales yesterday 8,000 bales, including 2,000 to speculators and exporters, closing quiet but steady.

Breadstuffs quiet but steady.

Provisions quiet.

LONDON, Saturday Evening.—Consols closed at 94⅛@92⅞ for money and account.

The Great Boat Race.

THE CHAMPION OF AMERICA FOR SINGLE SCULLS—WARD THE VICTOR.

From the Albany Express.

The great ten mile race for single sculls, for a purse of $500 and the Championship of America, came off yesterday afternoon at Poughkeepsie. Josh. Ward, of Newburgh, the present Champion, and Wm. Berger, of Poughkeepsie, were the contestants. The race was agreed on in consequence of a challenge issued by Berger, to row against any man in America for $500.

The attendance at the race was large, and the betting spirited, $100 to $25 being offered on Ward. The men came up in fine spirits, and both intent upon winning. Ward was dressed in white, Berger in light red, with head-dresses of the same color. The boats were precisely alike, having been made on the same model. They were each 26 feet long, and weighed about 55 pounds.

At 3 o'clock, the signal was given, and the boats shot away, Berger leading a little. On rounding the upper stake boat, five miles from the starting point, Ward was about five lengths ahead, and apparently making very little exertion. The return down the river was against a flood tide and strong head wind, which rendered it extremely difficult to keep the boats on an even keel, and when they reached the judges' boat, they were half full of water. Ward kept the lead throughout the last five miles, coming in four minutes ahead. His time for the first five miles was *thirty-two* minutes—the return time fifty-one minutes, or a total of ten miles in eighty-three minutes.

As Judge Douglas was bidding adieu to his friends at Montgomery, Ala., on Friday, the guards of the boat gave way with the pressure of the crowd. The Judge and Mrs. Douglas fell, but were not seriously injured.

TRIALS AND TRIBULATIONS OF A CANDIDATE FOR OFFICE.—The following "Journal of a Defeated Candidate" we commend to the consideration of those gentlemen who are desirous of serving their country. We think there are some people in this region who will find it is not altogether a fancy sketch. It has been published before, but it is good enough to read again:—

Thursday—Received the nomination for an office. Surprised and indignant. Remonstrated with committee. Was told I must place myself in the hands of my friends. Eventually did so.

Friday—Immense poster on a brick pile opposite house; my name in two foot letters.—Great anguish on the part of my wife and family, who believe that every officer in the city government, according to law, is indicted and tried at the end of his term. Friends meeting me in the street, say there is a rumor about town that I am up for office, a rumor which ought to be contradicted. Other friends offer ironical congratulations, and leave me in doubt whether the office is unfit for me, or I for the office. Old gentleman won't believe it; for he knew my father, and he was a very respectable man.

Saturday—Man on the stoop of my house with big whip and terrier. Broad-shouldered, slovenly person, with sanguinary eye. Come to advise me to beware of a class of ruffians that go round election times extorting money from candidates. Offers his services to tend polls. Customary, he says, to pay in advance. I refer him to my committee. He whistles to his dog. Engage him at $5, cash down. We part with mutual expressions of esteem.

Going in find six men smoking in my parlor; delegates from a target excursion. Customary, they say, for candidates to give prizes on these occasions. Refer them to my committee. Captain very polite—tells me he will give me time to think about it, and will come on Sunday with the whole guard in, to let me see what a fine looking set of fellows they are. Result, $10 for the prize.

Evening—Excited persons call for a subscription for a banner. Man come with a wooden leg—wants a new one. Three more banners. Clergymen for a subscription to deserving charity. Seventeen men to attend the polls. More cripples. Delegation wants their fire engine painted. Men without arms to post their bills. A woman with subscription for coffin. Children all crying up stairs. My wife in hysterics.—General terror and confusion.

Midnight — Torchlight procession; kettle drums; serenade; make a speech; rotten egg hits me in the eye; general fight; spanners, brickbats, clubs, banners, torches and fists.

Wednesday—Wake up defeated. Tell my friends I don't care for myself, but feel sorry for the city. My wife goes home to her mother; the children are sent where they cannot be under my influence. No home—no friends—no wife—no money—no office.

☞ James Huss, a Prussian chemist, formerly residing in this city, has been in Detroit lately, trying to make diamonds out of cornelians and agates. He was a singular customer, had no communication with any one, and only divulged his mysterious business when he was threatened with arrest as a counterfeiter. As soon as public attention was called to his operations, he disappeared. He had half a bushel or more of disintegrated agates, some of which were burned, and others showed the action of acids which seemed to have eaten out the impurities and left the flint as clear and transparent as crystal, which was, doubtless, the nearest he had come to the perfection of the sparkling diamond.

[N. Y. Ev. Post.

A hitherto Democratic Dutchman, of Ripley county, Indiana, gives the following reason for voting the Republican ticket: "I tinks I leaves de Democrats long time ago, but every year dey pulls de wool ober mine eyes, and so I goes mit dem again; but dis time dey pull it so tam far *dat I see right ober de top*. Dat ish vy I votes de Republican dicket."

See advertisement in to-day's paper of Prof Wood.

ALBANY EVENING JOURNAL.

TUESDAY EVENING, NOV. 6, 1860.

TO-DAY!

We anticipate our usual hour of going to press, both in order to give all hands in our establishment an opportunity of attending to their Political Duty, and in order to make a final appeal to every reader who may have neglected his.

IF YOU HAVE NOT VOTED,

Lose not another moment, but lay down this paper and go immediately to the Polls, and deposit your Ballot.

ONE VOTE

may turn the scale and decide not only the election of a Congressman, an Assemblyman or a County Officer, but may even decide the political character of the next Congress and the Policy of National Legislation.

DON'T BE SATISFIED WITH VOTING YOURSELF,

but go after any neighbor whom you know or fear to have neglected that duty, and bring him to the Polls.

BEWARE OF SPLIT TICKETS

and all kinds of frauds and forgeries, for there are dozens in circulation, at every Poll.

READ YOUR BALLOTS.

Scrutinize every name, and make sure there is no mistake or deception about a single letter.

DON'T STOP TO ARGUE.

Nobody can be convinced in the four hours that remain, by talk; but they are enough for active and effective *work*.

OFFER YOUR HELP

to those who are watching the Poll and bringing up Voters. There cannot be too many engaged in this work.

ATTEND TO THE UNREGISTERED.

Let no Republican lose his vote because he is not registered, but see that he is furnished with the necessary affidavit, of which blanks can be had at every Poll, thus securing his vote at the cost of very little trouble.

KEEP ORDER

In and around the Polls. Neither be concerned in any disturbance nor let others get up one, to to obstruct the access of Voters. All we want is a fair count of the honest verdict of the People.

BE "WIDE-AWAKE,"

like the admirable organization which is doing yeomans' service to-day. Our opponents are beginning to find that "Wide-Awakes" are good for something besides Parades.

WATCH FOR FRAUDULENT VOTERS.

There is a reward of FIFTY DOLLARS offered for the detection and arrest of any man attempting to vote fraudulently. This has doubtless frightened many, but it is always in the hurry and confusion of the latter part of the day that such attempts are most frequent.

CHALLENGE,

where there is the slightest doubt. Persons may have voted for years, and yet be disqualified. Look at the date of naturalization papers. If they were taken out since October 27th they do not entitle to a vote.

DON'T SWAP VOTES.

The Democrats will trade off Electors, State or anything, for a vote for their Congressional candidate. Make no such bargains. The State is safe, and so is the Electoral Ticket, but the County is close. We must

SECURE EVERY VOTE FOR OLCOTT,

that can be secured. This is the most important point of the whole contest in Albany County.

VOTE FOR THE CONSTITUTIONAL AMENDMENT.

It removes an absurd and unjust distinction, based on property. The Property Qualification for white men was abolished long ago, and it ought to be abolished entirely.

VOTE THE WHOLE TICKET.

There is not an objectionable name on the Republican ballots, nor one whose success will not add to or whose defeat would not detract from the effect of the triumph of our Principles.

THE CRISIS

of our political history as a Nation is this question of whether Free Labor or Slave Labor shall hereafter have possession of the Territories of the United States. The man who neglects to vote for Freedom now, leaves undone, in the hour of greatest need, an act that he will always wish he had performed. The man who votes against Freedom and for the three-headed hydra, will be ashamed to confess it a few years hence.

WATCH THE CANVASS,

both to ensure correct counting and to preserve order around the Polls.

SEND IN THE RETURNS,

and we will give you to-morrow, in return, the tidings of

A GLORIOUS VICTORY,

in the County, the State, and the Nation.

The Canvass.

The canvass of the votes by the Inspectors of Election will commence immediately upon the closing of the Polls, viz: at 13 minutes before 5 o'clock.

The Boxes will be taken up in the following order:—

1st. Electors.
2d. State.
3d. Assembly.
4th. School Commissioners and Suffrage Amendment.

The canvass of the Electoral Ballots in some districts will probably be finished by 7 o'clock. It will be late before the other boxes are completely canvassed.

The Returns To-Night.

Whatever returns are received by telegraph or otherwise to-night, will be announced simultaneously at the Headquarters of the Central Club, 356 Broadway, and at the 4th Ward Club Room (McClure's Building.)

PORTSMOUTH, Va., Nov. 5.—The greatest crowd that was ever witnessed in this city, gathered together on Saturday to listen to Hon. HENRY A. WISE. He spoke for four hours and was frequently interrupted with bursts of applause. HE DECLARED BEFORE GOD THAT HE WOULD NEVER SUBMIT TO THE ELECTION OF ABRAHAM LINCOLN.

This was telegraphed all over the Union yesterday, in hopes that WISE's crazy ravings would scare some timid voter. Now that there is no longer anything to be made by Disunion threats, the country will be amused to see how suddenly and ingeniously Disunionists can "back down" and "shuffle out" of their extravagant positions. Gov. WISE, as he has gone the farthest will probably recant the soonest. This may seem difficult, but he has done it so often before, that he will make nothing of it. In a few days he will probably publish a six column letter explaining that the word "never" in the above threat is to be understood not in its ordinary, but in its Virginia sense.

NEW YORK AND KINGS.—The Union Committee in New York telegraph to Mr. CAGGER that the majority against LINCOLN in that city and Kings will be FIFTY THOUSAND.—[*Atlas.*

This is one of the "last cards" intended for effect to-day. Fusion will get no such majority, and even if it did, it would be beaten by the rest of the State.

ENTHUSIASTIC RALLY AT IRELANDS' CORNERS. The Republicans of Irelands' Corners and vicinity had a fine meeting last night. Messrs. WATROUS & SMITH made forcible speeches to an audience of at least three hundred. The Wide-Awakes were out in force.

THE MOST INFAMOUS YET.—The Journal of Commerce parades a list of the killed and slaughtered men, women, and children, during the French Revolution of 1792, as an electioneering paragraph.

☞ The *Evening Journal Almanac* contains the Returns of the Election of 1859 for the whole state, by towns and districts.

☞ The Election is progressing quietly and peaceably in the several Wards. Thus far the weather has been unfavorable, rain falling almost uninterruptedly since sunrise; but notwithstanding this the vote is fully as large as usual, and in some Districts larger. As we go to press it is breaking away and looks as if the afternoon might be pleasant.

The Polls.

The Polls close at sunset. The sun sets at thirteen minutes before five o'clock.

The following are the places of holding the Polls in the several Election Districts:

1st Ward, N. D.—9 Franklin street.
S. D.—Hurst's, cor. S. Pearl and Alexander.
2d Ward, E. D.—77½ Church street.
W. D.—22 West Ferry street.
3d Ward, E. D.—27 Church street.
W. D.—129 Lydius street.
4th Ward, E. D.—10 Beaver street.
W. D.—Justice's Court Room.
5th Ward, E. D.—27 Maiden lane.
W. D.—City Hall.
6th Ward, 644½ Broadway.
7th Ward, M. D.—841 Broadway.
W. D.—258 North Pearl street.
8th Ward, N. D.—Northeast cor. Swan and Third sts.
S. D.—124 Orange street.
9th Ward, E. D.—43 Washington avenue.
M. D.—293 Washington avenue.
W. D.—Southwest cor. Bowery and Perry.
10th Ward, E. D.—At Ferguson's, southeast corner of Hawk and Hudson.
M. D.—Jno. O'Hagan's, Northwest corner of Elm and Swan.
W. D.—At Kirkpatrick's, Lydius street.

Send in the News.

The telegraph will give us the news on Election Night from towns along its line. After that we shall be gratified to receive further intelligence from our friends by letter. Not unfrequently, for several days after Election, we are in receipt of inquiries from all over the State, "how the State has gone," the writers of which forget to add what has been the result in their own County. But we can only tell the aggregate by combining the details. Send us local results and we will be enabled to send you general results in return.

The Wide-Awakes a Permanent Organization.

AMASA McCOY delevered the closing speech of the Campaign before the Albany Central Wide-Awake Club, last night. After which he offered the following resolutions which were adopted with great enthusiasm:—

Whereas, the Wide-Awake organization has rendered great and memorable service in the Presidential Campaign of 1860; in teaching the people sound political doctrine, and inciting to the performance of those political duties which every good citizen owes to the Republic; and

Whereas, Similar services, and similar means, will be desirable in the furture; not only for Presidential, but for State, and municipal elections;—therefore,

Resolved, That the Central Wide-Awake Club of Albany (whether the Republican Party is successful in to-morrow's election or not) hereby declares itself a permanent political body; and the officers are hereby instructed to hire a room for its permanent use; and to preserve the records, banners, torches, uniforms, and all other properties of the Club; as honorable memorials of the past, and incentives to patriotic service in the future.

Resolved, That we, the members of the Central Wide-Awake Club of the city of Albany, and the first which was organized in the State of New York, hereby tender our thanks and applause to our brethren of all other Wide-Awake organizations throughout the Union; for the great amount of time, energy, and zeal they have expended in the Campaign of 1860; and we cordially and respectfully invite them to unite with us in declaring for permanent organization; with a view to that "eternal vigilance" which is the "price of liberty."

Old Genesee.

Correspondence of the Evening Journal.

BATAVIA, November 5, 1860.

The last important meeting of the campaign, in this county, was held last Saturday night, at Le Roy. Through the generosity of DEAN RICHMOND, Esq., which, it is but fair to say, has been extended to his political opponents very freely in this campaign, an extra train was furnished to convey the Wide-Awakes of Batavia and Stafford to the meeting without any charge for fare. Notwithstanding the rain, about 100 Wide-Awakes embarked at Batavia and a large company at Stafford, besides many other Republicans. On arriving at Le Roy, we were received by the Wide-Awakes of that place and escorted to Starr Hall, where we had an opportunity to listen to a most eloquent German orator, GEORGE SAUL, Editor of the Syracuse German Democrat. The Wide-Awakes then proceeded to a large hall on the opposite side of the street, where was served up a great variety and profusion of cakes, pies, cold meats, biscuits, bread and butter, cider, &c., &c. After cheering the ladies of Le Roy and our candidates, the whole body of the Wide-Awakes marched around the Square with their torches lighted, three bands of music, banners, &c., and paid a complimentary visit to Hon. ALONZO S. UPHAM, at his residence. Although it was after eleven o'clock, with the first round of cheers from the Wide-Awake Battalion, the gallant Senator made his appearance, which was the signal for three cheers and a wide-awake. The Senator mounted the step-stone, in front of his residence, and was soon in the centre of a sea of torches, the Battalion forming about him as compactly as possible. He then delivered a very handsome speech, thanking the Wide-Awakes for their visit to him, assuring them that he was as wide-awake in the cause as they were, and urging them to do their whole duty on Tuesday. He concluded by proposing nine cheers for the candidates, which were given with a will, whereupon the Wide-Awakes marched to the Rail Road Depot, and were conveyed home.

Wide-Awake Song.

Now stand like brave men, one and all,
And gird your armor on;
The day of battle is at hand,
The victory must be won;
This is no time in idle dreams
Inglorious rest to take;
What man that loves the right and true
But must be Wide-Awake!

Hark! swells the song of triumph out
From old true-hearted Maine,
And Pennsylvania's peaceful shades
Take up the voice again;
And with that strain Ohio's waves
With joy the silence break,
And Indiana echoes back
"Forever Wide-Awake!"

No timorous, peaceful sounding Bells
Shall drown the exultant cry,
No Giant's threats of shadowy ills
Our hosts shall terrify;
What though sworn foes join hand in hand,
Unholy league to make,
God speeds the right, and speeds true men,
Whose hearts are Wide-Awake!

Come on, then, ye who see beyond
The strife of troublous days,
Nor barter Truth for selfish gains,
Nor stand in weak amaze;
When History, on undying page
Shall calm, sure records make,
Her voice shall bless the steadfast State
Whose sons were Wide-Awake! E.

The Electors.

There are 303 Presidential Electors apportioned among the States as follows:—

States.	Electors.	States.	Electors
Alabama	9	Minnesota	4
Arkansas	4	New Hampshire	5
California	4	New Jersey	7
Connecticut	6	New York	35
Delaware	3	North Carolina	10
Florida	3	Ohio	23
Georgia	10	Oregon	3
Illinois	11	Pennsylvania	27
Indiana	13	Rhode Island	3
Iowa	4	South Carolina	8
Kentucky	12	Tennessee	12
Louisiana	6	Texas	4
Maine	8	Vermont	5
Maryland	8	Virginia	15
Massachusetts	13	Wisconsin	5
Michigan	6		
Mississippi	7	Total	303
Missouri	9		

One hundred and fifty-two votes are necessary to an election.

To Editors, Reporters, and Telegraphers in the State of New York.

It is eminently desirable that the returns from the State at large on election night should be as reliable and succinct as possible, and in order to prevent the wires from being incumbered with a mass of useless matter, it will be well that the following ideas should be borne in mind: As far as practicable the press desire to obtain the vote by counties for Presidential Electors and Governor, but where it is impossible to give the full or a near approximation of the result by counties, the scattering returns which may come to hand will be acceptable; but that of fractional parts of cities or townships should not be allowed to pass over the wires, to the hindrance of more important matter. As to members of Congress and the Legislature, the name and politics of the parties chosen or probably elected is all that need be telegraphed. The vote for other officers on the State ticket is not required.

Attention to these points will, it is hoped, contribute largely to the publication, on the morning after the election, of an intelligible account of the result in the State.

The man who confines himself to the drink best for him is *well*-supplied.

TABLES FOR COMPARISON WITH ELECTION RETURNS.

In order to judge rightly of the indications of the scattered Election Returns as they come in, it is necessary to refer to former statistics. For the convenience of our readers we give below the official vote of the State, by counties, last Fall; the vote by Congressional Districts, the names of the Congressional and Assembly candidates, the Electoral Vote of the States, &c.

THE VOTE OF THE STATE LAST YEAR,

COUNTIES.	Secretary of State. Jones, Fusion.	Leavenw'h, R.
Albany	9215	7258
Allegany	2133	4771
Broome	2915	3491
Cattaraugus	2900	3978
Cayuga	3541	6180
Chautauqua	3211	5590
Chemung	2414	2452
Chenango	3614	4482
Clinton	3184	3252
Columbia	4123	3946
Cortland	2084	3018
Delaware	3484	3600
Dutchess	5070	5237
Erie	9416	7466
Essex	1519	2895
Franklin	2294	2292
Fulton	2446	2669
Genesee	2042	3309
Greene	3253	2500
Hamilton	396	213
Herkimer	2661	4426
Jefferson	5004	6860
Kings	18042	7971
Lewis	1918	2359
Livingston	2676	3215
Madison	2805	4676
Monroe	4793	7065
Montgomery	3069	2690
New York	38462	18272
Niagara	3303	3688
Oneida	7306	10288
Onondaga	6081	8830
Ontario	3104	3571
Orange	4988	4056
Orleans	2230	2848
Oswego	4850	7004
Otsego	4912	5469
Putnam	1210	1018
Queens	3547	1315
Rensselaer	7933	5002
Richmond	1659	678
Rockland	1751	749
Saratoga	4417	4352
Schenectady	1780	1779
Schoharie	3605	2503
Schuyler	1821	1884
Seneca	2363	1908
Steuben	4849	5759
St. Lawrence	3347	7846
Suffolk	2632	1694
Sullivan	3102	1670
Tioga	2580	3028
Tompkins	2514	3280
Ulster	5596	4034
Warren	1683	2183
Washington	2974	4735
Wayne	3210	4658
Westchester	6543	4330
Wyoming	1812	3128
Yates	1208	2236
Total	252954	251136

Jones over Leavenworth 1458

THE VOTE BY CONGRESSIONAL DISTRICTS.

Below we give the majorities in each Congressional District at the last election, on Secretary of State—the Fusion being represented by JONES and the Republican by LEAVENWORTH:—

FIRST DISTRICT.

	Republican.	Fusion.
Kings* (part)	160	—
Queens	—	2232
Richmond	—	981
Suffolk	—	938
		4151

Candidates in 1860—CARTER, Republican; SMITH, Breckenridge; SMITH, Douglas.

SECOND DISTRICT.

Brooklyn* (part)	—	4658

Candidates in 1860—HUMPHREY, Republican; ODELL, Fusion.

THIRD DISTRICT.

1st Ward, New York	—	860
2d " "	—	81
3d " "	—	170
5th " "	—	768
8th " "	—	1081
		2960

Candidates in 1860—WILLIAMSON, Republican, WOOD, Mozart; SAVAGE, Tammany.

FOURTH DISTRICT.

4th Ward, New York	—	1045
6th " "	—	1524
10th " "	—	616
14th " "	—	1429
		4614

Candidates in 1860—COMMERFORD, Republican; TUOMEY, Douglas; KERRIGAN, Breckenridge.

FIFTH DISTRICT.

7th Ward, New York	—	1242
13th " "	—	984
Williamsburgh	—	1000
		3226

Candidates in 1860—WALL, Republican; TAYLOR, Mozart; DUFFEY, Fusion.

SIXTH DISTRICT.

11th Ward, New York	—	1743
15th " "	—	145
17th " "	—	1472
		3360

Candidates in 1860—CONKLING, Republican; COCHRANE, Breckenridge; CHANLER, Douglas.

SEVENTH DISTRICT.

9th Ward, New York	—	744
16th " "	—	796
20th " "	—	1138
		2678

Candidates in 1860—DOW, Republican; WARD, Fusion.

EIGHTH DISTRICT.

12th Ward, New York	—	749
18th " "	—	1186
19th " "	—	900
21st " "	—	959
22d " "	—	564
		4358

Candidates in 1860—WAKEMAN, Republican; DELAPLAINE, Fusion; WILLET, Breckinridge.

NINTH DISTRICT.

Putnam	—	192
Rockland	—	1002
Westchester	—	2213
		3407

Candidates in 1860—NELSON, Republican; HAIGHT, Fusion.

TENTH DISTRICT.

Orange	—	932
Sullivan	—	1432
		2364

Candidates in 1860—VAN WYCK, Republican; ST. JOHN, Fusion.

ELEVENTH DISTRICT.

Greene	—	753
Ulster	—	1562
		2315

Candidates in 1860—SILVESTER, Republican; STEELE, Fusion.

TWELFTH DISTRICT.

Columbia	—	177
Dutchess	167	—

Candidates in 1860—BAKER, Republican; WAGER, Fusion.

THIRTEENTH DISTRICT.

Rensselaer	—	2931

Candidates in 1860—OLIN, Republican; McCONIHE, Fusion.

FOURTEENTH DISTRICT.

Albany	—	1962

Candidates in 1860—OLCOTT, Republican; CORNING, Fusion.

FIFTEENTH DISTRICT.

Hamilton	—	188
Saratoga	—	65
Warren	—	500
Washington	1761	—
	748	

Candidates in 1860—McKEAN, Republican; DAVIS, Fusion.

SIXTEENTH DISTRICT.

Clinton	—	68
Essex	870	—
Franklin	—	2
	70	

Candidates in 1860—WHEELER, Republican; HAND, Fusion.

SEVENTEENTH DISTRICT.

Herkimer	1765	—
St. Lawrence	2499	—
	4264	

Candidates in 1860—SHERMAN, Republican; FOOTE, Fusion.

EIGHTEENTH DISTRICT.

Fulton	223	—
Montgomery	—	379
Schenectady	—	1
Schoharie	—	1102
		1482
		223
		1259

Candidates in 1860—MIX, Republican; VIBBARD, Fusion.

TWENTIETH DISTRICT.

	Republican.	Fusion.
Oneida	2982	—

Candidates in 1860—CONKLING, Republican; GROVE, Fusion.

TWENTY-FIRST DISTRICT.

Broome	576	—
Chenango	868	—
Cortland	974	—
	2418	

Candidates in 1860—DUELL, Republican; NELSON, Fusion.

TWENTY-SECOND DISTRICT.

Madison	1871	—
Oswego	2154	—
	4025	

Candidates in 1860—LANSING, Republican; HITCHCOCK, Fusion.

TWENTY-THIRD DISTRICT.

Jefferson	1856	—
Lewis	441	—
	2297	

Candidates in 1860—CLARK, Republican; SHERMAN, Breckenridge; STARBUCK, Douglas.

TWENTY-FOURTH DISTRICT.

Onondaga	2751	—

Candidates in 1860—SEDGWICK, Republican; TEFFT, Douglas; MAY, Breckenridge.

TWENTY-FIFTH DISTRICT.

Cayuga	2639	—
Wayne	1440	—
	4087	

Candidates in 1860—POMEROY, Republican; BEARDSLEY, Fusion.

TWENTY-SIXTH DISTRICT.

Ontario	—	467
Seneca	—	460
Yates	1028	—
		927

Candidates in 1860—CHAMBERLAIN, Repub.; CLARK, Breckenridge; LEWIS, Douglas.

TWENTY-SEVENTH DISTRICT.

Chemung	38	—
Schuyler	63	—
Tioga	443	—
Tompkins	766	—
	1310	

Candidates in 1860—DIVEN, Republican; DOW, Fusion.

TWENTY-EIGHTH DISTRICT.

Steuben	910	—
Livingston	539	—

Candidates in 1860—VAN VALKENBURGH, Republican; WALKER, Fusion.

TWENTY-NINTH DISTRICT.

Monroe	2258	—

Candidates in 1860—ELY, Republican; REYNOLDS, Fusion.

THIRTIETH DISTRICT.

Allegany	2638	—
Genesee	1267	—
Wyoming	1314	—
	5219	

Candidates in 1860—FRANK, Republican; ROBERTSON, Fusion.

THIRTY-FIRST DISTRICT.

Niagara	385	—
Orleans	618	—
	1003	

Candidates in 1860—VAN HORN, Republican.

THIRTY-SECOND DISTRICT.

Erie	—	1950

Candidates in 1860—SPAULDING, Republican; HAVEN, Fusion.

*Congressional Vote of 1858.

VOTE OF ALBANY COUNTY LAST FALL.

From the Evening Journal Almanac.

		Sec. of State. Leavenworth. Rep.	Jones. Dem.
1st Ward,	N. D.	106	418
	S. D.	120	883
2d Ward,	E. D.	188	348
	W. D.	105	84
3d Ward,	E. D.	109	189
	W. D.	238	242
4th Ward,	E. D.	179	138
	W. D.	216	200
5th Ward,	E. D.	70	92
	W. D.	95	101
6th Ward		290	330
7th Ward,	E. D.	112	862
	W. D.	146	315
8th Ward,	N. D.	290	813
	S. D.	152	426
9th Ward,	E. D.	227	180
	W. D.	370	389
10th Ward,	E. D.	384	369
	W. D.	329	300
Total Wards		3736	5179
Bern	1st district	88	128
	2d district	188	88
	3d district	66	88
Bethlehem	1st district	239	286
	2d district	116	132
Coeymans	1st district	77	127
	2d district	57	152
	3d district	23	115
Guilderland	1st district	152	97
	2d district	93	140
	3d district	61	110
Knox	1st district	152	117
	2d district	91	57
New Scotland	1st district	106	79
	2d district	130	110
	3d district	149	79
Rensselaerville	1st district	124	145
	2d district	29	162
	3d district	44	84
Watervliet	1st district	204	149
	2d district	244	207
	3d district	140	312
	4th district	199	246
	5th district	228	180
	6th district	194	283
	7th district	115	110
Westerlo	1st district	65	111
	2d district	149	192
Total Towns		3517	4036
Total County		7253	9215

ASSEMBLY NOMINATIONS.

The Republican nominations for Members of Assembly are as follows:—

ALBANY.—1st, John I. Slingerland; 2d, Lewis Benedict, Jr.; 3d, Robert H. Pruyn; 4th, A. G. Sage.
ALLEGANY.—1st, Wilkes Angell; 2d, Lucius May.
BROOME.—Friend H. Burt.
CATTARAUGUS.—1st, Nelson J. Norton; 2d, Franklin Philbrick.
CAYUGA.—1st, Heman Benton; 2d, Smith Anthony.
CHAUTAUQUA.—1st, H. A. Prendergast, 2d, Hiram Smith, 2d.*
CHEMUNG.—Lucius Robinson.*
CHENANGO.—1st, Thomas Coster; 2d, S. E. Lewis.
CLINTON.—H. McFadden.*
COLUMBIA.—1st, Samuel Lasher; 2d, N. S. Collins.
CORTLAND.—Loomis Kennedy.
DELAWARE.—1st, Seymour E. Smith; 2d, Daniel Waterbury.
DUTCHESS.—1st, John B. Dutcher; 2d, Samuel J. Farnum.
ERIE.—1st, S. V. R. Watson; 2d, Victor M. Rice; 3d, Dexter Ewell; 4th, Wheeler Ferris.
ESSEX.—Martin Finch.*
FRANKLIN.—William Andrus.
FULTON AND HAMILTON.—James H. Burr.
GENESEE.—George W. Wright.
GREENE.—Ira Sherman.
HERKIMER.—1st, John Markell; 2d, Josiah Skull.
JEFFERSON.—1st, David Montague; 2d, P. D. Foster; 3d, W. T. Goodnough.
KINGS.—1st, Thomas McElrath; 2d, Marquis D. Moore; 3d, Nathan Comstock; 4th, John E. Cammeyer; 5th, Lucius C. Andrus; 6th, John M. Stearns; 7th, George H. Fisher.
LEWIS.—E. Baldwin.
LIVINGSTON.—1st, Martin Wiard; 2d, George Highland.
MADISON.—1st, Orrin B. Lord; 2d, Francis B. Hyatt.
MONROE.—1st, Martin Roberts; 2d, Lewis H. Morgan; 3d, Benjamin R. Wells.
NEW YORK.—1st, Joseph A. Gardiner; 2d, Ira H. Tuthill; 3d, John G. Gibson; 4th, Lewis Hopps; 5th, John J. Shaw; 6th, Edward A. Frazer; 7th, J. Wilson Greene; 8th, Andrew Craft; 9th, Horatio N. Sherwood; 10th, Robt. M. Boyd; 11th, Cummings H. Tucker, John Hooper; 12th, John Lambrecht, Charles Curtis; 13th, C. E. Birdsall; 14th, Jesse Fonda; 15th, Edward C. Johnson; 16th, Denis McCabe; 17th, John P. Cumming.
NIAGARA.—1st, Henry P. Smith; 2d, D. P. Scoville.
ONEIDA.—1st, James McQuade;* 2d, L. T. Marshal; 3d, Geo. H. Champlin; 4th, William Lewis.
ONONDAGA.—1st, Jeremiah Emerick;* 2d, Austin Myers;* 3d, Abner Chapman.
ONTARIO.—1st, Perez H. Field; 2d, S. H. Ainsworth.
ORANGE.—1st, S. Fullerton, Jr.; 2d, Howard Shaw.
ORLEANS.—Gideon Randall.
OSWEGO.—1st, D. W. C. Littlejohn;* 2d, Mason Salisbury.
OTSEGO.—1st, Elijah E. Ferry.
PUTNAM.—John Ordronoux.
QUEENS.—Edwin Mills.
RENSSELAER.—1st, Simon Mann; 2d, L. C. Ball; 3d, Anson Bingham.
RICHMOND.—Minthorne Tompkins.
ROCKLAND.—Edwin Marks.
ST. LAWRENCE.—1st, C. Richardson;* 2d, Edwin A. Merrit;* 3d, C. S. Chittenden.*
SARATOGA.—1st, Joel Seymour; 2d, James Sumner, Jr.
SCHOHARIE.—Samuel B. Briggs.
SENECA.—Ebenezer Munson.
STEUBEN.—1st, D. B. Bryan; 2d, Jeffrey Smith.
SUFFOLK.—1st, James H. Tuthill 2d, Edward C. Foot.
TIOGA.—C. S. Barker.
TOMPKINS.—Jeremiah W. Dwight.
ULSTER.—1st, Robert Loughran; 2d, George T. Pierce; 3d, Benj. Turner, Jr.
WARREN.—Walter C. Faxon.
WASHINGTON.—1st, Peter Hill; 2d, N. M. Catlin.
WAYNE.—1st, Thomas Robertson; 2d, Joseph W. Corning.
WESTCHESTER.—1st, Ethan Flagg; 2d, Samuel Hooper; 3d, Benj. F. Camp.
WYOMING.—John J. Doolittle.
YATES.—J. Hatmaker.

* Old members.

THE ELECTORAL TICKETS.

From the Rochester Democrat.

The following are exact copies of all the Electoral Tickets as originally nominated, and as they now stand. First we give the

REPUBLICAN TICKET.

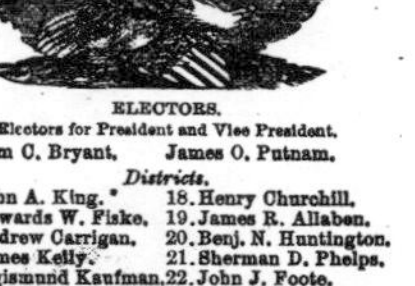

ELECTORS.

Electors for President and Vice President.

William C. Bryant. James O. Putnam.

Districts.

1. John A. King.*	18. Henry Churchill.
2. Edwards W. Fiske.	19. James R. Allaben.
3. Andrew Carrigan.	20. Benj. N. Huntington.
4. James Kelly.	21. Sherman D. Phelps.
5. Sigismund Kaufman.	22. John J. Foote.
6. Frederick Kapp.	23. Hiram Dewey.
7. Washington Smith.	24. James L. Voorhees.
8. William A. Darling.	25. William Van Marter.
9. Wm. H. Robertson.	26. John E. Seeley.
10. George M. Grier.	27. Frank L. Jones.
11. Rufus H. King.	28. James S. Wadsworth.
12. Jacob B. Carpenter.	29. Ezra M. Parsons.
13. John F. Winslow.	30. Charles C. Parker.
14. Jacob H. Ten Eyck.	31. Elisha S. Whalen.
15. N. Edson Sheldon.	32. John Greiner, Jr.
16. Robert S. Hale.	33. James Parker.
17. Abijah Beckwith.	

All of the candidates upon the above ticket will, if elected vote for Abraham Lincoln for President, and Hannibal Hamlin for Vice President.

THE BRECKENRIDGE TICKET.

The following ticket was nominated by the National (Breckenridge) Democrats:—

ELECTORS.

For Electors of President and Vice President.

Gideon J. Tucker. Henry S. Randall.

Districts.

1. John H. Brower.	18. Thos. B. Mitchell.
2. Daniel D. Miller.	19. John H. Gould.
3. Joseph W. Brown.	20. David Wager.
4. Charles Francis.	21. George B. rr.
5. J. A. Westervelt.	22. Jas. M. Blakeley.
6. James Lee.	23. Wooster Sherman.
7. Wm. N. McIntyre.	24. John L. Cook.
8. Stephen P. Russell.	25. Alex'r Thompson.
9. Aaron Ward.	26. George N. Clark.
10. Hudson Wells.	27. John Haggerty.
11. George Beach.	28. Wm. S. Hubbell.
12. Henry Snyder.	29. Mathew Rigney.
13. Geo. Van Santford.	30. Harry Wilber.
14. Hiram Perry.	31. John T. Murray.
15. Richard D. Davis.	32. Albert H. Tracy.
16. W. H. Payne.	33. Oscar F. Dickinson.
17. Joseph Lee.	

FUSION TICKET NO. 1.

The following ticket was nominated by the Douglas State Convention, after consultation with a Know-Nothing Committee, at whose request *ten* Know-Nothings pledged to Bell and Everett were placed upon the ticket. We separate them, so that the Douglas Electors and the Know-Nothing Electors may be distinguished:—

ELECTORS.

For Electors of President and Vice-President.

(DOUGLAS—25.)

Reuben H. Walworth, Heman J. Redfield.

District.

1. Selah B. Strong.	17. David C. Judson.
2. Charles H. Collins.	18. Charles Goodyear.
3. Francis R. Tillou.	19. George C. Clyde.
4. Elijah F. Purdy.	20. Ambrose S. Higgins.
5. Oswald Ottendorfer.	22. Lucius B. Crocker.
7. James Robinson.	23. Pierson Mundy.
8. John Anderson.	24. John M. Strong.
9. Edward Haight.	25. Edwin M. Anderson.
11. Elisha B. Strong.	29. Addison Gardiner.
13. Martin Springer.	30. John B. Skinner.
15. Isaiah Blood.	32. William Williams.

33. Stephen D. Caldwell.

(KNOW-NOTHINGS—10)

6. J. De Peyster Ogden.	20. Edward Huntington.
10. Daniel B. St. John.	26. James M. Pulver.
12. William Kent.	27. Miles Finch.
14. James Kidd.	28. Charles H. Carroll.
16. Henry H. Ross.	31. Lorenzo Burrows.

Mr. Huntington, in the 20th District, was struck off because he declared himself opposed to this fusion and in favor of Lincoln's election, and John Munn was substituted. Mr. Ottendorfer, in the 5th District, also avowed his opposition to running upon the ticket with Know-Nothings.

FUSION TICKET NO. 2.

The following ticket was made up by a self-constituted committee in the city of New York, by striking from the last named ticket seven Douglas men and substituting seven Breckenridge men, (retaining the ten Know-Nothings,) and this is the ticket which will be palmed off to Douglas men as a "Democratic Ticket," to Breckenridge men as a "National Democratic Ticket," and to Americans or Know Nothings as a "Union Ticket." It is very appropriately called

THE HYDRA TICKET!

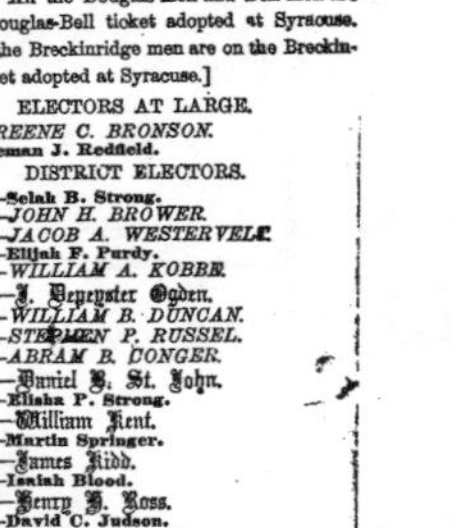

FUSION PICTURED & CLASSIFIED!

A Table Showing Honest Men where to Strike.

THE FUSION ELECTORS.

[Breckinridge men in *ITALIC CAPITALS*—Bell men in German—Douglas men in **Full Face.** All the Douglas men and Bell men are on the Douglas-Bell ticket adopted at Syracuse. Three of the Breckinridge men are on the Breckinridge ticket adopted at Syracuse.]

ELECTORS AT LARGE.

GREENE C. BRONSON.
Heman J. Redfield.

DISTRICT ELECTORS.

1—**Selah B. Strong.**
2—*JOHN H. BROWER.*
3—*JACOB A. WESTERVELT.*
4—**Elijah F. Purdy.**
5—*WILLIAM A. KOBBE.*
6—J. Depeyster Ogden.
7—*WILLIAM B. DUNCAN.*
8—*STEPHEN P. RUSSEL.*
9—*ABRAM B. CONGER.*
10—Daniel B. St. John.
11—**Elisha P. Strong.**
12—William Kent.
13—**Martin Springer.**
14—James Kidd.
15—**Isaiah Blood.**
16—Henry H. Ross.
17—**David C. Judson.**
18—**Charles Goodyear.**
19—**George C. Clyde.**
20—John Munn.
21—**Ambrose S. Higgins**
22—**Lucius B. Crocker.**
23—**Pearson Mundy.**
24—**John M. Strong.**
25—**Edwin M. Anderson.**
26—James M. Pulver.
27—Miles Finch.
28—Charles H. Carroll.
29—**Addison Gardiner.**
30—**John B. Skinner, 2d.**
31—Lorenzo Burrows.
32—**William Williams.**
33—**Stephen D. Caldwell.**

RECAPITULATION.

Douglas men,	18
Bell and Everett men,	10
Breckinridge men,	7
Total,	35

Three of the names in the last named list, to wit: John H. Brower, Jacob A. Westervelt and Stephen P. Russell, were on the original Breckenridge Ticket.

Those who wish to vote for LINCOLN and HAMLIN can do so by adopting the first of the above lists.

Those who wish to vote for none but "National Democrats" (Breckenridge and Lane) will take the second list, headed by Gideon J. Tucker and Henry S. Randall, and upon which Hiram Perry is the elector for this (14th) District.

Those who wish to divide their suffrage between Democrats and Know Nothings, giving Douglas and Johnson 25 votes and Bell and

"LET THE EAGLE SCREAM!"
A REPUBLICAN PRESIDENT OF THE U. S.
THE UNION IS REDEEMED!
"RIGHT MAKES MIGHT!"
LIBERTY AND UNION FOREVER!
A REPUBLICAN GOVERNOR
AND A
REPUBLICAN LIEUTENANT-GOVERNOR!
A REPUBLICAN LEGISLATURE!
CANAL COMMISSIONER AND STATE PRISON INSPECTOR!

HARPER'S WEEKLY.
A JOURNAL OF CIVILIZATION.
VOL. IV.—No. 202.] NEW YORK, SATURDAY, NOVEMBER 10, 1860. [PRICE FIVE CENTS.
Entered according to Act of Congress, in the Year 1860, by Harper & Brothers, in the Clerk's Office of the District Court for the Southern District of New York.

HON. ABRAHAM LINCOLN, BORN IN KENTUCKY, FEBRUARY 12, 1809.—[PHOTOGRAPHED BY BRADY.]

NEW YORK ILLUSTRATED NEWS.

No. 54.—Vol. III. NEW-YORK, SATURDAY, NOVEMBER 17, 1860. Price Six Cents.

THE PRESIDENTIAL STRUGGLE OVER.

ABRAHAM LINCOLN OUR NEXT PRESIDENT.

It is not known at what period the ancestors of Abraham Lincoln came to America. The first account that has been obtained of them dates back about one hundred and fifty years, at which time they were living in Berks County, Pennsylvania, and were members of the Society of Friends. Whence or when they came to that region is not known.

About the middle of the last century, the great-grandfather of Abraham Lincoln removed from Berks County, Pennsylvania, to Rockingham County, Virginia. There Abraham Lincoln, the grandfather, and Thomas Lincoln, the father of the subject of this sketch, were born. Abraham, the grandfather, had four brothers—Isaac, Jacob, John, and Thomas—descendants of whom are now living in Virginia, North Carolina, Kentucky, Tennessee, and Missouri. Abraham removed to Kentucky about the year 1780, and four years thereafter, while engaged in opening a farm, he was surprised and killed by Indians; leaving a widow, three sons, and two daughters. The eldest son, Mordecai, remained in Kentucky until late in life, when he removed to Hancock County, Illinois, where he shortly afterward died, and where his descendants still live. The second son, Josiah, settled many years ago on Blue River, in Harrison County, Indiana. The eldest daughter, Mary, was married to Ralph Crume, and some of her descendants are now living in Breckenridge County, Kentucky. The second daughter, Nancy, was married to William Brumfield, and her descendants are supposed to be living in Kentucky.

Thomas, the youngest son, and father of the subject of this sketch, by the death of his father and the very narrow circumstances of his mother, was thrown upon his own resources while yet a child. Traveling from neighborhood to neighborhood, working wherever he

[continued on page 26.

Abraham Lincoln, of Illinois, and Hannibal Hamlin, of Maine, President and Vice-President Elect. From a Photograph by Brady.

[Continued from first Page.]

could find employment, he grew up literally without education. He finally settled in Hardin County, where, in 1806, he was married to Nancy Hanks, whose family had also come from Virginia. The fruits of this union were a daughter and two sons. One of the latter died in infancy; the daughter died later in life, having been married, but leaving no issue. The sole survivor is the subject of this sketch.

Abraham Lincoln was born in Hardin County, Kentucky, February 12th, 1809. It would be difficult to conceive of more unpromising circumstances than those under which he was ushered into life. His parents were poor and uneducated. They were under the social ban which the presence of slavery always entails upon poverty. Their very limited means and the low grade of the neighboring schools, precluded the expectation of conferring upon their children the advantages of even a common English education. The present inhabitants of the Western States can have but a faint idea of the schools which fifty years ago constituted the only means of education accessible to the poorer classes. The teachers were, for the most part, ignorant, uncultivated men, rough of speech, uncouth in manners, and rarely competent to teach beyond the simplest rudiments of learning—"spelling, reading, writing," and sometimes a very little arithmetic. The books of study then in vogue, would not now be tolerated in schools of the lowest grade. The school-house, constructed of logs, floorless, windowless, and without inclosure, was in admirable harmony with teacher, text-books, and the mode of imparting instruction.

In his seventh year, Abraham was sent for short periods to two of these schools, and while attending them progressed so far as to learn to write. For this acquirement he manifested a great fondness. It was his custom to form letters, to write words and sentences wherever he found suitable material. He scrawled them with charcoal, he scored them in the dust, in the sand, in the snow—anywhere and everywhere that lines could be drawn, there he improved his capacity for writing.

Meanwhile, the worldly condition of the elder Lincoln did not improve. He realized in his daily experience and observation how slavery oppresses the poorer classes, making their poverty and social disrepute a permanent condition through the degradation which it affixes to labor. Revolving this matter in his mind, he wisely resolved to remove his young family from its presence. Accordingly, in the autumn of 1816 he emigrated to Spencer County, Indiana—one of the States consecrated forever to freedom and free labor by the Jeffersonian Ordinance of 1787, and which, with the States now comprising the territory included in that memorable instrument, has afforded asylum—an open field and fair play—to thousands upon thousands who have, in like manner, been driven from their homes by that great social scourge of the "poor whites" of the South.

Young Lincoln was in his eight year when the family removed to Indiana. They settled in an unbroken forest, gladly taking upon themselves all the privations and hardships of a pioneer life, in view of what they had left behind them. The erection of a house and the felling of the forest was the first work to be done. Abraham was young to engage in such labor, but he was large of his age, stalwart, and willing to work. An ax was at once placed in his hands, and from that time until he attained his twenty third year, when not employed in labor on the farm, he was almost constantly wielding that most useful implement.

Upon the arrival of the family in Indiana, the friends who were left behind were to be written to. The elder Lincoln could do nothing more in the way of writing than to bunglingly sign his name. The mother, though a ready reader, had not been taught the accomplishment of writing. In this emergency Abraham's skill as a penman was put into requisition, and with highly satisfactory results. From that time onward he conducted the family correspondence. This fact soon becoming public, little Abraham was considered a marvel of learning and wisdom by the simple-minded settlers; and ever afterward, as long as he remained in Indiana, he was the letter-writer for the neighbors generally, as well as for his father's family. That he was selected for this purpose was doubtless owing not more to his proficiency in writing than to his ability to express the wishes and feelings of those for whom he wrote in clear and forcible language, and to that obliging disposition that has always distinguished him in subsequent life. It cannot be doubted that something of Mr. Lincoln's style and facility of composition in later years, both as a writer and speaker, is to be traced back to these earlier efforts as an amanuensis for the neighborhood.

In the autumn of 1818, Abraham, in the loss of his mother, experienced the first great sorrow of his life.

After the removal of the family to Indiana, Abraham attended school a little, chiefly in the winter, when work was less pressing; but the aggregate of all the time thus spent, both in Kentucky and Indiana, did not amount to one year. He is therefore indebted to schools for but a very small part of his education. All men who become in any respect distinguished, are, in one sense at least, self-made; that is to say, the development and the discipline of the intellect can only be secured by self-effort. Without this, assistance on the part of teachers, however long and continuously offered, will yield no fruit. With it, assistance is valuable mainly in that it directs and encourages effort. He is said to be a self-made man who attains to distinction without having enjoyed the advantages of teachers and of institutions of learning; and in this sense Abraham Lincoln is peculiarly entitled to the appellation. His early teachers were men of scarcely any learning, and what he mastered through their assistance consisted only of the simplest rudiments of education. That subsequent training and disciplining of the intellect, that habit of close investigation, that power of intense thought, which enable him to master every subject he investigates, and that faculty of clear and forcible expression, of logical arrangement, and of overwhelming argument, by which he enforces his own well-grounded convictions—all this is the result of his own unaided exertions, and of a naturally sound and vigorous understanding. So far from being indebted to institutions of learning for any of the qualities which characterize him, he was never in a college or an academy as a student, and was never, in fact, inside of a college or academy building until after he had commenced the practice of the law. He studied English grammar after he was twenty-three years of age; at twenty-five he mastered enough of geometry, trigonometry, and mensuration to enable him to take the field as a surveyor; and he studied the six books of Euclid after he had served a term in Congress, and when he was forty years of age, amid the pressure of an extensive legal practice, and of frequent demands upon his time by the public.

Books were another means of education which young Lincoln did not neglect; but in a backwoods settlement of Indiana, forty years ago, books were somewhat rarer than now.

From 1829 until the financial revulsion of 1837-40, a vast flood of immigration poured into Illinois At the first-named date, the population of the State was only about 150,000—a number scarcely equal to the present population of the city of Chicago. This population was confined mostly to the southern part of the State. There were comparatively few people north of Alton, and these, as is always the case in the settlement of a new country, were scattered along the rivers and smaller water-courses or close to the edge of the timber-land. The large prairies, with the exception of a narrow belt along the fringes of the timber, were wholly uncultivated and without population. Indeed, at that time, and for many years after, it was the opinion of even the most intelligent people, that the larger prairies of Illinois would never be used for any other purpose than as a common pasturage for the cattle of adjacent settlers. It is only of late years, and since the introduction of railroads, that the true value and destiny of these prairies have come to be understood and appreciated. Thus, in 1829, only an infinitesimal portion of the better part of Illinois was occupied. At the same time, the people of other States entertained very imperfect notions of the character of the country and its wonderful natural resources. The first settlement by an indigenous American population had been the result of the accounts carried back to the old States by the soldiers who accompanied the gallant George Rogers Clark in that memorable expedition in 1778, which resulted in the conquest of Kaskaskia, Cahokia, and Vincennes.

Those who have come into Illinois since steamboats became numerous on the Western waters, and since the introduction of railroads, and the opening of the Illinois and Michigan Canal, have no correct idea how small an amount of business was transacted in the State so late as 1830, or of the great commercial revolution which has taken place since that time. At the period named there was but little inducement for growing surplus productions. The merchants of the country did not deal in corn, wheat, flour, beef, pork, lard, butter, or any of the great staples of the State. Beyond the purchase of a few furs and peltries, small quantities of feathers, beeswax, and tallow, the merchant rarely engaged in barter. The old United States Bank was then in existence, and through it the exchanges of the country were conducted at a rate so satisfactory that no Western merchant thought of shipping the products of the country to liquidate his Eastern balances. He bought his goods for cash, or on credit, and collected his debts, if so fortunate as to collect at all, in the same commodity, and never paid any of it out again except for goods. The dependence of the country for money was chiefly upon that brought in by new settlers. Occasionally an adventurer appeared who paid out money for sufficient of the products of the country to load a flat-boat, which he floated off to find a market.

Lincoln's first trip to New Orleans had been made from the Ohio River, while living in Indiana, and when he was in the nineteenth year of his age. On that occasion also he was a hired hand merely, and he and a son of the owner, without other assistance, made the trip A part of the cargo had been selected with special reference to the wants of the sugar plantations, and the young adventurers were instructed to linger upon the sugar coast for purpose of disposing of it. On one occasion they tied their boat up for the night near a plantation at which they had been trading during the afternoon. The negroes observing that the boat was in charge of but two persons, seven of them formed a plan to rob it during the night. Their intention evidently was to murder the young men, rob the boat of whatever money there might be on it, carry off such articles as they could secrete in their cabins, and then, by sinking the boat, destroy all traces of their guilt. They had not, however, properly estimated the courage and prowess of the two young men in charge. The latter, being on their guard, gave the would-be robbers and assassins a warm reception, and, notwithstanding the disparity in numbers, after a severe struggle, in which both Lincoln and his companion were considerably hurt, the former were driven from the boat. At the close of the fight, the young navigators lost no time in getting their boat under way. The trip, in the main, was successful, and in due time the young men returned to their homes in Indiana.

Lincoln and his associates for a second trip, Johnson and Hanks, were to join a Mr. Offut at Springfield, Illinois, as soon as the snow had disappeared, whence they were to go with him to Beardstown, the port of departure for New Orleans. When the snow melted, which was about the first of March, the whole country was so flooded as to render traveling impracticable. This led the party to purchase a canoe, in which they descended the Sangamon River to a point within a few miles of Springfield. This was the time and this the method of Lincoln's first entrance into Sangamon county—a county which was to be the field of his future triumphs, and which was to become proud of him as her most distinguished citizen, and which, in time, was to be honored through him with being the home of a President of the United States. On arriving at Springfield they learned from Offut that, not being able to purchase a boat in Beardstown, he had concluded to build one on the Sangamon River. Lincoln, Hanks, and Johnson, were hired for that purpose, at twelve dollars per month, and going into the woods, they got out the necessary timber and built a boat at the town of Sangamon, near where the Chicago, Alton, and St. Louis Railroad now crosses the Sangamon River, which they took to New Orleans upon the old contract.

The writer has not been put in possession of any of the incidents connected with this trip. It is sufficient for the present purpose, however, to know that so well did young Lincoln bear himself throughout—so faithful in all the trusts reposed in him by his employer; so active, prompt and efficient in all necessary labor; so cool, determined, and full of resources in the presence of danger—that before reaching New Orleans, Offut had become greatly attached to him, and on their return engaged him to take the general charge of a store and mill in the village of New Salem, then in Sangamon, now in Menard County.

In July, 1831, Lincoln was fairly installed in this new business. In those primitive times the country merchant was a personage of vast consequence. He was made the repository of all the news of the surrounding settlements, and as he "took the papers," he was able to post his customers as to the affairs of state and the news of the world generally. His acquirements in this last respect were as astounding to the country people as were those of Goldsmith's village schoolmaster to the simple rustics. His store was a place of common resort for the people on rainy days, and at those periods of the year when farm-work was not pressing, and nearly always on Saturday afternoons. There all the the topics of the neighborhood and of the times were discussed, the merchant usually bearing the leading part, and all disputed points of past history or of current events were always referred to him, as the ultimate tribunal, for decision. His word, and opinion, in these respects, were supreme, never disputed, and triumphantly repeated by the fortunate first-hearers at all casual meetings with the neighbors, and at all the little neighborhood gatherings at which the oracle was not present.

Early in the Spring of 1832, the Black Hawk war broke out in the northwestern part of the State. The previous year a part of the tribes of the Sac and Fox Indians had recrossed the Mississippi from its western bank, and taken possession of their old town on Rock River, a few miles above its mouth, and about four miles from where the city of Rock Island is now situated. The Indian title to the lands in that vicinity had been extinguished by a treaty made with the chiefs of the Sac and Fox Nations at St. Louis, in 1804, which treaty was afterwards confirmed by a portion of the tribes in 1815, and by another portion in 1816. Black Hawk always denied the validity of these treaties, and, in fact, of all the treaties made by his people with the whites. In the war of 1812, he had co operated with the British army, and had conceived an unconquerable hatred of the Americans. The lands on which the great town of his nation was situated, had recently been surveyed and brought into market, and a number of white settlers had gone upon them. This aroused the enmity of the old chieftain, and taking with him his women and children, and as many warriors as he could inspire with the same feeling, he returned to his former haunts, took possession of the ancient metropolis of his people, ordered the white settlers away, killed their stock, unroofed their houses, pulled down their fences, and cut up their growing grain. News of these outrages reaching Gov. Reynolds, at his request Gen. Gaines proceeded at once to Rock Island. Becoming convinced that Black Hawk meditated war on the settlers, Gen. Gaines called upon Gov. Reynolds for a small force of mounted volunteers. These were soon in the field, and in a short time, together with a few regular troops, appeared before Black Hawk's town. The latter, with his women and children and fighting men, retreated across the Mississippi without firing a gun; the volunteers destroyed the town, and encamped upon the Mississippi, on the site of the present city of Rock Island. Black Hawk, anticipating that the troops would follow him to the west side of the river, came into Fort Armstrong and sued for peace. A treaty was then made in which it was stipulated that Black Hawk's people should remain forever after on the west side of the river, never to recross it without permission of the President of the United States or the Governor of Illinois.

Prior to the adoption of the present constitution of Illinois, in 1847, elections for State officers and Members of the Legislature were held on the first Monday in August—for the former once in four years, for the latter once in every two years. Lincoln's return to New Salem was, therefore, but a few days before the election of that year for Members of the Legislature. The system of nominating candidates for office by county and State conventions had not then been introduced into Illinois. Indeed, party lines and party designations were at that time scarcely known in the State. There were "Clay Men," "Jackson Men," "Adams Men," "Crawford Men," and so on, but no clearly defined party creeds around which men of similar views rallied to make common cause against those holding opposite opinions. Men announced themselves as candidates for the various elective offices. It was a very rare circumstance that a contest for an office was narrowed down to two candidates More frequently a half dozen eager aspirants contested the prize.

The county of Sangamon was entitled to four members in the lower branch of the Legislature, and there were at the time of Lincoln's return, more than twice that number of candidates. Among the number were some of the ablest, best-known, and most popular men of the county, of whom may be mentioned John T. Stuart, afterwards Representative in Congress, Col. E D. Taylor, Peter Cartwright, the famous eccentric Methodist preacher, and others of considerable note. These gentlemen had been in the field some time before the return of Lincoln—had canvassed the county thoroughly, defining their position in local and other questions, and obtaining promises of support.

Lincoln had no sooner returned than he was urgently besought by his friends at New Salem to enter the lists for the Legislature against this array of strong men and old citizens. These entreaties, continued from day to day, together with the cordial reception he had just received at the hands of all his old acquaintances, induced him, against his better judgment, to give a reluctant assent, knowing very well that, under the circumstances, his election was entirely out of the question. It will be remembered that the county was a large one; that he had lived in it only from July to the following April; that he had but few acquaintances outside of the precinct of New Salem; and that the election was so near at hand as to deprive him of the opportunity of visiting other portions of the county, and making himself known to the people. Nevertheless, when the election came off, he was but a few votes behind the successful candidates. His own precinct—New Salem—gave him 277 votes in a poll of 284; and this, too, in the face of his avowed preferences for Mr. Clay, and notwithstanding the same precinct at the Presidential election, three months later, gave a majority of 115 for General Jackson. The result of this election, though practically a defeat, was, all circumstances considered, a most brilliant triumph, clearly presaging success in any future trial he might make And never since that day has Mr. Lincoln been beaten in any direct vote of the people.

In the summer of 1834, Mr. Lincoln was again a candidate for the Legislature. He had now become acquainted with the people throughout the county; and although they had not seen enough of him to have learned to appreciate him quite as highly as the people of New Salem precinct, nevertheles he was this time elected by an overwhelming majority, and by the largest vote cast for any candidate. Up to this period, and, indeed, for the two years after, Mr. Lincoln was not aware that he possessed any faculty for public speaking. His acquaintances knew him to be an admirable talker, full of original thought, a close reasoner, united to a matchless gift of illustration; and from their eager desire to get him into the Legislature, it is more than probable that they believed he would there develop into a forcible and ready debator. Whatever they had known him to undertake he had done well; and they therefore had faith in his success, should he enter this new and untried field of effort. In one of his memorable debates with Stephen A. Douglas, in 1855, the latter, in alluding to the early experience in life, as well as to the later efforts of his opponent, said:—"*Lincoln is one of those peculiar men who perform with admirable skill everything they undertake.*" Douglas had known and watched him closely for a quarter of a century—watched him not as an admirer and friend, but as a political opponent whom he always dreaded to encounter, and whose failure in anything would have given him sincere gratification—and this was the conclusion to which he had been forced to come contrary to his wishes. To be able to rise with the occasion, and to never fall below it, is one of the surest marks of genius; and we have the authority of the man, who, of all men in the world, is the least likely to be biased in Mr. Lincoln's favor, for saying that he has never failed to come up to this standard. The trait of character to which Mr. Douglas thus bore reluctant testimony, had been early remarked by Lincoln's friends It was not wonderful, therefore, that they had implicit faith in him—that, although young and wholly inexperienced in legislation, they cheerfully confided their interests to his keeping, for in his past life they had the strongest possible guarantee that in this new sphere he would make himself "master of the situation," and fully equal to all its duties.

But in the session of 1834-5, Mr. Lincoln did not attempt to make a speech. He was faithful in his attendance, watchful of the interests of his constituents, acquired the confidence of his fellow-members as a man of sound judgment and patriotic purposes, and in this manner he wielded a greater influence in shaping and controlling legislation than many of the noisy declaimers and most frequent speakers of the body. His constituents were satisfied—so well satisfied, indeed, that they re-elected him in 1836, again in 1838, and again in 1840, and would have continued electing him had he desired it; but by this time, as we shall presently see, his circumstances and position were greatly changed, and there were higher duties before him.

On retiring from the Legislature it was the intention of Mr. Lincoln to devote himself exclusively to the labors of his profession. His own convictions on the questions which divided parties were deeply-rooted and immovable. His party in the State were in a hopeless minority. There seemed but small opportunity for a man of his views to succeed in politics, while the qualities that he had by this time developed insured both an honorable fame and a lucrative income in his profession. To this he now turned with all the earnestness of his nature, and with a firm resolve to win laurels in it worth the wearing. But he was not permitted long to give his exclusive attention to professional pursuits. The groundswell of that political revolution which in 1840 carried the Whig party into power in the national government, had no sooner been felt, than there was a universal desire awakened among the Whigs of Illinois to make one more effort to carry the State over to the Whig column. Mr. Lincoln was assigned a place on the Electoral ticket—a position which he accepted with reluctance, but which he filled with great zeal and ability. In that memorable canvass he repeatedly met Mr. Douglas on the stump; and it is no disparagement to that gentleman to say, that then, as in later years, Mr. Lincoln proved himself to be immeasurably his superior—superior in logic, in argument, in resources as a debater, in broad and comprehensive views of national policy, in fairness and in gentlemanly courtesy toward his competitor.

After the election of that year, Mr. Lincoln returned to his professional duties. He had now attained a reputation at the bar which placed him in the front rank of the many able and profound jurists of the State. His services were eagerly sought in almost every case of importance; and perhaps no lawyer in Illinois, or any other State, has been more uniformly successful in the cases which he has undertaken. It is one of the peculiarities of Mr. Lincoln as a lawyer, that he holds himself bound in honor and in conscience, having accepted a fee, to thoroughly master the case of his client. In this regard he is noted among his professional brethren for the greatness of his labors. He not only studies the side of his client, but that of his opponent also. Consequently he is never taken unawares, but has ample resources for whatever turn the ingenuity, skill, or learning of the opposing counsel may give to the case. To this peculiarity, in part, is owing the well-known fact that whenever Mr. Lincoln is employed in connection with other eminent counsel, before the conclusion of the case the sole management of it is almost invariably surrendered to him. Not by any ostentatious thrusting of himself forward is this position obtained, for nothing could be more foreign to Mr. Lincoln's manner, either at the bar or elsewhere; but proving himself to be more completely master of the case than his associates, the latter voluntarily award the position to him, and even insist upon his taking it. Another peculiarity of Mr. Lincoln as a lawyer, is the fact that he is ever ready to give his assistance gratuitously to a poor client who has justice and right on his side. He has managed many such cases from considerations of a purely benevolent character, which he would have not have undertaken for a fee. More than this, in cases of peculiar hardship, he has been known, again and again, after throwing all of his power and ability as a lawyer, into the management of the case, without charge, or any other reward than the gratification of a noble nature, on bidding his client adieu, and when receiving his cordial thanks and the warm grasp of his hand, to slip into his palm a five or a ten dollar bill, bidding him to say nothing about it, but to take heart and be hopeful. Those who know him intimately will not be surprised at this relation, because it harmonizes well with his whole character; but so careful has he always been to conceal his charitable deeds that the knowledge of such actions on his part is confined to those who have come into possession of it without his agency.

In November, 1842, Mr. Lincoln was united in marriage to Miss Mary Todd, daughter of Hon. Robert S. Todd, of Lexington, Kentucky. The fruits of this union are three sons now living, and one dead. The eldest, now in his seventeenth year, is a student at Exeter Academy, New Hampshire, preparatory to entering Harvard University. The other sons are intelligent, promising lads. Mrs. Lincoln is a lady of charming presence, of superior intelligence, of accomplished manners, and, in every respect well fitted to adorn the position to which the election of her husband to the Presidency will place her. The courtesies and hospitalities of the White House have never been more appropriately and gracefully dispensed than they will be during the administration of Mr. Lincoln.

In 1846, Mr. Lincoln received the unanimous nomination for Congress by the Whig Convention for the Springfield District. In 1844 the district had given a majority of 914 to Mr. Clay, and the Democracy expected, in the Congressional election of 1846, to greatly lessen, if not entirely overcome, this majority. With the hope of securing the latter result, they put in nomination Rev. Peter Cartwright, the famous Methodist preacher, a man of great popularity with the people generally, and especially popular with his own denomination, which embraced a very large and influential population of the district. Mr. Lincoln spoke in the principal towns in the district, on the political issues of the day. His opponent did not meet him in discussion, but chose his own peculiar way of electioneering. The canvass resulted in the election of Mr. Lincoln by a majority of 1,511—a majority unprecedented in the district, and conclusive as to the estimation in which he was held by his immediate neighbors.

Mr. Lincoln took his seat in the National House of Representatives on the 7th of December, 1847—the beginning of the first session of the Thirtieth Congress. He met there such men as John Quincy Adams, George Ashmun, Jacob Collamer, John M. Botts, Washington Hunt, J. R. Ingersoll, T. Butler King, Henry W. Hilliard, George P. Marsh, Charles S Morehead, Meredith P. Gentry, James Pollock, Caleb B. Smith, Truman Smith, Robert C. Schenck, Alexander H Stephens, John B. Thompson, Robert Toombs, Samuel F. Vinton, and other prominent Whig leaders; and although a new man in Congress, and comparatively young, he at once took a prominent position among this brilliant array of distinguished men. Throughout his Congressional career, his record is that of a consistent Whig. On all the issues that divided parties which were brought before Congress for action, his name will be found recorded on the same side on which Clay and Webster had so often before recorded theirs.

When Mr. Lincoln took his seat in Congress, Gen. Scott had been nearly three months in possession of the city of Mexico. All the great battles of that war had been fought, and the negotiations which resulted in the treaty of Gaudalupe Hidalgo on the 2d of February, 1846, had progressed very far towards a favorable conclusion. The American Army, however, were still in Mexico; and various supply measures, resolutions of thanks, acts for extra pay, and for the relief of the widows and orphans of officers and soldiers who had fallen in the war, were brought before the Thirtieth Congress, and passed. *Mr. Lincoln voted in favor of every measure of this kind which came before Congress.* A careful examination of the Journals and the *Congressional Globe* discloses the fact that fourteen Acts and eight Joint Resolutions of the character referred to, were passed by this Congress. Of these, three Acts and two Joint Resolutions were passed under a call for the Ayes and Nays; the remainder without. We have the assurance of those who served in Congress with Mr. Lincoln—both his political friends and opponents—that he voted in favor of all the latter; while as to the former, the House Journal contains the proof.

After the Presidential election of 1848, Mr. Lincoln applied himself more closely than ever to the practice of his profession. In 1852 he was again placed by his Whig friends upon the Scott electoral ticket; but his professional engagements, together with the utter hopelessness of the cause in Illinois, deterred him from making as active and thorough a canvass of the State as he had done on former like occasions. In 1854 his profession had almost superseded all thought of politics. He had abandoned all political aspirations, content, as it seemed, with the honors which his profession brought him. The country was once more free from excitement. The agitation which grew out of the acquisition of territory from Mexico had been quieted by the compromise measures of 1850. Each of the political parties had expressed a determination to abide by that settlement of the slavery question. The status of all our unsettled territory was now fixed by law, so far as this subject was concerned. Sectional jealousies were obliterated, sectional strife healed, and concord and repose marked our enviable condition. From this peaceful and happy state the country was suddenly and unexpectedly aroused as "by the sound of a fire-bell at night," by the introduction of a bill into the United States Senate for the repeal of the Missouri Compromise. What followed is painfully fresh in the public recollection. The country was convulsed as it never had been before, and wise men clearly foresaw the evils that have since come upon us, and from which we have not yet recovered.

On his return to Illinois, after the passage of his Kansas-Nebraska bill, Mr. Douglas saw the mischief which that measure had wrought in the ranks of his party in his own State, and forthwith undertook to repair it. A Legislature was to be elected in November of that year, on which would devolve the duty of electing a successor to Gen. Shields in the U. S. Senate. It was a matter of great importance to Mr. Douglas to secure the re-election of Gen. Shields, as his defeat would be tantamount to a censure upon himself. He commenced his labors in Chicago, where he met with anything but a flattering reception from a constituency whom he had deceived, and whose moral sense he had grossly outraged. Thence he went to Springfield, the capital of the State. He arrived there at the time the State Agricultural Society was holding its annual fair. The occasion had brought together a vast multitude of people from all parts of the State. Hundreds of politicians had also assembled, among whom were many of the ablest men of the State. Much time was devoted to political speaking; but the great event of the occasion was the debate between Lincoln and Douglas. It had been nearly fourteen years since these gentlemen had been pitted against each other in a public discussion. In the canvass of 1840, Lincoln had proved himself more than a match for Douglas in debate.

In June 1856, a convention of those opposed to the Democratic party, was held at Bloomington, Illinois, at which time the Republican party was organized in that State, a Platform adopted, a State Ticket nominated, and delegates appointed to the National Republican Convention to meet at Philadelphia. Mr. Lincoln bore a leading part in securing these results. Perhaps no other man exerted so wide and salutary an influence in harmonizing differences, in softening and obliterating prejudices, and in bringing into a cordial union those who for years had been bitterly hostile to each other. His speech before that convention will ever be regarded by many of those who heard it, as the greatest effort of his life. Never was an audience more completely electrified by human eloquence. Again and again, during the progress of its delivery, they sprang to their feet and upon the benches, and testified by long-continued shouts and the waving of hats, how deeply the speaker had wrought upon their minds and hearts. It fused the mass of hitherto incongruous elements into perfect homogeneity, and from that day to the present, they have worked together in harmonious and fraternal union. It kindled also an enthusiasm in the bosoms of those who heard it, which they carried home with them, and with which they imbued their neighbors, and by which the Republican party of Illinois, in the first year of its existence, was carried triumphantly into power.

At the National Republican Convention of that year, Mr. Lincoln's name was presented by the Western delegates for nomination for the Vice-Presidency. Although, had his own wishes been consulted in the matter he would not have consented to this use of his name, it was nevertheless a well-deserved compliment, as well as a recognition of the fact that his reputation had now become national. Mr. Lincoln's vote on the informal ballot was 110—Mr. Dayton's, 259.

During the recess of Congress in 1857, Mr. Douglas made a speech at Springfield in further vindication of his Kansas-Nebraska Bill, known as his "Grand Jury Speech," from the fact that he was invited to deliver it by the Grand Jury of the U. S. District Court for Southern Illinois. In that speech, he first promulgated the doctrine that the framers of the Declaration of Independence, in asserting that "all men are created equal," simply meant to say that "British subjects on this continent were equal to British subjects born and residing in Great Britain." Mr. Lincoln, by invitation of a large number of his fellow citizens, replied to Douglas.

The Democratic State Convention met at Springfield on the 21st of April, 1858, and published a declaration of the principles on which they proposed to make their battle. They resolved—

"That the Democracy of Illinois are unalterably attached to, and will maintain inviolate, *the principles declared in the National Democratic Convention at Cincinnati, in June*, 1856."

Several supplementary resolutions were adopted, all tending to the same conclusion. Senator Douglas and his Democratic colleagues in the House of Representatives were warmly indorsed, and promised the "earnest and efficient support" of the party in the coming campaign. No rebuke was offered to the Administration for its course on Lecompton, except by a misty inference.

The election took place on the 2d of November. The excitement which had wrought the State up to a tempest during the progress of the fight, culminated on this eventful day. The whole number of votes cast for President in Illinois, in 1856, was 238,981; the whole number cast for members of the Legislature in 1858, was 251,145. A drenching and chilling rain poured down all day in the northern part of the State, extending southward, with more or less discomfort to voters, so far as Vandalia. It did not, however, reach "Lower Egypt." The result of the election is matter of history. Mr. Lincoln had a majority over Mr. Douglas, in the popular vote, of 4,085, while, by an unfair apportionment law, the latter had a small majority of the Legislature, and was therefore re-elected to the Senate.

The man whose history we have thus briefly traced now stands before the country the chosen candidate for President of the United States. Commencing life under circumstances the most discouraging, we have seen courageously and manfully battling his way upward from one position of honor and responsibility to another, until he now stands in an attitude to place his foot upon the very topmost round of honorable fame. He presents in his own person the best living illustration of the true dignity of labor, and of the genius of pure free American institutions, having been elevated through their instrumentality from poverty and obscurity to his present distinguished position.

Perhaps no more appropriathe conclusion can be given to this sketch of Lincoln's life, than the following, relative to his personal appearance, habits, tastes, &c., which is copied from the Chicago *Press and Tribune*, and for the correctness of which, in every particular, we can fully vouch:

"Mr. Lincoln stands six feet four inches high in his stockings. His frame is not muscular, but gaunt and wiry. In walking, his gait, though firm, is never brisk. He steps slowly and deliberately, almost always with his head inclined forward, and his hands clasped behind his back. In manner, he is remarkably cordial, and at the same time simple. His politeness is always sincere, but never elaborate and oppressive. A warm shake of the hand and a warmer smile of recognition are his methods of greeting his friends. At rest, his features, though they are those of a man of mark, are not such as belong to a handsome man; but when his fine, dark-gray eyes are lighted up by any emotion, and his features begin to play, he would be chosen from among a crowd as one who had in him not only the kindly sentiments which women love, but the heavier metal of which full-grown men and Presidents are made. His hair is black, and though thin, is wiry. His head sits well on his shoulders, but beyond that it defies description. It nearer resembles that of Clay than Webster's, but is unlike either. It is very large, and phrenologically well proportioned, betokening power in all its developments. A slightly Roman nose, a wide cut mouth, and a dark complexion, with the appearance of having been weather-beaten, complete the description.

In his personal habits, Mr. Lincoln is as simple as a child. He loves a good dinner, and eats with the appetite that goes with a great brain; but his food is plain and nutritious. He never drinks intoxicating liquors of any sort. He is not addicted to tobacco in any of its shapes. He was never accused of a licentious act in his life. He never uses profane language. He never gambles. He is particularly cautious about incurring pecuniary obligations for any purpose whatever; and, in debt, he is never content until the score is discharged. We presume he owes no man a dollar. He never speculates. The rage for the sudden acquisition of wealth never took hold of him. His gains from his profession have been moderate, but sufficient for his purposes. While others have dreamed of gold, he has been in pursuit of knowledge. In all his dealings he has the reputation of being generous but exact, and, above all, religiously honest. He would be a bold man who would say that Abraham Lincoln ever wronged a man out of a cent, or ever spent a dollar that he had not honestly earned. His struggles in early life have made him careful of money, but his generosity with his own is proverbial. He is a regular attendant upon religious worship, and, though not a communicant, is a pew-holder and liberal supporter of the Presbyterian Church in Springfield, to which Mrs. Lincoln belongs. He is a scrupulous teller of truth—too exact in his notions to suit the atmosphere of Washington, as it now is. His enemies may say that he tells Black Republican lies; but no man ever charged that, in a professional capacity, or as a citizen dealing with his neighbors, he would depart from the Scriptural command. At home, he lives like a gentleman of modest means and simple tastes. A good-sized house of wood, simply but tastefully furnished, surrounded by trees and flowers, is his own; there he lives, at peace with himself, the idol of his family, and for his honesty, ability and patriotism, the admiration of his countrymen.

If Mr. Lincoln is elected President, he will carry but little that is ornamental to the White House. The country must accept his sincerity, his ability, and his honesty, in the mould in which they are cast. He will not be able to make so polite a bow as Franlin Pierce, but he will not commence anew the agitation of the slavery question by commending to Congress any Kansas-Nebraska bills. He may not preside at the Presidential dinners with the ease and grace which distinguish the "venerable public functionary," Mr Buchanan; but he will not create the necessity for a Covode Committee and the disgraceful revelations of Cornelius Wendell. He will take to the Presidential Chair just the qualities which the country now demands to save it from impending destruction—ability that no man can question, firmness that nothing can overbear, honesty that never has been impeached, and patriotism that never despairs."

TEIN-TSIN AND THE PEIHO RIVER.

Small vessels only can approach the mouth of the Peiho River. Large ships are obliged to anchor just in sight of the low shores through which it flows into the sea of Pecheli. There is also a bar at the entrance, which can only be crossed by gun-boats at high tide. The forts which we took in 1858, and upon which, reconstructed by the Chinese, we suffered so severe a defeat in 1859, are just inside the entrance, within range of heavy guns from outside the bar. The village of Takoo is just above the forts, with a picturesque-looking building—the Governor's house.

The course of the river is winding up to Tien-Tsin; its depths regular; no shoal water in the center of the channel, and the banks gradually rise in hight on ascending the river. Tien-Tsin is about seventy miles from the mouth of the river, as miserable in appearance as most Chinese cities. The walls are in bad repair. No guns were mounted on them in 1858. The suburb, as usual in China, is in a far more flourishing condition than the town within the walls. It is situated on a large plain, dotted with villages, through which a fine road leads to Pekin. Apricots and other fruits are plentiful, and the vineyards are trained prettily in arches. The grapes seem inferior in quality.

At Tein-Tsin the Grand Canal, or, more properly, its continuation, the Eu-ho River, falls into the Peiho. This was the only place where the larger gun-boats could turn in 1858. This will give an idea of the breadth of the river. Four miles above Tien-Tsin the river becomes too shallow for gun-boats, but it is navigable for country boats as high as Tong-Chow-Fow, a city about twelve miles from Pekin, of which it is the port; and it will form a good depot for our stores when we advance to Pekin. The advance to that capital seems not a difficult matter to a far smaller force than ten thousand Europeans. It is about forty-five miles distant from Tien-Tsin—Tien-Tsin being about seventy-miles from the mouth of the Peiho.

KEEPING A SECRET.—The Newport *Mercury* relates a story of Stuart, the painter, which illustrates finely the power which a secret has to propagate itself, if once allowed a little airing, and to reach a few ears. Stuart had, as he supposed, discovered a secret art of coloring, very valuable. He told it to a friend. His friend valued it very highly, and came some time afterwards to ask permission to communicate it, under oath of eternal secrecy, to a friend of his who needed every possible aid to enable him to rise. "Let me see," said Stuart, making a chalk mark on a board at hand; "*I* know the art, and that is—"—"One," said his friend. "You know it," continued Stuart, making another mark by the side of the one already made; "and that is—"—"Two," cried the other. "Well, you tell your friend, and that will be—" making a third mark. "Three only," said the other. "No," said Stuart, "it's one hundred and eleven!" (111).

ELECTIONS OF PRESIDENTS.

Since the adoption of the Constitution we have had eighteen Presidential elections, but fortunately in no instance as yet has a President been chosen by the Northern or Southern States exclusively. The following table shows what number of Northern and what number of Southern States have voted for each of the successful candidates at each election:

Year. Candidates.	Northern States.	Southern States.
1788—Washington..........	5	5
1792—Washington..........	8	7
1796—Adams..............	7	2
1800—Jefferson	2	7
1804—Jefferson	8	7
1808—Madison.............	5	7
1812—Madison.............	8	8
1816—Monroe..............	8	8
1820—Monroe..............	12	12
1824—Adams...............	7	2
1828—Jackson.............	5	10
1832—Jackson.............	8	8
1836—Van Buren.	8	7
1840—Harrison............	10	8
1844—Polk	7	8
1848—Taylor	7	8
1852—Pierce..............	14	13
1856—Buchanan............	8	14
Total	129	143

No successful candidate except John Quincey Adams ever received less than a majority of all the States of the Union at the time of a given election, and it should be remembered that he was not chosen by the people, but by the House.

—A shrewd Wall street Republican has been trying to make some money by betting $50 that "*he could name* fifteen States which would vote for Lincoln, and $100 that his opponent could not name fifteen States which would vote against him." The bet being taken, the Lincoln man first named the fifteen Southern States for Lincoln, losing this part of the bet, and leaving the anti-Lincoln man to select fifteen of the eighteen free States. The Republican loses his bet of $50 and gains the bet of $100.

BY TELEGRAPH.

THE LATEST NEWS!

PRESIDENTIAL PROCLAMATION.

Washington, Dec. 15.—The President has issued a Proclamation, appointing the fourth of January as a day of Fasting, Humiliation and Prayer, in order to avert the alarming and immediate political danger and fearful distress and panic now threatening the country. He says that all hope now seems to have deserted the minds of men in this hour of calamity and peril, and to whom can we resort for relief but to God. His omnipotent arm alone can save us from the awful effects of our crimes and follies.—*Dispatch from the Chars. Mercury.*

Reports from Louisiana.

New Orleans, Dec. 14.—The unanimous action of the Louisiana Legislature in passing the Convention Bill, is considered here as establishing the policy of immediate separate action in this State.

After the State has resumed her sovereignty, a call for a general Convention of the slaveholding States will be issued.

The feeling in favor of secession is overwhelming. The Legislature has appropriated $500,000 for arming the State.

Highly Important from Washington.

Gen. Cass resigns—the alleged reason—President's banquet, etc., etc.

Gen. Lewis Cass, the Secretary of State, has resigned his place in the Cabinet. It is said that his resignation was caused by the refusal of the President to strengthen the garrison of the fortifications in the harbor of Charleston.

Gen. Cass contended that the present force there "was certain to be sacrificed to the fury of the secessionists."

The President, on the other hand, is said to be well assured that no attempt will be made against the forts unless reinforcements should be sent. He therefore considers that Major Anderson and his command are in no danger whatever.

The President, to-day, entertained the Diplomatic Corps and other high functionaries at what may be called a "State Dinner.

The Republicans are dispirited at the Union revulsion now sweeping over the Eastern, Northern, Middle and Southern States.

From the Southern Guardian.

AN APPEAL TO THE SOUTH.—NO. 1.

Whenever any measures are taken which involve the vital interests of the community in which I live, I speak out my opinions upon them, little thinking, and as little caring, whether in man's judgment they become my place and calling or not. This I have done repeatedly; and I have generally received for my pains unmerited reproof at first, and overmerited thanksgiving at last. So it may be in this instance.

South Carolina will certainly secede from the Union in a few months. Upon this momentos step hang issues of unspeakable importance and interminable consequences. This she knows full well; for her leading men are not all fools and desperadoes, as some would have the world believe they are. A faithful portrature of their character would be rather too complimentary for their taste, and quite too sentimental for this stolid, calculating age, in which the talk of "pledging *lives and fortune, and sacred honor,*" in defence of right, is regarded as ridiculous romance.—There is a something in them, I grant, that has made them the most restless people under the dealings of the General Government towards the South, of any people in the Union; but never have they manifested discontent without a sufficient cause. It may be the streak of French that is in them; it may be the Revolutionary spirit not yet extinguished within them; and it may be the peculiar endearment to their State institutions. When I enter their legislative halls, and notice the dignity, the gravity, the order, the comity in debate, and the respectful obedience yielded to the presiding officers, and go thence to the halls of Congress and see the tumult which prevails there, I glory in my just adopted State, and blush for the United States. When I enter their courts of justice, and observe the like dignity, gravity, order, comity and obedience there—see with what independence and impartiality justice is administered—particularly the criminal justice of the commonwealth, now almost lost in the Southern States—I do not wonder that they are tinged with a little more than ordinary State pride. When I consider their openhanded liberality in erecting public buildings, railroads, supporting schools, colleges, asylums, and other valuable and benevolent institutions; and remember the onerous burden of taxation which they have to endure to accomplish these ends, and the uncomplaining promptness with which they shoulder this burden—I say to myself "verily, citizens of South Carolina, ye are a peculiar people in this great Republic and worthy of something better than blame!" But these are not all—they are a *religious* people. Look into all her churches on the Sabbath day! They are all crowded; new ones are going up, old ones are being enlarged, and for about one hundred and sixty days union prayer meetings have been held in the capitol of the State, begun and prosecuted with no eye to the existing perils of the country.—When I consider all these things, I exclaim: "Well mayest thou, gallant, noble, generous, pious State, fire at every encroachment upon thy rights, for when they are gone, you will have lost more than any other State lost without a fault! From my soul I excuse thee for thy growing impatience at every new aggression upon thy prerogatives, thine honor, thy peculiar institution."

This is the State which has determined to withdraw from the Union, let the consequences be what they may, rather than to submit to the Black Republican rule She will triumph. I do not say that she will not have to go thro' tribulation.—That is one of the passports to a distinguished place in Heaven, and consequently no certain sighn of error. Two shots have been fired at her already froma press of a neighboring State and many more will come from quarters where she had a right to expect neutrality, if not sympathy and praise. But no matter; let her bear them unmurmuringly; and, without retort, move right ahead, in solid column, as she does move, and will move, in an atmosphere of prayer, asking no help, but receiving it thankfully and will she triumph gloriously. The ravages of seventy years but have left me but little physical strength, what remains is at her service. The evening haze is gathering on my mind, but there is light enough left to beacon other States to her help, and to this end I now begin to use it. But, to secure readers, I must say but little at a time. I therefore close for the present, with an earnest request that the Southern press give my brief articles a general circulation, for the sake of an old man who has done the South some service.

A. B. LONGSTREET.

TEH EAST FLORIDIAN.

WM. H. BABCOCK,
EDITOR AND PROPRIETOR.

FERNANDINA:

WEDNESDAY, DECEMBER 19, 1860.

THE SECESSION
OF THE
STATE OF FLORIDA.
THE DISSOLUTION
OF THE
UNION!
THE FORMATION
OF A
SOUTHERN CONFEDERACY.

TO OUR DEBTORS.

GENTLEMEN:—WE ARE IN NEED OF OUR LITTLE DUES.—You will not individually miss the small sums in which you are indebted, while the aggregate amount, is a matter to us, of very considerable importance, inasmuch as it provides the wherewithal to pay our Printers, purchase paper and other materials, and supply our own modest wants. We shall send you therefore a gentle reminder of your indebtedness, and hope that the demand will meet on the part of each and all of you, A PROMPT AND WILLING RESPONSE.

RELIGIOUS INTELLIGENCE!

We are informed that Rev. J. O. Branch: has been appointed by the Conference, to the Methodist Church of this place. Rev Mr. Timberlake, the late incumbent, has been appointed Sunday School Agent.

PERSONAL!

Hon G. W. Call, Senator from Nassau County, arrived last week, and received the hearty congratulations and unanimous "well-done" of his numerous friends.

LINCOLN HUNG IN EFFICY!

A correspondent, writing from Baldwin, informs us that one Abe Lincoln, who has been elected President of the Northern States, was recently hung in effigy in that town and was afterwards committed to the flames with due and appropriate solemnities.

TO THE POLLS ON THE 22D.

Let every voter deposite his ballot on the 22d inst. Vote for *straight out Secessionists*, and get your friends to do likewise. A large vote is essential, so that the views of Florida should be thoroughly understood.

SOUTH CAROLINA!

This state will secede this week. The land of flowers will entwine around the Palmetto on the 4ih day of next month.

SCOTT'S VARIETIES.

The above Company will appear in their dramatic representations at Cohen's Hall, uext Thursday and Friday evenings.

COUNTY CONVENTION.

A public meeting of the citizens of Nassau County, was held in this place on the 12th inst., for the purpose of nominating candidates for the State Convention.—Joseph Finegan, Esq., and Gen. J. G. Cooper, are the two gentlemen selected to represent the people of this county. They stand where they should, with their feet firmly planted upon the rock of secession, and will be sent to Tallahassee, with the fixed and avowed intention of voting the State of Florida out of the Union in the shortest possible time. They are gentlemen of the right stamp, honored and trusted members of this community, and will faithfully reflect the views and wishes of their constituents. Let's give them a rousing vote!

EXECUTION OF NEGROES.

We are informed that two negro men, the property of Wm. Strickland, Esq., of Alachua County, will be executed at Waldo on the 21st inst., in accordance with a resolution of the Vigilance Committee of that neighborhood. They have been convicted upon ample testimony and their own confessions, of having concocted a plan to murder their master and his family. No doubt whatever exists in the minds of the community as to their guilt. It is very much to be regretted that the infamous white scoundrels, who have doubtless lured these poor creatures to their merited doom, cannot be hung up at the same time and place.

SECESSION.

We publish an article under the above caption, not because we concur in the views which it presents, but through respect for the author, whom we know to be a gentleman of ability and the highest integrity, and thoroughly honest and conscientious in his convictions.

The demands of which he speaks, have been made time and again, and have been contemptuously disregarded. They are made by the highest authority of the land, the Constitution of the United States, and are ignored by the "higher law" of the Black Republicans—they are made by the master in quest of his property, aad are answered by murder, fine and imprisonment—they were made by Wigfall of Texas in the Senate only a few days since, and were received with scorn and derisive laughter. No, the demands which we should henceforth require, should be made and enforced, if needs be, at the point of the bayonet. Nothing but the sternest and most unflinching determination will avail the South at the present juncture. We are completely and utterly disgusted with the very name of compromise. It is a snare, a delusion, a device which can only serve to weaken our hands and strengthen those of the enemy. Has there been any *tangible* intimation of a change of feeling among the people of the North since the election of Lincoln? Does the action of the Vermont Legislature, in refusing to repeal the Personal Liberty Bill, by a vote of more than two to one, indicate a conciliatory spirit? Do the dissentions which prevail in the *panacea* Committee of thirty-three, and the dogged pertinacity which actuates a considerable number of the Northern members thereof, throw a gleam of hope upon the troubled sea of difficulties, or betoken a spirit of harmony and mutual confidence?

The Southern States should secede just so soon as their conventions can frame and pass the ordinances of secession, each for herself and separately. That separation from the non-slave-holding States should be *complete, final and irrevocable.* We may then again exchange the right hand of fellowship, but only as foreign powers, through the influence of mutual treaties and obligations. We are completely alienated, and are two nations in sentiment and interest. It is far better for both that we separete now. Each hour, each minute of our present condition, but deepens and intensifies the mutual jealousy which now exists.

If after separation, a collision takes place in consequence of a denial of our right to secede, we say, let it come. We cannot be conquered while fighting in defence of our liberty, our honor, our hearthstones, our all.

So far as Florida is concerned, we most fervently hope that on the 4th of January, 1861, she will forever, as a State, leave the present Confederacy. *Let the oonsequences be what they may,* she is bound in honor to herself, and in deference to the best interests of her citizens, to assume and exercise all the powers and rights of an independent sovereignty.

TO OUR PATRONS.

In accordance with a time-honored custom in vogue among the Press of this state, no paper will be issued from this office during the next week. With the close of 1860, a great Republic is breaking into fragments. One by one many of the component members thereof are making preparations to take their destinies into their own hands, and relying upon the God of battles and the truth and justice of their cause, to defend resolutely and to the last, those inalienable rights, life, liberty and the pursuit of happiness. These can never be acquired in the Union as it exists.—They are only to be regained in that form of government, which provides for the equality and protection of its citizens and ignores all sectional distinctions. Such a Confederacy, the Southern States are now forming, and the New Year will open upon one of the most glorious movements ever recorded upon the pages of History. A new Republic will spring into existence, strong and mighty, with all the elements of true greatness within her ample bosom. With no timid or vacillating step will she apply for admission among the sisterhood of nations, but with the assured and confident security of one who demands and who has the ability to occupy that position. *Esto perpetua!* With the utmost sincerity, do we invoke for you, our readers a merry Christmas and a happy New Year! God and the South!

FERNANDINA VOLUNTEERS.

A fine company, bearing the above title, was organized in this place, last week.—The following gentleman were elected officers:—Captain, Joseph Finegan: 1st. Lieut. J. G. Ashe: 2d do, W. B. Butler 3d do, H. C. Dozier: Surgeon, L. M. Butler, M. D: Orderly, P. H. Young. The company numbers abont seventy, rank and file, and embraces among its members, many of our oldest and most influential citizens. About thirteen hundred dollars have been raised for the purchase of arms Their uniform is to be made of cloth, manufactured South of Mason's and Dixon's line. We learn that their services have been tendered unconditionally to the Governor. *They are ready and await the word.*

Gleanings from the Florida Press.

—:o:—

The Key of the Gulf states that the residence of James Filor Esq, was recently totally destroyed by fire. The loss was very large.

A beautiful Secession Flag has been raised over the office of the St. Augustine Examiner. Many of the grey-haired citizens of the Ancient City have donned the blue cockade.

We learn from the Observer that the sailor Duggan, who killed Wallace in Pensacola a few weeks since, has been convicted of murder in the first degree.

T. E. Buckman Esq, says the Independent Press, has accepted the office of Superintendent of the Central Rail Road. A negro girl, the property of Mr. J. S. Wood, as we are informed by the same paper, was lately burnt to death.

A number of Northern fishermen have been compelled, as we learn from the St. Johns Mirror, to leave Mayport Mills.—They had rendered themselves quite obnoxious to the people in that locality.

☞The following is an extract of a letter from a gentleman high in position at Washington, and who is a close observer of the events now taking place at the Federal Capitol:

WASHINGTON, Dec. 8, 1860.

The work is going bravely on. Hale's speech no doubt reflects the *true sentiments* of the great mass of the Republican party. Very glad he made it—it will settle probably, North Carolina, Louisiana, and Arkansas.

Yours, very truly, **

FOR THE EAST FLORIDIEN.

MILITARY ORGANIZATION.

A meeting of the citizens of the City of Fernandina, convened together on the evening of December 15, 1860, at the Hall of Col. H. Timanus, for the purpose of organizing a Military Corps, when Mr. J. L. Harrington was called to the Chair and E. A. Papy requested to act as Secretary.

The object of the meeting having been explained by Mr. R. W. Murray, in a few appropriate remarks, the following Preamble and Resolutions were submitted by him and unanimously adoptod:

Whereas, The high regard we entertain for the institutions of the South—the land of our birth and the home of our adoption—renders it necessary, that we should, in times of threatened danger, exert our best endeavors to place ourselves in such a position as will enable us to protect her against the inroads of a foreign or domestic foe;—*And, whereas,* Such danger bidding fair to overtake us in the dismemberment of the Federal Union, we feel that it is the part of wisdom to marshall our forces and prepare for the struggle, by uniting together in the bonds of military amity and friendship. Be it therefore

Resolved, That we organize ourselves into a Military Corps, for the protection of Southern Rights, and that we will, to the fullest extent of our power, "protect, cherish, and defend," those rights, at all and every hazard.

Resolved, That in the selection of a uniform, we will seek to make it as purely of Southern manufactured goods as the nature of things will admit.

Resolved, That in withdrawing from the Company now organized in our City, we entertain no unkind feelings; but are simply actuated with the belief that we are old enough to think and act for ourselves.

Resolved, That we immediately tender to His Excellency Gov. M. S. Perry, our services, and whenever the time shall arrive, that we particularly desire "a place in the picture near the flashing of the guns."

The carrying into effect of the last resolve was postponed until the corps shall be more thoroughly organized.

After the enrolling of members the following gentlemen were elected Officers:

R. W. Murray............*Captain.*
J. L. Harrington.........*1st Lieutenant.*
J. W. Remley.............*2d* "
L. B. Chapman...........*3d* "
J. R. Schrimshaw.........*Ensign.*
Jno. Lang..................*Orderly Serg't.*

Mnch unanimity and good feeling prevailed during the meeting.

On motion, it was

Resolved, That the proceedings be published in the East Floridian.

J. L. HARRINGTON, *Chairman.*
E. A. PAPY, *Secretary.*

FOR THE EAST FLORIDIAN.

PUBLIC MEETING.

Pursuant to previous notice, a large number of the citizens of Alachua County, assembled in the Court House, in the Town of Gainesville, on Saturday the 9th inst., for the purpose of nominating suitable persons as candidates to represent Alachua County in the State Convention, to be held in Tallahassee, on the 2d day of January next, 1861.

On motion, Col. John C. Pelot was called to the Chair, and A. A. Maulden requested to act as Secretary.

The Chairman on taking his seat stated the object of the meeting in a few eloquent remarks.

The following Resolution was introduced by Col. J. B. Dawkins:

Resolved, That a Committee be appointed, consisting of one from each precinct in the County here represented, to report rules and regulations, and make apportionment to govern the votes of the different precincts represented in this meeting:

Which Committee was appointed as follows:

Henry Bradford..........Newnansville.
T. A. McDonell..........Gainesville.
William Strickland.........Waldo.
James C. Pelot...........Archer.
Col. Geo. Leitner..........Micanopy.
James Young..............Fort Walker.
B. T. Rives..................Providence.

The Committee after an hour's absence, returned the following report, which was adopted:

The Committee appointed to prepare rules and regulations for the government of this meeting, and to apportion the votes of the differents precincts for the nomination of Delegates to the State Convention, beg leave to submit the following:

That the rules governing the House of Representatives in the General Assembly, be adopted as the rules of this meeting.

That the nomination for Delegates be made by any member of this meeting.

That the voting shall be done by precinct, *viva voce.*

That each precinct shall be entitled to the following number of votes, in the following ratio:

That each precinct shall be entitled to one vote, and one vote for every twenty votes, and a fraction above one-half of twenty shall be so taken. And according to the above rules, each precinct shall be entitled to the following number of votes, to-wit:

Newnansville..............................10
Waldo...................................... 9
Gainesville................................. 7
Micanopy.................................... 5
Orange Creek.............................. 5
Archer....................................... 5
Fort Walker................................. 2
Providence.................................. 1

On motion, the meeting then proceeded to ballot for the different Candidates that had been nominated.

The result of the election was the choosing of Col. James B. Dawkins, and Col. John C. Pelot, as the candidates to represent Alachua in the State Convention.

During the meeting eloquent addresses were delivered by Hon. Tillman Ingram, Col. James B. Dawkins, Maj. James B. Bailey, and Col. John C. Pelot.

Gen. S. R. Pyles introduced the following Resolution:

Resolved, That the proceedings of this meeting be published in the Florida Dispatch, Peninsular Gazette, and East Floridian.

On motion, the meeting then adjourned.

JOHN C. PELOT, *Chairman.*
A. A. MAULDEN, *Secretary.*

[FOR THE EAST FLORIDIAN.]

SECESSION.

The word at the head of this article, Mr. Editor, is in every ones mind. We speak of nothing else, we think of nothing else. I apprehend, at no time, during the existence of this government, has anything like the degree of unanimity prevailed on any subject, as now pervades the whole people. For myself, I have yet to converse with the *first man,* who says, he is prepared to wait—for an "overt act."

The most important event that has ever occurred in our history, (not excepting the declaration of independence itself,) is about to take place—and it becomes us to aid coolly—dispassionately—and deliberately.

It is generally known by this time, who are to be the peoples representatives, to do this important work. In no instance I trust have the people of Florida failed to select the very best men for the service. For indeed, they have an important work before them—a work not for a day—or a year—but for *history*—a work that will be read of, and commented on by generations unborn.

There is a disposition, I fear under the excitement of the moment, how broad cast I know not, but judging from my own limited sphere of observation—all pervading for doing this solemn act, in a spirit of revenge, and spite. I trust the time intervening between this, and the assembling of the Convention, will afford opportunity for the members to think coolly upon the subject that they will take care that no such idea appears upon the record of their proceedings.

But rather, let the future historian, in making up the record of these times, be able to gather, from the proceedings of the Convention, that the people of the South were long forbearing, yea for thirty years they stood what no brave people could stand under different circumstances, hoping, against hope, that the people of the North would cease their encroachments, and come to an appreciation of our just rights. That they forbore until forbearance ceased to be a virtue, and in the end demanded only their just right, and they were refused them.

This is the character of record, which seems to me should be made up of these times.

Then I suggest, for the humblest of us may have our idears, and make suggestions.

That the Convention of the State of Florida, upon its assembling, draw up at once an ordinance of secession. Let the grievances of which we complain be enumerated: Let the clauses of the constitution which have been violated be recited. Let it be stated wherein the constitution is insufficient, and what would have made it sufficient, (for I apprehend no one will argue with the light of our experience, our fathers could not have made an instrument that would be binding.) Suppose for instance, it had been made high treason for any one to connive at the escape or attempt to rescue a fugitive slave, a clause requiring each State to make statutary laws for carrying out the provisions of the constitution, and twenty others that a moments reflection would suggest. I say, I apprehend no one will believe but that an instrument could have been made, that would have bound them provided they had signed it.

Then I say, let all these things be required. And let the last clause of the ordinance be—upon the Governor of this State, receiving *official information of all these things being done, between this and the third of next March,* then the Governor shall in that case answer by proclamation, that the State of Florida is back in the Union.

It may be said that the time is too short for the demands to be complied with. I grant that the time is short, but the occasion requires haste, and in these times of telegraphs, the thing is not impossible.

It may be asked, if it can be for one moment believed, that the North would grant the demand? I have no idea they would. Then why make the demand? I am not aware, that because we feel sure our enemy will refuse our *just demands,* that we are exonorated from making them, before taking the *ultima ratio.*

The idea seems to be popular, "Let us secede, and let advances be made by the North."

It strikes me, if the people of the South go out of the Union with that idea, we will stand a chance of not getting as much as by the plan suggested. Overtures doubtless will be made by the North—a Convention called to consider them—and it is just possible, terms may be agreed upon conceding some of our just claims for the sake of peace. By the plan suggested, *we get all* or none. Again, the very idea of listening to overtures at all, would imply a willingness to concede something.

The conquering General does not allow the vanquished foe to say upon what terms he will surrender; but he demands an unconditional surrender. So in this, let us DEMAND every thing to which we have a just claim, and let the North have the responsibility of refusing it.

Will any contend that our honor will be compromised by the plan suggested. A man's honor is never compromised in doing right; and is it not right to demand of your enemy reparation before taking to the last resort.

But a disunionist—who is a disunionist for the love of it—may ask. How, if the North should concede all we demand?—Then I say, if a wise Providence should cause so great a miracle to be wrought—that it is God's will this Union stand—and in God Almighty's name let it stand.

From appearances, a collision with the present administration seems inevitable.—Mr. Buchanan is our friend, and no doubt would be glad of any excuse not to strike. Let us try and give him that excuse, and it will afford us a breathing spell at least, to put our houses in order.

But the most practical reason for some such plan as suggested, and one most likely to be soonest called into use, is:—The masses I fear are going into this thing, as though when we secede, the work is done, when in reality, it is only just begun. Before we settle down into a firm working government, we will have to go through pain, tribulation, and hard times. This all history teaches.

When these hard times come, as assuredly they will come, we will have complaints. We will have grumblers—we will have men to say, these thiugs might have been avoided. We will have men to say, that we could have had all we required from the North for the asking.

Let us be in position to respond triumphantly to all such. "We did in the last resort demand only our just rights, and they were refused.

I would attach my name to this article, Mr. Editor, had I the conceit to believe it would add any thing to it. May I express the hope, however, that the ideas thrown out, may receive more than a passing thought, even though this article be signed only with one initial—that abler minds will elaborate them, and put in working shape something after the order of the ideas so crudely expressed; which, nevertheless, I feel through all the fibres of my system, to be just and right. B.

FOR THE EAST FLORIDIAN.

WALDO, Fla, Dec. 11th, 1860.

W. H. BABCOCK, Esq.:—*Dear Sir:*—At a meeting of the Santa-Fe Committee of Vigilance and Safety, held Nov. 24th, the following resolution offered by Dr. G. W. H. McRae, was adopted:

Resolved, That this Committee consider it dangerous to the peace and quiet of the country, for negroes to hire their own time, and that it shall be the duty of each member of this Committee, to bring to the notice of the Committee, any case of the kind, that may come to their knowledge.

At the last meeting of said Committee, held the 7th inst., the following resolution was adopted:

Resolved, That the resolution adopted by this Committee at its last meeting, in regard to negroes hiring their own time, be published in the East Floridian.

N. W. McLEOD, *Secretary.*

[FOR THE EAST FLORIDIAN.]

OCALA, December 3rd 1860.

MR. EDITOR:—Everything around us is encouraging. The most careless observer of surrounding things, can see that the people are aroused to their interests. Secession will soon go on, and the relief from suspense which we now experience (from merely anticipating a dissolution of the Union,) is indeed wonderful. And to speak of our remaining in the Union, is a death blow to all our hopes, and consequently "*Horrabile dictu.*" I have recently traveled over a great portion of two Southern States, Alabama and Georgia. The people of the empire State are almost unanimous in favor of secession, with their gallant leaders urging them to their interests, among whom may be named the patriot Toombs, Yancey the great Southern light to Liberty and Southern independence, is also making his mark, the best friend that the South has. The spirit which is now so predominant through the whole Southern States, will certainly perform the great work which is so much desired. Returning to my own State, the land of peace, and plenty, I found the most uncompromising secessionist. I ever saw all party names and prejudices are extinct.

"Gone glimmering through the things that were,"

'The school boy's tale the wonder of an hour.' All join to resist any further aggression. There may be seen in our little town banners floating in every direction, with inscriptions, such as "Let us alone." The blue badge is very much worn, not in "the hat," however, as some black hearted Abolitionist might suppose, but on the out side, or generally on the left side, nearest to the heart; and not until the last armed foe expires will they dishonor it. There are many remarks made respecting the resignation of Lincoln, which we hope will not be done, for it might be possible that some Southern man would be base enough to hold that position, and we ask for anything else, than a "compromise,"—the word is stricken from the Southern heart.

But, Mr. Editor, this is no time for talking, or time for writing, it is a time for action, and a firm and decisive step will bring peace and plenty to our doors.—Will we submit? No! not so long as that spirit of freedom and independence exists within the breast of the sons of the South, the grand characteristic of these who have long since been consigned to their tombs, who offered up their lives as a common sacrifice for their country's rights, whose motto was protection in the "Union, or independence out of it." It is a time for all union loving men, those who still sing peans to the Union, to be considered as traitors to our Southern institutions. It is a time, for all men, old and young, to openly avow their fidelity to the South, or leave.

We ask no quarter, and we grant none; for justice is our cause; heaven is our shield, is the motto of the

RED WHITE AND BLUE.

POSITION OF HON. EDWARD BATES.

Springfield, (Ill.,) December 16.—The Hon. Edward Bates, of Mo., called on Mr. Lincoln to-day, and they had a long interview. It is stated that Lincoln has formally tendered him the Secretaryship of the Interior under his Administration.—Thus a renegade Southerner will be rewarded for turning his back upon his section, and playing into the hands of her enemies. Mr. Bates, of course, is strongly against secession. He says it is treason, and *must be put down,* and the authority of the Government maintained at all hazards. [So much for Edward Bates.]

Address of Southren Congressmen.

Washington, Dec. 15.—Below is a reliable copy of the Southern address:

TO OUR CONSTITUENTS.

'The argument is exhausted." All hope for relief in the Union, through the agency of committees, Congressional legislation, or Constitutional amendments is extinguished; and we trust the South will not be deceived by appearances, or pretence, or guarantees.

In our judgment, the Republican party are resolute in their purpose to grant nothing that will, or ought, to satisfy the South.

We are satisfied that the honor, safety, and independence of the Southern people require the organization of a Southern Confederacy—a result to be obtained only by separate State secession—and that the primary object of each slaveholding State ought to be its speedy and absolute separation from a Union with hostile States.

Alabama.—(Signed) James L. Pugh, David Clopton, Sydenham Moore, Jabez L. M Curry, Jas. A. Stallworth.

Georgia.—J. W. Underwood, Lucius J. Gartrell, James Jackson, Jno. J. Jones M. J. Crawford, Alfred Iverson,

Florida.—Geo. S. Hawkins.

Arkansas —T. C. Hindman.

Mississippi.—Jefferson Davis, Albert G. Brown, Wm. Barksdale, Otho R. Singleton, Reuben Davis.

North Carolina.—Burton Craige, Thos. Ruffin.

Lonisiana.—John Slidell, Judah P. Benjamin, J. M. Landrum, L. T. Wigfall.

Texas.—John W. Hemphill, John H. Reagan.

South Carolina.—Millege Bonham, W. Porcher Miles, John McQueen, John D. Ashmore.

THE FORTIFICATIONS—TROUBLE AHEAD.

Washington, December 15.—Genl. Cass has resigned because the President refused to send more troops to the fortifications near Charleston. Col Huger has assured the President thet no more troops are needed. It is now conceded that no satisfactory compromise can be arranged, and dissolution and war are inevitable.

WASHINGTON ITEMS.

Attorney General Black to be Secretary of State—Caleb Cushing to get an Office—What Missourians say—Postmaster-General Holt recovered, ect.

Washington, December 15.—Mr. Buchanan has changed his Cabinet programme. Attorney-General Black will be Secretary of State in place of Gen. Cass, and Hon. Caleb Cushing will probably be appointed to the vacancy of the Supreme Court occasioned by the death of Judge Daniel.

Leading gentlemen from Missouri are privately discussing the question of Separate State Independence. They say the State of Missouri shall not be involved in the extreme Secession movement.

Postmaster-Genenal Holt is again convalescent.

Among the resolutions which are to be submitted to the House at an early day, is one of instruction to the Judiciary Committee, looking to an amendment to the Neutrality Laws for the prevention of hostile expeditions from our shores to foreign countries, and to restrain volunteer military forces from going from State to State for the purpose of aiding parties engaged in resistance to the Federal laws.

A number of Congressmen have already prepared speeches strongly in favor of coercion.—*Dispatch to the Charleston Courier,*

The Chair of State.—The exciting contest is over, and Francis W. Pickens, of Edgefield, has been elected Governor and Commander-in-Chief in and for the State of South Carolina for two years.

Mr. Pickens is too well known to many readers to require any particulars. He served acceptably in Congress from the "Old Ninety-six District," once represented by Calhoun and McDuffie, and now forming part of the Congressional District lately represented by Preston S. Brooks, and for the last time in the Congress of the United States by M. L. Bonham.

Mr Pickens, after retiring from Congress, remained some years in private life, and last appeared before his fellow-citizens, in this State as President of the Convention which nominated Delegates for the Cincinnati Convention of 1856.

He was appointed, by President Buchanan, to the Court of St. Petersburg, and has lately returned at his own request.—He bears a name conspicuous in the service of the State, in council and in arms, and his own record gives full guarantees that he will never err in want of devotion to the State.

W. W. Harlee, of Marion, has been elected Lieutenant-Governor—a worthy choice in all respects.—*Chas. Courier.*

THE SALE OF NEGROES (one hundred and sixty-five in nnmber) belonging to the estate of Sam Townsend, deceased, was commenced in this place on Monday, and will be continued to-day until concluded. The terms were twelve months credit, with interest from date. The prices were very high—negro men bringing one thousand five hundred, one thousand six hundred dollars, and upwards, and others in proportion. A large number of persons were in attendance from this and other counties,—*Huntsville (Ala.) Advocate, Dec. 5.*

THE CONSTITUTIONALIST FOR SECESSION.—We have stated that the position of our paper is in favor of secession. By that we mean that the State of Georgia, by herself, and upon her own corporate responsibility, should, on or before the fourth day of March, 1861, resume by the solemn voice of her people, in Convention assembled, all her sovereignty, aud dissolve every tie which binds her in the Federal Union.

Augusta Constitutionalist.

Obituary.—Died in Milledgeville Georgia, early in November, all the "overt act" gentlemen, who were few but noisy immediately preceding the election. They met their deserved fate at the hands of a unanimous resistance resolution.

Parties having claims against them are notified, that their estates are represented by the present co-operation.—*Columbus (Ga.) Times.*

The Southern students in Jefferson College, Cannonsburg, Pa., numbering about twenty, have determined to leave the institution on the 10th inst., and return to their homes.

The Secession of the Cotton States—Its Status—Its Advantages and Its Power.

A pamphlet bearing the above title has been sent to us by the author Major W. H. Chase of Pensacola. The pamphlet contains two excellent articles upon the subject of secession and deserves to be widely circulated.

CHARLESTON

MERCURY

EXTRA:

Passed unanimously at 1.15 o'clock, P. M., December 20th, 1860.

AN ORDINANCE

To dissolve the Union between the State of South Carolina and other States united with her under the compact entitled "The Constitution of the United States of America."

We, the People of the State of South Carolina, in Convention assembled, do declare and ordain, and it is hereby declared and ordained,

That the Ordinance adopted by us in Convention, on the twenty-third day of May, in the year of our Lord one thousand seven hundred and eighty-eight, whereby the Constitution of the United States of America was ratified, and also, all Acts and parts of Acts of the General Assembly of this State, ratifying amendments of the said Constitution, are hereby repealed; and that the union now subsisting between South Carolina and other States, under the name of "The United States of America," is hereby dissolved.

THE

UNION

IS

DISSOLVED!

Daily Advocate.

J. M. TAYLOR & TOM BYNUM.

EDITORS AND PROPRIETORS.

TUESDAY MORNING, JAN. 8, 1861.

THE ELECTION.—At the time of going to press we had not received the full returns of the election, but sufficient is known to insure the election of the whole Submission ticket.

DELAZON SMITH DEAD IN GOOD EARNEST. The overland dispatch which announced the death of Delazon Smith was shortly afterward represented to be true only in the qualified sense, that the late Senator's political prospects, in the state of his adoption, had become exceedingly poor. We learn, however, from the Portland (Oregon) *Daily News*, of Nov. 19, that Mr. Smith died in that city, on the previous day, at the age of forty-four.

CONVENTION OF SOUTH CAROLINA.—During the session of the 28th ult., the President read the following communication:

To the Honorable the President and Members of the Convention of the independent State of South Carolina:

Gentlemen—I am to-night informed that a resolution was this day adopted inviting me to a seat on the floor of your Convention. For the compliment thus paid my State, in my person, please accept my grateful acknowledgments. I regret that engagements elsewhere imperatively forbid the enjoyment of your proffered courtesy.

Intelligence received to-night makes "assurance doubly sure" that Alabama stands by the side of South Carolina, prepared to share with her a common destiny.

Information obtained on diligent inquiry in the last few days, justifies me in saying that the gallant sons of North Carolina and Virginia are now ready to rally around the standard of Southern rights and honor, which you have so gloriously reared, and that those two States will also be members, in all probability, of the great Southern Confederacy, by the 4th of next March. The other slave States must sooner or later take the same course, or be involved in inevitable ruin. To the bold, deliberate and decisive action of your body are the South indebted for the great movement which must end in the vindication of their rights—and the future historian must award to South Carolina the honor of leadership in carrying out the measures destined to release them from the wrongs and oppressions under which they have so long and so patiently suffered.

With sentiments of profound consideration, I am, most respectfully,

J. W. GARROT.

Charleston, December 26, 1860.

DEATH OF THE LAST KNOWN BLOOD RELATION OF GEN. JACKSON.—We find the following announcement of the death of James T. McCullough, the last known blood relation of the hero of Chalmette, in the Lake Providence *Herald*:

A JUST TRIBUTE TO DEPARTED WORTH.—Absence from home at the time of the death of our well beloved and respected friend, Jas. T. J. McCullough, prevented us from making early mention of the event in terms befitting the eminent excellence and worth of the deceased. Having known him well and intimately for several years, we can well appreciate, in common with all who knew him, the following tribute of respect to his memory, which we find in the last number of the Louisianian:

DIED.—At the residence of Geo. W. McCarrell, on the 1st inst., of pneumonia, James Thomas Jackson McCullough.

The deceased was the son of James McCullough and Mary Caffery, and was born near the Hermitage, in Tennessee. His father was cousin to Gen. Andrew Jackson, and his mother was the niece of Mrs. Rachael Jackson, wife of the General. With him has departed the last known blood relation of the old patriot, statesman, and soldier in the United States. It is a sad thing to record the death of our dear young friend, Jimmy McCullough. Although for several years past his health has been bad, he has preserved an equanimity of temperament and an amiability under his trials and afflictions which none but the true Christian can have. His generosity, kindness, and straightforward integrity had won for him a place in the affections of all who knew him, and has left a lasting monument to his memory. He did not seek the praise or honor of men, but was content to leave behind him the reputation of an honest man. He was devoid of envy and malice, and preferred to palliate, rather than expose the errors and foibles of others. So far as frailties of human nature will in any case allow, it is but justice to say that he performed all the obligations of the golden rule with sincerity and singleness of purpose. Modest and retiring, it was necessary to know him well in order to appreciate his many noble sentiments. His was a life of purity and goodness, and when the messenger came to call him "to that bourne whence no traveler returns," so great was his faith in the promise of his Redeemer, that he seemed to embrace death cheerfully rather than to fear and shun it. Many besides his friends and relatives will mourn his departure, and shed the tear of affectionate sorrow upon his grave. He died in the full hope of a blessed immortality, declaring that his peace with God was made. May his hopes be fully realized, is the fervent wish of his sincere FRIEND.

CONDITION OF FORT SUMPTER.—The Charleston *Evening News*, of the 29th, the latest date received from that city, says:

Some eighty mechanics and laborers reached this city from Fort Sumpter this morning, and will leave this afternoon in the Key Stone State for Philadelphia, Baltimore, etc., where they mostly belong. They do not feel disposed to take part in a battle, and as they could not remain without the chance of such a thing, they concluded to stay no longer.

They report about forty or fifty mechanics and laborers still there, and some seventy soldiers. About twelve casemate guns are mounted, mostly looking towards Sullivan's Island, and four or five barbette guns which work on pivots and can be worked facing in any direction. With their present force they can place several guns in position each day; and they have an abundant supply of shot and shell and provisions, and water to last them for months—the cisterns being large and amply supplied with good rain water. The guns of the largest calibre are not yet in position, and the number of cannon in the fort amounts to half its armament. On the night the soldiers took possession of Fort Sumpter the great body of the troops reached that place about 7 o'clock, and the workmen in the fort had no information or hint of it until it took place.

THE SPIKED GUNS.—The same paper adds:

We are happy to state that most of the cannon that were spiked at Fort Moultrie, are now in good condition, the metal pins that the United States officers were kind enough to leave in the touch-holes, being removed.

☞ The Secessionists of Tensas parish have nominated Samuel W. Dorsey and W. D. Anderson.

TELEGRAPH TO THE DAILY ADVOCATE.

MISSISSIPPI SECEDED!

NEW ORLEANS IN THE SOUTHERN COLUMN!

JACKSON, MISS., Jan. 7, 1861.—Mississippi Convention organized to-day, and resolution of Secession passed without a division.

NEW ORLEANS, Jan. 7, 1861.—Secession Senators and Representatives all elected, except five.

One hundred guns for the Queen City of the South!

LATEST DISPATCH.

Just as we go to press we learn that twenty Secessionists were elected in the city of New Orleans.

DISASTERS ON THE WESTERN RIVERS DURING THE YEAR 1860.—The St. Louis *Republican* publishes a list of disasters to steamboats, barges, canal and coal boats, and other river craft, during the year 1860. The number is unusually large, and the loss of life attending the disasters is also above the average of former years:

Number of steamboats destroyed and damaged	299
Number of canal boats and barges	48
Coal and flatboats	208
Steamboats totally destroyed	120

The disasters are attributed to the following causes:

Sunk	111
Burned	31
Explosion	19
Collision	24
Snagged and damaged	44
Damaged by storm	39
Breaking machinery	21
Collision with river bank	8
Total loss of life	254

The total loss in steamboat property, including canal boats, coal boats and barges, exceeds $2,000,000.

The loss on cargo could not be ascertained.

STARTLING FROM MOBILE.

THE UNITED STATES ARSENAL TAKEN.

Fort Morgan Probably Captured.

LATEST FROM WASHINGTON.

RETURN OF SOUTHERN MEMBERS HOME.

LATEST FROM SOUTH CAROLINA.

THIRTY-SIXTH CONGRESS—SECOND SESSION.

MOBILE, Jan. 4, P. M.—The United States Arsenal at this place was taken by Mobile troops this morning, at an early hour.

Twenty thousand stand of arms, fifteen hundred barrels of powder, three hundred thousand rounds of musket cartridges, with other munitions of war, fell into the hands of the Mobile soldiers.

No defense was made on the part of the Federal troops.

It is rumored that Fort Morgan, at the entrance of the bay, was also captured last night.

THE FLORIDA CONVENTION.—*Tallahassee*, Jan. 4.—A large number of delegates to the Convention have already arrived.

Judge McGhee, of Madison, is spoken of as President.

Resolutions will probably be adopted declaring the right and determination of the State to secede, which will be followed by the terms of the ordinance of secession.

Judge McIntosh, of the Federal Court, has resigned.

WASHINGTON, Jan. 5.—The members of the House of Representatives, from the Secession States, despairing of effecting an arrangement, are most of them preparing for a return to their respective homes.

Besides the departures already announced, Mr. Curry, of Alabama, left to-day, and others of that delegation will leave next week.

POSITION OF THE VIRGINIA DELEGATION. *Washington*, Jan. 5.—The Western members of the Virginia Legislature advocate the calling of a State Convention, and the passage thereby of declaratory resolutions against coercion.

The United States Senators and one Representative from Virginia acquiesce in this measure.

THE SLOOP-OF-WAR BROOKLYN.—*Washington*, Jan. 5.—The rumor that the sloop-of-war Brooklyn has been dispatched to Charleston, is officially denied.

THE EXCITEMENT IN CHARLESTON PASSING AWAY.—*Charleston*, Jan. 5.—Affairs here verge upon a state of quietude once more.

Fort Sumpter has not been besieged, as reported.

Major Anderson has been visited by his brother, and a conference has been held in the presence of three Carolinians.

SOUTH CAROLINA CONVENTION ADJOURNED. *Charleston*, Jan. 5, 7 P. M.—The State Convention adjourned this morning, subject to the call of the President.

CONGRESS OF THE SECEDING STATES.—Before adjourning, the Convention appointed delegates to a Congress, to be composed of representatives from the seceding States.

THE WORKINGMEN OF CINCINNATI.—*Cincinnati*, Jan. 5.—The meeting of the Workingmen's Association last night, was well attended.

Resolutions were passed to the effect that the Union must be preserved, and that upon its maintenance depended our safety and peace.

LINCOLN AND HIS FRIENDS.—*Pittsburg*, Jan. 5.—Mr. McClure, of this city, has been invited to Springfield to confer with the President-elect.

Duff Green, Esq., just returned from a visit to Mr. Lincoln, says that the future Executive would adjust the present difficulties satisfactorily.

Leading Republicans protest against the selection of Mr. Cameron as Mr. Lincoln's Secretary of State.

MAINE AND MASSACHUSETTS.—*Boston*, Jan. 5.—The annual message of the Governors of Maine and Massachusetts are strongly in favor of the Union. The latter denies the Constitutionality of the personal liberty bills, and the former says Maine is not the transgressor in this respect.

THE SOUTH CAROLINA FORTIFICATIONS.—*Washington*, Jan. 5.—In the United States Senate to-day, Mr. Mason's resolutions, asking the Secretary of War for a copy of the orders issued to the officers commanding the South Carolina fortifications; also, in reference to increasing the forces in the Virginia arsenals and forts—were laid over.

The House Pacific Railway bill was taken up and discussed, but no conclusion was arrived at.

THE ADMISSION OF NEW MEXICO.—Some of the representatives from the border slave States, said yesterday, that their people would be content with the admission of New Mexico, and Mr. Seward's Constitutional amendment against interfering with slavery in the States.

THE PACIFIC RAILROAD BILL.—In the Senate, Mr. Polk's amendment to the Pacific Railway bill to make the route run from the mouth of Kansas River was agreed to. Ayes 35, nays 23.

After the passage of this amendment, the Senate adjourned over till Monday.

COMMITTEE OF THE BORDER STATES.—*Cincinnati*, Jan. 5.—A special dispatch to the Commercial, from Washington, says the Congressional Committee of the Border States have agreed on a compromise. Mr. Sherman in assenting to this, renews the confidence of a final adjustment of the present difficulties.

THE SLOOP OF WAR BROOKLYN.—*New York*, Jan. 5.—The Post is in receipt of a private dispatch from Washington stating that if the sloop of war Brooklyn is sent to Charleston, she will be sunk in the harbor.

A FALSE REPORT.—*New York*, Jan. 5. The steamship Star of the West, of the New York, Havana and New Orleans line, coaled yesterday with unusual celerity. The report which says she is going to Charleston with troops was ridiculed at the company's office.

PENNSYLVANIA POLITICS—MEETINGS IN PHILADELPHIA.—*Philadelphia*, Jan. 5.—The adjourned meeting of the citizens on the state of the Union met again to-day. The committee on coercion and non-coercion resolutions made no report.

On motion, a Republican meeting adjourned and another was immediately called.

Resolutions were unanimously passed, denouncing the personal liberty bills of the North, and approving of Mr. Crittenden's resolutions.

The Black Republicans positively refused to take part in the proceedings.

LARGE FIRE IN CHICAGO.—*Chicago*, Jan. 5.—An entire block of buildings, bounded by Short, State and Levee streets, in this city, was entirely consumed by fire to-day.

The loss is estimated at $50,000, on which there was insurance of $25,000.

A SALUTE FROM WHEELING, VA.—*Wheeling, Va.*, Jan. 5.—A hundred guns were discharged to-day, in honor of Major Anderson, and his force.

NEW ORLEANS SYMPATHIZES WITH CHARLESTON.—*Charleston*, Jan. 5.—The President of the South Carolina Convention has received a telegraphic dispatch from the Mayor of New Orleans, saying that the Crescent City sympathizes with, and will support Charleston when the occasion demands her action.

Mr. Longstreet, President of the South Carolina College, implores the people to let the first shot come from the enemy.

NEW YORK MARKETS.—*New York*, Jan. 5.—Cotton firmer. Sales 750 bales at 12¾@13c. for Middling.

Flour closed dull, with sales of 250 bbls. at $3 30@5 40 for superfine state.

Corn declining. Sales 64,000 bushels at 70@72c.

Pork firm. Sales 950 bbls. at $16 37½@$16 50 for mess.

Lard firm. Sales 250 bbls. at 10¼@10½c. per pound.

Molasses—sales 110 barrels New Orleans at 34@37c., and 100 do., new crop, at 37c. the pound.

Sugar steady; sales 600 boxes Cuba at 5¼ to 5½c.

☞ Speaking of a debate in the Senate of North Carolina, upon the subject of sending Commissioners to South Carolina, asking her to suspend action on the matter of Secession, until a co-operation of the Southern States can be had, the Columbia (S. C.) *Carolinian* says:

A number of men in Georgia and Alabama are calling themselves resistance co-operation men. Let them act for resistance and act like men for themselves. He is a coward who fights only when he is sure of strong backing; he is no resistance man who waits for the co-operation of all the States by a simultaneous movement. Let Georgia, Florida, Alabama, Mississippi, Louisiana and Texas follow South Carolina, and there will be co-operation of all the Southern States. By separate State action alone can co-operation be attained. To get co-operation the Southern States must act of separate State movement; to get submission, they must each wait for a co-operative movement.

A MORMON KILLED.—A letter from Salt Lake to the *St. Louis Republican* has the following:

Reports reached the city yesterday of the murder of the son of one of the "Apostles," Geo. A. Smith, Jr., by the Novajo Indians, near the boundary line of the Territory and New Mexico. He was a young man of nineteen years of age, and one of a party of ten men from Washington and Iron counties, who had been on an exploring expedition. The Indians were "mad" with the pale faces for their losses further south, and this small party unsuspectingly coming upon them aroused the demon vengeance. Smith was half a mile from camp in search of a horse, when the Indians surrounded him, took his revolver, shot him four times with his own pistol, and fired into his body three arrows. Some of the explorers came up, and hurried off their wounded comrade, and had hardly time to mount with him before the Indians gave chase. Favored by good steeds the party kept ahead till the shades of evening, after a twenty mile run, gave them the advantage of concealment. Some things fell from a pack-horse which attracted the attention of the Indians, and stopping to gather them up, the pursued made good use of the advantage, and to that and the setting sun were they indebted for their preservation. From the great loss of blood and exhaustion in the chase, Smith only lived three hours, and at length had to be thrown into a bush, the only burial his comrades dare to give him. George A. Smith, Sr., the "Apostle," is one of the respected Mormons abroad, as well as at home.

DASTARDLY ASSASINATION.—*Three Brothers Murdered in Cold Blood.*—We learn of a most diabolical assassination that occurred yesterday morning early, at Lost Island, a point about six miles distant from the city, on the Louisville and Nashville Railroad. We are informed that about 2 o'clock Tuesday morning, a party of men called at the house occupied by two brothers named Hill, and demanded admittance. One of the brothers opened the door and was instantly shot dead. The party then entered and found the other Hill lying in bed with his wife, who had had a babe only a week since. He was ordered to get up, and was told that he had to die. He did not rise, and while his wife plead for him, was shot as he lay, several times, one bullet injuring the hand of his wife as she endeavored to shield him. Having accomplished the double murder, the assassins left, and proceeded to the house of a brother of the murdered Hills in the vicinity, and calling him up from his bed, shot him also in cold blood.

The treble murder having been completed, the villains fled, and as yet have not been discovered, although we understand that the wife of one of the Hills states that she can identify one of the assassins. Last Friday night, it will be remembered, the Hills were engaged in a difficulty at Sulphur Well, but whether there is any connection between the two affairs is, of course, unknown. We trust that so terrible a deed of violence will be sifted to the bottom and the guilty parties punished. A fight and an assassination are different things, and while the one might be looked leniently upon, an assassination, such as this is represented to be, cannot but be execrated by every man in the community. It was not easy to get at the facts of the case, but up to the time of this writing we have narrated all that we could learn of the affair.

William Hill was killed while in bed with his wife, and Jesse, a cousin, aged about twenty-two years, was also killed at the same house. The party then proceeded to the house of another brother of the Hills, and roused him up, but concluded not to molest him. They then went to the house of Russel Hill. When Hill heard them he aroused his wife and child and got them up into a loft with himself and arms. After he had his wife and child secure he came down, when he was killed. After he was dead they gave him several cuts in the neck and body.

The assassination resulted from a difficulty that occurred at a party in the neighborhood on Friday night last, in which one of the Walkers was shot. T. Jeff. Walker, of Bullitt county, and Herc. Walker were arrested on a Coroner's warrant last night, and lodged in jail on suspicion. Several other persons are implicated, who will, we hope, be ferretted out and brought to justice.—*Louisville Democrat, 2d.*

LETTER FROM MILLIKEN'S BEND.

MILLIKEN'S BEND, Dec. 30th, 1860.

Aditors Advocate—Now that South Carolina has declared herself fairly out of the Union, and it is a foregone conclusion that Mississippi and Louisiana will soon follow, we begin to look curiously forward and fain would anticipate the events that will next occur.

It is pretty generally considered that nothing like coercion will be attempted by the Federal Government, though the President still believes it his duty to continue to collect the customs in all the Southern ports; and if Mr. Buchanan still continues to practice this duty, it is hardly to be supposed that Mr. Lincoln will forego the same privilege. But as the use of a customhouse upon shore will certainly be deemed by the State authorities, the only plan of operations left open to the Government of the old Confederacy, will be to place a vessel off the harbor or the mouth of the Mississippi River, for the purpose of compelling all vessels coming in port to pay their dues before entering. Of course the seceding States will have to find some method of preventing this mode of procedure, else their advantages derived from a dissolution of the Union will be small. And here the question arises, how are we, without a navy, to operate against the customhouse forces, as of course, they will place themselves out of reach of land forces. There is but one practicable method presents itself to our view, by which we can prevent this monstrous imposition, and that is a very simple one, and will prove entirely successful, to-wit: Throw every article of merchandise which has passed through the hands of such customhouse officers, into the river. This, of course, will effectually put a stop to all collection of customs, though, of course, it will entail a little inconvenience upon ourselves; but how else can we defend ourselves—without a single ship of war with which to open the blockades, for, of course, it will require some little time, either to build a navy for ourselves, or to negotiate for the purchase of one from European powers. And if, in retaliation, the blockade should be so enforced as to prevent the egress of the cotton crop, then here is a nut to crack, which I will leave for those of more acuteness than myself. But as it behooves us to prepare for the worst, it would certainly be advisable for every planter to look to the loom and spinning wheel, else before next dog days come around his negroes may be able to make a plea of necessity for wearing less clothes than usual.

J. M. H.,
Milliken's Bend.

☞ On Saturday last, Mr. Provosty, according to appointment, addressed a large meeting at the Court House of this parish. His speech was made in French, as it was intended more particularly for those who were not able to understand him when he spoke in English on the preceeding Saturday. Mr. Provosty declared himself for immediate and separate secession, as the only remedy left for wrongs become unbearable by the election of Lincoln. Upon hearing his views fairly and squarely expressed, Judge Ebenezer Cooley, who had been a candidate for the Convention, with the most flattering prospects of success, withdrew from the contest; giving as his reason for so doing, his apprehension that the principles advocated by him, Mr. Provosty and Mr. McKneeley, being identical, the success of those principles might be endangered by having three candidates on the same side, while the Co-operationists put forward but two. Judge Ebenezer Cooley has thus displayed an instance of magnanimity, rare in these latter days, and which we hope to see appreciated by his parishioners on the first fitting occasion. *Point Coupee Democrat.*

REARING CHILDREN.—The following rules for rearing children are deserving the attention of every man and woman:

I. Children should not go to school until six years old.

II. Should not learn at home during that time more than the alphabet, religious teachings excepted.

III. Should be fed with plain, substantial food, at regular intervals of not less than four hours.

IV. Should not be allowed to eat anything within two hours of bed-time.

V. Should have nothing for supper but a single cup of warm drink, such as very weak tea of some kind, or cambric tea, or warm milk and water, with one slice of cold bread and butter—nothing else.

VI. Should sleep in separate beds, on hair mattresses, without caps: feet first well warmed by the fire or rubbed with the hands until perfectly dry; extra covering on the lower limbs, but little on the body.

VII. Should be compelled to be out of doors for the greater part of daylight—from after breakfast until half an hour before sundown—unless in damp, raw weather, when they should not be allowed to go outside the door.

VIII. Never limit a healthy child as to sleeping or eating, except at supper, but compel regularity as to both. It is of great importance.

IX. Never compel a child to sit still, nor interfere with its enjoyment, as long as it is not actually injurious to person or property, or against good morals.

X. Never threaten a child. It is cruel, unjust and dangerous. What you have to do, do it, and be done with it.

XI. Never speak harshly or angrily, but mildly, kindly, and, when really needed, firmly—no more.

XII. By all means arrange it so that the last words between you and you children at bed-time, especially the younger ones, shall be words of unmixed lovingness and affection.

UNTIMELY END OF FIVE MEN IN ONE DAY.—A letter from Santa Fe, New Mexico, of the 8th, says:

On the 4th inst., five men, all Americans, came to an untimely end in Albuquerque, under the following circumstances: A soldier, after carefully rolling himself up in his blankets, committed suicide by blowing his brains out with a pistol. Another soldier, to satisfy some old grudge, shot his sergeant, and he was lynched the same day. A gambler was killed in a fight with one of his companions, and the last was a victim in a duel between a soldier and a blacksmith, the soldier killing the blacksmith. I have not been able to learn the names of the parties, but they all rendered up their last accounts on the same day, in the manner I have stated.

☞ To attempt a recapitulation of the permanent and lasting good effects of Crookes' Invigorating Aromatic Vegetable Stomach Bitters, to the worn and debilitated, would be an endless task. They effectually preserve the system of the convalescent from internal disease. As well as purifying the blood, they preserve it in that state necessary to vigorous health, and are admirably adapted to the use of old and young, of both sexes, the bitter principle being hardly perceptible until it is felt in the good work of imparting tone and vigor.

Crookes' Invigorating Aromatic Vegetable Stomach Bitters can be had from grocers, druggists, and dealers generally throughout the United States, and is used as a medicinal drink at the bars of our principal saloons and hotels.

A SAD ACCIDENT.—Hinton Smith, Esq., was dangerously wounded on Monday last, by the discharge of a revolver which he was examining. The friction occasioned by the revolution of the cylinder caused an explosion; the ball escaping from the cylinder without passing through the barrel, entered his abdomen and lodged in the small of the back. He was in a most critical condition during the week.—*Caddo Gazette, 29th ult.*

MARRIED,

On Thursday evening 3d inst., at the residence of the bride, by the Rev. W. E. M. Linfield, Mr. EDWIN D. CHEATHAM to Miss CORDELIA VANLANDINGHAM, both of this parish.

PELICAN RIFLES.—The members of the Company are hereby ordered to assemble at the Armory on this (Tuesday) the 8th inst., at 9½ o'clock, A. M., precisely, in full uniform, to celebrate the Anniversary of the Battle of New Orleans.

W. F. TUNNARD, Captain.
F. D. TUNNARD, Orderly Sergeant.

AUDITORS OFFICE,
BATON ROUGE, December 19th, 1860.

IN accordance with Section 14 of the act entitled an act "Providing for runaway slaves, and establishing a General Depot for the same," approved March 19th, 1857, I hereby publish the list of runaway slaves turned over to the Internal Improvement Department of this State at the periods named, to-wit.

MADISON MASON, bright mulatto, 5 feet 7 inches high, hazel eyes, 28 or 30 years of age, weighs about 175 pounds, blacksmith by trade, marked with gunshot wounds in the legs, and says he belongs to John J. Winter, near Jackson, Mississippi; turned over to the Internal Improvement Service on the 12th of April, 1856. Amount of expenses paid by the State, $242 65.

DICK ODUM, black, 5 feet 4 inches high, eyes black, 28 or 30 years of age, weighs about 130 pounds, no trade, ruptured, and says he belongs to James Williams, on Bayou Lafourche; turned over to the Internal Improvement Service on the 12th of April, 1856. Amount of expenses paid by the State, $288 60.

GUILLARD BAKER, black, 5 feet 10 inches high, eyes black, 24 years of age, weighs about 155 pounds, stone-cutter by trade, marked with a burn on the right arm above the elbow, and says he belongs to Billy Baker, of South Carolina; turned over to the Internal Improvement Service on the 6th of August, 1856. Amount of expenses paid by the State, $201 35.

RICHARD JACKSON, black, 5 feet 10 inches high, eyes black, about 40 years of age, weighs about 160 pounds, no trade, marked with scar on the cheek, and says he belongs to Edmund Jackson, Knoxville, Tennessee; turned over to the Internal Improvement Service on the 2d of April, 1857. Amount of expenses paid by the State, $361 62.

JIM, black, 5 feet 3 inches high, eyes black, about 55 years old, weighs about 135 pounds, no trade, front teeth missing, and says he belongs to Wiley Thomas, West Feliciana, Louisiana; turned over to the Internal Improvement Service on the 25th of October, 1858. Amount of expenses paid by the State, $179 21.

JOHN, negro man, 5 feet 5¼ inches high, eyes black, about 45 years of age, weighs 128 pounds, two upper front teeth missing, ordinary beard, says he is a caulker by trade, and belongs to John Lee, of Norfolk, Virginia; turned over to the Internal Improvement Service on the 4th of August, 1859. Amount of expenses paid by the State, $182 50.

JESSY, (alias Warren,) dark griffe, 5 feet 3½ inches high, eyes black, about 34 years of age, weighs 141 pounds, heavy beard, no trade, completely paralysed and shrunk in right arm and shoulder, and part of the chest, and affected in hip and leg, says he belongs to Henry Williams, now supposed to be dead, or to his wife, also dead; turned over to the Internal Improvement Service on the 20th of August, 1859. Amount of expenses paid by the State, $166 80.

GEORGE HARRIS, black, 5 feet 6¾ inches high, eyes black, weighs 141 pounds, no trade, lump on the back of right hand, and stands badly on his feet, and has a scar from a burn on his breast, says he belongs to James McCullar, Holmesville, Mississippi, and is about 28 years of age; turned over to the Internal Improvement Service on the 27th of August, 1859. Amount of expenses paid by the State, $198 30.

DANIEL ALEXANDER, black, 5 feet 2½ inches high, black eyes, about 25 years of age, weighs about 135 pounds, calls himself a free man: turned over to the Internal Improvement Service on the 15th of November, 1859. Amount of expenses paid by the State, $168 25.

HENRY JACKSON, griffe, 5 feet 7 inches high, stout built, with one scar on the right cheek, near the mouth, and another scar over and in the right eyebrow, two grinders missing from the upper jaw, says he belongs to William Jackson, of Tennessee; turned over to the Internal Improvement Service on the 23d of January, 1860. Amount of expenses paid by the State, $164 25

JOHN, said to belong to Mr. Newton, of Vicksburg, Miss. Color, black; about 5 feet 7½ inches high, weighs 160 pounds, teeth good, and with no scar except one diagonally across his right temple, upper part; turned over October 6th, 1860. Amount of expenses paid by the State, $192 35.

ALBERT, said to belong to Robert Anderson, near Memphis, Tenn. Color, griffe, or dark mulatto; age 36, hight 5 feet 9 inches, front teeth good, no scars; turned over December 8th, 1860. Amount of expenses paid by the State, $272 40.

JOE LONG, color, mulatto: aged 49 years, hight 5 feet 8½ inches, teeth tolerably good, no scars, stout built and likely looking, says he is a free negro from Louisville, Ky.; turned over December 15th, 1860. Amount paid by the State, $268 46.

PETER DEWES, color, black, aged 40 years, hight 5 feet 5 inches, teeth tolerably good, no scars, active built, says he belongs to Henry Dewes, of Memphis, Tenn.; turned over December 15th, 1860. Amount paid by the State, $206 15.

E. W. ROBERTSON,
dec21-5tw Auditor.

In the matter of the Succession of MARY BILLS, dec'd—No. 687, Probate—Sixth Judicial District Court, parish of East Baton Rouge, Louisiana.

WHEREAS, Fielding Cooney, Administrator of said estate, has this day filed in said Court a final account of his administration of said estate;

Notice is hereby given to all persons interested, to show cause, (if any they can) within thirty days from the first publication of said notice, why said account should not be approved, homologated and made the judgment of the Court.

Given under my hand and the seal of said court, this 11th day of December, A. D., 1860.

JOS. NEPHLER,
dec12-4tw&1td Clerk.

Daily Advocate.

J. M. TAYLOR & TOM BYNUM.

EDITORS AND PROPRIETORS.

SATURDAY MORNING, JAN. 12, 1861.

IMPORTANT FROM ALABAMA!

SECESSION ORDINANCE PASSED!!

Hon. Wm. M. Brooks, President of the Alabama State Convention, telegraphed to Gov. Moore last night (11th) to this effect:

"I am instructed by the Convention to inform you that Alabama has this day seceded from the Union."

Nine cheers for the Southern Confederacy!

A Patriotic Offer.—The Southern Bank of New Orleans has tendered to Gov. Moore a loan of $50,000 on his own ter.ns. Such liberality de-deserves commendation.

Vote of Rapides.—The following is the vote of Rapides parish for Delegates to the Convention:

Senatorial—Elgee, 933. House—Manning 771, Texada 736, Smart 726. Co-operation ticket beaten by the above over 300.

Donaldsonville Cannoniers.—Pursuant to an order supposed to emanate from the Governor of this State, published in the *Evening Delta* of the 11th inst., the "Cannoniers of Donaldsonville" were called upon to make ready and embark on the steamboat *National*, chartered by the State to take up to Baton Rouge the troops necessary to take possession of the Barracks. The *National* DID NOT land at Donaldsonville, and this accounts for the absence of that corps.

A Donaldsonville Cannonier.

The Georgia Convention Election.—If the dispatches can be relied on, Georgia has gone for immediate Secession by a large majority. A dispatch from Augusta says that 104 counties had been heard from on the 7th inst., of which 70 were for immediate Secession, 29 for co-operation and 5 divided. There remain about 26 counties yet to be heard from. Among the counties which have elected immediate Secession candidates are several which have heretofore invariably been carried by the Conservative party. The majorities of the immediate Secession candidates is very heavy in their respective counties.

Virginia and Secession.—A letter from Hon. James M. Mason, United States Senator from Virginia, is published in the Winchester *Virginian*, in which he says the Union is already dissolved—that eight States will be out in thirty days—and that Virginia ought to secede as soon as possible. He thinks that Virginia, by secession now, might be able to assist in reconstructing a better Union.

Affairs in the West.—Our accounts from the various leading commercial cities of the West represent financial matters as being much easier than they have been since the present crisis set in. The Louisville *Courier* of the 7th says:

Since the heavy payments falling due on the 4th were all promptly met, the market has begun to ease up, and though matters are still tight, the feeling is much easier, and the banks will, in all probability, now expand and relieve the market to a great degree, and to-day the general feeling among the business men was that this depression cannot last long. The demand for money to-day was small, but the banks seemed more willing to discount, and a larger amount of paper than was usual taken.

Arming the North.—We take the following from the Alexandria (Va.) Gazette of yesterday:

There is talk about "arming," etc, in some of the Northern States—all to "enforce the laws." Hadn't they better turn their attention *first*, to the "enforcement of the laws" among themselves? Their disregard of their obligations—their legislative nullifications—the treasonable proceedings of their own people in the rescue of fugitive slaves, have all helped to bring on the present crisis. If they would "enforce the laws" at home, they would not have to complain of the efforts of their own evil example elsewhere. The inventors of bad precedents should be the last to complain, much less to "arm"—when their inventions come back "to plague them."

☞ R. C. Kerr, Esq., has been elected Mayor of Jackson, Miss.

THE TROOPS IN MOTION.

MOVEMENTS OF THE VOLUNTEERS.

DEPARTURE OF SEVEN COMPANIES.

Great Enthusiasm on the Streets.

RUMORS OF THEIR DOINGS, ETC., ETC.

Last evening our city was in a feverish state of excitement in consequence of the assembling of the volunteer militia at their various armories. Crowds of citizens thronged the streets, and speculation was rife as to the cause of this unusual activity among the troops. About half past nine o'clock, the Crescent City Rifles, a company of Minute Men, commanded by Col. Gladden, but on this occasion, owing to the absence of their commander, in charge of Lieutenant Commanding Wm. A. Metcalfe, and numbering forty-two men, marched down to the foot of Canal street. An hour later the second Company of Chasseurs-a-Pied, Capt. Meilleur, arrived at the same place, thirty-six strong, and fully equipped, with camp equippage.

The next company on the ground was the Louisiana Guards, Capt. S. M. Todd, under the immediate command of Lieut. Girardey. After they deposited their baggage on the steamboat National, they went back to the Washington Artillery Arsenal on Girod street, and armed themselves with muskets. Then came the Washington Artillery, Capt. Walton, under the immediate command of Lieut. ———, fifty-six strong, and presenting a splendid appearance, the men fully equipped and prepared for campaign service. After them appeared the Orleans Cadets, Capt. Charles D. Dreux, looking well in their fine gray suits. The Sarsfield Rifles, Capt. O'Hara, and the Louisiana Grays, Capt. W. T. Dean, then came down.

These seven companies, numbering about 250 altogether, went aboard the steamer National, which was chartered for the expedition, and came across the river to the foot of Common street in the evening. This force is, we understand, under the command of Col. J. B. Walton. Whither they are going is a matter of mystery; but when the National started off she went down the river.—*N. O. Delta.*

FRIDAY'S EVENTS.

SURRENDER OF UNITED STATES BARRACKS.

LOCAL EXCITEMENT!!

MILITARY DISPLAY!!

Friday, the 11th, was a day of excitement, novelty and turmoil on our streets. Six companies of troops from New Orleans arrived about 10 o'clock on Thursday night from that city on the steamer National, (chartered for the purpose) all under command of Col. J. B. Walton. They remained on board all night, and marched up to Boulevard street about 11 o'clock, where they formed into line with the companies from Grosse Tete, West Baton Rouge, the Pelican Rifles, National and Creole Guards and Louisiana Fencibles of this city. Altogether there were about six hundred men under arms, prepared and equipped for any service required of them. The display was indeed a fine one, and every way creditable to the officers and men in the respective companies. Gov. Moore, accompanied by a portion of his staff, passed the length of the line on foot, and was received by all with tokens of the highest regard.

The multitude that thronged the streets throughout the day was very large. All anticipated a collision at the United States Barracks, but about 12½ o'clock, when Col. Walton's command marched quietly in and took possession of the Arsenal enclosure, a feeling of relief immediately took the place of that of anxiety.

Maj. Haskin, commanding officer at this post—as gallant a soldier and as noble a gentleman as ever buckled on the sword—seeing that a useless effusion of blood would be the consequence of an attempt to defend his position, surrendered it to Gov. Moore in the name of the State. The demand was made upon him in writing through agents dispatched by the Governor on that mission on Thursday. Maj. Haskin consulted with his brother officers, and the agreement was unanimous that the surrounding circumstances necessitated the giving up of the place, and like experienced soldiers and humane men they acted accordingly on Friday morning.

Maj. Haskin was given the permission to remove his command with their arms and equipments at his own convenience, and he fixed upon this (Saturday) morning as the time for his departure. The forces, exclusive of the officers, stationed in the ordinance, as per agreement, were moved across to the Barracks where they remained yesterday through the day, the State troops meantime occupying the vacated ground. Everything was conducted with the strictest and most scrupulous regard for the feelings of Maj. H. and his officers and men. All seemed to appreciate the delicate position in which they were placed, and all commended the spirit which animated them in thus avoiding a collision which could only have resulted in the useless loss of life.

As to the policy pursued by Gov. Moore, in taking possession of this post, we can only say that it meets with universal approbation. It is a bold and responsible stroke, but on no ground can it be condemned. The perfidious treatment received by the people of South Carolina from the Federal Government, by which they to-day hold the key to her commercial city, pointed out to our people the absolute necessity of guarding themselves and preparing for the future. The people were becoming uneasy and excited at the existence and maintenance of a Federal force among them, having under their control such large materials for war; they were becoming restless, and of themselves might at an early day attempt to do that which the Governor has accomplished so honorably and peaceably. Major Haskin would never have surrendered his post to an attacking party. He could have been exterminated, but not conquered. The intervention, therefore, of Gov. Moore, is simply a peace measure. The State takes charge of the Federal property, and is responsible for its safe keeping. The troops that guarded it have bowed to the authority of Louisiana, in surrendering their trust, and by so doing have neither dishonored their flag nor themselves as soldiers.

Gov. Moore's course has been dictated by the very highest motives. He has anticipated the intentions of the people, and peaceably succeeded in doing that which would, sooner or later, have been done by more violent means. He deserves gratitude for conserving the peace between the Federal forces and the citizens of the State; he will command and receive the thanks of his fellow-Louisianians for the foresight and boldness with which he has anticipated events, and prepared for their protection and safety.

In conclusion, we cannot refrain from expressing our regret at an occurrence which took place in the afternoon of yesterday. Three of the companies that had been under arms for two days (Pelican Rifles, Creole Guards and Grosse Tete Rangers) considered themselves slighted because they were not detailed to march to the Arsenal and take quarters there with Col. Walton's command. There was no insult intended nor none given in the apparent but unreal preference to the New Orleans troops. Our friends in the companies named acted hastily and unreflectingly in leaving their positions, and we are sure they will be the first to discover and repair their mistake. They are all honorable gentlemen, and a little cool reflection will soon rectify a step taken under a momentary excitement. We are not wrong in our estimate of the character of those we refer to, and feel confident that they will be among the first to respond to the next summon "to arms" that is made upon all true sons of Louisiana.

"High Treason."—A New York sensation dispatch says the Cabinet is deliberating on the propriety of having Senators Toombs and Wigfall prosecuted for high treason. That would just about cap the climax of Administration folly and imbecility. By the time the Cabinet gets through with these two cases, there will be several millions more on hand who are proud to be called such traitors.

TELEGRAPHIC ITEMS.

IMPORTANT FROM MISSISSIPPI.

PASSAGE OF THE SECESSION ORDINANCE.

ILLUMINATIONS, FIRE-WORKS, ETC.

GREAT EXCITEMENT.

Jackson, Jan. 9.—The ordinance declaring the immediate secession of the State of Mississippi from the Federal Union, passed the Convention by a vote of 84 against 15.

The delegations from the States of South Carolina and Alabama took seats on the floor of the Convention amid great applause.

An effort to postpone the action of Mississippi was made, but afterwards voted down.

The fifteen opposing voters will sign the ordinance to-morrow, making it unanimous.

The most prominent places are brilliantly illuminated to-night, guns are being discharged, and rockets fired.

The most intense excitement prevails.

THIRTY-SIXTH CONGRESS—SECOND SESSION.

The President's Special Message. *Washington*, Jan. 9.—House.—The President's Special Message says, in regard to South Carolina, there is no other alternative but to collect the revenue and protect public property, that the right to use military and naval forces against illegal assaults is clear and indisputable. He says if the Union perishes it will be a calamity as severe in the Southern as well as in the Northern States. He recommends the transfer of the question to the ballot-box.

The President regrets that South Carolina did not reflect before having acted. He says that Major Anderson moved because he could not have held Fort Moultrie forty-eight to sixty hours. He ends his message by imploring Congress to settle the present difficulties.

Mr. Howard, of Michigan, moved the reference of the President's message to a special committee of five, asking whether forts had been seized, by whom the revenue cutters were held, etc.

Our Relations with Peru and Paraguay.—*New York*, Jan. 9.—Washington correspondents say that the President disavows Cave Johnson's award in the Paraguay case, and sustains Mr. Clay in regard to our relations with Peru.

Lincoln's Cabinet.—*Albany*, Jan. 9. The Albany Evening Journal says Hon. W. H. Seward has accepted the office of Secretary of State under Mr. Lincoln

The Louisville Conventions.—*Louisville*, Jan. 9.—The Union and Douglas Democratic Conventions adjourned, affirming and requiring the North to accede to Mr. Crittenden's resolutions.

The United States Cabinet.—*New York*, Jan. 9.—Hon. John A. Dix has been summoned to take a seat in the Cabinet.

The Tennessee Legislature.—*Nashville*, Jan. 9.—The Legislature to-day was occupied in the delivery of speeches by the commissioners from the States of Alabama and Mississippi.

THE WAR COMMENCED!

THE FIRST VICTORY OF THE SOUTH!

The Star of the West off Charleston Harbor.

SHE IS FIRED INTO FROM THE BATTERIES OFF MORRIS ISLAND.

SHE RECEIVES THREE SHOTS AND PUTS OUT TO SEA, SUPPOSED TO BE MUCH INJURED.

MAJOR ANDERSON SENDS A COMMUNICATION TO CHARLESTON!

Special Dispatches to the Delta.

Charleston, Jan. 9.—A constant watch has been kept for the last two days in expectation of the arrival of the steamship Star of the West, with reinforcements, fuel and provisions for Fort Sumpter. At 6 o'clock this morning the Star of the West hove in sight. As soon as she was discerned the new battery on Morris Island, lying outside of Sullivan's Island, was put in preparation for active measures. The drums beat to quarters, and the men were ordered to man the guns. In the meantime the steamer kept steadily approaching, and when she arrived within a distance of half a mile, she hoisted the American flag.

A warning gun was then fired across her bows, but elicited no attention whatever, the steamer keeping steadily on her course. As soon as it was perceived that she was determined to attempt an entrance into the harbor, the battery opened fire upon her. In a short time she was struck three times, when, finding it would be impossible to achieve her purpose, she put out to sea again, in a northeasterly direction.

In the meantime, Fort Moultrie had also opened fire on the steamer, but the distance was so great that the vessel could not be reached. Fort Moultrie fired nine shots, which, for the reason stated, were ineffectual.

The Star of the West was accompanied by a steam tender, heavily laden, supposed to be with provisions for Fort Sumpter. The Star of the West is known to be much injured by the fire from the battery.

These events have produced the greatest excitement here, and the city is in a perfect blaze of enthusiasm.

Major Anderson has just sent a communication to the Governor, with a flag of truce; but the nature of the communication has not yet been made public.

SECOND DISPATCH.

Charleston, Jan. 9.—Major Anderson's communication to the Governor inquired whether the firing at the steamer was by his order. The Governor replied that it was, when Anderson notified him that Fort Sumpter held command of the harbor and that no further communication by water would be allowed between the city and our forts. This will cut off all communication except by a circuitous land route.

The popular belief is that this must precipitate an attempt to storm Fort Sumpter. All the reserved regiments are under arms, and a general fight cannot be postponed many hours longer.

THIRD DISPATCH.

Charleston, Jan. 9.—As the State paid no heed to Major Anderson's threat, he sent another communication to the Governor to-night, saying he would defer the execution of his threat until his bearer of dispatches could return from Washington. Therefore all is quiet again, and the work of fortifying Morris Island is pushed forward with redoubled vigor.

Railways Blocked with Snow.—Official information has been received at the Postoffice Department, Washington, of the almost impassible condition of mail routes bordering on the Virginia and Tennessee, the Virginia Central, Orange and Alexandria, and Manassas Gap Railways. In many places the snow has reached a depth of three feet, rendering the most energetic, persevering efforts of the mail carriers to force their way through, in anything like schedule time, impossible.

AN IMPORTANT LETTER.

The Hon. John T. Monroe, Mayor of the city of New Orleans, has addressed the following letter to his Excellency, Gov. Moore, in relation to the rumored dispatch of United States troops to the South. The letter embraces topics worthy of the most serious consideration. It is a significant evidence of the feeling of Louisiana when Mayor Monroe—an avowed Co-operationist—is foremost in bringing to the knowledge of the Governor the perils we incur from the reckless policy of the Federal Administration:

Mayoralty of New Orleans,
City Hall, New Orleans, January 9, 1861.

To His Excellency, Thos. O. Moore, Governor of the State of Louisiana:

Sir—Intelligence received here this morning, and which, I presume, will have reached you before the receipt of this communication, informs us that the Federal Government has ordered United States troops to be sent to the South for the purpose of strengthening the garrisons of the fortifications along our sea-coast. A steamer is to leave Boston to-morrow with forces for Tortugas, a work of immense strength, which lies at the entrance of the Gulf of Mexico, and consequently commands the approaches to all the Gulf ports.

These movements leave no room to doubt that it is the intention of the Washington authorities to reinforce the garrisons in the neighborhood of New Orleans, thus assuming at once a hostile attitude in advance even of any State action on the part of the State in favor of secession from the existing Union. An attitude of this kind, involving threats of coercion and conquest, in case Louisiana should decide, in the exercise of her sovereign powers, to sever her connection with the North, not only justifies, but demands, the adoption of measures for averting the dangers to which we would be submitted should the fortresses alluded to be occupied by hostile forces. An enemy once in secure possession of those works would have the power to molest and even to destroy the commerce of New Orleans; and although they were constructed as defenses against foreign invasion, there seems little reason to doubt that the Federal Government is resolved to divert them from their legitimate purpose by converting them into hostile posts whence we may be assailed and annoyed, if not actually coerced into submission.

As the Chief Magistrate of the city of New Orleans, I would, on behalf of this community, and of the vast interests concentrated and represented within it, respectfully direct your attention to these facts, with the hope, which I trust may not long remain unfulfilled, that you will perceive the necessity of adopting speedy measures to avert the evils and the dangers with which we are menanced. I address you with the less hesitation from the fact that any precautionary movements of this kind should emanate from the highest authority of the State, in order to anticipate attempts which may be made by irresponsible organizations.

Very respectfully, your obedient servant,
John T. Monroe, Mayor.

THE EVENTS AT SAVANNAH.

The occupation of Fort Pulaski by the State troops—before mentioned by telegraph—is thus given in the Savannah journals. The *News* of the 4th says:

At an early hour yesterday morning detachments of men from the Chatham artillery, Capt. J. S. Claghorn, Savannah Volunteer Guards, Capt. John Screven and Oglethorpe Light Infantry, Capt. F. S. Bartow—fifty from each company—left the city by order of his excellency, Gov. Brown, for the purpose of taking possession of Fort Pulaski, on Cockspur island, about thirteen miles from the city. Adjutant-General Wayne and Col. A. R. Lawton accompanied the troops to the fort.

The *Republican* of the same date says:

From persons who came up the river last night, we learn that the troops dispatched by steamer yesterday arrived safely at their destination, and immediately went to work to prepare quarters and put the fortifications in a complete state of defense. They are a working as well as fighting body, and should trouble come they will give a good account of themselves.

Orders were sent up last night for reinforcement to be composed of further detachments from the Oglethorpes and the Guards. They will be sent down early this morning.

The following is the letter of Gov. J. E. Brown addressed to the Collector of the Port of Savannah, delivering into his charge the cutter Dobbin, which, at the time of her informal capture, was under orders to sail for Baltimore, said orders having been received by the Collecter fifteen days previous:

Pulaski House, Jan. 3, 1861.

John Boston, Esq., Collector of the Port of Savannah:

Sir—The revenue cutter J. C. Dobbin, which was seized by some unauthorized person or persons unknown to me, has, under the order given by me to Col. Lawton, now in command of Fort Pulaski, to protect Government property against injury, been recaptured and is now aground near Fort Pulaski. You will please send a revenue boat and take her into custody to-night, and I will have her hauled off to-morrow morning, and delivered to you at such place as you may designate. I much regret the lawless seizure of the vessel, and beg leave to assure you that I shall, from time to time, give such orders as will protect the Customhouse and other property belonging to the Federal Government till the action of this State is determined by the Convention of her people.

Very respectfully, etc.,
Joseph E. Brown.

MR. BENJAMIN'S PERORATION.

We have already published a synopsis of Senator Benjamin's speech. The following is the peroration:

And you, Senators of the Republican party, you assert, and your people assert that, under a just and fair interpretation of the Federal Constitution, it is right to deny that our slaves, which directly or indirectly involve a value of $4,000,000,000, are property at all entitled to protection in the Territories under and by the Government. You assert that by a fair interpretation of that instrument, it is right to encourage, by all possible means, the robbery of this property, and to legislate so as to render its recovery as dangerous and difficult as possible. You say that it is right and proper, under the Constitution, to prevent our mere transit across a sister State, to embark with our property on a lawful voyage, without being openly despoiled of it. You assert that it is right and proper to hold us up to the ban of mankind, in speeches and writings, as thieves, robbers, villains and criminals of the blackest dye, because we continue to own property which we owned at the time we all signed the compact. You say it is right that we should be disposed to spend our treasure in the purchase, and our blood in the conquest of foreign territory, and yet have no right to enter it for settlement, without leaving behind our most valuable property, under penalty of its confiscation. Your fathers interpreted this instrument to mean safety and peace to all, and you say it is eminently in accordance with the surety that our welfare and peace is to be preserved, that our sister States should combine to prevent our growth and development, and surround us with a cordon of hostile communities, for the express and avowed purpose of accumulating in dense masses, and within restricted limits, a population which you believe to be dangerous, and thereby forcing us to sacrifice a property nearly sufficient in value to pay the public debt of every nation in Europe. This construction of the instrument which was to preserve our security and promote our welfare, and which we only signed on your assurance that such was its object, you tell us now is a fair construction.

You don't propose to enter our States, you say, to kill and destroy our institutions by force. Oh, no! You initiate the faith of Phadamiscus, and you propose simply to enclose us in an embrace that will suffocate us. You don't propose to fell the tree—you promised not to. You merely propose to girdle it, and let it die; and then, when we tell you we don't understand this way, and your acting upon it in this spirit releases us from the obligations which accompany it, and under no circumstances can we consent to live together under that interpretation, and we say we will go, if you will let us go in peace, we are answered by your leading spokesman, "Oh, no, we cannot do that. We have no objection, personally, but we are bound by our oaths; if you attempt it, your people will be hanged for treason. We have examined this instrument thoroughly, and we cannot find any warrant in it for releasing ourselves from the obligation of giving you all these benefits, and our oaths force us to tax you for it. We can dispense with anything else, but we protest, upon our souls, that our consciences will be sorely worried if we do not take your money." That is the proposition of the Senator from Ohio (Mr. Wade), in plain language, "We can dispense with anything and everything else, but how to get rid of taking your money we cannot see." Now, Senators, this picture is not placed before you with any idea of acting upon any one of you, or that it will change the views or alter the conduct of any of you. All hope of that is gone. Our committee has reported this morning that no feasible scheme of adjustment can be devised. The day of adjustment has passed. If you propose to make one now, you are too late. And now, Senators, within a very few weeks we part, to meet again as Senators, in one common council chamber of the nation, no more forever. We desire, we beseech you, to let this parting be in peace. I conjure you to indulge in no vain delusion, that duty, or conscience, or interest, or honor, impose upon you the necessity of invading our States, and shedding the blood of our people. You have no possible justification for it. I trust it is from no craven spirit, or any sacrifice of the dignity or honor of my own State, that I make this last appeal, but from far higher and holier motives.

If, however, it shall prove vain—if you are resolute to pervert the Government, framed by the fathers for the protection of our rights, into an instrument for subjugating and enslaving us, then, appealing to the Supreme Judge of the Universe for the rectitude of our intentions, we must meet the issue you force upon us as best becomes freemen defending all that is dear to man. What may be the fate of this horrible contest none can foretell; but this much I will say: the fortunes of war may be adverse to our arms; you may carry desolation into our peaceful land, and with torch and firebrand may set our cities in flames; you may even emulate the atrocities of those who, in the days of the revolution, hounded on the bloodthirsty savage; you may give the protection of your advancing armies to the furious fanatics who desire nothing more than to add the horrors of servile insurrection to civil war; you may do all this, and more, but you never can subjugate us; you never can subjugate the free sons of the soil into vassals, paying tribute to your power; you never can degrade them to a servile and inferior race; never, never, never.

FLORIDA CORRESPONDENCE.

FLORIDA STATE CONVENTION.

Tallahassee, Thursday, Jan. 3, 1861.

The Convention met to-day, in the Capitol, at 12 o'clock.

On motion, Col. John C. Pelote, of Alachua county, was selected as temporary chairman, and Mr. B. G. Pringle, of Gadsden, was appointed temporary Secretary.

The delegates then came forward, presented their credentials, and enrolled their names, as follows:

Alachua—J. C. Pelote and J. B. Dawkins.
Brevard—Wm. B. Yales.
Calhoun—Simeon J. Baker.
Clay—Lewis C. Gaines was the member elected, but he died since his election, and Clay has no delegate at present.
Columbia, etc.—A. J. T. Might, G. H. Hunter and James A. Newman.
Dade and Monroe—Asa Tift, Winer Bethell and Wm. Pinckney.
Duval—J. P. Sanderson and J. M. Daniel.
Escambia—A. W. Nicholson and Sam. H. Wright.
Franklin—S. W. Spencer and McQueen McIntosh.
Gadsden—A. K. Alleson, S. B. Stephens, E. C. Love and T. G. Henry.
Hamilton—Joseph Thomas and Lewis A. Folsom.
Hernando—B. W. Saxon.
Hillsboro—James Gettes and Simon Turman.
Holmes—Richard D. Jordan.
Jackson—J. L. G. Baker, S. S. Alderman, Adam McNeeley and J. A. Collier.
Jefferson—T. B. Lamar, J. P. Anderson, T. M. Palmer and W. S. Dilworth.
Leon—G. T. Ward, John Beard, W. G. M. Davis and G. W. Parkhill.
Lafayette, etc.—J. C. McGehee, A. G. Lea, Henry S. Sevier and E. P. Barrington.
Levy—George Helvenston.
Liberty—W. T. Gregory.
Manatee—E. Glazier.
Marion—Jas. B. Owens, S. M. G. Gary and Wm. McGahagin.
Nassau—Joseph Finnegan and James G. Cooper.
New River—Isaac C. Coon and J. J. Lamb.
Orange—Isaac N. Rutland and William Woodruff.
Putnam—Jas. O. Devall.
Santa Rosa—Jackson Morton and E. E. Simpson.
St. John's—B. G. Mays and Matthew Solano.
Sumpter—D. G. Leigh.
Volusia—Jas. H. Chandler.
Washington—Freeman B. Irwin.
Watton—John Morrison and A. L. McCaskill.
Wakulla—Daniel Ladd and David Lewis.

The total number of delegates is 67.

Some of the old counties, now embraced in new counties, send delegates without respect to the new territorial organization, and hence the ambiguity which may appear in the list of counties above enumerated.

Col. Pelote, on taking the chair, as the temporary presiding officer of the Convention, said:

Gentlemen of the Convention—We meet together under no ordinary circumstances. The rapid spread of Northern fanaticism has endangered our liberties and institutions, and the election of Abe Lincoln, a wily Abolitionist, to the Presidency of the United States, destroys all hope for the future. We have, therefore, been sent by the people of our State, to devise the best means for our security. Their dearest interests are placed in our hands—to us is committed a high trust—upon us rests a heavy responsibility, and we are expected to meet the grave question before us with calmness and deliberation. Precipitation and rashness may prove disastrous. But, gentlemen, while prudence and a proper discretion should characterize all our deliberations, we must not forget that this important crisis demands great firmness. I trust we are fully prepared to meet the great issues before us as true patriots.

Our Legislature, through purely patriotic motives, has placed us in a conspicuous position. The eyes of the world are upon us, and our action will affect, for weal or for woe, not only our own State but perhaps our sister Southern States also.

And now, gentlemen, permit a word of admonition. Our interests are one, and we all desire to effect the same great end. Yet, there will, of necessity, arise a conflict of opinion as regards the best means to be used for its accomplishment. But I trust that strict courtesy will characterize your debates. We may honorably differ in minutiæ but we are engaged in a common cause. We are brethren and must stand shoulder to shoulder in the great work before us. And may the God of mercy and goodness direct us in our deliberations, that we may arrive at the best means to accomplish the desired end.

Judge McQueen McIntosh, of Franklin county, then arose and said:

Mr. Chairman—It is but seldom that men are called upon to discharge the grave and solemn duties about to devolve on us; and with nations as with men, there is a Providence that fashions their destinies. It is the blessing of that Providence that we should now implore to direct us in our future deliberations. When the night of storm and desolation had overtaken him, Euryalus exclaimed, in the language of supplication:

"*Tu oro solare inopem et seccurre relictæ.*"

If the heathen could thus implore the God of his mythology, we may appeal to the Christian's God to teach us to apply our hearts unto wisdom, that we may learn that which is right, and do that which is best for our unhappy country. I, therefore, move that the Right Reverend Bishop Rutledge be invited to take a seat by your side, and that this Convention be opened with prayer.

The motion was adopted unanimously, and Bishop Rutledge was conducted to the chair. He invoked the Throne of Grace to send its blessings upon the deliberations of the convention, and to enlighten the minds of its members, purify their hearts and conduct their proceedings in the way best calculated to promote the honor and interests of the state and the glory of God.

A motion was made that a committee of five be appointed by the chair, whose duty it shall be to select a suitable place for the sittings of the convention. The mover stated that the legislature will assemble here on Monday next, and it was necessary that a suitable place should be obtained for the convention to meet in. The Baptist church was named as a place which could be obtained. The resolution also provided that the committee should report to-morrow (Friday.) A member stated that to-morrow was Thanksgiving Day, and he proposed that the committee should report on Saturday and moved that the convention now adjourn until Saturday, twelve o'clock. The question was decided by the members rising—ayes 29, nays 24. So the convention adjourned until Saturday noon.

Friday Morning, Jan. 4, 1860.

L. W. Spratt just arrived.

Col. E. Bullock, the Commissioner from the state of Alabama, and the Hon. Edmund Ruffin, from Virginia, arrived here yesterday. It is reported that a consultation is now going on in regard to the policy of taking immediate possession of the forts and other Federal property in this State.

Judge McQueen McIntosh, of the Federal court, and Col. E. S. Blackburn, the United States Marshall, in Florida, have resigned.

It is probable that an ordinance of secession will be offered and passed about the middle of the ensuing week.

For the information of your commercial readers I state that the quantity of cotton shipped from this point annually is from 18,000 to 20,000 bales. The freight from here to Jacksonville is $1 65 per bale; to Fernandina $1 93, and to St. Marks 62 1-2 cents per bale. Cotton is transported from Tallahassee to New York (via Fernandina) for $4 50 per bale, and when not stored at Fernandina $4 38 per bale.

About 12,000 bales of cotton have been received here since the 1st of September.

WE THE UNDERSIGNED RESIDENTS of the parish of East Baton Rouge desirous of forming an Independent Company of Mounted Rangers, respectfully invite all those desirous of joining such a Company to meet at Academy Hall on Wednesday evening, January 16th, at 3 o'clock, to perfect the organization of the troops:

J. C. Stafford,	Gilbert Daigre,
A. V. Woods,	John Childs,
George Garig, Jr.,	G. F. White,
J. D. Stuart,	N. H. Phelps,
B. F. Bryan,	A. M. Kean,
Jos. Brady,	Dr. Duchien,
J. Bernard,	H. M. Pierce,
H. H. Walsh,	F. McHatton,
G. M. Pierce,	Jordan Holt,
H. A. Castle,	Samuel Oldfield,
M. Melton,	James Bogan,
Charles Harris,	Dr. T. J. Buffington,

W. C. McGimsey.

jan10

GENERAL ORDERS, NO 1.

Executive Office,
Baton Rouge, La., January 8, 1861.

I hereby appoint J. K. DUNCAN as my Aid-de-Camp and Assistant Adjutant General, with the rank of Lieutenant-Colonel.

He will be recognized and obeyed as such by all the volunteers and militia of the State of Louisiana.

Signed THOS. O. MOORE,
Commander-in-Chief Militia of Louisiana.

jan9-4td

Jacksonville Republican.

VOL. 25, NO. 3. | JACKSONVILLE, ALA. THURSDAY, January 17, 1861. | WHOLE NO. 1256

Jacksonville Republican

PUBLISHED EVERY THURSDAY MORNING BY

J. F. GRANT,

At Two Dollars within the year, or t re dollars at the end of the year.

A failure to give notice of a wish to dis- con inue will be consioered an engagement for the next year.

RATES OF ADVERTISING.

One dollar per square of 12 lines or less for the first insertion, & fifty cents per square for each continuance. Over one square counted as two, &c. Advertisements not marked, continued until forbid.

Yearly advertisements, $10 for one square and $5 for each additional square.

Annunciation of Candidates $5. Circulars of Candidates, 50 cents per square.

Interest charged on all accounts from the time they are due.

JACKSONVILLE FEMALE ACADEMY.

THE next session of this Institution, under the charge of Miss MARGARET A. COBB, will commence on the *Second Monday of January next,* (1861.)

Rates of Tuition.

FIRST CLASS.

PRIMARY STUDIES, embracing Primary Books in various branches, $8 00

SECOND CLASS.

General elements of Grammar, Arithmetic, Geography, and the Sciences, 12 00

THIRD CLASS.

Higher English branches and Mathematics. - - - - 16 00

FOURTH CLASS.

Languages. - - - - - - 20 00

Drawing, Music and ornamental branches. - - - - - - Extra.

Pupils should be sent in to commence with the session. No deduction will be made for absence, except in cases of protracted illness.

J. B. FORNEY. *Sec'y.*

Dec. 20, 1860.

A FRESH SUPPLY OF

Bacon,
Fish,
Rye,
and Flour.

Just received and for sale by

J. A. STEVENSON.

Sep't. 6 '60—tf.

Notice.

WE earnestly request all who have patronized us in the purchase of goods to settle by cash, if they can, and by note if they cant Save cost.

JNO. D. HOKE & BRO.

Dec. 20, 1860.

NEW FURNITURE STORE!

IN BECTON'S NEW BLOCK,
SELMA, ALABAMA

THE undersigned will have in store, on or about the 13th September next, the largest and most complete stock of CABINET FURNITURE. ever offered for sale in this place, and to which they would call the attention of buyers. Feeling confident that they can offer inducements that will justify them

BOGLÉ & DITMARS.

Selma, July 12, '60—tf.

DRS. J. C. & M. W. FRANCIS

RETURN their thanks to the public generally, for the liberal patronage heretofore extended to them, and will still continue the practice of Med cine, Surgery, &c. and devote their entire time and attention to the same. One or both, may be found at all times, when not professionally absent, at their old office, on the North-West corner of the public square, Jacksonville, Ala.

They will also keep constantly on hand a good supply of PURE DRUGS AND MEDICINES, for practice and for family use.

Aug. 16, 1860.—tf.

A BEAUTIFUL RESIDENCE,

AND

Town Lot For Sale.

IN the Town of Jacksonville Alabama, persons wishing to purchase, would do well to examine before purchasing elsewhere, for information call on A. WOODS, or J. F. GRANT.

June 26—'60.

VALUABLE LAND *FOR SALE.*

THE undersigned now offers for sale his two tracts of Land containing *FOURTEEN HUNDRED ACRES,* eight hundred of which is comprised in the tract upon which he now resides, situated in Choccolocco Valley, four miles south of White Plains, in Calhoun county, Ala.

Near five hundred acres are cleared, and in a fine state of cultivation—two hundred acres excellent bottom land, nearly all of which is cleared.

The place is well improved, having a large two story Frame Dwelling House, six rooms besides dining room and kitchen; all good out houses, Cotton Gin, and Screw, together with a large, young Orchard. All the upland is of good quality—fine for cotton and grain; and all the uncleared land is well timbered. Every field in the tract is well provided with water.

ALSO—**Six hundred and eighty acres,** known as the James A. Williams tract, situated eight miles from White Plains, on the Wedowee road, which is also well improved, having a large two story framed dwelling house, brick kitchen, and dining room; smoke house and negro houses, regularly and conveniently arranged—also, Cotton Gin, a Grist Mill, and a good site for a Saw Mill. About 400 acres cleared, lying level, and the greater portion first class bottom land; and the upland excellent. The entire tract is unusually well watered in every part—there is also on the place a good young orchard.

All the above described land will be sold on reasonable and accommodating terms.

Land buyers are respectfully invited to call and examine for themselves, and if they wish further information before doing so, they can obtain it by addressing a letter to me, at either White Plains or Corn Grove.

WASHINGTON WILLIAMS.

July 5, 1860.—tf.

TO THE PUBLIC.—The undersigned, being well known as a writer, would offer his services to all those requiring literary aid.—He will write Orations, Addresses, Essays, Presentation Speeches and replies; prepare matter for the press; write Acrostics, lines for Albums, Obituaries, and in fact attend to every species of correspondence. The utmost secresy maintained. Address,

FINLEY JOHNSON, Baltimore Md

DR. J. R. SLAYTON,

Having located permanently in Jacksonville, respectfully offers his services in the practice of

MEDICINE & SURGERY,

to citizens of Jacksonville & surrounding Country.

Can be found either at the Drug Store or Weir's Hotel

August 30 1860

DR. C. J. CLARK,
Surgeon & Practicing Physician,
JACKSONVILLE, ALA.

DR. CLARK will keep constantly on hand a supply of **Pure Medicines** for his own prescribing & to supply his patrons.

He will also take charge of Negroes suffering from Chronic Diseases, or requiring Surgical treatment, and board and treat them on reasonable terms. Jan. 18, 1859.—1y.

LIVERY AND SALE STABLE,
OXFORD, ALA.

J. A. DEARMON, is prepared at all times to furnish the public with VEHICLES and HORSES, at the following rates.

Horse per day.	$1 25
Buggy,	1 00
Horse and buggy per day	2 25
Horses Hack & driver,	5 00
Horse or Buggy, half a day	75

Damages to Horses or Vehicles must be settled for by person hirring them.

Transient persons can have their horses well taken care of at this Stable.

N. B. Persons who hire Horses and Buggies must not forget to pay up occasionally as corn is high and a cash article. If the fail 25 per cent will be added.

Feb. 22, 1860.—5t.

Special Notice.

HAVING determined to remove into the country, it becomes necessary for me to close up my business in Jacksonville. All persons indebted to me by note or account, are therefore, hereby notified to come forward and make payment. The notes and accounts of such as fail to do so will be placed in the hands of an officer for collection in the first part of January, 1861.

R. H. WYNNE.

J. H. STONE,
Wholesale & Retail Grocers,
WATER STREET,
SELMA, ALA.

nov. 8, '60.

RAILROAD and its Benefits!
J. G. SWAIN & CO.

KEEP constantly on hand, a large stock of FAMILY

GROCERIES
AND
PLANTATION SUPPLIES,

Which they are offering to sell upon terms as favorable as can be afforded anywhere.

They solicit an examination of their stock and prices, believing that they can make it to the interest of Alabamians to patronize their *own people.*

MR. D. M. ANDERSON, will be pleased to serve his friends and acquaintances from Calhoun county—and the undersigned will use his best endeavors to satisfy all who will favor him with a call. Respectfully,

N. D. JOHNSON.

Talledega, Ala. December 8, 1859.—tf.

JACKSONVILLE MALE ACADEMY.

THE Trustees of the Jacksonville Male Academy have procured the services of Rev. R. C. Hall for the year 1861.

The Academy will be opened for the reception of pupils on the 4th Monday in January 1861.

RATES OF TUITION.

Languages, and higher branches of Mathematics,	$20 00
Natural Sciences,	16 00
Common English,	12 50
Primary st dies,	10 00

WM. H. FORNEY, Sec.

Dec. 27, 1860—tf.

Committed

To the Jail of Jacksonville, Calhoun County, Alabama, by L. W. Cannon, J. P., on the 6th day of December, A. D. 1860, one Negro man, who says his name is JOE, He is of dark color, about five feet 8 or 9 inches high, and weighs about 189 pounds, and says he is 35 years old. He also says that he belongs to John Light, of Demopolis, Alabama or Mississippi. He further states that said Light bought him in Virginia from a man by the name of Hall Bates, and carried him to South Carolina, where he remained some three months, and was then brought into the State of Alabama, and that he left the said Light in Calhoun County, Alabama, some six weeks since.

The owner of the above described negro man, is hereby notified to come forward, prove property, pay charges and take him away, or he will be dealt with agreeably to the state in such cases made and provided.

FIELDING LOVE,
Sheriff of Calhoun County, Ala.

Dec. 13, 1830 —tf.

SELLING OUT
At Cost
FOR CASH.

THE undersigned having determined to change his place of business, now informs the public in general, that he will sell his present Stock of

GOODS
At Cost For Cash.

My Stock is new and full assorted, comprising **Dry Goods, Clothing, Boots & Shoes, Hats,** and a great many articles too tedious to mention.

All persons wishing to purchase great bargains, would do well to avail themselves of the opportunity immediately.

N. B. Those indebted for past purchases will confer a favor by calling in soon and paying up.

Remember, all accounts must be settled within the first part of December—therefore call in time.

AUGUST MEYERS.

Ladiga, Sept. 27, 1860.—tf.

Dr. JOHN M. TURK.
A REFORM PHYSICIAN,

OFFERS his professional services to the citizens of Oxford, Ala. and vicinity, and hopes to merit and share a liberal patronage. He proposes to treat all forms of disease, both chronic and acute, & that without the use of poisonous or depletive agents.

Dec. 22, 1859—tf.

JUST RECEIVED,
A SUPERIOR LOT OF

Bacon,
Salt,
Coffee.

For Sale by J. A. STEVENSON.

Oct. 11, 1860.

G. P. BURNETT, SOL. B. HENDRIX S. WALKER.

BURNETT, HENDRIX & WALKER,
WHOLESALE GROCERS,
Forwarding & Commission Merchants,
AND DEALERS IN
Foreign & Domestic Liquors, Cigars, Tobacco, &c.
No. 165, Main Street,
MEMPHIS, TENNESSEE.

Dec. 13, 1860—1y.

Particular Notice.

ALL persons indebted to C. G. Morgan & Co. of White Plains, will do well to call and settle, or they will other wise have to pay cost. (that is old debts past due.) Those owing on the book for 1860, will please call in and settle by note if not by money, for we must close up our old business immediately.

One of the firm will always be found at the old stand to attend to closing up the business. Nov. 29, 1866.—tf.

EXECUTOR'S SALE
OF
Personal Property.

UNDER and by virtue of an Order and Decree of the Probate conrt of Calhoun County, Alabamo, made on the 8th day of December, 1860, I will proceed to sell, on **Monday the 14th day of January, A. D. 1861,** at the late residence of Sims Kelly, deceased, the following Personal Property belonging to the Estate of the said Sims Kelly, deceased, to-wit:

NINE
LIKELY
NEGROES,

One Mare, six head of MULES,
Several hundred bushels CORN,
Wheat, Oats, Fodder,
2 Wagons, one Cart,
Cattle, Hogs and Sheep,
Blacksmith and Farming Tools,
One Buggy and Harness.

TERMS OF SALE, will be a credit of twelve months with interest from date. Note with two good and sufficient securities will be required to secuae the purchase money.

Cleared land will be rented at the same time and place.

SAMUEL C. KELLY, Exr.

Dec. 13, 1860—3t.

BLACKSMITH BUSINESS.

THE undersigned respectfully informs the citizens of Oxford and vicinity, that he has permanently located himself at that place, and is prepared to execute Blacksmith work in all its various branches; such as **Farm Work, Mill & Machine Irons,** Ironing and Repairing Buggies Carriages, Wagons, &c. &c.

Particular attention paid to horse shoeing, in the most approved and durable style.

Transient persons can have horses shod or other work done upon the shortest notice.

A good stock of iron &c. always on hand.

He may be constantly found at his place of business, ready to execute all work needed, which will be warranted by him, and executed on reasonable terms.

Ten per cent deduction for cash custom, from the usual credit prices

WM. P. PRICKETT.

Oxford, Ala., Mar. 8, 1860.—1y.

MERCHANT MILLS

THE undersigne takes this method to inform his friends and the public generally, that his MILLS, on Tallasseehatchee, five miles west of Jacksonville, are now in excellent running order, that he has two pair of French Burrs now in operation; and that he is prepared to make as good **Flour** and **Meal** as can be made in the up country.

He further informs his friends and old customers, that he has no connection with the Stephenson Mills, advertised over the signature of Abraham Adiholt.

J. A. ADIHOLD.

March 24, 1859.—tf

HOUSE AND LOT
FOR SALE

THE undersigned, having made arrangements to remove into the country, now offers for sale his house and lot in Jacksonville.

Ror information as to location, price, terms, &c. apply to John Francis, at Woodward's Store.

Dec. 6, 1860. R. H. WYNNE.

HIDES WANTED.

THE undersigned will take good dry Hides at 12½ cts per pound, and green Hides at 6¼ cts per pound, for all debts due him. Leather and Cash will also be paid for Hides at the same rates.

F. SNOW.

Jacksonville, July 10, 1860.

NEW STORE
AT OXFORD.
MORGANS & COOPER,

HAVE on hand a general stock of ***MERCHANDIZE,*** To which they invite the attention of the citizens of Oxford and vicinity. We sell for short profits, and prompt paying customers will find it to their interest to trade with us. All we ask is, to compare our Goods and prices with any in the County, and if you are not then satisfied, we will not ask you to trade with us.

COTTON YARNS always on hand for cash only. Oxford, Nov. 29, 1860.

S. MORGAN.
T. J. MORGAN,
C. J. COOKER,

THE BRICK CORNER
IS THE PLACE FOR YOU TO GO
IF YOU WANT
CHEAP GOODS.

BLUN & FRANK do not propose to sell Goods AT COST, but they will sell as

Cheap as the Cheapest.

They have always on hand a full assortment, and have just received a nice lot of **CALICOES** at 10, 10½ and 11 cents. Also a superior lot of **Chewing Tobacco.**

BLUN & FRANK want it distinctly understood, that they are settled here and are determined to stay. Dec. 23, '60.

NOTICE.
Ala. and Ten. River Railroad
WAREHOUSE,
By S. W. PETTIBONE, successor to W. Y. LUNDIE & CO.

Charge for receiving, weighing and shipping Cotton, twenty five cents per bale. When re-weighed. twenty five cents per bale will be charged to be paid by the purchaser. Cotton remaining over one month, will be charged ten cents a bale per month extra. Oct. 18, 1860—6m.

VALUABLE LAND & MILLS
To Rent.

I NOW offer to Rent my land two miles south of Jacksonville, either by the acre, or the usual share—possession given in time for wheat sowing. There are about 300 acres cleared, with houses and necessary improvements.

Also my Grist and Saw Mills, now in excellent order.

If preferred, I would sell my entire body of Land containing about **One Thousand Acres,** at a reasonable price and on accommodating terms.

J. A. STEVENSON.

Oct. 18, 1860.—tf.

English & Classical School.

The 3d session will open on Monday Jan 7th 1861. Terms same as heretofore.

L. H. PARSOMS, Principal.

FALL AND WINTER
GOODS.
J. A. STEVENSON

IS just receiving a large and well selected Stock of FALL & WINTER GOODS; consisting of

DRESS GOODS
OF EVERY DESCRIPTION.

Also, **Staple GOODS, Hats, Caps, Boots & Shoes, Factory Yarns & Osnaburgs,**

CLOTHING

Of every description for Men & Boys, of the most approved styles.

Crockery, Hardware, Cutlery, CASTINGS, CARPENTERS' and FARMERS' TOOLS of every description. Also a large and complete stock of ***GROCERIES,*** for sale at the lowest market prices

Also a good stock of **Sole Leather, Calfskins &c. &c.**

He would invite the attention of his friends and customers and the public to his Stock of Goods, which have been selected with great care and attention, and which is superior to any ever offered in this market. Purchasers will do well to call and examine before purchasing elsewhere.

Sept. 27, 1860.—tf.

J. A. STEVENSON.

Daily Stage Line
BETWEEN ROME AND TALLADEGA

THE Coaches now make close connections with the Railroads at both ends of the route. Distance 90 miles; time 22 hours.

Through passengers will find this an agreeable route.

Leaves Rome every morning at 6 1-2 o'clk
Leaves Talladega every evening at 6 "

POWELL & HUTCHINSON,
Proprietors.

NOTICE.

I HAVE my **Steam Grist Mills** in operation now and will be able to accommodate my customers and the public immediately. Everything connected with the ***Flouring Mill*** is of the best material, strict attention will be paid to all grain sent to these mills. All foreigners can be accommodated with a comfortable house and lot during their stay at the mills.

JAMES G. NISBET.

Feb, 3 1859.—tf

Dr. J. W. HICKS.
(*Lately of Rome Ga.*)

Having located permanently, offers his professional services to the citizens of Jacksonville and its vicinity. Office at Dr. T. N. Anglins Drug Store—residence the. house formerly occupied by Mr. Privett.

N. B. Particular attention given to diseases of women and children.

Sep't 6th, '60.—tf.

NEW CABINET SHOP.

THE undersigued respectfully informs the public that they have opened a New Cabinet Shop in Jacksonville on the east side of main street, next door south of Flemming's Carrirge shop; where they will make to order, and keep constantly on hand every description of

FURNITURE,
AND

which they will sell at lower prices than has ever been offered in this place. When they say they will sell their work cheap. they mean exactly what they say, and only ask of persons who may wish to purchase Furniture, to call upon them, and be convinced of the fact. They would call attention particularly to the fact that they will execute Coffin work of every size and qaality, unusually low.

C. R. LESTER

May 17.—1860.

Piles, Fistula, Tumours &c.

Dr. J. A. Clopton, of Huntsville Ala., treats with perfect success *Piles, Fistula, Tumours &c.*

Testimonials of the highest character will be forwarded to any that may wish them.

The patient is not confined to his bed or room, He has had the pleasure of treating an Old Govennor of the State, and the oldest Physician of Montgomery, and some of the first class of Mobile.

A three cent stamp must accompany all communications.

March, 1 1860.

ABNER WILLIAMS,
Cotton Factor
AND
Commission Merchant,
SELMA, ALA.,

Will continue to give special attention to the sale of *Cotton;* and to filling orders, when accompanied with *cash,* or its equivalent. *A liberal share of patronage is respectfully solicited.*

☞ Commissions: *same as heretofore.*

Sept. 27, 1860.—tf.

W. C. LAND,
WATCH MAKER AND JEWELER

HAS just returned from N. York and Philadelphia and is able to exhibit to the citizens of Jacksonville & adjoining country, a most splendid stock of

WATCHES

from all the celebrated Makers in Europe and America, also a fashionable stock of

JEWELRY,

For Ladies and Gentlemen, such as **Breast Pins, EarRings, Finger Rings, Chatalains, Vest Chains, Keys, Seals, &c.**

All of late style and good gold.

Also a fine lot of **Marine Lever Clocks,** in Rosewood and Enameled cases of superior make. Walking Canes, Silver Spoons, Silver Forks, Plated Castors and Fruit Baskets, Cake Trays, call Bells, &c &c. and numerous articles too tedious to mention.

My special attention will be paid to the repair of Watches and Jewelry as heretofore.

Engraving of every kind done in good style.

Jacksonville, Dec. 8, 1859.

POETRY.

Land of the South.

Land of the South!—imperial land!—
How proud thy mountains rise—
How sweet thy scenes on every hand—
How fair thy covering skies!
But not for this—oh, not for thee,
I love thy fields to roam—
Thou hast a dearer spell to me,
Thou art my native home!

Thy rivers roll their liquid wealth,
Unequalled to the sea—
Thy hills and valleys bloom with health,
And green with verdure be!
But not for thy proud ocean streams,
Nor for thy azure dome—
Sweet, sunny South!—I cling to thee—
Thou art my native home!

I've stood beneath Italla's clime,
Beloved of tale and song—
On Helvey's hills, proud and sublime,
Where Nature's wonders throng;
By temple's classic sunlight streams,
Where gods of old did roam—
But ne'er have found so fair a land
As thou, my native home.

And thou hast prouder glories too—
Than nature ever gave—
Peace sheds o'er thee her genial dew,
And freedom,s pinions wave—
Fair science flings her pearls around,
Religion lifts her dome,—
These, these, endear thee to my heart—
My own loved native home.

And "Heaven's best gift to man" is thine—
God bless thy rosy girls;
Like sylvan flowers, they sweetly shine—
Their hearts as pure as pearls!
And grace and goodness circle them,
Where'er their footsteps roam;
How can I then, whilst loving them,
Not love my native home?

Land of the South!—imperial land!
Then here's a health to thee—
Long as thy mountain barrier's stand
May'st thou be blest and free!
May dark dissension's banner ne'er
Wave o'er thy fertile loam—
But should it come, there's one will die,
To save his native home!

If, indeed, women were mere outside form and features only, and if mind made up no part of her composition, it would follow a ball room was quite as appropriate a place for obtaining a wife as an exhibition room for choosing a picture. But inasmuch as women are not mere potraits— their value not being determinable by a glance of the eye, it follows that a different mode of appreciating their value, and a different place for viewing them, antecedent to their being individually selected, is desirable. The two cases differ, also, in this, that if a man select a picture for himself from among all its exhibited competitors, and bring it to his own house, the picture being passive, he is able to fix it there; while the wife, picked up at a public place, and accustomed to incessant display, will not, it is probable, when brought home, stick so quietly to the spot where he fixes her, but will escape to the exhibition room again, and continue to be displayed at every subsequent exhibition, just as if she were not become private property, and never been definitely disposed of.—*Hannah More.*

Have you ever watched an icicle as it formed? You noticed how it froze one drop at a time until it was a foot long or more. If the water was clean, the icicle remained clear, and sparkled brightly in the sun; but if the water was but slightly muddy, the icicle looked foul, and its beauty was spoiled. Just so our characters are forming. One little thought or feeling, at a time adds its influence. If each thought be pure and right, the soul will be lovely, and will sparkle with happiness; but if impure and wrong, there will be final deformity and wretchedness.

The Gulf States and Fugitive Slaves. The idea prevails to some extent that the Gulf States have no reason to complain of the nullifying Acts of the North, because they do not lose any negros by escape. Well established facts prove this to be a mistake. According to the census of 1850, those States suffer nearly as much as the border States in this way. In 1850, the whole number of slaves which escaped was 1011, and they were from the several States as follows:—

Alabama	29	Maryland	279
Missouri	60	Mississippi	41
Arkansas	21	North Corolina	64
Delaware	26	South Carolina	16
Florida	18	Tennessee	70
Georgia	89	Texas	29
Kentucky	96	Virginia	83
Louisiana	90		
Total			1011

The New York Times thinks the number has since increased full fifty per cent., which would give 1500 a year, the aggregate value of which is $1,500,000. It will be seen, that while the loss of the border States is of course much the greatest, Georgia, in 1850, lost within seven as many as Kentucky, and Louisiana within six as many; so that the popular idea that the extreme Southern States do not suffer in this way is erroneous.—*Richmond Dispatch.*

A French writer has said that, "to dream gloriously, you must act gloriously while you are awake; and to bring annels down to converse with you in your sleep, you must labor in the cause of virtue during the day."

The sweetest, the most clinging affections are often shaken by the slightest breath of unkindness, as the delicate tendrils of the vine are agitated by the faintest air that blows in summer. An unkind word from one beloved, often draws the blood from many a heart, which would defy the battle-axe of hatred, or the keenest edge of vindictive satire. Nay, the shade, the gloom of the face, familiar and dear, awakens grief and pain. These are the little thorns which, though men of rougher form make their way through them without feeling much, extremely incommode persons of a more refined turn, in the journey through life, and make their travelling irksome and un-

---

A USEFUL MEDICINE.—It is now nearly twenty-five years since the firm of Fleming Brothers of Pittsburg, Pa., commenced the Manufacture of McLane's celebrated Nermifuge and Liver Pills, during which time they have paid over half a million of dollars for advertising the same. The great and growing popularity of this medicine is attested by the fact that during the past year they have sold the enormous amount of 1,500,000 boxes of the pills and vials of the vermifuge. This should be a satisfactory evidence of the usefulness and value of a medicine, the sale of which is every year increasing.

We have had frequent business transactions with Messrs· Fleming Bro's, and can truly say that we have never dealt with a more prompt and honorable house. Their payments are never deloyed longer than the time they are due, and their publishers are not subject to any annoyance in collecting—a fact which speaks volumes for the honorable character of their house.

Terrific Colliery Explosion—On Hundreb and Seventy Lives LOst.

On Saturday' December 1st, a minute explosion happened at Black Vein Pit, Wales. The colliery has been in work some years in the production of steam-coal; and as gas is in such pits more or less generated, the usual proventive measuros were adopted. The pit was examined according to custom on Saturday morning after which, between five and six o'clock, some two hundred men descended. About nine o'clock a terrific explosion occurred, which was heard far above the surfaco and upon inspection it was found that at some distance from the bottom of the pit the gas had fired—Considerable damage was done to the workings. As soon as the ventilation would allow, dead bodies were found in every direction. By twelve o'clock eleven had been sent up, and at four forty more had been collected at th bottom of the shaft, the whole being brought up in the course of the evening and in carts or hastily constructed bier conveyed to their respective home.

Additional particulars are given by the London *News* of the 4th: Instead of 120 persons having fallen vicsims, the probability is that at least fifty morv are dead, and that the fearful roll will swell to at least 170 names. During yesterday and the last two nights (says the *News*) the search in the workings was continued and corpses found and brought to the surface numbering, with those brought up on Saturday, about 100. One portion of the workings is now discovered to have fallen in, cutting off all communication with 60 or 70 persons who are beyond To reaco them will it is feared, occupy a considerable time but little or no expectation is entertained that one of the party will be discovered alive. When the explosion occured about two hundred men and boys were in the pit, of whom only about thirty have escaped.

INDIAN MASSACRE AT JACKSON, TEXAS.—A letter to a Western paper gives the particulars of the late tragedy in Jackson, Texas, which we have heretofore noted:

The Indians have murdered three families within four miles of our town, and proceeded in the direction of Brisco's, a mile from the others, and the presumption is, all are murdered at that place, as the smoke is plainly seen rising from their burning houses. Never before have we seen so much anguish; men, women and children, the mangled corpses at the houses of Mrs. Gage, Mr. Landman and Mr. Hays.

Another account states that four of the children of Mrs. Gage were dangerously, if not mortally wounded, and Mrs. Saunders, the mother of Mrs. G., killed and her body horribly mangled. A daughter of Mr. Landman, aged 12 years, was mortally wounded, and his wife and two children massacreed. Miss Matilda Gage and Miss Landman were made prisoners, but after being stripped of their clothing and ill treated, were released, and returned to their desolated homes in a state of nudity. A man named Sherman, missing his wife, went in search of her, and found her lying near a creek, with an arrow in her side and her scalp taken. After getting water and recovering somewhat, she was able to say that the Indians committed the most horrible brutalities upon her for an hour and a half, when one of them run his knife around her head, making an incision, then threw her upon the ground, and putting his foot upon her, tore her scalp from her head and left her. She lived three days, giving birth to a child a few minutes before her death. All the houses of the murdered were plundered of everything they contained.

DOES NEW ORLEANS SUFFER?—Says the New Orleans *Delta:* "Our Northern *friends* are solacing themselves with the idea that the South is suffering greatly from the present commercial distress, growing out of our political disorders. The only serious inconvenience and embarrassment which our people experience from this cause is due to a vassalage, the prospect of getting rid of which more than reconciles them to their present sacrifices. This is the vassalage to Northern brokers and capitalists. It would appear from the business of last week that our trade is rapidly releasing itself of this heavy yoke and asserting its independence. *Fifty seven thousand bales of cotton,* worth *two millions and a half dollars,* were sold last week for foreign account, The prices were remunerating, and the cotton will go abroad—not a bale io the northern spinners. Other trades exhibited a like revival; and, on the whole, the business of the week was very little behind that of last year. Let there be a peaceable secession, and the business of the same week next season will be double that of the present.

GREELEY ON COERCION.—But if the Cotton States generaly unite with South Carolina in seceeding we insist that they cannot be prevented and that the attempt must not be made. Five millions of people more than half a million are able and willing to shoulder a musket can never be subdued while fighting around and over their own hearthstones If they could be they would no longer be equal members of the Union, but conquered dependencies.

The End of the Rainbow.

BY L. VIRGINIA FRENCH.

"'Twas born in a moment, yet, quick as its birth,
It had stretched to the uttermost ends of the earth,
And, fair as an angel, it floated as free,
With a wing on the earth, and a wing on the sea.

How wide was the sweep of its beautiful wings!
How boundless its circle! how radiant its rings!
If I looked on the sky, 'twas suspended in air;
If I looked on the ocean, the rainbow was there;
Thus forming a girdle, as brilliant and whole,
As the thoughts of the rainbow that circled my soul;
Like the wing of the Deity, calmly unfurled
It bent from the cloud, and encircled the world."

So sang one whose spirit was as bright and full of beauty as the radiant bow that spans the summer heaven. There are those who spend the strength of youth for the glory of a laurel garland, or a crown of bays, and in mid age receive their reward; there are those who watch, and wait, and struggle through life for an earthly recompense which never comes; but few are they who, like "AMELIA," come singing with the morning from the portals of Paradise, and return thither with a lyre and crown ere the dew has gone up from its amaranthiue blossoms. Soft as the dreamy lull of chiming waters, light as the foot-fall of the summer wind, enchanting as some fairy-peopled vision, steals upon our spirits the music of her fyre. Poetical expression was not to her that "inner voice" interpreting the mysteries of our being; it was the simple "singing of the fountains" of her soul; and poetry was not to her an "ocean to the river of her thoughts," whereunto rolled great currents of reflection, and where swelled the tides of passion; it was the morning sun beam, looking daily down into her heart blossoms, until, like a bird amid the dawning, her impulsive spirit carolled forth its lays of joy and praise. If Ambition found a place within her soul, it was but as the star-shadow on the dreaming wave, for laurels bloomed upon her girlish brow, and when the maturity of womanhood brightened over it like a halo, she passed away into the Ideal World of which she has so often sung—now her radiant *reality!* And the "end of Earth" has been to her also the end of the Rainbow. For this bright arch is but a "bow of promise," which must needs have no existence in the land of eternal fruition. Have we ever though that there will be no rainbows in Heaven? For ah! it is but a beautiful child of earth, born of the cloud and sunshine, and *there* there are to be no clouds—"neither light of the sun, for the Lord God is the light thereof, and ye shall reign with Him forever and ever."

Time and again in our chidhood we have listened to old Nurse's tales of he treasures buried at the end of thet Rainbow. "Ah! child," she would say, with such a wise shake ef the thead, "if you *could* but run fast enough to catch it! and there, right under the end—just there, you see, where it comes down over the wood and rests on the meadow—hey! how bright the grass is!—well, *fust there* you would find the enchanted pot of gold, and all brimming over with jewels too—shining and sparkling—and great diamonds like drops of fire! Oh! honey, don't you wish you *could* catch the end of the rainbow?" And, then, how the child-heart would swell—how wide-open, eager eyes would measures the distance "away down into the meadow" where the light vision rested—how little pattering feet would bound off down the paths. and by the time they reached the gardan gate—the lovely, luring rainbow had faded into air!

THE SPEECH OF SENATOR PUGH—SENATORS IN TEARS—LADIES SOB ALOUD.—The correspondent of the Alexandria Gazette, alluding to the speech of the young Senator from Ohio, on Thursday last, says:

The scene in the Senate, to-day, at the conclusion of the speech of Mr. Pugh, of Ohio, was one that has never before been witnessed in the hall. The galleries were crowded to all their vast extent with a throng—on the one side of ladies, more than usualls attentive—and on the other, of men hanging upon the words of the orator. Having painted the horrors which would accompany civil strife, the young Senator, amid the eloquent words which thrilled the vast assemblage, in his closing sentences called up the vision of an unseen hand, writing on the walls of the Senate—"Thou hast been weighed in the balance and found wanting. THY KINGDOM IS DIVIDED." There was weeping in all parts of the chamber; ladies sobbed, tears shone in the eyes of many of the listeners in the galleries, and Senators Wigfall, Douglas, Davis and others were visibly affected. Mr. Douglas, during some proceedings a few minutes subsequent, declared that he saw a gleam of light for the country in the effect which the speech produced·

When our Northern enemies denounce us as cowards, thieves, and villians. they should remember that the South has produced a Marion, a Sumpter, a Washington, and a host of other renowned warriors; and that they have produced an Arnold and a Burr, whose names and deeds, will ever mar the brightest pages of our history.

LOUISIANA.—All our State exchanges, says the New Orleans *Bulletin,* are devoting themselves to the discussion of the mode of resistanco, and to the publication of the proceedings of public meetings. Not the faintest note of submission is heard·

POSTSCRIPT.

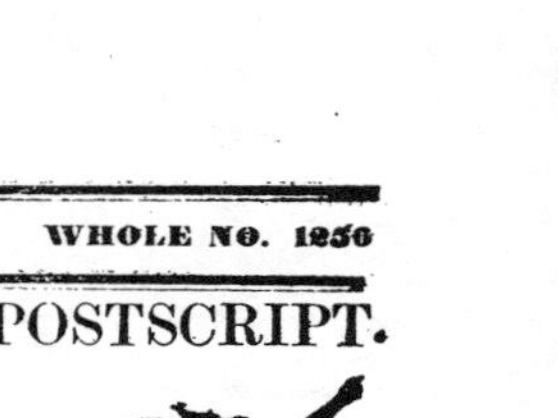

JACKSONVILLE, ALA.

January 14, 1861.

Alabama is Free!

Alabama to-day, is free and independent! She has taken her position among the sovereign nations of the earth, with not a link remaining of that galling chain of vassalage which bound her to the Union. The stain upon her escutcheons, which the past entailed, is wiped out forever, and her first step is taken in the grand procession of sister States whose motto is "liberty or death!" Side by side with the gallant commonwealth of South Carolina, she is her twain Star in the firmament of a new Confederacy to be built upon the ruins of the old. Looming up from the golden portals of the east, the sun throws his broad beams upon the landscapes of the very Eden of the South—the Palestine of a new Republic! Alabama is redeemed and disenthralled forever! The day of her redemption shall be embalmed in poetry, and consecrated by our children's children! The measure of her glory is full-orbed and complete, and language gives place to shouts of triumph!

JACKSONVILLE ALL ALIVE!!!

The glorious intelligence that Alabama had seceded on the 11t inst., reached here on Sabbath about 8 O'clock at night, and after 12 at midnight, a scene of general festivity was opened by the firing of Cannons and Small arms, with music and banners, which continued until broad daylight. Never was a scene witnessed wherein old and young participated so unanimously. We are all together! Three cheers for the gallant County of Calhoun!!!

This news was receieved after our first side was made up. Look out for important news in our issue on the day after to-morrow.

Special to the Advertiser.

ALABAMA OUT OF THE UNION!

The Vote sixty-one to Thirty-nine!!

A GLORIOUS DAY!!!

We have only time to announce, as our evening edition goes to press that the State Convention has withdrawn Alabama immediately and unconditionally from the Union.

The vote was taken about half-past two o'clock, and resulted 61 in favor to 39 against the Ordinance.

Truly, this is glory enough for one day. Our citizens are hailing the new era with demonstrations of profoundest emotion. The Capitol grounds and streets are alive with the moving mass of the cheering throng. Cannons are booming and bells ringing.

NEW ORLEANS, Jan. 8.—The election to day has given a large majority for the secession candidates in this city. The State has also gone largely for secession.—*Charleston Courier.*

WASHINGTON, JANUARY 8th.

Gen. Scott is now the ruling spirit of the Government, and is for war unless the South presents a United front, when he thinks war hopeless and impolitic.

Good News from New Orleans.

NEW ORLEANS, JAN. 7.

There are great rejoicings in this City over the result of the Convention election. All the secession candidates on the Senatorial ticket, and twenty-one out of twenty-four on the Representative ticket, are elected by a decided majority.

There is no doubt that the State has gone for secession by an overwhelming vote.

THE PECULIARITIES AND NECESSITY OF SLEEP. There is no fact more clearly established in the physiology of man than this, that the brain expands its energies and itself during the hours of wakefulness, and that those are recuperated during sleep; if the recuperation does not equal the expenditure, the brain withers—this is insanity. Thus it is that, in early English history, persons who were condemned to death by being prevented from sleeping always died raving maniacs; thus it is, also, that those who starved to death become insane; the brain is not nurished and they cannot sleep. The practical influences are these: 1. Those who think most, who do most brain work, require most sleep. 2. That time saved from necessary sleep is infalliblp destructive to mind, body and estate. 3. Give yourself, your children, your servants—give all that are under you—the fullest amount of sleep they will take, by compelling them to go to bed at some regular early hour and to rise the moment they wake, & in a fortnight nature, with almost the regularity of the rising sun, will unloose the bands of sleep the moment enough repose has been secured for the wants of the system. This is the only safe & sufficient rule; and as to the question how much sleep any one requires, each must be a rule for himself great nature will never fail to write it out to the observer under the regulations just given.

Daily Advocate.

J. M. TAYLOR & TOM BYNUM.

EDITORS AND PROPRIETORS.

TUESDAY MORNING, JAN. 22, 1861.

ADVOCATE EDITORIAL ROOMS.—In order to get out of the "noise and confusion" necessarily created in the business department of the *Advocate*, the editors have been compelled to seek a more quiet place to concoct and perfect their lucubrations. Our friends will always be welcome at our new *sanctum* on Third street, a few doors above our publication office.

THE LEGISLATURE—A full quorum of familiar faces challenged our attention as we entered the State House yesterday. Their proceedings, carefully jotted down by our admirable reporter, W. E. Cooke, Esq., will be found elsewhere.

The Convention meets on Wednesday; the Legislature meantime will probably adjourn for a couple of weeks, and give that body possession of the Hall of Representatives. By the time the Legislative committees are prepared to make their reports, the Convention will have already passed the ordinance of Secession and such other measures as necessity may dictate, and leave the other body to go on with such legislation as the interests of the State, under the new condition of things, may require.

Our columns will give a faithful history of everything that transpires in these exciting times.

☞ We commence to-day our annual reports of the proceedings of the State Legislature.

The hour is pregnant with importance to every citizen. The present position of public and national affairs, as well as the attitude in which the State of Louisiana now stands towards the Federal Government, must cause all to look with interest, if not anxiety, to the action of our legislative bodies. Upon this may hang the destinies of the future, in so far as concerns our State.

ALABAMA POSTAL REPORT—The special committee on postal affairs in the Alabama State Convention recommend that the means now in use for the service of the department be "permitted to continue until a postal treaty or treaties shall be concluded, or until otherwise ordered or provided by the authority of the State."

In the preamble it guarantees the protection of all mail contracts, as far as the Commonwealth is concerned.

ALABAMA STATE CONVENTION.—An ordinance authorizing the Governor to raise $1,000,000 for the defense of the State, was read and referred to the Committee on Finance, in the Alabama State Convention on the 12th. The money is to be raised by the issue of State bonds, to run not less than five nor more than twenty years, and the bonds not to be sold at a discount.

The same day, General Sanford, the commissioner from Georgia, addressed the convention. He said Georgia could have twenty thousand men in the field within thirty-six hours.

RESIGNATION OF CAPT. HARTSTENE.—It gives us pleasure, says the Savannah *News* of the 10th inst., to chronicle the fact that this gallant officer has resigned his position in the Federal Navy. Capt. H. entered the service at an early age, and has served long and faithfully, rising step by step from a young midshipman to his present exalted position in the front rank of American naval officers. No man has earned higher honors or wears them more gallantly. Long may he live to serve his native State.

SECESSION ORDINANCE OF FLORIDA.—The following is the ordinance of secession adopted by the late convention at Tallahasse:

We, the people of the State of Florida, in convention assembled, do solemnly ordain, publish and declare, that the State of Florida hereby withdraws herself from the confederacy of States existing under the name of the United States of America, and from the existing government of said States; and that all political connection between her and the government of said States ought to be and the same is hereby totally annulled, and said Union of States dissolved, and the State of Florida is hereby declared a sovereign and independent nation; and that all ordinances heretofore adopted, in so far as they create or recognize said Union, are rescinded, and all laws or parts of laws in force in this State, in so far as they recognize or assent to said Union, be and they are hereby repealed.

WILLIS ON SOUTHERN SOCIETY.—In a recent leading article for the *Home Journal*, Willis thus laments over the "estrangement of the South:"

Politics, trade and sectional differences quite out of the question (and "News" knows those branches of the question are sufficiently discussed in the other papers,) we are sustaining a great *social* loss in the estrangement of the South. In all the larger and more refined circles of our American society—at Saratoga and Newport, in our gayeties of the cities, and on our routes of fashionable travel and resort—the Southerners are unquestionably the class most sought and admired as "the nicest people." It would be hard to find a cultivated "society man," probably, anywhere at the North, who does not number many of his most valued friends and pleasantest acquaintances in this class. Explain it by what social alchemy you please, too, the infusion of the Southern amalgam in any alembic of politeness at the North, exceedingly improves the metal—partly, no doubt, from the corrective given by the more generous and graceful qualities of the South to the more angular and calculating qualities of the North. The American travelers who shine most at foreign courts and in foreign society, are from the South. They are, in fact, our country's natural patricians. And —abused though they are, at a distance, by some of the Northern newspapers as an offensive "oligarchy"—the tribute of preference and admiration is paid to them, by these very Northerners, at this very time, whenever they come personally in contact. And so, with all the "momentous issues" of secession left to more gregarious discussion, may we not fairly own, that, *individually*, Northern men are regretting exceedingly the *social estrangement* of the South?

HOLD HIM!—Gen. W. W. W. Wood, of the Natchez *Free Trader* has organized the Southern Confederacy by nominating the following ticket. We give his ticket and remarks in conjunction:

Southern United States of America.

OUR TICKET.

FOR PRESIDENT,
ALBERT GALLATIN BROWN,
of Mississippi.

FOR VICE PRESIDENT,
WM. L. YANCY,
of Alabama.

For Secretary of State,
J. P. BENJAMIN, of Louisiana.

For Lieutenant General (General-in-Chief) of the Army.
JEFFERSON DAVIS, of Mississippi.

For Generals of Division,
JOE LANE, of the South,
DAVID E. TWIGGS, of Georgia.

We have a host of the right sort of men in each and every Southern State for the various cabinet and Diplomatic positions.

This is our individual sentiment. We do not publish it as that of the party, or a party. We go heartily with Southerners for the South, knowing now, no party but that of the South. We throw out but a suggestion for the consideration of those who may organize the provisional or other government, to be had under the new regime about to be inaugurated.

We don't like to discriminate against true Southern men, but we must suggest to the *Free Trader* that Yancey, Benjamin, or Jeff. Davis would either supply the place of A. G. Brown without weakening the ticket.

THE PRESIDENT'S "FAST" REPUDIATED BY THE SOUTH CONGREGATIONAL CHURCH.

On Sunday morning last, Rev. Charles Beecher a brother of Rev. Henry Ward Beecher, preached a sermon to his Society at Georgetown, Mass., upon the condition of the country at the present time. It was a bold, vigorous production, stamped with the great intellectual force and freedom of thought so characteristic of the Beecher family. In the course of his remarks James Buchanan was handled without gloves, and the subject of slavery reviewed as only a Beecher can review this infernal system.

In the evening an adjourned church meeting was held, and the following resolutions, submitted at a former meeting, were discussed, and after considerable opposition were adopted by a close vote of 15 to 12. In the society and community at large, as we are informed, the majority in favor of the resolutions would be overwhelming.

Preamble and Resolutions of the South Congregational Church, Georgetown, Mass., Adopted Dec. 23 1860.

WHEREAS, the recent message of the President of the United States recognizing the existence of open rebellion at the South, advises to amend the Constitution so that the rebels may submit; and

WHEREAS, having laid the blame of this rebellion upon the "violent agitation of the slavery question at the North," the President now proclaims a National Fast, that we may confess our faults to God, and "implore him to remove from our hearts that false pride of opinion which would impel us to persevere in wrong for the sake of consistency," thus virtually summoning the people to repentance for the issues of the late Presidental canvass; therefore,

Resolved, That the President of the United States is in a treasonous conspiracy with rebels to overthrow the Government.

Resolved, That an amendment of the Constitution for the avowed purpose of propitiating armed rebellion is a thing unheard of in the annals of time, absurd, and impossible.

Resolved, That the only amendment which the age demands is an express repudiation of the slavery construction of the rendition and representation clauses of the Constitution.

Resolved, That the present distress is a judgment of God, not only upon our other sins but also and especially upon the sin of slavery, and that this people should immediately break off their sins by repentance, and daily seek forgiveness for the same.

Resolved, That viewed in connection with the charges and implications contained in his late message, the President's proclamation of a Fast, though verbally pious, is an act of hypocrisy and spiritual usurpation in the highest degree insulting and detestable, being nothing short of a virtual bull of excommunication against political adversaries, and that, under the circumstances, we must wholly decline the President's request. *Boston Atlas and Bee.*

That is the "concession" spirit of the North. Will the South longer parley with such enemies?

ANDY JOHNSON HUNG IN EFFIGY AT GRAND JUNCTION—*South Carolina Sustained.*—At a meeting of the citizens of Grand Junction, Tenn., and vicinity, on Friday night, the 28th of December, held for the purpose of denouncing the late speech of Andy Johnson, Dr. N. H. Prewitt was called to the chair, and a committee of five gentlemen appointed to draft resolutions. The following were unanimously adopted amid shouts of applause:

WHEREAS, Andrew Johnson, who was elected by the Legislature of Tennessee, to represent the State in the United States Senate, has, in the judgment of this meeting, misrepresented his constituents by his late speech delivered in the Senate, wherein he advocates coercing a sovereign State; and, whereas, we believe the said speech is calculated to further the aggression of our enemies, and was not an error of the head, but was actuated either by the promptings of a depraved heart, or from the hope of receiving office at the hands of a Black Republican administration; therefore, be it

Resolved, That we, a portion the people of Hardeman County, irrespective of party, do, for the purpose of expressing our indignation of Andy Johnson, hang him in effigy.

Resolved, That the Hon. W. W. Guy, our representative from this county, in the Legislature of Tennessee, be, and he is hereby requested to offer a bill before the Legislature, in extraordinary session assembled on the 7th day of January next, instructing Mr. Andrew Johnson out of the United States Senate.

Resolved, That a copy of these resolutions be sent, with the man of rags by us hung in representation of Andrew Johnson, to Mr. Cook of the city of Washington.

Resolved, That we hail with emotions of pride and satisfaction, each movement having for its object, resistance to Northern aggression and the safety of our homes and property.

Resolved, That while we desire and confidently expect the united co-operation of the slave States, in maintaining Southern rights and Southern honor, that we would sooner be sunk into the "ocean deep" than to utter one word of reproach against South Carolina for her act of secession, and that our hands and arm are now ready to defend her.

Resolved, That the papers of Tennessee be requested to copy these resolutions

N. H. PREWITT, Chairman.

WM. JENKINS, Secretary.

☞ Many a poor woman thinks she can do nothing without a husband; and when she gets one, finds she can do nothing with him.

☞ The N. Y. *Herald* boasts of enjoying a daily circulation of 82,000 which is read by 400,000 persons.

Louisiana Legislature.

January 21, 1861.

SENATE.—This body assembled, according to law, in their Hall at 12 o'clock, M., of to-day, the Lieutenant Governor, Hon. H. M. Hyams, in the chair.

On a call of the roll 21 Senators answered to their names.

The absentees numbered ten, and one vacancy has occurred since the last session, caused by the resignation of Hon. A. Malhiot, late Senator from the parishes of Assumption, Ascension and Terrebonne.

Mr. Goode introduced to the Senate the Hon. A. Tete, elected to fill the existing vacancy, and this gentleman, having been sworn, took his seat as Senator from the parishes above named.

The Secretary of the House informed the Senate of the organization of that body, and that it was ready to proceed to business.

A like message was sent from the Senate to the House,

Mr. Salomon presented a petition in regard to a certain marriage, which, on his motion, was referred to the Committee on the Judiciary.

He also offered a joint resolution relative to the adjournment of the two Houses after to-morrow, and the same was laid over under the rules.

This resolution, we presume, is introduced with a view to the assembling of the Convention, on the 23rd prox.

Mr. Shadburne introduced an act for the relief of James L. Crandell, Sheriff and Tax Collector of the parish of Madison.

Mr. Salomon offered a joint resolution providing for the appointment of a committee of both houses to investigate the affairs of the Rialroads of the State, and the same was, under a suspension of the rules, immediately taken up and adopted.

On motion of Mr. Lawrence the President appointed a committee of three, on the part of the Senate, to wait on the Governor and inform him of the organization of the two Houses, and of their readiness to receive any communication he might see fit to make. The committee named were Messrs. Lawrence, Moore, and Smart, who reported back that the Governor would on to-morrow communicate officially with the Senate.

Mr. Stevens offered a resolution allowing each member of the Senate, and its Secretaries, ten daily papers during the session, or their equivalent in weeklies, and the same was adopted.

On motion of Mr. Lawrence the number of members of the Committee on Militia was increased from five to nine.

On motion of Mr. Salomon, the Senate took recess for one half an hour.

At the expiration of this time, the Senate adjourned till 12 o'clock on to-morrow.

HOUSE.—This body assembled, in due course of law, in their Hall, at 12 o'clock, M., of to-day, the Speaker, Hon. C. H. Morrison, in the chair.

A call of the roll showed fifty-nine members present.

Mr. Voorhies of St. Martin introduced to the House, the Hon. Theogene Castille elected to fill the vacancy caused by the decease of Hon. G. B. Miller, late Representative of that parish, and this gentleman, having been sworn, took his seat.

Mr. Haynes offered a joint resolution appointing a committee of five on the part of the House and —— on the part of the Senate, to wait upon the Governor, in reference to any communications he might see fit to make, and the same having been adopted, the Speaker named on said committee: Messrs. Haynes, Lane of Jackson, Gantt, Adams and Bickham.

The Senate committee we have given above.

The chairman of the House committee reported back that the orders of the House had been duly executed and that the Governor would send in his communications on to-morrow.

On motion of Mr. Allen, the House proceeded to the election of a Doorkeeper.

The following nominations were made to-wit:

By Mr. Herron—James W. Beal.
By Mr. Brusle—Wm. Simmons.
By Mr. Bradley—Wm. Fletcher.
By Mr. Berry—Wm. Alexander.
By Mr. Coombs—Alfred Wilson.
By Mr. Allen—Frank White.

The vote was taken *viva voce*, and on the second ballot, 62 votes being cast, and Mr. Wm. Fletcher of Livingston, having received 34 votes, he was declared to be duly elected, and on motion of Mr. Bickham was sworn and entered upon the discharge of his duties.

Mr. Brusle offered a resolution providing that all investigating and traveling committees should transact their usual business during the recess of the session.

This resolution looks to the same event as that of the resolution offered in the Senate, for a temporary adjournment. It lies over under the rules until to-morrow.

On motion of Mr. Haynes, the Speaker was empowered to invite, alternatively, the officiating ministers of the city to open the House with prayer each day of the session.

Mr. Bradley offered a resolution appointing a joint committee to consist of five on the part of the House and —— on the part of the Senate, to investigate Railroad affairs, and to report on or before the 18th of February next, and the same was laid over.

The following unfinished business of the last session was taken up and placed on the regular calendar, to-wit:

On motion of Mr. Bush, bill No. 31, relative to the Supreme Court; No. 35, relative to crimes and offenses; No. 245, relative to the Barrataria and Lafourche Canal Company; No. 247, for the repeal of Article 2260 of the Civil Code; No. 248, relative to executory process; No. 249, relative to injunctions; No. 534, Harbor Masters; No. 282, relative to Births and Deaths.

On motion of Mr. Beggs, bill No. 73, of Senate, and of House 392, for the relief of John Roy; No. 577, relative to traveling agents.

On motion of Mr. Bartlett, bill No. 505, relative to the punishment of free persons of color remaining within the State in contravention of law.

The following acts were introduced and disposed of as follows, to-wit:

By Mr. Allen—An act appropriating $100,000 to pay the mileage and per diem of the members of the Legislature and the contingent expenses of the two Houses.

This act, under a suspension of the rules, went through its several readings and finally passed.

By Mr. Bush—An act repealing existing laws relative to the carrying of concealed weapons. Referred to the committee on the Judiciary.

By Mr. Drouett—An act authorizing the Judge of the Second District Court of New Orleans to appoint Harriet Rawles as Dative Tutrix of the minor Susan Prieur, on her taking the oath required and furnishing proper security. Referred to the Committee on the Judiciary.

By Mr. Bradley—An act for the relief of Adam Lobell, Sheriff and Tax Collector of the parish of Livingston. Referred to the Committee on Finance.

Mr. Allen offered a resolution allowing each member five daily newspapers, or their equivalent in weeklies, during the session.

Mr. Bradley moved to amend by inserting ten instead of five; and on this, the ayes and nays having been called by Messrs. McLelland and Bradley, resulted ayes 16, nays 40.

This motion was therefore lost, and the resolution adopted in its original form.

The Speaker presented a communication from the Auditor, containing a list of defaulters, and the same was referred to the Committee on Finance.

Mr. Bush introduced an act amendatory of acts incorporating the town of Thibodaux; referred to the Committee on the Judiciary.

On motion, the House adjourned till 10 o'clock to-morrow.

TELEGRAPHIC ITEMS.

THE GEORGIA CONVENTION.

PASSAGE OF THE SECESSION ORDINANCE.

REJOICING THROUGHOUT THE STATE.

The People Delirious With Excitement.

THIRTY-SIXTH CONGRESS—SECOND SESSION.

MILLEDGEVILLE, Jan. 19, P. M.—The ordinance for the immediate secession of the State of Georgia passed to-day, with the following vote: Ayes 208, nays 89; majority 119.

There is great rejoicing throughout the State. Guns are being fired, bells tolled, Lone Star flags unfurled to the breeze, and every manifestation of joy at the welcome verdict.

The Ordinance of Secession.

An ordinance to dissolve the union between the State of Georgia and other States united with her under the compact of Government, entitled "The Constitution of the United States."

WE, the people of the State of Georgia, in Convention assembled, do declare and ordain, and it is hereby declared and ordained, that the ordinance adopted by the people of the State of Georgia in convention assembled in 1788, whereby the Constitution of the United States was assented to, ratified and adopted; also, all acts and parts of acts of the General Assembly ratifying and adopting amendments to said Constitution, are hereby repealed, rescinded and abrogated.

We do further declare and ordain that the Union existing between the State of Georgia and other States, under the name and title of the "United States of America," is hereby dissolved; and that the State of Georgia is in full possession and exercise of all those rights of sovereignty which belong and appertain to a free and independent State.

REJOICING AT AUGUSTA.—*Augusta*, Jan. 19, 10 P. M.—The city is illuminated. Fireworks, the firing of cannon, ringing of bells, etc., are among the manifestations of joy, upon the reception of the news from the capital.

SENATE.—*Washington*, Jan. 19.—Senator Sumner offered a resolution, asking the President for the correspondence between the State Department and any foreign minister, relative to foreign vessels at Charleston; adopted.

The bill providing for the removal of the Red River raft, was made the special order for Thursday next.

The army bill, the bill providing for the payment of the California war debt, and one appropriating five hundred thousand dollars for the suppression of Indian hostilities, passed to-day.

WASHINGTON ITEMS.—*Washington*, Jan. 19.—Lieut. Terry is the challenger of Gen. Harney.

THE TREASURY LOAN.—*Washington*, Jan. 19.—The Treasury loan has reached twelve and a half millions, with an average of 10¼ per cent.

THE LEGISLAURE OF TENNESSEE.—*Time of the Convention fixed.—Nashville*, Jan. 19, 10 P. M.—The Senate has finally agreed to the House convention bill, with an amendment changing the date of the election for Delegates to February.

The convention is to assemble on the 25th of February next. The House has accepted the amendment.

THE MISSOURI LEGISLATURE.—*Passage of the Convention Bill.—St. Louis*, Jan. 19.—The bill providing for a convention of the people has passed both Houses of the Legislature, with the amendment requiring its submission to the people.

MISSISSIPPI STATE CONVENTION

REPORT OF THE COMMITTEE ON SOUTHERN CONFEDERACY.

Mr President—The committee to whom was referred the subject of the formation of a Southern Confederacy have had the same under consideration, and beg leave to make the following report:

In view of all the events of the last month, and the prospect before us, your committee is of opinion that it is a subject which should be acted upon with promptness and decision by the Convention. They furnish conclusive reasons for the necessity of an efficient Government for the seceding States of the late Union, before the 4th day of March next. They are now without a Federal form of Government, and an early and cordial Union among them is needed, to preserve peace, to promote order, to protect rights and avenge wrongs. Both at home and abroad its influence will be felt, and its formation and perfection was the great leading object for which this body was constituted.

To this end the committee recommends the election of seven Delegates to meet with delegates from other States, at Montgomery, Alabama, on the 1st Monday in February, 1861. This time and place meet the views of South Carolina and Alabama, and will dobtless be sanctioned by Florida, Georgia. Louisiana and Texas, and all other Southern States who may hereafter cooperate with us. The number of Delegates recommended is the same as that of our Senators and Representatives in the Congress of the late United States. It is believed that thus while we may secure ability of a varied character, we also avoid the confusion and delay sometimes incident to too large representation in point of numbers.

In the deliberations of such a body as is proposed, your committee think that each State should stand on a footing of perfect equality with every other State, and that each should cast one vote. Each will alike be sovereign, and as equals they should consider, act and unite for the common welfare of all.

For this Convention, your committee have thought it wise to instruct the Delegates to propose the Constitution of the late United States as a basis and outline of a Provisional Government for the seceding States. This instrument is familiar to us all, and while we have seceded from certain Northern political communities which are traitors to its provisions and false to its principles, we still admire the one and are true to the other. It is a guide which can safely be trusted and an adherence to it as far as possible, will lead to that which we now desire—the prompt erection of a Southern Federal Union.

And towards this end of pressing importance, your committee believe it proper that said Delegates should cast the vote of Mississippi for a President and Vice-President, under said Provisional Government. Without a doubt the Delegates who will be selected by this Convention, will be men of tried fidelity and worthy to fill this high trust.

It is proposed that the Provisional Government shall continue a short time and only until a Constitution and permanent plan of Government can be adopted by the intended Convention. As soon as such a plan is matured, it should forthwith be reported back to us by our Delegates for our ratification or rejection.

Your committee is not advised whether it is proper in them to recommend in regard to the nature or character of said Constitution and plan. Yet they will say that, in their opinion, the Constitution of the United States again should be mainly relied on as a precedent. Our experience will, however, suggest some changes to be made as well as some dangers to be avoided. Should the Convention believe it necessary to instruct the Delegates, that object can be obtained either by instructions to this committee to report the same by way of resolution or ordinance, or by way of a direct instruction from the Convention itself.

In conformity with these views we report the following resolutions to the Convention, and recommend their adoption:

CONVENTION RESOLUTIONS.

At a Convention of the people of the State of Mississippi, begun and holden at Jackson, in said State, in the year of our Lord, 1861.

Resolutions to Provide for the Formation of a Southern Confederacy.—We, the people of Mississippi, in Convention assembled, do declare and resolve, and it is hereby declared and resolved:

1st. That this Convention will, on the day of ——, at the hour of ——, proceed to the election, by ballot, of seven Delegates, whose duty it shall be when elected, to represent the State of Mississippi in a Convention of those States which have seceded, or which may hereafter secede, from the Government formerly known as the United States of America.

2d. That this Convention receives and adopts the suggestions that the Convention hereby contemplated shall meet and hold its sessions in the city of Montgomery and the State of Alabama, and that the time for said meeting shall be the first Monday and the 4th day of February, A. D., 1861.

3d. That this Convention accept the suggestion that each of the States seceding from the Government of the late United States, and concurring in the formation of a Southern Confederacy by said Convention, shall be entitled to one vote in the said Convention upon all questions which may be acted upon therein, and that each State send as many Delegates to said Convention as are equal in number to the number of Senators and Representatives to which it was entitled in the Congress of the late United States.

4th. That this Convention instruct said delegates to use all proper means to secure the formation of a Provisional Government of Union for such States as have seceded or may hereafter secede from the Government of the late United States, so as that the same may be organized and go into operation before the 4th of March next, and towards that end they are hereby further instructed to submit to said Convention, on the part of the people of the State of Mississippi, the Constitution of the late United States of America, as a basis and outline of such Provisional Government for the said seceding States; Provided, That said Provisional Government and the tenure of all offices and appointments arising under it shall cease and determine in one year from the first Monday and the fourth day of February, A. D., 1861, or when a Permanent Government shall have been organized as may be agreed upon.

5th. That this Convention do further instruct said delegates that they use all proper means to the end that the convention of said seceding States proceed forthwith to consider and propose a Constitution and plan for a permanent Government, establishing a Southern Confederacy among those States which have seceded or may hereafter secede from the late Federal Union, which Constitution and plan, when adopted, shall be referred back to this convention for its ratification or rejection.

6th. That in the event the convention of seceding States shall not for any cause assemble at the time and place indicated by these resolutions, then the delegates appointed by this convention shall be and they are hereby accreditted to any convention of seceding States which may meet at any other time and place and having for its object the formation of a Southern Confederacy.

An Ordinance concerning the Jurisdiction and Property of the United States of America in the sovereign State of Mississippi.

The people of the State of Mississippi, in convention assembled, declare and ordain, and it is hereby declared and ordained as follows, to wit:

SECTION 1. The title to the waste and unappropriated lands, fortifications, light-houses, hospitals, customhouses, and all other property owned or held by the said United States, within the limits of the State of Mississippi, on the 9th day of January, 1861, and all jurisdiction over the same, are hereby resumed and vested in the State of Mississippi.

SEC. 2. The Legislature shall have power to pass all laws necessary for the preservation and disposition of said lands, fortifications, lighthouses, hospitals, customhouses and other property, and the records pertaining to the same, and may provide for the adjustment of the claim of the said United States thereto.

SEC. 3. The Legislature shall have power to provide by law for the custody and preservation of the records and judicial proceedings of the Circuit and District Court of the United States in this State, and to prescribe the manner in which suits and proceedings, civil and criminal, now pending in said courts, shall be tried and determined, as well as to prescribe the manner in which the judgments of said courts, remaining unexecuted, and the judgments, mandates and decrees of the Supreme Court of the United States, in cases now pending therein, in which a citizen of this State may be a party, shall be carried into effect.

SEC. 4. The judicial power of this State shall extend in cases of admiralty and maratime jurisdiction, and the Legislature shall provide in what courts such jurisdiction shall be exercised.

SEC. 5. Nothing contained herein shall prevent the persons holding the office of Marshal of the United States, and their assistants in this State, from completing the census returns of the said United States.

AN ORDINANCE TO PROVIDE FOR POSTAL ARRANGEMENTS IN MISSISSIPPI.

WHEREAS, It is proper and necessary to avoid, as far as practicable, any disturbance of existing arrangements and contracts for carrying, delivering and distributing the mails; therefore,

The people of Mississippi, in Convention assembled, do ordain and declare, and it is hereby ordained and declared, that all laws, contracts and regulations made by the authority of the United States for conveying, delivering and distributing the mails, and for the protection thereof against depredations which were subsisting and in force at the date of an ordinance adopted by the people of Mississippi, in Convention assembled, on the 9th day of January, one thousand eight hundred and sixty-one, entitled, "An Ordinance to dissolve the Union between the State of Mississippi and the States united with her under the compact entitled 'The Constitution of the United States of America,'" be and the same are hereby continued in full force and effect so far as they are not incompatible with the terms and intent of said Ordinance, or with the provisions hereinafter made; and that persons charged with duties imposed by said contracts and regulations shall continue to discharge the same, and all violations of the penal laws aforesaid shall be prosecuted in the name and by the authority of the State of Mississippi, in the courts of said State having jurisdiction of crimes and misdemeanors in the same manner as other prosecutions are now conducted and determined by the laws of this State.

SEC. 2. *Be it further ordained*, That this Ordinance shall take effect from and after its passage, and shall continue in force until repealed by this Convention, or suspended by such laws or treaties as may be adopted or assented to for that purpose by the State of Mississippi.

ANOTHER JOHN BROWN RAID.—The New York *Herald* learns that John Brown, Jr., son of Old Ossawottomie, has recently been in secret session with some of the Abolitionists in Elmira, New York, and it is rumored that he is working up some plot for another insurrection.

LATEST FROM PENSACOLA.

PROBABLE BLOCKADE OF THE FORT

The Mobile Advertiser, of yesterday morning, announcing the return of the steamer Oregon from Pensacola, says:

We are informed by a gentleman who came over in the Oregon that as the steamer passed out of the harbor, she was in sight of a movement made by the Wyandotte and the revenue cutter, which looks as if the port of Pensacola was in a state of blockade. He says these vessels brought to a full rigged ship, which was standing in, and when the steamer ran them down out of sight the man-of-war and the cutter were lying alongside the merchantman, the latter lying to, with her fore-topsail to the mast. She was evidently in the temporary custody of the men-of-war.

The same informant advises us that when the Oregon ran into the jaws of Pensacola Bay with the troops, who were in the hold and elsewhere to keep them out of sight, the battlements of Fort Pickens were covered with men, the whole force evidently being at quarters for action. It must have been rather a ticklish moment for those on board the Oregon when running under the tremendous and well-manned batteries, which could have consigned them to destruction with a single broadside. The fort was evidently prepared for an attack from the force on the steamer, and would doubtless have fired on her if she had approached as if with the intention of an assault.

AFFAIRS AT THE FORTS AND NAVY YARD.

A passenger by the same steamer also communicates to the *Mercury* the following information as to the actual state of things at the forts and navy yard:

There are now about 1,000 men quartered at the barracks, navy yard, hospital, Forts Barancas and McRea, all of whom are in fine spirits and sanguine of success in ultimately taking Fort Pickens when they shall recieve orders to do so. They have plenty of provisions, arms and amunition, but are needing army engineers and artillerymen. For the lack of these latter, many important advantages are being lost, which, if early improved, will greatly aid in the taking and holding the fort, and especially in cutting off all reinforcements for it.

Fort Pickens is situated on Santa Rosa Island, on the point nearest the channel, and commands the whole of the fortifications. Santa Rosa Island is separated from the main land one and a quarter miles, there being two channels for the passage of vessels, one on the side of the main land and the other on the island side. Fort McRea is on a point of the main land, one half mile from Fort Pickens. Fort Barancas is just opposite Fort Pickens, on the main land, and the Barracks, Hospital and Navy Yard are also on the main land, within range of the guns from Fort Pickens. There are now at the latter fort about 80 men under the command of Lieut. Slimmer. There are already forty guns mounted, and the whole force of the fort is actively engaged in mounting others. They have provisions for six months, and ammunition to resist a siege of equal length. The officer in command declares his intention to hold out to the last, unless he is instructed by the authorities at Washington to give up the fort. Our informant thinks it would be an ugly job to attempt to take the fort with the means now at the command of our forces, but says they declare they will take it if ordered, even at the cost of one thousand men.

Our forces of the forts are under command of Col. Tennant Lomax, of Montgomery, and those at the navy yard are under command of Capt. Randolph, late a captain in the United States Navy.

The workmen who were engaged at the navy yard at the time it was taken possession of by our troops, have been organized into a military company under the command of Capt. Morrell.

Lieut. Slimmer, when he evacuated Fort McRae, destroyed about one hundred and fifty kegs of powder, by knocking out the heads and throwing them into the bay. His object appeared to be only to keep the guns from the fort being opened upon him while he retreated, as he left a large quantity of powder in the magazine. He not only spiked the guns, but rammed down the muzzle the wooden pieces used for stopping them, which had to be bored out by pump borers by our forces before they could be used. They have all been unspiked with the exception of two, and are now ready for use.

When the Oregon left yesterday, Com. Armstrong ran up the lone star flag of Alabama, which was saluted from the navy yard, and was then struck.

The U. S. storeship Supply left yesterday for New York, with the Forward officers and about forty of the sailors and thirty of the marines who were at the yard when taken.

There are a sufficient number of boats at the navy yard to land on the island five hundred troops in half an hour. A large number of sand bags are being made every day to more strongly protect our fortifications.

MORE REINFORCEMENTS FROM MOBILE.—The Oregon, however left Mobile again Thursday evening, with three hundred more troops, volunteers from Mississippi, for Pensacola. She was also to take another hundred from Fort Morgan, which would make a reinforcing force of four hundred. The whole number of volunteers now there, including the Mississippi and Alabama troops, cannot be less than two thousand.

PREPARATIONS FOR A FIGHT.—A special dispatch of Friday evening to the Mobile Advertiser says, "a fight seemes inevitable. We have twenty-five heavy guns mounted and ready for service. We can take Fort Pickens by losing three hundred men."

SHIP ASHORE NEAR FORT PICKENS.—A dispatch, of the same date, to the Tribune reports a ship ashore at Santa Rosa Island, about fifteen miles East of Fort Pickens. The U. S. steamer Wyandotte was alongside of her, and it was thought she might be the U. S. storeship Supply.

LETTER FROM VICE PRESIDENT BRECKINRIDGE.—The following letter has been received by some Baltimore gentlemen, in reply to one written by them, enclosing an article of Tuesday last from the *American's* Washington correspondent signed "F," and calling the Vice President's attention thereto without any comment:

Washington City, Jan. 2, 1861.

Gentlemen—I have your favor of yesterday, in which you call my attention to a letter from the Washington correspondent of the Baltimore American, in which it is stated that I "do not hesitate to openly and decidedly approve the course of your Governor" in refusing to convene the Legislature of Maryland.

My name was used by the letter writer without authority, and his statement is wholly untrue. Your friend and obedient servant,

JOHN C. BRECKINRIDGE.

Hon. J. V. L. McMahon, Peter W. Crane, and Wm Henry Norris, Esq.

THE RICHMOND ENQUIRER ON GEN. SCOTT. The Richmond *Enquirer* of the 3d inst., publishes a letter from Washington, from which we make the following extract:

Many good Southern people have fondly believed that Gen. Scott would propose measures of peace and compromise; but he has come to put an end to all possibility of peaceful accommodation, and to bring the military arm to bear upon the section which rejected him as Presi-

The Philadelphia Inquirer.

ESTABLISHED 1829. | PHILADELPHIA, SATURDAY, JANUARY 26, 1861. | PRICE TWO CENTS.

THE PHILADELPHIA INQUIRER,
PUBLISHED EVERY MORNING, BY
WILLIAM W. HARDING.
INQUIRER BUILDING, 121 SOUTH THIRD ST.

All letters to be addressed to the Publisher.

The daily INQUIRER will be served to subscribers in the City, at the reduced price of TWELVE CENTS a week, payable to the carriers—and mailed to subscribers out of the city at the rate of SIX DOLLARS a year, payable invariably in advance.

The tri-weekly INQUIRER will be mailed to subscribers out of the city on the mornings of Tuesday, Thursday and Saturday of every week, at the rate of FOUR DOLLARS a year, invariably in advance.

☞ Subscribers in the city desirous of paying for the paper by the year in advance can do so at the office.

TERMS—Cash, invariably in advance.

LOCAL INTELLIGENCE.

OUR WESTERN VISITORS.

THE BANQUET IN THEIR HONOR.

Festal Scene at the "Continental."

Liberal Speeches and Union Sentiments.

MERCANTILE HOSPITALITY IN FULL FLOWER.

Our readers have been fully posted on the movements of the delegation from the mercantile communities of the Northwest, now on a visit to this city, by invitation of the Board of Trade. The crowning event of the programme took place last evening, at the Continental. Our guests had previously had their receptions at Independence Hall, the Board of Trade rooms, and the Corn Exchange, and had passed through many of our most palatial stores and largest manufactories, and now they were to be entertained at the festive board by the gentlemen of the mercantile community, many of whom were the recipients of the hospitality of Chicago and Milwaukie, on the excursion of last fall.

The banquet was given at the Continental in a style of magnificence we have rarely seen equalled. The guests numbered about four hundred, representing the most prominent branches of business, together with a few of the professional men of prominence in our community. The banqueting room was just comfortably filled, there being one table extending the full length of the room, and nine other tables extending across the apartment at right angles from it. On the wall appeared a large American flag, and above it were placed the arms of Illinois, Pennsylvania, and Wisconsin. The tables were beautifully adorned with pieces of the finest confectionery, and every delicacy and luxury was provided, and we have never seen such abundance together with an equal proportion of good taste.

The discussion of the viands occupied over two hours, during which the utmost good feeling prevailed on all sides, and an animated conversation, witty repartees and genial interchanges of sentiment were interchanged "under the rose." A merry hum pervaded the hall, over which floated the streams of music, from BECK'S Philadelphia Band, conveniently placed in an ante-room.

HENRY BUDD, Esq., of the Corn Exchange, presided. On his right and left were the Presidents of the Chicago and Milwaukie Board of Trade, and the presiding officers of the Philadelphia City Councils. The following gentlemen acted as Vice Presidents:—

Vice Presidents—SAMUEL E. STOKES and E. C. BIDDLE.

The following gentlemen on the right and left of the President:—

IRA Y. MUNN, President Chicago Board of Trade.
SAMUEL C. MORTON, President Philadelphia Board of Trade.
HORATIO HILL, President Milwaukie Board of Trade.
A. G. CATTELL, President Philadelphia Corn Exchange.
STEPHEN CLAIRY, Chairman Board of Trade Committee of Chicago.
ALEXANDER HENRY, Mayor of Philadelphia.
The Mayor of Milwaukie.
THEODORE CUYLER, President of Philadelphia Select Council.
Commodore CHARLES STEWART, U. S. N.
C. B. TREGO, President Philadelphia Common Council.
J. EDGAR THOMSON, President Pennsylvania Central Railroad.
SAMUEL M. FELTON, President Baltimore and Philadelphia Railroad.
SOLOMON STURGES, merchant, Chicago.
GEORGE WATSON, banker, " "
L. P. HILLIARD, " "
WM. BLAIR, " "
WM. D HOUGHTELING, banker, "
B. CARPENTER, Water Commissioner, Chicago.
Dr. RAUCH, M. D., "
C. H. SPENCER, attorney, "
A. E. KENT, merchant, "
E. A. TUCKER, " "
O. LUNT, " "
C. H. RAY, editor *Tribune*, "
WATSON V. COX, merchant, "
Hon. ROBERT L. WILSON, Judge Recorder's Court, Chicago.
E. W. BLATCHFORD, Lead Works, Chicago.
JULIAN S. RUMSEY, merchant, "
S. N. GOODWIN, attorney, "
JNO. NAZRO, Chairman Committee Board of Trade, Milwaukie.
Gen. RUFUS KING, *Daily Sentinel*, Milwaukie.
J. A. NOONAN, merchant, Milwaukie.
J. W. DURAND, " "
L. H. KELLOGG, " "
DAVID FERGUSON, cashier bank, Milwaukie.
M. D. DENMAN, merchant, Quincy, Ill.
WM. WARDER, merchant, Ohio.
D. MILLER, merchant, Pittsburg.
J. A. WILSON, " "
DAVID S. BROWN, merchant, Philadelphia.
THOMAS NEWLIN, " "
SAMUEL V. MERRICK, Iron works, Vice President Board of Trade, Philadelphia.
M. MCMICHAEL, Editor *North American*, Philadelphia.
MORRIS L. HALLOWELL, merchant, "
WM. B. THOMAS, flour merchant, "
RICHARD PRICE, merchant, "
A. J. BUCKNOR, " "
WM. C. LUDWIG, " "
ED. A. SOUDER, " "

Mr. JOHN E. ADDICKS acted as Chairman of the Committee of Arrangements, and the happy manner in which the banquet passed off reflected no little credit upon his efforts. At half hast nine o'clock Mr. ADDICKS called the company to order.

Mr. BUDD then made a brief address as Chairman, in which he hoped the visitors had found their visit full of pleasure. The brief time of their present visit had not allowed them much opportunity for seeing and appreciating our city, but he hoped that in future they would make visits of greater length and equal pleasure. He would not long detain the company from the eloquence which awaited them, and he would, therefore, without further preface, announce the spicy toast—

1.—Our Guests.—We give them a hearty welcome, and hope the intimacy now formed may last forever.

This toast was responded to by F. AYER, Esq., of Chicago, as follows:—

SPEECH OF MR. AYER.

Mr. President—I rise to respond to this generous sentiment with mingled feelings of gratification and embarrassment. The opportunity afforded me on this festive occasion, in the presence of this large assemblage, comprising so much of the worth and respectability of Philadelphia, of signifying our grateful acknowledgments for these generous hospitalities, and the assiduous kindness and attention with which we have been greeted in your magnificent and delightful city, cannot be otherwise than gratifying. It would be doubly so, were I not disturbed by the painful consciousness of my inability to give adequate expression to the feelings which glow in all our hearts. It required not, Mr. President, the announcement of the sentiment you have just read, nor the enthusiastic applause with which it has been received, to assure us of the cordiality of our welcome here. We knew that well before. Nor is any assurance required from me, I trust, to convince you that we join you heartily in the hope you have expressed that "the intimacy now formed may abide forever."

The object of our visit here we conceive to be highly laudable and important. Most of us are, like yourselves, engaged in mercantile and commercial pursuits. Our two sister cities of Chicago and Milwaukie are, as you well know, the commercial centres of a vast and fertile tract of country devoted to the production of breadstuffs. My own city of Chicago has been for some years the largest primary grain market in the world, and in this respect Milwaukie is now, if I am not mistaken, second only to Chicago. The population of this great productive region is steadily and rapidly augmenting. Thousands of additional acres are brought into cultivation every successive season, and our surplus products must of course, as a general thing, keep steady pace with the progress of population and agricultural improvement. With these two cities you are now immediately and permanently connected by a continuous line of excellent railway.

Your city, so finely and centrally situated on the tide waters of the Atlantic, has become a great manufacturing, as well as a great commercial mart. You are located in the immediate vicinity of one of the richest mineral regions in the world. You have capital, and enterprise, and sagacity, and all the requisite facilities for building up here an immense and profitable commerce with the Northwest. We need your manufactures. We need, also, every year, a vast amount of your imported wares. We have grain to send you in abundance, and you can make for it here a ready market. Under these circumstances, it seems to us that no reason of an insuperable character can exist why an extensive and mutually profitable commercial intercourse cannot be established between us. To promote this object is, as you are well aware, the principal occasion of this visit.

Apart, however, Mr. President, from mere business considerations, there are other excellent reasons which might be suggested to justify this interchange of civilities. While we are anxious to preserve, and if possible, to increase and strengthen those commercial ties which have heretofore existed between you and us, we are also gratified at this opportunity of exchanging friendly salutations with our brethren of this ancient and time-honored commonwealth. We would cultivate with you those amicable and fraternal feelings which ought always to be cherished between the people of all the States composing our hitherto happy and prosperous Union. At this alarming and dangerous crisis, when some of our sister States are madly repudiating their constitutional obligations, and the Federal Government is menaced with destruction, it becomes those who remain loyal to the Constitution, to take temperate counsel together, and consider what can be done to allay sectional discord, to heal existing difficulties, and bring back the people of the disaffected States to the observance of their constitutional duties. If they have suffered any real injuries, let the cause of those injuries be removed.

If they have any real grievances of which to complain, let those grievances be redressed. If they entertain actual and serious alarm as to their future safety or the security of their rights under the Constitution, let all just and reasonable guarantees be given them that not one of those rights shall ever be invaded. Thus may we hope, by amicable means, to perpetuate this glorious Union, and preserve our country from the terrible calamities which must result from a hostile conflict between section and section.

Mr. President, we are not politicians, but men engaged in the peaceful and honorable pursuits of private life, having no further interest in public affairs than the laudable desire of maintaining the government established by our fathers, and securing always a wise, prudent and faithful administration of it. We are all true, I trust, to the Constitution and the Union, and would esteem that man as worthy of little honor who would not make some sacrifice to preserve them.

While, Mr. President, I avow these sentiments, which I trust are not liable to any just censure, as being partisan in their character, it is, perhaps, not improper for me to add, that I have seen no sufficient cause to justify the rash and revolutionary course which the disaffected States have seen fit to pursue. In this connection, a sentiment uttered by Mr. WEBSTER, in a speech delivered in this city in 1846, is not unworthy of repetition. "It may have happened," he said, "I think it has happened, on more than one occasion, that the spirit of the Constitution has been departed from; that serious violations of that spirit have taken place. What of that? Are we to abandon it on that account? Are we to abandon it? Why, I should as soon think," he said, "of abandoning my own father when ruffians attacked him. No! we are to rally around it with all our power and all our force, determined to stand by it or fall with it."

Mr. President, in conclusion I beg leave to offer the following sentiment:—

The City of Philadelphia—The abode of comforts, intelligence and refinement—the seat of industry, skill and enterprise—the birthplace of American Independence and of American Constitutional Liberty—We honor her for her loyalty to the Union, and trust that her counsels may aid in restoring peace to a distracted country. (Cheers.)

The second regular toast was:—

2.—The Great Northwest, the granary of the world.—We discover in the magnificence of her products and the spirit of her sons the promise of a glorious and ever brightening future.

General KING, of Milwaukie, responded to this toast in a speech full of eloquence and good feeling, and imbued with a strong Union spirit. He was loudly applauded.

The next regular toast was:—

3.—Chicago, the metropolis of the Northwest—the focus of enterprise and activity. She has called into existence the immense and dormant capabilities of vast regions, enriching, by her efforts, both East and West. (Great applause.)

This was responded to by Mr. J. P. CLARKSON, Esq., of Chicago:—

SPEECH OF MR. CLARKSON.

Gentlemen of the Board of Trade and Commerce of the City of Philadelphia—The honor and the pleasure have devolved upon me of responding on behalf of the city of Chicago and her representatives, to the sentiment you have just proposed. In doing so, it would scarcely be regarded as well timed or becoming in me, and I therefore do not propose to indulge in any eulogium or glorification of our young city, however worthy it might be of it, and however dear it is to us as the home of our adoption. Expressions of laudation will come with more fitness from some one who is not one of her citizens.

We thank you sincerely for the flattering language you have used with regard to her, and the more because we are vain enough to allow ourselves to believe that your language expresses the sentiments of your heart. For the rest, we are content that the city of Chicago shall write her own record. She has not thus far "hid her light under a bushel." She has told her past story well to the world, and we confidently trust that she will tell it well in the future.

The few words which I shall say shall, therefore, be rather *for* Chicago than *of* her, and I desire, in her name, to acknowledge her grateful appreciation of the courtesy on your part which is the occasion of the presence of her representatives amongst you at this time.

Thus far our visit has been one of unmixed gratification. At our first entrance into your beautiful State we were greeted by the citizens of Pittsburg with a cordiality which we shall not soon forget. We passed twenty-four hours with them amidst the smoke and din of the splendid manufactories which evidence their industry and their enterprise; and each moment opened to us a new scene of interest and delight. We met them comparative strangers, and left them with the warmth of old friendship. Sweeping over your noble Alleghenies, and speeding along your beautiful rivers, we came to you, at your request, with heartfelt satisfaction to exchange with you here the grasp of brotherly love.

Although to many of us your city and your faces are not familiar, yet the cordial welcome which you gave us has made us all feel now as though our acquaintance had been one of years instead of hours. Allow me then, gentlemen, in the name of the city of Chicago, one of whose delegates I am proud to be in this splendid monument of your enterprise, at this, the brilliant close of your public civilities to us, once more we thank you, from the bottom of our hearts, for the attentions and courtesies which, throughout our entire visit, have been so lavishingly bestowed upon us.

Chicago is no stranger to Philadelphia. It is but a short time since her merchants had the honor and gratification of entertaining a deputation from your number. It was even to them of a peculiarly interesting character. It was the inauguration of a new epoch in the history of our youthful city—we, scarcely out of our teens, so young that men in active business amongst us, in the prime of life, whose hairs are not yet frosted, have seen her both in her infancy and her development into early manhood; and yours, a city venerable and time-honored, proudly occupying a well merited position amongst the first in the new world. True, travelers had told, and the newspapers had published that the little trading post which, hardly a quarter of a century ago, feebly raised its head in the midst of a wild waste on the borders of Lake Michigan, had grown to be a large and thriving city.

But it was a matter as well of pride as of pleasure to us that you, dating back the beginning of your history to a period far beyond the memory of men now living, should have thought it worth your while to send a deputation representing the intelligence, the industry and the wealth of your city in the far West, to see whether what you had heard and read of us was indeed true, and to bid us God speed in our advances to prosperity and distinction.

You came amongst us. You saw with your own eyes, and heard with your own ears. You found, widely spread out upon the shores of our beautiful lake, the tramp and hum of a great and populous city. You saw on every side immense granaries, bursting with the accumulated products of our fruitful soil; wharves burdened with the wealth of our mighty Western forests, and streets and waters alive with the rush of busy and successful commerce.

We believed that you were both surprised and gratified with your visit. We have had no reason to change that belief since, and it is confirmed now by the manifestations upon your part of that friendly feeling which has induced our presence here.

We trust, gentlemen, that the interchange of civilities then begun—now continued—may never cease; that community of interests may accompany community of feeling, and that along the iron pathway which now so directly and intimately connects the two cities you shall send to us the products of your labor and skill, and shall bring back, in return from us, the fruits which spring in such luxuriant profusion from the teeming bosoms of our vast and fertile prairies.

Gentlemen—Reciprocal exchanges of fraternal good-will like the present, are always pleasing and beneficial to all concerned; but it is especially appropriate that ours should occur at this time, and in this place, of all others—now, when there is so much in the present condition and prospects of our common country to fill us with apprehension; and here, on this holy ground, this spot hallowed by so many solemn and thrilling associations of the past, and almost under the shadow of that edifice, your own priceless inheritance, which witnessed the birth of our Union, and where our glorious banner was first flung proudly to the sun in honor of the new and independent nation.

Chicago is singularly cosmopolitan. We fraternize in the rights and privileges of citizenship with nations of almost every country on the face of the globe. Amongst our most active and enterprising citizens are men whose homes are, or until recently were, in Maryland, Virginia, North Carolina, Kentucky, Tennessee, Missouri, and almost all the other Southern States. Many of us cherish the mighty Empire State as their loved "Alma Mater."—The dear family firesides of very many are in old New England, whilst hundreds of us, (and I thank God that I am able to add that I am among the number,) point with affection and pride to the hearthstones of our infancy upon the hills and in the valleys of your own noble Pennsylvania, the Keystone of the Arch; and in the delegation itself whom she has sent, on her behalf, to be the recipients of your hospitality, are gentlemen from the North and the South, the East and the West.

It is not, then, strange that the people of Chicago hold, as their brethren in language, in nationality, in blood, and in affection, every citizen of these United States.

Spurning from us all partisan and sectional animosities, recognizing no geographical lines of separation, we, of the great States of Illinois and Wisconsin,—speaking, too, for the entire Northwest,—desire here, on this spot of all others dear to the American heart, to record our unswerving and unalterable devotion—in heart and hand and fortune—to the welfare, the maintenance, and the perpetuity of the Union of the States.

God forbid that erring fanaticism or misguided ambition, from whatever quarter, should precipitate any irreparable sundering of the ties that have for so long bound us all together in a confederation, at once the admiration and the wonder of the whole civilized world, but rather let us unite in the sentiment—

> "The union of lakes, the union of lands!
> The Union of States none should sever;
> The union of hearts, the union of hands,
> And the flag of the Union forever!"

After the cordial applause at the close of this eloquent address, had ceased, the fourth toast was read, and received with great cheering:—

4.—Milwaukie—the worthy sister of Chicago; hospitable, vigorous and successful, we rejoice in her prosperity, continually increased.

Mr. JOHN NAZRO, of Milwaukie, responded as follows:—

SPEECH OF JOHN NAZRO.

Mr. President and Gentlemen of the Philadelphia Board of Trade:—It becomes my pleasing duty to respond to the sentiment just offered. I feel highly honored in having this privilege extended to me to answer in behalf of our city and in presence of so distinguished an assembly as the merchants of Philadelphia, and from the fact, Mr. President, of this being the city in which was passed the early life of my honored mother. The complimentary manner in which you have seen fit to refer to our city, and the kind and unlimited extension of your generous hospitality, meets in our hearts a warm response, and words are inadequate to express to you our most sincere thankfulness.

Milwaukie, as you well know, Mr. President, is situated on the western shore of Lake Michigan. In 1833 the first white inhabitant erected his solitary hut in the midst of Indian wigwams and hostile Indian tribes. Soon after, others began to seek their fortunes in the then far West, and in 1840 its population had increased to 1700. In 1847, the year in which myself emigrated from Massachusetts, that time-honored State, to seek my fortune in the far West, and take my chances with those who were struggling for advancement, Milwaukie contained about 9000, and from that period to the present time she has continued to advance in population, wealth and enterprise, until at this day she contains a thriving, industrious and energetic population of upwards of 50,000, composed of all nationalities, the Teutonic, Celtic, and in fact, Mr. President, I could say with truthfulness, she contains a fair representation from all parts of Europe, and many other parts of the world, and she will be ever ready to extend the right hand of fellowship and a hearty welcome within her borders to all who love and appreciate the principles of right, justice and humanity—love to God and love to man.

In 1852 the pioneer railroad was commenced, and at that time it was considered a doubtful enterprise. What has been the result since. We have now two complete lines of railroad, connecting the shores of Lake Michigan with the Father of Waters, with five other lines partially completed, and a steamboat connection, open at all seasons of the year, with the eastern shore of Lake Michigan, giving us an outlet for our products in midwinter.

Thus you see, Mr. President, we cannot be hemmed in, but shall go on and reap all the advantages which nature, prosperity and enterprise give to us.

You would naturally ask what foundation have we to sustain our future growth. I would point you to the golden fields of Iowa, Minnesota and Wisconsin, three great northwestern States, pouring their immense products into the lap of the fair white City of the Lakes, Milwaukie, the commercial emporium of Wisconsin, the natural outlet of these granaries of the West. I would call your attention for a moment to the exports of grain from our city for the past four years to show you what you may expect to see in the future. We exported of our surplus, in 1857, 4,000,000 bushels of wheat and flour reduced to wheat; in 1858, 6,000,000; in 1859, 7,000,000; in 1860, 10,000,000; in 1861 we expect to reach 15,000,000 bushels. Our reports of wheat and flour are now nearly, if not quite, equal to our enterprising sister of Chicago. Milwaukie has her common schools, her high schools, and other places of learning. By the wise forethought of the early settlers of Wisconsin, we have a school fund, second to none in the Union. Great attention is being paid to education, the great bulwark of freedom and civilization.

The wholesale trade of Milwaukie is increasing rapidly and, in face of all the commercial drawbacks for the past three years, it has been larger the past year than any previous one in her history.

Many of us, Mr. President, already have had the honor of commercial intercourse with your merchants, and I hope this visit may be the means of bringing us more frequently together, and of resulting to our mutual benefit. Mr President, I cannot permit this opportunity to pass without referring to your own noble State. My own business brings me in closer connection with you than any other delegate from the western cities—the manufacture of iron, that great staple of your commercial prosperity.

Many of our delegation are strangers to the manufacturing interests of your State, and have expressed their astonishment and surprise, and their infinite pleasure on viewing its extent and perfectness. You may well be proud of your sister city of Pittsburg as an evidence of certain wealth and prosperity, which is sure to follow when the manufacturing interests of a city and State is nourished and protected. Look at your own city, full of manufactories, the evidence of solid wealth everywhere, and the result of a full appreciation of the advantages by which you are surrounded.

Time will not permit me to occupy your attention any longer.

I must again, in behalf of the city of Milwaukie, and of the delegates here present, return to you our most heartfelt thanks for your very generous hospitality during our stay in your city, and trust the time may not be far distant when we may have the opportunity to return in part your kindness, and I extend to you now a hearty welcome to the commercial emporium of the Badger State.

In conclusion, Mr. President, permit me to offer the following sentiment:—

The State of Pennsylvania—She has within her borders the keystone to wealth, prosperity and happiness.

When the cheers which had frequently interrupted the progress of this address had ceased, the Chairman read the next sentiment, as below:—

5.—Philadelphia—the City of Brotherly Love. She seeks, by her iron bands, to unite herself permanently with her sister cities of the Northwest, and, upon this occasion, pledges to them her everlasting friendship.

THEODORE CUYLER, Esq., President of Select Council, responded in an address, brief, though full of eloquence and pith. It was loudly cheered on all sides.

The next sentiment was received with round after round of cheers, which seemed to increase in intensity for several minutes. It was as follows:—

6.—The Union!

The Star Spangled Banner was then sung in grand style by Mr. HUNNAKER, the vocalist, the entire company joining in cheering it and in keeping up the chorus.

The next sentiment was then given out:—

7.—The Breadstuffs Trade.—The Executive Power which dispenses the products of the soil and scatters them broadcast over a needy world. It is its sublime province to feed the hungry.

The reponse to this sentiment was by Mr. A. G. CATTELL. It was most enthusiastically applauded for its matter and its spirit.

The next sentiment was as subjoined:—

8.—Manufactures.—The just source of Philadelphia's pride; the enduring trophies of our industrial success; the permanent foundation of civic greatness.

REMARKS OF MR. MILLIKEN.

Mr. JAMES MILLIKEN, in answer to this toast, rose and said:—

Mr. Chairman and Gentlemen—The pride of Philadelphia in her manufactures is well grounded in their extent, and excellence in their commercial, social and political value. I speak by the book when I say that, in textile fabrics of every description, this city and its environs is the centre of a production larger than any other county in the Union. In iron work, our locomotive, marine and stationary engines, our railroad car-wheels and architectural castings, and all the multiform articles of household convenience, and of objects of vertu, hold the highest rank for quality and quantity; and especially in those tools and machines by which iron is shaped into all forms of use, like clay in the hands of the potter, do we particularly excel. Our cutlery, embracing the articles in common use by mechanics, asks no odds against the productions of Europe.

Philadelphia is the best ticket upon a hand-saw, or a drawing-knife, in a London hardware store, and our edge tools have now the market of Canada. Five years ago, the master cutler at Sheffield Hall, admitting the American triumph, accounted for it by saying that we use better steel. The true explanation is in the better material, the better machinery used in the manufacture, and above all, in the better character and condition of our workmen.

The great West, represented here to-night by your guests, knows the style of Philadelphia art in ornamental silver, gold and bronze work. Every agricultural fair of the Mississippi valley that bestows premiums liberally in the precious metals, appreciates and advertises it; and the South and southwest, unhappily not represented here to-night, hold as much of our handiwork of this kind as they could afford to buy in happier times, and more, mayhap than they can well preserve intact when their secretary of the treasure touches them up on the finances. By the time they are fairly in the hands of COBB at home and CORDEN abroad, I fear their plate will go in a lump into the patriotic melting pot.

We are no less distinguished as manufacturers of chemicals, carriages, agricultural implements, elegant furniture, clothing, and whatsoever else of use and luxury the civilization of the age demands. Standing as we do in the commercial focus of the iron and coal beds of Pennsylvania, with a system of internal communication with the granaries of the great West, and having direct and easy access to the raw materials for every form of fabrics that enter into common use, our energy and enterprise are invited, sustained and rewarded.

This success of Philadelphia is explained by her physical circumstances. The detailed proofs of her achievement may be found in the forthcoming statistical report of the able and intelligent Secretary of our Board of Trade, or may be inferred from the signs that are obvious to the most ordinary attention. This is not the time nor the place to load down the declarations with its proofs. Figures are more apt, when they run into millions, to overwhelm the understanding than to inform or convince it—more apt to weary attention than to entertain it.

I forbear, being determined to win that applause for what I do not say, which I shall probably deserve to lose for what I do say. I offer you this compromise, if you and this company will meet me with an equal concession. I will proceed; if not I will secede, after the high examples which I need not name; that is, after I shall have done my very best to break up the happy confederacy which now now surrounds this festive board. I am driven to compromise on this point because it is vain to attempt an inventory of our diversified manufactures; the index would exhaust the alphabet.

It would run through arms, alcohol, axes and anchors; boots, books, boats and fresh butter; clocks, cotton, cordage, crinoline and carpets; daguerreotypes, doctors, dollars and dinner speeches; everything elegant and everything else; flour, friction matches and forte pianos; gas, glass, glue and ground plaster; hats, hollow ware, hoops and hosiery; iron, India rubber and Declaration of Independence; jellies, jewelry and old junks; lamp black, leather, lead pipes, and lager; maps, marble monuments and political moderation; newspapers, but no nutmegs nor nonsense; opulence, oratory and civic orations to our friends out West; paints, paper, and political economy; quick lime, Quakers, and no wrangles but quadrangles; city railroads refinement and restoration of the Missouri Compromise; saddlery, common schools and anti-secessionists; telegraphic apparatus, tip-top tailor's "rhymes" (vide the Band of Tower Hall), and sound territorial adjustments; umbrellas and unfaltering devotion to the Union; vitriol, vinegar and vox populi; whips, wires (with the workers thrown in), wit and Wistar parties X, double X, and triple X pale ale, *ex*tended credits and *ex*tensive domestic *ex*changes; yarns, long and twisted, and yearnings for the good old times of yore. But I shall spare you the further pursuit of this zigzag rehearsal, least it lose its zest, before it runs down to zero.

The sentiment proposed proceeds to assume and assert that manufacturers of the rank and magnitude of ours secure our civic greatness, and hold the trophies won by an enduring tenure. I heartily concur. I think this confidence is equally well based in experience and in reason. The cities of the old world and the olden time, that have declined and perished, were either mere political capitals or exclusively commercial, or if manufacturing, as those of India, have suffered themselves to be overslaughed by greatly improved methods and agencies of converting science and skill.

A popular revolution can overturn a kingdom, a court and its capitol; for those who live upon tribute are themselves tributaries to power in the hand that grasp it. And a city of mere exchanges must sink into ruin whenever commerce, in its unsteadiness, finds new channels. But as husbandry recovers itself instantly from a season of drought, or the waste of invading armies, because it lives by the soil that retains its fruitfulness, so the city that lives by its own productive industry, has the creative power always in waiting, to restore and repair all damages when the storm has blown by.

Men may be conquered and killed, but their industrial arts survive. Their achievements remain as imperishable monuments for them, and imperishable forces for their survivors.

If Philadelphia were conquered by an army of barbarians, her machinery, with its comforts, would become necessities to her captors, and would conquer them.

Vandals may destroy the products of the fine arts, and reject the literature and philosophy of civilization; but the water works, the railroads, the engines, the mechanical machinery of an industrial community holds the rudest ravagers in dependence, and renders the science and skill of its engineers and artisans necessary to the victor and puts him into subjection.—Against the fluctuations of commerce, and the revolutions of government, the apparatus of the useful arts is equally resistant; business convulsions temporarily check its prosperity by calling off all that surplus of employment which happier times afford. But *its* occupation is not gone. Consumption still sustains supply as long and as far as labor of one kind, or its productions, are exchanged for those of another. While summer and winter, seedtime and harvest continue, and the earth holds its place in its orbit, the agriculturist, the fisherman and the miner will have that which will purchase and repay the labor of the artisan, and maintain his welfare and prosperity. Monetary revolutions that check and punish overtrading can temporarily abate the onward progress of the mechanic's wealth, but cannot shake the foundations of his reliance

A city with its territory all covered with buildings and pavements has no resource against foreign influence in the soil it holds. That grows nothing but rents and taxes, but with a wealth-producing skill and capital, its harvest is just as secure as the husbandman's, and even less dependent upon sunshine and fair weather.

Moreover, a great city, with thoroughly diversified productive or creative industry, supplies all its own needs except material and provisions, which it can always command, as surely as labor exchanges for labor, and products for products.

If Charleston lose her maritime commerce but a few years, she is irretrievably ruined. If Philadelphia were shut out from the sea, and all her banks were broken to boot, after the shock had spent its fury upon the trade and credit that was so interrupted, she would be self-sustaining and comfortable. India, Australia, Turkey, Egypt and Brazil already supply England with one-third of the cotton she consumes.

In thirty years the cotton exports of the South have risen from thirty millions of dollars' worth to one hundred and sixty millions, increasing four fold in quantity in that brief space. The effort which is now making in Europe for the increased cultivation of the staple in foreign lands may, in twenty years, fully meet the foreign demand.

But a city or a State depending upon those forms of production, which cannot thus be overrun by new enterprises, opened elsewhere, may well regard their industries in the language of the sentiment announced as the enduring, the only enduring trophies of success, the only permanent foundation of civic greatness.

Mr. MILLIKEN was loudly cheered throughout his able address.

The next toast was then read:—

9.—The Lake Trade.—Without a parallel in past experience. It tasks our imagination to appreciate its grandeur, and holds up its splendid prizes to competing States.

ADDRESS OF MR. KIMBER.

Mr. KIMBER, after expressing the pleasure with which he added his humble tribute to the honors of the guests of the evening, proceeded:—

For five or six years past, as chairman of the Inland Navigation Committee of our Board of Trade, it has been my lot to investigate the statistics of this great internal commerce, and thus, in some measure, to appreciate its wonderful growth and almost inconceivable magnitude.

Six hundred millions of dollars was the vast aggregate of the trade of all the ports of the lakes in 1856; and that of 1860, notwithstanding the decline in values, will doubtless be still greater.

$600,000,000!!! Why, Mr. Chairman, or gentlemen, did it ever occur to you to try to realize or to estimate that great sum?

It was a favorite saying of CANNING'S, that "There is nothing so false in the world as facts—except *statistics*." But let us look at the figures. They are within the reach of every one. Suppose this vast sum were invested in flour, at the market price of Chicago the past season—$4·50 per barrel—and we could range the barrels endwise, touching one another, do you know that you would have a line more than fifty thousand miles long; that you could encircle this globe with it more than *twice*, at its greatest diameter; that the swiftest bird could not fly over it in two months, flying at the rate of a mile a minute, from sunrise to sunset, in the longest weeks of the year.

Or, suppose the most accurate and accomplished bank teller were to attempt to pay off this vast tribute in gold dollars.

Let him commence on the day of his manhood's maturity, and let him count down with unerring precision, and unfailing strength, one dollar a second, telling every second in the minute, every minute of the hour, and ten hours a day for every working day of the year. Have you ever considered that his hand would be withered and trembling, his hair thin and white, and that he would have passed the limits of the life of man, threescore and ten years, before he had counted down the last dollar; that two generations of his fellow-men would have passed away, and more than half a century have closed over the graves of two thousand millions of his race while he was completing his mighty work? And if, for a moment, we attempt to estimate the enormous aggregate which this lake commerce would have that day reached—increasing as it is doing, with almost geometrical progression—the human mind recoils, confused and confounded, before a task possible to the Infinite alone.

But there is one remarkable feature of the lake trade which has come more immediately under my own observation of late years, to which I would like for a moment to call the attention of our friends at Chicago and Milwaukie, who are large shippers of grain and produce to the Atlantic markets. I allude to that remarkable law of trade by which the greatest facilities are afforded to westward bound shipments at extremely low rates, at the very time when freights eastward are the highest, and the trade in that direction most active.

This is more particularly the case with Coal and Iron; which, from a high rate of freight to Chicago five years ago, have been gradually carried at lower and lower prices each year, until during the past season the agents of the road in my charge have actually shipped largely iron and anthracite coal in ballast, paying merely to the vessel the cost of loading and unloading; and towards the close of the season even this expense was remitted, so anxious were the owners to hasten back, in order to secure the rich eastward freights.

Surely if this fact were more generally known, both in the Western and in the Eastern markets, it could not fail vastly to increase the traffic in these indispensable articles, thus laid down, as by the wand of a magician, noiselessly and freely, at the very doors of Western civilization and commerce, from the dark and rocky caverns of their native State.

But time would fail me to speak of other characteristic features of this great internal commerce; of the wonderful fact of the rich iron ore of Lake Superior being now brought to Buffalo, for manufacture in competition with iron of our own State; of the gradual tendency of the far Western trade towards Oswego, and the northern ports of New York on Lake Ontario; of the vast commerce suddenly created by the reciprocity treaty with the Canadas and the British provinces, amounting as it now does to $50,000,000 per annum.

I should like to have said a word, too, about the happy prospect of an early opening by way of the Sunbury and Erie road, of another great channel between Philadelphia and the great Lakes.

In conclusion, however, Mr. Chairman, I beg to give utterance to one impression which has been made on my mind, more deeply than any other, in contemplating these vast inland seas: and that is the conviction of their permanence—their unchanging, their almost eternal stability. What Lord BYRON has so beautifully said of the ocean, may well be spoken of them:—

"Time writes no wrinkle on their azure brow."

And now, gentlemen of the Northwest, if the storms that seem to threaten our beloved country shall not be stayed or turned aside by a higher and mightier Power; if the Cotton States, with all their vast and vaunted commercial exchanges are to leave us; if the Gulf of Mexico is to become to us a closed and foreign sea; if the golden gates of the Mississippi are to be bolted down, and its channels locked up to your magnificent commerce—thank God, we shall still have you and your majestic waters, forever *free* and open to us, and to you, and to all the world; that these glorious waters, drawing their farthest supplies from the tallest peaks of the Rocky Mountains, and those from Heaven, shall ever flow toward us, and to us, in one pure, deep, unfailing, unbroken and eternal current—fit emblem of that feeling which unites us all here this evening; and which, I hope and pray, may ever unite Philadelphia with the great Northwest.

The next toast was as below:—

10.—The Railroad System—Annihilating space and time.—It acts morally as well as physically; it binds together the hearts, the bodies, and the fortunes of our countrymen.

Mr. T. S. FARNUM responded in an energetic and spirited address, which was cordially applauded throughout.

The next toast was in the following words:—

11.—The Distributing Trade of Philadelphia.—The life from which fills the arteries of our commerce, and sends a healthy stream through all its veins.

MORTON MCMICHAEL, Esq., responded to this sentiment in ono of his most felicitous speeches. It was listened to with great interest, and frequently interrupted by rounds of applause.

The two next toasts were as follows. They were appropriately responded to:—

11.—The Lake Trade.—Without a parallel in past experience. It tasks our imagination to appreciate its grandeur, and holds up its splendid prizes to competing States.

Music—"Sail, Sail by the Midnight Gale."

12.—The Press.—The Intellectual Illuminator of the Age. May its light be ever clear and brilliant.

The concluding regular toast was—

13.—Woman. Heaven's last, best gift to man.

SPEECH OF D. DOUGHERTY, ESQ.

Mr. DOUGHERTY was peremptorily called for, and compelled to respond, which he did in the following graceful manner:—

Indeed, Mr. Chairman and gentlemen, I would have much preferred remaining a quiet sharer of this joyous scene than even the recipient of the honor now tendered—of responding to the toast complimentary to those to whom all true men own loving allegiance; whose golden chains, forged in the furnace of the heart, riveted in the dear days of life's young dreams, will ever clank in music round us until all is silent in the solemn stillness of the tomb. (Long continued applause.)

I trust that I too well know the proprieties of this festive occasion to descant at length even upon such a charming theme. To think of woman is to think of home—to think home is to think of country. (Vociferous applause.) And thus in one thought are blended the three dearest treasures upon earth. We live to enjoy them. We will die to defend them. (More applause.) In these degenerate days men prate of sections and of States. Our fair countrywomen, with a vivid remembrance of the revolution, true to the glories of the past, faithful to the mandates of the great Father of his Country, do not circumscribe their patriotism by artificial lines, but let it expand with generous emotions, until it embraces the *whole* of the republic, which God ever preserve! (Deafening applause.)

There are at least two places which every American can call his home. One is in our midst, and to which our welcome guests were yesterday escorted. I mean, of course, old Independence Hall. (Applause.) The other is the spot where repose the ashes of the dead WASHINGTON. Independence Hall and Mount Vernon are, and ever will be, the common property of all Americans. They cannot be torn into fragments, that each citizen may claim a share. (Applause.) The men of Pennsylvania will, with their lives, preserve the first for all their countrymen. The women of America, aye, led on by the matron of South Carolina, have purchased the last, and bequeathed it forever as the common heritage of the nation.

The festivities were kept up to a very late hour, and the speaking was interspersed with music from the band, which appeared to be highly enjoyed by all the participants. Nothing occurred to mar the pleasures of the evening, and the gentlemen from the West made the strongest expressions of eulogy in regard to the management of the entire excursion, and in particular the banquet, which thus delightfully closed the programme.

ANNUAL MEETING.—The Philadelphia Society for Alleviating the Miseries of Public Prisons, held its seventy-fifth annual meeting on Thursday evening last, and elected the following officers to serve the ensuing year:—

President—JAMES J. BARCLAY.
Vice Presidents—Townsend Sharpless, Dr. Wm. Shippen.
Treasurer—Edward H. Bonsall.
Secretaries—Wm. Parker Foulke, John J. Lytle.
Counsellors—Henry J. Williams, Saml. H. Perkins.
Members of the Acting Committee—Frederick A. Packard, Charles Ellis, Wm. S. Perot, Thos. Latimer, John M. Wetherill, Samuel Caley, Abram C. Brown, Benjamin H. Pitfield, John Horton, Isaac Barton, Richard Williams, James E. Kaighn, Alfred H. Love, Jeremiah Willits, William H. Burr, Jacob T. Bunting, John C. Farr, George Taber, Wm. Kederlen, Mahlon H. Dickinson, William Ingram, James Peters, Joseph Keen, Robert E. Evans, Albert H. Franciscus, Wm. R. McAdam, William Chapman, George Bringhurst, Charles Palmer, Charles P. Perot, William H. Dennis, Charles C. Lathrop, Thomas A. Robinson, Samuel Emlen, William Dorsey, George Vaux.

THE THIRD CONGRESSIONAL DISTRICT CASE.—The investigation of the ballot boxes of the Third Congressional District, in connection with the contest between Messrs. KLINE and VERREE, so far shows a gain of eighteen votes for Mr. VERREE, over the majority returned.

FORT SUMTER, CHARLESTON HARBOR, IN POSSESSION OF MAJOR ANDERSON.

The attention of the whole country is directed to this fortification, and the interest is becoming more and more intensified from the fact that a Commissioner from the State of South Carolina is at this moment in Washington, to demand a peaceful surrender of Fort Sumter to the State authorities. It is hardly likely that the President will accede to that demand, and it is understood that if it is refused, the people of South Carolina have determined to take it at any risk and at any cost.

We believe them to be terribly in earnest, and have no doubt that, as a last resource, they will bring every available force to bear in the endeavor to effect its capture. Whether they have commanding force enough in artillery to wrench it from its present occupants is a question which time alone can decide. The courage of the assailers cannot be called in question, and should an attack be made, the encounter will be obstinate and bloody. God grant that it may never take place! The following will give our readers an idea of the strength of Fort Sumter:—

It is built on an artificial island, immediately within the mouth of Charleston bay, between Fort Moultrie and the site of old Fort Johnson, of Revolutionary memory, and equidistant from those points about three-fourths of one mile. The ship channel leading from the sea to the city of Charleston is between Forts Sumter and Moultrie, and is entirely commanded within half range by them. Between Forts Sumter and Johnson the water is very shallow, only available for vessels of very light draft, and then only at high water. The artificial island on which Fort Sumter is built is constructed of the refuse from the granite quarries of New England. Ten years were consumed in its completion, at a cost of half a million of dollars. The fortification is of a pentagonal form, built of solid brick masonry. The walls are fifty feet in height, and from eight to ten feet in thickness, and are pierced for three tiers of guns, besides having necessary loop-holes for musketry, and designed for an armament of one hundred and forty pieces of ordinance of all calibres. Two tiers of the guns are under bomb proof casements, and the third or upper tier open, or, in military parlance, *en barrette*—the lower tier for forty-two-pounder Paixhan guns; the second tier for eight and ten-inch Columbiads, for throwing solid or hollow shot, and the upper tier for mortars and twenty-four-pound guns.

Daily Advocate.

J. M. TAYLOR & TOM BYNUM.
EDITORS AND PROPRIETORS.

SUNDAY MORNING, JAN. 27, 1861.

INDEPENDENT LOUISIANA

THE SECESSION ORDINANCE PASSED!

Only Seventeen Noes!!!

THE PELICAN FLAG UNFURLED!

The proceedings of the State Convention on Saturday the 26th of January mark an era in the history of the Commonwealth of Louisiana. On that day the representatives of the sovereignty of the State, ten minutes before the hour of 2 o'clock, P. M., declared and ordained the separation of Louisiana from the Government entitled the "United States of America." During the vote on the Ordinance the most solemn and profound interest and attention was impressed upon the members and the large concourse of spectators assembled to witness the ceremony. As each of those elected on the Co operation ticket rose in their seats and feelingly gave in their adhesion to the will of the majority, nothing could restrain the outbursts of applause from the audience.

When the last vote was recorded—when the name of York of Concordia was called—the crowd began to move and whisper, and when the result was announced that only *seventeen* out of one hundred and thirty members had responded in the negative, there was such a shout as never before went up from the floor of the Old Gothic Building.

At this moment Capt. H. W. Allen, walking in front of Gov. Moore, Col. Bragg, Rev. Mr. Linfield, Father Hubert and other distinguished gentlemen, came down the central aisle bearing the glorious Pelican Flag—the emblem of Independent Louisiana—which was received with waving of handkerchiefs by the daughters of Louisiana and perfect hurricanes of applause from her gallant sons there assembled.

An impressive prayer for the future prosperity and glory of the State having been delivered by Mr. Linfield, Father Hubert then, in an eloquent but brief address, dedicated the Flag and invoked the people of the State to its defense. The event was a solemn one; many an eye was dimmed with tears as they bid the long farewall to the glorious old Union which had once fostered and protected us, but which had finally passed into the hands of those who are sworn to oppress and crush us.

On the streets the feeling of gratification was equally deep, if not so demonstrative. A rocket went up from the State House grounds when the result of the vote on the Ordinance had been ascertained; this was the signal for a salute at the Garrison grounds, and soon the loud-mouthed cannon, under charge of Col. J. K. Duncan, thundered forth its glad-tidings to the people that Louisiana was a free and independent State.

The Ordinance, from the first day of the session was generally known to have been agreed upon by the majority; its passage therefore, was only a question of time. When its passage, therefore was announced in the Convention, the outside demonstrations were more hearty than boisterous. People met each other with beaming and joyful faces and cordial grasping of hands. They were all Louisianians, resolved to stand or fall together in support of the flag that now waves so cheerily and bravely from the topmost pinnacle of the Capitol.

Coming down to home matters, we cannot refrain from expressing our sincere gratification at the resolution finally agreed upon by our immediate representatives to vote for the Ordinance of Secession. They were elected by large majorities over the Secession Candidates, but with a liberal, enlightened and patriotic spirit they have nobly come forward and given their support to the measure which they saw the people of the State approved, and by so doing added materially to bringing about the almost unanimous result attained in the final vote.

Our space forbids any extended remarks as to the proceedings of yesterday. We must refer to our regular report for details.

ALMOST A PURCHASE.—A few days ago there came to our city a man named Brown, who advertised that he had $5,000 to invest in any good paying business. The drug business is a good business, especially when conducted by so enterprising a man as our friend Bogel; so Brown turned his attention in that direction for a trade. He most cordially purchased Bogel's establishment, gave a check on a Northern bank for $5,000 cash, and then took possession. The telegraph soon told the tale. The bank didn't have any of Brown's money; in fact, it didn't know Brown. Bogel very quietly ejected his successor yesterday, who, as he stepped out of the door, with the intention of leaving for some other locality, was nabbed by City Marshal Cousinard and taken off to Odom's boarding-house. Brown's wardrobe is a curious affair. Among the many articles of apparel is a dirty, greasy and ragged suit of old clothes, which a plantation negro would scarcely wear. Brown also had a plentiful assortment of cutlery about his person, when arrested, in the way of penknives and scissors of the choicest metal.

ARKANSAS STATE CONVENTION CALLED. On the 14th instant, the Convention bill passed the Legislature, and as there is no doubt of its approval by the Governor, a Convention will be held, should a majority of the people of the State conceive that their interests demand it. The bill provides for the people to vote upon the proposition of "Convention or no Convention," and at the same time for delegates thereto should the proposition for a Convention receive a majority of the votes cast. The election takes place on Monday, the 18th of February.—*Helena Shield.*

STATE CONVENTION.

FOURTH DAY'S PROCEEDINGS.

MORNING SESSION.

SATURDAY, January 26, 1861.

The Convention assembled at 10 o'clock, A. M.; 119 members present.

Mr. Provosty, of Point Coupee, submitted a resolution to accept a proposition from the City Council of New Orleans to hold the future sittings of the Convention in that city, and that, when the Convention adjourns to-day, it adjourn to reassemble in the city of New Orleans on Tuesday morning next; and that the President of the Convention appoint a committee of three to make such arrangements with the City Council as may be necessary to the carrying out of the purposes of this resolution.

Mr. Herron, of East Baton Rouge, opposed the adoption of the resolution in a few forcible remarks. He said that the course proposed would involve a wasteful expenditure of the public money; that the Deaf and Dumb Asylum in this city, the use of which had been tendered to the Convention, offered every necessary convenience; that there were members of the Convention who were also members of the State Legislature—working members of the latter body—and that the proposed change would result necessarily in the discontinuance of the session of that body.

Mr. Lawrence, of Plaquemines, thought the reasons for adjournment to New Orleans were overwhelming. The city of Baton Rouge was greatly wanting in those comforts and facilities needed by the members of the Convention.

Mr. Elam, of DeSoto, opposed the resolution for a number of reasons, but particularly, because it would result in the delay of pressing and important action of the Convention.

Mr. Moore, of St. Martin, proposed to amend the resolution by striking out "Tuesday," and inserting "the 31st inst." The Convention, he thought, should continue its sittings here until it had gotten through with all the business which, of necessity, required immediate action, such as the election of delegates to the Montgomery Convention, etc.

Mr. Fuqua, of East Baton Rouge, was glad that some question had risen to unseal the lips of the gentlemen. But, as to the change proposed, so far as he knew, every member had been made confortable. He well knew that the citizens of Baton Rouge had made every effort to provide agreeable quarters for the members. And, said he, is this a time to stickle about mere physical comforts? In the city of New Orleans, possibly, gentlemen may obtain more sumptuous dinners; drink better brandy; indulge in a greater number of luxuries; but was it becoming in those, who had been called together, under the mightiest responsibilities that could be imposed upon men, to decide the future destinies, for weal or woe, of the people of Louisiana, to talk about luxuries while engaged in the discharge of their vast trusts? He thought not. If he could see any good reasons for the removal he would not hesitate to vote for it. He saw none such: but there were many reasons against it. It would involve an additional expense of at least $10,000, and of $5,000 in the item of mileage alone. The Deaf and Dumb Asylum offered every convenience that was wanted for the sittings of the Convention. The use of the Methodist Church, also a large and commodious building, had been tendered; and though some members might feel themselves out of place there, he thought it in every way a suitable building, and that the tender of it deserved the consideration of the Convention.

Mr. Cannon, of Avoyelles, was opposed to any proposition having in view the use of either the Deaf and Dumb Asylum or the Methodist Church. In the former he feared, from the disposition to silence already shown by the members, that we should hear absolutely nothing more from them; and as to the use of the Church, unless its interior could offer much greater comforts than its steps, on which he had been under the necessity of passing a night, since his arrival in Baton Rouge, he should equally oppose it. As to the fact that there were some gentlemen who were members of both the Convention and the Legislature, they should have been less ambitious of office. It was certainly their privilege not to accept seats in the Convention. As for himself he had found in Baton Rouge neither sleeping nor eating quarters. It was of the first importance that the members should be well fed. He had learned from experience never to ask any thing of a hungry man. Differences among hungry men can never become reconciled. In view of the great interests at stake and the importance of harmonious action, the members should be well fed. He feared, if they should longer remain here, that they would furnish another illustration of the case of the Kilkenny cats by devouring each other. He himself was growing decidedly ravenous, and nothing but a timely removal would prevent the necessity of his falling upon some unlucky fellow-member.

There were loud calls for "The Question."

On motion of Mr. Elam, Mr. Moore's proposition to amend was laid on the table.

On motion of Mr. Herron, the Ayes and Nays were taken on the adoption of the resolution.

Mr. Fuqua asked for the consideration of the resolutions offered by Mr. Bienvenu, of St. Bernard, to refer the Ordinance of Secession, when passed, to the people of the State for ratification.

Mr. Perkins requested a moment's delay that he might move the reference to the Committee on the Judiciary and Public Property of the resolution of Mr. Polk, of Morehouse, submitted last evening in regard to the common domain of the Federal Government. The reference was made.

Mr. Bienvenu's resolutions were taken up.

Mr. Lewis, of Claiborne, proceeded to address the Convention in advocacy of the proposition to refer the Ordinance of Secession to the people.

He said he had no disposition to occupy the time of the Convention; but he felt that it was due to himself and others to state the reasons which impelled him and them to the course they would pursue on this question.

He had been elected as a Co-operationist. He was one of those that had hoped and believed that the rights of the South could be maintained and the Union of the States at the same time preserved. When this question was before the people of Claiborne, Co-operation he considered entirely practicable. But circumstances have greatly changed. Several States since then have dissolved their connection with the Federal Government. The only question now for our consideration was as to the effect that the same action on the part of Louisiana would have upon the interests of the people of the State. He would but assert the conviction of his judgment when he said that by immediate secession, we would place at hazzard the interests of a large portion of the people of Louisiana. He regarded it our solemn duty to protect the agricultural, commercial and other interests of the people, so long as not incompatible with the dignity, honor and safety of the State. He thought this might be done.

A few weeks of delay, that the people themselves might act on so grave a question, would not imperil the success of the great movement now in progress in the Southern States. He believed that if this question were submitted to them we shall have a united people in whatever action the Convention may determine on. And would it not be best that we should be united as one man in so great a crisis. It was his sincere conviction that such reference was due to the people. It was their right, and it ought not to be disregarded.

But he had been told by gentlemen that the people had already acted upon this subject in the recent election of delegates. He thought differently. That election was not a clear expression of their will. In the parishes of Madison, Tensas, and Concordia, having eight delegates on this floor, there had been cast only about 1,200 votes. In Orleans, having twenty-five delegates, there are 16,000 registered voters; yet only about 8,000 votes were cast. And so of other parishes. Can this be regarded as a full and satisfactory expression of the judgment of the people? He thought not.

The short delay asked for would not retard the progress of events to the final consummation of the formation of a Southern Confederacy, even before the inauguration of Abraham Lincoln's Administration; and Louisiana may still have her full voice in the formation of the Provisional Government at Montgomery.

And in regard to that Provisional Government may it not be important that we should know what character of Government that is to be, into which we are to go, before we abandon all connection with another? It is not impossible that we shall hereafter regret that we did not adopt the course set forth in the resolutions of the gentleman of East Feliciana (Mr. Fuqua) while we should loose nothing by a few weeks of delay, we should be enabled to place the cotton crop, a large portion of which is yet to be thrown into market, beyond the perils that might follow hasty action, and thus subserve in a measure the interests of our people.

He had no doubt of the ratification of the action of the Convention by the people; but on so grave a question, upon which hangs the destiny of hundreds of thousands, possibly millions, of human beings, it would seem that prudence, sound policy, would require its submission to the people. This decision would thus go forth to the country and to the world clothed with a moral force with which it could otherwise not be fully invested.

The speaker, after a few additional earnest and impressive remarks, concluded by saying that whatever may be the final action of the Convention, though that action be immediate and unqualified secession, there was no member of the Convention, no citizen, that would cleave with more devoted, more unfaultering fidelity than he to the fortunes of his adopted State, whether in sunshine or prosperity or in storms and adversity.

Mr. Perkins asked the indulgence of the Convention for a few remarks.

The course of the debate had made apparent the fact that there was but one spirit, one purpose, in the Convention. All, or nearly all, had the same object in view; but differed only as to form.

In the midst of peril and danger it was better always to pursue a regular and formal course. He thought he could show that such course had been pursued, and with no undue haste. He asked the reading of a portion of Gov. Moore's Proclamation, calling the Legislature into extra session. [It was read by Mr. Tappan of Orleans.] Thus, said Mr. P., it is perceived that the people were fully warned that they were in the presence of a great and imminent danger.

The Legislature came together under that call. The result was the passage of an act which he then held in his hand. The act states that in the opinion of the General Assembly of the State, there should be immediately called a Convention to take such steps as the safety and welfare of the people might demand. Such Convention was called and here we are to day with powers as broad as those of the Roman Dictator who was called to take the helm and guide the Roman people through every danger.

We are here not for a mere expression of our opinions to the people who sent us; nor to the Legislature of the State; nor to the world: but with powers broad enough, deep enough, and holy enough, if properly understood, to take decisive and final action upon the momentous question of our longer continuance in the Federal Union.

In his part of the State he felt assured the people expected no reference to them of the action of the Convention for their ratification or rejection. He himself had been sent there as a civilian to confront the dangers before us, with the courage of the soldier upon the battle-field who dies rather than turn his back to the foe. His people confided in his judgment and patriotism, and confirmed his acts in advance.

He regretted that any gentleman on the opposite side had conceived the idea that the silence of the majority was intended as a slight upon them. He believed that no member of the Committee of Fifteen could entertain such idea; and hoped that the whole house would see that this was the only proper course.

Sir, said he, we are not here for argument. That time has passed. Shall Louisiana be a laggard while her sister States are making haste to meet the dangers that are upon us? Shall we hesitate to act while others are preparing themselves to battle for the cause that is no less ours than theirs? For the maintenance of rights as dear to us as to them?

He would ask a little further indulgence to allude to a point raised last evening by the gentleman from Orleans, (Mr. Roselius.) That gentleman had stated that in no instance, in the history of the State, had the action of a Convention been withheld from the people for their final voice. There were present, said Mr. P., two distinguished gentlemen who were members of the Convention of '52, (one of them the President of that body,) who concurred in the statements in the memorandum just sent to him, and then in his hands. Its reading was asked for and was as follows:

"Mr. Roselius says that this Convention is irregular because it was called by virtue of an act of the Legislature, and that no Convention was ever before called in this State in this way."

Now the Convention of 1845 was called by such an act. If a Convention cannot be called by an act of the Legislature, it cannot be called at all. For no mode of calling one is provided by the present Constitution.

"Mr. Roselius also says that the proceedings of every Convention heretofore held in this State were submitted to the people." The Constitution of 1812 was *not* so submitted. That of 1845 was submitted; but why?

The Constitution of 1812 required that the law calling the Convention should "specify the alterations intended to be made". (Art. 7, Sec. 1.)

The law did so specify that the proposed amendments, but the Convention did not confine themselves to those specifications, but made an entirely new Constitution. A large party in the Convention opposed those additional amendments. They contended that the Convention could not go beyond the amendments specified in the act calling the Convention, but at all events they insisted that as many amendments which had been made that were not specified by the act by which it was called, that they should be submitted to the people. This, after some discussion, was determined on.

The amendments to the Constitution made in 1852, were submitted to the people because the Constitution of 1845 (Art. 140) requires such submission."

One word more, said Mr. P. in reference to our form of procedure. We are yet devisors. We have yet to take the first step towards providing against the dangers. We have yet to appoint Commissioners to aid in forming a Southern Federal Government. When these are all done, then it will be proper and necessary to place them before the people to ratify *in whole* and not *in part*.

Now, as to the policy of immediate secession, *Cui bono?* Is anything more wanted than merely a short delay to recommend the ordinance reported by the committee to the support of gentlemen? No, sir. Not one word of criticism has been passed on its phraseology. No doubt is entertained that the action of the Convention would be sustained by an almost unanimous vote of the people. Then why delay, when action, action, action is the cry that comes to us from all our sister States?

One thought more occurred to him—the inconsistency of referring the action of the Convention to the people. What did we say but two days ago? That our Governor was right in seizing the cannon that to-day might have been hurled against this very Convention. Sir, we should never have approved of such course unless we intended to show equal hereism in our present moment.

After a few additional remarks from Mr. Lewis, the vote was taken upon the resolutions of Mr. Bienvenu, which were rejected. Ayes 45, nays 84.

Notwithstanding the hour (12 o'clock) had arrived for the vote upon the Ordinance, on motion of Mr. Perkins the Convention extended to Ex-Governor Roman the courtesy of an opportunity to present his views.

The distinguished gentleman said that it was unnecessary to dwell upon the causes that had led to the condition in which we now are. It was sufficient to say that it was the result of the conflict on the subject of slavery.

We are, said he, in a condition similar to that of the Colonies when they rose to resist the oppression of the British Government. We are striving to rid ourselves from the power and oppressions of those who have undertaken to overthrow the Constitution of the country. We could not wish a better issue.

It was evident that in the Convention, nearly all had taken substantially the same position, and all were equally determined "to take no step backwards." The most popular policy was clearly for immediate Secession. He himself had entertained the belief that concerted action among the Southern States would better attain the objects all had in view; but a large majority of the Convention thought differently; and, without any waste of words, he desired to announce his purpose to acquiesce in their determination. All must follow the same destiny.

The solemnity of the proceedings of that body ought to be in keeping with the importance of its trusts. It is a high, a fearful responsibility by a single act to change the relations that we have heretofore sustained to the Federal Union. But it would seem we are left no other alternative.

The State of South Carolina (for which and for whose gallant citizens he had a high respect) had taken the lead. Other States have quickly followed. The vacillation and imbecility of President Buchanan, at one time almost favoring Secession, at another seeming determined on coercion, had helped "to precipitate the South into a revolution," to use the memorable words of the distinguished Mr. Yancey, of Alabama, who seems to have been gifted with nearly the powers of prophecy.

The question of co-operation, except with the States that have Seceded, is no longer a practicable one. It can no longer be considered as before us. Louisiana has no alternative but to follow the others that have led the way.

He deeply deplored the condition in which we are placed. He believed that, if the rapid swell of public opinion had permitted it, co-operative action of all the Southern States would have saved the Union. And to testify that conviction he should cast his vote against the Ordinance; but as soon as it has been passed he should subscribe to it as fully and as earnestly as if it had had his support from the beginning.

He hoped that the advantages of the new Government would be as great as have been those of the one we are about to abandon. But, whether they should be or not, his own fate was indissolubly connected with that of his State. Where she leads he must follow. We must present an unbroken front to the enemy.

Mr. Heron, being allowed the courtesy, spoke very briefly. He said that he had been elected as a Co-operationist. He had exhausted every effort in behalf of that policy. He felt that he had fully discharged the duty imposed by those at whose hands he held his position in that body. He now saw no other alternative than to vote altogether for unqualified, immediate secession.

Mr. Lewis of Claiborne, asked for the co-operation members the privilege of a few minute's retirement from the Hall of the Convention for consultation.

Mr. Perkins replied that he did not feel himself at liberty to assent to the request.

Mr. Dupre of St. Landry, made an impassioned and solemn appeal for a few moments of delay for consultation that all might unite on so momentous a question.

Mr. Perkins, with the general acquiescence, assented, and himself moved a recess of twenty minutes.

The Convention re-assembled at five minutes after 1 o'clock.

Mr. Lewis, of Claiborne, requested, for himself and other Co-operation members, the privilege of brief remarks, as the name of each should be called; which was assented to.

The President then announced that the Convention would proceed to vote upon the Ordinance of Secession.

As the roll was being called in the midst of the most impressive silence and solemnity, a large majority of the Co operation members in the order of their call, announced their purpose to vote for the Ordinance.

On the completion of the call the vote was found to stand—For the Ordinance, 113; against it, 17.

After stating the result, the President of the Convention rose and said:

"In virtue of the vote just taken, I do now announce that all connection of the State of Louisiana with the Federal Union is dissolved; and that she is now a free, sovereign and independent power."

This announcement was made at ten minutes before 2 o'clock.

The flag of the stars and stripes immediately disappeared, and that of the Lone Star and Pelican was displayed in ample folds above the President's chair.

It was greeted with irrepressible and tumultuous applause; on the subsidence of which a brief but eloquent prayer was delivered, in deep solemnity, by the Rev. W. E. N. Linfield, of the *Methodist Church*.

The Flag was then blessed, according to the form of the Catholic service, by the Rev. J. Hubert, of that church.

The following resolution, previously reported by the Committee of Fifteen, and intended to follow immediately the passage of the Ordinance of Secession, was unanimously adopted:

"*Resolved*, That we, the people of the State of Louisiana, recognize the right of the free navigation of the Mississippi River and its tributaries, by all friendly States bordering thereon. And we also recognize the right of egress and ingress of the mouths of the Mississippi by all friendly States and Powers; and we do hereby declare our willingness to enter into any stipulations to guarantee the exercise of said rights."

On the motion of Mr. Perkins, of Madison, the members of the Convention were requested to proceed to the Secretary's desk in alphabetical order, and sign the Ordinance, the President of the Convention signing first.

The signing was done upon an ample parchment sheet on which the Ordinance had been beautifully enrolled, each member being presented by the Sergeant-at-arms with a handsome gold pen for this special use.

The following are the names subscribed to the

ORDINANCE

To dissolve the union between the State of Louisiana and other States united with her, under the compact entitled "The Constitution of the United States of America."

We, the people of the State of Louisiana, in Convention assembled, do declare and ordain, and it is hereby declared and ordained, That the Ordinance passed by us in Convention on the 22d day of November, in the year 1811, whereby the Constitution of the United States of America, and the amendments of the said Constitution were adopted; and all laws and ordinances by which the State of Louisiana became a member of the Federal Union, be and the same are hereby repealed and abrogated; and that the union now subsisting between Louisiana and other States, under the name of "The United States of America," is hereby dissolved.

We do further declare and ordain, That the State of Louisiana hereby resumes all rights and powers heretofore delegated to the Government of the United States of America; that her citizens are absolved from all allegiance to said Government; and that she is in full possession and exercise of all those rights of sovereignty which appertain to a free and independent State.

We do further declare and ordain, That all rights acquired and vested under the Constitution of the United States, or any act of Congress, or treaty, or under any law of this State, and not incompatible, with this Ordinance, shall remain in force, and have the same effect as if this Ordinance had not been passed.

Hon. Alex. Mouton, of Lafayette, President; Messrs. W. R. Adams, Orleans; W. D. Anderson, Tensas; B. Avegno, Orleans; A. Barbin, Avoyelles; W. R. Barrow, West Feliciana; E. Bermudez, Orleans; *C.* Bienvenu, St. Bernard; P. E. Bouford, Orleans; A. Bonner, Franklin; *C. C.* Briscoe, Madison; W. Burton, St. Landry; L. Bush, Lafourche; E. G. W. Butler, Iberville; T. J. Caldwell, Bossier; F. Cannon, Avoyelles; W. *C.* Carr, Union; G. Clark, Orleans; T. A. Cook, St Landry; G. F. Connelly, Terrebonne; L. P. Conner, Concordia; S. S. Conner, St. Tammany; T. Cottman, Ascension; W. A. Davidson, Livingston; E. *C.* Davidson, Sabine; A. Declouet, St. Martin; A. DeBlanc, St. Martin; S. W. Dorsey, Teusas; E. Duffel, Ascension; L. J. Dupre, St. Landry; J. B. Elam, DeSoto; J. K. Elgee, Rapides; R. W. Estlin, Orleans; G. L. Fuselier, St. Mary; J. O. Fuqua, East Feliciana; A. H. Gladden, Orleans; F. Gardere, Jefferson; J. K. Gaudet, St. James; Y. W. Graves, DeSoto; A. M. Gray, Avoyelles; W. E. Gill, *Calcasieu*; M. E. Girard, Lafayette; S. H. Griffin, Union; J. Hernandez, Orleans; A. S. Herron, East Baton Rouge; B. L. Hodge, *Caddo*; R. Hodges, Bienville; S. Hollingsworth, St. John the Baptist; T. Johnson, Iberville; T. H Kennedy, Orleans; W. M. Kidd, Jackson; F. Labatut, Orleans; E. Lawrence, Plaquemines; *C.* T. Lagroue, Jefferson; *C.* O. LeBlanc, Orleans; L. S. LeBourgeois, St. James; F. Lewis, Bienville; J. L. Lewis, *Claiborne*; T. *C.* Manning, Rapides; H. Marshall, DeSoto; A. Marrero, St. Bernard; L. D. Marks, *Caddo*; I. N. Marks, Orleans; R. *C.* Martin, Assumption; J. H. Martin, *Carroll*; N. *Magee*, Washington; O. E. *Melancon*, Assumption; W. R. *Miles*, Orleans; J. J. *Michel*, Orleans; J. E. *Miller*, *Concordia*; J. *Moore*, St. *Martin*; J. *McCloskey*, Orleans; A. *McCollam*, Terrebonne; H. *McFarland*, Bossier; S. W. *McNeely*, Point *Coupee*; *M.* O. H. Norton, Orleans; J. G. Olivier, St. *Mary*; D. O'Bryan, Vermillion; W. Patterson, East Feliciana; J. S. Perkins, Lafourche; John Perkins, Jr., *Madison*; W. *M.* Perkins, Orleans; W. R. Peck, *Madison*; J. Pemberton, Orleans; A. H. Pierson, Natchitoches; W. S. Pike, East Baton Rouge; H. *M.* Polk, *Morehouse*; N. W. Pope, West Baton Rouge; A. Provosty, Point *Coupee*; W. Pugh, Assumption; H. Richardson, Washington; A. B. Roman, St. James; J. B. Slawson, Orleans; W. W. Smart, Rapides; E. C. Swayze, St. Landry; T. J. Semmes, Orleans; *C.* D. Stewart, Point *Coupee*; E. Sparrow, *Carroll*; J. Sompayrac, Natchitoches; N. G. Scott, *Claiborne*; T. W. Scott, West Feliciana; W. *M.* Smith, St. *Mary*; B. S. Tappan, Orleans; A. Talbot, Iberville; R. Taylor, St. *Charles*; J. A. Taylor, St. Landry; L. Texada, Rapides; J. S. Thomasson, *Claiborne*; R. B. Todd, *Morehouse*; J. T. Towles, West Feliciana; *C.* J. Tucker, Lafourche; *M.* Valentine, *Carroll*; A. Verret, Terrebonne; W. B. Warren, Jackson; A. Walker, Orleans; I. A. Williams, East Baton Rouge; J. A Williams, St. Helena; G. Williamson, *Caddo*; J. B. Wilkinson, Jr., Plaquemines; P. S. Wiltz, Orleans; Z. York, Concordia—121.

The members of the Convention who did not sign the Ordinance—nine in number—were Messrs. Garrett, of Ouachita; Lewis, of Orleans; Meredith, of Caldwell; Roselius, of Orleans; Rozier, of Orleans; Stocker of Orleans; Taliaferro, of Catahoula and Hough of Caldwell.

The Convention adjourned to meet in the city of New Orleans on Tuesday morning next.

RAISING THE FLAG AT THE GARRISON GROUNDS. About 5 o'clock yesterday evening the Pelican Flag was run up to the top of the flag-staff at the State Barracks, amid lound plaudits from the civilians and soldiers assembled. The troops of Captains Pierce and Farrar were drawn up in line for the occasion, and presented quite a soldier-like appearance.

☞ The Convention yesterday resolved to adjourn to New Orleans by a large majority. We trust they will not, in turn, become dissatisfied with their new quarters. They will soon discover the difference between the Hall of the Capitol and the Council and Concert Rooms of the metropolis. They have left us. We regret it—but be it so!

NAVIGATION OF THE MISSISSIPPI.—The resolution accompanying the report of the Committee of Fifteen relative to the free navigation of the Mississippi River was yesterday adopted by the State Convention. The resolution will be found in the report of the proceedings.

Thus, at the outset, Louisian has spiked the Abolition cry that the great stream is to be sectionalized, and that the Western people were to be cut off from their commerce with the Gulf States. Western steamboats, as heretofore, are to have free ingress and egress to and from the port of New Orleans, with no duty, tax or other discrimination against them than those previously existing of a municipal and police character.

PATRIOTIC.—As soon as the ordinance of secession was adopted our friend Roberts, of "Our House," hoisted the Pelican Flag, with a determination to stand or fall by the fate of the Pelican (his native) State. We refer his and our friends to the advertisement of "Our House" in another column, and speak for him a share of their patronage.

REMARKABLE SHOTS.—A friend informs us of three very remarkable shots, which were made a few days since, in this neighborhood by Mr. Silvent Marionneaux. He used a shot gun with No. 8 shot. The first fire, he killed 94 blackbirds—the second, 76, and the third 75. His gun weighs sixteen lbs.—*Iberville Gazette.*

FIRE.—The kitchen attached to the restaurant of Steve Basalisco took fire yesterday morning and was consumed in a few moments. A negro child was burnt in the conflagration.

TELEGRAPHIC ITEMS.

THE GEORGIA STATE CONVENTION.

MILLEDGEVILLE, Jan. 23.—It has been determined by the Convention to elect ten delegates to-morrow to the proposed Convention at Montgomery, Ala., on the 4th of February next. All Southern States will be invited to send delegates.

The Ordinance having reference to the African slave trade—which was made the special order of to-day—was amended, declaring it not piracy, but substituting imprisonment in the Penitentiary as a penalty for the violation of the former Federal laws bearing upon the subject.

The Ordinance passed unanimously, when another was offered by Mr. Hill of Troup, providing for the continuance and observance of the present postal revenue and other Federal laws.

It treats of the rights and privileges of non-residents, and mentions the probability of the speedy formation of a new Government upon the basis of the old one.

Judge Beming presented an Ordinance having reference to the inter-State slave trade.

A resolution prevailed for the appointment of Commissioners to all the slaveholding States, when Mr. Cobb reported an Ordinance revoking Federal jurisdiction over all lands ceded by the State of Georgia, and authorizing payment for arsenals, fortifications and stores. Laid over.

Many rumors are afloat relative to the representatives of Georgia to be sent to Montgomery. It is generally conceded, however, that Messrs. Toombs and Cobb will represent the State at large.

Much perplexity exists relative to delegates: little or no attention is paid to present Congressmen.

General satisfaction is expressed on the passage of the anti slave Ordinance.

ALABAMA STATE CONVENTION.—*Montgomery, Ala*, Jan. 23.—The State Convention passed an Ordinance to day annulling the offices of Military Commissioners and authorizing the Legislature to fill the vacancies created thereby. Much discussion ensued.

An Ordinance was presented authorizing the Governor to remove the arms and munitions of war from the Mount Vernon Arsenal and distribute the same to citizens of the towns throughout the State.

Another, vesting the Legislature with power to confiscate property belonging to enemies of the State and situated within its limits.

The Senate has passed a bill requiring all free negroes to leave the State of Alabama by the first of January next, under penalty of being sold.

LEGISLATURE OF NORTH CAROLINA.—*Raleigh*, Jan. 24.—The passage of the Convention bill is still doubtful.

MISSISSIPPI STATE CONVENTION.

Special to New Orleans Crescent.

JACKSON, Jan. 24, 1861.

Mr. Editor—The Convention of Mississippi to-day elected delegates to the Convention to be held at Montgomery, on the 4th of February next, to form a Southern Confederacy. The delegates were chosen from the State, irrespective of territorial or geographical lines, or of political affinities.

The following gentlemen were chosen to represent the State: Messrs. W. P. Harris, of Hinds; W. S. Wilson, of Claiborne; J. A. P. Campbell, of Attala; W. S. Barry and J. T. Harrison, of Lowndes; A. M. Clayton, of Marshall; and Walter Brooke, of Warren.

Two of the above named gentlemen (Brooke and Harrison) were strong and staunch Bell and Everett men.

The ordinance, as passed, looks forward to the speedy formation of a provisional or permanent Government.

Colonel D. C. Glenn, of Harrison, (well known in your city) was the nominee of the caucus of his Congressional District, and would certainly have been elected, but declined becoming a candidate for private and public reasons, the principal of the latter being that he thought no member of the Convention should fill any office which had been created by its act.

After the election of delegates, the Convention proceeded to the election of Major-General and Brigadier-Generals for the army proposed to be raised in accordance with the Military bill passed yesterday.

On the first ballot the Hon. Jefferson Davis received the unanimous nomination from, and election by, the Convention as Major-General.

Major Earl Van Dorn, formerly of the U. S. Cavalry, and noted for his gallant services, was then elected senior Brigadier-General.

Gen. Charles Clark, commander of the Second Mississippi Regiment in Mexico, was elected second Brigadier General.

Col. J. L. Allcorn, of Coahoma, was elected third Brigadier General, and C. H. Mott, of Marshall, was elected fourth Brigadier-General.

The regiment will be immediately raised, and in the course of four or five weeks Mississippi will have ten thousand men ready to take the field.

The only business of importance to be finished is the ordinance on citizenship and the ordinance providing for the raising of revenue. The Convention, in Committee of the Whole, adopted the *ad valorem* system of direct taxation, at the rate of thirty cents on the hundred dollars. The ordinance will be acted on to-morrow, and I will give you a sketch of the debate and proceedings, and then doff the office of correspondent.

The Convention is anxiously awaiting the action of Louisiana.

SHE STAR OF THE WEST AT FORT SUMTER.—*Interesting Statement of Lieut. Hall.*—A reporter of the New York *Herald* gleaned the following statement from Lieut. Hall, Major Anderson's bearer of dispatches:

He says Fort Sumter did not fire on Fort Moultrie or Morris Island because Major Anderson did not know that reinforcements had been sent in the Star of the West. He could only just discover a large vessel through the fog, it being impossible to ascertain her character or to learn her object or mission. It would have taken five or six hours to destroy Fort Moultrie, and half an hour or an hour to stop their firing upon the Star of the West, whereas this vessel could come as near Fort Sumter as she could get in five minutes. During the half hour she would have been in the fire from Fort Moultrie, and very likely have been sunk and many lives on board lost. Nothing would have been gained but the immediate opening of a civil war, loss of the ship and the lives of those on board. The men were all at the loaded guns, with matches lighted, expecting the word every minute to fire; but Major Anderson, after a struggle with his feelings, withheld the order to fire. He says the inhabitants of Charleston, and indeed of the whole State of South Carolina, have pledged all they have in the world—property, honor, lives—to maintain the independence of South Carolina. Some of the better and more cautious people admit that they have gone too fast, but they will keep their pledges to sustain her to the very last, even if they come out of the contest ruined. The stores in Charleston were all closed, except a few candy shops and provision stores. Fort Sumter does not need reinforcements. A ship of the size of the Star of the West could not now get into the harbor, as vessels have been sunk on the bar to prevent ingress.

The Charleston Mercury.

DAILY PAPER—TEN DOLLARS PER ANNUM, PAYABLE HALF-YEARLY IN ADVANCE.

VINDICE NULLO
SPONTE SUA SINE LEGE FIDES RECTUMQUE COLENTUR

VOLUME LVI. CHARLESTON, S. C., MONDAY, JANUARY 28, 1861. NUMBER 11,072

The Daily Mercury

IS PUBLISHED EVERY MORNING.

(SUNDAYS EXCEPTED.)

The Tri-Weekly Mercury

ON TUESDAYS, THURSDAYS AND SATURDAYS.

OFFICE, No. 4 BROAD-STREET, CHARLESTON, SOUTH CAROLINA.

TERMS: CASH IN ADVANCE.

DAILY MERCURY, for one year.......$10.00
" " for six months....... 5.00
" " for three months....... 2.50
" " for less than three months, $1 per month.

Newspaper Dealers and Retail Agents supplied on liberal terms.

TRI-WEEKLY MERCURY, for one year.......$5.00
" " for six months....... 2.50
" " for three months....... 1.25
" " for less than three months, 50c. a month.

FROM THIS DATE, no subscriptions out of the city will be received unless accompanied with the cash.

POSTMASTERS are authorised to act as our Regular Agents in obtaining subscribers and forwarding the money, for which they will be allowed 20 per cent. commission; only, however, when paid in advance.

Subscribers desiring their papers changed, must mention the Post Office FROM, as well as the one TO, which they desire the change to be made.

Gentlemen getting up Clubs of 5, 10, 20, or more, will be supplied at 20 per cent. less than the Regular Rates.

ADVERTISING RATES.

THE MERCURY has now the largest circulation of any paper in the State, and is second in this respect to but few papers in the South; it therefore offers great advantages to business men and others, whose interests require publicity.

ONE SQUARE of 12 lines, solid nonpareil, each insertion, 65 cents, and for each additional line 5 cents.

COMMUNICATIONS of personal interest will be charged as advertising matter.

Orders from without the city to publish Advertisements, Marriage Notices or Obituaries, will not be attended to unless the cash, or an acceptable city reference, accompany the order.

☞ On all bills of $50 and over, 20 per cent. discount is allowed.

The Charleston Mercury

Is for sale, daily, at the following places:

New York—At the newstands of the La Farge House and St. Nicholas Hotel.
Washington, D. C.—By FRENCH & RICHSTEIN, No. 278 Pennsylvania Avenue.
Memphis, Tenn.—By M. NEALIS.
Wilmington, N. C.—By T. J. WHITAKER.
Lynchburg, Va.—By J. J. CREED.
Clifton, Ala.—By V. J. GIBSON.
Baltimore—By M. H. UMBAUGH, Nos. 4 and 5 Jarvis Building, corner Baltimore and North streets.
Glenwood, Iowa.—By E. C. BLACKMAN.
Jackson, Miss.—By M. L. CARLISLE.
Richmond, Va.—By LEWIS L. SMITH.
Nashville, Tenn.—By R. H. SINGLETON.
Columbia, S. C.—By P. B. GLASS and S. TOWNSEND.
Rock Island, Ill.—By F. H. WARREN.
Chicago, Ill.—MCNALLY & Co.
New Orleans, La.—Newsman under the St. Charles Hotel.

☞ South Carolina Bank Bills taken in payment for subscription to the MERCURY.

TRAVELLER'S GUIDE.

Schedule of the South Carolina Railroad.

FOR AUGUSTA.		LEAVE.	FOR CHARLESTON.	
5.45 a.m.	2.30 p.m.	Charleston	3.30 p.m.	4.30 a.m
6.55	3.45	Summerville	2.22	3.05
7.25	4.15	Ridgeville	1.55	2.30
8.20	5.18	George's	1.08	1.35
9.20	6.20	Branchville	12.20	12.30
10.05	7.10	Bamberg	11.13 a.m.	11.25
10.50	8.05	Blackville	10.25	10.30
11.18	8.41	Williston	9.58	9.55
11.45	9.20	Windsor	9.32	9.22
12.25 p.m.	10.10	Aiken	8.52	8.33
12.48	10.3[illegible]	Graniteville	8.33	8.08
1.15	11.15 p.m.	Augusta	8.00 a.m.	7.30 p.m.
FOR COLUMBIA.			FOR CHARLESTON.	
8.20 a.m.	8.15 p.m.	Charleston	1.00 p.m.	10.30 p.m.
9.35	9.28	Summerville	11.45 a.m.	9.00
10.08	10.12	Ridgeville	11.15	8.24
11.05	11.17	George's	10.18	7.16
12.15 p.m.	12.25 a.m.	Branchville	9.35	6.20
1.08	1.25	Orangeburg	8.10	5.05
2.00	2.25	Lewisville	7.28	4.18
3.15	3.30	Kingsville	6.45	3.25
4.30 p.m.	5.20 a.m.	Columbia	5.00 a.m.	1.40 p.m.

CHARLESTON POST OFFICE.

DELIVERY AND CLOSING OF THE MAILS.

DELIVERIES.	MORNING.	EVENING.
Northern	9.00 a.m.	7.00 p.m
Columbia and Camden	9.00 a.m.	3.00 p.m
Country		3.00 p.m.
Augusta and Western	9.00 a.m.	5.00 p.m.
Offices on Greenville and Columbia Railroad	9.00 a.m.	
Offices on Charlotte and South Carolina Railroad	9.00 a.m.	

BEWARE!

THE MERCURY

MONDAY, JANUARY 28, 1861.

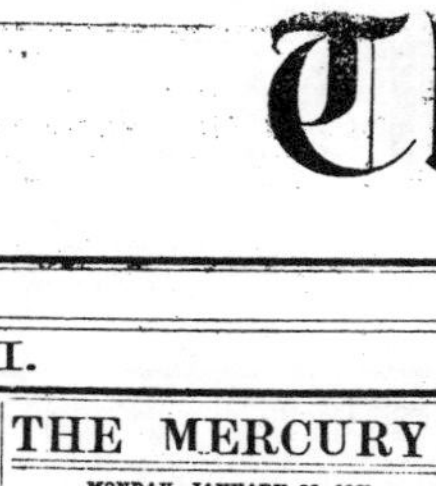

Our Flag.

On Saturday last both Houses of the General Assembly finally concurred in the design of the flag which is hereafter to represent the Sovereign State of South Carolina. The field is dark blue. Upon the upper inner corner of the flag is the crescent, in white, the horns pointing upward. In the middle of the flag is an oval, in white, emblazoned with a golden palmetto, upright. The cut we present will give an idea of the porportions of the new ensign.

No Federal Troops.

No Federal troops shall ever enter Virginia to operate against the South! Such was the solemn declaration of FLOYD, of Virginia, long ago. Yet we see that, contemplating the use of Federal troops against the South, the fortresses of Virginia are reinforced. Very beautiful, this! The Government of the United States, which left Harper's Ferry to the tender mercies of JOHN BROWN, arms it against Virginia herself. These fortresses, thus reinforced, are to be yielded, in March, to ABRAHAM LINCOLN. How many JOHN BROWNS are to be sheltered in Virginia, under the protection of United States troops, is a question in political arithmetic, which our sister State must answer for herself. There was a time, however, when Virginia could *snuff* tyranny in the breeze. Does she not *see* it in these bayonets of the Federal Government?

Temple Bar.

We are indebted to the attentions of a friend in New York for a copy of the first number of the new London magazine bearing this title. It is under the editorial control of Mr. GEORGE AUGUSTUS SALA, a gentleman who has obtained some credit in the literary world for a volume of sprightly travels. The contents of this first number of Mr. SALA's magazine, though generally in good taste and style, does not strike us with much show of saliency. There is nothing remarkable in its pages, though quite respectable. We note a brief paper on Lord BACON, reviewing a new work of Mr. HEPWORTH DIXON, the author of a life of WILLIAM PENN, in which PENN is defended against the assaults of MACAULAY. DIXON, in like manner, and from new materials, and the proper re-examination of old ones, undertakes to relieve the great English philosopher from the criminal aspersions which have darkened his honest fame for a hundred years. We have not seen his work, but Mr. SALA affirms and seems to show that the defence is conclusive, and that BACON has been the victim of a brutal slander.

Macaulay.

CRITICAL AND MISCELLANEOUS ESSAYS AND POEMS. By T. Babington Macaulay. New York: Appleton & Co.

These are the later writings, in prose and verse, of a writer of large, various and admirable powers; and it will not need any exhortation of ours to persuade our readers to seize eagerly upon this volume, and possess themselves of its contents. The collection includes a fine body of criticism on topics of singular charm and interest; many spirited and well versified poems; some keen satire; some classical sketchings, in form of fiction; papers on pure literature; on political economy; statistics; a biographical and critical sketch of MIRABEAU, and another of WILLIAM PITT. There are inscriptions, also, on the monuments of certain persons, which are all distinguished by their propriety and good taste, if wanting in any more remarkable features. Altogether, this volume will be found one of the pleasantest fireside books; suggestive to the thoughtful reader, and not wanting in attraction to the most desultory. MACAULAY's great excellence, indeed, *is as an essayist.* His histories are, in fact, essays, rather than histories; and labor under this disadvantage—that, like HUME, though differing from him politically, he still wrote as a partizan. It is as a body of essays that we are to read his writings. We can read them when we no longer care to read the *Tatlers*, the *Ramblers*, and the *Spectators*. We commend them as grateful reading to all parties.

Acknowledgments.

We have been favored with the following communication:

EXECUTIVE OFFICE, TREASURY DEPARTMENT, January 26th, 1861.

His Excellency the Governor:

SIR: I have the pleasure of reporting to your Excellency a donation of two thousand dollars for the service of the State, from "Another Combahee Planter."

This gentleman desires that his name should not be published. Whilst this desire indicates a modesty which adds grace to the donation, I have considered it not inconsistent with his direction, that I should express, in this public manner, your Excellency's high appreciation of his liberal and considerate patriotism.

I remain, with much respect,
Your obedient servant,
C. G. MEMMINGER.

FORTS MOULTRIE AND SUMTER IN NEW YORK.—Capt. EDWARD DALY received a letter from a friend in New York yesterday, from which, with the Captain's permission, we have been permitted to make the following extracts, which bear their own significance. Straws show the way the wind blows, and the actions of children generally portray the actions and feeling of their parents:

"I never laughed more on any occasion than I did on Friday last, in Brooklyn, at some ragged boys, divided into two parties, who were amusing themselves throwing snowballs opposite St. James' Church. Ten boys represented Fort Sumter, and eight of the smallest represented Fort Moultrie. There was a large crowd of children of older growth looking on, and after a hard battle, with three cheers for South Carolina, which was taken up by the bystanders, the Fort Moultrie boys charged on Fort Sumter, and gained a decisive victory."

THE GUNS OF THE FLORIDIANS.—The following guns are mounted at Barrancas, according to a correspondent of the *Pensacola Observer:*

11 thirty-two pounders, 3 Paixhan guns—8 inch, 2 eight inch Columbiads, 2 twelve pounders, 8 twenty-four pounders, 4 eighteen pounders, 8 twelve pounders.

Fort McRae has the following valuable armament unmounted:

22 forty-two pounders, 46 thirty-two pounders, 27 twenty-four pounders, 2 ten inch Columbiads.

MORE FALSEHOODS have been invented and circulated during the last four months about South Carolina, than have been told about any other subjects for the last twenty-five years. The forced loans, the tax of $16 a head on negros, the alleged exactions upon Gov. Aiken, the turbulent conduct of the volunteers, the suffering from want of food and coal, are but a few specimens of a thousand which have been manufactured out of the whole cloth, and never had the slightest shadow of foundation. It is humiliating to think that a class of writers exist in this country who earn their subsistance by deliberate slander, an article which they manufacture with no other care or scruple than to make it, like any other fabric, as complete as possible.—*Richmond Dispatch.*

THE ENGLISH PRESS ON AMERICAN AFFAIRS.—The comments of the English press on American affairs are the most amusing reading of the day. The combination of extraordinary ignorance and magnificent assumption is perfectly overwhelming.

Rashness of South Carolina.

Certain phlegmatics of the South, to call them by the tenderest name, have had a great deal to say about the rashness and hot haste of South Carolina in seceding from the Confederacy. But this is the language of cowardice borrowing the speech of impudence. South Carolina would not consult her sisters, quotha! as if her beautiful and indignant sisters did not refuse her appeal for consultation. They would neither act for themselves nor counsel with her. Such was the language and decision of the *politicians*, at least. We have great hopes that the *people* of these sister States will soon speak a different language. But South Carolina gave long notice before hand, that, with the election of LINCOLN, she had resolved on secession. Why did they not counsel with her when she declared that resolution? But we have some faint recollection that this sentiment, which looked to secession as the only remedy, was entertained and declared by some of these very politicians. It was understood among all of them that LINCOLN's election would endanger the Confederacy—so well understood that the New York merchants, who well knew what the danger was, devoted themselves to the one effort of defeating LINCOLN. Did these phlegmatics of the South feel less upon the subject than the New York merchants? One thing is certain—if, as our timid friends augur, this revolution shall turn out to be a bloody one, at least all the bloodshed will be on the hands of those tardy phlegmatics, who refused to counsel with South Carolina—who would do nothing themselves, and threw cold water on the zeal of those who strove to do. They had their warning—they should not be taken by surprise. The non-performance, in a time of national crisis, which shelters itself under the cloak of its dignity, is at once impudence and cowardice.

Letter from Georgia—One that Knows.

MILLEDGEVILLE, January 24, 1861.

Our business is progressing with good feeling and with energy. We have just gotten through our election for representatives to the Congress to be assembled at Montgomery on the 4th proximo. Before voting we required an assurance that none of these men were in favor of forming a Government having in view an immediate or ultimate Union with the Northern States. No such idea could be entertained. All are for the establishment of a Southern Confederacy on the basis of the old Constitution, and never, under any circumstances, connect ourselves with the Northern States. We are as strong on this point as you are.

Treaties of Amity and Commerce.

To the Editor of the Charleston Mercury:

By an accident, this question was neglected by the Convention at its late session. But it is not too late to repair the oversight. It was altogether appropriate, but not absolutely necessary, that *the Convention* should have acted in the premises. The constituted authorities of the State—the Legislature now in session, or the Governor—can appoint Commissioners to proceed to Europe and negotiate Treaties of Amity and Commerce with Foreign Powers in behalf of South Carolina, quite as well, and perhaps more appropriately, than the Convention. The importance of this measure cannot be overated. Georgia, with those farseeing, business-like, practical qualities which have ever characterised that noble State and earned for her the title of the Empire State of the South, has made an important move in this direction. Let us profit by her forecast and wisdom, and enter with all our zeal into the praise-worthy enterprise. It is absolutely necessary that treaties of this kind should be concluded at least with England, France and Belgium. The ports of Liverpool, London, Havre and Antwerp, should at once be placed in friendly commercial relations with Savannah, Charleston, Mobile and New Orleans. And South Carolina should take care that Charleston should not be behind the others. The commercial bondage that has held us in vassalage to the North for so many years, should be broken asunder. We can not be *a free people* so long as we are compelled *to pay toll* at the gates of New York, Boston and Philadelphia. They have been the factors of the South long enough. Religious affinity between the sections has been sundered for years, and on the 20th December, 1860, South Carolina sundered all political connection. Let her now follow up the stand so nobly taken, *and strike for Commercial Independence.* This mission should be in the hands of the intelligent merchant and the intelligent planter. We are fortunately situated in both respects: Mr. CHARLES K. PRIOLEAU, now residing in Liverpool, is deeply interested in the prosperity of his native State, and is heart and soul with her in her present action. He has the intelligence and hearty will (as are evidenced by his late communications to the MERCURY, and the London *Times*), and the practical knowledge of the commercial relations on both sides of the Atlantic, to render him eminently a fit and proper person, to act as one of the Commissioners of the State in this important mission. He is now residing, as we have said, in Europe. Let him be appointed. And who more fit to represent the planting interest than the Hon. WILLIAM ELLIOTT, of St. Paul's—a gentleman of experience in public affairs and great intelligence? As a producer of the raw material, he is personally interested to promote the commercial prosperity of the cotton-growing country. He is not wholly unknown in Europe, having been across the water more than once in a public as well as private capacity. He, if necessary, can disabuse the public mind abroad of prejudice against the domestic institutions of the South, which are "sinned against not sinning." He understands the whole question thoroughly, and has the intelligence and address to meet such difficulties as may be encountered. With such a combination of experience and intelligence, the mission must be successful and result in lasting benefit to the city of Charleston and to the Commonwealth. Let those in authority act wisely and well, and at once appoint this Commission, which will cost the State but a small amount; and let her co-operate with Georgia in securing to the *South* the trade and commerce of the *South*, which were *stolen* from her in an evil hour. The country that produces the four great staples of the world—rice, sugar, tobacco and cotton—should have her own independent commercial relations. If marble palaces and brown-stone fronts are to be erected from the fruits of Southern trade, let them be erected in New Orleans, Mobile, Savannah and Charleston. In conclusion, let us act and act promptly, before it is too late for us to be even in the race.

VERBUM SAT.

EXTRACT from the letter of a distinguished citizen of Alabama:

MONTGOMERY, January 22, 1861.

Alabama seceded unconditionally from the Union on the 11th inst., and the act requires nothing to give it validity. The signing of the Ordinance is a mere ceremonial, which it was intended should take place in public, but in consequence of the unwillingness of a portion of the minority to affix their names without first consulting their constituents, this plan was abandoned, and each member signs as he chooses. Between sixty and seventy, out of a hundred, have already signed, and there is every reason to believe that all the rest will follow their example. The press in North Alabama, where all the disaffection is supposed to exist, are unanimous in standing by the action of the State, and no fears are entertained of any serious division among our people. Some of the minority have been extremely bitter in their hostility to secession, but they are all loyal sons of Alabama, and not traitors, and will rally as one man to her standard. As a citizen of Alabama, I am mortified at the impression which has obtained in other States, as to the discord which prevails in our councils, for I am satisfied that it does the grossest injustice to a respectable and patriotic minority.

SECESSION DOWN EAST.—A Quebec paper says: "While the North and the South are on the eve of civil war, it is interesting to learn, as we do on unquestionable authority, that the leading men of the State of Maine are preparing the way for annexation to the British American Union. It is the most hopeful movement of the hour."

The memorable words of Old Hickory, "The Union, it Must and Shall be Preserved!" have been proven literally true, * * * for in spite of all appearances, the Union is certainly in a fine Pickle!—*Vanity Fair.*

The Irrepressible Conflict in the Navy.

JANUARY 21, 1861.

To the Editors of the National Intelligencer:

GENTLEMEN: In the Charleston MERCURY is a letter dated "Fort Moultrie, January 14, 1861," from J. R. Hamilton, of South Carolina, lately a lieutenant in the United States Navy, calling upon his former brother officers, especially those from the South, to espouse the cause of South Carolina and the other seceding Cotton States against the flag which has been hitherto their glory and boast, the Constitution they have sworn to support, and the country in whose service they are now engaged: to forget their oaths of allegiance, and not only to turn traitors themselves, but, by adding treachery to treason, to betray, if able to do so, the materiel of war entrusted to them by their country into the hands of their country's enemies.

I am persuaded that his appeal to the officers of the navy is a vain one. There does not exist a more loyal set of men than those who have given themselves to their country's service in the army and navy, or a set of men of more elevated ideas of honor and of right and wrong. The stuff of which traitors are made forms a meagre element in the construction of the character of a whole-souled sailor, chivalrous to an extreme, generous to a fault, and proverbially open-hearted. True, here and there may exist—late defections from our ranks have proved it—individuals ready to sacrifice honor to interest, and the vows their mouths have uttered when it becomes convenient to abjure them, but the great mass of officers of the navy are true to the Union and to the oaths of allegiance they uttered when they first accepted office under "the star-spangled banner" of our country, and the proposition of Mr. J. R. Hamilton will not only be ineffectual, but it is an offence to them.

I am not a Southerner by birth, but I married, twenty odd years ago, a daughter of Virginia, and by residence and association have been nearly ever since a citizen of a slaveholding State; my affections are with the South rather than with the North; but above South, above North, above all sectional partialities, is my love to our country, to the star-spangled banner that proclaims her sovereignty, and to her Constitution as accepted by Washington. Nor am I alone in this devotion to her cause; hundreds of my brother officers are equally ready to rally in her defence; and their motto, like my own, will be "Liberty and Union, now and forever, one and inseparable."

Respectfully, your obedient servant,
WILLIAM B. WHITING,
Lieutenant U. S. Navy.

CHARLESTON, S C., January, 26th 1861.

To the Editor of the Charleston Mercury:

I regret that it is necessary I should bring myself so directly before the public, but feel it due to myself to take some notice of a letter published in the Washington *National Intelligencer*, by Lieut. WILLIAM B. WHITING, United States Navy, and intended by him as a reply to my letter addressed to the Southern officers of the United States Navy, which you were kind enough to publish in your paper some ten days ago. Had Mr. WHITING addressed me directly I would not have troubled you with this communication, and would have been able to have noticed his assault through the medium of private hands. Since, however, he has chosen the press to ventilate his opinions, nothing is left to me but to notice him in the same way.

Mr. WHITING was placed upon the "Reserved List" in 1855, by the verdict of fifteen of his brother officers, he being considered by them "incapable of performing promptly and efficiently all his duty, both ashore and afloat." Upon this list he has remained ever since, although ample opportunity must have been given him by the Act of Congress, approved January 16, 1857, of appealing from this verdict to the Court of Inquiry, established by that Act, and even from such a court to the President of the United States.

Occupying, then, the equivocal position that he does, it is but fair to believe that Lieut. WHITING possesses no small share of assurance when he presumes to speak for the officers of the United States Navy. It ill becomes him to impugn the integrity and honesty of such men as DUNCAN INGRAHAM, HENRY HARTSTENE, and many others, from this and other Southern States, when the government he serves does not think him fit to be trusted with the honor of its flag afloat. For myself, then, this man's opinions of my actions are worth but little, but I decidedly object that he should make favor with his Abolitionized masters at my expense. If he makes friends with either this, or the next Administration by this letter of his, I will only regret that I have in the least way contributed to his restoration to the "Active List" of the United States Navy. For this end his letter was written. Otherwise Lieutenant WHITING might envelope himself to the extent of his pleasure in "the star-spangled banner," and if he had left me alone, might have remain in modest obscurity forever, so far as I was interested in him. As a Southern citizen, I must, however, protest against one statement in Mr. WHITING's letter. He says, "by residence and association" he has been for nearly twenty years, "a citizen of a slaveholding State." The United States Navy Register, printed by order of the Secretary of the Navy, in compliance with a resolution of the Senate, makes Lieutenant WILLIAM B. WHITING a citizen of New York; he has therefore either falsified the record of the Department under which he serves, or else his own words.

Mr. WHITING states that my letter of the 14th inst., to the Southern officers, is "an *offence*" to the navy officers generally. It may be to Consolidationists and Abolitionists; but since he is a navy officer, and has undertaken to speak for the service at large, I beg that he will understand that I will be most happy to give him satisfaction for that letter or for this. He knows where to find me, and has only to ask an interview, and I will grant it, under arrangements usual among gentlemen.

I trust that, in justice to me, the *National Intelligencer* will transfer this communication to its columns.

I am, Mr. Editor, your obliged and ob't serv't,
J. R. HAMILTON.

THE "WAR" AMONG THE NEW YORK MILITARY.—The dissatisfaction growing out of General SANFORD's offer of the services of the military to the Governor, to be used against the South, continues unabated in New York city. Capt LOVELL, of the City Guard, has thrown up his commission, and thus assigns his reasons:

"While I yield to none in my readiness to uphold and defend the constitution of my country, I am inflexibly opposed to the doctrine that the stronger section of the Union may place a new and unauthorized interpretation on that constitution, which, in the judgment of the weaker section, denies them complete security for their property, and then compel its unwilling recognition at the point of the bayonet. I decline to be made an instrument by the civil and military authorities of this State, under the specious and untenable plea of enforcing the laws, for inaugurating a policy which can only result in a sanguinary and protracted civil war."

THE ROBBERY OF ARMS BY THE NEW YORK POLICE.—CONTINUED OUTRAGES.—The seizure of a large quantity of arms and ammunition at New York, intended for Savannah, by the police authorities, is likely to give rise to a question of jurisdiction between the "State" police and the Federal authorities. The latter contend that if these goods were to be taken possession of at all, it was the duty of the United States Marshal and the United States District Attorney to move in the matter. The police, in stopping the shipment of the goods, it is held, stepped beyond the line of their duty, and must be held to their responsibility therefor.

The police commissioners, in answer, allege that the United States Marshal is an avowed secessionist, and is doing everything in his power to give aid and comfort to the disunionists, and that, therefore, it is considered expedient that the police take the business into their own hands. The police department is an Abolition institution.

The muskets seized on board the Savannah steamer *Monticello* on Tuesday, still remained at the arsenal, in Seventh avenue, and General Superintendent Kenneday says that no claimant has appeared with a view of recovering the same. The United States District Attorney was notified that a large quantity of powder and cartridges were shipped on board the Charleston steamer on Wednesday, but no steps were taken to prevent the departure of the alleged contraband goods to their destination.

The police, on Wednesday, by direction of Superintendent Kennedy, seized twenty-five cases, containing five hundred muskets, on board the schooner *Caspian*. These arms were intended for some point at the South, and were seized as contraband merchandize. They were consigned to Savannah.

Ex-President Pierce has sold out all his bank stocks and stocks of every description, and converted the proceeds into specie, which he has deposited specially in a bank in Concord, N. H.

Our Richmond Correspondence.

RICHMOND, January 24, 1861.

Richmond Redeemed—Meeting at the African Church—Botts Hissed—The Union in a Bad Way, etc., etc.

Richmond has redeemed herself! BOTTS is repudiated! Obedient to a call published in the city papers, a large meeting of the working men assembled at the African Church, last evening, for the purpose of taking into consideration the alarming state of the country, and nominating candidates to represent them in the Convention, if deemed expedient.

The meeting was called to order at 7 o'clock, Mr. THOMAS H. WYNNE, the Superintendent of the City Gas Works, was chosen to preside, and Mr. FRANK WEST, News Editor of the Richmond *Dispatch*, was elected Secretary. After a brief address, the Chairman pronounced the meeting ready for business.

On motion, a committee of fifteen was appointed to prepare resolutions for the action of the meeting. During the absence of the committee, PATRICK HENRY AYLETT, Esq., was called for, and responded briefly. He said he intended to speak after the committee had reported, as he preferred having some matter upon which to work. Captain O. JENNINGS WISE, of the Richmond *Enquirer*, was then called for. He announced his intention of speaking, also, as soon as the committe had reported. Some objection was made to Captain WISE, he not being considered a working man, although he declared himself in the printing trade.

A motion was then made and carried to appoint a Committee of Three to wait on Hon. JOHN M. BOTTS, and request him to address the meeting. While this Committee was absent on their errand, a motion was made to prohibit all persons from addressing the meeting, who were not mechanics, having served a regular apprenticeship at some trade, but owing to the confusion which prevailed, I was unable to ascertain whether or not it was carried. Motions were now made on every conceivable subject, and with a rapidity that would have baffled the efforts of a dozen chairmen to entertain. The Committee on resolutions having been absent some time, one man moved that a Committee of Three be appointed to wait on *them*. This made matters worse; the confusion and discord which reigned was unequaled by any I ever witnessed before; nearly every man in the house was speaking at once, and one or two gentlemen obtained the stand, and permission to speak for a few minutes, but owing to the din which momentarily grew worse and worse, I was unable to hear their names. As soon as they had left the stand, the confusion became terrific. The men rose from their seats, waved their hats, yelled, hooted and halloed at the tops of their voices. At this stage of the proceedings, Mr. BOTTS arrived, but as the Committee entered about the same time, very little notice was paid him.

It was with difficulty that the meeting could be brought to order, so that the resolutions could be read. They declared, in substance, that the duty of Virginia was to make common cause with her seceding sister States of the South, unless ample guarantees were tendered by the North, before the assembling of the Convention; and, also, deeming it inexpedient to nominate candidates for the Convention. Before the Chairman had finished reading the resolutions, he was interrupted, and it was with difficulty that he was allowed to go on. Before a vote could be taken, calls were made for BOTTS, mingled with hisses, and cries of "put him out," "break his neck," &c. BOTTS arose, and attempted to speak, but from my seat not a word could be caught. In a little interval, one gentleman moved that a committee of eight be appointed to request Mr. BOTTS to leave, which was seconded by several, but not acted on. Having vainly endeavored to make himself heard, for about one or two minutes, BOTTS deliberately put on his overcoat and hat, and left the meeting.

The confusion now became worse; no vote would be allowed upon the resolutions of the Committee, nor on those of Mr. HOPKINS, subsequently offered. A motion was at last made and carried, that the meeting of *working men* adjourn, and that immediately thereafter a meeting of *Union men* assemble in the Hall.

Mr. WYNNE was again called to the chair, but declined serving, as he understood it to be the duty of every man participating in the meeting to pledge himself to the support of the Union as it now stands, and that he was not prepared to do. (Applause.)

Several ineffectual efforts were made to organize a Union meeting, and, finally, the gas was turned off, leaving the vast hall lighted by only two candles on the Speaker's table.

The meeting now became thinned considerably. A few persons were left, however, who commenced singing:

"We won't go home till morning,
We won't go home till morning,
We won't go home till morning,
Till daylight doth appear."

But finally the house was cleared, the meeting breaking up without doing any business whatever.

I think the cause of the Union is in rather a blue way here now, and hope soon to see the day when there will not be a Union man in the State.

RUTLEDGE.

Our Florida Correspondence.

ST. AUGUSTINE, Fla., January 19, 1861.

The Facts of the Seizure of the Florida Forts.—The Garrison and Armament of Fort Marion.—The Secession News.—No Surrender Thought of, etc., etc.

In your paper of the 7th instant (which I have just seen) appears, in a letter to Messrs. W. M. LAWTON & Co., from their Fernandina correspondent, the following: "A order came from the Governor this afternoon, and the *Everglade* will leave here at midnight for St. Augustine, to have the forts there taken and bring us some guns, etc. We have since learned that the detachment of Fernandina Volunteers has executed promptly the wise order of Governor PERRY." For the credit of the Ancient City, I beg you will allow me to correct this statement. Governor PERRY, on the 4th instant, appointed Mr. GEORGE C. GIBBS, of this place, an aid-de-Camp, with orders to proceed to St. Augustine, seize the forts, arsenal, etc., and, if necessary, to call to his assistance such additional aid as might be necessary. On the 7th instant, this order was promptly executed by St. Augustine troops alone, and the Fernandina Volunteers had no more to do with it than they had with the capture of Fort Moultrie, in Charleston. Marion, which is the only fort at this place, is (as also the arsenal), in possession of the State, and is garrisoned by Capt. J. L. PHILLIP's Light Infantry, and by Capt. G. C. GIBBS' Artillery Company. The latter is occupied in mounting 32 pounders and 8 inch howitzers. An *unarmed* detachment of Fernandina Volunteers reached here per *Everglade* on Sunday, 6th inst., with an order for guns, &c., and after getting them on board, went to sea again on the 12th. This alone was the object of their visit. They were not even present when Major GIBBS demanded and received possession, nor were their services required, though had they been, they would have been promptly rendered. As there was no garrison to overcome, aid was not asked for. On the 12th inst., intelligence of the Secession of this State was received here. A beautiful flag, the work of the ladies of St. Augustine, was hoisted, and salutes fired by detachments from the Jacksonville Infantry, Capt. STEELE (here for arms), the St. Augustine Blues, Capt. PHILLIPS, and the Marion Artillery, Capt. GIBBS, while all the church bells rang a joyful peal. Under Spanish and under English rule, this old Fort has taken many a hard knock and may take many more; but never yet has its colors been lowered to an enemy, and please God they never will be.

C.

COERCION BALL.—Preparations are progressing for a grand "union" Inauguration Ball, to come off in Washington on the night of the 4th of March. Gen. Scott will head the list of managers, assisted by Commodore Stewart, Gen. Wool and other prominent officers of the army and navy. Messrs. Crittenden, Seward, and other Senators, are expected to participate in the management.

Our Washington Correspondence.

WASHINGTON, January 24, 1861.

The Union Destroyed by Andy Johnson, "Sanctified Jerusalem" Clemens, Emerson Etheridge, and that ilk—Northern Adulation of the Log-Mauler and his Son—Crittenden Again Down—More Plans—Who Douglas Belongs to—Party Lines kept up in the Border States—How they Work up the Union Agony at the North—South Carolina Hankerers After the Federal Flesh-Pots—Bad Spell of Weather, etc., etc.

From the South, the destroyers of the Union have always come. The cry is still they come! Led by ANDY JOHNSON, they are marching boldly before the eyes all mankind. Their names and their deeds of shame, are they not written in the Book of the Chronicles of the House of Representatives? Unto the immortal ANDY and unto "Sanctified Jerusalem" CLEMENS, is added the great EMERSON ETHERIDGE, of Tennessee. He goes a bow-shot beyond them all. If every man, woman and child in his State should declare for secession, he would lift on high the banner of stripes (the stars are virtually gone), and fight for the ber-lessed, the ger-lorious Union. In effect, this is what he said yesterday. He paid the thirty pieces of silver for a seat in LINCOLN's Cabinet, and now it is his by right of purchase.

If proof were needed of the monarchical tendency of the Northern mind, it could easily be found in two significant facts. First: The abject subserviency of the Republican leaders to LINCOLN's views and vagaries. Not a man of them—CAMERON, perhaps, excepted—dares to take a position without first ascertaining the Rail-splitter's wishes. Adherence to party—the bane of Democracy—has given place to submission to the will of the Autocrat. This is a striking fact, full of meaning, and must have attracted the notice of every one who has access to Northern newspapers. Second: The movements of LINCOLN's family are chronicled precisely in the style of the English Court Journal when mentioning the trifling goings to and fro, of a Prince of the royal household. Thus the New York papers tell of the presence of LINCOLN's son—christened "Prince of Rails" by the college boys—in that city. Where he went, what he did, and how he was honored by the city dignitaries, is all set forth in detail, as if it were a matter of the least consequence what a log mauler's boy did, more than any other sixteen-year-old stripling. This lick-spittle worship is characteristic of the North. People who have lived there tell me that a Justice of the Peace is more bowed down to than a President at the South.

Beyond the go-by, given, for the twentieth time yesterday in the Senate, to CRITTENDEN's amendment, there is little stirring in the way of news. A plan which looks to the resignation of the members of Congress on the 21st of February, and the election of successors "by the people who are to assemble here on the 22d," is mooted. BOCOCK, they say, has signed it. What this means, I cannot tell. It sounds like the veriest nonsense. DOUGLAS is out with his plan, which amounts to nothing more than adding two years to the Presidential term. Don't he wish he may get these two additional years? He is now, and has for a long time been in the hands of railroad capitalists. Last Spring they assumed his debts, amounting to more than $250,000, and had a twenty horse power engine and fifteen clerks here, directing, franking, and sending off Squatter Sovereignty documents. And there was then, as their is now, the best understanding between his fuglemen and those of Mr. BELL. I see that the DOUGLAS men in Richmond, Va., have nominated their man for the Convention. I don't think, though, that the BELL men can stomach him. But it is evident that party lines are being kept up in the Border States, and the road left open for the BELL-DOUGLAS coalition in the future.

Great efforts are being made by the Republicans to stimulate the Union feeling of the North to the point of fighting. The papers of this morning have in their telegraphic columns a bugaboo story about a man being stabbed at Pensacola, or thereabouts, for expressing Union sentiments. In town here, I have heard a report, which no doubt is busily circulated, especially among the Republicans and Submissionists, to the effect that one of your whilome Congressmen stated, as a fact, that he dared not open his lips in South Carolina in favor of the Union, lest it should cost him fifteen or twenty duels. And I suspect, though I do not know, that some of these same hankerers after the Federal flesh-pots, and delighters in Washington society, are writing to quasi-secessionists here, praying them to patch up the Union, so that they may once more get back to the joys of the Imperial Capital. Another dodge to stir up Union idolatry at the North is practiced in the picture papers—HARPER's *Weekly*, the *Illustrated News*, &c.—where Major ANDERSON and his men are represented in the attitude of prayer around the flag-staff of Fort Sumter, as the stripes are being raised aloft.

We are in the midst of another cold, slushy, sleety, rainy, muddy spell.

SEVEN.

Movements in Louisiana—The Governor's Message—Business at New Orleans.

The Governor of Louisiana, in his message sent to the Legislature on the 22d inst., says:

Our enemies will find that throughout Louisiana we are one people, one in heart, one in mind, and are not to be cajoled into an abandonment of our rights, and not to be subdued. All hopes are at an end that the dissensions between the North and South can be healed; all the propositions of moderate men have been contemptuously rejected, and the cry of the North is for coercion. There is no longer a doubt of the wisdom of the policy which demands that the conflict shall come and be settled now.

The New Orleans *Crescent*, of the 16th inst., thus speculates about business there, and the probable effect of secession:

Cotton is being hurried on shipboard as fast as the fifty presses of the warehouses and screws can prepare it, as well as the warehouse proprietors. There is a great deal of talk about what Collector Hatch will do after the 23d instant, or as soon as the act of Secession is passed. Merchants, shippers and others are in a state of betweenity. In the meantime, the representative of Queen Victoria, the Consul, is perplexed by the numerous interrogatories hourly put as to what he intends to do. When he receives instructions from his Government, or the British Minister at Washington, he will give public notice. Mr. Bull is too shrewd a diplomatist to allow our disturbances to interfere with his supply of cotton at this moment.

The movements in Cotton yesterday were large, that is, on the great levee, where several mammoth cargoes were being discharged. Among buyers and sellers there was not so much doing. After a storm comes a calm, applies to dealings in Cotton as in nature's movements. The sales of the staples for the last week, that is, from Monday to Saturday, inclusive, were 87,000 bales. This quantity having to be delivered, received and exchange negotiated, rather checked the movements yesterday. There was a disposition evinced by some buyers to await further advices from the other side.

The freight market continues somewhat excited. Rates have advanced to ⅝d. in British bottoms, and 23.32d. is a very close shave in an American vessel. Not so close, however, as a case in years gone by, say over a third of a century, when a shipper took up a vessel at 63.64 of a penny. We occasionally meet this old merchant on the flags, who, by the by, looks as hearty as he did in the eventful year of 1825, say 36 years ago.

The freight market is of course talked much of, and even the good Black Republican ship *William Singer*, has been cleared by Messrs. Meeker, Knox & Co., with a full cargo of cotton for Liverpool.

THE CATHEDRAL OF ST. DENIS, PARIS.—The works at the Cathedral of St. Denis are approaching completion. The most curious portion of the buildings is the crypt of the Carlovingian Kings, which formed a portion of the third church raised on the same spot, the first having been erected over the tomb of St. Denis before the invasion of the Franks; the second by Dagobert I., about the year 630; the third by Charlemagne, in 775; and the present structure in the twelfth century. This ancient crypt was found tolerably preserved, and has been repaired with great care. It contains at present the remains of Louis XIV., Marie Antoinette, and the aunts of the former, with those of the Duc de Berry and one of his children, the Prince de Conde, and Louis XVIII. The new crypt, which has been constructed to receive the ashes of the Bonaparte family, is placed beneath the transept and a small portion of the chancel, and immediately west of the Carlovingian tomb, thus bringing the two extremes into contact. It is very large, and consists of a central space and two side aisles; at the east end of the former in a small altar, lighted by means of a window or sky-light behind the high altar of the church.

Accounts from Fort Sumter.—What Captain Doubleday Says.

[*From the Washington Correspondence of the Baltimore Exchange.*]

I have been permitted to peruse a very interesting letter from Lieutenant DOUBLEDAY, of Fort Sumter, received last night, in which he says:

"While the leaders are becoming more pacific the mob is becoming more outrageous and ungovernable. I hear they are loud in threats about me. They say there may be some excuse for other officers, as they are supposed to be Southern men performing a duty disagreeable to them, but I am an open Republican and enemy. Some influential Southern men have written to Governor Pickens that his refusal to allow us to hold any communication with the city, and his interference with our mails, has made South Carolina enemies in many Southern States, and he has been urged to relax his severity. We have been living on our rations and a few vegetables laid in for Capt. Foster's workmen, who went away; and yet the MERCURY has the impudence to say we are fed by them. We have received no supplies of any kind from Charleston, with the single trifling exception of a box of candles smuggled in. If Major Anderson is allowed the privilege of contracting for fresh meats, as is done everywhere in the army, he will exercise it, but if it is proposed as a present from South Carolina, he will not receive it. The country people who never saw a gun or a fort, who have no education, and own little property, are raving mad to attack us.

"We may be too incredulous, but feel no apprehension, and don't believe the fort can be taken. Day before yesterday the Carolinians landed two or three mortars on Cumming's Point, on the nearest point of land for attacking the fort. There is not a particle of truth in the story of a mutiny. It was started in Charleston to induce the Government to surrender this place. There has been no prisoners in the guard house for a long time. The men are behaving admirably, are in good spirits, full of fun, and spoiling for a fight. As for surrendering, under any circumstances, they never dreamed of it. You need pay no attention to any thing you see in Charleston papers in reference to our affairs. If you reflect that when a boat comes with a white flag from Charleston, that none of our men are allowed to communicate with it, you will readily see that all their stories about us are mere inventions. The men bear their privations and severe guard duty very cheerfully. They miss their tobacco more than any thing else.

"P. S.—Two steamboats were on the watch over us all night, one in the direction of the bar and the other towards Charleston."

This is the substance of the letter which is dated the evening of the 20th. It gives a closer insight into matters concerning which there have been many contradictory statements.

Sentiment of Southern Officers of the Army.

To the Editor of the Constitution:

SIR: Several general officers of the army have lately favored the public with the information of their willingness to spill blood to keep sovereign States confederated together against the wishes of millions of their citizens. For one, I am not willing that the wordy outpourings of Major General Wool and the vaporings of Brigadier Harney shall go forth to the country as the uncontradicted sentiment of officers at this unfortunate juncture. I cannot permit the people of the country—the North as well as the South—to be thus deceived into the belief that any considerable number of the effective officers of the army regard it as either practicable or right to constrain the existence of the Federal Union one day after it shall cease to stand by and through the affection of its several members.

It is timely, therefore, for me to say in this way: I have as yet met with no officer of Southern birth who is not resolved, at the proper time, to cast his fortunes with his State, and, if need be, give his best services for the defence of her soil, the homes of his kindred, and the rights of his fellow statesmen from invasion or assault, even though made in the name of the Federal Union.

I can say further, I have seen no officer from a Southern State who is willing to be employed for the coercion of any State, whether South Carolina or Massachusetts. Some there are, I presume, who might accept such a service from a mistaken sense of duty, but I cannot hesitate to declare that those who can be found to act thus will prove few in number and exceptional cases. The great mass—if not, indeed, every single one—of Southern officers recognize their allegiance in times like these to their several States as clear and enforcing; and their countrymen may be assured they will not fail or falter in the discharge of their whole duty.

The army cannot be made the instrument of a central power, except for the defence of the whole country and against a foreign enemy—never for the subjugation of a sovereign member of the Confederacy formed by our fathers for purposes of common weal and common defence. It can never, under the Constitution, be legally employed against a State of the present Union; and those who think the officers of the army will lend the aid of their professional experience and training for the reduction of their own States and section into a condition of political vassalage to another section, will cherish a delusion.

In other and precise words:

The people of the Southern States need not distrust for one moment the loyalty of their kinsmen in the Federal army, as it is now organized. To a man, these officers—graduates of the Military Academy, as well as others—hold themselves ready at the call of their several States; when these need their professional services, they will not halt or hesitate; they will not remain in the service of a government of which their own States and section are not integral and equal parts. This is the fixed resolve of very many officers with whom the present writer has interchanged views, and whose ultimate course has been fully decided. That course has been the one absorbing question in the profession since the 6th day of November, because we have not failed to see that, in the event of any insensate attempt to preserve the Union by force, the army will at once be resorted to, and its officers, first of all Americans, be forced to choose sides in the terrible issue that must be joined when the sword shall be cast into the balance of the Federal Union.

A GRADUATE OF THE MILITARY ACADEMY.

The French bridges have permanent marks, with dates affixed, to show the heights of successive floods; they nearly all record this fact, that the floods are gradually and annually increasing in height. The bridge over the Loire, in the vicinity of the late disastrous inundation, especially indicate this; and it is not too much to affirm that the next great flood will be at least as disastrous as the last. The reason is obvious. The impetuous torrent from the high lands brings with it large quantities of stones and gravel, which are arrested by bridges, shoals, &c., so that the river beds are gradually becoming of a higher level, and navigation upon them is all but impracticable.

CELESTIAL ACCOUNT OF THE TAKING OF PEKIN.—A Chinese paper gravely relates that Lord Elgin, Baron Gros, all the officers and the whole allied army were enticed by the Emperor into Pekin, where a large palace was given to them to live in. After feasting them, and giving them samshoo of such excellent quality that the barbarians took too much of it, the Emperor caused the palace to be fired, and the whole army perished.

A "SELL."—Rockland, Me., was in a ferment last Saturday week over the rumor that General Scott had been killed in a duel with Toombs. "The bells were tolled and the streets filled with excited people," who finally went home, laboring under the impression that a "sale" had taken place.

AFFECTION IN MEN AND WOMEN.—Women are said to have stronger attachments than men. It is not so. Strength of attachment is evinced in little things. A man is often attached to an old hat; but did you ever know of a woman having an attachment for an old bonnet?—*Punch.*

W. M. Thomas, Esq., of Greenville, proffers to be one of twenty to raise ten thousand dollars for the benefit of the families of the poor men of the Greenville volunteers.

A few days ago 57 United States soldiers, who were compelled to evacuate the Arsenal at Baton Rouge, La., arrived at Newport (Ky.) barracks.

The State Bank of Louisiana proposes to loan the Governor of that State $100,000 without interest to arm the State.

A company of Minute Men was organized in Carrollton, Ky., last week, under the influence of the gallant old soldier, Gen. Wm. O. Butler.

Through the influence of the Emperor and Empress, shops in Paris are now shut on Sunday to a great extent.

The Petersburg (Va.) *Intelligencer* has been sold to R. C. Shell, of Dinwiddie County, Va., for $1560.

James Cook has been elected Mayor of Parkersburg, Va.

THE DAILY TRUE DELTA.

JOHN MAGINNIS, Proprietor. OFFICE--18 ST. CHARLES STREET. TERMS--TEN DOLLARS PER ANNUM.

VOLUME XXIII. NEW ORLEANS, TUESDAY MORNING, FEBRUARY 19, 1861. NUMBER 80

AUCTION SALES.

McCerren & Landry's Auction

Mart, Masonic Hall, St. Charles street.

REGULAR SALES HOUR, 11 o'clock A. M. Tuesdays and Saturdays for REAL ESTATE, SLAVES and STOCKS. Mondays and Thursdays for GENERAL MERCHANDISE, &c.

☞ FURNITURE, and other out-door Sales, will receive prompt attention. ja16tf

Valuable Improved Property

in New Carrollton, for sale on account of departure.

BY McCERREN & LANDRY — Auctioneers and Real Estate Agents, Masonic Hall, St. Charles street—

THAT VALUABLE PORTION OF GROUND, forming about two-thirds of the square No. 5, in New Carrollton, bounded by Milton, Upper Line, Dakin and Shakspeare streets, and measuring 272 feet front on Milton street, 180 feet front on Upper Line, and the same on Dakin street. The improvements consist of a beautiful COTTAGE DWELLING, of 10 Rooms, with Galleries, separate Kitchen Buildings, Cellars, Poultry Houses, Stables, Pigeon Houses, &c., 5 large Cisterns, and Outbuildings necessary. The Garden and Orchard are well cultivated, having some 60 Fruit Trees — comprising Plum, Orange, &c.

This property is beautifully situated, only six squares from the Carrollton Depot, and forms a very pleasant out-of-town residence. The grounds are tastefully laid out, and the premises are in good order.

For terms and further particulars, apply at the office of McCerren & Landry, where a descriptive plan of the property can be seen. fe1

C. E. GIRARDEY & CO.'S SALES.

A Double One-story Frame

House on Thalia street, between Liberty and Howard streets.

BY C. E. GIRARDEY & Co.—Office, No. 37 Magazine street—Will be sold on SATURDAY, Feb. 23, 1861, at 12 o'clock, at the City Hotel—

A CERTAIN LOT OF GROUND, in the square bounded by Thalia, Melpomene, Howard and Liberty streets, measuring 31 feet front on Thalia street, by 96 feet depth between parallel lines.

Improvements comprise a double one-story Frame DWELLING, having two rooms and kitchen and cistern to each tenement. Yard well filled and banquettes made.

Terms — One-third cash; balance at 12 and 18 months credit, for notes secured by mortgage on the property, bearing six per cent. current and eight per cent. eventual interest.

Property to be kept insured, and policy transferred to vendor.

Act of sale before M. Gernon, Notary Public, at the expense of purchasers. fe17

R. M. MONTGOMERY'S SALES.

Fine Stock at Auction.

BY R. M. MONTGOMERY, Auctioneer—Will be sold at auction on WDDNESDAY, the 20th inst., at 12 o'clock M., at the Tattersalls Stables, 164 Gravier street, without any reserve or limit—

28 head of fine HORSES, in pairs and single. Among the number are four fine St. Lawrence Colts. Also, one very fast team. Those in want of fast and fine stock can be accommodated.

Terms—Cash. fe19

JULIAN NEVILLE'S SALES.

James Nelligan's Sale of Fine

Horses.

JAMES NELLIGAN, Auctioneer, will sell EVERY DAY THIS WEEK, at 11½ o'clock A. M., at Dr. Elliott's Stables, corner Union and Baronne streets, without reserve or limit—

1 lot of fine A No. 1 Saddle and Harness HORSES.

Two New Rockaway CARRIAGES.

A lot of Fine New Rockaway BUGGIES.

Persons having Stock to dispose of will please call at Stables the day previous to the sale, and make entry of the same.

Terms—Cash. fe18¶

LEGAL NOTICES.

Mary Franc, wife of Charles

Falkenheiner, vs. her Husband.

THE STATE OF LOUISIANA—FOURTH DIStrict Court of New Orleans—No. 14,347.

I hereby certify, that on the 8th day of February, 1861, judgment was rendered in this Court in the following entitled suit, in the words and figures following, to wit:

In this case submitted for adjudication, the law and the evidence being considered, it is ordered, adjudged and decreed that a judgment of separation of property be entered in favor of plaintiff; and it is further ordered that plaintiff do recover of defendant the sum of five hundred dollars, with lien and privilege and legal interest from judicial demand, and costs.

Rendered February 8th, 1861.

Signed February 13th, 1861.

(Signed) J. W. PRICE, Judge.

In testimony whereof I have hereunto set my hand and affixed the seal of the said Court, at the city of New Orleans, on this 13th day of February, in the year of our Lord one thousand eight hundred and sixty-one, and the eighty-fifth year of the Independance of the United States.

J. O. CHALON, Clerk.

Marie Franc, epouse de Chas.

Falkenheiner, vs. son mari.

Je certifie par les présentes que le huitième jour de février 1861 jugement a été rendu par cette Cour, dans l'affaire ci-dessus, de la manière suivante, à savoir:

Dans cette affaire soumise pour une décision, la loi et les témoignages ayant été considérés, il est ordonné, adjugé et décrété qu'un jugement en séparation de biens soit enregistré en faveur de la demanderesse; et il est de plus ordonné que la demanderesse recouvre du défendeur la somme de cinq cents piastres, avec privilège et intérêt légal à dater de la demande judiciaire, et les frais.

Jugement rendu le 8 de février 1861.

Jugement signé le 13 février 1861.

(Signé) J. W. PRICE, Juge.

En foi de quoi j'ai apposé ma signature et le sceau de la dite Cour, en la ville de la Nouvelle-Orleans, ce 13me jour de février de l'année de Notre-Seigneur mil huit cent soixante-un, et la quatre-vingt-cinquième année de l'Indépendance des Etats-Unis.

J. O. CHALON, Greffier.

fe14 19 22

Succession of Jas. H. Riggin.

SECOND DISTRICT COURT OF NEW ORLEANS—No. 17,294.

Notice is hereby given to the creditors of this estate and to all other persons herein interested, to show cause within ten days from the present notification (if any they have or can) why the account presented by the testamentary-executor of the deceased should not be homologated and approved, the funds distributed in accordance therewith.

By order of the Court,

E. MICHOT, Deputy Clerk.

Succession de Jas. H. Riggin.

DEUXIEME COUR DE DISTRICT DE LA NOUvelle-Orléans—No. 17,294.

Avis est par le présent donné aux créanciers de la susdite succession et à toutes autres personnes que cela peut concerner d'avoir à déduire, sous dix jours à dater de la présente publication, les raisons pour lesquelles le compte présenté par l'exécuteur-testamentaire du défunt ne serait point approuvé et homologué, les fonds entre ses mains répartis conformément au dit compte.

Par ordre de la Cour,

fe10 14 18 E. MICHOT, Député-Greffier.

Chas. Boyle vs. his Creditors.

STATE OF LOUISIANA—SIXTH DISTRICT Court of New Orleans—No. 1832.

Notice is hereby given to the creditors of the insolvent that they have to meet at the office of Charles Stringer, notary public, on Monday, the 18th day of March, 1861, at 10 o'clock A. M., for the purpose of appointing a new syndic in place of Gerge W. Nettleton, deceased.

By order of the Court,

A. J. VILLERÉ, Deputy Clerk.

Chas. Boyle vs. ses Creanciers

ETAT DE LA LOUISIANE—SIXIEME COUR de District de la Nouvelle-Orléans—No. 1832.

Avis est par le présent donné aux créanciers de l'insolvable d'avoir à se réunir au bureau de Charles Stringer, notaire public, le lundi, 18me jour de mars 1861, à 10 heures du matin, dans le but de nommer un nouveau syndic en remplacement de George W. Nettleton, décédé.

Par ordre de la Cour,

A. J. VILLERÉ,

fe19 mr5 20 Député-Greffier.

SHERIFF'S SALES.

McIntosh's Executor vs. Mr.

and Mrs. Henning.

SECOND DISTRICT COURT OF NEW ORLEANS—No. 17,544.

By virtue of a writ of fieri facias to me directed by the Honorable the Second District Court of New Orleans, in the above entitled cause, I will proceed to sell at public auction, at my warehouse, No. 23 Jefferson street, in the Second district of this city, on Monday, the fourth day of March, 1861, at 10½ o'clock A. M.—

One lot of Household Furniture, as per inventory on file at my office.

Seized in the above suit.

Terms—Cash on the spot.

E. T. PARKER,

Sheriff of the Parish of Orleans.

L'executeur-testamentaire

de McIntosh vs. Sieur et Dame Henning.

DEUXIÈME COUR DE DISTRICT DE LA NOUvelle-Orléans—No. 17,544.

En vertu d'un writ de fieri facias à moi adressé par l'Honorable Deuxième Cour de District de la Nouvelle-Orléans, dans l'affaire ci-dessus, je procéderai le LUNDI, 4 de mars 1861, à 10½ heures A. M., à mon entrepôt rue Jefferson, No. 23, dans le Deuxième District de cette ville, à la vente publique et adjudication de:

Un lot de Meubles, suivant inventaire déposé en mon bureau pour recours.

Saisis dans l'affaire ci-dessus.

Conditions—Comptant au moment de l'adjudication. E. T. PARKER,

fe19 23 26 28 mr2 Shérif de la Paroisse d'Orléans.

E. J. HART & CO.,

Nos. 77 and 79 Tchoupitoulas street, Wholesale GROCERS, DRUGGISTS AND COMMISSION MERCHANTS, and dealers in

DURYEA'S IMPROVED STARCH AND MAIZENA.

no16 4m

THE TRUE DELTA

STEAM JOB PRINTING

ESTABLISHMENT,

18.........ST. CHARLES STREET.........18

We would call the particular attention of the Mercantile and Business Community to this Department of our Establishment, as we have made very extensive additions to it in the way of the

NEWEST STYLES OF POSTER AND GENERAL JOB TYPE, PRESSES, &C.,

WHICH ENABLE US TO

EXECUTE EVERY DESCRIPTION OF

PRINTING,

SUCH AS

MAMMOTH POSTERS,
FANCY SHOW CARDS,
VELVET WORK,
RAILROAD WORK,
LAWYERS' BRIEFS,
BOOK WORK,
STEAMBOAT WORK,
BUSINESS CARDS,
PROGRAMMES,
HAND-BILLS,

AND ALL KINDS OF

MERCANTILE WORK!

☞ The facilities we have in the way of ☜

STEAM, CARD AND HAND PRESSES,

ENABLE US TO

EXECUTE WORK RAPIDLY, NEATLY AND CHEAPLY!

RULING AND BOOK-BINDING,

OF EVERY DESCRIPTION, EXECUTED WITH DISPATCH!

no17 2dp tf

MANUFACTURES.

Machinery--Machinery.

STATIONARY & PORTABLE STEAM ENGINES,
CIRCULAR SAW MILLS,
SHINGLE MACHINES,
INDIAN RUBBER BELT,
CIRCULAR SAWS,
COTTON-SEED HULLERS,
CORN MILLS,
STEAM GAUGES,
IRON, GAS and
WATER PIPES,
POWER AND HAND PUMPS,

At the Machinery Depot of

RICHARD F. HARRISON,

au14 Nos. 40 and 42 St. Charles st.

Guns! Guns! Guns!

L. GERTEIS, No. 107 St. Charles street, Manufacturer of Guns, Rifles and Pistols, with all the latest improvements. Constantly on hand a general assortment of my own and European manufacture. Fire arms of all description neatly repaired. oc23 6m

Planters and Others

WANTING the BEST and CHEAPEST CORN and FLOURING MILLS in the world, can be supplied with that very article, by calling at 85 St. Charles street, New Orleans, where all the various sizes of these celebrated MILLS are for sale, or by addressing the undersigned by mail.

W. P. COLEMAN, Patentee,

oc5 d&W6m 8 St. Charles st., New Orleans.

NEGROES FOR SALE.

Negroes for Sale.

THE undersigned has re-opened the well-known Slave Depot, No. 47 Esplanade street, corner of Chartres, recently occupied by John B. Smith, with a very lively lot of field hands, house servants, washers and ironers, seamstresses, &c., on sale—all imported from Virginia and South Carolina.

Additional supplies will be received from those States during the season. Terms, reasonable for cash, or approved city acceptances.

THOS. E. MATTHEWS,

no1 6m¶ Office, 47 Esplanade st., cor. Chartres.

Arrival of Negroes for Sale.

I HAVE just arrived with ONE HUNDRED AND FIFTY NEGROES from Virginia and Maryland, such as Mechanics, House Servants, Cooks, Washers and Ironers and Field Hands. I will also receive during the season (every month) large supplies, exclusively from those States. I am determined to sell at prices to suit the times, for cash or approved city acceptances. They can be seen at my house, corner of Baronne and Gravier streets, New Orleans.

oc20 6m J. M. WILSON.

Negroes for Sale.

JOSEPH BRUIN, a regular trader in this city for the last twenty-six years, has just arrived with a large lot of Maryland and Virginia NEGROES—such as Mechanics, House Servants, Cooks, Washers and Ironers, and Field Hands, and will be receiving a fresh supply during all the season.

For sale on reasonable terms, for cash or approved city acceptances, at his old stand, corner of Esplanade and Chartres streets, Third District.

se19 d&W8m¶

Foster's Slave Depot,

NO. 76 BARONNE STREET, New Orleans. Keeps constantly on hand and for sale, Mechanics, Field Hands, Cooks, Washers, Ironers and General House Servants.

Also, Buys and Sells Slaves on Commission.

oc21

Carolina & Virginia Negroes.

THE subscriber has just arrived with a gang of very likely Carolina and Virginia NEGROES, consisting of Field Hands, House Servants, Cooks, Washers and Ironers, also, a No. 1 Bricklayer, and will be receiving fresh supplies during the season. Persons wishing to purchase will find it to their advantage to call, as they will be sold on accommodating terms.

H. F. PETERSON,

se27 6m¶ 15 Perdido street.

PINCKARD, STEEL & CO.,

CORNER GRAVIER & TCHOUPITOULAS STS.,

IMPORTERS AND DEALERS IN

LIQUORS, CIGARS, TOBACCO AND FINE GROCERIES,

INCLUDING

DURYEA'S IMPROVED PREMIUM GLEN COVE STARCH AND MAIZENA.

no16 4m

Coal! Coal! Coal!

THE undersigned is now prepared to furnish, at the shortest notice, to parties in all parts of the city, to steamboats, &c., ENGLISH CANNEL, PEYTONIA, ANTHRACITE (both egg size and lump) and PITTSBURGH COAL, at the lowest market prices.

Orders left at CREEVY & FARWELL'S, 29 Carondelet street; at R. & J. WATSON'S, 15 Commercial Place, or at the office of the undersigned, on the Levee, opposite Post No. 15, First District, will be promptly attended to.

ja20 1m WILLIAMSON SMITH.

Educational.

MRS. BRAND begs to inform her friends and the public that she has leased the residence of N. R. Jennings, Esq., No. 193 Camp street, first house above Julia. She is now prepared, in compliance with the desire of many parents, to receive more pupils than heretofore, though the number will continue to be limited. In addition to her day classes, she can accommodate a few young ladies as boarders. The best testimony she can give of her gratitude to those who may place their confidence in her, will be the devoted care she will bestow on the moral, intellectual and physical education of their daughters. All applications—which she requests may be early—made either in person or by letter to Mrs. BRAND, 193 Camp street, shall meet prompt attention.

References—Dr. Newton Mercer, John Watt, Esq., N. R. Jennings, Esq., Dr. G. W. Campbell and the Hon. J. P. Benjamin. 1y30 tf

EATON & BETTERTON,

New Levee, Common and Fulton streets, Wholesale GROCERS and COMMISSION MERCHANTS, and dealers in

DURYEA'S IMPROVED GLEN COVE STARCH AND MAIZENA.

no16 4m

BRADY, THOS. R. & CO., Lumber Merchants, Julia street, between Commerce and Levee streets.

WRIGHT'S REJUVENATING ELIXIR.

This is an all-powerful medicine, made upon the strictest pharmaceutical principles, by one of the ablest chemists of the age. Its object is to be a perfect specific for

Imbecility.
Disorganization of the Organs of Generation.
Sleeplessness,
Debility,
Nervous Affections, Feebleness,

And the destruction of the nervous system—the results of youthful indiscretion. It raises the sinking frame, it puts new life into the debilitated system and renews the entire man.

IT NEVER FAILS.

For sale in New Orleans, wholesale and retail, by

J. WRIGHT & CO.,

21 and 151 Chartres street,

Sole Proprietors.

THE CHIEF AMONG TEN THOUSAND.

DALLY'S MAGICAL PAIN EXTRACTOR has universally supplanted all other ointments and healing applications, in both the Eastern and Western Hemispheres, wherever introduced; and its intrinsic merits is the true secret of its success in all Cutaneous affections, whether the cause be accident or disease.

DALLY'S MAGICAL PAIN EXTRACTOR.

BURNS AND SCALDS

Are instantly relieved of their anguish, pain and inflammation by a timely application of this marvelous healer, and the flesh is renewed by a charm, no blemish or scar remaining.

THE FRIEND OF THE NURSERY.

Children are frequent sufferers from external injuries, especially from fluid and camphene explosions, therefore every mother should have this healing preparation constantly at hand. It heals sore breasts, and quickly removes the Tetter, or Ringworm, so prevalent in children.

TO TRAVELERS BY SEA AND LAND.

The machinist, the traveler, and every other individual whose lot in life throws him within the chance of accident from explosion, fire, or collision, should bear in mind that this Magic Extractor is his best and only friend. It is both portable and cheap, and should ever be his companion, as a friend in need. There are thousands of living witnesses to testify to its marvelous virtue, who owe their sound limbs and muscles to its saving efficacy.

The following are a few of the leading diseases for which DALLY'S MAGICAL PAIN EXTRACTOR is a Preventive, as well as Cure.

Burns,	Erysipelas,	Sores of all kinds,
Bruises,	Fistula,	Shot Wounds,
Boils,	Frost Bites,	Scrofula,
Broken Breast,	Fever Sores,	Scurvy,
Bites of Reptiles,	Felons,	Scalds,
Cancer,	Glandular Dis's,	Scurf,
Cracked Lips,	Mercurial Sores,	Scald Head,
Chapped Hands,	Pains generally,	Sprains,
Chilblains,	Pimples,	Small Pox,
Cramp,	Piles,	Tumors,
Contracted Cords,	Poison,	Tetter,
Chafes,	Rheumatism,	Ulcers,
Diseases of the Skin,	Rashes,	Venereal Sores, &c.

Sold at the principal Depots, 14 Broadway, New York, and 21 and 151 Chartres street, New Orleans, by J. WRIGHT & CO.,

General Agents.

It can also be obtained of all respectable druggist and merchants throughout the United States and Canadas.

DR. DAVIS' WILD CHERRY AND TAR.

HOW TO STOP A COUGH.

We continually hear the expression, "Oh! it is *only a Cough.*" Only, indeed! Yes, but that neglected cough will probably end in that fearful disease to think of—Consumption—that hurries without a hope such millions to their graves.

Will you take time by the forelock? Will you respite yourself from an untimely dissolution? If you will, be sure to have this faithful remedy at your hand. Every one knows what a specific is in the Wild Cherry, and then when combined with Tar, at once releases the mucus from the cells of the lungs, expectoration ensues, breathing becomes natural, and you are safe.

For sale in New Orleans by

J. WRIGHT & CO.,

21 and 151 Chartres street.

General Agents.

DR. OSGOOD'S INDIA CHOLAGOGUE

CURES

Fever and Ague, Chills and Fever, Dumb Ague, Intermittent and Remittent Fevers, Liver Complaint, Jaundice, Enlargement of the Spleen, and all the various forms of

BILIOUS DISEAES.

This invaluable medicine was prepared from an extensive practice of several years in a bilious climate, and is never known to fail curing Fever and Ague, or any of the diseases above named.

Those who are suffering from affections of this kind, and also those who have become invalids from their effects upon the constitution, will find the INDIA CHOLAGOGUE a most invaluable remedy for purifying the blood, and thoroughly cleansing from the system the morbid effects of a bilious climate.

The wonderful effects of Cholagogue in eradicating Bile from the human system can only explain its extraordinary agency in the speedy, thorough and permanent cure of Fever and Ague, and the various grades of intermittent and remittent fevers.

It has been tested in thousands of cases, and is pronounced by all who have used it, one of the greatest Fever and Ague remedies extant.

Be sure and ask for Dr. Osgood's India Cholagogue, as there are many counterfeits offered for sale.

For sale in New Orleans, wholesale and retail, at proprietor's prices.

J. WRIGHT & CO.,

21 and 151 Chartres street,

General Agents.

WINER'S CANADIAN VERMIFUGE.

This is the only sure remedy against worms in the human frame—things that are so fatal and destructive to children.

SAVE THE CHILDREN!

Let mothers be timely warned, and not allow these children murderers to remain in the systems of their offspring. Remember that

WINER'S CANADIAN VERMIFUGE

Will at once and for ever banish the reptiles, and the young will be saved. Think of this.

Colonel Vasser, of Mississippi, in a letter to J. W. Vesey. Esq., of the Aberdeen Conservative, thus winds up his communication on the value of this medicine to *his own family*—"My experience has convinced me that, in the experiment I have made with Winer's Canadian Vermifuge, it is due to suffering humanity, as well as to the manufacturer of the medicine, to make public the result of my observations. (Signed) "W. H. VASSER."

The Vermifuge is for sale, wholesale and retail, by

J. WRIGHT & CO.,

21 and 151 Chartres street.

Sole Proprietors.

MOTT'S

Invincible Cooking Ranges.

FOR SALE—The above

CELEBRATED RANGES,

Of different sizes, and at reasonable prices.

J. P. COULON,

au9 6m¶ 107 Poydras street.

Brashear City Saw Mill.

THIS SAW MILL, situated at Brashear City, is now prepared to furnish any quantity and quality of CYPRESS LUMBER. Orders addressed to the Saw Mill, or to the undersigned, will receive prompt attention.

ap19 1y BLANCHIN & GIRAUD.

Byrne's Patent Process

OF CLARIFYING SUGAR JUICES WITH SULPHUROUS ACID GAS.—This process, patented September 4th, 1860, (which is guaranteed,) is the only method by which Sulphate of Lime is not found in the Sugar, and the only process by which the quantity of Gas used can be ascertained. For further particulars apply to THOMAS BYRNE,

se23 Baton Rouge.

Double Cylinder Cotton Gins.

JUST RECEIVED—An invoice of all sizes, from 60 to 120 Saws, of the celebrated W. G. Clemons, Brown & Co., Columbus, Ga., make.

ALBERTSON & MUDGE,

au13 tf¶ 8 Union street

The Daily True Delta

LOCAL GOVERNMENT.

When the people of any state throw off by revolution, violently or, as at present, without resistance or opposition, the lines which politically bind them to a system of government subversive of the ends of its creation, one would suppose the first thing they would desire—if their free agency continued or if the change was the voluntary proceeding of a majority of their number—would be the adaption of their local government and regulations to the requirements of their new position, and the supercession of old and effete machinery for other better adapted to the successful working of the new order of affairs. When this is not done, the impression is irresistibly strong that in reality the changes initiated are not the work of the whole people or of any really considerable or influential number of them; but has been set on foot, matured and consummated without their consent, contrary to their real wishes and without sufficient cause or authorized warrant. So far, the revolution in these states seems the emanation of men in public office, of individuals whose official rule was, in the nature of things, soon forever to be terminated, and of those whose life-long ambition it has been to attain supreme dictation in the Union as it has heretofore existed, or over its broken and scattered fragments, as they now present it. This design, up to this time, seems to have encountered no check, moral or physical; scarcely provoked a protest; and the comforts and distinction enuring from the overthrow of one system of government, which would inevitably have produced a general rotation in office, have been secured apparently without an effort by those whom general execration and contempt had consigned to eternal oblivion for their ignorance, their venality and their worthlessness. So far the revolution has produced no fruits. The prosperity its authors promised the people so soon as they should be allowed the absolute control of their affairs, so far from being realized, appears to have passed away from the visions of the most sanguine, and in its stead uncertainty, doubt, alarm, paralyzation of everything and fearful depression prevail. One class only is prosperous, namely: the locust one which feeds and fattens upon the public extravagance and popular suffering. Offices, only required for the business of a great nation and to requite the convenient tools of ambitious and designing scoundrels, are kept up in full volume, and numerous others, civil and military, are being daily multiplied in order to prove the inexhaustible character of the public resources or the squeezeable plasticity of an unresisting and long-suffering population. If a voice of protest is heard like our own it is denounced as the mutterings of an unreasonable discontent, and the citizen so inconsiderate as to inquire whether the political changes we are undergoing require a sacrifice of the prosperity and substance of the people, as well as a loss of their legitimate control of their political affairs, is laughed at as a fool or denounced as a malcontent. If, then, any one asks himself whether the overthrow of our late government was caused by its encroachments upon our rights and invasion of our liberties, or to perpetuate office, power and wealth in the hands of an incapable and irresponsible body of men, the answer he will be obliged to make to himself cannot be a question of doubt or of speculation. In this state of things, is it too much to ask of those who have so much at stake, that they will initiate a movement to give to the tax-payers and the industrial bodies of the state a voice in and a control of its affairs, so that, in addition to revolution, we may not be obliged to add bankruptcy and ruin as its complement. If something be not speedily done, the severest suffering, and that, too, among classes ill able to endure it, will be experienced; our planters will be without supplies for the support of their people, and our merchants without credit—all of which, if a deliberate design be not harbored to deprive the people of their sovereignty, may be prevented by a wise administration of our local government and confidence in those charged with its administration. Tenderness of office-holders for each other, the sympathies so natural among those who have long been pensioners upon the public bounty, and who have cause to regard themselves as an exclusive and superior class, we can understand; but the time is rapidly approaching when even they will be compelled to relax their pretensions from lack of resources from the public industry to sustain them. Swimmingly as all so far has progressed, encouraging as seems the prospect of the entire brood being for aye quartered upon the people and their industry, it does seem to us that the enquiry will soon force itself upon the most reluctant, whether a vindication of southern rights must necessarily be accompanied by a sacrifice of personal liberty and a compulsory surrender of individual property for the support of men contributing nothing in return. The pecuniary condition of the state and city, if frankly stated, would make the most indifferent reflect, and that they do not now do so is only accountable for in the same manner as is done for those who shut their eyes for safety from approaching and inevitably injury.

New Orleans and Jackson Railroad.—In the Brookhaven (Miss.) Advertiser, of Saturday last, we find the following:

The flimsy structures erected after the late great break down on that part of the railroad running along the Tangipaho, gave way like reeds before the wind, last week, before the sudden floods occasioned by the great rain. It was predicted so by well-informed people, and we hope for the sake of the company's purse, slender as it is, that they will not resort to patch-work again, but build the necessary embankments, bridges, etc., in a substantial manner. Nothing but the most solid work will stand in that locality, as any one who has been around there will bear witness. The people living along the track are so impressed with the insufficiency of the present structures, and the necessity of doing away with the patch-work way of doing business, that even the wildest rumors find a willing ear among them; for instance, when, two or three weeks ago, it was noised about that a new route from the west end of Lake Maurepas to Crystal Springs was being surveyed, etc. There is no necessity for such extreme measures, but there is a necessity for permanency in the structures now about to be rebuilt. If it is patched up again the company will—burst.

Marine Disasters.

Further from the Brig James Madison. The total loss of the brig James Madison, of Baltimore, and all of the crew, except one, has already been published. In the Charleston Mercury of the 14th we find the following additional particulars:

Mr. Chas. G. Morton, (not Martin Lubec, as before reported,) mate of the brig James Madison, reached this city yesterday afternoon in the steamer Antelope, from Coles Island. He was picked up while clinging to a spar, on Tuesday last, about 9 A. M., about two miles from the beach, by a boat from the schooner Helen. When relieved he was much exhausted, and had given up all hope of assistance. He left the wrecked brig on Monday afternoon, in company with the cook and two seamen, all four of them clinging to the mainmast; but on Tuesday morning Mr. Morton found himself alone on the spar, the others having no doubt been washed off and drowned during the night by the violence of the sea. Capt. Travers was drowned near the vessel on Monday morning, and his body was found on the beach of Kiawah Island on Tuesday, and was identified by the mate, who has in possession the watch, bible, and other valuable little relics which were found on the person of the captain.

A Ship Sunk in the Delaware.—The ship John Trucks, Capt. Lindsay, from Liverpool to Philadelphia, 776 tons register, while on her way up the Delaware river on Sunday, was stove in by the floating ice. Through the assistance of the iceboat she reached Arch street wharf, in the comparatively shallow dock of which she was grounded. During the day, however, she slipped from this position into the deeper water of the river, and sank, carrying down with her, and consequently drowning, the steward, named Wilcox, who was in the cabin at the time. The John Trucks is owned by Bishop, Simons & Co., of Philadelphia, and valued at $60,000. Her cargo upon this voyage was said to be of 1800 tons burden. It consisted of Sheffield cutlery, iron, dry goods, salt, soda ash, &c. Of this large and costly amount, but about 80 tons were saved. She lay on Sunday evening in fifty feet water, the ice piled fifteen feet above her decks, and the three masts with frozen and dripping cordage, quivering under the ice flow. Her cargo is insured.

Loss of the Schooner Isabel.—The Baltimore Sun gives the annexed account of this vessel, the supposed loss of which was announced some time since:

The fact that the schooner Isabel, of this port, was missed, was announced several days ago. Her owners, Messrs. Friend, Ricketts & Co., have since received a letter from her commander, Capt. Milburn, dated Liverpool, January 26th. Capt. M. states that while on the passage from a guano island to Baltimore, his vessel sprung a leak and he was compelled to abandon her. On the 1st of January, in latitude 31°, longitude 75°, all hands were taken on board the ship North America, Capt. Lincoln, of Boston, bound from New Orleans for Liverpool. The vessel sprung a leak in a violent gale, and had her foresail and flying jib torn to pieces, on the last day of December. The men worked at the pumps steadily all night, but could not keep her free. They saw the ship the next day, with double-reefed maintopsail, a gale blowing from the north. Signal of distress was made, and the ship bore down and took the crew off. The Isabel was from St. Andreas, bound to Baltimore, with a cargo of guano.

Sloop of War Sunk.—The sloop of war Dale quietly sunk at her moorings, alongside of the wharf, at the navy-yard, on Thursday. Her deck abaft the main hatch is now under water. A gang of men were at work at her pumps during the day and gained a little on the leaks.—*Portsmouth (N. H.) Gazette.*

Compensation to Owners of Fugitive Slaves.—A memorial is in circulation for signatures in Philadelphia urging the legislature of Pennsylvania to pass a law compensating the owners of fugitive slaves where they are rescued by mobs, and also punishing every one engaging in such mobs. The Philadelphia Ledger says:

The passage of such a law as this would have a good effect. Nothing so effectually put a stop to the pro-slavery mobs, which in former days disgraced our city, as the passage of a law requiring the county to pay the cost of the property damaged. Under this law Pennsylvania hall, burned down by an anti-abolition mob, was paid for out of the county treasury. A Catholic church, burned in the time of the native American riots, was paid for in the same way. So soon as the tax-payers began to find these public amusements were growing expensive, they provided a police force to put a stop to them. A law which shall make the county liable for the value of a slave when he escapes through the interference of the citizens, would put a practical obstacle to the operation of any personal liberty bill. Every tax-payer would soon see the necessity of enforcing the constitutional provision, and those individuals that are now the most active on behalf of the fugitive would find their zeal in his cause diminish sensibly. Sentimental indulgence, when it costs nothing, may be liberally allowed, but when it touches the pocket its value is very soon properly estimated.

Peculating Officials.—Uncle Sam does not possess a clear monopoly of official swindlers, as the annexed paragraphs show:

Most of our citizens were surprised at the departure, on the express freight train on Friday last (says the Marietta, Ga., Advocate), of James M. Barnwell, clerk of the Superior court. It is supposed that he carried off some four or five thousand dollars in cash, besides some negroes. Some of our most worthy citizens are the sufferers. The books of fines and forfeitures and the accounts for court costs had been made the most of by him. It is believed that he had been for a considerable time past making his arrangements for this step. He is supposed to be accompanied by a woman with whom he had been on intimate terms, and that they will aim for Texas or California.

The Pittsburgh (Pennsylvania) people have just discovered that a large number of their tax collectors put the major part of their collections in their pockets; and that though this peculation has been going on for several years, the thieves have generally been reappointed. The grand jury of the county have indicted a whole batch of the delinquents.

The New York Senatorship—*Bribes Said to have been Offered on the Greeley Side.*—A correspondent of the New York Express, writing from Albany, alludes distinctly to alleged corruption on the part of the Greeley faction, during the late exciting senatorial canvass. To a New York member he says the attorneyship for the Northern district was offered, if he would vote for Greeley. This offer is said to have been made by a man in high position, who had just returned from Springfield, where he had left Greeley closeted with Mr. Lincoln. A lobbyist afterwards proposed to the same party an arrangement by which he would make $400, if Greeley obtained the election. On the day of the caucus he was treated to a sleigh ride, by some of the Greeley party, and feasted and moistened until it was supposed that he was in good condition for an operation, and an offer of $500 down was made to him, but he emphatically declined. The names of the operators are not given.

Texas Intelligence.

The Weatherford Whiteman learns that many families on the frontier are destitute of bread, and without the means of purchasing it. This is occasioned by the numerous Indian raids that have devastated the frontier.

The Hempstead Courier is informed that the damage, direct and indirect, resulting from the late smash-down at the Clear Creek bridge, etc., will not exceed $40,000.

Both houses of the legislature have passed a bill granting nine months stay in the collection of all debts by execution. It is not known whether the governor will approve the bill.

A resolution recognizing the importance of the completion of the New Orleans and Houston (Texas) railroad, as a matter of defence to the south, and calling the attention of the Louisiana legislature to the liberality of Texas towards said road, passed the legislature.

The Palestine Advocate states that the negro boy Martin, who was hung for the murder of Mr. Wm. D. Wesscott, of this city, at the Hunter house, in that place, confessed to having aided in the murder of Wesscott, but said that he was killed by a white man; that the two, the boy Martin and the white man, went into Mr. Wesscott's room to rob him; that Mr. Wesscott raised himself up in the bed, when the white man killed him by shooting him through the head with a pistol,—one of Mr. Wesscott's own pistols,—after which they robbed him of his money, pocket-book, watch and pistols. A meeting of citizens appointed a committee to arrest the individual implicated in the murder of Mr. Wesscott. The committee arrested in Freestone county a man by the name of Gilbert, and brought him back to Palestine, where he was surrendered to the civil authorities.

Martial Law Proclaimed.—The governor of South Carolina has issued his proclamation establishing martial law in and over Sullivan's island, and the waters and marshes adjacent. Some of the rules established are as follows:

No person or persons shall land upon the shore of Moultrieville, or depart therefrom, without the written permit of the commanding officer at that place, Gen. Dunovant.

No person or persons living at Moultrieville shall communicate with any of the posts established there, without a written permit of the officer.

No person or persons living at Moultrieville shall be at large in the streets or thoroughfares thereat, between the hours of tattoo and reveille, without the written permit of the commanding officer at that island.

No boat, or vessel, except those in charge of the quartermaster's department, shall visit Moultrieville without the written permit of Gen. Dunovant; and within the limits thus designated, the military power is made supreme in the enforcement of these regulations, and the officers in command are invested with full authority to govern and regulate all persons therein found, according to military law, and without any subjection or responsibility to the civil authorities and tribunals, or any process thereof; and all persons found within the said limits are strictly enjoined and commanded to obey and conform to the commands of the said officers in the aforesaid regulations, on pain of the military penalties otherwise to ensue.

☞ Greeley, of the New York Tribune, is wrathful. Is armed treason to be conciliated? shouts he. He talks just like George III. He thinks the demand of the slave states can't be granted; and that nothing any republican has thought of offering will be accepted; that if the Union is to be preserved by such means, the government will be humiliated; will submit voluntarily to digrace. So King George thought in 1776. If these concessions are made, then we have a Union; it is resisted, and concessions are made; nobody is hung or punished; and we are all disgraced, and have no government at all! Great idea of government the said Greeley has, to be sure. We never knew a government disgraced by concessions, whereby it maintained its various parts, retained its integrity and its power against other nations. On the contrary, it is the highest wisdom of government to make such an achievement.

Greeley thinks somebody ought to be punished, and so do we. We think Greeley, Wendell Phillips, Garrison, Wade, Yancey and others ought to be punished some, and when we settle this matter up, the punishment will follow. These parties will be mortified, disappointed, laid on the shelf as agitators and disturbers of the public peace, for whom God and the country have no further use. We shall not agree to hang any one of them. We can make better use of Kentucky hemp. We shall leave them all, God-forsaken set, to roll down the hill of life to the bottom, deploring the depravity of the times.—*Louisville Democrat.*

A Very Cool American.—A Frenchman recently eloped from Paris with the pretty wife of an American, and as soon as the latter learned what had taken place, he installed himself in the chateau of his rival, and wrote to the latter a missive, as follows:

You have appropriated my wife, and I have taken possession of your estate. By the time your love is squandered, I will try to have spent your fortune. I hope you will have an agreeable time in Switzerland, though December is a chilly month, I am told, in that country. I would recommend her to continue her singing lessons. I have had your orangery removed, as it intercepted the view of the pond. I dare say you will approve my course.

Naval Affairs—*The Cruise of the African Squadron.*—A letter dated St. Paul de Loando, Nov. 13, 1860, says:

The United States steamers Mohican and Sumter arrived at this port on the 9th; the former from Fernando Po, the latter from St. Helena. The Mohican brought the mails. The Sumpter has been to St. Helena to give her crew liberty. The men and officers seem to have enjoyed the visit well. The United States steamer Mystic, Lieut. Commanding Wm. E. Leroy, left this point on the 8th for St. Helena.

The yellow fever is raging at this place, and the strictest quarantine regulations exist. None of the officers of either ship are allowed to go on shore, except those attached to the paymaster's department, for stores, and the engineers for coal. Both vessels will leave in a few days to cruise off the Pengo.

Liberia Looking for Reciprocity.—President Benson, in his recent annual message to the legislature, complains much about the treatment of Liberia by our government, and makes the following suggestion:

It is for you to determine this session if, after its close, it can be regarded any longer politic or even just for this government to accord such commercial privileges to citizens of the most favored nations with which we have treaties of friendship and commerce, based upon principles of reciprocity, when the United States government refuses to accord to us similar privileges.

Suspension of a Dry Goods Firm.—Messrs. Jones, Brothers & Co., the oldest and one of the heaviest dry goods houses in Cincinnati, suspended payment yesterday. This disaster, the Gazette says, is attributable to unfortunate outside operations in railroad enterprises, stocks, &c., entered into some years ago, when matters in that line looked promising. The legitimate business of the firm always yielded handsome average profits, and the house was at one time quite wealthy.

XXXVIth CONGRESS---SECOND SESSION.

Invoking Blessings on the Outgoing and Incoming Administrations.

The House on Wednesday, the 13th, was opened with prayer by Chaplain Stockton, in which he said:

"Bless the outgoing administration; may it close its labors in peace without further violence and without any stain of blood; and we pray for the incoming administration, that Thy blessing may rest on the president-elect on his journey hitherward; that Thy good providence may be around him day and night, guarding him at every step; and we pray that he may be peacefully and happily inaugurated, and afterward by pure, wise and prudent councils, that he may administer the government in such a manner as Thy name may be glorified, and the welfare of the people in all their relations be advanced, and that an example of civil and religious liberty be followed in all the world."

The New Treasury Loan.

Mr. Sherman sent up the letter from the secretary of the treasury again urging speedy measures in view of the pressing demand on the treasury.

Mr. Sherman accordingly reported a bill authorizing the president, in place of any part of the recent loan, to issue coupon loans of a denomination not exceeding $50, and bearing not exceeding six per cent. interest, and running twenty years, and apply such bonds at par to the creditors who may receive them, the entire amount not to exceed that authorized by the recent loan act. He made an explanation showing the importance of the measure.

Mr. Garnett opposed, saying the speech of the president-elect at Indianapolis indicated coercion, and the inauguration of a military despotism. [Suppressed hisses.]

Counting the Electoral Vote.—At this stage of the proceedings the Senate was notified of the readiness of the House to have the electoral votes counted, when the senators entered the hall of representatives. Having given the full particulars of the "count" in our evening edition yesterday—which will be found on another page—we deem it unnecessary to reproduce it here.

The Pacific railroad bill was postponed until to-morrow.

A committee was appointed, in conjunction with the Senate, to wait upon the president-elect and notify him of his election.

Mr. Hindman suggested that General Scott be also informed that there was no further use of mercenaries around the capital.

Adjourned.

In the Senate on the 13th, after returning from the electoral count, the tariff bill came up.

Mr. Seward gave notice that he would move to erase that portion abolishing the warehouse system.

Mr. Simmons explained the amendments, when the bill was laid over.

The bill for the better organization of the military of the district of Columbia came up.

On motion of Mr. Lane it was recommitted to the military committee.

The bill providing that no extra numbers of any documents be printed without a joint resolution of both Houses, passed.

Mr. Bigler reported the patent bill, recommending that the Senate concur in all the amendments of the House except one. Agreed to.

Adjourned.

Republican Movements.—The Baltimore Exchange has the following in its leading column, double leaded. As the Exchange is not in the habit of publishing sensation items, we presume there is truth in this:

We learn that the active republicans in New York city, in their anxiety to prevent any movement on the part of Maryland prior to the Fourth of March, have offered to furnish from thirty to fifty thousand dollars to secure their object.

From the same source we have also the information that the army will be immediately increased, by the new administration, to from one hundred thousand to one hundred and fifty thousand men, and also close the southern ports.

Rebuke of Senator Wilson.—The city council of Newburyport, Mass., have unanimously passed resolutions rebuking Senator Wilson for the impertinent manner in which he presented a petition from over nine hundred citizens of that city in favor of the Crittenden compromise. The resolutions declare that "the city council of the city of Newburyport deem the manner in which the petition of our citizens was presented by Senator Wilson, a gross violation of their rights to be heard upon all matters touching the welfare of this Union; and that they have not received from the senator from Massachusetts the courtesy due them."

Tenders Refused.—Gen. Scott, in a letter to the officers of the Scott Life Guard, of New York, who tendered their services for the defence of the federal capital, states that the government does not contemplate calling any troops to Washington other than the militia of the district, and some detachments of regular troops. He further adds that it is desired by the friends of peace that no organized societies or clubs, even without arms, shall make their appearance in Washington until the tranquility of the public mind be restored.

Three Important Cases Pending.—Three cases of political importance will soon be before the United States Supreme court. These are: an appeal from the Territorial court of Kansas, on a decision as to the right of the people of a territory to exclude slavery therefrom; the controversy between Governor Magoffin, of Kentucky, and Governor Dennison, of Ohio; and the Lemmon case, from New York.

Profits of the Horse Railroads in New York.—The profits of the street railroads of the city are represented by enormous figures. The Third avenue road cost about $465,000. It is represented by a stock to the value of $1,250,000, which not long since was quoted at 170 per cent., or, in other words, it returns 20 per cent. on five times its original cost. The Sixth avenue road cost about $330,000, and is represented by a stock worth $800,000, which is valued at 170 per cent. The Eighth avenue road cost about $260,000, which is said to be worth 200 per cent.

Later from Hayti.—We have news from Hayti to January 22. Considerable anxiety was caused by Spanish policy and probable intentions in regard to the island of St. Domingo. It was said that some old claims were preferred by the Spanish goverment which would interfere materially with Haytien independence, and if time could be spared from affairs at home it might be well to watch affairs in that island. Coffee was still in demand, and commands high prices—from $132 to $134 per hundred lbs.

Cocoaine.—The ladies are delighted with Burnett's cocoaine. They describe with no slight enthusiasm its wonderful effects in promoting and preserving the beauty of the hair. Burnett's kalliston is equally admired as a cosmetic. It is Burnett & Co., who are also the propietors of the new perfume entitled Florimel, and of the Oriental tooth wash. All these preparations deserve the high reputation which they have already attained.—*N. Y. Home Journal.*

amendements proposés par eux, les commissaires en donneraient avis au Gouverneur de cet Etat, qui en ferait part à la Législature et à la Convention. Bien entendu, toutefois, que les commissaires susdits seront sou le contrôle de la Convention pendant son existence, et de l'Assemblée-Générale quand la Convention aura accompli son œuvre.

Résolu, Que dans l'opinion de cette Assemblée, les propositions renfermées dans la série de résolutions présentée au Sénat des Etats-Unis, par l'Hon. John J. Crittenden, modifiées de façon à ce que le premier article, relatif à l'amendement de la Constitution Fédérale, embrasse tous les Territoires des Etats-Unis, situés au Sud des 36° 30' de latitude, et protège l'esclavage dans ces Territoires pendant l'existence des gouvernements provisoires,—pourraient servir de base à un plan de conciliation, en ayant soin de modifier aussi l'article 4 des résolutions susdites, de manière à garantir aux propriétaires d'esclaves le droit de transiter avec leurs esclaves, sur tous les Territoires de l'Union, et sur le sol des Etats libres.

Résolu, Que l'ex-Président John Tyler est par ces présentes, et par le vote conjoint des deux Chambres de l'Assemblée Générale, chargé de se rendre auprès du Président des Etats-Unis, et que le juge John Robertson est aussi chargé de se rendre dans la Caroline du Sud et dans les autres Etats déjà séparés ou qui se sépareront de la Confédération, afin de prier le Président et lesdits Etats de s'abs tenir de tous actes tendant à provoquer un conflit entre les Etats scissionnaires et le gouvernement des Etats-Unis.

Résolu, Qu'avis sera immédiatement transmis par voie télégraphique, aux Gouverneurs des différents Etats et au Président des Etats-Unis, des résolutions précédentes, et que le Gouverneur de cet Etat informera lesdits commissaires susdits de leur nomination.

WM. F. GORDON fils.

Sur motion de M. Talbot le Sénat renvoie à un autre jour pour la reconsidération des résolutions précitées.

Sur la motion de M. Tucker, il est enjoint au Secrétaire de transmettre aux Représentants une copie de ces résolutions.

Les Sénateurs suivants, sans avis préalable et après la dispense des réglements, présentent les bills suivants, lesquels subissent deux lectures par leurs titres respectifs et sont envoyés devant les comités ci-après désignés :

M. Gardère,

Acte abrogeant la section 4 d'un acte intitulé : "Acte relatif aux ventes par le Shérif et aux ordres de *fieri facias*", approuvé le 15 mars 1855.—Cet acte n'aura de force que dans la paroisse de Jefferson.

M. Newell,

Acte autorisant David Bush et son épouse Mathilde Louisa Bush à adopter un enfant mineur et à changer son nom.

M. Pearce,

Acte pour amender et décréter de nouveau un acte intitulé : "Acte incorporant la Compagnie de navigation de la Louisiane, du Texas et de l'Arkansas."

M. Stevens,

Acte abrogeant la section 2 d'un acte intitulé : "Acte relatif aux patrouilles," approuvé le 15 mars 1855, en ce qui concerne la paroisse de Jackson.

M. Laidlaw,

Acte autorisant Jules Manouvrier et son épouse à adopter Joséphine Cristine Flagg.

Tous les bills précités sont envoyés devant le comité judiciaire.

M. Cottrell,

Acte augmentant le salaire de l'Assesseur de la paroisse de StLandry.

M. Moore,

Acte augmentant le salaire de l'Assesseur de la paroisse de Vermillion.

M. Laidlaw,

Acte venant en aide à Wm. M. Guni.

M. Lott,

Acte amendant un acte intitulé : "Acte pourvoyant à un revenu et à la manière de le collecter," approuvé le 15 mars 1855.

Les bills précédents sont envoyés devant le comité des finances.

M. Tucker,

Acte relatif à la construction de navires—envoyé devant le comité du commerce, de l'agriculture et des manufactures.

M. Goode,

Acte pourvoyant au desséchement des terres marécageuses et submergées dans la vallée de Terrebonne et de Lafourche.

La Chambre fait demander le concours du Sénat aux bills suivants :

Acte pourvoyant au remboursement d'une somme de $112 12 à Sosthène Thériot, Shérif de St-Jacques.

Résolution conjointe nommant un comité chargé de s'enquérir de l'utilité d'abolir le Bureau des travaux publics.

MM. Allen, Coleman, Phillips, Herron, Wilkinson, Beggs, White, Breithaupt, Bradley et Anderson font partie de ce comité de la part de la Chambre.

La Chambre fait aussi annoncer son concours aux bills et à la résolution qui suivent :

"Acte venant en aide à J. M. Serpas, Shérif et Collecteur de taxes de la paroisse de St-Bernard."

Acte autorisant le Gouverneur à nommer un notaire additionnel dans la paroisse de Claiborne.

Résolution conjointe relative au contrôle du bureau d'enrôlements des deux Chambres.

MM. Bush, Herron, LeBlanc, Rousseau et Kilbourne font partie de ce comité de la part de la Chambre.

Le Messager réclame ensuite la signature du Président du Sénat aux bills suivants des Représentants :

Acte venant en aide à Nathan Hass, Shérif et Percepteur de taxes de la paroisse de Caddo ;

Acte venant en aide à A. Lobbell, Shérif et Percepteur de taxes de la paroisse de Livingston ;

Acte pourvoyant à la nomination d'un Arpenteur additionnel pour la paroisse des Rapides.

L'Hon. Benjamin W. Pearce occupe le fauteuil.

Sur la motion de M. Stevens et après la dispense des réglements, le Sénat procède à la considération du bill du Sénat, intitulé :

Acte pourvoyant à l'impression et à la distribution d'un millier d'exemplaires, sous forme de brochures, des lois relatives aux écoles publiques dans cet Etat.

Ce bill, sur la motion du même Sénateur, est renvoyé devant le comité de l'instruction publique.

MESSAGES DE LA CHAMARE.—1RE LECTURE.

Résolution conjointe venant en aide à H. W. Allen.

Sur la motion de M. Gardère et après la dispense des réglements, la résolution précédente subit deux lectures et passe devant le comité des finances

Acte pourvoyant au remboursement d'une somme de $112 50 à Sosthène Thériot, Shérif de S-Jacques.

Résolutions conjointes relatives à l'abotition du Bureau des travaux publics.

Cette résolution subit deux lectures ; le blanc qui y avait été laissé est rempli par le mot "cinq" et le Sénat les adopte à la troisième lecture.

Le Président désigne les personnes suivantes pour faire partie du comité créé par ces résolutions, savoir: Messieurs Gardère, Moore, Tucker, Taylor, et Shadburne.

ORDRE DU JOUR.—2MES LECTURES.

Acte pour émanciper Victorine Melançon, femme de Jules Guidry, de la paroiste Ascension.

Sur motion de M. Goode, ce bill subit ses deuxième et troisième lectures et passe.

Acte pour venir en aide aux héritiers et représentants légaux de David Heran, décédé, et pour allouer une somme de de $2,954 16 dans ce but.

Sur motion de M. Goode, ce bill subit ses deux dernières lectures et passe.

Acte relatis aux Avocats de District.

Sur motion de M. Goode, ce bill est déposé sur le bureau, sujet à appel.

Acte relatif aux officiers publics.

Sur la motion de M. Goode, ce bill est déposé sur le bureau, sujet à appel.

Acte concernant les chemins publics.

Sur motion de Salomon, ce bill subit sa seconde lecture, et est référé au comité du judiciaire.

Acte autorisant l'Auditeur des comptes publics à à payer certaines sommes dues à la succession d'Augustin Eaplantier.

Sur motion de M. Salomon, ce bill subit ses deux dernières lectures et passe.

Acte incorporant la ville de Pontchitoulas, dans la paroisse de Livingston.

Sur motion de M. Womack, ce bill subit ses 2me et 3me lectures et passe.

BILL DU SENAT.

Sur motion de M. Goode les réglements sont suspendus, et le Sénat procède à la considération du bill du Sénat, intitulé :

Acte autorisant l'Auditeur des comptes publics et l'invitant à délivrer son mandat pour le paiement de la balance due sur certains mandats.

Ce bill subit ses deux dernières lectures et passe.

SESSION EXÉCUTIVE.

Sur motion de M. Goode le Sénat procède à huis-clos à l'examen des affaires de l'Exécutif, et, cet examen terminé, la réouverture des portes est ordonnée.

Sur motion de M. Gardère, le Sénat ajourne à demain, à 11 heures du matin.

VIRGINIA CONVENTION.—*Richmond, Va.*, Feb. 13. The Convention met at the Capitol. John Jenney of Loudon, was elected President, and made a Union Speech, but said he would insist on her rights as a condition to remaining in the Confederacy.

Daily Advocate.

J. M. TAYLOR & TOM BYNUM.

EDITORS AND PROPRIETORS.

THURSDAY MORNING, FEB. 21, 1861.

Messrs. Editors.—Please announce **Judge E. North Cullom**, of Avoyelles, as a candidate for the Judgeship of the District composed of the parishes of Avoyelles, West Feliciana, Point Coupee and West Baton Rouge. Election in April.

VOTERS FROM EACH PARISH.

Messrs. Editors—By request of many citizens, please announce the name of **L. A. Hernandez** for City Marshal. Election April next. CITIZENS.

Messrs. Editors—Please announce **Col. Sam Harbour** as candidate for City Marshal, at the ensuing April election.

MANY FRIENDS.

Messrs. Editors—You are authorized to announce **J. M. TRACY** as a candidate for City Marshal, at ensuing April election. VOX POPULI.

Mrs. Pickens, wife of the Governor of South Carolina, is at present in New Orleans.

EXHIBITION.—The inmates of the Deaf, Dumb, and Blind Asylum gave an interesting exhibition at the Capitol on Tuesday night. Everything went off to the greatest satisfaction of the large audience that attended to witness the performance.

COLUMBIADS.—Inquiries are made as to the nature of the cannon called Columbiads. A Columbiad is a heavy gun, capable of projecting a solid shot or shell with a large charge of powder, and at an angle of projection from five degrees below to thirty above the horizon ; it may be said, therefore, to combine the essential qualities of the gun, the howitzer and mortar, and may be used in place of either the one or the other of these in seacoast defense. It does not differ in its external shape from ordinary seacoast cannon. At present there are two sizes of Columbiads in use in our service, viz : the eight-inch and the ten-inch. The former weighs about 9,000 lbs., the charge of powder 10 lbs., the solid shot 64 lbs., and the shell 48 lbs. The latter weighs about 15,000 lbs., the charge of powder 16 lbs., the solid shot 128 lbs., and the shell 100 lbs.

THE PREPARATIONS AT CHARLESTON.—The Charleston correspondent of the Richmond *Dispatch* communicates the following intelligence under date of the 8th inst. :

A visit to Sullivan's Island yesterday satisfied me that there is no child's play in all this preparation. Sullivan's Island is about six miles long, and averages about two hundred yards wide. A few palmetto trees are the only growth on it, it being for the most part a sand bank. In Fort Moultrie they have everything in a state of readiness. Their magazine is well supplied with powder, and so completely secured that no shell or conflagration can possibly reach it. It is under ground, covered over with an arch of brickwork cemented, and full five feet of earth on that.

They have between fifty and sixty guns mounted, amongst them several Columbiads of the largest size, most of them bearing upon Sumter. The walls are most effectually protected by palmetto logs, all of which, it would seem, would bid defiance to any attack. The mortar battery is masked, and is protected by sand bags, raw hides and palmetto logs, and you would be astonished to see the great security of sand bags and hides. It is a heavy work, and no one can form any idea of its security without seeing it. In this battery they have four large mortars, and shells in abundance—all in place and ready for action. Higher up the island they have another battery, secured in the same way, with smaller guns, to protect the channel, which runs within a quarter of a mile of this fort. On the island are about two thousand soldiers, drilled constantly and regularly in the most rigid manner. Immediately in the rear of Sumter, and within five-eighths of a mile, is another formidable battery of the heaviest guns, which will play upon the weakest point of the fort. On Morris' Island are two other batteries, covered with railroad iron, placed in a slanting position, the balls striking which are compelled to glide overhead without doing the work of death. In all, they have eleven points of attack, all manned and the guns in place. Never did I expect to see my countrymen arrayed against each other in battle. I had almost wished that I had never lived to see such a sight as I saw yesterday.

HIBERNIAN INTELLIGENCE.—An Irishman who was standing on London Bridge, accosted a youth standing beside him, saying :

"Faith I think I know yer ; what's yer name ?"

"My name is Jones," replied the youth.

"Jones, Jones," said the Irishman, "I knew two ould maids by that name in Dublin, was aither of them yer muther ?"

THE NATIONAL (GERMAN) GUARDS.

Messrs. Editors—In your paper of this morning, I find copied from the Oswego (N. Y.) *Times*, a letter purporting to have been written by Mrs. Major Haskin to a relative in New York, concerning the seizure of the Barracks in this place. The letter is replete with misrepresentations or "mistakes," which are inexcusable even in a lady.

I beg to thank you for your prompt denial of the unwarranted assertion that "our German company belonging to the town had refused to go to the fort to fight against Maj. Haskin." But justice to the *only* German company in this place, demands something more than a mere denial of the accusation. A more loyal company than the German company alluded to, was not on the ground, nor can a more loyal company be found anywhere in the South, or on the face of God's earth. To prove this, it is only necessary to state a few facts.

In the first place, it is the only organized volunteer company which has never sought or received any aid from the State. Its uniform, arms, ammunitions and accoutrements were purchased by its own members at a cost of more than three thousand dollars, when other companies which had been fostered by the State and received their arms and accoutrements from the State, broke ranks and refused to serve, because we had not been properly treated, the German company stood firm and refused to follow the example. So far from refusing to go to the Barracks, we were anxious to do so, and, indeed, the only murmur which was heard, was that we were not allowed to do so.

By publishing this you will do justice to one of the most deserving companies to be found anywhere, and one, which, in the hour of trial, will be found foremost in the cause of the South and its adopted State. A GERMAN.

BATON ROUGE, Feb. 17th, 1861.

TELEGRAPHIC ITEMS.

Inaugural Ceremonies of President Davis OF THE CONFEDERATE STATES OF AMERICA.

THE INAUGURAL ADDRESS.

THE SOUTHERN CONGRESS.

Important from Washington—Virginia State Convention.

Special to the New Orleans Picayune.

MONTGOMERY, Feb. 18.—The Hon. Jefferson Davis of Mississippi, was inaugurated President of the Provisional Government of the Confederate States of America, as before arranged, to-day.

The inaugural ceremonies constituted, as a whole, the grandest pageant ever witnessed in the South.

The city was alive, from early morning, with delegations from the various States and people from the adjoining country, and long before the hour for the inauguration arrived, the Capitol Hill was filled with the beauty and chivalry of the South. A large number of military companies from this State, Mississippi and Georgia were also present, and gave eclat to the occasion.

The oath of office was administered to the President by the Chief Justice of Alabama in the principal hall of the Capitol. In his immediate presence were the members of the Southern Congress, now in session here, the delegations from the Confederate States and the chief civil and military authorities

President Davis commenced his address at precisely one o'clock. It is verbatim as follows :

PRESIDENT DAVIS'S INAUGURAL ADDRESS.

Gentlemen of the Congress of the Confederate States of America, Friends and Fellow-Citizens :

Called to the dificult and responsible station of Chief Magistrate of the Provisional Government, which you have instituted, I approach the discharge of the duties assigned to me with humble distrust of my abilities, but with a sustaining confidence in the wisdom of those who are to guide and aid me in the administration of public affairs, and an abiding faith in the virtue and patriotism of the people.

Looking forward to the speedy establishment of a permanent Government to take the place of this, which, by its greater moral and physical power, will be better able to combat with many difficulties that arise from the conflicting interests of separate nations, I enter upon the duties of the office to which I have been chosen, with the hope that the beginning of our career, as a Confederacy, may not be obstructed by hostile opposition to our enjoyment of the separate existence and independence we have asserted, and which, with the blessing of Providence, we will contend for and maintain.

Our present political position has been achieved in a manner unprecedented in the history of nations. It illustrates the American idea that governments rest upon the consent of the governed, and that it is the right of the people to alter or abolish them at will, whenever they become destructive of the ends for which they were established.

The declared purpose of the compact of the United States, from which we have withdrawn, was to "establish justice, insure domestic tranquillity, provide for the common defense, promote the general welfare, and secure the blessings of liberty to ourselves and our posterity ;" and now, when in the judgment of the sovereign States composing this Confederacy, it has been perverted from the purposes for which it was ordained, and ceased to answer the ends for which it was established, a peaceful appeal to the ballot-box has declared that, so far as they are concerned, the Government created by that compact should cease to exist.

In this they have merely asserted the right which the Declaration of Independence, July 4th, 1776, defined to be "inalienable." Of the time and occasion for its assertion and exercise, they, as sovereigns, were the final judges, each for itself.

The impartial and enlightened verdict of mankind will vindicate the rectitude of our conduct, and He, who knows all hearts, will judge of the sincerity with which we have labored to preserve the Government of our fathers in its spirit.

The right, solemnly proclaimed at the birth of the United States, and which has been solemnly affirmed and reaffirmed in the bills of rights of the States subsequently admitted into the Union of 1789, undeniably recognized in the people the power to resume the authority delegated to it for the purposes of government.

By this right the sovereign States, here represented, have seceded from this Confederacy, and it is an abuse of language that their act has been denominated revolutionary.

They have formed a new alliance, but, within each State, its government has remained the same, nor have the rights of person or property been disturbed.

The agent, through which they communicated with foreign nations, is changed, but this does not necessarily interrupt their international relations.

Sustained by the consciousness that this transition from the former Union to the present Confederacy has not proceeded from a disregard, on our part, of just obligations, or any failure to perform every Constitutional duty ; moved by no interest or passion to invade the rights of others ; and anxious to cultivate peace and commerce with all nations—if we may not hope to avoid war, we may at least expect posterity will acquit us from having needlessly made it.

Doubly justified, therefore, by the absence of wrong on our part, and by the wanton aggression of others, there can be no reason to doubt that the courage and patriotism of the people of the Confederate States of America will be found equal to any measure of defense which their honor and security will require.

An agricultural people, whose chief interest is the export of commodities, required in every manufacturing country, our true policy is peace and the freest trade which our necessities will permit.

It is alike our interest and that of all those to whom we would sell and from whom we would buy, that there should be the fewest practicable restrictions upon the interchange of these commodities.

There can, however, be but little rivalry between our people and any other manufacturing community, such as those of the Northern and Eastern States of the American Union.

It must follow, therefore, that mutual interests will invite to good will and kind offices on both parts.

If, however, passion or lust of dominion, should cloud the judgment or inflame the ambition of these States, we must prepare to meet the emergency, and maintain, by the final abitrament of the sword, the position which we have assumed among the nations of the earth.

We have entered upon a new career of independence, and must be inflexible in maintaining it, though pursued through many years of controversy with our late associates of the Northern States.

We have vainly endeavored to secure tranquillity and obtain respect for the rights to which we were entitled, and as a necessity, not as a choice, we have resorted to the remedy of separation, and henceforth our energies must be directed to the conduct of our own affairs and the perpetuity of the Confederacy which we have formed.

If a just percep permit us peaceably to pursue our separate political career, my most earnest desire will have been fulfilled. But if this be denied us, and the integrity of our territory and juris diction be assailed, it will but remain for us, with firm resolve, to appeal to arms, and to invoke the blessings of Providence on a just cause.

As a consequence of our new condition and relations, and with a view to meet anticipated wants, it will be necessary to provide for the speedy and efficient organization of branches of the Executive Department, having special charge of foreign intercourse, finance, military affairs and postal service.

For purposes of defense, the Confederate States may, under ordinary circumstances, rely mainly upon their militia ; but it is deemed advisable, in the present condition of affairs, that there should be a well instructed and disciplined army, more numerous than would usually be required for a peace establishment.

I also suggest that, for the protection of our harbors and commerce on the high seas, a navy be organized. But this, as well as other subjects appropriate to our necessities, has doubtless engaged the attention of the Congress.

With a Constitution differing from that of our fathers only so far as it is explanatory of our well-known intention to be freed from sectional conflicts, which have interfered with the pursuit of the general welfare, it is not unreasonable to expect that other States from which we have recently parted may seek to unite their fortunes with ours under the Government we have instituted.

For this your Constitution makes adequate provision, but beyond this, if I mistake not, the judgment and will of the people are that a reunion with States from which we have separated, is neither practicable nor desirable. To increase the power, develop the resources and promote the happiness of a Confederacy, it is requisite that there should be so much homogenity that the welfare of every portion be the aim of the whole.

When this does not exist, antagonisms are engendered, which must and should result in separation.

Actuated solely by the desire to preserve our own rights, and promote our own welfare, the separation of the United States has been marked by no aggression upon others, and followed by no convulsion. Our industrial pursuits have received no check. The cultivation of our fields has progressed as heretofore, and even should we be involved in war, there would be no considerable diminution in the production of staples which have constituted our exports, and in which the commercial world has interest scarcely less than our own.

This common interest of producer and consumer can only be interrupted by exterior force, which would obstruct the transmission of our staples to foreign markets, a course of conduct which would be as unjust towards us as it would be detrimental to manufacturing and commercial interests abroad.

Should reason guide the action of the Government from which we have separated, a policy so detrimental to the civilized world, the Northern States included, could not be dictated by the strongest desire to inflict injury upon us.

But if the contrary should prove true, a terrible responsibility will rest upon it, and the sufferings of multitudes will bear testimony to the folly and wickedness of our aggressors.

In the meantime there will remain to us, besides the ordinary remedies before suggested, the well known resources for retaliation upon the commerce of an enemy.

My experience in public stations of a subordinate grade to this, which your kindness has conferred upon me, has taught me that care and toil and disparagement are the prices of official elevation.

You will see many errors to forgive, many deficiencies to tolerate ; but you shall not find in me either want of zeal or fidelity to the cause that is to me highest and of most undying affection.

Your generosity has bestowed upon me an undeserved distinction ; one which I neither sought nor desired.

Upon the continuance of that sentiment, and upon your wisdom and patriotism, I rely to direct and support me in the performance of the duties required at my hands.

We have changed our political relations, but not our system of government. The Constitution framed by our fathers is that of these Confederate States. In their expositions of it, and in the judicial constructions it has received, we have a light which has revealed its true meaning.

Thus instructed as to the true meaning and just interpretation of that instrument, and ever remembering that all offices are but trusts, held for the people, and that powers delegated are to be strictly construed, I will hope, by due diligence in the performance of my duties, though I may disappoint your expectations, yet to retain, when retiring, something of the good will and confidence which welcome my entrance into office.

It is joyous, in the midst of perilous times, to look around upon a people, united in heart ; where one purpose of high resolve animates and actuates the whole ; where the sacrifices to be made are not weighed in the ballance against honor, liberty and equality.

Obstacles may retard, but they cannot long prevent the progress of a movement sanctified by its justice and sustained by a virtuous people.

Let us, therefore, invoke the God of our Fathers to guide and protect us in our efforts to perpetuate principles which, by His blessing, they were able to vindicate, establish and transmit to their posterity. With the continuance of His favor, ever gratefully acknowledged, we may hopefully look forward to success, to peace and to prosperity.

INAUGURATION OF FREE TRADE.—*Montgomery, Ala.*, Feb. 18.—Your correspondent has been permitted to forward to you, by telegraph, the following important act of the Southern Congress, which has been sent by mail to the Collectors of the Customs of the Confederate States, as also to all whom it may concern :

SECTION 1. *Be it enacted, by the Congress of the Confederate States of America*, That the following articles shall be exempt from duty and admitted free into said States, to wit : bacon, pork, hams, lard, beef, fish of all kinds, wheat, and flour of wheat, and flour of all other grains, Indian corn and meal, barley and barley flour, rye and rye flour, oats and oat meal, gunpowder and all the materials of which it is made, lead in all forms, arms of every description, and munitions and military accoutrements, percussion caps, and living animals of all kinds ; also, all agricultural products in their natural state.

SEC. 2. *It is also enacted*, That all goods, wares and merchandize, imported from any of the late United States of America, not being now a member of this Confederacy, into the Confederacy before the 4th of March next, which may have been *bona fide* purchased heretofore, or within ten days after the passage of this act, shall be exempt and free from duty.

SEC. 3. *It is also enacted*, That the State of Texas be and is hereby exempted from the operation of the tariff laws, heretofore passed or adopted by this Congress.

Signed, HOWELL COBB, President.

Passed on the 18th of February, 1861.

WASHINGTON, Feb. 18.—The Peace Convention has as yet done nothing. It is nearly equally divided whether to adopt Mr. Guthrie's plan of adjustment as recommended by the majority of the special committee, or to call a national convention, as recommended by the minority.

The Virginia delegation opposes both, and is strong against coercion, as also the Congress.

LINCOLN'S ADMINISTRATION.—It is still doubtful whether Seward or Chase will control Lincoln's administration. The former is against, the latter for coercion.

HOMESTEAD AND PACIFIC RAILROAD BILLS. ... sident will veto or pocket both the Homestead and Pacific Railroad bills.

SUGAR DUTY BILL.—The Senate is still engaged in the discussion of the House bill reducing the duties on sugars. It is believed it will not pass.

PROCEEDINGS OF THE FEDERAL CONGRESS. The Senate to-day was mainly occupied in the presentation of petitions, most of which were in favor of a settlement of the present difficulties in the country.

The report of the Committee of Conference on the deficiency bill was agreed to.

In the House Mr. Stanton reported a bill providing to call forth the militia for the execution of the law, to suppress insurrection, repel invasion, extending provisions to cases of insurrection against the authority of the United States, and authorizing the President to accept the services of volunteer cavalry, infantry and artillery.

Mr. Bocock said all force bills must be rejected, if peace was desirable.

Mr. Stanton demanded the previous question, which was not taken.

The report of the committee of thirty-three was resumed and postponed.

The bill authorizing the issue of fifty dollar treasury notes passed.

RESOLUTIONS OPPOSING COERCION.—*Richmon, Feb.* 18.—During the sitting of the Virginia State Convention on Saturday, several important resolutions were introduced, one of which opposes the retaking of the Southern forts ; another pledges the military resources of Virginia against any other mode of coercing the seceding States by the Federal Government ; and a third says that if compromises fail, Virginia will unite with her sister Southern States.

Ex-Governor Wise reiterated his policy of fighting in the Union, and counselled speedy action.

THE VOTE IN NORTH CAROLINA.—*Fayetteville, Feb.* 18.—A large number of the votes cast to-day were in opposition to the holding of a State Convention.

Great enthusiasm was mannifested over the stars and stripes, and to-night parties are parading the streets under the flag of the Union.

Louisiana Legislature.

WEDNESDAY, Feb. 20, 1861.

SENATE.—The Senate convened at 12 o'clock, pursuant to adjournment. Prayer was offered.

The journal of yesterday was read and approved.

Mr. Goode moved to reconsider the resolution by which the Secretary was ordered to spread upon the journal of the Senate the ordinances of the Convention ; said resolution was rescinded.

A message was received by the Senate from the Governor, transmitting a resolution of the Legislature of Texas, relating to the completion of the New Orleans and Texas Railroad.

On motion of Mr. Moore, the resolution was sent to the House, after retaining a copy for the use of the Senate ; and referred to the Committee on Public Works.

Mr. Patterson introduced a memorial from certain citizens of New Orleans, relative to changing the location of the First Justice's Court of New Orleans ; referred to the city delegation.

Mr. Goode, from the Committee on Railroads, reported favorably on a bill regulating the issuing of bonds to railroad companies.

On motion of Mr. Phillips, the bill was made the special order of the day for to-morrow.

On motion of Mr. Patterson, 250 copies of the bill were ordered to be printed for the use of the Senate.

The unfinished business of yesterday, viz : an act concerning the term of office of the commissioner of the second draining district, was then taken up and passed.

Mr. Phillips offered a substitute for the bill reported by the committee to amend the act providing for the levying, draining and reclaiming swamp lands in the parishes of Orleans and Jefferson ; adopted.

Mr. Phillips introduced, without previous notice, a bill relative to the Assessors of the parishes of Orleans and Jefferson ; referred to the Committee on Finance.

Mr. Phillips called up a bill relative to the establishment of a ferry across the Atchafalaya ; referred to the Committee on the Judiciary.

Mr. Phillips called up a bill in reference to abolishing the office of Superintendent of Public Education, and providing for the discharge of the duties of the office by the Secretary of State. After considerable debate in which Messrs. Tucker, Phillips and Talbot participated, the bill was referred to the Judiciary Committee.

Mr. Phillips, from the Committee on Enrollment, reported the correct enrollment of Senate bills.

A message was received from the Governor transmitting a report of the Military Board ; referred to the Committee on the Militia.

Mr. Patterson, leave having been granted, called up the resolution relative to the election of a State Printer. On motion of Mr. Patterson the resolution was laid on the table.

Mr. Pearce asked for a suspension of the rules in order to take up an act to amend an act to incorporate the Louisiana, Arkansas and Texas Navigation Company. On motion of Mr. Pearce the bill was passed.

HOUSE BILLS.

Joint resolution to appoint a joint committee for the purpose of inaugurating the flag of the State of Louisiana, on Friday the 22d of February. On motion of Mr. Taylor the resolution was laid on the table.

An act to amend Article 162 of the Code of Practice ; adopted.

Senate bill—An act relative to pratitioners of medicine. An amendment striking out that provision of the bill which restricts the privilege of practicing medicine to the graduates of regularly incorporated institutions of the late United States was debated at length by Messrs. Smith, Hough, Tucker and Buffington in favor of the amendment, and by Messrs. Goode, Phillips, Stevens and Smart in opposition to it. The amendment was adopted by a vote of 15 yeas to 11 nays.

After which the Senate took a recess until 6 o'clock this evening.

EVENING SESSION.

The Senate met at 6 o'clock, pursuant to adjournment.

On motion of Mr. Leefe the Senate when into Executive Session.

Upon the re-opening of the doors,

Mr. Laidlaw introduced a bill to authorize the Governor to issue patents to land ; referred to the Committee on Public Works.

Mr. Taylor introduced a report of the committee to which was referred the account of the Military Board,

Mr. Phillips introduced a bill for the relief of J. I. B. Kirk ; referred to the Committee on Claims.

Mr. Pearce from the Finance Committee, reported unfavorably concerning a bill to raise a revenue and collect the same.

The unfinished business of the morning was then taken up, viz : An act concerning medical practitioners.

Mr. Smith moved that the words "except midwifery," be striken out ; which was done. After considerable debate, in which Messrs. Shadburne, Delony, and Tucker participated, on motion of Mr. Shadburne, the fifth section was amended so that the provisions of the act shall not apply to persons who have been practising medicine in this State for the space of ten years previous to the passage of the act ; and the act passed.

Mr. Patterson offered a resolution, that when the Senate adjourn to-morrow, it stands adjourned until Monday, the 25th inst. ; laid over under the rules.

On motion, the Senate adjourned until to-morrow, at 11 o'clock.

HOUSE.—The House met at 10 o'clock, pursuant to adjournment, Hon. C. H. Morrison in the Chair.

On calling the roll, sixty members were found to be present.

Prayer by Rev. Mr. Linfield.

Minutes read and approved.

Mr. Allen presented a resolution that the Committee on Arrangements be allowed to draw $500 from the Treasury, to aid in inaugurating the flag of Louisiana ; laid on the table indefinitely.

Mr. Ewing presented a resolution to appoint a committee to inquire into the condition of the State Library ; resolution adopted.

A message was received from the Governor communicating report from Military Board ; report ordered to be printed and referred to Committee on Military Affairs.

Mr. Coleman presented a resolution relative to creditors ; referred to the Judiciary Committee.

The Committee on Finance presented a bill to regulate the pay of the pupils in the Deaf, Dumb and Blind Asylum ; bill re-committed to Finance Committee.

The Committee on Finance presented another bill to provide for the government of the Deaf, Dumb and Blind Asylum ; bill passed.

Committee on Internal Improvements reported favorably on an act providing for the sale of the slaves belonging to the Internal Improvement Department, and also providing for the sale of steamboats and barges, etc.

Same committee reported favorably on bill for the relief of J. F. Duggan.

Committee on Claims reported unfavorably on bill for the relief of Yateman, Ward & Co., of New Orleans.

Same committee reported unfavorably on bill for the relief of J. C. Prendergast.

By Mr. McFee—An act to repeal an act relative to the State Seminary of Learning at Alexandria ; referred to the Judiciary Committee.

By Mr. Fuller—An act defining the duties of Magistrates in Union parish ; bill passed.

By Mr. Beauvais—An act relative to Sheriffs in the parish of St. James; referred to Judiciary Committee.

By Mr. Robinson—An act to amend an act relative to trials of criminals in the parish of Caddo ; referred to Judiciary Committee.

By Mr. Beggs—An act relative to the Law Department of the University of Louisiana ; referred to the Finance Committee.

By Mr. Voorhies—An act to repeal an act relative to jury wards ; referred to Committee on Parochial Affairs.

By Mr. Bradley—An act to repeal an act providing for the payment for the correction of tax rolls in New Orleans ; referred to Committee on Finance.

By Mr. Knox of East Baton Rouge—A bill for the relief of Lewis Sanchez ; referred to Committee on Claims.

By Mr. Haynes—An act relative to fees and costs ; referred to Committee on Judiciary.

By Mr. Gantt—An act to amend an act relative to the Police Jury of St. Tammany ; referred to a special committee.

By Mr. Imboden—An act to create two additional Notaries Public in Carroll parish ; passed.

Mr. Tomkies, from Committee on Public Buildings, reported an act repealing an act paying the Sergeant-at-Arms for keeping a police over the State House grounds, and to appoint a gardner ; passed.

By Mr. Knox of Carroll—An act relative to sales made under writs of *fi. fa.*, referred to Judiciary Committee.

The rules were suspended to allow the taking up of several bills providing for the adoption of certain minors.

By Mr. Anderson—An act to incorporate the Opelousas Female College ; referred to the Judiciary Committee.

The order of the day—An act relative to the Judiciary—was then taken up and considered by paragraphs.

A motion was made to strike out the section of the bill relative to judgment on facts. House by a vote of 31 to 32 refused to strike out.

The bill was then laid on table until to-morrow at 1 o'clock.

By Mr. Allen, report of the University of Louisiana ; referred to the Committee on Education.

The appropriation bill then came up in its regular order.

The clause appropriating $25,000 for the support of the Jackson Insane Asylum, was recommitted to the Finance Committee.

The clause appropriating $6,000 for salary of Clerk of First District of New Orleans, was recommitted to Finance Committee. Bill was then passed.

A joint resolution from the Legislature of Texas was then read ; referred to Committee on Internal Improvement.

On motion the House then adjourned until 10 o'clock to-morrow.

THE CENSUS OF 1860.

Free States and Territories.

	1850.	1860.	Increase.
Maine	583,169	619,958	36,789
New Hampshire	317,976	326,072	8,096
Vermont	314,120	315,827	1,707
Massachusetts	990,514	1,231,494	236 980
Rhode Island	147,545	174,621	27,076
Connecticut	370,792	460,670	89,878
New York	3,097,394	3,851,563	754,169
New Jersey	489,333	676,084	187,751
Pennsylvania	2,311,786	2,916,018	604,232
Ohio	1,980,427	2,977,917	397,490
Michigan	397,657	754,291	356,637
Indiana	988,416	1,350,802	362,386
Illinois	851,470	1,691,238	889,768
Wisconsin	305,391	768,485	463,094
Iowa	192,214	682,003	489,789
California	92,597	384,770	292,173
Oregon	13,294	52,566	39,272
Minnesota	6,077	172,792	166,616
Kansas	......	143,645	143,645
Nebraska	......	28,893	28,893
Utah	11,354	50,000	38,646
Dakotah	......	4,839	4,839
Washington	......	11,624	11,624
	13,465,523	19,046,173	5,580,650

Slave States.

	1850.	1860.	Increase
Delaware	89,242	110,548	21,306
Maryland	492,666	946,183	153,517
Virginia	949,133	1,097,373	148,240
North Carolina	580,491	679,965	99,474
South Carolina	283,523	308,186	24,663
Georgia	524,503	615,336	90,838
Florida	48,135	81,885	33,750
Alabama	428,779	520,444	91,665
Mississippi	296,648	407,051	110,403
Louisiana	272,953	354,245	81,292
Texas	154,431	415,799	261,568
Arkansas	162,797	331,710	168,913
Tennessee	763,154	859,528	96,374
Kentucky	771,424	920,077	148,652
Missouri	594,622	1,085,595	490,973
District of Columbia	48,000	75,321	27,321
New Mexico	61,547	93,024	31,477
	6,522,048	8,602,470	2,080,422

Slave Population.

	1850.	1860.	Decrease.	Incr'se.
Delaware	2,290	1,505	785	......
Maryland	90,368	35,382	54,986	......
Virginia	472,528	495,826	......	23,298
North Carolina	288,548	328,377	......	39,829
South Carolina	384,984	407,185	......	22,201
Georgia	381,682	467,471	......	85,779
Florida	39,309	64,809	......	24,500
Alabama	342,892	435,463	......	92,581
Mississippi	309,878	479,607	......	169,729
Louisiana	244,809	312,186	......	61,377
Texas	58,161	184,956	......	126,795
Arkansas	47,100	109,065	......	61,965
Tennessee	239,460	287,112	......	47,652
Kentucky	210,981	225,400	......	14,419
Missouri	87,422	115,619	......	28,197
Dist. of Columbia	3,687	no returns	......	......
	3,203,999	3,990,953	55,771	743,375

Daily Advocate.

J. M. TAYLOR & TOM BYNUM,

EDITORS AND PROPRIETORS.

THURSDAY MORNING, FEB. 28, 1861.

CANDIDATES FOR DISTRICT JUDGE.

☞ We are authorized to announce Hon. **Thomas J. Cooley** as candidate for Judge in the Judicial District composed of the parishes of Avoyelles, Point Coupee, West Feliciana and West Baton Rouge.

Messrs. Editors.—Please announce **Judge E. North Cullom,** of Avoyelles, as a candidate for the Judgeship of the District composed of the parishes of Avoyelles, West Feliciana, Pcint Coupee and West Baton Rouge. Election in April.

VOTERS FROM EACH PARISH.

FOR MAYOR.

Editors Advocate—Please announce me as a candidate for the office of Mayor of the City of Baton Rouge, election second Monday, the 8th of April next

J. E. ELAM.

FOR MAYOR.

At the request of many of his fellow-citizens, we are authorized to announce **James H. Stith** as a candidate for Mayor of the city of Baton Rouge Election to take place on the second Monday in April.

CANDIDATES FOR CITY MARSHAL.

Messrs. Editors—You will please announce as a candidate for re-election to the office of City Marshal the present capable and efficient incumbent, **Edward Cousinard.** MANY VOTERS.

Messrs. Editors—By request of many citizens, please announce the name of **L. A. Hernandez** for City Marshal. Election April next. CITIZENS.

Messrs. Editors.—Please announce **Col. Sam Harbour** as candidate for City Marshal, at the ensuing April election.

MANY FRIENDS.

Messrs. Editors—You are authorized to announce **J. M. TRACY** as a candidate for City Marshal, at ensuing April election. VOX POPULI.

HON. J. P. BENJAMIN.—The telegraph brings us the gratifying intellligence that this distinguished and eloquent son of Louisiana has been appointed by President Davis to the high position of Attorney General of the Confederate States. No abler statesman, learned a lawyer and truer Southerner could have been found in the country, and in his selection the President adds another pillar of strength to the popular and vigorous administration of which he is the head. Mr. Benjamin has signified his intention to accept the appointment.

A CABBAGE.—Bowlin Chinn, of West Baton Rouge, sends us from Cypress Hall Plantation another monster of the vegetable kind. It is a cabbage something under the size of a negro cabin—at least it would make a barrel of "sour krout"—that is, provided the barrel be not *too* large.

☞ The friends of Charley McMain will be glad to learn that his wound assumed a better shape yesterday, and that the chances are now decidedly in favor of his recovery. Mr. Caldwell remains in prison awaiting an investigation.

DISGRACEFUL CONDUCT.—We have heard of several complaints recently of insults offered to respectable but unprotected ladies, of family, whose misfortune it is to be poor, from insolent scoundrels who knock for admission into their houses at night. Sometimes these calls are pretended to be through mistake, and at others impudent and senseless inquiries, are resorted to as an apology for the intrusion. There *are* such a thing as female virtue and respectability to be found under a lowly roof, and the nocturnal vagabond who expects to insult their possessors in this community with impunity will find himself mistaken whenever he is detected.

The occurrences we speak of are becoming too frequent to be accidental, and the complainants intend to take steps to have themselves protected from this species of scoundrelism. As a remedy, we recommend double-barrel shot guns and buckshot.

APPOINTMENTS BY THE GOVERNOR.—The following appointments were made yesterday by Gov. Moore, and confirmed by the Senate:

Thos. M. Jones—Asst. Adj't Gen. with the rank of Captain.

Geo. G. Garner—Aid-de-Camp and 1st Lieutenant.

John C. Moore—Captain of Artillery.

Somerville Burke—Assistant Surgeon.

John S. Moore—Notary Public—Rapides.

THE BALL.—How the little folks belonging to Prof. Lippard's dancing class did enjoy themselves at the fancy dress ball on Tuesday night at the Harney House! With what a *vim* the little courtiers, cavaliers, Highland Chiefs, Zouaves, Generals and Colonels of all countries, entered into the frolic and flirtation with their little partners, who were likewise converted into the tidiest representatives of court dames, flower girls, regimental daughters, etc., that it was ever our lot to behold. There was polished grace, etiquette and captivating sweetness in the dancing and intercourse of these children that exacted the spontaneous admiration of all. Prof. Lippard deserves both the thanks and the encouragement of parents for his proficiency as a teacher and instructor of their children in those accomplishments which adorn the social circle.

After the exhibition of the pupils, the "old folks" took the floor and kept it until 1 o'clock in the morning. Everybody had a fine time of it.

THE VIRGINIA CONVENTION.—In the Convention on the 19th the speech of Mr. Preston created great interest. He said the Union could never be reconstructed, and expressed full confidence that Virginia would join the Southern Confederacy. A resolution was introduced that Virginia has the legal right to secede, that the election of Lincoln was not a just ground, but since a portion of the South had seceded, leaving the border States in the minority in Congress, Virginia should demand additional guarantees and proper amendments to the Constitution. She should present an ultimatum to the Northern States, and fix a time beyond which she will not wait, and if it fails, then Virginia should take steps to secure her just rights out of the Union. Referred to Committee on Federal Relations.

THE JUDICIARY.

Whether or not the elective judiciary system has been a success in Louisiana, it is perfectly apparent that the prevailing sentiment of the day is opposed to it. The desire to have the appointing system restored by abolishing the elective is no longer confined to members of the bar, but has taken deep root in the mind of nearly all classes of the people. We frankly confess to having at one time been an advocate of the elective judiciary, but its results in Louisiana have not been what its friends expected of it. On the contrary, it has proven to be so near a failure that to not characterize it as such would almost do injustice to the truth.

The people of Louisiana have no particular reason to be proud of their Supreme Court, nor of the class of Judges elected to the bench in the various Judicial Districts. Mediocrity is alarmingly prevalent in both branches of the judiciary; native talent and legal knowledge are the exceptions, not the rule. That there *are* exceptions we are happy to acknowledge, and that those exceptions agree with us in our general estimate of the bench as at present constituted we have the satisfaction of knowing—at least from some of them.

It is not at all difficult to account for the great change in public sentiment in regard to this matter. People are becoming tired, disgusted and annoyed with the frequency with which they have to neglect their daily business and engage in the turmoils of political strife. So often are they called upon to go to the polls to vote for this officer and that, so rarely do they get a breathing spell from the importunities of candidates, that nothing short of an exciting Presidential or Gubernatorial canvass will bring out the full strength of the suffragans on election day. Wonderful and inconceivable, too, is the undeniable fact that no election excites so little attention and develops such a huge amount of indifference among the masses as the election for the important office of Judge. Look at the returns in the various Districts; look at the figures by which our Associate and Supreme Judges were put into office, and the secret of the failure of the elective system in our State is no longer a mystery. Taking the result in this District at the last election—and by which we secured the services of our present excellent and able Judge Avery—as an average vote (and it is largely over an average,) and we feel safe in asserting that it will be found that not over 20,000 votes are represented to-day on the Bench of Louisiana out of a total vote of 50,000.

The long and the short of it is, the people are heartily sick of so much voting, and are perfectly willing to be relieved of the burden of electing their judicial officers. Let them be appointed by the Governor or by the Legislature for a term of five or ten years, or during good behavior, and we venture to say it will receive the cordial approval of nine-tenths of the people of the State.

We could advance abundant reasons to sustain this position, but as we are simply giving form to what is conceded to be the public wish it is deemed unnecessary.

In the State Senate, on Tuesday, Senator Tucker introduced a proposition that will reach the case without any expense or trouble to the people. It is in the nature of Joint Resolution of the Legislature asking the State Convention to change the article of the Constitution relative to the election of Judges and give the power of appointing to the Governor. This seems to us the readiest and simplest mode of proceeding to effect the object. If the resolutions pass the Legislature, and go before the Convention, and the latter think the exercise of the power to be incompatible with their obligations to their constituency, let them attach the condition that the proposed amendment shall be null and void unless ratified by the popular vote. This would not only give satisfaction to the public, but would result in the success of the object contemplated in Senator Tucker's resolutions.

VERY IMPORTANT NEWS.

A large mercantile firm in New Orleans sends the evening *Picayune* of Tuesday the following dispatch just received by the house from a "reliable" source at Washington. We trust the source *is* "reliable," but thereupon we must be permitted to have our doubts:

WASHINGTON, Feb. 26.—The incoming Administration will not blockade the ports of the seceding States, nor will it attempt to collect duties in Southern ports.

It will also voluntarily surrender the forts and military posts still in the possession of the Federal Government, if they are not attacked before it comes into power and the negotiations to that end are completed.

In the meantime, I fear the border States will accept any compromise offered to them, if it be such as to quiet their people.

☞ Small Pox exists among the soldiers stationed at the St. Louis Arsenal.

☞ E. P. Willis, Esq., is announced for the Judgeship in the Livingston District. The name of George H. Martin, Esq., is mentioned in the same connection.

☞ President Felton, of Cambridge, asserts that the continued use of steel pens paralyzes the nerves of the arm. He advocates a return to the use of quills.

☞ The Grand Jury of Richmond, Va., have declared that the New York *World, Times* and *Tribune* are incendiary papers, and they propose to indict the publishers.

☞ Mortimer Thompson, ("Doesticks,") will, it is said, soon lead to the altar a beautiful daughter of Mrs. Parton, who has attained a world-wide celebrity by the *nom de plume* of "Fanny Fern." Mr. Thompson is at present a widower.

☞ The Memphis *Avalanche* says that Professor Wise, of æronautic fame, is at present engaged in selling apples and candy at the street corners in that city.

Louisiana Legislature.

WEDNESDAY, Feb. 27th, 1861.

SENATE.—The Senate met pursuant to adjournment.

On motion of Mr. Stevens the reading of the journal was dispensed with.

Mr. Goode from the Judiciary Committee, reported favorably the following bills, entitled An act relative to District Attorneys; an act to authorize Arthémise Chust, of the parish of Pointe Coupeé to adopt Octave Robellard and Ovide Robellard; an act to prohibit certain officers from practicing or receiving fees as Attorneys at law; an act amending an act entitled an act supplementary to the acts incorporating the town of Thibodaux, approved May 29th, 1846; an act authorizing Wenzel Reichelt to adopt Hellena Guisert; an act relative to the appointment of Notaries Public; an act to authorize William Alexander to adopt the minors Helen Jane and Mayo Spencer Duke; an act to recharter the ferry across the Atchafalaya River at Simmesport; with an amendment, an act granting additional powers to clerks of the District Courts; an act relative to the punishment of slaves; an act emancipating Julia A. Leollings, wife of John Row, of West Feliciana.

And he reported unfavorably the following bills:

An act to emancipate Volney E. Ogle and E. K. Ogle; an act to amend and re-enact the 11th section of an act relative to District Attorneys, approved March 15th. 1855.

Mr. Pearce, from Committee on Finance, reported favorably, with amendments, an act for the expenses of the Convention.

Mr. Pearce, from same committee, reported a bill making appropriation for purposes of State defense; made the special order of the day for to-morrow.

An act to amend an act to promote the formation of Military Companies, and to provide for the arming and equipment of the same; passed.

An act prescribing the manner in which money shall be drawn and accounted for, appropriated to the State for military purposes; adopted.

Mr. Pearce, from Committee on Finance, reported favorably on a bill for the government of the Asylum of the Deaf, Dumb and the Blind.

Mr. Shadburne, from Committee on Public Works, reported favorably on a bill authorizing the Governor to issue patents.

Also on joint resolutions from Texas, reported by bill, and recommended the printing of the report of the Board of Public Works.

Mr. Phillips introduced a joint resolution, instructing the Register not to issue any patents for sixteenth sections till further action of the Legislature; referred to the Joint Committee on the Land Office.

Mr. Laidlaw introduced without previous notice, a bill to make an appropriation to defray the expenses of the volunteer corps of New Orleans; referred to the Committee on Militia.

House bill for the relief of the Sheriff of the parish of St. Tammany; referred to the Committee on Finance.

Mr. Goode from the Special Committee on the Land Office, reported a joint resolution relative to the Land Office with amendments; adopted.

Mr. Pearce from the Finance Committee, reported the General appropriation bill; made special order for to-morrow.

House bill for the relief of Samuel M. Hyams, late Register of the United States Land Office at Natchitoches; referred to the Committee on Claims.

House bill for the relief of B. Melford; referred to Committee on Claims.

House bill relating to appeals in executory process; referred to Judiciary Committee.

House bill to prevent slaves hiring or letting their time; referred to Judiciary Committee.

Mr. Goode introduced without previous notice, an act to prohibit the Recorder of New Orleans to release persons confined as vagrants or suspicious characters; referred to the Judiciary Committee.

Mr. Goode introduced an act for the relief of L. D. Nichols, District Clerk of the parish of Ascension.

The special order of the day, viz:

An act to repeal an act entitled an act establishing a Board of Public Works; passed.

An act authorizing the Librarian to procure 250 copies each, of the Civil Code, and the Code of Practice, for destribution; an amendment, inserted by the Committee, substituting 400, for 250, was adopted; on motion of Mr. Stevens, the bill was laid on the table subject to call.

Mr. Buffington called up a bill for the relief of John F. Durgan; referred to the Committee on Public Works.

House bill to increase the per diem of the Policy Jury of the parish of Sabine; referred to the Committee on Parochial Affairs.

House bill to change the name of James P. McGee; referred to the Judiciary Committee.

Mr. Stevens gave notice that he should move to reconsider the vote abolishing the Board of Public Works.

Mr. Smart moved to re-consider the vote referring the bill to increase the per diem of the Police Jury of Sabine, to the Committee on Parochial Affairs, and the bill was taken up and passed.

Mr. Phillips called up the bill reported by the Judiciary Committee, relative to District Attorneys; adopted.

Mr. Phillips called up the bill authorizing Arthémise Chust to adopt Octave Robellard and Ovide Robellard; adopted.

Mr. Phillips called up the bill to re-charter the ferry across the Atchafalaya River; adopted.

Mr. Hough called up a bill relative to the punishment of slaves, reported by the Judiciary Committee; adopted.

Mr. Taylor called up the House bill, amendatory of the acts incorporating the town of Thibodaux; adopted.

Mr. Laidlaw called up the bill to emancipated Julia A. Leolling's wife of John Row; adopted.

After executive session the Senate adjourned till 11 o'clock to morrow.

HOUSE—The House met at 10 o'clock, and was called to order by Hon. C. H. Morrison, Speaker.

On calling the roll 57 members answered to their names.

Reading of the minutes was dispensed with.

Mr. Breithaupt introduced a bill to improve the navigation of Little River.

Mr. Bemiss introduced a memorial from the citizens of Jefferson relative to the District Courts.

Mr. Allen introduced a petition for the relief of Michael and John Tuesdale; referred to Committee on Claims.

Mr. Coleman introduced a resolution relative to the Military Board; adopted.

Mr. Gantt introduced a resolution to inquire into the condition of the Internal Improvement Fund, and report the same to the House; adopted.

Mr. Coleman introduced a resolution that the House hold evening sessions after Monday next; laid over under the rules.

The Committee on Propositions and Grievances reported unfavorably on the bill for the relief of Levi Priesley.

Committee reported favorably on the bill for the relief of Louis Sanchez.

Mr. Davidson, on behalf of the Judiciary Committee, reported favorably upon the resolution relative to judges of the State; and favorably upon the bill to fix the salary of the Judge of the Third Judicial District—a majority of the Committee *only* concurring in these reports.

Mr. Davidson, from the same Committee, reported adversely upon the following:

An act relative to the sale of property under writ of *fi. fa.*, and seizure and sale; an act to authorize the city of New Orleans to invest the McDonogh Fund in city bonds; an act relative to Sheriff sales in the parish of St. James; resolution concerning the creditors and receiver of an insolvent, introduced by the member from Madison, Mr. Coleman.

Mr. Davidson, from the same Committee, reported against Senate bill No. 42, being an act to emancipate Victorine Melangon of the parish of Ascension.

Mr. Lindsay, from a select committee, to whom was referred the bill for the relief of the New Orleans Medical College, reported favorably.

Mr. Allen, from the special committee to whom was referred the letter of Mr. George Williamson, Commissioner to Texas, relative to cannon which were used at San Jacinto and are now in possession of this State, reported in favor of appropriating $700 to mount the cannon and return them to the people of Texas: rules suspended and report adopted.

Mr. Allen, from the special committee to whom was referred the resolution authorizing the Governor to take possession and fit up one of the houses belonging to the late Ordnance Department, reported favorably; laid over under the rules.

Mr. Bickham made a motion to reconsider the vote by which a traveling committee was appointed to go to Jackson to examine the Insane Asylum; the vote was reconsidered, and the resolution creating the committee was laid on the table.

Mr. Bartlett obtained leave to withdraw a bill, for the relief of Charles Hatcher, from the files of last session.

Mr. Allen introduced a resolution authorizing the Governor to appoint an Engineer to take charge of the books, maps and charts belonging to the late Board of Public Works; referred to a special committee of three.

Mr. Marks introduced an act to incorporate the Baton Rouge Hebrew Eenevolent Society; referred to Judiciary Committee.

Mr. Fish introduced a bill relative to the collection of taxes in New Orleans; referred to Judiciary Committee.

Mr. Harper introduced an act to provide for the military defense of the State; referred to Committee on Finance.

Mr. Coleman introduced an act to regulate the power of Justices of the Peace in penal cases; referred to Judiciary Committee.

Mr. Wise introduced an act for the relief of G. W. Franklin, of the parish of Rapides; referred to Judiciary Committee.

Mr. Harper introduced an act relative to gambling; referred to Judiciary Committee.

Mr. Morrison introduced an act to grant additional powers to the municipal authorities of the town of Trenton, in the parish of Ouachita; rules suspended and bill passed.

Mr. G. P. Voorhies of Avoyelles, introduced an act to establish a ferry across the Atchafalaya at Cypress Point; referred to the Committee on Parochial Affairs.

Mr. Waggaman introduced an act creating a custodian for archives in New Orleans; referred to Judiciary Committee.

BILLS ON SECOND READING.

An act preventing slaves from hiring their own time; referred to Judiciary Committee.

An authorizing the sale of the slaves and steamboats belonging to the late Internal Improvement Department; passed.

An act for the relief of S. F. Harrison of the parish of Caddo; passed.

An act to refund moneys to the estate of Julius Ennis, deceased; passed.

Rules were suspended to allow a bill for the incorporation of Haynesville, in the parish of Claiborne; passed.

Bill for the relief of C. O. Moselle; laid on the table.

An act relative to the Charity Hospital, New Orleans, and the Deaf, Dumb and Blind Asylum, Baton Rouge; passed.

An act to create a Parish Prison Keeper in New Orleans; laid on the table.

Message from the Senate informing the House that they had concurred in House bill relative to Board of Public Works.

An act to incorporate the Ohio and Mobile Railroad; passed.

The order of the day—an act amending and re-enacting article 2,260 of the Civil Code.

This bill caused a long legal discussion in which Messrs. Gnatt, Dupuy, and Bartlett opposed the bill, and Messrs. Herron, Bush and Bemiss in favor.

Mr. Magioni introduced a resolution that the bill shall only apply to cases which shall occur after its promulgation; amendment adopted.

The ayes and nays were called on the engrossment of the bill which resulted, ayes 36, nays 25; bill ordered to be engrossed—House refused to suspend the rules to allow third reading of the bill.

Next order of the day—an act relative to the Judiciary came up for engrossment, and the ayes were called, resulting 27 ayes and 29 nays; House refused to engross bill.

BILLS ON SECOND READING.

An act authorizing Clerks of the District Courts to grant certain orders; passed.

An act relative to the judicial sales made at public auction; passed.

An act to authorize Wm. Ham and wife to adopt Caroline Wright, a minor; passed.

An act relative to seers, fortune tellers, etc.; laid on the table subject to call.

An act for the relief of John E. Testard; laid on the table subject to call.

An act for the relief of Adolph Lafargue, of Avoyelles.

Pending the consideration of this act the House adjourned until 10 o'clock to-morrow.

TELEGRAPHIC ITEMS.

THE SOUTHERN CONGRESS.

Public Lands--Further Cabinet Appointments--Permanent Constitution.

MONTGOMERY, Feb. 25.—During the sitting of the Congress to-day, a resolution was adopted instructing a committee to inquire into the present condition of public lands.

Mr. Rhett, of South Carolina, announced on behalf of the committee of which he is chairman, that a permanent Constitution would be reported on Wednesday.

Secrecy was removed from the bill on Postal Affairs, also the appointments of Messrs. Henry T. Ellet of Mississippi as Postmaster General, and J. P. Benjamin of Louisiana as Attorney General.

The Commissioners to Washington are Messrs. R. B. Roman of Louisiana, W. T. Crawford of Georgia, and John Forsyth of Alabama.

It is rumored that Mr. Mallory, of Florida, will be appointed Secretary of the Navy.

SHOOTING AFFAIR IN BATON ROUGE. *Baton Rouge*, Feb. 26.—Mr. Lafayette Caldwell, a member of the Board of Public Works, last night shot a young man by the name of Charles McMain. The wound inflicted is of a dangerous character. Mr. Caldwell was committed to jail, where he is visited by numerous friends. He insists that he was assaulted in his house.

PROCEEDINGS OF THE FEDERAL CONGRESS. *Washington*, Feb. 26.—The Senate yesterday was mainly occupied on the Miscellaneous Appropriation Bill. The Chiriqui amendment was rejected—ayes, 24; nays, 25.

The amendment was adopted repealing the act prohibiting the purchasing of patented articles by the Secretary of War.

In the House Mr. Sherman, in urging the necessity of concurring in the Senate amendments to the Tariff Bill, said on the advent of the present Administration the public debt consisted of $20,000,000, with $18,000,000 in the Treasury. He added that the public debt now amounted to $96,000,000, and that the Government must have $88,000,000 for the next fiscal year.

ATTEMPT TO SHOOT LINCOLN.—*Washington*, Feb. 26.—Proper authorities here have received information of an attempted plan to shoot Mr. Lincoln at his inaugural.

THE PEACE CONFERENCE.—*Washington*, Feb. 26.—The debate on the Peace Convention yesterday was very exiting. At one time Mr. Guthrie and some of his friends were so offended that they left the hall and threatened not to participate in the proceedings but subsequently returned.

DRAFT ON LOUISIANA.—*Washington*, Feb. 26.—Mr. King's draft on Mr. Guisott, Assistant Treasurer of Louisiana, for $300,000, was dishonored as Mr. Dix's had been.

TEXAS ELECTION.—*Galveston*, Feb. 23. The vote in the city of Galveston is as follows:

For Secession, 709; against Secession, 130; majority for Secession, 679.

HOUSTON, Feb. 23.—For Secession, 638; against Secession, 100; majority for Secession, 538.

PROCEEDINGS OF THE FEDERAL CONGRESS. *Washington*, Feb. 25.—In the Senate, Mr. Sumner, in presenting a petition from citizens in Massachusetts, asking the enactment of a law that no person be held to service by the laws of any State, and that such persons be declared free, said most emphatically that Congress had no right to interfere with slavery in the States.

The Postal bill came up. Mr. Hemphill of Texas, offered an amendment, empowering the Postmaster General to arrange with the seceding States in regard to postal affairs—lost. The bill passed by thirty-four against twelve.

The Tariff bill is being discussed in the House. All the Senate's amendments were concurred in with the exception of those relating to tea and coffee. A committee of conference was appointed on these two amendments.

THE SOUTHERN CONGRESS.

CAPITOL OF THE SOUTHERN CONFEDERACY,
MONTGOMERY, ALA., Feb. 21, 1861.

Eds. Pic.—The avaricious desire of the public to know who would receive Cabinet appointments has only been half gratified to-day; and inquisitive feeling will have food for thought a day or so longer, because no nominations have been made for the Navy, for Attorney General, nor for Postmaster General. As this letter goes off long before Congress meets to-morrow, I intend to hazard an opinion as to the nominations yet to be made. So here goes:

Postmaster General—Mr. Ellet of Mississippi.

Attorney General—Mr. Benjamin of Louisiana.

Secretary of the Navy—Mr. Perry of Florida.

If the news, by the wires, should materially overturn my speculations before this letter is printed, I hope that the compositor who "sets it up" will take care of my reputation for sagacity and fix things to suit, so as to induce the public to believe that your correspondent is not only marvelously accurate in his speculations, but has very superior means of knowing how milk gets into a cocoanut.

Everything appears to be going on smoothly in Congress. We hear of no jars. But it is just to state that the most important discussions, and those in which contrariety of opinion would be manifested, if at all, are all conducted in secret.

Below you will find the proceedings of Congress to-day.

SIXTEENTH DAY.

The Convention met to day at noon.

The journals of yesterday were read and confirmed.

Mr. Chilton of Alabama, said he had two communications sent to him by a scientific gentleman; one in relation to cast iron cannon, and the other in relation to patents. This gentleman has a plan by which he can render rifled cast-iron cannon fully equal to, and perhaps superior to the Armstrong gun. He desires to try the experiment, and demonstrate to the Committee on Military Affairs the excellency of his cast-iron guns. One of those communications was referred to the Military Committee, and the other to the Committee on Patents. The references were made.

Mr. Fearn of Alabama, presented a communication from Mr. Marshall, on the subject of metal castings, which, without reading, was referred to the Military Committee.

Mr. T. R. R. Cobb of Georgia, offered the following resolution of inquiry into the expediency of an export duty on cotton:

"*Resolved*, That the Committee on Finance be instructed to inquire into the expediency of laying an export duty on all raw cotton which may be exported from the Confederate States to any foreign country, by any other channel than through the seaports of this Confederacy."

Mr. Cobb said, I propose merely, Mr. President, to refer that resolution to the Finance Committee. At this time I am not prepared to discuss the policy of levying such a duty. That we have the power to do so there can be no doubt. I apprehend that we are conscious of the power we hold in our hands, by reason of our producing that staple so necessary to the world. I doubt not that power will exert an influence greater and mightier than armies and navies. We know that by an embargo we could soon place, not only the United States, but many of the European powers, under the necessity of electing between such a recognition of our independence as we require or domestic convulsions at home. The information in our possession seems to justify such an inquiry as the resolution proposes. It is a fact that some of the cotton now produced in this Confederacy is already seeking a new channel to the sea. We are informed that at Pittsburg, Pa., more than 20,000 bales of cotton have already been received and conveyed thither up the Mississippi and Ohio Rivers.

We are also informed that more than 20,000 bales of cotton from Rome, Georgia, have been sent by railroad to seek a port at Norfolk and Alexandria. We are further informed that the directors of the railroads communicating with the principal lines in our territory are now concerting schemes for the purpose of reducing freights on those roads, in order, in that way, to entice our cotton to markets in Northern ports. The result of such a course, if successful, would, in the first place, necessarily be to make the blockade of our ports a matter of no importance to foreign nations; secondly, it would destroy all commerce with our own sea ports, and thirdly, and most important of all, it would compel us to receive all the imported goods we might need after paying duties on them in New York city. These considerations have induced me to offer this resolution of inquiry. I do not think that the resolution should elicit discussion at the present time, but after the Committee on Finance have made their report, it may become a grave matter for the consideration of this body.

The resolution was adopted.

Mr. Shorter of Alabama, chairman of the Committee on Engrossments, reported as duly enrolled, and ready for the signature of the President, the following acts:

An act to determine the salaries of the Vice President and the heads of departments.

An act to organize the Department of State.

An act to establish the Navy Department.

An act to establish the War Department.

An act to organize and establish an executive department, to be known as the Department of Justice.

An act to establish the Postoffice Department.

On motion, Congress went into secret session.

Congress adjourned about 3 o'clock. None of the business transacted was made public, with the exception of the confirmation of a portion of the Cabinet. There were no other nominations made to Congress, to-day, by the President, than the following:

Secretary of State—Hon. Robert Toombs of Georgia.

Secretary of the Treasury—Hon. C. C. Memminger of South Carolina.

Secretary of War—Hon. L. Pope Walker of Alabama.

The foregoing nominations were confirmed, and Congress adjourned until to-morrow at 12 o'clock.

THE TARIFF.

The following is a synopsis of the Tariff of 1857, now in force in the Southern Confederacy, which comprises nearly all of interest to our merchants:

Manufactures of cedar wood, granadilla, ebony, mahogany, rose-wood, and satin-wood, per cent.,....30
Manufactures of the bark of the cork tree,....24
Manufactures of bone, shell, horn, pearl, ivory, or vegetable ivory,....24
Manufactures, articles, vessels, and wares, not otherwise provided for, of brass, copper, gold, iron, lead, pewter, platine, silver, tin, or other metal, or of which either of those metals or any other metal shall be the component material of chief value,....24
Manufactures composed wholly of cotton, bleached, printed, painted, or dyed,....24
Manufactures of cotton, linen, silk, wool, or worsted, if embroidered or tamboured in the loom or otherwise, by machinery, or with the needle or other process,....24
Manufactures, articles, vessels and wares of glass, or of which glass shall be a component material, not otherwise provided for,....24
Manufactures and articles of leather, or of which leather shall be a component part, not otherwise provided for,....24
Manufactures and articles of marble, marble paving tiles, and other marble more advanced in manufacture than in slabs or blocks in the rough,....24
Manufacturers of paper, or of which paper is a component material, not otherwise provided for,....24
Manufactures, articles and wares of papier mache,....24
Manufactures of wood, or of which wood is a component part, not otherwise provided for, 24
Manufactures of wool, or of which wool shall be the component material of chief value, not otherwise provided for,....24
Manufactures of hair,....19
Manufactures of fur,....24
Manufactures composed wholly of cotton, not otherwise provided for,....19
Manufactures of goat's hair or mohair, or of which goat's hair or mohair shall be a component material, not otherwise provided for, 19
Manufactures of silk, or of which silk shall be the component material, not otherwise provided for,....19
Manufactures of worsted, or of which worsted shall be a component material, not otherwise provided for,....19
Manufactures of flax, not otherwise provided for, 15
Manufactures of hemp, not otherwise provided for,....15
Manufactures of mohair cloth, silk twist, or other manufacture of cloth suitable for the manufacture of shoes, cut in slips or patterns of the size and shape for shoes, slippers, boots, bootees, gaiters, or buttons, exclusively, not combined with India rubber,.... 4
Manufactures of lastings suitable for shoes, boots, bootees, or buttons, exclusively,.... 4

Bagging, (Gunny) 15; Coffee free; Guano and other fertilizers, free; Iron in bars, etc., 24; Lime, 8; Molasses and sugar, 24; Books, Periodicals, Illustrated Newspapers, 8; Drugs in a crude state, 15; Medical preparations, 24; Dye Woods and extracts for dying, 4 per cent.

MR. HAMLIN EN ROUTE FOR WASHINGTON. *Speech at Bangor, Maine.*—*Bangor*, Feb. 18. Mr. Hamlin, the Vice President elect, accompanied by his wife, left for Washington this morning. He was escorted to the depot by thousands of his fellow-townsmen, who cheered and bade him farewell.

Previous to the starting of the train, Mr. Hamlin responded in a brief address, as follows:

"I go to discharge the official duties which have been conferred by a generous people, relying on Divine Providence. I trust that the confidence shall never be betrayed. I know full well that dark clouds are hovering around the political horizon, and that "madness rules the hour." But I am hopeful still. Our people are not only loyal to the Government, but are fraternal to all its citizens. And, when in practice it shall be demonstrated that the Constitutional rights of all the States will be respected and maintained by following the paths illumined by Washington, Jefferson and Madison, may we not reasonably hope and expect that quiet will be restored and the whole country still advance in a career which will elevate man in his social, moral, and intellectual condition?"

MARRIED,

On Monday the 18th inst., by the Rev. S. J. Larkins, Dr. M. W. GOLDSBY of Morehouse parish, to Miss DETTIE A. DUDGEON of Baton Rouge.

NEW YORK ILLUSTRATED NEWS

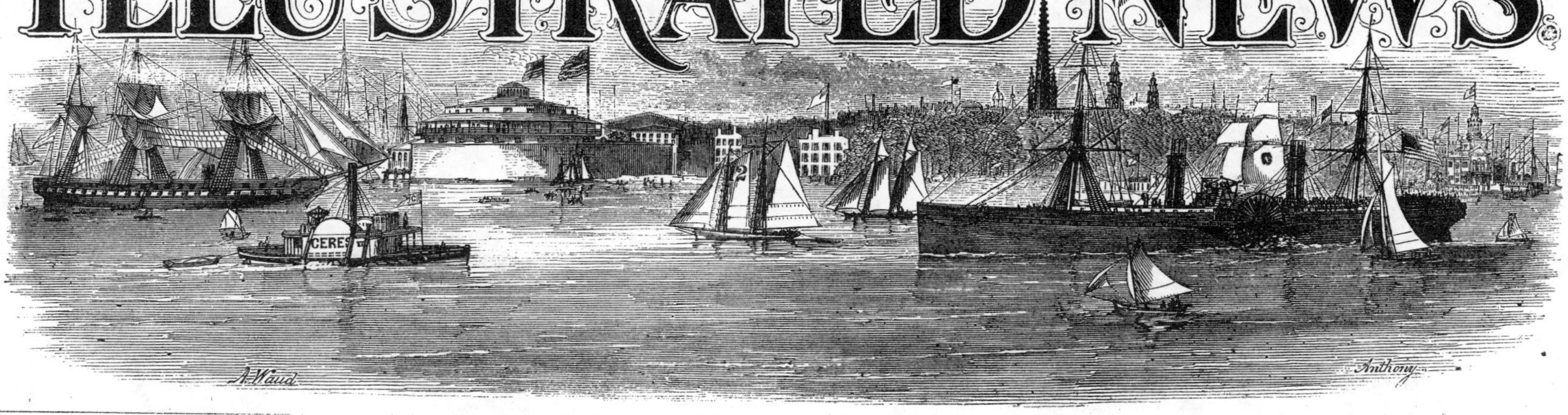

No. 69.—Vol. III. NEW-YORK, SATURDAY, MARCH 2, 1861. Price Six Cents.

MR. LINCOLN IN HIS NEW FACIAL APPOINTMENTS.

Now that kings, statesmen, and even handsome priests, whilst preaching of heavenly glories in general, and of their own glories in particular, have adopted the patriarchal fashion of beards and whiskers, as their highest and manliest adornment, there is no wonder that ambitious Americans—desirous of emulating such distinguished company—should cultivate their "mustaches" and "whiskeranders."

Our good President elect, "Honest old Abe," sets us a brave example in this respect, which all gentlemen, beardless from principle hitherto, will do well to adopt. "Honest Abe" has cultivated his whiskers, and looks as big and handsome now as the best and greatest of his contemporaries. We have the honor of presenting our readers with the first portrait of him taken with his new facial appointments, and we hope all patriotic ladies will fall in love with him.

MR. LINCOLN IN NEW YORK.

RECEPTION AT THE HUDSON RIVER RAILROAD DEPOT.

Mr. Lincoln's progress from Albany to New York was a continued ovation. All the people of the different localities round the railway stations turned out to welcome him with their vivats, and do honor to the brave old rail splitter. Hours before the train arrived in New York. crowds of people were waiting at Thirtieth street, where it was to stop, and where the uncrowned sovereigns of the Empire hoped to get a first glance at their future servant.

On the arrival of the train there were probably congregated some five or six thousand persons.

The police force were in large numbers on the ground, and the most perfect order was kept, though in this regard their labors were light, for the crowd were thoroughly good-humored. The hours preceding the time of the train were barren of incident. The new depot building was occupied by a detachment of police, and by a number of other favored gentlemen, including the omnipresent Reporters for the Press. A number of ladies, friends of the officers of the road, were also in the spacious rooms, which are as yet unurnished.

A peculiarity of the reception was the absence of all military display and the utter disregard of formal preparation. The City Authorities were not represented here, the Committee being on the train with Mr. Lincoln. The Mayor was not present, and the immense crowd were gathered together simply by their desire to see and to do honor to a single man—their choice, their hope, their reliance. There was no looking for a grand display, there was no promise, and no need of extraneous aids to attract the throng—no drums, no uniforms, no speeches from loud-mouthed cannon or soft-mouthed politicians, were promised, expected, or desired.

The telegraph had kept the people advised of the progress of the train, and it was known every half hour or oftener that no accident or hindering bother of any kind delayed the Presidential procession that was steaming down the Hudson at the rate of forty miles an hour. The weather was most favorable, all looked well, and the prospect was that the crowd would not be disappointed in their hopes.

The cars were due at 3 P. M, they kept their appointment to the minute—precisely as the hour was on the stroke the whistle and the engine bell announced the arrival of the visitors.

A hurried rush of eager spectators; a hurried forming of two hurried lines by the hurrying policemen; a hurried dash into the enclosure of a gasping, and gayly decorated locomotive engine; a hurried rising from sofa seats, and a hurrying step to the platform by happy passengers; a hurried grasping of a few hurrying hands; another hurried rush of the eager crowd to see the man of the hour; a hurried and exceedingly vigorous argument with the said hurrying crowd, by the police officers; a hurried rescue of Mr. Lincoln from the hand-shaking inflictions of admiring friends; a dozen hurried steps through the new depot building, a hurried passing into hundreds of carriages by the countless lucky ones, a hearty cheer from the now satisfied crowd, a five minute delay for an inscrutable something about the baggage, another cheer, a waving of innumerable white handkerchiefs from the hundreds of windows, a graceful raising of the hat by Mr. Lincoln in response thereto, a hurried order by a hurried Marshal, a hurried cracking of whips by many horses, and so, amid more cheers, more shouts of welcome, and more waving of more handkerchiefs, the procession began its march.

This universal waving of handkerchiefs was one of the most striking peculiarities of the whole scene; through the whole of the route, from first to last, from Thirtieth street to the Astor House, from the locomotive engine to the hotel parlor, the president progressed on the white breast of the most tremendous wave of handkerchiefs ever witnessed—his coming was anticipated by a white ripple of rectangular linen; he moved forward on the white bosom of a huge linen billow of colossal dimensions, and departing he left a wake of numberless handkerchiefs still gently tossing a multitudinous greeting—as if ev-

[See page 270

LATEST PORTRAIT OF MR. LINCOLN.—SKETCHED BY OUR OWN ARTIST.

MR. LINCOLN'S RECEPTION AT THE HUDSON RIVER RAILROAD DEPOT, THIRTIETH STREET, NEW YORK.

HON. JEFFERSON DAVIS, PRESIDENT OF THE SOUTHERN CONFEDERACY. See page 268.

HON. ALEXANDER H. STEPHENS, VICE-PRESIDENT OF THE SOUTHERN CONFEDERACY. See page 269.

A LIFE STORY.

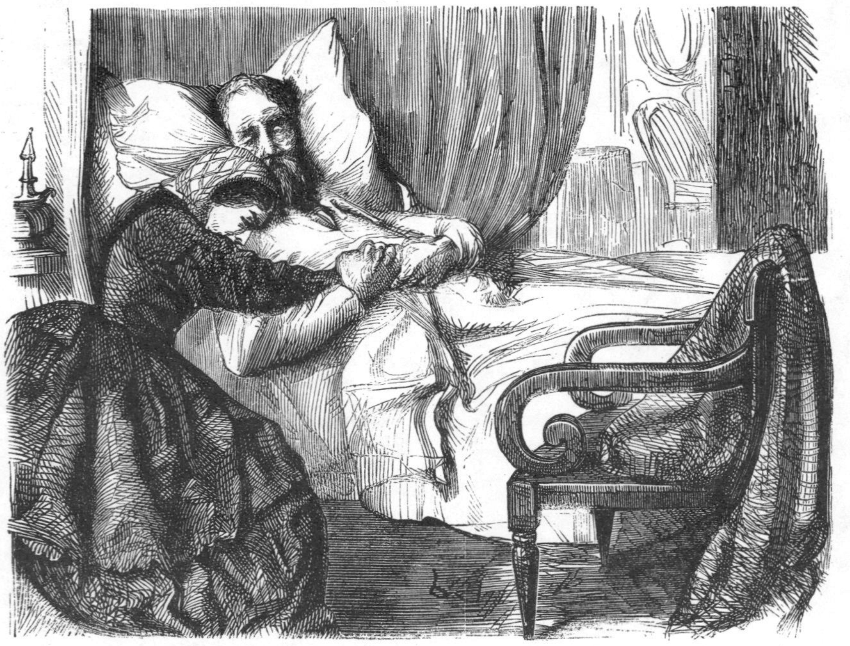

In haste I call'd him the light word
That darken'd life for ever ;
My pallid face nor moved nor stirr'd—
His lips but one short quiver.
He gave me that long yearning look,
And spake : "If such I be"—
And all his frame a shudder shook—
"I am not fit for thee."

We never met again—until
Long years had swept away :
His face was cold, and calm, and still—
My hair was tinged with gray.

Upon his arm a lady hung—
His voice was kind and free :
He did not know the blood-drops wrung
From my heart's agony.

We met but once again—the day
On which my darling died.
His wife and child had pass'd away
I bade farewell to pride.
We met—my face to his he drew—
He call'd me by my name ;
And in his dying hour we knew
Our love had been the same.

THE SILVER CORD.

BY SHIRLEY BROOKS.

CHAPTER XXIV.

On the day following that of Adair's interview with Henderson, at which he had extracted the scrap of paper from the reluctant hand of the lady's maid, Ernest, who had taken up his quarters at the little inn at Versailles, received an unexpected visitor. This was M. Silvain, who presented himself with considerable sternness of manner. The symptom was not lost on the observant Adair, but he had his own reasons for not being very little affected by any change of bearing in the usual polite and deferential perfumer.

"Ah, the dear Alphonse!" said Adair, in French, the language in which their subsequent conversation was conducted, and which Ernest Adair spoke with perfect facility.

M. Silvain bowed slightly, upon which Adair rose, mockingly returned an elaborate salute, and then resuming his seat, proceeded to make a cigarette.

"I wish to be favored with your attention, Monsieur," said Silvain, coldly.

"You have it, my good Alphonse. Have you discovered a new hair-dye, or does some confiding victim to your last invention in that line threaten you with the tribunals?"

"I am not here to *badiner*, Monsieur."

"Is that a grateful answer, when a friend anticipates your griefs, and prepares to solace them?"

"Before we separate you will need another preparation, M. Adair."

"For my hair?"

"I forbid you to jest at my profession, Monsieur, or on any other subject at the present moment."

"*Diavolo!*" said Adair, opening his eyes. "Let us hear more, and shall I order you some absinthe? It is very bad, but you are accustomed to deleterious liquids."

"I repeat to you, M. Adair, that I forbid jesting."

"Well, if you will neither be consoled nor treated, the tribune is to you. Speak."

"I had thought you, M. Adair, with certain drawbacks, for which I know how to make allowance, a man of honor."

"I swear to you that I have kept your secrets. Nobody has learned from me how you color the violet pomade. I only refuse to use it."

"You seek to enrage me, M. Adair, but you have already done so more effectually than by your coarse taunts."

"Enraged you, Alphonse?—you, the pattern of all that is soft and amiable. Nay, then I am a wretch, indeed, and miserable to the lowest extent. *De profundis* I implore you to tell me my crime, only break it to me gently, knowing the feminine tenderness of my heart."

"The word is well chosen, M. Adair, by a man who commits a brutal outrage upon a woman."

"And who has done such a truly shocking thing?"

"You, yourself, Monsieur, and in this very apartment."

"I begin to think, my fabulous Alphonse, that my hospitable offer of refreshment was something more than superfluous, and that you were wise to decline it. I would not presume to dictate, but I think that the interests of our trade may suffer if we indulge too freely in the sensuous pleasures, at least during business hours."

This was said very indolently, and the punctuation supplied by light puffs of smoke.

"Your insolence, Monsieur, will not deter me from the purpose I have come for," returned Silvain, who, though pale with anger, preserved much composure of deportment.

"I should be very sorry to deter you from anything, my dear Alphonse," replied Adair. "I cannot charge myself with habitually keeping you out of mischief. But tipsiness is such an exceedingly objectionable frailty, that a friend's ardor may be pardoned."

"A friend, M. Adair. That name is never again to be used between us."

"Exactly as you please, Alphonse. Perhaps you are right. Real friends need no parade of their affectionate sentiments."

Norwich Morning Bulletin.

EXTRA.

VOL. III. NORWICH, CONN., MONDAY, MARCH 4, 1861. No. 687.

Second Edition

REJOICINGS.—A salute of thirty-four guns was fired this noon, in honor of the incoming administration. The large Lincoln and Hamlin flag belonging to the Wide Awakes was suspended across Main street, and the vessels in port displayed their bunting. The church bells rang out a joyful peal, and knots of excited people gathered at every corner. Everybody breathed more freely at the thought that the term of James Buchanan and his corrupt officials had closed. May we never see such another.

BY TELEGRAPH TO THE MORNING BULLETIN.

XXXVIth CONGRESS—Second Session

SENATE, March 3d,—*Concluded.*—At the hour of going to press this morning, (3 o'clock,) our report closed with the Senate still in session, discussing the resolutions from the House Committee of Thirty-Three.

Mr. Pugh's amendment to substitute the Crittenden resolutions for those adopted by the House, was lost.

The House resolutions were then adopted—24 against 12.

The vote on the Crittenden resolutions was ayes 19, nays 20.

Recess was then ordered till 10 A. M., it being 7 o'clock, and the Senate having been in session all night.

HOUSE, March 4.—The House met at 10 The galleries were empty.

Speaker Pennington delivered a feeling farewell address.

After the delivery of the Speaker's address the House adjourned *sine die* in much good humor.

Mr. Lincoln's Inaugural Address.

FELLOW CITIZENS OF THE UNITED STATES:—In compliance with a custom as old as the Government itself, I appear before you to address you briefly, and to take in your presence the oath prescribed by the Constitution of the United States to be taken by the President before he enters on the execution of his office. I do not consider it necessary at present for me to discuss those matters of administration about which there is no special anxiety or excitement.

Apprehension seems to exist among the people of the Southern States that by the accession of a Republican Administration their property, and their peace and personal security, are endangered. There has never been any reasonable cause for such apprehension. Indeed, the most ample evidence to the contrary has all the while existed, and been open to their inspection.

It is found in nearly all the published speeches of him who now addresses you. I do but quote from one of these speeches, when I declare that I have no purpose directly or indirectly to interfere with the institution of slavery in all States where it exists. I believe I have no lawful right to do so, and I have no inclination to do so.—Those who nominated and elected me did so with full knowledge that I had made this and similar declarations, and had never recanted them. More than this they placed in the platform for my acceptance, and as a law to themselves and to me, the clear and emphatic resolution which I now read.

Resolved, That the maintainance involate of the rights of the States and especially the right of each State to order and control its own domestic institutions according to its own judgment, exclusively is essential to that balance of power on which the perfection and enduradce of our political fabric depend, and we denounce the lawless invasion by armed force of the social affairs of any State or Territory, no matter under what pretext as among the gravest of crimes.

I now reiterate these sentiments, and in so doing, I only press upon the public attention the most conclusive evidence of which the case is susceptible, that the property, peace, and security, of no section are to be in anywise endangered by the new incoming administration.

I add to that all the protection which, consistently with the Constitution and the laws, can be given, will be cheerfully given to all the States when lawfully demanded, for whatever cause, as cheerfully to one section as to another. There is much controversy about the delivering up of fugitives from service or labor. The clause I now read is as plainly written in the Constitution as any other of its provisions.

No person held to service or labor in one State under the laws thereof, escaping into another, shall in consequence of any law or regulation therein, be discharged from such service or labor, but shall be delivered upon claim of the party to whom such service or labor may be due."

It is scarcely questioned that that this provision was intended by those who made it for the reclaiming of what we call fugitive slaves, and the intention of the lawgiver is the law—all members of Congress swear their support to the whole Constitution—to this provision as much as to any other.

To the proposition then that slaves whose cases come within the terms of this clause shall be delived up, their oaths are unanimous. Now if they would make the effort in good temper could they not, with nearly equal unanimity, frame and pass a law by means of which to keep good that unanimous oath.

There is some difierence of opinion whether this clause should be enforced by national or by state authority; but surely that difference is not a very material one. If the slave is to be surrendered, it can be of but little consequence to him or to others how it is done. And should any one in any case be content that his oath shall go unkept on a merely unsubstantial controversy as to how it shall be kept?

Again, in any law upon this subject, ought not all the safeguards of liberty known in civilized and humane jurisprudence to be introduced, so that a free man be not in any case surrendered as a slave, and might it not be well at the same time to provide by law for the enforcement of that clause in the Constitution which guarantees that the citizens of each State shall be entitled to all privileges and imunities of citizens in the several States.

I take the official oath to-day with no mental reservations, and with no purpose to construe the constitution and laws by any hypercritical rules, and while I do not choose now to specify particular acts of Congress as proper to be enforced, I do suggest that it will be much safer for all, both in official and private stations, to conform to and abide by all those acts which stand unrepealed than to violate any of them, trusting to find impunity in having them held to be unconstitutional.

It is seventy two years since the first inauguration of a President under our National Constitution. During that period fifteen different and greatly distinguished citizens have in succession administered the executive branch of the government. They have conducted it through many perils, and generally with great success.

Yet with all other scope for precedent I now enter upon the same task for the brief constitutional term of four years, under great and peculiar difficulty. A disruption of the federal union, heretofore only menaced, is now formidably attempted. I hold that in the contemplation of universal law and of the constitution, the Union, of these states is perpetual.

Perpetuity is implied, if not expressed, in the fundamental law of all national governments. It is safe to assert that no government ever prospered which had a provision in its organic law for its own termination. Continue to execute all the express provisions of our national Constitution, and the Union will endure forever, it being impossible to destroy it, except by some action not provided for in the instrument itself. Again, if the United States be not a government proper, but an association of States, in the nature of a contract merely, can it, as a contract, be peaceably unmade by less than all the parties who made it. One party to a contract may violate it, break it, so to speak, but does it not require all to lawfully rescind it?

Descending from these general principles, we find the proposition that in legal contemplation the Union is perpetual, confirmed by the history of the Union itself.

The Union is much older than the Constitution. It was formed in fact by the articles of association in 1774. It was matured and continued in the Declaration of Independence in 1776. It was further matured, and the faith of all the then thirteen States expressly pledged and engaged that it should be perpetuated by the articles of confederation in 1778, and finally in 1789 one of the declared objects for ordaining and establishing the Constitution was, "to form a more perfect Union;" but, if the destruction of the Union by one or by a part only of the States be lawfully possible, the Union is less than before the Constitution, having lost the vital element of perpetuity.

It follows from these views that no state, upon its own mere motion, can lawfully get out of the Union: that resolves and ordinances to that effect are legally void, and that acts of violence within any state or states against the authority of the United States, are insurrectionary or revolutionary according to circumstances.

I therefore consider that in view of the Constitution and the laws, the Union is not broken, and to the extent of my ability I shall take care, as the Constitution itself expressly enjoins upon me, that the laws of the Union be faithfully executed in all the States.

Doing this I deem to be only a simple duty on my part, and I shall faithfully perform it so far as it is possible, unless my rightful masters, the American people, shall withhold the requisite means, or in some authoritative manner direct the contrary. I trust this will not be regarded as a menace, but only as the declared purpose of the Union that it will constitutionally defend and maintain itself.

In doing this, there need be no bloodshed or violence, and there shall be none, unless it is forced upon the national authority. The power confided to me will be used to hold, occupy, and possess the property and places belonging to the government, and collect the duties and imposts, but beyond what may be necessary for these objects there will be no invasion, no using of force against or among the people anywhere.

Where hostility to the United States shall be so great, and so universal as to prevent competent citizens from holding the federal offices, there will be no attempt to force obnoxious strangers among the people that object. While a strict legal right may exist for the government to enforce the occupency of these offices, the attempt to do so would be so irritating and so nearly impracticable withal, that I deem it better to forego for the time the uses of such offices.

The mails, unless repelled, will continue to be furnished in all parts of the Union. So far as possible the people everywhere shall have that sense of perfect security which is most favorable to calm, thought and reflection: the course here indicated will be followed unless current events and experience shall show a modification or change to be proper, and in every case and exigency my best discretion will be execised accordingly to the circumstances actually existing, and with a view and a hope of a peaceful solution of the national troubles, and the restoring of fraternal sympathies and affections.

That there are persons in one section or another who seek to destroy the Union at all events, and are glad of any pretext to do it, I will neither affirm nor deny. But if there be such, I need address no word to them. To those, however, who really love the Union may I not speak, before entering upon so grave a matter as the destruction of our national fabric, with all its benefits, its memories and its hopes? Would it not be well to ascertain why we do it?

Will you hazard so desperate a step while there is any portion of the ills you fly from which have no real existence? Will you, while the certain ills you flp to are greater than all the real ones you fly from? Will you risk the commission of so fearful a mistake,

All profess to be content in the Union, if all constitutional rights can be maintained. Is it true, then, that any right plainly written in the Constitution has been denied? I think not. Happily, the human mind is so constituted that no party can reach to the audacity of doing this, Think, if you can, of a single instance in which a plainly written provision of the Coustitution has ever been denied.

If by the mere force of numbers a majority should deprive a minority of any clearly written constitutional right, it might in a moral point of view, justify revolution. Certainly it would, if such right were a vital one, but such is not our case. All the vital rights of communities and of individuals are so plainly assured to them by affirmations and negations, guarantees and prohibitions in the Constitution, that controversies never arise concerning them. But no organic law can ever be framed with a provision sfiecifically applicable to every question which may occur in practical administration. No foresight can anticipate, nor any document of reasonable length contain express provisions for all possible questions. Shall fugitives from labor be surrendered by national or by State authority? The Constitution dors not expressly say. Must Congress protect slavery in the territory? The Constitution does not expressly say.

From questions of this class spring all our constitutional controversies, and we divide upon them into majorities and minorities. If the minority will not acquiesce, the majority must, or the government must cease. There is no other alternative for continuing the government but acquiescence on one side or the other. If a minority in such case will secede rather than acquiesce, they make a precedent which in turn will divide and ruin them; for a minority of their own will secede from them whenever a majority refuses to be controlled by such minority. For instance, why may not any portion of a new confederacy a year or two hence arbitrarily secede again, precisely as portions of the present Union now claim to secede from it? All who cherish disunion sentiments are now being educated to the exact temper of doing this. Is there such perfect identity of interests among the States which compose a new Union as to produce harmony only and prevent renewed secession?

Plainly, the central idea of secession is the essence of anarchy. A majority held in restraint by constitutional checks and limitations, and always changing easily with the deliberate changes of popular opinions and sentiments, is the only true sovereign of a free people. Whoever rejects it, does of necessity flag to anarchy or to despotism. Unanimity is impossible. The rule of a minority, as a permanent arrangement, is wholly impracticable, so that rejecting the majority principle, anarchy or despotism, in some form, is all that is left.

I do not forget the position assumed by some, that constitutional questions are to be decided by the Supreme Court, nor do I deny that such decisions must be binding in any case upon the parties to a suit, as to the object of that suit.—While they are also entitled to every high respect and consideration in all parallel cases by the other departments of the government, and while it is obviously possible that such decisions may be erroneous in any given case till the evil of following it being limited to that particular case, with the chance that it may be over ruled and never become a precedent for other cases, can better be borne than could the evils of a different practice At the same time the candid citizen must confess that if the policy of the govern ment upon the vital questions affecting the whole people is to be irrevocably fixed by the decisions of the Supreme Court, than the instant they are made an ordinary litigation between parties in personal actions, the people will have ceased to be their own, unless having to that extent practically resigned there government into the hands of that eminent tribunal.

Nor is there in this any new assault upon the court or the judges. It is a duty from which they may not shrink to decide cases of property brought before them, and it is no fault of their's if others seek to turn their decisions to political purposes. One section of our country believes that slavery is right and ought to be extended, while the other believes it is wrong and ought not to be extended. This is the only substantial dispute.

The fugitive slave clauses of the Constitution, and the law for the suppression of the foreign slave trade are each as well enforced, perhaps, as any law can ever be enforced where the moral sense of the people imperfectly supports the law itself. The great body of the people abide by their dry legal obligations in both cases, and a few break over in each. This, I think, can not be perfectly cured, and it would be worse in both cases after the separation of the sections than before. The foreign slave trade, now imperfectly suppressed, would be ultimately revived without restriction in one section, while fugitive slaves, now only partially surrendered, would not be surrendered at all by the other.

Physically speaking, we cannot separate. We cannot remove the respective sections from each other, nor build an impassable wall between them. A husband and wife may be divorced and go out of the presence and beyond the reach of each other, but the different parts of our country cannot do this. They cannot but remain face to face, and intercourse, either amicable or hostile, must continue between them. Is it possible, then, to make that intercourse more advantageous or more satisfactory after separation than before? Can aliens make better treaties than friends? Can they make laws? Can treaties be more faithfully enforced between aliens than laws can among friends? Suppose you go to war; you cannot fight always; and when, after much loss on both sides, and no gain on either, you cease fighting, the identical questions as to terms of interconrse are again upon you.

This country, with its institutions, belongs to the people who inhabit it. Whenever they shall grow weary of the existing government they can exercise their constitutional right of amending, or their revolutionary right to dismember or overthrow it; and I cannot be ignorant of the fact that many worthy and patriotic citizens are desirous of having the national Constitution amended.

While I make no recognition of any amendment, I fully recognize the full authority of the people over the whole subject, to be exercised in either of the modes prescribed in the instrument itself, and I should under existing circumstances favor rather than oppose a fair opportunity being afforded the people to act upon it. I will venture to add that to me the Convention mode seems preferable, in that it allows amendments to originate with the people themselves, instead of only permitting them to take or reject propositions originated by others not especially chosen for the purpose, and which might not be such as they would wish to accept or refuse.

I understand that a proposed amendment to the Constitution, which amendment, however, I have not seen, has passed Congress—to the effect that the federal government shall never interfere with the domestic institutions of States, including that of persons held to service. To avoid misconstruction of what I have said I depart from my purpose not to speak of particular amendments, so far as to say that holding such a provision to be already implied in constitutional law, I have no objection to its being made an express and irrevocable.

The Chief Magistrate derives all his authority from the people, and they have conferred none upon him to fix the terms for the separation of the States. The people themselves, also, can do this if they chose, but the Executive, as such, has nothing to do with it. His duty is to administer the present government as it came to his hands, and to transmit it unimpaired by him to his successor. Why should there not be a patient confidence in the ultimate justice of the people? Is there any better, or an equal, hope in the world? In our present differences, is either party without faith of being in the right?

If the Almighty ruler of nations with his eternal truth and justice be on your side of the Noath or on your's of the South, that truth and that justice will surely prevail by the judgment of this great tribunal. The American people, by the frame of the government under which we live, have wisely given their public servants but little power for mischief, and have with equal wisdom provided foa the return of that little to their own hands at very short intervals. While the people retain their virtue and vigilance, no administration, by any extreme wickedness or folly, can very seriously injure the government in the short space of four years.

My countrymen, one and all, think calmly and well upon this whole subjecteb. Nothing valuable can be lost by taking time. If there be an object to hurry any of you in hot haste to a step which you would never take deliberately, that object will be frustrated by taking time; but no good object can be frustrated by it, such of you as are now dissatisfied still have the old Canstitution unimpaired.

The laws are of your own framing under it, while the new administration will have no immediate power, if it would, to change either. If it were admitted that you who are dissatisfied hold the right side in the dispute, there still is no single good reason for precipitate action. Intelligence, patriotism, christianity, and a firm reliance on them who has never yet forsaken this favored land, are still competent to adjust in the best way all our present difficulty. In your hands, my dissatisfied fellow-countrymen, and not in mine, is the momentous issue of civil war. The government will not assail you. You can have no conflict without being yourselves the aggressors. You have no oath registered in heaven to destroy the government, while I shall have the most solemn one to preserve, protect and defend it. I am loth to close. We are not enemies but friends. We must not be enemies. Though passion may have strained, it must not break our bonds of affection. The mystic chords of memory sound from every battle field and patriot's grave to every living heart and hearthstone. All over this broad land will yet swell the chorus of the Union, when again touched as surely they will be by the better angels of our nature.

THE ALLYN HOUSE FIRE.—The losses by yesterday morning's fire are in some in stances not quite not quite as heavy as was at first supposed. The damage to the building will not exceed $1,000, fully insured; Abraham Rose, news office and tea store, loss about $3,000—insured for $1,900 in the New England; J. D. Bullard & Co., harness and trunks, loss about $250—their loss on the stock, aside from fixtures, is $183 25, which has been settled by the Phœnix office, who held a policy for $1,000 on the stock; Miller & Sedgwick, tailors, loss $1,000—insured in the Charter Oak office; Talcott & Goodman, the lesses of the hotel, are damaged a small amount by smoke and water. The whole loss will be about $6,000.—*Hartford Courant, 27th.*

REJOICINGS.—A salute of thirty-four guns was fired this noon, in honor of the incoming administration. The large Lincoln and Hamlin flag belonging to the Wide Awakes was suspended across Main street, and the vessels in port displayed their bunting. The church bells rang out a joyful peal, and knots of excited people gathered at every corner. Everybody breathed more freely at the thought that the term of James Buchanan and his corrupt officials had closed. May we never see such another.

Gazette & Sentinel.

PUBLISHED EVERY SATURDAY BY
W. P. BRADBURN,
EDITOR AND PROPRIETOR.

TERMS OF SUBSCRIPTION.

THREE DOLLARS AND FIFTY CENTS ($3 50) for one year, in advance. FIVE DOLLARS ($5 00) if not paid in advance.

SINGLE COPIES—Ten Cents.

No subscription will be discontinued unless a writte n notice to that effect is received from the subscriber himself, and all arrearges paid.

TERMS OF ADVERTISING.

ONE DOLLAR ($1 00) per square of ten lines, or less, of this space, ——————————, for the first insertion, and Fifty Cents for each subsequent insertion. A liberal discount, however, on these rates will be made on advertisements inserted for a longer time than two months, as follows:

	3 months.	6 months.	12 months.
1 square	$ 5 00	$ 8 00	$ 12 00
2 squares	8 00	12 00	20 00
3 squares	15 00	15 00	25 00
4 squares	12 00	20 00	30 00
5 squares	18 00	25 00	37 00
6 squares	20 00	30 00	45 00

For Professional or Business Cards, not exceeding one square, with paper, one year, $15.

Announcements of Candidates for office, $10. Cash in all cases, must accompany the announcement, whether handed in by a friend or the person announced.

The privilege of yearly advertisers is strictly limited to their own immediate and regular business.

Communications intended to promote the private ends or interests of individuals, corporations or societies, will be charged as advertisements.

All persons ordering Jobs or handing in advertisements on account of any local or political organization, will be held responsible for the payment of the same.

Marriages and Deaths published without charge. Obituaries inserted as other advertisements.

Advertisements not marked the length of time they are to be inserted, will be kept in the paper till forbid, and charged accordingly.

All advertisements by strangers or transient persons must be paid in advance.

Personal Cards, if inserted at all, will be charged two dollars per square.

☞Job Work always cash, and advertisementr are due when first inserted.

PLAQUEMINE:

Saturday, March 9, 1861.

FOR MAYOR.

MR. EDITOR—Please announce F. GALLAGHER, Esq., as the Democratic candidate for Mayor, to fill the unexpired term of P. E. Jennings. Election next Tuesday.

HIS PERSONAL AND POLITICAL FRIENDS.

☞We have placed all of our bills, without discrimination, in the hands of a collector, and as they are all small, the settling of which affecting so slightly one's finances, we trust that those indebted will make an effort to liquidate them, otherwise it will be impossible for us to meet our own bills. If we are forced we shall have to force others.

☞We trust that our subscribers will preserve their receipts for the payment of subscriptions, as we are liable to make mistakes, and should regret to ask payment wrongfully.

ELECTION FOR MAYOR.—It will be seen by advertisement that the election for Mayor, to fill the unexpired term of P. E. JENNINGS, will take place next Tuesday. The personal and political friends of Mr. F. GALLAGHER, it will be noticed above, have brought him out as a candidate for that office.

☞"The Travels of a Sugar Planter, or Six Months in Europe," is the title of a very interesting volume, which can be had in New Orleans or Baton Rouge. The author is an esteemed citizen of West Baton Rouge.—Those who have not read the letters of which this book is composed, (which originally appeared in the Baton Rouge *Advocate*,) have a rich treat before them if they will order it.

☞ Messrs. BEIHLER BROS. have left their old stand on Main street which they have occupied so long, and took that on Bank st. lately occupied by Mr. McWilliams as a grocery store, where they invite their old friends and the public to give them a call.

☞On the eve of his departure for Baton Rouge, Mr. B. GLAZER presents to his old friends his thanks for the patronage they have extended him. His brother continues the business here. See their cards.

☞It will be seen by advertisements in today's paper that, in consequence of the tariff of the Southern Confederacy, the prices of articles of medicine will be raised.

BAYOU PLAQUEMINE.—A resolution in the Legislature to drive piles across the mouth to prevent drift from entering, was lost. An attempt to close the Bayou will be made.

THE CONVENTION.—This body re-convened in New Orleans on the 5th. It attention so far has been mainly devoted to the public lands of the State. A Commissioner of Public Lands has been created.

☞See notice of a lost bundle.

Election of Judges.

The Governor of Louisiana has issued his proclamation for the election, on Monday the 1st of April next, of Judges for the District Courts of the State. It appears that Iberville, with East and West Baton Rouge, now compose the Fifth, instead of the Sixth District as formerly. As yet we have heard of no opponent to Judge AVERY, whose courtesy and strict attention to his official duties, having determined the people, apparently by acclamation, to retain him in the office he has conducted so well and filled so ably. The Baton Rouge *Advocate* says the friends of "the present able, popular and courteous Judge" will present his name to the voters of the District "for the position he now fills with so much impartiality and satisfaction to the public." The *Sugar Planter* has already announced him as the choice of West Baton Rouge; and we have no doubt that the other two papers of the District, will also endorse the eminent fitness of Judge AVERY for the position he fills, and the propriety of retaining him in it.

THE INAUGURAL.

The inauguration, of Abraham Lincoln as President of the United States of the North, took place at the city of Washington, on Monday last, with the usual ceremonies. Notwithstanding the pretended fears of his cowardly adherents that he would be assassinated either at Washington, or on his way thither, the "second Washington," by means of his "Scotch plaid and long military cloak," artfully escaped the snares laid for him by the Baltimore Plug Uglies, and arrived safely at his destination, where, surrounded by his armed cohorts, Black Republican Wide Awakes and hungry office seekers, he was, without the occurrence of anything extraordinary, duly inducted into the office to which he had been elected. It is the first time in the history ef the country that a President elect has been compelled to disguise himself on his way to assume the reins of government; the first time that a President of the United States has been inaugurated by the aid of a military escort.

The anxiety on the part of the whole country, to know the policy of the incoming Administration, in reference to the present state of affairs, has been fully satisfied by the inaugural address of Mr. Lincoln. The document is not amenable to the charge of that vagueness which characterized the silly, disgusting and disgraceful speeches he delivered at the different stopping places between Springfield and Washington. There is now no necessity for the credulous and the hopeful to speculate as to whether Mr. Seward, or Mr. Chase, Mr. Weed, or Mr. Greely, is to be the leading spirit of the Administration—whether Mr. Lincoln is for war or peace. Our hopes and our predictions are nullified—the future is WAR not PEACE. He has spoken plainly and unequivocally, and no man, with his eyes open, can fail to comprehend what he means. He is unquestionably for WAR. Although seven States have seceded from the Union, and have formed a government of their own, Mr. Lincoln holds that the Union is not dissolved, but that he is as much the President of these seven States, as he is of the six New England states, or the four middle States. Considering that the Constitution expressly enjoins upon him the duty of faithfully executing the laws, he will take care to execute them in South Carolina and Georgia, as well as in Maine and New Hampshire. And among other exercises of his Constitutional duty, he will "use the power confided to him to *hold and to occupy and possess the property and places belonging to the government, and to collect duties on imports.*" Yet Mr. Lincoln's friends tell us that he is not in favor of *coercion*, and he himself says there need not be any effusion of blood. Of course there need be no bloodshed if a brave and free people will consent to the quiet occupation of their own territory by the armed hirelings of a Black Republican government, and will submit to the levying of foreign tribute upon the commerce within their own ports. If we are a nation of cowards, if our spirits have been broken and subdued by Black Republican threats, we shall, most assuredly, no: lift our hands in defense of our rights, our homes, and our firesides, or spill the blood of those who invade our territory. But we mistake the temper of the Southern people, if they would quietly permit Mr. Lincoln to carry into execution the programme he has deliberately laid down in his inaugural address. The government of the Confederate States has sent Commissioners to Washington to negotiate the peaceful surrender of the forts within the limits of our territory. If their request be not complied with, nothing remains but the capture of those forts by force. And if any attempt be made to collect revenue in the Southern ports, it will undoubtedly be met by force on the part of this government. The Southern States have, all along, endeavoured to secede from the Union peaceably, and to avoid a collision with the North. For this reason they have acted with the utmost forbearance towards the North, whose armed soldiers occupy portions of our own territory. We still desire peace, but if Mr. Lincoln has determined to have war, then let there be war.

We shall look with considerable anxiety for the news of the effect produced by the inaugural address on the minds of our representatives at Montgomery. They can look upon it in no other light than a plain and direct declaration of war, and they will doubtless act upon it accordingly. They will see to it that we be prepared to meet our enemies when the conflict shall come. If some immediate change of Mr. Lincoln's policy be not announced, we do not see how hostilities can be avoided much longer, and if Maryland and Virginia go with the South—which they will certainly do—Mr. Lincoln might as well be preparing his "Scotch plaid and long military cloak," in order to conceal his precipitate flight from the capital in which he was so pompously inaugarated on Monday.

THE SKELETON OF LINCOLN'S SPEECHES—Reduced to their substance, says the Philadelphia Inquirer, all of Lincoln's speeches are this, and nothing more:

The proudest day of my life—[applause]—Feel it here—[vociferous cheering]—Can't express—[great excitement]—We are all brethren—[that's so]—Fatigued with travel and hoarse with speaking—['Go on.']—A great country, you are the people—[deafening applause]—Permit me to retire—[immense excitement.]

TEXAS.—The Secession act of Texas has been ratified by the people by a majority of forty or fifty thousand votes.

By Yesterday's Mail.

It is authoritatively stated that Mr. Lincoln will carry out anything the Cabinet decides upon. It is believed that he will refuse to hold any communication with the Commissioners of the Confederate States.

It is doubtfully asserted that John Bell considers the Inaugural a declaration of war, and that he will urge Tennessee to prepare for the conflict.

Thousands in Virginia, hitherto for Union, have come out warmly for Secession since the Inaugural was delivered. The papers of that State with scarcely an exception, say that it is now time for Virginia to declare her independence. In fact, the Inaugural, every where, is generally considered a declaration of war. In many places in North Carolina, it is turning the people in favor of secession. Arkansas will now secede. At Charleston, they are contented to await the action of President Davis and the government at Montgomery.

It is reported that President Davis has ordered Brigadier General Beauregard to proceed forthwith to Charleston, to take charge of the forces now raised for the investment of Fort Sumter.

The Steamship Empire City, chartered by the Government, was coaling with dispatch at New York, on the 6th, to proceed to the South.

Mr. Clingman, in consenting to the printing of the Inaugural, said he did not indorse the sentiments, which, if carried out, would lead to war.

Nooman B. Judd, of Illinois, has been appointed Minister to Berlin.

It is generally believed that Mr. Crittenden will fill the vacancy in the Supreme Court.

The Black Republican authority states that reinforcements will immediately be sent to Forts Pickens and Sumter.

On the 6th, a bill was introduced into the Southern Congress to prohibit the introduction of slaves from the United States into the Confederate States.

Later Still.

The opinion at Montgomery continues to prevail that war is inevitable.

Mr. Cobb has introduced a resolution into the Southern Congress, prohibiting the Federal Courts from taking cognizance of suits instituted by parties in the United States, unless the Government at Montgomery recognizes our independence.

Gen. Braxton Bragg, of the army of this State, has been appointed Brigadier General of the army of the Confederacy, and ordered to Pensacola, to take command of the troops there, and conduct the operations against Fort Pickens.

The flag of the Confederacy of the South, was hoisted for the first time at Montgomery, on the 4th, amidst the booming of cannou, the cheers of the people, the waving of handkerchiefs and every demonstration of enthusiasm.

Mr. Lincoln's Inaugural.

The Inaugural of Mr. Lincoln was received on Wednesday, and the choice, by the circumstances presented, was given us to publish it in full and leave out other and probably more interesting matter, or to publish the latter, and give of the first all that our readers, or Southern readers, are interested in, or what relates to our present position as a separate Confederacy. We choose the last. The extract below, from the *Picayune*, gives in a nut shell Mr. Lincoln's views and intentions with reference to all that relates to the seceded States. Of the Inaugural, the above journal says, "it may be separated into two marked portions—one, by far the larger, contains what is immaterial to the issues before us in the States. The other (which we give below) may be compressed into a few weighty sentences." He says we can have no conflict unless we are the aggressors. We have no oath, he says, to destroy the Government, while he has taken one to preserve it:

And this brings us to those portions of the inaugural which are material to us. We, of the seceded States, have nothing to care for Mr. Lincoln's personal opinions on the rights of States to secede from, or citizens to resist, the Union. That which concerns us is, what does he mean to do towards us, who are, in our own fixed estimate of our position, out of the Union; to the States which claim to be members of another distinct Confederacy? Here Mr. Lincoln is emphatic and intelligible, beyond mistake or peradventure.

Believing that no State is lawfully out of the Union, that all ordinances and decrees to that effect are null, and that all acts within a State against the authority of the United States are "insurrectionary or revolutionary, according to circumstances," he promises to take care to the extent of his ability, "that the laws of the Union be faithfully executed in all the States."

For the present he will not use force within a State for the purpose of supporting federal officers there, although the right to do so is advanced; nor will he oppose the transmission of mails when uninterrupted; but he will use all the power confided in him, "to hold, occupy and possess the property and places belonging to the Government, and to collect duties on imports."

This he will continue to do, "unless the American people shall withhold the requisite means, or in some anthoritative manner direct the contrary."

The President begs to have it understood that this is not a menance. He does not threaten to coerce; he is only protecting the rights and existence of the Federal Government, and will spill no blood but in self-defence.

But this is dealing with a grave public controversy by a juggle upon words. The qnestion which the Confederate States make is, that the Federal Government has no rightful authority within their limits, that the presence of its soldiers is military occupation by a foreign power, and that the collection of revenue on their commerce is the levying of foreign tribute. They say that the forcible intrusion of the Federal Government for these purposes is actual invasion and partakes of the character of war Mr. Lincoln says in reply that it will not be war if we submit unconditionally. It is not coercion to place a soldier with a loaded gun at your door with orders to shoot you if you attempt to go out. You may save bloodshed by staying within, locking your door and giving the soldier the key.

This determination of Lincoln to hold the forts and thus practically refuse to assent to the independence of the south and practically to hold the States in subordination by force after Congress has refused to do anything to conciliiate or to give any faith in future conciliation, is ominous of a speedy crisis in the only issue which is left to be contested, the right of peaceful separation. The government at Montgomery has already a mission at Washington with instructions to require the evacuation of the territory and the settlement of peaceful terms of separation.

Mr. Lincoln will probably refuse to receive and will certainly refuse to comply.

The question recurs to all thoughts—what then? Events may hurry faster than speculation, and the die cast before we could utter a prophecy.

Poisons.

Man is the most wonderful of all animals. Among other strange things which he can do, he can eat poisons with a certain degree of impunity. It is only necessary to be prudent, regular, and careful about the doses to survive for a considerable period.

A certain quantity of opium kills. Four or five grains is almost certain death to a person not in the habit of using it; but any one can learn to eat twenty and thirty grains at a dose. It becomes the necessity of a second nature, and though it shortens life, it does it so slowly that its operation in this respect is not alarming.

So coffee, tea, and tobacco are poisons. It requires some hardihood to get accustomed to the latter. A drop or two of the essential oil of either of these narcotics, or a very concentrated decoction, will kill; yet how many millions of men use all three every day of their lives. There is some derangement of the nervous system—some diminution of the strength—probably some shortening of life; yet how few hesitate to use these fascinating luxuries.

And arsenic is very decidedly a poison, yet there is at least one country in the world where it is habitually eaten. A young man of seventeen, say, begins by taking three grains at a dose, which is gradually increased until he gets up to twenty-three grains. It does not do to exceed this quantity, nor is it safe to leave off suddenly. When the arsenic-eater arrives at the age of fifty, he gradually diminishes the does. The immense quantity of poison constantly passing through his system does not prevent his reaching the age of seventy or eighty.

For all this, it is our opinion that the more simple our food, and the less poison we take of any kind or in any form, the better. Probably no man, at the end of his life, was ever sorry he had taken little opium, or brandy, or tobacco, though some may have been sorry for taking too much.

☞ An item of plunder carried away by an English officer, from the Emperor of China's palace, was a magnificent gold claret jug, valued at £128 sterling. A letter from Hong Kong says an artilleryman entered the summer palace, after the French had pillaged it, and finding a brassy-looking joss, which had been rejected for its appearance and weight, he shouldered it himself. On arriving at Hong Kong, he sold it for $33,000 for a very pure kind of gold, as it was; and the day after the purchaser again disposed of it for $9000 advance on his bargain.

NORTHERN AND SOUTHERN JOURNALS UPON THE QUESTIONS OF THE DAY.—The journals of the South, and those of Louisiana in particular, show themselves much superior to the press of the North in the manner in which they perceive the economical consequences of disunion. They bring to the discussion of this question, as delicate as it is essential, a spirit of moderation, a certainty of calculation, a knowledge of facts much superior to the disdainfully absolute conclusions which we see every day promulgated around us.—*N. Y. Courrier des Etats Unis.*

☞ By a transposition of letters, Punch make the United States, the *Untied* States.

Latest from Washington.

Lincoln's Cabinet in full Confirmed.

WASHINGTON, March 5th.—Mr. Lincoln sent into the Senate, to-day, the following Cabinet appointments:

Secretary of State—Hon. Wm. H. Seward, of New York.

Secretary of the Treasury—Hon. Salmon P. Chase, of Ohio.

Secretary of War—Hon. Simon Cameron, of Pennsylvania.

Secretary of the Navy—Hon. Gideon J. Welles, of Connecticnt.

Secretary of the Interior—Hen. Caleb B. Smith, of Indiana.

Attorney General–Hon. Edward Bates of Missouri.

Postmaster General—Hon. Montgomery Blair, of the District of Columbia.

The Senate immediately took up the appointments *seriatim*, and all of them were confirmed.

Opinions of the Inaugural.

It is Considered a Declaration of War.

Advice of Southern Men to Governor Pickens.

[From the Delta.]

WASHINGTON, March 5, 1861.—Southern men in this city, without distinction of party, regard Mr. Lincoln's inaugural as a declaration of war.

Hon. John Bell says he advises Tennessee to prepare for war as the only means of preventing it.

Hon. John Cochrane and many Northern Democrats, with some Republicans, say the same.

As soon as the coercion portion of the inaugural was read yesterday, dispatches were sent to Gov. Pickens advising him against attaking Fort Sumter, and to await the action of the Confederate States.

The Intelligencer this morning contains the reply of Mr. Holt to Mr. Thompson, denouncing the latter as a falsifier and infamous traitor, and eulogizing Gen. Scott.

The Intelligencer declines an opinion on the Inaugural, until it has an opportunity more deliberately to examine it.

Latest from Montgomery.

War considered Inevitable—The Standing Army—The War Strength.

MONTGOMERY, March 5th—Since the receipt of the Inagural address of Mr. Lincoln, it is universally conceded here that war between the Confederate States and the United States is inevitable. Mr. Benjamin said last night, that in his opinion, there would be a clash of arms within thirty days.

Mr. Conrad concurred in this view of the aspect of affairs. The standing army of the Confederate States will be fixed at ten thousand men. Congress is now engaged in organizing the army. Of course, in case of hostilities, the number of men put in the field will be greater. It is calculated that the States now composing the Confederacy can place 80,000 on a movable war-footing.

EPES SARGENT'S famous song—"A Life on the Ocean Wave"—has the romance taken out of it occasionally, as it seems by the following story in the Boston *Courier*:

A real jolly good old fellow was Dr. S. I was introduced to him just as the steamer Star was leaving her dock at New York for Europe. For the first twenty-four hours, "Richard was himself again;" but that fell destroyer, which neither spares age, sex, nor condition—sea-sickness—seized him, and nothing more was seen of the jolly old Doctor for several days. We had left the banks, and were steaming along beautifully, when one morning I saw the Doctor's head emerging from the lower regions. But what a face! long, lugubrious, distressed—his hair uncared for, dress untidy, eyes blood-shot. I could scarcely believe this apparition was the jolly old Doctor who had kept us all in a roar the first day out. "Well, my dear Dootor, how do you feel by this time!" "Feel!" said he, and there was an unmistakable earnestness in his eye; "feel! why I feel as though I had but two objects in life now. One is to put my foot once more on *terra firma*, and the other, to find out and whip the fellow who wrote "Life on the Ocean Wave!"

TIME AND PHOTOGRAPHY.—Sun pictures may be taken in various modes, some requiring several minutes, and others only an instant. Photographs of rapidly moving objects, as race horses, the waves of the sea, etc., are taken in the hundredth part of a second. In English experiments, an image was taken in the ten-thousandth part of a second; and a rapidly revolving wheel was taken in so brief a space, that it seemed perfectly well defined and stationary, being illuminated by a single discharge of an electric battery, occupying, according to Wheatstone, only the millionth part of a second.

☞ Mr. Rarey publishes a card relative to the claim of $100,000 damages by a person from the South, for an alleged breach of contract in exposing the system. He thinks that the first man who ever bridled a horse might as reasonably claim damages for an infringement of his system of horse-taming, and claims that he has attained his system only by a life-time of assiduous labor and study; and at the expense of sundry broken limbs. He considers the claim as an attempt to levy black-mail, an operation which has been repeatedly tried upon him in Europe.

COUNCIL PROCEEDINGS.

The Mayor and Board of Selectmen of the town of Plaquemine met at the Mayor's office this 5th day of March, 1861.

Present—P. E. Jennings, Mayor; J. L. Petit, N. Valega, J. E. Degelos, L. Charre.

A motion being offered that a committee be appointed to wait on Messrs. Desobry & Co. and Mrs. Edwards, and request them to clear the continuation ditch of the Corporation Canal, was adopted, and Messrs. J. L. Petit and J. E. Degelos were appointed on said committee.

A motion that a committee be appointed to examine the accounts of the Treasurer and Constable was adopted, and Messrs. Charre, Valega, Petit and Degelos appointed on said committee.

Mr. Degelos offered a resolution that the yearly salary of the Mayor be raised to the sum of four hundaed dollars, the same to take effect from and after the 1st Monday in May next, 1861, and the same having been put to vote was rejected.

P. E. Jennings, Mayor, tendered his resignation of office, to take effect as soon as his successor is elected and qualified, which on motion was accepted, and the Mayor ordered to hold an election to fill the unexpired term.

The following accounts were presented and allowed.

Sam'l. Warden, laborers on levee,	$27 00
Turin & Seiple, for lumber,	24 00
N. Valega, labor on levee,	12 00
R. A. Kearny, medicines for indig'ts.,	12 50
Jerome Blanchard, jailor's fees up to Jan. 15th, 1861,	20 25
Mme. Scott, [illegible] of hall up to 23d of February [illegible],	42 08
Total,	$137 75

There being no further business the Board adjourned till Saturday, 9th of March inst., at 9 o'clock A. M.

P. E. JENNINGS, Mayor.

JOHN MARCOT, Clerk.

GENERAL WINFIELD SCOTT, COMMANDER-IN-CHIEF OF THE AMERICAN FORCES.—See next page.

FRANK LESLIE'S ILLUSTRATED NEWSPAPER

No. 277.—VOL. XI.] NEW YORK, MARCH 16, 1861. [PRICE 6 CENTS.

THE HON. JEFFERSON DAVIS, PRESIDENT-ELECT OF THE NEW SOUTHERN CONFEDERACY, ADDRESSING THE CITIZENS OF MONTGOMERY, ALA., FROM THE BALCONY OF THE EXCHANGE HOTEL, ON THE NIGHT OF FEBRUARY 16TH, 1861, AND PREVIOUS TO HIS INAUGURATION.—FROM A SKETCH BY OUR SPECIAL ARTIST.—SEE PAGE 258.

NEW YORK ILLUSTRATED NEWS

No. 71.—Vol. III. NEW-YORK, SATURDAY, MARCH 16, 1861. Price Six Cents.

OPEN THIS PAPER WITH CARE BEFORE YOU CUT IT.

MR. LINCOLN TAKING THE OATH OF OFFICE IN THE FRONT OF THE CAPITOL. From a Sketch by Thos. Nast. See page 294.

INAUGURATION OF PRESIDENT LINCOLN IN FRONT OF THE CA

T WASHINGTON. FROM A SKETCH BY THOMAS NAST. SEE PAGE 294.

Gazette & Sentinel.

PUBLISHED EVERY SATURDAY BY
W. P. BRADBURN,
EDITOR AND PROPRIETOR.

TERMS OF SUBSCRIPTION.

THREE DOLLARS AND FIFTY CENTS ($3 50) for one year, in advance. FIVE DOLLARS ($5 00) if not paid in advance.

SINGLE COPIES—Ten Cents.

No subscription will be discontinued unless a written notice to that effect is received from the subscriber himself, and all arrearges paid.

TERMS OF ADVERTISING.

ONE DOLLAR ($1 00) per square of ten lines, or less, of this space, ——— ———————, for the first insertion, and Fifty Cents for each subsequent insertion. A liberal discount, however, on these rates will be made on advertisements inserted for a longer time than two months, as follows:

	3 months.	6 months.	12 months.
1 square	$ 5 00	$ 8 00	$ 12 00
2 squares	8 00	12 00	20 00
3 squares	15 00	15 00	25 00
4 squares	12 00	20 00	30 00
5 squares	18 00	25 00	37 00
6 squares	20 00	30 00	45 00

For Professional or Business Cards, not exceeding one square, with paper, one year, $15.

Announcements of Candidates for office, $10. Cash in all cases, must accompany the announcement, whether handed in by a friend or the person announced.

The privilege of yearly advertisers is strictly limited to their own immediate and regular business.

Communications intended to promote the private ends or interests of individuals, corporations or societies, will be charged as advertisements.

All persons ordering Jobs or handing in advertisements on account of any local or political organization, will be held responsible for the payment of the same.

Marriages and Deaths published without charge. Obituaries inserted as other advertisements.

Advertisements not marked the length of time they are to be inserted, will be kept in the paper till forbid, and charged accordingly.

All advertisements by strangers or transient persons must be paid in advance.

Personal Cards, if inserted at all, will be charged two dollars per square.

☞Job Work always cash, and advertisementr are due when first inserted.

New Advertisements.

PLAQUEMINE:

Saturday, March 23, 1861.

☞ Owing to the pressure upon our columns by the large number of advertisements demanding admission, we thought we would as an experiment make use of this small type for our locals. We doubt however if there are many of our readers who will thank us.

☞ We tender our warmest thanks to some unknown friend—for the frank looked as much like Morrison or Harrison as it did like Thompson or Fessenden—for Vol. XII, Part 1, Senate copy, for Surveys and Explorations of a Railroad Route from the Mississippi to the Pacific—a work copiously interspersed with colored quarto plates in the highest degree of art, of all descriptions of wild and romantic scenery between the points mentioned, and evidencing the extraordinary splendor in which such works were got up by authority of Congress. Again we thank the kind friend who sent us this magnificent work, destined some day to grace the Reading Room we now have in progress.

☞Doing as others do, we have taken the liberty to transfer to our columns so much of a letter from a friend, as relates to the proceedings of the Convention. Since the date of his letter, that body has been mainly engaged in debate upon the Banking Ordinance and with reference to the adoption of the Constitution of the Confederate States.

☞It will be seen by advertisement that VESSIER & DUBUCLET's cargo of Ice (and it is really of a very superior quality) has arrived, and that they will sell it to their town and deliver it to their country patrons at their usual rates—that is, as cheap as Ice can be delivered here from New Orleans.

☞ The Ladies will please take notice of the card of Mad'm. LORTIO, under the head of New Advertisements. Her services will doubtless meet with immediate requisition.

☞We present our thanks to Mr. JOSIAH BROWN for a copy of the Report of the Judiciary Committee of the Senate.

☞The Ohio and Mississippi above are falling. Old citizens think there will be no high water in Lower Louisiana this season.

The J. A. Cotton.

This, said to be magnificent, low pressure Mail and Passenger Steamer, intended to run between New Orleans and Bayou Sara, by day, we believe, is reported to have left Louisville for her native element in the lower Mississippi, and we may, therefore, see her at our wharf at any hour; if she does not in fact pass before the distribution of our paper. Capt. BERANCO, we understand, is to command her, while Mr. MUMFORD, his present able and courteous clerk, will take his place at her desk. Two more popular and appropriate officers to introduce the "Cotton" to the public, could not have been selected. Capt. Hooper brings her down. The citizens of Louisville have presented the boat with a fine portrait of this old Steamboatman. May the "Cotton" never "cotton" to anything that carrys wheels.

The Legislature.

The constitutional limitation of the session of the Legislature having expired last Thursday, the Governor, we understand, has porogued it for two weeks longer, that it may get through with the unfinished public business before it. The bill giving the Police Jury of this parish the right to drive piles across or near the mouth of Bayou Plaquemine, to prevent the drift from entering it, was defeated by the casting vote of the Speaker.

Since the above was in type we perceive no mention of the Legislature being prolonged, and conclude that the above information was erroneous. We see nothing of special interest in its concluding labors. We will soon give a list of its acts.

W. I. Hamilton, Esq.

After many years of absence and labor in a distant portion of the State—where he represented his parish in the Legislature with peculiar credit and distinction and was afterwards honored by his election to the office of Superintendent of Public Education—the above gentleman has returned to his native home, and has settled himself definitely among his old friends of Iberville, for the purpose of pursuing diligently the duties of his profession. See his card in another column.

A Natural Curiosity.

We were politely shown yesterday by Mr. T. Rudolph Verbois, a lamb which had to be killed to deliver it from its dam. It was of the full size at birth. It had two heads joined quarteringly, four eyes of the natural size, (the left eye of one head being about an inch from the rtght eye of the other,) and six legs of the same size. Had it not necessarily been killed in effecting its birth, there seemed nothing to prevent its living and growing.

Old Pictures into New.

If any of our friends have old pictures of themselves or family they desire to get renewed, and miniature and faded portraits they would like to have transformed into large and striking likenesses, they have but to step up into Bailey's Daguerrean and Artistic Saloon, and they can have their wishes soon gratified. We saw a miniature the other day on which the lineaments of the "face divine" were scarcely perceptible, so much had it faded, but in a few moments Mr. Bailey drew from it a large, clear and correct representation, which was originally the portrait of a well known gentleman of our town, now deceased.

Little Too Much of a Good Thing.

For some time past—even before the first adjournment of the Convention of this State, now in session in New Orleans—impressions crept into our mind from day to day as we glanced over its proceedings, that this political body was bestowing its attention upon matters of legislation not within its jurisdiction, or within the sphere of those duties for which it was specially convened by the voice of the people. Those impressions became more fixed perhaps, from the fact that the State Legislature was in session at the same time, and had constitutional cognizance of much public business which the Conventiou had assumed to take charge of or to appropriate to itself. When, therefore, a member of the Convention offered sarcastically a resolution to abolish the Legislature, we thought it not a bad idea, unless the Convention preferred to abolish itself by adjourning *sine die.*—The people were, it appeared, paying two bodies for the performance of duties which one could have accomplished, if they did not in fact legitimately belong to the Legislature; and such a state of things does not exactly tally with the economical ideas of a Democratic people. It was certainly extravagant for two political bodies, having similar functions, to be in operation at the same time.

But up to this time, ourself as well as many of our cotemporaries, we are convinced, who were warm advocates for the Convention, felt a delicacy in being the first to censure a body whose convocation they had been instrumental in bringing about, (at least such were our feelings,) trusting from day to day that the Convention would see the propriety of bringing its session to a close, till at length to be longer silent would be criminal, if the press assumes to itself the guardianship of the honor, rights and interests of the people.

We innocently supposed it to be the duty of the Convention to adjourn immediately after it had got through with the main and incidental duties for which it was convoked—to be called together again in any emergency which the Governor thought justified it, and which our Legislative body conld not legally take cognizance of. But we were disappointed. The Convention still pursued its course, legislating upon matters which either properly belonged to the Legislature or to a convention called to *revise the present organic law of the State.* At length there are murmurs arising from a Power before which all others in this Democratic land must bow. As the spokesman of that Power, or an Integral of it, we assume the responsibility of raising our voice in opposition to the course which the Convention is pursuing, but with a full knowledge of the humble and unpretending source from which such remonstrance springs.

The Convention was called together for a special and pressing necessity. It soon, nobly and patriotically, effected the purposes for which it was convoked. Freeing Louisiana from the hateful tyranny of Black Republican rule and persecution, providing for all possible contingencies that could grow out of such an act—taking possession of federal property, authorizing an inventory to be had, organizing an army, *&c.*, for protection—were about all the services required of the Convention. Had it adjourned after effecting these desideratums, it would have saved to the State at least $20,000 per week, and have merited the lasting gratitude of the State. It is to be lamented that it took a contrary course.

The Baton Rouge *Advocate*, in an article upon this subject, says:

Experimenting with our banking institutions, our railroads and the corporate institutions of individuals by a body elected to consider Federal relations *alone*, should and must be discontinued, or those engaged in it will meet a fearful condemnation when they lay aside the robes of power and return to their homes. The General Assembly is the tribunal to which the people look for legislation on matters of a strictly local character. That body is elected for this purpose—the present State Convention was not.

So say we—and we have but little doubt that our delegates from this parish are of the same opinion.

In his remarks upon the Banking Ordinance, on Wednesday, Judge WALKER, a delegate from New Orleans, takes occasion to say:

He had never expressed, either by words or by act, that the Convention possessed powers beyond those for which it was constituted. The Convention was called into existence exclusively for political purposes, arising from the triumphs of a policy fatal to our political existence, and the Convention was framed to meet this emergency.

This is unquestionably the correct understanding of the purposes for which the Convention was called into existence at the command of the masses. Let it do what it was called to do, and leave the rest to God and the People.

The "Home Guards," &c.

This company of volunteer soldiers had a turnout and parade in full uniform for the first time, on Monday last, in the vicinity of St. Gabriel Post-office, and, judging from the character of its rank and file, it was unquestionably a successful beginning. We regret that circumstances prevented us from gratifying our desire to be present. The uniform of this company is grey, jackets and trowsers, with a stripe and a cord of red down the outside seams of the latter.

There are now four volunteer military companies in this parish—the Grosse Tete Rangers, a cavalry company, Capt. C. W. KEEP; the Home Sentinels, of Plaquemine, Captain GERVAIS SCHLATRE; the Home Guards, of St. Gabriel, Capt. CHARLES A. BRUSLE; and the company at Bayou Goula, Capt. GUSTAVE LAUVE, the name of which we are not acquainted with. We should be pleased to be informed of the next parade of these companies of citizen soldiery, that we may from personal observation, speak of the force and appearance of Iberville's volunteer military arm—being already convinced, however, that it will compare favorably with similar military organizations in the State. We would also be pleased to be informed of the names of the officers in full of each company, if the sergeants or secretaries will be kind enough to furnish us with them.—The above companies were organized severally as they are mentioned.

We would respectfully suggest some appropriate day soon for a general parade and ball at some central point, say Plaquemine, by these combined companies of Iberville's gallant defenders. It would be a reunion of congenial spirits, with an admixture present of appreciative friends and fair admirers, and would undoubtedly be an occasion as pleasant as it would be appropriate.

If the precincts of the Island, and Grand River connected with Indian Village, were to act as gallant and patriotic (and we know these precincts have plenty of the right material at hand) as Grosse Tete, Plaquemine, the Oaks and Bayou Goula precincts have done, such force would undoubtedly reach to that of a battalion, and would be entitled to the officers and peculiar privileges pertaining to such military organization. We should be much pleased to see the accomplishment of such a design. It would highly redound to the reputation of our parish, and if the roar of battle should eventually reach the borders of our fair State, the fact that we had a battalion of organized soldiers in Iberville which could be mustered together at a given point at a few hours' notice, would bring a feeling of security and quiet slumbers to those fair but weak ones whom it is ever man's proud and sacred duty to shield from the horrors and sufferings of war, as from the rigors of want and the cruelties and oppressions of the world.

The Constitution.

As the Constitution of the Southern Confederacy is nearly the same as that of the United States, we thought it would be more to the taste and interest of our readers, in the present crowded state of our columns with advertisements, by showing them where or in what particulars the former differs from the latter, which has been read time and again by all who, hitherto, took an interest in the affairs of the old government. We have therefore given, in another column, the *Crescent's* review of the "*permanent* constitution of the *provisional* government," showing where it differs from the United States constitution and the advantages it possesses over the latter. Notwithstanding the somewhat informal manner of its creation, this constitution of our Confederacy cannot fail to meet the approbation of every true State Rights Democrat within its borders.

Casadavant, the Dentist.

This gentleman, of whom report speaks in such fabulous style of his extraordinary success in New Orleans, has removed to the commodious rooms, 107 Royal street, opposite the St. Louis Hotal, which are fitted up in a style to challenge the admiration of a prince, in which to receive his French, English and Spanish patrons. Certainly if one-half is true that is reported of this gifted and enterprising Dentist, his success in New Orleans has been unparalleled—and never have we heard a whisper derogatory to his private character or professional skill. A significant item is the fact (remember it) that he pays more annually for advertising, we know, than many a newspaper in this State realizes.

Chas. Byrne, 46 Tchoupitoulas st.

The Stove, Tin, Copper and Sheet-iron Manufactory of this gentleman, of the above number and street, New Orleans—the advertisement of which has been seen in our paper for nearly a year past—is the favorite establishment of all planters having business in that line, and who know the advantage of dealing with a man of integrity and punctuality, whose word with regard to his work and his wares can be implicitly relied upon. Such is Mr. CHAS. BYRNE, as all new customers will find. It is here where the celebrated "Byrne Stove" is to be found, which is so much prized by planters and steamboat men.

We Deem It Proper

As well as prudent, to say that we disclaim any local application by inserting the poetic lines on our fourth page. We would dislike to believe that Plaquemine was in the category of villages to which the plain-spoken and truthful poet alludes. A village exempt from such a trait *must be* a paradise and a home of love, indeed! Would'nt town lots be high in such a place, if the auctioneer could truly say:—

"In quietness with all around,
Here friendship, joy and peace abound,
And angry feelings perish?"

Would'nt they, now?

Correspondence of the Gazette & Sentinel.

NEW ORLEANS, March 16th, 1861.

Dear Sir:—By referring to the proceedings of the Convention, you will perceive that it has, this day, decided by a vote of 75 to 25, not to submit the Constitution of our Southern Confederacy for ratification by the people—deeming itself the impersonation of the people, and deputed by them not only to take the State out of the Union, but to provide for its welfare and government, in common with its confederate sister States.

The 2nd Section of the ordinance of the 29th of January, 1861, after directing the appointment of Delegates to the Montgomery Convention, ordains as follows—"That said delegates be instructed to aid in forming a Provisional Government, on the basis of the Constitution of the United States, for such States as have seceded, or may secede; to be established and put in operation before the 4th day of March, 1861; and the said Convention of seceding States shall proceed, forthwith, to consider and propose a Constitution and plan for a permanent Government for such States; which proposed plan shall be referred back to the several State Conventions, for their adoption or rejection."

Pursuant to the requirements of the foregoing section, the Congress of the Confederate States has considered and proposed a plan for a permanent Government for such States; the 1st section of the 7th article of the Constitution of which declares—"That the ratification of the Convention of five States, shall be sufficient for the establishment of this Constitution between the States so ratifying the same."

The Constitution will come up for adoption, day after to-morrow, and I am gratified in the conviction that it will be adopted by about the same vote as that upon the question of reference.

We will, probably, close our labors during next week, and I hope soon to see our admirable Confederate Government in full and successful operation.

Respectfully yours.

The Latest News.

The telegraphic despatches of the week relating to the all-absorbing subject of the Southern Confederacy *vs.* the United States Government, are such a mass of jumble and contradiction, that it is wholly unnecessary to give any—or a synopsis of any—except the very latest. We proceed then to give the substance of those depatches received by the morning and evening *Delta*, by the mail of yesterday.

The latest date from Washington, is the 20th, Montgomery the 20th, and Charleston the 21st.

The Southern Commissioners, it appears, expected no communication with Lincoln or Seward for eight or ten days; on the evening of the 20th, they were anxiously awaiting news from Charleston, to see if Lincoln was acting in good faith, in saying that Major Anderson's command had been withdrawn from Sumter.

Mr. Bayard had introduced a resolution into the Senate to recognize the independence of the Confederated States. He said that the Administration must either make war on the South or recognize its independence. It was probable that an extra Session of Congress would be called. In Washington 150 volunteers had offered their services to the Confederate States.

A despatch says that Major Anderson's command was to leave Sumter in the Steamer Columbia to-day.

It is reported that Mr. Crittenden will certainly be tendered the vacant seat on the Supreme Bench.

Despatches from New York, however, of the 21st, say that no order has been sent for the evacuation of Fort Sumter! Despatches from Anderson say that he has erected formidable sand batteries in the rear and weakest point of Sumter. This looks like evacuation!

The Secession ordinance in Arkansas has been voted down, amidst great excitement; the people were to vote on the first Monday in August for delegates to a Border State Convention.

The whole Democratic ticket had been elected in New Jersey!

Lord Lyons, Minister from England, expresses himself favorable to the Southern Confederacy. He has sent a Messenger home, detailing all our difficulties.

News from Mobile, say that a vessel from that city carrying provisions to the vessels off Pensacola harbor, had been seized.

The latest despatch from Washington says that it is supposed the Government will hold all the Southern forts at present occupied by Federal troops, except Fort Sumter. This despatch might be read two ways.

Very Important from Montgomery.

In the meantime, while the above news was flashing through the wires, there come a warlike despatch from Montgomery. Troops, so it reads, have been ordered immediately to Pensacola. This was on the 20th. This movement is supposed to be caused by news from Washington that Fort Pickens was to be reinforced at once.

The President of the Alabama Convention has requested the members to return immediately and prepare for war.

Late from Texas.

GALVESTON, March 19th.—Gen. Houston and the Secretary of State refused to appear on the 16th, before the Convention when summoned, after one notice, to take the oath of allegiance. The other State officers have taken the oath.

Lieut. Gov. Clark was to assume the Governor's powers on the 16th. It was not known what course Gen. Houston would pursue.

The Convention is rapidly maturing a defense for the frontier. The Indians in large numbers are committing depredations on the Western frontier.

Col. Ford is organizing a military force to protect the Rio Grande.

The Convention has passed an ordinance continuing the State Government officers who take the oath.

THE JUDGESHIP.—We are informed that the Hon. W. I. Hamilton, declines as a candidate for Judge in the new Judicial District. His many warm friends and admirers in this Parish regret to hear of his declination.—*Clinton Dem.*

☞ A German, at Frankfort-on-the Rhine, some weeks since, ate twenty-nine bologna sausages on a wager, and strange to say, lived three hours after.

BLUE EYES AND GREAT MEN.—The Court Journal says that all the American Presidents, except Gen. Harrison, had blue eyes. So had Shakespeare, Locke, Bacon, Milton, Goethe, Franklin, Napoleon and Humboldt.

The New Constitution.

From the Crescent.

We do not see what reasonable objection can be made to the Constitution of the Confederate States adopted by the Southern Congress now in Session at Montgomery. In the main it is but a copy of the Constitution of the old Union, with a few additions and changes, every one of which is, we think, an improvement.

The preamble differs from the preamble of the Constitution of the United States, in respect of its assertion of the doctrine of State Sovereignty. "Each State acting in its sovereign and independent character," is the language used, thus giving Constitutional sanction to a doctrine, the denial of which by the North, was the source of much trouble and confusion in the old Union. The preamble also recognizes our dependence upon a Supreme Being, which is something not found in the Constitution of the United States.

The Legislative Department of the Government is organized just as that of the Union was. The right of suffrage, however, is confined to citizens alone. In some of the Northern States they permit men to vote before they acquire citizenship—a most monstrous abuse, and one which our new Constitution wisely forbids. The ratio of representation in the lower House of Congress is fixed at not less than 50,000, and the three-fifths provision in regard to slaves is retained. Until otherwise ordered, Louisiana is to have six Representatives, South Carolina six, Geogia ten, Alabama nine, Florida two, Mississippi seven, and Texas, six.

The powers and duties of Congress are fully defined. In cases where several appropriations are embraced in one bill, the President is to have the right to veto any particular appropriations, and approve the others. This is a good provision. It will break up the logrolling system, whereby appropriations for unworthy objects were smuggled in at the close of Congress, and put into bills that were obliged to be passed. This will prevent anything like the fraud and stealage that prevailed in the old Union.

Congress is forbidden to grant bounties. No special legislation, no favoriteism to classes or any particular interests. This is good. We will have no swindling fishing bounties and navigation monopolies.

Then the post-office is to be self-sustaining. This is good again. it will prevent the squandering of the public money in all sorts of postal contracts, thus making the general treasury pay for the accommodation of mere local and particular interests.

The African slave trade is forbidden, but the importation of slaves from those States not members of the Confederacy is permitted, Congress, however, being granted the power to prohibit it at discretion.

No extra compensation to any contractor shall be granted. This is excellent. The Congress of the Union is bothered and badgered, every winter, with an innumerable caravan of contractors and old office-holders begging for extra pay. The members are button-holed and annoyed by them, past endurance—and many of these claims slip through and are paid, when there is not a shadow of justice in them.

The President is to be elected for six years, and is to be ineligible. Six years is short enough, and his being ineligible will prevent him from disposing of his patronage, or otherwise using his power, to retain himself in the office. No person shall be eligible to the office of President or Vice-President, except a natural born citizen of the Confederate States, or a citizen at the time of the adoption of the Constitution, or a citizen born in the United States prior to 20th December, 1860. A residence of fourteen years in the Confederate States, as they may exist at the time of the election, is also necessary. The duties of the President, and the organization of the Executive Departments, are about the same as in the Government at Washington.

The Judicial power is to be invested in a Supreme Court and such other inferior courts as Congress may establish, just as in the Northern Union.

The right of transit and sojourn with one's slaves, in any State or Territory, is affirmed and secured. Fugitive slaves are to be surrendered, and in all the Territories slavery is to be "recognized and protected." The framers of the present Constitution, are not so mealy-mouthed as our forefathers, and boldly use the words *slaves* and *slavery*, which was carefully excluded, for political reasons, from the Constitution of '87.

Other States may be admitted by a vote of two-thirds of the whole House of Representatives, and two-thirds of the Senate, the latter voting by States. The Constitution provides for its own amendment, and three States having the power to call a Convention for that purpose. The present Coustitution is to be considered in force, and the Government established, when ratified by five States, as to the States so ratifying it. Alabama has led the column, being the first State to ratify

On the whole, everybody—at least every Southern man—must admit that the constitution is essentially a good one, and a vast improvement upon the Constitution of the Northern Union. If there be some objections to it here and there, patriotism requires that they be surrendered rather than obstruct the Government in the beginning of its existence. We trust Louisiana will retain and strengthen the good impression she has already made at Montgomery, by promptly ratifying the Constitution by a unanimous vote of her Convention.

Gazette & Sentinel.

Flag of the Confederate States.

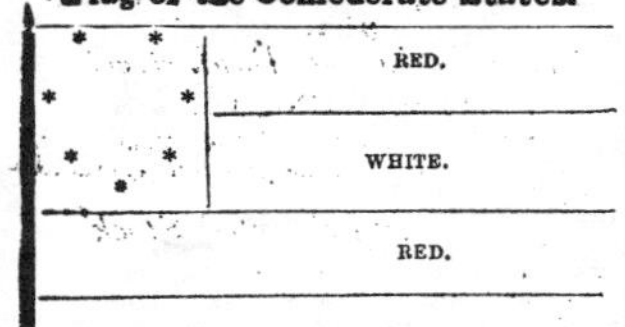

The Stars and Stripes.—The above flag has been unanimously adopted by the Southern Confederacy. It is composed of three stripes, the upper and lower red, and the middle white with a blue union containing a circle of seven stars, the union reaching down to the lower stripe.

How Can it be Done?

Collecting the Revenues in the Seceded States.—The collection of the revenue in ports in the Seceded States will, we opine, says the Richmond *Whig*, be no easy matter—a fact of which President Lincoln will doubtless be convinced when he comes to a critical examination of the several laws appertaining thereto. It should be remembered that the President has been clothed with no new power, even by the Republican Congressional majority. He cannot add to the regular army, and he cannot call out volunteers. Should he impartially "enforce the laws as they now exist, they will, to all intents and purposes, practically defeat all attempts to collect revenue." For an example of obstacles in the way of force, the N. York *Herald* puts the following case:—

Suppose that the ship Alliance arrives at Charleston from Havre, with a cargo of silks, laces, fancy goods, manufactured articles, etc., in all, say five hundred packages, consigned to fifty or more persons. In entering the harbor the Alliance is overhauled by a ship of war, with a collector on board. The master has nothing to show but his manifest, which does not particularize the quality of the articles shipped. It is for the consignees to produce their invoices and bills of lading, pay the duties and receive their goods. When the consignees fail to appear, the packages are to be sent to the public store, and in case they remain unclaimed during a stipulated time, they are sold at auction on account of the Government. According to maritime law, all duties must be collected within one marine league of the port, and bulk cannot be broken until the vessel has been regularly entered within the harbor. Should the Executive override all these provisions, and declare that in case the duties are not paid according to the new regulations, cargoes will be forfeited, a fresh obstacle arises. The machinery for the collection of the revenue is not alone executive. The judiciary has something to do with it. The Secretary of the Treasury cannot forfeit a pair of gloves without legal process to be had before a district judge and jury of citizens, to be empanneled from the district where the consignees reside. Where would the Government find a judge or jury in Charleston, Savannah, Mobile or New Orleans?

Diptheria.—This fatal throat disease has already, in the United States alone, resulted in the death of ten thousand persons. The disease comes on so suddenly, and runs its course so rapidly, that it proves fatal in a very few hours, unless the most active remedial measures are quickly resorted to. The following is a digest of a pamphlet just published on this disease by Dr. Snelling, of New York, he says:

Diptheria is a disease of the tonsils, palate, and back part of the throat; or in other words, it attacks pretty much the same parts as are involved in the common "sore throat." But its peculiarity consists in the fact that there is deposited upon the parts a peculiar whitish, or grayish, or *wash-leathery* looking deposit, which, as the disease goes on, spreads (according to its intensity) over the tonsils first, then to the palate down towards the larynx, up into the back nostrils, or forward upon the jaws. All these different varieties of spreading are attended with different degrees of danger. If it spread to the jaws, the patient will probably be very ill, but he will be in no danger of suffocation; if it spreads upwards into the back nostrils, his distress and discomfort will be greater, but his danger wiil be incomparably less than if it invade the respiratory passages. In these last cases the death is generally by suffocation.

The first symptoms are generally shivering and flushes of heart, fever, and some discomfort about the throat. The patient sickens rapidly, complains more and more of his throat, and, on examination, the peculiar deposit will be seen covering only a small part of one tonsil, or in one or two detached patches. The throat is vividly red and inflamed, generally of a rather dark red, however, and the parts more or less swollen. It might, possibly, in this stage, be mistaken for the simple sore throat, with white patches upon the tonsils, but the great prostration and debility, and the unmistakable illness of the patient will very soon undeceive. The tongue is also sometimes of a greyish, slaty, or blackish hue, which will help to determine the question. After the first febril onset, the disease is eminently one of debility and depression.

☞ French distillers are making brandy out of coal.

The Case of Mrs. Gaines.

The final decision in this case was delivered in the U.S. Court at Washington, a few days since. The New York *Herald*, in referring to it, says:

Associate Justice Wayne, in announcing the decision of the case of Mrs. Gaines, said it was of long standing and heretofore of doubtful result. The record covered three thousand pages, and at least eight of the ten points had been ruled by the Court with regard to it. At last it had been brought to a conclusion. The decision was, that she was the only legitimate child of Daniel Clark, and his universal legatee under his last will, and, as such, entitled to all the property, real and personal, of which Mr. Clark died possessed; and the defendant, Henning, having purchased certain property, with full notice of the nullity of the title under which he held, she is entitled to recover immediate possession of it, with the rents and profits. The Court said measures would at once be taken to enforce the decree; and Justice Wayne said in conclusion, the future writer of the history of Jurisprudence, would be obliged to register this celebrated case as the most remarkable.

From the nature of the controversy, the position of the defendants, and the obstinacy with which they have contested the claim of Mrs Gaines, the matter may now well be considered as finally and conclusively settled. Unless public information is very much at fault, Mrs. Gaines is undoubtedly tho richest woman on this side of the Atlantic, and if wealth could give it, ought to be the happiest.

It is understood that on the part of the ladies of Washington, New York, and of Memphis, Tennessee, a fitting testimonial in recognition of the indomitable faith and perseverance of Mrs. Gaines in this most remarkable and protracted case has already been agitated. Doubtless, too, the ladies concerned will carry out this idea as a tribute due to one of their own sex, who, against difficulties, delays, combinations and reverses that few men would have had the moral courage to face, has thus achieved one of the greatest legal triumphs of the country.

The State of Louisiana has seceded; but neither the State, nor the new Confederacy of which she is a member, has done anything to break the full force of this decision. The property involved amounts in value, some say five, some seven, some ten millions of dollars, and some put it at a still higher figure.

The decision in favor of Mrs. Gaines, creates a profound sensation. It is the absorbing topic of conversation in every circle, and those that know that lady and have watched the unparalleled perseverence and ability with which she has prosecuted her case, against the most extraordinary combination of talent and money that has ever been contended against, are rejoiced. Since the decision to-day, she has received the heartiest congratulations of her friends, culminating in a splendid ovation in the evening.—*New York Herald, 15th.*

Why Coffee Beaten in a Mortar is Better than Coffee Ground in a Mill.—It is not generally known that coffee which has been beaten, is better than that which has been ground. Such, however, is the fact; and in his brief article upon the subject, Savarin gives what he considers the reasons for the difference. As he remarks, a mere decoction of green coffee is a most insipid drink, but carbonization develops the aroma and an oil, which is the peculiarity of the coffee we drink. He agrees with other writers, that the Turks excel in this. They employ no mills, but beat the berry with wooden pestles in mortars. When long used the pestles become precious and bring great prices. He determined, by actual experiment, which of the two methods was the best. He burned carefully a pound of good Mocha, and separated it into two equal portions. The one was passed through the mill—the other beaten after the Turkish fashion in a mortar. He made coffee of each.

Taking equal weights of each, and pouring on an equal weight of boiling water, he treated them both precisely alike. He tasted this coffee himself, and caused other competent judges to do the same. The unanimous opinion was, that coffee beaten in a mortar was far better than ground in a mill. And after mentioning that any one may repeat the experiment, he tells a strange anecdote of the influence of one or the other kind of manipulation, viz: "Monsieur," said Napoleon, one day to Laplace, "how comes it that a glass of water into which I put a lump of loaf sugar tastes more pleasantly than if I had put in the same quantity of crusted sugar." "Sire," said the philosophical Senator, "there are three substances, the constituents of which are identical, sugar, gum, and amidon; they differ only in certain conditions, the secret of which nature has preserved. I think it possible that in the effect produced by the pestle some saccharine particles become either gum or amidon, and cause the difference." The remark became public, and Savarin says ulterior observations have confirmed the truth of it. *Boston Transscript.*

☞ The United States Supreme Court on the 14th, rendered a decision in the famous Gaines case; and, what is better, it has at last rendered justice to one of the noblest and most heroic woman—Mrs. Myra Clarke Gaines. The Court stood four to three in the decision, and Mrs. G. thus becomes possessor of the large estate involved.

Cure for In-Growing Nails.—It is stated by a correspondent of the *Medical and Surgical Journal*, that cauterization by hot tallow is an immediate cure for in-growing nails. He says: "The patient on whom I first tried this, was a young lady who had been unable to put on a shoe for several months, and decidedly the worst case I have ever seen. The disease had been of long standing. The edge of the nail was deeply undermined; the granulations formed a high ridge, partly covered with skin, and pus constantly oozed from the root of the nail; the whole toe was swollen, and extremely tender and painful. My mode of proceeding was this: I put a very small piece of tallow in a spoon and heated it over a lamp until it became very hot, and dropped two or three drops between the nail and granulations. The effect was almost magical. Pain and tenderness was at once relieved, and in a few days the granulations were all gone, the diseased parts dry and destitute of feeling, and the edge of the nail exposed so as to admit of being pared away without any inconvenience. The cure was complete and the trouble never returned. I have tried this plan repeatedly since, with the most satisfactory results. The operation causes but little if any pain if the tallow is properly heated. A repetition might in some cases be necessary, although I never have met with a case that did not yield to one application. Admitting the theory of Dr. Lorinner to be correct, the *modus operandi* is very plainly to be seen. The liquid cautery insinuates itself in every interstic under the nail, accomplishing in one minute, without pain, all that can be effected by the painful application of nitrate of silver for weeks.

Ladies Should Read Newspapers.—It is a great mistake in female education to keep a young lady's time and attention devoted to only the fashionable literature of the day. If you would qualify her for conversation you must give her something to talk about, give her education with the actual world and its transpiring events. Urge her to read newspapers and become familiar with the present character and improvement of our race.

History is of some importance, but the past world is dead, and we have little comparatively to do with it. Our thoughts and our concerns should be for the present world, to know what it is and improve its condition. Let her have an intelligent conversation concerning the mental, political, and religious improvements of our time. Let the gilded annuals and poems on the centre table be kept a part of the time covered with journals. Let the family—men, woman, and children—read the newspapers.

Thirst Worse than Hunger.—The disturbances to the general system which is known by the name of raging thirst, is far more terrible than that of starvation, and for this reason: During the abstinence from food, the organism can still live upon its own substance; but during abstinence from liquor, the organism has no such source of supply within itself. Men have been known to endure absolute privation of food for some weeks, but three days of absolute privation of drink (unless in a moist atmosphere) is, perhaps the limit of endurance. Thirst is the most atrocious torture ever invented by oriental tyrants. It is that which most effectually tames animals. Mr. Estly when he had a refractory horse always used thirst as the most effective power of coercion, giving a little water as the reward for every act of obedience. The histories of shipwrecks paint fearful pictures of suffering from thirst, and one of the most appalling cases known is the celebrated imprisonment of one hundred and forty-six men in the Black-Hole of Calcutta.—*Blackwood.*

Decisions of the Supreme Court.—We find in the *Delta* of Wednesday, the following decisions of the Supreme Court, relative to cases from this Parish:

Marcelin Landry, appellant, vs. Theodore Blanchard, Sheriff, et al., appellees. Appeal from the Sixth District Court of Iberville. Judgment avoided, and it is ordered that the defendant be perpetually enjoined from selling the raft of cypress trees described in plaintiff's petition, and that the possession thereof be restored to the plaintiff. Merrick, C. J.

Mrs. M. E. Boissac, appellee, vs. R. C. Downes, appellant. Appeal from the Sixth Judicial District Court, of the Parish of Iberville. Judgment affirmed. Merrick, C. J.

☞ It is rumored that Herring has received an order from Washington city for one of his largest and best patent safes for the White House. It is understood to be for Mr. Lincoln's personal use, not only for retreat to in time of danger, when assassins are supposed to be about, but if he should desire to travel, it is believed it will be safer to transport him from place to place in it, than in a Scotch cap and military cloak! Gen. Scott is to carry the key.—*N. Y. Day Book.*

MARRIED,

In this town on Tuesday last, by the Rev. Mr. Fallot, Mr. **CHARLES MARIONNEAUX** and Miss **ERNESTINE BELL**, all of this parish.

DIED,

In this parish, at the residence of Michel Hebert, Esq., on the evening of March 3d, 1861, at 9 o'clock, Mrs. **HELEN DUPUY**, widow of the late Zachary Hebert, the 80th year of her age.

THE NEW YORK HERALD.

WHOLE NO. 8982. MORNING EDITION—SATURDAY, APRIL 13, 1861. PRICE TWO CENTS.

THE WAR BEGUN.

Very Exciting News from Charleston.

Important Correspondence Between General Beauregard, Major Anderson and the Southern Secretary of War.

The Summons to Major Anderson to Surrender.

MAJOR ANDERSON'S REFUSAL.

Bombardment of Fort Sumter Commenced.

Terrible Fire from the Secessionists' Batteries.

Brilliant Defence of Maj. Anderson and His Gallant Garrison.

Reckless Bravery of the Confederate States Troops.

SIXTEEN HOURS FIGHTING.

Breaches in the Walls of Fort Sumter.

Several of Major Anderson's Guns Silenced.

Partial Cessation of the Firing for the Night.

Arrival of the Harriet Lane, Pawnee and Another Steamer Off Charleston.

THE HARRIET LANE FIRED INTO.

Anticipated Attempt to Reinforce Fort Sumter.

Maps and Plans of the Scene of Conflict,

&c., &c., &c.

OUR SPECIAL DESPATCHES FROM CHARLESTON.

CHARLESTON, April 12, 1861.

Civil war has at last begun. A terrible fight is at this moment going on between Fort Sumter and the fortifications by which it is surrounded.

In my last despatch I stated that negotiations had been reopened between General Beauregard and Major Anderson. This was done with a view to prevent an unnecessary effusion of blood.

The issue was submitted to Major Anderson of surrendering as soon as his supplies were exhausted, or of having a fire opened on him within a certain time.

This he refused to do, and accordingly, at twenty-seven minutes past four o'clock this morning Fort Moultrie began the bombardment by firing two guns. To these Major Anderson replied with three of his barbette guns, after which the batteries on Mount Pleasant, Cummings' Point, and the Floating Battery, opened a brisk fire of shot and shell.

Major Anderson did not reply, except at long intervals, until between seven and eight o'clock, when he brought into action the two tiers of guns looking towards Fort Moultrie and Stevens' iron battery.

Up to this hour (three o'clock Friday afternoon) they have failed to produce any serious effect.

Despatches received at headquarters from the various forts report that all is going on admirably, and no men hurt.

Major Anderson has the greater part of the day been directing his fire principally against Fort Moultrie, the Stevens and Floating Battery, these and Fort Johnson being the only five operating against him. The remainder of the batteries are held in reserve.

Some fifteen or eighteen shots have struck the Floating Battery, but made not the slightest impression upon its iron cased sides. The Stevens' Battery is also eminently successful, and does terrible execution on Fort Sumter.

Breaches, to all appearance, are being made in the several sides exposed to fire. Portions of the parapet have been destroyed, and several of the guns there mounted have been shot away.

Major Anderson is at present using his lower tier of casemate ordnance.

The fight is going on with intense earnestness, and will continue all night.

It is not improbable that the fort will be carried by storm.

The soldiers are perfectly reckless of their lives, and at every shot jump upon the ramparts, observe the effect, and then jump down, cheering.

A party on the Stevens battery are said to have played a game of the hottest fire.

The excitement in the community is indescribable. With the very first boom of the gun thousands rushed from their beds to the harbor front, and all day every available place has been thronged by ladies and gentlemen, viewing the solemn spectacle through their glasses. Most of these have relatives in the several fortifications, and many a tearful eye attested the anxious affection of the mother, wife and sister, but not a murmur came from a single individual.

The spirit of patriotism is as sincere as it is universal. Five thousand ladies stand ready to-day to respond to any sacrifice that may be required of them.

The brilliant and patriotic conduct of Major Anderson speaks for itself, and silences the attacks lately made at the North upon his character and patriotism.

Business is entirely suspended. Only those stores are open which are necessary to supply articles required by the army.

Governor Pickens has all day been in the residence of a gentleman which commands a view of the whole scene, a most interested observer. General Beauregard commands in person the entire operations, and thus far they have moved with the utmost system and success.

It is reported that the Harriet Lane has received a shot through her wheelhouse. She is in the offing. No other government ships are in sight up to the present moment, but should they appear the entire range of batteries will open upon them.

Troops are pouring into the town by hundreds, but are held in reserve for the present, the force already on the island being ample. People are also arriving every moment on horseback, and by every other conveyance. Within an area of fifty miles, where the thunder of the artillery can be heard, the scene is magnificently terrible.

CHARLESTON, April 12—6 P. M.

Captain R. S. Parker brings despatches from the Floating Battery, stating that up to this time only two have been wounded on Sullivan's Island. He had to row through Major Anderson's warmest fire in a small boat.

Senator Wigfall in same manner bore despatches to Morris Island, through the fire from Fort Sumter.

Senator Chesnut, another member of the staff of Gen. Beauregard, fired a gun, by way of amusement, from Mount Pleasant, which made a large hole in the parapet.

Quite a number have been struck by spent pieces of shell and knocked down, but none hurt seriously. Many fragments of these missiles are already circulating in the city.

The range is more perfect than in the morning, and every shot from the land tells.

Three ships are visible in the offing, and it is believed an attempt will be made to-night to throw reinforcements into Fort Sumter in small boats.

It is also thought, from the regular and frequent firing of Major Anderson, that he has a much larger force of men than was supposed. At any rate, he is fighting bravely.

There have been two rain storms during the day, but without effect upon the battle.

Everybody is in a ferment. Some of those fighting are stripped to the waist.

THE LATEST FROM CHARLESTON.

CHARLESTON, April 12—11 P. M.

A heavy rain caused a suspension of hostilities between seven and eleven o'clock, except an occasional gun.

THE SCENE OF OPERATIONS.

Charleston and Its Defences—Plan of the Harbor, Showing the Position of Forts Sumter and Moultrie, Cummings Point Iron Battery, Fort Johnson, the Floating Battery and Other Fortifications.

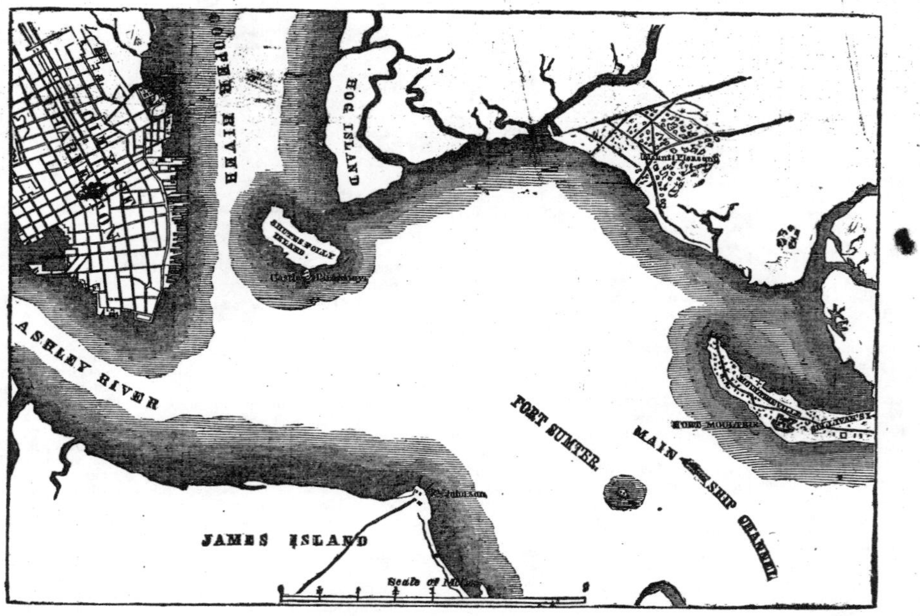

Major Anderson is busy repairing damages. He received twenty-nine full shots from Stevens' battery alone, making the bricks fly from the walls in all directions.

It is estimated that from twelve to eighteen hundred balls and shells were fired during the day. Over one hundred shells took effect inside the fort.

Orders have been issued to send Major Anderson a bomb from all the batteries every twenty minutes during the night, to keep him wide awake, making about two a minute.

Major Anderson fired only two barbette guns. Two more were dismounted. His shots at Fort Moultrie were generally bad, most of the balls going over. The same was the case with the Floating Battery, to which he was very particular in his attentions. A ball penetrated the Moultrie House, where a party of gentlemen were setting in the parlor, watching the fight. It entered the second story, and travelled into the kitchen. The gentlemen scattered miscellaneously.

The first shot was fired from Fort Johnson, on Morris Island, by Captain James, and the second by Lieutenant U. H. Gibbs. This was not answered until three o'clock this afternoon. The first shot from Stevens' Battery was fired by the venerable Edmund Ruffin, of Virginia. That ball will do more for the cause of secession in the Old Dominion than volumes of stump speeches.

It is a most remarkable fact that, after fifteen hours heavy cannonading, not one person has been placed *hors de combat*.

There are no tidings from Fort Sumter.

The schooner Petrel, Capt. S. F. Coste, received four shots, but no damage.

Three United States vessels are certainly outside. They were signalled by Major Anderson lowering and raising his flag.

The attempt will probably be made to reinforce him during the night. The mortar batteries are now blazing away. The scene is magnificent.

CHARLESTON, April 13—12:30 P. M.

It is utterly impossible to reinforce Fort Sumter to-night, as a storm is now raging.

The mortar batteries will be playing on Fort Sumter all night.

THE GENERAL PRESS DESPATCHES.

CHARLESTON, April 12, 1861.

The ball has opened—war is inaugurated.

The batteries of Sullivan's Island, Morris Island and other points were opened on Fort Sumter at four o'clock this morning. Fort Sumter has returned the fire, and a brisk cannonading has been kept up. No information has been received from the seaboard yet.

The military are under arms and the whole of our population are on the streets. Every available space facing the harbor is filled with anxious spectators.

The firing has continued all day without intermission.

Two of Fort Sumter's guns have been silenced, and it is reported that a breach has been made in the southeast wall.

Of the nineteen batteries in position only seven have opened fire on Fort Sumter. The remainder are held in reserve for the expected fleet.

Two thousand men reached this city this morning, and embarked for Morris Island and the neighborhood.

Intercepted despatches disclose the fact that Mr. Fox, who had been allowed to visit Major Anderson on the pledge that his purpose was pacific, employed his opportunity to devise a plan for supplying the fort by force, and that this plan had been adopted by the Washington government, and was in progress of execution.

The Floating Battery and Stevens' Battery are operating freely and Fort Sumter is returning the fire.

It is reported that three war vessels are outside the bar.

CHARLESTON, April 12—Evening.

The firing has ceased for the night, but will be renewed at daylight in the morning, unless an attempt is made to reinforce the fort, which ample arrangements have been made to repel.

The Pawnee, Harriet Lane, and a third steamer, are reported off the bar.

Troops are arriving by every train.

IMPORTANT CORRESPONDENCE.

COMMUNICATIONS BETWEEN THE CONFEDERATE SECRETARY OF WAR AND GEN. BEAUREGARD.

CHARLESTON, April 12, 1861.

The following is the telegraphic correspondence between the War Department at Montgomery and Gen. Beauregard immediately preceding the hostilities. The correspondence grew out of the formal notification by the Washington government, which is disclosed in Gen. Beauregard's first despatches:—

GEN. BEAUREGARD TO THE SECRETARY OF WAR.

CHARLESTON, April 8, 1861.

L. P. WALKER, Secretary of War:—

An authorized messenger from President Lincoln just informed Governor Pickens and myself that provisions will be sent to Fort Sumter peaceably, or otherwise by force. P. G. T. BEAUREGARD.

THE SECRETARY OF WAR TO GENERAL BEAUREGARD.

MONTGOMERY, April 10, 1861.

Gen. P. G. T. BEAUREGARD, Charleston:—

If you have no doubt of the authorized character of the agent who communicated to you the intention of the Washington government to supply Fort Sumter by force, you will at once demand its evacuation; and if this is refused, proceed in such manner as you may determine to reduce it. Answer.

L. P. WALKER, Secretary of War.

GENERAL BEAUREGARD TO THE SECRETARY OF WAR.

CHARLESTON, April 10, 1861.

L. P. WALKER, Secretary of War:—

The demand will be made to-morrow at twelve o'clock.

P. G. T. BEAUREGARD.

THE SECRETARY OF WAR TO GENERAL BEAUREGARD.

MONTGOMERY, April 10, 1861.

General BEAUREGARD, Charleston:—

Unless there are especial reasons connected with your own condition, it is considered proper that you should make the demand at an early hour.

L. P. WALKER, Secretary of War.

GENERAL BEAUREGARD TO THE SECRETARY OF WAR.

CHARLESTON, April 10, 1861.

L. P. WALKER, Secretary of War, Montgomery:—

The reasons are special for twelve o'clock.

P. G. T. BEAUREGARD.

GENERAL BEAUREGARD TO THE SECRETARY OF WAR.

CHARLESTON, April 11, 1861.

L. P. WALKER, Secretary of War:—

Demand sent at two o'clock; allowed till six o'clock to answer. P. G. T. BEAUREGARD.

THE SECRETARY OF WAR TO GENERAL BEAUREGARD.

MONTGOMERY, April 11, 1861.

General BEAUREGARD, Charleston:—

Telegraph the reply of Major Anderson.

L. P. WALKER, Secretary of War.

GENERAL BEAUREGARD TO THE SECRETARY OF WAR.

CHARLESTON, April 11, 1861.

To L. P. WALKER, Secretary of War:—

Major Anderson replies:—

I have the honor to acknowledge the receipt of your communication demanding the evacuation of this fort, and to say in reply thereto that it is a demand with which I regret that my sense of honor and my obligations to my government prevent my compliance.

He adds:—

Probably I will await the first shot, and if you do not batter us to pieces we will be starved out in a few days.

Answer. P. G. T. BEAUREGARD.

THE SECRETARY OF WAR TO GENERAL BEAUREGARD.

MONTGOMERY, April 11, 1861.

Gen. BEAUREGARD, Charleston:—

We do not desire needlessly to bombard Fort Sumter if Major Anderson will state the time at which, as indicated by him, he will evacuate, and agree that, in the meantime, he will not use his guns against us, unless ours should be employed against Fort Sumter.

You are thus to avoid the effusion of blood. If this or its equivalent be refused, reduce the fort as your judgment decides to be the most practicable.

L. P. WALKER, Secretary of War.

GENERAL BEAUREGARD TO THE SECRETARY OF WAR.

CHARLESTON, April 12, 1861.

L. P. WALKER, Secretary of War:—

He would not consent. I write to-day.

P. G. T. BEAUREGARD.

THE CONFEDERATE STATES CONGRESS.

MONTGOMERY, April 12, 1861.

An extra session of the Confederate States Congress has been called for April 29.

THE KENTUCKY VOLUNTEER REGIMENT.

LOUISVILLE, April 12, 1861.

Despatches have come here to hold the Kentucky volunteer regiment in readiness to move at a moment's notice, from the War Department at Montgomery.

CHARLESTON AND ITS DEFENCES.

The news of the bombardment of Fort Sumter by the Confederate forces, which we publish this morning, induces us to give a full description of the scene of operations, embracing the city of Charleston, its harbor and fortifications. The plans of the forts and batteries, showing the stronghold of Major Anderson and the position of the attacking forces under General Beauregard, cannot fail to interest our readers.

FORT SUMTER—THE STRONGHOLD OF MAJOR ANDERSON.

Fort Sumter is a modern truncated pentagonal fort, built upon an artificial island at the mouth of Charleston harbor, three and three-eighths miles from the city of Charleston. The island has for its base a sand and mud bank, with a superstructure, if we may so term it, of the refuse chips from several Northern granite quarries. These rocks are firmly embedded in the sand, and upon them the present fortification is reared. The island itself cost half a million of dollars, and was ten years in construction. The fortification cost another half a million dollars, and at the time of its occupancy by Major Anderson was so nearly completed as to admit the introduction of its armament. The walls are of solid brick and concrete masonry, built close to the edge of the water, and without a berm. They are sixty feet high, and from eight to twelve feet in thickness, and are pierced for three tiers of guns on the north, east, and west exterior sides. Its weakest point is on the south side, of which the masonry is not only weaker than that of the other sides, but it is not protected by any flank fire, which would sweep the wharf. Once landed, an entrance may, at the present state of the construction, be easily made; for the blinds of the lower embrasures, though six inches in thickness, may yet be easily blown away, and even if this was impossible, scaling ladders can reach those of the second tier, which are not protected in this manner. The work is designed for an armament of one hundred and forty pieces of ordnance of all calibres. Two tiers of the guns are under bombproof casemates, and the third or upper tier open, or, in military parlance, *en barbette;* the lower tier for forty-two pounder paixhan guns; the second tier for eight and ten-inch columbiads, for throwing solid or hollow shot, and the upper tier for mortars and twenty-four pound guns. The full armament of the fort, however, had not arrived there when Major Anderson took possession; but since its occupancy by the present garrison no efforts have been spared to place the work in an efficient state of defence, by mounting all the available guns and placing them in salient points. As we before remarked, the full armament of the fort is not in position, as only seventy-five of the one hundred and forty guns required for it are now mounted. Eleven paixhan guns are among that number, nine of them commanding Fort Moultrie, which is within easy range, and the other two pointing towards Castle Pinckney, which is well out of range. Some of the columbiads, the most effective weapon for siege or defensive operations, are not mounted. Four of the thirty-two pounder barbette guns are on pivot carriages, which gives them the entire range of the horizon, and others have a horizontal sweep of fire of 180 degrees. In addition to these weightier preparations for defence, the walls are pierced everywhere for muskets, of which there are endless numbers ready and loaded. The magazine contains seven hundred barrels of gunpowder and an ample supply of shot, powder and shells for one year's siege, and a large amount of miscellaneous artillery stores. The garrison is amply supplied with water from artificial wells, which are supplied by the frequent showers of rain. In a defensive or strategical point of view, Fort Sumter radiates its fire through all the channels from the sea approach to Charleston, and has a full sweep of range in its rear or city side. The fort is sufficiently out of range from a land artillery attack, so that all apprehensions for breaching it from that source may be put at rest, unless by guns of superior calibre. The maximum range of the guns from Sumter is three miles; but for accurate firing, sufficient to hull a vessel, the distance would require to be reduced one-half of that figure. The war garrison of the fort is six hundred men, but only seventy-nine of that number are within its walls, with the laborers—109 all told.

THE GARRISON IN THE FORT.

Names.	Rank.	Regiment or Corps.	Original Entry into Service.	Born in.
R. Anderson	Major	1st Art'y.	July 1, 1825	Ky.
S. W. Crawford	Asst. Sur'n.	Med. Staff	March 10, 1851	Penn
Abner Doubleday	Captain	1st Art'y.	July 1, 1842	N. Y.
Truman Seymour	Captain	1st Art'y.	July 1, 1846	Vt.
Theodore Talbot	1st Lieut.	1st Art'y.	May 22, 1847	D. C.
Jeff. C. Davis	1st Lieut.	1st Art'y.	June 17, 1848	Ind.
J. N. Hall	2d Lieut.	1st Art'y.	July 1, 1849	N. Y.
J. G. Foster	Captain	Engin'rs.	July 1, 1846	N. H.
G. W. Snyder	1st Lieut.	Engin'rs.	July 1, 1856	N. Y.
R. K. Meade	2d Lieut.	Engin'rs.	July 1, 1857	Va

Officers	9
Band	15
Artillerists	55
Laborers	30
Total	109

The embrasures for musketry on the side of the work exposed to the fire of the batteries of Cummings' Point and Fort Johnson have been filled with solid flagging, filled in with lead, and are now ball and bomb proof, adding materially to the strength of the work. Inside, the magazine and hospital have been protected by stone traverses, and the parade cleared.

FORT MOULTRIE.

Fort Moultrie, which first opened its batteries upon Major Anderson and his command, is one of the sentinels that guard the principal entrance to Charleston harbor. It is opposite to and distant from Fort Sumter about one and a half miles. It is, more properly speaking, a huge water battery, without any guns under cover. Its armament consists of eleven guns of heavy calibre and several mortars. The outer and inner walls are of brick, capped with stone and filled with earth, making a solid wall fifteen or sixteen feet in thickness. This work has been much strengthened recently, and presents a saucy front to Fort Sumter. It is now in command of Major Ripley, formerly of the United States Army, who has under his command several hundred experienced artillerists.

THE IRON FLOATING BATTERY.

This novel war machine, designed for harbor operations, is now anchored near Sullivan's Island, commanding the barbette guns of Fort Sumter. It is constructed of palmetto logs, sheathed with plate iron, and is supposed to be impregnable against shot. It is embrasured for and mounts four guns of heavy calibre. It requires sixty men to operate it. The first impression on seeing this machine is that of immense solidity. The outer or gun side is covered with six plates of iron—two of them of the T railroad pattern, placed horizontally, and the other four bolted one over the other, in the strongest manner, and running vertically. The wall of the gun side is full four feet thick, constructed of that peculiar palmetto wood so full of fibrous material that sixty-four pounders cannot pierce it. The main deck is wide and roomy. In nineteen open chambers, on the port side of the deck, we found a profusion of shot—thirty-four pounders—while just beyond them is an immense pile of sand bags, which protect an overhanging roof, under which is to be placed the hospital. This also protects the magazines (three in number), under which is the hold proper. There are six entrances to the hold, which will contain, if necessary, over three hundred men. It is kept in place by four heavy wedges, driven down by a species of ram, which will hold it fast, and prevent any swaying around by the tide.

CUMMING'S POINT IRON BATTERY.

The nearest point of land to Fort Sumter is Cumming's Point, distance 1,150 yards. On this point is the celebrated railroad iron battery, an illustration of which we give above. It consists of a heavy framework of yellow pine logs. The roof is of the same material, over which dovetailed bars of railroad iron of the T pattern are laid from top to bottom—all of which is riveted down in the most secure manner. On the front it presents an angle of about thirty degrees. There are three portholes, which open and close with iron shutters of the heaviest description. When open, the muzzles of the columbiads fill up the space completely. The recoil of the gun enables the shutters to be closed instantly. It is asserted, on high military authority, that this inclined plane will effectually resist guns of the heaviest calibre—first, because no shot can strike it except at an obtuse angle, which would cause the ball to glance; second, because its power of resistance is sufficient to withstand the fall of the heaviest shells. The columbiad guns, with which this novel battery is equipped bear on the south wall of Sumter, the line of fire being at an angle of about thirty-five degrees. This is not, of course, considered favorable for breaching; but owing to the fact that the wall is loop-holed for musketry throughout its entire length, which, of course, weakens it a great deal, the effect of shot upon it would, we think, even at the distance of 1,150 yards, effect a breach within a reasonable time. The work is in charge of several companies of the regular army of the Confederate States. If employed to reduce Fort Sumter, this battery will prove quite formidable.

THE INTERIOR OF FORT JOHNSON—GUN BATTERY.

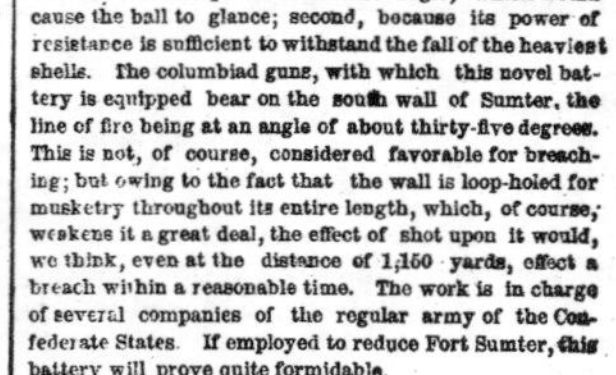

The Fort Johnson batteries consist of two hurge sand works, containing mortar and seige gun batteries, of which the above and the subjoined are good illustrations:—

FORT JOHNSON—MORTAR BATTERY.

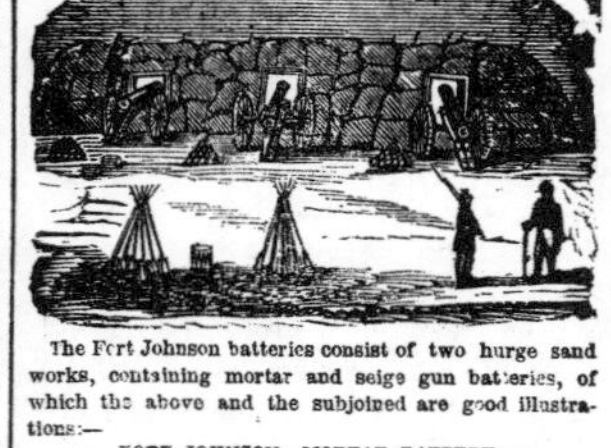

These works are one and one-fourth of a mile from Fort Sumter, and at present manned by two companies of regular artillery. The position of this old fort, which is of the utmost importance as a connecting point in the defence of the harbor, has been considered by the highest military authority as the key to all the defensive works in the harbor. Against the attack of forces by land, or a boat attack by the Stono river, it must be considered an essential element of defence.

CASTLE PINCKNEY.

Castle Pinckney is a small work, situated on the southern extremity of "Shute's Folly Island," between the Hog and Folly channels. Though in itself not a very considerable military work, yet, from its position, commanding as it does the whole line of the eastern wharves, it becomes of the utmost importance for it to be held by the State authorities. It is, in fact, the immediate outwork of the city, useful to annoy an invading fleet should it pass the outer forts, and to render their landing very difficult, if not impossible. In its plan it presents to the south a semicircular face; the eastern and western faces are formed by the line of rampart following the direction of the tangent to the circular arc at its extremity, and for a distance of twenty yards; the northern side is plain; at both the northeastern and northwestern angles are semicircular bastions, the outer extremities of the arcs being tangent respectively to the eastern and western sides of the fort. There are two rows of guns—the lower being in casemates (bombproof), the embrasures for which are about seven feet above low water mark, and the upper being *en barbette*. The height of the rampart is twenty, and the width thirty-two feet. The width of the outer wall and of the parapet is six feet; the depth of the casemates is twenty feet, height ten; the diameter (east and west) of the castle is one hundred and seventy feet. The entrance is on the northern side, on either side of which are the officers' and privates' quarters, messroom, &c. The ascent to the barbette is made on the northeastern and northwestern corners of the *terre-paradeplein*. In the centre of the latter is the furnace for heating shot. Around the foot of the scarp wall is a break water, about twelve feet in width, horizontally, which has its western side extended in a tangent direction to the south, to form the landing. The landing is protected by the fire of several guns sweeping its length. The armament of this castle consists of about twenty five pieces, 24 and 32 pounders, a few seacoast mortars and six columbiads—the latter not being mounted. In the magazine is a sufficiency of ammunition, including shot and loaded shell. This work has been of late put in as thorough repair as possible. Owing to the want of

[CONTINUED ON EIGHTH PAGE.]

NEW YORK HERALD.

JAMES GORDON BENNETT,
EDITOR AND PROPRIETOR.

OFFICE N. W. CORNER OF FULTON AND NASSAU STS.

TERMS cash in advance. Money sent by mail will be at the risk of the sender. None but Bank bills current in New York taken.

THE DAILY HERALD, two cents per copy, $7 per annum.

THE WEEKLY HERALD, every Saturday, at six cents per copy, or $3 per annum; the European Edition every Wednesday, at six cents per copy, $4 per annum to any part of Great Britain, or $6 12 to any part of the Continent, both to include postage; the California Edition on the 1st, 11th and 21st of each month, at six cents per copy, or $2 75 per annum.

THE FAMILY HERALD, on Wednesday, at four cents per copy, or $2 per annum.

VOLUNTARY CORRESPONDENCE, containing important news, solicited from any quarter of the world; if used, will be liberally paid for. OUR FOREIGN CORRESPONDENTS ARE PARTICULARLY REQUESTED TO SEAL ALL LETTERS AND PACKAGES SENT US.

NO NOTICE taken of anonymous correspondence. We do not return rejected communications.

ADVERTISEMENTS renewed every day; advertisements inserted in the WEEKLY HERALD, FAMILY HERALD, *and in the California and European Editions.*

JOB PRINTING executed with neatness, cheapness and despatch.

Volume XXVI..........................No. 102

New York, Saturday, April 13, 1861.

BOMBARDMENT OF FORT SUMTER.

Civil war has begun! General Beauregard, in accordance with instructions received on Wednesday, from the Secretary of War of the Southern confederacy, opened fire upon Fort Sumter yesterday morning, at twenty-seven minutes after four o'clock. Forts Johnson and Moultrie, the iron battery at Cummings' Point, and the Stevens Floating Battery, kept up an active cannonade during the entire day, and probably during the past night. The damage done to Fort Sumter had been, up to the last accounts, considerable. Guns had been dismounted, and a part of the parapet swept away.

Major Anderson had replied vigorously to the fire which had been opened upon him, but our despatches represent the injury inflicted by him to have been but small. The utmost bravery had been exhibited on both sides, and a large portion of the Charleston population, including five thousand ladies, were assembled upon the Battery to witness the conflict.

Down to our latest advices, the battle had been carried on solely by the batteries of the revolutionists and Fort Sumter. The Harriet Lane, Captain Faunce, the Pawnee, and another United States vessel, were off the harbor, but had taken no part in the conflict. The Harriet Lane is said to have received a shot through her wheelhouse.

The opinion prevailed in Charleston that an attempt would be made during the night to reinforce Fort Sumter, by means of small boats from the three vessels seen in the offing.

No one had been killed by the fire of Major Anderson, and the casualties among the Confederate troops in the batteries were inconsiderable. There is, of course, no account of the loss, if any, among the garrison of Fort Sumter.

The particulars of hostilities, as well as the correspondence and telegraphic despatches between General Beauregard, Major Anderson and the Secretary of War at Montgomery, will be found in the appropriate column.

It is not unlikely, in the present aspect of affairs, that hostilities will soon begin, if they have not already commenced, at Fort Pickens. The same policy that dictated the bombardment of Fort Sumter, before the arrival of reinforcements, no doubt directed similar operations at Pensacola.

Postscript.—Our reports to this hour—one o'clock A. M.—state that the bombardment had partially ceased for the night, unless an attempt should be made to throw men into Fort Sumter, for which the secessionists were fully prepared.

The News.

An extraordinary session of the Confederate States Congress has been called for the 29th inst.

Pennsylvania is preparing for the war. A bill was reported to the Legislature of that State yesterday appropriating half a million dollars for arming and equipping the militia, and subsequently passed in both houses, all the democrats voting against it. On the announcement of the beginning of hostilities, one democrat changed his vote.

The work at the Brooklyn Navy Yard is being carried on with unabated vigor. The Perry is nearly ready for sea. It is expected that the masts of the Wabash will be taken in to-day, while every factory and workshop resounds with the din of preparation. Similar activity prevails in the Philadelphia, Charlestown and other navy yards.

The New York Canal Board yesterday adopted a resolution to open the canals for navigation on the first day of May next.

The steamer North Star arrived at this port yesterday from Aspinwall, with $1,110,231 in treasure, and the Pacific mails and passengers. She brings no news from California, her advices having been anticipated by the overland expresses.

The North Star brings no news from the South Pacific or the Central American States. Advices from New Granada are meagre, but sufficient to indicate that the civil war is probably at an end, resulting in the triumph of General Mosquera over President Ospina. The former had his headquarters not more than six or eight hours' ride from Bogota, at a place called Guaduas, where he had gained a complete victory over a portion of Ospina's forces, in a battle which lasted two days. The general government sustained another defeat at the town of Buenaventura, and its cause is regarded as hopeless. There is great excitement in Panama in regard to the question of declaring that State independent of the confederation. The more influential portion of the community is apparently in favor of the movement.

Several appointments were yesterday made at the Custom House. In another column we give a list of the names. The business in that department still continues very dull. The Collector is expected back to-morrow evening, and on Monday will doubtless resume his afternoon reception of applicants.

The legislators at Albany were hard at work again yesterday, driving business through rapidly, in anticipation of an early termination to their labors. A large number of bills were acted on in both houses. In the Senate, among the bills passed were the New York Chamberlaincy bill, the Harlem Bridge bill, and the bill to submit the question of a revision of the constitution to the vote of the people of the State. The Supply bill was received from the Assembly, with the Senate's amendments non-concurred in, and the Senate resolved to adhere to its action thereon. The Senate adopted the concurrent resolution for the close of the present legislative session to-day at noon. The Assembly passed a large number of bills, among which was the half million appropriation bill for equipping the militia of the State. The Senate's amendments to the City Tax Levy were concurred in, and the bill is now in the hands of the Governor.

Yesterday was the eighty-fourth anniversary of the birthday of the illustrious Henry Clay, the conciliator in chief of the feuds which, in the troublous times of 1850, threatened to disrupt the Union. Strange and melancholy it is, that on this anniversary, that peace which the sage of Ashland secured to the country for a brief period has fled, and that the telegraph brought us the intelligence that fratricidal blood had been shed in the harbor of Charleston in a conflict between the army of the Confederate States and the troops of the United States. The morning had brought no news of the fray, and hope yet lingered in many a breast that hostilities would be averted, and on that feeling the minds of our citizens were anxious to do honor to the memory of the departed patriot. Flags were displayed in more than usual number from the City Hall, Custom House, the Battery, the Exchange, and from all the hotels and from numerous stores the flag of the old United States threw its broad folds to the breeze, and many a hopeful glance was directed to its flaunting, and many an aspiration, no doubt, went forth that it would again be the emblem of a reunited people. In the evening the usual Clay banquet was held at the St. Denis Hotel, to which upwards of a hundred gentlemen sat down. Patriotic toasts and speeches were the order of the night, while full justice was done to the bounteous spread prepared for the occasion.

The anxiety to hear later news from Charleston seemed to absorb the thoughts of commercial circles yesterday in nearly all branches of business, to the exclusion of almost everything else. Many bogus reports about despatches having come to hand were circulated—one declaring that Sumter was to be evacuated, another that it was to be provisioned. Another account reported the wires down and the mails stopped. It was not until after business hours, or between five and half-past five P. M., that the first despatch announcing the attack on Fort Sumter was received. The day's fighting soon after appeared in an extra edition of this paper. The news, though late, produced the greatest excitement.

The sales of cotton were confined to 500 a 600 bales, closing at about 12⅝c. for middling uplands. The flour market was less active and sales fair, including some lots for export. Wheat closed dull and 1c. a 2c. per bushel lower. Corn was without change of moment in prices. Pork was steady, with sales of mess at $17 50, and of prime at $13. Coffee was in fair request, with moderate sales. Freights were dull and rather easier, with fair engagements to Liverpool and London.

The Present Attitude of England and France Towards the United States.

Sir Robert Peel, a quarter of a century ago, considered that the expenditure of one hundred millions of dollars, would be a cheap price for sowing seeds of mischief upon the American continent, which might ultimately undermine our national greatness. The Father of his Country, had, long before, warned the citizens of the United States "against the insidious wiles of foreign influence," as "the most baneful foes of republican government," respecting which "the jealousy of a free people ought to be constantly awake." His caution "against the mischief of foreign intrigue," has been abundantly justified by the subsequent history of the country; for there has been no effort of diplomacy left untried to shake the foundations of institutions, which, by the rapid growth of their prosperity, have excited the alarm of governments guaranteeing less freedom to their subjects. In proportion as our territory has extended; its population, and the number of the States, has increased; the salutary working of a democratic system has been envied, admired, and emulated, by those who have been seeking to throw off a despotic yoke; and our power has become formidable, the hatred of the courts of Europe, but more particularly of England and France, has augmented, and our national downfall has been desired. The hour of tribulation has come at last, and nothing can be more humiliating and insulting to every patriotic heart, than the spirit in which it is contemplated abroad.

A recent article in the London *Times* contemptuously alludes to the fact that the "Northern and Southern States have entered into a race with each other for popularity, with the determination not to be outbid by a rival," and it adds, as a consequence over which Englishmen may rejoice;—"America must not suppose that she can enjoy, when divided into two hostile republics, all the great and unprecedented advantages, which she possessed, while she was content to dwell under the banner of one." The South and the North are alternately cajoled and insulted. In one breath we are told, by the press of London and Paris, that the slaveholding States deserve no sympathy, on account of the injustice of their cause, while, in the next, the North are assured that neither England nor France will recognise a blockade of the Southern ports, and that the Morrill tariff will compel them to enter into treaties of commerce with the Montgomery government. The London *Globe* exultingly proclaims, that "the prospects of the United States are not brilliant; that the broad track, made by the founders of the republic, is now definitely abandoned." "America," it continues, "enters on a new career, and some among us may live to see whether, like Europe, she will be divided into antagonistic nations, with fixed politics, or whether she will, like South America, be split up among a number of snarling communities, with here and there a bright spot shining brilliantly in the surrounding gloom."

The ministers accredited by President Lincoln to the different courts of Europe, will, most of them, soon arrive at their posts. Messrs. Wm. L. Yancey, Dudley Mann, and Judge Rost, the three special Commissioners selected by the federal government, at Montgomery, to negotiate a recognition, by Lord Palmerston and Louis Napoleon, of the independence of the seceding States, and permanent treaties, will appear in London and Paris at about the same time. Both England and France have, for six months, been contemplating with an anxious concern, inspired by selfishness, and the most sordid jealousy, the affairs of the United States. Whatever course they may resolve to pursue will be dictated by self interest, and a wish to perpetuate discord between the North and South for their own benefit. Not a ray of genuine sympathy is to be looked for. Well did the farsighted Washington declare, that "it is an illusion experience must cure, and a just pride ought to discard, to expect or calculate upon favors, from nation to nation." Therefore Northern and Southern organs degrade themselves when they boast that aid and assistance have been promised them from abroad. It is to be hoped that both the Washington and the Montgomery Cabinet will scorn those "entangling alliances" which have been ever considered as a great evil, to be carefully shunned, by every sound patriot and statesman of the country. Rival chieftains in Mexico and the South American States, may have found some temporary, doubtful advantages in the support of Powers like England and France; but neither the Gulf States, nor those that remain in the Union can be benefitted by their interference.

The United States, lately so defiant in its proud supremacy, in the Western hemisphere, will not descend to beggary at the doors of any foreign Powers. Dark and menacing as are the clouds that obscure the horizon, time will prove that we are abundantly able to settle our own differences. A nation of thirty millions of people, with resources that are unbounded, may indeed be crippled sorely by such disasters as seem to be impending; but it will not want energy to recover from the shock. The sober second thought of citizens, in the North and South, will return at last, and the remedy when applied, will be one that has been devised by ourselves. From England and France neither section needs to ask for favors, while we firmly believe that an injury inflicted upon either would, notwithstanding the inter-State animosities that now prevail, be resented by both.

The New Power in the State of New York.

The Hon. Hiram Barney, the new Collector of this port, bids fair to outstrip in sagacity and statesmanlike management, any of the leaders of parties here who have preceded him. He is a man of character and integrity, free from the mire and filth of existing organizations, and sufficiently detached from association with corrupt politicians to enable him to control them all. Federal officers, in past times, have contented themselves with apportioning spoils among their own immediate friends, for the aggrandizement or consolidation of some very second handed, unimportant piece of party machinery. Mr. Barney, we understand, aims at nothing less than to concentrate an influence which may rule not only the politics of the city, but, through it, of the State. He has ample means at hand to enable him to do so. The patronage under his control is immense, and both the Surveyor and Naval Officer, whoever they may be, will be compelled to act under his directions. New York is so divided and subdivided into political cliques, that, by a fair and judicious selection of officers, from among all of them who are willing to strike hands with the administration, and give it a hearty support, he can organize, from their ruins, a united party, which will bring chaos out of the present disorder.

Mr. Barney is a gentleman of the highest integrity, and will pay but small attention to applicants for place, merely because they howl, boisterously around the avenues to the Custom House. They will neither be accepted nor rejected, because they happen to be greedy or hungry; nor because they happen to belong to some Wide Awake club, or republican committee, with no higher merit. We are told that the number of individuals who have been heretofore democrats, who have applied to him for positions is immense. Tammany Hall is abundantly represented. Of those clerks who now occupy desks, given to them by Collectors Schell and Redfield, a very large number, probably a majority, have been converted to republicanism, since last November, and are known by the vehemence with which they advocate their new faith. Out of such elements, Mr. Barney will select, irrespective of past proclivities, subordinates who unite ability, industry, and official honesty, with zeal and influence to aid in consolidating the fabric he is desirous of creating. He need be in no hurry to make his appointments. The longer he waits, the greater the number of applicants will be, and the wider his range of choice. Delay will give him, also, the advantage of holding in suspense, and ascertaining from past good behavior, what the promises may be worth, of the thousands who are anxious for his favor. The price of Tammany men will hourly become cheaper, and the ranks will swell of those, who from street corners, if not from "house tops," are ready to pledge "lives, fortunes and sacred honor," in the great cause of party consolidation, which the statesmanlike tactics of the Collector are destined to achieve.

Whatever differences in opinion may prevail, there can be but small doubt that this scheme of the Collector is wise and far sighted, and that it will produce signal results. Merchants will be benefitted by it, and if any one suffers detriment, it will be of the class of impracticables, who choose to cling to their own opinions, or to keep alive unnecessary distinctions.

THE TAX LEVY IN THE SENATE—AN IMPORTANT OMISSION.—The Tax Levy, as it passed the Assembly, makes ample provision for useless jobs and worthless officials, but omits a matter as important and really necessary as a stationhouse for the new precinct north of the Central Park, a district of five miles in length. A police district without a stationhouse would be an absurdity too glaring to be intentional. It is doubtless owing to the sickness and absence of the Assemblyman of the district that the subject has been overlooked. Why will not the Senator for the upper district of the city remedy this blunder? A sum of ten thousand dollars is required for the purpose.

THE MORRILL TARIFF IN PENNSYLVANIA.—The Philadelphia *North American* closes a labored eulogium on the Morrill tariff as follows:—"As to the course of England and France, the folly of our own people may tempt them to some bluster; but it will result in nothing, not even in the apprehended throwing of European influence in favor of secession." We apprehend, however, that England and France will be apt to go to the most advantageous markets for their cotton and with their goods, without being very particular as to their duty of protecting the iron foundries of Pennsylvania. We dare say, too, that our high tariff men of that State will find out before the end of the year that their favorite hobby of home protection has become "an obsolete idea," and that this Morrill tariff cuts both ways.

NEWS FROM THE STATE CAPITAL.

ALBANY, April 12—9 P. M.

The county tax levy has been amended by adding two hundred and fifty thousand dollars for the Harlem bridge, and passed both houses.

The Senate has passed a resolution to adjourn to-morrow at twelve o'clock *sine die*. There is the most intense excitement and rejoicing in the lobby over the vote. The pulling and hauling that will take place to-night will astonish those not versed in the scenes of the closing hours of the Legislature at Albany. Should the House concur, a large number of the most important bills of the session will not be reached. The third House are, as a general thing, at least the money portion, working like beavers to have the Assembly concur in the Senate resolutions to adjourn. It is their interest to defeat legislation this year, and this is their mode for accomplishing that object. This is the very reverse from last year. Then they begged the members to stay; now they are praying for an adjournment forthwith.

The Assembly have been quarrelling over the Senate amendments to the Supply bill, and refused to concur in several of the amendments. The Senate, however, still insists, and there is a lively time brewing. The Assembly declare that they will not pay Lincoln's liquor bill at the Delavan.

The Vagrancy bill, relating to the city of New York, that passed the Assembly last night, is one of the greatest monstrosities that has gone through this Legislature. It has to-day gone to the Governor. There were a half dozen lines inserted by the committee in the Senate which raise the salary of the present Police Justices to five thousand per year, and continue them in office until a convention meets to provide for the election of their successors. This is the work of Justice Welsh, of the virtuous radicals, and Mr. Johnston. Its passage in the Assembly is one of the beautiful results of Robinson's relief resolutions. With the above exception the Vagrancy bill is a good one.

ALBANY, April 12—11:40 P. M.

The Assembly this evening concurred in the amendments of the Senate to the Supply bill, paying the full amount of the Delavan House bill to entertain the President, including the broken stoves, wines, &c. The republicans had a grand row there, and smashed things generally, and now the State pays the bill.

An effort was made to reconsider the vote by which the One-sixth Insolvent act was lost in the Assembly to-night; but it failed, not receiving the constitutional vote. That ends the matter for this session.

The bill taking the confirmation of contracts from the Common Council passed the Assembly this evening, receiving seventy-six votes. It has already passed the Senate. This is one of the hardest blows that the Common Council have received this winter. It destroys their profitable trade. Hardy, Hutchings, Varian and Arcularius, of New York, voted for it.

The Vagrancy bill, it seems, originated with the Commissioners of Charities and Correction. I am informed that the portions relative to the police justices was urged by them on account of the excellent management of the present Justices over vagrants, and it was thought that the public interests would be better served by continuing them in office rather than in trusting to the uncertainty of the ward politicians until the change by the apportionment under the new constitution. This, I find, since my afternoon despatch, to be the reason for inserting the amendment.

The most intense excitement prevails here this evening over the reported news of the commencement of hostilities at Charleston. The members and politicians are assembled at the hotels in groups, discussing the probable result and speculating over the fate of Anderson. The war spirit is in the ascendancy, and all rejoice over the fact that the Southerners commenced the fight. I hear but one expression from democrats as well as republicans, and that is, not to yield an inch now that war has commenced. Everything indicates that the feeling in Albany against the South will be a unit in less than twenty-four hours. Whilst it is deeply deplored that we have been drifted into civil war, no one now hesitates what to do.

NEW YORK LEGISLATURE.

Senate.

ALBANY, April 12, 1861.

The Senate is hard at work and doing a rushing business.

The amendments to the Coles or Harlem Bridge bill of the Assembly were concurred in.

The bill now goes to the Governor.

A large number of bills were reported from committees; among them the Telegraph Operators' bill; the Brooklyn Board of Education bill; a majority and minority report, for and against the Swill Milk bill; a majority and minority report, for and against the Metropolitan Health District bill.

A motion to make the latter bill the special order for half-past three o'clock, requiring unanimous consent, was objected to.

BILLS PASSED.

To widen Main street, Brooklyn.

Relative to the Chamberlaincy of New York city.

To submit the question to revise the constitution to the people of the State, by 19 to 8.

To amend the Bushwick Avenue act.

To confirm and legalize the grading of Eightieth street by contract.

THE NEW YORK CITY ANNUAL TAX LEVY.

Messrs. Truman, Lapham, Bell, Blood and Grant were appointed a committee to consider the claim bills and move them forward.

The PRESIDENT presented a communication from Hon. David Dudley Field, being a sharp and severe reply to the communication from the other Peace Commissioners, arraigning his conduct.

Laid on the table.

P. P. MURPHY asked unanimous consent to take up the resolution reported by the committee to examine the charges of malfeasance in office, requesting the Governor to remove John S. Anable, one of the Harbor Masters.

Mr. SPINOLA objected, and the motion was not entertained.

The Congressional Appointment bill was considered, and after several amendments had been proposed and rejected, the bill was passed by a vote of 17 to 9.

The negatives votes were Messrs. Abell, Blood, Calvin, Gardner, Hammond, Hillhouse, Montgomery, Spinola and Truman.

The concurrent resolution to adjourn *sine die* at twelve M., to-morrow, was adopted.

The Supply bill being received from the Assembly, with a message stating the items non-concurred in by that body, Mr. PROSSER moved to insist on the Senate's amendments. Carried, 22 to 8.

Mr. GOSS moved to reconsider the vote on the final adjournment.

Messrs. SPINOLA, TRUMAN and HAMMOND, in order to prevent a reconsideration, made motions and raised points of order until six o'clock, when, under the rule of fixing the hours of the session, the President declared the Senate adjourned till ten A. M. to-morrow.

Assembly.

ALBANY, April 12, 1861.

The Assembly is again hard at work to-day, with an evident intention to hurry up business.

Mr. MCDERMOTT, on a question of privilege, desired his vote recorded in the negative on the passage of the Coles or Harlem Bridge bill.

The feature of the morning was a spicy interlude, growing out of a quarrel in the select committee on the bill to amend the act of 1860 to open Madison avenue.

Mr. VARIAN, on a question of privilege, drew the attention of the House to the fact that Mr. Camp, another member of the committee, had seized on the bill, locked it up in a drawer and refused to deliver it up. A majority of the committee had chosen him (Varian) chairman, and instructed him to report the bill. He moved that Mr. Camp be directed to give up the bill.

Mr. CAMP replied, denouncing the bill, and declaring that he would never consent that such a bill should be passed in the small hours of the session, when legislation needed watching with extra vigilance.

Mr. VARIAN reported that the bill had been before the Legislature from an early day of the session, and the gentleman from Westchester (Mr. Camp) could have attended to it and opposed it before, had he not been running after the President elect from Springfield to Washington half the session.

The debate was carried on with considerable spice by other members—Messrs. Varian and Camp preserving good humor, and laughing at the propositions from Mr. Arcularius, that the desks be cleared away and the gentlemen be allowed to settle the difference between themselves.

The SPEAKER declared the motion not now in order, and the resolution instructing Mr. Camp to give up the bill was adopted.

A large number of reports were put in by committees.

The bill for the transfer of unclaimed dividends and funds from banks and courts of law to the State Treasury was reported for the consideration of the House. It is not likely to be reached again.

The select committee to report the bill to regulate milk freight on the Harlem road having failed to agree, Mr. DUTCHER moved that the bill be taken from their hands and sent to the first Committee of the Whole. Carried.

This insures action on the bill to-day.

The bill relative to contracts by the Mayor, Aldermen and Commonalty of New York was reported complete, and ordered to a third reading.

The bill relative to ferries between New York and Brooklyn was reported by the select committee for the consideration of the House.

Mr DARCY moved to disagree with the report, and order the bill to a third reading. Carried by a large majority.

Mr. BENEDICT, from the select committee, reported back the bill to appropriate half a million dollars to arm the militia of the State in substantially the same form as it was before, and it was passed—78 to 25. The bill now provides that the Governor, Lieutenant Governor, Secretary of State and Comptroller may, if they deem proper, expend money—not making the expenditure obligatory. This is the principle for which Messrs. Robinson and Kernan contended.

Mr. WATSON called up the Senate concurrent resolutions on the Reciprocity treaty, and they were adopted.

The bill to prevent the mutilation of the records of New York city was passed.

The bill to erect Highland county came up for a third reading.

Mr. BARNES moved to strike out the enacting clause, and spoke against the bill.

Mr. FULLERTON spoke in favor of the bill.

The motion to strike out the enacting clause was lost, and the bill passed by 68 to 26.

The Supply bill came down from the Senate, with a message that that body had concurred in the report of the Conference Committee on the bill. After a spirited debate the House agreed to concur in the following items:—Payment of extra compensation to the clerks and pages of the two houses.

An increased amount to the proprietors of the Delavan House for the reception of President Lincoln.

For the appropriation of $5 000 to the Lima College.

All the other amendments were concurred in.

The bill was returned to the Senate with an appropriate message.

The bill to amend an act to open Madison avenue was again brought before the House.

Mr. VARIAN made a majority report in favor of the bill.

Mr. CAMP presented a minority report against it.

After debate the House rejected the majority report and the bill was thus killed.

The House concurred in the Senate amendment to the New York county tax levy, which now goes to the Governor.

Recess till seven o'clock.

EVENING SESSION.

The bill to amend the Liquor law, requiring the Commissioners of Excise to give bonds, and making more stringent provisions as to the license to prohibit the liquor traffic on Sunday, and compelling the police to inform against all unlicensed houses, came up for a third reading.

Mr. WEBSTER moved to recommit the bill. Lost.

The bill was then read and lost—31 to 46.

The Annual Supply bill came from the Senate with the message that they insist on their amendments.

The House, after a debate, concurred in the full allowances to the proprietors of the Delavan House for the expenses of the entertainment to President Lincoln—66 to 38; also in the item of extra compensation to pages—65 to 36; and insisted on its non-concurrence in the remaining amendments of the Senate, being $5,000 appropriation to Lima College and extra compensation to clerks. The bill again goes to the Senate.

Mr. BIRDSALL called from the table the bill to amend the Insolvent law, requiring a petition of one-sixth of the creditors instead of two-thirds; to clear insolvents.

Messrs. Kernan and Ellingwood opposed the bill, and Messrs. Morgan, Bingham, Arcularius and Birdsall, supported it, and it was lost—54 to 35.

Pending the vote, Mr. TOWNSEND moved a call of the House, which was not ordered.

Mr. TOWNSEND then moved to take from the table the bill to amend the law relative to executions and other processes against insolvents. Lost.

The bill relative to contracts by the Mayor and Common Council of New York, requiring confirmation in fifteen days, came up for a third reading.

Mr. WOODRUFF moved to strike out the enacting clause.

Messrs. HUTCHINGS, VARIAN and BENEDICT supported the bill, and Mr. PRENDERGAST opposed it.

Under operation of the previous question the bill was passed—76 to 5.

Adjourned.

NEWS FROM THE NATIONAL CAPITAL.

WASHINGTON, April 12, 1861.

THE BIDS FOR TREASURY NOTES.

The treasury note loan is considered a great success. The difference between the rates for the treasury notes and the rates offered and declined for bonds last week, is about three hundred and fifty thousand dollars, which amount is saved to the government by the line of action adopted by Secretary Chase, which some thought too bold. The Secretary freely acknowledges the obligations of the Department to the capitalists of New York, Boston, Philadelphia and other cities, for the support given by them to the government notwithstanding the panic at the time of their bids.

The Treasury is now strong, having an available balance—counting the Treasury note loan as paid in—of over nine million dollars.

The President has made the following Massachusetts appointments:—

Charles A. Phelps, Surveyor of the port of Boston, in place of Fletcher Webster, who was removed at the earnest request of the Massachusetts Congressional delegation.

Eugene L. Horton, Navy Agent at Boston; Richard H. Dana, District Attorney; John S. Keyes, Marshal; John A. Goodwin, Postmaster at Lowell.

C. C. P. Baldwin, Marshal, and George Howe, Attorney for Vermont.

James C. Aiken, Marshal, and Ed. G. Bradford, Attorney for Delaware.

Lansing G. Vance, Postmaster at Norristown, Pa.

Harmon Bennett, Postmaster at Norwich, New York.

George L. Davis, of Milwaukee, will be appointed Paymaster in the navy.

The government is as yet without official advices of the murder of Mr. Haesken by Japanese highwaymen.

General Nye arrived here to-day, and is preparing to leave for Nevada. He had an interview with Colonel Lander to-day, who contemplates settling in that country.

It is denied that any portion of the Confederate States loan has been offered in New York. More than the entire amount has been arranged at par within the limits of the confederacy.

Senator Sumner called on Mr. Seward to day with James Redpath, the agent of the government of Hayti, and made known the passage of the resolution by the Legislature of Massachusetts instructing its Senators and representatives to use their influence to obtain the recognition of the Haytien independence. Mr. Sumner stated that this resolution was adopted on the petition of all the merchants of Boston having trade with Hayti, and added his own personal desires to those thus expressed by the Legislature. He also said that Governor Andrews warmly approved of this policy. It was also suggested that such a recognition was calculated to have a good effect in counteracting the reported Spanish movement against Dominica.

The Thatcher Comet.

OBSERVATORY OF HARVARD COLLEGE,
CAMBRIDGE, Mass., April 11, 1861.

ALBERT E. THATCHER:—

DEAR SIR—Your letter of the 9th inst., announcing the discovery of a comet in the constellation Draco has been received, and I beg to thank you for the favor. The notice in the NEW YORK HERALD of the 9th had already suggested an examination of that part of the heavens. The comet was readily found, and the following position determined with the aid of the micrometer of the great equatorial.

1861, April 10, 11h. 34m. 42s.
Comet's right ascension, 17h. 7m. 42.76s.
Comet's declination, × 59 deg. 30 min. 13.8 s.

The comet is bright for a telescopic object, but shows no tail. No information of a prior discovery in Europe has reached me. The latest astronomical intelligence from that quarter is up to the 29th of March.

Will you have the kindness to favor me with any early determinations of its position which you may have. If you have no precise observations, a diagram of its place among neighboring telescopic stars on the evening of its discovery would be useful for an early determination of the elements.

The new planet discovered at this Observatory by Mr. Tuttle, on the morning of the 10th, was again observed last evening. It had retrograded in right ascension thirty-six seconds, and had moved north in declination three minutes during an interval of twenty hours. Respectfully yours, G. P. BOND.

OBSERVATORY, WASHINGTON, April 11, 1861.

SIR—I have the honor to report the observations made last night by Mr. Ferguson, through the large equatorial, on a new comet:—

COMET 1861—III.

April 10—10 h. 10 min. 20.6 sec.—17 h. 17 min. 57.0 sec. × 59 deg. 26 min. 14 6 sec.

The comet is circular; two minutes in diameter, without any tail, condensed at the centre, with some trace of a nucleus. Its daily motion is 5 min. 12 sec., retrograde in right ascension, and × 46 min. in declination.

This comet was discovered at Mr. Rutherford's observatory in New York, April 4, by Mr. A. E. Thatcher, who reported it to this observatory by letter of April 9. Respectfully, M. F. MAURY, Superintendent.

Hon. GIDEON WELLES, Secretary of the Navy.

Superior Court.

Before Chief Justice Bosworth.

GEORGE MOUNTJOY UPON HABEAS.

APRIL 12.—At half-past four o'clock to-day the petitioner, George Mountjoy, was brought before the court, but the matter was further adjourned to next morning. Mr Anthon, on the part of the prosecution, said that he would contend that the writ of habeas was void, as it should have been issued by, and returnable to, the Court of Oyer and Terminer.

Mr. James T. Brady, associated with Mr. Larremore, said he would refer the Judge to the case of Quimbo Appo, where the Court of Appeals had decided that the Oyer and Terminer had no jurisdiction in the matter.

Chief Justice Bosworth said he would give the counsel half an hour each in the morning, commencing at ten o'clock, as he had to be at the General Term at eleven o'clock.

ACADEMY OF MUSIC.—"Linda di Chamounix" was sung last night for the concluding performance of the season. The distribution was the same, with one exception, as on a former occasion, when we reviewed the performance at some length. Miss Louise Kellogg was the Linda, Miss Phillips, Pierotto, and Brignoli as Carlo. Signor Ardavani replaced Ferri, invalided, in Antonia. There was a very large audience, and the performance seemed eminently satisfactory. Miss Kellogg's Linda, originally very good, is now much improved by study and practice. The others, Brignoli and Miss Phillips more particularly, were excellent. The opera closed with a new and clever polka by Muzio. To-day "Un Ballo in Maschera" will be given for the matinee—the last matinee till September. On Sunday night the religious portion of the community will have an opportunity to luxuriate in "Moses in Egypt" as an oratorio, at half the opera prices.

Arrivals and Departures.

ARRIVALS.

ASPINWALL, &c.—Steamship North Star.—H B Hubbard, Mrs J G Dow and daughter, Capt C P Patterson, wife and child; W D Powell, Mrs J P Haven, 3 children and servant; Mrs Judge McAllister and servant, Mrs P T Southworth, Madam Schulthess, Mrs Van Bokelin and 2 children, A J Case, wife and servant; Jas B Radcliffe, Mrs McAllister, child and servant; L D Hyman, Lieutenant Sturgeon, Lieutenant Wise, B Ross, Mrs Whitmore, G Mitchlen, J Cunningham, W H Brigham, wife and 2 children, A B Smith, E H Wakeman, G F Smith and wife, G H Crosseti, wife, child and servant, A H Tilden, H H Cohen, Mrs Belknap and servant, J L Dubois, Mrs L H Byer and child, C Scholtz, Mrs L Stevens, Miss M E Mulford, Moses Wicks, B A Farr, D W Corney, Mrs N Soule, Geo Clifford, Mrs Holbrook, J H Wade and family, E Creighton, Miss Smith, A Freilander, wife and child; Lieutenant G W Vanderbilt, A F Cooper, Mr Mocker, J A Boanke and wife, L W Moore, Jas Rhodes, H S Austin and wife, Mrs W B Johnson and daughter, Mrs D Phenix, Lieutenant F A Parker, M B Lillis, H Nathans, J M Hurtado, Messrs Batterly, Heatman and Jacobs, Mr and Mrs Ernos, A Gonzales, A Uribe, G Nareda, E Stribling, wife, 4 children and servant.

The Daily Delta.

VOL. XVI. NEW ORLEANS, SATURDAY, APRIL 13, 1861. NO. 130.

THE DAILY DELTA

AMUSEMENTS.

THE VARIETIES THEATER.—The theaters have presented only very meager results the present week. All eyes are turned to the stirring theater of war which is throbbing with dread artillery. The public mind is so much preoccupied with the drama whose scenes shift from Sumter to Pickens, from Pickens to Montgomery, and from Montgomery to Washington, as scarcely to heed the most seductive appeals of the mimic stage. The St. Charles, though backed by Miss Gougenheim and the Mobile company, has given up the contest. The Varieties holds out with laudable spirit. To-night, however, we may expect a more spirited mustering at the Varieties theater than on any previous night of the week. It is to be a benefit occasion, and the beneficiary is no less a person than that accomplished and versatile histrionic artist, Mr. Geo. Jordan. The bill comprises the comedy of John Bull, in which Jordan, Miss Thompson and Mrs. Chapman will figure in appropriate parts; and the Maid of Munster, in which Smith, Jordan, Owens, Miss Thompson and Mrs. Leighton will appear.

THE OPERA.—*Madame Frezzolini.*—This accomplished and brilliant Italian prima donna will make her third appearance at the New Opera House to-night The opera for the occasion will be Rigoletto.

THE ACADEMY OF MUSIC.—Prof. Heller will give one of his characteristic entertainments at this place to-day at noon, comprising legerdemain, magic, illusion, piano performance and ballad singing.

DRILL MASTER WANTED.—See the advertisement in another column for a good drill officer.

SLAVES FOR SALE.—See the advertisement of R. W. Long, offering some first-class slaves for sale.

Thanks to Purser De Costa, of the steamship Tennessee, for his polite attentions.

Messrs. C. E. Girardey & Co. sells this day, at the City Hotel, choice slaves, comprising cooks, washers and ironers. Full particulars in our auction column.

Messrs. H. M. Van Solingen & Co., will sell this day, at 10 o'clock A. M., at the New Basin, near Magnolia Bridge, the barge Kate, of New Orleans, her tackle, &c., as she now lies. See their advertisement.

The attention of buyers is called to the Port Wardens' sale of hats to be sold this day, at No. 47 Magazine street, by D. E. Morphy, auctioneer, at 11 o'clock A. M.

The attention of buyers is called to the unreserved sale of 350 packages and lots foreign and American dry goods this day, at 10 o'clock, by Vincent & Co., at their auction rooms, No. 28 Customhouse street.

FOR ST. LOUIS.—The regular passenger packet steamer New Uncle Sam will leave for St. Louis and intermediate landings this evening, at 5 o'clock. Thomas Keeffe, 25 Gravier street, is her agent.

FOR LOUISVILLE.—The fine passenger packet steamer Louisville, Capt. Hollcroft, will leave this evening, at 5 o'clock, for Louisville. Thos. Keeff, 25 Gravier street, is her agent.

NICARAGUAN SOLDIERS.—In another column will be seen a call from some of the officers of the late Nicaraguan army. At this time every Nicaraguan soldier should comply with this call. See it and respond.

FINE CLOTHING.—Our readers will find a very inviting advertisement from Alfred Munroe & Co., on the matter of fine clothing. To those who study dress and fashion, taste and economy, the stock of clothing of Alfred Munroe & Co. offers rare inducements.

R. W. Long, auctioneer, sold slaves to-day, ages from from 14 to 29 years, for from $1100 to $1400 cash—as high prices as have been obtained this season, which shows that the war news has not caused any decline in prices. See his advertisements.

TO COUNTRY PEOPLE—*Oil Light.*—Our country readers who want the real light, from pure kerosine oil, can get the same only at Covert & Hill's, No. 6 Chartres street. There the best and largest assortment of oil and lamps can be found at the lowest prices, and just suitable for our country readers.

A MODEL CRITICISM.—One Doctor Shaw has had the misfortune to be the author of a book, just published in London, under the title of "Travels in England: a Ramble with City and Town Missionaries," and has had the further ill fortune to provoke the following trenchant criticism from the London Athenæum. It is but a single paragraph, but savage enough to distress any timid author:

Dr. Shaw travels about England, but wherever he goes he searches for only one class of objects—the disfigurements of our social system. Set down in a magnificent town, he forthwith proceeds to inquire where the drunkards mostly congregate, in what street the wife beaters are found in the greatest numbers, what proportion of the juvenile community are addicted to blasphemy and theft, in what quarter the sewers are most offensive. The same spirit animates him in the tranquil lanes of a rural district. If, as he walks beneath the green canopy of a rustling avenue, he sees a little child playing on the verdant sward, he snatches it up, scares it into obstinate silence with a torrent of inquiries as to where it attends divine service, whether it knows the meaning of "salvation" and then, finding the terror stricken infant powerless to reply, walk away with a cheerful conviction that his young friend is in a dark state.

A MODEL CONSERVATIVE.—The following paragraph appears in that eminently conservative sheet, the Albany Evening Journal:

There are a thousand conjectures in regard to the apparent activity in the navy. One conjecture is that duties are to be collected on shipboard at Southern ports; and another, that those ports are to be blockaded. Either would be popular with the people, who desire some tangible demonstration of a purpose to vindicate the laws and dignity of the nation.

The receipts of the Associated Press of the State of New York for the last year, were $10 027 53. The expenditures were $8 735 45, exclusive of the payment for mails; leaving a balance of $575 75.

A little girl died, in horrible suffering, of hydrophobia, at Mountville, Pa., on Friday. She had been bitten six weeks before.

Three vessels were struck by lightning in Humboldt Bay on the 25th ult., the first cases of the kind in California.

The floor of a grain warehouse gave way at Fall River, Mass., on Friday night, and ten thousand bushels of grain went through.

The Queen of Spain is said to have offered the Pope her royal palace at Madrid, but the Pope announces his intention of remaining at Rome.

A London correspondent of the Cork Examiner says that "Charles Dickens wears stays like a woman." The "Dickens" he does!

At the cheaper opera house of London—the Surrey Theater—Verdi's Il Corsaro, an opera hitherto unheard in London, has been given with decided success.

A new paper has been started at Holly Springs. It is published weekly and semi weekly under the very suggestive and appropriate name of The Cotton States.

Ten thousand people in Newark, N. J., are out of employment, and many of them in a starving condition. "Nobody is suffering."

The United States steamer Sumter, Lieutenant Commanding Armstrong, was at Fernando Po on the 30th of January.

Mrs. Cora L. V. Hatch, "trance medium," says she has received a lecture on secession from Gen. Andrew Jackson, and has published it in a pamphlet form.

There are twenty daily papers—thirteen morning and seven evening—published in London.

HAYTI AND SAN DOMINGO.

THEIR POSITION AND HISTORY—THE DESIGNS OF SPAIN, AND HOW THEY HAVE BEEN CONSUMMATED.

From the Baltimore Exchange.

If any one will take the trouble to draw, on any good map of the United States, a line due South from the extreme point of the Peninsula of Florida, it will be found—after crossing the inlet, sixty miles wide, from the Atlantic Ocean to the Gulf of Mexico—to intersect the Island of Cuba at a point about one-third of its length. The northern shore of the remaining two-thirds of that island, winds, in a gentle curve, in a southeastly direction, finally terminating at Cape Maysi. What is known as the "Windward Passage"—a strait that connects the Atlantic Ocean with the Caribbean Sea—separates Cuba from Hayti—the distance between Cape Maysi, the eastern terminus of the former island, and Cape St. Nicholas, the western terminus of the latter, being not more than twenty-five miles. In the western portion of Hayti, covering about one-third of the area of the island, is established the Republic of Hayti, Port au Prince being its capital. The eastern division of the island, and by far the most mountainous, constitutes the Republic of Dominica, of which San Domingo is the capital. The Mona Passage, another entrance from the Atlantic to the Carribbean sea, separates on that side Hayti from the island of Porto Rico, the strait that divides them being about the same breadth as the Windward Passage—twenty five miles. It will thus be seen that Hayti lies exactly midway between Cuba and Porto Rico, both of which are Spanish dependencies, and any power holding these three islands would be in possession of the ocean gateways to the Gulf of Mexico, the Carribbean sea, and all the States of Central America.

We have been more particular in describing the geographical situation of these Islands, and their relative positions in regard to each other, because intelligence reaches us from Havana to the effect that Spain has seized upon that part of the Island of Hayti which is known to us as the Dominican Republic, or more popularly still, as San Domingo, and is about to annex it to the Spanish Crown. There is nothing at all improbable in this report, though it is not at all unlikely, if it should turn out to be true, that the fact of this reassertion of an authority which had been abandoned for nearly half a century will lead to great complications with this Government. Discovered by Columbus in 1492, and [illegible] by right of discovery, Hispaniola, San Domingo, or Hayti, for by [illegible] names the island has been known, [illegible] exclusive jurisdiction of Spain until [illegible] when the western part of it—that which is [illegible] Hayti—was ceded by the treaty of Ryswick to France. The remaining two-thirds—the present Dominican Republic—was a Spanish colony until 1785, when it too was ceded by the treaty of Basle to France, who thus acquired possession of the whole Island. It did not long remain under French rule. Shortly after the annexation took place, the negro slaves rose in insurrection under Toussaint L'Ouverture, Desalines and Christophe, and after a series of massacres scarcely paralleled anywhere, succeeded in either murdering or expelling all the white population, and in establishing a monarchy in the Northeast division of the Island, under Christophe, and a Republic in the Southwest, under Petion. In 1808 the Dominicans, oppressed by the tyranny of Desalines, called upon Spain for assistance, who seized upon the opportunity which was thus presented to her, to regain possession of her former colony. She held it but for a brief period. The following year the Dominicans again broke out into rebellion, declared their independence, expelled the Spanish Governor, abolished slavery, and established a republican form of government. The island continued divided for some years into three separate and distinct principalities—a republic, under Petion, in the Southwest; the monarchy, under Christophe, in the Northwest; and the Dominican Republic, under various chiefs, in the East. This distinction was kept up until after the death of Petion, in 1818, when the popularity of Boyer enabled him to unite all the governments under one rule, Boyer himself being chosen President of the Republic for life. In 1844, the negroes of what is now the Republic of Hayti obtaining the ascendancy, conferred the Presidency upon General Riviere. The Dominicans, fearing the expulsion or [illegible] of the Spanish [illegible] in maintaining their independence, chose [illegible] ana, the liberating chieftain for their President. His term of office expiring in 1849, Jimenes was elected Chief Magistrate in his stead, and Santana, who had become odious to the people, in consequence of the current belief that he had intrigued with the Court of Madrid to transfer San Domingo back to Spain, was banished from the Island. Jimenese, on the other hand, had scarcely been elevated to power before he conspired with Soulouque, the Emperor of Hayti, to unite the Dominican portion of the Island with that of the tawdry negro empire of the West. The near approach of Soulouque's army of invasion induced the Dominicans to recall Santana from exile, and to invest him with dictatorial powers. In the spring of 1849 he signally defeated the Haytien forces, and drove Soulouque back to his capital in disgrace. The following year Soulouque marched once more against the Dominicans; but was again encountered, and his forces were completely routed in a pitched battle. The independence of San Domingo being thus secured, Santana resigned his Dictatorship in favor of Baez, who was elected Constitutional President. Baez becoming unpopular, by reason of his favoring the policy of the Church party, Santana was re-elected to the Presidency in 1853; but, four years later, Baez again triumphed over his great rival. Baez had not, however, been more than six months in power, before the general dissatisfaction with his policy led in 1858 to a popular rising against his authority, which, being supported by Santana, resulted in the expulsion of Baez and the return of Santana to the Presidency. Theoretically, the Dominicans are as free as the people of the United States, after whose Constitution that of San Domingo is modeled. The laws in relation to the naturalization of foreigners are singularly liberal. "Free farm, farming utensils, and provisions for six months" are offered to settlers, and no distinction, as in Hayti, is made in favor of colored persons. These laws, it is now alleged, Spain has, for some years past, been taking advantage of, to introduce, under the auspices of Santana, large bodies of emigrants into the Island "with the view of promoting Spanish interests, and invoking the aid of the Spanish Government, at the first sign of resistance on the part of the native population." The plot is said to have succeeded. This disaffection of the mixed breeds, we are told, became gradually so menacing that on the 10th of last month, Spanish forces were disembarked from on board the vessels of war in the harbor; the Spanish flag was hoisted at St. Domingo, the capital, and at the last advices from Havana, a squadron of war steamers, carrying large reinforcements of troops, had been dispatched to support the movement which was so successfully inaugurated, and which, if report speaks true, is designed to re-establish the authority of Spain in Hispaniola, the most ancient of all her South American dependencies. We forbear from making any comment, at this time upon a movement which may have been misunderstood, and concerning which we have as yet but imperfect details. Until we know more in regard to the matter, the foregoing *resume* of the history of the island will serve, perhaps, to enlighten some of our readers, and will certainly enable us on any further occasion to render better understood such remarks as we may have occasion to make upon the question of Spanish occupation.

HOW HE "PASSED"—"Well," said the narrator, putting down his empty glass, and filling it again with Madeira, "I was shown into the examination room. Large table, and half a dozen old gentlemen at it. 'Big wigs,' thought I, 'and as sure as my name is Symonds, they'll pluck me like a pigeon.'" "Well, sir, what do you know about the science of your profession?" asked the stout man in the chair. "More than he does of the practice, I'll be bound," tittered a little wisp of a dandy—a Western ladies' doctor. I trembled in my shoes. "Well, sir," continued the stout man, "what would you do if a man was brought to you, during the action, with his arms and legs shot off? Now, sir, don't keep the Board waiting? What would you do? Make haste!" "By Jove, sir," I answered, a thought just striking me, "I would pitch him overboard, and go on to some one else I could be of more service to. By—" every one burst out laughing; and they passed me directly, sir—passed me directly."

The London Telegraph says emphatically: "Notwithstanding all the sympathy for the free States, we can not suffer our industry to be cut up by the roots in order that a slaveholding faction may be prostrated." Other journals express similar sentiments, and represent the business interests of the country as suffering serious injury from the state of incertitude as to the future in which they are kept by Mr. Lincoln's delay and indecision, and are discussing the propriety and necessity of recognizing our Confederacy.

Burch, the Chicago banker, and his wife will not live together, it is now said, but are negotiating for a "peaceful separation."

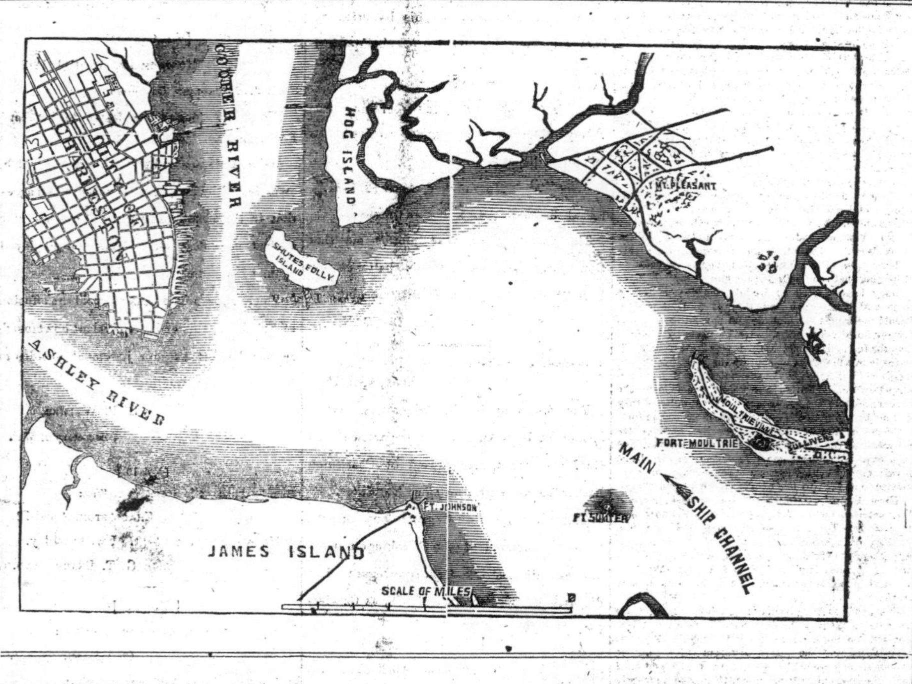

TELEGRAPHIC NEWS.

TELEGRAPHED TO THE NEW ORLEANS DAILY DELTA.

LATEST FROM MONTGOMERY.

An Extra Session of Congress Called.

SEVEN GUNS FIRED IN HONOR OF THE ATTACK.

LETTERS OF MARQUE TO BE ISSUED.

PROPOSED SEIZURE OF WASHINGTON.

MONTGOMERY, April 12.—An extra session of the [illegible] The Government has, up to 1½ o'clock to-day, received nothing later from Charleston. It is supposed that Major Anderson is returning the fire.

[Second Dispatch.]

Seven guns were fired to day in front of the Executive building, in presence of the Cabinet members, in honor of the attack on Fort Sumter by the Confederate forces. There is great rejoicing among the citizens. Three cheers were given for Gen. Beauregard, and three more for President Davis.

No further news from Charleston has been made public.

The Cabinet was in session all day, discussing important matters. Letters of marque and reprisal will be issued immediately.

Gov. Roman, in conjunction with Maj. Ben. McCulloch, proposes to this Government to have twenty five thousand men in Washington in ten days to take Lincoln and Gen. Scott prisoners of war.

Maj. McCulloch has ten thousand men now in Virginia, and purchased ten thousand stand of arms to circulate.

The President has issued his call for an extra session of Congress to convene on the 29th of April.

Rejoicing in Mobile.

MOBILE, April 12.—The most intense excitement prevails. There is great rejoicing among the citizens. Fifteen guns were fired in honor of the attack on Fort Sumter.

Steamer Vanderbilt Chartered as a Transport.

NEW YORK, April 12.—The United States Government has chartered the steamer Vanderbilt, of the New York and Southampton line, as a transport. She proceeded to the Brooklyn navy yard to-day to be fitted out in the required manner.

The Virginia Commissioners.

WASHINGTON, April 12.—The Commissioners appointed by the Virginia Convention to demand of Mr. Lincoln what policy he intends pursuing towards the seceded States, arrived in this city to-day, and will soon lay the object of their mission before the Administration.

Hostilities at Charleston.

WASHINGTON, April 12.—Private Southern dispatches leave no reasonable doubt that hostilities at Charleston commenced at an early hour this morning.

Gen. Beauregard telegraphed from Charleston on the 8th to Mr. Walker, the Secretary of War, "that Lincoln had notified Gov. Pickens and himself that provisions would be sent to Fort Sumter peaceably, or otherwise."

Mr. Walker (Montgomery, 10th,) responds "to demand the evacuation, and if refused, to proceed to reduce the fort."

Gen. Beauregard (Charleston, 10th,) replies "the demand will be made to-morrow, at 12."

Mr. Walker (Montgomery, 10th,) says to Gen. Beauregard, "Unless there are special reasons connected with your condition, it is considered proper for you to make the demand at an earlier hour."

Gen. Beauregard, (Charleston, 10th,) says, "The reasons are special for 12 o'clock."

Gen. Beauregard, (Charleston, 11th,) says, "The demand sent at 2 allowed till 6 to answer."

Major Anderson, (Fort Sumter, 11th,) replies that his sense of honor, and obligations to the Government, prevent his compliance. Adding, "Probably, I will wait orders from the President; and if you don't batter us to pieces we will be starved out in a few days."

Secretary Walker (Montgomery 11th) then telegraphs Gen. Beauregard, "We do not desire needlessly to bombard Fort Sumter, and if Major Anderson will state when he will evacuate, and in the meantime not use his guns against us until we fire, you are thus to avoid bloodshed. If something equivalent to this is not agreed to reduce the fort in the most practicable manner."

Gen. Beauregard, (Charleston 12th) telegraphs Secretary Walker: "He would not consent. I write to-day."

Firing on Sumter Certain.

AUGUSTA, April 12.—Passengers just arrived from Charleston announce that the firing on Sumter began this morning at half-past four o'clock.

HIGHLY IMPORTANT FROM CHARLESTON.

SULLIVAN AND MORRIS ISLAND BATTERIES AT WORK.

FORT SUMTER OPENED FIRE.

A BREACH MADE IN THE FORT.

WAR VESSELS REPORTED OUTSIDE.

CHARLESTON, April 12.—The batteries of Sullivan's Island, Morris Island and other points, opened on Fort Sumpter at 4 o'clock this morning. Fort Sumter returned the fire. A brisk cannonading is being kept up There is no information from the seaboard. The military are under arms. [illegible] bor is filled with [illegible] is on the streets, and the har-

[Second Dispatch.]

The floating battery is doing good service. Up to eleven o'clock there has been no loss on our side.

Fort Sumter replied at 7 o'clock this morning, and has kept up an astonishing fire ever since.

Steven's battery is slightly injured. Three shells are fired per minute. Four hundred in all have fallen.

A breach is expected to be made in Fort Sumter to-morrow.

Major Anderson's fire is principally directed against the floating battery.

War vessels are reported outside the harbor.

Only two soldiers are wounded on Sullivan's Island.

The range is now perfect from the land batteries. Every shot tells. It is thought, from Major Anderson's fire, that he has more men than was supposed.

Fort Sumter will succumb by to-morrow. It is raining at Charleston, but there is no cessation of the batteries. A continuous steady fire on both sides is being kept up.

The cutter Harriet Lane and the steam gun boat Crusader are reported off the bar, but have not entered the harbor.

The War Department have as yet no official dispatches.

Gen. Beauregard was at the batteries all day.

The Government expects Fort Sumter to succumb to-morrow.

[Third Dispatch.]

The firing continued all day. Two of Fort Sumter's guns are silenced, and it is reported a breach has been made through the south east wall.

No casualty yet happened to any of the forces.

Only seven of the nineteen batteries have opened fire on Fort Sumter. The remainder are held ready for the expected fleet.

Two thousand men reached the city this morning, and immediately embarked for Morris Island.

Fourth Dispatch.

CHARLESTON, April 12—11 P. M.—The bombardment of Fort Sumter is still going on every twenty minutes from the mortars.

It is supposed Major Anderson is resting his men for the night.

Three vessels of war are reported outside the bar. They can not get in on account of the roughness of the sea.

Every inlet to the harbor is well guarded.

Our forces are having a lively time of it.

No one has as yet received any injury.

The floating battery works admirably well.

Intercepted Dispatches

CHARLESTON, April 11.—Intercepted dispatches disclose that Mr. Fox, who visited Major Anderson on pledge of pacific purposes, devised a plan to supply Fort Sumter by force, and this plan has been adopted by the Federal Government, and is in progress of execution.

Volunteers from Kentucky.

LOUISVILLE, April 12.—Dispatches were received here to-day, to hold the Kentucky volunteer regiment in readiness to move at a moment's notice from the Montgomery War Department.

The Pennsylvania Militia

HARRISBURG, April 12.—The legislative bill was reported in the House to-day, appropriating $5,000,000 to arm and equip the Pennsylvania militia.

Cincinnati Markets.

CINCINNATI, April 12.—The Flour market closed dull at unchanged prices. Corn closed steady at 33c. ℔ bushel. Oats steady at 26c ℔ bushel. Whisky sales at 13½c ℔ gallon. Lard is quoted at 9¼c. to 9½c. ℔ lb. Sugar is selling at 6 to 7½c. ℔ lb. Molasses sales at 31 to 33c. ℔ gallon. Coffee is worth 13 to 14½c. ℔ lb

New York Markets.

NEW YORK, April 12.—The cotton market closed dull with sales of 850 bales at 12½@12⅝c. for middling uplands. Flour steady. Holders are pressing their stock on the market; sales 9 750 bbls. at $5 20@$5 30 for superfide State. Corn was steady, while the sales comprised 69 000 bushels at 63@70c. Pork buoyant; sales 825 bbls. at $17 50 for mess. Lard firm; sales 415 bbls. at 9¾@10½c. ℔ lb.

ST. LOUIS, April 12.—The Ohio river at this point is swelling with twenty feet water to Cairo. Upper Mississippi and the Missouri are rising rapidly.

GRAND SERENADE IN MONTGOMERY

Official Dispatches from Charleston.

FOUR GUNS IN FORT SUMTER DISMOUNTED

ANTICIPATED FALL OF SUMTER

Contemplated Expedition Against Washington.

Special Dispatch to the Daily Delta.

MONTGOMERY, April 12, 1861.

A grand serenade was given to-night to President Davis, Mr. Walker, Secretary of War, and Mr. Reagan, Postmaster General.

Mr. Walker made a speech in reponse to the compliment thus tendered to him. In the course of his remarks he informed the people that an official dispatch had just been received from Charleston.

The dispatch contained the gratifying information that the fire from the Confederate batteries had been vigorous and effective during the day—so much so that four of the guns in the fortress had been dismounted. On the side of the Confederate forces there had been no one killed or wounded, and none of the guns were injured.

Mr. Walker also stated it to be certain that Fort Sumter would be ours before to-morrow night. He likewise proclaimed that in less than three months the Confederate forces would be in possession of the City of Washington.

Mr. Reagan, on being serenaded, responded in a forcible and patriotic speech.

Mr. Toombs and Mr. Benjamin were likewise serenaded, and are now speaking.

Senator Bayard, of Delaware, is now here.

The regiments of Colonels Anderson and Patton have passed through this city on the way to Pensacola.

A dentist, whose skill at teeth pulling was well known, was recently met by a noted wag, who was carrying an old garden rake in one hand while he held the other to his face, which wore the lugubrious expression which the jumping toothache is so well calculated to produce on the sufferer. "Doctor," says he, "I want you to pull a couple of teeth for me." "Very well," replied the doctor, "just step into my office and I'll relieve you. There," continued he, as they entered, "take a seat on that chair and show me the teeth you wish extracted." "Well, doctor," says the wag, holding up the rake, "I want you to pull these two broken teeth out of this rake." For a moment the doctor was thrown off his guard by the joke that had been played upon him; but soon recovering himself, replied: "Well, let me have it; I might as well take the teeth out of one rake as another!"

The wife of William Stahl, a respectable German cabinet maker, in New Haven, Ct., killed her infant by drowning on Tuesday, and then destroyed her own life in the same manner. She had been ill for some time, became impressed with the idea that she would never recover, and during a fit of despondency she is supposed to have committed these acts.

UNTIMELY DEATH.—David Townsend, a printer, was killed at Como depot, Panola county, Miss., last week, by falling from a moving train of cars, which passed over his body. Mr. Townsend was a native of Massachusetts, but had been identified with Mississippi history for the last twenty-five years.

The Secessionists of Arkansas are making a noble and heroic struggle to carry the State out of the Union in August. If valor, energy and devotion to principle can win the victory, little Arkansas will soon be where she properly belongs—a star in the galaxy of the Confederate States.

In the historical collection at the palace at Berlin there are two cannon balls, each with one side flattened, said to have been fired by opposite parties at the siege of Magdeburgh, and to have met together in the air.

The body of John Page, who was attached to a train of emigrants, assaulted by Indians in Arizona, on the 28th of February, was found in the early part of March. He must have lived two weeks after the attack, and had evidently starved to death.

M. Paul de Musset, known in French literary circles from the paper war he carried on with George Sand, whence arose the two *brochures*, Elle et Lui and Lui et Elle, is engaged in preparing for publication the correspondence of his late brother, Alfred de Musset.

The Boston edition of Macaulay's fifth volume is to comprise a critical and biographical sketch of Macaulay and his writings, by S. Austin Allibone, and a double page fac-simile from one of Macaulay's latest manuscripts.

About every fifth store on Broadway is labeled "To Let." One year of Republican domination in our national affairs will bring the whole city "To Let."

[N. Y. Day Book.

Col. J. M. Sanborn, late Commissioner of the State of Michigan, has offered to take the contract to supply Fort Sumter with men and provisions for the sum of $500,000.

The choice ballads and poems that have appeared in Bentley's Miscellany have been collected and published in one volume. Among them are Longfellow's Village Blacksmith and Excelsior.

In a case before the Paris Civil Tribunal the fact was revealed that the person who contracts with the city of Paris for supplying funerals, is bound to have constantly on hand not fewer than 6,000 coffins.

George W. Steed, for several years Commissioner of Revenue at Norfolk, Va., died on last Wednesday.

A Card.

UNJUST MONOPOLY.

Editors Delta—When, some years ago, the public interests and necessities of New Orleans required the creation of the two Railroads which now run from this city to Jackson, Miss., and to Opelousas, in this State, respectively, the manifold advantages which these roads would confer on real estate owners, drivers of cab and carriages, hotel keepers, &c., of this city, were paraded before the public in speeches, reports and newspaper leaders, in the most logical, eloquent and convincing terms. The consequence was, that the people of this city *en masse* came forward and subscribed to the utmost of their means towards the organization of these Railroad Companies. Real estate owners not only subscribed, but voted to tax themselves heavily for the benefit of the enterprises. Every man interested, in any manner, in the cab, carriage and baggage business, contributed his earnings, and every one of that important and influential class of our citizens who own or conduct hotels or large boarding-houses ON THEIR OWN ACCOUNT, subscribed liberally, and encouraged and aided the movement, in the hope which had been held out to them by the managers of the companies, that, besides the patriotism and enterprise to which they could lay claim, the increased profits and benefits to their business would augment in wonderful proportions.

Well, thus it was, the road was built. Now what is the result. Have we, the people of New Orleans, the just, free and indiscriminate enjoyment of the advantages which were to flow so naturally from the successful construction of these roads? Or, are not the companies so managed as to divert these from the people to whom they legitimately belong—the permanent and tax-paying citizens of New Orleans—towards the enrichment of such as have no sympathy with our section, and have never contributed a dollar towards these enterprises? These are questions which the people desire answered, and which must, before long, be solved.

Many of our citizens, with great justice, complain bitterly of the wrong done them by the New Orleans, Jackson and Great Northern Railroad Company, in giving exclusive and vital privileges to Wilbur & Co., who run a line of omnibuses for the purpose of gathering up passengers and travelers on these roads for *certain hotels* in this city, and for them alone. Wilbur & Co. have the sole and important privilege of sending runners, free of expense, on the road, for the purpose of checking baggage and leading passengers (like innocent lambs) to their omnibuses, which are allowed a very convenient stand at the depot, and by means of which the passengers are conveyed and handed over to the tender mercies of certain hotel-keepers, (between whom and Wilbur & Co. there exists, of course, no particular privity or friendship,) and are not allowed to go where their own free will would lead them. Now, the question arises, was the Jackson Railroad built for the exclusive benefit of Wilbur & Co., and two or three hotels, whose owners have little or no identity with our city or State? Persons owning property in various parts of this city, tax-payers, stock holders in the company, and indeed, every man having a permanent home in this city, have an interest in this matter, and it is their duty to see that such unjust, discriminating, illiberal and unpatriotic monopolies should terminate. Let the managers of the company be brought to account. Let the republican principle—*the greatest good to the greatest number*—triumph; let there be fair play, and equal and impartial justice, and then no complaint will be heard. But these wrongs must cease; and the sooner the directors of the railroad act in the premises, the better.

mar23 Thur&W 1m* CITIZENS.

THE DAILY DELTA

FROM THE EVENING EDITION OF YESTERDAY.

Thanks to the purser of the steamship Florida for late Apalachacola papers.

We are pleased to meet in our city that eminent and eloquent divine and sincere and earnest Southern patriot, the Rev. C. L. Marshall, of Vicksburg, who is devoting his great talents and energies to the cause of the South.

First Regiment Louisiana Infantry.—We call attention to the fact that the Recruiting Officers of this regiment are paying two dollars premium to citizens or soldiers who may bring recruits to any one of the stations, the money being paid at the station so soon as the men are sworn into the service. The stations are advertised in another column.

We heard of one very notable exception to the general liberality of our merchants in aiding the equipment of our volunteers for Pensacola. This was the case of the head of one of our largest wholesale dry-good stores, whose annual sales exceed a million of dollars a year, who, when solicited for five dollars in aid of the volunteers, replied that he "could not afford to give for such a purpose." That man has made a quarter of a million of dollars from the trade of the South.

As an offset to this, we may relate an instance of the patriotic conduct of our neighbor, A. G. James, also a large wholesale dry goods merchant, who, hearing that one of his clerks, a young man, the only son of a widowed mother, had gone with our volunteers to Pensacola, informed the widow that her son's salary should be promptly paid to her during his absence, and that if he should fall in the defense of his country, that his salary should be paid to her weekly for five years. The same gentleman made the same offer to several of his clerks and warehousemen.

WHAT THE MORNING JOURNALS SAY.

The *Crescent* exposes the unparalleled duplicity of Seward in keeping our Commissioners at Washington with assurances of peaceful intentions, and in producing a general impression on the minds of Unionists in the Border States that the purposes of the Administration are pacific, and then suddenly commencing vigorous war measures. History does not record a more flagrant instance of low cunning. This treachery, however, had its Northern as well as its Southern victims. The former have greater reasons for complaint than the latter. We refer to the Northern bidders for the loan of the United States. These bidders were induced to make their offers by the most emphatic and positive assurance of peaceful intents on the part of the Executive.

The *Bee* shows up the absurdity of an article in the London Herald, in which the capacity of the South to defend itself against the old Government is dwelt upon:

The Herald says, with a dogmatic air, that the Southern States are deficient in all that can render their independence possible. Ay, indeed! Deficient in what? Are they deficient in numbers? The population of the South exceeds that of the United Colonies when they measured their might with that of Great Britain, and emerged triumphantly from the ordeal. Are they deficient in means? Why the South possesses boundless wealth in her agricultural products. She owes next to nothing—not one-tenth of the public debt ... She will [illegible] exportation of cotton, which European powers will take care to keep unchecked. Is she deficent in courage, determination or martial spirit? If the wrtier of the slur upon the South were among us, he would soon find occasion to retract his rash assertion.

The truth is that the North possesses neither the constitutional power nor the resources requisite for the subjugation of the South. Her hands are tied by defective powers, and her hostility measurably neutralized by the strife of factions in her midst, while the South, simply standing upon the defensive, and sustained by the cordial support, sympathy and aid of all her sons, occupies a vantage ground which will tell in every conflict. If we deprecate war, it is not that we entertain the smallest misgiving of the result, or fear the power of the adversary, but because we are loth to be driven to bloodshed, even for the protection of our dearest rights. Every right-minded and true-hearted man must hate war, and especially that most abhorrent form of it—civil strife, but there are evils of even greater magnitude and more intolerable than war—national shame, dishonorable submission, enforced obedience to a detested tyranny, are harder yet to be borne, and sooner than tolerate them the South is ready to accept the dread arbitrament of the sword.

The *Bulletin*, referring to the preparations at the North for hostilities against the South, says:

We conversed with a friend yesterday, who within a few days has had an interview with Mr. Chase, the Secretary of the Treasury. After expressing his sympathies for business men, who must suffer inconvenience and loss from the rigid observance of the revenue laws, he remarked, in emphatic language, that this state of things could not continue any longer; that the Government would act promptly and energetically in effecting a remedy.

The leading Republican journals every where are urgent and even importunate in pressing upon the Federal Government a prompt and decided course of action. The New York Tribune is ferociously truculent, and breathes nothing else but slaughter; they are impatient to let slip upon us the dogs of war. Gen. Webb, of the Courier and Enquirer, has been from the start for showing no quarter to the "traitors and rebels." "Hemp for traitors" has been his battle cry since Major Anderson was driven from Fort Moultrie. The New York Times, in a few of its last numbers, is striving to urge the laggard Administration to do something to vindicate the honor of the country, save its wasting revenues, and protect the New England manufacturers who are threatened with ruin. The Times invokes the intervention of the Government to enforce the revenue laws, and the arguments it uses are cogent, and its reasoning most persuasive—and its conclusions are irresistible, if only its premises and facts were true and tenable.

The *Picayune*, which a few days ago entirely discredited this news as published in the Delta, of the warlike movements of the North, now holds the following language:

The Northern journals, in the confidence of the Administration, are willing to accept this as the issue. We read in all their columns, with scarcely an exception, that the momentous question is, in their view, simply that, whether the Government can maintain itself against a discontented and resisting people, and contain none of the original questions, whether the South has been wronged, or needs guarantees and concessions. The New York Times frankly states this to be the issue, simply and singly, and it therein reflects, unmistakably, the predominant thought at Washington.

It tells us that "slavery has nothing to do with the tremendous issues now awaiting decision;" that "the question is precisely what it would be if there were not a negro slave on American soil;" and it proceeds to define whether the constitution created a government which has the right to preserve itself in every way against any portion of the people which renounces it. In simpler terms still, the question is to be made whether the people of the South shall not be subjugated to a government which they repudiate, whatever may be their convictions of its hostility to them, and its perilous purposes against their peace. There is to be no judgment but the judgment of the Government; and no power of self-protection but in the mercy of the Government.

This is the question which the Lincoln Administration will have undertaken to determine in their own way, by fire and sword, whenever they fire a musket in denial of the right of the seven Confederate States to the rights of self-government.

MONTGOMERY CORRESPONDENCE.

Special Correspondence of the Delta.

MONTGOMERY, April 9, 1861.

This town was yesterday thrown into unusual excitement by the news received from Charleston. A meeting of the Cabinet was called, and was in session the greater part of the afternoon. It is understood that up to the meeting yesterday, President Davis and Mr. Benjamin were the only two Executive officers here who believed we were to have war. Mr. Benjamin has, for a long time and frequently, expressed the opinion that war with the Black Republicans was inevitable; but until yesterday he was the only member of the Cabinet who entertained those views. But yesterday the Cabinet were unanimously and decidedly of the opinion that we were on the eve of a bloody contest, and that every preparation for it had already been made by Lincoln and his Cabinet. We, however, have not been idle, although hoping war might be avoided. President Davis and every member of his Cabinet have been preparing for it, and it is surprising how much has been done in so brief a period.

President Davis has called on the Confederated States for 19,000 men to be immediately equipped. Agents have been sent to Europe for more ammunition, and our supplies already on hand are very large. It is supposed by the Cabinet, that the war vessels sent from New York are destined for Fort Pickens. It is also supposed that reinforcements for this fort will not be landed from the island beyond the reach of our batteries, but at the wharf inside, purposely to draw Bragg's fire, and thus endeavor to create the ridiculous impression that we acted offensively and began the war. It is thought that all the vessels and all the troops from the North are intended for Fort Pickens, and at that point a bloody battle is to be fought. Indeed, I am informed, on reliable authority, that the President is in hourly expectation of hearing that the conflict has begun.

Bragg is instructed to fire into the vessels if they come within his reach and attempt to land troops. Should the troops be landed from beyond their reach, I think no attempt will at once be made by Bragg to take the fort. He is working day and night, and will be ready in a few days to capture the post, but the attempt will not be made at once, unless, as I have observed before, the United States vessels come inside the harbor, when in the emergency before mentioned they will be fired into, and the attack be made on the fort.

Official intelligence has been received here of the rejection of the Commissioners at Washington, and their expected return home. The delay has done us no harm; on the contrary, every hour has been of more service to us than to the people of the United States.

When events so important are so fast transpiring, correspondents for papers hardly know how to write. The news of the day and the predictions of the morrow may be old before their appearance in the public journals, but upon all I have written you may implicitly rely, as I have taken the greatest pains to substantiate all the facts I have stated.

Everybody is busy here working day and night for the coming event. The departments are all well organized; no time is lost; steadily, noiselessly, all pursue their labors, and the future historian will record the events passing around us in the acts of true and good men, conscious of restitution, gallantly and fearlessly preparing themselves for the great epoch of the 19th century.

TRANSIENT.

THE PERILS OF MINING—*A Man Buried Alive in a Shaft—Wonderful Escape.*—The Dubuque Times, of the 29th ult., records the following thrilling incident:

On Wednesday last an accident occurred in the mines, which borders on the marvelous, and is an illustration of the awful perils incident to the life of a miner. An old man named Day was at work alone in a deep shaft in Brunskill and Palmer's neighborhood. At about 1 o'clock in the afternoon, as he was busy at work, the rocks and earth caved in upon him. One huge stone, heavy enough to crush him to atoms, fell behind him, while another of still larger dimensions tumbled down in front of him, leaving a small crevice where he stood, and penning him tight against the side of the drift. These great boulders came up as high as his shoulders, and kept him from crawling out. The loose earth and sand kept constantly tumbling down for a long time, and filled the place about his body full. At last it began to fill up about his face and over his head. Slowly it rattled down piece-meal from above, filling up the space about his mouth and torturing him with distracting suspense. It was like being chained to a stake by the sea-shore and drowning by the tide.

He imagined that a few minutes would only elapse sometimes, but this old man maintained his self-possession entirely to the last minute, and by wagging his head from side to side, managed to get air enough for respiration. The earth ceased falling down after a while, so he no longer suffered anxiety from fear of being smothered, but how much worse fate was left for him. It would be by the merest chance that he was missed for a longtime, and if missed, no one would know where to seek him. He had just commenced on these diggings unknown to his neighbors, so slow starvation stared him in the face if he was not relieved. The long afternoon passed away, and, as the night approached, his wife began to look for him. The slow hours wore away, when she became alarmed, and sought the assistance of her neighbors. A party was soon collected; and with a vague idea where to look for the missing man, they started out.

Arriving at the right diggings by mere accident, they called out his name at the mouths of several shafts, and finally heard a faint response.

A man was let down by the windlass, and by the means of a tallow candle a small portion of the man's face was discovered. He stated that he was uninjured, but very much cramped in his position.

The men set to work to release him, and worked all the night through, not being able to get him out until 10 A. M. the next day. The first thing he asked for when he was raised to the surface was tobacco, and a few minutes after fainted. He slept several times during his confinement, and from all appearances he is unhurt.

A NORTHERN VIEW OF OUR LOAN.—From what we hear from the South, and from the confident tone of the Southern Press, it is safe to assume that the five million loan called for by the Southern Confederacy will not only be taken with promptitude, but nearly if not quite, at par. In this particular it will be in strong contrast with the eight millions called for by Secretary Chase, which, from present indications, is not likely to command over 93. One fact alone, which comes to us from a source entitled to credence, shows the confidence that Southern capitalists and business men repose in the Government. It is that every contractor who has furnished or undertaken to furnish the Southern Confederacy with any considerable quantity of supplies has agreed to receive a large per centage—in many instances, fifty per cent. of his pay in their Government securities. Indeed, one gentleman who has a large claim against the Government, which has been audited, and for which he can at any moment draw the money, declines to do so, preferring to wait and take the whole amount in bonds. We doubt not it will be found, when the time comes, that large numbers of patriotic and wealthy persons are ready and desirous of attesting their confidence in and satisfaction with the new Government by subscribing largely to this, its first call for pecuniary aid, and that they will have the gratification of being able to say to the people of the Old World: Our Confederacy, so much divided by the fanatics who have forced us into secession, possesses, in a far higher degree, the confidence of the people who compose it than is reposed in the Government of the United States; if proof be wanted, look at the loans—ours taken at par, or nearly par; yours at a discount of ten or twelve per cent. Republican journals and politicians may write sneeringly of it, and the London Times may turn up its nose and talk of the impossibility of raising five millions by a people who are "pledged to repudiation." Granted that President Davis is "the apostle of repudiation," and that the holders of Mississippi bonds have reason to remember his celebrated speech, delivered within the legislative hall built by British money, in which he ridiculed the "crocodile tears" of the "dupes who had ventured to petition for payment of their claims." This will not the less deter Southern men from coming forward to support a Government founded by themselves, and believed to be imperatively demanded to protect them from the detestable principles and aggressive action of the party which has accidentally found its way to power. [N. Y. Times.

Dante is to be further honored in Florence by the erection to his memory, in the Piazza della Signoria, of a noble statue. In May, 1865, there will be in that city a great national festival in honor of the poet, that being the sixth centennary commemoration of his birth. A similar festival will be held every five years, when medals will be awarded to the authors of the ten best works produced in the interval in relation to science, art and literature. It is also proposed to issue a new national edition of Dante, in six large royal octavo volumes, of six hundred pages each, with a supplementary volume containing lists of subscribers, and other matters. The text will be illustrated by the notes of the best living commentators on Dante.

This News is Official.

THE CONFLICT ACTUALLY COMMENCED.

BEAUREGARD OPENS HIS BATTERIES ON FORT SUMTER.

MONTGOMERY, April 12, 1861.

The conflict has commenced in Charleston.

Gen. Beauregard opened his batteries on Fort Sumter this morning at half-past 4 o'clock.

DISPATCH TO THE MAYOR.

Mayor Monroe this morning received the following dispatch:

MONTGOMERY, April 12, 1861.

Hon. J. T. MONROE, Mayor of New Orleans:

The Secretary of War informs me that Gen. Beauregard opened his batteries on Fort Sumter at 4½ o'clock this morning.

D. G. DUNCAN.

Special Dispatch to the Delta.

MONTGOMERY, April 12.

The following is the telegraphic correspondence between the War Department and Gen. Beauregard, in command of Charleston harbor, immediately preceding hostilities.

This correspondence grew out of the formal notification of the Washington Government, disclosed in Gen. Beauregard's first dispatch to the Secretary of War at Charleston.

[No. 1.]

CHARLESTON, April 8, 1861.

To L. P. WALKER, Secretary of War:

Authorized messengers from Lincoln just informed Gov. Pickens and myself that provision will be sent to Fort Sumter peaceably, if possible, but forcibly if necessary.

(Signed) G. T. BEAUREGARD.

[No. 2.]

Reply of Secretary of War to Gen. Beauregard:

MONTGOMERY, April 10, 1861.

If you have no doubt of the authorized character of the agent who communicated to you the intention of the Washington Government to supply Fort Sumter by force, you will at once demand its evacuation; and if this is refused, proceed, in such manner as you may determine, to reduce it. Answer.

(Signed) L. P. WALKER.

[No. 3.]

CHARLESTON, April 10, 1861.

To L. P. WALKER, Secretary of War:

The demand will be made to-morrow at 12 o'clock. Signed,

G. T. BEAUREGARD, Brig. Gen.

[No. 4.]

MONTGOMERY, April 10th, 1861.

The Secretary of War to Gen. BEAUREGARD:

Unless there are special reasons connected with your own condition, it is considered proper that you shall make the demand at an earlier hour. Signed, L. P. WALKER.

[No. 5.]

CHARLESTON, April 11, 1864.

To L. P. Walker, Secretary of War:

The reasons are special for 12 o'clock.

G. T. BEAUREGARD.

[No. 6.]

CHARLESTON, April 11, 1861.

To L. P. Walker, Secretary of War:

Demand sent at 2. Allowed till 6 to answer.

G. T. BEAUREGARD.

[No. 7.]

MONTGOMERY, April 11, 1861.

To Gen. Beauregard, Charleston:

Telegraph the reply of Anderson.

L. P. WALKER.

[No. 8.]

Gen. Beauregard to the Secretary of War:

CHARLESTON, April 11, 1861.

To L. P. WALKER, Secretary of War:

Major Anderson replies, "I have the receipt of your communication, demanding the evacuation of this fort, and to say in reply thereto, that it is a demand with which I regret that my sense of honor and of my obligation to my Government prevent my compliance."

He adds, verbally:

"I will await the first shot, and if you do not batter us to pieces, we will be starved out in a few days. Answer."

G. T. BEAUREGARD.

[No. 9.]

MONTGOMERY, April 11, 1861.

To G. T. BEAUREGARD, Charleston

We do not desire needlessly to bombard Fort Sumter.

Major Anderson will state the time at which, as indicated by him, he will evacuate, and agree that in the meantime he will not use his guns against us unless ours should be employed against Fort Sumter.

You are authorized thus to avoid the effusion of blood. If this or its equivalent be refused, reduce the fort as your judgment decides to be the most practicable.

L. P. WALKER,
Secretary of War.

[No. 10.]

Gen. BEAUREGARD to Secretary of War:

CHARLESTON, April 12.

He would not consent. I write to-day.

G. T. BEAUREGARD.

[No. 11.]

Gen. BEAUREGARD to the Secretary of War:

CHARLESTON, April 12.

I opened fire at 4:30 this morning.

G. T. BEAUREGARD.

NOTE.—An intercepted dispatch discloses the fact that Mr. Fox, who had been allowed to visit Major Anderson on the pledge that his purpose was pacific, employed his opportunity to devise a plan for supplying the fort by force, and that his plan had been adopted by the Washington Government and was in progress of execution.

Congress to Meet on the 29th Inst.

MONTGOMERY, April 12.

Announce in the Delta that President Davis has issued his proclamation convening Congress to meet on Monday, the 29th inst.

The above request is made at the instance of Attorney General Benjamin.

TELEGRAPHIC NEWS.

TELEGRAPHED TO THE NEW ORLEANS DAILY DELTA.

STARTLING INTELLIGENCE.

Fire Opened on Fort Sumter.

MONTGOMERY, April 12.—The Secretary of War says Gen. Beauregard opened fire on Fort Sumter this morning, at half-past four o'clock.

Vessels Prohibited to Pass Fort Pulaski.

SAVANNAH, April 11.—Orders have been issued prohibiting hostile vessels from passing Fort Pulaski.

Lieut. Talbot at Norfolk.

NORFOLK, April 11.—Lieut. Talbot and Mr. R. E. Chew have arrived here.

Change in Mr. Lincoln's Cabinet.

WASHINGTON, April 11.—There are rumors afloat, which are false, that a change is about to take place in Mr. Lincoln's Cabinet.

Border State Men in the Southern Army.

MONTGOMERY, April 11.—Upwards of 7000 men from the Border States have offered their services to the army of the Confederate States.

Charleston Affairs.

CHARLESTON, April 11.—Hon. Roger A. Pryor, of Virginia, has been appointed on General Beauregard's staff.

Major Anderson has declined to accede to Gen. Beauregard's summons for the surrender, with a reservation.

It is, however, currently reported that negotiations will be opened on the 12th between Major Anderson and Gen. Beauregard.

The Southern Commissioners.

WASHINGTON, April 11.—The Southern Commissioners charge the Administration with gross perfidy in attempting to reinforce Fort Sumter under pretext of evacuation.

They say the Montgomery Government earnestly desires peace. They return, convinced that war is inevitable, saying the responsibility rests upon the Administration.

United States Treasury.

WASHINTON, April 11.—The balance in the Treasury last month was $5,161,000.

The receipts from customs the week ending April 9, exceed those of the corresponding period last year by $29,400.

The Treasury bids exceed the demand by nearly $5,000,000. The Treasury is now in good condition.

Steamboats Passing Vicksburg.

VICKSBURG, April 12.—The Mars passed down at 4, and the H. R. W. Hill at 7 P. M. yesterday. The Yazoo at 2, and the Diana at 9 o'clock this morning.

Charles Reade publishes in the Literary Gazette a protest in regard to the way in which his Never Too Late to Mend has been ruthlessly dramatized without his consent. He signs himself "Charles Reade, sole author in all its forms of Never Too Late to Mend, of which seven nameless scribblers advertise themselves as the authors," and at the beginning of his protest premises that "an author is neither an outlaw, nor a dog, nor a disembodied spirit, nor even a mixture of the three, but a man and a citizen, with a citizen's claim to remuneration when he writes for another, and by inevitable consequence, a citizen's claim to be sole proprietor of his own production, when he creates it at his own cost, and honestly."

Mr. Frith, the academician, has added a new word to the English language—"skying," as applied to the ruthless maintop gallant-most hanging of the British Institution Committee. Some of our artists will find the participle applicable to the position of their pictures in the Academy.

CROPS IN ENGLAND.—The London Economist of the 9th ult., expresses apprehension concerning the coming crop:

We have arrived at a critical perid of the year as regards the produce of the next harvest. The season for sowing spring wheat is rapidly passing away, while the land has latterly not been in a favorable state for sowing. There was a great quantity of rain last week, which not only stopped all worh upon the land for some time, but left the soil so beaten down that wheat sowing became difficult. Mr. Caird, in the House of Commons recently, estimated the deficiency of last year's harvest at thirty-six per cent. In the same speech he gave an account of the successive agricultural disasters which, beginning in the autumn of 1859, prepared the way for the inadequate harvest of last year.

In October, 1859, the heaviest frost known for many years occurred, and not only prevented much such sowing, but extensively destroyed green fodder crops. A severer winter followed this short allowance, succeeded by a cold, wet, backward spring, and a cold, wet summer. Much grass was lost thereby, and the same bad weather continued through the harvest. Rain fell for thirty five of the forty days from July 21 to August 31, and the thermometer ranged 13° below the previous season. The crop was consequently lost, except in some of the earlier counties. At the same time the potato crop failed in Ireland, and corn had to be imported for that country as well as England. The wheat which was got in this spring before the rain looks well. There must be a deficiency, however, under the most favorable circumstances.

GUSTAVUS MODENA.—The same day, says our cotemporary, L'Eco d'Italia, that the Italian Parliament assembled at Turin, and proclaimed Victor Emanuel King of regenerated Italy, (Feb. 21,) a large concourse of people followed a great man to the grave—one who had contributed much by his words, his pen, and his sword, to the triumph of so noble a cause. This man was Italy's greatest tragic artist, Gustavus Modena, who, peacefully and resigned, closed his eyes to the light of day like a laborer ending his daily work. As an actor he was judged for what he was—a man of genius. As a writer, he handled the Italian language as the sculptor handles the facile clay, shaping it as he desires, and giving to it the most graceful forms. As a politician, he always fought the enemies of his country, whoever they were. As a citizen and a man, the historian will find in him an inexhaustible treasure of unique and incomparable traits of friendship and ineffable charity. When his name was announced as an acter in Alfieri's tragedies, or as a reader and declaimer of Dante, no theater, no concert hall was large enough to contain the crowds that flocked to hear him. His remains were followed to the grave by thousands of all classes, from the highest functionary of the government to the humblest citizen; men, women, children, all were there to pay the Roscius of Italy the last earthly tribute. Modena died in the faith of the Waldenses, and among his pall-bearers were many generals of the armies of Garibaldi and Victor Emanuel, several deputies, and his Excellency the Chevalier Lorenzo Valerio, Governor of Como, who represented the Italian Government. His remains were deposited in the cemetery of Turin, in the lot reserved for the community of the Waldenses.

INTERESTING TO YACHTSMEN.—It will be seen by the following paragraph from an English paper, that the grand British regatta of July next is open to comers from all the world:

The Royal Mersey Yacht Club having decided on holding a general regatta on the 4th and 5th of July next on the Mersey, her Majesty has graciously expressed through her Secretary, her intention of presenting a £100 cup to the club, to be sailed for by yachts belonging to any royal or national club—in other words, the competition will be open to all the world. A general subscription has been entered into by the members of the club, in order that the regatta may be conducted on the most liberal and extensive scale, and many liberal donations have already been received. A full programme will be issued in due time.

ESCAPE OF A MURDERER.—The Apilachicola Times says that James O'Connor, who was convicted of the murder of his wife, at the spring term of 1858, and afterward tried and sentenced to be hanged, made his escape from jail on Thursday. O'Connor was closely confined and heavily ironed to the floor of his cell, nevertheless with the aid of a knife he succeeded in cutting the two bolts which secured his irons. This being accomplished, the bolt of the lock of his cell door was next forced aside and his escape was easily effected.

In the cell was found a note, written by O'Connor, certifying that he had received no assistance from any one—that he had effected his escape by the use of a knife he found in a chink in the walls of his cell.

This convict made a similar escape last August, and after being at large two months, returned to the jail, and asked to be again placed in his old quarters.

THE ROTARY FORTRESS.—A French mechanic, by the name of Balbi, has lately invented a new kind of fortress, which works upon a plan that must astonish any hostile party that shall attempt to take it by assault. The new machine is in the shape of a round tower, ... non, the motive power which regulates its movements being steam. It is to be cased in a cuirass of iron plates, and so managed that on the first attempt at an escalade on the part of the enemy, the tower begins to revolve with a rapidity which renders it inaccessible, while, for the same reason, the picking off by an enemy of its defenders by the truest rifle becomes a matter of infinite difficulty. It can be propelled, like any conveyance moved by steam apparatus, from place to place, with similar speed. Its base is thickly set with pikes, which, once in rotation, would annihilate all who might approach it.

TWO MACAULYS.—Baron Macaulay is not the first English historian of that name. About a century ago flourished one Catherine Macaulay, who wrote and published a five-volume History of England, from the accession of James the First to the elevation of the House of Hanover. The book—clever, piquant and calumnious—was an immense success, and brought the author a profit of several thousand pounds, which aroused the envy of both Goldsmith and Johnson. Five years after Catherine Macaulay published her fifth volume Gibbon brought out the first of his Decline and Fall. He did not at the time meet with the success of his female rival; yet to-day everybody reads Gibbon, and very few have ever heard of Catherine Macaulay.

M. Garnier-Pages, who was formerly Mayor of Paris, and afterwards a member of the Provisional Government, will shortly publish a History of the Revolution of 1848, giving an account of all the political events of that memorable year. It will appear in four parts, under the following titles: The Revolution of 1848 in Europe, in three volumes; The Fall of Royalty, in one volume; The 24th of February, 1848, also in one volume; and The Provisional Government, in three volumes. The intimate knowledge which M. Garnier-Pages must necessarily have of the transactions of that period will enable him to produce a work of more than European interest.

The latest contributions to English Shakespeariana are entitled: Shakespeare's Puck and his Folk Lore; Illustrated from the Superstitions of all Nations, (second volume,) by William Bell; Shakespeare, his Birthplace and its Neighborhood," by John R. Wise; Shakespeare, a Critical Biography, and an Estimate of the Facts, Fancies, Forgeries, and Fabrications regarding his Life and Works which have appeared in Remote and Recent Literature, by Samuel Neil; and Proposed Emendations of the Text of Shakespeare's Plays, by Swynssen Jervis.

ENORMOUS PROFITS OF A RAILROAD.—The Cleveland and Erie Railroad, about 95 miles long, earned in 1860, $1 664,000, at a cost of $429 000, leaving a net profit of $1.233,000 on a capital—representing a cost of building and equipping the road—of only $4 602,000, showing a net profit of nearly twenty-seven per cent. The funded debt is only $1,602,000. The company could, therefore, after paying interest on the funded debt of seven per cent., declare a dividend of twenty-four per cent.

It is said that the celebrated San Carlos Theater at Naples will be placed under the management of Mr. Smith, lessee of Her Majesty's and Drury Lane theaters, London. Is is added that Mr. Smith can for several years offer the services of the following eminent singers: Of ladies, Grisi, Titiens, Lotti, della Santa, Borghi-Mamo, Gassier, Alboni, &c; and of gentleman, Mario, Giuglini, Mongini, Belart, Everardi, Vialetti and others.

The D'Aumale will occupy the chair at the next annual dinner of the Royal Literary Fund, London, on the 15th of May. Mr. Monckton Milnes, who announced the fact, eulogized the Duke for his royal descent, and congratulated the Society on the prospect of having a "foreign royal personage" to preside over them. The Duc d'Aumale, by-the-way, is a zealous biblio-maniac.

EFFECTS OF BAD WRITING.—It is stated that Mr. A. B. Dickinson, of New York, the newly-appointed Lincoln Minister to Nicaragua, was an applicant for the office of Marshal in Nebraska. His handwriting being indistinct, Seward thought he asked for the post of Minister in Nicaragua, and, being a friend, appointed him minister instead of marshal.

The London Literary Gazette for March 16th certains an elaborate review of Helper's "Impending Crisis," in the course of which it remarks: "We suppose this is the sort of book likely to further the good cause in America; for sixty-eight experienced senators, with Christian names ranging from Isaiah to Galusha, say so."

Owen Mahoney was found dead in a wood, at Franklin, Me., last week. In his pockets was a bottle of liquor and a bank-book showing a credit of $800.

CITY INTELLIGENCE.

INQUEST IN THE CASE OF THE MURDER OF JOHN RILEY BY WM. GALLAGHER—*Verdict Wilful Murder.* The inquest took place to-day before Coroner Beach:

Pat Conway sworn: On Thursday, at 2 o'clock P. M., at the corner of Notre Dame and Fulton streets, Wm. Gallagher and Pat Thompson were fighting in the street opposite my coffee-house, known as the Conway House, when a man named John Riley went between them to separate them, and as he did so Gallagher drew out a sheath knife and plunged it into the neck of John Riley, and then ran away immediately. Riley then came up to me and said he was killed, and asked me to take him to a doctor. He then lay down on the corner of the street and died.

Pat Thompson: I and the man who is killed were in company together, sitting in the coffee-house known as Conway's House, on Thursday, 11th April, in the afternoon. While we were sitting there, Gallagher and his partner came in, and stood leaning back to the counter. I was sitting on a chair. Gallagher's partner and one of the men sitting with me got into a scuffle. I got up from my chair to separate them; as I did so, Gallagher put his hand in his coat pocket, and pulled out a knife—a long and broad bladed one. As saw him pull out the knife, I stepped to one side of him and gave Gallagher a shove, and I shoved him outside of the door. Patrick McDermott halloed out to me, "Look out, Thompson, he is going to cut you." I ran into the street, and back again into the house, to avoid him; and as I ran to the house, I heard Riley say to him, "You should not draw a knife on any man." As Riley said this, Gallagher ran up to Riley and plunged the knife into Riley's neck. He then ran off, and I followed him, when I overtook an officer who was running after him; I then went with the officer, and saw Gallagher run into McDermot's house on New Levee street; as he ran in he closed the door; he then put his head up to a broken pane of glass in the door; the officer then waited for another officer to come up, when they went in and arrested the man in the privy; I am positive that Gallagher is the man who did the stabbing.

Pat McDermot testified to the same.

Police officer Berwin testified to his seeing Gallagher running and his following. The officer blew his whistle for aid, and still pursued Gallagher until he came to a coffee-house, where he went in, the officer still after him. The officer pushed the door open. Here Gallagher turned on the officer at the door, pushing the door to, and attempted to stab him with a sheath knife. The knife was stained with blood. He then ran into the rear yard, and the officer called for assistance, when officer Cregan came up, and they both went and arrested Gallagher, who said, "arrest me like a gentleman, and I'll go with you." The officers then searched for the knife, but could not find it.

This closed the evidence, and the verdict rendered was wilful murder.

MALICIOUS SCOUNDRELS BOGUS BULLETINS.—Some malicious scoundrels, evidently closely intimate with our enemies, the enemies of the South, are posting bulletins on the street corners announcing the most transparent falsehoods regarding the serious state of affairs in which our citizens, our sons and brothers' honor and lives are at present at stake.

We saw this morning a paper posted on the corner of Common and Carondelet streets, announcing a vilainous falsehood, and stating it emanated from a newspaper office. Had this reporter an opportunity of laying his hands on the rascally fabricator of the unmanly, mendacious *canard*, he would have placed the vagabond where he and all his Lincoln confederates should be.

This trifling with the feelings of a community in such serious times, is unpardonable, and we trust the police and good and loyal citizens will make an example of the first malicious rascal who publishes falsehoods knowingly. These are times when we want no internal feuds, when we all should be banded together against our common enemy, and he who is not with us, we repeat, is against us. Look to them, police; look to them, loya citizens.

The Charleston Mercury Extra.

Saturday Evening, April 13, 1861.

THE BATTLE OF FORT SUMTER!

END OF THE FIGHT!

MAJOR ANDERSON SURRENDERS!

All last night the mortar batteries were throwing shells into the Fort. At an early hour this morning the gun batteries re-opened their fire, which had been suspended during the night. Major ANDERSON replied about seven o'clock with a vigorous fire. It appeared that he had become convinced that his fire against the Cummings' Point Batteries was ineffectual, for he now devoted his attention almost entirely to Fort Moultrie, the Dahlgren Battery and the Floating Battery. At ten minutes after eight, A. M., a thick smoke was seen issuing from the parapet, and the roof of the southern portion of Fort Sumter barracks was soon in flames. The fire was produced either by a hot shot or a shell. During the progress of the fire, three explosions were produced by the fall of shells into the combustibles of the Fort.

At a quarter to one o'clock the flag and flag-staff of the United States was shot away. For some twenty minutes no flag appeared above the fort. Col. L. T. WIGFALL, in a small boat, approached it from Morris Island, with a white flag upon his sword. Having entered, he called for Major ANDERSON, stated that he was an Aid-de-Camp of Gen. BEAUREGARD; that seeing his distress and the impossibility of his holding the post, he claimed, in the name of his Chief, its surrender. In reply to the inquiry "what terms will be granted," he stated that Gen. BEAUREGARD was a soldier and a gentleman, and knew how to treat a gallant enemy, but that Major ANDERSON could not make his own terms, and must leave the details to Gen. BEAUREGARD.

Major ANDERSON then agreed to surrender to General BEAUREGARD, in the name of the Confederate States, and hauled down his flag, which he had again lifted, accompanied by a white flag.

The batteries then ceased firing, and Colonel WIGFALL reported to General BEAUREGARD, in Charleston.

The following are substantially the terms of the capitulation:

All proper facilities will be afforded for the removal of Major ANDERSON and command, together with company arms and property, and all private property.

The flag which he has upheld so long, and with so much fortitude, under the most trying circumstances, may be saluted by him on taking it down.

Major ANDERSON is allowed to fix the time of surrender, which is some time to-morrow (Sunday). He prefers going from Fort Sumter to the fleet off our bar.

A detachment of the regular army from Sullivan's island will be transferred to Fort Sumter; and one detachment from Morris Island.

No one has been killed or wounded upon our side. A few of the garrison of Fort Sumter were slightly wounded.

The Catawba will take Major ANDERSON to the fleet.

LATEST FROM MORRIS ISLAND.

HOSTILITIES SUSPENDED FOR THE NIGHT.

MORRIS ISLAND, Saturday, April 13, 6 P. M.

A boat sent in by the fleet of war vessels off the Bar, has just been brought to by a shot from one of our batteries. It contained, besides the oarsmen, Lieut. MARCY, of the Powhatan, bearing a flag of truce. He reports the vessels in the offing to be the Baltic, Illinois, Powhatan, Harriet Lane, and Pawnee.

Lieut. Marcy, in the name of his superior officers, has announced a suspension of hostilities until to-morrow morning.

It is rumored that he demands that Major ANDERSON and his men be allowed to join the fleet.

SOUTH CAROLINA
IS INDEPENDENT!

The Daily True Delta

SATURDAY, APRIL 13, 1861.

AMUSEMENTS TO-NIGHT.

VARIETIES THEATRE—John Bull—Perfection.
OPERA HOUSE—Rigoletto.
MAGNOLIA HALL—Free Concert by Twelve Talented Artistes.
ACADEMY OF MUSIC—Robert Heller, the Renowned Wizard.
VANNUCHI'S MUSEUM—Gallery of Art, 107 *St Charles street.*

TO OUR ADVERTISERS.

Our advertising friends will confer a great favor on us, and at the same time subserve their own interests by sending in all matter intended for Sundays publication, at as early an hour as possible this evening.

SUNDAY TRUE DELTA.

THE ONLY FIRST-CLASS LITERARY AND NEWS JOURNAL IN THE CITY—LARGEST CIRCULATION.

ORIGINAL CONTENTS. — Pen Sketches for Sunday, embracing literary and dramatic reviews; other editorials; the Pulpit of New Orleans; poetry, &c.

COMPILED AND SELECTED.—New anecdotes of the celebrated Richard Brinsley Sheridan; Household Receipts; Latest Fashions; Something of Gen. Sumter, after whom Fort Sumter is named; Women, North and South; Spice of Humor; Historic Sketch of Cleopatra; How beautiful eyes are kept beautiful; Extraordinary Scenes in the Pacific; poetry, &c.

NEWS.—The very latest news, political and otherwise, by mails and telegraph.

LOCAL, &c.—The very latest city, river and general commercial intelligence.

A SUGGESTION.—The fighting force, thus far, that has been organized in this city, and that have marched to the deadly breach, is composed of at least nine-tenths of those who voted the co-operation ticket. We now suggest that something like an equal division of the danger, as well as the glory, should be made. This can be easily done by the forming of a brigade of those who were the prime movers in the game of disruption. Let our ancient and war-like friend, Col. Slidell, be appointed to a brigadier-generalship; Col. Hatch, who is only a colonel by brevet, to a *de facto* colonel of the line; Major J. T. Semmes, to be lieutenant colonel, and several others that we might name, to the posts of sutlers, &c., &c. With such a brigade before Fort Pickens or elsewhere, the Zouaves would be no where.

☞ The purser of the steamship Tennessee, from Vera Cruz, has again laid us under obligations for his polite attentions, for which we return thanks.

☞ Messrs. James Hewitt & Co., Liverpool, have our acknowledgments for their circular per Africa.

☞ The purser of the Matagorda has our acknowledgment for late Texas papers.

GEN. TRACY'S BRIGADE.—The different companies of this brigade are ordered to assemble at their respective armories forthwith, and report themselves for active service in the field. See official notice in another column.

A CALL ON NICARAGUANS.—It will be seen by a notice in another column that a call is made by Major Dolan, late of the Nicaraguan army, on the old veterans who distinguished themselves under General Walker, to rally in defence of the south. Applications to be made at 99 Gravier street.

THE GENUINE KEROSINE OIL.—Covert & Hill, No. 6 Chartres street, have just received several large invoices of the genuine Downer Kerosine oil. Until recently it was impossible, owing to the great demand for this article, to obtain a full supply of it. Country merchants and planters should take a note of this.

THE WASHINGTON BATTALION ABOUT TO TAKE THE FIELD.—By reference to an official notice in another column, it will be seen the battalion of Washington Artillery is ordered to assemble at its arsenal at 9 o'clock this (Saturday) morning, fully equipped for active field service. The destination of the battalion is, we presume, Fort Pickens or Fort Jackson.

☞ R. M. Montgomery sells this day at 12 o'clock, at the Tattersalls stables, 164 Gravier street, a large lot of fine harness and saddle horses and mares, in pairs and single, good work mules, fine barouches and buggies. Persons wishing good stock can buy with as much confidence as at private sale, as they have the privilege of trying stock before paying for it. See advertisement.

SPRING AND SUMMER CLOTHING.—Our friends, Alfred Munroe & Co., of the palace clothing store, corner of Camp and Common streets, are now opening for the inspection of their customers, a fresh importation of spring and summer clothing, of the latest styles. Those requiring an outfit on economical terms, should lose no time in calling on Alfred Munroe & Co.

ATTENTION, MONTGOMERY GUARDS.—The members of this gallant company are ordered to appear at their armory at 9 o'clock this morning, preparatory to taking the field for active service. It is only necessary, we know, to pass the word along the ranks—"Montgomery Guards, prepare for action!" to bring every member of the corps into line of battle.

☞ McCerren & Landry will sell without reserve the following properties, at 11 o'clock this morning, at their auction mart, Masonic hall:

1. A certain lot of ground on Derbigny street, between St. Louis street and Carondelet walk, having a two-story frame house thereon—a double tenement.
2. A certain lot of ground in the Fourth district, fronting on Second street, between Division and Rousseau streets.
3. The residence of P. C. Perret, Esq., in Carrollton, with the grounds attached, forming about two-thirds of the square, bounded by Milton, Dakin, Upper Line and Shakspeare streets.

The above are all *to be* sold without reserve, as the owners are about departing from the city.

McC. & L. also sell this morning at their salesroom, Masonic hall, the boy Joseph, a black, aged 35, a good field hand.

☞ The number of agricultural societies in the United States, registered on the mailing book of the agricultural division of the patent office, March 29th, 1861, was as follows:

Alabama	9	Missouri	38
Arkansas	2	Nebraska Territory	12
California	16	New Hampshire	9
Connecticut	12	New Jersey	17
Delaware	4	New Mexico	1
District of Columbia	2	New York	115
Florida	0	North Carolina	9
Georgia	20	Ohio	111
Illinois	97	Oregon	5
Indiana	82	Pennsylvania	85
Indian Territory	1	Rhode Island	2
Iowa	95	South Carolina	14
Kansas	1	Tennessee	21
Kentucky	17	Texas	34
Louisiana	5	Utah Territory	2
Maine	23	Vermont	15
Maryland	11	Virginia	32
Massachusetts	45	Washington Territory	2
Michigan	29	Wisconsin	56
Minnesota	31		
Mississippi	19	Total	1101

☞ The New York Day Book, alluding to the opening of the spring book trade sales in that city, says the catalogue is larger this year than usual, but that "there is not a single purchaser present from the Confederate States."

THE SUPREME JUDGESHIP.—A Washington letter says a movement is on foot to induce Chase to take the Supreme judgeship, made vacant by the death of McLean. In that case Cameron would assume the treasury, and Robert C. Schenck, of Ohio, would be secretary of war.

MADAME CAPRELL,

The only great Natural CLAIRVOYANT, who has won the golden opinions of the world, and proved by her correct delineations of her visitor's life, that mysteries can be Clairvoyantly revealed, and the future predicted so perfect and reliably as to guard against many difficulties and casualties. No stranger should leave the city before visiting M'me Caprell, at her rooms, 127 Customhouse street, where much concerning one's self may be learned, for the powers of Clairvoyance are unbounded. Horoscopic charts of life forwarded by mail, upon receipt of day of birth. Satisfaction guaranteed. ap13 1t2dp&W*

Telegraphed to the True Delta.

LATEST AND IMPORTANT FROM CHARLESTON

Firing on Sumter Certain.

AUGUSTA, April 12.—Passengers just arrived from Charleston announce that the firing on Sumter began this morning at half-past four o'clock.

NEWS FROM MONTGOMERY.

AN EXTRA SESSION OF CONGRESS CALLED.

SEVEN GUNS FIRED IN HONOR OF THE ATTACK.

LETTERS OF MARQUE TO BE ISSUED.

PROPOSED SEIZURE OF WASHINGTON.

MONTGOMERY, April 12.—An extra session of the Confederate Congress is called for on the 29th of April.

The government has, up to half-past one o'clock to-day, received nothing later from Charleston. It is supposed that Major Anderson returned the fire.

[SECOND DISPATCH.]

Seven guns were fired to-day in front of the executive building in the presence of the cabinet members, in honor of the attack on Fort Sumter by the Confederate forces. There is great rejoicing among the citizens. Three cheers were given for Gen. Beauregard, and three more for President Davis.

No further news from Charleston has been made public.

The cabinet was in session all day discussing important matters. Letters of marque and reprisal will be issued immediately.

Gen. Roman, in conjunction with Major Ben. McCullough, proposes to this government to have twenty-five thousand men in Washington in ten days, to take Lincoln and General Scott prisoners of war.

Major McCullough has ten thousand men now in Virginia, and has purchased ten thousand stand of arms to circulate.

The president has issued his call for an extra session of Congress, to convene on the 29th of April.

Rejoicing in Mobile.

MOBILE, April 12.—The most intense excitement prevails. There is great rejoicing among the citizens. Fifteen guns were fired in honor of the attack on Fort Sumter.

Steamer Vanderbilt Chartered as a Transport.

NEW YORK, April 12.—The U. S. government has chartered the steamer Vanderbilt, of the New York and Southampton line, as a transport. She proceeded to the Brooklyn navy-yard to-day to be fitted out in the required manner.

The Virginia Commissioners.

WASHINGTON, April 11.—The commissioners appointed by the Virginia convention to demand of Mr. Lincoln what policy he intends pursuing towards the seceded states, arrived in this city to-day, and will soon lay the object of their mission before the administration.

Hostilities at Charleston.

WASHINGTON, April 12.—Private southern dispatches leave no reasonable doubt that hostilities at Charleston commenced at an early hour this morning.

Gen. Beauregard telegraphed from Charleston on the 8th to Mr. Walker, the secretary of war, "that Lincoln had notified Gov. Pickens and himself that provisions would be sent to Fort Sumter, peaceably or otherwise."

Mr. Walker, (Montgomery, 10th,) responds, "to demand the evacuation, and if refused, to proceed to reduce the fort."

Gen. Beauregard, (Charleston, 10th,) replies, "the demand will be made to-morrow at 12 o'clock."

Mr. Walker (Montgomery, 11th,) says to Gen. Beauregard, "Unless there are special reasons connected with your condition, it is considered proper for you to make the demand at an earlier hour."

Gen. Beauregard (Charleston, 10th,) says, "The reasons are special for twelve o'clock."

Gen. Beauregard (Charleston, 11th,) says, "The demand sent at 2. Allowed till 6 to answer."

Major Anderson (Fort Sumter, 11th,) replies that his sense of honor and obligations to the government prevent his compliance, adding, "Probably I will await orders from the president, and if you don't batter us to pieces, we will be starved out in a few days."

Secretary Walker (Montgomery, 10th,) then telegraphs Gen. Beauregard: "We do not desire needlessly to bombard Fort Sumter, and if Major Anderson will state when he will evacuate, and in the meantime not use his guns against us until we fire, you are thus to avoid bloodshed. If something equivalent to this is not agreed to, reduce the fort in the most practicable manner."

Gen. Beauregard (Charleston, 12th,) telegraphs Secretary Walker: "He would not consent. I write to-day."

Intercepted Dispatches.

CHARLESTON, April 11.—Intercepted dispatches disclose that Mr. Fox, who visited Major Anderson on pledge of pacific purposes, devised a plan to supply Fort Sumter by force, and this plan has been adopted by the federal government and is in progress of execution.

Volunteers from Kentucky.

LOUISVILLE, April 12.—Dispatches were received here to-day, to hold the Kentucky volunteer regiment in readiness to move at a moment's notice from the Montgomery war department.

The Pennsylvania Militia.

HARRISBURG, April 12.—The legislative bill was reported in the House to-day, appropriating $5,000,000 to arm and eqnip the Pennsylvania militia.

New York Markets.

NEW YORK, April 12.—The cotton market closed dull, with sales of 850 bales at 12½@12⅝c. for middling uplands. Flour steady; holders are pressing their stock on the market; sales 9750 bbls. at $5 20@$5 30 for superfine state. Corn was steady, while the sales comprised 69,000 bushels at 63 to 70c. Pork buoyant; sales 825 bbls. at $17 50 for mess. Lard firm; sales 415 bbls. at 9¾ to 10c. per lb.

Cincinnati Markets.

CINCINNATI, April 12.—The flour market closed dull at unchanged prices. Corn closed steady at 33c. ℔ bushel. Oats steady at 26c. ℔ bushel. Whisky—sales at 13½c. ℔ gallon. Lard is quoted at 9¼@9½c. ℔ lb. Sugar is selling at 6@7½c. ℔ lb. Molasses—sales at 31@33c. ℔ gallon. Coffee is worth 13@14½c. ℔ lb.

River Intelligence.

ST. LOUIS, April 12.—The Ohio river at this point is swelling, with twenty feet water to Cairo. The upper Mississippi and Missouri are rising rapidly.

HIGHLY IMPORTANT FROM CHARLESTON.

THE SULLIVAN AND MORRIS' ISLAND BATTERIES AT WORK.

FORT SUMTER OPENED FIRE.

A BREACH MADE IN THE FORT.

WAR VEESELS REPORTED OUTSIDE.

CHARLESTON, April 12.—The batteries of Sullivan's Island, Morris' Island and other points, opened on Fort Sumter at four o'clock this morning. Fort Sumter returned the fire. Brisk cannonading is being kept up.

There is no information from the seaboard.

The military are under arms.

The whole population is on the streets, and the harbor is filled with anxious spectators.

[SECOND DISPATCH.]

The floating battery is doing good service. Up to 11 o'clock there has been no loss on our side.

Fort Sumter replied at 7 o'clock this morning, and has kept up an astonishing fire ever since.

Stevens' battery is slightly injured.

Three shells are fired per minute. Four hundred in all have fallen.

A breach is expected to be made in Fort Sumter to-morrow.

Major Anderson's fire is principally directed against the floating battery.

War vessels are reported outside the harbor.

Only two soldiers are wounded on Sullivan's Island.

The range is more perfect from the land batteries. Every shot tells. It is thought rom Major Anderson's fire that he has more men than was supposed.

Fort Sumter will succumb by to-morrow.

It is raining at Charleston, but there is no cessation of the batteries. A continuous steady fire on both sides is being kept up.

The cutter Harriet Lane and the steam gunboat Crusader are reported off the bar, but have not entered the harbor.

The war department have as yet no official dispatches.

Gen. Beauregard was at the batteries all day.

The government expects Fort Sumter to succumb to-morrow.

[THIRD DISPATCH.]

The firing continued all day. Two of Fort Sumter's guns are silenced, and it is reported a breach has been made through the south-east wall.

No casualty has yet happened to any of the forces.

Only seven of the nineteen batteries have opened fire on Fort Sumter. The remainder are held ready for the expected fleet.

Two thousand men reached the city this morning and immediately embarked for Morris' Island.

[FOURTH DISPATCH.]

CHARLESTON, April 12, 11 P. M.—The bombardment of Fort Sumter is still going on every twenty minutes from the mortars.

No one has, as yet, received any injury.

The floating battery works admirably well.

Every inlet to the harbor is well guarded.

Our forces are having a lively time of it.

It is supposed Major Anderson is resting his men for the night.

Three vessels of war are reported outside the bar. They cannot get in on account of the roughness of the sea.

☞ HERRING'S PATENT CHAMPION FIRE AND BURGLAR-PROOF SAFES, Nos. 52 and 54 Gravier street, New Orleans.

LILLIE'S
FIRE AND BURGLAR-PROOF SAFES,
DAVIS BROS., AGENTS,
fe2 tf 93 Camp street.

WILCOX & GIBBS' SEWING MACHINES
ONLY $35!
Guaranteed to give Perfect Satisfaction.
DAVIS BROS., AGENTS,
fe2 tf 93 Camp street.

FAIRBANKS' SCALES!
ADAPTED TO EVERY BRANCH OF WEIGHING.
93 Camp street.
fe2tf FAIRBANKS & CO.

MADAME LA BLANCH,

The greatest Clairvoyant and Seeress in the known world, and the only Natural Spirit-Visionist that has ever existed within the present century—the unequaled revealer of all that relates to either the Past, Present or the Future. Her success as a Clairvoyant and Physician has established a reputation, in this city, which is acknowledged by all who visit her. Horoscopes or Charts of Life written by simply knowing date of birth. Madame La Blanch's residence No. 98 Baronne street, between Poydras and Perdido streets. ap13 1t2dp*

GENUINE
DOWNER KEROSINE OIL,
JUST RECEIVED AT
NO. 6 CHARTRES STREET.

☞ Several large invoices of the above unrivalled OIL, for sale wholesale and retail at the LOWEST PRICES.

COVERT & HILL.
ap13 2dptf

SPRING AND SUMMER CLOTHING!

FRESH IMPORTATIONS!

WE ARE CONSTANTLY IN RECEIPT OF NEW STYLES OF

Spring and Summer Clothing,

To which we invite the attention of our Friends and Customers.

SUMMER TWEED COATS, PANTALOONS AND VESTS.
S. M. CASSIMERE SUITS.
LINEN COATS, PANTALOONS AND VESTS.
ALPACA COATS.
BOMBAZINE COATS.
BARPOUR COATS.
FRENCH DRAP D'ETE COATS.
SINGLE-MILLED CLOTH COATS.
COATS, PANTALOONS AND VESTS—Of various New Styles.

GENTLEMEN'S
FURNISHING GOODS.

THE FAMOUS PATENT YOKE SHIRTS.
Gauze Merino, Gauze Cotton, Gauze FLANNEL UNDERSHIRTS.
SUMMER DRAWERS—of every description.
HALF HOSE, SUSPENDERS, GLOVES, &c.
ALL AT THE LOWEST POSSIBLE PRICES.
N. B.—All WINTER CLOTHING offered at VERY LOW PRICES.

ALFRED MUNROE & CO.,
STORY BUILDING,
CORNER OF CAMP AND COMMON STREETS.
ap13 3t2dp

Clothing!

MALARD & TOOKER,
CORNER OF CANAL & OLD LEVEE STS.,
OPPOSITE THE POSTOFFICE,

Offer to their numerous customers and the public in general, a well-selected assortment of

SPRING AND SUMMER CLOTHING!
CONSISTING OF

Tweeds and Summer CASSIMERE SUITS—of various qualities.
Fine Silk Warp Summer CASSIMERE SUITS.
French and English MERINO COATS, PANTS and VESTS.
Colored and Black Alpaca SACS and FROCTEES.
Fancy and White Drill Planters' LINEN, and White and Colored DUCK PANTS.
Planters' Linen, Gingham and White Linen and DUCK COATS.
Planters' Blouse LINEN DUSTERS.
Imitation Seersucker COATS, PANTS and VESTS.
White and Colored Marseilles VESTS, and Bombazine, Alpaca and Merino VESTS.

YOUTHS' AND BOYS' CLOTHING.

A General Assortment of Boys' and Youths' Spring AND SUMMER CLOTHING.

ALSO, A FULL STOCK OF
FURNISHING GOODS,
CONSISTING OF

Plain, Puff and Cross-Bosom SHIRTS—colored and White.
Gauze, Merino, Cotton and Lisle Thread UNDERSHIRTS.
Linen and Cotton DRAWERS,
SOCKS,
NECK-TIES,
SUSPENDERS, &c., &c.

MALARD & TOOKER,
ap7 6t2dp&W Corner Canal and Old Levee sts.

Plantation Clothing!

MALARD & TOOKER,
CORNER CANAL & OLD LEVEE STS.,
OPPOSITE THE POSTOFFICE.

We have in store an extensive assortment OF

SUMMER PLANTATION CLOTHING,
FOR MEN AND WOMEN,

With Boys' and Girls' Sizes, made up out of the best materials, and sewed in the strongest manner.

☞ Planters are solicited to call and examine our stock before purchasing, as they are sure of finding at our establishment all the varieties of CLOTHING necessary for fitting out their hands.

MALARD & TOOKER,
ap7 6t2dp&W Corner Canal and Old Levee sts.

LIGHT FOR THE MILLION!

20,000 GALLONS OF
GENUINE KEROSINE AND
COAL OIL,
(ON HAND AND EN ROUTE,)

From the best and largest manufactories, both North and South, for sale by the barrel or gallon, at the LOWEST PRICES, at the

GREAT SOUTHERN
COAL OIL AND LAMP EMPORIUM,
NO. 6 CHARTRES STREET,
Sole Agency for HALE'S Unrivalled Coal Oil Lamp.

Also on hand, the largest and only COMPLETE ASSORTMENT of

COAL OIL LAMPS
IN THIS CITY.

☞ For sale at LOWER PRICES than at any other house in the Southern States.

COVERT & HILL.

☞ N. B.—THE PUBLIC ARE CAUTIONED against endangering their lives by purchasing an adulterated article of COAL OIL, sold in this city. All Coal Oil sold at this establishment will be guaranteed PURE and perfectly SAFE in any hands.
ap12 2dptf

WISHART'S
PINE-TREE CORDIAL,
A CURE FOR
COUGHS, COLDS AND CONSUMPTION.

Consumption has destroyed more of the human family than any other disease, and the best physicians for many years have despaired of furnishing a cure or remedy that would heal the lungs; yet for more than two hundred years the whole medical world has been convinced that there is a mysterious power and efficacy in the Pine-Tree Tar to heal the lungs, therefore they have recommended the use of tar water, which in many cases had a good effect; but how to combine its medical properties so as to heal the lungs has ever been a mystery, until it was discovered by L. Q. C. Wishart, the proprietor of

WISHART'S PINE-TREE CORDIAL.

In this remedy you have a sure cure for Coughs, Colds, Inflammation of the Lungs, Consumption, Bronchitis, and all pulmonary complaints.

For sale in New Orleans, wholesale and retail, by
J. WRIGHT & CO.,
ma24 6t2dp&1tW 21 and 151 Chartres street.

TO HAVE A COLD IS ONE THING,

To cure a Cough is "another pair of shoes," as Madam Malaprop would say. We would most respectfully suggest as a happy experiment

DR. DAVIS' COMPOUND SYRUP OF WILD CHERRY AND TAR.

Its effects are expeditious and happy in the extreme.

For sale in New Orleans, wholesale and retail, by
J. WRIGHT & CO.,
ap7 6t2dp&1tW 21 and 151 Chartres street.

A WINK IS AS GOOD AS A KICK
TO A BLIND HORSE,

Is a very old adage, and applicable to all those who suffer from Exhaustion and General Debility, either caused by climate or dissipation. Why suffer and complain, when you have a restorative at your very door?

WRIGHT'S REJUVENATING ELIXIR

Is just the thing for your case. Sold at
J. WRIGHT & CO.'s,
21 and 151 Chartres street,
ap7 6t2dp&1tW Wholesale and Retail.

R. W. LONG,
AUCTIONEER AND APPRAISER,
Office, 115 Gravier st., opposite the St. Charles Hotel.
Slave Depot, 226 Common street, corner of Franklin street. ap7 6t2dp

GREAT SALE OF SILKS,
AT
TODD'S,
12 & 14.......... CHARTRES STREET ....12 & 14

The entire stock of
BLACK AND COLORED SILKS
IS NOW OFFERED
AT TWENTY-FIVE PER CENT. UNDER FIRST COST.

This Stock embraces all the New and Elegant Designs for

SPRING & SUMMER WEAR,
AND COMPRISES THE
GREATEST BARGAINS EVER OFFERED
IN NEW ORLEANS.

JOHN TODD,
ap11 3t2dp 12 and 14 Chartres street.

ROBERT PITKIN

Would again inform his Friends, and Strangers visiting the city, that his Assortment of

SUPERIOR
READY-MADE CLOTHING
AND
GENTLEMEN'S
FURNISHING GOODS

is now LARGE AND COMPLETE, embracing every article in his line of trade.

CITIZENS AND STRANGERS CALLING AT HIS
FASHIONABLE CLOTHING EMPORIUM,
NOS. 13 & 15......CAMP STREET......NOS. 13 & 15
Opposite Ladies' Entrance to City Hotel.

Will find EVERY ARTICLE suited to their wants, manufactured and selected with great care, elegance and taste.

ROBERT PITKIN,
no17 2dptf 13 and 15 Camp street.

JOHN G. LIGHTBODY'S NEWS INK.

This NEWS INK, from its acknowledged superiority over any other now manufactured in the United States, is used solely by all the principal newspapers in the Union.

The undersigned, being the Agents for its sale in the South and Southwest, would inform newspaper publishers that they keep always on hand a full supply, in kegs of 25, 50 and 100 pounds.

JOHN WRIGHT,
dec3 2dp tf and 151 21 Chartres st.

LAFAYETTE STEAM LAUNDRY,
APOLLO ST., BET. 3D & 4TH,

Is now prepared to Wash Hotel and Steamboat Clothing in a most superior manner, with quickest dispatch. Application to be made at
oc21 2dpti 57 CAMP STREET.

DR. O. ANFOUX
HAS REMOVED HIS OFFICE TO
No. 70 Baronne street,
oc26 2dptf Between Gravier and Union.

WIGS! WIGS! WIGS!

BATCHELOR'S WIGS AND TOUPEES surpass all. They are elegant, light, easy and durable, fitting to a charm. No turning up behind; no shrinking off the head. Indeed, this is the only establishment where these things are properly understood and made.

Manufactured at BATCHELOR'S, 16 Bond street, New York oc11 1y2dp

THE FOOL HATH SAID IN HIS HEART

Balsam Copaiva and other noxious drugs are the only cure for Gonorrhœa, either recent or chronic. Maybe it is, and maybe it ain't; but after you have used them, just try

VAN ZANDT'S DETERGENT,

and see which is the pleasantest and most rapid in its effects.

For sale in New Orleans, wholesale and retail, by
J. WRIGHT & CO.,
ap7 6t2dp&1tW 21 and 151 Chartres street.

"LADIES' BEAUTIFIER."

Phalon & Son's Liquid "Snow White Orienta Cream." Sold by all Druggists.

"BEAUTIFUL COMPLEXION."

Phalen's Liquid "Snow White Oriental Cream." Price 50 cents per bottle.

"BEAUTIFUL WOMEN"

Result from the use of PHALON'S Liquid "Snow White Oriental Cream."

"COCIN FOR THE HAIR."

Phalon & Son's "COCIN," or deodorized Cocoa Nut Oil, is the best and cheapest article for Dressing, Beautifying, Cleaning, Curling, Preserving and Restoring the Hair. Ladies, try it. For sale by all Druggists and Fancy Goods Dealers. Wholesale Agents for N. O., John Wright & Co. se20 1y2dp

DRS. KNAPP & McLAIN,
DENTAL SURGEONS,
154 CANAL STREET, NEAR BARONNE.

DENTAL NOTICE.

The undersigned takes pleasure to state that he has formed a copartnership in the practice of DENTAL SURGERY with A. F. McLAIN, M. D., a gentleman of scientific attainments and experience, in the practice of DENTISTRY, and whom he can commend to those who may require Dental aid.

The undersigned will still continue as usual to give his whole time to the practice of his profession.

no3 d&W2dptf FREDERICK H. KNAPP.

SEA SERPENTS,

Of a diminutive description, are frequently found in children, and when doctors fail to discover what ails the child, all you then have to do is to try the Worm Test, i. e., WINER'S CANADIAN VERMIFUGE, and that will fetch 'em, sure.

J. WRIGHT & CO., 21 and 151 Chartres street, sell it wholesale and retail, with full directions to each bottle. ap7 6t2dp&1tW

RATS AND ROACHES.

"But rats and mice and such small deer,
Have been Tom's food for many a year."

Shakspeare should have added roaches to this unique diet of "poor Tom's a cold."

DR. WILSON'S RAT AND ROACH EXTERMINATOR

would have been just the thing to bag such pestiferous game. See the state of despair the rats are in on a placard at J. Wright & Co.'s, 21 and 151 Chartres street, where this effective Exterminator is sold at wholesale and retail. ap7 6t2dp&1tW

CHARLES HEIDSIECK CHAMPAGNE.

The above WINE was awarded the first premium Medal at the great Bordeaux Exposition for 1859. It can be found at all the first-class Wine Merchants in this city.

T. W. BAYAUD & BERARD,
Sole Agents for North America, New York.
e25 2dpeowly

IMPORTANT TO FEMALES.

DR. CHEESEMAN'S PILLS.

The combination of ingredients in these Pills are the result of a long and extensive practice. They are mild in their operation, and certain in correcting all irregularities, painful menstruations, removing all obstructions, whether from cold or otherwise, headache, pain in the side, palpitation of the heart, disturbed sleep, which always arises from interruption of nature. They can be successfully used as a preventive. These pills should never be taken in pregnancy, as they would be sure to cause a miscarriage. Warranted purely vegetable, and free from anything injurious to life or health. Explicit directions, which should be read, accompanying each box. Price $1. Sent by mail by inclosing $1 to Dr. Cornelius L. Cheeseman, Box 4531, Postoffice, New York city.

☞ Sold by one druggist in every town in the United States.
R. B. HUTCHINGS,
General Agent for the United States,
20 Cedar street, New York.
Sold by JOHN WRIGHT & CO.,
and 151 Chartres street,
se27 6m2dp&W New Orleans.

MILITARY BOOKS!

MILITARY BOOKS!..........MILITARY BOOKS!

FOR SALE BY
THOS. L. WHITE,
BOOKSELLER,
105..........................CANAL ST..........................105

"HEAVY ARTILLERY,"

Just issued in Charleston, being a reprint of the work published by the old U. S. War Department.

FIELD ARTILLERY—By a Board of Artillery Officers.
GILLAM'S MILITARY MANUAL.
MAHAN'S FIELD FORTIFICATIONS.
GIBBONS' ARTILLERISTS' MANUAL.
BAYONET EXERCISE, AS USED IN THE ARMY.
ROBERTS' HAND-BOOK OF ARTILLERY.
WILCOX'S RIFLE PRACTICE.
DUNN'S MILITARY MANUAL FOR BEGINNERS.
ap11 3t2dp

DIRECT IMPORTATION.

JOHNS & DESSOMMES BROS.,
CORNER OF CHARTRES AND CANAL STREETS,
HAVE JUST RECEIVED, DIRECT FROM HAVRE,
A LARGE INVOICE OF VERY CHOICE
SPRING
DRESS GOODS!
CONSISTING OF
RICH ORGANDIES.

NEW STYLE OF ORGANDY ROBES.
PLAIN JACCONET MUSLIN—all colors.
FIGURED JACCONET MUSLIN—all colors.
Embroidered ENGLISH BAREGE—new style.
Plain and Figured ENGLISH BAREGE—at all prices.
GRENADINE BROCHÉ DE SOIE.
8-4 ENGLISH BAREGE—very fine.
PIQUE—all colors—very rich.
REAL JOUVIN KID GLOVES—$1 per pair.
FIGURED LINEN CAMBRIC—for Dresses.
ENGLISH PRINTS—at 12½c. per yard.

JOHNS & DESSOMMES BROS.,
fe12 2dptf Corner Chartres and Canal sts.

Boots and Shoes at Cost!

Having to remove from my present location, I now offer my entire stock

OF
BOOTS AND SHOES!
AT COST.

WALTER A. PECK,
No. 69 Canal street, corner of Dorseire street.
ap7 6t2dp

THE TRUE DELTA
STEAM JOB PRINTING
ESTABLISHMENT,
18.........ST. CHARLES STREET.........18

We would call the particular attention of the Mercantile and Business Community to this Department of our Establishment, as we have made very extensive additions to it in the way of the

NEWEST STYLES OF POSTER AND GENERAL JOB TYPE, PRESSES, &C.,
WHICH ENABLE US TO
EXECUTE EVERY DESCRIPTION OF
PRINTING,
SUCH AS

MAMMOTH POSTERS,
FANCY SHOW CARDS,
VELVET WORK,
RAILROAD WORK,
LAWYERS' BRIEFS,
BOOK WORK,
STEAMBOAT WORK,
BUSINESS CARDS,
PROGRAMMES,
HAND-BILLS,

AND ALL KINDS OF
MERCANTILE WORK!

☞ The facilities we have in the way of ☜

STEAM, CARD AND HAND PRESSES,
ENABLE US TO
EXECUTE WORK RAPIDLY, NEATLY AND CHEAPLY!

RULING AND BOOK-BINDING,
OF EVERY DESCRIPTION, EXECUTED WITH DISPATCH!
no17 2dp tf

OAK ORCHARD ACID SPRING WATER.

PAMPHLETS,

Containing the opinions of celebrated Chemists and Physicians respecting the use of this WATER, in the case of many diseases of the human system, will be supplied GRATIS, on application to

JAMES SYME,
WHOLESALE AND RETAIL DRUGGIST,
134 Canal street.

CALL FOR A PAMPHLET.
ma27 WeFr&Su 10t2dp

HAIR DYE! HAIR DYE!

BATCHELOR'S LIQUID HAIR DYE is the approved Dye of the age—the only reliable and harmless Hair Dye known. All others are mere imitations of this grand original. It produces instantly a splendid black or natural brown, without injuring the hair or staining the skin; the ill effects of bad dyes remedied, and the hair invigorated for life.

The genuine is signed WILLIAM A. BATCHELOR on the steel engraving, on each side of every box. All others are counterfeits, and should be avoided.

Sold by JOHN WRIGHT & CO.,
21 and 151 Chartres street, New Orleans.
Manufactory, 81 Barclay st., New York, late 233 Broadway. se29 1y2dp

FLAGGING.

1400 YARDS FLAGGING, PER SHIP EMPIRE,
FOR SALE BY
J. M. FORGAY.
ap6 6t2dp

WRIGHT'S REJUVENATING ELIXIR.

This is an all-powerful medicine, made upon strictest pharmaceutical principles, by one of ablest chemists of the age. Its object is to be a fect specific for

Imbecility.
Disorganization of the Organs of Generation.
Sleeplessness,
Debility,
Nervous Affections, Feebleness,

And the destruction of the nervous system—the results of youthful indiscretion. It raises the sinking frame, it puts new life into the debilitated system and renews the entire man.

IT NEVER FAILS.

For sale in New Orleans, wholesale and retail, by
J. WRIGHT & CO.,
21 and 151 Chartres street,
Sole Proprietors.

THE CHIEF AMONG TEN THOUSAND.

DALLY'S MAGICAL PAIN EXTRACTOR has universally supplanted all other ointments and healing applications, in both the Eastern and Western Hemispheres, wherever introdnced; and its intrinsic merits is the true secret of its success in all Cutaneous affections, whether the cause be accident or disease.

DALLY'S MAGICAL PAIN EXTRACTOR

BURNS AND SCALDS

Are instantly relieved of their anguish, pain and inflammation by a timely application of this marvelous healer, and the flesh is renewed by a charm, no blemish or scar remaining.

THE FRIEND OF THE NURSERY.

Children are frequent sufferers from external injuries, especially from fluid and camphene explosions, therefore every mother should have this healing preparation constantly at hand. It heals sore breasts, and quickly removes the Tetter, or Ringworm, so prevalent in children.

TO TRAVELERS BY SEA AND LAND.

The machinist, the traveler, and every other individual whose lot in life throws him within the chance of accident from explosion, fire, or collision, should bear in mind that this Magic Extractor is his best and only friend. It is both portable and cheap, and should ever be his companion, as a friend in need. There are thousands of living witnesses to testify to its marvelous virtue, who owe their sound limbs and muscles to its saving efficacy.

The following are a few of the leading diseases for which DALLY'S MAGICAL PAIN EXTRACTOR is a Preventive, as well as Cure.

Burns,	Erysipelas,	Sores of all kinds,
Bruises,	Fistula.	Shot Wounds.
Boils,	Frost Bites,	Scrofula,
Broken Breast,	Fever Sores,	Scurvy.
Bites of Reptiles,	Felons,	Scalds,
Cancer,	Glandular Dis's,	Scurf,
Cracked Lips,	Mercurial Sores,	Scald Head,
Chapped Hands,	Pains generally,	Sprains,
Chilblains,	Pimples,	Small Pox,
Cramp,	Piles.	Tumors,
Contracted Cords,	Poison,	Tetter,
Chafes,	Rheumatism,	Ulcers,
Diseases of the Skin,	Rashes,	Venereal Sores, &c.

Sold at the principal Depots, 14 Broadway, New York, and 21 and 151 Chartres street, New Orleans, by
J. WRIGHT & CO.,
General Agents.

It can also be obtained of all respectable druggist and merchants throughout the United States and Canadas.

WINER'S CANADIAN VERMIFUGE.

This is the only sure remedy against worms in the human frame—things that are so fatal and destructive to children.

SAVE THE CHILDREN!

Let mothers be timely warned, and not allow these children murderers to remain in the systems of their offspring. Remember that

WINER'S CANADIAN VERMIFUGE

Will at once and for ever banish the reptiles, and the young will be saved. Think of this.

Colonel Vasser, of Mississippi, in a letter to J. W. Vesey, Esq., of the Aberdeen Conservative, thus winds up his communication on the value of this medicine to *his own family*—"My experience has convinced me that, in the expeiment I have made with Winer's Canadian Vermifuge, it is due to suffering humanity, as well as to the manufacturer of the medicine, to make public the result of my observations. (Signed) "W. H. VASSER."

The Vermifuge is for sale, wholesale and retail, by
J. WRIGHT & CO.,
21 and 151 Chartres street,
Sole Proprietors.

DR. OSGOOD'S INDIA CHOLAGOGUE

CURES

Fever and Ague, Chills and Fever, Dumb Ague, Intermittent and Remittent Fevers, Liver Complaint, Jaundice, Enlargement of the Spleen, and all the various forms of

BILIOUS DISEAES.

This invaluable medicine was prepared from an extensive practice of several years in a bilious climate, and is never known to fail curing Fever and Ague, or any of the diseases above named.

Those who are suffering from affections of this kind, and also those who have become invalids from their effects upon the constitution, will find the INDIA CHOLAGOGUE a most invaluable remedy for purifying the blood, and thoroughly cleansing from the system the morbid effects of a bilious climate.

The wonderful effects of Cholagogue in eradicating Bile from the human system can only explain its extraordinary agency in the speedy, thorough and permanent cure of Fever and Ague, and the various grades of intermittent and remittent fevers.

It has been tested in thousands of cases, and is pronounced by all who have used it, one of the greatest Fever and Ague remedies extant.

Be sure and ask for Dr. Osgood's India Cholagogue, as there are many counterfeits offered for sale.

For sale in New Orleans, wholesale and retail, at proprietor's prices.

J. WRIGHT & CO.,
21 and 151 Chartres street,
General Agents.

DR. DAVIS' WILD CHERRY AND TAR.

HOW TO STOP A COUGH.

We continually hear the expression, "Oh! it is *only a Cough.*" Only, indeed! Yes, but that neglected cough will probably end in that fearful disease to think of—Consumption—that hurries without a hope such millions to their graves.

Will you take time by the forelock? Will you respite yourself from an untimely dissolution? If you will, be sure to have this faithful remedy at your hand. Every one knows what a specific is in the Wild Cherry, and then when combined with Tar, at once releases the mucus from the cells of the lungs, expectoration ensues, breathing becomes natural, and you are safe.

For sale in New Orleans by
J. WRIGHT & CO.,
21 and 151 Chartres street.
General Agents.

RATS! RATS! RATS!

THE PESTS OF HOUSKEEPERS

THOSE SHOCKING RATS.

The rats that eat up all our goods;
The rats that hate the coming floods;
The rats that terra firma seek,
From flooded sewer and flooded creek;
The rats—like all unearthly Gnomes—
Are now invading all our homes.
These rats must in the dust be laid,
Their debt of nature must be paid.
Oh! WILSON, thou alone can kill
The rats by thousands, at your will.

Wilson's Rat and Roach Destroyer.

Here we have the antidote. Dr. Wilson has been eminently successful in making his Destroyer so certain, so palatable too, to rats, that it kills them off at once. Thus, instead of scratching, boring holes, attacking pantries, and so on, "an awful stillness reigns around," much to the satisfaction and gratification of the household generally, but especially to the housekeepers. Remember, when you are besieged by rats, to ask for

DR. WILSON'S RAT AND ROACH EXTERMINATOR,

Use it, and your premises are clear.

For sale in New Orleans, wholesale and retail, by
J. WRIGHT & CO.,
21 and 151 Chartres street,
Sole Proprietor.

Gazette and Sentinel.

NEW SERIES--VOL. 4, NO. 9. PLAQUEMINE, PARISH OF IBERVILLE, LA., APRIL 13, 1861. OLD SERIES--VOL. 14 NO. 21.

PROFESSIONAL CARDS.

BENJ. N. DEBLIEUX,
Attorney at Law,
Plaquemine, Iberville Parish, Louisiana,

WILL devote his whole attention to the practice of their profession in all the Courts of the Sixth Judicial District. je23

DAVID N. BARROW, *Plaquemine, Iberville, La.* | N. W. POPE, *West Baton Rouge, Baton Rouge P. O., La*

Barrow & Pope,
Attorneys and Counsellors at Law,

WILL practice their profession in the parishes of West and East Baton Rouge, Iberville, Point Coupee and West Feliciana; the Supreme Court of Louisiana, and the United States District and Circuit Courts at New Orleans. my1-1y

OSCAR LAUVE,
Attorney at Law,

Will devote strict attention to the practice of his profession in all the Courts of the Sixth Judicial District.
Office with Zenon Labauve. ap24-1y

J. H. RILLS,
Attorney at Law and Justice of the Peace,
☞Office on Main street. aug6

Joseph Hotard,
Attorney and Counsellor at Law,
(*Office same as Zenon Labauve, Esq.,*)
jy16] PLAQUEMINE, LA.

GEORGE L. HILL,
Attorney at Law,
Tyler, Smith County, Texas,

WILL practice law and collect claims in the counties of Harrison, Panola, Rusk, Smith, Wood, Upshur, Cass, and Marion, and in the Federal and Supreme Courts at Tyler. my26

W. I. HAMILTON,
ATTORNEY AT LAW,

HAVING located at Plaquemine will devote his entire attention to the pratice of his Profession in the Parishes of
Iberville, East and West Baton Rouge.
He respectfully solicits the patronage of his old friends and the public generally, who can always find him at his Office on **Main Street** near the Court House, between the hours of 9 A. M. and 5 P. M., unless otherwise professionally engaged.
Plaquemine, La. oc16mh23.

E. GOURRIER,
Surveyor & Civil Engineer,
Baton Rouge, La.

WILL attend to calls in the Parish of Iberville, for surveying lands, mapping, Plant ations levelling, measuring canals and levees, draughting architectural designs, &c. nov24

J. H. SHANKS. JOHN KNEAL.
SHANKS & KNEAL,
HOUSE PAINTERS, GLAZIERS
—AND—
PAPER HANGERS,
sept1 PLAQUEMINE, LA

Hunenkamp & Hynes,
Wholesale Grocers and Commission Merchants,
ST. LOUIS, Mo.
☞Particular attention given to consignments of Sugar and Molasses, and to filling orders for Western Produce. jan6'58-tf

WM. H. POLSON,
House, Sign and Ornamental Painters, and Imitators of Wood and Marble. Paper Hanging and Glazing,
All done on the cheapest possible terms; and guaranteeing perfect satisfaction, he request the patronage of his friends and the public generally. my7-1y

Barber Shop.

NICOLAS BIEHLER respectfully informs his friends and the public that he still continues at his old stand on Main street, adjoining his brothers' Tailor-shop and Wine Store, where he still pursues SHAVING and HAIR CUTTING, as also CUPPING when called upon. s8

FRANK GLASER,
Boot and Shoemaker.

The business heretofore carried on by B. Glaser, will be conducted in future by Frank Glaser, at the old stand on Bank st., north of Main street, and he trusts that his attention to business, and endeavors to please his customers, and the manner in which his work is done, will merit him the continued patronage of his friends and the public.
my5-m9. FRANK GLASER.

LIVERY STABLE.

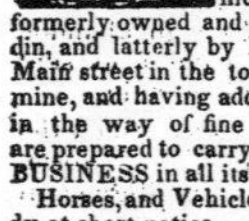

The Undersigned respectfully inform the public, that, having purchased and removed to the Livery Stable formerly owned and occupied by Sam'l. McFaddin, and latterly by Ira Orcutt, on Main street in the town of Plaquemine, and having added much to it in the way of fine Horses and Buggies, they are prepared to carry on the LIVERY STABLE BUSINESS in all its branches.
Horses, and Vehicles of almost every kind, ready at short notice.
Family Carriages supplied.
Customers can rely upon having their Horses well fed and taken care of. Give us a trial.
We also have fine large Lots for the accommodation of drovers.
JAMES BARKER,
my1-1y J. P. MARIONNEAUX.

Sewing Machines.
CHEAPER THAN EVER!

WE have a few SEWING MACHINES on hands, which we will sell at a great reduction of price to close out the lot.
sept1 ROTH, DEBLIEUX & CO.

MISCELLANEOUS.

THE GEM.

THE undersigned would respectfully announce to their friends and the public generally, that they have just purchased the Coffee-house and fixtures formerly kept by Phillip Heelein opposite the steamboat landing; and having been to considerable expense in papering all the rooms so that they are neat and pleasant, and having the *best brands of Liquors and Wines* to be had in New Orleans, and further, pledging ourselves to spare no pains to please all who call to see us, we shall expect a small share of the public patronage.
GEOGE TURIN, CHARLES SEIPPLE, } TURIN & SEIPPLE.
Plaquemine, May 19, 1860.

The Rainbow.

SOLOMON FREY presents his compliments to his friends and the public, and respectfully informs them that he has opened in the building on Main street, formerly occupied by Stockley & Delavallade, a
Coffee House and Lager Beer.
Saloon, where good liquors and good beer can be had, and where he hopes his old patrons and the public will call and see him. sep15

Rhine Wine.

The undersigned would say to his friends and to the public generally that he has just received a new supply of White and Red Rhine Wine, of a quality much superior to that received last year. The public may rely upon this wine being the true and actual juice of the grape, as it came from the vineyards on the Rhine. Call and try it.
aug11 GABRIEL BIEHLER.

Coffee House, Boarding House, Livery Stable.
MAURICE MARIX

INFORMS his friends and the public generally, that he has opened his new house, on Bank street, since the 4th of July, where he is finely situated to accommodate Boarders and transient visitors, on reasonable terms. His table shall always be furnished with the best the market affords.
His COFFEE HOUSE will always be supplied with the best of Liquors, Wine, Lager Beer, &c.
He has a BILLIARD TABLE kept in a separate room from the Bar, handsomely fitted up.
His STABLE cannot be surpassed; and all animals entrusted to his care shall meet with the most diligent attention.
He confidently hopes that his old friends will not forget him. Planters and others from the country will have their horses and buggies properly taken care of at all times, and as good a dinner and wine as the town affords, for themselves and friends. sep3

ANTHONY ASTREDO'S
OYSTER SALOON,
—AND—
RESTAURANT,
No. 16 Royal Street,
Next door to the Post Office, New Orleans.
Oysters in Barrels or Cans, Pickled or Spiced.
Fruit and Nuts of all kinds, wholesale and retail.
Always on hand a full supply of all the luxuries of the season.
Meals served in New York style.
City and country orders put up on the shortest notice. ap21-1y

New Butchery.

The undersigned respectfully informs the public that he has purchased the old and well known Butchery of F. Smith, and that he intends to keep his stall well supplied with the best of Beef, Mutton, Pork, &c. By a strict attention to his business in the above respect, he hopes to have a share of public patronage, and particularly the patronage of Mr. Smith's old customers.
P. S. The carts will run as usual down the Coast and to the Park,
dec25-1y BERTRAM BEYRIS.

HAASE BROS.
Ladies Dress Goods
AND
Plantation Goods
they particularly call attention to, as also their extensive stock of
Ready Made Clothing.
They will not pretend to give a list of their stock in the compass of an advertisement, but request all who are in want of
Cheap Goods,
to give them a call, as they feel fully satisfied that purchasers will not go away from their store dissatisfied.]oc23] HAASE BROS.

Millright, Engineer, &c.

THE undersigned, flattering himself that he is favorably known throughout the State as MILLRIGHT AND ENGINEER, would respectfully announce to the Sugar Planters and others, that he is prepared to contract to build
Sugar Mills and Engines
of the best build and finish, of any size required, and warranted in every case.
Contracts for next year respectfully solicited.

NOTICE TO BUILDERS AND OTHERS.
He is prepared to furnish IRON RAILINGS VERANDAHS, &c. Call and see his samples
aug25 A. ST. DIZIER.

At $10 per Thousand.
I HAVE FOR SALE,
192,000
Fine A No. 1 BRICKS.
jy [illegible]

WE have a large and fresh assortment of MEDICINES, which were purchased for cash in New York, and which we warrant in all cases, and will sell as low as any Hose in the South.
se8 STOCKLEY & DELAVALLADE.

Paints..............Oils.
LEAD, WHITE—White Zinc, Linseed Oil, Turpentine, &c., for sale by
se8 STOCKLEY & DELAVALLADE.

Just Received,
1 bbl. first quality Whiskey.
1 bbl common do.
10 gallons No. 1 Brandy.
Also, a lot of splendid Havana Cigars.
jy7 R. A. ORILLION.

MISCELLANEOUS.

F. LAGLEIZE,
Fancy Baker and Confectioner,

RESPECTFULLY informs families and others of Plaquemine and Iberville, that he is at all times prepared to furnish parties with *Cake and Confectionery* in every style, and manufactured in a manner not surpassed anywhere. He will furnish any thing that may be required in his line at the shortest notice, and on the most reasonable terms.—Bakery at the corner of Bank and Greaud streets. my12

ANTHONY WILBERT,
CABINET MAKER,

Takes this method of returning his thanks to his old friends and customers for the patronage heretofore received, and assures them that he will ever strive to accommodate them in his line.
He has now moved to the large and commodious building at the corner of Fenn's Alley and Bank street where he has a large stock of Furniture of every kind.
Old Furniture taken in exchange or repaired at very low prices.
He also makes COFFINS of every style at the shortest notice.
☞Fisk's Metallic Coffins supplied as heretofore.
Splendid Hearse. Price moderate. sep4

To Sugar Planters.
The Star Bagasse Furnace.
Patented 15th June, 1858.
Never Known to Fail!

PARTIES wishing to purchase the right to use please apply to
EVAN SKELLY.
—ALSO—
The Wood or Coal Furnace,
for either BOILERS or SUGAR KETTLES,
Patented December 21st, 1858.
☞Numerous references given. Apply as above. ap7

WAREHOUSE.
Forwarding and Commission Business.
Steamboat Landing, adjoining the Post-Office.

THE UNDERSIGNED have associated themselves together, for the purpose of doing a general Forwarding and Commission Business.
We will also Collect Monies due the merchants, and business men, of the North, East and West. All business intrusted to our care will be promptly attended to.
HEELEIN & JENNINGS.
PHILIP HEELEIN, } P. E. JENNINGS.
☞Refer to any reliable citizen of the Parish.
Iberville, La. dec31

NEW SADDLERY AND
Harness Establishment.

The undersigned respectfully announces to the citizens of Iberville and West Baton Rouge, that he has again returned to Plaquemine, with the intention of locating himself permanently, to carry on the
Saddlery and Harness Business
IN ALL ITS BRANCHES.
Those in want of SADDLES, HARNESS, or any article of PLANTATION GEARING, will find it to their interest to give him a call, before purchasing elsewhere.
Shop on Main street, lower story of the Old Masonic Hall. mh24 A. W. SCOTT.

Carriage and Harness Manufactory
AND
Carriage Trimming Establishment.
—:o:o:—
GUSTAVE RINGWALD,
Successor to Charles Veit & Co., at the old stand of A. W. Scott.

Respectfully informs the people of Iberville and West Baton Rouge that having purchased out the interest of his partner, he intends carrying on the same line of business, such as the manufacture of all kinds of
Saddles and Harness
And the Trimming and Painting of Carriages and Buggies.
And everything kept in a similar establishment
N. B.—No Repairing done on *CREDIT*.
Plaquemine, Nov. 12th, 1859. 1y

U. S. Mail Line,
BETWEEN PLAQUEMINE AND CHARENTON.

The steam propeller *VIRGINIA*, Rodolph Miller, Captain, will leave Plaquemine, carrying the mail, every Tuesday Morning, at 6 o'clock precisely—and returning leave Charenton every Wednesday Morning at 6 o'clock, and arrive at Plaquemine the same day. Leave Plaquemine again on Saturday morning at 6, and leave Charenton again on Sunday morning at 6 o'clock, connecting with the Iberville for Baton Rouge and Bayou Sara, and with the St. Mary for Franklin and New Iberia.
☞Shippers will please see that their freight is on board the boat the evening previous to her departure.—For further particulars apply to
dec22 J. McWILLIAMS & CO.

NOTICE.

THE undersigned having gone to Baton Rouge to engage in the BOOT and SHOE MAKING business, presents his thanks to his friends in this town and Parish, for the patronage hitherto extented to him, and trusts they will continue the same in favor of his brother, F. Glaser, who will continue the business here in the old stand on Bank street.
mar9 B. GLASER.

OYSTER SALOON:

The undersigned would respectfully inform his friends and the public generally that his Oyster Saloon is now in "full blast," where Oysters are served up in every style. Also—
Game and other Luxuries,
including "Ironsides Gumbo," and Gumbo, of every other description; Soups, Roasts, Stews, Frys, Broils—Salmon, Lobsters, Sardines, &c. &c.—
Desserts and Delicacies;
and WINES and LIQUORS of all kinds, and of the most superior quality. Give me a call.
nov12 H. LEBLANC.

CUTLERY—A new and beautiful assortment of Pen Knives just received and for sale low, by R. A. KEARNY

MISCELLANEOUS.

O. S. JENNINGS,
No. 20 CAMP STREET,
NEW ORLEANS, La.,
(Under the City Hotel Buildings,)
Watchmaker and Jeweler.
DEALER IN EVERY DESCRIPTION OF
FINE WATCHES,
Jewelry,
Silver and Plated Ware.
☞Watches and Jewelry repaired and warranted. oc15

PROSPECTUS.

Young Ladies Academy
AND
CONVENT OF HOLY CROSS,
Plaquemine, (Iberville,) La.

THIS INSTITUTION is beautifully situated in the centre of the town of Plaquemine, between Court, Church and Plaquemine streets. The buildings are large and commodious, and the grounds of good ample space for amusement and healthy exercise. The Institution being situated within a few minutes walk of the steamboat landing, enjoys the advantage of easy and frequent access. It is conducted by the Sisters of Holy Cross, who being wholly devoted to the important work of public instruction, spare no pains to improve the hearts of their pupils in virtue and store their minds with knowledge, and they pledge themselves to return the children to their parents improved in virtue and learning.
To impart a thorough education in the highest sense of the word—to train the moral and the intellectual being—to develope sound health and elegant manners, is an object of constant attention. The system of government is mild and maternal, aiming to guide rather than to drive the pupils along the path of duty. The comforts and dersonal habits of the young ladies, receive the same attention as in the most refined family circle.
Religion is the ground-work of education. The Institution is Catholic; but young ladies of all denominations are admitted, provided they are willing for the sake of order and uniformity to attend the exercises of public worship. The Academical year is of ten months. The course of Education embraces all the branches usually taught in Academies, with the facility of primary instruction in both the English and French languages, at the option of parents.

Terms for Boarders:

Entrance fee, Bed, $5,00,	$ 5 00
Board and Tuition, per annum, payments quarterly in advance,	80 00

Terms for half Boarders:

Tuition per month, payable monthly,	$10 00

Terms for Day Scholars:

Tuition, per month, payable monthly,	$4 00

Extra charges at the option of parents, iz Music, Medical Attendance, Board at Conven during Vacation, Washing and Mending, Bed Bedding, Mattrass, Stationery, Tapestry-work Embroidery, Artificial Flowers, &c. &c. Or Board, Tuition and Washing, Mending. Bed, Bedding, Mattrass. Stationery, Tapestry work, Embroidery, Artificial Flowers. &c. &c. Or Board, Tuition, Washing, Mending, Bed, Bedding, Stationery, complete, per annum, $240 00.

UNIFORM.
Winter—Green French Merinos.
Summer—Pink Gingham.
It is to be worn only on Sundays and Thursdays, and the other holidays when going to Church or Walk. Patterns of the make and the shade may be had at the Convent.

SPECIAL DIRECTIONS.
Each Boarder must be provided with six Sheets, Musquito Bar, six feet by three; twelve Chemises; ditto pairs of Hose; ditto of Handkerchiefs; six Pillow Cases; twelve Towels and Napkins; one Tumbler; Fork and Knife; table and desert Spoons, and all the requisites of Toilet.
Pocket money is to be deposited in the hands of the Superioress.
Visits are allowed to the Boarders from their Parents and Guardians on Sundays and Thursdays, and only from 9 o'clock A. M. to 4 o'clock P. M.
References—Plaquemine, Rev. Francois C. Fallot. New Orleans, Rev. P. F. Sheil, S. S. C., or
SISTER MARY OF CALVARY,
nov27-sep3 Superioress of the Convent.

PRESERVE YOUR TEETH.
J. A. CASADAVANT,
Surgeon Dentist,
107 *Royal Street, New Orleans.*
Opposite St. Louis Hotel.

CONTINUES to call the attention of those who need the services of a competent Dentist, and those persons whose Teeth have been injured by unskillful Dentists, whose gold drops out a short time after the Teeth are plugged, and whose Artificial Teeth cannot be worn with comfort, by applying to J. A. Casadavant, they can have all operations in the Dental Art performed conscientiously, and in the most scientific manner. He benumbs the gums, before Extracting Teeth, with a chemical preparation invented by him, which lessens the pain. Consultations in French, Spanish and English. dec31

ALLEN'S
Improved Stubble Shaver.

A number of the above important article, so useful in facilitating the culture of the sugar cane,—invented by J. Allen, and perfected by the undersigned—has been manufactured and is now on hand for sale in New Orleans by GEO. W. SISER, corner of Camp and Poydras, Agent for the sale of the machine in that city.
The undersigned has upwards of *seventy* certificates from the best planters in Louisiana, who have witnessed the operations of the *Stubble Shaver* in various soils; and there can be no questions of the fact that it meets—and fully meets—all the requirements and desideratums that could be needed or desired for performing cleanly, neatly and perfectly the work for which it was invented to perform, and in which performance it does the labor of at least *fifteen hands with the hoe!* It will also shave from 25 to 50 acres without sharpening. The price asked for them will be found to be surprisingly small considering the price paid for their manufacture.
Planters wanting the *Stubble Shaver* will please address GEO. W. SISER, New Orleans or to
oct 13 A. ST. DIZIER, Plaquemine:
Or to J. McWilliams.

Save your Fruit.

A NEW supply of Fruit Jars just receivedg every Jar warranted air tight—no sealin required. Call and see them at
R. A. KEARNY'S;,
aug11 Corner of Main and Bank sts.

MISCELLANEOUS.

SOUTHERN
MUTUAL INSURANCE
COMPANY.

Office of Southern Mutual Insurance Co., } of Baton Rouge.

IN CONFORMITY with the requirements of their charter, the SOUTHERN MUTUAL INSURANCE COMPANY publish the following statement:

Amount of premiums received from February 1st, 1860, to Febr'ry 1st, 1861.		$85,286,96
AS FOLLOWS:		
Premiums on Fire Risks......	$66.839 20	
" " Marine "......	13,760 49	
" " River "......	4,687 27	
	$85,286 96	
Premiums on unterminated Risks, February 1st, 1860.		$49,814 48
		$135,101 44
Less premiums on Risks not terminated		60,220 74
Nett earned premiums for the year ending 1st February, 1861.		$74,880 70
Losses paid during the same period:		
"NO LOSSES UNSETTLED."		
On Fire Risks............	$12,381 75	
" Marine Risks........	1,554 64	
" River Risks.........	3,440 17	
	$17,376 56	
Expenses during year as above	7,992 82	
		$25,369 39
Nett earned Profits for the year ending February 1st, 1861.		$49,511 32
The Company have the following Assets:		
Bills receivable, for premiums		$ 55,531 24
Bills receivable, for balance due on Stock Notes.		152 964 91
Cash, balance on hand		139,503 61
Balance due by New Iberia Agency		333 50
Balance due by New Orleans Agency ..		3,375 35
Total assets		$351,709 61

(Signed) WM. S. PIKE, Pres't.
F. E. Hebert, Sec'y.
Baton Rouge, February 2d, 1861.

STATE OF LOUISIANA, } Parish of E. Baton Rouge, Feb. 1. 1861.

Be it remembered, That on this first day of February, 1861, before me the subscriber, a Justice of the Peace in and for the parish aforesaid, personally appeared Wm. S. Pike, President, and F. E. Hebert, Secretary of the Southern Mutual Insurance Company, of Baton Rouge, who being duly sworn according to law do depose and say that the above accounts are just and true, and a correct transcript from the books of said Company.
(Signed) WM. S. PIKE, President.
F. E. Hebert, Secretary,
Sworn to and subscribed before me, this second day of February, 1861.
[Signed] P. A. WALKER, Justice of the Peace.
(Signed) P. A. WALKER, Justice of the Peace.

NOTICE.
Office Southern Mutual Insurance Co., } Baton Rouge, Feb. 4th, 1861.

At a meeting of the Board of Directors, held this day, it was *Resolved*, To pay *six per cent* interest on the outstanding Scrip, *eight per cent* to Stockholders on premiums paid by them for the year ending 1st February, 1861, and to declare a dividend of *fifty per cent* on the nett earned premiums of the Company for the year ending 31st January, 1861, for which certificates will be issued on and after the 1st day of March next.
It was further Resolved, To redeem the outstanding Scrip for the year 1858, on presentation at the office of the Company.
☞The Stockholders are hereby notified that an election for ten Directors and fifteen Trustees to serve for the ensuing year, will be held at the office of the Company, on Thursday, the 14th of March, 1861.
mh30 F. E. HEBERT, Sec'y.

KETTLE SETTING.
A Labor of Years Reduced to a Few Days.

HAVING been induced by frequent solicitation, to make public the science of Kettle Setting that I practice, I hereby give notice to all persons desiring to acquire a knowledge of the art, that I will give them instructions for the Setting of Kettles, for either wood or coal, on application to me.
My system is based upon principles, the plausibility and correctness of which admit of no contradiction, which are quickly and fully comprehended, and therefore not liable to be easily forgotten.
I have models for five different constructions of Kettles, and designs by which instruction is made easy, and the art soon acquired. Copies of designs or drawings are given to those whom I instruct. All those to whom I teach my system, are also assisted by my services, if required.
Instructions are only given to those who have been three or four years at the business of Kettle Setting, and are good workmen.
For further particulars, inquire, by letter or otherwise, of the undersigned.
JOHN TOWNSEND.
Plaquemine, (Parish of Iberville,) La., Feb. 25, 1860.
Refer to—Dr. C. Clement, Iberville.
" Louis Desobry, Sr., "
" Gervais & Roman Schlatre, "
" John Schlatre, "
" Sylvar Marionneaux, "
" Edward J. Gay, "
" Jas. C. Woods, West Baton Rouge.
" Dan. H. Hickey, do
" Thompson J. Bird, East Baton Rouge

DIRECT IMPORTATION
—OF—
HAVANA CIGARS!

WE are in receipt of a small invoice of HAVANA CIGARS imported by ourselves. These we can sell at New Orleans prices. We can furnish our customers with the GENUINE WEED at $35 per thousand—something very good at $40, as good as we could sell heretofore at $50.
By next steamship we shall receive a large invoice.
☞Call, examine and judge for yourselves
je30 STOCKLEY & DELAVALLADE

WADDELL'S PILLS.

THIS Purely Vegetable Pill, which is spoken off so highly by all who have used them, for Diarrhea, Dysentary, Piles, &c. &c., or any affliction of the Bowels and Stomach, can be had No. 93Camp street, New Orleans.

Gazette & Sentinel.

PUBLISHED EVERY SATURDAY BY
W. P. BRADBURN,
EDITOR AND PROPRIETOR.

Vice President Stevens.

The Montgomery correspondent of the Missouri (St. Louis) Republican gives the "Personel of Vice President Stephens" as follows:

Imagine the reanimated form of the remarkable, eccentric John Randolph, habited in a swallow-tail coat of black, badly cut pants, black vest, flowing silk neckerchief of the same sombre hue, flashy pendant watch chain, heavy seals, golden-rimmed eye-glasses, and a beaver cocked on the side of the head, and you have a faint idea of Stephens of Georgia. Until you look at the face a long time, however, you have no conception of the man. To picture the countenance with pen and ink is difficult. In its ordinary aspect of repose it is very common, yet even in its commonness, yet even it is unusual. At a a glance the impression it makes is but of pity for the "sufferer" to whom it belongs. The occasion when it was first my chance to see this remarkable man, I would have declared he was a Floridian. Mosquitoes, ague and fever, swamp and exhalations of the lowlands of the South recurred to me instantaneously.

"What in the name of wonder do they send such a man here for?" "What *did* he come from?" and "who is he, pray?" were questions that I promptly asked. "That's Stephens of Georgia," was the answer that astonished me. I need not say that my curiosity was fully aroused, and that I examined the face fully.—Minutely, then, I should say, it is excessively pale and almost corpse-like. The lips are thin, determined, of nearly an ashen hue. Heavy lines indent every part of it. Around the eyes are wrinkles run with the same regularity that spokes branch out from the hub of a wheel. The forehead is high, wide and full—yet the larger part of it is hidden by harsh, grayish hair, allowed to straggle about loosely.

The whole countenance is small, and emphatically effeminate. In youth it might have been prepossessing; though decidedly never good looking. Now it might readily be taken for an old lady's wrinkled face. The eye is the only redeeming feature; even in the repose it sparkles, fascinates and commands—in excitement it flashes. When conversing in an ordinary manner the voice, too, is boyish—womanish—but is, nevertheless, melodious and well modulated. As conversation merges into debate, and debate grows into an effort at oratory, excitement seems to change the entire man. His gestures become graceful, and the voice gains strength but not harshness. It has the clear ring of silver, and is so distinct that it can be heard by every man in the largest assembly.

Revaccination.

M. Hemincax has detailed to the Belgian Academy of Medicine the results of the revaccinations put into force at the prisons of Ghent and Vilvorde, the subjects amounting to one thousand six hundred and sixty. Of these, three hundred and seventy-nine, or sixteen per cent., were vaccinated with success; there were in seven hundred and sixteen manifest traces of a prior vaccination, and four hundred and seventy-one exhibited marks of small-pox. Of the seven hundred and sixteen, sixteen per cent., and of the four hundred and seventy-one, forty-six per cent. were vaccinated with success. The author's conclusions, from these and other cases, are as follows:

First, the revaccination of subjects who have been well vaccinated, produces generally but few useful effects; second, persons who have been the subjects of variola, have much more cause to be revaccinated than those who have undergone proper vacinnation; third, revaccination is successful in proportion to the length of time which has elapsed since the first vaccination or the attack of variola; fourth, until the age of twenty-five it is generally useless; fifth, from that age to thirty-five it gives rise to useless results in a certain number of individuals, but this number is so extremely small, that without proscribing it in such persons, it need not be warmly recommended to them; sixth, after thirty-five it becomes a sure preservative, and consequently necessary; seventh, its failure at one period furnishes no reason for not having recourse to it at other epochs, as there is no reason to suppose that the receptivity may not return between the one and the other operation.

Good for John Chinaman.—The 'loot' of the summer palace at Pekin, although productive of much plunder to the invaders, seems to have afforded them but little substantial benefit. The Chinese eagerly bought up a large quantity on the first days of the sale, giving in exchange counterfeit Mexican dollars.

Gazette & Sentinel.

The Supreme Court.

The following decisions upon appeals from the parish, we find in the *Picayune* of Thursday last:

Augustus Talbot *vs.* Julie E. Marionneaux, widow of Thos. Cropper, appellant. Appeal from the Sixth District Court of Iberville.

This is an action for professional services rendered defendant. Judgment for plaintiff affirmed.

Guillaume Regis *vs.* Michel Hebert, administrator, appellant. Appeal from Sixth District Court of Iberville. Suit on a letter of credit. Judgment reversed and rendered in favor of the defendant, with costs.

Succession of R. L. Schmitt, Wm. Creevy, administrator, appellant, *vs.* J. Marks, *et al.*, opponents. Appeal from Sixth District of Iberville. Judgment affirmed.

Austin and McWilliams *vs.* H. E. Moore. Decision in favor of plaintiff affirmed.

New Mexico Declares for the South.—In the St. Louis Republican we find the following letter:

Los Vegas, New Mexico,
March 12, 1861.

The stage arrived here this morning from Santa Fé, en route for the States, and as it was about leaving here on its way in, an express arrived from Col. Fauntleroy, commanding this Military Department, to the Commandant at Fort Union, ordering this officer to prepare for defense. On yesterday morning, about 11 o'clock, the people of the capital, (Sante Fé) Americans and Mexicans, en masse, seemed to have sprung up like "Cudmus' men," well armed and in great numbers, at once seized and now hold Fort Marcy. Col. F. declined to surrender the Fort, as was expected, and while in the act of remonstrating with the populace, the citizen soldiery rushed upon the works, and in ten minutes they were taken possession of.

Governor Rencher was the prime mover in these proceedings, and he now has charge of all the military equipments and public property. Everybody is surprised at this well concocted and efficient *coup d'armes.* In brief, New Mexico now has declared for, and practically affiliated with Texas and the South, and the United States as suddenly ignored and the allegiance changed.

Arizona also absolves her allegiance on the 16th inst.

Excuse haste,
Orcho Deoros.

Toby Tries his Gun.

Toby is high private in the first regiment of the Mississippi army. His company is armed with the breech-loading Maynard rifle, "warranted to shoot twelve times a minute, and carry a ball, effectively, 1600 yards." Men who fought at Monterey and Buena Vista, call the new fangled thing a "pop-gun." To test its efficiency, Toby's captain told his men "they must try their guns." In obedience to command, Toby procured the necessary munitions of war, and started with his "pop-gun" for the woods. Saw squirrel up a very high tree—took aim—fired. Effects of shot immediately and wonderful. Tree effectually topped, and nothing of the squirrel to be found except three broken hairs. "Pop-gun" rose in value—equal to a four-pounder. But Toby wouldn't shoot toward any more trees—afraid of being arrested for cutting down other people's timber. Walked a mile and a quarter to get sight of a hill. By aid of a small telescope, saw hill in distance; made ready; took aim at rock; shut both eyes—fired. As soon as breath returned, opened eyes; could see, just could; but couldn't hear; at least, couldn't distinguish any sounds; thought Niagara had broken loose or all out doors gone to drum-beating.—Determined to see if shot hit. Borrowed horse and started towards hill. After travelling two days and nights reached place; saw setting sun shining through the hill. Knew, right away, *that* was where the shot hit.—Went closer—stumbled over rocky fragments scattered for half a mile in line of bullet. Came to hole—knew the bullet hit there, because saw lead on the edges—walked in, walked right through; saw teamster on the other side, indulging in profane language; in fact, "cussin' considerable," because lightning had killed his team. Looked as his finger directed; saw six dead oxen in line with the hole through the mountain; knew *that* was the bullet's work, but didn't say so to angry teamster. Thought best to be leaving; in consequence, didn't explore path of bullet any further; therefore, don't know whether it stopped at all; in fact rather think it didn't. Mounted horse—rode back through the hole made by the bullet: came home; put gun away; but never told Captain a word about it; to tell truth, was little afraid he would think it a hoax. 'It is a right big story, boys,' said Toby in conclusion, 'but it's true, sure as shooting. Nothing to do with the Maynard rifle but load her up, turn her north, and pull trigger; if twenty of them don't clean out all Yankeedom, then I'm a liar, that's all.—*Oxford (Miss.) Intelligencer.*

☞ The manager of the Court street Menagerie, in Boston, has obtained a living white elephant, and will have it on exhibition in a few weeks.

☞ A sermon in four words on the vanity of earthly possessions: "Shrouds have no pockets."

Religion for the Times.

A writer in the *Congregationalist* describes a religion which the times require, in the following sensible and pointed language:

We want a religion that goes into the family, and keeps the husband from being spiteful when the dinner is late, and keeps the dinner from being late—keeps the wife from fretting when the husband tracks the newly-washed floor with his muddy boots, and makes the husband mindful of the scraper and the door-mat—keeps the mother patient when the baby is cross, and keeps the baby pleasant—amuses the children as well as instructs them—win as well as governs—projects the honeymoon into tho harvestmoon, and makes the happy hours like the eastern fig tree, bearing in its bosom at once the beauty of the tender blossom and the glory of the ripened fruit. We want a religion that bears heavily, not only on the "exceeding sinfulness of sin," but on the exceeding rascality of lying and stealing—a religion that banishes small measures from the counters, small baskets from the stalls, pebbles from the cotton bags, clay from paper, sand from sugar, chicory from coffee, otter from butter, beet juice from vinegar, alum from bread, strychnine from wine, water from milk cans, and buttons from the contribution box."

The religion that is to save the world will not put all the big strawberries on the top, and all the bad ones at the bottom It will not offer more baskets of foreign wines than the vineyards ever produced bottles, and more barrels of flour than all the wheat fields of New York grow, and all the mills grind. It will not make one-half of a pair of shoes of good leather, and the other of poor leather, so that the first shall redound to the maker's credit, and second to his cash. It will not put Govin's stamp on Jenkins' kid gloves, nor make Paris bonnets in the back rooms of a Boston milliner's shop, nor let a piece of velvet that professes to measure twelve yards, come to an untimely end in the tenth, or spool of sewing silk that vouches for twenty yards, be nipped in the bud at fourteen and a half, nor the cotton thread spool break to the yardstick fifty of the two hundred yards of promise that was given to the eye, nor yard wide cloth measure less than thirty-six inches from salvage to salvage, nor all wool delaines and all linen handkerchiefs amalgamate with clandestine cotton, nor coats made of old woolen rags pressed together, be sold to the unsuspecting public for legal broadcloth. It does not put bricks at five dollars per thousand into chimneys it contracted to build of seven dollar materials, nor smuggle white pine into floors that have paid for hard pine, nor leave yawning cracks in the closets, where boards ought to join, nor daub the ceiling that ought to be smoothly plastered, nor make window-blinds with slats that cannot stand the winds, and paint that cannot stand the sun, and fastenings that may be looked at, but are on no account to be touched.

The religion which is to sanctify the world, pays its debts. It does not consider that forty cents returned for one hundred cents given, is according to law. It looks upon a man who has failed in trade, and who coutinues to live in luxury, as a thief.

Our President.

The Journal of Commerce publishes a sensible letter, written from Savannah, to the editor of that paper, by a gentleman of New York, from which we make the following extract:

You would not be much surprised, were you here, to find how completely the new Federal Government is inaugurated, and how completely the old seems to be forgotten, except so far as the daily anxiety for a peaceable settlement is manifested by the hopes and fears inspired by sensation paragraphs and telegrams in the daily journals. Yet the business of life goes on socially, and on 'Change, except as interrupted by constant military exercises and preparations for defence. The public confidence in the military prowess of President Davis and accomplished and brave officers he is drawing around him, is marked and without exception. Indeed, Washington himself had not the confidence of Continentals more undividedly than has President Davis the hearts of the whole South. Even State pride and personal vanity seem to yield without a murmur. While the gallant and gifted graduates of West Point, who had earned their laurels in the bloody fields of Mexico, seem to revere him as Napoleon was loved by the old guard. Indeed, it is not extravagant to say, that they all believe in him, and invest him with every qualification as a soldier and statesman, let Republicans deride the rupture as they may, and hold out false hopes of speedy and easy settlement. I confess, aside from the horrors of civil war, always to be deprecated as the source of all national evils. I fear this popular leader, whose coolness and bravery cannot be doubted, will add a dangerous page to Republican history, should hostilities to the South induce, as was the case in classic history, this leader to "carry the war into Africa." The South has implored the North to grant them peace; and fearful will be the responsibility of those who counsel a destruction of those fraternal relations by the shedding of blood, as a mere abstraction of the right to govern an unwilling people, who desire peaceably to withdraw from a government found to be uncongenial to their peace and happiness; and who offer every other advantage which national reciprocity can give for mutual good.

Interior of the Earth.—It would appear from the theory of the earth's constitution, now very generally received, that the planet on which we live, contains within itself the elements of its own destruction. According to the theory in question, there exists within the outer crust—the cool temperature of which supports animal and vegetable life, and solidifies stone, coal and the various metallic ores—a mass of fluid igneous matter. Some of this matter occasionally escapes through the mouth of a volcano, or makes its presence felt by an earthquake; but neither the earthquake nor the volcano are considered as necessary to prove that fire exists in the centre of the earth. On descending beneath the surface, the heat gradually but steadily increases. At the depth of 2480 yards water will boil, and lead melts at the depth of 8400 yards. There is a red heat at the depth of seven miles, and by adopting the temperatures as calculated from Morveau's corrected scale of Wedgeworth's pyrometer, it is found that the earth is fluid at the depth of 100 miles. The discharge of melted earthy matter, called lava, from volcanoes, is thought to prove that the mass of the interior of the earth is in a state of fusion; while the hot springs in different parts of the world, show that a high temperature prevails at no very great depth. At the surface this internal heat is not perceptible, because the outer crust of the earth is a bad conductor.

Drinking Porter out of Pewter.—If porter be drunk out of a pewter pot, it will produce a more brisk sensation than when it is taken out of a glass vessel, which is ascribed to a galvanic effect. In this instance, there is a combination of one metal and two dissimilar fluids, which combination constitutes a galvanic circle. In the act of drinking, one side of the pewter pot is exposed to the action of the saliva, which moisten the lip, while the other metallic side is in contact with the porter; the circuit being thus completed, an agreeable relish is communicated to the beverage when it comes in contact with the tongue.

☞ Coughs. The sudden changes of our climate are sources of Pulmonary, Bronchial, and Asthmatic Affections. Experience having proved that simple remedies often act speedily and certainly when taken in the early stages of the disease, recourse should at once be had to "Brown's Bronchial Troches," or Lozenges, let the Cold, Cough, or Irritation of the Throat be ever so slight, as by this precaution a more serious attack may be effectually warded off. Public Speakers and Singers wil lfind them effectual for clearing and strengthening the voice. See advertisement.

DIED.

At his residence in this parish, last Thursday, at a quarter past 12, A. M., **WM. B. SAVORY,** in the 79th year of his age.

ESTRAY.

TAKEN up by J. P. CHENLEVILLE, one **MARE MULE,** no brands, right foot crooked, aged about 6 years.

The owner of the said animal can have the same by proving property and paying charges, otherwise she will be sold on Tuesday the 30th day of April next, 1861, at my residence on Grosse Tete.

mh30 J. E. BARGAS.

ESTRAY.

TAKEN up by Wm. BILLINGS, on Grosse Tete, one **GREY BEEF,** about two years old, no mark or brand.

The owner of the above animal will please come forward, prove property, pay charges and take it away, or it will be sold to the highest bidder on Tuesday, the 16th day of April, 1861, at the residence of Mr. Billings. mh30

J. E. BARGAS.

Succession Sale.

STATE OF LOUISIANA—Parish of Iberville—6th Judicial Dist. Court.

Succession of Pierre Durand,
DECEASED.

BY virtue of an Order or Decree to me directed from the Honorable the Sixth Judicial District Court of the State of Louisiana, in and for the Parish of Iberville, bearing date the **12th day of March, 1861,** ordering and decreeing the sale of the property belonging to the Succession of said PIERRE DURAND, dec'd, and situated in the Parish of Iberville, I will offer at Public Sale, to the highest and last bidder on

Thursday, the 18th of April, 1861, at 11 o'clock, A. M.,

And on the premises, the whole of the following described property, said property to be sold in block, to wit: A certain

PLANTATION,

Cultivated as a Sugar Plantation, lying and situated in the Parish of Iberville, on the right bank of the river Mississippi, at about fifteen miles below the Bayou Plaquemine, measuring twelve arpents, more or less front on Missisppi river, by sixty six arpents more or less in depth, except the four upper arpents which have a depth of seventy two arpents more or less, the side lines diverging—giving a superficie of about thirteen hundred arpents to said plantation. The said plantation is bounded above by land of John H. Randolph, below by land of Henry Rantiford, and in the rear by lands of Felix Dugar, Wm. M. and J. R. Thompson, and J. A. Hartman, together with all the buildings, improvements and appurtenances thereon, being and thereunto belonging; also, with the active servitudes of drainage thereunto belonging.

The following named and described

SLAVES, to wit:

John Bull, negro man aged 54 years, having an affection of the lungs; Rachelle, negro woman, aged 56 years, having the disease of the heart; George Parker, negro man, a cooper, aged 30 years; Adéle, negro woman, aged 26 years, a washer and ironer, and her 2 children, Fidélise, a girl, aged 8 years, and Henrietta, a girl aged 6 years; Kager, a negro man, aged 37 years; Louisa, negro woman aged 21 years, and her two children—John, a boy aged 3 years, and an infant child, a girl; Edmund, negro man aged 24 years; Angela, negro woman aged 18 years; Amédé, negro man aged 20 years; Paulin, negro man aged 36 years; Rachelle, negro woman aged 32 years; Sam Dison, negro man aged 33 years; Jackson, negro man aged 37 years; Mèlasie, negro woman aged 36 years, and her child Edward, a boy aged 7 years; Auguste, negro man aged 41 years; Peter, negro man aged 37 years; André, negro man aged 40 years; Modeste, negro woman aged 24 years; Ellen, negro woman aged 48 years, and her child Basilise, a girl aged 9 years; Ellena, negro woman aged 17 years; Joseph, negro man aged 42 years; Adeline, negro woman aged 37 years, and her two children, Antoine, a boy aged 8 years, and Prospére, a boy aged 7 years; Charles, negro man aged 42 years; Pauline, negro woman aged 47 years, ruptured; Steven, negro man aged 37 years; Ann Taylor, negro woman aged 32 years, and her child Mary, a girl aged 9 years; Martine, a negro woman aged 30 years, scrofulas, and her child Fanny, a girl aged 5 years; William, negro man aged 37 years; Elizabeth, negro woman aged 30 years, and her 2 children, Williamine, a girl aged 8 years, and Virginia, a girl aged 6 yrs.; Catherine, negro girl aged 10 years; Ephraim, negro man aged 40 years; Madelaine, negro woman aged 33 years and her three children, Sophia, a girl aged 8 years; Abraham, a boy aged 4 years, and Thomas, a boy aged 2 years; Alice, a negro girl aged 10 years; Hypolite, negro boy aged 14 years; Barker, negro man subject to rheumatism, aged 56 years; Henry, negro boy aged 19 years; Jack, negro man aged 56 years, ruptured; Martha, negro woman aged 52 years, ruptured; George Bell, negro man aged 37 years; Rosa, negro woman aged 29 years, and her two children, Clarissa, a girl aged 7 years, and an infant child; Dailey, negro girl aged 15 years; Rose, a girl aged 13 years; Soloman, negro man aged 65 years, infirm; Rachael, negro woman aged 52 years, ruptured; Nelson, negro man aged 80 years; Wilby, negro man aged 39 years; Rosalie, negro woman aged 56 years; Honoraé, negro man, sickly, aged 56 years; Jacinte, negro woman aged 33 years; Evariste, negro boy aged 12 years, cripple; Ines, negro woman aged 22 years; John, negro man aged 39 years; Nancy, negro woman aged 44 years, sickly; Augustin, negro man, cripple, aged 39 years; Hilaire, negro man aged 20 years; Louise, negro woman aged 18 years; Eole, negro boy aged 16 years; Artémise, negro woman aged 57 years; Sam, negro man aged 39 years; Willis, negro man aged 39 years; Agnes, negro woman aged 38 years; David, negro boy aged 19 years; Robert, negro man aged 32 yrs.; Lewis, negro man, sickly, aged 44 yrs.; Nancy, negro woman aged 57 years; Christophe, negro man aged 47 years; Jambart, negro boy aged 18 years; Pierre, negro man aged 24 years; Geo. Moreau, negro man aged 41 years, a Carpenter; Patsy, negro woman aged 35 years, and her three children—Eliza, a girl aged 6 years; Alfred, a boy aged 3 years, and an infant child; Paul, negro man aged 34 years.

Also, the following moveable Property, to wit:

41 mules; 1 horse; 1 mare; 6 oxen; 30 horn cattle; 40 hogs, 3 goats; 7000 fire bricks; 200,000 bricks; 1 timber wheel; 1 scale; 1 oil can; 60 gals. of oil; 1 scale; 100 hogsheads; one lot of hoop poles; 2500 barrels of corn more or less, one lot of hay; 2 corn shellers; 1 grinding machine; 10,000 feet of lumber; stove, 23 large plows; 10 small plows; 3 flueks; 1 subsoil; 5 shovels, 25 spades; 75 hoes; 32 pairs of gears; 40 bridles; 40 pairs of haims; 60 moss collars; 20 double-trees; 10 triple-trees; 50 single-trees; 32 axes; 40 cane knives; 11 cane carts; 4 bagasse carts, 2 kegs of nails; 45 bbls. of coal; 800 cords of wood; 8000 hogshead staves.

The one undivided fourth part of the whole of the herein above described property belongs to the Succession of said Pierre Durand, and the other three undivided fourth parts thereof belongs to Antoine Dubuclet, a resident of the said Parish of Iberville, and the share of said Antoine Dubuclet in said property, is sold with the consent of said Antoine Dubuclet, as it appears by the order of the said Sixth Judicial District Court of Louisiana.

TERMS OF SALE, CASH, payable on the day of sale.

G. S. ROUSSEAU, Auctioneer.
Iberville, March 15, 1861. mr15

Vente de Succession.

ETAT DE LA LOUISIANE—Paroisse d'Iberville—Cour du 6eme District.

Succession de feu Pierre Durand.

En vertu d'un ordre au decret a moi adressé par l'Hon'ble. Cour du Sixième District Judiciaire en et pour la paroisse d'Iberville, en date du 12ème. jour de Mars 1861, ordonant et decrétant la vente des propriétés appartenant à la succession de feu Pierre Durand, situeés dans la paroisse d'Iberville, J'offrérai en vente publique au plus offrant et dernier encherisseur,

Jeudi, le 18eme. jour d'Avril,

prochain, 1861, a 11 heures A. M., sur les lieux, toutes les propriétés ci-après décrites, lesquelles proprietiés seront vendues en bloc-savoir:

UNE CERTAINE HABITATION cultivée, en sucrerie, située dans la paroisse d'Iberville, sur le rive droite du fleuve Mississippi, a environ quinze milles plus bas que le Bayou Plaquemine, mesurant douze arpents, plus ou moins de face au fleuve Mississippi, sur une profondeur de soixante six arpents, plus ou moins, excepté les quatre arpents superieurs qui'ont une profondeur de soixante douze arpents, plus ou moins, les lignes superieures et inferieures divergeant, dounant à la susdite habitation une superficie de treize cents arpens, plus ou moins; la susdite habitation est bornée en haut par la terre de John H. Randolph, en bas par la terre de Henry Rantiford, et en arrière par la terre de Felix Dugas, William M. et J. R. Thompson et J. A. Hartman, avec toutes les batisses et ameliorations y appartenant, et avec toutes les servitudes certives d'egout qui appartiennant a la susdite habitation.

Les ESCLAVES ci après nommés et decrites avoir:

John Bull, negre agé de 54 ans, ayant une maladie de poumons.

Bachelle, negresse agée de 56 ans, ayant une maladie de cœur.

George Parker, tonnelier, negre agé de 30 ans;

Adele, negresse agée de 26 ans, blanchisseuse et repassieuse, et ses deux enfans—Fidelise, negritte agee de 8 ans; et Henriette, negritte agée de 6 ans;

Louisa, negresse agée de 21 ans, et ses deux enfans—John, negrillon agé de 3 ans, et une petite fille a la Manuelle;

Kager, negresse agée de 37 ans;
Edmund, negre agé de 24 ans;
Angela, negresse agée de 18 ans;
Amédé, negre agé de 20 ans;
Paulin, negre agé de 36 ans;
Rachelle, negresse agée de 32 ans;
Sam Dison, negre agé de 33 ans;
Jackson, negre agé de 37 ans;
Mélasie, negresse agée de 36 ans, et son negrillon Edward, age de 7 ans;
Auguste, negre agé de 41 ans;
Peter, negre agé de 37 ans;
André, negre agé de 40 ans;
Modeste, negresse agée de 24 ans;
Ellen, negresse agée de 48 ans, et son enfant Basilise, negritte agée de 9 ans;
Ellena, negresse agée de 17 ans;
Joseph, negre agé de 42 ans;
Adeline, negresse agée de 37 ans, et ses deux enfans—Antoine, negrillon age de 8 ans, et Prospère, negrillon agé de 7 ans;
Charles, negre agé de 42 ans;
Pauline, negresse agée de 47 ans, herniaire;
Steven, negre agé de 37 ans;
Ann Taylor, negresse agée de 32 ans, et son enfant Mary, negritte agée de 9 ans;
Martine, negresse agée de 30 ans, scrofuleux, et son enfant Fanny, negrette agée de 5 ans;
William, negre age de 37 ans;
Elizabeth, negresse agée de 30 ans, et ses deux enfans—Williamine, negritte agée de 8 ans, et Virginia, negritte agée de 6 ans;
Catherine, negritte agée de 10 ans;
Ephraim, negre agé de 40 ans;
Madelaine, negresse agée de 33 ans, et ses trois enfans—Sophie, negritte agée de 8 ans; Abraham, negrillon agé de 4 ans, and Thomas, negrillon agé de 2 ans;
Alice, negritte agé de 10 ans;
Hypolite, negrillon agée de 14 ans;
Barker, negre agé de 56 ans, sujet de rheumatis.
Henry, negre agé de 19 ans;
Jack, negre agé de 56 ans, herniaire;
Martha, negresse agée de 52 ans, herniaire;
George Bell, negre agé de 37 ans;
Rosa, negresse agée de 29 ans, et ses deux enfans—Clarisse, negritte agée de 7 ans, et une petit fille;
Dailey, negritte agée de 15 ans;
Rose, negritte agée de 13 ans;
Soloman, negre agé de 65 ans, inferme;
Rachel, negresse agée de 52 ans, herniaire;
Nelson, negre agé de 80 ans;
Wilby, negre agé de 39 ans;
Rosalie, negresse agée de 56 ans;
Honore, negre agé de 56 ans, inferme;
Jacinte, negresse agée de 33 ans,
Evariste, negrillon agé 12 ans, boiteux;
Ines, negresse agée de 22 ans;
John, negre agé de 39 ans;
Maney, negresse agée de 44 ans, inferme;
Augustine, negresse agée de 39 ans, boiteux;
Hilaire, negre agé de 20 ans;
Louise, negresse agée de 18 ans;
Eole, negrillon agé de 16 ans;
Artemise, negresse agé de 57 ans;
Sam, negre agé de 38 ans;
Willis, negre agé de 39 ans;
Agnes, negresse agée de 38 ans;
David, negre agé de 19 ans;
Robert, negre agé de 32 ans;
Lewis, negre agé de 44 ans, inferme;
Nancy, negresse agée de 57 ans;
Christophe, negre agé de 47 ans;
Jambart, negre agé de 18 ans,
Pierre, negre agé de 24 ans;
George Moreau, negre agé de 41 ans, charpentier;
Patsy, negresse agée 35 ans, et ses trois enfans—Eliza, negritte agée de 6 ans; Alfred, negrillon agé de 3 ans, et un enfant à la manelle;
Paul, negre agé de 34 ans.

Et aussi les proprietés mobiliers ci-après décrites, savoir:

Quarante et un mulets; 1 cheval; 1 jument, 6 bœufs; 30 bêtes a cornes; 40 cochons; 3 cabris; 7000 briques a feu; 200,000 briques; un diable; une balance; un bidou à huile; 60 gallons d'huile; une balance; 100 boucants; un lot de perches; 2500 barrils de maïs, plus ou moins; un lot de foin; deux machines pour egreuner de maïs; une machine pour eraser le maïs; 10,000 pieds de bois de charpente; un poïle; 23 grosses eharrues; 10 petites charrues; 3 flukes, un subsoil; 5 pelles pour jetter la terre; 25 pelles; 75 pioches; 32 pairs de traits; 40 brides; 40 pairs de bois de colliers; 60 colliers de mousses; 20 paloniers double; 10 paloniers triple; 50 paloniers simples; 32 haches; 40 conteaux à canes; 11 charrettes a canes; 4 charrettes a bagasses; 2 petits barrils de cloux; 45 barrils de charbon; 800 cordes de bois; 8000 douves a boucaut.

Le quart indivise de toutes les propriétés ci cedessus decrites appartient à la succession du dit feu Pierre Durand, et les autres trois quarts appartiennent a Antoine Dubuclet, un residant de la paroisse d'Iberville, et la part du dit Antoine Dubuclet dans les susdites propriétés saut vendues avec le un consentement du dit Antoine Dubuclet comme ii apparait par le decret de la susdite Cour du Sixième District Judiciaire de la Louisiane.

Conditions de la vente comptant, payable le jour de la vente.

G. S. ROUSSEAU, Encanteur.
Iberville, 15 Mars, 1861. mh16

State of Louisiana—Parish of Iberville—6th Judicial District Court.

Succession of **Charles McManus.**

WHEREAS: ADOLPHE GRASS has this day filed his final account of administration as Curator of the Estate of Charles McManus.

Notice is hereby given to all whom it may concern to show cause within thirty days from this date, why the final Tableau of Administration aforesaid, should not be homologated and made a judgement of this Court.

Iberville, March 28, 1861. mar30.
M. A. ESTEVAN, Clerk.

Etat de la Louisiane—Paroisse d'Iberville—Cour du 6eme District Judiciaire.

Dans la Succeston de feu

Charles McManus.

ATTENDU, que ADOLPHE GRASS a ce jour deposé au bureau d'Greffier de la Cour son compte à administration comme curateur de la susdite succession.

Avis est par le present donné à tous ceux que cela concerne de deduire sous trente jours de la date de ce present les raisons pour lesquelles le dit Tableau Final ne serait pas homologué et fait le jugement de cette Cour.

Iberville, le 28 Mars, 1861. m30.
M. A. ESTEVAN, Greffier.

EXTRA STANDARD.

Saturday Morning, April 13th, 1861.

THE WAR BEGUN.

FORT SUMTER ATTACKED.

The First Gun Fired by the South.

MAJOR ANDERSON PROMPTLY RETURNS THE FIRE!

The Bombardment Continues all Day and Night!

Breaches being effected in Fort Sumter, Part of the Parapet Destroyed, and Guns Shot Away.

SEVEN BATTARIES OPENED ON SUMTER.

The Pawnee, Harriet Lane, and another War Vessel off Charleston.

The War Vessels cannot enter the Harbor on account of a severe Storm.

NOBODY KILLED.

TWO MEN WOUNDED, SEVERAL KNOCKED DOWN BY SPENT BALLS.

Major Anderson will hold out until his Provisions are exhausted!

Great Excitement at the South!

The Military by Thousands pouring into Charleston!

The Floating Battery not a Failure.

Correspondence between the Secession Authories and Major Anderson.

OTHER NEWS BY TELEGRAPH.

NEW YORK, April 12.

A special dispatch from Washington to the *Commercial Advertiser* says the President to-day expresses confidence that a supply ship will be permitted by the Charleston authorities to land stores at Fort Sumter.

CHARLESTON, April 12.

The following is the telegraphic correspondence between the War Department at Montgomery and Gen. Beauregard immediately preceding hostilities. The correspondence grew out of the formal notification by the Washington government disclosed in Beauregard's first dispatch:

CHARLESTON, April 8.

To L. P. Walker, Secretary of War at Montgomery:

An authorized messenger, from Mr. Lincoln, has just informed Gov. Pickens and myself that provisions will be sent to Fort Sumter peaceably; otherwise by force.

(Signed) G. T. BEAUREGARD.

MONTGOMERY, April 10.

To Gen. Beauregard, Charleston:

If you have no doubt of the authorized character of the agent, who communicated to you the intentions of the Washington government, to supply Fort Sumter by force, you will at once demand its evacuation, and if this is refused proceed in such a manner as you may determine to reduce it. Answer.

(Signed) L. P. WALKER. Secretary of War.

[No. 3.]

CHARLESTON, April 10.

To L. P. Walker, Secretary of War:

The demand will be made to-morrow at 12 o'clock. (Signed) BEAUREGARD.

[No. 4.]

MONTGOMERY, April 10.

To Gen. Beauregard, Charleston:

Unless there are special reasons connected with your own condition, it is considered proper that you should make the demand at an early hour.

(Signed) L. P. WALKER, Secretary of War.

[No. 5.]

CHARLESTON, April 10.

To L. P. Walker, Secretary of War:

The reasons are special for 12 o'clock.

(Signed) BEAUREGARD.

[No. 6.]

CHARLESTON, April 11.

To L. P. Walker, Secretary of War:

The demand was sent at 2 o'clock; allowed till 6 o'clock to answer.

(Signed) BEAUREGARD.

[No. 7.]

MONTGOMERY, April 11.

To Gen. Beauregard, Charleston:

Telegraph reply of Anderson.

(Signed) L. P. WALKER.

[No. 8.]

CHARLESTON, April 11.

To L. P. Walker, Secretary of War:

Major Anderson replies: "I have the honor to acknowledge the reception of your communication demanding the evacuation of this fort, and say in reply that it is a demand with which I regret that my sense of honer and my obligations to my government prevent my complying with." He adds: "Probably I will await the first shot, and if you do not batter us to pieces, we will be starved out in a few days." Answer.

(Signed) BEAUREGARD.

[No. 9.]

MONTGOMERY, April 11.

To Gen. Beauregard, Charleston:

Do not desire needlessly to bombard Sumter. If Major Anderson will state the time at which, as indicated by him, he will evacuate and agree that in the mean time he will not use his guns against us, unless ours should be employed against Sumter, you are authorized thus to avoid the effusion of blood. If this, or its equivalent, be refused, reduce the fort us your judgment decides to be the most practicable.

(Signed) L. P. WALKER, Sec'y of War.

[No. 10.]

CHARLESTON, April 12.

To L. P. Walker, Secretary of War.

He would not consent. I write to-day.

(Signed) BEAUREGARD.

[NOTE.—Intercepted dispatches disclose the fact that Lieut. Fox, who had been allowed to visit Major Anderson on the pledge that his purpose was pacific, employed his opportunity to devise a plan for supplying the fort by force and that this plan had been adopted by the Washington government, and was in progress of execution.]

SECOND DISPATCH.

CHARLESTON, April 12.

The ball has opened! War is inaugurated!! The batteries of Sullivan's Island and Morris Island, and at other points, opened on Fort Sumter this morning.

Fort Sumter has returned the fire and a brisk cannonading has been kept up.

No information has been received from the seaboard as yet.

The military are under arms. The whole population is in the streets. Every available space facing the harbor, is filled with anxious spectators.

NEW YORK, April 12.

The *Herald* special despatch from Charleston, says Fort Moultrie began the bombardment with two guns, to which Major Anderson replied with three shots from his barbette guns, after which the batteries at Mount Pleasant, Cummings Point, and the Floating Battery opened a brisk fire with shot and shells.

Major Anderson replied only at long intervals, until between 7 and 8 o'clock, when he opened from the two tiers of guns looking towards Fort Moultrie and Stevens Battery, but at 2 o'clock had failed to produce any serious effect.

During the greater part of the day Major Anderson directed his shots principally against Forts Moultrie, the Stevens and Floating Batteries and fort Johnson, they being the only ones operating against him. Fifteen or 18 shot struck the Floating Battery without effect.

Breaches to all appearances are being made in the side of Fort Sumter exposed to fire. Portions of the parapet are destroyed, and several guns have been shot away.

The fight will continueall night.

The Fort will probably be carried by storm.

It is reported that the Harriet Lane has received a shot through her wheel house. She is in the offing.

No other government ships are in sight.

Troops are pouring into the city by thousands and all business is suspended.

THIRD DISPATCH.

CHARLESTON, April 12.

The firing was continued all day uninterruptedly.

Two of Fort Sumter's guns have been silenced, and it is reported that a breach has been made at the south-east wall.

The answer to Gen. Beauregard's demand, by Major Anderson, was that he would surrender when his supplies were exhausted, and was not reinforced.

Not a casualty has yet happened to any of the forces. Of 19 batteries only 7 have been opened on Fort Sumter. The remainder are held in reserve for the expected fleet.

Two thousand men reached the city this morning and embarked for Morris Island and neighborhood.

[FOURTH DISPATCH.]

CHARLESTON, April 12.

The bombardment of Fort Sumter continues.

The Floating Battery and Stevens' Battery are operating freely.

Sumter is returning the fire.

Three war vessels are outside the bar.

[FIFTH DISPATCH.]

The firing has ceased for the night, but will be renewed at daylight in the morning, unless an attempt is made to reinforce, for which ample arrangements are made to repel.

Only two have been wounded during the day.

The Pawnee, Harriet Lane, and another steamer, are reported off the bar.

Troops are arriving by every train.

[SPECIAL DESPATCH FROM CHARLESTON.]

6 o'clock, Evening.

Dispatches from the Floating Battery state that two men had been wounded on Sullivan Island.

Quite a number have been struck by spent pieces of shells and knocked down, but none hurt seriously.

Three ships are visible in the offing, and it is believed an attempt will be made to throw reinforcements into Sumter by boats.

It is also thought, from the regular and frequent firing of Anderson, that he has a much larger force of men than was supposed.

There have been two rain storms to-day, but they had no effect on the battle.

SIXTH DISPATCH.

CHARLESTON, April 12.

The bombardment is still going on every twenty minutes from mortars.

It is supposed that Anderson is resting his men for the night.

Three vessels of war are reported outside.

They cannot get in the sea is so rough.

Nobody hurt.

The floating battery works well.

Troops arrive hourly.

Every inlet is guarded.

Lively times!

SEVENTH DISPATCH.

CHARLESTON, April 12.

The firing on Sumter continues!

Reviving times on the Palmetto Coast!!

EIGHTH DISPATCH.

CHARLESTON, April 13, 12.30 A. M.

It is utterly impossible to reinforce Fort Sumter to-night.

The mortar batteries will be playing on Sumter all night.

VIRGINIA COMMISSIONERS.

WASHINGTON, April 12.

The Virginia Commissioners visited the President this afternoon, but not in an official capacity. They were received directly after the Cabinet meeting.

APPOINTMENTS.

The following appointments have been made: Charles A. Phelps, Surveyor of Boston, in place of Fletcher Webster, who was removed at the urgent request of the Massachusetts Congressional delegation.

Richard H. Dana, District Attorney, and John Keyes, Marshal of Massachusetts.

John A. Goodwin, Postmaster at Lowell.

O. P. Baldwin, Marshal, and Gen. Howe, District Attorney, of Vermont.

J. C. Aiken, Marshal, and E. G. Bradford, District Attorney, of Delaware.

GEN. SCOTT WANTED FORTS SUMTER AND PICKENS EVACUATED.

The expedition for the relief of Fort Sumter is said to be undertaken against the advice of Gen. Scott, he having urged the evacuation of both Forts Sumter and Pickens.

THE RECOGNITION OF HAYTIEN INDEPENDENCE.

Mr. Sumner called on Mr. Seward to-day, with Mr. Redpath, and made known the passage of the resolution of the Massachusetts Legislature, instructing its Senators and Representatives to use their influence to obtain the recognition of Haytien independence. Mr. Sumner stated that this resolution was adopted on the petition of all the merchants of Boston, having trade with Hayti, and added his own personal desire to those expressed by the legislature. He also said Governor Andrew warmly approved of this policy. It was also suggested that such recognition was calculated to have a good effect in counteracting the reported Spanish movement against Dominica.

THE CONFEDERATE LOAN.

It is denied that any portion of the Confederate State Loan has been offered in New York. More than the entire amount has been arranged for at par within the limits of the confederacy.

FROM THE PACIFIC—OVERLAND TELEGRAPH.

Among the passengers in the North Star is J. H. Wade, Esq., who returns after perfecting arrangements on the Pacific side for the immediate construction of a telegraph line from San Francisco to Salt Lake, to which point the lines are now being constructed by the Western Union Telegraph Company from St. Louis.

ONE OF THE CHARTERED STEAMERS BOUND SOUTH.

NEW YORK, April 12.

Steam tug Uncle Ben was seen on the afternoon of the 9th, ten miles south of Barnegat, bound south.

EXTRA SESSION OF THE CONFEDERATE CONGRESS.

MONTGOMERY, April 12.

An extra session of Congress has been called for the 29th.

SOUTHERN REJOICINGS.

MOBILE, April 12.

There is intense excitement and rejoicing here. Fifteen guns have been fired in honor of the attack on Fort Sumter.

KENTUCKY VOLUNTEERS FOR THE SOUTH.

LOUISVILLE, April 12.

Dispatches have come here to hold the Kentucky volunteers in readiness to move at a moment's notice, from the War Department at Montgomery.

THE PENNSYLVANIA WAR BILL PASSED.

HARRISBURG, April 12.

The War bill passed both Houses to-night, without amendment. Gov. Curtin waited at the executive office to sign it, and has signed it.

The Charleston dispatches about hostilities were received in both Houses, producing profound sensation.

THE FEELING IN BALTIMORE.

BALTIMORE, April 12.

The Charleston news was not generally promulgated until after night fall. It produced a profound sensation. There was a general impression of regret at bloodshed, and great diversity of views, but the general feeling was in favor of the government.

THE VIRGINIA CONVENTION.

RICHMOND, April 12.

The fourteenth resolution was adopted, with Totte's amendment, this being the last resolution of the proposed amendments to the Constitution. Wise's substitute was rejected. Adjourned.

Official dispatches between Beauregard, Anderson and Walker, have been circulated in the Convention this afternoon.

There was considerable sensation, but there was no indications that the Union men would consent to secede, without the coperation of the Border States. The public is greatly excited.

FROM MEXICO—JUAREZ ELECTED PRESIDENT.

NEW ORLEANS, April 12.

Dates from Vera Cruz are to the 9th.

A conducta with three millions in specie arrived at Vera Cruz March 30th.

De Lajada is dead.

The roads to the Capitol are newly patrolled.

Juarez had been elected President.

It is reported that Minister Weller has resigned.

ADJOURNMENT OF THE NEW YORK LEGISLATURE.

ALBANY, April 12.

A resolution was adopted by the Legislature to adjourn *sine die* at 12 o'clock to-morrow.

FIRE.—About 4 o'clock this morning fire was discovered in the counting room of S. Thomas & Co., in the lower story, east end of Taber's Block, head of Taber's wharf. The alarm was promptly responded to by the fire department, and the flames were extinguished before doing much damage. The fire took under the stove.

LOSS OF A HORSE.—This morning, after the horses belonging to steamer Onward were detached from the engine, they became frightened at the approach of No. Six hand engine, and ran into the company, one of the horses coming in contact with the pole of the engine with such force as to break one of his shoulders. The animal ran on three legs up Union street two or three squares, when he fell. A large crowd of sympathizers gathered around, until the horse was killed, by being knocked in the head. It was a very fine animal, valued at $250.

☞ We understand that orders have been given for the working of a few papers for the mail at the *Mercury* office, and the balance to be struck off after the issue of our extra. Of course the first copies will not have the stirring Southern news. An enterprising sheet that *Mercury!* There is a statute law against larceny.

The game of sending a copy of the *Mercury* to this office at an early hour this morning didn't work. We could see through as small a grindstone as that.

The Charleston Mercury.

DAILY PAPER—TEN DOLLAR PER ANNUM, PAYABLE HALF-YEARLY IN ADVANCE.

VINDICE NULLO
SPONTE SUA SINE LEGE FIDES RECTUMQUE COLENTUR.

COUNTRY PAPER—THRICE A WEEK—FIVE DOLLARS PER ANNUM IN ADVANCE.

VOLUME LVI. CHARLESTON, S. C., MONDAY, APRIL 15, 1861. NUMBER 11,126

The Daily Mercury

IS PUBLISHED EVERY MORNING.

(SUNDAYS EXCEPTED.)

The Tri-Weekly Mercury

ON TUESDAYS, THURSDAYS AND SATURDAYS.

OFFICE, No. 4 BROAD-STREET, CHARLESTON, SOUTH CAROLINA.

TERMS: CASH IN ADVANCE.

DAILY MERCURY, for one year........$10.00
" " for six months........ 5.00
" " for three months........ 2.50
" " for less than three months, $1 per month.

Newspaper Dealers and Retail Agents supplied on liberal terms.

TRI-WEEKLY MERCURY, for one year........$5.00
" " for six months........ 2.50
" " for three months........ 1.25
" " for less than three months, 50c. a month.

FROM THIS DATE, no subscriptions out of the city will be received unless accompanied with the cash.

POSTMASTERS are authorised to act as our Regular Agents in obtaining subscribers and forwarding the money, for which they will be allowed 20 per cent. commission; only, however, when paid in advance.

Subscribers desiring their papers changed, must mention the Post Office FROM, as well as the one TO, which they desire the change to be made.

Gentlemen getting up Clubs of 5, 10, 20, or more, will be supplied at 20 per cent. less than the Regular Rates.

ADVERTISING RATES.

THE MERCURY has now the largest circulation of any paper in the State, and is second in this respect to but few papers in the South; it therefore offers great advantages to business men and others, whose interests require publicity.

ONE SQUARE of 13 lines, solid nonpareil, each insertion, 65 cents, and for each additional line 5 cents.

COMMUNICATIONS of personal interest will be charged as advertising matter.

Orders from without the city to publish Advertisements, Marriage Notices or Obituaries, will not be attended to unless the cash, or an acceptable city reference, accompany the order.

☞ On all bills of $50 and over, 20 per cent. discount is allowed.

The Charleston Mercury

for sale, daily, at the following places:

New York—At the newstands of the La Farge House and St. Nicholas Hotel.
Washington, D. C.—By FRENCH & RICHSTEIN, No. 278 Pennsylvania Avenue.
Memphis, Tenn.—By M. NEALIS.
Wilmington, N. C.—By T. S. WHITAKER.
Lynchburg, Va.—By J. J. CREED.
Clifton, Ala.—By V. J. GIBSON.
Baltimore—By M. H. UMBAUGH, Nos. 4 and 5 Jarvis Building, corner Baltimore and North streets.
Glenwood, Iowa.—By E. C. BLACKMAN.
Jackson, Miss.—By M. L. CARLISLE.
Richmond, Va.—By LEWIS L. SMITH.
Nashville, Tenn.—By R. H. SINGLETON.
Columbia, S. C.—By P. B. GLASS and S. TOWNSEND.
Rock Island, Ill.—By F. H. WARREN.
Chicago, Ill.—MCNALLY & CO.
New Orleans, La.—Newsman under the St. Charles Hotel.

☞ South Carolina Bank Bills taken in payment for subscription to the MERCURY.

THE MERCURY.

MONDAY, APRIL 15, 1861.

April 13. 1861.

Throughout the whole of Friday night the various mortar batteries continued their iron rain upon Fort Sumter. At an early hour on Saturday morning the gun batteries, which had been silent during the darkness of the night, reopened their fire. About seven o'clock Fort Sumter vigorously returned their compliments. The Cumming's Point Batteries were uninjured by any shots which had been fired against them, had not effected anything like a breach, although battering considerably and to the depth of a foot, the pancoupee on the southeast corner. Major ANDERSON devoted his attention to the Sullivan's Island batteries, Fort Moultrie especially, and the Floating Battery. Forty rounds of hot shot were poured into him from Fort Moultrie, and this fire was returned by a rapid and heavy cannonade from the sea-girt fortress, riddling the quarters. In the emphatic language of an officer, "the quarters were knocked to h——l, but nobody hurt." During the morning thirty or forty successive shots, from Sumter, were fired at the Dahlgren Battery, occasioning so much danger to the men at the gun that Capt. HAMILTON temporarily removed them. The Floating Battery, commanded by Capt. HAMILTON, and in charge of Lieutenants YATES and HARLESTON, in its turn, received appropriate attention. Twelve indentions are visible; one ball going through the edge of the roofs, lodged in the sand bags, producing a slight contusion on the head of a private. The four-gun battery commanded by Lieut. VALENTINE, and Capt. HALLONQUIST's very effective mortar battery, were earnestly attended to. We learn that Capt. HALLONQUIST was covered with dirt spattered upon him by ANDERSON's fire; no damage, however, was done to a single man, officer or private, anywhere, and all performed their duties with the same spirit and alacrity. BUTLER's mixed battery, beyond the Moultrie House, was also busy, and was responded to now and then. The Mortar Batteries at Fort Johnson, under command of Captain JAMES and Lieutenant GIBBES, worked steadily and efficiently, attracting an occasional shot from their frowning antagonist.

At ten minutes after 8 a. m. a thick smoke was seen issuing from the southern portion of Fort Sumter's barracks; the flames broke out visible to the eye. At times the fire appeared to be almost extinguished, and then again would rise. Whilst it was in progress, two explosions occurred from the fall of shells among the service magazines or combustibles of the fort. The concentrated fire of all the batteries were steadily kept up, the progress of the flames continued, and all the quarters were involved in conflagration; a dense cloud of black smoke issued.

The fire from Fort Sumter became irregular and weak; towards midday it almost entirely ceased. Still the flag flew, and shot and shell fell regularly and steadily upon the beleagured fortress.

At noon, on Friday, during the heat of the engagement, Maj. ANDERSON made a signal of distress to the men of-war lying off of our bar, and on Saturday again, while under fire from all the batteries, and troubled with the heat and smoke of the burning barracks, again lowered the flag of the United States, as a signal for assistance to his naval allies; the ships were only from three to five miles off, the day was bright and clear, the water smooth. But discretion was the better part of valor. The Northern officers in command, having been so carefully selected, for their fidelity to their section and superior trustworthiness in a hostile crusade against the South, were unwilling to incur the risk of running their ships into the harbor, and engaging our batteries. They thought it prudent not to attempt reinforcements in launches. The soldiers of Abolitionism were left to their fate, without an attempt to relieve their perilous condition. Their idle allies had the pleasure of seeing them strike their colors to the Confederate States. They are commendable for their gallantry, and we trust that these brave mariners will receive a suitable commendation from their no less gallant JACKSON the Second and his magnanimous Cabinet.

At a quarter to 1 o'clock the flag of the United States on Fort Sumter went down with its staff. For some twenty minutes no flag appeared above the fort. Col. L. T. WIGFALL, accompanied by private H. GOURDIN YOUNG, of the Palmetto Guard, got into a small boat pulled by negros. They approached it from Morris Island, Col. WIGFALL holding up his sword with a white handkerchief tied upon it. Before they reached the fort, however, the United States flag, accompanied by a white flag, was held up on the rampart, which Col. WIGFALL did not see. The Sullivan's Island batteries, not perceiving the boat, continued their fire upon the United States flag, the boat approached the wharf. Col. WIGFALL having entered the fort, called for Major ANDERSON, and stated that he was Aid-de-Camp to General BEAUREGARD—that, seeing his distress, and the impossibility of holding the post, and that, as no flag was flying, he had come to claim a surrender, in the name of his chief. He replied to the enquiry what terms would be granted, stating that Major ANDERSON could not make his own terms, but that General BEAUREGARD, a soldier and a gentleman, knew how to treat a gallant enemy. Major ANDERSON must leave the details of the surrender to General BEAUREGARD. Major ANDERSON then agreed to surrender to General BEAUREGARD, in the name of the Confederate States, and at one o'clock and five minutes struck the United States flag which had been standing in company with the white flag. The Sullivan's Island batteries ceased firing, and Colonel WIGFALL started to report to General BEAUREGARD in Charleston.

Soon after the United States flag first disappeared, three Aids-de-Camp had been despatched from Headquarters; but Col. WIGFALL had anticipated Capt. LEE and Cols. MILES and PRYOR.

When the report was made of what had occurred, Major JONES, the Chief of Gen. BEAUREGARD's staff, accompanied by Colonel CHARLES ALSTON, was sent with authority to arrange the terms given. These were to the following effect:

All proper facilities will be afforded for the removal of Maj. ANDERSON and command, together with company arms and property, and all private property.

The flag which he has upheld so long, and with so much fortitude, under the most trying circumstances, may be saluted by him on taking it down.

Major ANDERSON is allowed to determine the precise time of yielding up the post, and is permitted to go by sea or land, according to his election.

At seven Major JONES returned to Fort Sumter, and the final arrangements and terms were definitely fixed.

We understand that a detachment of regulars from Sullivan's Island, and a detachment of Major DE SAUSSURE's command from Morris Island, have been detailed by Col. RIPLEY to occupy the captured fort.

We learn that Fort Sumter is uninjured in its capacity for defence, no breach being made in the walls, but that the quarters are completely destroyed, notwithstanding the Palmetto Fire Company was despatched to put out the fire. The quarters on Friday caught three times, and were extingushed by the soldiers; on Saturday this was impossible. At one time the smoke within the fort was so distressing that the men in the casemates were constrained to place their mouths to the floor for breathing. Maj. ANDERSON has expressed admiration and surprise at the perfection of practice by our batteries. He was almost entirely prevented, by this cause, from using his barbette guns. But for the paucity of his force, and their consequent ability to retire within the casemates, destruction of life must have been frightful. Thus protected, they escaped with only five wounded — none killed. We understand four casemate and five barbette guns have been dismounted by our guns. We also learn that Maj. ANDERSON and Lieut. DAVIS have expressed their opinion that, had they been allowed to use their hundred and twenty-eight four pounders in barbette, bearing upon the iron battery, they might have destroyed it. The accurate fire of the rifle cannon was very annoying, and materially assisted in the defence of Morris Island, and in battering the southeast wall.

The Battle of Fort Sumter is a marvellous affair in the bloodlessness of an engagement of thirty-two hours and a half. It is surely the merciful finger of God. But to no human agencies engaged in the business is greater praise due than to those who conceived and planned our defences, and who have erected them in so faithful and substantial a manner. To these causes—the admirable efficiency of our defensive preparations, and the handsome manner in which the guns have been used to annoy and cripple the enemy—is the wonderful, unprecedented result due.

We have not, and do not pretend to do justice to the officers and men engaged in the combat. We feel our incompetence to do it—a task of necessary discrimination, delicacy and difficulty. Many, we know, are worthy of notice, and will receive it at the proper hands, whom we, through our ignorance, have not named in our very imperfect notes. They, as well as the public, must excuse such unintentional short-comings.

THE BOMBARDMENT OF FORT SUMTER.

Surrender of Major Anderson.

Full Particulars.

We closed the report of the grand military diorama in progress on our Bay amid the clouds and gloom and threatening perils of Friday night. The firing, abated in the early evening, as though for the concentration of its special energies, commenced again at ten o'clock, and amid gusts of rain, and clouds that swept the heavens, the red hot shot and lighted shells, again streamed from the girt of batteries around, and concentrated in fearful import over Fort Sumter. Of the effects little was visible, of course, and anxious citizens, who from battery, spire and housetop, had bided the peltings of the storm, mute spectators of the splendid scene, could only wait the opening of the coming day for confirmation of the hopes and fears with which the changes in the scene successively inspired them.

As dawn approached, the firing again abated, and when the rising sun threw its flood of light over the sparkling waters from a cloudless sky, it was but by random shots from outlying batteries, with scarce an answer from Fort Sumter, that spectators were assured the contest still continued, and that human feeling was not in harmony with the grace and glory of the scene. It was but a little while, however, before the energy of action was restored, and as the work of destruction still went on, it was feared that still another day of expectation and uncertainty was before us. But at 8 o'clock the cry arose from the wharves, and rolled in one continuous wave over the city, "FORT SUMTER IS ON FIRE!" The watchers of the night before, who had retired for a few moments, were aroused, occupations were instantly suspended, and old and young, either mounted to their points of observation, or rolled in crowds upon the Battery, to look upon the last and most imposing act in this great drama.

The barracks to the south had been three times set on fire during the bombardment of the day before, but each time the flames were immediately extinguished. Subsequently, however, a red-hot shot from Fort Moultrie, or a shell from elsewhere, found a lodgment, when the fact was not apparent, and the fire, smouldering for a time, at length broke forth, and flames and smoke rose in volumes from the crater of Fort Sumter. The wind was blowing from the west, driving the smoke across the fort and into the embrasures, where the gunners were at work, and pouring its volumes through the port holes; the firing of Fort Sumter appeared to be renewed with vigor. The fire of the Fort, long, fierce and rapid, however, was gradually abated, and although at distant intervals a gun was fired, the necessity of preserving their magazines and of avoiding the flames, left the tenants little leisure for resistance. But the firing from without was continued with redoubled vigor. Every battery poured in its ceaseless round of shot and shell.—The enthusiasm of success inspired their courage and gave precision to their action; and thus, as in the opening, so in the closing scene, under the beaming sunlight, in view of thousands crowded upon the wharves and house tops, and amid the booming of ordnance, and in view of the five immense ships sent by the enemy with reinforcements, lying idly just out of gun shot on the Bar, this first fortress of despotic power fell prostrate to the cause of Southern Independence.

At about 9 o'clock the flames appeared to be abating, and it was apprehended that no irreparable injury had been sustained; but near 10 o'clock a column of white smoke rose high above the battlements, followed by an explosion which was felt upon the wharves, and gave the assurance that if the magazines were not exploded, at least their temporary ammunition were exposed to the element still raging. Soon after the barracks to the east and west were in flames, the smoke rose in redoubled volume from the whole circle of the fort, and rolling from the embrasures, it seemed scarcely possible that life could be sustained. Soon after another column of smoke arose as fearful as the first. The guns had long been completely silenced, and the only option left to the tenants of the fortress seemed to be whether they would perish or surrender.

At a quarter to one o'clock, the staff, from which the flag still waved, was shot away, and it was long in doubt whether, if there were the purpose, there was the ability to re-erect it. But at the expiration of about twenty minutes, it again appeared upon the eastern rampart, and announced that resistance was not ended. In the meantime, however, a small boat started from the city wharf, bearing Colonels LEE, PRYOR and MILES, Aids to Gen. BEAUREGARD, with offers of assistance, if perchance the garrison should be unable to escape the flames. As they approached the fort the flag appeared, and, as the firing from our batteries was unabated, they started to return, and had progressed, perhaps, the larger portion of the way when a shout arose from the whole circle of spectators on the islands and the main land, announced that the white flag of truce was waving from the ramparts. A small boat had already been seen to shoot out from Cumming's Point, in the direction of the fort, in which stood an officer with a white flag upon the point of his sword. This officer proved to be Col. WIGFALL, Aid to the Commanding General, who, entering through a port hole, demanded the surrender. Major ANDERSON replied, that "they were still firing on him." "Then take your flag down," said Col. WIGFALL; "they will continue to fire upon you so long as that is up." And further intercourse, resulting in a surrender of the fort, upon terms definitely arranged by Major JONES, the Chief of Gen. BEAUREGARD's staff, was held, which will be more distinctly set forth in other portions of the paper. The boat, with other Aids from Charleston, had returned, and, receiving Col. WIGFALL, they all came over to the city; and thus was inaugurated the closing act in the military drama.

In the afternoon Major JONES, Cols. CHESNUT and MANNING, with other officers and the Chief of the Fire Department and the Palmetto Fire Company, went down to Fort Sumter, and the details were concluded. We have not now the time to make a detailed description of the fort. It is enough to state at present that the walls are uninjured. Upon one of the faces (to the west), exposed to the water battery, it had received eighty shots; the other, equally exposed to this battery and to Fort Moultrie, had received more. Many of the doors to the embrasures had been driven in, but the permanent injury was slight; the balls penetrated but about 8 or 10 inches, removing about a half bushel of material. The cornice of the parapet in many places was knocked off, but all the parapet guns dismounted had been restored to their positions, and their carriages seemed then but little injured by the flames. The wall was most disfigured by the balling from Cummings' Point, but then there was little progress to a breach. Some of the casement guns were dismounted, and the devastation within the fort was great; the gunners were covered with fragments of shells. The barracks were swept entirely away, and there was nothing left but a loose mass of brick and mortar. A more detailed account of the effect of the bombardment upon the fort will be found in another column.

The Fight as Seen from Cummings' Point.

[FROM A SPECIAL CORRESPONDENT ON MORRIS ISLAND.]

On Thursday morning, when I came to Morris Island, it was evident that the term of preparation and practice was soon to close. The men all expected the order to open fire that night. And, indeed, there were reasons enough to justify the belief that it would be given. It was generally known that a fruitless demand for the surrender of Fort Sumter had been made that afternoon. And, from what was known of Gen. BEAUREGARD, nobody imagined that he would delay action many hours after such a refusal. Besides, the unusual proceedings at the batteries bearing on Fort Sumter showed plainly that we were upon the eve of battle. The sandbags, which screened from ANDERSON's view the 42 pounders at the Point Battery, were hastily removed as soon as it was dark; the works in the neighborhood of the Point were all lit up with lanterns; the guns were loaded, shotted and sighted, and the men were kept at their posts long after their usual time for retiring. Thus matters stood until a few minutes after 8 o'clock, when, to the great chagrin of the impatient young gunners, their officers gave the order to return to their quarters. The companies accordingly filed off, as usual, to their camps, the tattoo resounded over the dark sand hills, the tents were soon tenanted, and the men forgot their disappointment in sleep.

THE BOMBARDMENT OPENED.

A light rain commenced falling soon after midnight and continued, with intermissions, for several hours. At half-past four o'clock in the morning of Friday the more wakeful of our men were aroused by the distant boom of a shell. We afterwards learned from the sentinels that it came from the Fort Johnson mortar battery. In a moment the camps were all astir. The long roll summoned a few drowsy ones to the ranks, and the eager squads, convinced that the time for action had at last arrived, trotted off at a quick pace towards their respective posts. Everything being in readiness, the three batteries of Morris' Island bearing upon Fort Sumter, opened immediately. It was not yet daybreak, and the scene, which at that moment was novel, was picturesque as well. The course of the shells on their fiery way could be easily traced until they exploded in a white cloud of smoke, followed by a dull detonation, over the parapets of Fort Sumter. The effect of the solid shot was also perceptible with the naked eye. At each discharge of the guns, either the water adjacent to the fort would be dashed up in great sheets of spray, or the dense brown cloud of crumbling brick and mortar would mark the spot upon the ramparts hit by the balls. Meanwhile we could see that the batteries at other points in the harbor were as actively employed as our own. Ever and anon the shells flew out from the mortar batteries at Fort Johnson, Sullivan's Island, and Mount Pleasant. The Floating Battery, stationed in the Cove, was quite hidden from our view by the smoke from its own guns, but it was not difficult to see the effective execution of its 42 pounders upon the north parapet of Fort Sumter. Quite a large portion of the Sullivan's Island shore was also wrapped in the white smoke, but the incessant flashing from the merlons of Fort Moultrie assured us that RIPLEY was hammering away with characteristic vigor. At first the Morris Island batteries alternated regularly with the others, but later this arrangement was found embarrassing, and our batteries fired at the discretion of the officers commanding them.

HOW THE GUNS WERE MANNED.

Here, perhaps, I ought to give some account of the men who worked the guns in this portion of the harbor. The batteries which bore upon Fort Sumter from Morris Island are three in number, mounting in all six guns and six mortars. The outermost of these is the now famous TRAPIER Battery, in itself a monument of engineering science and energy. It is composed of massive beams and sandbags, and contains at this time three eight inch mortars. When the work was first built, it also mounted some heavy guns; but these have been removed, their carriages and closed embrasures remaining to show the position which they occupied. The TRAPIER Battery was manned by the Marion Artillery, Captain KING, assisted, towards the close of the bombardment, by the Sumter Guards, Captain RUSSELL. The former company labored incessantly at their pieces, from the opening of the bombardment until Saturday morning. Their fire was skillful, and but very few of their shells failed to explode either in or over the fort.

The next work, and nearer to the city than the TRAPIER battery, is the STEVENS, or Iron Battery—a novelty in military engineering—planned by and constructed under the supervision of an estimable son of this State. The efficiency of this unique fortification was a matter of no little concern to many previous to the action: but all doubts were immediately dispelled by Major ANDERSON's tests, as I shall presently relate. The Iron Battery contains three heavy Columbiads. It is flanked by immense slopes of sand bags, and these are burrowed very curiously, but securely, with places to retreat, which the soldiers call "rat-holes," but which are in reality very dry, capacious and comfortable chambers, except, perhaps, that the ceiling might be a trifle higher. And here I may as well say that all the fortifications have one or more of these rat-holes, to be used as a magazine, a hospital or as quarters for the relief according to circumstances.

Passing from the Iron Battery, we come to the Point Battery, a large work containing three ten-inch mortars, two 42 pounders, and the newly arrived rifle cannon, presented to the State by CHARLES K. PRIOLEAU, Esq., now in Liverpool, and junior partner in the firm of JOHN FRASER & Co. It will, doubtless, be a great satisfaction to that gentleman to know that his timely gift was so serviceable to our troops. The gun has patent side sights attached, by means of which the greatest accuracy of range was obtained, and each of its conical balls crashed through its mark with telling effect.

Both these last named important posts, the Iron and Point Batteries, were held by the Palmetto Guards, Capt. CUTHBERT—a gallant corps, which, for numbers, alertness, efficiency and unexampled coolness in action, won the respect and admiration of all who saw them during the fight. I think that their officers must be proud of such men and I know that those officers are not unworthy of their command. The two batteries manned by the Guards were commanded by Major STEVENS, of the Citadel Academy. Capt. CUTHBERT devoted himself especially to the direction of the Iron Battery. The rifled cannon was worked by a squad of the Palmetto Guards, under the superintendence of Capt. THOMAS, of the Citadel Academy.

I should not omit to mention the fine looking companies in charge of the long line of batteries pointing to the Ship Channel and extending along the whole extent of the Morris Island beach, although they were not called into action, we cannot forget that it is to their sleepless vigilance we must attribute the indisposition of the fleet to reinforce ANDERSON's garrison. Perhaps through the foolhardiness of our enemies, they may yet have an opportunity of vindicating their valor in the fight as well as their vigilance on the watch.

ANDERSON OPENS HIS BATTERIES.

At half-past six o'clock a dull unpleasant drizzle began to fall, and the leaden sky betokened a dreary day. Our guns kept pounding indiscriminately at the walls, parapet and quarters of Fort Sumter, but for nearly two hours no reply came. The Fort seemed as if all within were asleep; not a casemate was opened, and there was no movement noticeable in any portion of the post, excepting the flapping of the United States flag, floating defiantly from a very lofty staff. Thus things continued until a few minutes after 7 o'clock, when a shout from the hundreds peeping over the sandbags announced that ANDERSON had opened fire. He began with his heavy casemate guns bearing upon Cumming's Point. His first efforts were directed to batter down the Iron Battery. For a time his shots were watched with intense interest, but after fifteen minutes' firing it became apparent that he could make no serious impression upon the iron-cased roof. Ball after ball rebounded from the close layers of railroad iron, and splashed their way harmlessly through the marsh beyond. Most of his shots were aimed too high, and whizzed above the battery without striking it. These went ricochetting over the surface of the water, tearing up vast masses of the sea-weed, and giving a terrible fright to hundreds of the sea-fowl, which rose in every direction from the marsh. The effect of the shots which hit the iron battery was not perceptible to those within, except by the noise of the concussion, and even this was not so loud as we had expected.

At half-past 7 o'clock the flash from the parapet of Fort Sumter announced that ANDERSON had begun to work his barbette guns. This, however, did not continue very long, for the continual explosion of our shells in every direction, on and around the parapets, soon admonished him of the risk of exposing his men in that position.

At twenty minutes before 8 o'clock an alarm from our guard boats cruising about the Bar announced a steamer in the offing. Looking out from the crest of the sand hills with my glass I could descry, in the far distance, a large steamer very similar in appearance to those which ply between Charleston and New York. It was afterwards ascertained to be the *Nashville*. Later in the day three other vessels were seen—two of them evidently men-of-war. They made no attempt, however, to come in, but lay together in the offing throughout the day.

About half-past 10 o'clock a shot from ANDERSON struck the middle port of the Iron Battery, crushing in the iron plates that protected the guns, making an indenture of several inches. The ball did not penetrate, but glanced off like the others over the marsh. The force with which it struck the door, however, unfortunately so disarranged the lever by which the port was opened and closed, that it was found impossible, during the remainder of the day, to work that gun. The other two kept up a brisk fire throughout the whole of the bombardment.

The firing from all the batteries on both sides of the harbor was maintained steadily until nightfall. Major ANDERSON, during the afternoon, appeared to have become convinced that his efforts to riddle the Iron Battery were ineffectual, for the steady fire which he had kept up against Cummings' Point was transferred to Fort Moultrie, the Dahlgren and the Floating batteries on the other side of the Bay. He took care, however, at irregular intervals of fifteen or twenty minutes, to send a shot whizzing over our heads, and this kept our men upon the *qui vive*. At one time I noticed that the direction of his shots against Morris Island was changed from the Point batteries to those farther out. Perhaps he meant to rake the camps, the sight of which was plainly enough indicated by our flags. If such was his design, his aim was very creditable, for the balls—some said grape—whistled a few feet above the heads of the Sumter Guards, who had been detached from the 17th Regiment, and posted as a reserve at the head of the line of tents to act as a relief to the Marion Artillery at the TRAPIER Battery. Whenever a flash from the southeastern casemate announced that a shot was coming, it was somewhat ludicrous to notice the sudden dodge of hundreds of heads behind the sand hills, and the abject prostration of such of the darkeys as had not already betaken themselves to the other extremity of the Island.

A few minutes before 7 o'clock, the fire from Fort Sumter ceased. Shortly afterwards our guns also stopped firing. At half-past 7 the rain, which had been lowering all day, began to fall in torrents, and most of our men sought such shelter as was to be had. The storm was a trying one. The wind howled drearily over the sand hills, and the rain descended with a force and volume, against which the slight tents and leaky sheds—the only available cover—were a poor protection. The storm continued, with an occasional lull, until near morning. Meantime our gallant young gunners at the Mortar Batteries, nothing daunted by the disagreeable rain, had kept up their firing of shells during the entire night, though at somewhat longer intervals than before. The Sumter Guards deserve special mention for the alacrity with which they performed the laborious and unpleasant duty of strengthening the foot of the Iron Battery with sandbags. For many hours of the night during the worst of the storm they worked steadily, lifting the wet and heavy bags into position, and when day broke the face of the work was even stronger than on Friday.

SECOND DAY OF THE BOMBARDMENT.

Saturday morning, the 13th of April, a day long to be remembered in our annals as marked by the close of the most extraordinary bombardment on record, came in bright and glorious. The clouds had cleared away, but the rain had left the ground moist, and the air pleasantly cool. About sunrise a vigorous fire was re opened from our guns. The effects of the first day's bombardment could now be easily seen without the aid of a glass. The south and east facades of Fort Sumter were completely pitted by balls, and from what we had seen of the fire from Sullivan's Island and the Cove, we knew that the north facade could not be in much better condition. The edge of the parapet was in many places cut off, a number of the guns were dismounted, and the embrasures of the casemates were so battered, that the regularity of their outline could hardly be distinguished. The chimneys and roof of the barracks were also perforated in many places by our balls. The guns of Fort Sumter did not re open fire until seven o'clock, when the shots began to pour in quick succession from the casemates pointing towards Fort Moultrie. RIPLEY's men returned shot for shot, and at each discharge from Sullivan's Island, we could see great fragments of the parapet of Sumter toppling over into the water.

FORT SUMTER ON FIRE.

At ten minutes after 8, a. m., a thick black smoke was seen issuing from the southern portion of Fort Sumter, and a moment later a wild shout of triumph rang along the sand hills, and was heartily echoed across the water from Sullivan's Island and Fort Johnson, as we saw the red flames piercing the top of the barracks and borne eastward by the high wind, wrapping the entire parapet in dense clouds of smoke. The sight infused new confidence into our men, and the bombardment immediately became far more rapid and fierce than at any previous time. The singular coolness with which our gunners had, until then, performed their duty, seemed for a moment to have given way to the excitement of the novel scene. The bombs flew so thick and fast that we could see them exploding in groups over the flaming fortress, while only a few seconds intervened between the hammering fire of the heavy ordnance.

The fire blazed furiously, until the whole line of the barracks on the south side of Fort Sumter was swept away, leaving only some of the crumbled, blackened and tottering chimneys towering over the ramparts. Then the fire burned lower, the flames sank behind the parapet, and we were left in ignorance as to their further progress. In the course of the forenoon we noticed several violent explosions, apparently doing serious damage to the fort, but whether these were caused by the fire communicating to hand-grenades and like combustibles, or to the magazines, we could only conjecture. During the progress of the conflagration, for a long time Maj. ANDERSON maintained a steady and terrible firing against Fort Moultrie, but very few guns were fired towards Morris Island.

THE FLAGSTAFF SHOT AWAY.

At a quarter before 1 o'clock another tremendous cheer from the watchers upon our batteries called me to my point of observation, just in time to see the flagstaff of Fort Sumter bearing the flag of the United States falling heavily inside the Fort. From this auspicious moment the impression became general among our men that the fortress would be ours before night fall.

For fifteen or twenty minutes I could see no ensign over the fort, but, at the end of that time, I descried a large United States flag elevated amid the smoke close on the north wall of the fort. Meantime a small boat had shot out from the beach of Cumming's Point towards the wharf of Fort Sumter. I afterwards learned that it contained Col. LOUIS T. WIGFALL, Aid to Gen. BEAUREGARD, and Private GOURDIN YOUNG, of the Palmetto Guards. Col. WIGFALL bore a flag of truce upon his sword. A white flag also waved upon Fort Sumter, and in a short time the conclusion of the negotiations was announced to us by the disappearance of the United States flag from the fort.

THE SURRENDER ANNOUNCED.

The rest is briefly told. Col. WIGFALL returned and notified the Captains of the several companies to inform their respective commands that the fort was unconditionally surrendered.

The scene that followed was altogether indescribable. The troops upon the hills cheered and cheered again. A horseman galloped at full speed along the beach, waving his cap to the troops near the Lighthouse. These soon caught up the cry, and the whole shore rang with the glad shouts of thousands.

The first burst of exultation over, all eyes were turned to the fleet in the offing, and the guards resumed their wonted rounds upon the batteries which have so nobly vindicated the independence of the State.

INCIDENTS OF THE BATTLE.

Although during the thirty-four consecutive hours through which the bombardment lasted, not a man was in any way injured upon our side, it cannot be said that our men altogether escaped Major ANDERSON's balls. As Captain JONES was standing in the Point Battery a spent ball, which had struck the sand bags above, rolled over striking him upon the back of the neck, but not with sufficient force to hurt him. The ball—a 32 pounder—was preserved as a memento of the occasion.

The first gun fired from the Iron Battery at Cumming's Point was discharged by the venerable EDMUND RUFFIN. He subsequently shot all the guns and mortars used during the action.

The bright-quartered flag of the Marion Artillery floated proudly over the TRAPIER Battery during the whole of the bombardment. On Saturday morning, when the men at these mortars were relieved by the Sumter Guards, the splendidly broidered blue banner, presented by some ladies a short time ago to the latter Company, was placed side by side with the ensign of the Marion's, and the rest of the action was fought with both flags waving overhead. It was noticed as a singular coincidence that at the very moment when the emblems of the Game Cock and the Swamp Fox were first fluttering together from the crest of the battery, the fire was discovered issuing from the parapet of Fort Sumter.

During the drenching rain Friday night, an alarm was given owing to a boat having attempted to pass the beach batteries on Morris Island. It was finally overhauled, and found to contain two sailors on a drunken frolic, who were dismissed with a reprimand for their rashness.

The Scene at Fort Sumter.

An officer who visited the fort soon after the terms of evacuation were made, states that the scene there presented is beyond conception. Without, the walls have the appearance, at a distance, of having been covered with an immense number of brick poultices spattered in every direction. This is the shattering effect of the shot. Within, the entire fort wore an aspect as if the hand of the destroying angel had swept ruthlessly by and left not a solitary object to relieve the general desolation. The blackened walls of the officers' and soldier's quarters were yet smoking, ashes and embers met the eye at every turn, while the shot and shell which had been rained upon the stronghold lay in great quantities upon all portions of the parade ground.

The appearance of both Major ANDERSON, his officers and the men, indicated the terrible nature of the ordeal from which they had just emerged. Deprived of sleep for many hours, fatigued with their labors at the guns, and prostrated by their battle with an element which waged beyond control, they looked worn, haggard and ready to drop with sheer exhaustion.

When the fire was at its greatest height Major ANDERSON stated that the only manner in which they could breathe was by laying flat upon the ground within the casemates, with their faces to the earth, while, added to the danger, was the occasional explosion of the piles of shells collected for service at different points within the fort.

It is to the fact that so few men were in the fortification, that is due the preservation of life. Major ANDERSON himself stated that had there been two hundred more, not less than one half of them must have been killed, owing to the absence of sufficient room, under the circumstances, for their protection.

As it was, their provisions would have given out in two days more, when an unconditional surrender would have necessarily resulted.

He also remarked that yesterday was one of the proudest days of his life, for while he had endeavored to do his duty as an officer, he had not taken the life of a fellow being.

The interview between Major ANDERSON and our informant was not a long one, and consequently many interesting incidents connected with Fort Sumter, which belong to the memorable occasion, must for the present remain unknown.

During the evening, a boat arrived at Morris Island from one of the Northern vessels in the offing, bearing a Lieutenant and a flag of truce, his object being to arrange for the evacuation of the soldiers with their property. He also assured the commanding officer at that point (Gen. SIMONS), that hostilities would not take place during the night. The matter was referred to Gen. BEAUREGARD.

Meanwhile Major ANDERSON had himself addressed a letter to the latter officer, requesting that the steamship *Catawba* should be at the wharf of Fort Sumter at nine o'clock this (Sunday) morning.

She accordingly proceeded to this destination at the hour designated, since which time further occurrences have not transpired to us.

Steamers and small boats are to-day busily plying between the city and the Islands, carrying soldiers and spectators, but none are admitted to either Fort Sumter or the other fortifications without the usual permits from Headquarters, which, at the present writing, are more difficult, from prudential reasons, to be obtained than ever before.

THE LATEST.

The Evacuation of Fort Sumter—Embarkation of Major Anderson.

We closed our town report in the extra of yesterday with the surrender of Fort Sumter, and with a brief account of its battered appearance, and give this morning the scene and circumstances of its evacuation. At half-past 12 o'clock his Excellency Governor PICKENS, with his Aids, and Messrs. JAMISON and MAGRATH, of his Executive Council, and General BEAUREGARD, with his Aids, Messrs. MILES, PRYOR, MANNING, CHESNUT, and JONES, and many distinguished gentlemen, invited to be present, took their departure in a steamer from Southern wharf, and were borne in the direction of the Fort. As we advanced it was apparent, however, that the evacuation was not completed. Though the steamer *Isabel*, at the request of Major ANDERSON, had been present from 9 o'clock, and the expectation had been occasioned that very soon thereafter his command would be under way, still causes of delay had intervened. To avoid the embarrassments of a premature arrival, the party was landed upon Sullivan's Island. Availing themselves of the opportunities thus afforded, they visited the floating battery, the Dahlgren battery, the enfilading battery, and were ascending the mortar battery, when the booming of the guns upon the parapets of Fort Sumter, announced the lowering of the "stars and stripes." In the terms of capitulation, it was allowed to Major ANDERSON to salute his flag, and it was perhaps expected that he would fire the usual complement of twenty-one guns; but reaching that number, he still went on to fire, and the apprehension was that he might exhibit the discourtesy of numbering thirty-four. But he continued still to fire up to fifty, and then slowly lowering his flag, the shouts from assembled thousands upon the shores and the steamers, and every species of water craft, announced that the authority of the late United States upon the last foot of Carolina's soil was finally withdrawn.

It had been noticed, that at the firing of the seventeenth gun, there was the sound as of two reports, and the impression was that two guns had been fired together; but, as the party, re-embarking, were on their way to Fort Sumter, they were met by a boat, which announced that one of the casons had exploded, and made the earnest request that the boat would return to Sullivan's Island for a fire engine, from the apprehension that the magazine might be in danger. This obtained, the party again started for the fort, and made their entrance.

It were vain to attempt a detailed description of the scene. Every point and every object in the interior of the fort to which the eye was turned, except the outer walls and casemates, which are still strong, bore the impress of ruin. It were as if the Genius of Destruction had tasked its energies to make the thing complete, brooded over by the desolation of ages. It could scarce have been developed to a more full maturity of ruin. The walls of the internal structure, roofless, bare, blackened, and perforated by shot and shell, hung in fragments, and seemed in instant readiness to totter down. Near the centre of the parade-ground was the hurried grave of one who had fallen from the recent casualty. To the left of the entrance was a man who seemed to be at the verge of death. In the ruins to the right there was another. The shattered flag-staff, pierced by four balls, lay sprawling on the ground. The parade-ground was strewn with fragments of shell and of the dilapidated buildings. At least four guns were dismounted on the ramparts, and at every step the way was impeded by portions of the broken structure. And so it was that the authorities, compelled to yield the fortress, had at least the satisfaction of leaving it in a condition calculated to inspire the least possible pleasure to its captors.

Of all this, however, the feeling was lost when, ascending to the parapet, the brilliant panorama of the bay appeared—when from this key to the harbor the view expanded to the waving out line of main and island, and when upon this key the flag of the Confederacy, together with the Palmetto flag, were both expanded to the breeze. And when the deafening shouts arose from the masses clustered upon boats and upon the shores, and when the batteries around the entire circuit shook the fortress with the thunders of their salutation the feeling that the victory was indeed complete, that the triumph was a fact accomplished, that liberty had indeed been vindicated, and that the State had established her claim to the skill and courage necessary to the cause she had the intellectual intrepidity to avow, thrilled in the breast of every one of Carolina's sons, as seldom has such feeling thrilled in the breasts of any men before.

Shortly after the arrival, the garrison marched out, and were received on board the *Isabel*; which, however, from the condition of the tide, was unable to move off, and it was a somewhat unpleasant circumstance that Major ANDERSON and his command should have been made unwilling spectators of the exultations inspired by their defeat.

Of those suffering from the casualty we have mentioned, one was killed upon the spot; two were wounded, it is supposed mortally, and were left for medical treatment; and two others badly wounded, also, at their earnest solicitation, were carried off.

The occasion was not without the charm and interest afforded by the presence of the fair. The lady of His Excellency Governor PICKENS, and the wife and daughter of Attorney-General HAYNE, witnessed the ceremony from the boat, and Mrs. HENRY BONNETHEAU has the distinction of being the first in the fort under the flag of the Confederacy. She was down to attend the sister of Lieut. DAVIS, her guest during the period of her brother's confinement to the fort, and with the eye and genius of an artist, it was doubtless with a feeling of especial pleasure that she was favored with the opportunities of this occasion.

Colonel RIPLEY was put in command. The departments of the service necessary to bring the fort to order were distributed. The men were preparing such rude appliances for comfort as the dreary place admitted of; and as, at twilight, we steamed off for the city, of those standing upon the ledge around the base of the fort, the last to be seen was the venerable EDMUND RUFFIN, of Virginia, who, with canteen and blanket strapped upon his shoulder, seemed to be submitting with exemplary complacency to the experience of a volunteer.

The party started in the *Clinch*, but were changed to the *Nina*, to whose hospitable master we are indebted for an entertainment which, though speedily extemporized, was gratefully accepted by his guests.

Other Facts.

The arrangements for the departure of Major ANDERSON were completed yesterday morning. At the early hour of 5 o'clock, Commodore HARTSTENE, and Messrs. JONES, Chief of the Staff, and PRYOR and MILES, Aids to Gen. BEAUREGARD, accompanied by Lieut. SNYDER, of Major ANDERSON's command, proceeded in the *Clinch* to the fleet off the bar. They found the commanding officer, Capt. GILLIS, on board the *Powhatan*. Lieut. SNYDER obtained an interview with Capt. GILLIS, who asked, and obtained permission to visit Major ANDERSON, for the purpose of arranging for his departure. Accordingly, about 9 o'clock, Capt. GILLIS and Lieut. SNYDER were deposited at Fort Sumter, when it was decided that Major ANDERSON and his command would accept the offer of the *Isabel*, which had been made to him.

Major ANDERSON and his command marched out to the tune of "Yankee Doodle." They were dressed in full uniform, and carried their arms. Major ANDERSON looked care-worn and deeply despondent, produced, no doubt, among other circumstances, by the sad accident which happened whilst saluting his flag.

On the return from the fleet, it was observed that Capt. GILLIS closely examined the batteries on both shores with his glass, and made several attempts to glean information from persons on board the steamer. In short, he exhibited a disposition to take every advantage of his accidental entrance into the harbor.

The *Atlantic*, standing furtherest seaward, was yesterday morning brought up with the other vessels. As she contains the largest number of the hostile troops, together with the flying artillery, it was thought possible an attempt would be made to effect a landing last night, on the supposition that our forces would be less vigilant in consequence of the surrender of Fort Sumter. One hundred and fifty horses are divided between the *Baltic* and *Atlantic*.

The funeral of the private named HOWE, who was killed by the explosion, was attended by a portion of the Palmetto Guard, Capt. CUTHBERT, and portions of Company B, Capt. HALLONQUIST, and Capt. HAMILTON's Company. Mr. HOWE was buried with the honors of war.

Fort Sumter is now garrisoned by the detachment of Company B, under Capt. HALLONQUIST, and a portion of the Palmetto Guard, Captain CUTHBERT. The command has been given to Col. RIPLEY, who won bright laurels at Fort Moultrie in the recent engagement.

The rockets thrown up at Stono on Saturday evening caused unnecessary alarm in this city. By order of Gen. BEAUREGARD, two of the Aids of Gov. PICKENS, with a detachment of volunteers, composed principally of Virginians and Georgians here on a visit, went on board the *Lady Davis*, to proceed to Wappoo Cut; but, before they got under way, the order was countermanded, as it was discovered that there was no cause for apprehension.

The Flag of the Confederate States and the Palmetto, were raised on Fort Sumter simultaneously—the former by Col. JONES, Chief of Gen. BEAUREGARD's Staff, and Col. FERGUSON. The Flag of the Confederate States was manufactured in this city. It was the intention to have made use of the flag that was first hoisted on the Capitol, at Montgomery, but unfortunately it had been mislaid. The flag-staffs were about fifteen feet high, and were lashed to two of the big guns by Commodore HARTSTENE.

Four hundred and seven shots were fired from the Floating Battery, and one hundred from the Dahlgren Battery. Both are under the command of Capt. J. R. HAMILTON.

A Night in the Harbor—A Cruise after the Enemy.

[FROM OUR OWN REPORTER.]

STEAMER SEABROOK, STONO INLET, April 12, 1861.

About seven o'clock on Thursday evening last, the Navy of South Carolina, Commodore HARTSTENE, left Charleston for a cruise off the Bar. Our reporter was so fortunate as to obtain permission to accompany the expedition.

His interview with Commodore HARTSTENE, was brief and pointed. Approaching a middle-aged, weather beaten, hardy gentleman, who bore the appearance of having seen service, he inquired for Captain HARTSTENE. "I am that gentleman," was the reply. "I have a permit to visit Sullivan's Island to write an account of the battle for THE MERCURY," urged the reporter. "We are not going to Sullivan's Island, sir," returned the veteran, "we're going to sea, and the steamer will leave in a moment, and so you had better go ashore." "I must make a report, sir, and I'll go to sea with you, if I can obtain your permission," was next urged. "Well, you can go, sir," was the reply, "but we expect warm work, and you may be landed at Stono to-morrow morning, or find yourself shortly in New York with a halter round your neck." "Aye, aye, sir, I'll take my chance," was the ready answer, and the reporter waved his hand to the crowd, for the steamer was even then casting off, and he could not have remained behind had he chosen.

The squadron consisted of the steamers "Clinch" and "Seabrook." The former was the flag ship. Both have been fitted up with a view to service in the harbor, and are furnished with twelve pound howitzers, and a force sufficient to serve them. There was no want of ammunition. In short, every preparation was made for a successful cruise. The following are the officers of the "Clinch": Lieut. PELOT, Commanding; Lieut. PORCHER; Midshipmen R. H. BACOT and G. D. BRYAN. The "Seabrook" was commanded as follows: Lieutenant Commanding J. M. STRIBBLING; Lieutenant EVANS; First Assistant Engineer, J. H. LOPER; Assistant Surgeon R. W. GIBBES, Gunner CUDDY, and Midshipmen INGRAHAM and WILKINSON. The "Lady Davis" also forms a part of the squadron, but she was not on duty last night. Her officers consist of Lieut. DOZIER, Commanding; Lieut. GRIMBLE; First Lieut. HENRY A. MULLINGS acting Pilot; First Assistant Engineer GEDDES; Third Assistant Engineer YATES, and Midshipman THOMAS.

The "Clinch" had taken her position near the bar early in the afternoon, and accordingly it was the "Seabrook" that left Charleston at 7 o'clock, cheered by the large crowd at the wharf. About half past seven, under easy head of steam, the various conjectures in regard to what would be the probable reply of Major ANDERSON to the summons to surrender, were suddenly cut short by the look-out reporting a rocket seaward. All eyes were instantly turned in that direction, and two red rockets burst in the air, followed by the burning of a blue light. Fort Johnson promptly recognized the signal that our enemy had made his appearance, sending up the answering rocket almost the instant the blue light, displayed by the Clinch, disappeared. Excitement and preparation for whatever might occur immediately succeeded. The howitzers were manned, the decks were stripped, guns, revolvers and ammunition were distributed. When all that could be had been done, silently sped the steamer on her course; steadily she approached Fort Sumter, all blackness in the distance. Suddenly a hail was heard, and a hoarse voice shouted "the pirates are off the bar." "What steamer?" was asked. "The Harriet Lane, twelve miles out," shouted the same gruff voice, and we were then informed that she alone, of all the expected cruisers, had been seen. Great eagerness was at once manifested to reach our destination. It was fully expected an attempt would be made to land troops in boats. This it was the purpose of the expedition to prevent.

Finally, at 8 o'clock, the Steamer lay off the "Clinch," when a pilot boat brought a confirmation of the approach of the "Harriet Lane." Commodore Hartstene then took possession of the flag ship, and twenty men were transferred from the "Clinch" to the "Seabrook."

The hour at which Major ANDERSON was to indicate his decision by the firing of a shell, having arrived, all eyes were strained in the direction of Fort Sumter. As minute after minute elapsed, and the stillness and blackness of Fort Sumter remained unbroken, the belief became general that Major ANDERSON had surrendered.

In the meantime the squadron lost not sight of its duty. Both vessels cruised all night in search of the expected war boats, just within the bar. It was the original intention of the Commanding Officer to have proceeded out to sea, but as the wind increased, and there was every indication of a "heavy blow," the pilots said it could not be done with safety. In this manner an hour passed, supper was eaten—10 o'clock arrived, and yet Fort Sumter had given no signal, nor had the slightest appearance of hostilities been noticed on the part of our batteries. Belief now became certainty, and not one of us but expected to steam into Charleston for breakfast, after saluting the Palmetto waving over that much coveted "four acres of land."

The expedition, however, redoubled its vigilance, in order to prevent the possibility of sur

[CONTINUED ON FOURTH PAGE.]

CLOTHING AT WHOLESALE

W. T. LEITCH, JR., & CO.,

No. 151 MEETING-ST.,

OPPOSITE THE MAIN ENTRANCE TO THE CHARLESTON HOTEL.

W. T. Leitch, Jr., & B. W. Burnet

ANNOUNCE THAT THEY HAVE JUST OPENED A LARGE AND WELL ASSORTED STOCK OF

FASHIONABLE

READY MADE CLOTHING

AT THE ABOVE LOCATION, WHICH THEY WILL BE PLEASED TO EXHIBIT TO THEIR FORMER FRIENDS AND BUYERS IN GENERAL.

A liberal Discount to CASH PURCHASERS.

Orders solicited and faithfully executed.

W. J. LEITCH, JR. B. W. BURNET.

March 27

GREAT REDUCTION

IN THE PRICE OF

CARPETS, OIL CLOTHS,

AND

CURTAIN GOODS.

JAS. G. BAILIE,

Importer, Jobber and Dealer,

No. 234 KING-STREET,

RESPECTFULLY INVITES THE ATTENTION OF PURCHASERS to his extensive STOCK OF NEW AND BEAUTIFUL PATTERNS, which has been selected with great care, and will be sold at GREATLY REDUCED PRICES FOR CASH. The Stock consists of:

MEDALLION VELVET CARPETS
WILTON CARPETS
Royal Velvet Carpets
Tapestry Brussels Carpets
Wire Brussels Carpet
Extra Imperial Three-ply Carpets
English, Scotch & American Imperial Carpets
English and American Venetian Carpets
Cotton and Hemp Carpets
16-4 & 12-4 Druggets and Crumb Cloths

Mosaic, Velvet, Axminster, Tourney, Wilton, Brussels, Tapestry, Tufted and Mottled Rugs

Irish Cocoa, Manilla, Velvet, Adelaide, Jute, Skeleton, Alicante and India Rubber Door Mats

Stair Carpets and Stair Rods

Hair and Straw Brooms, &c., &c.

In the

CURTAIN DEPARTMENT,

I HAVE A LARGE AND BEAUTIFUL ASSORTMENT, and can confidently commend my Goods for inspection, as affording the very best assortment ever offered in this market. BROCATELLES, SATIN DeLAINES, SATIN DAMASKS in new designs, DAMASKS in all qualities and colors, Lace, Muslin and Nottingham CURTAINS.

SOME VERY CHEAP

CENTRE TASSELS, LOOPS, GIMPS
PICTURE TASSELS, CORDS, &c.
CORNICES, PINS AND BANDS
A full assortment

Window Shades,

In every Design, Trimmed and put up with dispatch.

FLOOR OIL CLOTHS,

In English and American Manufacture, of all widths, which will be cut and put down, and guaranteed in every respect.

WHITE, AND RED AND WHITE CANTON MATTINGS, in all widths, qualities and brands.

COCOA MATTINGS, in Calcutta and American make, and in all qualities and widths.

I respectfully invite the inspection of my Goods, and can safely promise that the Goods are fresh and new. Owing to the unsettled state of affairs, I am determined to dispose of my stock at unprecedented low prices

FOR CASH.

☞ Orders from the country solicited, and will have my prompt attention.

☞ Carpets and Curtains made up with dispatch, and warranted to please.

JAMES G. BAILIE,

IMPORTER, JOBBER AND DEALER,

New Carpet Store, No. 234 King-st., Charleston.

January 18

C. D. CARR & CO.,

30 BROAD-STREET,

CHARLESTON, S. C.,

HAVE OPENED THEIR FALL STOCK OF ALL DESCRIPTIONS OF

COATINGS,

CASSIMERES AND VESTINGS,

ALSO,

A full and varied assortment of
SHIRTS,
ROBES DE CHAMBRE,
ENGLISH HOSIERY,
NECK TIES,
SCARFS, &c., &c.

JOUVINT CIE MEDAILLE D'OR KID GLOVES, ENGLISH BUCK AND DOE TAFFETA PLUSH GLOVES.

Ten Per Cent. Discount for Cash.

October 22 mwf [Oct. 16]

BROWN'S BRONCHIAL TROCHES. Cure Cough, Cold, Hoarseness, Influenza, any Irritation or Soreness of the Throat, Relieve the Hacking Cough in Consumption, Bronchitis, Asthma and Catarrh, Clear and give strength to the voice of

PUBLIC SPEAKERS AND SINGERS.

Few are aware of the importance of checking a Cough or "Common Cold" in its first stage; that which in the beginning would yield to a mild remedy, if neglected soon attacks the Lungs. "*Brown's Bronchial Troches*," containing demulcent ingredients, allay Pulmonary and Bronchial Irritation.

BROWN'S Troches.	"That trouble in my throat (for which the '*Troches*' are a specific) having made me often a mere whisperer." N. P. WILLIS.
BROWN'S Troches.	"I recommend their use to PUBLIC SPEAKERS." REV. E. H. CHAPIN.
BROWN'S Troches.	"Great service in subduing HOARSENESS." REV. DANIEL WISE.
BROWN'S Troches.	"Almost instant relief in the distressing labor of breathing peculiar to ASTHMA." REV. A. C. EGGLESTON.
BROWN'S Troches.	"Contain no opium or anything injurious." DR. A. A. HAYES, Chemist, Boston.
BROWN'S Troches.	"A simple and pleasant combination for COUGHS," &c. DR. G. F. BIGELOW, Boston.
BROWN'S Troches.	"Beneficial in BRONCHITIS." DR. J. F. W. LANE, Boston.
BROWN'S Troches.	"I have proved them excellent for WHOOPING COUGH." REV. H. W. WARREN, Boston.
BROWN'S Troches.	"Beneficial when compelled to speak, suffering from COLD." REV. S. J. ANDERSON, St. Louis.
BROWN'S Troches.	"Effectual in removing Hoarseness and Irritation of the Throat, so common with SPEAKERS and SINGERS." PROF. M. STACEY JOHNSON, La Grange, Ga. Teacher of Music Southern Female College.
BROWN'S Troches.	"Great benefit when taken before and after preaching, as they prevent Hoarseness. From their past effect, I think they will be of permanent advantage to me." REV. E. ROWLEY, A. M., President of Athens College, Tenn.

☞ Sold at TWENTY-FIVE CENTS A BOX.

Sole Wholesale and Retail Agents for South Carolina,

VAN SCHAACK & GRIERSON

DRUGGISTS, 221 KING-STREET,

At the Sign of the Negro and Golden Mortar.

January 19

JOHN ARTMAN,

MANUFACTURER of

CARRIAGES, BUGGIES,

SULKIES, WAGONS, CARTS, &c, ALSO, WHEEL WRIGHT

BUSINESS, IN ALL ITS BRANCHES, at No. 5, Archdale street, Charleston, S. C. tuthsly October 27

ENCOURAGE

SOUTHERN PREPARATIONS.

CLEVELAND'S

PREMIUM COLOGNE.

THIS COLOGNE IS COMPOSED OF SUBSTANCES, carefully purified, and of a gentle and beneficial action; to the most agreeable perfume it unites the most efficacious properties. It has thus established for itself a reputation, without eclat and without advertisement, and it has never ceased to increase until it has at length acquired a place on the toilet of the fashionable world, which it can never lose.

Under all these considerations, the superiority of this EAU DE COLOGNE OF CLEVELAND'S, over all others cannot be contested; and it has also a decided advantage in point of economy, as it can be obtained in any quantity, from one ounce to one gallon; also put up in pint and quart bottles at 50 cents and $1 each, and in bottles of every variety, shade and color.

Prepared and sold only at

W. Y. PAXTON'S,

DRUG AND CHEMICAL ESTABLISHMENT,

CHARLESTON, S. C.

March 18

CLEVELAND'S TOOTH POWDER

CLEVELAND'S PREMIUM COMPOUND ORRIS AND MYRRH DENTIFRICE FOR CLEANSING, BEAUTIFYING AND PRESERVING THE TEETH AND GUMS.—Having been engaged for years in endeavoring to discover a chemical preparation, resulting from a combination of ingredients that might prove beneficial, and at the same time safe in its action, the proprietor has at length the pleasure of presenting the above, the only scientific compound which has stood the test of chemical analysis, and what is more satisfactory, of twenty years experience in an unexampled extent of Dental Practice. If the durability of the Teeth, and the preservation of their beauty, be objects of importance, any article that will promote those ends must be a desirable acquisition; and this preparation, which has stood not only the tests of experience, but those of science, cannot fall of obtaining a share of public patronage.

It will not be amiss to mention a few of its most prominent qualities—such as removing all tartarous adhesions without injuring the teeth, interposing its antiseptic qualities to Scorbutic affections of the Gums, restoring them to firmness and pleasing color, and contributing largely to establish the pearly whiteness of the teeth, and a pure and salubrious breath.

DIRECTIONS.—Use with a harsh brush night and morning.

A Diploma awarded by the South Carolina Institute, 1850 to J. A. CLEVELAND, for the best Dentifrice.

N. B.—Tooth Brushes (manufactured and imported expressly for this establishment) always on hand.

Prepared and sold at

W. Y. PAXTON'S,

DRUG AND CHEMICAL ESTABLISHMENT,

No. 215 KING-STREET.

March 18

CLEVELAND'S COUGH MIXTURE.

THE PROPRIETOR, IN OFFERING THIS PREPARATION to the public, would embrace this opportunity to state upon what grounds he puts forth its merits, and he reason upon which it founds its superior claims to the attention of the afflicted. Thus all who require its use, may repose full confidence in the curative powers.

It is now over fifteen years since it was first prepared and offered for sale; although it has been used in a large private practice by an eminent Physician, and it is confidently offered to the public as a remedy without parallel for the relief and cure of all Diseases for which it is recommended, from the many testimonials of persons at standing, we only offer the following, from THE CHARLESTON MERCURY:

COUGH MIXTURE.—We have, unfortunately, had occasion recently to try a variety of remedies for a severe Cold, and we unhesitatingly bear testimony to the superior efficacy of the Cough Mixture, prepared by Dr. CLEVELAND, King-street. Its effect in soothing the irritation of the throat was immediate, and in promoting and easing expectoration most decided. We have no doubt of its usefulness as a remedy or palliative for Croup, Cold and other diseases of the throat and lungs, and of its safety as a Family Medicine.

Prepared only at

W. Y. PAXTON'S,

DRUG AND CHEMICAL STORE,

No. 215 KING-STREET, CHARLESTON, S. C.

March 18

CLEVELAND'S

ESSENCE OF JAMAICA GINGER,

25 CENTS A BOTTLE.

Sold at

W. Y. PAXTON'S,

DRUG AND CHEMICAL STORE,

No. 215 KING-STREET.

March 18

CLEVELAND'S YEAST POWDER

37½ CENTS A POUND.

CLEVELAND'S NE PLUS ULTRA YEAST POWDER, warranted to make good Bread, without fail, if good flour is used, and to keep in any climate.

No ingredient is used in the manufacture of this Yeast which is not pure, and, as it is manufactured on Chemical principles, it will not fail to raise Bread, Cakes, Buckwheat Cakes, &c., when used according to the directions. It is particularly recommended for sea voyages and for exportation to hot countries. The low price at which it is offered should recommend it to every family, especially at the present unsettled state of affairs, as it is the cheapest article now in use.

DIRECTIONS.—To every quart of Flour used put three teaspoonsful of the Powder, and mix it well while dry. Then mix, as usual, with water, milk, &c., and it is ready to bake at once, but it receives no injury by standing one or two hours. In order to have Bread with a fine grain it should be well kneaded.

It is important that the Dough, Butter or any article made, should not be too stiff or thick, and to every quart of Flour used add one table-spoonful of Lard, Butter or any kind of shortening, which will greatly improve and add to the lightness of the article made.

N. B.—Keep the Bottle or Canister well closed, and never dip a wet spoon in the Yeast.

Prepared and sold at 37½ cents a pound, only, at

W. Y. PAXTON'S,

No. 215 KING-STREET.

March 18

Dr. BENNETT'S

BOWEL COMPLAINT MIXTURE.

A SOVEREIGN REMEDY

FOR

BOWEL COMPLAINT.

Sold at

W. Y. PAXTON'S,

DRUG AND CHEMICAL STORE,

No. 215 KING-STREET.

March 18

Dr. PEARSON'S

RHEUMATIC RELIEF

AND

FIRE EXTRACTOR

IS HIGHLY RECOMMENDED TO THE PUBLIC B[Y] many families who have used it, and know it to be as with great success, when applied according to directions.

The RELIEF AND FIRE EXTRACTOR is put up in 25, 37½ and 75 cents bottles.

Prepared and sold at

W. Y. PAXTON'S,

DRUG AND CHEMICAL STORE,

No. 215 KING-STREET.

March 18

SCOTCH PIG IRON.

100 TONS NO. 1 PIG IRON, TO ARRIVE PER brig F. J. Nevins, from Glasgow, for sale by R. T. WALKER, Boyce & Co.'s Wharf.

April 12

SALT AFLOAT.

2000 SACKS LIVERPOOL SALT, IN SEAMLESS Sacks, landing this day per W. H. Gilliland, and for sale by HOLMES & STONEY, Boyce & Co.'s wharf.

March 27

TOBACCO.

We are exclusively in the

TOBACCO COMMISSION BUSINESS,

WE SELL FOR ALMOST EVERY RESPECTABLE MANUFACTURER IN VIRGINIA AND NORTH CAROLINA. WE OFFER TO THE TRADE OVER

5000 PACKAGES,

OF EVERY DESCRIPTION, GRADE, STYLE AND COLOR,

AT THE LOWEST PRICES.

ALSO,

SMOKING TOBACCO,

IN EVERY STYLE AND PACKAGE. AND

200 Boxes Virginia Powhatan Pipes

☞ Dealers cannot get such an assortment in any house South of Baltimore.

S. WYATT & CO.,

March 27 1mo No. 163 EAST BAY.

STEAM ENGINES, BOILERS AND MACHINERY

THE SUBSCRIBER IS NOW PREPARED TO BUILD, on the most reasonable terms, STEAM ENGINES, BOILERS, and MACHINERY of all descriptions, to order; also his improved HORSE POWER, 18 and 24 inch; VERTICAL CORN MILL, RICE PESTLES, SUGAR MILLS and BOILERS, COTTON SEED MILLS (for manure), and one of the best PORTABLE SASH SAW MILLS ever offered for Planter's use. I am also prepared to furnish all parts of the McCARTHY GIN, and to repair old ones equal to new IRON AND BRASS CASTINGS made at the shortest notice.

William S. Henerey.

January 31 No. 313 MEETING-STREET, NEAR LINE. tuth

KEROSENE OIL,

PURE AND LIGHT COLOR.

JUST RECEIVED A FRESH SUPPLY OF KEROSENE OIL, pure, and is free from smoke.

For sale by

J. R. WILTBERGER,

March 11 No. 245 KING STREET.

LIGHT! LIGHT! LIGHT!

THE MOST BEAUTIFUL ASSORTMENT OF "JONES' COAL OIL LAMPS" of every variety, including some splendid CHANDELIERS, etc., etc., suitable for Stores, Dwellings, Churches and Assembly Rooms. ALSO, A large supply of finest quality COAL OIL, very light colored. Just received, and for sale by B. SCHUR, Agent, No. 129 Meeting-st., next to corner Market-st.

October 18

Kettlewell's Renovator.

25 TONS OF THIS POPULAR FERTILIZER NOW Landing. It can be as profitably applied in the drill as under and after the plant is up.

Price $33 per Ton.

For sale by

RHETT & ROBSON,

NOS. 1 AND 2 ATLANTIC WHARF.

April 10 c wfm3

LAND PLASTER!

LAND PLASTER! LAND PLASTER! ROSENDALE CEMENT! ROSENDALE CEMENT! ROSENDALE CEMENT! CALCINED PLASTER, CALCINED PLASTER, CALCINED PLASTER. Manufactured and for sale by the HUDSON RIVER CEMENT COMPANY, Jersey City, New Jersey.

P. S.—This is now the only Cement Manufactory in New Jersey. February 26

GUANO

OF DIRECT IMPORTATION,

FROM JARVIS' AND BAKER'S ISLANDS.

THE RAPIDLY INCREASING FAVOR WHICH THIS Guano has met at the hands of practical Planters, who base their opinions of its merits upon their own experience in its use—in connection with the highest scientific testimony of its value as a permanent fertilizer, particularly commend it to the attention of all who are desirous of obtaining the best and cheapest, which is much the most economical of the concentrated manures in the market, being sold at forty per cent. less than Peruvian Guano. WARRANTED PURE AND UNADULTERATED. For Sale by

Wardlaw, Walker & Co.

February 7 c

READ

WHAT THE NEWSPAPERS SAY

ABOUT

HEIMSTREET'S

INIMITABLE

RESTORATIVE.

"A superior Hair Restorative."—*Boston Journal.*

"It takes precedence of all others."—*Springfield Republican.*

"Has triumphantly won for itself the name INIMITABLE."—*Saratogian.*

"We would advise our readers to buy nothing but the ORIGINAL INIMITABLE HAIR RESTORATIVE."—*Troy Whig.*

"It is the most reliable article for restoring the hair to its ORIGINAL COLOR."—*Family Journal.*

"We have been using it for years."—*Boston Saturday Evening Gazette.*

"When people can protect their hair from the tell-tale marks of age; when they can luxuriate in glossy black locks at an advanced period of their lives; when white and gray hair can be turned to a beautiful black or auburn; when the hair can be made to grow in profusion; all this can be done, it cannot do any harm to tell what will do it. HEIMSTREET'S HAIR RESTORATIVE will do it. This Hair Restorative is vastly superior to anything of the kind ever invented. The facts in our possession, in regard to this wonderful preparation, lead us to unqualifiedly recommend it."—*Cleveland (Ohio) Plain Dealer.*

[*From the St. Louis News.*]

The following "home" certificate was handed to us this morning for publication. The writer, as well as the druggist, is well known in St. Louis. We are inclined to believe that HEIMSTREET'S HAIR RESTORATIVE possesses merit of no low order:

ST. LOUIS, Mo., June 1st, 1859.

I hereby certify that my hair having become gray and partially *bald*, I bought from Henry Reynolds, druggist, corner Vine and Third streets, one four bottle of HEIMSTREET'S INIMITABLE HAIR RESTORATIVE (prepared by W. E. Hagan & Co.) By its use my hair was restored to its original color and thickness; it removed all dandruff, arrested its falling, and gave it a rich, glossy appearance. Its effects were entirely different from any hair preparation I ever used. I have heard of several ladies and gentlemen, my intimate friends, who all speak of the "Inimitable" as being one of the best and cheapest hair preparations in use. I refer to Henry Reynolds, druggist, for the truth of my statements.

WILLIAM BOSBYSHALL.

[*From the St. Louis Republican.*]

☞ The following extract speaks volumes in favor of HEIMSTREET'S INIMITABLE HAIR RESTORATIVE, as it comes from one of the most extensive drug houses in Mississippi, and from a high-toned and honorable gentleman:

JACKSON, MISS., May 29th, 1860.

W. B. MERWIN, 61 Market-st., St. Louis, Mo., Advertising Agent for Heimstreet Hair Restorative.

Dear Sir—The medicines you introduced in our city last winter are all having a large sale, and giving in every case satisfaction. Mr. James Henderson (one of our first citizens) is 67 years old, and has used all the hair dyes and restoratives of the day, but has never used an article equal to HEIMSTREET'S INIMITABLE HAIR RESTORATIVE IN COLORING. That it far surpasses any preparation that he has ever used. It has restored the hair of the bald and gray to its original luxuriance and beauty.

You can write the proprietors, W. E. Hagan & Co., Troy, N. Y., that they have the best selling article for Hair Restorative in our market, and that it gives satisfaction in every case. Respectfully yours,

J. S. SIZER, Wholesale Druggist.

We would add, that many of our first citizens in St. Louis are speaking in glowing terms of this article. We can refer to Henry Reynolds, druggist, corner Third and Vine streets, opposite City Hotel, and to nearly all the druggists in our city.

This article is NOT A DYE, but restores Hair to its *original color and greatly strengthens the roots of the Hair.*

AVOID IMITATION!

Price 50 cents and $1 a bottle, the large bottles holding three times as much as the small ones.

Orders should be addressed to the Wholesale and Retail Agents for South Carolina,

VAN SCHAACK & GRIERSON,

DRUGGISTS, No. 221 KING-STREET

At the Sign of the Negro and Golden Mortar.

January 24

TRENCH'S NEW WORK—A SELECT Glossary of English words, used formerly in sense, different from the present. By Richard Chenevix Trench, D. D. 1 volume. 75 cents.

Just published and for sale by RUSSELL & JONES, 251 King-st.

LATEST by TELEGRAPH.

MONDAY, APRIL 15, 1861.

LINCOLN DECLARES WAR.

A Call Issued for Seventy-five Thousand Volunteers.

The Proclamation in Full.

PREPARATIONS IN WASHINGTON,

etc., etc., etc.

[FROM OUR OWN CORRESPONDENT.]

WASHINGTON, April 14.—The Cabinet has been in session during the whole of to-day (Sunday). It is said that Major ANDERSON is strongly suspected of treachery. The Abolitionists say that the despatches from Charleston are all one sided, and profess not to believe them. A proclamation will be issued to-morrow, calling for 75,000 volunteers. 15,000 are called for from New York; 13,500 from Pennsylvania; 5000 from Massachusetts, and the residue from the other States.

The Proclamation, it is understood, will suspend the mail service in the seceded States, stop the telegraph, and declare Washington under martial law.

The excitement here is intense. A company of cavalry was sent to-day to Fort Washington, down the Potomac, twelve miles from this city.

The North is becoming a unit in favor of a war, and many think that the approaching struggle will be purely sectional. Several leading Democrats of New York have published a card in favor of sustaining the Government.

It is now admitted that the Administration intentionally deceived the Southern Commissioners.

Rumor says that Gen. SCOTT will resign; but this is doubtful. LINCOLN will refuse to accept any more resignations.

LINCOLN yesterday told members of the *Corps Diplomatique* that he would exhaust, if necessary, the whole power of his government in the attempt to retake Fort Sumter.

SEWARD, the other day, assured RUSSELL, the correspondent of the London *Times*, that the United States Government would regard the recognition of the Southern Confederacy by any European power as a *casus belli*. RUSSELL quietly replied, that the Administration had better reinforce Fort Sumter before threatening Europe.

LINCOLN has answered the Commissioners from Virginia in writing. He copies first that portion of his Inaugural in relation to the forts, property and the collection of the revenue, which he reaffirms. But he regrets the uncertainty attached to his Inaugural. He meant when it was delivered to refer only to the property in the possession of the Federal Government. If the attempt on Sumter is verified, he will repossess all places previously held by the Government, and will repel all cases of force by force. If Sumter be attacked, he will withdraw all the mails, and assume that war has been commenced. He regards all military force as much in the Union now as before secession. He will not invade to collect the revenue, but he will land to relieve the forts. He repeats that he will adhere to his entire Inaugural.

SUMNER to-day called on SEWARD, and urged the recognition of the independence of Hayti.

Two companies of United States cavalry arrived here this morning from Texas.

[FROM THE ASSOCIATED PRESS.]

WASHINGTON, April 14—10 p. m.—LINCOLN will to-morrow issue the following Proclamation:

BY THE PRESIDENT OF THE UNITED STATES—A PROCLAMATION.

Whereas, The laws of the United States have been for some time past and now are opposed, and the execution thereof obstructed, in the States of South Carolina, Georgia, Alabama, Florida, Mississippi, Louisiana, and Texas, by combinations too powerful to be suppressed by the ordinary course of judicial proceedings, or by the powers vested in the Marshal by law—

Now, therefore, I, ABRAHAM LINCOLN, President of the United States, in virtue of the power in me vested by the Constitution and the laws, have thought fit to call forth, and hereby do call forth, the militia of the several States of the Union to the aggregate number of seventy-five thousand, in order to suppress said combinations and to cause the laws to be duly executed. The details for this object will be immediately communicated to the State authorities by the War Department. I appeal to all loyal citizens to favor, facilitate and aid this effort to maintain the honor, the integrity and the existence of our National Union and the perpetuity of popular government, and to redress the wrongs already long enough endured. I deem it proper to say that the first services assigned to the forces called forth will probably be to reposses the forts, places and property which have been seized from the Union, and in such an event the utmost care will be observed, consistently with the objects aforesaid, to avoid any devastation and destruction of, or interference with, property, or any disturbance of peaceful citizens in any part of the country; and I hereby command the persons composing the combinations aforesaid to disperse and retire peaceably to their respective abodes within twenty days from this date.

Deeming that the present condition of public affairs present on extraordinary occasion, I do hereby, in virtue of the power in me vested by the Constitution, convene both Houses of Congress. Senators and Representatives are therefore summoned to assemble at their respective Chambers at 12 o'clock, noon, on Thursday, the 4th day July next, then and there to consider and determine such measures as, in their wisdom, the public safety and interest may seem to demand.

In witness whereof, I have hereunto set my hand, and caused the seal of the United States to be affixed.

Done at the City of Washington, this 15th day of Christ, in the year of our Lord one thousand eight hundred and sixty-one, and of the independence of the United States the eighty-fifth.

ABRAHAM LINCOLN.

By the President.

WILLIAM H. SEWARD, Secretary State.

The War Department is very busy to day in the preparation of the details to be communicated to the State authorities.

An additional force of Federal troops arrived here to-day by special train.

SECOND DESPATCH.

WASHINGTON, April 14.—It is reliably reported that two Regiments of Pennsylvania troops are now on their way to Washington.

Five officers of the United States Navy tendered their resignations yesterday, which were refused by the Department. It is probable that their names will be stricken from the Navy list, as dismissed. This has been done in recent cases in the army under similar circumstances.

The National Volunteers, last night, passed resolutions severely denouncing the military operations of the LINCOLN Government, and expressing sympathy with the cause of the Confederate States.

It is said that the Volunteers number several hundred men. The military guard at the several Government departments, was largely increased last night.

THIRD DESPATCH.

It is privately stated that eight thousand troops will be called from Virginia, and three thousand from Maryland, to co-operate in LINCOLN's schemes of coercion.

The Abolitionists generally blame ANDERSON, and many are still incredulous about the surrender.

ANDERSON's gallantry and the admiration which he seems to have excited among the Carolinians, are warmly commended by fair minded men.

Virginians here of all shades of political opinion think that the State will secede.

THE SURRENDER OF FORT SUMTER.

Reception of the News.

HALIFAX, April 13.—Intelligence of the bombardment of Fort Sumter has been received. The Legislature, amid intense emotion, passed the following resolution:

Resolved, That we have heard, with the deepest sorrow and regret, of the outbreak of civil war among friends—neighbors—in the United States; and, without expressing an opinion upon the points of the controversy, we seriously lament that those who speak our language, and have our civilization, should be shedding each other's blood, and we desire to offer our fervent prayer to the Father of the Universe for the restoration of peace.

NEW YORK, April 13.—There is great excitement here. Business is entirely suspended. Stocks are down. Fears are entertained that the tug-boats sent out have foundered in the gale. The *Kangaroo* is detained to carry the news about Fort Sumter to Europe.

MOBILE, April 13.—The news of the surrender of Fort Sumter was received with immense cheering. The streets are crowded, the Confederate and Palmetto flags are flying, cannon booming, bells ringing and there is general rejoicing.

AUGUSTA, April 13.—One hundred guns have been fired in honor of the surrender of Fort Sumter.

NEW ORLEANS, April 13.—The news of the surrender of Fort Sumter, this afternoon, is hailed with great joy. One hundred guns are firing. The flag of the Confederacy has been unfurled, and the eyes of all beam with gratification.

A general muster of the city volunteer companies took place this morning. Preparations are being made for a more complete defence of the city.

THE NEWS FROM MONTGOMERY.

MONTGOMERY, April 13.—Lieut. WERDEN is a prisoner here, and has been compelled to give up to the Secretary of War his despatches from Lieut. SLEMMER to the Government at Washington. The Attorney-General, whose opinion has been asked, declares that Lieut. WERDEN had violated his promise to report to Gen. BRAGG, and had carried secret despatches to Fort Pickens, after showing other despatches to Gen. BRAGG, and failing to report himself on his return.

Fort Pickens was reinforced last night. It is understood that Charleston is blockaded.

Major CHAMBERS, of the Alabama Army, has just arrived from Pensacola. He brings Lieut. REED WERDEN, of the United States Navy, prisoner of war. He was bearer of despatches to Fort Pickens and the Federal fleet at Pensacola bay. He is held by the Secretary of War, who sent a detachment on the railroad to arrest him.

The President has appointed E. WARREN MOISE Judge of the District of Louisiana.

General BEAUREGARD telegraphed to the Secretary of War, late last night, that there was heavy firing all Friday, that four guns on Fort Sumter had been dismounted, that the Confederate batteries were all safe, that nobody was hurt, that four steamers were off the bar, and that the sea was rough. Nothing has been received from Charleston this morning by the War Department.

The President and the Secretary of War were serenaded last night at the Exchange Hotel. The latter being called out, said the Confederate flag would soon be waving over Fort Sumter, and from the Federal Capitol at Washington, if the independence of the Confederate States was not recognized, and hostilities were continued.

THE NEWR FROM VIRGINIA.

RICHMOND, April 14.—The Commissioners of Virginia have to-day returned from Washington. They are cautious in expressing any opinion relative to the reply they received from LINCOLN.

The attack and surrender of Fort Sumter is the all-engrossing topic of conversation here. The matter was yesterday brought up in the Convention, when the Secessionists were cheered most enthusiastically, and the Unionists condemned.

A resolution was offered that Virginia should at once unite with the South, but no action was taken upon it. The Convention then adjourned.

There were great rejoicings last night over the surrender of Fort Sumter. Bonfires were blazing throughout the city, cannons fired salutes, and the speeches, music, processions, etc., were kept up until after midnight.

PREPARATIONS IN THE NORTH.

NEW YORK, April 14.—The U. S. Government has chartered the steamers *Philadelphia* and *Ericsson*. The former vessel is being rapidly filled with provisions, army stores and munitions of war. It is now generally believed here that the LINCOLN Government means to blockade every port in the Confederate States.

BOSTON, April 14.—On Saturday the Adjutant General's office was crowded all the forenoon. The officers of the State military have tendered their respective commands to the Government.

An extreme war feeling is at length arrived.

Governor ANDREWS, of this State, leaves for Washington this afternoon.

PROVIDENCE (R. I.), April 14.—Governor SPRAGUE has tendered his services to the Government. He offers a Marine Battery and a thousand infantry, which he will accompany himself.

HARRISBURG, Pa., April 13.—The War Bill passed both Houses without amendment, and the Governor signed it. A despatch from Charleston about hostilities, on being announced in both Houses, produced a profound sensation. In the House SMITH, a Democrat, changed his vote to aye on the War Bill. All the other Democrats voted against it.

LOUISVILLE, KY., April 13.—A despatch from the War Department, at Montgomery, has been received, directing that the Kentucky Regiment of Volunteers be held in readiness to march at a moment's notice.

NORFOLK, April 13.—Orders have been received to fit out the steamer *Merrimac* for service immediately. It it reported that the Guard Ship on the coast of North Carolina has been wrecked, and seventeen lives lost.

NEW YORK, April 14.—Advices from Albany say that Governor MORGAN, of this State, will tomorrow issue a call for 25,000 men to assist LINCOLN in coercion.

Markets.

NEW ORLEANS, April 13.—Sales of Cotton 1700 bales. Freights ⅝d.

NEW YORK, April 13.—Cotton dull. Midling Uplands at 12⅛@12⅝c. Flour quiet; Southern at $5.30@$5.65. Wheat steady. Corn steady; Mixed at 61½@68c; Southern White at 70c; Yellow at 69c. Turpentine firm at 36@37c. Rosin steady at 32½c. Rice firm at 3¾@4¼c. Freights unchanged.

MILLS' BOURBONIA

FIRST PREMIUM

BOURBON WHISKY.

DISTILLED IN BOURBON COUNTY, KENTUCKY, AND a pure and wholesome article, recommended by many Physicians as an excellent remedy in PULMONARY COMPLAINTS.

"It is possessed of an excellent flavor and fine aroma."

KENIFICK & SKRINE,

January 15 No. 260 KING-STREET, AGENTS.

AIMAR'S

SPORTSMAN'S OINTMENT

WILL PRESERVE

Gun Barrels and all Steel Mountings

FROM RUST, AND RENDER

Boots and Shoes Water-Proof.

Sold at Wholesale by

HAVILAND, STEVENSON & CO.

RUFF & DOWIE.

G. W. AIMAR.

At Retail, by

ALL DRUGGISTS AND HARDWARE DEALERS.

October 24

THE NEW BOOKS.—1. LECTURES OF LOLA MONTEZ, including her "Autobiography," "Wits and Women of Paris," "Comic Aspect of Love," "Beautiful Women," "Gallantry," &c., &c. Muslin, steel portrait. Price $1.

2. WOMEN'S THOUGHTS ABOUT WOMEN.—The latest and best work by the author of "John Halifax, Gentleman," "Agatha's Husband," "The Ogilvies," "Olive," &c. Bound in Muslin. Price $1.

3. FOLLOWING THE DRUM; or, Glimpses of Frontier Life. Being brilliant sketches of recruiting incidents on the Rio Grande, &c. By Mrs. Egbert L. Viele. Muslin. Price $1.

4. LIFE OF HUGH MILLER, author of "Schools, and Schoolmasters," "Old Red Sandstone," &c. From the Glasgow edition. Prepared by Thomas H. Brown. Muslin. Price $1.

5. TRUE LOVE NEVER DID RUN SMOOTH, an Eastern Tale, in Verse. By Thomas Bailey Aldrich, author of "Bable Bell." Elegantly printed and bound in Muslin. Illustrated Price 50 cents.

6. DEAR EXPERIENCE. c. By G. Ruffini, author of "Doctor Antonio," "Lorenzo Benoni," &c., with illustrations by Leech, of the London Punch. Muslin. Price $1.

For sale by SAM. HART, sr., 300 King-street, Importer Foreign Books.

NAUTICAL CATECHISM FOR THE use of the Marine School of Charleston, South Carolina—25 cents. This work is not only intended as a Text Book for Marine Schools, but a Manual of Instruction for those who would know somewhat of a ship and sailor craft. Proceeds of the sale are appropriated to the Marine School Fund. RUSSELL & JONES.

Clarified and Crushed Sugar LANDING.

950 BBLS. CLARIFIED AND CRUSHED SUGAR, landing per Maria Morton and Ida Della Torre. ALSO, 1500 coils Choice MANILLA ROPE. For sale by GEO. W. WILLIAMS & CO., Nos. 1 and 3 Hayne-street.

April 11 6

New Crop Cuba Molasses Landing.

350 HHDS. NEW CROP CUBA MOLASSES LANDING on Exchange and Adger's wharf. For sale by GEO. W. WILLIAMS & CO., Nos. 1 and 3 Hayne-street.

April 14 6

New Crop Rio Coffee Landing.

2100 BAGS NEW CROP RIO COFFEE LANDING, and in Store. For sale low by GEO. W. WILLIAMS & CO.

April 9 6

Bacon Sides Shoulders, etc.

150 CASKS BACON SIDES. 100 Casks Bacon Shoulders. 10,000 Hams averaging 11 lbs. 200 Barrels Prime Leaf Lard. 100 Tierces "Neffs" Sugar Cured Hams. For sale by GEO. CASSARD, No. 46 South-street, Baltimore, Who keeps constantly on hand a large Stock of Provisions of all kinds. February 16

Hams, Sides and Shoulders.

50 TIERCES CHOICE FAMILY HAMS. 40 hhds. Second Quality Hams. 30 hhds. Prime Bacon Sides. 42 hhds. Second Quality Shoulders. For sale by R. & A. P. CALDWELL & CO.

March 25

Flour, Sugar and Candles.

300 BARRELS SUPERFINE FLOUR. 150 barrels B. and C. Yellow Sugar. 200 boxes Adamantine Candles. For sale by R. & A. P. CALDWELL & CO.

March 25

Syrup and Molasses.

40 BARRELS CHOICE FLORIDA SYRUP. 75 barrels Prime N. O. Molasses. For sale by R. & A. P. CALDWELL & CO.

March 25

HAVANA SEGARS!

WE ARE DIRECT IMPORTERS OF THE ABOVE, AND make it a specialty. Steamer twice per month give us the facility of maintaining a Stock of the latest and most approved brands.

We propose to forward to DEALERS, desiring to test our Stock, samples of such Styles as they may designate.

Should any particular Brand be desired, and not comprised in our usual Stock, we will import specially, in quantities not less than 5000.

F. C. & S. C. BLACK,

SUCCESSORS TO FRANCIS C. BLACK,

No. 11, Rear of the Exchange.

September 21 c f

The South Carolina

WHITE LEAD, ZINC AND COLOR WORKS.

100 TONS OF WHITE LEAD, ZINC AND COLORS manufactured at our Works. For sale three per cent. below Northern prices, and of warranted superior quality, by CARMALT & BRIGGS, No. 97 East Bay.

September 24

J. E. SUARES,

282 AND 284 KING-STREET

OFFERS HIS LARGE AND WELL SELECTED STOCK OF FASHIONABLE FURNITURE, which he is constantly receiving by every arrival from the North, and principally from the best manufactories in New York, consisting of Rosewood, Walnut, Oak and Mahogany FURNITURE PARLOR SETTS, in Brocatelle, Reps and Hair Cloth; also a large assortment of ENAMEL CHAMBER SETTS; together with a general assortment, which he offers on as good and reasonable terms as any other house.

All orders attended to with despatch. Goods carefully acked for the country. 1yr April 4

BRADENBAUGH & POPE

DEALERS IN

METALS,

AND

MANUFACTURERS OF COPPER,

No. 75 SMITH'S WHARF,

BALTIMORE, MD.

MANUFACTURE AT THE "GUNPOWDER COPPER WORKS," and keep in store, Copper Sheets (Braziers and Sheathing), Rods, Rivets, Nails, etc. Pattern Sheets and Bottoms made to order. Dealers in Pig Iron Sheet, Rod, and Hoop Iron; Wrought Iron Tubes—Plain and Galvanized—for Gas, Water, or Steam; Malleable Iron Hittings; Lead Pipe and Sheet Lead; Gas Fitters' Tools Fooks, Cement, etc., Copper Ingots, Tin, Lead, Spelter Founders' Facings, Fire Bricks, etc., etc. March 8

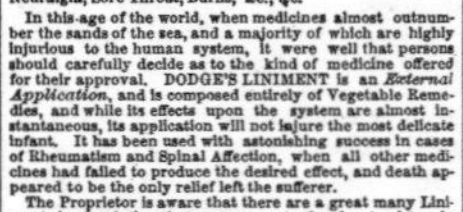

DODGE'S

AMERICAN LINIMENT

Has proved itself an invaluable remedy for Rheumatism Pains in the Back and Chest; Inflammation of the Kidneys and Bowels, Contraction of the Muscles, Spinal Affections, Neuralgia, Sore Throat, Burns, &c., &c.

In this age of the world, when medicines almost outnumber the sands of the sea, and a majority of which are highly injurious to the human system, it were well that persons should carefully decide as to the kind of medicine offered for their approval. DODGE'S LINIMENT is an *External Application*, and is composed entirely of Vegetable Remedies, and while its effects upon the system are almost instantaneous, its application will not injure the most delicate infant. It has been used with astonishing success in cases of Rheumatism and Spinal Affections, when all other medicines had failed to produce the desired effect, and death appeared to be the only relief left the sufferer.

The Proprietor is aware that there are a great many Liniments in circulation that possess not the least virtue in healing they disease the are warranted to cure, and are only sold by means of high-sounding advertisements. Suffice it to say that this medicine is modestly brought before the public as TRULY VALUABLE, and as such, is recommended to the afflicted.

For sale by all respectable Druggists in this City.

The Trade will be supplied by

JOHN ASHHURST & CO.,

DIRECT IMPORTERS OF CHOICE DRUGS & MEDICINES,

No. 29 HAYNE-STREET.

October 6 c

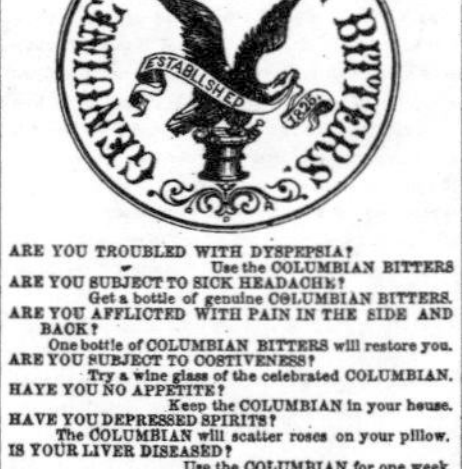

ARE YOU TROUBLED WITH DYSPEPSIA? Use the COLUMBIAN BITTERS.

ARE YOU SUBJECT TO SICK HEADACHE? Get a bottle of genuine COLUMBIAN BITTERS.

ARE YOU AFFLICTED WITH PAIN IN THE SIDE AND BACK? One bottle of COLUMBIAN BITTERS will restore you.

ARE YOU SUBJECT TO COSTIVENESS? Try a wine glass of the celebrated COLUMBIAN.

HAVE YOU NO APPETITE? Keep the COLUMBIAN in your house.

HAVE YOU DEPRESSED SPIRITS? The COLUMBIAN will scatter roses on your pillow.

IS YOUR LIVER DISEASED? Use the COLUMBIAN for one week.

HAVE YOU GIDDINESS OF THE HEAD? Don't fail to try the COLUMBIAN BITTERS.

Habitual Costiveness is cured by these Bitters, connected with feeble constitutions and persons of Sedentary habits, which often excite a very unfavorable influence upon the general health of the subject, and is particularly manifested by a restless and desponding state of mind, irregular, if not a loss of appetite.

Whoever is subject to the horrors of Constipation should at once purchase this sure remedy. In the train of Costiveness follow disordered Local Congestion, very frequently Mania or Hypochondria, violent Headaches, Palpitations and other affections of the Heart and Rheumatic Swellings.

The COLUMBIAN BITTERS are a combination heretofore unknown in the history of Medicine, differing entirely from all other preparations from the various preparations, in their effect upon the patient, at different times, offered to the public. They act specifically upon the digestive organs, thereby bringing it under their direct and immediate influence. Although possessed of powerful and controlling effects, yet they are entirely harmless, and cannot injure the most delicate constitution. Nothing will be more certain to effect a cure for all these ills. Loss of appetite, produced by Disease is seated in the frame, and hurrying fast its victims along the path of life, then their mysterious influence is felt and seen; they enkindle new life and vigor, and bring Health and Strength back to the sufferer.

Purchasers of the COLUMBIAN BITTERS should be careful to procure the same from a regular agent.

Every bottle of the COLUMBIAN BITTERS is prepared under the immediate supervision of an experienced member of our firm, hence we are able to guarantee that every ounce is of uniform Strength and Excellence.

For sale by the following respectable Druggists:

KENIFICK & SKRINE.	GEO. W. AIMAR.
E. M. CAREY.	W. Y. PAXTON.
CHARLES H. PANKNIN,	DAWSON & BLACKMAN.
STONEY & WILTBERGER.	Dr. P. M. COHEN.
W. G. TROTT.	Dr. GEO. CAULIER.
JULIUS ROUMILLAT.	C. F. SCHWETTMAN.
NELSON CARTER.	T. W. SPEISSEGGER.
	RUFF & DOWIE.

The trade supplied by

HAVILAND, STEVENSON & CO.,

No. 23 HAYNE-STREET.

January 18 3mo

FOR FORT PALMETTO AND BATTERY ISLAND.

QUARTERMASTER-GENERAL'S DEPARTMENT, CHARLESTON, April 15, 1861.

THE STEAMER EXCEL, CAPTAIN O'LARY, WILL leave for the above posts THIS DAY, at 10 o'clock, a. m., from Chisolm's Mill.

April 15 1 L. M. HATCH, Quartermaster-General.

EXCURSION.

THE

CAROLINA,

Capt. THOMAS J. LOCKWOOD,

WILL MAKE AN EXCURSION AROUND THE Harbor THIS DAY, 15th inst., leaving Southern Wharf at TEN o'clock. She will run sufficiently near Fort Sumter to give an opportunity to those who may wish, to see the exterior of the Fort. Fare $1. April 15

TO LEAVE ON WEDNESDAY MORNING, AT 6 O'CLOCK,

FOR FLORIDA, SAVANNAH,

BEAUFORT AND BLUFFTON.

THE SUPERIOR IRON

CECILE,

Captain F. PECK,

WILL LEAVE SAVANNAH STEAM PACKET WHARF as above, on WEDNESDAY MORNING, at 6 o'clock.

E. LAFITTE & CO., Agents, Savannah Steam Packet Wharf.

April 15 2

FOR FLORIDA, VIA SAVANNAH.

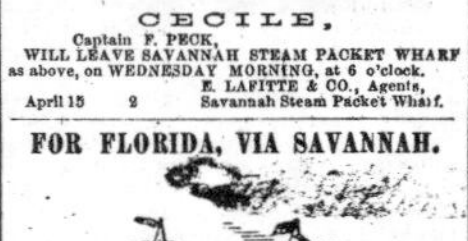

CAROLINA,

CAPT. T. J. LOCKWOOD,

WILL LEAVE SOUTHERN WHARF EVERY TUESDAY MORNING, at 7 o'clock, for Savannah, which port she will leave at 6 p. m. same day, for Fernandina, Jacksonville, and Palatka, touching at the intermediate Landings on the St. John's River.

Returning will leave Palatka THURSDAY, at 5 a. m., Jacksonville at 5 p. m., and Savannah FRIDAY, at 6 p. m., arriving at Charleston SATURDAY MORNING.

Passage from Charleston to Savannah	$3.00
Passage from Charleston to Fernandina	6.00
Passage from Charleston to Jacksonville	8.00
Passage from Charleston to Picolata and Palatka	10.00

Freight received on SATURDAY and MONDAY.

For engagements of Freight or Passage, apply to

H. L. CHISOLM, Agent, Florida Steam Packet Company, Southern Wharf.

March 15 fsm13

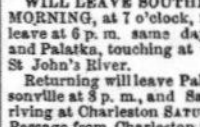

STEAM—NEW YORK, SOUTHAMPTON AND HAVRE.—THE VANDERBILT EUROPEAN LINE OF STEAMSHIPS WILL SAIL BETWEEN NEW YORK, SOUTHAMPTON AND HAVRE, CARRYING THE UNITED STATES MAILS.

FROM NEW YORK, FOR SOUTHAMPTON AND HAVRE.	RETURNING FROM HAVRE AND SOUTHAMPTON.
ILLINOIS, Terry, Saturday, April 6	Wednesday, April 24
VANDERBILT, Lefevre, " May 4	Wednesday, May 22
ILLINOIS, Terry, " May 18	Wednesday, June 5
VANDERBILT, Lefevre, " June 15	Wednesday, July 3
ILLINOIS, Terry, " June 29	Wednesday, July 17
VANDERBILT, Lefevre, " July 27	Wednesday, Aug. 14

These ships have Watertight and Fire-Proof Compartments.

Certificates of Passage issued from Europe to America. Specie delivered in London or Paris.

Dr. TORRANCE, Agent, No. 5 Bowling Green, New York.

Sight Drafts on London, Paris and Frankfort.

March 15

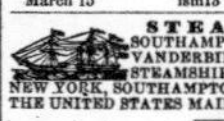

FOR SALE.—THE STEAMER HUNTER WOODS, built of iron, is 183 feet on deck, 8 feet hold, 28 feet beam, will carry the bulk of 1600 barrels, or 400 bales cotton on her main deck, which is flush from stem to stern; has more deck room than most steamers of 600 tons. Cabin on upper deck; burns less than half a cord of wood per hour; low pressure engine, 26 inches cylinder, 6 feet stroke; draws light, only 3 feet; loaded, 5 feet; speed, 10 miles per hour. She is in perfect order; was built of the very best materials, without regard to cost. For further particulars apply to J. BRANDT, jr., Baltimore.

March 15

IF YOU WANT

ANY OF THE

RELIABLE

PATENT MEDICINES

OR YOUR

PRESCRIPTIONS

PREPARED

WITH CARE,

AT

VERY REASONABLE PRICES,

CALL OR SEND YOUR ORDERS

TO

Van Schaack & Grierson's

FAMILY MEDICINE STORE,

221 KING STREET,

AT THE SIGN OF THE NEGRO AND GOLDEN MORTAR.

January 19 c

THE GREAT VIRGINIA DISCOVERY.

Some four months since our excellent townsman, NAPTHALE EZEKIEL, informed us that he had prepared a HAIR RESTORER, with which he was experimenting on his own head, whose top was entirely bald. We saw him two days since, and on the place so bald four months since, a fine crop of hair has sprung up with a vigorous growth. So convinced is Mr. Ezekiel of the efficacy of his discovery that he has named it the

INFALLIBLE VIRGINIA HAIR RESTORER.

Mr. E. is about going into an extensive manufacture of a article that is destined to prove of anxious interest to old bald-pated friends.—*From the Richmond Enquirer* Dec 1859.

I, N. EZEKIEL, take oath on the holy Bible, that I have been bald for the past twelve years, and have restored my hair by using EZEKIEL'S VIRGINIA HAIR RESTORER.

NAPTHALE EZEKIEL.

This day sworn to before me, by Napthale Ezekiel.

JOS. MAYO, Mayor of Richmond.

THE GREAT VIRGINIA DISCOVERY is for sale in Charleston by all respectable Druggists.

Price, One Dollar per Bottle.

All orders should be addressed to

JOHN ASHHURST & Co.,

IMPORTERS AND WHOLESALE DRUGGISTS,

No. 29 HAYNE-STREET.

SOLE AGENTS FOR SOUTH CAROLINA.

February 27

AGRICULTURE AND GARDENING.—Loudon's Arboretum Britannicum, History and Description of the Forest Trees and Shrubs of Britain, 8 vols., 8vo, including 4 of Plates, with nearly 3000 Illustrations, $22.50; Loudon's Encyclopedia of Agriculture; Loudon's Encyclopedia of Gardening; Loudon's Encyclopedia of Plants; Loudon's Hortus Britannicus; Loudon's Ladies Companion to the Flower Garden; Hooker's Muscologia Exotica; Smith's English Flora, 4 vols; Illustrated Botany, 2 vols; Coleman's European Agriculture; Paxton's Botany, beautifully illustrated; Lindley's Horticulture; Stephen's Book of the Farm; The Wheat Plant and Indian Corn, its Culture, Origin and Development, &c., &c.; Davy's Agricultural Chemistry, Grapes and Manures, &c., &c. For sale by SAM'L HART, sen., No. 300 King-street

ITALY AND FRANCE IN THE SIXTEENTH CENTURY, or Ettore Fieramosca, or the Challenge of Barletta. By Massimo D'Azeglio. $1.

THE VICISSITUDES OF ITALY SINCE THE CONGRESS OF VIENNA. By A. L. V. Gretton. $1.25.

For sale by RUSSELL & JONES, 251 King-st.

AUCTION SALES.

Estate sale, by order of the Executor and consent of the Ordinary.—515 acres of land, near Summerville Depot, South Carolina Railroad.

BY J. E. BOWERS.

Will be sold on WEDNESDAY next, 17th instant, at eleven o'clock, in front of the Exchange,

All that TRACT OF LAND, containing 515 acres, about half a mile above Summerville Depot, adjoining J. R. Stall, McClaren, Ferguson and Easterling's land, as per plat now divided into two tracts of 257¼ acres each, through the centre of the plot, and to be sold as two separate tracts of 257¼ acres each. This land is well adapted to raising stock, for turpentine and for planting purposes.

ALSO,

All that LOT OF LAND, with the buildings thereon, situated in Spring street, next to the corner of Meeting, on the south side, lot measuring and containing 37 feet deep, by 51 feet front and back lines, be the same more or less, with a very neat two story wooden HOUSE, on brick foundation, containing four square rooms, pantry, and fine piazza to the west; a good kitchen, and out buildings, and a good well of water.

Conditions—Half cash; balance in one year, secured by bond and mortgage; house insured, and policy assigned. Purchasers to pay J. E. B. for papers.

April 10 thsnwd

AUCTIONEERS' PRIVATE SALES.

Cook and Washer.

BY WILLIAM SIMONS.

At Private Sale, FLORA, a complete Meat Cook and Plain Washer. She belongs to an Estate, and is sold by order of the Executors. Apply as above, at

April 9 No. 26½ BROAD-STREET.

Tract of Superior Bottom Lands, in Wharton County Texas.

BY HUTSON LEE.

At Private Sale, 1960 acres of superior BOTTOM LAND, above overflow, situated in Wharton county, Texas. This tract is six (6) miles below the county town of Wharton, on the Colorado river, in the immediate neighborhood of "Peach Creek" and "Old Caney," where lands are celebrated for their fertility and fine average crops, often yielding (2) two bales of cotton to the acre. A railroad, now being constructed, will run within one mile of the tract.

To those in search of superior planting lands, having every facility for transportation, and an exhaustless supply of good water, a rare opportunity is here offered for making a profitable investment.

Negroes, at a fair valuation, will be taken in payment for a part or the whole of the purchase money.

Titles clear and indisputable.

For terms and further particulars apply at

No. 51 BROAD-STREET, Next door to Telegraph Office,

January 10 1s Charleston, S. C.

WHARTON & PETSCH,

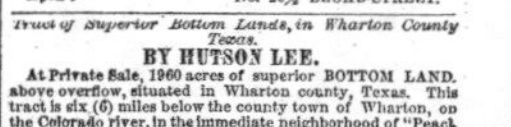

CAR WORKS

CHARLESTON, S. C.

ARE PREPARED TO BUILD CARS OF ALL KINDS on reasonable and accommodating terms, short notice, and deliver to any point in the Union.

THOMAS J. WHARTON.............A. H. PETSCH

August 2 tuths

★ ★ ★

DR. SWEET'S

INFALLIBLE LINIMENT,

THE

GREAT EXTERNAL REMEDY.

FOR RHEUMATISM, GOUT, NEURALGIA, LUMBAGO, STIFF NECK AND JOINTS, SPRAINS, BRUISES, CUTS AND WOUNDS, PILES, HEADACHE, AND ALL RHEUMATIC AND NERVOUS DISORDERS.

For all of which it is a speedy and certain remedy, and never fails. This Liniment is prepared from the recipe of Dr. Stephen Sweet, of Connecticut, the famous bone setter, and has been used in his practice for more than twenty years with the most astonishing success.

As an Alleviator of Pain, it is unrivalled by any preparation before the public, of which the most skeptical may be convinced by a single trial.

This Liniment will cure rapidly and radically, **Rheumatic Disorders** of every kind, and in thousands of cases where it has been used it has never been known to fail.

For Neuralgia, it will afford immediate relief in every case, however distressing.

It will relieve the worst cases of **Headache** in three minutes and is warranted to do it.

Toothache also will it cure instantly.

For Nervous Debility and General Lassitude arising from imprudence or excess, this Liniment is a most happy and unfailing remedy. Acting directly upon the nervous tissues, it strengthens and revivifies the system, and restores it to elasticity and vigor.

For Piles.—As an external remedy, we claim that it is the best known, and we challenge the world to produce an equal. Every victim of this distressing complaint should give it a trial, for it will not fail to afford immediate relief, and in a majority of cases will effect a radical cure.

Quinsy and Sore Throat are sometimes extremely malignant and dangerous, but a timely application of this Liniment will never fail to cure.

Sprains are sometimes very obstinate, and enlargement of the joints is liable to occur if neglected. The worst case may be conquered by this Liniment in two or three days.

Bruises, Cuts, Wounds, Sores, Ulcers, Burns and Scalds, yield readily to the wonderful healing properties of DR. SWEET'S INFALLIBLE LINIMENT, when used according to directions. Also, **Chilblains, Frosted Feet, and Insect Bites and Stings.**

Every Horse Owner

should have this remedy at hand, for its timely use at the first appearance of Lameness will effectually prevent those formidable diseases, to which all horses are liable, and which render so many otherwise valuable horses nearly worthless.

Over four hundred voluntary testimonials to the wonderful curative properties of this Liniment have been received within the last two years, and many of them from persons in the highest ranks of life.

CAUTION.

To avoid imposition, observe the Signature and Likeness of Dr. Stephen Sweet on every label, and also "Stephen Sweet's Infallible Liniment" blown in the glass of each bottle, without which none are genuine.

RICHARDSON & CO., Sole Proprietors, Norwich, Ct.

For sale by the Wholesale and Retail Agents,

VAN SCHAACK & GRIERSON,

Druggists, No. 221 King street, sign of the Negro

September 6 c and Golden Mortar.

OAK ORCHARD ACID SPRINGS

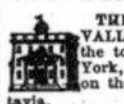

THESE SPRINGS ARE SITUATED IN THE VALLEY OF THE OAK ORCHARD CREEK, in the town of Alabama, Genessee county, New York, eight miles South of the village of Medina, on the Erie Canal, and fourteen miles from Batavia.

The principal Acid Springs are three in number; besides these, there are six others. They are all located within a circuit of about fifty rods. The Medicinal qualities of these Waters are fully shown in the subjoined testimonials. They contain a very large amount of Sulphuric Acid, Sulphate of Iron, Sulphate of Lime, and Proto-Sulphate of Iron. The great Medicinal virtues possessed by the Waters depend very largely upon the presence, in such unusual quantities, of these curative substances.

Hundreds of cases of disease, especially those resulting from the Scrofulous Diathesis, have been cured by their use. IN SKIN DISEASES—even in confirmed LEPROSY—the Waters have been signally successful.

Opinions of medical and scientific gentlemen are given in the circular. The following gentlemen speak in strong terms of the Medicinal value of these Waters: Professor Emmons, T. Romeyn Beck, M. D., of Albany; James McNaughton, M. D., of Albany; Edward Spring, M. D., of New York; Dr. R. Campbell, of Pittsfield, Mass.; Dr. J. S. Shuler, of Lockport, N. Y. They recommend the Waters confidently. Dr. Spring refers to a case of Chronic Diarrhea, of several years standing, which was cured by the use of the Water. Dr. Beck says, "I am satisfied that these Waters are highly valuable as a Medicinal Agent." Dr. Campbell says, "They must be highly beneficial for all Chronic Diseases of the Stomach and Bowels."

Dr. S. F. Wells read a paper on the subject of these Waters, before the Academy of Physicians, in the city of New York. In which he stated that the Waters possess decidedly tonic, refrigerant, and astringent properties; and that the class of diseases to which they are more particularly adapted are chronic affections of the digestive and urinary organs, and some of the cutaneous diseases; chronic dyspepsia; chronic diarrhea; chronic dysentery, chronic dyspepsia, chronic cystitis; diabetes; cases of passive hemorrhage, such as purpura hemorrhagica, and the colliquative sweats of Hectic fever. The Water may also be often used with advantage, he says, in cases of low typhoid fevers; in convalescence from protracted fevers, to excite the appetite and promote digestion; in diarrhea, particularly such as are dependent on a relaxed or ulcerated state of the mucous membrane of the intestines. In catarrhs, affections, or illness attended with phosphatic sediments. It is the suitable remedy, being preferable to muriatic acid, as being more palatable, and just as fit combined with digestion of the stomach. In febrile diseases it can be used freely, diluted, as a refrigerant to diminish thirst and preternatural heat. In skin diseases—in those forms of dyspepsia connected with an alkaline condition of the stomach, as in Pyrosis, or waterbrash—it will prove better than hydrochloric acid. In cases of Colica pictonum, and other injurious consequences arising from the action of lead, this water will prove to be an invaluable antidote. In chronic pharyngitis, laryngitis, chronic mucous catarrh, and gangrenous sore mouth, chronic ophthalmia (externally), as a gargle in ulcerated sore throat, in cases of salivation, and in gonorrhea and gleet; and in adult piles. When taken internally, a wine-glassful, or a tumbler, diluted, taken three times a day, is sufficient for an adult.

Other testimonials from physicians, and other respectable individuals, may be seen on application to the Agent.

Dealers supplied on liberal terms.

No Water genuine unless procured from

H. W. BOSTWICK, Sole Agent, No. 574 Broadway, New York.

Sold in Charleston by PHIN & DORN.

VAN SCHAACK & GRIERSON, Druggists, No. 221 King-street, Sign of the Negro and Golden Mortar.

May 8 tuths 1y

THE LARGEST AND CHEAPEST ASSORTMENT OF THE BEST MANUFACTURED Umbrellas, Parasols and Walking Canes,

Ever offered for sale in this market, Wholesale and Retail.

B. JOHNSON & CO.,

UMBRELLA MANUFACTURERS,

263 KING-STREET, NEAR WENTWORTH,

CHARLESTON, S. C.

We would most respectfully call the attention of our friends, and the public of the city and country to our stock of SILK and other UMBRELLAS.

We are now manufacturing and offering for sale one of the best Umbrellas ever offered to the trade. It is made in constant receipt of Silks and Ginghams, manufactured in England under our own special direction, by which means we are enabled to produce a better article than can be procured elsewhere; we have a fine assortment of Gingham Linen and Cotton Umbrellas, and Silk Parasols, Folding Umbrellas for gentlemen, &c. We also have a large stock of fine Ginghams, Linens and Cottons, and Buggy Umbrellas, with and without joints.

A large assortment of WALKING CANES.

P. S.—We have also added to the above establishment the Manufacture of WIRE SAFES, for keeping Provisions, which are warranted superior to any imported. All orders will be punctually attended to. February 10

BLAKEY'S (R.) HISTORY OF THE PHILOSOPHY OF MIND—Embracing the opinion, all writers on Mental Sciences, from the earliest period to the present time. 4 volumes, 8vo. Longmans, 1850. $9.

For sale by RUSSELL & JONES, 251 King-st.

THE MERCURY.

BY R. B. RHETT, JR.

[CONTINUED FROM FIRST PAGE.]

prise. Lieut. STRIBLING sleeplessly paced the deck all night. His energy and perseverance overcame all obstacles. Lieut. EVANS took the first watch as officer of the deck; Midshipman INGRAHAM took the second; First Assistant Engineer LOPER the third; Gunner CUDDY the fourth; and Midshipman WILKINSON the morning watch. Scarcely, however, had the latter officer entered upon the discharge of his duties, before he made a report that cleared up all doubt as to the decision of Major ANDERSON and the determination of General BEAUREGARD.

At 4.40 A. M., the signal shell was thrown from Fort Johnson, and shortly afterwards the contest—a contest that will make the 12th of April, 1861, a memorable day in history—for the possession and occupation of Fort Sumter commenced. Shell followed shell in quick succession; the harbor seemed to be surrounded with miniature volcanoes belching forth fire and smoke. Still Major ANDERSON gave no sign of resentment, save the defiance expressed at his flag-staff. But a shell from Cumming's Point bursts on the parapet—the brave Cummings' Pointers are getting the range! Another falls quite within, and now Fort Moultrie seems to have got the range, and the Floating Battery, which the North believed a humbug, begins to indicate her position. She's not exactly at her wharf in Charleston, nor is it positive she will not take a position nearer still to Fort Sumter. It is getting to be warm work for Major ANDERSON.

There, I see a flash—there goes the first shot from Fort Sumter, right plump at Cummings' Point. A considerable interval elapses, which is improved by all the batteries within range of Fort Sumter, and then the question of whether Major ANDERSON will keep up the fire is definitely settled. Casemate follows casemate with dogged deliberation.

But whilst all this was transpiring, we were rapidly steaming out to sea. There goes the whistle of the General Clinch, and we haul up close and receive orders to follow in her wake. We come to anchor, and presently Lieut. STRIBLING starts from his seat, seizes a glass, and looks eagerly eastward. He reports a steamer, and what he supposes to be a brig, standing straight in. The vessels are at a great distance, however; but when we see them more plainly we are almost satisfied that we have had a sight of the LINCOLN squadron or at least a portion of it. The General Clinch makes another signal, and we haul in our anchor and follow straight for Cumming's Point. As we steam by battery after battery, we can see the men on the beach waving their hands to us, and distinguish a faint cheer. At last we come to anchor close in, just below Cummings' Point, where an excellent view of the firing was obtained. In a brief period the steamer which had been seen off the bar became plainly visible at Cummings' Point. She was taken for the Harriet Lane, and Cummings' Point threw two shells at her. The squadron immediately steamed out to sea, and as we neared the strange steamer, she run up the Palmetto flag. It is believed to have been the Nashville, Captain MURRAY, from New York. At first she made for the squadron, but afterwards changed her course, and when last seen was heading for Charleston.

Stono was reached about 10 o'clock, a. m., without any further adventure, and as the vessel came to anchor, Fort Palmetto fired a gun. Commodore HARTSTENE went on shore, and made a report. It appears that this was the first intelligence of the commencement of hostilities that had been received; the firing of the guns not being audible at this distance, in consequence of the wind.

Commodore HARTSTENE, in the Clinch, has left for Cummings' Point, to report to General BEAUREGARD, leaving orders for the Seabrook to wait further orders. The officers and men are all dissatisfied. They know that some hard fighting is being done, and regret that they have no hand in it. Their only consolation is the hope, that the orders they are waiting for will be to service on Morris' Island.

STONO, 3½ o'clock, April 12.

The Clinch returned, but brought no orders.

It is reported there is a man-of-war around the Point. An attack in boats is expected to-night.

CHARLESTON, April 13.

At 7 o'clock, I left Fort Palmetto. All was quiet there. No steamers were in sight, and the Edisto had arrived with Captain SHEDD's command, consisting of eighty tall, stout, fighting men. The men are in the best of spirits, and have made up their minds to fight to the death. Captain POPE and the Lafayette Artillery have been at this fortress for the last three months, and they have made it almost impregnable. Their battery fully commands Stono Inlet, and woe to the unlucky vessel with Yankee colors that escapes the breakers and gets within range. "Uncle Ned" has a pet gun, that he says will sink any vessel that approaches. "Uncle Ned" claims the first shot.

Your correspondent returned by the mail route, which is an admirable means of transportation for a limited number. You travel partly on land and partly on water, and, if he is allowed to express an opinion, the sentinels are very faithful in the discharge of their duty. In short, reader, don't attempt the journey unless you are ticketed through.

On the way I saw a portion of Col. HAGOOD's regiment disembark from the Chesterfield, for Morris Island. The entire regiment will be in position before night.

The firing was audible for miles, and the large volume of smoke issuing from Fort Sumter created almost universal belief that Major Anderson had surrendered.

The Official Correspondence.

The following is a copy of the official correspondence which took place before the bombardment commenced:

[No. 1.]

Gen. Beauregard's Despatch to the Secretary of War.

CHARLESTON, April 8, 1861.

To L. P. WALKER:

DEAR SIR: An authorized messenger from Lincoln has just informed Gov. Pickens and myself that provisions will be sent to Fort Sumter, "peacably if they can, forcibly if they must." [Signed] G. T. BEAUREGARD.

[No. 2.]

Reply of the Secretary of War to Gen. Beauregard.

MONTGOMERY, April 10, 1861.

To Gen. BEAUREGARD, Charleston:

If you have no doubt of the authorized character of the agent who communicated to you the intention of the Washington Government to supply Fort Sumter by force, you will at once demand its evacuation; and if this is refused, proceed in such a manner as you may determine to reduce it. Answer.

[Signed] L. P. WALKER.

[No. 3.]

Gen. Beauregard to the Secretary of War.

CHARLESTON, April 10, 1861.

To L. P. WALKER:—The demand will be made to-morrow at 12 o'clock.

[Signed] G. T. BEAUREGARD, Brigadier-General.

[No. 4.]

The Secretary of War to Gen. Beauregard.

MONTGOMERY, April 10, 1861.

To Gen. BEAUREGARD, Charleston:

Unless there are special reasons connected with your own condition, it is considered proper that you should make the demand at an earlier hour.

[Signed]. L. P. WALKER.

[No. 5.]

Gen. Beauregard to the Secretary of War.

CHARLESTON, April 10, 1861.

To L. P. WALKER:—The reasons are special for twelve o'clock.

[Signed] G. T. BEAUREGARD.

[No. 6.]

Gen. Beauregard to the Secretary of War.

CHARLESTON, April 11, 1861.

To L. P. WALKER: Demand sent at two o'clock. Allowed till 6 o'clock to answer.

[Signed] G. T. BEAUREGARD.

[No. 7.]

The Secretary of War to Gen. Beauregard.

MONTGOMERY, April 11, 1861.

Gen. BEAUREGARD, Charleston:—Telegraph reply of Anderson.

[Signed] L. P. WALKER.

[No. 8.]

Gen. Beauregard to the Secretary of War.

CHARLESTON, April 11, 1861.

To L. P. WALKER: Major Anderson replied: "I have the honor to acknowledge the receipt of your communication demanding the evacuation of this fort, and to say in reply thereto that it is a demand with which I regret that my sense of honor and of my obligation to my government prevent my compliance." He adds verbally: "I will await the first shot, and if you do not batter us to pieces, we will be starved out in a few days." Answer.

[Signed,] G. T. BEAUREGARD.

[No. 9.]

The Secretary of War to Gen. Beauregard.

MONTGOMERY, April 11, 1861.

To Gen. BEAUREGARD, Charleston: We do not desire needlessly to bombard Fort Sumter. If Major Anderson will state the time at which, as indicated by him, he will evacuate, and agree that in the meantime he will not use his guns against us, unless ours should be employed against Fort Sumter, you are authorized thus to avoid the effusion of blood. If this, or its equivalent, be refused, reduce the Fort as your judgment decides to be the most practicable.

[Signed] L. P. WALKER.

[No. 10.]

Gen. Beauregard to the Secretary of War.

CHARLESTON, April 12, 1861.

To L. P. WALKER: He would not consent. I will write to-day.

[Signed] G. T. BEAUREGARD.

[No. 11.]

Gen. Beauregard to the Secretary of War.

CHARLESTON, April 12, 1861.

To L. P. WALKER: We opened fire at 4.30, a. m.

[Signed] G. T. BEAUREGARD.

NOTE.—Intercepted dispatches disclose the fact that Mr. Fox, who had been allowed to visit Major Anderson on the pledge that his purpose was pacific, employed his opportunity to devise a plan for supplying the Fort by force, and that this plan had been adopted by the Washington Government, and was in progress of execution.

Our New York Correspondence.

NEW YORK, April 10.

The Serpent Seward—Audacity of the Tribune—The Virginia Unionists—Schemes About Texas—The Real Strength of the Expedition Against the South—Anderson's Provisions—Grumbling at Paying Duties—Stoppage of the Mails, etc., etc.

The *Tribune*, in a double-leaded leader, says this morning:

We are enabled to state with positive certainty that the principal object of the military and naval expedition which has sailed from this harbor within the past four days is the relief of Fort Sumter.

The satanic cloven foot of Abolitionism is at length displayed. The serpent SEWARD, who, beneath his wreathed smiles to the Commissioners who represented your Confederacy, secreted the deadly poison whose venom now breaks forth in invasion of your soil, is revealed in his true light. His oily speech at the New England dinner, and his subsequent speech in Congress, were only intended to deceive, as "the old serpent, the devil and satan," beguiled our first parents in the Garden of Eden. But he did not deceive the great body of the Southern people, nor the intelligent friends of freedom in the North. The *Tribune* says the Cabinet is a unit, and that SEWARD was always of the same opinion as he is now. Whence, then, the violent attacks in the *Tribune* from day to day upon the Secretary of State on the ground that he was pacific? It says:

Mr. Seward has uniformly said, in reply to inquiries as to the policy of the Administration, that its acts would disclose its policy. On all the questions that have come before the Cabinet in relation to the course to be pursued in suppressing the rebellion of the slaveholders, and particularly in regard to the recent warlike measures of the Administration, the President and Mr. SEWARD are entirely agreed in opinion. He was in close conference with the President yesterday, and several times to-day, and is known to have been greatly instrumental in shaping the very policy and programme for which the newsmongers would have him retire from office.

So then the honied words of Mr. SEWARD were, from the beginning, designed to lead the country astray, and to lull the people into a false security, that there was peace when there was no peace, and when war was in his heart. At this moment, indeed, when the government have sent a hostile expedition against the South, and the *Tribune* in every column rejoices that the rebels will be put down by the sword, and that the slaveholders will be crushed, says the government means "peace," but that it is the South who is making war! "Mr. SEWARD," says the *Tribune*, "has at length replied to the communication of the Rebel Commissioners in a courteous note, declining to receive them in official capacity, *but assuring them of the pacific intentions of the President.*" This is the insidious language under which the atrocious designs of the Abolitionists are cloaked. Had they avowed these designs at first, they never could have gained the ascendant; and even now they are afraid to say what they really mean—a war against the domestic institutions of fifteen States. Hence, like LOUIS NAPOLEON, who said "the empire is peace," at the very time when he had planned war, the cunning of the serpent suggests that the armed squadron sent to the South, with its bomb shells and other deadly missiles, is on an errand of peace and humanity—no less than to relieve the hunger of one ANDERSON and one SLEMMER. It seems that even the crew of the *Brooklyn* are, or lately were, in a bad way, for, says the *Tribune*:

We print this morning an interesting letter from a correspondent on board the steamer *Brooklyn*, off Fort Pickens. He states that the crew of the vessel had been nearly in a state of starvation from the cutting off of their usual supplies by order of Gen. Bragg, and that to the date of his writing, April 2, no orders had been received for the reinforcement of Lieut. Slemmer's command.

If the philanthropic intentions of the government to feed the hungry are thwarted, then woe to the Southern savages who would starve these men! Their blood must flow like water. Such is the unmitigated insult offered to every understanding, in the editorial columns of the *Tribune*.

But there is one thing for which that journal deserves credit—its outspoken audacity. Yesterday's number contained a letter from HORACE GREELEY to Mr. SUMMERS, of Virginia, in which he denounces the Union men of the State in terms which their forbearance and vacillating policy have richly earned. This is this their reward for bowing and cringing at the footstool of Black Republican power. They are now spurned, execrated and spat upon, and they have the sympathy of no party, North or South. It is believed in this city that the leaders who have interfered with the natural action of the State wanted offices from LINCOLN, and I have no doubt that many of these gentlemen would be mean enough to accept it if were only offered to them. Now that they are disappointed, perhaps they will find it convenient to chime in with the rising storm, lest it sweep them away. Quoth GREELEY, the principal organ of the Administration to Mr. SUMMERS:

But your Union majority has wasted weeks in hair-splitting talk, whilst the secessionists have steadily acted; you have waveringly held an equivocal position, while they have had a definite purpose, and marched straight towards their object; and the necessary result is that they are far stronger to-day, and their prospect far brighter, than if they had carried the State at your late election. *And if the Union shall be finally wrecked, very much of the blame will justly fall on the shilly shally Unionists in the Virginia Convention.*

There is a good deal of truth in this; and if the action of the so-called Unionists in Virginia have not broken up the Union, it has materially contributed to civil strife. Had Virginia taken her stand in the beginning with South Carolina, there would be no war to-day, and no menaces of war against the South. But now, not only is war inaugurated against the slaveholding States, but worst of all for Virginia, there is the danger of civil convulsion in Virginia. The *Tribune* denounces the Secessionists of the State as having an insurrection against the State authorities in contemplation, while the same journal hounds on the Federal Government to the stirring up of insurrection in Texas against the State authorities there in favor of a deposed traitor Governor. The argument of GREELEY is like a two-edged sword—it cuts either way, and cuts against himself. The following from the *Evening Post* indicates the hopes of the Republican party in exciting civil war in the Southern States:

There is reason to believe that Gov. Houston will prove himself neither without energy nor foresight, and that he will yet make a good stand against the Secessionists in Texas. The Convention which deposed him acted without a shadow of authority, and the Governor has the right to resume the duties of the office to which the people chose him at any time when he can collect forces of loyal men. There is no doubt at all that a very large proportion of the people of Texas are in favor of preserving the Union, which has for sixteen years given them protection from foes without and within. *There is in Western Texas a not inconsiderable free-labor element, which will not suffer itself to be carried into a Confederacy where labor is debased by slavery.*

Here is the doctrine of HELPER's book. Now, that the fanatics believe themselves so near the attainment of their long-cherished object, some of them scarcely care to wear disguise any longer.

The Republican journals have greatly magnified the number of forces in the expedition to the South. Their object is to keep up the courage of their party and to intimidate the Southern Government. The troops were sent away in the darkness of the night, or taken on board as the vessels were just leaving, in order to conceal their numerical weakness. As for the discipline of three-fourths of the men, it is no better than that of a mob. They are perfectly raw. The *Tribune* admits that those on Governor's Island were "new recruits," but adds with great *naivete* that "some of these men are almost giants in size and muscle." It seems there are giants in these days. A rifle bullet or a grapeshot, nevertheless, would make a hole through the best of them. The *Tribune* did well to qualify its encomium by saying "some," for such a miserable set as most of these troops are, I have never seen.

In another place the *Tribune* says of them:

Of the recruits on the Island, it may be said that their ease and precision of movement, as well as their numbers when altogether, rendered their appearance quite formidable, and they looked like a little army. Their officers, too, showed indications of being able military men. The following troops left the Island:

	Men.		Men.
Company G	68	Company F	100
Company C	67	Company D	100
Company E	47		
Company B. (left since 8.)	15	Total	397

These soldiers, except the 15 men of Company B, are recruits, nominally better to facilitate transportation. The regiments to which they are to be assigned are not known.

The return of Captain MERCER from the *Powhatan* has greatly mortified the Republicans.—They pretend that he was superseded after the ship went to sea; but the more probable version is that suspecting the destination of the ship, he ordered the tug boat to remain alongside till he was 35 miles at sea, the point at which he was permitted to open the sealed orders. As soon as he saw what these orders were he returned in the tug, and immediately resigned. No doubt he will be court-martialed, like Capt. JOHNS. The *Illinois* did not start till yesterday morning at six o'clock. One of the journals gives the following exaggerated account of the numbers:

As near as we can make out, the strength of the fleet, chartered for special (but as yet unknown) service, South, is as follows:

Coatzacoalcos	1,000	Illinois	1,500
Fashion	1,900	Ocean Queen	1,500
Atlantic	2,000	Yankee	400
Baltic	2,000	Thomas Freeborn	320
Total			9,720

The *Coatzacoalcos* and *Fashion* are expected here every day; the *Ocean Queen* and steamships *Yankee* and *Freeborn* were chartered yesterday. The *Baltic*, *Atlantic* and *Illinois* have sailed, as already stated.

The *Ocean Queen* now lies at the wharf, opposite King street, North river. Workmen are engaged in putting a new bowsprit in her, but that seems to be the only preparation in progress. One of the officers professed to be totally ignorant of her being chartered by the Government, and there are no indications that she will be ready to proceed to sea in less than three or four days.

Notwithstanding all the braggadocio of the Republican journals, they are thoroughly appalled at the preparations at Charleston to give a reception to their expedition. Hence they now say that ANDERSON has four months' provisions, because they fear a repulse. If that be so, then, what becomes of the pretence about his starvation in the *Tribune*? The heading of its despatches from Washington to-day is:

DISPATCHES FROM LIEUTENANT SLEMMER.

HE HAS FOUR MONTHS' PROVISIONS.

THE FORT ABLE TO WITHSTAND THE REBELS.

NO NEED OF REINFORCEMENTS.

THEY CAN BE PUT IN THE FORT AT ANY TIME.

THE REBELS UNABLE TO PREVENT IT.

Liars ought to have good memories.

Yesterday Collector BARNEY was again served with a protest from certain merchants, who claim that, under the Constitution, they cannot be compelled to pay duties until the revenue laws are enforced in all parts of the country alike.

As the *Tribune* informs us that the mails to South Carolina are to be stopped as soon as communication with Major ANDERSON is cut off, I know not whether this letter will ever reach you.

CAVALIER.

Our Washington Correspondence.

WASHINGTON, April 9, 1861.

Treatment of the Southern Commissioners—Their Departure—The Virginia Convention—Ben McCulloch—The Southern Forts—Botts—What Lincoln Means to Do, etc., etc.

Ere this reaches you, you will have learned by telegraph that the Administration have finally refused to treat with the Ministers from the Confederate States, assigning as a reason that they regard their authority as complete over them, and that they cannot recognize secession. They have kept back their answer to the last moment. Meantime, they have got their armament ready, and it has, at length, sailed from New York. They now think to take the South at a disadvantage. But the able statesman and soldier at the head of the Montgomery Government understands Northern perfidy too well to become its dupe. I have reason to know that he has at no time been deceived by the double dealing of SEWARD, and that he has employed his best energies to put the South in a state of defence.

I understand the Ministers have addressed to-day a final communication to the government, setting forth the purposes of their mission, and the grounds upon which the South bases her action. They will probably take their departure from the city to-morrow. Their mission has been conducted with a great deal of discretion. They have been chary of their confidence to strangers or news mongers, and where they have given it to gentlemen, it has been to men who respected it. They have not acted rashly, but have exhausted moderation, patience and diplomacy in an effort to settle peaceably the pending questions. Nor have they been the dupes of a false and treacherous government, which held itself bound by no principle of honor, and looks to no result but success.

The Virginia Convention has deputed three Commissioners to come here to learn the President's policy. They have not yet gotten here. The Secessionists are daily gaining ground in that State. They are conducting the contest with an energy and spirit worthy of true men, and are certain to succeed. There is a feeling among the people to get rid of the Submission Convention, this LINCOLN Government, and JOHN LETCHER, the wretched sot and traitor who fills the Governor's chair, by one and the same movement. It would be a glorious riddance.

Major BEN. MCCULLOCH's movements have created a good deal of speculation and some alarm. His purpose was a business instead of a political one, but the story has been started that he had a band of 5000 men to seize this city. These Black Republicans are a wretched set of poltroons, and have no idea of fighting themselves. Their plan is to pay Irishmen and Germans to do it for them at so much per day. They do not care how many of *them* are killed or maimed.

It has now become a general impression in Washington that an attempt will be made to reinforce ANDERSON. You will notice my letters some time back pointed to this. We are looking here every day to hear the news of the attempt—its success or failure. Southern men sincerely trust it may be repelled, and have no doubt that in anything like an equal contest the brave sons of Carolina will give a good account of themselves. Great faith, too, is put in the science and resources of your commander, Gen. BEAUREGARD. Nothing is so dear an object to the Black Republican heart as to relieve ANDERSON's command and keep possession of Sumter.

It is pretty generally avowed now that it is intended to reinforce Fort Pickens at the risk of a fight, and the Texas "blind" is pretty well abandoned.

Mr. JOHN MINOR BOTTS, one of the basest of the Virginia Unionists, is here. He is looking out for spoils, and impudently defends the coercive policy of Mr. LINCOLN.

I look for an immediate call of Congress by the President, a proclamation by LINCOLN against the seceding States as "rebels," &c., and an additional proclamation putting this District under martial law. The object of the latter will be to inspire a reign of terror, to compel men to serve in the militia, and to give a pretext for persecuting, imprisoning and murdering those in this city who dare to express sympathy with the South.

I do not believe that the persons of your Embassadors will be violated, though it has been strongly urged by the Republican press of the North. Certain it is that in the Senate Republican caucus it was gravely advocated that the Indians in Northern Texas should be incited to make incursions on the whites. That and JOHN BROWN raids show that they are ready for any diabolical conduct. And though international law may forbid violence to the persons of Embassadors, SEWARD and LINCOLN have their "higher law" at hand for any emergency.

I learn the officers of the Army identified with the South by long residence or marriage look with horror at this most wicked war on the South. The Northern Democrats, or most of them, reprobate it without stint. Even Mr. DOUGLAS condemns it in conversation, and predicts it will end in the capture of Washington by the South.

Mr. LINCOLN has no special fears as to the Border States. He is an obstinate and very ignorant man, and looks on BOTTS and SUMMERS as types of Virginia sentiment, and of the Border States. The wretched apathy of the people has suffered this delusion to grow in his mind, and it is now so firmly rooted in his head that nothing but experience can dethrone it. So LINCOLN is indifferent and careless about the matter, and feels about the war pretty much as a boy does with a holiday and a new kite—little realizing that it will be any thing more than a few rounds and a hasty submission of the South to his orders. The Border States he does not count in at all. He now speaks more freely as to his purposes, and shows his teeth in his talk. As for the Black Republicans generally, of the radical sort, they just begin to show their hate and demoniac rage as they think they see a chance of gratifying it. They are like an adder warmed into fresh life. What fools we were to hug him so long! What idiocy to take him again to our bosom! SOUTH.

—o—

WASHINGTON CITY, April 10, 1861.

The Perfidious Administration—Destination of the Armada—A Doubtful Point—Mustering the Volunteers—Anxiety About Sumter, etc., etc.

The public conviction has settled down to the belief that the Government armada is destined for Charleston, and the whole of it will be combined in the effort to subjugate your State. It is no part of Gen. Gen. SCOTT's tactics to divide up his forces, but to concentrate all for a great blow. My conjecture is, that an experimental steamer will be sent up the Bay, laden with men, and provisions and fuel. If fired on, as she undoubtedly will be, then the Federal forces will be landed to attack the Confederate State forces in the rear, and simultaneously ANDERSON will begin to fire, and the war vessels to press up the Bay.

The doubtful point about the business would seem to be, whether the Government troops will land south of Morris' Island or some point north of Charleston. The former is the one most plausible, and best calculated to aid the ships, but still the Government would much desire to take the city of Charleston and hold it.

This Government is occupied by your enemies; men who hate your people, and would crush them, if they could, to the earth for the crime of wishing and daring to be free. The Administration labor under the delusion that they will soon strike terror to the South, and that the war thus begun will be a small and a little one. They have been deceived by BOTTS, of Virginia, and others, and made to believe by Southern traitors that they will have nothing to do up hereabout.

Let your people be of good cheer. There are hundreds of thousands of true and brave men in the Border States, who at the first news of a conflict in Carolina, will buckle on their armor, and haste to give the Northern Government occupation on the border. Nor will they stop there. The enemy's country must be made to bear the burden of the war.

The Government began to day the work of mustering in the military of the District, and putting the test oath to them. Few were willing to go it. Most of the people here will be unwilling to fight against Maryland and Virginia, though a large majority have no marked sympathies with either party. I suppose the uniformed and drilled militia of the District are about a thousand in number, and, of this number, perhaps a fourth may be ready to fight against the South.

We are all looking with intense anxiety to hear news from Charleston. Business is suspended for the most part. I presume martial law will be proclaimed here in a day or so. At all events, my correspondence will soon become unsafe, and perhaps impossible, from this point.

SOUTH.

COMMERCIAL.

Latest Dates.

LIVERPOOL	Mch. 30
HAVRE	Mch. 29
HAVANA	Mch. 27

EXPORTS—APRIL 13.

NEW YORK—Schr B N Hawkins—651 bales Upland Cotton, 100 tons Old Iron, and 56 Empty Ale Bbls.

The Market—Saturday Evening, April 13.

COTTON.—The only transactions during the last two days amounted to 110 bales, at 18⅛c. sold on Friday.

WILMINGTON, April 13.—TURPENTINE.—Sales yesterday of 250 bbls. and this morning of 80 do. at 2.00 for yellow dip, 1.60 for Virgin, and 1.00 for Hard, per 280 lbs. Spirits Turpentine and Cotton—No sales. Rosin.—Sales yesterday of 1500 bbls. Common at 90 cents, per 310 lbs. Pea Nuts.—We note the sales yesterday of 2,000 bushels at 1.15@1.20, as in quality. Corn.—A cargo of 1460 bushels received from Hyde county changed hands at 60 cents per bushel cash.

Consignees per South Carolina Railroad, April 13.

1612 bales Cotton, 65 bbls Flour, Naval Stores, Mdse, Cattle, &c. To Drake & Moses, Bowie, Lafitte & Co, Colcock, McCally & Malloy, J J Cohen, Caldwell, Blakely & Co, A Gardelle, O'Neale & Crawford, E H Rodgers & Co, Graeser & Smith, Smith & Dullin, Wardlaw, Walker & Co, Cothran, Jeffers & Co, W C Dukes & Sons, W M Lawton & Co, Capt Thomas, Caldwell & Robinson, Mazyck & Howard, Holmes & Stoney, Adams, Frost & Co, W C Bee & Co, C N Averill, Horsey, Auten & Co, Rhett & Robson, J W Zehe, L M Hatch, W B Smith & Co, P F Stevens, Miss G Bay, Moise & Co, T J & C H Moise, and Order.

PASSENGERS.

In steamship Nashville, from New York—C S Webster, F Anderson, A F Rudler, F Witheiman, Miss E Barney, M L Graves, J Lyon, Henry Dee, Dr E S Adler, Wm Appleton and servant, A Elias, J Bayley and lady, Miss Stiles, Wm Amory, J Kauffer, J Kauffer, J Cohen, Mrs A Clayton and servant, P O'Conner and lady, E A Leland, M Greenan, W Kernan, A Dugan, and M Cohen.

In steamer Carolina, from Fernandina via Savannah—Mrs J E Spears, Hamilton, and J B Preg.

MARINE NEWS.

Charleston.—Lat. 32.47 N. Lon. 79.27 W.

SUN RISES 5H. 34M. SETS 6H. 26M.—HIGH WATER, 11H. 6M.

WIND—E.

ARRIVED.

April 13.

Schr Morning Star, Evers, Euhaw. 2600 bushels Rough Rice, and 60 bales Sea Island Cotton. To O'Hear, Roper & Stoney, Ingraham & Webb, and Coffin & Pringle.

Schr William & John, Leonard, Combahee. 2100 bushels Rough Rice. To E Barnwell & Son.

Schr Rob Roy, Cannon, East Point Mill. 98 bbls Rice. To Adams, Frost & Co.

Sloop Shamrock, Magrath, St Paul's. 105 bales S Island Cotton. To O'Hear, Roper & Stoney, and Fraser & Dill.

Steamer Carolina, Lockwood, Fernandina via Savannah. 120 bales Sea Island and 5 bales Upland Cotton, and Mdse. To H L Chisolm, Hanckel & Nowell, Fraser & Dill, Caldwell, Blakely & Co, Wardlaw, Walker & Co, Ingraham & Webb, S C Railroad Agent, E H Rodgers & Co, W M Lawton & Co, Chafee, Croft & Chafee, J & J D Kirkpatrick, P C Gaillard & Co, Cothran, Jeffers & Co, Nickerson & Purcell.

Prioleau's boat, from Dean Hall Mill. 77 bbls Rice. To Mazyck & Howard.

April 14.

U S M steamship Nashville, Murray, New York, — hours. Mdse. To H Missroon & Co, Adams' Express Co, R Arnold, C N Averill, J Ashhurst & Co, J E Adger & Co, D A Amme, H Ash, J Armstrong, C D Ahrens, Burckmyer & Moffett, C H Bird, W G Bancroft, T M Bristoll & Co, E Bates & Co, A Bischoff, E M Carey, N Carter, A Carter, J F Church, Cadow, McKenzie & Co, Jas Cantwell, Crane, Boylston & Co, Carmalt & Briggs, G F Cole, Geo S Cooke, T M Cater, Chamberlain, Miler & Co, Courtney, Tennent & Co, F Dupont, J Dothage, W F Dodge, J & F Dawson, C C Drake, Dewing, Thayer & Co, Albert Eife, Evans & Cogswell, Jno Fraser & Co, Foley & Fitzparick, I L Falk & Co, G D Grice, Force & Mitchell, Gilliland, Howell & Co, J H Graver, Cyrus Gill, Graeser & Smith, Gantt & Stoney, L M Hatch, Geo S Hacker, Hyatt, McBurney & Co, J Hurkamp & Co, Horton & Shepherd, Hastie, Calhoun & Co, Hamilton & Smith, Hayden & Whilden, Haviland, Stevenson & Co, Harral, Nichols & Co, Horsey, Auten & Co, Johnston, Crews & Co, J Kuck, Kinsman Bros, G W King, Kerrison & Leiding, F Kressell, Klinck, Wickenberg & Co, J Kennard, D Lopez, E P Lemman, Lillienthal & Klatte, A Lengnick, James Murphy, Thos Murphy, J G Milnor & Co, E Mantoue, C S Maule, J E Meyer, B Mordecai, Wm Marscher, J F Martin, E H Marjenhoff, G F Meldau, Mazyck & Howard, B Myerhoff, Jas R Mood, McCarter & Dawson, Marshall, Burge & Co, Nayler, Smith & Co, C Nohrden, L Orcutt, Order, O'Hear, Roper & Stoney, B O'Neill, J D Otis, D Paul & Co, People's Bank, A Robbins, H Panzerbeter, N M Porter & Co, S Rosenbluth, B Schur, Ruff & Dowie, Russell & Jones, G W Steffens & Co, J W Stoy, A S Smith, A Spellmann, Sims & Barksdale, W Steele & Co, E B Stoddard & Co, Seedorff & Schuchert, Thos Stenhouse, C Tatem, A Tobias' Sons, A Trager & son, A R Taft & Co, W G Trott, J Von Hollen, H E Vincent, Jas Walker, G A Wheaton, J R Wiltberger, D R Williams & Co, Jos Walker, Waldron, Egleston & Co, D Welters, Williams & Brown, Robt Wince, Wardlaw, Walker & Co, Railroad Agent, and others.

Schr W W Starr, Steedman, Pon Pon. 2400 bushels Rough Rice and Hay. To O'Hear, Roper & Stoney.

Doar's sloop, from Santee. 2000 bushels Rough Rice. To Robertson, Blacklock & Co.

IN THE OFFING.

A Ship, Herm Brig and several Schooners—unknown.

CLEARED.

April 13.

Schr C S Carstairs, Robinson, Georgetown (S C)—Master.

Schr J Clark, Scull, Georgetown (S C)—Master.

Schr B N Hawkins, Wyatt, New York—Jno Fraser & Co.

WENT TO SEA.

April 13.

Schr N M Tanner, Paty, Baltimore.

April 14.

Schr Deborah Jones, Tatem, Wilmington (N C).

MEMORANDA.

The schr Village Gem, Baker, for Georgetown, SC, cleared at Wilmington April 13.

NOTICE TO MARINERS.

WRECK IN BARROW DEEP.

Trinity House, London, March 22, 1861.

Notice is hereby given that a Green Buoy marked with the word Wreck has been laid 10 fathoms south of a barge sunk in Barrow Deep.

The buoy lies in 7 fathoms at low water spring tides, with the following bearings:

Barling Church, in line with the preventive vessel at Haven Gore Creek, N W.

The Easternmost of two trees: East of Hern High Mill, in line with the Mill at Hern Bay, S⅜E.

Mouse Lightvessel, NE⅜N.

East Oaze Buoy, SE⅜E.

By order. P. BERTHON, Secretary.

Office Lighthouse Board, Portland, April 5, 1861.

The Spar Buoy on Webster Rock, off Broad Sound, at entrance from Casco Bay, is gone from her moorings. A new Buoy of the same class will be set immediately.

By order of the Lighthouse Board.

WM. ROGERS TAYLOR, Lighthouse Inspector, First District.

LIST OF VESSELS

SAILED, CLEARED AND UP FOR CHARLESTON.

COASTWISE PORTS.

BOSTON.	
Schr Aid, Endicott	cleared April 3
Schr Mary Haley, Haley	cleared April 4
NEW YORK.	
Schr Mary P Hudson, Hudson	cleared Mch. 18
Schr Ida Della Torre, Jones	cleared Mch. 14
Schr Cherokee, Myers	cleared Mch. 22
Schr D B Warner, Carrow	advertised Mch. 16
Schr Helene, Derrickson	advertised Mch. 26
Schr May, Smith	advertised Mch. 26
Schr Sunny South, Weeks	advertised Mch. 27
PHILADELPHIA.	
Schr C A Heckscher, Stubbs	cleared April 4
Schr Ida, Wormwood	cleared April 9
BALTIMORE.	
Schr G W Grice, Harrington	sailed April 6
Schr Minnehaha, Young	advertised April 4
NEW ORLEANS.	
Schr Col Lester, Delano	cleared Mch. 28
Schr Mary Clinton, Ryan	advertised Mch. 27
Schr Aid, Gooding	advertised April 1
Schr H Blackman, Corson	advertised April 2
Schr John Aumack, Pierce	advertised April 9

FOREIGN PORTS.

LIVERPOOL.	
Ship Mary Crocker, Williams	sailed Feb. 24
Bark Eilwan, Swann	sailed Feb. 24
Ship Jno Fraser, Herbest	sailed Mch. 5
Bark Alabama, English	sailed Mch. 21
Ship Chas Cooper, Jordan	cleared Feb. 21
Ship Alliance, DeForrest	cleared Feb. 28
Ship Monmouth, Jones	cleared Mch. 14
Ship Sir Alan McNab, Chapman	cleared Mch. 19
Bark Hilja, Henderson	cleared Mch. 18
Ship Metropolis, Foster	loading Feb. 18
Ship Elisa Bonsall, Michaels	loading Feb. 21
Ship Assyria, Delano	loading Feb. 21
Ship Montezuma, Atkins	cleared Mch. 21
Ship Albert Gallatin, Storer	loading Mch. 15
LONDON.	
Ship War Eagle, Taylor	cleared Mch. 18
CLYDE.	
P. J. Nevins, ——	loading Mch. 28
CARDIFF (WALES).	
Bark Ann & Catharine, Hughes	sailed Feb. 26
HAVRE.	
Schr Walter Raleigh, Phillips	sailed Feb. 6
BREMERHAVEN.	
Bark Gauss, Wieting	sailed Mch. 14
BROUWERSHAVEN.	
Ship Henry, Wilson	sailed Feb. 6
HAVANA.	
Schr C C Smith, Westmoreland	cld Mch. 20

OFFICE CLERK OF COUNCIL, APRIL 8, 1861.—The following persons have filed their applications in this Office for RETAIL AND TAVERN LICENSES, to date from this day:

LICENSE NO. I.

J. A. COOK & CO., corner King and Mary-streets. Sureties—James McCarey and H. Stender.

J. F. FICKEN, corner Archdale and Beaufain-streets. Sureties—Henry Cobia and Charles H. West, jr.

JOHN HURKAMP, corner King and Broad-streets. Sureties—J. L. Tobias and Parker J. Holland.

C. TIEDEMANN, corner Calhoun and Washington-streets. Sureties—John Marshall and J. T. Ellsworth.

JAMES WILEY, King, above Spring-street. Sureties—Jas. McCarey and Oswell Reeder.

LICENSE NO. II.

N. AHRENS, corner Woolfe and Nassau-streets. Recommended by John Tiencken, A. Linstedt, J. F. Ritter, C. Sahlman, J. Spellman and C. Dunneman. Sureties—A. Linstedt and John A. Cook.

J. J. BREDENBERG, corner Marsh and Inspection-streets. Recommended by B. Bollmann, J. G. Lynch, John Moran, M. Luhy, J. H. Bredenberg and J. H. Petermann. Sureties—John Moran and J. H. Bredenberg.

H. BLAKEN, Judith-street. Recommended by C. H. Harbers, James Kennedy, A. Koennecke, John H. Thee, C. Dieckhoff and W. H. Norris. Sureties—John H. Thee and C. Dieckhoff.

JOHN BEHR, corner Coming and Radcliffe-streets. Recommended by J. H. Renneker, Charles Kanapaux, C. Whittemore, J. N. Tiedemann, J. B. Washington and G. W. Olney. Sureties—J. A. Cook and J. N. Tiedemann.

JOHN BUGGLE, corner King and Line-streets. Recommended by H. Fincke, P. Buchheit, W. C. Stall, H. A. Duc, John Hogan and J. H. Bucking. Sureties—C. Lilienthal and R. Stemmermann.

J. D. BULLWINKLE, corner East Bay and Laurens-streets. Recommended by J. J. McPherson, C. W. Seignious, A. J. White, H. L. Lyall, W. M. Martin and J. B. Morgan. Sureties—C. Sahlman and H. Hagermann.

D. BULLWINKLE, corner Amherst and America streets. Recommended by D. B. Haselton, R. Tobin, J. W. McMillan, P. O'Connell, J. F. Ritter and John Tiencken. Sureties — John H. Thee and John Tiencken.

J. H. BORNEMANN, corner Washington and Vernon-streets. Recommended by C. Tiedemann, M. Luhrs, J. H. Petermann, P. Woodward, J. T. Ellsworth and C. Nohrden. Sureties—J. A. Cook and William Brunges.

C. H. EBERHARDT, corner St. Philip and Wentworth-streets. Recommended by H. Z. Laurey, W. C. Horlbeck, J. Kruse, P. Moran, R. Caldwell, Wm. Schnierle and F. Roessler. Sureties—L. Bredenberg and J. H. Bredenberg.

A. FINCKE, corner Mary and America streets. Recommended by John C. Miller, D. Keenan, George H. Brown, A. Koennecke, P. O'Connell and C. Dieckhoff. Sureties—C. Lilienthal and A. Koennecke.

A. FARRELLY, corner Cumberland and Philadelphia-streets. Recommended by P. Fogarty, R. Gannon, John Molony, J. D. Kennedy, T. L. Quackenbush and James Cosgrove. Sureties—Philip Fogarty and John Molony.

E. J. H. FISCHER, corner Church-street and Stoll's Alley. Recommended by Thomas Daniels, F. Entelman, M. T. Ryan, Charles Love, B. S. Aldert and C. T. Craig. Sureties—Henry Gerdts and C. Lilienthal.

WM. GREER, 274 King-street. Recommended by B. Johnson, F. Von Santen, O. E. Johnson, S. N. Brown, A. Falk and M. Shalloe. Sureties—B. Johnson and Abraham Falk.

B. GERKEN, corner Meeting and Calhoun-streets. Recommended by B. Bollmann, D. Hiffernan, J. H. Scheper, P. Rahal, James Gibbes and J. H. Mashburn. Sureties—F. Entelmann and D. Kohlmann.

JOHN C. GRUBE, 63 Market-street. Recommended by E. Davis, D. A. Amme, Theo. Cordes, F. Lampe, R. Gannon and J. D. Kennedy. Sureties—F. Lampe and G. Chas. Schmetzer.

JOHN GEDDES, Market-street. Recommended by R. Gannon, Wm. R. Huron, Michael Gratton, Wm. McKay, James Cosgrove and Patrick Collins. Sureties—Michael Gratton and James Cosgrove.

F. HISCH, Line-street, near South Carolina Railroad. Recommended by F. O'S. Seyle, P. Buchheit, W. Bredeman, D. H. Schwecke, G. H. Rumple and D. Apeler. Sureties—W. Bredeman and H. H. Funke.

J. H. HEYER, corner Bogard and Percy-streets. Recommended by A. Poppen, G. Engelbert, F. Vanderlippe, H. Wragge, J. H. Fedtke and T. Gifford. Sureties—D. Kassens and G. Engelbert.

H. HASTEDT, corner Rutledge and Spring-streets. Recommended by P. J. Sires, T. M. Cater, Wm. Ferguson, R. C. Millings, George R. Richards and James Cannaday. Sureties—George R. Richards and James Cannaday.

H. HOFFMANN, corner Spring and Ashley-streets. Recommended by John McElroy, Wm. Ferguson, G. Chas. Schmetzer, Walter Cade, T. L. Rodgers and B. Bargmann. Sureties—G. Charles Schmetzer and B. Bargmann.

S. HARBERS, corner Spring and Chesnut-streets. Recommended by H. Schwartz, J. Tolle, Thomas L. Rodgers, C. Brener, H. H. Funke and J. H. Jones. Sureties—J. D. Osterholtz and C. H. Harbers.

A. HERNHOLM, corner Spring and Norman-streets. Recommended by H. H. Funke, H. Schwartz, John H. Jones, A. W. Muckenfuss, J. Tolle and H. Bulcken. Sureties—J. C. H. Claussen and B. O'Neill.

W. D. HINNERS, corner Coming and Wentworth-streets. Recommended by S. K. Brown, M. B. Ruder, J. M. Walton, G. P. Williams, Edward Winslow and William Brunges. Sureties—F. Roessler and B. Lilienthal.

J. F. L. HABERNICHT, No. — Elliott-street. Recommended by D. H. Furst, F. Entelman, J. C. Blohm, William Callahan, H. W. Schroder and Moses Levy. Sureties—Dan'l H. Furst and H. Bischoff.

C. KLINTWORTH, corner Washington and Charlotte-streets. Recommended by C. H. Harbers, Jas. Kennedy, A. Koennecke, J. H. Thee, C. Dieckhoff and W. H. Norris. Sureties—John H. Thee and C. Dieckhoff.

P. C. KARRIGAN, 77 Market-street. Recommended by Jas. Cosgrove, N. F. Petit, R. S. Millaer, B. Foley, P. Moran and G. Follin. Sureties—B. Foley and P. Moran.

F. LEHMHUHL, corner Meeting and Water-streets. Recommended by Thos. E. Ryan, Wm. C. Miller, J. Legare Yates, Henry McLeod, John Sloman and Thos. Thompson. Sureties—H. Bischoff and J. C. H. Claussen.

H. D. LUBS, corner Hanover and Columbus-streets. Recommended by W. C. Stall, J. L. Fitts, F. Dawson, H. Hagermann, P. Buchheit and Job Dawson. Sureties—H. Hagermann and P. Buchheit.

DANIEL MIXER, Meeting-street. Recommended by J. J. McCarter, E. J. Dawson, G. C. Selman, T. Kelly, E. W. Marshall and Edwin Bates. Sureties—Thaddeus Kelly and E. W. Marshall.

L. F. MEYER, No. 143 King-street. Recommended by J. B. P. Alley, C. F. Schwettman, C. D. Ahrens, George Kriete, H. Campsen and F. Wehmann. Sureties—Jas. W. May and M. P. O'Connor.

WM. MARSCHAR, corner State and Market-streets. Recommended by A. Canale, A. Bianchi, A. Robins, A. McLeish, J. C. H. Claussen and Joseph Pattini. Sureties—A. Robins and J. C. H. Claussen.

C. MENSING, corner of Bull and Rutledge streets. Recommended by A. Calder, H. Meyer, Wm. Whaley, F. Richards, Thad. Street and Wm. M. Lawton. Sureties—C. H. Klincke and O. Tiedemann.

M. MONSEES, corner Church and Elliott-streets. Recommended by D. H. Furst, M. Levy, F. Wienholtz, F. Entelmann, H. Runken and Wm. Callahan. Sureties—Daniel H. Furst and F. Wienholtz.

C. MORMIER, corner Church and Elliott-streets. Recommended by [illegible]

[illegible]

Forbes and M. Levy. Sureties—W. A. Wilson and Moses Levy.

J. H. THIELE, corner St. Philip and Line-streets. Recommended by Jas. McCarey, W. Hutwalcker, A. Eddie, J. H. Hartz, L. Brandt and Jacob Wredan. Sureties—Henry Gerdts and F. Wienholtz.

HENRY THEE, corner East Bay and Elliott-streets. Recommended by F. Wienholtz, H. Wittschen, Moses Levy, Joseph Samson, W. A. Wilson, and J. C. Otjen. Sureties—W. A. Wilson and H. Wittschen.

M. A. THOMPSON, 7 Elliott-street. Recommended by Moses Levy, D. H. Furst, H. Runken, Wm. Doran, J. D. Kennedy and F. Wienholtz. Sureties—John D. Kennedy and C. C. Trumbo.

W. TIEDEMANN, King, above Shepherd-street. Recommended by James Kennedy, F. Charlon, Dennis Hogan, C. W. Wrede, L. Rimrodt and M. Schmalgemeier. Sureties—James Kennedy and James Melvin.

HENRY THOMAS, 22 Calhoun street. Recommended by James Carroll, D. Hiffernan, Thomas Darcy, G. W. Nickerson, J. H. Scheper and A. Von Dohlen. Sureties—P. Hogan and James Moorhead.

H. A. TORCK, Chapel-street. Recommended by C. Lilienthal, E. P. Leman, W. J. Robinson, P. M. Doucin, Dieckhoff and O. Tiedemann. Sureties—J. C. Claussen and C. Lilienthal.

H. A. TORCK, corner Market and East Bay streets. Recommended by D. L. McCarthy, A. Bianchi, Oliver Farnum, A. Robins, J. Campsen and J. C. H. Claussen. Sureties—J. Campsen and J. C. H. Claussen.

J. H. VOLLERS, corner King and Queen-streets. Recommended by H. Campsen, John O'Mara, Robert Wing, A. Leprince, W. Heins and J. Morello. Sureties—Henry Campsen and W. Heins.

C. VOLMER, corner Rumney and King-streets. Recommended by F. Wittpenn, V. M. Salvo, C. F. Lubs, P. Buchheit, J. H. Graver and H. Hagermann. Sureties—H. Hagermann and P. Buchheit.

D. WERNER, corner Anson and Pinckney-streets. Recommended by J. Campsen, W. Hockaday, Thomas Kenny, F. Lampe, T. C. Speissegger and E. Collins. Sureties—J. Campsen and J. C. H. Claussen.

F. WEINHOLTZ, — East Bay. Recommended by F. P. McGary, Charles Love, Thomas Costello, R. Forbes, H. Runken and D. H. Furst. Sureties—E. H. Marjenhoff and H. Runken.

C. D. WAGENER, corner East Bay and Pinckney-streets. Recommended by C. W. Seignious, J. C. H. Claussen, F. Lampe, C. Lilienthal, T. Cordes and B. Bollmann. Sureties—John T. Elsworth and J. H. Bredenberg.

C. WATERMAN, corner Market and Church-streets. Recommended by A. Speiman, J. D. Kennedy, G. Charles Schmetzer, F. Lampe, R. Gannon and J. Oberhauser. Sureties—F. Lampe and G. Chas. Schmetzer.

JOHN WELDON, corner Laurens and Washington streets. Recommended by P. O'Connell, James Kennedy, John Moran, James Melvin, P. Brady and P. Duffie. Sureties—John Moran and P. Brady.

G. H. ZERBST, corner Duncan and Pitt-streets. Recommended by C. D. Brahe, D. McQueen, George William Walker, F. Nihaus and F. Jager. Sureties—D. Apeler and B. O'Neill.

JOHN H. ZEHE, corner King and Warren-streets. Recommended by F. Salvo, J. Wirth, Jos. H. Oppenheim, G. W. Wescott, Charles Dunn and H. H. Bolger. Sureties—F. Salvo and H. H. Bolger.

A. COOK, No. 113 East Bay. Recommended by William L. King, M. McBride, J. H. Murrell, A. S. Willington & Co., W. J. Crafts and William A. Wilson. Sureties—M. McBride and James H. Murrell.

THOMAS CAREW, No. 21 Queen-street. Recommended by J. C. Blohme, John Graham, Philip Fogarty, John Kenny, Thomas Finigan and H. Bollmann. Sureties—John Kenny and John Graham.

J. C. OYERMANN, corner King and George-streets. Recommended by A. J. Moses, J. Van Winkle, George Prince, B. Strauss, A. Montgomery and H. W. Dorre. Sureties—J. F. Streckfuss and H. W. Dorre.

JOHN R. HORSEY, Clerk of Council.

April 10 5

The Philadelphia Inquirer.—EXTRA.

GREAT NATIONAL TRAGEDY.

Details of the Bombardment of Fort Sumter.

THE FINAL SURRENDER.

Major Anderson on his Way to New York.

THE PRESIDENT'S PROCLAMATION ISSUED.

SEVENTY-FIVE THOUSAND MEN CALLED FOR.

A Special Session of Congress.

WAR [illegible]MENTS ON FOOT.

ENROLLME[illegible]

[St]rong Union Feeling in Baltimore.

[T]HE ACTION OF THE VIRGINIA STATE CONVENTION.

[S]ECESSION DEMONSTRATION AT RICHMOND, VA.

CONTEMPLATED ATTACK ON WASHINGTON.

FORT DELAWARE TO BE SEIZED.

The Despatches from Charleston.

FIRST DESPATCH.

CHARLESTON, S. C., April 13.—At intervals of twenty minutes, the firing was kept up all night on Fort Sumter.

Major ANDERSON ceased to fire at 6 o'clock in the evening.

All night he was engaged in repairing the damages done to the fort, and protecting the guns in [bar]bette on the parapet.

[He] commenced to return the fire this morning [at] o'clock, but seemed to be greatly disabled.

The battery on Cummings' Point is doing Fort [Sum]ter great damage.

At 9 o'clock this morning, a dense smoke pour[ed] out from the walls of Fort Sumter.

SECOND DESPATCH.

[CH]ARLESTON, April 13.—*The Federal flag at Sumter is at half-mast, signalling distress.*

[The] shells from Fort Moultrie and Morris [Islan]d fall into ANDERSON'S stronghold thick [and] fast. They can be seen in their course from Charleston battery.

[T]he breach made in Fort Sumter is on the side [op]posite Cummings' Point. Two of its port-holes [are] knocked into one, and the wall from the top [is] crumbling.

Three vessels, one of them a very large-sized [illegible] bar, and [illegible] preparing to participate in the conflict.

The fire of Morris Island and Fort Moultrie is divided between Fort Sumter and the ships-of-war. The ships have not as yet opened fire.

An explosion has occurred at Fort Sumter. A dense volume of smoke was seen suddenly to rise.

Major ANDERSON has ceased to fire for about an hour. It is thought that the officers' quarters in Fort Sumter are on fire.

THIRD DESPATCH.

CHARLESTON, April 13.—Two of Major ANDERSON'S magazines have exploded. It was thought that they were only the smaller magazines.

Only occasional shots are now fired at Fort Sumter from Fort Moultrie.

The Morris Island battery is doing heavy work.

The greatest excitement prevails in the city.—The wharves, steeples, housetops, and every available place are packed with people. The ships in the offing have not yet aided ANDERSON.

It is now too late for them to come over the bar, as the tide is ebbing.

CHARLESTON, April 13—Noon.—The ships in the offing appear quietly at anchor, and have not fired a gun.

The entire roofs of ANDERSON'S barracks are in a vast sheet of flame.

Shells from Cummings' Point and Fort Moultrie are bursting in and over Fort Sumter in quick succession. The Federal flag still waves over the fort. Major ANDERSON is only occupied in putting out the fire. Every shot appears to tell, and the spectators are anxiously expecting the striking of the flag.

FOURTH DESPATCH.

CHARLESTON, April 13.—Fort Sumter is undoubtedly on fire.

The flames are raging.

ANDERSON has thrown out a raft loaded with men, who are passing up buckets of water to extinguish the flames.

The fort is scarcely discernable for the smoke.

The men on the raft are now the objects of fire from Morris Island.

W[ith] good glasses the balls can be seen skip[pin]g the [water and striking] the unprotected raft.

Great havoc is created among the poor fellows.

It is surmised that ANDERSON is gradually blowing up the fort. He scarcely fires a gun.

The flames are bursting from all the port holes of Fort Sumter, and destruction is inevitable.

The few shots that ANDERSON fired this morning knocked the bricks off the chimneys on the officers' quarters at Fort Moultrie like a whirlwind.

It seems that ANDERSON'S only hope is to hold out for aid from the ships.

CHARLESTON, April 13.—Two war ships are making in towards Morris Island, with the view to land troops to silence the batteries.

FIFTH DESPATCH.

CHARLESTON, April 13.—Four vessels, two of them being large war steamers, are in sight over the bar. The largest of the vessels appears to be engaging Morris Island.

The flames have nearly subsided in Fort Sumter, but ANDERSON does not fire any guns.

Gen. BEAUREGARD left the wharf, just now, in a boat, for Morris Island.

SIXTH DESPATCH.

CHARLESTON, S. C., April 13—P. M.—The bombardment has ceased. Major ANDERSON has drawn down the Stars and Stripes, and displayed a flag of truce. This has been answered from the city, and a boat is now on the way to Fort Sumter.

SEVENTH DESPATCH.

CHARLESTON, April 13.—The Federal flag was again hoisted at Fort Sumter, when PORCHER MILES, under cover of a flag of truce, went over to the fort.

In a few moments after his arrival there, the Federal flag was hauled down by ANDERSON, and a white one unfurled.

The Federal flag was shot away by the Palmetto Guards at Morris Island. In all, two thousand [sh]ots were fired. No South Carolinians were hurt.

FORT SUMTER AFTER THE BOMBARDMENT.

Fort Sumter.

We present the readers of THE INQUIRER this representation of the fort at the termination of the bombardment.

The Topographical Plan.

In the topographical plan the dangerous proximity of the soldiers' barracks to the powder magazines will be observed. The barracks, according to our report, were nearly or quite destroyed by fire, and to subdue the flames in this quarter appears to have been the principal object of Maj. ANDERSON during the morning of Saturday.

The Fort After the Engagement.

The representation of the Fort after the engagement tallies as near as possible with its actual state.

Throughout the whole exciting period during which Fort Sumter has been the theme of conversation, competent military men have doubted its ability to stand a protracted bombardment. Neither Sumter nor Pickens were constructed to sustain a siege, but rather to defend harbors against hostile fleets. For the latter purpose they are admirably adapted; no "wooden walls" could withstand the fire from their batteries, or do themselves harm; but a well-sustained fire from different points on the adjacent shores it has been shown has effectualty silenced Sumter, whatever might be the effect of a similar ordeal to Pickens.

The exterior of the Fort presents a sorry appearance. The portion which suffered most was that exposed to the iron battery at Cummings' Point. The walls, not constructed in a very durable manner (in despite of all heretofore said), were honeycombed, and several breaches were made. A portion of one of the corners was completely carried away. The heavy columbiads at Cummings' Point, capable of throwing balls of eight or ten inch calibre for a distance of two miles, did terrible execution.

It has been seen also that the forces of Major ANDERSON were entirely inadequate to effectually work the guns, and attend to the incidental requirements. It is not to be wondered at, under the circumstances, that Fort Sumter surrendered.

The men were on duty thirty-six hours, with balls or shells striking the casemates and guns of the fort constantly. Competent military men [say] that the intense vibration or shock produced on the brain and nervous system of those in the vicinity is terribly exhausting.

At the siege of Sevastopol the men who worked the guns were relieved every twenty minutes, and groomed with whisky and flannel to enable them to endure the concussion produced by the firing of their own guns and the shock of the enemy's balls and shells striking the fortification. The fearful hardships which Major ANDERSON'S small band underwent, during the awful day and night of Friday last, may well have driven Capt. DOUBLEDAY insane, as our reporter telegraphs.

The concussion attending the firing of a columbiad in [a] [illegible] casemate of a fort, is said to

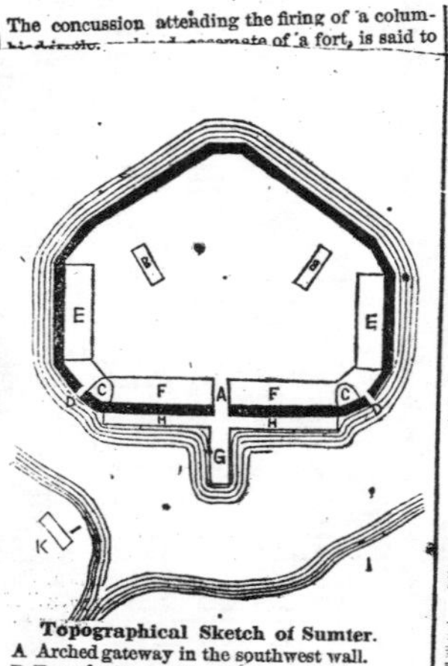

Topographical Sketch of Sumter.

A Arched gateway in the southwest wall.
B Furnaces for heating shot.
C Powder magazines.
D Sally ports.
E Barracks for the soldiers.
F Officers quarters.
G Wharf—depth of water on east side sixteen to eighteen feet.
H Principal landing—extending along the entire soutwest wall.
I Morris Island beach.
K Fort Johnson, on James Island.

We would mention that the position of Morris and James Islands, owing to the small size of the ennraving, is not intended to be considered as more than indicating their proximity to Fort Sumter.

Cummings' Point Iron Battery.

Cummings' Point Iron Battery was three-fourths of a mile distant from Sumter, and brought three Columbiads to bear against the Federal stronghold. It consisted of a heavy framework of yellow pine logs. The roof was of the same material, over which dovetailed bars of railroad iron of "T" pattern were laid from top to bottom—all of which was riveted down in the most secure man[ner]. On the front it presented an angle of [about] thirty degrees. There were three port-holes which opened and closed with iron shutters of the heaviest description. When open, the muzzle of the columbiads filled up the space completely. The recoil of the gun enabled the shutters [to be] closed instantly. It will thus be seen with [what] security the parties working the three heavy pieces of ordnance could operate upon Sumter. The shot of Major ANDERSON might fall like [ha]il upon the inclined plane of railroad iron, and produce no impression beyond a slight indentation. Several companies of the Confederate troops worked this battery both day and night. The ship channel was commanded by this battery, although it does not appear that it devoted much of its attention to the war vessels—their distance probably being too great.

Fort Johnson Mortar Battery.

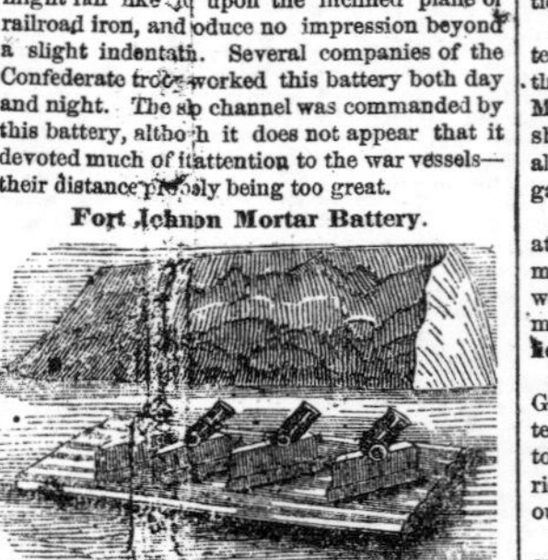

By reference to our topographical plan, the position of Fort Johnson (of which we also give a profile representation,) will be seen at a glance. The mortar battery was a huge sand work, thrown up by the Confederate forces in haste, but afterwards improved so as to present quite a formidable front to the enemy. It contained four mortars, manned by two artillery companies.

Fort Johnson Gun Battery.

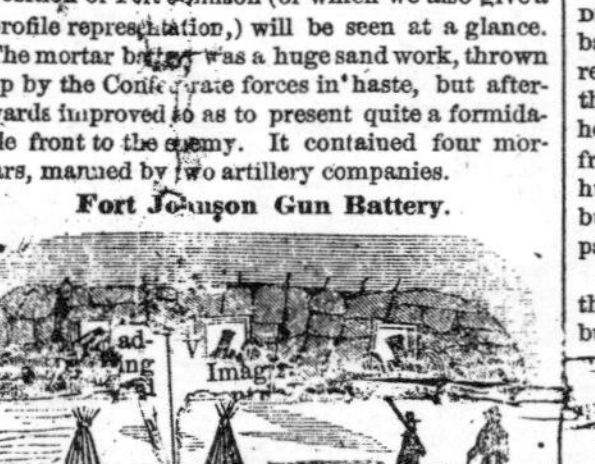

The gun battery consists of sand bags, and is of more finished construction than its associate—the mortar battery alluded to. It was erected upon the site of an old fort. It contains seige guns and several mortars. The interior is represented in our view of the Gun Battery. The fort is in one of the best possible positions for the defence of the harbor.

This news is reliable, and puts to rest all my previous reports about Fort Sumter. The bells are ringing a merry peal and our people are engaging in every demonstration of joy.

Our people generally sympathize with Major ANDERSON, but express abhorrence for those who were in the steamers off our bar and in sight of us, and did not even attempt to reinforce him.

Judge MAGRATH, who has just returned from Fort Sumter, reports that the wood-work of the fort and the officers' quarters were all burnt out.

The fort will be taken possession of to-night by the Confederate troops. Gen. BEAUREGARD, with two aids, have left for Fort Sumter. Three fire companies of Charleston were on their way to Fort Sumter to quell the fire before it reaches the magazine.

EIGHTH DESPATCH.

CHARLESTON, April 13—Evening.—A boat from one of the war vessels on the outside has communicated with General SIMMONS, in command of the forces on Morris Island, and made the request that one of the steamers be allowed to enter the port for the purpose of taking away ANDERSON and his command.

An arrangement has been agreed upon by the parties to stay further proceedings until nine o'clock to-morrow.

CHARLESTON, April 13.—Evening.—The Fairfield regiment, 1000 strong, have just passed the *Courier* office, on their way to Morris Island There are now 10,000 men under arms in the harbor and on the coast.

NINTH DESPATCH.

CHARLESTON, April 13.—Evening.—Fort Sum[ter news] has been received in a reliable shape.

Ex-Senator CHESNUT and ex-Governor MANNING, and W. PORCHER MILES have just landed, and marched to the Governor's house, followed by a dense crowd of people, who are wild with joy. They bring the particulars.

It was reported that ten of the garrison at Fort Sumter had been killed, but your reporter has just had an interview with W. PORCHER MILES, who has just returned from a visit to Fort Sumter, and is assured by him that no one was killed.

Major ANDERSON stated that he surrendered his sword to General BEAUREGARD as the representative of the Confederate Government. Gen. BEAUREGARD said he would not receive it from so brave a man. He says Major ANDERSON made a staunch fight, and elevated himself in the estimation of every true Carolinian.

During the fire, when Major ANDERSON'S flagstaff was shot away, a boat put off from Morris Island, carrying another American flag for him to fight under.

The Conflict of Friday.

Major ANDERSON, during the greater part of Friday, directed his fire principally against Fort Moultrie, the Stevens and Floating Batteries—these and Fort Johnson being the only five operating against him. The remainder of the batteries were held in reserve.

Some fifteen or eighteen shots struck the iron Floating Battery, but made not the slightest impression upon its iron cased sides. The Stevens Battery was eminently successful, and did terrible execution on Fort Sumter.

The soldiers were perfectly reckless of their lives, and at every shot jumped upon the ramparts to observe the effect, and then jumped down cheering.

A party on the Stevens Battery are said to have played a game of cards during the hottest fire.

The excitement in the community was indescribable. With the very first boom of the gun thousands rushed from their beds to the harbor front, and all day every available place was thronged by ladies and gentlemen, viewing the solemn spectacle through their glasses. Most of these had relatives in the several fortifications, and many a tearful eye attested the anxious affection of the mother, wife and sister.

Business was entirely suspended. Only those stores were open which were necessary to supply articles required by the army.

Governor PICKENS remained all day in the residence of a gentleman commanding a view of the whole scene, a most interested observer. Gen. BEAUREGARD commanded in person the entire operations.

Troops were pouring into the town all day by hundreds, but were held in reserve for the present, the force already on the island having been considered ample. People also arrived every moment on horseback, and by every other conveyance.

The flag of Fort Sumter floated to the breeze all day. It was not struck by a single shot.

Quite a number of the contestants at the different Secession forts were struck by spent pieces of shell, but not seriously injured.

About six o'clock on Friday evening it became necessary to convey despatches from Sullivan's Island to Charleston. Capt. R. S. PARKER undertook the mission, and started in a small boat. He delivered the despatches to Gov. PICKENS, after having rowed through the warmest fire of Major [ANDERSON]. [illegible] spatches to Morris Island, through the [illegible] Fort Sumter.

Two rain storms occurred during the day, but did not interrupt the firing. Many of those engaged worked in their shirt sleeves. The excitement was intense.

The regularity of the replies of Major ANDERSON during the day led to the belief on the part of the assailants that by some means he had received reinforcements of men.

About eight o'clock in the evening the rain commenced to pour, and the uncovered batteries on the islands were obliged to cease firing regularly, and content themselves with occasional guns.

The interval is believed to have been made use of by Major ANDERSON to repair damages. He is said to have received twenty-nine full shots from the Stevens battery alone, making the bricks fly from the walls in all directions.

It is estimated that from twelve to eighteen hundred balls and shells were fired during the day. Over one hundred shells took effect inside the fort.

The shots from Sumter to Fort Moultrie generally went rather wide of the mark. They were from two of ANDERSON'S barbette guns. The same was the case with the Floating Battery, to which he was very particular in his attentions.—A ball penetrated the Moultrie House, where a party of gentlemen were sitting in the parlor, watching the fight. It entered the second story, and traveled into the kitchen. The gentlemen scattered miscellaneously, and sought a better position.

Vessels were stationed at different points in the harbor. One of these, the schooner *Petrel*, Capt. S. F. COSTE, received four shots, but suffering no material damage.

It was known before evening that at least three, and perhaps four, Government vessels were outside the bar, and signals were believed to have been exchanged between them and Major ANDERSON.

The first shot was fired from Fort Johnson, on Morris Island, by Capt. JAMES, and the second by Lieutenant U. H. GIBBS. This was not answered until three o'clock this afternoon. The first shot from the Stevens Battery was fired by the venerable EDMUND RUFFIN, of Virginia.

It was anticipated by the Secessionists that the Government vessels would make an effort to reinforce Sumter during the night of Friday. To prevent this, extra forces were detailed to Morris and Sullivan's Islands, and guards were stationed both on the shores and in boats in the harbor, with orders to signal at once, if any reinforcement was attempted.

Orders were issued to send Major ANDERSON a bomb from all the batteries every twenty minutes during the night, to keep him wide awake, making about two a minute.

So passed the night of Friday.

The Conflict of Saturday.

Early on Saturday morning the regular cannonade was resumed with increased energy on the part of those in the shore batteries.

Lights were visible in motion on Fort Sumter all night, and Major ANDERSON was, doubtless, engaged in protecting his guns and making necessary repairs. He did not reply to any fire during the night.

Soon after the firing was commenced on Saturday morning, it was evident that some of the woodwork [of Fort Sumter had caught fire. The Sec]essionists were delighted. It was conjectured that the magazine of the Fort would explode. This was also feared by Major ANDERSON, for his guns remained silent and it is believed that efforts were made to subdue the flames.

The principal antagonist of Fort Sumter was the battery on Cummings' Point. The shells were thrown into and around the fort almost without intermission. From Moultrie and Morris Island there was no abatement.

Finally it appeared as though ANDERSON had yielded to the difficulties of his position. The flag of Sumter was put at half-mast—a signal of distress. It is believed that several of the smaller magazines exploded, as sudden clouds of smoke were seen to rise from Sumter. No aid was rendered by the Federal ships in the offing. It is not known whether they were able to cross the bar. The vessels were signalled, however, quite frequently by Major ANDERSON.

The wharves, steeples, housetops, and all available points within sight of the forts, were crowded with many women and children. Several of the Secession batteries opened upon the war vessels, but with what result is not known.

Finally the flag of truce was displayed on the ramparts of Sumter about half-past one o'clock.

The Fort surrendered.

Details of the Surrender.

VISIT OF OUR CORRESPONDENT TO THE FORT—EXPLANATION OF THE EXPLOSIONS—THE INTERIOR A MASS OF RUINS—THE WALLS HONEYCOMBED BY SHOT—DAMAGE TO FORT MOULTRIE—THE BARRACKS IN RUINS—DWELLINGS SHATTERED.

CHARLESTON, April 13—Evening.—Hostilities have for the present ceased, and the victory belongs to South Carolina.

With the display of the flag of truce on the ramparts of Fort Sumter at half-past one o'clock, the firing ceased, and an unconditional surrender was made. The Carolinians had no idea that the fight was at an end.

So soon after the flagstaff of Major ANDERSON was shot away, Colonel WIGFALL, the Aid of General BEAUREGARD, at his commander's request, went to Fort Sumter with a white flag, to offer assistance in extinguishing the flames. He approached the burning fortress from Morris Island, and while the firing was raging on all sides he effected a landing at Sumter. He approached a port-hole, and was met by Major ANDERSON, the commandant of the fort. The latter said that he had just displayed a white flag, but the firing was kept up nevertheless.

Col. WIGFALL replied that Major ANDERSON must haul down the American flag—that no parley would be granted—surrender or fight was the word.

Major ANDERSON then hauled down his flag and displayed only the flag of truce. All firing instantly ceased, and two officers of Gen. BEAUREGARD'S staff, ex-Senator CHESNUT and ex-Governor MANNING, came over in a boat, and stipulated with Major ANDERSON that his surrender should be unconditional for the present, subject to the terms of Gen. BEAUREGARD.

Major ANDERSON was allowed to remain with his men in actual possession of the Fort, while Messrs. CHESNUT and MANNING came over to the city, accompanied by a member of the Palmetto Guards, bearing the orders of his company. These were met at the pier by hundreds of citizens, and as they marched up the street to the General's quarters, the crowd was swelled to thousands. Shouts rent the air, and the wildest joy was manifested on account of the welcome tidings.

After the surrender a boat with an officer and ten men was sent from one of the four ships in the offing to Gen. SIMMONS, commanding on Morris Island, with the request that a merchant ship, or one of the vessels of the United States, be allowed to enter and take off the commander and garrison of Fort Sumter.

Gen. SIMMONS replied that if no hostilities were attempted during the night, and no effort was made to reinforce or retake Fort Sumter, he would give an answer at 9 o'clock on Sunday morning. The officer signified that he was satisfied with this, and returned to his vessel.

Your correspondent accompanied the officers of Gen. BEAUREGARD'S staff on a visit to Fort Sumter. None but the officers, however, were allowed to land. They went down on a steamer, and carried three fire engines for the purpose of putting out the flames.

The fire, however, had been previously extinguished by the exertions of Major ANDERSON and his men. The visitors reported that Major ANDERSON surrendered because his quarters and barracks were destroyed, and he had no hope of reinforcements, as the fleet lay idly by during thirty hours, and either would not or could not help him. Besides this, his men were prostrated from over exertions. There were but five of them hurt, four badly, and one, it is thought, mortally; but the rest were worn out and physically incapable of continuing the fight.

The explosions that were heard and seen from the city in the morning, were caused by the bursting of loaded shells ignited by the fire which could not be removed quick enough.

The [fire] in the barracks was caused by the [illegible]

Within Fort Sumter everything but the casemates is an utter ruin. The whole interior looks like a blackened mass of ruins. Many of the guns are dismounted. The side opposite the iron battery at Cummings' Point is the hardest dealt with. The rifled cannon from the battery played great havoc with Fort Sumter, and the walls look like a honeycomb. Near the top is a breach as large as a cart. The side opposite Fort Moultrie is also honeycombed extensively, as is that opposite the floating battery.

Fort Moultrie is badly damaged. The officers' quarters and barracks are torn to pieces. The frame houses on the Island are riddled with shot, and in many instances the whole sides of the houses are torn out.

The fire in Fort Sumter was put out, and recaught three times during the day.

Dr. CRAWFORD, Major ANDERON'S Surgeon, is slightly wounded in the face.

It is positively asserted that none of the Carolina troops are injured.

Major ANDERSON and all his officers and men still remain in Fort Sumter. I approached near enough to the wall to see him bid his visitors adieu. In addition to this, conversations that were had with him were repeated to me.

A boat was sent from the Fort to-night, to officially notify the fleet that Major ANDERSON had surrendered.

It is not known when the Carolinians will occupy Fort Sumter, or what is to be done with the vanquished.

Every one is satisfied with the victory and happy that no blood was shed.

In the city, after the surrender, the bells were rung and salutes fired.

[The above is from a special correspondent of of the Associated Press, who reached Charleston early on Saturday, and may be relied on as entirely correct.—REPORTER.]

Departure of Anderson and His Men for New York.

THE FLEET STILL OUTSIDE.

CHARLESTON, April 14.—Major ANDERSON and his men will leave to-night, at eleven o'clock, in the [Isabel], for New York.

The war fleet is still outside.

[The] scene when ANDERSON and his men took formal leave of Fort Sumter was a thrilling and impressive one.

[Beaure]gard's Report of the First Day's Engagement.

[Montgomery, April 13.—General BEAURE]GARD telegraphed late hour last night, that [the firing had been] going on all day, and that four guns of [Fort] Sumter had been dismounted.

The Confederate batteries were all safe, and none of his men were hurt. Four steamers were in the offing, with a rough sea.

Nothing was received from Charleston, this morning, by the War Department.

Letter from Fort Moultrie.

CHARLESTON, April 13.—Your correspondent has just read a letter received from S. C. BOYLESTON, dated Fort Moultrie, 6 o'clock this morning.

He says not one man was killed or wounded during yesterday's engagement.

The iron battery has been damaged.

The rifled cannon of the battery did great execution on Fort Sumter. They were all aimed into Major ANDERSON'S port holes.

Three of Fort Sumter's barbette guns were dismounted. One of them was a ten-inch Columbiad.

A corner of Fort Sumter, opposite Fort Moultrie, was knocked away.

The *Water Witch*, *Mohawk*, and *Pawnee*, it was thought were the three first vessels seen in the offing.

Reception of the News in the South

AT MOBILE, ALA.

MOBILE, April 13.—The announcement of the surrender of Fort Sumter was received with immense cheering by the crowds who have been gathering in the vicinity of the newspaper offices all day. The Confederate and Palmetto flags are flying everywhere. Salutes are firing and bells ringing. The people are greatly rejoiced.

AT AUGUSTA.

AUGUSTA, April 13.—A hundred guns were fired here to-day in honor of the victory of the Confederate army.

AT MONTGOMERY.

MONTGOMERY, Ala., April 13.—Despatches from Governor PICKENS, to the Secretary of War were read by the clerk of the War Department from the Executive buildings during the day in the presence of President DAVIS and his Cabinet. They gave rise to general rejoicing in all circles. Seven guns were fired in honor of the [surrender] of Fort Sumter.

War Spirit in New Orleans—Defence of the Mississippi.

NEW ORLEANS, April 13.—There was a grand muster of the city volunteer companies this morning. Preparations are being made to defend the Mississippi river in the best possible manner.

The War News at Boston.

BOSTON, April 13.—An intense excitement was created in this city this afternoon, by the news of the Charleston telegrams.

The announcement of the surrender of Fort Sumter is not believed by many. Others pronounce it a hoax. A more detailed account of this bloodless battle and surrender is anxiously awaited.

[This was received previous to the confirmatory despatches from Charleston.]

The War Spirit in Massachusetts.

BOSTON, April 13.—The Adjutant General's office was crowded this forenoon with officers of the State military, tendering their commands to the Governor. An extreme war feeling has been aroused.

Governor ANDREW left for Washington this afternoon.

Arrest of a U. S. Naval Officer by the Confederate Government.

DESPATCHES OF LIEUT. SLEMMER INTERCEPTED.

MONTGOMERY, April 13—Major [illegible] of the Alabama army, arrived from Pensacola to-day, bringing Lieut. REED WERDEN, of the United States navy, as prisoner of war. He was bearer of despatches to Fort Pickens and the United States fleet off Pensacola bay. He is held by the Secretary of War, who sent a detachment of troops to arrest him.

MONTGOMERY, April 13.—Lieut. WERDEN has been compelled to give up his despatches from Lieut. SLEMMER, of Fort Pickens, to the Government at Washington. The Attorney-General's opinion as to the law in his case has been requested.

It is charged against Lieut. WERDEN that he violated his promise to report to Gen. BRAGG and carried in secret despatches to Fort Pickens, while he showed other despatches to Gen. BRAGG; and also, that he failed to report himself on his return.

From the Montgomery Government.

WAR TO BE DECLARED.

WASHINGTON, April 14.—Official advices from Montgomery indicate that the Confederate Congress will, on re-assembling, at once declare war against the United States.

It is believed that in the act of declaration a distinction will be made between alien friends and alien enemies, the former including the Border States and such citizens of the North as oppose the coercion policy of the Administration. All obligations to this class are so much to be respected as though in time of peace.

The War Feeling in Lancaster.

LANCASTER, April 13.—The war news has created an intense excitement here. The stars and stripes are displayed at different points in favor of ANDERSON. A call for a public meeting on Wednesday has already been issued to sustain the Government. It is numerously signed. Volunteers are being enroled.

Reinforcement of Fort Pickens.

MONTGOMERY, April 13.—Fort Pickens was reinforced last night. It is understood that Charleston is to be blockaded.

Excitement at Baltimore.

BALTIMORE, April 13.—The intelligence from Charleston has produced great excitement, and the anxiety to obtain further news is intense.

A man made his appearance in the streets with a large secession cockade on his hat. He was pursued by a mob, and was only protected from violence by the interference of the police.

Aid to Government from Rhode Island.

PROVIDENCE, April 13.—Governor SPRAGUE has tendered to the Government the services of the Marine Artillery and one thousand infantry, and offers to accompany them himself.

New York for the Union.

TWENTY-FIVE THOUSAND MEN TO BE CALLED OUT.

NEW YORK, April 14.—Advices from Albany state that Governor MORGAN will to-morrow issue a call for twenty-five thousand men for the assistance of the Federal Government.

A private letter from Governor CURTIN states that Pennsylvania can furnish one hundred thousand men and have them in Washington in forty-eight hours, if required.

DAVID DUDLEY FIELD has gone to Washington, on an invitation, for the purpose of consulting with the Administration.

The New York Regiments Volunteering for the Defence of Washington.

NEW YORK, April 14th.—The Seventh and Sixty-ninth Regiments have volunteered for the defence of Washington, but have not yet started. The Twelfth Regiment will hold a meeting to-morrow.

Excitement in New [York].

[illegible] body of policemen are on duty at the [Herald] office to guard against a rumored attack. There will probably be no disturbance [illegible]

More Transport Steamers Chartered.

NEW YORK, April 13.—The Government has chartered the steamers *Philadelphia* and [illegible]. The former is rapidly filling with provisions, army stores, and munitions of war. The [illegible] will be held in reserve for any emergency.

[The telegraph [illegible] closed at 11 o'clock, the lines being down [illegible] South.]

[Extra Session] of the Illinois Legislature.

CHICAGO, April 14.—Governor YATES will issue a proclamation to-morrow, calling for an extra session of the Legislature, to meet at Springfield, one week from next Tuesday, the 23d inst.

Sailing of the Steamer New York.

NEW YORK, April 13.—The steamer *New York* has sailed with 177 passengers.

Satisfactory Result.

It will be seen from the following article from the Richmond *Enquirer*, one of the most violent of the Secession organs, that the commencement of hostilities by South Carolina has hastened the passage of the Stuart proposition offered in the Virginia Convention by Mr. SCOTT :—

"By reference to our telegraphic column it will be seen that war has actually commenced in South Carolina. It is a significant fact, that before *this news was announced in the Virginia State Convention*, then in Committee of the Whole, that body proceeded at once, by a large majority, to adopt the proposition of Mr. ROBERT E SCOTT, substantially providing for the assemblage of a National Convention—through which, of course, Virginia will be handed over to the tender mercies of a Black Republican majority."

THE TEXAS TROOPS AT NEW YORK.—It is understood that the disposition of the cavalry companies brought by the *Coatzacoalcos* will be made as soon as possible, and that two companies will be sent to Washington and the rest to Carlisle, Pa., barracks. They will probably be sent to-day.

CLEVELAND DAILY PLAIN DEALER.

VOLUME XVII. CLEVELAND, MONDAY EVENING, APRIL 15, 1861. NUMBER 88.

CLEVELAND PLAIN DEALER,

PUBLISHED

DAILY, TRI-WEEKLY, AND WEEKLY,

BY

J. W. GRAY,

AIN DEALER BUILDINGS, CORNER OF SUPERIOR AND VINEYARD STREETS, CLEVELAND.

TERMS OF SUBSCRIPTION.

Daily per Year	$5 00
Less than a year, per Month	50
Tri-Weekly, per Year	3 00
two copies, one year	5 00
" five " "	12 00
" " 20 " "	40 00

No Paper will be sent unless Paid in Advance.

The DAILY PLAIN DEALER is one of the oldest daily papers in the Northwest, and being the only Democratic Daily in Northern Ohio it affords advantages to advertisers unequaled by any paper in this vicinity. It contains the latest news and market reports received by Telegraph up to the time of going to press, and 30 hours in advance of the New York Dailies. It is published every afternoon (Sundays excepted) at 3 o'clock, and is sent to Mail Subscribers at the low price of $5 00 per year, or 50 cents per month, payable in advance. Delivered to City Subscribers at 12½ cents per week.

The TRI-WEEKLY is printed every Tuesday, Thursday and Saturday evening at $3 00 per year to Mail Subscribers, invariably in advance. Delivered to City Subscribers at eight cents per week.

The WEEKLY is printed every Wednesday Morning and contains the News of the Week, choice original and selected Miscellany, Editorials, Correspondence, the latest Telegraph Reports, and carefully prepared Market Reports, of this and the Eastern Markets. It has the largest circulation of any paper in Ohio, and is furnished to

Single Subscribers, per year	$1 50
Clubs of Ten	12 00
Clubs of Twenty and upward, per year	00

and one copy gratis to the getter up of a club.

Invariably in Advance

THE SEIGE OF FT. SUMTER

A Battle Without a Parallel.

SEBASTOPOL OUTDONE.

Seven Batteries Engaged--Twelve Held in Reserve.

3,000 Shot and Shells Fired in 36 Hours.

FT. SUMTER ON FIRE.

The American Flag Fired On by the Secession Rebels when Displayed as a Signal of Distress.

WAR VESSELS IN THE OFFING.

NO RELIEF FROM THEM.

MAJ. ANDERSON SURRENDERED.

Stars and Stripes Hauled Down.

THE FLAG OF THE CONFEDERATE STATES RUN UP.

Great Joy in Charleston.

THE SOUTHERN STATES IN A BLAZE OF EXCITEMENT.

The North Arousing--The President's Voice still for War.

ALL FOR THE "POOR NIGGER."

Treason has at last put on the horrid front of war. The flag of our country trails in the dust. Forbearance ceases any longer to be a virtue. Peace purchased at any price is not the policy of wisdom. In the language of PATRICK HENRY, "*We must fight!*" The crisis has come when we must determine whether secession is right and rebellion wrong; whether treason to the government is to be openly tolerated or forcibly resisted, and whether we have any government at all.

The following despatches tell the story of our country's disgrace. They are in the main reliable. Read them, reflect upon them, and then be prepared to act upon them:

CHARLESTON, April 13.—Two of Anderson's magazines exploded. Only occasional shots are fired at him from Moultrie. The Morris Island Battery is doing heavy work. It is thought that only the smaller magazines have exploded. The greatest excitement prevails. The wharves, steeples and every available place is packed with people. U. S. Ships are in the offing, but have not aided Major Anderson.

It is too late now to come over the bar, as the tide is ebbing.

CHARLESTON, April 13.—The ships in the offing appeared to be quiet at anchor. They have not fired a gun yet.

The entire roof of the barracks at Sumter are in a vast sheet of flames.

Shells from Cumming's Point and Fort Moultrie are bursting in and over Fort Sumter in quick succession.

The Federal flag still waves.

Major Anderson is only occupied in putting out the fire.

Every shot on Fort Sumter now seems to tell heavily.

The people are anxiously looking for Major Anderson to strike his flag.

It is stated from reliable authority that up to 10 o'clock to to day that no one at Moultrie was killed.

Eleven shots fired from Fort Sumter penetrated the floating battery below the water line.

Shots fired by Major Anderson early this morning, knocked the chimneys from the officers quarters at fort Moultrie like a whirlwind.

Major Anderson's only hope now is to hold out for aid from the ships.

The ships are making in toward Morris Island with a view to land troops and silence the batteries there.

CHARLESTON, April 13.—Fort Sumter is unidoubtedly on fire. The flames are raging all round it.

Major Anderson has thrown out a raft loaded with men who are passing up buckets of water to put out the fire.

The Fort is scarcely discernable. The men on the rafts are now objects of fire from Morris Island with glasses. Balls can be seen skipping over the water, striking the unprotected rafts.

Great havoc is created among the poor fellows.

It is reported that Major Anderson is gradually blowing up the Fort. He scarcely fires a gun.

CHARLESTON, April 13, A. M.—The batteries on Sullivan's Island, Cumming's Point and Steven's Battery are pouring shot and shell into Fort Sumter.

Major Anderson does not return the fire.

Fort Sumter is still on fire.

There has just been two explosions at Fort Sumter.

At half-past 11 o'clock flames were seen bursting from the port holes. The destruction of Fort Sumter is inevitable. Four vessels, two o them large steamers, are in sight over the bar. The largest appears to be engaging with Morris Island.

The flames have nearly subsided in Sumter, but Maj. Anderson does not fire any guns.

Gen. Beauregard left the wharf just now in a boat for Morris Island.

The excitement, if anything, is increasing.

I have read a letter from S. S. Baylston, dated Moultrie, 6 o'clock this A. M. He says not one man was killed or wounded. The iron battery had been damaged. The rifled cannon of the battery did great execution on Sumter, and were all aimed into Anderson's port-holes. Three of Sumter's barbette guns were dismounted, one of which was a ten-inch Columbiad. A corner of Ft. Sumter opposite Moultrie was knocked off.

The steamers *Water Witch, Mohawk and Pawnee*, it was thought, were the three first vessels seen in the offing.

Another correspondent says the bombardment has closed. Maj. Anderson has drawn down the stars and stripes, and displayed a white flag, which has been answered from the city, and a boat is on the way to Sumter.

CHARLESTON, April 13.—Beauregard has just gone to Sumter; also three fire companies, to quench the fire before it reaches the magazine.

Third Dispatch.—Sumter is unconditionally surrendered. The people are wild with joy. No Carolinians hurt—two thousand shots fired altogether.

Anderson and his men were conveyed to Morris Island, under guard.

Anderson reached the city as the guest of Beauregard.

The people sympathise with Anderson, but abhor those in the steamer in sight, who did not even attempt to reinforce him.

The wood work and officers' quarters at Sumter are all burnt.

No officers are wounded. The Fort will be taken possession of to-night.

The breaches made in Fort Sumter are on the side opposite Cummings' Point. Two of its port holes are knocked into one, and the wall from the top is crumbling.

Three vessels, one of them a large sized steamer, are over the bar, and seem to be preparing to participate in the conflict.

The pier of Morris Island and Fort Moultrie is divided between Fort Sumter and the ships of war.

The ships have not yet opened fire.

CHARLESTON, April 13, via Augusta.—Fort Sumter has surrendered, and the Confederate flag floats over its walls. None of the garrison confederate troops hurt.

CHARLESTON, April 13—1 P. M.—The Federal flag was again hoisted over Fort Sumter, when Porcher Miles with a flag of truce, went to the Fort. In a few minutes the Federal flag was again drawn down by Maj. Anderson, and the white flag again unfurled.

MONTGOMERY, Ala., April 13.—The President and Secretary of War were serenaded last night, and the latter was called out. He said that the Confederate flag would soon be waiving over Fort Sumter and from the Federal Capitol at Washington if the Independence of the Southern States was not recognized and hostilities continued.

The only despatch received last night was from Gen. Beauregard, and is believed to be favorable.

MONTGOMERY, April 13.—Major Chambers arrived here, bringing Lieut. Warden, of the Federal Navy, prisoner of war from Pensacola. He was bearer of despatches to Pickens.

Guns were fired here, and great rejoicings in honor of their "victory."

Gen. Beauregard telegraphed to the Secretary of War late last night that there had been heavy firing all Friday, that four guns on Fort Sumter had been dismantled, that the Confederate batteries were all safe, that nobody was hurt, the four steamers were off the bar and that the sea was quite rough. Nothing of to day's date has been received by the War Department from Charleston.

HALIFAX, April 13—News of the bombardment has caused a profound sensition.

The Legislature passed a resolution expressing deep sorrow and regret for war among neighbors, without expressing an opinion, and offered prayers for reconciliation.

NASHVILLE, April 13—The enthusiasm is very great.

At a public meeting resolutions were adopted condemning the Administration for causing the present state of affairs, and sympathizing with the South.

Zollicoffer and others spoke.

MEMPHIS, April 13—Great excitement. Cannon and rockets firing, bonfires, music and speeches.

BOSTON, April 13—Intense excitement is caused by the surrender, but it is not believed by many.

LANCASTER, Pa., April 13—Stars and stripes displayed in honor of Anderson. Volunteers are being rapidly enrolled.

PHILADELPHIA, April 13.—The war feeling is rampant. The people are incredulous about Sumter's news. Two regiments of militia will be ready to march in a few days.

NEW YORK, April 13—The Government has chartered the steamers Philadelphia and Ericsson.

The former is being rapidly filled with provisions, army stores and munitions of war. The latter is held in reserve.

WASHINGTON, April 13—The Commissioners from Virginia had a pleasant interview with the President this forenoon. The result was simply a statement that he would act according to the Inaugural programme—hold the public property and maintain the defensive.

The President's reply was given in writing.

It will be recollected that the Commissioners came under instructions to respectfully ask the President to communicate to the Virginia State Convention the policy to be pursued in regard to the Confederate States.

WASHINGTON, April 13.—The reply of the President to the Virginia Commissioners repeats the purpose to hold, occupy and possess the property and places belonging to the government, and collect the duties and imports, but not use force except what is necessary for this object.

An unprovoked assault has been made upon Sumter, and I shall repress it if I can, and take places which have been seized, I shall, to the best of my ability, repel force by force. If the war news proves true, I shall probably withdraw the mails from seceded States. I consider the forts and property in those States yet belonging to the United States. I shall not attempt to collect duties by armed invasion. I don't mean however, and may not land force to relieve the Fort.

He re-affirms the Inaugural, except about mails.

BALTIMORE, April 14—A man made his appearance in this city to-day with a secession cockade. He was pursued by a crowd and had to be protected by the police.

Intense excitement prevails and there is great anxiety to learn the news from Charleston.

NEW ORLEANS, April 13—A grand muster of the city volunteers took place this morning to make preparation to defend the Mississippi in the best possible manner.

RICHMOND, April 13.—In the Convention Carlisle and Early deprecated the action of South Carolina in firing on Sumter, and expressed devotion to the stars and stripes.

The Secessionists replied applauding the gallantry of South Carolina, and claimed that whatever the Convention did the State would go out of the Union.

The Governor communicated a dispatch from Gov. Pickens giving an account of the bombarding and saying, there is a furious fire on us from Sumter. We will take the fort and can sink the fleet. If they attempt to land elsewhere we can whip them. We have nearly seven thousand of the best troops in the world, and a reserve of ten thousand. We will triumph or perish. Let me know what Virginia will do.

In debate it was said that the Southern army would march through Virginia and thousands would join it.

COLUMBUS, O., April 14.—Adj't Gen. Carrington has just issued orders carrying into effect the Militia Laws just enacted by the General Assembly of Ohio, and providing for 6000 regular militia besides all the militia of the reserve of not less than 35,000 men, to be subject to be immediately transferred into the regular force. The regular militia has been organized into twenty five regiments, which upon a war basis would make 25,000 men.

On Saturday the Adjutant's office was thronged by persons eagerly inquiring for the news, and offering their services, irrespective of party, in support of the General Government.

DETROIT, April 14.—The war news created a profound sensation. The unanimous sentiment is that the position assumed by the government must be maintained. Impromtu meeting of the Detroit Bar and influential citizen was held yesterday, and was composed of all parties. It passed resolutions denouncing rebellious organization called the Confederate States, and declared their intention to stand by the flag at all hazards.

Another meeting of the citizens will be held to-morrow night.

RICHMOND, April 14.—There were demonstrations of joy during the night. A party hoisted a Southern flag on the Capitol, but it was subsequently removed by the guard.

PHILADELPHIA, April 14.—Gov. Curtin has gone to Washington. He says Pennsylvania can send 100,000 men to defend Washington.

The Surrender of Fort Sumter confirmed.

An unconditional surrenderde.

Fort Sumter set on Fire Three Times by hot shot from Ft. Moultrie.

The Fleet Fired not a Shot.

Presidents' Proclamation.

75,000 *Volunteers called for service.*

Extra Session of Congress called to meet the 4th of July.

THE STRENGTH OF THE GOVERNMENT TO BE TESTED.

THE COUNTRY RESPONDING!

Stock in the "Star Spangled Banner" on the rise.

NO LONGER PARLEY WITH TRAITORS.

An Extra Session of the Illinois Legislature called.

THE PRESIDENT NOT SURPRISED AT THE NEWS OF THE SURRENDER.

Lincoln's Reply to Virginia Commissioners not satisfactory to the ramrod Rebublicans.

CHARLESTON, April 13.—At ½ past one o'clock the firing ceased and an unconditional surrender was made.

The Carolinians were much surprised that the fight was over so soon.

After the flag staff was shot away, Wigfall was sent by Beauregard to Sumter with a white flag to offer assistance to subdue the flames. He was met by Anderson who said he had just displayed a white flag, but the batteries had not stopped firing.

Wigfall replied that Anderson must haul down the American flag. "Surrender or fight" was the word.

Anderson then hauled down the flag.

Gen. Beauregard's staff went over and stipulated that the surrender must be unconditional, for the present subject to the terms of Gen. Beauregard.

Anderson was allowed to remain in actual possession for the present.

CHARLESTON, April 14.—Negotiations were completed last night. Anderson's command will evacuate in the morning and embark on the war vessels off the harbor.

Five of Anderson's men were wounded; one thought mortally.

After the surrender a boat with ten men was sent from the ships of war outside to Morris Island, requesting permission for the vessel to enter and take off Anderson's command.

It is reported that Anderson surrendered because his quarters and baracks were destroyed and he had no hope of reinforcements as the fleet lay by 30 hours and couldn't or wouldn't help him.

The explosions heard at Fort Sumter were caused by hot shots igniting the wood.

The Barracks caught fire three times from hot shot from Fort Moultrie. Everything is in ruins but the casemates. Many guns are dismounted.

Fort Moultrie was badly damaged. The houses on the Island are riddled.

A boat was sent from the Fort to-night to officially notify the fleet of the surrender of Fort Sumter.

It is not known what will be done with Fort Sumter or the vanquised.

CHARLESTON, April 14.—Anderson and his men leave to-night on the Isabel for New York.

WASHINGTON, April 14.—The President will issue to-morrow a proclamation calling for seventy-five thousand militia to suppress combinations in the seceding States. The first service will probably be to repossess the Forts that have been seized from the Union.

Also call Congress together on the 4th of July.

The War Department is busy preparing details to communicate to the States.

WASHINGTON, April 14—Arrangements were made to concentrate the military on any threatened point.

The greatest anxiety is manifested to hear further Southern news.

It is rumored that an attack is to be attempted on Fort Delaware, Md. The War Department have taken steps to prevent it.

Five officers in the Navy tendered their resignations and were refused. Their names will probably be stricken from the list.

The National Volunteers passed resolutions denouncing the military operations of the Government, and expressing sympathy for the Secessionists.

The guard at the department has been largely increased.

BUFFALO, April 14.—Accounts received from numerous Eastern cities represent intence excitement. The militia are volunteering their services, and there is a general determination to support the government.

The President's proclamation says; Whereas, the laws of the United States have been and are now opposed in several States by a combination too powerful to be suppressed in the ordinary way, I therefore call forth the militia of the several States of the Union, to the aggregate number of 75,000, to suppress said combination and execute the laws. I appeal to all loyal citizens to facilitate aid to this effort to maintain the laws and the integrity of the national Union and the perpetuity of popular government, and redress the wrongs long enough endured.

The first service assigned the forces will probably be the repossession of the forts, places and property that have been seized from the Union. The utmost care will be taken consistent with the object to void devastation, destruction and interference with property of peaceful citizens in any part of the country; and I hereby command the persons composing said combination to disperse within twenty days from date.

I hereby convene both Houses of Congress for the 4th of July next, to determine upon measures for the public safety which interests demands.

Signed, ABRAHAM LINCOLN, Pres.,
By WM. H. SEWARD, Sec'y of State.

ALBANY, April 14.—It is rumored that Governor Morgan has received despatches from the President asking aid from this State.

Lincoln's reply, to the Virginia Commissioners is decidedly unsatisfactory to Republicans and Democrats. The former think it is not decided enough, and the latter believe it is an indication of civil war.

The Herald's despatch says Lincoln received the news of Anderson's surrender with the remark, "He wasn't surprised."

The Seventh and Sixty-ninth Regiments have volunteered for the defence of Washington.

NEW YORK, April 14.—The *Times'* Charleston correspondent, Jasper, was arrested as a spy and ordered to quit the State.

ERIE, April 14.—The news from the South greates the most intense feeling. Men of all parties express their determination to stand by the government and fight for the supremacy of the the U. S. flag. All our volunteer companies will offer their services to the government tomorrow.

CHICAGO, April 14.—Gov. Yates will issue a proclamation to-morrow calling an extra session of the Legislature, to meet in Springfield one week from next Tuesday.

The News.

There is little room for anything else than war news in our paper and less in the public mind for the extraordinary condition of the country very naturally and very properly absorbs all minds and fills all hearts with sadness. But we have no alternative—no election. The war is actually and vigorously begun by our enemies, and we see signs now of a vigorous response by our Government, and we say amen. for "we join ourselves to no party that does not carry the flag and keep step to the music of the Union."—Patrick Henry asked—"Shall we gather strength by irresolution and inaction?—by lying supinely on our backs and hugging the delusive phantom of hope till our enemies have bound us hand and foot?" We now can answer it. We now see what delay has lost us rather than gained us. Our enemies have rejoiced at our delay and turned the time to good account by unremitting efforts and preparation for war. They are the worst enemies of the country and the most efficient aiders and abetters of the rebels who urge us to receive but give no blows—to be attacked without resistance.

Look to the telegraph columns for startling news. Big events crowd thick upon us. Armies are in active service, new regiments are called for and

"With trilling fife and pealing drum
And clashing horn they come, they come."

Our readers can rely on us for the latest and fullest news, for, at whatever cost, the PLAIN DEALER will come to time.

Letter From Gen. Jo Lane.

Vanity Fair publishes the following letter, supposed to have been received from Gen. Jo LANE, who, it is scarcely necessary to say, is much noted for his spelling abilities:

March the third, 18 & 60 onct.

EDS. VANNURTY FAIR: if god spairs my life i shall seceed with in 20 dase. johnson of tennysea is fornenst me, but he haint got no intelect into him. Sivil war is certain & i wants to hear the Cannin Rore. Hist the Palmettoe banner from on top your offis & let it waive to the brees. Dont mucillate this mannerscript and be particlar not to make Misstaiks in the spellin and punktooate it proper, amerykan Staitsman suffers from scrofulus papers which tries to bring them into ridicool by mucilatin their mannerscripts. On to the frey! the god of Bottles upon the palmettoe flag. yours respectably.

GOSEF LANE.

"COME REST IN THIS BOSOM."—One of the fullest bosoms of ancient or modern times, has exhibited at the first station last evening, when a woman, who had been picked up drunk on the sidewalk, was brought in.—There was an unusual fullness in the region of her bosom, which induced suspicions that it was not nature's handiwork, and voluntarily she commenced revealing the mysteries of that portion of her person, not, however in such a manner as to shock the sensitive nature of the officer. She removed from her dress a bottle of Champaine, two plates, half a dozen oranges, ten doughnuts, four pieces of cake, a pound of butter, a pound of sugar, quarter of pound of tea, a coffee-pot. gridiron, and so would have brought to light a cooking-stove, if the officers had not tired of receiving the articles drawn from their seclusion, and begged of her to desist. That woman would be a treasure to a man about to start to California by the overland route, as she could carry such a quanity of refreshments in her bosom, and always have them handy.—[Boston *Herald*.]

Fatting Sheep.

Oil cake comes rather high now in market.—Next to oil cake the best food is a mixture of Indian meal and oat meal, about equal parts, bulk for bulk, say a bushel of oats and a bushel of corn ground together. In this mixture the weight of corn-meal will be greater than the oat meal. A pound of the mixture per day, with two or three pounds of good hay according the size of the sheep, will make good feed. Beans are very fattening to sheep, but rather costly. Let the sheep have all the water they want. They are the best judges whether they need water or not.—*Maine Farmer.*

THE SIEGE OF SUMTER.

View of the Battle Scene--Position of Forts Sumter, Moultrie, Iron Battery, Floating Battery, Cummings Point and Fort Johnson.

The above cut is a view of Fort Sumter, at 11 A. M., the 2d day of the seige, as described by the despatches. The few men in the Fort, not half enough to man the guns, after fighting all the day before from 4 o'clock in the morning until the evening, then ceased firing only to clean their guns, repair breeches and if possible take a little rest, were kept awake by the continued shelling from the mortar batteries, until at last they had to contend with fire within as well as without the Fort.

It was in this condition that a signal of distress was hoisted to induce the war steamers to come to their relief. But it would seem from President LINCOLN's reply to the Virginia Commissioners, that said war vessels had no orders to land troops, and with his men thus exhausted and seven batteries bearing upon him from without Major ANDERSON had to surrender.

The walls of Sumter were sixty feet high, from eight to twelve feet in thickness, built of brick and concrete. It was pierced for two tiers of guns besides the barbettes on the top wall. The work was designed for an armament of one hundred and forty pieces of ordnance of all calibres. Two tiers of guns are under bomb proof casemates, and the third or upper tier open, or in military parlance, *en barbette;* the lower tier for forty-two pounder paixham guns; the second tier for eight and ten inch columbiads, for throwing solid or hollow shot, and the upper tier for mortars and twenty-four pound guns. The full armament of the Fort, however, had not arrived there when Major Anderson took possession; but since its occupancy by the present garrison no efforts have been spared to place the work in an efficient state of defense, by mounting all the available guns and placing them in salient points. As we before remarked, the full armament of the Fort was not in position, as only seventy-five of the one hundred and forty guns required for it were mounted. Eleven paixham guns were among that number, nine of them commanding Fort Moultrie, which is within easy range, and the other two pointing towards Castle Pinckney, which is well out of range. Some of the columbiads, the most effective weapon for siege or defensive operations, were not mounted. Four of the thirty-pounder barbette guns were on pivot carriages, which gives them the entire range of the horizon, and others have a horizontal sweep of fire of 180 degrees.

The magazine contains seven hundred barrels of gunpowder and an ample supply of shot, powder and shells for one year's siege and a large amount of miscellaneous artillery stores. The war garrison of the fort is six hundred men, but only seventy-nine of that number were within its walls, with the laborers—103 all told.

All that was wanting to have made the Fort impregnable was its full compliment of men and provisions. Through the imbecility and treason of the late administration and the cowardice and want of statesmanship of the present, the key of the South has been surrendered, our nation disgrace and rebellion made rampant.

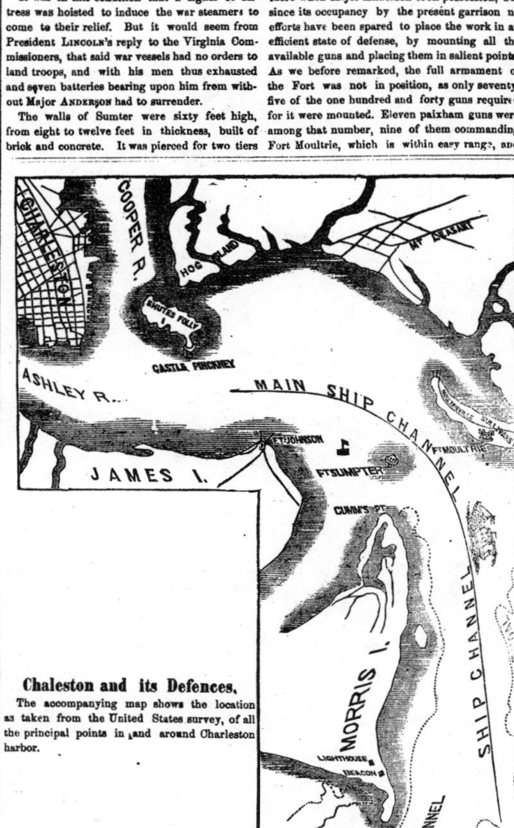

Chaleston and its Defences,

The accompanying map shows the location as taken from the United States survey, of all the principal points in and around Charleston harbor.

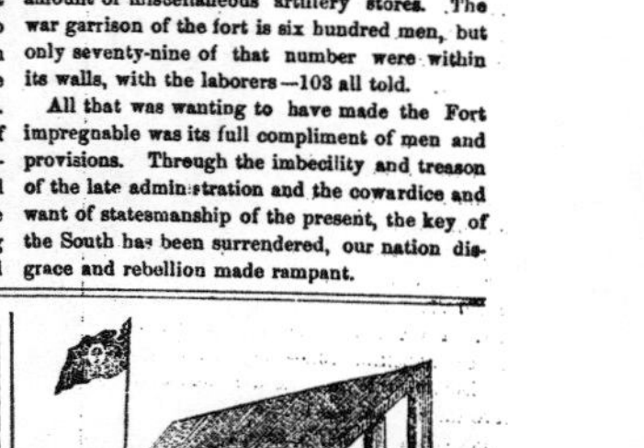

Cumming's Point Iron Battery.

The nearest point of land to Fort Sumter is Cuming's Point; distance 1,150 yards. On this point is the celebrated railroad iron battery, an illustration of which we give above. It consists of a heavy framework of yellow pine logs. The roof is of the same material, over which dovetailed bars of railroad iron of the T pattern are laid from top to bottom—all of which are riveted down in the most secure manner. On the front it presents an angle of about thirty degrees.—There are three port-holes, which open and close with iron shutters of the heaviest description.—When open the muzsles of the Columbiads fill up the space completely. The recoil of the gun enables the shutters to be closed instantly. It is asserted on strong military authority, that the inclined plane will effectually resist guns of the heaviest calibre—first, because no shot can strike it except at an acute angle, which would cause the ball to glance, second, because its power of resistance is sufficient to withstand the fall of the heaviest shell. The Columbiad guns, with which this novel battery is equipped, bear on the south wall of Sumter, the line of five being at an angle of thirty-five degrees.

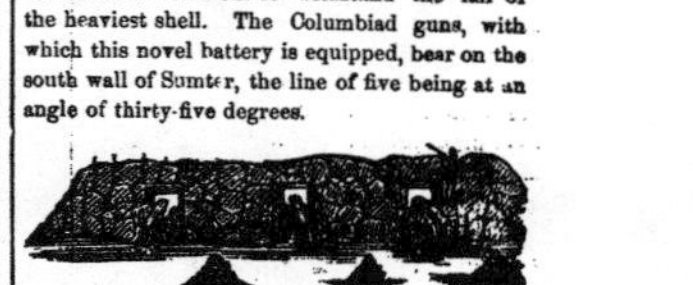

Interior of Ft. Johnson--Gun Battery.

The Fort Johnson Batteries consist of two huge sand works, containing mortar and siege gun batteries, of which the above and the subsequent cuts are good illustrations.

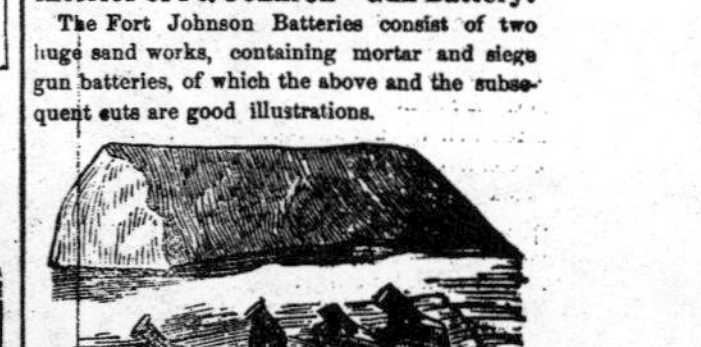

Fort Johnson--Mortar Battery.

These works are one and one-fourth of a mile from Fort Sumter and were manned by two companies of regular artillery. The position of the old Fort has given Maj. ANDERSON great annoyance, as it was from this Mortar Battery, thus protected, that Sumter was so successfully shelled as to set it on fire. It is passing strange that amidst all the late improvements in the art of war, a Fort cannot be constructed fire proof.

THE EXACT DISTANCES OF THE FORTS.

Fort Sumter is three and three-eighths miles from Charleston, one and one-eighth mile from Fort Moultrie, three fourths of a mile from Cummings' Point, one and three-eighths from Fort Johnson, and two and five-eighths miles from Castle Pinckney. The city of Charleston is entirely out of the range or the guns of Fort Sumter.

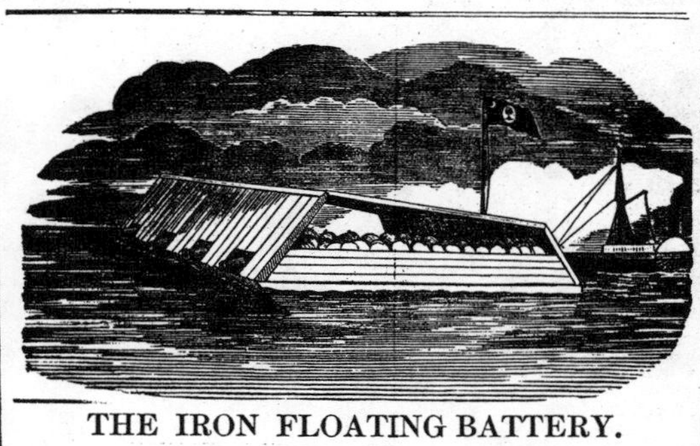

THE IRON FLOATING BATTERY.

This novel war machine, designed for harbor operations was anchored near Sullivan's Island, commanding the barbette guns of Fort Sumter. It is constructed of palmetto logs, sheathed with plate iron, and impregnable against shot. It is embrasured for and mounts four guns of heavy calibre. It requires sixty men to operate it.—The first impression on seeing this machine is that of immense solidity. The outer or gun side is covered with six plates of Iron—two of them of the T. railroad pattern, placed horizontally, and the other four bolted one over the other, in the strongest manner, and running vertically. The wall of the gun side is full four feet thick, constructed of that peculiar palmetto wood so full of fibrous material that sixty four pounders cannot pierce it. The main deck is wide and roomy. In nineteen open chambers, on the port side of the deck, was put a profusion of shot—thirty-four pounders—while just behind them is an immense pile of sand bags, which protect an overhanging roof, under which is placed the hospital. This also protects the magazines (three in number), under which is the hold proper. There are six entrances to the hold, which will contain, if necessary, over three hundred men It is kept in place by four heavy wedges, driven down by a species of ram, which holds it fast, and prevents any swaying around by the tide.

A SENSIBLE LANDLORD.—An exchange says: "A little incident traspired some weeks ago, at one of our Frankfort hotels, which is worthy of notice. A little girl entered the bar-room, and in pitiful tones told the keeper that her mother had sent her there to get eight cents. 'Eight cents,' said the keeper. 'Yes sir.' What does your mother want with eight cents? I don't owe her anything.' 'Well,' said the child, 'father spends all his money here for rum, and we have had nothing to eat to-day. Mother wants to buy a loaf of bread.' A loafer remarked to the barkeeper to 'Kick the brat out.' 'No said the keeper, 'I'll give her the money and if the father comes back again I'll kick him out

—"Ah, how do you like my mustache, Mith Laura?" lisped a dandy to a merry girl. "Oh, very much. It looks like the fuz on the back of a catterpillar."

CHEAP BEER.—A very good, palatable, wholesome beer, may be obtained from acorns and hops. It is sightly sparkling, eminently tonic, and a febrifuge. The acorns are steeped in water for fifteen or twenty days, the water being renewed four or five times; they are then transferred to a cask, hops are added, the cask filled up with water, and the bunghole lightly covered, but not stopped, as there is an escape of gas. In fifteen or twenty days the beer is fit to drink; and, as fast as it is drawn off, fresh water may be poured on. The cost is less than three-pence per gallon. It would supply four or five persons for eight months with a very excellent beverage.—*London Paper.*

—If the gentleman who keeps a shoe shop with a red head, will return the umbrella of a young lady with an ivory handle he will hear of something to her advantage.

BOMBARDMENT OF FORT SUMTER BY THE BATTERIES

E CONFEDERATE STATES, APRIL 13, 1861.—[See Page 257.]

Lynchburg Virginian.

Friday Morning,............April 19, 1861.

☞ MR. THOS. J. BAGBY is our authorized Agent in Richmond, to procure advertising and subscriptions. We commend him to the attention of our friends.

Harper's Ferry.

The great interest attaching just now to this important town, may serve to render a description of it acceptable to our readers. In its topography it is one of the most remarkable localities on the face of the globe—a Thermopylæ, that a scientific engineer with a sufficiency of heavy ordnance, and four or five regiments, could hold against the world. The town lies just above the mouth of an opening in the Blue Ridge, and at the confluence of the Shenandoah and Potomac rivers, whose united waters, in the opinion of Mr. Jefferson, forced the passage and "tore down the mountain from its summit to its base." Just between those two rivers that flow on either side along the base of the mountain, rises gradually, a high promontory upon which the town, for the most part, is built. Extending up some half mile or more to Camp Hill, (so called from the fact that troops of the United States were encamped there during the Administration of John Adams,) the apex of the acclivity is reached, and thence a corresponding declivity is seen on the other side. The slope from East to West is, as we have said, gradual, but the sides of the hill facing North and South are rugged and precipitous. The summit of the hill, therefore, can only be reached from East and West; from the former by passing the narrow gorge between the mountains, on the Maryland side, which could be swept by cannon from the hill above, or from the point below—or, from the latter by passing through Virginia territory in the Shenandoah valley; and the approaches in that direction also could be swept by cannon planted on the hill. The Potomac, which is about a fourth of a mile wide at the Ferry, is crossed by a substantial railroad bridge which could be destroyed, and thereby cut off all access from the Maryland side. When it is considered that the troops that would be conveyed from Washington or from the Northern States, could not approach the town from any other quarter than this, (except those that might be sent from the West, and that would have to come through nearly three hundred miles of Virginia territory,) where they would have to pass a narrow defile of not more than thirty feet, at the base of the mountain, and could be raked by batteries from the hill before mentioned and from the plain below, some conception may be formed of the impregnable character of the position. We know of but one means by which the town could be taken in the face of a strong military force. The mountain on the Maryland side might have batteries planted upon it to dislodge the forces from the hills of the town, if they were not properly protected with earth works; but the besiegers would not be able to damage the musket factory, which is erected along the Potomac, and upon which their guns could not be brought to bear; nor the rifle factory, on the Shenandoah, which would be completely covered and protected from the point indicated by the hills alluded to. Taken altogether, we know not a position any where that could so easily and effectually be held by a small force against a large one. We have little doubt that the several regiments of volunteers, to the number of two or three thousand men, that could be had in the thickly populated counties of Jefferson, Frederick, Berkeley and Loudoun, at a few hours notice, have already been concentrated at Harper's Ferry, unless Lincoln had anticipated such a movement and thrown in large bodies of his mercenaries previously. He has had some ninety dragoons there, bequeathed him by the late Administration, but they could have been easily overcome if not reinforced. We know the men of that country, their courage, and expertness in the use of fire arms, and feel assured that they will render a good account of themselves when engaged with the Northern hordes. But if, unfortunately, the hirelings of the Administration first occupied the ground, we may expect to hear of bloody work. A report was circulated here yesterday, though we had no telegraphic communication with Washington,—that a conflict was raging at Harper's Ferry.—The intelligence purported to have come from a member of the Convention, and may be reliable, though we are not warranted in saying so.

Down With Lincoln!

Let this be the war cry that shall animate all the sons of the South, in the war for liberty which has been forced upon them by the tyranny of Abraham Lincoln. The revolution has begun, and no alternative is left us but to accept the gauge of battle in vindication of our rights and honor. Down with Lincoln! and death to the invader! From the mountains to the seaboard, and all over the broad savannahs of the South—let this be our rallying cry! Down with the man who has cursed his country with civil war. Death to the tyrant and all his mercenaries!

To Arms! To Arms!

Let all the youth whose ages range from fourteen to eighteen, and who are, therefore, not eligible for the active service, be organized into companies, and placed under proper commands, to act as a *corps de reserve*, and to protect our homes. Scores of chivalric youths who are able to do service in this way, will enter the ranks and act efficiently in case of necessity, in conjunction with the "Silver Grays." The calmness of age could check the ardor of youth, whilst the zeal of the latter would fire the hearts of the former, if this incentive were wanting. Organize! organize!

Gov. Hicks of Maryland.

We take the following from the Baltimore Sun of yesterday. The only inference we can draw from it, is that Gov. Hicks has not yet responded to Mr. Simon Cameron:

The Excitement in the City—The excitement in the city had considerably abated yesterday, if the comparatively meagre assemblage on the corners of the streets was indicative of such a result. The subject of the probable response of Gov. Hicks to the requisition of Mr. Lincoln formed a general topic of conversation, and the presence of the Executive of the State in the city added to the anxiety to know his conclusion in the matter. The contemplated action of Virginia was much talked of, and many expressed their impatience at the tardiness of her convention in arriving at some definite result.

Lincoln proposes to "maintain the Union with all the means at his disposal;" and by extraordinary means not lawfully at his disposal. How much easier he could have accomplished this great and blessed object. Had he applied none other than peaceful remedies, and freely conceded to the South her rights, as the Union men advised—his country would not have been disrupted to-day, nor the earth been called upon to drink the blood of his fellow-citizens, slain in fratricidal strife. A peaceful, conciliatory policy would have conquered, but war has alienated all the affection we ever entertained for the Union. It can never be restored. We will never again consort with men who have shown a desire to invade our soil and shed our blood. Never! Never! can the Union be restored. The voice of our brother's blood to be shed in this terrible and unnatural conflict would cry out against it. The Union is gone and gone forever.—Abraham Lincoln has done it. He is responsible, and let every man cry out,

> "Oh, for a tongue to curse the slave,
> Whose treason, like a deadly blight,
> Comes o'er the council of the brave,
> And blasts them in their hour of might."

The Military Force in Washington.

The Washington correspondent of the Petersburg Express says:

"Certain it is, that there are over 10,000 secretly well-equipped gentlemen in the city, and the surrounding cities and country, ready, at a moment's notice, to flock to the standard of a certain military man whose name I had rather not mention. This is no surmise, but certain knowledge. When to expect the call to be made, or what will be deemed sufficient cause for making it, I do not know. But should this secret force be called out, there is danger of there not being much bloodshed, for the city force will make scarcely a decent resistance. The oath required previous to the enlistment of volunteers has occasioned much difficulty. Not only have two of the finest companies in the District been completely broken up, but there is scarcely a company whose number has not been greatly reduced by this requirement.—Besides this fact, there is great dissatisfaction manifested in the ranks of the Federal troops.—Scarcely a day passes without an instance of desertion. Over 200 men, from the 900 that have been stationed in the city since the inauguration of the revolution, have deserted. A day or two since 20 marines left at once for the South, and the officers privately assured the citizens of their real intentions and determination as to carrying out Lincoln's policy."

Help the Volunteers!

As it now seems probable that most if not all of the Volunteer Companies of the city will soon be called into active and perhaps actual service, and as many of our young men who have already joined, and others who are both willing and anxious to join one or another of the Companies, are unable to equip themselves, I believe it is only necessary for the fact to be known, for our people to step forward at once, and generously, munificently provide for all of their wants—The Ladies—God bless them!—are doing all that they can,—let our men imitate these glorious and unselfish examples.

The writer begs to suggest that all contributors for the purpose be handed over to the Commandants of the respective Companies.

As many ladies who are willing to aid have not yet had an opportunity of doing so, it is suggested that they furnish the Comandants with their names and what they are willing to contribute.—Do this for OUR COUNTRY.

E. C. BURKS, OF BEDFORD.—A friend, writing from this county, informs us that the late constituents of this gentleman will insist upon his return to the House of Delegates. We are pleased to hear it.

"Of the last Legislature, Mr. B. was one of the most attentive, enlightened and useful members. We but express the opinion of every one who knew him here last winter, when we say that he possesses all the characteristics of the useful legislator.—*Richmond Enquirer.*

The Famine in India—Two Millions of People Starving.

The news from India is frightful in the extreme; "famine is devastating the country." The London Times of the 29th, in an article on the subject, after alluding to the fact that the famine is created by draught, says:

It is drought in a land where the sun bakes up the soil almost to the hardness of pottery, and where the earth, without rain in the accustomed season, is an impenetrable crust. Where irrigation works exist the scanty waters will suffice to produce scanty crops, but where there are no such works there is no vegetation to be found. Mr. Edmonstone, the Lieutenant Governor of the North western Provinces, had himself seen that in a march of twenty miles there was not a green blade in any direction. Families were fleeing away from the death which threatened them. Emaciated multitudes were drooping and dying by the way. And all this, we are told, is but the beginning of the terrible calamity which threatens to involve a population reckoned by one of the speakers at the Mansion-house at seven millions and a half. Of these it is stated that two millions and a half are actually starving.

A great meeting was held in London on the 25th ult. to promote subscriptions for the relief of the famine caused by the drought in the North-western provinces of India. Liberal amounts have already been given by many leading institutions and private firms, the Bank of England leading with £500, and a heavy total is likely to be expeditiously raised. It is to be regetted, however, that the broader and more prompt course has not been adopted of meeting the emergency by an ample state contribution to be furnished by means of a special loan. The population of the suffering district is estimated at four millions, and according to the latest advices the lives of one million five hundred thousand were actually at that moment dependant on the arrival of charitable aid. No relief in the shape of new crops can come before June. For three or four months, therefore, there must be prolonged assistance. It is stated that a single pound sterling will suffice for the support of a Hindoo peasant for three months.

Tobacco.

It seems the Virginia weed is never to be allowed to rest. It has enemies on all sides. The last "counterblast" is from Sir Benjamin Brodil, the physician of Queen Victoria, and we suppose, all the royal family. This gentleman hates the Virginia weed, as the old fashioned Federalists hated the Virginia resolutions of '98—'99. He tells all sorts of stories about its naughty doings. The habitual use of it, in smoking, has made one man blind, another deaf, a third crazy, and all nervous. Whole nations have been known to degenerate into semi-idiots by habitual indulgence in it. One generation smokes excessively. Their children are degenerate, from this vice of their parents. In turn the children smoke a little harder than their fathers, and their offspring are a little more degenerate than they are themselves. Thus it goes on, until the race finally becomes extinct. The Turks, four centuries ago, were the terror of Christendom. They have smoked themselves into perfect nonentities. They are filthy beasts, not fit to live in Europe. It is news to us, to be sure, that tobacco did all this. We thought opium had some share in the mischief. But Sir Benjamin says it was tobacco, and he is physician to the Queen.

Now, we are very much afraid Sir Benjamin, with all his learning and experience, will no more be able to abolish the use of tobacco than was King James I. of glorious memory, the same after whom our magnificent river is called, having been changed from Powhatan. The "counterblast" of the monarch had the direct opposite effect to what had been expected. It set half the civilized world to inquire about this then comparatively unknown weed. Men are perverse by nature. They love all manner of sin, but they love that which is forbidden the best. They take their disposition from Eve. Nobody, we presume, supposes that venerable old lady would ever have thought of stealing the fruit, if she had not been told it was wrong to do it. Now, Sir Benjamin thinks school boys and other lads indulge in the luxury of smoking partly because they think it manly and partly because they have nobody at hand to admonish them of its evil tendency. Both these causes may have their effects to a certain extent; but we believe much the greater number smoke because they know it is wrong. That is, in general, reason enough for a boy, and to say the truth, it is in most cases, reason enough for a man, too.—*Rich. Dispatch.*

ACQUISITIVENESS AND ASSININITY LARGE.—An office seeker at Auburn, N. Y., rests his hopes upon a flattering chart of his phrenological developments from O. S. Fowler, which, with other credentials he has forwarded to Washington.

Who is Responsible?

The Toronto (Canada) Leader justly holds the Government at Washington responsible for the war which has just begun. It says:

The Cabinet at Washington, in the calm judgement of the world, committed a serious error in appealing to the arbitrament of the sword; but it is now too late to adopt the only statesmanlike policy—to recognize secession as a fact—and act accordingly. What has now to be done is for the two Confederacies to do each other as much harm as possible, in the least possible time; to kill as many men, to sink as many ships, to cripple as much as possible one another's resources. It will be a war of brothers, and of brother's enraged against one another with an intensity of hatred that only brothers can feel. A less edifying spectacle could hardly be presented to the world; and while the general sympathy of mankind has been with the North, the Government at Washington will generally be responsible for the issue of blood.

And such will be the impartial judgment of the whole civilized world.

Attack on Fort Sumter—Another Account.

The fort is burned into a mere shell, not a particle of woodwork can be found. The guns on one side of the parapet are entirely dismounted; others split, while the gun carriages are knocked into splinters.

Major Anderson says the accuracy of the firing surprised him, and that if he had two hundred more men, one half would have been killed for want of suitable protection.

When Colonel Chesnut, aid of General Beauregard, went to offer assistance after the fire, he says the fort was like an oven, and he could hardly breathe. It was so hot that Major Anderson received him in one of the casements. Inquiry being made how many were killed he said, "None" "How many on your side?" "None," was the response. "Thank God," replied Major Anderson, "there has been a higher Power over us."

Major Anderson says it is preposterous to fight such a people. One of the officers in the fort remarked that they had endeavored not to fire on exposed individuals. "Yes," said Major Anderson, "I gave orders not to sight men, but to silence batteries."

As regards harbor defence, the fort is just as good as ever. The casement are perfect, the guns there in prime condition and bear on both sides.

Major Anderson was obliged to throw overboard a large quantity of powder to prevent explosion, and it was floating around the fort to day.

The fort has been garrisoned by the Palmetto Guards, and put under command of Lieutenant-Colonel Ripley, who commanded Fort Moultrie after the departure of Major Anderson.

The Major's feelings were spared in every respect, and no person except authorized aids allowed inside.—The harbor is full of boats sailing around the fort. But no parties without business are permitted to land.

Before going into action Major Anderson sent word, by an Aid of Gen. Bearegard, to the Governor, thanking him for kind attentions during the past two months, and very solemly said, "Farewell, gentlemen. If we do not meet again here, I hope we shall meet in a better world."

The Confederate flag and Palmetto flag were hoisted on seperate spars simultaneously.

The fire has broken out afresh in the ruins of the fort. Two engines have gone down to operate, and, if necessary to flood the magazine.

The Washington *States and Union* says: 'STAMPEDE.—There is a general stampede of office seekers from here during the past two days. This afternoon a large number will leave, mostly from Pennsylvania. The distress which prevails among this unfortunate people is truly lamentable. A number who came here with bright anticipations, find themselves, after a two weeks sojourn, out of money and without friends. The proprietors of the hotels can attest this fact. They have now over four hundred carpet bags and valises, which have been left by the pilgrims in search of office, for their boarding bill. As far as heard from, there is only one valise that contains anything valuable, and in that one, was found a well-executed twenty dollar bill on the State Bank of Ohio. It is said that there will be an auction sale in the latter part of next week, just to get rid of the rubbish.

MEETING LAST NIGHT.—There was a very large and enthusiastic meeting last night at Exchange Building, at which resolutions were passed in favor of calling the Legislature, and of putting the city in a state of defense. A number of our citizens made spirit-stirring speeches; and the greatest unanimity of sentiment prevailed to the bad faith of the Lincoln Government in adopting a coercionary policy.—*Memphis Tenn. Bulletin.*

COMING EVENTS CASTING THEIR SHADWS BEFORE.—The Republicans in Washington, according to the correspondent of the New York Evening Post, are already canvassing where the capital of the Northern Confederacy is to be after Lincoln gives up Washington to Jefferson Davis. The Western Republicans, it says, warmly supports Columbus; Ohio.

FREE TRADE IN NEW YORK.—We learn from the New York Evening Post that the idea of the necessity of forming a free trade league in New York has already been acted upon; and one is in process of formation, counting among its co-operators some of the most influential merchants of that city.

COMMERCIAL.

LYNCHBURG MARKETS,
REPORTED BY
A. B. RUCKER,
PRODUCE BROKER,
133 MAIN STREET.

☞ These quotations, it will be understood, represent whole sale prices generally.

APPLES.—Good supply. $1.50@$3 per barrel.
BACON.—I notice an improved feeling in the market, and quote 10½ to 11.
BEANS—White 1 25 to 1 50.
BEESWAX.—30@31 cents.
BUTTER—Full suppy—For table use 18 to 25c; cooking 10@15
CORN.—Stock accumulating. Yellow 60 cents; White 65.
CORN MEAL.—70@75 cents.
CEMENT.—James River $1.80@$2.00.
DRIED FRUIT.—Dried Apples 40 to 45c per busheld. Unpeeled 1.10 to $1.20, pealed peaches $2.75@3.50.
FLOUR.—I quote superfine $6 25@6 37; extra $6 50@6 62; family $7.
FLAXSEED.—1.05 to 1.10 cents.
FEATHERS.—Plenty and dull—40@42 cents.
FERTILIZERS.—Supply ample. No. 1 Peruvian Guano $65 ₱ ton of 2,000 lbs; Reese's Manipulated Guano $52.50; Sombrero Guano $35.00; Mexican Guano $25.00; American Guano $40.00; Rhodes Sup. Phosphate of Lime $50.00; Ruffin's Phospho Peruvian Guano $52.50; Ruffin's Bone Ash Guano $52.50; Ruffin's Tobacco Manure, $47.50; Ruffin's Ground Bone Ash $47.50; Fowle & Co.'s Soluble Phosphated Peruvian Guano, $52.50; Diuguid's Bone Dust, $30.00; Ruffin's Tobacco Manure, $47.50; Ground Plaster in bulk $9.00; in bags or barrels $11.00. Langhorne's Manipulated Guano $50.00 per ton.
GRASS SEEDS.—Orchard Grass $1.50@$1.75; Randal $1.00; Timothy $3.25@$3.50; Clover Seed $6.50 to $6.75.
GINSENG.—35@40 cents.
HAY.—Baled $1.00@$1.10; ₱ wagon load 80@$1.00
IRON.—Mountain $90@$100 ₱ ton.
LARD.—Receipts increasing—11@11½ cents.
LIME.—Thomastown $1.50@$1.60; Mountain $1.00@$1.10
ONIONS.—75 to 80c.
PEAS.—$1@1.25 per bushel.
POTATOES.—75c to $.
OATS.—Sheaf—80@$ 0c—shelled ₱ bus. 33 lbs. 34@37c.
WHEAT.—For prime Family Flour Wheat there is an improved feeling, and I quote $1 20 to $1 35, for Red; $1 25 to $1 45, for White—for choice. Low grades wheat from $1.20@$1.00—according to quality.
WOOL.—Unwashed 20@24c.; washed 33@37.
TOBACCO.—I have to notice an improved feeling—note sales lugs at 1 50 to $3 50; inferior leaf $3 to $5; working $6 to $10.
PORK.—No stock. Last sales $8 00 cash.

CANDIDATES FOR OFFICE.

CANDIDATE FOR CONGRESS.

☞ We are authorized to announce WALLER R. STAPLES, of Montgomery, as a candidate for Congress, in the 12th Congressional District. mar. 29-d & w tde.

To the Voters of Campbell and Lynchburg.

☞ I was nominated at last Campbell Court, by the then Union party of this county, as a candidate to represent the county, in part, in the next General Assembly of Virginia.

I accepted the position with the hope, at that time, that something might be done to restore the Union to its original purity, with the rights of the South satisfactorily guaranteed, and if a demonstration was made to coerce the Seceding States, we should at once dissolve our connection with the North, and defend our rights to the last. That step has been taken, and the duplicity and treachery of Lincoln, together with his warlike demonstrations and consummate impudence toward the South, have forever defeated the laudable and patriotic object had in view by our more hopeful fellow-countrymen; and I now stand on a common platform with all the friends of the South—that of resistance to the presumptious tyranny of Abe Lincoln.

As it has been reported that I have withdrawn from the canvass, I deem it proper to state that such is not the fact. I am still, a candidate. A. J. CLARK.
apl 19 dac1w

A CARD.

AS I shall not be able to canvass all parts of the County, I deem it proper to take this method of announcing to the people of Campbell and Lynchburg, that I am before them as a candidate for a seat in the next Legislature. As one of the nominees of the Southern Rights Party, it is hardly necessary for me to say that I have been, and am still, an advocate of the immediate resumption, on the part of the State of Virginia, of those powers delegated by her to the Federal Government, and an immediate bestowment of the powers thus withdrawn, upon the Confederate States Government. Whilst I have been ever firm in the support of my own opinions, I have never denounced those of my fellow-citizens who differ with me, but have always felt assured that whenever the proofs became as clear to them, as to me, that it was the deliberate purpose of the Federal Government to deprive us of our Constitutional rights, we would unite as one man in their defence. That day has now come. To day, fellow-citizens, I cannot believe we differ, and have only to say that, should it be your pleasure to make me one of your Representatives, I will endeavor faithfully and honestly to discharge the duties of the office.
apl 18-dac3t ROBERT C. SAUNDERS

Attention Rifle Grays!

PARADE at your Armory FRIDAY morning at 9 o'clock, in undress uniform (with gray pants,) and all accoutrements, for the purpose of attending Regimental parade and Inspection. Members will come prepared to stand a rigid inspection of arms and accoutrements. Also attend the regular weekly drill, THURSDAY evening at ½ to 8, in undress uniform.
By order of Capt. Langhorne.
apl 17-2t JOS. A. KENNEDY, O. S.

Attention Militia!

IN compliance with the order of Col. Langhorne and Adjutant Blackford, the 8th Company of the 131st Regiment, will parade in front of the Court house, on FRIDAY next, at 10 o'clock, A. M. A punctual attendance requested.
By order of the Adjutant.
apl 17-3t JAMES McGOWEN, Captain.

Attention Artillery!

YOU will meet at your Gun House, on THURSDAY night at 8 o'clock. It is expected of all who have their names on the Roll, and LOVE VIRGINIA, will ANSWER to WHEN CALLED.
By order of Lieut. in Command.
C. H. TAYLOR, O. S.
You will also meet at the same place, on FRIDAY morning, at 10 o'clock—black pants, grey shirt and cap. (See his order.)
By order of Col. Langhorne.
apl 17-2t

Attention Troop!

CALL at N. GUGGENHEIMER'S and leave your measures for undress shirts and caps.
By order
apl 17 3t A. D. WARWICK, 1st Sergt.

Cavalry Recruits Wanted!

RECRUITS for ACTIVE SERVICE are wanted at once for the Troop. Persons wishing to enlist will please call at the office of Mr. Charles (Lieut.) Blackford and do so.
The attention of country gentlemen, in the neighborhood, is particularly called to the above.
apl 17-3t THE OFFICERS OF THE TROOP.

Attention Company 5!

YOU will meet on Corner of 10th and Court Streets, FRIDAY, 19TH inst., at 10 o'clock, precisely. Every member is expected to be out, as it is ordered by D. A. Langhorne, Colonel of the Regiment.
Also, election for Lieutenants will be held.
apl 17-3t JOHN B. SHANER, Captain.

Attention! 131st Regiment of Va. Militia!!

ALL the Companies, Volunteer and Militia of this Regiment, are required to assembled for inspection and drill on FRIDAY morning at 10 o'clock, in front of the Court-house.
This order is designed to embrace every person in the bounds of the Regiment, not specially exempted by law
By order of Col. D. A. Langhorne.
apl 16-4t B. L. BLACKFORD, Adjt.

SPECIAL NOTICES.

☞ REV. J. LANSING BURROWS, D. D., of Richmond, will deliver the Anniversary Address before the Philomathean and Jefferson Societies, of Allegheny College, on the 26th of June next.
apl 16-ts

Stockholders' Meeting.

☞ There will be a meeting of the Stockholders of the Merchants' Bank of Virginia, at their Banking House in the city of Lynchburg, on Wednesday, the 8th day of May next, at 11 o'clock, A. M., the object of which is to consider the propriety of accepting the amended charter of the said Bank, in accordance with the provisions of the late act of the Legislature. A full meeting of stockholders is desired. By order of the Board. JNO. F. BAUGH, Cashier.
april 5-dacw4w

To my Friends and Customers!

AS it is necessary that I should pay my *own* debts and as I intend to do it at all hazards, I deem it but courtesy to those that owe me by bond or account, due and past due January 1st, 1861, to inform them of the deliberate intention which, in justice to those I owe, has FORCED itself upon me, to place in the hands of a COLLECTOR all claims remaing in my hands unpaid on the 15th day of April next, with instructions to COLLECT. My reasonable friends will appreciate, hence I have no fears of giving offence. I greatly prefer giving this my personal attention, but other departments of my business renders it impossible. Hoping to hear from you in a practicable and tangible way very soon, I am yours truly, L. L. ARMISTEAD,
march 12 No. 140 Main street, Lynchburg.

SALES BY AUCTION

THIS DAY.

House and Lot, Negro Woman, Horses, Waggons and Drays for Sale.

BY virtue of a deed of trust executed to me on the 31st day of August, 1860, by R. F. Sims and wife, I shall proceed, on FRIDAY, the 19TH day of April, 1861, to sell the property conveyed in said deed, to wit: A House and Lot on Diamond Hill, in rear of Captain Samuel McCorkle's (now occupied by said Sims,) fronting 85 feet on —— alley, running back 85 feet; subject to a lien of the Citizens' Building Fund Association of $—. On the lot is a good well of pure water, and the improvements are good. I shall sell at the same time a NEGRO WOMAN, Sarah, used to house work, six horses, and four Waggons or Drays.

The sale will take place in front of the Market-house, commencing at 11 o'clock, a. m.

TERMS:—On the Real estate about $100 in cash will be required, and a credit of four and eight months on the balance of the purchase money, negotiable paper, satisfactorily endorsed, and the title retained until the notes are paid. A credit of sixty days on the personal property, negotiable notes, satisfactorily endorsed. Interest added on all the notes.
apl 13-dtds J. N. GORDON, Trustee.

FUTURE DAYS.

IN pursuance of a decree of the Circuit Court of Amherst, pronounced on the 3d day of April, 1861, in the chancery case of Sale vs. Sale, the undersigned Commissioners, will proceed to sell to the highest bidder, at PUBLIC AUCTION, on the 3RD DAY OF MAY NEXT, at the Market house, in the city of Lynchburg, on a credit of six months, with interest from date, to be secured by negotiable notes satisfactorily endorsed, *NINETEEN LIKELY AND VALUABLE SLAVES*, men, women and children.
RO. M. BROWN,
JNO. O. L. GOGGIN,
LEWIS S. CAMPBELL,
apl 9-d20t Commissioners.

The Charleston Mercury.

TRI-WEEKLY.

DAILY PAPER—TEN DOLLARS PER ANNUM, PAYABLE HALF-YEARLY IN ADVANCE. | VINDICE NULLO SPONTE SUA SINE LEGE FIDES RECTUMQUE COLENTUR. | COUNTRY PAPER—THRICE A WEEK—FIVE DOLLARS PER ANNUM IN ADVANCE.

VOLUME LVI. CHARLESTON, S. C., SATURDAY, APRIL 20, 1861. NUMBER 11,130

The Daily Mercury

IS PUBLISHED EVERY MORNING.

(SUNDAYS EXCEPTED.)

The Tri-Weekly Mercury

ON TUESDAYS, THURSDAYS AND SATURDAYS.

OFFICE, No. 4 BROAD-STREET, CHARLESTON, SOUTH CAROLINA.

TERMS: CASH IN ADVANCE.

DAILY MERCURY, for one year....................$10.00
" " for six months.................. 5.00
" " for three months................. 2.50
" " for less than three months, $1 per month.

Newspaper Dealers and Retail Agents supplied on liberal terms.

TRI-WEEKLY MERCURY, for one year............$5.00
" " for six months............ 2.50
" " for three months.......... 1.25
" " for less than three months, 50c. a month.

FROM THIS DATE, no subscriptions out of the city will be received unless accompanied with the cash.

POSTMASTERS are authorised to act as our Regular Agents in obtaining subscribers and forwarding the money, for which they will be allowed 20 per cent. commission; only, however, when paid in advance.

Subscribers desiring their papers changed, must mention the Post Office FROM, as well as the one TO, which they desire the change to be made.

Gentlemen getting up Clubs of 5, 10, 20, or more, will be supplied at 20 per cent. less than the Regular Rates.

ADVERTISING RATES.

THE MERCURY has now the largest circulation of any paper in the State, and is second in this respect to but few papers in the South; it therefore offers great advantages to business men and others, whose interests require publicity.

ONE SQUARE of 13 lines, solid nonpareil, each insertion, 65 cents, and for each additional line 5 cents.

COMMUNICATIONS of personal interest will be charged as advertising matter.

Orders from without the city to publish Advertisements, Marriage Notices or Obituaries, will not be attended to unless the cash, or an acceptable city reference, accompany the order.

☞ On all bills of $50 and over, 20 per cent. discount is allowed.

The Charleston Mercury

for sale, daily, at the following places:
New York—At the newstands of the La Farge House and St. Nicholas Hotel.
Washington, D. C.—By FRENCH & RICHSTEIN, No. 278 Pennsylvania Avenue.
Memphis, Tenn.—By M. NEALIS.
Wilmington, N. C.—By T. S. WHITAKER.
Lynchburg, Va.—By J. J. CREED.
Clifton, Ala.—By V. J. GIBSON.
Baltimore—By M. H. UMBAUGH, Nos. 4 and 5 Jarvis Building, corner Baltimore and North streets.
Glenwood, Iowa.—By E. C. BLACKMAN.
Jackson, Miss.—By M. L. CARLISLE.
Richmond, Va.—By LEWIS L. SMITH.
Nashville, Tenn.—By R. H. SINGLETON.
Columbia, S. C.—By P. B. GLASS and S. TOWNSEND.
Rock Island, Ill.—By F. H. WARREN.
Chicago, Ill.—MCNALLY & Co.
New Orleans, La.—Newsman under the St. Charles Hotel.

☞ South Carolina Bank Bills taken in payment for subscription to the MERCURY.

TRAVELLER'S GUIDE.

Schedule of the South Carolina Railroad.

FOR AUGUSTA.		LEAVE.	FOR CHARLESTON.	
5.45 a.m.	2.30 p.m.	...Charleston...	3.30 p.m.	4.30 a.m
6.55	3.45	...Summerville...	2.22	3.05
7.25	4.15	...Ridgeville...	1.55	2.30
8.20	5.13	...George's...	1.03	1.25
9.20	6.20	...Branchville...	12.20	12.30
10.05	7.10	...Bamberg...	11.13 a.m.	11.25
10.50	8.05	...Blackville...	10.25	10.30
11.18	8.41	...Williston...	9.58	9.55
11.45	9.20	...Windsor...	9.33	9.22
12.25 p.m.	10.10	...Aiken...	8.52	8.38
12.43	10.33	...Graniteville...	8.32	8.08
1.15	11.15 p.m.	...Augusta...	8.00 a.m.	7.30 p.m.
FOR COLUMBIA.			FOR CHARLESTON.	
8.20 a.m.	8.15 p.m.	...Charleston...	1.00 p.m.	10.30 p.m.
9.35	9.38	...Summerville...	11.45 a.m.	9.00
10.08	10.12	...Ridgeville...	11.15	8.24
11.05	11.17	...George's...	10.18	7.16
12.15 p.m.	12.25 a.m.	...Branchville...	9.25	6.20
1.08	1.25	...Orangeburg...	8.10	5.05
2.00	2.25	...Lewisville...	7.28	4.18
3.15	3.30	...Kingsville...	6.45	3.25
4.30 p.m.	5.20 a.m.	...Columbia...	5.00 a.m.	1.40 p.m

TRI-WEEKLY MERCURY.

SATURDAY, APRIL 20, 1861.

For What Are We Contending?

For more than thirty years the people of South Carolina have been contending against the consolidation of the Government of the United States. Created a Confederation of Republics whose central power, authority and jurisdiction, were carefully limited by the compact of the Constitution, and made conformable to, and within its proper limits, co-ordinate with the original and reserved powers, authority and jurisdiction of the several States of which it was composed, the United States Government has steadily usurped powers not granted—progressively trenched upon State Rights. Not a bald, irresponsible, unchecked, vulgar democracy of mere numbers, was organized by the instrument of Federation between the States; but a well adjusted, duplicate system, harmonious and complementary—the central common Government performing its allotted functions within its prescribed sphere, and each State Government performing all other functions of Government not expressly yielded to the other. If that Government became practically omnipotent, it was clear that it must be a most fearful despotism—a despotism of one section of the Union over the other—a despotism of Manufacing over Agricultural States—of Free States over Slaveholding States. Earnestly and faithfully have our public men at Washington contended against this fatal consummation. It was not for free trade only in 1833—it was not against anti-slavery fanaticism only in 1852—it is not now against our preclusion from our Territories, or the vulgar crew who fill the high places at Washington, that we have set up for ourselves a separate destiny. These are all effects of one great cause—the consolidation of the Federal Government. As *facts*, we have been obliged to meet them—but the facts themselves were comparatively insignificant. They were like the ship money which HAMPDEN refused to pay—like the three pence a pound on tea, which our fathers resisted. They proved to us that we were the slaves of a consolidated despotism—that self government, and the security which self government alone can impart—and liberty, and the princeless self-esteem and proud repose, which liberty only can inspire—were no longer our inheritance or possession. It was in vain that South Carolina endeavored to prove that this despotism existed. We had the forms of a free representative government. There was a party in the Northern States *professing* those principles of limitation and restriction, which might yet be restored to ascendency in the government, and make it again a free government. There was a deep reverence and attachment to the Union, which blinded the understandings of some of the brightest intelligences of the South. These all conspired to carry the South on in the chains of a sectional despotism, which looked, in its final consummation, to nothing short of our absolute subjection and ruin. South Carolina, by her secession, forced the test of the nature of the government under which we lived. It has proved itself. As one scale of hypocrisy after another fell off of its poisonous surface, it stood forth a pure, fierce monster of despotism. The *National Intelligencer*, of Washington, for forty years the central organ of Consolidation, identifies its policy with the New York *Tribune*. BLAIR, the mouth-piece of JACKSON Democracy in 1833, and JOHNSON, of Tennessee, its modern prototype, and DOUGLAS and BUCHANAN, now join with LINCOLN and CHASE and SEWARD in the grand effort to establish, *by the sword*, what has long existed as a policy—*the despotism of a consolidated government under the Constitution of the United States.* The matter is now plain. State after State in the South sees the deadly development, and are moving to take their part in the grand effort to redeem their liberties. It is not a contest for righteous taxation. It is not a contest for the security of slave property. It is a contest for freedom and free government, in which everything dear to man is involved. Shall we submit to the sectional and remorseless despotism of a majority of the Northern States, with no restraints on their lawless will, no checks on their omnivorous rapacity? That is the question. Every man, every boy in the South answers No! And they will fight the foul usurpers and tyrants, if they dare the issue of war, as long as the streams run and the sun shines on our vallies.

Washington City.

We sincerely hope that no effort will be made by citizens of the South to take possession of the city of Washington, and to expel the officials of the Government of the United States from their abodes or offices. If any such effort is made before Virginia and Maryland shall have seceded from the Union of the United States, it will be very disastrous to the cause of secession. It will raise the State pride of the citizens of these proud Commonwealths, who will not be able to see, with indifference, their territories lawlessly invaded and used for an unlawful purpose. And when these States have seceded, it will be for *them* to settle their relations towards Washington. The course of JAMES the Second, we think, will be followed. That Scotch cap and military cloak will again be called into service; and the Black Republican horde, who now defile the high places at Washington, will fly like rats out of a burning barn. Let them go. Do not pollute the soil of Virginia or Maryland with their mean blood. Let them go. To keep them in Washington, after Virginia and Maryland have seceded, you will have to put them in a three-story jail. Do not dignify them by chasing them—much less killing them.

HENRY WARD BEECHER ON WAR.—Rev. HENRY WARD BEECHER preached a war sermon in Brooklyn on Sunday. Of course the South and slavery were denounced. Here are a few extracts from his sermon:

"We must draw the lines close. Let men take sides one way or the other; let every man show his hand; we want no middle men, no shufflers; all must now stand each for himself on this great question. He who is not with us and for us is against us. Great men have spoken on this subject eloquently and feelingly, but the guns of Sumter have spoken more than them all. As for me, I am determined. I'll have no commerce nor dealings henceforth with a foe to liberty. No man shall come to my house, or receive my hospitality, or break my bread, or share my roof, who has feelings of hostility to liberty, unless he comes as a converted sinner, and I shall treat any and every one who comes in my way, who is false to his country and the hour we live in, as a traitor, for such he is.

"Let this matter be settled now. Let it never come up again. If war must come, let us meet it; it's better to brave it thoroughly now; to brave, if necessary, a protracted war, so that it is a final one, than for twenty years to come be troubled with an intermittent breaking out at every period. It has got to be settled one way or the other. The North has the population, the means, and the courage—for there is no such breadth of courage at the South as there is at the North. "The Northern men," said that illustrious general—that tried patriot—that noble man—Gen. Scott—"are hard to get into a fight, but most terrible fellows when once in." [Applause, suppressed.] The North abhors war, but if it enters upon a contest, I can wish its detractors no more punishment than that they stand in the ranks of their opponents.

"Yesterday morning affairs looked blue enough: but last night we slept peaceably, believing that all was well. Again this morning we hear of the striking of our flag, and this evening doubts were thrown upon the wisdom of the action of that gallant soldier, Anderson. I came hither with a sorrowful heart, sad and somewhat cast down; but since I have reached this desk, a despatch has been handed me, coming through the hands of one of our country's most illustrious defenders, saying that "Sumter is reinforced, and Moultrie is the fort which lies in ruins." [To describe the scene which ensued, says the *Times*, surpasses our ability—it beggars description—cheers, huzzas, and shouts made the building ring—the waving of hats and handkerchiefs, and the simultaneous uprising of many hundreds of people made the scene a most remarkable one. Mr. Beecher was, of course, wrongfully informed.]

THE MERCHANTS of New Orleans are quite patriotic. Many of them hearing of the wishes of clerks to enlist in the service of the Confederate States, informed them that their salaries would be continued and their places reserved for them on their return. A large grocery house furnished four of its employees for Pensacola on these liberal conditions.

Privateering.

We publish in our issue to day the Proclamation of President DAVIS in reference to the issue of Letters of Marque and Reprisal. To avoid any misunderstanding and prevent comment arising from the supposition that the President intends to assume the authority and responsibility of issuing these himself, without the action of Congress, we would say that the Proclamation is merely a *preparatory* indication of what he intends to recommend to Congress, and what we have no doubt Congress will do and ought to do, in the event that war becomes *inevitable*. The secession of Virginia and the Frontier Southern States may command the peace even from the silly fanatics who at present rule Washington. The South does not want war. We stand on the defensive. But, if the Northern Government choose to have war, they can and will have it, they may rest assured.

In view of the recent proclamation of President DAVIS, the extract which we give below from KENT'S Commentaries, in which the subject of privateering is ably treated, will be read with interest. The United States Government has persistently refused to surrender the right to resort to "this licentious practice," and Mr. MARCY, while Secretary of State under President PIERCE, resisted the attempt of the European powers to abolish it, with great determination, and in very cogent reasoning. He repulsed the pretences of England and France, on this subject, in a masterly manner. It will not, therefore, excite the indignation of those great commercial nations that the Southern Confederacy should administer a taste of this physic to the Yankee shipping interest. In fact, it will not be difficult to find in their ports vessels and crews who will accept commissions of marque and reprisal. It is certain that there will be no difficulty in finding Northern capitalists who, in the dull times fast coming upon Northern shipping interests, will be willing to organize freebooting expeditions to prey on the commerce of their own fellow-citizens. When an honest penny can be turned in the slave-trade, Yankee ship-owners have not been slow to engage in it, notwithstanding the vulgar prejudices of Faneuil Hall. It is not likely, therefore, that patriotic scruples will deter the same class of men from going into a business which, while enriching them individually, will punish the section which has helped so much to destroy their country's prosperity:

It was the received opinion in ancient Rome, in the times of Cato and Cicero, that one who was not regularly enrolled as a soldier, could not lawfully kill an enemy. But the law of Solon, by which individuals were permitted to form associations for plunder, was afterwards introduced into the Roman law, and has been transmitted to us as a part of their system. During the lawless confusion of the feudal ages, the right of making reprisals was claimed and exercised, without a public commission. It was not until the fifteenth century that commissions were held necessary, and began to be issued to private subjects in time of war, and that subjects were forbidden to fit out vessels to cruise against enemies without license; and there were ordinances in Germany, France and England to that effect. It is now the practice for maritime states to make use of the voluntary aid of individuals against their enemies as auxiliary to the public force; and Bynkershoeck says that the Dutch formerly employed no vessels of war but such as were owned by private persons, and to whom the government allowed a proportion of the captured property, as well as indemnity from the public treasury. Vessels are now fitted out and equipped by private adventurers, at their own expense, to cruise against the commerce of the enemy. They are duly commissioned, and it is said not to be lawful to cruise without a regular commission. Sir Matthew Hale held it to be depredation in a subject to attack the enemy's vessels, except in his own defence, without a commission. The subject has been repeatedly discussed in the Supreme Court of the United States, and the doctrine of the law of nations is considered to be, that private citizens cannot acquire a title to hostile property, unless seized under a commission, but they may still lawfully seize hostile property in their own defence. If they depredate upon the enemy without a commission, they act upon their peril, and are liable to be punished by their own sovereign, but the enemy are not warranted to consider them as criminals, and as respects the enemy, they violate no rights by capture.

Such hostilities, without a commission, are, however, contrary to usage, and exceedingly irregular and dangerous, and they would probably expose the party to the unchecked severity of the enemy, but they are not acts of piracy. Vattel, indeed, says, that private ships of war, without a regular commission, are not entitled to be treated like captures made in a formal war. The observation is rather loose, and the weight of authority undoubtedly is, that non-commissioned vessels of a belligerent nation may at all times capture hostile ships without being deemed, by the law of nations, pirates. They are lawful combatants, but they have no interest in the prizes they may take, and the property will remain subject to condemnation in favor of the government of the captor, as *droits of the admiralty*. It is said, however, that, in the United States, the property is not strictly and technically condemned upon that principle, but *jure reipublicæ*; and it is the settled law of the United States, that all captures made by non-commissioned captors, are made for the government.

In order to encourage privateering, it is usual to allow the owners of private armed vessels to appropriate to themselves the property, or a large portion of the property they may capture; and to afford them and the crews other facilities and rewards for honorable and successful efforts. This depends upon the municipal regulations of each particular power, and as a necessary precaution against abuse, the owners of privateers are required, by the ordinances of the commercial states, to give adequate security that they will conduct the cruise according to the laws and usages of war, and the instructions of the government, and that they will regard the rights of neutrals, and bring their prizes in for adjudication. These checks are essential to the character and safety of maritime nations. Privateering, under all the restrictions which have been adopted, is very liable to abuse. The object is not fame or chivalric warfare, but plunder and profit. The discipline of the crews is not apt to be of the highest order, and privateers are often guilty of enormous excesses, and become the scourge of neutral commerce. They are sometimes manned and officered by foreigners, having no permanent connection with the country, or interest in its cause. This was a complaint made by the United States, in 1819, in relation to irregularities and acts of atrocity, committed by private armed vessels, sailing under the flag of Buenos Ayres. Under the best regulations, the business tends strongly to blunt the sense of private right, and to nourish a lawless, and fierce spirit of rapacity. Efforts have been made, from time to time, to abolish the practice. In the treaty of amity and commerce between Prussia and the United States, in 1785, it was stipulated that, in case of war, neither party should grant commissions to any private armed vessel to attack the commerce of the other. But the spirit and policy of maritime warfare will not permit such generous provisions to prevail. That provision was not renewed with the renewal of the treaty. A similar attempt to put an end to the practice was made in the agreement between Sweden and Holland, in 1675, but the agreement was not performed. The French legislature, soon after the breaking out of the war with Austria, in 1792, passed a decree for the total suppression of privateering, but that was a very transitory act, and it was soon swept away in the tempest of the revolution. The efforts to stop the practice have been very feeble and fruitless, notwithstanding that enlightened and enlarged considerations of national policy have shown it to be for the general benefit of mankind to surrender the licentious practice, and to obstruct as little as possible the freedom and security of commercial intercourse among the nations.

THE MILITARY FORCE IN WASHINGTON.—The Washington correspondent of the Petersburg *Express* says:

"Certain it is, that there are over 10,000 secretly well-equipped gentlemen in the city, and the surrounding cities and country, ready, at a moment's call, to flock to the standard of a certain military man whose name I had rather not mention. This is no surmise, but certain knowledge. When to expect the call to be made, or what will be deemed sufficient cause for making it, I do not know. But should this secret force be called out, there is danger of there not being much bloodshed, for the city force will make scarcely a decent resistance. The oath required previous to the enlistment of volunteers has occasioned much difficulty. Not only have two of the finest companies in the District been completely broken up, but there is scarcely a company whose number has not been greatly reduced by this requirement. Besides this fact, there is great dissatisfaction manifested in the ranks of the Federal troops. Scarcely a day passes without an instance of desertion.—Over 200 men, from the 900 that have been stationed in the city since the inauguration of the revolution, have deserted. A day or two since 20 marines left at once for the South, and the officers privately assure the citizens of their real intentions and determination as to carrying out Lincoln's policy."

UNACCOUNTABLE.—Nothing could more strongly illustrate the madness which rules the hour than the fact that a considerable number of the citizens of Washington, some of them holders of real property, are rabid secessionists.—*Washington Star.*

Current Literature.

We say *current* literature, but we opine that literature of all kinds, save that of war, has but little currency, and commands but little, in the shape of cash, at this moment. Most of the publishers have either gone by the board, or have safely housed themselves under it, hiding from the storm. Several have made very shocking failures. Few continue to publish, and these only do so sparingly, to keep their hands in practice. Of these, the most active are HARPER & BROTHERS, APPLETON & Co., TICKNOR & FIELDS, and LIPPINCOTT & Co. There may be others, but we do not get their issues. From HARPER & BROTHERS we get five volumes of their very pretty pocket and school edition of the Classics, including "Euripides," "Virgilius" and "Thucydides." They also send us volume *five* of MACAULAY'S "History of England," all that he left in manuscript, except a few detached and blotted fragments. The volume is edited by his sister, Lady TREVALYAN. It brings the narrative down to the death of King WILLIAM, March, 1702. The portions we have read are clear, forcible, picturesque and highly interesting, showing no falling off in the resources of the writer. We owe, to the same publishers, a duodecimo entitled "The Ordeal of Free Labor in the British West Indies," by Wm. G. SEWALL. This work consists of letters on free labor in the British West Indies, originally written for that most scoundrelly sheet, the New York *Times*, but subsequently enlarged and revised. The author in his preface tells us that "it is not designed, in this work, to draw from the results of British emancipation any inference, or to point any conclusion, favorable or unfavorable, to slave labor in the United States," &c. Of course, then, the value of the publication will depend wholly upon the fidelity of the writer in his report of the facts. In regard to these, as we have not examined the volume, we shall venture to say nothing. But we cannot but regard it as quite a suspicious circumstance that the writer should have chosen such a medium as the New York *Times* for his original publication of letters designed to be honest of statement and forbearing of opinion, when the subjects were slavery and emancipation. How any sort of truth should seek such an organ for utterance, is surprising enough. To HARPER & BROTHERS we also owe a very pretty and pleasant volume, entitled "The Wits and Beaux of Society," by that clever couple, GRACE and PHILIP WHARTON, to whom we are indebted for a work of similarly pleasant reading, called "The Queens of Society," which, no doubt, most of our readers have dawdled over gratefully, in moments of pleasant idlesse and reverie. The conspicuous "*centres*," in the present volume, gathering around them a host of satellites, are GEORGE VILLIERS, DE GRAMMONT, ST. EVREMOND, ROCHESTER, Beau FIELDING, CONGREVE, Beau NASH, Duke of WHARTON, Lord HARVEY, STANHOPE (CHESTERFIELD), Abbé SCARRON, ROUCHEFOUCAULT, ST. SIMON, HORACE WALPOLE, SELWYN, SHERIDAN, BRUMMELL, HOOK, SYDNEY SMITH, Bubb DODDINGTON, &c. A full book; racy; teeming with anecdote, and copious in biographical detail; with good life portraits occasionally, and some figures at full length; illustrated by numerous pictures, showing groups, costume of the time, &c. A book to last one through the longest day or journey.—"*Trumps*, a novel," by Mr. GEORGE CURTIS—whose opinions of Southern men and women are so unfavorable, that his chance is to receive more *kicks* from the one than *kisses* from the other;—has been gathered up, from the serial into the book form; but as nobody seems to have any opinion of *it*, why should we be at the trouble of making one?—especially as we have never read it—and—never mean to read it.

APPLETON & Co., we perceive, have published volume *eleven* of their great Cyclopedia, but the copy sent us (as we are advised) has not yet come to hand.

LIPPINCOTT & Co., Philadelphia, have assumed the publication, *serially*, of the English-American-German Conversations-Lexicon, began in this country by the APPLETONS, in whose hands it reached some twenty numbers. No doubt a most valuable Cyclopedia, for the people of universal knowledge. Oh! if making people universally learned, *could* make them universally clean, decent, truthful and honest, we might, from these admirable works, anticipate the rapid coming of the millennium! The same publishers announce a new and complete work on the "Birds of North America," to be edited by SPENCER F. BAIRD, Assistant Secretary of the Smithsonian Institution, with the help of the Ornithologists. Text and Atlas will be separate; and sold together, or separately. The volume of text will contain more than a thousand pages; the Atlas will include 100 plates quarto; the specimens, chiefly from the Smithsonian Museum; the price of the former $5, the latter $15. See RUSSELL & JONES for all these works.

FOR THE MERCURY.

Has the President of the Confederate States a Right to Issue Letters of Marque and Reprisal?

"*Inter arma silent leges.*"

Your paper of this morning contains President DAVIS' Proclamation, "inviting all those who may desire service in private armed vessels on the high seas, to make application for commissions or letters of marque and reprisal to be issued under the Seal of these Confederate States." The question I propose for your consideration, is this: Has the *President* of the Confederate States the power to issue "letters of marque and reprisal under the Seal of these Confederate States?"

There cannot be two opinions upon the subject. He has no such power. The Provisional Constitution of the Confederate States, under which he is acting, has distinctly and unequivocally vested this power in "the Congress" alone, and has no where given a particle of power over this subject to the President.

In the sixth section of the First Article of the Constitution, granting powers to *Congress*, are the following words: "To declare war, *grant letters of marque and reprisal*, and make rules concerning captures on land and water." Here, the power to grant letters of marque and reprisal is vested in Congress alone, and follows the power "to declare war." President DAVIS has just as much power "to declare war" against the United States as to grant letters of marque and reprisal. He has power to do neither. Both are exclusively within the authority of the Congress of the Confederate States.

If you will turn to the second section of the Second Article of the Constitution, ordaining the powers vested in the President, you will find that his whole military power consists in the following clause: "The President shall be Commander-in-Chief of the Army and Navy of the Confederacy, and of the militia of the several States when called into actual service of the Confederacy."

I suppose it requires no argument to show that where a power is not granted in the Constitution to the President, he cannot have it; and that where it is *expressly granted to Congress*, that of itself is an absolute negation of it to any other department of the Government.

A CAROLINIAN.

STEAM AS A DEFENSIVE AGENT.—All the U. S. vessels are provided with engines for pouring volleys of hot water upon their assailants. We trust that the Southern defences will all be supplied with this efficient agent. We are naturally a hospitable people in the South, and ought to give the new comers a reception appropriate to their merits. Scalding and skinning is the very least mark of distinction we can bestow upon these invading swine.

A NOTEWORTHY FACT.—The New York *Tribune*, of the 13th, speaking of the despatches from General Beauregard to President Davis, which were received in New York a few hours after they were sent to Montgomery, says this is doubtless the first instance in the history of war where a despatch from a general in the field to his own government was read on the day it was written, in a hostile city nearly 800 miles distant.

DEATH OF A DISTINGUISHED ALABAMIAN.—The Eufaula *Spirit of the South* announces the death of Major B. F. Treadwell of that city, after a short illness. Major T. represented Barbour County in the State Legislature in the session of 1844, and was a prominent participant in the exciting scenes in Kansas in 1856.

FORT SUMTER.

Official Correspondence Between General Beauregard and Major Anderson, Previous to the Bombardment.

[Copy.]

HEADQUARTERS PROVISIONAL ARMY, C. S. A.,
Charleston, S. C., April 11, 1861—2, p. m.

SIR: The Government of the Confederate States has hitherto forborne from any hostile demonstration against Fort Sumter, in the hope that the Government of the United States, with a view to the amicable adjustment of all questions between the two Governments, and to avert the calamities of war, would voluntarily evacuate it. There was reason at one time to believe that such would be the course pursued by the Government of the United States, and under that impression my Government has refrained from making any demand for the surrender of the fort.

But the Confederate States can no longer delay assuming actual possession of a fortification commanding the entrance of one of their harbors, and necessary to its defence and security.

I am ordered by the Government of the Confederate States to demand the evacuation of Fort Sumter. My Aids, Colonel CHESNUT and Captain LEE, are authorized to make such demand of you. All proper facilities will be afforded for the removal of yourself and command, together with company arms and property, and all private property, to any post in the United States which you may elect. The flag which you have upheld so long and with so much fortitude under the most trying circumstances, may be saluted by you on taking it down.

Colonel CHESNUT and Captain LEE will, for a reasonable time, await your answer.

I am, sir, very respectfully,
Your obedient servant,
(Signed) G. T. BEAUREGARD,
Brigadier General Commanding.

Major ROBERT ANDERSON, Commanding at Fort Sumter, Charleston Harbor, S. C.

[Copy.]

HEADQUARTERS, FORT SUMTER, S. C.,
April 11th, 1861.

GENERAL: I have the honor to acknowledge the receipt of your communication demanding the evacuation of this fort; and to say in reply thereto that it is a demand with which I regret that my sense of honor and of my obligations to my Government prevent my compliance.

Thanking you for the fair, manly and courteous terms proposed, and for the high compliment paid me,

I am, General, very respectfully,
Your obedient servant,
(Signed) ROBERT ANDERSON,
Major U. S. Army Commanding.

To Brigadier General G. T. BEAUREGARD, commanding Provisional Army C. S. A.

[Copy.]

HEADQUARTERS PROVISIONAL ARMY, C. S. A.,
Charleston, April 11, 1861—11 p. m.

MAJOR: In consequence of the verbal observations made by you to my Aids, Messrs. CHESNUT and LEE, in relation to the condition of your supplies, and that you would in a few days be starved out if our guns did not batter you to pieces—or words to that effect;—and desiring no useless effusion of blood, I communicated both the verbal observation and your written answer to my communication to my Government.

If you will state the time at which you will evacuate Fort Sumter, and agree that in the meantime you will not use your guns against us, unless ours shall be employed against Fort Sumter, we will abstain from opening fire upon you. Colonel CHESNUT and Captain LEE are authorized by me to enter into such an agreement with you. You are therefore requested to communicate to them an open answer.

I remain, Major, very respectfully,
Your obedient servant,
(Signed) G. T. BEAUREGARD,
Brigadier-General Commanding.

Major ROBERT ANDERSON, Commanding at Fort Sumter, Charleston Harbor, S. C.

[Copy.]

HEADQUARTERS, FORT SUMTER, S. C.,
2.30, a. m., April 12, 1861.

GENERAL: I have the honor to acknowledge the receipt of your second communication of the 11th inst., by Col. CHESNUT, and to state, in reply, that cordially uniting with you in the desire to avoid the useless effusion of blood, I will, if provided with the proper and necessary means of transportation, evacuate Fort Sumter by noon on the 15th instant, should I not receive, prior to that time, controlling instructions from my Government, or additional supplies; and that I will not, in the mean time, open my fire upon your forces, unless compelled to do so by some hostile act against this fort or the flag of my Government by the forces under your command, or by some portion of them, or by the perpetration of some act showing a hostile intention on your part against this fort or the flag it bears.

I have the honor to be, General,
Very respectfully,
Your obedient servant.
(Signed) ROBERT ANDERSON,
Major U. S. A. Commanding.

To Brigadier General G. T. BEAUREGARD, Commanding Provisional Army C. S. A.

[Copy.]

FORT SUMTER, S. C., April 12, 1861,
3.20 a. m.

SIR: By authority of Brigadier General BEAUREGARD, commanding the Provisional Forces of the Confederate States, we have the honor to notify you that he will open the fire of his batteries on Fort Sumter in one hour from this time.

We have the honor to be, very respectfully,
Your obedient servants,
(Signed) JAMES CHESNUT, jr,
Aid-de Camp.
STEPHEN D. LEE,
Captain S. C. Army and Aid-de-Camp.

Major ROBERT ANDERSON, United States Army, Commanding Fort Sumter.

Webb.

To the Editor of the Charleston Mercury:

SIR: As a Northern man, I have been delighted to hear on all sides "curses loud and deep" upon the blasphemous and cowardly attack of WEBB, of the *Courier and Enquirer*, upon Major ANDERSON, and *par contre coup* upon General BEAUREGARD. The many past turpitudes of this buckram general of the New York press, who embodies all of Falstaff's vices, and some modern ones unknown to that poor knight, without one of his few redeeming traits, although known to your older inhabitants, have been left too far in the past by this swift age to familiarize the present generation with those acts of venality, cowardice and bestiality in his past life, which have prepared those who know him to feel no surprise at any enormity he may strive to perpetrate.

Mr. BIDDLE has long since disappeared in the grave; yet who has forgotten the bribe of fifty-two thousand dollars he paid out of the pockets of the unfortunate stockholders of the United States Bank to produce a somerset of Colonel WEBB'S organ in his favor?

There are two other subsequent atrocities which stamp the Buckram Colonel. The first of these was the prostitution of his journal to the persecution of the lovely and accomplished Mrs. WOOD (LADY LENOX), against whom he stimulated a riotous mob, to gratify his resentment against her husband. The next was his pitiless diatribe against a poor English actor named ANDERSON, with the same motive and result. I do not know what part he took in the Astor Place riot against MACREADY.

Rest assured that this hoary debauchee does not represent any respectable portion of the citizens of New York, and is solely the exponent of his own perverse opinions and soured temper. His sheet is now but a huge advertising almanac, which its subscribers take from habit. After all his bitterness and invective during the late campaign, it would seem that the degrading offer of the post at Constantinople must have so wounded his vanity as to have bereft him of all his slender remaining stock of sense or decency.

But the hand of God has not been idle—age, disease and infirmity are now the just portion of this foul-mouthed disgrace to your profession. His racked frame, which still retains a Luciferian will, if not power, for evil, is now but a plague-hospital—the den of an impotent Caliban.

I trust, therefore, that your readers will not identify the atrocity to which I have alluded with the feelings and opinions of any decent social or political faction in New York. In his ardor to defend the Administration, and perhaps the prudent fleet, this reckless and thoroughly unscrupulous partisan would be ready to slander his own father, if by so doing he could produce a "diversion" in public opinion, and buy his way into office and emolument.

Yours respectfully,
CHARLESTON, April 18, 1861. VIATOR.

ARRIVAL OF BIG GUNS.—Yesterday four of the immense Columbiads that were captured at Baton Rouge when our State authorities took possession of the Arsenal, arrived here, and will be placed in positions to defend the approaches to the city as soon as practicable. There are a few more of the same sort yet to arrive. Hurry up these "baby-wakers."—*New Orleans Bee, 15th.*

FORT SUMTER.

Official Correspondence Between General Beauregard and Major Anderson, Previous to the Bombardment.

[Copy.]

HEADQUARTERS PROVISIONAL ARMY, C. S. A.,
Charleston, S. C., April 11, 1861—2, p. m.

SIR: The Government of the Confederate States has hitherto forborne from any hostile demonstration against Fort Sumter, in the hope that the Government of the United States, with a view to the amicable adjustment of all questions between the two Governments, and to avert the calamities of war, would voluntarily evacuate it. There was reason at one time to believe that such would be the course pursued by the Government of the United States, and under that impression my Government has refrained from making any demand for the surrender of the fort.

But the Confederate States can no longer delay assuming actual possession of a fortification commanding the entrance of one of their harbors, and necessary to its defence and security.

I am ordered by the Government of the Confederate States to demand the evacuation of Fort Sumter. My Aids, Colonel CHESNUT and Captain LEE, are authorized to make such demand of you. All proper facilities will be afforded for the removal of yourself and command, together with company arms and property, and all private property, to any post in the United States which you may elect. The flag which you have upheld so long and with so much fortitude under the most trying circumstances, may be saluted by you on taking it down.

Colonel CHESNUT and Captain LEE will, for a reasonable time, await your answer.

I am, sir, very respectfully,
Your obedient servant,
(Signed) G. T. BEAUREGARD,
Brigadier General Commanding.

Major ROBERT ANDERSON, Commanding at Fort Sumter, Charleston Harbor, S. C.

[Copy.]

HEADQUARTERS, FORT SUMTER, S. C.,
April 11th, 1861.

GENERAL: I have the honor to acknowledge the receipt of your communication demanding the evacuation of this fort; and to say in reply thereto that it is a demand with which I regret that my sense of honor and of my obligations to my Government prevent my compliance.

Thanking you for the fair, manly and courteous terms proposed, and for the high compliment paid me,

I am, General, very respectfully,
Your obedient servant,
(Signed) ROBERT ANDERSON,
Major U. S. Army Commanding.

To Brigadier General G. T. BEAUREGARD, commanding Provisional Army C. S. A.

LATEST by TELEGRAPH.

SATURDAY, APRIL 20. 1861.

THE WAR DECLARED.

Proclamation by the President.

FIRST BLOW AT NORTHERN COMMERCE.

Letters of Marque and Reprisal to be Issued immediately.

&c., &c., &c.

THE NEWS FROM MONTGOMERY.

MONTGOMERY, April 17.—The Proclamation of LINCOLN having at last been received here in a form sufficiently authentic to leave no doubt of its being genuine, President DAVIS has in turn issued to-day the following highly important and spirited Proclamation.

PROCLAMATION.

BY THE PRESIDENT OF THE CONFEDERATE STATES OF AMERICA.

Whereas, ABRAHAM LINCOLN, the President of the United States, has, by Proclamation, announced the intention of invading this Confederacy with an armed force for the purpose of capturing its fortresses, and thereby subverting its independence, and subjecting the free people thereof to the dominion of a foreign power; and *whereas* it has thus become the duty of this Government to expel the threatened invasion, and to defend the rights and liberties of the people by all the means which the laws of nations, and the usages of civilized warfare, place at its diiposal:

Now, therefore, I, JEFFERSON DAVIS, PRESIDENT OF THE CONFEDERATE STATES OF AMERICA, do issue this my Proclamation, inviting all those who may desire, by service in private armed vessels on the high seas, to aid this Government in resisting so wanton and wicked an aggression, to make application for commissions or Letters of Marque and Reprisal, to be issued under the Seal of these Confederate States.

And I do further notify all persons applying for Letters of Marque, to make a statement in writing, giving the name and a suitable description of the character, tonnage and force of the vessel, and the name and place of residence of each owner concerned therein, and the intended number of the crew, and to sign said statement and deliver the same to the Secretary of State, or to the Collector of any port of entry of these Confederate States, to be by him transmitted to the Secretary of State.

And I do further notify all applicants aforesaid that before any commission or Letter of Marque is issued to any vessel, the owner or owners thereof, and the commander for the time being, will be required to give bond to the Confederate States, with at least two responsible sureties, not interested in such vessel, in the penal sum of five thousand dollars; or if such vessel be provided with more than one hundred and fifty men, then in the penal sum of ten thousand dollars, with condition that the owners, officers and crew who shall be employed on board such commissioned vessel, shall observe the laws of these Confederate States and the instructions given to them for the regulation of their conduct. That they shall satisfy all damages done contrary to the tenor thereof by such vessel during her commission, and deliver up the same when revoked by the President of the Confederate States.

And I do further specially enjoin on all persons holding offices, civil and military, under the authority of the Confederate States, that they be vigilant and zealous in discharging the duties incident thereto; and I do, moreover, solemnly exhort the good people of these Confederate States, as they love their country, as they prize the blessings of free government, as they feel the wrongs of the past and these now threatened in aggravated form by those whose enmity is more implacable because unprovoked, that they exert themselves in preserving order, in promoting concord, in maintaining the authority and efficacy of the laws, and in supporting and invigorating all the measures which may be adopted for the common defence, and by which, under the blessing of Divine Providence, we may hope for a speedy, just and honorable peace.

In testimony whereof, I have hereunto set my hand, and caused the Seal of the Confederate States to be affixed, this *seventeenth* day of April, 1861.

By the President.

(Signed) JEFFERSON DAVIS.

R. TOOMBS, Secretary of State.

NEWS FROM WASHINGTON.

[FROM OUR OWN CORRESPONDENT.]

WASHINGTON, April 17—9½ p. m.—The Administration is exultant over the war feeling in the North, and LINCOLN says, bluntly, that the South shall have war just as long as the Free States will furnish the "sinews"—men and money.

Gen. SCOTT proposes to concentrate 35,000 men at this point; 25,000 at St. Louis; 5000 in Western Texas; 25,000 at Fort Pickens; and 1000 to cruise off the coast of the Carolinas. It is generally believed that his suggestions will be acted on.

The most feverish anxiety is manifested to hear news from Richmond. LINCOLN fully anticipates the secession of the Old Dominion, and fears that from that quarter the thunder and the lightning may come together.

The necessary orders will be issued to-morrow to throw heavy reinforcements in Fort McHenry, near Baltimore. This move, it is hoped, will keep Maryland quiet.

WASHINGTON, April 18.—A despatch just received by the Secretary of War (Mr. CAMERON), states that the United States Arsenal at Harper's Ferry, one of the finest in the country, and made famous by being the scene of the JOHN BROWN raid, was seized this morning by the Virginia troops.

Also that the Custom House at Norfolk has been broken into by Governor LETCHER's orders, and the arms carried off.

Also that the Norfolk harbor entrance is effectually blocked up with sunken boats.

The news of the secession of Virginia is generally believed here, and has caused great consternation among the friends of the Administration. A Cabinet meeting is now in session, and the coercionists look very blue.

LATER.

It is rumored and credited here that a formidable force is now marching from Central Virginia ta hold Harper's Ferry.

The *National Intelligencer* of this morning says that "the telegraph yesterday was constantly conveying despatches between the Governors of South Carolina and Virginia, and we are deprived of the use of the wires between Washington and Richmond."

The Northern pepers and despatches are filled with accounts of war preparations on all sides. It is said by the military men here that a few hours hence Washington City will be fully defensible against any force.

THE LATEST.

Ten o'clock, p. m.—The Pennsylvania Regiment arrived here to night. The soldiers are quartered in the old Hall of Representatives. Two more trains loaded with Northern troops are expected to-night.

The most intense excitement prevails here, owing to a very general impression that the Virginia troops will attack the city to-night

Reliable intelligence received here indicates that the Virginia Convention has, in secret session, passed the Ordinance of Secession.

LINCOLN and SCOTT are both surrounded with strong guards.

Markets.

NEW ORLEANS, April 17.—Sales of Cotton to-day, 3500 bales, at 12c. Freights to Liverpool ⅝d.

THE WARLIKE REPORTS.

GREAT NEWS FROM VIRGINIA.

Norfolk Harbor Obstructed.

BALTIMORE, April 18.—Capt. PEARSON, of the Norfolk steamer, just arrived here, reports that the main entrance to the harbor of Norfolk has, *by order of Gov* LETCHER, been obstructed, so as to prevent the U. S. war vessels from leaving, as ordered, upon their mission of coercion. This was effected by sinking boats across the mouth of the channel. Capt. PEARSON was obliged to come up across the flats.

Seizure of Arms, etc.

NORFOLK, April 18.—The U. S. Custom House was broken into last night, and a large quantity of guns, ammunition, etc., stored there, was taken out. The Federal Revenue Cutter was also boarded, and her guns seized.

Effect of the Virginia News.

IN AUGUSTA.

AUGUSTA, April 18.—The news of the secession or reported secession of Virginia, was received here with immense cheering, ringing of bells and general joy. The news was communicated to Mr. PRYOR as he was on the cars departing for Montgomery.

IN MOBILE.

MOBILE, April 18.—The news from Virginia was received here with immense cheering, a salute of an hundred guns and a general ringing of the bells. The people are frantically joyous, and impromptu speeches are being made on the occasion.

THE NEWS FROM MONTGOMERY.

[FROM OUR OWN CORRESPONDENT.]

MONTGOMERY, April 18.—Everybody here is excited and rejoiced at the glorious news from the Old Dominion. The event has been celebrated here in spirited style. The Montgomery True Blues fired a salute of eleven guns—seven for the Confederate States, one for Virginia, one for Memphis, one for Arkansas and one for North Carolina.

The Virginians here are particularly jubilant. They have fired a salute of one hundred guns on their own hook.

The city is a-blaze to night with bonfires, illuminations, fireworks, etc., and speeches are being delivered.

Several letters of marque have already been issued.

REPLIES TO LINCOLN'S PROCLAMATION.

From Tennessee.

NASHVILLE, April 18.—Governor HARRIS, of this State, replies to LINCOLN's call on Tennessee for two regiments of troops, by saying that "Tennessee will not furnish a single man for coercion, but fifty thousand, if necessary, for the defence of our rights or those of our Southern brothers.

From Missouri.

ST. LOUIS, April 18.—Governor JACKSON answers CAMERON by telling him that his "requisition is illegal, unconstitutional, revolutionary, inhuman, diabolical, and cannot be complied with." Missouri won't furnish a single man for such an unholy crusade.

NEWS FROM TEXAS.

GALVESTON, April 17.—The Convention of Eastern Arizona met at Mesilla on yesterday (16th inst.) There was a very numerons attendance. P. T. HERBERT, the Texas Commissioner, was cordially welcomed. A resolution was adopted cordially endorsing the action of the seceding States, declaring that Arizona's interest is with the Southern Confederacy; that she will not recognize LINCOLN's Administration, nor his officers; that the people of Western Arizona be invited to join in this movement; and that a vote be taken on these resolutions on the second Monday in April.

On Sunday last the *Star of the West* was still off Indianola. The *Empire City* and *Mohawk* left on Friday evening, with troops. Their destination was unknown.

Six companies of United States troops under Majors SMITH and SIBLEY, were near Indianola, awaiting reinforcements from the upper frontier.

Major RHETT, late U. S. A., has resigned, and has offered his services to the Confederate States.

Active preparations are making here for defence.

Important from Europe.

War Preparations on the Continent—Cotton Buoyant and Advancing, etc.

HALIFAX, April 17.—The new steamship *Kedar* has arrived from Liverpool with dates to the 6th instant.

GENERAL NEWS.

The appearance of matters on the Continent betokened speedy war.

The French Army, by direction of the Emperor, was drilling constantly for active service.

All the Marshals of France were summoned to attend a Council of War on the 8th inst.

Military operations were about commencing in Italy.

The *Niagara* took out £35,000 in coin.

COMMERCIAL NEWS.

LIVERPOOL, Saturday, April 6.—The sales of Cotton to-day were 20,000 bales.

The market was buoyant, and advancing. The news by the steamship *America* caused ⅛d advance. Breadstuffs and provisions steady. Consols 91⅝@91¾c.

HAVRE, Friday, April 5.—*Tres Ordinaire* quoted at 104. *Bas* 99. Market dull and steady. Sales of the week 4500 bales. Stock on hand 277,000 bales.

THE CONFEDERATE LOAN.—The subscription was continued Thursday with great activity. The total amount subscribed in Charleston is two millions two hundred and sixty thousand dollars. In New Orleans, on the first day, two millions seven hundred thousand dollars were subscribed. These two cities alone will take more than the amount offered. On Wednesday, Savannah subscribed $187,000, and Hamburg, S. C., $72,000. Reports from other places will exhibit a large excess of subscription.

AN ELEGANT SILK FLAG, manufactured for the ladies of Camden, is to be presented to Captain KENNEDY's Company of Volunteers now in service.

FIRST REGIMENT RIFLES, S. C. M.—This fine command, after a prolonged absence from their homes on active duty, will, we learn, be furloughed for a time. Col. M. JENKINS' regiment, we believe, is to relieve them.

REGIMENTAL CHAPLAIN APPOINTED. — Rev. A. J. STAFFORD, private of Capt. HARRINGTON's Company, has been offered, and accepted, the position of Chaplain in the Eighth Regiment South Carolina Volunteers, Col. CARTE, and is now on duty with the detachment, on Sullivan's Island, under command of Lieut.-Col. HENIGAN

REPRIEVE GRANTED.—RICHARD WHITE, who was sentenced to be hung to-day for murder, was Thursday reprieved by his Excellency the Governor, until May 7th. We have heard many express the hope that in view of the late glorious and bloodless victory achieved by our troops, the death penalty in this case might be commuted. Many circumstances are urged besides, which would seem to warrant the exercise of Executive clemency.

PERSONAL.—Rev. Dr. CUMMINGS, of St. Stephen's Church, New York, is now in Charleston, the guest of Bishop LYNCH. Dr. CUMMINGS visits our city for the purpose of fulfilling a promise to preach the sermon at the dedication of Saint Joseph's Church, which was to have taken place next Sunday, but which, in view of the disturbed condition of affairs, has been postponed. The Rev. LEO FILLION, we understand, is to have the pastoral charge of St. Joseph's Church.

TROOPS FROM SOUTH CAROLINA.—The President of the Confederate States has made a requisition on South Carolina for eight thousand troops from this State.

HELP FROM TENNESSEE.—Gov. PICKENS has received from Hon. C. G. MEMMINGER, a despatch stating that Tennessee has offered fifty thousand troops to defend the South, and not one man for LINCOLN. Tennessee is all a-blaze. Tennessee is arming.

THE FIRST GUN.—We are informed that Lieut. H. S. FARLEY, of Captain JAMES' Company, had the honor of firing the alarm or first gun of the battle on the morning of Friday last.

A MEETING was held in the Catholic Church at Columbia yesterday to aid in relieving any of the families of any absent soldiers who may be destitute.

Exciting News from Baltimore.

THE FIRST BLOODSHED.

Resistance to Northern Troops, etc., etc., etc.

BALTIMORE, April 19.—A terrible conflict has occurred this afternoon between the people of this city and a portion of the soldiers of the New York Seventh Regiment.

Several have been killed and wounded.

The whole volunteer military force of the city is under arms, and Governor HICKS has proclaimed martial law.

[The city was considerably excited yesterday afternoon by the above rather meagre despatch, which appeared upon the bulletin boards. Owing to the wires having been cut or otherwise disarranged, no further particulars of this exciting news was sent to us by the agent of the Associated Press; but from a number of conflicting private despatches, which have been kindly furnished us, we glean the following information:

It appears that such detachments of the New York Seventh Regiment as were willing to become the tools of Coercion (the Regiment, as a whole, being opposed to such a cause) reached Baltimore to-day. An excited mob met them upon their arrival at the President-street Station, and began throwing stones at the car containing them. The newly arrived companies abstained from resenting the attack, and thanks to their own prudence, combined with the efforts of the police, succeeded in reaching the Camden Station, whence they were to start for Washington.

A Massachusetts Regiment arriving about the same time was also stoned, and in reply fired upon the populace, killing a number of citizens, and among others several highly esteemed in the community. We hear that Mr. DAVIS, of the firm of DAVIS, PAYNTER & Co., was among those killed At the last accounts the firing was still going on The number of the killed is variously stated from twenty to two hundred.

The city volunteers, who sympathize with the South, had immediately mustered, and Governor HICKS had proclaimed martial law.

JOHN W. GARRETT, the President of the Baltimore and Ohio Railroad Company, had issued orders that the trains upon the Company's road were, upon no pretext, to transport troops either to or from Washington.

The populace had torn up the railroad track to prevent the passage of the trains, and there is reason to believe that the telegraph wires were cut—both those connecting with the North and with the South.]

We have received no further intelligence of the outbreak up to the moment we go to press.—EDITOR MERCURY.]

News from Washington.

WASHINGTON, April 19.—The Alexandria *Gazette* of this morning confirms the rumor, prevalent here yesterday, to the effect that a body of Virginia troops were marching upon Harper's Ferry this morning.

About 400 Pennsylvania troops and Sherman's battery of flying artillery arrived here to-night.

The Proclamation of Gov. LETCHER, of Virginia, denouncing LINCOLN's course, acknowledging the independence of the Confederate States, calling out the whole volunteer force of the State to be ready for immediate service, and refusing to furnish any quota to LINCOLN's coercion army, has caused a great sensation here.

The rapid increase in the number of the Southern resignations is very perplexing to the Administration.

Rejoicings in Mobile.

MOBILE, April 18.—An immense meeting called by the citizens of Virginia, is now progressing. There is the greatest enthusiasm and rejoicing in consequence of the glorious news from the Old Dominion. An effigy representing LINCOLN and ridden upon a rail, has just passed the meeting, causing uproarous merriment. The city is brilliantly illuminated, and the band is playing "Carry me back to Old Virginia's shore."

Rejoicings in New Orleans.

NEW ORLEANS, April 18.—The news of the Secession of Virginia has been received here with great demonstrations of joy, and a salute of one hundred guns. All the newspaper offices are flying the Southern flag.

Kentucky Legislature Convened.

LOUISVILLE, KY., April 19.—Gov. MAGOFFIN, of this State, has issued his proclamation, convening the Legislature in extraordinary session on the 27th instant.

The Confederate States Loan.

MONTGOMERY, April 19.—The Treasury Department has thus far heard that the bids for the new Five Million Loan have reached eight millions. The smaller towns are yet to be heard from.

Montgomery has taken two millions, of which four hundred dollars is taken by two negros, belonging to Gen. HARDAWAY and Col. BIBB.

The defences of Texas and Louisiana are engaging the especial attention of the Government today.

Markets

NEW ORLEANS, April 18.—Sales of Cotton 1000 bales, at 11½ to 12¼. Freights in American vessels ⅝d; in British bottoms ⅝d. Sterling Exchange 4@5 ℘ cent. premium. Exchange on New York par@¼ discount.

REBELS AND TRAITORS.—This is the common epithet bestowed by the Lincoln's press upon the people of the seceded States. The same title was applied by the British and Tories in the Revolution to our ancestors. Even George Washington was styled the "rebel leader, Mr. Washington." It took the "rebels" some time to teach the Tories good manners, but they succeeded at last; nor do we despair altogether of improving the Republican mode of speech, and that at no distant day. George the Third never perpetrated a thousand part of the wrongs against the colonies which Lincoln meditates against the Southern States, and there is no other difference between the two tyrants, except that the one was a getleman and the other is a blackguard.—*Richmond Dispatch.*

JOHN HEART, ESQ.—We were pleased a day or two since, to receive a call from this gentleman, formerly one of the proprietors of THE CHARLESTON MERCURY, but more recently Superintendent of Public Printing at Washington, which latter position he resigned some time since. Mr. Heart is a staunch friend of the Confederate States, and we are glad to see him among us. —*Montgomery Advertiser.*

APPOINTMENTS.—A. G. Hudgins, and John F. Holden, Esqs., resigned cadets from Annapolis, have been appointed midshipmen in the navy of the Confederate States. Lieutenant Ingraham, of Mississippi, has been appointed by the Secretary of War to a First Lieutenancy in the army. Mr. I. belonged to the United States army, and is a relative of Commodore Ingraham.

THERE is much opposition in the Italian Parliament to the idea of making Rome the capital. One deputy said that philosophical ideas would be changed to religious ones if they went there.

A FRENCH EDITOR, criticising the style of the speeches of Jules Favre, says it reminds him "of an ancient orator accompanied by a flute."

ON THE 24th of February last an ærolite fell in Dordogne, of considerable size, in a state of ignition. It has been preserved in the museum of the department.

THE New York papers call upon the loafers, vagrants and rowdies of New York, and also all industrious, but unfortunate men, to seize the present golden opportunity to enlist, receive bounty and soldiers' pay, and become serviceable patriots.

A YOUNG MAN by the name of Samuel Barker, from Washington, D. C., is raising recruits in Terre Haute, Indiana, to join the Southern army.

Immense quantities of rain and snow have recently fallen in the Holy Land. The cisterns at Jerusalem have been filled, to the great satisfaction of the inhabitants, as they have not been before in two hundred years.

Black laces, Cambrai and Lama, the former as good as Chantilly, are now the mode in Paris for trimming. Lama shawls are worn at morning calls, visits to the theatre, and evening toilets.

MESSRS. FORSYTH AND ROMAN, two of the Southern Commissioners to Washington, returned to Montgomery on Monday.

COMMERCIAL.

Latest Dates.

LIVERPOOL .... April 3
HAVRE .... April 1
HAVANA .... April 6

EXPORTS OF THE WEEK.

FOREIGN.

BARCELONA—Spanish brig Sebastian—302 bales Upland Cotton.

RIO DE JANEIRO—Bark Indus—200,000 feet Lumber.

COASTWISE.

BOSTON—Schr Julia Grace—33,000 feet Lumber.

NEWPORT (R I) AND A MARKET—Schr Mediator—13 bales Upland Cotton, 48,195 feet Lumber, &c.

PORTLAND (ME)—Schr Grecian—58,320 feet Lumber.

NEW YORK—Schr Emily—439 bales Upland Cotton, 1000 Hides, 79 tierces Rice, 28 Empty Bbls..... Schr M Y Davis—338 bales Upland Cotton, 311 tierces Rice..... Schr B N Hawkins—681 bales Upland Cotton, 100 tons Old Iron, and 56 Empty Ale Bbls.....Schr Van Name—100 bbls Rosin, and 180,000 feet Lumber.....Steamship Marion—157 casks Rice, 518 bales Upland Cotton, and 50 pkgs Sundries.

PHILADELPHIA—Schr Ney—8 bales Upland Cotton, 6 do Samples, 50 tierces Rice, 28 bales Rope Cuttings, 18 hhds Iron, 37 pkgs Furniture, 125 Empty Bbls.

BALTIMORE—Schr Maryland—65 tierces Rice.....Schr N M Tanner—55,114 feet Lumber.

NEW ORLEANS—Bark Cherokee—510 tierces Rice, 1550 sacks Peas, &c.

ELIZABETH CITY (N C)—Schr Planter—1 tierce Rice and 100 sacks Salt.

COLUMBIA (N C)—Schr Best—1 bbl Flour, 100 sacks Salt.

GEORGETOWN (S C)—Schr C T Smyth—2 tierces Rice, 5 casks Ale, 6 bbls Molasses, 7 bbls Whisky, 200 sacks Salt, &c.

JACKSONVILLE AND FERNANDINA—Steamer Cecile—40 bbls Flour, 20 sacks Salt, 10 casks Cutlery, &c.

IMPORTS—APRIL 18.

MATANZAS—Brig Matron—100 hhds Sugar, 174 hhds, 32 tierces and 42 bbls Molasses, 20,000 Segars, to Mordecai & Co.

CHARLESTON MARKET.

Ending Thursday Evening, April 18.

COTTON.—Received the past week by Railroad, 4041 bales; by water and wagons, 221 bales—together 4262 bales—corresponding week last year, 4236 bales. Exported in the same time to foreign ports, 302 bales; coastwise, 1992 bales; making the total exports of the week 2294 bales, and leaving on hand a stock of 21,921 bales, inclusive of 1342 bales on shipboard not cleared, against a stock of 35,385 bales, and 4720 bales on shipboard same time last year.

The total receipts since our last report amount to 40,887 bales (against 50,533 bales same time last year), making a grand total from the 1st September to the latest dates, of 3,865,821 bales against 4,161,485 bales the same time last year, and 3,409,956 bales the year previous. Decrease since last year, 795,664 bales.

Cleared since, and not included in the above:

RIO DE JANEIRO—Brig West Indian—29 tierces Rice, 127,202 feet Lumber.

NEW YORK—Brig J H Jones—676 bales Upland Cotton, 180 tierces Rice, 79 boxes Copper Ore, &c.

In our last review for the week ending on Thursday evening, the 11th inst., we reported the market as having closed in a very depressed and unsettled state, buyers towards its close having almost entirely withdrawn on account of the threatening political aspect of affairs. The total sales of the week amounted to 2644 bales, of which some 449 bales sold during the last three days at a decline of about a ¼ on previous prices.

The stirring and exciting events with which the past week commenced, and more or less continued up to its close, barred the market almost entirely of purchasers, only two or three English buyers remaining, who, with a very restricted enquiry, confined their operations to 385 bales, at the following particulars: 40 bales at 11¾; 62 at 12; 40 at 12¼; 176 at 12½; 30 at 12¾; 46 at 13¼; and 124 at 13½ cents. Prices having ranged very irregular, we are compelled to omit quotations, with the remark that purchasers were offering at the close of the market about 12c. for Middl ng.

The market for LONG COTTONS has remained at a dead stand, and without a solitary transaction throughout the entire week.

RICE.—The market, which, in consequence of the great events occurring in the beginning of the week, had come to a complete stand, opened yesterday with great activity, and continued so up to its close to day, resulting in the sales of all the available store lots, amounting to some 1500 tierces, at an irregular advance of $⅛ ℘ 100 ℔s. The extremes of sales were from $3⅞ to $3⅞; the bulk at $3½ to $3¾ ℘ 100 ℔s.

ROUGH RICE.—No arrivals.

NAVAL STORES.—The transactions of the past week have been principally in Spirits, for which there was a good demand equal to the receipts. The sales amounted to some 300 casks at 38 cents. We were not apprised of any sales of the old crop of Rosin; and of the new the arrivals were very few. About 30 barrels received, sold at $4.50 ℘ 250 ℔s. Three vessels now loading for British ports have about 4400 barrels Rosin and 700 barrels Spirits on shipboard not cleared.

GRAIN.—There have been no arrivals of any description, and we have consequently no cargo sales to report, either of Corn or Oats. As dealers continue amply supplied for the retail trade, we continue our former quotations, based upon the last sales. Corn ranging from 67@70 cents, and Oats at 38c.

HAY.—The arrivals of the week, amounting to some 300 bales North River, sold on landing on the wharf at $1.40 ℘ 100 ℔s. Holders of store lots appear not anxious to duplicate sales at those figures.

FLOUR.—The receipts of the week have been light, and with a decreasing stock holders have been able to realize during the past week firmer and advancing prices. The sales to bakers and city dealers have ranged at from $7 to $7¾ for Baltimore Super, Charleston inspection, and a lot of 100 barrels Country Super brands sold at $7¾.

BACON.—During the week previous the past the market was nearly swept by the demand by government contractors. The market during the past week has in consequence been almost bare of saleable meat, and no sales to establish a market have been reported to us. We would quote Shoulders nominally, at 10@10½; and Sides at 12@12½, as prices which might be realized in a retail way.

SALT.—There have been no arrivals since our last, but the market remains well supplied. We hear of sales during the past week at from 70@75c. ℘ sack from on shipboard, holders of store lots not offering below 80c.

GROCERIES.—We were informed that there had been quite a lively demand during the past two or three days for the leading articles, in the way of supplying the demand for country orders in particular. Some 50 or 60 hhds. Louisiana Sugars sold from 6¼@8¼c., including common to clarified qualities. Louisiana Molasses at 40c., and Cuba Clayed at 25c. For Coffee there was also a good demand at 16c. for prime Rio.

For other articles, including Bagging, Bale Rope and Domestic Liquors, we have no sales to report, there being no demand whatsoever for either.

STOCKS.—This branch of business has continued during the past week at a perfect stand.

EXCHANGES.—The week previous the past closed upon an entirely unsettled market, inasmuch that we found ourselves compelled to omit quotations. During the past week confidence has been restored, and our Banks at its close negotiating Sterling Bills at from 8@8½ ℘ cent. premium, and Francs 5.27½@5.30—Checking on the North at 2½ @3 per cent. premium.

FREIGHTS—To Liverpool have advanced rapidly since our last, commencing with the engagement of a British vessel at the opening of the week at 5-16d. for square bales, and followed subsequently by two others at ⅜d. and ½d.; the market closing at upward tending rates and with no room at those quoted above. Coastwise rates are entirely nominal, and consequently unquotable, there being so little offering either by steamers or sail vessels.

NEW ORLEANS, April 13.—COTTON.—Arrived since the 9th inst., 7896 bales. Total receipts of the week 14,522 bales. Cleared since the 9th inst., 30,053 bales. Total exports of the week 52,981 bales. Stock on the 12th instant 149,420 bales.

We noticed in our last semi-weekly report a very quiet market, with sales on a limited scale at irregular prices, indicating towards the close a decline of ¼@½c., but we stated at the same time that as factors generally adhered to their previous pretensions, we would make no change in our quotations. On Wednesday, however, there was more disposition to meet the demand at the concessions demanded, and 2250 bales changed hands, at irregular prices, but mostly on the basis of the reduced figures of 12½@12¾c. for Middling. On Thursday the market continued dull and the business was again on a very moderate scale, embracing only 1500 bales, while prices showed increased irregularity, the advantage, if any, being still more on the side of buyers. Yesterday we noticed some enquiry, but it was mostly at figures below the views of factors, and the sales barely reached 2000 bales, while prices were still cheaper. This makes an aggregate for the three days of 5750 bales, and a total for the week of 11,250 bales, buyers for England, France, the Continent and the North participating in the business. With the remark that a considerable portion of the stock is held above the ruling rates, but that in the absence of competition among buyers, the prices actually paid lean to inside figures, we reduce our quotations as below:

Quotations.—Inferior 6½@8; Ordinary 9@9½; Good Ordinary 10@10½; Low Middling 11¼@11½; Middling 12@12¾.

Statement—Stock on hand Sept 1, 1860....bales..73,934
Arrived past three days........7,896
Arrived previously........1,784,114—1,792,010

1,865,944

Exported past three days........30,053
Exported previously........1,686,471—1,716,524

Stock on hand and on shipboard........bales...149,420

SUGAR.—*Louisiana*—We noticed in our last report sales during the early part of the week of 2100 hhds. without any material change in prices, since which, with moderate receipts, the market has continued firm until yesterday, when the demand was slack and the advantage on the side of the buyer, the sales comprising 600 hhds. on Wednesday, mostly on the basis of 5@6c. for Fair to Fully Fair, 600 hhds. on Thursday at the same figures, and 390 yesterday within the range of our quotations. This makes an aggregate of about 1500 hhds., and a total for the week of 3600, taken for the West, our neighboring ports and the city trade, the market closing heavy at the following quotations: Inferior, 3@4; Common to Good Common, 4½@4¾; Fair to Fully Fair, 5@6; Prime to Choice, 6½@7; Centrifugal, 5½@7½. Arrived since the 9th inst. 2570 hhds. 106 bbls. Total receipts of the week 4704 hhds. 118 bbls. Cleared since the 9th inst. for Texas 26 hhds., Florida 4; together, 30 hhds. Total exports of the week 392 hhds. 3 bbls.

FREIGHTS.—Since our semi-weekly report, the European Freight market has exhibited but little activity. The engagements comprise four ships taken for Havre, at ⅞c. for Cotton, one for Marseilles at $11 for Tobacco, and one for Liverpool at 12d for Corn. A British and an American ship laid on for Liverpool. Filling up in American at ⅝d., and a British ship taking Cotton at ⅝d. Coastwise there is nothing doing.

MOLASSES.—The demand has been moderate, but prices have continued steady, the sales since our last report comprising 900 barrels on Wednesday, mostly at 22@24 cents for Fermenting, and 25@26c for choice Reboiled; 800 bbls on Thursday at about the same figures, and 600 yesterday at 12½@16c for Inferior, 18@24 for Common and Fermenting, and 24@26 for Prime. This makes an aggregate for the three days of 2300 bbls, and for the week of 6100, the market closing at the above figures. There has been only a limited demand for half barrels, the sales of which comprise less than 500 packages—closing at 26@28c for Fermenting. Arrived since the 9th instant, 2635 bbls. Total receipts of the week, 4096 bbls. Cleared since the 9th instant, for Texas, 107 bbls; Charleston, 200; Pensacola, 37; together, 844 bbls. Total exports of the week, 529 bbls.

BACON.—The receipts have been more moderate, the demand is fair, and the market has been firm, with an upward tendency in prices. Round lots may be quoted at 7⅞c for Shoulders, 10¼@10½c for Ribbed Sides, and 11@11¼c ℘ ℔ for Clear. The retail demand is met at 8 for Shoulders, 10¾ for Ribbed Sides, 11¼@11½ for Clear Sides, 9½@10 for plain Hams, and 11@12c ℘ ℔ for fancy Sugar-cured. We notice sales of 250 casks in many lots, of which 45 casks Shoulders at 7¾, 57 at 8, 60 do. Ribbed Sides at --, 55 at 10¾, and 30 casks Clear Sides at 11¼c ℘ ℔. Arrived during the past three days 2286 casks, 210 boxes. Cleared for Florida 69, Texas 58, St. Thomas 11 casks.

LARD.—The receipts have been more moderate and the market has remained quiet. We noticed sales early in the week of 300 tierces Prime at 10c, and 175 kegs at 11c, and since then 120 tierces at 10c ℘ ℔. Prime in tierces may be quoted at 9¾@10, and in kegs at 10¾@11c ℘ ℔. The retail demand is supplied at 10¼c for tierces and 11c ℘ ℔ in kegs. Arrived during the past three days 1691 bbls, 1390 kegs. Cleared equal to 14,119 kegs, viz: Boston 294, Texas 825, Bordeaux 1600, Havana 11,200, St. Thomas 200.

WHISKY.—The receipts have been light, the demand is very limited, but the market is well supplied and so dull and unsettled that prices for Rectified are almost nominal. There have been no sales of any importance, excepting 40 bbls Rectified at 20c ℘ gallon. The retail demand for Rectified has been supplied at 22c ℘ gallon. Arrived during the past three days 1144 bbls. Cleared for Florida 83, Texas 184, St. Thomas 40 bbls.

NAVAL STORES—The supply of Spirits Turpentine is moderately fair, but the demand is limited. We quote at 28@30c for that in prime shipping order, and noticed early in the week sales of 50 bbls prime at 29c, and since then 125 bbls at 30c ℘ gallon. Of Rosin the supply on sale is moderate. The lower grades have been in fair demand, and the finer grades are scarce. There have been sales of 2000 bbls at 90c@$1.00 for common and No. 2, and $1.20 ℘ bbl for No. 1.

GUNNY BAGS—We quote as the range 13@15c for light to extra heavy. The market remains quiet but firm.

BAGGING AND BALE ROPE—At retail we quote Kentucky Bagging at 11@14c ℘ yard for hand loom to the best power loom. The last sales reported of hand loom were at 10 cts cash, and 10½ on time, and of power 12c, cash. Of India, 140 bales sold early in the week at the advanced rate of 12c ℘ yard. Rolls retail at 12 and bales at 12½c, and we quote at whoesale 11¾c ℘ yard cash. Of Bale Rope, hand made may be quoted at 7@7½, and machine 7¾@8¼c ℘ ℔. Iron Cotton Ties sell at 5½@6c ℘ ℔.

COFFEE.—The demand during the past week has been more active but at slightly easier prices, the market closing quiet but firm. The sales comprise 7423 bags Rio at a range for extremes of 10¾@13¾c. ℘ ℔. We quote Ordinary at 10½@11, Fair 11½@12¾, Good Fair 13¼@13½c. ℘ ℔. There is no Prime in the market. There have been no arrivals during the past three days. The stock now on hand is about 10,735 bags, against 20,209 at the same date last year.

RICE—*Carolina.*—The supply is fair and the demand is met at 4¼@4½c. ℘ ℔. according to quantity and quality.

MONEY MARKET.—The dangerous aspect of political affairs, which culminated yesterday in actual hostilities at Charleston, has influenced the Money market in an adverse direction, and scarcely anything of importance has been done during the last few days. The few transactions that have come under our notice were at 10@12 ℘ cent., but yesterday there was no disposition to operate at all. The Banks discount most of the prime short paper that is offered.

EXCHANGE.—The Foreign Exchange market has again given way, and drawers meet with obstacles in making negotiations. Clear Sterling has been sold at a range of 106½@107, the latter for the most preferred names. Drafts with Bill-of-Lading, fully equal to Clear, were taken yesterday at 106, and the range for these now is from 105@106. Francs have ruled from 5f.87½@5f.27½, but yesterday the highest offer for the best Bills was 5f.30. A limited business has been done in Sixty-day Bills on New York at a range of 1@1¼ ℘ cent. discount. Strictly prime names were sold yesterday at 1¼. Sight has been in fair request at ¼ premium for Bankers' Drafts, and ⅛@¼ for Bank Checks. Short Sight has sold at par to ¼ premium.

NEW ORLEANS WEEKLY COFFEE STATEMENT.

Arrivals since July 1, direct........bags..267,947
" " " coastwise........267,947
Same time last year, direct........248,417
" " " coastwise........16,278—264,695

Increase of imports this year........3,252
Stock in first hands this day........10,735
Stock in second hands this day........10,735
Same time last year........20,209

Decrease of stock this year........9,474

Sales of the week—683 bags at 13¾c; 528 at 13¼; 359 at 13; 823 at 12¾; 402 at 12½; 407 at 12¼; 1650 at 12; 267 at 11¾; 880 at 11½; 1319 at 11¼; 472 at 11¼; 100 at 10¾; 32 at 11½c Skim'g. Total 7423.

Stock on hand last week........17,855
Received since........17,855
Stock on hand this day........10,735

Taken for consumption........7,120

Market—Ordinary 10½@11; Low Fair to Fair 12½; Good Fair 13¼@13½; Prime — cents.

H. T. LONSDALE, SON & Co.

Comparative Statement of Receipts, Exports and Stocks of Cotton at the following places to the latest dates.

PORTS.	Stocks on hand 1st Sept'r, 1860	1859	Received since 1st September, 1860	1859	Exported to Great Britain since Sept. 1, 1860	1859	Exported to France since Sept. 1, 1860	1859	Exported to Oth'r For. Ports since Sept 1, 1860	1859	Total Exports to For. Ports since Sep. 1, 1860	1859	Shipments to Northern Ports, 1860	1859	Stock on hand and on shipboard, 1860	1859
NEW ORLEANS, April 12	73984	26092	1712868	2008652	1029152	1140108	356877	273841	207637	207927	1587166	1621876	[illegible]	[illegible]	[illegible]	[illegible]
MOBILE, April 12	41682	20106	[illegible]	[illegible]	[illegible]	[illegible]	[illegible]	[illegible]	[illegible]	[illegible]	[illegible]	[illegible]	[illegible]	[illegible]	[illegible]	[illegible]
FLORIDA, April 12	864	907	[illegible]	[illegible]	[illegible]	[illegible]	[illegible]	[illegible]	[illegible]	[illegible]	[illegible]	[illegible]	[illegible]	[illegible]	[illegible]	[illegible]
TEXAS, April 6	8168	2655	[illegible]	[illegible]	[illegible]	[illegible]	[illegible]	[illegible]	[illegible]	[illegible]	[illegible]	[illegible]	[illegible]	[illegible]	[illegible]	[illegible]
SAVANNAH, April 16	[illegible]	[illegible]	[illegible]	[illegible]	[illegible]	[illegible]	[illegible]	[illegible]	[illegible]	[illegible]	[illegible]	[illegible]	[illegible]	[illegible]	[illegible]	[illegible]
Sea Island	[illegible]	[illegible]	[illegible]	[illegible]	[illegible]	[illegible]	[illegible]	[illegible]	[illegible]	[illegible]	[illegible]	[illegible]	[illegible]	[illegible]	[illegible]	[illegible]
CHARLESTON, April 18	[illegible]	[illegible]	[illegible]	[illegible]	[illegible]	[illegible]	[illegible]	[illegible]	[illegible]	[illegible]	[illegible]	[illegible]	[illegible]	[illegible]	[illegible]	[illegible]
Sea Island	[illegible]	[illegible]	[illegible]	[illegible]	[illegible]	[illegible]	[illegible]	[illegible]	[illegible]	[illegible]	[illegible]	[illegible]	[illegible]	[illegible]	[illegible]	[illegible]
NORTH CAROLINA, April 13	600	300	[illegible]	[illegible]	[illegible]	[illegible]	[illegible]	[illegible]	[illegible]	[illegible]	[illegible]	[illegible]	[illegible]	[illegible]	[illegible]	[illegible]
VIRGINIA, March 1	850	875	[illegible]	[illegible]	[illegible]	[illegible]	[illegible]	[illegible]	[illegible]	[illegible]	[illegible]	[illegible]	[illegible]	[illegible]	[illegible]	[illegible]
NEW YORK, April 8	64891	43452	[illegible]	[illegible]	[illegible]	[illegible]	[illegible]	[illegible]	[illegible]	[illegible]	[illegible]	[illegible]	[illegible]	[illegible]	[illegible]	[illegible]
OTHER PORTS, April 6	20204	20416	[illegible]	[illegible]	[illegible]	[illegible]	[illegible]	[illegible]	[illegible]	[illegible]	[illegible]	[illegible]	[illegible]	[illegible]	[illegible]	[illegible]
TOTAL SALES	218997	140445	3865821	4161485	1872828	2175706	583614	516979	315512	388272	2729954	3075957	[illegible]	[illegible]	[illegible]	[illegible]
TOTAL LAST SEASON	140445		4161485		2175706		516979		388272		3075957		[illegible]		[illegible]	
INCREASE	78552						[illegible]						[illegible]		[illegible]	
DECREASE			295664		302878				67760		355003		[illegible]		[illegible]	

We have deducted from New Orleans, 30875 bales; from Mobile .. bales; Charleston 255 bales Sea Islands and 2378 bales Upland Cotton, and from Savannah ... bales Sea Island Cotton and ... bales Uplands—the quantity received at those ports from Florida, Mobile, Texas and Savannah.

Comparative Statement of Cotton and Rice, EMBRACING STOCK ON HAND, RECEIPTS AND EXPORTS.

	1860. Cotton S. I.	Upl'd.	Rice. Bbls.	Same time last sea'n Cotton S. I.	Upl'd.	Rice. Bbls.
Stock on hand Sept. 1	1836	7585	[illegible]	1362	16237	1145
Received since April 11	258	4260	[illegible]	[illegible]	[illegible]	[illegible]
Received previously	19988	291750	[illegible]	[illegible]	[illegible]	[illegible]
Total receipts	[illegible]	[illegible]	111164	27632	447285	[illegible]
Exported since April 11	[illegible]	2294	1172	[illegible]	[illegible]	[illegible]
Exported previously	[illegible]	[illegible]	91079	[illegible]	[illegible]	[illegible]
Total exports	17591	281650	92251	22806	441958	112166
On shipboard not cleared	[illegible]	[illegible]	[illegible]	[illegible]	[illegible]	[illegible]
Consumption and Export by land	90	1842	[illegible]	[illegible]	[illegible]	[illegible]
Burnt	[illegible]	[illegible]	16000	[illegible]	[illegible]	[illegible]
Deduction from total receipts	[illegible]	[illegible]	108589	22939	436673	130206
Remaining on hand April 18	3941	20579	1575	4634	80015	2496

Statement of Cotton and Rice.

EXPORTED TO	From Sept. 1, 1860, to April 18, 1861. S. I.	Upl'd.	Rice.	From Sept. 1, 1859, to April 19, 1860. S. I.	Upl'd.	Rice.
Liverpool	6754	100935	8367	11187	190777	3051
Scotland				50	1443	2
Other Br. ports	24					
Total G. Britain	6778	100935	8367	11237	192220	3053
Havre	3475	25433	3327	6250	56002	6550
Marseilles					214	245
Other Fr. ports		978	709		1922	510
Total France	3475	26411	4036	6250	58138	7305
Holland		5601	222		8245	748
Belgium			1345		1008	1787
North of Europe	16	17179	5924	48	34785	9687
Total N. of Eur'e	16	22780	7491	48	43988	12217
South of Europe		21724	382		22873	405
W. Indies, &c			6681			14691
Total For. ports	10269	171850	21957	17535	317214	37671
Boston	538	27495	7008	289	26682	5781
Rhode Island, &c					2372	
New York	6784	73032	36866	4965	76738	35034
Philadelphia		4242	2880	24	12998	6586
Balt. & Norfolk		5027	7312		5049	7466
New Orleans, &c			12772			16669
Other U. S. ports		13	3416			2959
Total coastwise	7322	109800	70294	5271	124739	74495
Grand Total	17591	281650	92251	22806	441958	112166

Bank Shares, Stocks, &c.

NAMES OF INSTITUTIONS.	Orig'l Cost.	Present Prices.	Last ½ An. Div.
Bank of Charleston, shares..$	100	96 @ ..	$3 50
Do. new issue....do	50	.. @ ..	1 50
South Carolina....do	45	.. @ ..	1 75
State....do	25	.. @ ..	
Union....do	50	.. @ ..	1 75
S. W. Railroad Bank..do..25 / S. Carolina Railroad..do.100	125	97 @ ..	4 25
New Issue	50	35 @ 36	1 75
Planters & Mechanics' Bank	25	23 @ ..	87½
Farmers & Exchange do	25	23 @ ..	1 00
People's Bank	25	25½ @ 26	87½
Commercial (Col'bia) Bank	25	.. @ ..	1 25
Exchange Bank, do	25	.. @ ..	1 25
Charleston Ins. & Trust Co	25	.. @ ..	5 00
South Carolina Insurance Co	25	.. @ ..	1 50
Fireman's Insurance Co	10	.. @ ..	60
Gas Light Company	25	.. @ ..	
State 6 Per Cent. Stock	100	.. @ ..	
State 5 Per Cent. Stock	100	.. @ ..	
City 6 Per Cent. Stock	100	.. @ ..	
City 5 Per Cent. Stock	100	.. @ ..	
Hamburg Bank	50	.. @ ..	2 00
Camden Bank	50	.. @ ..	2 00
Bank of Georgetown	100	.. @ ..	1 00
Merchants' Bank, Cheraw	100	.. @ ..	5 00
Bank of Chester	25	.. @ ..	1 25
Dry Dock	25	.. @ ..	87½
Bank of Newberry	25	.. @ ..	1 00

Purchasing Rates of Exchange by the BANKS.

Bills on England, 8@8½ ℘ cent. prem.
Bills on France, 527½@530.
Bills on New York, 5@10 days, @— ℘ ct. off.
Bills on New York, 30 days, @— do.
Bills on New York, 60 days, @— do.

Comparative Export of Rough Rice and LUMBER FOR THE PORT OF CHARLESTON.

EXPORTED TO	From Sept. 1, 1860, to April 18, 1861. R. Rice, bushels.	Lumber, feet.	From Sept. 1, 1859, to April 19, 1860. R. Rice, bushels.	Lumber, feet.
Liverpool	12905			
London				
Other Br. ports		4100		
Total Gr. Britain	12905	4100		
Havre			8750	
Bordeaux				
Other Fr. ports				
Total France			8750	
North of Europe	65063	14582	82487	43885
South of Europe		778866		1350851
West Indies, &c		559000		1418090
Total For. ports	77968	1356417	91237	2812826
Boston	56286	75591	24853	
Rhode Island		48200		165060
New York	14510	259500	11126	1100478
Philadelphia				894500
Balt. and Norfolk		339731		369020
Other U. S. ports	580	596758		842000
Total coastwise	71276	1319780	35979	3373998
Grand Total	149244	2776197	127216	6186324

Statement of Exports of Wheat, Flour AND NAVAL STORES FOR THE PORT OF CHARLESTON.

EXPORTED TO	From September 1, 1860, to April 18, 1861. Wheat, bushels.	Flour, barrels.	N. Stores barrels.
Liverpool			23756
Other British Ports			4263
Total Great Britain			28019
Havre			68
Other French Ports			
Total France			68
North of Europe			3600
South of Europe			
So. America and West Indies		572	20
Total Foreign Ports		572	31707
Boston			5673
New York		11	20264
Philadelphia			1078
Baltimore and Norfolk			8215
Other United States Ports		1098	972
Total Coastwise		1109	37202
Grand Total		1681	68909

Exports of Cotton and Rice, FROM THE 11TH APRIL TO THE 18TH APRIL, TO WHERE EXPORTED.

	S. I.	Upl'd.	Rice.
Barcelona		302	
Total Foreign		302	
New York		1971	547
Philadelphia		8	50
Baltimore			65
Newport, R. I		13	
New Orleans			510
Total Costwise		1992	1172
Grand Total		2294	1172

List of Vessels loading for Foreign Ports

PORTS.	1860. Gr. Britain	France	Other Ports	1859. Gr. Britain	France	Other Ports
New Orleans, April 14	27	11	8	46	11	21
Mobile, April 14	7	0	4	18	4	6
Florida, April 12	1	0	0	6	0	0
Savannah, April 16	16	0	6	6	0	1
Charleston, April 18	6	0	0	6	0	3
New York, April 8	26	8	80	14	4	92
Other Ports, April 12	10	0	13	8	1	10
Total	93	19	111	99	20	189

Wholesale Prices.

ARTICLES.	$ cts.	$ cts.
BAGGING, Gunny	12	12¾
BALE ROPE, Western and Northern	9	9¾
BACON, Hams	14	14¾
Shoulders	10	10½
Sides	12	12¾
COFFEE, Rio	15	16
CANDLES, Adamantine	18	22
Charleston, Tallow	..	15
FLOUR. Baltimore	7	7¾
GRAIN, Corn, No. Carolina and Baltim'e. Western in bags, bags included.	66	70
Oats	38	..
GUANO, Peruvian, long ton	70	..
Do. Mexican	25	..
Jarvis and Baker's Island—short ton	40	..
Kettlewell's Renovator do	..	..
Do Plaster—long ton	..	..
Manipulated Guano, Nos 1 and 2	..	..
Rhode's Super-Phosphate Lime	..	..
Ichaboe	50	..
Sombrero	30	..
Elide	50	..
HAY, North River	1 40	..
LARD, barrels and kegs....℔	12	13
MOLASSES, New Orleans...gal	38	40
Cuba Clayed	25	26
Do. Muscovado	..	..
NAILS, 4d. to 20d....℔	3¼	3¾
NAVAL STORES.		
Turpentine, Virgin	..	..
Pale Rosin	..	..
Rosin, No. 1	1 75	..
Do. No. 2	1 20	..
Do. Common	1 ..	..
Spirits Turpentine...gal	..	33
RICE	3½	3¾
SUGAR, Louisiana, raw...℔	6¼	8
Do. Clarified	8¼	8¾
Cuba Muscovado	..	7½
Crushed	..	..
Do. do. Loaf	..	..
SALT, Liverpool Coarse...sack	70	80
SHOT, all sizes	7¼	8
SPIRITS—Gin, Holland	..	..
Rum, Northern	..	..
Whisky, Western	53	..

Stock of Cotton in the Interior Towns, NOT INCLUDED IN THE RECEIPTS.

TOWNS.	1860.	1859
Augusta and Hamburg, April 1	24241	34964
Macon, Ga., April 1	4874	11527
Columbus, Ga., April 1	7922	21112
Montgomery, Ala		
Memphis, Tenn		
Columbia, S. C		

Consignees per South Carolina Railroad, April 18.

432 bales Cotton, 30 bbls Flour, 138 bushels Wheat, Naval Stores, Mdse, Cattle, &c. To J & J D Kirkpatrick, L M Hatch, Caldwell, Blakely & Co, Reeder & DeSaussure, Graeser & Smith, Colcock, McCally & Malloy, Smith & Dulin, Sims & Barksdale, E Barnwell & Son, Shingler & Hale, Jacobs & G, Claussen, E B Stoddard & Co, W B Smith & Co, C Froneberger, J E Adger & Co, Capt Thomas, Deveaux & Heyward, Ravenel, Huger & Milliken, and Order.

MARINE NEWS.

Charleston.—Lat. 32.47 N. Lon. 79.27 W.

SUN RISES 5H. 30M. SETS 6H. 29M.—HIGH WATER, 1H. 59M.

WIND—S. W.

ARRIVED.

April 18.

Spanish brig Vencedor, Millet, Matanzas, 12 days. Ballast. To Hall & Co.

IN THE OFFING.

Ship John Fraser, from Liverpool.

CLEARED.

April 18.

Brig West Indian, Arnet, Rio de Janeiro—Brown & Hyams.
Brig J H Jones, Mills, New York—Holmes & Stoney.
Schr Pennsylvania, Munroe, Georgetown (S C)—Master.
Schr C T Smyth, Westerlund, Georgetown (S C)—Master.

WENT TO SEA.

April 18.

Schr F C Smith, Anderson, Georgetown (S C).

FROM CHARLESTON.

Ship Samoset, McNear, Havre, March 29.
Schr Lewis S Davis, Alden, New York, April 15.
Schr John Aumack, Pearce, New Orleans, April 14.

LIST OF VESSELS IN THE PORT OF CHARLESTON APRIL 18, 1861.

Steamships........8
Ships........8
Barks........5
Terns........0
Brigs........6
Schooners, over 100 tons........13

Total........40

MEMORANDA.

The brig Roamer, Thompson, from Georgetown, S C, arrived at Boston April 13.

The schr F F Randolph, Miller, which arrived at New York April 15, from Georgetown, S C, had very heavy east and northeast gales the entire passage. 12th inst, of Cape Hatteras, fell in with schr Wave, of Great Egg Harbor, Capt Barrett, from Philadelphia for Savannah March 17, with a cargo of slate, and took from her the officers and crew, six in number. The Wave had experienced a constant succession of heavy gales, during which sprung a leak. The W went down a short time after they were taken off.

THE WAR DECLARED.

Proclamation by the President.

FIRST BLOW AT NORTHERN COMMERCE.

Letters of Marque and Reprisal to be Issued immediately.

&c., &c., &c.

THE NEWS FROM MONTGOMERY.

MONTGOMERY, April 17.—The Proclamation of LINCOLN having at last been received here in a form sufficiently authentic to leave no doubt of its being genuine, President DAVIS has in turn issued to-day the following highly important and spirited Proclamation.

PROCLAMATION.

BY THE PRESIDENT OF THE CONFEDERATE STATES OF AMERICA.

Whereas, ABRAHAM LINCOLN, the President of the United States, has, by Proclamation, announced the intention of invading this Confederacy with an armed force for the purpose of capturing its fortresses, and thereby subverting its independence, and subjecting the free people thereof to the dominion of a foreign power; and *whereas* it has thus become the duty of this Government to expel the threatened invasion, and to defend the rights and liberties of the people by all the means which the laws of nations, and the usages of civilized warfare, place at its diiposal:

Now, therefore, I, JEFFERSON DAVIS, PRESIDENT OF THE CONFEDERATE STATES OF AMERICA, do issue this my Proclamation, inviting all those who may desire, by service in private armed vessels on the high seas, to aid this Government in resisting so wanton and wicked an aggression, to make application for commissions or Letters of Marque and Reprisal, to be issued under the Seal of these Confederate States.

And I do further notify all persons applying for Letters of Marque, to make a statement in writing, giving the name and a suitable description of the character, tonnage and force of the vessel, and the name and place of residence of each owner concerned therein, and the intended number of the crew, and to sign said statement and deliver the same to the Secretary of State, or to the Collector of any port of entry of these Confederate States, to be by him transmitted to the Secretary of State.

And I do further notify all applicants aforesaid that before any commission or Letter of Marque is issued to any vessel, the owner or owners thereof, and the commander for the time being, will be required to give bond to the Confederate States, with at least two responsible sureties, not interested in such vessel, in the penal sum of five thousand dollars; or if such vessel be provided with more than one hundred and fifty men, then in the penal sum of ten thousand dollars, with condition that the owners, officers and crew who shall be employed on board such commissioned vessel, shall observe the laws of these Confederate States and the instructions given to them for the regulation of their conduct. That they shall satisfy all damages done contrary to the tenor thereof by such vessel during her commission, and deliver up the same when revoked by the President of the Confederate States.

And I do further specially enjoin on all persons holding offices, civil and military, under the authority of the Confederate States, that they be vigilant and zealous in discharging the duties incident thereto; and I do, moreover, solemnly exhort the good people of these Confederate States, as they love their country, as they prize the blessings of free government, as they feel the wrongs of the past and these now threatened in aggravated form by those whose enmity is more implacable because unprovoked, that they exert themselves in preserving order, in promoting concord, in maintaining the authority and efficacy of the laws, and in supporting and invigorating all the measures which may be adopted for the common defence, and by which, under the blessing of Divine Providence, we may hope for a speedy, just and honorable peace.

In testimony whereof, I have hereunto set my hand, and caused the Seal of the Confederate States to be affixed, this *seventeenth* day of April, 1861.

By the President.

(Signed) JEFFERSON DAVIS.

R. TOOMBS, Secretary of State.

TRI-WEEKLY MERCURY.

BY R. B. RHETT, JR.

FOR THE MERCURY.

Song.

NINE CHEERS FOR THE BOYS AT THE GUNS.

AIR—"*Let the Toast be Dear Woman.*"

I.

Bright were the beams of the morning sky
On the day of the fight o'er the sea,
When the Palmetto boys raised the battle-cry,
As they fought for the Land of the Free;
When the boys at the guns stood defying
The threats of their insolent foe,
And the Palmetto Banner was flying
From the forts all around and below.
Then the toast, then the toast be "*Fort Johnson*,"
Hurrah for Carolina's sons;
Let the toast, let the toast be "*Fort Morris*,"
Nine cheers for THE BOYS AT THE GUNS!
Hip, hip, hurrah! Hip, hip, hurrah!
Hurrah! hurrah! hurrah!
Nine cheers for the boys at the guns!

II.

Bright was the glare of the raging flame
When Fort Sumter was held by the foe;
Hot was the shell and the shot that came
From the batteries around and below;
When the boys at the guns stood defying
The fire of their insolent foe,
And the Palmetto Banner was flying
From the forts all around and below.
Then the toast, then the toast be "*Fort Moultrie*,"
Carolina is proud of her sons;
Let the toast, let the toast be "*Fort Stevens*,"
Nine cheers for THE BOYS AT THE GUNS!
Hip, hip, hurrah! &c.

III.

Bright were the beams of the patriot's eye
When *Fort Sumter again was ours!*
Loud were the shouts that arose on high,
When we planted our flag on its towers!
When the boys at the guns stood defying
The flag of the conquered foe,
And the Palmetto Banner was flying
From the forts all around and below.
Then the toast, then the toast be "*Fort Sumter*,"
Hurrah for our brave-hearted sons;
Let the toast, let the toast be "*Fort Sumter*,"
NINE CHEERS FOR THE BOYS AT THE GUNS!
Hip, hip, hurrah! &c.

CLAUDE.

CHARLESTON, S. C., April 15, 1861.

The Fall of Fort Sumter.

WHAT THE PAPERS SAY ABOUT IT.

The Northern papers are filled with very amusing comments upon the result of the bombardment of Fort Sumter by our troops. From some of the leading journals of various shades of opinion we make the following extracts:

THE RESULT.

[*From the New York Tribune.*]

Fort Sumter is lost, but Freedom is saved. There is no more thought of bribing or coaxing the traitors who have dared to aim their cannon balls at the flag of the Union, and those who gave their lives to defend it. It seems but yesterday that at least two-thirds of the journals of this city were the virtual allies of the Secessionists, their apologists, their champions. The roar of the great circle of batteries pouring their iron hail upon devoted Sumter, has struck them all dumb. It is as if one had made a brilliant and effective speech, setting forth the innocence of murder, and, having just bidden adieu to the cheers and the gas-light, were to be confronted by the gory form and staring eyes of a victim of assassination, the first fruit of his oratorical success. For months before the late Presidential election, a majority of our journals predicted forcible resistance to the Government as the natural and necessary consequence of a Republican triumph; for months since they have been cherishing and encouraging the Slaveholders' Rebellion as if it were a very natural and proper proceeding. Their object was purely partisan—they wished to bully the Republican Administration into shameful recreancy to Republican principle, and then call upon the people to expel from power a party so profligate and cowardly. They did not succeed in this; they *have* succeeded in enticing their Southern *proteges* and some time allies into flagrant treason.

There cannot be a rational doubt that every man who aided or abetted the attack on Fort Sumter is involved in the guilt of treason. That all the besiegers of Forts Sumter and Pickens have incurred the penalty of Treason—which is Death—is indisputable.

Most of our journals lately parading the pranks of the Secessionists with scarcely disguised exultation, have been suddenly sobered by the culmination of the slaveholding conspiracy. They would evidently like to justify and encourage the traitors further, but they dare not: so the Amen sticks in their throat. The aspect of the People appals them. Democrat as well as Republican, Conservative and Radical, instinctively feel that the guns fired at Sumter were aimed at the heart of the American Republic. Not even in the lowest groggery of our city would it be safe to propose cheers for Beauregard and Gov. Pickens. The Tories of the Revolution were relatively ten times as numerous here as are the open sympathizers with the Palmetto Rebels. It is hard to lose Sumter; it is a consolation to know that in losing it we have gained a united people. Henceforth, the loyal States are a unit in uncompromising hostility to Treason, wherever plotted, however justified. Fort Sumter is temporarily lost, but the Country is saved. Live the Republic!

MAJOR ANDERSON'S COURSE APPROVED.

[*The Tribune's Washington Despatch.*]

No blame is imputed to Major Anderson by the Administration, and no whisper affecting his fidelity and loyalty is tolerated. His action was necessarily contemplated by his orders, [illegible] overpowered by an overwhelming force, or reduced to an extremity for the want of provisions. [illegible]

FIRST DEFEAT OF THE REBELS.

[*From the New York Evening Post.*]

[illegible] The rebels have chosen war. [illegible]

WAR DECLARED.

[*From the New York Herald.*]

At all events, the relinquishment of Fort Sumter and this manifesto of President Lincoln are equivalent to a declaration of war on both sides between the Confederate and the United States. [illegible]

These questions will irresistibly impress themselves upon the mind of every thinking man, North and South. Earnestly laboring in behalf of peace, from the beginning of these sectional troubles down to this day, and for the maintenance of the Union through mutual concessions, we do not even yet utterly despair of arresting this civil war before it shall have passed beyond the reach of reason.

THE BULLET *vs.* THE BALLOT.

[*From the New York Express.*]

The "irrepressible conflict," started by Mr. Seward, and endorsed by the Republican party, has at length attained to its logical, foreseen result. That conflict, undertaken "for the sake of humanity," culminates now in inhumanity itself, and exhibits the afflicting spectacle of brother shedding brother's blood.

Refusing the ballot, before the bullet, these men, flushed with the power and patronage of the Federal Government, have madly rushed into a civil war, which will probably drive the remaining Slave States into the arms of the Southern Confederacy, and dash to pieces the last hope for a reconstruction of the Union.

To the gallant men, who are so nobly defending the flag of their country within the walls of Fort Sumter, the nation owes a debt of eternal gratitude—not less than to the equally gallant and patriotic spirits, who, in like obedience to the demands of duty, are perilling their lives and shedding their blood in the heroic, but, as yet, unsuccessful endeavor to afford them succor. But, to the cold-blooded, heartless demagogues, who started this civil war—themselves magnanimously keeping out of the reach of bodily harm—we can only say, you must find your account, if not at the hands of an indignant people, then in the tears of widows and orphans. The people of the United States, it must be borne in mind, petitioned, begged and implored these men, who are become their accidental masters, to give them an opportunity to be heard, before this unnatural strife was pushed to a bloody extreme, but their petitions were all spurned with contempt, and now the bullet comes in to decide the issue!

MAJOR ANDERSON A TRAITOR.

[*From the New York Courier and Enquirer.*]

Sumter has fallen—surrendered, we fear, by a traitor; and that traitor Major Robert Anderson. This is harsh language; but it is the language of truth demanded by what appears to be the grossest act of treason ever perpetrated in this or any other country. The treason of Twiggs is admitted by all to have exceeded that of Benedict Arnold; but the names of both Arnold and Twiggs will sink into insignificance—indeed, are almost rendered respectable, when compared with the more damning infamy which from present appearances must forever attach to that of Robert Anderson.

The circumstances of this abominable treason are so palpable and transparent, that no man who reads them can hesitate in arriving at the conclusion that Anderson arranged with Beauregard for the surrender of Sumter, before it was assaulted; that the defence was but a sham; and that it was deemed important the surrender should take place before relief could be afforded by the government fleet, hourly expected to arrive with troops, provisions and munitions of war.

WASHINGTON IN DANGER.

[*From the New York World.*]

When the first gun was fired from Fort Moultrie, all hope of compromise, conciliation and peace perished. The United States has now to put down rebellion by force of arms. Though there are many loyal patriots within the limits of the seven seceded States, we are now at war with the revolutionists who have tied those States together into a rebellious confederacy. With war comes all the dangers, risks and hazards of war; and of these the greatest is the loss of Washington. To the revolutionists, the possession of Washington is more to be desired, and easier to be had, than the possession of Fort Sumter.

Washington, then, the capital of the nation, is our weakest point.

We do not wish to act the part of alarmists, and dare say the Administration has a full appreciation of whatever danger there may be. But the continued possession of the Federal Capital is of such vital consequence that the Government will be derelict if it does not make Washington secure against all possible attacks, whether the preparation is open or covert. The Capital must be held at all hazards and at whatever cost.

LINCOLN'S POLICY AN "IMBECILE BOTCH."

The bombardment of Fort Sumter is certainly a battle by itself, and the whole affair a transaction without a parallel. Except the glorious career of Anderson in Charleston harbor, now sadly but to him honorably terminated, we need not remark that we have no single point of satisfaction to dwell upon as American citizens. The whole conduct of affairs at that point on the part of the United States, is one tissue of unmitigated mortification and disgrace. As if it were not enough for us to smart under the pity of the world and the humiliation of our own reflections, we must be subjected to the scorn of perjured traitors, who if they have neither truth nor honor nor love of country, have mettle, audacity and force of arms, to redeem even them from pure contempt. To think that *a petty State, inferior to one of our considerable towns*, revolted for purposes that poor humanity itself abhors, has advanced in three months to swollen and menacing success, with swift and unchecked stride, conquering and to conquer, over the dishonored constitution and laws, the cowed government and the overpowered forces of the once glorious and great American Republic! To think of five thousand "confederate" felons, without one gun, or shot, or ounce of powder, which they had not stolen with treachery and violence from the United States in time of profound peace, deliberately getting ready nineteen tremendous batteries of our own best guns, and pouring a forty hours' storm of shot and shell upon a faithful United States officer and sixty men, while a United States fleet, loaded down with land and sea artillery, lay quietly in the offing, looking on at the horrid *battue!* Every true American heart is this day sick with shame.

It would be a premature judgment to censure unconditionally, at present advices, the conduct of the officers of the expedition, whose cool inaction, in sight of his desperate extremity, told upon the noble-hearted Anderson more heavily than all the guns of the enemy, and forced even the bold outlaws who beleaguered him, to send cheers of admiring sympathy mingled with their shot, and to vent curses and groans for the pusillanimity of the comrades who should have succored him or fallen with him to a man. We cannot help thinking there was an opportunity for an act of daring heroism, which might or might not have been successful, but which the world would have admired forever. Instead of this, it is the impression, from present appearances, that whoever held the responsibility at sea on Saturday has earned perhaps the reputation of "a discreet and prudent officer." The singular description—"a bloodless victory"—which the Confederates are enabled to apply to this affair, is a scathing sarcasm upon the efficiency of our boasted "relief fleet." It is safe enough to say there is blame and disgrace resting somewhere. If the force was so small that any attempt to raise the siege would have been sheer madness, why was it sent, with notice two or three days ahead of its arrival of the intention to provision the fort peaceably, or, failing that, to reinforce it by arms? Either the Government or its officers appear to have made an imbecile botch of it.

THE BEGINNING OF THE END.

[*From the New York Times.*]

The curtain has fallen upon the first act of the great tragedy of the age. Fort Sumter has been surrendered, and the stars and stripes of the American Republic give place to the felon flag of the Southern Confederates. The defence of the fortress did honor to the gallant commander by whom it was held, and vindicated the Government under which he served. Judging from the result, it does not seem to have been the purpose of the Government to do anything more. The armed ships which accompanied the supplies took no part in the contest. Whatever may have been the reason for it, their silence was probably fortunate. They could scarcely have forced their way through the heavy batteries which lined the coast, nor could their participation in the fight have changed the result. The preparations of the enemy were too complete, and their forces too numerous, to warrant any hope of success with the number of guns at our command. The fort was bravely defended. It has fallen without loss of life—the ships are on the spot to enforce the blockade of Charleston harbor—Fort Pickens, according to a despatch from Montgomery, has already been reinforced—and everything is ready for unrolling the next and the far more terrible scene of this great drama.

The Government of the United States is prepared to meet this great emergency with the energy and courage which the occasion requires, and which the sentiment of the nation demands. The President issues his proclamation to day, convening Congress for the 4th of July, and calling for *seventy-five thousand volunteers* for the defence of the Union, and the protection of the rights and the liberties of the American people. The people will respond to this demand with alacrity and exultation. They ask nothing better than to be allowed to fight for the Constitution which their fathers framed. Whatever may have been their political differences, there has never been a moment when they were not ready to sink them all in devotion to their common country, and in defence of their common flag. The President's proclamation will be hailed with an enthusiasm which no event of the last twenty years has called forth—with a high-hearted determination to exterminate treason, which will carry terror into the hearts of the Confederates, who have conspired for the destruction of the freest and best government the world has ever seen.

THE RUBICON PASSED.

[*From the Philadelphia Press.*]

The spirit which has been manifested since the assault upon Fort Sumter commenced shows that the anomaly we have too long witnessed, of peace upon one side, and war upon the other, will very speedily be destroyed. Henceforth we shall no longer strive to see how little we can do to strengthen forts, to maintain armies, to fit out fleets, to enforce the laws, and protect the honor of the nation, but how much. We will no longer seek to tie the hands of the Government—to cripple its powers—to unman and degrade it—to strengthen and encourage treason, and to dishearten and humiliate loyalty. The issue is now made up—either this great Republic or its desperate adversaries must be overthrown—and may God defend the right!

Henceforth each man, high and low, must take his position as a patriot or a traitor—as a foe or a friend of his country—as a supporter of the flag of the stars and stripes or of the rebel banner. The contest which is impending will doubtless be attended with many horrors, but all the facts show that it has been forced upon us as a last resort, and war is not the worst of evils. Since the startling events of the last five months have been succeeded by a brutal bombardment of a fort erected at vast expense for the defence of Charleston harbor, which would have been peaceably evacuated if the rebels had not insisted upon the utter humiliation of the Government, and since the Secretary of War of the Southern Confederacy has threatened to capture Washington, and even to invade the Northern States, while a formal declaration of hostilities is about to be made by the Confederate Congress, we should be wanting in every element of manhood, be perpetually disgraced in the eyes of the world, and lose all self-respect, if we did not arouse to determined action to re-assert the outraged dignity of the nation.

A JUSTIFICATION.

[*From the Baltimore Sun.*]

Were the Confederate States now a foreign foe, and we had declared war against them, with the *status* of Sumter as it was in the present case, we should regard them as the veriest fools and cowards, had they failed to make the attack before reinforcements could arrive, and so to secure the advantages of their position. And by this estimate they must be judged in this thing. For although the administration at Washington does not regard them as a foreign foe, yet the Confederate States constitute a nation, with its independence declared, and therefore they regard the United States as a foreign foe. In the attack upon Sumter they have done just what the United States would have done with respect to England at the opening of the Revolutionary war; just what any nation would do under the same circumstances. And in fact they have done that thing, which, had they not done, they would have been the subject of scoff and ridicule up and down the whole gamut of Black Republican insolence. The questions which now arises are all with respect to the future. The inflamed and warlike spirit accredited to the Northern cities and free States generally, must not be taken into the account, or we shall plunge into a prolonged, sanguinary, and indecisive conflict in which the border States will soon become the "dark and bloody ground." A war of conquest and subjugation against the Southern Confederacy, will terminate in inevitable disaster, whatever may be the actual termination of the strife. Such a war must begin, as it has really been anticipated, by a positive purpose on the part of the administration at Washington to reduce the Southern States to political inequality in the Union. Consequently, the alternative of submission to this administration at any time, includes assent to political inequality, and the recognition of a power which has avowed an "irrepressible conflict" with Southern institutions. Whatever successes may attend the United States, therefore, as against the Confederate States, the end must be the recognition of the independence of the latter, or the holding them by military power. In the latter case all union is at an end; peace and harmony will be unattainable; and the utter prostration of all business will continue indefinitely. On the other hand, the recognition of the independence of the Confederate States will at once end the strife, restore public confidence, and relieve the enterprises of industry and capital from the embarrassment which now hinders their prosperity, and must in the end overwhelm them with calamity.

AMERICAN TOPICS ABROAD.

[*From the London Times March 26.*]

Ever since Mr. Lincoln delivered his Inaugural Address the American public has been engaged in the effort to understand it. Whether it means war or peace has not yet been decided by the most acute commentators; and their embarrassment is pardonable, for it is plain that Mr. Lincoln's Cabinet is equally at fault, and some people say that Mr. Lincoln himself knows no more of his own intentions than his supporters know. In fact, circumstances will give the explanation of this mysterious document. Like the popular divines who profess to interpret the Apocalypse, we must wait for the event, and then it will be easy to show that such and such a passage of the "Inaugural" had such a meaning, and no other. In the meantime, two high authorities differ wholly in their anticipations of the Presidential policy. Mr. Douglas, the most zealous and able advocate of local rights—the man who would allow the first emigrants into a territory to decide on the institutions of the future State, and who, consequently, condemns to the uttermost the doctrine of coercion, declares himself satisfied with the President's language, which he is sure means nothing but peace. On the other hand, President Davis and the Mongomery Congress are equally sure that war is impending. The military preparations at the South are on a scale which indicates serious forebodings and strong determination. A very large force is under arms—much larger than any which the North is likely to have at its command, unless, indeed, a crusade be proclaimed and the Northern Militia be brought into action.

* * * * * * * * *

It is with no wish to elevate them (that is, the seceding States) unduly in the eyes of Englishmen that we have called attention to the decorous and statesmanlike proceedings of their Congress. As a nation we are too much accustomed both to praise and censure to be flattered by the soft words of the Southerners. We see clearly the aim of these politicians; it is to gain the good will of foreign nations, and particularly England, by placing Southern liberality in contrast with the grasping and narrow-minded legislation of the Free States. But surely it is no small thing that even for their own advantage the Southerners should pay a tribute to the true principles of international intercourse. *Whatever be their motives, it is not for us to sneer when an American community abolishes its Navigation Laws, declares it a fundamental principle that duties shall never be levied so as to foster particular branches of industry, and adopt a resolution for the establishment of international copyright.*

[*From the London Examiner, March 23.*]

There is a bird which is said to provide for its safety by putting its head into a hole so as not to see its enemy. A bird of this feather is President Lincoln. His method of dealing with a great evil is not to see it, and to deny its existence. The Union is intact. The Union is unbroken, because it is theoretically indissoluble. No State can have seceded from it, because no State has the right to secede, and consequently the Union exists, and must forever exist, in all its integrity. There is no Southern Confederacy, it is a mere name, a titular pretension, no reality. "We are seven," persists the child in Wordsworth's poem, the death of two of the number not disturbing the idea fixed in the affections.

The little Maid would have her will,
And said, "Nay, we are seven."

We are thirty-four, in like manner fondly persists the American President. And in every respect but one he intends to act as if the Southern Confederacy was a sham and the Union a reality, instead of the reverse, which is the notorious fact.

What can be expected, what can be hoped of a policy based on an enormous and notorious fiction? The Pope declares the encroachments on his temporalities null and void, and that his authority remains sacred and intact; but these are mere words thrown into the air, as they say in the East, the harmless consolations of impotence. The American President's assertions of the infallibility of the Constitution are more serious, as they entail consequences in action. Accordingly the President pledges himself to hold, occupy and possess the property and places belonging to the Federal Government, to collect the duties and imposts, but not to use force, except such as may be necessary for these objects, for which, he says, no bloodshed or violence is needed. More cunning than Shylock, Mr. Lincoln contemplates some mode of cutting the pound of flesh nearest to the heart of the South without spilling a drop of blood. Does he suppose that Fort Sumter can be retained or the other forts recovered, that the Federal property can be restored, the customs duties collected in the Gulf States, without coming to blows? He does not, indeed, propose to insist on all the Federal obligations. He will not attempt to enforce the discharge of Federal duties where people refuse to fill the offices, and as little, when it comes to the point, will he attempt to re-occupy forts, recover property, and levy customs. For such comparatively trumpery objects, what people would consent to a civil war? The preservation of the Union, if practicable, might be deemed worth a civil war, but President Lincoln starts with the assumption that the Union is undissolved, and consequently his civil war would appear to be not for the great object of saving the Union itself, but for the recovery of its poor furniture.

THE CINCINNATI TIMES has a pleasant article on "the "Rush for Office at Washington," and heads it with these mottos, which embody the whole matter in a most remarkable manner:

"The combat deepens—on, ye brave,
Who rush to office, or the grave!"
* * * * * * * *
"Let those *now* seek that never sought before,
And those that *always* seek, *now seek the more!*"

JUDGE DOUGLAS has prepared a tariff which will secure free trade between Canada, the United States, the Confederate States and Mexico, yet ensure the collection of uniform duties on goods imported from abroad. This he proposes to introduce if an extra session of Congress is called.

JUDGE G. W. LANE, recently appointed United States Judge of the Northern District of Alabama, and confirmed by the Senate to that position, has thrown up his commission, and volunteered as a private in the Confederate army.

MAJOR WM. MONTGOMERY GARDNER, late Captain in the Second Infantry, U. S. Army, and more recently Major in the Georgia Army, has been appointed a Major in the army of the Confederate States. He has been ordered to Savannah.

The *Day Book* says New York, at present, presents a highly illumined appearance, being placarded all over with bills of "to let," "for sale," and "selling off at cost." Delightful Black Republican times.

GEN. CHAZEL, Belgian Minister of War, said, in a recent speech in the Chambers, that escarpments of masonry were now abandoned in his system of fortifications.

HOE, the printing press maker, while he was in Paris, concluded not to have his press patent renewed. The papers in that city are such slow coaches they don't need double cylinders.

During Mr. Charles Dickens' last English provincial tour it is stated that he cleared upwards of £20,000 after paying all expenses.

Vice President Alexander H. Stephens and Gen Gideon J. Pillow passed through Atlanta on Sunday last, *en route* to Montgomery.

The Southern people welcome their new guns from the Tredegar works with the shout of "Hail Columbiads!"

A LAD named J. T. Pratt was crushed to death in Morehead's factory, at Leaksville, N. C., a few days ago.

THE KING and Queen of Naples held a levee in Rome a few weeks since, which was attended by *eighteen* persons! How like the world.

The New York *Tribune* is very much hurt because the Richmond *Examiner* speaks of Mr. Lincoln as a "low and obscure Illinois baboon."

MAJ. L. D. FRANKLIN, one of the most wealthy and influential farmers of Jefferson county, Tenn., died suddenly last week.

THE New England Methodist Conference have passed anti slavery resolutions in the most offensive terms.

The War News.

The news conveyed in our despatches this morning is important. While the LINCOLN Administration is rapidly concentrating the hungry hordes with which it proposes to subjugate the South, and draining the pockets of the anxious stock jobbers who have staked their all in the success of the mad scheme of coercion, the President of the Confederate States meets the threatened invasion promptly and with vigor. In a Proclamation issued yesterday, he announces that letters of marque and reprisal will immediately be issued, under the authority of the Government, to armed vessels cruising as privateers upon the high seas. Northern cupidity is thus arrayed against Northern fanaticism, and it is not difficult to predict the result.

The valorous Yankee, led by the scent of the rich prey, will not long scruple, under the sanction of the Southern flag, to sweep from the seas the commercial marine of his Yankee neighbors. How long the shipping interest of the North will care to sustain the terrible risk which begins to-day remains to be seen.

If, however, this measure should not suffice to check the impudent pretensions of the abolitionized North to hold a free people in subjection, the Confederate States are ready to try other and more direct remedies.

Publications of the late United States.

Among the few persons whom we envy, as still in the possession of the late Government of the United States, is the worthy descendant of BENJAMIN FRANKLIN, Professor A. D. BACHE, the able and eminent Superintendent of the United States Coast Survey. He is too good a man to be in such bad company—to toil for such a nefarious Government, and his proper place is with ours. We confess to a great yearning to have him—an honorable officer, in an honorable office, in an honorable Government like ours. We did not need to be reminded of his deserts or our desires by the receipt of his "Report of the Progress of the Survey of the Coast during the year 1859," which we owe to the courtesy of the Assistant in charge of the Survey office. This is an additional quarto to the already large and valuable series which delineate the entire line of coast, rivers, bays, harbors and inlets of the Atlantic and Gulf, from the farthest east to the remote south and west. The labor has been stupendous; the work done, not only wonderful in extent, but in value. Science, art, enterprise and commercial industry, proclaim this collection one of the noblest and most useful ever executed for, and by, the late Confederacy.

2 *Military Commission to Europe*—1855—'56.

This quarto is by Major MORDECAI, of the Ordnance Department of the late United States. It consists of his report of the results of his military observations in the Crimea, and in other parts of Europe, made as member of a Military Commission sent out under the orders of JEFFERSON DAVIS, then Secretary of War of the United States, now the honored President of the Confederate States. It affords an excellent companion volume to that of Capt McCLELLAN, of the same Commission, published some time ago. The contents show what are the military organizations of Russia, Prussia, Austria, France and Great Britain; describe the ordnance used in the Crimea; the arsenals, and military establishments of most of the Great Powers of Europe; and particularly addresses its inquiry to cannon and artillery, including rifle cannon and ordnance of largest calibre. The detail is very various, and is copiously illustrated by excellent drawings and engravings, with proper scales of measurement.

3. *Explorations and Surveys* for a Railroad Route from the Mississippi to the Pacific.

We have here the first and second parts of volume twelve of this very elaborate work, tributary to a grand scheme, which was to cost—possibly—several hundreds of millions of dollars, and which, we take for granted, is knocked on the head forever, by the rapid rush of Cotton States to independence. Scientific and literary men will congratulate themselves upon the results of the surveys, as embodied in these twelve volumes, which describe the country, its soil, rocks, rivers, beasts, birds, fish, reptiles—all that could be seen, or drawn, and all drawn well, and well printed, and here on record, but at a most enormous expense drawn out of the pockets of the Southern planter. We approve of the books, and congratulate the explorers and editors upon the work they have done, but curse the spoilsmen of the country who have thought, in this expense, only of providing jobs for tools and retainers. The cost of this publication alone, simply for printing and engravings, would cover any one of our States with all the railroads which it will need for a hundred years. The cost of the surveys is, perhaps, incomputable.

ALARM IN WASHINGTON.—A correspondent of the Baltimore *Sun* gives the following interesting account of the condition of things in Washington City under the LINCOLN dynasty:

The note of military preparation here resembles that of a European town just upon a great and long war. Outposts are extended and strengthened, sentries are posted at public buildings, cavalry horses are being purchased, and groups of citizens gather about the military quarters, which are so rapidly augmenting that they may be seen from all points. The numbers of lookers on convey an idea of the want of employment that must have existed here for some time back. Such persons as enlist get twenty dollars per month as privates, and the distribution of this sum may be the means of helping some distressed families.

It is stated to-day that a considerable number of Baltimoreans have come down here to enlist; also that orders have gone North for volunteers there not to "stand upon the order of their coming, but to come at once." Some persons who reside across the river, in Virginia, have the impression that a military reconnoisance has been made of the heights commanding this city, by officers in the service of the Confederate States, and this idea may be urged as a ground for occupying them by the government troops. Indeed, it is stated that pickets will be pushed out in that direction. A very large force is to be concentrated at this *key* position, those heights will probably be seized by one party or another as soon as Virginia acts. As I write, a full company of Washington Light Infantry are marching past, and some post in the vicinity looking towards Maryland is their probable destination. Things are conducted here in the most secret manner possible. At some of the Departments intercourse with subordinate clerks is entirely cut off.

THE WAY THEY BRAG.—The *Tribune* of Saturday said:

"Fort Sumter is one of the strongest fortresses on our seaboard, and there is not the slightest probability that serious damage could be done to it by one day's fire of batteries so distant as those of the Rebels."

This is on a par with most of their vaporing. When the "Rebels" get nearer to you they will try and do better.

FORT PICKENS REINFORCED.—A brief line in a telegraphic despatch a day or two since, announced that Fort Pickens had been reinforced. Some doubt has been felt in relation to this announcement, but the following telegram, in the Richmond *Enquirer*, sets the matter at rest by confirming the report:

MONTGOMERY, April 13.

To the Hon. Henry A. Wise:

By authority of the Hon. L. P. Walker, Secretary of War, I have to inform you, for general publicity, that on last night reinforcements were thrown into Fort Pickens, by the Government at Washington, in violation of the convention existing between that Government and this Confederacy.

JOHN TYLER, jr.

NORTHERN TELEGRAPHIC DESPATCHES.—In the New York *Herald*, of the 14th inst., appears a despatch from the Associated Press reporter in this city, stating—

First. That cannonading "is going on fiercely from vessels outside and along our coast."

Second. That "Major ANDERSON has thrown out a raft loaded with men, who are passing up buckets of water to extinguish the fire; that balls are to be seen skipping over the water and striking the unprotected raft, creating great havoc among the poor fellows."

Third. "That eleven shots penetrated the Floating battery below the water line."

Fourth. "That Fort Sumter had unconditionally surrendered."

Fifth. "That Major ANDERSON and his men, under guard, were conveyed to Morris Island."

Sixth. "That Major ANDERSON had reached the city and was the guest of Gen. BEAUREGARD."

The truth of these despatches is too well known to require a refutation before a Charleston public, but it is due to the special correspondent of the New York *Herald*, whose statements thus far have been entirely in accordance with the circumstances, to state that a distinction should be made between the facts sent by him and those sent by the reporter of the Associated Press.

IMPROMPTU SERENADE.—A large crowd of our citizens, with a band of music, assembled in front of the Mills House, on Wednesday evening. Appropriate and stirring speeches were made by the Hon. JNO. A. MCQUEEN and Hon. ROGER A. PRYOR.

It was stated in THE MERCURY of Wednesday that Mr. PRYOR had left the city. It was his intention to have done so, but he was detained for the purpose of carrying despatches from General BEAUREGARD to the Government at Montgomery. He left Thursday morning at 6 o'clock.

CHAPLAIN OF THE SECOND REGIMENT.—Rev. E. J. MEYNARDIE, Pastor of the Methodist Church at Camden, having been tendered by Col. KERSHAW the appointment of Chaplain in his Regiment and accepted the same, left on Saturday morning for Charleston.

LINCOLN'S MEN-OF-WAR.—The schooner *G. D. & R. F. Shannon*, which arrived here yesterday from Boston, was off this bar during the bombardment, and was boarded by the sloop-of-war *Pawnee*, the officer of that vessel taking her for the schooner *E. Waterman*, of this port. They scrutinized her papers very closely, and made threats of what they would do had she been that vessel. Their courage certainly did not display itself when they had a fitting opportunity.

THE NEW LOAN.—The subscription for the first Confederate State Loan was carried on Wednesday with quiet spirit, and the Commissioners were busily engaged to the latest hour. The total amount so far subscribed in Charleston, was $2,080,000. The books will be open again to-day.

CAPTAIN B. J. JOHNSON'S company of volunteers, "The Coast Guard," reported themselves to Lieut. Col. BRANCH, at the east end of Sullivan's Island, on Thursday night, numbering, rank and file, 88, all in health and good spirits, but disappointed at the indisposition of the LINCOLN forces to land.

NORTHERN VESSELS ORDERED HOME.—A report prevailed along the wharves yesterday, that most of the vessels here owned in Baltimore and north of that, had been ordered home.

NUMBERS of our brave volunteers, who took part in the bombardment of Fort Sumter, have returned to the city on furlough. They report all well at the different posts, and, as everybody says now-a-days, "nobody hurt." There is no lack of vigilance, however. A constant lookout is maintained at all the posts.

CHARLESTON PREPARATORY MEDICAL SCHOOL. The Lectures in this School begun under the most favorable auspices; but, interrupted by recent events, will be again resumed, of which due notice will be given.

VISIT TO FORT SUMTER.—Wednesday morning Mr. RUSSELL, the correspondent of the London *Times*, now in this city, visited Fort Sumter. He was accompanied by Colonel MILES, Colonel CHESNUT, Colonel MANNING and Colonel WHITING, Aids to General BEAUREGARD, and Colonel LUCAS, Aid to Governor PICKENS. Mr. FONTAINE, of the New York *Herald*, and others, were of the party.

J. B. FRENCH, Esq., a young lawyer of Virginia, recently proffered his services and was elected a member of the "Lancaster Greys." Since the secession of his State he has received permission and determined to return.

ASSISTANCE FOR NORTH CAROLINA.—Colonel MCRAE, of North Carolina, returned last night with the Columbiads for which Gov. ELLIS asked. We learn that Gov. ELLIS expects an attack in less than two days, and that he is making every possible preparation for it. Already a number of guns have been obtained from Virginia and placed in position.

AN UNPLEASANT ACCIDENT.—A boat, with four members of the military companies stationed at Battery Island, was capsized in a squall on Monday evening last, about half-past six o'clock, during the passage from Coles' Island to the former place. At the time the accident happened, the boat was about one mile from its destination. After the capsize the soldiers were fortunate enough to get hold of the bottom of the boat, to which they clung for three hours. Their cry for help was heard by their comrades at Battery Island, but they could render them no assistance. They were finally rescued, however, by Mr. P. H. GRIMBALL, who paid them every attention which their distressing situation required.

A FATAL ACCIDENT occurred Wednesday on the South Carolina Railroad, at Lee's Turnout. As Mr. WILLIAM LEE was crossing the track to obtain a paper, the down train from Augusta struck him with such terrible force as to kill him instantly.

AN INQUEST was held Wednesday, by Coroner WHITING, over the body of an unknown negro, who was found drowned near Vanderhorst's wharf. The verdict of the Jury was, that he came to his death from causes unknown. He was well-built, apparently about forty-five years of age, and had a scar, as if from a cut, over the left eye. The body was found about 11 o'clock yesterday morning.

MILITARY ARRIVALS.—The Secession Guards, Capt. PERRYMAN, 100 men, and the Southern Guards, Capt. MADISON, also 100 men, came down Wednesday night by the late train on the South Carolina Railroad. Both these fine companies belong to the 7th Regiment.

PERSONAL.—Mr. WILLIAM H. WILSON, editor of the Washington (Ga.) *Independent*, has been for several days stopping in our city. Merchants and business men, who desire to extend their business in the counties of Wilkes, Oglethorpe and Lincoln, will find the *Independent* a first-rate medium for advertising.

SALES OF REAL ESTATE.—J. E. BOWERS, Auctioneer, yesterday sold the tract of land, containing 515 acres, about half a mile from Summerville Depot, adjoining J. R. STALL, McCLAREN, FERGUSON and EASTERLING'S land, for $1.15 per acre. Also, the lot in Spring-street, next to the corner of Meeting, on the south side, measuring 87 feet deep, by 51 feet front, with a two-story wooden house, containing four square rooms and improvements, for $2025.

GODEY'S LADY'S BOOK.—The May number of this interesting Magazine has been received by SAMUEL HART, sr., 300 King street.

THE FLOATING BATTERY, we understand, will be placed in position at Stono Inlet.

THE NEW COMMANDER AT PICKENS.—We have it from good authority, says the Pensacola *Observer*, of the 12th, that Lieut. Slemmer has been superseded in the command of the above fortification by the appointment of Major Tower, who is there in the discharge of his duties.

The New York *Day Book* (secession) of Saturday is dressed in mourning over the inauguration of civil war.

THE Government, it appears, had considerable difficulty in getting its $5,000,000 Treasury notes taken on Thursday.

Dumas and a newspaper editor, an Italian, were about to fight a duel at last accounts.

A horse's affirmative is always expressed by a neigh.

The Fall of Fort Sumter.

WHAT THE PAPERS SAY ABOUT IT.

The Northern papers are filled with very amusing comments upon the result of the bombardment of Fort Sumter by our troops. From some of the leading journals of various shades of opinion we make the following extracts:

THE RESULT.

[*From the New York Tribune.*]

Fort Sumter is lost, but Freedom is saved. There is no more thought of bribing or coaxing the traitors who have dared to aim their cannon balls at the flag of the Union, and those who gave their lives to defend it. It seems but yesterday that at least two-thirds of the journals of this city were the virtual allies of the Secessionists, their apologists, their champions. The roar of the great circle of batteries pouring their iron hail upon devoted Sumter, has struck them all dumb. It is as if one had made a brilliant and effective speech, setting forth the innocence of murder, and, having just bidden adieu to the cheers and the gas-light, were to be confronted by the gory form and staring eyes of a victim of assassination, the first fruit of his oratorical success. For months before the late Presidential election, a majority of our journals predicted forcible resistance to the Government as the natural and necessary consequence of a Republican triumph; for months since they have been cherishing and encouraging the Slaveholders' Rebellion as if it were a very natural and proper proceeding. Their object was purely partisan—they wished to bully the Republican Administration into shameful recreancy to Republican principle, and then call upon the people to expel from power a party so profligate and cowardly. They did not succeed in this; they *have* succeeded in enticing their Southern *proteges* and some time allies into flagrant treason.

There cannot be a rational doubt that every man who aided or abetted the attack on Fort Sumter is involved in the guilt of treason. That all the besiegers of Forts Sumter and Pickens have incurred the penalty of Treason—which is Death—is indisputable.

Most of our journals lately parading the pranks of the Secessionists with scarcely disguised exultation, have been suddenly sobered by the culmination of the slaveholding conspiracy. They would evidently like to justify and encourage the traitors further, but they dare not: so the Amen sticks in their throat. The aspect of the People appals them. Democrat as well as Republican, Conservative and Radical, instinctively feel that the guns fired at Sumter were aimed at the heart of the American Republic. Not even in the lowest groggery of our city would it be safe to propose cheers for Beauregard and Gov. Pickens. The Tories of the Revolution were relatively ten times as numerous here as are the open sympathizers with the Palmetto Rebels. It is hard to lose Sumter; it is a consolation to know that in losing it we have gained a united people. Henceforth, the loyal States are a unit in uncompromising hostility to Treason, wherever plotted, however justified. Fort Sumter is temporarily lost, but the Country is saved. Live the Republic!

EXTRA

NEW YORK ILLUSTRATED NEWS.

NEW-YORK, SATURDAY, APRIL 20, 1861.

PORTRAIT OF MAJOR ANDERSON, FROM A PHOTOGRAPH TAKEN IN FORT SUMTER.

This, the last portrait of the hero of Fort Sumter, will be particularly acceptable to our readers at the present time, from the circumstance that it is from a sketch taken within the walls of the fortress he has so nobly defended against vastly superior forces. The patriotism of the gallant Major forms a brilliant contrast to the conduct of those who have done so much to dishonor our army, and will cause his name to be remembered with reverence for all time.

MAJOR ANDERSON LOOKING OUT FOR THE RELIEF SQUADRON PREVIOUS TO THE ATTACK.

For Major Anderson's sake, we are glad that himself and his gallant command are relieved from their trying position before Charleston. The anxieties attendant upon their situation, supplies rapidly diminishing, the increasing power and vigilance of the besiegers, added to uncertain knowledge of the intentions of the Government, must have weighed heavily upon the mind of the gallant Major, as he vainly scanned the horizon for the expected supplies and reinforcements, upon which depended the continued occupation of the fortress, but which, alas, he was never destined to receive.

MAJOR ANDERSON

OPENING OF THE WAR!

IMPORTANT CORRESPONDENCE.

First Shot Fired from Fort Moultrie!

MAJOR ANDERSON SURRENDERS.

FORT SUMTER EVACUATED.

THE LATEST DISPATCHES.

OUR EXTRA SHEET.

We present our readers with a sketch of the bombardment of Fort Sumpter, taken on the spot by an artist who saw the first gun fired from Fort Moultrie.

We have hastened to supply the eager demand of the public for a pictorial representation of the first act in the terrible drama which is before us.

See page 371.

MAJOR ANDERSON ON THE RAMPARTS OF FORT SUMTER, LOOKING OUT FOR THE SQUADRON OF RELIEF PREVIOUS TO THE ATTACK.

SUPPLEMENT TO THE

GAZETTE & SENTINEL.

MONDAY, April 15, 10, A. M.
PLAQUEMINE:

Saturday, APRIL 20, 1861.

From our Bulletin of Last Saturday.

WAR BEGUN!

FORT SUMPTER TAKEN.

Plaquemine, Saturday Morning 13th. Our obliging postmaster has just furnished us with the Evening Delta of yesterday, containing the following important news. We shall condense it all we can, without leaving out any important items.

There is a despatch from Montgomery, stating that Gen. Beauregard opened his fire on Fort Sumpter yesterday morning at 4 o'clock.

The next despatch is from Col. Duncan, at Montgomery, to the Mayor of New Orleans, confirming the above.

The next despatch from Montgomery introduces the following correspondence which we give in full:

No. 1.] Charleston, April 8th.
To L. P. Walker, Sec'y War.

Authorized messengers from Lincoln just informed Gov. Pickens and myself that provisions will be sent to Fort Sumpter peaceably, if possible, but forcible if necessary.

(Signed.) G. T. Beauregard.

No. 2.] Reply of Sec'y of War to Gen. Beauregard.

Montgomery, April 10th.

If you have no doubt of the authorized character of the agent who communicated to you the intention of the Washington Government to supply fort Sumpter by force, you will at once demand its evacuation; and if this is refused, proceed, in such a manner as you may determine, to reduce it.

(Signed) L. P. Walker.

N. 3.] Charleston, April 10th.
To L. P. Walker, Sec'y War.

The demand will be made to-morrow at 12 o'clock. (Signed)
G. T. Beauregard.

No. 4.] Montgomery, April 10th.
The Sec'y War to Gen. Beauregard.

Unless there are special reasons connected with your own condition, it is considered proper that you shall make the demand at an earlier hour.

(Signed) L. P. Walker.

No. 5.] Charleston, April 11th.
To L. P. Walker, Sec'y War:

The reasons are special for 12 o'clock.
G. T. Beauregard.

No. 6.] Charleston, April 11th.
To. L. P. Walker, Sec'y War:

Demand sent at 2. Allowed until 6 to answer. G. T. Beauregard.

No. 7.] Montgomery, April 11th.
To Gen. Beauregard:

Telegraph the reply of Anderson.

No. 8.] Gen. Beauregard to the Sec'y of War.

Charleston, April 11th.

Major Anderson replies; "I have the receipt of your communication, demanding the evacuation of this fort, and to say in reply thereto, that it is a demand with which I regret that my sense of honor and of my obligation to my Government prevent my compliance."

He adds verbally:

"I will await the first shot, and if you do not batter us to pieces, we will be starved out in a few days. Answer."

G. T. BEAUREGARD.

Montgomery, April 11.
To G. T. Beauregard, Charleston.

We do not desire needlessly to bombard Fort Sumpter.

Major Anderson will state the time at which, as indicated by him, he will evacuate, and agree that in the meantime he will not use his guns against us unless ours should be employed against Fort Sumpter.

You are authorized thus to avoid the effusion of blood. If this or its equivalent be refused, reduce the Fort as your judgment decides to be the most practicable. L. P. WALKER,
Secretary of War.

Gen. Beauregard to Sec. of War.
No. 10.] Charleston, April 12.

He would not consent. I write today. G. T. BEAUREGARD.

Gen. Beauregard to Secretary of War.
No. 11.] Charleston, April 12.

I opened fire at 4:30 this morning.
G. T. BEAUREGARD.

NOTE.—An intercepted dispatch discloses the fact that Mr. Fox, who had been allowed to visit Major Anderson, on the pledge that his purposes were pacific, employed his opportunity to devise a plan for supplying the fort by force, and that his plan had been adopted by the Washington Government and was in progress of execution.

A despatch to the Delta, says, on the authority of Mr. Benjamin, that President Davis had issued his proclamation re-assembling Congress on the 29th.

It is telegraphed that a change is to take place in Lincoln's Cabinet.

The Latest!

A gentleman who arrived this morning on the Mary Keene, which left New Orleans last evening at 5 o'clock, several hours after the Delta went to press, informs us that a dispatch had been received, stating that FORT SUMPTER HAD BEEN TAKEN!

From our Bulletin of Monday.

Fort Sumpter Surrendered!

Terrible Effects of the Batteries!

THE CONFLAGATIONS!

Great Rejoicings in Montgomery!

Knowing the great interest of our subscribers and the public to know the first results growing out of the conflict forced upon us by a sectional President and his myrmidons, we shall continue to lay before our readers, in extras daily, whatever occurs with reference to the trial by arms, of the great questions of freedom or slavery of the people of the Confederate States, which the present contest determines.

The following glorious news, with reference to the hostilities at Charleston, (the intelligence of the commencement of which we gave in an Extra on Saturday,) is contained in all the New Orleans papers of yesterday, and may be relied upon as correct:
Special Despatch to the Delta.

Montgomery, April 13th.

Major Anderson has hauled down the United States flag on Fort Sumter, and has run up a white flag. The effect of the vigorous and steady firing from the Confederate States batteries has been terrific. The shell, especially, have been very effectively directed—so much so, that they have set the works on fire in several places. The conflagration resulting from this cause has continued for several hours. The fire of our batteries continued till the moment when the white flag was displayed from the Fort. Aids have been sent by Gen. Beauregard to Major Anderson.

The dispatch from Gov. Pickens to the Secretary of War, announcing the surrender of the Fortress, was read by the Clerk of the War Department, from the front of the Executive building, in the presence of President Davis and the members of the Cabinet.

Seven guns were fired for the surrender, one for Gen. Beauregard, and one for the Confederate States.

There is great rejoicing here.

Flag of the Confederacy flies over Fort Sumpter.

CHARLESTON BLOCKADED!

Montgomery, April 13.—Our flag flies over Fort Sumpter. Charleston is now blockaded by the United States fleet which lies off the harbor.

Arrest of an Emissary of Lincoln.

Montgomery, April 13th.—An emissary of Lincoln was arrested to-day on the train en route for Pensacola. He was bearing despatches to Lieut. Slemmer, in command of Fort Pickens. His name is Worden, and he is a Lieut. in the U. S. Navy.

Another despatch dated Charleston, April 13th, says:

The Fort has been burning several hours, from the effect of the shells thrown into it. Two explosions have been produced.

Another despatch says four.

Anderson has ceased firing for some time.

Major Anderson in the City—Sumpter Garrisoned by Confederate Troops.

Charleston, April 13th.—Gen. Beauregard takes possession of Fort Sumpter to-morrow morning.

Major Anderson has the privilege to salute his flag.

No one was killed on our side.

The surrender was unconditional. Gen. Beauregard prescribes the terms.

Fort Pickens Reinforced.

Pensacola, April 13.—Reinforcements were thrown into Fort Pickens last night.

Dispatches from Washington state that the war news creates much regret. The regular troops were ordered to the outskirts and the volunteers to protect the public buildings.

Massachusetts sustains Lincoln—also Rhode Island, which offers her artillery and a thousand infantry, and Governor Sprague says he will accompany them whereyer ordered.

A great Southern sympathy meeting has been held in Nashville.

Business partially suspended in Cincinnati.

Vessels continue to be chartered, and war vessels are actively being prepared for sea.

Lincoln's answer to the Virginia Commissioners was, that he would act in accordance with the language of his Inaugural address.

[Remainder will be found on the Third Page of the Paper.

CURIOUS SIATISTICS.—We learn from the annual report of the New York Metropolitan Police force the following items:

Actors arrested during the year 1860, 58; artists, 201; aldermen, 1, (only one—there must be a mistake somewhere!); bar-tenders, 114; clerks, 1,491; custom-house officers, 9; deputy sheriffs, 6; editors, 5 (bad men!); hotel-keepers, 641 (awful!); printers, 54 (exceedingly moderate!); prostitutes, 4473; priests, 3; proof-readers, 2 (better than priests!); reporters, 11; servants, 3598; lawyers, 80 (more than all the editors, proof-readers, reporters, and printers combined); telegraph operators, 5 (exactly as bad as editors); vocalists, 4. The total number of all sorts and conditions of people arrested by the police force during the year, was 65,806, of which over 50,000 were under 40 years of age, and 20,000 of them females.

DESERTED TO THE SOUTH.—It is stated that twenty of the rank and file of the army left Washington on Thursday for Montgomery, for the purpose of enlisting in the Southern army. These desertions make an aggregate of two hundred and eighty army recruits for the Southern Government from the federal capital, since they have been stationed there by Gen. Scott.

Gazette and Sentinel.

NEW SERIES--VOL. 4, NO. 10. PLAQUEMINE, PARISH OF IBERVILLE, LA., APRIL 20, 1861. OLD SERIES--VOL. 14 NO. 22.

PROFESSIONAL CARDS.

BENJ. N. DEBLIEUX,
Attorney at Law,
Plaquemine, Iberville Parish, Louisiana,

WILL devote his whole attention to the practice of their profession in all the Courts of the Sixth Judicial District. je23

DAVID N. BARROW, *Plaquemine, Iberville, La.* | N. W. POPE, *West Baton Rouge, Baton Rouge P. O., La*

Barrow & Pope,
Attorneys and Counsellors at Law,

WILL practice their profession in the parishes of West and East Baton Rouge, Iberville, Point Coupee and West Feliciana; the Supreme Court of Louisiana, and the United States District and Circuit Courts at New Orleans. my1-1y

OSCAR LAUVE,
Attorney at Law,

Will devote strict attention to the practice of his profession in all the Courts of the Sixth Judicial District.
Office with Zenon Labauve. ap24-1y

J. H. RILLS,
Attorney at Law and Justice of the Peace,
☞Office on Main street. aug6

Joseph Hotard,
Attorney and Counsellor at Law,
(*Office same as Zenon Labauve, Esq.,*)
jy16] *PLAQUEMINE, LA.*

GEORGE L. HILL,
Attorney at Law,
Tyler, Smith County, Texas,

WILL practice law and collect claims in the counties of Harrison, Panola, Rusk, Smith, Wood, Upshur, Cass, and Marion, and in the Federal and Supreme Courts at Tyler. my26

W. I. HAMILTON,
ATTORNEY AT LAW,

HAVING located at Plaquemine will devote his entire attention to the pratice of his Profession in the Parishes of

Iberviile, as tand West Baton Rouge.

He respectfully solicits the patrouage of his old friends and the public generally, who can always find him at his Office on Main Street near the Court House, between the hours of 9 A. M. and 5 P. M., unless otherwise professionally engaged.
Plaquemine, La. oc16mh23.

E. GOURRIER,
Surveyor & Civil Engineer,
Baton Rouge, La.

WILL attend to calls in the Parish of Iberville, for surveying lands, mapping, Plant ations levelling, measuring canals and levees, draughting architectural designs, &c. nov24

J. H. SHANKS. JOHN KNEAL.
SHANKS & KNEAL,
HOUSE PAINTERS, GLAZIERS
—AND—
PAPER HANGERS,
sept1 PLAQUEMINE, LA

Hanenkamp & Hynes,
Wholesale Grocers and Commission Merchants,
ST. LOUIS, Mo.

☞Particular attention given to consignments of Sugar and Molasses, and to filling orders for Western Produce. jan6'58-tf

WM. H. POLSON,
House, Sign and Ornamental Painters, and Imitators of Wood and Marble. Paper Hanging and Glazing,

All done on the cheapest possible terms; and guaranteeing perfect satisfaction, he request the patronage of his friends and the public generally. my7-1y

Barber Shop.

NICOLAS BIEHLER respectfully informs his friends and the public that he still continues at his old stand on Main street, adjoining his brothers' Tailor shop and Wine Store, where he still pursues SHAVING and HAIR CUTTING, as also CUPPING when called upon. s8

FRANK GLASER,
Boot and Shoemaker.

The business heretofore carried on by B. GLASER, will be conducted in future by FRANK GLASER, at the old stand on Bank st., north of Main street, and he trusts that his attention to business and endeavors to please his customers, and the manner in which his work is done, will merit him the continued patronage of his friends and the public.
my5-m9. FRANK GLASER.

LIVERY STABLE.

The Undersigned respectfully inform the public, that, having purchased and removed to the Livery Stable formerly owned and occupied by Sam'l. McFaddin, and latterly by Ira Orcutt, on Main street in the town of Plaquemine, and having added much to it in the way of fine Horses and Buggies, they are prepared to carry on the LIVERY STABLE BUSINESS in all its branches.
Horses, and Vehicles of almost every kind, ready at short notice.
Family Carriages supplied.
Customers can rely upon having their Horses well fed and taken care of. Give us a trial.
We also have fine large Lots for the accommodation of drovers.
JAMES BARKER,
my1-1y J. P. MARIONNEAUX.

Sewing Machines.
CHEAPER THAN EVER!

WE have a few SEWING MACHINES on hands, which we will sell at a great reduction of price to close out the lot.
sept1 ROTH, DEBLIEUX & CO.

MISCELLANEOUS.

THE GEM.

THE undersigned would respectfully announce to their friends and the public generally, that they have just purchased the Coffee-house and fixtures formerly kept by Phillip Heelein opposite the steamboat landing; and having been to considerable expense in papering all the rooms so that they are neat and pleasant, and having the *best brands of Liquors and Wines* to be had in New Orleans, and further, pledging ourselves to spare no pains to please all who call to see us, we shall expect a small share of the public patronage.
GEOGE TURIN, CHARLES SEIPPLE, } TURIN & SEIPPLE.
Plaquemine, May 19, 1860.

The Rainbow.

SOLOMON FREY presents his compliments to his friends and the public, and respectfully informs them that he has opened in the building on Main street, formerly occupied by Stockley & Delavallade, a

Coffee House and Lager Beer.

Saloon, where good liquors and good beer can be had, and where he hopes his old patrons and the public will call and see him. sep15

Rhine Wine.

The underigned would say to his friends and to the public generally that he has just eceived a new supply of White and Red Rhine Wine, of a quality much superior to that received last year. The public may rely upon this wine being the true and actual juice of the grap, as it came from the vineyards on the Rhine. Call and try it.
aug11 GABRIEL BIEHLER.

Coffee House, Boarding House, Livery Stable.
MAURICE MARIX

INFORMS his fiends and the public generally that he has opened his new house, on Bank street, since the 4th of July, where he is finely situated to accommodate Boarders and tansient visitors, on reasonable terms. His table shall always be furnished with the best the market affords.
His COFFEE HOUSE will always be supplied with the best of Liquors, Wine, Lager Beer, &c.
He has a BILLIARD TABLE kept in a separate room from the bar, handsomely fitted up.
His STABLE cannot be surpassed; and all animals entrusted to his care shall meet with the most diligent attention.
He confidently hopes that his old friends will not forget him. Planters and others from the country will have their horses and buggies properly taken care of at all times, and as good a dinner and wine as the town affords, for themselves and friends. sep3

ANTHONY ASTREDO'S
OYSTER SALOON,
—AND—
RESTAURANT,
No. 16 Royal Street,

Next door to the Post Office, NEW ORLEANS.
Oysters in Barrels or Cans, Pickled or Spiced.
Fruit and Nuts of all kinds, wholesale and retail.
Always on hand a full supply of all the luxuries of the season.
Meals served in New York style.
City and country orders put up on the shortest notice. ap21-1y

New Butchery.

The undersigned respectfully informs the public that he has purchased the old and well known Butchery of F. Smith, and that he intends to keep his stall well supplied with the best of Beef, Mutton, Pork, &c. By a strict attention to his business in the above respect, he hopes to have a share of public patronage, and particularly the patronage of Mr. Smith's old customers.
P. S. The carts will run as usual down the Coast and to the Park,
dec25-1y BERTRAM BEYRIS.

HAASE BROS.
Ladies Dress Goods
AND
Plantation Goods

they particularly call attention to, as also their extensive stock of

Ready Made Clothing.

They will not pretend to give a list of their stock in the compass of an advertisement, but request all who are in want of

Cheap Goods,

to give them a call, as they feel fully satisfied that purchasers will not go away from their store dissatisfied.]oc23] HAASE BROS.

Millright, Engineer, &c.

THE undersigned, flattering himself that he is favorably known throughout the State as MILLRIGHT AND ENGINEER, would respectfully announce to the Sugar Planters and others, that he is prepared to contract to build

Sugar Mills and Engines

of the best build and finish, of any size required, and warranted in every case.
Contracts for next year respectfully solicited.

NOTICE TO BUILDERS AND OTHERS.
He is prepared to furnish IRON RAILINGS VERANDAHS, &c. Call and see his samples
aug25 A. ST. DIZIER.

At $10 per Thousand.

I HAVE FOR SALE,
192,000
Fine A No. 1 BRICKS.
jy THEO. BLANCHARD.

WE have a large and fresh assortment of MEDICINES, which were purchased for cash in New York, and which we warrant in all cases, and will sell as low as any Hose in the South.
se8 STOCKLEY & DELAVALLADE.

Paints..............Oils.
LEAD, WHITE—White Zinc, Linseed Oil, Turpentine, &c., for sale by
se8 STOCKLEY & DELAVALLADE.

Just Received,
1 bbl. first quality Whiskey.
1 bbl common do.
10 gallons No. 1 Brandy.
Also, a lot of splendid Havana CIGARS.
jy7 FR. A. ORILLION.

MISCELLANEOUS.

F. LAGLEIZE,
Fancy Baker and Confectioner,

RESPECTFULLY informs families and others of Plaquemine and Iberville, that he is at all times prepared to furnish parties with *Cake and Confectionery* in every style, and manufactured in a manner not surpassed anywhere. He will furnish any thing that may be required in his line at the shortest notice, and on the most reasonable terms.—Bakery at the corner of Bank and Greaud streets. my12

ANTHONY WILBERT,
CABINET MAKER,

Takes this method of returning his thanks to his old friends and customers for the patronage heretofore received, and assures them that he will ever strive to accommodate them in his line.
He has now moved to the large and commodious building at the corner of Fenn's Alley and Bank street where he has a large stock of Furniture of every kind.
Old Furniture taken in exchange or repaired at very low prices.
He also makes COFFINS of every style at the shortest notice.
☞Fisk's Metallic Coffins supplied as heretofore.
Splendid Hearse. Price moderate. sep4

To Sugar Planters.

The Star Bagasse Furnace.
Patented 15th June, 1858.
Never Known to Fail!

PARTIES wishing to purchase the right to use please apply to
EVAN SKELLY.
—ALSO—
The Wood or Coal Furnace,
for either BOILERS or SUGAR KETTLES,
Patented December 21st, 1858.
☞Numerous references given. Apply as above. ap7

WAREHOUSE.
Forwarding and Commission Business.
Steamboat Landing, adjoining the Post-Office.

THE UNDERSIGNED have associated themselves together, for the purpose of doing a general Forwarding and Commission Business.
We will also Collect Monies due the merchants, and business men, of the North, East and West. All business intrusted to our care will be promptly attended to.
HEELEIN & JENNINGS.
PHILIP HEELEIN, P. E. JENNINGS. }
☞Refer to any reliable citizen of the Parish Iberville, La. dec31

NEW SADDLERY AND
Harness Establishment.

The undersigned respectfully announces to the citizens of Iberville and West Baton Rouge, that he has again returned to Plaquemine, with the intention of locating himself permanently, to carry on the

Saddlery and Harness Business
IN ALL ITS BRANCHES.

Those in want of SADDLES, HARNESS, or any article of PLANTATION GEARING, will find it to their interest to give him a call, before purchasing elsewhere.
Shop on Main street, lower story of the Old Masonic Hall. mh24 A. W. SCOTT.

Carriage and Harness Manufactory
AND
Carriage Trimming Establishment.
—:o:o:—
GUSTAVE RINGWALD,
Successor to CHARLES VEIT & Co., at the old stand of A. W. SCOTT.

Respectfully informs the people of Iberville and West Baton Rouge that having purchased out the interest of his partner, he intends carrying on the same line of business, such as the manufacture of all kinds of

Saddles and Harness
And the Trimming and Painting of Carriages and Buggies.

And everything kept in a similar establishment
N. B.—No Repairing done on *CREDIT*.
Plaquemine, Nov. 12th, 1859. 1y

U. S. Mail Line,
BETWEEN PLAQUEMINE AND CHARENTON.

The steam propeller *VIRGINIA*, RODOLPH MILLER, Captain, will leave Plaquemine, carrying the mail, every Tuesday Morning, at 6 o'clock precisely—and returning leave Charenton every Wednesday Morning at 6 o'clock, and arrive at Plaquemine the same day. Leave Plaquemine again on Saturday morning at 6, and leave Charenton again on Sunday morning at 6 o'clock, connecting with the Iberville for Baton Rouge and Bayou Sara, and with the St. Mary for Franklin and New Iberia.
☞Shippers will please see that their freight is on board the boat the evening previous to her departure.—For further particulars apply to
dec22 J. McWILLIAMS & CO.

NOTICE.

THE undersigned having gone to Baton Rouge to engage in the BOOT and SHOE MAKING business, presents his thanks to his friends in this town and Parish, for the patronage hitherto extented to him, and trusts they will continue the same in favor of his brother, F. GLASER, who will continue the business here in the old stand on Bank street.
mar9 B. GLASER.

OYSTER SALOON!

The undersigned would respectfully inform his friends and the public generally that his Oyster Saloon is now in "full blast," where Oysters are served up in every style. Also—

Game and other Luxuries,

including "Ironsides Gumbo," and Gumbo, of every other description; Soups, Roasts, Stews, Frys, Broils—Salmon, Lobsters, Sardines, &c. &c.—

Desserts and Delicacies;

and WINES and LIQUORS of all kinds, and of the most superior quality. Give me a call.
nov12 H. LEBLANC.

CUTLERY—A new and beautiful assortment of Pen Knives just received and for sale low by R. A. KEARNY

MISCELLANEOUS.

O. S. JENNINGS,
No. **20** *CAMP STREET,*
NEW ORLEANS, La.,
(Under the City Hotel Buildings,)
Watchmaker and Jeweler.
DEALER IN EVERY DESCRIPTION OF
FINE WATCHES,
Jewelry,
Silver and Plated Ware.
☞Watches and Jewelry repaired and warantd. oc15

PROSPECTUS.

Young Ladies Academy
AND
CONVENT OF HOLY CROSS,
Plaquemine, (Iberville,) La.

THIS INSTITUTION is beautifully situated in the centre of the town of Plaquemine, between Court, Church and Plaquemine streets. The buildings are large and commodious, and the grounds of good ample space for amusement and healthy exercise. The Institution being situated within a few minutes walk of the steamboat landing, enjoys the advantage of easy and frequent access. It is conducted by the Sisters of Holy Cross, who being wholly devoted to the important work of public instruction, spare no pains to improve the hearts of their pupils in virtue and store their minds with knowledge, and they pledge themselves to return the children to their parents improved in virtue and learning.

To impart a thorough education in the highest sense of the word—to train the moral and the intellectual being—to develope sound health and elegant manners, is an object of constant attention. The system of government is mild and maternal, aiming to guide rather than to drive the pupils along the path of duty. The comforts and dersonal habits of the young ladies, receive the same attention as in the most refined family circle.

Religion is the ground-work of education. The Institution is Catholic; but young ladies of all denominations are admitted, provided they are willing for the sake of order and uniformity to attend the exercises of public worship. The Academical year is of ten months. The course of Education embraces all the branches usually taught in Academies, with the facility of primary instruction in both the English and French languages, at the option of parents.

Terms for Boarders:

Entrance fee, Bed, $5,00,	$ 5 00
Board and Tuition, per annum, payments quarterly in advance,	80 00

Terms for half Boarders:

Tuition per month, payable monthly,	$10 00

Terms for Day Scholars:

Tuition, per month, payable monthly,	$4 00

Extra charges at the option of parents, iz Music, Medical Attendance, Board at Conven during Vacation, Washing and Mending, Bed Bedding, Mattrass, Stationery, Tapestry-work Embreidery, Artificial Flowers, &c. &c. Or Board, Tuition and Washing, Mending, Bed, Bedding, Mattrass. Stationery, Tapestry work, Embroidery, Artificial Flowers. &c. &c. Or Board, Tuition, Washing, Mending, Bed, Bedding, Stationery, complete, per annum, $240 00.

UNIFORM.
Winter—Green French Merinos.
Summer—Pink Gingham.

It is to be worn only on Sundays and Thursdays, and the other holidays when going to Church or Walk. Patterns of the make and the shade may be had at the Convent.

SPECIAL DIRECTIONS.

Each Boarder must be provided with six Sheets, Musquito Bar, six feet by three; twelve Chemises; ditto pairs of Hose; ditto of Handkerchiefs; six Pillow Cases; twelve Towels and Napkins; one Tumbler; Fork and Knife; table and desert Spoons, and all the requisites of Toilet.

Pocket money is to be deposited in the hands of the Superioress.

Visits are allowed to the Boarders from their Parents and Guardians on Sundays and Thursdays, and only from 9 o'clock A. M. to 4 o'clock P. M.

References—Plaquemine, Rev. Francois C. Fallot. New Orleans, Rev. P. F. Sheil, S. S. C., or
SISTER MARY OF CALVARY,
nov27-sep3 Superioress of the Convent.

PRESERVE YOUR TEETH.

J. A. CASADAVANT,
Surgeon Dentist,
107 *Royal Street, New Orleans.*
Opposite St. Louis Hotel.

CONTINUES to call the attention of those who need the services of a competent Dentist, and those persons whose Teeth have been injured by unskillful Dentists, whose gold drops out a short time after the Teeth are plugged, and whose Artificial Teeth cannot be worn with comfort, by applying to J. A. CASADAVANT, they can have all operations in the Dental Art performed conscientiously, and in the most scientific manner. He benumbs the gums, before Extracting Teeth, with a chemical preparation invented by him, which lessens the pain. Consultations in French, Spanish and English. dec31

ALLEN'S
Improved Stubble Shaver.

A number of the above important article, so useful in facilitating the culture of the sugar cane,—invented by J. ALLEN, and perfected by the undersigned—has been manufactured and is now on hand for sale in New Orleans by GEO. W. SISER, corner of Camp and Poydras, Agent for the sale of the machine in that city.

The undersigned has upwards of *seventy* certificates from the best planters in Louisiana, who have witnessed the operations of the *Stubble Shaver* in various soils; and there cau be no questions of the fact that it meets—and fully meets—all the requirements and desideratums that could be needed or desired for performing cleanly, neatly aud perfectly the work for which it was invented to perform, and in which performance it does the labor of at least *fifteen hands with the hoe!* It will also shave from 25 to 50 acres without sharpening. The price asked for them will be found to be surprisingly small considering the price paid for their manufacture.

Planters wanting the *Stubble Shaver* will please address GEO. W. SISER, New Orleans or to
oct 13 A. ST. DIZIER, Plaquemine:
Or to J. McWILLIAMS.

Save your Fruit.

A NEW supply of Fruit Jars just receivedg every Jar warranted air tight—no sealin required. Call and see them at
R. A. KEARNY'S,
aug11 Corner of Main and Bank sts.

MISCELLANEOUS.

SOUTHERN
MUTUAL INSURANCE
COMPANY.

Office of Southern Mutual Insurance Co., OF BATON ROUGE. }

IN CONFORMITY with the requirements of their charter, the SOUTHERN MUTUAL INSURANCE COMPANY publish the folowing statement:

Amount of premiums received from February 1st, 1860, to Febr'ry 1st, 1861.	$85,286,96
AS FOLLOWS:	
Premiums on Fire Risks......	$66,839 20
" " Marine "......	13,760 49
" " River "......	4,687 27
	$85,286 96
Premiums on unterminated Risks, February 1st, 1860......	$49,814 48
	$135,101 44
Less premiums on Risks not terminated	60,220 74
Nett earned premiums for the year ending 1st February, 1861......	$74,880 70
Losses paid during the same period:	
"NO LOSSES UNSETTLED."	
On Fire Risks......	$12,381 75
" Marine Risks......	1,554 64
" River Risks......	3,440 17
	$17,376 56
Expenses during year as above	7,992 82
	$25,369 39
Nett earned Profits for the year ending February 1st, 1861......	$49,511 32
The Company have the following Assets:	
Bills receivable, for premiums......	$ 55,531 24
Bills receivable, for balance due on Stock Notes......	152 964 91
Cash, balance on hand......	139,503 61
Balance due by New Iberia Agency....	333 50
Balance due by New Orleans Agency ..	3,375 35
Total assets......	$351,709 61

(Signed) WM. S. PIKE, Pres't.
F. E. HEBERT, Sec'y.
Baton Rouge, February 2d, 1861.

STATE OF LOUISIANA, PARISH OF E. BATON ROUGE, Feb. 1. 1861. }

Be it remembered, That on this first day of February, 1861, before me the subscriber, a Justice of the Peace in and for the parish aforesaid, personally appeared Wm. S. Pike, President, and F. E. Hebert, Secretary of the Southern Mutual Insurance Company, of Baton Rouge, who being duly sworn according to law do depose and say that the above accounts are just and true, and a correct transcript from the books of said Company.
(Signed) WM. S. PIKE, President.
F. E. HEBERT, Secretary,
Sworn to and subscribed before me, this second day of February, 1861.
[S gned] P. A. WALKER, Justice of the Peace.
(Signed) P. A. WALKER, Justice of the Peace.

NOTICE.

OFFICE SOUTHERN MUTUAL INSURANCE Co., Baton Rouge, Feb. 4th, 1861. }

At a meeting of the Board of Directors, held this day, it was *Resolved*, To pay *six per cent* interest on the outstanding Scrip, *eight per cent* to Stockholders on premiums paid by them for the year ending 1st February, 1861, and to declare a dividend of *fifty per cent* on the nett earned premiums of the Company for the year ending 31st January, 1861, for which certificates will be issued on and after the 1st day of March next.

It was further Resolved, To redeem the outstanding Scrip for the year 1858, on presentation at the office of the Company.

☞The Stockholders are hereby notified that an election for ten Directors and fifteen Trustees to serve for the ensuing year, will be held at the office of the Company, on Thursday, the 14th of March, 1861.
mh30 F. E. HEBERT, Sec'y.

KETTLE SETTING.
A Labor of Years Reduced to a Few Days.

HAVING been induced by frequent solicitation, to make public the science of Kettle Setting that I practice, I hereby give notice to all persons desiring to acquire a knowledge of the art, that I will give them instructions for the Setting of Kettles, for either wood or coal, on application to me.

My system is based upon principles, the plausibility and correctness of which admit of no contradiction, which are quickly and fully comprehended, and therefore not liable to be easily forgotten.

I have models for five different constructions of Kettles, and designs by which instruction is made easy, and the art soon acquired. Copies of designs or drawings are given to those whom I instruct. All those to whom I teach my system, are also assisted by my services, if required.

Instructions are only given to those who have been three or four years at the business of Kettle Setting, and are good workmen.

For further particulars, inquire, by letter or otherwise, of the undersigned.
JOHN TOWNSEND.
Plaquemine, (Parish of Iberville,) La, Feb. 25, 1860.
Refer to—Dr. C. Clement, Iberville.
" Louis Desobry, Sr., "
" Gervais & Roman Schlatre, "
" John Schlatre, "
" Sylvar Marionneaux, "
" Edward J. Gay, "
" Jas. C. Woods, West Baton Rouge.
" Dan. H. Hickey, do
" Thompson J. Bird, East Baton Rouge

DIRECT IMPORTATION
—OF—
HAVANA CIGARS!

WE are in receipt of a small invoice of HAVANA CIGARS imported by ourselves. These we can sell at New Orleans prices. We can furnish our customers with the GENUINE WEED at $35 per thousand—something very good at $40, as good as we could sell heretotofore at $50.
By next steamship we shall receive a large invoice.
☞Call, examine and judge for yourselves
je30 STOCKLEY & DELAVALLADE

WADDELL'S PILLS.

THIS Purely Vegetable Pill, which is spoken off so highly by all who have used them, for Diarrhea, Dysentary, Piles, &c. &c., or any affliction of the Bowels and Stomach, can be had No. 93Camp street, New Orleans.

Gazette & Sentinel.

PUBLISHED EVERY SATURDAY BY
W. P. BRADBURN,
EDITOR AND PROPRIETOR.

A Queer People.

Chamher's Journal, discussing a recent book of missionary travels in Africa, thus alludes to one of the tribes which are found in that *terra incognita*:

But the strangest of all are the stories told of the Dokos, who live among the moist, warm bamboo woods to the south of Kaffa and Susa. Only four feet high, of a dark olive color, savage and naked, they have neither household temples, neither fire nor human food. They live only on ants, mice, and serpents, diversified by a few roots and fruits; they let their nails grow long like talons, the better to dig for ants, and the more easily to tear in pieces their favorite snakes.

They do not marry, but live indiscriminative lives of animals, multiplying very rapidly, and with very little maternal instinct. The mother only nurses her child but a short time, accustoming it to eat ants and serpents as soon as possible; and when it can help itself it wanders away where it will, and the mother thinks no more of it. The Dokos are invaluable as slaves, and are taken in large numbers. The slave hunters hold up bright colored cloths as soon as they come to the moist, warm bamboo woods, where these human monkeys live; and the poor Dokos cannot resist the attraction offered by such superior people. They crowd around them and are taken by thousands.

In slavery they are docile, attached, obedient, with few wants and excellent health. They have only one fault—a love of ants, mice and snakes, and a habit of speaking to Yer with their heads on the ground and their heels in the air. Yer is their idea of a superior power, to whom they talk in this comical nature when they are dispirited or angry, or tired of ants and snakes, and longing for unknown food. The Dokos seem to come nearest of all people yet discovered to that terrible cousin of humanity—the ape.

The Utility of Refuse Things.

The prussiate of potash is made in large quantities in Cincinnati from the hoofs, horns and other refuse of slaughtered cattle.

Cow-hair, taken from the hides in tanneries, is employed in making plastering-mortar, to give it a fibrous quality.

Sawdust is sold for sprinkling the floors of markets. It is also used for packing ice for shipping.

The rags of old. worn out skirting, calico dresses, and the waste of cotton factories, are employed to make the paper upon which these lines are printed.

Old ropes are converted into fine note paper, and the waste paper itself, which is picked up in the gutter, is again reconverted into broad, white sheets, and thus does duty in revolving stages.

The parings of skins and hides, and the ears of cows, calves, and sheep, are carefully collected and converted into glue.

The finer qualities of gelatine are made from ivory raspings and the bones and tendons of animals.

Bones converted into charcoal, by roasting in retorts, are afterwards employed for purifying the white sugar with which we sweeten our coffee.

The ammonia obtained from the distillation of coal in making gas, is employed for saturating orchil and cudbear, in making the beautiful lilac colors that are dyed on silk and the fine woolen goods.

Carbonic acid, obtained in the distillation of coal tar, is employed with other acids to produce beautiful yellow colors on silk and wool.

The shavings of cedar wood, used in making pencils, are distilled to obtain the otto of cedar wood.

Brass filings and old brass kettles are remelted, and employed to make the brass-work of printing presses and pumps.

Old copper scraps are used in the construction of splendid bronze chandeliers, for illuminating our churches and the mansions of the wealthy.

Old horseshoe nails are employed to make the famous steel and twist barrels of fowling-pieces.

☞An Irishman who was standing on London Bridge, accosted a youth standing beside him, saying:

"Faith I think I know yer; what's yer name?"

"My name is Jones," replied the youth.

"Jones, Jones," said the Irishman, "I knew two ould maids by that name in Dublin, was aither of them yer muther?"

NATIONAL MADNESS.—"Except God keep the minds of men," Bishop Butler once asked, "what is to prevent a nation from going crazy any more than an individual.

Gazette & Sentinel.

PUBLISHED EVERY SATURDAY BY
W. P. BRADBURN,
EDITOR AND PROPRIETOR.

TERMS OF SUBSCRIPTION.

THREE DOLLARS AND FIFTY CENTS ($3 50) for one year, in advance. FIVE DOLLARS ($5 00) if not paid in advance.

SINGLE COPIES—Ten Cents.

No subscription will be discontinued unless a written notice to that effect is received from the subscriber himself, and all arrearges paid.

TERMS OF ADVERTISING.

ONE DOLLAR ($1 00) per square of ten lines, or less, of this space, ———— ————, for the first insertion, and Fifty Cents for each subsequent insertion. A liberal discount, however, on these rates will be made on advertisements inserted for a longer time than two months, as follows:

	3 months.	6 months.	12 months.
1 square	$ 5 00	$ 8 00	$ 12 00
2 squares	8 00	12 00	20 00
3 squares	15 00	15 00	25 00
4 squares	12 00	20 00	30 00
5 squares	18 00	25 00	37 00
6 squares	20 00	30 00	45 00

For Professional or Business Cards, not exceeding one square, with paper, one year, $15.

Announcements of Candidates for office, $10. Cash in all cases must accompany the announcement, whether handed in by a friend or the person announced.

The privilege of yearly advertisers is strictly limited to their own immediate and regular business.

Communications intended to promote the private ends or interests of individuals, corporations or societies, will be charged as advertisements.

All persons ordering Jobs or handing in advertisements on account of any local or political organization, will be held responsible for the payment of the same.

Marriages and Deaths published without charge. Obituaries inserted as other advertisements.

Advertisements not marked the length of time they are to be inserted, will be kept in the paper till forbid, and charged accordingly.

All advertisements by strangers or transient persons must be paid in advance.

Personal Cards, if inserted at all, will be charged two dollars per square.

☞Job Work always cash, and advertisementr are due when first inserted.

New Advertisements.

FOR CONGRESS.

We are authorized to announce **Col. H. W. ALLEN,** of West Baton Rouge, as a candidate for Congress of the Confederate States for the Fourth Congressional District, composed of the Parishes of West Feliciana, Point Coupee, St. Landry, Lafayette, Vermillion. West Baton Rouge, Iberville, St. Mary and St. Martin. Election first Monday in November.

FOR AUDITOR.

We are authorized to announce **H. PERALTA,** of East Baton Rouge, as a Candidate for Auditor of Public Accounts—subject to a nomination by a Democratic State Convention, if one iscalled.

FOR ASSESSOR.

Mr. Editor: Please announce the name of **T. RODOLPH VERBOIS,** Esq., as a Democratic Candidate for Assessor for the parish of Iberville, subject to the State Rights Democratic Convention.

We are authorized to announce **ERNEST CALLERY,** the present incumbent, as a Candidate for re-election to the office of Assessor, subject to the decision of the State Rights Democratic Convention.

SHERIFF AND RECORDER.

Mr. Editor: You will plea-e announce the following gentlemen for the offices which precede their respective names, subject to the decision of the State Rights Democratic Convention, viz:

For Sheriff, - - - - J. L. PETIT.
For Recorder, - - - J. H. ERWIN.

FOR RECORDER.

Mr. Editor: You will please announce the name of **ADOLPHE HEBERT,** Esq., as a Candidate for the office of Recorder of the parish of Iberville, subject to the decision of the State Rights Democratic Convention.

FOR SHERIFF.

Mr. Editor: Please announce my name in your paper as a Candidate for the next Sheriffalty of this parish.

GUSTAVE LAUVE.

Bayou Goula, April 18th, 1861.

To Corporation Claimants.

☞As the undersigned has a "small pile" of Corporation funds in his hands, unappropriated, these who have claims which have been allowed, and are duly signed by the Mayor, with the order "to pay," would do well to present them and get their money. "First come, first served."

WM. P. BRADBURN,
ap20 *Corporation Treasurer.*

NOW IS THE TIME

TO BUY CHEAP GOODS!

HAVING returned from New Orleans with the finest and best selected stock of

DRY GOODS

That has ever been brought to this Market, I take pleasure of informing my friends and old Customers, that the following is a part ot my stock:—

Ladies' Dress Goods,

In every quality of the latest styles.

Rich English Barege Robes, Organdy Robes, Jaconets, Muslins, Ladies' Shawls, and Lace Mantillas, real and imitation, Parasols, Corsets, Hosiery, Ladies' Embroidered Handkerchiefs, and Valencienne Collars and Sleeves.

A splendid assortment of Linen Goods, Towels and Napkins, and Irish Linen; Ladies' Bonnets and Ribbons of all the latest styles.

Ladies' and Childrens' Shoes,

Of the best manufacturies, &c., &c.,

☞TO PLANTERS—A large stock of Staple Goods for sale at very low prices.

☞Also, a lot of English Barege at 15 cts. per yard. Call at

ap20] LEOPOLD KAHN'S.

CHOICE GROCERIES.

CHAS. N. ROTH & CO..

RESPECTFULLY invite the public to call and examine their stock of

Groceries and Produce,

Being satisfied that they can show them a stock inferior to none ever brought to this market, which they offer at **Lower Prices than have been paid heretofore.** The following are among the leading articles generally required, all of which are of a superior quality—viz:

Mess Beef,	Hay,
Mess Pork,	Flour,
Clear Sides,	Rice,
Smoked Meats,	Coffee,
Breakfast Bacon,	Sugar,
Beef, Lard, Beans,	Dried Apples,
Corn, Oats,	Sweet Oil,
Old Burbon Whisky,	Oils, Paints.
Old Family Brandies,	&c., &c., &c.

Besides many other articles too numerous to mention—together with a spendid stock of Fancy Groceries.

ap20] C. N. ROTH & CO,

New Advertisements.

SCHOOL NOTICE.

THE undersigned would informs parents and others that

HIS SCHOOL IS REMOVED,

From the original location, to the house belonging to Mr. Comaux, opposite the residence of Mr. Ross, late J. Bte. Roth's, at the head of Bank street. The public is informed that he will give his entire time and attention to those entrusted to his care. He instructs in both languages, English and French.

ap 20] A. DOMINIQUE.

The Right Place to Buy Jewelry.

W. A. HAYWARD,

Manufacturing Jeweler,

208 Broadway, New York.

NO one purchasing Jewelry of any description should fail to call upon W A. HAYWARD, before purchasing, or send him an order for samples. Any person wishing samples to order from, can have the same sent with the privilege of returning anything they may not want.

☞N. B. Full assortment of Goods for the $1 Stores and Jewelery Envelopes. [ap20

ELECTION NOTICE.

MAYOR'S OFFICE,
April 20th, 1861.

PURSUANT to a resolution of the Board of Selectmen of the Town of Plaquemine, an Election will be holden at the Court House, on MONDAY, the 6th day of May next, 1861, for the purpose of electing a Mayor and Five Selectmen to serve for the ensuing year.

The polls to open at 10 o'clock, A. M., and to close at 2 P. M.

THOS. E. GRACE, *Mayor.*
Plaquemine, La. ap20

WANTED,

A SITUATION as GARDENER, by a man who understands Gardening in all its branches, and the management of Green Houses and the propagating of their plants. He is acquainted with the cultivation of Fruits, Flowers, Shrubs, Bulbs, Grape Vines, and Vegetables in all their variety—the laying out of Gardens in Fourteen different plans. He has attended to the above business for many years in the South, and is able to take charge of a large place. Any person requiring such a Gardener, can find him by addressing a letter to "W. C., Gardener," at the office of this paper, between this day and Monday, the 22d. [ap20

PLAQUEMINE:

Saturday, APRIL 20, 1861.

☞Holders of accepted claims against the Corporation will find a notice interesting to them in the adjoining column.

☞LEOPOLD KAHN comes before his customers this week in a card, detailing an outline of the rich and extensive stock of Ladies' Goods, which he has opened, fresh from the importers' rooms in New Orleans. Give him a call.

☞Messrs. CHAS. N. ROTH & Co. give a list of a few of their leading articles this week—all of which are first class articles, the prices of which are placed at exceedingly low figures; of their canvassed hams we can "speak by the book"—being sweet, juicy and of a fine flavor, and sold much cheaper than we have been able to purchase hams of first quality for many years past. In fact their stock is allnew and cheap, and appears to be going "like hot cakes." Their liquors are very superior.

☞We are requested by Father FALLOT to say that the Pews in the Catholic Church will positively be rented to-morrow, the 21st.

The News.

Our paper this week contains a correct synopsis of the important news received by telegraph in the city since the attack on Fort Sumpter. We consequently issue a supplement. Papers in wrappers can be lad at the office. The week has been an eventfulone the histoty of this continent.

A Daily Bulletin.

Ever desiring to do all that lays in our power, and in oursphere as an Editor, to merit the approbation and support of our patrons, we have determined to contiue issuing a Bulletin daily *while the war lasts,* or when news received is of sufficient importance to justify it. These Bulletins will be sent regularly to our town and parish subscribers, without any extra charge. We shall be enabled to get the New Orleans evening papers almost daily, and in a few hours afterwards our subscribers will receive whatever they contain that is important.

We would therefore suggest that the present is an inviting time to subscribe for all who are not already on our list, and who feel any interest in the events which may be anticipated from the position of affairs at this time. As this enterprise will cost us much additional work and expense, the dues of those in arrears would be most appropos and thankful at the present time. Will they please bear this in mind.

Weather, Crops, &c.

Since the storm last Sunday night, the weather has been balmy and beautiful. The rain was just what was wanted for the crops; since then, we are told, the crops seem fairly to jump out of the ground!—It is not in the memory of the oldest inhabitant that the crops of cane, cotton and corn promised a more fruitful harvest than they do at present. It is the same with fruits, with potatoes, and every thing else that a wise creator has adapted for the consumption and benefit of us all. Surely the blessings of Providence are with us in our present struggle.

Highway Robbery and Nearly Murder.

We learnt from Mr. LOUVARIRE yesterday morning, that on the previous night about 9 o'clock, he was attacked by negroes in the Cut-off Road between this parish and West Baton Rouge, knocked known, beaten and robbed of fifty dollars. He shows evidences of terrible blows upon his person. He had been at work in West Baton Rouge—was on foot at the time, with his clothes in a bundle, (which was also taken,) coming in this direction. Mr. L. says he is of St. James parish, and has relatives in Donaldsonville.

For the Seat of War.

The steamer Louis d'Or, from Shreveport, passed down on Wednesday, having on board the Shreveport Greys, Capt. BAIRD, 110 strong, destined for the seat of war. GEO. WILLIAMSON, 1st Lieut., L. D. MARKS, 2d do., B. L. HODGE, 3d do., LAWRENCE L. BUTLER, 1st Corporal. All of the three Lieutenants were members of the Convention, and the First Lieutenant and First Corporal are the son-in-law and son of Col, E. G. W. BUTLER, of this parish. This reminds us that the third generation of "the Butlers" of the Revolution will soon be in the choice element of their race. The above company turned out within twenty-four hours after due notice was served upon them to prepare for the field. And, to the immortal honor of Capt. JOHNSON, of the Louis d'Or, he brought the company down free of charge!

The Military Display last Monday.

Owing to the severe storm that visited us lst Sunday night, (which it seems, was as violent in Baton Rouge and New Orleans as here,) our streets on the following day were in rather an uncomfortalle condition for the marchings and evolutions of the military turn-out on that day. Notwithstanding, the Home Sentinels, Capt. SCHLATRE, and the Iberville Greys, Capt. BRUSLE, with their respective bands of music, (after the first had received the latte on its landing on this side the river,) marched through our town and elicited the admiration of our citizens.—We were pleased to see present, but not in parade, a number of "Capt. Keep's mounted dare-devils," who however appeared very modest and orderly—he characteristics of brave men. It has been a long time if ever, since Plaquemine has seen so much of the "pride and circumstance of war." At night, the weather being fair and pleasant, a ball came off at LeBlanc's Hall, and what with the gay unifoms and sparkling eyes, served to make of it an exciting, harmonious and brilliant affair. We can say, in the language of the poet:

> "Hearts beat happily; and when
> Music arose with its voluptuous swell,
> Soft eyes look'd love to eyes which spoke again,
> And all went merry as a marriage-bell."

A New Fire Engine.

We are glad to perceive that the Union Fire Co. engine has at length arrived. It came on Sundy last, and appears to be of the right size and lightness for the rough and often muddy and almost impassable streets of a country town. We are confident, from the patience, the energy and the perseverance of the above Company for the long period they kept organized, without the pride of a "merchine to run with," that its future will be garlanded with many brave and heroic acts of its individual members; for in case of fire, they and their engine, we know, will be in the hottest of it.

While upon this subject we would suggest to the Town Council the propriety of making some proffer to any company which should organize as a Fire Company and take in their charge the fine fire engine belonging to the Corporation, which is now nothing but an expense to it. Surely, one fire engine company in successful operation ought to stimulate the organization of another, particularly when a fine engine is in readiness for such company. If that could be effected, then we would suggest that the combined companies unite, as in New Orleans, as a military force (say of the artillery arm) for home protection.

Struck by Lightning and Consumed.

We learn that, during the storm last Sunday night or Monday morning, a house used as a stable and corn-crib, on the plantation of Judge COLE, about five miles below this on the river, was struck by lightning, which set fire to and consumed it. All the corn was lost, and a horse perished in the flames.

Bailey's Atela and Picture Saloon.

We hear of very little jewelry, few watches, &c., being now sent from here to the city for repair. A visit to Bailey's Atela, adjoining his Picture Saloon, will tell the reason. All that kind of work required here is now done by BAILEY, and in the best style. But that is not all he does. As the tocsin of war is now sounded, and no one knows how soon he may be on his "winding way" to the field of strife, would it not be well to let BAILEY take a fac simile of our features, in case of "casualties," and the natural desire of our country to have portraits of its heroes?

More Candidates.

It will be seen by reference to the adjoining column, that two more popular gentlemen of this parish are out as candidates for two of the best and most responsible offices in the parish.

The Black Republican Autocrat.

The rail splitter autocrat has just got his dander up since the taking of Fort Sumpter, and in defiance of the Constitution which he swore but a few days since to observe and preserve, has issued a proclamation for volunteers to subdue the Confederacy—as he has it, to "redress wrongs that have long been endured." He requires seventy-five thousand men to do this, and also to repossess the forts, &c., which he says, belongs to the "Union." Seventy-five thousand to do all that work! Why, the yellow-fever will kill off that number of Black Republicans, to say nothing of what Southern valor, gunpowder and shot will do. This proclamation, says the *Picayune,* is clearly in opposition to the Constitution and laws of the United States. That paper says:

> Neither the constitution of the United States, nor the laws which have been passed to execute its provisions, ever designed to give the President the awful power of summoning, on his own motion, the whole physical power of the country within his reach, to institute war upon one-fourth of the Union, under the plea of suppressing an insurrection. The constitution gave Congress the power to pass laws to provide for calling forth the militia "to execute the laws of the Union, to suppress insurrections, and repel invasion."
>
> Congress, in compliance with that direction, passed a law in which they empowered the Ppresident to call out any number of militia which he may think sufficient, when needed to suppress "combinations too formidable to be suppressed by the ordinary course of judicial proceedings, or by the powers vested in the marshals" of the United States.

This is evidencing plainly the influences of a first error. The Black Republican party insisted that their course, principles and programme were right, by that "Higher Law," which they pretend to obey or to be governed by, and which is nothing else than red Republicanism double-distilled, and which places the interests and intentions of its proselytes ahead of and superior to all laws and constitutions stamped on parchment. It was this sort of thing which made the Republicans defy the Fugitive Slave Act—which caused them to swear destruction to the slave property of the South in defiance of all laws upon that subject, or the rights of States to manage their own internal affairs; and it is that same despotic spirit which now causes old Abe to play the bravo, in subjugating (if he can) the free people of the Southern Confederacy, and despoiling them of the property baqueathed to them by their revolutionary fathers and sustained and guaranteed to them and their children, and children's children for all time to come, by the statutes of '78.

Having been wrong in the outset—having built up their organization upon principles antagonistical to law and justice—the Black Republican party, in the person of its President, is acting in a manner which, being in defiance of law, will, like the common transgressor, keep going on from bad to worse, making each act more heinous or arbitrary than the last, till the perpetrator himself is brought to the scaffold, his party annihilated, and the Government becomes an anarchy or military despotism—eventually with its own hands, wiping itself from the family of nations! Such will be the fate, we predict, of Lincoln, his party and his Government.

But the acts of this lawless "Higher-Law' Executive are for his own people to contemplate, not ours. If they are satisfied that Lincoln shall take the law into his own hands, it is for them to reap the reward of their folly. They were told that the Black Republican party could alone save the country. They believed it. They placed it in power by their united votes; and now, the *saviour* it will prove, will be that which the wolf gives to the lamb—*"covering and devouring!"*

Lincoln, too, clearly acknowledges his lawlessness in the calling Congress together at the expiration of eighty days. Why this delay? Why not convene it at once? By placing the assembling of Congress at such distant day, clearly evinces his doubt that Congress would sanction the measures he is now taking. Consequently, Lincoln and his abolition supporters are fearful that the opportunity now presented will never occur again.

What opportunity? The opportunity of marshalling a gigantic army, not so much for the purpose of coercing the seceded States as *it is a raid on a magnificent scale, and with all the appliances of Government at his command, to free the slaves which the Southern Confederacy contains!* This it is which stimulates Lincoln to his lawless measures. Napoleon won and lost an Empire in a hundred days. *He wishes to free four millions of slaves within eighty days! and before there is a competent body in power to check [illegible]n by the reins of law!*

Ah! little does he know of the metal of the Southern people. Next to their liberties, the institution of slavery is their pride and their boast. It is to preserve these jewels in her escutcheon—all her sons care to live for—which unites them as one man, and which calls them now to the field of strife and of honor to defeat the plans and the arms of this harlequin-Nero who presides at Washington.

War! War!! War!!!

Events have been crowding thick and fast upon us since our last issue. On the 12th the news was heralded through the land that our gallant forces had taken Fort Sumpter without bloodshed. This was the signal for the men of the South everywhere to rush to arms; every day brings the tidings that volunteers are offering their services by the legion, and that patriotic men are ready to give of their substance for the defense of the liberties of our country. The patriotic fires which have been lying dormant in the hearts of the people of the Border Slave States, have burst forth in all their splendor, and soon we shall see the whole South united to repel the fanatical myrmidons of the Black Republican Confederacy. Old Virginia is on the brink of secession;* the patriotic Governor of Kentucky has refused to respond to Lincoln's call for volunteers, and noble Tennessee, the home of the traitors Johnson and Etheridge, has offered her invincible soldiers to our President, who will march as soon as their services shall be needed. Unionism and "Reconstructionism," are dead forever at the South, and buried beyond hope of resurrection. Every man is resolved to fight in defense of his home and fireside, and will die in his tracks rather than surrender or retreat from the Black Republican army. In the meantime the Lincoln administration is also moving, and, if we may believe the telegraph, is fast concentrating an army of occupation and subjugation. According to that veracious vehicle of information, troops, in fabulous numbers, have offered their services, who will soon be upon us, as thick as blackberries, ready to perform miraculous and unheard of feats of valor. We do not believe that there has been any such uprising of the people of the North, as the hirelings of the press have telegraphed abroad, for the purpose of intimidating the Southerners and causing them to ground their arms and "disperse." We know that there are many at the North who are opposed to the insane measures of the Black Republican administration, which are destined to bankrupt the country, and then to end in a humiliating and disgraceful defeat. But even supposing that the whole North is united, we are abundantly able to defend ourselves against any army that it can support in the field. Although the North is much more populous than the South, we still have more men than we can conveniently make use of—many more than will be required to carry on the war to a successful termination. The men of the south have borne the brunt of the battle, in all the contests through which the old Union has passed, and have achieved the glory which has caused its flag to be respected by all nations; with much more bravery and energy will they fight now, when not only their honor, but their homes and property, nay, their very existence, are at stake. That the North may do us great injury in a long and bloody war, we do not deny; but they never can subjugate us—NEVER. In the language of our eloquent Vice President, "seventy-five times seventy-five thousand men cannot conquor us?"

We say, then, to our spirited and patriotic men, war is upon us, and is destined to last for some time; seize your arms and defend your homes, yonr families and your property. The war blast has sounded—it is no time for idleness and inaction.

*Since this was written, the booming of "Black Bess" on Thnrsday night and the hurrahing of the "b'hoys," were in honor of the act Old of Virginia, declaring that her destiny was with the South.

Synopsis of the Police Jury Proceedings.

The Police Jury assembled at a regular meeting in this town, on Monday, 8th of April inst. All the members were present, except Mr. Hyde, of the 8th Ward.

The session being opened, it was ordered that an election be held for members of Police Jury, from the 2nd (Plaquemine) Ward, and from the 3rd (Village) and 6th (Grand River) Wards.

A 10th School District was formed of the Bayou Alabama and Marangouin, and back settlements of Bayou Grosse Tete.

The sum of $300 was appropriated to the Union Fire Company No. 1, of this place, to purchase an engine.

The sum of $200 was appropriated to road and bridges on Bayou Paul, and $75 to repair the road and bridges of Manchac Cut Off.

The sum of $4 per day was fixed as the salary of members of Police Jury for each day they attend, and 10 cents per mile for coming and returning

The Polls on Gross Tete, was ordered back to the old store of Tho. Johnston.

The sum of $741 0[illegible] was appropriated to cancel certain bills.

The account of W. P. Bradburn, for advertising notices for sale, to lowest bidder, to make road and levee, ordered by Parish Commissioners, amounting n full to $20, was rejected. The Jury then adjourned.

Next day, the 9th, the Police Jury re-assembled—Present as before, except J. A. Sigur.

The accounts of the Parish Treasurer were examined and found corect, and a cash balance of $28,274 23 in his hands.

The account of Ernest Callery of $60, for making Tableaux of Parish Tax, and extension of same furnished to Sheriff, was read and rejected.

A tax of $15 was imposed upon all persons holding shows, concerts, and such like, in the Court House.

The report of Mr. Keep, as Secretary of the Grosse Tete and Marangouin Road, was adopted.

Commissioners were appointed to fully repair the Island Cut-Off road, and put it in good travelling order.

A resolution offered by Mr. Keep, was passed, repealing the Act relative to the Fire-Proof Building, and the monies appropriated therefor, be given to the various military companies of Iberville, viz: $750 to the Gross Tete Rangers, $500 to the Bayou Goula Guards, $500 to the Iberville Grays, $500 to the Home Sentinels, $500 to the Grosse Tete Fencibles, and $500 to an Artillery Company, when such is thoroughly organized; and the balance be placed in the Contingent Fund.

The resolution allowing hogs to run at large on the right [illegible]nk of Plaquemine, between the lands of V. J. Dupy and Victor Dupuy, be repealed.

No April Term of Court.

Editor Gazette and Sentinel:

Dear Sir—You will please give publication to the following letter from our worthy Judge, and oblige,

Yours Respectfully,
THEO. BLANCHARD.

BATON ROUGE, April 15th, 1861.

Mr. Blanchard, Sheriff of Iberville.

Dear Sir—Sustained by the general opinion of ten members of the bar, that, under the present legislation on the subject, it would be the exercising and exceedingly doubtful authority to hold the next term of the District Court in Iberville, on Monday next, and believing that the law authorizing the same, has been appealed and ceased to have any effect on and after the first Monday of April, 1861, the District Court will not be held next Monday.

Please say as much for the information of the public in the papers next Saturday, and oblige, Very truly your friend, &c.,

DAN'L D. AVERY,
Judge Fifth Judicial District.

COUNCIL PROCEEDINGS.

The Mayor and Board of Selectmen of the Town of Plaquemine, met at the Mayor's Office this 12th day of April, 1861.

Present—Thos. E. Grace, Mayor; J. E. Degelos, A. Talbot, and N. Valega, Selectmen.

The Mayor suggested the necessity of repairing the streets and cleaning the ditches within the Corporation, and the Board considering that their term of office has nearly expired, it was therefore determined to delay taking any action in the matter for the present.

On motion, the Constable was authorized to expend the price received for the fence around St. Johns's square, [$19 50], in levelling and grading said square.

There being no further business, the Board adjourned.

[Signed] T. E. GRACE,
JOHN MARCOT, *Clerk.* *Mayor.*

The Mayor and Board of Selectmen of the Town of Plaquemine, met at the Mayor's Office this 18th of April, 1861.

Present—Thos. E. Grace, Mayor; L. Charre, J. E. Degelos, A. Talbot, Selectmen.

Upon the application of several indigent persons within the Corporation for relief, the Board rejected the same, expressing it as their opinion that the said applications should be presented to the Police Jury.

On motion, A. Talbot and L. Chare, were appointed a committee to confer with the Officers of the Union Fire Company No. 1, for the purpose of making arrangemnets for transferring the engine belonging to the Corporation, to the said Fire Company.

The Mayor was authorized to order an election to be holden on the first Monday in May next, 1861, to elect a Mayor and five Selectmen, to serve for the ensuing year.

The bill of Dr. C. Ward for services as Physician and Medicines furnished to indigents, being considered, the sum of $75, was allowed in full payment of same.

There being no further business, the Board adjourned.

[Signed] T. E. GRACE,
JOHN MARCOT, *Clerk.* *Mayor.*

A Faithful Allay Suspended.

It is mortifying to see such a journal as that time-honored and Democratic one, the Philadelphia *Pennsylvanian,* stop the lever and machinery of its publication, in consequence of that usual cause, *failure of its party to support it.* Nothing perhaps shows more conclusively the state of society North, when such dirty-mouthed abolition sheets as the Philadelphia *News* can prosper, and so old and able a journal must succumb for want of funds to maintain it. When able sheets like the above, are forced to be discontinued because of a lack of the Democracy to come to their support, we may bid farewell to the preeminence of the principles which unite and prosper us as a State Rights Democratic people:

> Thankful as we are to those patrons who have come forward to our aid, and to the kind friends who have interested themselves in our behalf, we must for the present cease the further prosecution of so unequal a task. When the Democratic party of this city shall be left unrepresented by an organ, and shall have its time-honored principles assailed without a defender, and when the opposition shall have a clear field, with no Democratic sentinel to detect their wickedness, and no faithful champion to resist their fatal march, the democratic masses who could sustain a paper prosperously, will perhaps awaken to their dereliction and their folly. They may perhaps be then willing to assume their part of the responsibility, and by sustaining the journal which sustains them and their principles, enable its publisher to do battle in their cause,

☞The following article which we take from the Vidalia *Intelligencer,* speaks the sentiments which have frequently been uttered by the press in all parts of the State, and are as true as they are deserved:

The St. Charles Hotel.

> A few days' sojourn in the glorious Crescent—that "horn of plenty" which crowns the vast vale of the Mississippi, and introduces her incalculable wealth into the bosom of foreign commerce—has given us our first experience of the St. Charles—that "hotel of hotels," all the world over.
>
> We pass by the gorgeous, massive and artistic architecture, wich reminds one of the Grecian temples of old The heaven-aspiring columns without, indicate only a heaven of earthly comfort, security, order and luxury within.
>
> The rotunda, where all the guests are received, on first entrance, is but a vestibule of a city within a city. Let gloom or glory, storm or sunshine reign abroad, all is peace, sociality, joy, within. From a thousand guests, the elite of the east, south, west, north, and the wide world abroad, enough can be gathered for pleasure, instruction, gaiety, and solid improvement within those massive walls, no matter how the world goes without. The ladies and gentlemen's parlors are all that the most select soirees and reunions anywhere can be, except that the openness and geniality of Southern manners give an indescribable charm to Southern intercourse.
>
> We cannot speak too highly of the table luxuries. They cannot be exceeded the world over, and command the rarities of the tropical as well as the temperate climes. The movement of the hundreds of servants; the cleanliness and silence of the family and gentlemen's rooms; the strict, yet always unnoticeable police and watch over person and property, exercised all over the pyramid of human habitation, make the stranger feel, while, in his quiet and retired room, to which scarce the thunder of the vexed streets can ascend, only as a murmur, that he is, indeed, in "home, sweet home."
>
> The conclusion we came to, on this first visit to the St. Charles, was, that Hildreth, the arch-genius directing the whole—his amiable and accomplished brother, Hildreth the younger, the ever placid treasurer M——, and Monroe, the Mercury of the Sphere, can "keep a hotel."
>
> The management of the office resembles the operations of a bank. The deposits daily are tens of thousands. The board bills, daily, more than half the year, are more than three thousand dollars, or twenty thousand dollars per week. This is a concern.

COULDN'T DO IT.—An exchange paper tells a story of a man in London, who determined to spend all he made during the first year in advertising. He soon found that it was impossible, for the simple reason that the more he advertised the more he made, and after a strenuous effort to get rid of his money in advertising, he had to give it up. If you don't believe it, try it.

Gazette & Sentinel.

From Tuesday's Bulletin.

Important from Washington.

CITY IN GREAT EXCITEMENT!

Lincoln's Proclamation for Troops!

Extra Session of Congress Called.

The City Strongly Guarded.

Washington, April 14.—The City of Washington is in a perfect uproar of excitement over the proclamation just issued by Lincoln, calling forth the militia of the several States, and convening the Federal Congress for the 4th of July. Thirty thousand men have already been tendered. The city is very strongly guarded at every point. The cavalry is on the road, and the militia inside. More troops have been ordered.

The following is Lincoln's

PROCLAMATION.

Whereas, The laws of the U. States have been, and are now, opposed in several States, by combinations too powerful to be suppressed in the ordinary way:

I, therefore, call forth the militia of the several States of the Union to the aggregate of seventy-five thousand, to suppress said combinations and execute the laws.

I appeal to all loyal citizens to facilitate and aid this effort to maintain the laws and integrity of the National Union and the perpetuity of popular government, and redress wrongs that have long been endured.

The first service assigned to the forces will be to repossess the forts, places and property that have been seized from the Union.

The utmost care will be taken, consistent with the object, to avoid devastation and destruction, or interference with the property of peaceful citizens, in any part of the country; and I hereby command persons composing the aforesaid combinations to disperse within twenty days from this date.

I hereby convene both Houses of Congress for the Fourth of July next, to determine upon measures which the public safety and interest demand.

(Signed) ABE LINCOLN.

W. H. SEWARD, Secretary of State.

Telegrams from Erie, Pa., Chicago, Detroit, Buffalo, Indianopolis and Madison, Ind., say great excitement is manifested, and that offers of volunteer companies are made to sustain Lincoln's Government; 50,000 men, it is thought can be had at once.

Gov. Curtin of Pennsylvania has gone to Washington to say that 100,000 men from that State can be had to defend the Capitol.

The Governor of Illinois has convened the Legislature of that State for the 24th inst.

From Ohio, people irrespective of party, are offering their services to the Government.

Lincoln's Reply to Virginia Commissioners.

Washington, April 14.—Lincoln, in his reply to the Virginia Commissioners, says an unprovoked assault was made on Fort Sumpter, and that consequently he will retake alike seized places to the best of his ability, and repel force by force—that it will probably cause the mails to be withdrawn from the seceded States. He will not collect duties by armed invasion, but may land forces to relieve forts on the border country.

Albany, April 15.—It is rumored that Gov. Morgan has received despatches from Lincoln, asking aid. Lincoln's reply to the Virginia Commissioners has dissatisfied both the Democrats and Republicans. The Seventh and Sixty-ninth regiments have offered their services to defend Washington.

Demonstrations of Joy in Richmond.

Richmond, April 14.—The news of the surrender of Fort Sumpter was received with demonstrations of joy. A Southern flag was hoisted upon the capitol, but subsequently hauled down.

From Montgomery.

Maj. Anderson Allowed to Depart—The Southern Forces to Concentrate at Fort Pickens—Lincoln Denounced by the National Volunteers—The Offer of Troops by Tennessee—Dispatch from Mr. Sanders!—Fort Pickens easily Taken—State Sovereignty Recognized—Kentucky with the South—New Orleans Takes the Whole Loan!

Montgomery, April 14.—It is stated upon authority of Sec'y. Walker, that Anderson and his force are allowed to depart.

Ex-U. S. Senator Wigfall, as General Beauregard's aid, received Anderson's sword, and immediately returned it to him.

The Southern forces are to concentrate at Pensacola.

Twenty regiments are offered by Tennessee for our service.

The Confederate Congress, on re-assembling, will declare war if our ports are blockaded.

Seven hundred National volunteers at Washington refuse to serve under Lincoln, and denounce him.

Montgomery, April 14.—George N. Sanders has sent the following dispatch to Dean Richmond, Mayor Wood and August Belmont:

"One hundred thousand mercenary soldiers cannot occupy and hold Pensacola. The entire South is under arms. Negroes strengthen the militia. Fort Pickens quickly conquered. Northern Democrats are standing by the South. The Northern States and people are not held responsible for Lincoln's acts unless endorsed by them. State sovereignty is fully recognized. New York, protect your social and commercial ties by resisting Republican and Federal aggression. Philadelphia should repudiate the action of her Legislature. The commerce of Rhode Island and New Jersey is safe when distinguishable.

(Signed) G. N. SANDERS.

An offer has been made to the Treasury Department to take the whole Confederate loan of fifteen millions at par by parties in New Orleans.

Secretary Toombs has received a dispatch from Hon. J. C. Breckinridge and Gov. Magoffin, of Kentucky, stating that greatly excited sympathizers are entirely with the South. Seven thousand men of the Border States are under arms, and have offered to move at a moment's notice.

In reply to a message asking what was the feeling at Montgomery, President Davis says, rough and curt:

"Fort Sumpter is ours, and nobody is hurt. With mortar, paixhan and petard, we tender old Abe our Beauregard."

The fleet was still in sight off Charleston, to-day.

Virginia State Convention.

Richmond, April 13.—In the State Convention an amendment to the fifth section was ordered and adopted, not to affect the Southern separated States.—At a meeting in Alexandria to form a home guard, resolutions were adopted to resist aggression.

The Feeling in Baltimore.

Men with secession emblems have been chased by crowds and protected by the police.

The bark Fenshaw hoisted the secession flag.

A crowd compelled a boy to take it down. The captain rehoisted and required thirty police to protect it. The indignation was intense.

From Thursday's Bulletin.

Later from Montgomery!

VIRGINIA HEARD FROM.

Secession about to Triumph!

Secretary Toombs in Receipt of Dispatches from Virginia Convention.

The papers from the city to-day, are filled with important despatches. We give below a faithful synopsis of the whole:

Montgomery, April 15th.—Great gratification is felt here in Government as well as private circles, in consequence of news received in regard to the course of the Virginia Convention on the question of secession.

It is stated positively that the Unionists of the Virginia Convention will, on to-morrow, [the 16th,] bring in a Secession Ordinance, and cordially unite with the Secessionists in passing it immediately.

The chief authority for this statement is a dispatch to that effect received by Mr. Toombs, Confederate Secretary of State, from Mr. Robert G. Scott, a distinguished member of the Virginia Convention, and one of the leading secessionists in that State

Montgomery, 16th.—The Cabinet received Lincoln's Proclamation amid bursts of laughter. The Secretary of War will call out thirty-two thousand more troops to-day to meet Lincoln's forces.

It is positively stated in a despatch to the Associated Press (the above is to the Delta solely) that Virginia will pass the Ordinance of Secession in two days.

The Secession feeling now is at boiling heat in Virginia.

Lincoln's Proclamation was received with contempt at Wilmington, N. C.

In all the free or Black Republican States, the Governors are either issuing proclamations for troops, in accordance with Lincoln's call, or convening the Legislatures—to put the States on a war footing—the people offering money and volunteering—and an enthusiasm generally, so the dispatches state, to sustain the Government.

Gov. Magoffin indignantly refuses to supply the Kentucky quota of troops, agreeably to Lincoln's proclamation.

There is great excitement in Philadelphia, and citizens of secession proclivities have been warned by the so-called Vigilance Committee. Gen. Patterson's residence has been threatened by the mob. Fillmore, Buchanan and Cass are with Lincoln.

The Philadelphia Steamship at New York, was about to leave with troops, &c., for the South. At a meeting held it was resolved to ask the Legislature for funds to sustain Lincoln.

A number of troops from various points are on their way to Washington.

At a large meeting at Paducah, Ky., resolutions were passed to sustain the South.

A large meeting was held at Louisville. That city is with the South. It endorsed Gov. Magoffin's action—and uniting her destiny with the South.

It is said that no orders as yet have been issued to blockade the Southern ports; and yet there are eleven vessels reported to be off Charleston, and not permitting any kind of a craft to enter

A Massachusetts and New York regiment goes to Fort Monroe.

A report prevailed that Gen. Scott had resigned, and was engaged with Cameron and Ajutant Gen. Thomas.

Letcher is for a Central Confederacy, but conforms to the will of Virginia.

A hundred guns were fired at Norfolk in rejoicings for the fall of Sumpter.

The Memphis and Ohio Railroad offers to transport Southern troops free. The Union flags of the Steamers was hauled down at Memphis. The citizens are arming and volunteering rapidly.

Gen. Pillow, from Tennessee, has arrived at Montgomery. President Davis will make his head quarters at Richmond in ten days. So it is believed.

FURTHER!

From the Delta of Yesterday Afternoon.

News from Richmond Alarms Lincoln and his Cabinet.

Republicans Startled!

Lincoln Indignant at the Reception of his Proclamation.

Davis, Pillow, Breckinridge and Beauregard to Take the Field!

&c. &c. &c. &c.

Washington, April 16.—News has been received here of the reinforcement of Fort Pickens. The Administration is greatly encouraged in consequence.

Lincoln and Cabinet are profane and emphatic in their expressions relative to the manner in which the Proclamation was received at Montgomery.

Reinforcements are being effected at Fort Pickens in daylight, without reserve. Gen. Bragg is also preparing vigorously for the onset. Nearly all the New Orleans troops had arrived. all

Washington, April 17.—The Intelligencer came out this morning in favor of coercion; this is suggestive. It is thought that if the Border States had acted promptly, no collision would have taken place. The Republicans are startled at the effect of their own policy.

Montgomery, April 17.—It is now stated on the best authority, that as soon as Virginia moves, DAVIS, PILLOW, BRECKINRIDGE and BEAUREGARD will take the field.

In a speech of Alex. H. Stevens, at Atlanta, he said it would take seventy-five times seventy-five thousand men to intimidate us.

Gen. Pillow guarantees to raise ten thousand men for the Confederacy in twenty days.

The fleet off Charleston has left.

Richmond, April 17.—The Convention has been in secret session for some time. It is believed that the Ordinance of Secession has passed.

Gov. Hicks, of Maryland, responds to the call of Lincoln for troops.

New Orleans, April 17.—A great run was made on the Citizens' Bank to take the Southern Loan. Two millions was taken at par before 12 M.

Gov. Moore, of this State, has issued his proclamation for 3000 more troops, in conformity to the call of President Davis.

From Friday's Bulletin.

The War Spirit North.

100,000,000 DOLLARS OFFERED

The Revolution to be Crushed Out!

New York, April 17.—It is rumored that the Seventh Regiment of Volunteers, recently called into the service of the United States, has been ordered to Fort McHenry, Va.

It is also stated that, notwithstanding the refusal of the Governors of Kentucky and Missouri to respond to Lincoln's call, independent volunteer companies are organizing in those States to support the Federal Government.

The Republican papers also say that the Government has been offered a hundred millions of dollars to prosecute the war.

The New York Herald is also out this morning in nearly the same tone. It denounces the people of the Confederate States as rebels, and says the revolution will speedily be put down.

It is stated that 20,000 men have been ordered to Washington in case that Virginia secedes; but this is doubtful.

Excitement in New York!

A mob in New York has compelled the secession papers to display the Union flag. Money is being liberally subscribed to equip the 7th Regiment.

FROM MONTGOMERY.

Call for 32,000 Troops.

Montgomery, April 17th.—The loan is being rapidly taken up. President Davis has issued a call for 32,000 troops. Georgia, Alabama, South Carolina, Mississippi, Louisiana and Texas, 5,000 each, Florida 2,000.

Further from Montgomery.

Montgomery, April 17th.—A proclamation will be issued to-morrow for letters of marque and reprisal—Cabinet has had a long session. A call will probably be issued for 150,000 more troops—man for man with Lincoln.

Charleston takes 2,000,000 of the loan.

Gov. Ellis, of North Carolina, telegraphs to Secretary of War, that he has taken possession of all the forts in that State.

Fifty thousand Tennessee and Kentucky troops were offered this morning to the War Department.

Great Excitement in Cincinnati.

Cincinnati, April 17th.—Guns and powder marked for Memphis, has been seized by Chief of Police. No Steamboats are allowed to bring provisions south. Two armed steamboats search all boats leaving in this direction. A large quantity of bacon, for Charleston via Nashville, was seized.

Louisville, April 17th.—This city has appropriated $50,000 for its defense.

The resistance feeling is unanimous in Memphis. The casting of cannon has commenced.

In New York recruiting is going on briskly. Sailors applying for naval service.

Gen. Scott is with Lincoln, and has laid before him an elaborate plan for conquering the south. The Administration fears that Virginia will strike with vigor, if she secedes. The Cabinet is very nervous about the way Virginia will act.

LATER FROM THE CITY.

GLORIOUS NEWS!

VIRGINIA SECEDED!!!

From the Evening Delta of Yesterday.

Montgomery, April 18.—A despatch has been received here that Virginia has seceded. The Ordinance of Secession passed to-day.

The above is fully confirmed by various sources.

She has seized the Navy Yard at Norfolk and the Arsenal at Harper's Ferry.

One hundred guns were fired in New Orleans yesterday in hornor of these events.

Nashville, April 18.—Gov. Harris replies to Lincoln's call for two regiments thus: "Tennessee will not furnish a man for coercion, but fifty thousand if necessary for the defence of our rights and those of our Southern brethren."

St. Louis, April 18.—Gov. Jackson tells Lincoln that his requisition is illegal, unconstitutional, revolutionary, inhuman, diabolical, and cannot be complied with.

Montgomery, April 18.—President Davis has issued a proclamation inviting privateers to make war on Northern commerce by letters of marque.

Intelligence from Charleston says that President Davis will take command at Pensacola.

It is said that Old Abe is highly exultant by the reports of enthusiasm North. He says the seceded states will soon be subdued—that the south can have war as long as the free states will provide men and money. That won't be long.

Cincinnati Boats Seized.

We learn by the steamer Quitman that the steamboatmen, yesterday afternoon in New Orleans, seized all the Cincinnati boats in port, as a retaliation for stopping the boats in Cincinnati having provisions on board for New Orleans.

LOAN

For the Defense of the Confederate States.

FIVE MILLIONS of the most advantageous investment will be offered to the public on the 17th APRIL ensuing, and every citizen throughout the Confederate States will have the opportunity of taking a share of the benefit, at the same time of sustaining the cause of his country.

Bonds with coupons will be issued in sums from $1000 to $50; and where it is preferred, stock certificates in the usual form may be had. The interest is at 8 per cent. per annumn, payable every six months at all our principal cities.

The debt has the very unusual and important security of a duty of one-eighth of a cent per pound, or about 62 cents per bale on all cotton exported. This duty, under all circumstances of peace or war, secures the punctual payment of the interest, and furnishes a sinking fund for the redemption of the principal. The coupons when due, are receivable in payment of the duty on cotton, and are thus made available as coin, everywhere in our country. In order to enable all portions of our people to take part of this valuable investment and to exhibit their common interest in raising funds for the common defense, books of subscription will be opened at the cities and principal interior towns; five per cent. must be paid in cash at the time of subscription, and the remainder on or before the 1st of May—interest to run from the date of such payment. Persons desiring to secure their subscriptions, may pay in cash the whole amount, and take a receipt for the delivery of bonds or stock. To equalize the rate of subscription at all points, and to enable all persons conveniently to subscribe, current bank notes of the place will be received at their market value in coin.

In case of an over-subscription, preference will be given to those who pay down the whole subscription; next to subscribers of $50; next to subscribers of $100.

C. G. MEMMINGER,

Secretary of t Treasury.

MONTGOMERY, March 16, 1861.

For more ample information to all concerned, a copy of the act of Congress is subjoined:

AN ACT to raise money for the support of the Government, and to provide for the defense of the Confedervte States of America.

SECTOIN 1. The Congress of the Confederate States of America do enact, That the President of the Confederate States be and he is hereby authorized at any time within 12 months after the passage of this act, to borrow, on the credit of the Confederate States, a sum not exceeding Fifteen Millions of Dollars, or so much thereof as in his opinion the exigencies of the public service may require, to be applied to the payment of appropriations made by law for the support of the Government and for the defense of the Confederate States.

SEC. 2. The Secretary of the Treasury is hereby authorized, by the consent of the President of the Confederate States, to cause to be prepared certificates of Stock or Bonds, in such sums as are hereinafter mentioned, for the amount to be borrowed as aforesaid, to be signed by the Register of the Treasury, and sealed with the seal of the Treasury; and the said certificates of Stock or Bonds shall be made payable at the expiration of ten years from the first day of September next; and the interest thereon shall be paid semi-annually, at the rate of Eight per cent. per annum, at the Treasury and such other places as the secretary of the Treasury may designate. And to the bonds which shall be issued, as aforesaid, shall be attached coupons for the semi-anuual intrrest which may accrue, which coupons may be signed by officers to be appointed for the purpose by the Secretary of the Treasury. And the faith of the Confederate States is hereby pledged for the due payment of the principal and interest of said stock and bonds.

SEC. 3. At the expiration of five years from the first day of September next, the Confederate States may pay up any portion of the bonds or stocks, upon giving three months previous public notice, at the seat of Government, of the particular stocks or bonds to be paid, and the time and place of payment; and from and after the time so appointed, no further interest shall be paid on said stock or bonds.

SEC. 4. The certificates of stock or bonds shall be issued in such form and for such amounts as may be determined by the Secretary of the Treasury, and may be assigned or delivered under such regulations as he may establish. But none of them shall be for a less sum than fifty dollars; and he shall report to Congress, at its next session, a statement in detail of his proceedings, and the rate at which the loans may have been made, and all expenses attending the same.

SEC. 5. From and after the first day of August, 1861, there shall be levied, collected and paid, a duty of one-eighth of one cent per pound on all cotton in the raw state exported from the Confederate States; which duty is hereby specially pledged to the due payment of interest and principal of the loan provided for in this act; and the Secretary of the Treasury is hereby authorized and required to establish a sinking fund to carry into effect the provisions of this section. Provided, however, that the interest coupons issued under the second section of this act, when due, shall be receivable in payment of the export duty on cotton; provided also, that when the debt and interest thereon, herein authorized to be contracted, shall be extinguished, or the sinking fund provided for that purpose, shall be adequate to that end, the said export duty shall cease and determine.

Approved 28th February, 1861.

Referring to the above advertisement for a loan of Five Millions of Dollars to the Confederate States, together with the act of Congress creating it, the undersigned, appointed Commissioners, give notice to the public that books of subscription for said loan, will be opened at the Branch of the Louisiana State Bank, at Baton Rouge, on the 17th of April, 1861.

Apart from other considerations, this loan offers to subscribers a high rate of interest—Eight per cent. per annum—payable semi-annually, and the highest order of security—a special appropriation of an export duty on cotton of one-eighth of a cent per pound—thus presenting inducements which cannot fail to commend the loan to public favor, as a sound and profitable investment.

H. W. ALLEN,
W: RUFFIN BARROW,
DANIEL D. AVERY,
W. S. PIKE.
Commissioners.

Baton Rouge, April 1st, 1861. [ap13

Lynchburg Virginian.

Tuesday Morning,..........April 23, 1861

☞ Mr. Thos. J. Bagpy is our authorized Agent in Richmond, to procure advertising and subscriptions. We commend him to the attention of our friends.

We have had no Northern mails since Saturday, and it is rumored that Lincoln has prohibited their passing through Washington; though we do not credit the rumor.

The National Intelligencer.

This journal, for which we entertain the highest respect, as well as for its editors, whom we have the honor to know, still clings to a hope of reconstructing the Union, and appeals to Virginia to use her good offices in the work of mediation. We can well appreciate the motives that influence the ancient surviving editor of that paper, who has been so long associated with much that was great and glorious in the history of the country. It would be strange if he, at least, did not feel anxious to restore the government to its original condition. We have had opportunity to see how his patriotic heart was stirred when speaking of the disruption of his country.—But, the deed is done. His counsels, and those of thousands of humbler co-laborers all over the Union have been disregarded. When it might have been easy to speak the word that would have saved the Union, that word was not spoken. It is too late now. Bayonets and blood will not restore it. Such a result is impossible. We assure our honored cotemporary that Virginia will never consent to re-unite her destiny with the men who have relied upon their superior military resources to preserve the Union, and have taken up arms to crush us. We accept the arbitrament to which they have appealed, and now, relying upon the favor of the God of battles, and convinced of the rectitude of our intentions, we calmly and firmly await the result. We will never, never, never, consent to live again under one government with the States that have taken up arms against us. We do assure our friends of the *Intelligencer* that this is the predominant, we may say, universal feeling in Virginia. No more Union with the fanatics who were not content to let us live in peace with them. Henceforth, we are no longer to be one people, *and do not desire to be.* If we have friends left in the North, let them come to us and we will receive them kindly; or, if they stay where they are we will do them no harm; but, with the restless agitators who overawe them, we can never consort again. For the Massachusetts that is ruled by Andrew, Sumner, Wilson, Burlingame, &c., we have no more use forever. And let all the people of the South say Amen!

Tennessee.

This patriotic State seems to be all on fire, and as its legislature is convened in extraordinary session for Thursday next, we may expect that measures for resistance will be immediately adopted. In all parts of the State her people are manifesting the spirit of '76, and are determined to overthrow the Lincoln tyranny.—From the Nashville *Patriot* of the 19th inst., we learn that the home of Jackson, and the place of his sepulchre, is not behind others in the determination to dissolve a Union such as the immortal patriot himself, with all his love of Union, would not countenance. The *Patriot* was an ardent Whig and Union paper almost to the last, and it now says:

The political excitement in the city continues unabated. The most sanguine are less and less confident with the developments of each succeeding hour, and now the feeling and belief are almost universal that there is no possible escape from a bloody and desolating war. If that fearful issue is inevitable,—and we can see no reason to disbelieve it—we feel assured that Tennessee will stand as one man. Business here is in a measure suspended. The people are congregated on the streets, and speeches being made at many points. Every night large meetings are held, in which the general sentiment is that the Union is irretrievably at an end. Several volunteer companies are in process of formation, and enlistments are rapid. From all the surrounding counties in this division of the State, the people generally accept the issue of war as already determined, and are prepared to accept the consequences, whatever they may be.—In the Western District the people have almost reached the point of entire unanimity; while from East Tennessee the masses are rapidly coming to the conclusion that it is worse than unless to longer cling to the Union whose substance has already departed.

The Memphis *Bulletin* too, one of our most valuable exchanges, and until within a week past one of the firmest Whig and Union papers in the country, submits the following correct views;

The South, united, is impregnable to the unjust and cruel war that the perfidious Administration proposes to wage upon us under the boyish, the worse than puerile pretext of showing that we "have a Government." Infamous beyond expression—atrocious to a degree that has no computation in language—is this war, this horrible civil war, inaugurated needlessly, recklessly, savagely, by the Lincoln Administration.

As we said a few days ago, these men have alike misunderstood and betrayed the friends of the Constitution in the South. They promised peace, and they hypocritically enter upon measures that could lead to nothing else but war.—They professed to reverence the Laws, and they outrage all laws in the pretence of maintaining them.

The Union, so devotedly worshiped, is pratically at an end. A union held in place by brute force, is no union. It is a despotism—a despotism to be sternly resisted, to the last extremity, by freemen.

To make that resistance effectual, there must be union of sentiment, and unanimity of action. He is the worst enemy of the State, who would devide the one or distract the other. It is a time—demanding unselfish sacrifices—an offering of individual prejudices upon the alter of the general good and the common safety. It is not a time to stickle about *any* minor points. "Let the dead past bury its dead." He is the best patriot who *now* stands truest and adds most to the solid strength of his section in resisting this lawless and outrageous invasion of Southern homes and Southern firesides.

The Alexandria *Sentinel* says that, "among the men who rushed to Harper's Ferry was a company of unarmed men from Rappahannock County. When asked what they could do, they replied that they were splendid fellows for throwing stones."

"Du tell! Why, I want to know," Jonathan will say, "what business we have with men who will stand before bayonets with nothin' but *stuns* in their hands? We had better get to hum." Appropos of this Harper's Ferry incident, we find the following in the Washington *States* of Saturday evening. Says that paper:

Those in conversation with the Massachusetts soldiers to-day, say they accord a meed of praise to the bravery of the Baltimoreans. When they fired a volley into the mob, it was thought that they were scattered in every direction; but the smoke had barely cleared away ere the Baltimoreans closed on them and fought desperately, their weapons comprising paving stones and a few pistols.

If the brave Baltimoreans had been armed not one of those Yankee mercenaries would have reached Washington, or ever seen their homes again. And this is the spirit they will find everywhere evinced by the men they have undertaken to conquer. We hope that they will not be permitted to set foot upon the soil of Virginia, but if, through force of numbers they overpower the brave men sent to protect our frontier, they will find a guerilla war waged upon them to an extent that was not equalled at any time in the Tyrol. Even the women of our mountains will roll down rocks upon them, whilst our marksmen will decimate their ranks at every turn. With the feeling now burning in the breasts of an outraged people, it may be impossible to restrain them from annihilating the invader. The further they penetrate into the interior, the more certainly do they cut off all hope of ever getting out again. Death to the invader!

Capt. Robert E. Lee.

We rejoice that this distinguished officer and worthy son of Virginia, has withdrawn from Lincoln's army and thrown himself upon the bosom of his native State. It was what we expected of the man. Capt. *Maury* has done likewise; and thus, these two noble men, the very flower of the Army and Navy of the late United States, respond to the call of their glorious old mother. Sparta never had worthier sons. All honor to them and to the State that furnished them. Let no Coriolanus be found in the army of mercenaries that shall besiege the cities of Virginia. If there should be—even though it were a Scott, whose laurelled brow has towered like the sons of Saul, long a conspicuous object amongst his countrymen—the women may not entreat them, but will execrate their memory. Virginia expects every son of hers, no matter where he has been in the past, to do his duty now in this her hour of trial. If they be true Virginians they will act like Lee and Maury and Forrest have done.

The Alexandria *Gazette*, of Saturday last, and before the fact of Col. Lee's resignation had transpired, thus referred to him:

It is probable that the Secession of Virginia will cause an immediate resignation of many officers of the Army and Navy from this State. We do not know, and have no right to speak for or anticipates the course, of Col. Robt. E. Lee. Whatever he may do, will be conscientious and honorable. But if he *should* resign his present position in the Army of the U. S. we call the immediate attention of our State to him, as an able, brave, experienced, officer:—no man his superior in all that constitutes the soldier, and the gentleman—no man more worthy to head our forces and lead our army. There is no one who would command more of the confidence of the people of Virginia, than this distinguished officer; and no one under whom the volunteers and militia would more gladly rally. His reputation, his acknowledged ability, his chivalric character, his probity, honor and—may we add, to his eternal praise—his christian life and conduct—make his very name a "tower of strength." It is a name surrounded by revolutionary and patriotic associations and reminiscences.

Kentucky.

This gallant State is moving. Her legislature meets on the 27th, and will, no doubt, act promptly. "The Hunters of Kentucky" will again go forth to do battle for the South. Old Kentucky will be right, and respond to the call of the Old Dominion.

LATE NEWS.

We are indebted to our interprising cotemporary the Alexandria *Gazette* for the following summary of late news contained in its extra, received on Sunday.

Latest and important news from Baltimore!—General Scott's Position!—Seizure of the Steamer St. Nicholas!—Removal of Ammunition!—Military Spirit in Maryland.—Troops to prevent the passage of Northern Forces through the City of Baltimore.—Excitement in Washington.—Northern Troops en route for Washington.—Bridges Destroyed!—Latest and reliable from Harper's Ferry!—Fifteen Thousand? Stands of Arms and the Buildings destroyed. The Troops at Carlisle Barracks.—Five Thousand best Minnie Muskets secured by State Troops!—Position of Kentucky!—&c., &c.

BALTIMORE AFFAIRS.

Baltimore, April 20.—p. m.

A gentleman just from Baltimore reports that the city was quiet and orderly, the irritating cause of the excitement having been removed, the people are calm. The city is in charge of the Baltimore soldiery. He also reports that the Canton Bridge, on the Baltimore and Wilmington Railroad a short distance from Baltimore, has been destroyed.

The returned Massachusetts troops are, it is said, at Havre-de-Grace, where are also the Pennsylvania troops, which were on their way to Washington. They are there by order of President Lincoln, who has ordered all the Administration troops now in Maryland, to its Northern border.

Washington, April 20.—p. m.—W. W. Watson, formerly a resident of Alexandria, the Washington correspondent of the New York Express, has been put in charge of the telegraph office by the Secretary of the War Department. Everything sent over the wires must undergo his inspection.

GEN. SCOTT.

Washington, April 20, P. M.—Gen. Scott it is said is now on friendly terms or even holds verbal communication with three members of the Cabinet, viz: Seward, Chase, and Cameron.

SEIZURE OF THE ST. NICHOLAS.

Washington, April 20, P. M.—The Steamer St. Nicholas, of the Baltimore and Washington line of steamers, was this morning seized by order of the Administration.

MOVEMENTS OF AMUNITION.

Washington, April 20,—P. M.—Two large schooners are now loading with amunition at the Arsenal. Destination unknown.

MILITARY SPIRIT IN MARYLAND.

Marlboro', April 20, P. M.—Every available man that could be raised in the county, and mustered with military Companies, has gone this morning to Baltimore, to aid in repressing the Northern troops.

BURNING OF A BRIDGE ON THE NORTHERN CENTRAL RAILROAD.

Baltimore, April 20, P. M.—The Melville Bridge between Woodbury and Mount Washington, on the Northern Central Railroad has been burnt down.

It is reported that the Northern troops are at the Relay House, a station on the Northern Central Railroad. The Melville Bridge is a short bridge—60 feet span.

It is reported that the Railroad Ferry Boat at Havre-de-Grace, has been seized by the Marylanders, in order to prevent the passage of Northern troops. The only two possible land routes by which the Northerners who are reported to be on the north side of the Susquehanna, to the number of from three to seven thousand, can now possibly reach Baltimore, and consequently Washington, are by returning to Philadelphia and taking the Pennsylvania Central road, or to march up to Port Deposit, a distance of 12 miles from Havre-de-Grace, where there is as yet an unobstructed passage, and from there to reach the Baltimore and Wilmington road.

The troops, however, by themselves, or reinforced by the N.Y., Seventh Regiment may be advancing on Washington by water.

CAPTURE OF HARPER'S FERRY AND 5,000 STAND OF MINNIE MUSKETS.

We have the following reliable intelligance from Harper's Ferry, from the lips of our townsman Surgeon C. W. Chancellor, who arrived in this city this morning *direct from* Harper's Ferry:

The flag of the free Commonwealth of Virginia is now flying over the works.

The Virginia troops took possession of the Armory after the United States forces had retreated. They found there five-thousand Minnie muskets, uninjured, as well as the machine shop and the machinery, which will be of great service to the State.

The Armory buildings and two carpenter shops at the Ferry were destroyed by fire, but all else is saved.

Seven of the U. S. Soldiers, who had been stationed at the post, have deserted and joined the forces of Virginia.

This is certainly relable, and is the only definite account yet published.

ARRIVAL OF THE HARPER'S FERRY TOOOPS AT CARLILE.

Carlile, Pa., April 20.—Lieut. Jones and 43 men, lately of the Harper's Ferry Garrison arrived here yesterday evening. In consequence of the approach of 2500 men ordered by Gov Letcher to take possession of the armory, they destroyed all the buildings, together with 15,000 stand of arms, and made a forced march to Hagerstown during the night.

POSITION OF KENTUCKY.

Louisville, April 19.—A Union meeting was held here last night, at which Mr. Guthrie and other prominent men made speeches. Resolutions were adopted that the Confederate States having commenced the war, Kentucky assumes the right to choose her position, or that she will acknowledge loyalty till the Government becomes the aggressor. She opposes the call of the President for volunteers for the purpose of coercion, or the raising of troops for the Confederacy; asserts that secession is no remedy for the pending evils, and that Kentucky will not take part with either side, at the same time declares her soil sacred against the hostile foot of either.

The Governor is endeavoring to induce the banks to take a loan of $500,000 for the defence of the State.

LATER.

BURNING OF GUNPOWDER BRIDGE &C., &C.

Washington, April 20, P. M.—Gunpowder Bridge, on the Baltimore and Wilmington Railroad, over Gunpowder river has been burnt by the Marylanders.

VIRGINIA STATE STOCKS

New York, April 20, 3 P. M.—Virginia State Stocks were sold in New York to-day at 36.

VIRGINIA MONEY.

Washington, April 20, 4 P, M.—There is no market for Virginia money here to-day.

ANOTHER PROCLAMATION.

By the President of the U. S. of America.

A PROCLAMATION.

Whereas an insurrection against the Government of the United States has broken out in the States of South Carolina, Georgia, Alabama, Florida, Mississippi, Louisiana, and Texas, and the laws of the United States. for the collection of the revenue cannot be effectually executed therein conformably to that provision of the Constitution which requires duties to be uniform throughout the United States:

And whereas a combination of persons, engaged in such insurrection, have threatened to grant pretended letters of marque to authorize the bearers thereof to commit assaults on the lives, vessels, and property of good citizens of the country lawfully engaged in commerce on the high seas, and in waters of the United States:

And whereas an Executive proclamation has been already issued, requiring the persons engaged in these disorderly proceedings to desist therefrom, calling out a militia force for the purpose of repressing the same, and convening Congress in extraordinary session to deliberate and determine thereon:

Now, therefore, I, Abraham Lincoln, President of the United States, with a view to the same purposes before mentioned, and to the protection of the public peace, and the lives and property of quiet and orderly citizens pursuing the lawful occupations, until Congress shall have assembled and deliberated on said unlawful proceeding, or until the same shall have ceased, have further deemed advisable to set on foot a blockade of the ports within the States aforesaid, in pursuance of the laws of the United States and of the law of nations in such case provided. For this purpose a competent force will be posted so as to prevent entrance and exit of vessels from the ports aforesaid. If, therefore, with a view to violate such blockade, a vessel shall approach, or shall attempt to leave any of the said ports, she will be duly warned by the Commander of one of the blockading vessels, who will endorse on her Register the fact and date of such warning, and if the same vessel shall again attempt to enter or leave the blockaded port, she will be captured and sent to the nearest convenient port, for such proceedings against her and her cargo as prize as may be deemed advisable.

And I hereby proclaim and declare that if any person, under the pretended authority of the said States, or under any other pretense, shall molest a vessel of the United States, or the persons or cargo on board of her, such person will be held amenable to the laws of the United States for the prevention and punishment of piracy.

In witness whereof, I have hereunto set my hand, and caused the seal of the United States to be affixed. Done at the City of Washington, this nineteenth day of April, in the year of our Lord one thousand eight hundred and sixty-one, and of the Independence of the United States the eighty-fifth.

[L. S.] ABRAHAM LINCOLN.

By the President:
William H. Seward,
Secretary of State.

Maryland.—The Baltimore American of Saturday says:—"In the afternoon on Friday, an immense town-meeting was held, at which addresses were made by Mayor Brown, Governor Hicks, and other gentlemen, and assurances given that no more troops would be allowed to pass through the city. Assurances, it is stated, have also been given by the Philadelphia Railroad Company that no more troops will be transported over that road without advising with the Governor and Mayor. The military were immediately called out, and they took charge of the city last night, relieving the police who have been worn out by exertions and constant watchfulness to which the last four days have subjected them. The city was quiet and orderly during the afternoon, and night."

President Lincoln's war policy has created intense excitement in St. Mary's county. The Leonardtown Beacon says the evacuation of Sumter was greeted with the firing of cannon and ringing of bells. A call has been issued for a county mass meeting to adopt measures of an effective character.

A great excitement was occasioned in Annapolis, and a determination expressed to stand by the authorities of the State in preventing the passage of Northern troops through its limits.

At Frederick, the telegraphic news from Baltimore of the conflict with armed Northern troops passing through to the South, created a great furore. The "Union" gun is silenced.

There was to have been at Marlboro' last Saturday, a large meeting of the military.

Mr. N. S. Bennett.—Mr. N. S. Bennett who has been residing in Alexandria for some time past, was yesterday notified by a crowd of citizens that he was the subject of just suspicion, and that the safety of the community required him to leave the city within five hours. He promised compliance with the demand and left.

The troops at Harper's Ferry were composed of the Staunton Artillery and West Augusta Guards, Albemarle Rifles, the Monticello Guards, the Southern Guards, the Sons of Liberty from the University Scott's and Parran's companies from Gordonsville and Barboursville, a company from Louisa, the Orange Montpelier Guards, two Culpeper Rifle companies, the Winchester Continentals, the Winchester Rifles, a Charlestown company and a portion of the Fauquier Cavalry.

Capt. Paulding, Commander Emmons, and Lieut. Woodhull constitute the Board of Detail through whom all the naval preparations are made.

The Chief Clerk's room is the only one in the Navy Department accessible at this time to the public.

It appears that neither the Powhatan nor the transport steamship Atlantic were off Charleston at the Sumter affair.

Latest from Harper's Ferry.

We have, from a most reliable source, definite information that the Federal troops left Harper's Ferry before the arrival of any of the Virginia forces. Knowing, perhaps, that some of the State troops were in the neighborhood, the U. S. forces fired the armory buildings, and destroyed them, together with some 3000 condemned muskets, being all that remained in the building—the others having been conveyed away by the Federal authorities at different periods for months past. A train laid to blow up the workshop failed, and as a consequence Virginia gets the machinery uninjured. A train was, also, laid to blow up the bridge but in the haste of departure the retiring troops neglected to apply the match.—*Alex, Gazette of yesterday.*

Washington Items.

We take the following Items from the Washington States of Saturday:

The Capitol Building.

We this morning, by the courtesy of a friend in authority, got into the Capitol, and made a reconnoissance of the building and its present condition. It has been converted into regular barracks. A large body of men were engaged in throwing up breastworks made of barrels of cement, heavy iron castings, and other weighty materials used in the extension work. The Massachusetts regiment, several companies of Pennsylvania troops, and also, some of our city military, in all numbering over fifteen hundred troops, are quartered in the building.

The Pawnee.

The U. S. sloop of war Pawnee steamed up the Potomac yesterday morning, with all her guns out, evidently having on board a considerable force. A short time after, the Anacostia, also steamed up to Washington. Both vessels sailed down the river again last night. Report says their destination was Norfolk.

Germans for the South.

A well informed German citizen informs us that he is in receipt of intelligence to-day from Baltimore, which represents that the German population there, to a very considerable extent, have determined to take up arms in defence of the South.

Mail Boats Locked.

The mail boats for the South were detained here last night by order of the government.

Telegraph Embargo.

The government has seized the telegraph offices here, and allow no despatches to come or go over the wires except those that meet the views of its policy.

Resignation.

Bernard C. Crook, mail agent on the Orange and Alexandria railroad, has resigned.

Appointment.

George Wm. Brent has been appointed by the Governor, a Major of Artillery in the 2d division of Virginia militia.

Declination.

It was announced some day ago, that J. Keith Marshall, esq., has withdrawn his name from all connection with the collectorship of Alexandria, and would not accept the same if it was tendered him.

Capt. Robert E. Lee.

We rejoice that this distinguished officer and worthy son of Virginia, has withdrawn from Lincoln's army and thrown himself upon the bosom of his native State. It was what we expected of the man. Capt. *Maury* has done likewise; and thus, these two noble men, the very flower of the Army and Navy of the late United States, respond to the call of their glorious old mother. Sparta never had worthier sons. All honor to them and to the State that furnished them. Let no Coriolanus be found in the army of mercenaries that shall besiege the cities of Virginia. If there should be—even though it were a Scott, whose laurelled brow has towered like the sons of Saul, long a conspicuous object amongst his countrymen—the women may not entreat them, but will execrate their memory. Virginia expects every son of hers, no matter where he has been in the past, to do his duty now in this her hour of trial. If they be true Virginians they will act like Lee and Maury and Forrest have done.

The Alexandria *Gazette*, of Saturday last, and before the fact of Col. Lee's resignation had transpired, thus referred to him:

It is probable that the Secession of Virginia will cause an immediate resignation of many officers of the Army and Navy from this State. We do not know, and have no right to speak for or anticipates the course, of Col. Robt. E. Lee. Whatever he may do, will be conscientious and honorable. But if he *should* resign his present position in the Army of the U. S. we call the immediate attention of our State to him, as an able, brave, experienced, officer:—no man his superior in all that constitutes the soldier, and the gentleman—no man more worthy to head our forces and lead our army. There is no one who would command more of the confidence of the people of Virginia, than this distinguished officer; and no one under whom the volunteers and militia would more gladly rally. His reputation, his acknowledged ability, his chivalric character, his probity, honor and—may we add, to his eternal praise—his christian life and conduct—make his very name a "tower of strength." It is a name surrounded by revolutionary and patriotic associations and reminiscences.

Richmond Dispatch.

FRIDAY MORNING.......APRIL 26, 1861.

We understand that some newsboys and others have been charging *five* and *ten cents* for the *Daily Dispatch*. This is extortion, as there is no increase of the price of the paper at our counter. While it is an extortion that we cannot prevent, the public might well refuse to submit to it.

Accident to the Dispatch Press.

The press on which the *Dispatch* is printed was disabled Wednesday night by the breaking of a part of its machinery. The paper was therefore late in making its appearance yesterday, as we had to transfer its forms to another press, which, a few years since, would have been amply expeditious to supply all demand for newspapers in this city; but it is altogether unable to press off the daily edition of the *Dispatch* within many hours of the time when it should be distributed throughout the city. The damage, we hope, (so it was written yesterday,) will be repaired in time to issue the paper of Friday (to-day) with usual promptitude.

The Daily Dispatch.

The circulation of the *Daily Dispatch* continues rapidly to increase, and has reached so large a number that it is with difficulty that the edition can be printed with our present machinery. It has attained a daily issue within a fraction of THIRTEEN THOUSAND. This large issue unavoidably and frequently delays the appearance of the paper in some portions of the city until a late hour. The exciting events of the day make the paper more than ever sought for, and it is a great disappointment to its city readers not to get it before breakfast. The means of the establishment are exerted with all possible speed to accommodate them; but it is sometimes absolutely out of the power of printers and pressmen to issue the paper in due time. We make this statement in explanation of the occasional delays which have caused complaint.

The large circulation of the *Dispatch* demands an increase of its machinery in the press room; but as there is yet no Southern manufactory of presses, and we are cut off from communication with the North by the war, we do not know when we shall be able to supply ourselves with what is so much needed from the New York manufacturer. We shall continue our exertions to do the best that is possible with our present facilities.

Virginia and the Southern Confederacy.

Our whole community was electrified with delight yesterday upon learning that the Virginia Convention had passed an Ordinance applying for admission to the Southern Confederacy, and placing all the troops and military resources of the State at the disposal of the Confederate Government. We congratulate the people of Virginia on this decisive and glorious movement. It introduces us to a Union of men of the same family, who are bone of our bone and flesh of our flesh; whose institutions, habits and blood are one; whose rights and interests are the same, and who can depend on each other in life or death, in peace or war, now and forever.—The old Union contained in itself the seeds of its own dissolution; this has the germ of imperishable life. From the very beginning there were the signs of an "irrepressible conflict" between the two sections, and the arbitrament of that conflict by the sword has only been adjourned to the present time because of the "irrepressible conflict" in the North between fanaticism and self-interest; the one prompting an armed crusade against slavery, the other dreading the results of that crusade upon its pocket. The first principle has triumphed, but its triumph is over the Union, and not over slavery. The South is now free from its Republican tyrants; it defies them; it bids them howl on and do their worst. A new Confederacy has risen, which will be purer and more glorious than the first; a Confederacy which the North shall look at hereafter as the lost spirits look upon the inestimable joys of Heaven, which they have sacrificed at the shrine of their own evil passions. The glory and prosperity of this Confederacy will one day be acknowledged abroad; the commerce of the world will fill its seaports; we shall drive the Yankees to fill our nations of Christendom in preference to those barbarians who are forcing civil war upon us. Virginia will become the first commercial and manufacturing State of the American continent, and Norfolk, Baltimore and Richmond equal to New York, Boston and Philadelphia. We may not live to see the day, but come it will. Out of the sabres of civil war will rise a Phœnix, beautiful and glorious beyond the vision of the most fervid enthusiasm.

Proposition from Lincoln.

Again was a report rife on the streets yesterday that LINCOLN had sent a proposition to Virginia for a truce till the assemblage of Congress. We do not believe this report.—Were he to make such a proposition, it would amount simply to a confession of weakness, which none but idiots could be expected to make. What could he expect to gain by it, but to avail themselves of. It would amount simply to this: That he is not quite ready to cut our throats, but will be obliged to us if we would be polite enough to wait till he is ready. What could he expect to gain by it? If he were ready, and we were not, who that knows LINCOLN believes he would make such a proposition? Who can believe that he, who has deceived Virginia so completely in those repeated peaceful assurances of his, which lulled the Virginia Convention to sleep till the enemy was already at our very gates and about to lay his hands upon our doors? Who can believe him, after his repeated lies about withdrawing reinforcements from Fort Sumter? Who can believe him, knowing that he and his Cabinet are all depraved, unprincipled scoundrels, personally as well as politically? Who can believe, in a word, that Virginia is a fool, or that the acceptance of such a proposition would not rouse a revolution in Virginia in less than twenty-four hours after it was known? No! The acceptance of any proposition, of any kind, from ABRAHAM LINCOLN, except the unconditional surrender of Washington and every Southern fort now in his possession, and the acknowledgment of Southern Independence, would be sure to be followed by REVOLUTION!

But it is useless to argue about such reports. We have already been assured upon the highest authority that there will be no truce between Virginia, thank Heaven, has gone forever from the base dominion of ABRAHAM LINCOLN, and he can neither deceive her with his lying tongue, nor with his double back with the sword. Better that every man, woman and child upon her soil should die, than live a vassal of that vile and vulgar tyrant who has usurped the seat of WASHINGTON.

Tories and Traitors.

We have heard, though we can scarcely credit the statement, that there are men in some parts of Virginia who are endeavoring to persuade them the spirit of the State by circulating slanders as infamous as that gotten up at the beginning of the troubles about the $16.00 tax on Carolina negroes. Among other things, that the South Carolina Government has no fleet sent to Charleston for the purpose of reinforcing Fort Sumter, and that therefore the attack upon that fort was wholly unnecessary. That such lies should be circulated by the insatiable villains who conceived it. In the North, every man is put in peril of his life who does not sustain their murderous onslaught upon the South. The South can scarcely afford to be more merciful to tories and traitors in her own borders. Give all such wretches fair warning before executing upon them the justice they deserve,—continue to watch them, and if they do not leave, let the punishment be dealt them by being honest men; and, our word for it, they will learn in a short time discretion,—whatever their base natures is capable.

Amherst County.

The example of this glorious county is beyond all praises. It is reliably reported that Amherst, which has but fifteen hundred voters, will contribute one thousand volunteers.

LIBERAL APPROPRIATION.—The Farmers' Bank of Lynchburg made an appropriation of one thousand dollars towards the equipment of the volunteer companies.

Important Financial Measures.

We are gratified to learn the Board of Public Works have ordered the suspension of all work upon the railroads of the State. The Board wisely concluded that to put any more State bonds upon the market, while the Abolitionist brokers of New York city are running them down sixty per cent. below par, would be to prostrate the market for a long time to come. They also felt it to be their duty to reserve all the resources and credit of the State for the exigencies of a war, the end of which no man can now foresee.

It was expected yesterday that the Convention would adopt an ordinance establishing a union of Virginia with the Confederate Government, under the Constitution as amended at Montgomery; and that the military organization and operations of the State would at once be placed under the direction of the Confederate authorities; at the same time that she would come under the operation of the Southern tariff and general civil jurisdiction. Such a measure would be permanent, and final in fact; though it would, of course, be provisional in form until after the vote of the 24th May next. In a financial point of view, such a measure would be of immense value to Virginia. Of all the Southern States, she is the most heavily burdened with debt; her aggregate annual taxes being alone one-third the gross amount paid by the whole fifteen Southern States. At the same time that her debt is the heaviest of all, the entire brunt of the war will most likely fall upon her. She is the bulwark of the South; the South sends to her aid; and the disgraceful conflict of her own deliverance through a position of distrustful isolation; and of course, also, the whole cost of the war would fall upon her treasury.—Union with the Confederate States brings military co-operation at the same time that it brings a division of the expenses of the war. The latest advices from Montgomery represent President DAVIS as ready to proceed to Richmond, and to march from twenty to fifty thousand Confederate troops into the State so soon as this Commonwealth becomes a part of the Confederacy. The annexation would secure the immediate co-operation of this force, the consummate Generalship of the Confederate officers, and the transfer of the forces of Virginia to the Confederate Army, to be paid from the Confederate fisc.

It is of the highest importance, therefore, that this annexation should be made at once. The submissionists must waive their aversions to the South in the presence of a common danger and in deference to the pressing financial necessities of the Commonwealth. The people of Virginia would cheerfully pay all the expenses of the war, however heavy, if the honor or the safety of the State required her incurring them alone; but this war is for the benefit of the whole South; it is a war in the burdens and glories of which the whole South are anxious to participate, and Virginia can ill afford to refuse this generous assistance for the sake of gratifying the unreasonable antipathies of a few discredited politicians with whom she has no sympathy. Besides, the cordial union of the whole South would have a moral effect at the North that would tend strongly to shorten the war, and thus may save a vast expenditure to the Southern treasury. In a word, this continued isolation is a luxury of which the State has had enough, and it is time to renounce it forever.—She is for the policy of the Revolution, the policy of union between all the States engaged in the same great struggle, and, in spite of the opposition and stubborn resistance of Tories.

The stoppage of the public works of the State will throw large numbers of laborers out of employment, and thus supply a valuable addition to the *personnel* of the army.—President DAVIS might obtain some fifteen hundred or two thousand recruits who might be taken to the vacated barracks at Lexington and drilled in a few weeks into well disciplined regiments. The negroes released from the public works would make valuable laborers in the entrenchments and fortifications now going on upon our Eastern waters. They would be proof against the miasma of the lowlands, and so effectively employed, be let loose upon any free negro regiments that might be sent down against us from the North.

P. S.—Since writing the above, we learn that the Convention yesterday passed an Ordinance applying for admission to the Southern Confederacy, and placing all the troops and military resources of the State at the disposal of the Confederate Government.

Gen. Pierce.

The fiery furnace of the times is testing patriots everywhere. Gen. PIERCE, the loudest of all men in his professions of devotion to the Constitution, has gone over soul and body to the enemy. For our own part, we never had any faith in politicians, no matter what party they belong to. Human nature is corrupt enough at its best, and a politician's human nature is worst of all. There is a class of unfortunate women whom all the world execrates; they are not as bad as the politicians. Both are equally corrupt, but the one class is driven to their calling from misfortune; the other from selfish and deliberate calculation. The rank and file of the people of all parties are honest and patriotic, but the leaders would in general sell their own country and their souls for a mess of pottage. We have more respect for an out and out Abolitionist than for the hypocritical Conservatives of the North. The Abolitionist is an honest man; the Conservative is a dishonest man. The Conservative is a sordid and sneaking knave. May Heaven's indignation and blast annihilate them both!

The Rev. W. G. Starr.

The Rev. W. G. STARR, of the Virginia Annual Conference, and formerly President of the Virginia Military Institute to deliver a poem before the young ladies of the Warrenton Female College, North Carolina, at its next commencement. The bestowment of such an honor upon one so young is a rare instance of meritorious genius, and is no small tribute to the proprietry of such a selection. Mr. STARR's poems—a collection of which we have had the pleasure of reading some of them before several years past, appeared over his signature in many papers and periodicals of the South. They possess peculiar delicacy of sentiment in union with classic simplicity of style, and not unfrequently appeal to the affections with a touching sensitive nature. They indicate an intimate acquaintance with the human heart—its vices and virtue, its strength and weakness—and reveal not only high attainments in classic scholarship, but a correct knowledge of the power of Poetry, founded upon an accurate taste.

All Hail, Tennessee.

Rev. Dr. LEE, of Norfolk, who has lately returned from Tennessee, informs us that the whole State is for secession with one voice, and that the people are wild with enthusiasm.

SERENADE.—A number of citizens complimented our gallant brothers of the South Carolina Regiment with a serenade, at the Exchange Hotel, at 9 o'clock last night. An immense number of persons were in attendance to testify their respect to the recipients of the compliment. Among the prominent gentlemen present, were delivered by the true Southern-hearted (Brigadier-General BONHAM, Gen. THOS. J. GREEN, (of N. C.,) Col. ALDRIDGE, of the S. C. volunteers, Hon. A. H. STEPHENS, Vice-President of the Southern Confederate States, and others.—We noticed at the Hotel the venerable Edmund RUFFIN, his Honor the Mayor, besides a number of military and civic dignitaries of the city and elsewhere.

BALLOON VOYAGE EXTRAORDINARY.—Lowe, the aeronaut, it is reported, has arrived in Columbia, S. C., having left Cincinnati early on Saturday morning. His destination was Richmond, but after nine hours' journey he arrived in Union District, S. C.

We are requested by Mr. J. F. GIBSON, Agent of the Adams Express Company, to give notice that all parcels and letters enclosed in Government envelopes will be forwarded by the Adams Express Company, free of charge, to the various Volunteer companies of the Southern Confederacy.

BY THE GOVERNOR OF VIRGINIA.

A PROCLAMATION.

Whereas, the Convention of this Commonwealth has, on this, the 25th day of April, 1861, adopted an ordinance "for the adoption of the Constitution of the Provisional Government of the Confederate States of America;" and has agreed to a "Convention between the Commonwealth of Virginia and the Confederate States of America," which it is proper should be made known to the people of this Commonwealth and to the world: Therefore, I, JOHN LETCHER, Governor of the Commonwealth of Virginia, do hereby publish and proclaim that the following are authentic copies of the Ordinance and Convention aforesaid.

[L. S.] Given under my hand as Governor, and under the seal of the Commonwealth, at Richmond, this 25th day of April, 1861, and in the 85th year of the Commonwealth. JOHN LETCHER.

By the Governor:
GEORGE W. MUNFORD,
Secretary of the Commonwealth.

AN ORDINANCE
For the Adoption of the Constitution of the Provisional Government of the Confederate States of America.

We, the delegates of the people of Virginia, in Convention assembled, solemnly impressed by the perils which surround the Commonwealth, and appealing to the searcher of hearts for the rectitude of our intentions in assuming the grave responsibility of this act, do, by this Ordinance, *adopt and ratify* the Constitution of the Provisional Government of the Confederate States of America, ordained and established at Montgomery, Alabama, on the eighth day of February, eighteen hundred and sixty-one; provided that this ordinance shall cease to have any legal operation or effect, if the people of this Commonwealth, upon the vote directed to be taken on the Ordinance of Secession passed by this Convention, on the 17th day of April, eighteen hundred and sixty-one, shall reject the same. A true Copy,
JNO. L. EUBANK, Secretary.

Convention between the Commonwealth of Virginia and the Confederate States of America.

The Commonwealth of Virginia, looking to a speedy union of said Commonwealth and the other slave States with the Confederate States of America, according to the provisions of the Constitution for the Provisional Government of said States, enters into the following temporary convention and agreement with said States, for the purpose of meeting pressing exigencies affecting the common rights, interests and safety of said Commonwealth and said Confederacy.

1st. Until the union of said Commonwealth with said Confederacy shall be perfected, and said Commonwealth shall become a member of said Confederacy, according to the Constitutions of both powers, the whole military force and military operations, offensive and defensive, of said Commonwealth, in the impending conflict with the United States, shall be under the chief control and direction of the President of said Confederate States, upon the same principles, basis and footing as if said Commonwealth were now, and during the interval, a member of said Confederacy.

2d. The Commonwealth of Virginia will, after the consummation of the Union contemplated in this Convention, and her adoption of the Constitution for a permanent Government of the said Confederate States, and she shall become a member of said Confederacy under said permanent Constitution, if the same occur, turn over to the said Confederate States all the public property, naval stores, and munitions of war, &c., she may then be in possession of, acquired from the United States, on the same terms and in like manner as the other States of said Confederacy have done in like cases.

3d. Whatever expenditures of money, if any, said Commonwealth of Virginia shall make before the Union, under the Provisional Government as above contemplated, shall be consummated, shall be met and provided for by said Confederate States.

This Convention entered into and agreed to, in the city of Richmond, Virginia, on the twenty-fourth day of April, 1861, by Alexander H. Stephens, the duly authorized Commissioner to act in the matter for the said Confederate States, and John Tyler, Wm. Ballard Preston, Saml McD. Moore, James P. Holcombe, James C. Bruce, and Lewis E. Harvie, parties duly authorized to act in like manner for said Commonwealth of Virginia—the whole subject to the approval and ratification of the proper authorities of both Governments respectively.

In testimony whereof, the parties aforesaid have hereto set their hands and seals, the day and year aforesaid, and at the place aforesaid, in duplicate originals.

ALEX'R H. STEPHENS, [Seal.]
Commissioner for Confederate States.

JOHN TYLER, [Seal.]
WM. BALLARD PRESTON, [Seal.]
S. MCD. MOORE, [Seal.]
JAMES P. HOLCOMBE, [Seal.]
JAMES C. BRUCE, [Seal.]
LEWIS E. HARVIE, [Seal.]
Commissioners for Virginia.

Approved and ratified by the Convention of Virginia, on the 25th of April, 1861.
JOHN JANNEY, President.
JOHN L. EUBANK, Sec'y.

WILL REMAIN IN RICHMOND A FEW DAYS LONGER.

THE ONLY SAFE AND PERMANENT CURE FOR CORNS, BUNIONS, SOFT CORNS, AND ALL DISEASES OF THE FEET, IS THE UNERRING SYSTEM PRACTICED BY DR. M. A. SCHLOSSER, AUTHOR OF SEVERAL WORKS ON THE DISEASES OF THE FEET, AND SURGEON CHIROPODIST, BY SPECIAL APPOINTMENTS, TO HIS IMPERIAL MAJESTY, NAPOLEON III., AND HIS MAJESTY THE KING OF BAVARIA.

READ. READ. READ
THE FOLLOWING
RICHMOND TESTIMONIALS.

From Dr. E. Powell, M. D.
This is to certify that Dr. SCHLOSSER eradicated two Corns for me, without any pain, and entirely to my satisfaction.—with entire relief to me from all pain. E. POWELL, M. D.
Richmond, April 16th, 1861.

From John M. Speed, Member of the Convention.
Dr. SCHLOSSER has extracted two Corns from my foot, without giving any pain, and to my entire satisfaction. JNO. M. SPEED, Lynchburg.
Richmond, April 18th, 1861.

From J. M. G. Dickinson, Esq.
Dr. SCHLOSSER has extracted a number of Corns from my feet, without any pain, giving perfect satisfaction. T. M. G. DICKINSON.
Richmond, April 20th, 1861.

From B. M. Harris.
Dr. SCHLOSSER has extracted five Corns from my feet, without the slightest pain. B. M. HARRIS.
Richmond, April 20th, 1861.

From John S. Angel, Esq.
This is to certify that Dr. SCHLOSSER extracted two Corns for me, without pain, and with great skill. JOHN S. ANGEL.
Richmond, April 17th, 1861.

In addition to the above, a great number more, from Richmond, are in Dr. SCHLOSSER's possession. The Doctor's method has not only been successful in this country, but also in Europe, as may be seen by the numerous certificates, from which he has been favored by

His Imperial Majesty, NAPOLEON, the Emperor of the French.
His Majesty, the KING OF BAVARIA.
His Imperial Highness Prince JEROME NAPOLEON BONAPARTE.
His Royal Highness Prince ALEXANDER, of Wurtemburg.
His Imperial Highness ARCH DUKE OF AUSTRIA.
His Royal Highness DUKE OF SACHSON-MEININGEN.
His Royal Highness DUKE B., of Sax Weimar.
His Highness Prince RICHARD METTERNICH.
†F. H. CARDINAL, Archbishop of Paris.
†ALAXIS, Bishop of Nancy, first Chaplain to Napoleon III.
Marechal CANROBERT.
A. H. ARNETH, Physician in Ordinary to the Grand Duchess Helena, of Russia.
BERNARD ROSSER, Physician in Ordinary to H. M. the Queen of Greece.

The signatures and seals of the above names, with several thousand more, from Sovereigns, Diplomatists, Clergymen, Physicians, Merchants, Military Men and Editors, of this country and Europe, may be seen at Dr. SCHLOSSER's office, where he may be consulted daily from 10 o'clock, from 9 A. M. till 6 P. M., at the SPOTSWOOD HOTEL, Parlors No. 111 and 113, near the Ladies' Drawing Rooms.

Private entrance on Main street.
No professional connection with any one. Dr. S.'s method is different from others. He does not pretend to cure corns by cutting or plastering.—These give only a short relief, but not a permanent cure.

A FEW DAYS LONGER IN RICHMOND.
ap 24—6t

FOR SALE.—One of HOE'S LARGE CYLINDER PRINTING PRESSES, 40x57. This Press is in good order, and warranted in perfect condition. Apply at this office. mh 19—ts

MARINE INTELLIGENCE.

PORT OF RICHMOND, APRIL 25, 1861.

High Water this day (Friday) at 5½ o'clock.

SAILED.

Schr. Willard Saulsbury, Hudson, down the river, light.
Schr. Mary Willis, North, Baltimore, light.
Schr. Leader, Gardner, down the river, light.
Schr. Casper Hitt, Shoe, "
Schr. New York, Cordival, "
Schr. Jos. English, Nickerson, "
Schr. Geo. Marion, Griffin, "
Schr. St. Cloud, Swanney, "
Schr. Shields, Warren, "
Schr. Baltimore, Phillips, Baltimore, mdze., W. D. Colquitt & Co.
Schr. Amphes, Cates, Wilmington, N. C., mdze., W. D. Colquitt & Co.
Steamer Belvidere, Keen, Baltimore, mdze. and passengers, D. & W. Currie.

AT A MEETING OF THE JUSTICES OF THE COUNTY OF HENRICO, held at the Court-House, on the 25th day of April, 1861,—present, John R. Garnett, (Presiding Justice,) S. S. Waldrop, John Nottles, John W. Lee, John T. Childrey, John R. King, Elijah Baker, Robert H. Henley, Joseph C. Burton, Thos. Hobson, Geo. M. Savage, and Thos T. Duke:

Ordered, that in view of the present crisis of the affairs of our State, and in accordance with the Convention of the State Convention requesting the counties to aid and equip such portion of the volunteers as may be needed; that the County of Henrico will raise the sum of ten thousand dollars for that purpose.

Ordered, that to enable us to raise this amount immediately, this Court will issue the bonds of this county payable, and of sums, to be loaned on a sum of $50 each, and fifty bonds for the sum of $100 each, which bonds shall bear interest, and the amount of each respective bond, and a levy for that purpose ... by law; and that this Court will make a levy for the redemption thereof in the next county levy.

Ordered, that inasmuch as the bonds cannot be issued till the Court actually sits and enters this order of record, citizens who desire to aid in raising the amount be requested to pay the money to the treasurer of the Committee of Disbursement hereinafter provided for, such sum not less than $100, as they may be willing to invest in the bonds to be issued, and the treasurer, or agent, shall give receipts for the same, and shall be authorized to receive a bond or bonds of this county equal to the amount so paid, which shall bear interest from the time such money is so paid to said Committee until the redemption thereof.

Ordered, that John T. Childrey, John Nottles, George H. King, John W. Lee and John R. Garnett, be appointed a Committee to receive the sums so paid, and to disburse the same.

Ordered, that F. Saunders, Henry Cox and John W. Fussell, be appointed a Committee in District No. 1, to solicit subscriptions for the benefit of those persons or families who are suffering by the absence of volunteers called into service, and that said Committee be authorized to disburse the same to such persons in the district, as they in their discretion may deem proper, upon whom they are dependent.

Ordered, that Dr. John Knox, E. Baker and Jno. P. Harrison, be appointed a similar Committee in District No. 2.

Ordered, that Fendall Griffin, N. F. Bowe and John Hudgins be appointed a similar Committee in District No. 3.

Ordered, that James A. Moore, F. Mayo and John A. Hutcheson, be appointed a similar Committee in District No. 4.

Ordered, That it be recommended that all commandants of Volunteer Companies in this county, will meet at the Court-House TO-MORROW at 12 o'clock.

Copy—Teste: [Signed,] WM. FOLKES, C. H. C.
ap 26—1t

SUIT OF DIVORCE.—The suit brought in the Circuit Court of the city of Richmond, by MARY FRANCES KIRBY and THOMAS EDWARD, her infant, for divorce from her husband, ROBERT F. KIRBY, was decided in her favor on the 20th day of March last, and the judge awarded to her one-third of the proceeds of the sale of Robert F. Kirby, for her life. ap 26—3t*

LEE GUARD.—RALLY, VOLUNTEERS, RALLY! All persons disposed to join a company, will call and see us. Serving GUARD, during the war, forming, and make his mark as a member. Mj. James LEE, will report promptly at Headquarters, corner of 9th and Main sts., opposite Bosher's Hall.

CORNS, BUNIONS, NAILS, &c.—Persons troubled with the above, can, in a few seconds, by Dr. SCHULTZ, the resident Surgeon Chiropodist. Office Wall Street Hotel, 9th st.

Dr. S. is a Southern gentleman, and those ladies who have not been to him will find it to their interest, [having previous engagements to fulfill,] will be so at the earliest opportunity.
ap 25—2t*

RALLY, VIRGINIANS!—HAMPDEN GUARD.—I report company to be ready for immediate service, to be formed after the English pattern. Hamden, will report promptly at the offices of Lawrence S. Marye and James Pleasants, on 11th street.
No expense has been made for furnishing horses and all equipments; and also for the subsistence of the company, as soon as formed. Can accommodate the first. ap 26—3t

FIGHT FOR YOUR COUNTRY.—All those wishing to co-operate with us in organizing a Volunteer Company, will meet at BEAVER DAM DEPOT, Hanover County, on Saturday next, 27th April, at 11 o'clock.
WM. NELSON,
C. ST. GEORGE NOLAND,
CHARLES COOKE,
LEWIS F. TERRELL,
HILLARY JONES,
WM. FONTAINE.
ap 23—4t*

NOTICE.—The Books for subscription to the Capital Stock of the "FARMERS' AND MECHANICS' INSURANCE COMPANY OF THE CITY OF RICHMOND," will be opened at the office of JAS. M. TAYLOR & SON, on the 10th day of MAY next, under the direction of THE COMMISSIONERS.
ap 26—1m

SERVANTS FOR SALE & HIRE

SPECIAL NOTICE.—FOR SALE—100 yards BLACK DRILL, for making Knapsacks. ALSO, FOR HIRE—Two or three BLACKSMITHS, by the month or for the balance of the year. Apply immediately to JOHN POPE, 13th st., between Main and Cary.
ap 26—1t*

FOR HIRE.—A No. 1 middle aged COOK, WASHER and IRONER, without encumbrance. Apply to JOS. STERN, Broad street.
ap 26—2t*

FOR HIRE—A No. 1 female HOUSE SERVANT; also, one BOY, accustomed to house work. Apply to REDWOOD & KEACH, 34 Main street.
ap 22—1t

GEORGE B. STEEL, DENTIST.
Office and residence on Main, between 7th and 8th streets, (five doors above the Spotswood Hotel,) Richmond, Va. Having been engaged in the practice of his profession in this, his native city, since the year 1836, he would respectfully solicit a continuance of that liberal patronage.
ap 26—2w

NOTICE TO INDIVIDUALS WHO PROPOSE TO PASS ON VIRGINIA STATE BUSINESS ON THE VIRGINIA CENTRAL AND ORANGE AND ALEXANDRIA RAILROADS.—The Virginia Central and Orange and Alexandria Railroad Companies, the latter to have the cars been heretofore, not to be made a claim upon the Companies for passage, but in order that the individual travelling for the State must exhibit the permit, or certificate from the proper officer or authorized person, to be exhibited to the conductor.
THOS. DODAMEAD, Gen'l Supt. Va. Central Railroad.
H. W. VANDEGRIFT, Gen'l Supt. O. & A. Railroad.
ap 26—2w

RICHMOND AND YORK RIVER RAILROAD.—Passenger Train leaves Richmond daily, at 4 A. M. Leaves West Point, MONDAYS, WEDNESDAYS and FRIDAYS, at 12 M.; TUESDAYS, THURSDAYS and SATURDAYS, at 10 A. M.
Freight Train leaves Richmond TUESDAYS, THURSDAYS and SATURDAYS, at 4 P. M.; leaves West Point MONDAYS, WEDNESDAYS and FRIDAYS, at 12 P. M.
Sunday Train leaves Richmond at 8 A. M.—leaves West Point at 4 P. M.
R. H. TEMPLE, Sup't.
ap 26

NOTICE.—On and after this day, the night Trains will run as usual, leaving Richmond and Fredericksburg at their regular trips to Fredericksburg, leaving Richmond Depot at 7 o'clock P. M.
The Passenger Trains of this Company will stop going and returning at the Hermitage Fair Grounds.
SAM'L RUTH, Sup't.
Office R., F. & P. R. R. Co., Richmond, April 26, 1861.
ap 26—3t

FOR LYNCHBURG.—To leave on FRIDAY, the 26th inst., at 12 M., from the Basin, the canal boat SATURDAY EVENING.—The steamer ELLA SCOTT will leave as above. For freight, apply to GUY & COX, Agents, at Cox's Bluff, Dock street.
ap 26—2t

FOR PHILADELPHIA.—The A No. 1 steamship CITY OF RICHMOND is now loading for the above port, and will leave on FRIDAY, 26th inst., at 6 o'clock P. M. For freight, apply to GUY & COX, Agents, at Cox's Bluff, Dock street. For freight or passage, apply to the Captain on board.
Freight for Boston taken through as usual.
ap 26—1t C. P. CARDOZO, Agent, Rocketts.

HOUSE AND LOT IN SIDNEY FOR RENT.—An excellent two-story LOT, with a good BRICK HOUSE, in Sidney, on the Westham Plank-Road, just opposite the Toll Gate. Possession given immediately. Any one desiring to lease this valuable property on very low terms. Apply to GODDIN & APPERSON.
ap 26—3t

DOVE LODGE, No. 51.—The stated meeting of DOVE LODGE, No. 51, is postponed on account of War. F. J. BOGGS, Master. GEORGE H. TOMPKINS, Sec'y.
Richmond, April 26, 1861.

THE MILITARY.—The sewing Machine Company have this day received extensive JAPAN ROOMS to the undersigned for the exclusive use of making up military clothing for the soldiers of the SOUTHERN STATES and ready to JAPAN CANTEENS and CAMP CUPS, LETTER KNAPSACKS, &c., &c., and to do any work in that line. M. DAVIS, On Cary street, below 15th.
ap 26—3t*

LIVERPOOL FINE SALT.
5,000 sacks LIVERPOOL FINE SALT, per ship Hiawatha, in James river, direct from Liverpool.
For sale by
EDMOND, DAVENPORT & CO.
ap 26—1t

NOTICE.—The SOUTH CAROLINA soldiers can have their SOUTH CAROLINA BANK NOTES translated into VIRGINIA BANK NOTES at par at the office of
R. H. MAURY & CO.
Office under the St. Charles Hotel.
ap 26—1t

SOLDIERS' PIPES.
SWEET BRIAR ROOT.
For sale by
F. HOELDECKE, Broad st., Third door from 7th st.
ap 26—3t*

SPECIAL NOTICES.

Premium Photographs.—GREAT REDUCTION IN PRICE. PHOTOGRAPHS FOR ONE DOLLAR, PHOTOGRAPHS FOR ONE DOLLAR, PHOTOGRAPHS FOR ONE DOLLAR, Made only at VANNERSON'S Gallery, No. 77 Main street, Formerly Whitehurst's Gallery.
ap 25—3t*

Soldiers, Attention.—If any of you wish your NAMES OR INITIALS engraved on brass, to wear on your caps, or to be placed on your guns, you can have it done in the best style, and at short notice, by application to J. WEIGHT, at the Type Foundry, on Franklin st. ap 22—3t*

Science of War. THE BOOK FOR THE TIMES! TACTICS FOR OFFICERS OF INFANTRY, CAVALRY AND ARTILLERY! Arranged and Compiled by Capt. L. V. BUCKHOLTZ. Price 75c. Just published by J. W. RANDOLPH, 121 Main st.
ap 25—3t

My own customers are respectfully informed that my stock of SILK and COTTON is nearly exhausted. If I succeed in getting more, it will be at an advanced price.
E. R. CRAIG, 227 Main st., Richmond, Va.
ap 25—3t

Notice.—To Merchants, Grocers, Physicians, and OTHERS ENGAGED IN BUSINESS IN THE THIRD DISTRICT.—The undersigned has been appointed by the Sergeant of the City, to assess the LICENSES for business in the Third District of the city, in accordance with the ordinance, on the 1st of May, which includes the Hay Scales, at the Law Office of Mr. Tyler, ... from 9 o'clock A. M., till 5 o'clock P. M., for the purpose of issuing LICENSES to all who have not obtained the same for the current year.
If licenses are not obtained before the 1st day of May, I am required by law to assess for double the amount, and all parties violating the law are subject to a penalty of from $20 to $100.
For G. W. H. TYLER, Com. 3d Dist. City of Richmond.
ap 24—7t*

War!
BALLS FOR NAVY PISTOLS, and for sale by C. D. YALE & CO., Iron Buildings, Governor st.
ap 23—6t

Merchants, Attorneys, Keepers of BOARDING-HOUSES, and all others required by law to obtain Licenses, are notified that the Commissioner of the Revenue for Madison Ward, and the 2d District of the city, at the Sheriff's office, 125 Main st., every day this week, from 9 A. M. to 5 P. M., prepared to issue LICENSES and take the oaths of all who have not obtained them, and who are required by the act of the General Assembly of April 2d, 1861, provides that all who do not obtain their licenses on or before the 30th last, shall pay double the tax on their license, and shall be subject to a penalty for doing business without a license.
JOHN JOHNSON, Com. Rev. 2d District City of Richmond.
ap 22—6t*

Great Bargains.
FIVE THOUSAND YARDS OF BEAUTIFUL BAREGES, BAREGE ANGLAIS, FOULARDS, CHALLIES, FRENCH JACONETS, &c.
Many of this Spring's importation, BOUGHT AT PANIC PRICES, To sell at 25 CENTS PER YARD.
Call and see them before they are all sold.
SAM'L M. PRICE & CO.
ap 12—ts

Second Supply.
NEW GOODS!
Opening by Steamer this day—
BLACK SILK MANTLES, newest styles and patterns.
Beautiful HERNANI SHAWLS.
Full SHAWLS, a rare article.
Elegant hooped Silk, very cheap.
Splendid HERNANI SUITS for dresses.
Most beautiful ORGANDIES, very cheap.
FRENCH JACONETS in great variety, very cheap.
MOURNING GOODS
In variety, among which are cheap—
BAREGES, GRENADINE BAREGES, CHALLIES, &c.
SAM'L M. PRICE & CO.
ap 9—ts

Great Sale AT REDUCED PRICES, OF A LARGE PORTION OF OUR STOCK OF RICH DRESS GOODS!
On our own counters, in the large Shawl Room attached to our store.
In order to reduce our stock and business to a scale demanded by the altered condition of the times.
Among the GOODS Now offered are—
Beautiful SILK DRESSES, at 10, 12, 15 and $20.
Beautiful SILK ROBES at $20.
BAREGE ROBES, $8 and $10.
Splendid BAREGES, DUSTERS, &c., &c.
A great variety of BAREGES, GRENADINES, CHALLIES, POPLINS, ORGANDIES, LAWNS, to be sold without regard to cost.
SAM'L M. PRICE & CO.
N. B.—The NEW GOODS of the season receiving by every steamer.

Spring Importation—1861.
RIBBONS, MILLINERY AND STRAW GOODS.
ARMSTRONG, CATOR & CO., Importers and Jobbers of RIBBONS, BONNET SILKS AND SATINS, VELVETS, RUCHES, FLOWERS, FEATHERS, STRAW BONNETS, FLATS, &c., No. 237 and Lofts of 239 Baltimore st., BALTIMORE, Md.
Offer a stock unsurpassed in the United States in variety and cheapness.
Orders solicited and prompt attention given. Terms—six months, 6 per cent. off for cash, par funds.
mh 5—ew*

Cod Liver Oil of several brands—Just to hand and for sale by JNO. W. GARLICK, Apothecary, Franklin street.
ap 5

Rock's Good Samaritan—For Rheumatism, NEURALGIA, &c. For sale by JNO. W. GARLICK, Apothecary.

Bed Bug Poison—A Speedy Extermination. For sale by JNO. W. GARLICK, Apothecary, &c.

ATTENTION, VOLUNTEER COMPANIES.—I am now ready to furnish on sale cheap, 2 cases Ashland Grey Tweeds, suitable for military clothing. I have 150 SADDLES for sale and for sale—50 Saddles and Bridles, complete.
ap 22 ALEX. NOTT.

POCKET COMBS, with Brush and Looking-Glass—a convenient and necessary article for the Volunteers; Leather and India Rubber Drinking Cups, Flasks, &c. just received and for sale by A. BODEKER & CO., 137 Main st.
ap 20

MATTRESSES, COTS, &c.—On hand, a stock of every kind of Matrasses, such as Wool, Matrasses, Cots, and Single and Double Bedsteads, &c., for sale, at low prices.
ALEX. NOTT.

WINES, BRANDY, &c.—Champagne Wine; Claret Wine; superior Port Wine; Madeira Wine; Sherry Wine; Cognac Brandy; the celebrated brands; Wine; superior Old Whiskey, for sale by I. & G. B. DAVENPORT.

GREY MERINO SHIRTS.—Received, a lot of Grey Merino Under Shirts; also, a lot of good Gray Merino Drawers, for sale by JOHNSON & HARWOOD.
ap 23

CROCKERY AND GLASSWARE, &c.—I have on hand a large lot of low price Crockery and Glassware, for sale cheap.
ALEX. NOTT.

SYRUP AND MOLASSES.—Superior clarified syrup; Sugar-house Molasses, for sale by I. & G. B. DAVENPORT.
ap 26

NOTICE.—For the present, we shall offer our stock of Goods low for cash.
JOHNSON & HARWOOD.
ap 23

WESTERN LARD, White Greasy; Tanners' Oil, for sale by I. & G. B. DAVENPORT.

CANDLES.—400 Boxes Adamantine Candles, for sale by I. & G. B. DAVENPORT.

TO HEADQUARTERS ARMY OF THE SOUTHERN CONFEDERACY.—The subscriber having on hand a large amount of BREAD, would be pleased to receive orders for the same. Can furnish five to forty barrels per day. Having superior workmen engaged with me, I will sell at reasonable rates.
JOHN G. BRIDGES, Corner Broad and 3d streets.
ap 23—6t*

MERCHANTS AND OTHERS, IN JEFFERSON WARD, (which composes all between Broad and Main streets,) who have not obtained their licenses on or before the 30th of April, they will be subject to double the amount of taxes. I will be found at my store on E. B. Cook's every day, from 9 till 4, to receive license from them.
JOHN W. WRIGHT, C. R.
JOHN M. FRANCISCO, Comm'r Revenue.
ap 25—2t*

TENT CLOTH.—The James River Manufacturing Company can furnish a very good article of Tent Cloth. Persons in want will please apply to the above purpose, if nothing better can be had.
P. B. BENTLEY, Agent.
ap 26

ATTENTION, MILITARY.—Call at MONTAGUE'S shop, corner Bank and 12th streets, and have your CUTTING SPOONS for Shooting.
ap 22—6t

FRESH BUTTER.
COOKING BUTTER 20 CENTS.
For sale at retail, by J. S. ROBERTSON.
ap 25

NOTICE.—All persons indebted to the late firm of Mr. S. P. COCKE, at "Dover Mills," Goochland county, where I may be found.
R. WOOD.
ap 26—3t*

FOR SALE.—A fine English, single barrel SHOT GUN. For sale by TYLER & SON, Cary st.
ap 26—3t*

GOODS FOR VOLUNTEERS FOR THE WAR.—20 pieces Grey Cloths, 6-4 wide, at $1.25 per yard; 3,000 Colored Blankets, cheap.
ALFRED MOSES, 63 Main st.
ap 25

CORN.—135 bags prime White Corn in store and for sale by BLAIR & MARVIE, Cary and 12th streets.
ap 25

NAPLES FIGS, NAPLES FIGS.—Received per express, 100 drums of Naples Figs, a fine article, for sale by WM. G. DANDRIDGE.
ap 25

PEACH BLOW AND MERCER POTATOES.—600 bushels Peach Blow and Mercer Potatoes, in store and for sale by WM. G. DANDRIDGE, No. 100 Broad st.
ap 12

BLACKBURN'S HENNESSY BRANDY.—Various vintages for sale by DUNLOP, MONCURE & CO.
ap 8

WANTS

WANTED—DRUMMER.—Company B, Lieut. D. G. MCINTOSH, First Regiment South Carolina Volunteers, wish to employ a KETTLE DRUMMER. Apply at their quarters, at the New Poor House Building, north end of 3d street.
ap 26—3t*

WANTED—IMMEDIATELY—Three good TAILORS, to work either by the week or by the piece. None but good workmen need apply.
N. STOCKDALE, No. 114 Main st.
ap 26—1t*

WANTED—ROOMS.—Wanted, immediately, in a central and genteel part of the city, a suit of THREE ROOMS, furnished or unfurnished, for a family of three persons. Address "G." Dispatch office.
ap 26—3t*

WANTED—IMMEDIATELY—Two good COOPERS. Apply to WM. N. TINSLEY.
ap 26—1t*

WANTED—SOUTHERN [illegible] ... A few more recruits wanted for a company. All joining will be furnished with uniform. Apply at Headquarters, in the Old United States Hotel, corner of Main and 19th streets.
ap 26—1t*

WANTED.—A middle-aged gentleman, of good habits and business qualification, is desirous of obtaining a SITUATION to some mercantile house in the city.
Reference—E. H. Chamberlayne, Esq., and Dr. J. N. Powell. Address, "E. G. M.," at this office.
ap 26—2t*

WANTED—A second-hand SODA WATER PUMP, and one or two iron fountains. Address, "MICHAEL."
Care of Box 862, Richmond P. O.
ap 26—2t*

WANTED.—Men for immediate active service in LIGHT ARTILLERY. Apply over Woodhouse & Co., on Main street.
ap 25—3t J. PEYTON, Captain.

WANTED—Three or Four FURNISHED ROOMS, for a small family, or for House. Address "R." care of Dispatch office.
ap 25—3t*

WANTED—TO TINNERS.—Wanted, TIN PLATE and SHEET-IRON WORKERS. Apply at once.
ap 22—3t C. D. YALE & CO.

WANTED—To hire, a number of HANDS to assist in manufacturing cloth for the Confederate Army. The workmen ... manufacturing WORKS are hereby notified that they can get employment again by calling at the Works immediately. Also, those who have enlisted as they may be about to be working at the works ... P. RAHM.
ap 26—1t

WANTED—THREE HUNDRED HANDS—To work on Jackets, Pants, Shirts and Overcoats. None need apply except those accustomed to that kind of work.
WM. IRA SMITH, 114 Main st.
ALSO—FOUR CUTTERS WANTED, at 114 Main street.
WM. IRA SMITH.
ap 22—1t

WANTED—DRUMMERS.—Wanted 16 BOYS, DRUM CORPS of the 1st Regiment Va. Volunteers for immediate service. Boys must come prepared, with the written permission of parents or guardians. Apply, with that permission, to the DRUM MAJOR, at Military Hall, over the Old Market, from 11 to 2 o'clock, and from 4 to 6 o'clock.
ap 25—3t

WANTED—THREE CUTTERS who understand cutting Jackets and Pants by measurement.
WM. IRA SMITH, 114 Main street.
ap 20—ts

WANTED—HANDS for SEWING MACHINE WORK wanted by
KENT, PAINE & CO.
ap 23—3t

WANTED—A few able NEGROES at the Carbon Hill Mines, for the balance of the year, or by the month.
JOHN J. WERTH, Agent.
ap 18—ts

WANTED—CHECKS on NEW YORK, BALTIMORE and PHILADELPHIA. Also, GOLD and SILVER, for which the highest rates will be paid.
C. W. PURCELL & CO.
ap 11—dtf

WANTED—To purchase, a few likely NEGROES. Any person having Servants to sell, can find a purchaser by addressing "Cox 225," Richmond Post-Office, giving a full description of them, and the prices.
Dealers in the city or country, thus enabling collectors to save commissions and trouble.
mh 28—1m*

WANTED—All persons to know that I manufacture all styles and qualities of TRUNKS, and having a large stock on hand, I can sell at the lowest prices, as good as any other article. A first-class, Home-made Sole Leather Trunks, Ladies' French Dress Trunks, Bonnet Boxes; also, all the common styles, all sold at manufacturers' prices, wholesale and retail. Call at my Factory and Wholesale room, opposite Dispatch office. Factory Cary street, above 8th.
Trunks Repaired.
fe 26—ts JAMES KNOTTS.

WANTED—SIGHT EXCHANGE on Baltimore, Philadelphia and New York. ALSO—GOLD and SILVER, for which the highest rates will be paid by
R. H. MAURY & CO.
de 7—ts

WANTED.—The subscriber wishes to employ a first-class CONFECTIONER, to whom he will give the highest price.
ANDRE ANTONI, St. Nicholas Saloon.
fe 22—ts

WANTED—TIME BILLS on BALTIMORE, PHILADELPHIA, NEW YORK and BOSTON, for which a liberal premium will be paid by
R. T. BRADLEY & CO.
fe 22—ts

DIVIDEND NOTICE.

OFFICE R., F. & P. R. R. COMPANY, Richmond, April 18, 1861.

DIVIDEND NOTICE.—At a meeting of the Board of Directors of this Company, held at this office, a DIVIDEND of FIFTY DOLLARS and FIFTY CENTS per share, out of the net profits of the Company for the past six months, was declared, payable to the Stockholders, or their legal representatives, on and after the 1st of May next. Transfer books will be closed on SATURDAY, 27th April.
C. W. MACMURDO, Treasurer.
ap 18—1t

DIVIDEND NOTICE.—At a meeting of the Board of Directors of this Company, held at their office, a DIVIDEND of 3½ per cent., out of the net profits of the Company for the last six months, was declared, payable to the Stockholders, or their legal representatives, on the 1st day of May next.
Transfer Books will be closed on SATURDAY, April 27th.
C. W. MACMURDO, Treasurer.
ap 17—ts

NOTICE.—In accordance with the 23d section of the Act fully passed by the Council of the City of Richmond on the 4th March, 1861, I hereby give notice to all persons to the Committee on Finance have classified all persons and firms ... merchants, traders, shop-keepers, manufacturers, keepers of ordinaries, brokers, &c., which classification is now completed ... the Auditor's office, where all interested can see the classification of their ... the Commissioners of the Revenue have ... The Committee of Finance will meet in the Council Chamber on TUESDAY, the 6th day of this month, (April,) at 4 o'clock P. M., to hear applications from all persons who may think they are aggrieved by said classification, and if any such persons who shall fail to appear before the Committee ...
M. L. GRATTON, A. C. R.
ap 23—8t

AN ORDINANCE CONCERNING SUSPICIOUS CHARACTERS.
[Passed April 22d, 1861.]

Be it Ordained by the Council of the City of Richmond, That when any person believes or suspects any one to be a free negro or a slave without his presence, continuance of any such person may ... suspicious or unsafe, as it is to remain in the city, it shall be the duty of the Mayor ...
That it shall be the duty of the Mayor to have such person so suspected, brought before him for examination, and he shall have power to send such person to jail ... and if found guilty, or of any person ... if the Mayor shall be of opinion that such suspected person shall be directed ...
This ordinance shall go in force from its passage.
A Copy—Teste:
THOS. LAWSON, C. C. R.
ap 23—1t

AN ORDINANCE CONCERNING THE GOOD ORDER OF THE CITY OF RICHMOND.
[Passed April 22d, 1861.]

Be it Ordained by the Council of the City of Richmond, That every Hotel Keeper, Keepers of Restaurants, Keepers of Lager Beer Saloons, or of any places in which ardent spirits, porter, beer, or cider is sold, are hereby prohibited from selling to any soldier any intoxicating drink after the hour of 10 o'clock ...
Any person violating this Ordinance may be fined twenty dollars by the Mayor, and every day shall constitute a separate offence.
This Ordinance shall go in force from its passage.
A Copy—Teste:
THOS. LAWSON, C. C. R.
ap 24—1w

EXECUTIVE DEPARTMENT, Richmond, April 23, 1861.

THE GOVERNOR of the Commonwealth of Virginia, acknowledging the prompt and patriotic manner in which the telegraphs ... to the communication by the ... so important ... any of the Telegraph offices, or conveying any of the business, the facilities of the Telegraph for the purpose of transmitting ... it is desired to the ... in military operations, therefore ... who ... in the order of the Governor.
JOHN ECHOLS, Aid to Gov. Letcher.
ap 24—ts

ORDNANCE DEPARTMENT, Richmond, Va., April 21, 1861.

PROPOSALS will be received for the furnishing of Ammunition to be delivered by ... Proposals ... the prices for ... at the Armory as ... the Department ... the months, nor does it know ... be delivered.
C. DIMMOCK, Col. of Ordnance.
ap 21—ts

COMMISSIONER WATSON'S OFFICE, Richmond, April 23, 1861.

THE CREDITORS OF BROOKE PLEASANTS, under his deed of 6th October, 1860, to James & Taylor & Son, Trustees, will present their claims, properly vouched, to me, at my office, on Monday, the 6th day of May, 1861, that I may state an account of the same, agreeably to a decree of the Circuit Court of Richmond.
WM. F. WATSON, Commissioner.
ap 24—1m

SHINGLES.
100 M Heart and Sap CYPRESS SHINGLES
For sale by A. S. LEE.
fe 12—ts

FRESH GOSHEN AND PACK BUTTER.—Prime Goshen and Pack Butter, EXTRA RICH SUGAR CURED HAMS, excellent FAMILY FLOUR, &c., for sale by P. McGARTHY, 117 Broad street.
ap 17

GROUND PLASTER.—100 tons superior Ground Plaster. It is ground at the Quarries in New Brunswick, and we would respectfully ask the attention of farmers to this superior article. For sale by BRIDGFORD & CO., On the Dock.
ap 18—1m

IRON—250 tons English Railroad Iron, comprising a full assortment of Rounds, Squares, Flats, Ovals, Scrolls, Horse-Shoe, Bands, &c., &c.; also, 80 tons Swedes Iron, for sale by EDWIN WORTHAM & CO.
ap 3

MILITARY NOTICES.

VERINA TROOP.—Meet at Rockettes Old Field, for Drill, THIS MORNING, at 10 o'clock.
H. MYERS, O. S.
By order of Capt. AKIN.
ap 26—1t

ATTENTION, HENRICO LIGHT DRAGOONS.—Meet at the Court-House, on SATURDAY, the 27th FEBRUARY, at 10 o'clock, in fatigue uniform, except officers, who are required to wear dress uniform. By order of Capt. MCGRUDER.
JAS. R. BRISBE, O. S.
ap 26—1t

HEADQUARTERS ARTILLERY COMPANY.—HOWITZER ... TODAY, at 2 o'clock, and report promptly. By order. J. PEYTON, Captain Commanding.

ATTENTION, ARTILLERYMEN.—All who desire to join the HENRICO ARTILLERY COMPANY, will meet at the Court-House on ... and enroll their names at Headquarters, on Main st., two doors below the Exchange Bank.
ap 24—3t

179TH REGIMENT VIRGINIA MILITIA.—ATTENTION! COMPANY NO. 1.—All persons belonging to this company, will assemble at the corner of Broad and 17th streets, on THIS AFTERNOON, at 4 o'clock, to attend the semi-annual Company muster.
By order of the Colonel.
Lieut. A. W. NOLTING, Jr.

HEADQUARTERS RICHMOND GRAYS, BOSHERS' HALL.
I. A Box for the depository of letters for the Richmond Grays will be placed at this store.
II. Persons desiring to send bundles to the Grays, will leave them at this store by 3 o'clock each day, until further notice.
III. The families will call for letters addressed to them, by calling at this store.
By order of F. M. BONAVITA.

ATTENTION, VIGILANT GUARD.—The company will meet EVERY EVENING, at the office of Lieut. STERN, on Franklin street, between 13th and 14th, at 7 o'clock, until further orders.
By order of the Captain.
Capt. BAYLY.
ap 26—ts

CHANGE OF HEADQUARTERS.—The HEADQUARTERS OF COMPANY "F," 1st REGIMENT VA. VOLUNTEERS, is established at the MECHANICS' INSTITUTE, second story. All members of the Company who are anxious to report themselves immediately.
By order of Capt. Lay.
ap 24—3t J. S. TOWER, 1st Serg't.

THE FOLLOWING ORDERS have been issued to Gen. PHILIP ST. GEORGE COCKE, of the 1st Brigade, Gen. WM. B. TALIAFERRO, of the 4th; Gen. SALLOW, of the 11th; Gen. JONATHAN RICHMOND, of the 19th; Gen. C. MOORE, of the 9th; Gen. R. G. PEYTON, of the 20th; and Gen. J. A. EARLY, of the 13th:

GENERAL HEADQUARTERS, ADJ'T GENERAL'S OFFICE, Richmond, April 22, 1861.

You will forthwith send to this place all the armed volunteer companies, Artillery, Light Infantry and Riflemen, in your brigades, for active service. Employ messengers, if necessary, for this service. The Cavalry Companies will hold themselves in readiness.
By command.
WM. H. RICHARDSON, Adj't.
ap 24—3t

GENERAL HEADQUARTERS, ADJ'T GENERAL'S OFFICE, April 22, 1861.

VOLUNTEER COMPANIES, now in Richmond, or on their way to the City, will report in person to Lieut. CUNNINGHAM, at the Hermitage Fair Grounds. The Captains will report in person to Lieut. CUNNINGHAM, Acting Assistant Adjutant General.
By command.
WM. H. RICHARDSON, Adj't.
ap 24—3t

ADJUTANT GENERAL'S OFFICE, April 22d, 1861.

FOR GENERAL INFORMATION.—Requisitions for ARMS, EQUIPMENTS and AMMUNITION, must be direct to the State ... in the ... must be sent.
By command.
W. H. RICHARDSON.
ap 24—ts

HEADQUARTERS COMPANY "K," ... The Headquarters of this company are established at the old (until lately so called) UNITED STATES HOTEL, corner of Main and 19th streets, where all ... from 11 A. M. to 1 P. M. Any one wishing to join the company can at the same time during the hours stated.
By order of the Captain.
FRED'K LEMKUL, Quartermaster.

LOST.

LOST—On Monday evening, either in Richmond, or on the road from Richmond to Fair Grounds, a ... PERS. Any person finding said papers, and ... them to the Dispatch office, will receive a reward of $5.
PARTHENIA PARSONS, A few wanted of color.
ap 25—3t*

LOST—A MEERSCHAUM CIGAR TUBE between Amelia Court-House and Jetersville. The finder will be suitably rewarded by leaving it at this office.
It belongs to one of the Farmville Guards.
ap 26—1t

STRAYED—From the Fair Grounds, on Tuesday last, a medium size BLACK HORSE. Has four white feet, a white blaze in his forehead, and has a ... and ... Any information leading to his recovery, ... ATKINSON, in Manchester.
ap 25—1t

TWO TRUNKS were brought to my house with soldiers' ... for which the owner ... ROBERT E. LEFEBVRE. Grace st., East of Pantheon.
ap 26—1t*

TRUNKS LOST.—Were taken from the Steamer "Glen Cove," on Saturday last, two TRUNKS and a BONNET BOX, which the owner is anxious to recover. The articles were evidently taken by mistake, those who have them will confer a favor by returning the same to H. R. O. HARKINS, in Rocketts, opposite the Steamboat Wharf. They are marked...
ap 24—3t*

LOST—TEN DOLLARS REWARD.—Lost Monday, on the way from 5th to the Fair Grounds, a BLACK BOOK, with thirty-five dollars in bills of the Exchange Bank, ... in the hands of ... Union Savings Bank for ... reward ... to the Armory.
A. E. ZEHLE, Soldier, near the Armory.

LOST—On the Brooke Turnpike, near the first Toll-Gate, a Dress Skirt ... will be paid.
ap 25—1t*

LOST—BOND.—Notice is hereby given of the loss of a BOND made to Miss Emily F. Guna, by John Foe, Jr., with Wilson Williams as surety, for five hundred dollars, and dated August, 1846, and interest has been paid thereon up to the month of March, 1861—and application will be made for the renewal of said Bond.
ap 22—6t*

LOST.—A CERTIFICATE OF REGISTERED STOCK OF THE STATE OF VIRGINIA No. 2,640, for $600, payable to Lewis F. Kidd. Notice is hereby given that application will be made to the Second Auditor of said State for a renewal of the same.
L. T. KIDD.
ap 9—lawim

LOST.—A CERTIFICATE OF STOCK OF THE CITY OF RICHMOND No. 2,, dated February, 1859, for TWO HUNDRED DOLLARS, issued to the undersigned, and application will be made for its renewal.
WM. H. VERNON.
Richmond, Feb. 11, 1861.

LOST.—A NEGOTIABLE NOTE, dated March 4th, 1861, on eight months, amounting to $794, same being payable to the order of ... and ... the payment of the same ...
J. F. HELLER & CO.
ap 15—ts

HORSES, &c., FOR SALE.

FOR SALE.—A HORSE, BRIDLE and SADDLE, (new) Price $150. Apply to J. C. HUDSON, at J. J. Dornin's Tobacco Factory.
ap 25—3t

FOR SALE—A No. 1 MILCH COW, with a very fine Calf, 2 weeks old. Also—One of those fine Durhams, a 3 years old, and very gentle. Just in from the country of Hanover. Inquire of OWENS & MILES.
ap 26—ts

NOTICE.—As I do not know at what moment I may be called off, with the volunteer company of which I am a member, I would offer to the public generally, my whole stock of FURNITURE of any description ... low for cash.
THOS. TAYLOR OWENS, Broad street, between 6th and 7th.

NOTICE.—I will wish to buy a second-hand CARRIAGE or BAROUCHE. Confer with BARKSDALE & BRO., 18th and Cary streets.
JAS. E. GILLESPIE.

DON JUAN.—The proper ... will stand for the ... at the ... stables of his proprietor, near Drake's Branch.
TERMS—$30 the season; $50 insurance. Mares kept on usual terms.
PEDIGREE.—By Imp. Glencoe, dam Darkness by Wagner; 2d, Lady Grey, by Sir Richard; 3d, Ogle's Lady, 4th, Imp. Hurricane, ... &c.
DON JUAN is a rich blood bay, ... 16 hands high, ...
T. W. GAINES, Drake's Branch.
ap 1—1m*

TO ALL SHERIFFS, COMMISSIONERS OF THE REVENUE AND TELEGRAPH OPERATORS IN THE COMMONWEALTH.—Notice is hereby given that all persons ... are ... specially ... in the ... circumstances ... orders ...
By order of the Governor,
GEO. W. MUNFORD, Secretary of the Commonwealth.

KEROSINE OIL LAMPS.—A large assortment of the very best quality, with extra Wicks, Chimneys, &c., for sale low by THOS. A. BRANDER & CO., 127 Main street.
mh 27

COAL OIL.—A supply of the best Coal Oil, for sale by the gallon or quart, by JAS. P. DUVAL, Druggist, Opposite the Post-Office.
mh 26

Richmond Dispatch.

FRIDAY MORNING.......APRIL 26, 1861

TO THE SOUTHERN FLAG!

Lines read at the raising of a Secession Flag at Lanesville, Va., on the 1st of April, 1861.

BY MRS. S. G. NEALE.

Hail! emblem of honor, and freedom; all hail!
Thou beauteous flag of the South:
Though tyrants may hate thee, and Yankeedom rail,
We are proud of thy honor and truth.

The land that conceived thee shall honor thy birth,
Though envy may curse and defame;
The spirit of freedom abroad in the earth
Shall speak of thy honor and fame.

Virginia, the mother of States, shall awake
To the call of freedom and right,
And justice, and honor, and interest shall make
A Union of spirit and might.

Her sons who now sit in a Council of State,
We invoke in honor's fair name,
To gather the jewels and leave to its fate
The casket now severed in twain.

With our sister States of the South we will form
A casket more beauteous and rare,
Where honor, and justice, and freedom shall come,
To lighten the burdens of care.

Virginia's fair daughters shall bless her proud sons,
Who tyrants' devices o'erturn,
And place in its orbit the eighth glorious State
To revolve around freedom's bright sun.

May the God of all wisdom approvingly look
On this contest for justice and right,
And help us to rear in a South sisterhood
A union of spirit and might.

BY THE GOVERNOR OF VIRGINIA.

A PROCLAMATION.

The Convention of the Commonwealth of Virginia having adopted, on the 17th day of April, 1861, an ordinance "to repeal the ratification of the Constitution of the United States of America, by the State of Virginia, and to resume all the rights and powers granted under said Constitution;" and by the schedule thereto annexed, required polls to be opened for the ratification or rejection of the same by the people of this State, on the 4th Thursday in May next: Now, therefore, I, John Letcher, Governor of the Commonwealth of Virginia, do hereby proclaim that the annexed is an authentic copy of said Ordinance and Schedule, and that all officers designated therein are required to conform to its provisions, in every respect.

{ L.S. } Given under my hand, as Governor, and under the seal of the Commonwealth, at Richmond, this 24th day of April, 1861, and in the 85th year of the Commonwealth. JOHN LETCHER.

By the Governor:
George W. Munford,
Secretary of the Commonwealth.

AN ORDINANCE

To repeal the Ratification of the Constitution of the United States of America, by the State of Virginia, and to resume all the rights and powers granted under said Constitution.

The people of Virginia, in their ratification of the Constitution of the United States of America, adopted by them in Convention, on the twenty-fifth day of June, in the year of our Lord one thousand seven hundred and eighty-eight, having declared that the powers granted under the said Constitution were derived from the people of the United States, and might be resumed whensoever the same should be perverted to their injury and oppression, and the Federal Government having perverted said powers, not only to the injury of the people of Virginia, but to the oppression of the Southern slaveholding States:

Now, therefore, we, the people of Virginia, do declare and ordain that the Ordinance adopted by the people of this State, in Convention, on the twenty-fifth day of June, in the year of our Lord one thousand seven hundred and eighty-eight, whereby the Constitution of the United States of America was ratified—and all acts of the General Assembly of this State ratifying or adopting amendments to said Constitution—are hereby repealed and abrogated; that the Union between the State of Virginia and the other States under the Constitution aforesaid is hereby dissolved, and that the State of Virginia is in the full possession and exercise of all the rights of sovereignty which belong and appertain to a free and independent State. And they do further declare that the said Constitution of the United States of America is no longer binding on any of the citizens of this State.

This Ordinance shall take effect and be an act of this day when ratified by a majority of the votes of the people of this State, cast at a poll to be taken thereon on the fourth Thursday in May next, in pursuance of a Schedule hereafter to be enacted.

Done in Convention, in the city of Richmond, on the seventeenth day of April, in the year of our Lord one thousand eight hundred and sixty-one, and in the eighty-fifth year of the Commonwealth of Virginia.

A true Copy. Jno. L. Eubank, Secretary of Convention.

[SCHEDULE.]

It shall be the duty of the officers conducting the elections directed by law to be held on the fourth Thursday in May next, at the places appointed for holding the same, to open a poll to take the sense of the qualified voters of this Commonwealth, upon the ratification or rejection of "An ordinance to repeal the ratification of the Constitution of the United States of America, by the State of Virginia, and to resume all the rights and powers granted under the said Constitution," adopted in Convention, at the city of Richmond, on the seventeenth day of April, one thousand eight hundred and sixty-one.

2. The poll-book shall be headed "The Ordinance of Secession," and shall contain two columns, one headed "For Ratification," and the other "For Rejection," and the names of those who vote for the ratification of the said Ordinance shall be written under the former heading, and the names of those who vote for its rejection shall be written under the latter heading.

3. The said officers shall make return of the number of persons voting for each proposition at the time and in the manner provided by law in the case of other elections, and shall forthwith deliver the returns, together with the poll-books, to the Clerks of their respective counties and corporations; and it shall be the duty of such Clerks respectively to transmit immediately to the Governor of the Commonwealth copies of the said returns so delivered to them.

4. The Governor shall, without delay, make proclamation of the result, stating therein the aggregate vote for and against the ratification, to be published in such newspapers in the State as may be deemed requisite for general information; and if a majority of said votes be cast for the ratification of the said Ordinance, he shall annex to his proclamation a copy thereof, together with this Schedule.

5. The Secretary of the Commonwealth shall cause to be sent to the Clerks of each county and corporation as many copies of this Schedule and Ordinance aforesaid as there are places of voting therein, and three copies to each of the military commanders, hereinafter referred to, using special messengers for that purpose when necessary. And it shall be the duty of said Clerks to deliver the same to the Sheriffs for distribution, whose duty it shall be forthwith to post the said copies at some public place in each election district.

6. The expenses incurred in providing poll-books, and in procuring writers to enter the names of the voters therein, shall be defrayed as in the case of the election of members to the General Assembly.

7. The qualified voters of the Commonwealth, who may be absent from the counties or corporations of their residence, on the day of election, in the military service of the State, may vote for the ratification or rejection of the said Ordinance at such place or places within their encampment, or, as the commander at such encampment shall designate, whether the said encampment shall be within the limits of this State or not. For each place of voting he shall appoint a superintendent, three commissioners, and as many clerks as shall be necessary, who, after having been first duly sworn by him, shall perform the duties required of, and be liable to the penalties imposed upon, such officers under the election laws of this State.

8. The officers conducting the said election shall, on the day after the election, or as soon thereafter as may be, deliver the poll-books to their said commander, who shall forthwith forward the same to the Governor of this Commonwealth, who shall count the said votes in ascertaining the result of the said election in the State.

9. That the election for members of Congress for this State to the House of Representatives of the Congress of the United States, required by law to be held on the 4th Thursday in May next, is hereby suspended and prohibited until otherwise ordained by this Convention.

Done in Convention in the city of Richmond on the 24th day of April, eighteen hundred and sixty one, and in the eighty-sixth year of the Commonwealth of Virginia.

A true Copy, John L. Eubank, Secretary of Convention.

BY THE GOVERNOR OF VIRGINIA.

A PROCLAMATION.

Whereas, in the emergency which was supposed to exist during the past week, arising from information that an invasion of the rivers of the State was about to be made, and the movements of the vessels of the United States with troops into the waters of this Commonwealth, and the unusual destruction of public property by the agents of that Government, both at Harper's Ferry and at the Gosport Navy-Yard, gave ample reason for such belief; and whereas, under such circumstances, sundry vessels in the waters of the James River, the Rappahannock, York, and Potomac Rivers, and their tributaries, have been seized and detained by the authorities of the State, or officers acting under patriotic motives without authority, and it is proper that such vessels and property should be promptly restored to the masters in command, or to the owners thereof: Therefore,

I, John Letcher, Governor of the Commonwealth, do hereby proclaim that all private vessels and property so seized or detained, with the exception of the steamers Jamestown and Yorktown, shall be released and delivered up to the said masters or owners. Proper officers of the State Navy have been assigned to each of the rivers herein mentioned, with orders to release such vessels and property, and give certificates for damages incurred by the seizure and detention.

I felt it my duty, furthermore, to advise the people of the Commonwealth (not in the military service of the State,) to return to their usual avocations, in connection with the trade and commerce of the country, assuring them protection and defence. If war is to be inaugurated by an attempt to invade this Commonwealth, or to use coercion against the Southern Confederated States—a contingency dependent on the action of the Government of the United States—it shall be met and conducted by this Commonwealth upon principles worthy of civilized nations and of this enlightened age. I appeal to all our people not to interfere with peaceable, unoffending citizens of others, who preserve the peace and conform to our laws; and I do hereby especially discountenance all acts of seizure of private property without authority of law, and require that order shall be restored, and that all the laws be administered and executed by the tribunals especially assigned for the purpose.

{ L.S. } Given under my hand, as Governor, and under the seal of the Commonwealth, at Richmond, 24th April, 1861, and in the 85th year of the Commonwealth. JOHN LETCHER.

By the Governor:
George W. Munford,
Sec'y of the Commonwealth.

The following officers of the State Navy are assigned to the duties required by this Proclamation:

For James River—Capt. Cocke and Commander Tucker.
For Potomac River—Capt. Forrest and Lieut. Semmes.
For Rappahannock River—Lieut. Lewis.
For York River—Commander J. L. Henderson and Lieut. J. S. Maury. ap 25—d&c3t

BY THE GOVERNOR OF VIRGINIA.

A PROCLAMATION.

Whereas, Volunteers are simultaneously tendering their services, in person, from all parts of the State, without waiting for orders, as they were required to do by a former proclamation, and are repairing to Richmond, without previous notice, at great expense to the Commonwealth, and before suitable provision has been made for their accommodation, and before their services are required; these are, therefore, to require all companies not now in Richmond and not ordered here or elsewhere, to remain at their homes, holding themselves simply in readiness for service, until ordered by competent authority. All persons engaged in making artillery harness or other equipments, or on any other special duty for the State, are exempted from military service, without express orders to the contrary.—And no company will be mustered into service unless the complement of men prescribed by law shall have been obtained.

Given under my hand, &c.
JOHN LETCHER.

By order of the Governor:
George W. Munford,
ap 25—d&c3t Sec'y of the Commonwealth.

COMMERCIAL.

Richmond Markets, April 25, 1861.

APPLES.—Northern $2.50@3.50, Virginia Pippins $2.50 to $4.

BACON.—Market firm. We quote to-day: Sides 11 cts.; Shoulders 9 cts.; plain Hams 11½@12 cts.; Sugar-cured 13@13½ cents; Todd's Hams 14 cts.

BAGS.—Seamless Bags, 25c.; Manchester do., 19@23c.; Gunny do., 12@14c.

BEANS.—White $1@1.10 ℔ bushel.

BEESWAX.—27 cts.

BROOMS.—$2@3, according to quality.

BUCKETS, &c.—Painted Buckets $1.87½@$2 ℔ dozen; three-hoop Painted Pails $2.25@2.50 ℔ dozen; heavy Cedar Tubs, neat, $3.50@$5 ℔ nest; heavy Cedar Feed Buckets $6.50 ℔ dozen.

BUTTER.—We quote good Butter at 20 to 25c.; inferior 8 to 10c.

CANDLES.—Tallow 13½@14c. ℔ lb.; Jackson's 14c.; Hull's 16c.; Adamantine 18@20c.; Sperm 45c.; Patent Sperm 54@56c.

CEMENT.—James River $1.70@1.80 ℔ bbl.; Northern Rosendale at $1.70@1.80.

COAL.—White and Red Ash Anthracite Coal, for grates, $7.50 ℔ cart load of 25 bushels, ℔ ton of 2,240 lbs. $8; Foundry do. $7 ℔ ton of 2,240 lbs.; Bituminous Lump $5 ℔ load of 25 bushels; Hail $4.50; Smiths' Coal 12@14c. ℔ bushel.

COFFEE.—We quote Rio 14½@15 cts.; Laguayra, 15½@16 cts.; Java 18½@19 cents; Mocha 20 cts.

COKE.—For city consumption $5 ℔ cart load of 25 bushels, for sof [t] lump; soft hail $4.50. Hard lump and hail $4.50.

CORN.—We quote 75@80 cts. per bushel.

CORN MEAL.—City Bolted Meal 90@95 cents; country 70@75 cts.

COTTON.—8½ to 12 cts.

COTTON YARNS, &c. Cotton Yarns 21@22 cts.; Cotton Cordage 24 cts.; Seine Twine 27 cts.; Carpet Warp 22 cts.; Wrapping Twine 22 cts.

DRIED FRUIT.—No arrivals. Dried Apples from 40 to 50c. ℔ bushel.

FEATHERS.—Dull at 44@45 cts

FERTILIZERS.—Demand light. We quote Peruvian Guano $62½ ℔ ton; Ruffin's Tobacco Manure $45 ℔ ton; AA Mexican $25; Elide Island $48; Patagonian $25; Sombrero $30; Nevassa or Brown Columbian $30; Reese's Manipulated Guano $50; Rhodes' Super Phosphate of Lime $43; Robinson's Manipulated Guano $50; Hartman's (Richmond) Amoniated Super Phosphate Lime $40; do. Manipulated Guano $50; do. Bone Dust $38 ℔ ton.

FISH.—New Nova Scotia Herrings, gross, $2.75@$3; a cargo of new No. 1 Halifax Cut Herrings arrived and sold at $4, on 4 mo.'s time. No North Carolina in market. Mackerel, large No. 3, new, $8.50; small do. $5.

FLAXSEED.—$1.20@1.40 ℔ bushel.

FLOUR.—There are no sales for shipment. The stock of country is very limited, and sales confined to home consumption. We quote Superfine at $8; Extra $8.50; Family $9.

FLOUR BARRELS.—45 to 50 cts. for city made; Country have sold recently at from 20 to 30 cts.

FRUIT.—Oranges: Messina $2.50 ℔ box. Lemons: $4 ℔ box. Raisins: Bunch $2.50@$3; layers $3@3.25. Prunes 10 to 40 cents ℔ box, according to quality. Figs 10@20 cents per lb.

GINSENG.—35@40 cents, and in demand.

GRASS SEEDS.—We quote prime Clover Seed $6.50 for new; $6@6.25 for old. Timothy $4@4.25 per bushel. Orchard Grass $2.

GUNPOWDER.—Dupont's and Hazard's Sporting $5.75; Blasting $3.75; Eagle Canister $14.25; FFF Canister $8.25. In quantities of twenty kegs and upwards, 50 cents a keg less.

HAY.—$1.20@1.25 per cwt.

HIDES.—Salted 8½@9 cents; dry 11@13 cts. Calf Skins, green, $1@1.12. South American, none.

HOOP POLES.—Flour bbl. $7.50@9 ℔ 1,000; hhd. poles, $15.

IRON AND NAILS.—Pig Iron $28@34, as in quality and quantity; Swedes $400 per ton; English Refined $70; Tredegar $85; Common English $60; American country $95. Cut Nails 3¼@3½ cts. ℔ lb.

LARD.—Prime Western Leaf, in bbls., 11½@12 cents; kegs 12@12½ cents—all for new.

LEAD.—We quote 6¼@6½ cents ℔ lb. for pig; bar 6½@7 cts.

LEATHER. We quote good stamp, middle weights, 23@24 cts. ℔ lb.; over weights 22@23 cts.; light 23@23½c.; good damaged 21c.; poor 16@18c; upper leather $2.00@3.50, as to size, weight and quality; Harness 35@36c.; Skirting, in the rough, 25@28c.; finished 31@35c.

LIME.—85c. to $1 from wharf. From store, we quote Northern $1.12½; Virginia 90c.@$1.

LIQUORS.—Brandy: Otard, Dupuy & Co., $3.25@7 ℔ gallon; A. Seignette, $2½@4½; Sazerac $3½@7; Hennessey $3½@7½; Peach scarce at $1½@2½; Virginia Apple 60@85 cts.; do., old, 75c.@$1.50; Northern do. 55@85 cts.; Imitation 45@47½ cts. Rum: New England 40@45c. for mixed; 50@55c. for pure. Gin: Holland $1.20@1.75.

LUMBER.—Clear White Pine $45; refused do. $29; merchantable $20@25 ℔ M. One inch Yellow Pine Plank $10@12; three-quarter do. $9@11; 1½ do. $14@16; 1¾ do. $13@14; 2 do. $12.50@15. Flooring $18@20, face measure; Scantling $11@13 for heart and sap; all heart $18@20, according to size. Garden Rails, heart and sap, 12½@13 cts. each; all heart 18@25 cts. Shingles $5@6 ℔ M. Weather Boarding $13@16. Inch Oak Plank $30@35. Buttonwood ⅞ inch $25@30. Inch Cherry $35; ⅞ Poplar $20@25 ℔ M. Dressed Flooring, Virginia, $25@28. Dressed Flooring, Southern, $28@30. Laths $2.25 to $2.37 ℔ M for sawed, on the wharf

MOLASSES.—New Orleans 40 cts.; Cuba Muscovado, in bbls., 30@33 cts.; in hhds., 25@30 cts.; English Island 30@33 cts.; Ochenhousen's 28 cts.

OATS.—40 to 45 cts. per bushel.

OFFAL.—Bran 20 cts.; Shorts 25 cts.; Brown Stuff 35 cts.; and Ship Stuff 65 cts. ℔ bus.

ONIONS.—Red $2 ℔ bbl. of near three bushels; Silver-skin $2½.

PEAS.—None in market.

PLASTER.—Lump—We quote sales at $4 ℔ ton. Claiborne's Richmond Ground $8.50 ℔ ton packed; Sharpe's do. packed $8.50; loose $7.50.

POTATOES.—We quote Northern 60@65 cts. ℔ bushel.

RICE.—5@5½ cts.

ROSIN.—$1.70@1.75 ℔ bbl.

RYE.—We quote 60@65 cts. ℔ bus.

SALT.—Last sales from wharf $1.40; from store $1.60 ℔ sack.

SALTPETRE.—9@10 cts. ℔ lb.

SENECA ROOT.—35@37½ cts.

SHOT.—7@7½ cts. cash, and time as to quantity, for drop and buck.

STARCH.—Corn 6@6½ cts.; Pearl 7@8½ cts.

STAVES.—Good oak, for flour barrels, we quote at $5 ℔ thousand; Machine cut $7@8.

SUGARS.—New Orleans Sugar we quote 7@8 cents; Cuba 7@8 cents; Porto Rico 7@8 cents; Loaf 10½@11 cents; Crushed and Powdered 10 cents; Coffee Sugar: A 9 cents; B and Extra C 9c.

TOBACCO.—Sales still limited, at former quotations. *Lugs* $1.50 to $3; *Leaf* $4 to $10. No fine manufacturing in market. Stock on hand of the old crop very light, and mostly of inferior quality.

WHEAT.—Receipts light and market firm at $1.50@$1.60 for White; $1.30@$1.37½ for Red.

WHISKEY.—Richmond Rectified 29@30 cents; Stearns' Old Malted Rye $1.50; other qualities 75 cts.@$1.50 ℔ gallon.

WINES.—Port, Burgundy $1@$2.50 ℔ gallon; Port Juice $2 50@$4. Madeira, Sicily 45c.@$1.75; Old Madeira $2.50@$4. Sherry, Permartin, Duff and Gordon, Amontilado, $2@$6.

WOOD.—Wholesale: Oak $3.50@$3.75 ℔ cord; Pine $2.75@$3. Retail Oak $5; Pine $4.50.

WOOL.—Tub Washed sold at 35@37c.; unwashed third less. Fleece as in quality.

FREIGHTS.

FOREIGN.—Nothing to add relative to foreign freights.

DOMESTIC.—All shipping stopped coastwise.

CATTLE, HOGS, SHEEP, &c.

BEEF.—Sales this week at $3@4.25 for good to prime cattle. A very few bought at the latter price. Market well supplied.

SHEEP.—We quote sales at $2.50 to $3 per head for ordinary sheep, and $4.50 to $5 per cwt. gross for the best quality.

HOGS.—Sales of corn-fed at $8@8.50 per cwt.; distillery-fed $7.50@8.

MONEY MATTERS.

We give below the best quotations we can obtain:

Nothing whatever doing in Exchange North.

South Carolina and North Carolina Bank notes, Planters' and Miners' Bank of Murphy (N. C.) 20 per cent. discount.

Specie—Quotations nominal.

LIST OF VIRGINIA BANK NOTES BANKABLE IN RICHMOND.

All the Banks located in Richmond, and the branches of such as have branches.
Bank of Commerce, Fredericksburg.
Bank of Howardsville, Howardsville, Albemarle.
Bank of the Old Dominion, Alexandria.
Bank of Rockbridge, Lexington.
Bank of Rockingham, Harrisonburg.
Bank of Scottsville, Scottsville.
Central Bank of Virginia, Staunton.
Danville Bank, Danville, Va.
Farmers' Bank of Fincastle, Fincastle.
Merchants' Bank, Lynchburg.
Monticello Bank, Charlottesville.
Southwestern Bank, Wytheville.
Branch of the Bank of the Valley, Staunton.
Do. do. do., Christiansburg

LIST OF VIRGINIA BANK NOTES UNBANKABLE IN RICHMOND.

Bank of the Valley and branches, save at Staunton and Christiansburg.
Bank of Wheeling, Wheeling.
Manufacturers' and Farmers' Bank of Wheeling and branches.
Northwestern Bank of Virginia, Wheeling, and branches.
Merchants' and Mechanics' Bank of Wheeling and branches.
Bank of Charleston, Malden, Kanawha.
Bank of Berkeley, Martinsburg.
Branch Bank of the Old Dominion, at Pearisburg.
Bank of Phillippi, Phillippi, Barbour county.
Bank of Winchester, Winchester.
Fairmont Bank, Fairmont.

The notes of the foregoing Banks are bought by the brokers of this city at 1 per cent. discount.

VIRGINIA BANK NOTES THAT ARE AT TWENTY-FIVE PER CENT. DISCOUNT.

The notes of the following Banks are at 25 per cent. discount:
Bank of Manassas, Front Royal.
Bank of Weston, Lewis county.
Trans-Alleghany Bank of Jeffersonville, Tazewell.

There are probably few, if any, of the notes of the last named Bank afloat, as it has been discredited for some years.

SALES OF STOCKS IN RICHMOND,

Reported by John A. Lancaster & Son, *for the week ending April 25th,* 1861.

Virginia 6 per cents., sales [illegible]$60.
Richmond City Bonds, last s[ales] $94.
Bank of Virginia Stock, sales $70.
Farmers' Bank Stock, sales $100.
Exchange Bank Stock, $102 offered.
Virginia Fire and Marine Insurance Stock, last sales $38.
Merchants' Insurance Stock, last sales $72½.
Richmond Fire Association Stock, sales $58.
Richmond, Fredericksburg & Potomac Railroad Stock, $80 offered.
Virginia Central Railroad Stock, last sales $45.
Richmond & Petersburg Railroad Stock, last sales $57½
Richmond & Danville Railroad Stock, last sales $55.
James River & Kanawha Stock, last sales $17½.

PROFESSIONAL CARDS.

GEORGE C. EGGLESTON, ATTORNEY AT LAW, Will practice regularly in all the COURTS of AMELIA and the adjoining counties. N. B.—COLLECTIONS promptly made. Address, Amelia Court-house. fe 21—law3m*

DR. PICOT has removed his office to No. 8 Wall street. ap 20—1m

LAWRENCE S. MARYE, ATTORNEY AT LAW, Practices in the Courts of the city of Richmond and the counties of Henrico, Hanover and Caroline. He is also Notary Public and Commissioner of the United States Court of Claims. The partnership between Mr. Chastain White and himself being dissolved, his office is now on 11th st., just below Goddin's Hall. fe 13—1y

DR. GEO. W. BRIGGS offers his professional services to the citizens of Richmond and vicinity. Office next door to Ed. Eacho's, on 14th street, between Main and Franklin. Residence—27th and Broad sts., Church Hill. ja 29—3m

A CARD. WM. F. WATSON, ATTORNEY AT LAW UNITED STATES COMMISSIONER. AND COMMISSIONER IN CHANCERY. Note.—In the latter capacity, will attend to the making up and reporting the accounts of Executors, Administrators, Curators and Trustees. Office, Custom-House, Bank st. no 12—1y

CHAS. H. DIMMOCK, ATTORNEY AT LAW. Office, No. 3 Law Building, Franklin street, Richmond, Va. mh 30—3m*

J. WELCH, DESIGNER AND ENGRAVER ON WOOD, At Pelouze's Type Foundry, Law Building, Franklin street, Richmond, Va. mh 29—1m

DRY GOODS, &c.

WET GOODS! WET GOODS!!—DAMAGED BY FRESH WATER AT THE WHARF AT ROCKETTS.—Receiving this day:—1 case Bleach Cottons, at 12½c, worth 20c; 10,000 yards of Spring Prints, at 6d a yard, fast colors, worth 12½c; 50 pieces blue Denins, at 10½c; 50 pieces Cotton Pants stuff, at 15c; 50 pieces Tuckapaws stuff, at 20c; French Jaconets and Organdies, worth 75c, at only 25c; Huckaback Towels at $2 a dozen; Silk Veils at 62½c, worth $1; 5 pieces Black Silk, great bargain; Berages, &c., &c. The above Goods are desirable, and worthy the attention of all who want cheap goods. They will be sold exclusively for cash, being bought on those terms, and offered at profits so small I cannot afford to charge to any party. ALFRED MOSES, ap 23 63 Main st.

GOLDEN'S WINDOW SHADE DEPOT, 230 BROAD STREET. Having disposed of my old stock of Shades at auction, I have just opened a large and beautiful assortment, all new styles: 900 Gold Border SHADES, only 75 cents, with fixtures; 600 Gold and Velvet, $1.00, worth $2.00; 400 Gold and Velvet Centre, $1.25, very rich; 800 Light and Dark Landscapes, 37½ cents only; 450 large Gilt-Framed PARLOR PICTURES, different scenery, at the low price of $2.00, worth $6.00; 1,000 FIRE SCREENS, at 25 cents each; 800 WINDOW CORNICES, from 75 cents to $5.00; English, German and American OIL CLOTHS, all widths, and very cheap. Call at the Dry Goods and Window Shade Depot of [ap 5—3m] M. GOLDEN, 230 Broad st.

GREAT BARGAINS FOR CASH.—I am still closing out my present stock of DRY GOODS at a great sacrifice for cash. Those having the ready cash will find it greatly to their interest to call and examine my stock before purchasing elsewhere, as I am determined to sell every article without regard to cost. ap 1—1m JNO. L. SMITHER, No. 29 Main st.

GREAT BARGAINS IN SILKS.—500 yards Checked Silks at 50 and 75 cts.; 500 dress patterns Red Silk at $12, $15 and $20; 100 rich Silk Robes at $20 and $25, worth double the money; 100 Berege and Organdie Robes at half price; 1000 yards Berege Anglais at 12½c. per yard; rich Embroidered and Printed Berege Anglais; Broche Challies and Mozambiques; plain Crape Berege and Berege at 25c., worth 37½ and 50c. For bargains in all styles of Dress Goods, call at 99 Main street. [ap 9] CHRISTIAN & LATHROP.

SPRING DRY GOODS.—We have received our Spring stock of Fancy and Staple Dry Goods, and invite the public to examine our stock and prices before purchasing, as we are offering great inducements for cash. JOHNSON & HARWOOD, ap 12 No. 77 Main street.

A PROCLAMATION OF THE GOVERNOR, issued on the 17th inst., calls for all the volunteers to hold themselves in readiness. 'Tis therefore necessary that they should supply themselves with Blankets—a large assortment of which can now be found at the lowest prices at LEVY'S.

MANTILLAS, MANTILLAS.—We are now in receipt of new styles of Black Silk, Barage, Anglais, and black Lace MANTILLAS, which we are selling at prices to suit the times. ap 12 JOHNSON & HARWOOD, 77 Main st.

200 MORE HANDSOME SPRING MOUSLINS, opening this morning, at only a ninepence the yard, at EZEKIEL'S, mh 29 41 Main st., Mallert's old stand.

BLACK SKIRT BRAID.— RUBBER COAT and VEST BUTTONS; GOLD BRAID; COMBINATION CORSETS, all sizes; SEWING SILKS; COATS' SPOOL COTTON; LINEN CAMBRIC HANDKERCHIEFS; WOVEN SKIRTS, 25 to 50 hoops. Full lines of the above Goods just received and for sale to the trade by fe 27 GINTER, ALVEY & ARENTS.

PANIC PRICES, IN EARNEST, At WHOLESALE and RETAIL, By JOSEPH STRAUSE, No 27 Main street. Just bought at less than 40 cents on the dollar, a large stock of rich Lawns at 6¼, 8, 10 and 12 cts.; Fine Jaconets and Organdies, 12½c, 1s. &c.; Debages, 8 cts., 10 cts., and higher; Bereges, all colors, at 1s., 25cts., &c.; 500 handsome Berege Stella Shawls, with Chenille Embroidery, at $1.50, worth $5.00; Black and Colored Silk Parasols, from 75 cents and upwards; fast-colored Calico, at 6¼ and 8 cents, cheap at 10; Ladies' Silk Thread Gloves and Gauntlets, at 12½ and 25 cents; short and long Silk Mits, at 37½ and 50 cents, worth double the money; Hoseries, Linen Handkerchiefs, Irish Linen, and Bosoms; Brown and Black Shirting and Sheeting; Pillow Case Muslin and Toweling; French Needle-Worked Collars from 12½ to 25 cts.; Cambric and Swiss Bands, the finest work in the city; Cassimeres and Linen Goods for Men and Boys' wear; Black and Colored Silks, and great many more Goods, too numerous to mention, will be found at prices that astonish every body that calls at No. 27 Main street. Look out for the right place. [ap 1] JOSEPH STRAUSE.

SPRING GOODS—MARCH, 1861.— KENT, PAINE & CO., Importers and wholesale dealers in FOREIGN and DOMESTIC DRY GOODS, No. 163 and 165 Main street, Richmond. We are receiving, and have now in store, a large and desirable stock of fresh Spring Goods, consisting of the usual variety, and embracing every desirable style of Foreign and Domestic Goods, which we are prepared to offer to our customers upon the most favorable terms. We shall, in consequence of the disturbed condition of commercial matters, confine our sales to cash and prompt six months' buyers, for negotiable paper; and to such, great inducements will be offered. Our stock will be kept up during the season, and not be surpassed, in variety and extent, by any house in the Southern States. In our CLOTHING DEPARTMENT we are prepared to exhibit a large, fashionable and fresh stock, of our own manufacture, and gotten up expressly for our own trade. BROWN SHEETINGS and SHIRTINGS will be sold at nett prices, for cash, in bankable funds. Orders are solicited, and will receive our prompt and personal attention. [mh 8] KENT, PAINE & CO.

BARGAINS, BARGAINS, BARGAINS.—Just received, a large lot of English Berege, at very low prices for the times. I shall offer them at the low figure of 10 cents per yard. Also, a lot of those Embroidered ditto, at one shilling. All ladies in want of cheap Dress Goods, will do well to give me a call before purchasing, as I am confident that I can offer great inducements. I have a great many Goods in store that I can offer bargains in, such as Handkerchiefs, Collars, Irish Linen Shirt Fronts, and various other goods. Call and look for yourselves at my stock. ap 2 ALFRED MOSES, 63 Main st.

SPRING GOODS AT A GREAT SACRIFICE, TO CLOSE BUSINESS.—CHARLES A. GWATKIN, 8th and Main streets, north side, will sell the whole of his spring stock at a great sacrifice—a large assortment Lawns, Cambrics, Collars, Poplinetts, &c. Families may rely upon getting bargains. Also, a large lot French Bereges and English Bereges, at a great loss. House for rent. CHAS. A. GWATKIN, ja 21 8th and Main streets.

CHEAP SILKS—FOULARDS.—Just received a lot of low-priced Silks; Foulard Silks, and other Dress Goods. Our Goods have been bought at a great reduction from usual prices, and to cash and prompt-paying customers we are willing to sell at very small profits. ap 11 CHILES & CHENERY.

MILITARY FATIGUE SHIRTS.—Military Fatigue Shirts of blue, grey and red Flannel, manufactured at short notice. ap 16 KENT, PAINE & CO.

STUART'S WHISKEY.—This celebrated brand of Whiskey is distilled in the county of Augusta, Va., and stands unrivalled as the purest Whiskey in Virginia. We invite the especial attention of the trade, with the perfect assurance that it is second to no Whiskey in this or any other market. For sale by BRIDGFORD & CO., ap 8 Commission Merchants, on the Dock.

STORAGE.—We can store the bulk of 10,000 barrels, on accommodating terms. [illegible] BRIDGFORD & CO.

MEDICAL HOSPITALS.

HOSPITAL OF THE MEDICAL COLLEGE OF VIRGINIA.—This Hospital erected by the liberality of the State, at a cost of more than $20,000, is now completed, and open for the reception of patients. It is admirably adapted by its plan for the accommodation of the sick, and is furnished with every convenience requisite for their comfort and successful treatment. Its situation, on Marshall street, east of 12th, immediately adjacent to the Medical College, while retired and airy, is at the same time central, and convenient of access from all parts of the city.

The patients are under the immediate charge of the Professors of the College, (who make daily visits,) assisted by a competent Resident Physician.

All persons requiring Medical or Surgical treatment are admitted, except the Insane, and those laboring under Small-Pox and other infectious disorders.

Lying-in Women, both white and colored, receive special care and attention.

CHARGES,
Including Board, Medical Attendance, &c.:
White patients.........$6 per week,
Slaves.................. 5 " "

And at the same rate for fractions of a week. For less than one week, $1 per day, up to the charge for a full week.

Several neatly furnished Private Rooms have been provided for those desiring separate accommodations. The charge for these will vary from $7 to $15 per week.

For Surgical operations, a fee ranging from $2 to $30 will be required, in addition to the above weekly rates.

All charges payable on the removal of the patient.

A limited number of beds placed at the disposal of Charitable Associations, at $150 per annum, payable semi-annually, or at a corresponding rate for six months.

Patients conveyed to or from the Hospital in a suitable vehicle, provided expressly for the purpose.

Citizens and strangers are invited to visit the Hospital, and inspect its arrangements.

President—Dr. L. S. JOYNES.
Attending Physicians—Drs. TUCKER, CONWAY, and McCAW.
Attending Surgeons—Drs. GIBSON, PETICODAS, and WELLFORD.
Resident Physician—Dr. ISAIAH H. WHITE.
Steward—F. M. PARISH. ap 22—1y

BELLEVUE HOSPITAL, CHURCH HILL, RICHMOND, VA. White Patients—In wards, $6 per week; in private rooms, $7 to $15 per week. Slaves—$5 per week. Less than a week, $1 per day; but not to exceed $5 per week. Fractions over the first week 71 cents per day. *No extra charges* except for surgical operations, and then an additional fee ranging from $2 to $30 will be charged. *Bills payable on the removal of the patient.* No small-pox admitted.

A covered spring wagon will convey patients to and from the Hospital when desired. Orders may be left at the Hospital, or at the office of A. L. Holladay, 12th street, between Main and Cary.

The subscriber, who has been connected with the institution since its foundation, having taken it under his exclusive charge, aided by competent assistants, solicits a continuance of the liberal patronage of his friends and of the public generally.

Attending Physician and Surgeon, JAMES BOLTON, M. D., Grace street, between 4th and 5th.
ASSISTANTS: C. W. P. BROCK, M. D., Church Hill, cor. 25th and Marshall sts
C. M. HUNTER, ja 18—1y Resident Physician.

MAIN ST. HOSPITAL FOR SLAVES.—This Hospital is situated near the corner of Main and 26th streets, and is admirably adapted in airiness, privacy and healthfulness of position, to the purposes for which it has been instituted, namely: For MEDICAL, SURGICAL and OBSTETRICAL treatment of SLAVES. The rules and regulations governing this institution have already been published. A circular containing full particulars will be furnished those who may desire further information.

Terms.—Patients per week, $5; less than a week, $1 per diem; *but the aggregate shall not exceed the charge for a full week.* Patients attending the daily examinations (not fit subjects for HOSPITAL CONFINEMENT,) charged the regular fee adopted by the profession at large. The above charges include board, medicine, medical attendance and nursing. Surgical operations charged according to rules of other Hospitals of the city. For further information, apply to the Physician resident at the Hospital, or to either of the undersigned Physicians and Proprietors.

FRS. W. HANCOCK, M. D., Main st., bet. 3d and 4th, or No. 130 Main st.
ST. GEO. PEACHY, M. D., Exchange Hotel, or Grace st., bet. 5th and 6th.
R. S. VEST, M. D., Franklin st., Near Ballard House, or cor. Main and 7th sts.
PHILIP S. HANCOCK, M. D., Resident Physician.
J. G. TREVILIAN, M. D., ap 19—1y Resident Assistant.

HOTELS.

EXCHANGE HOTEL, HARRISONBURG, VA. Dr. WILLIAM WILLIAMS, Proprietor. P. H. WOODWARD, Superintendent. This House, pleasantly situated, is in every respect a FIRST-CLASS HOTEL, and is now ready for the reception of all who may visit the Valley. It is especially a desirable stopping place for those who pass to and from the Watering Places in this vicinity. The House and Furniture are both entirely new, and the Rooms large and comfortable and handsomely furnished.

TERMS:
Board, (including room, &c.,) per day.......$1 75
" " " per week...... 7 00
" " " per month..... 25 00
mh 1—1awtMay15&t3tawtJuly15

VIRGINIA HOTEL, STAUNTON, VIRGINIA. The VIRGINIA HOTEL, so extensively known to the traveling public as one of the very best Hotels in the State, is now owned solely by Messrs. WM. H. & THOS. P. PEYTON, who will devote their whole attention to the purpose of increasing, if possible, the high reputation which it at present sustains, and will leave no exertion unemployed to render their guests satisfied and comfortable. The recent additions put to this establishment enable the proprietors to accommodate a much larger number of guests than formerly.—The whole building, in the interior and exterior, has been recently REFITTED and PAINTED, and looks now GOOD AS NEW.

The proprietors have secured the services of Mr. WM. D. GILKESON, Sr., an experienced landlord, and formerly of the Taylor Hotel, Winchester, as SUPERINTENDENT, who will pay every attention to those stopping at the Hotel.—Capable and faithful servants are also provided, to ensure the comfort of guests. The table will continue, as heretofore, to equal that of any hotel in the State.

Connected with the Hotel are extensive STABLES, under the management of BYERS & CO., well known for their experience and efficiency in this department. Horses will be taken on livery, and Horses, Buggies, and Hacks will be afforded to guests on reasonable terms.

The Proprietors are well prepared to accommodate families who wish to spend the Summer months in this healthy portion of the State.

This Hotel is well furnished, and contains as good and comfortable bedding as any house in the State.

In this Hotel there are two of Fielding's new and excellent marble-bedded, and patent-cushioned BILLIARD TABLES. New and comfortable BATHING ROOMS have just been neatly fitted up.

Wm. H. Peyton, who has been so long connected with this Hotel, will devote his whole attention to the accommodation of the guests. He is thankful for the liberal patronage heretofore bestowed, and would respectfully ask a continuance of the same.

WM. H. PEYTON, THOS. P. PEYTON, } Proprietors.

N. B.—The office of all the STAGE LINES is at this House; also, the office of ADAMS & CO'S EXPRESS. WM. H. PEYTON & BRO. Staunton, March 15, 1861. ap 17—tf

EXCHANGE HOTEL AND BALLARD HOUSE. RICHMOND, January 14th, 1861. The proprietors of this well-known and popular establishment beg leave to return their heartfelt thanks to their friends and the public generally, for the liberal patronage they have at all times been favored with; and it affords them pleasure to announce that the recent changes, removals, and a thorough renovating of the entire establishment, makes it one of the most pleasant and comfortable Hotels (for permanent boarders, as well as transient company,) that can be enjoyed anywhere in the country. It is due to the liberality of the Stockholders of the EXCHANGE to say that everything has been done which could add to its value and increase the comfort and convenience of its guests.

Among the important changes and improvements in the BALLARD HOUSE, they have added a well-arranged and convenient RESTAURANT, which is now open for the patronage of the public. In arranging this part of their business, a handsome room has been provided for the ladies of the Hotel, with a private entrance from the parlor floor of the Ballard House.

In view of the large expenditures, and renewed energy, and strict attention on their part, they hope to merit a continuance of that patronage so long enjoyed by them. ja 15—ts JOHN P. & THOS. E. BALLARD.

SPOTSWOOD HOTEL, RICHMOND, VA. This new HOTEL, at the corner of Main and 8th streets, just finished and elegantly furnished, is now open for the accommodation of guests. The location is the best in the city and every effort will be made to please the patrons of the House. I have secured the services of Mr. T. W. Hoeniger, late of the Everett House, New York. no 5—1y JOSEPH H. CRENSHAW

VIRGINIA SAVINGS BANK. *Chartered by the Legislature of Va.* CAPITAL...............................$100,000. MONEY received on deposit in sums of FIVE DOLLARS and upwards, on which interest at the rate of six per centum per annum is paid for sums remaining six months or longer; for shorter periods, interest at the rate of 5 per centum. The whole joint stock bound for the deposits. Deposits received and certificates issued by the Cashier, T. B. STARKE, at the store of Spence & Garey, corner of Main and Governor streets, Richmond, Va. SAM'L S. COTTRELL, Pres't T. B. STARKE, Cashier, oc 24—12m DAVID BAKER, Jr., Secretary.

FINE ARTS, FINE ARTS, FINE ARTS.—WM. SATTLER & CO., 142 Main street, beg leave to inform their patrons, Artists, Teachers, and the public generally, that they have received an extensive and entirely new collection of fine Oil Prints, Line and Mezzotint Engravings and Lithographs, both plain and colored, amongst them a great variety of studies for the various branches of Ornamental Drawing and Painting. They will be pleased to show their Goods, and respectfully solicit a visit to their establishment, a few doors below the Exchange Bank. N. B.—Having a Frame Factory connected with their business, orders for the same will receive immediate attention. ap 11

THORLEY'S FOOD FOR CATTLE AND HORSES increases the milk of each cow from two to six quarts daily, and improves the quality; restores worn-out and broken-down horses in a short time, and may be used with great benefit for saddle, carriage and dray horses. It has given general satisfaction. For sale by BLAIR & HARVIE, mh 5 Cary and 11th streets.

200 BBLS. CINCINNATI COMMON WHISKEY, for sale by WM. WALLACE SONS.

STEAMBOATS, SHIPPING, &c.

STEAM WEEKLY BETWEEN NEW YORK AND LIVERPOOL, landing and embarking passengers at QUEENSTOWN, (Ireland.) The Liverpool, New York and Philadelphia Steamship Company intend dispatching their full-powered Clyde-built Iron Steamships as follows: GLASGOW, SATURDAY, April 27. CITY OF WASHINGTON, SATURDAY, May 4. VIGO, SATURDAY, May 11. And every Saturday, at noon, from Pier 44, North River.

RATES OF PASSAGE:

First Cabin	$75	Steerage	$30
Do. to London	80	Do. to London	33

Steerage Return Tickets, good for six months, $60. Passengers forwarded to Paris, Havre, Hamburg, Bremen, Rotterdam, Antwerp, &c., at reduced through fares.

Persons wishing to bring out their friends can buy tickets here at the following rates, to New York: From Liverpool to Queenstown, First Cabin, $75, $85 and $105. Steerage from Liverpool $40. From Queenstown $30.

These steamers have superior accommodations for passengers, and carry experienced Surgeons. They are built in water-tight iron sections, and have Patent Fire Annihilators on board.

For further information, apply at the Company's offices. JOHN G. DALE, Agent, 15 Broadway, New York; or, ap 19—ts W. BELL, Agent, Richmond.

SUMMER ARRANGEMENT—TO PORTSMOUTH AND NORFOLK.—The Steamer CURTIS PECK, Capt. Jno. H. Freeman, will, on and after MONDAY next, April 1st, leave the Wharf at Rocketts regularly every MONDAY, WEDNESDAY and FRIDAY MORNINGS, for the above places, at 6 o'clock precisely, leaving NORFOLK each alternate morning (except Sunday) at the same hour, 6 o'clock, and touch at all the regular Landings on the River, going and returning. Passage to Portsmouth or Norfolk, $2.00; Meals extra, 50 cts. each. Freight taken as usual; but all goods sent to be landed on the River must be paid for when sent down to the Boat, and will not be responsible for any damage or loss after delivering it on the wharf to which it is directed. mh 29—ts R. O. HASKINS.

STEAMSHIPS JAMESTOWN AND YORKTOWN.—The ROANOKE has been withdrawn from the line again, between RICHMOND and NEW YORK. The JAMESTOWN, Captain Skinner, and the YORKTOWN, Capt. Parrish, will continue their regular trips between the two places, stopping at Norfolk each way. They will leave New York for Richmond every TUESDAY and SATURDAY AFTERNOON, at 3 o'clock. Returning, they will leave Richmond for New York every TUESDAY and FRIDAY, at 4 P. M. Passage to New York, including meals and state-room accommodations, only $10. Steerage passage only $5. For further information apply to the undersigned. LUDLAM & WATSON, ap 9 Opposite Steamers' Wharves.

COX'S LINE.—FREIGHT BOATS TO LYNCHBURG THREE TIMES A WEEK—TUESDAYS, THURSDAYS AND SATURDAYS.
Boat MERCHANT, Capt Thos. T. Emett.
Boat JAS. J. IRBY, Capt. L. Mayo.
Boat OLIVIA, Capt. H. W. Guy.
Boat ELLA SCOTT, Capt. J. W. Stratton.
Boat FAME, Capt. W. H. Parsons.
Boat ——, Capt. ——.
These Boats are all of the first class, commanded by careful Captains and hands, and leave promptly as advertised. For freight, apply to GUY & COX, Agents, fe 7—ts At Cox's Shed, Dock street.

HATS, CAPS, &c.

SPRING TRADE. 1861. ELLETT & WEISIGER, MANUFACTURERS AND WHOLESALE DEALERS IN HATS, CAPS AND STRAW GOODS, *No. 167 Main st., opposite Exchange Bank, Rich'd,* Have ready, and are now offering to the merchants of Virginia, North Carolina, and Tennessee, at prices to suit the times, a complete stock of SPRING and SUMMER GOODS, which for variety and style cannot be excelled. Buyers will do well to give us a call before purchasing elsewhere. mh 23 ELLETT & WEISIGER.

SPRING TRADE. 1861. HATS, CAPS, AND STRAW GOODS. ROBERT L. DICKINSON, (Successor to Binford, Dickinson & Weisiger,) No. 78 Main Street, Richmond, Va., Has open and in store a full and complete stock of HATS, CAPS, and STRAW GOODS, of the latest and most fashionable styles, which will be sold at Wholesale and Retail, on the most favorable terms. The attention of merchants is most respectfully solicited to call and examine for themselves. MILITARY HATS and CAPS made to order at the shortest notice. Cash purchasers will find it to their interest to call and examine my stock before purchasing.

LIFE AND FIRE INSURANCE.

LIFE, FIRE AND MARINE INSURANCE. *RICHMOND FIRE ASSOCIATION.* Office, No. 158 Main (N. E. Corner of 11th) St., RICHMOND, Va. *Chartered 29th March,* 1837. This old and reliable Institution, with ample capital, and contingent fund carefully invested, continues to insure SLAVES, BUILDINGS, MERCHANDIZE, of every description; HOUSEHOLD FURNITURE and Family WEARING APPAREL, VESSELS, CARGOES and FREIGHT, at the lowest current rates. Losses adjusted and paid with all possible dispatch.

DIRECTORS:
David Currie, Robert M. Burton,
C. T. Wortham, Francis J. Barnes,
John H. Claiborne, John T. Sublett,
John J. Wilson, Thos. A. Rust,
Alex. Garrett. Geo. N. Gwathmey.
Peter C. Warrick.
DAVID CURRIE, President.
John J. Wilson, Treasurer.
R. T. Brooke, Secretary. de 27—1y

JAS. B. MACMURDO, Agent MANHATTAN LIFE INSURANCE COMPANY, of New York. Office at the Insurance Agency of Thomas M. Alfriend, on 11th street, nearly opposite Goddin's Hall, where applications will be received. au 13—1y

FIRE INSURANCE. MARINE INSURANCE. (Incorporated 1832.) THE VIRGINIA FIRE AND MARINE INSURANCE COMPANY. Office No. 131 Main Street, Richmond. CAPITAL and SURPLUS, $230,000. This Company has the advantage of *twenty-seven years'* experience in the Insurance business, and having enjoyed the favor of the public during all of that period, needs no special recommendation to the citizens of Virginia. It effects Fire Insurance in city and country, and Marine Insurance to all parts of the world. Its cash capital and surplus are as above, and its affairs are managed prudently, but liberally, and its rates are as low as those of any other good institution.

DIRECTORS:
W. L. Cowardin, J. E. Wadsworth, Patrick Cullen,
Joseph Allen, Wm. Beers, Geo. W. Smith,
Horace L. Kent, Thos. Samson, B. L. Winston,
Wm. Palmer, Chas. W. Purcell, Jno. N. Gordon,
Alex. R. Parker, Jos. P. Winston, Arch. Thomas,
Jas. A. Inloes, H. A. Claiborne.

Apply to the President or Secretary, in person or by letter. W. L. COWARDIN, President. Wm. Willis, Jr., Secretary. je 9—ts

AS AGENT of several first class FIRE INSURANCE COMPANIES, the undersigned is prepared to issue SHORT-TERM POLICIES. to protect increased stocks of goods during the coming season. MERCHANTS desiring additional insurance are solicited to call on J. H. MONTAGUE, sa 1—3tawts Merchants' Insurance Co.

RICHMOND CLOTHING MANUFACTORY.—The subscribers have on hand a large and complete assortment of SOUTHERN MANUFACTURED GOODS—Cloths, Cassimers and Vestings, of all grades, from the following noted mills: Crenshaw Mills, Richmond, Va.; Miller & Co.'s Mills, Culpeper county, Va.; Kelley, Ford & Co.'s Mills, Fredericksburg, Va.; Thomas & Aimes' Mills, Marion, Smith county, Va.; Rock Island Mills, Charlotte, N. C.; which we are prepared to make to measure at the shortest notice, and in the latest and most approved styles—goods that will compare in every respect with the best Northern manufactured goods, and many of the Crenshaw goods equal in quality to French. There can be no longer an excuse for buying goods manufactured out of the State. In addition, we keep always on hand a stock of FRENCH AND ENGLISH CLOTHS AND CASSIMERES, not to be surpassed by any house in the city. We have the best of Cutters, and a corps of workmen not to be surpassed by any house in the Union, with a determination to furnish our patrons with Southern Clothing—material raised South, goods wove South, cut and made South, and we trust to be sold and worn South, as we are determined to do all in our power to push forward Southern institutions. SPENCE & GAREY, Clothiers and Merchant Tailors, fe 25 Corner of Main and 13th streets.

ELIXIR PROPYLAMINE.—A NEW REMEDY FOR RHEUMATISM. We invite the attention of the Medical Profession, and persons suffering with Rheumatism, to the "ELIXIR PROPYLAMINE," as a most valuable and eligible preparation of the Chloride of Propylamine, which has been successfully and extensively used in Europe and America, in the treatment of this disease. It is *not a quack nostrum,* and full directions as to dose, &c., accompany each bottle. MEADE & BAKER, Pharmaceutists, 186 Main street, mh 26 Corner above the Post-Office.

ELIXIR PROPYLAMINE, FOR RHEUMATISM.—This valuable agent is now presented in a form ready for immediate use, which will commend itself to the suffering patient, and to the medical practitioner who may feel disposed to test its valuable remedial powers. It will be seen by the circular that accompanies it, that it has stood the most rigid test at the Pennsylvania Hospital, and elsewhere. EDWARD T. ROBINSON, ap 5—1m 4th and Franklin streets.

RHEUMATISM.—Physicians, and persons suffering with Rheumatism, should give the "Elixir of Propylamine" a trial. It has been highly extolled in the hospital reports of Europe and America as an efficacious remedy for this disease. For sale, with all new pharmaceutical preparations, at MEADE & BAKER'S Drug Store, ap 2 186 Main st., corner above P. O.

LEONARD'S INSTANT RELIEF; Ayer's Cherry Pectoral; Wistar's Balsam of Wild Cherry and Lozenges; Mrs. Gardner's Balsam Liverwort; Radway's Ready Relief; Rock's Good Samaritan; Indian Chologogue; Mrs. Winslow's Soothing Syrup; Rose's and Hartshorne's Cough Syrup, &c. L. WAGNER, Druggist, mh 29 Corner 6th and Broad streets.

PURE LEAD—Linseed Oil; Colors, ground in oil and dry; Paint Brushes; Sand Paper; Putty; Spirits Turpentine and Varnishes—all of good quality, and at prices compelled to give satisfaction. Just received by R. W. POWERS Druggist, ap 13 Corner Main and 15th sts.

SPRING CLOTHING—ALL NEW.—I am now prepared to show my new SPRING STOCK, which is gotten up after the latest reported styles, and made by the best workmen—something stylish, durable and cheap. Crenshaw Goods ready-made. IRVING HULL, Agent, [illegible] Main, corner 14th street.

APOTHECARIES, &c.

J. W. FRAYSER, APOTHECARY AND DRUGGIST, *Seventeenth, between Grace and Broad Streets,* RICHMOND, VA., Dealer in Drugs, Medicines, Chemicals, Fancy Articles, Toilet Soaps, Perfumery, &c. Also, Paints, Oils, Dye-Stuffs, Burning Fluid, Kerosene Oil, Alcohol; Garden and Flower Seeds; Cigars, Snuff and Tobacco, of various brands; Brushes, Combs, &c.; all the popular Patent Medicines of the day, and all other articles usually kept in Drug stores, which will be sold on the most reasonable terms. Physicians and others can rely on having their PRESCRIPTIONS carefully and accurately compounded at all hours of the DAY and NIGHT. J. W. FRAYSER, Druggist, mh 23 17th street.

E. T. ROBINSON, GRADUATE OF THE PHILADELPHIA COLLEGE OF PHARMACY, (Successor to Laidley & Robinson,) Fourth and Franklin streets, Richmond, has in store a large, fresh and well-selected stock of Medicines, Chemicals, Perfumery, Fancy Articles, &c., which he offers at low prices. Strict personal attention will be given to all the departments of the business. Orders for shipment will be promptly attended to and most carefully packed. no 27

JOHN W. GARLICK, M. D., APOTHECARY AND DRUGGIST, Market Place, Franklin St., *Richmond, Va.* DRUGS, MEDICINES, PAINTS, OILS, WINDOW GLASS, VARNISHES, DYE-STUFFS, FANCY ARTICLES, &c. PROPRIETOR AND MANUFACTURER OF SEMPLE'S INFALLIBLE BAKING POWDER.

NEW DRUG STORE. ROBERT W. POWERS, Apothecary and Druggist, Begs leave to inform his friends and the public that he has taken and re-fitted in a new and handsome style, the store formerly occupied by J. B. Wood, and more recently by C. S. Dawson, No. 48, corner Main and Wall streets, one door above the St. Charles Hotel, Richmond, Va., and has just opened with an entirely new stock of DRUGS, MEDICINES, CHEMICALS, FANCY and TOILET ARTICLES, PERFUMERY, &c., Comprising every article usually kept in his line, selected in person by himself, with especial reference to their freshness, purity, and entire reliability. Physicians will find his stock of DRUGS, CHEMICALS, STANDARD PHARMACEUTICAL PREPARATIONS, SURGICAL INSTRUMENTS, &c., very complete, embracing many new and desirable articles. Prescriptions carefully compounded at any hour of day or night. Orders promptly attended to. oc 5—ts ROBT. W. POWERS.

PURCELL, LADD & CO., WHOLESALE DRUGGISTS, *No. 122, corner of Main and 13th Streets,* Dealers in DRUGS, MEDICINES, INDIGO, MADDER and other DYES, WINDOW GLASS, PAINTS, OILS, BURNING FLUID, KEROSINE and COAL OILS, &c., &c., Comprising a large and general assortment of Goods in their line, which we offer to Merchants and others very low for cash, or on time to strictly punctual customers. PURCELL, LADD & CO., Druggists, Corner Main and Governor streets, mh 21 Richmond.

FIRST-CLASS MEDICINES. MEADE & BAKER, PHARMACEUTISTS AND VENDORS OF PURE AND RELIABLE MEDICINES, CHEMICALS, PHARMACEUTICAL PRODUCTS, Surgical Instruments and Appliances; Medicine Chests for plantations, families and travelers; Physicians' Saddle Bags; London Elastic Stockings, Trusses and Supporters; Porte-Monnaies, Combs, Brushes, Toilet Mirrors; first quality Perfumery, Pomades and Soaps; Mineral Waters, bottled at the Springs; Medicinal Wares and Apparatus; Magnetic Machines, &c., all of the best quality and at the lowest rates. MEADE & BAKER, 186 Main st., corner above Post-Office, de 29 Richmond, Va.

JOSEPH LAIDLEY, CHEMIST, GRADUATE OF PHARMACY, (Late Laidley & Robinson,) *Main and Fifth Streets, Sign of the Red Mortar,* RICHMOND, VA., Manufacturer of and Dealer in pure and reliable MEDICINES, selected and prepared by himself, expressly for physicians', plantation and family use. All new and rare Remedies, pure Chemicals and Pharmaceuticals, Medicine Chests, Saddle Bags, Surgeons' Instruments, Implements, &c., at manufacturers' prices. Bandages, Braces, Supporters, Trusses, London Elastic and Laced Stockings. Perfumery, Soaps, Brushes and Combs, of all kinds; Fancy Goods, pure Spices, pure White Kerosine Oils, Oils of all kinds, Burning Fluid, Paints, Glass, Dye Stuffs and Varnishes. Prime Smoking and Chewing Tobacco, genuine Havana Cigars. Pure Medical Brandy, Wines and Whiskey. Flavoring Extracts for Cooking, Cooking Wines, and all other articles kept in a first-class Drug Store, and on as good terms as similar articles can be bought for, either North or South. mh 5

L. WAGNER, APOTHECARY AND DRUGGIST, keeps on hand and for sale only fresh and reliable Drugs, the most popular genuine Patent Medicines, all the latest approved Pharmaceutical Preparations, Chemicals, Dye Stuffs, Oils, Paints, Window Glass, Putty, Brushes of all kinds, Turpentine, the best of Coal Oil, Sperm Oil, Burning Fluid, Alcohol, Perfumery, Fancy Articles, Cigars, and Tobacco. Corner Broad and 6th streets, Richmond, Va. fe 21

FALL TRADE. 1861. W. PETERSON & CO., Wholesale Druggists and Dealers in Indigo, Spices, Madder, Logwood, Bi. Carb. Soda, Starch, Sal Soda, Tobacco, Snuff, Cigars, Nutmegs, Salad Oil, Saltpetre, Sponges, Saleratus, Flor. Sulphur, Copperas, Brimstone, Alum, Cochineal, White Lead, Zinc Paint, Linseed Oil, Colors, Paraffine Oil, Solar Oil, Lard Oil, Castor Oil, Tonqua Beans—invite the attention of merchants visiting Richmond, to an examination of their stock, which, in variety and price, is not surpassed in this or any Northern city. Orders promptly attended to. W. PETERSON & CO., ja 14 Druggists, 155 Main street, corner 12th.

A. BODEKER & CO., APOTHECARIES AND DRUGGISTS, No. 10 Main Street, near Old Market, Richmond, Va., will keep on hand a general assortment of pure Drugs, Medicines, Chemicals, Oils, Paints, Window Glass, Putty, Dye Stuffs, Patent Medicines, Brushes, of all kinds; Surgical Appliances, Burning Fluid, Alcohol, Soaps, Perfumery, Fancy Articles, Garden Seeds, Glue, Sand Paper, Tobacco, Cigars, Snuff, Medicinal Liquors, &c. Prescriptions prepared at all hours, with special care, by members of the firm alone. Physicians' orders from the country executed promptly, and the most reliable medicines furnished. ja 9

CHINA, GLASSWARE, &c.

EXCITING NEWS!—IMPORTANT TO THE SOUTH!—In these desperate times it will be cheering news to our friends and the public in general to be informed that we have just opened, at our new establishment, especially built for our trade, at No. 205 Broad street, between 4th and 5th, a splendid stock of CHINA and GLASSWARE, HOUSE FURNISHING and FANCY GOODS, assuring them that many goods being bought only recently for cash, at panic prices, will be offered to them at prices suiting these difficult times admirably. We specially recommend our Dinner, Tea and Toilet Sets, etc., etc.; Dr. Kane's Refrigerators, and others; Water Coolers; four-minute Ice Cream Freezers; Bird Cages; Children's Carriages; Table Cutlery; Silver-Plated, Aibata, Britannia, Block Tin, and Japanned Ware; Tea Trays; Looking-Glasses and Picture Frames, (which we manufacture to order;) Wooden and Willow Ware, and a general assortment of Fancy Goods.—Please call at our new store, 205 Broad street. ap 22 SCHAAP & CO.

CHINA, GLASS AND EARTHENWARE *WHOLESALE AND RETAIL.* O. B. TAYLOR, 117 Main Street. Has now in store, and on storage, a LARGE and FULL ASSORTMENT of ARTICLES IN HIS LINE OF BUSINESS. He has lately ENLARGED his FACILITIES for DOING BUSINESS, and has INCREASED HIS STOCK. He is prepared to sell upon as reasonable terms as any of the repacking houses of the North. Thankful for the liberal patronage heretofore bestowed on him, he will endeavor, by prompt attention to business, to merit a continuance of the same. mh 18—2m

GLASSWARE.—Just opened, a fine stock of Goblets, Tumblers, Wines, Champagnes, Lemonades, Ale Glasses, Lager Beer Glasses, Salvers, Fruit Bowls, Pickle Stands, Glass Tubes, Salt Cellars, &c., &c. Our stock is full and complete. THOS. A. BULKLEY & CO., ap 15 157 Main street.

RICHMOND POTTERIES, foot of Main street, Rocketts, and corner Cary and 12th streets, Richmond, Va. KEESEE & PARR, Proprietors.—The subscribers respectfully inform the merchants of Virginia, North Carolina and Tennessee, that they are manufacturing the best quality of STONEWARE, which they will sell at the very lowest prices, *with a liberal discount for cash.* All ware sold by us will be delivered in any part of the city free of charge. THOS. W. KEESEE, de 7 DAVID PARR.

SPRING STOCK OF CHINA, GLASS AND QUEENSWARE.—We have on hand, and are receiving daily, of direct importation, a large stock of China, Glass and Queensware, consisting of fine decorated Dinner Setts; Tea Setts; Chamber Setts, &c.; fine buff and pink decorated Dessert Setts; white French China, in large variety, sold by the sett or piece; white Granite and fancy printed Dinner Ware, Chamber Setts, Tea Ware, &c. of various styles and patterns. Glassware of every description of Cut, Pressed, Blown, Bohemian, French, &c. Also, a large variety of Kerosene Lamps, with the latest improved Burners. Also, a large stock of Japanned Waiters, of various styles and qualities; Papier Mache Waiters, in setts, beautifully decorated. Silver-Plated Ware, consisting of Waiters, Castors, Spoons, Forks, Cake Baskets, Card Baskets, Pickle Forks, Butter Knives, Water Dippers, Candlesticks, Ice Pitchers, Goblets, Mugs, &c.—Also, a fine stock of Table Cutlery, of the best manufacture. All of which will be sold at very low prices. We would ask our friends and the public generally to call and examine our stock before purchasing elsewhere, as we think we can make it to their interest to purchase of us. We would also call their attention to our large stock of Fancy Goods, which we shall offer at greatly reduced prices from this date, (March 11.) GEO. J. SUMNER & CO., mh 12 Iron Front Buildings, Governor st.

REDUCTION IN PRICE.—STEBBINS, PULLEN & CO. will, from this day, offer their entire stock of FANCY GOODS, VASES, &c., at greatly reduced prices for cash. Now is the time to make your purchases for the holidays. Call early. STEBBINS, PULLEN & CO., ja 8 Corner 9th and Broad sts.

ALE AND BROWN STOUT IN BOTTLES.—25 bbls. Blood's superior Bottled Ale; 25 bbls. Blood's superior Bottled Brown Stout, on consignment and for sale low, to close, by [illegible] BRIDGFORD & CO.

TRAVELERS' GUIDE.

SPECIAL NOTICE. VIRGINIA CENTRAL RAILROAD. *CHANGE OF HOURS.* The MAIL and PASSENGER TRAIN will leave RICHMOND daily, at 6 o'clock A. M., for GORDONSVILLE, CHARLOTTESVILLE, STAUNTON, ALEXANDRIA, LYNCHBURG, &c. THOS. DODAMEAD, Gen'l Sup't. Office Va. Central Railroad } April 23d, 1861. } ap 24—1w

GEN'L SUPT.'S OFFICE VA. CENT'L R. R., Richmond, April 20, 1861. THE PASSENGER TRAINS will commence running regularly on MONDAY next. THOS. DODAMEAD, ap 20—ts General Sup't.

VIRGINIA CENTRAL RAILROAD—CHANGE OF HOURS.—The MAIL and PASSENGER TRAINS leave RICHMOND daily, except Sundays, at 6 A. M. In consequence of injury to the road by high water, near Hanover Court-House, Passengers will take the Cars of the R., F. & P. R. R. to the JUNCTION, where they take the Central Trains. THOS DODAMEAD, General Sup't. Gen'l Supt's Office Va. Cen. R. R., } Richmond, April 16, 1861. } ap 17—ts

NOTICE—RESUMPTION OF TRAVEL.—The damage occasioned by the late heavy rains having been repaired, our Trains are now running regularly, and have been since Sunday, 14th inst. SAML. RUTH, Supt. Office R., F. & P. R. R. Co., } Richmond, April 17th, 1861. } ap 17—ts

IMPORTANT CHANGE OF SCHEDULE.—On and after SUNDAY, 14th instant, the MORNING MAIL TRAIN will leave Richmond Depot at 6.00 A. M., instead of 6.30 A. M., as heretofore. The EVENING MAIL TRAIN will leave at 7.00 P. M., as before. SAM'L RUTH, Superintendent. Office R., F. & P. R. R. Co., } Richmond, April 11, 1861. } ap 12—ts

OFFICE RICH'D & PET'G R. R. CO., } Richmond, Nov. 29th, 1860. } ON AND AFTER MONDAY, the 3rd day of December, the TRAINS on this Road will run as follows:

TRAINS LEAVE RICHMOND FOR PETERSBURG.
Express daily, (except Sundays,) at.... 4 30 A. M.
Accommodation, (tri-weekly) Monday, Wednesday and Friday, at............ 8 00 A. M.
Mail *daily*, at............................ 2 45 P. M.

TRAINS LEAVE PETERSBURG FOR RICHMOND.
Express *daily* at......................... 3 45 A. M.
Accommodation (tri-weekly,) Monday, Wednesday and Friday, at............ 8 00 A. M.
Mail daily, (except Sundays,) at........ 5 15 P. M.
de 3—ts THOS. H. WYNNE, Superintendent.

TRAVELERS TO THE NORTH.—1861. NORTHERN CENTRAL RAILWAY.—Trains leave Calvert Station, Baltimore, daily, (except Sunday,) at 8.30 A. M., and at 5.30 P. M., for Niagara Falls, (fare only ten dollars,) Buffalo, Owego, Oswego, Toronto, Hamilton, all parts of Western New York and Canada, for Detroit, Chicago, Cincinnati, St. Louis, and all parts of the West, Northwest and Southwest. Travelers can go to Detroit, Chicago, Milwaukie, &c., via Niagara Falls, at the same cost as by any other route. A new route to New York is now open by this Road, via Harrisburg and Jersey City, with only one change of cars. Fare, $6. Take the 8.30 A. M. train and go through by daylight, over first-class Roads and through a beautiful country. Try it. Buy tickets only to Baltimore. JAS. C. CLARKE, Sup't. John T. Rigney, Assistant Sup't. je 13—1y

NOTICE. TO PASSENGERS 1861. GOING NORTH.—NEW ARRANGEMENT.—IMPORTANT TO TRAVELERS.—THROUGH TICKETS AND THROUGH CHECKS.—GREAT NORTHERN ROUTE—Carrying the great United States Mail. Twice daily, (Sunday night excepted) between Richmond, Alexandria, Washington, Baltimore, Philadelphia, New York, and all important points West, via Acquia Creek and Washington, over the Richmond, Fredericksburg & Potomac Railroad, to the Potomac river, 75 miles, and by splendid and comfortable steamers thence to Washington, 55 miles—in all 153 miles in seven hours, being a comfortable and perfectly safe rate of speed. Hours of departure: 6.30 A. M., and 7 P. M. BAGGAGE, under charge of Special Agents, CHECKED THROUGH to Washington, Baltimore, Philadelphia and New York. Through Tickets can be secured to the following points, viz: Baltimore, Philadelphia, Cincinnati, Columbus, Indianapolis, Cairo, Dayton, Jeffersonville, Rock Island, Zanesville, Washington, New York, St. Louis, Chicago, Pittsburg, Louisville, Decatur, Newark and Vincennes. Passengers breakfast and sup at Ashland, and dine on board the comfortable steamer between Acquia Creek and Washington. Persons wishing to obtain tickets for *servants* for Washington city and points further North, must, in *all cases,* be vouched for by some responsible white citizen of Richmond, *in person,* known to the officers of the Road, *as no Tickets will be sold if applied for by them.* For further information, apply at this office, Broad Street, Shockoe Hill. JAS. B. WINSTON, Gen'l Ticket Ag't. Sam'l Ruth, Sup't. ja 9—ts

NOTICE TO THE PUBLIC. NEW AND IMPORTANT ARRANGEMENT, 1861.—The ADAMS EXPRESS COMPANY respectfully announce to the public that they have arranged to run their Express TWICE DAILY from NEW YORK, PHILADELPHIA and BALTIMORE to RICHMOND, thereby affording unusual facilities for obtaining their freight and packages in the shortest possible time. Expresses leave New York at 1, 5 and 6 o'clock P. M. Expresses leave Philadelphia at 8 A. M., and 11 P. M. Expresses leave Baltimore at 4.20 A. M. and 4.20 P. M., arriving in Richmond at 3.30 A. M. and 2 P. M. Expresses leave Richmond for New York, Philadelphia and Baltimore, and all points North and West, at 6.30 A. M. and 6.30 P. M. Freight and packages should in all cases be at our office ONE HOUR before the departure of the Trains. EXPRESSES FOR THE SOUTH leave Richmond TWICE DAILY, at 4.30 A. M., 2.45 P. M. The Adams Express Company feel that they can guarantee to the public civility, attention and satisfaction in all their intercourse with their officers in Richmond, and nothing will be left undone on their part to meet the wants of their customers. Freight and packages arriving by the Express from the North at 3 o'clock P. M., will be delivered immediately, thereby giving to our customers an advance of twelve hours over our arrangements heretofore. STEAMER EXPRESSES, TO AND FROM NEW YORK, SEMI-WEEKLY. Freights delivered immediately upon the arrival of the ship. HEAVY AND LIGHT FREIGHTS, PACKAGES, MONEY, BONDS, LEGAL DOCUMENTS, &c., forwarded with safety and dispatch to all parts of the United States, Canadas, and Europe. NOTES, DRAFTS AND BILLS, with or without Goods, collected at all accessible points throughout the United States, and prompt returns guaranteed. SLAVES forwarded by each of our Expresses, in charge of careful and reliable messengers. TOBACCO and other samples carried at unusually low rates. All freights promptly called for and delivered without extra charge. For further information, please call at our office, 202 Main street. "ADAMS EXPRESS COMPANY," au 7—ts W. H. TREGO, Sup't.

RESTAURANTS, &c.

THE FRANKLIN HOUSE, On 6th Street, Between Marshall and Broad, will be open to the public TO-DAY. SNACKS will be furnished in the best style, at all hours of the day, and the BAR will be constantly supplied with superior LIQUORS, WINES, LAGER BEER, ALE and CIGARS. ap 8—1m* JAMES KIRK.

THE GRAPES RESTAURANT AND READING ROOM, 76 Main street, (four doors below the "Dime,") is daily becoming more popular, and is pronounced by the citizens of Richmond, Norfolk and Petersburg, to be second to none in the city. The BRANDIES, WINES, CIGARS and EDIBLES, are of the best, and at prices to suit the times. E. W. USSHER, Proprietor. N. B.—FREE LUNCH, of SOUPS, &c., from 11 to 1 o'clock. mh 30—1m*

ATTENTION, ANGLERS!—FRESH SUPPLY OF FISHING TACKLE, 1861.—I am now opening the most complete assortment of FISHING TACKLE ever offered in Richmond. Amongst my assortment may be found all the variety of HOOKS, such as Virginia, Limerick, Aberdeen, Kerby, Sockdologers, &c., besides a full assortment of HOOKS on Gut and Gimp; also, Gut and Gimp extra; Rigged Lines, with Floats and Hooks complete; Sea Grass, Floats and Sinkers extra; Cotton, Linen and Flax Lines; Silk Lines, in great variety, and of superior quality; Trout Flies and Reels; Walking-Cane Fishing Rods, &c. Also, just received, a fine assortment of COLT'S celebrated FIVE-SHOOTERS, all sizes. JAMES WALSH, Maker and Importer of Guns, Rifles, &c. ap 15—1m

ARTIFICIAL TEETH.—THE CHEOPLASTIC AND VULCANITE PROCESS.—G. W. JONES, Dentist, having the right for the above mode of making Teeth, and being satisfied of its absolute superiority over all other methods, can with confidence commend it to those desiring full or partial sets of teeth, and especially such as may be dissatisfied with those they are now using.—The perfect adaptation of the plate to the mouth, and the suction thereby secured, enables him to insert one or more teeth *without clasps.* This method having been adopted by those standing highest in the profession, North and South, testimonials will be given and specimens exhibited to those wishing to see them. Sets of Teeth, on gold or any other plate, will, of course, be made for those preferring them. Filling, Cleansing, Extracting, and all other operations gently and thoroughly performed. Teeth extracted by ELECTRICITY, *without pain.* Office on Main street, opposite Corinthian Hall. de 1—1y

IMPROVE YOUR EYESIGHT. FRANKLIN & CO., OPTICIANS, Offer to the public their improved CRYSTAL PERISCOPIC SPECTACLES, for preserving and restoring the impaired vision to its prime vigor. Also, a very fine assortment of MICROSCOPES, TELESCOPES, MARINE and OPERA GLASSES, and the finest collection of STEREOSCOPES and STEREOSCOPIC PICTURES. CRYSTAL GLASSES set in old frames. No. 148 MAIN STREET, ja 21—d1y Richmond, Va.

RICHMOND-MADE PIANOS FOR SALE BELOW NORTHERN PRICES.—The subscriber has on hand three new, very superior 7 octave PIANOS, which he warrants to be equal, if not superior, to any instrument of the same quality from Northern manufactories. He also offers his services to the public as TUNER and REPAIRER OF PIANOS, at reasonable rates. CONRAD FREIMANN, North side Broad st., between 2d and 3d. References.—H. P. Lefebvre, Esq.; Prof. E. W. Thilow; Prof. W. F. Graber, &c. [illegible]

ANGLO-AFRICAN, EXTRA.

Wendell Phillips on the War.

VOL. II. NO. 41. NEW YORK, APRIL 27, 1861. WHOLE NO. 93.

WENDELL PHILLIPS ON THE WAR.

Phonographic report by J. M. W. Yerrinton.

On Sunday last, April 21st, not less than four thousand people were crowded within the walls of the spacious Music Hall, in Boston, to listen to a Discourse on the War, by Wendell Phillips, Esq., before the Twenty-Eighth Congregational Society; and almost an equal number were excluded, because of the impossibility of finding even an inch of standing room. The platform was most profusely, yet tastefully decorated with the "stars and stripes," for the first time seeming to symbolize the cause of impartial freedom, under the extraordinary circumstances of the times. Other parts of the hall were also handsomely adorned. The desire to hear Mr. Phillips was of the gravest and intensest character. On entering the hall, he was greeted with hearty, irrepressible rounds of applause, which were frequently repeated during the delivery of his thrilling remarks. The following selection of Scripture, from the 50th and 51st chapter of Jeremiah, was first read by him, and produced a marked sensation, in consequence of its extraordinary applicability to the state of the times in our land. It was loudly cheered at its conclusion!

"The word that the Lord spake against Babylon, and against the land of the Chaldeans, by Jeremiah the prophet. Lo, I will raise, and cause to come up against Babylon, an assembly of great nations from the north country; and they shall set themselves in array against her; from thence she shall be taken: their arrows shall be as of a mighty expert man; none shall return in vain. And Chaldea shall be a spoil: all that spoil her shall be satisfied, saith the Lord. Put yourselves in array against Babylon round about: all ye that bend the bow, shoot at her, spare no arrows; for she hath sinned against the Lord. Shout against her round about; her foundations are fallen, her walls are thrown down; for it is the vengeance of the Lord: take vengeance upon her: as she hath done, do unto her.

A sound of battle is in the land, and of great destruction. The Lord hath opened his armory, and hath brought forth the weapons of his indignation: for this is the work of the Lord God of hosts in the land of the Chaldeans. Woe unto them! for their day is come, the time of their visitation.

Behold, I am against thee, O thou most proud, saith the Lord God of hosts: for thy day is come, the time that I will visit thee. And the most proud shall stumble and fall, and none shall raise him up: and I will kindle a fire in his cities, and it shall devour all round about him.

Thus saith the Lord of hosts, The children of Israel and the children of Judea were oppressed together; and all that took them captives held them fast, and refused to let them go. Their Redeemer is strong; the Lord of hosts is his name; he shall thoroughly plead their cause, that he may give rest to the land, and disquiet the inhabitants of Babylon.

A sword is upon the Chaldeans, saith the Lord, and upon the inhabitants of Babylon, and upon her princes, and upon her wise men. A sword is upon the liars, and they shall dote; a sword is upon her mighty men, and they shall be dismayed; a sword is upon their horses, and upon their chariots, and upon all the mingled people that are in the midst of her; and they shall become as women; for it is the land of graven images, and they are mad upon their idols. Thus the slain shall fall in the land of the Chaldeans, and they that are thrust through in her streets. For Israel hath not been forsaken, nor Judah of his God; though their land was filled with sin against the Holy One of Israel.

Flee out of the midst of Babylon, and deliver every man his soul; be not cut off in her iniquity; for this is the time of the Lord's vengeance; he will render unto her a recompense. We would have healed Babylon, but she is not healed: forsake her, and let us go every one into his own country; for her judgment reacheth unto heaven, and is lifted up even to the skies.

One post shall run to meet another, and one messenger to meet another, to shew the king of Babylon that his city is taken at one end, and that the passages are stopped, and the reeds they have burned with fire, and the men of war are affrighted. For thus saith the Lord of hosts, the God of Israel, The daughter of Babylon is like a threshing-floor; it is time to thresh her. The violence done to me and to my flesh be upon Babylon, shall the inhabitant of Zion say; and, My blood upon the inhabitants of Chaldea, shall Jerusalem say. Then the heaven and the earth, and all that is therein, shall sing for Babylon: for the spoilers shall come unto her from the north, saith the Lord."

DISCOURSE OF MR. PHILLIPS.

"Therefore thus saith the Lord: Ye have not hearkened unto me in proclaiming liberty every one to his brother, and every man to his neighbor: behold, I proclaim a liberty for you, saith the Lord, to the sword, to the pestilence, and to the famine."—Jer. 34: 17.

Many times this winter, here and elsewhere, I have counselled peace—urged, as well as I knew how, the expediency of acknowledging a Southern Confederacy, and the peaceful separation of these thirty-four States. One of the journals announces to you that I come here this morning to retract those opinions. No, not one of them! (Applause.) I need them all—every word I have spoken this winter—every act of twenty-five years of my life, to make the welcome I give this war hearty and hot, Civil war is a momentous evil. It needs the soundest, most solemn justification. I rejoice before God to-day for every word that I have spoken counselling peace; and I rejoice with an especially profound gratitude, that for the first time in my anti-slavery life, I speak under the stars and stripes, and welcome the tread of Massachusetts men marshalled for war. (Enthusiastic cheering.) No matter what the past has been or said; today the slave asks God for a sight of this banner, and counts it the pledge of his redemption. (Applause.) Hitherto, it may have meant what you thought, or what I did; to-day, it represents Sovereignty and Justice. (Renewed applause.) The only mistake that I have made was in supposing Massachusetts wholly choked with cotton dust and cankered with gold. (Loud cheering.) The South thought her patience and generous willingness for peace were cowardice; to-day shows the mistake. She has been sleeping on her arms since '76, and the first cannon-shot brings her to her feet with the war-cry of the Revolution on her lips. (Loud cheers.) Any man who loves either liberty or manhood must rejoice at such an hour. (Applause.)

Let me tell you the path by which I, at least, have trod my way up to this conclusion. I do not acknowledge the motto, in its full significance, "Our country, right or wrong." If you let it trespass on the domain of morals, it is knavish and atheistic. But there is a full, broad sphere for loyalty; and no war-cry ever stirred a generous people that had not in it much of truth and right. It is sublime, this rally of a great people to the defence of what they think their national honor! A "noble and puissant nation rousing herself like a strong man from sleep, and shaking her invincible locks." Just now, we saw her "reposing, peaceful and motionless; but at the call of patriotism, she ruffles, as it were, her swelling plumage, collects her scattered elements of strength, and awakens her dormant thunders."

But how do we justify this last appeal to the God of Battles? Let me tell you how I do. I have always believed in the sincerity of Abraham Lincoln. You have heard me express my confidence in it every time I have spoken from this desk. I only doubted sometimes whether he were really the head of the government. To-day he is at any rate Commander-in-chief.

The delay in the action of Government has doubtless been necessity, but policy also. Traitors within and without made it hesitate to move till it had tried the machine of Government just given it. But delay was wise, as it matured a public opinion definite, decisive, and ready to keep step to the music of the Government march. The very postponement of another session of Congress till July 4th plainly invites discussion—evidently contemplates the ripening of public opinion in the interval. Fairly to examine public affairs, and prepare a community wise to coöperate with the Government, is the duty of every pulpit and every press.

Plain words, therefore, now before the nation goes mad with excitement, is every man's duty. Every public meeting in Athens was opened with a curse on any one who should not speak what he really thought. "I have never defiled my conscience from fear or favor to my superiors," was part of the oath every Egyptian soul was supposed to utter in the Judgment Hall of Osiris, before admission to heaven. Let us show, today, a Christian spirit as sincere and fearless. No mobs in this hour of victory, to silence those whom events have not converted. We are strong enough to tolerate dissent. That flag which floats over press or mansion at the bidding of a mob, disgraces both victor and victim.

All winter long, I have acted with that party which cried for peace. The anti-slavery enterprise to which I belong, started with peace written on its banner. We imagined that the age of bullets was over; that the age of ideas had come; that thirty millions of people were able to take a great question, and decide it by the conflict of opinions; and, without letting the ship of State founder, lift four millions of men into Liberty and Justice. We thought that if your statesmen would throw away personal ambition and party watchwords, and devote themselves to the great issue, this might be accomplished. To a certain extent, it has been. The North has answered to the call. Year after year, event by event, has indicated the rising education of the people,—the readiness for a higher moral life, the patience that waits for a neighbor's conversion. The North has responded to the call of that peaceful, moral, intellectual agitation which the anti-slavery idea has initiated. Our mistake, if any, has been that we counted too much on the intelligence of the masses, on the honesty and wisdom of statesmen as a class. Perhaps we did not give weight enough to the fact we saw, that this nation is made up of different ages; not homogeneous, but a mixed mass of different centuries. The North *thinks*—can appreciate argument—is the nineteenth century—hardly any struggle left in it but that between the working class and the money kings. The South *dreams*—it is the thirteenth and fourteenth century—baron and serf—noble and slave. Jack Cade and Wat Tyler loom over the horizon, and the serf rising calls for another Thierry to record his struggle. There the fagot still burns, which the Doctors of the Sorbonne called, ages ago, "the best light to guide the erring." There men are tortured for opinions, the only punishment the Jesuits were willing their pupils should look on. This is, perhaps, too flattering a picture of the South. Better call her, as Sumner does, "the Barbarous States." Our struggle, therefore, is no struggle between different ideas, but between barbarism and civilization. Such can only be settled by arms. (Prolonged cheering.) The Government have waited until its best friends almost suspected its courage or its integrity; but the cannon shot against Fort Sumter has opened the only door out of this hour. There were but two. One was Compromise; the other was Battle. The integrity of the North closed the first; the generous forbearance of nineteen States closed the other. The South opened this with cannon shot, and Lincoln shows himself at the door. (Prolonged and enthusiastic cheering.) The war, then, is not aggressive, but in self-defence, and Washington has become the Thermopylæ of Liberty and Justice. (Applause.) Rather than surrender it, cover every square foot of it with a living body (loud cheers); crowd it with a million of men, and empty every bank vault at the North to pay the cost. (Renewed cheering.) Teach the world once for all, that North America belongs to the stars and stripes, and under them no man shall wear a chain. (Enthusiastic cheering.) In the whole of this conflict, I have looked only at Liberty—only at the slave. Perry entered the battle of the Lakes, with "Don't give up the ship," floating from the masthead of the Lawrence. When with his fighting flag he left her crippled, heading north, and mounting the deck of the Niagara, turned her bows due west, he did all for one purpose,—to rake the decks of the foe. Acknowledge secession, or cannonade it, I care not which; but "Proclaim liberty throughout all the land unto all the inhabitants thereof." (Loud cheers.)

I said, civil war needs momentous and solemn justification. Europe, the world, may claim of us, that before we blot the nineteenth century by an appeal to arms, we shall exhaust every concession, try every means to keep the peace; otherwise, an appeal to the God of Battles is an insult to the civilization of our age; it is a confession that our culture and our religion are superficial, if not a failure. I think that the history of the nation and of the Government both, is an ample justification to our own times and to history for this appeal to arms. I think the South is all wrong, and the Administration is all right. (Prolonged cheering.) Let me tell you why. For thirty years, the North has exhausted conciliation and compromise. They have tried every expedient, they have relinquished every right, they have sacrificed every interest, they have smothered keen sensibility to national honor, and Northern weight and supremacy in the Union; have forgotten they were the majority in numbers and in wealth, in education and strength; have left the helm of Government and the dictation of policy to the Southern States. For all this, the conflict waxed closer and hotter. The Administration that preceded this was full of traitors and thieves. It allowed the arms, ships, money, military stores of the North to be stolen with impunity. Mr. Lincoln took office, robbed of all the means to defend the constitutional rights of the Government. He offered to withdraw from the walls of Sumter everything but the flag. He allowed secession to surround it with the strongest forts which military science could build. The North offered to meet in Convention her sister States, and arrange the terms of peaceful separation. Strength and right yielded everything—they folded their hands—waited the returning reason of the mad insurgents. Week after week elapsed, month after month went by, waiting for the sober second thought of two millions and a half of people. The world saw the sublime sight of nineteen millions of wealthy, powerful, united citizens allowing their flag to be insulted, their rights assailed, their sovereignty defied and broken in pieces, and yet waiting, with patient, brotherly, magnanimous kindness, until insurrection having spent its fury should reach out its hand for a peaceful arrangement. Men began to call it cowardice, on the one hand; and we, who watched closely the crisis, feared that this effort to be magnanimous would demoralize the conscience and the courage of the North. We were afraid that, as the hour went by, the virtue of the people, white-heat as it stood on the 4th day of March, would be cooled by the temptations, by the suspense, by the want and suffering that were stalking from the Atlantic to the valley of the Mississippi. We were afraid the Government would wait too long, and find, at last, that instead of a united people, they were deserted, and left alone to meet the foe.

All this time, the South knew, recognized, by her own knowledge of Constitutional questions, that the Government could not advance one inch towards acknowledging secession; that when Abraham Lincoln swore to support the Constitution and laws of the United States, he was bound to die under the flag on Fort Sumter, if necessary. (Loud applause.) They knew, therefore, that the call on the Administration to acknowledge the Commissioners of the Confederacy was a delusion and a swindle. I know the whole argument for secession. Up to a certain extent, I accede to it. But no administration that is not traitor, can ever acknowledge secession. (Cheers.) The right of a State to secede, under the Constitution of the United States—it is an absurdity; and Abraham Lincoln knows nothing, has a right to know nothing, but the Constitution of the United States. (Loud cheers.) The right of a State to secede, as a revolutionary right, is undeniable; but it is the nation that is to recognize that; and the nation offered, in broad convention, at the suggestion of Kentucky, to meet the question. The offer was declined. The Government and the nation, therefore, are all right. (Applause.) They are right on constitutional law; they are right on the principles of the Declaration of Independence. (Cheers.)

Let me explain this more fully, for this reason; because—and I thank God for it, every American should be proud of it—you cannot maintain a war in the United States of America against a constitutional or a revolutionary right. The people of these States have too large brains and too many ideas to fight blindly—to lock horns like a couple of beasts in the sight of the world. (Applause.) Cannon think in this 19th century; and you must put the North in the right—wholly, undeniably, inside of the Constitution and out of it—before you can justify her in the face of the world; before you can pour Massachusetts like an avalanche through the streets of Baltimore, (great cheering,) and carry Lexington and the 19th of April south of Mason and Dixon's Line. (Renewed cheering.) Let us take an honest pride in the fact that our Sixth Regiment made a way for itself through Baltimore, and were the first to reach the threatened Capital. In the war of opinions, Massachusetts has a right to be the first in the field.

I said I knew the whole argument for secession. Very briefly let me state the points. No government provides for its own death; therefore there can be no constitutional right to secede. But there is a revolutionary right. The Declaration of Independence establishes what the heart of every American acknowledges, that the people—mark you! THE PEOPLE!—have always an inherent, paramount, inalienable right to change their governments, whenever they think---whenever *they* think, that it will minister to their happiness. That is a revolutionary right. Now, how did South Carolina and Massachusetts come into the Union? They came into it by a convention representing the people. South Carolina alleges that she has gone out by convention. So far, right. She says that when the *people* take the State rightfully out of the Union, the right to forts and national property goes with it. Granted. She says, also, that it is no matter that we bought Louisiana of France, and Florida of Spain. No bargain made, no money paid betwixt us and France or Spain could rob Florida or Louisiana of her right to remodel her government whenever the people found it would be for their happiness. So far, right. The People---mark you! South Carolina presents herself to the Administration at Washington, and says, "There is a vote of my convention, that I go out of the Union." "I cannot see you," says Abraham Lincoln. [Loud cheers.] "As President, I have no eyes but constitutional eyes; I cannot see you." [Renewed cheers.] He was right. But Madison said, Hamilton said, the Fathers said, in '89, "No man but an enemy of liberty will ever stand on technicalities and forms, when the essence is in question." Abraham Lincoln could not see the Commissioners of South Carolina, but the North could; the nation could; and the nation responded, "If you want a Constitutional Secession, such as you claim, but which I repudiate, I will waive forms---let us meet in convention, and we will arrange it." [Applause.] Surely, while one claims a right within the Constitution, it may without dishonor or inconsistency meet in convention---even if finally refusing to be bound by it. To decline doing so is only evidence of intention to provoke war. Everything under that instrument is peace. Everything under that instrument may be changed by a National Convention. The South says, "No!" She says, "If you don't allow me the Constitutional right, I claim the revolutionary right." The North responds---"When you have torn the Constitution into fragments, I recognize the right of THE PEOPLE of South Carolina to model their government. Yes, I recognize the right of the three hundred and eighty-four thousand white men, and four hundred and eighty-four thousand black men to model their Constitution. Show me one that they have adopted, and I will recognize the revolution. [Cheers.] But the moment you tread outside of the Constitution, the black man is not three-fifths of a man---he is a whole one" [Loud cheering.] Yes, the South has a right to secede; the South has a right to model her government; and the moment she shows us four million of black votes thrown even against it, I will acknowledge the Declaration of Independence is complied with, [loud applause]—that the PEOPLE, south of Mason's and Dixon's Line, have re-modeled their government to suit themselves: and our function is only to recognize it.

I say, the North had a right to assume this position. She did not. She had a right to ignore revolution until this condition was complied with; and she did not. She waived it. In obedience to the advice of Madison, to the long history of her country's forbearance, to the magnanimity of nineteen States, she waited: she advised the Government to wait. Mr. Lincoln, in his inaugural, indicated that this would be the wise course. Mr. Seward hinted it in his speech, in New York. The *London Times* bade us remember the useless war of 1776, and take warning against resisting the principles of Popular Sovereignty. The *Tribune*, whose unflinching fidelity and matchless ability make it, in this fight, "the white plume of Navarre," has again and again avowed its readiness to waive forms and go into Convention. We have waited. We said, "Anything for peace." We obeyed the magnanimous statesmanship of John Quincy Adams. Let me read you his advice, given at the "Jubilee of the Constitution," to the New-York Historical Society, in the year 1839: he says, Recognizing this right of the *people* of a State,—mark you, not a State: the Constitution knows no States; the right of revolution knows no States: it knows only THE PEOPLE. Mr. Adams says, "The PEOPLE of each State in the Union have a right to secede from the confederated Union itself.

Thus stands the RIGHT. But the indissoluble link of union between the people of the several States of this Confederated Nation is, after all, not in the *right*, but in the *heart*.

If the day should ever come (may Heaven avert it) when the affections of the people of these States shall be alienated from each other, when the fraternal spirit shall give way to cold indifference, or collisions of interest shall fester into hatred, the bands of political association will not long hold together parties no longer attracted by the magnetism of conciliated interests and kindly sympathies; and far better will it be for the people of the disunited States to part in friendship from each other, than to be held together by constraint. Then will be the time for reverting to the precedents which occurred at the formation and adoption of the Constitution, to form again a more perfect union, by dissolving that which could no longer bind; and to leave the separated parts to be reunited by the law of political gravitation to the center."

The North said "Amen" to every word of it. They waited. They begged the States to meet them. They were silent when the cannon-shot pierced the flag of the "Star of the West." They said "Amen," when the Government offered to let nothing but the bunting cover Fort Sumpter. They said "Amen," when Lincoln stood alone, without arms, in a defenceless Capital, and trusted himself to the loyalty and forbearance of thirty-four States.

The South, if the truth be told, *cannot* wait. Like all usurpers, they dare not give time for the people to criticise their title to power. War and tumult must conceal the irregularity of their civil course, and smother discontent and criticism at the same time. Besides, bankruptcy at home can live out its short term of possible existence only by conquest on land and piracy at sea. And, further, only by war, by appeal to popular frenzy, can they hope to delude the border States to join them. War is the breath of their life.

To-day, therefore, the question is, by the voice of the South, "Shall Washington or Montgomery own the continent?" And the North says, "From the gulf to the pole, the Stars and Stripes shall atone to four million of negroes whom we have forgotten for seventy years; and, before you break the Union, we will see that justice is done to the slave." [Enthusiastic and long continued cheers.]

There is only one thing that those cannon shot in the harbor of Charleston settled, and that is, that there never can be a compromise. [Loud applause.] We Abolitionists have doubted whether this Union really meant Justice and Liberty. We have doubted the honest intention of nineteen million of people. They have said, in answer to our criticism,—"We believe that the Fathers meant to establish justice. We believe that there are hidden in the Armory of the Constitution weapons strong enough to secure it. We are willing yet to try the experiment. Grant us time." We have doubted, derided the pretence, as we supposed. During these long and weary weeks, we have waited to hear the Northern conscience assert its purpose. It comes at last. [An impressive pause.] Massachusetts blood has consecrated the pavements of Baltimore, and those stones are now too sacred to be trodden by slaves. [Loud cheers.]

You and I owe it to those young martyrs, you and I owe it, that their blood shall be the seed of no mere empty triumph, but that the negro shall teach his children to bless them for centuries to come. [Applause.] When Massachusetts goes down to that Carolina fort to put the Stars and Stripes again over its blackened walls, [enthusiasm,] she will sweep from its neighborhood every institution that hazards their ever bowing again to the Palmetto. [Loud cheers.] All of you may not mean it now. Our fathers did not think in 1775 of the Declaration of Independence. The Long Parliament never thought of the scaffold of Charles the First, when they entered on the struggle; but having begun, they made thorough work. [Cheers.] It is an attribute of the Yankee blood—Slow to fight, and fight once. [Renewed cheers.] It was a holy war, that for Independence: this is a holier and the last—that for Liberty. [Loud applause.]

I hear a great deal about Constitutional liberty. The mouths of the Concord and Lexington guns have room only for one word, and that is Liberty. You might as well ask Niagara to chaunt the Chicago Platform, as to say how far war shall go. War and Niagara thunder to a music of their own. God alone can launch the lightning, that they may go and say, Here we are. The thunder-bolts of His throne abase the proud, lift up the lowly, and execute justice between man and man.

Now, let me turn one moment to another consideration. What should the Government do? I said "thorough" should be its maxim. When we fight, we are fighting for Justice and an Idea. A short war and a rigid one, is the maxim. Ten thousand men in Washington! it is only a bloody fight. Five hundred thousand men in Washington, and none dare come there but from the North. [Loud cheers.] Occupy St. Louis, with the millions of the West, and say to Missouri, "You cannot go out!" [Applause.] Cover Maryland with a million of the friends of the administration, and say, "We must have our Capital within reach. [Cheers.] If you need compensation for Slaves taken from you in the convulsion of battle, here it is. [Cheers.] Government is engaged in the fearful struggle to show that 89 meant Justice, and there is something better than life in such an hour as this." And, again, we must remember another thing—the complication of such a struggle as this. Bear with me a moment. We put five hundred thousand men on the banks of the Potomac. Virginia is held by two races, white and black. Suppose those black men flare in our faces the Declaration of Independence. What are we to say? Are we to send Northern bayonets to keep Slaves under the feet of Jefferson Davis? [Many voices, "no," "never."] In 1842, Gov. Wise, of Virginia, the symbol of the South, entered into argument with Quincy Adams, who carried Plymouth Rock to Washington. [Applause.] It was when Joshua Giddings offered his resolution stating his Constitutional doctrine that Congress had no right to interfere, in any event, in any way, with the Slavery of the Southern States. Plymouth Rock refused to vote for it. Mr. Adams said, (substantially,) "If foreign war comes, if civil war comes, i insurrection comes, is this beleaguered Capital, is this besieged Government to see millions of its subjects in arms, and have no right to break the fetters which they are forging into swords? No; the war power of the Government can sweep this institution into the Gulf." [Cheers.] Ever since 1842, that statesman-like claim and warning of the North has been on record, spoken by the lips of her most moderate, wisest, coolest, most patriotic son. [Applause.]

When the South cannonaded Fort Sumpter the bones of Adams stirred in his coffin. [Cheers.] And you might have heard him, from that granite grave, at Quincy, proclaim to the nation, "The hour has struck! Seize the thunder-bolt God has forged for you, and annihilate the system which has troubled peace for seventy years!" [Cheers.] Do not say that it is a cold-blooded suggestion. I hardly ever knew Slavery go down in any other circumstances. Only once, in the broad sweep of the world's history, was any nation lifted so high that she could stretch her imperial hand across the Atlantic, and lift, by one peaceful word, a million of slaves into liberty. God granted that glory only to our mother land.

How did French Slavery go down? How did the French Slave-trade go down? When Napoleon came back from Elba, when his fate hung trembling in the balance, and he wished to gather around him the sympathies of the liberals of Europe, he no sooner set foot in the Tuilleries than he signed the edict abolishing the Slave-trade, against which the Abolitionists of England and France had protested for twenty years in vain. And the trade went down, because Napoleon felt that he must do something to gild the darkening hour of his second attempt to clutch the sceptre of France. How did the Slave-system go down? When, in 1848, the Provisional Government found itself in the Hotel de Ville, obliged to do something to draw to itself the sympathy and liberal feeling of the French nation, they signed an edict—it was the first from the rising republic—abolishing the death-penalty and Slavery. The storm which rocked the vessel of State almost to foundering, snapped forever the chain of the French slave. Look, too, at the history of Mexican and South American emancipation; you will find that it was, in every instance, I think, the child of convulsion.

That hour has come to us. So stand we to-day. The Abolitionist who will not now cry, when the moment serves, "Up, boys, and at them," is false to liberty. [Great cheering.] [A voice—"So is every other man."] Say not it is a hard lesson. Let him who fully knows his own heart and strength, and feels, as he looks down into his child's cradle, that he could stand and see that little nestling borne to Slavery, and submit—let him cast the first stone. But all you, whose blood is wont to stir over Naseby and Bunker Hill, will hold your peace, unless you are ready to cry with me—*Sic semper Tyrannis!* So may it ever be with Tyrants! [Loud applause.]

Why, Americans, I believe in the might of nineteen million of people. Yes, I know that what sowing machines and reaping machines and ideas and types and school-houses cannot do, the muskets of Illinois and Massachusetts can finish up. [Cheers.] Blame me not that I make every thing turn on liberty and the slave. I believe in Massachusetts. I know that free speech, free toil, school-houses, and ballot-boxes are a pyramid on its broadest base. Nothing that does not sunder the solid globe can disturb it. We defy the world to disturb us. [Cheers.] The little errors that dwell upon our surface, we have medicine in our institutions to cure them all. [Applause.]

Therefore there is nothing left for a New England man, nothing but that he shall wipe away the stain that hangs about the toleration of human bondage. As Webster said at Rochester, years and years ago, "If I thought that there was a stain upon the remotest hem of the garment of my country, I would devote my utmost labor to wipe it off." [Cheers.] Today that call is made upon Massachusetts. That is the reason why I dwell so much on the Slavery question. I said I believed in the power of the North to conquer; but where does she get it. I do not believe in the power of the North to subdue two million and a half of southern men, unless she summons justice, God, and the negro to her side; [Cheers] and in that battle we are sure of this---we are sure to rebuild the Union down to the Gulf. [Renewed cheering.] In that battle, with that watchword, with those allies, the thirteen States and their children will survive---in the light of the world, a nation which has vindicated the sincerity of the Fathers of '87, that they bore children, and not pedlars, to represent them in the nineteenth century. [Repeated cheers.] But without that---without that, I know also, we shall conquer. Sumpter annihilated compromise. Nothing but victory will blot from history that sight of the Stars and Stripes giving place to the Palmetto. But without justice for inspiration, without God for our ally, we shall break the Union asunder; we shall be a confederacy, and so will they. This war means one of two things----Emancipation or Disunion. [Cheers.] Out of the smoke of the conflict there comes that---nothing else. It is impossible there should come anything else. Now, I believe in the future and permanent union of the races that cover this continent from the Pole down to the Gulf. One in race, one in history, one in religion, one in industry, one in thought, we never can be permanently separated. Your path, if you forget the black race, will be over the gulf of Disunion,—years of unsettled, turbulent, Mexican and South American civilization, back through that desert of forty years to the Union which is sure to come.

But I believe in a deeper conscience, I believe in a North more educated than that. I divide you into four sections. The first is the ordinary mass, rushing from mere enthusiasm to

"A battle whose great aim and scope
They little care to know,
Content like men-at-arms to cope,
Each with his fronting foe."

Behind that class stands another, whose only idea in this controversy is sovereignty and the flag. The seaboard, the wealth, the just-converted hunkerism of the country, fill that class. Next to it stands the third element, the people; the cordwainers of Lynn, the farmer of Worcester, the dwellers on the prairie---Iowa and Wisconsin, Ohio and Maine---the broad surface of the people who have no leisure for technicalities, who never studied law, who never had time to read any further into the Constitution than the first two lines---"Establish *Justice* and secure *Liberty*." They have waited long enough; they have eaten dirt enough; they have apologized for bankrupt statesmen enough; they have quieted their consciences enough; they have split logic with their Abolition neighbors long enough; they are tired of trying to find a place between the forty-ninth and forty-eighth corner of a Constitutional hair, [laughter;] and now that they have got their hand on the neck of a rebellious aristocracy, in the name of the PEOPLE, they mean to strangle it. That I believe is the body of the people itself. Side by side with them stands a fourth class---small, but active---the Abolitionists, who thank God that he has let them see his salvation before they die. [Cheers.]

The noise and dust of the conflict may hide the real question at issue. Europe may think, some of us may, that we are fighting for forms and parchments, for sovereignty and a flag. But really, the war is one of opinions: it is Civilization against Barbarism: it is Freedom against Slavery. The cannon shot against Fort Sumpter was the yell of pirates against the DECLARATION OF INDEPENDENCE: the war-cry of the North is its echo. The South, defying Christianity, clutches its victim. The North offers its wealth and blood in glad atonement for the selfishness of seventy years. The result is as sure as the throne of God. I believe in the possibility of Justice, in the certainty of Union. Years hence, when the smoke of this conflict clears away, the world will see under our banner all tongues, all creeds, all races---one brotherhood---and on the banks of the Potomac, the Genius of Liberty, robed in light, four-and-thirty stars for her diadem, broken chains under feet, and an olive-branch in her right hand. [Great applause.]

THE ANGLO-AFRICAN.

PROSPECTUS.

THE WEEKLY ANGLO-AFRICAN, to whose management the undersigned has recently succeeded, was started nearly two years ago, to afford a medium of communication whereby we, the people of color, might become better known to each other and to the community at large. It aimed to hold, as it were, a mirror before our people, wherein, seeing themselves reflected, they might detect and remedy their defects, or discover and improve their advantages.

In this endeavor it has, so far, met the approbation and patronage of our people, which it is our desire that it should continue to merit and attain. Therefore, in order to guard against misrepresentation and disarm prejudice, we take this occasion to assure our patrons and the public generally, that the aim of the paper will be in the future, as it has been in the past, the elevation and progress of the colored race. We shall endeavor to widen its field of vision and to extend its sphere of action, in order to ally our movements and identify our sympathies with the efforts of black men everywhere in their attempts to overthrow slavery, achieve their liberties and effect the complete rehabilitation of the race. To aid in the dissemination of the knowledge and the promotion of the culture necessary to accomplish that end, the Weekly Anglo-African will be devoted to a vigilant scrutiny and careful exposition of the condition and prospects, primarily, of the colored population of the United States, free and enslaved, and incidentally with that of the race abroad.

In the prosecution of this work, it will need, and earnestly solicits, the assistance of every well-wisher of our people, and all information and suggestions of a practical nature will be gratefully received.

It will endeavor to furnish reliable statistics relative to our moral, economic and social attitude: also, biographical sketches of distinguished men of color.

We intend to furnish a reliable "History of the Revolutions of Hayti," written by M. de St. Armand, a distinguished advocate and citizen of Port-au-Prince, translated expressly for the Anglo-African. It is now appearing in our columns. Subscribers can receive it from the commencement, if they so desire.

By the aid of intelligent correspondents, both at home and abroad, we hope to keep our readers advised on matters of local interest, as well as those of general import. We desire that this paper should be a reflex of the mature thought, and a proof of the mental ability of our people; and we hope by the aid of their good wishes and kind coöperation to make it instrumental in the overthrow of Slavery and the establishment of Liberty, Equality, and Fraternity.

Terms.

For one year, payable in advance,	$2 00
" six months, " " "	1 00
" three " " " "	50

Address GEORGE LAWRENCE, Jr.,
Publisher,
No. 48, Beekman St., New York.

WHAT THE WAR IS---NO COMPROMISE

Let it be clearly understood by men of all parties, what the war is—not a war of aggression, or of its own seeking, on the part of the National Government, but purely of self-defence and for SELF-PRESERVATION—a war not to subjugate THE PEOPLE of the South, but to crush a desperate and traitorous SLAVE OLIGARCHY, who despise popular rights, and who have not dared to submit the Constitution of their new Confederacy to the verdict of Southern voters—a war for the illimitable extension and unending existence of a system which turns millions of God's rational creatures into beasts and merchandize, and for the overthrow of all free institutions, and the subversion of the Declaration of Independence, on the part of the conspirators! Surely, all honest, upright, patriotic citizens can have but one opinion about it. Surely, never before could a people, in taking up arms to defend all that is dear to them, and to put down a tyrannical usurpation, more appropriately use the words of the immortal Burns:—

"Who would be a traitor-knave?
Who would fill a coward's grave?
Who so base as be a slave?
Let him turn, and flee!

Lay the proud USURPERS low!
Tyrants fall in every foe!
LIBERTY'S IN EVERY BLOW!
LET US DO OR DIE!"

THE NEW YORK HERALD.

WHOLE NO. 8997. SUNDAY MORNING, APRIL 28, 1861. PRICE THREE CENTS.

THE WAR.

Highly Important News from Washington.

The Capital Garrisoned by Eighteen Thousand Northern Troops.

The City Considered Safe from Attack.

MORE TROOPS POURING IN.

OUR MAP OF THE SEAT OF WAR.

Description of the March of the Soldiers through Maryland.

IMPORTANT NEWS FROM BALTIMORE.

Revival of the Union Feeling Among the Inhabitants.

The Message of Gov. Hicks to the Legislature.

REPORTED NEUTRALITY OF VIRGINIA

The War Movements in the Metropolis,

&c., &c., &c.

IMPORTANT FROM WASHINGTON.

Reliable Report of the Condition of Affairs at the Capital—Eighteen Thousand Northern Troops on the Ground—The Capital Safe, &c.

WASHINGTON, (Via Perrysville and Havre de Grace,) Saturday Morning, April 27, 1861.

I left Washington this morning, shortly after midnight, and hence am able to furnish you the very latest news from the national capital.

Washington is safe! No less than eighteen thousand armed men are at this moment congregated within its limits. The fearful suspense and apprehension under which all its inhabitants, from the President down to the lowliest citizen, labored, was ended by the safe arrival on Thursday afternoon of the Seventh regiment, and of the Fifth and Eighth Massachusetts regiments, and the Rhode Island infantry, under command of Governor Sprague and the Seventy-first of New York, safe and sound, on yesterday afternoon. These, with the Massachusetts and Pennsylvania regiments that preceded them, represent an aggregate of over six thousand volunteers from the North, to which two more regiments from New York—the Twelfth and Sixty-ninth, and the Fifth from Pensylvania, a rifle battalion and artillery from Massachusets, that had arrived at Annapolis junction last evensng, were to be added by rail this morning.

All the above troops had marched from Annapolis to the junction.

Yesterday afternoon the breaks in the road had been all repaired, and a train was sent clear through to Annopolis to bring over the remainder of the Northern troops, landed at that point, but after it had passed the track was again torn up by secession sympathisers, about two miles from the junction, so that on the return in the evening, of the train, it ran off, and a New York officer, whose name I was unable to learn, was seriously injured by the accident.

The track was at once relaid, and there is no doubt that the communication by rail between Washington and Annapolis is perfect to-day. The road hereafter will be strictly guarded, and no more secession outrages are likely to occur.

Most of the Northern troops suffered greatly from want of provisions and water while off and at Annapolis; but their sick list is nevertheless small, and their enthusiasm and devotion unaffected.

The Trip of the Seventh and other Regiments through Maryland.

WASHINGTON, (Via Perrysville and Havre de Grace,) Saturday morning, April 27, 1861.

The five days of isolation from the remainder of the world, which to Washington seemed a month, have ended. The Seventh regiment, reported now to have been cut to pieces; now to be coming up the Potomac in the old Constitution, towed by steam-tugs; now to be marching across the country; and now to be aground in a vessel off Annapolis, reached the railroad station here about noun yesterday. The whistle, not heard for many hours in our isolated position, brought an excited crowd to welcome them to the city and the welcome extended along Pennsylvania avenue to the White House, where they were reviewed by the President and Secretaries Seward and Cameron.

As you will see when I tell you the history of the previous thirty-six hours, it required no little spirit to march that hot, dusty two miles, over heated pavements. One of the most stalwart men in the regiment, a man who weighs one hundred and eighty pounds, and has always been a leader in gymnastics and boating, told me this morning that his feet felt at every step as though knives were running through them. A sergeant's feet were a mass of blisters, and many others were in a bad plight. Yet, with true Seventh regiment pluck, after such a march as regular troops seldom make—a march worse, says one of the band, who served in the Mexican war, and at other times in the regular army—than any forced march within his experience, every man, except three or four who were sunstruck on the previous day, and had not then entirely recovered, was in the ranks. All are well now, and presenting their usual fine appearance.

After dining at Willard's, Brown's and the National Hotels, they marched to the Capitol, and were quartered for the night in the hall of the House of Representatives and adjacent appartments.

This morning they were all at work writing letters upon desks which have never been put to so good a use before, or cleaning their belts and other parts of the uniform. They look none the worse to-day for the touch of sunburn on cheek and nose, and are apparently in the best possible spirits and health.

The history of their journey from Annapolis to Washington, derived from the best sources, is this. The regiment left Philadelphia, as you are doubtless aware on Saturday afternoon, in the steamer Boston, which barely held them. On Sunday their Chaplain performed service on the quarter deck. On Monday morning, before daylight, they reached Annapolis, where they found the Massachusetts troops, under General Butler, aground in the Maryland, and spent the day endeavoring to get them off.

On Monday evening they disembarked, and went into quarters at the Naval School, sleeping on the bare floor, supping and breakfasting from a rather scanty stock of provisions of crackers, ham and raw pork.

Tuesday they spent in their quarters, whence they sent out scouts to investigate the state of the country. It was reported that, at a town meeting held on Monday, in Annapolis, the citizens voted to hang the first man who harrassed the troops on their advance, and the scouts reported rails torn up, but no signs of a disposition to oppose them on the part of the country people.

THE SEAT OF WAR.

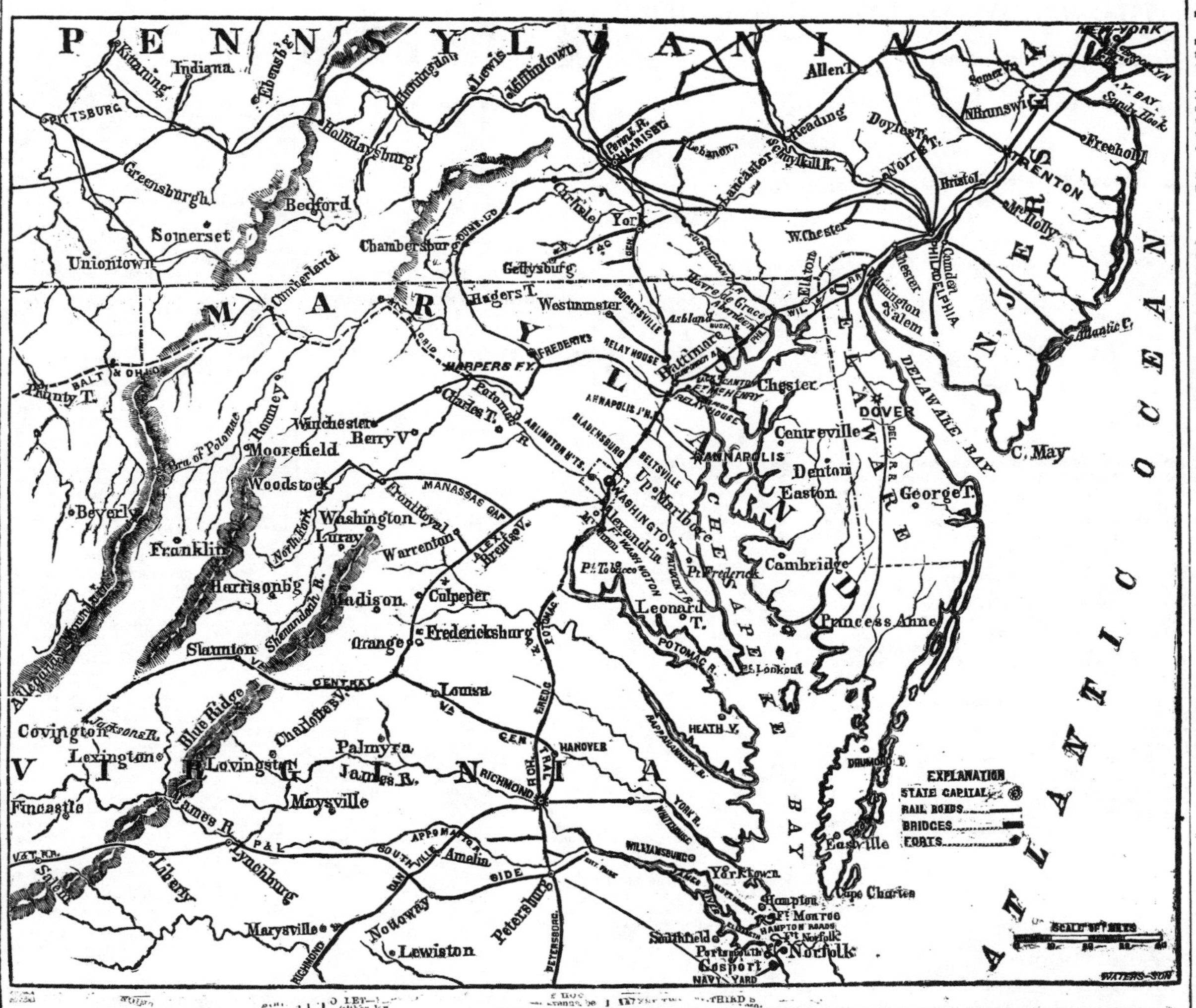

At about eleven or twelve o'clock Tuesday night, lights were reported outside the harbor, and the regiment, which was about going to bed, was mustered to arms. The lights belonged to ships bringing more federal troops, and the regiment got to bed again at one or two o'clock.

At four A. M. Wednesday, Company 2, Captain Clark and Company 6, Captain Nevins, forming the advanc guard, marched to the railway station, where they found an engine and two or three passenger cars, ready to start. This was the work of the Massachusetts regiment, with General Butler, who had found the engine dismantled. "Who knows how to make an engine?" asked General Butler. Six practical machinists stepped from the ranks, but one claimed the privilege of making repairs. "I made that engine," said he, and pointed out his private mark.

The Sixth and Second companies were unable to proceed in the cars more than three or four miles, because the rails were torn up. Then commenced the march. Scouts and skirmishers were thrown out in front and on each side. Rails torn from switches at Annapolis, too short for use and having to be pieced out with joists of timber, replaced the missing rails, excepting where they could be found in the bushes besides the track. The rails and timber were carried on baggage cars, which were pushed by the men. On the front car was a howitzer, with guards and and gunners. All day they marched, mending the track wherever it needed mending, pushing along the cars under a sun which brought the thermometer up to eighty-nine, occasionally hearing shots in the distance, but in no wise molested.

About sunset they reached the remains of the bridge near Millersville, twenty feet high and sixteen feet long, which had been burnt, and the engineer corps of the regiment, assisted by the Massachusetts men, who had done good service throughout the day in repairing the track, rebuilt the bridge and relaid the rails, so that after a heavy shower, which wet the men through, they were enabled to proceed. After nightfall the march continued, through swamps and mist, out of which chill blasts came. Company 6 had been ordered to roll up its overcoats, and had only blankets. Occasional rails had to be replaced. The baggage cars were still to be pushed on by men, who had no sleep for twenty-four hours, who had experienced unusual heat and unusual chilness by turns for twenty hours, and who were wet and exhausted.

About three A. M. twenty feet of the railroad or more—rails, sleepers and all—were found at the bottom of a a high embankment, appearing to have been thrown down there very recently. The advance scouts, indeed, saw the men who did it running away. This section of railroad was hauled up by the howitzer ropes and replaced.

Towards daylight the advance companies halted unti the regiment closed up, when the whole body marched to within two miles of the Annapolis junction, where they awaited the arrival of the cars from Washington.

I have described the march of the advance corps. That of the residue of the regiment was similar. They did not have the labor of laying rails and pushing cars, but marched the twenty-five miles, after a sleepless night and scanty breakfast, under a broiling sun, in a day so hot that a large portion fell out of the ranks.

After the halt the rails of the neighboring fences made sufficient fires. In all cases they were paid for. One secessionist farmer charged $40, and on receiving that sum declared that he had always heard that the Seventh regiment were gentlemen, and that now he knew it.

A few of the men managed to breakfast at farmers' houses, for which they uniformly paid. The country people of Maryland, whom some secessionists, had endeavored to convince that the Northern troops were little better than Indians, and would treat them accordingly, were agreeably disappointed.

Every one expresses surprise that no one in the regiment has been attacked with fever and ague. Every one is full of admiration at the pluck which the kid glove regiment displayed. Only sheer pluck could have carried them through so much fatigue and exposure.

Every one in the regiment; with whom I have talked, praises the Massachusetts regiment, whose services were invaluable.

At about noon to-day the Fifth and Eighth Massachusetts regiments, and the Rhode Island regiment, arrived. They had come by rail to the junction, and had thence marched all night—as they met no cars—about twelve miles, to within six miles of the city. They looked hot and fatigued, but, emulating the Seventh, marched in review before the President at the White House.

The Rhode Island regiment is quartered in the Patent Office.

A number of wagons, containing the families of Virginians, who have been driven out because they refused to take the oath of allegiance to the State imposed by the secessionists, arrived this morning. The other day fifty or more from the same neighborhood came in. Some of the women were forced to leave, if report may be be lieved, in male attire. Such is chivalry.

WASHINGTON, April 27, (Via Perryville, April 27—9 P. M.), 1861.

The train that ran off the track night before last, in consequence of the removal of several ties by the secessionists, consisted only of a locomotive and one car. Col. Vosburgh was the person hurt; but his injury are not of a serious character, as first supposed.

Gallagher, a member of the Providence, R. I., Cadets, broke a leg on the way to Washington.

It is a positive fact that troops from the Confederate States, to the number of about fifteen hundred, have arrived at Norfolk and Richmond. I learn, also, from the very best authority, that the General commanding the rebels in Virginia, at Harper's Ferry, has applied to the Baltimore and Ohio Railroad for means of transportation. But, on the other hand, there is no truth in the report that batteries are being erected on the Virginia side, opposite Washington.

The following recently issued proclamation also shows anything but a haste for war:—

BY THE GOVERNOR OF VIRGINIA.

Whereas, volunteers are simultaneously tendering their services, in person, from all parts of the State, without waiting for orders, as they were required to do by a former proclamation, and are repairing to Richmond, without previous notice, at great expense to the Commonwealth, and before suitable provision has been made for their accommodation, and before their services are required; therefore this proclamation is to require all companies not now in Richmond, and not ordered here or elsewhere, to remain at their homes, holding themselves simply in readiness for service until ordered by competent authority.

Given under my hand, &c., JOHN LETCHER.

Jeff Davis is in Richmond, believed to be on a secret visit to the Governors of North Carolina, Virginia and Tennessee, for purposes of consultation.

A secession flag, waving from a housetop in Alexandria, is distinctly visible from the President's room at the White House.

Our Map of the Immediate Seat of War.

This map covers an area of some five hundred by four hundred miles, embracing the immediate field of warlike operations of which Washington is the centre. The important military points surrounding it, beginning at the South and coming round through Virginia and Maryland, are indicated in the following schedule:—

	Miles.
The great Fortress Monroe, at the outlet of James river and Chesapeake bay, and distant from Washington, down the Potomac and bay	225
From Washington to Richmond, Va., via Potomac and railway from Acquia creek	130
From Washington to Acquia creek, down the Potomac	55
From Washington to Alexandria, below Washington	7
From Washington to Arlington Heights, across the Potomac from President's House, as the bird flies	2½
From Washington to Harper's Ferry, by rail 80, by way of canal, along Potomac river	60
Havre de Grace, down Chesapeake bay and thence via Annapolis Railroad to Washington	85
Do. via Baltimore to Washington	64
From New York to Havre de Grace	169
From Philadelphia to Havre de Grace	62
From New York to Washington, by rail	233
From New York to Washington, by sea and by Chesapeake bay and Potomac river direct, about	530
Via the sea, the bay and Annapolis Railroad, about the same.	

From a glance at the map, it will be seen while the Potomac river forms an important defensive line to Washington against Virginia, the State of Maryland, by land and water, is completely at the mercy of the North.

SERVICES TO-DAY AT CASTLE GARDEN.

Rev. Thomas W. Conway, Chaplain to the New York Zouaves, will preach to the regiment in Castle Garden, this (Sunday) morning, at nine o'clock. The friends of the young men and strangers will be provided with seats.

IMPORTANT FROM MARYLAND.

Meeting of the Legislature—Special Message of Governor Hicks—Important Action of the Senate.

BALTIMORE, April 27, 1861.

GENTLEMEN OF THE SENATE AND HOUSE OF REPRESENTATIVES:—

The extraordinary condition of affairs in Maryland has induced me to exercise the constitutional prerogative vested in the Governor, to summons the Legislature in special session, in the hope that your wisdom may enable you to devise prompt and effective means to restore peace and safety to our State. I shall detail briefly the startling events which have induced me to summon you together, and which have so suddenly placed us in the state of anarchy, confusion and danger, from which I sincerely trust you may be able to extricate us. Believing it to be the design of the administration to pass over our soil troops for the defence of the city of Washington, and fearing that the passage of such troops would excite our people and provoke a collision. I labored earnestly to induce the President to forego his purpose. I waited upon him in person, and urged the importance of my request. I subsequently communicated with him and his Cabinet by special despatches, entreating an abandonment of his designs. To all my requests I could get but the reply that Washington was threatened with attack; that the government had resolved to defend it; that there was no other way of obtaining troops than by passing them over the soil of Maryland, and that the military necessity of the case rendered it impossible for the government to abandon its plans, much as it desired to avoid the dangers of a collision. My correspondence with the authorities at Washington is therewith submitted. The consequences are known to you. On Friday last a detachment of troops from Massachusetts reached Baltimore, and was attacked by an irresponsible mob and several persons on both sides were killed. The Mayor and Police Board gave to the Massachusetts soldiers all the protection they could afford acting with the utmost promptness and bravery. But they were powerless to restrain the mob. Being in Baltimore at the time, I co-operated with the Mayor to the fullest extent of my power in his efforts. The military of the city were ordered out to assist in the preservation of the peace. The railroad companies were requested by the Mayor and myself to transport no more troops to Baltimore city, and they promptly acceeded to our request. Hearing of the attack upon the soldiers the War Department issued orders that no more troops would pass through Baltimore city provided they were allowed to pass outside its limits. Subsequently a detachment of troops were ascertained to be encamped at or near Cockeysville, in Baltimore county. On being informed of this the War Department ordered them back. Before leaving Baltimore, Colonel Huger, who was in command of the United States Arsenal at Pikesville, informed me that he had resigned his commission. Being advised of the probability that the mob might attempt the destruction of this property, and thereby complicated our difficulties with the authorities at Washington. I ordered Colonel Petherbridge to proceed with sufficient force and occupy the premises in the name of the United States government, of which proceeding I immediately notified the War Department. On Sunday morning last I discovered that a detachment of troops, under command of Brigadier General Benjamin F. Butler, had reached Annapolis in a steamer, and had taken possession of the practice-ship Constitution, which during that day they succeeded in getting outside of the harbor, of Annapolis, where she now lies. After getting the ship off, the steamer laid outside the harbor, and was soon joined by another steamer having on board the Seventh regiment, from New York city. Brigadier General Butler addressed me, asking for permission to land his forces. It will be seen from the correspondence herewith submitted, that I refused my consent. The Mayor of Annapolis also protested. But both steamers soon afterwards landed and put off with the troops. Subsequently other large bodies of troops reached here in transports, and were landed. I was notified that the troops were to be marched to Washington. They desired to go without obstruction from our people, but they had orders to go to Washington, and were determined to obey these orders. In furtherance of their designs they took military possession of the Annapolis and Elk Ridge Railroad, in regard to which act I forwarded to Brigadier General Butler the protest, and see the reply herewith submitted. On Wednesday morning the two detachments landed took up the line of march for Washington. The people of Annapolis, though greatly exasperated, acting under counsel of the most prudent citizens, refrained from molesting or obstructing the passage of the troops through the city. Seriously impressed with the condition of affairs and anxious to avoid a repetition of events similar to those which had transpired in Baltimore, I deemed it my duty to make another appeal at Washington. Accordingly I sent a special messenger to Washington, with a despatch to the administration, advising that no more troops be sent through Maryland; that the troops at Annapolis be sent elsewhere, and urging that a truce be offered with a view of a peaceful settlement of existing difficulties by mediation. I suggested that Lord Lyons, the British Minister, be requested to act as mediator between the contending parties. The result of the mission will be seen from the correspondence herewith submitted. These events have satisfied me that the War Department has concluded to make Annapolis the point for landing troops, and has resolved to open and maintain communication between this place and Washington. In the brief time allowed it is impossible for me to go more into detail. The documents accompanying this message places before you all the information possessed by me. I shall promptly communicate such other information as may reach me. Notwithstanding the fact our most learned and inteligent citizens admit the right of the Govrnment to transport its troops across our soil, it is evident that a portion of the people of Maryland are opposed to the exercise of the right. I have done all in my power to protect the citizens of Maryland and to preserve peace within our borders. Lawless occurrences will be repeated I fear unless prompt action be taken by you. It is my duty to advise you of my own convictions of the proper course to be pursued by Maryland in the emergency which is upon us. It of no consequence now to discuss the causes which have induced our troubles. Let us look to our distressing present and to our portentous future. The fate of Maryland, and perhaps of her sister Border Slave States, will undoubtedly be seriously affected by the action of your honorable body. Therefore should every good citizen bend all his energies to the task before us, and therefore should the animosities and bickerings of the past be forgotten and all strike hands in the bold cause of restoring peace to our State and to our country. I honestly and most earnestly entertain the Convention that the only safety of Maryland lies in preserving a neutral position between our brethren of the North and of the South. We have violated no right of either section. We have been loyal to the Union. The unhappy contes, between the two sections has not been commenced or encouraged by us, although we have suffered from it in the part. The impending war has not come by any act or any wish of ours. We have done all we could to avert it. We have hoped that Maryland and other border slave States by their conservative position and love for the Union might have acted as mediators between the extremes of both sections, and thus have prevented the terrible evils of a prolonged civil war. Entertaining these views, I cannot counsel Maryland to take sides against the general government until it shall commit outrages on us which would justify us in resisting its authority. As a consequence I can give no other counsel than that we shall array ourselves for Union and peace, and thus preserve our soil from being polluted with the blood of brethren. Thus, if war must be between the North and South, we may force the contending parties to transfer the field of battle from our soil, so that our lives and property may be secure. It seems to me that, independently of all other considerations, our geographical position forcees us to this, unless we are willing to see our State the theatre of a long and bloody civil war, and the consequent utter destruction os every material interest of our people, to say nothing of the blood of brave men and innocent women and children, which will cry out from our soil for vengeance upon us, if we fail to do all that in us lies to avert the impending calamity. The course I suggest has all the while been the sole groundwork of my policy; and but for the excitement prevailing among our people during the past few days, I believe the object I have kept steadily in view during my administration would have been consummated. If it has failed, I have the full consciousness that throughout the whole of my harrassing and painful incumbency of the gubernatorial chair, I have labored honestly and faithfully for the peace, the safety and the interests of Maryland, and of our common country. This consciousness has fully sustained me in all my troubles, and has enabled me to endure patiently all the cruel, unmerited and heartless attacks that have been made upon my integrity. I have also comfort in the conviction that my policy has been sustained by a large majority of the people, and nothing that has transpired since the recent lamentable occurrences within our State has shaken that conviction. A momentary frantic excitement took the place of reason and good judgment, and men for the time threw aside all prudent thoughts of the future in the burning desire to avenge what they considered wrongs. I submit my suggestions to your wisdom, and I appeal to you not only as devoted citizens of Maryland, but as husbands and fathers, to allow that prudence and christianlike temper, so honorable to all men to guide your counsels, and I implore you not to be swayed by the passions which seem to be so fully aroused in our midst to do what the generations to come after us will ever deplore. In conclusion, gentlemen, I ask your indulgence, if I have omitted to present to you any other matter of interest in connection with the important subject which you are summoned to consider. The short time I have had in which to prepare this communication, and the turmoil and excitement around me, may have caused omissions; but, if so, they will be promptly supplied when indicated by you.

T. HALLIDAY HICKS.

All the Governor's correspondence accompanies the message.

Ten thousand copies were ordered to be printed.

The Senate has just passed a bill to repeal the 19th section of article 12 of the Code of Public General Laws, and enacting the following as a substitute:—

No bank shall issue any note, certificate, or other device, to circulate as currency, of a less denomination than one dollar, under the penalty prescribed in the article on currency.

The act is to take effect from the date of its passage.

The House has referred the bill to a committee, consisting of Messrs. Pitts, Harrison and Briscoe.

On motion of Mr. Wallis the above committee were instructed to consider and report in regard to the legalization of the existing suspension of specie payments by the banks.

The Senate has adopted an address to the people of Maryland, stating that the Legislature will not pass an act of secession; but if they believe the people desire it, they will give them an opportunity of declaring for them their future destiny. The House has not acted on it.

The House has appointed a committee to report an act for the call of a convention of the people, of which Mr Scott, of Baltimore, is chairman.

MOVEMENTS OF TROOPS.

ANNAPOLIS, April 25—Evening.

Troops from Perrysville have been disembarking at this point all of to-day. They come down in steam transports, and the grounds of the Naval Asylum are now filled with them. The steamers Cuyler and Columbia arrived here from New York last night with troops on board. The Seventh New York regiment, and the Massachusetts regiment left here on Wednesday morning for Washington To-day the Seventy-first New York regiment and 4,000 other troops left for Washington.

COMMUNICATION WITH WASHINGTON.

The railroad communication between here and Washington is not yet opened, and no trains have yet been run. It is expected that the troops will have to march to Washington on foot. All the troops here are under marching orders, and expect to start every moment. The depot of the railroad leading to Washington is filled with Massachusetts troops.

NAVAL ACADEMY.

The Naval Academy here has been completely broken up. The midshipmen have been compelled to vacate their quarters for the military. All the midshipmen have been sent on board the Constitution, which will sail for New York to-morrow, (Friday.) On their arrival at New York the midshipmen will be sent to sea.

SCARCITY OF PROVISIONS.

There is great scarcity of provisions here. Flour is $20 per barrel, and other things in proportion. The hotels are "cleaned out," and can give travellers nothing to eat.

MILITARY MOVEMENTS.

General Keim, of the Pennsylvania Volunteers, has just arrived, and is now in consultation with General Butler, chief in command here. The Massachusetts battalion of Flying Artillery, Major Cook commanding, one hundred men, are stationed at the Naval Academy, and will hold that point.

The following corps are to be retained here for the present:—The Massachusetts Light Artillery, the Third battalion Massachusetts Rifles, and Sixth New York regiment.

TROOPS EN ROUTE TO WASHINGTON.

The following regiments have left here for Washington:—

Seventh New York regiment ... men	961
Eighth Massachusetts regiment	780
Fifth Massachusetts regiment	780
Twelfth New York regiment	1,000
Seventy-first New York regiment	1,000
Fourth Pennsylvania regiment	780
Fifth Pennsylvania regiment	780
Tenth Rhode Island regiment	780
First Rhode Island regiment	1,000
Total men—nine regiments	7,880

LATE ARRIVALS.

The Fifth Massachusetts regiment, the Boston Light Artillery and the Third battalion of Rifles have just arrived.

HIGHLY IMPORTANT NEWS FROM PERRYVILLE, MARYLAND.

PERRYVILLE, Md., April 27, 1861.

J. S. Potter, of Massachusetts, just from Washington, and who left last night, bearing important despatches from General Scott, furnishes the following news of interest:—

General Harper, Commander of the forces at Harper's Ferry, had given the assurance that Virginia would allow no attack on the capital from her soil. The authority for the above assertion is confirmed by a gentleman just from Richmond, as being the sentiment expressed by Governor Letcher.

There was a grand flag demonstration in the city of Baltimore last evening, which threatened a serious difficulty between the police, under Marshal Kane, and the Unionists, but the latter kept up the flag. To-day no flags of any description are allowed.

The Eighth regiment of Massachusetts arrived at Washington yesterday at noon.

WASHINGTON, (Via Perrysville and Havre de Grace). Saturday Morning, April 27, 1361.

Baltimore is apparently quiet. But it would be a great mistake to suppose that the secession fever, that seized so suddenly upon a large portion of her people, had altogether died away. It is still raging with all its furor among the dominant elements of her population. The brutal and barbarous demonstration of its virulence on the 19th inst. will surely be repeated, should a like occasion offer. It is true, several Union flags made their appearance in various parts of the city in the course of yesterday, but there can be no doubt as to the nature of the sympathies of those that have always shaped the political destinies of Baltimore. They want her to join the fortunes of the South, and will stretch every nerve and run every risk to accomplish their traitorous purposes. I have had occasion to become familiar with the feelings of the rural population of Maryland during the last week. Like the people of the slaveholding Seates farther South, it has been infused by an incendiary press with frightful conceptions of the intents of the republicans at present to be invasion and devastation of the slave States, and the abolition of slavery by force of arms. Hence the secession pestilence finds easy and numerous victims. I am firmly convinced, and with me many of the most intelligent Union men of the State, that Maryland will link her fortunes with those of Virginia. The result of the deliberations of her Legislature will doubtless prove this belief to be well grounded within the next ten days.

Baltimore is already paying the penalty of her wickedness. Business is at an absolute stand still, money is hourly growing scarce and provisions are steadily advancing in price. The proposition to create a circulating medium, in the shape of municipal notes of a small denomination, is a symptom of an impending collapse. Should the secession folly be realized, Baltimore is doomed to eternal ruin.

There is a general wide spread belief in secession circles that the guns of Fort McHenry will never be used against Baltimore. Many allusions to a recent understanding between its late commander and certain members of the garrison, aiming at its betrayal into the hands of the traitors, have reached my ear. I trust there are no facts to warrant them.

THE REIGN OF TERROR IN VIRGINIA.

CHAMBERSBURG, Pa., April 27, 1861.

A number of residents of Virginia have passed through here *en route* for the North in the last twenty-four hours. Many of them have left everything behind, and are obliged to depend upon the charities of the people to continue their journey.

All who come from as far south as Richmond, could get out of the State only by a special permit from Gov. Letcher. Their statements show that a reign of terror exists in the interior of Virginia. The mob everywhere appropriate to their own use whatever they may fancy; farmers are stopped on the road, their horses taken from under the plea that they are for the defence of the South; graneries are searched, and everything convertable for food for either man or beast carried off.

This has been carried to such an extent that along the northern border of Virginia a reaction is taking place and instructions are being sent from Western Maryland, to the delegates at Annapolis, that if they vote for secession the people will hang them on their return home. The news of the unanimous sentiment of the North, the prompt and decisive action on the part of the State governments in enlisting men has strengthened the Union men of Western Maryland and the border counties of Virginia.

A number have found their way here, and joined the federal army to fight against Jefferson Davis' troops.

The Mayor of Hagerstown was here this morning, and states that the Stars and Stripes were this morning hoisted in that place. There is but a handful of secessionists there, and he says these will be driven out of town.

REPORTED ASKING OF AN ARMISTICE BY SECRETARY CAMERON.

RICHMOND, VA., April 23, 1861.

It is reported here that a despatch has been received

[CONTINUED ON EIGHTH PAGE.]

HARDEE'S TACTICS.

MAY, 1861. MILITARY SUPPLEMENT to the PHILADELPHIA INQUIRER. PRICE SIX CENTS.

INTRODUCTION TO THE STUDY OF HARDEE'S TACTICS.

DESCRIPTION OF ARMS.

RIFLES AND RIFLE SHOOTING.

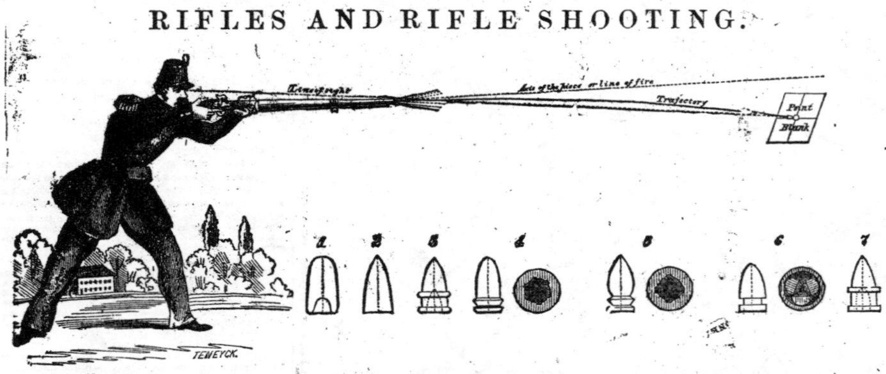

Rifles and Shooting.

We wish to disseminate among the people useful and accurate information on this subject. The great essentials of modern infantry tactics are quick and steady movements, combined with rapid and accurate rifle shooting. A complete revolution has been effected in the army exercises in Europe within ten years, and few of our citizen soldiery seem to be aware of the fact. Every soldier and citizen should now make himself acquainted with field exercises, by shooting at targets at various distances, from 200 up to 1200 yards, while performing rapid evolutions. All our citizen soldiers require considerable severe drilling in the field, so as to become quick and accurate marksmen. Some general and plain instructions on this topic will be useful to all.

The first thing necessary for a soldier is a trusty rifle. It should be easily and conveniently charged, and its fire should be certain and effective. It should be capable of destroying an enemy at the distance of 1200 yards with its bullet, and it should be effective in hand-to hand combat with a sword or bayonet attached to it. A soldier should, therefore, know what his rifle can do, and what he can do with it, at certain distances. If he is ignorant of these, let him be taught before sending him to fight.

The accompanying figure represents a light infantry soldier firing point blank. The trajectory of the projectile or bullet is shown, together with the several forms of bullets used in European armies; also the American picket bullet and army cartridge.

The Bullets and Bores.

Bullet No. 1 is that of the British Enfield rifle. Its form is defective. The front is too blunt, and the cylinder too long without a groove. No. 2 is the American picket bullet, without a chamber [illegible] carries more accurately. No. 3 is the French Delvigne bullet—it is good. The friction is but limited, as it comes only upon the two rings, and the groove is wound with a greased cord. This lubricates the missile, and tends to keep the bore clean. Sections 4 and 5 are views of the famous Swiss bullets, with sections of their rifles. Their accuracy is remarkable. At 800 yards distance they strike targets of four by six feet 66 times out of 100 shots. No. 6 is the most highly approved French bullet, with a section of its hollow chamber, which is a three-sided pyramid. This bullet was adopted after a great many experiments as being the best. No. 7 is a double-ringed bullet with a chamber; it is good for rapid loading. No. 8 is the American cartridge, with a conical ball having three grooves. Formerly, the United States cartridges contained a ball and three buck shot.

The hollow chamber in a bullet is to admit of rapid loading. The powder expands the lead, fills the bore, and prevents windage, therefore they are not required to fit so snugly at the muzzle. A heavy bullet has the greatest range. By making it long-cylindrical in form, greater weight is secured, but such bullets must have rings or grooves in proportion to the length of the cylinder, so as to lessen the friction.

Principles of Shooting.

The general principles of firing, applicable to all rifles and fire-arms, are deduced from the positions of three lines relatively to one another, namely, line of fire, line of sight, and the trajectory. The line of fire is the axis of the barrel prolonged indefinitely; it is the line along which the centre of the ball is directed. The line of sight passes through the bottom of the notch in the rear sight of the rifle and the upper edge of the front sight. To *aim* is to direct the line of sight upon an object, as shown in the figure. To do this correctly, the rear and front sights of the rifle and the point or object aimed at must be in the same straight line. If the rifle has been properly tested, if it is accurate in projecting its missile, a man with a clear eye, a steady hand, and a cool head, will soon make a good marksman by carefully sighting his object, if he loads his rifle carefully.

The trajectory is a curved line described in the atmosphere by the center of the bullet in its flight. The trajectory and the line of fire become more separated as the distance of flight increases. The line of fire is above the trajectory. The bullet, during its flight, is subjected to the action of three forces, viz.: the impulse of the powder, the resistance of the air, and the action of gravity. The air tends to divert it from its right line of flight and shortens its range; gravity gradually brings it to the ground. The more flat the trajectory line, the more dangerous is the shooting. In order, therefore, to obtain accuracy of fire, it is necessary that the soldier should be able to judge of his distance from the object to be struck,

Fig. 8.

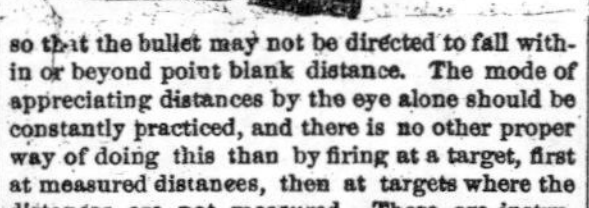

so that the bullet may not be directed to fall within or beyond point blank distance. The mode of appreciating distances by the eye alone should be constantly practiced, and there is no other proper way of doing this than by firing at a target, first at measured distanees, then at targets where the distances are not measured. There are instruments for measuring distances by inspection, such as the "tige" and "stadia," but soldiers have no time to use them in an engagement. They may be sometimes very useful in skirmishing, and each officer should carry one; but the great effort of the soldier should be the cultivation of the sight and judgment for rapid firing with the fewest and most simple devices.

American Army Rifles.

The rifle muskets in our regular army have their grooves with a twist of one turn in six feet, and decreasing in depth from breech to muzzle. This makes the cartridge a little stiff to leave the muzzle, but its shooting is more accurate on this account. The ball has three grooves around the cylindrical part and no wedge or capsule is used inside. The weight of the ball is 730 grains, the charge of powder is 70 grains. The barrel of the rifle-musket is 40 inches long, and entire, with bayonet, 73 85 inches. The army rifle (not the rifled musket) is 33 inches long; with bayonet the weapon is 71·8 inches long. The total weight of the rifle-musket is 9·90 pounds; that of the rifle, with bayonet, 12·98 pounds.

The United States rifles are fired without patches. The rifles and rifle muskets of our army compare favorably with those of the Europeans. They are like those of England; the latter were adopted from American models. No target practice in our army has, however, been ever reported to equal that of the Swiss, English, Austrian or French soldiers.

Breech-Loading Rifles.

A Board met at West Point, four years ago, to test breech-loading rifles. They experimented with quite a number, subjecting them to target firing. A Sharpe's rifle was fired 18 times in 50 seconds; but Colonel BURNSIDE's was considered the best. A second Board met in 1858, and again decided in favor of BURNSIDE's, but did not recommend it. COLT's revolving rifle is like his pistol in the principle of its construction. It has seven grooves of uniform depth and increasing twist. There are very few breech-loading rifles in the army; they are not so accurate as those which load at the muzzle, and they are more complex in construction.

Schools for Rifle Practice.

Shooting schools have been established in all the European armies, and at West Point the cadets are also regularly instructed in firing at the target, but only at short distances. In England the shooting school is at Hythe. The term in it occupies two and a half months. Detachments of the regiments succeed each other there during the entire year. In France the term of practice occupies four months. Practical instruction is given to the soldiers in estimating distances by the eye, and in rapid accurate firing. Such an establishment should be commenced in New York at once.

Old Firing.

It has been said that "the battles of the American Revolution were gained by the rifle." British soldiers were not then instructed to shoot at a mark; but those days are all past forever. At the battle of Vittoria, in Spain, 800 balls were fired for every man that was killed. At the battle of Cherubusco, in Mexico, 125 American balls were fired for every Mexican that was killed; this was better firing then that of the enemy, who fired 800 balls for every man killed on our side. This, however, will not do now. In England a party of 30 skirmishers can destroy a battery of light artillery, at 800 yards distance, in one minute.

New Military Tactics.

In the olden times, the solid columns and the desperate charge generally won the battle; but light, active troops, spread over an extended field with good rifles, would soon slaughter the best drilled columns in the world, armed with smooth-bored muskets and handled in the old-fashioned pasteboard style. Modern tactics require a more extended field for manœuvering, hence greater care is necessary in handling the soldiers, and more intelligence on the part of the soldier is necessary for taking up proper positions, to save themselves and harass the enemy to the greatest advantage. Formerly, the position of an army could be approached within 300 yards, without experiencing injury from infantry fire. With the modern rifles, they could not approach nearer than 1000 yards. Cavalry must now keep at a respectable distance until they can dash in under cover of the smoke, or be preceded with riflemen and artillery.

INTRODUCTORY ARTICLE.

GENERAL INFORMATION.

In an emergency like the present, everybody is inquiring for the best book on *Infantry Tactics*, and the relative merits of COOPER, SCOTT, HARDEE GILHAM, and others, are discussed by thousands who are putting them to practical use. Only a few words, after careful examination, are needed to settle their claims. COOPER was the manual many years ago. SCOTT's improved manual, in three volumes, entirely superseded this, and was appointed by law as the regulation drill for the army.

General SCOTT's excellent work was, almost without alteration, translated from the French, from whom all the world has drawn, and is constantly drawing, the most improved military instruction. In arrangement and exactness, it exhibits General SCOTT's characteristic care and precision.

Finding, however, that French invention and ingenuity had made further important improvements, the United States Government appointed Colonel HARDEE to superintend the translation of the new French system for Light Infantry, and it was at once adopted by the Secretary of War for all infantry regiments of the United States army. The movements are simplified and rendered much more rapid, and the system, as a whole, is far preferable to SCOTT's. There is a complete drill for infantry of the line as well as light infantry.

Now, it is a disagreeable fact that Col HARDEE, who *translated* the book, and has no other merit in the matter, and JEFFERSON DAVIS, who, as the Secretary of War, ordered its use, are both in the ranks of the enemy. But to denounce its use, as one of our cotemporaries has done, on that account, is like refusing to study EUCLID's geometry or to apply the principle of the lever, because EUCLID and ARCHIMEDES were heathen.

The simplest remedy, if one be needed at all, is to let Secretary CAMERON issue a new order, and change the disagreeable name to "Authorized Tactics for the United States Infantry." Meanwhile, let no one care for the name, but *use the best for its own sake*, and thank, not the translator, but the French, for their excellent instruction.

The Manual of Arms in SCOTT's Tactics is no suited to the improved rifle musket, while HARDEE's is. The movements in SCOTT are too slow, and require many halts in formation, while HARDEE makes many manœuvres in double quick time, and without halting between two.

HARDEE is *the* book for the use of the troops now drilling. By all means let the Government and State authorities look to this, and not put us fifty years back in this matter.

ORGANIZATION OF A COMPANY.

In an organization, the smallest number complete in itself, is the *company*, which varies in number from 50 to 100 rank and file.

A *captain*, two or more *lieutenants*, from four to six *sergeants*, and as many *corporals*, are attached to each company. The captain and lieutenants are the *officers*, and the sergeants and corporals are the *non-commissioned officers* of the company.

The captain is responsible for the instruction discipline, general efficiency, and moral tone of the company.

Posts of Field Officers and Regimental Staff.

The field officers, colonel, lieutenant-colonel, and major, are supposed to be mounted, and on active service shall be on horseback. The adjutant, when the battalion is manœuvring, will be on foot.

The colonel will take post thirty paces in rear of the file closers, and opposite the centre of the battalion. This distance will be reduced whenever there is a reduction in the front of the battalion.

The lieutenant colonel and the major will be opposite the centres of the right and left wings respectively, and twelve paces in rear of the file closers.

The adjutant and sergeant major will be opposite the right and left of the battalion, respectively, and eight paces in rear of the file closers.

The adjutant and sergeant-major will aid the liutenant-colonel and major, respectively, in the manœuvres.

The colonel, if absent, will be replaced by the lieutenant colonel, and the latter by the major. If all the field officers be absent, the senior captain will command the battalion; but if either be present, he will not call the senior captain to act as field officer, except in case of evident necessity.

The quartermaster, surgeon, and other staff officers, in one rank, on the left of the colonel, and three paces in his rear.

The quartermaster sergeant, on a line with the front rank of the field music, and two pass on the right.

Posts of Field Music and Band.

The buglers will be drawn up in four ranks, and posted twelve paces in rear of the file closers, the left opposite the centre of the left centre company. The senior principal musician will be two paces in front of the field music, and the other two paces in the rear.

The regimental band, if there be one, will be drawn up in two or four ranks, according to its numbers, and posted five paces in rear of the field music, having one of the principal musicians at its head.

Color-Guard.

In each battalion the color-guard will be composed of eight corporals, and posted on the left of the right centre company, of which company, for the time being, the guard will make a part.

The front rank will be composed of a sergeant, to be selected by the colonel, who will be called for the time *color-bearer*, with the two ranking corporals, respectively, on his right and left; the rear rank will be composed of the three corporals next in rank; and the three remaining corporals will be posted in their rear, and on the line of file closers. The left guide of the color-company, when these three last named corporals are in the rank of file closers, will be immediately on their left.

In battalions with less than five companies present, there will be no color-guard, and no display of colors, except it may be at reviews.

The corporals for the color-guard will be selected from those most distinguished for regularity and precision, as well in their positions under arms as in their marching. The latter advantage, and a just carriage of the person, are to be more particularly sought for in the selection of the color-bearer.

General Guides.

There will be two *general* guides in each battalion, selected, for the time, by the colonel, from among the sergeants (other than first sergeants) the most distinguished for carriage under arms, and accuracy in marching.

These sergeants will be respectively denominated, in the manœuvres, *right general guide*, and *left general guide*, and be posted in the line of file closers; the first in rear of the right, and the second in rear of the left flank of the battalion.

The lieutenants assist the captain in the maintenance of discipline, and in the instruction.

The company is divided into two equal parts, which are designated as the first and second *platoon*, counting from the right; and each platoon is, in like manner, divided into two *sections*.

HARDEE'S RIFLE AND L[illegible]T INFANTRY TACTICS.

SCHOOL FOR THE SOLDIER, SCHOOL FOR THE COMPANY, AND INSTRUCTIONS for SKIRMISHES COMPLETE.

Prepared Under the Direction of the War Department.

PUBLISHED BY PERMISSION OF MESSRS. J. B. LIPPINCOTT & CO.

TITLE FIRST.

ARTICLE FIRST.

Formation of a Regiment in order of battle or in line.

1. A REGIMENT is composed of ten companies, which will habitually be posted from right to left, in the following order: first, sixth, fourth, ninth, third, eighth, fifth, tenth, seventh, second, according to the rank of captains.

2. With a less number of companies the same principle will be observed, viz: the first captain will command the right company, the second captain the left company, the third captain the right centre company, and so on.

3. The companies thus posted will be designated from right to left, *first* company, *second* company, &c. This designation will be observed in the manœuvres.

4. The first two companies on the right, whatever their denomination, will form the *first division*; the next two companies the *second division*; and so on, to the left.

5. Each company will be divided into two equal parts, which will be designated as the first and second platoon, counting from the right; and each platoon, in like manner, will be subdivided into two sections.

6. In all exercises and manœuvres, every regiment, or part of a regiment, composed of two or [illegible] companies, will be designated a battalion. [illegible] be posted on the left [illegible] the right centre battalion company. That company, and all on its right, will be denominated the *right wing* of the battalion; the remaining companies the *left wing*.

8. The formation of a regiment is in two ranks; and each company will be formed into two ranks, in the following manner: the corporals will be posted in the front rank, and on the right and left of platoons, according to height; the tallest corporal and the tallest man will form the first file, the next two tallest men will form the second file, and so on to the last file, which will be composed of the shortest corporal and the shortest man.

9. The odd and even files, numbered as one, two, in the company, from right to left, will form groups of four men, who will be designated *comrades in battle*.

10. The distance from one rank to another will be thirteen inches, measured from the breasts of the rear rank men to the backs or knapsacks of the front rank men.

11. For manœuvring the companies of a battalion will always be equalized, by transferring men from the strongest to the weakest companies.

Posts of Company Officers, Sergeants and Corporals.

12. The company officers and sergeants are nine in number, and will be posted in the following manner:

13. The *captain* on the right of the company, touching with the left elbow.

14. The *first sergeant* in the rear rank, touching with the left elbow, and covering the captain. In the manœuvres he will be denominated *covering sergeant*, or *right guide* of the company.

15. The remaining officers and sergeants will be posted as file closers, and two paces behind the rear rank.

16. The *first lieutenant*, opposite the centre of the fourth section.

17. The *second lieutenant*, opposite the centre of the first platoon.

18. The *third lieutenant*, opposite the centre of the second platoon.

19. The *second sergeant*, opposite the second file from the left of the company. In the manœuvres he will be designated *left guide* of the company.

20. The *third sergeant*, opposite the second file from the right of the second platoon.

21. The *fourth sergeant*, opposite the second file from the left of the first platoon.

22. The *fifth sergeant*, opposite the second file from the right of the first platoon.

23. In the left or tenth company of the battalion, the second sergeant will be posted in the front rank, and on the left of the battalion.

24. The corporals will be posted in the front rank, as prescribed No. 8.

25. Absent officers and sergeants will be replaced—officers by sergeants, and sergeants by corporals. The colonel may detach a first lieutenant from one company to command another, of which both the captain and first lieutenant are absent; but this authority will give no right to a lieutenant to demand to be so detached.

NOTE.—Paragraphs 26 to 41 inclusive, relate merely to posts of Field Officers and regimental staff, and will be found fully set out in the introduction.

ARTICLE SECOND.

Instruction of the Battalion.

42. Every commanding officer is responsible for the instruction of his command. He will assemble the officers together for theoretical and practical instruction as often as he may judge necessary, and when unable to attend to this duty in person, it will be discharged by the officer next in rank.

43. Captains will be held responsible for the theoretical and practical instruction of their non-commissioned officers, and the adjutant for the instruction of the non-commissioned staff. To this end, they will require these tactics to be studied and recited lesson by lesson; and when instruction is given on the ground, each non-commissioned officer, as he explains a movement, should be required to put it into practical operation.

44. The non-commissioned officers should also be practised in giving commands. Each command, in a lesson, at the theoretical instruction, should first be given by the instructor, and then repeated, in succession, by the non-commissioned officers, so that, while they become habituated to the commands, uniformity may be established in the manner of giving them.

45. In the school of the soldier, the company officers will be the instructors of the squads; but if there be not a sufficient number of company officers present, intelligent sergeants may be substituted; and two or three squads, under sergeant instructors, be superintended, at the same time, by an officer.

46. In the school of the company, the lieutenant colonel and the major, under the colonel, will be the principal instructors, substituting frequently the captain of the company, and sometimes one of the lieutenants; the substitute, as far as practicable, being superintended by one of the principals.

47. In the school of the battalion, the brigadier general may constitute himself the principal instructor; frequently substituting the colonel of the battalion, sometimes the lieutenant colonel or major, and twice or thrice, in the same course of instruction, each of the three senior captains. In this school, also, the substitute will always, if practicable, be superintended by the brigadier general or the colonel, or (in case of a captain being the instructor) by the lieutenant colonel or major.

48. Individual instruction being the basis of the instruction of companies, on which that of the regiment depends, and the first principals having the greatest influence upon this individual instruction, classes of recruits should be watched with the greatest care.

49. Instructors will explain, in a few clear and precise words, the movement to be executed; and not to overburden the memory of the men, they will always use the same terms to explain the same principles.

50. They should often join example to precept, should keep up the attention of the men by an animated tone, and pass rapidly from one movement to another, as soon as that which they command has been executed in a satisfactory manner.

51. The sabre bayonet should only be fixed when required to be used, either for attack or defence; the exercises and manœuvres will be executed without the bayonet.

52. In the movements which require the bayonet to be fixed, the chief of the battalion will cause the signal *to fix bayonet*, to be sounded; at this signal the men will fix bayonets without command, and immediately replace their pieces in the position they were before the signal.

Instruction of Officers.

53. The instruction of officers can be perfected only by joining theory to practice. The colonel will often practise them in marching and in estimating distances, and he will carefully endeavor to cause them to take steps equal in length and swiftness. They will also be exercised in the double quick step.

54. The instruction of officers will include all the Titles in this system of drill, and such regulations as prescribe their duties in peace and war.

55. Every officer will make himself perfectly acquainted with the bugle signals: and should, by practice, be enabled, if necessary, to sound them. This knowledge, so necessary in general instruction, becomes of vital importance on actual service in the field.

Instruction of Sergeants.

56. As the discipline and efficiency of a company materially depend on the conduct and character of its sergeants, they should be selected with care, and properly instructed in all the duties appertaining to their rank.

57. Their theoretical instruction should include the School of the Soldier, the School of the Company, and the Drill for Skirmishers. They should likewise know all the details of service, and the regulations prescribing their duties in garrison and in campaign.

58. The captain selects from the corporals in his company those whom he judges fit to be admitted to the theoretical instruction of the sergeants.

Instruction of Corporals.

59. Their theoretical instruction should include the School of the Soldier, and such regulations as prescribe their duties in garrison and in campaign.

60. The captain selects from his company a few privates, who may be admitted to the theoretical instruction of the corporals.

61. As the instruction of sergeants and corporals is intended principally to qualify them for the instruction of the privates, they should be taught not only to execute, but to explain intelligibly every thing they may be required to teach.

Commands.

There are three kinds.

62. The command of *caution*, which is *attention*.

63. The *preparatory command*, which indicates the movement which is to be executed.

64. The command of *execution*, such as *march* or *halt*, or, in the manual of arms, the part of command which causes an execution.

65. The tone of command should be animated, distinct, and of a loudness proportioned to the number of men under instruction.

66. The command *attention* is pronounced at the top of the voice, dwelling on the last syllable.

67. The command of *execution* will be pronounced in a tone firm and brief.

68. The commands of caution and the preparatory commands are herein distinguished by *italics*, those of execution by CAPITALS.

69. Those preparatory commands which, from their length, are difficult to be pronounced at once, must be divided into two or three parts, with an ascending progression in the tone of command, but always in such a manner that the tone of execution may be more energetic and elevated; the divisions are indicated by a hyphen. The parts of commands which are placed in a parenthesis, are not pronounced.

TITLE SECOND.

SCHOOL OF THE SOLDIER.

General Rules and division of the School of the Soldier.

70. The object of this school being the individual and progressive instruction of the recruits, the instructor never requires a movement to be executed until he has given an exact explanation of it; and he executes, himself, the movement which he commands, so as to join example to precept. He accustoms the recruit to take, by himself, the position which is explained—teaches him to rectify it only when required by his want of intelligence—and sees that all the movements are performed without precipitation.

71. Each movement should be understood before passing to another. After they have been properly executed in the order laid down in each lesson, the instructor no longer confines himself to that order; on the contrary, he should change it, that he may judge of the intelligence of the men.

72. The instructor allows the men to rest at the end of each part of the lessons, and oftener, if he thinks proper, especially at the commencement; for this purpose he commands REST.

73. At the command REST, the soldier is no longer required to preserve immobility, or to remain in his place. If the instructor wishes merely to relieve the attention of the recruit, he commands, in *place*—REST; the soldier is then not required to preserve his immobility, but he always keeps one of his feet in its place.

74. When the instructor wishes to commence the instruction, he commands—ATTENTION; at this command the soldier takes his position, remains motionless, and fixes his attention.

75. The *School of the Soldier* will be divided into three parts; the first, comprehending what ought to be taught to recruits without arms; the second, the manual of arms, the loadings and firings; the third, the principles of alignment, the march by the front, the different steps, the march by the flank, the principles of wheeling, and those of change of direction; also, long marches in double quick time and the run.

76. Each part will be divided into lessons, as follows:—

PART FIRST.

Lesson 1. Position of the soldier without arms: Eyes right, left and front.
Lesson 2. Facings.
Lesson 3 Principles of the direct step in common and quick time.
Lesson 4. Principles of the direct step in double quick time and the run.

PART SECOND.

Lesson 1. Principles of shouldered arms.
Lesson 2. Manual of arms.
Lesson. 3. To load in four times, and [illegible]
Lesson 4 Firings, direct, oblique, by file, and by rank.
Lesson 5 To fire and load, kneeling and lying
Lesson 6 Bayonet exercise.

PART THIRD.

Lesson 1. Union of eight or twelve men for instruction in the principles of alignment
Lesson 2 The direct march, the oblique march, and the different steps.
Lesson 3. The march by the flank.
Lesson 4. Principles of wheeling and change of direction.
Lesson 5. Long marches in double quick time, and the run, with arms and knapsacks.

PART FIRST.

77. This will be taught, if practicable, to one recruit at a time; but three or four may be united, when the number be great, compared with that of the instructors. In this case, the recruits will be placed in a single rank, at one pace from each other. In this part, the recruits will be without arms.

LESSON I.

Position of the Soldier.

78. Heels on the same line, as near each other as the conformation of the man will permit;
The feet turned out equally, and forming with each other something less than a right angle;
The knees straight without stiffness;
The body erect on the hips, inclining a little forward;
The shoulders square and falling equally;
The arms hanging naturally;
The elbows near the body;
The palm of the hand turned a little to the front, the little finger behind the seam of the pantaloons;
The head erect and square to the front, without constraint;
The chin near the stock, without covering it;
The eyes fixed straight to the front, and striking the ground about the distance of fifteen paces.

Remarks on the position of the Soldier.

Heels on the same line;

79. Because, if one were in rear of the other, the shoulder on that side would be thrown back, or the position of the soldier would be constrained.

Heels more or less closed;

Because, men who are knock-kneed, or who have legs with large calves, without constraint, make their heels touch while standing.

The feet equally turned out, and not forming too large an angle;

Because, if one foot were turned out more than the other, a shoulder would be deranged, and if both feet be too much turned out, it would not be practicable to incline the upper part of the body forward without rendering the whole position unsteady.

Knees extended without stiffness;

Because, if stiffened, constraint and fatigue would be unavoidable.

The body erect on the hips;

Because it gives equilibrium to the position. The instructor will observe that many recruits have the bad habit of dropping a shoulder, of drawing in a side, or of advancing a hip, particularly the right, when under arms. These are defects he will labor to correct.

The upper part of the body inclining forward;

Because, commonly, recruits are disposed to do the reverse, to project the belly, and to throw back the shoulders, when they wish to hold themselves erect, from which result great inconveniences in marching. The habit of inclining forward the upper part of the body is so important to contract, that the instructor must enforce it at the beginning, particularly with recruits who have naturally the opposite habit.

Shoulders square;

Because if the shoulders be advanced beyond the line of the breast, and the back arched (the defect called *round shouldered*, not uncommon among recruits), the man cannot align himself, nor use his piece with address. It is important, then, to correct this defect, and necessary to that end that the coat should set easy about the shoulders and arm-pits; but in correcting this defect, the instructor will take care that the shoulders be not thrown too much to the rear, which would cause the belly to project, and the small of the back to be curved.

The arms hanging naturally, elbows near the body, the palm of the hand a little turned to the front, the little finger behind the seam of the pantaloons:

Because, these positions are equally important to the *shoulder arms*, and to prevent the man from occupying more space in a rank than is necessary to a free use of the piece; they have, moreover, the advantage of keeping in the shoulders.

The face straight to the front, and without constraint;

Because, if there be stiffness in the latter position, it would communicate itself to the whole of the upper part of the body, embarrass its movements, and give pain and fatigue.

Eyes direct to the front;

Because, this is the surest means of maintaining the shoulders in line—an essential object, to be insisted on and attained.

80. The instructor having given the recruit the position of the soldier without arms, will now teach him the turning of the head and eyes. He will command:—

1. *Eyes*—RIGHT. 2. FRONT.

81. At the word *right*, the recruit will turn the head gently, so as to bring the inner corner of the left eye in a line with the buttons of the coat, the eyes fixed on the line of the eyes of the men in, o supposed to be in, the same rank.

82. At the second command, the head will resume the direct or habitual position.

83. The movement of *Eyes*—LEFT will be executed by inverse means.

84. The instructor will take particular care that the movement of the head does not derange the squareness of the shoulders, which will happen if the movement of the former be too sudden.

85. When the instructor shall wish the recruit to pass from the state of attention to that of ease, he will command:

REST.

86. To cause a resumption of the habitual position, the instructor will command:

1. *Attention*. 2. SQUAD.

87. At the first word, the recruit will fix his attention; at the second, he will resume the prescribed position and steadiness.

LESSON II.

Facings.

88. Facing to the right and left will be executed in one *time*, or pause. The instructor will command:

1. *Squad*. 2 *Right* (*or left*)—FACE.

89. At the second command, raise the right foot slightly, turn on the left heel, raising the toes a little, and then replace the right heel by the side of the left, and on the same line.

90. The full face to the rear (or front) will be executed in two *times*, or pauses. The instructor will command:

1. *Squad*. 2. ABOUT—FACE.

91 (*First time*.) At the word *about*, the recruit will turn on the left heel, bring the left toe to the front, carry the right foot to the rear, the hollow opposite to, and full three inches from, the left heel, the feet square to each other.

92 (*Second time*.) At the word *face*, the recruit will turn on both heels, raise the toes a little, extend the hams, face to the rear, bringing, at the same time, the right heel by the side of the left.

93. The instructor will take care that these motions do not derange the position of the body.

LESSON III.

Principles of the Direct Step.

94. The length of the direct step, or pace, in common time, will be twenty-eight inches, reckoning from heel to heel, and in swiftness, at the rate of ninety in a minute.

95. The instructor, seeing the recruit confirmed in his position, will explain to him the principle and mechanism of this step—placing himself six or seven paces from, and facing to, the recruit. He will himself execute slowly the step in the way of illustration, and then command:

1. *Squad, forward.* 2. *Common time.*
3. MARCH.

96. At the first command, the recruit will throw the weight of the body on the right leg, without bending the left knee.

97. At the third command, he will smartly, but without a jerk, carry straight forward the left foot twenty-eight inches from the right, the sole near the ground, the ham extended, the toe a little depressed, and, as also the knee, slightly turned out; he will, at the same time, throw the weight of the body forward, and plant the left foot, without shock, precisely at the distance where it finds itself from the right when the weight of the body is brought forward, the whole of which will now rest on the advanced foot. The recruit will next, in like manner, advance the right foot and plant it as above, the heel twenty-eight inches from the heel of the left foot, and thus continue to march without crossing the legs, or striking the one against the other, without turning the shoulders, and preserving always the face direct to the front.

98. When the instructor shall wish to arrest the march, he will command:

1. *Squad.* 2. HALT.

99. At the second command, which will be given at the instant when either foot is coming to the ground, the foot in the rear will be brought up, and planted by the side of the other, without shock.

100. The instructor will indicate, from time to time, to the recruit, the cadence of the step by giving the command *one* at the instant of raising a foot, and *two* at the instant it ought to be planted, observing the cadence of ninety steps in a minute. This method will contribute greatly to impress upon the mind the two motions into which the step is naturally divided.

101. Common time will be employed only in the first and second parts of the School of the Soldier. As soon as the recruit has acquired steadiness, has become established in the principles of shouldered arms, and in the mechanism, length and swiftness of the step in common time, he will be practiced only in quick time, the double quick time and the run.

102. The principles of the step in quick time are the same as for common time, but its swiftness is at the rate of one hundred and ten steps per minute.

103. The instructor wishing the squad to march in quick time, will command:

1. *Squad, forward.* 2. MARCH.

LESSON IV.

Principles of the Double Quick Step.

104. The length of the double quick step is thirty-three inches, and its swiftness at the rate of one hundred and sixty five steps per minute.

105. The instructor, wishing to teach the recruits the principles and mechanism of the double quick step, will command:

1. *Double quick step.* 2. MARCH.

106. At the first command, the recruit will raise his hands to a level with his hips, the hands closed, the nails towards the body, the elbows to the rear.

107. At the second command he will raise to the front his left leg bent, in order to give to the knee the greatest elevation, the part of the leg between the knee and the instep vertical, the toe depressed; he will then replace his foot in its former position; with the right leg he will execute what has just been prescribed for the left, and the alternate movement of the legs will be continued until the command:

1. *Squad.* 2. HALT.

108. At the second command, the recruit will bring the foot which is raised by the side of the other, and dropping at the same time his hands by his side, will resume the position of the soldier without arms.

109. The instructor, placing himself seven or eight paces from, and facing the recruit, will indicate the cadence by the commands, *one* and *two*, given alternately at the instant each foot should be brought to the ground, which at first will be in common time, but its rapidity will be gradually augmented.

110. The recruit being sufficiently established in the principles of this step, the instructor will command:

1. *Squad, forward.* 2. *Double quick.*
3. MARCH.

111. At the first command, the recruit will throw the weight of his body on the right leg.

112. At the second command, he will place his arms as indicated No. 37.

113. At the third command, he will carry forward the left foot, the leg slightly bent, the kn[illegible] somewhat raised—will plant his l[illegible] foot, [illegible] thirty-three inches from the ri[illegible], and with the right foot will then execute what has just been prescribed for the left. This alternate movement of the legs will take place by throwing the weight of the body on the foot that is planted, and by allowing a natural oscillatory motion to the arms.

114. The double-quick step may be executed with different degrees of swiftness. Under urgent circumstances the cadence of this step may be increased to one hundred and eighty per minute. At this rate a distance of four thousand yards would be passed over in about twenty-five minutes.

115. The recruits will be exercised also in running.

116. The principles are the same as for the double quick step, the only difference consisting in a greater degree of swiftness.

117. It is recommended in marching at double quick time, or the run, that the men should breathe as much as possible through the nose, keeping the mouth closed. Experience has proved that, by conforming to this principle, a man can pass over a much longer distance, and with less fatigue.

PART SECOND.

GENERAL RULES.

118. The instructor will not pass the men to this second part until they shall be well established in the position of the body, and in the manner of marching at the different steps.

119. He will then unite four men, whom he will place in the same rank, elbow to elbow, and instruct them in the position of shouldered arms, as follows:

LESSON I.

Principles of Shouldered Arms.

120. The recruit being placed as explained in the first lesson of the first part, the instructor will cause him to bend the right arm slightly, and place the piece in it, in the following manner:—

121. The piece in the right hand—the barrel nearly vertical and resting in the hollow of the shoulder—the guard to the front, the arm hanging nearly at its full length near the body; the thumb and fore-finger embracing the guard, the remaining fingers closed together, and grasping the swell of the stock just under the cock, which rests on the little finger.

122. Recruits are frequently seen with natural defects in the conformation of the shoulders, breast and hips. These the instructor will labor to correct in the lessons without arms, and afterwards, by steady endeavors, so that the appearance of the pieces, in the same line, may be uniform, and this without constraint to the men in their positions. much in the beginning, but labor by degrees to render this position so natural and easy that they

123. The instructor will have occasion to remark that recruits, on first bearing arms, are liable to derange their position by lowering the right shoulder and the right hand, or by sinking the hip and spreading out the elbows.

124. He will be careful to correct all these faults by continually rectifying the position; he will sometimes take away the piece to replace it the better; he will avoid fatiguing the recruits too may remain in it a long time without fatigue.

125. Finally, the instructor will take great care that the piece, at a shoulder, be not carried too high nor too low: if too high, the right elbow would spread out, the soldier would occupy too much space in his rank, and the piece be made to waver; if too low, the files would be too much closed, the soldier would not have the necessary space to handle his piece with facility, the right arm would become too much fatigued, and would draw down the shoulder.

126. The instructor, before passing to the second lesson, will cause to be repeated the movements of *eyes right, left,* and *front,* and the *facings.*

LESSON II.

Manual of Arms.

127. The manual of arms will be taught to four men, placed, at first, in one rank, elbow to elbow, and afterwards in two ranks.

128. Each command will be executed in one *time* (or pause), but this time will be divided into motions, the better to make known the mechanism.

129. The rate (or swiftness) of each motion, in the manual of arms, with the exceptions herein indicated, is fixed at the ninetieth part of a minute; but, in order not to fatigue the attention, the instructor will, at first, look more particularly to the execution of the motions, without requiring a nice observance of the cadence, to which he will bring the recruits progressively, and after they shall have become a little familiarized with the handling of the piece.

130. As the motions relative to the cartridge, to the rammer, and to the fixing and unfixing of the bayonet, cannot be executed at the rate prescribed, nor even with a uniform swiftness, they will not be subjected to that cadence. The instructor will, however, labor to cause these motions to be executed with promptness, and above all, with regularity.

131. The last syllable of the command will decide the brisk execution of the first motion of each time (or pause). The commands *two, three,* and *four,* will decide the brisk execution of the other motions. As soon as the recruits shall well comprehend the positions of the several motions of a time, they will be taught to execute the time without resting on its different motions; the mechanism of the time will nevertheless be observed, as well to give a perfect use of the piece, as to avoid the sinking of, or slurring over, either of the motions.

132. The manual of arms will be taught in the following progression: The instructor will command:—

Support—ARMS.
One time and three motions.

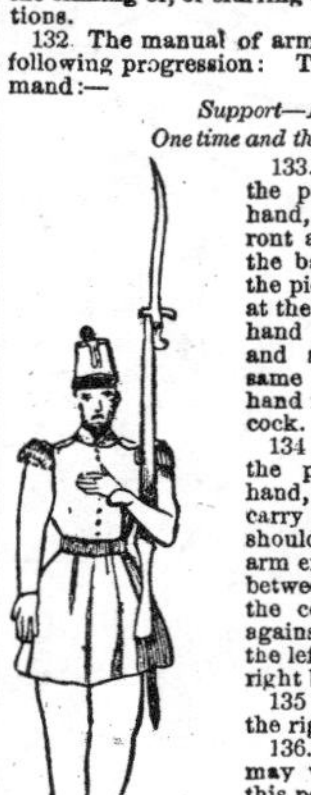

133. (*First motion.*) Bring the piece, with the right hand, perpendicularly to the front and between the eyes, the barrel to the rear; seize the piece with the left hand at the lower band, raise this hand as high as the chin, and seize the piece at the same time with the right hand four inches below the cock.

134. (*Second motion.*) Turn the piece with the right hand, the barrel to the front; carry the piece to the left shoulder, and pass the fore-arm extended on the breast between the right hand and the cock; support the cock against the left fore-arm, the left hand resting on the right breast.

135. (*Third motion.*) Drop the right hand by the side.

136. When the instructor may wish to give repose in this position, he will command:—

REST.

137. At this command, the recruits will bring up smartly the right hand to the handle of the piece (small of the stock), when they will not be required to preserve silence, or steadiness of position.

138. When the instructor may wish the recruits to pass from this position to that of silence and steadiness, he will command:—

1. *Attention.* 2. SQUAD.

139. At the second word, the recruits will resume the position of the third motion of *support arms.*

Shoulder—ARMS.
One time and three motions.

140. (*First motion.*) Grasp the piece with the right hand under and against the left fore-arm; seize it with the left hand at the lower band, the thumb extended; detach the piece slightly from the shoulder, the left fore-arm along the stock.

141. (*Second motion.*) Carry the piece vertically to the right shoulder with both hands, the rammer to the front, change the position of the right hand so as to embrace the guard with the thumb and fore-finger, slip the left hand to the height of the shoulder, the fingers extended and joined, the right arm nearly straight.

142. (*Third motion.*) Drop the left hand quickly by the side.

Present—ARMS.
One time and two motions.

143. (*First motion.*) With the right hand bring the piece erect before the centre of the body, the rammer to the front; at the same time seize the piece with the left hand half way between the guide sight and lower [illegible] along the barrel and against the stock, the fore-arm horizontal and resting against the body, the hand as high as the elbow.

144. (*Second motion.*) Grasp the small of the stock with the right hand below and against the guard.

Shoulder—ARMS.
One time and two motions.

145. (*First motion.*) Bring the piece to the right shoulder, at the same time change the position of the right hand so as to embrace the guard with the thumb and fore-finger, slip up the left hand to the height of the shoulder, the fingers extended and joined, the right arm nearly straight.

146. (*Second motion.*) Drop the left hand quickly by the side.

Order—ARMS.
One time and two motions.

147. (*First motion.*) Seize the piece briskly with the left hand near the upper band, and detach it slightly from the shoulder with the right hand; loosen the grasp of the right hand, lower the piece with the left, reseize the piece with the right hand above the lower band, the little finger in the rear of the barrel, the butt about four inches from the ground, the right hand supported against the hip, drop the left hand by the side.

148. (*Second motion.*) Let the piece slip through the right hand to the ground by opening slightly the fingers, and take the position about to be described.

Position of order arms.

149. The hand low, the barrel between the thumb and fore-finger extended along the stock; the other fingers extended and joined; the muzzle about two inches from the right shoulder; the rammer in front; the toe (or beak) of the butt, against, and in a line with, the toe of the right foot, the barrel perpendicular.

150. When the instructor may wish to give repose in this position, he will command:—

REST.

151. At this command, the recruits will not be required to preserve silence or steadiness.

152. When the instructor may wish the recruits to pass from this position to that of silence and steadiness, he will command:—

1. *Attention.* 2. SQUAD.

153. At the second word, the recruits will resume the position of *order arms.*

Shoulder—ARMS.
One time and two motions.

154. (*First motion.*) Raise the piece vertically with the right hand to the height of the right breast, and opposite the shoulder, the elbow close to the body; seize the piece with the left hand below the right, and drop quickly the right hand to grasp the piece at the swell of the stock, the thumb and fore-finger embracing the guard; press the piece against the shoulder with the left hand, the right arm nearly straight.

155. (*Second motion.*) Drop the left hand quickly by the side.

Load in Nine Times.

1. LOAD.*

One Time and One Motion.

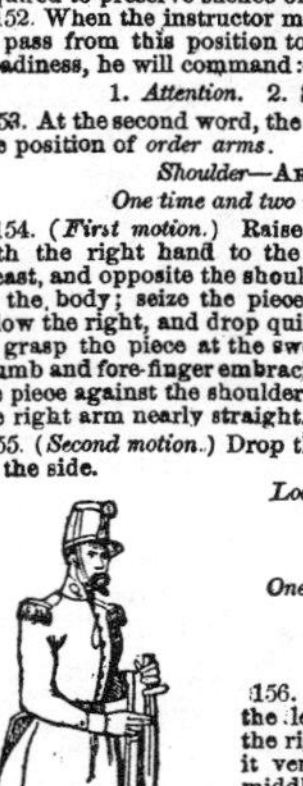

156. Grasp the piece with the left hand as high as the right elbow, and bring it vertically opposite the middle of the body, shift the right hand to the upper band, place the butt between the feet, the barrel to the front; seize it with the left hand near the muzzle, which should be three inches from the body; carry the right hand to the cartridge box.

2. *Handle*—CARTRIDGE.
One time and one motion.

157. Seize the cartridge with the thumb and next two fingers, and place it between the teeth.

3. *Tear*—CARTRIDGE.
One time and one motion.

158. Tear the paper to the powder, hold the cartridge upright between the thumb and first two fingers, near the top; in this position place it in front of and near the muzzle—the back of the hand to the front.

4. *Charge*—CARTRIDGE.
One time and one motion.

159. Empty the powder into the barrel; disengage the ball from the paper with the right hand and the thumb and first two fingers of the left; insert it into the bore, the pointed end uppermost, and press it down with the right thumb; seize the head of the rammer with the thumb and fore-finger of the right hand, the other fingers closed, the elbows near the body.

5. *Draw*—RAMMER.
One time and three motions.

(160. *First motion.*) Half draw the rammer by extending the right arm; steady it in this position with the left thumb; grasp the rammer near the muzzle with the right hand, the little finger uppermost, the nails to the front, the thumb extended along the rammer.

161. (*Second motion.*) Clear the rammer from the pipes by again extending the arm; the rammer in the prolongation of the pipes.

162. (*Third motion.*) Turn the rammer, the end of the rammer passing near the left sh[illegible]; place the head of the rammer on the ba[illegible], the back of the hand to the front.

6. *Ram*—CARTRIDGE.
One time and one motion.

163. Insert the rammer as far as the right, and steady it in this position with the thumb of the left hand; seize the rammer at the small end with the thumb and fore-finger of the right hand, the back of the hand to the front; press the ball home, the elbows near the body.

7. *Return*—RAMMER.
One time and three motions.

164. (*First motion.*) Draw the rammer half-way out, and steady it in this position with the left thumb; grasp it near the muzzle with the right hand, the little finger uppermost, the nails to the front, the thumb along the rammer; clear the rammer from the bore by extending the arm, the nails to the front, the rammer in the prolongation of the bore.

165. (*Second motion.*) Turn the rammer, the head of the rammer passing near the left shoulder, and insert it in the pipes until the right hand reaches the muzzle, the nails in front.

166. (*Third motion.*) Force the rammer home by placing the little finger of the right hand on the head of the rammer; pass the left hand down the barrel to the extent of the arm, without depressing the shoulder.

8. PRIME.*

One time and two motions.

167. (*First motion.*) With the left hand raise the piece till the hand is as high as the eye, grasp the small of the stock with the right hand; half face to the right; place, at the same time, the right foot behind and at right angles with the left; the hollow of the right foot against the left heel. Slip the left hand down to the lower band, the thumb along the stock, the left elbow against the body; bring the piece to the right side, the butt below the right fore-arm—the small of the stock against the body and two inches below the right breast, the barrel upwards, the muzzle on a level with the eye.

168. (*Second motion.*) Half cock with the thumb of the right hand, the fingers supported against the guard and the small of the stock—remove the old cap with one of the fingers of the right hand, and with the thumb and fore-finger of the same hand take a cap from the pouch, place it on the nipple, and press is down with the thumb; seize the small of the stock with the right hand.

[illegible]—ARMS.
One time and two motions.

169. (*First motion.*) Bring the piece to the right shoulder and support it there with the left hand, face to the front; bring the right heel to the side of and on a line with the left; grasp the piece with the right hand as indicated in the position of *shoulder arms.*

170. (*Second motion.*) Drop the left hand quickly by the side.

READY.
One time and three motions.

171. (*First motion.*) Raise the piece slightly with the right hand, making a half face to the right on the left heel; carry the right foot to the rear, and place it at right angles to the left, the hollow of it opposite to, and against the left heel; grasp the piece with the left hand at the lower band and detach it slightly from the shoulder.

172. (*Second motion.*) Bring down the piece with both hands, the barrel upwards, the left thumb extended along the stock, the butt below the right fore-arm, the small of the stock against the body and two inches below the right breast, the muzzle as high as the eye, the left elbow against the side; place at the same time the right thumb on the head of the cock, the other fingers under and against the guard.

173. (*Third motion.*) Cock, and seize the piece at the small of the stock without deranging the position of the butt.

AIM.
One time and one motion.

174. Raise the piece with both hands, and support the butt against the right shoulder; the left elbow down, the right as high as the shoulder; incline the head upon the butt, so that the right eye may perceive quickly the notch of the hausse, the front sight, and the object aimed at; the left eye closed, the right thumb extended along the stock, the fore-finger on the trigger.

175. When recruits are formed in two ranks to to execute the firings, the front rank men will raise a little less the right elbow, in order to facilitate the aim of the rear rank men.

176. The rear rank men, in aiming, will each carry the right foot about eight inches to the right, and towards the left heel of the man next on the right, inclining the upper part of the body forward.

*If MAYNARD'S primer be used, the command should be, *load in eight times*, and the eighth command will be, *shoulder arms*, and executed from *return rammer*, in one time and two motions, as follows:—

(*First motion.*) Raise the piece with the left hand, and take the position of shoulder arms, as indicated No. 76.

(*Second motion.*) Drop the left hand quickly by the side.

FIRE.

One time and one motion.

177. Press the fore-finger against the trigger, fire, without lowering or turning the head, and remain in this position.

178. Instructors will be careful to observe, when the men fire, that they aim at some distinct object, and that the barrel be so directed that the line of fire and the line of sight be in the same vertical plane. They will often cause the firing to be executed on ground of different inclinations, in order to accustom the men to fire at objects either above or below them.

LOAD.
One time and one motion.

179. Bring down the piece with both hands, at the same time face to the front and take the position of *load* as indicated No. 87. Each rear rank man will bring his right foot by the side of the left.

180. The men being in this position, the instructor will cause the loading to be continued by the commands and means prescribed No. 87 and following.

181. If, after firing, the instructor should not wish the recruits to reload, he will command:—

Shoulder—ARMS.
One time and one motion.

182. Throw up the piece briskly with the left hand, and resume the position of *shoulder arms*, at the same time face to the front, turning on the left heel, and bring the right heel on a line with the left.

183. To accustom the recruits to wait for the command *fire*, the instructor, when they are in the position of *aim*, will command:—

Recover—ARMS.
One time and one motion.

184. At the first part of the command, withdraw the finger from the trigger; at the command *arms*, retake the position of the third motion of *ready*.

184. The recruits being in the position of the the third motion of *ready*, if the instructor should wish to bring them to a shoulder, he will command:

SHOULDER—ARMS.
One time and one motion.

185. At the command *shoulder*, place the thumb upon the cock, the fore-finger on the trigger, half-cock, and seize the small of the stock with the right hand. At the command *arms*, bring up the piece briskly to the right shoulder, and retake the position of shoulder arms.

187. The recruits being at shoulder arms, when the instructor shall wish to fix bayonets, he will command:—

Fix—BAYONET.
One time and three motions.

188. (*First motion.*) Grasp the piece with the left hand at the height of the shoulder, and detach it slightly from the shoulder with the right hand.

189. (*Second motion.*) Quit the piece with the right hand, lower it with the left hand, opposite the middle of the body, and place the butt between the feet without shock; the rammer to the rear, the barrel vertical, the muzzle three inches from the body; seize it with the right hand at the upper band, and carry the left hand reversed to the handle of the sabre-bayonet.

190. (*Third motion.*) Draw the sabre-bayonet from the scabbard and fix it on the extremity of the barrel; seize the piece with the left hand, the arm extended, the right hand at the upper band.

Shoulder—ARMS.
One time and two motions.

191. (*First motion.*) Raise the piece with the left hand and place it against the right shoulder, the rammer to the front; seize the piece at the same time with the right hand at the swell of the stock, the thumb and fore-finger embracing the guard, the right arm nearly extended.

192. (*Second motion.*) Drop briskly the left hand by the side.

Charge—BAYONET.

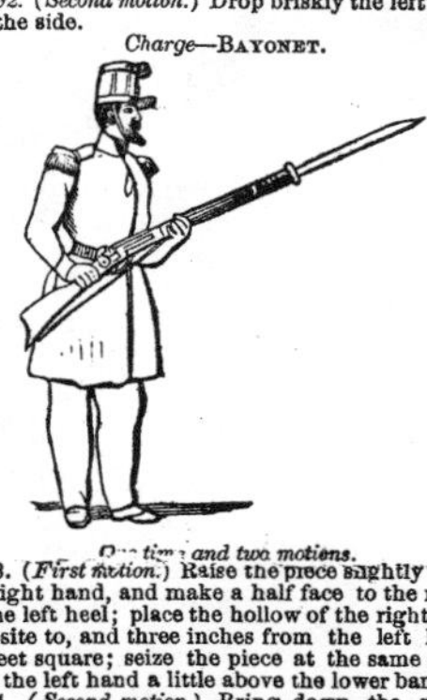

One time and two motions.

193. (*First motion.*) Raise the piece slightly with the right hand, and make a half face to the right on the left heel; place the hollow of the right foot opposite to, and three inches from the left heel, the feet square; seize the piece at the same time with the left hand a little above the lower band.

194. (*Second motion.*) Bring down the piece with both hands, the barrel uppermost, the left elbow against the body; seize the small of the stock, at the same time, with the right hand, which will be supported against the hip; the point of the sabre-bayonet as high as the eye.

Shoulder—ARMS.
One time and two motions.

195. (*First motion.*) Throw up the piece briskly with the left hand in facing to the front, place it against the right shoulder, the rammer to the front; turn the right hand so as to embrace the guard, slide the left hand to the height of the shoulder, the right hand nearly extended.

196. (*Second motion.*) Drop the left hand smartly by the side.

Trail—ARMS.
One time and two motions.

197. (*First motion.*) The same as the first motion of *order arms.*

198. (*Second motion.*) Incline the muzzle slightly to the front, the butt to the rear and about four inches from the ground. The right hand supported at the hip, will so hold the piece that the rear flank men may not touch with their bayonets the men in the front rank.

SHOULDER—ARMS.

199. At the command *shoulder*, raise the piece perpendicularly in the right hand, the little finger in rear of the barrel; at the command *arms*, execute what has been prescribed for the *shoulder* from the position of *order arms.*

Unfix—BAYONET.
One time and three motions.

200. (*First and second motions.*) The same as the first and second motions of *fix bayonet*, except that, at the end of the second command, the thumb of the right hand will be placed on the spring of the sabre-bayonet, and the left hand will embrace the handle of the sabre-bayonet and the barrel, the thumb extended along the blade.

201. (*Third motion.*) Press the thumb of the right hand on the spring, wrest off the sabre bayonet, turn it to the right, the edge to the front, lower the guard until it touches the right hand, which will seize the back and the edge of the blade between the thumb and first two fingers, the other fingers holding the piece; change the position of the hand without quitting the handle, return the sabre-bayonet to the scabbard, and seize the piece with the left hand, the arm extended.

Shoulder—ARMS.
One time and two motions.

202. (*First motion.*) The same as the first motion from *fix bayonet*, No. 191.

203. (*Second motion.*) The same as the second motion from *fix bayonet*, No. 192.

Secure—ARMS.
One time and three motions.

204. (*First Motion.*) The same as the first motion of *Support arms*, No 133, except with the right hand seize the piece at the smalll of the stock.

205. (*Second motion.*) Turn the piece with both hands, the barrel to the front; bring it opposite the left shoulder, the butt against the hip, the left hand at the lower band, the thumb as high as the chin and extended on the rammer; the piece erect and detached from the shoulder, the left fore-arm against the piece.

206. (*Third motion.*) Reverse the piece, pass it under the left arm, the left hand remaining at the lower band, the thumb on the rammer to prevent it from sliding out, the little finger resting against the hip, the right hand falling at the same time by the side.

Shoulder—ARMS.
One time and three motions.

207. (*First motion.*) Raise the piece with the left hand, and seize it with the right hand at the small of the stock. The piece erect and detached from the shoulder, the butt against the hip, the left fore-arm along the piece.

208. (*Second motion.*) The same as the second motion of *shoulder arms from a support.*

209. (*Third motion.*) The same as the third motion of *shoulder arms from a support.*

Right shoulder shift—ARMS.
One time and two motions.

210. (*First motion.*) Detach the piece perpendicularly from the shoulder with the right hand, and seize it with the left between the lower band and guide-sight, raise the piece, the left hand at the height of the shoulder and four inches from it; place, at the same time, the right hand on the butt, the beak between the first two fingers, the other two fingers under the butt plate.

211. (*Second motion.*) Quit the piece with the left hand, raise and place the piece on the right shoulder with the right hand, the lock plate upwards; let fall, at the same time, the left hand by the side.

Shoulder—ARMS.
One time and two motions.

212. (*First motion.*) Raise the piece perpendicularly by extending the right arm to its full length, the rammer to the front, at the same time seize the piece with the left hand between the lower band and guide sight.

213. (*Second motion.*) Quit the butt with the right hand, which will immediately embrace the guard, lower the piece to the position of shoulder arms, slide up the left hand to the height of the shoulder, the fingers extended and closed. Drop the left hand by the side.

214. The men being at support arms, the instructor will sometimes cause pieces to be brought to the right shoulder. To this effect, he will command:—

Right shoulder shift—ARMS.
One time and two motions.

215. (*First motion.*) Seize the piece with the right hand, below and near the left fore-arm, place the left hand under the butt, the heel of the butt between the first two fingers.

216. (*Second motion.*)—Turn the piece with the left hand, the lock plate upwards, carry it to the right shoulder, the left hand still holding the butt, the muzzle elevated; hold the piece in this position, and place the right hand upon the butt as is prescribed No. 210, and let the left hand fall by the side.

Support—ARMS.
One time and two motions.

217. (*First motion.*) The same as the first motion of *shoulder arms*, No. 212.

218. (*Second motion.*) Turn the piece with both hands, the barrel to the front, carry it opposite the left shoulder, slip the right hand to the small of the stock, place the left fore-arm extended on the breast as is prescribed No. 134, and let fall the right hand by the side.

Arms—AT WILL.
One time and one motion.

219. At this command, carry the piece at pleasure on either shoulder, with one or both hands, the muzzle elevated.

Shoulder—ARMS.
One time and one motion.

220. At this command, retake quickly the position of shoulder arms.

221. The recruits being at ordered arms, when the instructor shall wish to cause the pieces to be placed on the ground, he will command:—

Ground—ARMS.

One time and two motions.

222. (*First motion.*) Turn the piece with the right hand, the barrel to the left, at the same time seize the cartridge box with the left hand, bend the body, advance the left foot, the heel opposite the lower band; lay the piece on the ground with the right hand, the toe of the butt on a line with the right toe, the knees slightly bent, the right heel raised.

223. (*Second motion.*) Rise up, bring the left foot by the side of the right, quit the cartridge box with the left hand, and drop the hands by the side.

Raise—ARMS.
One time and two motions.

224. (*First motion.*) Seize the cartridge box with the left hand, bend the body, advance the left foot opposite the lower band, and seize the piece with the right hand.

225. (*Second motion.*) Raise the piece, bringing the left foot by the side of the right; turn the piece with the right hand, the rammer to the front; at the same time quit the cartridge box with the left hand, and drop this hand by the side.

Inspection of Arms.

226. The recruits being at *ordered arms*, and having the sabre-bayonet in the scabbard, if the instructor wishes to cause an inspection of arms, he will command:

Inspection—ARMS.
One time and two motions.

227. (*First motion.*) Seize the piece with the left hand below and near the upper band, carry it with both hands opposite the middle of the body, the butt between the feet, the rammer to the rear, the barrel vertical, the muzzle about three inches from the body; carry the left hand reversed to the sabre-bayonet, draw it from the scabbard and fix it on the barrel; grasp the piece with the left hand below and near the upper band, seize the rammer with the thumb and forefinger of the right hand bent, the other fingers closed.

228. (*Second motion.*) Draw the rammer as has been explained in *loading*, and let it glide to the bottom of the bore, replace the piece with the left hand opposite the right shoulder, and retake the position of *ordered arms.*

229. The instructor will then inspect in succession the piece of each recruit, in passing along the front of the rank. Each, as the instructor reaches him, will raise smartly his piece with his right hand, seize it with the left between the lower band and guide sight, the lock to the front, the left hand at the height of the chin, the piece opposite to the left eye; the instructor will take it with the right hand at the handle, and, after inspecting it, will return it to the recruit, who will receive it back with the right hand, and replace it in the position of *ordered arms.*

230. When the instructor shall have passed him, each recruit will retake the position prescribed at the command *inspection arms*, return the rammer, and resume the position of *ordered arms.*

231. If, instead of *inspection of arms*, the instructor should merely wish to cause bayonets to be fixed, he will command:

Fix—BAYONET.

232. Take the position indicated No. 227, fix bayonets as has been explained, and immediately resume the position of *ordered arms.*

233. If it be the wish of the instructor, after firing, to ascertain whether the pieces have been discharged, he will command:

Spring—RAMMERS.

234. Put the rammer in the barrel as has been explained above, and immediately retake the position of *ordered arms.*

235. The instructor, for the purpose stated, can take the rammer by the small end, and spring it in the barrel, or cause each recruit to make it ring in the barrel.

236. Each recruit, after the instructor passes him, will return rammer, and resume the position of *ordered arms.*

Remarks on the Manual of Arms.

237. The manual of arms frequently distorts the persons of recruits before they acquire ease and confidence in the several positions. The instructor will therefore frequently recur to elementary principles in the course of the lessons.

238. Recruits are also extremely liable to curve the sides and back, and to derange the shoulders, especially in loading. Consequently, the instructor will not cause them to dwell too long, at a time, in one position.

239. When, after some days of exercise in the manual of arms, the four men shall be well established in their use, the instructor will always terminate the lesson by marching the men for some time in one rank, and at one pace apart, in common and quick time, in order to confirm them more and more in the mechanism of the step; he will also teach them to mark time and to change step, which will be executed in the following manner:—

To mark time.

240. The four men marching in the direct step, the instructor will command:—

1. *Mark Time.* 2. MARCH.

241. At the second command, which will be given at the instant a foot is coming to the ground, the recruits will make a semblance of marching, by bringing the heels by the side of each other, and observing the cadence of the step, by raising each foot alternately without advancing.

242. The instructor wishing the direct step to be resumed, will command:—

1. *Forward.* 2. MARCH.

243. At the second command, which will be given as prescribed above, the recruits will retake the step of twenty-eight inches.

To change step.

244. The squad being in march, the instructor will command:—

1. *Change step.* 2. MARCH.

245. At the second command, which will be given at the instant either foot is coming to the ground, bring the foot which is in rear by the side of that which is in front, and step off again with the foot which was in front.

To march backwards.

246. The instructor wishing the squad to march backwards, will command:—

1. *Squad backward.* 2. MARCH.

247. At the second command, the recruits will step off smartly with the left foot fourteen inches to the rear, reckoning from heel to heel, and so on with the feet in succession till the command *halt*, which will always be preceded by the caution *squad.* The men will halt at this command, and bring back the foot in front by the side of the other.

248. This step will always be executed in quick time.

249. The instructor will be watchful that the recruits march straight to the rear, and that the erect position of the body and the piece be not deranged.

LESSON III.

To load in four times.

250. The object of this lesson is to prepare the recruits to load at will, and to cause them to distinguish the times which require the greatest regularity and attention, such as *charge cartridge, ram cartridge,* and *prime.* It will be divided as follows:—

251. The first time will be executed at the end of the command; the three others at the commands, *two, three* and *four.*

The instructor will command:—

1. *Load in four times.* 2. LOAD.

252. Execute the times to include charge cartridge.

TWO.

253. Execute the times to include ram cartridge.

THREE.

254. Execute the times to include prime.

FOUR.

255. Execute the time of *shoulder arms.*

To load at will.

256. The instructor will next teach loading at will, which will be executed as loading in four times, but continued, and without resting on either of the times. He will command:

1. *Load at will.* 2. LOAD.

257. The instructor will habituate the recruits, by degrees, to load with the greatest possible promptitude, each without regulating himself by his neighbor, and above all without waiting for him.

258. The cadence prescribed No. 129, is not applicable to loading in four times, or at will.

LESSON IV.

Firings.

259. The firings are direct or oblique, and will be executed as follows:—

The direct fire.

260. The instructor will give the following commands:—

1. *Fire by squad.* 2. *Squad.* 3. READY. 4. AIM. 5. FIRE. 6. LOAD.

261. These several commands will be executed as has been prescribed in the *Manual of Arms.* At the third command the men will come to the position of *ready*, as heretofore explained. At the fourth they will aim according to the rank in which each may find himself placed, the rear rank men inclining forward a little to the upper part of the bo[illegible] in order that their pieces may reach as m[illegible] beyond the front rank as possible.

[illegible] will load their pieces and return immediately to the position of *ready.*

263. The instructor will recommence the firing by the commands:—

1. *Squad.* 2. AIM. 3. FIRE. 4. LOAD.

264. When the instructor wishes the firing to cease, he will command:—

Cease firing.

265. At this command, the men will cease firing, but will load their pieces if unloaded, and afterwards bring them to a shoulder.

Oblique Firings.

266. The oblique firings will be executed to the right and left, and by the same commands as the direct fire, with this single difference—the command *aim* will always be preceded by the caution, *right* or *left oblique.*

Position of the two ranks in the Oblique Fire to the right.

267. At the command *ready*, the two ranks will execute what has been prescribed for the direct fire.

268. At the cautionary command, *right oblique*, the two ranks will throw back the right shoulder and look steadily at the object to be hit.

269. At the command *aim*, each front rank man will aim to the right without deranging the feet; each rear rank man will advance the left foot about eight inches towards the right heel of the man next on the right of his file leader and aim to the right, inclining the upper part of the body forward and bending a little the left knee.

Position of the two ranks in the Oblique Fire to the left.

270. At the cautionary command *left oblique*, the two ranks will throw back the left shoulder and look steadily at the object to be hit.

271. At the command *aim*, the front rank will take aim to the left without deranging the feet; each man in the rear rank will advance the right foot about eight inches towards the right heel of the man next on the right of his file leader, and aim to the left, inclining the upper part of the body forward and bending a little the right knee.

272. In both cases, at the command *load*, the men of each rank will come to the position of load a prescribed in the direct fire; the rear rank men bringing back the foot which is to the right and front by the side of the other. Each man will continue to load as if isolated.

To Fire by file.

273. The fire by file will be executed by the two ranks, the files of which will fire successively, and without regulating on each other, except for the first fire.

274. The instructor will command:—

1. *Fire by file.* 2. *Squad.* 3. READY. 4. COMMENCE FIRING.

275. At the third command, the two ranks will take the position prescribed in the direct fire.

276. At the fourth command, the file on the right will aim and fire; the rear rank man in aiming will take the position indicated No. 176.

277. The men of this file will load their pieces briskly and fire a second time; reload and fire again, and so on in continuation.

278. The second file will aim, at the instant the first brings down pieces to reload, and will conform in all respects to that which had just been prescribed for the first file.

279. After the first fire, the front and rear rank men will not be required to fire at the same time.

280. Each man, after loading, will return to the position of ready and continue the fire.

281. When the instructor wishes the fire to cease, he will command:—

Cease—FIRING.

282. At this command, the men will cease firing. If they have fired they will load their pieces and bring them to a shoulder; if at the position of *ready*, they will half-cock and shoulder arms. If in the position of *aim*, they will bring down their pieces, half-cock, and shoulder arms.

To fire by rank.

283. The fire by rank will be executed by each entire rank alternately.

284. The instructor will command:—

1. *Fire by rank.* 2. *Squad.* 3. READY. 4. *Rear rank.* 5. AIM. 6. FIRE. 7. LOAD.

285. At the third command, the two ranks will take the position of *ready*, as prescribed in the direct fire.

286. At the seventh command, the rear rank will execute that which has been prescribed in the direct fire, and afterwards take the position of *ready.*

287. As soon as the instructor sees several men of the rear rank in the position of ready, he will command:—

THE GATHERING.

Forward! onward! far and forth!
An earthquake shout awakes the North!
Forward!

Massachusetts hears that cry—
Hears and gives the swift reply,
Forward:

Pennsylvania draws her sword,
Echoes from her hills the word,
Forward!

Brave New York is up and ready
With her thirty thousand steady,—
Forward!

Small Rhede Island flies to arms,
Shouting at the first alarms,
Forward!

Illinois and Indiana
Shriek as they unroll our banner,
Forward!

Not behind the rest in zeal,
Hear Ohio's thunder-peal,
Forward!

From Vermont, New Hampshire Maine,
Comes the same awakening strain,
Forward!

Old Connecticut is hence,
Ready to give back the cheer,
Forward!

Minnesota, though remote,
Swells the free inspiring note,
Forward!

Iowa and Michigan,
Both are ready to a man,—
Forward!

Not the last in honor's race,
See Wisconsin come apace—
Forward!

Delaware, New Jersey rise,
And pu[illegible] their martial guise.
Forward!

Onward! On! a common cause
Is yours—your liberties and laws.
Forward!

Forward in your strength and pride!
God himself is on your side.
Forward!

Suggestions from an Old Soldier.

Allow an old soldier who has seen service to offer a few practical suggestions to our men who are marching South.

Avoid drinking water as much as possible while marching. When you feel dry rinse your mouth with water, but do not swallow it. Water alone should not be drank, but mixed with vinegar; or a little cold coffee is the only wholesome beverage in a campaign.

While marching or on sentry never sit down for a second—bear up! The change of posture will affect your powers more than the actual marching.

Have plenty of buttons, needle and thread, rags of linen and some strong twine in your knapsack—you will want it

White linen gaiters over brogans are the best, boots offering too much reflection to the sun's rays. The gaiters are made white and shiny again by applying a mixture of common chalk with a rag or sponge, and let the gaiter get dry under the air or sun.

If you have a long march in warm weather before you, cut off the body of your pantaloons to the middle of the thigh and sew the legs to your drawers, fastening the suspenders to the drawers, it will relieve you greatly. Drawers are essential.

Keep a vial of sweet oil, and every night rub your gun with a rag dipped in oil. In the morning, or with starting, rub it clean; it is the best way to preserve it from rust and keep it in working order. When not using it put a piece of cork or something else in the mouth of your gun to keep out the dust, rain, &c.

When marching, put some of the weight you have to carry on your breast—for instance, part of the cartridges—so as to relieve and counterpoise the weight to be carried.

Have some lard in a small tin box, to grease your boots or shoes with, to keep them smooth and soft, particularly in wet weather, or passing through a swampy country.

When on the march, never let a weak comrade get behind the company—assist him in carrying his load. When once left behind he is at the questionable mercies of the rear guard, and may perish before the ambulance comes up.

Finally, avoid spirituous liquors as you would poison.

The Armstrong Gun.

We have now precise information, says the London *Journal*, respecting the experiment conducted recently with an Armstrong gun against a martelle tower at Eastbourne. The guns employed were a 40 pounder of 63 cwt., and a short 100 pounder, weighing only 54 cwt. The distance was 1032 yards, and the projectiles employed were partly solid shot and partly percussion shells. The tower was built of very strong brick work, the thickness of the wall being 7 feet 3 inches on the land side, and 9 feet on the side next the sea. The roof or platform consisted of a massive vault of great strength, supported by the walls and by a solid pillar of brick work occupying the centre of the tower. The 80 pounder shot was found to pass quite through the wall into the tower, piercing 7 feet 3 inches of brick work; the other lodged in the wall at the depth of about five feet Five shells were then fired, and with so much effect that after eight or ten rounds from each gun the interior of the tower became exposed to view. The centre pillar supporting the bomb proof was speedily knocked away, but the structure was so compact that the vault continued to stand, and was only brought down by a succession of shells exploded in the brick work. Nothing could exceed the precision with which these shells were thrown. The broken section of the vault was itself but a small object to hit, but this was done with such unerring certainty that the very spot selected was almost invariably struck. The total number of shot and shell fired against the tower was 170, of which only a small proportion was from the 100 pounder. The 100 pounder gun used on this occasion throws shells which weigh 100 lbs. and contain 8 lbs. of powder, and yet the weight of the gun with which these tremendous projectiles are discharged is less than that of the ordinary 32 pounder, the weight of which is 5600

Soldiers' Exemption in Pennsylvania.

Those who desire to serve their country will see that their families and property are fully protected by the annexed section of the Pennsylvania act of 1812:—

"No execution or other process shall issue against any officer, non-commissioned officer or private of the militia, when called into actual service, under a requisition of the President of the United States, or in pursuance of the orders of the Governor of this Commonwealth; nor shall any such process issue against him until thirty days after he shall have returned from duty, to his usual place of residence, or until forty days after he shall have been discharged; and the court, alderman or justice of the peace from which or from whom any such process shall have issued, shall quash the same, as soon as the fact of any such person being ordered on public duty shall have been proven, and all the costs which shall have accrued in commencing or conducting any such process shall be paid by the person or persons who shall have applied for the said execution or other process."

Important to Foot Soldiers.

HOW TO CLOTHE THE FEET AND KEEP THEM COMFORTABLE.

1. Blistering, burning, soreness and tenderness of the soles of the feet may almost invariably be prevented, even when marching for days together and over a heated road, by soaping the sole of the stocking—that is, covering it with a thin coating of the cheapest brown soap. This, at the same time, keeps the skin of the sole cool, hardens it, and prevents inflammation. Coarse cotton socks are the best for walking.

2. Don't wear woolen socks when marching, not even thin ones, no matter in what climate.

3. The boot or shoe should have a thick sole; it is not sufficient that they should be simply "doubled soled." The soles should be at least half an inch thick; if three-fourths of an inch or an inch, all the better; they are more expensive, but if well made will last a long time, and even in the warmest weather will be found easy to walk in, the feet easily becoming accustomed to their weight.

SOLDIERS' EQUIPMENTS.—The following are allowed to each soldier, to be placed in the knapsack or bundle. We publish it as useful to volunteer companies formed or in process of formation:—One fatigue cap, two flannel shirts (one on), two pairs drawers (one on), four pairs socks (one on), one pair pants, one overcoat, one blanket, one pair shoes (broad soled, low heels, and well saturated with oil), one towel, one comb, one piece of soap, one black silk neckcloth, one colored silk handkerchief, one pair slippers (for use when heavy shoes are drying), one flannel sack, one tooth brush. No other baggage will be allowed, except pipes, segars, and tobacco.

APPROACHES TO THE CITY OF WASHINGTON

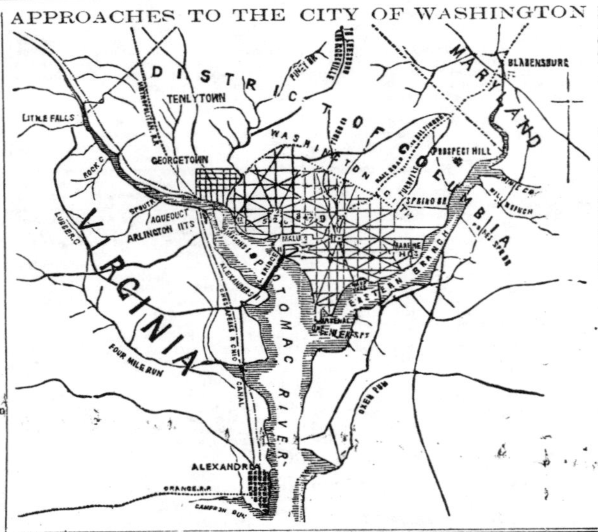

CHESAPEAKE BAY, FORT MONROE, AND NORFOLK HARBOR

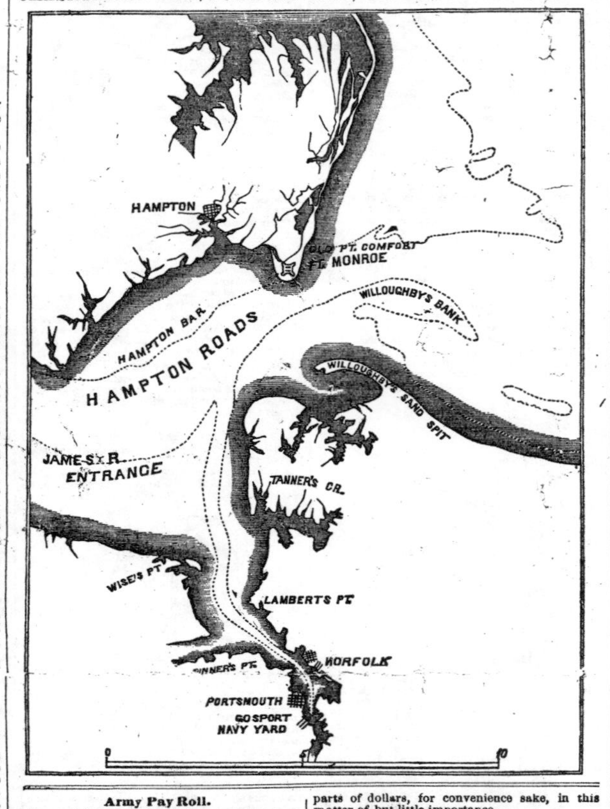

Army Pay Roll.

As much interest is felt in the pay of the army, we subjoin a list, taken from last year's edition of the Army Register, of the pay and subsistence of all the grades in the army.

In the first column will be found the net salary per month, and in the second the total salary per month, which includes rations, servant hire, forage, etc, etc.

	Per Month.	Total.
GENERAL OFFICERS.		
Lieutenant-General	$270	$770
Aids-de-Camp and Military Secretary to Lieutenant General, each	80	194
Major-General	220	469
Senior Aid-de-Camp to General-in-Chief	80	187
Aid-de-Camp, in addition to pay, etc., of Lieutenant	24	32
Brigadier-General	124	323
Aid-de-Camp, in addition to pay, etc., of Lieutenant	20	19
ADJUTANT-GENERAL'S DEPARTMENT.		
Adjutant-General—Colonel	110	235
Asst. Adjutant-General—Lieut-Col.	95	211
" " " —Major	80	187
" " " —Captain	70	137
Judge Advocate—Major	80	187
INSPECTOR-GENERAL'S DEPARTMENT.		
Inspector-General—Colonel	110	235
SIGNAL DEPARTMENT.		
Signal Officer—Major	80	187
QUARTERMASTER'S DEPARTMENT.		
Quartermaster-General—Brig. General	124	323
Asst. Quartermaster-General—Colonel	110	235
Dept. Quartermaster-General—Lt.-Col.	95	211
Quartermaster—Major	80	187
Assistant-Quartermaster—Captain	70	137
SUBSISTENCE DEPARTMENT.		
Commissary General of Subsistence—Colonel	110	235
Assistant Commissary-General of Subsistence—Lieut. Colonel	95	211
Commissary of Subsistence—Major	80	187
Assistant Commissary of Subsistence—Captain	70	137
Asst. Commissary of Subsistence, in addition to pay, etc., of Lieutenant	20	111
MEDICAL DEPARTMENT.		
Surgeon-General $2740 per annum	..	228
Surgeons of ten years' service	80	223
Surgeons of less than ten years' service	70	173
Asst. Surgeons of ten years' service	70	173
Asst. Surgeons of five years' service	70	137
Asst. Surgeons of less than five years' service	53	120
PAY DEPARTMENT.		
Paymaster-General $2740 per annum	..	228
Deputy Paymaster-General	95	211
Paymaster	80	187
OFFICERS OF THE CORPS OF ENGINEERS, CORPS OF TOPOGRAPHICAL ENGINEERS AND ORDNANCE DEPARTMENT.		
Colonel	110	235
Lieut.-Colonel	95	211
Major	80	187
Captain	70	137
First Lieutenant	53	120
Second Lieutenant	53	120
Brevet Second Lieutenant	53	120
OFFICERS OF MOUNTED DRAGOONS, CAVALRY, RIFLEMAN AND LIGHT ARTILLERY.		
Colonel	110	235
Lieutenant-Colonel	95	211
Major	80	187
Captain	70	145
First Lieutenant	53	128
Second Lieutenant	53	128
Brevet Second Lieutenant	53	128
Adjutant and Regimental Quartermaster, in addition to pay of Lieutenant	10	10
OFFICERS OF ARTILLERY AND INFANTRY.		
Colonel	65	218
Lieutenant-Colonel	80	194
Major	70	175
Captain	60	118
First Lieutenant	50	108
Second Lieutenant	45	103
Brevet Second Lieutenant	45	103
Adjutant, in addition to pay, etc., of Lieutenant	10	18
Regimental Quartermaster, in addition to pay, etc., of Lieutenant	10	26

In the above we have not inserted the fractional parts of dollars, for convenience sake, in this matter of but little importance.

BELOW THE GRADE OF LIEUTENANT.

The first column denotes the pay per month of artillery and infantry, and of dragoons and riflemen, when serving on foot. The second column denotes the pay per month of light artillery, and of dragoons and riflemen when mounted; Sergeant-Major, Quartermaster, Sergeant.

Principal Musician, and Chief Bugler, each	$21	$21
First Sergeant of a company	20	20
Ordnance Sergeants	22	..
Hospital Stewards	22	..
All other Sergeants, each	17	17
Corporals	13	14
Buglers	12	13
Musicians	12	..
Farriers and Blacksmiths	15	15
Artificers	15	..
Privates	11	12

In addition to the pay as above stated, one ration per day and an abundant supply of good clothing is allowed to every soldier. Quarters, fuel and medical attendance are always provided by the Government, without deduction from the soldiers' pay. If a soldier should become disabled in the line of his duties, the law provides for him a pension, or he may, if he prefer it, obtain admission into the Military Asylum, which will afford him a comfortable home so long as he may wish to receive its benefits.

RATIONS FOR THE ARMY.

The intention is good to properly provision our volunteers, and if no dearth of the things necessary therefor should take place, the following is the list of rations:—

For breakfast, at seven o'clock, A. M., there will be furnished for each man provisions in the following quantities:—

One quart of good coffee.
Eight ounces of bread.
Three-eighths of a pound of beef.
At twelve o'clock, M., for dinner:—
Five-eighths of a pound of beef or mutton, well cooked, with potatoes.
One quart baked beans to every ten men, and every other day, in lieu of baked beans, rice, bean or vegetable soup will be furnished at the rate of one pint per man.
At five o'clock P. M., for supper—
Three pints of coffee.
One quarter pound of cold beef or mutton.

The coffee to be furnished will be properly sweetened, and milk in due proportion will also be provided.

What is Martial Law?

At the present crisis the significance of a term so much used and with so little accurate sense of its meaning, becomes unusually important.

Martial law is generally and vaguely held to be a suspension of all ordinary civil rights and process, and as such approximates closely to a military despotism. It is an arbitrary law, originating in emergencies. In times of extreme peril to the State, either from without or within, the public welfare demands extraordinary measures. And martial law being proclaimed, signifies that the operation of the ordinary legal delays of justice is suspended by the military power, which has for the time become supreme. It suspends the operation of the writ of *habeas corpus*—enables persons charged with treason to be summarily tried by court martial, instead of grand jury; justifies searches and seizures of private property, and the taking possession of public highways and other means of communication. Involving the highest exercise of sovereignty, it is, of course, capable of great abuse, and is only to be justified on emergencies of the most imperative and perilous nature.

THE AMOUNT OF LEAD REQUIRED TO KILL A SOLDIER.—At the meeting held on Monday, at Cooper Institute, Doctor CHURCH addressed the audience upon the mortality incident to war. Disease and exposure constituted, he said, the great causes of death among soldiers. There had been obtained careful statistics at the Crimea and other places, of the amount of metal employed, and the number of the killed and wounded. The result was that they had ascertained with mathematical certainty, that 270 pounds of lead were shot away to every man that was killed. Prevention against disease was, therefore, what the soldier chiefly needed.

MAP
OF
THE RAILROAD AND WATER ROUTES TO WASHINGTON.

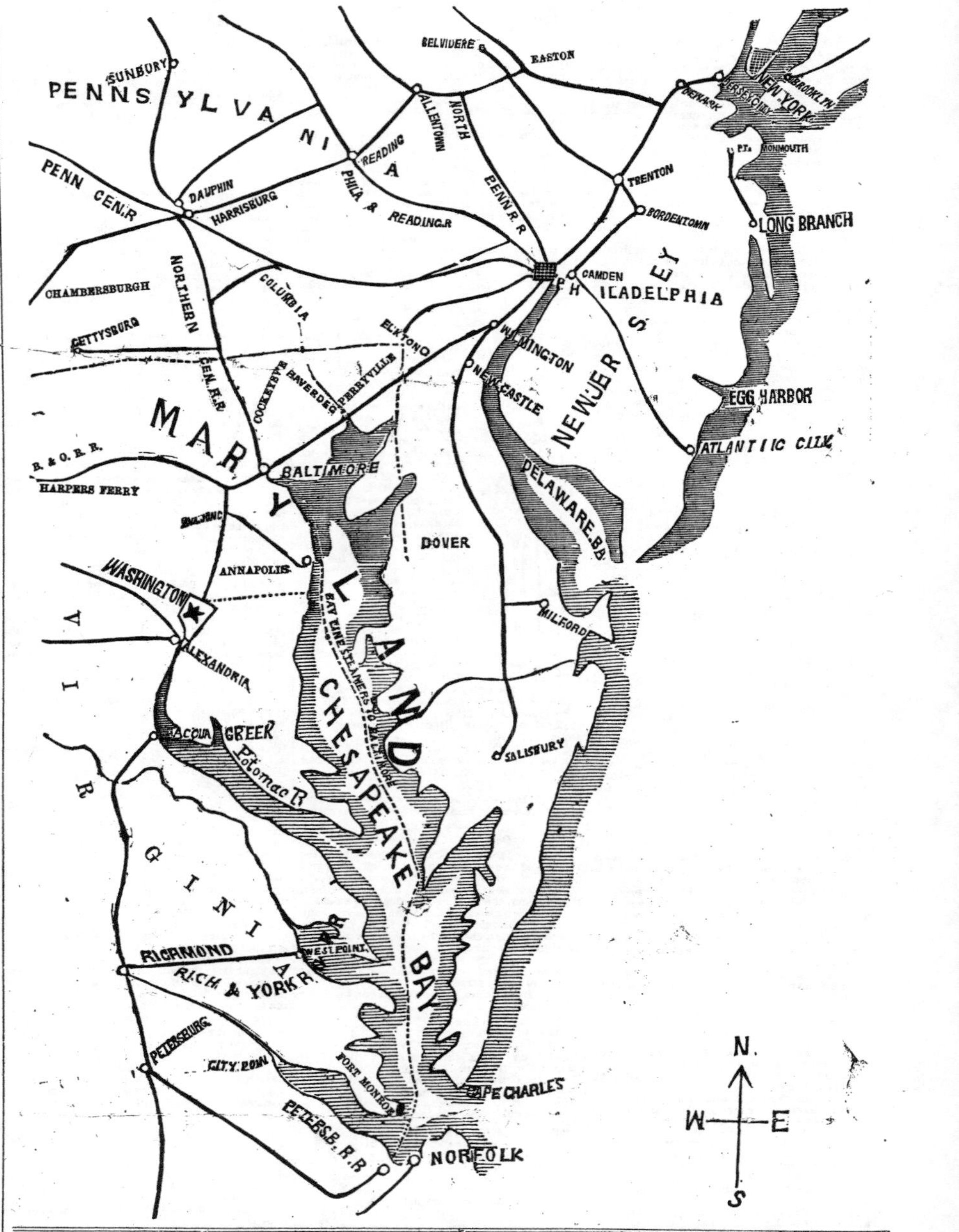

WHAT IS PIRACY?

Privateers and their Punishment.

We propose briefly to consider the effect of accepting and acting under such commissions as are offered by the recent proclamation of JEFFERSON DAVIS.

By an act of Congress passed April 30th, 1790, every citizen of the United States who commits any robbery or act of hostility against the United States, or any citizen thereof, upon the high seas, under color of any commission from any foreign prince or State, or *on pretence of authority from any person*, is to be deemed a pirate, and, on conviction, is to suffer death. The citizen who offends under color of such commission, is thus guilty of piracy just as much as if no such commission or authority existed. (U. S. agt. WILTBERGER, 5 Wheat., 100.

By the same act, any person who shall, on land or sea, assist, procure, or counsel any person to commit any piracy affecting life, is made accessory to such piracy when committed, and is liable to the punishment of death.

By the same act, any person, who, knowing of the commission of any such act of piracy, shall receive or conceal any such pirate, or any vessel or goods by him piratically taken, is declared an accessory after the fact, and is made liable to imprisonment not exceeding three years, and fine not over five hundred dollars.

But lest it should be imagined that the citizens of foreign nations may accept and act under the commission of JEFFERSON DAVIS with impunity, we call attention to the law on this subject also It is a principle of national law that it is inexcusable and base for any one to take a license from a foreign government to prey upon the subjects of a State in amity with his own country. (1 Kent Comm., 99.) The law of France, from an early date, treated any French subject as a pirate who engaged in such a way against the property of a nation at peace with France. Modern nations have universally adopted the same rule in their own laws, and in their treaties with each other, for over two hundred years.

The treaties now existing between the United States and England, France, Spain, Prussia, Holland, Sweden, Chili, Brazil, Venezuela, Bolivia, Ecuador, and probably other nations, all contain a provision expressly declaring that no subject or citizen of either nation shall accept a commission or letter of marque to assist an enemy in hostilities against the other, under penalty of being deemed and treated as a pirate. And by act of Congress passed March 3d, 1847, any alien found on the sea cruising against the vessels and property of the United States, or of any citizen thereof, contrary to the treaty with such alien's government, when by such treaty such acts are declared piratical, may be tried and convicted of piracy in any Circuit Court in the district into which he may be brought.

These treaties and this statute apply, it will be observed, in cases where the party or power assuming to grant the privateer's license to an alien is an acknowledged power, and has been, to some degree, at least, recognized among nations. Should a long civil war ensue between the Federal Government and its rebellious subjects, foreign nations might in time recognize the existence of such a civil war, and the rebels might be admitted, in their character of an actual power at war, to a sort of *quasi* existence, so far as a rebel ship, cruising against us, would not be deemed piratical by the courts of such foreign nation, although it would be so deemed in our own courts.

A pirate is one who robs on the high seas; and he is considered a common enemy of man. As such he is convicted and punished with death by the courts of any and every nation where he may be captured or brought. By the treaties above alluded to the several Governments of the civilized world have bound themselves, while at peace with us, thus to treat any of their own subjects who cruise against the United States in any case; whether the power granting the commission be an established Government or only a rebellious community waging a long civil war against us.

But at present even the stringent provisions of these treaties are not needed to fasten upon aliens who venture out under the piratical flag of JEFF. DAVIS the pirate's doom. As long as there is no acknowledgment of the Southern Confederacy by foreign nations, its so-called privateers are pirates in every sense. Pirates by the law of nations and the acknowledged rules of national intercourse, pirates by the statute law of their own outraged Government, they are equally pirates, whether natives or aliens, and will be condemned as pirates in the courts of any nation.

If foreign governments should even hasten to treat with JEFF. DAVIS and admit him and his band of conspirators into their alliances, his foreign-born privateers would still be pirates under our treaties and by the settled law of nations, while his native-born privateers would be pirates by our own laws, and the whole nest of villains find the way short from the deck to the gallows or yard-arm.

Let it not be forgotten that under the acts of Congress referred to it is piracy and a capital offence for any one to assist, procure or counsel any piracy resulting in death. Any owner furnishing a vessel, or any one who aids in furnishing or equipping her for a privateer, or any one who shares in the speculation, or even counsels it, knowing it for a privateering cruise, may, if death results from the cruise, be indicted and convicted of the piracy, and shall suffer death.

It is more than likely that in the course of the conflict we shall capture some of the *respectable merchants*, or some of the ship-furnishers, or, perhaps, some of the advisers and counsellors who get up these piratical expeditions and share the plunder. If so, let short work be made of these wretches, who begin by repudiating their honest debts and proceed to fatten themselves on robbery and piracy. Let vigilance be also exercised over our own ports, that no secret sympathizer here may escape the penalty of furnishing or fitting out a private craft. Our laws are full enough and stringent enough, as has been fully shown; but "*leges vigilantibus, non dormientibus, subveniunt.*"

DAILY TELEGRAPH.

Vol. 1. Thursday, May 2, 1861. No. 4.

The Painesville Daily Telegraph

IS PUBLISHED EVERY MORNING (MONDAYS EXCEPTED) AT PAINESVILLE, OHIO.

L. S. ABBOTT, Editor & Proprietor.

TERMS.—One shilling per week invariably in advance.

☞ A limited number of advertisements will be inserted at moderate prices.

HOW ABOUT BUSINESS?

Many are apprehensive that all business will be brought to a stand still by the present disturbed condition of the country. We are inclined to think that it will be checked but temporarily at the North. As soon as our people have become a little used to the times and volunteering shall have been finished up we shall have nothing to do but to go to work. The abundance of grain in the country must move off soon, at highly remunerative prices, and the farmer has everything to encourage him to cultivate just as many acres as he has the farm to cultivate with, and almost certain promise of good prices for the year to come. A vast amount of money must necessarily be spent to buy goods, mechanics' manufactures, for "riding on the rail," &c., just as in times past. Why can't we have good times?

☞ New Orleans seems to be terror stricken with the prospect of a negro insurrection.

☞ The volunteers of Benwood, Va., in answer to Governor Letcher's requisition for troops are said to have replied that they "would see him d——d first."

☞ Thomas Francis Meagher is raising an Irish regiment in New York.

☞ The Conneaut *Reporter* denies the report that appeared in the Cleveland *Herald* stating that John Brown was at the head of 400 negroes near Virginia, and that he meditated a raid into that State. The *Reporter* says that Brown has a commission from the U. S. Government to raise a company of Sharp Shooters and is now busy in getting up his company.

DAILY TELEGRAPH.

THURSDAY MORNING, MAY 2, 1861.

The Oil Well Catastrophe.

We glean from the *Erie Dispatch* the following particulars in relation to the calamity which occurred at or near Titusville, recently:

"The accident occurred while thirty-two or thirty-three persons were immediately around the derrick in the shanty, with large numbers in the vicinity, observing the oil spouting at the rate as is supposed of eighty barrels per hour.

"When the gas and oil, from some yet unexplained cause, took fire and exploded, the effect of which was like that of applying a match to a powder magazine. Some were thrown off their feet and immediately suffocated by the gas and flames, while those who were not, rushed forth with their clothing all in a blaze. The clothing of those who fell was immediately saturated with oil, and burned much more rapidly for that cause. Some of the men were burned black before the flames of their clothing could be put out. Only three of those who fell were rescued."

Nineteen persons it is known to have been killed, and nineteen others more or less injured. The *Dispatch* remarks further:

"The shanties adjoining the well took fire, and communicated to some eight derricks. A large barn, which had just been erected, was burned, with all its contents. The horses and cattle were taken out before the fire reached it. Over a thonsand barrels were burned, a number of which were filled with oil. Several vats filled with oil were destroyed. The flames of burning gas and oil, according to the testimony of all who witnessed them, reached to the height of at least two hundred feet in one column. It was a grand sight. Words can not describe the magnificence of such a scene as this, presented in the night."

The amount of oil which it was thought was thrown out of the well per hour, was not less than 80 barrels.

The well seems at last to have exhausted itself, and the fire was extinguished on Sunday before last.

☞ The Louisville *Journal* speaks in terms of the most scathing rebuke of the backing down of John Bell. In speaking of his apostacy it says: "It is a burning scandal to the cause of Constitutional Liberty."

TELEGRAPHIC DISPATCHES.

Reported for this Paper.

Secessionists Shot and Hung!

NO ARMISTICE!!

THE KILLED AT MOULTRIE!

New York, May 1st.

Captain Carson of the Schooner B. B. Pitts, from Charleston, states that he was at the wharf near Fort Moultrie during Sumter's bombardment, and that 60 dead bodies were carried across his track to land, and Monday 40 more were carried out at one time and 60 at another. Captain Carson and mate saw and counted the bodies, and that all the soldiers were sworn to deny any loss of life.

Washington special to the *World* says:—Arrangements have been made for the resumption of travel by rail via Baltimore and York, Pa.

All Southern journals received to day state that a large number of troops are gathering there, and the free negroes are being pressed into the service.

Nearly every portion of Washington and the District is connected by telegraph.

Letters received to-day from Paris state that the French Government is fully posted in American affairs, and no sympathy is felt for the Confederate States.

The *Post's* special says: Arrangements are being made for the resumption of the Northern mail service.

Scott will soon move his head-quarters to Philadelphia. 30,000 troops are to be concentrated.

Gen. Bonham is reported as in command of the rebel troops in Va.

Lord Lyons denies the report that he had solicited an armistice.

A letter from a member of the 7th regiment says six secessionists were caught on the 27th, and two were shot on the morning of the 28th; another was to be shot on the next morning Several had been arrested for tearing up the railroad track.

A private letter from Annapolis says, the brig Caledonia has two men hanging from her yard, one for smuggling powder and provisions to Charleston—the other for piloting the 7th regiment into the Chesepeake bay with the intention that the Baltimorean secessionists should capture Annapolis before the 7th reached there.

DAILY TELEGRAPH.

Vol. 1. Friday, May 3, 1861. No. 5.

The Painesville Daily Telegraph

IS PUBLISHED EVERY MORNING (MONDAYS EXCEPTED) AT PAINESVILLE, OHIO.

L. S. ABBOTT, Editor & Proprietor.

TERMS.—One shilling per week invariably in advance.

☞ A limited number of advertisements will be inserted at moderate prices.

Camp Perry.

A camp for the drilling of military has been established on the Fair Grounds just above town. The Geauga companies, amounting to 200 will be detained here until orders are given to march for active operations. It is the intention to secure the quartering of one regiment here if possible. Booth furnishes the fare. This camp will be under the control of Brigadier General Cadwell. The Geauga Rifle Company, Capt. Geo. E. Paine, arrived here last evening accompanied by the Chardon Brass and Fife Bands. They bore several banners bearing the following inscriptions, "The Geaugas are Coming," "Geauga Rifles", and "Have you seen the Cheese Makers?" They made a fine appearance and were heartily cheered as they passed through our streets.

We also learn that a company of a hundred men has organized at Burton, E. A. Ford, Captain. It is expected that they will soon receive orders to join the rifle company at Camp Perry.

☞ It is expected that the 7th Regiment of Ohio Volunteers, in which is included the Union Guards of Painesville, will leave Cleveland for Camp Dennison to-day.

☞ Gov. Corwin was received with distinguished consideration at Cuba by the Gov. General. Gov. Corwin dined with him on Sunday the 21st. The Confederate States have "no sight" in Cuba.

☞ At a flag raising in Boston, the other, day, Edward Everett made a patriotic speech. He and John Bell do not seem to be driving teams together any longer.

☞ In Tennessee Senator Johnson still denounces secession. Parson Brownlow says in the Knoxville *Whig*:

"We are for the Union as it is first; for a Border State Confederacy next; and for the Southern Confederacy, never, in any contingency or under any circumstances that may arise."

TELEGRAPHIC DISPATCHES.

Reported for this Paper.

WAR NEWS!

Western Virginia Still Loyal to the Union!

N. Y. ZOU[illegible]NAPOLIS.

Later from Pensacola and Cairo!

VIRGINIA BLOCKADED.

SPIES ARRESTED AT ANNAPOLIS!

Annapolis, May 2d,—4 p. m.

The steamship Baltic has arrived with the New York Zouaves on board. A great demonstration was made on their landing.

The Zouaes were greatly disappointed in not being permitted to pass through Baltimore.

The Baltic reports all quiet in the bay. Gun boats cruising up and and down constantly.

The 69th regiment from New York is stationed on the road to Washington, in squads, within hailing distance of each other.

A Captain of the 9th regiment arrested a spy the night before last at Annapolis, just from Montgomery, with important papers. He is a brother of the Grandvall of Hoboken, N. J., killed by a Cuban sometime ago. He will probably be hung.

A son of an influential farmer here is under arrest as a spy. He opened dispatches delivered to him at Washington.

The correspondent of the Batlimore *Sun* has left, fearing an arrest. The populace were desirous to lynch him.

I learn at the State House that the Legislature of Maryland will doubtless order a State Convention, probably May 30th. It is said that the Union feeling is gaining ground. One week of Secession rule has disgusted many of its former advocates.

[CONTINUED ON FOURTH PAGE.]

DAILY TELEGRAPH.

FRIDAY MORNING, MAY 3, 1861.

How to Do It.

If it be the purpose of the Powers that be, at Washington, as it is the wish and determination of the people, that the military preparations of the country now going on shall crush out effectually the rebellion in the Southern States, the course to be pursued is clear. The Southern States must be invaded by forces large enough to overawe and crush down all opposition. It is evident to our mind that when suitable forces are sent into the South, at p[illegible]hat the Union people will be nu[illegible]ugh to assume the reins of Government and put its wheels going in the right direction. Thorough work must be done in this matter. We don't want another job of the kind for long years to come. Let them, the traitors, feel "That the way of the transgressor is hard" in the most strictly literal sense, and we shall have heard of the last of rebellion in our day.

Privateering.—It is pretty certain that the Montgomery despotism intends to encourage a vigorous business in the way of privateering off their coast. These pirates should be caught and hung without ceremony. This piratical operation may thus be speedily rendered a scary business.

☞ Carl Schurz has obtained leave of absence from his mission for three months, and will leave Washington for the West to enter upon active military operations.

☞ The Southern Commissioners say that they gained the main object in going to Washington, which was to gain time for the South to arm themselves.

☞ The Richmond *Examiner* and the Richmond *Enquirer* both say that the negroes offer to enlist to fight for the State of Va. After the fighting is over the State will probably remove them by passage of laws to repel them from its precincts or to sell them into slavery.

The Killed at Charleston.

It is stated on the authority of a soldier who has reached New York, and who was in Fort Moultrie during the fight that for a time the carnage in Moultrie was terrible. This was in the forenoon of the first day. He states that between 300 and 400 men were killed. The killed were tumbled into boxes, many of them before they were scarcely dead, and then hurried off for burial. Many of the people who had friends in the fort did not believe that none were killed, and were constantly inquiring for them. They were told that the absent were on Sullivan's Island.

Hurrying off by night of the dead for burial, was the result of the Charleston authorities to disguise the slaughter from the people. The number of the murdered was very large.

It is also stated upon credible authority that one hundred and fifty men were killed at Morris' Island.

TRI-WEEKLY MERCURY.

BY R. B. RHETT, JR.

God Save The South.

God bless our Southern land!
Guard our beloved land!
God save the South!
Make us victorious,
Happy and glorious;
Spread thy shield over us;
God save the South!

God of our sires, arise!
Scatter our enemies,
Who mock Thy truth;
Confound their politics,
Frustrate their knavish tricks;
In Thee our faith we fix;
God save the South!

In the fierce battle hour,
With Thine almighty power,
Assist our youth;
May they, with victory crowned,
Joining our choral round,
With heart and voice resound,
"God save the South!"

THE WAR NEWS.

All doubt of a fierce war of sections seems now to be dispelled. The North has thaown off its disguise. The breaking loose of the pent-up mails furnishes us with an avalanche of exchanges, from which we make some interesting selections.

THE TERMS OF PEACE.

The New York *Tribune* of the 1st, mildly tells us what we are to expect. It says:

The only terms of peace, which would not provoke a revolution in all the loyal States, would be the unconditional submission of the traitors, the abandonment of the Montgomery Government, the surrender of the stolen Federal property, and the return of all the seceding States to obedience to the laws. We have no doubt this will be done at last; but not until the main question has been debated in one or two considerable battles. Until they are beaten in war, the Seceders will never abandon their great conspiracy; and the sooner and the more decidedly they are beaten, the better for all concerned. On the other hand, the people of the North and West are resolved that the business shall now be disposed of forever; that rebellion shall be crushed, and the integrity of the Republic maintained. * * *

We mean to conquer them—*not* merely to defeat, but to *conquer*, to SUBJUGATE them—and we shall do this the most mercifully, the more speedily we do it. But when the rebellious traitors are overwhelmed in the field, and scattered like leaves before an angry wind, it must not be to return to peaceful and contented homes. They must find poverty at their fire sides, and see privation in the anxious eyes of mothers and the rags of children. It is little enough the slaves will do when masters are at the wars, and to be idle and wasteful is the least harmful thing in which they are likely to engage themselves. There will be little cotton raised in the Southern States this year, and that little must pay the enhanced expense of a new route to market, if allowed to go at all, the price thereof to be returned in the bare necessaries of life, in limited quantities, at starvation prices. The whole coast of the South, from the Delaware to the Rio Grande, must be a solitude, save from the presence of a blockading squadron, so that no relief shall come in to the beleagured people from the sea. The other great highway, the Mississippi, it is the duty of the West to hold, and to prohibit its use, either partially or totally, as the obstinacy of these infatuated rebels shall promise to be of a shorter or longer duration. The West can drown or starve the lower country, as it pleases, if a continued rebellious obstinacy shall compel the North to accept the alternative. If Maryland goes out of the Union, and Baltimore continues contumacious, the same means of coercion should be resorted to. If Baltimore should be anything more than the name of an extinct city after the secession of that State, not another barrel of flour, not another bushel of corn, not another hog, not so much as a spring chicken, should be allowed to approach her by land or water. Half way measures will not do with an enemy who will conquer us and desecrate all this fair land with their accursed barbarism, unless we conquer them.

PLANS OF THE ENEMY.

The telegraphic correspondent of the New York *Tribune* at Washington professes to be thoroughly informed upon the progress of events in Virginia. After giving his narration of the movements of troops in this quarter, he goes on to say:

I have excellent authority for stating that the Administration purposes to strike a decisive blow before many days, probably within a fortnight. The Northern line of defence will doubtless be moved further South, in season for the people of Virginia to have fair play in voting on the *Ordinance*, and protection in the enjoyment of their liberty and property. It is not unlikely that the Alexandria Custom House, the Gosport Navy Yard, and perhaps Harper's Ferry, will be re-possessed. It is doubtful whether Richmond will be attacked, although this stroke is strongly urged upon the Administration from several quarters. There is reason to think, however, that the advance upon Virginia will be made from several quarters at once with overwhelming forces.

A design of making a demonstration on Florida and South Carolina at the same time was once, it is said, entertained; but this part of the plan has probably been relinquished. The policy which has been most pressed upon the President within the last few days is substantially as follows: To hold Virginia, as Maryland is held, with a strong hand, and await Mr. Jefferson Davis in the Old Dominion until the hot weather is over; meantime to seal hermetically every Southern port, and see what comes of it, and if, when the cool months begin, Davis and Company have not been disposed of by their own people, to treat them as they deserve. Of course, time must be allowed for properly equipping, arming and disciplining the volunteer forces. No General can muster an army and put it in the field in a week. I am afraid that the North is in too great a hurry, and expects a decisive blow to be struck before the national arm has been fairly raised.

The *Herald* of the same date says:

With regard to the movement of troops, there has been little change at the seat of war since our news of yesterday; the military *status quo* is preserved, but the course of the Government is still decided upon, and it is a vigorous one. General Patterson is to march two *corps d'armee* through Maryland, each ten thousand strong; one body is to go from Harrisburg by the Northern Central Railroad, and the other by the Wilmington and Baltimore Road, through the city of Baltimore. An army of ten thousand men is to be concentrated at Annapolis, ready to march on Baltimore in case of resistance. The New Jersey troops, three thousand strong, left Trenton yesterday for Annapolis, to form part of this *corps a'armee*. This movement will effectually settle the question of free travel to the National Capital.

WHAT THE HERO OF THE MINCIO SAYS.

Ever since RAYMOND, of the New York *Times*, ran away from the elbows of the Mincio, he has been prolific of military plans. Gen. SCOTT, having disregarded his advice, lost Fort Sumter. We hope more respect will be paid to RAYMOND'S advice about the impending abolition invasion. He says:

That the United States must invade Virginia and become possessed of Richmond, is most certain. That Jeff. Davis will be delighted to hear it, is also true, because we have sketched his programme of the campaign to the letter, just as he wants it. But while he thinks to offer battle on the Northern line of Virginia, and to make a feint of retreating towards Richmond and tempting on the elated army of the Union until he can flank it from Norfolk and York River on the east, and from Harper's Ferry and Winchester on the west, and then annihilate it, he forgets that his whole army, his people, his country, are *already flanked by the seacoast and the Gulf*, and that no army will advance upon Richmond until every soldier of the Gulf States is fully employed at home, in saving from Union armies that will hang upon their coasts, the plantations and the *animate property* on whose products the South expects to live! Here is a flanking movement that ends the war, if we may so speak, before it has fairly begun. It serves the double purpose, too, of blockade and invasion. It forces the Secession Armies to gather and encamp in the lagoons and morasses of the coast, while the Union Armies *have good health on shipboard*. It transfers the theatre of war to a region that the Northern half of the Gulf States dare not risk their lives in; and yet if the invasion is unresisted there, the Confederate States must fall in remediless ruin. With a vigorous prosecution of the war in this direction, Mr. Jeff. Davis is a lost man—his petty despotism is doomed. England and France have failed him. His King Cotton has proved to be King Log. The navies of England and France will not keep his ports open. His cotton (what little may be grown) will not be exported, and the first coupon on his recent loan, secured by the export duty on cotton, will never be paid. The seas and the Gulf are still ruled by the glorious Stars and Stripes, and just where Jeff. Davis is merely a pirate, to be hung at the yard arm, the Union is one of the mighty nations of the earth, ready to pour out on his exposed flank, among his helots and against his homes, armies great enough to appal and paralyze a half million of his swordsmen.

THE REINFORCEMENT OF FORT PICKENS.

The United States steamship *Atlantic*, Government transport, arrived at New York on Wednesday, from Pensacola, bringing a confirmation of the reported reinforcement of Fort Pickens. The *Atlantic* sailed from New York on April 7, having on board troops, provisions and war munitions. She arrived at Fort Taylor, Key West, on the 13th, and at Fort Jefferson, Tortugas, on the 14th, at both of which places she took on board additional troops and government stores, and sailed for the mouth of Pensacola harbor, joining the fleet stationed there, and anchoring off Santa Rosa Island, on which is Fort Pickens, on the evening of the 16th. Immediately on her arrival, during the night of the 16th, the reinforcement of the Fort by the fleet commenced, in which the *Atlantic* took a prominent part.

The operation of reinforcements continued up to April 28, during which time a large number of troops, horses, cannon, provisions, workmen, firearms and great quantities of various kinds of military stores were safely landed, and placed securely within the walls of Fort Pickens. The steam transport *Illinois*, also arrived off Santa Rosa Island on the 19th, and her troops and stores were also landed. During all these operations not a gun was fired by the Southerners from their fortifications. Fort Pickens is now amply supplied with men and guns to successfully resist any attack, there being now in the Fort and on Santa Rosa Island together about one thousand men, with provisions and stores sufficient to last for six months; and from the advantageous position in which this late reinforcement places both the garrison and the fleet, further supplies of men, provisions, &c., can hereafter be thrown in at pleasure.

Among the passengers by the *Atlantic* were Captains Meiggs and Walker, and Lieutenants Reed, Parker, Gordon and Saint, United States navy.

IMPORTANT FROM MISSOURI.

A despatch from St. Louis, dated Friday, May 3d, says:

The Governor's message was delivered to both Houses this morning, after which the House went into secret session.

Governor Jackson says the President, in calling out the troops to subdue the seceded States, has threatened civil war, and his act is unconstitutional and illegal, and tending toward consolidated despotism. While he evidently justifies the action of the Confederate States in seceding, he does not recommend immediate secession, but holds the following language:

"Our interests and sympathies are identical with those of the slaveholding States, and necessarily unite our destinies with theirs. The similarity of our social and political institutions, our industrial interests, our sympathies, habits and tastes, our common origin, territorial contiguity, all concur in pointing out our duty in regard to the separation now taking place between the States of the old Federal Union. He further adds, that Missouri has at this time no war to prosecute. It is not her policy to make an aggression, but in the present state of the country she would be faithless to her honor, recreant to her duty, were she to hesitate a moment in making the most ample preparations for the protection of her people against the aggression of all assailants. I therefore recommend an appropriation of a sufficient sum of money to place the State, at the earliest practicable moment, in a complete state of defence."

In conclusion, he says: "Permit me to appeal to you, and through you to the whole people of the State, to whom we are all responsible, to do nothing imprudently or precipitately. We have a most solemn duty to perform. Let us, then, calmly reason one with another, avoid all passion and tendency to tumult and disorder—obey implicitly the constituted authorities, and endeavor ultimately to unite all our citizens in a cordial co-operation for the preservation of our honor, the security of our property, and the performance of all those high duties imposed upon us by our obligations to our families, our country, and our God.

LEXINGTON, MO., May 3.—The Union demonstration held here last night was broken by up the Secessionists. One Union man was shot, but not seriously injured. There was to be a Union meeting here at 2 o'clock this afternoon, but it has been suppressed by the Secessionists. The Secession flag now waves in front of the Court House.

MOVEMENTS IN KENTUCKY.

A Cairo correspondent writes that about a dozen volunteers, belonging to a Chicago company, had refused to take the oath and left the ranks.

Major Buckner, Commander-in-Chief of the Kentucky militia, had a conference with Col. Prentiss, Commander of the forces at Cairo. There was much excitement at Paducah, Ky., and companies were constantly drilling. Four pieces of artillery had been received from Nashville.

It was understood that the Governor of Tennessee had made a demand upon the Governor of Illinois for the arms and munitions of war taken from a steamer. The boat had been given up to the owners and taken to Paducah.

The war feeling was high at Nashville, and several companies were drilling day and night.

A twenty-four pounder and a considerable number of troops were stationed at Columbus, Ky. The town was carefully guarded and all strangers closely watched, as the people feared an attack from the Cairo forces. The steamer *Julius H. Smith* had slipped by Cairo and landed 450 Colt's rifles.

MOVEMENTS IN DELAWARE.

From the following, it appears that there has been some excitement lately at Wilmington, Delaware:

WILMINGTON, May 2.—There has been much excitement here for a day or two past. Captain McMullen, of the Philadelphia Independent Rangers, has been in the city for the purpose of detecting some suspected parties here from Baltimore. It was rumored that an attack was to be made on the Powder Works of the Messrs. Dupont. Our Home Guards were called out, and after marching part of the way to the Works, were met by the Mayor of Wilmington, who directed them to return, as there was no occasion for their services. Every stranger is closely watched in this vicinity. On Monday night, two shots were fired at the guard on the Brandywine Railroad Bridge.

Messrs. Quigley & Stone have the contract for rebuilding the bridges between the Susquehanna and Baltimore. A sufficient force will accompany them to secure their protection.

MOVEMENTS IN MASSACHUSETTS.

With regard to Massachusetts affairs we learn from Boston that—

There is talk of calling an extra session of the Legislature to make an appropriation and authorize the Governor to establish a camp in Massachusetts, where all the newly organized volunteers can rendezvous until called into active service, the privates in the meantime to be paid $20 per month by the State.

Lieutenant Collier, of the United States Marines, attached to the *Minnesota*, raised the American flag to-day on the steeple of the Old South Church. Lieut. Collier is a native of Maryland.

MOVEMENTS IN CONNECTICUT.

The Connecticut Legislature convened on Wednesday. A despatch says:

Gov. Buckingham, in his message, recommends an efficient State militia; says that forty-one volunteer companies have already been accepted, and that the Fifth Regiment will be full in a few days. The regiments will not leave the States until they are fully equipped with camp and baggage train, and prepared to take care of themselves on all occasions.

The Legislature will make liberal appropriations for war purposes. All parties are acting in harmony on that question. The State is out of debt, and owns some $400,000 Bank stock.

The Governor has accepted the tender by Col. Colt of a regiment of ten companies, armed with rifles and sabre bayonets at his own expense. Col. Colt also furnishes officers to drill the men in the use of these arms, likewise at his own expense.

MOVEMENTS AT PHILADELPHIA.

From Philadelphia, May 3d, the telegraph advises us that:

All travel to the South is stopped to-day. No communication with Baltimore or Washington is permitted by the military authorities. General Patterson refused to give travellers his pass, and holds the roads exclusively for the transport of troops and munitions of war.

Three hundred passengers from Washington reached this city to-day. They have occupied thirty hours in the journey from that capital to this point.

Nineteen members of the Seventh Regiment of New York, have just arrived here, and leave immediately to join their comrades at Washington. They go by the way of Perryville and Annapolis.

Commodore Gregory, of Rhode Island, accompanies this detachment of the Seventh to the capital. He intends, notwithstanding his advanced years, to offer his services to the Government. He has been in the navy for fifty-two years.

NORTH CAROLINA.

The Legislature of North Carolina on Thursday, unanimously repealed the 5th section of the 76th chapter of the Revised Code, which requires all officers in that State to take an oath to support the Constitution of the United States before entering on their duties.

The Act further provides that it shall not be lawful to administer any such oath or affirmation to any officer, civil or military.

THE "FIRE ZOUAVES."

The brutal New York Zouaves seem to be amusing themselves hugely at the expense of the Washington people. The *Star* says:

Restaurants, cigar stores and hack and omnibus drivers, were levied upon, and, in settling, coolly told to charge it to Uncle Sam, Jeff. Davis, or some imaginary captain. One party entered a house and called for breakfast, and having swept the table and done some injury to the house, told the lady to call on the Colonel for damages, &c. It is probable these tricks will cease in a short time, as the officers are determined to expel from the regiment every man who does not behave himself becoming a soldier. In fact, we hear that ten rather incorrigible 'b'hoys have been promptly headed towards home by their officers.

The subdued method of announcing the above outrages will strike the attention of the reader.

WHAT THE B'HOYS SAY.

The first inquiry made by the firemen, on landing from the cars, was, with grave-faced earnestness, "Can you tell us where Jeff Davis is? we're lookin' for him." "Yes," said another, "we're bound to hang his scalp in the White House before we go back." Another one, whose massive under-jaw and breadth of neck indicated him "some in a plug muss," remarked that they had expected to have arrived by the way of Baltimore. "We would have come through Baltimore like a dose of salts," he added, with an air of disappointment. One of them beckoned a citizen, confidentially, to his side and inquired, "Is there any secession flags about here?" He was assured that secession bunting was an article that did not prevail here. He nodded, and added, "I only wanted to know."

On coming down the Avenue, the Franklin fire company reel passed them at a sharp run, on its way to a fire; and the familiar apparatus was saluted with such a yell of recognition along the entire line as must have fairly astonished the staid old reel.

Somebody remarked to one of the b'hoys that his hair was cut *rayther* short. "Oh, yes," was the reply, "we all had our heads *filed* before we left New York." They all look like fighting boys; but one company seems to have a special prestige that way. "If there's any mischief done, lay it onto Company 83," seemed to be a pet phrase amongst the b'hoys.

Some of the Zouaves, in emerging from their quarters (Columbian market building) this morning, disdaining the tedious, common-place mode of exit by the stairway, let themselves down to the street from the third story by a rope, like so many monkeys.

END OF UNIONISM IN ARKANSAS.

The Little Rock *Gazette*, probably the ablest, and certainly hitherto a most uncompromising opponent of secession, thus defines its position in the present conflict:

We fairly and deliberately, in the light of day, and in the exercise of our calm and cool judgment, take upon ourself the position of resistance to, and rebellion against, the present Government of the United States; and if there be any who wish to denounce us for this as treason against Lincoln's government, or war against Lincoln, we are willing and ready to furnish them the testimony, by the commission of an overt act whenever an opportunity offers.

THE RESPONSE OF VIRGINIA.

The Richmond *Examiner* states that the proclamation of Governor Letcher for volunteers in Virginia has been responded to by over *seventy thousand soldiers*.

"Young men from every class and profession throughout the State, all of them raised with arms in their hands from earliest boyhood, form Virginia's army. They are all said to be good marksmen, enured to fatigue by hunting and farming, riding and exercise of all kinds; eager to rush to the defence of their homes, fathers, mothers, rights and liberties—such are the defenders of Virginia. All of the State has not yet been heard from, and when it is, the number will be swelled to *one hundred thousand* of the best soldiers that ever stood forth to defend their country from oppression. Such an army, officered from the flower of the late United States army, and commanded by the brave and gallant Lee, the noble son of Light Horse Harry, conquest will be impossible, and the invader that has the hardihood to trespass upon the soil of Virginia will meet a sure and speedy death."

MOVEMENTS IN MARYLAND.

FREDERICK, Md., May 3.—A bill to create a Military Board of Seven, including ex Governor Lowe and Thomas Winans, with full power over purse and sword, is about to pass the Senate. It virtually supersedes the Governor, though he is to be one of it. The object is to fully arm the secessionists, and put the State on a war footing.

The excitement in this city and portion of the State is intense. There is trouble brewing, as the passage of the bill will revolutionize the State.

BALTIMORE.

Affairs remain quiet in Baltimore. Fort Madison, an earthwork fortification commanding the city and harbor, is in possession of government troops. The steamer *Maryland* landed a force of the Massachusetts troops from Annapolis, and large quantities of stores at Fort McHenry on Friday, and afterwards steamed up to the city with the stars and stripes flying.

MISCELLANEOUS WAR NEWS.

The New York *Express*, of Saturday, regards the telegrams from Missouri and Kentucky as of great importance. The message of the Missouri Governor sounds secessionist, and it does not like the way the Union men are going to the wall here and there in Old Kentucky.

Embarrassment in commercial circles appear to multiply. Sixty-nine failures for the week, of which thirty-nine are in New York.

It is a suggestive circumstance that most of the ships arriving at New York from Europe come in *empty*. The war is having a crushing effect upon the Northern shipping interest. The imports of foreign goods show a woeful falling off.

Two hundred men of the 8th New York Regiment have entrenched themselves on an eminence ten miles from Annapolis, commanding the Baltimore road. They have two pieces of artillery.

Should the Federal forces attempt to invade the State of Virginia, military men say that three routes only, lie open to them. These three are, one from Harrisburg, by railroad, through Harper's Ferry to Winchester; one from Washington, over the long bridge, and through Alexandria to Richmond; and the last by water, from any Northern port up the James River to the capital of the State.

Warnings to leave Washington are not only given by rowdies and unauthorized persons, but also by high officials. A few days since, Commodore Paulding notified Charles H. Winder, Esq., that if he continued to visit the Navy Department, as he was wont to do on business, he would be arrested, as it was understood that he was a secessionist.

American Topics Abroad.

The English papers have a good deal to say about American affairs, but the pressure upon our columns will not permit us to quote from them as fully as we could wish. The London *Telegraph*, of April 5th, in alluding to LINCOLN'S blockade, says shrewdly enough:

There appears, for the time, no danger of misapprehensions on the subject of the contemplated blockade, for the naval forces of the New World Republic, if they cannot rescue Fort Sumter, cannot surely undertake to lock up a prodigious seaboard, penetrable by large and accessible harbors, and open for hundreds of miles to the commerce of the world. The time has not come then, for Great Britain to express any diplomatic opinion upon the politics of the United States.

The London *Times*, of the same date, speaking of a war of coercion, says:

Such a war, we are well convinced, would come too late to undo the mischief that has already been done. It might, indeed, aggravate and envenom the wound, but could not heal it. The object is, if possible, to retain a diseased limb, but the knife is only useful when amputation has been resolved on. If nothing be done to make matters worse, it is quite conceivable that America may contain two confederacies, which, when relieved from a bond which both have hitherto borne with so much impatience, may cultivate friendly relations with each other, may enter into intimate alliances, and if not possessed of that influence in the world which a single confederation might exercise, may at least be able to exercise a power sufficient for all legitimate ends. Let American statesmen ponder well over the Fourth of July orations, to which they have listened from their early youth, and they will find there abundant proof how great is the error, where two nations speak the same language and belong to the same race, of striving to perpetuate by force and bloodshed a Union which has ceased to be one of friendship and good will. If the English Government had been content not to tax the Colonies, or if, having fallen into that great error, it had been content to allow them to depart peaceably as soon as it found that their connection with the Mother Country had become distasteful to them, how much of the bitterness and the evil of the separation would have been spared!

The Liverpool *Times*, in a long article, speculates upon the probable results of the coming war. We quote:

As war, then, between the two Republics seems to be regarded as certain, the question that remains to be asked is, What will the principals gain by it? It is evident that President Lincoln has neither an army nor a navy at hand to make the South submit, and it is equally certain that the South is even more anxious than the North to test it by a trial of strength. The old Government has certainly one alternative to which it may resort; but is so terrible in conception, and would prove so malignant in practice, that we will do Mr. Lincoln the justice of expressing our disbelief in his ever having recourse to it. The South is so strong on its own ground that no amount of Federal force which can be brought into the field, within any reasonable period, would stand a chance of success; but the Washington Government might readily make the slaves the instruments of vengeance, by putting arms into their hands to be turned against their masters. A servile war, thus inaugurated, would probably be one of the bloodiest and fiercest in the whole records of mankind, and while the men of the South were engaged in putting it down, their seaboard might be scoured, their cities ravaged, their property confiscated or destroyed, by the Unionist party. An extreme and desperate alternative like this would test the strength of the South, but the probability is that, even against such accumulated difficulties and odds, the South would ultimately triumph. We cannot, as we have said, suppose that Mr. Lincoln and his supporters, after their recent declarations, would have recourse to this diabolical policy; and yet, short of it, we can see no reasonable prospect of success in soliciting an encounter with the South.

If civil war has really commenced between the North and the South, we hope that the representatives of England and France at Washington have been instructed by their respective governments to tender their aid as mediators before the struggle has roused all the fierce passions which, if continued for any length of time, are certain to be called into play.

The *London American*, of the 10th ult., under the head, "Commercial Independence of the South," confesses:

While we have always deprecated the secession movement as a political mistake, we have never doubted that a separation would develope the commercial energies of the South with a rapidity unknown to her past history. Events have already confirmed this view, and the progress recently made in the establishment of direct steam communication between Europe and the Southern Republic shows the change that has been effected in the spirit of the people. Charleston alone raised more capital for the establishment of a steamship line with Europe in three weeks, under the inspiration of a commercial independence, than all the South could have done in the same number of years in the Union. The Southern Commercial Convention assembles year after year, but had never been able to obtain subscription to the proposed line to a larger amount than $10,000. While we have opposed the political separation of the States, it has always seemed to us desirable, for the interests of all sections of the country, that there should be less commercial dependence upon the North.

AMONG THE LATE RESIGNATIONS from the U. S. service, we notice the following;

Hon. John A. Campbell, of Ala., Associate Justice of the Bench of the Supreme Court of the United States.

Taliaferro Hunter, of Va., late Fourth Auditor.

Major H. B. Tyler, of Va., United States Marine corps.

Surgeon Dinwiddie B. Phillips, of Va., late U. S. A.

Lieut. G. H. Hill, of N. C., late of Sherman's Battery, Third Artillery.

Lieut. McGary, of the U. S. Navy, has also resigned and returns to North Carolina, waiting orders.

Alex. W. Lawrence, Professor of Mathematics in the United States navy, Lieut. B. W. Frobel, of Virginia, Capt. Robert K. Hudgins, and Second Lieutenant Wm. E. Hudgins, of the United States revenue service, have resigned.

CAPT. W. F. LYNCH, of Virginia, late of the United States navy, has resigned.

Lieutenant Anderson Jackson, United States army, grandson of the old hero, has resigned and joined the army of the South.

WHO IS HE?—The Washington correspondent of the New York *Herald* says:

A patent for an improved mode of training horses was granted to-day to Commodore Daniels, of Barnwell Court House, South Carolina. The thing was done as expeditiously, and with no more trouble than if he had belonged to New England.

WAR DECLARED!

The Act of Congress in Full.

From Our Own Correspondent.

MONTGOMERY, ALA., May 6, 1861.

The following Act has been passed by the Congress of the Confederate States in secret session. The injunction of secresy has been removed therefrom:

AN ACT RECOGNIZING THE EXISTENCE OF WAR BETWEEN THE UNITED STATES AND THE CONFEDERATE STATES, AND CONCERNING LETTERS OF MARQUE, PRIZES AND PRIZE GOODS.

Whereas, The earnest efforts made by this Government to establish friendly relations between the Government of the United States and the Confederate States, and to settle all questions of disagreement between the two Governments upon principles of right, justice, equity and good faith, have proved unavailing, by reason of the refusal of the Government of the United States to hold any intercourse with the Commissioners appointed by this Government for the purposes aforesaid, or to listen to any proposal they had to make for the peaceful solution of all causes of difficulties between the two governments; and, *whereas*, the President of the United States of America has issued his Proclamation, making requisition upon the States of the American Union for 75,000 men, for the purpose as therein indicated of capturing forts, and other strongholds within the jurisdiction of, and belonging to, the Confederate States of America, and has detailed naval armaments upon the coasts of the Confederate States of America, and raised, organized and equipped a large military force to execute the purpose aforesaid, and has issued his other Proclamation, announcing his purpose to set on foot a blockade of the ports of the Confederate States; and *whereas*, the State of Virginia has seceded from the Federal Union and entered into a convention of alliance, offensive and defensive, with the Confederate States, and has adopted the Provisional Constitution of the said States, and the States of Maryland, North Carolina, Tennessee, Kentucky, Arkansas, and Missouri have refused, and it is believed that the State of Delaware and the inhabitants of the Territories of Arizona and New Mexico, and the Indian Territory south of Kansas, will refuse to co-operate with the Government of the United States in these acts of hostilities and wanton aggression, which are plainly intended to overawe, oppress, and finally subjugate the people of the Confederate States; and *whereas*, by the acts and means aforesaid war exists between the Confederate States and the Government of the United States, and the States and Territories thereof, except the States of Maryland, North Carolina, Tennessee, Kentucky, Arkansas, Missouri, and Delaware, and the Territories of Arizona and New Mexico, and the Indian Territory south of Kansas: Therefore,

SECTION 1. *The Congress of the Confederate States of America do enact*, That the President of the Confederate States is hereby authorized to use the whole land and naval force of the Confederate States to meet the war thus commenced, and to issue to private armed vessels commissions, or letters of marque and general reprisal, in such form as he shall think proper, [illegible] of the Confederate States, against the [illegible] goods and effects of the Government of [illegible] States, and of the citizens or inhabitants of [illegible] and Territories thereof, except [illegible] Territories hereinbefore named. [illegible] however, that property of the [illegible] contraband of war) laden on [illegible] vessel, shall not be subject to seizure [illegible] *and provided further*, that [illegible] citizens or inhabitants of the United States [illegible] ports of the Confederate States, [illegible] have been since the 5th of April last, or may hereafter be, in the service of the Government of the United States, shall be allowed thirty days after the publication of this Act to leave said ports and reach their destination; and such vessels and their cargos, excepting articles contraband of war, shall not be subject to capture under this Act, during said period, unless they shall have previously reached the destination for which they were bound on leaving said ports.

SEC. 2. That the President of the Confederate States shall be, and he is hereby authorized and empowered to revoke and annul, at pleasure, all letters of marque and reprisal which he may at any time grant pursuant to this Act.

SEC. 3. That all persons applying for letters of marque and reprisal, pursuant to this Act, shall state in writing the name, and a suitable description of the tonnage and force of the vessel, and the name and place of residence of each owner concerned therein, and the intended number of the crew; which statement shall be signed by the person or persons making such application, and filed with the Secretary of State, or shall be delivered to any other officer or person who shall be employed to deliver out such commissions, to be by him transmitted to the Secretary of State.

SEC. 4. That before any commission or letters of marque and reprisal shall be issued as aforesaid, the owner or owners of the ship or vessel for which the same shall be requested, and the commander thereof for the time being, shall give bond to the Confederate States, with at least two responsible sureties, not interested in such vessel, in the penal sum of five thousand dollars; or if such vessel be provided with more than one hundred and fifty men, then in the penal sum of ten thousand dollars; with condition that the owners, officers and crew, who shall be employed on board such commissioned vessel, shall and will observe the laws of the Confederate States, and the instructions which shall be given them according to law, for the regulation of their conduct; and will satisfy all damages and injuries which shall be done or committed contrary to the tenor thereof, by such vessel, during her commission, and to deliver up the same when revoked by the President of the Confederate States.

SEC. 5. That all captures and prizes of vessels and property shall be forfeited, and shall accrue to the owners, officers and crews of the vessels by whom such captures and prizes shall be made; and on due condemnation had, shall be distributed according to any written agreement which shall be made between them; and if there be no such written agreement, then one moiety to the owners, and the other moiety to the officers and crew, as nearly as may be according to the rules prescribed for the distribution of prize money, by the laws of the Confederate States.

SEC. 6. That all vessels, goods and effects, the property of any citizen of the Confederate States, or of persons resident within and under the protection of the Confederate States, or of persons permanently within the territories, and under the protection of any foreign prince, government, or State in amity with the Confederate States, which shall have been captured by the United States, and which shall be recaptured by vessels commissioned as aforesaid, shall be restored to the lawful owners, upon payment by them of a just and reasonable salvage, to be determined by the mutual agreement of the parties concerned, or by the decree of any court having jurisdiction, according to the nature of each case, agreeably to the provisions established by law. And such salvage shall be distributed among the owners, officers, and crews of the vessels commissioned as aforesaid, and making such captures, according to any written agreement which shall be made between them; and in case of no such agreement, then in the same manner and upon the principles hereinbefore provided in case of capture.

SEC. 7. That before breaking bulk of any vessel which shall be captured as aforesaid, or other disposal or conversion thereof, or of any articles which shall be found on board the same, such captured vessel, goods or effects, shall be brought into some port of the Confederate States, or of a nation or State in amity with the Confederate States, and shall be proceeded against before a competent tribunal; and after condemnation and forfeiture thereof, shall belong to the owners, officers, and crew of the vessel capturing the same, and be distributed as before provided; and in the case of all captured vessels, goods and effects, which shall be brought within the jurisdiction of the Confederate States, the District Courts of the Confederate States shall have exclusive, original cognizance thereof, as in civil causes of admiralty and maritime jurisdiction; and the said courts, or the courts, being courts of the Confederate States, into which such causes shall be removed, and in which they shall be finally decided, shall and may decree restitution, in whole or in part, when the capture shall have been made without just cause. And if made without probable cause, may order and decree damages and costs to the party injured, for which the owners and commanders of the vessels making such captures, and also the vessels shall be liable.

SEC. 8. That all persons found on board any captured vessels, or on board any recaptured vessel, shall be reported to the Collector of the port in the Confederate States, in which they shall first arrive, and shall be delivered into the custody of the Marshal of the District, or some court or military officer of the Confederate States, or of any State in or near such port, who shall take charge of their safe keeping and support, at the expense of the Confederate States.

SEC. 9. That the President of the Confederate States is hereby authorized to establish and order suitable instructions for the better governing and directing the conduct of the vessels so commissioned, their officers and crews, copies of which shall be delivered, by the collector of the customs, to the commanders, when they shall give bond as before provided.

SEC. 10. That a bounty shall be paid by the Confederate States of $20 for each person on board any armed ship or vessel, belonging to the United States, at the commencement of an engagement, which shall be burnt, sunk or destroyed by any vessel commissioned as aforesaid, which shall be of equal or inferior force, the same to be divided as in other cases of prize money—and a bounty of $25 shall be paid to the owners, officers and crews of the private armed vessels, commissioned as aforesaid, for each and every prisoner by them captured and brought into port, and delivered to an agent authorized to receive them, in any port of the Confederate States; and the Secretary of the Treasury is hereby authorized to pay or cause to be paid to the owners, officers and crews of such private armed vessels, commissioned as aforesaid, or their agent, the bounties herein provided.

SEC. 11. That the Commanding Officer of every vessel having a commission, or letters of marque and reprisal, during the present hostilities between the Confederate States and the United States, shall keep a regular journal, containing a true and exact account of his daily proceedings and transactions with such vessel and the crew thereof; the ports and places he shall put into, or cast anchor in; the time of his stay there, and the cause thereof; the prizes he shall take, and the nature and probable value thereof; the times and places, when and where taken, and in what manner he shall dispose of the same; the ships or vessels he shall fall in with; the times and places, when and where he shall meet with them, and his observations and remarks thereon; also, of whatever else shall occur to him, or any of his officers or marines, or be discovered by examination or conference with any marines or passengers of, or in any other ships or vessels, or by any other means, touching the fleets, vessels and forces of the United States; their posts and places of station and destination, strength, numbers, intents and designs: and such commanding officer shall, immediately on his arrival in any port of the Confederate States, from or during the continuance of any voyage or cruise, produce his commission for such vessel, and deliver up such journal so kept as aforesaid, signed with his proper name and handwriting, to the collector or other chief officer of the customs at or nearest to such port; the truth of which journal shall be verified by the oath of the commanding officer for the time being, and such collector or other chief officer of the customs shall, immediately on the arrival of such vessel, order the proper officer of the customs to go on board and take an account of the officers and men, the number and nature of the guns, and whatever else shall occur to him on examination, material to be known; and no such vessel shall be permitted to sail out of port again until such journal shall have been delivered up, and a certificate obtained under the hand of such collector or other chief officer of the customs, that she is manned and armed according to her commission; and upon delivery of such certificate, any former certificate of a like nature which shall have been obtained by the commander of such vessel, shall be delivered up.

SEC. 12. That the commanders of vessels having Letters of Marque and Reprisal, as aforesaid, neglecting to keep a journal as aforesaid, or wilfully making fraudulent entries therein, or obliterating the record of any material transactions therein, where the interest of the Confederate States is concerned, or refusing to produce and deliver such journal, commission or certificate, pursuant to the preceding section of this act, then and in such cases, the commissions or Letters of Marque and Reprisal of such vessels shall be liable to be revoked; and such commander, respectively, shall forfeit for every such offence the sum of $1000, one moiety thereof to the use of the Confederate States, and the other to the informer.

SEC. 13. That the owners or commanders of vessels having letters of marque and reprisal as aforesaid, who shall violate any of the acts of Congress for the collection of the revenue of the Confederate States, and for the prevention of smuggling, shall forfeit the commission or letters of marque and reprisal, and they and the vessels owned or commanded by them shall be liable to all the penalties and forfeitures attaching to merchant vessels, in like cases.

SEC. 14. That on all goods, wares and merchandise captured and made good and lawful prize of war, by any private armed ship having commission or letters of marque and reprisal under this act, and brought into the Confederate States, there shall be allowed a deduction of 33 1 3 per cent. on the amount of duties imposed by law.

SEC. 15. That five per centum on the net amount (after deducting all charges and expenditures) of the prize money arising from captured vessels and cargos, and on the net amount of the salvage of vessels and cargos recaptured by the private armed vessels of the Confederate States, shall be secured and paid over to the Collector or other chief officer of the customs, at the port or place in the Confederate States at which such captured or recaptured vessels may arrive, or to the consul or other public agent of the Confederate States, residing at the port or place, not within the Confederate States, at which such captured or recaptured vessel may arrive. And the moneys arising therefrom shall be held and are hereby pledged by the Government of the Confederate States as a fund for the support and maintenance of the widows and orphans of such persons as may be slain, and for the support and maintenance of such persons as may be wounded and disabled on board of the private armed vessels commissioned as aforesaid, in any engagement with the enemy, to be assigned and distributed in such manner as shall hereafter be provided by law.

THE CHARLESTON RIFLEMEN send us the following complimentary resolution. It gratifies us to know that we have in any way contributed to the comfort of that gallant corps, which has done the State such faithful service:

MILITARY HALL, May 6, 1861.

A meeting of the Charleston Riflemen was held this evening, when the following resolution was unanimously adopted:

Resolved, That this corps do tender their sincere thanks to the Editors of THE CHARLESTON MERCURY, for their kindness in forwarding to them THE DAILY MERCURY, which has been a great source of pleasure and comfort during their encampment at Fort Pickens, Battery Island.

Respectfully submitted.

J. C. R. TAYLOR, Secretary *pro tem*.

AT A MEETING of the Washington Light Infanty Volunteers (who intend, about seventy strong), to go to Virginia, held last evening at Military Hall, the following gentlemen were elected officers;

JAMES CONNER, Captain.
JAMES LOWNDES, 1st Lieutenant.
T. M. LOGAN, 2d Lieutenant.
T. KLINK, 3d Lieutenant.
W. A. DOTTERER, 1st Sergeant.
J. H. GARDNER, 2d Sergeant.
J. COPES, 3d Sergeant.
J. A. CONDY, 4th Sergeant.
C. S. ATKINSON, 5th Sergeant.
W. C. DAVIS, 1st Corporal.
R. H. BOMAR, 2d Corporal.
THOMAS FORD, 3d Corporal.
H. G. BAKER, 4th Corporal.
H. ROUX, 5th Corporal.
A. M. LLOYD, 6th Corporal.

CHARLESTON:

THURSDAY, MAY 9, 1861.

Demoniac Howlings.

The howlings of the beast sufficiently betray his parts. Those of the Northern press, especially the philanthropist, are absolutely hellish. They roar like devils, and they rage like wolves. They begin to feel the truth, in a terrible experience of loss and ruin, of the thousand warnings which we gave them long ago. We said to them, "You grin and leer and gibber now—but you will soon howl in desperation." In their blind vanity—in their remorseless cupidity, they took no counsel from wisdom, or thought, or the experience of nations, or the warnings of history. Their lusts blinded them to the light, their appetites deafened them to all honest and warning voices, and the ruin falls upon them like a thunderbolt. They roar with hate and terror. They threaten with a fiendish malice, which would be something terrible, did it not declare rather for their sufferings, and agonies and terrors, than their powers. The spear is in the throat of the wolf, and he writhes upon it; the heel is upon the head of the snake, and his wriggles are death

Our Montgomery Correspondence.

MONTGOMERY, May 6, 1861.

War—Terms of the Act—Letters of Marque—Sand Bags—Military Movements—Soldiers Fund—The South Carolina Regiments—Distinguished Strangers, etc., etc.

The act recognizing the existence of war between the United States and the Confederate States, which I wrote you was passed on the 3d inst., was made public to-day. As will be seen, the act commences with a brief review of the course of the Federal Government since the formation of this government, and recognizes the existence of war between the Confederate States and all the States and Territories of the United States, except the slaveholding States and the Territories of Arizona and New Mexico, and the Indian Territory south of Kansas. By it the President is authorized to use the entire land and naval force to meet the war thus commenced by the LINCOLN government, and also authorizes the issuance of letters of marque and general reprisal, under the seal of the Confederate States, against the vessels of the United States and the property of its citizens. Vessels now in port will be allowed thirty days after the publication of this act to leave and to

THE WAR NEWS.

All doubt of a fierce war of sections seems now to be dispelled. The North has thaown off its disguise. The breaking loose of the pent-up mails furnishes us with an avalanche of exchanges, from which we make some interesting selections.

THE TERMS OF PEACE.

The New York *Tribune* of the 1st, mildly tells us what we are to expect. It says:

The only terms of peace, which would not provoke a revolution in all the loyal States, would be the unconditional submission of the traitors, the abandonment of the Montgomery Government, the surrender of the stolen Federal property, and the return of all the seceding States to obedience to the laws. We have no doubt this will be done at last; but not until the main question has been debated in one or two considerable battles. Until they are beaten in war, the Seceders will never abandon their great conspiracy; and the sooner and the more decidedly they are beaten, the better for all concerned. On the other hand, the people of the North and West are resolved that the business shall now be disposed of forever; that rebellion shall be crushed, and the integrity of the Republic maintained. * * *

We mean to conquer them—*not* merely to defeat, but to *conquer*, to SUBJUGATE them—and we shall do this the most mercifully, the more speedily we do it. But when the rebellious traitors are overwhelmed in the field, and scattered like leaves before an angry wind, it must not be to return to peaceful and contented homes. They must find poverty at their fire sides, and see privation in the anxious eyes of mothers and the rags of children. It is little enough the slaves will do when masters are at the wars, and to be idle and wasteful is the least harmful thing in which they are likely to engage themselves. There will be little cotton raised in the Southern States this year, and that little must pay the enhanced expense of a new route to market, if allowed to go at all, the price thereof to be returned in the bare necessaries of life, in limited quantities, at starvation prices. The whole coast of the South, from the Delaware to the Rio Grande, must be a solitude, save from the presence of a blockading squadron, so that no relief shall come in to the beleagured people from the sea. The other great highway, the Mississippi, it is the duty of the West to hold, and to prohibit its use, either partially or totally, as the obstinacy of these infatuated rebels shall promise to be of a shorter or longer duration. The West can drown or starve the lower country, as it pleases, if a continued rebellious obstinacy shall compel the North to accept the alternative. If Maryland goes out of the Union, and Baltimore continues contumacious, the same means of coercion should be resorted to. If Baltimore should be anything more than the name of an extinct city after the secession of that State, not another barrel of flour, not another bushel of corn, not another hog, not so much as a spring chicken, should be allowed to approach her by land or water. Half way measures will not do with an enemy who will conquer us and desecrate all this fair land with their accursed barbarism, unless we conquer them.

a force of fifty thousand men at such points in Virginia as Harper's Ferry, Alexandria, Richmond and Norfolk, and still retain twenty-five thousand men to guard Washington and suffocate secession in Maryland, and within a week we trust that some such plan of operations will be made manifest.

The N. Y. *Herald* makes a very good hit, and the South must "acknowledge the corn." THE MERCURY, however, is out of the scrape. We don't profess to be quite so enthusiastic as some of our brethren, and we are poor believers in such late converts. Had the report been true, we should have had little confidence in the vain old dotard.

IT IS REPORTED that an English steamer will leave here in a short time for Liverpool. She has fine accommodations for passengers, and is a favorable opportunity to [illegible] many of our merchants who are here arranging to visit Europe for the purchase of their fall supplies.

NEW MUSIC.—We have received a piece of music entitled "The [illegible] of Fort Sumter Polka March." It is very handsomely gotten up.

IT HAS BEEN REPORTED that Governor HAMMOND of this State gave five thousand dollars to the State to be used for her defence, and that [illegible] We are authorized to say that if any thing has been given or tendered from Governor HAMMOND, it has not [illegible] Executive Department.

A FORT SUMTER OFFICER RESIGNS.—Lieutenant RICHARD K. MEADE, late of the United States Army, and on duty at Fort Sumter during the siege by the South Carolina troops, has resigned his position, and returned to his native State, Virginia.

THE NEW YORK HERALD, we notice, is still offered for sale in Charleston. Ought this to be permitted?

AT A MEETING of the Hibernian Society, held last night, the name of THOMAS FRANCIS MEAGHER was unanimously stricken from the roll of the honorary members of that Society.

THE BUTLER GUARDS, of Columbia, left that city for Virginia Monday afternoon, by a special train on the Charlotte Railroad. They were escorted to the depot by the whole regiment to which they were attached, and by the Richland Volunteer Rifle Company.

charge my duty. We were boys at college together, and I trust we will be spared to travel through life, bound together as friends, by associations connected with a period of great peril, as well as of high and intrepid daring in the policy and cause of South Carolina.

May God bless you.

Yours, with great regard,

F. W. PICKENS.

To Hon. D. F. JAMISON.

THE CATHOLICS AND THE CRISIS.—The New York *Freeman's Journal* contends that "Catholics have done nothing to bring on this war," and urges them to speak out and call once more for counsels of peace. The *Journal*, alluding to the *Tribune's* exhortation [illegible]

[illegible]

RUMORED REVOLT ON BOARD THE FEDERAL FLEET AT PENSACOLA.—A letter from a gentleman connected with the Medical Department of the Florida Army, dated Warrington, April 26th, says:

"There was evidently a violent commotion amongst the [illegible] steamers. One, the *Sabine*, commanded by Capt. Adams, the first Lieutenant of which is Mr. Murdough, and the Surgeon, [illegible] Dr. Minor, all Southern men, [illegible]"

A SALIENT PARAGRAPH.—A young damsel in Worcester, Mass., has written to the editor of the New York *Tribune*, "There's that Morrill tariff [illegible]"

Mr. Russell's Letters to the London Times.

We find in the London *Times*, of the 22d ult., the second letter from its special correspondent in America, Mr. RUSSELL. It was written on the 5th of April, while he was yet sojourning at Washington. The fact that these letters may have some influence in giving direction to British sentiment, induces us to give place to the subjoined extracts. It must be borne in mind that events of a stupendous nature have occurred since it was written, and for the purpose of informing himself correctly on the points at issue, Mr. RUSSELL is now at the South:

Without the means of enforcing an authority which many of its own adherents, and most of the neutral parties, denied to it, Mr. Lincoln's Administration finds itself called upon to propound a policy and to proceed to vigorous action. The demand is scarcely reasonable. The policy of such men suddenly lifted to the head of affairs, which they cannot attempt to guide, must be to wait and watch; and their action must be simply tentative, as they have no power to put forth with moderate hope of success any aggressive force.

Be satisfied of this, the United States Government will give up no power or possession which it has at present got. By its voluntary act, it will surrender nothing whatever. No matter what reports may appear in the papers, or in letters, distrust them if they would lead you to believe that Mr. Lincoln is preparing either to abandon what he has now or to recover that which he has not.

The United States Government is in an attitude of protest; it cannot strike an offensive blow. But if any attack is made upon it, the Government hopes that it will be strengthened by the indignation of the North and West to such an extent that it can not only repel the aggression, but possibly give a stimulus to a great reaction in its favor.

On these principles Fort Sumter and Fort Pickens are held. They are claimed as Federal fortresses. The Stars and Stripes still float over them. Whatever may be said to the contrary, they will remain there till they are removed by the action of the Confederate States. * * * *

Mr. Lincoln has no power to make war against the South; the Congress alone could give it to him; and that is not likely to be given, because Congress will not be assembled before the usual time, unless under the pressure of an imperious necessity.

Why, then, hold these forts at all? Why not give them up? Why not withdraw the garrisons, strike the flag, and cease to keep up a useless source of irritation in the midst of the Southern Confederation? The answer to these questions is: These forts are Federal property. The government does not acknowledge the existence of any right on the part of the people of the States to seize them as appertaining to the individual States. The forts are protests against the acts of violence to which the Federal authority has yielded elsewhere. They are, moreover, the *points d'appui*, small as they are, on which the Federal Government can rest its resistance to the claims of the Southern Confederation to be acknowledged as an independent Republic. If they were surrendered without attack, or without the existence of any pressure arising from the refusal of the Southern authorities to permit them to get supplies, which is an act of war, the case of the United States Government would be, they consider, materially weakened. If it be observed that these forts have no strategetic value, it may readily be replied that their political value is very great. But, serious as these considerations may be, or may be thought to be, with respect to foreign relations, there are, in reference to domestic politics, still more weighty inducements to hold them. The effect produced in the North and Northwest by an attack on the forts while the United States flag is floating over them would be as useful to the Government at Washington as the effect of abandoning the forts or tamely surrendering them would be hurtful to them in the estimation of the extreme Republicans. A desperate attack, a gallant defence, the shedding the blood of gallant men, whose duty it was to defend that entrusted to their keeping, and who yielded only to numbers—the outrage on the American flag—would create an excitement in the Union which the South with all its determination and courage is unwilling to provoke, but which the Government would be forced to use in its own service.

Such an event must lead to war—a very terrible and merciless war, and both parties pause before they resort to that court of arms. Unless the Border States join in the South, Mr. Jefferson Davis could scarcely hope to carry out the grand projects which are attributed to his military genius of marching Northwards and dictating terms on their own soil to Republicans. He could scarcely venture to leave the negro population unguarded in his rear, and his flanks menaced by the seaborn Northerners on one side, and by such operations as the water-sheds significantly indicate on the other. It is idle to speculate on the incidents of that which may never occur, and which, occurring, may assume the insignificant aspect of border skirmishes, or the tremendous proportions of a war of races and creeds, intensified by the worst elements of servile and civil conflict. The Government of Mr. Lincoln hope and believe that the contest may be averted. The Commissioners of the South are inclined to think, also, there will be a peaceful solution—obtained, of course, by full concession and recognition. But inaction cannot last on the part of the South. Already they have begun the system of coercion. The supplies of the garrison at Sumter will be cut off henceforth, if they are not already forbidden. They do not fear the moral effect of this act, for some of their leading men actually believe that nothing can stop the progress of a movement which will, they fondly think, absorb all the other States of the Union, and leave the New England States to form an insignificant Republic of its own, with a possible larger destiny in Canada.

* * * * * *

The Government is elated at the success of the loan, and Mr. Chase has taken high ground in refusing offers made to him yesterday, and in resolving to issue Government securities for the balance of the amount required to complete the amount. Mr. Forsyth, one of the Southern Commissioners, who has just returned from New York here, is equally satisfied with the temper of parties in that city, and seems to think that the New Yorkers are preparing for a secession. But, though States may be sovereign, it has never been asserted that cities or portions of States are so, and in the Western and Northern portions of the State of New York there is a large agricultural population, which, with the aid of Government, would very speedily suppress any attempt to secede on the part of the city, if men are to be believed who say they know the circumstances of the case. Virginia is claimed by both sides, but accounts this morning are to the effect that the secessionists have been defeated on a division, by a vote of two to one, in favor of the Union; and, although General Houston appears to be forced to accept the situation for a time, there are many who think he will organize a strong reaction against the dominant secessionists.

Whatever may be the result of all these diverse actions, the Great Republic is gone! The shape of the fragments is not yet determined any more than their fate. They may reunite, but the cohesion can never be perfect. The ship of State was built of too many "platforms;" there were too many officers on board; perhaps the principles of construction were erroneous—the rigid, cast iron old Constitution guns burst violently when tried with new projectiles; any way, those who adhere with most devotion to the vessel admit that it is parted right amidships, and that its prestige has vanished.

English Trade and the American Troubles.

The New York "*Shipping and Commercial List*," of May 1st, gives extracts from the London *Times* of April 17th, which contains nearly two columns of reports from the manufacturing districts, exhibiting in a most striking light the ruinous depression of trade there, consequent upon the prospect of civil war in the United States. All branches appear to be alike affected. The result of the *Times'* statements may be condensed as follows: In Wolverhampton, trade is about as bad as bad can be, but under the impression that the American (Morrill) tariff will be speedily repealed, and that the separation of the North and South can be peacefully effected, there are many of the iron masters who are confident of a speedy renewal of orders from the United States. (The impression alluded to, seems to have been created by private letters from this side, the writers of which appear to have been blind to the true meaning of the events in progress here.) From Sheffield, the reports are of the most discouraging character. Some of the cutlery manufacturers, exclusively employed in the American trade, have closed their establishments altogether; but the diminished likelihood of war was raising hopes that the crisis would come to an end sooner than was generally anticipated. At Nottingham, the wholesale houses have been buying more freely, and some few orders from America are reported—enough to revive a feeling of confidence as to the future, and to justify manufacturers looking forward to increased demands. At Birmingham, stagnation in every department is the order of the day. From America the orders are entirely nominal. The long continued depression in trade is at last becoming serious as far as the artisans are concerned, so many of them having been employed not more than three or four days in the week, and the number of those who are unemployed has been on the increase of late.

A number of heavy failures are announced. At Bradford, also, the American houses are either out of the market altogether, or if they buy at all, their purchases are insignificant in amount. At Newcastle-on-Tyne it was thought that when the new American tariff came into operation it would entirely stop the exportation of coals thence for the United States; but in consequence of the low freights that now prevail, a large quantity is being shipped. Of course, by the operation of the tariff the American consumer loses all the advantages of the low freights.

The New York *Commercial Journal*, which makes these quotations, adds:

"We need not continue these citations. We have submitted enough to show that, severe as the blow is, which our political troubles have dealt to trade and commerce at home, our foreign relations are staggering under it even worse than we are; a fact which will engender with many a hope that self interest may yet prompt her Majesty's Government to tender its good offices as mediator between the two sections of our unhappy country, to put a period to a strife which, if it go on, bids fair to inflict injuries upon the commerce of the whole world, from which it will take many long years to recover. We have no idea, ourselves, that the offer of any such mediation, at present, would be accepted; but, when mutually exhausted by a desolating conflict, who shall say that an olive branch, coming from the parent country, in a spirit of genuine kindness and good will, would be rejected with scorn?"

It is said that Gen. Scott will change his headquarters from Washington to Philadelphia.

SOUTHERN PROVISIONAL CONGRESS.

EXTRA SESSION.

MONTGOMERY, ALA., May 6, 1861.

The Congress met at 12 o'clock, m., and was called to order by the President, Hon. HOWELL COBB, of Georgia. After prayer by the Rev. Mr. MANLY, the Journal of yesterday was read and approved.

RESIGNATION OF A MEMBER.

The PRESIDENT laid before the Congress the following letter from Mr. ANDERSON, late a member of Congress from Florida:

NEAR PENSACOLA, FLA., May 1, 1861.

Hon. Howell Cobb, President, etc., Montgomery, Ala.:

SIR: On the 8th of April last, I addressed to you a communication, formally resigning the seat in the body over which you preside which I had the honor of holding for the State of Florida. I have this day learned, that up to a late date, that communication had not been received. I desire, therefore, to repeat its tenor as indicated. The new relations I have voluntarily assumed with another branch of the Government renders this course proper, that a successor may supply my place in the Congress. With many of the liveliest and most pleasing recollections of my brief association with the memorable body over which you worthily preside, and with sentiments of the highest regard for yourself personally,

I am, sir, very respectfully,
Your obedient servant,
J. PATTON ANDERSON.

On motion of Mr. MORTON, of Florida, the communication was ordered to be spread on the journal.

PRESIDENTIAL AND CONGRESSIONAL ELECTIONS.

Mr. CURRY, of Alabama, on leave, introduced the following bills, which were severally read twice by their titles, and referred to the Committee on the Judiciary.

A bill to be entitled, "An Act to fix the time for the election of Representatives to Congress, and the time for the assembling of Congress."

A bill to be entitled "An Act to provide for the election of President and Vice President."

THE FEELING IN LOUISIANA.

Mr. PERKINS, of Louisiana. Mr. President: I ask the indulgence of the House to have read from the desk, a resolution passed by one of the interior parishes of Louisiana. The question has often been asked as to the feeling pervading that State, especially among those originally opposed to secession. I hold in my hand a resolution passed at a public meeting composed chiefly of those who originally opposed the movement. It is not a very large parish, but it has already three hundred soldiers at the disposal of the Government. At a public meeting hastily called, $12,000 were subscribed and paid on the spot, and the following resolution passed, which I am assured is the sense of that parish, and but indicates the feeling pervading the entire State.

The PRESIDENT. The gentleman from Louisiana calls for the reading of the following resolution. It will be read if there be no objection.

There being no objection, the resolution was read, as follows:

Resolved, by the Planters of the Parish of Feliciana in general meeting assembled, That we hereby stand pledged to tender to the State of Louisiana and the Government of the Confederate States, should it be needed, the whole annual proceeds of our crops, deducting only what may be necessary for our current expenses, during the continuance of the present hostilities.

The PRESIDENT. What motion does the gentleman make?

Mr. PERKINS. Mr. President, I make no motion, but simply desire the favor of having the resolution read at the desk.

PENSACOLA AND GEORGIA RAILROAD.

Mr. MORTON, of Florida. Mr. President, I beg leave to present a memorial of the Pensacola and Georgia Railroad Company, and I ask that the memorial, together with the accompanying papers, be referred to the Committee on Finance. The memorial is not to remit the duties, but to obtain credit for the railroad iron now in bond in the Custom House.

The question being taken, the motion was agreed to, and the memorial was accordingly referred without being read.

And then the Congress proceeded to sit with closed doors.

The War Cloud in Europe.

In the midst of the threatening events on this side of the water we are apt to overlook the progress of affairs in Europe, from whence the mutterings of a dreadful contest, soon to commence, come to us by every arrival. The Paris correspondent of the Boston *Traveller* writes, under date of the 11th inst., as follows:

Whether it be the 1st of April which casts its ludicrous shadow upon us, or that we feel the quiverings which forerun the earthquake, certain it is the political atmosphere was never more agitated than it is now by all manner of alarming rumors—some long faces vow Russia and France entered into a secret treaty for the partition of Turkey—a poor country, which is certainly in a most deplorable condition—on the 13th of March last; other faces, no ways shorter, whisper mysteriously of negotiations between Russia, Austria, Italy and France for the dismemberment of Turkey, for the extension of French territory to the Rhine, for the destruction of Belgium, for the obliteration of all the minor powers of Germany under Prussia, to whom Austria would concede its German provinces, and surrender its Italian provinces to Italy, receiving in exchange the Roumain and Sclave Provinces on the Lower Danube, which consolidated with Hungary, Bohemia, &c., would make it a powerful and united Sclavonic Power of the first magnitude, while Prussia, rewarded by Holland, the Hanseatic towns, all the minor kingdoms, principalities and powers of Germany, would relinquish its Polish provinces; Russia rewarded by Greece and Constantinople, would imitate Prussia's example, and the Kingdom of Poland would be reconstituted.

England would be driven from the Mediterranean, and the Continent would attempt to ruin her. *You may rest assured some such scheme is on foot. Louis Napoleon is exerting every influence intrigue and corruption can bring into play against England.* Mons. Mores, the poor banker's, arrest, was chiefly due to his active exertions to sustain Turkey, and thereby counteract these designs. Frenchmen here insist that Austria is, or soon will be, obliged to make its election between being the monarch of German dynasty in an Empire where the Germans are in a minority, or the monarch of a Sclavonic dynasty well consolidated and consequently powerful. It is asserted here upon excellent authority that the French Ambassador at Vienna has offered to the Austrian Government to surrender Venetia to Vittore Emmanuele and gain a close alliance with Italy and France against the Hungarians and other discontented provincials within its borders, together with territory on the Adriatic and the Lower Danube. Rumors of changes in the Cabinet are still current (nobody believes what the *Moniteur* says); the most accredited place Mons. Baroche as Minister of the Interior, Mons. Rouher taking his place as Minister without a portfolio and President of the Council of State; while Mons. de Persigny becomes Minister of Foreign Affairs in place of Mons. Thouvenel, sent to Constantinople or to St. Petersburg, while Mons. Fould becomes Minister of Finance and negotiates the loan of $200,000,000 or $300,000,000.

But the war rumors are most numerous, and if they are to be believed, Marshal McMahon has been summoned to Paris by telegraph, and has had a long conference with Louis Napoleon. There has been a long council at which all the Marshals were present, at the Tuileries. The Lyons camp is to receive reinforcements. The Cabinet of Turin had requested Louis Napoleon to send a garrison to Ancona. Four men-of-war are victualling at Toulon, and are immediately to be sent to the Syrian coast. The reason Louis Napoleon removed the ashes of Napoleon early in April, instead of waiting for the 5th of May, is, he knows that by the 5th of May all his time and attention will be absorbed by the gravest cares. Everybody in Paris believes war at hand—inevitable—and this a great European war. The last letters received from Rome represent the Pope as contemplating a departure from the Eternal City. He has already sent his most valuable pontifical ornaments, relics, and the costly presents made him by sovereigns, carefully packed in boxes, to Spain. The Cardinals are expecting to be forced to a general flight; a French Bishop has received a letter from a Cardinal, in which the latter says: "The situation of affairs grows worse daily, and I foresee new misfortunes, which will force us to leave Rome; perhaps I shall be glad to find with you a refuge from the tempest. Several of the Cardinals think of retiring to the south of France or to Nice, for as that town no longer belongs to Piedmont, we may reside there with something like security."

The French Government makes its soldiers take long marches every day, and they carry with them several days' provisions; this is to inure them to war's fatigues. It is said Louis Napoleon has invented a new musket, which will carry a ball three thousand yards, and pierce the thickest obstacles; the barrel is said to be very short and the stock very thick. Russia is said to be endeavoring to secure a basis of operations against English India, at Samarkand. Louis Napoleon has written a severe letter to Prince Murat, touching the latter's obstinate pretensions to the Neapolitan throne. Louis Napoleon warns him that if he persists there will be a rupture between them. The French Minister of Public Works was not present at the recent opening of the bridge across the Rhine at Kehl; a sign of war, for it was Louis Napoleon who forbade his appearance; and contrary to all usage no decorations were distributed to the German engineers. The French Government has issued $60,000,000 of treasury bonds; its floating debt is now at the least $300,000,000. It is said 8400 Savoyards have elected to remain Italians, notwithstanding the annexation of Savoy to France.

MR. JOHN CALVIN MCDANIEL, of Pickens District, who was severely wounded at the regimental muster last summer, by the accidental discharge of the cannon, died on the 27th ult.

Celibacy clubs are rife in New York now, says the *Home Journal*. Companies to insure against Matrimony are talked of.

GEORGE WILKES, editor of *Wilkes' Spirit*, has left New York to join Cassius M. Clay's regiment at Washington.

LEONARD CAPEHART, a well known citizen of Pickens District, died on the 23d ult., aged nearly 100. He was a native of Virginia.

Thirteen of the New York Banks on Saturday week contributed nearly half a million of dollars for the defence of the Government.

The Mobile Cadets, now in Virginia, are possessed of property worth in the aggregate between three and four millions of dollars.

THE State of Missouri has obtained 12,000 kegs of powder from the mills above that city.

FORTRESS MONROE.

Plan of the Fortress--An Interesting Description--Its Means of Defence and Points of Attack--The Garrison--Practicability of Reducing it, etc., etc.

The great stronghold at Old Point Comfort, Va., known as Fortress Monroe, at this juncture is justly esteemed by far the most important of the various points which are likely soon to become the theatre of war. Commanding the entrance of Hampton Roads, its guns effectually blockade the James and Elizabeth rivers, stopping all vessels bound either to or from Richmond, Petersburg or Norfolk. Great annoyance is thus given to the trade of Virginia and North Carolina; but as the same blockade could be made by vessels of war, within or without the Capes, it may be a question with the authorities whether Fortress Monroe should be reduced by investment or conquered by forcing the capitulation of Washington City.

The form and site of the Fortress are accurately represented in the following cut:

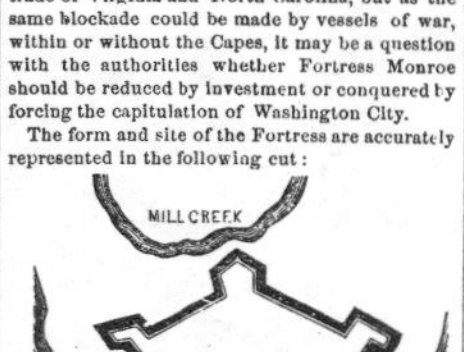

HAMPTON ROADS

HISTORY OF THE POST.

Fortress Monroe is situated on that point of land formed by the extreme western bank of the Chesapeake, and the extreme eastern bank of Hampton Roads, and at the junction of the two waters. It was discovered during the war of 1813–14, that Chesapeake Bay was the key to all the waters of Virginia and Maryland, and all who are at all familiar with the history of the country, will remember that British vessels came into Hampton Roads and not only took the town of Hampton, but threatened to apply the torch to Norfolk, that Phœnix-like, had sprung from the ashes of a former war with that power. Peace was declared in 1815, and when the next Congress met they took into consideration the subject of coast and harbor defences; accordingly a board of engineers was appointed, and an appropriation made for the prosecution of such plans as might be decided upon.

About this time the grand army of Napoleon was quiet, and several of his principal officers made our republican country their home; among them was Gen. Bernard, an experienced soldier, and one of the most skillful engineers then existing. He was accordingly invited to assist in the work of arranging our system of coast and harbor defence; and, in 1816, in company with several American officers, projected Fortress Monroe and Fort Calhoun, more generally known as the "Rip Raps." The work was laid off, and both forts commenced in 1819. From that time to this there has been more or less work going on at Fort Monroe, and while that work is sufficiently advanced to be placed in a state of defence, it is far from being finished.

DESCRIPTION OF THE FORT.

The extent of the work may be judged from the fact that it is over a mile around the ramparts; the wall covers a space of twenty or twenty-five acres, and there is about fifteen acres inside of the garrison. The casemates commence in the vicinity of the postern, behind the water battery, and extend with little intermission, to the arched doorway. On either side of that entrance are casemates which are used as quarters for the officer of the day, guard house and barracks for the guard. Those nearest the port-cullis have embrasures which are intended to protect that point from attack. Indeed all the casemates are supplied with embrasures, behind which are mounted forty-two-pounders.

On the ramparts, at those points where there are no casemates, are mounted guns, upon wooden carriages, whose saucy looking muzzles are plainly to be seen above the green turf that caps the fortification. At the extreme southern bastion floats the stars and stripes, while just below it, on the inside of the garrison, is a neat little Episcopal Church where the Chaplain, Mr. Cheevers, still continues to offer up his prayers for the Union and its President. A deep moat surrounds the whole work; this moat is supplied with water from Mill creek, and, while the gates are open, ebbs and flows with the tide.

THE WATER BATTERY.

The water battery, like all the masonry on this fort, is a beautiful piece of work; it is built of stone, and is sufficiently thick to withstand any shot that can be projected against it from the bay beyond. It is finished with casemates, the arches of which are turned with brick, and rest upon granite columns in the rear. This battery has forty-two embrasures, and is supplied with a like number of 42-pounders, which, like all the rest of the guns in the garrison, are fully mounted and ready for action. It covers all that face of the garrison that fronts upon the channel of the bay, and is only intended as a means of offence and defence when attacked by a force on the water. This portion of the work, like the ramparts, is covered with a green turf, and presents a beautiful and pleasant promenade in the summer afternoons.

THE WEAKEST POINT.

At the upper or northern extremity of the battery commences a redoubt or breastwork that extends around to the point of that bastion in which the magazine is situated; in the middle of this redoubt is a sally-port or postern that leads out to an outer work (not yet finished) that is intended to protect the fort from the land side. From the water battery to the magazine is decidedly the weakest portion of this fortress, and a well organized force of one thousand men could readily carry the fortification at this point. Besides the fact that there are no casemate guns on these two faces, the gates that supply the moat with water are on this side, and at the low tide might be closed to prevent the water from coming in on the change of the tide, and thus could a land force reduce the draught of water to such an extent as to enable them to wade across and scale the walls, which, of course, could only be done under a murderous fire. The gun from only one shoulder could be brought to bear upon the scaling party, and that one, or even two, would be so depressed as to render its effect doubtful. Besides this, a storming party could reduce the garrison to submission in a short while, unless the elements conspired to furnish them water, for there is not a spring, or well, or pump on the work; but, like the good people of Norfolk, the soldiers at Old Point have to depend on the clouds for their drink.

IS THE FORT IMPREGNABLE?

We were led into the above remarks, because of the fact that Fortress Monroe is considered impregnable, but such is not the fact; it lacks much of it as it now stands, and, even if it was completed, we give our idea of the work when we remind our readers that Sebastopol and Gibraltar fell before a resolute enemy.

As no fortification is impregnable to a well-appointed army of resolute and determined men, the question of reducing Fortress Monroe is one to be determined by the wisdom and judgment of the civil and military authorities of the Confederate States, taking into consideration the necessary loss of life that must ensue in its successful capture. Upon this point we venture no opinion, leaving it to the wisdom and discretion of President Davis and his able officers in command of the State and Confederate forces.

The garrison at Fortress Monroe is, doubtless, very large and well appointed at this time, with the capacity, on the part of the United States authorities, to increase it to a larger amount. We have no idea that the reports as to the number of troops now at Fortress Monroe, variously estimated at from three to five thousand, are correct. But that a large and strong garrison is now within the fort we have no doubt.

What Will England Do?

[*From the New York Express, May 4.*]

The silly story, started by some Washington correspondent of the Philadelphia *Press* (and copied into other journals, far and wide), that the British Minister had tendered the use of his government to aid in putting down the revolution, South, has brought out Lord Lyons himself, in a flat denial.

There is one thing we may as well make our minds up to first as last, we think—and that is, the British Government will be very careful to avoid taking sides with either North or South, in this war, until such times as the progress of hostilities shall disclose on which side its material interests lie, and as soon as it can discern that, it will not be slow to act—and the action, depend upon it, will be adopted with a sole eye to its own advantage, and without respect to any abstract anti-slavery sentiment. The very haste of the British Minister to deny the statement the Philadelphia journal imputed to him is, in itself, a proof of his position. Not to have denied it, was to break with the South; and breaking with the South is, just now, not the thing desired in Downing street.

It will be a long time before the English forgive the North its Morrill Tariff; and it will be a still longer time before they consent to forget the muss we made in New York, Cincinnati, and other Northern cities, about their enlistments for the Crimean war. Yet, forgiveness for the one and forgetfulness of the other, must precede any such affectionate overtures as those ascribed to, but denied by, Lord Lyons.

But, if any of our readers are still inclined to question the correctness of these assumptions, we may with perfect propriety invite their attention to the extracts we make from the leading London, Liverpool, and Manchester journals, just to hand by the *Arabia*. If there be any sentiments of sympathy with the North in these journals, we are unable to see them. The Cotton Lords of Manchester, the Money Kings of London, the shipping merchants and shop-keepers of Liverpool, all sing but one song, and that is, "Separation it must be, Mr. Lincoln,"—but "under no circumstances civil war." One of them (the Liverpool *Times*), even goes so far as to characterize the President's declaration of a more vigorous policy towards the seceding States, as absolutely "diabolical," while another alludes to it in terms which would seem to indicate that the writer had been studying the recent style of THE CHARLESTON MERCURY or the Richmond *Examiner*.

LATEST by TELEGRAPH.

THURSDAY, MAY 9, 1861.

THE IMPENDING STRUGGLE!

Congress Recognises the Existence of War with the United States.

ARKANSAS SECEDES FROM THE UNION.

News from the Seat of War.

HIGHLY IMPORTANT FROM MONTGOMERY.

War Officially Declared against the United States--Letters of Marque and Reprisal--Free Ships make Free Goods--Thirty Days Grace to Federal Vessels--Fund for Widows and Orphants of Privateers.

MONTGOMERY, May 6.—Senator CURRY, of Alabama, to day presented a bill fixing the time for the election of Representatives to Congress.

Also a bill providing for an election for President and Vice-President, under the Permanent Constitution. The bills were referred to the Judiciary Committee.

Secrecy has been removed from an Act passed by Congress, recognizing the existence of war between the United States and the Confederate Statess and serving letters of marque, prizes and prize goods.

The preamble to the Act recites LINCOLN's acts and proclamations, and the necessity for the Confederate States accepting the war thus commenced by him.

The Act authorizes the granting of Letters of Marque and Reprisal, on certain conditions. A proviso announces the doctrine that "free ships make free goods." Thirty days are allowed United States vessels now in ports of the Confederate States, for lawful commerce, to return to their home ports.

Five per cent. of the prize money is reserved as a fund in aid of the widows and orphans of those killed on private armed vessels, and for the support of the wounded and disabled.

The Arkansas News--Rush for Letters of Marque--Doings in Congress, etc., etc., etc.

MONTGOMERY, May 7.—Salutes are now being fired in front of the government buildings in honor of the secession of Arkansas.

Hon. W. H. HILLIARD telegraphs that the Tennessee Legislature has passed the Act of Secession.

The *Confederation* newspaper of this morning says that over three hundred applications have been made to the State Department for letters of marque and reprisal.

Congress to-day met at noon.

Mr. BROOKE, of Mississippi, presented the ordinance of the Virginia State Convention, adopting the Confederate States Provisional Constitution; also the resolutions appointing Commissioners to Congress—two of whom, Messrs. BROCKENBOROUGH and STAPLES were present.

Mr. BROOKE moved that they be qualified, and take their seats; pending which—

Mr. RHETT moved that Congress go into secret session, and the Virginia Commissioners be invited to remain.

Carried.

IMPORTANT FROM RICHMOND.

A Federal Steamer Reconoitering within Forty Miles of Richmond.--Arrival of Louisiana Troops, etc., etc., etc.

[FROM OUR OWN CORRESPONDENT.]

RICHMOND, May 6.—A steamer in the service of the LINCOLN Government came up the York River yesterday to West Point, distant only forty miles from Richmond, and which, in military parlance, is the key to the city. There is no doubt that she had on board a reconnoitering party. She came directly up to the wharf. The people here are much excited about it.

FORTIFYING WEST POINT.

Hitherto no precautions have been taken for the defence of West Point, and there is no telegraphic communication with that place. Many say that the enemy might, by a vigorous move, have landed there and marched within fifteen miles of Richmond without our knowing it.

Whether this was so or not, Gen. LEE is now actively guarding against such a surprise. Yesterday, by his orders, six 9-inch Dahlgren guns were sent down, and one thousand men. Others will immediately follow. It is now confidently believed that Richmond will be attacked by water approaches.

ARRIVAL OF LOUISIANA TROOPS.

The Caddo Rifles, from Shreveport, La., and the Louisiana Guards, Emmett Guards and Montgomery Guards, from New Orleans—in all 500 men—have just arrived.

FROM ALEXANDRIA.

Seward's Instructions to Dayton.--Arms and Supplies for Washington, etc.

ALEXANDRIA, May 7.—SEWARD's instructions to DAYTON (LINCOLN's Minister to England) are peremptory in their opposition to the Southern Confederacy, and announces the determination of the Government to wage civil war.

Large quantities of ammunition, supplies and troops are passing up to Washington in ships.

THE NINTH STAR.

Secession of Arkansas from the Federal Union.

LITTLE ROCK, May 7.—The Ordinance of Secession has been passed, and Arkansas is out of the Abolition Union.

Tennessee Moving.

NASHVILLE, May 7.—The Ordinance of Secession adopted here, is to be submitted to the people of the State for ratification, on the 8th of June.

Enthusiastic Reception of the Clinch Rifles.

MILLEN, GA., May 7.—Never has such a sight been seen as was witnessed this evening. The Clinch Rifles were greeted at every station and cross roads between Augusta and Millen by enthusiastic crowds. At several points young and beautiful ladies, numbering from sixty to eighty, were ranged along the railroad with rifles in their fair and delicate hands, and presented arms to the Clinch Rifles as they passed, with showers of bouquets. The Clinch Rifles have taken Millen, virtually; never did Zouave or other soldiery win greater applause; in fine, their progress thus far has been attended with that appreciation ever manifested for this favorite and universally popular military corps.

GEORGE N. SAUNDERS.—People in Montgomery are getting suspicious of the famous George N. Saunders. But George, they say, has such an easy, devil-may-care way about him, button-holing the President, and sliding oilily in the Cabinet meetings, that it will be difficult to convict him of an overt act. It is very certain that he isn't wanted, but the difficulty is to get rid of him. He doesn't take hints; laughs and says they are not intended for him.

PATRIOTIC LADIES.—The ladies of the little town of Pendleton, hearing that some of the volunteers were in need of uniforms, have offered to make up 500 uniforms in five days, or 1000 in ten days, if needed. Besides this, they have raised a subscription for a handsome flag, to be presented to Captain Kilpatrick's company, now encamped in Columbia, and another for a company in Pickens District, under the command of Capt. J. L. Shanklin.

HAMLET AMENDED.—Fechter, the French actor, in playing Hamlet wears a flaxen, instead of dark hair, as all other Hamlets do. His costume, too, is entirely different from the traditional semi-court dress worn by English and American representatives of the part. It is loose and flowing, and richly trimmed with furs. As the Danes are a northern people, the propriety of the attire, and of the getting up adopted by the truthful Parisian, is apparent. His innovations have been very much applauded in London.

INSURRECTION IN RUATAN.—The schooner *Aramenata*, from Ruatan, reports an insurrection in Ruatan by the Indians. Fifteen British officers are said to have been killed by the insurgents. Capt. Dunn's West India Regiment had left for the scene of action. The English Government is to give up the island on the 1st of June, positively, whether Honduras accepts it or not.

Virginia has hit Washington in a weak point. No oysters can be had for love or money, as none came up the river this week.

THE FIRST attempt to cast a cannon in Nashville war made on Saturday last, with perfect success.

THE NEWS FROM ALEXANDRIA.

[FROM OUR OWN CORRESPONDENT.]

ALEXANDRIA, May 7.—Aggressive movements of the United States forces on Harper's Ferry are looked for at any moment. The Virginia troops are well posted there, with a strong reserve of Kentuckians. They are ready for fight.

No movement on Alexandria has yet been made. The Washington *Star* says, that it is not probable that any such movement will be made at all.

About 2500 troops left Washington for the Relay House to-day. This point is the junction of the main stem of the Baltimore and Ohio Railroad with its Washington branch, and would be the starting point of troops moving towards Harper's Ferry.

The number of troops in Washington is now estimated at 25,000.

The steamers *Roanoke, Cambridge and John S. Thrift* passed up to Washington to-day loaded chiefly with provisions.

SEWARD, in his instructions to DAYTON, Minister to France, says:

"The insurgents have instituted revolution with open, flagrant, deadly war to compel the United States to acquiesce in the dismemberment of the Union. The United States have accepted this civil war as an inevitable necessity. The constitutional remedies for all the complaints of the insurgents are still open to them, and will remain so; but, on the other hand, the land and naval forces of the Union have been put into activity to restore the Federal authority and to save the Union from danger."

"You cannot be too decided or too explicit in making known to the French Government that there is not now, nor has there been, nor will there be, the least idea, existing in this Government, of suffering a dissolution of this Union to take place in any way whatever."

Senator BAYARD, of Delaware, arrived in Wilmington on Monday, having returned from Montgomery. It was feared that he would be mobbed.

THE NEWS FROM RICHMOND.

[FROM OUR OWN CORRESPONDENT.]

RICHMOND, May 7.—The excitement here to-day is greater than at any previous time. Simultaneous attacks are expected by land and water upon Harper's Ferry, Norfolk and Richmond.

Col. KERSHAW's South Carolina Regiment have received orders to hold themselves in readiness to move at a moment's notice. They now await marching orders from Montgomery.

Col. BLANCHARD's Louisiana Regiment has received orders to move on Harper's Ferry.

The Butler Guards, Capt. HOKE, of Greenville, S. C., arrived this evening, and have attached themselves to KERSHAW's Regiment.

Governor LETCHER has returned from Norfolk. There is an universal clamor here for the presence of President DAVIS.

THE NEWS FROM MONTGOMERY.

[FROM OUR OWN CORRESPONDENT.]

MONTGOMERY, May 7.—There are several rumors prevalent in this city to-night. Among them is one that a number of Federal troops have been landed at Princess Anne County, Virginia, preparatory to a march to retake the Gosport Navy Yard.

Also, that Gen. BEAUREGARD will be ordered to Norfolk to-morrow.

Also, that the steamer *Heighly*, of the New Orleans and Mobile Line, laden with freight, has been stopped by United States war vessels.

A bill bearing on the service of South Carolina troops, is now pending in Congress.

THE NEWS FROM TENNESSEE.

[FROM OUR OWN CORRESPONDENT.]

NASHVILLE, TENN., May 7.—The Legislature to-day passed the ordinance by which the State of Tennessee separates from the Union. It is to be submitted to the people on the 8th of June for ratification. There will be no serious opposition to it.

The Legislature has also concluded an offensive and defensive league with the Confederate States Commissioners.

An appropriation has been made of $5,000,000 to arm and equip 56,000 volunteers.

The greatest enthusiasm prevails here for the cause of independence.

Hon. John Cochran, private in the Eufaula Rifles, has been appointed Aid-de-Camp to General Bragg. He is not the New York John.

Henry Ward Beecher, it is said, is going to the war as a chaplain. He would do well to keep beyond the range of Southern rifles.

Hon. C. C. Clay, jr., late U. S. Senator from Alabama, has returned home from Minnesota in somewhat improved health.

Samuel R. Glen, special correspondent of the New York *Herald*, was arrested in New Orleans on a despatch from Mobile, but was shortly released.

There was a provision panic in Louisville on Monday, but it turned out that there was upwards of 3,000,000 bbls. of bacon alone in the city.

A letter from a well-informed man in Missouri expresses the confident opinion that that State will be with the South in a very short time.

Capt. Theodore Fink, U. S. A., died of apoplexy, at Detroit, on the 3d instant.

Three thousand troops were encamped at New Orleans on the 1st instant.

The President and Directors of the Bank of North Carolina have tendered to the State a loan of $500,000 for purposes of defence.

The Amoskeag Veterans, of Manchester, N. H., have voted to tender their services to the Governor for the war.

We have amidst the gloom of civil war, cheering accounts of the growing crops in Maryland and Virginia.

Lieutenant Jones, who burned Harper's Ferry Arsenal, has been promoted to the rank of Captain.

Over 1000 men are now employed in the Philadelphia Navy Yard in fitting out vessels of war.

Miramon, late President of Mexico, is expected to fix his residence in Spain.

CHARLES A. GREINER, of Georgia, has been arrested in Philadelphia as a Secessionist.

The Meagher Guards.

At a Meeting of the Meagher Guards, held at the Military Hall, on the evening of the 6th inst., the following preamble and resolutions were unanimously adopted:

The Report of the Committee, appointed to inquire into the truth of the rumors, that THOMAS FRANCIS MEAGHER, Esq. (in honor of whose patriotic efforts for the liberation of Ireland this company was named), had joined the crusade against the Southern States, having been heard—

1. *Resolved*, That the same be confirmed.

And, whereas, from the said Report, it appears to be true that Mr. MEAGHER has been carried away by the fanaticism of the North, and has enrolled himself in the ranks of our enemies, taking arms against us in this most unholy war, in support of usurpation and oppression, thus proving himself recreant to the sacred principles of liberty, of which he was hitherto so uncompromising an advocate; therefore,

2. *Resolved*, That, remembering the services of Mr. MEAGHER in the cause of freedom in Ireland, this Company have learned, with infinite disappointment and regret, that he, too, should have joined the oppressors of this their adopted land.

3. *Resolved*, That under these circumstances this Company can no longer, consistently with its position and dignity, bear his name, and that the same be and hereby is repudiated by them.

4. *Resolved*, That the name of THOMAS FRANCIS MEAGHER be erased from the roll of the honorary members of this Company.

5. *Resolved*, That it be referred to a Committee to suggest some suitable name by which this Company shall hereafter be known.

6. *Resolved*, That a copy of these preamble and resolutions be published in the daily papers of this city, and in the New York *Day Book*.

[From the minutes.]

JOHN P. DALY,
Secretary *pro tem.*

MARRIED.

On the 4th inst., at St. Michael's Church, by the Rev. P. T. KEITH, WM. HENRY ARMSTRONG, of New York, to SARAH MATILDA, youngest daughter of the Hon. W. J. GRAYSON, of this city. *

In Aiken, S. C., on the morning of the 5th inst., at the residence of the Bride's father, by J. M. C[illegible], Esq., Mr. ELBERT HARDING, of Beech Island, S. C., to Miss JANE, eldest daughter of Rev. A. FRANKLIN.

At the residence of her father, in Allendale, Barnwell District, by the Rev. CHAS. A. LAWTON, Miss MARTHA BAYNARD, eldest daughter of Dr. JAMES S. LAWTON, to Mr. EDWARD S. RILEY, of Beaufort District.

OBITUARY.

DIED, on the 25th of April, 1861, KATE BENNET, only daughter of Mrs. H. J. WATERS, aged 8 years and 5 months.

When age moves trembling to the tomb,
The heart pours forth its bitter sighs;
But, oh! how mournful is the gloom,
That shrouds the hearth when children dies.

And oh! the bitter tears that roll
In silent sorrow on the sod;
Yet why not calm the troubled soul,
The child will meet thee with her God. *

COMMERCIAL.

Latest Dates.

LIVERPOOL	April 23
HAVRE	April 20
HAVANA	April 18

EXPORTS—MAY 7.

LIVERPOOL—Br brig Mary—404 bales Upland Cotton and 98 bbls Rosin.

BARCELONA—Spanish bark Olimpia—1444 bales Upland Cotton and 3 00 Staves.

BOSTON—Schr Caliope—363 bales Upland Cotton, 210 tcs Rice and 10 bbls Turpentine.

The Market—Tuesday Evening, May 7.

COTTON.—There were but a very few buyers out to-day, and the sales amounted to 307 bales only, at unchanged prices. The following comprise the particulars: 28 bales at 10¾; 17 at 10½; 58 at 11¼; 150 at 12; 38 at 12¼; 1 at 13; and 15 bales at 13¾ cents.

The Market—Wednesday Evening, May 8.

COTTON.—We have no change to report in the market to-day. With a quiet demand, and at former prices, the sales amounted to 406 bales at the following particulars: 35 bales at 10¼; 19 at 10½; 42 at 10¾; 48 at 11; 78 at 11¼; 30 at 11¾; 7 at 12; and 147 at 12¾c.

GALVESTON, April 27.—*Cotton Statement.*

Stock on hand 1st September...bales	3168
Received this week at this port	1718
Received previously at this port	106647
Received at other Texas ports	26097
Total	137630
Exported to Great Britain to date..bales .. 42846	
" France	3640
" Other Continental Ports	11191
" New Orleans	27878
" New York	24359
" Boston	25991—135905
Remaining on hand and on shipboard, not cleared, bales	1725

SORLEY, SMITH & Co.

MOBILE, May 4.—COTTON.—The receipts since April 26th have been 1376 against 4078 for the corresponding week last year. The exports have been 7282 bales—against 8296 bales last year. The stock on hand and on shipboard not cleared is 26,010 bales, against 104,525 bales at the same date last year.

Our last weekly review closed with an unsettled market, the sales of the week ending Friday, April 26th, amounting to 1450 bales, our quotations for Middlings being nominally 10¾@11c. On Saturday sales were made of 300 bales, on Monday 400, on Tuesday 150, on Wednesday 150, on Thursday 150, and on Friday (yesterday) 50 bales, at nominal prices, the quotation for Middling being generally stated at 11c. The sales of the week foot up 1200 bales, taken mostly on English, and some on Spanish account.

FREIGHTS.—Nothing is doing with the exception of some little business for Liverpool, to which port British ships, the only ones in port, are filling up at ¾d.

BAGGING AND ROPE.—We quote without change India Bagging at 12 cents. Kentucky hand loom 13 cents, and power loom 16 cents. Manilla *Rope*, of superior quality, is offered at 9@9½ cents. Hemp, 8½@9 cents ℔ lb. Market dull.

BACON.—The demand for this and other articles of provisions continues active, and prices are firmer. We quote Shoulders, 9 cents. Sides, 11½ cents. Clear do., and Hams, 13 cents ℔ lb.

BUTTER.—Extravagant prices are asked for the small stock in market, and no quotations can be given.

NAVAL STORES.—We quote Spirits Turpentine 28c ℔ gal.; Rosin $1.25 ℔ bbl for No 1, and 80@90c and $1 for No 2. The Southern Oil Company quotations are: for Navy Pitch $2.50@$3 ℔ bbl; Deck Oil 37½c ℔ gallon; Bright Varnish 30c ℔ gallon; Machinery Oil 75c; Paint Oil 40c ℔ gallon; Gas Oil 25c ℔ gallon; Crude Naphtha 20c; Refined do 25c ℔ gallon, Patent Wheel Grease 5c ℔ lb.

RICE.—There has been considerable retail business doing at former quotations, viz: 5¼@5½c ℔ lb. Stock reduced

SAILING OF THE OCEAN STEAMERS.

FROM THE UNITED STATES.

SHIPS.	LEAVES.	FOR	DATE
Asia	New York	Liverpool	May 8
Bremen	New York	Bremen	May 11
Hammonia	New York	Southampton	May 15
Great Eastern	New York	England	May 24
Canadian	Portland	Liverpool	May 30
FROM EUROPE.			
Arabia	Liverpool	New York	April 20
Adriatic	Galway	New York	April 23
City Baltimore	Liverpool	New York	April 24
North American	Liverpool	Quebec	April 25
Africa	Liverpool	New York	April 27
Arago	Southampton	New York	May 1
Great Eastern	Milford Haven	New York	May 1
Nova Scotian	Liverpool	Quebec	May 2
Saxonia	Southampton	New York	May 4
Hibernia	Galway	Boston	May 7
Canadian	Liverpool	Quebec	May 9
Teutonia	Southampton	New York	May 14
New York	Southampton	New York	May 15
Fulton	Southampton	New York	May 20
North Briton	Liverpool	Quebec	May 16

Consignees per South Carolina Railroad, May 7.

156 bales Cotton, 235 sacks Flour, Naval Stores, Mdse, Cattle, &c. To Sims & Barksdale, T E Ryan, B O'Neill, J H Vollers, L M Hatch, G W Williams & Co, Graeser & Smith, R Spriggs, E B Stoddard & Co, and Order.

Consignees per South Carolina Railroad, May 8.

27 bales Cotton, 414 bbls Flour, Naval Stores, Mdse, Cattle, &c. To Jno Fraser & Co, G W Williams & Co, J C H Claussen, Matthiessen, O'Hara & Co, H L P McCormick, J E Ficken, Brown & Hyams, E H Myers, J A Burckmyer, and Order.

Consignees per Charleston and Savannah Railroad, May 8.

Merchandise, &c. To Col Lowndes, Fraser & Dill, O'Hear, Roper & Stoney, E Barnwell & Son, Horton & Shepherd, S C Railroad Agent, and Order.

PASSENGERS.

In steamer Nina from Georgetown—Miss Weston, Miss A Weston and servants, Mrs M A E Sparkman and servant, Miss Watles, Miss Alston and servant, Mrs R J Middleton, two Misses Middleton, Master Middleton and servant, Mrs Withers, Dr A M Foster, son and servant, Master S Coachman, Dr W M Post, W Green, J J P Alston, H L Pinckney and two daughters, and fourteen on deck.

In steamer General Clinch, from Santee Steam Mill—Mrs Trapler, Master Trapler and three servants, E S Horry and two servants, Miss Choiseul, Miss Long and servant, and fifteen on deck.

MARINE NEWS.

Charleston.—Lat. 32.47 N. Lon. 79.27 W.

SUN RISES 5H. 14M. SETS 6H. 46M.—HIGH WATER 6H. 24M.

WIND—S. W.

ARRIVED.

May 7.

Schr E Waterman, Chadwick, Georgetown. 270 tcs Rice. To J & S P Ravenel, Robertson, Blacklock & Co, Middleton & Co, and W C Bee & Co.

Schr Zaidee, Hadley, Combahee. 4200 bushels Rough Rice. To T G Simons & Sons.

Schr Rutherford, Bennett, Bennett's Mill. 58 bbls Rice. To Middleton & Co.

May 8.

Schr R S Hawley, Pritchett, Elizabeth (N C). 3200 bushels Corn and 50 bushels Peas. To Butler & Bee.

Schr Saml Adams, Prince, Darien (Ga). 410 bbls Rosin, 50 bbls Spirits Turpentine and 25 bbls Rosin. To Geo E Pritchett.

Schr Santee, Kroag, Pon Pon. 300 bushels Rough Rice and 24 bales Sea Island Cotton. To Robertson, Blacklock & Co, and O'Hear, Roper & Stoney.

Schr Geo Washington, Finagin, Pon Pon. 1070 bushels Rough Rice. To Coffin & Pringle.

Schr Joanna Ward, Peterson, Back River. 3610 bushels Rough Rice. To Coffin & Pringle.

Schr Elizabeth, Stewart, Back River. 2700 bushels Rough Rice. To J A Winthrop & Son.

Schr Rob Roy, Cannon, East Point Mill. 132 bbls Rice. To T G Simons & Sons, and J A Winthrop & Son.

Schr Rutherford, Bennett, Bennett's Mill. 104 bbls Rice. To Middleton & Co.

Schr Geo Chisolm, Misdorff, Chisolm's Mill. 175 bbls Rice. To E Barnwell & Son.

Steamer Nina, Davis, Georgetown. 200 tierces Rice, 110 bags Pea Nuts and Sundries. To J & S P Ravenel, Robertson, Blacklock & Co, Mazyck & Howard, and others.

Steamer Gen Clinch, Relyea, Santee Steam Mill. 240 tcs Rice and Sundries. To H L P McCormick, Adams, Frost & Co, Robertson, Blacklock & Co, Mazyck & Howard, Mott A Pringle, Herckenrath, Lesesne & Huger, and Mrs M S Lamb

Deveaux's boat, from Wando. 29 bales Sea Island Cotton. To Deveaux & Heyward.

CLEARED.

May 7.

Spanish bark Olimpia, Barcelo, Barcelona—Hall & Co.

British brig Mary, Moorehouse, Liverpool—G A Hopley & Co.

Schr Callope, O'Neill, Boston—Holmes & Stoney.

WENT TO SEA.

May 7.

Ship R H Tucker, Clark, Liverpool.

Br ship Gondar, Gooding, Liverpool.

Br bark Walton, Jones, Liverpool.

Schr Calliope, O'Neill, Boston.

Steamer Carolina, Lockwood, Fernandina via Savannah.

May 8.

Spanish bark Olimpia, Barcelo, Barcelona.

FROM CHARLESTON.

Bark Cronos, Valentin, Svendborg, April 13.

Bark Meteor, Ohlsen, Queenstown, April 16.

LIST OF VESSELS

SAILED, CLEARED AND UP FOR CHARLESTON.

COASTWISE PORTS.

NEW YORK.

Schr Cherokee, Myers	cleared Mch. 22
Schr May, Smith	advertised Mch. 26
BALTIMORE.	
Schr Minnehaha, Young	cleared April 21
NEW ORLEANS.	
Schr H Blackman, Corson	advertised April 2
Schr John Aumack, Pierce	advertised April 9

FOREIGN PORTS.

LIVERPOOL.

Ship Sir Alan McNab, Chapman	sailed Mch. 25
Ship Gen Parkhill, ——	sailed Mch. 26
Ship Albert Gallatin, Storer	sailed Mch. 26
Bark Hilja, Henderson	sailed Mch. 23
Ship Eliza Bonsall, Stalker	sailed Mch. 27
Ship Avon, Munce	sailed April 1
Ship Monmouth, Jones	sailed Mch. 24
Ship Montezuma, Atkins	sailed Mch. 28
Ship Chas Cooper, Jordan	cleared Feb. 21
Ship Alliance, DeForrest	cleared Feb. 28
Ship Metropolis, Foster	loading Feb. 13
Ship Assyria, Delano	loading Feb. 21
Ship Amelia, Bishop	loading April 18
LONDON.	
Brig P J Nevins, Cole	loading Mch. 28
NEWPORT.	
Ship Alliance, Trefiro	sailed April 1

MAJOR ANDERSON OF THE UNITED STATES' ARMY, LATE COMMANDANT OF FORT SUMTER, CHARLESTON HARBOUR.—SEE PRECEDING PAGE.

THE DAILY DELTA

PUBLISHED BY THE NEW ORLEANS DELTA NEWSPAPER COMPANY

TERMS—PER ANNUM.

DAILY DELTA, (invariably in advance)......$10
WEEKLY DELTA, do. do. 3
SUNDAY DELTA, do. do. 2

For any time less than one year the DAILY DELTA will be delivered to City Subscribers at 20 cents a week.

ADVERTISING RATES

Advertisements $1 a Square for the first insertion. Every subsequent insertion 50 cents.
Advertisements on the Second Page $1 per measured Square each insertion.
Advertisements at intervals $1 a Square each insertion.
Marriage and Funeral Notices $1 each insertion.
A Liberal Discount made to regular Advertisers.

WEDNESDAY MORNING, MAY 15, 1861.

J. E. BOULIGNY.—We are informed by members of the family of Mr. J. Edward Bouligny, that the telegraphic statement of his having been at Perryville, drilling Northern volunteers, is entirely false. He left this city for Washington with the intention of bringing home his wife. The following dispatch was received from him a few days ago:

"WASHINGTON, May 7th.

Louis Bouligny, Esq., New Orleans:
Arrived yesterday. Wife's health bad. Will leave in a few days. J. E. BOULIGNY."

We are likewise informed that Mr. Bouligny is heartily with the South in her struggle with the Lincolnites. It gratifies us to make this statement, and we only hope it is well founded. It would be a source of profound regret that in a family which is distinguished for its gallantry, its chivalry and its devotion to the South, there could be found one recreant member.

In addition to the above dispatch, we have been furnished with the following extract from a letter just received from Mr. Bouligny:

"When I arrived in Washington I found every thing upside down. All the public buildings, churches, &c., are occupied by the Federal troops, and the place in general is a '*hog pen*.' Give my inquiring friends the reasons of my delay in not returning home earlier."

IS IT THE DUTY OF THE SOUTH TO PAY NORTHERN DEBTS DURING THE EXISTENCE OF THE WAR?

Editors Delta—As the above question seems to be deserving of more attention than it has received from the press of New Orleans during the present financial crisis, this communication is respectfully addressed to you for the purpose of eliciting discussion on the all-important subject.

It is a well known fact that the trading and mercantile community of New Orleans and other large cities in the South, have, during every crisis and at all times, whether there might be a stringency or easiness in the money market, shown an ability and willingness to meet all their engagements honestly and promptly, far surpassing that of any large city in the Northern or Eastern States. Compare the number of failures in the Northern and Eastern cities during the crisis of 1857 and of the present one, with those at home. How very few failures have occurred here or in the South with the wholesale breaking up of business, and suspension of payments in the North, West and East. It cannot, therefore, be charged to the South that she has ever had an idea of shirking or avoiding the payment of her honest debts, or to defraud her creditors of a single penny under ordinary circumstances. But at the present time, when the whole country is convulsed by the proclamation of Lincoln and his Black Republican Cabinet, that war has been waged against circumstances the question arises, whether the South should continue to furnish the North, an avowed enemy, with the means whereby she may carry on a deadly warfare against us, and for the accomplishment of their diabolical and unholy designs?

Citizens of the South, in paying their debts to the North at present, are of course but furnishing supplies to an alien enemy, greatly assisting in the prosecution of their intended work. Thus far there has been scarcely if any let up in the South as to her regular and large remittances of money to the North.

Placing it at a small estimate, there can be no less than five hundred thousand dollars paid to the North and West weekly! from this city alone. It then becomes a question whether his Excellency, the Governor, or the proper authorities, should not interfere and forbid this suicidal policy at once. Individuals are willing to incur the slight injury and apparent disgrace of being protested rather than aid the enemy. But the great bulk of our commercial and trading community and throughout the South, will continue to pay their obligations, thinking it an honor to do so, and to get through the present extraordinary crisis unprotested. Indeed, it is an honor which the large cities of the South have always sustained; but, besides this, there are here, and throughout the seceded States, a great many agents and members of commercial houses in the North, East and West, daily remitting large sums to their respective homes, all of which goes to sustain their friends; and unless this practice is at once put a stop to by the intervention of our authorities, it will of course continue so until the South has almost completely depleted herself. Indeed, we have always shown to the North a spirit of liberality and generosity altogether too great, and which has never been reciprocated; but now, by the recent demonstrations, we see clearly enough how our liberality has been appreciated. With these facts staring us in the face, what then have we to expect from the North? Nothing but the severest blow she can deal upon us.

Has not already the U. S. District Attorney for New York issued an official notification to the banks and private banking institutions in New York city, forbidding them to make any remittances whatsoever to cities in the seceded States, under penalty of proscription for treason! But this order was revoked at the solicitation of New York merchants, and they were still allowed to hold commercial intercourse with the South, it being for their own pecuniary benefit, and for fear the South (then owing the North, in all probability, a sum exceeding one hundred millions,) would retaliate. But why should not the South retaliate at once? Their intention and the unholy designs which they are waging upon us ought to be sufficient and just cause.

So far as international law is concerned, it has been the decision of the very highest authority in America. Chancellor Kent and others, besides also the most eminent British jurists, that it is an act of *high treason* to pay debts to, or to hold or carry on friendly communication and intercourse whatsoever with an enemy whereby he may be benefited during the existence of war.

In a word, the South is at present to a very great degree aiding the Northern foe by furnishing them with sums of money, although it be in payment of debts due. We do not by any means advocate the repudiation of debts, but in self-defense and justice to our country, we advocate the cause of postponement of all payments and remittances to the North until this wild delirium of their people, and of Lincoln and his Cabinet at Washington, is subdued and peace once more established. Had this course been adopted immediately after Lincoln's proclamation of war, it would, no doubt, have had a very decided effect in our favor; and even now, if it can be adopted, can not fail to assist materially in bringing the poor deluded wretches and mad fanatics of the North to their sober senses.

CITIZEN.

Special Dispatches to the Delta.

LINCOLN'S BLOCKADE

The Niagara Ordered to the Mouth of the Mississippi.

REPORTED CAPTURE OF PRIVATEERS

LINCOLN THINKS HIS BLOCKADE SUFFICIENT.

Probable Movement Towards Harper's Ferry.

THE VOYAGE of the GREAT EASTERN.

LONDON TIMES FOR THE SOUTH.

MOVEMENTS OF THE WHEELING TRAITORS

RICHMOND, May 14th.

The Lincoln Secretary of the Treasury at Washington says that the ports of Charleston, Savannah, Mobile and New Orleans will be blockaded in a few days. The steam frigate Niagara is ordered to the mouth of the Mississippi.

The United States steam sloop-of-war Pawnee still lies off Alexandria.

There are reports that two privateers were captured to-day, by a frigate, after a stout resistance, off Gardner's Island, New York.

[This must be a mistake, as no letters of marque had yet been issued.—*Eds. Delta.*]

The Washington authorities seem to consider that their blockade will be sufficient, together with the recapture of the forts, to effect the subjugation of the South.

Indications point to a movement of the U. S. forces toward Harper's Ferry; but the Confederate forces are too strongly posted at that place to be dislodged.

An editorial in the London Times, of May 1st, is favorable to the South. It says that Lincoln may well hesitate to begin the war and repeat the British enterprise of 1814-15 at New Orleans.

The Great Eastern made her trip to New York in nine and a half days. She encountered heavy gales and rolled tremendously, but there was no pitching movement.

The Wheeling traitors are continuing their movement for a division of the State. They propose to call their State New Virginia. They profess to have

RICHMOND, May 14th.

A special messenger who has just arrived, informs the Governor and Council of the advance of a large body of troops, with horses and mules, out of Fort Monroe. They have crossed the creek and advanced a considerable distance into Virginian territory.

REMOVAL OF THE CAPITAL.

Goods from lately Seceded States to pay no Duty

A SPY SHOT AT PENSACOLA.

The New York Seventh Homeward Bound.

MONTGOMERY, May 14, 1861.

It is now considered certain that Congress will adjourn within a week, to meet at Richmond in July next. Capital to be removed then. Congress has passed an act exempting from duty goods imported into the Confederacy from States that have recently seceded. All is well at Pensacola, and no fight expected for the next two or three weeks.

The spy Anthony has been shot by order of Gen. Bragg.

It is reported that the Seventh Regiment will return to New York after the expiration of their thirty days enlistment.

TELEGRAPHIC NEWS.

TELEGRAPHED TO THE NEW ORLEANS DAILY DELTA.

FOUR DAYS LATER FROM EUROPE.

ARRIVAL OF THE STEAMSHIP EUROPA.

Effect of the American News in England.

ALL LIVERPOOL MARKETS EXCITED.

COTTON ADVANCED 3-8d.

HALIFAX, May 14.—The Cunard Royal Mail steamship Europa, Captain Leitch, arrived at this port to day *en route* for Boston.

She left Liverpool at noon, Saturday, the 4th, and touched at Queenstown the evening of the 5th, and brings four days later news than was received by the Great Eastern at New York.

Liverpool Cotton Market.

LIVERPOOL, May 4.—The Brokers' circular reports the sales of the week ending with Friday, at 90,000 bales, 22,000 of which are reported as having been taken by speculators, and 16,500 for export.

Holders offer freely. All qualities of Cotton advanced ⅛ to ¼d. during the week.

The sales Friday comprised 15,000 bales, at full rates. The following are the authorized quotations:

Fair Orleans..........8¾d.	Middling Orleans 7 13 16d.
Fair Mobile..........8½d.	Middling Mobile.....7¾d.
Fair Uplands..........8⅜d.	Middling Uplands. 7 9 16d.

The stock of Cotton in port sums up 990,000, of which 818,000 are of American production.

Manchester Trade.

The accounts from Manchester are not of a favorable character.

Sales of goods and yarns unimportant.

Breadstuffs and Provisions.

Messrs. Richardson, Spence & Co. say the week's business in Breadstuffs closed steady.

Provisions ruled steady.

London Money Market.

LONDON, May 4.—The closing quotations for Consols were 91¼@91⅜.

The amount of bullion in the Bank of England decreased £277,000 during the week.

The Money market is more stringent.

LATEST FROM LIVERPOOL.

[Via Queenstown.]

Cotton Market.

LIVERPOOL, May 5, P. M.—The news from America received here yesterday by the steamer Persia, produced great excitement. All markets are thereby excited and unsettled.

The sales of cotton yesterday (Saturday) included 20,000 bales, of which 10,000 were taken by speculators and for export, the market closing at a partial advance of ⅛d. Heavy stocks were withdrawn.

Breadstuffs and Provisions.

The breadstuffs and provisions closed steady.

London Money Market.

LONDON, May 5, P. M.—Quotations for consols closed at 91⅛ to 91⅜c.

EUROPEAN POLITICAL INTELLIGENCE.

Great Britain.

In the House of Commons Lord John Russell, in answering to Mr. Evart, said that England had directed a naval force to America for the protection of British shipping. He said England would use every possible means to avoid taking part in this lamentable contest. He advised his Government to keep out of it.

The betrothal of Princess Alice to Prince Louis of Hesse has been formally announced.

The London Times says the excitement between the Northern and Southern sections of America has not been paralleled since the early days of the French Revolution.

Underwriters ask 20 to 25 shillings from New Orleans; 10 to 15 from New York on British and 1 to 2 per cent extra on American vessels from India, China, &c. War risks on American vessels detained in Southern ports advanced from 5 to 10 guineas.

The Globe says it was Thiers wrote the Duc d'Aumale.

France.

The pamphlet the Archbishop of Tours is writing to the Minister of Justice, says the temporal power of the Pope is abolished, and that the Catholic world will hold Napoleon responsible therefor.

Paris Bourse firm. Rentes 69f. 15c.

Spain.

Spanish correspondents say that all the San Domingo towns have pronounced in favor of being annexed to Spain.

Italy.

Large bodies of Italian troops had embarked at Genoa for Southern Italy, and three thousand had reached Naples.

The official journal of Rome denies that Sardinia will make conciliatory proposals to Rome.

THE CONFEDERATE CONGRESS.

A Day of Prayer and Fasting to be Observed.

MONTGOMERY, May 14.—In Congress to day, Judge Oldham, of Texas, offered a resolution inquiring into the expediency of making the city of Houston a port of entry and delivery.

Mr. Clingman presented resolutions of the House of Commons of North Carolina, placing that State in an independent position and in opposition to the Lincoln Government.

Mr. Thomas R. R. Cobb offered the following resolution in reference to a day of fasting and prayer:

The dependence of nations as of individuals upon an overruling Providence, at all times, we fully recognize, but when perils surround and national existence is threatened, it peculiarly becomes a people to manifest their submission to the will and guidance of the Omnipotent Ruler of the Universe. If the cause be righteous and the quarrel just, we may confidently rely on Him who reigneth alike over the armies of earth and the hosts of heaven; at the same time we recognize our duty to appeal humbly to Him who hath said, "I will be inquired of of my people to the end."

Therefore, That the whole people of these Confederate States may in unison and with one accord, approach the throne of the Most High to invoke his blessing upon us in our defensive struggle for the right of self government, and the enjoyment of the liberty He vouchsafed to our fathers, and to protect us from those who threaten our homes with fire and sword, our domestic circles with ruthless lust, our fathers' graves with invaders' feet, and our altars with infidel desecration,

Resolved, By the Congress of the Confederate States, that the President be requested to issue his proclamation appointing a day of fasting and prayer, in the ob-

The preamble and resolution was unanimously adopted.

The Oglethorpe Light Infantry of Savannah, Capt. Bartow, ranking among the first companies of the South, has volunteered its services for the war, which have been accepted. The company leaves soon for Virginia.

The flag of the Confederate States, which waved over Fort Moultrie during the bombardment of Fort Sumter, now hangs in full length in the rear of President Cobb's chair.

Northern Governors and Western Virginia.

HARRISBURG, May 14.—It is understood that Governors Curtin and Dennison have pledged the Union men of Western Virginia all the Pennsylvania and Ohio forces to protect them against the Secessionists.

Indiana and Illinois have made the same promise to the Union men of Kentucky and Maryland.

The Governors of all the free States from Pennsylvania westward have asked and obtained a pledge from Lincoln, that no compromise nor cessation of war should take place until the National flag floats over all Federal property.

Tender of Volunteers to the Federal Government—Position of U. S. Troops.

NEW YORK, May 14.—The 69th Regiment has been accepted during the war.

Another Zouave regiment and a Boston regiment are ready to march to Washington.

General Butler has been ordered to the outposts. Col. Jones' camp at the Relay House has been extended ten miles towards Harper's Ferry.

The Capitol is surrounded by a circle of encampments, controlling all the roads to Virginia and Maryland.

Address of Brigadier-General Harney.

ST. LOUIS, May 14.—Brigadier-General Harney has published an address, in which he says that undoubtedly the whole power of the Government will be exerted to keep Missouri in the Union. He deems it his duty to suppress all unlawful combinations of men—military or otherwise.

Capt. Lyon has been elected Brigadier-General over the first four regiments of Federal volunteers, with the concurrence of the President.

Virginians Fortifying the Potomac, &c.—Affairs in Maryland.

BALTIMORE, May 14.—It is reported that the Virginians have strongly fortified the Maryland heights overlooking Harper's Ferry, and don't intend to evacuate them. On Sunday 7,000 stand of arms and twelve cannon arrived.

A bitter feeling exists in Washington county against the Virginians. A collision is considered probable.

Mr. Thomas Winans has been cordially received by the Virginians.

The Legislature of Maryland has adjourned till June 4.

Orders by the Secretary of Treasury.

WASHINGTON, May 14.—The Secretary of the Treasury directs all officers of customs to prohibit the transmission of munitions of war and supplies for the South, including telegraphic instruments and materials

Schooner Seized at Baltimore.

BALTIMORE, May 14.—A schooner, with pikes manufactured by Mr. Thomas Winans, has been seized.

Federal troops have fully established themselves at Federal Hill.

Federal Troops Ordered in All Directions.

WASHINGTON, May 14.—A detachment of regulars and volunteers has gone to Baltimore. A New Jersey regiment has been ordered to Alexandria.

Resignation.

PHILADELPHIA, May 14.—Mr. Robert Tyler has resigned his office in the Pennsylvania Supreme Court and left the city.

Gen. Wool to Command Fort Monroe.

WASHINGTON, May 13.—Brig. Gen. John E. Wool has been ordered to the command of Fortress Monroe.

Rhode Island Banks.

PROVIDENCE, May 14.—The banks of Rhode Island take $500,000 of the Federal loan.

TWO DAYS LATER FROM EUROPE.

ARRIVAL OF THE STEAMER PARANA.

ENGLAND AND THE AMERICAN DIFFICULTIES

Liverpool Cotton Market Firm.

ST. JOHN'S, May 14.—The steamer Parana, of the Galway line, from Galway on the 7th inst., has arrived here, bringing two days later news from Europe.

Liverpool Cotton Market.

LIVERPOOL, May 7.—The Cotton market continues to exhibit a tone of firmness. The sales are not given.

London Money Market.

LONDON, May 7.—There has been barely any change in the English funds since Saturday.

Quotations for Consols to-day closed at 91¼@91⅜.

EUROPEAN POLITICAL INTELLIGENCE.

Lord John Russell made an important statement in the House of Commons relative to American affairs. As to the Federal Government committing infringement on international law by collecting duties from foreign ships before breaking the bulk, the law officers of the Crown said [illegible] much depended on circumstances, that no definite instructions had been given to cruisers.

He believed collection impracticable.

Relative to a blockade of the S[illegible]rts, they said it could only be recognized wh[illegible]ve.

Regarding letters of marque, the Government was of opinion that the Southern Confederacy must be [illegible]nized as belligerents.

Other important questions were still under consideration.

Arrivals from Europe.

NEW YORK, May 14.—The ship Kangaroo, from Liverpool the 1st and Queenstown the 2d inst., and the Arago, from Southampton and Havre the 1st inst., have arrived. News anticipated.

New York Markets.

NEW YORK, May 14.—Cotton steady; sales to-day 1800 bales at 14c. Flour, $4 95@$5 10. Corn declined 1c. Pork, $17 [illegible]. Cuba Sugar, 4@6½c. New Orleans Molasses, 34c.

Cincinnati Markets.

CINCINNATI, May 14.—Flour $4 50 to $4 60. Corn 34c. Oats 28c. Whisky 12½c. Pork $16 50. Sugar 5½ to 7c. Coffee 13 to 14½c. Molasses 30 to 34c.

River Intelligence.

LOUISVILLE, May 14.—The river is still falling, with 11 feet water in the canal.

JUDGE CAMPBELL'S EXPLANATION.

The following is the correspondence alluded to in our dispatches a few days ago. It was laid before Congress on the 11th inst.:

WASHINGTON CITY, April 13, 1861.

SIR—On the 15th March ult., I left with Judge Crawford, one of the commissioners of the Confederate States, a note in writing to the effect following:

"I feel entire confidence that Fort Sumter will be evacuated in the next five days. And this measure is felt as imposing great responsibility on the Administration.

"I feel entire confidence that no measure changing the existing status, prejudicially to the Southern Confederate States, is at present contemplated.

"I feel an entire confidence that an immediate demand for an answer to the communication of the Commissioners will be productive of evil and not of good. I do not believe that it ought at this time to be pressed."

The substance of this statement I communicated to you the same evening by letter. Five days elapsed, and I called with a telegram from Gen. Beauregard to the effect that Sumter was not evacuated, but that Major Anderson was at work making repairs.

The next day, after conversing with you, I communicated to Judge Crawford, in writing, that the failure to evacuate Sumter was not the result of bad faith, but was attributable to causes consistent with the intention to fulfill the engagement; and that as regarded Pickens I should have notice of any design to alter the existing status there. Mr. Justice Nelson was present at these conversations, three in number, and I submitted to him each of my written communications to Judge Crawford, and informed Judge C. that they had his (Judge Nelson's) sanction. I gave you, on the 22d of March, a substantial copy of the statement I had made on the 15th.

The 30th of March arrived, and at that time a telegram came from Gov. Pickens, inquiring concerning Col. Lamon, whose visit to Charleston he supposed had a connection with the proposed evacuation of Fort Sumter.

I left that with you, and was to have an answer the following Monday, (1st of April.) On the 1st of April I received from you the statement in writing: "(I am satisfied) the Government will not undertake to supply Fort Sumter without giving notice to Gov. P." The words "I am satisfied" were for me to use as expressive of confidence in the remainder of the declaration.

The proposition as originally prepared was, "The President may desire to supply Sumter, but will not do so," &c., and your verbal explanation was that you did not believe any such attempt would be made, and that there was no design to reinforce Sumter.

There was a departure here from the pledges of the previous month, but with the verbal explanation, I did not consider it a matter then to complain of. I simply stated to you that I had that assurance previously.

On the 7th of April I addressed you a letter on the subject of the alarm that the preparations of the Government had created, and asked you if the assurances I had given were well or ill founded. In respect to Sumter your reply was "Faith as to Sumter, fully kept—wait and see." In the morning's paper I read, "An authorized messenger from President Lincoln informed Governor Pickens and myself that I was invited to wait for and see." In the same paper I read that intercepted dispatches disclosed the fact that Mr. Fox, who had been allowed to visit Major Anderson, on the pledge that his purpose was pacific, employed his opportunity to devise a plan for supplying the fort by force, and that the plan had been adopted by the Washington Government, and was in process of execution. My recollection of the date of Mr. Fox's visit carries it to a day in March. I learn he is a near connection of a member of the Cabinet. My connection with the Commissioners and yourself was superinduced by a conversation with Justice Nelson. He informed me of your strong disposition in favor of peace, and that you were oppressed with a demand of the Commissioners of the Confederate States for a reply to their first letter, and that you desired to avoid it if possible at that time.

I told him I might perhaps be of some service in arranging the difficulty. I came to your office entirely at his request, and without the knowledge of either of the Commissioners. Your depression was obvious to both Judge Nelson and myself. I was gratified at the character of the counsels you were desirous of pursuing, and much impressed with your observation that a civil war might be prevented by the success of my mediation. You read a letter of Mr. Weed to show how irksome and responsible the withdrawal of troops from Sumter was. A portion of my communication to Judge Crawford, on the 15th March, was founded upon these remarks, and the pledge to evacuate Sumter is less forcible than the words you employed. These words were: Before this letter reaches you (a proposed letter by me to President Davis) Sumter will have been evacuated.

The Commissioners who received those communications, conclude they have been abused and overreached. The Montgomery Government hold the same opinion. The Commissioners have supposed that my communications were with you, and upon the hypothesis were prepared to arraign you before the country in connection with the President. I placed a peremptory prohibition upon this as being contrary to the term of my communications with them. I pledged myself to them to communicate information upon what I considered as the best authority, and they were to confide in the ability of myself, aided by Judge Nelson, to determine upon the credibility of my informant.

I think no candid man who will read over what I have written, and considers for a moment what is going on at Sumter, but will agree that the equivocating conduct of the Administration, as measured and interpreted in connection with these promises, is the proximate cause of the great calamity.

I have a profound conviction that the telegrams of the 8th of April of Gen. Beauregard, and of the 10th of April of Gen. Walker, the Secretary of War, can be referred to nothing else than their belief that there has been systematic duplicity practiced on them through me. It is under an impressive sense of the weight of this responsibility that I submit to you these things for your explanation.

Very respectfully,

[Signed] JOHN A. CAMPBELL,
Associate Justice of the Supreme Court of the U. S.

Hon. WM. H. SEWARD, Secretary of State.

DISPATCHES

To L. P. Walker, Secretary of War:

An authorized messenger from President Lincoln just informed Gov. Pickens and myself that provisions will be sent to Fort Sumter peaceably, or otherwise by force.

Gen. P. G. T. Beauregard:

If you have no doubt as to the authorized character of the agent who communicated to you the intention of the Washington Government to supply Fort Sumter by force, you will at once demand its evacuation, and if this is refused, proceed in such manner as you may determine to reduce it.

WASHINGTON CITY, April 20, 1861.

Sir—I inclose you a letter, corresponding very nearly with one I addressed to you one week ago, (13th April,) to which I have not had any reply. The letter is simply one of inquiry in reference to facts concerning which, I think, I am entitled to an explanation. I have not adopted any opinion in reference to them which may not be modified by explanation, nor have I affirmed in that letter, nor do I in this, any conclusion of my own unfavorable to your integrity in the whole transaction.

All that I have said and mean to say is, that an explanation is due from you to myself. I will not say what I shall do in case this request is not complied with, but I am justified in saying that I shall feel at liberty to place these letters before any person who is entitled to ask an explanation of myself.

Very respectfully,
JOHN A. CAMPBELL,
Associate Justice of the Supreme Court U. S.

Hon. WM. H. SEWARD, Secretary of State.
No reply has been made to this letter.
April 24, 1861.

MONTGOMERY, May 7, 1861.

Sir—I submit to you two letters that were addressed by me to the Hon. W. H. Seward, Secretary of State of the United States, that contain an explanation of the nature and result of an intervention by me in the intercourse of Commissioners of the Confederate States with that officer. I considered that I could perform no duty in which the entire American people, whether of the Federal Union or of the Confederate States, were more interested than that of promoting the counsels and policy that had for their object the preservation of peace. This motive dictated my intervention. Besides the interview referred to in these letters I informed the Assistant Secretary of State of the United States (not being able to see the Secretary) on the 11th of April, ult., of the existence of a telegram of that date from Gen. Beauregard to the Commissioners, in which he informed the Commissioners that he had demanded the evacuation of Sumter, and if refused, he would proceed to reduce it.

On the same day, I had been told that President Lincoln had said that none of the vessels sent to Charleston were war vessels, and that force was not to be used in the attempt to supply the fort. I had no means of testing the accuracy of this information, but offered that if the information was accurate I would send a telegram to the authorities at Charleston, and it might prevent the disastrous consequences of a collision at that fort between the opposing forces. It was the last effort that I would make to avert the calamities of war. The Assistant Secretary promised to give the matter attention, but I had no other intercourse with him or any other person on the subject, nor have I had any reply to the letters submitted to you.

Very respectfully,
JOHN A. CAMPBELL.

Gen. Davis, President of the Confederate States.

The attention of those in want of every description of household furniture, fresh drugs, medicines, perfumery, etc., is particularly called to the large sale, this day, at 10½ o'clock, at the corner of Camp and Girod streets, by R. M. Montgomery, auctioneer. See advertisement.

We are under many obligations to Dr. Clarke, of this city, for a St. Louis Republican of the 11th. It was brought down by a lady of St. Louis.

FOR STATE AUDITOR.—It will be noticed that the Hon. Wm. L. Knox, of Carroll, is announced as a candidate for Auditor of Public Accounts. Col. Knox was for eight or nine years sheriff and for the last four years has been Representative of the parish of Carroll. We know him to have been, and that he is now, "after the straightest sect of his religion," a dyed-in-the-wool Southern Rights man. Two years ago he was a candidate before the Democratic Convention for the Treasurer's office, but was defeated by a very small majority. He is well and favorably known throughout the State. The man who has sufficient energy, tact and popularity to beat Knox, will be very apt to be the next Auditor.

MARRIED:

On the 11th inst., by the Rev. S. Hedges, Mrs. CORNELIA B. WHIPPLE to ADOLPH SCHEFFER, both of this city.

DIED:

On the 25th December, 1860, at Woodford Plantation, Louisiana, SYDNEY, youngest son of Gen. Felix Huston, deceased, and Mary E. Daingerfield, aged eight years and five weeks.

On the 2d May at Hardingsburg, Breckinridge county, Ky., Mrs. MARGARET HUSTON, mother of Gen. Felix Huston, deceased, aged 85 years and 10 months.

"Blessed are the dead which die in the Lord."

In Berne, Switzerland, March 3d, 1861, of heart disease, ALICE AMELIA, a native of Charleston, S. C., 18 years of age, and only daughter of Dr. C. W. Johnson.

New-York Semi-Weekly Tribune.

VOL. XVII. NO. 1,670. NEW-YORK, TUESDAY, MAY 28, 1861. THREE DOLLARS A YEAR.

COLONEL ELMER E. ELLSWORTH,
ASSASSINATED AT ALEXANDRIA, MAY 24, 1861.
[A Biography of Col. Ellsworth was printed in THE TRIBUNE of Saturday.]

THE MURDER OF COL. ELLSWORTH.

TEARING DOWN THE REBEL FLAG.

PUNISHMENT OF THE MURDERER.

MINUTE AND ACCURATE ACCOUNT.

From Our Special Correspondent.

WASHINGTON, Friday, May 24, 1861.

I have already given by telegraph a brief account of the successful movement of to-day, and of our sorrowful calamity, and I hasten to send such details as my own observation enables me to supply. The part of the expedition with which I moved was that under command of the late Col. Ellsworth. His Regiment of Zouaves was certainly the most actively employed, and was the earliest upon the hostile ground; and with him were associated the most startling events of the day. Of the general forces which are now assembled in Alexandria, others can speak better than I, for their operations were wholly distinct, until the time of the junction, when they were combined under one command. The exact nature of the inroad, as well as the means by which it was to be effected, were of course withheld from the public up to the latest hour, and the only sure method of gaining accurate knowledge of the result was by joining what seemed likely to be the leading body in the movement.

It was generally understood in Washington, on Thursday evening, that an advance of some sort was contemplated, though the rumors fixed no exact time or point of assault. But as the night advanced, the slight fever of excitement which the half-authorized intelligence created, wore away, and the city fell into its usual tranquillity. The contrast between its extreme quiet and the bustle which pervaded some of the expectant camps, was very remarkable. I crossed the Potomac, from Seventh street, in a little boat, and before I had half reached the Zouave camp, unusual indications of busy preparation came echoing over the water. The night was peculiarly still and clear, and the moon so full and lustrous, that the camp was almost visible from the opposite shore. Above the slight murmur caused by the rustle of arms and the marching, a song would occasionally be heard, and once the whole regiment burst out into "Columbia, the Gem of the Ocean," with all the fervor they could bring to it. It was not early when I reached the camp, but the exercise was still progressing under the vigilance of the Colonel, who threw in now and then clear and energetic counsels for the guidance of his men in the morning's work. Before midnight everything needful had been done, and the troops were scattered to their tents for two hours of rest. The Colonel did not sleep until much later. He sat at his table completing the official arrangements which remained to him, and setting carefully before his subordinates the precise character of the duties they were to be charged with. After this he was alone, and I thought, as I entered his tent a little before he turned to his straw and blankets, that his pen was fulfilling a tenderer task than the rough planning of a dangerous exploit. He was so much a stranger to fear, this brave little Colonel, that his friends sometimes wondered at him; but it seemed, then, that he was not insensible to the awful hazards of his station. I hope that those who were nearest to him will find a touch of consolation in the assurance that the last moments he passed alone were given to them.

For more than an hour the encampment was silent. Then it began to stir again, and presently was all alive with action. At 2 o'clock, steamboats appeared off the shore, from one of which Capt. Dahlgren, the commander of the Navy-Yard, came to announce that all was ready for the transportation. The men marched forward in line, and were drawn up by companies to the beach. At this time, the scene was animated in the highest degree. The vivid costumes of the men—some being wrapped from head to foot in their great red blankets, but most of them clad in their gray jackets and trowers and embroidered caps; the peaks of the tents, regularly distributed, all glowing like huge lanterns from the fires within them; the glittering rows of rifles and sabers; the woods and hills, and the placid river, which here meet in exquisite proportion, enfolding all—and all these suffused with the broad moonlight, were blended in such novel picturesqueness that no man among the throng could fail to be moved by it. The embarkation was rapidly conducted, and, although the spot chosen was not apparently the most advantageous, was completed in less than two hours. The entire regiment, excepting the small guard necessarily left behind, nearly one thousand men, were safely bestowed and on their way down the river by 4 o'clock, just as the dawn began to shine over the hills and through the trees.

The night had passed without any noteworthy incident. It had been thought possible that the rebels, who could by some means undoubtedly have gained premonition of the movement, might fire the bridge by which other regiments were to advance upon them, and thus diminish the attacking force for a time. Nothing of this kind, however, had been attempted, and as we steamed down the river (very slowly, for the boats were heavily laden), there was no sign that we were expected, or that any inroad was provided against. This seemed at first suspicious, especially as on nearing Alexandria we found it sharing the same appearance of repose. It could hardly be credited that at least a rumor of warning should not have reached them. But if it had, it would appear that their enormous self-confidence was not to be even thus disturbed, for it afterward was found that no preparations either for resistance or for evacuation had been made until early in the morning, when, if I am rightly informed, the sloop-of-war Pawnee had sent ashore a summons to surrender the town, which I believe the garrison were considering, or had partially assented to, when we arrived. It was not until our boats were about to draw up to the wharf that our approach was noticed in any way; but at the latest minute a few sentinels, whom we had long before discerned, fired their muskets in the air as a warning, and, running rapidly into the town, disappeared. Two or three of the Zouaves, fancying that the shots were directed toward them (which they certainly were not), discharged their rifles after the retreating forms, but no injury to anybody followed. The town was thus put on its guard, but yet so early was the hour, and so apparently unlooked for our arrival, that when we landed, about half-past 5 o'clock, the streets were as deserted as if it had been midnight.

Before our troops disembarked, a boat, filled with armed marines, and carrying a flag of truce, put off from the Pawnee, and landed ahead of us. From the officer in charge we learned that the Pawnee had already proposed terms of submission to the town, and that the Rebels had consented to vacate within a specified time. This seemed to settle the question of a contest in the negative; but in the confusion of mustering and forming the men, the intelligence was not well understood, and received but little attention. Indeed, I am quite sure that the Pawnee's officer did not seek Col. Ellsworth, to communicate with him, and that the Colonel only obtained a meager share of information by seeking it directly from the bearer of the flag of truce himself. No doubt this omission arose from the confused condition in which affairs then stood. But it would have caused no difference in the Colonel's military plans. No attack was meditated, except in case of a forcible resistance to his progress. On the other hand, the idea of the place being under a truce seemed to banish every suspicion of a resistance either from multitudes or individuals. It was just possibly this consideration that led Col. Ellsworth to forego the requisite personal precautions, which, if taken, would have prevented his unhappy death. But I am sure none of us at that time estimated the probability of the danger which afterward menaced us. Perhaps the thought of actual bloodshed and death in war was too foreign to our experiences to be rightly weighed. But it certainly did not enter our minds then, as poor Ellsworth's fate has since taught us it should have done, that a town half waked, half terrified, and under truce, could harbor any peril for us. So the Colonel gave some rapid directions for the interruption of the railway course, by displacing a few rails near the depot, and then turned toward the center of the town, to destroy the means of communication southward by the telegraph; a measure which he appeared to regard as very seriously important. He was accompanied by Mr. H. J. Winser, Military Secretary to the Regiment, the Chaplain, the Rev. E. W. Dodge, and myself. At first he summoned no guard to follow him, but he afterward turned and called forward a single squad, with a Sergeant from the first company. We passed quickly through the streets, meeting a few bewildered travelers issuing from the principal hotel, which seemed to be slowly coming to its daily senses, and were about to turn toward the telegraph office, when the Colonel, first of all, caught sight of the Secession flag, which has so long swung insolently in full view of the President's House. He immediately sent back the Sergeant, with an order for the advance of the entire first company, and, leaving the matter of the telegraph office for a while, pushed on to the hotel, which proved to be the Marshall House, a second-class inn. On entering the open door, the Colonel met a man in his shirt and trowsers, of whom he demanded what sort of flag it was that hung above the roof. The stranger, who seemed greatly alarmed, declared he knew nothing of it, and that he was only a boarder there. Without questioning him further the Colonel sprang up stairs, and we all followed to the topmost story, whence, by means of a ladder, he clambered to the roof, cut down the flag with Winser's knife, and brought it from its staff. There were two men in bed in the garret whom we had not observed at all when we entered, their position being somewhat concealed, but who now rose in great apparent amazement, although I observed that they were more than half dressed. We at once turned to descend, Private Brownell leading the way, and Colonel Ellsworth immediately following him with the flag. As Brownell reached the first landing-place, or entry, after a descent of some dozen steps, a man jumped from a dark passage, and hardly noticing the private, leveled a double-barreled gun square at the Colonel's breast. Brownell made a quick pass to turn the weapon aside, but the fellow's hand was firm, and he discharged one barrel straight to its aim, the slugs or buckshot with which it was loaded entering the Colonel's heart, and killing him at the instant. I think my arm was resting on poor Ellsworth's shoulder at the moment. At any rate, he seemed to fall almost from my own grasp. He was on the second or third step from the landing, and he dropped forward with that heavy, horrible, headlong weight which always comes of sudden death inflicted in this manner. His assailant had turned like a flash to give the contents of the other barrel to Brownell, but either he could not command his aim or the Zouave was too quick with him, for the slugs went over his head, and passed through the panels and wainscot of a door which sheltered some sleeping lodegrs. Simultaneously with this second shot, and sounding like the echo of the first, Brownell's rifle was heard, and the assassin staggered backward. He was hit exactly in the middle of the face, and the wound, as I afterward saw it, was the most frightful I ever witnessed. Of course Brownell did not know how fatal his shot had been, and so before the man dropped, he thrust his saber bayonet through and through the body, the force of the blow sending the dead man violently down the upper section of the second flight of stairs, at the foot of which he lay with his face to the floor. Winser ran from above crying, "Who is hit?" but as he glanced downward by our feet, he needed no answer.

Bewildered for an instant by the suddenness of this attack, and not knowing what more might be in store, we forbore to proceed, and gathered together defensively. There were but seven of us altogether, and one was without a weapon of any kind. Brownell instantly reloaded, and while doing so perceived the door through which the assailant's shot had passed, beginning to open. He brought his rifle to the shoulder, and menaced the occupants, two travelers, with immediate death, if they stirred. The three other privates guarded the passages, of which there were quite a number converging to the point where we stood, while the Chaplain and Winser looked to the stair-case by which we had descended, and the adjoining chambers. I ran down stairs to see if anything was threatened from the story below, but it soon appeared there was no danger from that quarter. However, we were not at all disposed to move from our position. From the opening doors, and through the passages, we discerned a sufficient number of forms to assure us that we were dreadfully in the minority. I think now that there was no danger, and that the single assailant acted without concert with anybody; but it is impossible to know accurately, and it was certainly a doubtful question then. The first thing to be done was to look to our dead friend and leader. He had fallen on his face, and the streams of blood that flowed from his wound had literally flooded the way. The Chaplain turned him gently over, and I stooped and called his name aloud, at which I thought then he murmured inarticulately. I presume I was mistaken, and I am not sure that he spoke a word after being struck, although in my dispatch I repeated a single exclamation which I had believed he uttered. It might have been Brownell, or the Chaplain, who was close behind me. Winser and I lifted the body with all the care we could apply, and laid it upon a bed in a room near by. The rebel flag, stained with his blood, and purified by this contact from the baseness of its former meaning, we laid about his feet. It was at first difficult to discover the precise locality of his wound, for all parts of his coat were equally saturated with blood. By cautiously loosening his belt and unbuttoning his coat, we found where the shot had penetrated. None of us had any medical knowledge, but we saw that all hope must be resigned. Nevertheless, it seemed proper to summon the surgeon as speedily as possible. This could not easily be done, for, secluded as we were in that part of the town, and uncertain whether an ambush might not be awaiting us also, no man could volunteer to venture forth alone, and to go together, and leave the Colonel's body behind, was out of the question. We wondered at the long delay of the first company, for the advance of which the Colonel had sent back before approaching the hotel, but we subsequently learned that they had mistaken a street, and gone a little out of their way. Before they arrived we had removed some of the unsightly stains from the Colonel's features, and composed his limbs. His expression in death was beautifully natural. The Colonel was a singularly handsome man, and, excepting the pallor, there was nothing different in his countenance now from what all his friends had so lately been accustomed to gladly recognize. The detachment was heard approaching at last, a reënforcement was easily called up, and the surgeon was sent for. His arrival, not long after, of course sealed our own unhappy belief. A sufficient guard was presently distributed over the house, but meanwhile I had remembered the Colonel's earnestness about the telegraph seizure, and obtained permission to guide a squad of Zouaves to the office, which was found to be entirely open, with all the doors ajar, yet apparently deserted. It looked a little like another chance of a surprise. The men remained in charge. I presume it was not wholly in order for me, a civilian, to start upon this mission, but I was the only person who knew the whereabouts of the office, and the Colonel had been very positive about the matter. When I returned to the hotel, there was a terrible scene enacting. A woman had run from a lower room to the stairway where the body of the defender of the Secession flag lay, and recognizing it, cried aloud with an agony so heart-rending that no person could witness it without emotion. She flung her arms in the air, struck her brow madly, and seemed in every way utterly abandoned to desolation and frenzy. She offered no reproaches—appeared indeed almost regardless of our presence, and yielded only to her own frantic despair. It was her husband that had been shot. He was the proprietor of the hotel. His name was James T. Jackson. Winser was confident it was the same man who met us at the door when we entered, and told us he was a boarder. His wife, as I said, was wild almost to insanity. Yet she listened when spoken to, and although no consolation could be offered her by us for what she had lost, she seemed sensible to the assurance that the safety of her children, for whom she expressed fears, could not possibly be endangered.

It is not from any wish to fasten obloquy upon the slayer of Col. Ellsworth, but simply because it struck me as a frightful fact, that I say the face of the dead man wore the most revolting expression of rage and hatred that I ever saw. Perhaps the nature of his wound added to this effect, and the wound was something so apalling that I shall not attempt to describe it, as it impressed me. It is probable that such a result from a bullet-wound could not ensue once in a thousand times. Either of Brownell's onslaughts would have been instantaneously fatal. The saber-wound was not less effective than that of the ball. The gun which Jackson had fired lay beneath him, clasped in his arms, and as we did not at first all know that both barrels had been discharged, it was thought necessary to remove it, lest it should be suddenly seized and made use of from below. In doing this, his countenance was revealed.

As the morning advanced, the townspeople began to gather in the vicinity, and a guard was fixed, preventing ingress and egress. This was done to keep all parties from knowing what had occurred, for the Zouaves were so devoted to their Colonel that it was feared if they all were made acquainted with the real fact, they would sack the house. On the other hand, it was not thought wise to let the Alexandrians know thus early the fate of their townsman. The Zouaves were the only regiment that had arrived, and their head and soul was gone. Besides, the duties which the Colonel had hurriedly assigned before leaving them had scattered some companies in various quarters of the town. Several persons sought admission to the Marshall House, among them a sister of the dead man, who had heard the rumor, but who was not allowed to know the true state of the case. It was painful to hear her remark, as she went away, that "of course they wouldn't shoot a man dead in in his own house about a bit of old bunting." Many of the lodgers were anxious to go forth, but they were detained until after I had left. All sorts of arguments and persuasions were employed, but the Zouave guards were inexorable.

At about 7 o'clock, a mounted officer rode up, and informed us that the Michigan 1st had arrived, and had captured a troop of rebels, who had at first demanded time for reflection, but who afterward concluded to yield at discretion. Not long after this, the surgeon made arrangements for the conveyance of Col. Ellsworth's body to Washington. It was properly vailed from sight, and, with great tenderness, taken by a detachment of the Zouaves and the 71st New-York Regiment (a small number of whom, I neglected to state, embarked in the morning at the Navy-Yard, and came down with us), to the steamboat, by which it was brought to the Navy-Yard. It now remains in the care of Capt. Dahlgren.

Washington is greatly excited over the strange news, and there seems to be much doubt among the citizens as to what has really been accomplished. I am as yet ignorant of the movements of other troops sent to occupy the place, but there can be no question but that an ample force, for all the purposes we need to carry out, is now there. I only attempt to furnish a record of that part of the expedition which I witnessed, and to supply the particulars, which would surely be sought after, of the bereavement which has caused our grievous sorrow. I am sure that no young officer in our Northern land could be more sincerely and universally mourned than Col. Ellsworth will be. Perhaps none so much so, for his name was a familiar token for all that was brave, and loyal, and true. There is not a town that did not know him, and could not speak of him to his honor. His friends, while lamenting his early fall, may assure themselves that he perished in performing a daring and courageous action—in resenting a shameful and long undredressed insult to his Government and the Chief Magistrate of his country. It may be said that his deed was rash, but I should not like to hear this reproach too hardly urged against him. He was young, and ardent, and full of ambition, and perhaps knew not that sense of caution which a colder nature would possess. But it would be well for many of us if we were as free from faults, and as rich in manly virtues, as was this gallant, noble and devoted soldier.

I find that I have been free in speaking of my own very slight connection with the events of this morning. It certainly was not from any anxiety on my part to do so; but because I could not, in making a rapid and yet particular narration of a matter in which so few persons acted, avoid alluding to each incident precisely as it occurred, without pausing to consider, at this time, the question of personality.

The following is the card of the proprietor of the Marshall House, whose death is recorded in the above letter:

MARSHALL HOUSE,
JAMES W. JACKSON, Proprietor,
Corner of Pitt and King streets,
ALEXANDRIA, Virginia.

Virginia is determined, and will conquer under the command of JEFF. DAVIS.

The subjoined plan shows the position in which the late gallant Colonel Ellsworth fell. Only a section of the Marshall House is represented. There are wings on either side, and at the back, a number of passages converging at the point "C." It was from one wing through the door K that Jackson's wife appeared, to seek her husband:

A Office of Marshall House.
B B Lodging-rooms.
C Passage in which Jackson was concealed.
D Chamber in which Col. Ellsworth's body was laid.
E Attic—the beds in which were occupied.
F Ladder by which Col. Ellsworth obtained the flag.
G Where the man, supposed to be Jackson, was first met.
H Spot or staircase where Col. E. stood when shot.
I Platform where he fell.
J Platform where Jackson dropped.
K Door through which Jackson's wife appeared.

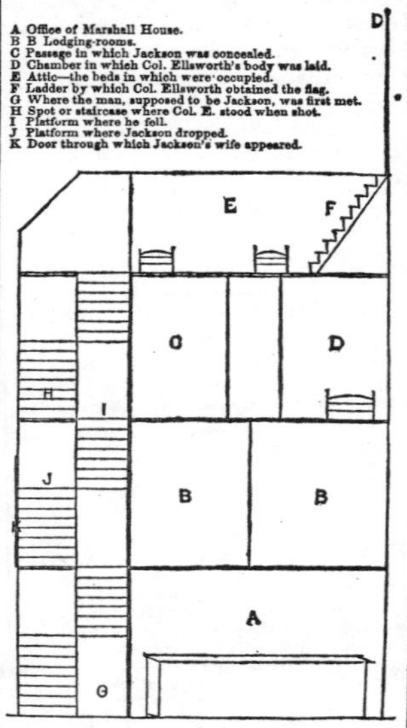

HOW THE NEWS WAS RECEIVED.

The news of Col. Ellsworth's murder was received everywhere with a thrill of horror and sorrow and indignation. The flags were at once put at half-mast, and in almost every city and town resolutions appropriate to the event were passed. On Saturday morning the remains of Col. Ellsworth were conveyed to the east room of the President's house, where for several hours they lay in state. The coffin was draped with the American flag, and adorned with choice flowers. The face was exposed to the public. Many persons, principally soldiers, visited the White House to take a farewell look at him.

Owing to the immense throng of anxious gazers on the remains of the deceased, the funeral cortege delayed moving from the Executive mansion till near 1 o'clock. All along the line of Pennsylvania avenue flags were displayed at half-mast and draped in mourning.

Every available point, including the windows, balconies, and house-tops, were thronged with anxious and sorrowful spectators. Various testimonials of respect were paid. All the bells of the city were tolled, and the heads of the soldiers and troops uncovered.

Several companies of the City corps, followed by the New-York 71st Regiment, Marines, and the local cavalry corps formed the military escort, with their arms reversed and colors shrouded.

The hearse was followed by a detachment of Zouaves, one of whom, the avenger of Col. Ellsworth, carried the identical Secession flag torn down by the deceased.

Then followed the President, accompanied by Secretaries Seward and Smith, and the rear of the procession was composed of carriages containing the captains of the Zouave Regiment.

The special train bearing the body arrived at New-York on Sunday morning, and the remains were at once attended to the Astor House. At 9 o'clock priaate services were there held, after which the coffin was taken to the Governor's Room in the City Hall. The building, within and without, was draped in mourning. For three hours the multitude poured into the Hall, anxious to look upon the face of the dead. The coffin was literally buried beneath the floral offerings which had been laid on it. A large and splendid military escort, the firemen in a body, distinguished military and civic officials, and a large concourse of citizens formed the procession which attended Ellsworth's remains to the steamer waiting to take them to his home, in Mechanicsville. The occasion was one of the most oppressive solemnity, and the sorrow of a was unfeigned and poignant.

The following is a copy of the last letter written by Col. Ellsworth, except one to his affianced bride, written at the same time, just before moving on Alexandria:

HEADQUARTERS 1ST ZOUAVES, CAMP LINCOLN,
WASHINGTON, D. C., May 23, 1861.

My Dear FATHER and MOTHER: The regiment is ordered to move across the river to-night. We have no means of knowing what reception we are to meet with. I am inclined to the opinion that our entrance to the City of Alexandria will be hotly contested, as I am just informed a large force have arrived there to-day. Should this happen, my dear parents, it may be my lot to be injured in some manner. Whatever may happen, cherish the consolation that I was engaged in the performance of a sacred duty; and to-night, thinking over the probabilities of the morrow and the occurrences of the past, I am perfectly content to accept whatever my fortune may be, confident that He who noteth even the fall of a sparrow will have some purpose, even in the fate of one like me.

My darling and ever-loved parents, good bye; God bless, protect, and care for you. ELMER.

SKETCH OF COL. ELLSWORTH'S LIFE.

The announcement on Friday of the assassination of Col. Ellsworth by one of the retreating enemy, who lingered on the spot after the capture of Alexandria, was the signal for profound and intense excitement throughout the city. His name had been familiar to all classes of our population, since the military visit which called forth such universal enthusiasm; and his recent energy, boldness, and determination in organizing a regiment for the defense of the country has been the theme of applause and admiration from every tongue. He fell in the exercise of a characteristic trait, which has often been the subject of remark. Not content with assuming the direction of the soldiers under his command, he was always foremost in action—attending with his own eye to the execution of details which are usually left to subordinates, and as far as possible performing with his own hands the services which he had a right to demand from his subalterns. Fired with this impetuous zeal, he rushed forward on gaining the soil of the rebels, to tear down in person the waving emblem of Secession, but before he could return to his comrades he was slain by a dastardly shot from a Virginian, who met with summary retribution at the hands of an incensed soldier of the deceased, before he could slink away to boast of his ignoble deed. The death of Ellsworth, like that of Warren on Bunker Hill, will send a thrill of indignant rage throughout the land. His blood will cement the covenant to which our armed hosts have sworn, to count their lives as nothing in support of their cause. Henceforth his name will be a watchword in the camp, a war cry on the battle field, and as a flame of fire in the hearts of his brave Zouaves who burn to avenge his death.

Col. Elmer E. Ellsworth was a native of Malta, Saratoga County, N. Y., where his bereaved parents are now living, and although he had attained so prominent a position in our military service, was yet in early youth at the time of his death, having scarcely completed the twenty-fourth year of his age.

For the last few years he had been a resident of Chicago, where he was engaged in the practice of law, but was distinguished for his love of military affairs and his remarkable zeal and efficiency as an officer and disciplinarian. Previous to his entering the service of the United States, with his regiment of New-York Zouaves, he held the office of Quartermaster of the Northern Division of Illinois and Paymaster-General of the militia of that State. His first company of Zouaves was formed in Chicago in the Spring of 1859, and soon became famous for their admirable drill and wonderful feats of activity. In the course of a year, their peculiar tactics had excited so much attention that a strong desire was expressed that they should visit the East, and accordingly, in July, 1860, they left Chicago for a military tour to New-York and other cities of the seaboard. Their reception in this city formed a new era in the history of the militia. The enthusiasm which was excited by their strange and picturesque costume, the astonishing precision of their drill, and their reckless exhibition of strength and skill, pervaded the whole country, and received a fresh impulse on the recent call to arms for the suppression of rebellion. Col. Ellsworth himself was prompt in his answer to the summons of the Government. He lost no time in the offer of his services, and in less than three days after his proposal to form a Zouave Regiment from the Fire Department of New-York, over a thousand brave fellows had enlisted under his command. Since they were mustered into actual service, there has been but one opinion of their value and effectiveness. Amply have they redeemed their brilliant promise, by the noble performance of their late duty. Devoted to their gallant commander, whose personal qualities were as winning as his military genius was remarkable, his death has been the occasion to them of overwhelming grief, that can only be appeased by their share in the triumph which his cowardly assassination did not permit him to witness.

Col. Ellsworth was a man of exemplary moral habits, and a model of temperance and integrity. It is said that he never tasted a drop of liquor, nor smoked a cigar in his life. At the time of his martyr's death, he was engaged to be married to Miss Spofford, an estimable young lady of Rockford, Illinois. The personal sorrow for his untimely loss can hardly be more poignant than the indignant national grief, which is pledged both to honor the memory and avenge the murder of the departed.

ELLSWORTH.

We mourn, alas! thy hapless fate!
And yet 't was glorious thus to die;
Thine eye with victory's gleam elate,
And Freedom's banner floating high.

Thy hand the rebel flag had torn
From off its pinnacle of pride;
And we, alas! can only mourn
That one so young, so brave, has died!

For now thy noble hopes are crushed,
Thy glowing dream of conquest o'er;
The pulses of thy being hushed
Amid the coming battle's roar.

Yet we will still remember thee,
And round thy pallid brow still spread
Sweet garlands, to thy memory,
Thou first among our glorious dead!

Troy, N. Y., May 24. J. L. Y.

THE MOVEMENT UPON VIRGINIA.

CAPTURE OF ALEXANDRIA.

Arlington Hights Occupied.

FLIGHT OF VIRGINIANS.

The following dispatches from our Washington correspondents will give the reader a clear idea of the capture of Alexandria:

WASHINGTON, Friday, May 24, 1861.

Ten thousand United States troops breakfast in Virginia this morning. As I telegraphed last night, Alexandria was occupied by Federal troops at an early hour this morning. A movement as successfully executed as it was skillfully planned, has resulted in the capture of a troop of horse, the complete possession of Alexandria, and the Potomac line of hills thence to points opposite Georgetown.

About 10 o'clock last night four companies of picked men moved over the Long Bridge as an advanced guard. They were sent to reconnoiter, and if assailed were ordered to signal, when they would have been reënforced by a corps of regular infantry and a battery.

At 12 o'clock Col. Ellsworth's regiment of Zouaves embarked in steamers from the Navy-Yard for Alexandria.

At 12 o'clock also the infantry regiment, artillery and cavalry corps began to muster and take marching order. As fast as the several regiments were ready they proceeded to the Long Bridge, those in Washington being directed to take that route. The troops quartered at Georgetown, the 69th, 5th, 8th, and 28th New-York Regiments proceeded across the chain bridge, under the command of Gen. McDowell.

The achievement is clouded by the assassination of a gallant officer. About 1½ o'clock six companies of District Volunteers, including the National Rifles and Turners, stepped from the Long Bridge upon Virginia soil. It had been intended to capture the first patrols by boats, but the bright moonlight prevented it. The patrols crossing the first hill, took to their horses' heels. Nothing else hostile was seen until they arrived at Alexandria.

This vanguard was commanded by Inspector-General Stone, under whom Capt. Smead led the center, Adjutant Abbott the left, and Capt. Stewart, son of Sir Charles Stewart, the right wing. They stopped within half a mile of the town, waiting for the main body, having made sure that the coast was clear.

The rest of the army crossed the bridge in the following order:

12th Regiment, New-York.
25th Regiment, New-York.
1st Regiment, Michigan.
1st, 2d, 3d, and 4th, New-Jersey, in the order named.

Two regular cavalry corps, of 86 men each, and Sherman's two batteries; next and last came the New-York 7th. Following these was a long train of wagons filled with wheelbarrows, shovels, &c. Altogether there were at least 13,000 men in the advancing army.

Maj.-Gen. Mansfield commanded the movement of the troops until the last corps left the District. The first regiment of the main body that crossed the Long Bridge started at twenty minutes past 2, and the last corps left the District at about a quarter to 4 o'clock.

At 4 o'clock, Maj.-Gen. Sandford and staff left Willard's, and proceeded to Virginia to take command of the advancing forces.

At 4 o'clock in the morning, the Captain of the Pawnee demanded the surrender of the town. A Major, in command of the Virginia troops, refused. The Captain then said the consequences would be terrible to the village and all its inhabitants, and prolonged the time till 8 o'clock.

Not far from 5 o'clock, the fleet of boats with Zouaves on board, came up to the wharf at Alexandria. Some twenty or thirty shots were fired upon the boats by the Secession forces as they came up to the wharf, but none were killed or wounded. The Zouaves disembarked, and literally took the city.

The first of the troops who crossed the Long Bridge to enter the town were the Michigan Regiment accompanied by Senator Chandler, to whose courtesy I am indebted for interesting particulars.

They were accompanied by two guns from Sherman's Battery and a company of United States cavalry. As they marched into the street a whistle saluted them, and a train of cars steamed away, probably bearing most of the Secession forces. One company of horse, however, numbering thirty-five men, were captured, with their horses, accouterments, and flag, mounted, mounting, and preparing to mount.

Sherman's Battery came up the street like a whirlwind, and they had no choice but to surrender, alive or dead.

After this bloodless capture, the Secession flag, to which Col. Ellsworth had attended, appearing nowhere, the Michigan men proceeded to tear up the rails leading out of the city, while other detachments did the same office for the road at distant points. Gen. Scott and Secretary Seward were at the Long Bridge when the troops filed over it.

WASHINGTON, Friday evening, May 24, 1861.

The District volunteers are entitled to great credit for their readiness to march into Virginia. The understanding, when they were sworn in, was that they were not to be marched out of the District. Of all the volunteers enrolled, only one man refused to go when requested by Col. Stone. This man is not in good odor among his comrades here, and is very sorry now that he did not go.

The real brunt of the land expedition fell upon the six companies from the District, led by Col. Stone, forming the advance guard. On the march over the bridge a single howitzer might have swept them away, and at other points the passage was so narrow that it was easily defended, or, being flanked by thickets, easily ambushed.

One detachment went along the Alexandria road, another along the road by the river, while another dropped down in a boat to cut off the patrol, which the moonlight prevented. Small bodies guarded the road about half way to Alexandria. The rest of the distance was reconnoitered within half a mile.

This morning, after the other troops took position, the District militia, having been relieved, returned to Washington. They had been on duty the whole night, and many of them on severe scouting service, which sunk them neck-deep in the morasses of the Virginia shore. On returning, toil-worn and covered with mud, this morning, past the New-York 7th Regiment, they were heartily cheered. All the soldiers of the different regiments were to-day enthusiastic at the movement.

To-day the Federal troops were occupied in throwing up entrenchments along the Hights. No official reports have yet been received, the officers being too busy to send them. Only one Colonel has been over to the city, and he was here but a few minutes on an errand.

At 4 o'clock this morning a large number of Government wagons went across Long Bridge, loaded with picks, shovels, and all manner of tools of that description, and accompanied with a full corps of carpenters and workmen. Train after train of wagons, carrying Government tools and fortification implements, have crossed since. At noon to-day, Rickett's Light Artillery, six pieces, went over the river. Col. Wilcox, of the Michigan Regiment, is now in command at Alexandria. We hear that the line of steam ferry-boats will soon resume their trips between this city and Alexandria.

Jackson, who shot Col. Ellsworth, is the same man who headed the gang who attacked the Republican liberty-pole at Occoquan, Fairfax County, before the Presidential election. He cut down the pole with his own hand.

The town is full of rumors of fighting at Alexandria to-day. But they are utterly unfounded. Rumors are also afloat of a simultaneous attack last night at Norfolk and Harper's Ferry. The War Department has no such information. These reports show the feverish excitement of the town. I have just returned from Virginia, having ridden from the Georgetown Aqueduct down to the Arlington House and back again, and am enabled to give you a precise statement of the condition of affairs there up to 5 o'clock this afternoon. Four regiments—the 5th, 28th, and 69th, from New-York, and one from Pennsylvania—had crossed from Georgetown over the Aqueduct, and taken up positions which I will hereafter specifically state. I found four ferries busily plying below the Aqueduct, carrying wheelbarrows and other implements of fortification and stores. One-half of the 69th were still on Analostan or Mason Island, which is half-way across the river, opposite Georgetown, and connected with the Virginia shore by a causeway. The other half is engaged in throwing up square earthworks in Mr. Cass's wheat field, about half a mile due south of the end of the Aqueduct, upon the Virginia Hights which slope up from the river. This eminence is about three quarters as high as Georgetown Hights. On the table land, along the road running south, is a line of pickets extending a mile and a half to the bivouac of the 5th New-York and 28th Brooklyn Regiments, who lie scattered along a distance of several hundred yards east and west from that point. In a farm-yard near by is a battery of artillery. The Pennsylvania Regiment is encamped at the Chain Bridge, some three miles above.

Returning to the Aqueduct, and following down the course of the river, I found no troops or pickets for the distance of two miles. I visited Arlington Hights, and the Arlington House, the residence of Col. Lee. I found no troops, either Federal or Confederate, on the Hights, and could learn nothing of their movements from the servants of the house. I was told that the family of Col. Lee had only left there last week. From this point the encampments of our troops between Long Bridge and Alexandria were plainly visible.

WASHINGTON, Saturday, May 25, 1861.

I have just returned from a visit to Alexandria, made in company with two gentlemen who were in that city during the early part of this week, before the Secession spirit had been laid. Virginia begins to assume an active military appearance at the termination of the bridge leading from Washington, which is closely guarded, no crossing being permitted without special passes. The first guards stationed are taken from the New-York Seventh and another Regiment, which are encamped at Hunting Park Race Course, a short distance from the shore. The hotels and refreshment booths along the main road were all under watch, the proprietors taking frequent opportunities to affirm themselves the strongest Union men in the world. When it was suggested that it might have been safe to express such sentiments a week ago, they said, if it would they hoped they might die.

Just beyond the Seventh's camp a formidable fortification, commanding the head of the bridge, is about completed. The trenches were dug and the earthworks raised by detachments from the Seventh and the New-Jersey troops. The men all working vigorously with pick and shovel, in spite of a fierce sun. A thick grove which had surrounded the spot had been entirely levelled, and the trunks of trees removed. The works are progressing under the direction of Major Barnard, Engineer-in-Chief. The officers under him are Captains Alexander and Blunt, and Lieutenants Prime, Hunter and Robert, all of the regular engineer corps. The last named is a South Carolinian by birth, and has ten uncles in the Confederate army; one of them a General in Georgia. Other requisite fortifications are forming at strong points about Washington, one of them covering the aqueduct bridge at Georgetown.

Among the captures yesterday morning was one made by the President's Mounted Guard, which stopped a train of two cars which were returning from Leesburg, on the Loudon and Hampshire Road, as it reached Riley's Hill, just beyond Ball's Crossroads, and arrested the passengers, three in number, named H. Nevitt, D. Porter, and J. W. Quinton, and brought them to this city, where they were placed in Jail. The squad destroyed no less than six bridges, four above and two below the place where the train was stopped.

WASHINGTON, May 26, 1861.

I visited Arlington House this afternoon. The beauty. The garden is a mass of flowers. trees and turf are in June. luxuriance and The prospect of the river and city is charming. General Sanford was not there. The headquarters were in charge of Colonel Alex. Hamilton, of the staff of General Sanford, and Colonel Lyons of the New-York 8th, which marched from Washington, and whose tents are in the woods about the house. Gen. Sanford told them that this was emphatically the post of honor.

The telegraph is nearly completed from Washington and Alexandria to Arlington House. Among the visitors to-day was Leutze, the painter. Gen. Sandford was courteous in taking possession of the house. He yesterday sent to inquire whether the family of Gen. Lee was there, and to offer a guard if so. When assured that thay had left a fortnight ago, he sent to Gen. Lee to say that he was obliged to make Arlington House his quarters, and would see that the premises received no damage. Twelve or fifteen servants were in the house, with a month's provisions. Most of the furniture was removed. I subsequently visited the 69th's intrenchments at Georgetown, which are of a character to defy assault.

MILITARY EQUIPMENTS.

To the Editor of The N. Y. Tribune.

SIR: Allow me to make some suggestions in relation to the equipment of our volunteers. They are all to be instructed as light infantry, to maneuver in double quick time, to run, and to fence with the bayonet. They should have an easier, lighter, and healthier equipment than United States troops have heretofore had.

I. A well-made light felt (not wool) U. S. regulation hat. A reddish-gray color is better than black, but a linen or cotton cover doubled or trebled at the band would overcome that objection. These hats should not be of wool, because wool hats are hotter, absorb moisture, and won't keep their shape.

II. Loose, and, for Summer, light clothes. The regulation clothing is too heavy for a Summer campaign in Virginia. I recommend that our volunteers be all furnished with a fighting suit, to consist of our all-wool hunting shirt, with a sack back, or an ordinary sack coat to be always kept buttoned over the stomach, and all-wool, but heavier, "peg-top" pantaloons.

III. Gutta-percha shelter-tent knapsacks. These knapsacks make the soldier very independent of the baggage train, &c. The soldier is always sheltered at a halt, and never lies on the damp ground.

IV. High (just above the ankle bone) Oxford shoes. As activity upon the feet is the very gist of bayonet fencing, a good shoe is of the very first importance. The subject is worthy of a separate article, and I will write you again about it.

V. Enfield muskets. They are lighter than any others that I know, and more accurate. Above all things let the troops be well armed. We all know, in muscular contests, how much depends upon confidence. There is nothing that gives the soldier so much confidence as the possession of a superior arm.

VI. The whole equipment as light as is consistent with the comfort of the men.

Allow me to add that the State ought to insist upon having good soldiers at the head of the brigades; those who know how to attack a strong position and how to defend one, and who know how to take advantage of ground both for attack and defense; in short, men of scientific military instruction and clear heads.

I have the honor to remain your obedient servant,
———, of three campaigns.

No. 60 Wall-street, May 25.

The screw-steamship Etna, Capt. Kennedy, which sailed from Liverpool at 11 a. m. on the 15th, and from Queenstown on the 16th inst., arrived here on Monday, bringing passengers and a million and a half of specie.

FROM FORT PICKENS.

Arrival of Lieut. Slemmer and his Command.

The U. S. transport Philadelphia, Capt. Kittridge, arrived here on Sunday morning from Fort Pickens, via Tortugas and Key West, making the passage from the latter place in six days and twelve hours, with Lieut. Slemmer and his command, and twelve women and children, and twelve mechanics. Everything was quiet at Fort Pickens when the P. left. The fleet lay at anchor off the fort, in readiness to coöperate with Col. Brown, keeping up a constant watchfulness and intercepting all vessels bound in, thus cutting off all supplies from the Secession forces by water. The fleet consists of the U. S. ship Sabine, H. A. Adams, Commander; steam sloop-of-war Brooklyn, C. H. Poor, Commander; steam-sloop Powhatan, D. D. Porter, Commander; steamer Water-Witch, W. Rockendoff, Commanding. The steamer Mohawk, J. H. Strong, Commanding, was at the east end of Rosas Island, to prevent any vessels of light draft from entering at the eastern channel.

Lieut. Slemmer's company are very much worn down by fatigue and constant labor and watchfulness. Several of them have the scurvy, and others are suffering from attacks induced by over-exertion and want of proper food. Lieut. Gillman of this company is also a passenger, and from the appearance of both officers and privates it is evident that the change of locality was necessary to restore the health of all. The P., in passing the Sabine and sloop-of-war Brooklyn, fired a gun for each ship, and exchanged salutes by dipping ensign, which was returned by both ships; and to show their appreciation of Lieut. Slemmer, their rigging was manned, and three cheers were given by the crew, which were returned by Lieut. Slemmer's men and the crew of the Philadelphia with right good will. The Philadelphia sailed hence April 19, with sealed orders, having on board a large cargo of army and ordnance stores. Arrived at Key West at 1 a. m. on the 29th; communicated with Major French, commander at Fort Taylor, and proceeded to Fort Jefferson, Tortugas Island; landed a large amount of subsistance stores, and sailed at 9 a. m. of the 30th for Fort Pickens, where she arrived at 8 p. m. of the 2d, and anchored inside the fleet. On the 3d approached within ¾ of a mile of the fort and landed mules and beef cattle in safety and discharged most of the remainder of the cargo. During this time the Philadelphia lay within range of the guns of Forts McRae and Barrancas and the land batteries, but no disposition was manifested to attack her. The weather was so bad that she was delayed 3 days in discharging. On the 14th proceeded to Fort Jefferson, Tortugas, and landed the rest of the cargo there. May 16, 11 p. m. arrived at Tortugas, discharged ordnance stores and sailed for Key West at 10 p. m. of the 17th, where she arrived on the 18th at 8 a. m., and sailed for New-York on the 19th, having ascertained that the greater part of the troops expected from Havana on their way from Texas for New-York had previously sailed in two sailing vessels.

STATEMENT OF A YOUNG MAN FROM PENSACOLA.

A young gentleman, named G. A. Kerbey, who, a few weeks ago, visited the quarters of some of the rebels, saw their condition and heard their murmurings, has been represented in the Southern papers as being on their side, and for that reason had been held at Fort Pickens as a prisoner and sent home in double irons. It may be well to state that this is a slight mistake, inasmuch as Mr. Kerbey came a first-class passenger in the Philadelphia, which brought Lieut. Slemmer to this port, and gives us the following brief statement:

PREPATIONS OF THE SECESSIONISTS AT PENSACOLA.

Up till the 25th of April, only five sand batteries had been completed. Seven more were in process of erection. The guns for the latter had not at that time arrived, and could not arrive until the completion of the Montgomery and Pensacola Railroad which would not be finished before the 10th of the present month. They were pushing the work with all speed when I left.

General Bragg remarked one evening, in conversation with some of his officers, that he would not be ready in two months, and he was confident that Col. Brown would wait for him. There were about 7,000 troops encamped in and about Warrington Navy-Yard, Forts, and the village of Warrington, the inhabitants having entirely deserted it. Reënforcements had almost ceased to arrive. There was great dissatisfaction among the men who were there already in camp. Desertions were very frequent, and particularly after the reënforcement of Fort Pickens. The discipline among the citizen soldiers is very poor. The grounds which they have for dissatisfaction may be set down: 1st, As Bragg; 2d, Provisions; 3d, The climate.

They are obliged to work in a fine white sand which swarms with fleas; in another month yellow fever will probably drive them away or kill them. The provisions are principally from the North, being chiefly cornflour. With Gen. Bragg's generalship the men are dissatisfied; they think he goes too slow. They assert quite freely that Lieut. Slemmer out-generaled him at every move.

The whole of Santa Rosa Island is in full possession of the U. S. troops. No men can now be landed on the island with a view to attacking Fort Pickens from that quarter.

Batteries have been erected close to the Fort bearing on Bragg's batteries, which were intended for the formerly *weak* side of Pickens.

U. S. soldiers have been landed at the extreme end of Santa Rosa Island, from the Fort, to erect batteries to guard the entrance to Pensacola by Santa Rosa sound.

A strict blockade is now on the harbor. The U. S. ship Powhatan, Captain Porter, stands guard and does his work effectually. Nothing whatever is allowed to pass in or out. Several steamers, and scores of sailing craft have been sent off. There was some disturbance with some of them which were inclined to be factious.

ELMER E. ELLLSWORTH.

Died May 24, 1861.

WEEP, weep, Columbia! Death with traitorous hand
Has slain a Hero, quenched a manly flame,
Cast heartfelt sorrow o'er a throbbing land,
And carved, for future years to read, a name
On the grand altar of our country's fame.
Strew roses o'er his corpse—a Soldier's vow
He took—a Soldier's pall enwraps him now;
At Glory's portal Death's red summons came.
Chant, O ye Land, the Soldier's burial hymn
O'er ELLSWORTH'S bier; and as ye sadly turn,
With falt'ring voice, and eyes with tear-drops dim,
Swear ye that Retribution's torch may burn
In every breast! A martyr's youthful blood
Cements your oath. Strike! for your cause is good!
A. A.-A.

From California.

FORT KEARNEY, Monday, May 27, 1861.

The Pony Express passed at 12 o'clock on Friday night (24th), but by some mistake our budget of news was taken out between here and Fort Laramie, reaching us by coach yesterday.

There has been but little incident in California this week except the Union meetings, which continue to be held almost nightly in the principal towns and cities. The speeches and resolutions invariably favor a vigorous war policy on the part of the Administration until every foot of the Union acknowledges the Stars and Stripes.

An effort is making in San Francisco to organize a company of volunteers to tender their services to the General Government, on the supposition that the Pacific Mail steamship will give them a free passage East. A similar organization has been commenced in Sacramento, the members holding themselves in readiness to obey the first call of the President.

The arrangements for a grand patriotic demonstration on the coming anniversary of American Independence was initiated by a meeting of citizens of Sacramento on the 13th.

The Republican State Central Committee have issued a call for a Convention composed of delegates of Union men irrespective of party, to meet in Sacramento on the 18th of June. The Republicans do not design giving up their organization, but adopt the Union test simply and purely without reference to other issues.

A resolution has been offered in the Assembly instructing our Senators in Congress and requesting our Representatives there to offer California as a mediator in the present difficulties, and in favor of a Convention to revise the Constitution of the United States.

HUMBUG DISPATCHES.

NASHVILLE, Monday, May 27, 1861.

A private dispatch to *The Daily Gazette* says there was fighting at Harper's Ferry on Saturday evening, at which the Federal troops were repulsed. On Sunday a fight occurred at Hampton. Near Fortress Monroe 600 Lincoln troops were killed and wounded, while the Southern loss was only 50.

Partial returns from 18 counties of Virginia show only 13 votes against Secession.

HEALTH OF SENATOR DOUGLAS.—The friends of Mr. Douglas in Washington are in receipt of late news from Chicago, justifying the hope that he will speedily be restored to his usual good health.

MARRIED.

ADAMS—DOTY—At Carrollton, Mississippi, on Thursday, April 11, by the Rt. Rev. Bishop Green, the Rev. John Charles Adams, M. D., to Miss Helen M. Doty of Lockport, New-York.

BRACKETT—BLUNT—In Brooklyn, on Sunday, May 19, by the Rev. T. Franciolli, Samuel Brackett to Ellen M. Blunt, all of Brooklyn.

BALDWIN—HOOKER—In New-Haven, Conn., on Tuesday, May 21, at St. Paul's Church, Albert Baldwin of Newark, N.J., to Jennet P. Hooker, daughter of Chaarles Hooker, M. D., of New-Haven.

CLARKE—ROBERTSON—In Brooklyn, on Wednesday, May 8, at St. Luke's Church, by the Rev. J. D. Vermilye, John A. Clarke of Armonk, N. Y., to Lizzie H., second daughter of John W. Robertson, esq., of Brooklyn.

CREARY—MIDDLETON—In Brooklyn, on Monday, May 20, by the Rev. J. H. Perry, George Creary of Keyport, New-Jersey, to Miss Eliza Jane, daughter of late Captain Nathaniel Middleton of New-London, Conn.

FRAZIER—ELDRIDGE—In this city, on Wednesday, May 22, by the Rev. H. H. Garnet, Lewis Frazier of Milan, Dutchess County, New-York, to Ellen Eldridge of this city.

HEMINWAY—ROGERS—In Jersey City, on Thursday, May 23, by the Rev. Dr. Rogers, Homer Heminway of Watertown, Connecticut, to Susan R. K., daughter of the late Captain William T. Rodgers of the former place.

HAGERTY—HUGHES—In East Cambridge, Mass., on Thursday, May 23, by the Rev. Joseph Coyle, Michael H. Hagerty of Brooklyn, to Sarah E., daughter of Alexander Hughes, esq., of East Cambridge.

HOVER—SWARTS—On Thursday, May 23, by the Rev. Dr. J. M. Krebs, Ira W. Hover, late of San Francisco, to Emma, daughter of Aaron Swarts of this city.

LORD—STRICKLAND—At the Astor House, on Friday evening, May 24, by the Rev. Mr. Burlingham, Lieutenant Charles V. Lord, Quartermaster 2d Regiment Maine Volunteers, and Miss Fanny E. Strickland, daughter of General S. P. Strickland of Bangor, Maine.

RHEUTAN—YOUNG—On Wednesday, May 22, by the Rev. Ira R. Steward, Abram A. Rheutan to Miss Mary H., daughter of the late Robert Young, all of this city.

DIED.

BAILEY—In this city, on Friday, May 24, Daniel Drew Bailey.

BUELL—In Hartford, Conn., on Sunday, May 19, Fisher A. Buell, aged 25 years.

CLAYTON—In Brooklyn, on Saturday, May 25, Lizzie Lindley Louise, aged 4 years, adopted daughter of James H. and Sarah B. Clayton.

CAREY—In Brooklyn, on Friday, May 24, in her 20th year, Anne, daughter of Bernard and Anne Carey.

COEY—On Friday, May 24, Thomas Coey, son of the late William J. Coey, in the 23d year of his age.

DUNN—In this city, on Saturday, May 25, John Dunn, jr., aged 18 years.

DELANY—In this city, on Saturday, May 25, after a long and severe illness, Rosamond, the beloved wife of James Delany, aged 42 years.

DEVLIN—On Friday, May 24, Ann, wife of John Devlin, in the 40th year of her age.

DANIELS—In this city, on Friday, May 24, Frances Daniels, second daughter of Patrick and Eliza Daniels, aged 6 years, and 3 months.

FREEL—In Brooklyn, on Friday, May 24, Ellen Freel, daughter of Edward and Elizabeth Freel, aged 28 years and 24 days.

GREENVAULT—In Brooklyn, E. D., on Saturday morning, May 25, 1861, of consumption, Daniel D. Greenvault, aged 32 years, 6 months and 9 days, eldest son of Daniel Greenvault of this city.

GRUBER—On Wednesday, May 22, Esther Gruber, daughter of John and Esther Gruber, aged 19 years, 4 months and 8 days.

GUINIVAN—In this city, on Friday, May 24, after a lingering illness, Bridget, wife of Martin Guinivan, aged 34 years, a native of the Parish of Lismore, County Waterford, Ireland.

GLOVER—On Friday, May 24, Erastus W. Glover, aged 39 years, 5 months and 20 days.

HERBST—On Monday, May 20, Theodore N. Herbst, son of John W. Herbst, aged 39 years.

HOWARD—On Thursday, May 23, William C. Howard, a native of this city, in the 49th year of his age.

HEINS—In this city, suddenly, on Saturday, May 25, Mrs. Anna Margaretta Heins, beloved wife of Cord Heins, aged 44 years and 3 months.

KLAUBERG—In Williamsburgh, on Saturday, May 25, after a lingering illness, Emma C. Klauberg, youngest child of Carl and Emma Klauberg, jr., aged 1 year, 6 months and 23 days.

LUBKEMANN—In this city, on Saturday, May 25, Hermann H. son of the late Henry N. and Maria Lubkemann, aged 2 years, 3 months and 8 days.

LIVINGSTON—In this city, on Thursday, May 23, after a short but painful illness of bilious colic, William Bichford, youngest son of William H. and Mary C. Livingston, in the 16th year of his age.

MACKINTOSH—In this city, on Saturday, May 25, Harry M., eldest child of W. H. and Abba B. Mackintosh, aged 10 years.

McLEAN—In this city, on Friday, May 24, Catharine McLean, aged 18 years and 3 months.

McA. LEER—In this city, on Saturday morning, May 25, James, son of Patrick McA. Leer, aged 18 years and 7 months.

MARTIN—In this city, on Friday, May 24, Charles Martin, aged 13 years and 6 months.

NEVIN—In Brooklyn, on Friday, May 24, Mary, wife of James Nevin, aged 35 years.

POTTER—In this city, on Saturday, May 25, Mr. George Potter, aged 52 years.

PAPE—In this city, on Friday, May 24, Charles W. Pape, only son of Dr. Ernst D. and Catharine Pape, aged 9 years and 2 months.

PEARSALL—Suddenly, at Ithaca, on Wednesday, April 17, Charles W. Pearsall, formerly of Manhasset, Long Island, in the 59th year of his age.

RYAN—In this city, on Saturday, May 25, Mary Ellen Ryan, only daughter of James and Bridget Ryan, aged 4 months and 23 days.

RICE—In this city, on Thursday, May 23, Joseph Rice, in the 26th year of his age.

ROGERS—At sea, on board the Aspinwall steamer Champion, on Friday, May 17, Edmund Rogers of this city, aged 36 years.

SEACORD—In Naples, Ontario County, N. Y., on Monday evening, May 20, 1861, A. T. Seacord, in the 38th year of his age.

SECOR—In this city, on Thursday, May 23, Margaret Louisa, wife of Frank Secor, aged 33 years.

SMITH—On Thursday, May 23, at Williamsburgh, Margaret Smith, wife of John Smith, aged 27 years.

SHERIDAN—In this city, on Saturday, May 25, Rosey, the beloved wife of Andrew Sheridan, in the 35th year of her age, a native of the Parish of Cerrick Macross, County Monaghan, Ireland.

TOBIAS—In this city, on Friday, May 24, T. J. Tobias, aged 75 years.

TWITCHINGS—On Sunday, May 26, after a lingering illness, Anna M., the beloved wife of Thaddeus Twitchings, aged 25 years and 6 days.

UDALL—At Great Neck, Long Island, on Saturday, May 25, Richard Udall, aged 80 years and 9 months.

VAN LOAN—On Sunday, May 26, Isabell Van Loan, eldest daughter of Bronk and Ellen Frances Van Loan, in the 6th year of her age.

WILSON—In this city, on Saturday, May 25, John Wilson, sr., aged 75 years.

YOUNG—In Brooklyn, on Sunday, May 26, Susan Augusta, youngest daughter of Robert and Elizabeth Young, aged 5 years, 2 months and 26 days.

COMMERCIAL MATTERS.

Sales at the Stock Exchange........MAY 27.

8,000	U. S. 6s '81 coupon..	86	150	N. Y. Central RR......	71⅛
5,000	U. S. 5s '71 registered	79	550	do............	71⅛
3,000	U. S. 6s '81 registered	88	200	do..........s60	70⅞
11,500	Treas. 12 ₱ c. Notes.	102	50	do............c	71⅛
12,000	Tenn. State 6s '90....	44	150	Erie Railroad........	21⅞
4,000	do...........s10	44	150	do...........s5	21⅞
2,000	Virginia State 6s.....	47½	100	Harlem RR. Pref......	26
13,000	do..............	47⅝	50	Hudson River RR......	34½
3,000	Virginia 5s Ster. Bs..	40	15	do............	34½
1,000	N. C. State 6s.......	56½	50	Mich. Cen. RR........	41⅛
5,000	do..........s30	55	400	do............	41
1,000	Louisiana State 6s....	51½	50	Ill. Cen. RR. Sc'p, p & c	66½
2,000	Chi. & Rock Isl. Bs..	92	100	do..........opg	67
2,000	Missouri State 6s....	40½	100	do..........s30	65
5,000	do..............	40⅝	300	do..........s10	66½
10,000	do..............	40¾	50	do..........opg	67½
32,000	do..............	41	100	Gal. & Chi. RR....p&c	57
12,000	do..............	41½	100	Cleve. & Tol. RR......	21⅞
5,000	do..........s30	41	100	Chi. & R. I. RR....opg	31½
1,000	do..............	41¼	15	N. J. RR.............	113
15	Bank of New-York.....	80	50	Chi. Bur. & Qu'y RR..	54
5	Bank of Commerce.....	79	50	do............	54½
35	Park Bank............	88			

SECOND BOARD.

2,000	U. S. 6s '61 Coupon..	86¼	250	N. Y. Cen. R. R......b4	71⅛
2,000	do..............	86½	150	do............	71⅛
15,000	do..............	86	25	Hudson River R. R....	34½
5,000	U. S. 6s '81 Regist'd.	88	*5	Panama R. R.........	103
1,000	U. S. 6s '74 Coupon.	78½	50	Erie Railroad........	21⅞
7,000	N. Car. State 6s.....s3	56	50	do..........s10	21⅞
3,000	Virginia State 6s...s3	47½	100	do............	21⅞
1,000	do...........s3	47½	250	do............	22
7,000	do..............	47⅝	100	Harlem R. R. Pref....	26
10,000	do...........s5	47½	100	do............	26½
15,000	do..............	48	200	Ill. Cen. R.R. Scrip opg	67¼
8,000	Tenn. State 6s '90...	44	100	do..........opg	67⅞
15,000	Missouri State 6s....	41½	50	Cleve. & Tol. R. R.....	21⅞
4,000	Mic. Cen. 8 ₱ ct. 1st Mge. S. F'd Ct. Bs.	93½	25	Chi. & R. I. R. R......	32
50	Pac. Mail Steam Co..s5	62	150	do............	32½

MONDAY, May 27—P. M.

There was no prominent feature in the stock movement to-day, but evidently a more cheerful tone among operators. The transactions at the morning Board were quite restricted, excepting in Border-State bonds, but a general advance was established by the necessities of the shorts, who compete with each other for the moderate quantites of cash stock offered. The successes of the Federal troops have undoubtedly some favorable influence upon the market, as also has the taking of the nine million loan; but the strongest element of the rise is that of the over sales of the bears, and the consequent demand for cash stock. The few sellers' options put out are at the large differences which have ruled for the past month, showing the difficulty the bears find in carrying forward their shorts. The widest difference is in Illinois Central, which sold at 67 for the opening, 1st of June, and 65, seller thirty. The difference in New-York Central is about 1 ₱ cent for sixty days. Between the Boards the market was steady, but without activity. At the Second Board, with a fair amount of transactions, there was a very firm feeling, and a further advance was established. There appeared to be an increased amount of orders among the commission houses, and some of the bulls took heart, and bid freely for buyers' option. Central sold as high as 71⅞, and closed at that. Pacific Mail was in demand, and after the regular session 63½ was bid, against 61½ on Saturday. Illinois Central sold up to 68¼, an improvement of 1¾ ₱ cent on Saturday. Hudson River advanced ½ ₱ cent, Harlem ¼ ₱ cent, Rock Island ½ ₱ cent, Erie ¼ ₱ cent, &c. The transactions in State Stocks to-day add up $175,000, in nearly every case at an advance of Saturday's prices. Virginias sold up to 48, which is ½ ₱ cent better. Missouri 6's advanced 1 ₱ cent, and Tennessees ½ ₱ cent. The advices from St. Louis indicating that Missouri will be kept in the Union, strengthens the bonds of this State, although there is little or no expectation that the July interest will be paid. The other State stocks sympathize, and, being in moderate supply, the quotations have an improving tendency. In Railroad bonds there is no movement worthy of notice. The market generally is firm. Government securities are without important change, but were heavy at the Second Board, under the false impression that the new loan had not all been taken. After the board the market was firm in the street at the annexed quotations: Virginia 6s, 47⅞@48; Missouri 6s, 41⅝@41¾; Canton Co., 5; Pacific Mail, 63½@63⅝; New-York Central Railroad, 71¾@71⅞; Erie Railroad, 22@22¼; Hudson River Railroad, 34½@35; Harlem Railroad, 10¾@11; Harlem Railroad Preferred, 26@26½; Reading Railroad, 30¾@31; Michigan Central Railroad, 40¾@41; Michigan Southern and Northern Indiana Railroad, 11@11½; Michigan Southern and Northern Indiana Guaranteed, 24½@24¾; Panama Railroad, 103@103½; Illinois Central Railroad, 67¾@68; Galena and Chicago Railroad, 56¼@57; Cleveland and Toledo Railroad, 21⅞@22¼; Chicago and Rock Island Railroad, 32¼@32½; Chicago, Burlington, and Quincy Railroad, 54@55.

There is a firmer feeling in foreign Exchange, as is usual after the arrival of gold for the purchase of bills. The transactions have yet been moderate at 104@105¾ for Sterling, and 5.40@5.35 for Francs.

Freights—The market is more active. To Liverpool, 50 tuns Starch, at 30s; 160 bales Cotton, at 3-16d.; 60,000 bush. Wheat, at 8d. in bulk and 8½d. in bags; 24,000 bush. Corn, at 8@8½d. in ships' bags; 2,000 bbls. Flour, at 2s.; 45 hhds. Tallow, at 45s.; 200 bbls. Pork, at 3s. 3d. To London, 6,000 bush. Wheat, per British vessel, at 11d. in bulk; 3,500 bbls. Flour, at 2s. 6d.@3s.—the latter rate by foreign vessel; 500 bbls. Pork, at 3s. 3d.; 130 hhds. Tobacco, at 32s. 6d.; 14,000 bush. Wheat, part at 9½d., in ships' bags. To Glasgow, by British vessel, 800 bbls. Flour, at 2s. 9d.; 15 tuns Grease Butter, at 32s. 6d. To Havre, 5,000 bush. Wheat, in ships' bags, at 17c. A British bark to Cork, for orders, with 20,000 bush. Corn, at 11d. in bulk. A vessel, with 30,000 bush. Corn, to Cork and a market, at 10½d. in bulk and bags. A vessel of 300 tuns, from Lisbon to Rio Grande, with salt, at 40s. A vessel of 220 tuns, from an Eastern port to a Windward Island, with Lumber, at $10 per M. feet; one of 150 tuns, to the West Indies and back, for $1,250.

The Secretary of the Treasury has awarded the loan the bids for which were opened on Saturday—$6,753,000 to bidders for bonds or stock, and $2,241,000 to bidders for Treasury Notes at par. The stock was awarded at 85 up to 93, there being $2,397,000 at 85, $1,795,000 at 85.05, and $1,773,000 at 86. The Treasury Notes were bid for from Boston and Providence. A few bids were made below 85, but these were rejected. There have been resales of about $200,000 of this loan at 86½. When it was supposed that the whole loan had not been taken, Mr. Cisco had an application for the whole amount not awarded at 85. Nearly three millions of dollars have already been paid into the Treasury on this loan, and the Secretary is now provided with ample means to meet the Treasury Notes maturing in June, and the July interest on the public debt. The difficulty in regard to the Boston bid appears to be that it was put in for the Treasury Notes to be awarded on the 30th inst. We presume enough of it was transferred to complete the loan awarded on Saturday.

The following is a comparative statement of the condition of the banks of New-York City, May 18 and May 25:

	May 18.	May 25.		
Loans..............	$120,007,806	$118,141,356	Dec.	$1,866,450
Specie.............	39,537,980	38,622,791	Inc.	24,811
Circulation........	9,061,131	8,798,882	Dec.	267,249
Deposits...........	93,179,527	91,334,879	Dec.	1,844,648

Markets—CAREFULLY REPORTED FOR THE N. Y. TRIBUNE.

MONDAY, May 27, 1861.

ASHES—The inquiry is fair for Pots at $5 37½@$5 43½. Pearls are steady at $5 62½.

COTTON—The market has been a little more active; sales of 3,000 bales. We quote nominally at 14@14½c. for Middling Orleans, and 13¾@14c. for Gulfs.

COFFEE—Rio is steady; sales of 500 bags at 12@13½c., and 150 bags Maracaibo at 13½@14c.

FLOUR AND MEAL—The demand for Western Canal Flour is fair, more especially for State brands; these are not plenty, and are well sustained. The medium grades are unsalable, and are heavy. Family Extras are quiet, but prices are sustained; the sales are 15,400 bbls. at $4 91@$5 05 for superfine Western; $5@$5 07½ for superfine State; $5 20@$5 40 for the low grades of Western Extra; $5 20@$5 27½ for Extra State; $5 30@$5 40 for choice do.; $5 55@$5 65 for shipping brands of round-hoop Extra Ohio; and $5 70@$7 50 for trade brands of do. Canadian Flour is steady, and in fair request; the low grades are more plenty; choice brands are firm, and not plenty; sales of 670 bbls. at $5 20@$7 60 for Extras. Southern Flour is less active, but with moderate arrivals and a reduced stock, prices are sustained; the sales are 1,166 bbls. at $6@$6 60 for mixed to good superfine Baltimore, &c., and $6 65@$9 for the better grades. Rye Flour is quiet; the supply good; sales of 170 bbls. at $3@$4. Corn Meal is steady, the supply not large; sales of 321 bbls. at $3 for Jersey, and $3 20 for Brandywine.

FISH—All kinds are dull and heavy. We quote St. Georges Bank at $3 25@$3 50; Mackerel, for No. 2, at $4 50, and $3 25@$3 50 for No. 3; Herring, scaled and No. 1, 10@22c.

GRAIN—There is a good export demand for prime Wheat; this is very firm, but unsound and ordinary qualities are very difficult of sale, and prices are very irregular; fair White is firmer and in good demand, in part for export; very choice White is very firm and in request for milling; the sales are 26,400 bush. Chicago Spring at $1@$1 15; 71,200 bush. Milwaukee Club at $1 09@$1 21; 16,700 bush. Amber Iowa at $1 22@$1 24; 3,100 bush. Red State at $1 28 afloat; 32,700 bush. choice Canada Club at $1 22; 13,300 bush. White Ohio and Indiana at $1 40@$1 45; 4,700 bushels White Canadian at $1 45; 6,000 bushels North-Western Club at $1 17; 1,400 bushels White Michigan at $1 67@$1 75; 8,400 bushels White Kentucky at $1 80. Barley is in fair demand and is less plenty; the sales are 1,466 bush. State at 60@62½c. Barley Malt is quiet at 75@80c. Oats are inactive, but steady; sales of Western at 31@33c., and State at 33@34c. Rye is in limited demand at 68c. for Northern. Corn is quite firm and in brisk demand for export and the trade; the supply of inferior is not so large; this is firmer; the sales are 148,000 bush. at 41@42c. for unsound; 43@45c. for new mixed Western; 45@46c. for old do.; 56c. for old Western Yellow; 48@50c. for new do.; 50c. for old and new mixed together, and 47c. for new round Yellow.

HOPS—The market is quiet, and prices rule in the buyers' favor. We quote nominally at 11@18c.; the latter rate for very choice.

HAY—The inquiry is moderate for shipments, and the market is heavy; sales of 600 bales at 60@70c. ₱ 100 lb.

LIME—The market for Rockland is quiet, but prices are steady, at 60c. for Common, and $1 for Lump.

MOLASSES—The demand is very moderate; prices are steady. Sales of 180 hhds. Cuba Muscovado at 15c. for refining. By auction, 28 hhds. Porto Rico at 18c.

NAVAL STORES—The market for Spirits Turpentine is inactive at 70@72½c. Crude is held firmly at $5. Common Rosin is quiet at $2 12½@$2 20, we do not hear of any sales. Fine do. is steady at $2 25@$4 for No. 1, and Strained in yard and delivered. We quote low No. 2 at $2@$2 25, in yard and delivered. Tar is dull at $2 25 for Wilmington. Pitch is nominal.

OILS—Whale is quiet at 40@41c.; we only hear of sales of 200 bbls. at New-Bedford on private terms. Linseed is quiet at 56@57c.; small sales are making at the above price. Sperm is dull at $1 30@$1 40; we do not hear of any transactions; other descriptions are dull and nominal.

PROVISIONS—The inquiry for Pork is limited, and the market is heavy for Prime, but firm for Mess; the arrivals are fair; the sales are 521 bbls. at $16 75@$17 for Mess, and $12 25@$12 50 for Prime. Beef is dull, and hardly so firm; the supply is good; sales of 170 bbls. at $9 50@$11 for repacked Mess, and $11 50@$12 50 for extra. Cut Meats are more plenty, and are lower; sales of 120 hhds. and tcs. at 4¼@5½c. for Shoulders and 6@7c. for Hams. Beef Hams are dull at $14@$16, the latter rate for extra Chicago. Smoked Meats are in good supply, and steady. Lard is less active, and is quite heavy; the supply is not large; sales of 280 bbls. and tcs. at 8⅞@9c. Butter is in fair demand at 10@15c. for Ohio, and 12@16c. for State. Cheese is in steady demand at 5@8c.

RICE—Is quiet; sales of 200 tcs. at $5 50@$6 50 ₱ 100 lbs.

SUGARS—The market is steady, but quiet; sales of 675 hhds., mainly Cuba, at 4@4½c., over one-half at 4c.; 80 boxes Havana on private terms. By auction, 300 hhds Porto Rico at 4⅜@5⅛c.

TEAS—Green and Black are both steady, with a moderate demand.

TALLOW—The demand is good, and the market is firm; sales of 38,000 lb prime a 9½c., cash.

WOOL—There is a fair demand prevailing for low medium Wools, suitable for military clothing. The market for Fine is neglected; there is very little inquiry for Foreign Fine Wools. The trade in California Wools since our last comprise sales of 5,000 lb at 31c., and 100 bales of Black ditto at 11@20c., cash. In Pulled there has been very little doing. We only hear of 6 bales being sold at 27@30c. We give quotations with all the extreme rates: Domestic Fleeces, 23@52c.; Domestic Pulled, 20@46c.; California, 12@33c.; Cape, 18@30c.; South American, 9@25c.; Smyrna, 10@26c.; Donskoi, 18@21c.; East India, 9@30c.

WHISKY—The market is firm, the demand fair; sales of 800 bbls. at 16½c.

THE SEMI-WEEKLY

Gazette & Sentinel.

Published every Wednesday and Saturday by
W. P. BRADBURN,
EDITOR AND PROPRIETOR.

TERMS OF SUBSCRIPTION.

THREE DOLLARS AND FIFTY CENTS ($3 50) for one year, in advance. FIVE DOLLARS ($5 00) if not paid in advance.

SINGLE COPIES—Ten Cents.

No subscription will be discontinued unless a written notice to that effect is received from the subscriber himself, and all arrearges paid.

TERMS OF ADVERTISING.

ONE DOLLAR ($1 00) per square of ten lines, or less, of this space, ——— ————————, for the first insertion, and Fifty Cents for each subsequent insertion. A liberal discount, however, on these rates will be made on advertisements inserted for a longer time than two months, as follows:

	3 months.	6 months.	12 months.
1 square	$ 5 00	$ 8 00	$ 12 00
2 squares	8 00	12 00	20 00
3 squares	15 00	15 00	25 00
4 squares	12 00	20 00	30 00
5 squares	18 00	25 00	37 00
6 squares	20 00	30 00	45 00

For Professional or Business Cards, not exceeding one square, with paper, one year, $15.

Announcements of Candidates for office, $10. Cash in all cases, must accompany the announcement, whether handed in by a friend or the person announced.

The privilege of yearly advertisers is strictly limited to their own immediate and regular business.

Communications intended to promote the private ends or interests of individuals, corporations or societies, will be charged as advertisements.

All persons ordering Jobs or handing in advertisements on account of any local or political organization, will be held responsible for the payment of the same.

Marriages and Deaths published without charge. Obituaries inserted as other advertisements.

Advertisements not marked the length of time they are to be inserted, will be kept in the paper till forbid, and charged accordingly.

All advertisements by strangers or transient persons must be paid in advance.

Personal Cards, if inserted at all, will be charged two dollars per square.

☞Job Work always cash, and advertisementr are due when first inserted.

FOR CONGRESS.

We are authorized to announce **Col. H. W. ALLEN,** of West Baton Rouge, as a candidate for Congress of the Confederate States for the Fourth Congressional District, composed of the Parishes of West Felicians, Point Coupee, St. Landry, Lafayette, Vermillion. West Baton Rouge, Iberville, St. Mary and St. Martin. Election first Monday in November.

FOR AUDITOR,

We are authorized to announce **BYTHELL HAYNES,** of Clinton, as a Candidate for Auditor of Public Accounts at the ensuing Fall election.

We are authorized to announce **H. PERALTA,** of East Baton Rouge, as a Candidate for Auditor of Public Accounts—subject to a nomination by a Democratic State Convention, if one is called.

FOR ASSESSOR.

Mr. Editor: Please announce the name of **T. RODOLPH VERBOIS,** Esq., as a Democratic Candiate for Assessor for the parish of Iberville, subject to the State Rights Democratic Convention.

We are authorized to announce **ERNEST CALLERY,** the present incumbent, as a Candidate for re-election to the office of Assessor, subject to the decision of the State Rights Democratic Convention.

SHERIFF AND RECORDER.

Mr. Editor: You will please announce the following gentlemen for the offices which preede their respective names, subject to the decision of the State Rights Democratic Convention, viz:

For Sheriff, - - - J. L. PETIT.
For Recorder, - - J. H. ERWIN.

FOR RECORDER.

MR. EDITOR: You will please announce the name of **ADOLPHE HEBERT,** Esq., as a Candidate for the office of Recorder of the parish of Iberville, subject to the decision of the State Rights Democratic Convention.

FOR SHERIFF.

MR. EDITOR: Please announce my name in your paper as a Candidate for the next Sheriffalty of this parish.

GUSTAVE LAUVE.

Bayou Goula, April 18th, 1861.

New Advertisements.

Grand Concert.

THE LADIES OF THE

CATHOLIC CHOIR,

Will give another of their interesting Concerts, on

Thursday, June 6th, 1861.

One-half of the proceeds to be devoted to MILITARY PURPOSES.

Come One! Come All!!

Plaquemine, June 1.

BARROW & POPE,

Attorneys at Law.

DURING the absence of Lieut. N. W. POPE, David N. Barrow will be at West Baton Rouge Court House every Monday, unless professionally engaged elsewhere.

By request he attends to the legal business of Capt. H. M. Favrot.

Address him at Plaquemine. (ju1

DR. M. E. DEMARET,

HAVING located himself about five miles below the Ferry on the opposite bank of the River, in Iberville, offers his professional services to the citizens of the Parish on that side. jun1

Called Meeting of Town Council.

The Mayor and Board of Selectmen met at the Mayor's Office, this 28th of May, 1861.

Present—T. E. GRACE, Mayor.

Selectmen—A. Talbot, M. Marix and James Carlin.

The object of the Meeting being for the purpose of opening and considering the proposals received for the cleaning of the ditches, &c., and cleaning out and deepening the Corporation Canal; and the same being done, the cleaning of the Ditches and repairing of the streets was given Henry Cushing at the price of $3 per arpent; and the cleaning out and deepening of the Corporation Canal, to M. Brusnihan, for $8 per acre. Said parties to furnirh security for the faithful completion of said work.

All persons in the habit of throwing trash, slop, etc., into the streets and gutters, are hereby warned to discontinue the same, otherwise severe measures will be taken against them.

Account of Louis Protalong for pickets, allowed $16,85.

No further business Council adjourned.

T. E. GRACE, Mayor.

C. A. ROTH, Clerk.

New Advertisements.

State of Louisiana—Parish of Iberville—5th Judicial District Court,

In Matter of Estate of Rosalie Melancon and Dorville LaCroix.

WHEREAS: CLEOPHAS BARBAY has this day filed in this Court his final account of administration of the Estate of Rosalie Malançon and Dorville LaCroix, both dec'd.

Notice is hereby given to all whom it may concern to show cause within Thirty days from this date, why the final Tableau of Administration aforesaid, should not be homologated and made a judgement of this Court, and the bond of the administrator cancelled and annulled.

Iberville, May 29, 1861.

ju1 M. A. ESTEVAN, Clerk.

Etat dela Louisiane—Paroisse d'Iberville—Cour du 5eme District Judiciaire.

Dans la Successton de feus

Rosalie Melancon & Dorville LaCroix.

ATTENDU, que CLEOPHAS BARBAY a ce jour enliassé en cette Cour son Tableaux final d'administration de la succession de fues Rosalie Melançon and Dorville LaCroix.

Avis est par le present donné à tous ceux que cela concerne de deduire sans trente jours de la date de ce present les raisons pour lesquelles le dit Tableaux final ne serait pas homoloqué et fait le judgment de cette Cour et le cautionnement annullè.

Iberville, le 29 Mai, 1861.

ju1. M. A. ESTEVAN, Greffier.

PLAQUEMINE:

SATURDAY, JUNE 1st, 1861.

☞ Col. L. HEBERT, 3rd Louisiana Regiment, is still at the St. Charles Hotel, New Orleans.

☞It is not true that BAILEY has been elected Captain of the "Red Shirts." But it is true that he is prepared to take the phiz of all who expect to immortalize themselves or perish, whether or not he may be engaged with the eye-glass and screw, in soldering and repairing.

The Red Shirts.

This military company, originating with Mr. A. ST. DIZIER, we believe, and which he and Captain VERBOIS were instrumental in getting up so far, had an addition to its number a few days since of some eight or ten, which were procured at Bayou Goula, where the company had gone on the *Herron*, by the invitation of Mr. GUSTAVE LAUVE, as we learn, of whose hospitalities it partook. The company now numbers between forty and fifty, mostly natives of the "Gem of the Ocean," which is alone sufficient guarantee that hard licks from them may be expected in the cause of Liberty; and as our friend PIKE, G., of Baton Rouge, would say—a class, than which none know better the *value*—so much per foot—of the soil of the South, or the inestimable blessings which flow from its level surface.

The Jackson Avengers.

This is the name the above company has adopted, in honor of the brave man who sacrificed his life to slay the notorious Ellsworth, who hauled down the flag he had hoisted over his own house. It was well named. An election for officers took place on Thursday—Mr. A. St. DIZIER withdrawing—when GUSTAVE LAUVE, Esq., was elected Captain, by acclamation; JOSEPH ST. DIZIER was elected 1st Lieutenant, and OSCAR LAUVE, Esq., 2nd Lieut. The company, we think, has been fortunate in the selection of its Captain. Gallant, generous and high-spirited, his men have but to follow him if they would distinguish themselves; while in camp they will have in Capt. LAUVE, a sincere friend, whose eye will ever, we are sure, be directed to their comfort and their wants.

The Vigilance Committee.

Our citizens must not forget the meeting called for 10 o'clock this morning at the Court-house, for the purpose of forming a Vigilance Committee, to watch over and guard the peace, quiet and welfare of this community. Its organization, we are sure, will not lead to any harsh or violent measures against the rights and liberties of any person or persons; but a ready and decisive action on its part may be expected when any outrage upon the laws, jeopardizing the safety and interests of society, comes authenticated indisputably before it. The very knowledge that such an association exists, with its spies in every direction, will alone be sufficient, in a great measure, to prevent acts and abuses detrimental to the peace and interests of our citizens.

The Little Virginia.

This little propeller, Capt. MILLER, will run in future, we learn, twice a week to Grosse Tete, returning the same day. This is good news to lower Grosse Tete. She is a most comfortable little boat, and her commander a most obliging gentleman, as all who travel on her will discover.

The Weather

Is becoming unusually sultry; a fine shower now would be of vast advantage; and it looks as if we have not long to wait for one.

☞ It is a favorite remark of the Black Republicans, that the Secessionists of the South are afraid of the people, because several of the States did not see fit to submit their Secesson Ordinances to the popular vote. What do they think of Virginia? While her Convention hesitated so long to pass a secession ordinance, her people have ratified it by nearly a unanimous vote. In Texas, the vote for secession was two to one against it; and so would it have been in all the other States, had there been any necessity for taking a vote on the question. The people are a long way ahead of their leaders in resistance to Black Republican rule.

THE VIRGINIA ELECTION.—The returns from the Virginia election, held on Thursday, show that the State has gone overwhelmingly for the ratification of the Secession Ordinance. The majority is estimated, from dispatches received in the city of Richmond, at 150,000.

The vote in Richmond stood 4000 for Secession, and only 16 against it. At Alexandria, 915 for it, 102 against it. It is said that with the exception of the above two cities, and Portsmouth, the returns from Eastern Virginia gave no votes against ratification.

☞ The subsoription in New Orleans for the family of James W. Jackson, the brave man who slew Ellsworth at Alexandria, bids fair to realize a handsome sum for his needy widow and orphans.

Are they Mad?

The *Crescent*, alluding to the gigantic scale on which the North is preparing for war, and the talk of getting up a quarrel with England and France, asks if all the Northern editors are mad? We do not think they are mad; if they are, "there is method in their madness." The North has been cherishing for years a deadly and vindictive hatred against the South and now thinks there is an opportunity to inflict an irreparable injury upon the rights of the South, and to destroy its existence as a people. It is evident to these fanatics that it will take men and money to accomplish their purposes, and they are willing to make the sacrifice for the sake of success. They know, moreover, how to play the game of brag; and they think that their blustering and bravado while enrolling their troops, their pretensions of being able to wipe out the South at a single blow, will have the effect of intimidating us and forcing us to sue for an immediate peaee. They will continue their game until they are well whipped in two or three great battles, when they will find out that fear is something of which the people of the South have no personal experience, and will be perfectly willing to treat of the difficulties between the two countries in a rational manner. As for their threats against all those foreign powers that sympathize with the Confederate States, it is all for the same purpose—to impress us with the power and importance of the Lincoln Government. So far from getting into a war with foreign nations, the Black Republicans are not so "mad" as not to see that they have their hands full already, and will doubtless back down as soon as their high-handed measures shall provoke anything like resistance on the part of the governments of Europe.

The News of the Fighting.

The battles at Harper's Ferry and Hampton. Va., reported in our Extra on last Saturday, and given in our Wednesday's edition, have not yet been confirmed by any previous dispatches from Virginia. The report we gave was in all the New Orleans papers. It is no proof that such report had no foundation, for the reason that no further intelligence of such fights has been received. It must be recollected, that the President, at the present time, has charge over all the telegraph offices in the Confederacy; and it may be, for reasons we have no right to enquire into, that a report of these battles have been prohibited, besides much other war news that we *don't get*, and without considering the evil of making such public, weary ourselves very much about it—many, probably, coming to the conclusion that Jeff. Davis and our leading Generals, are either very dilatory, or paralyzed by the immensity of the enemy's preparations, of which we hear plenty of news. Of course, the enemy or their operators send us "plenty of news," and they are very sure to color it so as, they hope, to create consternation among our people. Yes, such consternation as they did'nt bargain for—such as makes men grasp the firmer the sword handle, and makes them the more eager to meet the dastard foe. It is possible, nevertheless, that false reports may come among us, and that the report we allude to is premature; but under the facts such as we state, it is no proof that those battles have not occurred, because we have no further intelligence of them. A dispatch from Washington, states that the *Star* acknowledged to a battle having been fought at Harper's Ferry, and says that the Federal forces suffered defeat and great loss—this is the only confirmation we have had, but this is strong.

Since the above was in type, we find the following in the Evening *Picayune* of Thursday:

THE FIGHT AT HARPER'S FERRY CONFIRMED.—A private dispatch to the Mobile Tribune, dated Harper's Ferry, May 26, confirms the report of a fight at that place and the repulse of the enemy. It says:

"The Abolitionists were repulsed at Harper's Ferry. Sixty Confederates and six hundred Abolitionists were killed. No details."

☞ There have been no telegraphic dispatches of importance during the past week Occasional a sensation dispatch comes from the North, which remains good only until the the next promptly contradicts it.

PADUCAH, May 27.—A company of Forty men, from Carbondale, Ill., passed through here to-day to offer their services to Jeff. Davis. More of them are expected to-night The citizens provided them with money and a flag.

THE INTEREST GREAT BRITAIN HAS IN THE CONFEDERATE STATES.—English authorities have recently estimated the capital invested by their countrymen, in spinning and weaving cotton alone, at about $326,250,000, and that a further sum of $150,000,000 must be added for the processes of dyeing, printing and bleaching. The floating capital of the importers of the raw material is estimated at $32,500,000; that of the ship owners, at $15,000,000—making a total, independent of all subsidiary trades ministering indirectly, of $522,750,000. These are the estimates of Mr. J. A. Mann, in his "Cotton Trade of Great Britain," published in London last year. The *Westminister Review* for April, adopts these figures, and although large, does not think there is any reason for believing them to be exaggerated.

TELEGRAPH LIES.—The Associated Press dispatches all pass through the hands of Northern officials, and are as full of lies as an egg is full of meat.

The Iberville Greys.

As we find there are several alterations in the list of this company, as published last in our paper, we have determined again to publish it, particularly as Captain BRUSLE requests it. Its rank and file are now as follows:

OFFICERS:

CHARLES A. BRUSLE, CAPTAIN,
THOMAS C. BROWN, 1st Lieutenant,
THOS. G. STRINGER, 2nd " Sr.
T. RODOLPH VERBOIS, 2nd " Jr.
FRANK W. GOODWYN, 1st Sergeant,
J. AMEDEE LANDRY, 2nd "
URSIN BABIN, Jr., 3rd "
J. OSCAR TERRELL, 4th "
J. B. RAMOIN, 1st Corporal,
OCTAVE BEVIN, 2nd "
ERNEST GOURRIER, 3rd "
H. OSCAR VERBOIS, 4th "

PRIVATES:

Jos. Alsbatch,	V. A. Hebert,
M. Arceneaux,	W. Hall,
S. Allain,	A. J. Johns,
S. Aucoin,	A. Joly,
T. Aucoin,	W. H. Johnson,
Ben. Berry,	J. Kinney,
E. M. Boissac,	L. Kahn,
E. C. Belfield,	E. D. LeBlanc,
Edw. Barlow,	F. Lanoue,
E. L Breaux,	F. Leonard,
J. H. Breaux,	H. LeBlanc,
J. Bell,	M. LeBlanc
M. R. Broussard,	John McManus,
L. D. Blanchard,	J. Macready,
N. Blanchard,	N. Minter,
P. Burns,	W. B. McGinnis,
D. Bridges,	C. Norton,
J. C. Braun,	C. Nichols,
N. Beard,	C. Pruet,
S. Breaud,	W. H. Polson,
C. D. Craighead,	E. Richard,
J. Crowell,	A. S. Randolph,
M. Coughlan,	Felix Roth,
J Connor,	J. Richard,
J. Chastant,	N. Richard,
C. G. Dupuy,	P. Richard,
J. Dennis,	P. Slaven,
S. D. Davis,	J. Schairer,
J. A. Ellis,	P. F. St. Amant,
H. E. Gindier,	N. Schade,
N. Gayard,	W. Saunders,
P. Gleason,	G. R. Terrell,
F. Gourrier,	K. Willhert,
A. A. Hebert,	P. C. Willis,
A. O. Hebert,	P. White.
H. P. Hirsch,	J. L. Hebert,

Letter from Capt. Brusle.

Knowing that every thing relating to the "Iberville Greys," now on its way to Fort Smith, Ark., however unimportant, is devoured with eager interest by the friends and relatives of the young men composing the Company, we append the following extract from a letter of Capt. Brusle to the editor of this paper, dated—

S. B. ARKANSAS, below Napoleon, May 25th, 1861.

Our destination is Fort Smith, Ark. The object of our expedition, is to have a little engagement with Montgomery or Lane, for the amusement of the boys. By-the-by, I never saw young men in better spirits, or any more gay and cheerful. I procured tobacco for them at Vicksburg, and at every town we stopped provisions of the very best, were obtained for them."

TOO LATE.—The New York Herald says that the Gorilla Government at Washington, gave notice, a month ago, to the Powers of Europe, that it now accepts the code adopted at the Congress of Paris in 1856, which declared privateering to be piracy. Too late. When that code was proposed, the United States promptly and emphatically rejected it. The Powers of Europe will understand why Seward is in such hot haste to accept it now, and they will spurn the proposition contemptuously, knowing, as they do, the motive which prompts it. The Gorrilla Government at Washington, will hereafter find itself baffled at every turn.

☞ The U. S. Steamer Brooklyn, now engaged in blockading the mouth of the Mississippi, undertook, a few days since, to stop some French and English vessels loaded with valuable cargoes, as they were proceeding to sea. The French and English Consuls in New Orleans, having notified the Captain of the Brooklyn, that their governments would not submit to such treatment, that officer was suddenly frightened into submission and promptly released the vessels. Old Abe will find that he is likely to get into a pretty quarrel yet with foreign powers that trade with the Confederate States.

HURRAH FOR DAN.—We perceive in the New York *Herald* of the 25th, kindly loaned us by Mr. BAILEY, a paragraph respecting Dan Rice. It appears that he was at Cincinnati, when the mob collected, ordered him to pull down the flag he had flying at his fore, and to hoist the "stars and stripes." Dan told them he "would see them d——d first," and uncovering a howitzer on his forecastle, told them to come on! But the mob mizzled, and during the confusion, Dan and his boat had got over on the Kentucky side.

☞ MR. R. D. Shepherd, one of the survivors of the battle of New Orleans, who has the largest income from the rent of houses of any person in New Orleans, has, we learn by the *Delta*, devoted the whole of that income to the use of the Government of the Confederate States.

☞ No man is always wrong. A clock that does not go at all, is right twice in the twenty-four hours.

The Police Jury.

This parochial body meets at the Court House in this town on Monday next. It is composed of the following gentlemen:

J. A. SIGUR, Bayou Goula Ward.
P. T. COLLE, Island "
AUG. CHRISTIN, St. Gabriel "
B. MARIONNEAUX, Plaquemine "
J. A. DARDENNE, Ind. Village "
C. W. KEEP, Grosse Tete "
S. B. ROANE, Grand River "

Hard Volunteers.

The following description of a company of Arkansas volunteers, shows the kind of fighting men found in the Swamps of Arkansas. We copy from a letter in the *Picayune*, dated Vicksburg, May 15th.:

Arkansas is in arms and eager for the fray. Men are pouring in from all directions. The State can be relied on to put in the field one-half of her voting population. Lawyers, doctors, planters, and mechanics respond—the great trouble being that the Governor does not receive them as fast as offered on account of not having received requisitions from the President. One witnessed the other day, when visiting Fort Randolph, above Memphis, will give an idea of the *esprit* which pervades Arkansas. An Arkansas river boat arrived with about fifty rough-looking characters headed by a man of iron frame, who stood full six feet four inches in his brogans; each man was armed with a rifle, powder flask slung over his shoulder and a knife in belt.—Walking up to the edge of the camp, the leader addressed the sentinel on guard: "Say, stranger, whar's the Captin, Kurnel, or Gineral, for me and the boys has come along for a fight." The sentinel, surprised, called the Captain of the guard, who, learning the character of his visitors, asked the leader what company he had the honor of receiving. "Now Cap'n you have us thar; we ain't belonging to no company; we hearn thar was some fitin' to be dun agin them ar Yankees, and we up rifle and come." Cap. R. ventured to say that it was necessary to be accepted by the Governor before he could receive them into camp, when he was interrupted by six footer, saying, "look here, Cap'n, we are nuthin' but a crowd of bar hunters; nary a one but can hit his mark at five hundred yards; and and you see that ar place," pointing to a clump of trees, "well, as you don't want us inside your place thar, our boys 'ill just scatter ourseles around thar, and when the Gineral tells you to march, we march; when he says, 'boys, there's fitin' to be dun,' we're thar; and if we cant whip a regiment of them blue bellied cusses, may we never set fut in Arkansas swamp agin. What say you, boys?" The boys responded with a yell that resembled a crowd of catamounts or Comanches. Whereupon the Cap'n "caved," and told them to walk in to camp, he'd take them, orders or no orders.

GEN. LEE OF VIRGINIA.—This officer is thus described by the Richmond correspondent of the Charleston *Courier:*

Speaking of Gen. Lee, he appears to be every inch a gentleman and officer. Personally, in many characteristics, he is a second edition of General Beauregard, bound in a larger volume—being, perhaps, three or four inches taller. He has a broad, expansive forehead, which loses itself in locks of iron grey hair, well developed intellectual organs, especially the perceptive faculties; a fine profile; a keen, expressive dark brown eye, which undisturbed by anything behind it would not be unbecoming to a Quaker, but aroused, looks as if he might penetrate a two inch plank—a face which in repose has an air of military rigidity, but lit up with a smile seems to contain a sort of intelligent benediction; a nose slightly on the Roman style of architecture; and a mouth which if one may judge from the lines around it, for it is concealed by a heavy, iron grey moustache, is full of spirit and determination.

Like Beauregard, his manner is affable, courteous and refined, combining so nicely the *bonhommie* of a man of the world with the dignity of his position, that you can hardly tell where the one begins and the other ends. He dresses in plain black clothes, wears an old felt hat, which, nine times out of ten, is knocked in on one side, and in this attire, is the last man in the world who would be taken for Gen. Lee, the Commander-in-Chief of the Virginia army.

☞ Four boxes of earth, alike in quality and exposure to light and heat, were planted at the same time with corn from a single ear placed recently in a physician's office. In one box dry corn was planted; in another the seed was soaked in clean warm water; in the third the seed was soaked in a solution of lime water; in the fourth the seed was soaked in the chloride of lime and copperas water, equal parts. One week afterward the box planted with dry corn had not germinated, the second box had just commenced to germinate, the third box was just showing its green blades, and in the fourth box the blades were nearly three inches high. Copperas will keep birds and worms from eating the seed, and one pound will soak enough for twenty acres.

HARPER'S WEEKLY.
A JOURNAL OF CIVILIZATION.

VOL. V.—No. 233.] NEW YORK, SATURDAY, JUNE 15, 1861. [SINGLE COPIES SIX CENTS. $2 50 PER YEAR IN ADVANCE.

Entered according to Act of Congress, in the Year 1861, by Harper & Brothers, in the Clerk's Office of the District Court for the Southern District of New York.

Publisher's Notice.

OF the last number of *Harper's Weekly* we published ONE HUNDRED AND FIFTEEN THOUSAND COPIES.

This extraordinary circulation, and the character of *Harper's Weekly*, render it superior as an Advertising medium to any other journal published in the United States. It is probable that each number of *Harper's Weekly* is read by at least ten adults. It circulates among the classes which advertisers desire to reach. A very large proportion of its circulation is preserved for future reference and bound. The space allotted to advertisements is very limited: the price, 75 cents a line on the last page; 50 cents a line on the page preceding.

THE MURDER OF ELLSWORTH.

WE publish herewith a picture showing the manner in which Colonel Ellsworth was murdered. It is from a rough sketch by Brownell, the gallant young Zouave who avenged his Colonel's death. The circumstances of the murder were fully detailed in our last number.

We also give a view of the MARSHALL HOUSE AT ALEXANDRIA, where the murder took place. It is, as our picture shows, a second-rate tavern: its keeper Jackson, who murdered Ellsworth, and was so instantly punished for the deed, was notorious as a secessionist leader, and a man of violent habits. He had been engaged in several street frays growing out of the secession question, and like too many Southerners, was prompt with the knife and pistol. We notice that he is becoming a martyr among the Southerners; at Mobile alone, $1100 have been collected for his widow.

Accompanying these pictures we publish a portrait of a secessionist prisoner caught at Alexandria with a rifle of preposterous length and make.

All these pictures are from sketches by our special artist accompanying the troops into Virginia.

SECESSIONIST PRISONER CAPTURED AT ALEXANDRIA.—THE MARSHALL HOUSE AT ALEXANDRIA.—THE MURDER OF COLONEL ELLSWORTH.—[SEE ARTICLE ABOVE.]

Gazette & Sentinel.

[From the Evening Delta.

THE BATTLE OF BETHEL.

DETAILED ACCOUNTS.

Yorktown, June 11th, 1861.

An engagement, lasting four hours, took place yesterday, (Monday) between five regiments of the troops from Old Point, and 1100 Confederates troops, consisting of Virginians and North Carolinians, under Gen. Magruder. at Bethel Church, York county. Before telling you of the battle, I will give you some circumstances preceding it. About two weeks ago, a party of 300 Yankees came up from Hampton and occupied Bethel Church, which position they held a day or two, and then retired, leaving written on the walls several inscriptions, such as "Death to the Traitors !" "Down with the Rebels!" etc. To these excursions into the interior, of which this was the boldest, Gen. Magruder determined to put a stop to, and accordingly sent a few companies of his own troops into Bethel, In addition to this, he determined to carry the war into the enemy's country, and on Wednesday last, Stanard's battery of the howitzer batallion was ordered to the Church, where it was soon joined by a portion of Brown's battery, of the same corps. The North Carolina regiment under Col. Hill, was also there, making in all about 1100 men and seven howitzer guns.

On Saturday last the first excursion of considerable importance was made. A detachment of 200 infantry and a howitzer, under Major Lane, of the N. C. regiment, started different routes to cut off a party which had left Hampton. The party was seen and fired at by Maj. Randolph's detachment, but made such fast time that they escaped. The troops under Major Lane passed within sight of Hampton, and as they turned up the road to return to Bethel, encountered the Yankees, numbering 90, who were entrenched behind a fence in the field, protected by a high bank. Our advance guard fired on them, and in another moment the North Carolinians were dashing over the fence in regular French Zouave style. The Yankees fled for their lives, leaving behind them three dead and a prisoner. The fellow was a stout, ugly fellow from Troy, N. Y. He said that he had nothing against the South, but somebody must be soldiers. None of our men were hurt.

On Monday morning, about 600 infantry and two guns, under Gen. Magruder, left the camp and proceeded towards Hampton; but after advancing a mile or two, received information that the Yankees were coming in large force. We then retired, and after reaching camp, the guns were placed in battery, and the infantry took their places behind their breastwork.

About 9 o'clock the glittering bayonets of the enemy appeared on the hill opposite, and above them waved the Star Spangled Banner. The moment the head of the column advanced far enough to show one or two companies, the Parrot gun of the Howitzer Battery opened on them, throwing a shell right into their midst. Their ranks broke in confusion, and the column, or as much of it as we could see, retreated behind two small farm houses. From their position a fire was opened upon us, which was replied to by our battery, which commanded their route of approach. Our firing was excellent, and the shells scattered in all directions when they burst. They could hardly approach the guns which they were firing for the shells which came from our battery.—Within our encampment fell a perfect shower of canister shot, bullets and balls. Remarkable to say, not one of our men was killed inside of our encampment. Several horses were slain.

Finding that bombardment would not answer, the enemy tried to carry the position by assault, but met a terrible repulse at the hands of the infantry as he tried to scale the breastworks. The men disregarded sometimes the defences erected for them, and leaping on the embankment, stood and fired at the Yankees, cutting them down as they came up. One company of the New York Seventh regiment, under Capt. Wardrop. or Winthrop, attempted to take the redoubt on the left The marsh they crossed was strewn with their bodies. Their Captain, a fine-looking man, reached the fence, and leaping on a log, saying "Come on, boys; one charge and the day is ours." The words were his last, for a Carolina rifle ended his life the next moment, and his men fled in terror. At the redoubt on the right a company of about 300 New York Zouaves charged one of our guns, but could not stand the fire of the infantry and retreated precipitately.

During these charges the main body of the enemy on the hill, were attempting to concentrate for a general assault, but the shell from the howitzer battery prevented them As one regiment gave way, another would be marched to the position, but with no better success, for a shell would scatter them.

About 1 o'clock their guns were silenced, and a few moments after their infantry retreated precipitately down the road to Hampton.

Our cavalry, numbering three companies, went in pursuit, and harassed them down to the edge of Hampton. As they retreated many of the wounded fell along the road and died, and the whole road to Hampton was strewn with haversacks, overcoats, canteens, muskets, &c., which the men had thrown off in their retreat.

After the battle, I visited the position they held. The houses behind which they had been hid had been burnt by our troops. Around the yard were the dead bodies of the men who had been killed by our cannon, mangled in the most frightful manner by the shells. The uniforms on the bodies were very different, and many of them were dressed like the Virginia soldiery. A little farther on we came to the point which they had carried some of their wounded, who had since died. The gay-looking uniforms of the New York Zouaves contrasted greatly with the paled, fixed faces of their dead owners. Going to the swamp through which they attempted to pass to assault our lines, presented another bloody scene. Bodies dotted the black morass from one end to the other. I saw one boyish, delicate looking fellow lying in the mud, with a bullet hole through his breast. His hand was pressed on the wound from which his life blooded had poured, and the other was clenched in the grass. Lying on the ground was a Testament which had fallen from his pocket, covered with blood. On opening the cover I found the printed inscription, "Presented to the Defenders of their Country, by the New York Bible Society."

Among the haversacks picked up along the road, were many letters from the Northern States, asking if they liked the Southern plantations, and if the Southern barbarians had been whipped out yet.

The force of the enemy brought against us was about 4000, according to the statement of the six prisoners we took. Ours was 1100. Their loss in killed and wounded must be nearly 200. Our loss is one killed and three wounded.

The Louisiana regiment arrived about one hour after the fight was over. They are a fine-looking set of fellows.

As there was force enough at Old Point to send up to Bethel and surround us, we took up the line of march and come up to Yorktown, where we now are.

I hear to day that troops from Old Point are now marching up to attack us, but can not say whether it is so or not.

I should have written you more fully, but as the boat is now in sight, I will have to close my letter.

The British Naval Force on the American Station. — The Manchester Guardian, of the 22d ult., has the following:

Although we have a considerable naval force on the North American and West India station, it is clear in the face of the war between the Northern and Southern States, that our Government cannot too soon reinforce the squadron. We have at present in the American waters, two 90-gun ships, two vessels carrying 21 guns, and one carrying 11 guns; with fourteen others of smaller size. The total number of guns is 339, and the number of men 4196. The 40-gun frigate Mersey left last week to join the squadron; the Challenger, 22, the Rinaldo, 17, and the Driver, 6, are being speedily equipped for the same destination; while the Ariadne, 26, has been ordered home from the Mediterranean to refit, preparatory to being sent out to assist in the protection of British interests.

Loss of the Big Gun.—The sinking of the big gun "Union" at Baltimore last week, has caused much regret—"over the left." This gun was intended for Fortress Monroe, where it was to have been placed in a position which would have commanded Sewell's Point Battery. It weighs 60,000 pounds, and carries a 400-pound ball, and will reach with deadly effect, a distance of nine miles. It was lost in removing it from the wharf to a steamer, and is said to have sunk in six feet-water, with six feet of soft mud below that. Such an immense bulk of avoirdupois has probably gone down to a distance that will defy all efforts to reclaim it. It will be remembered that two enormous Columbiads, intended for Fort McHenry, were effectually spiked in Baltimore week before last. It is now hinted that some rascally secessionists, who were employed to place the monster gun on board, purposely let her slip into the depths below. It matters but little, however.—*Peterburg Express.*

The Grain Crop.—The Intelligencer says that wheat is being offered at 60 cents per bushel at Austin. There are three fine steam mills in the county, and it is believed that flour will be sold at from $2 to $3 per hundred, and perhaps less. The LaGrange True Issue says that corn is selling on Caney at 23 cts. per bushel, and that it is believed that enough corn and small grain would be grown this year in Texas to do the State three years. A large number of new settlers will be necessary to consume the supplies.—*Galveston Civilian.*

How the "Thunderer" Snubs Them.—The London *Times* compares the march of the Massachusetts soldiers to Washington, to the occupation of Boston by Gen. Gage in 1775. It finds analogies between the proclamation of Lincoln and those of George III., and more than hints that the attrocities of the French Revolution are not so culpable as the military proceedings of the Federal Government.

The Richmond correspondent of the Charleston Courier says the secretary of State will resign his present position.

Mrs. Emily Tubman, of Augusta, Ga., formerly of Frankfort, Ky., has armed a regiment in this State.—*Savannah News.*

An Arkansas Heroine.—The Pocahontas (Ark.) Advertiser, of the 31st ult., has the following:

Miss Williams, a daughter of Isaac Williams, living in Black River swamp, about seven miles from this place, heard the report of the approach of troops to this place on Sunday evening. Her father was not at home, but she immediately caught a horse, and was soon off in search of him. She found him at a neighbor's house and told him to hurry on home and get his gun and come here and help to drive back the enemy. She then returned home, got down her father's rifle, moulded his lead all into bullets, took the gun, powder and bullets, and hid them under the house, and again got upon the horse and rode to several houses and spread the alarm, returned home in time to give the old man his gun and ammunition, and started him with a crowd of ten men, whom she had collected for the scene of action. All this was accomplished in less than two hours.

Success a Matter of Will.—Success has no more eccentricity, than the gingham and muslin we weave in our mills. I know no more affecting lesson to our busy, plotting New England brains, than to go into one of the factories with which we have lined all the water-courses in the States. A man hardly knows how much he is a machine until he begins to make telegraph, loom, press, and locomotive, in his own image.—But in these, he is forced to leave out his follies and hindrances, so that when we go to the mill the machine is more moral than we. Let a man dare go to a loom, and see if he be equal to it. Let machine confront machine, and see how they come out. The world-mill is more complex than the calico-mill, and the architect stooped less. In the gingham-mill, a broken thread or a shred spoils the web through a piece of a hundred yards, and is traced back to the girl that wove it, and lessens her wages. The stock holder, on being shown this, rubs his hands with delight. Are you so cunning, Mr. Profitloss, and do you expect to swindle your master and employer, in the web you weave? A day is a more magnificent cloth than any muslin, the mechanism that makes it is infinitely cunninger, and you shall not conceal the sleezy, fraudulent, rotten hours you have slipped into the piece, nor fear that any honest thread, or straighter steel, or more inflexible shaft will not testify in the web.—*Emerson.*

DIED.

Died on the 19th inst., Antonia Stark, only daughter of John N. Stark, and Celanie Derousell, aged 1 year and 6 months.

Morte le 19, Antonia Stark, fille unique et John N. Stark, le Celanie, Deroussell.

State of Louisiana—Parish of Iberville—5th District Court.

In matter of Estate of DANIEL HOY, deceased.

WHEREAS: Ann Wailey, Administratrix of the above succession, has filed in this Court her account of Administration of the same.

Notice is hereby given to all whom it may concern to file in writing within thirty days from the date hereof, any opposition they may have, why the said account should not be homologated and approved, and her bond as Administratrix of said Estate cancelled and annulled.

Clerk's office, Iberville, June 7, 1861.

je8 E. A. MARIONNEAUX, Dep. Clerk.

Etat de la Louisiane, Paroisse d'Iberville—Cour du 5me. District Judiciaire.

Dans la Succession de feue DANIEL HOY.

ATTENDU que Ann Wailey a ce jour enléassé en cette cour son compte d'Administration de la succession de feu Daniel Hoy.

Avis est par le present donné à tous ceux que cela concerne de deduire sous trente jours de la date de ce present les raisons pour lesquelles le dit tableau ne serait pas homologué et fait le jugement de cette cour et son cautionnement, comme tel annullé.

Iberville, 7th Juin, 1861.

E. A. MARIONNEAUX,

je8. *Dep. Greffieir.*

State of Louisiana, Parish of Iberville—Fifth District Court.

In matter of Estate of Narcisse P. Landry, dec'd.

WHEREAS: George Harrison, in his capacity of Tutor and ex-officio Administrator of the estate of Narcisse P. Landry, has this day filed his Final account of distribution.

Notice is hereby given to all whom it may concern to show cause within thirty days from the date hereof, why said account should not be homologated and made a judgment of this court.

M. A. ESTEVAN, Clerk.

Iberville, June 6th, 1861. [je8

Etat de la Louisiane—Paroisse d'Iberville—Cour du 5eme District Judiciaire.

Dans la Succession de feu Narcisse P. Landry.

ATTENDU que GEORGE HARRISON en sa capacité de Tuteur et d'ex-officio Administrateur de la succession de fue Narcisse P. Landry, a ce jour deposé son compte Final de distribution.

Avis est par le present donné à toux ceux que cela concerne de deduire sous trente jours de la date de ce present les raisons pour lesquelles le dit compte ne serait pas homologué et fait le jugement de cette Cour.

M. A. ESTEVAN, Greffier.

Iberville, Juin 6, 1861. [je8.

NOTICE.

ALL person Indebted to the Clerk's Office of this Parish for fees, who will not settle their bills on demand, are hereby notified that writs of fieri facias will issue against them or their sureties at once.

je8 M. A. ESTEVAN, *Clerk.*

An Estimate,

EXHIBITING the various items of expenditure required for the parish of Iberville for the year ending June next. 1862, and made in conformity with a resolution passed at a session of the Police Jury of the parish of Iberville. held on the 4th of June, 1861, to wit:

Payment of Jurors,	$2,000
Inspectors of Roads & Levees,	1,000
Parish Printing,	400
Coroner's Inquest,	500
Members of Police Jury,	600
Clerk of Police Jury,	300
Parish Attorney,	300
Parish Constable;	150
Parish Treasurer,	800
Incidental Expenses,	4,000
Special Tax,	16,000
Total,	$27,000

By order of the Police Jury.

je8 J. H. RILLS, Clerk.

POLICE JURY,
Parish of Iberville.

On Monday the 3d June, 1861, at a regular meeting of the Police Jury of the Parish of Iberville, the following members were present, to wit:

J. ADOLPHE SIGUR, *Member of 1st Ward.*
AUGUSTE CHRISTIN, " " *4th* "
P. T. COLLE, " " *5th* "
C. W. KEEP, " " *7th* "

The Police Jury was called to order by J. H. Rills, the Clerk.

Then came Mr. BELFORT MARIONNEAUX, member elect from the 2d Ward—

Mr. JOHN A. DARDENNE, member elect from the 3d Ward, and—

Mr. S. B. ROANE, member elect from the 6th Ward—

Who presented their certificates of election, and took their seats, after having taken the oath required by the Government of the Confederate States of America, and of this State, the members held over were also sworn accordingly.

Then the Police Jury proceeded to the election of a President for one year from the date hereof; and Mr. John A. Dardenne having been proposed was unanimously elected President for one year from the date hereof.

On motion, the Police Jury proceeded to the election of a Police Jury Constable for one year from the date hereof, and Mr. Ernest Marionneaux was unanimously elected.

Mr. Allen Jumel, Parish Treasurer, was unanimously re-elected for one year from the date hereof.

Then the Police Jury proceeded to the election of a Parish Attorney for one year from the date hereof.

Mr. Colle put in nomination the name of John Marcot.

Mr. Keep put in nomination the name of Benj. Deblieux—and the votes having been taken, resulted as follows:

For Mr. Deblieux, 4 votes.

Messrs. Colle and Christin voted for Mr. Marcot, 2 votes.

Mr. Deblieux having received a majority of the votes, was declared duly elected Parish Attorney.

Then the Police Jury proceeded to the appointment of Road and Levee Inspectors for one year from date, and the following persons were duly appointed, to wit:

1st Road and Levee District,	Theodore Sigur;
2d " "	Antoine Toffier;
3d " "	Lucien Landry;
4th " "	Hyppolite Broussard;
5th " "	Joissin Robert;
6th " "	Hortaire Orillion;
7th " "	H. J. Hyde;
8th " "	John Schlatre;
9th " "	Valsey Hebert;
10th " "	T. J. Papineau;
11th " "	Joseph Hebert;
12th " "	Adolphe Babin;
13th " "	Alexis Pochet;
14th Road District,	F. A. Hudson;
15th Road and Levee District,	N. Kleinpeter;
16th " "	David Flynn;
17th Road District,	Jean Pardo;
18th Road and Levee District,	Wm. Thompson;
19th " "	Theodule Tuilier;
20th " "	John S. Whitney;
21st Road District,	E. A. Ellis;
22d Road and Levee District,	Wm. Cushman.

Then the Police Jury proceeded to appoint Commissioners of Election to serve for one year from the date hereof, and the following persons were appointed, to wit:

First Precinct, at the Buena Vista Hotel, Bayou Goula—Nathaniel Cropper, Ernest Comeaux and Austin Hunt.

Second Precinct, Court-House, Plaquemine—Paul Deblieux, Edward Savory and Homer Marionneaux.

Third Precinct, House of Michael Schlatre—Alfred Greaud, Silvert Marionneaux and Michel Hebert.

Fourth Precinct, store of Bissell & Schlatre, Indian Village—Oscar Dupuy, Aubry Nereaux and Amilka Dupuy.

Fifth Precinct, house of Pierre Richard. Oaks—Samuel Gourrier, Ulger LeBlanc and Henry S. Browne.

Sixth Precinct, house of Edouard Dupuy, Island—Victor Blanchard, Jules Bonecaz and Edgar Dupuy.

Seventh Precinct, Ives' Mill, Bayou Sorrell—Lucien LeBlanc, James Clark and Geo. Mitcheltree.

Eighth Precinct, house of Keep & Schlatre, Gsosse Tete—Adolphe Dupuy, Adolphe Grass and Wm. Briggs.

Tho Police Jury then appointed Commissioners of Patrol, to serve for one year from this date, to wit:

1st Patrol District,	Theodore Sigur;
2d " "	Nathaniel Cropper;
3d " "	Oscar Hebert;
4th " "	Henry Desobry;
5th " "	Homer Marionneaux;
6th " "	Sebastian Schlatre;
7th " "	Philogene Marionneaux;
8th " "	James Ventriss;
8th " "	Rene LeBlanc;
9th " "	Pierre Miermont;
10th " "	Eugene LeBlanc;
11th " "	Charles Mather;
12th " "	Zenon Blouin;
13th " "	John Hobly;
14th " "	Augustin LeBlanc;
15th " "	Olivia Daigre;
16th " "	William Patrick;
17th " "	W. J Bogan;
18th " "	Theodule Guidry;
19th " "	Joseph LeBlanc.

On motion, Resolved, That the present Board of Examiners of Public Schools be composed of Messrs. V. J. Dupuy, Samuel Matthews and Jos. H. Balch. for the right bank of the Mississippi river; and Messrs. J. Trasimond Dupuy, H. S. Browne and W. R. Boote, for the left bank of the Mississippi, to serve for one year from the date hereof.

The Report of P. T. Colle, one of the Commissioners of the Island Cut-off Road, was presented, read and laid over until next meeting.

The petition of the inhabitants of Marangouin and Point Coupee, praying for relief, was rejected.

On motion, Resolved, That the parish Recorder be ordered to annul and cancel the bond furnished by G. S. Rousseau, late parish Treasurer, as keeper of the parish School Fund for the year ending June 28th, 1859; and further, that a copy of this Resolution be furnished to said Recorder.

Resolved, That from and after this date the salary of the parish Constable be one hundred and fifty dollars per annum; and further Resolved, that E. A. Marionneaux, the present parish Constable, be entitled to have and receive the sum of fifty dollars, extra compensation, for work done and services rendered during the past year—said sum to be paid upon the warrant of the President of the Police Jury.

Resolved, That in consequence of a portion of the Grosse Tete Road being under water, there-made a Road District, to be known as District No. 23, and that George Mitcheltree be, and he is hereby appointed Road Inspector in and for said District.

Mr. Keep offered the following preamble and ordinance which were unanimously adopted—

Whereas, the State Legislature at its last regular Session, repealed the Act establishing the Board of Public Works—thereby paralysing the arm to which we have looked for protection and security; and, whereas Bayou Plaquemine in its present condition, its mouth unprotected from the entrance of drift wood, Grand River, its main outlet, being closed with drift and sediment, will be the cause as surely as it exists, of the inundation and ruin of the most settled and flourishing portions of the Parish; and, whereas with such facts and certainty at hand, it becomes the duty of the Parochial authorities to take measures to protect and guard the Parish against an impending danger threatening its most vital interests; Therefore, be it ordained by the Police Jury of the Parish of Iberville, that Messrs. Belfort Marionneaux, Michael Schlatre, jr., and Dr. T. S. Garrett, be and they are hereby appointed Commissioners with full power to devise and superintend the execution of a plan to prevent effectually the drift wood from going down Bayou Plaquemine.

Be it further ordained, &c., That as soon as the water will have fallen sufficiently to allow said Commissioners to commence operations, they are hereby empowered to call upon the Parish negroes, who they shall employ in executing the plan they may devise—returning said negroes under the direction of the Grosse Tete Road Commissioners, as soon as the work will be completed.

Be it further ordained, &c., That the sum of $500 be, and the same is hereby appropriated to purchase materials, &c., for the executing of said work.

Be it further ordained, &c., That the Commissioners are authorized and instructed to communicate with the aurhorities of the Parish of West Baton Rouge, to obtain their concurrence and assistance in the above work.

Be it further ordained, &c., That in authorizing the said work at the mouth of Bayou Plaquemine, the Police Jury does not pretend to assume any power not delegated to it, but is only acting in self-defence and for the protection of the Parish, in a case for which the Legislature has failed to provide, and for which it cannot provide in time to save the Parish from ruin and devastation.

On motion, resolved, that Articles 101 and 105 of the Patrol Ordinance be, and the same are hereby repealed and the following enacted in their stead.—1st. The Patrol shall be armed and equipped as directed, or deemed proper by the Chief or Patrol. 2nd, The Patrol shall meet at any place or rendezvous designated by the Chief.

The round shall commence at 9 o'clock in the summer, and 8 o'clock in winter, and continue until 3 o'clock in summer, and 4 o'clock in winter; but the hours may be changed whenever the Chief may deem it necessary. The Patrol on duty shall run over the District or be distributed and posted in such a manner by its chief as to render it most efficient, and shall visit all negro quarters and search all cabins deemed suspicious by the Chief.

Resolved further, That the following articles be, and they are hereby incorporated in the Police regulations,—

1st. No slave shall be allowed to own a skiff, or boat of any kind, or traffic with his fellow slaves in any manner whatsoever; and if found so offending, and at the complaint of any one either before a justice of the Peace, or to the commissary of the patrol, he shall receive fifteen lashes.

2nd. Any Planter owning a tract of land at a distance from his home place, and worked or cultivated by the same negroes, or enjoying the privilege of working or using the timber on any land. shall at all times keep a white man with them, and in their transit from one place to the other, they shall be accompanied by the Overseer or any other white person employed for the purpose. Any Planter failing to comply with the above regulation, shall upon conviction thereof, be subject to a fine of not less than $25 and not more than $100, recoverable before any Court of competent jurisdiction.

3rd. Whenever a negro wishes to take a wife on a neighboring plantation, he shall only do so with a written permission, both of his owner and that of the woman. He shall be allowed to visit her only twice a week, and then with a pass from his master specifying the nights upon which he has permission to visit her—at what time he must go at night and return in the morning. Any negro found in contravention of the above, shall receive the same punishment as prescribed for the one found without a pass.

On motion of Mr. Roane, it was Resolved, That Arvillian Raffrey, an indigent person, be allowed a pension of $6 per month, payable upon the warrant of the member of the 6th Ward.

[From the Evening Delta.

THE BATTLE OF BETHEL.

DETAILED ACCOUNTS.

Yorktown, June 11th, 1861.

An engagement, lasting four hours, took place yesterday, (Monday) between five regiments of the troops from Old Point, and 1100 Confederates troops, consisting of Virginians and North Carolinians, under Gen. Magruder. at Bethel Church, York county. Before telling you of the battle, I will give you some circumstances preceding it. About two weeks ago, a party of 300 Yankees came up from Hampton and occupied Bethel Church, which position they held a day or two, and then retired, leaving written on the walls several inscriptions, such as "Death to the Traitors !" "Down with the Rebels!" etc. To these excursions into the interior, of which this was the boldest, Gen. Magruder determined to put a stop to, and accordingly sent a few companies of his own troops into Bethel, In addition to this, he determined to carry the war into the enemy's country, and on Wednesday last, Stanard's battery of the howitzer batallion was ordered to the Church, where it was soon joined by a portion of Brown's battery, of the same corps. The North Carolina regiment under Col. Hill, was also there, making in all about 1100 men and seven howitzer guns.

TO THE PUBLIC.

HAVING made arrangements with the School Directors of the Fourth School District of this Parish, for the purpose of teaching a Public School for the young ladies in said District, I hereby give notice to the Parents that the same will be opened on

On Monday, June 17th.

jun15 WIDOW P. JUMEL.

ALLEN JUMEL in Account with the PARISH OF IBERVILLE.

Dr.		Cr.	
April 9—To balance on hand,	$6,122 39	June 3—By Amt. sundry drafts	$10,882 79
Amt. transferred from Acct. of Fire-proof Building as per ordinance passed by the Policy Jury this day	7,600 00	By Commission on amt. received this Quar., say 20 pr ct.	60
May 27—Amt. from J. H. Rils for fines collected of J.A. Hebort	10 00	By bal. forwarded	7,659 00
" 29—J. H. Rils fines C.N. Roth & Wilcox	10 00		
June 3—Amt. transferred from Acct. of Grosse Tete R. & L. Fund, per ordinance passed April 9, '61	4,800 00		
	$18,542 39	Total	$18,542 39
" 3—Bal. on hand	$7,659 00		

Amt. Cr. of the School Districts.

Nos. 1	$1,164 36
" 2	993 75
" 3	135 60
" 4	2,749 25
" 5	1,222 14
" 6	954 02
" 7	909 80
" 8	1,332 93
" 9	1,152 33
Total	$10,614 19

Recapitulation.

Amount subject to drafts	$7,659 05
" Credited to School Districts	10,614 19
" " Road and Levee Fund.	682 22
" " Iberville School Soc.	311 50
Total amount in Treasury	$19,266 91

Respectfully submitted to the Police Jury, this 3d day of June, '61.

ALLEN JUMEL, Treasurer.

Approved June 4th, '61.

(Signed) Jno. A. Dardenne, Prest.

NOTICE TO TAX-PAYERS.

SHERIFF'S OFFICE,
Parish of Iberville, May 25, 1861.

ALL persons who have not yet paid their State and Parish Taxes, are hereby notified to make payment of the same to me, at my office, or to my Dep'y, T. E. Grace, in his rounds in the Parish, between this and the **First of July next,** otherwise legal measures will positively be taken to enforce their immediate payment.

All persons requiring Licences—State or Parish—will certainly be denounced to the proper authorities unless they at once provide themselves with the same.

No further indulgence need be expected, as none can or will be given.

THEO. BLANCHARD,

my25) Sheriff.

SUPPLEMENTARY·SHEET.

Plaquemine, La., Wednesday, June 19, 1861.

Supplement to the

Gazette & Sentinel.

Published every Saturday by

W. P. BRADBURN,

EDITOR AND PROPRIETOR.

TERMS OF SUBSCRIPTION.

THREE DOLLARS AND FIFTY CENTS ($3 50) for one year, in advance. FIVE DOLLARS ($5 00) if not paid in advance.

SINGLE COPIES—Ten Cents.

No subscription will be discontinued unless a written notice to that effect is received from the subscriber himself, and all arrearges paid.

TERMS OF ADVERTISING.

ONE DOLLAR ($1 00) per square of ten lines, or less, of this space, ——— —————————, for the first insertion, and Fifty Cents for each subsequent insertion. A liberal discount, however, on these rates will be made on advertisements inserted for a longer time than two months, as follows:

	3 months.	6 months.	12 months.
1 square	$ 5 00	$ 8 00	$ 12 00
2 squares	8 00	12 00	20 00
3 squares	15 00	15 00	25 00
4 squares	12 00	20 00	30 00
5 squares	18 00	25 00	37 00
6 squares	20 00	30 00	45 00

For Professional or Business Cards, not exceeding one square, with paper, one year, $15.

Announcements of Candidates for office, $10. Cash in all cases must accompany the announcement, whether handed in by a friend or the person announced.

The privilege of yearly advertisers is strictly limited to their own immediate and regular business.

Communications intended to promote the private ends or interests of individuals, corporations or societies, will be charged as advertisements.

All persons ordering Jobs or handing in advertisements on account of any local or political organization, will be held responsible for the payment of the same.

Marriages and Deaths published without charge. Obituaries inserted as other advertisements.

Advertisements not marked the length of time they are to be inserted, will be kept in the paper till forbid, and charged accordingly.

All advertisements by strangers or transient persons must be paid in advance.

Personal Cards, if inserted at all, will be charged two dollars per square.

☞Job Work always cash, and advertisements are due when first inserted.

CANDIDATES FOR ELECTION.

FOR CONGRESS.

We are authorized to announce **Col. H. W. ALLEN,** of West Baton Rouge, as a candidate for Congress of the Confederate States for the Fourth Congressional District, composed of the Parishes of West Feliciana, Point Coupee, St. Landry, Lafayette, Vermillion, West Baton Rouge, Iberville, St. Mary and St. Martin. Election first Monday in November.

FOR AUDITOR.

We are authorized to announce **BYTHELL HAYNES,** of Clinton, as a Candidate for Auditor of Public Accounts at the ensuing Fall election.

We are authorized to announce **H. PERALTA,** of East Baton Rouge, as a Candidate for Auditor of Public Accounts

FOR ASSESSOR.

Mr. Editor: Please announce the name of **T. RODOLPH VERBOIS,** Esq., as a Democratic Candidate for Assessor for the parish of Iberville, subject to the State Rights Democratic Convention.

We are authorized to announce **ERNEST CALLERY,** the present incumbent, as a Candidate for re-election to the office of Assessor, subject to the decision of the State Rights Democratic Convention.

FOR SHERIFF.

☞ We are authorized to announce **Joseph H. Erwin, Esq.,** as a candidate for the office of Sheriff of this Parish at the next November election.

Mr. Editor: You will please announce **J. L. PETIT,** as a candidate for Sheriff, subject to the decision of the State Rights Democratic Convention.

FOR RECORDER.

Mr. Editor: You will please announce the name of **ADOLPHE HEBERT,** Esq., as a Candidate for the office of Recorder of the parish of Iberville, subject to the decision of the State Rights Democratic Convention.

FOR SHERIFF.

Mr. Editor: Please announce my name in your paper as a Candidate for the next Sheriffalty of this parish.

GUSTAVE LAUVE.

Bayou Goula, April 18th, 1861.

We are authorized to announce **J. M. RILS** as a Candidate for Sheriff at the ensuing Fall election.

New Advertisements.

SPECIAL NOTICE.

To the Editor of the Gazette and Sentinel.

You will please publish the following order of Judge D. D. Avery, granted upon the petition of the members of the bar and citizens of this Parish:

"For the reasons set forth in the foregoing petition, it is ordered that the ensuing term of the Fifth Judicial District Court for the Parish of Iberville, to be held on the 4th Monday of July, 1861, be and the same is hereby adjourned for that term *sine die*, and it is further ordered that the said petition, together with this order, be filed and spread on the Minutes of the Court, and be published in the Gazette & Sentinel for the information of the public."

(Signed) DAN'L D. AVERY.
Judge of the Fifth Judicial District.

Filed June 14th, 1861.
M. A. Estevan, Clerk.

Grosse Tete, June 13, 1861.

To W. P. Bradburn, Esq.

Dear Sir: My name having been announced several times in your paper as a candidate for the office of Recorder without consultation with me, you will please discontinue said announcement, and announce me as a candidate for Sheriff, and oblige

Yours, very respectfully, etc.,
JOS. H. ERWIN.

PLAQUEMINE:

Wednesday, June 19, 1861.

☞ We would call attention to the advertisements of Mr. F. X. Lurk, who has a fine lot of Dry Goods for sale cheap for Cash. He also has liquors of the finest brand. He invites his friends to test their genuineness.

THE VERY LATEST NEWS.

AFFAIRS IN MISSOURI.

Governor Jackson at Boonville.

Convention Called Together.

Secessionists in Full Sway of the Missouri.

Skirmish Near Independence.

St. Louis, June 17.—Gov. Jackson will make his first stand at Boonville, a town situated on the right bank of the Missouri river, forty-eight miles northwest of Jefferson City.

Rumors are current that the Missouri State Convention will be called together immediately.

Ben. McCulloch is said to be at Fort Smith, Ark., with 10,000 men.

Twelve Illinois regiments are stationed within two hours march of St. Louis.

Two thousand State troops are at Boonville. The Secessionists have full sway of both sides of the Missouri river from Kansas to Boonville, and are well prepared for a fight.

A skirmish occurred near Independence, in which the Federalists were beaten.

Patriots are burning all the railroad bridges.

Hagerstown, June 17.—Six hundred troops are still at Harper's Ferry.

The Southern pickets are again opposite Williamsport. The Confederate troops have burned seventy locomotives.

Fortress Monroe, June 15th.—Gen. Butler demands 15,000 additional men.

Louisville, June 17.—It is reported that Gov. Magoffin orders no Tennesseeans to occupy the Kentucky islands in the Mississippi. It is also reported that a detachment of the State Guard has been ordered to Columbus.

Richmond, June 16.—Passengers from Winchester, who arrived here to-day, confirm the report of the evacuation, or rather partial evacuation, of Harper's Ferry.

The evacuation is considered provisional, and is approved here.

Interesting.—The N. Y. Tribune in speaking of the subjugation of the South, says:

It is evident that strong measures *must* be used. It is sheer nonsense to think of keeping an immense army to keep them in subjection after we conquor them, they must be driven from the South. To this end, we propose that the Federal government make a grant of the Utah Territory to them. They will certainly choose banishment to aunhilation.

PROGRESS OF THE WAR.

(From the Delta of the 16th.)

THE WAR IN MISSOURI.

Illinois Volunteers Entering the State.

GOV. JACKSON AT WORK!

Confederates Joining Missouri!

St. Louis, June 15th.—Illinois volunteers have entered Missouri at Hannibal.

Gov. Jackson, with cars and locomotives, is going West, burning the bridges as he proceeds.

It is said that a large number of Confederates from Arkansas and Northern Texas, are ready to move on Gov. Jackson's invitation.

Mr. Tucker, of the State Journal, has been arrested.

Hermann, June 15th.—The Steamer Louisiana, the third of the invading fleet, is here to take on Col. Bœrnstein's regiment.

Postal Matters.

Washington, June 15th.—Blair has dispatched to the Postmaster at Louisville, as follows:

"Orders requiring mail matter coming from disloyal States to be held for postage, does not imply to prevent delivery on payment of postage."

Evacuation of Harper's Ferry.

Frederick, Md., June 15.—A special agent of the Associated Press just from the Maryland Heights over looking Harper's Ferry, says the Ferry has been mainly evacuated, only about 2000 troops remaining.

The route of the main body was by turnpike towards Charleston and Shepherdstown.

The bridge at Shepherdstown has been burned.

The Southern pickets have been withdrawn from Williamsport.

Federal Military Movements.

Alexander, June 14th.—Active military movements are progressing in consequence of the evacuation of Harper's Ferry.

An effort will be made to prevent concentration.

Washington, June 15th.—General Schenck has been ordered to cross the Potomac with his brigade.

An attack from Gen. Beauregard is apprehended.

Virginia State Convention.

Richmond, June 15.—The vail of secrecy has been removed from yesterday's proceedings in the Convention.

The vote on Virginia's act of secession of April 17th, stood as follows: For secession, 88; against, 55.

The journal show changes, and the final vote stood 103 in favor of the passage of the ordinance.

On the 14th inst., the Ordinance was signed by 91 members, several delegates being absent in the war, sickness having deterred others, and one, Capt Marr, having been killed by the Federalists at Fairfax.

Various rumors are current of battles and movements of the Federal troops, but nothing has as yet been authentically ascertained.

Capture of the Privateer Savannah.

New Nork, June 15th,—The privateer Savannah, in charge of Midshipman Cook, has arrived here. Her crew numbering 35, were put in irons on the Minnesota.

Rendezvous of Federal Forces.

Chicago, June 15th.—Orders have been issued for twelve regiments to rendezvous as follows: Four at Qunicy, four at Alton, and three at Careyville, on the 18th.

From Fortress Monroe.

Fortress Monroe, June 14th.—No information has been received here about the movement of the Southerners.

The Fortress in reality is invested, except by sea. No egress or ingress is safe. Movements are impossible.

A Noble Act.—Maj. James Freeman, one of the wealthiest men in Georgia, says that he will give all his negroes can make (over his family support) for the benefit of the Confederate States during the war, and that if it be found necessary, he will sell his lands and negroes, and give the proceeds to the Confederacy.

He has contributed considerably to the volunteer companies of his county, and is willing and waiting a chance to give more. When (pertinently asks the Charleston Courier) will the glorious cause of freedom lag, when Georgia and the South are full of such men?

[Communicated.]

Mr. Editor.—You will render the friends of Col. Louis Hebert a service, by publishing the subjoined "Special Orders" from Head Quarters of the C. S. A. The object of this is to prove the falsity of certain charges brought against the Colonel. As is generally the case with all such reports, the originators are careful not to let themselves be known. In order to justify the Col. entirely in the estimation of the public, these Special Orders and the Certificate are published:

(Special Orders—No. 45.)

Head Quarters, Milt. Dis. of La. C.S.A.
New Orleans, May 27, '61.

II. Leave of absence for four days for the benefit of his health, is granted to Col. Louis Hébert, 3rd Regt. La. Vols.

By order of Col. P. O. Hebert,
D. Beltzhouver,
Maj. Regt. Art., A. A. A. G., C. S. A.

(Special Orders—No. 46)

Head Quarters, Milt. Dist. La., C.S.A.
New Orleans, May 30, 1861.

IV. The leave of absence granted to Col. Louis Hebert, 3rd Regt. La. Vols., C. S. A., on account of his health, by Special Orders, No. 45, May 27th, 1861, is extended until June 2nd, 1861

By order of Col. P. O. Hebert,
D. Beltzhouver,
Maj. Regt. Art., A. A. A. G., C. S. A.

New Orleans, La.,
June 8th, '61.

I hereby certify that Col. Louis Hebert, 3rd Regt. La. Vol., was for several days during the latter part of May last, sick and under my charge, confined to his room and bed, and that he was to unwell at the time to join his regiment.

John M. Haden,
Surg. C. S. A., Med. Dis. Dept., La.

By the above it will be seen that instead of being absent without leave, and spending his time to no purpose in New Orleans, whilst his regiment was on its way to the seat of war, Col. Hebert was sick; it is proper to state that during his convalescence, he was employed in making purchases to complete the equipment of his regiment. In conclusion, I will also state that the Col. has recovered his health and joined his regiment, at the head of which he will prove himself equal to any emergency.

A. FRIEND.

Spiking Negroes.—The New York Tribune has an article recommending that the slaves taken by the Abolition soldiers from their masters, should be put to hard work in making batteries, and then makes this mysterious proposition:

"Then, too, if the exigencies of the campaign require so summary a proceeding, these contraband bipeds might be destroyed—*as property*. For example, when cannons are about to be abandoned to the enemy, a prudent General causes them to be spiked, and so thoroughly spiked as to be forever worthless, as cannon to the foe. So, as to negroes who had served in the Union camp, if our army were compelled to let them fall into the enemie's hands, they must first spike them, as property, so that they would be good for nothing to the foe; and, to make thorough work of it, the negroes must be instructed to tell the rebels, who might try to use them, that they were spiked."

Spiking negroes as they spike cannon! What does the wretch mean? Does he propose to cut off the hands and feet, to maim and mutilate the slaves when they can no longer make use of them? No crime is too horrible for the New York Tribune, and it would not suprise us if this is really what it means.—*Richmond Dispatch.*

More Outrages by the Lincolnites—A letter to the Richmond Dispatch, dated Norfolk, June 4th, says:

The Lincoln hirelings are still bent on carrying out their fiendish ends. Besides their deeds of plunder, may resort to other and more vile and inhuman crimes in the outrages of our women and children. A young lady, daughter of a respectable farmer living in the vicinity of Newport News, was taken by these reckless villains and imprisoned in Fortress Monre, where, judging from what has already been done, a most foul and inhuman outrage will be perpetrated. Already have poor and helpless women and children been treated in this manner, too revolting to think of. Besides Miss Lee, several other ladies are prisoners at this fort, where, helpless and alone, the mercy of God can only release them.

In Hampton, also, a young man, formerly of this city, was taken, divested of his clothing, and compelled to walk the distance of three miles to Fortress Monroe, where he was confined as prisoner. Does not the heart shrink at such deeds of criielty; and must the offenders go unpunished?

☞ Lazy girls make rich men poor, and industrious girls make poor men rich.

Complaining.—We see no reason why the Virginian rebels should complain so bitterly of the atrocities perpetrated upon them, their rebellious conduct deserves all the tortures that can be ingeniously applied.—*Louisville Journal.*

This Sepoy editor should be immediately shipped to Delhi, D. C., where his natural sympathies for his fellow-man should have full scope in a practical sense. We can find no words for commentation. However, we sympathize with this poor deluded creature, and bespeak for him comfortable quarters in some far distant *hot-house.*

Well Pictured.—An exchange speaking of Geo D. Prentice, the editor of the Louisville Journal, says:

He has widsom but it is mightily perverted. Ever since he began his political career, it has been one perpetual stride of hypocrisy and personal abuse. His moral character is below par, and has been so ever since he commenced to dabble in politics. He is a man of debased habits—intemperance and licentiousness are conspicuouly stamped upon every feature, especially the latter. His vicious habits and oft-repeated ill-treatment of his wife, drove her from him to become an outcast upon society at large. He is a political weather-cock, and a man whose slander is no disgrace—a man of low cunning—a creaping coward, and dishonest citizen. His popularity is spurious and ill-gotten; famed for billingsgate, and doubly renowned for his natural licentiousness; a mouldering mass of iniquity—such is Geo. D. Prentice.

Gov. Jackson's Proclamation.

St. Louis, Mo., June 13th.—The following is Governor Jackson's Proclamation:

A series of unlooked-for and unparalleled acts have been inflicted upon the peace and dignity of this commonwealth, and upon the right and liberties of its people, by wicked and unprincipled men, professing to act under the authority of the Federal Government. Solemn enactments of your Legislature have been nullified. Your volunteer soldiers have been arrested; commerce with her sister States have been suspended; trade with your own fellow-citizens has been subject to the harassing control of armed soldiery; peaceful citizens have been imprisoned without warrant; unoffending and defenceless men, women and children have been ruthlessly shot down and murdered, and other unbearable indignities heaped upon your State and yourselves.

To this you have submitted with patriotic forbearance, which has only encouraged more daring usurpations. My object has been to preserve peace and avert war from our borders. With that view, Gen. Price arranged with Gen. Harney. The State Government faithfully adhered to the agreement. The Federal Government manifested its disapprobation by the dismissal of Gen. Harney, and commenced a proceeding utterly hostile to the agreement waiving the dignity of Missouri.

I solicited an interview with General Lyon, and made propositions more honhorable to the Federal Government than to Missouri, that if the Federalists would withdraw, I would pledge to disband the militia, forbid the introduction of arms into the State, protect all citizens (regardless of their political opinions), repress all insurrections, maintain a strict neutrality; and if necessary to carry out these pledges, I would call for Federal assistance. Nothing but the desire to avert civil war could have induced these humiliating proprositions. These propositions were rejected.

Governor Jackson calls for 50,000 militia to repel the invaders.

Gazette & Sentinel.

PROGRESS OF THE WAR.

(From the Delta of the 12th.)

THE WAR IN VIRGINIA!

Highly Important from Virginia!

ANOTHER BATTLE!

THE ENEMY REPULSED THREE TIMES!

HE LEAVES 100 KILLED ON THE FIELD.

RICHMOND, VA., June 11, 1861.—A battle took place yesterday at Bethel Church, which is situated between Newport News and Yorktown, the former point being in possession of the enemy, and the latter held by our forces. Newport News is a point projecting into James river, directly opposite Norfolk harbor, and is accessible to the Federal fleet.

Our force in the engagement consisted of twelve hundred men, under the command of Col. J. Bankhead Magruder, formerly of the United States Artillery.

The Bethel Church, where the conflict occurred, is on high ground, and being occupied by the Confederate troops, was assaulted by three thousand of the enemy. They were repulsed three several times, suffering a heavy loss. Our loss was trifling.

The Confederate troops in the action were the First North Carolina Regiment, the Hampton (Va.) Battalion, and one company of the Richmond Howitzers.

The enemy retreated to Newport News, leaving about one hundred dead bodies on the road, and our men in possession of the Church.

Still Later.

Enemy's Loss at Bethel Church!

A Federal Colonel Killed!

Our Loss but Five.

Bethel Church Burnt Down!

RICHMOND, June 11, 1861.—One report received here since my first dispatch is that the loss of the enemy in killed and wounded at the battle of Bethel Church was two hundred.

A Federal Colonel, name unknown, is among the killed.

Our casualties are stated as numbering but five in all.

The enemy had several pieces of artillery. Our troops had six pieces.

The enemy fired very badly.

The number of our troops in the battle is now said to have been two thousand.

Baltimore, June 11.—General Butler moved several regiments to dislodge the Southerners at Great Bethel, nine miles from Hampton.

At Little Bethel a German regiment mistook the signal, and fired on Colonel Townsend's column, marching in close order, with two pieces of artillery. Other accounts say that Townsend fired first, but did no harm. The Germans' fire killed one and wounded two.

At daybreak two regiments moved from Fortress Monroe to support the main body. Little Bethel was burned down, and the army advanced towards Great Bethel. Arriving there, they could see no men, no batteries—only flashes and comrades falling.

Lieut. Grebble, U. S. A., and twenty-five others were killed, besides one hundred wounded.

Intense indignation is manifested against Gen. Pierce for not having ordered an earlier flight of the Federalists.

Another Victory of the Southerners.

The Engagement at Hampton.

Three Hundred Federalists Killed!

RICHMOND, June 11.—On Saturday, a scouting party of Confederates near Hampton, encountered scouting parties of Federalists numbering 200.

The Federalists mistook the Confederates and claimed to be their friends, saying they belonged to the 2d New York Regiment.

The Southerners fired on the Federalists, killed ten, wounded twelve or fifteen, and took one a prisoner. The Confederates received no injury. Although the Federalists returned the fire both sides withdrew.

On Monday a body of Federal troops, about 4,000 strong, attacked the entrenched Confederates, numbering about 1,000, at Bethel Church. The Confederates repulsed the Federalists three times. The latter then withdrew. The former held their position until this morning, when they also withdrew.

The loss on the Federal side amounted to about 300 in killed and wounded. One Confederate was killed and five or six wounded.

Washington Gossip.

WASHINGTON, June 11.—The Tribune says that an army officer had an interview with Gen. Scott, and was positively informed that no important attack would be made on the enemy's position until the fortifications around Washington are entirely completed.

But for the want of vessels, a steamer would go for Mr. Harvey, the U. S. Minister to Portugal, to bring him home a prisoner.

At 3 o'clock this morning, a large force marched through Georgetown, D. C., towards Point of Rocks.

The Southerners are in possession of information regarding the Federal movements.

The Government has advices that the cannon at Manassas Gap are planted in the form of a semi-circle, with the railroad station in the center.

The Southerners talk of flanking the Federal lines, and capturing the city without going via Baltimore.

Gen. Scott's horse was sent to Baltimore to-day. It is believed that Scott will leave to-night for Frederick, to take command in person.

Affairs in Missouri.

ST. LOUIS, June 12.—Gen. Price and Gov. Jackson had a conference with Gen. Lyon and Col. Blair, during which the former proposed the removal of the Federalists from Missouri soil and the disbandment of the militia.

Gen. Lyon refused to consent, and after four hours' session, the conference, without coming to an agreement, adjourned.

Gen. Price and Gov. Jackson went to Jefferson City in a special train.

ST. JOSEPH, June 12.—A battalion under Major Culley, made up from the regulars at the forts, is coming here.

Another brigade is going to Kansas City.

Important Correspondence.

The following dispatch is published in the papers:

To Governor Magoffin:

"CINCINNATI, June 11, 1861.

"I have received information that Tennessee troops are under orders to occupy Island No. 1, six miles below Cairo. In accordance with my understanding with Gen. Buckner, I call upon you to prevent this step. Do you regard the islands on the Mississippi river above the Tennessee line as within your jurisdiction? And if so, what ones?

"Respectfully,

"GEO. B. MCCLELLAN,
"Adjutant General, U. S. A."

Federal Troops in Georgia.

Great Excitement.

SAVANNAH, June 12.—The Republican, of this morning, says that Federal troops, in large numbers, landed yesterday at Hilton Head. Their object in having effected this landing is not known, but causes great excitement.

Com. Tattnal is in command of the State troops.

The Maryland Vote.

In Henry Winter Davis's district, the vote will be close. It is thought the Bethel victory will greatly strengthen the Southern Rights vote.

Speech of President Davis.

President Davis, at the serenade given him the other night at Spottswood House, Richmond, appeared and addressed the crowd as follows:

Friends and Fellow-Citizens: I thank you for the compliment that your presence conveys. It is an indication of regard, not for the person, but for the position which he holds. The cause in which we are engaged is the cause of the advocacy of rights to which we were born, those for which our fathers of the Revolution bled—the richest inheritance that ever fell to man, and which it is our sacred duty to transmit untarnished to our children. Upon us is devolved the high and holy responsibility of preserving the Constitutional liberty of a free Government. (Applause.) Those with whom we have lately associated have shown themselves so incapable of appreciating the blessings of the glorious institutions they inherited, that they are to-day stripped of the liberty to which they were born. They have allowed an ignorant usurper to trample upon all the prerogatives of citizenship, and to exercise power never delegated to him; and it has been reserved for your own State, so lately one of the original thirteen, but now, thank God, fully separated from them, to become the theater of a great central camp, from which will pour forth thousands of brave hearts to roll back the tide of this despotism. Apart from that gratification we may well feel at being separated from such a connection, is the pride that upon you devolves the task of maintaining and defending our new government. I believe that we shall be able to achieve the noble work, and that the institutions of our fathers will go to our children as sacred as they have descended to us. (Applause.) In these Confederate States we observe those relations which have been poetically ascribed to the United States, but which there never had the same reality—States so distinct that each existed as a sovereign, yet so united that each was bound with the other to constitute a whole; or, as more beautifully expressed, "distinct as the billows, yet one as the sea." (Applause.) Upon every hill which now overlooks Richmond, you have had, and will continue to have, camps containing soldiers from every State in the Confederacy; and to its remotest limits every proud heart beats high with indignation at the thought that the foot of the invader has been set upon the soil of old Virginia. (Great cheering.) There is not one true son of the South who is not ready to shoulder his musket, to bleed, to die, or to conquer in the cause of liberty here. (Cheers.)

Beginning under many embarrassments, the result of seventy years of taxation being in the hands of our enemies, we must at first move cautiously. It may be that we shall have to encounter sacrifices; but, my friends, under the smiles of the God of the just, and filled with the same spirit that animated our fathers, success shall perch on our banners. (Great cheers.) I am sure you do not expect me to go into any argument upon those questions which for twenty-five years have agitated the country. We have now reached the point where argument being exhausted, it only remains for us to stand by our arms. (Cheers, and cries of we will.) When the time and occasion serve, we shall smite the smiter with manly arms, as did our fathers before us and as becomes their sons. To them we leave the base acts of the assassin and incendiary—to them we leave it to insult helpless women; to us belongs vengeance upon man. (Tremendous applause.)

Now, my friends, I thank you again for this gratifying manifestation. (A voice: "Tell us something about Buena Vista.")

Well, my friends, we will make the battle field of Virginia another Buena Vista, and drench them with blood more precious than that shed there. We will make a history for ourselves. We do not ask that the past shall shed our luster upon us, bright as our past has been, for we can achieve our own destiny. We may point to many a field over which has floated the flag of our country when we were of the United States—upon which Southern soldiers and Southern officers reflected their brave spirits in their deeds of daring; and, without intending to cast a shadow upon the courage of any portion of the United States, let me call it to your remembrance that no man who went from any of these Confederate States, has ever yet, as a general officer, surrendered to an enemy. (Great applause.)

Pardon me if I do not go into matters of history; and permit me, again, to thank you for this kind manifestation of your regard, to express to you my hearty wishes for the individual prosperity of you all, with the hope that you will all pray to God to crown our cause and our country with success.

His Excellency then retired from the window amid long cheers.

MARRIED,

On the 10th of June, by the Rev. Father Fallot, CHAS. N. ROTH to Mrs. ZULMA MARIONNEAUX, all of this place.

State of Louisiana—Parish of Iberville—5th District Court.

In matter of Estate of DANIEL HOY, deceased.

WHEREAS: Ann Wailey, Administratrix of the above succession, has filed in this Court her account of Administration of the same.

Notice is hereby given to all whom it may concern to file in writing within thirty days from the date hereof, any opposition they may have, why the said account should not be homologated and approved, and her bond as Administratrix of said Estate cancelled and annulled.

Clerk's office, Iberville, June 7, 1861.

je8 E. A. MARIONNEAUX, Dep. Clerk.

Etat de la Louisiane, Paroisse d'Iberville—Cour du 5me. District Judiciaire.

Dans la Succession de feue DANIEL HOY.

ATTENDU que Ann Wailey a ce jour enléassé en cette cour son compte d'Administration de la succession de feu Daniel Hoy.

Avis est par le present donné à tous ceux que cela concerne de deduire sous trente jours de la date de ce present les raisons pour lesquelles le dit tableau ne serait pas homologué et fait le jugement de cette cour et son cautionnement, comme tel annullé.

Iberville, 7th Juin, 1861.

E. A. MARIONNEAUX,
je8. Dep. Greffeir.

State of Louisiana, Parish of Iberville—Fifth District Court.

In matter of Estate of Narcisse P. Landry, dec'd.

WHEREAS: George Harrison, in his capacity of Tutor and ex-officio Administrator of the estate of Narcisse P. Landry, has this day filed his Final account of distribution.

Notice is hereby given to all whom it may concern to show cause within thirty days from the date hereof, why said account should not be homologated and made a judgment of this court.

M. A. ESTEVAN, Clerk.
Iberville, June 6th, 1861. [je8

Etat de la Louisiane—Paroisse d'Iberville—Cour du 5eme District Judiciaire.

Dans la Succession de feu Narcisse P. Landry.

ATTENDU que GEORGE HARRISON en sa capacitè de Tuteur et d'ex-officio Administrateur de la succession de fue Narcisse P. Landry, a ce jour deposé son compte Final de distribution.

Avis est par le present donné à toux ceux que cela concerne de deduire sous trente jours de la date de ce present les raisons pour lesquelles le dit compte ne serait pas homologué et fait le jugement de cette Cour.

M. A. ESTEVAN, Greffier.
Iberville, Juin 6, 1861. [je8.

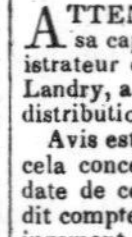

NOTICE

TO THE MILITIA!

ALL the free white males, who have resided in the State Sixty Days, and are Eighteen and under Forty-five years of age, and are not exempt under the laws of the Confederate States, or of this State, from Militia duty, are requested to give their names to the respective captains or orderly Sergeants of their beats without delay—in order that I may make my return to the Adjutant General.

ERNEST CALLERY,
my25) Assessor.

FIGHTING MEN WANTED.

THE undersigned is in want of SIXTY-FOUR men (Irishmen), able and willing to do service for their country.

my22 OSCAR DUPUY.

MISCELLANEOUS.

An Estimate,

EXHIBITING the various items of expenditure required for the parish of Iberville for the year ending June next. 1862, and made in conformity with a resolution passed at a session of the Police Jury of the parish of Iberville, held on the 4th of June, 1861, to wit:

Payment of Jurors,	$2,000
Inspectors of Roads & Levees,	1,000
Parish Printing,	400
Coroner's Inquest,	500
Members of Police Jury,	600
Clerk of Police Jury,	300
Parish Attorney,	300
Parish Constable;	150
Parish Treasurer,	800
Incidental Expenses,	4,000
Special Tax,	16,000
Total,	$27,000

By order of the Police Jury.

je8 J. H. RILLS, Clerk.

POLICE JURY,

Parish of Iberville.

On Monday the 3d June, 1861, at a regular meeting of the Police Jury of the Parish of Iberville, the following members were present, to wit:

J. ADOLPHE SIGUR, *Member of 1st Ward.*
AUGUSTE CHRISTIN, " " *4th* "
P. T. COLLE, " " *5th* "
C. W. KEEP, " " *7th* "

The Police Jury was called to order by J. H. Rills, the Clerk.

Then came Mr. BELFORT MARIONNEAUX, member elect from the 2d Ward—

Mr. JOHN A. DARDENNE, member elect from the 3d Ward, and—

Mr. S. B. ROANE, member elect from the 6th Ward—

Who presented their certificates of election, and took their seats, after having taken the oath required by the Government of the Confederate States of America, and of this State; the members held over were also sworn accordingly.

Then the Police Jury proceeded to the election of a President for one year from the date hereof; and Mr. John A. Dardenne having been proposed was unanimously elected President for one year from the date hereof.

On motion, the Police Jury proceeded to the election of a Police Jury Constable for one year from the date hereof, and Mr. Ernest Marionneaux was unanimously elected.

Mr. Allen Jumel, Parish Treasurer, was unanimously re-elected for one year from the date hereof.

Then the Police Jury proceeded to the election of a Parish Attorney for one year from the date hereof.

Mr. Colle put in nomination the name of John Marcot.

Mr. Keep put in nomination the name of Benj. Deblieux—and the votes having been taken, resulted as follows:

For Mr. Deblieux, 4 votes.
Messrs. Colle and Christin voted for Mr. Marcot, 2 votes.

Mr. Deblieux having received a majority of the votes, was declared duly elected Parish Attorney.

Then the Police Jury proceeded to the appointment of Road and Levee Inspectors for one year from date, and the following persons were duly appointed, to wit:

1st Road and Levee District,	Theodore Sigur;
2d " "	Antoine Toffier;
3d " "	Lucien Landry;
4th " "	Hyppolite Broussard;
5th " "	Joissin Robert;
6th " "	Hortaire Orillion;
7th " "	H. J. Hyde;
8th " "	John Schlatre;
9th " "	Valsey Hebert;
10th " "	T. J. Papineau;
11th " "	Joseph Hebert;
12th " "	Adolphe Babin;
13th " "	Alexis Pochet;
14th Road District,	F. A. Hudson;
15th Road and Levee District,	N. Kleinpeter;
16th " "	David Flynn;
17th Road District,	Jean Pardo;
18th Road and Levee District,	Wm. Thompson;
19th " "	Theodule Tuilier;
20th " "	John S. Whitney;
21st Road District,	E. A. Ellis;
22d Road and Levee District,	Wm. Cushman.

Then the Police Jury proceeded to appoint Commissioners of Election to serve for one year from the date hereof, and the following persons were appointed, to wit:

First Precinct, at the Buena Vista Hotel, Bayou Goula—Nathaniel Cropper, Ernest Comeaux and Austin Hunt.

Second Precinct, Court-House, Plaquemine—Paul Deblieux, Edward Savory and Homer Marionneaux.

Third Precinct, House of Michael Schlatre—Alfred Greaud, Silvert Marionneaux and Michel Hebert.

Fourth Precinct, store of Bissell & Schlatre, Indian Village—Oscar Dupuy, Aubry Neveaux and Amilka Dupuy.

Fifth Precinct, house of Pierre Richard, Oaks—Samuel Gourrier, Ulger LeBlanc and Henry S. Browne.

Sixth Precinct, house of Edouard Dupuy, Island—Victor Blanchard, Jules Bonecaz and Edgar Dupuy.

Seventh Precinct, Ives' Mill, Bayou Sorrell—Lucien LeBlanc, James Clark and Geo. Mitcheltree.

Eighth Precinct, house of Keep & Schlatre, Gsosse Tete—Adolphe Dupuy, Adolphe Grass and Wm. Briggs.

The Police Jury then appointed Commissioners of Patrol, to serve for one year from this date, to wit:

1st Patrol District,	Theodore Sigur;
2d " "	Nathaniel Cropper;
3d " "	Oscar Hebert;
4th " "	Henry Desobry;
5th " "	Homer Marionneaux;
6th " "	Sebastian Schlatre;
7th " "	Philogene Marionneaux;
8th " "	James Ventriss;
8th " "	Rene LeBlanc;
9th " "	Pierre Miermont;
10th " "	Eugene LeBlanc;
11th " "	Charles Mather;
12th " "	Zenon Blouin;
13th " "	John Hobly;
14th " "	Augustin LeBlanc;
15th " "	Olivia Daigre;
16th " "	William Patrick;
17th " "	W. J Bogan;
18th " "	Theodule Guidry;
19th " "	Joseph LeBlanc.

On motion, Resolved, That the present Board of Examiners of Public Schools be composed of Messrs. V. J. Dupuy, Samuel Matthews and Jos. H. Balch, for the right bank of the Mississippi river; and Messrs. J. Trasimond Dupuy, H. S. Browne and W. R. Boott, for the left bank of the Mississippi, to serve for one year from the date hereof.

The Report of P. T. Colle, one of the Commissioners of the Island Cut-off Road, was presented, read and laid over until next meeting.

The petition of the inhabitants of Marangouin and Point Coupee, praying for relief, was rejected.

On motion, Resolved, That the parish Recorder be ordered to annul and cancel the bond furnished by G. S. Rousseau, late parish Treasurer, as keeper of the parish School Fund for the year ending June 28th, 1859; and further, that a copy of this Resolution be furnished to said Recorder.

Resolved, That from and after this date the salary of the parish Constable be one hundred and fifty dollars per annum; and further Resolved, that E. A. Marionneaux, the present parish Constable, be entitled to have and receive the sum of fifty dollars, extra compensation, for work done and services rendered during the past year—said sum to be paid upon the warrant of the President of the Police Jury.

Resolved, That in consequence of a portion of the Grosse Tete Road being under water, therefore cutting off travel by said road, therefore—

Be it Resolved, That the keeper of the Ferry at the Indian Village be released from the payment of his obligations to the parish, commencing from the 1st day of April, 1861, and extending to 1st day of September, 1861.

Resolved, That the pension allowed the families of soldiers who absent themselves in defence of our country, be so amended as to read—That the family of every soldier in needy circumstances be allowed not less than $10 nor more than $25 per month.

Mr. Dardenne, at the special request of Capt. Charles A. Brusle, of the "Iberville Greys," presented a detailed account of the expenditures of the money appropriated by the Police Jury for the use of said company.

Whereupon, the Police Jury unanimously opposed the examination of the details of said expenditures, having the most implicit confidence in Capt. Brusle and knowing that every cent appropriated for the use of said company would be well and properly spent when it passed through the hands through the hands of their gallant Captain; and in order to provide for any further contingency that may arise and also to reassure Capt. Brusle and his gallant soldiers, that though absent they are not forgotten. Now be it—

Resolved, That the Police Jury of the parish of Iberville do hereby appropriate the additional sum of Fifteen Hundred Dollars for the use of the "Iberville Greys," said sum to be subject to the order of the Captain of said Company, whenever called for by him or his authorized agent.

On motion, the Police Jury adjourned till tomorrow 10 o'clock, A. M.

JUNE 5.—The Police Jury met pursuant to adjournment. Same members present.

On motion of Mr. Christin, Resolved, That from and after this date the Ferriage across the river opposite Plaquemine is hereby increased to twenty cents for foot passengers.

On motion of the same member, Resolved, That the Resolution passed on the 25th day of last May, at the extra session of the Police Jury, allowing the sum of Two Thousand Dollars to any company offering its services either to the State or Confederate States, be and the same is hereby amended, so as to read as follows, to wit:

Resolved, That hereafter no money shall be drawn under said resolution from the Parish Treasury by any company whose services have not been accepted by the Confederate States, and said money to be drawn by draft, signed by the President of the Police Jury.

The petition of Capt. Pardo, of the Pellican Guards, having been presented, was read and unanimously rejected.

On motion of Mr. Christin, Resolved, That the Parish Printing be done by each of the two papers printed in the parish, and that the sum of four hundred dollars, appropriated for that purpose, be equally divided between them,

Said Resolution having been put to vote, was carried by five votes to one, Mr. Roane voting in the negative.

The petition of Mr. Ephraim Lanier praying for relief, was reconsidered and again rejected.

Upon which, Mr. Morionneaux offered the following, to wit:

Whereas, the Corporation of the town of Plaquemine has failed to support Ephraim Lanier, one of its paupers, and blind at that—

Therefore be it Resolved, That the sum of fifty dollars for one year from this date, be allowed him as a gratuity from the parish. Said resolution having been put to vote, was rejected.

The petition of the inhabitants of Lower Grand River, praying for a division of the Road and Levee Dist. No. 7, having been presented, was read and accepted; and on motion of Mr. Roane, it was Resolved, That the Road Leeve District No. 7, of this Parish, be changed and limited as follows—said District to begin at the "Park," and to extend along the East side of Grand River, to the lower line of the land belonging to the widow and heirs of L. J. Sigur—and that portion of said Dist. No. 7, extending from the upper line of said Sigur tract, to the Southern Parish boundary, together with the western side of said Grand River, (known as Lower Grand River) extending from said boundary up to Bayou Pigeon, opposite to the mouth of Little Pigeon, be created and made a Road District, to be known as District No. 23, and that George Mitcheltree be, and he is hereby appointed Road Inspector in and for said District.

Mr. Keep offered the following preamble and ordinance which were unanimously adopted—

Whereas, the State Legislature at its last regular Session, repealed the Act establishing the Board of Public Works—thereby paralysing the arms to which we have looked for protection and security; and, whereas Bayou Plaquemine in its present condition, its mouth unprotected from the entrance of drift wood, Grand River, its main outlet, being closed with drift and sediment, will be the cause as surely as it exists, of the inundation and ruin of the most settled and flourishing portions of the Pariah; and, whereas with such facts and certainty at hand, it becomes the duty of the Parochial authorities to take measures to protect and guard the Parish against an impending danger threatening its most vital interests; Therefore, be it ordained by the Police Jury of the Parish of Iberville, that Messrs. Belfort Marionneaux, Michael Schlatre, jr., and Dr. T. S. Garrett, be and they are hereby appointed Commissioners with full power to devise and superintend the execution of a plan to prevent effectually the drift wood from going down Bayou Plaquemine.

Be it further ordained, &c., That as soon as the water will have fallen sufficiently to allow said Commissioners to commence operations, they are hereby empowered to call upon the Parish negroes, who they shall employ in executing the plan they may devise—returning said negroes under the direction of the Grosse Tete Road Commissioners, as soon as the work will be completed.

Be it further ordained, &c., That the sum of $500 be, and the same is hereby appropriated to purchase materials, &c., for the executing of said work.

Be it further ordained, &c., That the Commissioners are authorized and instructed to communicate with the authorities of the Parish of West Baton Rouge, to obtain their concurrence and assistance in the above work.

Be it further ordained, &c., That in authorizing the said work at the mouth of Bayou Plaquemine, the Police Jury does not pretend to assume any power not delegated to it, but is only acting in self-defence and for the protection of the Parish, in a case for which the Legislature has failed to provide, and for which it cannot provide in time to save the Parish from ruin and devastation.

On motion, resolved, that Articles 101 and 105 of the Patrol Ordinance be, and the same are hereby repealed and the following enacted in their stead.—1st. The Patrol shall be armed and equipped as directed, or deemed proper by the Chief or Patrol. 2nd, The Patrol shall meet at any place or rendezvous designated by the Chief.

The round shall commence at 9 o'clock in the summer, and 8 o'clock in winter, and continue until 3 o'clock in summer, and 4 o'clock in winter; but the hours may be changed whenever the Chief may deem it necessary. The Patrol on duty shall run over the District or be distributed and parted in such a manner by its chief as to render it most efficient, and shall visit all negro quarters and search all cabins deemed suspicious by the Chief.

Resolved further, That the following articles be, and they are hereby incorporated in the Police regulations,—

1st. No slave shall be allowed to own a skiff, or boat of any kind, or traffic with his fellow slaves in any manner whatsoever; and if found so offending, and at the complaint of any one either before a justice of the Peace, or to the commissary of the patrol, he shall receive fifteen lashes.

2nd. Any Planter owning a tract of land at a distance from his home place, and worked or cultivated by the same negroes, or enjoying the privilege of working or using the timber on any land shall at all times keep a white man with them, and in their transit from one place to the other, they shall be accompanied by the Overseer or any other white person employed for the purpose. Any Planter failing to comply with the above regulation, shall upon conviction thereof, be subject to a fine of not less than $25 and not more than $100, recoverable before any Court of competent jurisdiction.

3rd. Whenever a negro wishes to take a wife on a neighboring plantation, he shall only do so with a written permission, both of his owner and that of the woman. He shall be allowed to visit her only twice a week, and then with a pass from his master specifying the nights upon which he has permission to visit her—at what time he must go at night and return in the morning. Any negro found in contravention of the above, shall receive the same punishment as prescribed for the one found without a pass.

On motion of Mr. Roane, it was Resolved, That Arvillian Raffrey, an indigent person, be allowed a pension of $6 per month, payable upon the warrant of the member of the 6th Ward.

On motion, Resolved, That the Clerk of the Police Jury, be and he is hereby authorizsd to make out an estimate exhibiting the various items of expenditures required for the Parish of Iberville, for the current year, 1862, and to cause the same to be published at least 60 days before the next meeting of this Body, to fix and decide on the amount of Parish taxes to be assessed in said Parish, in conformity with the 6th Section of an Act of the Legislature, entitled an Act relative to Police Juries," approved March 9th, 1847.

Then came Allen Jumel, Parish Treasurer, who presented his accounts and vouchers, and the same, after having been examined by the Committee, were found just and correct; and that there is in the hands of the Treasurer a cash balance of $19,266—91 100; whereupon it was Resolved, That said Treasurer's account and vouchers be accepted and approved, and said Treasurer's bond cancelled.

Then the following accounts were allowed, after being approved by the Committee, to wit:

Antoine Blanchard for act of sale....	$12 50
M. T. Snee, fees in criminal matters,	16 80
Theo. Blanchard, Sheriff, to fees &c.	44 63
J. H. Rills, fees in criminal matters,	28 75
James L. Barker	12 50

On motion the Police Jury adjourned until its next regular meeting, 1st Monday of September, 1861.

P. T. COLLE,
S. B. ROANE,
AUG. CHRISTIN,
C. W. KEEP,
B. MARIONNEAUX,
JOHN A. SIGUR,
J. A. DARDENNE, Prest.

Attest—J. H. RILLS, Clerk Police Jury.

The Golden Era.

BROOKS & LAWRENCE, PUBLISHERS, No. 123 CLAY STREET.

SAN FRANCISCO, CALIFORNIA, SUNDAY, JUNE 30, 1861. VOL. IX.---NO. 30.

Poetry.

[Original.]

NATIONAL ODE.

FOR THE

Eighty-Fifth Anniversary of American Independence.

BY CORNY QUILLS.

My Native Land! my Native Land!
It is to thee my Muse would bring
The thoughts, the words, the fire, the deeds,
That from a patriot's bosom spring.
With thrilling lips, on bended knee,
I pledge my fealty to thee.

To be a child of thine is more
Than royal despot ever knew;
There is a largeness in the thought,
That moves me ever to be true.
A freedom broader than a throne,
Has grown in me as thou hast grown.

First in the cause of human weal,
First in the freeman's dauntless heart;
First in the championship of right,
First in the world's commercial mart.
I am a king where'er I view
Thy flag of red, and white and blue.

Unto what grandeur thou hast grown,
Stretching thy arms from sea to sea;
Perfect in form and matchless power,
The world-wide idol of the free;
Dearer and dearer in the sight,
Of Him whose Arm is in thy might.

Long have thy heroes' swords been sheathed,
And long thy reveilles unheard;
Not dumb, but willing to be mute,
From peace unwilling to be stirred.
Alas! alas! the word has sped,
And arm'd the ashes of the dead!

On this thy natal morn they rise,
From Freedom's grave and glory's tomb;
And marshall to thy threatened front,
With scar and never healing wound.
With spirit tread and hand unseen,
They smile where Memory's banners gleam.

From Concord and from Lexington,
From Cambridge and from Bunker Hill;
From Lundy's Lane and Monmouth Bridge,
The heart can hear them tramping still;
With rallying cry and charge forlorn,
Above the dust of Washington!

The blood that stains full many a field,
Grown green beneath the tears of Time,
Blushes beneath the traitor feet,
That desecrate a right divine,
And brings a sternness to the eye
Of those now marching on to die.

Thank God there still is something left,
Of olden fire and noble pride;
To stay the madness of the hour,
When Freedom's progress is denied.
Thank God! there yet is blood and true,
To stripe with *red* the white and blue.

From brawny hills and slumbering vales,
Thy waiting heroes quickly spring;
Columbia! when thy bugles call,
They're swifter than the eagle's wing.
The plough forgot, forsook the mill,
To battle for a nation's will.

Not long the clouds of war shall hide,
The stars that rush to ruin now;
The storm shall pass and with it take
The blasting darkness from thy brow.
Thou canst not fall, thou canst not fail,
While God is just and truth avail.

Too strongly wove with human good,
Too closely twined with human weal;
Thou hast no pause, thou hast no end,
While hearts are true and swords are steel.
More than a mortal curse will fall
On him who dares to weave thy pall.

It cannot, cannot, ever be,
So great a glory so shall end;
No, no, with treach'rous green and black,
The tints of Heaven will not blend.
Still shall thy constellation shine,
Land of the Evergreen and Pine.

On this thy glorious natal day,
With double love and double pride,
I pledge thee as did they of yore,
Who past away but never died;
Life, soul and honor in thy need,
Thy stars and stripes my only creed.

O! not to empty sound I pledge;
Eternal principles are thine;
Howe'er beset—howe'er belied,
Thy future will be more sublime
Than sweetest poet, wisest sage,
Have said or sung of any age.

Thy course may wander wild at times,
And backward lapse to barb'rous shame;
The motto of thy shield is "ON,"
And soon thou goest on again.
Thy fate, thy destiny, decree—
But end, O, Liberty! with thee.

Beloved theme, endearing spell,
I rise from utt'rance unto thought;
Too faint for speech, but free to see,
The glory without shadow wrought;
That slowly dawns, and brightly glows,
Beyond thy Rubicon of foes.

Higher and higher still shall soar,
The Eagles of the freegrown land;
Broader and broader yet shall wave,
The pennons of the Union Band.
All foes shall melt like mist of night,
Before the red, and blue and white.

Whene'er thy grand armorial shows,
The Vulture in the Eagle's nest;
Whene'er thy mighty ensign stoops,
To kiss a craven traitor's crest;
Farewell to hope, farewell to right,
For death and everlasting night.

Thou dost not need a pen like mine,
To paint thy deeds or tell thy fate;
Thy prestige overrunneth Time,
Thy greatness will be more than great.
March on! march on! to matchless might,
God speeds the blue, and red and white. K.

OUR COUNTRY.

Who dies in vain
Upon his country's war fields and within
The shadow of her altars? Feeble heart!
I tell thee that the voice of patriot blood,
Thus pour'd for faith and freedom, hath a tone
Which from the night of ages, from the gulf
Of death shall burst and make its high appeal
Sound unto earth and heaven!—*Mrs. Hemans.*

THE AMERICAN FLAG.

BY JOSEPH RODMAN DRAKE.

I.

When Freedom from her mountain height
Unfurled her standard to the air,
She tore the azure robe of night,
And set the stars of glory there.
She mingled with its gorgeous dyes
The milky baldrick of the skies,
And striped its pure celestial white
With streakings of the morning light;
Then from his mansion in the sun
She called her eagle bearer down,
And gave into his mighty hand
The symbol of her chosen land

II.

Majestic monarch of the cloud,
Who rear'st aloft thy regal form
To hear the tempest trumpings loud,
And see the lightning lances driven;
When stride the warriors of the storm
And rolls the thunder-drum of heaven!
Child of the sun! to thee 'tis given
To guard the banner of the free!
To hover in the sulphur smoke,
To ward away the battle stroke,
And bid its blendings shine afar,
Like rainbows on the cloud of war—
The harbingers of victory!

III.

Flag of the brave! thy folds shall fly,
The signs of hope and triumph high;
When speaks the trumpet's signal tone,
And the long line comes gleaming on,
Ere yet the life-blood, warm and wet,
Has dimm'd the glistening bayonet,
Each soldier's eye shall brightly turn
To where the sky-born glories burn,
And as his springing steps advance
Catch war and vengeance from the glance;
And when the cannon-mouthings loud
Heave in wild wreaths the battle-shroud,
And gory sabers rise and fall
Like shoots of flame on midnight's pall—
Then shall thy meteor glances glow,
And cowering foes shall sink beneath
Each gallant arm that strikes below
That lovely messenger of death!

IV.

Flag of the seas! on ocean's wave
Thy stars shall glitter o'er the brave;
When death careering on the gale,
Sweeps darkly round the bellied sail,
And frighted waves rush wildly back
Before the broadside's reeling rack,
Each dying wanderer of the sea
Shall look at once to Heaven and thee,
And smile to see thy splendors fly
In triumph o'er his closing eye!

V.

Flag of the free heart's hope and home,
By angel hands to valor given,
Thy stars have lit the welkin dome,
And all thy hues were born in heaven!
Forever float that standard sheet
Where breathes the foe but falls before us,
With Freedom's soil beneath our feet,
And Freedom's banner streaming o'er us!

THE STAR-SPANGLED BANNER.

BY FRANCIS S. KEY.

O, say, can you see, by the dawn's early light,
What so proudly we hail at the twilight's last gleaming?
Whose broad stripes and bright stars, through the perilous fight,
O'er the ramparts we watched, were so gallantly streaming?
And the rocket's red glare, the bombs bursting in air,
Gave proof through the night that our flag was still there.

CHORUS.

O, say, does that star-spangled banner yet wave
O'er the land of the free and the home of the brave?

On the shore, dimly seen through the mist of the deep,
Where the foe's haughty host in dread silence reposes,
What is that which the breeze, o'er the towering steep,
As it fitfully blows, half conceals, half discloses?
Now it catches the gleam of the morning's first beam,
In full glory reflected, now shines in the stream.

CHORUS.

'Tis the star-spangled banner—O, long may it wave
O'er the land of the free and the home of the brave!

And where is that band who so vauntingly swore,
Mid the havoc of war, and the battle's confusion,
A home and a country they'd leave us no more?
Their blood has washed out their foul footsteps' pollution;
No refuge could save the hireling and slave
From the terror of flight, or the gloom of the grave.

CHORUS.

And the star-spangled banner in triumph doth wave
O'er the land of the free and the home of the brave.

O, thus be it ever, when freemen shall stand
Between their loved home and war's desolation!
Blessed with victory and peace, may the Heaven-rescued land
Praise the power that hath made and preserved us a nation.
Then conquer we must, when our cause it is just,
And this be our motto: "In God is our trust!"

CHORUS.

And the star-spangled banner in triumph shall wave
O'er the land of the free and the home of the brave.

STAND BY THE FLAG.

Stand by the flag! its stars, like meteors gleaming,
Have lighted Arctic icebergs, Southern seas,
And shone responsive to the stormy beaming
Of old Arcturus and the Pleiades.

Stand by the flag! its stripes have streamed in glory,
To foes a fear, to friends a festal robe;
And spread, in rhythmic lines, the sacred story
Of Freedom's triumph over all the globe.

Stand by the flag!—on land and ocean billow,
By it your fathers stood, unmoved and true;
Living defended—dying, from their pillow.
With their last blessing, passed it on to you.

Stand by the flag! immortal heroes bore it
Through sulphurous smoke, deep moat and armed defence;
And their imperial shades still hover o'er it—
A guard celestial, from Omnipotence.

Stand by the flag! it is a holy treasure;
Though wrong may dim some stars which should be light,
A steady, gentle and persistent pressure
Kindly exerted, yet will set them right.

Stand by the flag!—though death shots round it rattle,
And underneath its waving folds have met
In all the dread array of sanguine battle,
The quivering lance and glittering bayonet.

Stand by the flag—all doubt and treason scorning—
Believe, with courage firm, and faith sublime,
That it will float until the eternal morning,
Pales, in its glories all the lights of time!

Then up with our flag! let it stream on the air!
Though our fathers are cold in their graves,
They had hands that could strike, they had souls that could dare,
And their sons were not born to be slaves!

Up, up with that banner! where'er it may call,
Our millions shall rally around;
A nation of freemen that moment shall fall
When its stars shall be trailed on the ground.

COLUMBIA, THE GEM OF THE OCEAN: OR, THE "RED, WHITE AND BLUE."

O Columbia! the gem of the ocean,
The home of the brave and the free,
The shrine of each patriot's devotion,
A world offers homage to thee.
Thy mandates make heroes assemble,
When Liberty's form stands in view,
Thy banners make tyranny tremble,
When borne by the red, white and blue!

When war waged its wide desolation,
And threatened the land to deform,
The ark, then, of Freedom's foundation,
Columbia, rode safe through the storm!—
With her garlands of victory around her,
When so proudly she bore her brave crew,
With her flag proudly floating before her,
The boast of the red, white and blue!

The wine-cup, the wine-cup bring hither,
And fill you it true to the brim;
May the wreaths they have won never wither,
Nor the star of their glory grow dim!
May the service united ne'er sever,
But they to their colors prove true;
The Army and Navy forever—
Three cheers for the red, white and blue!

HAIL, COLUMBIA!

BY JUDGE HOPKINSON.

Hail, Columbia, happy land,
Hail, ye heroes! heaven-born band,
Who fought and bled in freedom's cause,
Who fought and bled in freedom's cause,
And when the storm of war had gone,
Enjoyed the peace your valor won;
Let independence be your boast,
Ever mindful what it cost,
Ever grateful for the prize,
Let its altar reach the skies;
Firm united let us be,
Rallying round our liberty,
As a band of brothers joined,
Peace and safety we shall find.

Immortal patriots, rise once more!
Defend our rights, defend our shore;
Let no rude foe with impious hand,
Let no rude foe with impious hand,
Invade the shrine where sacred lies
Of toil and blood the well-earned prize;
While offering peace sincere and just
In heaven we place a manly trust,
That truth and justice may prevail,
And every scheme of bondage fail;
Firm united let us be, etc.

Sound, sound the trump of fame!
Let Washington's great name
Ring through the world with loud applause,
Ring through the world with loud applause,
Let every clime to freedom dear
Listen with a joyful ear;
With equal skill, with steady power,
He governs in the fearful hour
Of horrid war, or guides with ease
The happier time of honest peace.
Firm united let us be, etc.

ADAMS AND LIBERTY.

AN OLD NATIONAL SONG.—BY THOMAS PAINE.

[Whatever were his religious errors, he bowed devoutly at the altar of his country.]

Ye sons of Columbia, who bravely have fought,
For those rights, which unstained from your sires had descended,
May you long taste the blessings your valor has bought,
And your sons reap the soil which their fathers defended.
'Mid the reign of mild peace
May your nation increase,
With the glory of Rome and the wisdom of Greece;
And ne'r may the sons of Columbia be slaves,
While the earth bears a plant, or the sea rolls its waves.

In a clime whose rich vales feed the marts of the world,
Whose shores are unshaken by Europe's commotion;
The trident of commerce should never be hurled
To incense the legitimate powers of the ocean.
But should pirates invade,
Though in thunder array'd,
Let your Cannon declare the free charter of Trade.
For ne'er shall the sons of Columbia be slaves,
While the earth bears a plant, or the sea rolls its waves.

The fame of our arms, of our laws the mild sway,
Had justly ennobled our nation in story;
Till the dark cloud of faction obscured our young day,
And enveloped the sun of American glory.
But let the Traitors be told,
Who their country sold,
And bartered their God for his image in gold—
That ne'er shall the sons of Columbia be slaves,
While the earth bears a plant, or the sea rolls its waves.

While France her huge limbs bathes recumbent in blood,
And society's base threats with wide dissolution;
May Peace, like the dove who returned from the flood,
Find an ark of abode in our mild constitution!
[illegible]
Yet the boon we disclaim,
If bought by our Sovereignty, Justice or Fame.
For ne'er shall the sons of Columbia be slaves,
While the earth bears a plant, or the sea rolls its waves.

'Tis the fire of the flint each American warms,
Let Rome's haughty victors beware of collision!
Let them bring all the vast aid of Europe in arms,
We're a world by ourselves, and disclaim a division!
While with patriot pride,
To our laws we're allied,
No foe can subdue us, no faction divide.
For ne'er shall the sons of Columbia be slaves,
While the earth bears a plant, or the sea rolls its waves.

Our mountains are crowned with imperial Oak,
Whose roots, like our liberties, ages have nourished;
But long ere our nation submits to the yoke,
Not a tree shall be left on the field where it flourished.
Should invasion impend,
Every grove would descend;
From the hilltops they shaded our shores to defend.
For ne'er shall the sons of Columbia be slaves,
While the earth bears a plant, or the sea rolls its waves.

Let our patriots destroy Anarch's pestilent worm,
Except liberty's growth should be checked by coercion,
Then let clouds thicken round us, we heed not the storm;
Our realm fears no shock, but the earth's own explosion.
Foes assail us in vain,
Though their fleets bridge the main,
For our altars and laws with our lives we'll maintain.
For ne'er shall the sons of Columbia be slaves,
While the earth bears a plant, or the sea rolls its waves.

Should the tempest of war overshadow our land,
Its bolts could ne'er rend Freedom's temple asunder;
For, unmoved, at its portal would Washington stand,
And repulse, with his breast, the assault of the thunder!
His sword from the sleep
Of its scabbard would leap,
And conduct with its point, every flash to the deep.
For ne'er shall the sons of Columbia be slaves,
While the earth bears a plant, or the sea rolls its waves.

Let Fame to the world sound America's voice;
No intrigue can her sons from their Government sever;
Her pride is her Adams—her laws are her choice,
And shall flourish, till Liberty slumbered forever!
Then unite heart and hand,
Like Leonidas' band,
And swear to the God of the ocean and land,
That ne'er shall the sons of Columbia be slaves,
While the earth bears a plant, or the sea rolls its waves.

E PLURIBUS UNUM.

BY CAPTAIN J. W. CUTTER.

Though many and bright are the stars that appear,
In that flag by our country unfurled,
And the stripes that are swelling in majesty there,
Like a rainbow adorning the world;
Their lights are unsullied as those in the sky,
By a deed that our fathers have done;
And they're leagued in as true and as holy a tie
In their motto of "Many in one."

From that hour when those patriots fearlessly flung
That banner of starlight abroad,
Ever true to themselves, to that motto they clung,
As they clung to the promise of God.
By the bayonet traced at the midnight of war,
On the fields where our glory was won,
O, perish the heart or the hand that would mar
Our motto of "Many in one."

Mid the smoke of the contest—the cannon's deep roar—
How oft it hath gathered renown!
While those stars were reflected in rivers of gore,
When the cross and the lion went down:
And though few were the lights in the gloom of that hour,
Yet the hearts that were striking below
Had God for their bulwark, and truth for their power,
And they stopped not to number the foe.

From where our green mountain-tops blend with the sky,
And the giant St. Lawrence is rolled,
To the waves where the balmy Hesperides lie,
Like the dream of some prophet of old,
They conquered, and, dying, bequeathed to our care,
Not this boundless dominion alone,
But that banner, whose loveliness hallows the air,
And their motto of "Many in one."

We are many in one while there glitters a star
In the blue of the heavens above;
And tyrants shall quail 'mid their dungeons afar,
When they gaze on that motto of love.
It shall gleam o'er the sea, 'mid the bolts of the storm,
Over the tempest, and battle, and wreck;
And flame where our guns with their thunder grow warm,
'Neath the blood on the slippery deck.

The opressed of the earth to that standard shall fly,
Wherever its folds shall be spread;
And the exile shall feel 'tis his own native sky,
Where its stars shall float over his head;
And those stars shall increase till the fulness of time
Its millions of cycles has run;
Divide as we may in our own native land,
To the rest of the world we are one.

THE BATTLE-FIELD.

A thousand hearts are great within my bosom;
Advance our standards, set upon our foes;
Our ancient word of courage, fair saint George,
Inspire us with the spleen of fiery dragons!
Upon them! Victory sits on our helms.
Shaks. Richard III.

[Written for the Golden Era.]

FIGHTING FOR HIS COTTON.

BY HIDALGO.

Among the earliest and wealthiest of the settlers of St. Louis, was John Mulanthey, Esq., an Irish gentleman of good birth and better education. Possessed already of a large fortune, he invested largely in real estate on and about the site of the now vast western metropolis, and with the foresight of a good financier, calmly awaited a "rise," in property. A tide of emigration flowed more than it ebbed toward the great commercial centre of the Mississippi Valley, but its days of repletion had not yet come. The more tangible lands of Western New York, Pennsylvania and Ohio, attracted the eye of the hardy pioneer, and even Indiana was as yet a wilderness where the red deer bounded in joyous freedom through green lawns hitherto untramped save by the beaded moccasin of the warlike Shawnee. The palmy days of Missouri had not yet come, and the great capitalist, the hero of our narrative, was biding his time.

Mr. Mulanthey was, at the date of the circumstance we are about to relate, already a man past the meridian of life, and had a large family growing up about him. One of his daughters has since married Col. John O'Fallon, a soldier and a gentleman, who now enjoys his *otium cum dignitate* in the city of St. Louis. Another married that rough diamond of the American army, Gen. William Harney, the best abused man and the most honest soldier in the service—(long life and better luck to him.) Mrs. Harney died about a year ago, and left all her property, valued at three millions of dollars, to her husband, his heirs and executors. Her father was a man who was close and shrewd, without being downright miserly; hospitable, but not lavish in his mode of living; stern and dignified in his mien, avoiding the disagreeable extreme of cold *hauteur* which repels cordiality, and deadens friendship. On Change, small as was the St. Louis "Bourse" in those days, his deportment was affable and gentlemanly, and no money-lender was as popular as Mr. Mulanthey, who loaned money at rather easy terms, only he never took aught save the best of security. [Like neighbor King, of the gold escutcheon marked "Money Cheap," he wanted the collateral, and moreover he always ses it.]

By-and-bye there came rumors of war. The Union Jack of England stooped to boarding the peaceful, being merchant vessels owned and commanded by [illegible], and commenced the piratical [illegible] under the asserted "Right of Search." The blood that had warmed at Bunker Hill, Saratoga, Yorktown and Cowpens, was not yet chilled. England had tried (this was not the first time) to rule her fractious daughter with a rod of iron; Miss Columbia had armed herself with a long one of "Old Hickory."

And so the war began. The farmer left his unscoured plow in the mould, the grazier deserted his peaceful lowing flock on the hill-side, and the sombre visaged smithy dropped the massive sledge beside his anvil.

From the Chattahoochee to the Penobscot, from the turbulent foaming, crested Chesapeake, to the calm, polished bosom of Huron, went up the cry of "To arms!" as if a single voice had raised its tone in freedom's name. The whole country was on the war path, and the very schoolboy snatched down "dad's" yager from the elkhorns above the fireplace, while his mother, with choking sobs, slung the powder horn around his neck, kissed his beardless cheek, and bade him go where Liberty and Honor had "blazed the trail."

Provisions naturally began to rise in value, and money was hard to acquire. Planters were obliged to sell off crops for little or nothing, in order to support their families and servants. This offered the shavers new chances, and among those to avail themselves of this emergency, was Mr. Mulanthey. He descended the mighty main artery of America—the Mississippi, and bought up cotton at ten dollars per bale, which he "flatted" to New Orleans, and stored along the levee, awaiting the withdrawal of the blockading squadron in the Gulf. But fortifications were wanted to prevent the incursions of the forces of Gibbs and Packenham. Bricks and mortar were scarce, and there was no time to make them; besides they were expensive and Uncle Sam was poor. In the midst of this emergency, General Jackson, in command of the South-western division, hit on a plan to build a fort of bales of cotton. As he had none of his own, he took those of Mr. John Mulanthey, and commenced the erection of breastworks. I believe that cotton breastworks are by no means unfashionable at this very day, and think there is often considerable danger from being exposed to the fire of beautiful eyes from behind them.

This seizure of cotton was accomplished in the temporary absence of Mulanthey, whose rage, on learning the circumstance, knew no bounds. He devised a dozen expedients for revenge on "Old Hickory," but as readily abandoned them. At last, he hit upon the plan of calling on the merchants and property-holders of New Orleans to sustain him in the loss of his property, the aforesaid cotton. More or less must certainly be damaged; and as it would be ruined in defence of their houses, goods and chattels, it was but fair they should proffer some remuneration. But they all gave him one answer: "Go and see General Jackson; whatever is right, in his opinion, that we will do."

That afternoon, a messenger informed the commander that a gentleman was awaiting an audience with him. In reply to the hasty "Show him up," a gentleman, with white hair done up in a queue, black knee breeches and white silk stockings, entered the general's marquee. General Jackson motioned him to a seat:

"Your name is—"

"John Mulanthey!"

"Of St. Louis?"

"The same; I am the owner of the cotton you seized to fortify this place. As much of it will be necessarily injured for sale, I have petitioned the merchants to give me some bond of indemnity or security for the loss of my cotton in the preservation of their buildings and storehouses. They referred me to you, General, saying they would abide by your decision in the matter."

"You shall have it," said the General, as he drew aside the curtains and snatched a musket from the hands of a sentry, "here it is. Indemnity for the past—shoulder arms; security for the future—shoot down every Englishman you see, by the Eternal?"

It was in vain that the *millionaire* objected to this indemnity. Jackson made him drill with his corps, and take up the regular duty of the camp. He was too good an Irishman not to fight, and cowardice was not one of his failings.

It is not my intention to speak of the glorious affair of the 8th of January, 1815, for it is "familiar as a household word everywhere, from where the still undimmed Stars and Stripes float over the sandy bluffs of Michilmackinack, to the spot where a horde of traitors have raised the filthy palmetto and rattlesnake rag on the banks of the Rio Grande. Every man in America honored and praised Andrew Jackson as the salvator of his country, but *one.* That man was John Mulanthey; he didn't go a picayune on General Jackson, he didn't. But what cared the hero of Orleans for his hate; he valued him as lightly as did Sampson the men of Askelon.

Ten years had rolled away, and St. Louis had grown fourfold. The rise in real estate had made Mulanthey's wealth great enough to fill the coffers of a mogul. But now he had got old and childish, and so afraid was he that his negro servants would murder him for his money, that he caused them to be locked up at sundown each night, in a dungeon constructed for that purpose. He crossed about the streets daily, loaning money and shaving notes, although he was too infirm to walk very far at a time. Overcome with fatigue he strolled into a bookstore to rest himself. The stock was being sold at auction, [*a la Roman,*] and an auctioneer held up a book, saying:

"Here's the life of Gen. Andrew Jackson, gentle*men*; how much am I bid for it?" asked the knight of the red flag.

"Fufty cints," said Mr. Mulanthey, in a thin voice, "that's two bits more than its worth."

"Who the divil said that?" cried a stout Irish grocer from Second street. "Ah Misther Mulanthey, is that you? now, I'll bid five dollars. I say, gintlemen, d'yes know the raison why Misther John Mulanthey don't like Gineral Jackson? I'll tell yees; he made him shouldher a mushket, be Jasus, an' fight for"—here he hesitated, and a gentleman in the crowd asked—"his country?"

"Not a divil an' inch iv it," said Duffy, the grocer, "Misther Mulanthey was *fightin for his cotton.*"

Who could deny that "Cotton was King" after that? Surely not a HIDALGO.

The "Fourth" in our National History.

The fourth day of the month is a great day in our history as a nation. The instances cited to prove this fact—eight in number—are as follows.

April 4, 1609—Hudson discovered the Bay of New York.

July 4, 1776—Declaration of Independence.

Oct. 4, 1777—Battle of Germantown.

Oct. 4, 1777—Articles of Confederation signed.

[illegible] a great service [illegible] the colonies. [illegible] me weeks after, Washington resigned command [illegible] army, and retired to private [illegible] line.

July 4, 1815—The Algerine Admiral captured by an American squadron; the Dey makes advantageous terms of peace to America.

March 4—Presidential Inauguration.

August 4, 1858—Arrival of the Atlantic Telegraph fleet both upon the British and American shores.

This enumeration ignores many prominent and striking events in American annals associated with the fourth day of the month, as the following more extended list will show. We place the items in their chronological order:

August 4, 1492—Columbus, with his adventurous companions, lost sight of the last peak of the old world in their wondrous voyage in search of the new.

Nov. 4, 1493—Columbus discovered Guadaloupe.

August 4, 1609—Hudson discovered Cape Cod.

Oct. 4, 1609—Henry Hudson completed his exploration of the "Hudson" River, and sailed for home to report his discovery.

March 4, 1629—Massachusetts Patent confirmed by Charles I.

March 4, 1638—Massachusetts Patent demanded by the British Crown.

March 4, 1681—The Charter of Pennsylvania signed by Charles II.

April 4, 1704—The first newspaper in the United States estaplished at Boston, called the Boston *News Letter.* It was published seventy years.

July 4, 1754—The Commissioners of the American Colonies met at Albany.

August 4, 1759—Crown Point taken from the French.

March 4, 1776—The American army took possession of Dorchester Heights.

February 4, 1783—Cessation of hostilities with Great Britain.

January 4, 1784—Treaty of Peace signed between the United States and Great Britain.

March 4, 1789—The first Congress of the United States assembled in New York, and the Federal Constitution went into effect.

March 4, 1791—Vermont admitted into the Union.

June 4, 1791—First Legislature of Kentucky met.

June 4, 1801—The American prisoners at Tripoli liberated.

February 4, 1808—First Legislative proceedings in relation to the New York canals.

July 4, 1817—The construction of the Erie Canal commenced.

Dec. 4, 1819—Alabama admitted into the Union.

Nov. 4, 1825—First boat down the Erie Canal arrived at New York.

July 4, 1826—John Adams and Thomas Jefferson died.

July 4, 1831—James Munroe died.

July 4, 1845—Texas annexed to the United States.

July 4, 1848—Treaty of Peace with Mexico proclaimed. The corner stone of the Washington Monument, at the Federal city, was laid this date.

YANKEE DOODLE.

THE ORIGINAL VERSES OF THE REVOLUTION.

Father and I went down to camp, along with Captain Goodwin;
And there we saw the men and boys as thick as hasty pudding.

CHORUS.

Yankee Doodle keep it up, Yankee Doodle dandy,
Mind the music and the step, and with the girls be handy.

And there was Captain Washington, upon a slapping stallion,
A-giving orders to his men,—I guess there was a million.
CHORUS.—Yankee Doodle, etc.

And there they had a swamping gun, as big as a log of Maple,
On a deuced little cart—a load for father's cattle.
CHORUS.—Yankee Doodle, etc.

But I can't tell you half I see, they kept up such a smother;
So I took my hat off, made a bow, and scampered home to mother.
CHORUS.—Yankee Doodle, etc.

HISTORY OF OUR FLAG.

Rev. Dr. Putnam, of Roxbury, Mass., in a late sermon, gave the subjoined sketch of our flag:

The history of our glorious old flag is of exceeding interest, and brings back to us a throng of sacred and thrilling associations. The banner of St. Andrew was blue, charged with a white saltier or cross, in the form of the letter X, and was used in Scotland as early as the eleventh century. The banner of St. George was white, charged with the red cross, and was used in England as early as the first part of the fourteenth century. By a royal proclamation dated April 12th, 1706, these two crosses were joined together upon the same banner, forming the ancient national flag of England. It was not until Ireland, in 1801, was made a part of Great Britain, that the present national flag of England, so well known as the Union Jack, was completed. But it was the *ancient* flag of England that, constituted the basis of our own American banner. Various other flags had indeed been raised at different times by our colonial ancestors. But they were not particularly associated with, or at least, were not incorporated into, and made a part of the destined "stars and stripes." It was after Washington had taken command of the fresh army of the Revolution, at Cambridge, that January 2, 1776, he unfurled before them the new flag of thirteen stripes of alternate red and white, having upon one of its corners, the red and white crosses of St. George and St. Andrew, on a field of blue. And this was the standard which was borne into the city of Boston when it was evacuated by the British troops and was entered by the American army. Uniting, as it did, the flags of England and America, it showed that the colonists were not yet prepared to sever the tie that bound them to the mother country. By that union of flags they claimed to be a vital and substantial part of the empire of Great Britain, and demanded the rights and privileges which such a relation implied. Yet it was by those thirteen stripes that they made known the union *also* of the thirteen colonies, the stripes of white declaring the purity and innocence of their cause, and the stripes of red giving forth defiance to cruelty and oppression.

On the fourteenth day of June, 1777, it was resolved by Congress, "That the flag of the thirteen United Sates be thirteen stripes, alternate red and white, and that the union be thirteen white stars in a blue field." The resolution was first made public, Sept. 3, 1777, and the flag that was made and used in pursuance of it was that which led the Americans to victory at Saratoga. Here the thirteen stars were arranged in a circle, as we sometimes see them now, in order better to express the Union of the States. In 1794, there having been two more new States added to the Union, it was voted that the alternate stripes, as well as the circling stars, be fifteen in number, and the flag as thus altered and enlarged, was the one which was borne through all the contests of the war of 1812. But it was thought that the flag would at length become too large if a new stripe should be added with every freshly-admitted State. It was therefore enacted, in 1818, that a permanent return should be made to the original number of thirteen stripes, and that the number of stars should henceforth correspond to the growing number of States. Thus the flag would symbolize the Union as it might be at any given period of its history, and also as it was at the very hour of its birth. It was at the same time suggested, that these stars, instead of being arranged into a circle, be formed into a single star—a suggestion which we occasionally see adopted. In fine, no particular order seems now to be observed with respect to the arrangement of the constellation. It is enough, if only the whole number be there upon that azure fold—the blue to be emblematical of perseverance, vigilance, and justice, each star to glorify the glory of the State it may represent, and the whole to be eloquent forever, of a union that must be "one and inseparable."

Time would fail me to enter more largely into the details of this history. Enough has been said to show, in some satisfactory measure, the sources whence the materials of our flag were drawn. The old banner of England contributed its colors. Great men made it their study. Washington, Adams, Franklin, Morris, Sherman, and many more of their immortal compeers gave it their thought and care. And then it had to be made a fact in the world by the conflicts, bloodshed, and victories, of a seven years' war. It is the flag that was gazed upon by the patriots of "the times that tried men's souls." It is the flag which they bore and followed into the thickest of the fight. It is the flag which they loved and honored, and which at last they compelled their proud enemies to acknowledge and respect. It is the flag which became the symbol of our national independence and glory.

And what precious associations have clustered around it since! Not alone did our fathers set up this banner in the name of God over the well-won battle-fields of the Revolution, and over the cities and towns which they rescued from despotic rule; but think where also their descendants have carried it and raised it in conquest or protection. Through what clouds of dust and smoke it has passed—what storms of shot and shell—what scenes of fire and blood—Not alone at Saratoga, at Monmouth, and at Yorktown, but at Lundy's Lane and New Orleans, at Buena Vista and Chepultepec. It is the same glorious old flag which inscribed with the dying words of Lawrence, "Don't give up the ship," was hoisted on Lake Erie by Commodore Perry just on the eve of his great naval victory—the same old flag which our great chieftain bore in triumph to the proud city of the Aztecs and planted upon the heights of her national palace. Brave hands have raised it above the eternal regions of ice in the Arctic seas, and have set it up on the summits of the lofty mountains in the distant west. Where has it not gone, the pride of its friends and the terror of its foes? What countries and what seas has it not visited? Where has not the American citizen been able to stand beneath its guardian folds and defy the world? With what joy and exultation seamen and tourists have gazed upon its stars and stripes, and read in it the history of their nation's glory, and received from it the full sense of security, and drawn from it the inspiration of patriotism! By it, how many have sworn fealty to their country! What bursts of magnificent eloquence it has called from Webster and from Everett! What lyric strains of poetry from Drake and Holmes! How many heroes its folds have covered in death! How many have lived for it, and how many have died for it! How many, living and dying, have said, in their enthusiastic devotion to its honor, like that young wounded sufferer in the streets of Baltimore, "Oh! the flag—the Stars and the Stripes!" And wherever that flag has gone, it has been the herald of a better day. It has been the pledge of freedom, of justice, of order, of civilization, and of Christianity. Tyrants only have hated it, and the enemies of mankind alone have trampled it to the earth. All who sigh for the triumph of Truth and Righteousness, salute it."

PENNSYLVANIA AVENUE, WASHINGTON—THE GRAND PARADE OF THE UNITED STATES ARMY.

4th of JULY EXTRA--PICTORIAL EDITION.

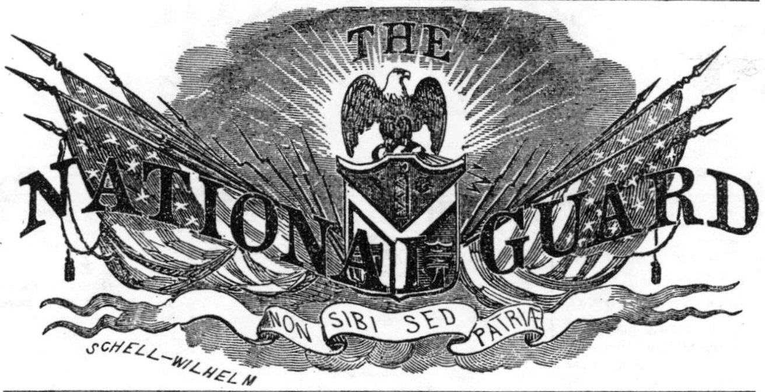

"Hemp Cravats for all Disunionists."

VOL. 2. CAMP PENNSYLVANIA, BALTIMORE, MD., JULY 4, 1861. NO. 3.

It being a custom for all patriotic citizens, as well as of all public bodies, to celebrate the glorious Anniversary of our Nation's Independence, and as the Newspaper press universally indulge in patriotic editorials of an elaborate and comprehensive character,—and as we feel ourselves entitled to credit for a certain amount of patriotism, have, since our organization, been a public body, and are now extensively engaged in the Newspaper business, we felt that we should not allow the day to pass by, without celebrating it in some way. As the article of money has become with us, "*among the things of the past*," not having received a cent of pay since we left home, many of our men now being engaged in the solution of the problem how to support a family at home without money—we at once abandoned the idea of a pyrotechnic display. As we live upon the "*fat of the hog*," and not the "*fat of the land*," a very small margin was allowed for a "fete champetre." A dress parade was next thought of,—but as rags are not usually considered as emblematic of elegance and full dress—that was also condemned, we not caring to have our men appear in *undress* upon such a glorious occasion. Speeches and orations were at once pronounced as "*played out*." At length we determined that we would publish a Special Number of our extensive sheet, expressly for the occasion—and not wishing to expose ourselves to the severe criticisms of "The Press," by exciting their envy with one of our elaborate, chaste, elegant and patriotic effusions, we determined to issue a "Jubilee Edition," that our boys might be able to enjoy a laugh, without the aid of them $10,000 appropriated for the celebration of the day by the "Home Guard." After immense toil and severe labor, sleepless nights and deep research, and the employment of the most distinguished and extraordinary talent, we submit the result of our labors to the inspection of our patrons and an admiring world.

"Au Reservoir."

Principal occupation of "**HOME GUARD**."—"The Girls we left behind us."

Kane Man.

Man Merry.

Capt. Co. I.—Boy, where's that Sirloin of Beef.
Boy.—Warm weather hurried it off before the appointed hour, Sir.

Vinyard, or Gunpowder—Te mpest.

Red Brigade Muster—
Jakes' superior Pruned Relief.

Marshall Kane.

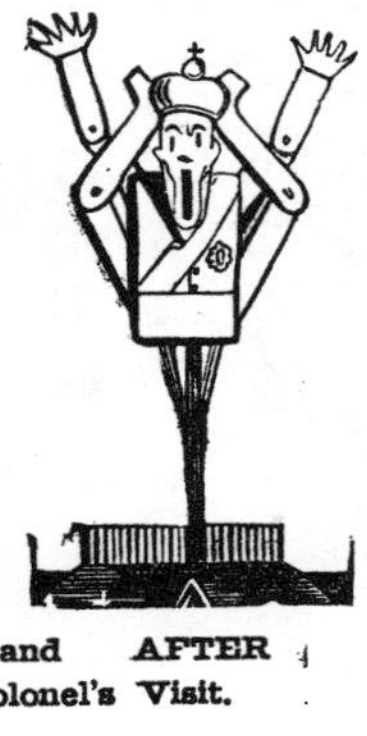

BEFORE and AFTER
The Colonel's Visit.

Kane at Fort McHenry.

Sergeant Wickedshad.—Tell the General, that I put up that broom, and that if he has any objections to it—to send one of my size to take it down.

A HOME GUARD—"At Home."

Drawing supplies from the Patapsco.

McBride the Rash, reconnoitering the village, in obedience to special orders: supposed intention of the rebels to make a sortie upon the caravan, for legal exchange demanded at Fort Vinyard.

From Daguerreotype, by Bones & Myers.

A HOME GUARD "In Battle."

Doestick's Zouave Drill—Right-winged.

Theatrical troupe—Wood, manager.

The Lady that lost her Portmonnaie.

Gen. Beauregard at Fort Sumter,

At Fort Pickens,

At Manassas Gap,

At Richmond.

The Philadelphia Inquirer.

ESTABLISHED 1829. | PHILADELPHIA, SATURDAY, JULY 13, 1861. | PRICE TWO CENTS.

THE REBELLION.

HIGHLY IMPORTANT NEWS.

FROM GEN. McCLELLAN'S COLUMN.

GREAT BATTLE IN WESTERN VIRGINIA.

REBELS ROUTED WITH HEAVY LOSS.

CAPTURE OF HORSES, WAGONS, CAMP EQUIPAGE, &c.

Official Report of the Battle at Rich Mountain.

ROUT OF THE REBELS IN MISSOURI.

HOSTILE ATTITUDE OF FRANCE.

MOVEMENTS OF THE ENEMY.

THE TROOPS CROSSING THE POTOMAC.

THE PRIVATEER JEFF. DAVIS AT WORK.

FOUR VESSELS CAPTURED

A Rebel Newspaper Suppressed.

ARREST OF POTOMAC PIRATES.

ANOTHER ATTEMPT TO SEIZE A STEAMER.

THE PIRATE SCHOONER CAPTURED

ARREST OF A SPY.

THE LATEST FROM WASHINGTON.

Special Despatches to the Inquirer.

Our Relations with Spain.

WASHINGTON, July 12.—The domestic troubles by which the country is convulsed are of such engrossing interest that it is no wonder that our foreign relations are kept somewhat out of sight. Yet they cannot be overlooked, for they are, in fact, closely connected with the progress of the suppression of the rebellion. If the blockade of the Southern ports, for instance, is made really effective, (as Mr. SEWARD says it shall be) there is not the slightest danger of English or French interference. While it is just as certain that English and French merchant vessels *will* run the blockade, under the guns of their men-of-war, if the blockade is *not* made effective. In a word, this whole matter of blockade will be conducted upon the strict principles of international law. But France and England are not the only troublesome neighbors that we have. Spain, also, is taking advantage of this critical time to annoy us. Spain now is ruled by a young and ambitious Queen, whose ministers find her determined to attempt to recover to the Spanish crown all of the ancient possessions of that monarchy in America, among which is the whole of Mexico. A warm friend of our late Minister, Mr. SOULÉ, and well informed through him of the state of affairs here, Queen ISABELLA has doubtless formed a prejudice against the North, and a preference for the cause of the Southern States. She knows, at all events, that if she wishes to prosecute her designs on Mexico, she can never have so favorable a time as the present, when we are distracted with our civil war. And accordingly we find her agents stealthily at work, and the Dominican affair is the first step in her programme.

It was in reference to this matter that the resolution passed the House on Wednesday, calling upon the President for information upon the subject, and asking him what protest, if any, our Government has made against this insolent and aggressive conduct on the part of Spain. It will soon be time now, too, to hear from CARL SHURZ. It has been intimated that his notorious radicalism, and the fact of his being an avowed infidel, while ISABELLA is a devout Catholic, will cause the latter to refuse to receive him. If this should be the case, it will be indicative, on the part of the Queen, of a desire to come to an open rupture with this country. If he is received, however, we may soon look for some energetic action on his part. Mr. SEWARD has, doubtless, furnished him with instructions equally decided in tone as those furnished to Messrs. ADAMS and DAYTON.

Position of France.

In case of an imbroglio with Spain, however, where will France be found? The answer to this question is found in the recent conduct and language of NAPOLEON; in the fact that four French officers of high rank are now serving in the Confederate army; in the further fact that Prince CAMILLE DE POLIGNAC, who has recently had an interview with JEFF. DAVIS, evidently desirous of playing the *rôle* of LAFAYETTE, and in the still further fact that numerous agents of the French Government are at this moment engaged in buying up cotton and tobacco in the Southern States.

Movements of the Enemy.

The recent singularly dilatory movements of our forces across the river seem to have inspired the enemy with renewed courage and activity. It is reported this morning, that our scouts near Fairfax have discovered that the enemy was largely reinforced there last night, and that among the new arrivals were four brass field pieces, in addition to those known to have arrived there on Wednesday. The statement that the enemy have retreated from Fairfax is incorrect. It arose from the marching backwards and forwards on the roads of several newly arrived regiments, who were going through battalion and field manœuvres.

And here I may mention another fact. If Gen. SCOTT believed the ridiculous stories that have been so industriously circulated, that the Rebels were decimated by the measles, that they are badly fed and worse armed, that they were deserting by whole companies, that they have no *esprit du corps*, that there is not more than 15,000 of them between here and Manassas, (some accounts say even less than 10,000), he would have attacked and routed them long ago. With 30,000 of our troops, including SHERMAN'S Battery and that of the Rhode Island Regiment, he could, in a single day, rout and utterly exterminate *such* a horde, and, planting our victorious eagles at Manassas Junction, hold the intervening country with the remaining 60,000 troops now here. The moral effect of such a victory would be worth more than the victory itself. It would at once revive the drooping spirits of our soldiers; it would silence the croakings of a carping press in New York; it would give us such prestige abroad that we would hear no more about English or French interference, or about the recognition of a Southern Confederacy by France.

But General SCOTT is too old a soldier to base his movements upon hearsay, or upon such weak inventions of the enemy as exaggerated reports of their weakness, circulated by themselves and their agents in this city, for the very purpose of leading us, through blind, vain confidence, into an ambuscade. His movements are based upon actual knowledge of the enemy's strength, obtained by himself in his own way. This knowledge prevents him from being led into any such snare. With the whole of his comprehensive plan for the suppression of the rebellion clearly marked out, he will not deviate from it to appease the noisy clamor of any clique. His plan cannot fail, and in due time it will be executed.

A Knotty Question.

It is said that the question will be soon raised whether we shall continue to extend to the Rebels the privileges attendant on a flag of truce. There is more in the question than at first appears.

According to the acknowledged principles of international law, and the practice of modern warfare, the privileges of a flag of truce are to be granted only to "nations" at war with us, or to belligerents occupying that position. Now, the men whom we are fighting do not constitute a nation; and it is to prevent them from becoming a nation that we are fighting them. They are *rebels* against our and their own National Government, and are not therefore entitled to any of the rights of "nations" or of belligerents.

Therefore it is wrong, not only to grant them the privileges of a flag of truce, but also to treat with them for an exchange of prisoners. The true doctrine is that expressed by the President himself, "no compromise with traitors; and no argument but at the cannon's mouth." Congress has shown an unmistakable intention to sustain the President in this line of policy. If we give the Rebels the rights of belligerent nations by receiving their flags of truce, and exchanging prisoners with them, we cannot complain of European nations for giving them the other rights of belligerent nations.

Naval Affairs.

The Special Committee of the Senate, appointed to prepare a bill for promoting the efficiency of the Army and Navy, is in session today. Nothing is known as to the result of their labors, but from the well-known character of the members of the Committee, it is believed that they will avoid all measures such as those adopted by the Naval Retiring Board some years ago, which broke the hearts of so many brave men, and brought such disaster on the Naval service. They will probably conclude their labors at an early day, and report immediately.

More Troops Crossing.

Five more regiments crossed the Potomac today with their baggage trains and camp equipage. They will take the place of those regiments which were advanced this morning towards Fairfax.

Evils of Hasty Legislation.

Already the evils of hasty legislation are apparent. The House seems disposed to hurry through the whole business of the session in a few days, and to pass, or refuse to pass, the most important measures, with the least possible consideration. This is all wrong, and will so be seen when it will be too late to remedy the evils that such a course will entail. The more haste the less speed, always. The true maxim in legislation, as in other matters, is to make haste slowly.

Yesterday, when Mr. LEHMAN moved to appropriate the paltry sum of $50,000, in order to place Fort Delaware in a suitable state of defence, the motion was contemptuously rejected. If Mr. LEHMAN had been allowed to explain how urgent was the necessity for this appropriation, it would have passed. Mr. SPAULDING, of New York, to his honor be it said, did attempt to speak in its favor, and began to demonstrate how necessary such an expenditure was, but he was not allowed to continue. The motion of Mr. TROWBRIDGE, of Michigan, also, to appropriate a million of dollars for the completion of the defensive works on the right bank of the Potomac, and for the construction of other works on this side, was in the same summary manner voted down.

"To Speak, or Not to Speak?"

To speak, or not to speak, on the great measures now before Congress, that is the question. Whether 'tis better in blind haste to pass them, and repent of the mischief so done hereafter; or to examine them carefully, make them *right*, and then pass them, is the question that every representative ought to consider. It seems to be the disposition in both Houses, to listen patiently to the speeches of the half-dozen members *against* the bills, and then contemptuously disdain to reply to them, but to pass the bills over their heads, without a word of explanation. Such a course would indeed be the most cutting rebuke that could be administered to the disaffected members. But such a course would not satisfy the country. There is not—at least there ought not to be—anything in any of the bills now pending, that will not bear the closest scrutiny and the minutest investigation. Let the bills then be discussed at moderate length; let their provisions be fully explained, and their purposes fully set forth.

Washington Rumors.

The city has been filled with a rumor to day, in relation to the objects and purposes of the Government with regard to the war, which it is right that you should have, although I do not credit it. The impression has been gaining ground ever since the end of last week, that it is a political, and not a military reason, that now keeps our troops inactive. The mysterious letter from JEFF. DAVIS, and the studied care of the Administration to keep its contents secret, are now said to be directly connected with this continued inactivity. The talismanic word "Peace" is now whispered, startling as it is to hear it amid the constant tramp of armed squadrons, the ceaseless roll of drums, and all the pride, pomp and circumstance of glorious war. It is impossible to give these rumors any definite shape, because they have no shape.

They float in the air and permeate everywhere. In the camps the officers are gloomy, and the men discontented. "Why are we not led against the enemy?" they ask. "In a few days," continue the three months men, "our time will be up, and we have not, and will not have, a shot at the enemy before we go home."

Really, the loss to the service of these three months' regiments will be very great. They are the best and most effective regiments in the field.

No Abolitionism.

A great deal of bad feeling has been created among the more moderate Republicans by the introduction of the irrepressible negro, in the shape of Mr. LOVEJOY'S resolution in regard to fugitive slaves. LOVEJOY is a most violent and radical Abolitionist. In conversation he does not hesitate to declare openly that he chiefly rejoices in this war because it will free the slaves. LOVEJOY has private griefs to avenge, but he ought not to bring them into Congress. His resolution is looked upon as an attempt to drag the slavery question into Congress, and as affording proof of the assertion made by the enemies of the Administration, that this is a war primarily against slavery and slaveholders.

The Cavalry Regiments.

An order has been issued from the War Department that horses and equipments for the several Cavalry Regiments being organized, be purchased by the Government, and that the regiments report themselves in Washington immediately. ANDREW F. McREYNOLDS, W. H. YOUNG, and FITZ HENRY WARREN, have been sworn as Colonels. McREYNOLD, for the New York and Pennsylvania Regiments,—YOUNG for the Kentucky Regiment, and WARREN for the Western. Colonel McREYNOLDS has left to bring on his, but it is said Colonels YOUNG and WARREN will remain here to receive theirs, as their several companies shall come on.

Arrival of Recruits.

A delegation of 150 recruits, with two howitzers, for the New York Fourteenth Regiment, now at Arlington Heights, arrived here yesterday.

The Second Regiment howitzer corps, with four howitzers and a six-pounder field-piece, also arrived.

Arrival of Horses and Wagons.

At an early hour yesterday morning, a train arrived, bringing 200 horses and a large number of baggage wagons. A large number of horses also arrived during the day, which are to be used for the cavalry.

Navy Yard Matters.

Everything continues as busy as ever at the yard.

In the anchor shop, the hands, under the superintendence of master-workman JOHN TUCKER, are busily engaged in making the heavy anchors for the sloop-of-war *Pensacola*, now lying at the dock. She is to be provided with five seven thousand-pound anchors, besides eight small ones, varying from one thousand pounds down to fifty pounds.

Congressional Matters.

The Senate this morning adopted an amendment to the Volunteer bill (authorizing the enlistment of five hundred thousand men), directing the acceptance of all artillery, cavalry and infantry regiments that may be tendered for three years.

The peace proposition introduced by Senator SAULSBURY in the Senate, this morning, is substantially the old CRITTENDEN compromise—that and nothing more.

Arrest of Potomac Pirates.

ATTEMPTS TO SEIZE A STEAMER FOILED.

BALTIMORE, July 12.—Another bold plot to seize one of our river steamers by the Rebels, has just transpired. The steamer *Chester*, as before stated, was sent by the Government, a few days since, down the bay in search for a schooner fitted out by Colonel THOMAS, the French lady, but returned unsuccessful.

Yesterday morning the steamer *Pioneer* left here for her usual trip to Annapolis, West River, Cambridge and Easton; and on returning this evening, landed four prisoners at Fort McHenry, upon the charge of piracy; having, as is alleged, been concerned in the seizure of the steamer *St. Nicholas*. The *Pioneer* left Cambridge this afternoon. The prisoners came to Cambridge in a canoe about 12 o'clock on Thursday night, having with them a large box filled with carbines, Colt's revolvers, cutlasses, sabre bayonets, cartridge boxes, buck shot, &c.

The circumstances being suspicious, they were arrested by the civil authorities and taken into custody by a platoon of the Dorchester Home Guards, who had charge of them till they reached the Fort. Two of the prisoners were recognized as Baltimoreans, and are said to have belonged to Colonel THOMAS' expedition.

THE PIRATE SCHOONER SEIZED—A FIGHT AT CAMBRIDGE, MD.

BALTIMORE, July 12.—The steamer *Arrow*, which left here yesterday with a detachment of troops, made another search for the pirate schooner, and found her aground on a shoal off Egg Neck Narrows. She had been abandoned by the crew. A guard was left on board, and a tug has been sent to tow her up.

There seems to be no doubt from various circumstances, that the design was to seize the steamer *Chester*. When the steamer *Pioneer* left Cambridge, a prominent Secessionist on the wharf gave three cheers for JEFF. DAVIS, which was the signal for a regular free fight between the Secessionists and Union men there gathered. Pistols and bowie knives were freely used, and it is the opinion of some of the passengers that several parties sustained serious injury.

Governor HICKS was seen standing on the wharf at the time.

Arrest of a Spy.

A RELATIVE OF SENATOR MASON.

WASHINGTON, July 12.—The steamer *James Guy* went to Port Tobacco, Md., yesterday, at 4½ P. M., after TALIAFERRO, a late clerk in the Navy Department, a Virginian, and son-in-law of ex-Senator MASON, of that State. He went thither by land yesterday, and Captain DARLING, of the Capitol police, discovering the fact, charged him with being a spy of JEFF. DAVIS. The latter obtained the *James Guy* and went in pursuit. The *Guy* arrived at Port Tobacco in the night, and found TALIAFERRO, who was arrested, taken on board and brought hither a prisoner, arriving here at 4½ to-day.

A large bundle of letters, addressed to prominent citizens in the South, was found on him; also plans of the locations of our camps in and around Washington.

Boarded by a Privateer.

BOSTON, July 12.—The ship *Mary Goodell*, Captain McGILVERY, from New York bound to Buenos Ayres, arrived at Portland this afternoon, and reports that she was boarded on the 9th, in lat. 39, long. 67, by a full rigged pirate brig, which released the former after putting on board Captain ENFIELD, of the brig *John Welsh*, of Philadelphia; Captain SMITH, of the schooner *S. J. Waring*, of Brookhaven, and Captain DEVEREUX, of the schooner *Enchantress*, of Newburyport; which had been taken this week.

The privateer brig was evidently the *Jeff. Davis*. The cargo of the *Goodell* being British property, she was released; but the privateer took from the *Goodell* five of her crew and a supply of water.

Great Battle in Western Virginia,

THE REBELS ROUTED WITH GREAT LOSS.

Stars and Stripes Triumphant.

ROARING RUN, Va., July 12.—A battle was fought yesterday afternoon at Rich Mountain, about two miles east of this place, where the enemy, numbering about two thousand, under the command of Col. PEGRAM, were strongly entrenched.

About three o'clock in the morning, Gen. ROSENCRANTZ, with a portion of the Eighth, Tenth and Thirteenth Indiana Regiments, and the Nineteenth Ohio, left this place, and, after a very difficult march of seven or eight miles, cutting a road through the woods, succeeded in surrounding the enemy.

About three o'clock P. M. a desperate fight ensued, lasting about an hour and a half, resulting in a loss of sixty of the enemy killed, a large number wounded, and many prisoners, some of whom are officers.

The enemy retreated precipitately, leaving behind them six guns, a large number of horses, wagons, camp equipage, etc.

The loss on our side is about twenty killed and forty wounded. Among the latter was Captain CRISMILLER, of the Indiana Tenth.

SECOND DESPATCH.

ROARING RUN, July 12.—This has been a glorious day for the old flag and our brave fellows who have rallied under it. The utmost confusion prevails here, and it is impossible to send a report of the names of the killed and wounded. As soon as the drenching rain ceased we struck our tents, and took up our line of march from Buckhannon in a southeasterly direction, on the main road to Staunton. The Rebels, about twenty-five hundred strong, with heavy earthwork batteries, were entrenched on the western slopes of the Rich Mountain, about seventeen miles east from Buckhannon, and two miles west from Beverly, which is on the east side of the mountain.

They had selected the forks of the Roaring Creek, which empties, after a northerly course, into the Tygart's Valley River, a branch of the Monongahela. The creek crosses the road in two places about a mile apart. The morning was cool and bracing, and our men were in capital spirits. General ROSENCRANZ ordered the brigade to cut a path through a thick growth of mountain pine trees and heavy undergrowth of brush, for nearly nine miles, which occupied about ten hours.—After resting at noon we came in sight of the Rebels at about four o'clock, and at once opened a heavy fire upon them with our artillery, under cover of which our men stormed their batteries.

They made a vigorous resistance, but were unable to resist the desperate assault of our Indiana troops. We have possession of their baggage, field pieces, tents and ammunition. We have also a number of prisoners. The wounded are being cared for in our hospital, and our surgeons are attending to all alike. General ROSENCRANZ had his horse shot from under him, and the hair-breadth escapes are numerous. The loss of the Rebels is about two hundred killed and wounded. Our loss is about twenty. The prisoners give gloomy accounts of the condition of their forces, and many of them seem satisfied with their capture.

OFFICIAL REPORT OF THE BATTLE OF RICH MOUNTAIN.

WASHINGTON, July 12.—The following despatch was to-day received at the head-quarters of the army here:—

HEAD-QUARTERS DEPARTMENT OF OHIO, RICH MOUNTAIN, 9 A. M., July 12.

Col. E. D. TOWNSEND:—We are in possession of all the enemy's works up to a point within eight miles of Beverly. We have taken all his guns, a very large amount of wagons, tents, etc., as well as everything he had, and a large number of prisoners, many of whom were wounded. Several officers are prisoners. They lost many killed. We have lost in all, perhaps twenty killed and fifty wounded, of whom, all but two or three, were in the column under ROSENCRANZ, which turned the position. The mass of the enemy escaped through the woods entirely disorganized.

Among the prisoners is Dr. TAYLOR, formerly of the army. Colonel PEGRAM was in command. ROSENCRANZ'S column left the camp yesterday morning, and marched some eight miles through the mountains, reaching the turnpike some two or three miles in the rear of the enemy, and defeating an advance force, and taking a couple of guns. I had a position ready for 12 guns near the main camp, and as the guns were moving up I ascertained that the enemy had retreated.

I am now pushing on to Beverly, a part of ROSENCRANZ'S troops being now within three miles of it. Our success is complete, and almost bloodless. I doubt whether WISE and JOHNSTON will unite to overpower me. The behavior of the troops in the action and towards the prisoners was admirable. (Signed) G. B. McCLELLAN,
Major Gen'l Commanding.

The Blockade of the Potomac.

ATTEMPT TO BLOW UP THE FLEET FRUSTRATED.

WASHINGTON, July 12.—The steam gun-boat *Freeborn*, Lieutenant LOWRY commanding, arrived up from Aquia Creek at 6 o'clock this morning. She has been cruising at nights up and down between that point and the mouth of the river, preventing any communication between Lower Maryland and Virginia. The service has been active, arduous and dangerous.

On Sunday, at noon, the *Freeborn* was at Aquia Creek, with the *Resolute*, *Pawnee* and *Pocahontas*, and two large oil casks were discovered floating down towards the fleet with the ebb tide. When within a quarter of a mile, a small boat was sent from the *Pawnee* to reconnoitre them. The *Resolute* supported the small boat, and it was discovered that they were infernal machines. One struck the rudder of the *Resolute*, and became detached from its buoy and sank. The other careened over, and its fuse was extinguished by dipping it in the water. The latter was hauled on board the *Pawnee*. It had a cylinder made of boiler iron, five feet long and eighteen inches in diameter, filled with all sorts of destructive elements, designed to blow the Potomac squadron to atoms.

The machine weighed about four hundred pounds. Connecting the cylinder with the cask or buoy, which was full of a coil of slow match, was an india rubber coated fuse.

The machine has a devilish-looking appearance. The *Freeborn* brought it up to the Navy Yard, where it attracts great attention. Thousands have visited it to-day.

Death of Gov. Ellis, of North Carolina.

LOUISVILLE, July 12.—The *Picayune* has a special despatch dated Richmond, 8th inst., announcing the death of Governor ELLIS, of North Carolina, at the Red Sulphur (Va.) Springs on Sunday last.

BATTLE AT MONROE, MISSOURI.

TWELVE HUNDRED REBELS ROUTED.

A GUN CAPTURED.

TWENTY OR THIRTY REBELS KILLED.

None Killed on the Union Side.

From Missouri.

ROUT OF THE REBELS AT MONROE.

ST. LOUIS, July 12.—A gentleman from Hannibal last night says that Col. SMITH'S command at Monroe was reinforced by three hundred mounted men from Illinois, yesterday afternoon, when the Rebels were attacked and dispersed. Gen. HARRIS, in command of the Rebels, was forced to leave his horse and take to the woods. A large number of the Rebels were captured.

Capt. McALLISTER, who was reported killed, was only severely wounded. He will probably recover.

The Hannibal Home Guards arrived home safely last night.

CHICAGO, July 12.—Three companies sent to the relief of Colonel SMITH, at Monroe, Missouri, returned last night, and report the road unobstructed between Hannibal and Monroe. On arriving at the latter place, they formed a junction with Col. SMITH'S force, which was entrenched in the Academy Buildings.

The Rebels, twelve hundred strong, were grouped over the prairie out of reach of Colonel SMITH'S rifles. They had two pieces of artillery, which were brought to bear, but the distance was so great that the balls were almost spent before reaching our lines. SMITH'S artillery was of longer range, and did considerable execution. The fight lasted until dusk, and the last shot from our side dismounted one of the enemy's guns.

Just at that moment Gov. WOOD, of Illinois, fell on their rear with the cavalry sent from Quincy on Wednesday, and completely routed them, taking 75 prisoners, one gun, and a large number of horses. About 20 or 30 of the Rebels were killed. Not one man on our side was killed, although several were severely wounded.

Col. SMITH is determined to shoot some of the most prominent Rebels.

Gen. TOM HARRIS, the Rebel leader, escaped.

The Volunteer Bill.

INQUIRY INTO THE WAR DEPARTMENT CONTRACTS.

WASHINGTON, July 12.—The Volunteer bill, which passed the House to-day, has yet to be acted upon by the Senate. The President is authorized to accept the services of 500,000 volunteers. The appropriation of $500,000,000 was stricken out, for the reason that the money for their support will be provided for in some other bills.

Mr. VAN WYCK'S amendment was voted down. It proposed that the Chaplain, or other competent person of every regiment, be appointed Postmaster, to frank letters and papers for all officers, musicians, and privates, the matter so franked to be carried free of postage, and also received without charge. Similar privileges were likewise proposed to be extended to those in the service of the Navy and Marine corps. The House, however, adopted an amendment that letters to or from soldiers be exempted from the pre-payment of postage, leaving it to be paid by the recipient. The bill provides liberal bounties for re-enlistments.

The House Select Committee, to examine into the War Department contracts, will immediately proceed to business. The first subject of inquiry will be in reference to the chartering of the steamer *Cataline*.

It appears, by an order just issued, that the Quartermaster's Department will provide horses, and the Ordnance Department will furnish horse equipments for volunteer cavalry companies, upon the requisition of the mustering officer, as fast as such companies are mustered into the service.

Interesting from Northern Missouri.

QUINCY, Ill., July 11.—A messenger just arrived from Hannibal, brings intelligence that the railroad bridge between that place and Palmyra was burned last night, and the bridge on the Quincy and Palmyra road, across the same stream, has also been destroyed.

General MATHER has sent a detachment of one company of artillery, with infantry and cavalry, by steamboat, to Marion city, six miles south, with orders to push from thence by land to aid Col. SMITH. By the route taken, they will avoid the bridges that have been destroyed, but will have to march 30 miles. General MATHER has also sent a strong detachment by the Quincy and Palmyra road, with orders to open the route by to-night at all hazards.

Colonel PALMER arrived this evening with 800 men. He routed a camp of the Rebels yesterday, taking a lieutenant prisoner.

One regiment has been ordered from Alton, and one from Chicago, to this place.

The circumstances of the skirmish in which Captain PETERS' company was engaged, are reported to be as follows:—The forces stationed at Monroe made an incursion into the country, for the purpose of capturing a party of Rebels. The officers neglected to leave a sufficient force behind, and upon returning were fired on by the Rebels, who killed eight. The Rebels had, in the meantime, burned the cars and the station house.

SEWARD, who killed Captain HOWELL, was taken to St. Louis last night.

Pennsylvania Troops at Camp Wayne.

WEST CHESTER, July 12.—The troops at Camp Wayne, Col. R. BIDDLE ROBERTS commanding, were inspected to-day by Lieutenant-Colonel COPPEE. The examination of the men, their arms, accoutrements and quarters was very thorough and complete. The inspecting officer expressed himself highly gratified. Col. COPPEE was well received by both the officers and men.

Col. ROBERTS' Regiment is now fully uniformed, and presents a fine appearance. The men are in high spirits and good health.

A Rebel Newspaper Suppressed.

ST. LOUIS, July 12.—About four hundred men of Colonel McNEIL'S Regiment, Reserve Corps, visited the *State Journal* office, early this morning, and removed the type, paper, &c., and read an order from General LYON, prohibiting the further publication of that sheet. The proprietors will respect the order, and lay the whole matter before General FREMONT, on his arrival here.

Arrest of a Correspondent.

MARTINSBURG, July 10.—All is quiet in the Camp. SAMUEL J. REA, a well-known correspondent, was arrested by order of General PATTERSON, probably to prevent communication with the Eastern press. All access to him is denied.

A post office has been established here, and letters to this division are nightly delivered.

Late from Cairo and Memphis.

CAIRO, Ill., July 11.—A gentleman from Memphis reports that a Rebel Regiment left there yesterday for Missouri. He also reports that two thousand Rebels are at Point Pleasant, Missouri, making preparations to attack Bird's Point.

General PILLOW has been superseded by Colonel ADKINS, at Memphis. All is quiet there.

LETTER FROM MARTINSBURG.

Correspondence of the Inquirer.

MARTINSBURG, Va., July 11, 1861.

The Seventeenth Pennsylvania Regiment and the New York Ninth have no tents with them, as they were ordered to travel light, and they therefore left them with one company as guard. They are encamping in the open air.

Two men broke into Mrs. KANE'S house last night, beat and cut the old lady with a butcher knife, and frightened her daughter, Miss MARY KANE, so badly, that she was soon afterwards found dead. Two men are under arrest, and every means are being used to bring the perpetrators to an account.

One of the men under arrest is HENRY FISHER, of Capt. TOWER'S Company, Sixth Regiment. He had been detailed as guard for the Brigade-Quartermaster's Department, and a pass belonging to him, from Lieut. BAUGH, was found near the house; the knife also belonged to him. He professes to have proof of his innocence. The perpetrators of the deed, if found and convicted, will be either hung or shot. A teamster is also under arrest. The prisoners are strongly guarded, and hold no communication with each other.

I saw a number of the members of the different regiments in town to-day in dress parade clothes. Everything is come to a stand-still in regard to a march. The Rhode Island battery moved this morning to a more pleasant encampment, a mile or two nearer Winchester. The prisoners from "Secesh" have taken off their uniforms, and their friends have furnished them with plain clothes and good eating. Some were being measured for new clothing when we were in this morning. The military stock market is so low that we have not heard any rumors or false alarms for two days past. The people look as if some panic had come, and stare at each other in astonishment. It is the first time it has been so still from the first call for volunteers up to the present time.

The First New York, Col. SWARTZWELDEN, and the Twelfth, Colonel BUTTERFIELD, eleven hundred strong, arrived yesterday morning, having made the march from Hagerstown, fording the Potomac, in less than twelve hours from starting.

The rumors of an armistice is believed by some, but the few who believe it are three months men, and are determined, if no other way offers, to enlist for three years, as they will not be drilled for three months and have no fight. So you can count them in.

C.

Affairs in Missouri—Lawless Outrage.

ST. LOUIS, July 12.—Col. McNEIL publishes a proclamation to the people of Missouri, stating that the suppression of the *State Journal* was in consequence of its giving aid and comfort to those in active rebellion against the authority of the United States Government, encouraging the people to take up arms against that authority to commit acts of violence and oppression against loyal citizens, and by fabrications of false reports respecting the United States troops, also inciting disaffected citizens to the commission of overt acts and treason, with a view of entirely subverting the Federal authority in the State.

The Clinton County (Mo.) *Journal*, published by the printers in Major STURGIS' command, states that outrages are being committed along the western border of Missouri by lawless banditti, led on by MONTGOMERY and JARRISON. It is also authorized to state that they are acting without the authority or sanction of the United States, and will be treated as outlaws by all good citizens and soldiers wherever found.

Virginia Legislature at Wheeling.

WHEELING, July 12.—The debate in the House of Delegates during the last day or two have been very interesting. They occurred mainly on the resolution of Mr CROTHERS, of Brooke county, to instruct Senators and Representatives to vote men and money without stint to the Government, and to oppose all compromise until rebellion was crushed, and upon a resolution of Mr. VANCE, of Harrison, to protest against Mr. LOVEJOY'S proposition to repeal the Fugitive Slave law. Mr. CROTHERS' proposition was passed with only one dissenting voice, Mr. ARNOLD, of Lewis county, who is regarded as a doubtful Union man. Mr. VANCE'S resolution was tabled by a large vote.

From Fortress Monroe.

FORTRESS MONROE, July 11.—J. T. SONGSTER, of Col. BAKER'S Regiment, a native of Philadelphia, was shot by mistake by a sentry, on Sunday night, and died yesterday.

Thirty men of Col. WARDROP'S Regiment had made a reconnoissance within nine miles of Yorktown. They went up between James river and Great Bethel. At the latter place there are posted two hundred Confederate cavalry and one hundred artillery.

One hundred recruits from New York, for Col DURYEA'S Regiment, have arrived here.

The time of the Massachusetts regiments will expire on the 16th, and that of the First Vermont a few days later.

LATEST FROM OLD POINT COMFORT

COL. MAGRUDER REPORTED KILLED

The *Clipper* Extra, of yesterday, gives the following interesting letter from Old Point Comfort:—

By the arrival of the steamer *Louisiana*, at half-past six o'clock, we have gathered the following facts and rumors concerning events at Fortress Monroe and vicinity:—

From an officer of the Federal army, who came passenger on the boat, we were informed that it was reported and generally believed at the Fortress, that Colonel MAGRUDER, of the Confederate forces, had been killed a few days since during a short engagement with the Federal forces at Newport News.—The rumor was more fully strengthened yesterday by a negro making his way to Newpoint in a small boat, and stating that such was the case, and that the body of the Rebel chieftain had been taken to Norfolk.

Throughout yesterday the woods on Sewall's Point were burning briskly, a dense volume of smoke completely enveloping the Point. It is now thought that the woods were set on fire by shells thrown from the Sawyer gun, placed on the Rip Raps.

During yesterday the most powerful glasses were brought to bear upon the point to ascertain if the Rebels still held possession of the place. After a careful survey of the place not a Rebel could be seen. The rascals have either deserted their stronghold, or are playing some devil's trick.

Just as the *Louisiana* was quitting the Old Point wharf, the *St. Lawrence*, from Philadelphia, in tow of the *Quaker City*, came into the Roads, and was saluted by the vessels comprising the blockade.

From scouts sent out yesterday, intelligence was received at head-quarters that the Rebels had evacuated Great Bethel, and had retired to Yorktown, where they intend to make a stand. Whether the Rebels intended the place for an oyster stand, or a stand to be whipped, our informant did not say. The latter, however, appears to us to be the most reasonable.

On Wednesday night, J. G. SANGSTON, a member of the California Regiment, while in his tent, was accidentally killed by a comrade, from the careless use of his musket. The body was brought to this city this morning, in charge of the brother of the deceased, and was taken to New York.

Colonel BUTLER, brother to the commanding officer of the Fortress, arrived by the boat and proceeded direct to Washington, as bearer of despatches to the Government. Captain KILPATRICK, who left this city on Wednesday afternoon for Fortress Monroe, in charge of 100 Zouaves, returned this morning, and will visit New York for the purpose of raising a battalion of mounted men.

The Captain is still suffering intensely from the wound which he received at Great Bethel, but notwithstanding, he bears up under the fate of war, and is nobly battling in the cause of his country. So great is the regard entertained for the gallant Captain in New York, that weeks will not elapse before he has under charge the men whom he is in quest of.

In consequence of many of the soldiers becoming intoxicated and abusing their officers, General BUTLER has notified the dispensers of intoxicating drinks that hereafter they will be prohibited from selling or giving liquor to the soldiers. All persons so offending will be severely punished.

The weather still continues very hot, and the troops are so sun-burnt that when they reach home their friends will scarcely recognize them.

A picket, while reconnoitering a mile and a half from Newport News, yesterday, came across the body of a Confederate soldier. He had been shot in the high, and, from appearances, died from loss of blood

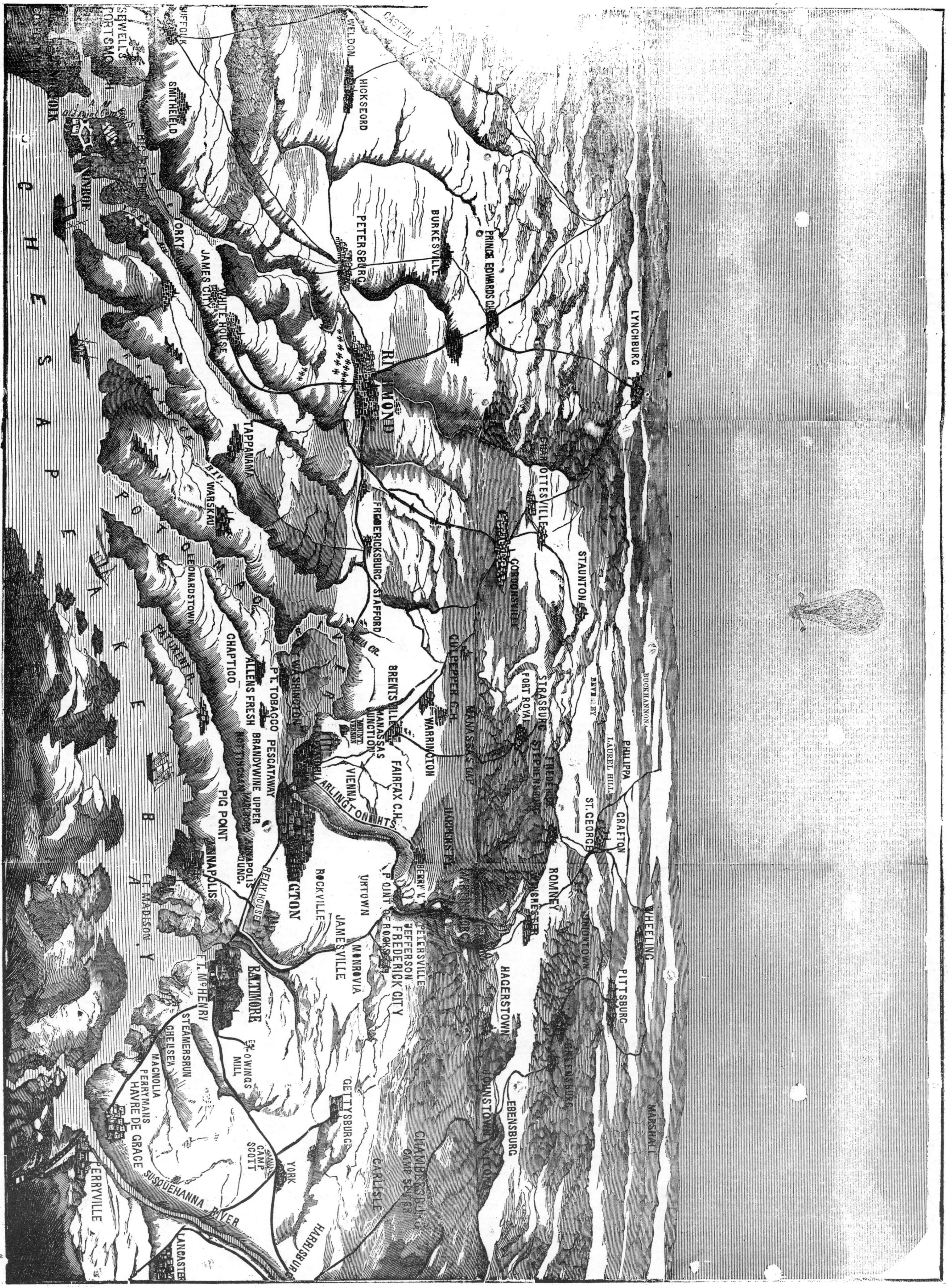

BIRD'S-EYE VIEW OF THE SEAT OF WAR.

Entered according to Act of Congress.

The Daily Delta.

VOL. XVI. NEW ORLEANS, THURSDAY, JULY 18, 1861. NO. 197.

THE DAILY DELTA

FROM OUR EVENING EDITION OF YESTERDAY.

We are indebted to the Adams Express for late papers.

ARMS.—It has been wisely suggested that instead of sending all our artisans, mechanics and laborers to Virginia, steps should be taken to retain them here at home, to manufacture arms. There are several foundries in the city that might be set to work in this business, and an abundance of material can be obtained to manufacture any description of arms. The Belleville Iron Foundry at Algiers might be used as an armory. Our planters usually have a large quantity of old iron on hand which they would contribute to our cause, and the excellent iron of Tennessee can be readily obtained for this purpose. That arms can be manufactured here has been most satisfactorily shown. This is a practical suggestion and ought to be carried into effect. No patriotic mechanic who could be useful in carrying out this plan, ought to abandon a sphere in which he can be made useful to our cause, to enter the ranks of the army. We have soldiers enough, but not enough of the proper arms to render them effective. Let the Confederate Government send an ordnance officer and armorer to superintend the organization and establishment of such an armory in this city, and let all our mechanical skill be directed to this work.

The Baltimore Sun thus states the war programme of the Lincolnites:

> The plan of offensive operations embraces the employment both of the army and navy in the occupation of some of the principal commercial cities on the Atlantic and Gulf coasts. But this plan will not be carried out before winter. It is intended, however, that Memphis shall be taken by an army and armed flotilla early in the fall, and from that great depot the growing cotton crop will come forward to market through the interior. Trade, both foreign and domestic, will then, it is supposed, be revived, and as prosperous as ever.

This is a pretty bold and big plan. If the enemy is twice as strong as he claims to be, he may be able to carry out this grand scheme. It will involve a vast expenditure of blood and money, and it is quite possible, if not highly probable, that it may fail. But assume that it is successful, how will it advance the design of the enemy? If they capture Memphis, will they get the growing crop of cotton? They will do so when the South abandons its position, and then there will be no use of continuing the war. Every man who should send a bale of cotton to Memphis while in the occupation of the enemy, would be a traitor to the South. The idea indicated in the above proceeds on the theory—a false one—that our people, especially our cotton producers, are not perfectly united and earnest in this war. The enemy will find this delusion a very expensive and disastrous one.

WHAT THE MORNING JOURNALS SAY.

The *Bulletin* quotes the New York News to show the vile system of fraud and falsehood which the Abolition leaders and their coadjutors have inaugurated and are keeping up.

The Bulletin quotes also the following from a speech of Edward Everett delivered not five months ago:

> To expect to hold fifteen States in the Union by force is preposterous. The idea of a civil war, accompanied as it would be, by a servile insurrection, is too monstrous to be entertained for a moment. If our sister States must leave us, in the name of heaven, let them go in peace.

There would be no better proof of the miserable pusilanimity of Everett than is presented in a comparison of his recent declarations in a speech to a New York mob in favor of a war to the knife against the South with the foregoing and similar utterances in previous speeches.

The *Bee* has some just and edifying suggestions relative to the disaster in Western Virginia, cautioning our people not to underrate the courage and prowess of the enemy, nor to be dismayed or cast down by one or many disasters.

The *Picayune* refers to our relations with Spain, showing that the Government of that nation has recognized the belligerent rights of the Confederate States, and that whilst prohibiting the entrance of privateers into her ports, she is bound to recognize the right of a ship-of-war like the Sumter to take her prizes into Spanish ports:

> Whatever prizes the Sumter may have sent into Havana or any other Spanish port must, therefore, be confirmed to the captors; and we judge further, that the right of the Sumter herself to enter and remain in those ports will be conceded to be as perfect as that of any war steamer of the United States, until the Spanish Government decides, with the same impartial neutrality, that neither shall be admitted.
>
> Just now the authorities of Spain are not likely to make any concessions of mere favor to the Government of Mr. Lincoln. It has given them just cause of offense by sending to the court of a Catholic sovereign and a slaveholding monarchy a foul-mouthed infidel and a brawling, fanatical Abolitionist. It has taken offense at the Spanish occupation of St. Domingo, and called the Spanish Government to account, with some audible mutterings from those who speak for its purposes, of warlike intentions, to prevent the consummation of that stroke of Spanish policy. It is a bad time, and they are a very unsuitable set at Washington to look for any stretch of Spanish courtesy to help them harass the Confederate States, which can be to Spain a useful ally and a harmonious neighbor.
>
> Mr. Secretary Seward is said to be getting ready to make a quarrel out of this, by demanding of Spain the delivery to the Federal authorities of the prizes which the Sumter sent into Havana. The pretension for this must be that the Confederate States have no belligerent rights, but are to be treated as mere insurgents. The capture of an armed public vessel of the Confederate States will not be allowed to divest the right of property. This makes the question which Spain will have virtually decided by the decree of neutrality. She has pledged strict impartiality between the two parties, as belligerents, and Secretary Seward will only get himself and his Government into a new scrape by making a foolish quarrel with Spain.

The *Crescent* takes high grounds as to the peace which the Confederate States seek to secure and establish North:

> The North must be made to sue for peace, and be compelled to accept the terms which we will propose. This is the only way this war ought to be ended, and it is the only way it will be ended, unless the enemy in the meantime, as is highly probable, breaks down for the want of means wherewith to carry on the contest.
>
> The "peace party" in the North is not, however, exactly that sort of peace party which the South would like to see there. They are for peace merely because the war has prostrated business, and threatens to involve them in a fearful national debt. They are not for peace because they believe the South to be right. What we want is for them to declare for peace on the broad ground that the South is right on principle. When they take the position that the provocation of the South was more than sufficient; that the right of secession, under our form of government, is undoubted; that it is a correct theory that all governments ought to derive their existence from the consent of the governed; in short, that the South not only had the right to resist, but was fully and amply justified in so doing—then, and only then, will there be a peace party at the North worth talking about.

FUNERAL ORATION

DELIVERED BY LIEUT. COL. ADOLPHUS OLIVIER, AT THE OBSEQUIES OF

LIEUT. COL. CHARLES DIDIER DREUX.

Soldiers and Citizens—When the Lacedemonian mothers buckled the armor on the willing limbs of their sons and sent them forth to battle, it was their wont in giving them their shields to use the words famous in history: "Come back *with it*, or *upon it*." I believe the heart of this great city, when it sent forth its sons to repel the invasion of fanaticism, must have been filled with the same proud confidence in the spirit of its youth. They went forth to the onset with the heroic determination to be worthy their lineage and the cause which kindled before them like a beacon set on high. Like the body of a Lacedemonian hero carried through the mournful streets on a floor of shields, Charles Didier Dreux comes to his last resting place escorted by the brave hearts of his fellow-soldiers beating in unison with the heart of the State, while the tears of the people fall like dew upon his grave.

It must have been sad for him to have engaged in this war; and I feel the woe which must have entered his great heart as the memories of his youth, the struggles and triumphs of other days crowded thick and fast upon his soul. He venerated, almost idolized the American Union; and he looked upon her gorgeous ensign with the feeling of the servant of the Lord as his eyes were bent on the pillar of fire as it rose in the wilderness. He held the Constitution to be a covenant between universal man and his nation for the security of liberty, regulated and determined by constitutional law. Yet, alas! how the cause for which he so devotedly labored has fallen. The Union was becoming hateful to our people; the name of *American* was being lost, or was to be shared with the foe; the flag of the Republic, desecrated by the rude hand of grasping power, was being carried in the van by mercenary hordes; the very Genius of Liberty was fleeing the sanctuaries of the Capitol, and methinks it must have been with a noise similar to that of the flapping of wings of the guardian angels as they hurried from the *sanctum sanctorum* as the hour for the final destruction of the Temple of Jerusalem had tolled—*simul ingens motus exedentium*; the black flag was casting its shadow upon the brow of the nation, and the musket buts of a hireling soldiery were ringing on the floor of the Temple of Justice; while the letter of the Constitution glowed and flashed under the very eyes of those who had violated its spirit; we of Louisiana had suffered and endured for years the taunts and jeers of the oppressors; the confidence of the world was being shaken as regards the capacity of man for self-government; the destinies of freedom and of humanity had fallen into the hands of men, the miserable predicants of a cause without a creed and without a faith, until galled and forced to choose between resistance and submission, the State, appealing to God, resolved to be free. As these things were transpiring, stretched on the couch of sickness and suffering, the gloom which had settled upon my land clouded my aching heart; and I saw dark-veiled shapes rising with the darkness over the horizon of my country, and I thought of those who had been the partners of the trials and joys of my youth, and the eye of my soul saw a flock of young eagles soaring through the darkness [illegible] mounting upward, and I thought of him whose remains now lie mouldering before you. There were then words of anger and menace; the sea began to darken with threatening vessels, our frontiers bristled with bayonets and the tramp of armed men was heard on our borders—the South with one voice crie[illegible] "to arms!" The spirit of Charles Dreux never could [illegible] submission to wrong when accompanied with insult. In the full gush of his youth and of his usefulness; with the brand of genius, reeking and perfumed, all over him; the head of a young and dearly beloved family; engaged in the pursuit of a profession which, wide open before him, held up to his eye the choicest rewards and honors; esteemed and beloved, he left father, wife, child, brothers and sisters to bare his breast for his mother South. He made Louisiana's cause his own; and the first in the lead of our volunteer troops, and surrounded by his devoted followers, he left the pleasures of home and entered the tented field. With the firm, elastic steps of the knightly warrior he was ascending the heights of fame and glory, when he poured out his heart's blood in a libation to Liberty.

Born in New Orleans on the 11th of May, A. D. 1832, Charles Didier Dreux, from early youth, gave promise of eminent success in life.

The issue of one of our oldest Creole families, after preliminary studies, he was sent to Amherst College, Mass., then under the superintendency of Mr. Hitchcock, who is now a Peter the Hermit in the unholy crusade against the South; after a short visit to his native city, he and his two younger brothers became cadets of the Western Military Institute at Blue Lick Springs, Ky.; becoming a member of the Frankfort Military Institute, his talents and aptitude as an officer soon elevated him to the rank of Captain in the battalion. When the Scott campaign fairly opened, he went with the Kentucky delegation to attend the great Whig Convention at Niagara, and we have still in our possession the letter which he wrote us, in the full gush of his youth's success. His return home was one continuous ovation.

To speak of his career in New Orleans during that canvass would be unnecessary. The trials and triumphs of those days are green in the memory and hearts of the people. His life as an orator, as District Attorney, member of the Legislature, Captain and Lieut. Col., is known to all. The versatility of his genius was marvelous; he spoke with the utmost facility and correctness the English, French and Spanish languages, while his conversation glittered and sparkled with the choicest gems of classic lore. As a man, none could know him without being drawn toward him by irresistible sympathetic influences: his friendship was passion's essence—it kindled and warmed you with its own congenial heat; did the gloom of sadness light upon your soul, like sunshine upon the face of the waters would his heart mirror forth its own sunny hopes; in the domestic circle or the festive board, the sparkle of his wit, his unrivaled powers of illustration captivated the attention of all near him; his capacity of physical endurance was almost incomprehensible; as we laid down side by side in early youth, or after the long canvassing day, I have often wondered how nature could have blended such extraordinary faculties in one being. As an orator he towered among his peers; his countenance bespoke the presence of self-confiding power; his voice at times was soft and melting as the memory of early days, then filled with unspeakable pathos; anon hissingly breathing of irony, then loud and thundering as ocean's tongue; but when his countenance would be lit by the glow and fire of his soul, and his large hazel eye would dilate and his nostrils expand, as though he "smelt the battle afar off," then 'twas a noble sight to see him, and one could appreciate the *gaudia certaminis* as, gladiator-like, he rose and towered before you in the arena of political discussion. But his was not only the eloquence freshly gathered in the flowery gardens of rhetoric, it was

> Like the clear brook's stone of luster, and gave
> With the flash of the gem, its solidity too.

These remarkable faculties of mind, combined with the breathing influences of heart and soul, drew all men toward him, and he held fast their affections as with hooks of steel. Never did man in so brief a career achieve such a wide spread and deeply deserved popularity. His soldiers must have idolized him. Leaving New Orleans as a Captain of the Orleans Cadets, in the brief space of a few weeks the eye of his superiors singled him out from among his peers and the responsible position of Lieutenant Colonel was assigned him. He took the head of his command on a field which would have been rendered famous by his deeds of valor had not death marked him for a victim. There are souls which can feel that the end of life is approaching. In his letters to his wife he often spoke of the uncertainty of life, yet sought to cheer her to bear that which he must have felt was drawing near. His heart must have been filled with ineffable sadness. He must have seen the light of eternity stealing through the gates of heaven as he slept under the broad canopy of the firmament, and seen with the eyes of his home-wandering soul the loved forms at home hovering over his slumbers. Yet never did he falter in the pursuit of his profession. It was on the night of the fifth of the present month that he led a reconnoitering party in the vicinity of Newport News. It must have been a noble sight to have seen him, as the light of the battle was on his brow, marshaling his force into line, the metallic notes of his iron voice sounding in the fastnesses of the forest, then when he felt the gush of his life-blood through the lips of a mortal wound, stilling his proud and dauntless heart, and startling the echoes of eternity with the last adieu of his departing soul, as Lawrence when the grapeshot was in his ear, crying: "Boys, don't surrender;" afterward pillowing his drooping head on the breast of his valiant soldiers kneeling beside him.

He has fallen, and at the hands of whom. I know the mind of Gen. Scott to be of too martial a cast to be easily moved; but, when the news of this death reached his ears, he must have thought of him who caused to blaze all the deeds of his life; who from Niagara to the shores of the Gulf filled the brazen throat of fame with the tale of his prowess. He must have remembered the days when he paraded the streets of this city, amid the shouts of our people, the magic of the young warrior's eloquence, hanging as a mantle of glory over his shoulders. Oh! General Scott, 'twas you who armed the hand which snapped his heart-strings, and that, too, on the soil of your mother State. Yet,

> "Like the day star in the wave
> Sank the hero in his grave,
> 'Midst the dewfal of a nation's tears."

So young to be dead. I feel that half my heart will lie buried in his tomb; the voice of early days comes stealing out of this cold tenement, and speak to my heart. God of the patriot and the warrior, comfort his aged and venerated father—solace the bleeding, broken heart of his young and disconsolate wife, in this the hour of her bereavement and woe—cast the shadow of thy wings over the head of his orphan child—let the rays of thy morning and evening sun linger around this sepulchre, that the last resting place of the gallant dead be crowned with the reflects of the glory of thy face.

> "——tho' sweet are our home recollections,
> Tho' sweet are the tears which in tenderness fall,
> Tho' sweet are our friendships, our hopes, our affections,
> Revenge on dire foes is sweetest of all."

Soldiers! let the spirit of the departed warrior fill your breasts; let his last death shout be your rallying cry, and the memory of his valor stiffen the sinews of your arms; and when the hour for the l[illegible] inevitable conflict shall have arrived, when [illegible] face, breast to breast, steel against steel, [illegible] will meet the foe, oh! then, strike home; strike [illegible]very sword be fleshed to the hilt, and let his [illegible]e, riding on the wings of the battle-storm, min[illegible] with your shouts of victory. Like him remember "'Tis the cause makes all, degrades, or hallows [illegible] in its fall;" that we must not weigh in the [illegible] arms; but [illegible] the chivalrous motto, "If God be with us what boots who the aggressor?" and that we must write for our mother South with the point of our swords an Illiad which will be worthy of the past. The South must be free, else become a black Golgotha, rivalling the Calvary upon which were stretched the limbs of the God man for the eternal teachings of generations. If, in a cause like ours, fall we must, fall we like him! and when the legions whose conquering tramp is heard in the distance, "like the rush of mighty waters," will pause on the scene of carnage and inquire after their comrades gone before them, throughout the sounding corridors of all time the proud reverberations of Fame's echoes will answer, as did the soldiers of France on the honored grave of Latour D'Auvergne—"Fallen on the field of honor!"

Let the blood of the martyred hero ascend as a holy holocaust to heaven, and draw blessings upon our nation, and his name live embalmed in the veneration and love of our people.

SPEECH OF COL. SEYMOUR IN THE CONNECTICUT LEGISLATURE.—On the 3d inst. a series of war resolutions which had passed the Senate of Connecticut came up in the House, when Ex-Governor Seymour opposed them in a brief speech, as follows:

> Sir, I am on this floor as the advocate of peace measures! I will not sanction this war, except so far as it can be waged on constitutional grounds. This question now wears a totally different aspect from that which it presented when the President issued his call for volunteers. Then it was for "the protection of the capital and the repossession of the forts." I am heartily glad that the capital is protected. I would protect the Federal capital and the archives.
>
> But nothing has been done to recapture the forts. But a movement of invasion has been commenced—an invasion of a sovereign State. I think the gentleman from Stratford was right in saying there is a movement—a growing sentiment among the people, in favor of a peaceable settlement, of an honorable peace! I go with him and with all who are for peace measures instead of war measures! There seems to be a radical mistake on the part of many people: they seem to think the South can be conquered. Sir, this is impossible. It can no more be done than the South can conquer the North! There are brave men there as well as here.
>
> In revolutionary days we knew something of them. In the war of 1812 they rallied around our flag and protected our commerce. Now it is not well to underrate the prowess of these enemies, as you call them, though I recognize, even in this state of things, some there whom I knew, and who are still our brothers in heart. This mistake cost Braddock a galling defeat in the old French war; it cost the British many a humiliating defeat in the war of the Revolution. Do you think you can secure their loyalty and affection by force? Two or three sovereign States have been overrun and trampled under foot already.
>
> You have got a kind of foothold which you call "peace;" but it is not peace—it is smothered war. Maryland is in a volcanic condition to-day, and the same spirit will rise at all times, in spite of all the chains you can put upon it, and of all the ruin that is wrought. You may destroy their habitations, devastate their fields, and shed the blood of their people, still you cannot conquer them. "Even in their ashes live their wonted fires."
>
> I shall vote against these resolutions. I hope Congress will adopt some peace measures which shall hold the Border States and draw back those that have gone out—so that, in some future day, we may have the South again under the banner of the Union.

The Lafourche Union is informed that Lincoln vessels have been seen cruising in the neighborhood of Caillou Island, and that Mr. Douglas, who keeps the light-house on Timbalier Island, was visited by a party of eighteen from one of the enemy's men of war, about three weeks ago, who left on his table a bottle containing a notice of blockade. We didn't know the chaps bottled their wrath.

TELEGRAPHIC NEWS.

TELEGRAPHED TO THE NEW ORLEANS DAILY DELTA.

THE RICH MOUNTAIN AFFAIR.

Number of Troops Engaged.

Retreat Admirably Conducted.

LOUISVILLE, July 16.—We are advised that Gen. Garnett's forces numbered 5000, and the Federalists under McClellan amounted to 22,000, who were advancing in three columns.

Morris had flanked the Confederates on the north, and McClellan on the south, while Rosencrants approached through the centre.

The patriots stood their ground to the last possible moment of safety, and the retreat must have been admirably managed, as the pursuers had no opportunity of using their small arms.

So well was the rear guarded, that though in retreat it was outflanked twice by the converging columns, but twenty were killed.

At last accounts the Confederates were retreating towards St. George. The Federalists hope that Gen. Hill, now at Oakland, will harass the Confederates in their retreat towards Hardy county.

It must be remembered that these troops have kept McClellan's columns in check for weeks.

FROM MISSOURI.

Missourians Becoming Bold.

Military Train Fired Into.

ST. LOUIS, July 16.—A military train was fired into twelve miles above St. Charles, severely wounding two Federalists.

The mail carrier reports that Major Harris is twelve miles beyond Fulton, with 3000 men. The Federal Colonel, McNeill, is expected to reach Fulton to night.

The houses along the route are deserted.

Hon. J. W. Tucker is making speeches throughout the country, arousing the Missourians.

Col. Steifail, at Lexington, reports having discovered two hundred kegs of powder and machinery for making cannon.

Steamers are prevented from passing Jefferson City, unless carrying the United States flag.

FROM WESTERN VIRGINIA.

Piedmont Occupied by Federals

HARRISBURG, July 16.—The reserve force at Cum-[illegible] but were repulsed.

CINCINNATI, July 16.—Col. Woodruff attacked a Virginia force between Mad river and Barboursville, killing and wounding several. Only one Federalist was killed.

IMPORTANT FROM WASHINGTON.

Early Advance of McDowell's Column.

SCOTT VISITS THE TROOPS IN VIRGINIA.

WASHINGTON, July 16, 12 M.—Gen. McDowell will certainly advance to-night.

Gen. Scott and staff visited the troops on the Virginia side to-day.

[Second Dispatch].

McDowell Advancing.

WASHINGTON, July 16, P. M.—The army has advanced. Gen. McDowell left at 3:30 this afternoon. The destination of his column is not known.

His advance guard is at Hunting Creek, ten miles from Washington.

U. S Congress.

WASHINGTON, July 16.—In the House the bill to increase the efficiency of the volunteer force has passed.

The Navy bill has passed the Senate.

Capture of a New Orleans Vessel.

NEW YORK, July 16.—The schooner Ella, of New Orleans, from Tampico to New York, is the vessel which has been captured.

Rev. James Turner Leftwich, Pastor of the Presbyterian Church in Alexandria, having prayed for the success of the Southern cause, in the Sabbath services in his church, was arrested on coming out of the pulpit, by an orderly named Fairbanks, and, being taken before the Colonel of Fairbanks's regiment, named Heintzelman, a demand was made upon the reverend gentleman that he should discontinue his prayer for the South, and offer up orisons "for the Union and the President of the United States." Mr. Leftwich maintained his right of "free prayer," and declared his unalterable purpose to continue to ask the blessings of Divine Providence upon the Southern people and their cause. His church was closed. In the evening, however, a dispatch from Washington was received, under instructions of which Mr. Leftwich was unconditionally released, and his church reopened.

Holt, the ex-Secretary of War, is in Kentucky, endeavoring to convince the people that they ought to surrender their liberties and cheerfully support the despotism inaugurated at Washington by the present higher law Administration.

A deserter, named W. H. Wilson, from the 6th Louisiana Regiment, arrived at Alexandria on the 13th. He is an Indianian, and says he enlisted to get North as soon as he could desert.

SNAKE TAMING.—We witnessed on Tuesday morning last an extraordinary instance of snake taming. A boy belonging to Mr. John T. Davis, of this place, went early in the morning for a load of wood, found a large rattlesnake, caught him, and brought him home in his wagon, exhibiting him lying across his lap, holding him up first by his head and then his tail, making him coil up in his arms, rattle and cease at pleasure of the boy. A number of our citizens witnessed this strange feat. The rattlesnake had eight rattles, and was about four and a half feet long, and large in proportion—was tamed completely in about two hours. The boy says he can do the same with any snake, and has been in the habit of catching and taming them all his life. We could scarcely believe it when we saw this venomous death dealing serpent made as tame as a lady's lap dog in a few hours.

Mariana (Fla.) Patriot.

REMARKABLE SUICIDE OF A BOY.—A few days ago a lad named George Vanniman, aged nineteen years, and a son of V. H. Vanniman, of Jeromeville, Ashland county, Ohio, committed suicide, under the following circumstances: While out gunning with a comrade he shot and crippled one of his neighbor's cattle. Complaint was made to the father of the lad by the owner of the animal, and when the guilty party was questioned about the offense, he at first denied, but finally confessed it. He was then reproved for his conduct, and exhibited considerable feeling. He soon after went up stairs, and taking his gun, left the house. He was followed by the members of the family, but before they overtook him he placed the muzzle of the gun to his head and moved the trigger with his toe, killing himself instantly.

ARRIVAL OF A SPY.—A man whose name we were unable to learn, and who belonged to one of the companies in our army, was brought to the city yesterday as a spy. When detected, he had concealed on his person a number of files for spiking guns, and after discovering that it was useless to deny his guilt, he confessed that he had, under promise of large remuneration from the Yankee authorities at Washington, joined our army with the intention of spiking all of our guns, and when the feat was accomplished, of giving the necessary intelligence to the enemy to enable them to march on us. Happily the rascal was prevented from consummating his purpose. He was handed over to the military authorities, and will, we trust, meet his deserts. [Richmond Enquirer, 13th.

JOHN MERRYMAN INDICTED FOR TREASON.—We learn by the Baltimore papers of the 11th, that John Merryman, a citizen of Baltimore, a man of influence, public spirited, and a true patriot, has been indicted by the Grand Jury of the United States District Court for treason. He has been held a prisoner of war at Fort McHenry for weary weeks, and now is indicted for "levying and carrying on war, insurrection and rebellion against the United States, on the 23d of April;" also, that he broke down telegraph wires and bridges, all to hinder and delay the passage of United States troops. Similar indictments were found against Chas. Cockney, Lewis Bitter, James McCartney, Philip Casmire, Michael Hooper and Richard H. Mitchell. [Louisville Courier.

STOPPING A SOURCE OF INFORMATION.—We understand some of the faithful of Old Abe's followers hereabouts have been earning a little of Abe's secret service money, by contriving dispatches to his fleet in the Roads, by means of putting such little favors as they may have in a bottle, and setting it adrift on the proper tide, to be floated down. They put a little flag or signal in the cork, so as to attract the attention of the enemy, who cruise about the Roads in pursuit of these dispatches. Capt. John Young, of the Harbor Police, however, has put a quietus on this amusement, as his operations in the river and Roads will intercept all such dispatches. [Norfolk Day Book.

TROOPS FOR CANADA.—Armstrong artillery from India have been ordered to Canada. They go overland 1500 miles. This is the first time artillery has been ordered overland from India. Two hundred horses for artillery are on the way out for Canada. All the guns being sent out are Armstrong cannon. The headquarters of the Rifles will be at London; and, a very unusual thing, a detachment will be sent to St. Catherines. In this city, the old Parliament buildings will be used as the officers' quarters; and the new barracks and the fort is to be put into order for the men. [Toronto Leader, 6th.

in our own correspond[illegible] of firing upon [illegible] guns.—The two accounts refer to different affairs, but telegraphic dispatches [illegible] place, near the mouth of Perdido river. The first was by mounted men with pistols, about 9 o'clock on Saturday morning, and did not do execution; the second did, but we are not positive when it took place. [Mobile News.

The Champlain Citizen learns that Fort Montgomery, at Rouse's Point, is to be placed on a war footing at once, and that active preparations to that end are in progress. The Government probably thinks it well, in view of the "precautionary" increase of British forces in Canada, to take some precautionary measures for the protection of the frontier.

The Republican papers are publishing with, we are sorry to say, not a little gusto, the report that the Queen of England is insane. The British press returns the compliment, and declares that not only Lincoln but his whole Cabinet is mad. [New York Day-Book

THE CITY.

LADY MANNERS IN THE CARS.—In the absence of a more interesting topic, this question is becoming quite important now to that portion of the moving community which avails itself of the convenience of city railroad cars. Women have privileges, and why should'nt they enjoy them? This reporter thinks they should, and to the fullest extent. He goes up Camp and comes down Magazine two or three times every day, on the cars; knows every brick in every building on the way, from the mutilated sign of the Judson bankers, going up, to that infernal word "Blood," (in red letters,) on a certain three story building, coming down. Knows all the regular customers, male and female, who patronize the line, and can tell, with his eyes shut, who gets off and who gets on. He sides in this contest with the weak—the ladies, of course—and intends to back them up to the best of his ability.

He contends that the ladies have the right to take up the seats in the cars, in a matter-of-course way, without acknowledging the courtesy of gentlemen who are green enough to get up for them. Whenever he sees a lady with small ideas and large skirts occupy two seats which have been vacated, without a nod recognizing the courtesy, he inwardly exclaims, "bully! that girl knows her prerogative, right, privilege, immunity and due, and has the grit to exercise it." He thinks, too, hat her parents had the sound sense, when she was young, not to addle her pate with any of those silly, romantic notions about "manners" which your "Victims" and "Beverlys" would have inculcated. She is the kind of a woman who can stand her hand with the world, and meet difficulties on their own ground in a way of her own, claiming as rights what your softer and gentler women acknowledge as courtesies. She is the kind of woman to make your masculines "stand round," and whenever this reporter sees one of them enter a car in which he is seated, a mixed feeling of awe and admiration crawls through his entire system from hat to boots; he assumes a perpendicular position and economises space to his smallest diameter. She challenges his respect and esteem with all the emotions of deference which of right is due a bear in petticoats.

And yet there are ladies who so far forget their privileges and the respect to which they are entitled, as to acknowledge with a sweet smile what they have been taught to consider a courtesy from gentlemen. They are surely not aware of the hopeless minority of their class, or they would rise in the might of their right and show the masculines that they have every thing to receive and nothing to bestow.

We shall advocate the giving up of the cars entirely to the ladies—permit no gentlemen in the cars—and have the charter of the railroad company so amended as to allow six ladies to take up an entire car, making it a penal offense for any driver to even notice by a nod the hailing of a masculine, though he be a cripple.

Gazette & Sentinel.

PROGRESS OF THE WAR.

THE WAR IN MISSOURI.

LATE AND IMPORTANT!

BATTLE OF SPRINGFIELD, MO.

McCulloch with 12,000 Men, Attacks 14,000 Federalists.

Kills 900 and Takes the Balance Prisoners.

Southern Loss 200!

MEMPHIS, July 15th.—News reached Little Rock yesterday, via Pocahontas, that Gen. McCulloch, with 12,000 men, attacked 14,000 Federalists at Springfield, Mo., killing 900.

The Federalists surrendered unconditionally.

Two hundred Southerners are killed.

The "Iberville Greys," were engaged in the above conflict, if true that it has really occurred, and it looks plausible. Let us hope the good news is indeed true.

St. Louis, July 17.—The Missourians under Magoffin, attacked the Federalists between Cedalia and Georgetown, killing seven. The Missourians lost three. Magoffin had 700 men.

Bœrnstein announces that he will administer no more oaths of allegiance, but will keep suspected persons confined.

THE WAR IN VIRGINIA!

The Latest News.

Patterson Advancing on Winchester!

Federal Advance Guard at Fairfax—Southerners Falling back to Centreville.

Arrival of McDowell at Germantown.

He Moves Toward Manassas.

Bunker Hill, July 17.—General Patterson moved on Winchester on Tuesday, with a force of 21,000 men, and would be able to reach that point on Tuesday night.

It is supposed that Gen. Johnston will skirmish heavily, but not risk a pitch battle.

Washington, July 17.—The advance guard of Gen. McDowell's column reached Fairfax at noon. The Confederate pickets retired an hour before falling back on Centreville, where the Confederates will probably make a stand.

Germantown, July 17.—Taylor's division moved early yesterday morning. The Southerners fell back towards Centreville.

Four divisions will move toward Manassas Junction to-morrow.

We stop the Press to announce the latest news received by the Delta. We heartily wish it may be true.

A Great Victory!

BATTLE AT BULL'S RUN.

The Enemy Repulsed Three Times!

RETREATED IN DISMAY!

Washington Artillery Distinguished Themselves.

Our Hospital Fired Upon.

Pitched Battle near Fairfax.

17,000 Troops Engaged in It!

Immense Slaughter of The Federalists!

Richmond, July 18.—Gen. Beauregard has achieved a great victory.

At daybreak this morning the enemy appeard in force at Bull's Run. They attempted to cross, when a battle ensued, three miles northwest of Manassas Junction.

The Federalists were repulsed three times with immense loss.

Our loss is small in comparison.

The 1st and 17th Virginia Regiments were prominent in the fight.

The Washington Artillery, of New Orleans, did great execution.

Wm. Singstor, a rifleman, killed a Federal officer of high rank, and took $700 in gold from his person.

A shot passed through the kitchen house where Gen. Beauregard was sitting at dinner.

The enemy fired into our hospital, where the yellow flag was flying.

Richmond, July 18.—Reliable advices from Fairfax say that the Federalists advanced this morning with 10,000 strong. After many hours fighting they were driven back by 7000 Confederates with great loss.

From Western Virginia we have accounts of the surrender of Col. Heck's command and four companies of the Georgia regiment.

Confederate States of America.

President—JEFFERSON DAVIS, of Miss.
Vice-President—A. H. STEVENS, of Ga.
Sec'y of State—ROBT. TOOMBS, of Ga.
Sec'y of the Treasury—C. C. MEMMINGER, of South Carolina.
Sec'y of War—L. P. WALKER, of Ala.
Attorney-Gen.—J. P. BENJAMIN, of La.
Postmaster-Gen.—J. A. REGAN, of Texas.
Sec'y of Navy—S. B. MALLORY, of Fla.

Population of the Confederate States.

States.	Free.	Slave.	Total
S. Carolina,	308,186	407,185	715,371
Georgia,	615,336	467,461.	1,082,797
Florida,	81,885	63,809	145,694
Alabama,	520.444	437,473	957,917
Mississippi,	407,551	479,607	887,158
Louisiana,	354,245	312,186	666,431
Texas,	415,999	184,956	600,955
Virginia,	1,105,196	590,884	1,595,080
N.Carolina,	661,586	331,081	992,667
Arkansas,	324,313	111,104	435,427
Tennessee,	834,068	275,784	1,109,852
Total,	5,608,556	8,539,150	9,137,606

Area of the Confederate States.

Texas...	237,504	N. Carolina...	50,704
Virginia,	61,362	Mississippi...	47,156
Florida..,	59,268	Tennessee....	45,500
Georgia..	50,000	Louisiana....	41,255
Arkansas.	52,198	S. Carolinia..	29,985
Alabama..	50,722		

Lincoln's Calculations.

The *Picayune*, in an article showing up the absurdities of Lincoln's message calculations, says:

On these principles the expenditure of the North, during Mr. Lincoln's war, cannot cost the people of the Northern States less than $380,500,000 per annum. For the period of a seven years war, this would be $2,663,500,000, which is $500,000,000 more than all the revenues which have been collected by the Federal Government from all sources whatsoever, including the proceeds of all public loans and Treasury notes, from the beginning of the Government in 1789 to the 30th of June, 1861. The sum is greater by nearly a *Thousand Millions of Dollars* than all the money which the Government has received from all sources whatever, exclusive of what it has borrowed, from the first day of its existence.

In a subsequent issue the same paper adds:

By a slip of the pen, the sum which Mr. Lincoln, in his message, pledges the willingness of the North to raise for the purpose of subjugating the South, was stated, this morning, to be "four times the whole amount of all the expenditures of the United States, for all purposes whatever, from the 4th of March, 1789, to the 30th of June, 1861." It is, roughly speaking, nearly three times that amount, being in the proportion of 60 to 22.

It is, however, nearly four times the amount of all the sums raised by the Federal Government during that whole period, from all sources whatever, exclusive of loans and treasury notes—all the money which it ever got without borrowing it. The actual sum of all their collections down to fractions of a dollar, was $1,535,570,454 28, which is but little over one-fourth of what Mr. Lincoln promises the world that the Northern people will be willing to pay to conquer the South!

The amended computation does not, however, affect the absurdity of Mr. Lincoln's gasconade. A handful of millions or so are as feather weights with him. A tenth part of what he promises, would be as much out of his reach as to pluck down the moon and coin it into dollars. It would make no difference if he should throw in for *lagniappe* an odd thousand or two of millions.

A BEAR CRUSHED.—The Petersburg Express says that on Sunday morning last, as a provision train from Norfolk was proceeding up the railroad, a big black bear emerged from the Dismal Swamp at a point below Suffolk, and ran up the track. Not being quite so fleet in his movements as the locomotive, bruin was overtaken, and coming in contact with the cowcatcher, soon spread himself on the side of the road, rolled up his eyes and breathed his last. He was taken to Suffolk and divided among the soldiers, who had a royal dinner on bear meat Sunday.

☞ The man who would not take a paper because he could borrow one, has invented a machine with which he can cook his dinner by the smoke of his neighbor's chimney.

WHAT THE ARKANSAS WOMEN ARE DOING.—The Little Rock Gazette hopes it will not be considered boastful when it states that the Ladies of that city, since the war began, have performed an extraordinary amount of patriotic labor. They have made nearly or quite three thousand military suits, upwards of fifteen hundred haversacks, and probably five thousand shirts, and have also covered twelve hundred canteens.

DESIRE OF SOLDIERS FOR WATER ON THE BATTLE FIELD.—A Yankee participator in the fight at Great Bethel, gives the following idea of the risk a soldier will run to obtain water upon the battle field:

Some of us have had very narrow chances for life. In the course of the fight several of us ran across a road along which the cannon of the enemy were constantly playing, in order to get water. (I find, by the way, that on the battle field a man will risk his life without hesitation for water.) Having got it, we were waiting to rush back again, dodging the balls in order to do so.—Our First Lieutenant sang out, "Don't so many of you come at once!" I, with some others, stopped to allow the next lot to pass. They made a rush, and when nearly across, a cannon ball came whizzing along and killed four men, mowing them down instantly.

THRILLING SNAKE STORY.—The St. Joseph (Michigan) Traveler, says:

We learn that James Graham, Esq., our up-and-dressed Sheriff, whose adventure with the wolf, which, it will be recollected, he skated down and caught on the river last winter, an exploit, by the way, that has been copied into almost every paper in the United States, yesterday was the hero of another adventure more wonderful than the one alluded to. While crossing a piece of marshy ground bordering on northern bayou, near this village, in company with a small boy, he discovered two extraordinary large blue racer snakes just ahead of him, and, although armed with nothing but an insignificent stick, he resolved at once to endeavor to dispatch the monsters. Therefore, by describing a circle, he headed them off and hemmed them in next the water, which this specie of reptile dislikes exceedingly, but as he approached nearer and nearer, the largest one with head erect, turned upon him, and in an instant, coiled himself about his legs with such tenacity that it was impossible for him to move from his tracks without falling over.

But in spite of this predicament the Sheriff was not much alarmed, until he saw the other snake, which had been running from side to side, suddenly dart towards him, and with the quickness of lightning, leaped upon him, catching his right arm in his embrace and binding it to his body as firmly as if it had been secured with chains of steel, and, of course, notwithstanding he strained every nerve in the effort, he could not release it. With his left hand he drew a sheath-knife from a breast pocket of his coat, and made short work of severing the coils of his adversaries. The largest of these monsters measured seven feet four inches in length. The Sheriff says that it seemed to him that the terrible embrace of the large reptile was equal to the strength which two men could bring to bear on a rope about a person's limbs, and was extremely painful, while the quickness of their movements was indeed astonishing. He brought away their heads as trophies of his victory.

MARRIED,

In this town on Monday evening, the 8th inst., by the Rev. Mr. Fullot, M. R. HAGGERTY, Esq., Merchant of New Orleans, to Miss VIRGINIA LABAUVE, daughter of the Hon. Zenon Labauve, of this place.

We tender our thanks for the evidence of regard had for us, as embraced in the handsome present of a portion of the luxuries which followed the above occurrence—the uniting of two hearts in love and harmony, we trust, in many, many happy years to come.

Also, in this parish, on the evening of Tuesday, the 8th inst., at the residence of the bride's mother, Mr. ADEDMA LANDRY to Miss VICTORIA DUPUY, daughter of the late Paulin Dupuy, all of this parish.

We were remembered here also, in the manner usual on such occasions, and while we return our greatful acknowledgements, cannot avoid breathing within a hope that long years of happy, sunny days will gleam upon the future of the young couple who have thus pledged to each other their love, their constancy and their faith, while journeying on together through the changing vistas of this world's ways.

DIED.

In this Town, on the 2nd inst., M. BOONE, infant son of Francois and Elodie Boone, aged 13 months.

Also, on the 17th inst., in this town, Mr. MORIS MARIX, in the 46th year of his age.

State of Louisiana—Parish of Iberville—Fifth District Court.

In matter of Estate of CHARLES LOUIS PETIT, dec'd.

WHEREAS Joseph Lucien Petit has this day petitioned this Court for letters of administration in the Succession of Charles Louis Petit, dec'd:

Notice is hereby given to all whom it may concern, to show cause within TEN days from the date hereof, why the prayer of said petition, should not be granted.

E. A. MARIONNEAUX,
Clerk's Office, July 12, 1861. Dp. Clerk.

Etate de la Louisiane—Paroisse d'Iberville Cour du 5me. District Judiciaire.

Dans la Succession de fue Charles Louis Petit.

ATTENDU que Joseph Lucien Petit à ce jour presenté une petition en cette Cour, a l'effet d'obtenir des lettres d'administration dans la succession de feu Charles Louis Petit:

Avis est par le present donné à tous ceux que cela concerne de deduire sous dix jours de la date de ce present les raisons pour lesquelles il ne serait pas fait droit à la dite petition.

Bureau du Greffier Juilet 12, 1861.
E. A. MARIONNEAUX,
jy13 Dp. Greffier.

Sheriff's Sale.

HELENE BARBET, vs. ALEXANDER ROTH. } No. 1241.

PARTITION SALE.

STATE OF LOUISIANA—PARISH OF IBERVILLE, 5th JUDICIAL DISTRICT COURT.

By virtue of an order or decree to me directed from the Honorable the late 6th District Court, and now the 5th District Court of the State of Louisiana, in and for the Parish of Iberville, bearing date the 11th day of Feb., 1861, ordering and decreeing the sale of the property belonging to the Succession of Eloise L. Langlois, deceased wife of Alexander Roth. I will offer at PUBLIC SALE to the highest and last bidder, on

SATURDAY, the 3rd day of August Next, 1861, at 11 o'clock, A. M.,

On the premises, the following described property—to wit:

Seperate Property of Deceased.

1st. A TRACT OF LAND situated in the said Parish of Iberville on the left bank of the Bayou Plaquemine, whereon the said Alexander Roth resides, containing four arpents front on the said Bayou, by forty arpents in depth of the first concession, with a double concession in the rear of said tract, containing the same quantity of land in superfices as the front tract or first concession, both said tracts forming the Plantation which is established and cultivated as a Sugar Estate, which is bounded above by land belonging to Joseph Kleinpeter, and below by lands belonging to Widow Paulin Dupuy.

2nd. A TRACT OF LAND (uncultivated) situated in said Parish, on the Island of Plaquemine, containing six arpents on said Bayou, by the depth extending from the lower to the upper branch of the Bayou Plaquemine, bounded above by land of Joseph Kleinpeter, and below by land of Etienne Robert.

SLAVES.

Pauline, negro woman (sickly) aged about 47 years.
Paul, negro man, aged about 24 yrs.
Joseph, " " 22 "
Major, " " 20 "
John, negro boy " 16 "
Aspasie, negro woman, aged 31 "
and her child Louisa, girl, 11 "
Clementine, negro woman,—"Cook," (sickly) aged 46 years, and her child Sophy, aged 9 years.
Desirée, mulatto woman (sickly), house servant, aged 25 years, and her child Isadore, aged 4 years.
Euphrosine, mulatto woman, house servant, aged 23 years, and her child Charles, aged 4 years.
Mary Jane, negro woman, aged 18 yrs., and her child George, aged 8 months.
Amy, Orphan child, aged 6 months.
Henry, negro boy, aged 16 years.

Community Property—(SLAVES.)

Bill or William, negro man, aged 44 years.
Tom, negro man, aged 37 years.
Ben, negro man, aged 36 years.

Community Property—MOVEABLES.

One lot of Plantation and farming utensils, such as Carts, [Cane and Bagasse,] Flukes, Double and Single Ploughs, Hoes, Cross Cut Saws, Axes, Spades, Shovels, &c., &c. Also, a lot of Carpenters', Coopers' and Blacksmiths' tools; about 350 cords of wood; 7 Mules, 3 Horses, 3 Cows and Calves; one lot of Household Furniture—a full description of which will be given on the day of sale.

TERMS---CASH.

Plaquemine, Parish of Iberville,
July 1st, 1861. july6
THEO. BLANCHARD, *Sheriff.*

Vente de Sherif.

HELENE BARBET, vs. ALEXANDER ROTH. } No. 1241.

Vente en Partage.

ETAT DE LA LOUISIANE—PAROISSE D'IBERVILLE—COUR DU 5ème DISTRICT.

En vertué d'un ordre on decret à moi addressé par l'Honb'l autrefoe's Cour du 6ème, District and maintenant la 5ème Cour de District Judiciere de l'etat de la Louisiane, en et pour la Paroisse d'Iberville, en date du 11me jour de Fevrier, 1861. Ordenant la vente des proprietrés appartenant à la Succession de feu Eloise L. Langlois, epouse d'Alexander Roth, J'offrirai, en vente publiquean plus offrant et dennier en cherisseur

Samedi, le 3 Aout prochain, 1861, a 11 heures, a. m.

Sur les lieux les proprietés suivantes, savoir:

Bien propres de defunte.

1—UN MORCEAU DE TERRE situé dans la Paroisse d'Iberville, sur la rive gauche du Bayou Plaquemine, sur lequel demeure Alexander Roth, contenant quatre arpents de face sur le dit Bayou, et quarante de profondeur de la premiere concession, avec une double concession en arriere du dit morceau de terre contenant la méme quantité de terre que la premiere concession les deux morceaux de terre formant l'habitation qui est établie, et cultivé en sucre—et qui est borné en haut, par terre appartenant à Joseph Kleinpeter, et en bas par terre appartenant à Veve Pauline Dupuy.

2o—UN MORCEAU DE TERRE (inculte) situé dans la Paroisse d'Iberville, sur l'isle Plaquemine, contenant six arpents sur le dit Bayou, par la profondeur s'etendant du Bayou Jacob au Bayou Plaquemine, borné en haut par terre de Joseph Kleinpeter, et en bas par terre d'Etienne Robert.

ESCLAVES.

Pauline, (maladive) negresse agcéde 47 ans.
Paul, negre homme, agé 24 ans.
Joseph, " " 22 "
Major, " " 20 "
John, " " 16 "
Aspasiè, negresse " 31 "
et son enfant Louise agé 11 "
Clémentine, negresse (maladive), Cuisiniere, agé 46 ans.
et son enfant Sophié, agé 9 "
Desireé, mulatresse (maladive) domestique de maison, agé 25 ans,
et son enfant Isidore, agé 4 "
Euphrosine, mulatresse, domestique de maison, agé 23 "
et son enfant Charles, agé 4 "
Mary Jane, negresse " 18 "
et son enfant George, " 8 mois
Aimé, orphelinè " 6 ans.
Henry, " 16 ans.

Biens de Communeanté—(ESCLAVES.)

Bill ou William, negre homme, agé de 44 ans.
Tom, " " " 37
Ben, " " " 36

Biens de Communeanté—MOBELE'RS.

Un lot d'outils Aratoires tel que Charrettes, Charrues, Prirhes, outils de Charpentiers de Forgeron, et de Tonnelièr, àpenprés, 350 cordes de bois, Sept Mulets, trois Cheveaux, trois Vaches et Veaux; un lot de Meubles, etc., etc.

Conditions---Comptant.

THEO BLANCHARD, *Sherif.*
Plaquemine, Paroisse d'Iberville.
Juillet 1er, 1861. july6

Runaway in Prison.

Was committed to the Parish prison, negro TOM, claiming to belong to Thos. Powell, of New Orleans. Tom is about 30 years old, 5ft. 9 in. high, slender, wears moustache and goatee; is nearly a griff. The owner is hereby notified to reclaim him as required by law.

THEO. BLANCHARD Sheriff.

AETE conduit à la geole de cette Paroisse le TOM, disant appartenir à Thos Powell de la New Orleans. Tom est agé d'environ 30 ans; 5 pieds 9 pouces de taille; porte la barbe, et est de couleu moyen griff. Le proprietaire est notifié de la eclamer comme la loi le requiert.

ly6 THEO. BLANCHARD, Sherif.

Runaway in Prison.

Was committed to jail negro boy HENRY, claiming to belong to James Devalle of W. B. Rouge. Henry is about 23 years old; 5 ft. 9 in. high; black, inclined to griff—large white eyes and bushy hair. The owner is hereby notified to reclaim him in the manner required by law.

THEO. BLANCHARD, Sheriff.

AETE conduit à la geole de cette Paroisee, negre HENRY, disant appartenir à James Devalle la Paroisse d'Ouest Baton Rouge. Henry est agé d'environs 23 ans; 5 pieds 9 pouces de taille; noir; yeux blanco.

Le proprietaire est notifié de la reclamer comme la loi le requiert. THEO. BLANCHARD,
july13 Sherif.

SPECIAL NOTICES.

NOTICE.

MR. LOUIS DESOBY, you are hereby notified to repair your road from your saw mill down to your lower line, and also all your cross bridges, and cut down the weeds from your Levee, within your enclosure, from your saw mill to your lower line; this work to be completed according to law, by the 15th of October, 1861.

JOHN SCHLATRE,
jly6 Inspector of 8th District.

MR. V. J. DUPUY, you are hereby notified to make your road 6 feet wider, and to raise it to the same height of the old road, little above Pratalongo's house, where there has been a crevasse some years' back; this work to be completed by the 15th of October, 1861.

JOHN SCHLATRE,
jly6 Inspector of 8th District.

MR. B. DUPUY, you are hereby notified to dig out your ditches so as to drain your road on your lower tract of land; repair your cross Bridges, cut down all deadened timber within reach of your road, remove them therefrom and cut down the weeds; this work to be completed according to law, by the 15th of October, 1861.

JOHN SCHLATER,
jly6 Inspector of 8th District

Inspector's Notice

To Non-Residents of the 17th District.

TO Laurent Millaudon, Daniel Holliday. Augustin LeBlanc, Estate Charles A. Slack, George W. Campbell, Dr. Thos. S. Garret, Isaac Erwin, Estate C. H. Dickinson, Mrs. E. Woolfolk,—

Each and every one of you are hereby notified to deliver your road 25 feet wide, free of obstructions; said road to be raised in the middle, with a ditch on each side, all weeds, briars, roots and stumps whatsoever, to be removed, holes to be filled. Your Cordelle Road to be cleared of all obstructions. The above works to be accomplished on or before the 15th day of October, 1861, according to law.

J. PARDO,
Inspector 17th District.
Grosse Tete, June 14, '61—jun28.

To Sosthene Allain.

YOU will repair your bridges forthwith; you will level your road wherever neccessary, and clean your ditches so as to drain said road; this to be completod according to law by the 15th of October, 1861.

J. V. HEBERT,
jun29 9th Dist. Road and Levee Inspector.

TO LAURENT MILLAUDON, Eugene Robosse and ——LAURIOT, You are hereby notified to repair your road and levee on your lots of land, lying on Bayou Maringouin, in the parish of Iberville, by cutting the weeds and brush from said lots according to law, by the 15th October.

D. P. FLYNN,
jun29 Inspector.

Notice.

MY wife, Leontine Chaudoer, having left my domicile, and instituted suit for separation from bed and board from me, I hereby notify the public not to credit her on my account.

jly13 VALLERY ROTH.

State of Louisiana—Parish of Iberville—5th Judicial District Court.

In Matter of Estate of Rosalie Melancon and Dorville LaCroix.

WHEREAS: CLEOPHAS BARBAY has this day filed in this Court his final account of administration of the Estate of Rosalie Malançon and Dorville LaCroix, both dec'd.

Notice is hereby given to all whom it may concern to show cause within Thirty days from this date, why the final Tableau of Administration aforesaid, should not be homologated and made a judgement of this Court, and the bond of the administrator cancelled and annulled.

Iberville, June 20, 1861.
ju22 M. A. ESTEVAN, Clerk.

Etat dela Louisiane—Paroisse d'Iberville—Cour du 5eme District Judiciaire.

Dans la Successton de feus

Rosalie Melancon & Dorville LaCroix.

ATTENDU, que CLEOPHAS BARBAY a ce jour enliassé en cette Cour son Tableaux final d'administration de la succession de fues Rosalie Melançon and Dorville LaCroix.

Avis est par le present donné à tous ceux que cela concerne de deduire sans trente jours de la date de ce present les raisons pour lesquelles le dit Tableaux final ne serait pas homoloqué et fait le judgment de cetté Cour et le cautionnement annullè.

Iberville, le Juin 20, 1861.
ju22. M. A. ESTEVAN, Greffier.

$60 REWARD!

A REWARD of $60 will be given for the apprêhension of Runaways **Charles, Joe** and **Josh,**—or $25 for the arrest and delivery of each of said slaves to the undersigned.

CHARLES is about 35 years old—5 ft. 9 in high, black, stout, with heavy, ugly looking countenance, and long, bushy head of hair, and belongs to Charles Nettleton.

JOE is a griff—about 19 yrs. old—5 ft. 5 in. high, stout, speaks in a very slow, drawlling manner, and has a large mole on one side of his neck; and JOSH, his father, a good looking old darkey, aged about 50 years, 5 ft. 8 in. high—will weigh about 145 lbs., and belongs to Mrs. Mary Laughlin.

As these negroes are supposed to have been harbored, all persons are hereby notified that the penalties of the law will be strictly enforced against any one concealing or harboring same.

LAUGHLIN & NETTLETON,
"Down Home" Place,
my25 Grand River, Iberville, La.

Richmond Dispatch.

MONDAY MORNING.......JULY 22, 1861.

Terrific Fight at Manassas!

VICTORY AGAIN PERCHES ON OUR BANNER.

Yesterday was a day long to be remembered in the annals of Richmond. During the whole afternoon groups could be seen gathered around the newspaper offices and the hotels, anxiously inquiring whether any news had been received from the scene of expected conflict. Towards the hour at which the Central cars generally arrived, crowds could be seen wending their way to the depot, expecting that news would be received from passengers from the neighborhood of the engagement.

On inquiry, we ascertained that when the cars left Manassas, (7 o'clock, A. M.,) heavy firing was heard in the vicinity of Bull's Run, about three miles from that place, and where the battle of Thursday occurred. Our informant could not distinguish anything like the report of cannon, and therefore concluded the fight was confined principally to skirmishers. Before the train reached this city, however, information had reached them at Gordonsville that the engagement had become general, and that a terrific battle was progressing.

Private dispatches of the most reliable character were received at a late hour in the evening, informing us that the attack was made by our forces about four o'clock, in consequence of an attempt of the enemy to throw up breastworks under the disguise of burying their dead. In the general engagement President DAVIS led the centre, Gen. BEAUREGARD the right wing, and Gen. JOHNSTON the left wing of our army.

The Lincoln army was completely routed. Hampton's Legion suffered considerable loss.

Sherman's celebrated Battery of Light Artillery was taken by our troops.

The fight was very severe and fatal on both sides. Among the prominent officers who are reported to have been killed are Col. BARTOW, of Georgia; Gen. BEE, of South Carolina; Gen. KIRBY SMITH, and Col. JOHNSON, of the Hampton Legion.

The following dispatch was received by Mrs. President DAVIS late last evening:

"We have won a glorious but dear bought victory—the night closed with the enemy in full flight, pursued by our troops.

"JEFF. DAVIS."

The reader is referred to our telegraph column for intelligence from the scene of action.

The Fight At Manassas, Thursday.

FURTHER PARTICULARS.

[FROM OUR OWN CORRESPONDENTS.]

BULL'S RUN, July 19, 1861.

While our boys are leaning on their muskets and discussing the events of yesterday, I retire a few paces in the woods to give you a few outlines of the battle of yesterday, fought, and as a matter of course, won chiefly by the boys of the 1st Regiment, aided by the Washington Artillery, of New Orleans, and some Alexandria Artillery. Not knowing the exact position the other regiments of our brigade occupied, and as the heat of the fire was chiefly conducted against and sustained by us, I will strictly confine myself to the part we bore in the fight, leaving it to the others to state their share in it. Our brigade left Camp Pickens on the 17th, at 10 A. M.—No pen can describe the mortification our company (Company I) experienced, when we (who, with the rest, stood ready to march off,) got orders to stay behind and guard the camp until further orders, and I shall not even attempt it. Luckily for us, at about 11 P. M., (I just stood on guard,) a horseman rode into camp, halted in front of Capt. Taylor's tent, and brought the orders from headquarters to strike our tents and keep ourselves in readiness to join our regiment at daybreak. In the joy of my heart I ran about twenty paces beyond my post (don't tell it to the officer of the guard) to impart the tidings to the next sentinel. The drum was rolled, and in a second our fellows were out of their tents and went to work with a will, so that in two hours all our knapsacks were packed, haversacks filled, and our tents, as well as those of the departed companies, were struck. But don't let me keep the news longer from you. Suffice it to say, that we marched off at about 8 A. M., and our regiment drawn up in line at Bull's Run, with the exception of Company D, who were posted already as skirmishers.

At about 12 o'clock we heard the first volley of musketry, and Company I was ordered to post themselves beyond Company D on the right. We marched towards the banks of the creek and threw ourselves behind the trees, in the bushes, flat on the ground, on our knees, standing, sitting—in short, every possible position or attitude which human nature possibly can assume. It was about half an hour before one of our men spied the first Yankee, and popped him down most unceremoniously, and shortly after that the ball opened for good. True, Companies I and D had very little to do with it, as our post was not attacked during the day; and thus, besides sending now and then a Yankee, who was inquisitive enough to pry in our affairs, reeling down the hill, (where they were posted,) we comparatively kept far from the enemy's fire, only a few musket balls, or a piece of shell, now and then lodging in and near the trees and bushes behind which we were deployed. The other companies figured more conspicuously, and had a glorious time of it. Smith's Band, splendidly as it executes their pieces, and fond as we are to listen to them, could not give us a nicer piece of music than that played by our Artillery. It is a style quite new to us, *but it beats Yankee Doodle altogether to pieces*. Col. Moore was wounded in the left arm, in the commencement of the fight, and had to be carried from the field; whereupon Major Skinner, aided by Capt. Mitchell, took the command, (Lieut. Col. Fry being at the time quite busy in another part,) and nobly did they acquit themselves of their task. Where the fire was the hottest, there you were sure to see our brave commanders, cheering and commanding our boys alternately. Company H fought side by side with the Alexandria Rifles, (of the 11th Regiment,) and vied with each other in the display of courage and intrepidity. They (Company H) deplore the loss of one man, and had two men slightly wounded; but dearly did they make the enemy pay for their loss. Almost out of the very ranks of the enemy they dragged the man who shot their brave comrade, and Lieut. Vaughan possessed himself of his arms, (a splendid rifle, by the bye.) The man is now a prisoner. Besides this one, they took two or three more prisoners, and any quantity of rifles and Minnie muskets, most of which they dropped again, as they obstructed their movements. Capt. Sherman and his Washington Volunteers (Company E,) had a good chance of wreaking their vengeance upon their foes and grasped at it with both hands. The Captain himself fired both his pistols five times, which we may safely believe as having killed ten men, he being a dead shot. They, too, lost one man and had four more wounded. Company B was unfortunate enough to have their Captain (Lee) and Lieutenant (Harrison) wounded, which fact added, if possible, to their courage—besides they lost one man and five slightly wounded. Company K, too, deplore the loss of one man and two wounded, and from their side made a perfect slaughter in the enemy.

Apropos—When the regiment left on the 17th, eight of Company K's men were on guard, and as orders were given from headquarters not to let anybody pass out of camp after the regiment left, it was to be expected that they had to stay behind; but Lieut. Loman took his men when they came back, and stating plainly that where his company was, there too was their place. They passed in spite of the sentinels and joined their boys.—Well done Rifles!

Company C, too, showed that they are the boys who relish a fight. They were lucky enough to carry every man of their camp safe and sound back again, except three or four who were slightly wounded, amongst whom Lieut. English. Company G unfortunately lost their 2d Lieutenant, Miles, and his loss is deeply felt by the whole regiment. He was an efficient officer and highly estimated by his men and fellow-officers. His death and the loss of the other five noble fellows throw a gloom over the triumph of yesterday, which we cannot shake off entirely, in spite of us. But the recollection how and when they fell and the thought that we expect hourly to get called upon to avenge their death, cheers us greatly and makes us bear our loss.

Don't think that I placed the companies in this sketch according to their valor, (for as Lieut. Col. Fry exclaimed this morning: "our boys, one and all, have done bravely,") but I just put them down as I was able to take notes down. Altogether it was the most decided down-right whipping the Yankees ever received on Virginia soil. They had the advantage of ground and the advantage of numbers. Not that we had not men enough, but we never had more than 1200 men in the field at the same time, while they were leading 15,000 men on at one charge. Their famous Sherman battery did not intimidate us in the least, and we had the pleasure to send to-day two of their most splendid rifle cannon to Manassas. I believe we got muskets enough to equip a good-sized battalion, and there is no end to the haversacks and canteens which they threw away in their flight. Amongst other things, our wagons brought us to-day a load of caps and hats, which shows that after all they must have great respect for us, or they would not have taken them off for us. Well, at 7 o'clock P. M. we stopped firing, but they did not stop retreating, and there the fun ended for that day.

N. B.—Gen. Longstreet showed himself in the most conspicuous part of the fight, and had his horse shot from under him.

COMPANY I.

P. S.—Honor to whom honor is due. The color guard acted most heroically. While the fight was the hottest Serg. Reeves, with Corp. Norvell and four privates, passed the creek with flying colors, having to wade up to their waist through the water, and planted the glorious bars and stars on the hill under an incessant fire from the enemy, whilst Reeves roared out to Turner to rally to their colors After repeated orders to retreat only, he fell back with his men to the main body.

Company G lost two men more than I stated first—thus three in all.

The dead are buried. A large apple tree shades their graves, and McLane's farm, which received their noble bodies, will forevermore be a sacred place in the memory of the whole South. They are carefully wrapped up in their blankets, and papers with their honored names attached to each of them. Peace be to their ashes.

COMPANY I.

MANASSAS JUNCTION, }
July 19, 1861, 9 P. M. }

Well, one of the long-looked for "big fights" to come off at this place, as the first step towards the destruction of Richmond, has taken place, and resulted in a complete frustration of the enemy and his plans. A more complete and glorious victory we could not have asked, and must add another leaf to the chaplet of Gen. Beauregard's fame. When 7,000 men are thrice repulsed by less than two thousand, with over ten times the loss sustained by the attacked; when the 2,000 attacked has no peculiar advantage of position, nor breastworks to protect them, it certainly proves either uncommon skill in the management of the defence, or extraordinary weakness in the plan of attack.

On yesterday, about noon, Gen. McDowell, with twelve or fourteen regiments and one battery, in which there were at least two rifle cannon, attempted to force a passage across Bull's Run, at Mitchell's Ford, about 3½ miles from Manassas Junction. General Longstreet's Brigade, composed of the First Virginia Regiment, under Col. Moore, the Seventeenth Virginia and one Louisiana Regiment, being situated near the Ford, received the attack, principally the First Virginia Regiment, and repulsed them three times, with a loss of only 12 men killed and about 60 wounded, while the loss of the enemy is stated by their own men to be not less than 300 killed and 600 wounded. There were not more than 1,000 of our men engaged, including a battery of two or three guns, while there could not have been less than 3,000 of the enemy actually engaged, besides a battery of at least two rifle cannon. We expected the attack would be renewed to-day, but this morning the enemy hoisted a white flag and asked permission to bury their dead, which was granted; and it was from these men who have been burying the dead, and the prisoners, ten in number, that we learn there were 900 missing this morning at roll call. They have been all day burying their dead, and we don't know whether they are done yet or not. It is rumored just now, at 11, A. M., that Gen. Beauregard was hourly expecting a night attack.

Besides the killed and wounded, and the ten prisoners we took, we have taken two 32-pound rifle cannon, some four or five hundred muskets, and as many hats. Our men behaved with the utmost coolness. firing irregularly, but taking good aim. The battle lasted three and a half hours. The musketry firing by the enemy was done with remarkable regularity, but with little effect, as the result proved.

A rifle cannon ball went through the house occupied by our men as a hospital, near Gen. Beauregard's quarters.

DAN.

P. S.—July 20, 6 A. M.—There was no firing this morning in the direction of our line.—The reports this morning from the killed and wounded of the enemy are so contradictory that I cannot say anything is reliable. There is do doubt they have met with a severe loss, and a most extraordinary defeat in their attempt to cross Bull's Run.

D.

Correspondence of the Richmond Dispatch.

Fight at Rich Mountain.

STAUNTON, July 19, 1861.

I will attempt to give you a description of the fight at Rich Mountain as far as I saw and participated in it. We were attacked about 12 o'clock, M. When the firing commenced I was at the camp cooking dinner for our company that were in the trenches on the mountain. When I heard the first gun I caught up my musket and ran up to the trenches where I left my company, but found they had left for a point farther up the mountain. I followed on to overtake my company and found them in a ravine, stationed behind trees, to tickle the enemy's rear if they attempted to come down that way; but they didn't come. After waiting some time our captain marched up to the road, intending to march us up to aid those on the mountain.—We had gone about twenty feet up the road when we were fired upon by the enemy from the bushes. After the first volley our men fell back and sheltered themselves behind trees to gain time to rally the men for another charge. We again emerged into the road and marched up through the fire of the enemy within ten feet of the enemy's bayonets, when the fire became so hot that we had to retreat. We retreated about twenty yards down the road, where we again formed a line, but concluded not to advance again as we had only 83 men and the enemy between four and five hundred men, and the most of them were in ambush. We marched down the mountain about two hundred yards, when we met Col. Pegram with about three hundred men to reinforce us. He then led us up to the top of the mountain for the purpose of driving the enemy from that position; but after getting there and finding the enemy in such force he abandoned the idea and placed us under the command of Major Tyler, to join Col. Garnett's command, but after getting to Beverly we heard that Gen. Garnett was retreating from Laurel Hill. We then marched to Huttonville and joined Col. Scott's regiment. Col. Pegram is now a prisoner in Beverly and Gen. Garnett is dead.

A SURVIVOR OF RICH MOUNTAIN.

Correspondence of the Richmond Dispatch.

Affairs in King George.

PORT CONWAY, VA., July 18, 1861.

Notwithstanding the call was anticipated, our militia was considerably "flurried" upon the appearance of Gov. Letcher's late proclamation. While there is no lack of proper zeal for the cause, nor want of nerve to meet the conflict in which they have been called upon to engage, yet there are many who find themselves surrounded by such circumstances as render it next to impossible for them to leave their homes. Great indeed will be the sacrifice in many individual cases, but all personal interests and considerations must now be made to yield to the higher service we owe to our country. The various militia companies of the county will rendezvous at our Court-House on Monday next, where they will remain to await further orders.

At Mathias' Point all has been quiet for the past ten or twelve days. There have been some cases of sickness among the soldiers there, but none have as yet proved fatal.

A most melancholy accident occurred in our midst on Monday last. Mr. Wm. J. W. Greer and C. B. Spilman, the former a resident of this county and Postmaster at Shiloah, the latter a son of Mr. Wm. L. Spilman of Westmoreland, while bathing with a party of other gentlemen in Rosier's Creek, were swept off by the current and drowned. Their bodies have since been recovered. Mr. Greer leaves a large family, upon whom the saddest affliction has fallen by this melancholy occurrence. He was a man of the most generous impulses, kind and affectionate in his family, and highly esteemed as a friend and neighbor. Young Spilman, though but a lad, was universally beloved. Brave almost to a fault, yet so amiable in his disposition and exhibiting such manly and noble traits of character as to endear himself to all with whom he was brought in contact.

REKAB.

Correspondence of the Richmond Dispatch.

From Gaully Bridge.

GAULLY BRIDGE, July 17, 1861.

It is pretty well understood now that there has been a sharp engagement about fifteen miles below Charleston, at a place called Coles, between Gen. Wise's forces and a detachment of about 5,000 of the enemy, who have certainly landed and advanced on Charleston. This force landed at two points, Buffalo and Guyandotte, about 1,500 at the latter place, on Saturday last. The detachment which landed at Guyandotte was opposed at a point called Sun Up by Captain Jenkins' company and about 500 militia. All the militia fled on the appearance of the enemy except about 150, who, with Capt. Jenkins' command, gave battle. The result was forty killed and sixty wounded of the enemy, and one killed on our side. This was an old patriarch eighty years old, who used his spectacles and fired with his rifle from an ambuscade until he was discovered and put to death, not however until he had killed six.

Captain Jenkins' company behaved most gallantly, and fired from a cross road on the enemy with the most deadly effect. Nearly an entire platoon fell from the first company fire. The enemy immediately retreated, but have rallied, and it is thought joined their comrades who landed at Buffalo.

Col. J. Lucius Davis has just arrived from Lewisburg with several noble companies raised for the Wise Legion. *

The War in Missouri—The State of Affairs as Reported by the Enemy.

We find the following dispatches from Black Republican sources, (of course not altogether to be relied on,) in the latest Tennessee papers:

ST. LOUIS, July 16.—The Washington correspondent of the *Anzeiger* says Captain Sweeney's appointment as Brigadier General of the St Louis Home Guard was never confirmed by Government, and orders have been issued calling him and his company of regulars to join his regiment, the 2d U. S. Infantry, at Washington.

Respectable authority says Colonel Siegel will be promoted to be a Brigadier General.

The train on the North Missouri Railroad conveying a detachment of Colonel Smith's Regiment of Zouaves, were fired into yesterday from the woods skirting the road twenty miles above St. Charles, and two troops severely wounded.

The report that Senator Green had violated his parole is untrue. J. W. Tucker, the late editor of the State Journal, is making violent Secession speeches in the country. Colonel Steifli, of the 5th Regiment of reserve corps, arrived from Lexington to-day, and reports having captured 200 kegs of powder, 30 muskets, 1 cannon, a quantity of machinery for boring, and a mould for casting cannon, and several other contraband articles.

Orders have been issued prohibiting steamers from passing Jefferson City unless they have the American flag flying.

ST. LOUIS, July 17.—Mr. Hayward, Superintendent of the Hannibal and St. Joseph railroad, just from Hannibal, received the following dispatch previous to leaving that place:

HUDSON, Mo., July 16.—800 Federal troops came up ahead of the passenger train as far as Melville, thirty miles above St. Charles, on the North Missouri Railroad, where the track was torn up and the troops fired into. An engagement ensued, resulting in the loss of seven rebels killed and several prisoners One man caught with a gun in his hands was immediately hung.

Another, attempting to escape, was riddled with balls. The fighting still continued when the passenger train passed up. Federal loss, three killed and seven wounded. Thirty horses were captured. The strength of the rebels is not known.

FROM SOUTHWESTERN MISSOURI.

The St. Louis Democrat, of the 16th, has the following news from the Southwest, fully confirming our previous reports of the movements of the Arkansas troops:

Capt. Conrad's command, which had been left at Neosho, report that on the 5th of July they were surrounded by 1,500 Arkansas troops, and were given fifteen minutes' time to surrender. Before the time expired the enemy's force was increased to 3,000. Capt. Conrad then surrendered his command. Ben. McCullough was present.

Gen. Price and Gov. Jackson then demanded that their men and arms be delivered to the Missouri troops. The Arkansas officers refused this demand. Afterwards Capt. Emmett McDonald passed among them and inquired if they were not St Louis boys. They replied they were. The Captain then treated a number of them to lager beer. They were then sent off, after taking the obligation not to bear arms against the Southern Confederacy, under the escort of Arkansas troops, as it was understood that the Missourians intended to murder them.

The escort accompanied them some thirty miles, when they were left to find their way to Springfield.

A large number of Indians was present in the camp at Neosho.

Volunteering for Twelve Months and for the War—A Patriotic Letter from a Son to his Father.

[From the Atlanta Southern Confederacy.]

Messrs. Editors: The following letter was written by a son, 19 years old, to his father, who, whilst he was willing that his son should volunteer for twelve months, was reluctant to give him up during the war. If you think this letter breathes the right spirit—if you think it will touch the hearts of *other* fathers and of *other* sons in the right place, please give it a place in your valuable paper:

DEAR FATHER: The Lester Volunteers are now preparing to start for the seat of war, and I feel it to be my duty to ask your consent before I go. When I volunteered for one year, you seemed perfectly willing; but when I saw you last, you appeared dissatisfied that I had agreed to go during the war. It is needless for me to say anything in regard to the change which the Congress of the Confederate States has made. Let it suffice to say that I think it is nothing but right, and if I did not, I would be willing to go anyhow.—Nothing can be too hard, no sacrifice too great, when Liberty is at stake. But a father's love will foresee dangers, and urge a *cause*. You point me to the toils, hardships and dangers of a soldier's life. These I know are great; but is the strong right arm of God too weak to protect, too short to defend me from the vices and crimes which surround the soldier?—the only enemies I fear. Shall I not trust Him? "Ah! but death is almost certain," you respond. Would you teach me to fear to die in defence of right, of truth and of justice?—Fighting for the land of my birth, for the rights guaranteed to us by the Eternal God, for the home I love? I feel that death, in its most horrid and ghastly form, would have no terrors for me. "But perhaps you will not be needed; wait until you are called for again," you reply. I have heard this advanced often, and have as repeatedly inquired, *when will that be?* Will it be when our land is invaded and laid waste with fire and sword; our homes desolated; our loved ones butchered—when the Confederate flag trails in the dust, our army defeated and disorganized? No, Father: the first gun that boomed from Fort Sumter called in thunder tones upon me to rally to the standard of my country, and I burn to answer that call.

But I feel that I cannot go without your consent, for you are my father, and as such you have the right to say whether or not I shall go. I beg you, as you love me, withhold not your consent. If you refuse, I must obey; but when it is done, life will have lost all charms for me, even if the South should, by a vigorous campaign, soon end the war by driving from our land the vandals of the North.

Oh! call me not back. Rather immure me in some loathsome dungeon; let me be the cringing vassal of some heartless tyrant; bind, rivet the clanking chains of an ignoble, perpetuated slavery upon me, rather than shower on my head the blessings of a liberty bought by the blood of others. Let me pour out the gushing fountain of my own heart to secure my own rights, and I am content. I want no liberty but *my own*, achieved by my own exertions and purchased by my own blood. Call me not a blind enthusiast. Does love of country need a stimulant to call it into action? Must reason be dethroned that the fires of patriotism may be aroused? No idle dream of fame, no slavish love of money actuates me. All I ask is to fight for my country. I want no remuneration. Give me a few tattered rags to hide my nakedness, a crust to appease the gnawings of hunger, and Liberty, and I am happy.

You want me to continue to my studies.—Do you suppose I can forget a bleeding country and devote my time and attention to the study of the law? Impossible! I sometimes take up my books, determined to forget everything else, but, soon my mind is wandering over the plains of the Old Dominion, and, in my imagination, I hear the thunder of cannon on our borders, and I see the smoke of battle ascend in dense columns towards Heaven, and books, home, self, are all forgotten, and I long for the hour of departure to arrive.

I know it will wring my heart to bid you perhaps a last farewell. Were I the only one to regret my leaving, I could go without a sigh; but to see my friends in tears is too much for me. Every day I think of that sad, sad hour, and my heart swells with grief; tears flow unrestrained. I sit down sometimes in my room, at the lone hour of the night, when all eyes save those of an all-seeing God are closed in sleep, sometimes in the depths of the forest, beneath the overshadowing branches of some monarch of the woods, and give vent to the long pent-up feelings of my heart. Do not, however, suppose that this or anything else will keep me from going. Tell mother to make what clothes she wants me to have.—We expect to start in two or three weeks.

Now, father, let me entreat you, with all the earnestness of my heart, to give your consent willingly, and a father's parting blessing. I cannot go without them; I cannot live and stay at home. Your son,

W. E. ROGERS.

HUNG.—We noticed last week that a most brutal murder had been committed on the person of Mrs. Holand, an old lady 70 years of age, of Chattooga county. We have since learned that a negro woman belonging to Mrs. H. and who lived with her did the black deed with an axe.

The negro made a full and voluntary confession, she said no one was concerned in it but herself; she did not know why she did it unless the devil was in her."

On last Friday evening, after exhorting the negroes present to be obedient to, their owners, she was hung by the citizens.

We learn also that Mrs. H. was an exceedingly kind lady. She had given the woman no cause of offence except that she complained a very little that the chicken pie was not as good as it might have been.—*Rome (Ga.,) Southerner, 18th.*

Hon. J. H. Jewett, a distinguished citizen of Shelbyville, Ky., died on Saturday, the 13th, at that place.

Highly Interesting from Pensacola—Particulars of the Firing on the Federal Launch.

[Corr. of the Mobile Advertiser and Register.]

PENSACOLA, Sunday night, July 14.—The Advertiser and Register was telegraphed last night the fact, that a detachment of the Montgomery Mounted Rifles had fired upon a boat filled with Federal sailors. The Rifles, under Capt Clanton, have for some time been performing the laborious and dangerous duty of guarding the coast in the neighborhood of the East Pass of Santa Rosa Island, but without incident until Friday morning. About seven in the morning of that day, a detachment of the company under Capt. Clanton, discovered approaching the Island ashore, a small boat or launch from the blockading steamer lying a mile or two distant.

The men immediately concealed themselves behind a mound of sand and awaited their approach to within a very short distance of the ambuscade, when they were discovered by the crew. The launch immediately stopped, and attempted to pull round, when Capt. Clanton demanded their approach to the shore For a moment it seemed the intention of the launch to obey his summons, when the officer in charge of the boat drew his sword and ordered a return to the ship. Capt. Clanton a second time ordered their approach to the shore, accompanied with a threat to fire on them if disobeyed, which was disregarded. The Rifles then opened fire at a short distance, when the officer in command—supposed to be a midshipman—reeled and fell across the guards of the boat.

He is supposed to be killed or desperately wounded. Several others in the launch were thought to be hurt or killed, as the boat (an eight oared one) got out of the scrape with the assistance of only two oars. Nineteen shots were fired at not over a hundred yards Some of them, it is thought, must have been killed. The gun of one of the men missed fire the first volley; he claimed the privilege of a fire, however, which was granted, and it was thought with success. These are all the particulars of the affair I have been able to gather.

These fellows, it seems, have been in the habit of running about in their boats, for some time, near the shore, with the purpose of supplying themselves with water, as well as dropping the lead, and Capt. Clanton determined to put a stop to their audacity, and set the trap into which they came very near marching. Molten lead must have been a poor substitute for the cool spring water with which the rascals have been in the habit of slaking their thirst. The result of this, some think, may be a serious matter, and that their small boats may retaliate on our coast guard Let them try it, if they want Captain Lovell's little fleet to make 'em "scratch gravel."

There has been no addition to the squadron for the last day or two at the anchorage. Like old Patterson, the fleet is inactive.

LATER.—Capt. Clanton, with nearly all his command, has returned to this side. They are confident of having killed five or six. They fired at about one hundred yards. The flags of the steamer were at half-mast when they left their retreat for camp. Three guns were discharged from her, which they suppose were summons to other launches to return or "look out."

HEADQUARTERS OF THE FORCES, }
RICHMOND, July 4, 1861. }

GENERAL ORDERS, No. 30.—

I.—The Court of Inquiry which convened at Beverly on the 20th ult., at the request of Col. G. A. Porterfield, of the Virginia Volunteers, to examine into the circumstances of the retreat of the Virginia Forces from Philippi on the 3d of June, under his command, has reported the following facts in the case:

A force of Virginia troops, consisting of some six hundred effective Infantry, (or thereabouts,) and about one hundred and seventy-five Cavalry, (or thereabouts,) sufficiently well armed, but badly and insufficiently supplied with the necessary accoutrements and ammunition, was stationed at Philippi, Barbour county, Va., on the morning of the 3d June, 1861, (where they had been for some six or seven days,) under the command of Colonel Geo. A. Porterfield, of the Virginia Volunteers.

On the morning of the day just indicated, at between daybreak and sunrise, this command was attacked, and taken by surprise; no alarm or intimation of the enemy's approach having been given by the guard, or infantry pickets, until the enemy was within some four hundred yards of the place, and had commenced the fire from his Artillery. By the examination, it is shown, that a main and picket guard, as strong as was consistent with the effective infantry force present, was regularly detailed and posted at distances sufficiently far out to accomplish the object in view, provided they knew and did their duty; which latter is strongly to be suspected, from the fact, that although in advance, they failed to give any intimation of the enemy's approach: a conclusion which is strengthened by the official report of the mounted officers, out with the scouting parties on the night of the 2d of June, that they had neither seen an infantry picket, nor been challenged by its sentinels, going from, or returning to, the town that night. It appears, that immediately upon the arrival of the command at Philippi, the officer in command, Colonel Porterfield, took measures to place his force, which was raw, and new in service, under a course of instruction, and to select those, in his opinion, best fitted to instruct the sentinels and guards in their duties. The testimony shows, that while there was a certain degree of confusion in some quarters, a portion of the command moved from the town in good order; and that the whole force, nearly, after passing some distance from the town, was re-formed and proceeded in order.

It is shown in the evidence, that an expectation of attack, or movement upon Philippi shortly to be made, was entertained generally among the officers and others of the command, and that intelligence (how well founded is not known) was brought, from time to time, of the strength and supposed intent of the enemy

The testimony sets forth, that this had so far produced its effect, as to induce the officer in command to call a meeting of his officers; that the result of their consultations and deliberations was an almost, if not unanimous decision in favor of immediate retreat; that when Col. Porterfield returned to the room, (from which he had been absent a short time,) their opinion was conveyed to him, to which he seemed loth to accede; yet, determined to make a further examination of the ammunition on hand, and to prepare the baggage and train for removal at a moment's notice

No orders to march, at any particular time, were given, so far as can be gathered from the testimony, although it appears that an understanding or impression was had or entertained by some, that the movement would not take place until morning, while some believed it contingent upon the weather.

The record will disclose the fact of a difference of construction, (as to the hour of return,) of the orders given to the officer in command of the Cavalry company, from which the scouting party or parties was taken for duty on the night of 2d inst.

The testimony of several witnesses bears evidence of the cool, deliberate and self-possessed conduct of Col. Porterfield, on the morning of the 3d June.

The Court having been directed to express its opinion, as well as report the facts, present the following:

1st. That the commanding officer having received information deemed by him sufficient to prepare for an early retreat, erred in permitting himself to be influenced by the weather, so far as to delay the execution of his plan.

2d. That the commanding officer did order dispositions to be made to prevent surprise; but a misunderstanding as to the time at which the scouts were to be called in, and a total want of proper vigilance on the part of the infantry pickets, caused a surprise, which distinct and definite instructions, properly executed, would have avoided.

3d. That the commanding officer erred in not advancing and strengthening his picket beyond the usual limits, under the circumstances.

4th. That the commanding officer exhibited upon the occasion decided coolness, self possession and personal courage, and exerted himself, as far as possible, to effect a retreat in good order.

II.—The Commanding General having attentively considered the proceeding of the Court of Inquiry in the foregoing case, concurs in the opinion expressed by the Court in the statement of facts deduced from the testimony.

These facts show, that the position at Philippi was seriously threatened by a superior force of the enemy, distant only four hours' march; that Colonel Porterfield was aware of the danger of his position, and prudently prepared to evacuate it. His desire to prevent the occupation of the town by the enemy was worthy of all praise; and had he prudently sent back his baggage and ineffective men, arranged his plan of defence, and taken proper measures to secure information of the advance of the enemy, he might safely have retained his position, and either given battle or retired, as circumstances might dictate. It does not appear from the record of the Court, that any plan of defence was formed; but it does appear that the troops retired without his orders, and that the instructions to his advance guard were either misconceived or not executed.

To these circumstances must be attributed the disaster that followed; and they call for heavy censure upon all concerned.

The Commanding General remarks with pleasure upon the coolness, self-possession, courage and energy displayed by Colonel Porterfield at the moment of attack; but he cannot exonerate him from blame in not taking proper precautionary measures beforehand. Yet, in consideration of all the circumstances of the case, he does not think it necessary to do more than to express the opinion of the Court, in the hope that the sad effects produced by the want of forethought and vigilance, as exhibited in this case, will be a lesson to be remembered by the Army throughout the war.

III.—The Court of Inquiry, of which Colonel Wm. B. Taliaferro, Virginia Volunteers, is President, is dissolved.

By command of General LEE.
jy 22—1t* GEO. DEAS, A. A. G.

FOURTH COMPANY, HOWITZER BATTALION.—This command having been received and commissioned by the Governor of Virginia, is now at the New Fair Grounds. Thirty more good RECRUITS can be received into it, to make full number complete. Apply at the Fair Grounds, or former Barracks, 13th and Cary sts.
jy 22—1w* N. B. BINFORD, Capt.

TELEGRAPHIC NEWS.

Reported for the Richmond Dispatch.

TERRIFIC BATTLE!

Our Army Again Victorious!!

GREAT SLAUGHTER ON BOTH SIDES.

BEAUREGARD'S HORSE SHOT FROM UNDER HIM.

General McDowell Mortally Wounded.

THE ENEMY IN FULL RETREAT.

&c, &c., &c.

MANASSAS JUNCTION, July 21.—A battle, lasting ten hours, was fought at Stone Bridge today.

Gen. Beauregard is again victorious.

The slaughter on both sides is tremendous.

Gen. Beauregard had a miraculous escape from death. He had his horse shot from under him while leading Hampton's Legion into action.

Gen. Johnston seized the colors of a wavering regiment and rallied them to the charge.

It is impossible to estimate the number of the dead and wounded.

It is reported that the Federal Commander, Gen. McDowell, was mortally wounded.

On our side, Col. and acting General, Brigadier General Francis Bartow, of Georgia, was mortally wounded, and is since reported dead.

The battle commenced at 8 o'clock A. M., and closed at 6 P. M., with the enemy in full retreat, pursued by our cavalry.

President Davis arrived on the battle field after the action had commenced.

THE LATE BATTLE AT MANASSAS.

THE ENEMY'S ACCOUNT.

WASHINGTON, July 19, (via Mobile, July 20.)—Full particulars of the fight at Bull Creek near Manassas, received at Washington, state that three companies of Federal troops, while crossing a ravine, received a raking fire from the Confederates, killing a number of them; but they stood their ground, covering the retreat of a brass cannon and Sherman's battery, the horses of which were disabled. Four regiments, supported by cavalry joined in the battle. The Southerners used their guns well. The Federalists again advancing encountered a raking fire from the Southerners. The Federal guns, after being put in position, poured grape and canister shot into the Southerners until their ammunition was exhausted. Several of the Federal guns were disabled.—The total loss of the Federalists is estimated at *forty* killed.

Gen. Tyler ordered the Federalists to fall back. Wilcox's division were ordered to attempt to outflank the Bull Creek batteries.

A dispatch received at the War Department to-day says that fighting is still going on at Bull's Creek.

[SECOND DISPATCH.]

WASHINGTON, July 19, (via *Mobile, July* 20.) The New York *Commercial* says that information has been received at the War Department that the Bull Creek battery had been taken. No particulars have been received.

The New York *Times* says the loss on the side of the Federalists is *one hundred* (100) killed and wounded. It says this will hasten the attack on Manassas, which will doubtless occur to-morrow. (Saturday.) The Confederates, the *Times* says, lost but few.

The *Tribune* states that the Secretary of War says that more than *fifty* of the Confederates were killed, including five Captains and six Lieutenants. From another source it is reported that Bull Creek has been carried by the Zouaves and the Massachusetts Fifth.

Mr. Craig, of Illinois, (member of Congress,) and Col. Richardson, who left Bull Creek at 8 o'clock this morning, report no general fight since Thursday, when the Federalists fell back; but early in the morning occasional firing from skirmishers was heard.

Gen. McDowell told Col. Richardson he should hereafter first examine the location of the enemy's batteries before engaging the enemy.

NEW YORK, July 20.—The "World" newspaper says there is no truth in the reported fighting at Bull's Point to-day. Gen. Scott says that the army will make no new movement to day, nor is it likely that it will before Saturday.

The Evening Post says that the official report says *twelve* were killed and *forty* wounded, but it is supposed that more were killed in the woods near the creek.

[THIRD DISPATCH.]

WASHINGTON, July 20.—An official dispatch dated at Bull's Creek, at seven o'clock P. M., on Friday, says "there has been no fighting since yesterday." At the time of closing the dispatch the armies were in sight of each other.

[FOURTH DISPATCH.]

BULL'S CREEK, Friday afternoon, 4 o'clock.—There has been no fighting to-day. The Confederates are still in possession of their three principal batteries.

With the assistance of glasses, large bodies of the Confederates are seen moving on the right and left.

There are no indications of a retreat, and there will probably be no forward movement before Sunday.

FROM MISSOURI.

The Unreliability of Intelligence from that State

LOUISVILLE, July 20.—Dispatches from St. Louis and other points in Missouri, are utterly useless—private letters equally so. The indications are plain that the entire State is in a blaze, and nothing is allowed to be published or go through the mail tending to encourage the patriots Nothing but items stating that McCulloch has quarreled with Gen. Jackson, and gone home, the impossible annihilation of Secession camps in districts where all are Secessionists, and where no St Louis Dutch or Illinois soldiers have arrived, are allowed to be published.

From Gen. Wise's Legion—Capture of Federalists.

WASHINGTON, July 20.—An official dispatch from Gen. McClellan, dated Beverly, July 19th, says: "Gen Cox decoyed 600 of Gen. Wise's Legion out to Barboursville."

The Kanawha correspondent of the Cincinnati *Gazette*, in a letter dated July 18th, at noon, says that two regiments, with two guns and the Trenton Cavalry, were ordered to reconnoitre Pope's Creek. On reaching the Creek they found the Virginians, 1,500 strong, well entrenched with masked batteries and two guns. The Federal troops fired forty rounds and silenced the batteries, but their ammunition giving out, they retired. Captain Allen and Lieut Pomeroy were killed. Col. Norton of the 21st Ohio Regiment was badly wounded and captured.

Col. Woodruff, Lieut. Col. Neff (bogus Ky.) and Col De Villiers, of the 11th Ohio Regiment, left Cox's camp on the 17th inst., and are believed to have been either killed or captured.

From Washington.

WASHINGTON, July 20.—Gen. Mansfield has issued orders that no fugitive slave, on no pretext whatever, shall be permitted to reside in or march with the Federal Army.

The bill appointing an Assistant Secretary of War and enlarging the War Bureau has been passed.

The name of the steamship Keystone State is to be changed to the Northern Light.

Proclamation of a Yankee General.

ST. CHARLES, Mo., July 19.—Brigadier General Pope, of Illinois, has issued a proclamation in which he says that offenders against the laws of the United States will be dealt with in the most summary manner, without waiting for a civil process to be issued.

Cotton Sales in New York.

NEW YORK, July 20.—Sales of cotton at 15½c.

RICHMOND LIGHT GUARD, Having mustered into service and now going into camp, WILL RECEIVE A FEW MORE MEMBERS Before leaving. Apply at once at HEADQUARTERS, 13th street, Betw'n Main and Cary sts.
jy 22—ts

PERSONAL.

NOTICE.—All persons are forbid to credit my wife HENRIETTA S. BRILL. She having left my home, and deserted from me, I will be no longer responsible for any bills she may contract. [jy 20—2t*] HENRY BRILL.

CHANCERY NOTICES

CITY OF RICHMOND, to wit:—At Rules held in the Clerk's Office of the Court of Hustings for the said city, on Monday the 1st day of July, 1861:

Lawson Nunnally..........Plff, }
against } IN DEBT
George W. Jordan, John Q. Winn and Robert S. Jordan, late partners under the firm of Jordan, Winn & Co. Dfts, }

The object of this suit is to recover against the defendant the sum of Four Hundred and Twenty-Five Dollars, with legal interest thereon from the 9th day of December, 1860, till paid. Affidavit having been made that the defendant, Robert S. Jordan, is not a resident of the State of Virginia, he is hereby required to appear in the said Clerk's Office within one month after due publication hereof, and do what may be necessary to protect his interest. A Copy—Teste:
jy 4—law4w RO HOWARD, Clerk.

CITY OF RICHMOND, to wit:—At Rules held in the Clerk's Office of the Court of Hustings for the said city, on Monday, the 1st day of July, 1861:

Peter J. Archer..........Plff, }
against } IN DEBT.
Thomas H. Ellis, Powhatan Ellis, Jr., Margaret K. Ellis, Matthew P. Taylor and R. M. Nimmo,.........Dfts. }

MANASSAS JUNCTION, }
July 19, 1861, 9 P. M. }

Well, one of the long-looked for "big fights" to come off at this place, as the first step towards the destruction of Richmond, has taken place, and resulted in a complete frustration of the enemy and his plans. A more complete and glorious victory we could not have asked, and must add another leaf to the chaplet of Gen. Beauregard's fame. When 7,000 men are thrice repulsed by less than two thousand, with over ten times the loss sustained by the attacked; when the 2,000 attacked has no peculiar advantage of position, nor breastworks to protect them, it certainly proves either uncommon skill in the management of the defence, or extraordinary weakness in the plan of attack.

On yesterday, about noon, Gen. McDowell, with twelve or fourteen regiments and one battery, in which there were at least two rifle cannon, attempted to force a passage across Bull's Run, at Mitchell's Ford, about 3½ miles from Manassas Junction. General Longstreet's Brigade, composed of the First Virginia Regiment, under Col. Moore, the Seventeenth Virginia and one Louisiana Regiment, being situated near the Ford, received the attack, principally the First Virginia Regiment, and repulsed them three times, with a loss of only 12 men killed and about 60 wounded, while the loss of the enemy is stated by their own men to be not less than 300 killed and 600 wounded. There were not more than 1,000 of our men engaged, including a battery of two or three guns, while there could not have been less than 3,000 of the enemy actually engaged, besides a battery of at least two rifle cannon. We expected the attack would be renewed to-day, but this morning the enemy hoisted a white flag and asked permission to bury their dead, which was granted; and it was from these men who have been burying the dead, and the prisoners, ten in number, that we learn there were 900 missing this morning at roll call. They have been all day burying their dead, and we don't know whether they are done yet or not. It is rumored just now, at 11, A. M., that Gen. Beauregard was hourly expecting a night attack.

Besides the killed and wounded, and the ten prisoners we took, we have taken two 32-pound rifle cannon, some four or five hundred muskets, and as many hats. Our men behaved with the utmost coolness. firing irregularly, but taking good aim. The battle lasted three and a half hours. The musketry firing by the enemy was done with remarkable regularity, but with little effect, as the result proved.

A rifle cannon ball went through the house occupied by our men as a hospital, near Gen. Beauregard's quarters. DAN.

P. S.—July 20, 6 A. M.—There was no firing this morning in the direction of our line.—The reports this morning from the killed and wounded of the enemy are so contradictory that I cannot say anything is reliable. There is do doubt they have met with a severe loss, and a most extraordinary defeat in their attempt to cross Bull's Run. D.

The Philadelphia Inquirer.

ESTABLISHED 1829. PHILADELPHIA, MONDAY, JULY 22, 1861. PRICE TWO CENTS.

VICTORY!!

ADVANCE OF THE UNION FORCES.

A TERRIFIC BLOODY BATTLE.

COLONELS CAMERON AND SLOCUM AMONG THE KILLED.

The Rebel Batteries at Bull's Run Captured.

Gallant Charge of the New York Thirteenth, Sixty-ninth and the Seventy-ninth Regiments.

Union Troops Shelling Manassas Junction!

Reinforcements of Rebels Arriving at Manassas Junction.

General Patterson Superseded by Gen. Banks in Command of the Upper Potomac.

GEN. DIX TO COMMAND THE DEPARTMENT OF ANNAPOLIS.

The Order of General McClellan to his Troops Congratulating them on their Victories.

MESSAGE OF JEFF. DAVIS, THE REBEL PRESIDENT.

Recapture of Prize Schooners from Pirate Prize Crews.

The Battle at Bull's Run.

GREAT SLAUGHTER AND BRILLIANT VICTORY.

This has indeed been a glorious day for the Union. From morning till night the battle has been progressing, and on both sides have the troops shown their courage and fearless impetuosity. Hundreds on both sides have been slain and now sleep in death on the gory field of battle. The slaughter was indeed terrific, and the sight appalling to one unaccustomed to the horrors of war. General McDOWELL telegraphed at five o'clock this afternoon, that he had taken the batteries at Bull Run. A complete victory has been gained over the Rebels at this place, and they are now in full retreat towards Manassas, with our troops following them closely. The firing was so heavy that it has been heard in Washington for an hour past.

Still Later—The Rebels Driven to Manassas

Our troops have compelled the Rebels to retreat until they have reached Manassas, and our artillery are now triumphantly engaged in shelling the left of the enemy's entrenchments there. The bravery of our boys is the theme of praise, and it is believed by those competent to judge that more desperate valor was never seen; and it is plainly evident that it must have been so, considering the immense advantage of the Rebels in having everything fully prepared that time and labor would allow.

A Fierce and Bloody Battle—Our Troops Masters of the Field.

This has been the bloodiest battle of modern times. An officer who has just arrived here from the battle field, says our loss is very heavy, but we remain masters of the field. The column of Acting Major General HUNTER did the most fighting, and suffered the most. Col. SLOCUM was killed. The shelling of Manassas has again been renewed. The excitement attendant upon it is very great here.

Visit to Centreville.

The Secretary of War, accompanied by Colonel SCOTT, Superintendent of the military railroads and telegraph, and Colonel CULLUM, one of Gen. SCOTT's aids, returned this evening from the head-quarters of Gen. McDOWELL, at Centreville.

General McDOWELL had been actively engaged in making a reconnoissance all day. The scouts sent out from the left wing reported about noon that they heard the locomotives and movements of trains of cars all the morning and forenoon in the direction of Manassas Junction. This information led to the belief that either reinforcements had come up from Richmond, or else Gen. JOHNSTON's forces had arrived from Winchester and Strasburg; and the latter seemed to Gen. McDOWELL most probable.

Since the engagement on Thursday afternoon, the Union troops have been exceedingly busy in erecting batteries and mounting long range thirty-two pound guns.

Reported Death of Col. Cameron.

It is reported that Colonel CAMERON, of the Seventy-ninth New York Regiment, (Highlanders) brother of the Secretary of War, has been killed.

The Rebel Forces.

It has been ascertained that the Rebel forces number about thirty-eight thousand in and about Manassas. General SCOTT received this information to-day, and was asked by a member of Congress what was the strength of the Union force? "It is enough," was the laconic reply of the General. He said he now had men enough. He was assured that the loyal people of the whole country were looking with anxiety to him, as the chief agent in putting down the rebellion. He replied, that the uprising of the American people in defence of freedom was a sublime spectacle, and an example to the civilized world, and the moral effect of it would do more to quell the rebellion than the arms they bore.

Rebel Hung.

A Rebel was observed stabbing some of our men who fell in battle. He was captured and hung to a tree, in sight of the Rebel pickets, and remained there, dangling in the air, with his face as black as any negro.

POSITION OF THE UNION AND REBEL ARMIES

On the Morning of July 21st, before the Victory at Bull's Run, Recorded in our News Columns.

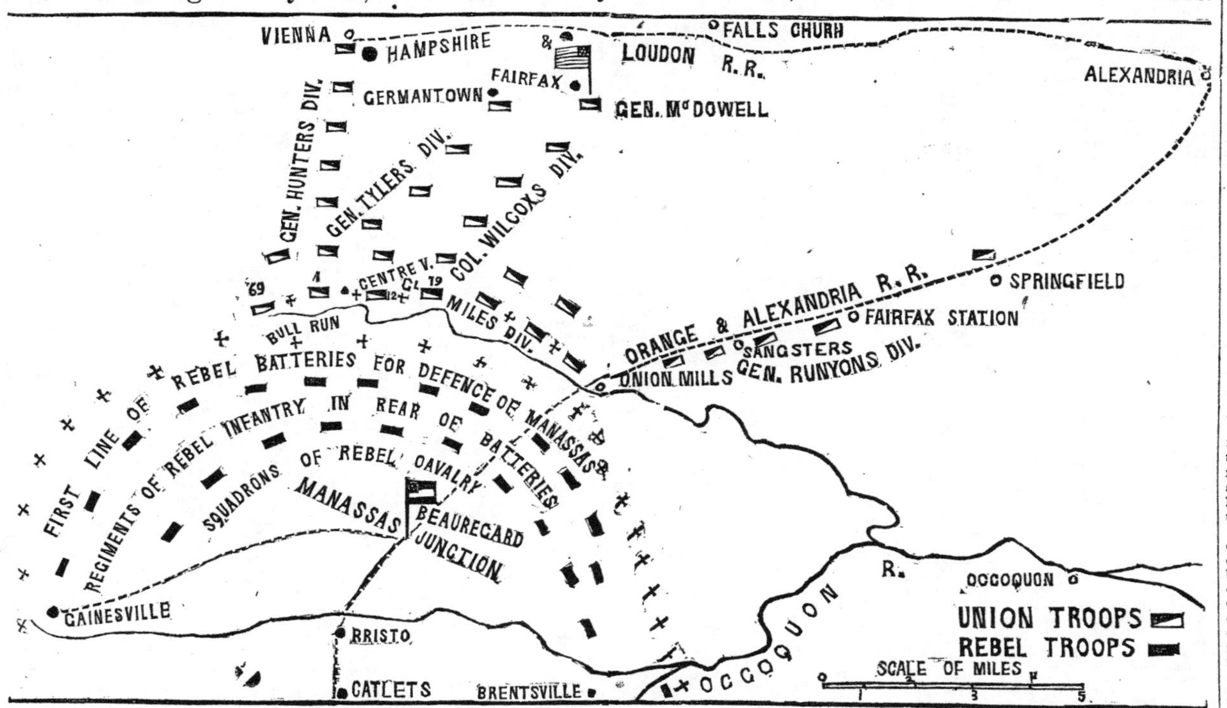

Burned Down.

The largest house in Centreville has been burned down. The neighbors say that it was set on fire by the owner himself.

The Killed and Wounded.

The number who were killed and wounded in the battle and have since died of their wounds, is now said to have been 59 in all, 17 of them belonging to the Massachusetts First, and two to the New York Twelfth.

Statement of a Deserter.

A Connecticut man, who had been pressed into the Rebel army, came into one of our camps to-day. He estimates the enemy at from 70,000 to 80,000, of whom 17,000 are the army of Gen. JOHNSTON. This deserter also says that twenty-seven companies of cavalry form a part of this force, useless within intrenchments. He also says that a very large number of the Rebels were killed in the action. The first shell fired from our batteries burst at the feet of Gens. LEE and BEAUREGARD, who were talking together, and killed a number of officers.

Rebels Gone from the River.

Lieut. CRAVEN, in his despatch to the Navy Department, states that, having been informed that the steamer *Sophia* was fired into by the Rebels at Mathias Point on Sunday morning, he ran the *Yankee* close under the land at the Point and threw several shells among the underbrush, but discovered no enemy. He adds that he is satisfied that the enemy have been moving the greater part of their forces from the heights behind Aquia Creek. Their camp, which was conspicuous some days since, is now broken up. No doubt they are moving to reinforce BEAUREGARD.

Refugees and their Stories.

Refugees continue to pour into Washington from the eastern counties of Virginia, and report that the Secession troops are suffering much from want of provisions, having been compelled to withdraw their pickets from many points, in consequence of the miserable condition of their commissariat.

The New York Twenty-fifth.

The New York Twenty-fifth Regiment, Col. ROGERS, was yesterday still stationed inside of the entrenchments of Fort Runyon, and Capt. SEYMOUR, who was with Major ANDERSON at Sumter, had been detailed to instruct the regiment in artillery practice with the heavy guns now in position there.

More Contraband.

The Navy Department has received a despatch from Com. STRINGHAM, stating that nine slaves were picked up near the mouth of the Rappahannock river, a few days since, by a Government vessel. They had made their escape in a row-boat. According to their account, all the able-bodied male negroes in Essex and Middlesex counties, Va., were being armed. The only Union man in the latter county, who had dared to express his sentiments, was murdered a short time since. Com. STRINGHAM, in view of this new position in which the contraband has been placed by its owners, has written to the Department for instructions.

Ordered to Charleston, Va.

Four New York Regiments have been ordered to Charleston to take the place of four Pennsylvania Regiments, whose term has expired.

England asks One Open Cotton Port.

It is rumored that the British Government, acting in concert with that of France, is about to request the exemption of one Southern cotton port from the blockade, so that they may get needful supplies of the staple. The idea has been discussed for some time past among leading English journals; but the Administration will, under no circumstances, concede to the request if made.

Fears of a Rebel Judge.

Judge CAMPBELL, late of the Supreme Court, in a recent letter, says that the flower of the South is at Manassas Junction, and that whichever way the events of the battle turn, it cannot but be productive of disastrous results. He also says that he fears it may go against the Confederate States.

Prize Vessels Arrived.

The propeller *Reliance* arrived at the Navy Yard yesterday, having in tow a couple of prize schooners—the *Brunette* and the *Ringdove*—captured a short time since, near City Point, by the steamer *Yankee*. Their cargoes consisted of pig iron, nails and vitriol, and were valuable. The *Brunette* was loaded at Philadelphia, the *Ringdove* at Baltimore. The cargo of the former was consigned to Richmond, that of the latter to Norfolk and Petersburg.

A Narrow Escape.

Lieut. PRIME, of the Engineers, narrowly escaped falling into the enemy's hands after the battle of Bull's Run. He rode up to a party of soldiers to inquire of the whereabouts of some of the officers engaged, from whom to learn the particulars of the affair. "Where is Col. SHERMAN's brigade?" he asked. "Don't know." "What regiment are you?" "Fifth North Carolina." Lieut. PRIME had the presence of mind to continue the conversation, until, finding out where to water his horse, he rode away for the purpose, and then put spurs to his horse.

The Roanoke Fired Into.

Despatches received at the Navy Yard from Commodore PENDERGRAST, of the *Roanoke*, states that while cruizing near Hatteras Inlet, on the 10th inst., a Rebel battery opened fire on his vessel from the beach, but every shot fell short The fire was returned with good effect. On the 12th the *Roanoke* anchored in the mouth of Cape Fear River, and found a Rebel flag flying over Fort Caswell and the town of Smithville. There was a battery at the south of the fort, where were a number of men drilling. Fort Caswell was manned with fourteen barbette guns and several field pieces. A red flag was flying from Bald Head Lighthouse. The *Roanoke* arrived off Charleston Bar on the 14th, where were the *Wabash*, the *Vandalia* and the *Union*.

No Water at Manassas.

The importance of Bull's Run to the enemy is very great. The people in the vicinity affirm that there is no water at Manassas Junction, except what is brought from the Run. That lost, the Rebels must abandon their position.

Order About Prisoners, etc

The following order has just been issued:—

GENERAR ORDERS, NO. 44.

WAR DEPARTMENT, ADJT.-GENERAL'S OFFICE,
WASHINGTON, July 13, 1861.

First:—In compliance with a resolution of the House of Representatives, the Secretary of War directs that officers report to this office, the names and residence of all prisoners that may hereafter be taken, and released upon their oath of allegiance to the United Ssates. In like manner, officers will report the names and residences of all prisoners who have been taken and released upon their oath of allegiance to the United States previous to this date.

Second:—Chaplains appointed to Volunteer Regiments in accordance with general orders No. 15, current series, from the War Department, will, in all cases, be duly mustered into the service, in the same manner as prescribed for commissioned officers.

Third:—Volunteer regiments about to be discharged will be returned to the States in which they were raised in time to be there mustered out at the expiration of their service.

Fourth:—First Lieutenant J. F. SLAUGHTER, First Artillery, having left his regiment without authority, and being now in arms against the Government of the United States, is dismissed from the army, to date from May 14, 1861.

Fifth:—Second Lieut. JOHN M. KERR, Regiment of Mounted Riflemen, having overstayed his leave of absence, and failed to report to this office, is dropped from the rolls of the army.

By order. L. THOMAS, Adjutant-General.

Twenty-third Regiment Homeward Bound —Evacuation of Johnston.

Special Despatch to the Inquirer

SANDY HOOK, Md., July 21.—The Twenty-third Regiment of Pennsylvania Volunteers have reached this point on their way to Philadelphia, where they will arrive to-morrow. Upon their arrival they will be received by Colonel ELLMAKER's Regiment of Grey Reserves, who will escort them from the depot.

They return home to recruit their ranks, and will immediately return to the seat of war, under the command of Col. BIRNEY.

We have received advices that JOHNSTON has evacuated Winchester, and will unite his forces with those of BEAUREGARD.

Recapture of the Brig Cuba.

NEW YORK, July 21.—The brig *Cuba*, which was captured by the *Sumter*, and retaken by Capt. STROUT and crew from the prize crew, made a desperate resistance. On the 14th, the midshipman of the *Sumter* went into the maintop, and when Capt. STROUT came on deck he said he wanted to speak with him; but seeing a pistol in his hand, the captain procured a revolver and ordered him down—but refusing to comply, the Captain fired at him twice. One of the shots taking effect in his shoulder, he came down.

Another Vessel Recaptured from the Pirates.

NEW YORK, July 21—Arrived, the schooner *S. J. Waring*, captured by the privateer *Jeff. Davis*, on the night of the 16th. When fifty miles south of Charleston, the colored steward, WILLIAM TILLMAN, killed three of the prize crew with a hatchet. The other two were captured, but set at liberty on promising to work the vessel. Their names were JAMES MILNOR and JAMES DAWSETT, of New Jersey. TILLMAN, with the aid of the rest of the crew, except one man, named DONALD McLEOD, who refused to assist in the recapture of the vessel, brought her to this port.

Later from the Battle Field at Manassas Junction.

THE ENEMY DRIVEN FROM BULL'S RUN.

Union Reinforcements Thrown Forward.

WASHINGTON, July 21st—Received 9 P. M.—The orders to Gen. McDOWELL to move forward at 6 o'clock yesterday, were suspended until early this morning. Our troops in the meantime were employed in cutting a road through the woods, in order to flank the enemy's batteries.

The Secretary of War has received a despatch that the fighting was renewed at Bull's Run this morning. Our troops engaged the enemy with a large force, silenced their batteries, and drove the Secessionists to the Junction.

The city of Washington is wild with excitement and joy. The firing was distinctly heard here in the direction of Bull's Run, from eleven till about three P. M., when a cessation took place till nearly five P. M. At seven this evening the reverberation was still audible.

A gentleman who arrived here to-night says that at three this afternoon the Second and Third New Jersey Regiments were ordered to march forward from Vienna, first sending back their baggage to Camp Trenton. Other troops were hurrying forward to the scene of hostilities. There is great military bustle and excitement in the direction of all the camps.

From the Head-quarters of the Army.

ARRIVAL OF JOHNSTON'S CORPS D'ARMEE AT THE JUNCTION.

Orders to Attack the Enemy's Stronghold.

WASHINGTON, July 21.—It is not doubted in high military quarters that the Rebel General JOHNSTON, recently at Winchester, was enabled to effect a junction, sometime yesterday, with Gen. BEAUREGARD, at Manassas Junction.

Official despatches were sent at two o'clock this morning from head-quarters to General McDOWELL.

General McDOWELL was to have moved upon the enemy at six o'clock last evening.

The Thirty-seventh New York passed over into Virginia this morning, the band playing "Dixie" amid the cheers of the soldiers and citizens.

Every possible arrangement has been made by the Associated Press agent to get the earliest reliable news of any result at Manassas Junction. It is the impression in well-informed circles here that the action is progressing there at this hour.

FROM THE SEAT OF THE WAR.

ADVANCE OF THE GRAND ARMY.

BEAUREGARD OUTFLANKED.

APPROACH OF GEN. McCLELLAN'S DIVISION.

A Decisive Battle Momentarily Expected.

RE-ENLISTMENT OF THE NEW YORK REGIMENTS.

CENTREVILLE, July 21.—[By telegraph from Fairfax Court House.]—We have successfully outflanked the enemy. At half-past two this morning the various regiments about Centreville were formed for the march, and at three they were in motion in the direction of Perryville, leaving Bull's Run to the left.

At six o'clock the first shot was fired by one of the 32-pound rifled cannons, which was sent ahead to batter any masked batteries that might be encountered on the road. There was no reply from the enemy, and the advance guard moved on. Gen. McDOWELL's head-quarters were three miles beyond the town of Centreville.

The greater part of the army moved to the right to avoid a bridge some distance beyond, said to have been undermined. They will pass over the stream on pontoons prepared by Captain ALEXANDER, of the Engineers, who has previously reconnoitered the country minutely, and to whom, in a great measure, the plan of the campaign is due.

A general battle is expected to-day or to-morrow, which will probably decide the fate of the whole campaign. If General JOHNSTON has not yet effected a junction with General BEAUREGARD, he will be entirely cut off by this manœuvre, and thrown back upon the mountains, his army utterly demoralized, and will probably fall into the hands of General McCLELLAN, who is now advancing beyond the Blue Ridge. If he has succeeded in reaching BEAUREGARD's camping ground, it offers a communication with General PATTERSON's division, and, thus reinforced, the Federal army can crush out the opposition. If we are driven back, the army can retreat upon Centreville, and keep an open communication with Washington.

If Gen. BEAUREGARD remains where he is his communication with the rear is endangered, and Manassas being situated in the apex of a triangle formed by the railroads, a movement in his rear would destroy his communication with Richmond.

The only danger our troops run by this flank march would be by the sudden advance by BEAUREGARD upon Centreville, thus interfering with our rearward communication, and cutting off supplies. But this manœuvre would indicate a desperation on his part, as cutting himself off from supplies, and placing himself in an exhausted country between the Federal troops and the Potomac.

The Sixty-ninth New York was assigned the post of honor in the advance movement. The members of this Regiment have unanimously agreed to remain in the service, although their time has expired. All the New York regiments will follow their example.

For five hours one steady column of troops has been passing through Centreville. The morale of the soldiers is excellent. All are anxious for a battle, and when informed of the purpose to advance, the enthusiasm was beyond description.

It is supposed that BEAUREGARD's forces considerably outnumber our own.

A battle is imminent at any moment, but it may not take place before to-morrow night.

The telegraph wires are rapidly following the army, and offices were opened this morning at Fairfax Court House, with Messrs. BUELL and BENTON as army operators.

[It is believed the foregoing was written about 10 o'clock this morning.—PHILA. REPORTER.]

Great Battle at Manassas

GOVERNMENT BULLETINS.

STARS AND STRIPES VICTORIOUS!

WASHINGTON, July 21—[Received at 11 P. M.]—The following bulletins were received in official quarters to-day, during the progress of the battle, from the telegraph station, about four miles from Bull's Run.

FAIRFAX, 11 A. M.—Rapid firing from heavy guns and frequent discharges of musketry.

11·40.—Fighting very heavy and apparently on our left wing.

11·50.—There is evidently a battle towards our left, in the direction of Bull's Run, and a little north. The firing is very rapid and heavy.

1·45.—Heavy guns again, apparently nearer. Musketry heavy and nearer.

2 P. M.—The musketry very heavy, and drawing much nearer. There is evidently a movement nearer to our left.

2·45 P. M.—Firing a little further off, and apparently in the direction of the Junction. Less heavy guns and more light artillery, as near as I can judge.

3 P. M.—The firing ceased ten minutes since.

3·55 P. M.—The firing has almost entirely ceased, and can only be heard with difficulty. I shall telegraph no more, unless there should be a renewal of the battle which has been so gloriously fought for the old Stars and Stripes. From all indications here, our troops have at least stood their ground.

FAIRFAX C. H., 3·50.—Our courier has not returned. Quartermaster BARTON, of the Second Michigan, has just passed, and says that the officers, men and citizens of Centreville say that a general engagement of the whole line has taken place three and a half miles this side of the Junction, and that our troops have driven and forced the Secession lines back to the Junction. We expect the courier now every moment.

CENTREVILLE, 4 P. M.—Gen. McDOWELL has ordered the reserves now here, under Col. MILES, to advance to the bridge over Bull's Run, on the Warrenton road, having driven the enemy before him. Col. MILES is now about three or four miles from here, directing the operations near Blackburn's Ford.

FAIRFAX, July 21, 4 45 P. M.—Two of our couriers have returned, but were unable to communicate in person with General McDOWELL. One of the couriers was on the field of battle. He says our troops have taken three masked batteries, and forced the Rebels to retire. He says the battle was general on Bull's Run for some distance. One of the batteries taken was in a wheat field, and the other some distance from it. The third battery was still further on.

5 20 P. M.—Another despatch says that the Federals have won the day. The loss on both sides is very heavy, but the rout of the Rebels is complete. The batteries at Bull's Run are silenced, and two or three others taken.

5·40 P. M.—The firing has ceased. We shall send another courier there in a few minutes. The Colonel went at four o'clock and will be back soon.

STILL LATER.

A report, not official, but from an apparently reliable source, says that the column under Col HEINTZELMAN has followed the Rebels to Manassas Junction, and has opened fire on their entrenched camp, and was then shelling them.

The cannonading can occasionally be heard in Washington and on Georgetown Heights.

The head-quarters of the army are inaccessible to-night, the President and the Cabinet being privately with Gen. SCOTT and other distinguished gentlemen.

ANOTHER WASHINGTON DESPATCH

WASHINGTON, July 21, 12 o'clock, P. M.—The most intense excitement is everywhere existing to hear the news from the field of battle. Every returning spectator is immediately surrounded, and the demand for intelligence is insatiable. Many unauthorized rumors prevail, which serve to confuse the truth.

The smoke of the battle could be seen from the eminences in Washington. Numbers of Members of Congress, and even ladies, went to the neighborhood of Bull's Run to witness the battle. One of them reports that Col. HUNTER, of the Third Cavalry, but acting as Major General, was seriously, if not mortally wounded. It is stated with confidence in all quarters that Col. CAMERON, of the Seventy-ninth New York, and brother to the Secretary of War, and Col. SLOCUM, of the Second Rhode Island, were killed.

STILL LATER—DETAILS OF THE BATTLE.

WASHINGTON, July 21—Midnight—A most severe battle was fought to-day at Bull's Run bridge. The conflict was desperate, lasting over nine hours. The programme, as stated in the first despatch, was carried out until the troops met with a succession of masked batteries, which were attacked with vigor and success.

Our troops advanced as follows:—Col. RICHARDSON proceeded on the left with four regiments of the Fourth Brigade, to hold the Battery hill on the Warrenton road, in the vicinity of the ground where the last battle was fought. The flank movements have been previously described. SCHENCK's and SHERMAN's Brigades, of TYLER's Division, advanced by the Warrenton road, while HEINTZELMAN's and HUNTER's Divisions took the fork of the Warrenton Road to move between Bull's Run and the Manassas Junction. Col. KEY's Brigade remained at Centreville.

Information was received by Gen. TYLER's command of the existence of the enemy's battery commanding the road. Our troops were then formed in battle array. The Second New York and Second Ohio on the left, the — Ohio and Second Wisconsin, and Seventy-ninth, Thirteenth and Sixty-ninth New York on the right. Col. MILES' Division followed in the rear.

The first range gun was fired by SHERMAN's Battery at 10 minutes of 7. The Rebels did not return his shot until an hour and a half afterwards. When Colonel HUNTER's Division came up the battle became general. The latter's movement to gain the enemy's rear was almost a success.

The enemy's position was opened on by several of Captain CARLISLE's howitzers, followed by slight skirmishing. The Rebels rapidly received reinforcements from Manassas Junction after the attack was opened. The battle consisted in a succession of fires from the masked batteries, which opened in every direction; when one was silenced, its place was supplied by two, and in the daring charges of our infantry in unmasking them.

The Second Ohio and Second New York Militia were marched by flank through the woods, by a new made road, within a mile of the main road, when they came on a battery of eight guns, with four regiments flanked in the rear.

Our men were immediately ordered to lie down on either side of the road, in order to allow two pieces of artillery to pass through to attack the work, when this battery opened upon us, and killed, on the third round, Lieut. DEMPSEY, of Company G, New York Second, and WM MAXWELL, a drummer; also seriously wounding several others. Our troops were kept for fifteen or twenty minutes under a galling fire, not being able to exchange shots with the enemy, although within a stone's throw of their batteries. They succeeded in retiring in regular order, and with their batteries.

The most gallant charge of the day was made by the New York Sixty-ninth, Seventy-ninth and Thirteenth, who rushed upon one of the batteries, firing as they proceeded with perfect eclat, and attacking it at the bayonet's point.

The yell of triumph seemed to carry all before it. They found that the Rebels had abandoned the battery, taking only one gun; but this success was acquired only after a severe loss of life, in which the 69th were the greatest sufferers, and it was reported that the Lieut. Colonel was among the first killed. The Zouaves also distinguished themselves by their spirited assaults on the batteries at the point of the bayonet, but it is feared that their loss is immense.

Up to three o'clock, P. M., it was generally understood that we had hemmed in the enemy entirely, and that they were gradually retiring; that HUNTER had driven them back in the rear; that HEINTZELMAN's command was meeting with every success; and that it required but the reserve of TYLER's division to push on to Manassas Junction.

A Mississippi soldier was taken prisoner by HASBROUBK, of the Wisconsin Second. He turned out to be Brigade-Quartermaster PRYOR, a cousin of ROGER A. PRYOR. He was captured with his horses, he by accident riding into our lines. He discovered himself by remarking to HASBROUCK, "We are getting badly cut to pieces." "What regiment do you belong to?" asked HASBROUCK. "The Nineteenth Mississippi," was the answer. "Then you are my prisoner," said HASBROUCK.

Continued on Eighth Page.

Continued from the First Page.

From the statements of this prisoner it appears that our artillery has created great havoc among the Rebels, of whom there is from 30,000 to 40,000 in the field, under the command of BEAUREGARD, while they have a reserve of 75,000 at the Junction. He describes an officer most prominent in fight, distinguished from the rest by his white horse, as JEFF. DAVIS.

He confirms the previous report of a negro regiment in the Rebel ranks, but says that it is difficult to get them into proper discipline in battle array.

The positions of the enemy extended in three lines in the form of a triangle, the apex fronting the centre of our column. The area seems to have been filled with masked batteries.

At 7 o'clock this evening guns were still heard firing at short intervals.

MESSAGE OF JEFF. DAVIS TO THE CONGRESS AT RICHMOND.

NEW ORLEANS, July 20.—DAVIS' Inaugural Message called attention to the causes which formed the Confederacy, and he says, it is now only necessary to call attention to such facts as have occurred during the recess, and to matters connected with the public defence. He congratulates the Congress on the accession to the Confederacy of three equal sovereign States. The several States deemed it advisable to remove the departments and archives to Richmond, to which place Congress had already removed the seat of Government.

After the adjournment of the last Congress the aggressive movements of the enemy induced prompt and energetic action. The accumulation of the enemy's force on the Potomac sufficiently demonstrated that his efforts were to be directed against Virginia, and from no point could her defense and protection be so efficiently directed as from her own capital. The rapid progress of the last few months has stripped the vail behind which the true policy and purposes of the LINCOLN Government had previously been concealed. It is now fully revealed.

The message of their President, and the action of their present Congress, confess their intention of subjugating the Seceded States by a war of folly, equalled only by its wickedness—a war by which it is impossible to attain the proposed result, whilst its dire calamities will fall doubly severely on themselves. Commencing last March with an affectation of ignorance of the secession of seven States which had organized a Confederate Government, persisting, in April, in the absurd assumption of the existence of a riot which was dispersed by a *posse comitatus*, continuing in several successive months, in false representations that these States intended an offensive war, in spite of the conclusive evidence to the contrary, furnished as well by official action as by the basis of the Constitution, the President of the United States, and his advisers, succeeded in deceiving the people of those States into the belief that the purpose of this Government was not peace at home, but conquest abroad, not the defence of our liberties, but the subversion of the people of the United States. The series of manœuvres by which this impression was created, and which were devised in perfidy, are already known. Fortunately for the truth of history, Mr. LINCOLN'S message minutely details the attempt to reinforce Fort Pickens in violation of an armistice, which he confessed he had been informed of only by rumors too vague and uncertain to create any attention.

The hostile expedition despatched to supply Fort Sumter was admitted to have been undertaken with a knowledge that its success would be impossible. The sending of a notice to the Governor of South Carolina of an intention to use force to accomplish the object, and quoting from his inaugural that there would be no conflict unless these States were the aggressors. He proceeds to declare that his conduct, as in the past, will be in the future. This promise, which could not be misunderstood, gave notice of the approach of a hostile fleet. He charges these States with being the assailants of the Union. The world cannot misunderstand this unfounded pretence.

Mr. LINCOLN expresses concern lest some foreign nation had so shaped its actions as if it supposed an early destruction of the Union was probable, and he abandons further disguise, and proposes to make the contest short and decisive. He confesses, even by an increased force and these enormous preparations, that the United States is engaged in a conflict with a great and powerful nation. He is compelled to abandon his pretence of dispersing rioters and suppressing insurrection. He is driven to the acknowledgment that the Union is dissolved. He recognizes the separate existence of the Confederate States by interdiction, embargo and blockade.

All commerce between the two sections are cut off, repudiating the foolish idea that the inhabitants of the Confederate States are still citizens of the United States. DAVIS compares the present invasion with that of Great Britain in 1781, but which was conducted in a more civilized manner. Mankind will shudder at the outrages now being commited on defenceless females by those pretending to be fellow citizens, who depict the horror with which they regard deliberate malignity, and which, under the pretext of suppressing insurrection, make special war upon sick women and children by withholding the medicines necessary for their cure. The sacred claims of humanity, respected by all nations even in fury of battle, by a careful deviation of attack on hospitals, are now outraged by the Government which pretends to desire a continuance of fraternal connections. Such outrages admit of no retaliation, unless the actual perpetrators are captured.

Mr. TAYLOR'S mission to Washington was for the purpose of effecting an exchange of the prisoners taken on the privateer *Savannah*. He informed Mr. LINCOLN of our determined purpose to check all barbarities on prisoners of war by such retaliation as would effectually put an end to such practices. Mr. LINCOLN'S promised reply is not received.

In reference to the peculiar relations existing between this Government and the States usually termed the Border Slave States, some of them would have united with us, as they are, with almost entire unanimity, oppose to the prosecution of a war with us, but these States which regard us as brethren, are restrained by the actual presence of large armies, the subversion of civil authority, and the declaration of martial law, the President declaring that in order to execute the laws, some single law, made in extreme tenderness of citizens' liberty, may, to a limited extent, be violated.

We may well rejoice that we have forever severed connection with a Government that thus tramples on all principles of constitutional liberty, and with a people in whose presence such an avowal may be paraded.

Operations in the field will be greatly extended by reason of a policy which, heretofore secretly entertained, is now avowed and acted on by the United States. The force hitherto raised, proved ample for the defence of the seven States which originally organized the Confedergcy. Excepting on those fortified islands which the enemy's naval force enabled them to retain, he has been driven entirely out. Now, at the expiration of five months from the formation of this Government, not a single hostile foot presses their soil. Our forces, however, must necessarily prove inadequate to the reported invasion by half a million of men now proposed by the enemy. A corresponding increase of our forces, therefore, becomes necessary.

Our crops are now the most abundant ever known in our history. Many believe the supply adequate to two years' consumption. Our citizens manifest a laudable pride in upholding their independence, unaided by any resources other than their own, and subscriptions to the loan proposed by the Government cannot fall short of $50,000,000, and will probably exceed that sum.

The Latest from the Seat of War.

CENTREVILLE, July 20, 6 P. M.—The whole division has just commenced to advance, leaving the Bull's Run batteries to the left. Their destination is supposed to be a point on the Manassas road, above the Junction, thus cutting off communication and supplies from JOHNSTON, who is now believed to be approacning the Junction from Strausburg.

Nothing else has transpired this afternoon.

CHANGED.—The head-quarters of the Fifteenth Regiment of the United States Infantry has been changed from Wheeling to Cleveland.

LATEST FROM CENTREVILLE.

ADVANCE OF THE WHOLE DIVISION.

JOHNSTON APPROACHING.

CENTREVILLE, July 20, 1 P. M.—The affair at Bull's Run of the 18th, which has been magnified into a terrible battle, has not resulted so disastrously to our army as has been represented in some quarters. The list of killed and wounded cannot, however, as yet, be accurately ascertained. The inmates at the hospital at Centreville are increased by those who have suffered from exhaustion, and not by the wounded. This fact gives rise to exaggerated stories as to the large number wounded.

A flag of truce, which was sent by General MCDOWELL to the enemy's line, in order to recover our dead and wounded, was refused by the enemy, for the reason, possibly, that they wish to conceal the position of their batteries.

It may be well to state that Gen. MCDOWELL, at the commencement of the action, was at Sangster's Point, on a visit to Col. HEINTZELMAN'S command; and while on his way to Centreville was informed of the battle. He immediately proceeded to the scene, but did not arrive there until the firing had ceased.

The movement towards Manassas Junction from Centreville was unauthorized, the order of march of Gen. TYLER'S division being limited to the latter point (Centreville), in order to await a flank movement by Col. HEINTZELMAN'S division, which was at that time at Sangster's, on the line of Manassas Railroad. Gen. TYLER, having ascertained that masked batteries were in the vicinity, he ordered a reconnoissance on his own responsibility. The result of this reconnoissance, in discovering the battery (although acquired by a loss of life), will probably be an adequate compensation, besides a large body of our troops have been tried, and by no means found wanting.

The order to retire was given in consequence of the Federal battery having exhausted its shot and cannister, and the exhaustion of the cavalry, which, under the command of Capt. BRACKETT, performed the most efficient services in the action. The gallant captain was at all times in advance of his command, his men following him in a fearless and determined spirit; but the want of water for the horses—a difficult which is feared will be encountered from Centreville to Manassas Junction—prevented him from continuing his efforts to unmask the enemy.

It is regretted by some military men that the infantry was not called into more active service during the engagement, the best part of the fight devolving on the artillery and cavalry.

The entire portion of Colonel HEINTZLEMAN'S command, which, it is understood, was to flank the enemy on the south of Manassas Junction, at Brentsville, has been removed to the vicinity of Centreville, and this portion of the country is now crowded with our troops. The publication of more definite information regarding their strength and numbers would be injurious to the service.

Last night passed quietly, with the exception of a few instances of the pickets firing.

The changes in the position of the troops have led many to suppose an advance was intended immediately, but it rather indicates a preparatory and defensive arrangement.

Reports that the enemy's batteries were assaulted last night are entirely without foundation; but it is supposed that Brentsville will be entered to-night. This, however, is mere conjecture, as it is probable that Gen. MCDOWELL is still awaiting instructions from Washington.

A deserter from the Rebels, who arrived here this evening, states that our fire of the 18th created great havoc among the enemy, and but for the fact that they were rallied continually by Gen. LEE, they would have retired.

It is understood here that heavy guns have been brought from the Junction to the scene of action by the Rebels.

There is some good reason to suppose from the large number of baggage wagons on the road coming from Strausburg to Manassas Junction, as observed through glasses and a reconnoissance made by Lieutenant TOMPKINS, that General JOHNSTON had succeeded in making his retreat from Winchester, and is on his way to the Junction, to join the army at the latter place. At all events, such is the opinion in military circles here. Although this will largely increase the Confederate Army there, it does not in the least deter, but only changes our military operations in that direction, as it hems in the main forces of the enemy between the advance of Generals MCDOWELL'S and PATTERSON'S commands.

Secretary CAMERON, to-day, in company with Colonel SCOTT, of the military railroad, paid a visit to Centreville, and reviewed the several brigades. He returned to Washington this evening.

At the hour of writing, Capt. GRIFFITH'S battery is moving up the Manassas road, probably to take a position on the hill.

Operations of General Patterson's Army.

CHARLESTON, Va, July 20, 1861.—In consequence of the complaints from numerous commanders that their men were without shoes, clothing, &c, and could not now be supplied, as the time for which they had been sworn in was nearly expired, General PATTERSON visited the different brigades and plead earnestly with the men to stand by him, for the love of their country and the honor of our flag, for a few days longer, but failed to gain support.

The good behavior of the soldiers is having an excellent effect upon the townspeople. Many of the families were prepared to leave on the arrival of our army, but now are going to remain, feeling that their property and persons are secure.

Three members of the New York Ninth Regiment yesterday arrested Lieut. HARLETT, of the Rebel cavalry force, while secreted in a house here. This officer is said to have commanded the troops that fired from Harper's Ferry upon Col. STONE'S brigade when passing opposite that point.

The jail where JOHN BROWN was imprisoned, and the scene of his execution, are constantly visited by our volunteers.

Capt. MCMULLIN'S Rangers have found numerous secreted arms.

Major JOSEPH KNIPE, of General WILLIAMS' staff, has recruited a new rifle regiment for the war from those about to disband. He will assume command.

Colonel WALLACE, of the Indiana Zouaves, has a new regiment ready for him at Indianapolis, to be armed with the sabre bayonet and Enfield rifle.

Colonel CLARK, of the New York Nineteenth (Cayuga) Regiment, is under arrest, upon charges made by his officers. He will be court martialed soon.

A mail bag belonging to our army, and filled with matter, has been found here. Indications show it to have been stolen, while on the way to Martinsburg, a week since.

Major LEDLIE, of the New York Nineteenth Regiment, this morning, at one o'clock, was fired on, when making the grand rounds, by a man named WELCH. The latter was arrested, and his arms taken from him. WELCH says, in excuse, that he did not see LEDLIE, but hearing a noise, thought foxes were robbing his roosts.

The Indiana Eleventh Regiment, Col. WALLACE, marched to head quarters to-day, and informed General PATTERSON of their willingness to serve ten days extra.

The Second Regiment Pennsylvania Volunteers left this morning for Harrisburg, via the Baltimore and Ohio Road, from Sandy Hook.

The railroad bridge across the Potomac, at Harper's Ferry, will soon be rebuilt.

Latest from Missouri—All Quiet.

JEFFERSON CITY, July 20.—A messenger from Col. MCNIEL, at Fulton, arrived here this evening, having left there at noon to-day. He reports everything quiet there and the wounded doing well. Col. HAMMER is seven miles beyond there.

Lieut.-Col. BROWN, who arrived here yesterday, will take his command here, and Col. BOERSTEIN will leave with his command for St. Louis on Monday.

Several companies of the Home Guard are stationed at the Fair Grounds at St. Louis, and all is quiet there.

Post Office for Gen. Patterson's Command.

HAGERSTOWN, July 20.—The Post Office for Gen. PATTERSON'S head quarters, and also for his command, is now Sandy Hook, Maryland, on the Baltimore and Ohio Railroad, near Harper's Ferry.

Naval Intelligence.

BOSTON, July 20.—The corvette *Vincennes*, (20 guns) arrived below last night. She has been cruising a week south of Nantucket for privateers. The revenue cutter *Crawford*, on a cruise, has also put in here.

Return of Captain Varian's Battery.

WASHINGTON, July 21.—Gen. MCDOWELL has caused the following order to be issued:—

"Captain VARIAN'S Battery of Light Artillery, attached to the New York Eighth Regiment, State Volunteer Militia, having completed the period of its enlistment, is honorably discharged from the service of the United States, and will march to Alexandria and report to General RUNYON, to be mustered out of the service.

"The materiel of the battery will be turned over to the ordnance officer of this command."

This battery, it will be recollected, started from New York within 24 hours' notice. It has at all times rendered prompt, willing and efficient service and gained the approval of high military gentlemen.

The body of Private CLACK, of the New York Fourteenth State Volunteers, who was accidentally shot two months ago, went forward to-day, under escort, to his relations in Brooklyn.

Forward to Washington.

HARRISBURG, July 21.—The Fourth Regiment, Colonel MARCH, were mustered into the United States service yesterday, and left at five o'clock for Washington. All were well and in good spirits.

PITTSBURG, July 21.—The Eighth Pennsylvania Reserve Corps, Colonel GEO. M. HAYS, left this city for Hagerstown this morning.

Col. BLACK'S Regiment, Scott Legion No. 2, was ordered to be mustered in, and proceed to the main army in Virginia.

Operations of Gen. M'Clellan's Army.

GEN. M'CLELLAN'S ADDRESS TO HIS SOLDIERS.

BEVERLY, Va., July 20, 1861.

HEAD QUARTERS ARMY OF OCCUPATION, WESTERN VIRGINIA, BEVERLY, Va., July 19, 1861.

SOLDIERS OF THE ARMY OF THE WEST—I am more than satisfied with you. You have annihilated two armies, commanded by educated and experienced soldiers, intrenched in mountain fastnesses, and fortified at their leisure. You have taken five guns, twelve colors, fifteen hundred stand of arms, one thousand prisoners, including more than forty officers. One of the second commanders of the Rebels is a prisoner; the other lost his life on the field of battle.

You have killed more than two hundred and fifty of the enemy, who has lost all his baggage and camp equipage. All this has been accomplished with the loss of twenty brave men killed and sixty wounded on your part. You have proved that Union men, fighting for the preservation of our Government, are more than a match for our misguided and erring brothers. More than this, you have shown mercy to the vanquished. You have made long and arduous marches, with insufficient food, frequently exposed to the inclemency of the weather. I have not hesitated to demand this of you, feeling that I could rely on your endurance, patriotism and courage. In the future I may have still greater demands to make upon you—still greater sacrifices for you to offer.

It shall be my care to provide for you to the extent of my ability; but I know that, by your valor and endurance, you will accomplish all that is asked. Soldiers—I have confidence in you, and I trust you have learned to confide in me. Remember that discipline and subordination are qualities of equal value with courage. I am proud to say that you have gained the highest reward that American troops can receive—the thanks of Congress and the applause of your fellow citizens.

GEO. B. MCCLELLAN, Major-General.

Southern News, via Louisville.

LOUISVILLE, July 20.—Several military resignations in this State are currently reported, viz:—SIMEON B. BUCKNER, Inspector General, has resigned, and probably BEN. HARDIN HELM, Assistant Inspector General, will do so. Also, that Colonel HUNT, of the Second State Guard Regiment, and Major SYMES, of the same line, have resigned. The impression is that these resignations will cause the disbanding of the State Guard.

In consequence of repeated midnight disturbances at the Louisville depot of the Nashville road, in reference to contraband freight, during the past week, the falling off of business has induced the Directors to run but one train daily southward, and that to leave here at 9 o'clock in the morning.

Changes in Military Commands.

BALTIMORE, July 21.—General DIX arrived here to-day, and will to-morrow supersede General BANKS, who supersedes General PATTERSON in command of the Northeast Department of Virginia and Pennsylvania.

The railroad bridge at Harper's Ferry will be completed to-morrow, making a connection with Winchester and Charleston, as well as Western Virginia.

Return Home of Col. Dare's Regiment.

SANDY HOOK, Md., July 21.—Before leaving Charlestown, Gen. PATTERSON addressed the Twenty-third Pennsylvania as follows:—

Officers and men of the Twenty-third:—I cannot part from you without expressing my sentiments in relation to your conduct as a regiment. It has been satisfactory in every respect, from the time you came out to perform a difficult duty guarding the railroad up to the present time. When complaints were made against regiments for pillaging private property, I heard none against you, the Twenty-third, and you have had less men in the guard house than any other regiment in my command.

At the affair of Hock's Run you behaved in a most admirable manner; in fact, no regiment could have come up better, even if they had been regulars, and you were indeed taken for regulars by many on that occasion.

In returning to your homes you take with you my best wishes, and I hope you will receive in Philadelphia a cordial reception, which your bravery and patriotism has earned.

Three cheers were given for Gen. PATTERSON, three for Col. DARE, and three for Lieut.-Col. BIRNEY.

The Regiment marched to this point, and left in the Sunday evening train for Philadelphia.

Marine News.

NEW YORK, July 21.—Arrived, ship Harriet, from Cardenas; barques Ninevah, do; Mercy, Ellen, Cinade, and Bolivar, and brigs Stella, from Minatillan; Marshal Ney, from Vera Cruz; barque Ferdinand and Louis, from Penang; schr. Wm. Stairs, from Matanzas.

The gunboat *Iroquois* was spoken yesterday, 40 miles from Sandy Hook. She had been on a cruise off Nantucket, and proceeded again in the same direction. The brig *Stella*, of Richmond, from Minatillan bound to London, reports having left there schooner *G. F. Kelland*, of New Orleans, fitting out as a privateer.

LATE SOUTHERN NEWS.

New Orleans Items of the 16th instant.

We are indebted to a friend for copies of the New Orleans *Delta* and *Picayune* of the 16th instant, *only five days old*, from which we glean the following items:—

THE DEATH OF GARNETT.—The death of General GARNETT had been received at New Orleans. The manager of the Telegraph line requested that the despatch should be suppressed, but they did not obey the request.

MORE VESSELS.—The flag officer of the Confederate Navy, at Savannah, advertises for contracts for building five vessels, of about 160 tons each, for the Confederate Navy.

ANOTHER RENEGADE.—Major H. H. SIBLEY, late of the United States Army, has been appointed Brigadier-General in the Confederate Army, and is *en route* for Texas, via Berwick's Bay and New Iberia, to raise a Brigade of Mounted Cavalry for service on the northeastern frontier of that State. The following officers are attached to his staff:—First Lieut. H. C. MCNEIL, Acting Assistant-General; Surgeon, E. N. COVEY; First Lieutenant THOS. OCHELTREE, Aid-de-camp; and Capt WM H. HARRISON, Quartermaster. The General has given permission to Southern manufacturers to manufacture his tents, regardless of the patent he received from the United States Government.

POST AGENT.—The Hon. Mr. ASHMORE, of South Carolina, has been appointed Agent of the Post Office Department.

THE THIRD NORTH CAROLINA PRIZE.—The Charleston *Courier* has a letter dated Newbern, N. C, July 8, which says:—"Our third prize, the schooner *Herbert Manton*, 199 tons, of Barnstable, Mass., we captured on the 2d instant. Her cargo consists of 70 hhds. molasses and 198 hhds. sugar. She was bound to New York.

PRIZES TO BE SOLD.—The barque *Ocean Eagle*, ship *Milan*, and schooners *Ella*, *Mermaid* and *John Adams*, and the brig *Panama*, with their cargoes, are advertised for sale on the 27th instant, by the Confederate States Marshal.

COLONEL WIGFALL.—Colonel LEWIS T. WIGFALL has accepted the command of a battalion of Texans.

GENERAL LEE.—General LEE is commander of the Confederate forces, with his head-quarters at Richmond.

THE CROPS.—The crops in Louisiana it is said were never more favorable. It is expected that there will be more corn and potatoes than was ever before known, and an equally abundant crop of sugar is also anticipated.

ANOTHER REGIMENT.—Major M. C. M. HAMMOND, of Athens, Ga., and formerly of the U. S. Army, is raising another Georgia regiment.

LOCAL INTELLIGENCE.

A GIFT TO GENERAL KELLEY.—A magnificent sword and pistols have been presented by the merchants and citizens of Philadelphia, to Gen. B. F. KELLEY. They were sent to Wheeling, Va., and from thence to the recipient. Upon the scabbard of the sword is inscribed the following:—

"Presented by the Merchants and Citizens of Philadelphia, to Gen. B. F. KELLEY, Commanding the First Regiment of Virginia Volunteers against the Great Rebellion of 1861.
Commemorable of his engagement with and total rout of fifteen hundred Rebels, at Phillippi, Va., June 3, 1861."

There is a splendid gold foil tassel attached to the sword, which will doubtless be highly valuable, as being the gift of a personal friend, WM. MILLER, Esq.

The pistols are splendid weapons, (of BEALL'S Patent Navy,) splendidly finished and beautifully mounted.

The presentation took place by correspondence. The members of the Corn Exchange participated largely in the subscription necessary to purchase the gifts, the committee being Messrs. HUGH CRAIG, RICHARD PRICE, Jr., and JOHN P. KILGORE. The following is an extract from the note which was sent to Gen. KELLEY:—

"In testimony of the gallant conduct of our honored fellow-citizen, Gen. B. F. KELLEY, commanding the First Virginia Regiment of United States Volunteers, in an engagement with the Confederate Rebels at Phillippi, Barbour county, Virginia, on the morning of June 3d, 1861, in which action he was severely wounded whilst in pursuit of the routed Rebels, we, the undersigned merchants, members of the Corn Exchange and citizens of Philadelphia, do herewith direct to be procured and presented to the said General B. F. KELLEY, a dress sword, suitably inscribed; also, one pair of pistols, for holster service."

The reply of Colonel KELLEY contains the following:—

I am embarrassed for the want of language adequately to express my emotions of gratitude for the flattering and provident kindness and attention of yourselves and other friends in Philadelphia whom you represent. I can only thank you, with the assurance that I am, by such acts as these, more than repaid for all that I have been able to accomplish. My earnest hope now is that I may be speedily so far restored to health as to be able to enter upon the active duties of the command of the First Brigade of Virginia Volunteers in the service of the United States, to which I have been recently promoted by my State, and have further opportunities of proving my zealous devotion to the honor and interests of our beloved country.

The opportune presents with which you have honored me shall be most jealously guarded and preserved, and, I need hardly add, will be worn in honor, so that you and my other friends may ever have the assurance that they have been worthily bestowed. I am, gentlemen, your very obedient servant and fellow citizen, B. F. KELLEY.

A STERN CHASE AND ITS RESULT.—The transport schooner *Narragansett*, Captain HALL, which arrived at this port on Saturday last, from Key West, had an adventure, a few days previously, which for a time, rather startled the hardy sons of Neptune on board of her. When off Cape Hatteras, and proceeding slowly under easy sail, a steamer was discovered heading for the *Narragansett*. The stranger was "long, low and black," and her flag, seen but indistinctly, wore much the appearance of the barred rag of Secessia. Not caring to visit any disloyal port at this juncture, Capt HALL clapped on all sail, and his good craft was soon bounding rapidly over the foam-capped billows. The steamer fired a gun, and started in pursuit. For about five hours the chase continued, the pursuer slowly gaining upon the schooner, and finally came up with and boarded her. The stranger proved to be the United States gun-boat *Albatross* and had given chase to the *Narragansett* on the supposition that she was a privateer. Mutual explanations were made, and the two vessels separated amid the hearty cheers of their respective crews.

ARREST OF AN ALLEGED SECESSIONIST.—On Friday last a man named JOHN F. CLARK, having taken too much liquor, made his appearance in Chesnut street, near Third, and accosting some persons who were standing there, gave utterance to alleged treasonable sentiments. He was immediately knocked down by a gray haired gentleman, and was then taken to the lock-up by two policemen. On Saturday morning he was fined by Alderman OGLE for being intoxicated, and received a reprimand.

THE ATLANTIC MONTHLY.—The ever-welcome *Atlantic Monthly* for August has reached us from Messrs. TICKNOR & FIELDS, Boston, and we have rarely seen it better supplied with useful and interesting information. A well-written article on *Fabrilia*, so much talked about since the cotton emeute, will pay perusal. Mail clad steamers also have an interesting hearing. Reminiscences of STEPHEN A. DOUGLAS also help to make up this number.

PROTECTION OF THE MAILS.—On many of the railroads of the State, the rules of the Post Office Department, prohibiting strangers from riding in the mail cars, have been very little regarded. Postmaster WALBORN has called the attention of the Department to this matter, and hereafter the rules will be strictly enforced at every hazard. This is necessary in order to protect the valuable packages.

IMPROVEMENT IN THE COURT ROOM OF QUARTER SESSIONS.—This room will be much improved during the recess. The prisoners' dock will be moved back against the wall, where the hall door now opens. That door will be replaced by one opening only into the dock, and the passage for spectators there will be closed. This will add to the convenience of those attending the Court.

MAJOR RAWLINGS.—Major RAWLINGS, who met his death last week near Fortress Monroe, while on a scouting party, was a young man, well known to many Philadelphians. Immediately after the attack upon the troops in Baltimore, he left that city for the North, and since that time has participated, more or less, in different military movements. He left Philadelphia but a few days before his death.

THE HAY AND STRAW MARKET.—During the past week, 225 loads of hay and 49 loads of straw were weighed and sold at the Farmers' Hay and Straw market, North Seventh street. The supply was light and the prices were better than those last quoted. Best quality old timothy hay sold at 75@80c. ₩ 100 lbs; inferior at 65@70c.; new hay at 55@60c. Straw was abundant, and sold at 65@70c. ₩ 100 lbs.

U. S. STEAMSHIP "SUSQUEHANNA."—This vessel having broken a shaft near Fortress Monroe, entered our port last Saturday for repairs. Her officers are embellishing Chesnut street with their uniforms. In addition to them are a number of red-capped members of the band. These young men are, in most part, swarthy natives of Cuba.

DRILL OF THE GREY RESERVES.—The Third Regiment of this Brigade, under command of Colonel PETER C. ELLMAKER, will drill upon the grounds of J. DICKINSON LOGAN, M. D., on Second street road above Nicetown lane, to-morrow afternoon, 23d inst.

SKULL FOUND.—On Saturday afternoon, some boys who were fishing in the Delaware, opposite Eleventh Ward, brought up a man's head. There were marks upon the skull which seemed to denote that its proprietor had met a violent death.

NEW TELEGRAPH LINE.—Telegraphic communication has just been opened between this city and Franklin, via Butler, in Western Pennsylvania. This brings the celebrated oil region within speaking distance. Individual enterprise has constructed the new line.

PENNSYLVANIA RAILROAD.—The President and Directors of the Pennsylvania Central Railroad Company, with their families, have been sojourning at Cresson for some time past. Major ANDERSON is also there.

ACCIDENT.—Yesterday a man, named NIEL KELLY, had his right leg fractured by a kick of a horse, near the Navy Yard. He was an employee in the foundry of Merrick & Sons. He was admitted to the Pennsylvania Hospital.

THE NAVY.—Fifteen men-of-war of the United States Navy were constructed at this city.

CITY MANUFACTURING INTERESTS—THE MILLS AT MANAYUNK.—There are at Manayunk twenty-one mills for woolen and cotton goods, and two paper mills. Of the former, six only are running, viz:—the mill of JAMES M. PRESTON, manufacturing jeans, which has been running only three weeks, and will again cease, if no further demand occurs for goods; that of BOLTON WINPENNY, which has been running for two weeks past on a Government order for army pantaloon stuffs; the mill of SYDNEY SOLMS, working jeans and twills, which has been running steadily through the season, and will probably continue to do so; and that of LAYCOCK & HOLT, for cotton goods, which has been running for one month. In addition to these, Messrs. ARCHIE CAMPBELL & Co., have been using three mills for cotton goods, on half time, employing one-third only of their former hands.

Several additional mills are daily in hopes of procuring Government work. Men earn from six to ten dollars, and women from three to six dollars, by the week of sixty hours. More money can be made by working on jeans than on other descriptions of goods. About five hundred operatives only have now employment.

The paper mills of Messrs. NIXON & Co., and Mr. MCDOWELL, have been continually running.

No reduction has taken place in wages.

Four military companies from Manayunk, composed almost entirely of operatives, have gone to the war; two went directly from the place, and two became allied with BAKER'S and the Mozart Regiment in New York. In all about four hundred men have left this great manufacturing Ward.

There is much privation among operatives out of employ, which is in a measure relieved by the charitable weekly distribution among them, at Temperance Hall of two hundred dollars' worth of provisions. This is obtained by subscription in the neighborhood. Some assistance is also given by a committee for the relief of soldiers' families, and also from the pay of the soldiers themselves. Notwithstanding all this, many families can seldom afford to purchase meat, and live on an amount scarcely sufficient to sustain them in health. To the credit of the district be it said, that good order and patience under trial everywhere prevail. All are in hopes of a speedy change, and in the meantime are anxious for Councils to order the commencement of the contemplated water works at Flat Rock, a mile above the village. It is expected, also, that Councils will make an additional appropriation for a culvert leading from Levering street to Cotton street, through George street, for the purpose of relieving this street of the damaging floods which ensue upon each heavy rain. $3500 was appropriated for the purpose last February, and consumed. $7000 more are required.

Very few buildings are going up beyond the new Masonic Hall, which approaches completion.

The population of Manayunk is about 10,000. The business of stores throughout the place is very dull. Beyond the dry goods and paper mills there, no others exist, except a sawmill, which has long ceased running, and a machine shop, with a small foundry, which employs a dozen hands.

A NARROW ESCAPE OF SIX PERSONS FROM BURNING.—An exciting scene was witnessed, early yesterday morning, at No. 219 Race street. Six persons narrowly escaped death by burning.

At two o'clock, A. M., as Sergeant DOUGHERTY and officer SHOURDS, of the Sixth Ward, were passing the three-story brick dwelling of ADAM KOOB, they discovered smoke issuing from the cellar. This, of itself, was not of unusual occurrence, inasmuch as the cellar was used as a bakery. Two men were found to be at work at the oven in the subterranean apartment. These were KOOB and his brother-in-law. No improper fire, however, was discovered.

A slight investigation on the part of the officers, developed the fact, that a fire was raging in the front room above the cellar, used as a sales-room, and opening into the street. The alarm was immediately given. KOOB hurried back through the cellar, and made an effort to force a passage upward, by a back staircase. This was found to be impossible, and, meantime, the flames were gathering headway, and roaring and cracking almost beneath his wife and child, who were asleep. Not discouraged, KOOB hurried through an alley to the rear of the premises, sprang upon a shed, and by an ingenious adjustment of boards, managed to transfer his family (wife, child, and sister,) from the burning building into the windows of an adjoining house, occupied by WILLIAM STEFFE. The sister, however, either through fright, or with an idea of obtaining a readier egress, passed up to the roof of the building, and descended through the trap-door of the adjoining premises.

The third story of the structure was partially occupied by JAMES LUNNEY, wife and daughter. They proceeded to the third story back room, and after having thrown a bed upon a shed which was beneath, ultimately reached the ground in safety, being assisted by the police and citizens.

The escape of these six persons can only be attributed to the alertness of the officers who gave the alarm. Had the fire remained undiscovered for five minutes longer, rescue would have been almost impossible. Fortunately, the flames were checked before very serious damage was inflicted, the loss probably not exceeding $500. The origin is unknown, but it is possible that the furnace in the cellar was instrumental. The premises were owned by Dr. A. R. KINKELIN, and insured in the Green Tree Company, while KOOB has an insurance of $1000 in the Royal Insurance Company. The fire had evidently been burning for one hour before it was discovered.

A PHILADELPHIA FIRE ZOUAVE REGIMENT.—It is stated in certain quarters, that upon the return of the three months Philadelphia Regiments, an effort will be made to send out a Fire Zouave Regiment from Philadelphia, for service during the war. With this end in view, one HERR F. LINSKY, formerly a captain in the Polish service, will endeavor to introduce the HARDEE (or French) drill into the broadsword, exercise and artillery practice. He intends to pick one thousand men from the Philadelphia Fire Department, and train them in such a manner as to be irresistible, either in an offensive or defensive movement. The allegation is also made that Lieut. Col. BAXTER has accepted the Colonelcy of the new corps.

RETURN OF THE TWENTY-THIRD REGIMENT.—By the following despatch, which was received last evening from one of the Reporters of THE INQUIRER now with Colonel DARE at Sandy Hook, near Harper's Ferry, it will be seen that the Twenty-third Regiment is about to return to this city:—

SANDY HOOK, July 21.

"The Twenty-third Regiment, Colonel DARE, has reached this point on its homeward march. It will recruit in Philadelphia, and return to the war under Colonel BIRNEY. It will reach Philadelphia on Monday evening or Tuesday, and, it is expected, will be received at the depot by the Third Regiment Grey Reserves, Colonel P. C. ELLMAKER."

THE HOME FOR THE FRIENDLESS.—This institution is for children. None of them have been guilty of delinquencies, however. They are from 3 to 12 years of age. They number 175 in all, and are chiefly boys. No labor is performed, except in a garden, and much time is given to their schooling, if of suitable age. Late arrivals there are mostly children of volunteers. Most ragged and woeful photographs of some of them are exhibited, taken on their first entrance. The building is very handsome, was built in 1854, and cost $20,000. The institution is situated near the House of Refuge.

SAILING OF THE KEYSTONE STATE.—The steamer *Keystone State* sailed yesterday. She passed Lewes, Delaware, about two o'clock, P. M., the wind being North. She is to convoy home the California steamer *Northern Light*, which has $1,000,000 in specie. This task having been successfully accomplished, she will proceed in search of the *Sumter*, as we stated on Saturday. She carries six eight inch guns, two thirty-two pounders, and one rifled cannon.

MAGAZINES, &c.—We have received from J. B. LIPPINCOTT & Co. *Harper's Monthly* for August. As usual, it contains an abundance of choice things, beginning with "The Central Park," by T. ADDISON RICHARDS, whose name is a sufficient guarantee of the excellence of the article. The illustrations, and large amount of reading matter in this number, will abundantly repay the outlay of twenty-five cents.

CLASSIFICATION OF PAUPERS.—The plan proposed, some time since, for the classification of the paupers in the Almshouse, has been commended by the Resident Physicians to whom it was referred, with one or two slight modifications. The matter has now been referred to the Hospital Committee, by whom the details will be perfected.

PHILADELPHIANS SAILED FOR EUROPE.—The following Philadelphians sailed on Saturday from New York for Europe:—Mr. and Mrs. DAVID THOMPSON, Miss BALDWIN, Mr. SERRILL, Mrs. ROB'T WATTS and three children, MAC ARTHUR STEWART, Mrs. BIDDLE, Mr. JOHNSTON, Rev. H. VIDAUER.

CITY MILITARY INTELLIGENCE.—It has been expected that the two regiments at Easton would visit this city en route for Washington. An order to this effect was issued on Thursday last, but was countermanded on Saturday. The regiments in the eastern part of the State will now concentrate at Camp Curtin, at Harrisburg.

Certain contractors in this city are about to remodel the arms which have been collected from the old volunteer organizations in the State. O. H. WHEELER, of Mauch Chunk, has been appointed agent by Governor CURTIN for their collection.

The Cameron Light Guard Regiment is rapidly filling up. Fourteen companies now at the seat of war have made application to be admitted into the regiment, seven of which have been accepted by the Colonel, GEORGE P. MCLEAN. There are now three companies recruiting in this city, one of which was inspected on Thursday evening last; one will be inspected to-day, and one on Tuesday evening, by the Brigade Inspector, B. F. WEEKS. As soon as these three companies are full they will be mustered into the U. S. service.

A company of sixty-five volunteers arrived in the city on Saturday morning, in charge of Capt. KEENAN, for Col. CHORMANN'S Regiment of Rifle Rangers. They are from the lumber regions of the west branch of the Susquehanna, and will make good soldiers.

A party of young men, from the ages of 17 to 20 years, have just organized a Cadet company under the title of the Jourdon Cadets, Company A. They number at present fifty men.—At an election held on Saturday the following were elected officers:—Captain, DANIEL HARRINGTON; First Lieutenant, JAS. MCHOCKLING; Second Lieutenant, JOS. MCGITTAGAN; Orderly-Sergeant, JOHN RODGERS.

W. H. STERR, No. 719 Filbert street, is purchasing horses in large quantities for Government use. The next inspection takes place at STERR'S establishment this afternoon, at 4 o'clock.

Colonel MARSH'S Fourth Reserve Regiment was sworn in on Saturday last, at Camp Curtin, by Captain HASTINGS, U. S. A.

Captain S. E. COHEN has received instructions to have the two companies for the "Independent Maryland Brigade" ready to be mustered in on Thursday next, when they will immediately move to "Camp Carroll," Baltimore.

A sermon was preached to the soldiers of Colonel MURPHY'S Regiment yesterday, by Dr. NATHANIEL WEST, at the Camp near Hestonville.

Colonel JAMES MILLER is now forming a regiment for the war. He served with distinction in the Mexican war.

A Camp has been formed by Captain FRIEDMAN'S Cavalry Company, near the upper depot of the Girard College Passenger Railway Company.

The Cameron Dragoon Regiment, commanded by Colonel M. FRIEDMAN, has been accepted by the Secretary of War. The men are going into camp as fast as mustered in, on a beautiful lot opposite the depot of the Ridge Avenue Railway Company. As this is the only cavalry encampment in the neighborhood of the city, the drill, &c., will be new to a large portion of our citizens. The cars of the Ridge Avenue Company, via Arch, Ninth and Ridge avenue, run directly to the spot.

ALLEGED ROBBERY OF WESTERN MAILS.—JOSEPH LIST and JOSEPH HUNTER, the former a messenger of Adams' Express and the latter a Baggage Master on the Pennsylvania Railroad, were arrested a few days since on the charge of having robbed the mails, on the Pennsylvania Railroad, during their transit between Pittsburg and Harrisburg.

For some time past robberies of the Western mail have been so frequent, that the Postmaster, Mr. WALBORN, has called the attention of the Post Office Department to the facts, and an investigation has been made. That inquiry resulted in their arrest.

Messrs. LIST and HUNTER had a hearing before United States Commissioner HEAZLITT, on Saturday morning, when the following facts were gathered from the testimony of Mr. S. N. PENN, of Ohio, special Post Office agent, who conducted the investigation, and tracked the alleged thieves.

It appears that the robbery the parties are charged with was committed on the night of the 1st, or morning of the 2d of July, somewhere between Pittsburg and Harrisburg, on the Pennsylvania Railroad. Several pouches, from towns in Ohio, destined for Philadelphia and New York, were rifled, together with a pouch from St. Joseph, Mo., to Washington city. The robbery was discovered by the depredators tumbling back into the St. Joseph pouch a quantity of opened letters, drafts and envelopes, which belonged to pouches from Ohio, and destined for Philadelphia and New York.

It was shown by Mr. PENN in his evidence that the pouches which had been tampered with were never in the same car on any portion of the route, except between Pittsburg and Harrisburg, because they came by different railroads as far as Pittsburg, and then the St. Joseph pouch went down the Northern Central from Harrisburg, while the pouches from Ohio kept on the Pennsylvania Railroad until they reached Philadelphia. The accused were, according to the testimony, the only persons in charge of the mail between Pittsburg and Harrisburg, on the train which left Pittsburg at 4.10 P. M., on the 1st instant, and arrived in Philadelphia on the 2d inst. at an early hour, and they were arrested under instructions from the Department. At the close of Mr. PENN'S testimony, the prisoners were held for a further hearing on the 2d of August.

MARRIAGE OF ARMSTRONG.—Recently a notice of the marriage of THOMAS J. ARMSTRONG to Miss ISABELLA MCCLEHAN appeared in the newspapers. The notice set forth that the marriage was solemnized on the 6th of October, 1859, by Rev JOHN G. WILSON, of the First Independent Church, Marlborough street, Kensington. The groom is the unfortunate young man who is now under sentence of death for the murder of ROBERT CRAWFORD.

DROWNED.—Yesterday afternoon, a man named MICHAEL BURNS, aged twenty three years, was drowned while bathing at Petty's Island. The body was not recovered.

CAMDEN AFFAIRS.

RELIEF AND PAY TO FAMILIES OF VOLUNTEERS.—Another month's State pay to the families of volunteers will be due and paid this week by the Committee. Letters from some of the officers, however, indicate that the three months volunteers will not return home as long as their services are needed. Next Monday evening, 29th inst., a public meeting of citizens will be held at the Court House to receive the report of the Committee.

THE NEXT MAYOR.—Mayor ATKINSON having accepted the position of Quartermaster of the Camden Regiment, his office will be vacant when he leaves. E. J. TORAM, the City Recorder, will act in his place until his return, or until the expiration of the term.

THE WEST JERSEY RAILROAD.—This road is now opened to Bridgeton, thirty-eight miles from this city. Travel will, we learn, commence in two weeks from this. The officers of the road will make an excursion to that place on Wednesday next.

CAMDEN REGIMENT.—This regiment, which is nearly full, has, we learn, been accepted by Gov. OLDEN. The companies, as soon as full, will proceed to Trenton to be mustered in, when the pay will commence, and the men be equipped and armed.

CHIPPEWA REGIMENT.—This regiment is rapidly filling. Several companies will be equipped this week, when they will encamp at the Diamond Cottage.

FOWL TRADE.—The hennery of Mr. G. BRITTIN, near Seventh and Federal sts., was visited on Thursday night last, and relieved of its occupants.

LEGAL INTELLIGENCE.

SATURDAY'S PROCEEDINGS.

NISI PRIUS—Judge STRONG.—The Minehill and Schuylkill Haven Railroad Company vs. The Mahonoy and Broad Top Mountain Railroad Company.—The point involved in this case, which has been heretofore argued, is as to the right of the defendants, under their charter and supplements, to connect with complainants' road.

QUARTER SESSIONS—Judge ALLISON.—In this Court the business of the term was pretty well closed up, and a number of sentences of parties convicted during the week were imposed.

RICHARD MAYBERRY, who pleaded guilty to stealing a horse, was sentenced to an imprisonment of two years and three months.

L. HICKMAN, for passing a counterfeit note, was imprisoned for six months.

JOHN BRANNAN, convicted of assault and battery, was sentenced to three months.

GEO. BETZEL, for keeping a disorderly house, No. 3 Penn street, was sentenced to four months in the County Prison.

The World

THE FIELD IS THE WORLD

MORNING COURIER AND NEW-YORK ENQUIRER.

VOL. II.—NO. 343. NEW-YORK, MONDAY, JULY 22, 1861. NO. 11,519.

LATEST NEWS BY TELEGRAPH.

THE SOUTHERN REBELLION.

TERRIFIC ENGAGEMENT.

GRAND NATIONAL VICTORY.

A Death-Blow to the Rebellion.

STORMING OF THE BULL RUN BATTERIES.

COMPLETE ROUT OF THE REBELS.

HEAVY LOSS OF LIFE.

The Fight Commenced at Manassas.

MANASSAS TO BE STORMED TO-DAY.

FROM WASHINGTON.

[SPECIAL DISPATCH TO THE WORLD.]

WASHINGTON, July 21.

The federal forces have taken all the batteries at Bull Run to-day, and are pressing on to Manassas. There is terrible loss on both sides. The cannonading was heard here. This is from official information telegraphed to the Department.

Hon. C. B. Hoard, member of the last Congress, is just in, having witnessed four hours' of to-day's battle. He describes it as terrific, and reports an immense loss of life. The enemy attempted, with an immense force, to turn our right flank, which came near being successful, when our large siege gun—a 32-pounder—opened fire, causing tremendous havoc on the enemy, and routing them. Hoard was obliged to get out of the way, and left for here at 2 P.M, while the fight was progressing.

WASHINGTON, July 21.

The last official dispatch, dated Fairfax, 5:30 P.M., which says, "A courier just in confirms the taking of Bull Run, with great loss of life, and says that Col. Heintzelman was on the left of the Junction shelling the intrenchments when the courier left."

WASHINGTON—11 P. M.

The excitement which prevails in Washington to-night beggars all description. It may be safely stated that its equal was never witnessed. There are ten thousand rumors prevailing, based apparently on such authoritative sources as to leave no doubt of their correctness, but of so contradictory a character that it would be idle to transmit them. Those who have arrived from the scene of battle describe it as so terrific and frightful that it is a human impossibility to get anything out of their over-excited minds. Persons in the same party make such contradictory statements that the public yield in despair of obtaining anything which they can believe. The Department is likewise troubled by these couriers giving their most absurd stories. It is therefore useless to send you the thousands of rumors.

Dr. Ray, of the Chicago *Tribune*, reached here after eleven o'clock, leaving Bull Run at four P. M. He says the day's battle "exceeds everything of the kind in the history of this country." When he left, our troops were in between Bull Run batteries and Manassas. One of the New-York correspondents is just in. He left the scene of battle at five P. M. when our column had been reinforced and the Union forces were pressing on Manassas.

When this last gentleman left we had the Bull Run batteries, and were fighting at five miles to the right in advance of them. There is great rejoicing here. Colonel Hunter was wounded in the face and has been brought in here.

WASHINGTON—midnight.

Col. Hunter's column did all the fighting at Bull Run for the first hour, and was used up badly. The Rhode Island and three Connecticut regiments were in the fight. Col. Slocum, of the Rhode Island Second, was killed.

The rumored death of Col. Cameron, of the Seventy-ninth, is not confirmed, nor is the wounding of Col. Heintzelman settled.

The members and senators who come in, as well as the civilians, vary in their estimates of the number of killed from three hundred to three thousand. The facts cannot yet be ascertained.

WASHINGTON, July 22—12:15.

The New-York Zouaves charged gallantly three times with bayonets on the rebels, when their ranks were broken by a charge of Virginian cavalry.

At seven P. M. couriers returning from Manassas heard cannonading.

Gen. Scott's headquarters, the War Department and President's house, are crowded to-night with anxious spectators.

Troops have been sent from here to reinforce Gen. McDowell, and if we have not possession of Manassas to-night the fight will be renewed in the evening. All the civilians who have come in agree that the rebels have an immense force.

1:30 A. M.

The New-York Sixty-ninth, Ellsworth Zouaves, New-York Fourteenth, New-York Seventy-first, New-York Eighth, and New-York Seventy-ninth, are the regiments which stood the brunt of the battle in Col. Hunter's Division, and are severely cut up.

WASHINGTON, July 21.

The orders to move yesterday evening at 6 o'clock were countermanded till early this morning, our troops meantime cutting a road through the woods in order to flank the enemy's batteries.

The Secretary of War has received a dispatch that the fighting was renewed at Bull Run this morning. Our troops engaged the enemy with a large force, silenced their batteries, and drove the secessionists to the Junction.

The city is wild with joy.

Firing was heard in this city to-day from the direction of Bull Run from 11 till about 3 o'clock. There was a cessation till nearly 5 o'clock, and at seven this evening the reverberation of cannon was still audible.

A gentleman, who arrived to-night, says, at 3 o'clock this afternoon the Second and Third New Jersey Regiments were ordered to march forward from Vienna, the first sending their baggage back to Camp Trenton. Other troops were hurrying forward to the scene of hostilities, and there is much military excitement and bustle in the direction of all the camps.

WASHINGTON, July 21.

The following bulletins were received in official quarters during the progress of the battle from the Telegraph Station, about four miles from Bull Run:

FAIRFAX COURT HOUSE, July 21—11 A. M.

There is rapid firng from heavy guns, and frequent discharges of musketry.

11:40 A. M.

The fighting is very heavy, and apparently more on our left wing.

11:50 A. M.

There is evidently a battle toward our left, in the direction of Bull Bun and a little north. The firing is very rapid and heavy.

1:45.—Heavy guns are heard again, and apparently nearer. The musketry is heavy and nearer.

2 P. M.—The musketry is very heavy, and drawing much nearer. There is evidently a movement more to our left.

2:45 P. M.—The firing is a little further off, and apparently in the direction of the Junction. Less heavy guns and more light artillery, as near as I can judge.

3 P. M.—The firing has ceased ten minutes since.

3:35 P. M.—The firing has almost entirely ceased, and can only be heard with difficulty. I shall telegraph no more unless there should be a renewal of the battle, which has been so gloriously fought for the old stars and stripes, and from all indications here our troops have at least stood their ground.

FAIRFAX C. H.—3:50 P. M.

Our courier has not yet returned. Quartermaster Barton, of the Second Regiment of Michigan, has just passed, and says that the officers, men, and citizens at Centreville say a general engagement of the whole line had taken place three and a half miles this side of Manassas, and that our troops had driven and forced the secessionists' lines back to Manassas. We expect a courier now every moment.

CENTREVILLE—4 P. M.

Gen. McDowell has ordered the reserves now here under Col. Miles to advance to the bridge over Bull Run, on the Warrenton road.

FAIRFAX COURT HOUSE, 4:45 P.M.

Two of our couriars have returned, but are unable to communicate in person with Gen. McDowell. One of the couriers was on the field of battle. He says our troops have taken three masked batteries, and forced the enemy to fall back and retire. He says the battle was general on Bull Run for some distance. One of the batteries taken was in a wheat field, and the other some distance from it, and the third still further on.

5:20 P. M.—Another dispatch says that the federals have won the day. The loss on both sides is heavy, but the route of the rebels is complete. The batteries on Bull Run are silenced, and two or three others taken.

5:45 P.M.—The firing has ceased. We shall send another courier there in a few minutes. The courier went at 4 o'clock, and will be back soon.

A still later report, not official, but from apparently reliable source, says that the column under Colonel Heintzelman has followed the rebels to Manassas Junction, and has opened fire on their intrenched camp and was then shelling them.

DETAILS OF THE BATTLE.

WASHINGTON, July 21.

A most severe battle was fought to-day at Bull Run Bridge. The conflict was desperate, lasting over nine hours.

The programme, as stated in the first dispatch from Fairfax Court House, was carried out, until the troops met with a succession of masked batteries batteries which were attacked with vigor and success after a severe loss of life. Our troops advanced as follow:

Col. Richardson, who distinguished himself in the previous engagement, proceeded on the left with four regiments of the Fourth Brigade, to hold the battery on the hill on the Warrenton road in the vicinity of the place where the last battle was fought. The flank movements were described in the first dispatch.

Schenck's and Sherman's brigades of Gen. Blair's Division advanced by the Warrenton road, while Colonels Heintzelman's and Hunter's division took the fork of the Warrenton road to move between Bull run and Manassas Junction.

Col. Keyes's Brigade remained at Centerville.

Information was received by Gen. Tyler's command of the existence of the enemy's battery commanding the road. Our troops were then formed in battle array.

The Second New-York and First Ohio on the left, and the Second Ohio and Second Wisconsin, and Seventy-ninth, Thirteenth and Sixty-Regiments, of New-York, on the right. Col. Miles's regiment followed in the rear.

The first range gun was fired by Sherman's battery at ten minutes of seven.

The rebels did not return his shot until an hour and a half afterwards. When Col. Hunter's Division came up, the batttle became general. Col. Hunter's movement, to gain the rear of the enemy, was almost a sucess. The enemy's position was opened on by several of Carlisle's howitzers, followed by slight skirmishing. The rebels rapidly received reinforcements from Manasses Junction after the attack was opened. The battle consisted of a succession of fires from masked batteries, which opened in every direction. When one was silenced, its place was supplied by two) and in the daring charges of our infantry in unmasking them, the Second Ohio and Second New-York Militia were marched by flank through the woods by a new-made road within a mile of the main road, when they came on a battery of eight guns, with four regiments flanked in the rear. Our men were immediately ordered to lie down on either side of the road, in order to allow two pieces of artillery to pass through and attack the work, when this battery opened upon us, and killed on the third round Lieutenant Dempsey, of Company G, New-York. second and Wm. Maxwell a drummer, and seriously wounding several others. Our troops were kept for fifteen or twenty minutes under a galling fire, they not being able to exchange shots with the enemy, although within a stone's throw of their batteries. They succeeded in retiring in regular order and with their battery.

The most gallant charge of the day was made by the New-York Sixty-ninth, Seventy-ninth, and Thirteenth. who rushed up upon one of the batteries, firing as they proceeded, with perfect *eclat*, and attacking it with the bayonet's point. The yell of triumph seemed to carry all before it. They found that the enemy had abandoned the battery and only taken one gun, but this success was acquired only after a severe loss of life, in which the Sixty-ninth most severely suffered, and it was reported Lieutenant-Colonel Nugent was among the first killed.

The Zouaves also distinguished themselves by their spirited assaults on the batteries at the point of the bayonet, but it is feared that their loss is immense.

Up to the hour of 3 o'clock P.M. it was generally understood that we had hemmed in the enemy entirely, and that they were gradually retiring; that Col. Hunter had driven them back in the rear, that Col. Heinzelman's command was meeting with every success, and that it required but the reserve of General Tyler's division to push on to Manassas Junction. A Mississippi soldier was taken prisoner by Hasbrouck, of the Wisconsin Second Regiment. He turned out to be Brigadier-Quartermaster Pryor, cousin to Roger A. Pryor. He was captured, with his horse, as he by accident rode into our lines. He discovered himself by remarking to Hasbrouck, "we are getting badly cut to pieces." "What regiment do you belong to?" asked Harbrouck. "The Nineteenth Mississippi," was the answer. "Then you are my prisoner," said Harbrouck.

From the statements of the prisoner, it appears that our artillery has created great havoc among the rebels, of whom there are from 30,000 to 40,000 in the field under command of General Beauregard. While they have a reserve of 75,000 at the Junction.

He describes an officer most prominent in the fight distinguished from the rest by his white horse as Jeff. Davis. He confirms the previous reports of a regiment of negro troops in the rebel forces, but says it is difficult to get them in proper discipline in battle array.

The position of the enemy extended in three lines in the form of a triangle, the apex fronting the center of our column. The area seems to have been filled with masked batteries. At 7 o'clock this evening guns were still heard firing at short intervals.

THE GRAND ADVANCE.

CENTREVILLE, July 21, via FAIRFAX COURT HOUSE, July 21.

We have successfully outflanked the enemy. At 2½ o'clock this morning the various regiments about Centreville were formed for march, and at 3 o'clock they were in motion in the direction of Perryville, leaving Bull Run to the left. At 6 o'clock the first gun was fired by a 30-pound rifled cannon sent ahead to batter the masked batteries that might be encountered on the road. There was no reply from the enemy, and the advance moved on.

At Gen. McDowell's headquarters, three miles beyond Centreville the greater part of the army moved to the right to avoid a bridge, some distance beyond, said to have been undermined. They will pass over upon pontoons prepared by Capt. Alexander of the engineers corps, and who has inspected the country minutely in a previous reconnoissance, and to whom, in a great measure, the plan of the campaign is due.

A general battle is expected to-day or to-morrow, and which will probably decide the fate of the whole campaign.

If Gen. Johnson has not yet formed a junction with Gen. Beauregard, he will be entirely cut off by this manouver. Thrown back upon the mountains, his army will become utterly demoralized, and probably fall into the hands of Gen. McClellan, who is advancing beyond the Blue Ridge; and if he has formed a junction with Gen. Beauregard, it opens our communication with Gen. Patterson's column, and thus reinforced, the federal army can crush out opposition.

If we are driven back, the army can retreat upon Centreville and keep open communication with Washington. If Gen. Beauregard remains where he is, his communications in the rear are endangered, and Manassas Junction being situated in a apex of a triangle formed by railroads, a movement in his rear would destroy his communications with Richmond.

The only danger the federal troops run by this flank march would be by a sudden advance of Gen. Beauregard upon Centreville, interrupting communications and cutting off our supplies. But this manouver would be desperate, as cutting himself off from supplies and place himself in an exhausted country, and between the federal troops and the Potomac.

The Sixty-ninth New-York Regiment was assigned the post of honor in advance. The members of this regiment have agreed unanimously to serve, although their time is now out.

All the New-York regiments will follow this example.

For five hours one steady column of troops passed through Centreville.

The morale of the soldiers is excellent, and all are anxious for a battle, and when informed of the purpose to advance the enthusiasm was beyond all description.

It is supposed that Gen. Beauregard's forces are larger than ours.

Telegraphic wires are rapidly following the army, and offices were opened this morning at Fairfax Court House, with Messrs. Buell and Benton as army operators.

WASHINGTON, July 21.

Gen. McDowell has caused the following order to be issued:

Captain Varian's battery of light artillery, attached to the Eighth Regiment of New-York Volunteers, State Militia, having completed the period of its enlistment, is honorably discharged from the service of the United States, and will march to Alexandria and report to Gen. Runyon, to be mustered out of the service of the United States.

The *materiel* of the battery will be turned over to the ordnance officer of this command.

This battery, it will be remembered, started from New-York within twenty-four hours' notice. It has at all times rendered prompt, willing and efficient service, and gained the approbation of high military gentlemen.

The body of Private Black, of the Fourteenth New-York regiment, state militia, who was accidentally shot two months ago, went forward today, under an escort, to his relatives in Brooklyn.

It is not doubted in military quarters that General Johnson was enabled to effect a junction with the confederates some time during yesterday.

Official dispatches were sent to General McDowell at 2 o'clock this morning. General McDowell was to have moved upon the enemy at 6 o'clock last evening.

They New-York Thirty-seventh Regiment passed over into Virginia this morning, the band playing "Dixie," amid the cheers of the soldiers and citizens.

WASHINGTON, July 20.

Fifteen secessionists were captured at Bull Run on Thursday and brought to this city to-day under a strong guard. One was a South Carolina sergeant, the others Alabamians. General Mansfield sent them to the old capitol building, which has been fitted up as a prison. The prisoners are rough looking and were objects of much interest as they marched through the streets.

MORE TROOPS EN ROUTE.

PITTSBURG, July 21.

Colonel Black's Regiment, Scott's Legion numbee two, have been ordered to be mustered into service, and proceed directly to the main army in Virginia. Six of his companies are in Pittsburg, and four in Philadelphia.

NON-ARRIVAL OF THE NORTH AMERICAN.

FARTHER POINT, Sunday, July 21—3 P.M.

There are no signs of the steamer North American, now due. Weather clear.

The North Briton passed down at 2.20 P.M., having been detained by a dense fog, head winds and heavy rains.

GEN. PATTERSON SUPERSEDED.

General Banks his Successor.

GEN. DIX IN COMMAND AT BALTIMORE.

WASHINGTON, July 20.

Gen. Banks has been transferred from the command of the Department of Annapolis to that of Virginia, vice General Patterson. General Dix, of New-York, will take the place of General Banks.

BALTIMORE, July 21.

Gen. Dix arrived here to-day, and will to-morrow supersede Gen. Banks, who will supersede Gen. Patterson.

The bridge across the Potomac at Harper's Ferry will be up to-morrow, making connection with the Winchester road to Charleston.

FROM MISSOURI AND ARKANSAS.

KANSAS CITY, MO., July 19.

The Fort Scott *Democrat*, of the 13th, furnishes the following items:

General Lyon, who is marching south toward Springfield, has about 6,000 men, including Major Sturges's command. He has also twenty-four pieces of field artillery of various descriptions, an abundance of ammunition, and a full train of baggage wagons.

McCullough and Jackson have retreated across the Arkansas line, for the purpose of drilling their troops. Their available force is estimated at 17,500, including the Texan Rangers and a Mississippi regiment. Gen. Lyon's strength will be between 10,000 and 12,000.

The Jayhawkers, under Jamison, have been stationed on the state line below this place some days. Jamison will maintain a force of 200 or 300 men in that region until the United States troops arrive.

A train which passed through this place about a month since with the families and property of the United States soldiers from the Indian country, was intercepted and searched by him a few days' since, and a quantity of ammunition, wagons, &c., taken possession of. Jamison gave his receipt for the articles seized, to be held subject to the order of the United States government. The owner of the property taken stated in this place, on the way up, that half of the profits of the trip should be used to purchase arms for the southern confederacy. He was not with the train on its return.

JEFFERSON CITY, MO., July 18.

A sergeant belonging to Captain Cook's company of Home Guards arrived at Syracuse this evening. He reports that Captain Cook had captured eight secessionists, among them a messenger from Jackson, bringing letters to different persons. In one of these letters Jackson begs for more men, and admits having lost 500 killed in the battle of Carthage.

Colonel Boernstein has ordered another expedition into Calloway county, to open the road to Fulton, where Col. McNeill's command is posted.

ST. LOUIS, July 19.

The Santa Fe correspondent of the *Republican* says that it is probable that Col. Camby will soon send a force to recapture Fort Bliss, Texas, where there is a large amount of army stores belonging to the federal government.

Dr. Porter, from Springfield on the evening of the 16th inst., arrived here to-night. He reports that Governor Jackson and Ben. McCullough's forces are at Camp Walker, ten miles south of the Missouri line, and at Yellowville, Arkansas. Their pickets extended as far as Neosho, thirty miles north of Camp Walker.

General Pope left to-day for St. Charles, where he establishes his headquarters. His command in North Missouri will be 7,000 strong, and so posted that Jefferson City, Booneville, Lexington and all the principal points in the northern part of the state be within easy striking distance. The federal troops and the Home Guards at Jefferson City will encamp outside of the city limits during the session of the State Convention.

JEFFERSON CITY, July 20.

A messenger from Col. McNeil at Fulton arrived this morning, having left there at noon to-day. He reports everything quiet there, and that the wounded are doing well. Col. Hammer is seven miles beyond there.

Lieut.-Col. Brown, who arrived yesterday, will take command here. Col. Boernstein will leave for St. Louis with his command Monday. Several companies of Home Guards are stationed at the Fair grounds. The city is quiet.

FROM FORTRESS MONROE.

FORTRESS MONROE, July 19, via Baltimore, July 20.

The Minnesota has steam up, but her destination is not known.

The Monticello yesterday fired into a body of confederates a short distance above Newport News.

The confederates fired some heavy guns last evening from the Pig Point battery.

The Quaker City last night picked up a man in a sail boat from Norfolk. He reports only what was well known before, namely—the raising of the three United States ships of war in Norfolk harbor and the rifling of cannon at the navy yard. There are not 10,000 troops in Norfolk and vicinity. He says that the confederates feel sure of success, and they are determined to fight to the last extremity.

Jefferson Davis is in Richmond. There was much depression on account of the rebel defeat in Western Virginia.

BOSTON ITEMS.

BOSTON, July 20.

The Third and Fourth Massachusetts, from Fortress Monroe, will be dismissed this afternoon on furlough, that the members may visit their families. There is some necessary delay in mustering them out of service, but it will be done early next week.

The Vincennes arrived below last night. She has been cruising a week, south of Nantucket, for privateers.

The revenue cutter Crawford, also on a cruise for privaeers, has put in here.

The large wooden building on Causeway street, used as the inward freight depot of the Boston and Maine Railroad was destroyed by fire this morning. A considerable quantity of merchandise which was stored therein was badly damaged, including forty bales of cotton, a small quantity of flour, cases of shoes, &c.

THE PENNSYLVANIA TROOPS IN BALTIMORE.

BALTIMORE, July 20.

The Pensylvania troops in Baltimore have all been reclothed at the expense of that state, and paid off by the general government, and are also re-inlisted and accepted by the War Department for three yeas, or during the war.

FROM LOUISVILLE.

LOUISVILLE, KY., July 20.

Military resignations are current. It is reported that Simon P. Buckner, Inspector-General of Kentucky, has resigned, and that Ben. Hardin Helm, Assistant Inspector-General is about resigning, that Col. Hunt, of the Second Regiment of the State Guard, and Major Symmes of the State Guard had also resigned. The impression is that the resignations will cause the disbanding of the State Guard.

In consequence of repeated midnight disturbances at the Louisville depot of the Louisville and Nashville Railroad in reference to contraband freight during the past week, and the falling off of business, the directors have concluded to run but one train southward per day hereafter, to leave Louisville at 9 A. M.

TAKE CARE OF THE WOUNDED.—Gov. Randall, of Wisconsin, has addressed a letter to the governors of the Northern States calling their attention to the need for proper care of the soldiers who are wounded or otherwise disabled in the war. He says he has appointed a special agent to look after such of the Wisconsin soldiers as are thus afflicted, and recommends the other governors to do likewise. The agents could accomplish much real good by co-operation.

JEFF. DAVIS'S MESSAGE TO THE SOUTHERN "CONGRESS."

RICHMOND, Va., via New Orleans, July 20.

In my inaugural I called attention to the causes which formed the confederacy. It is now only necessary to call attention to such facts which have occurred during the recess and to matters connected with the public defense.

He congratulates Congress on the accession to the confederacy of three equal sovereign states (mentioning the several states). It was deemed advisable to remove the several departments and archives to Richmond, to which place Congress already removed the seat of government. After the adjournment of Congress, the aggressive movements of the enemy induced prompt and energetic action. The accumulation of the enemy's forces on the Potomac sufficiently demonstrated that his efforts were directed against Virginia, and from no point could necessary measures for her defense and protection be so efficiently directed as from our own capital.

The rapid progress of the last few months stripped the vail, behind which the true policy and purposes of the Lincoln government were concealed, and they are now fully revealed. The Message of their President and the action of their Congress at the present session, confess the intention for the subjugation of the seceding states by a war; a folly which is equaled only by its wickedness. It is a war by which it is impossible to attain the proposed result. While the dire calamity cannot be avoided by us, it will fall with double severity on themselves. Commencing in March last, with an affectation of ignorance of the secession of seven of the states which organized the confederate government, persisting in April in the absurd assumption of the existence of a riot, which was dispersed by a *posse comitatus*, and continuing in the successive months the false representations that these states intended an offensive war, in spite of conclusive evidence to the contrary, furnished as well by official action as by the basis of the Constitution, the President of the United States succeeded in deluding the people of those states into the belief that the purpose of this government, not peace at home but conquest abroad; not the defense of our liberlies, but the subjugation of the people of the United States. The series of maneuvers by which the impression was created, the act by which they were devised, and the perfidy by which they were executed, are already known. Could it be supposed they would make openly their success a subject of boast and self laudation in the executive Message? Fortunately for the truth of history, Lincoln's Message minutely details the attempt to reinforce Fort Pickens, in violation of an armistice, of which he confesses to have been informed only by rumors too vague and uncertain to create any attention. The hostile expedition dispatched to supply Fort Sumter is admitted to have been undertaken with a knowledge that its success was impossible. The sending of a notice to the governor of South Carolina of an intended *ruse* for the accomplishment of the object, and quoting from the inaugural, there could be no conflict unless these states were the aggressors, he proceeds to declare that his conduct, as in the past for the future, was the performance of this promise, which could not be misunderstood. In defiance of our statement that he gave notice of the approach of the hostile fleet, he charges these states with being the assailants of the union of the states. The world cannot misunderstand this unfounded pretense. Lincoln expresses concern that some foreign nations have so shaped their actions as if they supposed the early destruction of the Union probable. He abandons the further disguise, and proposes to make the contest short and decisive, and confesses even an increased force might be demanded. These enormous preparations, a distinct avowal that the United States are engaged in a conflict with a great and powerful nation; compelled to abandon the pretense of dispersing rioters and suppressing insurrection, and driven to the acknowledgment that the Union is dissolved, they recognize the separate existence of the Confederate states by indirection. By the embargo and blockade by which all commerce between the two is cut off, they repudiated the foolish idea that the inhabitants of the confederacy are still citizens of the United States, for they are now waging an indiscriminate war upon them with a savage ferocity unknown to modern civilization.

He compares the present invasion to that of Great Britain of 1781, which was conducted in a more civilized manner. Mankind will shudder at the outrages committed on defenseless females by those pretending to be our fellow citizens, and will depict the horror which they regard the deliberate malignity, which, under the pretext of suppressing insurrection, make a special war on the sick, women and children, by carefully devised measures to prevent their obtaining medicines necessary for their cure.

The sacred claims of humanity, respected by all nations even in the fury of battle, by a careful deviation of an attack from hospitals, are now outraged by the government, which pretends to desire to continue fraternal connections. Such outrages admit of no retaliation unless the actual perpetrators are requited.

Col. Taylor's mission to Washington was to propose an exchange of the prisoners taken on board the privateer Savannah, and to inform Mr. Lincoln of our determined purpose to check all barbarities on prisoners of war by such retaliation as would effectually put an end to such practices. Mr. Lincoln's promised reply has not yet been received.

Reference is made to the peculiar relations existing between this government and the states usually termed "Border Slave States," which cannot properly be withheld from notice. Our people are animated by sentiments toward the inhabitants of those states, which found expression in your enactment refusing to consider them enemies, or authorize hostilities against them. A large portion of the people of those states regard us as brethren, and if they were unrestrained by the actual presence of large armies, the subversion of civil authority and a declaration of martial law, some of them, at least, would joyfully unite with us. But they are, with almost entire unanimity, opposed to the prosecution of the war waged against us. These are facts of which the daily recurring events warrant the assertion that the President of the United States, in refusing to recognize in those, our late sister states, the right of refraining from an attack on us, justifies his refusal by the assertion that the states have no other power than that reserved to them in the Union by the Constitution.

This new constitutional relation between the states and federal government is a fitting introduction to another assertion of the Message, that the executive possesses the power of suspending the *habeas corpus*, delegating that power to military commanders at discretion; and both these propositions claim respect equal to that which is felt for the additional statement of opinion of the same paper, that it is proper in order to execute the laws, that the same single law made to meet the extreme tenderness of the citizens for liberty; that practically it relieves more of the guilty than the innocent, should to a very limited extent be violated. We may well rejoice that we have forever severed the connection with a government that thus trample on all principles of constitutional liberty, with a people in whose presence such avowals could be paraded.

Our operations on the field will be greatly extended by reason of the policy which, heretofore secretly entertained, is now avowed and acted on by the United States. The forces hitherto raised have proved ample for the defence of the seven states, which originally organized the confederacy. With the exception of those fortified islands whose defense is effectually aided by the preponderation of naval force, the enemy has been driven completely out of those states, and now at the expiration of five months from the formation of the government, not a single hostile foot presses their soil. The forces, however, must necessarily prove inadequate. On account of the invasion by half a million of men now proposed by the enemy, a corresponding increase of our forces becomes necessary.

The Message refers to the abundant crops with which we have been cheered, the most abundant known in our history. Many believe the supply addequate to two years' consumption. The citizens manifest laudable pride in upholding their independence, unaided by any resources other than their own, and the subscription to the loan proposed by the government cannot fall short of fifty millions of dollars, and will probably largely exceed that sum.

[Owing to some unexplained cause, the remainder of this "Message" has failed to come to hand.]

THE EIGHTH PENNSYLVANIA REGIMENT.

PITTSBURG, Pa., July 21.

The Eighth Pennsylvania Regiment, reserve corps, Col. George M. Hays, left the city for Hagerstown this morning.

THIRTY-SEVENTH CONGRESS.

EXTRA SESSION.

SENATE.

WASHINGTON, July 20.

Mr. WADE (Ohio) offered a joint resolution that the President be authorized to appoint a commissioner at the coming World's Fair in London. Referred to the Committee on Foreign Relations.

Mr. COWAN (Pa.) presented a memorial from citizens of Pennsylvania, in favor of a national armory in that state.

Mr. KING (N. Y.) presented resolutions from the Legislature of New-York in relation to the reciprocity treaty with England. Referred to the Committee on Foreign Relations.

Mr. HALE (N. H.) reported [illegible] to increase the medical corps of the navy.

Mr. HALE offered a res[illegible] the Naval Committee be empowered [illegible] into the circumstances of the surrend[illegible] the navy yard at Pensacola and at Norfolk, with power to call for persons and papers. Referred to the Committee on Naval Affairs.

Mr. TRUMBULL (Ill.), from the Judiciary Committee, reported back the bill to confirm the bonds of postmasters, with a recommendation that it do not pass. If the bonds are good no bill is needed. Laid on the table.

Mr. FESSENDEN (Me.) from the Committee on Finance, reported back the bill to allow the Secretary of the Treasury to remit certain fines, and it was passed.

Mr. JOHNSON (Tenn.) introduced a bill to provide for the transportation of arms and munitions of war to loyal citizens in the states now in rebellion, and to provide for organizing them into regiments, &c. He said that the loyal citizens in those states felt that the government was bound to protect them against invasion and insurrection. It was referred to the Committee on Military Affairs.

Mr. TRUMBULL introduced a bill to provide for the holding of the Circuit and District courts in certain districts during the temporary insurrection. Referred to the Committee on Judiciary.

The bill in relation to the police force of Washington was taken up. It provides for the appointment of the police by the President of the Senate and the Speaker of the House. Passed.

The bill to reimburse the Seventy-first regiment's expenses for employing a band was taken up and passed.

The bill for the construction of one or more iron-clad ships of war was taken up. It provides that the Secretary of the Navy appoint a board of naval officers to examine, and if the board report favorably, the secretary be authorized to have said ships built. Laid over.

The resolution approving the acts of the President was taken up.

Mr. LATHAM (Cal.) proceeded to speak. He said there was such marked discrepancy in the opinions of the senators with whom he held friendly relations, that he felt it his duty to explain his own opinions. Some gentlemen on the floor differ from those who heretofore recognized and listened with pleasure to the eloquence of his friend from Kentucky (Mr. Breckinridge). And, also, to the senator from Delaware (Mr. Bayard). But he was pained that he did not hear one single word of denunciation of the treacherous infractions committed on the Constitution by the states now arrayed in hostility against the government. The gentleman could find with logical reasoning infinitesimal flaws in the conduct of the President, but not one word in condemnation of those who openly trample the Constitution under foot. Whatever necessity required the President to do to enforce the law and the government, was right and proper, even though he might have committed an infraction of the authority delegated to him. But he would not sanction the writ of *habeas corpus* in Maryland, because he thought that state showed her allegiance by sending members to Congress, and that there was no necessity for such a suspension, except it was evident that the judiciary of that state was disloyal. No man doubts the loyalty of the Chief Justice. His character is pure and unstained. Neither could he justify the President for increasing the regular army, for the object could have been accomplished by a volunteer force. In regard to the blockade of the ports and suspension of the writ of *habeas corpus* in Florida, and all the other acts enunciated in the resolution, he gave the President his most cordial support; and he would say here, as a representative of a sovereign state of a loyal people, if the President, when assured that traitors threatened the capital and the overthrow of the government, had not resorted to every means in his power to preserve the government, he would have deserved the execration and scorn of every honest man, now and to all posterity. The senator from Indiana (Bright) says there are three parties here. In fact, there are four; one is in the majority; those on the other side are prosecuting the war merely to sustain and uphold the government; another, a minority, seek to make this the occasion to raise a hue and cry against slavery, under a plea for the Constitution and Union. On this side of the chamber are those who belong to the Democratic party, who cannot find condemnation for the acts of the southern states, and are not willing to support the government; but there are still others here, myself among the number, who never changed an opinion as to the duties of the government in regard to slavery, but believe it to be their bounden duty to give their voices and votes to sustain the government by all constitutional means.

Mr. RICE (Minn.) said he wished to indorse all that had been said by his friend from California.

On motion of Mr. JOHNSON (Tenn.) the subject was postponed till Monday.

Executive Session.—Adjourned.

THE FIGHT ON THE KANAWHA.

[From the Cincinnati Commercial.]

The steamer Dunleith, Captain A. D. Wilson, arrived from Parkersburg yesterday, bringing the latest intelligenee from the Kanawha River.

Captain Hugh Campbell, of the government transport steamer Mary Cook, who came passenger in the Dunlieth, reports that a severe action took place on Thursdry afternoon between the rebels, and the federal troops under Colonel Lowe, of the Twelfth Ohio Regiment, and seven companies of Colonel Norton's Regiment.

Capt. Campbell did not learn any satisfactory details, but states that our troops exhausted all their ammunition, and retired, after severe loss, with their two field pieces. The federal fleet was lying below Potatella Creek, and the action took place at "Scarey," some distance in the interior. It appears that our troops were sent out with orders to make a reconnoisance, but not to attack the enemy, who were in a strongly intrenched position, numbering 1,500 strong, unless it appeared the position could be easily carried.

Capt. Campbell reported that Col. Norton was severely wounded while gallantly encouraging his men to charge, and he was left on the field and captured by the enemy.

The extent of our loss is not known, but we infer that it was quite serious. The enemy also suffered severely. Col. Lowe sent back during the action for ammunition, and Gen. Cox sent it forward with reinforcements, but our troops were met returning from the field. Lieut. Pomeroy, of Ottowa, O., was mortally wounded, and he was sent to this city on the steamer Dunleith, but he expired at Gallipolis. One private in the cavalry company which forms part of Gen. Cox's brigade, was killed. Col. Woodruff and Lieutenant-Colonel Neff, of the Second Kentucky Regiment, and Major De Villiers, of the Eighth Ohio, were at the engagement as spectators, and when Captain Campbell left Pocatelia creek, twenty hours after the conflict, they had not returned. The inference is strong that they were taken prisoners, and we are afraid our troops met with a severe reverse. Capt. Campbell reports that they fought gallantly, and did not retire until their ammunition was completely exhausted.

A REVEREND REBEL.—Rev. Dr. Stiles, of New Haven, and secretary and agent of the Southern Aid Society, is gazetted as a chaplain in the rebel army. His two sons are also in arms against their country. Whether he still receives money for "southern aid" is not stated.

THE LATE GEN. GARNETT.—The ball which caused the death of Gen. Garnett was from a minie musket and the wound produced is said to be a most terrible one, tearing the body like a cannon ball. The ball entered the middle of the back and came out just above the breast, tearing through two coats, a vest and underclothing.—*Wheeling Intelligencer.*

We still receive occasional complaints of the difficulty of obtaining a full supply of THE WORLD AND COURIER AND ENQUIRER on some of the railroad trains running from this city. We are endeavoring to effect satisfactory arrangements on all the routes, and if our friends just at this time will aid and co-operate with us by insisting on having this paper, if it be the one which they prefer, we think it will not be long before all complaints of this nature will entirely cease.

Persons wishing to have THE WORLD AND COURIER AND ENQUIRER left at their residences in the city will please leave their address at the publication office.

The large and increasing circulation of this journal, its unequaled variety and extent of commercial and other advertisements, commend it to business men as the best medium of advertising in this city.

We are happy to announce to our friends that all classes of our readers and advertisers, with hardly a single exception, are more than satisfied with the changes and improvements which we are effecting in the publication of this paper.

As a medium of commercial intelligence and of general news, it combines the features of both classes of newspapers, and yields to neither in the extent and accuracy of its information.

It is the only paper which a business-man can take without the necessity of buying another.

The WEEKLY WORLD, containing all the news of the week, can be obtained in wrappers, with postage stamps, at the counter of the publication office. Price five cents.

The World

MONDAY, JULY 22, 1861.

THE DAY'S NEWS.

The Senate, on Saturday, passed the bill authorizing the Secretary of the Treasury to remit fines incurred by vessels having improper clearances; and, after a speech from Mr. Latham in in support of the administration, adjourned. The House not in session.

The rebel congress met at Richmond on Saturday. Jeff. Davis's message was communicated, and will be found in another column.

The rebel batteries at Bull Run were carried yesterday by our troops, after a severe fight; the troops pressed rapidly forward to Manassas, and at the latest advices were in position before the rebel intrenchments.

Our dispatches from Charlestown, Virginia, state that on Saturday the Second Regiment Pennsylvania Volunteers left for Harrisburg. The Indiana Eleventh Regiment had informed Gen. Patterson of its willingness to serve ten days extra. Its commander, Col. Wallace, has a new regiment ready for him at Indianapolis. Major Joseph Knipe, of Gen. Williams's staff, has recruited a new rifle regiment for the war from those about to disband.

General Banks has been appointed in place of General Patterson, and has been succeeded in Baltimore by General Dix, who arrived there last night to assume command.

The schooner S J. Waring arrived yesterday. On July 7 she was taken a prize by the privateer Jeff. Davis, and a prize crew of five men put aboard, together with three of the schooner's crew. One of the latter, the steward, a colored man named William Tillman, July 16, killed three of the prize crew, and took command of the vessel, bringing her to this port. The brig Cuba also arrived here yesterday, having been recaptured from a prize crew of five men from the privateer Sumter. The prize crew are locked up in the Tombs.

The Pony Express brings news from San Francisco to the 10th inst. The Union Democratic convention at Sacramento adjourned on the 9th, having nominated John Conners for governor. The Broderick element controlled the ticket. It is understood that the Breckinridge convention will reassemble and nominate for all the state offices, for the purpose of defeating the Union democracy. This opposition strengthens the Republicans.

Rev. Dr. Hoge, associate pastor with Dr. Spring, yesterday afternoon read his resignation and delivered a farewell discourse, before leaving for Richmond this week. He said that in this war his sympathies had been with the South.

The Money Market has been more active during last week, from increased transactions in the Stock Exchange. On call the supply is abundant at five to six per cent. First class mercantile paper is scarce, and passes at six to seven per cent. for short, and seven to nine per cent. for long dates. The foreign exchange market is firm for bankers' sixty-day sterling bills at 107, and some quote 107⅛. The stock market was less buoyant to-day. The New-York Banks hold about $48,000,000 in specie to-day, and the weekly average will be nearly $47,000,000, the largest amount they have ever held.

Cotton has fallen off a fraction in price under a pressure to sell one or two large lines. Breadstuffs were dull and heavy. Groceries were inactive, but we notice some little excitement in drugs, based upon tariff prospects. In provisions "hog products" continued dull and drooping, but beef was rather firmer. Other merchandise was inactive, and freights dull to all leading ports.

THE VICTORY.

Our dispatches this morning tell the story which the people have waited and longed to hear. After a bloody and terrible, but glorious day's fighting, we have turned the enemy's position, and taken his batteries at Bull Run, and promptly following up this advantage, while our brave troops were flushed with the ardor of victory, we have encountered and driven back the whole force of the enemy. BEAUREGARD had been reinforced by JOHNSTON'S command, which, by a rapid retreat from Winchester, had been able to join him; and we have met, and, after a desperate and determined struggle, to which there are few parallels in the annals of modern warfare, have routed the combined rebel hosts.

It appears that Gen. McDOWELL had orders to set his troops in motion at 6 o'clock Saturday night, but the orders were temporarily countermanded. But at 2½ yesterday morning, in the soft light of a splendid full moon, they commenced their march, which they continued through a new-cut road in the woods, in the cool of a Virginia morning, till the advance of day brought them face to face with the foe. There has been no such protracted and vigorous fighting as followed during the day since Waterloo. At Solferino the battle was equally terrible, but it was sooner decided. The rebels truly felt that the fate of their new fangled confederacy was staked on the issue of yesterday's contest, and they disputed the ground inch by inch, fighting with the desperation of devils. But the steady bravery of the national troops was incapable of repulse. They have taught the vaunting and braggart "chivalry" a needed lesson as to the quality of northern pluck.

At Manassas there will still be some desperate fighting; but the great battle yesterday relieves the result of all uncertainty. It demonstrates that the war will be short. The rebels have nearly reached the end of their resources; we are but just beginning to draw on ours. This battle forbids them to think of any aggressive movement, and allows us to make a general concentration of our forces for the advance on Richmond. PATTERSON'S column, under the command of General BANKS, can hasten forward to join General McDOWELL, while the invincible McCLELLAN brings his brave fellows across the mountains, both together reinforcing the main body of the army by forty or fifty thousand men. BEAUREGARD can confront them by no such force as the national army thus reinforced will consist of; and, although he may have advantages of ground and skillfully constructed intrenchments, the superiority of our numbers will enable us to move upon his flank and menace his rear, and compel him to retreat to avoid the danger of being hemmed in and compelled to surrender at discretion. He has the disadvantage, too, of fighting with troops a large portion of which are forced levies, whose heart is not in the rebel cause, and who will have still less disposition to fight in behalf of treason when they find themselves driven from post to post before the victorious armies of the Union. Our troops, on the other hand, are all volunteers, who are fighting in a cause they love, and who will go on from strength to strength, renewing their confidence with each successive victory.

As the news of this great victory flies across the ocean and is spread over Europe, the public opinion of the world will turn definitely and finally against the success of the rebels, and cut off their last hope of sympathy or recognition. The statesmen of Europe will easily draw the conclusion that an upstart and spurious nation, who are virtually imprisoned *en masse* by a blockade, who have neither money nor credit for putting a second army in the field, who have been compelled to retreat before the national troops till they at last made a stand in a position strong by nature and fortified by all the resources of modern engineering, and there, in their own chosen stronghold, have been beaten and routed—European statesmen will at once see that this bogus and mushroom nation is already on its last legs, and that it is for the interest of the world that no hand shall be interposed to hold it up. The present cotton supply in England will last till December, and no English statesman will doubt, after hearing to-day's news, that before the beginning of winter the United States will hold the chief ports for the exportation of cotton. This battle, then, begins to snap the spine of the rebellion, and we shall shortly witness its utter collapse.

ALECK-A-DAY!

"Monsieur Tonson" has come again. ALECK STEPHENS has turned up with another speech. His oratorical functions seem to revolve in four-monthly cycles. Every third of a year he faces us with a new display of eloquence. He is as regular as the moon. Yet there is a difference. ALECK does not, moonlike, in his periodic returns, come back with the same disc. He changes unaccountably. There is never any telling how he is going to show next. He beats ENCKE'S comet all to pieces. In his November speech, he held forth as follows: "The first question that presents itself is, shall the people of the South secede from the Union in consequence of the election of Mr. LINCOLN to the presidency of the United States? My countrymen, *I tell you frankly, cordially, and earnestly, that I do not think that they ought.*" Four months roll round, and ALECK again presents himself. But in this March speech he beams out on another side altogether. He there maintains that a southern confederacy founded upon the idea that "slavery is the natural and moral condition of the negro" is a necessity; that "it is capable of giving the world the highest type of civilization ever exhibited by man," and that "if we are true to ourselves, our destiny and our high mission, it must become the controlling power of the continent." ALECK, throughout this speech, is luminous for the confederacy—full orbed, resplendent. Now, after another four months, he comes back again, but another change has come over him. He is no longer radiant. He has a strange dull, streaked, overcast, dubious aspect. We hardly know what to make of him.

He appears, it seems, on a mission from the Confederate Congress for war funds. He wants fifty millions certain; but how much more he cannot tell. He says, "the probability is that we shall have to raise one hundred millions, and it may be, if the war goes on and increases, that we shall have to raise more;"—that "the war will go on;"—that "there is no hope for us, no prospect for an early and speedy termination of the war, until we drive the enemy back;" but when that will be he cannot tell. All that he can vouch for is that "cotton is the tremendous lever by which we can work out our destiny under Providence." Cotton is to raise the wind, that is to feed the men who are to make head "against four hundred thousand, or against four times four hundred thousand"—and "to the cotton planters he would say, come up with the cotton to-day." He wants every planter to "lend, not give," a portion—say a half—of his crop to his government, and take confederate bonds as security. But the awkward question has met him, whether these bonds are worth anything. "I have been frequently asked," he says, "if these bonds are good." He answers with an *if*. "If we succeed, if we establish our independence, if we are not overridden, if we are not subjugated, I feel no hesitancy in telling you it is the best government stock in the world that I know of. But candor also compels me to state that if LINCOLN overruns us, if we are subjugated, these bonds will *not be worth a single dime.*" This certainly is not a very flattering prospect for the investment. We don't hear that there was any rush towards the subscription paper. It seems people will be putting questions. Of course this cotton is worthless unless it can be sold out of the country, and the planters naturally inquire how that is to be done. Well, he frankly owns that he don't know himself—only some how. "I meet," he says, "many asking about the blockade. I cannot to-day tell you how the blockade is to be raised. But there is one thing certain—in some way or other it will be obliged to be raised, or there will be revolution in Europe—there will be starvation there." That dilemma is the only guarantee the vice-president can offer. But England, unfortunately, don't recognize any such necessity. Its government has given ours the most explicit assurance that it will not meddle with the blockade. The vice-president himself has a creeping sensation that these inducements don't "stand to reason." In fact he acknowledges that he don't want reason to determine the matter. "If the men are in doubt how much to subscribe, I am perfectly willing they shall go home and ask their wives. A woman always acts from impulse, and her impulses are generally right; but a man ponders and thinks and doubts." That is just it. Impulses are to be trusted. Pondering and thinking would play the mischief.

Are we to look for another oratorical display from the vice-president in November? The present prospect is against this. The signs are that he is suffering "disastrous eclipse." His revolutions are about over. By the autumnal equinox, we calculate, he will have been wound up altogether.

NATURE AND OBJECT OF THE WAR.

It is not so much an act of *war* as of family *government* in which our nation is now engaged. Its object is not to assail foreign foes, but to subdue rebellious children. It seeks only the restoration and protection of loyalty. Its end is salvation, not destruction. All southern rights and privileges, as truly as all northern, it aims to protect. This gives great peculiarity to the present war, and reflects distinguished honor on our civil and military leaders. They have conducted it on the *paternal plan*, contemplating the ultimate welfare of the entire Union. It is this truly liberal and patriotic course that has secured to the administration the confidence and support of all parties. It is indeed essential to the very existence of our republic that its rulers have a single eye to the exact object of the contest, and pursue it in a strictly constitutional way. It is only by doing this that they can save us from military despotism on the one hand or anarchy on the other, and avoid festering a spirit of indomitable rebellion in all the seceded states. The rebellion can never be put down and kept down, under a republican government, but by a strictly constitutional course. Let all the people of the Southern States be assured to-day that the government has no designs against their constitutional rights and privileges—that it seeks only their loyalty and protection under the broad and generous folds of the flag of the Union, and the battle—a bloodless but triumphant one—would be nearly fought. Uncounted treasures, lives, agonies, would be spared. To this understanding all must come at last; why not at once? In this view, the injury done by those fanatical journals who aim to subvert confidence in our leaders, and who intensify and prolong the rebellion by presenting to the South a false issue of the contest, is beyond calculation. They embarrass the government, fortify rebellion, and mislead the northern mind. Their course is treasonable. The Union has enemies at the North as well as at the South. We at the North have no partialities for slavery; but, for the sake of the constitutional government under which we exist as a nation, we agree to let the South have it, and take all the responsibility and management of it to itself. This we still agree to do, even in the midst of war and bloodshed, and despite of all the evils it has brought upon us. The South shall know, the world shall know, all future history shall record, that President LINCOLN and the government of the United States have been true to their pledges in every iota. Should the South then, by persistent rebellion, bring destruction upon its own favorite institution, the blame will rest just where it ought to. That the South has *no* cause for disaffection is more than we can say. The long continued attacks upon its favorite institution from northern presses, pulpits, churches, state legislatures, and individuals even in Congress, are not to be set down as nothing. By some they were intended to sunder the Union; by more, however, only to exterminate slavery—as though the latter could be peaceably done without the former. But *the government of the United States* has ever been true to the South. President LINCOLN, in his inaugural, and in all his subsequent acts, and all the doings of Congress sustaining his administration, have maintained a strict adherence to the letter and spirit of the Constitution. Moreover, the great body of the northern people have no desire that the government should invade a single constitutional right. The Southern States have therefore no *justifiable* cause for the course they have taken. The civilized world will forever hold them guilty of a most treasonable and wicked rebellion against the most mild and beneficent government ever known on earth. A false notion, long cherished by capitalists and inculcated by some political economists at the South, that the material interests of the Southern States would be promoted by a separate confederacy; a cherished ambition to have a seat and center of political power among them; the treasonable teachings and influence of JOHN C. CALHOUN; the aspirations of political demagogues—all stimulated by the anti-slavery agitations of the North—have at last culminated in the maddest rebellion and most gigantic public outrage ever known upon earth. This stupendous folly and horrible wickedness is doomed to shame and everlasting contempt. Much as we are disposed to favor, in all constitutional ways, the "peculiar institution," if it is made the occasion of persistent rebellion against the federal government—if it is arrayed against the Union—let it be driven forever from the land, as by the blast of the breath of the Almighty. The decree has gone forth—it is recorded on high, and written in twenty million hearts—*the Union must and shall be preserved, at all events and all hazards!* Never was defeat more certain, more deserved, and, if the rebellion is persisted in, more awful, than that awaiting the rebellious states.

It is stated that General PATTERSON is to be succeeded in the command of his division by General BANKS, and that General DIX is to go to Baltimore. A better disposition of the men at its service the government could not have made. General BANKS is too energetic and vigorous an executive officer to be so much as suspected of tardiness and inaction. General DIX at Baltimore will hold all the advantage which has been gained by his predecessor's prompt and decisive action, and suffer no detriment to the republic from the hands of the traitors in Baltimore.

LIEUT. SMITH.—Second Lieutenant Wm. H. B. Smith, of the Independent Boston Fusileers, First Regiment, killed at Bull Run, was thirty-eight years of age, and leaves a wife and child. He joined the Fusileers in 1857, and had been previously a member of the New-York Seventh Regiment. He was a printer by profession, and was formerly publisher of the *Signal*, a Boston penny paper.

FROM McDOWELL'S COLUMN.

THE FIRST DAY AT BULL RUN.

[FROM OUR SPECIAL CORRESPONDENT.]

CENTREVILLE, Friday Morning, July 19.

The *rationale* of our ill-success at Bull Run is plain enough. No attack should have been made by us until the nature of the enemy's preparations had been thoroughly investigated. From the great length of the forest and range intersected by Bull Run, and the signs of forces and intrenchments visible through all this length, such an investigation might be the work of a week. We had driven scattered bodies of the rebels before us for fifteen miles; we knew they were retiring on Manassas Junction. Night before last we learned that the heaviest resistance would not be made at the Junction, but at the dangerous passes of the Run. Reconnoissances in force are bad affairs always, and especially so when made on a road directly in front of the perspected position. Our attacking numbers were either too many or too few. Gen Tyler very properly halted his fifteen thousand at Centreville, and rode forward with the cavalry to reconnoiter the ground. When he sent back for the rifled artillery, it was merely intended that a few 20-pound shells should be thrown among the fastnesses across the valley, in order to stir up the hive and show us where and how many the enemy were. The result was obtained, and the day's proceedings should have then and there ended—all our forces being brought up for a resistless attack from every side, to be made to-day or to-morrow.

As it was, the clever ruse of the rebels, who bore our fire for some time, then gave us eight guns in rapid succession, and again were perfectly silent and apparently retreating to the south (our left), warmed the blood of our staff to such a degree that a full battery of guns was ordered up (consisting of two field 6-pounders, two 12-pound howitzers, and two 12-pound rifled guns), and Richardson's Fourth brigade, which chanced to lead the day's column.

In fact, one thing leading to another, we drifted into an engagement. Our hill battery saved the day for us, interchanging tremendous broadsides with the enemy across the intervening valley. The sight and sound were wonderfully grand. No spot could be better adapted for the scenic display of a great battle, and, when the contest is renewed by our entire force, it will present such a spectacle as one may live many lifetimes and yet not have a chance to see.

The following diagram will give a correct idea of the position:

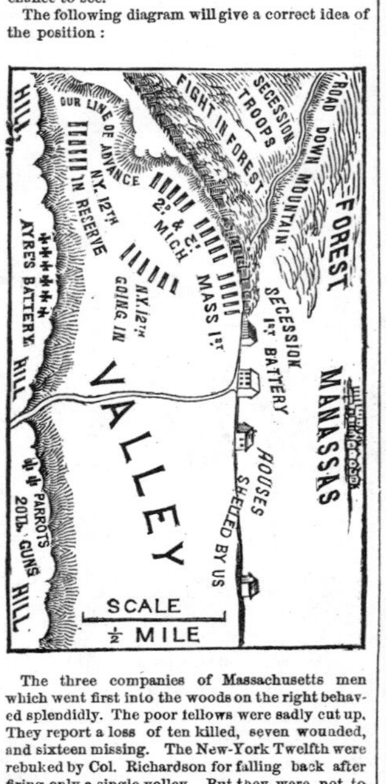

The three companies of Massachusetts men which went first into the woods on the right behaved splendidly. The poor fellows were sadly cut up. They report a loss of ten killed, seven wounded, and sixteen missing. The New-York Twelfth were rebuked by Col. Richardson for falling back after firing only a single volley. But they were not to blame. Sent in to cover our two howitzers, they advanced within a rod of the enemy's ambuscade, and were then saluted with a continuous stream of the most galling fire experienced during the action. To load, fire, or shelter under such deathful volleys, was impossible. If their colonel had not ordered them back when he did, few of them would have come out alive. The most gallant part of the whole affair was the manner in which Capt. Ayre and Lieut. Lorraine took their howitzers into those woods—pieces of all the most difficult to save, and to lose which would be the deepest disgrace a soldier could experience. Brackett, of the cavalry, accompanied them, simply because fighting is to him a luxurious and natural enjoyment. After the artillery horses were all shot down he helped to drag out the guns, and then galloped his company up the hill. On the way a rifled cannon ball passed between his men and knocked a hole straight through the body of a Michigan private in front.

Col. Richardson and his aid were constantly passing backward and forward through the fire, and did all that unsupported men could do. And when the Michigan troops retired, it was in good order, under cover of our hill battery.

I have heard a deal about the peculiarly unpleasant sound of the rifled cannon balls as they pass over one's head, or by your right and left, and yesterday, for the first time, obtained a practical knowledge of its character. Before these weightier visitors came along the minie balls fell thick and fast about the "press-brigade" (the leading New York and Boston journals were well represented on the ground), and the disagreeable minor whistling was enhanced by the knowledge that they could not well be dodged. But it so chanced that we got into the direct range of the cannonade, and furthermore that we could not get out of it. So we stood and took it. All agreed that the noise made by the heavy rifled balls was of a totally different quality from our previous conception. Round shot and grape emit a friendly greeting in comparison. Some who were mounted became targets for a sharp-shooter, who had worked himself into into an appropriate position, and were willing to descend from consequential elevations, and not be above their neighbors for the nonce.

This morning, as I have said, the whole army is concentrated at Centreville, Heintzelman's and Miles's divisions having arrived from the left. When the advance is made it will be by three roads leading to Bull Run—the one pursued yesterday being directly in front, the others flanking it on both sides. This is what should have been done yesterday. Richardson's brigade is now forming in marching order on yesterday's road—which they now know so well. Sherman's (3) Brigade has taken the right, Col. Keys in command; Heintzelman and Miles will probably go to the left. I do not know to which columns the remaining forces will be assigned, but we can throw, if all are used, nearly 40,000 men on Bull Run and the Junction. Our line of battle will be six miles in extent. The wings of our encampments are now that distance from each other, and the whole landscape smokes with our occupation. Gen. McDowell is here arranging the advance in person.

THANKS TO GEN. McCLELLAN.—The Virginia Legislature, now in session at Wheeling, has just passed a series of resolutions thanking Gen. McClellan and the officers and troops under him for liberating them from the oppression of the Confederate States government.

FROM FORTRESS MONROE.

[FROM OUR OWN CORRESPONDENT.]

OUTPOSTS AT HAMPTON, July 19, 1861.

AN AMATEUR SCOUTING PARTY SURPRISED BY THE REBELS.

Last evening, at about 10 o'clock, a small party of the Naval Brigade, accompanied by Major T. E. Rawlings, brother of Dr. Augustus Rawlings, a visitor here, left the camp at Hampton on an amateur scouting expedition. They passed on to Newmarket bridge, crossing there at about 3 o'clock this morning. When half a mile beyond, and just as day was breaking, they saw not far away on the left a small company of mounted dragoons. Turning to escape, they ran toward a negro house in the opposite direction, but were surprised to be met near the door, and just before they had reached it, by a party of dragoons, mounted and unmounted, who fired upon them to cut them off and assist the company first seen in surrounding them. The scouting party returned the fire with pistols, their distance from the rebels only being from five to ten paces, and two of them dropped from their horses. The rebels first seeing them coming up fired up the scouts One of the balls passed directly through the head of Major Rawlings, killing him instantly. Capt. Jenkins, of the Naval Brigade, was severely wounded and fell. A private named Shurtleff was also wounded, and both were taken prisoners. The remainder of the party fled into the house and then through into the woods. Capt. Halliday, who was the leader of the expedition, sent his secretary, N. P. Small, from the place where they halted in the woods, around on his way to the camp for a company who should come to their relief. They were not pursued, and from the spot to which they had fled they could see considerable confusion among the rebels, when, soon after, they went away, bearing their dead (as it is supposed) and wounded and prisoners. Mr. Small has not since been heard from, and it is supposed that he too has been taken a prisoner. A negro and his wife, occupying the cabin near where the shooting occurred, were severely frightened and fled to the woods in terror. The body of Major Rawlings was recovered, being left on the spot by the rebels.

AMONG THE REBELS.

A scouting party from the Tenth Regiment, who this week crossed Harris Creek, and encamped on the bank of Back River, opposite the rebel camp, think the number of rebels said to be located there greatly exaggerated, and that there are no facilities by which their cavalry can be transported to this side to aid in an attack. There are not more than six or eight hundred, where previous reports have represented from two to three thousand. It is reported that they have moved down to join the forces from Yorktown, now back from Newport News.

The people inhabiting the country through which the party passed, were mostly "poor whites" and negroes. Many of the whites were communicative, and others most morose and reserved. One woman, who was asked by the captain of the company where they could go to get information, replied: "*Go to Yorktown! There's where you'll get information—a right smart of it, too, I reckon!*"

At night they camped near a windmill on Mesech's Point, and in sight of the rebel camp fires. At evening they saw a number of pickets, and a most vigilant guard was kept. The signal lights, red and blue, was seen by one of the sentries in the tower of the windmill, and the very man who ferried them across Harris Creek was implicated in giving them. The boats of the rebels frequently come out for the purpose of seizing the blacks who resort to the river for fishing. Knowing this fact, Capt. White, who led the expedition, arranged a decoy. He exchanged clothes with a laborer, and in this attire, accompanied by several contrabands, went out into the stream, intending to provoke a pursuit, and then draw the enemy under the guns of his men ambushed on the shore A rain, however, set in just as the boat started, which made it impossible to see but a short distance, and the plan was accordingly abandoned. Returning toward the house of the ferryman, whom they had resolved to arrest, the commander of the party assumed the character of a captain, with a company of rebel Zouaves from Louisiana. They made several calls under this guise, and obtained in this way a considerable insight into the feelings of the people. Calling upon one Dennis, and announcing themselves, he expressed himself delighted at seeing them, and quite exhausted his supply of prepared food in his ardor to demonstrate devotion to the rebel cause. He laughed in supreme contempt at the "oath of allegiance," saying that "not a single Virginian in this vicinity, who has taken it, feels himself in the least bound to keep it." He said they were "in the lion's jaws, and if they would not lose all they had they must pretend to be Union men." At the close of the interview Captain White said, being a perfect stranger, he desired to find some good secessionists, in whom he could put perfect confidence, to aid him in obtaining information of the movements of the "Yankees." Mr. Dennis replied that almost any of the Virginians were reliable, and then gave him, upon a paper, the names of six farmers in the vicinity of our picket lines. Among them was the name of the ferryman, and the other five, as well as he, hold "oaths of allegiance to the United States."

They called once more as Louisiana Zouaves, and found a woman at home. She talked rabid secession a few moments, then eyeing one of her listeners carefully, cried out: "I've seen you before, sir. I've seen you at Old Point" (the Fortress)! Then turning to the captain: "Yes, and you, too, sir!" She immediately became strangely unsociable, and thus remained until they left.

The party arrested the ferryman on their way back, and he is now in custody within the Fortress

AFFAIRS AT THE FORTRESS.

Several points along the opposite side of the Roads are being fortified by the rebels actively, and an attempt to throw shells into the fort is anticipated. If the right kind of artillery can be obtained by the rebels, as it is reported, from Richmond, they can accomplish it.

Col. Allen is still under arrest; the court martial, in which Gen. Butler will appear in person as his accuser, is to be convened next Monday morning, by order from the War Department.

SPEECH OF A. H. STEPHENS, AT AUGUSTA, GA.

On the 11th inst. the rebel vice-president addressed a large audience at Augusta, urging the immediate subscription of the cotton loan. He said:

My business to-day is to unfold to you the exigencies of this war and its requirements. The Congress, it is known to you, provided for raising 100,000 men. Nobly, gallantly, and patriotically has that call been responded to, and is now being responded to. Thousands and tens of thousands have gone to the battle-field. These men, however, must be clothed; they must be fed; they must be armed; they must be equipped. Wars can be sustained not by men alone; it requires men and money. The questions upon which I am to address you to-day relate to the importance of raising the necessary amounts of money to meet these requisitions.

Upon the adjournment of the Congress from Montgomery to Richmond, the estimate was for 100,000 men for the first fiscal year. The amount estimated by the Secretary of the Treasury to meet the requirements to support an army of this number was $50,000,000—a large amount. This amount must be raised. How to do it, is the question. But since that adjournment—since that estimate, this war has assumed a wider and broader range. It has taken on larger and more gigantic proportions, and instead of 100,000 men, we may have to send 200,000 to meet the enemy; instead of $50,000,000, we may have, and the probability is, that we shall have to raise $100,000,000; and it may be, if it goes on and increases, that we shall have to raise more. The estimate, however, of the Secretary of the Treasury was $50,000,000, and whatever number of men, and whatever amount of money shall be necessary must be raised. We do not intend to be subjugated. Mr. Lincoln has increased his call from 75,000 to 400,000 men. He has increased his demand for money from the $5,000,000 first asked for (the amount I do no exactly recollect), and asks his Congress, now in session, for $400,000,000. Whether he will raise his men or his money, I know not. All I have to say about it is, that if he raises his 400,000 men, we must raise enough to meet him, and if he raises his $400,000,000, we must raise enough to meet it.

It is a war of political and social existence, and unless we intend to be overriden and beaten down and subjugated, and to become the vassals of his mercenaries and myrmidons, we must, every one of us—every man, every boy, and every woman—be prepared to do our duty. Our means in men and money are ample to sustain our independence. We have, upon a reasonable estimate, at least 700,000 fighting men. Whether all these will be required to drive back his armed myrmidons, I know not; but, if they are, every man must go to the battle-field. He may think, and doubtless does, that 400,000 men will intimidate, subjugate and overrun us. He should recollect, however, as we should, and reverentially, too, that "the race is not to the swift, nor the battle to the strong," but it is God that gives the victory. * *

The object is to get along with as little tax as possible; but, my countrymen, do not suppose the government will not tax you, if necessary; for I tell you the government does not intend to be subjugated, and if we do not raise the money by loans, if the people do not contribute, I tell you we intend to have the money, and taxation will be resorted to if nothing else will raise it. Every life and every dollar in the country will be demanded rather than you and every one of us shall be overrun by the enemy. On that you may count. The government, while it desires to carry on the war, establish your independence, and maintain the government, at the same time wishes to do it in such a way as not to cripple industry; and while our men are in the field fighting the battles of their country, their brethren at home are discharging an equal duty, so that no serious detriment to public property will be sustained; and we have the element to do this that no other people in the world have.

Now, then, if four millions of bales of cotton are made, upon an average price, they will bring two hundred millions of dollars. If the cotton-planter will but lend, not give—lend to the government the proceeds of but one half, that will be one hundred millions of dollars, double what the government wants, or did want when we adjourned—quite enough to keep two hundred thousand men in the field—the balance you can use as you please.

It is not asking a donation; the government simply wishes to control the proceeds of your cotton. The government proposes to give you a bond bearing eight per cent. interest, paying the interest also semi-annually. It is not a gift or donation, but simply your surplus cotton, as much as you can spare. This is the proposition:

"We, the subscribers, agree to contribute to the defense of the Confederate States that portion of our crop set down to our respective names; the same to be placed in warehouse or in the hand of our factors, and sold on or before the —— next."

Fix the day of sale as soon as you please; the first of January, the first of February, or the first of March, if you please; though I am aware the government wishes you to sell it as soon as convenient; but let each planter consult his interest, and in the meanwhile consult the market. But to proceed—

"And the net proceeds of the sale we direct to be paid over to the Treasurer of the Confederate States for bonds for the same amount, bearing eight per cent. interest."

I understand that a committee will be appointed before this meeting adjourns, to canvass this county. Every planter, therefore, of Richmond county, will be waited upon and afforded an opportunity to subscribe. I wish, therefore, to say to that committee, and everybody, subscribe. I prefer you putting down, first, your name; second the number of bales; and I prefer your putting down the proportion of your crop. I want, especially, the number of bales, but would like also to know the proportion it bears to your crop. Let everybody, those with small crops as well as large, give evidence, in this way, of their patriotism, and I believe that the patriotism that puts down two bales, if it be half their crop, gives more, and more patriotically, than the man who grows one thousand and put down one-half of his, because, as the Savior said, the woman who gave her mite, gave more than all the rest. Let everybody, therefore, put down a portion of their crop, if it be but two bales, or fifty bales, or one hundred bales, or five hundred bales.

Inquiries have been made of me, and I take this opportunity to answer them: "Whether these bonds will circulate as money—will they pay debts?" On this point I wish no mistake. They are not intended as currency; they are unfitted to answer the purpose of circulation. The bonds are larger than this paper. (A letter sheet.) The obligation is on the upper part of it, and the whole of the lower part is divided into forty squares or checks. In each one of these checks the interest is counted for each six months for twenty years. The checks are called coupons, and all the party holding them has to do, is every six months to clip off the lower coupon, send it to the treasury, and get his interest. The bond is not suitable to carry in your pocket-book and use. It would wear out. It is intended to represent a fixed capital, or permanent investment—just so much as you can spare from your cotton crop. That is all. Instead of putting your surplus in lands, negroes, houses, furniture, useless extravagance or luxuries, just put it in confederate bonds.

But while I said it was not intended to circulate or to pay debts, I have not the least doubt that anybody who will sell his crop entire for bonds will find no difficulty in getting the money for them, for they draw interest, and are better than money; and any man holding a note will give it up and take a bond, for a note draws but seven per cent., and this draws eight. I have no doubt that all minors' and trust property will soon be invested in it. The entire amount of private funds in the State of Georgia, on private loans, I suppose is ten or twenty millions of dollars, at seven per cent. All that amount will immediately find its way into these bonds, and hence a planter who sells his entire crop, and needs money, can get it from the money-lenders on these bonds.

I have been frequently asked if these bonds were good. Well I want to be equally frank upon that point. If we succeed, if we establish our independence, if we are not overridden, if we are not subjugated, I feel no hesitancy in telling you it is the best government stock in the world that I know of. It is eight per cent. interest; and if we succeed in a short time, in a few years, if not more than one hundred millions, or two hundred millions are issued, I have but little doubt they will command a considerable premium. The old United States stock (six per cent. bonds), five years ago, commanded fifteen and sixteen per cent., and went as high as twenty per cent. Take the central railroad. The stock of that company commands fifteen per cent. premium now. These bonds pay eight per cent., semi-annually; therefore, if there is a short war, these bonds very soon will command fifteen or twenty per cent.; but candor also compels me to state that if Lincoln overruns us—if we are subjugated, these bonds will not be worth a single dime, and nothing else you have will be worth anything. If we are overrun, they will be worth just as much as anything else you have, and nothing else you have will be worth anything. So that is the whole of it.

Let us, then, come up and contribute what we can. I say to the planters that I do not wish to urge anybody, but let everybody discharge his duty to the country as he feels it. But upon this subject of the war, I will detain you a few minutes, because it is a common inquiry with me, how long I think the war will last—whether or not it will be a short one? Well, my countrymen, I will tell you this, that it is known only to the Ruler of events. It is curtained from mortal knowledge and mortal vision. I know not; I would not know if I could. It is the mysterious future; but there is one thing I can tell you with confidence, and that is, it is going to last until the enemy is whipped and driven from our soil. And it will require men and money to do it, and the best way to make it a short war is to send men into the field, and to raise means enough to support them in the field to drive the enemy out. When I tell you it is an uncertain war I cannot account for its duration upon any rational principle. It is a fanatical war, and whenever fanaticism gets control of reason, you can make no speculation in regard to it. * * * *

What is to be the result of this war? I am not a prophet, but I look upon it as fraught with the most momentous consequences, not unto us, but the people of the North. I have always believed that if the Union were destroyed, the North would run into anarchy and despotism. We are the salt of the concern, and it is only questionable whether or not we have quit too soon. That is the only doubt I have. Where it will end I do not know, but never again will they enjoy constitutional government at the North. They never understood it. Constitutional liberty is a plant of southern growth, watered by southern hands, nurtured by southern hands, and if it is to be maintained, to live to light the world; it is to be done in the Southern Confederacy. At the North there is anarchy. Property will migrate just as it did in France. That is the end.

How long will they be able to war against us? I tell you it will be until we drive them back. There is no hope for us, there is no prospect for an early and speedy termination of the war until we drive them back, and my wish, my idea, my desire and my counsel would be to raise men enough immediately from the mountains to the seaboard to do it. Let all send up men to drive the enemy out; and to the cotton planters I would say, come up with the cotton to-day. I do not want to embarrass any one, but I would say to you, tell your debtors to wait until you are out of danger.

THE NEW YORK HERALD.

WHOLE NO. 9081. NEW YORK, MONDAY, JULY 22, 1861. PRICE TWO CENTS.

A GREAT BATTLE.

BRILLIANT UNION VICTORY!

Capture of Bull's Run Batteries.

The Rebels Routed and Driven Back to Manassas.

The Most Sanguinary Battle Ever Fought in America.

One Hundred and Twenty-five Thousand Men Engaged.

Twelve Hours Terrific Fighting.

Frightful Loss of Life on Both Sides.

The Rebel Army Seventy Thousand Strong.

Exciting Account of the Advance of the Union Army to Battle.

The Men Go Into Action Singing Patriotic Songs.

The New York Sixty-Ninth Go Into the Fight Stripped to their Pants.

Colonel Cameron, of the Higland Regiment, and Lieut. Col. Nugent, of the Sixty-Ninth Killed, and Cols. Hunter and Heintzelman Wounded,

&c., &c., &c.

THE GREAT BATTLE.

FAIRFAX COURT HOUSE, July 21, 1861.

I am *en route* to Washington with details of a great battle.

We have carried the day.

The rebels accepted battle in their strength, but are totally routed.

Loss on both sides considerable.

Bull's Run is silenced and two or three other batteries taken.

WASHINGTON, July 21, 1861.

The city is full of exaggerated rumors. It is difficult to tell what is reliable. Cannonading recommenced at four o'clock this afternoon, and ceased at five, probably occasioned by attempts of our troops to carry some rebel batteries between Bull's Run and Manassas Junction. Official despatches state that we have taken three batteries in the form of a crescent, numbering nineteen guns.

It is known that Manassas Junction was supplied with water by a canal from Bull's run. This, of course, will now be cut off, leaving the rebels without water for their cavalry.

Very few reliable details have yet reached us. That a most brilliant victory has been achieved by our gallant troops there is no doubt. Many encomiums are bestowed upon the Fire Zouaves and the Sixty-ninth. It is reported that the former met the Louisiana Zouaves, routed them and captured their colors; that the men of the Sixty-ninth stripped to the skin, except pants, and pitched into the fight regardless of fatigue or personal safety.

LATER.

Gen. McDowell telegraphs that *the enemy are completely routed from Bull's Run, and retreating towards Manassas, leaving their batteries in possession of the Union forces*

WASHINGTON, July 21—3 P. M.

Col. Miles' division proceeded this morning, at four o'clock, to cut a road through the woods, to order to flank the rebel battery—a feat which he gallantly accomplished, and carried the position. This movement, however, brought on a general engagement. *Cannonading has been distinctly heard at the Arsenal and on Long Bridge—a distance of twenty miles—from an early hour this morning until two o'clock this afternoon*, when it ceased. The firing was from guns of the heaviest calibre to those of the lightest weight, and was almost incessant.

WASHINGTON, July 21—6 P. M.

The War Department has information by telegraph of the capture of Bull's Run battery, the taking of which brought on a general engagement of the most desperate and sanguinary character.

Despatches from General McDowell to General Scott announce the capture of Bull's Run by the Union troops and the retreat of the rebels on Manassas.

Fighting commenced at three this morning and continued most desperately till after two o'clock this afternoon.

The rebels were driven back inch by inch, leaving their dead on the field.

The loss of life on both sides is frightful.

Couriers are now on their way to Washington with such details as have been gathered, which will be forwarded to the HERALD at once upon arrival.

Our troops behaved most gallantly, and our guns were very effective.

The whole force on both sides is said to have been engaged, General Johnston having joined the rebels, as previously stated, making General Beauregard's army amount to some seventy thousand men.

It is supposed that the rebels will suffer greatly at Manassas for lack of water.

WASHINGTON, July 21—8 P. M.

I have just arrived in Washington. I have been on the battle field all day, up to twenty minutes past four, at which time I left.

The fight has been a terrible one.

A despatch, just received, says that Colonel James Cameron, brother of the Secretary of War, and Colonel of the Seventy-ninth (Scotch) New York regiment, is killed.

Colonel David Hunter, commanding the centre division, is mortally wounded.

Colonel S. P. Heintzelman, commanding the third division, is slightly wounded.

I saw the rebels flying in vast numbers before leaving the field of glory and carnage.

Lieutenant Colonel J. J. Porter made an effort to procure the body of Lieutenant Smith, of Boston, but was fired upon by the artillery of the enemy.

The best estimate we can make of the rebel forces around Manassas in about fifty thousand. The greatest enthusiasm prevails throughout the Union ranks.

Report has gained credence among Union officers that General Johnston has effected a junction of his forces with those of General Beauregard.

We can distinctly see Beauregard's house, two miles distant.

Jefferson Davis is understood to be at Manassas Junction.

Colonel Cowdin's Massachusetts First regiment were fired on by rebel pickets several times last night as they slept in the road on their arms.

THE SKIRMISHING BEFORE THE GREAT BATTLE.

WASHINGTON, July 21—1 P. M.

The HERALD'S correspondent at Bull's Run sends the following, dated Bull's Run, Saturday evening, half past four o'clock:—

Five or six thousand of the enemy are seen retreating in the direction of Manassas Junction.

Generals Tyler, Richardson, Lieutenant Colonel Porter and Major Horton have reconnoitered all day, and were fired upon by the enemies pickets.

The Massachusetts First, under Colonel Cowdin, Lieutenant Colonel Welles, Major Chandler and Lieutenant Colonel Porter, detailed from the Missouri Fifteenth, are in the advance. At one o'clock Senator Wilson and Congressman Alley arrived on the ground, and were received with great enthusiasm.

Our pickets and those of the enemy are within gunshot of each other.

At this moment the advance are proceeding, sustained by several batteries, to regain Bull's Run.

ADVANCE OF THE GRAND ARMY.

CENTREVILLE, July 21, Via FAIRFAX COURT HOUSE, July 21, 1861.

We have successfully outflanked the enemy. At half-past two o'clock this morning the various regiments about Centreville were formed for marching, and at three o'clock they were in motion in the direction of Berryville, leaving Bull's Run to the left. At six o'clock the first gun was fired by a thirty pound rifled cannon, sent ahead to see after the masked batteries that might be encountered on the road. There was no reply from the enemy, and the advance moved on.

At Gen. McDowell's headquarters, three miles beyond Centreville, the greater part of the army moved to the right to avoid a bridge some distance beyond, said to have been undermined. They will pass over upon pontoons, prepared by Capt. Alexander, of the Engineer corps, and who has inspected the country minutely in a previous reconnoissance, and to whom, in a great measure, the plan of the campaign is due.

A general battle is expected to-day or to-morrow, and which will probably decide the fate of the whole campaign.

If General Johnston has not yet formed a junction with General Beauregard, he will be entirely cut off by this manœuvre, and thrown back upon the mountains. His army will become utterly demoralized, and will probably fall into the hands of General McClellan, who is advancing beyond the Blue Ridge. And if he has formed a junction with General Beauregard, it opens our communication with General Patterson's column; and, thus reinforced, the Union army can crush out opposition.

The only danger the Union troops run by this flank march would be by a sudden advance of General Beauregard upon Centreville, interrupting communications and cutting off our supplies. But this manœuvre would be desperate, as cutting himself off from supplies and placing him in an exhausted country, and between the Union troops and the Potomac.

The Sixty-ninth New York regiment was assigned the post of honor in advance. The members of this regiment have agreed unanimously to serve, although their time is now out.

All the New York regiments will follow this example.

For five hours one steady column of troops passed through Centreville.

The *morale* of the soldiers is excellent, and all are anxious for a battle, and when informed of the purpose to advance the enthusiasm was beyond all description.

It is supposed that General Beauregard's forces are larger than ours.

Telegraphic wires are rapidly following the army, and offices were opened this morning at Fairfax Court House, with Messrs. Buell and Benton as army operators.

THE BATTLE.

OPERATIONS OF THE LEFT WING.

WASHINGTON, July 21, 1861.

The HERALD'S special correspondent from the Left Wing of the Grand Army sends in the following despatch:—

CAMP AT CENTREVILLE, July 20—Midnight.

At the headquarters of the most advanced division—the Fifth, Colonel Dixon S. Miles—we have a sight of the Grand Army at midnight, upon the eve of battle The order has been given for the advance at half past two o'clock A. M., upon the formidable batteries in front of us, one of them only two miles distant. The enemy's pickets are within rifle shot of where we are sitting; but in the lines of this division all is quiet.

An hour ago we passed along the lines. Lights are burning elsewhere; but, under the supervision of the veteran at the head of this division, all is dark and still. Not a tent is to be seen, but upon the slope of a hillside extending half a mile towards Centreville, seven thousand men are lying upon their arms, and ready at the tap of the drum to rally to the rescue of the Republic. Here and there in an adjacent camp the sky is lighted up with the glare proceeding from the burning of a shade of boughs, erected in lieu of tents, of which only a few have as yet arrived. This is inconsiderate, for to practised soldiers, like General Joe Johnston and General Beauregard, it will plainly indicate an intention to abandon the camp and move forward. In the front of a wary enemy all these little details must be cared for. The slightest indication from which information can be obtained in regard to intended movements should be guarded against. Except these burning shades, and the white covers of the wagons, not a sign of the grand army is visible, and not a sound is heard except the measured tread of the sentinels and the occasional snort of a horse. Yet we are on the eve of a grand battle—perhaps the battle that is to make the bloodiest picture in the book of time.

The army has bivouacked here two days. The camp stretches for nearly a mile northeast and south of the hamlet of Centreville. Two miles to the southwest the enemy is posted in a force at present estimated at sixty thousand. There are numerous batteries to be taken.

The reconnoitering party sent out by General Taylor on Thursday discovered three in a bunch. This reconnoissance was a mistake. It was made not only without orders, but against the positive protest of the officers o engineers attached to the division.

After all the extravagant reports that have gone forward, it appears that there were only three companies of infantry and one section, two pieces of artillery, in that engagement. This was a slender force with which to attack five thousand men behind three formidable batteries.

As I write, the buglers at Gen. McDowell's headqurrters are sounding the "Assembly." It is time for the men to be getting under arms. The whole army is to move at from two to half-past two o'clock. The battle is expected to begin at daybreak. At ten o'clock I was at the headquarters of General McDowell. He was then holding a council of war around a table in his tent, at the head of which he sat. Cool and imperturbable, were gathered the Commanders of Divisions. Outside, mounted upon their horses, each surrounded by his staff, were the Commanders of Brigades. Conspicious among these we noted Col. Burnside, accompanied by Governor Sprague, who takes a lively interest in all that is to be done, and Colonel Andrew Porter, and they receive their instructions. The dangling sabres rattle against the horses' sides, the sentinels present arms as they hurry off to prepare their brigades for the movement in the morning.

It has been ascertained by careful reconnoisances that the rebels have planted batteries on the Warrentown turnpike, to oppose the passage of Bull's run. These are in addition to the famous Bull's run batteries. They have also mined the stone bridge across the run, and made a heavy abbatis on the right bank, to intercept the advance of the Union troops in that direction. The ford above the bridge is guarded by a strong force; but it has not been positively ascertained if they have a battery there. It is, however, evident that The grand stand on the part of the rebels is to be made here, and a serious fight must ensue.

It is the intention of General McDowell to turn this position of the rebel's and force them to abandon it, and also to seize the railroad leading from Manassas Junction to the valley of Virginia, and cut off reinforcements from that quarter.

The whole army encamped here will take part in the movement, but one division—the Fifth, under Colonel Miles—will be held in the neighborhood of Centreville as a reserve to reinforce and relieve any point where cool courage and experience and ability shall be required to insure success.

General Richerdson's brigade has been encamped since Thursday in the same position held by it since the skirmish on Thursday. This brigade is, for the present, attached to the division. The whole of this division will make a demonstration upon Blackburn's ford, and meanwhile erect such defensive works in the neighborhood of Centreville as the Engineer corps shall direct.

General Tyler's division, except Richardson's brigade, is to make a feint upon the bridge across Bull's run, but is not to open fire until daybreak unless assaulted,

Hunter's division will be in the advance, and will cross Bull's run above the ford, at Ludley's spring, and make an attack upon the rebel force guarding the lower ford.

Heintzelman's division will follow Hunter's, but cross Bull's run at the lower ford after it has been cleared by Hunter's division.

In this way the rear of the enemy will be reached, and his reinforcements cut off. The fate of the contest hangs upon the result of this battle. If it be decided by a victory of the federal forces the war will be of short duration.

The troops are all in good spirits and eager for the opportunity to prove their mettle. They recognize to-night the reality and responsibility of the duty in which they are engaged.

The drums of Hunter's division are sounding the reveille. In half an hour more the grand army will be in motion, and before night to-day, July 21, its first great success will be announced to the world.

The route from Washington hitherward by moonlight was full of Romantic incidents. It was a bright, beautiful night. The pale goddess had hung her silver lamp in the mid heavens to light our way. As far as Fairfax Court House we met a number of carriages conveying back to the city visiters to the camp. Arrived at the Court House, which is occupied by a battalion of the Fourth Michigan regiment. We were kindly cautioned by an officer that the rest of the road, some seven or eight miles, was dangerous at night without an armed escort, but a Sergeant of the First Rhode Island and the Quartermaster of the Thirty-first New York regiments agreed to go on, as they were willing to make the trip and on he went, accompanied by a guide, who had been some weeks ago driven from Manassas by the rebels. We had given the countersign and passed the Union pickets at the village of Providence, Fairfax Court House about one mile, when our guide called attention to some dozen or more men collected at the top of a hill ahead, who began to run into the woods on each side. With weapons drawn and ready for use we proceeded slowly, but when the point was reached there was no one visible. Five miles more of the road was cautiously traversed, closely watching the houses and thick woods by the wayside, when we struck upon the picket of General McDowell's army. The road from Fairfax Court House to Centreville is not just now the safest in the world for Union men at night, for the rebels in their wantonness creep in behind our lines and take delight in pepping away at visitors to General McDowell's army who happen to be belated.

A romantic story is told here of an officer upon Col. Hunter's staff. He was riding out yesterday, and got some distance outside of our lines, when suddenly, in a turn of the road, he found himself in the midst of a regiment marching along. Thinking it was one of our own volunteers, he inquired of the men what regiment it was, and was answered that it was the Seventh North Carolina. With admirable nonchalance he asked what other regiments were on the way, and was told there were several, but they did not know what they were. He proceeded with them a few rods until he came to a cross road, down which he turned his horse, but was cautioned not to go in that direction as it would take him to the place where some of their men were killed the day before and right into the lines of the Lincoln men. He replied that he only wanted to water his horse, and as soon as he got out of sight spurred back to our lines delighted to have escaped. The similarity of the uniform of the rebel officers with that of our own alone enabled him to escape detection.

This army is paying damages for the land it occupies as it passes along. To-day an assessment of damages in this neighborhood was made by the Board of Examiners, and the amounts assessed were paid. One man, whose house was occupied as the headquarters of The commander of one of the divisions which was bivouacked upon his land, received three hundred and fifteen dollars. A neighbor, whose oat field and house was similarly occupied, received one hundred, and another one hundred and fifty dollars, all in gold. One of them was heard to say he had not for a long time seen so much real money, and that he would willingly give all he had received to be allowed to go back of Manassas and tell his friends how much they were deceived about the Union army, and that it was not coming among them to ravish their women, and destroy their property and carry off their negroes, but to protect the people and pay their way in gold. His only fear was that if he went back to Manassas he would be impressed into the service of the rebel army, and either hung for having received federall gold, or prevented from returning to his family.

The sounds of the advance are in my hears. I go to join it. God protect the right. May He who has made and preserved us a nation bring victory to our proud banner to-day.

OPERATIONS OF THE CENTRE.

WASHINGTON, July 21, 1861.

The HERALD'S special correspondent furnishes the following despatch from the seat of war of the early proceedings of the grand army to-day:—

ON THE HILLSIDE OVERLOOKING Bull's run, Sunday, July 21—10 A. M.

It was broad daylight when the divisions of Cols. Hunter and Heintselman were fairly *en route* for their respective positions.

The movements of these columns were watched anxiously from a high hill south of Centreville. The men moved forward briskly, singing patriotic songs, and with such spirit as would lead an uninitiated looker on to suppose they were going to a feast instead of to a desperate fight. Their long lines of glittering bayonets reflected the sun's rays from the two roads they were following, and there were anxious listeners as they passed out of sight in the woods that skirted the banks of Bull's run. General McDowell accompanied Colonel Hunter's column.

At a quarter past six o'clock four guns were heard in the direction taken by the head of Gen. Tyler's column, but whether fired by his batterses or those of the rebels is not yet ascertained.

The columns pressed on, regiment after regiment, attended only by ammunition and hospital wagons and ambulances.

The time wore wearily away, and your correspondent concluded to turn his attention to the Left wing, which was facing the batteries at Bull's run, attacked on Thursday.

It is the opinion of experienced officers that the enemy will attempt to turn our left flank and get between General McDowell's column and the city of Washington. This would give the hardest fighting to Colonel Miles' division, which is on the extreme left.

Colonel Richardson's brigade occupies the same position it occupied on Thursday, when the Bull's run reconnoissance was made.

Colonel Davies' brigade is in his rear, between Bull's run and Centreville, and Colonel Blenker's brigade is supporting them at Centreville.

The outposts of Colonel Richardson's brigade are within musket range of the edge of the woods, in which are concealed the rebel batteries discovered on Thursday. Their pickets are protected by trees.

Every sentinel had been instructed to take a tree and keep his body well covered by it.

About seven o'clock large bodies of rebel infantry were seen filing into the thick wood surrounding these batteries, as if to turn the left flank of Colonel Miles' division. Lieut. Edwards opened upon them from an adjoining eminence with shell and shrapnal from two twenty pounder rifled cannon. After a few rounds the evidences of the presence of the enemy ceased, and firing was suspended.

Soon afterwards your correspondent and another proceeded some rods beyond the outpost picket accompanying Colonel Richardson, and discovered large bodies of infantry in the wood, within musket range. Two pieces of Major Hunt's battery of light artillery had been placed in position, and opened fire with shell and shot, which drove them back from the point where they were so saucily showing themselves.

The enemy have not fired a single answering shot. The silence upon the right of the columns advancing by way of the Warrenton bridge and the ford at Ledly's Spring would indicate that the heads of our advancing columns must most assuredly have reached ere this the points upon which they were advancing.

The rebels seem to be equally active in preparing. From the high hill overlooking the masked batteries at Bull's run large bodies of cavalry, artillery and infantry have been all the morning moving rapidly towards the heads of Hunter's and Heintzleman's and Tyler's columns. They have not, however, abandoned their batteries at Bull creek. Their silence may be a ruse to invite attack, but it is evident to all that a grand battle is to be fought to-day, perhaps along the whole of our lines. The rebels are bringing to bear all their available strength; they have an abundance of artille ry, and have disposed of it skillfully. Two hospitals have been established, and detachments of the First Massachusetts, Twelfth New York Volunteers, and Second and Third Michigan regiments, have been detailed as a quartermaster's guard.

DETAILS OF THE BATTLE.

WASHINGTON, July 21, 1861.

A most severe battle was fought to-day at Bull Run Bridge. The conflict was desperate, lasting over eleven hours.

The programe, as stated in the first despatch from Fairfax Court House was carried out until the troops met with a succession of masked batteries, which were attacked with vigor and success, after a severe loss of life. Our troops advanced as follows:—

Colonel Richardson, who distinguished himself in the previous engagement proceeded on the left, with four regiments of the Fourth brigade, to hold the battery on the hill on the Warrenton road, in the vicinity of the place where the last battle was fought. The flank movements were described in the first despatch.

Schenck's and Sherman's brigades, of General Tyler's division, advanced by the Warrenton road, while Colonels Heintzelman's and Hunter's division took the fork of the Warrenton road to move between Bull's Run and Manassas Junction.

Colonel Keyes' brigade remained at Centreville.

Information was received by General Tyler's command of the existence of the enemy's battery commanding the road. Our troops were then formed in battle array.

The Second New York and First Ohio on the left, and the second Ohio and Second Wisconsin, and the Seventy-ninth, Thirteenth and Sixty-ninth regiments of New York on the right. Colonel Miles' division followed in the rear.

The first range gun was fired by Sherman's battery, at ten minutes to seven o'clock. The rebels did not return his shot until an hour and a half afterwards. When Col. Hunter's division came up another battle became general. Colonel Hunter's movement to gain the rear of the enemy was almost a success. The enemy's positio was opened on by several of Carlisle's howitzers, followe by slight skirmishing. The rebels rapidly received reinforcements from Manasses Junction after the attack was opened.

The battle consisted of a succession of fires from masked batteries, which opened in every direction (when one was silenced its place was supplied by two) and in the daring chrrges of our infantry in unmasking them. The Second Ohio and Second New York militia were marched by flank through the woods by a new made road within about a mile of the main road, when they came on a battery of eight guns, with four regiments flanked in the rear. Our men were immediately ordered to lie down on either side of the road, in order to allow two pieces of artillery to pass through and attack the work, when this battery opened upon us and killed on the third round Lieutenant Dempsey, of Company G, New York Second, and Wm. Maxwell, a drummer, and seriously wounding several others.

Our troops were kept from fifteen to twenty minutes under a galling fire, they not being able to exchange shots with the enemy, although within a stone throw of their batteries. They succeeded in retiring in regular order, and with their battery.

The most gallant charge of the day, was made by the Sixty-ninth, Seventh-first and Thirteenth, who rushed upon one of the batteries, firing as they proceeded with perfect *eclat* and attacking it with the bayonets point. The yells of triumph seemed to carry all before it. They found that the rebels had abandoned the battery and only taken one gun, but this success was acquired only after a severe loss of life, in which the Sixty-ninth most severely suffered, and it was reported that Lieutenant Colonel Nugent was amongst the first killed.

The Zouaves also distinguished themselves by their spirited assaults on the batteries at the point of the bayonet, but it is feared that their loss is immense.

Up to the hour of three o'clock, P. M., it was generally understood that we had hemmed in the enemy entirely, and that they were gradually retiring, that Colonel Hunter had driven them back in the rear, that Colonel Heinzelman's command was meeting with every success, and that it required but the reserve of General Tyler's division to push on to Manassas Junction.

A Mississippi soldier was taken prisoner by Hasbrouck, of the Wisconsin Second regiment. He turnied out to Brigade Quartermaster Pryor, cousin to Roger A. Pryor. He was captured with his horse as he by accident rode idto our lines. He discovered himself by remarking to Hasbrouck, "We are getting badly cut to pieces." "What regiment do you belong to?" asked Hasbrouck. "The Nineteenth Mississippi," was the answer "Then you are my prisoner," said Hasbrouck.

From the statements of this prisoner it apperrs that our artillery has created greas havoc among the rebels, of whom there are from thirty thousand to forty housand in the field, under command of General Beauregard, while they have a reserve of seventy-five thousand at the Junction.

He describes an officer most prominent in the fight, distinguished from the rest by his white horse, as Jeff. Davis. He confirms the previous reports of a regiment of negro troops in the rebel forces, but says it is difficult to get them in proper discipline in battle array.

The position of the enemy extended in three lines in the form oi a triangle, the apix fronting the centre of our column. The area seems to have been filled with masked battories.

At seven o'clock this evening guns were still heard firing at short intervals.

RESERVES ORDERED FORWARD.

CENTREVILLE, July 21—4 P. M.

General McDowell has ordered the reserves now here, under Colonel Miles, to advance to the bridge over Bull's run on the Warrenton road.

EFFECTS OF THE BATTLE IN WASHINGTON.

WASHINGTON, July 21, 1861.

The most intense excitement is everywhere existing to hear further from the field of battle. Every returning spectator of the events is immediately surrounded to relate his observations.

The demand for intelligence is insatiable, and many unauthenticated rumors prevail, which serve to confuse the truth. The smoke from the battle could be seen from the eminences in Wasnington.

A number of members of Congress, and even ladies, went to the neighborhood of Bull's Run to witness the battle. One of them reports:—Colonel Hunter, of the Third cavalry, acting as Major General, was seriously, if not mortally wounded.

It is stated with confidence in all quarters, that Colonel Cameron, of the Seventy-ninth regiment, and brother of the Secretary of War, and Colonel Slocum, of the Second Rhode Island regiment, were killed.

The destination of Colonel McCunn's Thirty-seventh regiment has been changed to Manassas Junction, by way of Alexandria.

SKETCH OF COL. DAVID HUNTER, UNITED STATES ARMY,

Acting Major General of the Second division of the grand army, under General McDowell, fell, as will be seen from our despatches, mortally wounded at the battle of Bull's run yesterday. Major General Hunter commanded the centre division of the attacking Union force at the moment he received his death wound. David Hunter was born in the District of Columbia. He entered the United States Army as a cadet from the State of Illinois, in the month of September, in the year 1818; was commissioned as Second Lieutenant of the Fifth regiment of infantry on the 1st of July, 1822; First Lieutenant in June, 1828, and Captain of the First regiment of dragoons in March, 1833. Captain Hunter resigned his commission on the 4th of July, in the year 1836, and was appointed a temporary paymaster of the army on the 31st of November, 1841. He received his commission as paymaster on the 14th of March, in the year 1842 Major General Hunter held the commission of Colonel of the Third regiment of United States cavalry when the war commenced, and was promoted to the rank in which he so gloriously distinguished himself as hostilities progressed.

SKETCH OF COLONEL CAMERON.

Among the persons who have fallen in the first great battle for the suppression of the present rebellion, we have to record Colonel James Cameron, Commander of the Seventy-ninth (Scotch) regiment. Colonel Cameron is a brother of the present Secretary of War, and was elected to take command of the regiment on account of the strong Scotch feeling which he possessed, and his Cameronian sentiments

At the time of the resignation of Col. McLeay, the command of the regiment devolved upon Lieut. Colonel Elliott, who acted as Colonel for a short time, and would have gallantly led his men to face any danger, backed as he was by the confidence of the whole regiment, had he not had a desire to place at the head of the corps, to use his own expression, "a Cameron in every respect worthy to lead our clan."

Colonel Cameron has been described in the following manner at the time of his taking command of his new charge:—

Of splendid proportions, standing over six feet high and straight as an arrow, he is still in full vigor, time having touched him but lightly as he passed. Of most courteous demeanor, and always considerate of the wants of his men, he is at the same time an admirable soldier, having commandeda Pennsylvania regiment for some years. The day of his in- auguration was a gala day in our camp When the ballot had been proceeded with and the result announced, the acceptance by Colonel Cameron of the position to which he had been elected was received with the greatest enthusiasm.

The election took place in the city of Washington on the 20th of June, and the agreeable news was instantly transmitted by telegraph to this city, where it was received with great satisfaction, the friends of the regiment predicting all sorts of success for the Seventy-ninth while under the command of two such officers as Cameron and Elliott.

The sad intelligence of his death will be received with unfeigned sorrow both by his numerous friends and by the people generally, as we can ill afford at any time, much less at the present, to lose such a man as Colonel Cameron has proved himself to be.

Colonel Elliott will now take command of the regiment, which will in no manner suffer, beyond the simple fact of losing an officer that they all loved and respected.

Colonel Cameron was a native of Pennsylvania, in which State he commanded a regiment for many years, as stated above.

THE HEROES OF THE BATTLE.

We give a list of the generals, and field and line officers commanding the various divisions, brigades, regiments and detachments engaged at the great battle of yesterday. We have compiled the list from the records kept in the HERALD office, with a desire to perpetuate on the roll of fame the names of those who so gellantly fought in this momentous contest in the war to suppress rebellion and preserve the integrity of the greatest republic of the world.

COMMANDER OF THE GRAND ARMY.
BRIGADIER GENERAL IRVIN M'DOWELL, U. S. A.
STAFF OF THE DEPARTMENT COMMANDER.
ADJUTANT GENERAL'S DEPARTMENT.
Captain James B. Fry, Assistant Adjutant General.
AIDES DE CAMP.
First Lieutenant H. W. Kingsbury, Fifth Artillery.
Major Clarence S. Brown, New York State Militia.
Major James S. Wadsworth, New York State Militia.
ACTING INSPECTOR GENERAL,
Major W. H. Wood, Seventeenth infantry.
ENGINEERS.
Major J. G. Barnard.
First Lieutenant F. E. Prime.
TOPOGRAPHICAL ENGINEERS.
Captain A. W. Whipple.
First Lieutenant Henry L. Abbott.
Second Lieutenant Haldimand S. Putnam.
QUARTERMASTER'S DEPARTMENT.
Capt. O. H. Tillinghast, Assistant Quartermaster.
SUBSISTENCE DEPARTMENT.
Capt. H. F. Clark, Commissary of Subsistence.
MEDICAL DEPARTMENT.
Surgeon, W. S. King.
Assistant Surgeon, David L. Magruder.

FIRST DIVISION.

ACTING MAJOR GENERAL, BRIGADIER GENERAL DANIEL TYLER OF THE CONNECTICUT MILITIA.

FIRST BRIGADE.
Acting Brigadier General, Colonel E. D. Keyes, Eleventh Infantry.

FIRST REGIMENT CONNECTICUT VOLUNTEERS.
Colonel.....George S. Burnham, of Hartford.
Lieutenant Colonel.....John L. Chatfield, of Waterbury.
Major.....Theo. C. Bacon, of New Haven.
Adjutant..... —
Quartermaster.....Justin Hodge, of Barkhamstead.
Surgeon.....C. P. Stearns.
Surgeon's Mate.....Frederick Dibble.
Sergeant Major.....John S. Spalding.
Quarterm'ter's Sergeant.J. V. B. Williams.
Captains.
Company A, Hartford Light Guard—J. C. Comstock.
Company B, Hartford—Ira Wright.
Company C, Windsor Locks—Levi N. Hillman.
Company D, Waterbury City Guard—Marcus Coon.
Company E, Wooster Guard, of Danbury—E. E. Wildman.
Company F, of West Meriden—Theodore Byxbee.
Company G, of New Britain—Frederick W. Hart.
Company H, of Bridgeport—Richard Fitzgibbons.
Company I, Rifle Company, of Hartford—J. R. Hawley.
Company K, Bridgeport Rifles—John Speidel

SECOND REGIMENT OF CONNECTICUT VOLUNTEERS.
Colonel.....Alfred H. Terry, of New Haven.
Lieutenant Colonel.....David Young, of Norwich.
Major.....Robert O. Tyler, of Hartford.
Adjutant..... —
Surgeon.....A. [illegible] Douglas, M. D., of New London.
Surgeon's Mate.....Francis Bacon, of New Haven.
Captains.
Company A, Middletown—David Dickinson.
Company B, Winchester, Canton and New Hartford—Abram G. Kellogg.
Company C, New Haven—E. W. Osborn.
Company D, Derby—C. D. Russell.
Company E, South Norwalk— ——
Company F, Norwich Rifles, A—Frank S. Chester.
Company G, Norwich Rifles, B—Henry Peale.
Company H, New London Rifles—E. C. Chapman.
Company I, Hartford Rifles—James W. Gore.
Company K, Winstead Rifles—Sherman T. Cook.

THIRD REGIMENT CONNECTICUT VOLUNTEERS.
Colonel.....John Arnold, of New Haven.
Lieutenant Colonel.....Allen P. Brady, of Torrington.
Major.....Alexander Warner, Woodstock.
Adjutant.....Fred'k. J. Peck, of New Haven.
Quartermaster.....Richard E. Holcomb, of Granby.
Surgeon.....John McGreggor, of Thompson.
Assistant Surgeon.....Matthew T. Newton, of [illegible]
Sergeant Major.....Wm. E. Brady, of Torrington.
Assistant Quartermaster.....J. H. Alexander, of [illegible]
Colonel's Aid.....Joseph Ridley, of New Haven.
Second Colonel's Aid.....Edwin Gavitt, Jr., of Norwich.
Captains.
Company A, South Norwalk—Douglas Fowler.
Company B, New Haven—Samuel J. Root.
Company C, Bridgeport—Frederick Frye.
Company D, New Haven—Daniel Klein.
Company E, Danbury—James E. Moore.
Company F, Hartford Rifles, A—George N. Loots.
Company G, Meriden Rifles—Jared R. Cook.
Company H, Norwich Rifles—Edward Harlan.
Company I, Hartford Rifles, E—John A. Nelson.
Company K, Stamford Rifles—Albert Stevens.

SECOND REGIMENT MAINE VOLUNTEERS.
The Bangor Regiment.
Colonel.....C. D. Jameson, of Bangor.
Lieutenant Colonel.....C. W. Roberts, of Bangor.
Major.....George Varney, of Bangor.
Adjutant.....John E. Reynolds, of Bangor.
Quartermaster.....Charles V. Lord, of Bangor.
Sergeant Major.....Edward L. Appleton, of Bangor.
Quartermaster Sergeant.....Luther H. Pierce, of Bangor.
Surgeon.....William H. Allen, of Orono.
Surgeon's Mate.....A. O. Hamlin, of Bangor.
Captains.
Company A, Bangor—Herman Bartlett.
Company B, Castine—S. K. Devereaux.
Company C, Brewer—Elisha N. Jones.
Company D, Milo—John S. Sampson.
Company E, Bangor—Levi Emerson.
Company F, Bangor—David Chaplin.
Company G, Bangor—Daniel F. Sergeant.
Company H, Bangor—T. Merricke.
Company I, Bangor—John Carrell.
Company K, Old Town—F. C. Foss.

EIGHTH REGIMENT NEW YORK STATE MILITIA BATTERY.
Captain.....Joshua M. Varian.
First Lieutenant.....Robert Brown.
Second Lieutenant.....Stephen H. Cornell.

UNITED STATES CAVALRY.
Section of Company B, of the Second regiment.....Lieutenant Tompkins.

SECOND BRIGADE.
Brigadier General Robert C. Schenck, of the Ohio Volunteers.

FIRST REGIMENT OF OHIO VOLUNTEERS.
Colonel.....A. D. McCook.
Lieutenant Colonel.....E. S. Parrott.
Major.....J. Hughes.
Adjutant.....J. S. Parrott.
Sergeant Major.....T. McKinsey.
Quartermaster.....James Hill.
Quartermaster Sergeant.....M. Steele.
Color Sergeant.....C. C. Smyth.
Captains.
Company A, Lancaster Guard—Stafford.
Company B, Dayton Lafayette Yagers—Deisher.
Company C, Dayton Light Guard—Pease.
Company D, Dayton Montgomery Guard—Crowe.
Company E, Cleveland Grays—Paddock.
Company F, Franklin Blues—Kell.
Company G, Light Guard—Bayley.
Company H, Zanesville Guard—Hazlett.
Company I, Mansfield Guard—McLaughlin.
Company K, Jackson Guard—Brook.

SECOND REGIMENT OHIO VOLUNTEERS.
Colonel..... — Harris.
Lieutenant Colonel..... — Mason.
Major..... — Parry.
Adjutant..... —
Captains.
Company A, Rover Guard—Finch.
Company B, Columbus Videttes—Sprall.
Company C, State Fencibles—Mitchell.
Company D, Cincinnati Zouaves—Baldwin.
Company E, Lafayette Guard—Haldenhoff.
Company F, Springfield Zouaves—Mason.
Company G, Pickaway Guard—Black.
Company H, Steubenville Guard—Cook.
Company I, Cincinnati Harris Guard—Harrold.
Company K, Urbana Rifles—Baldwin.

[CONTINUED ON EIGHTH PAGE.]

BATTLE OF CARTHAGE, MISSOURI—GALLANT ATTACK OF COLONEL SIEGEL'S D

N ON A SUPERIOR FORCE OF REBEL TROOPS. SKETCHED BY J. S. SCHEIBEL. SEE PAGE 186.

DAILY DISPATCH--Extra.

TUESDAY, JULY 23d, 1861.

Richmond Dispatch.

ACCOUNT FROM WASHINGTON.

"We Have met the Enemy and They are Ours!"

THE FEDERALS ACKNOWLEDGE THEIR DEFEAT!

Awful Slaughter of Troops!

ELLSWORTH'S "PET LAMBS" CUT TO PIECES!

ALL THE FEDERAL BATTERIES TAKEN.

Gloom in Washington and Evident Apprehensions of an Invasion.

A GLORIOUS VICTORY FOR THE SOUTHERN CAUSE!

&c., &c., &c.

WASHINGTON, July 22—*Noon.*—Our troops, after gaining a great victory on yesterday, were repulsed, and commenced a retreat on Washington.

After this information was received last night from Centreville, a series of events took place here in the highest degree disastrous. Many confused statements prevail, but enough is positively known to warrant the statement that the Federal forces have suffered to a degree which casts a deep gloom over the remnants of the army, and excites the deepest melancholy throughout Washington.

The carnage was tremendously heavy on both sides, and on the Federal side it is represented to have been frightful.

The Federals advanced gradually among the masked batteries, and were surely driving the Confederates towards Manassas, when the Southerners seemed reinforced by Gen. Johnston. The Federals were immediately driven back, and a panic among them suddenly occurred, and a regular stampede took place.

It is understood that Gen. McDowell undertook to make a stand near Centreville, but the panic was so fearful that the whole army became demoralized. It was impossible to check them either at Centreville or Fairfax C. H. Large numbers of troops, on their retreat, fell on the way-side from exhaustion, and the dead, wounded and exhausted are all along the route to and from Fairfax C. H. The road from Bull's Run is strewn with arms and knapsacks, which were discarded by the Federals in order to facilitate their retreat.

Gen. McDowell was in the rear of the retreating forces and endeavored to rally them, but with only partial success.

Only two hundred of the Fire Zouave Regiment are left from the slaughter.

The 69th and other New York Regiments suffered frightfully.

Sherman's, Carlisle's, Griffin's and the West Point Batteries were taken by the Confederate troops.

They also took the eight siege 32-pounders, rifle cannon.

Col. Wilcox, who commanded a Brigade, was killed.

Capt. McCook is also among the killed.

Col. Heintzelman was wounded.

Washington presents a scene of most intense excitement. Wagons are continually bringing in the dead and wounded, and the feeling is awfully distressing. Both telegraph and steamboat communication with Alexandria has been suspended. Fortifications are being strongly reinforced with fresh troops. It is understood that Gen. Mansfield will take the command.

Fortifications on the Virginia side of the river are being improved and reinforced, and large rifled cannon and mortars are being rapidly sent over.

RECEPTION OF THE NEWS IN LOUISVILLE.

THE SOUTHERN-RIGHTS MEN REJOICING.

LOUISVILLE, July 22.—The news of the victory of the Confederate forces, near Manassas, on the 21st inst., creates the most intense excitement here. This news has startled the public mind, as the morning papers here published dispatches from Washington which proclaimed a brilliant victory for the Federal army.

There is great and unbounded rejoicing here among the Southern-Rights men.

SAD ACCIDENT.—An accident occurred last Saturday on the railroad near Weldon, N. C. by which two privates in Capt. Brevard's Company, of the Second Florida Regiment, lost their lives. Their names were Searcey and Russell. They were on the top of one of the cars, and the unfortunate soldiers were knocked off as the train passed under a bridge. The practice of riding on the top of cars is unsafe, even when travelers are acquainted with the road over which they may be passing; and warnings like that above noticed should be heeded by our troops whose lives are now valuable to the country.

MR. BRECKINRIDGE'S SPEECH.—From the Washington correspondent of the Cincinnati Gazette, we learn that the speech of Hon. J. C. Breckinridge, in the Senate, Tuesday, was bold, fearless, and severely denunciatory of the Administration. As an oratorical effort it was fine, attracting an audience far exceeding the capacities of the Senate Chamber.—The unconstitutional acts of the President were the burden of his remarks. He proclaimed his opposition to the war and his belief in the propriety of the ultimate destruction of this system of Government.

MELANCHOLY COINCIDENCE.—Lieut. John P. Nisbet, who raised and organized the Orleans Cadets with Col. Dreux, died in New Orleans of consumption, while the remains of his old friend and companion were on their way to the tomb. His illness commenced just before the company volunteered for the war. He was universally esteemed in New Orleans.

REPORTED CONFLICT BETWEEN FOREIGN STEAMERS.—On Friday morning last, heavy firing was heard off the Charleston bar, and a pilot who came up reported that a French war steamer passing the blockading fleet had been fired at, possibly with the intention of bringing her to. She promptly returned the fire, injuring her assailant severely.

A GALLANT OFFICER GONE.—Captain D'Laguel, who was killed at Rich Mountain while standing so gallantly at his guns, was the same gentleman formerly holding the position of Lieutenant at the Fayetteville (N. C.) Arsenal, under the United States Government. He was evidently a brave, high toned gentleman, and a true son of the South.

SINGULAR EXPERIMENT.—Take a round piece of pasteboard and insert it in a quill open at both ends, and lay this on another piece of pasteboard of the same shape, in which is stuck a pin, so that the pin will enter the quill. Blow through the quill as hard as you may, but the lower piece cannot be blown off.

A common spool, such as is used for sewing cotton, forms a suitable apparatus for trying this wonderful experiment. Take a bit of smooth writing paper a little larger than the head of the spool, and run a pin through the paper and into the bore of the spool. Now, by blowing down it will be found impossible to blow the paper off. By observing closely, it will be seen that the paper does not quite touch the head of the spool. It is, of course, necessary to hold the paper up with your hand until you begin to blow.

The explanation is this: When currents of air are established, radiating from the central tube horizontally between the disk and the paper, the greater area of the disk as compared with that of the tube causes the air above the paper to be rarified, when the pressure of the air below, not being counterbalanced, holds the paper up. The pin acts as an anchor to prevent the paper from being blown away horizontally.

MASSACHUSETTS TROOPS GOING HOME.—Baltimore papers of a recent date furnish the subjoined news from Fortress Monroe:

The steamer Adelaide, Capt. Cannon, arrived Wednesday morning from Old Point Comfort. She brought a number of passengers, among whom were several of Duryea's Zouaves, wounded in the battle of Great Bethel.

The Third Massachusetts Regiment left on Tuesday afternoon, on the steamer Cambridge, and the Fourth was to have left yesterday by the Spaulding, for Boston. Gen. Pierce, who commanded at Great Bethel, returns with them.

A battalion had been sent out from Newport Newspoint, in search of a squad of Confederate cavalry, but had not returned when the A. left. The following is the letter from the correspondent of the Associated Press:

The Third Massachusetts Regiment sails for Boston this evening, in the steamer Cambridge. They were reviewed by General Butler to-day. The Fourth Massachusetts Regiment follows to-morrow. Col. Max Webber's and Colonel Butler's Regiments were to occupy Hampton; but this plan has been somewhat changed. Brigadier General Pierce retires from the Massachusetts Regiments.—Col. Duryea will probably be Acting Brigadier General in Hampton.

FOREIGN CONSULS IN THE SOUTH.—The Jackson *Mississippian*, in a strong article in reference to the foreign policy of the Confederate States, says:

Let us demand of all foreign nations that they accredit their consuls and other agents to the *Confederate States* of America, and not to the United States, or recall them at once. To let these agents remain among us in their official capacity, as we are now doing, is misplaced courtesy, altogether unbecoming an independent and self-reliant people.

HAD A CONVERSATION WITH HIM.—A letter from Harper's Ferry to a Mississippi paper relates the following:

"Occasionally a merry burst of laughter is heard as some ridiculous incident is related. 'See here, boys,' said one of the men, the other day, 'I had a conversation with Gen. Johnston, just now.' 'The devil you did!—What did he have to say to you?' inquired a dozen voices. 'Why, he told me if I didn't get out of that garden, and let alone those onions, he'd have me tied up behind a wagon.'"

DESTRUCTIVE FIRE AT LINDSAY, CANADA.—*Great Destruction of Property.*—A dispatch dated Buffalo, July 9, says:

Advices from Toronto report the occurrence of a destructive fire at Lindsay, a village in the county of Peterboro', which consumed some seventy buildings, over one-half of which were stores. The fire occurred on the 5th inst., and the destruction of property was complete.

Price of Subscription.

IN THE CITY, single copy, TWO CENTS; served by Carriers for *Twelve Cents* per week, payable to the carriers.

OUT OF THE CITY, single copy, THREE CENTS; one month, *Fifty Cents;* two months, *One Dollar;* four months, *Two Dollars;* six months, *Three Dollars;* one year, *Six Dollars*, payable invariably in advance.

Orders for the paper, will be received at the office of Publication, No. 74 BALTIMORE STREET, NEAR GAY.

The usual deduction in favor of Newsmen and Agents.

All communications should be addressed to the Publisher of *The South.*

The South.

Price of Advertisements.

One Square—one insertion		50
" "	twice	75
" "	three times	1.00
" "	one week	1.50
" "	two weeks	2.00
" "	one month	4.00
" "	three months	10.00
" "	six months	15.00
" "	one year	30.00

Six lines or less make a square. Contracts to be subject of special agreement. Marriage and Obituary notices, 25 cents.

Advertisements will be received at the office of Publication, No. 74 Baltimore street, near Gay.

Advertisements should be sent in early.

Vol. 1. No. 79. Baltimore, Wednesday Evening, July 24, 1861. Th. W. Hall, Jr. Editor.

The South.

"Before St. Mark still glow his steeds of brass,
Their gilded collars glittering in the sun;
But is not Doria's menace come to pass?
Are they not *bridled?* Venice, lost and won,
Her thirteen hundred years of freedom done,
Sinks, like sea-weed, into whence she rose!
Better be whelm'd beneath the waves, and shun,
Even in destruction's depth, her foreign foes,
From whom submission wrings an infamous repose.'

The following verses were written during the war in the Crimea, and finding them so beautifully suited to our own South, a lady of this city has taken the liberty to alter them slightly, trusting that, if they ever meet the eye of the author, he will pardon her for adapting them to present circumstances, and regard her doing so as a sincere compliment to him:

What will they say down South, when the story there is told,
Of deeds of might for Southern right, done by the brave and bold;
Of Lincoln, proud in Spring time, humbled ere Summer's sun?
They'll say 'twas like our noble South—they'll say 'twas bravely done!

What will they say down South, when hush'd in awe and dread,
Fond hearts thro' all our happy homes, think of the mighty dead;
And muse in speechless anguish, on father, brother, son?
They'll say in our gallant South: God's holy will be done.

What will they say down South, the matron and the maid,
When wither'd, widow'd hearts, have found the price that each has paid:
The gladness that their homes have lost, for all the glory won?
They'll say in our dear noble South: God's holy will be done.

What will they say down South? our names both night and day,
Are in their hearts, or on their lips, when they laugh, or weep, or pray:
They watch on earth, they plead with heav'n, then forward to the fight!
Who droops or fears when Davis cheers, and God defends the right?

THE WAR.

From Washington.

The *Associated Press* telegrams contain the following intelligence from Washington, under date of July 23:

The President and Secretary of War are vigorously at work reorganizing a powerful army. Within the last twenty-four hours over 60,000 fresh troops, with a number of batteries of artillery, have been accepted. A number of regiments have arrived here, and every day will bring immense reinforcements to the National Capital. Ten new regiments will be in Baltimore by this evening. The Federal losses have been greatly exaggerated. It is now well ascertained that the killed will fall short of *one thousand*. The Secession troops did not follow our retreating forces after they passed Bull Run. Col. Einstein, of the Pennsylvania Twenty-sixth Regiment, returned to the battle-field about eleven o'clock on Sunday night and brought off six pieces of cannon, which he delivered to the commanding officer on the Potomac yesterday evening. The Colonel reports that the field was clear, and not an enemy in sight.

This afternoon Dr. Belt, of Prince George's county, Md., was arrested in Washington on the charge of treasonable language against the Government. He would have been hung by the mob but for the active interference of some army cavalry, a squad of whom assisted in taking him to jail. Henry Barron and J. D. Cattlin, of Georgetown, D. C., were also arrested and committed to jail on the charge of conspiring against the Government.

Ten prisoners of war were brought in to-day by our cavalry, among whom is Lieut. Col. Boone. They are Georgians, North Carolinians, South Carolinians and Virginians.

Col. A. Schimmelfemning, of Philadelphia, arrived here to-day and offered the services of his regiment of one thousand and forty men, a large portion of whom have seen service in Europe. Nearly all the officers are Prussians who distinguished themselves in the service. The regiment has been accepted by the Government.

General McClellan is expected here to-morrow. His presence is awaited with much anxiety. The appointment is highly popular, both among the troops the distinguished civilians here congregated.

But fifty men of Company E, Captain Leveride, of the Fire Zouaves have returned out of ninety-seven members. The loss of the Seventy-first New York Regiment will not be more than fifty killed. One hundred of their wounded were mustered out of service to-day, their term having expired on Sunday.

On the battle field balls were found of the pattern used in the English army, showing that the Confederates use arms of English manufacture.—Dr. B. Buckstine, of the Fifth Maine Regiment, Dr. Allen, of the Third, and Dr. A. A. C. Williams, of the First Maine, whose regiment was not in the action, but volunteered to go with the Fire Zouaves, were taken prisoners; the two first at the hospital, and the latter on the battle field after being wounded.

The following letter was received this morning by Capt. Tyler, at Alexandria, which seems to indicate that some of the Federal troops must have stood their ground at Centreville, and that the Confederates could not have advanced immediately, if at all:

"HEADQUARTERS, NEAR CENTREVILLE, July 22.
Capt. Tyler, Assistant Commissary General, Alex.

"For God's sake send me some forage. I have three hundred and twenty-five horses, and nothing for them to eat.

(Signed) "CAPTAIN GIBSON,
of Franklin's Brigade."

The state of affairs at Alexandria does not seem to indicate that we hold a position more advanced than that before the march commenced. No persons are allowed to pass beyond the lines, which seem to be within four or five miles. So stringent is this regulation that a lady in the perils of child-birth was refused a pass this afternoon to go to her home in Fairfax county, where she had left her children.

The utmost excitement continues to prevail in Alexandria. The citizens generally seem to anticipate an advance of the Confederates within forty-eight hours. It is known, however, that the Manassas Railroad is not obstructed as far as Springfield, and the Loudoun Road as far as Camp Upton.

The following is a later despatch than the foregoing:—

WASHINGTON, July 24—2 A. M.—General Tyler is in the city to-night. He says he knows nothing about the Federal troops throwing up entrenchments at Centreville. He cannot explain Captain Gibson's letter. All the hotels are crowded with guests. Many soldiers from the battle field, not beirg able to find out their rendezvous, are lying about the streets, on door steps, etc.

The war steamers *Pawnee* and *Perry* are lying opposite Alexandria.

Private intelligence from Washington altogether discredits the idea that any portion of the Federal forces have been able to make a stand at Centreville, or at any point beyond Fairfax C. H. The best opinion seems to be that except stragglers who have been unable to make good their escape, and are hiding in the woods to avoid capture, there are no Federal troops outside of the Alexandria lines which are not extended more than four or five miles from that city. Most of the regiments are within the intrenchments on Arlington Heights. The condition of those who remain in Washington is deplorable in the extreme—many of them hatless, coatless, shoeless, and in some instances without pantaloons—mostly unarmed, having flung away everything in their flight—standing, limping, lying or sitting upon the corners of streets, or the stoops of houses, and appealing to the charity of passengers for means to buy food and tobacco. Much blame is attached to their officers for not making greater efforts to collect these disorganized wrecks of the "Grand Army," but the difficulty in many cases is that the officers themselves are among the missing.

Army Officers of capacity and intelligence do not hesitate to pronounce the present army demoralized beyond the possibility of successful reorganization, and express the conviction that the attempt to supply its place with another, will prove an utter failure. The rank and file of the new army, they say, will be worse than that of the old one, which comprised nearly all the uniformed volunteer corps of the Northern cities, and was consequently of the best material, so far as intelligence and some previous knowledge of tactics went, that the country could afford—and as for the officers, they ask, how does the Government expect to find better? To fill the new regiments with the same class of incapables, who received commissions before, is to incur the certainty of similar defeat, while, if Government proposes to appoint none but educated military men to positions in its new army, it will have to wait for a few years until West Point can furnish them; for at present, there is not a sufficient number of such in the country to officer properly an army of 100,000 men. The old army was but 12,000 or 18,000 strong, and many of its best officers are now in the Confederate ranks—those who were tried in the late battle were the best that Government had to oppose to these—and the result is seen. Such, at least, is the talk in military circles.

A very bitter feeling against secessionists is said to exist at present in Washington, which has been inflamed by the accounts which have been disseminated in regard to barbarities alleged to have been committed by the Confederate troops. To such an extent has this feeling arisen, especially among the Federal soldiers, that apprehensions were felt that the few Confederate prisoners who were in the city would be massacred. A violent assault was yesterday made by a mob upon a party of four prisoners, who were brought into the city under an escort of soldiers, and after a hearing before Gen. Mansfield, were being taken to the old Capitol building, which is now used as a guard-house. The crowd threatened to hang them and attempted to take them from the hands of the soldiers. "In front of Willard's," says this morning's *Republican*, "the excitement was very great: one gentleman (*sic*) pushed his way through the crowd, and dealt one of the prisoners a powerful blow, nearly knocking him down; at other places on the route there was great trouble in getting them through the crowd." In like manner a Dr. Belt, a citizen of Prince George's county, Md., who was arrested for uttering "seditious language," only escaped being lynched by the mob, through the active interference of some U. S. cavalry who charged upon the crowd with drawn sabres.

Beyond additional lists of the killed and wounded, and Munchausen-like stories of the feats of valor performed by individuals during the battle, the Washington papers of this morning contain absolutely nothing; in regard to the present and future plans of the Administration, they are ominously silent. As an illustration of the means which are used to inflame the popular passions, and create another war-fever at the North, we may quote the statement of the official paper, *The Republican*, that the Confederates, in the late battle, used balls coated with a substance, "supposed to be of a poisonous nature," of which large numbers were found. In like manner the *Associated Press* lends itself to the same infamous purpose, by giving currency to the story of a Zouave about the cruelties practised upon his comrades—whom he pretended to have seen tied to trees, as the Indians used to serve their captives, and tortured with bayonets in lieu of arrows.

A deception of a different kind and of a less revolting nature is that attempted to be practised on the people in regard to the amount of the Federal loss in the late battle. It having been found that the capture of Sherman's battery, on account of the *prestige* which has always attached, in this country, to that particular arm of the service, was having a peculiarly depressing effect, six pieces of artillery, which had not been in the battle at all, were produced and are now exhibited on Capitol Hill, as Sherman's guns, to satisfy the people that they have not been taken. It is impossible for such a paltry piece of deception to countervail the concurrent statement of every correspondent who witnessed the battle, or has been at any pains to ascertain the facts, that the guns were among the first that fell into the hands of the enemy. In addition to the foregoing, gleaned chiefly from private but altogether reliable sources, we subjoin the following, which appeared in part of our last edition yesterday evening, not having been received in time to appear in the entire edition, part of which had already been worked off:

An officer of the army who arrived from Washington at half-past 4 o'clock this afternoon states that not less than 1,000 wounded were brought into the various hospitals in Washington to-day. He further states that during the retreat from Bull's Run, a rumor having gained currency that all the Fire Zouaves taken by the Confederates were put to death, a party of Zouaves broke into the hospital at Centreville, and killed the few wounded Confederate prisoners who were there.

A letter from a gentleman in high position in Washington, to a friend in this city, after characterizing the defeat of the Federal army as a complete rout, says that Mr. Russell, of the London *Times*, gives the following account of the engagement. He says that the Confederate forces completely deceived the Federal Generals. They had thrown up works at Centreville which they never intended to use, and as soon as the army arrived, they would retreat leaving baggage and provisions, &c., to indicate a hasty retreat. This course was pursued up to Bull's Run, when masked batteries without number played upon the Federal right, left and centre. If a battery was taken, another opened upon its flank, and the captured battery was soon retaken by the Confederates. The fight continued thus for nine hours, when the Confederate forces charged upon the left wing of the Federalists, and the whole were routed. Mr. Russell says that the loss in killed, wounded and prisoners on the Federal side must be at least 12,000. He calls it a disastrous defeat.

The same writer says that at the muster of the Fire Zouaves last night, only 103 answered to their names. The 69th brought home 256 out of 1,000, and the 71st, 329 out of 1,100. Col. Gorman, of the Minnesota Regiment, says that the Federal forces actually engaged were 40,000, with heavy reserves at Centreville.

It is positively stated that the army moved not only against the advice but the wish of General Scott. The writer adds: "It is acknowledged that the defeat must have a most damaging effect in Europe, as those governments were only waiting to see the result between the centre of the army and the main division of the Confederates."

EUROPE.

The telegraph reports the arrival of the steamer *Washington* at New York yesterday, with Liverpool advices to the 13th inst., and of the *Arabia* at Halifax with advices *via* to Queenstown, to the 14th. The *Arabia* brings £117,000 in specie.

In the House of Commons Lord Palmerston denied the rumor that the English minister at Vienna had recommended the Emperor of Austria not to receive the address of the Hungarian Diet, unless it recognized his sovereignty as King of Hungary. Lord Elgin is spoken of as the successor of Lord Herbert as Secretary of War.

Baron de Videl, a well known foreign nobleman, attempted to murder his son in the streets of London. The latter is said to be entitled to a large fortune on coming of age, which the Baron was unable to pay him.

The Indian four million loan bill was taken at above the fixed minimum price.

Prince Napoleon was to leave London for New York on the 8th.

The *Siecle* says that the Emperor, by advocating processes which lead to liberty against those which directly or indirectly favors slavery, very clearly shows the sympathies of the French Government in the conflict now raging in the American Union.

Judgment had been rendered in the affair of Mires, the French banker, declaring Count Simon responsible for the losses of the depositors.

The Marquis Lavalette has been nominated to the Grand Cross of the Legion of Honor.

Advices from Italy assert that the Dutch Government has resolved to recognize the Kingdom of Italy.

Cardinal Vannicello, Archbishop of Ferrara, is said to be likely to succeed to the Papal chair in case of the Pope's death.

The army of Denmark is to be reduced to the peace footing.

The Sultan has dismissed the seraglio and retained only one wife!

The Liverpool cotton market closed quiet but steady.

Flour closed quiet. Wheat firm. The weather continued wet. Corn was firm at extreme rates.

Provisions closed steady.

LONDON, Saturday evening.—Consols closed at 90a90½ for money, and 90¼a90¾ for account.

LIVERPOOL MARKETS.—Flour closed dull at 25a 28s. Wheat is dull at a decline of 2a3d. Western Red 9s 6da 11s; Southern 11sa11s 6d; White 12sa12s 6d. Corn is quiet and less firm; mixed 26s 6da29s; yellow 29sa29s 6d; white 31sa32s.—The weather has been unsettled and wet.

Provisions.—Beef closed dull for inferior qualities. Pork is stead. Bacon is dull, but an improved demand at an advance of 1sa2s. Lard steady with more doing at 28s 9da50s. Tallow is dull.

Produce.—Rosin closes firm at 6s 4da6s 6d.—Spirits Turpentine closed firm and all qualities slightly advanced. Coffee quiet. Rice steady.—Carolina has advanced. Philadelphia Bark 10s 6d. Cloverseed 42s for American red.

LONDON MARKETS.—Wheat steady. Flour dull 26sa28s 6d.

Metals.—Iron is dull; Bars at £5 to £5 2s 8d; Pig Iron 49s.

Coffee closed firm; Rio quiet. Tea generally unchanged. Spirits Turpentine closed firm and active at 5s. Tallow very dull at 49s 6d.

Baring Brothers report generally an improved demand in the Stock market; United States Fives 72½ extra dividend; Maryland Fives, bonds, 58 to 60.

THE THIRTY-SEVENTH CONGRESS.
Extra Session.

WASHINGTON, July 23.

SENATE.

Mr. Ten Eyck introduced the following resolution:—

Resolved, That the President of the United States be requested to inform the Senate under what circumstances Lieutenant John W. Worden, of the United States Navy has been imprisoned at Montgomery, Alabama; whether he is still in prison, and whether any, and if any, what measures have been taken by the Government of the United States for his release. Agreed to.

On motion of Mr. Sumner the Senate went into executive session. Adjourned.

HOUSE OF REPRESENTATIVES.

Mr. Thaddeus Stevens reported from the Committee on Ways and Means a bill to provide additional revenues to defray the expenses of the Government by the assessment and collection of direct taxes. Referred to the Committee of the Whole.

Mr. Conkling, of New York, reported a bill respecting bills of exchange and promissory notes.—Referred.

Mr. Blair reported back the Senate bill providing for the better organization of the military establishment of the United States. Referred.

Mr. Sedgwick, of New York, reported back Senate bill providing for the better organization of the Marine Corps, with amendments. Passed.

The same gentleman also reported back for reference the Senate bills appointing an Assistant Secretary of the Navy; inquiring into the expediency of procuring iron-clad ships and floating batteries, and providing for the increase of the medical staff of the navy.

Mr. Curtis, of Iowa, reported a bill appropriating a sum not exceeding $8,500 for the payment to Captain McConnell of certain expenses incurred in the organization of the First Regiment of Maryland Volunteers, and asked that the Committee be discharged, and asked the reference of this bill to the Committee of the Whole.

Mr. Burnett objected to the discharge of this Committee.

Mr. Eliott, of Massachusetts, introduced a bill to increase the consular representation of the United States during the present insurrection. Referred.

SPECIAL SESSION OF THE CITY COUNCIL.

FIRST BRANCH.—*Tuesday, July 23d*, 1861.—Mr. Dixon offered the petition of Mary E. Seguin, administratix of John F. Seguin, asking compensation for damages sustained by a mob attacking the drug store of the deceased, on Brown street, on the 16th of September, 1859—referred to the committee on claims. Mr. Allen offered a resolution requesting the register to furnish the branch with a detailed statement of the expenses incurred under the ordinance appropriating $500,000 for the defense of the city. During the discussion of the resolution, Mr. Nicholas stated that it was understood that about $24,000 had been expended, and that the whole expenditure would probably reach about $50,000. The resolution was adopted by yeas 10, nays 9. Messrs. Nicholas and Hay afterwards changed their votes from affirmative to negative, and Mr. Thomas changed his vote from negative to affirmative, and the resolution was finally rejected by

Yeas—Messrs. Yeisley, Wolfe, Meyers, Thomas, Phelps, Drakeley, Allen, Chase and Phelps—9.

Nays—Messrs. President, Bandel, Bolgiano, Staylor, Brown, Nicholas, Blanchard, Hay, Tegmeyer and Crout—10.

Mr. Blanchard called up the report and resolution from the select committee to which was referred the special message of the mayor in reference to the police authorities of the city, including the memorial of the city council to the Congress of the United States for a redress of existing grievances. The report was discussed at length, and the resolution to memorialize Congress adopted by the following vote:

Yeas—Messrs. President, Bandel, Bolgiano, Staylor, Brown, Nicholas, Blanchard, Hay, Tegmeyer and Crout—10.

Nays—Messrs. Yeisley, Wolfe, Meyers, Thomas, Phelps, Drakely, Allen, Chase and Dixon—9.

The branch adjourned to Thursday.

SECOND BRANCH.—An ordinance making an appropriation for the expense of State election was received from first branch and passed.

——The Washington *Republican* of this morning says: The statement in yesterday's issue that the railroads between Baltimore and New York had been taken possession of for the transportation of troops, though obtained from the best authority accessible to us, proves to be incorrect.

The South.

WEDNESDAY AFTERNOON, JULY 24, 1861.

A Well-Regulated Militia being Necessary to the Security of a Free State, the Right of the People to Keep and Bear Arms shall not be Infringed.—*Constitution U. S., Amendments, article* 2.

No Soldier shall in time of peace be quartered in any house, without the consent of the Owner, nor in time of war, but in a manner to be prescribed by law.—*Const. U. S., Amendments, art.* 3.

The right of the people to be secure in their persons, houses, papers and effects, against unreasonable searches and seizures, *shall not be violated*, and no Warrant shall issue, but upon probable cause, supported by Oath or affirmation, and particularly describing the place to be searched, and the persons or things to be seized.—*Constitution U. S., Amendments, art.* 4.

"To secure these rights, governments are instituted among men, deriving their just powers "from the consent of the governed."—*Declaration of Independence, July* 4, 1776.

It is idle to say that the power of taxation (or, by parity of reasoning, any other power) rests on consent, provided there be a right claimed for the government to compel that consent by force.—*Say, Political Economy, Chapter on Taxation.*

"That *in all cases, and at all times*, the military "ought to be under strict subordination to, and "control of the civil power."—*Declaration of Rights of the People of Maryland.*—*Art.* 27.

Can anybody show a different principle in the Constitution of the United States?

"That no man ought to be *taken, or imprisoned*, "or disseized of his freehold, liberties or privi-"leges, or outlawed, or exiled, or in any manner "destroyed, or deprived of life, liberty, or pro-"perty, but by the judgment of his peers, or by "the law of the land."—*Declaration of Rights of the People of Maryland, Art.* 21.

Notice to Correspondents.

In consequence of the multitude of anonymous communications received every day, it is found necessary to remind correspondents, that in no case can any notice be taken of any communication, unless accompanied by the name and address of the writer, not necessarily for publication, but as an evidence of good faith.

The South is published every afternoon, after the arrival of the mails, and consequently contains all the latest news by mail and telegraph, up to the hour of publication, and fully twelve hours in advance of the morning papers.

For Sale by all the principal newsmen in this city and throughout the South. Persons desiring Agencies for the sale or distribution of the Paper in any particular Town or neighborhood, will apply to the Publisher.

Orders for the Paper will be received at the Office of Publication, No. 74 Baltimore street. If sent by mail, must be accompanied by the cash.

The usual discount in favor of Newsmen and Agents. Postmasters and others forming Clubs of Ten will be furnished with one Copy *gratis*, or *ten* copies will be sent to one address, upon receipt of the subscription price for *nine*, for the time ordered.

A gentleman who arrived in this city this morning from Virginia, and who was detained at Manassas Junction on Sunday during the battle, thinks that the Confederate loss will probably *not exceed six hundred*—that of the Grand Army, he says, must be immense, as the ground occupied by the different regiments during the fight, and wherever the Confederate batteries opened upon them, was strewn with corpses, piled one upon the other, two and three deep. From 7,000 to 10,000 he thinks a moderate estimate of their loss upon the field. The report of Gen. Johnston's death is entirely unfounded. The Army of the Shenandoah was moving to attack Patterson at latest accounts.

MANASSAS.

It will be remembered that some two months ago, immediately after the first occupation of Alexandria by the Federal troops, the Hon. William C. Rives, of Virginia, made a speech at Atlanta, Georgia, which was reported in the newspapers. The people wished to know why Alexandria had been left undefended, and Mr. Rives explained that it had been done designedly, and that if ever the Federal army left Alexandria it would find a trap set for it, into which it would surely fall. The remark at the time was thought highly imprudent, and would undoubtedly have been so, if it could have been supposed that Mr. Rives was in possession of the plans of the Southern Generals, or was capable of betraying their confidence. It is more likely that Mr. Rives spoke entirely fro his own head, and that them remark was prompted solely by the desire to offer a satisfactory excuse for the failure to provide for the defence of Alexandria, and suffering the enemy to obtain a footing upon Virginia soil. If we remember aright, at the time Mr. Rives spoke, General Beauregard had not assumed the command at Manassas Junction, and the seat of government had not been transferred from Montgomery to Richmond. It is very certain that the plans which have resulted so triumphantly in the total discomfiture of the Federal army, must have been the fruit of long deliberation, careful study and thorough knowledge of the ground and all its capabilities of attack and defence. They were necessarily the growth of time and circumstance, and it is difficult to imagin either that they were so far matured or had been so freely communicated, at the time Mr. Rives alluded to the "trap" into which the Federal army was destined to fall, as to justify the inference that he spoke by authority. Be this as it may—the hint, prophetic as it has turned out to be, given by Mr. Rives, appears to have been entirely unheeded by the Government at Washington, and it is literally a "trap" into which its army has fallen.

We have seen ducks tolled within range of gunners lying bidden behind "masked batte-"ries," by the scampering of a dog, trained for the purpose, along the shore, and turkeys baited with a little corn scattered in a trench; the "Grand Army" has been lured to its destruction by means equally simple and almost identical. A few pickets hastily scrambling out of the way of the army, riding off in plain view of its advancing columns—a mess of hot rice left smoking upon a table, a broiled chicken or two, three quarters of fresh beef—sufficed to delude the Federal Generals into the notion that the "Rebels" were not going to fight—that they were retreating, and that they would make no stand this side of Richmond, if they made one there. Not even the lesson received at Bull's Run on Thursday evening, was sufficient to dissipate this illusion. They thought—McDowell in his carriage, and Scott in his chamber—that this was but a feint to cover the retreat of the Confederate army to Richmond, and consequently the latter were enabled to repeat the artifice on Sunday, with precisely the same effect as if they had never tried it before. A few guns left purposely in an exposed position, inviting attack, served repeatedly to draw the Federal troops within range of the batteries, which were "masked," and whose unmasking cost them so dear—a gradual slackening or cessation of fire, the sudden abandonment of a position which a few moments before had been obstinately contested, a simple movement of baggage-wagons to the rear, inviting pursuit, time and again lured them within that deadly *entourage* of rifles and cannon, from which so few came out alive, and into the track of that splendid cavalry, whose path through the Federal ranks carried death and destruction with it. Winding paths had been cut through the woods, which tempted the Federal commanders to follow them, under the impression that they led to the rear or by the flank of the Confederate batteries—and were found enfiladed by artillery and musketry, and terminating at the mouths of cannon and before breastworks and rifle-pits filled with riflemen. The rapidity and frequency with which the Confederate batteries changed their position, and the suddenness with which they opened fire from points where the Federal soldiers were willing to swear that none existed twenty minutes before, added to the perplexity of the "Grand Army," the bewilderment of its officers, and the apprehensions of the men. After fighting nine hours in a labyrinth of masked batteries and rifle pits, and manifesting a degree of steadiness under fire and against cavalry, which none but veteran troops could have been expected to exhibit—the "Grand Army," out-generalled and out-manœuvered, fairly beaten and routed, commenced a retreat under circumstancts which soon changed it into a flight. The particulars of that night of horrors, following upon a day of carnage are already partially known. Whenever they come to be fully disclosed, they will prove two things—first, that the retreat of the Grand Army was occasioned not by a senseless panic, but its complete defeat and discomfiture,—and secondly, that the loss sustained in the battle and in the rout which followed, in killed, wounded and prisoners, and in material of war, arms, equipage, accoutrements, provisions and baggage, exceeds anything of which the public has yet received positive information.

There is another circumstance, which in reviewing the results of the battle ought not to be left out of consideration; we do not think that there is any occasion to detract from the glory of the victory which the Confederate army has won, by accusing the soldiers of Northern cowardice. The length of time that the action lasted, and the number of the killed and wounded, sufficiently indicate the contrary; no doubt, had the troops been under better discipline, or their officers been better qualified for their position, many of the mistakes upon the field, and much of the confusion and disaster in the retreat would have been prevented; no doubt also, that many of the stories of individual acts of gallantry, of hair-breadth escapes, and desperate encounters with the bayonet and the knife, are sheer fabrications, the result of the soldier's natural desire to exaggerate the dangers through which he has passed, and so diminish what he feels to be the disgrace of his defeat. But we prefer to attribute the victory rather to the *superior* courage and discipline of the Southern troops, and above all, to the superior generalship displayed by their commanders, than to any absolute want of courage on the part of the Northern troops. We believe this conclusion to be not only more strictly in accordance with the actual facts, but it is a more srtisfactory foundation upon which to base our expectations for the future. Now that the quality of the two armies has been fairly tested, we can await with tranquil hearts the issue of any future battle—if the Government shall insanely insist upon such another trial of its ability to conquer the South.

What price the Confederates have paid for their victory, we are yet without the means of stating. By comparison with the loss sustained at Bull's Run, where it is now definitely ascertained that the number killed on the Confederate side did not exceed *three*, and the wounded *thirty*, the Confederate loss at Manassas must have been in proportion exceedingly light. Bull's Run, although a much smaller affair, was fought in precisely the same manner—the Southern troops being chiefly under cover and screened from the fire of the enemy, who was even in ignorance of their exact position. A gentleman of this city—represented to be a highly intelligent and perfectly truthful man—and who has just arrived, states that he was at Manassas Junction the whole of Sunday, during the battle, and that the Confederate loss *will not exceed six hundred*. That of the Grand Army, he estimates at from seven to ten thousand. Private information from Washington of the most reliable character, based upon the statements of Federal officers who were in the battle, and npon the condition of the army as it presents itself to the eye of the observer, put the entire Federal loss in killed, wounded, and missing, at double the above figures. As the Confederates were left to bury the Federal dead, and for the most part to take care of the wounded, our first definite account of the Government's loss, as well as of their own, will come from the Southern papers.

The disparity which will undoubtedly be found to exist between the loss of the two armies will be owing chiefly, if not altogether, to the peculiar strategy adopted by Beauregard, and especially to his employment of masked batteries, for inflicting heavy loss upon the enemy without greatly exposing his own men in return. The use made of "masked batteries" at Manassas was greater than in any battle of like magnitude which has ever been fought—the reason probably being that the sparsely inhabited thickly-wooded character of our country offers greater facilities for their successful employment than has been the case in Europe, at any time since the introduction of light artillery.

What the effect of the battle will be upon the continuance of the war, it is as yet premature to determine. In spite of all its parade about organizing another army—the helpless, uncared for condition of the one which is now in Washington, as described elsewhere in to-day's paper, seems to justify the assertion that the Government is stunned by the magnitude of its disaster, and has not recovered sufficiently to know what it means to do—while the Northern papers are too busy in settling who is to blame for this Waterloo defeat, to be able to afford anything like a correct indication of the state of feeling which the news has awakened at the North.

Among the Confederate prisoners at Beverly, Va., is said to be the Rev. Mr. Atkinson, President of Hampden College, Prince William county. He was Captain in a company in Pegram's command.

Mr. Atkinson is, we believe, a Presbyterian clergyman, Hampden College belonging to that denomination, and a brother of the Rt. Rev. Dr. Atkinson, Bishop of North Carolina.

Position of Senator Pearce.—The *Kent Conservator* denies that Senator Pearce voted for the Administration war measures, as reported by the Washington Republican papers. It says he did not vote at all upon the Force Bills, for the reason that he was sick and confined to his room. It says the same reason has thus far prevented him from speaking against the usurpations of the President, but that as soon as his health will permit, his voice will be heard in the Senate, rebuking the violators of the Constitution.

Gen. Dix has a Command.—The people of Baltimore have gotten rid of Banks, "the Union slider," and Gen. John A. Dix is now Lincoln's "Governor General of Maryland." General Dix is personally a gentleman—Banks is simply a Yankee dancing master, of no education, and with just sense enough to conceal his deficiencies. We predict for him a miserable career as a soldier. Gen. Dix is somewhat of the latter, but we think must feel deeply humiliated in being used by this abolition administration for their wicked purposes. We should not like to live in history as one of "Lincoln's Generals."—*N. Y. Day Book.*

From Fortress Monroe.

[*Correspondence of the Associated Press.*]

Fortress Monroe, July 23d.—An important military movement from Old Point was to have taken place to-day, but has been deferred in consequence of the unfortunate news from Washington. A feeling of gloom pervaded the camps on the receipt of the news from Washington, but there is no despondency, however, or any doubt as to the result of the war.

The gun boat *Penguin*, stationed at Newport News, yesterday allowed a heavily ladened schooner from Norfolk pass up the James River. She was probably ladened with cannon for Richmond. Only 6 shots were fired at her.

La Mountain is at Old Point, and will make an ascension day after to-morrow to reconnoitre the position of the enemy. Capt. Dyer, of the Ordnance Department, had arrived from Washington.

Abolition Congressmen in Battle,

A correspondent of the New York *Daily Times* has the following:

"Congress adjourned Friday until Monday expressly to allow the members to see the show. Neither Congress nor the Union wish to see another such a sight. At the grand stampede civilians were awfully scared; and I think several of them were taken prisoners. I witnessed some terrific feats of running among them. Many lost their carriages, and for aught I know are skulking about the woods now. One very fat Congressman offered an artilleryman $20 for a horse, but after he had the horse, he found it so hard to mount that he turned pale all over. He John Gilpined along, near my legs, until his horse threw him, when his agony was fearful. Three of us boosted him up, and he cut again as though the d—l was after him. That M. C. will never go to the wars again."

Despatch from the Secretary of War.

The following despatch from the Secretary of War was received by the Union Defence Committee of New York yesterday:

Washington, July 22, 1861.—*Moses H. Grinnell, S. Draper and Alexander Hamilton:*—In reply to telegram will say—Cheer our friends to active exertions, that we may speedily retrieve our fortune of yesterday. We are making most vigorous efforts to concentrate a large and irresistible army at this point. Regiments are now arriving, and many have left for the Capital, and our works on the South bank of the Potomac are being well manned with reinforcements. *The Capital is safe.* Simon Cameron, Sec. of War.

The Feeling in New York.

The New York *Day Book* of yesterday afternoon contains the following items:

A man was at the barracks in the Park yesterday, charged with desertion. When asked why he deserted he replied: "I learned that since I left for the war, that my two children had been sent to the Almshouse, and my wife turned a beggar in the street. I deserted to rescue them. Do your worst with me."

A hard working mechanic of this city recently asked a prominent Republican politician—"What have we working men got by voting for Lincoln! We are totally ruined, and there is nothing left for us, but to leave our families to starve, and go to the war to be shot like dogs."

How Near the Grand Army Came to Being Surrounded.

The following account of the battle of Manassas, taken from the correspondence of a Philadelphia paper, proves conlusively that the retreat of the Grand Army was *not* the result of a panic, but that it was the only means of saving Gen. Schenck's brigade from being surrounded and cut to pieces—the Southern cavalry having partially succeeded in getting in his rear:

Taking a short cut through the woods, I reached the rear of Gen. Tyler's division. On my way I came upon Club Creek, a small stream with steep banks. There the rebels had cut trees for a long distance, to impede the progress of the troops. Subsequent events indicate that the plan of the battle had been long considered, and that it was one of the suppositions of the enemy that the attack would be made by Gen. McDowell as it was made.

Reaching the left wing of Gen. Tyler's division, I found four pieces of Sherman's battery at rest, having been engaged all the morning, with the loss of three men. At a small house a hospital had been established. Many civilians were here in carriages. Further on was General Schenck's brigade, which had also been engaged, but had been withdrawn after severe loss.

Passing to an elevation in the rear of Schenck's Brigade, a wide view was obtained. A mile or two in rear of Burnside I could see a cloud of dust. What could it mean? Inquiries gave no satisfaction. Also, in the same direction a mass of infantry were in view. Not liking the appearance of things, I returned to the left flank.

Exhausted from heat and thirst, in company with some civilians, we went for water to a spring, a hundred yards to the left. Suddenly there was a commotion, a noise as of men in confusion. A bullet went spinning past, and then there came musket shots, and one or two cannon discharges. Looking in the direction of the Warrenton road, there was a scene of indescribable confusion. Everybody ran. A portion of Sherman's battery thundered by. There were baggage wagons, private carriages, ambulances, artillery wagons, and crowds of men, fleeing in indiscriminate confusion, all crowding across the bridge at Club creek, or passing through it. Half way up the hill, toward Centreville, the troops were forming. A line of skirmishers were thrown out. Behind them were the Garibaldians. Beyond was Miles' reserve.

Richardson's brigade came in from its position, and notwithstanding the confusion, a formidable front was already presented with the batteries which had been saved from the enemy.

Then commenced the retreat of the baggage train, and the unwarranted destruction of property which followed. Soon after, the two New Jersey regiments, which had been stationed at Vienna, came up, and materially aided in the subsequent retreat to Fairfax.

There is reason to believe that we had no pickets thrown out on our right flank, and that to this cause, in connection with others, may be traced the terrible rout. The first intimation Gen. Schenck's brigade had of the cavalry charge was the reception of shots in their backs It is plain that this flank movement in our rear was a part of a game of strategy elaborately planned and consummately enacted. The abbatis on our creek was doubtless intended as a *cul de sac*.

If the movement of the enemy had been more rapidly made, if the bridge at Club Creek had been seized, Gen. Schenck's entire brigade with all the civilians would have been swept into the woods, where, hemmed in by the deep, rocky ravines, with the abbatis along its banks, they could have been completely cut off.

The Horrors of War.

The Washington correspondent of the *Daily Times* has the following description of the horrors of war:—

To read of a battle, with its poetry of heroism, is a very fine thing. All men applaud the bold fellow, and all women throw laurels on the gallant soldier who is ready to throw down his life for his country's flag. If one sees it, the thing is different. I was at the defeat of our forces yesterday near Centreville, and as I witnessed the hot shot and the terrible shell tearing through the air; as I saw the horrible grape and shrapnel doing its too certain work all around; as I saw my friend storming, heroically, masked batteries, which the terrible incompetence of their leaders did not allow them to silence, owing to insufficient reinforcements being sent in proper time; when I saw these heroes at 11 dollars a month losing heads, legs and arms, in thick profusion around me; when I witnessed the horrible rout brought about by a masterly flank movement of their picked cavalry and sharp-shooters, and when I saw our artillerymen unlimber their guns, cut loose the traces of their horses and flee, leaving the pieces behind; when I saw, too, our boasted cavalry flying in the same mad haste, with regiment after regiment pushing after them like so many sheep, throwing for three miles guns, bayonets, cartridge-boxes and provisions of every kind away—dragoons riding over infantry in their flight, and the ground absolutely covered for three miles with bodies, then I realized as only those can who see it, the actual horrors of war.

——The U. S. sloop of war *Portsmouth*, Com. Calhoun, arrived at St. Helena, May 18th, from Loando, and sailed again on the 15th for the same port. The U. S. steamer *Lancaster* was at Honolulu, June 8, from Panama, to sail for San Francisco soon.

THE THIRTY-SEVENTH CONGRESS.

Extra Session.

TO-DAY'S PROCEEDINGS.

SENATE.

Mr. Grimes, of Iowa, offered a resolution that the Committee on the Judiciary be instructed to inquire into the expediency of requiring an oath of allegiance to be administered to each military, naval officer and employee of the Government.—Agreed to.

Mr. Trumbull, from the Committee on the Judiciary, reported back to the House bill to define and punish conspiracies, recommending that it pass.

Mr. Bayard, of Delaware, said he wished to make a minority report against the bill.

Mr. Trumbull objected to his report being received as a report from the Committee when the majority make no report. It was not according to usage. He had no objection to the Senator stealing his news.

The Senate discussed the question at some length, and the motion to print was disagreed to.

The joint resolution to approve of the acts of the President was postponed till Friday next.

The bill for the better re-organization of the military establishment was returned from the House with an amendment as a substitute for the bill. The Senate refused to concur.

HOUSE OF REPRESENTATIVES.

Mr. Elliott, from the Committee on Commerce, reported a bill, which was passed, authorizing the President, by and with the advice of the Senate, to appoint Consuls at any foreign ports where he may deem advisable, for the preventing of piracy, at a salary not exceeding $1,500 per annum, their offices to cease when internal peace shall be restored.

Mr. Sedgwick, from the Committee on Naval Affairs, reported the Senate bill providing for the appointment of a Board of three skillful Naval officers, to report on the construction or completion of an iron or steel or iron clad steamship or battery; and if the report be favorable that the Secretary of the Navy be authorized to construct one or more. A million and a half dollars is appropriated to carry the act into effect. The bill was passed.

Mr. Sedgwick also reported the Senate bill authorizing the appointment of an Assistant Secretary of the Navy, at $3,000 per annum, and eight additional clerks. Passed.

Also, the Senate bill providing for the increase of the Medical Corps of the Navy. Passed.

Mr. Blair, from the Committee on Military Affairs, reported the Senate bill authorizing the President to accept the services of 500,000 volunteers.

Mr. Bingham, from the Committee on the Judiciary, reported a resolution, which was passed, requesting the President to communicate to the House, if in his judgment it be not incompatible with the public interests, grounds, reasons and evidence on which the Police Commissioners of the city of Baltimore have been arrested and detained as prisoners at Fort McHenry.

Mr. Stevens from the Committee on Ways and Means reported a bill appropriating $100,000, with which to pay the Police organized by the United States authorities in the City of Baltimore.

Mr. Burnett, of Kentucky, attacked the bill, and spoke of the President usurping power and trampling on the rights of Maryland, etc.

Mr. Richardson, of Illinois, accused Mr. Burnett of helping to produce the present disastrous condition of affairs, by aiding to break up the Democratic party.

Mr. Burnett, of Kentucky, denied the charge.—He wished to have no personal controversy with him here, but could have one elsewhere, if he desired it.

Mr. Richardson, of Illinois, declared himself in similar terms, and great excitement ensued. Mr. Richardson spoke about the recent battle as against the judgment of Gen. Scott, and related a conversation to prove it.

Mr. Stevens, of Pennsylvania, explained the bill. He spoke of the Maryland Legislature as a "nest of traitors," and the Chief of Police as a traitor.

A long and highly exciting interesting debate ensued, after which the bill was passed.

From the South.

New Orleans papers of the 10th inst. contain a few items of interest, with extracts from other Southern journals, which we subjoin:

Gov. Pickens, of Sonth Carolina, has issued a proclamation convening the State Legislature on the first Wednesday in November next, for the purpose of choosing electors for President and Vice-President, and two Senators in Congress. He has also issued writs of election for members of Congress from the several districts, the electiou to be held on the same day.

Ninety days ago (says the *Avalanche*) he would have been a dreamer who would then have predicted the casting of cannon, grape and canister shot and shells at Memphis, yet Col. Hunt has, by his large contracts for these implements of warfare, satisfied the community that Memphis has the basis laid for becoming the great foundery and machine shop of the Mississippi valley. She will be to the West what Richmond is to the East.

The editor of the Montgomery (Ala.) *Post* acknowledges the receipt of an open ball of cotton, taken from the stalk on the 10th inst.

The corporation of New Orleans have offered a reward of five hundred dollars for the detection and conviction of any person who may be engaged in furnishing provisions to the blockading squadron. The Petersburg (Va.) *Express* says that the Confederate troops now in Virginia, and under arms, is estimated at 170,000.

The Raleigh (N. C.) *Standard* calls the attention of the Confederate Congress to the immense beds of coal and iron on Deep River, North Carolina, and zealously urges the establishment of a national foundry there. The coal, it is said, is equal to the best Cumberland, and the iron ore, by a cheap process, can be easily rendered equal, for gun and cannon purposes, to the Marshal iron of England, or the importations from Norway, formerly used at Harper's Ferry.

Memphis papers of the 17th quote flour at $7.50 a$8 per bbl.; Pork at $27 per bbl.; butter at 20 a24 cents per lb.; corn in large supply at 55a60 cents, and wheat at $1a$1.15 per bushel.

At Charleston the supply of corn is large, and selling at $1a$1.10 per bushel; flour at $6a$6.75 per bbl., and bacon at 13½a18 cents per pound.

The Memphis *Avalanche* of Tuesday last makes the following report: "At a moderate calculation, ten thousand chickens were received in this city yesterday. The steamer *Kentucky* had four thousand, the *Rose Douglas* five, and the *Kanawha Valley* one thousand." The pot-pie business is not very effectually blockaded.

Reception of the Rev. Dr. Hoge.—This gentleman having resigned his position as associate pastor with Dr. Spring, last evening received his friends previous to his departure. A large crowd of Republicans congregated, it is supposed to insult him, but they contented themselves with placing on the stairway leading to Dr. Hoge's room, the following inscription:—"A live secessionist on exhibition up stairs. Admission free. Walk up." This very "smart" proceeding was all they did. Dr. Hoge saw his friends, and then withdrew.—*N. Y. Day-Book.*

The South.

HABEAS CORPUS.

"Next to personal security," says Mr. Justice Blackstone, "the law of England regards, asserts "and preserves the personal liberty of individuals. "This personal liberty consists in the power of "locomotion, of changing situation or moving "one's person to whatsoever place one's own "inclinations may direct, without imprisonment "or restraint, unless by due course of law.

"By the Petition of Right, 3 Car. 1st, it is en-"acted that no person shall be imprisoned or de-"tained without cause shown, to which he may "make answer according to law. By 16 Car. 1st, "ch. 10, if any person be restrained of his liberty "by order or decree of any illegal court, or by "the command of the KING'S MAJESTY in person, "or by warrant of the council board, or of any "of the privy council, he shall upon demand of "his counsel, have a writ of *habeas corpus* to "bring his body before the Court of King's Bench "or Common Pleas, who shall determine whether "the cause of his commitment be just, and here-"upon to do as to justice shall appertain.

"To bereave a man of life or by violence to "confiscate his estate without accusation or trial "would be so gross and notorious an act of des-"potism as must at once convey the alarm of "tyranny throughout the whole kingdom, but "confinement of the person by secretly hurrying "him to jail where his sufferings are unknown or "forgotten is a less public, a less striking and "*therefore a more dangerous engine of arbitrary "government*. And yet sometimes, when the State "is in real danger, even this may be a necessary "measure. BUT THE HAPPINESS OF OUR OWN CON-"STITUTION IS THAT IT IS NOT LEFT TO THE EXECU-"TIVE POWER TO DETERMINE WHEN THE DANGER OF "THE STATE IS SO GREAT AS TO RENDER THIS MEASURE "EXPEDIENT; FOR IT IS THE PARLIAMENT ONLY, OR "LEGISLATIVE POWER THAT WHENEVER IT SEES PRO-"PER CAN AUTHORIZE THE CROWN, BY SUSPENDING "THE HABEAS CORPUS ACT FOR A SHORT AND LIMI-"TED TIME, TO IMPRISON SUSPECTED PERSONS WITH-"OUT GIVING ANY REASON FOR SO DOING."—*Commentaries on the Laws of England, Vol. 1. pp. 135—136.*

So our own Chief Justice Marshall, in the case of Bollman, 4 *Cranch*, 100, says: "If at any time "the public safety should require the suspension "of the power vested by this act (the power to "grant writs of *habeas corpus*) in the Courts of "the United States, *it is for the Legislature to say "so*. That question depends on political consid-"erations on which the Legislature is to decide. "Until the Legislative will be expressed, this "Court can only see its duty and *must obey the "laws*." This was in a case of Treason.

So Judge Story in his *Commentaries on the Constitution*, sec. 1336, says: "It would seem as the "power is granted to Congress to suspend the "writ of *habeas corpus* in case of rebellion or inva-"sion, that the right to judge whether the exigency "had arisen must exclusively belong to that body."

So in 1807, when great alarm existed as to Burr's conspiracy, a bill was brought before the Senate in secret session to suspend the writ of *habeas corpus*. When brought into the House of Representatives, that body refused to consider it in secret session, and by a vote of 113 to 19 rejected the bill on its first reading. On that occasion Mr. Dana of Connecticut used the following language: "This bill authorizes the arrest of per-"sons not merely by the President or other high "officers, but by any person acting under him. "*I imagine this to be wholly without precedent. If "treason was marching to force us from our seats, I "would not agree thus to destroy the fundamental "principles of the Constitution, or commit such an "act either of despotism or pusillanimity*."

HISTORICAL PARALLELS.

"We hold these truths to be self-evident, that all men are created equal; that they are endowed by their Creator with certain unalienable rights; that among these, are life, liberty, and the pursuit of happiness. That, to secure these rights, governments are instituted among men, deriving their just powers from the consent of the governed; that, whenever any form of government becomes destructive of these ends, it is the right of the people to alter or to abolish it, and to institute a new government, laying its foundation on such principles, and organizing its powers in such form, as to them shall seem most likely to effect their safety and happiness. Prudence, indeed, will dictate that governments long established, should not be changed for light and transient causes; and, accordingly, all experience hath shown, that mankind are more disposed to suffer, while evils are sufferable, than to right themselves by abolishing the forms to which they are accustomed. But, when a long train of abuses and usurpations, pursuing invariably the same object, evinces a design to reduce them under absolute despotism, it is their duty, to throw off such government, and to provide new guards for their future security."—*Declaration of Independence.*

Yes, sir, we wish for peace, but how is that blessing to be preserved? I shall repeat here a sentiment I have often had occasion to express. In my opinion there is nothing worth fighting for but national honor: for, in the national honor is involved the national independence. *I know that a State may find itself in such unpropitious circumstances, that prudence may force a wise government to conceal the sense of indignity. But the insult should be engraven on tablets of brass, with a pencil of steel.* AND WHEN THAT TIME AND CHANCE, WHICH HAPPEN TO ALL, SHALL BRING FORWARD THE FAVORABLE MOMENT, THEN LET THE AVENGING ARM STRIKE HOME. It is only by avowing and maintaining this stern principle of honor, that peace can be preserved.—*Gouverneur Morris, Speech in the Senate of the U. S., Feb. 24*, 1803.

"A town meeting of Boston had been called at the Old South Church, in consequence of some new aggression upon the rights of the people. The different orators of the patriot party had in turn addressed the meeting, loud in complaint and accusation, but guarded and cautious on every point which might look like an approach towards treasonable expressions, or direct exhortations to resistance. Adams placed himself in the pulpit, and sat quietly listening to all their harangues; at length he rose and made a few remarks, which he closed with the following pithy apologue: "A Grecian philosopher who was lying asleep on the grass, was suddenly roused by the bite of some animal on the palm of his hand. He closed his hand quickly as he awoke, and found he had caught in it a small field mouse. As he was examining the little animal which had dared to attack him, it bit him unexpectedly a second time: he dropped it, and it escaped. Now, fellow-citizens, what think you was the reflection which this trifling circumstance gave birth to, in the mind of the philosopher? It was this: *That there is no animal, however weak and contemptible, which cannot defend its own liberty, if it will only* FIGHT FOR IT."—*Samuel Adams, Memoir in American Eloquence, Vol. I.*

Guard with jealous attention the public liberty. Suspect every one who approaches that jewel. *Unfortunately, nothing will preserve it but downright force.* WHENEVER YOU GIVE UP THAT FORCE, YOU ARE INEVITABLY RUINED.—*Patrick Henry, Speech in the Virginia Convention, June 4*, 1788.

The honorable gentleman who presided, told us, that to prevent abuses in our government we will assemble in convention, recall our delegated powers, and punish the servants for abusing the trust reposed in them. Oh, sir, we should have fine times, indeed, if to punish tyrants it were only sufficient to assemble the people. *Your arms wherewith you could defend yourselves are gone; and you have no longer an aristocratical, no longer a democratical spirit.* Did you ever read of any revolution in any nation brought about by the punishment of those in power, inflicted by those who had no power at all? You read of a riot act in a country which is called one of the freest in the world, where a few neighbors cannot assemble without the risk of being shot by a hired soldiery, the engines of despotism. *We may see such an act in America. A standing army we shall have also, to execute the execrable commands of tyranny*, and how are you to punish them? Will you order them to be punished?—Who shall obey those orders? Will your mace-bearer be a match for a disciplined regiment? In what situation are we to be?—*Patrick Henry, Speech in Virginia Convention, June 4th*, 1788.

Where are your checks in this government?—Your strongholds will be in the hands of your enemies. *It is on the supposition that your American Governors shall be honest that all its good qualities are founded, but its defective and imperfect construction puts it in their power to perpetrate the worst of mischiefs should they be bad men.* And, sir, would not all the world, from the Eastern to the Western hemisphere, blame our distracted folly in resting our rights upon the contingency of our rulers being good or bad? Show me that age and country where the rights and liberties of the people were placed on the sole chance of their rulers being good men without a consequent loss of liberty. I say that the loss of that dearest privilege has ever followed, with absolute certainty, any such mad attempt, If your American chief be a man of ambition and abilities, how easy will it be for him to render himself absolute! The army is in his hands, and, if he be a man of address, it will be attached to him; and it will be the subject of long meditation with him to seize the first auspicious moment to accomplish his design. And, sir, will the American spirit solely relieve you when this happens? I would rather, infinitely, and I am sure most of this convention are of the same opinion, have a king, lords and commons, than a government so replete with such insupportable evils. If we make a king, we may prescribe the rules by which he shall rule his people, and interpose such checks as shall prevent him from infringing them: *but the president in the field, at the head of his army, can prescribe the terms on which he shall reign master so far that it will puzzle any American ever to get his neck from under the galling yoke.* I cannot, with patience, think of this idea. If ever he violates the laws, one of two things will happen: he will come at the head of his army to carry every thing before him; or, he will give bail, or do what Mr. Chief Justice will order him. If he be guilty will not the recollection of his crimes teach him to make one bold push for the American throne? Will not the immense difference between being master of every thing, and being ignominiously tried and punished, powerfully excite him to make this bold push? But, sir, where is the existing force to punish him? Can he not, at the head of his army, beat down every opposition?

Away with your president, we shall have a king; the army will salute him monarch; your militia will assist in making him king, and fight against you; and what have you to oppose this force?—What will then become of you and your rights?—WILL NOT ABSOLUTE DESPOTISM ENSUE?—*Patrick Henry, in the Virginia Convention, June*, 1788.

"'The glorious spirit of liberty is vanquished and left without hope but in a miracle,' said desponding patriots. 'I confess,' said Samuel Adams, 'we have, as Wolfe expressed it, a choice of difficulties. Too many flatter themselves that their pusillanimity is true prudence; *but in perilous times like these, I cannot conceive of prudence without fortitude.*' He persevered; but John Adams retired from the service of the people, and devoting himself to his profession, for a time ceased even to employ his pen in their defence. Otis who had returned to the Legislature, disordered in mind, and jealous of his declining influence, did but impede the public cause. In Hancock, also, vanity so mingled with patriotism, that the Government hoped to separate him from its uncompromising opponents."—*Bancroft's U. S., vol. 6, page* 402, *year* 1771.

"'Here,' said Mayhew, as he lamented the cold adhesion of the timid good, and for himself, trod the thorny path of resistance to the grandeurs of the world—'here, there are many who see the right, and yet the wrong pursue. But it is my fixed resolution, notwithstanding many discouragements, in my little sphere, to do all I can for the service of my country, that neither the republic nor the churches of New England may sustain any injury.' And every where men began to enter into a solemn agreement not to use a single article of British manufacture; not even to wear black clothes for mourning. To encourage the growth and manufacture of wool, nearly all Boston signed a covenant to eat no lamb."—*Bancroft's U. S., vol. 5, p. 206, year* 1771.

The King, in his reply, pledged himself *speedily and effectually to enforce "obedience to the laws and the authority of the supreme legislature."* His heart was hardened. *Having just heard of the seizure of ammunition at the fort in New Hampshire*, he intended that his language should "open the eyes of the deluded Americans." "If it does not," said he to his faltering minister, "it must set every delicate man at liberty to avow the propriety of the *most coercive measures.*' "*The New England governments are now in a state of rebellion. Blows must decide whether they are to be subject to this country or to be independent.*"—*Bancroft's U. S., vol. 7, p.* 177–227.

They rushed on with headlong indiscretion, thinking not to involve the empire in a civil war, but to subdue the Americans by fear. The first step towards inspiring terror was, to declare Massachusetts in a state of *rebellion*, and to pledge the parliament and the whole force of Great Britain to its reduction; the next, by prohibiting the American fisheries, to *starve* New England; the next, to call out the savages on the rear of the Colonies; the next, *to excite a servile insurrection.*—*Bancroft's U. S., vol. 7, p.* 322.

In the Congress of 1774, there was not one member, except Patrick Henry, who appeared to me sensible of the precipice, or rather the pinnacle on which we stood, and had candor and courage enough to acknowledge it. America is in total ignorance, or under infinite deception concerning that assembly. To draw the characters of them all would require a volume, and would now be considered as a caricatured print. One-third Tories, another Whigs, and the rest mongrels.

There was a little aristocracy among us of talents and letters. Mr. Dickinson was *primus inter pares*, the bell-wether, the leader of the aristocratical flock.—*John Adams, Letter to Jefferson, Nov.* 12, 1813.

As to the history of the Revolution, my ideas may be peculiar, perhaps singular. What do we mean by the Revolution? The war? That was no part of the Revolution. It was only an effect and consequence of it. *The Revolution was in the minds of the people, and this was effected from 1760 to 1775, in the course of fifteen years, before a drop of blood was drawn at Lexington.* The records of thirteen Legislatures, the pamphlets, newspapers, in all the colonies, should be consulted during that period, to ascertain the steps by which the public opinion was enlightened and informed concerning the authority of Parliament over the colonies. *The Congress of 1774 resembled, in some respects, though I hope not in many, the Council of Nice in Ecclesiastical history.* It assembled the priests, from the east and the west, the north and the south, who compared notes, engaged in discussions and debates, *and formed results by one vote and by two votes which went out to the world as unanimous.*—*John Adams, Letter to Jefferson, August* 14, 1815.

Truth, being known, will prevail over artifice and misrepresentation. In such case *no man, who is worthy of life, liberty or property, will or can refuse to join with you in defending them to the last extremity*, disdaining every sordid view, and the mean, paltry considerations of private interest and present emolument, when placed in competion with the liberties of millions; *and, seeing that there is no alternative but absolute, unconditional submission, and the most abject slavery, or a defence becoming men born to freedom, he will not hesitate about the choice.* Although superior force may, by the permission of Heaven, lay waste our towns and ravage our country, it can never eradicate from the breasts of freemen, those principles which are ingrafted in their very nature. *Such men* WILL DO THEIR DUTY, NEITHER KNOWING NOR REGARDING CONSEQUENCES; but submitting them, with humble confidence, to the omniscient and omnipotent Arbiter and Director of the fate of empires, and trusting that his Almighty arm, which has been so signally stretched out for our defence, will deliver them in a righteous cause.—*John Rutledge, in the South Carolina Assembly, April 11th*, 1776.

It was a maxim of the Roman people, which eminently conduced to the greatness of that State, never to despair of the commonwealth. THE MAXIM MAY PROVE AS SALUTARY TO US NOW, AS IT DID TO THEM. Short-sighted mortals see not the numerous links of small and great events which form the chain on which the fate of kings and nations is suspended.—Ease and prosperity, though pleasing for a day, have often sunk a people into effeminacy and sloth. Hardships and dangers, though we for ever strive to shun them, have frequently called forth such virtues as have commanded the applause and reverence of an admiring world. Our country loudly calls you to be circumspect, vigilant, active and brave. Perhaps, (all gracious heaven avert it,) perhaps the power of Britain, a nation great in war, by some malignant influence, may be employed to enslave you; but let not even this discourage you. Her arms, 'tis true, have filled the world with terror; her troops have reaped the laurels of the field; her fleets have rode triumphant on the sea; and when, or where, did you, my countrymen, depart inglorious from the field of fight? You, too, can show the trophies of your forefathers' victories and your own; can name the fortresses and battles you have won; and many of you count the honorable scars of wounds received, whilst fighting for your king and country.—*Joseph Warren, Boston, March 6th*, 1775.

But, pardon me, fellow-citizens, I know you want not zeal or fortitude. *You will maintain your rights, or perish in the generous struggle. However difficult the combat, you never will decline it when freedom is the prize.* An independence of Great Britain is not our aim. No, our wish is, that Britain and the colonies may, like the oak and ivy, grow and increase in strength together. *But whilst the infatuated plan of making one part of the empire slaves to the other is persisted in*, the interest and safety of Britain, as well as the colonies, require that the wise measures recommended by the honorable the Continental Congress be steadfastly pursued; whereby the unnatural contest between a parent honored and a child beloved, may probably be brought to such an issue, as that the peace and happiness of both may be established upon a lasting basis. *But if these pacific measures are ineffectual, and it appears that the only way to safety is through fields of blood, I know you will not turn your faces from your foes, but will, undauntedly, press forward, until tyranny is trodden under foot.*—*Joseph Warren, Boston, March 6th*, 1775.

Upon the whole it has been the policy of the British authority to oblige us to supply our wants at their market, which is the dearest in the known world, *and to cramp and confine our trade so as to be subservient to their commerce, our real interest being ever out of the question.*—*Chief Justice Drayton, Charge to the Grand Jury, Charleston, May* 23, 1776.

Our liberties and safety cannot be depended upon if the King of Great Britain should be allowed to hold our forts and cannon, or to have authority over a single regiment in America or a single ship of war in her ports. For if he holds our forts he may turn them against us, as he did Boston against her proprietors; if he acquires our cannon he will effectually disarm the colony; if he has a command of troops among us, even if we raise and pay them, shackles will be fixed upon us—witness Ireland and her national army. The most express act of Parliament cannot give us security, for acts of Parliament are as easily repealed as made. Royal proclamations are not to be depended upon, witness *the disappointments of the inhabitants of Quebec and St. Augustine.* Even a change of ministry will not avail us, because, notwithstanding the rapid succession of ministers, for which the British Court has been famous during the present reign, *yet the same ruinous policy ever continued to prevail against America.* In short, I think it my duty to declare, in the awful seat of justice and before Almighty God, that in my opinion the Americans can have no safety but by the Divine favor, their own virtue, and their being so prudent as NOT TO LEAVE IT IN THE POWER OF THE BRITISH RULERS TO INJURE THEM. *Indeed the ruinous and deadly injuries received on our side, and the jealousies entertained, and which in the nature of things must daily increase against us, on the other, demonstrate to a mind the least given to reflection upon the rise and fall of empires, that true reconcilement can never exist between Great Britain and America, the latter being in subjection to the former.*—*Chief Justice Drayton, Charge to the Grand Jury, Charleston, April* 23, 1776.

"Of the inhabitants of Boston, six thousand seven hundred and fifty-three still remained in the town, pining of sorrow; deprived of wholesome food; confined to their houses after ten o'clock in the evening; liable to be robbed without redress; ever exposed to the malice of the soldiers, and chidden for tears as proofs of disloyalty.—*Bancroft's U. S., vol. 8, p. 42, year* 1775.

"They closed their statement in the words of their new member, Jefferson: 'These Colonies now feel the complicated calamities of fire, sword and famine. We are reduced to the alternative of choosing an unconditional submission to irritated ministers, or resistance by force. The latter is our choice. We have counted the cost of this contest and find nothing so dreadful as voluntary slavery.'" —*Bancroft's U. S. vol. 8, p. 36, year* 1773.

"The loss of officers was observed to be disproportionably great; and the gloom in the quarters of the British was deepened by the reflection that they had fought not against an enemy, but against their fellow-subjects and kindred; not for the promotion of civil or religious freedom, *but for the supremacy of one part of the empire over another.*"—*Bancroft's U. S., vol. 8, pp. 25-26, Battle of Bunker Hill.*

"Here too, as every where else, preparations for resistance had been deferred; no more than four barrels of powder could be found in the city. While Washington was borne toward Cambridge on the affectionate confidence of the people, Congress which had as yet supported its commander-in-chief with nothing beyond a commission," &c., &c.—*Bancroft U. S., vol. 8, p. 24, "Not Prepared for Resistance."*

The wife of Colonel Pinckney is distinguished as one of those heroic and self-sacrificing women of the revolution, "whose intrepidity and fortitude lent so able a support to the cause of their country." An incident in her life is recorded in Garden's interesting *Anecdotes of the Revolution.* "A British officer of rank once said to Mrs. Pinckney—'It is impossible not to admire the intrepid firmness of the ladies of your country. Had your men but half their resolution, we might give up the contest. America would be invincible.'"—*American Eloquence, Vol.* 1.

"But in truth the cry of Dunmore did not rouse "among the Africans a passion for freedom. To "them bondage in Virginia was not a lower condi-"tion of being than their former one; they had no "regrets for ancient privileges lost; their memo-"ries prompted no demand for political changes; "no struggling aspirations of their own had invited "Dunmore's interposition; no memorial of their "grievances had preceded his offices."—*Bancroft's U. S., vol. 8, p. 225—year* 1775.

"When Washington learned the fate of the rich "emporium of his own 'country,' for so he called "Virginia, his breast heaved with waves of anger "and grief; 'I hope,' said he, 'this and the threat-"'ened devastation of other places will unite the "'whole country in one indissoluble bond against a "'nation which seems lost to every sense of virtue "'and those feelings which distinguish a civilized "'people from the most barbarous savages.'"—*Bancroft U. S., 8 vol., 232—Burning of Norfolk.*

"Yet the majority of Congress, scrupulous not "to outrun the convictions and sympathies of their "constituents, and pleasing themselves by confiding "ing in the speedy restoration of peace, not only "made no adequate preparations for resistance, but "would not even consent to relieve the states from "anarchy by sanctioning the institution of Govern-"ments in the several colonies. The hesitancy of "so many members, especially of Dickinson, in-"censed John Adams, who maintained that the "fifty or sixty men composing Congress should at "once form a constitution for a great empire, pro-"vide for its defence, and, in that safe attitude, "await the decision of the King. His letters to "New England, avowing these opinions, were in-"tercepted; and so little were the central colonies "prepared for the bold advice, they were published "by the royalists as the surest way of destroying "his influence, and heaping obloquy on his name." *Bancroft U. S., 8 vol., 55—year* 1775.

"The people of Maryland, happier than that of Pennsylvania, escaped intestine dissensions and insured unanimity, by passing over the proprietary government, and intrusting the conduct of resistance to a series of conventions. The prudent, the slow, the hesitating were allowed an influence; but from the first, all parties acquiesced in the principle of deriving all power from the people; and the province, however its movement was sometimes retarded, proceeded courageously in an unbroken line. In November, 1774, it adhered to the association, adopted in the general Congress, and its patriotism was confirmed by the austerity of religious zeal. At an adjourned session in December, the Maryland convention, fifty-five members being present from sixteen counties, resolved unanimously to resist to the utmost of their power, taxation by Parliament, or the enforcement of the penal acts against Massachusetts. To this end they voted with equal unanimity a well regulated militia, to be composed of all the freemen of the colony, between fifteen and sixty. They resolved also, that all former difficulties about religion or politics from henceforth should cease, and be forever buried in oblivion; and the benign aurora of the coming republic lighted the Catholic to the recovery of his rightful political equality in the land which a Catholic proprietary had set apart for religious freedom. Charles Carroll of Carrollton, who, under the British government, had not had so much as a vote at the polls, was placed unanimously on the committee of correspondence.

"It was throughout the continent a subject of regret that the zeal of Dulany had grown cool. As he kept silent, the foremost man in Maryland was Samuel Chase, like Dulany a lawyer; less circumspect and less careful of appearances; but strong, downright, brave and persevering; capable of error from rashness or self-will, but not capable of faltering in the cause which he approved. Vehement even to a fault, he did not always speak softly or shun coarse invective; but his undaunted spirit, his fierce independence of mind, his unbending energy, his scorn of semblance without substance, of servility, of plausible hypocrisy that glossed servility over, his eloquence, which sprung from his heart and expressed the vigor of his nature, his uncompromising energy, justly won for him the confidence of Maryland."—*Bancroft's U. S., vol. 8, p.* 75-7.

Gen. Washington's Advice.

Upon the evacuation of Boston by the British, General, Washington wrote a letter, from which the following is an extract, to his brother, John Augustine Washington. The letter is dated "Cambridge, 31 March, 1776," and is contained in the third volume of Spark's Writings of Washington, p. 339:

"The enemy left all their works standing in Boston and on Bunker's Hill; and formidable they are. The town has shared a much better fate than was expected, the damage done to the houses being nothing equal to report. But the inhabitants have suffered a good deal in being plundered by the soldiery at their departure. All those who took upon themselves the style and title of government-men in Boston, in short, all those who have acted an unfriendly part in this great contest, have shipped themselves off in the same hurry, but under still greater disadvantages than the King's troops, being obliged to man their own vessels, as seamen enough could not be had for the King's transports, and submit to every hardship that can be conceived. One or two have done, what a great number ought to have done long ago, committed suicide. By all accounts, there never existed a more miserable set of beings, than these wretched creatures now are. Taught to believe, that the power of Great Britain was superior to all opposition, and, if not, that foreign aid was at hand, they were even higher and more insulting in their opposition than the regulars. When the order issued, therefore, for embarking the troops in Boston, no electric shock, no sudden explosion of thunder, in a word, not the last trump could have struck them with greater consternation. They were at their wits' end, and, conscious of their black ingratitude, they chose to commit themselves, in the manner I have above described, to the mercy of the waves at a tempestuous season, rather than meet their offended countrymen."

FROM OUR SECOND AND THIRD EDITIONS OF YESTERDAY.

BY THE PHILADELPHIA TRAIN.

Additional Details of the Battle of Manassas.

The Philadelphia papers furnish us with additional details of the great fight, from which we make the following selections. The *Inquirer's* correspondent says:

At 10.45 General Schenck led his column, headed by the Eighteenth and Second Ohio and New York, within a few hundred feet of a masked battery of six guns.

They waited till our men got up close, and then opened on them, firing in rapid succession. A retreat was ordered and our men fell back.

Schenck failed to rally his column in any order. The Ohio and New York men scattered through the woods in pursuit of shelter and water. The sun was broiling hot, and almost suffocating, for the men were now out of water.

Up to about three P. M., our army was victorious, *but the men had a dread of the masked batteries, that could not be overcome;* they were placed all over the hill-tops and on sides of ravines, and would open fire upon us when least expected.

We were in the centre of Tyler's division, on the hill just east of Bull's Run on the Warrenton road. About 2 P. M. we saw clouds of dust rising to our left, as though they were trying to outflank us and come on us in the rear. We called several officers' attention to it, but there seemed to be no man who could have reinforcements sent for to cover our flank.

On the left of the road were Sherman's and Carlisle's batteries, drawn up for fight; on the right were some three thousand men, consisting of parts of the Ohio and New York Regiments, and the New York Sixty-ninth. About three o'clock P. M. their batteries opened on us; every ball was well fired; the first fell in front of the batteries, and the next one took of the heads of two men, a few yards below us, where Messrs. S. R. Smith, Sheriff J. Harper, Mr. Shaw, of the New York *Herald*, and ourself, were standing. Orders were now given for the men to lie down, and let the balls pass over; and just as the order was given, another one swept over our heads, and ploughed the field a few steps in our rear. Our battery did not fire a gun. The enemy were not to be seen, owing to dense woods between them and us. Our heavy siege gun was lying to the right, disabled by the carriage being broken down; the balls flew faster and faster, and the batteries were apparently being brought closer. We then went back to the edge of the woods where our hospitals were located.

The following is the best and most connected narrative of the battle, in brief, that we have met with—it is from the Philadelphia *Inquirer:*

I have spent this morning in hearing the accounts of the battle from officers who actually participated in it in all parts of the field and during the whole day, and can, therefore, give you full particulars. The conflicting reports of last night arose from the fact that no less than three separate and distinct engagements took place during the day, in different parts of the field, and that the field of battle covers a space of ten miles in extent. The reconnoissances that had been made on Friday and Saturday must have been made under such circumstances as to render the results uncertain and unsatisfactory. But whatever were the results, General McDowell determined to advance from Centreville and to attack the enemy's batteries on Bull's Run, hoping to be able to turn them on the right, to silence them, and then by a further advance to strike the Manassas Gap Railroad at a point near Bull's Run Mountain, and so cut off Johnston, and prevent his communication with Beauregard. The attempt has been made, and it has resulted in a complete failure.

At 2 o'clock Sunday morning the troops were roused from their slumbers, and formed in marching columns. The Second Division, Col. Hunter, led the advance. The West Point Battery; a part of the Fifth Regiment U. S. Artillery; the Second Rhode Island Regiment with their battery; a part of the Second Regiment U. S. Artillery, and Capt. Seymour's siege train of eight 32 pounder rifled cannon, headed the column. The moon was full, the sky without a cloud, and it was nearly as light as day. The First Division, General Tyler, advanced at the same time, in a nearly parallel column; the Third Brigade, Col. Sherman, in advance; the Sixty-ninth New York, Col. Corcoran, leading the van. The Seventy-ninth, Col. Cameron, followed, and the Second Brigade, General Schenck, (the Ohio Regiments,) were close behind. By daybreak Bull's Run was reached. The batteries were placed in position, and our guns opened on the enemy's works. The firing was responded to by three batteries, and was kept up on both sides till 11 A. M. The enemy's fire then slackened, and afterwards entirely ceased. It was supposed, therefore, that their guns had been silenced, and a charge was ordered to carry the batteries. The charge was made, at a run, by the above regiments. There was a little, though not much, resistance made by the musketry of the foe, and in a few minutes the batteries were ours, the few gunners there bayoneted at their guns, the Confederate flag torn down, and the Stars and Stripes raised. It was then that McDowell sent that despatch to Gen. Scott, announcing a glorious victory and the batteries in our possession. But our triumph was of short duration. The enemy had abandoned these batteries in order to lead us into a snare. In half an hour after we had taken the batteries, and while the men were resting from their fatigue, a terrific fire was opened upon them with musketry and cannon. The latter were in other masked batteries, the very existence of which was unknown. The riflemen who were firing at us were also unseen.

The fire was so hot that our men found it impossible to stand it, and were compelled reluctantly to abandon the batteries. They retired in good order, however, under cover of our artillery, which now again began to open upon the enemy, throwing shells towards their masked batteries, but without effect. At 3 P. M. our loss had been fearful. Colonel Cameron had been killed, General Schenck killed, Colonel Slocum killed, and Colonel Hunter wounded. Many other of our officers had been killed and whole regiments decimated. The enemy had not once showed himself up to this time. At three, however, having silenced many of our guns, the enemy charged upon us in an overwhelming force. The troops stood gallantly, but the charge was irresistible, and we were compelled to retire. The artillerists spiked their guns.

The excitement in the city was intense. A despatch had been received by Gen. McDowell at the War Department, at 8 P. M., Sunday, requesting immediate reinforcements. All the regiments in the city were immediately ordered over, and by 2 o'clock this morning, crossed the Long Bridge. All night long drums beat in the streets, and recruiting parties paraded the avenues, calling for volunteers to defend the capital. The firing of the heavy guns was distinctly heard in Washington during the evening.

This morning, soon after daylight, it became known that the disasters of Sunday had not ended with the light, but that new reverses had been experienced during the night. All this morning, up to the time of writing, (2 P. M., Monday,) straggling squads of soldiers have been pouring over the Long Bridge, and along Pennsylvania avenue. They are all unwounded, but in every case covered with a thick coating of dust and sweat, their hair matted, their clothes torn and blood-stained, some armed and some unarmed. There are no less than 10,000 of them here, up to this time, and they are still coming. I have seen among them men from the following regiments:—Seventy-first New York; Second Maine; First and Second Ohio; Sixty-ninth and Seventy-ninth New York, (the latter the Highlanders;) Second and Third Michigan; Twenty-Seventy New York; Second New Hampshire; Eleventh New York, (the Zouaves.) Many of the men throw themselves down on door steps, on curb-stones, and on the pavement, and faintly cry for water.

Since 10 o'clock Pennsylvania avenue has been crowded with them, and since that time measures have been taken for their relief. From many of the cross streets, people are running, bringing baskets of refreshments, bread, milk, water, coffee, &c. Elegantly dressed ladies, side by side with negro women, are carrying wine, coffee and water to the soldiers, unheeding the rain that is fast falling. The ladies don't stop to draw the corks of the bottles of Catawba wine, but knock the necks off, and pour out the contents in new tin cups. A soldier has just died. The men state that for three days they have had nothing to eat except crackers, and were all day yesterday without water. The men state that last night, after ten o'clock, the enemy advanced on Centreville in strong force, with mortars for throwing shells. That we were unprepared to resist them, and were compelled to retreat. That our army made a stand at Fairfax, but were driven out of that place, the shells pouring in upon them like hail; and that the whole army is now in full retreat upon Washington.

The result of the battle yesterday has been the entire and complete defeat of our whole army.—The loss of life in the battle alone will reach fully three thousand, and two thousand more will die of their wounds. The slightly wounded, severely wounded, and those wounded who will recover after amputation, amount to fully five thousand more. We have lost hundreds of prisoners, among them Colonel McCook, First Regiment Ohio.—Sherman's splendid battery had to be abandoned to the enemy. Previous to its abandonment, however, the gunners say they spiked the pieces. The splendid battery of the Second Rhode Island Regiment is said to be dismounted and rendered entirely useless. The enemy captured our two large 32-pounders, and then turned them on our retreating columns. The horses attached to all the foregoing guns were cut loose, and brought off the field safely.

The retreat is thus described by another correspondent:

About 4 P. M. a report flew from man to man that Simon Cameron's brother, Col. of the 79th, was shot through the breast by a cannon ball, and instantly killed. Lt.-Col. Elliott, of the 79th, rode towards his regiment, having been after reinforcements, when a ball cut his horse's head off, and threw him down, bruising him so that he could barely escape. All the stragglers now commenced to run towards Centreville, and the caissons, ambulances, and sutlers' wagons were ordered to be taken back at once towards Centreville.

The batteries were ordered around to cover our retreat, and keep the Rebels from cutting us off from Centreville, which was about three miles in our rear, and where we had about four or five thousand of a reserve force; the batteries wheeled off and took up the road, and were retreating in good order, when, about a half a mile out, one of the gun carriages was upset. *A portion of Sherman's and Carlisle's were left in the roadside, the gunners cutting the traces and running their horses. This put the infantry in a perfect panic;* they broke ranks indiscriminately and commenced to run; knapsacks, haversacks, guns, cartrige boxes, hats, coats and everything, being thrown in all directions. The men were parched for water and were falling in every direction. Officers were equally panic-stricken with the privates, and in vain we endeavored to stop the retreat. The enemy appeared in sight, firing their guns, the balls raining upon us thick.

Our friends had now all left, and the troops were flying, and at the cry that the cavalry were riding them down and butchering all, we started for Centreville. We mounted a wounded horse, and clinging to his mane, made for the road again leading to Centreville.

Here the road was strewn with wrecks of wagons, provisions, muskets, blankets, ammunition, and everything the men could divest themselves of. *The ground was full. The fields in all directions were full. The fire of the enemy was kept up in the rear. Part of Sherman's battery breaking down, the men cut the traces and fled.* The ammunition wagon was left on the ground. We should judge that *ten thousand guns and rifles* were lost on the way, while the cartdge boxes, bayonets, sabre bayonets and swords were innumerable. About a mile from Centreville, an attempt was made to rally the men, but with little success. A few thousand were stopped, but many without weapons. On the high hill top at Centreville a column of infantry was seen, with their gleaming bayonets. On the top the artillery were also drawn, up, prepared to fire.

The Garibaldians, Einstein's and Blenker's regiments were drawn up at the foot of the hill, and escaping men ordered to fall in. Loud cheering was done, and the rallying cry given, but it was but little or no use—men had no officers when they did halt, and so they kept on retreating; "water, water!" was the cry: "give me water or I'll sink," was heard from all sides; not a drop was to be had fit to drink; the wells were all drained, and the clouds of dust filled the air at every point. We got in the rear of a negro hut, and there secured water thick with filth, but it was the best to be had; a number of buildings were used for hospitals, *and on every side cries were made for surgeons.*

Orders were now circulated for the men to gather at their last camping ground, around Centreville; it was heeded by some, but most neglected it and continued their stampede towards Fairfax.

The firing of the enemy was kept up on our rear with artillery, *and their cavalry rode through and through, cutting and slashing with perfect fiendishness.*

Our wounded and dead are nearly all on the battle field in the hands of the enemy; such as could crawl or walk were trying to get away, and such pitiable spectacles were seen as made our heart sick; but we could not help them; the few ambulances were started off early with the wounded and never returned. We saw a number lying on the roadside, with medicine chests and bandages.

The immense baggage train, consisting of some six hundred or a thousand wagons, lined the road for a mile and a half on the Warrenton road towards Bull's Run, two miles back of Centreville. When the panic started the wagons tried to fall back on Centreville, but a number were upset and broken down; the drivers would immediately leave them and escape on the horses. Others would throw out their load of provisions and stores, and fill up with soldiers and muskets; the body of the luggage, however, got in the rear of Centreville.

Our greatest loss is in the thorough demoralization of our army. It will take weeks to gather the scattered forces in the condition we had them.

The cowardly retreat on the morning of the fight, by the Pennsylvania Fourth, and various batteries, had a depressing effect upon our force, and encouraged the Rebels by the story that *our men were running.* That their "time was up" is an excuse that will not answer; they fled ignominiously when our country needed them.

Col. Corcoran of the 69th was once captured, and the colors of the regiment taken.

From Washington.

The Washington correspondent of the Philadelphia *Inquirer* writes lugubriously. He says:

After a pedestrian tour of fourteen miles, I am able to furnish you with the following items:

I left Fairfax Court House this morning about 5 o'clock, and at that time every white person had deserted the village and the telegraph office was closed. The troops from Centreville were marching rapidly towards Alexandria.

As I walked along the road, I passed Colonel Tyler's command and other Michigan and New Jersey regiments, on their way from Centreville to Fairfax Court House. The road was lined with military stores and soldiers' equipments, as though their owners had left in a desperate hurry.

The rumor now is that Fairfax Court House is in the hands of the Rebels.

Governor Dennison, of Ohio, left here last night for home, with orders to raise several regiments of troops for immediate service. He expresses himself as confident of a rally to the standard of the Union.

From New York.

The correspondent of the Philadelphia *Ledger* says that New York has been panic stricken by the great defeat, and adds:

The city has been in a state of indescribable excitement all day. The anxiety to see the lists of the killed and wounded, and to know the worst is painful and universal. The newspaper offices are thronged with mothers and sisters, as well as fathers and brothers, waiting in agonizing suspense the publication of each successive bulletin, and grief, for the moment, is everywhere.

The moral effect of this disaster is more dreaded even than its physical results. Merchants and business men fear that its first result abroad will be the recognition of the rebel Government by England and France. The first steamer to take out the news will be the *Canada*, from Boston, on Wednesday.

Wall street, you will see, has received a staggering blow. Government securities went down from 5 to 6 per cent. in the course of the afternoon, and the entire market, it is scarcely necessary to say, was greatly depressed.

It was rumored that a meeting of the 7th regiment was to be held this afternoon, at 3 o'clock, to tender their services at once to the Government—but, on repairing to their armory, I discovered the armory doors closed, and the report entirely without foundation.

Circulars are out calling for a special meeting of the Union Defence Committee at an early hour tomorrow morning.

The Latest News.

The New York papers groan sadly over their defeat. The *Tribune* insists that the victory was theirs, but somebody ordered a retreat, and instanter everybody ran. It grumbles terribly, and thinks General Scott should not have moved without more men. It is also insolent upon General Patterson, and throws a large share of the disgrace upon him.

The Herald thinks the Capital is now really in danger, and that all the troops should be concentrated there without delay. The defeat is attributed to the unfortunate teamsters! As these men were necessarily in the rear of the "Grand Army," we are at a loss to conceive how they could have produced the result.

The details of the battle, as contained in the New York papers, do not differ from those which we give elsewhere.

The Killed and Wounded, etc.

WASHINGTON, July 23d.—The weather is bright and beautiful after the heavy rain of yesterday, and this morning the streets present a lively appearance. Soldiers in various garbs are either wending their way to their respective places of rendezvous, or entertaining still anxious and curious persons with additional incidents of the battle and subsequent retreat. Some of the soldiers are almost sinking under their severe pedestrian fatigue; those who were more fortunate in flying to Washington either on horses cut from the baggage wagons or in vehicles, make a comparatively neat appearance. Amid the hasty gathering of so many odds and ends of regiment under the distressing circumstances it is no wonder the charities of our citizens are solicited.

This morning is occupied in putting affairs in order on the Virginia side within the original Federal lines. The business of repairing the commissariat and ordnance damages is in lively progress. The boats are again running to Alexandria. The Fire Zouaves will rendezvous at the headquarters of the Twelfth Regiment to-day, when some accurate knowledge of their losses may be ascertained.

The last seen of Col. Wilcox, of Michigan, he was lying wounded on the battle-field, and he is either dead or taken prisoner; Captain Worthington, Company B; —— Butterworth, Company C; Lieutenant Casey, Company G; —— Monck, Company F; Orderly Sergeant Lewis Hartmeyer, Company A; privates Richard Jones, Company A; Jas. Kelly, Company F, and both color bearers—all killed. —— Cunningham, Company A; John Stafford, Company G, are among the wounded. Major Bidwell took the place of Col. Wilcox and managed to bring this regiment out of the field in the best possible order.

A Zouave drummer boy, who was taken prisoner but escaped, reports that the secessionists have an immense number of prisoners, supposed principally those picked up on the way.

Another Fight in Missouri.

KANSAS CITY, Mo., July 20.—By a special messenger just arrived, we learn the following: On the 18th, at 2½ P. M., Major Van Horn's command of United States Reserve Home Guards, of this place, numbering one hundred and seventy men, were attacked by five hundred Confederates, under Capt. Duncan, three miles north of Harrisonville. The fight lasted four hours, during which time a continual firing was kept up on both sides. At 6½ o'clock the Confederates withdrew, leaving the Union men victorious. The loss of the Confederates was fourteen killed, including two officers. The Union men continued their march, crossing Grand river, but they were compelled to leave three of their baggage wagons on the bank of the river, owing to the high water. Major Van Horn left this city on the morning of the 17th, for the purpose of reinforcing Major Dean, now holding West Point, Mo., with a small force, having routed one hundred Confederates at that place. Maj. Van Horn's force was attacked while at dinner. They planted their flag staff on the ground, never giving way an inch, nor moving the flag till after the Confederates withdrew. The enemy attempted to flank them on the left, with a company of cavalry, but were completely routed.

Latest from Harper's Ferry.

HARPER'S FERRY, July 22.—There has been no recent movement of troops at this point. Great excitement prevails in consequence of reports from the vicinity of Manassas Junction. There is much indignation among the soldiers at the supposed superseding of Gen. Patterson by Gen. Banks. News from Winchester states Gen. Johnston's forces on Wednesday last at 34,000, among them two Maryland Regiments numbering 1,200 men. On Wednesday, the 18th, he commenced to move towards Manassas Junction with 30,000 men, leaving the remainder at Winchester. Those left were principally Virginia Militia. The main column crossed the Shenandoah at Mills Ford. None of the Confederates, nor even their cavalry, has been seen or heard of in this region for several days.

Southern Account of the Battle of Manassas.

RICHMOND, July 22.—In the victory at Manassas, Gen. Beauregard commanded the right wing, President Davis the centre, and Gen. Johnston the left wing of the Confederate army. The hottest attack was upon Gen. Johnston's wing, but was successfully resisted, when Davis attacked the Federals with the centre, and the rout became complete.—Our loss cannot now be known. Gen. Beauregard and Staff are safe. The General's horse was shot under him.

Fatal Affray in Louisville.

LOUISVILLE, July 22.—John W. Tompkins, formerly a clerk of the Board of Aldermen, a violent Secessionist and a recruiting officer for the Southern Confederacy, was shot dead this afternoon by Henry Green, a city watchman. Tomkins was halloing for Jeff. Davis, and was requested to desist by Green, when he drew a knife on Green, but was retreating when Green shot him. The Coroner's verdict just rendered, says that Green shot Tompkins without sucfficient cause.

Two Union Men Hung in Missouri.

ST. CHARLES, Mo., July 21.—By train to-day we have confirmation of the report that Colonel Benj. Sharpe, of Montgomery county, and Lieut. Jaegar, of the Federal forces, were wounded by the Confederates, and subsequently hung. Lieut. Jaegar had been wounded in the arm a day or two previous by the Secessionists, near Wellsville, and was being taken by Col. Sharpe to the latter's home in a buggy, when they were fired upon by parties concealed in the bushes by the roadside.

The Daily Delta.

VOL. XVI. — NEW ORLEANS, FRIDAY, JULY 26, 1861. — NO. 203.

THE DAILY DELTA

FROM OUR EVENING EDITION OF YESTERDAY.

For the past two or three days the Picayune has published the dispatches of the Associated Press, sent to all the city papers, under the head of "Special to the Picayune." Is this not a mistake on the part of our neighbor?

WHAT THE MORNING JOURNALS SAY.

The *Bee* dilates upon the consequences of the great victory at Manassas, the loss of prestige of the Federalists, the contempt of European Governments and people, and the unbounded confidence and heroic resolve of the Southern soldiery. The previous vaunting and grand demonstrations of the enemy reserve to render this defeat more crushing and disgraceful.

The *Picayune* refers in appropriate terms to the sorrowful aspects of our great victory in the many bereavements it has caused:

The sternest warrior might pause at such a sight, and reckon up the cost of noble blood, the waste of vigorous life, and the desolation of a thousand loving households, which make up the terrible price exacted of the South, in her resistance to the ferocious crime of the North. And the softest nature can not dwell on the wickedness out of which all this bloodshed and misery have come, without being hardened into implacable resentment.

Freedom's battle has had its hecatomb of martyrs. While we have reason to be glad that few Louisianians have fallen, there are painful expections in many bosoms yet for the lists of slain and wounded. Bitter tears have already been shed over kindred and friends who are known to have fallen on that field. Names, too, have reached us, of gallant soldiers of our sister States, who, dying in the cause of us all, have watered the tree of Southern liberty with their life streams. These are lost jewels of the South, for whom the robber enemy will be called to a rigid account. The deaths of a regiment of Northern invaders would be dearly bought by the death of a single one of these.

To each one of them there is son, brother or kindred to start forth as the avengers of blood, and to hunt out the men who, in pursuit of their own lusts of ambition and rapine, have forced themselves into a peaceful country, to slaughter its sons for defending their own hearthstones from the spoiler, for punishment as murderers of the innocent and assassins of liberty.

Feelingly and gratefully has the Congress of the Confederate States recorded their tribute of affection and honor to these martyrs. The laying down of their lives to their country gives them immortality in history.

The *Bulletin* quotes, with appropriate comments, the article of the New York Tribune, urging that the present war be closed with one grand fight on equal terms, and that the beaten party shall submit. Here is its language:

In short we believe the patriot soldiers are to-day able and eager to whip the rebels, and we want to see them allowed to try. If they are not able to thrash the traitors in fair stand-up fight, our pride revolts at the idea of slowly starving them into subjection, or whipping them by virtue of money borrowed in Europe. We say, challenge them to meet the patriot volunteers in fair fight; if they quail, they are ruined; if they fight, and are beaten, they must give it up; while, if they beat us, we ought to do the same. Let us have this matter decided forthwith, so that our brave men may quit soldiering and return to more profitable vocations.

Who ever trusts to the faith and declarations of such convicted liars as Greeley? Did he not, when secession first commenced, advocate the policy of letting the seceding States go in peace, and did he not afterwards employ all his diabolical demagoguery to arouse and stimulate the ignorant and fanatical masses to embark in this war, and prosecute it with a fury and barbarity unparalleled in modern warfare? He will again prove himself the renegade—false to all truth and honor—by new and more fanatical appeals to the passions of the multitude, whom he is leading to such ruin and misery. What cares he about the consequence? It is not he or his who will suffer any of the horrors of the war. The base wretch stays at home and hounds on poor ignorant people, fire boys and city rowdies, to a bloody death, that he may promote the integrity of his political party and promote the hellish conspiracy of abolition.

RANK IN THE CONFEDERATE SERVICE.—The Picayune has the following in regard to rank in the Confederate Army:

Will the Picayune oblige the undersigned by giving the highest military grade or rank attainable in the Confederate States Army? A controversy having arisen respecting it, and an agreement to rely upon your decision, prompts him to trespass upon your generosity in making the request. A SUBSCRIBER.

The president is *ex officio* commander-in-chief of the army. After that rank, the highest is that of Major-General.—*Eds Pic.*

We understand the matter differently. In the regular Confederate service there is but one rank—that of General. There are no Major or Brigadier Generals in that service. Before the adoption of the act creating the regular army of the Confederate States, the old plan of the United States army was adopted, and the ranks of Major and Brigadier Generals were created. It is under this bill that Gens. Twiggs and Polk are Major Generals; and Bragg, Walker, Bonham and others are Brigadiers. Beauregard being at the head of the Brigadier Generals of the Provisional army, was promoted for his gallantry and generalship to the grade of General in the regular army of the Confederate States. He is ranked, however, by Johnston, Lee and Cooper, and with them makes up the four Generals in the Confederate Army. It was doubtless to prevent any conflict of rank, and the superseding of Beauregard in command at Manassas by Johnston, that President Davis appeared on the field, ranking both, as Commander-in-Chief.

Capt. Swain having telegraphed to Col. Hays or Capt. Jett, to send a list of the killed and wounded belonging to Company B, Crescent Rifles, received the following reply:

To Capt. Richard Swain:

MANASSAS, July 24.

Stacker Brooks was killed, Charles V. Fischer slightly wounded in the leg.

W. P. HARPER,
Crescent Rifles, Company B.

To David Kemper, care of A. D. Kelly & Co.:

MANASSAS, July 24.

Stacker Brooks was killed in the engagement of the 18th.

Gen. W. W. Loring, late Colonel of the U. S. Rifle Regiment, we learn from the Richmond Dispatch, has been assigned by President Davis to the command in Northwestern Virginia, and was to have left Richmond for his post on Monday last. The Dispatch adds that in the course of a week or ten days he would have a force under him of fifteen thousand men, and would be able to cope with Gen McClellan.

Zollicoffer and Cheatham, of Tennessee, have been appointed Brigadier Generals in the Provisional Army of the Confederate States.

BATTLE OF BULL RUN.

From the Richmond Examiner, July 20.

For more than a week the commanding General of the Confederate forces at Manassas has been anticipating an advance of the enemy, and had so arranged his troops as to be prepared at all points. At Fairfax Court House Gen. Bonham was stationed, with six regiments of infantry, composed of four from South Carolina, (Kershaw, Cash, Williams and Bacon,) and two from Virginia, (Preston and Withers,) and two batteries of light artillery, (Shields's Howitzers and Kemper's Company,) and about five hundred cavalry, under command of Col. Bradford, of Virginia.

At Fairfax Station, about four miles distant from the Court House, and on a line with it, Gen. Ewell, of Virginia, was posted with three regiments of infantry, two Alabama, (Sieble's and Rhodes's,) and one from Louisiana, (Seymour's.) These regiments were stationed at intervals of a mile from each other, Rhodes's 5th Alabama Regiment guarding the Braddock Road approach from Alexandria, which intersects the country road between the Court House and the Station. At both places, infantry works had been thrown up for the protection of the troops, and at the Court House, particularly, extended lines of defense, including two or three masked batteries, had been constructed.

At Centreville, a commanding eminence on the turnpike road, between Fairfax Court House and Bull Run, Col. Cocke was stationed with his regiment and Latham's Light Battery. The object of these preparations was to resist the incursion of anything short of a large army into the interior, and in the event of the approach of a force under twenty thousand men, to give battle and drive them back. At the same time, orders had been issued, in case of an overwhelming demonstration of the enemy, to fall back on Bull Run, the selected battle ground. To provide for this contingency, the troops, for more than a week past, have been trimmed of all superfluous baggage, and been under orders to keep on hand constantly three days' provisions in advance. Quartermaster and Commissary supplies have been kept in limited amounts, and the wagons held in constant readiness to move off with camp equipage, &c., &c.

We are particular in stating these minute details to give the reader an idea of what was anticipated by the commanding general, and of his arrangements to meet the contemplated contingency.

On Thursday, the enemy felt his way cautiously up from Alexandria and Washington, in three separate columns, of probably fifteen thousand each—one down the railroad, another the Braddock road, and the third from the direction of Falls Church. Our pickets were driven in about 2 o'clock, and our troops, after firing several hundred rounds, withdrew in order before the advancing foe, and fell back on the banks of Bull Run, a stream about four miles from Manassas and eight from the Court House.

The "Run" is about sixty feet wide and easily fordable for infantry at this season of the year; but its points of defense against an adversary attempting to cross are inviting to the military eye. Here the retiring forces were met by Gen. Longstreet's Brigade, consisting of the 11th, 17th and 1st Virginia Regiments, under the command respectively of Cols. Garland, Corse and Moore, together with artillery from New Orleans. We bivouacked for the night in expectation of the fight opening at daybreak. But the enemy approached cautiously, beating the roads and woods in advance of them with skirmishers, until about four o'clock in the afternoon, when their main body arrived within a half mile of the Run, and made three several attempts to advance on it, and each time were repulsed with great slaughter.

The reports of the loss of the enemy are conflicting, varying it from five to fifteen hundred. Certain it is, their retreat had every appearance of a signal rout, leaving, as they did, their dead behind them, and losing six pieces of their artillery. Two of the Virginia regiments pursued them for some distance, and captured quite a number of prisoners. The Confederate loss is estimated at about one hundred killed, wounded and missing. It is said the enemy, in their several advances, behaved at first with much spirit, quickly rallying and closing up their mowed columns, but finally broke, and gave way under the murderous execution

On Wednesday afternoon, dispatches were sent to Gen. Johnston to repair with a portion of his command to reinforce Gen. Beauregard at Manassas. Johnston had his entrenchments at Winchester strongly fortified and defended with heavy artillery, as to be able to spare at least half his command without any risk. The propriety of these instructions is vindicated by the dispatch in another column announcing that Patterson has left Martinsburg, and is on his way across the Potomac. Johnston by this time is at Manassas, prepared to take part in the fight to day, should it occur.

The enemy, as they advanced, displayed their accustomed Vandalism, burning and destroying as they went. The villages of Fairfax Court-House, Germantown and Centreville were reduced to ashes, and men and women were fleeing in every direction. Such are the well-authenticated accounts of passengers by the Central train of yesterday.

FURTHER PARTICULARS.

Information derived from gentlemen who left Manassas Junction at 9 o'clock yesterday morning enables us to lay before our readers the important particulars of the great victory achieved by our troops on Thursday last.

At dawn on that day, the enemy recommenced their advance upon our lines. The Washhington Artillery went out to meet them, and a skirmishing fight between the opposing forces of flying artillery immediately began and lasted until 11 A. M. At this hour their whole front, infantry and artillery, continuing still to advance, our infantry also pushed forward and the fight became general.

The battle continued with unabated fury for three hours, when, about two o'clock, P. M, the enemy's center giving way before the fire of our artillery and the charge of our infantry, their whole force fell back precipitately and in disorder.

But, after an interval of an hour, during which there was some unimportant skirmishing, at three o'clock P. M., the enemy again returned to the charge with redoubled impetuosity, and again, after severe fighting, were they driven back at the point of the bayonet.

A third time they were rallied and brought up, but only to be repulsed quickly and with great slaughter.

It was now five o'clock P. M., and the enemy made no attempt to renew the fight, but retreated hastily, leaving the field, strewn with the bodies of their dead and wounded, in possession of the Confederates.

The battle extended along the creek. Bull Run, a distance of over a mile, and within this space the enemy had left 986 of their men dead or mortally wounded.

Our loss, as counted that night, was 137 killed, wounded and missing, but by the next morning, this number was reduced to less than sixty by the return of stragglers, who had been scattered and lost in the woods during the night.

The famous Sherman battery, upon which the enemy evidently based so much hope and success, was almost utterly annihilated. Some say there is scarcely a corporal's guard of them left. Our 1st Regiment of Virginia Volunteers, under Col. P. T. Moore, is said to have fought desperately. Three seperate charges were made by it with the bayonet, and in each instance the enemy fled like sheep. Among the enemy's dead were many officers, whose uniforms indicated high rank, though their names were unknown. Before the departure of the train for Richmond, yesterday morning, the enemy had sent in a flag of truce to Gen. Beauregard, asking permission to bury their dead, which was of course, granted.

The number of the enemy actually engaged in this battle is variously estimated at between five and ten thousand, whilst our force little exceeded three thousand five hundred.

Only eight of our men are certainly known to have been killed, which, with those who are so severely wounded as to leave little or no hope for their recovery, will, perhaps, bring our actual loss up to twenty. Few of our men who were struck are dangerously hurt. About twenty of them came down last evening by the Central cars, the most severely wounded of whom was a Captain of the Washington Artillery, who was wounded in the leg by the explosion of a shell. Col. P. T. Moore, who was struck early in the fight, arrived by the same train. His wound had not been dressed, and from the loss of blood and the jolting of the cars, he was very much exhausted when he reached home, but he is considered in no danger. The ball took effect on the inner side of his arm, and, glancing from the bone—which is not thought to be broken—came in contact with one of his ribs, producing a very painful but not dangerous wound.

Lieut. Wirt Harrison, wounded in the instep by a buckshot, and Mr. Knauff having received a musket-ball through the hand, also reached home yesterday evening. Major Carter Harrison and Capt. James K. Lee were so severely wounded as to render their removal to Richmond dangerous. We could not ascertain the character of Major Harrison's injuries, but Capt. Lee is said to have been struck in the back, near the spinal column, by a bullet, which passed entirely through his body. He is thought to have been accidentally shot by one of his own men.

The remains of Lieut. Humphrey Miles, of Company G, 1st Regiment of Virginia Volunteers, were brought down and delivered to his friends. He is thought to have been shot by a member of Company I, of the same regiment.

One of the Washington Artillery, whose name we did not learn, was killed, and seven wounded. The most of these latter were struck during the explosion of a shell, which was thrown by the enemy after the battle was over, and whilst they were in retreat.

It was reported that seven guns of the Sherman battery had been captured by our troops, but others, who seem to have had good opportunities of information deny the truth of this statement. But all agree that we secured many hundred rifles and muskets, besides a vast quantity of side-arms.

We learn from a gentleman who left Gordonsville yesterday, and who had previously conversed with an intelligent friend directly from Manassas, that the result of the battle at Manassas has not been accurately given in the dispatches received from that quarter. Our informant states that not more than ten were killed on our side, and that our whole loss in killed, wounded and missing, will not exceed fifty or sixty. The loss on the Federal side, he thinks, was not so large as represented in our dispatches, and will hardly go over two hundred.

ANOTHER ACCOUNT.

Other passengers from Manassas, who reached here last night, state that the killed, wounded and missing of the Cenfederate Army number 142, and the number of the Federals left dead on the field, 986.

It will be seen that there are very wide discrepancies in the accounts given of the battle in our paper of this morning. We have presented the several statements, and leave our readers to sift the truth of the matter.

BATTLE OF MANASSAS.

THE NORTHERN ACCOUNTS.

BULL RUN, July 19—P. M.—From careful inquiry and personal observation, the number of wounded on the Federal side amounts to sixty, and the killed to forty.

There has been no firing. The Confederate are still in possession of their principal battery.

With a spy glass large bodies of Confederates were seen moving at right and left, apparently finding their base line of operations, and not retreating.

Batteries are being erected on our side, commanding theirs, which are of a substantial character.

WASHINGTON, July 21.—The following bulletins were read in official quarters during the progress of the battle from the telegraph station, about four miles from Bull Run:

FAIRFAX, 12 A. M—Rapid firing from heavy guns and frequent discharges of musketry.

11:40 A. M—Fighting very heavy and apparently more on our left wing.

11:50 A M.—There is evidently a battle toward our left in the direction of Bull Run and a little north. The firing is very rapid and heavy.

1:45 P. M.—Heavy guns again, and apparently musketry; heavy and nearer.

2 P. M.—The musketry is very heavy and drawing much nearer. There is evidently a movement more to our left.

2:45 P. M.—The firing is a little farther off and apparently in the direction of the Junction. There are less heavy guns, and more light artillery, as far as I can judge.

3 P M.—The firing ceased ten minutes since.

3:35 P. M.—The firing has almost entirely ceased, and can only be heard with difficulty.

I shall telegraph no more unless there should be a renewal of the battle, which has been so gloriously fought for the old stars and stripes, and from all indications here our troops have at least stood their ground.

3:50 P. M.—Our courier has not yet returned. Quartermaster Barton of the 2d Michigan regiment has just passed, and says that the officers, men and citizens at Centreville report that a general engagement of the whole line has taken place 3½ miles this side of Manassas, and that our troops had driven and forced the Secessionists back to Manassas. We expect our courier now every moment.

4:45 P. M.—[illegible] in person with Gen. McDowell. One of the couriers was on the field of battle. He says our troops have taken three masked batteries and forced the rebels to fall back and retire. He says the battle was general on Bull Run for some distance. One of the batteries taken was in a wheat field and another at some distance from it, and a third still further off.

The Tribune's dispatch says that a deserter reports the rebels nearly 80,000 strong, and that Johnson, with 17,000 men, marchad in last night. They have 27 companies of cavalry. He says that the first shell from our batteries burst near Lee and Beauregard, killing a number of officers.

5:20 P. M.—The Federal troops have won the day. The loss on both sides is heavy, but the route of the rebels is complete.

The batteries at Bull Run are silenced, and two or three others taken.

5:40 P. M.—The firing has ceased. We shall send another courier there in a few minutes. The Colonel went at 4 o'clock and will be back soon.

STILL LATER.—A report, not official, but from an apparently reliable source, says that the column under Heintzelman has followed the rebels to Manassas Junction, and has opened fire on their entrenchments and camps and was then shelling them. The cannonading can occasionally be heard in Washington and from Georgetown Heights.

The headquarters of the army are inaccessible to-night, the President and Cabinet being privately with Gen. Scott and staff and other distinguished gentlemen.

Intense excitement exists in this city. The smoke from the battle could be seen from eminences in Washington.

It is reported that Col. Hunt is seriously—perhaps mortally wounded—also, Col. Cameron, brother of the Secretary of War, is reported killed at Bull's Run.

The battle lasted nine hours. The first range gun was fired by Sherman's battery at ten minutes of seven. The rebels didn't return the fire for an hour, and as soon as Col. Hunter's division came up the engagement became general. The rebels rapidly received reinforcements from Manassas, and as fast as masked batteries were silenced more sprang up, our infantry charging on and silencing them gallantly.

The most brilliant charge was made by the New York 69th, 79th and 13th regiments, at the point of the bayonet, capturing a battery, but with severe loss. The Zouaves greatly distinguished themselves.

A Mississippian taken prisoner by the Wisconsin 2d, turns out to be Q. M. Pryor, a cousin of Roger Pryor. He acknowledges our cavalry made great havoc among the rebels, who were nearly 40,000 strong in the field, commanded by Beauregard, with a reserve of 75,000 at Manassas. He also says Jeff. Davis was in the fight, mounted on a white horse, and confirms the report of a regiment of negroes in the rebel army.

At 7 P. M. guns were still heard at intervals.

Judge Campbell, late of the Supreme Court, writes that the flower of the South is at Manassas, but he fears that the battle goes against the Confederates.

The Herald says it is believed that Manassas has been reinforced from Richmond, or by Johnston, though Gen. Scott does not believe Johnston has left Winchester. Gen. Scott is reported to have said that the Union forces were sufficient.

CENTREVILLE, July 20, 1 P. M—The affair at Bull Run, of the 18th, which has been magnified into a terrible battle, has not resulted so disastrous to our army as has been represented in some quarters. The list of killed and wounded can not, however, as yet be accurately ascertained. The inmates of the hospital at Centreville are increased by those who have suffered from exhaustion and not by wounds. This fact gives rise to exaggerated stories as to the large numbers of wounded.

A flag of truce, which was sent by Gen. McDowell to th eenemy's line, in order to recover our dead and wounded, was refused by the enemy, for the reason, probably, that they wished to conceal the position of their batteries.

It may be well to state that Gen. McDowell, at the commencement of the action, was at Langster's Point on a visit to Col. Heintzleman's command, and while on his way to Centreville, was informed of the battle. He immediately proceeded to the scene, but did not arrive there until the firing had ceased.

The movement towards Manassas Junction from Centreville was unauthorized, the order of march of Gen. Tyler's division being limited to the latter point, in order to wait a flank movement by Col. Heintzleman's division, which was at that time at Langster's Point on the line of the Manassas railroad.

Gen. Tyler having ascertained that masked batteries were in the vicinity he ordered a reconnoissance on his own responsibility. The result of this was the discovering of the battery, and although acquired by the loss of life will probably be advantageous. Besides a large body of our troops have been tried and by no means found wanting. The order to retire was given in consequence of the Federal battery having exhausted its shot and cannister, and the exhaustion of cavalry, which, under command of Capt. Brackett, performed most efficient service in the action. The gallant Captain was at all times in advance of his command, and his men followed him in fearless and determined spirit, but want of water for horses (a difficulty which it is feared will be encountered from Centreville to Manassas Junction) prevented him from continuing his efforts to unmask the enemy.

It is regretted by some military men that the infantry was not called into more active service during the engagement, the best of the fight devolving on the artillery and cavalry.

The entire portions of Col. Heintzleman's command, which it is understood was to flank the enemy on the south of Manassas Junction at Brentsville, has been removed to the vicinity of Centreville, and this portion of the country is crowded with our troops. The publicity of more definite information regarding their strength and their numbers would be injurious to the service.

A deserter from the rebels, who arrived here this evening, states that our fire on the 18th created great havoc among the enemy, and but for the fact that they were rallied continually by Gen. Lee they would have retired.

It is understood here that heavy guns have been brought from the Junction to the scene of action by the rebels.

There is some good reason to suppose, from the large number of baggage wagons on the road coming from Strasburg to Manassas, as observed through glasses and a reconnoissance made by Lieut. Tompkins, that Johnston has succeeded in making his retreat good from Winchester, and is on his way to the Junction to join the army at the latter place. At all events, such is the opinion in military circles here. Although this will largely increase the Confederate army, it does not in the least deter, but only changes our military operations in that direction, as it hems in the main forces of the enemy between the advances of Gen. McDowell and Patterson's command.

Secretary Cameron to-day, in company with Col. Scott, of the military railroad, made a visit to Centreville, and reviewed several brigades. He returned to Washington this evening.

LATER—20th, 6 P. M.—The whole division has just commenced to advance, leaving Bull Run batteries to the left. Their destination is supposed to be a point on Manassas road above the Junction, thus cutting off communication and supplies from Johnston, who is now believed to be marching upon Manassas Junction.

CENTREVILLE, July 21.—We have successfully outflanked the enemy at half-past two o'clock this morning.

The various regiments about Centreville were formed for marching at three o'clock in the morning, in the direction of Perryville, leaving Bull Run to the left.

6 O'CLOCK A. M.—The first gun was fired by the 30-pounder rifled cannon sent ahead to batter the masked batteries that might be encountered on the way. There was no reply from the enemy, and the advance moved on to Gen. McDowell's headquarters, three miles beyond Centreville.

The greater part of the army moved to the right to avoid a bridge some distance beyond, said to have been undermined. They will pass over on pontoons prepared by Capt. Alexander of the engineer corps, and who has inspected the country minutely on a previous reconnoissance, and to whom, in a great measure, the plan of the campaign is due.

A general battle is expected to-day or to-morrow, and which will probably decide the fate of the whole campaign. If Johnson has not formed a junction with Beauregard he will be entirely cut off by this maneuver, thrown back upon the mountains, his army, utterly demoralized, will probably fall into the hands of McClellan, who is advancing beyond the Blue Ridge. If he has formed a junction with Beauregard, it opens our communication with Patterson's column, and thus reinforced the Federal army can crush out opposition.

If we are driven back the enemy can retreat upon Centreville and keep open communication with Washington. If Beauregard remains where he is his communication in the rear is endangered, and Manassas being situated in the apex of the triangle formed by the railroads, a movement in his rear would destroy his communication with Richmond.

The only danger the Federal troops run by the flank march would be a sudden advance of Beauregard upon Centreville, interposing communications and cutting off our supplies, and placing him in an exhausted Potomac. [illegible] the Federal troops and the

The 69th New York regiment [illegible] position in advance. The members of this regiment have agreed unanimously to serve, although their time is now out. All the New York regiments will follow their example.

For five hours one steady column of troops passed through Centreville. The *morale* of the soldiers is excellent. All are anxious for a battle, and when informed of the purpose to advance, the enthusiasm was beyond all description.

It is supposed Beauregard's forces are larger than ours. A battle is imminent at any moment. It may not take place till to-morrow night.

The telegraphic wires are rapidly following the army, and offices were opened this morning at Fairfax Court House, with Messrs. Buell and Burton as army operators.

The orders to move yesterday evening at six o'clock were countermanded till early this morning. Our troops meantime were cutting a road through the woods in order to flank the enemy's batteries.

The Secretary of War has received a dispatch saying that fighting was renewed at Bull Run. Our troops engaged the enemy with a large force and silenced their batteries and drove the Secessionists to the Junction.

The city is wild with joy.

Firing was heard in this city to-day from the direction of Bulls Run, from 11 till 3 o'clock—then a cessation till near 5, and at 7 this evening the vibration of cannon was still audible.

A gentleman arrived to-night says at 3 o'clock P. M. the 2d and 3d New Jersey Regiments were ordered to march forward from Vienna, sending their baggage to Camp Trenton. Other troops were hurrying forward to the scene of hostilities, and there is much military excitement and bustle in the direction of all the camps.

CENTERVILLE, July 21, 4 P. M.—Gen. McDowell has ordered the reserve, now here, under Col. Miles, to advance to the bridge over Bull Run, on the Nawenton Road, having driven the enemy before him. Col. Miles is now about three or four miles from here, directing operations near Blackburn Ford.

THE BATTLE OF MANASSAS.—From the Richmond Examiner we learn that our cavalry at Manassas numbered fifteen hundred, and that all were engaged in pursuit of the retreating enemy.

From the same paper we take the subjoined extract:

The armies under Patterson and Johnston both arrived on the field in time to take part in this general action. Patterson's column had marched from Martinsburg to the neighborhood of Winchester, and pretended to offer battle; but decamped in the night, recrossed the Potomac, and made its way to the scene. Johnston learned his retreat next morning, and marched twenty regiments directly to Manassas. The enemy were also reinforced by ten thousand new troops the evening before the battle, and brought out fifty additional pieces of artillery from Washington, among which were two Dahlgren guns of a large size.

REPUBLICANS STILL FISHING FOR OFFICE.—An amusing instance, as undeniable as funny, is as patent here as the Patent Office itself. An Illinois Republican was sent for by a Republican member of Congress to come on to Washington to get an office in the Post Office Department in this city. He came, and after innumerable pros and cons, a meeting was at last effected between the Congressman, the expectant to office, and the Postmaster General. The out-of-office man received a line from the head official to a subordinate to examine the applicant touching his competency, who, among other arithmetical questions, gave him the following: Find the interest of $637 28 for 17 months, 19 days, at 8 per cent. The question was a puzzler—he figured and he sweat—he perspired and he figured—but the correct amount of interest he could not get. The office is not yet obtained, but he is fishing for another one less abstruse, which, if he gets, I will with pleasure inform you. This is a true relation, and, if needs be, more full particulars could be given. [Washington letter.

The Governor of Virginia has amended his proclamation, calling out the militia, by requiring but ten per cent. of the white population of the entire State, and exempting from the call those localities which may have already sent forward that quota as volunteers.

Extract of a letter dated one hundred and sixty miles southwest from Chicago, Illinois: "Everything looks as blue as a whetstone out here, and a man who should be caught paying a note would be an object of public curiosity. The market price of corn is ten cents a bushel. Only think, a dinner at a hotel costs five bushels good yellow corn."

CITY INTELLIGENCE.

INCENDIARISM.—A fine prospect for a conflagration and very probable loss of life, presented itself at the drug store of Dr. Wood, 150 Tchoupitoulas street, last night. The fire department was summoned at about 11 o'clock, on account of a dense smoke which was seen issuing from the drug store, under the Western Veranda Hotel. Upon breaking open the doors, it was discovered that some fiend had placed a lot of kindling pine, paper, baskets saturated with turpentine, and other combustibles, in a corner in the back part of the store, and had set fire to the pile. Immediately over this pile was the stairway, which led up into the upper stories of the building, and forming the only means by which those who occupy the upper part could escape. Had the discovery of the fire been delayed five minutes longer, there is little doubt that the conflagration would have been attended with considerable loss of life. It is a mystery how the incendiary could have succeeded in placing the fire there, as the only two doors which lead into that portion of the building were locked, and Dr. Wood had, as usual, closed the store at 6 o'clock, P. M., and had gone home. We hope Capt. Jack Adams, and his associate, Capt. Younnes, may succeed in ferreting out the fiend who planned this frightful scheme.

JOHN STACKER BROOKS.—We sincerely regret to learn that young Brooks, a member of the Crescent Rifles, Capt. Jett's company, was killed in the battle at Manassas, last Sunday. He was a young man of great promise, a model soldier, and the idol of his parents. His father and mother had indulged in the brightest hopes of his future; and his employer, who patriotically claimed the privilege of equipping him for the war and furnishing him with every comfort which money could purchase, loved him as his own son. He was in his eighteenth year; the son of Capt. M. D. F. Brooks, of the Brooks House, and his death will be deeply mourned by his parents, brothers and sisters.

Letters received from Virginia, which can be had by applying at this office:

Miss Josephine Bayol,	Miss Calice Badin,	Mrs. Daniel Dorley,
Miss Caroline Cariz,	Mrs. E. W. Israel,	Mrs. C. F. Windle,
Mrs. Mary J. Ward,	N. B. Baker,	John Breen,
John Brogniens,	J. W. Carroll,	J. B. Duran,
Isaac Francis,	Michael Gernon,	Louis Jos. Guerin,
Jacob Groveson,	N. Messenger,	Mr. Joseph Queyron,
Capt. R. N. Smith,	Joseph Thompson.	

MORE TROOPS.—The Pointe Coupee Volunteers arrived last night, on the steamer Laurel Hill, consisting of 66 men, fully armed and equipped. They are commanded by Willie Barrow, Captain; T. J. Bird, 1st Lieutenant; C. D. Lancaster, 2d Lieutenant; C. D. Favrot, 2d Jr. Lieutenant.

POSTPONED.—In consequence of the very short notice given of the mass meeting to have been held in Lafayette Square this afternoon, the matter has been postponed. Due notice will be given of the time when it will take place.

POSTPONED.—Mr. Thos. L. Mills' departure for Yorktown has been postponed to Friday morning. Mr. Mills will take charge of any letters for our friends in Yorktown. Letters should be left at the City Hotel before 7 o'clock to-morrow morning.

STEALING A MUSKET.—Peter Kelley is charged by Robert Teller, all in the Fourth District, with stealing a musket. He must have wanted to shoot something.

LIST OF LETTERS

Remaining in the Post Office at New Orleans July 26, 1861.

Ladies' List.

A		
Abbott H miss	Allman E A mrs	Anderson A mrs
Appalona E mrs	Anderson E S mrs	Atkinson A E mrs
B		
Blake M mrs	Baily M A Bridget	Brady E mrs
Balmer A mrs	Branch M mrs	Barrow G M mrs
Barrett R mrs	Barton E miss	Beck Theresia
Beard E L C mrs	Benson C mrs	Berlia A mrs
Bremernan C mrs	Betterly M mrs	Bryan Maria miss
Birch J miss	Brinkman Widow	Britton F mrs
Brown S miss	Bowers A miss	Boyne M A mrs
Burbank J mrs	Burke M miss	
C		
Clarke A miss	Clarke M A miss	Caldwell G H mrs
Calvert W H Dr mrs	Cammack H mrs	Carroll M A miss
Carrick E mrs	Carroll Catherine	Cary A M mrs
Castright M J miss	Carey mrs	Crayon W mrs
Cavanagh Mary	Cheal L mrs	Cleary mrs
Cohen R miss	Coffer M A mrs	Coffee J mrs
Conen Barbara miss	Comstock J H widow	Conners R miss
Connall M mrs	Coleman A E mrs	Conwell A H mrs
Connor M mrs	Commins M mrs	Cooper S S miss
Corcoran C mrs	Copeland M A miss	Cox M J mrs
Cox N miss	Coach Rebecca	Culligan M L miss
Curlet mrs	Curry M A mrs	
D		
Dantel C mrs	Danson J A mrs	Davis C J miss
Davis F mrs	Davis Ann mrs	Davidson C
Davis M S mrs	Dever R mrs	Dewar E A mrs
Driver A mrs	Dixon S J mrs	Dickins C miss
Diber Hosan miss	Donlan M A mrs	Doyl Bridget mrs
Dawson M A mrs	Doherty E miss	Donlon mrs
Dunn M mrs	Dumont E miss	Du Shane A E mrs
E		
Edwards M E mrs	Elsbury E miss	Elliott J miss
Elliott E miss	Ewing M A mrs	Evins Maria
F		
Farley M miss	Fairfax H mrs	Francis C miss
Flanders F mis	Fassmann D mrs	Fay M miss
Fath M mrs	Feeny Mary	Freborgh L M mrs
Fletcher L A miss	Fentress E G miss	Firney A miss
Finnegan B mrs	Friedrich G J mrs	Fitzhenry M miss
Foley E miss	Ford L miss	Forstall mrs
Fortier M A mrs	Fox A mrs	Fuller C mrs
Fuller E mrs		
G		
Graham H M miss	Grace T mrs	Gallagher O
Grady Mary	Gray F miss	Graves A miss
Gray F miss	Green A mrs	Gillespie J mrs
Ginn A mrs	Glidden M E miss	Gibson T mrs
Griffin J miss	Good S miss	Golway J miss
Gordon S miss	Gorraly C mrs	Groos E mrs
Grogen H miss	Gillespie J miss	
H		
Hall J H mrs	Hall E miss	Hall A miss
Hammond E	Hanlon M mrs	Hastigan M mrs
Hastnett M mrs	Harris R miss	Heard A E miss
Healy C miss	Hemp S miss	Henson E mrs
Hickey Catherine	Hogan J mrs	Holt M E miss
Hoitzman E miss	Hopkins Eliza	Howell A mrs
Hoskins J M miss	Harper C J mrs	Hoyle dr mrs
Huddleston M mrs	Hughes A mrs	Hull S miss
Hudson A mrs	Hughes E A mrs	
J		
Jacobs E mrs	Jones L B miss	Jones mrs or Cath Collins
Jordan M E mrs	Joubert J J miss	
Jewell J S		
K		
Kane R miss	Kavanagh C miss	Krause A miss
Krail M A mrs	Kean S A mrs	Kelly E mrs
Kerley Catherine	Kennerly S A mrs	Kibbe A miss
Kilpatrick M mrs	Kuhn K mrs	
L		
Larker L A mrs	Lindin M miss	Lewis J miss
Lanimore J Mrs	Lyttle L miss	Louis Johanna
Lathrop E mrs	Lyons M J mrs	Leonard E mrs
Latham A miss	Lockett Clara	Leo M miss
Laughlin M mrs	Logan H M mrs	Levy F mrs
Lonergan Mrs	Love E W miss	Lynch M Frs
Leake I miss	Lloyd J A mrs	Lydon J mrs
Leavell L V	Lukeley Mrs	Lee J L miss
Leaf A P mrs		
M		
Moready Mrs	Morrisey B mrs	Meyers M miss
Madden C mrs	Moore Bernard mrs	Meyers L miss
Maddux L T mrs	Morrison L A miss	Miltrons M J miss
Macriade Miss	Morrison Catherine	Miller M mrs
Mansfield Morgant	Morris E mrs	Misle M mrs
Marsh S mrs	Murphy K miss	Mitchell J miss
Morton E H mrs	Murphy S miss	Monahan E miss
Martin Anne	Murphy M miss	Montgomery B H mrs
Markey Mrs	Murphy Bridget	Moses H miss
Mathews E mrs	Murphy Patrick mrs	Morse E A miss
Meagher M miss	Murdock A A	Morris E mrs
Mealia E mrs		
Macs		
McCrohan Catherine	McCabe R miss	McKeef mrs
McCaherry R mrs	McDonnell T mrs	McKennon E mrs
McCan M miss	McDonald K miss	McManus M J miss
McClelland C E mrs	McEnerny Sarah	McMullen miss
McClelland E mrs	McGarry Ann	McMullen Mary miss
McCoy H J mrs		
N		
Nelson J mrs	Noblet madame	Norman E J miss
Newcomb J G mrs	Norman L miss	Nugent Bridget
Nolen A mrs		
O		
O'Brien C J miss	Oliver M J miss	Orr H mrs
O'Brien Honora	O'Neil M miss	O'Rourke miss
O'Brien A miss	O'Neil E O miss	O'Sullivan Mary
O'Keefe H miss		
P		
Palmatory O mrs	Preston mrs	Plough H miss
Parmalee A N mrs	Peterson E miss	Poole F E miss
Parton C miss	Preston M miss	Pouliot C mrs
Pierce Sarah H	Phillips C miss	Powell L K mrs
Pierson M J miss	Prise M miss	Posey Scotty miss
Pierce W J mrs	Pocock mrs	Power Bridget
Pettis M miss	Pohlman L mrs	
Q		
Quirk A mrs	Quirk S E mrs	Quill M miss
Quinn M miss		
R		
Randolph T A mrs	Ripley S G mrs	Roberts E miss
Reid A miss	Ritchie M P mrs	Roscoe C J miss
Reid M mrs	Ridgely G mrs	Rogers M T mrs
Reiser P miss	Rhodes mrs	Rowan Bridget
Ryder E mrs	Rhodes A M T mrs	
S		
Sladden L miss	Stillman L O mrs	Shepard A B miss
Sprague La miss	Smith M R mrs	Shepard L A miss
Stannmyre N mrs	Smith C miss	Sexton Margaret
Sparks S miss	Simmonds A J mrs	Stewart M B miss
Shaw M A mrs	Singlin Kate mrs	Silvy E M mrs
Savage M miss	Spence T mrs	Sterry M A miss
Sweeney M miss	Stewart M A miss	Selden T mrs
Sweam A mrs	Seymour M J mrs	Spronle A A miss
Sullivan miss 242 Prytania street	Summers J miss	Sutcliff R mrs
T		
Taylor M S mrs	Typhine L mrs	Thomas J miss
Taylor John mrs	Tilman H miss	Thomsen L mrs
Tyrell H miss	Thorp E J mrs	Tumbelly mrs
V		
Von Phil H mrs		
W		
Welch E mrs	Webster J mrs	Wilson R miss
Ward Maria	Wright W H mrs	Wingard M J mrs
Warfield P S mrs	Wilson mrs	White M mrs
Washington U miss	Williams Annette	White W H mrs
Wheatly mrs	Williams L miss	Wikoff E
Wolf M mrs	Woods M E mrs	
Initials.		
Mellie W miss		

Gentlemen's List.

A		
Adams J	Allen Jos	Anderson L
Adams Z	Addison Jos	Armour Chas
Alas Joseph	Addison Paul	Arnot W
Adams H C	Adrian J	Armor James
Abram Morris	Aycock J	
B		
Bancroft P B	Britten C	Beck M
Barnes T G	Briste J	Berry J G
Baxter Jerry	Breckel M	Berry J S
Balfour L	Buckner Jos	Berry L S
Blackman J W	Buckner J	Browden D
Blackman J	Briggs C F	Baylor W
Baker Nicholas	Brierly Tho R	Bethea J P
Baker M	Balsai A	Beck C M
Baker Henry	Black C B	Buttler W
Baker W	Black J	Bruning H
Bartells H L	Black M	Buchanan W
Barrow A D	Balor Jas	Buckwood J H
Barrow W	Barroun J B	Burritt J J
Barrett Joe	Brown A M	Burke Pat
Barrett J	Brown W	Burke R A
Barden H F	Brown M	Burke M
Barrett T	Brook Jno capt	Burke Jas
Bennett J P	Brothers Jas	Burke J
Bennett A	Brackett G	Burns J dr
Bennett J	Broker F	Burns W
Bein H H	Bowers G P	Burns P W
C		
Cain Mike	Cannon J W capt	Caley Jas
Cannell Jno	Cassady F A	Campbell, Ellis & co
Cassin H	Casey H F W	Carrett J N
Carey P C	Carter R D	Clair H
Carpenter M S	Carter D C	Chambers W A
Caroll Thos	Chamberlain Jas	Clark Andrew
Clark Thos	Crawford W D	Cheatham J A
Clark A H	Crawford R H	Cleal G E
Crane W R	Crane A dr	Crevey W J
Crenflow H	Christman mr	Coyne Jno
Cheeny L C	Cabren Jacob & co	Cofield J
Clifford J J	Cocks J G	Cook J B
Cronen Denis	Cross F C	Colby J M
Corbia E	Collins J K	Connor M
Crowley E	Collins J A	Conway Pete
Cunningham M		
D		
Darrell J L	Davis rev	Dean J
Day W C	Deffenbrook T	Drews W
Davis J H	Downs S T	Dennison D A
Dillon Pete	Doyle C	Dunphy M
Ditmay J W	Donohoe J H	Dunn Thos
Dixon G D	Donels P C	Dunbar N H
E		
Evans E D	Evans T J	Evans C F
Erber Henry		
F		
Flash Jno	Franklin Ben	French J
Fagin Pal	Fall J S	Fitzpatrick Jas
Farrow W L	Farrell J	Fitzpatrick H M
Fitzgerald Paul	Fitzsimmons H	Foley J S
Findley T M	Fisher Ceo	Fulton O J
Furman J L		
G		
Gains L	Giffian M	Gerkesker E G
Gavisk M H	Grider Rube	Gentry A M
Gaisser G	Gooch H B	Green A A
Gallagher Wm	Gormly F	Greenwood A G
Gardner F col	Gust H L	Green Elijah
Grant Jno	Gunmer Jo	Gillick J J
H		
Harth E M R	Harding Jno	Hodgkiss B B
Hasting Thos	Hart J J	Houghton G P
Halick G H	Hart A W	Hogg Thos
Hammond F G	Harris R M	Holmes J H
Hamlett C	Hays W T	Hoey Jno
Hamilton Alex	Hamilton T J	Huser Jacob
Hanson A	Heard D M	Hunter Jno
Hart C M	Heath Jno	Huyter J W
Hart W A	Henrick R	Huston R C
Hardesty E	Higham Jas	Humphrey B D
Hartz Chas	Hinegan Ed	
I		
Irwin J R	Ivy Jacob	
J		
Janter Jno lieut	Johnson Ruben	Jewell J W
Jackson B F	Johnson A H	Jerrille R
Jackson Jas	Jones J C K	Job Herman
James mr	Jones J C	Jordan Mike
Jerrison J	Jones Jas S	Jorden A H
K		
Kane Mike	Kelly Alex	Kinly Jno
Kearr L	Kirby C	King V
Keenan J G		
L		
Langridge Jno	Lewis A J	Langhoff C W
Lary Chas	Lewis T R	Lanier C S
Law Jno	Lee T B	Lenard Henry
Laughlin A S	Loret F C	Lenke Jas
M		
May O G	Mason W J	Martin Jno
Mestar Ed	Mason H W	Morris R J
Merkel A C	Mahar J M C	Morton Henry
Melat Jos	Malard S L	Moulte Jno
Meyer A	Mannery F C	Mulligan M W
Miles W H	Mackay Thos	Mulligan H
Mufelin C	Mater C	Murphy C A
Mullard Geo	Man S C	Murphy Andrew
Munes M	Martin Jno	Murphy F T
Miller Geo M	Martin Wm	Murphy Jno
Mitchell W H & B A	May Jno H	Murry Sol
Maniac J C	Moore Jno J	Murry E
Moore S E & co		Murry W C
Macs		
McBride Jno	McKinney M B	McDermott A
McCarty Alex	McManus L	McGuire Jno
McCauly F	McLeny Saml	McGuinness J K
McDannold T A	McMaster M	McGonaz J
McFarland J T	McPeake Saml	McHalle, Pike & co
McFenney H		McRee W J dr
N		
Nelson Thos F	Norton Jas	Norsis J
Noble R H		
O		
Olente D B	O'Connor Jas	Otto H
O'Donnell H		
P		
Pauley rev J A	Patterson L A	Patton A A
Patton Jothan	Parham Jno M	Parker Jacob
Parker Abram	Parsons John	Penny Chas T
Petitt Chas	Phelps E G B	Percer Francis
Perkins A S	Pierson H	Pierson Alfred H
Pindell Wm H	Phifer Chas	Philips Ed col
Power K H	Power Louis	Power James
Poindexter J B	Postell P S dr	Porter P L
Paul James	Plumer T W	
Q		
Quant Johann		
R		
Rappold John	Regan Tim	Reed Thos
Reed Mr	Rosch E C	Rose Jeff
Rosenthal U J	Roter F K & co	Roberts J B
Rogers W N	Rhoades Z	Russell M
Russell Geo H	Ryder capt	Roberts Edgar
S		
Sawer J P	Saunders J M	Sargean Patsy
Sauer Jacob	Salleau & co	Scanlen Wm
Schacton Norbert	Shamburger Thos	Shaw John
Shaw P Henry	Slaughter E	Strangham John
Stansbury W A	Stafford Henry	Starkes Wm
Seaver Geo L	Seers Henry	Seavers A
Seppelt Joseph	Sheahan Pat	Sheard Henry
Sneed John T	Stewart Geo H	Steubick B C
Stevens M O	Stevens G F D cap.	Street Saml A
Stemhart B	Singleton Joseph	Sibley John T
Sibley H H brig	Shilling Benedict	Shields mr rev
Spitts mr	Stickney L D	Smith Thos
Smith W P	Smith Chas T	Smith Henry H
Scott Saml R	Scott Robt	Scott John
Shroud Adam	Sloan Jas A	Stott Allen T
Scruggs Dan E	Sturges Theadore	Sylvester & Son
T		
Talbot W H	Tardy H H	Tharp James
Trainor John	Tegder B H	Terrell M E
Thiberge Hy R	Todd T P col	Todd T G
Thomas H J	Thomas F A	Tom James
Thomassy R	Thompson Richd	Trowbridge N
Turner J B	Tulane Paul	Thole Henry
U		
Uzee Charles		
V		
Venn Jas	Vreller J	Van Houten G D
W		
Wallace J C	Warne Ed	Warner Paul
Warner S J	Warner Wm	Warner John W
Well Geo	West Wm	Wiggins J C
Wingate E H	Wicks Edw	Wickliffe Nat
Willingham R M	Wild Andrew	Wilder M
Whitman Geo	Whittaker Wm	Wright Edw
Wright Jos W	White James	Williams Jos
Williams Joe	Williamson Jas	Williams A C
Y		
Youngblood W C	Yodd J H	Yantis R H

Initials

Keeper Parish Prison....To Police Jailer....Clerk Anna Perre ....Superintendent Workhouse....Pastor First Baptist Church.... Mrs P H A.

New Orleans, July 26, 1861.

J. L. RIDDELL, P. M.

Gazette and Sentinel.

NEW SERIES--VOL. 4, NO. 28. PLAQUEMINE, PARISH OF IBERVILLE, LA., JULY 27, 1861. OLD SERIES--VOL. 14 NO. 39.

PROFESSIONAL CARDS.

W. I. HAMILTON,
ATTORNEY AT LAW,

HAVING located at Plaquemine will devote his entire attention to the practice of his Profession in the Parishes of

Iberville, East and West Baton Rouge.

He respectfully solicits the patronage of his old friends and the public generally, who can always find him at his Office on **Main Street**, near the Court House, between the hours of 9 A. M. and 5 P. M., unless otherwise professionally engaged.

Plaquemine, La. oc16mh23.

DAVID N. BARROW, Plaquemine, Iberville, La.	R. W. POPE, West Baton Rouge, Baton Rouge P. O., La

Barrow & Pope,
Attorneys and Counsellors at Law,

WILL practice their profession in the parishes of West and East Baton Rouge, Iberville, Point Coupee and West Feliciana; the Supreme Court of Louisiana, and the United States District and Circuit Courts at New Orleans. my1-1y

J. H. RILLS,
Attorney at Law and Justice of the Peace,

☞Office on Main street. aug6

GEORGE L. HILL,
Attorney at Law,

Tyler, Smith County, Texas,

WILL practice law and collect claims in the counties of Harrison, Pasola, Rusk, Smith, Wood, Upshur, Cass, and Marion, and in the Federal and Supreme Courts at Tyler. my26

BENJ. N. DEBLIEUX,
Attorney at Law,

Plaquemine, Iberville Parish, Louisiana,

WILL devote his whole attention to the practice of their profession in all the Courts of the Sixth Judicial District. je23

Joseph Hotard,
Attorney and Counsellor at Law,

(*Office same as Zenon Labauve, Esq.,*)

jy16] *PLAQUEMINE, LA.*

E. GOURRIER,
Surveyor & Civil Engineer,

Baton Rouge, La.

WILL attend to calls in the Parish of Iberville, for surveying lands, mapping, Plantations levelling, measuring canals and levees, draughting architectural designs, &c. nov24

G. M. WILHOIT,
Cotton and Sugar Factor and Commission

MERCHANT,

No. 60 Carondelet St., New Orleans.

Prompt attention given to all consignments. may4

J. M. SHANKS.	JOHN KNEAL.

SHANKS & KNEAL,
HOUSE PAINTERS, GLAZIERS —AND— *PAPER HANGERS,*

sept1 PLAQUEMINE, LA

Hanenkamp & Hynes,
Wholesale Grocers and Commission Merchants,

ST. LOUIS, Mo.

☞Particular attention given to consignments of Sugar and Molasses, and to filling orders for Western Produce. jan6'58-tf

Madam Jumel's SCHOOL.

Mrs. P. JUMEL hereby informs her friends and the public in general, that she has opened a **School for Young Ladies** at her residence on Plaquemine street.

The Musical Department is under the charge of **Mrs. Angelina Jumel.**

The Classes will be taught by the Principal, aided by competent teachers.

The course of studies will be complete in the English and French languages, and other branches of Education.

Terms of Boarders.

Board per Month.	$15 00
Half Boarders,	6 00
Washing,	3 00
Tuition—French and English—	4 00
Music—Instrumental and Vocal,	7 00

At the request of parents, Embroidery, and other Fancy Needle Work, will be taught by **Mrs. P. Jumel.**

☞For further particulars apply to the Principal, on the premises. mh16-ap11

Segar and Tobacco Store.

THE undersigned respectfully informs his friends and the public generally of Iberville that he has opened a Store in Plaquemine, adjoining Leopold Kohn's Fancy Dry Goods Store, for the **Manufacture and Sale of Segars,** and also to keep constantly on hand the best brands of

IMPORTED SEGARS.

He will also keep the best quality of *CHEWING AND SMOKING TOBACCO*

By always keeping on hand an excellent stock of the above, he hopes to receive a liberal share of public patronage.

aug26 GUSTAVE NEDIT.

New Butchery.

The undersigned respectfully informs the public that he has purchased the old and well known Butchery of F. Smith, and that he intends to keep his stall well supplied with the best of Beef, Mutton, Pork, &c. By a strict attention to his business in the above respect, he hopes to have a share of public patronage, and particularly the patronage of Mr. Smith's old customers.

P. S. The carts will run as usual down the Coast and to the Park,

dec25-1y BERTRAND BE[illegible]RIS.

FOR SALE.

A fine Residence, situated in about the centre of this town. For further particulars apply at this office. feb23

MISCELLANEOUS.

GABRIEL BROWN'S
DRY GOODS AND *CLOTHING STORE.*

HE is again on hand with the first and finest stock of

DRY GOODS.

April 11th, 1861.

Goods for Ladies' Dresses, New and Splendid Jewelry.

AN EXTENSIVE STOCK OF

Ready Made Clothing,

AND ARTICLES OF

Gentlemen's Wardrobe,

in all their variety,

And a splendid supply of

FANCY GOODS GENERALLY,

A description of which is impossible in the limits of this advertisement. Call an examine is all I desire—buying is certain to result.

☞Dry and Fancy Goods Department in room nearest the corner.

☞Ladies are particularly requested to give us a call that we may show them the handsomest and cheapest goods they have yet seen.

GABRIEL BROWN,

ap13 Double Store, Main near Bank st.

NEW GROCERY STORE.
WHOLESALE & RETAIL!

CHAS. N. ROTH & CO.,

TAKE this method of informing their friends and the public generally of the Parish of Iberville, that they have just opened and established a

Wholesale & Retail PRODUCE & GROCERY STORE

In the Double Brick Store, in Desoboy's Row, recently occupied by J. McWilliams & Co., on the corner of Main and Plaquemine streets.

Their stock comprises a complete list, as well as it could be made at the start, of all articles for

Family & Plantation Use,

usually found in a Grocery store, besides a large and splendid assortment of

FANCY GROCERIES.

At a more convenient time, a list of the leading articles in their Establishment, such as families generally require, will be given.

The public may rely upon it, that these articles are all fresh and perfect, and will be put at the lowest possible figure to our customers. ap13

FRANK HIPPLER,
Boot and Shoe Maker,

Take this occasion to thank his patrons for their past patronage, and to inform them that he is at present located on Main street, first house above Ross & Gallagher's store, in the house recently occupied by Beihler Bros., Tailors, where customers will find that he will continue his work with the same punctuality, perfection and dispatch that has hitherto characterized it. He guarantees that no work can surpass his in point of style, finish, fit and durability. oct27

KETTLE SETTING.
A Labor of Years Reduced to a Few Days.

HAVING been induced by frequent solicitation, to make public the science of Kettle Setting that I practice, I hereby give notice to all persons desiring to acquire a knowledge of the art, that I will give them instructions for the Setting of Kettles, for either wood or coal, on application to me.

My system is based upon principles, the plausibility and correctness of which admit of no contradiction, which are quickly and fully comprehended, and therefore not liable to be easily forgotten.

I have models for five different constructions of Kettles, and designs by which instruction is made easy, and the art soon acquired. Copies of designs or drawings are given to those whom I instruct. All those to whom I teach my system, are also assisted by my services, if required.

Instructions are only given to those who have been three or four years at the business of Kettle Setting, and are good workmen.

For further particulars, inquire, by letter or otherwise, of the undersigned.

JOHN TOWNSEND.

Plaquemine, (Parish of Iberville,) La., Feb. 25, 1860.

Refer to—Dr. C. Clement, Iberville.
Louis Desobry, Sr., "
Gervais & Roman Schlatre, "
John Schlatre, "
Sylvar Marionneaux, "
Edward J. Gay, "
Jas. C. Woods, West Baton Rouge.
Dan. H. Hickey, do
Thompson J. Bird, East Baton Rouge.

F. LAGLEIZE,
Fancy Baker and Confectioner,

RESPECTFULLY informs families and others of Plaquemine and Iberville, that he is at all times prepared to furnish parties with *Cake and Confectionery* in every style, and manufactured in a manner not surpassed anywhere. He will furnish any thing that may be required in his line at the shortest notice, and on the most reasonable terms.—Bakery at the corner of Bank and Greaud ets. my12

ICE! ICE!

WE are happy to inform our friends and patrons and the public generally, that the schooner "Argus Eye," containing our cargo of Ice has arrived, and our

ICE ESTABLISHMENT

is now ready to meet orders. The article is of the purest and best description, and will be sold and delivered to our customers as usual. Our Ice Depot is now fitted up in a style second to no similar establishment in the State.

VESSIER & DUBUCLET.

feb23

Barber Shop,

NICOLAS BIEHLER respectfully informs his friends and the public that he still continues at his old stand on Main street, adjoining his brothers' Tailor shop and Wine Store, where he still pursues SHAVING and HAIR CUTTING, as also CUPPING when called upon. s8

Plaquemine Saw Mill.

THIS popular Mill is now in the zenith of its prosperity, and prepared to fill orders for Lumber of every description. So bring your bills if you want them filled out with good sound Lumber, at the usual prices,

mh10 HEBERT & MAYOT.

MISCELLANEOUS.

R. A. KEARNY,
Apothecary, Chemist and Druggist,

Corner Main and Bank streets,

PLAQUEMINE, La.,

Begs leave to call the attention of his friends and the public in general to his

Newly Selected Stock

—OF—

Drugs, Medicines, and Chemicals,

which he guarantees *pure*.

Physicians' prescriptions will receive particular attention at all hours of the day or night.

The Patronage of the public is respectfully solicited.

Plaquemine, July 10, 1860.

CLARET—Lafitte, Levillo, Château Margaux, &c., for sale by

jy14 R. A. KEARNY.

OLD RYE WHISKEY—Old Jamaica Rum, Anisette, Fine Cordials, &c., for sale by [jy14] R. A. KEARNY.

CIGARS—For those requiring a fine Cigar, I can offer inducements seldom met with, for sale by

jy14 R. A. KEARNY.

GARDEN SEEDS—New Crop—every Variety—Turnip, Red Top, and Flat Dutch, for sale by

jy14 R. A. KEARNY.

CUTLERY—A new and beautiful assortment of Pen Knives just received and ale low by R. A. KEARNY

PAINTS, Oils, Varnishes, Brushes, Window Glass, Putty, &c., for sale by

jy14 R. A. KEARNY.

TOBACCO—Smoking and Chewing, several qualities, for sale by

jy14 R. A. KEARNY.

NEW ORLEANS
—AND—

Bayou Sara Mail Line Company.

Summer Arrangement.

FOR Bayou Sara and the Coast, the new low-pressure passenger packet

J. A. Cotten,—Capt. V. B. Beranco,

Leaves New Orleans
Every Sunday morning at 9 o'clock,
" Wednesday " 9 "
" Friday " 9 "

Returning—leaves Bayou Sara every Monday, Thursday and Friday, at 8 a. m.

For Fort Adams, Tunica, Morganza, Bayou Sara and the Coast,

The fine Passenger Packet

ACADIA..........Capt. E. F. GROSS.

Leaves New Orleans every Monday and Thursday Evening, at 5 o'clock, extending her trips on Thursday as far up as Fort Adams. my5

Carriage and Harness Manufactory
AND

Carriage Trimming Establishment.

GUSTAVE RINGWALD,
Successor to CHARLES VEIT & Co., at the old stand of A. W. SPOTT.

Respectfully informs the people of Iberville and West Baton Rouge that having purchased out the interest of his partner, he intends carrying on the same line of business, such as the manufacture of all kinds of

Saddles and Harness

And the Trimming and Painting of Carriages and Buggies.

And everything kept in a similar establishment N. B.—No Repairing done on *CREDIT.*

Plaquemine, Nov. 12th, 1859. 1y

HAASE BROTHERS'
Ladies Dress Goods

AND

Plantation Goods

they particularly call attention to, as also their extensive stock of

Ready Made Clothing.

They will not pretend to give a list of their stock in the compass of an advertisement, but request all who are in want of

CLOTH GOODS.

to give them a call, as they feel fully satisfied that purchasers will not go away from their store dissatisfied. [oc23] HAASE BROS.

MATTHEW PARK.	MATTHEW M'CLINTOCK.

PARK & McCLINTOCK,
—DEALERS IN—

Foreign and American Marble, Mantels, Monuments, Statuary, *Tombs, Headstones, &c.,*

S. W. Corner of Washington Avenue and 5th st., and 95 Washington Avenue, between 4th and 5th streets,

je2 ST. LOUIS, MO.

Refer to—Zenon Labauve, Plaquemine,
Michel Hebert, Iberville,
Roth, Deblieux & Co., do.
Capt. Trinidad, West Baton Rouge.

SOUTHERN FIRE-PROOF ROOFING.

Patented by R. Glennon, March 23d, 1858.

THE Cheapest and most durable **Roofing** in use. Sent to any part of the country with Directions for application.

REFERENCES

Can be seen, and information by letter or in person obtained on application to the office,

No. 57 St. Charles Street, N. O.

For specimens or further particulars. enquire at the Post Office of PHILIP HEELEIN, Esq., Plaquemine, La. mar30

STATIONERY—Letter, Cap and Note Paper; Envelopes, all kinds; Blank Books, a large assortment, for sale by

jy14 R. A. KEARNY.

INSURANCE, &c.

SOUTHERN. MUTUAL INSURANCE COMPANY.

Office of Southern Mutual Insurance Co., of Baton Rouge.

IN CONFORMITY with the requirements of their charter, the SOUTHERN MUTUAL INSURANCE COMPANY publish the following statement:

Amount of premiums received from February 1st, 1860, to Feb'ry 1st, 1861.	$85,236,96
AS FOLLOWS:	
Premiums on Fire Risks........$66,839 20	
" " Marine " 13,710 49	
" " River " 4,687 27	
	$85,236 96
Premiums on unterminated Risks, February 1st, 1860	$49,814 48
	$135,101 44
Less premiums on Risks not terminated	60,220 74
Nett earned premiums for the year ending 1st February, 1861	$74,880 70
Losses paid during the same period: "NO LOSSES UNSETTLED."	
On Fire Risks..........$12,331 75	
" Marine Risks..........1,554 64	
" River Risks..........3,440 17	
	$17,376 56
Expenses during year as above	7,992 83
	$25,369 39
Nett earned Profits for the year ending February 1st, 1861	$49,511 32
The Company have the following Assets:	
Bills receivable, for premiums	$ 55,531 24
Bills receivable, for balance due on Stock Notes	152 964 91
Cash, balance on hand	139,503 61
Balance due by New Iberia Agency	333 50
Balance due by New Orleans Agency	3,375 35
Total assets	$351,709 61

(Signed) WM. S. PIKE, Pres't.

F. E. HEBERT, Sec'y.

Baton Rouge, February 2d, 1861.

STATE OF LOUISIANA, PARISH OF E. BATON ROUGE, Feb. 1, 1861.

Be it remembered, That on this first day of February, 1861, before me the subscriber, a Justice of the Peace in and for the parish aforesaid, personally appeared Wm. S. Pike, President, and F. E. Hebert, Secretary of the Southern Mutual Insurance Company, of Baton Rouge, who being duly sworn according to law do depose and say that the above accounts are just and true, and a correct transcript from the books of said Company.

(Signed) WM. S. PIKE, President.

F. E. HEBERT, Secretary,

Sworn to and subscribed before me, this second day of February, 1861.

[Signed] P. A. WALKER, Justice of the Peace.

(Signed) P. A. WALKER, Justice of the Peace.

NOTICE.

OFFICE SOUTHERN MUTUAL INSURANCE Co., Baton Rouge, Feb. 4th, 1861.

At a meeting of the Board of Directors, held this day, it was *Resolved*, To pay *six per cent* interest on the outstanding Scrip, *eight per cent* to Stockholders on premiums paid by them for the year ending 1st February, 1861, and to declare a dividend of *fifty per cent* on the nett earned premiums of the Company for the year ending 31st January, 1861, for which certificates will be issued on and after the 1st day of March next.

It was further Resolved, To redeem the outstanding Scrip for the year 1858, on presentation at the office of the Company.

☞The Stockholders are hereby notified that an election for ten Directors and fifteen Trustees to serve for the ensuing year, will be held at the office of the Company, on Thursday, the 14th of March, 1861.

mh30 F. E. HEBERT, Sec'y.

ALLEN'S
Improved Stubble Shaver.

A number of the above important article, so useful in facilitating the culture of the sugar cane,—invented by J. ALLEN, and perfected by the undersigned—has been manufactured and is now on hand for sale in New Orleans by GEO. W. SISER, corner of Camp and Poydras, Agent for the sale of the machine in that city.

The undersigned has upwards of seventy certificates from the best planters in Louisiana, who have witnessed the operations of the *Stubble Shaver* in various soils; and there can be no questions of the fact that it meets—and fully meets—all the requirements and desideratums that could be needed or desired for performing cleanly, neatly and perfectly the work for which it was invented to perform, and in which performance it does the labor of at least *fifteen hands with the hoe!* It will also shave from 25 to 50 acres without sharpening. The price asked for them will be found to be surprisingly small considering the price paid for their manufacture.

Planters wanting the *Stubble Shaver* will please address GEO. W. SISER, New Orleans or to

oct 13 A. ST. DIZIER, Plaquemine: Or to J. McWILLIAMS.

NEW BOY'S SCHOOL.

Opposite O. Lauve's, at the residence of the late Mr. Thomas.

THE undersigned having established himself here permanently, for the purpose of Teaching, offers his services to the citizens of Plaquemine and vicinity, for conducting a BOY'S SCHOOL, in the FRENCH and ENGLISH LANGUAGES.

He expects to commence about the 21st of this month. Being determined to devote his energies to the instruction of those under his care, he trusts to receive a liberal share of the patronage of parents and guardians.

ANTHONY DOMINIQUE.

Nouvelle Ecole Anglaise & Française.

LE SOUSSIGNÉ s'étant établi d'une maniere permanente à Plaquemine, respectueusement offre ses services aux citoyens de l'endroit et du voisinage dans les capacités de maître d'ecole enseignant la langue Anglaise, et la langue Française. Le Local est situé vis-a-vis Mr. Oscar Lauve, autrefois la residence de M. Thomas. jan12

NOTICE.

ALL person indebted to the Clerk's Office of this Parish for fees, who will not settle their bills on demand, are hereby notified that writs of fieri facias will issue against them or their curities at once.

je8 M. A. ESTEVAN, *Clerk.*

J. McWILLIAMS & CO.

J. M'WILLIAMS.	CHAS. CLEMENT, JR.

J. M'WILLIAMS & CO.,
PLAQUEMINE, LA.

NEW FALL GOODS.
September 8, 1860.

To the People of Iberville and West Baton Rouge.

WE have now open and ready for exhibition a LARGE AND VARIED ASSORTMENT OF

Fall and Winter Goods,

bought direct from importers and manufacturers. We enumerate a few articles only, among them will be found—

Bleached Cotton Shirtings and Sheetings;

All widths, and some very fine quality; English and French Cottons, best make, fine, soft and undressed; Unbleached Shirtings and Sheetings; Heavy Plain and Twilled Lowels.

Prints.

French, English and American, 6from to 7 ct. per yard—the finest made.

Furniture Prints.

desirable patterns.

Dress Goods.

In this department our stock is large and the assortment varied, consisting of Silks and Poplins, new styles; DeLaines and Cashmere, plain and printed; Black Silks, plain and figured.

Ladies and Misses' Cloaks.

We have in this line a large and varied assortment, precluding all possibility of a description. They were purchased direct from the manufacturers, and are offered at prices varying from $5 to $35.

Ready-Made Clothing.

The largest, best and cheapest stock ever bro't to the parish. Men's suits compose—from $5 50 to $60. Call and see them.

Boys' & Youths' Clothing.

Suits, for Boys from 3 to 20 years of age, ranging in price from $5 to $18.

Shirts and Drawers.

Nearly every size and style made.

Embroideries.

We have in the above a very large and varied assortment, comprising the latest and most fashionable styles. Among them are—
Richly Embroidered Valencienne Setts;
do do Linen and Pique Setts;
Plain Linen Setts and Collars;
Japanese do new styles;
Richly Embroidered L. C. Handkerchiefs;
Plain Hem-stitched do;
Mourning do do—some extra fine
Ladies' Plain do, from 10c to the finest quality
Gentlemen's do, a large assortment.

Carpets and Rugs.

The most complete lot ever brought to this section of the country—some very rich—which can be seen in the third story of our store, and for sale very cheap. Call and see.

Fancy Notion Department

In this we defy competition, both for variety and price. Among them are Fans, some extra rich; Puff and Powder Boxes, extra rich; Ladies' Portmonaies; Work Boxes and Dressing Cases; Writing Desks, assorted sizes.

Hats and Caps.

Men's Hats, from 50 cents to $8 50, new styles; Boys' Hats and Caps, from 25 cents to $2 50.

Ladies' Riding Hats, &c.

Misses' Hats, at about Manufacturers' prices.

☞Expecting to be in our NEW STORE for the early Fall trade, we purchased a large lot of the above, but having no convenient place to keep them, are offering them at a bargain.

Ladies', Misses' and Children's Shoes.

We have a lot of the above made specially for us.

Men's and Boys' Boots and Shoes.

Creole style, and made to order.

Hardware and Cutlery.

In this department we are constantly making additions to our assortment, keeping up with the improvement of the age in every article new and desirable.

Jewelry.

The Best and Richest ever bro't to Iberville.

Among the stock we have ten of the best Stoddard Gold Watches, made to order; 20 setts Pins and Ear Rings; Bracelets, Finger Rings; $3,000 worth of Diamond Rings and Pins, some very rich; Gold Vest and Fob Chains, Thimbles and Buckles.

Brushes and Baskets.

The best lot ever seen in any country store.

Paints and Oils.

The best made in the United States.

Brandies,

Direct from the New York Customhouse, from $3 50 to $14 a gallon. Champagne—15 baskets of the Duke of Montibello.

Groceries.

A complete assortment always on hand.

J. McWILLIAMS & CO.,

sep22 Bank st., Plaquemine, La.

FRANK GLASER,
Boot and Shoemaker.

The business heretofore carried on by B. GLASER, will be conducted in future by FRANK GLASER, at the old stand on Bank st., north of Main street, and he trusts that his attention to business and endeavors to please his customers, and the manner in which his work is done, will merit him the continued patronage of his friends and the public.

my5—m9. FRANK GLASER.

At $10 per Thousand.

I HAVE FOR SALE,

192,000

Fine A No. 1 BRICKS.

jy THEO. BLANCHARD.

CHINA WARE—Vases—a large variety, which I will sell at and below cost.

jy14 R. A. KEARNY

Gazette & Sentinel.
Published every Saturday by W. P. BRADBURN,

EDITOR AND PROPRIETOR.

AS GOOD FOR BEAST AS MAN.—Mr. Jno. B. Robertson, who writes to the Picayune from the Parish of St. Mary—speaking of the disease among cattle known as the Charbon, says;

Charbon, I think, arises from poverty of blood in the animal, and this poverty of blood may occur in every condition of flesh from fat to lean. The disease usually manifests itself by external swellings on the under parts of the animal's body, from the throat to the flanks. These tumors soon become insensible to pain, and mortify, owing to the want of action and vitality in the blood. With this diagnosis of the disease, I directed my search for some blood-nourishing stimulant, and I soon found that good common whisky or brandy was the best; it at once gave increased and stronger action to the heart, and, by restoring a powerful circulation of enriched blood to the diseased parts, soon brought away all traces of the tumors, and effected a perfect cure.

Good whisky should be administered three or four times during the twenty-four hours, say every six hours, for four or five days. For each dose, a pint of whisky and a pint of water put into a quart bottle and drench.

It is essential that a steady stimulation should be kept up by frequent drenching for several days.

The remedy is a simple one—not hard to find, and hence worth a trial.

ONE OF THE HORRORS OF BATTLE.—We learn that on Thursday last, two of the dead bodies of Lincoln's men were found in the woods in the neighborhood of the Bethel battle ground, in a state of decomposition. They were traced out by means of the buzzards hovering over the spot. One of the corpses had in his haversack a quarter of baked shoat. It is supposed they had crawled away from the scene of battle after being wounded, and died on the spot on which they were discovered. From their uniforms it is presumed that they were members of the Zouave regiment.

It is said that all along the route from Bethel to Hampton, a most intolerable stench prevails, and that from the appearance of the buzzards circling round about, there must be numbers of putrifying carcasses in the woods.—*Norfolk Day Book.*

A GOOD NAME.—The name of Jackson seems to be gaining an enviable distinction in the present war. First, James W. Jackson, of Alexandria, Va., slew Col. Ellsworth for interfering with a flag, private property, when he knew his own death would follow. Second, Gov. Jackson, of Missouri, has taken a bold, patriotic stand for the South, against heavy odds. Third, Mrs. Jackson, of Tazewell, drove Andy Johnson, the traitor, from her hotel, assuring him that money could not purchase her provisions for such an ingrate. Hurrah for the Jacksons!—*Fayetteville Observer.*

ROTH, DEBLIEUX & CO.

T. ROTH.......PAUL DEBLIEUX.......O. MARIONNEAUX

NEW FIRM.

ROTH, DEBLIEUX & CO., Commission Merchants,

AND DEALERS IN

Dry Goods, Clothing, Jewelry, Boots and Shoes, Hardware, Crockery, Saddelry,

AND

GROCERIES.

Plaquemine, La.

Carpets and Mattings.

IN STORE always a fine assortment of Carpets and Mattings, which we offer at city prices. Carpets at 30c to $1 50 per yard—Mattings at 25 to 50c.

sep15 ROTH, DEBLIEUX & CO.

Lime. Lime.

100 BBLS. Richards' Cape Lime; 50 do. Thomaston Lime. The above is fresh, and a superior article for making sug

sep15 ROTH, DEBLIEUX & CO.

500 Monkey Jackets,

400 PAIRS Kersey Pants; 2000 pairs Russets; 25 bbls. best Lard Oil; do best bleached Whale Oil. Now in store and for sale by

sep15 DEBLIEUX & CO.

Boots and Shoes.

WE have now in store a large assortment of various styles for Ladies, Misses, Gents, Youths and Children, received direct from manufactories, which we can offer at low prices.

aug96 ROTH, DEBLIEUX & CO.

Jewelry! Jewelry! Jewelry!!

WE are now opening a fine lot of new styles. Any one wishing anything in this line, will find it to their advantage to call and examine our stock.

aug 26 ROTH, DEBLIEUX & CO.

100,000 FIRE BRICK FOR SALE, Cheap for Cash. Apply to

my4 CHAS. N. ROTH &

Gazette & Sentinel.

PROGRESS OF THE WAR.

THE WAR IN VIRGINIA!

The Great Slaughter at Manassas!

Richmond, July 22—9 a. m.—The reports of the killed and wounded were so unreliable last night, and the statements in such confusion following the victory at Manassas, that the agent of the Associated Press refrains from mentioning them, being fearful of giving causeless pain to anxious hearts.

It is now ascertained that among the distinguished dead, are Generals Bartow, of Georgia, Bee, of South Carolina, Kirby Smith, of Florida, and Col. Johnson, of Hampton's South Carolina Legion.

Gen. Beauregard and all his staff are safe, although Beauregard had his horse shot from under him.

Gen. Joseph E. Johnston commanded on the left, where the enemy made their fiercest attack.

Gen. Beauregard commanded the right.

President Davis reached the field of battle at noon, and took command of the center.

When the left was pressed the severest, the center disengaged a portion of the enemy's force, thus deciding the fortunes of the day.

It is stated that the enemy was commanded by Gens. Scott, Patterson and McDowell, and it is also reported that the latter was seriously wounded.

(Second Dispatch.)

Receipt of the News of the Defeat at Washington City.

TERRIBLE PANIC THROUGHOUT WASHINGTON!

The City Overspread with Gloom!

Washington, July 22d, 12 p. —Our troops, after gaining a great victory, were eventually repulsed, and commenced a retreat on Washington.

After the latest information from Centerville last night, a series of events took place proving in the intensest degree disastrous.

Many confused statements are prevalent, but enough is known to warrant the statement that we have suffered to a degree which casts a gloom over the remnant of the army and excites the deepest melancholy throughout Washington.

The carnage was tremendous, heavy on both sides, and on our side it is represented as frightful.

We were advancing, taking masked batteries, and gradually, but surely, driving the enemy towards Manassas, when the enemy seemed to be reinforced by Gen. Johnston, We were immediately driven back and a panic among our troops suddenly occurred.

A regular stampede, in fact, took place.

It is understood that Gen. McDowell undertook to make a stand near Centerville, but the panic was so fearful that the whole army became demoralized, and it was impossible to check them, either at Centerville or Fairfax Court-House.

Large numbers of the troops, in retreat, fell on the wayside from exhaustion, and are scattered all along the route all the way from Fairfax Court-House.

The road from Bull Run is strewed with arms and knapsacks, discarded by the troops.

Of the celebrated Ellsworth New York Fire Zouaves, only 200 escaped from the slaughter.

The 69th and other N. Y. regiments suffered frightfully.

Sherman's, Carlisle's, Griffin's and the West Point batteries were taken by the Confederates, as were also the eight thirty-two pound siege cannon.

Col. Wilcox, commander of a brigade, and Capt. McCook were killed.

Washington is the scene of the intensest excitement. Wagons are continually arriving bringing in the dead and wounded. The feeling in the city is awfully distressing.

Both telegraphic and steamboat communication with Alexandria are suspended to the public.

The fortifications are being strongly reinforced by fresh troops.

It is supposed that Gen. Mansfield will take command of the fortifications on the other side of the river.

Large rifled cannon and mortars are being rapidly sent over.

From Western Virginia!

General Wise gains a Decided Victory.

Richmond, July 22.—Lieut. Hood, of Crump's Company, arrived here last evening, and says that the company and regiment are safe at Monterey

Pssengers state that Gen. Wise won a decided victory in the Kanawha Valley last week, killing 150 of the enemy, and losing but few.

(Further Particulars.)

Retreat of the Lincolnites Cut Off at Bull's Run!

FEDERAL LOSS FROM 4000 *to* 5000!

Rumoured Recommencement of the Battle by Patterson.

Washington, July 22.—The Rhode Island Battery was captured at Bull's Run Bridge, where the retreat was cut off. Their horses were all killed.

The Seventy-Frst New York Regiment lost half their men.

Among the list of Officers killed, we find the following additional names :—Capt. Gordon, of Massachusetts; Col. Slocum, of the 22nd, and Lieut. Col. Fowler, of the 14th New York Regiments.

The last estimate of the killed and wounded on our side is put down at from 4000 to 5000.

A rumor says that Geu. Patterson arrived this morning in the vicinity of Manassas, and commenced an attack on the Confederates. The exhaused condition of his men prevented his coming to Gen. McDowell's aid during the battle.

Still Later—Glorious News.

The Enemy Eighty Thousand Strong!

Their Loss 10 to 15 Thousand!

Gallant Conduct of the Lsuisiana Troops!

MAJOR WHEAT'S BATTALION SUFFERED SEVERELY.

Culpepper Courthouse, July 22nd.—The enemy at Manassas was 80,000 strong, and was completely routed with immense loss, estimated at from 10,000 to 15,000.

Our loss has been considerable.

Wheat,s battalion suffered severely. Maj. Wheat and many of his men were wounded. The rest of the Louisianians suffered lightly.

The Washington Artilery and the La. Infantry did splendid execution.

The enemy was pursued all night.

Centreville is occupied by our troops.

President Davis arrived here last night.

Still Further Particulars.

Glorious Charge of Louisianians, Virginians and Mississippians under Gen. Beauregard.

Our Dead to be Sent Home.

THE WOUNDED WELL CARED FO R

Culpepper C. H., July 22.—Early in the morning the enemy, having obtained our badges and countersign, had got forward in front.

The enemy fought obstinately. The battle begun early in the morning. Abont 11 a. m., the enemy suffered a repulse, but being reinforced, made another effort for the mastery. At two, they were again repulsed. They renewed the struggle, and was finally routed at five, fleeing in all directions, and pursued by our cavalry and by Jeff Davis at the head of a body of fresh troops, which had been held in reserve, to Centreville.

Our army captured very many cannon, a large number of rifles, an immense number of prisoners, and a vast qnantity of baggage.

Gen. Beauregard charged Sherman's battery, in person, at the head of his gallant men. Our whole army covered itself with glory.

The slaughter of the enemy was horrible. For miles the ground was strewed with the dead and dying.

A large number of officers and New York politicians were taken prisoners.

Despatches from President Davis to the Secretary of War.

It states that the Confederate force immediately engaged, was 15,000, and the Federalists are estimated at 35,000. This refers to the left wing, where the battle was principally waged, and don't include the right and centre, which was but partially engaged.

The entire Confederate force amounted to about 40,000 and the Federalists nearly 80,000.

The Confederate Congress.

Richmond, July 22.—Congress met at noon, opening with prayer.

The following dispatch to Gen. S. Cooper, Adjutant-General, was read by the Clerk:

"Manassas, Sunday night.—Night has closed upon a hard bought field. Our forces have won a glorious victory. The enemy has been routed, leaving a large amount of arms, munitions, knapsacks and baggage. The ground was strewn for miles with the dead, and the farm houses and grounds around are filled with his wounded. The pursuit was continued until darkness covered the fugitives. We have captured several field batteries and regimental stand of arms, and one U. S. Flag. Many prisoners have been taken. Too much praise cannot be bestowed, whether for the skill of the principal officers, or for the gallantry of the troops. The battle was mainly fought on our left, several miles from our field works. Our forces engaged, did not exceed 15,000. That of the enemy is estimated at 35,000. [Signed]

JEFF. DAVIS."

[Resolutions were then adopted, recognising the hand of the Most High in this great victory, requesting Ministers in the forthcoming Sabbath, to offer up thanksgiving and praise for the mighty deliverance, and expressing sympathy for the families of those whose blood has been shed on the altar of liberty.]

A Large Meeting in Richmond.

A large public meeting was held in Richmond, and a committee appointed to go to Manassas and receive all the wounded able to be transported to that city.

It is impossible to obtain details of the dead and wounded yet.

The battle ground extended over a space of ten miles.

United States Congress.

In the House, Mr. Wright offered a resolution that the reverses at Bull's Run, no way impair the ultimate success, &c, of the Federalists; which was abled.

Army News from Washington.

Gen. McClellan has been ordered to the command of the forces on the Potomac, and is succeeded in Eastern Virginia by Gen. Rosencrantz.

The Federal army will be immediately reorganized and increased.

Gen McDowell is at Headquarters at Arlington. His division will resume its former position.

The cavaly of the Confederates was the terror of our volunteers, who kept to the woods to avoid their murderous charges.

Reports from Baltimore.

Baltimore, July 22.—There is great excitement here. The Southerners are rejoicing exceedingly, and the efforts of their friends to quiet their delirum is of no avail. It is said that a considerable force will be required to keep them down. Thirty arrests have been made for attempts to incite revolts.

The defeat at Manassas is attributed to the inactivity of Patterson, who had received a dozen official orders to engage Johnston at any odds.

New York, July 23.—The Herald's special correspondent says that the retreat was nothing more or less than a stampede. McDowell displayed great bravery, but his efforts to arrest the panic were unavailing.

The New York 71st, 14th, and 27th, Maine regiments were mowed down like grass.

The list of killed and wounded embrace a large number of officers.

From Louisville.

A Citizen Murdered for Shouting for Jeff. Davis.

Louisville, July 22.—John W. Tompkins, formerly clerk of the Board of Aldermen, while shouting for Jeff. Davis to-day, was ordered to desist by Green, a city watchman, which resulted in the watchman killing Tompkins instantly. The Coroner's verdict was that Tompkins was killed without sufficient cause.

The Very Latest.

We condense the copious telegraphic reports which came to hand yesterday. After the battle, our army advanced its lines to Fairfax C. H. and Centreville. Our loss is estimated at 500 killed and 1000 wounded; that of the enemy from ten to fifteen thousand. We captured nine millions worth of arms, ammunition, &c.

The loss on the part of the Louisiana troops is not large. The Tiger rifles made a desperate charge with the bowie knives.

LATER STILL.—The New Orleans papers of yesterday contain nothing additional relative to the battle of Manassas, nor any telegraphic items of interest.

Gazette & Sentinel,

Published every Saturday by

W. P. BRADBURN,

EDITOR AND PROPRIETOR.

TERMS OF SUBSCRIPTION.

THREE DOLLARS AND FIFTY CENTS ($3 50) for one year, in advance. FIVE DOLLARS ($5 00) if not paid in advance.

SINGLE COPIES—Ten Cents.

No subscription will be discontinued unless a written notice to that effect is received from the subscriber himself, and all arrearges paid.

TERMS OF ADVERTISING.

ONE DOLLAR ($1 00), per square of ten lines, or less, of this space, ———————, for the first insertion, and Fifty Cents for each subsequent insertion. A liberal discount, however, on these rates will be made on advertisements inserted for a longer time than two months, as follows:

	3 months.	6 months.	12 months.
1 square	$ 5 00	$ 8 00	$ 12 00
2 squares	8 00	12 00	20 00
3 squares	15 00	15 00	25 00
4 squares	12 00	20 00	30 00
5 squares	18 00	25 00	37 00
6 squares	20 00	30 00	45 00

For Professional or Business Cards, not exceeding one square, with paper, one year, $15.

Announcements of Candidates for office, $10. Cash in all cases must accompany the announcement, whether handed in by a friend or the person announced.

The privilege of yearly advertisers is strictly limited to their own immediate and regular business.

Communications intended to promote the private ends or interests of individuals, corporations or societies, will be charged as advertisements.

All persons ordering Jobs or handing in advertisements on account of any local or political organization, will be held responsible for the payment of the same.

Marriages and Deaths published without charge. Obituaries inserted as other advertisements.

Advertisements not marked the length of time they are to be inserted, will be kept in the paper till forbid, and charged accordingly.

All advertisements by strangers or transient persons must be paid in advance.

Personal Cards, if inserted at all, will be charged two dollars per square.

☞Job Work always cash, and advertisementr are due when first inserted.

THE FALL ELECTION.

FOR CONGRESS.

We are authorized to announce **Col. H. W. ALLEN,** of West Baton Rouge, as a candidate for Congress of the Confederate States for the Fourth Congressional District, composed of the Parishes of West Feliciana, Point Coupee, St. Landry, Lafayette, Vermillion. West Baton Rouge, Iberville, St. Mary and St. Martin, Election first Monday in November.

FOR AUDITOR.

We are authorized to announce **BYTHELL HAYNES,** of Clinton, as a Candidate for Auditor of Public Accounts at the ensuing Fall election.

We are authorized to announce **H. PERALTA,** of East Baton Rouge, as a Candidate for Auditor of Public Accounts

FOR ASSESSOR.

Mr. Editor: Please announce the name of **T. RODOLPH VERBOIS,** Esq., as a Democratic Candidate for Assessor for the parish of Iberville, subject to the State Rights Democratic Convention.

We are authorized to announce **ERNEST CALLERY,** the present incumbent, as a Candidate for re-election to the office of Assessor, subject to the decision of the State Rights Democratic Convention.

We are requested to announce **JOHN A. DANOS,** Esq., as a Candidate for the office of Assessor of this parish. jun29

FOR SHERIFF.

☞ We are authorized to announce **Joseph H. Erwin, Esq.,** as a candidate for the office of Sheriff of this Parish at the next November election.

Mr. Editor: You will please announce **J. L. PETIT,** as a candidate for Sheriff, subject to the decision of the State Rights Democratic Convention.

PLAQUEMINE, June 26, 1861.

To W. P. Bradburn, Esq.

Since my friend, Capt. GUSTAVE LAUVE, declines unning for the Sheriffalty of this parish, for reasons expressed by him in your paper, I wish you to announce me to the people of Iberville, as a caudidate for Sheriff at the ensuing fall election.

ALLEN JUMEL.

FOR RECORDER.

We are authorized to announce **EMILE RIVIERE,** as a candidate for Recorder, of this Parish, at the ensuing Fall election.

MR. EDITOR: You will please announce the name of **ADOLPHE HEBERT,** Esq., as a Candidate for the office of Recorder of the parish of Iberville, subject to the decision of the State Rights Democratic Convention.

Superintendent of Public Education.

We are requested to announce **HENRY AVERY,** the present Superintendent of Public Education, as a Candidate for re-election.

New Advertisements.

Extra Meeting of Police Jury.

THE Members of the Police Jury of the Parish of Iberville, are requested to attend an extra meeting to be holden on next Thursday, the 1st day of August, 1861. By order of

J. A. DARDENNE,

J. H. RILLS, Sec. Prest. of the Police Jury.

Plaquemine, July 25th, 1861—jy27

NOTICE.

THE Commissoned and Non-Commissioned Officers of the Iberville Regiment, are requested by Major-General Commanding the 2nd Division La. Militia, to meet on Monday, the 29th inst., at 5 o'clock, P. M., at the Court House of this Parish, for the purpose of organizing a School of Instruction.

Iberville, July 25th, '61.

NOTICE.

ALL persons indebted to the undersigned, will please call and settle, as the Mail Contractors need the money due them from this office, and must have it.

P. E. JENNINGS, Postmaster.

Plaquemine, July 27th—jy27-5in.

RUNAWAY IN PRISON.

WAS committed to jail, boy JOHN WAKER, claiming to belong to Robert Wilkinssu, of the English Turn, Parish of Plaquemines. John is about 26 years old; 5 ft. 7 or 8 in. high; sprightly; plain spoken; griff; will weigh about 135 lbs.

The owner is hereby notified to reclaim said Slave in the manner required by law.

THEO. BLANCHARD, Sheriff.

A ETE conduit à la geole le negre JOHN WAKER, d'isant appartenir à Robt. Wilkinson, du "Toor des Anglais," Paroisse de Plaquemines. John est un griff; agé de 26ans; 5 pieds 7 à 8 pouces de taille; de bel apparence et d'un poids d'environs 135 livres.

Le propriétaire est notifié de le reclamer comme la loi le requiert.

jy27 THEO. BLANCHARD, Shérif.

NEW TEXAS AND TENNESSEE FLOUR, just received and for sale by

jy27 CHAS. N. ROTH & CO.

New Advertisements.

SPECIAL NOTICES.

FRANCOIS ALLAIN, you are hereby notified to dig out the crawfish holes in your levee, and to stop all the leaks in the same; to increase the base of your levee where the greatest depth of water stands against it in high water, and raise the same two feet above the high water mark; to remove from your levee all stumps, logs, trees and weeds. Your road must be raised with earth across a low place near the upper line. Your road ditches must be cleaned, the ditch on the opposite side of the levee requires deepening—slope both ditches on the road side, and throw the earth to the centre of the road. A number of draining ditches must be cut, running back sufficiently to thoroughly drain your road. Your road must be made 20 feet wide between the ditches, and raised in all the low places. The above work must be completed by the 15th of October next, 1861, in conformity with the Road and Levee Ordinances of the Parish of Iberville.

H. J. HYDE, Inspector of 7th Road and Levee Dist.

Grand River, July 17th, 1861. jy27.

FFRAN. MARIONNEAUX, you are hereby notified to insrease the base of your levee, and raise it two feet above the high water mark; to dig out the crawfish holes in your levee, and to stop all the leaks in the same; to clear your road and levee of all weeds, stumps, logs, trees and other obstructions; to clean out the ditches next the levee, and deepen and widen the other ditch and throw the earth in the centre of the road; all the low places in your road to be raised with earth, and the road to be 20 feet wide between the ditches. A sufficient number of ditches and bridges must be made across your road, to thoroughly drain the water from the levee ditch. Leading ditches must be cut, running back a sufficient distance to drain your road. The bridges must be made of good substantial material, and 18 feet in length. The above work must be completed by the 15th of October next, 1861, in conformity with the road and levee ordinances of the parish of Iberville.

H. J. HYDE, Inspector of the 7th Road and Levee Dist.

Grand River. July 16th, '61.

FELIX GREAUD, you are hereby notified to dig out the crawfish holes in your levee, and stop all the leaks in the same; to increase the base and raise the levee two feet above the high water mark; to remove from your levee all stumps, logs, trees and weeds; also to clean out your road ditches, deepen the ditch on the road side, slope both ditches on the road side, and throw the earth to the centre of the road; to raise the low places in your road with earth; to cut leading ditches running back a sufficient distance to drain your road. Your road must be made 20 feet between the ditches. The above work must be completed by the 15th of October next, '61, in conformity with the road and levee ordinances of the parish of Iberville.

H. J. HYDE, Inspector of the 7th Road and Levee Dist.

Grand River, 16th, '61.

JOHN SLIDELL, you are hereby notified to make the necessary repairs to your road and levee. Your road must be cleared of all weeds, stumps, trees and other obstructions; the levee ditch must be cleaned out, and the ditch on the opposite side of the road must be widened and deepened, and the earth thrown in the centre of the road. Both of the ditches must be sloped on the road side. A sufficient number of ditches and bridges must be made across the road to thoroughly drain the water from the foot of the levee. The bridges must be made of good and substantial material, and 18 feet in length. Leading ditches must be cut, running back a sufficient distance to drain your road. Your road must be raised with earth in all the low places. All weeds and bushes must be cut on your levee. The above work must be completed by the 15th of October next, '61, in conformity with the road and levee ordinances of the parish of Iberville.

H. J. HYDE, Inspector of the 7th Road and Levee Dist.

Grand River, July 16th, '61.

J. M. RILS, you are hereby notified to increase the base of your levee; to dig out the crawfish holes and stop the leaks in your levee, and to raise it two feet above the high water mark; to remove all stumps, trees, logs and weeds from your levee. Also to clear your road of all stumps, logs, weeds and other obstructions; to clean out your road ditches; slope them on the road side, and throw the earth in the centre of the road; to make a sufficient number of ditches across your road to drain the water from the levee, and to make good and substantial bridges across the ditches, 18 feet long; to cut a number of leading ditches running back a sufficient distance to drain your road. The low places in your road must be raised with earth. The above work must be completed by the 15th of Octoher next, '61, in conformity, with the road and levee ordinances of the parish of Iberville.

H. J. HYDE, Inspector of the 7th Road and Levee Dist.

Grand River, July 15th, '61.

J. D. DENEGRE, you are hereby notified to make the necessary repairs to your road and levee. Your road must be cleared of all weeds, stumps, trees and other obstructions. The levee ditch must be cleaned out, and the ditch on the opposite side of the road, must be widened and deepened, and the earth thrown in the centre of the road; and both of the ditches must be sloped on the road side. A sufficient number of ditches and bridges must be made across the road to thoroughly drain the water from the foot of the levee. The bridges must be made of good and substantial material, and 18 feet in length. Leading ditches must be cut, running back a sufficient distance to drain your road; your road must be raised with earth in all the low places. All weeds and bushes must be cut on your levee. The above work must be completed by the 15th of October next, '61, in conformity with the road and levee ordinances of the parish of Iberville.

H. J. HYDE, Inspector of the 7th Road and Levee Dist.

Grand River, July 16th, 1861.

LUCIEN LANDRY, you are hereby notified to dig out the crawfish holes in your levee, and stop the leaks in the same; to increase the base and raise the levee two feet above the high water mark; to remove from your levee all stumps, logs, trees and weeds; also to clean out your road ditches, deepen the ditch on the wood side, slope both ditches on the road side, and throw the earth in the centre of the road; to raise the low places in your road with earth; to make ditches across your road to drain the water from the levee; and to make good and substantial bridges over the same, 18 feet long; to cut leading ditches running back a sufficient distance to drain your road. The above work must must be completed by the 15th of October next, 1861, in conformity with the road and levee ordinances of the Parish of Iberville.

H. J. HYDE, Inspector of the 7th Road and Levee Dist.

Grand River, July 16th, '61.

WIDOW JOHN BAPTISTE TUILLIER, you ars hereby notified to increase the base of your levee, and to raise it two feet above the high water mark, and to dig out all the crawfish holes; to clear your road and levee of all weeds, stumps and other obstructions; to clean your road dtches, and deepen the outside road ditch, and to slope both ditches on the road side, and throw the earth in the centre of the road; also to make a substantial bridge 18 feet in length across your road, and to make a leading ditch running back a sufficient distance to thoroughly drain your road. The above work must be completed by the 15th of October next, 1861, in conformity with the road and levee ordinances of the Parish of Iberville.

H. J. HYDE, Inspector of the 7th Road and Levee Dist.

Grand River, July 16th, '61. jy27

New Advertisements.

SOSTHENE LEONARD, you are hereby notified to increase the base of that portion of your levee from the house to the lower line, four feet, and to raise it two feet above the high water mark. The other portion of your levee must have the base increased and raised to the same height; to clear your road and levee of all weeds, logs, trees and other obstructions; to fill up the low places in your road, and make your road 18 feet wide. The above work must be completed by the 15th of Oct. next, 1861, in conformity with the Road and Levee Ordinances of the Parish of Iberville.

G. T. TUILLIER, Commissary of Road & Levee—19 Dist.

Grand River, July 9th, '61. jy27

A. J. POWELL and JOHN SLIDELL, you are hereby notified to clear your road and levee of all weeds, bushes, trees, and other obstructions; and to fill up with earth the low places in your road, and to make your road 18 feet wide between the ditches. The above work must be completed by the 15th of Oct. next, '61, in conformity with the Road and Levee Ordinances of the Parish of Iberville.

G. T. TUILLIER, Commissary of Road & Levee—19 Dist.

Grand River, July 9th, '61. jy27

A. J. POWELL, you are hereby notified to repair your road and levee on Lot. No—, by the 15th of Oct. next, in conformity with the Road and Levee Ordinances of the Parish of Iberville.

G. T. TUILLIER, Commiss'y of Road & Levee—19 Dist.

Grand River, July 9th, '61. jy27

MICHEL HEBERT, you are hereby notified to repair your levee; to clear your road & levee of all weeds, logs, trees, and other obstructions; and to make your road 18 feet wide. The above work must be completed by the 15th of October, '61, in conformity with the Road and Levee Ordinances of the Parish of Iberville.

G. T. TUILLIER, Commiss'y of Road & Levee—19 Dist.

Grand River, July 9th, '61. jy27

J. H. RILS, you are hereby notified to increase the base of your levee and raise it two feet above the high water mark; to clear your road and levee of all weeds, bushes, trees, logs and other incumbrances, and to make your road 18 feet wide between the ditches. The above work must be completed by the 15th of October next, '61. in conformity wtth the road and levee ordinances of the parish of Iberville.

G. T. TUILLIER, Commiss'y of the 19th Road and Levee Dist.

Grand River, July 9th, '61 jy27

FLAVIEN TUILLIER, you are hereby notified to increase the base of your levee, and raise it two feet above the high water mark; to clear your road and levee of all weeds, logs, trees, and other obstructions; and to make your road 18 feet wide, between the ditches. The above work to be completed by the 15th of October next, 1861, in conformity with the road and levee ordinances of the parish of Iberville.

G. T. TUILLIER, Commiss'y of Road and Levee—19th Dist.

Grand River, July 9th, 1861.

MRS. CHRISTOPHER ADAMS, you are hereby notified to drain and repair your road, and repair bridges on same, in compliance with the law, by the 15th of October next, '61.

GEO. MITCHELTREE, Road Inspector—23rd Dist.

Grand River, July 11th. jy27

HENRY E. LAWRENCE, Esq., you are hereby notified to drain and repair your road and bridges by the 15th of Oct. next, '61, in accordance with the law.

GEO. MITCHELTREE, Road Inspector—Dis. 23.

Grand River, July 11th. '61 jy27

TO the Heirs of Estate of A. G. Stringer—you are hereby notified to drain and repair road and bridges of the above Estate, by the 15th of Oct. next, in accordance with the law.

GEO. MITCHELTREE, Road Inspector—Dis. 23.

Grand River, July 11th, 61. jy27

To the Citizens of Iberville.

I HAVE been ordered by Adjutant-General GRIVOT, to collect all the OLD MUSKETS, RIFLES, CARTRIDGE BOXES, and other arms and equipments belonging to the State, that may be found in this parish, and them placed in some safe depot, ready for use or transportation whenever orders are received from Headquarters.

There are 60 or more old U. S. Flint Muskets, formerly used by Capt. Hacker's Company, that are now scattered throughout the parish. It is expected that all those who may have one or more of them in their poseession, will deliver them up immediately

I am also requested to obtain all the old arms that may be in the hands of private individuals, that they do not want, provided they will sell them at a reasonable price, or provided their patriotism shall prompt them to give them to the State. None are desired unless they can be made, by repairing, fit for the field.

The Government will not be in a condition to pay for these arms immediately. Such persons as are not disposed to give their old shot guns, rifles, &c., to the government, will receive a certificate of the kind of arm furnished by them, and its value, and at the end of the war, will be paid on presentation of the certificate, or have the arm returned to them with repairs.

It is to be hoped that this appeal from the Governor to the good people of our parish, will cause every true and patriotic man to come forward and offer what is now so much needed in defense of our cause.

Messrs. Roth & Deblieux will take charge of all that is left with them, and the names of the donors.

GERVAIS SCHLATRE, Col. Commanding—Iberville Regt.

july 27. La. Militia

State of Louisiana—Parish of Iberville—5th Judicial District Court.

In Matter of Estate of G. Theodule Babin, dec'd.

WHEREAS: Euphemie Oreline Babin has this day filed in this Court her account of administration of the Estate of G. Theodule Babin, dec'd, in her capacity of natural tutrix and ex-officio Administratrix.

Notice is hereby given to all whom it may concern to show cause within Thirty days from this date, why the said Tableau of Administration aforesaid, should not be homologated and made a judgement of this Court.

Iberville, July 25, 1861.

ju22 M. A. ESTEVAN, Clerk.

Etat de la Louisiane—Paroisse d'Iberville—Cour du 5eme District Judiciaire.

Dans la Successton de feu

G. THEODULE BABIN.

ATTENDU, que Euphemie Oreline Babin a ce jour deposé en cette Cour son Tableaux d'administration de la succession de fue G. Theodule Babin, en sa capacitè ce tutrice naturalle et ex-officio administratrice.

Avis est par le present donné à tous ceux que cela concerne de deduire sans trente jours de la date de ce present les raisons pour lesquelles le dit Tableaux ne serait pas homoloqué et fait le judgment de cette Cour.

Iberville, le Juillet 25, 1861.

jy27. M. A. ESTEVAN, Greffier.

PLAQUEMINE:

SATURDAY, JULY 27th, 1861.

OUR WAR TERMS.

As the necessaries of life, and material for conducting our paper, cannot now be obtained without cash, we are forced to publish the following as our INVARIABLE TERMS, until business gets back into its accustomed channel, and confidence is once more restored:

All miscellaneous or transient advertisements—of persons not advertising by the year—must be paid for when presented for insertion.

Job Work of every description (save Funeral Tickets), must be paid for before leaving the office.

Legal advertisements, such as Sheriff's and Succession Sales, are due on the day of sale.

Petitions for Administratorships, and advertisements of homologation notices, must be paid in advance, or guaranteed by a responsible name,—the first, that they will be paid *some time or other*, and the latter, at the end of the thirty days for which they are advertised.

☞Continued indisposition of the editor, makes it impossible for him to issue such a paper as he would desire. An enlargement to a size greater than any ever issued in this place, will follow his restoration to the duties of his office. There are evidences that this will occur in a short time. Will our friends bear with us.

Thanksgiving.

When the news of the battle of Manassas reached Richmond, the Confederate Congress passed a set of beautiful resolutions recognising the hand of Providence, and recommending the people to observe to-morrow as a day of thanksgiving, by appropriate religious ceremonies. We hope that our people will engage in the services of the day with humble and reverent hearts, and offer up their sacrifice of thanksgiving to Him who has showered upon us so many blessings in our holy struggle for independence.

YOUNG MR. MCILHENY.—This young gentle man from Woodville, Miss., and lately engaged in this place as a teacher, it is feared, is one of the victims on the late hard-fought field of Manassas. He left here to join Capt. STAMP'S (a Nephew of Jeff. Davis) Woodville Company, all of whom excepting 16, including its Captain, sacrificed their lives in the holy cause in which they were engaged. This company was a portion of Wheat's, all but a hundred of which was killed, and the Commander probably mortally wounded.

☞ Our friends will please send in their advertisements early in the week —a number coming in at the end of the week, causing the present delay in the issue of our paper.

THE GREAT VICTORY.

Our columns to day contain as full accounts of the great battle fought at Manassas Junction on Sunday last, as we could glean from the repocts that have come to hand. The details of the engagement so far are but partial. The number of troops engaged on each side, and the number of killed and wounded, cannot be known with certainty until further accounts are received. Enough is known, however, to make it certain, that both armies were very large; that the loss on both sides, particularly on the part of the Federalists, was frightful; and that our gallant soldiers have achieved a complete victory which has never had its parallel on this continent, and seldom in the history of modern warfare. The Southern troops under the command of our loved and honored President, and our gallant Generals, have scattered the hireling myrmidons of the Black Republican government, and have driven them back, over the bodies of their own dead and wounded, to the position they held before the commencement of that boasted march, which they fondly hoped would lead them into the heart of the Southern Confederacy.

It is impossible to overestimate the importance of this engagement. For months the Federalists have been concentrating an army composed of the flower of the Northern manhood, until it had reached such dimensions that their most sagacious generals believed it impregnable by any force that the South was able to bring against it. The gloom that overcasts the whole North, shows that the proud spirit of the people has been subdued; that they have lost the prestige of victory, and that it will be an uphill work with them until the end of the war. It is useless for Mr. Cameron to tell them to take courage and repair their misfortunes; they can never again fight with earnestness, with the vision of the terrible carnage at Manassas before their eyes. The country will lose its credit in the eyes of the world; the enlistment of 500,000 men and the raising of $400,000,000, will be a much more difficult matter than the passage of a resolution by a servile Congress.

We can hardly hope that the end of the war is near at hand, even though the enemy has met with such a severe repulse. As long as there are left any hopes of accomplishing their purposes they will carry on this war and no longer. They will submit only when the South has whipped them into submission.—But whether they fight or not, whether the war be long or short, let us take fresh courage and, with a firm reliance upon a beneficient Providence, let us not entertain a doubt that we shall bring this war to a triumphant termination, and be recognized by the world as a sovereign, free and independent nation.

SOME OF THE MEN IN WISE'S LEGION.—The Richmond Dispatch says there are some very notable gentlemen in Wise's Legion, who will be of the greatest advantage to that remarkable military organization, which is destined to make a powerful impression in the western portion of the State. It gives the names of the following gentlemen and their antecedents:

Mons. Pardigon, a very learned Frenchman, who is a master of infantry tactics, and especially skilled in bayonet exercise. He has given most valuable instruction to the followers of Gen. Wise. Mons. P. is an admirable teacher of modern languages, and one of the best writers of the day. He is ardently devoted to the Southern cause, and we saw him the other day marching westward through Lewisburg, armed and equipped in the most approved style as a foot soldier.

Capt. Buckholtz, a German, and a highly accomplished artillery officer. He has written a work on the subject. His knowledge and practical skill are very thorough in the department of the military science to which he has devoted himself.

Col. Adler, an Italian, from Garibaldi's army. He is a magnificent cavalry officer. A commission was tendered him by Lincoln, as Colonel of cavalry; but he preferred to serve the Southern Confederacy. He declares that he "never fights for the Government, but for the people; never for perogative, always for liberty."

He is a man of great physical prowess, and an officer of great experience.

Gen. Henningsen and Col. Frank Anderson. These officers have a fresh and extensive fame in our own country. Their exploits on the Isthmus are no doubt remembered by our people.

They are important acquisitions to Gen. Wise's column.

A CHAPTER UPON CIRCUMLOCUTION.—A day or two since an unsophisticated darkey waited upon a certain military gentleman with a bill of $1 15 for washing done at the camp hospital, which, after undergoing a rigid scrutiny by the officer, was returned with the following explanation, which the artonished son of Ethiopia listened to with an equal amount of wonder and perplexity:

"This bill," said the military gentleman, "will first have to be sent to the Quartermaster-General at Washington, and he will report to Adjutant-General, who will lay it before the Secretary of War, for his approval. The Adjutant being satisfied, it will be sent to the Auditor of State, who will approve of it and send it to the Secretary of the Treasury, who will at once dispatch an order to the Collector of this port to pay the bill."

The darker relieved himself of a long drawn sigh. "Then massa," he remarked, "dat last gemblam you spoke of pays for de washin', does he?"

"No," continued the other, "he will hand it to the Quartermaster; but as there is no such officer here at present, some proper person must be appointed by the Secretary of War, under the direction of the President, and his appointment must be approved by the Senate. Congress not being in session now, the commission cannot be issued until after it meets. When this commission is received the Quartermaster will show it to the Collector and demand the funds. You will then call upon him; he will pay it, you giving your receipt."

The unfortunate nigger first scratched his head, then shook it, and finally said, "I guess I'll hab to let dis washing slid, but it am de last job I does for Uncle Sam, shure!"—*Cin. Enq.*

A BRAVE BEAUTY.—The Alexandria correspondent of the N. Y. Express, sends the following very interesting war item:

I have to chronicle the arrest of another spy, at the fortification on this side of the river. This time, however, it is no bearded knight, no enterprising draughtsman, or rabid Southern States Rights man, but a beautiful, blushing damsel, of some eighteen summers, who claims to have been born in Washington, and that her name is Alice Kingsbury. She was arrested by some of the Michigan Regiment, who thought it strange to see so lovely a female so oft around the camps, "solitary and alone." Upon the dress of the lady, I am informed, there was found an accurate diagram of the fortifications on Shuter's Hill. The positions of the guns were strictly delineated, and all the weak spots marked in red pencil. The lady, for such, by her deportment and language, she undoubtedly is, is of course in close custody.

☞ A country paper, in an obituary notice, speaks of the deceased as being "a most estimable young man, and devout christian *until* the day of his death." Pity the young man had not died sooner, to save his reputation.

☞ Old Mrs. Pilkins was reading the foreign news by a late arrival. "Cotton is declining," exclaimed the old lady. "Well, I thought as much,—the last thread was remarkably feeble—dear me."

☞ A man from the country, whose wife had eloped and carried off the feather-bed, was in Louisville in search of them—not that he cared anything about the wife, "but the feathers," says he, "them's worth forty-eight cents a pound."

☞ A fellow lately contracted in writing with a wood dealer for a quantity of "tip-top-wood." The man began to deliver it; but it was so full of limbs that the purchaser demurred, saying that it was not good. The woodman replied: "It was just what I agreed to deliver, 'tip-top wood," and I believe this grew on that part of the tree."

☞ An enraged gentleman addressing from his chamber window a youth who had been serenading his daughter half an hour, said: "You are a great boar, and I think you mean to keep on boaring until you get water," adding, "here it is," emptying a pitcher full upon his head.

☞ I say, Cuffy, why you no come to see dis darkey? If I hab lib as so close as you does to me, I'd come to see you ebry day." "O, 'cause my wife patch my trouserloons all to pieces, I'se too shamed to go nowhar."

☞ The Charlottsville Review says the women "are the frieze and carvings around the temple of humanity—the sauce which gives all its sweetness to the dumpling of life."

☞ An enthusiastic girl says that the first time she ever locked arms with a young man, she felt like "Hope leaning on an anchor." What a delightful feeling!

Head Quarters, 2nd Division,
Louisiana Militia.
PLAQUEMINE, July 18th, 1861.

GENERAL ORDERS.

No. 1.

1. PURSUANT to orders from the Governor of Louisiana, and in virtue of my appointment as Major General of the 2nd Division of Louisiana Militia, I hereby assume command of the same.

2. The following Officers will constitute my Division Staff, and will be obeyed and respected accordingly:

VALSIN J. DUPUY, Colonel and Inspector of Division.

JOHN A. SIGUR, Lieutenant-Colonel and Quartermaster of Division.

AUGUSTUS TALBOT, Major and Aide-de-Camp.

MARK A. ESTEVAN, Major and Aide-de-Camp.

AUGUSTE LEVERT, Jr., Major and Paymaster of Division.

PIERRE M. LAMBREMONT, Major and Surgeon of Division.

3. Generals of Brigade will immediately organize their Brigades, and the Regiments and Companies which pertain thereto; and will report the same to my Head Quarters, at Plaquemine, that I may be enabled to appoint the time and place for their respective review and inspection.

4. Captains of Companies will prepare complete muster Rolls of the same for inspection, at the times appointed; and will make to the Colonels of their Regiments, quarterly returns of the same—forwarding to my Head Quarters duplicates thereof.

5. Colonels of Regiments will consolidate their Company Returns, and make to the Commanders of their respective Brigades, Quarterly Regimental Returns,—forwarding to my Head Quarters duplicates thereof.

6. In this time of peril to our country and our institutions, every man is expected to do his duty; and he who aspires to Military command for the sake of title only, has mistaken his vocation, and cannot too soon give place to those inspired by patriotism and courage; for a strict compliance with all the requirements of law and military usage, is expected and will be enforced.

GUSTAVE S. ROUSSEAU,
Maj. Gen. 2nd Division, Louisiana
jly20 *Militia, Commanding.*

State of Louisiana, Parish of Iberville—Fifth District Court.

In matter of Estate of Paul Pelissier, dec'd.

WHEREAS: Joseph H. Rils has this day petitioned this Court for letters of Curatorship of the vacant Estate of Paul Pelissier, dec'd.

Notice is hereby given to all whom it may concern, to show cause within ten days from the publication hereof, why the prayer of petitioner should not be granted.

M. A. ESTEVAN, *Clerk of Court.*

Iberville, July 19, 1861. jly20

Etat de la Louisiane, Paroisse d'Iberville—Cour du 5me. District Judiciaire.

Dans la Succession de feue Paul Pelissier.

ATTENDU que Joseph H. Rils, a ce jour presenté sa petition en cette Cour à l'effet d'obtenir des lettres de curatelle de la Succession vacante de feu Paul Pelissier.

Avis est par le present donné à tous ceux que cela concerne de deduire sous DIX jours de la date de ce present les raisons pour lesquelles il ne serait pas fait droit à la dite petition.

M. A. ESTEVAN, Greffier.

Iberville, Juillet 19.

The Daily Delta.

VOL. XVI. NEW ORLEANS, TUESDAY, JULY 30, 1861. NO. 205.

THE DAILY DELTA

FROM OUR EVENING EDITION OF YESTERDAY.

Wm. L. Cushing, Esq., has courteously favored us with a Memphis paper of the 28th inst.

On Thursday last the weather was so cool at Baton Rouge that winter clothing was worn, and the Gazette and Comet says fires were not uncomfortable.

Capt. P. H. Thomson, of Col. Gladden's regiment, will leave for Warrington on Wednesday morning. Any letters for officers or men of that command left at R. Nugent & Co.'s, 155 Common street, to-morrow, will be taken.

No More Nurses Wanted.—We are informed that Gov. Moore has received a dispatch from Richmond, stating that no more nurses are required there to take care of the sick and wounded.

We have received yesterday's Memphis Appeal from Ellis's Post-office News Depot. No New York papers came through by express yesterday, and the quotations we make in other columns relative to the battle of Manassas are taken from the Appeal.

[illegible] Prentice [illegible] ing to revive the [illegible] of his brother Abolitionists after the great route at Manassas, says that the United States can furnish a greater army than that of Xerxes. Yes, and a more unfortunate one. Manassas has proved their Marathon. The next great battle will be their Platea.

The collection yesterday at the Methodist Church, on Carondelet street, Rev. Mr. Walker, for the benefit of our wounded soldiers, amounted to $550. There were collections at all the Churches, and it is thought that at least $5000 were thus raised in furtherance of the suggeston which we had the pleasure of making in this paper.

It is suggested that the New York politicians and members of Congress, who were captured by our troops at Manassas, be exchanged for the captive and contraband negroes held by Butler at Fortress Monroe, and that the rank and file, who are now held as prisoners at Richmond be sent south, to work on our fortifications, in order to afford the Yankees an opportunity of refuting the Southern theory that the white man is not adapted to hard labor in this climate.

WHAT THE MORNING JOURNALS SAY.

The *Crescent* rejoices that the appeal to the arbitrament of arms has so widened the breach between the Northern and Southern people that for centuries to come they never can be friends. Thus the South will be released from all the bonds that have heretofore held our States and people to the Northern communi- [illegible] will be made to rely upon herself. [illegible] rism of Northern [illegible] the brutality and barba- [illegible] the [illegible] burning of the thriving little villages of Germantown and Halifax. In regard to these infamous barbarisms we have [illegible] testimony of their own Generals. There could not be a better commentary on their professions of fraternity and good feeling for the South than these incidents afford. It happens that the country through which they passed was chiefly inhabited by persons from the North, many of whom were friendly to the Federalists. In their blind fury, however, no distinction was made between friend and foe. The property of all was given to the flames, and every species of outrage which barbarism could conceive or practice was perpetrated. McDowell regrets these violences, at least he says so, but it does not appear that anybody was punished for it. We can not say that we regret such occurrences. They will serve a great purpose. They will open the eyes of those deluded individuals, of whom there are a few in the Border States—in Kentucky there are a great many—who have been led astray by the pretense of good feeling, brotherly kindness and love of the Union, on the part of the hypocritcal Lincolnites. They show that this war is one purely of passion, revenge and brutal destructiveness. Henceforth the Southern man, who gives his countenance or sympathy to such a cause, must sink in baseness and degradation even below the ruffians whom he encourages in their career of desolation and barbarism.

The *Bulletin* shows the importance of curing our own meats in the South and the facility with which it can be done. We have reason to know that all our planters are fully alive to the importance of this subject, and that unusual attention has been given to the raising of hogs and stock this season. It is only necessary for every planter to raise a hog for every negro on his plantation to render the home supply of meat equal to the demand. Our planters are all laboring with great zeal to this end.

Meanwhile Texas is doing wonders towards supplying the neighboring States with meats. The supply of beef was never so cheap and abundant as it has been this summer.

The Bulletin quotes the following plan of attack of this city, proposed by that enlightened warrior, Raymond, of the New York Times:

We are aware that a force is being organized at Cairo, to move down the river, under the command of Gen. Fremont. But the vulnerable side of the city is not in that quarter. By approaching it through Lake Pontchartrain, we could plant batteries to command it without encountering previous resistance save at one point. In going down the Mississippi we should have to fight our way at every step through the very hot-bed of secession. The English Government might be notified of our purpose. Its Cabinet would instantly see that the success of the plan proposed would solve the whole difficulty, would relieve it of all apprehension, and lay again the foundation of an *entente cordiale* between the two countries, now thoroughly shaken by the indiscreet manifestations of satisfaction of the English people and press over the downfall of the Great Republic.

John Bull having had some experience of the practicability of this plan, will no doubt give it his warm approval and cordial aid!

That silly demagogue, Cassius M. Clay, signalized his appearance on his new field of diplomacy, by writing a letter to the London Times, menacing Great Britain with the direst vengeance of the "great Republic" if it did not openly espouse the cause of the subjugation of the South; and by a speech in Paris, in which he reminded the Frenchmen of their defeat at Waterloo, and of their duty to avenge that great disaster. We trust that Cassius remained in Paris long enough to afford the wit and revenge of the French an opportunity of suggesting the remarkable similitude of Waterloo and Manassas.

OUR ARMY IN TENNESSEE.

Special Correspondence of the Delta.

JACKSON, Tenn., July 26, 1861.

Messrs. Editors—In my last I stated that the malcontents of East Tennessee, as I shall continue to designate them, had put forward the name of one Trigg for Governor. This gentleman, it now appears, has not been long enough in the State to be eligible for the office. So Brownlow's Whig, the chief organ of the malcontents, advises them to support Col. Wm. H. Polk, who has been sometime canvassing the whole State for the office in opposition to the incumbent, and who is of course more acceptable [illegible] Gov. Harris, who continues to thwart their designs by every means in their power. Polk has [illegible] appointment to speak here, when I shall notice particularly any allusion he may make to the indorsement of him by the malcontents. The Governor has already stationed a large portion of the troops so as to protect East Tennessee, not from the malcontents of course, but from any possible invasion to which the Lincolnites may be invited. Cumberland Gap in that section will no doubt be fortified to keep out the army of McClellan.

Gen. Patterson, of the Lincoln Army, has two brothers in East Tennessee, one of them a Captain of a secession company, and the other Postmaster at the Cumberland Gap, by appointment of President Davis, and both said to be true to the South as the needle to the pole. By the way, the General himself, so largely interested in mortgages in Louisiana plantations, had to be very roughly persuaded, under a threat of a mob of violence to his person and property in Philadelphia, to assume his present position towards us, and the Yankees have doubtless more than one cause to be suspicious of his movements, and especially, if true, his refusal or neglect to "engage Johnston at all hazards, despite a dozen official orders to do so," before the great battles near Manassas.

A lady who passed through this place yesterday, had a St. Louis paper, which stated that our Gen. Hardee had gotten into Missouri, within twenty miles of Pilot's Knob, the southern termious of the Iron Mountain Railroad, extending 87 miles south from St. Louis. At our last accounts Hardee, with a well appointed army of not less than 12,000 men, was in Randolph county, Ark., on Black river, near Martinsburg, on the boundary line of S. E. Missouri, about 80 miles from Bird's Point, 80 from Pilot's Knob, and 60 from New Madrid. As Gen. Polk has in the last few days rapidly concentrated forces from various points of this State to some unknown quarter on the river, probably Madrid Bend, whence they could easily join Hardee at Suffington, or Ogden, only 40 to 50 miles from Bird's Point by a railroad, I am inclined to think the main object is to surprise and capture the enemy's forces at perhaps cut off the retreat of the Federals from the army of the Border Chieftain. I would not as a cautious correspondent, intimate from this point of observation our movements, were it not for the fact that they speak for themselves, and by some strange espoinage seem known in Cairo almost as soon as they happen. A spy was caught in Kentucky the other day, near the camp at Union City, the one doubtless who has been so regularly posting the Cairoites. One was arrested here this evening, claiming to be from Galveston, Texas, but having his baggage marked New York. He seemed very much frightened, and will, I presume, be allowed time to prove his assertions, if true.

The most stirring movements in the army are indicated by the recent orders of Gen. Polk, one of them having prevented every train of cars from leaving Memphis this morning, so that the train from Canton, Miss., and that from Columbus, Ky., reached here without the respective connections at Grand Junction and Humboldt. It is the opinion of the majority, as he is also controlling the telegraph, that the General is moving forward forces from Memphis, Randolph, New Madrid and other points, and is determined to keep his movements beyond the possibility of communication to the enemy by spies. It can hardly be, as some here imagine, that the object is to prevent too great a rush to Virginia on the railroads, or the transmission of too much information as to the truth of our casualties in the great battle.

JULY 27.—Martial law has certainly been proclaimed in Memphis. A gentleman of this place has just arrived from there, and so reports. He was permitted to leave by passport only, and was put under oath, I learn, to intimate nothing of military movements. We have had no papers from there now for two days, and the gentleman who was permitted to pass on account of very urgent business, says no papers are allowed to go out of the place. It is rumored here that the General had concentrated from 12,000 to 15,000 troops in Memphis, and that they have all been moved forward to attack some point. By the time this communication is given to your readers the telegraph possibly may inform you of another important battle. The enemy having been foiled at our strongest defences, will try to surprise us now, no doubt, at some imagined weak point. The spy caught up near Union City had a letter, which he had just written, yet in his pocket I learn, informing the army at Cairo when several thousand of our forces would leave Union City, saying then would be the time for attack. It may be the object on our side to invite attack by apparently weakening our army at Union City. I have not heard what was done with this spy, but the fellow caught up as one here has been released. If any of the troops are taken from Union City, they will be removed Sunday, the 28th instant, consisting of three regiments of Tennesseeans, one of them the regiment from this county. This latter most of the citizens here seem to object to very much, as Jackson will be left quite open to attack, should the enemy make any advance by railroad from Columbus.

As I estimated would be the case, matters are growing gradually more interesting at this point, and the battles near Manassas will no doubt lead to thrilling events all along the border.

J. J. L.

A Vile Calumny.—The New York Herald contains the following vile calumny against this paper:

Trouble in the Secession Camp.—Read the very suggestive and instructive extracts which we publish to-day from the New Orleans Delta. It will thus be seen that among the thinking men of the South the Jeff. Davis despotism has become the next thing to an intolerable public nuisance. "If such things are done in the green tree what will be done in the dry?" If such outspoken denunciations, even in New Orleans, are now indulged in against a "body which, without popular warrant, has constituted itself the Government" of the revolted States, while yet they believe in New Orleans that Virginia is perfectly safe under the care of Beauregard, what may we not expect to hear from the far South with the expulsion of Davis and his confederates from Richmond? We are more than ever encouraged to believe that with the loss of Virginia to the secessionists the work of suppressing this Southern rebellion will be substantially accomplished. Let the good work for the Union go on.

We need not warn the readers of this paper that no such articles ever appeared in its columns.

THE GREAT BATTLE AT MANASSAS.

Defeat Acknowledged by the Northern Papers.

The statements of the Northern press relative to the battle at Manassas are beginning to reach us, and, from extracts which we subjoin, it will be seen that they acknowledge their defeat to have been of the most disastrous character.

The New York Tribune says:

The engineers were about constructing a bridge for the artillery, the regular stone bridge having been mined, and the two columns under Gens. Tyler and Hunter, the latter of which was led by Gen. McDowell, had actually completed the junction, when the order to retreat was given. Why it was given, no person who witnessed the battle, and saw the condition in which affairs stood, can attempt to comprehend. The only point positively held by the enemy was in a hollow to our left, and although an attempt was undoubtedly made to overreach us at the left, an ample force—one entire brigade—was ready to receive them, and did receive and repulse them afterward, in spite of the panic which reigned. But at the beginning of the retirement, a few ambulances and baggage wagons were driven hurriedly away, which seemed to spread terror among the troops within hearing, who instantly broke ranks and ran, pell-mell, toward Centreville.

This contagion caught the rest, and in less than ten minutes our army was flying in the utmost disorder. Everything was abandoned. The wounded were deserted in the hospitals, and the only thought was of individual safety. Guns were thrown aside, and blankets and knapsacks were lost and trampled upon. The artillery shared the panic; the guns were cut loose and the gunners used the horses to escape the more swiftly. Those on foot begged piteously to be allowed to share the horses of those who rode. Many strove to clamber into wagons, and were pushed back by the bayonets of those who occupied them.

The ground was strewed with food, weapons and clothing of every kind. Many of our guns were left to fall into the enemy's hands, including the large 32-pounders, which had done so much service during the fight. All courage, all manliness seemed to have forsaken our terror stricken men.

The last stand upon the field was made by one of the Ohio regiments, under Col. McCook, I believe, but about three miles back the reserve brigade of Gen. Blenker was drawn up in line to cover the retreat and effect whatever service was needed. The stand of Gen. Blenker saved us from great losses.

The disorder of our men continued during the night. There was no army, only a vast rabble. By midnight they were all scattered in the road to Fairfax Court House, and soon after Gen. Blenker, with the Eighth New York Regiment, took up his retreat in perfect order—the only body that so retreated.

I left Centreville at 8 o'clock this morning. The last fragments of our force had all been long gone; even the hospitals were nearly deserted, all who could limp having started forth with crutches and canes. The rebel scouts were passing through the town, and apparently endeavoring to ascertain in which way they could best succeed in cutting off the stragglers. I do not know, however, that any serious attempt to do this was made.

The road from Centreville to Fairfax was thick with [illegible] tinued.

Still Another Account.

The Philadelphia Inquirer publishes a description of the battle and the retreat, by a person who was present during the whole day. We extract the following statements:

Ten men were killed and wounded belonging to the New York Second Regiment, and also four in the Second Ohio Regiment, by the premature discharge of our own muskets in their hands. A retreat was ordered, and our men fell back.

Schenck failed to rally his column in any order. The Ohio and New York men scattered through the woods in pursuit of shelter and water. The sun was broiling hot, and almost suffocating, for the men were now out of water.

We were in the center of Tyler's division, on the hill just east of Bull Run, on the Warrenton road. About 2 P. M. we saw clouds of dust rising to our left, as though they were trying to outflank us and come on us in the rear. We called several officers' attention to it, but there seemed to be no man who could have reinforcements sent for to cover our flank.

On the left of the road was Sherman's and Carlisle's batteries, drawn up for the fight; on the right were three thousand men, consisting of parts of the Ohio and New York Regiments, and the New York Sixty-ninth. About three o'clock P. M., their batteries opened on us; every ball was well fired; the first fell in front of the batteries, and the next one took off the heads of two men, a few yards below us, where Messrs. S. R. Smith, Sheriff J. Harper, Mr. Shaw, of the New York Herald, and ourself, were standing. Orders were given for the men to lie down, and let the balls pass over; and just as the order was given another one swept over our heads, and plowed the field a few steps in our rear. Our batteries did not fire a gun. The enemy were not to be seen, owing to the woods between them and us. Our heavy siege gun was lying to the right, disabled by the carriage being broken down; the balls flew faster and faster, and the batteries were apparently being brought closer.

About 4 P. M. a report flew from man to man that Gen. Cameron's brother, Colonel of the Seventy-ninth, was shot through the breast by a cannon ball and instantly killed.

Lieut. Col. Elliott, of the Seventy-ninth, rode toward his regiment, having been after reinforcements, when a cannon ball cut his horse's head off, and threw him down, bruising him so that he could barely escape. All the stragglers now commenced to run toward Centreville, and the caissons, ambulances and sutler's wagons were ordered to be taken back at once toward Centreville.

The batteries were ordered around to cover our retreat and keep the rebels from cutting us off from Centreville, which was about three miles in our rear, and where we had about four or five thousand of a reserve force; the batteries wheeled off and took up the road, and were retreating in good order, when, about half a mile out, one of the gun carriages was upset.

A portion of Sherman's and Carlisle's were left on the roadside, the gunners cutting the traces and running their horses. This put the infantry in a perfect panic; they broke ranks indiscriminately and commenced to run; knapsacks, haversacks, guns, cartridge boxes, hats, coats and everything being thrown in all directions. The men were parched for water and were falling in every direction. Officers were equally panic stricken with the privates, and in vain we endeavored to stop the retreat.

Charles Ogden, George R. Smith, Sheriff Harper, Russell Ernett, of Pittsburg, begged our men not to retreat, and pleaded with tears for them to go back and get Col. Cameron's body; we took muskets and threatened to shoot them down if they did not, but we might as well have pleaded with the winds to cease blowing.

The enemy appeared in sight, firing their guns, the balls raining upon us thick. Emerging from the valley, we saw the reporter of The World, with the standard of the Massachusetts 5th, waving it over him and pleading for the men to rally around him; but it was in vain; they heeded him not. An officer asked the privilege of riding behind him. It was granted, and before they had gone a hundred yards a shot from the thicket struck the officer in the head and he reeled off. Mr. Stedman wrapped up the standrrd, and galloped about a mile ahead, and afterwards succeeded in rallying a large force.

Our friends had now all left, and the troops were flying, and at the cry that the cavalry were riding them down and butchering all, we started for Centreville. In the edge of the woods we noticed Mr. Villard, of the New York Herald, trying to pacify the men, telling them it was only a panic. He was mounted, but could not take any passengers. Our thirst was now painful, the dust filling our nostrils till we could scarcely get breath. Finding no headway could be made on foot, and being liable to be shot or hewn down momentarily, we made for a horse we heard rushing through the woods and caught him; he had a shot through him in the flank, and was bleeding profusely, and had no saddle or brible. We mounted him, and clinging to his mane, made for the road again leading to Centreville.

Here the road was strewn with wrecks of wagons, provisions, muskets, blankets, ammunition, and everything the men could divest themselves of. The ground was full. The fields in all directions were full. The fire of the enemy was kept up in the rear. Part of Sherman's battery breaking down, the men cut the traces and fled. The ammunition wagon was left on the field. We should judge that ten thousand guns and rifles were lost on the way, while the cartridge boxes, bayonets, sabre bayonets and swords were innumerable. About a mile from Centreville an attempt was made to rally the men, but with little success. A few thousand were stopped, but many without weapons. On the high hill top at Centreville a column of infantry was seen, with their gleaming bayonets. On the top the artillery were also seen drawn up, prepared to fire.

The Garibaldians, Einstein's and Blenker's regiments were drawn up at the foot of the hill, and escaping men ordered to fall in. Loud cheering was done, and the rallying cry given, but it was little or no use—men had no officers when they did halt, and so they kept on retreating. "Water, water!" was the cry; "give me water, or I'll sink," was heard from all sides. Not a drop was to be had fit to drink. The wells were all drained, and the clouds of dust filled the air at every point. We got in the rear of a negro hut, and there secured water thick with filth, but it was the best to be had. A number of buildings were used for hospitals, [illegible] side cries were made for surgeons.

All the inhabitants nearly had fled from Centreville, expecting it to be stormed by the rebels. Guards were stationed at the few wells not dry, to allow no water except to the wounded and sick. A house on the top of the hill had been burnt the previous night, and what few men could be induced to work were engaged in throwing up an embankment, some eight feet thick, out of the ruins and of dirt; it was about two hundred feet square. Orders were now circulated for the men to gather at their last camping ground, around Centreville; it was heeded by some, but others neglected it and kept up the stampede. No provisions were to be had, and the men were all hungry, having had nothing to eat since 2 o'clock, A. M., and but little or no water. At 6½ o'clock, P. M., when we started for Washington, the troops were coming in, and no one of any coolness or self possession supposed our forces would retreat from Centreville.

As the hours passed on, the fight became more and more terrific. The fortunes of the day began to waver, especially as the Federal troops did not seem to gain any material advantage, and only made their advances slowly, laboriously, and at great loss of life. The rebels were strongly entrenched behind masked batteries of rifle cannon. They seemed to be innumerable. Again and again our men charged upon them, only to find when they had dislodged them in one place they had reappeared in another, until at last the Federal soldiers were compelled to fall on their faces to avoid the swift messengers of death. It was found, too, that the rebel forces largely outnumbered those of the Federals. I have no means of knowing the exact strength of either of the armies, but the best authorities state that the Secessionists numbered 70,000, while at no time had Gen. McDowell in action as many as 40,000. Our troops were mainly infantry; our batteries, as a general thing, were small though well managed; they were no match for the cannon of larger calibre manned by the rebels.

The fight continued until after 5 o'clock, without exhibiting any material result. The rebels had most decidedly the advantage in position and guns, and they used it with fearful effect. The bravery of our troops was superhuman, but what bravery could meet the unerring and unceasing cannon which came sweeping from almost every tree or heap of brush? Our men unmasked them, battery upon battery, only to find their lessened ranks were unequal to the task. A retreat was commenced by a New York regiment, and very soon became general.

The firing of the enemy was kept up on our rear [illegible] fight, for Gen. McDowell, which he had orders to deliver immediately. He at once, without making any attempt to do so, said if Gen. Scott wanted to get his head blown off let him take them himself; he would not do so, and so they never went.

We left Centreville with the cheering news that Gen. Mansfield, with artillery and an immense force, was coming up to turn the rebels back. About a mile east of Centreville, we met the 1st New Jersey, with their Colonel leading at their head, and his staff, pleading for the men to return; his drummer corps were playing Yankee Doodle, and their colors were flying; the men kept cheering all the time, and urging one another to return; they were nearly worn out with their forced march from Vienna. They were followed by the New Jersey Third.

They inspired courage into the retreating soldiers, but many fell exhaused by the way-side, considering it safe to remain a few minutes longer to rest. Large numbers of the men fell into their old camp grounds, and the baggage wagons drove in the fields all along the road; but the most sorrowful sight was the loss of provisions and all kinds of stores, that lined the road for five miles.

The cowardly retreat on the morning of the flight, by the Pennsylvania 4th, and various batteries, had a depressing effect upon our force, and encouraged the rebels by the story that our men were running. That their time was up, is an excuse that will not answer.

Incidentals.

Members of the 71st says that 200 of that regiment has been captured, but that its loss, killed and wounded, is not severe.

The Zouaves have probably suffered most. Their conduct was beyond praise.

Of 300 marines only 45 were counted at the Long Bridge this morning.

The sight which met the eyes of Col. Hunter's brigade when, after marching through the woods and taking one battery, it came in sight of the enemy, is described as a grand one. Their line of battle had been formed in splendid order, and fresh troops were brought in by rail constantly.

A New Orleans Zouave captured yesterday by the Fire Zouaves, boasted that the rebels had shown no quarter to the Federal troops, having in many instances cut the throats of the wounded. He had no sooner made this disgusting disclosure than he was suspended in the air.

During the retreat Heintzelman's columns were followed by the rebel cavalry, who literally butchered our men. It is reported that when the left wing reached the batteries a second time they took them and routed the rebel forces.

The rebels, however, being reinforced again, came up and retook them. When the retreat of the left wing commenced, the enemy made an attack on Gen. Schenck's men, who were still in command, defeating them and causing them to retreat. Most of the fighting of the enemy at this point was done with bowie knives.

It has been ascertained that the rebel forces number about 38,000 in and about Manassas. Gen. Scott received this information to-day, and was asked by a member of Congress what was the strength of the Union force. "It is enough," was the laconic reply of the general.

A rebel was observed stabbing some of our men who fell in battle. He was captured and hung to a tree, in sight of the rebel pickets, and remained there, dangling in the air, with his face as black as any negro.

From the Baltimore American.

Enough has been gathered, however, and from reliable sources, to render it certain that the battle was most bloody, but not in its general result, but in the character of its individual conflicts. In some instances the conflict is said to have been carried on with hand-to-hand desperation, entrenchments being lost and won again at the point of the bayonet, and in one instance, at least, at the point of the knife. Thus the Second Michigan are said to have been driven out of a small battery which they had entered, by a desperate bayonet charge by a regiment (of Mississippians, it is supposed,) armed with rifles without bayonets, and with bowie-knives, one of which, captured by a member of the Second Michigan, and triumphantly exhibited by its captor, was in size and weight not much unlike a saber bayonet.

An officer of the Sixty-ninth (Irish) Regiment states, in illustration of the desperate charater of the attack and of the repulse, that the battery attacked during the day by them, and defended, as was ascertained by two youthful prisoners, by a regiment of South Carolinians, was taken and retaken at the point of the bayonet *eight times in succession*, the Carolinians at last retaining possession of the work by the aid of a fourth battery which was unmasked at the critical period of the fight.

A Confederate soldier and a member of a Wisconsin regiment were found upon the field locked in a deadly embrace, the former clutching the hair of his antagonist, in whose breast a bowie knife was found buried to the hilt, he himself having died apparently from a ghastly wound in his breast.

The batteries of the Confederates, it is generally conceded, were planned with consummate skill, and so closely concealed or masked that not until they opened fire could their deadly neighborhood be detected. They were so arranged as to entirely command each other, and the Federal troops found that the deadliest portion of their gallantry and enterprise was that which gained them entrance to a masked battery. They were also covered with rifle pits, so contrived as to afford a swift retreat by the rear, and from these a deadly fire was poured upon the advancing columns. It was from these shelters that the Confederate riflemen inflicted the heaviest losses upon the Fire Zouaves.

In the effort during the early part of the day to outflank the enemy, the Federal officers found paths leading, as they supposed, to the desired positions in the rear of the batteries, and these were followed with zeal and daring, but in more than one instance they are said to have proved mere traps, deliberately devised for the destruction of those who should attempt it, and from which, once entered, egress was prohibited by the splendid cavalry which formed a conspicuous feature of the Southern force, and the strength of which has been estimated in round numbers at from 3000 to 15,000.

The crisis of the day was reached about four o'clock, when the Confederates, suddenly emerging from the batteries, behind which they had previously sheltered, dashed upon the Federal lines, and the assault being followed by an irresistible shower of leaden hail, two regiments acting, it is said, under a misunderstanding of a general order, commenced a retrograde movement, which was quickly followed by the remainder of those in action, until soon the entire column was in retreat. The movement at first began with deliberation, and might have continued in good order, but for an unfortunate alarm, which, commencing on the left of the column, spread rapidly over the field until the entire army, with a few honorable exceptions, broke into a flight which became a general stampede. When at a portion of Bull Run, where a small bridge was placed, they encountered the unexpected opposition of an apparently newly erected battery, supported by a column of infantry.

right wing under the command of Col. Conner, and the left under that of Capt. Garey—the command of the intrepid Watson Guards, who had so distinguished themselves in the opening of the action, being devolved upon Lieut. W. D. Jennings, until joined by Lieuts. Bates and Tompkins, who had undertaken the brave mission of bringing water to the suffering men through the thickest of the fire.

The slaughter of the enemy at the battery, as the combined charge of the Virginia Regiment and the Hampton Legion swept over it, is said to have been terrific. The fugitives were pursued by the companies of the Legion to near Centreville. For four or five miles the pursuit is described to have been over dead bodies, which strewed the retreat of the enemy.

The Legion reports about thirty killed and mortally hurt, with the immense number of nearly three hundred wounded—truly a gallant record. Neither its cavalry companies nor artillery arrived in time for the action; had they done so, quicker work would have been made by the Legion. As it is, with the gallant record it has made, and the compliments of Beauregard given it the day after the victory, it may boast, indeed, to have had a distinguished part in the glorious day.

The names of Captains Conner, Garey, Adjutant Barker and Surgeons Darby and Taylor are mentioned among those who distinguished themselves heroically in the fight.

The escapes of many of the men through the storm of fire are described as almost miraculous. The South Carolinians were better shots than the enemy. At three fires from one of the Corporals, J. W. Tompkins, two Yankees were seen to bite the dust; and at one time of the action, Lieut. Jennings, with a revolver, fired into the enemy a number of shots, nearly each one of which struck its man. Many of the Legion had their clothes torn through with bullets.

Mr. Pritchard, the general telegraphic agent has kindly furnished us with the following:

From a very intelligent and reliable gentleman from South Carolina, who was on the battle field, and who held a prominent position there, I have obtained the following statement:

[illegible] Hampton Legion) on the battle ground near Manassas on Sunday last.

The 2d Regiment, commanded by Col. Kershaw, was in the hottest of the fight. Col. Cash, of the 8th Regiment, was with Col. Kershaw, and those regiments brigaded together.

Col. Sloan's 4th Regiment was the first which engaged the enemy—it opened the ball. It was stationed three miles to the left of the other South Carolina regiments, and, with the Louisiana troops, suffered considerably. Adjutant Wilkes, Lieut. Earle and other officers were killed. Capt. Poole was severely, if not mortally wounded. Capt. Kilpatrick was also wounded,

Defeat Acknowledged by the Northern Papers.

The statements of the Northern press relative to the battle at Manassas are beginning to reach us, and, from extracts which we subjoin, it will be seen that they acknowledge their defeat to have been of the most disastrous character.

The New York Tribune says:

The engineers were about constructing a bridge for the artillery, the regular stone bridge having been mined, and the two columns under Gens. Tyler and Hunter, the latter of which was led by Gen. McDowell, had actually completed the junction, when the order to retreat was given. Why it was given, no person who witnessed the battle, and saw the condition in which affairs stood, can attempt to comprehend. The only point positively held by the enemy was in a hollow to our left, and although an attempt was undoubtedly made to overreach us at the left, an ample force—one entire brigade—was ready to receive them, and did receive and repulse them afterward, in spite of the panic which reigned. But at the beginning of the retirement, a few ambulances and baggage wagons were driven hurriedly away, which seemed to spread terror among the troops within hearing, who instantly broke ranks and ran, pell-mell, toward Centreville.

This contagion caught the rest, and in less than ten minutes our army was flying in the utmost disorder. Everything was abandoned. The wounded were deserted in the hospitals, and the only thought was of individual safety. Guns were thrown aside, and blankets and knapsacks were lost and trampled upon. The artillery shared the panic; the guns were cut loose and the gunners used the horses to escape the more swiftly. Those on foot begged piteously to be allowed to share the horses of those who rode. Many strove to clamber into wagons, and were pushed back by the bayonets of those who occupied them.

The ground was strewed with food, weapons and clothing of every kind. Many of our guns were left to fall into the enemy's hands, including the large 32-pounders, which had done so much service during the fight. All courage, all manliness seemed to have forsaken our terror stricken men.

The last stand upon the field was made by one of the Ohio regiments, under Col. McCook, I believe, but about three miles back the reserve brigade of Gen. Blenker was drawn up in line to cover the retreat and effect whatever service was needed. The stand of Gen. Blenker saved us from great losses.

The disorder of our men continued during the night. There was no army, only a vast rabble. By midnight they were all scattered in the road to Fairfax Court House, and soon after Gen. Blenker, with the Eighth New York Regiment, took up his retreat in perfect order—the only body that so retreated.

I left Centreville at 8 o'clock this morning. The last fragments of our force had all been long gone; even the hospitals were nearly deserted, all who could limp having started forth with crutches and canes. The rebel scouts were passing through the town, and apparently endeavoring to ascertain in which way they could best succeed in cutting off the stragglers. I do not know, however, that any serious attempt to do this was made

MILITARY.

HEADQUARTERS CARONDELET GUARDS, No. 12 Gravier street.
Mr. R. H. Y-LS, of the firm of C. Yale, Jr., & Co, having been appointed Treasurer of this Company, no one is authorized to solicit subscriptions for said Company except those holding lists signed by him and Capt N. J. WILSON. jy30 tf

GLADDEN RIFLES. — All able-bodied young men, wishing to volunteer for immediate active service, will apply at No. 91 Gravier street. Uniforms and equipments furnished.
WM. A. METCALFE, Captain,
jy27 1m late 1st Lieut. Crescent Rifles, Company A.

FOR VIRGINIA!—Company C, Continental Guards.—A few more men wanted to complete the roll of this Company, for immediate active service in Virginia. Uniforms and equipments furnished free.
Apply at the Armory, which is open daily from 9 A. M. until 9 P. M., corner of St. Charles and Lafayette streets, opposite the City Hall
Squad drills every evening at 7½ o'clock. jy27 1w

NOTICE.—The members (active and honorary) of the Louisiana Guard are notified that a meeting will be held on TUESDAY EVENING, the 30th inst., at 6½ o'clock, at the Armory, corner of Natchez and New Levee streets. As business of importance will be brought up, every member is earnestly requested to be present.
GUS. A. BREAUX,
jy26 Acting for Louisiana Guard.

HEADQUARTERS HARDEE RIFLE GUARD, corner of Carondelet and Common streets.—Wanted, a few more men, of good character, to fill the ranks of his company, for immediate State service. Apply on nights of drill, TUESDAY, THURSDAY and SATURDAY EVENINGS. Uniforms free. By order.
JOSEPH ANDREWS, Jr., Captain.
CHAS. E. DIRMEYER, 1st Lieutenant. jy25 1w

HEADQUARTERS SOUTHERN NAVAL BRIGADE, 705 Tchoupitoulas street, between Josephine and Adele streets—WANTED, Thirty good, active men, for immediate service. Uniform, equipments and board furnished. Apply immediately.
JAMES HILL, Captain.
H. L. LEVY, Lieutenant.
S. WHITE, O. S. jy24 2w

HEADQUARTERS LOUISIANA GUARD.—The members of the Louisiana Guard are notified that the Armory has been removed to the corner of New Levee and Natchez streets, where they are respectfully invited to attend their usual drills.
GUS. A. BREAUX,
jy14 1m Acting for Battalion La. Guard.

HEADQU[illegible] CELTS, Corner St. Mary and Tc[illegible] streets, July 13, 1861.—The following [illegible] have consented to collect funds to aid in the equipment of Company A Southern Celts:

G. Farrell, Esq.,	Hon. W. R. Miles,
T. L. Lemly, Esq.,	J. P. Higgins, Esq.,
Hon. T. J. Semmes,	John Gorman, Esq.,
M. Hynes, Esq.,	W. C. Budd, Esq.,
W. J. Ahern, Esq.,	Thos. Hanly, Esq.,
W. J. Castell, Esq.,	Dr. W. G. Austin.

Contributions will be duly acknowledged by Mr. M. O'Rourk, Treasurer, on behalf of the Company.
jy14 1m S. O'LEARY, Captain.

All parties desirous of communicating with Company A, American Rifles, now in Virginia, can have their letters safely transmitted by leaving them with the undersigned, at the office of A. THOMSON & CO., 48 Tchoupitoulas street, on or before SATURDAY of every week, until further notice.
jy5 2m R. T. BOYLE, Lieut. Am. Rifles Co. B.

ATTENTION, DELTA RIFLES.—The above Company meets for Drill Exercise every WEDNESDAY and SATURDAY EVENINGS, at 7½ o'clock, at their Armory, corner of St. Charles and Lafayette streets. The members are requested to be punctual. By order of
H. BREEN, Captain.
WM. H. MCLORINAN, Orderly Sergeant. apr23 6m

HEADQUARTERS OF AMERICAN RIFLES, Company B—Armory, 33 Carondelet street—Attention!—You are hereby ordered to attend drill every WEDNESDAY and SATURDAY EVENINGS, at 7 o'clock. By order of the Captain.
may11 1m* D. FITZPATRICK, O. S.

HEADQUARTERS MARION RANGERS, No. 57 St. Charles street. New Orleans, July 27. ATTENTION.—Company drills MONDAY, WEDNESDAY and FRIDAY EVENINGS, at 5 o'clock. Punctual attendance required.
By order of the CAPTAIN.
R. B. L. SORRY, O. S. jy27 tf

HEADQUARTERS CARONDELET GUARDS, New Orleans, July 25, 1861.
FOR THE SEAT OF WAR—For Immediate Active Service—A few more good Men will be accepted in the Carondelet Guards by applying at Headquarters, No. 12 Gravier street. Clothing and equipments furnished. jy26 tf N. J. WILSON, Captain.

ARMORY MARION RANGERS—NEW ORLEANS, July 17th, 1861.—Attention!—Company drills MONDAY and FRIDAY EVENINGS at Wood Cotton Press, at 5 o'clock. Business meetings every WEDNESDAY EVENING at the same hour. Punctual attendance required.
By order of the Captain.
y17 tf R. B. L. SOREY, O. S.

HEADQUARTERS LOUISIANA RIFLES, Company A—Merchants' Exchange, Royal street, Room No. 5.—You are hereby ordered to attend Company drills every TUESDAY and FRIDAY NIGHTS, and Squad drills every morning, from 8 to 10. Meetings every MONDAY and SATURDAY NIGHTS, and it [illegible] requested that every member be present.
R. K. LAUGHLIN, Captain.

HEAD[illegible] JACKSON REGIMENT, July 6, 1861—Two or three Com[illegible] Jackson Regiment, to complete its organization [illegible] accepted by the Secretary of War. Captains of Companies [illegible] [illegible] Confederate States service will [illegible] Jackson [illegible] Exchange.

WANTED FOR COMPANY B, LOUISIANA RIFLES—A few more good men to fill up the ranks of the above company. To those enlisting a good bounty will be paid.
Good pay, board and lodging and uniforms furnisheed free of expense.
Apply at No. 3 Front Levee street.
jy6 tf JOHN DEPAS, Lieutenant Commanding.

HICKORY GUARDS, ATTENTION!—The Hickory Guards drill EVERY EVENING, at the Engine House of No. 18, on Calliope street. Regular meetings every Monday, Wednesday and Friday.
All persons of good character who desire to engage in military life are requested to join.
AUG. RICHARDS,
JOHN KAVANAUGH,
WM. MOYNAN,
june30 tf Committee.

HEADQUARTERS SLIDELL VOLUNTEERS—June 23, 1861.
At a meeting held this evening, the following gentlemen were appointed to receive subscriptions for the above company:
R. JOHNSON, 114 Camp street.
J. REARDON, 7 Chartres street.
JOHN MURRAY, at D. H. Holmes's, Canal street.
WILLIAM SMEDLEY, 424 Poydras street.
No other parties are authorized to collect any money for this company. june29 tf THOMAS H. WASSON, Secretary.

RIPLEY RIFLE RANGERS—Members of this company will attend drill EVERY EVENING, at 7½ o'clock, punctually.
Headquarters—No. 8 New Levee and Tchoupitoulas streets, corner of Common. By order.
june28 tf F. G. RANDOLPH, Secretary.

FOR THE WAR!—Bonford Guards—A few more able bodied young men are wanted to fill the ranks of the Bonford Guards, to go into immediate active service. Uniforms and equipments will be furnished. Apply at the Armory, 61 Customhouse street, up stairs. june11 tf

HEADQUARTERS OF THE POLISH BRIGADE, First Regiment, 57 St. Charles street—Companies and individuals wishing to be mustered without delay, in the service of the Confederate States, will apply from 9 A. M. to 6 P. M.
V. SULAKOWSKI, Colonel,
je11 tf Commanding First Regiment.

The title of the SEYMOUR GUARDS will be henceforth changed to the CARVIN GUARDS. Ten more able bodied men will be enrolled, to complete the full company. Good board, clothing and bounty will be given. Apply at the rendezvous, 69 Tchoupitoulas street.
jy19 M. HANLY, Captain.

FOR THE WAR IN VIRGINIA!—The MORSE GUARDS want twenty able-bodied men, of good character, to complete the ranks of this Company, bound for the seat of war. Those wishing to join us in the Southern Cause will please call at the Armory, No. 66 St. Charles street, where they can be uniformed and equipped, free of expense. Good board and lodging furnished. jy10

DELTA RIFLE COMPANY—June 21, 1861. Twenty able bodied men wanted to complete the ranks of the above Company for immediate active State service. Uniforms and equipments furnished free of cost. Apply on WEDNESDAY and SATURDAY EVENINGS at their Armory, corner of St. Charles and Lafayette streets.
The following gentlemen are authorized by the above Company to solicit and receive contributions for the purpose of enabling the Company to proceed immediately on active duty.
JOHN BREEN,
WM. MILLER,
J. T. McFARLANE,
J. C. SMITH.
Committee.
By order of H. BREEN, Captain.
W. H. MCLORINACE, O. S. june22

VOLUNTEERS WANTED.—The undersigned is authorized by Colonel V. SULAKOWZKY, of the 1st Regiment of the Polish Brigade, to raise a Company for active service for the Confederate States. The Company will be called a Polish Company. Uniforms and equipments will be such as used by the Polish nation and will be neat. Board furnished free.
All able bodied men of good character, irrespective of nationality, will be received in this Company at No. 66 St. Charles and No. 102 Poydras street. jy12 F. BEUTER, Captain.

VOLUNTEERS! VOLUNTEERS!!—Board, Uniforms and Equipments furnished Free!—RACE GUARDS!—Twenty men are wanted to fill the ranks of this Company, for immediate service in Virginia Apply at once at the Armory, corner of Julia and Tchoupitoulas streets.
june15 HENRY N. SORIA, Captain.

FOR THE WAR—SLIDELL VOLUNTEERS. A few more able bodied Volunteers wanted to complete the company of Slidell Guards, the company to join the Polish Brigade, First Regiment, for immediate active service in Virginia. Arms and equipments to be furnished as soon as the company is mustered into service. Armory, No. 8 Front Levee street, between Customhouse and Crossman streets.
june12 WILLIAM SMEDLEY, Captain.

CONFEDERATE GUARDS, Company C, Attention!—You are hereby ordered to attend company drills every TUESDAY, THURSDAY and SATURDAY, at 6 o'clock P. M., at the Armory, corner of Camp and North streets, "Moresque Building." Punctual attendance is requested.
By order JOS. ELLISON, Captain.
CHAS. W. PESCAY, O. S. june14

SPECIAL NOTICES.

BANK OF LOUISIANA, New Orleans, July 22, 1861.—At a meeting of the Board of Directors, held this day, a semi-annual dividend of five per cent., and an extra dividend of five per cent., were declared, out of the profits o the last six months, payable to the stockholders, or to their legal representatives, on or after Monday, 5th August next.
jy23tf AUG'T MONTERUIL, Cashier.

MERCHANTS' BANK, NEW ORLEANS, July 1, 1861.—The dividend, declared THIS DAY, of FOUR PER CENT., out of the profits of the last six months, will be paid on and after MONDAY, July 8th. jy1 1m W. S. MOUNT, Cashier.

NOTICE TO STOCKHOLDERS OF SOUTHERN PACIFIC RAILROAD—That those stockholders who have subscribed to the new books, but have not closed up their subscriptions by payment, and others who have expressed a desire to subscribe, may have an opportunity, each, to protect their interests in this enterprise, I will keep the subscription book open for one week longer, at No. 84 Common street.
The sum of money which is now imperatively needed to protect the interests of the stockholders is not very large, and it is hoped that stockholders at New Orleans, who are so peculiarly interested in the success of this work, will not permit themselves to be cut off from it by withholding the very small increased subscription necessary to protect their interests. It must be borne in mind, too, that Mr. Stevenson, the President, pledges to the stockholders who now increase their subscriptions, full and complete protection for both their old and new stocks.
apr28 R. V. RICHARDSON, Agent.

SOUTHERN PACIFIC RAILROAD COMPANY. I have opened books for subscription to the Capital Stock of this Company, under the Louisville Resolutions of 15th inst., at No. 84 Common street, where I may be found from 9 A. M. to 3 P. M., for a few days. I desire to meet there all friends and stockholders. Please be prompt. mar28 tf R. V. RICHARDSON, Agent.

NOTICE.—The South-western Express Company is now prepared to forward freight and packages to all parts of Louisiana and Texas. Office 96 Camp street. nov18 tf

THE ELECTION.

EDITORS DELTA—Please announce HENRY AVERY, the present Superintendent of Public Education, as a Candidate for re-election. jy19

PROMOTE HIM—Messrs. Editors: Please announce H. PERALTA as a candidate for AUDITOR OF PUBLIC ACCOUNTS, at the election in November.
Mr. Peralta is the present efficient Chief Clerk in the Auditor's Office, and served under Bordelon and Marks. He should be promoted. apr3 ted&w LOUISIANA.

FOR STATE AUDITOR—WM. L. KNOX, of Carroll parish, is a candidate for State Auditor at the next election. He will be supported by
may15 A MAJORITY OF VOTERS.

WANTS—WANTS.

DICTIONARIES WANTED IN ALL LANGUAGES.—Persons having also FRENCH and SPANISH BOOKS to sell, should bring them to
Prof. BRETTE'S
jy28 2t 13 St. Charles street.

ANY PERSON having the command of $20,000, will be conferring a great benefit on the Government, by making a loan, payable in three years, April, 1864, on unincumbered mortgage, with 8 per cent. interest. The borrower will apply the entire amount of such loan, when obtained, for the organizing and equipping of military companies to serve during the war. For information, apply at this office. je21 tf

WANTED—Drummers, Fifers and Buglers, for the Polish Brigade. Apply at No. 57 St. Charles street. june11 tf

NEW ADVERTISEMENTS.

E. CONERY, GROCER AND DEALER IN WESTERN PRODUCE,
Nos. 2 Front and 10 Fulton Streets,
Has constantly on hand a full supply of Groceries, Wines, Brandies, and Liquors of the very best quality, and for sale in lots to suit purchasers, at the lowest market price. june22 1y

NOTES ON DEAFNESS—An Instructor and Guide for Deaf Persons, by W. L. DAVIS, M.D. The work can be had on application, or it will be sent free on receipt of stamps to pay postage.
N. B.—Dr. Davis has removed his office from 127 Carondelet street to No. 11 Bourbon street. jy11 tf

CANNONS.....CANNONS....CANNONS.
CANNONS FOR SALE.
TWENTY PIECES OF CANNON, of the best and most approved manufactory in the world, ranking from SIX to TWENTY-FOUR POUNDERS.
Apply to N. J. WILSON,
54 Magazine street,
jy25 tf

[illegible] SOUTHERN HOUSE [illegible] [illegible] ventilated, [illegible] the rooms fronting on Railroad Avenue would be very hot, were there not 334 feet of veranda of ten feet in depth.
Even these verandas would be hot were they not shielded from the sun by 5486 feet of blue and white striped canvas curtains.
The water would be two warm for the glowing faces of its guests were it not fresh from the coolest springs of pure free stone water instead of a cistern standing in the sun.
The reflection of the sun's rays would add greatly to the heat of the place, did they not descend upon the richest verdure of forest green instead of a bed of sand.
The position of Proprietor of the CENTRAL HOUSE would be uncomfortably warm did he not offer in this Southern House a few more real comforts than can be found in any Country Hotel in the South.
Distance from New Orleans—two dollars. april1 tf

STATE OF LOUISIANA, Sixth District Court of New Orleans—I hereby certify, that on 3d day of July, 1861, judgment was entered in this Court in the suit of Maria Roux, wife of Herman Mehrtens, vs. her husband—No. 9557—in the words and figures following, to wit: In this case submitted to the Court on the written argument of counsel, the Court having duly considered the pleadings and evidence, it is ordered, adjudged and decreed, that there be judgment decreeing a separation of property between plaintiff and defendant herein; and it is further ordered that the plaintiff, Maria Roux, wife of Herman Mertens, recover from said defendant the sum of two hundred and forty dollars, and costs of suit, with five per cent. per annum interet on said sum of two hundred and forty dollars from the 10th June, 1861, until paid.
Judgment rendered July 3, 1861. Judgment signed July 15, 1861.
(Signed) R. K. HOWELL, Judge.
In testimony whereof, I have hereunto set my hand and affixed the seal of the said Court, at the city of New Orleans, on this 19th day of July, in the year of our Lord one thousand eight hundred and sixty-one. A. J. VILLERE,
jy21 3tin10d Deputy Clerk.

ETAT DE LA LOUISIANE—Sixieme Cour de District de la Nouvelle Orleans—Je certifie par le present que jugement a ete enregistre en cette cour le 3 de juillet 1861, dans l'affaire de Maria Roux, epouse de Herman Mehrtens, vs. son epoux No. 955; en mots et formes comme suivent: Dans cette affaire, soumise a la Cour en argument ecrit de l'avocat, la cour ayant considere la plaidoirie et l'evidence, il est ordonne, adjuge et decrete, que jugement soit rendu decretant une separation de propriete entre la demanderesse et le defendeur; il est de plus ordonne que la demanderesse, Maria Roux, epouse de Herman Mertens, recouvre du dit defendeur la somme de deux cent quarante piastres et les frais de cour, avec interet de cinq pour cent par an sur la susdite somme de deux cent quarante piastres, a partir du 10 de juin jusqu'au paiement.
Jugement rendu le 3 de juillet 1861. Jugement signe le 15 de juillet 1861.
(Signed) R. K. HOWELL, Juge.
En temoignage duquel j'ai ici pose ma signature et attache le sceau de la dite cour, a la ville de la Nouvelle Orleans, le 19me jour de uillet de l'annee de Notre Seigneur mil huit cent soixante-et-un.
A. J. VILLERE,
jy21 3tin10d Depute Greffier.

NOTICE—MARSHAL'S OFFICE, CONFEDERATE STATES OF AMERICA, District of Louisiana.
S. C. McLellan et al. vs. Ship Abaellino—In the District Court of the Confederate States, District of Louisiana—In Prize No. 8.
The proceeds of the sale of the prize ship Abaellino having come into my hands for distribution, all persons interested therein are hereby notified to present their claims at my Office for adjustment and payment within ten days from this date.
C. B. BEVERLEY, C. S. Marshal,
jy24 10t Office, New Custom House.

NOTICE.—The interest of MR. WILLIAM BUCHANAN, in the firm of JOSEPH R. SHANNON & CO., ceased on the 1st inst. The undersigned will continue the business in his own name and for his own account, and will liquidate the affairs of the late firm. JOS. R. SHANNON.
New Orleans, July 22, 1861. jy28 3t

LIME! LIME! LIME! LIME!
2000 bbls. Alabama and Thomaston.
I. S. HOLDEN & CO.,
jy9 1m Corner Magazine and Poydras streets.

LOGWOOD—A superior article, for sale by
J. B. VALENTINE & CO.,
jy28 tf No. 51 Common street.

JEANS AND LINSEYS—Alabama and South Carolina manufactured, for sale by
J. B. VALENTINE & CO.,
jy28 tf No. 51 Common street.

MEXICAN WOOL—For sale by
J. B. VALENTINE & CO.,
jy28 tf No. 51 Common street.

300 CASES AND TRUNKS OF BOOTS AND SHOES, suitable for city or country trade, for sale by J. B. VALENTINE & CO.,
jy28 tf No. 51 Common street.

TO THE MILITARY.—Call and see Williams's Folding MUSQUITO BARS, got up expressly for camp use. Prices low, at the sole agency,
WELLS'S Southern Coal Oil and Lamp Depot,
a2 tf corner Carondelet and Poydras streets.

INSURANCE.

CITIZENS' MUTUAL INSURANCE COMPANY.
O. GAILLARD, President.
A. SCHREIBER, Secretary

TRUSTEES:

GEO. W. WEST,	AR. MILTENBERGER,	MARTIN GORDON, JR.
JAMES A. WHITE,	J. LEISEY,	NUMA AUGUSTIN,
DOUGLAS WEST,	R. P. HUNT,	OMSAIRE OLIVIER,
D. JAMISON,	M. MUSSON	A. BORN,
ISMAR GAILLARD,		

The Company continue to insure against the perils of the seas and rivers, and loss and damage by fire, at the current rates of premium.
Office—No. 3 Carondelet street. dec15-1y

AMUSEMENTS.

ST. CHARLES THEATER.
Grand Dramatic Performance
MONDAY EVENING, August 5th, for the Benefit of the
ALLEN GUARDS,
By the Amateurs of this city, assisted by several Ladies of the Profession, on which occasion will be presented the domestic Drama in three acts, by Douglas Jerrold, entitled
THE RENT DAY.
After which a
SONG..........................by...........Miss Fanny Pierson.
The whole to conclude with the pleasing Comedy in one act, of
FAINT HEART NEVER WON FAIR LADY.
Box office open on Saturday, August 3d, and Monday, August 5th, from 10 o'clock A. M. to 3 P. M. each day, where seats may be secured.
Prices of Admission as usual. jy30-1w

ARMORY HALL...............Camp street.
For one Week, commencing on MONDAY NIGHT, July 29th—Benefit for the aid of Families of Absent Volunteers.
The Panopticon of the South,
A Mechanical Exhibition of life-like moving figures, representing scenes in the present War, including the BOMBARDMENT OF FORT SUMTER, with perfect views of the principal Forts in the South.
For particulars see programmes.
Grand Matinee on Saturday, for the accommodation of Families and Schools.
Tickets, 50c.; Children and Servants, 25c.; Children and Servants, to Matinee, 15c.
Doors open at 7½, commence at 8 o'clock. Box Office open for sale of Tickets from 10 to 12 A. M., and 3 to 5 P. M. jy26 1w

SOUTHERN CONFEDERATION GARDEN, In Algiers, above the Canal street Ferry.
Open Every Sunday During the Season.
The proprietors of this Garden respectfully wish to inform the public, that this Garden will be open every Sunday during the season, and that everything will be carried on in a way to give entire satisfaction to all who may visit this Garden.
A large Ball Room has been built for dancing. Good Lager Beer and Liquors can be had at the Bar, &c.
ADMISSION—Gentlemen 25 cents; ladies, accompanied by gentlemen, free; ladies not accompanied by gentlemen will not be admitted. JOHN JASKE & HENRY H. LEOPOLD,
ap26 fri sat sutf Proprietors.

LOUIS CONTI BEGS TO ANNOUNCE to the public that he has started a LINE OF HORSE BOATS, which are running in Bayou St. John, from the Terminus of the City Railroad, conveying Passengers TO AND FROM THE LAKE, at the rate of TWENTY CENTS for the Excursion.
The boats will leave every day from 6½ to 10½ A. M. and from 2 to 9 P. M. On Sunday will run EVERY HOUR. jy14 1m

MUSICAL AND ATTRACTIVE.—A Musical Entertainment will take place at BOUDRU'S late Restaurant, on the Pontchartrain Railroad, every MONDAY, THURSDAY and SATURDAY EVENINGS. An excellent band of music, from the French Opera Orchestra, has been engaged. Visitors will be regaled with everything which will conduce to their comfort and pleasure. jy21 1m

EDUCATIONAL.

UNIVERSITY OF LOUISIANA.
MEDICAL DEPARTMENT.
The Annual Course of Lectures in this Department will commence on MONDAY, November 11, 1861, and will terminate in the ensuing March.
JAMES JONES, M. D., Professor of Practice of Medicine.
J. L. RIDDELL, M. D., Professor of Chemistry.
WARREN STONE, M. D., Professor of Surgery.
A. H. CENAS, M. D., Professor of Obstetrics.
GUSTAVUS A. NOTT, M. D., Professor of Materia Medica.
T. G. RICHARDSON, M. D., Professor of Anatomy.
THOMAS HUNT, M. D., Professor of Physiology and Pathology.
S. E. CHAILLE, M. D., W. C. NICHOLS, M. D., } Demonstrators of Anatomy.
The Rooms for Dissecting will be open on the second Monday in October.
The Faculty are Visiting Physicians and Surgeons of the Charity Hospital.
The Students accompany the Professorts in their visits, and, free of expense, enjoy extraordinary practical advantages.
Preliminary to the Course, Lectures will be delivered daily in the Amphitheater of the Hospital, from the 7th of October, on Clinica Medicine and Surgery, and other subjects, without any charge to students.
THOMAS HUNT, M. D., Dean.
The Administration of the Charity Hospital elect annually, in April, fourteen Resident Students, who are maintained by the institution. jy13 d&Wtd

KENNER ACADEMY—
VICTOR SCHELIHA, PRINCIPAL.
The Fifth Session of this Institution commenced on MONDAY October 1. Its location, on the New Orleans and Jackson Railroad within half an hour's ride of the city, combines the advantages of perfect seclusion, and being easy of access.
For Prospectus, address the Principal.
REFERENCES IN THE CITY—Capt. J. J. Brown; Dr. D. C. Holliday; Messrs. L. Hellwig, at Reilly & Co.'s; Samuel Locke; Chas Newman [illegible] ing no more to the establishment, and will only be re-admitted his paying the final regular quarter of said year.
No student above the age of fifteen years can be admitted without having obtained the consent of the Committee on Admission, through the President.
Copies of rules and prospectus may be obtained by applying to the Trustees and President, or to A. D. VOISIN, Esq., 98 Gravier street, N. O. oct27tf C. O. DUGUE, President.

MR. T. M. H. LAFONT, Bachelor of Arts in the French University, ex-Professor in the Imperial Lyceum of Bordeaux, Professor of the French Tongue, and Literature, Latin, Greek, Geography, History and Spanish Language, will spend some hours in private lessons. Apply No. 157 Baronne street
Mrs. H. LAFONT, provided with diploma of capacity, formerly Directress of an Academy in Bordeaux, and lately in the Island of Cuba, will spend some hours a day in teaching the [illegible] branches of education in French and Spanish tongues. Apply at No. 157 Baronne street. [illegible]

DENTISTRY.

ARTIFICIAL TEETH—The best, cheapest and most replete Dental Establishment in New Orleans, is DR. FIELDING'S, 194 Canal street.
His facilities for manipulating Artificial Teeth are unsurpassed by any Practical Dentist in the Southern States, defying competition and at prices charged by the inexperienced.
Persons requiring superior Dentistry, should procure it where they can rely upon the experience, skill and integrity which Dental Science can produce.
Every Artificial Tooth is of surpassing beauty, which can not be detected from the very productions of nature, gradually restoring that uniformity to the features so essential to youth and beauty, and warranted satisfactory for mastication and articulation.
PAINLESS TOOTH EXTRACTOR, for readily extracting Teeth without pain, superseding anything before attained by the profession, astonishing all who witness it.
All operations in Dentistry performed with care and skill, and for cheapness and utility are unsurpassed by others. Unskillfully applied Teeth remodeled and a sure fit guaranteed at moderate charges. At the following prices, a written guarantee accompanying each set, if desired, and if not found as represented after two months' trial, their money will be returned.
Full sets on Sterling Silver base............$25
Full sets finest finish gums, bound............40
Full sets vulcanized Rubber, equal to gold, from....$40 to 80
Full sets on 18 caret gold base, beautiful, from....50 to 80
Full sets on 22 caret gold base, from........75 to 125
The most perfect gems that can be produced.
Those requiring Artificial Teeth are cordially invited to call and examine before engaging elsewhere.
DR. FIELDING, Dental Surgeon,
feb27 1y 194 Canal street.

KNAPP & McLAIN,
DENTAL SURGEONS,
154..............CANAL STREET..............154
Teeth extracted without pain—new improvement on chloroform.
All operations performed according to the latest scientific improvements in the art.
Artificial Teeth, with gold, platina, or the new and cheap Vulcanit Base.
Prices to suit the times. tan9 d&wly

ATTENTION!!!—NOTICE TO THE PROFESSION.
No. 13 Baronne street, near Canal.
The NEW ORLEANS SOUTHERN DENTAL DEPOT is fully supplied with superior Gold and Tin Foils of Southern manufacture, a fine lot of Teeth, and all other articles required by the Profession, at the lowest market prices.
N. B.—The public is hereby notified that Mr. ISAAC CHANDLER is in no way connected with the Dental Depot, No. 13 Baronne street june16 tf TH. ANFOUX.

MEDICAL.

DR. JAMES BURNS—Office and residence 359 Common street, between Claiborne and Derbigny streets
feb8 tf

VACCINATION—DR. DALTON has just received a small supply of GENUINE VACCINE MATTER, and would advise all who are not protected from Small Pox, to call at No. 166 ST. CHARLES street and be vaccinated. dec19 tf

MRS. FRANCES BURRITT, M. D., still continues the practice of her profession in this city. Ladies wishing to consult her will please call before 10 o'clock A. M.; or from 4 to 5 P. M. Residence, 118 Prytania street, corner of Euterpe. Ladies in confinement can have treatment and board at her residence, if desired. jy18'61 1y*

SOUTHERN MEDICAL HOUSE—Founded in 1845.
The attention of strangers and others visiting New Orleans is called to this MEDICAL ESTABLISHMENT.
Those requiring surgical or medical aid can rely on prompt attention, permanent cure and moderate charges.
Particular attention paid to the treatment of all Acute and Chronic Diseases of the Nervous System and Genito-Urinary Organs, comprising Spinal Affections, Paralysis, Chorea, Urethritis, Gravel, Strictures in every form, Diseases of the Kidneys, Bladder and Prostrate Gland, Mercurial Affections, Scrofula and Diseases of the Skin, also comprising Primary, Secondary, Tertiary and Hereditary Syphilis, causing in their different stages ulceration of the Head and Throat, destruction of the Palate, Nodes on the Bones, Alopecia, (loss of hair,) Pains, (nocturnal) resembling and often treated for rheumatism, blotches, &c.
SPERMATORRHŒA.
Special attention paid to cases of Spermatorrhœa, arising from Onanism, (self-abuse,) or other causes. For full particulars, see "Treatise," to be had at the office.
Patients treated for this unfortunate malady by the most recent and effective method, comprising the ELECTRO-MAGNETIC applications to the Spine, Acupuncture, and, if necessary, Cauterization.
Surgical operations performed for Fistula in Ano, Urinary in the Perineum, communicating with the Urethra, Hydrocele, Congenital and Accidental, Phymosis Varicocele, (by pressure,) Callous Impassable Strictures, False Passages, &c.
Persons applying on the first symptoms of any Acute Specific diseases, cured in many cases by the Abortive Method, in forty-eight to seventy-five hours.
City references given, as well as the recommendations of many years' practice in New Orleans.
L. C. THOMSON, M. D., 118 Carondelet street, between Poydras and Lafayette streets, FIFTH house above Poydras.
Office hours—From 7 A. M. to 8 P. M. may10 1y

THE DAILY DELTA

SOUTHERN BANK CONVENTION.

The adjourned session of the Convention of Southern Banks commenced at Richmond on the 24th inst., the following delegates presenting themselves:

ALABAMA.—Central Bank of Alabama, Wm. Knox, Charles T. Polland.

FLORIDA.—None.

GEORGIA.—Planters' Bank of the State of Georgia, R. R. Cuyler; Central Railroad and Banking Company of Georgia, R. R. Cuyler; Bank of Commerce, G. B. Lamar; Bank of Columbus, G. B. Lamar; Mechanics' Bank of Augusta, Thomas S. Metcalf.

LOUISIANA.—Crescent City Bank, W. C. Tompkins, J. O. Nixon.

NORTH CAROLINA.—Bank of the State of North Carolina, G. W. Mordecai; Bank of Cape Fear, W. A. Wright; Farmers' Bank of North Carolina, W. A. Caldwell; Bank of Yanceyville, Thos. D. Johnston; Bank of Clarendon, John D. Williams; Commercial Bank of Wilmington, O. G. Parsley; Bank of Washington, James E. Hoyt; Miners' and Planters' Bank, A. T. Davidson.

SOUTH CAROLINA.—Bank of the State of South Carolina, C. M. Furman; Bank of South Carolina, C. V. Chamberlain; State Bank, Wm. C. Bee, George B. Reid, Robert Mure and George Coffin; Union Bank of South Carolina, W. B. Smith; Planters' and Mechanics' Bank, J. J. McCarter, C. H. Stevens and C. T. Mitchell; Bank of Charleston, J. K. Sass and George A. Trenholm; Southwestern Railroad Bank, James Rose, J. K. Holmes; Farmers' and Exchange Bank, John S. Davies; People's Bank, D. L. McKay and James S. Gibbes; Merchants' Bank of South Carolina, at Cheraw, Allen Macfarlan; Bank of Georgetown, J. G. Henning; Bank of Chester, George S. Cameron.

TENNESSEE.—Bank of Tennessee, G. C. Torbett; Branch Bank of Tennessee, Memphis, Jos. Lenow; Branch Bank of Tennessee, Knoxville, J. G. M. Ramsey.

VIRGINIA.—Farmers' Bank of Virginia, W. H. Macfarland; Bank of Virginia, James Caskie, Alfred T. Harris and John L. Bacon; Exchange Bank, L. W. Glazebrook, and W. P. Strother; Bank of the Commonwealth, L. Nunually, J. B. Norton and James Alfred Jones; Merchants' Bank of Virginia, C. R. Slaughter; the Danville Bank, W. T. Sutherlin; Bank of Richmond, Alexander Warwick; Traders' Bank of Richmond, Hector Davis, E. Denton and Andrew Johnson.

On motion of R. A. Cuyler, Esq., the Secretary read the resolutions adopted by the Convention at Atlanta, Georgia, June 3, 1861, as follows:

Resolved, That this Convention do recommend to all the Banks in the Southern Confederacy to receive in payment of all dues to them the Treasury notes of the Government, to be issued under the act of Congress of May 16, 1861, and also to receive the same on deposit and pay them out again to customers.

Resolved, That, until the said Treasury notes can be prepared and issued, it be recommended to all the Banks that they do agree to advance to the Government, in current notes, such sums severally as may be agreed upon between them and the Secretary of the Treasury. The said advance to be made on the deposit with the Banks of Treasury notes of large denomination or 8 per cent. stock or bonds.

Resolved, That all the Banks in the Southern Confederacy are earnestly urged to take immediate action on the foregoing resolutions, as a measure of the greatest importance to the Government and the people, and communicate the same without delay to the Secretary of the Treasury at Richmond.

Resolved, That it be recommended to all the railroad companies in the Southern Confederacy to receive the Treasury notes in payment of fares and freights.

Resolved, That the Legislatures of the several States be recommended to make it lawful for their Tax Collectors and other officers to receive the Treasury notes in payment of taxes and all other public dues.

Resolved, That all the States, cities and corporations having coupons payable in the city of New York, or elsewhere in the enemy's country, be requested, during the continuance of the war, to appoint some place of payment within the Confederate States, and to give their creditors notice of the same.

Resolved, That the committee recommend that when this Convention adjourns, it adjourn to meet again on the 24th day of July, at Richmond, Va., and that all the Banks not represented in the Convention be requested to send delegates to the adjourned meeting at Richmond.

The President informed the meeting that the Secretary of the Treasury authorized him to state that he had received letters from the various Banks represented in the last meeting of the Convention, agreeing to conform to the above resolutions.

On motion of James G. Holms, Esq.

Resolved, unanimously, That this meeting, representing a large proportion of the banking capital of the Confederate States, avail themselves of this occasion to express their hearty approval of the policy of the Government, in prosecuting with the utmost vigor the war of our independence.

Resolved unanimously, That it is the duty of the banks, capitalists, and property-holders generally, to give the Government all the support in money and other means demanded by the war.

Resolved unanimously, That it is the opinion of this meeting that the capital resources of the country are abundantly adequate to supply all the demands created by the war, and that this Convention will cheerfully contribute its aid, to render those resources available to the people and the Government.

Resolved, That a committee of one from each State be appointed to receive and report upon any measures that may be proposed for the adoption of this meeting.

The President appointed the following committee in accordance with the above resolution:
George A. Trenholm, of South Carolina.
Thomas S. Metcalf, of Georgia.
G. W. Mordecai, of North Carolina.
C. T. Pollard, of Alabama.
G. C. Torbett, of Tennessee.
W. H. Macfarland, of Virginia.
W. C. Tompkins, of Louisiana.

CONFEDERATE CONGRESS.

RICHMOND, July 24, 1861.

Congress met at 12 o'clock M., and was opened with prayer by Rev. George Woodbridge.

Hon. Howell Cobb in the chair.

The journal of the preceding day was read and approved.

The arrival of Hon. George R. Mason and Hon. Roger A. Pryor, members elect from the State of Virginia, was announced; whereupon they came forward and were duly qualified.

Mr. Macfarland, from a Special Committee, made the following report.

The Committee to whom was referred the resolutions approving the prompt and patriotic efforts of the Mayor of the city of Richmond in behalf of the wounded in the glorious victory of Manassas, and tendering the co-operation of Congress in his beneficent plan, respectfully report that, in a public meeting of the citizens of Richmond, convened by the Mayor on Monday, the 22d inst., the following proceedings were had:

[The proceedings have been already published in the newspapers.]

These proceedings meet the exigency in a spirit of broad and considerate sympathy. There is no duty to which our fellow-citizens, or their representatives and agents, are prepared to respond more spontaneously and liberally than to that which summons them to the consolation and relief of their intrepid defenders. It would not become the Congress of the Confederate States to permit the city of Richmond to take to herself the whole charge of providing for the wounded and sick of the army, which, under the blessing of Providence, triumphed gloriously at Manassas.

It behooves Congress to provide the funds necessary to meet the outlay which may attend the execution of this beneficent design; therefore

Resolved, That the sum of five thousand dollars be placed at the disposal of the Secretary of the Treasury, to be expended in securing the comfort of the officers and men of the army who were in the battle of Manassas, and may be removed to the city of Richmond under the resolution of the Common Council.

The report was agreed to, and resolution adopted.

Mr. Thos. R. R. Cobb, of Georgia, delivered an eloquent and affecting eulogy of the late Col. Bartow, killed at Manassas, and submitted the annexed resolutions:

Resolved, That Congress has heard with unfeigned sorrow of the death of the Hon. Francis S. Bartow, one of the delegates from the State of Georgia; that the natural exultation for a glorious victory achieved by our arms, is checked by the heavy loss sustained by the Confederacy, in the death of one of her most efficient counsellors; and that, as his colleagues, we feel a peculiar loss to ourselves, in one who had won our esteem, and gained much of our affection.

Resolved, That with pleasure we record our admiration of his heroic defense, on the field of battle, of the action of Congress, in which he participated so largely, and find some consolation for his death in the conviction that his noble self-sacrifice will serve to establish the work which he so boldly aided to begin.

Resolved, That we appreciate the loss which Georgia, his native State, has sustained in the death of one of her noblest sons, and that we tender to the bereaved family the sympathy of hearts, to some extent, stricken by the same blow which has crushed their own.

Resolved, That a copy of these resolutions be communicated to the family of the deceased.

Resolved, That in testimony of our respect for his memory, the Congress do now adjourn.

The resolutions were unanimously adopted.

Appropriate remarks in reference to the character of the deceased, were made by Messrs. Hill, of Georgia, Mason, of Virginia, and Chesnut, of South Carolina.

In accordance with the resolutions adopted, the President announced Congress adjourned.

A GRAPHIC SKETCH OF THE BATTLE OF MANASSAS.

The following sketch, taken from a letter to the Southern Confederacy, Atlanta, Ga., contains, besides a brief but comprehensive account of the battle, the most lucid view of the topography of the battle-field which we have seen:

Gen. Johnston had arrived the preceding day with about half of the force he had, detailed from Winchester, and was the senior officer in command. He magnanimously insisted, however, that Gen. Beauregard's previous plan should be carried out, and he was guided entirely by the judgment and superior local knowledge of the latter. While, therefore, Gen. Johnston was nominally in command, Beauregard was really the officer and hero of the day. You will be glad to learn that he was this day advanced from a Brigadier to the rank of a full General. But to the battle.

At half past 6 in the morning, the enemy opened fire from a battery planted on a hill beyond Bull Run, and nearly opposite the center of our lines. The battery was intended merely to "beat the bush," and to occupy our attention, while he moved a heavy column towards the Stone Bridge, over the same creek, upon our left. At 10 o'clock, another battery was pushed forward, and opened fire a short distance to the left of the other, and near the road leading north to Centreville. This was a battery of rifled guns, and the object of its fire was the same as that of the other. They fired promiscuously into the woods and gorges on this, the southern, side of Bull Run, seeking to create the impression thereby that our center would be attacked, and thus prevent us from sending reinforcements to our left, where the real attack was to be made. Beauregard was not deceived by the maneuver.

It might not be amiss to say that Bull Run, or creek, is north of this place, and runs nearly due east, slightly curving around the Junction, the nearest part of which is about 3½ miles. The Stone Bridge is some seven miles distant, in a northwesterly direction, upon which our left wing rested. Mitchel's Ford is directly north, and distant four miles, by the road leading to Centreville, which is seven miles from the Junction. On our right is Marion Mills, on the same stream, where the Alexandria and Manassas Railroad crosses the Run, and distant four miles. Proceeding from Fairfax Court House, by Centreville, to Stone Bridge, the enemy passed in front of our entire line, but at a distance ranging from five to two miles.

At 9 o'clock, I reached an eminence nearly opposite the two batteries mentioned above, and which commanded a full view of the country for miles around, except on the right. From this point I could trace the movements of the approaching hosts by the clouds of dust that rose high above the surrounding hills. Our left, under Brigadier Generals Evans, Jackson and Cocke, and Col. Bartow, with the Georgia Brigade, composed of the 7th and 8th Regiments, had been put in motion, and was advancing upon the enemy with a force of about 15,000, while the enemy himself was advancing upon our left with a compact column of at least 50,000. His entire force on this side of the Potomac is estimated at 75,000. These approaching columns encountered each other at 11 o'clock.

Meanwhile, the two batteries in front kept up their fire upon the wooded hill where they supposed our center lay. They sent occasional balls from their rifled cannon to the eminence where your correspondent stood. Gens. Beauregard, Johnston and Bonham reached this point at 12 o'clock, and one of these balls passed directly over and very near them, and plunged into the ground a few paces from where I stood. I have the ball now, and hope to be able to show it to you at some future day. It is an eighteen pound ball, about six inches long. By the way, this thing of taking notes amidst a shower of shells and balls is more exciting than pleasant. At a quarter past 12 o'clock, Johnston and Beauregard galloped rapidly forward in the direction of Stone Bridge, where the ball had now fully opened. Your correspondent followed their example, and soon reached a position in front of the battle-field.

The artillery were the first to open fire, precisely at 11 o'clock. By 11½ the infantry had engaged, and there it was that the battle began to rage. The dusky columns which had thus far marked the approach of the two armies, now mingled with great clouds of smoke, as it rose from the flashing guns below, and the two shot up together like a huge pyramid of red and blue. The shock was as tremendous as were the odds between the two forces. With what anxious hearts did we watch that pyramid of smoke and dust. When it moved to the right we knew that the enemy were giving way; and when it moved to the left we knew that our friends were receding.

Twice the pyramid moved to the right, and as often returned. At last, about 2 o'clock, it began to move slowly to the left, and thus it continued to move for two mortal hours. The enemy was seeking to turn our left flank, and to reach the railroad leading hence to [illegible] This was unfortunate for us, as it required a corresponding extension of our own lines to prevent his extreme right from outflanking us—a movement on our part which weakened the force of our resistance along a space of two miles. It also rendered it the more difficult to bring up reinforcements, as the farther the enemy extended his right, the greater the distance our reserve forces had to travel to counteract the movement.

This effort to turn our flank was pressed with great determination for five long, weary hours, during which the tide of battle ebbed and flowed along the entire line with alternate fortunes. The enemy's column continued to stretch away to the left like a huge anaconda, seeking to envelope us within its mighty folds and crush us to death; and at one time it really looked as if he would succeed. But here let me pause to explain why it was our reinforcements were so late in arriving, and why a certain other important movement miscarried.

The moment he discovered the enemy's order of battle, Gen. Beauregard, it is said, dispatched orders to Gen. Ewell, on our extreme right, to move forward and turn his left or rear. At the same time he ordered Generals Jones, Longstreet and Bonham, occupying the center of our lines, to co operate in the movement, but not to move until Gen. Ewell had made the attack. The order to Gen. Ewell unfortunately miscarried. The others were delivered, but as the movements of the center were to be regulated entirely by those on the right, nothing was done at all. Had the orders to Gen. Ewell been received and carried out, and our entire force brought upon the field, we should have destroyed the enemy's army almost literally. Attacked in front, on the flank and in the rear, he could not possibly have escaped, except at the loss of thousands of prisoners and all his batteries, while the field would have been strewed with his dead.

Finding that his orders had in some way failed to be executed, Gen. Beauregard at last ordered up a portion of the forces which were intended to co-operate with Gen. Ewell. It was late, however, before these reinforcements came up. Only one brigade reached the field before the battle was won. This was led by Gen. E. K. Smith, of Florida, formerly of the United States army, and was a part of Gen. Johnston's column from Winchester. They should have reached here the day before, but were prevented by an accident on the railroad. They dashed on the charge with loud shouts, and in the most gallant style. About the same time, Maj. Elzey, (formerly of the Augusta Arsenal, I may have his title wrong,) coming down the railroad from Winchester with the last of Johnston's brigades, and hearing the firing, immediately quit the train and struck across the country, and as a gracious fortune would have it, he encountered the extreme right of the enemy as he was feeling his way around our flank, and with his brigade struck him like a thunderbolt, full in the face. Finding he was about to be outflanked himself, the enemy gave way after the second fire. Meanwhile Beauregard rallied the center and dashed into the very thickest of the fight, and after him rushed our own brave boys with a shout that seemed to shake the very earth. The result of this movement, from three distinct points, was to force back the enemy, who began to retreat, first in good order, and finally in much confusion. At this point the cavalry were ordered upon the pursuit. The retreat now became a perfect rout, and it is reported that the flying legions rushed past Centreville, in the direction of Fairfax, as if the earth had been opening behind them. It was when Gen. Beauregard led the final charge, that his horse was killed by a shell.

HEROISM OF GEN. BEE.—A correspondent of the Charleston Mercury, narrating the battle of Manassas, says:

The name of this officer deserves a place in the highest niche of fame. He displayed a gallantry that scarcely has a parallel in history. The brunt of the morning's battle was sustained by his command until past 2 o'clock. Overwhelmed by superior numbers and compelled to yield before a fire that swept everything before it, Gen. Bee rode up and down his lines, encouraging his troops by every thing that was dear to them, to stand up and repel the tide which threatened them with destruction. At last his own brigade dwindled to a mere handful, with every field officer killed or disabled. He rode up to Gen. Jackson and said: "General, they are beating us back."

The reply was, "Sir, we'll give them the bayonet."

Gen. Bee immediately rallied the remnant of his brigade, and his last words to them were, "There is Jackson standing like a stone wall. Let us determine to die here, and we will conquer. Follow me!"

His men obeyed the call, and at the head of his column, the very moment when the battle was turning in our favor, he fell, mortally wounded. Gen. Beauregard was heard to say he had never seen such gallantry. He never murmured at his suffering, but seemed to be consoled by the reflection that he was doing his duty.

United States fives feel one and a quarter per cent. at New York on the 19th, in consequence of the pause at Bull Run. Of course the bears used the paws.

ARRIVAL OF THE WOUNDED AT RICHMOND, VIRGINIA.

From the Richmond Examiner, 25th inst.

A special train was started from Manassas Junction yesterday, freighted with over two hundred of our wounded troops, who had been struck in the late battle. They were distributed at the various stopping places along the line of the railroad, in the neighborhood of their homes, and a number were transferred to the train going westward toward Staunton. Between thirty and forty were brought on to this city and properly cared for and disposed of by the relief committee.

THE NEW YORK ZOUAVES.

Two cars in this train were appropriated to the transportation of wounded Yankees, twenty-three in number, the majority of whom belonged to Ellsworth's Fire Zouaves. There were among them, however, a great variety of uniforms. One fellow, with bright red pants and a blue jacket, told us he belonged to the 14th Regiment of New York militia. They were all wounded in the most horrible manner, and as their wounds had received no attention, they were in a truly pitiable condition.

Their friends having run off and deserted them, they had lain on the field just where their injuries were received until picked up by our troops, and our surgeons being more than busy attending to our own wounded, their cases were, of necessity, postponed till after their arrival in this city. The most of them had been shot in the lower extremities. One fellow had both his legs crushed, and several had one leg broken. One of the Zouaves presented a most dreadful spectacle. A rifle ball had entered just below his right eye. His whole face and head were so swelled and distorted by inflammation that it is no great stretch of language to say that "his own mother would not have known him."

From another of Ellsworth's Zouaves, whose left leg had been shattered by a musket ball, but who seemed at the time to be suffering but little pain, we derived considerable information. He is a very intelligent fellow, and disposed to talk. He told us that there were not ten Zouaves in the regiment who did not rejoice when Ellsworth was killed; that he was one of the most brutal and tyrannical men that ever lived; that he never issued an order without accompanying it with an oath or a kick. He also said that the Southerners had done great injustice to Ellsworth's and Duryea's Zouaves, by supposing them to be composed of the same material as Billy Wilson's "pet lambs."

On inquiring at what time during the action he was hurt, and by what regiment the Zouaves were opposed, he said he had been wounded during the second hour of the battle, and was captured by and carried to the rear of the 2d Regiment of the South Carolinians. This regiment it was, he reports, that annihilated the Zouaves. He said he had been but a few moments behind the South Carolinians before he was fully convinced that the Yankees could never whip these people.

He says that no description could do justice to the coolness and nonchalance of the Palmettos during the most terrible carnage of the fight. He says that as the wounded fell and were borne to the rear, though they, in many cases, must have been suffering agony, they jested and laughed as though nothing had happened, and they were in the midst of peace and security.

One demure looking fellow seemed to think his fate an uncommonly hard one, as the moment he arrived on the field, before he had even cocked his gun, a bullet struck him full in the belly, and passed entirely through him.

These men were carried temporarily to Harwood's factory, where their wounds received the attention they so much required.

FROM TEXAS.

We have Galveston dates to the 20th inclusive.

Gen. Van Dorn arrived at Galveston on the 19th, from Houston.

The Indians are somewhat troublesome, driving off stock in San Saba county. Henry Cames was shot by them and supposed to be mortally wounded. They had also appeared in considerable numbers on the Sandias, and stolen sixty horses from Mr. Crowervan.

The Austin Gazette says Gov. Clark will tender Missouri 10,000 Texan troops.

The Gazette says the twenty companies called for by President Davis, will be taken according to priority of their organization. It says:

The following are now ordered to march to Brenham, to be there mustered into the Confederate service: [illegible] Gonzales; Ed. H. Cunningham [illegible] Martin, Henderson; W. P. Townsend, Robertson; G. M. Whaley, Leon, and R. M. Powell, Montgomery.

Orders have been sent Gen. Van Dorn to furnish the [illegible] The troops will go by railroad to the Sabine.

A letter from Fort Chadbourne to the Austin Gazette says that on the 23d ult., a scout under charge of Lieut. Robt. Cotter, Capt. Davidson and Lieut. Col. Frost, struck an Indian trail near the head waters of the Colorado, and after following it for several miles, got in sight of the Indians. After a chase of about five miles, part of the Rangers got among the Red Skins, when a desperate fight ensued for about fifteen minutes. Capt. S. G. Davidson, of Company H, from Bell county, and private A. J. McCarty, of Lockart, were killed. Three Indians were killed and one wounded. The rest escaped; but at night the Indians appeared in large bodies, some distance off from the camp. They made no attack. Lieut. Lambert, who writes to the Gazette, says it is believed they are Reserve Comanches.

The fort at the mouth of the Brazos is completed. It is well and solidly built.

S. L. S. Ballowe's Coast Defense company is in charge of the coast from San Luis to the head of Matagorda Bay.

The Columbia Democrat has seen two samples of good blasting and rifle powder, made in Brazoria by the Messrs. Chirouge.

Major Wm. A. Irwin, a native of Brook county Virginia, died at Crockett, Houston county, on the 2d inst., aged 65 years. He was one of Stephen F. Austin's companions, when he came to Texas in 1821; served in the wars that achieved Texan independence; and was the messenger dispatched from the Alamo by Fannin, to inform Gen. Houston of the investment of that fortress.

Lieut.-Gov. Reynolds, of Missouri, was at Memphis on Saturday last, on his way from Richmond.

COMMERCIAL.

OFFICE OF THE DAILY DELTA,
NEW ORLEANS, MONDAY EVENING, July 29, 1861.

COTTON—Sales to-day 59 bales. Received 16 bales.

TOBACCO—Nothing reported

SUGAR—About 100 hhds. sold. Fair to fully fair, 3¾@4¼; clarified, yellow, 5½@6¼c. ℔ lb.

MOLASSES—150 bbls. sold at 16c. for inferior, and 22c. ℔ gallon for prime reboiled.

FLOUR—100 fair extra sold at $9, and 100 choice at $9 50 ℔ bbl.

CORN—64 sacks white sold at 60c., and 40 at 65c. ℔ bushel.

OATS—220 sacks sold at 60c. ℔ bushel.

SHEAF OATS—39 bales sold at $30 ℔ ton.

BACON—25 casks Shoulders sold at 11½c. ℔ lb.

LARD—200 tierces sold at —.

PORK—Mess is retailing slowly at $24@$24 50 ℔ bbl.

WHISKY—Rectified is retailing at 37½c. ℔ gallon.

CATTLE MARKET.

JEFFERSON CITY, MONDAY EVENING, July 29.

Arrived to-day 25 Hogs, and 260 Veal Cattle. Sales 134 Texas Cattle, 14 Hogs and 130 Veal Cattle. Stock on sale 902 Texas Cattle, 28 Hogs, 442 Sheep and 380 Veal Cattle. Prices:

Beef Cattle, Western, first quality	℔ lb. net	—	@ —
Beef Cattle second quality	℔ lb. net	—	@ —
Beef Cattle, Texas, first quality	℔ head	$20 00	@30 00
Beef Cattle, Texas, second quality	℔ head	10 00	@18 00
Hogs, Western	℔ lb. gross	8	@ 8½
Sheep, choice	℔ head	3 50	@ 5 00
Sheep, in lots	℔ head	— 00	@ 2 75
Milch Cows, first class		— 00	@— 00
Milch Cows, second quality		00 00	@00 00
Veal Cattle		7 00	@10

Confederate States of America.

TREASURY DEPARTMENT,
RICHMOND, June 26, 1861.

Proposals will be received, in conformity with the Act of Congress, for the PURCHASE OF THE BONDS OF THE CONFEDERATE STATES, (bearing annual interest at 8 per cent., payable semi-annually,) with the proceeds of sales of Raw Produce or Manufactured Articles.

The proposals shall specify the quantity to be delivered, the time and place of delivery, and the Factor or Warehouseman to whom the delivery is to be made. The proceeds of sales may be paid in Bills of Exchange, or other funds, rated at their current value, in Coin or in Treasury Notes, at par.

The proposals will be addressed to the "Secretary of the Treasury," at Richmond, either singly or in lists, embracing several names.

C. G. MEMMINGER,
yl 3taw6w2p Secretary of the Treasury

The London American.

MAP OF THE SEAT OF WAR,

POSITIONS OF THE REBEL FORCES, BATTERIES, ENTRENCHMENTS AND ENCAMPMENTS IN VIRGINIA—THE FORTIFICATIONS FOR THE PROTECTION OF RICHMOND.

THE "LONDON AMERICAN," AN INTERNATIONAL NEWSPAPER, PUBLISHED EVERY

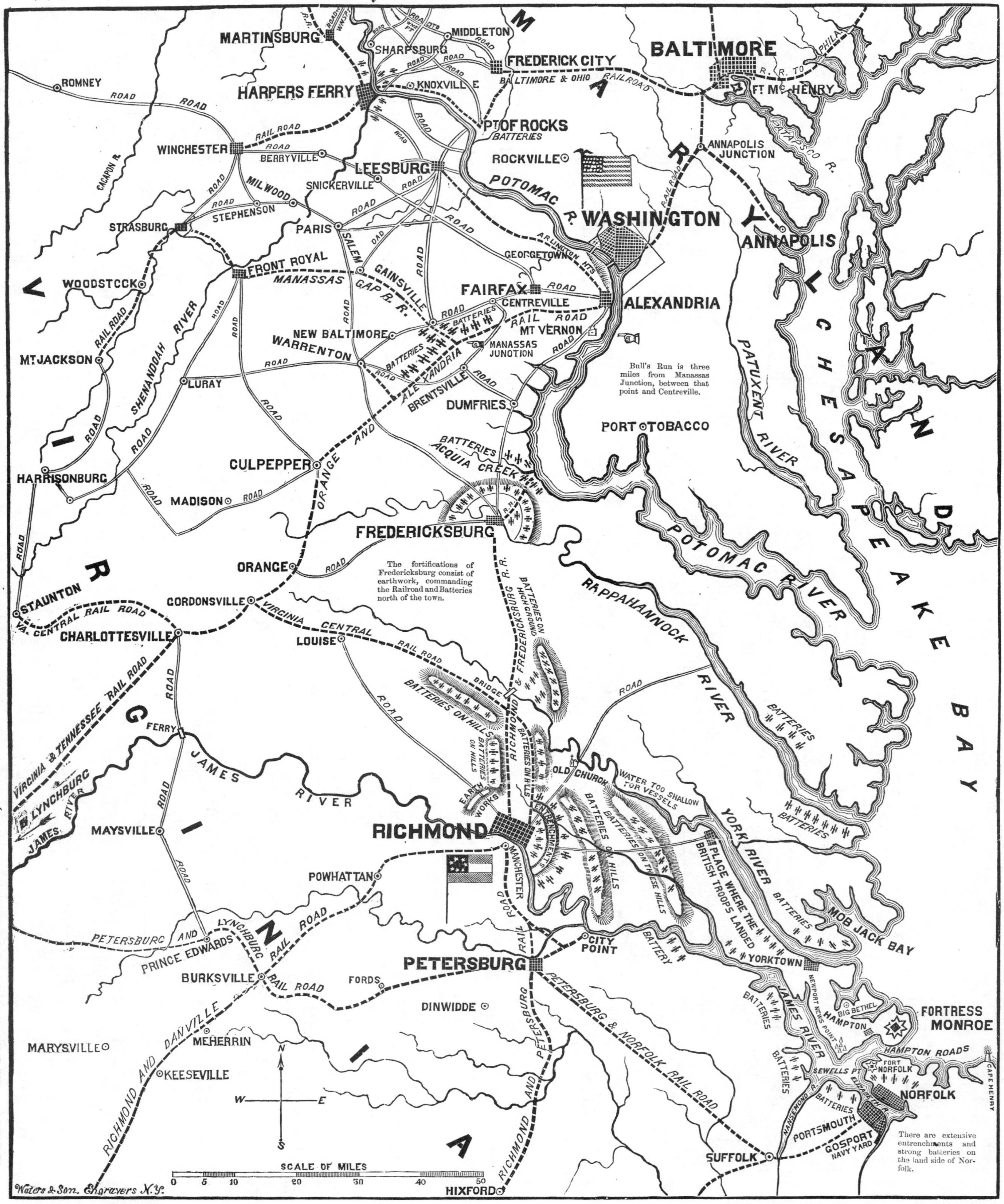

WEDNESDAY MORNING, PRICE 3d. OFFICE, 9, EXETER CHANGE, & ALL NEWSMEN.

From Washington to Alexandria .... 8 miles.
" " " Mount Vernon ....16 "
" " " Acquia Creek ....55 "
" " " Fredericksburg .....70 "
" " " Richmond ....130 "
" " " Petersburg ....152 "
" " " Norfolk ....230 "

From Washington to Manassas Junction....35 miles.
" " " Warrenton...........49 "
" " " Culpepper ....70 "
" " " Charlottesville ......118 "
" " " Fairfax ....14 "
" " " Leesburg.............31 "
" " " Harper's Ferry .....51 "

From Washington to Baltimore ....38 miles.
" " " Annapolis ....23 "
From Baltimore to Frederick City.........60 "
" " " Point of Rocks.........70 "
From Manassas Junction to Front Royal....51 "
" " " Strasburg......61 "

At the Battle of Bull's Run, fought on Sunday, the 21st July, about 22,000 Unionists and about 60,000 Rebels were in the engagement. After a contest of twelve hours, the Unionists were repulsed, with a loss of nearly five hundred men killed and wounded. The Rebels sustained a much greater loss.

Daily Alta California.

FRED'K MacCRELLISH & CO.

FRED'K MacCRELLISH............WM. A. WOODWARD

DAILY ALTA CALIFORNIA..........Is published Every Morning, and delivered to subscribers in the city at 50 cents per week, payable to the Carriers; single copies 10 cents. Mail subscribers, $18 per annum, in advance; for six months, $9; three months, $5.

PUBLICATION OFFICE:
124 Sacramento street—Alta California Building

SAN FRANCISCO, SATURDAY, AUGUST 3.

CITY ITEMS.

How the News was Received.—Though no extra was issued from the *Alta* office announcing it, the painful news received by last night's Pony Express soon spread throughout the lower portion of the city, and a terrible state of excitement prevailed. It was almost impossible to procure either egress from or ingress to our office, so dense was the mass of anxious and excited people who thronged about it soliciting still further particulars. The remarks of the various groups who stood upon the street-corners and in public places showed the feeling that prevailed. It was one of intense bitterness. Men with pale faces, compressed lips and clenched fists were heard to exclaim, "This must be avenged; they were in greater numbers and behind entrenched camps; they dare not meet us face to face in the open field."

Others of more nervous temperament seemed almost frantic, and gave utterance to very forcible expressions, natural, but scarcely fitted for print. Everywhere the feeling evinced was not of fear as to the final result, but of regret and indignation.

Daily Alta California.

VOL. XIII. SAN FRANCISCO, SATURDAY MORNING, AUGUST 3, 1861. NO. 4186.

ARRIVAL OF THE PONY

St. Louis Dates to the 25th of July.

General Battle at Bull's Run.

Federal Troops Defeated

Retreat of M'Dowell's Army to the Potomac.

Dreadful Carnage on both sides

Patterson's Inactivity the Cause of the Disaster.

Desperate Valor of the Fire Zouaves and N. Y. 69th.

McClellan ordered to Washington.

RENEWED ENTHUSIASM FOR THE WAR

200,000 Men Ordered to Washington.

"LITTLE RHODY" AGAIN IN THE VAN.

Second Attack upon the Fortifications at Bull's Run ...... The Rebels Driven Back inch by inch..... The Rebels Reinforced by Gen. Johnson...... Panic and Route of our Army......Excitement in Washington......Recall of Patterson......

California Troops Accepted!

A Regiment of Infantry and Five Companies of Cavalry Called Out.

OUR FORT KEARNY SUMMARY.

The American Rebellion.

Congressional.

BY TELEGRAPH.

WASHINGTON, July 21st.

The fighting at Bull's Run commenced at three o'clock, A. M., and continued most desperately until two P. M.

The rebels were driven back inch by inch, leaving their dead on the field.

The loss of life on both sides was frightful. Our troops behaved most gallantly. The guns were served effectively.

It is said the whole force of the Rebels were engaged, Gen. Johnston having joined the Rebels, as previously stated, making Beauregard's force about 70,000.

WASHINGTON, 21st—midnight.

The battle has been one of the most severe ever fought on this continent. Up to 2 o'clock the enemy was driven nearly two miles, falling back from one position to another equally strong.

At every point fresh reinforcements poured in, almost without numbers.

The Fire Zouaves were terribly cut up. While drawing up to make an attack, they were assailed by a concealed battery, with a strong pressure on their rear, and were forced to break.

WASHINGTON, July 22.

After the latest information from Centreville, 7:30 last night, a series of events took place in this city.

Many confused rumors were afloat. Enough was known to warrant the statement that we suffered in a degree which casts gloom over all, and excited the deepest melancholy throughout Washington. The carnage was tremendous on both sides; ours is represented as frightful.

We were advancing, taking their masked batteries, slowly but surely, driving the enemy towards Manassas, when the enemy seemed to be reinforced by General Johnston, who, it is understood, took command. He immediately commenced driving us back, when a panic among our troops suddenly occurred, and a regular stampede took place all through.

Gen. McDowell attempted to make a stand at Centreville, but the panic was so fearful that the whole army became demoralized and it was impossible to check them at Centreville or Fairfax Court House. Retreat continued until the regular entrenchment was reached; a large number fell by the way from exhaustion.

Gen. McDowell was on their rear, exerting himself to rally the men with only partial effect. The latter part of the army, it is said, made their retreat in good order.

Miscellaneous.

FRANK LESLIE'S ILLUSTRATED NEWSPAPER

Entered according to the Act of Congress in the year 1861, by FRANK LESLIE, in the Clerk's Office of the District Court for the Southern District of New York.

No. 298—VOL. XII.] NEW YORK, AUGUST 3, 1861. [PRICE 6 CENTS.

THE BATTLE AT BULL'S RUN, SUNDAY, JULY 21.

THIS terrible and disastrous battle has absorbed the attention of the country during the past week. The accounts which have come to us from time to time have by degrees cleared away the extra horrors which surrounded it, and have happily lessened the calamitous results which were at first supposed to have attended it. It is now known that the defeat was only a repulse; that the flight was only a partial panic, and that the troops in advance retreated in good order by command of General McDowell. Our loss is ascertained to be two hundred and eighty killed, seven hundred and twenty-nine wounded, and four hundred and seventy-seven missing, instead of from four to five thousand killed, as at first reported. The loss of the rebels is admitted to be nearly two thousand, among them several high military officers. Their army in action and in reserve numbered over ninety thousand men, led by Davis in person, supported by Beauregard and Johnston, while our force in action was less than twenty thousand. The rebels took but few guns and but little of our war material, but they took many prisoners. Notwithstanding their immense force, they were in no condition to pursue the advantage they had gained; had they done so they might have converted a repulse into a disastrous and total defeat. As it is, our army has withdrawn into its lines on the Potomac, and the rebels have advanced their pickets within two miles of the Federal lines.

Of the future operations of the campaign by the Federal Government nothing is known. Regiments are constantly arriving at

THE BATTLE AT BULL'S RUN, ON SUNDAY, JULY 21, 1861—GALLANT AND SUCCESSFUL ASSAULT OF THE N. Y. FIRE ZOUAVES ON A REBEL BATTERY, WHICH THEY TAKE AT THE POINT OF THE BAYONET.—FROM A SKETCH BY OUR SPECIAL ARTIST ACCOMPANYING MAJOR-GENERAL M'DOWELL'S COMMAND.

NEW YORK ILLUSTRATED NEWS.

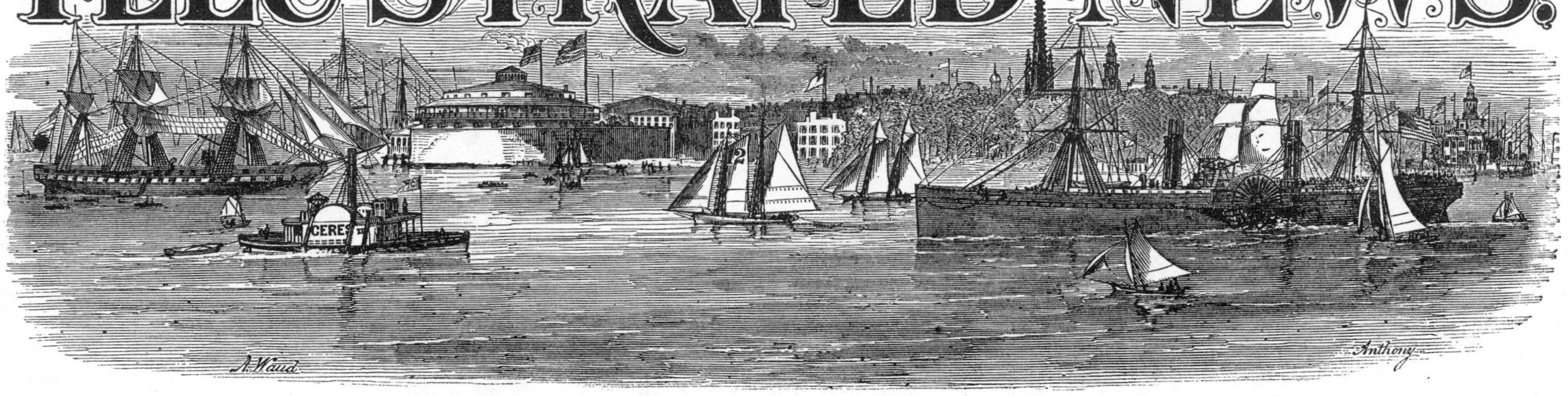

No. 93.—Vol. IV. NEW-YORK, MONDAY, AUGUST 12, 1861. Price Six Cents.

MAJOR-GENERAL McCLELLAN, COMMANDING THE TROOPS NOW ON THE POTOMAC. From a Photograph. See page 234.

Infantry. UNIFORMS OF REGULAR CONFEDERATE TROOPS. Cavalry. Artillery.

Volunteer Infantry of Virginia. 1st Regiment Maryland Line. South Carolina Light Infantry. Hampton Legion. Rockingham Battery Artillery. Gentlemen of the Road Independent Cavalry.

UNIFORMS OF T

Louisiana Zouaves. Washington Artillery of New Orleans. Mississippi Rifles. Heavy Infantry of Georgia. Alabama Light Infantry. Marine Battery, Manassas Junction.

Black Horse Cavalry. Dragoon Gu·rds, 4th Regt., Va. Cavalry. Mounted Rifles, North Carolina. Virginia Cadets. Greyson Dare-devils. Kentucky Rifle Brigade. Tennessee Sharp-shooters.

FEDERATE ARMY.

DAILY NASHVILLE PATRIOT.

PUBLISHED DAILY, TRI-WEEKLY, AND WEEKLY, BY A. S. CAMP & CO., NO. 16 DEADERICK STREET.

VOL. XXII. | NASHVILLE, TENN., SUNDAY, AUGUST 25, 1861. | NEW SERIES—NO. 1756

THE BATTLE OF MANASSAS PLAIN.

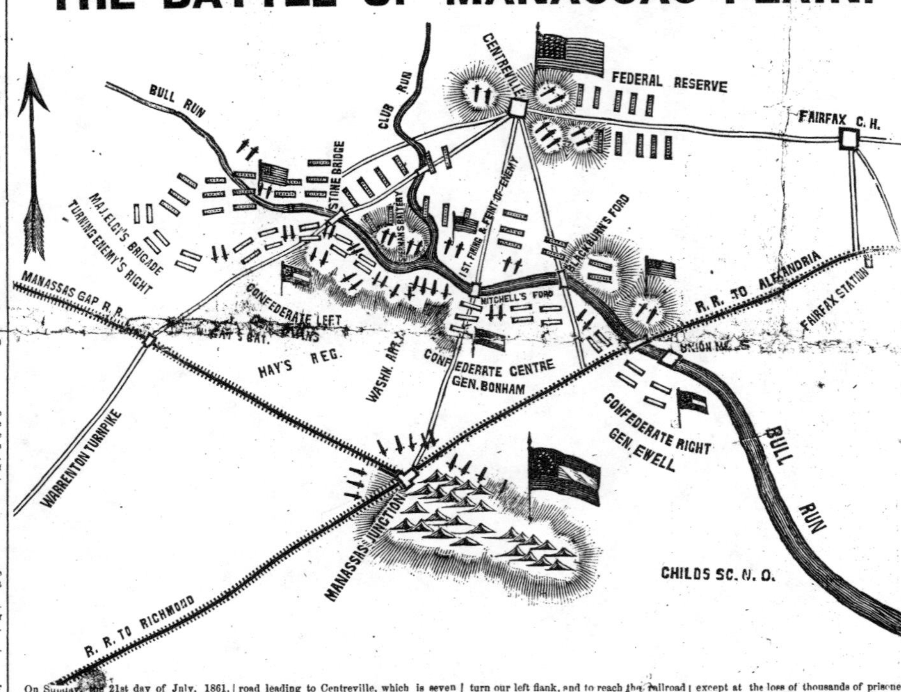

On Sunday, the 21st day of July, 1861, this great battle was fought, and a great victory won by the Confederate troops. Heaven smiled on our arms, and the God of battles crowned our banners with laurels of glory.

Gen. Johnston had arrived the preceding day with about half of the force he had detailed from Winchester, and was the senior officer in command. He magnanimously insisted, however, that Gen. Beauregard's previous plan should be carried out, and he was guided entirely by the judgment and superior local knowledge of the latter. While, therefore, Gen. Johnston was nominally in command, Beauregard was really the officer and hero of the day.

At half-past six in the morning the enemy opened fire from a battery planted on a hill beyond Bull Run, and nearly opposite the centre of our lines. The battery was intended merely to "beat the bush," and to occupy our attention, while he moved a heavy column towards the Stone Bridge, over the same creek, upon our left. At ten o'clock, another battery was pushed forward, and opened fire a short distance to the left of the other, and near the road leading North to Centreville. This was a battery of rifled guns, and the object of its fire was the same as that of the other. They fired promiscuously into the woods and gorges on this, the Southern, side of Bull Run, seeking to create the impression thereby that our centre would be attacked, and thus prevent us from sending reinforcements to our left, where the real attack was to be made. Beauregard was not deceived by the manœuvre.

It might not be amiss to say that Bull Run or creek is North of this place, and runs nearly due East, curving around the Junction, the nearest part of which is about 3½ miles. The Stone Bridge is some seven miles distant, in a North-westerly direction, upon which our left wing rested. Mitchel's ford is directly North, and distant four miles, by the road leading to Centreville, which is seven miles from the Junction. On our right is Union Mills, on the same stream, where the Alexandria and Manassas railroad crosses the Run, and distant four miles. Proceeding from Fairfax Court House, by Centreville, to Stone Bridge, the enemy passed in front of our entire line, but at a distance ranging from five to two miles.

At 9 o'clock our left under Brigadier Generals Evans, Jackson and Cooke, and Col. Bartow, with the Georgia Brigade, composed of the 7th and 8th regiments, had been put in motion, and was advancing upon the enemy with a force of about 15,000, while the enemy himself was advancing upon our left with a compact column of at least 30,000 These approaching columns encountered each other at 11 o'clock.

Meanwhile, the two batteries in front kept up their fire upon the wooded hills where they supposed our centre lay. At a quarter past 12, Johnston and Beauregard galloped rapidly forward in the direction of Stone Bridge, where the ball had now fully opened.

The artillery were the first to open fire, precisely at 11 o'clock. By half-past 11, the infantry had engaged and there it was that the battle began to rage. The dusky columns which had thus far marked the approach of the two armies, now mingled with great clouds of smoke, as it rose from the flashing guns below, and the two shot up together like a huge pyramid of red and blue. The shock was as tremendous as were the odds between the two forces. With what anxious hearts was watched that pyramid of smoke and dust! When it moved to the right, we knew the enemy were giving way; and when it moved to the left, we knew that our friends were receding. Twice the pyramids moved to the right, and as often returned. At last, about 2 o'clock, it began to move slowly to the left, and thus it continued to move for two mortal hours. The enemy was seeking to turn our left flank, and to reach the railroad leading hence in the direction of Winchester. To do this, he extended his lines, which he was enabled to do by reason of his great numbers. This was unfortunate for us, as it required a corresponding extension of our own lines to prevent his extreme right from outflanking us—a movement on our part which weakened the force of our resistance along the whole line of battle, which finally extended over a space of two miles. It also rendered it the more difficult to bring up reinforcements, as the further the enemy extended his right, the greater the distance our reserve forces had to travel to counteract the movement.

This effort to turn our flank was pressed with great determination for five long, weary hours, during which the tide of battle ebbed and flowed along the entire line with alternate fortunes. The enemy's column continued to stretch away to the left, like a huge anaconda, seeking to envelope us within its mighty folds and crush us to death; and at one time it really looked as if he would succeed.

The moment he discovered the enemy's order of battle, Gen. Beauregard, it is said, dispatched orders to Gen. Ewell, on our extreme right, to move forward and turn his left or rear. At the same time he ordered Generals Jones, Longstreet and Bnoham, occupying the centre of our lines, to co-operate in this movement, but not to move until Gen. Ewell had made the attack. The order to Gen. Ewell unfortunately miscarried. The others were delivered, but as the movements of the centre were to be regulated entirely by those on the right, nothing was done at all. Had the orders to Gen. Ewell been received and carried out, and our entire force brought upon the field, we should have destroyed the enemy's army almost literally.—Attacked in the front, on the flank, and in the rear, he could not possibly have escaped, except at the loss of thousands of prisoners and all his batteries, while the field would have been strewn with his dead.

Finding that his orders had in some way failed to be executed, Gen. Beauregard at last ordered up a portion of the forces which were intended to co-operate with Gen. Ewell. It was late, however, before these reinforcements came up. Only one brigade reached the field before the battle was won. This was led by Gen. E. K. Smith, of Florida, formerly of the United States Army, and was part of Gen. Johnston's column from Winchester. They should have reached here the day before, but were prevented by an accident on the railroad. They dashed on the charge with loud shouts and in the most gallant style. About the same time, Maj. Elzey (formerly of the Augusta Arsenal)—coming down the railroad from Winchester with the last of Johnson's brigades, and hearing the firing, immediately quit the train and struck across the country, and, as a gracious fortune would have it, he encountered the extreme right of the enemy as he was feeling his way around our flank, and with his brigade struck him like a thunder-bolt, full in the face. Finding he was about to be out-flanked himself, the enemy gave way after the second fire. Meanwhile, Beauregard rallied the centre and dashed into the very thickest of the fight, and after him rushed our own brave boys, with a shout that seemed to shake the very earth. The result of this movement from three distinct points, was to force back the enemy, who began to retreat, first in good order, and finally in much confusion. At this point, the cavalry were ordered upon the pursuit. The retreat now became a perfect rout, and it is reported that the flying legions rushed past Centreville in the direction of Fairfax, as if the earth had been opening behind them. It was when Gen. Beauregard led the final charge, that his horse was killed by a shell.

CONSTITUTION

OF THE

Confederate States of America.

We, the people of the Confederate States, each State acting in its sovereign and independent character, in order to form a permanent federal government, establish justice, insure domestic tranquility, and secure the blessings of liberty to ourselves and our posterity—invoking the favor and guidance of Almighty God—do ordain and establish this Constitution for the Confederate States of America.

ARTICLE I.

SECTION 1.

All legislative powers herein delegated shall be vested in a Congress of the Confederate States, which shall consist of a Senate and House of Representatives.

SECTION 2.

1. The House of Representatives shall be composed of members chosen every second year by the people of the several States; and the electors in each State shall be citizens of the Confederate States, and have the qualifications requisite for electors of the most numerous branch of the State Legislature; but no person of foreign birth, not a citizen of the Confederate States, shall be allowed to vote for any officer, civil or political, State or Federal.

2. No person shall be a Representative, who shall not have attained the age of twenty-five years, and be a citizen of the Confederate States, and who shall not, when elected, be an inhabitant of that State in which he shall be chosen.

3. Representatives and Direct Taxes shall be apportioned among the several States, which may be included within this Confederacy, according to their respective numbers, which shall be determined, by adding to the whole number of free persons, including those bound to service for a term of years, and excluding Indians not taxed, three-fifths of all slaves. The actual enumeration shall be made within three years after the first meeting of the Congress of the Confederate States, and within every subsequent term of ten years, in such manner as they shall, by law, direct. The number of Representatives shall not exceed one for every fifty thousand, but each State shall have at least one Representative; and until such enumeration shall be made the State of South Carolina shall be entitled to choose six—the State of Georgia ten—the State of Alabama nine—the State of Florida two—the State of Mississippi seven—the State of Louisiana six, and the State of Texas six.

4. When vacancies happen in the representation from any State, the Executive authority thereof shall issue writs of election to fill such vacancies.

5. The House of Representatives shall choose their speaker and other officers; and shall have the sole power of impeachment; except that any judicial or other federal officers resident and acting solely within the limits of any State, may be impeached by a vote of two-thirds of both branches of the Legislature thereof.

SECTION 3.

1. The Senate of the Confederate States shall be composed of two Senators from each State, chosen for six years by the legislature thereof, at the regular session next immediately preceding the commencement of the term of service; and each Senator shall have one vote.

2. Immediately after they shall be assembled, in consequence of the first election, they shall be divided as equally as may be into three classes. The seats of the Senators of the first class shall be vacated at the expiration of the second year; of the second class at the expiration of the fourth year, and of the third class at the expiration of the sixth year; so that one-third may be chosen every second year; and if vacancies happen by resignation, or otherwise, during the recess of the legislature of any State, the executive thereof may make temporary appointments until the next meeting of the Legislature, which shall then fill such vacancies.

3. No person shall be a Senator who shall not have attained the age of thirty years, and be a citizen of the Confederate States; and who shall not, when elected, be an inhabitant of the State for which he shall be chosen.

4. The Vice President of the Confederate States shall be President of the Senate, but shall have no vote, unless they shall be equally divided.

5. The Senate shall choose their other officers; and also a President *pro tempore* in the absence of the Vice President, or when he shall exercise the office of President of the Confederate States.

6. The Senate shall have the sole power to try all impeachments. When sitting for that purpose, they shall be on oath or affirmation. When the President of the Confederate States is tried, the Chief Justice shall preside; and no person shall be convicted without the concurrence of two-thirds of the members present.

7. Judgment in cases of impeachment shall not extend further than to removal from office, and disqualification to hold and enjoy any office of honor or profit, under the Confederate States; but the party convicted shall, nevertheless, be liable and subject to indictment, trial, judgment and punishment according to law.

SECTION 4.

1. The time, place and manner of holding elections for Senators and Representatives shall be prescribed in each State by the legislature thereof, subject to the provisions of this Constitution; but the Congress may, at any time, by law, make or alter such regulations, except as to the times and places of choosing Senators.

2. The Congress shall assemble at least once in every year; and such meeting shall be on the first Monday in December, unless they shall by law, appoint a different day.

SECTION 5.

1. Each House shall be the judge of the elections, returns and qualifications of its own members, and a majority of each shall constitute a quorum to do business; but a smaller number may adjourn from day to day, and may be authorized to compel the attendance of absent members, in such manner and under such penalties as each House may provide.

2. Each House may determine the rules of its proceedings, punish its members for disorderly behavior, and, with the concurrence of two-thirds of the whole number, expel a member.

3. Each House shall keep a journal of its proceedings, and from time to time publish the same, excepting such parts as may in their judgment require secrecy, and the yeas and nays of the members of either House, on any question, shall, at the desire of one-fifth of those present, by entered on the journal.

4. Neither House, during the session of Congress, shall, without the consent of the other, adjourn for more than three days, nor to any other place than that in which the two Houses shall be sitting.

SECTION 6.

1. The Senators and Representatives shall receive a compensation for their services, to be ascertained by law, and paid out of the treasury of the Confederate States. They shall, in all cases, except treason, and breach of the peace, be privileged from arrest during their attendance at the session of their respective Houses, and in going to and returning from the same; and for any speech or debate in either House, they shall not be questioned in any other place.

2. No Senator or Representative shall, during the time for which he was elected, be appointed to any civil office under the authority of the Confederate States, which shall have been created, or the emoluments whereof shall have been increased during such time; and no person holding any office under the Confederate States shall be a member of either House during his continuance in office. But Congress may, by law, grant to the principal officer in each of the Executive Departments a seat upon the floor of either House, with the privilege of discussing any measures appertaining to his department.

SECTION 7.

1. All bills for raising revenue shall originate in the House of Representatives; but the Senate may propose or concur with amendments as on other bills.

2. Every bill which shall have passed both Houses, shall, before it becomes a law, be presented to the President of the Confederate States; if he approve, he shall sign it; but if not he shall return it with his objections to the House in which it shall have originated, who shall enter the objections at large on their journals, and proceed to reconsider it. If, after such reconsideration, two-thirds of that House shall agree to pass the bill, it shall be sent, together with the objections, to the other House, by which it shall likewise be reconsidered, and if approved by two-thirds of that House, it shall become a law. But in all such cases, the votes of both Houses shall be determined by yeas and nays, and the persons voting for and against the bill shall be entered on the journal of each House respectively. If any bill shall not be returned by the President within ten days (Sundays excepted) after it shall have been presented to him, the same shall be a law, in like manner as if he had signed it, unless the Congress, by their adjournment, prevent its return; in which case it shall not be a law. The President may approve any appropriation and disapprove any other appropriation in the same bill. In such case he shall, in signing the bill, designate the appropriations disapproved; and shall return a copy of such appropriations, with his objections, to the House in which the bill shall have originated, and the same proceedings shall then be had as in case of other bills disapproved by the President.

3. Every order, resolution or vote, to which the concurrence of both Houses may be necessary (except on a question of adjournment) shall be presented to the President of the Confederate States; and before the same shall take effect, shall be approved by him; or being disapproved by him, may be re-passed by two-thirds of both Houses according to the rules and limitations prescribed in case of a bill.

SECTION 8

The Congress shall have power—

1. To lay and collect taxes, duties, imposts, and excises, for revenue necessary to pay the debts, provide for the common defence, and carry on the government of the Confederate States, but no bounties shall be granted from the treasury; nor shall any duties or taxes on importations from foreign nations be laid to promote or foster any branch of industry; and all duties, imposts, and excises shall be uniform throughout the Conederate States:

2. To borrow money on the credit of the Confederate States:

3. To regulate commerce with foreign nations, and among the several States, and with the Indian tribes; but neither this, nor any other clause contained in the constitution, shall ever be construed to delegate the power to Congress to appropriate money for any internal improvement intended to facilitate commerce; except for the purpose of furnishing lights, beacons, and buoys, and other aids to navigation upon the coasts, and the improvement of harbors and the removing of obstructions in river navigation, in all which cases, such duties shall be laid on the navigation facilitated thereby, as may be necessary to pay the costs and expenses thereof:

4. To establish uniform laws of naturalization, and uniform laws on the subject of bankruptcies, throughout the Confederate States, but no law of Congress shall discharge any debt contracted before the passage of the same:

5 To coin money, regulate the value thereof and of foreign coin, and fix the standard of weights and measures:

6. To provide for the punishment of counterfeiting the securities and current coin of the Confederate States:

7. To establish post offices and post routes; but the expenses of the Postoffice Department, after the first day of March in the year of our Lord eighteen hundred and sixty-three, shall be paid out of its own revenues:

8. To promote the progress of science and useful arts, by securing for limited times to authors and inventors the exclusive right to their respective writings and discoveries:

9. To constitute tribunals inferior to the Supreme Court:

10 To define and punish piracies and felonies committed on the high seas, and offences against the law of nations:

11. To declare war, grant letters of marque and reprisal, and make rules concerning captures on land and water:

12. To raise and support armies; but no appropriation of money to that use shall be for a longer term than two years.

13. To provide and maintain a navy:

14 To make rules for government and the regulation of the land and naval forces:

15. To provide for calling forth the militia to execute the laws of the Confederate States, suppress insurrections and repel invasions:

16. To provide for organizing, arming, and disciplining the militia, and for governing such part of them as may be employed in the service of the Confederate States; reserving to the States, respectively, the appointment of the officers, and the authority of training the militia according to the discipline prescribed by Congress:

17. To exercise exclusive legislation, in all cases whatsoever, over such district (not exceeding ten miles square,) as may, by cession of one or more States, and the acceptance of Congress, become the seat of the Government of the Confederate States; and to exercise like authority over all the places purchased by the consent of the legislature of the State in which the same shall be, for the erection of forts, magazines, arsenals, dockyards, and other needful buildings: and

18. To make all laws which shall be necessary and proper for carrying into execution the foregoing powers, and all other powers vested by this Constitution in the government of the Confederate States, or in any department or officer thereof.

SECTION 9.

1. The importation of negroes of the African race, from any foreign country, other than the slaveholding States or Territories of the United States of America, is hereby forbidden; and Congress is required to pass such laws as shall effectually prevent the same:

2. Congress shall also have power to prohibit the introduction of slaves from any State not a member of, or Territory not belonging to, this Confederacy.

3. The privilege of the writ of habeas corpus shall not be suspended, unless when, in cases of rebellion or invasion, the public safety may require it.

4. No bill of attainder, or *ex post facto* law, or law denying or impairing the right of property in negro slaves shall be passed.

5. No capitation or other direct tax shall be laid unless in proportion to the census or enumeration hereinbefore directed to be taken.

6. No tax or duty shall be laid on articles exported from any State, except by a vote of two-thirds of both Houses.

7. No preference shall be given by any regulation of commerce or revenue to the ports of one State over those of another

8. No money shall be drawn from the Treasury, but in consequence of appropriations made by law; and a regular statement and account of the receipts and expenditures of all public money shall be published from time to time.

9. Congress shall appropriate no money from the treasury except by a vote of two-thirds of both Houses, taken by yeas and nays, unless it be asked and estimated for by some one of the heads of the Departments, and submitted to Congress by the President; or for the purpose of paying its own expenses and contingencies, or for the payment of claims against the Confederate States, the justice of which shall have been judicially declared by a tribunal for the investigation of claims against the Government, which it is hereby made the duty of Congress to establish.

10 All bills appropriating money shall specify in federal currency the exact amount of each appropriation and the purposes for which it is made; and Congress shall grant no extra compensation to any public contractor, officer, agent or servant, after such contract shall have been made or such service rendered.

11. No title of nobility shall be granted by the Confederate States; and no person holding any office of profit or trust under them, shall, without the consent of the Congress, accept of any present, emoluments, office or titles of any kind whatever, from any king, prince, or foreign State.

12. Congress shall make no law respecting an establishment of religion, or prohibiting the free exercise thereof; or abridging the freedom of speech, or of the press; or the right of the people peaceably to assemble and petition the Government for a redress of grievances.

13. A well regulated militia being necessary to the security of a free State, the right of the people to keep and bear arms shall not be infringed.

14. No soldier shall, in time of peace, be quartered in any house without the consent of the owner; nor in time of war, but in a manner to be prescribed by law.

15. The right of the people to be secure in their persons, houses, papers, and effects against unreasonable searches and seizures, shall not be violated; and no warrant shall issue but upon probable cause, supported by oath or affirmation, and particularly describing the place to be searched, and the persons or things to be seized.

16. No person shall be held to answer for a capital or otherwise infamous crime, unless on a presentment or indictment of a grand jury, except in cases arising in the land or naval forces, or in the militia, when in actual service, in time of war or public danger; nor shall any person be subject for the same offence to be twice put in jeopardy of life or limb; nor be compelled, in any criminal case, to be a witness against himself; nor be deprived of life, liberty, or property, without due process of law; nor shall private property be taken for public use, without just compensation.

17. In all criminal prosecutions the accused shall enjoy the right to a speedy and public trial, by an impartial jury of the State and district wherein the crime shall have been committed, which district shall have been previously ascertained by law, and to be informed of the nature and cause of the accusation; to be confronted with the witnesses against him; to have compulsory process for obtaining witnesses in his favor; and to have the assistance of counsel for his defence.

18. In suits at common law where the value in controversy shall exceed twenty dollars, the right of trial by jury shall be preserved; and no fact so tried by a jury shall be otherwise re-examined in any court of the Confederacy, than according to the rules of the common law.

19. Excessive bail shall not be required, nor excessive fines be imposed, nor cruel and unusual punishments be inflicted.

20. Every law or resolution having the force of law, shall relate to but one subject, and that shall be expressed in the title.

SECTION 10.

1. No State shall enter into any treaty, alliance, or confederation; grant letters of marque and reprisal; coin money; make anything but gold and silver coin a tender in payment of debts; pass any bill of attainder, or *ex post facto* law, or law impairing the obligation of contracts; or grant any title of nobility.

2. No State shall, without the consent of the Congress, lay any imposts or duties on imposts or exports, except what may be absolutely necessary for executing its inspection laws; and the net produce of all duties and imposts, laid by any State on imports or exports, shall be for the use of the treasury of the Confederate States; and all such laws shall be subject to the revision and control of Congress

3. No State shall, without the consent of Congress, lay any duty of tonnage, except on sea going vessels, for the improvement of its rivers and harbors navigated by the said vessels; but such duties shall not conflict with any treaties of the Confederate States with foreign nations; and any surplus or revenue, thus derived, shall, after making such improvements, be paid into the common treasury; nor shall any State keep troops or ships of war in time of peace, enter into any agreement or compact with another State, or with a foreign power, or engage in war, unless actually invaded, or in such imminent danger as will not admit of delay. But when any river divides or flows through two or more States, they may enter into compacts with each other to improve the navigation thereof.

ARTICLE II.

SECTION 1.

1. The executive power shall be vested in a President of the Confederate States of America. He and the Vice President shall hold their offices for the term of six years; but the President shall not be re-eligible.—The President and Vice President shall be elected as follows:

2. Each State shall appoint, in such manner as the legislature thereof may direct, a number of electors equal to the whole number of Senators and Representatives to which the State may be entitled in the Congress; but no Senator or Representative, or person holding an office of trust or profit under the Confederate States, shall be appointed an elector.

3. The electors shall meet in their respective States and vote by ballot for President and Vice President, one of whom, at least, shall not be an inhabitant of the same State with themselves; they shall name in their ballots the person voted for as President, and in distinct ballots the person voted for as Vice-President, and they shall make distinct lists of all persons voted for as President, and of all persons voted for as Vice-President, and of the number of votes for each, which list they shall sign and certify, and transmit, sealed, to the government of the Confederate States, directed to the President of the Senate; the President of the Senate shall, in the presence of the Senate and House of Representatives, open all the certificates, and the vote shall then be counted; the person having the greatest number of votes for President shall be the President, if such number be a majority of the whole number of electors appointed; and if no person have such majority, then, from the persons having the highest numbers, not exceeding three, on the list of those voted for as President, the House of Representatives shall choose immediately, by ballot, the President. But in choosing the President, the vote shall be taken by States, the representation from each State having one vote; a quorum for this purpose shall consist of a member or members from two-thirds of the States, and a majority of all the States shall be necessary to a choice. And if the House of Representatives shall not choose a President, whenever the right of choice shall devolve upon them, before the fourth day of March next following, then the Vice President shall act as President, as in case of the death or other constitutional disability of the President.

4. The person having the greatest number of votes as Vice President shall be the Vice President, if such number be a majority of the whole number of electors appointed: and if no person have a majority, then, from the two highest numbers on the list the Senate shall choose the Vice President; a quorum for the purpose shall consist of two-thirds of the whole number of Senators, and a majority of the whole number shall be necessary to a choice.

5. No person constitutionally ineligible to the office of President shall be eligible to that of Vice President of the Confederate States.

6. The Congress may determine the time of choosing the electors, and the day on which they shall give their votes; which day shall be the same throughout the Confederate States

7. No person except a natural born citizen of the Confederate States, or a citizen thereof, at the time of the adoption of the Constitution, or a citizen thereof born in the United States prior to the 20th of December, 1860, shall be eligible to the office of President; neither shall any person be eligible to that office who shall not have attained the age of thirty-five years, and been fourteen years a resident within the limits of the Confederate States, as they may exist at the time of his election.

8. In case of the removal of the President from office, or of his death, resignation, or inability to discharge the powers and duties of the said office, the same shall devolve on the Vice President; and the Congress may, by law, provide for the case of removal, death, resignation, or inability both of the President and Vice President, declaring what officer shall then act as President, and such officer shall act accordingly until the disability be removed or a President shall be elected.

9. The President shall, at stated times, receive for his services a compensation which shall neither be increased nor diminished during the period for which he shall have been elected; and he shall not receive within that period any other emolument from the Confederate States, or any of them.

10. Before he enters on the execution of his office, he shall take the following oath or affirmation:

"I do solemnly swear (or affirm) that I will faithfully execute the office of President of the Confederate States, and will, to the best of my ability, preserve, protect and defend the Constitution thereof."

SECTION 2.

1. The President shall be commander-in-chief of the army and navy of the Confederate States, and of the militia of the several States, when called into the actual service of the Confederate States; he may require the opinion, in writing, of the principal officer in each of the Executive Departments, upon any subject relating to the duties of their respective offices; and he shall have power to grant reprieves and pardons for offences against the Confederate States, except in cases of impeachment.

2. He shall have power, by and with the advice and consent of the Senate, to make treaties, provided two-thirds of the Senators present concur: and he shall nominate, and by and with the advice and consent of the Senate, shall appoint ambassadors, other public ministers and consuls, Judges of the Supreme Court, and all other officers of the Confederate States, whose appointments are not herein otherwise provided for, and which shall be established by law; but the Congress may, by law, vest the appointment of such inferior officers, as they think proper, in the President alone, in the courts of law or in the heads of Departments.

3. The principal in each of the Executive Departments, and all persons connected with the diplomatic service, may be removed from office at the pleasure of the President. All other civil officers of the Executive Department may be removed at any time by the President, or other appointing power, when their services are unnecessary, or for dishonesty, incapacity, inefficiency, misconduct, or neglect of duty; and when so removed, the removal shall be reported to the Senate, together with the reasons therefor.

4. The President shall have power to fill all vacancies that may happen during the recess of the Senate, by granting commissions which shall expire at the end of their next session; but no person rejected by the Senate shall be re-appointed to the same office during their ensuing recess.

SECTION 3.

1. The President shall, from time to time, give to the Congress information of the state of the Confederacy, and recommend to their consideration such measures as he shall judge necessary and expedient; he may, on extraordinary occasions, convene both Houses, or either of them; and in case of disagreement between them, with respect to the time of adjournment, he may adjourn them to such time as he shall think proper; he shall receive ambassadors and other public ministers; he shall take care that the laws be faithfully executed, and shall commission all the officers of the Confederate States.

SECTION 4.

1. The President, Vice President, and all civil officers of the Confederate States, shall be removed from office on impeachment for, and conviction of, treason, bribery, or other high crimes and misdemeanors.

ARTICLE III.

SECTION 1

1. The judicial power of the Confederate States shall be vested in one Superior Court, and in such Inferior Courts as the Congress may from time to time order and establish. The judges, both of the Supreme and Inferior Courts, shall hold their offices during good behavior, and shall, at stated times, receive for their services a compensation, which shall not be diminished during their continuance in office.

SECTION 2.

1. The judicial power shall extend to all cases arising under this Constitution, the laws of the Confederate States, and treaties made or which shall be made under their authority; to all cases affecting ambassadors, other public ministers and consuls; to all cases of admiralty and maritime jurisdiction; to controversies to which the Confederate States shall be a party; to controversies between two or more States; between a State and citizens of another State where the State is plaintiff; between citizens claiming lands under grants of different States, and between a State or the citizens thereof, and foreign States, citizens or subjects; but no State shall be sued by a citizen or subject of any foreign State.

2. In all cases affecting ambassadors, other public ministers, and consuls, and those in which a State shall be a party, the Supreme Court shall have original jurisdiction. In all the other cases before mentioned, the Supreme Court shall have appellate jurisdiction, both as to law and facts, with such exceptions, and under such regulations, as the Congress shall make.

3. The trial of all crimes, except in cases of impeachment, shall be by jury, and such trial shall be held in the State where the said crime shall have been committed; but when not committed within any State, the trial shall be at such place or places as the Congress may by law have directed.

SECTION 3.

1. Treason against the Confederate States shall consist only in levying war against them, or in adhering to their enemies, giving them aid and comfort. No person shall be convicted of treason unless on the testimony of two witnesses to the same overt act, or on confession in open court.

2. The Congress shall have power to declare the punishment of treason, but no attainder of treason shall work corruption of blood, or forfeiture, except during the life of the person attainted.

ARTICLE IV.

SECTION 1.

1. Full faith and credit shall be given in each State to the public acts, records and judicial proceedings of every other State. And the Congress may, by general laws, prescribe the manner in which such acts, records, and proceedings shall be proved, and the effect thereof.

SECTION 2.

1. The citizens of each State shall be entitled to all the privileges and immunities of citizens in the several States, and shall have the right of transit and sojourn in any State of the Confederacy, with their slaves and other property; and the right of property in said slaves shall not be thereby impaired.

2. A person charged in any State with treason, felony, or other crime against the laws of such State, shall, on demand of the Executive authority of the State from which he fled, be delivered up to be removed to the State having jurisdiction of the crime.

3. No slave or other person held to service or labor in any State or Territory of the Confederate States, under the laws thereof, escaping or lawfully carried into another, shall, in consequence of any law or regulation therein, be discharged from such service or labor; but shall be delivered up on claim of the party to whom such slave belongs, or to whom such service or labor may be due.

SECTION 3.

1. Other States may be admitted into this Confederacy by a vote of two-thirds of the whole House of Representatives, and two-thirds of the Senate, the Senate voting by States; but no new State shall be formed or erected within the jurisdiction of any other State; nor any State be formed by the junction of two or more States, or parts of States, without the consent of the legislatures of the States concerned as well as of the Congress.

2. The Congress shall have power to dispose of and make all needful rules and regulations concerning the property of the Confederate States, including the lands thereof.

3. The Confederate States may acquire new territory; and Congress shall have power to legislate and provide governments for the inhabitants of all territory belonging to the Confederate States, lying without the limits of the several States; and may permit them, at such times, and in such manner as it may by law provide, to form States to be admitted into the Confederacy. In all such territory, the institution of negro slavery as it now exists in the Confederate States, shall be recognized and protected by Congress, and by the territorial government; and the inhabitants of the several Confederate States and Territories, shall have the right to take to such territory any slaves, lawfully held by them in any of the States or Territories of the Confederate States.

4. The Confederate States shall guaranty to every State that now is or hereafter may become a member of this Confederacy, a republican form of government, and shall protect each of them against invasion; and on application of the legislature (or of the Executive when the legislature is in session) against domestic violence.

ARTICLE V.

SECTION 1.

1. Upon the demand of any three States legally assembled in their several conventions, the Congress shall summon a convention of all the States, to take into consideration such amendments to the Constitution as the said States all concur in suggesting at the time when the said demand is made; and should any of the proposed amendments to the Constitution be agreed on by the said convention—voting by States—and the same be ratified by the legislatures of two-thirds of the several States, or by conventions in two-thirds thereof—as the one or the other mode of ratification may be proposed by the general convention—they shall thenceforward form a part of this Constitution. But no State shall, without its consent, be deprived of its equal representation in the Senate.

ARTICLE VI

1. The Government established by this Constitution is the successor of the Provisional Government of the Confederate States of America, and all the laws passed by the latter shall continue in force until the same shall be repealed or modified; and all the officers appointed by the same shall remain in office until their successors are appointed and qualified, or the offices abolished.

2. All debts contrated and engagements entered into before the adoption of this Censtitution shall be as valid against the Confederate States under this Constitution as under the Provisional Government.

3. This Constitution, and the laws of the Confederate States, made in pursuance thereof, and all treaties made, or which shall be made under the authority of the Confederate States, shall be the supreme law of the land; and the judges in every State shall be bound thereby, anything in the constitution or laws of any State to the contrary notwithstanding.

4. The Senators and Representatives before mentioned and the members of the several State legislatures, and all executive and judicial officers, both of the Confederate States and of the several States, shall be bound by oath or affirmation, to support this Constitution; but no religious test shall ever be required as a qualification to any office or public trust under the Confederate Ssates.

5. The enumeration, in the Constitution, of certain rights, shall not be construed to deny or disparage others retained by the people of the several States.

6. The powers not delegated to the Confederate States by the Constitution, nor prohibited by it to the States are reserved to the States, respectively, or to the people thereof.

ARTICLE VII.

1. The ratification of the conventions of five States shall be sufficient for the establishment of this Constitution between the States so ratifying the same.

2. When five States shall have ratified this Constitution in the manner before specified, the Congress under the Provisional Constitution, shall prescribe the time for holding the election of President and Vice President; and for the meeting of the Electoral College; and for counting the votes, and inaugurating the President. They shall, also, prescribe the time for holding the first election of members of Congress under this Constitution, and the time for assembling the same. Until the assembling of such Congress, the Congress under the Provisional Constitution shall continue to exercise the legislative powers granted them; not extending beyond the time limited by the Constitution of the Provisional Government.

Adopted, unanimously, March 11, 1861.

Nashville Patriot.

DAILY $8; TRI-WEEKLY $5; WEEKLY $2.

ANTHONY S. CAMP, THOS. CALLENDER, IRA P. JONES, H. EDMUNDSON

BY A. S. CAMP & CO.

W. HY. SMITH, IRA P. JONES, } Editors.

No. 16 Deaderick Street.

SUNDAY MORNING, AUGUST 25, 1861.

The Battle of Manassas Plains.

We make room this morning for the letter of Mr. RUSSELL, the correspondent of the London *Times*, descriptive of the disgraceful retreat of the Federal forces from the battle-field on Manassas Plains. It is exceedingly graphic, and will be read with interest. He was not sufficiently enterprising to get within seeing distance of the battle, and therefore does not attempt a description of it. It appears, however, that he had enterprise enough get away, after the retreat had fairly degenerated into a panic, about as fast as any of the fleet-footed Yankees. Indeed, he seems to have had a laudable desire to keep as far in advance of the flying squadrons as possible; of course, not because he apprehended any danger to himself, but simply on account of his personal comfort. After perusing his letter, the reader's mental pictures of the Manassas Races, however grotesque, would be incomplete without the burly RUSSELL and his bobtail nag, struggling for the lead, forming a very prominent part.

We also publish comments of the *Times* and other English Journals on the battle; which has produced a considerable sensation "over the waters." The Southern people have convinced the British that they are made of "true metal," and however much the Yankees may be derided, they will respect those who have shown themselves capable of commanding it.

LIEUT. COL. BRAZELTON.—The second battalion of East Tennessee Cavalry was organized at Knoxville on the 22d inst. WM. BRAZELTON, Jr., was elected Lieut. Colonel and J. C. BRADFORD, Major. The *Register* says—"This, although the first battalion of cavalry organized, is the second in order of the reception of the companies. Lieut. Colonel Brazelton, was elected to that position from the ranks, where he had patriotically taken his stand as a private. He has occupied a prominent position heretofore in the politics of East Tennessee. He gave his whole soul to the work of getting up a splendid cavalry company from Jefferson, and took his chance for promotion with all who joined his company."

COL. N. G. TAYLOR HEARD OF.—A correspondent of the Knoxville *Register*, writing from Carter county, under date of August 21, says:—

"Nat. Taylor took to the woods on Monday morning 12th inst., and has not been in since. He is now said to be in the "Crab Orchard" surrounded by a body guard of 100 faithful and obedient Lincolnites who guard him by turns. How true this is, I am not able to say, but I have no doubt he is badly alarmed. Thus far the Lincoln army has acted upon Taylor's philosophy, and taken to their heels at the approach of danger.

"Messengers pass from here to Taylor's retreat in the Crab Orchard every day or two, and it is told on the authority of a preacher who turned States' evidence, that a plan was concerted by Taylor and his associate Lincolnites, to tear up the railroad from Knoxville to Bristol in one night, burn the property of Southern men, and take all the leading ones prisoners. This may be true as to their resolve, but I doubt their ability to accomplish it."

Confederate Congress.

RICHMOND, Aug. 22.—In Congress to-day an act was passed authorising to be paid to Charles P. Pollard, Esq., President of the Alabama and Florida Railroad, the sum of [illegible] being the difference between [illegible] per cent. duty on railroad iron paid by him for his road.

An act was also passed establishing a mail line from Station No. 19 on the Savannah, Albany and Gulf railroad to Monticello, Fla., but the Post Master General will not be required to [illegible] mail on said route unless, in his opinion, the public interest demands it.

The President has approved the following acts:—

An act establishing a uniform rule of naturalization for persons enlisted in the armies of the Confederate States.

An act to increase the corps of artillery.

An act making an appropriation of $50,000 to pay for the service of physicians employed in conjunction with the medical staff of the Confederate army.

An act authorizing the Secretary of War to employ cooks and nurses for the military service, and appropriating for such service the sum of $130,000.

An act appropriating the sum of $57,000,000 for payment of the Military, Quarter Master's supplies, and transportation, and for the purchase of subsistence and ordnance stores and medical supplies and service.

An act appropriating $50,000 for the establishment and support of military hospitals.

A resolution authorizing the Secretary of War in his discretion to furnish volunteer cavalry companies with all the necessary equipments.

An act to provide for local defence and special service.

Together with some few other acts of no general interest.

A Steamer Captured by a Gunboat—A Good Haul in Turn.

At daylight on yesterday morning, the packet *W. B. Terry*, running from Paducah (Ky.) on the Tennessee river, owned at Eastport, (Miss.), and commanded by Capt. JOHN JOHNSON, was unexpectedly seized whilst laying near the wharf at Paducah, by the LINCOLN gunboat *Conestoga* and an armed force of 250 armed federal troops, and taken as a prize to Cairo. This feat was no doubt performed by way of retaliation for the recent capture of the steamers *Equality* and *Cheeney* by our men. But the captain and crew of the *Terry* were not to be so easily outdone, as the sequel proved. Accordingly in the afternoon they managed by some means to seize the steamer *Samuel Orr*, which was a regular packet between Paducah and Evansville, and owned at the latter place. They succeeded in hurrying her up the Tennessee river to Fort Henry, as we learn, on the Kentucky and Tennessee line, where she was safely secured with a heavy cargo of groceries, consisting principally of coffee, bacon, whisky, etc. Her cargo was to be paid for only on delivery at Paducah, a circumstance which saddles the loss on the shippers and not the consignees.

The *Orr* is one of the fleetest packets on the river, and, with her contents, is a valuable "haul."—*Memphis Appeal*, 23.

ARREST OF A. R. BOTELER.—The Clarke county (Va.) *Conservator* is reliably informed that a number of Federal troops went to the residence of Hon. A. R. Boteler, near Shepherdstown, on last Tuesday morning, and forcibly carried him off. They went to his house before daybreak, and took him out of his bdd.

Since the above was written, we have received the Winchester *Republican*, which confirms the report of Mr. Boteler's arrest, but says he ways subsequently released by order of Gen. Banks. The *Republican* says that some two hundred abolitionists surrounded Mr. B.'s house, when one his daughters, a beautiful young lady, demanded to know their business there. She was responded to by the most genteel looking of the ruffians, who politely told her unless she immediately withdrew her brains would be blown out. Mr. Boteler, as soon as he could dress, presented himself at the door, and demanded to know by whose authority this outrage upon his person and family was committed. This they declined to give, and ordered him to immediately accompany them. As he was unarmed and surrounded by 200 armed men, resistance was out of the question; but as they appeared apprehensive of an attack from him, to quiet their fears he suggested that they had best handcuff him, in order to insure their safety. He was taken on immediately through Shepherdstown, across into Maryland, to the headquarters of General Banks, where he was courteously treated, and released as above stated.—*Richmond Dispatch.*

Mr. Russell's Letter on the Battle of Manassas Plains.

Special Correspondence of the London Times.

WASHINGTON, July 22, 1861.

I set down to give an account—not of the action yesterday, but of what I saw with my own eyes, hitherto not often deceived, and of what I heard with my own ears, which in this country are not so much to be trusted. Let me, however, express an opinion as to the affair of yesterday. In the first place, the repulse of the Federalists, decided as it was, might have had no serious effects whatever beyond the mere failure—which politically was of greater consequence than it was in a military sense—but for the disgraceful conduct of the troops. The retreat on their lines at Centreville seems to have ended in a cowardly rout—a miserable, causeless panic. Such scandalous behavior on the part of soldiers I should have considered impossible, as with some experience of camps and armies I have never, even in alarms among camp followers, seen the like of it. How far the disorganization of the troops extended I know not; but it was complete in the instance of more than one regiment.

Washington this morning is crowded with soldiers without officers, who have fled from Centreville, and with "three month men," who are going home from the face of the enemy on the expiration of their term of enlistment. The streets, in spite of the rain, are crowded by people with anxious faces, and groups of wavering politicians are assembled at the corners, in the hotel passages, and the bars. If, in the present state of the troops, the Confederates were to make a march across the Potomac above Washington, turning the works at Arlington, the capitol might fall into their hands. Delay may place that event out of the range of probability. The North will, no doubt, recover the shock. Hitherto he has only said, "Go and fight for the Union." The South has exclaimed, "Let us fight for our rights." The North must put its best men into the battle, or she will inevitably fail before the energy, the personal hatred, and the superior fighting powers of her antagonist.

On Saturday night I resolved to proceed to Gen. McDowell's army, as it was obvious to me that the repulse at Bull Run and the orders of the General directed against the excesses of his soldiery indicated serious defects in the army; not more serious, however, than I had reason to believe existed. Curiosity was aroused by the story that *McDowell had been actually ordered to make an attack on Manassas, and that Gen. Scott had given him till 12 o'clock to be master of Beauregard's lines.* If General Scott ordered the attack at all, I venture to say he was merely the mouthpiece of the more violent civilians of the Government, who mistake intensity of feeling for military strength. The consequences of the little skirmish at Bull Run, ending in the repulse of the Federalists, were much exagerated and their losses were put down at any figures the fancy of the individual item who was speaking suggested. *"I can assure you, Sir, that the troops had 1,500 killed and wounded; I know it."* I went off to the headquarters, and there Gen. Scott's aid informed me Gen. McDowell's official report gave 60 killed and 37 wounded.

When I spoke with officers at General Scott's headquarters of the expedition, it struck me they were not at all sanguine about the result of the day, and one of them said as much as induced me to think he would advise me to remain in the city if he did not take it for granted it was part of my duty to go to the scene of action. An English gentleman who accompanied me was strongly dissuaded from going by a Colonel of cavalry on the staff, because, he said, "the troops are green, and no one can tell what may happen." But my friend got his pass from Gen. Scott, who was taking the whole affair of Bull Run and the pressure of the morrow's work with perfect calm, and we started [illegible] Sunday morning for Centerville, [illegible] at twenty-five miles southwest [illegible] ton. The long and weary [illegible] by different pickets along [illegible] by the [illegible] masses at different points [illegible] country looked vacant in spite of crops of Indian corn, for the houses were shut up, and few indigenous people whom we met looked most blackly under their brows at the supposed Abolitionists.

On turning into one of the roads which leads to Fairfax Court House and to Centerville beyond it, the distant sound of cannon reached us. That must have been about 9·30 A. M. It never ceased all day, at least whenever the rattle of the gig ceased the booming of guns rolled through the woods on our ears. One man said it began at 2 o'clock, but the pickets told us it had really become continuous about 7½ or 8 o'clock. In a few minutes afterward a body of men appeared on the road, with their backs toward Centerville and their faces toward Alexandria. Their march was so disorderly that I could not have believed they were soldiers in an enemy's country—for Virginia hereabouts is certainly so—but for their arms and uniform. It soon appeared that there was no less than an entire regiment marching away, singly or in small knots of two or three, extending for some three or four miles along the road. A Babel of tongues rose from them, and they were all in good spirits, but with an air about them I could not understand.

Dismounting at a stream, where a group of thirsty men were drinking, and halting in the shade, I asked an officer, "Where are you men going, Sir?" "Well, we're going home, Sir, I reckon, to Pennsylvania." It was the 4th Pennsylvania regiment, which was on its march, as I learned from the men. "I suppose there is severe work going on behind you, judging from the firing?" "Well, I reckon, Sir, there is." "We're going home," he added after a pause, during which it occurred to him, perhaps, that the moment required explanation, "because the men's time is up. We have had three months of this work." I proceeded on my way, ruminating on the feelings of a General who sees half a brigade walk quietly away on the very morning of action, and on the frame of mind of the men, who would have shouted till they were hoarse about their beloved Union—possibly have hunted down any poor creature who expressed a belief that it was not the very quintessence of everything great and good in government and glorious and omnipotent in arms—coolly turning their backs on it when in its utmost peril because the letter of their engagement bound them no further.

Wherever there was a house by the roadside the negroes were listening to the firing. All at once a terrific object appeared in the wood above the trees—the dome of a church or public building, apparently suffering from the shocks of an earthquake and heaving to and fro in the most violent manner. In much doubt we approached as well as the horses' minds would let us, and discovered that the strange thing was an inflated balloon, attached to a car and wagon, which was on its way to enable Gen. McDowell to reconnoitre the position he was then engaged in attacking—*just a day too late.* The operators and attendants swore as horribly as Anna's warriors in Flanders, but they could not curse down the trees, and so the balloon seems likely to fall into the hands of the Confederates.

At about 11 o'clock we began to enter on the disputed territory which had just been abandoned by the Secessionists to the Federalists in front of Fairfax Court House. It is not too much to say that the works thrown up across the road were shams and makebelieves, and that the Confederates never intended to occupy the position at all, but sought to lure the Federalists to Manassas Gap, where they were prepared to meet them. Of course the troops of the enemy did not wish to be cut off, and so they had to cut down trees, to place across the road, and put fieldpieces in their earthworks to command it. On no side could Richmond be so well defended. The Confederates had it much at heart to induce their enemy to come to the strongest place and attack them, and they succeeded in doing so. But if the troops behaved as ill in other places as they did at Manassas, the Federalists could not have been successful in any attempt whatever.

It was noon when we arrived at Fairfax Court House—a poor village of some 30 or 40 straggling wooden and brick houses. The village was held by a part of the reserve of McDowell's force, possibly 1,000 strong. The inhabitants were, if eyes spoke truth, Secessionists to a man, woman and child, and even the negroes looked extra black, as if they did not care about being fought for. A short way beyond this village, Germantown, the scene of the recent excesses of the Federalists, afforded evidence, in its blackened ruins, that Gen. McDowell's censure was more than needed. Centreville was still seven miles ahead. The guns sounded, however, heavily from the valleys. Rising above the forest tops appeared the blue masses of the Alleghanies, and we knew Manasses was somewhere on an outlying open of the ridges, which reminded me in color and form of the hills around the Valley of Baidar. At last Centreville appeared in sight—a few houses on our front, beyond which rose a bald hill, the slopes covered with bivouac huts, commissariat carts and horses, and the *top crested with spectators of the fight.*

The road on each side was full of traces of Confederate camps; the houses were now all occupied by Federalists. In the rear of the hill was a strong body of infantry—two regiments of foreigners, mostly Germans, with a battery of light artillery. Our buggy was driven up to the top of the hill. On the hill there were carriages and vehicles drawn up as if they were attending a small country race. They were afterwards engaged in a race of a different kind. In one was a lady with an opera glass in and around and on others were legislators and politicians. There was also a few civilians on horseback, and on the slope of the hill a regiment had stacked arms, and was engaged in looking at and commenting on the battle below. The landscape in front was open to the sight as far as the ranges of the Alleghanies, which swept around from the right in blue mounds, the color of which softened into violet in the distance. On our left front a gap in the lowest chain of the hills showed the gap of Manassas, and to the left and nearer to us lay the Junction of the same name, where the Alexandria railway unites with the rail from the west of Virginia, and continues the rout by rails of various denominations to Richmond.

The scene was so peaceful a man might well doubt the evidence of one sense that a great contest was being played out below in bloodshed, or imagine, as Mr. Seward sometimes does, that it was a delusion when he wakes in the morning and finds there is civil war upon him. But the cannon spoke out loudly from the green bushes, and the plains below were mottled, so to speak, by puffs of smoke and by white rings from bursting shells and capacious howitzers. It was no review that was going on beneath us. The shells gave proof enough of that, though the rush of the shot could not be heard at the distance. Clouds of dust came up in regular lines through the tree tops where infantry were acting, and now and then thier wavering mists of light blue smoke curled up, and the splutter of musketry broke the booming of the guns. With the glass I could detect now and then the flash of arms through the dust clouds in the open, but no one could tell to which side the troops who were moving belonged, and I could only judge from the smoke whether the guns were fired toward or away from the hill. It was evident that the dust in the distance on our right extended beyond that which rose from the Federalists.

The view toward the left was interrupted, but the firing was rather more heavy there than on the front or right flank, and a glade was pointed out in the forest as the beginning of Bull or Poole's Run, on the other side of which the Confederates were hid in force, though they had not made any specific reply to the shells thrown into their cover early in the morning. There seemed to be a continuous line, which was held by the enemy, from which came steady, solid firing against what might be supposed to be heads of columns stationed at various points or advancing against them. The soldiers, who followed each shot with remarks in English or German, were not as eager as men generally are in watching a fight. Once, as a cloud of thick smoke ascended from the trees, a man shouted out, "That's good; we've taken another battery; there goes the magazine." But it looked like, and I believe was, the explosion of a caisson.

In the midst of our little reconnoisance an Englishman came up and told us the action had been commenced in splendid style by the Federalists, who had advanced steadily, driving the Confederates before them—a part of the plan, as I firmly believe to bring them under the range of their guns. He believed the advantages on the Federalist side were decided, though won with hard fighting, and he had just come up to Centerville to look after something to eat and drink, and to procure little necessaries, in case of need. Suddenly up rode an officer, with a crowd of soldiers after him from the village. "We've whipped them on all points!" he shouted. "We've taken their batteries, and they're all retreating!" Such an uproar as followed! The spectators and the men cheered again and again, and cries of "Bravo!" 'Bully for us!' "Didn't I tell you so?" and guttural "hochs" from the Deutschland folk, and loud "hurroos" from the Irish. Soon afterward my horse was brought up to the hill, and my friend and the gentleman I have already mentioned set out to walk toward the front.

As I turned down into the narrow road or lane, already mentioned, there was a forward movement among the four wheeled tilt wagons, which raised a great deal of dust. I had met my friends on the road, and after a few words rode forward at a long trot as well as I could past the wagons and through the dust, when suddenly there arose a tumult in front of me at a small bridge across the road, and then I perceived the drivers of a set of wagons with the horses turned toward me, who were endeavoring to force their way against the stream of vehicles setting in the other direction. By the side of the new set of wagons there were a number of commissariat men and soldiers, whom at first sight I took to be the baggage guard. They looked excited and alarmed, and were running by the side of the horses—in front the dust quite obsured the view.

At the bridge the currents met in wild disorder. "Turn back! Retreat!" shouted the men from the front, 'we're whipped! we're whipped!' They cursed and tugged at the horse's heads, and struggled with phrenzy to get past. Running by me on foot was a man with the shoulder straps of an officer. 'Pray, what is the matter, sir?' 'It means we're badly whipped, and that's a fact,' he blurted out in puffs, and continued his career. I observed that he carried no sword. The teamsters of the advancing wagons now caught up the cry.—'Turn back—turn your horses,' was the shout up the whole line, and, backing, plunging, rearing, and kicking, the horse, which had been proceeding down the road reversed front and went off toward Centreville. Those behind them went madly rushing on, the drivers being quite indifferent whether glory or disgrace led the way provided they could find it.

In the midst of this extraordinary spectacle an officer, escorted by some dragoons, rode through the ruck with a light cart in charge. Another officer, on foot, with his sword under his arm, ran up against me. 'What is all this about?' 'Why, we're pretty badly whipped.—We're all in retreat. There's General Tyler there, badly wounded.' And on he ran. There came yet another, who said, 'We're beaten on all points. The whole army is in retreat.' Still there was no flight of troops, no retreat of an army, no reason for all this precipitation. True, there were many men in uniform flying toward the rear, but it did not appear as if they were beyond the proportions of a large baggage escort.

I got my horse up into the field out of the road, and went on rapidly toward the front. Soon I met soldiers who were coming through the corn, mostly without arms; and presently I saw firelocks, cooking tins, knapsacks, and greatcoats on the ground, and observed that the confusion and speed of the baggage carts became greater, and that many of them were crowded with men, or were followed by others, who clung to them. The ambulances were crowded with soldiers, but it did not look as if there were many wounded. Negro servants on led horses dashed frantically past; men in uniform, whom it were a disgrace to the profession of arms to call 'soldier," swarmed by on mules, chargers, and even draught horses, which had been cut out of carts or wagons, and went on with harness clinging to their heels, as frightened as their riders. Men literally screamed with rage and fright when their way was blocked up.

On I rode, asking all, "What is all this about?" and now and then, but rarely receiving the answer, "We're whipped;" or "We're repulsed." Faces black and dusty, tongues out in the heat, eyes staring—it was a most wonderful sight. But where was the fiend? I looked in vain. There was, indeed, some cannonading in front of me and in the rear, but still the firing was comparatively distant, and the runaways were far out of range. As I advanced the number of carts diminished, but the mounted men increased, and the column of fugitives became denser. A few buggies and light wagons filled with men, whose faces would have made up "a great Leporello" in the ghost scene, tried to pierce the rear of the mass of carts, which were now solidified and moving on like a glacier. I crossed a small ditch by the roadside, got out on the road to escape some snake fences, and looking before me saw there was still a crowd of men in uniforms coming along.

The road was strewn with articles of clothing—firelocks, waist-belts, cartouch boxes, caps, greatcoats, mess tins, musical instruments, cartridges, bayonets and sheaths, swords and pistols—even biscuits, water bottles, and pieces of meat. Passing a white house by the roadside, I saw, for the first time, a body of infantry with sloped arms marching regularly and rapidly toward me. Their faces were not blackened by powder, and it was evident that they had not been engaged. In reply to a question, a non-commissioned officer told me, in broken English, "We fall back to our lines. The attack did not quite succeed." This was assuring to one who had come through such a scene as I had been witnessing.

I had ridden, I suppose, about three or three and a half miles from the hill, when I came out on an open piece of ground, beyond and circling which was forest. Two field pieces were unlimbered and guarding the road; the panting and jaded horses in the rear looked as though they had been hard worked, and the gunners and drivers looked worn and dejected. Dropping shots sounded close in front through the woods, but the guns on the left no longer maintained their fire. I was just about to ask one of the men for a light, when a sputtering fire on my right attracted my attention, and out of the forest or along the road rushed a number of men. The gunners seized the trail of the nearest piece to wheel it round upon them; others made for the tumbrils and horses, as if to fly, when a shout was raised "Don't fire! they are our own men!" and in a few minutes on came, pell mell, a whole regiment in disorder.

I came across an officer and stopped him. "We're pursued by cavalry," he gasped: "They've cut us all to pieces." As he spoke a shell burst over the column; another dropped on the road, and out streamed another column of men, keeping together with their arms, and closing up the stragglers of the first regiment. I turned, and to my surprise saw the artillery-men had gone off, leaving one gun standing by itself. They had retreated with their horses. It was now well established that the retreat had really commenced, though I saw but few wounded men, and the regiments which were falling back had not suffered much loss. No one seemed to know anything for certain. Even the cavalry charge was a rumor.

Several officers said they carried guns and lines, but then they drifted into nonsense which one reads and hears everywhere about "masked batteries." One or two talked more sensibly about the strong positions of the enemy, the fatigue of their men, the want of a reserve, severe losses, and the bad conduct of certain regiments. No one spoke as if he thought of retiring beyond Centreville. The clouds of dust rising above the woods marked the retreat of the whole army, and the crowds of fugitives continued to steal away along the road. The sun was declining, and some thirty miles yet remained to be accomplished ere I could hope to gain the shelter of Washington.

No one knew whether any corps or regiment was marching, but there were rumors of all kinds—"the Sixty-ninth are cut to pieces," "the Fire Zouaves are destroyed," and so on. Presently a tremour ran through the men by whom I was riding, as the sharp reports of some field pieces rattled through the woods close at hand. A sort of sudden roar, like the voice of distant breakers rose in front of us, and the soldiers who were, I think, Germans, broke into a double, looking now and then over their shoulders. There was no choice for me but to resign any further researches; so I put my horse into a trot, keeping in the fields alongside the roads as much as I could, to avoid the fugitives, till I came once more on the rear of the baggage and store carts, and the pressure of the crowd, who, concious of the aid which the vehicles would afford them against a cavalry charge, and fearful, nevertheless, of their proximity clamored and shouted like madmen as they ran. The road was now literally covered with baggage. It seemed to me as if the men inside were throwing things out purposely.

On approaching Centreville a body of German infantry of the reserve came marching down and stemmed the current in some degree; they were followed by a brigade of guns and another battalion of fresh troops. I turned up on the hill half a mile beyond. A battery of fields guns was in position where we had been standing. The men looked well. As yet there was nothing to indicate more than a retreat, and some ill-behavior among the wagoners and the riff raff of different regiments. I turned my horse's head and rode away through the village, and after I got out upon the road the same confusion seemed to prevail. Suddenly the guns on the hill opened, and at the same time the thuds of artillery from the wood on the right rear. The stampede then became general.

What occurred at the hill I cannot say, but all the road from Centreville for miles presented such a sight as can only be witnessed in the track of the runaways of an utterly demoralized army. Drivers flogged, lashed, and beat their horses, or leaped down and abandoned their teams and ran by the side of the road; mounted men, servants, and men in uniform, vehicles of all sorts, and commissariat wagons thronged the narrow ways. At every shot a convulsion, as it were, seized upon the morbid mass of bones, sinew, wood, and iron, and thrilled through it giving new energy and action to its desperate efforts to get free from itself. Again the cry of "Cavalry" arose. "What are you afraid of?" said I to a man running beside me. "I am not afraid of you," said the ruffian, levelling his piece at me and pulling the trigger. It was not loaded or the cap was not on, for the gun did not go off. I was unarmed, and I did go off as fast as I could, resolved to keep my own counsel for the second time that day. And so the fight went on.

At one time, a whole mass of infantry, with fixed bayonets, ran down the bank of the road, and some falling as they ran must have killed and wounded those among whom they fell. As I knew the road would soon become impassable or blocked up, I put my horse to a gallop and passed on toward the front. But mounted men still rode faster, shouting out, "cavalry are coming." Again I ventured to speak to some officers whom I overtook, and said, if these runaways are not stopped the whole of the posts and pickets into Washington will fly also!" One of them, without saying a word, spurred his horse and dashed on in front. I do not know whether he ordered the movement or not, but the van of the fugitives was now suddenly checked, and, pressing on through the wood at the roadside, I saw a regiment of infantry blocking up the way, with their front toward Centreville. A musket was levelled at my head as I pushed to the front. "Stop, or I'll fire." At the same time the officers were shouting out, "don't let a soul pass." I addressed one of them and said, "Sir, I am a British subject. I am not, I assure you, running away. I have done my best to stop this disgraceful rout, (as I had) and have been telling them that there are no cavalry within ten miles of them." "I can't let you pass, Sir!" I bethought me of Gen. Scott's pass. The Adjutant read it, and the word was given along the line, "let that man pass!" And so I rode through, uncertain if I could now gain the Long Bridge in time to pass over without the countersign.

It was about this time I met a cart by the roadside surrounded by a group of soldiers, some of whom had "69" on their caps. The owner, as I took him to be, was in great distress, and cried out as I passed, "Can you tell me, sir, where the Sixty-ninth are? These men say they are cut to pieces." "I can't tell you." "I'm in charge of the mails, sir, and I will deliver them if I die for it. You are a gentleman, and I can depend on your word. Is it safe for me to go on?" Not knowing the extent of the *debacle*, I assured him it was, and asked the men of the regiment how they happened to be there. "Shure, the Colonel himself told us to go off, every man on his own hook, and fly for our lives," replied one of them. The mail agent, who told me he was an Englishman, started the cart again. I sincerely hope no bad result to himself or his charge followed my advice.

I reached Fairfax Court House; the people, black and white, with anxious faces, were at the doors, and the infantry were under arms. I was besieged with questions, though hundreds of fugitives had passed before me. Washington was still eighteen miles away. The road was rough and uncertain, and again my poor steed was underway; but it was no use trying to outstrip the runaways. Once or twice I imagined I heard guns in the rear, but I could not be sure of it in consequence of the roar of the flight behind me. It was most surprising to see how far the foot soldiers had contrived to get on in the advance.

After sunset the moon rose, and among other acquaintances, I jogged alongside an officer who was in charge of Col. Hunter, the commander of a brigade, I believe, who was shot through the neck, and was inside a cart, escorted by a few troopers. This officer was, as I understand, the Major or second in command of Col Hunter's regiment, yet he had considered it right to take charge of his chief, and to leave his battalion. He said they had driven back the enemy with ease, but had not been supported, and blamed—as bad officers and good ones will do—the conduct of the General: "So mean a fight I never saw." Now, what is to be thought of an officer—gallant he may be as steel—who says, as I heard this gentleman say to a picket, who asked him how the day went in the front: "Well, we've been licked into a cocked hat; knocked to ——." This was his cry to teamsters, escorts, convoys, the officers and men on guard and detachment, while I, ignorant of the disaster behind, tried to mollify the effect of the news by adding, "Oh, its a drawn battle. The troops are re-occupying the position from which they started in the morning." Perhaps he knew the troops better than I did.

As I approached Washington, having left the Colonel and his escort at some seven miles on the south side of the Long Bridge, I found the grand guards, pickets, posts, and individual sentries burning for news, and the word used to pass along, "What does that man say, Jack?" "Begorra, he tells me we're not beat at all—only retreating to the ould lines for the convaniency of fighting to-morrow again. Oh, that's illigant!" On getting to the *tete de pont*, however, the countersign was demanded; of course I had not got it. But the officer passed me through on the production of Gen. Scott's safeguard. The lights of the city were in sight, and reflected on the waters of the Potomac, just glistened by the clouded moon, shone the gay lamps of the White House, where the President was probably entertaining some friends. In silence I passed over the Long Bridge. Some few hours later it quivered under the steps of a rabble of unarmed men. At the Washington end a regiment with piled arms were waiting to cross over into Virginia, singing and cheering. Before the morning they received orders, I believe, to assist in keeping Maryland quiet. For the hundredth time I repeated the cautious account, which, to the best of my knowledge, was true. There were men, women and soldiers to hear it.

The clock had just struck 11 P. M., as I passed Willard's. The pavement in front of the hall was crowded. The rumors of the defeat had come in, but few of the many who had been fed upon lies and the reports of complete victory which prevailed could credit the intelligence. Seven hours had not elapsed before the streets told the story. The "Grand Army of the North," as it was called, had representatives in every thoroughfare, without arms, orders or officers, standing out in the drenching rain. When all these most unaccountable phenomena were occurring I was fast asleep, but I could scarce credit my informant this morning when he told me that the *Federalists, utterly routed, had fallen back on Arlington to defend the Capital, leaving nearly five batteries of artillery, 8,000 muskets, an immense quantity of stores and baggage, and their wounded and prisoners in the hands of the enemy.*

Let the American journals tell the story their own way. I have told mine as I know it. It had rained incessantly and heavily since early morning, and the country must be unfit for operations; otherwise, if Mr. Davis desired to press his advantage, he might now be very close to Arlington Heights. He has already proved that he has a fair right to be considered the head of a "belligerent *power*." But though the North may reel under the shock, I cannot think it will make her desist from the struggle, unless it be speedily followed by blows more deadly even than the repulse from Manassas. There is much talk now (of "masked batteries," of course) of outflanking and cavalry, and such matters. The truth seems to be that the men were overworked, kept out for twelve or fourteen hours in the sun exposed to long-range fire, badly officered, and of deficient regimental organization. Then came a most difficult operation—to withdraw this army, so constituted, out of action in face of an energetic enemy, who had repulsed it. The retirement of the baggage, which was without adequate guards and was in the hands of ignorant drivers' was misunderstood and created alarm, and that alarm became a panic, which became frantic on the appearance of the enemy and on the opening of their guns on the runaways. But the North will be all the more eager to retrieve this disaster, although it may divert her from the scheme, which has been suggested to her, of punishing England a little longer.

The exultation of the South can only be understood by those who may see it, and if the Federal Government perseveres in its design to make a union by force, it may prepare for a struggle the result of which will leave the Union very little to fight for. I pity the public across the water, but they must be the victims of hallucinations and myths it is out of my power to dispel or rectify just now. Having told so long a story, I can scarcely expect your readers to have patience, and go back upon the usual diary of events; but the records, such as they are, of this extraordinary repulse must command attention. It is impossible to exaggerate their importance. No man can predict the results or pretend to guess at them.

The London Press on the Battle of Manassas Plains.

The London *Times* of Monday, August 5, says:

The army of the United States, which has just been routed, has had all its spirit broken, and as a military body has ceased to exist; but there are ten times as many ready to come on, perhaps to the same fate. We wish we could find something in this victory upon which we could congratulate either the victors or the vanquished. We wish we could see in it the probable cause of that humility or that contentment which might facilitate peace. We can, however, unhappily, see in it nothing but what must stimulate the evil passions of both combatants. It is a complete victory—as much a victory as Austerlitz.

The *Daily News* says:

The defeat of the North shuts the door to compromise or to acquiescence in any terms the South can offer. The Union is bound to conquer now. The spirit of New England and the Northwest will rise to the occasion, and we of the old race, dried and strengthened by many reverses, shall not be surprised if our kinsmen never rest until they have turned defeat into victory.

The *Daily Telegraph* says:

The battle of Bull Run was a battle which, if second to Magenta or to Solferino in actual slaughter, was marred by more envenomed hostility. The dominant feeling in England on this unhappy quarrel is one of unfeigned and bitter sorrow. If Americans labor for one moment under the impression that the successes or reverses of one or of the other section of the combatants will awaken anything like partisan feeling in this country, they are most grievously mistaken.

The *Daily News* says:

In the Exchange Rooms of Manchester, when the defeat of the Unionists became known, there was much excitement among those present, principally American captains and brokers.

[From the London Times, August 7.]

The dissensions which arose some months ago in the United States of North America have unfortunately assumed the character of open war. Such is the tranquil comment of the Royal Speech upon the event in the New World which have fallen so unexpectedly upon the ear of Europe. Our Queen has reflected with an excellent fidelity the feelings of our people. After the first surprise was over, and when the "God bless me! you don't say so!" had been said, we think we never heard of a battle in which 75,000 men seem to have been engaged on each side, and which fell so blank upon the public ear, and engaged so little European interest. The fact is, we do not like to laugh, and the scene of the ridiculous comes too strongly over us when we would be serious. It is a great battle without the dignity of danger or the painful interest of great carnage. There are all the ridiculous incidents of stark fear and rabid terror, without much real peril and with very little actual suffering. We begin to feel that we have been cheated out of our sympathies.

When this war broke out we English all pictured to ourselves two earnest sections of the same population interlaced in mortal combat, warring to the knife and to the death. We received by every mail little samples of an atmosphere of blood and thunder and war and wounds. All America appeared to us, poor dupes! like a fresh exploded mine—all smoke, and fragments, and torn limbs. We fancied our kinsmen reckless, furious, flying at each other's throats, and careless of their own safety. At the same time that they were shaking their knives at each other, they were shaking their fists at us. We trembled for what we were fated to see. We held our breath for the first shock of battle between these two young giants. We shut our eyes against the deadly struggle. We are calmer now. We are all calmer. We are satisfied with these warlike athletes, who were issuing such dire threats against any one who should dare to offer to separate them, are not so very reckless. Since their dissensions have assumed "the character of open war," they have been carried on upon strictly humanitarian principles.

If we are to believe the American press, an American battle has never yet been so dangerous as an American passenger boat, and not much more so than an American railway. The hostile forces shell each other out of strong fortresses without losing a single life. They fight a battle in Western Virginia which determines the fate of a district at the expense of less than a score of casualities; and a great stand up battle is fought between 150,000 men, ending in a panic and a twenty miles run; and when the "Grand Army of the Potomac" reaches Alexandria, the New York Herald reports that "the killed on our side will be between three and five hundred."

It is very difficult to guage the solidity of anything American—even of a great battle. We know that there was a great rout in front of that gap which runs up into the hills, for we were represented in the ruck, and may say that we saw it with our own eyes and heard the cannonade with our own ears.—There is a probability, also, that the number of men present at the battle mounts to the high figure of 150,000, for both accounts seem to agree upon this. Beyond these facts, however, everything seems vague and uncertain.

The advance of the "Grand Army of the Potomac" reads in the American papers like a burlesque of the progress of Xerxes to the Hellespont. The great Federal victory of Bull Run, which was flashed over the Northern States and recorded in the Northern papers, was a thing hovering for hours, while yet in print upon the confines of fancy and possibility. The abject rout, the ultimate reality, was what we could have least believed. Perhaps we ought to have anticipated that the same ferocious men who had burnt up the homesteads on their line of march would speed back over the embers with pale faces in their panic flight. But this never did occur to us. It requires the testimony of the Americans themselves and the witness of our own correspondent to suggest to us that 75,000 American patriots fled for twenty miles in an agony of fear, although no one was pursuing them, and that 75,000 other American patriots abstained from pursuing these 75,000 enemies because they were not informed how stark frightened these were. Even the artillery were not captured, but picked up.—The guns were left behind because they impeded the flight of the artillerymen, and they might have been to a great extent carried off if the apprehensions of the gunners would have allowed them to take advantage of the leisure which the prudent conqueror was so ready to afford. On the other hand, our correspondent thinks that the panic had gone so right to the heart of the North, that if Gen. Beauregard had the enterprise to follow up his advantage, he might have gone almost unresisted into Washington City itself. All that the Northern press says upon this subject is to congratulate themselves that the enemy did not know in what a fright they were.

This is not our account of this battle. It is the American account. It is the account of the New York papers, alternating as they do between shrieks of victory, of agony, [illegible]. If [illegible] between three hundred and five hundred men, it seems to us to be a very cheap lesson. See what they have gained by it. They have found out now that the spirit of patriotism, and even the instinct of combat, does not prevent Northern volunteers from going off in a body under pretense of their time of enlistment being up, although the morning of the combat may be come, and the cannon may be sounding in their ears.—They have found out also that even a Northern army can, without much good military reason given, lose its attraction of cohesion, and dissolve into a mob. They have also *found out that the Southerners are not to be walked over like a partridge manor, and that they have some military heads among them.*

Of course, we must expect them to meet these hard facts by a certain quantity of bluster. They must call out a few more millions of volunteers, and they must make a confident demand upon an incredulous world for a few more hundred millions sterling. But behind all this there must rise a gathering doubt that this Southern nut is too hard to crack, and that the military line, as a matter of business, does not answer. The North has now made its experiment, and not only has it not answered, but the process has not been encouraging. As matter of habit and to ease the American mind, a certain quantity of threats and tall words may be necessary and they may pass. But they will be of small avail against the facts as they now stand. In the face of the picture of that screaming crowd—the Grand Army of the Potomac, &c.—these great words from the expectant gentleman at Washington lose their every charm.

These people do all in their power to alienate our sympathy, for they are amenable neither to courtesy nor to misfortune. Nothing civilizes them. They seem to think that at all seasons and upon all occasions England is a safe target for their insults and threats. They either feign very well or else they positively think they can influence our policy by their bluster. There was a moment, on the 21st of July, when victory was supposed to be with the "Grand Army of the Potomac," and the most popular newspaper in New York seized the opportunity to show what use our excellent friends proposed to make of their victory. The first thought was revenge upon England.

After some taunts at what are supposed to be our recent recantations, the organ of New York moderation continues: "And now, forsooth, because the Queen's Government sees fit to stultify itself, not daring to carry into execution its implied threats, and prohibits the entry of Southern privateers into British ports, we are required to let bygones be bygones, and evee to ignore that any cause of displeasure has existed! The absurdity and inconsistency of acknowledging the 'equal belligerent rights' of the rebel States, and then snubbing them from sheer cowardice and fear of the consequences, bestows no title to consideration, nor will leisurely repentance for hastily offered indignities be considered the slightest atonement when the time shall have come to resent them. Both England and Spain may rest assured that just retribution will be visited upon them for taking advantage of our domestic disturances to fur ther their own selfish schemes of aggrandizement.

"For the outrage offered in the Queen's Proclamation, the United States will possess itself of Canada, and for the invasion of St. Domingo Her Catholic Majesty will certainly have to pay with the sacrifice of Cuba. We have first to put down rebellion at home, but every hour proves that the war that has begun will prove a short one, and that ere the lapse of another half year armies will exist on the American Continent of over half a million of men thirsting for a foreign foe upon whom to expend their strength. When the Union element at the South shall have been fairly emancipated, and the forces of the Republic shall have been united, let Great Britain and Spain beware. Our armies never will consent to lay down their arms while a vestige of European domination remains in the Western hemisphere. Causes of war we have enough, and they will not cool for keeping."

If this is what we are to receive from the supremacy of the North, the North can scarcely expect that we should put up very ardent vows for their conquest of the South. If the conquest of the Southern States means also the conquest of Canada and Cuba, and the establishment of a great military aggressive power in North America, we may learn to bear more patiently the scene that occurred at Bull Run. We are not, however, fearful enough to be ferocious. On the contrary, we cordially and even sincerely congratulate our would-be enemies that they have escaped with such small loss from the sword of General Beauregard, and, much as they tell us it would be against our interest, we sincerely advise them to make up their quarrel, and avoid all serious effusions of blood. When they have returned to the habits of peace they will not be nearly so bloodthirsty as they think they will be; or, if they should be, they will not be so mischievous as they say they will be. Spain will know how to keep in check a navy which is now terribly embarrassed by two small privateers, and the Canadas have in other days given a very good account of invaders from the other side of the river. The United States are a very great nation, and we wish them all lawful prosperity; but they are not half so capable of mischief as their newspapers think they are.

By Telegraph.

M. W. BARR, at Louisville, Ky., is the special and recognized agent of the Southern Associated Press, at that point, the New York Associated Press having ceased to have any control of matter telegraphed to newspapers south of Louisville.

No telegraph operator or agent is permitted to make up such reports. The Telegraph Company has no agency whatever in the preparation of dispatches for the press, nor is it in any manner responsible for the character or truth of this kind of news.

From Ohio.

CLEVELAND, Ohio, Aug. 24.—The Stark County Democrat has been totally gutted by volunteers.

From Cairo.

CAIRO, Aug. 24.—It is reported that the Paducahans sent to Union City for cannon. 4,000 Missourians are reported at Benton, Mo., fortifying.

From Washington.

WASHINGTON, Aug. 24.—The passport system does not apply to persons going or returning from Canada by Rail.

Hayti advices of the 8th say that a formidable conspiracy to overthrow the Government by the blacks has been discovered.—Several arrests have been made. San Domingo advices represent the inhabitants reconciled to the Spanish Government.

The line from Alexandria to London is dotted with Confederate camps. At Leesburg there are 3,000 Infantry and six cannon. At a point six miles below, there are 6,000 men and six cannon; and four miles beyond, 3,500 men. There are also 2,000 cavalry in Loudon county. The Potomac remains too high to be forded even by cavalry.

WASHINGTON, Aug. 24.—Senator Johnson expects to head the army on his return to Tennessee.

Lincoln will do his utmost to sustain the Union cause in that State.

The rumor that Banks had reached Winchester is false. He is not in Virginia.

The Postmaster-General directs that the papers presented by the New York Grand Jury as dangerous, shall not be forwarded.

Major Barrett has been arrested and taken to Fort Lafayette.

The Townsend county, Maryland, Court House and records are burned.

The Post says that Johnson declares he will not return to Tennessee unless he accompanies a Union army.

From Louisville.

LOUISVILLE, Aug. 24.—The crisis in Kentucky is probably reached. Eighty armed men left this morning as a posse for the Collector by a special train to capture nine wagons of contraband goods on the Rocky Fork. They left the main line at Lebanon Junction and captured the train. At the latest advices the capturers were [illegible]. Persons interested in the adventure are said to consider the property safe.

The Lebanon branch train did not reach the Junction. It is supposed that the track is destroyed.

LOUISVILLE, Aug. 24.—The Collector's posse have returned with the plunder. Printer McCarty was killed by accidentally falling from the train. Only one rail was pulled up on the Lebanon branch road. The plunder filled 25 freight cars.

Fortress Monroe.

FORTRESS MONROE, Aug. 24.

The Seminole, from the blockade off Charleston, has arrived, bringing the schooner Albion, with a cargo of Sugar, Coffee and Fruits, sailing under British colors.

The Seminole will coal and repair.

The blockade off Charleston consists of the Roanoke and Vandalia.

From Boston.

BOSTON, Aug. 24.—The following officers of the frigate Congress have resigned: Capt. of Marines, Robt. Francis, of Virginia; Second Lieut. Thos. S. Wilson, of Missouri; Midshipman H. B. Claybourne and Hilary D. Cass, of New Orleans.

From New York.

NEW YORK, Aug. 24.—Cotton sales 1,800 bales; upland middling 18½.

From Connecticut.

DANBERRY, Conn., Aug. 24.—At the raising of a peace flag at Fairfield to-day, about 400 persons were present. An attempt to raise the Stars and Stripes was successfully resisted. A fight ensued, in which two peace men, Messrs. Weldman and Gorman, were seriously injured. Shovels, pickaxes and stones were used, but no fire arms. The peace flag is flying. Great excitement.

From Missouri.

JEFFERSON CITY, Aug. 24.—The bogus State Government has appointed George R. Smith Adjutant General of the State, and John How Police Commissioner for St. Louis.

PROCLAMATION

BY

ISHAM G. HARRIS,

GOVERNOR OF THE STATE OF TENNESSEE,

To the Sheriffs of the several Counties of said State—GREETING:

YOU are hereby commanded to open and hold an election at all the places of holding elections in your respective Counties, on the 5TH DAY OF OCTOBER NEXT, after giving the notice required by law, for the election of a Supreme Judge for said State, to fill the vacancy occasioned by the resignation of Robert L. Caruthers, and due return thereof make to me according to law.

In testimony whereof, I have hereunto set my hand and caused the Great Seal of the State, to be affixed at the Department in Nashville, on this 1st day of August, A. D. 1861.

{ L. S. }

By the Governor: ISHAM G. HARRIS.

J. E. R. RAY, Secretary of State.

aug7–dtw&wtd.

HOMES FOR THE INDUSTRIOUS

IN THE

GARDEN STATE OF THE WEST.

THE ILLINOIS CENTRAL RAILROAD CO., HAVE FOR SALE

1,200,000 ACRES OF RICH FARMING LANDS,

IN TRACTS OF FORTY ACRES AND UPWARD,

ON LONG CREDIT AND AT LOW PRICES.

MECHANICS, FARMERS & WORKING MEN. THE attention of the enterprising and industrious portion of the community is directed to the following statements and liberal inducements offered them by the

ILLINOIS CENTRAL RAILROAD COMPANY. which, as they will perceive, will enable them, by proper energy, perseverance and industry, to provide comfortable homes for themselves and families, with comparatively speaking, very little capital.

LANDS OF ILLINOIS.

No State in the Valley of the Mississippi offers so great an inducement to the settler as the State of Illinois. There is no portion of the world where all the conditions of climate and soil so admirably combine to produce those two great staples, CORN and WHEAT, as the Prairies of Illinois.

RICH ROLLING PRAIRIE LANDS.

The deep rich loam of the prairies is cultivated with such wonderful facility that the farmers of the Eastern and Middle States are moving to Illinois in great numbers. The area of Illinois is about equal to that of England, and the soil is so rich that it will support twenty millions of people.

EASTERN AND SOUTHERN MARKETS.

These lands are contiguous to a railroad 700 miles in length, which connects with other roads and navigable lakes and rivers, thus affording an unbroken communication with the Eastern and Southern markets.

APPLICATION OF CAPITAL.

Thus far, capital and labor have been applied to developing the soil; the great resources of the State in coal and iron are almost untouched. The invariable rule that the mechanic arts flourish best where food and fuel are cheapest, will follow at an early day in Illinois, and in the course of the next ten years the natural laws and necessities of the case warrant the belief that at least five hundred thousand people will be engaged in the State of Illinois in various manufacturing employments.

RAILROAD SYSTEM OF ILLINOIS.

Over $100,000,000 of private capital have been expended on the railroad system of Illinois. Inasmuch as part of the income from several of these works, with a valuable public fund in lands, go to diminish the State expenses; the TAXES ARE LIGHT, and must consequently every day decrease.

THE STATE DEBT.

The State debt is only $10,105,398 14, *and within the last three years has been reduced* $2,959,746 80, *and we may reasonably expect that in ten years it will become extinct.*

PRESENT POPULATION.

The State is rapidly filing up with population; 868,025 persons having been added since 1850, making the present population 1,723,663, a ratio of 102 per cent. in ten years.

AGRICULTURAL PRODUCTS.

The Agricultural Products of Illinois are greater than those of any other State. The products sent out during the past year exceeded 1,500,000 tons. The wheat crop of 1860 approaches 35,000,000 bushels, while the corn crop yields not less than 140,000,000 bushels.

FERTILITY OF THE SOIL.

Nowhere can the industrious farmer secure such immediate results for his labor as upon these prairie soils, they being composed of a deep rich loam, the fertility of which is unsurpassed by any on the globe.

TO ACTUAL CULTIVATORS.

Since 1854 the Company have sold 1,300,000 acres. They sell only to actual cultivators, and every contract contains an agreement to cultivate. The road has been constructed through these lands at an expense of $30,000,000. *In 1850 the population of forty-nine counties, through which it passes, was only 335,598 since which 479,293 have been added; making the whole population 814,891, a gain of 143 per cent.*

EVIDENCES OF PROSPERITY.

As an evidence of the thrift of the people, it may be stated that 600,000 tons of freight, including 8,600,000 bushels of grain, and 250,000 barrels of flour were forwarded over the line last year.

EDUCATION.

Mechanics and workingmen will find the free school system encouraged by the State and endowed with a large revenue for the support of schools. Their children can live in sight of the church and schoolhouses, and grow up with the prosperity of the leading State in the Great Western Empire.

PRICES AND TERMS OF PAYMENT.

The prices of these lands vary from $6 to $25 per acre, according to location, quality, &c. First class farming lands sell for about $10 to $12 per acre; and the relative expense of subduing prairie land as compared with wood land is in the ratio of 1 to 10 in favor of the former. The terms of sale for the bulk of these lands will be

ONE YEAR'S INTEREST IN ADVANCE,

at six per cent per annum, and six interest notes at six per cent., payable respectively in one, two, three, four, five and six years from date of sale; and four notes for principal, payable in four, five, six and seven years from date of sale; the contract stipulating that one-tenth of the tract purchased shall be fenced and cultivated, each and every year, for five years from date of sale, so that at the end of five years one-half shall be fenced and under cultivation.

TWENTY PER CENT. WILL BE DEDUCTED.

from the valuation for cash, except the same should be at six dollars per acre, when the cash price will be five dollars.

Pamphlets descriptive of the lands, soil, climate, productions, prices, and terms of payment, can be had on application to

J. W. FOSTER, Land Commissioner,
CHICAGO, ILLINOIS.

For the names of the Towns, Villages, and Cities situated upon the Illinois Central Railroad, see pages 188, 189 & 190, APPLETON'S RAILWAY GUIDE.

HARD WARE.

A. W. M'CALL. G. W. FALL
A. B. MONTGOMERY, Special Partner

M'CALL & FALL,

Wholesale and Retail
DEALER IN
GUNS, CUTLERY, EDGE TOOLS,
Plows, Rakes, Cultivators,
AND
BUILDING HARDWARE
KIRKMAN & ELLIS' OLD STAND
34, Public Square,
NASHVILLE, TENN.

HAVING added to our already large stock of HARD WARE and CUTLERY, a fine assortment of FIRST QUALITY

RETAIL GOODS

Embracing—
FINE TABLE AND POCKET KNIVES,
EDGE TOOLS,
BUILDING HARDWARE,
FARMERS, CARPENTERS,
COOPERS, SMITHS, and
MACHINISTS' Tools, Implements, &c., &c.

We respectfully solicit a call from our friends, former patrons of "M'CALL & CO." and the public generally.

M'CALL & FALL,
Kirkman & Ellis' Old Stand,
34 PUBLIC SQUARE
Nashville, Tennessee.
121-dtf

REMOVAL.

Howe Sewing Machine Office,
Removed to
34 UNION STREET.

First Floor, recently occupied by J. C. Harvey & Co.
In calling the attention of our numerous patrons and the public to our removal to more accessible quarters, we deem it unnecessary to refer to the merits of the Howe Machine, as their good qualities are already "household words."
A full stock of Silk, Spool Cotton, and Machine Findings always on hand. CONE BROS., Agents,
34 Union Street,
jan17-tf Nashville, Tenn.

STOVE AND HOLLOW WARE FOUNDRY.

(Broad Street, beyond N. & C. Railroad.)
Nashville, Tennessee.

THE undersigned has purchased the above Foundry of Mr. H. P. Dorris, and is prepared to fill all orders for STOVES, HOLLOW WARE and other CASTINGS, at the shortest notice, and at prices which will make it an object for dealers to patronize him. His work will not only be executed in the best and most substantial manner, but cheaper than the same articles can be bought abroad and imported, or manufactured here. He respectfully solicits orders.
apr6—tf J. LOVELL.

FIRST CLASS BOARDING HOUSE

No. 26 Cherry Street,
[Six doors below the Postoffice.]

THIS House is kept by W. W. SUMMERS, and the Table is always supplied with the best the market affords: The rooms are large and commodious, well furnished, and lighted up with gas. Give me a call, and if you are not satisfied your money will be refunded. Transient custom respectfully solicited.
feb16-tf W. W. SUMMERS.

South Nashville Bakery.

NOW open and ready to furnish parties, private or public, at shortest notice. Every kind of Bread, Cake and Confections constantly on hand, and any extras furnished at short notice.
dec18-3m

Potatoes.

100 BBLS. No. 1 POTATOES just received and for sale by
may14 B. R. CONNOR & BRO.

BROOKS & ORR'S & McNAUGHT'S

SPOOL COTTONS, all sizes, in Black, White and Colors, at 50 cents per dozen, at
HOWE SEWING MACHINE OFFICE,
mar15-tf 34 Union street.

Miscellaneous.

Willimantic Linen Company's
PATENT FINISH
Spool Thread.

THIS Thread is made expressly for Sewing Machines and is pronounced by competent judges to be the best thread in the market for Machine or hand sewing
For sale by the case or dozen at factory prices at the office of Wheeler & Wilson. C. R. PARSONS.
dec11-tf

B. B. CONNOR & BRO,

No. 5 College Street,
GENERAL PRODUCE
AND
Commission Merchants

Orders filled at the Lowest Cash Price.

PERSONAL ATTENTION GIVEN TO
CONSIGNMENTS.

PRODUCE

We are daily receiving and will sell for the lowest Cash Price,

Hay, Corn,
Oats, Bran,
Shorts, Flour,
Meal, Onions,
Potatoes, Apples,
Bacon, Lard,

And all other kinds of Produce and Seeds
April 7—1ydw

NEW YORK
KEROSENE OIL CO.,
AT PRICES TO COMMAND THE MARKET!

KEROSENE ILLUMINATING OIL.
PARAFFINE ILLUMINATING OIL.
PETTOLEUM ILLUMINATING OIL.
MACHINERY OILS.

DEPOT,
COZZENS & CO., 89 Water St.,
apr4—3m NEW YORK.

Dr. G. R. Bond's French Preventives.

THIS article enables those whose health or circumstances do not permit an increase of family, to regulate or limit the number of their offspring without injuring the constitution. It is the only safe and sure preventive against *Pregnancy* and *Disease*. The above article can be sent to any part of the United States or Canada, two for $1 or $5 per dozen.

DR. G. W. BOND'S SPANISH FEMALE MONTHLY PILLS—These Pills are the only medicine married or single ladies can rely upon with safety and certainty for the immediate removal of obstructions, irregularities, &c, *They should not be used during Pregnancy.* Price $2 per box—each box contains 72 Pills. *Sent by mail.*

The Doctor can be consulted on all diseases of a private nature. *Scientific treatment, a quick cure and moderate charge guaranteed.*

GEORGE R. BOND, M D, Office corner of Grand and Orchard streets, *over the Shoe Store.* Entrance No 65, Orchard street, New York. Established in 1832.
sept12-w9m

Hotels, &c.

THE ST. CLOUD HOTEL,
Enlarged and Refurnished.

THE undersigned having taken the ST. CLOUD HOTEL, has enlarged it materially, and refurnished it throughout in the most elegant style, will open the house to the public on Thursday the 5th inst.
SAMUEL J. CARTER.
July 2 dtf. U G

FRENCH'S HOTEL
On the European Plan,
CITY OF NEW YORK.
Single Rooms 50 cents per Day.
City Hall Square, corner of Frankfort st.,
(Opposite City Hall.)

Meals, as they may be ordered, in the spacious Refectory. There is a Barber's Shop and Bath Rooms attached to the Hotel.
N. B.—BEWARE OF RUNNERS and HACKMEN who say we are full. R. FRENCH,
july18-1y Proprietor.

RESTAURANT TORTONI.

NO. CEDAR STREET, Nashville.
H. V. BASSET, PROPRIETOR.

THIS establishment has newly been opened, and is fitted up "with all the modern improvements." The tables are supplied with all the luxuries that can be procured, prepared in the very best style.
The Bill of Fare, indeed, will challenge comparison with that of any house in the Southwest.
The finest Wines and Brandies are kept constantly on hand. Dinners or Suppers furnished in any part of the city on short notice. dec11-tf

ADAMS, EVES & CO.'S
EATING
AND
Drinking Saloon.
NO. 3 DEADERICK ST., NASHVILLE, TEN.

THIS popular *cafe* is kept open day and night. It is well stocked with Wines, Brandies and Liquors of all kinds, Cigars, Tobacco, &c. The Table is always well-supplied with the best the market affords, served up in excellent style. Lunch or meals can be had at any hour during the day or night: also Hot Coffee every morning at 5 cents per cup. The proprietors respectfully ask a continuance of the liberal patronage hitherto extended them. may3-tf

"METROPOLITAN"
EATING HOUSE,
CORNER CEDAR AND CHERRY STREETS,
Nashville, - - - - Tennessee.
J. MOORE, Proprietor.

I HAVE made extensive arrangements for the receiving of all the delecacies of the coming season, of Fish, Flesh and Fowl; our Oysters will be from the most celebrated beds. Pickels and condiments from the celebrated establishments of Cross & Blackwell and Lea & Perrin, with a large and well selected stock of

Wines, Liquors, &c., &c.

Excellent COOKS and attentive Waiters, the whole under the superintendance of that well known Epicure, Mr. CHARLES PICLES.
On and after the 15th of September we will be prepared to wait upon our customers, DAY AND NIGHT. Railway travelers will find this arrangement to their advantage.
REMEMBER THE METROPOLITAN.
sep3-tf

THE BARNES HOUSE,

J. T. Barnes & Co., Proprietors,
No. 43, Union Street,

FURNISHES Meals at all hours, day and night, and has extensive arrangements for regular supply of Game of every description, Fish, Oysters, the very best Wines, and every other article of luxury which can possibly be obtained in Nashville. The house is provided with the best of Cooks, and the best apparatus for cooking. Eating Hall fitted up in handsome, comfortable style. sep3-tf

Southern Trunk Manufactory.

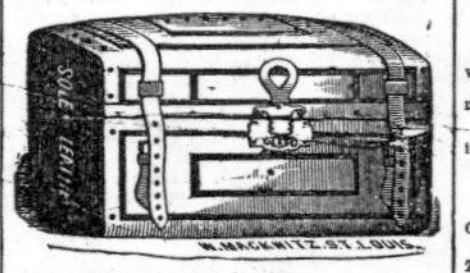

FASSETT & CROSSMAN,
NO. 51 MARKET STREET, NASHVILLE, TENNESSEE
Manufacturers and Wholesale and Retail
DEALERS IN ALL KINDS OF
LADIES' AND GENTS' TRAVELING TRUNKS,
BONNET BOXES,
Valises, Carpet Bags, &c., &c.,

DESIRE to call the attention of all those in want of anything in our line, (wholesale or retail,) to examine our stock before purchasing elsewhere, as we are confident that we can sell as low as any other house in the city. Our stock is all of our own manufacture and is made of the best materials and by first-class workmen. All must admit the wisdom of buying work made at home, in preference to buying that made at the East expressly for jobbing.
We especially invite the attention of the Ladies to our

PATENT TRUNK FOR LADIES.

It has compartments for Bonnets, Dresses, Parasols Brushes, and a water-proof compartment for Sponges Oils, &c.
All kinds of Trunks made to order covered or repaired, at short notice. Give us a call, at 51 Market street, two doors South of the Square.
june23-d1y. FASSETT & CROSSMAN.

DR. JOHN W. MORTON,
Residence; Cor. College and Watkins' Avenue
(FORMERLY LINE STREET,)
OFFICE NO 63 NORTH CHERRY STREET.
jan27-tf

Shelton's Marble Works!
Church street, next door to Cornelius's Cabinet shop
Nashville, Tenn.,

THE undersigned would inform his friends and the public generally that he will continue the MARBLE BUSINESS in this city, at his shop, next door to Cornelius's Cabinet shop, on Church street, and calls attention to the stock of

Marble Monuments, Tombs, etc.

Which he has on exhibition and for sale, embracing great variety, finished in the most superb manner He is prepared to manufacture on the shortest notice **Marble Mantles**; and every description of **Marble Work**, of the finest American and Italian Marble. His work will, as heretofore, be waranted, and his prices to suit the times. M. L. SHELTON.
jan9—tf

M'FERRAN'S
NORTH MARKET STREET.

THE undesigned begs leave to inform his friends and the public that he has still on hand a number of handsome vehicles of all kinds, and a splendid stud of buggy and saddle horses, for the use of fast young gents on COURTING EXPEDITIONS, or for the accommodation of Young America and Young America's Sweetheart.
What man living, of any sort of progressive spirit, would be content to snail it behind a SLOW HORSE when he knows that an ANIMAL OF SPIRIT could be obtained

AT THE LEVIATHAN STABLES.

Parties desiring Coaches for "PIC-NICS," and safe and careful Drivers, should not forget what the papers said about THE NEW COACH, from the LEVIATHAN LIVERY STABLES, on North Market street.
J. C. McFERRAN,
an20-tf Proprie

A. HEINRICH

HAS ON HAND a supply of Lining Leather for the manufacture of

Boots, Shoes and Caps,

which he is offering for sale. may23-1w

R. T. FLEMING,
HOUSE, SIGN
AND
Ornamental Painter,
62 Union Street, NASHVILLE,
(Between Cherry and Summer streets.)
Orders from the country promptly attended to.

Valuable Business House for Sale.

I PROPOSE to sell, for the purpose of closing a copartnership business, the new three-story Brick House, situated on Cherry Street, a few doors South of Broad, now occupied by Messrs. Buss Bros'., as a Grocery Store. The property fronts 25 feet on Cherry St., and runs back 91 feet. The third story is fitted up as a family residence, and affords ample room for a large family; and is free from taxation, State, county and city. It is one of the most elligible business locations in that part of the city, and will be sold AT A BARGAIN. For particulars as to the location and terms apply on the premises or to ISAAC PAUL.
mar29-tf UAA

DR. J. H. McLEAN'S
Strengtnening Cordial and Blood Purifier!
The Greatest Remedy in the World, and the most delicious and delightful Cordial ever taken.

It is strictly a scientific and Vegetable Compound, procured by the distillation of Roots, Herbs and Bark, Yellow Dock, Blood Root, Black Root, Sarsaparilla, Wild Cherry Bark and Dandelion enters into its composition. The entire active remedial principle of each ingredient is thoroughly extracted by my new method of distilling, producing a delicious, exhilerating spirit, and the most Infallible remedy for renovating the diseased system, and restoring the sick, suffering and debilitated Invalid to Health and Strength.

Before taking. After taking.

McLean's Strengthening Cordial
WILL EFFECTUALLY CURE
Liver Complaint, Dyspepsia Jaundice,

Chronic or Nervous Debility, Diseases of the Kidney and all diseases arising from a disordered Liver or Stomach, Dyspepsia, Heartburn, Inward Piles, Acidity or sickness of the Stomach, Fullness of Blood to the Head, Dull Pain or swimming in the Head, Palpitation of the Heart, Fullness or Weight in the Stomach, sour Eructations, Choking or suffocating feeling when lying down, Dryness or Yellowness of the Skin and Eyes, Night Sweats, Inward Fevers, Pain in the small of the Back, Chest or Side, sudden flush of Heat, Depression of spirits, Frightful Dreams, Languor, Despondency, or any Nervous Disease, Sores or Blotches on the skin, and Fever and Ague (or Chills and Fever.)

Over a Million of Bottles

Have been sold during the last six months, and in no instance has it failed in giving entire satisfaction. Who then, will suffer from Weakness or Debility when *McLean's Strengthening Cordial* will cure you?
No language can convey an adequate idea of the immediate and almost miraculous change produced by taking this Cordial in the diseased, debilitated and shattered nervous system, whether broken down by excess, weak by nature, or impaired by sickness the relaxed and unstrung organization is restored to its prestine health and vigor.

MARRIED PERSONS

or others conscious of inability, from whatever cause will find McLean's Strengthening Cordial a thorough regenerator of the system, and all who may have injured themselves by improper indulgence, will find in the Cordial a certain and speedy remedy.

TO THE LADIES,
McLean's Strengthening Cordial
Is a sovereign and speedy cure for
Incipient Consumption, Whites,
Obstructed or Difficult Menstruation, Incontinence of Urine or Involuntary Discharge thereof, Falling of the Womb, Giddiness, Fainting and all Diseases incident to Females.

There is no Mistake About It.

Suffer no longer. Take it according to directions. It will stimulate, strengthen and invigorate you and cause the bloom of health to mount your cheek again. Every bottle is warranted to give satisfaction

FOR CHILDREN.

If your children are sickly, puny or afflicted, McLean's Cordial will make them healthy, fat and robust. Delay not a moment, try it and you will be convinced.

It is Delicious to Take.

CAUTION.—Beware of Druggists or Dealers who may try to palm upon you some Bitter, or Sarsaparilla trash, which they can buy cheap, by saying it is just as good. Avoid such men. Ask for McLean's Strengthening Cordial, and take nothing else. It is the only remedy that will purify the Blood thoroughly, and at the same time strengthen the system.
One tablespoonful taken every morning fasting, is a certain preventive for Cholera, Chills and Fever, Yellow Fever, or any prevalent disease. It is put up in large bottles.
Price only $1 per bottle, or 6 bottles for $5
J. H. McLEAN,
Sole Proprietor of this Cordial. Also, McLean's Volcanic Oil Liniment.
Principal Depot on the corner of Third and Pine sts., St. Louis, Mo.
Sold by W. W. BERRY & DEMOVILLE, Nashv and all respectable Druggists everywhere
may10-dinsawly

HELMBOLD'S
GENUINE PREPARATION

HELMBOLD'S BUCHU for the Bladder.
HELMBOLD'S BUCHU for the Kidneys,
HELMBOLD'S BUCHU for the Gravel,
HELMBOLD'S BUCHU for the Dropsy,
HELMBOLD'S BUCHU for Nervousness,
HELMBOLD'S BUCHU for Loss of Memory,
HELMBOLD'S BUCHU for Dimness of Vision,
HELMBOLD'S BUCHU for Difficult Breathing,
HELMBOLD'S BUCHU for Weak Nerves,
HELMBOLD'S BUCHU for Universal Lassitude,
HELMBOLD'S BUCHU for Horror of Disease,
HELMBOLD'S BUCHU for Night-sweats,
HELMBOLD'S BUCHU for Wakefulness,
HELMBOLD'S BUCHU for Dryness of skin,
HELMBOLD'S BUCHU for Eruptions,
HELMBOLD'S BUCHU for Pain in the Back,
HELMBOLD'S BUCHU for Heaviness of the Eye with temporary suffusation and loss of sight,
HELMBOLD'S BUCHU for Mobility and Restlessness, with want of attention and horror of society,
HELMBOLD'S BUCHU for Obstructions
HELMBOLD'S BUCHU for Excesses arising from indiscretion, and all diseases of

FEMALES—FEMALES—FEMALES
FEMALES—FEMALES—FEMALES
FEMALES—FEMALES—FEMALES
OLD OR YOUNG, SINGLE, MARRIED, OR CONTEMPLATING MARRIAGE,
TAKE NO MORE PILLS,
TAKE NO MORE PILLS,
THEY ARE OF NO AVAIL,
THEY ARE OF NO AVAIL
HELMBOLD'S EXTRACT BUCHU
IS THE VERY BEST REMEDY IN THE WORLD

For all complaints incident to the sex, whether arising from indiscretion, habits of Dissipation, or in the

DECLINE OR CHANGE OF LIFE!
SEE SYMPTOMS ABOVE!
NO FAMILY SHOULD BE WITHOUT IT!
TAKE NO MORE BALSAM, MERCURY, OR UNPLEASANT MEDICINES FOR UNPLEASANT AND DANGEROUS DISEASES.
HELMBOLD'S EXTRACT BUCHU
Cures

Secret Diseases

In all their stages, At little expense
Little or no change in Diet; No inconvenience

AND NO EXPOSURE

Use *HELMBOLD'S EXTRACT BUCHU* for diseases arising from habits indulged in

BY YOUNG AND OLD
" " " "
" " " "
" " " "
" " " "

And for diseases arising from habits of dissipation. It removes all improper discharges; and will restore the patient in a short time to a state of health and purity
Use *Helmbold's Extract Buchu* for diseases and affections of the most distressing character.
Use *Helmbold's Extract Buchu* for all affections and diseases of the

Urinary Organs.
" "
" "
" "

Whether existing in
MALE OR FEMALE.
" " "
" " "
" " "

From whatever cause originating and no matter of
HOW LONG STANDING
" "
" "
" "

All the above diseases and symptoms admit of the same treatment and may originate from the same cause

READ! READ!! READ!!!

HELMBOLD' BUCHU is safe and pleasant in taste and odor, but immediate in action.
Personally appeared before me an Alderman of the city of Philadelphia, H. T. HELMBOLD, Chemist, who being duly sworn, does say that his preparation contains no narcotic, mercury, or injurious drugs, but is purely vegetable.
H. T. HELMBOLD, Sole Manufacturer.
Sworn and subscribed before me, the 23d day of November, 1854.
WM. P. HIBBARD, Alderman.
Price $1 per bottle, or six for $5, delivered to any address.

ONE THING CERTAIN,

A Trial Costs but a Dollar—Try it!

And be convinced of its efficacy. And it is accompanied by reliable and responsible certificates from Professors of Medical Colleges, Clergymen and others
Prepared by
H. T. HELMBOLD,
Practical and Analytical Chemist,
104 South Tenth street, below Chestnut,
Philadelphia
NECESSARY CAUTION—should unprincipled Dealers try to palm off another article, which pays a better profit and is worthless,—ask for Helmbold's, take other.
CURES GUARANTEED.
RAINS & BROWN,
Wholesale and Retail Agents, Nashville;
Sold by all Druggists everywhere.
aug6-dawly

A. RIVA & CO.,
IMPORTERS
Direct through the Custom-house of Nashville
AND DEALERS IN
Wines, Brandies, &c.,
From France, Spain, Portugal, Germany and Italy!
Havana Cigars, Olive Oil,
Vermicilli, &c., &c.,
No. 30 North Market street,
(Next door above the Watson House,)
NASHVILLE, TENNESSEE.

WE have established a house in this city for the purpose of carrying fine WINES, BRANDIES, CIGARS, &c., &c We keep constantly on hand several qualities of Wines and Brandies, which have never before been imported into this State.
We import our Goods direct, (one of our firm being in Europe much of his time,) and PAY THE CUSTOM-HOUSE DUTIES ON ALL THE FOREIGN ARTICLES HERE in the city, which fact, we think, alone should prove that we have imported goods.

Notice to Shippers.

SUPERINTENDENT'S OFFICE,
NASHVILLE & CHATTANOOGA R. R. Co.,
Nashville, April 16th, 1861.

HAVING caught up with the accumulated freights at Nashville, the extra charges on Through Freights for Storage and extra Drayage, has been removed. E. W. COLE, Sup't.
apr16—dtf

Music.

New Steinway Piano
At Luck's Music Store,
No. 45 Union street.

THIS Instrument is warranted new and not sixty days from the manufactorry as will be seen on examination. I will sell at manufacturer's price, without additional charge for freight. Those in want of a Piano will find it to their interest call and examine it before purchasing.
JOHN LUCK,
mar17-tf Music Dealer, 45 Union

FLAGS! FLAGS!!
Hang out your Banners!

I AM now prepared to furnish Flags of any style or size. JOHN LUCK,
apr19—tf 45 Union street

Secession Flag Badges,
At LUCK'S,
rpr27 45 Union Street

CHILDREN'S CABS,
CHILDREN'S CABS,

Just received at LUCK'S, 45 Union street, the largest assortment in the city. feb28

Bugles! Drums!
PALMETTO SONG!

JUST Published by J. A. McClure, the Palmetto Song, destined (from its name and merit,) to be the most popular song ever printed. Price 40 cents—sent to any address post paid.
ARMY BUGLES and DRUMS furnished at the lowest prices, and satisfaction guaranteed.
Call at the Southern Music Store, 33 Union street.
J. A. McCLURE,
july4 Music Publisher.

Southern Music Store.

JAS. A. McCLURE takes pleasure in announcing to the public that he has now associated with him Prof. O. BECKER, the popular Musician and Author. His many friends and the public generally, can now have his aid in selecting Sheet Music and Musical Instruments. My stock of Sheet Music and Pianos is the largest in the South-west, to which will be added daily all the New Music published
I am still manufacturing Drums and Bugles, which are pronounced the best in use. Give us a call before purchasing elsewhere.
J. A. McCLURE & CO.
N. B.—Just issued second edition of the Palmetto Song; the most popular song ever published in the South. In press, Prof. Becker's new song, Star of Liberty, which will be ready about 1st August Send your order. Only 40c.
Suly 26.

DRUMS! DRUMS!

J. A. McCLURE 33 Union street, having completed his facilities to manufacture as many as 200 Wood Bass and Snare Drums per day, has reduced the price to $10 for first class Snare, $18 for 24 inch Bass, and $20 for 26 inch. Persons in the country can have the above sent them by remitting the above amount.
Also received, the fourth edition of the "Song of the South," the most popular song ever published.—Sent post-paid on receipt of 50 cents.
N. B.—No Iron Drums made by me.
may29-tf

SCHUETZE & LUDOLFF,

MANUFACTURERS OF IRON FRAME, GRAND, SQUARE and PARLOR GRAND PIANO FORTES, made with all the improvements conductive to superiority of tone, touch and durability, GOLD MEDALS awarded at the Fairs in New York, 1855 '56 and '55, and in St. Louis, 1859 Dealers, School and Families will save money by calling before purchasing. All instruments guaranteed for three years Warerooms 452 BROOME ST, (a few doors West of Broadway,) New York. feb21-6m

"CASH" IS "KING!"

An opportunity that can never occur again to purchase
Fashionable and Elegant
GOLD AND GOLD-PLATED
JEWELRY,

At prices that never entered into the wildest dreams of the Manufacturer a month ago, but which the present stagnation of Trade makes an unfortunate *necessity*, is now offered at the

AGENCY
OF THE
Association of Manufacturing Jewelers,
108 North Fourth Street,
SAINT LOUIS, MO.

Where in order to make rapid sales and clear out goods as fast as possible, you are offered

YOUR CHOICE FOR 1 DOLLAR.

The Stock Consists, in Part of

Gold Coral Sets	Ladies' Gold Coral Breast Pins
Cameo "	Revolving Breast Pins
Lava "	Cameo " "
Jet "	Jet " "
Florentine "	Mosaic " "
Mosaic "	Minature " "
Plain "	Gents' Gold Etruscan Breast Pins
Minature "	Gents' Gold Plain Breast Pins
Gold Stone "	Gents' Cross Breast Pins
Grape "	" Minature " "
Enameled "	" Cluster " "
Painted "	Gold Tooth Picks
Carbuncle "	Ladies' Gold Pencils
Wire "	Ladies Plain and Engraved Gold Bracelets
Fine Gold Pens and Cases	Ladies' Gold Neck Chains
Fine Gold Pens and Silver Holders	" Long Guard Chains
Gents' Vest Chains	Gold Studs, plain and with settings
Gold Lockets	Gold Sleeve Buttons, plain and with settings
Gold Thimbles	Full sets Carbuncle Studs and Buttons
Fine Silver Plated Cups	Fine Silver-Plated Table, Dessert and Tea Spoons
Fine Silver Plated sets of Forks	Napkin Rings
Dessert and Dinner Knives, Ivory Handles, in sets	Fine Pearl-handled Six Bladed Pocket Knives, &c., &c.
Coral Necklaces	
Fine Silver Plated Salt Cellars lined with Gold	
Plain, Enameled and Engraved Cold Finger Rings	

IN SHORT
EVERYTHING IN THE WAY OF JEWELRY!
All in the most magnificent styles and in bewildering variety, and
ANY ARTICLE YOU MAY CHOOSE, FOR

ONE DOLLAR

All WARRANTED to be worth at
Retail from 300 to 400 Per Cent More

Than the price at which they are now offered, the whole having been originally manufactured for the Retail Trade, and now disposed of because CASH MUST BE REALIZED.
Send the Dollar by Mail or Express, and upon receipt of it we will forward any one of the beautiful articles above named. State whether you wish us to forward by Mail or Express, and your directions will be complied with faithfully and promptly
E. ADAMS
Agent for the Manufacturing Jewelers' Association,
april 3—tf 108 N. Fourth Street, St. Louis.

PHOTOGRAPHIC CARD.

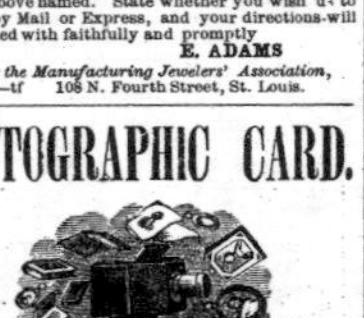

I TAKE pleasure in announcing to my old friends and customers that after an absence of two years, I have again returned to resume the practice of the PHOTOGRAPHIC ART in all its branches, having purchased the interest of my brother in the old established Gallery in Union street, and having spent four months in New York the past Summer to obtain fully all the late improvements in the art. I have painted, renovated and enlarged the suite of Rooms throughout. That my facilities are now better to produce first-class work than most Galleries can boast of, and conduce to the comfort of our patrons. I trust not only to sustain the proud position the Gallery has heretofore sustained, but to elevate it to a still higher standard. I have also engaged the services of Mr. COOK, one of the best Photographers in the world, who took the Pictures which obtained the first premium at the World's Fair in London, in 1851, and I am determined not only to make this the leading Gallery in the State, but my work shall not be surpassed North or South, and now introduce to the public the following new styles:
Imperial Phothgraph, India Ink,
Vigenette, plain or colored,
Ivorytypes,
Pastel Portal Pictures, life size,
Photographs on Canvass, life size,
Visiting Cards, full length plain,
Autograph Photographs, 18 taken at one sitting.
Stereoscopes, on glass or paper,
I still continue to make the Melainotype and Ambrotype as heretofore. The above styles are all entirely new in this city, except the Autograph Card, when but one made at a sitting. All who are in want of anything in my line are politely invited to give my a call before visiting elsewhere, when I will prove by occular demonstration the above facts.
Respectfully, F. N. HUGHES.
oct20-tf B. G. D. U. A. A.

A Thousand Babies Wanted.

CHILDREN of any age can now have their pictures taken perfect, as we have built a Room expressly for their use. Groups of Children also taken in a fraction of a second, in clear weather. Mothers need not now have the trouble to take them to a Gallery a dozen times, and at last put up with a caricature, if they will but go at once to
feb18-tf HUGHES' PREMIUM GALLERY.

TOYS & FIREWORKS
Wholesale and Retail.

COUNTRY MERCHANTS and all others desiring anything in the above line, will find the best assortment in the city at LUCK'S
dec4-tf 45 Union street

For Rent.

ON the Ewing Avenue, a very convenient Brick Cottage, with seven rooms Rent $250. Likewise a very desirable Frame Dwelling house, with cistern, stable and carriage house, Rent $300. Apply at Hughes' Art Gallery, corner of Union and College streets. C. C. HUGHES.
dec5-tf

FASTEST LINE EAST!
VIA
Cincinnati.
COMMENCING APRIL 14th, 1861.
Little Miami and Columbus and
Xenia and
CIN'TI, HAMILTON & DAYTON
1861. 1861.
RAILROAD!

From CINCINNATI to

Boston in 32¼ hours.	New York in 31 hours.
Philadelphia in 27½ hours.	Baltimore in 29 hours.
Saratoga Springs in 25¾ hrs.	Albany in 25¾ hours.
Buffalo in 15¼ hours.	Dunkirk in 14 hours.
Cleveland in 8¾ hours.	Pittsburg in 13¼ hours.
Wheeland in 11¼ hours.	Steubensville in 11 hours
Crestline in 6 hours.	Zanesville in 7 hours
Sandusky in 8¾ hours.	Toledo in 9¾ hours.
Detroit in 12¾ hours.	

Through Trains leave Cincinnati as follows:

6:15 A. M. EXPRESS From Cincinnati, Hamilton and Dayton Depot, connects via. Toledo, Detroit and Canada.

7:00 A. M. CINCINNATI EXPRESS From Little Miami Depot, connects via. Columbus, Cleveland Dunkirk and Buffalo; via. Columbus, Crestline and Pittsburg; via. Columbus, Steubensville and Pittsburg; via. Columbus, Bellair and Benwood.

9:25 A. M. EXPRESS MAIL From Little Miami Depot, connects via. Columbus, Bellair and Pittsburg; via. Columbus, Crestline and Pittsburg; and via. Columbus, Cleveland, Dunkirk and Buffalo.

5:45 P. M. EXPRESS From Cincinnati, Hamilton and Dayton Depot, connects via. Toledo, Detroit and Canada.

10 P. M. NIGHT EXPRESS From Cincinnati, Hamilton and Dayton Depot, connects via. Columbus Steubensville and Pittsburg; via. Columbus, Crestline and Pittsburg; via. Columbus, Cleveland, Dunkirk and Buffalo; via. Columbus, Belliar and Benwood; and via Columbus, Belliar and Pittsburg;

Modern Sleeping Cars on this Train.

Passengers or Lake Steamers, will take the morning Train.

The 5:45 p. m. Express Saturdays for Toledo only.

The Night Express runs Daily, Saturdays excepted. All other Trains run Daily, Sundays excepted.

Trains run by COLUMBUS TIME, which is 7 Minutes faster than CINCINNATI TIME.

Baggage Checked Through to all Eastern Cities.

Passengers should bear in mind that the "CINCINNATI" is the OLD and FAVORITE ROUTE. Connections are made promptly, the Roads are thoroughly BALLASTED, and all modern improvements adopted—insuring SPEED COMFORT and SAFETY.

THROUGH TICKETS

Are sold at all the PRINCIPLE RAILROAD TICKET OFFICES in the WEST and SOUTH. Ask for Tickets via. CINCINNATI.
P. W. STRADER, General Ticket Agent, Cin'ti.
may17-tf

Groceries.

M. A. PARRISH & CO.,
Produce, Commission
AND
FORWARDING MERCHANTS,
Fronting on College and Market Sts.,
South of Broad,
Nashville, Tennesssee.

HAY.
500 bales prime Timothy just received and for sale low by M A PARRISH & CO.

BALED OATS.
100 bales prime Sheaf Oats, just received and for sale by M A PARRISH & CO.

CRUSHED CORN.
100 bags Crushed Corn just received and for sale by M A PARRISH & CO.

WHITE AND BLACK OATS.
1000 bushels White Oats;
800 " Black "
Just received and for sale by M A PARRISH & CO.

NESHANNOCK POTATOES.
200 barrels Northern Potatoes, just received and for sale by M A PARRISH & CO.

WHEAT BRAN.
300 bags Wheat Bran, just received and for sale by M A PARRISH & CO.

CORN
4000 bushels Shelled Corn;
1000 " Ear "
Just received and for sale by M A PARRISH & CO.

CORN MEAL.
250 bags fine Corn Meal;
100 " Bolted "
Just received and for sale by M A PARRISH & CO.

SEED RYE.
100 bags No 1 Rye, just received and for sale cheap by M A PARRISH & CO.

Most of the above articles are on consignment, as well as many others not mentioned in the above list, all of which will be sold cheap in order to close consignments as speedily as possible. Those wishing goods in our line would do well to call and examine our stock before purchasing elsewhere.
oct3-tf M A PARRISH & CO

Just received by M. A Parrish & Co.
200 BAGS Crushed Corn;
100 bags Family Meal;
350 bags White Meal Corn.
apr18-tf

50,000 Copies already sold.
EVERYBODY'S LAWYER
AND
COUNSELLOR IN BUSINESS,
BY FRANK CROSBY,
Of the Philadelphia Bar.

It Tells You How to draw up *Partnership Papers* and gives general forms for *Agreements* of all kinds, *Bills of Sale, Leases and Petitions.*
It Tells You How to draw up *Bonds* and *Mortgages, Affidavits, Powers of Attorney, Notes and Bills of Exchange, Receipts and Releases.*
It Tells You The Laws for the *Collection of Debts*, with the *Statutes of Limitation*, and amount and kind of property *Exempt* from *Execution* in every State.
It Tells You How to make an *Assignment* properly, with forms for *Composition* with *Creditors*, and the *Insolvent Laws* of every State
It Tells You The legal relations existing between *Guardian* and *Ward, Master* and *Apprentice*, and *Landlord* and *Tenant.*
It Tells You What constitutes *Libel* and *Slander*, and the Law as to *Marriage Dower*, the *Wife's Right in Property, Divorce and Alimony*
It Tells You The Law for *Mechanics' Liens* in every *State*, and the *Naturalization Laws* of this country, and how to comply with the same.
It Tells You The Law concerning *Pensions* and how to obtain one, and the *Pre-Emption Laws to Public Lands.*
It Tells You The Law for *Patents*, with mode of procedure in obtaining one, with *Interferences, Assignments* and *Table of Fees.*
It Tells You How to make your *Will* and how to *Administer on an Estate*, with the law and the requirements thereof in every *State.*
It Tells You The meaning of *Law Terms* in general use, and explains to you the *Legislative, Executive and Judicial Powers* of both the *General* and *State Governments*
It Tells You How to *keep out of Law*, by showing how to do your business legally, thus saving a vast amount of property, and vexatious litigation, by its timely consultation.

Single copies will be sent by mail, postage paid, to *Every Farmer, Every Mechanic, Every Man of Business, and Everybody in Every State*, on receipt of $1,00 or in law style of binding at $1,25.

$1000 A YEAR can be made by enterprising men everywhere, in selling the above work, as our inducements to all such are very liberal.
For single copies of the Book, or for terms to agents with other information, apply to or address
JOHN E. POTTER, Publisher,
No. 617 Sansom st., Philadelphia, Pa.
sept7-w3m

"WAR NOTICE."

FROM and after this date, we will not fill orders for any description of Goods unless accompanied by the "CASH."
Being obliged to pay cash for every article we purchase, our friends and the public generally will at once see the necessity of this course on our part.
Our Stock of GROCERIES and CONFECTIONARIES is now full and well assorted, and Cash dealers will find our house the place to purchase.
THOMPSON, SPERRY & CO.,
No. 24 Market street,
apr20-tf Nashville, Tenn.

A War of Extermination

WILL be waged by the undersigned against la competition in the

TOBACCO AND SEGAR TRADE,

determined to let no
CASH CUSTOMER
Go without the Goods J W. LANGLEY,
apr19-tf 44 Union street.

BUSINESS.

WANTED, a partner, in a well established and paying cash business, to take the place of one retiring on account of ill health. From one to two thousand dollars will be required. This is an excellent chance for an active business man, single or young. Married man preferred. Address 516 P. O. Nashville,
mar27—tf

Transportation.

Nashville and Chattanooga R. R

Change of Schedule.
ON AND AFTER
Wednesday, May 1st, 1861,

Passenger trains on the Nashville and Chattanooga Railroad, will run as follows:—

GOING EAST.
Leave Nashville at 8:30 A. M. and 3:15 P. M.
Arrive at Chattanooga 6:00 P. M. and 1:20 A. M.

COMING WEST.
Leave Chattanooga at 9:15 A. M. and 7:20 P. M.
Arrive at Nashville at 3:15 P. M. and 7:30 A. M.

THE Trains leaving Nashville at 8:30 A. M., connect at Wartrace with Shelbyville Branch, at Tullahoma with McMinnville and Manchester Railroad, and at Docherd with Winchester and Alabama Railroad.
The Trains leaving Nashville at 3:15 P. M., connect at Wartrace with Shelbyville Branch, at Stevenson with Memphis and Charleston Railroad, and at Chattanooga with East Tenn. and Geo., and Western and Atlantic Railroads.
Through Tickets to the following points, and at prices annexed, can be had at all hours, on application to the Ticket Agent, at Office, at Depot:

Richmond, Va.	$27 35
Petersburg,	27 00
Lynchburg,	23 75
Knoxville,	10 50
Charleston,	21 00
Savannah,	21 00
Macon,	15 00
Augusta,	16 50
Atlanta,	11 00
Columbus,	16 50
Montgomery,	18 00
Huntsville,	5 90
Grand Junction,	10 00
Memphis,	10 50
Holly Springs, Miss.,	11 00
Canton,	17 50
New Orleans,	24 00
Bersheba Springs,	7 50
McMinnville,	4 30

july20-tf E. W. COLE, Superintendent.

Nashville, Edgefield & Kentucky
RAILROAD.

New Route to the West and South, Memphis, Jackson, New Orleans, Vicksburg, Mobile, &c., &c.

Commencing SUNDAY, JULY 21st, 1861. Trains will leave as follows:
3.30 A. M.—LOUISVILLE ACCOMMODATION.—Runs daily (Sundays excepted) making direct connection at State Line with Trains to Louisville.
3.30 P. M.—MEMPHIS EXPRESS.—Runs daily.—Makes direct connections with all points South and West. Distance shorter and time less than by any other Route.
The **3.30 A. M.** Train is the only one leaving Nashville that makes direct connection for Louisville.
Through tickets for sale at the Ticket Office in L. & N. R. R. Depot, to Memphis, Hickman, Paris, Humboldt, McKenzie, Jackson, New Orleans and Mobile.
A. ANDERSON,
aug4—tf Receiver.

Nashville and Decatur Railroad.

Change of Schedule.
THROUGH TO MEMPHIS IN 17 HOURS

ON and after SUNDAY, July 21st, 1861, the Mail Train will leave Nashville DAILY at 7 P. M.
Returning, arrive at Nashville 1.15 A. M.
Way Passenger Train will leave Nashville DAILY, except Sundays, at 6 A. M.
Returnidg, arrive at Nashville 6.10 P. M.
The 6 A. M. train connects with trains to Huntsville and Chattanooga.
The 7 P. M, train connects with trains to Corinth, Grand Junction, Memphis and New Orleans.
W. O'N. PERKINS,
july19—tf General Superintendent.

Louisville and Nashville
RAILROAD.
NASHVILLE TO RICHLAND, (CAMP TROUSDALE,)
CHANGE OF TIME.
TO TAKE EFFECT FRIDAY, JULY 19TH, 1861.

LEAVING NASHVILLE at 4.30, P. M., arriving at RICHLAND (Camp Trousdale) at 7 P. M
Returning—leave RICHLAND at 7 A. M., arriving at NASHVILLE at 9.30, A. M.
J. C. BALDWIN,
july18-1w Agent L. & N. R. R.

Louisville and Nashville
RAILROAD.

1861. Spring and Summer Schedules, 1861.

Commencing SUNDAY, APRIL 28TH, 1860, Trains will run as follows:

	Train No. 1.	Train No. 2
Leave Nashville,	4 A. M.,	3 P. M
Arrive at Louisville,	12:30 P. M.	11:20 "
RETURNING.		
Leave Louisville,	12 M.,	12 P. M.
Arrive at Nashville,	9:00 P. M.,	9:35 A. M

TRAIN NO. 1 runs daily—all other trains daily, Sunday's excepted.
TRAIN NO. 1 makes direct connection at Louisville for Cincinnati, Indianapolis, Pittsburg, Baltimore, Washington City, Philadelphia, New York and Boston
Both Trains make direct connection for Cincinnati, Indianapolis, Chicago, St. Louis, and all points North and Northwest.
Through Tickets for sale at the Depot for all principal points East, North and West.
april 16-dtf J. B. ANDERSON, Superintendent.

NOTICE TO CONSIGNEES.
Louisville & Nashville
RAILROAD.

ON and after April 1st, 1861, no Freight will be delivered by the Louisville and Nashville Railroad until charges thereon are paid Consignees will be notified of the arrival of their Goods, together with the amount of charges. This system will facilitate the adjustment of all claims for loss, damage, or overcharge, and has been found necessary, in order to enable all Agents to make returns to the General Office, as required by the regulations of the Company.
mar28-2w J. B. ANDERSON, Sup't.

Notice to Shippers.

IT being of the utmost importance for the proper protection of the Track, and to keep out of the way of gravel and other trains, that freight trains be run at regular uniform rate of speed, which can only be accomplished by running on schedule time; therefore, in order that the freight trains may be run on the time laid down in the schedule, it is ordered that after thirty days from this date, freight will be received by the Nashville and Chattanooga Railroad Company at schedule stations only.

Rates on Flour Reduced.

THE Nashville and Chattanooga Railroad will receive at Nashville, Wartrace, Shelbyville and Stations on N. & C. R. R. between Nashville and Wartrace, and give through receipts for Flour by Car load to Charleston or Savannah, at One Dollar per barrel through.
E. W. COLE,
jan22-tf Sup't of Transportation N. & C. R. R.

Notice to Shippers.

SUPERINTENDENT'S OFFICE,
NASHVILLE & CHATTANOOGA R R. Co.,
Nashville, April 1st, 1861.

THE Agency at Shellmound, on the Nashville and Chattanooga Railroad, has been discontinued. Therefore freights must be prepaid on Goods destined for that Station. The Company will not be responsible for such freights after being unloaded in good order at the station.
apr14-tf E. W. COLE, Superintendent.

Express to Clarksville.

THE Southern Express Company respectfully announce that they are now running MESSENGERS through to Clarksville, via. E. & K. and M. C. & L. Rail cars, and are prepared to forward to that place and intervening points with promptness and dispatch all goods usually sent by express. They will also forward to all places on stage routes, connecting with the above Railroads. Bills, notes, drafts, etc., collected and prompt return made.
Office No. 19 Public Square.
feb17-tf A. K. HOLT, Superintendent.

Notice to Passengers.

THE Passenger Train on the Nashville & Chattanooga R. R., heretofore leaving Nashville at 3:30 A. M., and arriving at 5:30 P. M., has been discontinued until further notice. For the accommodation of way passengers a Passenger Car will be attached to the Cowen Way Freight Train leaving Nashville daily, Sunday's excepted, at 6 A. M., and arriving at 6:30 P. M. E W. COLE, Superintendent.
feb5—tf

Charleston and Savannah
FREIGHT LINES.
Rates Reduced and Speed Increased.

EXPRESS Freight Trains on all the roads. On and after the 24th of December, 1859, through rates from New York to Nashville

First Class, per 100 pounds	$1 64
Second Class, " "	1 35
Third Class, " "	1 16
Fourth Class, " "	99
Hats, Caps and Bonnets	2 25

Time from Savannah and Charleston to Nashville three, three and a half and four days.
Time from New York and Philadelphia, seven and a half, eight and nine days.
Intervening Sabbaths cause the above variations in time, as no freight trains are run on Sunday over three lines.
No detentions by ice or snow. Overcharges and damages (except damages occurring at sea) promptly adjusted by the Nashville and Chattanooga Railroad on delivery.
dec23-tf C. W. ANDERSON.

Great National Route.

To Baltimore Philadelphia,
NEW YORK AND BOSTON,
AND ONLY ROAD TO
Washington City.
CENTRAL OHIO
AND BALTIMORE AND OHIO
RAILROADS

TERMINATE at Baltimore and Washington City on the East, and Columbus on the West, at which places it connects with Railroads for and from all points in

The West, Southwest and Northwest.

Passengers by this route can visit the cities of Baltimore, Philadelphia, New York and Boston at the cost of a ticket to New York or Boston alone by other lines.
Through tickets can be procured via Washington City to the Eastern Cities at an additional charge of two dollars only.
Sleeping cars attached to all night trains.

TICKETS GOOD UNTIL USED,

With the privilege of stopping off at all principal points.
Business men or Travelers, for pleasure or information, can visit all the eastern Cities at a comparatively small expense. The scenery is celebrated for its wonderful beauty and sublimity; it is unequalled in the world. Its system of Day and Night track Police; its splendid equipment. its exclusive Telegraph Lines; its large amount of double track; its fine Hotels (under the surveillance of the Company) ensures to the passenger

SPEED, SAFETY AND COMFORT.

Through Tickets and baggage checks can be obtained at all the principal Railroad and Steamboat offices in the West.
Ask for Tickets via, Baltimore and Ohio Railroad.
W. P. SMITH, Master of Transportation.
L. M. COLE, General Ticket Agent.
E. F. FULLER, General Western Agent.
J. W. BROWN, Gen'l Ticket Agent, C. O. R. R
april18

Georgia Western Railroad.

OFFICE GEORGIA WESTERN RAILROAD Co
Atlanta, Nov. 17th, 1860

AT a meeting of the Board of Directors, held this day, it was
Resolved, That taking into consideration the threatening aspect of political affairs, and the consequent stringency in the money market, the Board of Directors deem it prudent to postpone the proposed letting of contracts on the Georgia Western Railroad until March or April next, of which due notice will be given.
Resolved, That an instalment of one dollar per share be called in, payable on the first day of December next, at the office of the Company in Atlanta, in lieu of the ten per cent. called in, payable at the aforesaid time and place.
Resolved, That the Chief Engineer be instructed to continue in service the corps of Assistant Engineers, in order to prepare the whole work for letting between Atlanta and the Western terminus. W. P. ORME,
nov24-tf Secretary

EXPRESS FREIGHT.

THE Nashville and Chattanooga Railroad Company in connection with the Roads below, are running an Express Freight Train from Charleston and Savannah to Nashville, at slower speed, but with the same certainty as their passenger Trains. No delay to freights by this route. E. W. COLE,
jan27-tf Supt.

Notice to Shippers.

OFFICE SUPERINTENDENT, N. & C. R. R.
Nashville, March 7, 1861.

UNTIL further notice, Freights for Memphis and Charleston Railroad, and local stations on the Nashville and Chattanooga Railroad, will be recived on Mondays and Fridays. E. W. COLE,
mar7-tf Superintendent.

$3,000,000 in Gold!
Pike's Peak and the Golden City!

TRAVELERS FOR
Missouri,
Illinois,
Iowa,
Kansas,
Nebraska,
Wisconsin,
New Mexico,
California and
Utah Territory,

WILL please take notice that the first class passenger steamers

C. E. HILLMAN, CORBITT, Master,
Leaves here every TUESDAY, at 4 o'clock, connecting at Cairo with Illinois Central Railroad, and at St. Louis with all the Railroad and Steamboat Lines to all Western points.
AND on every SATURDAY, the famous and fleet packet
B. M. RUNYAN, MILLER, Master,
Leaves this port, connecting as above.
This Route for all persons going West is the cheapest and most expeditious. For Freight or Passage apply on board or to A. HAMILTON, Agent.
nov23-tf

1860. REGULAR 1861.

Nashville and Cincinnati Packet,
THE FINE STEAMER
CLIPPER,
TOM. BRUCE, Captain, JOHN T. HOPKINS, Clerk.

THE steamer CLIPPER has entered, as a regular packet, between this city and all intermediate ports and Cincinnati, and will continue during the entire season. Having superior accommodations for Passengers, she offers every inducement for the safe and speedy conveyance of the traveling public. The utmost attention will be paid to the interest of all shippers. H. H. HARRISON, Agent.
nov23-tf

NASHVILLE & NEW ORLEANS
Regular Packets.

The good and reliable Steamers
RED ROVER, STRONG, Master,
JAMES WOODS, BOYD, Master.
JAMES JOHNSON, JOHNSON, Master.

WILL make regular trips in the Nashville and New Orleans Trade throughout the Season. These Boats are in fine order, and offer superior inducements to the traveling and shipping public. For Freight or Passage apply on board, or to.
nov23-tf A. HAMILTON, Agent.

Season's Arrangement
FOR
1860-61
Cincinnati and Nasville Pioneer Line.

The following Boats comprise a regular line, and will remain permanently in the trade during the entire season, and in all cases shippers may rely on the punctual departure of these Boats as advertised:
Steamer NASHVILLE, P. K. BARCLAY, Master
Steamer GLENWOOD, J. A. FRAZIER, Master
Steamer LADY PIKE, J. S. HERD, Master.
Steamer IDA MAY, RENO, Master
A. HAMILTON,
dec21-6m H. H. HARRISON, } Agents.

BARGAINS! BARGAINS!!
BARGAINS.
Dry-Goods at Auction Prices!!

STILL a few more of those fine and desirable DRESS GOODS left, at HARDY BRO'S., to be sacrificed. We invite the city and country buyers to this Stock of Goods, as it is a rare thing to find so fine a lot of Goods outside of a regular house. The stock consists of Ginghams, Plain and Cross Barred Muslins, Bareges, Challys, Brilliants, fine Mulls, Muslins, Tarletons, Musquito Nettings, Irish Linens, and various other goods, too numerous to mention. The goods must be closed out this week, regardless of price; so call early if you want Bargains. HARDY BROS'.
No. 42 Public Square, Nashville, Tenn.
July5—tf

TRAVELERS,

WHEN you go to New York, drive direct to the SMITHSONIAN HOUSE, Broadway, corner of Houston street, conducted on the European plan. Good Fare, good Rooms, prompt attendance, and moderate charges. Single rooms, 50 cents, 75 cents and $1 per day. Double rooms and parlors $1.50 to $3; meals as ordered. This Hotel has all the appointments of the best hotels, a most central location, and is heated throughout by steam.
feb28-d3m SAMUEL E. MEAD, Proprietor.

BLACKSMITHING.
IN ALL ITS BRANCHES,
Shop on Church between Cherry and College sts.,
Nashville, Tenn.

THE undersigned respectfully informs the public that he has recently taken the above stand and is prepared to do Blacksmithing in all its branches, such as Horse-Shoeing, Buggy-Repairing, &c., &c., &c., the best manner and at short notice. He solicits a share of public patronage.
JAS TARPLEY,
Agent

NEGROES TO HIRE.

WE have a lot of good Negroes to hire, Men, Girls and Boys. [jan3-tf] H. H. HAYNES & CO.

JOHN BULL AND THE AMERICAN LOAN.

No, Shylock—we did not come about the loan—we have money enough, and to spare, at home. But we thought, since our English brethren had come to be ruled by such as you, and your hirelings, yonder, that we had better keep an eye on you.

GEMS OF THOUGHT.

The design of Heaven in lopping off the under branches is that the parent stem may shoot higher in the direction of Heaven.

It is better to dwell in a forest haunted by tigers and lions, the trees our habitation, flowers, fruit, water for food, the grass for a bed, and the bark of the tree for garments, than live among relations after the loss of wealth.

Never be afraid to own the truth, let the consequences be what they may. Ever keep truth for your motto and guide and you will surely be the gainer in the end.

BEN McCULLOCH, THE REBEL GENERAL COMMANDING THE TRAITORS IN SOUTHERN MISSOURI. From a Photograph. See page 267.

SPECIAL NOTICES.

MILITARY.

AMUSEMENTS.

WANTS—WANTS.

NEW ADVERTISEMENTS.

THE SUNDAY DELTA.

FROM OUR ARMY IN THE WEST.

Special Correspondence of the Delta.

JACKSON, TENN., Aug. 29, 1861.

Editors Delta—Your readers thus far will have missed nothing by my involuntary inactivity more than a change of mere local observations; for army matters have remained very much *in statu quo*, fruitful only of such myths as the reported capture of Cape Girardeau, which, instead of being in our hands, is severely guarded by about 12,000 Lincolnites.

By return yesterday of the special mail carrier to this point I am favored with the most reliable intelligence, as late as the 24th inst., from Gen. Pillow's "Army of Liberation" in Missouri. Most of the army were still at New Madrid, having done nothing "notable." But I am advised not to be surprised to hear at an early day of an advance and the total rout of the Republicans from all their strongholds on the river. The want of transportation had been the principal cause of delay. That having been since provided, you may confidently expect to hear of as speedy movement as possible upon Cape Girardeau, whence the army will proceed to form a junction with Hardee's command, which, on the 24th inst., were about three days' march north-west of Pillow's. All the regiments but the 6th and 9th Tennessee, and Col. A. K. Blythe's Mississippi battalion, had moved forward from New Madrid toward Charleston, a station of the Cairo and Fulton (Ark.) Railroad. The recent victory at Springfield had infused great spirit and eagerness into the troops, but the Army of Liberation, though generally welcomed, had not met with that special enthusiasm among the people which might have been expected about New Madrid. There were evidences of reaction, however, in this respect, and it was expected that shortly they would more actively assist, when the ignorant among them became satisfied that the army was really one of liberation and not invasion in freeing the State from the odious influences that now control it. The enemy were making great and hasty preparations to meet Pillow, but they were doubtless in a quandary to determine whether Old Gid would attack Bird's Point, or, giving it the go-by, really make his demonstration upon Cape Girardeau; and so far as my intimations go, let me assure them that such is the reticence of our leaders, they must remain in continued dubiety as to our movements. It was expected that the balance of our army would move forward last Sunday.

Garrett Davis, the Union Commissioner from Kentucky to Washington, having returned, reports that the Union encampments of that State will be increased, (and not disbanded,) in accordance with the wishes of the Union members of the Legislature and the Union delegation in Congress; and a meeting of this delegation has been called to assemble next Monday at the State capital, for the purpose, no doubt, of giving direction to State legislation so as to disband the State Guards, etc., and give the State more completely over to the wishes and rule of the Submissionists.

Gen. Rousseau's (of Louisville) Brigade, it is believed, in some parts of that State, and it is in fact rumored, will move to Bowling Green or some other part of the State to form the neuclus of the Lincolnite's army of invasion. All this works well, as I conceive, to the point of satisfying the quasi-Submissionists of Old Kentucky, those who have been operating with the Republican Unionists, that there is no such thing as Kentucky neutrality, and that all along nothing but their subjugation has been intended. The quasis have joined with the radical Unionists in the cry of neutrality, to keep war off their land, not because they approved of the radicals now apparent intentions. When the matter comes to taking sides, these quasis are for the South, I have not the least shadow of a doubt, almost to a man, and will yet turn the scales as heavily on our side as they have heretofore turned them on the side of the radical Unionists or Submissionists.

One of the great outrages of the times was the tearing up last Saturday of a portion of the track of the Nashville Railroad in Simpson county, Kentucky, near the Tennessee line, by the regular employees of the road, and by order, it is said, of President Guthrie and the directors. The citizens of Simpson, maugre the Union Submissionists, resisted this rather singular proceeding, and with those of Franklin made the conductor return with the hands and replace the rails torn up. This quieted the people, but the train was detained in order to make some investigation into the matter. The burning of the bridge of the Mississippi Central Railroad over the Forked Deer river, near this town, (Sunday night!) was supposed to have resulted from accident, or the falling of the sparks of a locomotive, and no arrest has been made; but the almost simultaneous destruction on the Nashville road, would seem to indicate that there was some general system of annoyance, if not actual demolition of this most important means of transportation, intended. About the time of the destruction of this bridge reinforcements were being pretty actively conveyed over the Mississippi Central to Union City.

You will doubtless have seen the address of Thomas A. R. Nelson to the East Tennesseeans, counseling them to acquiescence in the action of the majority of the State. Hon. George W. Bridges, who has been so intensely for the Union, and ran in the late election for the United States Congress, has signified his intention to raise a regiment of volunteers from the Unionists of his district for the Confederate service; while Col. Nat. G. Taylor, (late Bell and Everett elector for the State at large,) who has been second to none, and perhaps boldest of all, in the treasonable scheme intended, of tearing up the railroad beyond Knoxville, has escaped from the State, and sought protection among the Submissionists, in their encampment at Crab Orchard, Kentucky. Thus peace seems to be restored to East Tennessee. J. J. L.

THE ONLY WAY TO LEARN FRENCH.
Not at school,
Not by painful rules,
Not by routine,
Not by memorizing the fictiticus and unspoken French of Ollendorff, Manesca, Fasquelle, Bolmar, etc.
But by practice,
By oral conversation, in relation, in proportion and well adapted to the student's capacity,
In a word, by a good habit.
Ladies, gentlemen and children, who wish to be at once taught the true daily spoken French, get a pure pronunciation, a natural ease, fluency and elegance, should apply at Prof. Brette's, 13 St. Charles street, where an abundance of practice is daily afforded.
N. B.—The English is not allowed to be spoken after the first week.

ORLEANS FEMALE ACADEMY.—We would direct the special attention of parents and guardians to the advertisement in another column, announcing that the nineteenth annual session of the Orleans Female Academy commences to-morrow. This institution is under the direction of President M. D. Dimitry, as President of the College Board, and has become celebrated for combining a substantial education with elegant accomplishments. Mr. Dimitry himself is one of the most thorough scholars on the Continent, and a remarkable educational tact, possessed by him, has been improved by an experience of half a life time, unremittingly devoted to the profession. Under his supervision, he has trained and able teachers for every branch of knowledge taught in the college, and the building itself, in light and ventilation, and spaciousness in the apartments, is one of the very best the city contains.

MUSIC.—Messrs. P. P. Werlein & Halsey send us from their large collection of music the following beautiful pieces: "President Jefferson Davis's Grand March," by Mrs. Flora Byrne; "Nelly was Bright and Happy"—words by 'Amelia,' the Virginia Poetess, music by Jas. H. Newman; "Flowers from Foreign Lands;" and "Ellen Bayne," arranged with brilliant variations for the piano, by Ernst W. Muller.

We have also received from the publisher Mrs. L. Fanshaw's translation of de Lagrave's popular and favorite romance, "Il va partir." The English and French words of the music are attached.

The recent Paris census shows that no fewer than 23,000 persons are employed on photography and photographic processes in that city.

RUSSELL'S SECOND LETTER

ON THE

Disaster at Manassas Plains.

WASHINGTON, July 24, 1861.

As no one can say what a day or a night may bring forth, particularly in time of war, I avail myself of a chance of probable quiet, such as it is, amid the rolling of drums, the braying of trumpets and bands, the noise of marching men, rolling of wagons, and general life and activity in the streets, to write some remarks on the action at Manassas or Bull Run.

Of its general effects abroad, and on the North and South, a larger and perhaps a better view can be taken from Europe than on this side of the Atlantic. There is a natural and intense anxiety to learn what impression will be made abroad by the battle; for notwithstanding the vulgar and insolent arrogance of the least reputable portion of the press in the United States, generally conducted by aliens or persons who have left Great Britain *from cause*, it is felt that the result of the action must have very strong influences over the fortunes of the contending parties, particularly in the money market, to which recourse must be had in fear and trembling.

It would be well not to arrive at hasty conclusions in reference to the bearing of the defeat on the actual struggle. Those who are persuaded that the North must and will subjugate the South, see in the disaster merely a prolongation of the war, a certain loss of material, or even an increment of hope in the spirit it will arouse, as they think, among the Unionists. Others regard it as an evil omen for the compromise they desire to effect, as it will give the North another insult to avenge and inspire the South with additional confidence. The Confederates will accept it as proof demonstrative of their faith that the North can not conquer them, and may take it into their heads to corroborate it by an attempt to inflict on the North that with which they have been menaced by the Cabinet of Washington and its supporters.

Of the Cabinet, Mr. Chase, the Secretary of the Treasury, is perhaps the only man who bore up against the disheartening intelligence of Monday morning; but Mr. Seward and others are recovering their spirits as they find that their army was more frightened than hurt, and that the Confederates did not advance on the capital immediately after their success. It was a sad, rude sweep of the broom to the cobweb-spinners—to the spider politicians, who have been laying out warps in all directions, and are now lying in frowsy heaps among the ruins of their curious artifices. Nothing can restore them to their places in the popular estimation; nothing could have kept them there but the rapid, complete success of their policy, and the speedy fulfillment of their prophecies. The sword they have drawn is held over their heads by the hands of some coming man whose face no one can see yet, but his footsteps are audible, and the ground shakes beneath his tread.

If Mr. Lincoln were indeed a despot, with the genius to lead or direct an army, now would be his time. All the odium which could be heaped upon him by his enemies, all the accusation that could have been preferred North and South, have been fully urged, and he could not add to them by leading his army to victory, while with victory would certainly come the most unexampled popularity, and perhaps an extraordinary and prosper us tenure of power. The campaign would be one worthy of a Napoleon, nor could it be determined by even $500,000,000 and 500,000 men, unless they were skillfully handled and well economized. If popular passion be excited by demagogues, and if it be permitted to affect the council of the State, it is easy to foresee the end, though it is not so easy to predict by what steps ruin will be reached at last.

The great question to be decided just now is the value of the Union sentiment in the North. Will the men and the money be forthcoming, and that soon enough to continue the war of aggression or recuperation against the seceded States.

While Congress has been passing bills of pains and penalties, confiscating rebel property and amending sundry laches in the penal code, as well as filling up fat holes, through which conquered and runaway Secessionists might escape, in the laws and body of the Constitution, the conquest is suddenly deferred, and Cotton stands King of the battle field. "We are glad of it," cry the extreme Abolitionists, "actually delighted, because now Slavery is doomed."

If the bulk of the capital and population of the North is thrown into this struggle, there can be but one hope for the Confederates—brilliant victories on the battle-field, which must lead to a recognition from foreign Powers. The fight can not go on forever, and if the Confederate States meet with reverses—if their capital is occupied, their Congress dispersed, their territory (that which they claim as theirs) occupied, they must submit to the consequences of defeat. Is that equally true of their opponents? On what ground can the United States, which were founded on successful rebellion, claim exemption from the universal law which they did so much to establish?

Whatever the feelings of the North may be now, there can be no doubt that the reverse at Manassas caused deep mortification and despondency in Washington. Gen. Scott, whether he disapproved, as it is said, the movement onward or not, was certain that the Confederates would be defeated. Every hour messengers were hurried off from the field to the end of the wire some miles away, with reports of the progress made by the troops, and every hour the telegrams brought good tidings up to 4 o'clock or so, when the victory seemed decided in favor of the Federalists; at least the impression was that they had gained the day by driving the enemy before them. Then came the news of the necessary retirement of the troops; nevertheless it is affirmed that up to 8 o'clock in the evening Gen. Scott believed in the ultimate success of the United States troops, who under his own immediate orders had never met with a reverse.

The President, the Secretary of War, and other members of the Government, were assembled in the room where the telegraph operator was at work far into the night, and as the oracles of fate uncoiled from the wires, gloom gathered on their faces; and at last, grave and silent they retired, leaving hope behind them. It must have been to them a time of anxiety beyond words; but of old the highest honors were given to him who in calamity and disaster did not despair of the Republic. And it is to the credit of the President and his advisers that they have recovered their faith in the ultimate success of their cause, and think they can subjugate the South after all.

But the raw levies are not likely to be fit for much for months to come, and it is difficult to see how they will be fit for anything until they get proper officers. Some of the so-called regiments which have recently come in are mere mobs, without proper equipments, uniform, or arms; others are in these respects much better than the troops who were beaten. It is not courage (need it be said?) which is wanting—it is officers; and without them men are worth little or nothing. The men of some regiments fought well: others did not. There was little or no difference between the privates of the one and those of the other. There was probably a marked distinction between the officers. The West Point Cadets will all be used up by the increase of the regular army of the United States to 40,000 men, just agreed upon by Congress; and the bulk of the officers with military experience and education are provided for already.

The President is not exempt from the fate of the unfortunate in all republics, but he has yet a good deal of the future to draw upon, and the people are amused by changes among the military commanders and by threats and promises, for which they will all have to pay before the quarrel is adjusted. It is so generally ascertained that Gen. Scott did not approve the advance, for which his plans were not matured, (and it is so probable, too,) that it may be believed by those who have not the greatest faith in the firmness of his character, and who think he might be induced to give orders for the execution of ill-conceived and hasty projects, or, at all events, to precipitate operations without the necessary conditions of success. It is certain the country was becoming fretful and impatient, and that men, like Mr. Wilson, Chairman of the Military Committee of the Senate, were loud in their complaints of the delays and inactivity of the army and of its chief.

The schism which must always exist between professionals and quacks, between regular soldiers and volunteers, has been greatly widened by the action on Sunday. The volunteers indulge in severe reflections on the generalship of the commander; the regulars speak with contemptuous bitterness of the inefficiency and cowardice of the volunteer officers. The former talk learnedly of the art of war, and of the cruelty of being led like sheep to the slaughter. The latter, without detracting from the courage of the men, inveigh against those who directed their regiments on the field; and the volunteer privates are glad to add their testimony against many of the officers, whose pride in uniforms and gold lace did not permit them to soil them in the smoke of gunpowder. It is remarkable that so much hankering after military reputation should be accompanied, in some instances at least, by absence of any military spirit.

There are various statements in reference to the conduct of the regular cavalry and infantry. The regular officers admit that at one time the cavalry gave way, but they did not break or fly; they were rallied, drew up in line again, and showed front to the enemy. The regular officers declare that it was the infantry which saved the retreat, covering it steadily in conjunction with the Germans; and the losses of the United States Marines argue that they had a large share of the enemy's fire. The artillery, who lost their guns, speak, as artillery will do under the circumstances, of the infantry which deserted them; and the general officers, who must after all be the best judges, bear strong testimony to the good services and general steadiness of the regulars engaged in the action.

When the statements in the American papers are compared with the facts, I am aware it will be necessary to rely a little on "character," in asking faith for what I report. There was not a bayonet charge made by the Federalist infantry during the day; there was not a charge of any kind made by the Confederate cavalry upon any regiment of their enemy until the latter broke. There was not a hand-to-hand encounter between any regiments. There was not a single "battery charged" or taken by the Federalists. There were no masked batteries in the play by the former. There was no annihilation of rebel horse by Zouaves, Fire or other.

A volley fired by one battalion emptied three saddles among a body of horse who appeared at some distance, and the infantry, which performed the execution then retired. There were no desperate struggles except by those who wanted to get away. The whole matter in plain English amounts to this: The Federalists advanced slowly but steadily, under the fire of their artillery, driving the enemy, who rarely showed out of cover, in line before them, and gradually forced them back on the right and center for a mile and a half towards Manassas. As the enemy fell back they used their artillery also, and there was a good deal of pounding away at long ranges with light field guns and some heavier rifled ordnance, the line on both sides being rarely within 500 yards of each other.

On one occasion the regiments on the right were received by a musketry fire from the enemy which induced them to fall back, but they were rallied and led forward towards the front. The Confederates again gave way, and the Federalists advanced once more. Again the line of the enemy appeared in front and delivered fire. The Zouaves, as they are called, and the 11th New York, which were on the flank, fell into confusion not to be rallied, and eventually retired from the field in disorder, to use the mildest term, with a contagious effect on their comrades and with the loss of the guns which they were supporting.

Nothing would, or could, or did stop them. In vain they were reminded of their oaths to "avenge Ellsworth's death." Their flag was displayed to the winds; it had lost its attractions. They ran in all directions with a speed which their fortune favored. "I tell the tale as it was told to me" by one who had more to do with them, and had better opportunity of witnessing their conduct than I had, for, as I have already stated in a previous letter, I was late on the ground, and had not been able to see much ere the retreat was ordered. Though I was well mounted, and had left Washington with the intention of returning early that night, I found fugitives had preceded me in masses all the way, and when I crossed the Long Bridge about 11 o'clock, I was told that the city was full of those who had returned from the fight.

But, if the miserable rout and panic of the Federalists have produced such deplorable results to their cause, they have still much to be thankful for. Had the Confederates been aware of their success, and followed up their advantage early on Monday morning, there was no reason on earth why they should not have either got into Washington or compelled the whole of the Federal army that kept together and could not escape, as it was all on one road, to surrender themselves prisoners with all they possessed. If the statements of the Federalist papers as to their strength be correct, the rebels could have easily spared 30,000 men for that purpose, with a reserve of 10,000 or 15,000 in their rear.

The Chain Bridge, the fords above the Falls, were open to them—at least there could be but little or no opposition from the disorganized forces. The columns moving round from Fairfax to their left by Vienna, would have been able certainly to cross at Matildaville; others could have got over at the Falls, and still there would have been enough to permit Beauregard to occupy Manassas, and to send on a heavy column to cover Alexandria, and to shut up the Federalists in the earthworks and *tete du pont*, if not to wrest them from troops deeply affected by the rout they were witnessing.

If the Confederates had the cavalry of which so much has been said, they were scandalously handled. A detour by a cross road from Centreville to the Germantown road would have placed the horse in the rear of the retreating mass in half an hour, and it is not too much to say that mass would have thrown itself on the mercy of the pursuers. If Beauregard or Lee's force was small, as they say, and suffered as much as the Federalists aver, the flight is the more incomprehensible. But still it is very strange that the victors should not have been aware of their victory—that is, of the utter rout which followed their repulse.

The attempt to form line on the top of Centreville, only partially successful as it was, might have imposed on the enemy, and saved McDowell from the pursuit which he did his best to evert. The journals, which at first boated of the grand Union army of 45,000 men, are now anxious to show that only 20,000 were engaged. Why did the other 25,000 run away? The German Regiment under Col. Blucker, and perhaps some other corps, may have retired in good order, but eventually few withstood the incessant alarms. The rain, which commenced on Monday morning early, may have had much to do with the undisturbed retreat of the Federalists, as the enterprise and activity of the enemy would be much diminished in consequence, and as for the beaten army, it has been always observed that troops hold together and march well in rain. But with all allowance and excuses, it is still mysterious inactivity. Johnston, whose junction with 40,000 men is said to have taken place (if he had half the number it is more than I gave him credit for) on the morning of the battle, must have swelled the force under Lee and Beauregard to 70,000 men at the least. He is the best officer in the Confederate army.

Before breakfast I rode over the Long Bridge to Arlington. There were groups of soldiers, mostly without arms or belts, some few shoeless, a good many foot sore, going along the ground, or standing in the streets of the city, engaged in the occupation called "loafing" in these parts. Several of the men stopped me to inquire after the different regiments to which they belonged. They were dejected and broken down looking fellows, but at all events their mein was more becoming than that of their officers, who are crowding about the hotels and talking of their "whipping" with complacency and without shame.

Great exertions were requisite yesterday to prevent the mob of disorganized soldiers and the rabble from murdering the Confederate prisoners, and it was necessary to rescue them by patrols of dragoons. Gen. McDowell has been much distressed by the dastardly conduct of some of the beaten troops toward their prisoners, and there has been strange scenes in consequence.

"General," said one man, "had I known this, I would have died a hundred times before I fell into those wretches' hands. Let me go free, and let any two or four of them insult me then!" The soldiers are, however, greatly irritated, not only by defeat, but by reports of the most horrible cruelties and atrocities toward prisoners and wounded by the Confederates. For one, I am loth to credit these stories, but it is only right to say that there are many such current, particularly in reference to the New Orleans Zouaves.

Gen. McDowell is a man in the prime of life, some forty and odd years of age, very powerfully built, with a kindly, honest, soldierly expression in face and manners, and it was pleasant to see that, though he was not proud of being "whipped," there was no dejection other than that a man should feel who has been beaten by his enemy, but who knows he has done his duty. Originally he had proposed a series of operations different from those which were actually adopted, and his disposition for the advance of his columns, after the scheme of attack was decided upon, were careful and elaborate.

But he miscalculated somewhere the powers of the regular troops. All his subsequent operations were vitiated by the impossibility of gaining the points fixed on for the first day's march, and General Tyler, who engaged somewhat too seriously with the enemy on the left at Bull Run on the Thursday before the battle, in making what was a mere reconnoisance, put them on the alert and hastened up Johnston.

The officers all agree that the Federalists had advanced steadily on the right and center, and that they had driven back the Confederates with considerable loss for a mile and a half, when the panic took place in the regiments on the flank of the right, which necessitated the issue of an order for the retirement of the whole force, and the advance of the reserve to cover it.

The volunteers who had broken could not be rallied. The movement, always dangerous with such materials, under such circumstances, was misunderstood by the wagon drivers and by other regiments, and the retreat became finally the shameful rout, which was only not utterly disastrous because of the ignorance and inactivity, or the weakness of the enemy. Maj. Barry, an officer of the regular United States Artillery, told me he could not stop the runaways who ought to have protected his guns, though the gunners stood by them till the enemy were fairly upon them, and that as for the much talked-of cavalry, two round shots which were pitched into them by his battery sent them to the right-about at once.

The regular officers spoke in only one way of the conduct of the officers of the volunteers and of certain regiments. Indeed, what could be said of men who acted after and in action as others acted before it, and went away as fast as they could? Thus the men of a volunteer battery marched off, leaving their guns on the ground the very morning of the engagement, because their three months' term of service was up; and the Pennsylvania regiments exhibited a similar spirit. The Sixty-ninth Irish volunteered to serve as long as they were required, and so did some other corps, I believe; but there must be something rotten in the system, military and political, which generates such sentiments, and developes neither the sense of military honor nor any of that affectionate devotion for the Union which is called by one party in America patriotism. McDowell's corps were ordered to march with three days' food cooked, not including, of course, the day of marching. The food was, however, issued inclusive of that day, and the next day the men had eaten up or wasted the two days' rations in one, and had nothing. They were badly provided with food and with water on the very day of the action, and some men told me that evening they had eaten nothing since 2:30 A. M. Indeed, the General witnessed the disorder which was caused by the regiments rushing out of the ranks to drink at a small stream before they went into action, though their canteens were filled before they set out.

Mr. Bernel, the British Consul, came over to-day to consult with Lord Lyons on certain matters connected with our interest in the city of Baltimore. As the truth is developed the Secessionists in Washington become radiant with joy, and can not conceal their exultation whenever it is safe to indulge it.

Their ears are erect for the sound of the cannon which is to herald the entrance of the enemy into the capital of the United States. The Unionists, on the other hand, speak of the past hopes of the enemy—of the great reinforcements arriving—of the renewed efforts of the North, and of its determination to put down rebellion. There must be an infatuation which amounts to a kind of national insanity in a portion of the North, or is it possible that they believe what the journals tell them—that they are the strongest, bravest, richest, mightiest people in the world, and that they only have to will and the world—including the Confederate States—is prostrate before them. The exaggerations and misstatements of part of the American press would certainly lead those who believed it to such conclusions.

The name of the German General who has made himself so conspicuous in Missouri is the subject of a paragraph in the St. Louis Republican, which, noticing the various ways his name is spelt, says it is correctly written Franz Sigel.

THE CITY.

PRESENTMENT OF THE GRAND JURY.—The Grand Jury yesterday reported on the following cases:

Chas. McCormick, charged with the murder of John Higgins, at the Half-way House—a true bill.

Joseph Jolly, charged with assault upon a little girl ten years old, with intent to commit rape—a true bill.

RETURNED.—Dr. Felix Formento, one of those noble-hearted gentlemen who went to Missouri to assist in the work of administering to the sick and wounded of the Southern troops, has returned to the city. We are authorized to state that his report, which is of great interest, will be made to the Relief Committee at their next meeting.

GONE TO ARKANSAS.—Messrs. C. S. Hewes and W. E. Parham, who are duly authorized to do so, have gone into the interior of the State of Arkansas for the purpose of soliciting from the citizens as many guns as they can spare, under the recent request of the Confederate Government. It is stated that there are a great many guns in the interior of that State which may be had for the asking.

FIRE.—At fifteen minutes past 11 o'clock last night a fire broke out in a two-story wooden building on the corner of Bienville and Tonti streets, occupied, the lower part by Mrs. Coleman as a grocery store. The upper portion was used as a dwelling house. The building, with the greater portion of its contents, was destroyed. No insurance. It is supposed that the fire was the work of an incendiary.

CAPT. J. B. WEAVER BEFORE THE C. S. COMMISSIONERS.—It will be remembered that His Honor Mayor Monroe, before whom an affidavit was made charging Capt. J. B. Weaver with treason, turned the case over to the Confederate States Court for decision. Yesterday afternoon the accused was brought before C. S. Commissioner Lusher for a hearing, the C. S. District Attorney, H. D. Miller, being present. Capt. Weaver was accompanied by his counsel, Col. G. W. Race.

After a patient hearing of the case the Commissioner discharged the accused, upon the ground that he was a citizen of Missouri, and as such owed no allegiance to the Southern Confederacy, and was, therefore, not amenable to the charge of treason.

Mr. Black, of the firm of R. W. Estlin & Co., of this city, stated that the dinner eaten by the accused near Baltimore, during his Northern tour, (of which mention was made in our report yesterday morning,) was at the residence of his (Black's) brother-in-law, one of the strongest secessionists in the South, whose house is guarded by two hundred soldiers.

We learn that after his discharge by the C. S. Commissioner, Capt. Weaver demanded that the oath of allegiance to the Southern Confederacy should be administered to him immediately, and that Commissioner Lusher proceeded to administer it.

It may not be improper here to state, in connection with this case, that the steamboat D. A. January, one-fourth of which is owned by Capt. Weaver, is still in the hands of the Lincoln Government—that the owners are to receive for her the sum of $1500 per month, and $26,000 if she is lost.

A very large class of our community is engaged in the steamboating business, directly and indirectly, and it seems very hard that they should suffer the loss of hundreds of thousands of dollars on account of the war, because of their loyalty to the South, whilst others engaged in the business can make a good thing of it with their boats by letting the U. S. Government have them as transports for troops to come and bring desolation to our hearths, or use them to carry provisions to feed those troops.

QUARTERLY REPORT OF THE CORONER.—Inquests held by the Coroner of the Parish of Orleans from the 1st day of June to the 31st day of August—*Homicides*.—June 6th, Thomas Jones, 30 years old, native of Boston, killed by an unknown person; 8th, slave Sally, killed by slave Cornelius; 11th, unknown man, killed by unknown person; 15th, Chas. Haerrig, 3 years old, crushed by a milk cart; 17th, James Ging, 32 years old, Ireland, killed by unknown person; Michael Fellingher, 22 years old, Germany, killed by Henry Loomis; John W. West, 45 years old, Kentucky, killed by Thomas Shaw; 22d, C. McLeod, 30 years old, Tennessee, killed by James Dillon and other unknown persons.

July 1st, William O'Brien, 40 years old, Ireland, killed by John Rejshback; 8th, John Dougherty, 22 years of age, Kentucky, killed by John Kennedy; 20th, Michael Farrell, 44 years old, Ireland, killed by Patrick Boyle.

August 6th, John Higgins, 30 years of age, Ireland, killed by Charles McCormick; 13th, Wm. Adams, 38 years old, Buffalo, killed by persons unknown; 19th, J. B. Haughton, 52 years old, North Carolina, killed by Bob Johnson.

Suicides.—June 24th, Wilhelm Therft, 33 years old, Germany, by hanging; July 19th, Henry Trewinsky, 50 years old, Poland, by pistol shooting; 23d, Lewis Kramer, 61 years old, Germany, by poisoning.

Total, 14 homicides, 13 suicides, 3 accidental deaths by shooting, 2 by burning, 2 by falling, 2 by falling in privies, 4 by being run over by carts, 1 by being crushed by the fall of a safe, 21 drowned persons, 6 deaths from intemperance, and 58 from various diseases. Grand total, 116 deaths.

Forty-seven of those persons were natives of the Confederate States, 9 of the Federal States, 13 of Germany, 19 of Ireland, 4 of England, 1 of France, 2 of Switzerland, 1 of Poland, 1 of Africa, 2 of Hayti, 1 of Havana, 1 of Portugal, 1 of Italy, and 14 of an unknown nativity.

RECORDER GASTINEL'S COURT.—Wm. Jones, charged with vagrancy and supposed to be a dangerous and suspicious character, and not one of those citizens who spend their time in erecting church edifices, was sent to the Workhouse for three calendar months.

Mrs. Jones gave bond to appear and answer the charge of insulting and abusing Lizzie Miller, with the intention of getting her "mad" up and raising a big row.

Phillip Nellick, one of those precious young scamps who get under the wharves, where flour, sugar, coffee, &c., is stored, and bore holes in the barrels, having a basket to catch the leakage, thus stealing quite a large quanty of stuff, was arrested by special Ben. Leggett. He was sent to the Parish Prison to await a hearing.

Charles, a slave of Mrs. Dorson, forgetting the respect due to a white person, undertook to insult and abuse officer Alvarez, whilst the latter was on duty in the French Market. Sent to prison to await examination.

RIVER INTELLIGENCE.

OFFICE OF THE DAILY DELTA,
NEW ORLEANS, SUNDAY, Sept. 1.

Yesterday was the last of a dull week and a dull month in the steamboating line. It can be justly noted for the small quantity of business done and the great quantity of rain that fell. It is to be hoped that the coming week may prove more active, and, if possibly convenient, a little less rain would do......The boats advertised all got off, except the Gen. Hodges. The General will leave for Red River on Tuesday next......The Lizzie Simmons was drawing nine feet, which might be considered a heavy up stream freight......The Lafourche and the Sallie Robinson also had a fair quantity of freight......The only arrival we have to note is the Prince of Wales from Memphis. The Prince's down trip consisted principally of flour and corn......

The arrivals of river steamers in this port for the week ending Friday at noon last were sixteen in number, classed as follows:

Coast Lower	1	Red River	1
Coast Upper	7	Memphis	4
Vicksburg	2	Barataria	1

MEMPHIS, Aug. 29.—The river opposite this point rose six inches in the twenty-fours ending at dark last night.

Business at the landing yesterday was moderately brisk. The weather was warm and cloudy with occasional rain.

The Louisville arrived from New Orleans yesterday moring with an excellent trip, including 1000 sacks salt, 210 hhds. sugar, 60 tons pig iron, 150 bales gunny bags, and a lot of miscellaneous freight, besides a cavalry company from Providence, Louisiana.

The Gen. Quitman cleared for New Orleans last evening on one wheel, carrying 1200 bbls. flour, 30 hhds. tobacco, 40 bales coston, 100 bbls. apples, and a large quantity of miscellaneous freight.

LOUISVILLE, August 28.—The river is still falling, with scant 7 feet water in the canal, a decline of about 4 inches in 24 hours. The weather is clear and pleasant. The river at Cincinnati, yesterday, had fallen 14 inches. It was also falling at Pittsburg. We see it stated that Capt. Montgomery, with the Jas. Montgomery, went to Mound City with a lot of carpenters and laborers. The boat, on arrival at Mound City, is to be converted into a floating hotel.

BOATS LEAVING.

FOR THE COAST.—*On Monday*.—The Laurel Hill, Captain S. Heno, will leave on Monday evening at 5 o'clock for Bayou Sara. Geo. Wilkinson is her clerk.

PRINCE OF WALES—*For Memphis*—The Prince is to leave as above at 5 o'clock Monday afternoon. Capt. James Lee is in command, and Mr. A. G. Folger is in the office.

MONETARY AND FINANCIAL.

OFFICE OF THE DAILY DELTA,
NEW ORLEANS, SATURDAY EVENING, August 31, 1861.

The official Bank statement of to-day compares as follows with that for last Saturday:

	Aug. 31.	Aug 24.	Difference.
Short Loans	$11,781.601	$11,192,066	Increase....$589,535
Specie	14,325,014	14,438,709	Decrease,... 113,695
Circulation	6,470.681	6,420,016	Increase,... 50,665
Deposits	15,364,471	15,512,763	Decrease.... 148,292
Exchange	3,515,289	3,482,260	Increase.... 33,029
Dis. Bal	549,879	624,211	Decrease.... 74,332
Long Loans	7,759,246	7,387,133	Decrease.... 627,887

The net variation in long and short Loans for this week is a decrease of 38,000, and the aggregate transfer from the former to the latter column falls but little short of $600,000. Circulation has been slightly augmented, and there is a nominal addition to Exchange, while specie and Deposits exhibit an unimportant reduction as compared with the returns for the previous week.

OFFICIAL WEEKLY STATEMENT OF THE BANKS OF NEW ORLEANS
CASH ASSETS.

Banks.	Loans.		Specie.	
	Aug. 31.	Aug. 24.	Aug. 31.	Aug. 24.
Citizens'	2.408.723	2.253.689	4.074.448	4.104.560
Canal	809.737	723.210	941.799	935.141
Louisiana	1.458.904	1.3 0.616	2.710.15'	2.704.594
Louisiana State	2.640.873	2.524.796	2.731.487	2.711.110
Mechanics' & Traders'	706.588	684.849	830.353	843.890
Bank of New Orleans	1.033.253	1.002.805	942.374	1.042.135
Southern	99.909	99.689	483.619	480.425
Union	1.015.950	934.450	476.045	508.819
Merchants'	430.078	423.741	106.197	123.369
Crescent City	691.187	696.748	179.505	171.738
America	486.399	487.473	849.030	812.928
Total	11.781.601	11.192.066	14.325.014	14.438.709
	Increase......589.535		Decrease.....113.695	

CASH LIABILITIES.

Banks.	Circulation.		Deposits.	
	Aug. 31.	Aug 24.	Aug. 31.	Aug. 24.
Citizens	1.981.185	1.956 280	3.534.416	3.561.235
Canal	632.565	638.290	853 259	849.763
Louisiana	771.176	774.631	3.401.867	3.396.843
Louisiana State	1.461.415	1.417.630	3.354 723	3.411.505
Mechanics' & Traders'	263.710	256.780	895.451	918.090
Bank of New Orleans	418.690	417.405	915.680	995.353
Southern	37.195	37.275	469.418	470.045
Union	423.390	431.780	616.394	626.982
Merchants	214.705	221.130	295.482	298.107
Crescent City	102.530	102.520	124.929	119.124
America	163.720	166.295	902.852	865.716
Total	6.470.681	6.420.0 6	15.364.471	15.512.763
	Increase.......50.665		Decrease......148.292	

COMPARATIVE STATEMENT OF EXCHANGE HELD BY THE VARIOUS BANKS, AND BALANCES DUE DISTANT BANKS, FOR TWO WEEKS; THE LATTER BEING COMPRISED IN TABLE OF DEPOSITS PUBLISHED ABOVE.

Banks.	Exchange.		Due Distant Banks.	
	Aug. 31.	Aug. 24.	Aug. 31.	Aug. 24.
Citizens'	704.747	697.655	149.504	138.440
Canal	1,466.437	1.466.437	82.076	75.955
Louisiana	526.458	532.337	32.200	35.626
Louisiana State	657	657	87.329	117.553
Mechanics' & Traders'	249.458	249.458	8.808	9.198
Bank of New Orleans	20.000	....	47.110	58.206
Southern	508.837	512.215	....	....
Union	29.548	11.095	124.349	167.475
Merchants	9.357	12.343	10.060	13.708
Crescent City	....	....	4.602	4.209
America	63	63	3.841	3.841
Total	3.515.289	3.482.260	549.879	624.211
	Increase.......33.029		Decrease.......74.332	

Nothing has transpired [illegible] our last to materially alter the condition of the market, and [illegible] ations have continued restricted throughout in every department of business. As heretofore, there was some movement noticeable daily in second-class paper, secured by strong collaterals, and in country mortgage names, both of which went off freely at previous figures—2@3 per cent. per month, according to date of maturity; but strictly A1 signatures were, for the most part, exceedingly inactive, owing to the limited character of the supply, although they could have been readily placed at 1@1½ per cent per month, and the lower descriptions may still be considered wholly unsalable.

Stocks and Bonds have exhibited but little, if any, animation since the date of the previous review, and the market for this description of securities must still be represented as in an unusually unsettled condition. The better classes of shares are in moderate request, and sales to a considerable extent could be readily effected at prices to suit the views of buyers, but the tendency of rates is still upward for all dividend paying stocks, and the various other grades are entirely overlooked. Bonds also attract less attention than usual, but there is no disposition manifested to press sales except at extreme figures. Confederate Bonds and Treasury Notes are rapidly gaining in public favor and heavy operations are looked for in both, at their full value, in a brief space of time. As stated in our last, most of the Banks receive heavy notes on special deposit, and to-day one at least reported an amount taken in regular deposit in its weekly statement to the Board of Currency. In fact, they are fast becoming the circulating medium of the whole of the Confederate States, and must soon cause the principal Banks to retire their whole regular issues. But the city of Mobile is thus far considerably ahead of all others in its efforts to popularise the Treasury Notes of the Southern Confederacy, and its Bank Managers deserve especial praise for coalescing in a movement to receive them in payment of all classes of obligations, whilst they promptly discharge their own liabilities in specie, whenever it is called for. Such should be the course adopted in every State where no constitutional impediment exists, and even the latter ought to be removed as soon as practicable.

Exchange is still very plenty, and rates have further receded within the present week. As may be seen on reference to the Bank aggregate, the total has been slightly increased since our last by accessions from other Southern seaports, but the demand has, for the same time, been still further diminished. Transactions are rigidly confined to small amounts for direct remittance purposes, and the market closes unsettled at the subjoined quotations: Clear Sterling Bills, 2@4 ⅌ cent. premium; Bank Notes, 6@7 ⅌ cent. premium; Francs, 5.20@5.10 per dollar.

PUBLIC DEBT.—A. J. Guirot, Esq., Assistant Treasurer C. S. A., notifies holders of Confederate Bonds, in another column, that the September coupons of interest due to citizens and corporations of Louisiana and Mississippi, will be paid at his office in this city on and after Monday, the 2d prox. Thus, it will be seen, that notwithstanding the magnitude of the requirements for carrying on our war of independence against an unrelenting and tyrannical foe, our Government is found equal to every responsibility devolving upon it, and is alike mindful of the integrity and the defenses of the nation.

ROBBING PETER TO PAY PAUL.—The last St. Louis Republican says:

There was some little excitement in bank circles to-day, in consequence of the arrival in the city of Major John McDonald, of the American Zouave Regiment, with $58,650 of coin taken from the vaults of the St. Genevieve branch of the Merchants' Bank. On its arrival the coin was deposited in the office of the Assistant United States Treasurer. It seems that this seizure of coin was at the order of Gen. Fremont, and intended as a mere precautionary measure, to prevent its falling into the hands of the rebel armies now in the southeast.

On the same day of its deposit in the Sub Treasury it was, by order of Gen. Fremont, turned over to the Merchants' Bank.

COMMERCIAL.

OFFICE OF THE DAILY DELTA,
NEW ORLEANS, SATURDAY EVENING, Aug. 31, 1861.

COTTON—We did not hear of a sale to-day.

TOBACCO—Nothing reported. Receipts 8 hhds.

SUGAR—The sales comprise about 150 hhds. at previous rates. Fair to fully Fair 5¾@6c. ⅌ ℔.

MOLASSES—No sales have been reported.

FLOUR—100 bbls. good Extra sold at $8 ⅌ bbl.

CORN—300 sacks Yellow sold at 54c. ⅌ bushel.

OATS—300 sacks sold at 75c. ⅌ bushel.

BRAN—225 sacks Bran and Shorts sold at $1 30, and 925 Bran at $1 35 ⅌ 100 ℔s.

WHEAT—325 sacks poor Red Wheat sold at 95c.; 342 prime Red at $1 20, and 44 Red at $1 15 ⅌ bushel.

WHISKY—Rectified is retailing at 40@42c. ⅌ gallon.

LARD—Prime in tierces is retailing at 20c. ⅌ ℔.

PORK—Mess is retailing at $30 ⅌ bbl.

BACON—Shoulders are retailing at 15c., ribbed sides at 17c., and sugar-cured hams at 17@20c. ⅌ ℔.

CATTLE MARKET.

JEFFERSON CITY, SATURDAY EVENING, August 31, 1861.

Arrived to-day, 270 Texas Cattle, 25 Hogs, 321 Sheep, and 113 Veal Cattle. Sales 176 Texas Cattle, 20 Hogs, and 50 Veal Cattle. Stock on sale 538 Texas Cattle, 51 Hogs, 321 Sheep and 113 Veal Cattle.

Beef Cattle, Western, first quality	⅌ ℔. net	—	@ —
Beef Cattle second quality	⅌ ℔. net	—	@ —
Beef Cattle, Texas, first quality	⅌ head	$30 00	@45 00
Beef Cattle, Texas, second quality	⅌ head	20 00	@30 00
Hogs, Western	⅌ ℔. gross	8	@10
Sheep, choice	⅌ head	3 50	@ 5 00
Sheep, inferior	⅌ head	—	@ 3 00
Milch Cows, choice			—@—
Milch Cows, ordinary			—@—
Veal Cattle		8	@11

THE NEW YORK HERALD.

WHOLE NO. 9133. NEW YORK, THURSDAY, SEPTEMBER 12, 1861. PRICE TWO CENTS.

THE NATIONAL BATTLE GROUND.

The Armies of the Potomac---Encampments of Over Three Hundred Thousand Armed Men---Scene of the Coming Decisive Conflict.

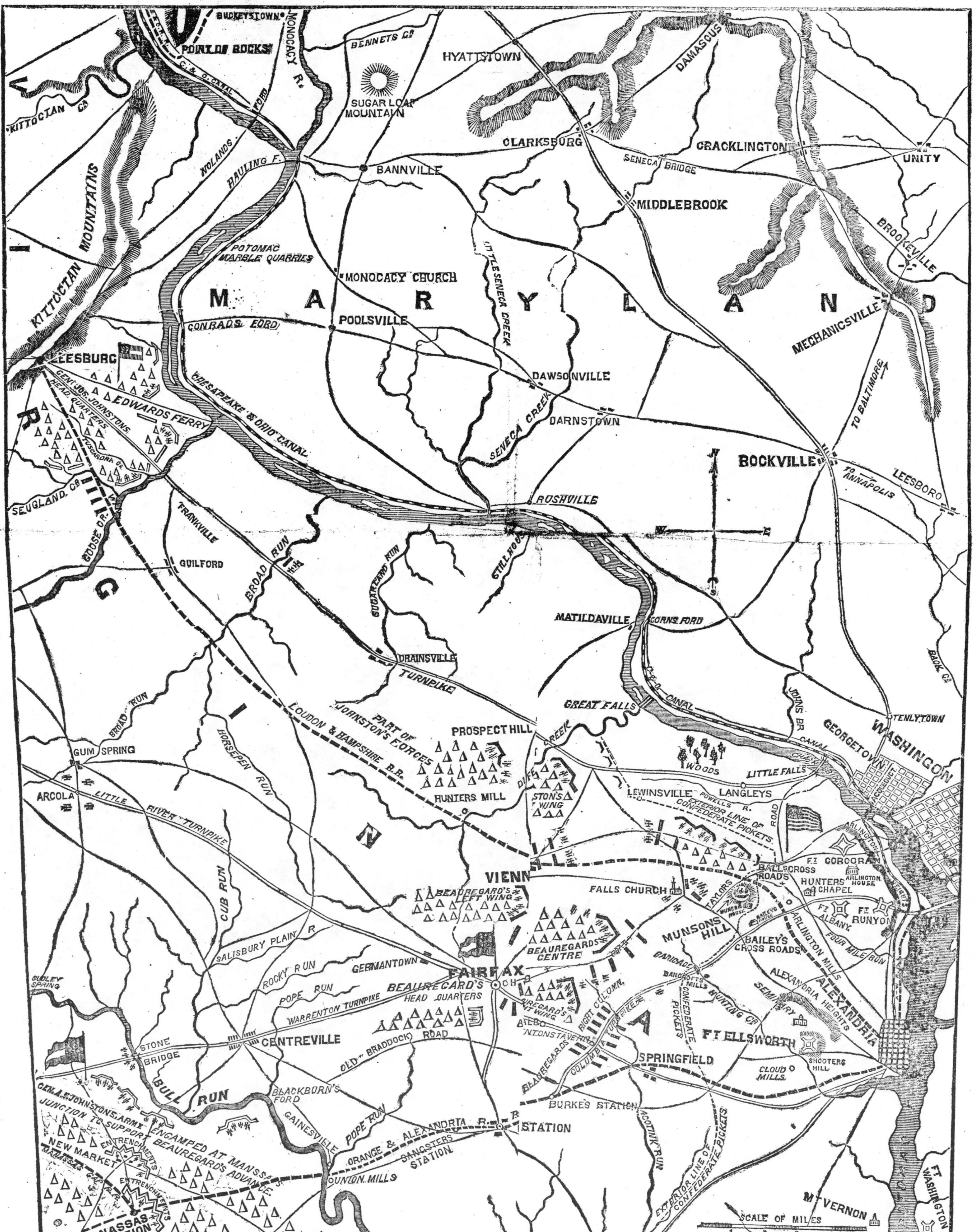

THE ILLUSTRATED LONDON NEWS

No. 1108.—VOL. XXXIX.] SATURDAY, SEPTEMBER 14, 1861. [WITH A SUPPLEMENT, FIVEPENCE

MEETING OF THE BRITISH ASSOCIATION AT MANCHESTER.

SCIENCE, like Wisdom, is justified of her children. Time was when the annual sessions of the British Association were held to be a capital theme for ridicule, and when journalists who cater for the instruction and amusement of men of business thought it became them to raise an uproarious laugh at what they described as talking, peripatetic, and wool-gathering philosophy. It is not the first time by a good many that the shadows which herald the approach of a majestic success, misinterpreted by men who believe that "there is nothing like leather," have excited wondrous ebullitions of noisy merriment, of which subsequent events have made the said men sheepishly ashamed. The British Association has not merely outlived the jeers of its early assailants—it has seen them converted into acclamations of praise.

THE WAR IN AMERICA: TEXAN RANGERS (FEDERALISTS) RECONNOITRING BETWEEN ALEXANDRIA AND FAIRFAX, VIRGINIA.—FROM A SKETCH BY OUR SPECIAL ARTIST.

SEE SUPPLEMENT, PAGE 282.

THE NEW YORK HERALD.

WHOLE NO. 9135. NEW YORK, SATURDAY, SEPTEMBER 14, 1861. PRICE TWO CENTS.

THE NATIONAL POPULAR LOAN.

Fac Simile of a Hundred Dollar Treasury Note, with Coupons Attached---Interesting Financial Intelligence for the People.

THE REBELLION.

IMPORTANT FROM WASHINGTON

Rebel Reconnoissance in Force of the Union Lines.

A Great and Decisive Battle Near at Hand.

The Reported Trouble with Major General Fremont.

The Main Difficulty a Personal One with Col. Frank Blair.

Action of President Lincoln on Gen. Fremont's Proclamation.

IMPORTANT FROM BALTIMORE.

Arrest of Members of the Maryland Legislature and Other Secessionists.

A Bold Rebel Plot Overthrown by Gen. McClellan.

IMPORTANT FROM KENTUCKY.

The Legislative Act Driving Out the Rebels Passed Over the Governor's Veto.

Another Skirmish and Rebel Defeat in Western Virginia,

&c., &c., &c.

OUR SPECIAL WASHINGTON DESPATCHES.

WASHINGTON, Sept. 13, 1861.

REBEL RECONNOISSANCE IN FORCE OF THE UNION RIGHT AND CENTRE—A GREAT AND DECISIVE BATTLE NEAR AT HAND.

At about half-past four o'clock this afternoon, the enemy, in pretty strong force, with infantry, artillery and cavalry, appeared in front of the Union pickets on the centre and right wing of our forces on the Virginia side of the Potomac. They made their first demonstration on the road leading from Fall's Church" to Ball's Cross Roads, driving in our pickets with heavy bodies of skirmishers and scouts, immediately followed up by planting a section of artillery near Mary Hill's house. From this point they directed a sharp fire of grape, canister and shrapnel, on the Union pickets at Ball's Cross Roads, directing their fire at every point along the road wherever they thought our pickets were established between Ball's Cross Roads and the Chain Bridge. The Union pickets retired in order.

Intelligence was immediately communicated to General McDowell, at Arlington House. After the demonstration on our pickets near Ball's Cross Roads, the rebels paid their respects to several places to the right of our works, near the Chain Bridge. They made a direct onset on Van Desburger's house, two miles from the Union camp, where we had a picket stationed. They fired ten or twelve shells, doing no damage.

Soon after a body of one hundred cavalry, and about the same number of infantry, appeared, when our picket of twenty men retired to Van Dennerten's house, one-eighth of a mile distant, when they were shortly after reinforced with a battery of artillery. A column of infantry, cavalry and artillery, including Captain Mott's and Captain Griffin's batteries, took position at important points, awaiting the appearance of the enemy. Brigadier General William F. Smith commanded the whole force, and with the assistance of his able Chief of Engineers, Lieutenant Orlando M. Poe, will await any demonstration that the enemy may make in the morning.

The astonishing alacrity with which the Union troops got under arms on the right wing was truly commendable, moving as they did in twenty minutes after the long roll "To arms" was beat.

Night intervening by the time our troops got into position, no progress could be made either to ascertain the strength of the enemy or the intention of this movement.

After dark the rebels turned incendiaries, burned the houses and barns of Mr. Basil Hall, Mrs. Mary Hall, Mr De Kay, Mr. Samuel Birch, Mr. Tabers and others.

Private James Lowry, of Company A, Kentucky Cavalry, who was on picket duty when the enemy approached, had his horse shot from under him and barely escaped with his life.

The Union pickets were re-established during the night.

The advance of the enemy upon our lines to-night is known to but few of the citizens of Washington. There is little doubt that a battle will occur at daybreak, at some point between Washington and Point of Rocks.

It is believed by many that the movement upon our centre will prove a feint, and that the enemy will attack either the column of General Banks or General Stone.

General McClellan and staff have been very active all night, are confident in our strength, and do not doubt the result. [illegible] tar necessity. It is now or never with him. Rely upon it the capital cannot be taken.

THE REPORTED TROUBLE WITH MAJOR GENERAL FREMONT.

All sorts of reports are in circulation relative to General Fremont and the visit of Postmaster Blair and Quartermaster General Meigs to St. Louis. These reports are not only current here, but are telegraphed all over the country. I have ascertained the facts in the case.

The gravest difficulty at St. Louis was personal, between General Fremont and Colonel Frank P. Blair, Jr. It arose from different causes, and was manifested on various occasions, public and private. Confident hopes are entertained that it has now been substantially adjusted.

Complaints are made, from sources which have received consideration, against General Fremont, for alleged inaccessibility to persons having important business with him, and an indisposition to co-operate cordially with the State officials. It is probable that the ground for such dissatisfaction will be removed.

General Fremont's proclamation, which was written and promulgated without consultation with anybody, will be modified to a certain extent by the President. He requires, or requests, General Fremont, in a letter already written, to be made public in a few days, to interpret his proclamation so as to make it accord with the law of Congress passed at the recent session. This is the substance. I do not undertake to give you his language; but my authority for all these statements is the highest that the case admits of.

The relations between President Lincoln and General Fremont continue amicable.

The President sent Postmaster General Blair out to St. Louis as a friend of General Fremont's. Quartermaster General Meigs went on other business—simply to investigate the Quartermaster's Department there.

No other charges, except those mentioned, which have any weight at all with the President, have been made against General Fremont.

Mrs. Fremont left Washington in good spirits to-day, on her return to St. Louis.

CAUSE OF THE ARREST OF SECESSIONISTS IN BALTIMORE—THE PLOT TO CARRY MARYLAND OUT OF THE UNION—FORTUNATE FRUSTRATION OF THE SCHEMES OF THE REBELS.

The arrest at Baltimore of the secession members of the Legislature of Maryland has exploded a plot of the rebels which will prove of vast importance to the government. It is known that some of the arrested secession members of the Legislature had a programme all prepared, by which an act was to be passed declaring Maryland out of the Union and a State in the Southern confederacy. The movement of the rebel army up the river was preparatory to a contemplated movement across. The attempt was to be made on the day the Legislature acted. At the same time the Mayor of Baltimore, who was also arrested to-day, was to co-operate by the best demonstration he could make. By the arrest of the leaders of this conspiracy the Legislature is without the power to act, and the rebels of Baltimore have lost their chief.

A simultaneous movement of rebels was to take place along the eastern shore of Maryland, under the supposed direction and leadership of ex-Commander Buchanan, of the navy, to aid the rebel army of Virginia in crossing to Maryland. This movement under Buchanan was to be made to distract our centre.

The plot is exploded by the prompt action of General McClellan, in directing the arrests made in Baltimore to-day.

THE CONDITIONS OF MAYOR BERRET'S RELEASE.

Mayor Berret was released only upon the condition that he would take the oath of allegiance and resign formally the office of Mayor.

A PRUSSIAN PRINCE VOLUNTEERING IN THE UNION ARMY.

Prince Salm Salm, of the Prussian army, arrived here to-day, and was presented to the Secretary of State by the Prussian Minister. The Prince is highly recommended by the Prussian government, as an experienced and capable military officer, who has distinguished himself in the field in his own country. He has tendered his services to our government, and will probably be commissioned and detailed upon the staff of one of our generals, in order that his military experience and skill may be made available. This tender of so distinguished a military officer of the Prussian army, coming, as he does, recommended by his government, and fortified and endorsed here by the chief representative of that Power, is taken as a good omen.

A BRITISH MAJOR GENERAL'S OPINION OF THE FORTIFICATIONS AROUND WASHINGTON.

Yesterday General McClellan was accompanied in his inspection of the grand army before Washington by a distinguished Major General of the British army, who was highly pleased with the fortifications and the appearance of the troops. He expresses the opinion that Washington cannot be taken.

ARRIVAL OF ESCAPED UNION PRISONERS FROM RICHMOND—NARRATIVE OF THEIR EXPERIENCE WHILE IN THE HANDS OF THE REBELS, AND THE MANNER IN WHICH THEY ESCAPED, ETC.

The steamer Resolute, of the Potomac flotilla, arrived this evening at the Navy Yard, having on board Captain John R. Hurd, Quartermaster Charles I. Murphy, and Lieutenant Raynor, who had recently escaped from Richmond. Captain Hurd was attached to the Kentucky Volunteers, and was taken prisoner in Northwestern Virginia. Quartermaster Murphy was of the New Y[illegible] Raynor of the First [illegible] Volunteers. Both the latter were taken prisoners at Bull run.

Lieutenant Murphy was engaged caring for the wounded at Sudley's Church, when a detachment of Colonel Stewart's cavalry came up and took the wounded and those in attendance in custody. They were treated with great kindness, Lieutenant Cummings of the cavalry, only eliciting from them a promise that they would not attempt to escape, and giving them assurances that they would be treated as prisoners of war. They were left without any guard during the night, a few of the cavalry occasionally visiting the church to see that there was no movement for escape. On Monday night an order came from General Beauregard to have all the prisoners, except the wounded, removed at once to Manassas, and though they left two hundred and eighty wounded uncared for, they were compelled to leave. Three men, not surgeons, were left to give the wounded water, while the remainder, including nine surgeons, were taken to Manassas. On learning the condition of things at Sudley's Church Colonel Preston, of the rebel army, regretted that the order had been sent, and he gave permission to the whole party to return, provided they would take an obligation not to bear arms against or to aid the enemies of the Confederate States. This obligation, however, Mr. Murphy refused to take, and he, with others, was sent to Richmond. He states that at Manassas parallel earthworks had been thrown up in every direction as far as the vision could reach. They were well supplied with artillery. On their way to Richmond the prisoners were treated with kindness by the officers in charge, though they were the subject of great curiosity to the multitude on the way. They suffered no insult, except from the women, who eagerly questioned them as to their intentions, making insulting allusions to the Yankees. Arrived at Richmond, the prisoners were taken to Liggon's tobacco factory, where they are still confined. They were all treated as well as the rebel soldiers were, being furnished with an abundance of food. Mr. Murphy, until a fortnight before his escape, being an attendant upon the sick, was permitted to go about the city, but this permission was subsequently withdrawn, and he remained a close prisoner until he made his escape. Learning that his wife was in deep distress at his imprisonment, he determined to effect his escape, and in concert with Lieutenant Raynor and Captain Hurd, devised a plan.

They observed that the surgeons were permitted to pass in and out without obstruction, they being distinguished by a bit of red ribbon, and as the sentinels were changed every two hours they thought they could pass by the guard as surgeons, provided they could get the necessary badge. Tearing a bit of red flannel from one of their shirts, and putting it on his coat, Lieutenant Raynor passed out without difficulty, and by a previous arrangement he made a purchase of a pocket compass and a map of Virginia. Mr. Murphy and Captain Hurd passed out on the next relief by the same means, and met Lieutenant Raynor on the corner of a neighboring street. This was about eight o'clock on the 5th instant.

Their purpose in the escape was to leave Richmond, following a northeasterly direction, crossing the Rappahannock, to reach the Potomac, where they expected to reach our fleet. This they successfully accomplished, after great privation and suffering, extending through several days, of which the following is a brief narrative:—

After going half a mile beyond the city limits they struck the Union turnpike, which they followed out. Owing to the darkness they successively ran upon a tollgate guarded with soldiers, and a breastwork with cannon, from which they retreated, and succeeded in turning unperceived through neighboring fields. They met country wagons, all of which they avoided. After travelling fifteen miles they went to sleep as daylight dawned in the woods. At nine o'clock in the morning they resumed their march, keeping in the woods, however, as long as daylight lasted. They eat during the day their only food, a sandwich each, which they had brought with them. The second night they crossed the Chickahominy river on a milldam, and continued their march until daylight, when they reached a large plantation, and nearly encountered a number of negroes going to their work. They succeeded in avoiding them, and continued their journey during the day, crossing the Pamonkey river by means of a raft, which they constructed. They then built a fire in the woods, and made a good meal of roasted corn and potatoes, both of which they had secured in fields on their route. During their whole route the roads not unfrequently took them out of their course, in which case they would abandon them, and, guided by their compass, would go across the country until they struck another road which suited their destination. Generally they slept during the day, doing most of their travelling by night, and of course at times suffering terribly from hunger, thirst and insects.

On Saturday they succeeded in crossing the bridge over the Matapony river without observation.

Their map, of course, was of little value to them as regards the detail of the country throrgh which they were travelling, and they were at a loss to determine where they were. On one of the roads they came to a country store on which they discovered by the moonlight a notice posted, which they tore off and took with them to the woods. On lighting a piece of candle, they discovered it to be a notice to the creditors of the late General Garnett, who was killed in Western Virginia, to present their claims at Bowling Green, in Carolina county. This saved them the risk of making personal inquiries as to where they were, which they had determined to do the next morning.

On that night they met a negro in the woods, but they passed by each other without salutation. They were assisted, too, by an inspection of a guideboard, and at this point a negro suddenly came upon them unawares, but in a seeming fright he ran away. Fearing that he might give the alarm, they ran for a long distance, that they might be beyond the danger of pursuit.

On Wednesday morning, about two o'clock, they reached the Rappahannock, where they were fortunate in finding a small boat. Mr. Murphy took off his shoes in passing through a small village near the river, that he might avoid making any noise, and in getting into the boat he accidentally left his shoes on the bank. This was the occasion of much suffering subsequently, as he had to perform the remainder [illegible] journey in bare feet, which were terribly blistered and swollen. Having crossed the Rappahannock they started for the Potomac. They had travelled but a short distance when they found themselves upon the margin a deep swamp through which they were compelled to wade with mud knee deep for [illegible] a mile. They continued on their course until they came within sight of the Potomac. They encountered a party of negroes unexpectedly, and were compelled to speak or be the subject of suspicion. They inquired for a boat to carry them across the river, announcing themselves to be Confederate officers.

THE REBEL LOSS IN THE LEWINSVILLE AFFAIR.

It has been ascertained that the enemy's loss in the affair at Lewinsville, the day before yesterday, is thfrty killed and between sixty and seventy wounded. A resident near the same place says that after Captain Mott arrived, one of the shells from his thirty-two-pounder howitzer dismounted one of the rebel guns and put nine men *hors du combat*.

ASSAULT ON A UNION OFFICER BY A SECESSIONIST.

About half-past eleven to-night, a man named Galt was arrested, for having struck a Union officer over the head because the latter denounced Galt for having proclaimed, in the street and elsewhere, for Jeff. Davis. Galt was accompanied by another fellow, who also declared his secession sympathies. The companion of Galt was secreted in Brown's Hotel, and up to midnight had not been arrested, the police not daring or caring to make a search for him. This is the first demonstration of the kind that has happened, and will probably be the last. The officer assaulted, fortunntely, was not seriously injured.

THE ARMY.

Lieut. George H. Butler, of the regular army, has been detached from Gen. Butler's staff, and detailed as Aid-de-Camp to General Lander's staff.

THE COTTON EXCITEMENT ABATING IN ENGLAND.

Private letters in this city from England and the Continent show that the fever created in England, growing out of a fear that cotton would become scarce, in consequence of the blockade of our Southern ports, is subsiding, and that a decided reaction is taking place. A large amount of cotton, procured before the blockade by the manufacturers of New England, that cannot now be used in consequence of the hard times, has been offered to England.

THE PAYMENT OF VOLUNTEERS.

The following order has been addressed to Paymaster General Larned by the War Department:—

You will arrange for the payment of volunteers as directed by the provisions of the act of Congress relating thereto, dated July 24, and as amended August 6, 1861, viz:—When organized and accepted by the Governors of the several States, without regard to the date of mustering into the service of the United States, provided payment has not been made by the respective States, for which the government will eventually be liable. Where volunteer regiments have been accepted by the War Department, upon what is termed independent acceptances, you will allow pay from the date of organization of each company with the minimum number of men, satisfactory evidence in each case to be furnished your department before payment is made. SIMON CAMERON, Secretary of War.

THE MAIL SERVICE IN MISSOURI.

A despatch to the Post Office Department from St. Louis says that no mails have yet passed over the Hannibal and St. Joseph Railroad, and that the prospect of renewal of the service on that route is bad.

SERENADE TO MR. FOSTER, OF NORTH CAROLINA.

Hon. Charles Henry Foster, of North Carolina, who it is understood returns in a day or two to that State to participate actively in the war for the Union, was to-night complimented with a serenade to which he appropriately responded.

CASSIUS M. CLAY'S WASHINGTON GUARD CELEBRATION.

Cassius M. Clay's Washington Guards, who rendered such efficient service in the defence of the capital in the dark days in April, held a meeting to-night, at their headquarters, and unanimously resolved to celebrate the 17th of September, the anniversary of the adoption of the Constitution of the United States, and the delivery of Washington's Farewell Address. Professor Amasa McCoy, of the Clay Guards, was invited to deliver the oration. Professor McCoy accepted the invitation, and announced that the theme of his lecture would be—"Mr. Russell and the London *Times* on the rebellion and the war against the national constitution." The President of the United States, General McClellan, Mr. Holt, the Secretary of State, and two or three hundred of the most distinguished civil and military characters now at the national capital, are to be specially invited to attend.

NEW MEXICO APPOINTMENTS.

Albert W. Archibald, of Fort Union, New Mexico, was to-day appointed United States Marshal for that Territory.

Captain J. W. Holmes, the new appointed Secretary, left Washington to-day for New Mexico.

IMPORTANT ORDER FROM GENERAL M'CLELLAN.

General McClellan has issued the following order:—

First—The attention of brigades and regimental commissaries of subsistence, and of officers acting as such, are directed to paragraphs 20, 21 and 22 of Subsistence Regulations, or paragraphs 1,073, 1,074 and 1,075 of the Army Regulations of 1857. Subsistance officers must make issues to the hospital, and keep the accounts of hospital funds in strict conformity with the requirements of the regulations cited.

Second—All changes of the station of medical officers to be promptly reported to the Medical Director at these headquarters, and the authority given by which the change was made.

Third—Leaves of absence to medical officers are prohibited unless granted at these headquarters.

Fourth—Patients will not be sent from the regimental to the general hospitals without the authority of the Medical Director. Applications for this authority must be made in writing, the names and diseases of the patients, and be handed into the office of the Medical Director between the hours of nine and ten A. M.

Fifth—When a soldier is sent to the general hospital his company commander shall certify and send with him his descriptive list and account of pay and clothing.

Sixth—Male nurses and cooks for the general hospitals are to be detailed from the privates of the army, regular and volunteer. The allowance will be one nurse to ten patients and one cook to thirty. Where women are employed the number of men to be called for will not exceed a number sufficient to make up the whole force to the allowance above authorized. Hired nurses and cooks will be forthwith discharged.

Seventh—Men reported at the general hospitals for duty will be sent by the surgeon in charge to the office of the Medical Director at ten o'clock A. M. for the passes necessary to enable them to rejoin their regiments.

Eighth—Medical officers joining this army for duty, with or without troops, will report promptly to the Medical Director in person. If with troops, they will report the number of men, the state of their supplies and ambulance transportation.

Ninth—Ambulances will not be used for any other than the specific purpose for which they are designed, viz.:—The transportation of the sick and wounded, except by the written authority of the brigade commander, the Medical Director of the army, and the Quartermaster in charge of them in the city of Washington. The Provost Marshal is directed to see that the provisions of this order are carried out and will arrest every officer and confine every private or non-commissioned officer who is found violating it. All government ambulances now in possession of regiments or separate corps will be turned in to the chief Quartermaster, with the exception of one two wheeled ambulance to each regiment. One two wheeled transport cart will be allowed to each general hospital for the conveyance of marketing and hospital stores.

Tenth—The practice of bringing communications in person to the officers at their headquarters, with a view to obtain immediate attention to the matter involved, proves a serious hindrance to the prompt transaction of business and must be discontinued. Unless under extraordinary circumstances, all communications for the General commanding are to be transmitted to his headquarters by the ordinary modes; and the person concerned will await replies to be furnished them in the same manner.

Eleventh—Persons having official business at these headquarters will transact the same between the hours of nine A. M. and three P. M.

Twelfth—The arms of the troops must be thoroughly inspected by the company officers at least once a day.

Thirteenth—The reveille will not be beaten until after sunrise, and hot coffee will be issued to the troops immediately after the reveille roll call, as a preventative of the effects of malaria.

Fourteenth—Troops on the march or changing positions will move without music. Drums are not to be beaten, nor trumpet sounded, except for the stated exercise and calls.

Fifteenth—All requisitions for ordnance and ordnance stores and supplies for the troops serving in this army will be transmitted through the appropriate commanders to the chief of ordnance at their headquarters.

Sixteenth—Officers belonging to this army are directed to wear their uniforms at all times at their stations.

Seventeenth—The small fort near Fort Corcoran, thrown up by the Fourth regiment of Michigan Volunteers, will be known as Fort Woodbury.

By command of

Major General McCLELLAN,

S. WILLIAMS, Assistant Adjutant General.
RICHARD B. IRWIN, Aid-de-Camp.

ADDITIONAL PROTECTION TO THE POSTAL REVENUE.

The Postmaster General has directed, as an additional protection to the postal revenue, the exclusive issue of the stamped envelope, containing the new improvement of the dissolving lines. This envelope cannot be manufactured by the ordinary machinery, and is not, therefore, liable to imitation by the insurgents. It is found that but few, if any, of the letters enclosed in this new envelope have occasioned trouble to the Postmasters in deciphering illegible superscriptions or postmarks, (the proper position of both on the envelope being indicated by the lines, so as to prevent their mutual obliteration), thus obviating the most frequent cause of miscarriage. These and other considerations have induced the Postmaster General to assume the expense of this important invention, and to supply the new envelope on the same terms as the old. The department will not probably issue proposals for a new contract for some time.

ALLEGED FRAUDS OF ARMY CONTRACTORS.

The government is about to investigate the alleged frauds committed upon it in the sale of horses furnished by Pennsylvania contractors. The inspector at Perryville, Maryland, within the last ten days has condemed between four and five hundred army wagons, and notified the manufacturers to remove them.

IMPORTANT FROM NORTH CAROLINA.

Arrival of Ships-of-War Off Fort Macon—Rebel Troops Hurrying to Beaufort, &c.

LOUISVILLE, Sept. 13, 1861.

A Newbern (N. C.) special despatch to the Charleston *Mercury* of the 8th says that "a Yankee war vessel appeared off Beaufort last night. When the train left last night it was reported that four vessels were in the Sound and others coming in. Only one, however, is known to be here. A number of detached companies have already left for Beaufort, and General Gatlin, with the Seventh regiment of North Carolina troops, Colonel Campbell, will leave this morning for the same destination. Colonel Barnes' regiment is already at Beaufort. General Gatlin thinks Fort Macon cannot be taken."

WILMINGTON, N. C., Sept. 9, 1861.

Four United States vessels had anchored off Fort Macon at seven o'clock Saturday afternoon. Their object is not known.

THE PRIVATEER SUMTER.

BOSTON, Sept. 13, 1861.

Captain King, of the brig Northman, before reported condemned at Surinam, came passenger in the brig Muscovado, which arrived at Baltimore September 11. He states that the privateer Sumter arrived at Surinam August 11, and was at anchor inside of Fort Amsterdam on the 23d of August.

THE NATIONAL POPULAR LOAN.

Operations in the American Bank Note Establishment.

Rapid Manufacture of Treasury Notes.

FAC SIMILE OF A TREASURY NOTE,

&c., &c., &c.

The American Bank Note Company of this city is now engaged, with nearly the whole machinery of its vast establishment, in the manufacture of United States Treasury notes for the subscribers to the popular loan. As we stated before, the demand upon the energies and productive powers of the company has never been so great, and all the operatives are consequently compelled to work on extra hours of the day and far into the night to keep pace, as far as possible, with the pressure of the government for the new notes.

The thousands of persons who daily pass through Wall street and round about the Merchants' Exchange little know that there is such an extensive establishment, affording employment to many scores of persons, in full operation in the upper stories of the Exchange. The upper story was built expressly for the American Bank Note Company, and extends over the whole length and breadth of the main building. It is constructed of the most solid materials, in the safest and most substantial manner. Every department of the building is burglar and fireproof, and it is impossible to conceive how security and strength could be better attained. The rooms are all wide, lofty and airy, and the machinery adjusted and fitted with mathematical precision. Every department operates in a distinct branch of the establishment, and there is little or no communication between the operatives of one division and those of another.

On the first floor we have the business office and the director's rooms, fitted up with great taste and refinement, and extensively ornamented with engravings, bank note specimens, and artistic designs for bank notes. These are most varied and beautiful, including drawings by Darley, Herrick, Casiler, Edmonds and others. When one of these sketches is chosen for a note, it is reduced by the photograph to the size required, after which it passes into the hands of the engraver, who, by a very delicate and ingenious process, transfers it to the steel plate, where it is fixed by his little sharp pointed tools. When every line of the portrait or drawing has thus been transferred—which can easily be ascertained by means of the powerful magnifying glasses that are used—and the background is put on with the aid of a machine, the plate is subjected to a process called case-hardening, which renders the steel so hard and tough that it will resist any amount of pressure without injury to the engraving. This is necessary, as the engraving in this hardened state is easily transferred from the flat steel plate to a cylindrical roller of soft steel, by the agency of presses of immense power; and when perfectly transferred these rollers are hardened in their turn, so that any number of reproductions of the original engraving is by this means placed at the disposal of the operators, and also enables the company to preserve the plates so that all future impressions might be uniformly like the original. The process is altogether a most intricate but interesting one, and a very inadequate idea can be given of it in this brief sketch.

On the second floor is the art department, so called from the fact that here the various designs and models are prepared. Here may be seen every kind of model and drawing that the skill of the artist could invent or the photographer reduce to miniature proportions. On the third floor are the depositories of paper, of the very finest description, accumulated in immense quantities. The plate vaults, or repositories for printed plates, are also situated on this floor. They are secured by ponderous doors, bolted, barred and locked against the idea of burglarious entrance. Watchmen, tried and skilful, guard the portals, and keep eternal vigils over the wealth of the company. And the burglar's occupation, like Othello's, is forever "gone," so far as this establishment is concerned. In other apartments of this floor are the drying and finishing rooms, hydraulic presses, machines for numbering the notes, drying racks, and the steam engine and boiler which heats the building in cold weather. The drying process is a peculiar feature of this department. The notes all come from the printers wet or damp, and before they can be folded or packed they must be perfectly dry, to avoid the otherwise inevitable blurring and besmearing of the impressions. Sometimes, as at present, there are from forty to fifty thousand sheets to be dried every day in a room where many other operations are in progress, without interference with any branch of the business. To secure this desideratum and to promote celerity in the movements of the establishment, moveable racks are constructed in an inner apartment, into which large numbers of the damp sheets are inserted. Beneath the racks are pipes, heated by steam to a given temperature, and a cold current of air, which is allowed free access to these racks, passing over the steam pipes, becomes heated, and is thus converted into a valuable agent for the drying of the bank notes. The notes, thus dried, are put into the hands of the folders and finishers, after passing through hydraulic presses to make them flat and smooth. There are large iron safes in which to keep the finished notes, and the walls surrounding them are as sound and solid as those of a fortress.

The fourth story, extending around the entire square, is occupied by the actual working department, and three-fourths of it by the printing division alone. The several engraving departments, such as the pictorial, lettering and transferring (properly the engraving department), occupy the north front of the Exchange, as here there is a more regular and unchanging light. The room from the floor to the ceiling is upwards of fifteen feet high, and the ventilation as perfect as it can possibly be.

There are sixty presses engaged in printing the United

[CONTINUED ON EIGHTH PAGE.]

THE DAILY DELTA

PUBLISHED BY THE NEW ORLEANS DELTA NEWSPAPER COMPANY.

TERMS--PER ANNUM.

DAILY DELTA, (invariably in advance)......$10
WEEKLY DELTA, do. do. 3
SUNDAY DELTA, do. do. 2

For any time less than one year the DAILY DELTA will be delivered to City Subscribers at 20 cents a week.

ADVERTISING RATES

Advertisements $1 a Square for the first insertion. Every subsequent insertion 50 cents.
Advertisements on the Second Page $1 per measured Square each insertion.
Advertisements at intervals $1 a Square each insertion.
Marriage and Funeral Notices $1 each insertion.
A Liberal Discount made to regular Advertisers.

The SEMI-WEEKLY DELTA is issued every Tuesday and Friday morning, at $5 per annum.

SATURDAY MORNING, SEPTEMBER 21, 1861

THE SUNDAY DELTA.

The Delta of to morrow will contain editorials on topics of interest; original contributions, prose and poetical; a miscellany of selected reading matter; the latest news, foreign and domestic; local intelligence and gossip, &c., &c.; the whole forming a collection of varied, amusing and instructive reading matter.

THE SEMI-WEEKLY DELTA.

This paper, which is published every Tuesday and Friday mornings, and contains the latest news up to hour of publication, can be had, in wrappers, at the office, No. 94 Camp street, and at all the newspaper depots in the city. Terms of subscription, five dollars per annum.

THE WEEKLY DELTA.

The Weekly Delta contains leading editorials; the latest news, foreign and domestic, by mail and telegraph; a miscellany of selections, original poetry and communications, of the Daily Delta; and as a record of passing events is unsurpassed by any similar publication.

The Weekly, issued every Saturday, and the Sunday Delta every Sunday morning, can be had, folded in wrappers for mailing, at the office counter, No. 94 Camp street, and at all the newspaper depots and agencies in the city.

MARTIAL LAW.

War, in any of its aspects, is a thing so remote from the experience of the great mass of our people that it is not surprising that many of them are mentally disturbed and confused when compelled to face its actual exigencies, vicissitudes and dangers. Nor is it wonderful that some of them should be profoundly impressed with the idea that the present war is extraordinary, exceptional, and anomalous in its character. Such persons are in the habit of characterizing it as an unnatural war, as one replete with unusual horrors, charged to the point of explosion with elements of social disturbance and convulsion. In thus thinking and speaking, they confound national war with civil war, and virtually endorse the theory of the Lincoln Administration which up to this moment has insisted on treating the Southern Confederacy as a rebellious and insurrectionary combination, and not a nationality engaged in defending its independence. Nothing like this fatal concession is called for by the emergency. Those who are capable of calmly surveying the true political and military position of the Confederacy, must perceive clearly enough that there is no rebellion, no insurrection, none of the circumstances and conditions of civil war within its limits. The only apparent exceptions to this general observation exist in places which are occupied by armies of the enemy. They are cases growing out of the existence of the war, and do not by any means qualify its original and essential character.

No people ever exhibited more spirit of unanimity, more spirit of patriotic co-operation, as a nation, more confidence in one another and in their common Government, than the people of the Southern States composing the Confederacy, exhibit at the present hour. There is no need for them to resort to extraordinary expedients for preventing domestic dissensions and troubles, and compelling the public, with the iron hand of military power, to put on the guise of a harmony of feeling and purpose which does not exist. Such things they can afford to leave to their frenzied and desperate enemies at the North. It has been the pride of the South that her people were as composed as determined in all situations of the war which was forced upon them, while their enemies were wildly oscillating between bravado and panic, between ferocity towards Southerners and a cowardly dread, expressed in the worst forms of intolerance and oppression, of defection and revolution in their own midst. Let this still be the pride of the South. Let it still be her glory to stand in shining contrast with the moral, social and political characteristics of the North.

We regret to see martial law suggested for New Orleans at this time by persons who can hardly have acquainted themselves with the nature of that law and the conditions which justify its enforcement. They have evidently lost their composure, and are haunted by visions of tremendous Northern armadas sweeping down the Southern coast, and, after pulverizing Pensacola, Mobile, and other minor places, consummating their mission by a swoop upon New Orleans. A grand army under Fremont, assisted by a countless fleet of gunboats, moving down the Mississippi valley against New Orleans, is also playing the mischief with their morbid imaginations, and intensifies the picture they draw of the dangerous, almost desperate situation of the city. According to these men, there is but one refuge from the approaching doom. They have heard of martial law; they have no precise notion of what it means; but the very mystery of the institution is a ground of their belief that it possesses incalculable virtues. Therefore they are for seeking safety in martial law.

Now, martial law may be a very useful thing in its place, but is unquestionably a very foolish, and possibly very pernicious thing out of its place. But let us see what it is. Martial law must not be confounded with military law. Military law consists of the code enacted by the legislative authority of a country for the government of its army and navy, together with such regulations as may be prescribed by competent military authority respecting discipline. Military law does not set aside municipal law. Emanating originally from the same authority, they are co-ordinate, not antagonistic. Martial law is the abrogation of all law in the usual sense of the word, and, as Blackstone observes, is really no law at all. It is simply the assumption of absolute power by one or more persons exercising military authority. The Confederate Constitution, like that of the United States, makes no mention of martial law, though it impliedly sanctions its virtual existence in certain exigencies, by providing that Congress may suspend the writ of *habeas corpus* when, in cases of rebellion or invasion, the public safety may require the suspension. But there would seem to be no implied sanction whatever for the suspension of that writ, which is the most essential feature of martial law, by any single military commander, by the Governor of a State, or the President of the Confederate States. It must follow, then, that nothing but the argument of of *ex necessitate rei* can justify the establishment of martial law. There must be rebellion or invasion, and its establishment must appear to be the only condition of the public safety. Do the circumstances of New Orleans furnish an argument based upon such facts? Is there rebellion in New Orleans, is there an invasion almost at her door? There is neither. Rebellion we certainly shall not have. Invasion may or may not come. But, meantime, let us wait for the actual exigency, for the necessity of the case, before we think of abrogating all law and appealing for safety to a military dictatorship. Our civil and military authorities, acting in happy unison, seem quite able to protect us from spies and traitors for the present, and we can see no immediate cause for disturbing this satisfactory state of affairs, but only danger of undue alarm and perhaps panic among the population in seriously urging the expediency of martial law. Since martial law will not create new armies for us, or guns, or forts, and since we have no rebellion or invasion at this moment, why talk about it?

SPECIAL DISPATCHES TO DAILY DELTA.

LATEST FROM RICHMOND.

Col. Washington's Death Confirmed.

Promotion of General Bragg.

The President's Health.

SKIRMISHES ON THE POTOMAC.

RICHMOND, Sept. 19, 1861.

We are still without official reports from Gens. Floyd and Lee in regard to the late important operations of our armies in Western Virginia; but the Examiner has authentic confirmation of the report that Col. John A. Washington, aid to Gen. Lee, was killed while reconnoitering. Col. Washington was a great grand nephew of President Washington, and late owner of the Mount Vernon homestead. He was not a professional military man. His loss is deeply regretted.

Mr. Benjamin is now acting as Secretary of War. Generals Polk and Lee, and Mr. Branch, of North Carolina, are spoken of in connection with the office.

Gen. Bragg has been promoted, by being transferred from the provisional to the regular service, with the rank of General.

Major G. W. Smith, formerly a distinguished officer of the United States Corps of Engineers, has lately arrived here, and, it is thought, will be appointed a Major General.

President Davis was out yesterday, and his health is improving.

Skirmishes are constantly occurring on the Potomac, and almost invariably result in our favor.

SUPPLIES FOR OUR SOLDIERS.—We would caution the friends of our soldiers, who may be engaged in raising supplies for their support and comfort, against the danger of serious loss and waste, by sending such directly to the camps, instead of to some central depot. A great many things have been sent directly to camps which have either not reached their destination or have been thrown away in the movements of the troops. The greatest want of our army is that of transportation. It is found extremely difficult to procure the teams and cattle for the necessary transportation of the army, much less for any surplus supplies that may be sent to our soldiers by their friends. The consequence is that a great many things of value, comfort, and even of necessity, are thrown away. To avoid this it would be wise to establish a depot for our soldiers in Richmond—where all the donations of our citizens might be kept—and from which they could easily be transmitted where immediately required. It would be well for the friends of our volunteers to bear in mind that there are but a dozen wagons allowed to each regiment, to carry their tents, provisions, munitions, &c., and that everything they personally need has to be carried on their backs. It would be better, even, to be stinted in certain comforts than to have to add to their burdens, or to overload the teams, and thus impair the efficiency and celerity of movement of the army. It is a question, too, whether our soldiers are any the better for many things which are sent to them. The sick and convalescent need extra comforts and delicacies; but the healthy soldier is a great deal better adapted to his work when he subsists upon plain and substantial diet, and is provided with coarse, strong and warm clothing.

RHEUMATISM, DIARRHEA AND DYSENTERY.—We invite particular attention to the certificates in our advertising columns attesting the efficacy of the remedies for rheumatism and diarrhea to be obtained at No. 117 St. Ann street, New Orleans.

FOR PASS CHRISTIAN.—The Creole will leave for Pass Christian and other places, at 8 A. M. to-day.

TELEGRAPHIC NEWS.

TELEGRAPHED TO THE NEW ORLEANS DAILY DELTA.

IMPORTANT FROM KENTUCKY.

Occupation of Muldrough's Hill by the Confederates.

Prominent Kentuckians for the South.

MEMPHIS, Sept. 20.—Quartermaster Phillips, who has just arrived here from Muldrough's Hill after stores, reports that that point fell into the hands of the Confederates, without meeting any opposition.

The Confederate force, 4000 strong, he says, are busily occupied in throwing up fortifications to repel attack.

It is reported that Gen. Rousseau is not in Louisville, and also that Guthrie and other prominent Kentuckians, who have heretofore upheld the Lincoln Government, have declared themselves for the South.

[To Mr. Jones, of the Southwestern office, we are indebted for the above.]

FURTHER FROM KENTUCKY.

Arrest of Ex-Gov. Morehead.

Proceedings of the Legislature.

Suppression of the Louisville Courier.

Movements of Gen. Rousseau.

GREEN RIVER, Ky., Sept. 20.—A number of Southerners passed here this afternoon from Louisville, in various conveyances. They report that Ex-Governor Morehead had been arrested and sent to Bastile Lafayette.

The Kentucky Legislature, now in session at Frankfort, calls the Kentuckians and Tennesseans invaders, and that they must be expelled; that the Federalists only came to Kentucky to preserve the tranquility of the State. The Legislature requests the Governor to place Thomas L. Crittenden in command of the State Guards.

Mr. Underwood was unable to suppress his emotions, and spoke against the passage of such infamous resolutions.

These proceedings are taken from yesterday's Louisville Journal.

The Louisville Courier has been suppressed for advocating the Southern cause.

Rousseau, yesterday morning, was crossing Rolling Fork in flats. Not liking the mustering of the Hardin county boys, he suddenly recrossed the six hundred that had got over.

Muldrough's Hill is not occupied. [As the information given in the Memphis report was brought by an official, this statement is likely to be incorrect.]

[The above was kindly furnished us by the officers of the Southwestern telegraph line.]

News from the Confederate Capital.

RICHMOND, Sept. 20.—E. A. Banks, formerly of the Montgomery Confederation, has been appointed Quartermaster at Yorktown.

The body of Col. John A. Washington, aid to Gen. Lee, reached here this afternoon.

Six Hessian prisoners, taken in the mountains of Virginia, and fifteen from Manassas, arrived this afternoon by the Central train.

We have no news of interest from the camps. The reported shelling of Leesburg is bosh.

Ex Secretary Walker is now Brigadier General, and will have for his command Watts's, Judge's and Bullock's Infantry Regiments and Clinton's Cavalry Regiment, all from Alabama, with the Columbus (Ga.) Light Artillery Battalion.

The Richmond Examiner was sold, by the consent of its owners, at public outcry, to-day, for $15,000. The paper was purchased by Jno. M. Daniel, who will continue its publication as heretofore.

Truce-flagged Federal Vessel at Norfolk.

NORFOLK, Sept. 20.—The passengers by the Federal steamer Fanny Cadwallader, which arrived yesterday with a flag of truce, were searched in New York, Philadelphia and Old Point. These passengers report that it was believed in New York that Lincoln and Seward were there.

A letter brought by the steamer from a prisoner at the Rip Raps, to his family, had $20 abstracted from it by the Federals, and had endorsed on it: "$20 taken out and returned to owner."

The War in Western Virginia.

RICHMOND, Sept. 20.—We have received no confirmation of the capture of Gen. Reynolds, and the statement begins to lose credence.

The Enquirer of this morning in reporting intelligence from Western Virginia says that Lee has cleared out an old and long unused road leading to a strong position between Rosencrantz's and Reynolds's force. Reynolds's force can not retreat, for Jackson guards the ford of Cheat river, and can not advance, for Lee's forces are compelled to arrest them. Starvation or surrender is the alternative of Reynolds's forces. It is highly probable that an engagement is over ere this, but it will take some days to know the result.

Various Interesting Items.

The Examiner says that Bragg has been made full General of the Confederate Army, and L. P. Walker Brigadier-General.

Major G. W. Smith, of Kentucky, a resigned major in the Federal corps of engineers, has arrived, and will probably soon enter the Confederate service.

It is understood that the Federals were reinforced at Arlington by 10,000 men on Tuesday.

All communication with the North has been cut off since the 13th.

About 500 Yankee prisoners will be soon sent to New Orleans.

Still Further from Richmond.

RICHMOND, Sept. 20.—The sequestration of Yankee effects has been going on at the rate of nearly half a million the past few days. The general inquiry is: "What's doing in other cities?"

The report of Lee's capturing Reynolds was telegraphed to Governor Letcher, and from sources the Governor regarded reliable. Subsequent intelligence does not sustain the capture.

We are glad to learn that our theatrical friend, Mr. W. H. Crisp, is in the Southern army at Manassas Junction, in command as 1st lieutenant of the Dixie Artillery. He played well his part in many mimic battles, and is now in readiness to act well his part in dread war's reality. His two sons, Harry and Charles, who were in the battle of Manassas, were unhurt, and are now in the advanced columns near Washington. The many friends of Mrs. and Mr. W. H. Crisp and the boys will be pleased to hear of their patriotic devotion to the South. [Huntsville Advocate.

Gen. Grayson, in entering upon his duties in command of the Florida department, has made Tallahassee his headquarters, and appointed his staff as follows: Lieut. John B. Grayson, Aid and Assistant Adjutant General; Assistant Surgeon E. T. Sabal, Medical Director; Lieut. Mayo, Topographical Engineer; Lieut. L. M. Butler, Instructor of Infantry Tactics; Lieut. Wood, Aid-de-Camp, and Lieut. D'Anson, Asst. Quartermaster. In a special order, the General directs that personal property, in such exposed situations as to invite depredations by the enemy, be removed to more secure places.

A FAMILY OF GIANTS.—The Montgomery mail publishes the following:

Eds. Mail—Seeing the boast of the great and tall Georgia soldier who was six feet ten inches high, I ask you in some part of your valuable journal, to which I have been a subscriber for the last six years, to give this a publication:

I have in the Confederate States army five sons. I will now give their ages, height and weight: My eldest son, M. J. Horn, is 28 years old, six feet three inches high, weighs 156 pounds; Josiah J. Horn, 26 years old, six feet seven inches high, weighs 178 pounds; Isaac J. Horn, the third, is six feet seven inches high, weighs 202 pounds, 24 years old; Edward L. Horn is 22 years old, six feet three inches high, weighs 175 pounds; Rowlen W. T. Horn is in his 20th year, is six feet two inches high, weighs 168 pounds.

And I further say, that there are in the Coffee Rangers 25 men who will average six feet five inches high, and will weigh 150 pounds.

Now, if Georgia can beat this, and every family in the Confederacy can or will do likewise, what number will be in the Confederate army?

Yours, &c., H. K. H. HORN.

Arrival from Europe.—The friends of Mr. Meredith Calhoun were agreeably surprised by his arrival here, one day last week, in good health and spirits, after an absence of over twelve months in Paris. He evaded espionage, and run the gauntlet of Northern rebel hunters, by studiously ignoring the English language after his arrival in Canada, and communicating with persons of the English tongue through his French attendant, who speaks English pretty well, and acted as his interpreter.

He brings intelligence of the rapid progress of public opinion in favor of the recognition of the Confederate Government, especially since our victory at Manassas. As he passed through London, he says Mr. Yancey told him he anticipated the breaking of the blockade by England and France between the 15th of October and the 15th of November, at farthest, in which opinion Mr. C., whose opportunities for acquiring information were very favorable, fully concurs. [Huntsville (Ala.) Democrat.

Died in Germany.—The New York papers announce the death of Mrs. Charles Astor Bristed, the excellent and accomplished wife of the well-known "Carl Benson." Mrs. Bristed expired at Baden Baden, Germany, on Monday, August 5, of a complicated heart disease. She was a woman of great personal and mental attractions, which she inherited from both her parents, (the late Henry Brevoort, of New York, and Laura Carson, of South Carolina,) as well as those of a most enchanting sweetness and gayety of disposition. In Baden she was universally loved and respected. The inhabitants and residents attended her funeral with almost regal honors. Members of the diplomatic corps came from a distance to be present at the ceremony, and ladies of the highest aristocracy followed the procession to the grave. She was but 37 years of age.

Another Doubtful Bishop.—Bishop Odenheimer, of New Jersey, has issued a form of prayer for the use of the Protestant Episcopal clergy of his diocese on the day of the national fast, in which there is no intimation of a desire for the success of the nation in its struggle for life. The whole thing is devoted to the personal wants and trials of the members of the army, and can be used by a Secessionist with at least as much satisfaction as by a true loyal Christian. The patriotic clergy of the Episcopal Church will spue it out of their mouths, or add petitions of their own more suitable to the occasion. [New York Express.

Resignation of an Old Pastor.—Rev. Dr. Spring is about to resign his pastoral charge of the old Brick Church, in New York, where he has held position for over fifty-one years. He is quite infirm, and the recent troubles in his church with Dr. Hoge, who was an anti-Union man and went heart and soul for the South, and the recent marriage of the Doctor, gave him as much as he can attend to. So his resignation is probable, though most persons suppose that he would prefer to live and die pastor of his old charge. [New York Correspondence of the Boston Journal.

Harry Macarthy, the Arkansas Comedian, gives one of his rich and entertaining personation concerts at the Academy of Music at 12 o'clock to-day. This will be for the express convenience of ladies and children, who find it impracticable to attend in the evening. This evening, too, at the usual hour, the Academy will be open for the reception of those who are fond of a good thing.

MARRIED:

On the 12th September, at the residence of the bride's father, W. F. O'ROURKE to GEORGIA L. ROUSSEAUX, all of the parish of St. Tammany.

DIED:

On the 15th of August, of dropsy, Mrs. R. F. JONES, in the 67th year of her age, at the residence of her son, in Franklin parish, Louisiana.

"Our Mother will rise with the just."

Cincinnati and St. Louis papers please copy.

CONFEDERATE AND STATE FLAGS made of Silk, complete with Staffs, Spears, &c., always on hand. Also Flags of all kinds made to order and for sale by

MRS. A. E. OBER,
jy14 tf 2p at the Sewing Machine Office, No. 11 Camp street.

FOR CONGRESS.—We are authorized to announce SAM. C. REID, Esq., as a candidate for the Second Congressional District, composed of the First and Fourth Municipal Districts of New Orleans and the parish of Jefferson, to represent said Congressional District in the first regular Congress of the Confederate States, subject to the approval and ratification of the electors thereof, at the election to be held on the first Monday of November next. sep12 2p4t&Su,Wed

UNIVERSITY OF LOUISIANA.

MEDICAL DEPARTMENT.

The Annual Course of Lectures in this Department will commence on MONDAY, November 11, 1861, and will terminate in the ensuing March.

JAMES JONES, M. D., Professor of Practice of Medicine.
J. L. RIDDELL, M. D., Professor of Chemistry.
WARREN STONE, M. D., Professor of Surgery.
A. H. CENAS, M. D., Professor of Obstetrics.
GUSTAVUS A. NOTT, M. D., Professor of Materia Medica.
T. G. RICHARDSON, M. D., Professor of Anatomy.
THOMAS HUNT, M. D., Professor of Physiology and Pathology.
S. E. CHAILLE, M. D., } Demonstrators of Anatomy.
W. C. NICHOLS, M. D., }

The Rooms for Dissecting will be open on the second Monday in October.

The Faculty are Visiting Physicians and Surgeons of the Charity Hospital.

The Students accompany the Professors in their visits, and, free of expense, enjoy extraordinary practical advantages.

Preliminary to the Course, Lectures will be delivered daily in the Amphitheater of the Hospital, from the 7th of October, on Clinical Medicine and Surgery, and other subjects, without any charge to students.

THOMAS HUNT, M. D., Dean.

The Administration of the Charity Hospital elect annually, in April, fourteen Resident Students, who are maintained by the institution. jy13 d&Wtd

NEW ORLEANS AND MOBILE MAIL LINE.

NOTICE.—No Mobile freight will be received by the Pontchartrain Railroad for this line until further notice, the line having ceased running to Mobile for the present.

R. GEDDES, Agent.
NEW ORLEANS, September 20, 1861. sep20 2pe&m

UNIFORMS OF ALL KINDS made to order at low prices. Also, sewing of all kinds done on the Grover & Baker Sewing Machines. Apply to MRS. A. E. OBER, at the Southern Sewing Machine Depot, No. 11 Camp street. jy14 tf 2p

Launch at Algiers.

The Confederate States Steam Gunboat will be launched from the Ship Yard of Messrs. John Hughes & Co., THIS AFTERNOON, at 3 o'clock.

The contract for building this boat was signed only sixty days ago. sep20 1t*

Notice.

At a meeting of the Board of Directors of the Southern Oil Company, held Friday, the 20th inst., the President reported interruption of water communication between this city and Mobile, thereby requiring the various products of the factory transported by rail, incurring heavy expense, which the former prices would not warrant sales, the following resolutions were adopted:

Resolved, Owing to the interruption in the navigation of Mississippi Sound, the manufactured products of this Company must now be transported by rail, the following prices will be charged:

No. 1 Refined and Car Box Oil..............65c. per gallon.
Nos. 2 and 3 refined Tanners' and Gas Oils 4?c. per gallon.
Wheel Grease..............................6c. per lb.

Resolved, The old prices remain the same for all deliveries and sales from the factory at Mobile.

SIMEON TOBY, JR., President.
GEO. C. BOGERT, Secretary. sep21 2p1w

To the Public.

The undersigned having received a military education, and as an attack upon New Orleans is expected, I prefer to raise a company to serve as artillery—believing this to be the most effective arm of our service, and as the time approaches, we must have drilled men. Delay breeds danger, and experience is necessary to perfect the soldier. In order that the expense may be as small as possible, I propose a uniform, of gray fatigue cap, with a red band around the base or outer border; a gray jacket, with red facings; together with black pants, will complete the outfit. Each member is expected to furnish said equipment. Those who are desirous to join said company will leave their names at Messrs. Belden & Eames', corner of Magazine and Gravier streets. The officers of this company will be composed of men who have received a military education. sep21 2t* HENRY F. WADE, JR.

Headquarters Second Brigade

FIRST DIVISION LOUISIANA VOLUNTEER STATE TROOPS.—NEW ORLEANS, Sept. 20, 1861.

General Order No. 7.

1. In obedience to General Order No. 33 from Division Headquarters, the Volunteer Companies attached to this Brigade are hereby ordered to parade for review and inspection on WEDNESDAY, the 25th inst., at 4 o'clock P. M., at the Place d'Armes.

2. The Major General commanding the Division, wishing to see under arms the full force of the Volunteer Corps of this Brigade, to examine and inspect the condition and quality of their arms and equipments, it is expected that the Commanders will bring out their Companies with full ranks, and at the same time be prepared to furnish the Inspector of Division with a detailed return of the condition and efficiency for active service of the troops under their commands.

3. The Commanders of Companies are charged with the execution of this order. By order, DANIEL EDWARDS, Col. Comd'g.

G. BREDOW, JR., Aid-de-Camp. sep21

Notice.

The Southern Pacific Railroad having been sold, and a new Company having been formed, ALL holders of PAID-FOR old Stock, residing within the Confederate States, who desire to become connected with the new Company, can, by applying to the undersigned, at No 84 COMMON STREET, learn the terms upon which RECOGNIZED old Stock will be admitted to the books of the new Company.

The terms proposed will commend themselves to all just-minded persons. The cheerful co-operation of every honest Stockholder of the old Company, friendly to our Government is earnestly desired. The Board indulges in no unbecoming threats. In arranging with unprotected Stockholders, due regard will be had to the deranged state of the finances of the country.

J. S. HOLMAN, Esq., President of the new Company, is in the city, and will remain several days. He will be pleased to see the friends of the enterprise at the office. He desires to confer with them—to learn their views, and to present to them the views of the Board of Directors, as to the future policy of the Company.

H. S. FULKERSON, Agent.
New Orleans, Sept. 20, 1861. sep21 1t2p"u&1tW*

Notice.

Persons having GUNS to sell or donate, can make disposition of the same by calling at No. 15 CAMP STREET, up stairs.

During my temporary absence, ROBERT PITKIN will take charge of the Confederate Agency in this city.

sep19 tf BALLARD S. DUNN, Agent C. S.

Washington Artillery.

HEADQUARTERS FIFTH COMPANY, Battalion Washington Artillery, New Orleans, Sept. 19, 1861.

Messrs. U. D. TERREBONNE and WM. R. NORCOM are empowered to ask and receive subscriptions from the friends of this Battalion for the purpose of providing that portion now in Virginia with heavy serviceable Tents. Contributions to the same, also, of warm Under Garments, Socks, Shoes, Blankets, &c., will be cheerfully accepted, if left at No. 40 Camp street, and will be forwarded to Headquarters without delay.

sep20 2p3t W. IRVING HODGSON, Captain.

Notice

To Masters of Vessels, Importers and Others

CUSTOM-HOUSE, NEW ORLEANS, COLLECTOR'S OFFICE, Sept. 20, 1861.

Notice is hereby given, for the information of Masters of Vessels and others interested, that the Hon. Secretary of the Treasury has issued to me, under date of 22d August, 1861 Treasury regulations, authorizing vessels from foreign countries, in view of the inefficiency of the blockade, to enter any harbor on the coast of the Confederate States, and to discharge their cargoes thereat, without regard to the same being an established port of entry, on the master or owner of said vessel reporting to the Collector of the nearest collection district, and conforming to the requirements of the revenue laws under his supervision.

sep20 1w2p F. H. HATCH, Collector.

Citizens' Bank.

CITIZENS' BANK OF LOUISIANA, NEW ORLEANS, Sept. 16, 1861.

At a called meeting of the Board of Directors of this Bank, held this day at 9 o'clock A. M., the President laid before the Board a proclamation of the Governor of this State, dated this day, recommending the banks of New Orleans to suspend specie payments, with the object and under regulations therein set forth. Said proclamation was read; whereupon it was unanimously

Resolved, That the Citizens Bank of Louisiana hereby accedes to the recommendation of the Governor to suspend specie payment forthwith on all its liabilities, and that the four regulations proposed by his Excellency in his proclamation of this day for the government of the several banks during the suspension, be and they are hereby adopted, as follows to-wit:

1st. The circulation of the chartered banks—that is, the Canal, Citizens', Bank of Louisiana, and the Louisiana State Bank—shall not exceed the amount of coin held by them respectively, and the circulation of the Free Banks shall be restricted to the amount of bonds at present deposited with the Auditor of the State, and in accordance with existing laws.

2d. The suspension of specie payments will not interfere with the weekly and monthly returns to the Board of Currency, nor with the fundamental rules governing the Banks, nor in opposition to the recommendation herein made.

3d. The Banks will receive on deposit and in payment of debts due them, the notes of the Confederate States of America, and pay them out at their counters.

4th. The usual weekly statements must be made through the Board of Currency, and all balances paid in Confederate notes or coin. By order: E. ROUSSEAU,
sep16 2p Cashier.

CITIZENS' BANK OF LOUISIANA, NEW ORLEANS, September 16.

Parties having paper on collection in this Bank, are hereby notified and requested, unless they consent to receive Treasury notes of the Confederate States, or local bank notes, in payment of said paper, to withdraw the same; and no paper shall hereafter be received on collection where the owners require other than Treasury notes or local bank notes in payment of same. By order.

sep16 2p E. ROUSSEAU, Cashier.

Union Bank.

UNION BANK OF LOUISIANA, NEW ORLEANS, Sept. 17, 1861.

Parties having notes in collection are notified to withdraw the same, unless they consent and authorize the Bank to receive Confederate or local Notes in payment of their collections, and for the future no paper will be received in collection except on this condition. sep17 2p6t GEO. A. FRERET, Cashier.

Headquarters First Brigade

FIRST DIVISION LOUISIANA VOLUNTEER TROOPS. NEW ORLEANS, September 17, 1861.

General Order No. 32.

1. In obedience to General Orders No. 33 from Division Headquarters, the Volunteer Companies of this Brigade will parade for inspection and review at Lafayette Square on MONDAY, 23d September at 4 o'clock P. M.

2. The Major General commanding the Division being desirous of seeing under arms the full force of this Brigade, inspect its condition and know its wants, it is hoped and expected that Commanders of Companies will endeavor to parade with full ranks, and be prepared to furnish the Inspector with a statement of the condition and wants of their respective companies.

3. The Commanders of Companies attached to this Brigade are charged with the execution of this order.

By order of L. A. CHARBONNET, Colonel Comd'g.
JOHN F. CALDWELL, Major and Brigade Inspector. sep13

Headquarters First Division,

LOUISIANA VOLUNTEER TROOPS. NEW ORLEANS, Sept. 16, 1861.

General Orders No. 33.

1. The Major General commanding wishing to see under arms the full force of the daily increasing volunteer corps of his Division, and at the same time examine and inspect the condition and quality of their arms, equipments, &c., orders that the several Brigades and unattached corps of the Division will prepare to parade for review and inspection on the days and at the hours herein fixed, and at such places as may be hereafter designated.

2. The Louisiana Legion Brigade, Col. Numa Augustin commanding, in the absence (on leave) of Brig. Gen. James Trudeau, will parade on SATURDAY, the 21st of September, at 4 o'clock P. M., at such a place, in the vicinity of the city convenient and suitable for the purpose, as the Colonel commanding may select.

3. The 1st Brigade, Col. L. A. Charbonnet commanding, in the absence (on detached duty) of Brig. Gen. E. L. Tracy, will parade on MONDAY, the 23d of September, at 4 o'clock P. M., at a convenient and proper place within the limits of the Brigade, to be selected by the Colonel commanding.

4. The 2d Brigade, Col. D. Edwards commanding, in the absence (on detached duty) of Brig. Gen. Charles A. Labuzan, will parade on WEDNESDAY, the 25th of September, at 4 o'clock P. M., at such proper and convenient place in the Brigade as the Colonel commanding may select.

5. All other organized corps, whose officers have been commissioned as belonging to the 1st Division, but which corps are not attached to any particular Brigade, will parade under their proper officers on Lafayette Square, First District, on FRIDAY, 27th September, at 4 o'clock P. M.

6. The Regiment of Native Guards, Col. Felix Labatut commanding, will parade on the Place d'Armes, Second District, on SUNDAY, the 29th September, at 4 o'clock P. M.

7. The officers in command of the above named corps are charged with the execution of this order in their respective commands.

8. The Major General relies with confidence on the zeal and activity of the officers in bringing out on this occasion their several commands with full ranks, and hopes that they will likewise be prepared to furnish the Inspector of the Division with a complete and detailed return of the condition and efficiency for active service of the troops under their commands.

By order of JOHN L. LEWIS, Maj. Gen. Comd'g.
L. E. FORSTALL, Inspector 1st Division L. V. T. sep17 tf

Military Goods.

MUSKET CAPS;
ALSO,
CAPS FOR COLT'S REVOLVERS.
Cartridges.
GOLD AND WORSTED TRIMMINGS.
SWORDS, WITH FINE BLADES,
BELTS AND SASHES
FINE BLUE, SKY-BLUE, GRAY and RED BROADCLOTH.
Buttons for Military Uniforms,
GOLD LACES, and SILK OIL-CLOTH. For sale at
H. FRANKO'S,
Next to the corner of Poydras and Carondelet sts.
sep10 2dp Fri,Sun,Wed tf

To Buyers.

People from this and other States visiting this city would do well to give the undersigned a call, as they have a

Very Large and Well Assorted Stock
OF
FANCY AND STAPLE DRY GOODS,
Which will be disposed of
AT VERY REASONABLE PRICES
For Cash.
U. LAROUSSINI & CO.,
sep3 1m 137 Canal street.

Now Ready,

A COMPLETE MAP OF THE SEAT OF WAR,
Comprising
All of the Confederate States,
Together with
MISSOURI, KENTUCKY, MARYLAND AND DISTRICT OF COLUMBIA.
Price..................................75 cents.
Published and for sale, wholesale and retail, at
THE EXCHANGE BOOK-STORE,
E. EZEKIEL,
J. C. Morgan's Old Stand.
A liberal discount to the trade. je28

New Military Goods.

BLUE CLOTH,
GRAY JEANS,
SWORDS,
GOLD BRAID,
EAGLE BUTTONS, &c.,
FLANNEL SHIRTS.
To be had at reasonable prices, at
HOFFMAN & MARKS'S,
aug18 2ptf 63 Chartres street.

Proceedings

OF THE
LOUISIANA STATE CONVENTION,
IN ENGLISH AND FRENCH,

Together with the ORDINANCES passed by said Convention, (in both languages) and the CONSTITUTION OF THE STATE as amended.

For sale by

BLOOMFIELD & STEEL,	PETER O'DONNELL,
T. L. WHITE,	HERBERT & ESCOUSSE,
GEO. ELLIS,	W. F. GOLDTHWAITE,
P. HAWES & CO.,	E. EZEKIEL,

T. FITZWILLIAM.

Orders from the country filled at a liberal discount. may28 tf

Mrs. C. E. Da Ponte

Respectfully announces that she is prepared to give lessons at the residences of her pupils, or at her own Studio.

DRAWING AND PAINTING,
IN OIL OR WATER COLORS,
HEADS, LANDSCAPES AND FLOWERS.
ALSO,
GRECIAN PAINTING, WAX AND PAPER FLOWERS,
197 Camp street,
Between Julia and St. Joseph streets.
ja13 2ptf

The Throat, Lungs and Heart.

A CARD.

Dr. ROBERT HUNTER desires to make known to all persons suffering from any affections of the Throat, Lungs or Heart, to the treatment of which his practice is exclusively confined, that his Office, No. 156 Canal street, is still open, under the personal attendance of Dr. A. FOLLIN, a practitioner of enlarged experience, who is conversant with his views and practice.

Persons in the country can consult him by letter, if unable to attend personally.

Office hours, 9 A. M. to 3 P. M.

Consultations in English, French and Spanish. sep8 2wd&W2p

Fassmann's Iron Tie.

The subscribers are receiving weekly supplies of IRON from Tennessee, which they will sell at a small advance for CASH only.

H. FASSMAN & CO.
41 Carondelet street.
R. J. LATTING & CO.,
aug21 2ptf 15 Union street.

Military.

HEADQUARTERS FIRST BRIGADE, FIRST DIVISION L. M., New Orleans, August 14, 1861.

The Headquarters of this Brigade has been removed from Exchange Alley to No. 40 PERDIDO STREET.

By order. L. A. CHARBONNET,
Colonel Commanding.
JOHN F. CALDWELL, Major and Brigade Inspector.
aug14 2ptf

Public Debt.

Coupons upon the Bonds for the Confederate Loan, issued to citizens and corporations of the States of Louisiana and Mississippi, for interest payable 1st September ensuing, will be paid on presentment at the office of the Assistant Treasurer, New Orleans, La.

A. J. GUIROT,
au30 3taw3w Assistant Treasurer, C. S. A.

Notice.

Contributions for the Sick and Wounded Soldiers of our Army are to be left at WILLIAM H. SMITH'S Store, No. 58 Gravier street.

By order of the Committee.

W. A. ELMORE, President.
D. I. RICARDO, Secretary. sep1 2ptf

Carpet Warehouse—19 Chartres st.

We have a large assortment of Carpetings, such as Wilton, Medalion, Velvet, Brussels, Tapestry, Three Plys, Ingrains, Dutch, Venetians, &c. Also, Floor Oil Cloth, of all widths and qualities; White, Colored and Cocoa Mattings; Window Shades, Table Covers Rugs and Mats, Drugget and Linen Crumb Cloths, &c., &c., which we offer for cash at moderate prices.

sep15 1w2p A. BROUSSEAU & CO.

The Philadelphia Inquirer.

ESTABLISHED 1829 | PHILADELPHIA, SATURDAY, SEPTEMBER 21, 1861. | PRICE TWO CENTS.

THE REBELLION.

IGHLY IMPORTANT FROM MISSOURI.

LATEST FROM LEXINGTON.

The Battle Continued on Tuesday and Wednesday.

Heroic Defence by Colonel Mulligan and his Brave Soldiers.

REINFORCEMENTS CLOSE AT HAND!

Ben McCulloch Advancing on Jefferson City!

PREPARATIONS TO REPEL HIM.

A Reconnoissance of Hardee's Position.

SEVERAL SKIRMISHES WITH THE REBELS.

LATEST FROM KENTUCKY.

Governor Magoffin Vetoes the Bill inviting Gen. Anderson to take Command of the Troops.

The Bill Passed Over the Veto!

A REGIMENT FROM THE HAWAIIAN ISLAND.

Sickness in the Rebel Camp.

THE BERDAN SHARP-SHOOTERS.

President Lincoln a Good Shot.

The Latest News from General Banks' Column.

NARROW ESCAPE OF A SCOUTING PARTY.

Rebel Encampment Shelled!

Two Rebel Defeats in Hardy County, Virginia.

THE CAPTURE OF CORN, GUNS, UNIFORMS, ETC.

THE LATEST FROM WASHINGTON.

Special Despatches to the Inquirer.

WASHINGTON, Sept. 20.

The Prisoner from Munson's Hill.

The escaped soldier from Munson's Hill, who came into our pickets at Bailey's Cross Roads, yesterday morning, is still closely incarcerated at the Thirteenth Street Jail. Positive orders have been issued by Gen. PORTER that no one be allowed to see him until his statement has been handed into the Government. I doubt, however, whether he is possessed of much information relative to the condition of the enemy, other than that telegraphed to THE INQUIRER last evening. A gentleman who had a short conversation with him at Bailey's Cross Roads, gave me the principal points of his narrative, which, with much that I omitted, was but a recapitulation of the story of the prisoner from Fairfax Station. A close watch is kept over all the prisoners who thus desert the Rebel army, and they are always incarcerated until the Government has had an opportunity of ascertaining the real motive prompting such escape.

Washington not to be Attacked.

One strong point of his story, you will remember, is his testimony relative to the long expected attack upon Washington. This idea, the prisoner states, has been entirely abandoned, not only by the officers of the Rebel army, but also with the men. The chain of strong forts which has been thrown around Washington since the Bull Run conflict, has entirely dissipated any hope that the enemy has heretofore possessed of effecting an entrance into the Federal City, and now it would appear from the fact that a large force of men have been marched into Western Virginia, that they seek to make that portion of the country the field of their immediate operations. The narrative, however, must be taken with every grain of allowance, as it is not out of reason to presume that the prisoner *may* be a traitor of the blackest dye, and is endeavoring to relax our vigilance on the other side of the Potomac, by the circulation of such a story as the one we have just quoted.

Why Isn't There a Fight?

This is the daily interrogatory of hundreds of visitors to the Federal city, who have journeyed hither under the impression that a battle is at hand, and who are unwilling to leave until that belief is verified by an actual conflict. In the meantime, the board bills of these individuals are running up at a fearful rate, and the fact is evident, to not a few, that unless the armies of the two sections soon come together, they will be obliged to "vamoose the ranch" without gratifying their blood thirsty propensities. Such men talk of "the killed and wounded" with as much sang froid as they would of reed bird shooting, and say in an off-hand way, backed by a large oath, that a victory would be cheap at the loss of ten thousand men!

The sight of one-tenth of that number of men slain upon the battle field would sicken them for the remainder of their lives, and render the word "gunpowder" a contraband upon their lips. Neither ten thousand nor one thousand men are to be sacrificed by the Government to pander to the morbid appetites of such a clan, nor will the life of a single man be endangered, until an absolute necessity exists for it. Even though the glove has been thrown down to us from Munson's Hill; though the property of good Union men has been devastated by the traitor's torch, yet we are content to bide our time, and when that momentous epoch arrives to grasp and wear that glove as becomes a strong and mighty nation.

A Little Courtesy, Gentlemen!

The good spirits help the man who is obliged to ask even the slightest courtesy from some of our new-fledged military officers who have lately fallen into such good fortune as to be the possessors of a little brief authority. The impudent and silly replies of these soldier-clad civilians operates upon a man something in the manner of a trepanning of the brain is represented to act upon one's constitution. The style in which some of these upstarts flounder about in a little pool of glory of their own creation, is too ridiculous to laugh at. Men who are known, root and branch, at their own homes, to be gentlemen in every sense of that term, are treated with the greatest indignity where these fellows hold office, and youth and gray hairs meet with a similar reception.

Men who are acquainted with military life, who have been tutored in military academies, and have seen service upon the battle-field, are almost always distinguished for their easy and affable style, used as they are, to command those who are around them; but in the case of some of those who wear the shoulder-bands and buttons for the first time, they have put far from them even the common courtesies of life, and reduce themselves to the level of cowards and tyrants. Such conduct also has its proper effect upon the soldiers of their command, and it is no wonder that insubordination and mutiny is often the result.

The Berdan Sharp-Shooters—The President a Good Shot.

The BERDAN sharp-shooters gave a highly satisfactory evidence of their skill this afternoon at the encampment, having previously been reviewed by the President Among the many spectators were Secretaries SEWARD, CAMERON and SMITH, Assistant Secretary SCOTT, the Prince DE JOINVILLE and his son and nephew, Generals MCDOWELL, MANSFIELD and other military officers. Gen. MCCLELLAN and his staff and body guard were also on the ground during the firing, which was at a distance of five hundred yards. Two hundred and sixty shots were fired, and the target was completely riddled. The President tried his hand and made a most excellent shot.

Rebel Forces in Virginia.

You may rely upon it, that the boasts of the Rebels, that they have two hundred and fifty or three hundred thousand men in Virginia, so circumstanced as to be able to aid in attacking Washington are fabulous. Mr. KENNEDY, Census Superintendent, corroborates the truthfulness of my statement, made a few days since. He has recently visited Virginia, and states that they have not a force exceeding one hundred thousand men.

Unconditional Union Association.

Meetings called by the above title, are held in Alexandria weekly. They are largely attended by ladies and gentlemen of the highest positions. Soul-stirring speeches and music always delight the audience.

Work on the Public Buildings Resumed.

The work upon the new Treasury building and the dome of the Capitol has been recommenced, and there is not much doubt but what it will soon go along steadily. It will astonish some of the foreign folks to see us going forward so deliberately with improvements, and putting down the greatest Rebellion the world has ever seen, at the same time.

The Prince de Joinville.

The Prince DE JOINVILLE and his son and nephews are receiving unofficial but hospitable attentions from the President and Secretary of State.

Cavalry from Colorado Territory.

A regiment of cavalry is authorized to be raised in Colorado Territory. One of its leading citizens says it will furnish three or four if necessary.

A number of prominent gentlemen are now here on business connected with the supplying of arms to regiments in their respective States.

Garibaldi's Adjutant.

The Adjutant of GARIBALDI, who arrived in the last steamer, visited Secretaries CAMERON and SEWARD this afternoon.

Suspected Rebel Arrested.

A man named KIRBIE, was brought in to Gen. SMITH's head-quarters this afternoon, on the supposition of being a Secessionist. All is quiet along the outposts to-night.

Horrible Accident in Berks County.

TWO MEN INJURED BY THE EXPLOSION OF A BOMB SHELL.

Special Despatch to the Inquirer.

READING, Sept. 20.—A horrible accident occurred to-day, in Douglas township, this county. As Mr. CHARLES B. WEAVER, of Colebrookdale Foundry, was experimenting with a bomb-shell, which had just been cast, it prematurely exploded, a piece of the missile striking him in the forehead, between the eyebrows and the root of the nose, penetrating to the brain. He is not expected to live.

At the same time, Mr. SAMUEL WEIDNER was terribly burned in the face, and will probably lose his eye-sight. The WEAVERS have a contract for making a large number of shells for the Government.

The different nominees of the Union Party have accepted the nominations tendered by the Convention, and are sanguine of success.

Two Rebel Defeats in Hardy County, Va.

BALTIMORE, Sept. 20.—The Cumberland papers received here state that Capt. KEDD's cavalry from New Creek, and a company of infantry from Fort Pendleton, made a descent upon a camp of Rebels in Hardy county, Virginia, on the 12th inst. One shot from their 12-pounder scattered the Rebels like chaff. Several were killed and wounded, and a number of prisoners taken, and their camp with all its equipage captured and destroyed. A large quantity of corn, with guns, uniforms, &c., were also secured.

The same day Col. ZEIGLER attacked some two hundred and fifty Rebels drilling near Barboursville. The Rebels fled at the first fire. Their leader and two others were made prisoners. Several were killed and wounded.

A Contradiction.

LANCASTER, Sept. 20.—The *Express* publishes an authoritative contradiction of BAYARD TAYLOR's statement in the New York *Tribune*, in relation to Ex-President BUCHANAN sending a portrait of Miss LANE to the *Almanach de Gotha*. There are reasons for believing that the publisher of the Almanach has been hoaxed by a German artist recently traveling through this country. There is no other foundation for the story whatever.

IMPORTANT FROM MISSOURI.

LATER FROM LEXINGTON.

The Fight Continued on Tuesday and Wednesday.

Brave Defence by Colonel Mulligan.

ST. LOUIS, Sept. 20.—A gentleman named KING, who left a point on the Missouri river opposite Lexington, on Wednesday night, who arrived here this morning, reports that a severe fight occurred on Tuesday for the possession of three ferry boats which lay at the levee. The Rebels, under PRICE, advanced on the boats in two bodies, one from above and the other from below the town, and after a very sharp engagement they were repulsed. The boats were not in a fair range of Col. MULLIGAN's guns, his fortifications being so situated as to prevent him from commanding them completely, and his force was too small to admit of his making a sortie against PRICE's overwhelming numbers. Mr. KING says he saw twelve wagons loaded with killed and wounded Rebels taken off after the fight.

He also says that PRICE assaulted MULLIGAN's forts four or five times on Wednesday, but was repulsed each time with a loss of from three to four hundred.

The reinforcements from the North, probably under Gen. STURGIS, were expected to arrive late on Wednesday, but as PRICE had obtained possession of the ferry boats they would not be able to cross the river, and of course, could be of little or no service in relieving Col. MULLIGAN.

Mr. KING's account is quite incoherent, and entire reliance is not placed on it here. There is but little question, however, that a battle had taken place, but the details are as yet unknown.

[If any portion of the above account is correct, the reported capture of Lexington received *via* Booneville is evidently false.]

FURTHER PARTICULARS.

ST. LOUIS, Sept. 20.—The following additional particulars in reference to affairs in Lexington have been ascertained:—

The first attack upon the fortifications is said to have been made on Thursday of last week, but this is certainly a mistake, as PRICE did not leave Warrensburg, forty miles south of Lexington, until Wednesday night. The attack was probably made on Monday, as previously stated, with about 8000 men. The engagement lasted two hours, when the Rebels were repulsed with the loss of 100 killed and between 200 and 400 wounded. Our loss stated at five killed and several wounded.

The fortifications are situated at the edge of the town, on a bluff overlooking the river. The works are of earth, seven feet high and twelve feet thick, with a ditch six feet deep and twelve feet broad, surrounding them. Another and smaller work is erected inside, defended by a ditch—the whole works being capable of holding ten thousand troops.

The attack on Wednesday was a determined one, and lasted nearly all day.

The reinforcements from the North, under Gen. STURGIS, probably number 3000, but should they be unable to cross the river, which is quite likely, the only aid they can render will be to sweep the Rebels with their artillery. It is confidently hoped, however, that the 6000 troops that left Jefferson City on Wednesday, by steamers, will be able to land at or near Lexington, and cut their way through the Rebel forces and join Colonel MULLIGAN. It is said that Colonel MULLIGAN expressed confidence in being able to hold his position against any force not more than ten times greater than his own.

It was believed at Booneville that LANE had reached Lexington with reinforcements.

McCulloch Advancing on Jefferson City.

PREPARATIONS TO REPEL HIM AT OSAGE BRIDGE.

ST. LOUIS, Sept. 20.—The following special despatch has been received by the *Republican*.

JEFFERSON CITY, Sept. 20.—A report received here this morning, states that General MCCULLOCH, with probably 20,000 Rebels, was on the Osage river, seventy miles hence, date not stated, marching on Jefferson City. The commanding officer is inclined to credit the report.

Colonel RICHARDSON took a position to-day with his Home Guards at the Osage Bridge, where the first attack will no doubt be made. He says that he will not desert the post until the last man falls.

Lieutenant MONTGOMERY, of General FREMONT's staff, has just arrived from Georgetown, and says that heavy firing was heard at Booneville, all day Wednesday and late in the night, in the direction of Lexington, thus disproving the story that that place had been taken on Tuesday. It is believed at Booneville that PRICE could not take Lexington, but if he should it would only be with terrible slaughter.

JACKSON, it is said, has no more than nine hundred and fifty men, and is surrounded on every side. He cannot escape if defeated, nor hold Lexington if he captures it.

In Pettis county all the Rebels have gone off in squads to join JACKSON.

Nearly all the Unionists have also left from fear. The country is perfectly desolate. Fine crops are standing ungathered everywhere.

No boat has arrived from above but is hourly expected.

The Secessionists are greatly alarmed at the position of affairs at Lexington.

Reconnoissance of Hardee's Position—A Skirmish.

WASHINGTON, Sept. 20.—Gen. FREMONT telegraphs to the head-quarters of the army, dated yesterday, giving the following information:—

Major GAVITT, of the First Indiana Regiment of Cavalry, who was sent on a reconnoissance towards HARDEE's position at Greenville, met the enemy's pickets, drove them in, killing two and taking two of the enemy prisoners. He also captured sixty muskets and twenty-five horses."

A Skirmish on Black River.

IRONTON, Mo., Sept. 20.—A skirmish occurred on Thursday at Black River, twelve or fifteen miles southward of here, between three companies of Indiana cavalry, under Major GAVITT, and a body of Rebels, under the notorious BEN TALBOT, in which five of the Rebels were killed and four taken prisoners, and thirty-five horses and a quantity of arms captured. The Rebels scattered in all directions, and being familiar with the country escaped pursuit.

Military Movements on the Southern Border

LEAVENWORTH, Sept. 20.—The latest accounts from the Southern border represent the Rebels under RAINS as marching northward and Gen. LANE's command following him. It is difficult to obtain information of the movement of troops, owing to the necessity of secrecy.

About one thousand Rebels were at Platte City, eight miles east of this place, yesterday, supposed to be on the march to join RAINS or PRICE, crossing the river at or near Liberty. A portion of this force has been engaged in the recent bridge burnings on the western division of the Hannibal and St. Joseph Railroad. A column of Federal troops from points on the Hannibal road, were in pursuit of them. The militia of the counties in Kansas bordering on the river, have been under arms during the last two weeks to repel any invasion. The Second Kansas Regiment, which arrived here on the 15th from Rolla, have been continually on the move for nearly three months. They had an enthusiastic reception by the citizens and military of this city, and were given a dinner at the hotel.

Excitement at Kansas City.

BRILLIANT SKIRMISH AND ROUT OF THE REBELS—ATTEMPT TO CROSS THE RIVER—THEIR BOAT SUNK.

KANSAS CITY, Mo., Sept. 17.—Considerable excitement was occasioned here on Saturday last, by the appearance of the Rebel scouts on the opposite banks of the river. A company of twenty-five mounted men was sent over from this place, who discovered a Rebel camp of from 200 to 300, six miles distant from the river. An additional force was detailed in the afternoon, who made a successful attack, killing seven of the Rebels, capturing six prisoners and their horses, and destroying their barracks. Only one of the Federal troops was wounded.

Yesterday a large force of Rebels, supposed to be a part of the band recently encamped in St. Joseph, made their appearance four miles below, on the opposite shore, and attempted to cross the river on an old flat-boat, sending a part of their force to attract the attention of the Federal troops by firing into this city and Wyandotte. They were, however, repulsed, and the boat sunk. It is believed that they succeeded in crossing at Zibley Ferry, sixteen miles below, which they had possession of last evening. The city was alive with reports of skirmishes of both parties. Several shots were heard, but it is believed no damage was done.

FROM THE LOWER POTOMAC.

From Gen. Banks' Column.

CLAIMS FOR DAMAGES—NARROW ESCAPE OF A SCOUT—A REBEL ENCAMPMENT SHELLED—COL JOHN K MURPHY'S REGIMENT.

DAWSONVILLE, Md., September 18.—There has been no serious demonstration on the part of the Rebels within the past forty-eight hours, and as far as can be learned, everything along the Upper Potomac remains in a state of quiet to-night.

The Division-Quartermaster to-day protested in the name of the War Department, against the payment, in coin, of any bills for damages sustained by owners of property where encampments are located; but he will certify to such claims, based on principles of equity, leaving it to Congress or the Court of Claims to authorize the payment. The cause of this procedure is supposed to have arisen from the fact that much of the United States coin heretofore disbursed for this purpose has found its way to the Secession side of the Potomac. It is understood, however, that supplies for forage and subsistence are not included in this protest.

Yesterday an unauthorized scout of the Thirty fourth New York went across the Potomac, near the mouth of the Senaca, and were attacked by a superior party of the enemy. One of our men was killed outright, and several wounded. One of the latter was shot through the cheek, but fled, pursued by the attacking party. On reaching a creek, he threw in his gun and plunged in himself. Lying on his back and resting his head upon a stone, with his mouth and nostrils above the water, he evaded his pursuers; and after three hours' submersion, he crawled to the shore of the river. His companions, who were concealed on the Maryland side, discovered and rescued him, while making a vain attempt to swim across. These incursions, which can be productive of no good to our cause, are condemned by experienced officers.

The Second Rhode Island battery, stationed near the mouth of the Senaca, yesterday shelled an encampment of the Confederates nearly opposite, and it is believed several were killed. The enemy did not respond, probably for the want of artillery.

It is reported that a Lieutenant and several men belonging to one of the River Guard regiments, crossed the river secretly, and are believed to have deserted to the Rebels The names of the officer and regiment are withheld until the report can be verified, but the authority is conceded to be reliable.

Our own and the enemy's pickets are said to frequently meet on one or the other shore of the Potomac, and pass time in social intercourse, occasionally partaking of each other's hospitality.

This morning, at daylight, it was discovered by Gen. STONE's pickets, near Conrad's ferry, that the enemy, during the previous night, had commenced and partially constructed an entrenchment on the Virginia side, about five hundred yards from the shore, upon a slope facing the river. One of our light batteries opened upon them about nine o'clock, and after twenty or thirty rounds nothing was to be seen of the enemy, and but little of the results of their labors. For some days past conversations have been held between our own and the Rebel pickets, from which it has been discovered that the latter belong to the Second Richmond Cavalry, who were anxious to exchange late Richmond papers for the leading Union journals, but our pickets declined to reciprocate.

Lieutenant-Colonel SEWARD, nephew of the Secretary of State, recently, from serious indisposition, withdrew from the command of the New York Nineteenth and proceeded to Washington, where he tendered his resignation; but before its acceptance a rumor reached him that a battle between a superior force of the enemy and the division to which his regiment was attached was imminent, and, notwithstanding his physical debility, he withdrew the resignation and immediately rejoined his command.

Your correspondent hopes to be excused for particularizing, among the efficient regiments of General BANKS' command, the Pennsylvania Twenty-ninth, under the veteran Colonel MURPHY. This officer rose to the grade of a Lieutenant-Colonel in the war of 1812-15, and still retains the vigor of early manhood. This regiment joined the army at Sandy Hook, and its commander, as well as his officers, have performed all the arduous marches on foot. His encampment, drills and discipline are considered models by competent military authorities.

There is a general complaint in regard to mail facilities in this division of the army. Numerous letters never arrive, while others are days and weeks behind their time. This is attributed to local offices and carriers more than to the department at Washington.

Sickness in the Rebel Army.

BALTIMORE, September 20.—A recent copy of the Charleston *Mercury* contains an editorial article, in which it speaks of the bad food furnished by the Commissariat at Richmond. It speaks of "fifteen thousand troops now lying sick, scattered all around Manassas." It adds that the Commissary Department "furnish raw wheat flour, and leave the poor soldiers to work it into dough, which has proved more fatal to the army than Yankee rifles and cannon." In the same paper it also stated that "the number of disabled volunteers in Richmond increases with each day's arrival from Manassas. On Sunday the Central cars brought down one hundred of the sick, who were immediately distributed to the different hospitals. An arrival on Monday morning added one hundred and fifty patients to the list.

From Fortress Monroe.

BALTIMORE, Sept. 20.—The Old Point boat brings no news of importance.

THE LATEST FROM KENTUCKY.

COLONEL CRITTENDEN'S REGIMENT.

LOUISVILLE, Sept. 20.—Colonel CRITTENDEN, from Indiana, who was the first to bring a regiment from another State into Western Virginia, in aid of the Federal Government, and the first to come to the aid of Kentucky, passed through here with his regiment well armed and equipped. He passed through our streets towards the Nashville depot this afternoon, and proceeded immediately southward. They were enthusiastically received at different points on the route.

Brigadier-General WARD arrived to-day from Washington and will immediately take command in Central Kentucky.

A portion of General ROSSEAU's forces are in possession of Muldrough's Hill.

Justice CATRON, of the U. S. Court, issued, to-day, writs of habeas corpus in the case of Ex-Governor MOOREHEAD, DARRETT and BARR, returnable on Monday next.

Kentucky Legislature.

ANOTHER VETO BY GOVERNOR MAGOFFIN.

FRANKFORT, Sept. 20.—The bill which passed both houses requesting General ANDERSON to take command of the Kentucky Volunteers, was vetoed by Governor MAGOFFIN, and passed over his veto. The vote in the House was 68 against 22.

Unionists Joining the Federal Forces.

LOUISVILLE, Sept. 20.—Nothing of importance has been received from points south of here. Passengers from Lebanon report that the people from the country are coming in to join the Federal forces.

Nothing has as yet been ascertained of movements in Southern Kentucky, the telegraphic communication being still interrupted beyond Lebanon Junction.

W. N. HALDEMAN, the principal proprietor of the *Courier*, will publish a card in the *Journal* to-morrow, asking a modification of the interdict against the publication of the *Courier*, and agreeing to avoid the publication of matter prejudicial to the Federal Government, and to be loyal to that Government while Kentucky remains in the Union.

Prisoners En Route for Fort Lafayette.

INDIANAPOLIS, Sept. 20.—Ex-Governor MOORHEAD, MARTIN W. BARR and R. T. DARRETT, arrested at Louisville yesterday, for treason, were brought here to-day, and are to be sent to Fort Lafayette by order of the War Department.

OUR NEW YORK LETTER.

Correspondence of the Inquirer.

NEW YORK, Sept. 20, 1861.

It is a difficult matter now-a-days to get all the stirring news afloat, in this great metropolis, within the compass of an ordinary letter. You commonly expect a word or two in reference to the most important subjects now passing in fact. The New York Fire Zouaves undertook a start for Fortress Monroe yesterday afternoon, but the steamer came back with them after going down the bay a ways. The principal trouble among the boys appears to be their back pay. An understanding has been had with them by Colonel LOSIER, and he expects to get off this afternoon, with 400 of them. Much of the trouble in this regiment is due to the bad management of some of its subordinate officers.

The British brig *Mystery*, which was seized on suspicion of having run the blockade into Georgetown, S. C., with a cargo of ice and butter, has been brought up to the city. According to the story of her Captain, the shipper of her cargo gained a very light profit on his venture. He states that he left Boston for Havana with a load of ice, and was thirty-nine days making the passage; and in that period his cool commodity became reduced by heat to eighty tons, (a considerable reduction from two hundred,) which he sold at Matanzas for four dollars per ton, and afterwards loaded there with sugar, for New York. No doubt the vessel will be libelled.

The schooner *Kensington*, lying in Gowanus Creek, Brooklyn, has been seized to-day. She is registered in the name of F. TORRANS, Charleston, S. C., and is partly owned in Havana, Cuba.

Up to last night the city post office had exchanged $12,000 worth of postage stamps. Strange as it may appear, also, large numbers of letters continue to be dropped in the mails for places in the Rebel States. Many of them are received in the foreign despatch. More than one thousand three hundred have been stopped within the past week. A burglar attempted to enter the store No. 24 Walker street, just before daylight this morning. He succeeded in getting inside, but was astonished to meet a colored porter, who slept there. The porter fired his pistol at him, receiving, at the same time, a return of the compliment from the robber. The ball from the thief's pistol passed through the colored man's shirt. The rascal escaped through the adjoining building.

As this was the day PETER TOUTANT, alias BEAU-

The Berdan Sharp-Shooters—The President a Good Shot.

The BERDAN sharp-shooters gave a highly satisfactory evidence of their skill this afternoon at the encampment, having previously been reviewed by the President Among the many spectators were Secretaries SEWARD, CAMERON and SMITH, Assistant Secretary SCOTT, the Prince DE JOINVILLE and his son and nephew, Generals MCDOWELL, MANSFIELD and other military officers. Gen. MCCLELLAN and his staff and body guard were also on the ground during the firing, which was at a distance of five hundred yards. Two hundred and sixty shots were fired, and the target was completely riddled. The President tried his hand and made a most excellent shot.

She was built in 1851, by P. & S. SPRAGUE & Co., of Boston, and was then named the *Telegraph*. While at Savannah, in 1859, she was burned, and there rebuilt, when her name was changed to the one she now bears. She is a clipper model, registered 1000 tons, and her value estimated at $30,000. Her 200 tons cargo, and freight money on the balance, after paying seamen's wages, and probably captain's wages also, are confiscated.

The ship *Benefactor* was also seized, on the ground that one-eighth of the vessel is owned by parties residing in Virginia. She was, however, promptly released on filing the proper bonds at the Custom House Seven-eighths of this ship are owned by LOWE Brothers, of New York, and is now under charter to sail for China, carrying a large and valuable cargo.

The Sinking Fund in the State Treasury has been used to redeem $96,000 of the California 7 per cent bonds at 99⅝ on the dollar.

Los Angelos papers continue to notice the arrival, in the southern part of the State, of emigrants from Texas. They report a terrible condition of affairs as existing in that unhappy State, and that large numbers are leaving for California, who are sick of Secession; there is no security for life or property there, either against the Indians or the Secessionists. The latter find that if men, even of their kind, want money, they demand it, and if it is refused they threaten to shoot him. All the Union men were disarmed at the first, and they are powerless, but there are large numbers of them, and if they had arms and assistance from the Government, would bring the Secessionists to a terrible retribution. There are many on the road to California They all hope that, when they get through, they will find at least peace and quiet here.

Advices from Washoe say that emigrants are pouring in from the plains every day. It is estimated that the number coming to California across the plains, this season, will reach 25,000 or 30,000. They come from Indiana, Illinois, and Iowa—the greatest number by the central route. Letters are also reaching Oregon from emigrants on their way, overland, to that state. There were some 2000 wagons traveling in a compact body. Captain MAINADEER and an escort were in company. It is stated that there would be a scarcity of provisions, as the supply on hand could be made to last only six weeks Parties have started out from Walla Walla with pack trains of provisions, to meet their friends.

The steamer *Carrie Ladd* arrived at Portland, September 2d, bringing 27,000 in gold dust from the Nez Perces mines. The Indians are reported as peaceable and the recent alarm sounded about the danger of Indian hostilities on a large scale is evidently an exaggeration.

The correspondent of the *Doll Mountaineer* says it is demonstrated beyond dispute that the whole region of country embraced between the Cascade and Rocky Mountains is one vast gold field, and only required development to revolutionize that entire coast. An area of 32,000 square miles has been sufficiently prospected to establish the existence of mineral wealth Exploring parties have been fitted out for the Elk country and Bitter Root valley, where large prospects are anticipated. The near approach of winter renders a postponement of emigration to that quarter advisable, but in the spring there will probably be another gold rush.

Operations of the Scouts.

A letter from Lewinsville, Virginia, says:—The Rebels have turned out of their homes all the women and children belonging to the Union men in this vicinity. They have also taken all their household effects, driven off their stock, and have carried away all the hay, corn and oats, they could get their hands upon.

Last night the Union troops, not far from here, captured about forty head of cattle, which had been stolen by the Rebels, who were caught in the act of driving them off.

The scouting parties sent out from General SMITH's division have been very successful in finding the precise location of the Rebel pickets.

They are, for the most part, picked men, selected from the Sixth Maine, and are commanded by Lieutenant ROBERTS, with O. G. SAGE as a guide. Mr. SAGE is so well acquainted with this part of the country that he has never failed to conduct our scouts safely through the most dense forests and thickets, and sometimes when the nights are so dark that a man could not be seen at a distance of ten feet; and all this he accomplishes without the aid of a compass.

We have unmistakable evidence that the Rebel army is advancing towards our camps Their pickets are being doubled on all their most important posts, and are constantly taking advanced positions.

Captain FLOYD and Mr. SAGE succeeded, yesterday, in capturing five prisoners, most of whom will, doubtless, be detained until after the war.

ties at the Corn Exchange, last week, that the steamship *Great Eastern* would make the passage to New York in ten days. The ten days were "up" at noon to-day, and the money, of course, is lost I have heard $5000 mentioned as the figure risked in one case. Verily, fools and their money are soon parted.

The Board of Aldermen have a special session this evening, with a view, it is supposed, to appoint a Street Commissioner in the place of the present incumbent, SMITH, who is mysteriously absent at the South, and supposed to be acting with the Rebels in Tennessee or Kentucky. (He is first cousin to BRECKINRIDGE.) The office of Street Inspector is one of the "fattest" in the gift of the Municipal Government, and there is, of course, a great scramble for it on the part of the "mousing politicians." Its expenditures are about three millions per annum, and has some six hundred men in its employment.

A well known Democratic politician, named RICHARD BRADLEY, proprietor of a saloon called "The Capitol," in Jerolamon street, Brooklyn, committed suicide last evening, by jumping off one of the ferry boats, while in a state of intoxication.

General trade continues to improve, though not at a rapid pace. There were heavy operations of a speculative character in Breadstuffs this morning, at a further improvement in prices The private letters from the Continent are understood to be even more favorable for the trade than the published advices. The Grocers, too, are doing an active business, not only in the way of supplying domestic wants, but in reshipments to the West Indies and South America.

In money there is no new movement worth mentioning. The recent activity has been followed by comparative indifference. Call loans are easy at 4½@5 ℔ cent., and prime short-dated paper at 6@7. The latter, however, is very scarce. Sterling bills for to-morrow's packet steady at 108¾@109.

There has been a very active demand all day for Federal stocks and Treasury notes, and all that could be had were snapped up at 98½@98⅝ for the latter. Some business is said to have been done in the 6's of '61, on European account. The subscriptions to the Treasury loan for the day foot up $300,000. ARGUS.

NEW YORK STOCK EXCHANGE, SEPTEMBER 20.

$32,600 U.S 6's '81 reg...	90⅜	20 sh Metrop'n Bank..	85¼
$1,000 U.S. 6's '81 coup.	90⅝	25 sh Corn Ex. Bank..	80
$1,000 U. S. 5's '65......	87½	10 sh Penn'a Coal Co..	76
$7,000 U. S 5's '74 coup.	80½	5 sh Pacific M. S. S. Co	83
$25,000 do..........	80¼	200 do..............	82½
$23,000 Tr'y 12 p c Notes.	101	100 do..............	82¾
$12,000 Tr'y 6 p c Two Y.	98⅝	100 sh N. Y. Cent'l R R.	73¾
$1,000 Ind. Canal b's, '60	80	200 do..........s10	73⅛
$1,000 Ill. Sterling bs...	80	100 do..........s15	73⅜
$600 Ind'a State 5's...	79	450 do..............	73½
$1,000 Virg'a State 6's.	52	300 do............s5	73⅜
$5,000 do........s15	51¼	65 sh Erie Railway....	26
$8,000 Tenn. St 6's '90.	43	25 sh Hud. River R. R.	34
$10,000 Mo. State 6's...	43⅝	100 do..........s30	33¼
$10,000 do..........	43¼	9 sh Panama R. R.....	110
$2,000 Miss. 6's, iss. to		100 sh Gal. & Chic...b30	69¼
H. & St J. R. R.	47	18 do..............	69
$1,000 Erie R. 1st m. bs.	103	59 do............s3	69¼
$2,000 Erie R. 4th m. bs.	70	50 do..........s10	69
$4,000 N.Y.C c.v bs, '76,	100¼	50 do.............c	69⅝
$1,000 Hud. Riv S F. bs,	96	50 sh Clev. & Tol. R. R.	29⅜
$1,000 Mich Cen. 6. p.c.		200 do..............	29¾
1st m S F cvt. bs	98	300 do..............	29⅝
$500 Ill Cen. R.R. bs.	93	100 do...........b30	29¾
$1,000 Gal. & Chi. 1st m	98	250 sh Chic. & R. I. R. R.	43¾
$1,000 L.E.&W 1st m b.	66½	100 do..............	44
$2,000 LaC. & Mil. 1 g.bs.	11	250 do..............	43¼
10 sh National Bank...	89	50 do..........s10	43¾
10 sh Bank of Com.....	80	73 sh Mil. & P. D. Ch. R.	18
10 sh Mer. Exc. Bank	78	16 sh New Jersey R. R.	112
5 sh Metropoli an Bk.	87½		

SECOND BOARD.

$6,000 U. S. 6s, '81....reg	90⅝	150 sh P. M. S. S. Co...	83
$1,000 U. S. 6s, '67.....	90⅜	25 do..............	83¼
$5,000 U. S. 6s, '62.....	95	215 sh N. Y. Cen. R....	73¾
$2,000 Michigan 6s.....	81½	300 do..............	73⅝
$1,000 Minnesota 8s.....	80	300 sh Cleve. & Tole...	29⅜
50 sh Erie Railway.....	26¼	100 sh Chi. & R. Is. R...	43¾

The Money market continues to grow easier. On call the supply is abundant at 5 ℔ cent, while strictly prime paper is selling at 6@7 ℔ cent. In Foreign Exchange the business is moderate, at 108¾@109 for banker's sterling, and 5f.25⅝@5f.27½ for bills on Paris. Stocks are a little easier. Harlem and Cleveland & Toledo have declined ⅛; Michigan Southern Guarantied and Reading, ¼; Hudson, ⅜; and Illinois Central, ⅝.

CLOSING PRICES—*Reported by H. Toland & Son, Exchange Place.*—Erie, 26@26¼; Reading, 35@35¼; New York Central, 73⅛@73½; Michigan Southern, 13½@14; Michigan Southern Guarantied, 30½@31; Illinois Central, 65½@66; Canton, 9@10; Harlem, 10¼@10½; Harlem Preferred, 25@25½; Hudson, 33½@33¾; Cleveland and Toledo, 29¼@29⅝. Market steady.

OFFICE OF THE ASSISTANT TREASURER, UNITED STATES, New York, September 20, 1861.

Total Receipts..................	$453,890 00
" Payments..................	516,500 26
" Balance..................	15,918,901 87
For Customs..................	8,600 00
Treasury Notes..................	413,000 00

Daily Democrat.

PRINTED AND PUBLISHED BY
HARNEY, HUGHES & CO.
Office—East side Third Street, between Market and Jefferson.

TO ARMS! TO ARMS!

Proclamation of General Robert Anderson.

Kentuckians! called by the Legislature of this, my native State, I hereby assume command of this Department. I come to enforce, not to make laws, and, God willing, to protect your property and your lives. The enemies of our country have dared to invade our soil. Kentucky is in danger. She has vainly striven to keep peace with her neighbors. Our State is now invaded by those who professed to be her friends, but who now seek to conquer her. No true son of Kentucky can longer hesitate as to his duty to his State and country. The invaders must, and, God willing, will be expelled. The leader of the hostile forces who now approaches, is, I regret to say, a Kentuckian, making war on Kentucky and Kentuckians. Let all past differences of opinion be overlooked.

Every one who now rallies to the support of our Union and of our State is a friend.

Rally, then, my countrymen, around the flag our fathers loved, which has shielded us so long. I call you to arms for self-defense, and for the protection of all that is dear to freemen. Let us trust in God, and do our duty, as did our fathers. (Signed,)

ROBERT ANDERSON,
Brig. Gen. U. S. A.

To the Militia of Kentucky.

By the authority which you yourselves have appointed, you are called upon to defend your State. Misguided countrymen, whom you loved too well to fight, despite their wrongs to you, waging unnatural war, have tarnished the bright fame of Kentucky; and for the first time, since your sires bequeathed you this noble State, its soil is polluted by the tread of hostile armies.

I will not impugn the patriotism and courage of my countrymen, by supposing that any appeal, however eloquent, could so rouse them to energy and prompt action as this simple statement.

But to the State Guard I must add a word. Now is your opportunity to wipe out every reproach that has been put upon you. You owe it not only to your duty as men and citizens, but to that solemn obligation of soldiers which you cannot forget without dishonor, to respond at once to this call.

The State Guard will rendezvous as soon as possible at Louisville and report to me. The residue of the militia and such of the Home Guard as choose to volunteer will rendezvous as soon as possible at Louisville, Frankfort, Camp Dick Robinson, Gen. Sherman's camp, New Haven, and Henderson.

Come in battalions, regiments, companies, or come as individuals, and you shall be mustered into service under pay at once.

T. L. CRITTENDEN,
Brig. Gen. Ky. State Guard.

General Pope's Proclamation.

FELLOW-CITIZENS: I call you to arms for the defense of the city. The engine bells will be tapped at 5 o'clock to call the people of each Ward to the enginehouse thereof, where it is earnestly asked that you will enroll yourselves into companies for the defense of our city.

After doing so you are requested to report to me at my office, and also, to report the number of guns, public or private, of each company.

My office is on Fifth street, opposite the Courthouse. HAMILTON POPE,
Brigadier-General Home Guard.

☞ The following gentlemen are requested to act as a committee to attend to providing a lunch at the Nashville Depot for soldiers, as they may arrive from time to time: W. H. Goddard, John Graham, Andrew Graham, J. Callahan, J. Smith Speed, W. J. Cornell, A. B. Semple, George G. Fetter, John H. Haywood, E. A. Holyoke.

J. M. DELPH, Mayor.

Contributions in money can be sent in to any member of the committee. Provisions should be sent to the depot, to W. H. Goddard, and all baskets and packages of provisions should be marked with the name of the family sending them.

W. H. GODDARD, Chairman.

FEDERAL TROOPS.—The arrival of Federal troops by the river yesterday morning, and their departure over the Nashville road, has created considerable excitement.

The men were well uniformed and disciplined, and attracted the admiration of all who saw them march through our streets.

NOTICE.—To enable us give to the public the latest war news, we will publish the Bulletin this afternoon at half-past four o'clock. The telegraph news will be obtained if possible.

PRENTICE, HENDERSON & OSBORNE.

☞ Up to two o'clock this morning nothing of importance was received from General Sherman's Command.

☞ Quite a number of the members of the Legislature reached our city by last night's train.

☞ Wm. H. Grainger, Union candidate for a seat in the City Council, was elected from the Sixth ward yesterday.

☞ We learn that a new postofficer has been established in this county to be called the "Falls of Harrod." C. A. M. Yarbra is appointed postmaster.

☞ The Henry Fitzhugh arrived yesterday afternoon loaded with troops from Newport barracks, who took passage on the Louisville and Nashville Railroad.

☞ The Frankfort Yeoman is "still harping on my daughter." We trust the considerate friends of the old woman who edits it will indulge her in her scolding.

☞ The new made Home Guard paraded the streets last night. We learn that some six or eight hundred men promptly enrolled their names. As many more should come forward by 12 o'clock Monday.

MORE TROOPS.—The Thirty-seventh Indiana Regiment, Col. Scribner, from Camp Noble, crossed the river last evening, and departed on the train to join Col. Rousseau's brigade.

☞ Gen. McClellan has issued an order instructing soldiers performing picket duty not to fire on the pickets of the enemy unless provoked, or in self-defense. Colonels have been directed to arrest soldiers violating this order.

ATTENTION, ANDERSON ZOUAVES.—You are hereby requested to meet at your armory, on Preston street, below Washington, (tobacco warehouse) on Monday night at 7½ o'clock. All good Union men from 18 to 30 years old, are invited to join.

☞ Mr. C. C. Spencer requests us to say that he has in store a large lot of new and second-hand furniture, which he is peremptorily ordered to sell on Monday morning at his auction rooms. Sale by order of constable for families removing from the city.

☞ The ladies were out in force at the Nashville depot, yesterday, with coffee and provisions for the troops. This is right—this is the patriotic aid the better portion of creation can properly render in such times as these.

☞ Mr. F. A. Wichelman, whose place is opposite the Nashville Depot, will keep a coffee stand. His coffee will be furnished free to volunteers. Others wishing a cup of coffee will be served at the usual price Mr. Wichelman is a worthy gentleman, and deserves the patronage of the public.

☞ We were informed late last night that Capt. Fish Henry, a well known conductor on the Nashville Railroad, has been seized by a party of Secessionists and taken to Tennessee. We trust the scoundrels may not vent their malice in this way further without a thorough retaliation.

☞ Capt. J. Ruckstuhl has gone into Camp Sherman with seventy-five able-bodied men. Capt. R. is a war veteran, having been bred a soldier and served our country in the war with Mexico. His body is covered with scars received there, which are silent witnesses of the hot service he has seen.

☞ Col. Bayles has secured the services of Capt. C. C. Gilbert, of the regular army, to aid him in instructing his regiment of cavalry, and hopes to obtain his appointment as Lieutenant Colonel. The regiment is now encamped at the Fair Ground, and is named, after the General, Camp Anderson. Capt. Gilbert is known for his gallant conduct at Springfield, Mo. This will be a fine regiment. Fill it up fast.

CITIZENS OF THE FOURTH WARD.—There being no engine-house in the Fourth Ward, it is desired that the citizens thereof will meet to morrow morning, at nine o'clock, at Beck's coffee-house, corner of First and Jefferson streets, and organize themselves into companies, elect their officers, and report to the same, as well as the number of guns, public and private, to

HAMILTON POPE,
Brigadier General Home Guard.

TO THE UNION CITIZENS OF LOUISVILLE. Three regiments are expected early this morning. The committee respectfully request that all contributions be sent to the Nashville depot as early as possible. Meat and bread, in the form of thick sandwiches, is preferred, although acceptable in any form. Any merchant wishing to contribute will find cheese, tobacco (in small plugs), and burnt and ground coffee acceptable.

The committee return their thanks for the very liberal contributions made yesterday, which were gratefully received and duly appreciated by the gallant men who have gone to our defense.

Every basket or package must be plainly labelled with the donor's name, and accompanied by some responsible person.

Contributions in money may be sent to the undersigned. W. H. GODDARD,
Chairman Citizens' Committee.

P. S.—The committee will meet at half-past seven o'clock this morning at the depot.

LETTER FROM FRANKFORT.

CAPITAL HOTEL,
FRANKFORT, Sept. 21, 1861.

MESSRS. HARNEY, HUGHES & CO.:

Gentlemen: A resolution was passed appointing a committee of two in the House, or two in the Senate, to wait on Major Anderson, informing him of the resolutions which passed requiring him to call out the militia, &c.

The Representative Chamber is gradually thinning out. Nearly every one of the Southern Rights members have left on account of the disturbed condition of their section of the country. There was a rumor here last night that from Owen and Scott counties many thousands of men were coming into the Capital to take possession and tear things. About eight o'clock a company of cavalry from camp Dick Robinson rode into the city. They came after some cannon and ammunition at the arsenal. They are about as hard set of looking men to fight, I expect, as you ever saw. They have the finest looking horses, generally speaking, that I ever saw together. There is a small encampment on the railroad below here, protecting some bridges. I do not know, but I believe it is composed of young men belonging to no regular military organization, but who have volunteered to protect the road.

Sam Gill is one of the most indefatigable men I ever saw. He is seemingly everywhere. And while you have scarcely missed him from his accustomed place, you hear of some movement he has made which shows that he, as a member of the Military Board, sees at once, and appreciates quick and energetic action. Sam Gill, since I have been here so that I can see and watch him, has become one of my weaknesses.

YOURS, &c.

Beware of Traitors!

At a meeting of some of the leading Knights of the Golden Circle, on Friday night, we understand they suggested an organized guerrilla party, for the purpose of burning and murdering through the city and country. The Castles through the country were to follow in their action. We make this publication that the people may be apprized of their machinations, and keep a watch accordingly. A party that will resort to such hellish means can never triumph, as God is just.

☞ Mr. James Cronan, to keep from being impressed into the Confederate army, fled from his home, his family, his all, in Elizabethtown. If his wife, Mary Cronan, should be so fortunate as to reach the city she can find something to her advantage by calling at the Galt House.

THE SICK AMONG THE SOLDIERS.—It is to be expected that the various troops reaching here from other points will have some persons on the sick list. In order to provide for this contingency, the city authorities should see that the Hospital is in a suitable condition to provide all possible accommodations and comforts for the sick, and we hope that the Collector of this Port will see that similar means are provided at the United States Marine Hospital for ample benefits for our friends in need. And we take this occasion to suggest to the Regimental Surgeons that it is not necessary for them to stop here with their sick friends. There are numbers of physicians in the city, whose duties compel them to remain here, who will gladly bestow every possible attention upon the sick soldiers. Professors Palmer, Flint, and Bell, and Dr. Geo. W. Ronald, will be happy to contribute all in their power to the welfare of the invalid soldiers.

SIXTH WARD AWAKE.—At a meeting held at the city court room yesterday evening, a company of Home Guard, numbering 80 men, was formed, being composed of many of our most influential citizens. Among the privates, we learn that Judge William Bullock stands almost among the very first enrolled. Such unpretending patriotism is worthy of all commendation. An election of officers resulted as follows: Captain, W. S. Clements; First Lieutenant, Joseph Odell; Second Lieutenant, —— Taylor. The remaining officers will be elected at the next meeting on Monday evening, at 7 o'clock.

☞ We understand that on Friday evening last a lot of arms, amounting to some one hundred and two guns, belonging to the State Guard at Lexington, were stolen, and the parties having them in charge had proceeded out about ten miles on the Versailles Pike, when they were overtaken by a party of cavalry and the whole of them captured and brought back. The Union men are wide awake in that section.

WINCHESTER, KY., Sept. 20, 1861.

MESSRS. HARNEY, HUGHES & CO.:

Gentlemen: The glorious old county of Clarke has given us an infallible assurance of the loyalty and veneration of her people to the Federal Union. A tremendous barbecue was given to-day at the Fair Grounds, near Winchester. The procession was one of the grandest pageants I have ever witnessed. The people were addressed by Andy Johnson, Col. Carpenter, Judge Emory, and other eloquent speakers. The tables were sumptuous, such as the hospitable people of Clarke alone know how to prepare.

Yours, in haste, B.

MESSRS. HARNEY, HUGHES & CO.:

Gentlemen: The city authorities providing refreshments for soldiers as they arrive at the Nashville depot, I will not put up my stand, but request those who promised donations to me, to send them to Mr. Goddard, at the Nashville depot.

F. A. WICHELMAN.

☞ Modesty, like virtue, must be its own reward.

Meeting in the Second Ward.

At a meeting, held in pursuance of a call upon the citizens of the Second ward, at the engine-house, Esq. Connell took the chair, and W. H. C. Dryden acted as Secretary. The meeting being called to order and the object thereof explained by W. H. Watts, Esq., the citizens, after enrolling their names to the number of one hundred, proceeded to the election of the following officers:

Captain—Lewis Ferrell; First Lieutenant—E. M. Buchanan; Second Lieutenant—J. M. Coward; Third Lieutenant—Geo. W. Johnston; First Sergeant—James H. Kendall; after which, on motion of James W. Osborne, the meeting adjourned.

J. M. CONNELL, Chairman.
W. H. C. DRYDEN, Secretary.
LOUISVILLE, Sept. 21, 1861.

A Word to Newspaper Readers.

The Daily Morning Democrat and Evening News supply all the dispatches, local and general news. Those who wish to keep posted with the stirring events of the times, should be supplied with both editions. The morning edition costs twenty-five (25) cents for every two weeks, and the evening edition fifteen (15) cents for two weeks. This places a paper within the reach of all.

INFORMATION WANTED.—If Mr. Abraham Lunsford, who was to have left Crittenden county, Missouri, and meet his wife, from Laurel county, Kentucky, in this city on the 15th instant, is in the city, or if any one can give any information of him by calling at the corner of Green and Eighth streets, where his wife and children may be found, the information will be thankfully received. se20 3t

CLIFFORD & CO., GENERAL COMMISSION MERCHANTS.—50 casks clear bacon sides, 20 casks ribbed bacon sides, 10 casks bacon shoulders, 200 packages butter, 50 bbls. krout, and 50 bbls. beans in store and for sale low, to close consignment, by Clifford & Co., commission merchants, 226 Main street, between Second and Third, Louisville, Ky.

ATTENTION, CLOTHING MERCHANTS!—To-morrow morning, Saturday, September 21st, we shall open samples of an invoice of men's jeans pants, men's sattinet and cassimere coats, overcoats, plush and velvet vests, for sale at private sale, at low prices, at auction rooms. S. G. HENRY & CO.,
se20 3t Opposite Louisville Hotel.

ARTILLERISTS.—There will be a meeting at the Hope Engine House, on Monday night, at 7½ o'clock, for the purpose of filling up a company of Home Artillery. Good Union men, who wish to help to protect their homes and the city from the hands of our foes, can now have an opportunity of joining a good company.

☞ Rev. George C. Lorimer will preach at the Walnut-street Church this day, Sunday, at eleven o'clock A. M., and at half-past seven P. M. d2&n1

☞ He who is voluntarily false will soon be so involuntarily; from deceiving others he will get to deceive himself.

☞ Happiness must arise from our own temper and actions, and not immediately from any external conditions.

QUESTION AND ANSWER.—Is John Bull's motive in befriending the South, one of mercy? Mercy? Nary!—*Vanity Fair.*

☞ Most men have in their souls no locomotive strong enough to draw a train of thought.

☞ If we carry not the beautiful within us, we may travel over the world in vain search of it.

☞ Every art is best taught by example; good deeds are productive of good friends.

☞ Men generally make way for him who is determined to push boldly past them

To the Young Men of Kentucky.

By the authority, and for the service of the Government of the United States, I propose to organize in Kentucky a regiment of cavalry, to serve three years, or during the war, to consist of ten companies, each company to contain not less than eighty-four, nor more than one hundred and four, rank and file.

Horses and all equipments to be furnished by the Government.

Volunteers owning good horses can have them appraised, mustered into the service, and paid for by the mustering officer.

The Captains and Lieutenants are to be elected by the companies, respectively.

Captains of companies will report to me at the Galt House, in Louisville, as soon as practicable. No company must be removed from its point of organization until ordered into camp. Transportation to the point of rendezvous will be furnished. None but active, vigorous men, and men of steady habits, will be received.

Capt. Richard W. Johnson, of the regular army, has been detailed to act as Lieutenant Colonel. I intend to make this regiment, in all respects, equal to the best drilled and disciplined corps in the regular army.

I know this call will be patriotically answered. The soil of Kentucky has been wantonly invaded. J. S. JACKSON.
LOUISVILLE, KY., Sept. 6, 1861. tf

COL. ORMSBY'S REGIMENT.

To the Young Men of Kentucky.

By the authority and for the service of the Government of the United States, I propose to organize in Kentucky a regiment of Infantry, to serve three years or during the war, to consist of ten companies, each company to contain not less than eighty-four, nor more than one hundred and four, rank and file.

Captains of companies will report to me, at the Galt House, in Louisville, as soon as practicable. No company must be removed from its point of organization until ordered into camp. Transportation to the point of rendezvous will be furnished. None but active, vigorous men, and men of steady habits, will be received.

Pay will commence on the day of enlistment. Most of the gallant fellows who served with me in Mexico, are still able and willing, thank God! to bear arms for their country. Rally, freemen! Companies will go into camp immediately.

se13 dtf STEPHEN ORMSBY.

Railroad Matters.

DEPARTURE OF TRAINS.

LOUISVILLE, NEW ALBANY AND CHICAGO RAILROAD.

On and after Monday, August 12, passenger trains will leave New Albany as follows:

LEAVE NEW ALBANY.

Chicago Express (daily except Sundays)	5:00 A. M.
St. Louis Night Express (daily)	7:45 P. M.

ARRIVE AT NEW ALBANY.

St. Louis Express	4:30 A. M.
Reaching Louisville	5:15 A. M.
Chicago Mail	6:40 P. M.
Reaching Louisville	7:30 P. M.

JEFFERSONVILLE RAILROAD.
FROM JEFFERSONVILLE.

Cincinnati and Eastern Express	2:30 P. M.
Connection Train (at Seymour with O. and M. Railroad) East and West	11:00 P. M.

LOUISVILLE AND LEXINGTON R. R.

Passenger Train No. 1	6:00 A. M.
Passenger Train No. 2	2:50 P. M.
Accommodation Train	5:20 P. M.

LOUISVILLE AND NASHVILLE R. R.

Lebanon Train (Sundays excepted)	7:00 A. M.
Bardstown and Elizabethtown (Sundays excepted)	4:00 P. M.

SOUTH BRANCH INTELLIGENCER.

VOL. XXXII. Romney, Hampshire County, Va., September 25, 1861. NO. 5.

From the Southern Advocate

VOLUNTEER'S SONG.

To arms, ye brave, the battle lowers;
The South from danger never cowers;
Our chieftains come from freedom's towers!
To fight for liberty.
Along Virginia's classic shores
A plund'ring horde its legions pours;
In Bethel's wood our cannon roars,
Achieving victory.

But still they come from hill and plain,
Insulting foes our soil profane,
Our towns are burned, our people slain,
By Northern chivalry;
And Northern leaders boldly swear,
To make the South a desert drear,
Unless her sons consent to wear
A bondman's livery.

What though Manassas' fight is done,
The battle fought, the vict'ry won,
Our foes drove back on Washington,
Retreating shamefully;
What though our brothers won a name
Immortal as that field of fame,
Shall we by future action claim
No name won manfully!

Shall we at home in peace remain,
No laurels win, no honors gain,
Our heroes leave to die in vain,
In old Virginia?
It must not be! arise ye brave,
And march to glory or the grave;
Our brethren and our country save
From Lincoln's Tyranny!

Awake, arise! ye men of might,
Gird on your armor for the fight,
March forth to battle for the right
And rout the enemy.
[illegible] rallying cry,
With blades of battle raised on high,
Around our standard we will die,
Or hail our country free.

MAYSVILLE.

INTELLIGENCER:

ROMNEY, FRIDAY, SEPT. 20, 1861.

THE PREACHERS' REGIMENT.—A regiment of Arkansas troops, from the southern part of the State, says the Helena *Shield*, passed up last Sunday, *en route* for the seat of war, that should properly be styled the Preachers' Regiment. The Col, Bradley, from Pine Bluff, is a Methodist Minister, and besides him there are no less than eight preachers in the regiment, one of whom is over seventy years of age!

INDIANS JOINING McCULLOCH.—The Helena (Ark.) *Shield*, of the 10th inst., learns that on last Monday *thirteen hundred* Indian warriors—Southern allies—crossed the Arkansas river near Fort Smith, *en route* for McCulloch's camp. These Indians were armed with rifle, butcher knife and tomahawk, and had their faces painted, and seemed eager for the fight.

☞ Several prisoners confined in the Richmond jail for various offences have presented a petition to the Mayor, representing that they claim to be citizens of the United States, and are therefore anxious to obey President Davis's Proclamation requiring them to leave the Confederate States, but are prevented by the bars, bolts and walls of their prison.

MARYLAND.—A gentleman, who was recently in Maryland, gives the editor of the Richmond *Whig* a very interesting account of the state of feeling among the people and of the horrible despotism of the Yankee mercenaries. Arrests are nightly made of the most respectable citizens; and in large districts of country, men never sleep at home. They seek safety in the woods.—Rogueries and outrages of all kinds are constantly perpetrated. The negroes, almost without an exception, are true to their masters, and have an intenser hate of the Yankees than even their mistresses have. Very often, through their vigilance their masters have been enabled to escape the myrmidons of Lincoln. The wish, the prayer of the whole population, white and black, men women and children, is for the [illegible] Army of DELIVERANCE. When that day does arrive, it will witness such an uprising—such an exterminating fury as the world has never seen. The New York *Herald* states that the Maryland population is so intensely Rebellious that a Confederate army could march from the Potomac to Baltimore without the fact being made known to the Federal authorities by any of the inhabitants. Surely, such a people, outraged and panting for liberty, have a right to all our sympathies and to all the aid our arm can give them.

A GOOD THING FOR OUR NEGROES.—It cannot be denied that a number of diseases must result from the wearing of leather shoes by our negroes, when engaged in outdoor operations during the cold weather, or in wet situations. In Germany, Belgium and France, in order to prevent these evils, at least to some extent, the use of wooden shoes has long since been introduced, and are extensively worn by the whole farming and laboring population.

The Governments of Europe have very much encouraged the manufacture of the same, and their preference over leather shoes is much recommended by all Boards of Agriculture and of Health. There is hardly an operation on the farm and about the farm houses, the garden, &c., in which they could not be most profitably used.—They are perfectly secure against the penetration of water, and being always dry, will keep the feet warm and thereby prevent many diseases.

They are light and easy to wear, of a pleasant appearance, and may be blackened or varnished. They can be worn with or without stockings, and, with many other advantages, they combine such durabilities as to last almost a whole life-time, at a cost of from twenty-five to thirty-seven cents.

They are certainly entitled to the attention of the farming and laboring population of the South. The wood for their manufacture is to be had, in great abundance, in most of our Southern States.—*Farmer and Planter.*

FUNNY LETTERS FROM MANASSAS.—Mr. J. PRYOR furnishes the Memphis *Appeal* the following letters found on the field of Manassas after the hegira of the Grand Army; the first being evidently from an impatient young lady to her martial sweetheart:

DEAR BILL—I want you to come back home as quick as you ever can get off, and we will get married the very first night after you arrive. I wish you was at home now, and I had one arm round your neck and you had both yours round mine, what a glorious squeese we'd have!

Alas! says Pryor, poor Bill will return no more to his ardent lady love. With two thousand others of his deluded comrades, he sleeps quietly beneath the sod of Manassas.

[Verbatim copy of a letter written by a Yankee soldier the night before the fight at Manassas, said letter having been found in his haversack, which he ran off and left upon the field:]

CENTREVILLE, July 20.—*Dear Friends:* It is with pleasure that I seat myself to wright a few lines to let you know that I am well and hope that these few lines will find you the same. I chased a rebel and took his rifel from him and the rifel was worth about forty dollars we don't make eney thing of going out and taking a ox or a pig and if we want to wride we take a horse we don't know but what we shall be cauled into battel a moment warning and I am redey foor them *we don't calkerlate to Show any favers to the Sons of bichis* I want you to give my love to all the folks and tel them to wright as soon as they can our ordley Sargent was Shot through the foot and had to have his toes taken off I want you to tel meria to wright for I haven heard from her I want you to wright to
from your friend
STILMAN WRINK.
Wright soon.

WHAT A MAINE WOMAN THINKS OF THE WAR.—Among the letters picked up after the battle of Manassas Plains, was one addressed by a lady of Bangor, Maine, to a Federal soldier. The following is an extract:

"Mary Benson came to see me last week for the first time for two months. 'The Stars and Stripes' have surely divided us for our sympathies are in opposite directions. I am not afraid to say that mine is for the South decidedly. I haven't a doubt that the North will get one tremendous whipping. It is true the North boasts of its strength, but 'the race is not always to the swift, nor the battle to the strong.'

"I read a most beautiful letter written by Mrs Andrew J Donnelson, daughter-in-law of Andrew Jackson, to General Scott, beseeching of him to avert the civil war already begun. It was one of the most touching letters I ever read. How could he withstand such an appeal? I can't feel at all reconciled to the war; it is so unnatural. Those who have the largest contracts to fill are the ones that cry loudest for the war, and swing the largest banners to the breeze; such things are wrong, and the right must and will triumph.

THE PRISONERS AND THE JUVENILE YANKEES.—The Richmond correspondent of the Memphis *Appeal* relates an incident which we consider worth copying:

The prisoners still remain in their old quarters at Harwood's factory at the lower end of Main street. A gentleman who visited them a day or two ago has related to me a short dialogue as having occurred in his hearing at the prison, which is so good that I will give it to you. A group of grinning little negroes, just discharged from their daily labor, had gathered around a window of the factory and were amusing themselves with comments upon the appearance of the captives. One of these latter, annoyed at being thus stared at and discussed by young Sambo, broke out at the largest of them:

"Go away, you d—d little cuss; if it hadn't been for the like of you, I'd have never been in this pesky place."

"Well, boss," says small ebony, "what you come 'ere for? We all never ax you to come 'ere—nobody want you come 'ere—lemme 'lone."

The ocean behind us
Is dark with its strife.
We have reached calmer seas,
From the conflict of life;
And the lights of the fair land
Are gleaming before,
We are nearing the shore, mother
Nearing the shore.

THE CASE FAIRLY STATED.—The Charleston "Courier" says:

"We must conquer or be conquered," say the war compelling organs of the North. The motto is true for the South, and we

A RESPONSE TO FREMONT

HEADQUARTER'S 1ST MILITARY DISTRICT,
Missouri State Guard,
Camp Hunter, Sept. 2, 1861.

Whereas, Major General John C. Fremont, commanding the minions of Abraham Lincoln in the State of Missouri, has seen fit to declare martial law throughout the whole State, and has threatened to shoot any citizen soldier found in arms within certain limits; also, to confiscate the property and free the negroes belonging to the Missouri State Guard:

Therefore, know ye, that I, M. Jeff Thompson, Brigadier General of the first military district of Missouri, having not only the military authority of Brigadier General, but certain police powers, granted by acting Governor Thomas C. Reynolds, and confirmed afterwards by Governor Jackson, do most solemnly promise that for every member of the Missouri State Guard, or soldier of our allies, the armies of the Confederate States, who shall be put to death in pursuance of the said order of Gen. Fremont, that I will *hang, draw and quarter* a minion of said Abraham Lincoln.

While I am anxious that this unfortunate war should be conducted, as far as possible, upon the most liberal principles of civilized warfare, and every order that I have issued has been with that object, yet, if this rule be not abandoned, (and it must first be done by our enemies) I intend to exceed General Fremont in his excesses, and will make all tories that come within my power rue the day that a different policy was adopted by their leaders.

Already mills, barns, warehouses and other private property has been wastefully destroyed by the enemy in this district, while we have taken nothing except articles strictly contraband, or absolutely necessary. Should these things be repeated I will retaliate tenfold, so help me God.

M. JEFF THOMPSON,
Brigadier General Commanding.

COL. TURNER ASHBY.—This gallant officer (rumor has it,) has an independent command of cavalry and infantry. He is stationed in Jefferson county, where he is rendering important and efficient service. On Friday night last he planted a cannon on the bluffs below Shepherdstown, opposite the camp of the enemy, and as the fog cleared away in the morning, exposing the enemy to full view and just as they were gathered in a group in answer to the morning REVEILLE, the torch was applied to his "black devil," which belched forth such a shower of grape as to cause a general stampede of the Abolition vandals from the Maryland heights. Eight were killed by the first fire, and a large number wounded. The strength of the enemy in the immediate vicinity of Shepherdstown is estimated at 3000. We trust that Colonel Ashby may be immediately placed in command of a full regiment of cavalry, with at least a regiment of infantry. This with the militia now in service in this and the adjoining counties, is all that we ask for the defence of the lower Valley.—*Winchester Rep., Sept. 20.*

☞ A correspondent of the Lynchburg Virginian writing from CAMP GAULEY, Floyd's Brigade, under date of the 4th inst. says:

A most intelligent and reliable friend related to me yesterday an incident of recent date, which deserves to be handed down to history as one of the most striking instances on record of female patriotism and courage. A few days after the fight at Scary near Charleston, Kanawha, two or three Yankee officers visited the house of a Mrs Fry, who had been driven from his home by the enemy. A daughter of Mr. F. saw them approaching through the gate, and confronted them in the porch, with a demand to know their business.—They stated they were looking for Secession flags, and heard there were some there. Her reply deserves to be hung as an "apple of gold in a picture of silver." "Brave men," said she, in scorn, "take flags on the field of battle—cowards only hunt them at the house of defenceless women. Mine is in the hands of our brave volunteers; go and take it from them." This rebuke was crushing. "Tom," said the one to the other, "we had better leave her," and off they went, with the blushes of shame mantling their cheeks, if, indeed, they were not dead to the feeling which occasion them.

A few days ago I rode past the freshly made graves of some of the Yankees, and at the head of one of them, I discovered, written by some wag, upon a piece of white paper, the following significant lines:

"The Yankees came in serried bands
To take possession of our lands,
But this very small, contracted spot,
Shows all the land *these* Yankees got."

This is very good poetry, I think, and better sentiment. The Yankees would do well to profit by the hint.

LOVELY SALLIE BELL.

In a lonely, silent valley,
Near a shady dell,
Sweetly slumbers dearest Sallie,
Lovely Sallie Bell;
She was pure, for nature made her
Smiling as the sunny noon,
Fairer far than all the flowers
Blushing o'er her early tomb.
CHORUS.—In a lonely, silent valley,
Near a shady dell,
Sweetly slumbers dearest Sallie,
Lovely Sallie Bell.

Years have sped since last we parted,
I and Sallie Bell;
I to wander broken-hearted,
She to joys unspeakable.
Other forms around me hover,
Other voices greet mine ear;
While sighing winds are whispering over
Sallie! lost and dear.
CHORUS.—In a lonely, silent valley,
Near a shady dell,
Sweetly slumbers dearest Sallie,
Lovely Sallie Bell.

Thus have all my visions banished
Of the loved and fair,
And hope's sweet blossom's banished
Like the fleeting air:
How I long to rest beside her
Near the shady dell,
Where oft we met in childhood's hours,
I and Sallie Bell.
CHORUS.—In a lonely, silent valley,
Near a shady dell,
Sweetly slumbers dearest Sallie,
Lovely Sallie Bell.

From the Richmond Whig.

To the Editor of the Whig: The following lines accidentally came into my hands, and without the knowledge of the fair authoress, I take the liberty of sending them to your paper, and dedicating them *to the Alabama Volunteer Regiments now in Virginia.*

THE APPEAL.

Let me go! the war-drum soundeth,
And the bugle screams afar;
Hark! now, louder far resoundeth
Deadlier music from the war.
See! my countrymen lie bleeding—
On the parching sand they lie—
Messengers of death still speeding—
O'er them bends a torrid sky.

List! those open wounds have voices,
Louder than the stirring drum;
From their gory lips they call us—
Southern daughters, mothers, come!
Can we sit at home, white handed,
Sheltered from the wind and sun,
Roughest hands, with clumsy kindness,
Doing what ours should have done?

On his couch of straw extended,
Faint, a youthful hero lies,
By the soldier's friend attended,
Who my place, yes mine supplies—
For a woman should be near him
Aiding through the lonely path,
'Tis her accents that should cheer him
As he falters "This is death."

"Is there no one can repeat me
Verses that I used to hear?
Words my mother used to teach me,
Bending at her knee in prayer?
Ah! my mind grows dim and dimmer,
And my sight is fading too,
Yet I think I see you, comrade,
Would, I saw my mother too?"

But alas! no tender mother
Bends above that anguished brow!
Ah! young soldier, O my brother!
Would, I were beside thee now!
Let me go! too long I linger,
Harder-hearted than the foe.
Hark! my country, duty calls me
Dear companions let me go!

GREENE CO., ALA., July 6 1861.

SOAP.—We urge upon the attention of farmers and house keepers the importance and necessity of making soap. The old fashioned home made soap—the best in the world for laundry purposes—can be made with ease by every house wife, and, at this time, will pay handsomely for the trouble. The article is becoming very scarce and high. This great "civilizer" should not be neglected. The common turpentine soap, which usually costs 2½ a 3 cents per pound to make, is now selling in our market at from 15 to 20 cents per pound.—This should not be for an article so easily made. The price, however, is not so important as that the demand should be promptly furnished.—*Enquirer.*

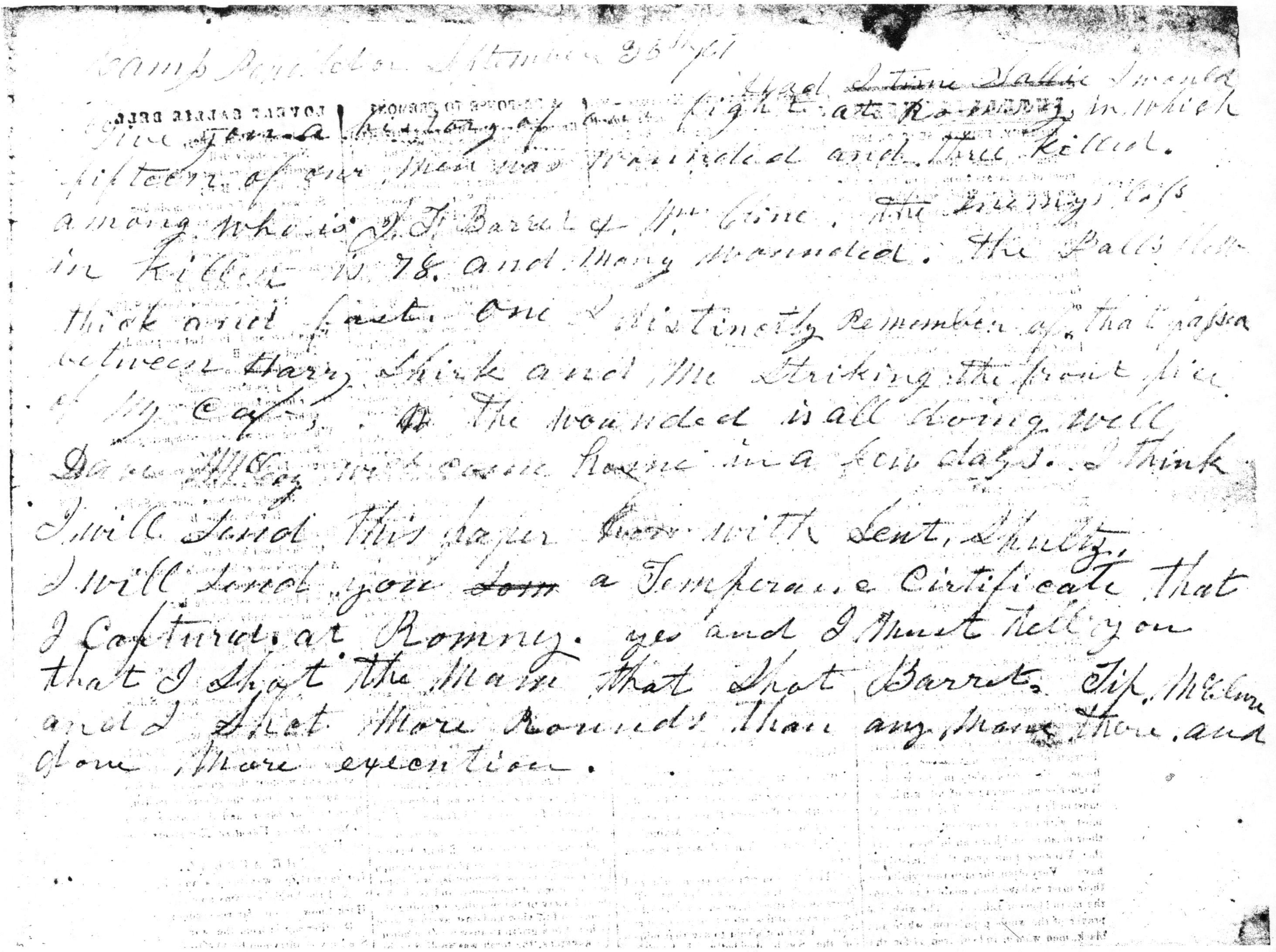
Camp Pendleton September 30th/61
Had I time Sallie I would
Give you a history of our fight at Romney, in which
fifteen of our men was wounded and three killed.
among who is J. F. Barret & Wm Cline. The Enemy's loss
in killed is 78. and many wounded. The Balls flew
thick and fast. One I distinctly Remember of that passed
between Harry Shirk and Me Striking the front piece
of my cap. The wounded is all doing well
Dave McCloy will come home in a few days. I think
I will send this paper ~~here~~ with Sent. Shultz.
I will send you ~~some~~ a Temperance Certificate that
I Captured at Romney. yes and I Must tell you
that I Shot the Man that Shot Barrett. Tip McClure
and I Shot More Rounds than any Man there and
done More execution.

*The letter inside is as follows....."Camp Pendleton (Md.), September 30th/61.....Had I time Sallie I would give you a history of our fight at Romney, in which 15 of our men was wounded and 3 killed. Among who is J.F. Barrett and Wm Cline. The Enemy's loss in killed is 78 and many wounded. The Balls flew thick and fast. One I distinctly remember of that passed between Harry Shirk and me striking the front piece of my cap. The wounded is doing well. Dave McCloy will come home in a few days. I think I will send this paper with Sent. Shultz. I will send you a temperence certificate that I captured at Romney. Yes and I must tell you that I shot the man that shot Barret. Tip McClure and I shot more rounds than any man there and done more execution....." (unsigned)

Certainly a unique item for the Civil War Collector. I believe Shirk was probably with the 4th OVI at the Battle of Romney - Reid - "Ohio In The War" p. 36 says - "Lt. Col Cantwell with six companies (of the 4th O.V.I.) moved on Romney (Va.) leaving Pendleton on the 24th of Sept. and after a brisk engagement, drove the Rebels from that place. The loss of the regiment in this action was 32 men wounded....."

LATEST NEWS.

From the Richmond Examiner.

Critical Situation in Western Virginia—Rosencranz Marching on the Big Sewell.

Intelligence of the most important and critical nature has reached here from the seat of war in the West, by special express arrived yesterday evening. The news from our camps on the Gauley line is as late as Wednesday last, furnishing a most uncommon instance of the dispatch of intelligence from that quarter.

On Friday last Gen. LEE arrived at FLOYD'S camp at Meadow Bluff. He was accompanied by an escort of twenty men and three baggage wagons. On the Sunday following Gen LEE proceeded to WISE'S encampment, on the Big Sewell, and made a thorough reconnoissance of the position.

It was known that ROSENCRANZ had crossed the Gauley, and was making his way towards our lines. It was reported that he had crossed the Gauley at Hughes' Ferry, taking up his line of march on the Wilderness road, but, learning the position of FLOYD'S forces, had retraced his march, crossing the river again at Carnefax (the locality of the late battle) and directing his movements towards WISE'S position on the Big Sewell,

Gen. Lee had taken four regiments of Floyd's command to reinforce Gen. Wise. The juncture of these two forces would not it is said, amount to more than 5,000 men, and it had been determined to give battle ... approach of the enemy. Rosencranz' force was estimated at 14,000 men.

It was understood that the position of Gen. Wise was exceedingly strong. The dispositions of the forces had been made by Col. Henningsen; and it was ... they would be able to check Rosencranz, notwithstanding the considerable superiority of his numbers.

On Wednesday last Gen. Floyd had prepared dispatches to hurry up reinforcements on points from the route to Richmond Col. Russell's Mississippi Regiment had arrived out, as had Col. Phillips' Legion or Battalion, 600 strong.

At the time of the preparation of these dispatches it was reported in Gen. Floyd's camp that an engagement had already taken place, or was in progress, between Gens. Lee and Wise and the enemy. Meadow Bluff is about 15 miles distant from Wise's position. If an action had taken place, or was being contested, its result was not known or certainly anticipated at the last reliable accounts which have reached through special express.

The "hotel rumors" which were in circulation last night are not subjects of notice, as we are satisfied that we have the last reliable accounts which have reached here yesterday from the seat of war, and that they do not contain any information of the result of an engagement with the enemy.

If it should become necessary for our forces to fall back from the Big Sewell, it is understood that they will do so upon Gen. Floyd;s position, which is said to be impregnable, defended as it is, on one side by a mountain bluff, and on the other by a considerable stream. Our forces, in the position now occupied by Floyd's command, could not be outflanked. They would command the Wilderness road and the Boyer's Ferry road, both of which connect with the pike and guard the only passable approach to Lewisburg,

We take the above from the Richmond *Examiner* of yesterday, but the following from the *Dispatch*, of same date, contains an army order, which states that General Wise was engaged with the euemy on the 24th. Says the *Dispatch* :

The position of affairs in Western Virginia is full of interest. We have dates from Meadow Bluff on the 25th instant, (Wednesday last.) In an order to Major Dunn, Brigade Quartermaster, Gen. Floyd's Adjutant uses the following language, which we extract:

HEADQ'R ARMY OF THE KANAWHA, }
Meadow Bluff, Sept. 25, 1861. }

The enemy have concentrated their entire available force in Western and Northwestern Virginia on this road, and it is absolutely necessary to the command of Gen. Floyd and to the cause that he should have reinforcements. The enemy have already appeared before Gen. Wise in large force Gen. Lee went to his succor with four of General Floyd's regiments, which leaves the latter with a very small force. Hence you see the necessity of rapid reinforcements.

P. S.—Gen. Wise was fighting yesterday but with what success is not learned.

Gen. Lee had brought with him from Huntersville no troops, and was attended only by an escort of twenty men and three baggage wagons.

Meadow Bluff is a strong position, commanding the approach to Lewisburg, whether by the main turnpike road from Gauley Bridge, or the Wilderness road from Summersville, or the road from Bowyer's ferry on New River. At this point Gen. Floyd is stationed with what of his command is left after the four regiments taken forward by Gen. Lee, and is very strongly fortified.

Gen Wise is west of Meadow Bluff ... teen miles, on Sewell mountain, in a very strong position. The four regiments taken up to him by Gen. Lee will increase our force there to about five thousand men.—This number was doubtless attacked by Rosencranz on Wednesday last at the head of fourteen thousand. It was hoped that Generals Lee and Wise would be able to hold the position and check the enemy; if not, they would withdraw to Meadow Bluff, where no doubt is entertained but that the united force of the two commands could repel the enemy. The public will look with intense interest for the result of these attacks of Rosencranz. A fine Mississippi regiment, under Col. Russelll, and four hundred of Col. Phillips' Legion, of Ga., reached Gen. Floyd, respectively, Monday and Wednesday.

[*Correspondence of the N. Y. Herald.*]

PROBABLE EARLY RECOGNITION OF THE REBEL CONFEDERACY BY SPAIN.

WASHINGTON, Sept. 18.—There are sound reasons for believing that the Spanish government have taken the initiatory steps to recognize the rebel government of the Confederate States. It is believed here that the reports about the conduct of the Captain-General of Cuba have been thrown out by the Spanish authorities to feel the public pulse, and that the Spanish Minister is really in possessession of instructions to recognize the Southern Confederacy in a few days. Whether this order is contingent upon another defeat of the Union arms is not clear. That the Spanish government naturally entertains an unkind feeling towards the government of the U. States is an easy matter to understand, on account of the Ostend manifesto, but when it is remembered that the authors of that piratical document are the leaders of the present rebellion, it is strange that Spain should so much admire them as to desire to recognize their bogus government over and above the present genuine government, composed of the old and firm friends of Spain, and particularly that class of men who fought the Buchanan Government in its attempt to steal Cuba. [That something is going on in the Spanish kingdom, of a mysterious character, is evident from the fact that to-night the Spanish Minister gave a dinner at his residence to six of the prominent foreign ministers. It was not only a mysterious, but a highly important affair. The parties present, and the points discussed, will serve for further consideration. That the dinner came off is sufficient.

EFFECT OF NEWSPAPER REVELATION OF NAVAL MOVEMENTS.

The conduct of the New York "Tribune" ... exposing, or attempting to expose the programme of secret naval expeditions, has become very embarrassing ... and in some instances caused a change ... orders heretofore issued. It is to-day a subject of inquiry by the Government where the leak in the Navy Department is, by which means the "Tribune" has been supplied with the secrets of the department. The unpatriotic disposition of the "Tribune" managers" in attempting to expose the operations of the Navy, is a subject of severe comment here.

LOYALTY IN CONNECTICUT—GREAT UNION DEMONSTRATION AT HARTFORD.

Hartford, Sept. 17.—A large concourse of citizens from all parts of the State assembled here to-day, to listen to Hon. D. S. Dickinson and others.

Major. Gen. Jas. T. Pratt presided. All the political parties of the State were represented, and places of business were closed during the meeting. Mr. Dickinson's speech was one of his best efforts, and had a powerful effect.

Senator Latham, of California, sent a letter of apology for his absence, full of patriotic spirit.

Thomas Francis Meagher sent a dispatch as follows:

"I cannot go to Hartford to-day. I go to the war. Talking is over. Fight is the word!"

The loyal sentiment of the State is fully aroused.

MASSACHUSETTS DEMOCRATIC STATE CONVENTION.

Worcester, Sept. 18.—The Democratic State Convention met here to-day. Moses Bates was elected President, and after some preliminary business the following nominations were made: Isaac Davis, of Worcester, for Governor; Edwin C. Bailey, Lieut. Governor.

Resolutions were adopted giving as the motto of the Convention. "The Federal Government: It must and shall be maintained." Sustaining heartily the Administration in the vigorous prosecution of the war; asserting as their principles, "Separation never—Union forever."

GENERAL WOOL AND THE CONTRABAND NEGROES.

Major Cannon, of General Wool's Staff, has arrived with despatches. Gen. Wool wants to know what to do with the negroes, upward of two thousand of whom are now at Fortress Monroe. Gen. Wool is ordered to send to Washington all whom he can spare—the men to be put on the intrenchments, and the women in the camp kitchens, to be paid for their services. Beside two thousand at the fort, there are ten or fifteen on each of our men-of-war which sail from Hampton Roads, who get $8 a month and found.

We are informed that on the 14th of September, Mr. G. M. Emack, of Prince George county, Maryland, was arrested by a party of Sickles's Brigade, and carried before General Walker, commanding the Brigade, during the sickness of Sickles. Seizing an opportunity, he suddenly drew his knife and stabbed Walker twice, mortally wounding him. He was then fired upon by the soldier who was guarding him, who fortunately missed him. He then struck at the ... cutting off three of his fingers. Mr. ... rushed by the rest of the guard, and ... his flight succeeded, after a toilsome journey, in reaching the Potomac and crossing into Virginia ... near this city. ... that Gen. Walker has died of his wounds,—*Richmond Enquirer.*

The Washington "Star" says that a conversation with Mr. Buchanan, the ex President fully indorsed the policy of Mr. Lincoln's Administration.

ATTENTION.

THE subscriber having just received twenty bundles of the first quality of AMERICAN IRON, is now prepared to fill all orders for Camp Kettles, Mess-Pans, &c., with dispatch.

jy12-ts C. S. BLISS,
No. 121, Main Street.

BY TELEGRAPH.

FROM WILMINGTON, N. C.

WILMINGTON, Sept. 26.—The same two Yankee war steamers are reported to be off the coast below this morning.

[SECOND DISPATCH.]

WILMINGTON, Sept. 26, P. M.—Reliable information reports five Yankee war vessels off New Inlet at 12 o'clock to-day, and two off Western Bar.

IMPORTANT FROM WESTERN VA.

RICHMOND, Sept. 26.—Passengers from Western Virginia by the train this afternoon, report that Gen. Wise refuses to fall back from Sewell's mountain, and expects a fight every moment.

THE POTOMAC BATTERIES.

RICHMOND, Sept. 26.—It is reported that two Federal steamers were fired upon today by our batteries on the Potomac and completely riddled.

THE YANKEE PRISONERS BOUND SOUTH.

WILMINGTON, Sept. 26.—Two hundred and fifty prisoners arrived here at 6.30 this evening on their way to New Orleans.

[*From the Rich. Dispatch.*]

We are indebted to Mr. Smallwood, a former resident of this city, but for a long time engaged at Harper's Ferry, who called on us yesterday morning, direct from Winchester, for the following summary, from the Baltimore *Clipper*, of Tuesday, the 24th inst.

THE BATTLE AT LEXINGTON, KENTUCKY.

The *Clipper* gives an account of the battle fought at Lexington, Ky., on Monday, the 16th, between Gen. Price, in command of the Confederate forces, and Col ... gan, commanding the Federal troops in their entrenchments. It is described as being a most bloody contest, lasting for two days, ending with the repulse of the Confederates, whose loss is estimated at 3,000. Federal loss 800.

GEN. ANDERSON ISSUES A PROCLAMATION.

General Anderson has issued a stirring Proclamation to the people of Kentucky, in which he calls upon the Union men to rally around the flag of their country and aid in putting down the rebellion.

REPORTED OCCUPATION OF PADUCAH BY THE CONFEDERATES.

The *Clipper* contains a dispatch stating that the Confederates had taken possession of Paducah, Ky.

SEWARD ON THE SUPPRESSION OF THE LONDON TIMES.

A committee of Federal citizens, indignant at the articles in the London *Times*, which alluded to the Federal Government loan as worthless, have written to Wm. H. Seward, suggesting the suppression of the London *Times* in America. Seward replies that the best way to effect this object will be for the American journals to shut down on the republishing of the articles from the columns of that offensive but influential sheet.

THE FEDERALS CROSSING NEAR MARTINSBURG.

Mr. Smallwood informs us that a few days ago some eight hundred Federal soldiers crossed over from the Maryland shore at Falling Waters, three miles from Martinsburg. It is supposed that they intend to destroy the property of the Union refugees, which would otherwise be confiscated to the Confederate Government.

THE AMERICAN PONY EXPRESS, EN ROUTE FROM THE MISSOURI RIVER TO SAN FRANCISCO.—FROM A SKETCH BY G. H. ANDREWS.

Some of our readers may possibly be puzzled, when reading American news, to find most important intelligence from California, Oregon, British Columbia, and the Pacific side of the continent of North America contained in a short paragraph headed "By Pony Express;" and the questions naturally arise, What is meant by a pony express? where does it come from? where does it go? and why is it a pony express, and not a horse, or a stagecoach, or a railway express? For the purpose of giving some information on this point, our Special Artist has taken the trouble to visit the locale of the pony express, to see it arrive and depart at its eastern terminus, and also to get a view of it en route on the plains.

The great importance of maintaining a rapid communication between the States of the American Union situated on the Atlantic and Pacific seaboards has long been felt, and numerous projects for connecting them by railways have been continually before Congress, but to the present time scarcely anything has been done either towards the railway or telegraph. Between the Missouri River and California—a distance of 2000 miles—there exists a huge wilderness of prairies, arid plains, mountains, forests, and two huge mountain-chains—the Rocky and the Cascade Ranges. Through the whole of this must an Atlantic and Pacific railway be carried when it is made, if it be made through United States' territory. The railway works were extraordinary in perforating and climbing the Alleghanies. Railways are now being made through the mountains in India, and in other places where tremendous obstacles have to be overcome, yet on none of the lines made or being made do such formidable barriers exist as are found between the Atlantic and Pacific States of the American Union. The present unhappy state of affairs—the waste of war—is draining the national exchequer dry, and deferring to a distant date the completion of the most important work the United States' Government has had in hand since the declaration of independence—the binding their eastern and western territory together with a band of iron.

Mr. W. H. Russell, of the firm of Russell, Major, and Waddel, extensive Government contractors for the conveyance of stores overland to the States on the west side of the Rocky Mountains, having observed the daily-increasing importance of a more rapid means of communication than then existed, hit upon the exceedingly bold idea of running a pony express from the Missouri River to the Pacific Ocean, carrying a telegram from New York, or any other part of the States, to San Francisco in eight days, and a letter in thirteen. Those who knew the country through which the express must pass shook their heads, and said it would never do; the route was far north, the winter severe, the roads impassable, the snow lying often fifteen feet deep on the ground. It then took 115 days to make a quick passage between New York and San Francisco.

Mr. Russell was not the man to set aside a plan he had made up his mind he could carry out by any multiplication of difficulties: he therefore prepared to make the attempt. First he built stations all along the route and stocked them well and plentifully, then engaged a corps of fearless and trustworthy riders, and purchased about six hundred horses, the very best that money could procure. Having done all this and a great deal more that was necessary, on April 9, 1860, two ponies started simultaneously, one from San Francisco, and the other from St. Joseph, on the Missouri; and, although the season was most unfavourable, the mud being in some places two or three feet deep, yet the entire distance, one thousand nine hundred miles, was run in seven days and a half, carrying despatches from New York and San Francisco. This performance is the more remarkable because the early part of April is considered the very worst season of the year: the snows on the mountains are deep, and on the plains the rivers are swollen and filled with floating ice. Old mountaineers consider April as bad as any winter month on the mountains, and worse on the plains. The pony express, being "un fait accompli," continued to run regularly with letters once a week from each end, travelling invariably to a time schedule, until the month of June, when a source of trouble appeared which had long given cause for anxiety. The wild Indians of the western plains began to meddle with the express, and shot dead from his horse one of the couriers. His body was found a few days after, stripped of everything; but the bag of letters remained beside him untouched. The horse and the firearms are what the Indians want, and they wisely consider that meddling with the letters would only unnecessarily irritate Uncle Sam without doing them any good.

The dangerous ground extended about three hundred and fifty miles from Salt Lake, in Utah territory, west to Carson city. In this district the inter-

LOCAL AND STATE NEWS.

Read the interesting letter of our *Beauregard* correspondent.

As we anticipated, there was no truth in the report that the enemy had taken possession of Leesburg. The Richmond Dispatch of yesterday says:

We learned at a late hour last night that the President had received a dispatch contradicting the report that our forces had fallen back from Leesburg.

ROBBED THE LANDLORD.—The store room of the Norvell House, immediately in rear of the hotel building and situated on 11th street, was entered on Thursday night and plundered of a sack of coffee, some bacon, and a lot of soap. The thief entered through a window, from which he sawed a bar, making an aperture large enough to admit his body.

THE EXTORTIONER.—The Marion (Smyth) *Visitor* says:

We learn that there will be a public meeting held in this place, on the first day of next Nov. Court, to take this subject into consideration, and particularly the great advance lately made in the price of Salt at the salt works in this county, where it is now sold at 75 cents per bushel, when it only costs from 8 to 10 cents per bushel to manufacture it. A more particular notice of this meeting will be given hereafter.

We trust that the people of Smythe will handle the extortioners, of which the *Visitor* complains. The army worm is certainly "the worm that never dies." Let it be subjected to "the fire that is not quenched." Men who will avail themselves of the opportunity now afforded them to grind the faces of the poor and the suffering deserve no sympathy.

We published in our last, an account of the Leesburg fight which was taken from the Richmond *Dispatch*, and not credited, through inadvertance of the compositor.

W. RILEY CLARK.—This young man, a private in Capt. W. W. Blackford's company—"The Washington Mounted Rifles," from this county, whilst out on picket a few days ago, was shot by Federal pickets, and very narrowly escaped with his life. Several balls were fired at him—one completely shattering his right arm above the elbow, another taking ffeect in the palm of his left hand. His horse was shot in the head—five or six balls hitting him. As the horse fell, young Clark jumped off and made his escape; and strange to say, his horse came into camp soon after he reached it. Young Clark was a brave and excellent soldier, and his loss to his company will be much regretted. His arm was amputated.—*Abingdon Virginian.*

LATEST NEWS BY THE MAILS.

ARRIVAL OF FEDERAL PRISONERS.

Yesterday morning, it was rumored about the streets that the Federal prisoners captured at Leesburg, would arrive in this city on an extra train at 10 o clock a. m. Long before that hour, people began to assemble in the vicinity of the Central depot, and the crowd received constant accessions until the arrival of the train. A detachment of Regulars, under the command of Lieut. *Bradford*, were posted to keep the crowd off from the track, and the adjacent space between Broad and Marshall streets. About half-past 10 o'clock, the train arrived, and as soon as practicable, the prisoners were removed from the cars to Broad street, where they were formed into a column, eight abreast, and surrounded by a guard, forming a "square." The commissioned officers, twenty-five in number, were placed at the head of the column. Their names and rank, and the Regiments to which they were respectfully attached, are as follows:

Colonels—Cogsbell, 42d New York; W R Lee, 20th Massachusetts.

Major E J Revere, 20th Mass.

Adjutant Charles L Pearson, 20th Massachusetts.

Assistant Surgeon E H R Revere, 20th Massachusetts.

Captains—Francis J. Keffer, 1st "California;" John McKral, do; J M Studley, 15th Mass.; Henry Bowman, do; Chas S Simmons, do; Timothy Omairo, 42d, New York—6 in all.

Lieutenants—G B Perry, 20th Mass., S Gibberson, 42d N Y; Henry Van West, do; J E Green, 15th Mass; J H Hooper, do.; R B Vassall, do; W C Harris, 1st Cal.; C M Hooper, do; Frank A Parker, do; W H Kearns, do; and G W Kearrey, do—11.

The whole number of prisoners brought down on the train was *five hundred and twenty-five*, viz: 183 of the 1st California, 150 of the 15th Mass., 93 of the 42d N Y, 73 of the 20th Mass; including one negro, and one each from the 40th N Y, 1st N J, 3d R I, and Pennsylvania cavalry. The so called "California Regiment" was composed of eight companies raised in Philadelphia, and two in New York.

The guard which accompanied the prisoners to this city consisted of 84 men, detailed from the 4th North Carolina, 17th Georgia, and 49th Virginia Regiments, under the command of Lt Col T C Johnson, of the 19th Ga., and Capt J B Andrews, of the 4th N C.

The only incident that occurred before the prisoners left the cars was a quarrel between two of them, which the guard promptly suppressed One of them was drinking water from a bucket, when another kicked him in the bread-basket, which evoked a volley of oaths and a violent threat to duck the kicker with the remnant of the water in the bucket. The kicker merely replied, in Bwoery vernacular, "Well, what do you slobber in der burkit for, say?" The first squad of prisoners which were marched to the front, embraced a few insolent dogs, who remarked aloud in our hearing, "We can whip you like Irish potatoes" "Damn you, you will see us again," etc. After this impertinence we did not regret that the crowd, on Broad street halted them, a minute afterwards, with a cheer of exultation. The squad which followed behaved with more decorum. The prevailing opinion of the by-standers, in regard to the prisoners, is that they are in the aggregate the best looking set of "YANKEES" that has yet been brought to the city, but according to our notion, there was nothing to warrant so favorable a conclusion, unless it be that a majority of the gang had on the new winter uniform with which they were recently furnished; but their apparel could not disguise their foreign nativity and rough, repulsive, personal appearance. The officers were mostly good looking men.

The prisoners were conducted to the tobacco factory of Mr. Robert A. Mayo at the corner of Cary and 25th strees, which had been appropriated for the purpose, by order of Gen. Winder. The procession was viewed with great interest and satisfaction by crowds of persons, who thronged the side-walks, but there was no exultations, except the cheering near the depot, as the prisoners were brought into view, and the gleeful laughter of the spectators, whilst conversing with one another.

The regular mail train, which arrived about 4 o'clock, P M., brought down one hundred and thirty-two more prisoners captured at Leesburg, Among them were two commissioned officers, Capt. G. W. Rockwell, of the 18th Massachusetts Regiment and Lieut. Chas. McPherson, of the —th N. Y. ("Tammanys" Regiment. They were marched to prison, guarded by a detachment of the 18th, Georgia Regiment, Lieut. Laws commanding.—*Richmond, Whig.*

LINCOLN'S ORGAN ON THE WAR.

"There cannot and there never will be peace again in what once formed the U. S., *as long as slavery exists in the South.* This is the decree of God himself, who has declared an eternal antagonism between right and wrong!!!"

"To talk of peace, therefore, *as long as slavery exists on this continent*, in conjunction with freedom, is both foolish and impracticable!!!"

"If we intend to be free, *the sooner we go to work to overthrow and banish the institution of slavery* the longer our freedom will last and the nobler it will become!!!' —*Harrisburg (Penn.) Telegraph—Lincoln's Organ.*

Among the papers in Lincolndom that continue to denounce the war are the Albany *Argus* the Patterson (N. J.) *Register*, the Dubuque (Iowa) *Herald*, and the Hartford *Times*.

THE BATTLE AT LEESBURG.

We have obtained some further and intelligent particulars of the late brilliant engagement, on our side, near Leesburg, and of the extent and glorious incidents of our victory. These details are from the intelligent testimony of eye witnesses of the battle, and may be taken as a reliable version of it. They represent our victory to have surpassed even the accounts heretofore published by us, and to have given a manifestation of the ardent and desperate courage of our troops, such as seldom has been exhibited in the history of any campaign.

The fighting on our side is described as terrific. In the thickest of the fight, the Mississippi troops throwing aside their muskets, knapsacks and even hats, charged upon the Yankees with Bowie knives, making the attack with yells of rage and excitement.

The enemy made three distinct attacks upon our lines. At one time in the action, for the space of about twenty minutes, the battle raged, with the two opposing forces within thirty feet of each other, amid the stunning reports of musketry and occasional essays of the enemy to reach us with the bayonet. The attempts to charge bayonets on our lines was held in check each time by the steady fire of our troops; and, when their turn came to charge, they rushed into the enemy with a fury that is said have swept them into the most indiscribable disorder and panic-stricken confusion.

Great credit in the action is awarded to the Eighth Virginia Regiment, commanded by Col. EPPA HUNTON. This regiment is said to have assailed the enemy on the flank at a critical point of the action, and to have completed his disorder by the effect of their attack.

General Baker is said to have behaved with the most extraordinary gallantry, and the generosity of even his enemy accords the highest praises to the courage and devotion displayed by him in the thickest of the fight. His body was pierced through and through by bullets. He fought on, without drawing the least notice to his wounds, until, at last, he fell dead by a shot from a Mississippi rifleman, that pierced his temple.

Of the large number of the prisoners taken by us, the most considerable portion are said to be Irish and Germans, but few of the "irrepressible conflict" Yankees showing their faces in the lot.—*R. Examiner.*

The Greensburg Expedition.

PRECIPITATE FLIGHT OF THE LINCOLNITES.

The Nashville *Patriot* of Tuesday last, says:

Gen. Hardee, who started on Wednesday last with 1,500 men to Greensburg to break up Ward's encampment of Lincolinites there has returned to Munfordsville.

He was delayed in his march by a sudden rise in Little Barren river, which prevented his force crossing, thus giving the enemy time to effect their escape, which they did in real Bull Run style.

Some 250 of Gen. Hardee's cavalry, who succeeded in effecting a crossing, proceeded to Greensburg, but the Lincolnites, some 1,400 in number, having been advised of the movements, precipitately fled towards Lebanon.

Our cavalry then occupied Greensburg, where they still remain.

But for the inopportune rise in Little Barren, the surprise of the enemy would have been complete, and their entire force would have been captured.

THE BAGGAGE OF WM. C. PRESTON CONFISCATED.—The New York *Commercial* of Thursday says, This morning Mr. George Bisbee give information to the Surveyor of the Port that two or more large cases, belonging to Wm. C. Preston, late United States Minister to Spain, and now a General in the Rebel army, had been brought to this port by the ship *Germania* from Havre. The cases were discovered while the cargo of the ship was being discharged yesterday One of the packages is very large, probable containing Preston's diplomatic carriage. The others are of less pretentions size. The cases have all been removed to the public stores where they will without doubt be confiscated as Rebel property.

THE CHAMELEON.—An officer in Africa thus writes of the habits of this animal.

As some of the habits of the chameleon may not be generally known, I will take the liberty of mentioning a few of them which came under my own observation. One morning on my return from parade, I saw, close to my tent a very large chameleon hanging on a bush. I immediately secured him and provided a box for him to stay in. In the course of a few days he became quite familier, and having seen them before, I knew how to gain his affections which, in the first place was by feeding him well, in the next place by scratching his back with a feather. I used to put him on my table at breakfast, and in the course of a very few minntes I have seen him devour fifty flies, catching them in the most dexterous manner with his long slimy tongue. Nor does he ever move from his position, but so sure as an unfortunate fly comes in reach, so sure is he caught, and that with the rapidity of thought.

In the forenoon I always give him a large slice of bread, which he devoured, and he generally supped on as many flies he could manage to entrap, setting at defiance the noble Hamlet's theory of the chameleon's death. Promiser would not have suited at all, being at the end of each day considerably more like a crammed capon than an air-fed chameleon. It is not true that this animal will change color according to what he is put upon; but he will change hade aeccording as he is pleased or displased. His general hue is bright green, with small golden spots all over his body. He remains in this state when he is highly pleased by being in the sun or being fed or scrached, which he delights in. When angry and he is very easily made so, his hue changes to a duskey green, almost black, and the golden spots are not to be seen; but I never could perceive any other color on his body but green in a variety of shades. The spots enlarge very much when he is in a good humor, so much, indeed, as to give a yellow tinge to the upper part of the animal but, in general they are merely little yellow spots here and there on the back and sides.

BY TELEGRAPH.

Telegraphed expressly for the "Lynchburg Virginian."

FURTHER FROM THE FIGHT AT LEESBURG.

The Confederate Loss.

DEPARTURE OF THE FLEET FROM OLD POINT.

REMOVAL OF GEN. FREMONT.

ELECTION IN TENNESSEE.

RICHMOND, Oct. 25.

The following Confederates have been ascertained to be among the killed and wounded in the Leesburg fight. 18th Mississippi, John J. Cooper, killed. Frank Clark, mortally wounded Privates Short, Sanders, Willis, Maddox, John Devine and Capt. A. P. Hill, badly wounded

The 13th Mississippi was not in the fight.

The last charge was made by the 8th Virginia and 17th Mississippi Regiments, in which 60 of the enemy were killed

Col. Richard Taylor, of Louisiana, has been appointed a Brigadier General. [Col Taylor is a son of Ex-President Taylor

No later official intelligence has been received from Leesburg.

Gen. Beauregard telegraphed the President that our loss in the recent engagement at Leesburg was 28 killed and 70 wounded.

The loss of the enemy is not definitely ascertained, but the total amount will reach 1300.

The fleet at Old Point has left, it is supposed, for the South. Twenty-nine steamers and transports, however, are still there.

NASHVILLE, Oct. 25.

Langdon C. Haynes has been elected Confederate States Senator by the Tennessee Legislature on the 1st Ballot.

The Cincinnati Gazette says that Fremont has positively been removed by Lincoln's order. Gen. Hunter is appointed as his successor.

No. 83. November, 1861 Price One Penny. Registered for Transmission Abroad.

Electrotyped by Knight & Hawkes, Clerkenwell Close, London.

AMERICAN SLAVERY.

A FEW months ago, we had before us at "Lloyd's," a file of American newspapers. They were from the chief cities in the Southern States. Amongst the varied advertisements of goods and chattels for sale, we read several, of which the two following extracts are samples :

On the first Tuesday in February next, in front of the Court House, during the legal hours of sale, will be sold:

A Negro Woman, 50 years old, | A Negro Girl, 13 years old,
A Negro Boy, 15 years old. | A Negro Boy, 10 years old,
A Negro Boy, 4 years old.

These negroes are *country-raised*, sound and healthy, and sold for *no fault*. Also, a woman, 50 years old, nurse, her grandson, 15; daughter, 13; son, 10; boy, 5 years.

"Under, and by virtue of an order and decree of the Hon. Judge of Probate, will be sold for *cash*, in front of the Court House, on Thursday, 28th February, at 12 o'clock, the following slaves—

Bob, aged about 19 years,
Angeline, aged about 21, and her *two children* (!)
Webb, aged about 2 *years* (!)
Frank, aged about 6 *months*." (!)

Some of our readers will probably inquire, "Were not the newspapers a century old?" We regret to add, that they all bore the date, not of 1761, but 1861. Yes, in the land of boasted liberty, these horrible slave-auctions have long been matters of daily occurrence.

Not content with continuing the curse of slavery in the present Slave States, the Southerners, who have long carried the elections for President, have of late years, used every effort to extend its withering influence, into the newly-added States. The *free-soil* party, although not professed advocates for the abolition of slavery in the States where it *now* exists, have set their faces like flint against the New States being other than *Free* States. This feeling, we rejoice to say, has happily been spreading like leaven during the last few years. The election of Mr. Lincoln as President, was a great triumph. He was the first "Free-soiler" ever elected to fill the presidential chair. The whole civilised world hailed his election as a step in the onward progress of humanity.

Jealous of the rising power of the friends of freedom, the Southern States have revolted, and are now struggling not only to retain, but to strengthen the chains of the oppressed.

It is not, we think, generally understood in England, that the Federal Government stands pledged to give *freedom* to those slaves who may escape to the "lines" of the Northern Army, and holds itself responsible to give "compensation," in cases where the slaves have belonged to masters who are "loyal" to the government. This is a great step towards emancipation.

We earnestly entreat all our readers to pray that the issue of the American struggle may be so overruled by Divine Providence, that the dark stain of slavery, which has so long marred the glory of America, may be for ever wiped away, and that advertisements, such as the above-named, may not continue to pollute the press of a professedly Christian land.

SCENE AT A SLAVE-MART.

A VALUED friend of mine, in America, who was once a slaveholder, but under the ennobling influence of Christianity, had emancipated his slaves, told me, that, on going once into a slave-mart, he saw among those to be sold, a remarkably fine slave. When put up for sale, the auctioneer described him as a man of much physical power, and a skilful worker in iron. Such a man it was expected would bring a large price ; and such was the case. There was a slave purchaser present, an itinerant trafficker in the bodies of men, who, as the bidding proceeded, kept ahead of the rest, which the poor slave observed. After a time, the slave stepped off the block, and said to his bidder : "Well, master, I perceive that you intend to buy me. But, Sir, if you buy me, you must buy my wife too : there she stands, crying yonder." "I don't know that I shall purchase you," said he : "get upon the block." The bidding went on, this person still keeping in advance. The slave again in great anxiety stepped off the block, and made a similar request, and met with a like repulse. In a short time after, this slave-dealer bought the slave, who then said, "Master, my wife and I are much attached to each other ; she will be of little use to her master when I am gone ; you may buy her cheap ; do, master, buy my wife, and I will be a faithful slave to you. I am a skilful worker in iron, and will bring you good wages : do, master, buy my wife." "I came not," said he, "to buy your wife, but you." On this, the slave turned and embraced her tenderly, clasping her in his arms ; when, as if a new thought had struck him, he came again to his master, and said, "You must buy my wife, and I will be to you a faithful slave." His master sternly refused his request. "Well," said he, "If you will not buy my wife, I will never be your slave ;" and immediately killed himself with a weapon which he drew from his pocket."—JNO. SCOBLE, ESQ.

THE SLAVE'S ADDRESS TO BRITISH LADIES.

NATIVES of a land of glory,
Daughters of the good and brave,
Hear the injured negro's story,
Hear, and help the kneeling slave.
Think how nought but death can sever,
Your loved children from your hold,
Still alive, but lost for ever,
Ours are parted, bought, and sold!

Seize, then, every favouring season,
Scorning censure or applause ;
Justice, truth, religion, reason,
Are your leaders in the cause!
Follow! faithful, firm, confiding,
Spread our wrongs from shore to shore ;
Mercy's God your efforts guiding,
Slavery shall be known no more!

O, PITY THE SLAVE MOTHER.

I PITY the slave mother, careworn and weary,
Who sighs as she presses her babe to her breast ;
I lament her sad fate, all so hopeless and dreary,
I lament for her woes, and her wrongs unredressed.
O who can imagine her heart's deep emotion,
As she thinks of her children about to be sold ;
You may picture the bounds of the rock-girdled ocean,
But the grief of *that mother* can never be known.

THE LATE JAMES NISBET, ESQ.,

THE Rev. Dr. David Brown, at a public meeting recently held in the City of Aberdeen, said—"I have rarely met with such a striking and beautiful illustration of the value of Christian principle in relation to the observance of the LORD'S-DAY, than that which the late James Nisbet, the eminent publisher, of London, told me of himself. He said his father was a soldier, and after the battle of Waterloo, was discharged with a small pension. He rented a small cottage and croft, in his native county in the South of Scotland, but when the rage for large farms began there, his father's croft was taken from him, and he had to make the best of a rough world by other means of gaining a livelihood. Having given his boy James a fair education, and instilled into his mind the religious principles of the family—which were very sound and very practical — he told James that he must make the best of his way to London, and do for himself in the world. James, or rather *Jamie* as he was familiarly called, went to London, and soon found employment, though it was rather of a menial description. Having been taught to respect the Lord's-day, and the House of Prayer, James regularly attended Swallow Street Presbyterian Church, where he received saving good. His employer now insisted that he should work on the Sunday for some part of the day, but this he refused to do, and was then discharged without a friend in the world. Two weeks after, his first employer met him in one of the streets at the West-end of London, and inquired what he was doing. He told him that he had supported himself for two weeks by driving a baker's cart, and that he had no fear of being provided for without breaking the Lord's-day. His master asked him to return to his employment, and he would not require him to do any work on the Sunday. This he agreed to do, and while in that situation he married, and his wife attended to a little shop of stationery and books. They had a very happy home, which was much frequented by pious people from Scotland. About that time, the London Missionary Society had accepted several young men from Scotland as Missionaries, and having to prepare them in London, Mr. Nisbet was requested to board and lodge them. This he cheerfully agreed to do, and his home then became quite a mission-house, for when the young men went abroad they used to write to Mr. Nisbet, and his family, for the encouragement of other young men who were under training. Meanwhile, his business increased, and he devoted himself wholly to it. Thenceforward his shop was, to a great extent, the resort of the religious world connected with the foreign mission enterprise ; his business connexion multiplied, and the foundation of the great publishing concern, which bears his name was then permanently laid—all through Mr. Nisbet's love of Christian principle, and his observance of the Lord's-day."

If thou turn away thy foot from the Sabbath, from doing thy pleasure on My holy day; and call the Sabbath a delight, the holy of the Lord, honourable; and shalt honour Him, not doing thine own ways, nor finding thine own pleasure, nor speaking thine own words: Then shalt thou delight thyself in the Lord; and I will cause thee to ride upon the high places of the earth, and feed thee with the heritage of Jacob thy father: for the mouth of the Lord hath spoken it.

ISAIAH lviii. chapter, 13 and 14 verses.

REASONING OF A DOG.

EXTRAORDINARY as the following anecdote may appear to some persons, it is strictly true, and shows the sense, and, I am strongly inclined to add, reason of the Newfoundland dog :—A friend of mine, while shooting wild fowl with his brother, was attended by a sagacious dog of this breed. In getting near some reeds by the side of a river, they threw down their hats, and crept to the edge of the water, where they fired at some birds. They soon afterwards sent the dog to bring their hats, one of which was smaller than the other. After several attempts to bring them both together in his mouth, the dog at last placed the smaller hat in the larger one, pressed it down with his foot, and thus was able to bring them both at the same time.—*Jesse's Anecdotes of Dogs.*

A FRIEND TO FLY TO.

A SHORT time since, I was awakened by the sound of footsteps in my chamber, and a confused noise in the streets. I soon became aware that an alarm of fire was lending its peculiar terrors to the dead of night, and that a startled child was hurrying to nestle in a parent's arms. A few gentle words, and a few loving caresses, and the tumultous throbbings of that little heart were soon again in a sweet, sound sleep. "What a blessing to have a friend to fly to!" was the thought that came at once to my mind ; and what a lesson for us all, is this simple incident. "For we have not an high priest which cannot be touched with the feeling of our infirmities ; but was in all points tempted like as we are, yet without sin. Let us therefore come boldly unto the throne of grace, that we may obtain mercy, and find grace to help in time of need." We may not always have an earthly parent or friend to fly to. But a sympathising Saviour we have always. Times of need will come, when neither father nor mother will be able to help us. He always will, who has gone to appear in the presence of God before us. Reader! remember your Friend. He has given you this gracious promise, "I will *never* leave thee nor forsake thee."

Recompense to no man evil for evil. Provide things honest in the sight of all men. If it be possible, as much as lieth in you, live peaceably with all men. Dearly beloved, avenge not yourselves, but rather give place unto wrath: for it is written, Vengeance is mine; I will repay, saith the Lord. Therefore if thine enemy hunger, feed him; if he thirst, give him drink: for in so doing thou shalt heap coals of fire on his head. Be not overcome of evil, but overcome evil with good.

ROMANS xii. chapter 17—21 verses.

LUCIFER MATCHES.

MANY of our readers, no doubt, remember, the old-fashioned tinder-box, and the way in which, by striking flint and steel, a spark was caught in the tinder, and after two, three, or even five minutes, a light was obtained. Among the many improvements of the present time, not the least useful is the Lucifer match—expeditious, cleanly, cheap—*and with care, safe.*

But is the lucifer-box used with care? We fear we must answer NO. The lucifer-box stands on the mantleshelf in many houses where the children can get at it, and they often amuse themselves with striking lights, and the consequence is, that they not only set fire to themselves and perish by the most terrible of deaths, but they also imperil the lives and property of others. A farmer in Kent, this year, had his entire rick-yard, and farm burned down and was completely ruined, entirely through some children playing with lucifer-matches. But the evil is by no means confined to children. The working-man carries lucifer-matches in his pocket to light his pipe. He enters the workshop, throws off his jacket, and the mere act of throwing it, or anything striking against his pocket is enough to cause the combustion of the matches—and if his jacket only were burned, it would be the just punishment of his carelessnes—but, unfortunately, a fire once kindled, no one knows where it may end. And there is no doubt in the minds of those best able to form a judgment, that the fires caused by the careless use of lucifer-matches cost the insurance offices many thousands a-year—to say nothing of the lost lives that cannot be restored or compensated—and the ruin that comes to multitudes of poor people who are not insured.

There never was a year more memorable for its dreadful and fatal fires than that which is now drawing to a close. In most cases, there is the greatest mystery as to how these fires originated, but all agree that the unhealthy and expensive custom of smoking, and the consequent frequent and careless use of the lucifer-match has had much to do with the terrible increase of fires.

Death by fire was once a rare calamity, it is now one of our most frequent occurrences. We are paying dear, indeed, for our advancement in art and science, when one of the most useful implements of modern civilization has become, by abuse, a frequent emissary of death. Let us resolve to be careful in the use of the lucifer match. Let all make conscience of keeping lucifers in a safe place, using them at a right time, and for a right purpose.

THE USE OF BIRDS.

FOUR petitions have been presented to the French Senate asking the influence of that body in preserving birds which destroy insects hurtful to agriculture, and a committee of the Senate have drawn up a report on these petitions. Many of the facts mentioned are very curious, and highly in favour of the preservation of birds. Sparrows, rooks, owls, and birds of that class are *specially valuable* according to this report, and it is proposed, for the preservation of birds, to prohibit bird-nesting and the destruction of the eggs and young of birds, and also to prohibit the destruction of all birds, except by fire-arms, with such exceptions as are named in the report.

A SEASONABLE REPROOF.

A GENERAL Officer, then in a high command, and no less justly famed for his liberality of spirit and urbanity of manners, than for his military and other distinguished talents, had laid it down as a rule that his doors should be locked, and his servants in bed before midnight. A young aid-de-camp who had lately arrived in the family, having more than once infringed this wise regulation, the general took the following method to correct him.

One morning the gentleman arrived, and with a gentle rap, made no doubt of his being admitted as heretofore, but what was his surprise and confusion, when instead of beholding John, the servant, he found his General standing before him with the latch in his hand. The young officer was beginning to make the best apology in his power, when the General stopped him short by saying, "Pray, sir, come in, I beg you will not think of making any apology ; the fact is, as I knew you were out of the house, and as I have ever since I have had the honour of being in this command, made it a rule to send my servants to bed at twelve o'clock, I was apprehensive they might keep you waiting at the door ; I therefore thought it best to sit up for you, that you might not suffer so unpleasant an inconvenience." A better lesson could scarcely have been given. It produced the desired effect.

"A word spoken in due season, how good it is." "The words of the wise are as goads, and as nails fastened by the Master of Assemblies." T. H. W.

SHORT PIPES & SHORT SMOKERS.

I WONDER who invented smoking? One would like to know by what means the idea first came into a man's mind. We can imagine how the idea was improved upon, and how the help of art has made the practice what we now see it—smoking made easy. But the original idea, and where it came from, is the puzzle. How it ever came into a man's thoughts to suck smoke into his mouth and then puff it out—this is the mystery. Did the general idea of taking in and giving out hot smoke suggest itself, or was some one smitten with the fragrance of burning tobacco? Was smoke the first thought, and something to smoke an after thought? Or was tobacco first, and how to make the most of it second?

Smoke, however, is a fact, and smoking is a wide-spread habit. Men smoke, and women smoke, youths smoke, and children smoke. And I fancy the practice has grown in this direction—downward, from men to boys. Good is to grow the other way, and the knowledge of God is to go "from the least to the greatest ;" but evil and the knowledge of it grows downward, and goes from the greatest unto the least.

As we see little urchins, sitting in a group at the mouth of some court or alley, and puffing away with the gravity of grandfathers, we cannot help asking, "Who is to blame for this? *Would boys smoke if men did not?* There cannot be at the first any natural liking for it. As a rule, it is utterly disagreeable, makes the stomach as uneasy as the troubled sea, and it is only after several attempts that a lad can smoke with comfort. Why do young folks take these pains? Because they think it manly to smoke."

This is the key to other practices beside smoking. Boys get tired prematurely of boys' apparel, and their hearts yearn after long coats and stand-up collars. On the same ground, they strain their eyes to catch the first dawn of coming whiskers, and begin to shave before others see any need for that operation. All this, and much more, because boys wish to look like men.

Even in the excuses given for smoking, boys copy their betters. I knew a family that was always poor. The father and mother earned money, but where it went was not quite clear. The children starved and begged. One forenoon, about ten, I met, in the Seven Sisters' Road one of these children, a boy not more than nine years old, puffing away with a short pipe in his mouth. This very boy had been to my house, not many days before, begging for broken victuals, and I was startled at finding him transformed into a practised smoker. I took him to task, and showed him how unseemly it was to spend money on tobacco and pipes when his little brothers and sisters were wanting bread. He drew himself up to his full height, looked a reproachful look, and, with the air and tone of injured innocence, replied, "The doctor recommended me to smoke, sir." He felt wronged because I had misunderstood his case. He did not smoke because he liked it, or for any other selfish reason. It was out of regard to his health that he had taken to the pipe ; he smoked by doctor's orders!

The power to break up this habit amongst boys lie in the hands of men. If there were no long smokers there would soon be no short ones. Let it not be a mark of manhood to smoke, and the pipe would lose its charms for boyhood. If fathers and masters would sacrifice the cigar, and burn the carved tobacco-box instead of burning its contents, their sons and apprentices would not long care to smoke. I do not think that authority need be used, or the law laid down. Let smoking be confined to youngsters, and they will soon tire of it. Make it a boyish practice, and its doom is sealed, and its days numbered.

The fashions are fixed by the upper ten thousand. What they do and how they dress *is* the fashion. This is copied gradually by the lower ten million ; and when any particular style of dress gets into the kitchen, it soon passes out of fashion amongst gentlefolk. What is worn by the housemaid is not long in favour with the mistress. On the other side, what is not worn by the mistress is not long in favour with the housemaid. Let anything be common amongst servants, and peculiar to them, and its charm is gone. They don't like to have a fashion to themselves. Let crinoline be laid aside by all mistresses, and in six months hoops would be no more seen. Servants would not wear what *only* servants wore.

I say nothing about this principle, good or bad ; only that it is a power in the hands of rich folks, and grown-up men. And leaving dress to come back to smoking, let *men* play the man. By not doing this thing themselves, it is in the power of men to make smoking unmanly. Do that, and you break the neck of the practice amongst boys and youths. Let it have to be said, "Only *boys* smoke," and short pipes and short smokers would soon disappear.

In this lies the only hope we have of seeing the habit put down. Lads will never see that what is proper in men is unsightly in them ; and so long as fathers and masters, and grown-up brothers smoke, so long will boys smoke when they can find time and money. And they smoke some other things beside tobacco. A lad fills his pipe, he sees only tobacco ; but I see going into that pipe, head, money, time, health, books, brains, prospects. The pipe is filled at last, and a light is struck ; and things which the lad ought to set a high price upon, he puffs away in smoke. J. B.

NOTICES TO CORRESPONDENTS.

BOOKSELLERS, SECRETARIES OF BUILDING SOCIETIES, &c.—We shall feel much obliged to any of our friends who will kindly send us the names and addresses of Booksellers, also of the Secretaries of Building and Land Societies, in the towns where they reside.

CANVASSING CARDS—Cards adapted for entering the names of Subscribers to the *British Workman*, together with a supply of Canvassing-bills, may be had by any of our readers, gratis and post-free, on application to the Editor, 9, Paternoster Row, London. E.C. If *each* reader were to get one of these Cards filled up with subscribers' names, it would at once increase the circulation of the "British Workman" to twelve times its present amount! Cards for entering the names of 12, 50, or 100 subscribers may be had.

THE abolition of the Paper Duty will, we hope, enable us before long, to improve the appearance of our publication.

PACKETS BY POST.

☞The Publisher will forward packets of the "British Workman" to any part of the United Kingdom, Channel Islands, Shetland and Orkney Isles, France, or Belgium, POST FREE, as under :—

4 copies for	4d.,	or for one year	4s.	
8 ,,	8d.,	,,	8s.	MUST BE
12 ,,	1s.,	,,	12s.	
16 ,,	1s. 4d.,	,,	16s.	PAID IN
20 ,,	1s. 8d.,	,,	20s.	
24 ,,	2s. 0d.,	,,	24s.	ADVANCE.
50 ,,	4s. 2d.,	,,	50s.	

All orders, with remittances, to be addressed to MR. SAMUEL W. PARTRIDGE, *No. 9, Paternoster Row, London. E.C.*

THE EFFECT OF PARDON.

In the garrison town of Woolwich, a few years ago, a soldier was about to be brought before the commanding officer of his regiment, for some misdemeanor. The officer entering the soldier's name said, "Here is ——, again, what *can* we do with him, he has gone through almost every ordeal?" The sergeant-major, M. B., apologized for intruding, and said, "There is one thing which has never been done with him yet, sir." "What is that, sergeant-major?" "Well, sir, he has never yet been *forgiven*." "Forgiven!" said the colonel, "Here is his case entered." "Yes, but the man is not before you, and you can cancel it." After the colonel had reflected for a few minutes, he ordered the man to be brought in, when he asked what he had to say relative to the charges brought against him. "Nothing, sir," was the reply, "only that I am sorry for what I have done." After making some suitable remarks, the colonel said, "Well, we have resolved to forgive you." The soldier was struck with astonishment, the tears started from his eyes—he wept. The colonel, with the adjutant, and others present felt deeply, when they saw the man so humbled. The soldier thanked the colonel for his kindness, and retired. The narrator had the soldier under his notice for two years and a-half after this, and never during that time was there a charge brought against him, or fault found with him. Mercy triumphed! Kindness conquered! The man was won!

This is just the method God adopts with us in the everlasting gospel. We are guilty. The charges are brought against us. The case is entered. But the Lord delighteth in mercy. He seeks to melt us by his love. He is ready to forgive: He sends to us, saying, "Only acknowledge thine iniquities." And then offers us a pardon—a pardon which cost Him the life of his only begotten Son. A pardon, not of one sin, but of all our sins. A pardon that will bring peace to the conscience on earth, and entitle us to eternal rest in heaven. The soldier, in the case before us, gladly accepted the pardon, was melted down by the kindness of his colonel, and wept as a child would weep. But sinners, too often hear of God's forgiving love without emotion, and instead of humbly confessing their sins, aud gladly embracing the pardon offered, they treat it with neglect or contempt. What can be the reason of this? The reason is, they do not realize their criminality, or the danger to which they are exposed—they do not believe in an eternal hell, as the punishment which their sins deserve, and therefore they treat the gospel as if it were a fable, or a subject of no importance.

Reader, have you felt that you are guilty before God? Guilty of breaking his law, which is holy, just and good. Guilty, not of breaking the law once, but ten thousand times—not in one form but in a multitude of ways—so that if God were to punish you according to your desert, he must sentence you to hell for ever. Have you understood the gospel, which tells you that God is loath to punish you, that he has no pleasure in the death of a sinner; to prove which, he spared not his Son, but delivered him up, the just for the unjust; to bear our sins, to atone for our guilt; that so God may be just, and yet pardon and justify every sinner that believes on Him? Do you see that God offers to pardon you, invites you to come to his throne of grace, that you may obtain mercy—and has long been, and is now, waiting to be gracious unto you. What would you have said, if the soldier referred to, had insulted his colonel, when he told him, that he had made up his mind to forgive him; and had told him he did not want his pardon,—but that he was a most hardened and ungrateful wretch? Yet if you refuse, or neglect, to humble yourself before God, and ask for the pardon promised in his word, you are acting just such a part before God. O, the folly, the consummate folly of the man, who trifles with eternal punishment—who rejects the Saviour of sinners—who refuses to come to God by Him, that he may be pardoned, sanctified, and saved!

Grace teaches good works. The pardoned soldier became a changed man—mercy did, what punishment could not, for it thoroughly reformed him. So, if we believe the love that God has to us, if we receiye the message of his mercy, the promise of his grace, and come to him for pardon and obtain it; we shall find that the grace of God, that bringeth salvation to us, will teach us to deny ungodliness and worldly lusts, and to live soberly, righteously, and godly, in this present evil world. Nothing softens the heart like kindness, and therefore in the gospel, the kindness of God our Saviour, is set before us. Nothing inspires the soul with gratitude like love, nor will anything make us desire so to walk as to please God like gratitude; and therefore the gospel minister cries "Herein is love, not that we loved God, but that he loved us, and gave his Son to be the propitiation for our sins!" If the grace that presents a free, full, and everlasting pardon of all sin, will not melt our hard hearts, and reform our vicious lives, nothing will. The law with its rigid requirements and terrible threatenings, only hardens the sinner's heart, and renders him obdurate and sullen; but the gospel with its sweet invitations, gracious provision, and glorious promises, melts, humbles, and re-models every heart that believes and receives it, and as it melts, humbles, and re-models the heart, it consequently reforms, regulates, and consecrates the life to God's glory and praise. Once more, reader, that gospel, speaks to you. Once more, the God of all grace addresses you. After living so long in sin, after hardening yourself against him so often, after treating him with such criminal contempt, he says, "Come *now*, and let us reason together: though your sins be as scarlet, they shall be white as snow; though they be red like crimson, they shall be as wool." That is, they shall be blotted out, they shall be all forgiven, and you shall be white as the driven snow, and clean as the well-washed wool. And even if my reader be a desperate sinner, one of the foulest transgressors, one of the basest of Adam's race; yea, if you are the vilest that ever breathed God's air, or blasphemed God's holy name, or injured your fellow-men, if you deserve the lowest and hottest hell, yet to you, to you at this moment, to you after all that you have done, God speaks, not in a voice of thunder—speaks not in wrath, but in mercy—speaks, as if he were not willing that any should perish, but that all should come to repentance—and what, think you, are his words? "Wonder, O heavens! Be astonished, O earth!" God, the infinitely holy! God, the inflexibly righteous! God, says to the vilest out of hell, "Seek ye the Lord while he may be found, call ye upon him while he is near; let the wicked," the desperately wicked, "forsake his way, and the unrighteous man his thoughts;" the man of no character, the most depraved, "and let him return unto the Lord, and he will have mercy," yea, he will have mercy, for he delights to do so, He will have mercy upon him; "and to our God, for he will abundantly pardon." Abundantly pardon! Yes, he will pardon like a God. Pardon all sin, pardon all sin completely. Pardon with his whole heart, and with his whole soul. Pardon so as to cover sin, so as to annihilate the charge of sin, so as to free from all the penal consequences of sin, and from the consequences of sin for ever. He will forgive all, not only forgive but forget. Hear his own precious words, "I will be merciful to their unrighteousness, and their sins, and their iniquities will I remember no more." O, blessed assurance, that God will not only blot our sins out of his book, but out of his memory, so that they shall be remembered against us no more for ever.

By permission of the 'Weekly Tract Society,' we are enabled to print the foregoing, as one of our series of *Illustrated Tracts*.

"If we confess our sins,
He is faithful and just to
forgive us our sins."

SIN LEAVES ITS MARK.

Mr. Gough, in a lecture before the Young Men's Christian Association, of London, in dwelling on the corrupting influences of bad associates, alluded to the inevitable penalty of mental suffering which every transgressor incurs:—

"What you learn from bad habits and in bad society," said he, "you will never forget, and it will be a lasting pang to you. I tell you in all sincerity, not as in the excitement of speech, but as I would confess and have confessed before God, I would give my right hand to-night if *I could forget* that which I have learned in evil society—if I could tear from my remembrance the scenes which I have witnessed, the transactions which have taken place before me. You cannot, I believe, take away the effect of a single impure thought that has lodged and harboured in the heart. You may pray against it, and, by God's grace, you may conquer it, but it will, through life, cause you bitterness and anguish."

THE SWEARER REPROVED.

An officer much addicted to profane swearing, visited one of the deep mines in Cornwall. He was attended by a pious workman, who was employed in the works. During his visit to the pit, the officer uttered many profane and abominable expressions; and as he ascended, in company with the pious miner, finding it a long way, he said to him. "If it be so far down to your work, how far is it to hell?" The miner promptly replied, "I do not know how far it is to hell, sir; but I believe, that if the rope by which we are drawn up should break, you would be there in a minute."

AN AFRICAN MERCHANT.

Is all the money spent by Great Britain in the suppression of the slave-trade lost? Let the following fact reply. Years ago, a little black boy was stolen from his home in Africa, and carried away captive into the Yeruba Country. After enduring much suffering, and narrowly escaping being offered as a human sacrifice, he was, when about sixteen years of age, sold as a slave to the Portuguese. No one can describe the horrors of the slave-ship into which the young African, was forced, with hundreds of fellow-slaves. After being some days at sea, the slaver was seen by a British man-of-war, and, after a good chase, was secured as a prize. The vessel was taken to Sierra Leone, and the slaves were liberated. The poor boy, to whom we refer, was apprenticed to a European merchant. By diligence, attention and perseverance, he proved a valuable servant, and, on the expiration of his apprenticeship, he was employed in various stations of trust by English merchants. Step by step, he advanced. He sought and found Divine help and guidance. Through the kindness of the Rev. Thos. Dove, he was enabled to begin business on his own account, and God has prospered the work of his hands. He is now one of the most influential of the Sierra Leone merchants. He is one of England's best customers, importing into Africa as he does *many thousands of pounds'* worth of our manufactures. John Ezzidio, Esq., of Sierra Leone, for such is the name of the gentleman whose career we have briefly sketched, is not only promoting commerce, but we rejoice to add, is using his influence and his money in extending the blessings of the Gospel amongst his countrymen. Let America emancipate her slaves, and we feel assured that, even in a commercial point of view, she will be the gainer.

JOHN EZZIDIO, ESQ., WHO, WHEN A BOY, WAS SOLD TO THE PORTUGUESE SLAVE-TRADERS.

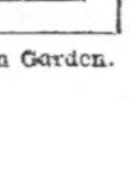

London: Published monthly, at the Office, No. 9, PATERNOSTER ROW; also by W. TWEEDIE, 337, Strand; and A. W. BENNETT, 5, Bishopsgate Street Without.

London: George Watson, Printer, Kirby St., Hatton Garden.

D'EPINEUIL ZOUAVES—COSTUME OF OFFICER AND PRIVATE. See page 10.

THE GREAT NAVAL EXPEDITION.

Perhaps there never was an epoch in the history of a mighty nation that was fraught with greater interest than the event which has been so graphically delineated by the artist, in the accompanying engraving. On the morning of the 29th of October, 1861, the Great Naval and Military Expedition, which had been in course of preparation for several months past, set sail from Hampton Roads on its mission. The following was the

ORDER OF SAILING.

†
Wabash.
Ottawa. Unadilla.
Pawnee. Seneca.
Isaac Smith. Pembina.
Curlew. R. B. Forbes.
Penguin.

Baltic, towing	Atlantic.	Empire City.
Ocean Express.	Vanderbilt, towing	Ericsson.
Pocahontas.	Great Republic.	Philadelphia.
Illinois, towing	Ocean Queen, towing	Florida.
		Roanoke.
		Matanzas.
Golden Eagle.	Zenas Coffin.	Ben. Deford.
Locust Point.	Potomas.	Ferryboat ——.
Star of the South.	Winfield Scott.	Daniel Webster.
Parkersburg.	Union.	Augusta.
Belvidere.	Oriental.	Ariel.
Coatzacoalcos.		Marion.
Alabama.	Gunboat O. M. Pettit.	Gunboat Mercury

Gunboat Mohican. Gunboat Seminole.
Cahawba.

The Expedition was fitted out under the joint auspices of the Army and Navy Departments, Major-General THOMAS W. SHERMAN having control of the military matter connected with it, and Commodore SAMUEL F. DUPONT, organizing the naval portion of it.

The fleet cleared from Annapolis in three columns on the morning of Monday, October 21, and anchored in Hampton Roads, off Fortress Monroe, next day. From thence it sailed under sealed orders, and with increased strength, on Tuesday, the 29th inst. The order of embarkation at Annapolis, was as follows:—

1. First brigade, Brigadier-General VIELE commanding.

Third New Hampshire Volunteers, steamer *Atlantic*.

Forty-sixth New York Volunteers, steamer *Daniel Webster*.

Forty-seventh New York Volunteers, steamer *Roanoke*.

Forty-eighth New York Volunteers, steamer *Empire City*.

Eighth Maine, steamer *Ariel*.

The horses and wagons pertaining to the First Brigade were assigned to the steamers *Belvidere* and *Philadelphia*

2. The Second Brigade, Brigadier-General I. J. STEVENS, (late Governor of Oregon,) viz:—

The Roundhead (Pennsylvania) Regiment, Colonel LANSURE, steamer *Ocean Queen*.

Five companies Fiftieth Regiment, steamer *Ocean Queen*.

Five companies Fiftieth Regiment, steamer *Vanderbilt*.

Eighth Michigan Regiment, steamer *Vanderbilt*.

The horses and wagons of the brigade were assigned to the steamer *Ben De Ford*.

III. Third Brigade, Brigadier-General H. G. WRIGHT, commanding.

Fourth Regiment New Hampshire Volunteers, to steamer *Baltic*. Sixth Regiment Connecticut Volunteers, to steamers *Marion* and *Parkersburg*.

Seventh Regiment Connecticut Volunteers, to steamer *Illinois*.

Ninth Regiment Maine Volunteers to steamer *Coatzacoalcos*.

The horses and wagons pertaining to the Third Brigade were assigned to the steamer *Baltic*.

IV. HAMILTON'S Light Battery to steamer *Ericsson*.

V. The Battalion of Volunteer Engineers, (from Fortress Monroe, Va), to the steamer *Star of the South*.

VI. The regiment of Rhode Island Volunteers (from Fortress Monroe, Va.), to the steamer *Cahawba*.

VII. Division Head-quarters to the steamer *Atlantic*, and the horses pertaining thereto to the steamer *Ericsson*.

VIII. Each Brigade Commander will select from the transports assigned to his Brigade, the one upon which the Head-quarters will embark; the names of the transports thus selected to be reported to these Head-quarters.

IX. The horses and equipments of mounted officers will, as far as practicable, be so placed as to be disembarked at the shortest notice.

There were numerous regiments which joined the expedition at Fortress Monroe and other points, of which we have no definite information. Subjoined is a sketch of the flag-ship *Wabash*:—

The steam frigate *Wabash* is the flag-ship of Flag Officer SAMUEL F. DUPONT, of the South Atlantic blockading squadron. She is a screw frigate of 3200 tons burthen, mounting forty guns; she was built at Philadelphia, in 1855. Previous to the blockade of the Southern ports she was lying in ordinary at the Brooklyn Navy Yard, but was then immediately fitted out, and has been doing active service ever since. Her present armament is twenty-eight 11 inch Dahlgren guns; one 10-inch Dahlgren, one 80-pound rifled Dahlgren, one 30 pound Parrot, fourteen 8 inch shell guns and three boat howitzers. The crew includes about 650 men and marines.

The following are the principal military officers of the expedition:—

CHIEF OF THE EXPEDITION.

Acting Major-General—Brigadier-General T. W. SHERMAN.

STAFF.

Assistant Adjutant-General—Captain Louis Pelouze, Fifteenth Infantry.
Chief Quartermaster—Captain Rufus Saxton, Assistant Quartermaster United States Army.
Assistant Quartermaster—Captain H. A. Hascall, Assistant Quartermaster United States Army.
Assistant Quartermaster—Captain Charles E Fuller, Assistant Quartermaster United States Army.
Chief Commissary—Captain Michael Morgan, Assistant Commissary Subsistence United States Army.
Chief Engineer—Captain Quincey A. Gilmore, United States Engineers.
First Assistant Engineer—First Lieutenant John A. Tardy, Jr., United States Engineers.
Second Assistant Engineer—Second Lieutenant Patrick O'Rorke, United States Engineers.
Topographical Engineer—Second Lieutenant Jas. H. Wilson, United States Engineers.
Chief of Ordnance—Captain John McNutt, Ordnance Department United States Army.
Assistant Chief of Ordnance—First Lieutenant Frances J. Shunk, Ordnance Department United States Army.
Medical Director—Surgeon George E. Cooper, United States Army Medical Department.
Signal Officer—First Lieutenant Theodore L. Dumont, United States Volunteers.
Aid-de-Camp—Lieutenant George Merrill, United States Volunteers.
Aid-de-Camp—Lieutenant James Magner, Twenty-eighth Massachusetts Volunteers.
Additional Paymaster—Major Z. K. Vaughborn.
Additional Paymaster—Major J. L. Hewitt.

FLAG OFFICER OF THE SQUADRON.
Commodore SAMUEL F. DUPONT.

STAFF.

Flag Captain—C. H. Davis.
Fleet Lieutenant—S W. Preston.

SHIP'S OFFICERS.

Lieutenant Commanding—C. P. R. Rodgers.
First Lieutenant and Executive Officer—Thomas G. Corbin.
Second Lieutenant—John H Upshur.
Third Lieutenant—Stephen B. Luce.
Fourth Lieutenant—John Irwin.
Fifth Lieutenant—E Q Matthews.
Sixth Lieutenant—John S Barnes.
Surgeon—Edward Gilchrist.
Major Commanding Marines—J. T. Doughty.
Paymaster—John J. Gulich.
Chief Engineer—J. W. King.
Doctor—James Magee
Chaplain—George W. Dorrance.
Acting Masters—Townsend Stiles, John W. Bentley, John E. Rockwell.
Midshipmen—James P. Robertson, R. John H. Rowland, H. Lamson.
Captain's Clerk—J. Henry Bulkley.
Assistant Engineer—R W. McCleery.
Second Assistant Engineers—F. J. Lovering, Thos. A Stevens.
Third Assistant Engineers—Philip R Voorhees, Harris H. Molony, W. C. Williamson, Hillary Messimer.

The Marines.

Accompanying the expedition is a battalion of United States Marines, under the command of Major JOHN GEORGE REYNOLDS.

Sketches of the Commanders.

SKETCH OF COMMODORE SAMUEL F. DUPONT.

Commodore SAMUEL F. DUPONT, the commander of the naval forces of this great expedition, is a native of the State of New Jersey, but received his appointment into the navy from the State of Delaware, of which he is a citizen. An original entry into the service of his country was on the 19th of December, 1815; he has been, therefore, nearly forty-six years in the service. Up to the present time Commodore DUPONT has spent nearly twenty-two years on sea, eight and a half years in active duty on shore, and the balance of his time has been unemployed. His present commission bears date September 14, 1855.

THE GREAT NAVAL EXPEDITION—FROM FORTRESS MONROE, OCT. 29.

He was last at sea in May, 1859, and since time he has been commandant of the Navy Yard in this city, where his kindness of manner, together with his strict discipline won for him many friends. The many important positions which Com DUPONT has filled, since he has been in the Navy, has already been given in the columns of THE INQUIRER.

GENERAL THOMAS W. SHERMAN.

Acting Major-General THOMAS W. SHERMAN in charge of the expeditionary corps—was born in Rhode Island, and graduated at the West Point Military Academy in 1836, standing number eighteen in a class of forty-six cadets—an unusually large proportion—and was appointed Second Lieutenant in the Third United States Artillery, in July, 1836. In March, 1837, he became Assistant Commissary of Subsistence, and in the same month of the following year was promoted to a First Lieutenancy. Just at the breaking out of the troubles with Mexico, he was promoted to a Captaincy, his commission bearing date May 28, 1846.

He served with distinction previously in the Florida wars, and accompanied General TAYLOR to Mexico, rendering himself conspicuous for the zeal and efficiency with which he performed his duty. He was breveted Major for his gallant and meritorious conduct at the battle of Buena Vista, February 23, 1847. Since the close of the Mexican war he has been on duty in various parts of the country. On the formation of the Fifth Artillery, he was appointed Lieutenant-Colonel of the regiment, a portion of which was engaged in the Bull Run fight, under the name of SHERMAN'S, and, subsequently, AYRES' Battery. He was made Brigadier-General May 17, 1861.

ARRIVALS AT THE HOTELS
UP TO MIDNIGHT.

CONTINENTAL HOTEL—Ninth and Chesnut streets.

G. W. Buck, N. Y.	H O. Freeman.
Peter Halderman, Colum'a.	Maj Gedding, U. S. A.
N. C. Erdley.	Geo. T De Ford & la., Balt.
C. D. Bigelow, N. Y.	Homer Franklin, N. Y.
B. R. Petriken, L. Haven.	G. A Jessup, Montrose, Pa.
J. S. Rhodes, Wheeling, Va.	Chas. Hancock, U S. M.
Mrs. Allen, Belmont, Ohio	James Harvey, Wash, D. C.
F. E. Snow, St. Paul.	C. W. P. Nichols, Boston.
J. N. Church, N. Y.	Hon. D. Todd, Ohio.
E. Tweedy, N. Y.	M. Taylor, Wash., D. C.
Geo. Pearson. Baltimore.	Mrs. J. Fisk, Pottsville.
Geo. B. Williams, Boston.	Pliny Fisk, Pottsville.
R S. Patterson. Wash, D. C.	John C. English, Zanesville.
Geo Strawbridge & la., Pa.	Geo B. Wright, Ohio.
Capt. Baldwin, U. S. N.	W. H Higbee, Trenton.
Geo. Gibbs.	Mrs Gen. D. Tyler, Conn.
Dr. D A. Edgar, N. Y.	C R Merrill, Ohio.
E. W. Leavenworth, N. Y.	G. Pike & wife, N. Y.
E Perry, New Bedford.	Miss Town, New York.
John L. Coffin, Iowa	J. Duval & wife, N. York.
I. M. Denson & la, Balt.	John P Durbin, New York.
N W. Stuyvesant, Jr, Balt.	Mr Mullany, New York.
M. F. Wentworth, Me.	R. W. Coryell, St. Clair, Pa.
P. Van Renssalear, N. Y.	John E. Giddings, U. S. N.
G. Brady, New York.	E. S. Sanford, New York.
J. B. Bradford, Milwaukie.	S T. Baker, New York.
Maj. J. H. Jennings & lady, Mass.	W. C. Churchill, N. York.
	A. H. Ringlord, Conn.
Mr. Hayht, New York.	D. Rodney, Del.
Dr. Nancrede & l, Torrisd'e.	J. B. McCreary & l, Mauch Chunk.
Hon. A. H Reeder, Easton.	
H W. Crothers, Va	J. B. Palmer, Prov., R. I.
W W. Clapp, Sr, & l, Boston	B. Wall, Providence, R. I.
J. P. Marquard, Boston	W. C. Codman, Boston.
John H. Neall, New York.	Geo. Whitney, Boston.
Geo Ashman, Mass.	R. W Emmons, Boston.
W. Coleman, Pittsburg.	W. H Lumberton & l, Phil.
D S. Briggs & la.	G. Beebe, Portsmouth, N H.
F. Miller & lady, Xenia, O.	H. Webster, California.
C. T. Davenport, N. Y.	S. R. Wiles, Boston.
W. Seligman, N. Y.	Paul Smyth, Boston.
H S Wells, N. Y.	T. B. Hobbs & lady, N. Y.
J. O Frost, N. Y.	Capt. Jas. Lawless, Wilm'tn.
J. S Barry, Boston.	Chas Hughes, Albany.
W. M Shuster Wash'n, D.C.	Mrs Col. Lord, Wash'n.
Geo H C. Neal Balt.	John M. Boteler, Wash'n.
B. Bateman, N. Y.	A. N. Rankin, Chambersb'g.
T. J Halpin, N. Y.	Miss Ada Rankin, Chambs'g.
J. F Connor & lady, Md.	Com C. H. Poor, U. S. N.
F. F. Dorr, N. Y.	N. J. Beacock, Gloversville.
G. B. Dorr, N. Y.	A Judson, Gloversville.
J. Jaroslawski, N. Y.	P. Lippman, N. Y.
T. W. Jordan, Washington.	E S Taylor, Boston.
M. T. Seymour, N. Y.	M. S Wilkinson, Minnesota.
G. W. Bostick, N. Y.	W. H. Forbes, Minnesota.
Mr. Fridge & l, Wash., D. C.	Mr. Holdrege, N. Y.
Jos Perkins. Cleveland.	H S. McCombe, Del.
S. Welt & daughter, Clevel'd	Thos. Briggs, Cincinnati, O.
D. F. Bacon, Oxford.	Robt. M Kirkland, Balt.
A. S. Porter, N. Y.	James Perrine, Dayton.
A. B. Wetmore, N. Y.	W. Corliss, Providence, R.I.

MERCHANTS' HOTEL—Fourth street, above Market.

J. M. Carr, Allegheny.	John Evans, Baltimore.
J R. Hedges N. Y.	Wm. N Masterson, Ripley O.
J. Myers Waverly, O.	Geo H Davenport, Ohio.
L Dodge, New Haven.	R W. Derickson, U. S. A.
W M. Lloyd. Hollidaysburg	Is. Painter, Wesmorel'd Co.
Miss Lloyd, Hollidaysburg.	H Watson, N. Y.
John Darner, Canton, O.	David Blair, Jr., Lancaster.
Rev. Dr Paxton, Pittsburg	Isaac Addams & dau, Reading
W J. Sibley, Wash. D C	W H Harlow, Rockford.
Thos G. Lewis, Buffalo.	J. B Nash, Jr, Rockford.
Dr Suessecott, Chambers'g.	G. W. Hathaway, Rockford.
Rev W. S Plumner, Alleg'y	J. M. Sanderson. N. Y.
W Dunlap, Steubenville.	J H. Young, Mifflinsburg.
Lieut. E. S Ulman, Pa.	Richard Fincken, N Y.
T. J. Wilcoxson, Ill.	F L. Williams, N Y.
J C Bates, Ill	Jos Penn, Boston.
D. H. Snyder & son, Easton.	B. N. Miller. Pittsburg.
J. Coldwell, Connersville.	J. H Brightman, Peoria, Ill.
R E. Hendricks, Pa	R. H. Hartley, Pittsburg.
J. D. Jacobs, Chambersburg	

AMERICAN HOTEL—Chesnut street, above Sixth.

B. P. Woods, Md.	W Harris, Philad.
J. E Jones, Smyrna, Del.	John A. Moore, Del.
Jos B. Fenby. N. Y.	Jas F Smith, Reading.
J. G. Jones Philad.	W. Verner, Minersville.
Warren Mansfield, Mass.	A. R Terry, Erie, Pa.
Geo J. Radford. N. Y.	Moses Heider, Erie, Pa.
W. B. Bastord, N. Y.	W. W. Laman, Mich.
Jeff. Fowler, Brooklyn.	H B Decker Rochester, NY.
E Burrell, N. Y.	G. L. Boyd, Tamaqua.
W. McEvoy, N. Y.	W. Asaland, Pa.
F. B. Stewart, N. Y.	F. A Curtis, Del.
P. J. O'Rourk, Albany.	James Baynes, Balt.
Chas Shoener, Tamaqua.	W. Wolff, Pottsville.
J. L. DuBois, Doylestown.	Lott Dean, Boston.
E. Harvey, Princeton, N. J.	F. C. Eanes, Beardstown.
G. T. Harvey, Pa.	

BLACK BEAR HOTEL—Third street, above Callowhill.

D. Housam, Reading.	James Tomlinson, Byberry.
F. Fleger, Pa.	Geo. H. Kohler, Easton.
B. Krubb, Pa	M Richard, Hamburg.
James Slack, Yardleyville.	Benj T mlinson. Byberry.
Isaac L Trexler Yardley'e.	Casper Roads, Somerton.
W. R Neals Yardleyville	Silas Roads, Somerton.
Thos Williard. Yardleyv'e.	James M. Thomas, Pa.
Wm Paff, Yardleyville.	A. Roads, Somerton.
F T Beals, Yardleyville.	Isaac Tomlinson, Byberry.
R. Burroughs, Yardleyv'e.	A. Delp, Doylestown.
F Vansant, Bensalem.	G. Clemens, Chester Val'y.
Wm. Eddons, Pa	Jos. Whital, Northampton.
E. Cadwalader, Pa.	Jacob K Hill, Earlsville.
A. Buckman, Pa.	Lyle Nelson, Attleboro.

ST LOUIS HOTEL—Chesnut street, above Third.

J. Bigler, N. Y.	J. W Storey & w., Wis.
J. J Rockwell, N. Y.	T C. Faxon & la., N. Y.
Saml W. Thompson, N. Y.	S Landsberg, N. Y.
J. Haldeman. Penna.	A L Fleury. N. Y.
S Hopkins, N. Y.	W H. Swope, N. Y.
A. M. Sackett & son, do.	S. Hopkins, N. Y.
B Hamill, Mercer co, N. J.	Clark Pierson, Lambertv.
G Barnes, Hamilton, C. W.	Chas Underwood, Conn.
W. S. Brown, Buffalo.	A S Kidder. N. Y.
R. McNamee, N. Y.	Ed H Brownson, Phila.
F. A. Hollester, Albany.	E. Adams, Philada.
H.G. Andress, Mich.	

UNION HOTEL—Arch street, above Third.

J. Belding, Randolph. O.	J. Logan, Marion, Iowa.
H O. Carter, Granville O.	Jas P Bowman, Ohio.
G J. Stout, Wheeling, Va.	N. Byers, Marion, Iowa.
L G Crane. U. S. N.	L. B. Hawley, Phœnixville.
W. M McLachlon, N. Y.	A J. Epley & sis., St. Louis.
S. D Taber, N. Y.	Miss E.E Harrison, St. Louis.
W. Ward, Ohio.	L. A. McCord, St. Louis.
J. Q Northrop, N. Y.	Mrs. Depew, Easton.
Lieut. E. Drake, N. Y.	Miss E. Depew, Easton.
Jonas J Wortman, N. J.	W. H. Thompson, Bridgeton, N. J.
Bryan Markey. N. J.	
Patrick Mooney, N. J.	A. B. Stewart, Orangev., Pa.
Mrs. Stackhouse Philad.	S. E. Blake, Worces., Mass.

MOUNT VERNON HOTEL—Second street, above Arch.

Miss E. Harding, Chester co., Pa.	A L. Stevens, Boston.
	G. E. Scott, Boston.
Wm. Worthington, Montg'ry co., Pa.	Col. T. H. Conner, Philada.
	O. Goodwin, Boston.
Thos. M. Horton, Wilkesb're.	F. S. Edwards, Churchville.
Geo. Jones, Philadelphia.	James S. Doran, U. S. A.
N. Shaw. Philadelphia.	G. Dusenbury, N. Y.
J. de Banes N. Y.	Benj. C. Bromade, Boston.
C. S. Deeker, Boston.	

MADISON HOUSE—Second street, above Market.

Mrs. W. P Henry, Rocky.	James H. Sutton, Del.
John Gordan, Pemberton.	Franklin P. Gilbert, Del.
W Evans. Moorestown, N.J.	Maj Thos. Jamey, Phila.
A.H. Reeder, Bucks co., Pa.	Daniel Poor, Brownsburg.

REVERE HOUSE—Third street, above Race.

L. B. Pierce, Doylestown.	Jno. A. Weiser, York, Pa.
T. T. Worth, Lebanon.	Jacob Stair, Gettysburg.
M. Ware. Philada.	E. Miller, Trout Run.
W. Weaver, Penna.	Benj. M. Peck, Towanda.
J. T. Kline, Penna.	W. A. Peck, Camp Lacy.

BALD EAGLE HOTEL—Third street, above Callowhill.

J. T. Berger, Quakert'n, Pa.	Benj. Beans, Bucks co.
Peter Seibert. Easton	Wm. Beans, Bucks co.,
G. V. Tracenick Bethlehem,	R V Glover, Hazleton, Pa.
O Balderston, Bucks co.	Lieut. R. Roberts, Doylest'n.
Saml. Smith, Bucks co.	

AMUSEMENTS, MUSIC, &c.

THE PRESTIDIGITATUER.—Mr. HERRMANN was greeted with a crowded house last evening. Of all his feats, the multiplication of bowls of gold fish is probably the most astonishing. The second sight is wonderful, and the magnetic dance of silver coin in a tumbler, at the word of command, is incomprehensible. Mr. HERRMANN has never been excelled—he is the Prince of Prestidigitatuers

WALNUT STREET THEATRE.—The *Hidden Hand*, with Mrs. COWELL as "Capitola," and *Black Eyed Susan*, with ADAMS as "William," ALICE GREY as "Susan," and Miss JEFFERSON as "Dolly Mayflower."

CONTINENTAL THEATRE.—The *Siren of Paris*, with its fine scenery, good acting and striking tableaux, followed by an amusing afterpiece.

ARCH STREET THEATRE.—The *House on the Bridge at Notre Dame*—the greatest play ever produced at the Arch Street Theatre.

SIGNOR BLITZ, our distinguished friend, gives afternoon and evening exhibitions to-day, at the Assembly Buildings.

Daily Alta California.

VOL. XIII. SAN FRANCISCO, WEDNESDAY MORNING, NOVEMBER 6, 1861. NO. 4279.

Daily Alta California.

FRED'K MacCRELLISH & CO.

FRED'K MacCRELLISH............WM. A. WOODWARD

DAILY ALTA CALIFORNIA.........Is published Every Morning, and delivered to subscribers in the city at 50 cents per week, payable to the Carriers; single copies 10 cents. Mail subscribers, $18 per annum, in advance; for six months, $9; three months, $5.

EVENING ALTA CALIFORNIA.........Is published Every Evening (Sundays excepted,) for circulation in the interior, and contains the latest news up to the hour of going to press.

WEEKLY ALTA CALIFORNIA.........Is published on Thursday Morning, and furnished by mail to subscribers, at $5 per annum, in advance; also, mailed to the address of persons in any part of the world. For six months, $3; single copies, 12½ cents.

PUBLICATION OFFICE:
536 Sacramento street—Alta California Building

SAN FRANCISCO, WEDNESDAY, NOV. 6.

CITY ITEMS.

THE DASHAWAYS—LAYING THE CORNER-STONE OF THEIR NEW HALL.—The event of yesterday was the laying of the corner stone of the new Dashaway Hall, on the south side of Post street, near Dupont street, by his Excellency Governor Downey. The ceremonies attendant thereon began at half-past one o'clock P. M., and were witnessed by large numbers of both sexes. Stretching across the street were national and other flags and extending from the rear to the front of that part of the building already nearly erected—the first story—was a large quantity of other bunting, procured for the occasion. The exercises were had upon what will be the flooring of the second story, leading to which was the banner of the Society, having on one side its name and date of organization—January, 1859—and on the other, "Death to King Alcohol." The music was furnished by Walcott's Brass Band. President Wainwright briefly explained the objects of the gathering, after which Rev. Mr. Lacy made an impressive prayer. An ode was then sung by the Dashaway choir, and then Gov. Downey was introduced. He said he felt proud of the honor that had been conferred in permitting him to perform so grateful a task as that of laying the corner-stone of a building [illegible]

[BY PONY EXPRESS.]

LETTER FROM ST. LOUIS.

[FROM OUR OWN CORRESPONDENT.]

Revelations by the Congressional Investigating Committee.

Particulars of the Recapture of Lexington.

OTHER VICTORIES IN MISSOURI.

ST. LOUIS, October 22, 1861.

A report has been received by telegraph from Atchison, that the President of the Central Overland California and Pike's Peak Express Company has given orders for a suspension of the Pony Express service to California, as soon as the Telegraph is completed to the Pacific, which will be in a few days hence. By this dispatch it will appear that Mr. W. H. Russell still has authority over this important branch of the California overland communication, although it has been repeatedly stated that his company was only working under a subcontract with the Butterfield Overland Company, on that section between St. Joseph and Salt Lake City. Whether the Butterfield Company will consent to abandon the Pony Express or not, remains to be seen. There is a legal objection involved in this question which affects the Daily Overland Mail contract. As the bill for a daily mail passed Congress, provision was made for a Pony Express, as part of the service to be performed by the contractors, the time, as well as the maximum of compensation, being fixed by the bill. Now, if the Pony Express be withdrawn, the question arises, will it vitiate the Daily Overland Mail contract? There will probably be considerable of an uproar in California when this is known, and although the telegraph is the most important of the two interests, the stoppage of the Pony will be likely to create indignation.

The Pacific Telegraph Nearly Finished.

It will be no occasion for surprise if the telegraph is completed, in working order, all the way from the Mississippi River to San Francisco many days before these lines appear in print. The opening of the line to Salt Lake, on the 16th, was followed by the exchange of congratulatory messages between Brigham Young and J. H. Wade, President of the Pacific Telegraph Company, and President Lincoln and acting Governor Fuller, of Utah. The fact that the loyal States were in communication by telegraph with Mormondom, seems to have been the first evidence in the minds of Eastern and Western editors that a Pacific Telegraph has been building for several months past. It is now spoken of as a great triumph, and the enterprise of the company is properly praised. It has been a source of great satisfaction to the Pacific Telegraph folks that their end of the line is first finished. From the energy displayed by Mr. Street, of your city, in building west from Salt Lake City, it was feared the section between there and Fort Churchill would be done first. Although beaten as to time, there is every disposition to award the contractors on the Californian end great credit for their exertions to overcome the difficulties of the work. Mr. Creighton, who superintended the work between Julesburgh and Salt Lake, is deserving of praise for his exertions, and last, though not least, the Mormons themselves have been efficient allies in the enterprise.

[illegible]

TELEGRAPHIC

BY OVERLAND TELEGRAPH

Preparations of the Army of the Potomac to Move.

NEWS FROM ROSEKRANS' COMMAND

CASE OF THE PIRATES IN PHILADELPHIA

Reported Repulse of Floyd with Great Loss.

What McClellan is Doing.

MISCELLANEOUS NEWS.

Later from Europe.

The Washington special dispatch to the *Commercial* says the New Jersey Brigade marched on Saturday morning. They will doubtless complete the perfect preparations for preventing the passage of the rebels over into Maryland, under cover of the guns of their Potomac batteries.

The same authority says that all regiments of the Army of the Potomac have their camp equipments, wagons, ambulances, horses and mules, and other appurtenances ready for taking the field at an hour's notice. [illegible]

THE DAILY SUN.

VOLUME VII.} COLUMBUS, GA., NOVEMBER 8, 1861. {NUMBER 93.

THE DAILY SUN.

DeWOLF...R. J. YARINGTON...T. GILBERT.
THOS. GILBERT & CO.,
Editors and Proprietors.

SUBSCRIPTION RATES:

The Sun is published daily at $5 a year, payable strictly in advance. Subscriptions for less than a year at the rate of 50 cents per month, in advance.

ADVERTISING RATES:

All advertisements of five lines or less, inserted at 50 cents for the first insertion and 25 cents for each additional insertion.

Advertisements exceeding five lines (except by special contract) will be charged 10 cents a line for the first insertion, and 5 cents a line for each additional insertion.

A card not exceeding six lines, not renewable, will be inserted three months for $5, six months for $8, and twelve months for $12.

Ten lines, not renewable, will be inserted three months for $8, six months for $12, eight months for $16, and twelve months for $20.

Advertisements of ten lines, renewable at pleasure, inserted for $25 a year.

Contract advertisements exceeding ten lines to be charged at the rate of $10 for each additional ten lines.

For announcing candidates the charge is Five Dollars invariably, to be paid in advance.

THE DAILY SUN.

From yesterday's One O'Clock Edition.

Receipts.—*The reception of the Sun, when ordered by mail, will be our receipt for the money; especially to those subscribing for a less time than a year.*

When subscribers receive the paper with this paragraph marked, they will understand it as informing them that their subscription is about to expire, and that the paper will certainly be stopped unless they make a remittance.

The Daily and Weekly Sun.

We would call the attention of those wishing a good newspaper from this place to our terms in another column, where our rates for a month to a year's subscription can be seen. We would also call attention to the very low rates at which we offer the WEEKLY SUN to clubs. The WEEKLY is a large sheet, containing *thirty-two columns, almost entirely reading matter*—☞ *very few advertisements being allowed to encumber its columns.* ☜

☞ Copies of the DAILY SUN can be obtained. Price, five cents

It is stated that the Lincoln Government has now within the lines of the army of the Potomac, in round numbers, 30,000 horses, purchased at $120 apiece; 700 mules at $141 apiece, and 5000 wagons at $110. Should the Confederates ever get them into a general engagement, there is but little doubt that most of this useful property will fall into their hands.

Sketch of the Rebel Gen. Evans.

A New York paper has the following sketch of General Evans.

Brigadier-General Nathaniel George Evans is a native of South Carolina, and graduated at West Point in 1844. He was appointed to a second Lieutenancy in the First United States Dragoons in July, 1848, and was transferred to the Second Dragoons in September, 1849.—In March, 1855, he became first Lieutenant of the Second Cavalry, and was promoted to a Captaincy in the following year, which position he held under Major Van Dorn when the latter commanded the expedition against the Camanches in 1858, winning no little distinction for his bravery in the severest battle of the campaign, near Wachita village, in Texas. His connection with the rebels is contemporaneous with the secession of South Carolina, by whose Governor he was appointed Adjutant-General of the regular forces of the State. He was subsequently appointed Brigadier General, and, in conjunction with Generals Jackson and Cooke, commanded the left wing of the rebel forces at the battle of Bull Run, in which engagement he was in immediate command of the Brigade composed of Wheat's Battalion, Col. Hay's Seventh Louisiana Volunteers and the Washington Artillery.

Correspondence of the Nashville Union.

BOWLING GREEN, Nov. 2, 1861.—Just such a dark muskyday as is said to invite Londoners to commit suicide was yesterday, the gloom and discontent of which was perfected by the non arrival of the train from Nashivlle, and the variable reports of the skirmish at Woodbury, a small town 21 miles below Bowling Green, at the confluence of the Big Barren and Green River, where it was reported the day previous that 800 of the enemy had made an attack upon 100 of our cavalry, cutting them to pieces; the departure on Thursday of several regiments of Infantry, and three or four squads of mounted men, caused excitement to rise to fever heat, and the reports reaching here from time to time, alone rendered the day sufferable.

In summing up the expedition, the facts are, from the best information to be had, as follows: The Federals ventured as far as Morgantown, which is five miles below Woodbury. Our pickets at the latter place threw out twelve men as scouts who were caught in an ambuscade, about a mile from the main body of the enemy, and were fired upon. Four of their number being wounded; all however, save one, escaped, he was carried off by them. After returning to Woodbury, a courier was dispatched here for reinforcements which was promptly sent off, the report reaching here mean while that the Federals were coming up Green River, in strong force, our cavalry dashed forward hoping to intercept them, but only succeeded in taking a portion of the rearguard, as they were retreating towards Owensboro, and returned bringing twenty-five prisoners.

Thus has a very unimportant affair been magnified into huge dimensions.

The falling back of our troops from the railroad bridge over Green river, has also given rise to the report that Rousseau's forces had come south of that stream, via turnpike through the town of Munfordsville, which report cannot be traced to any reliable source; and a gentleman who left Elizabethtown on Wednesday, states that none of Rousseau's men are south of Nolin creek, which is only ten miles south of the last named town.—With the exception of 1,000 Dutch Zouaves camped at Elizabethtown, the whole of the Federal force on the Northern line is at Nolin bridge, where there are fifteen regiments, with a few pieces of artillery, but no fortifications whatever.

Passengers on the train coming from Cave City on Thursday night, report several shots at that place, made by straggling Lincolnites, no one was injured.

Fugitives just in from Breckinridge and Grayson counties confirm previous reports of many depredations committed by irregular bodies of troops from Indiana in Meade and other border counties.

The convention at Russellville adjourned on Wednesday to meet again on the 18th, when there will be representatives from all the counties and such action will doubtlessly be taken as will place the State in her proper position.

LEXINGTON.

Paris papers assert that, in consequence of late events in Japan, the British vessels on China stations have been ordered to Jeddo.

From the New York Times, Oct. 29.

The Great Expedition—Important General Order.

The following general order was issued on Saturday, and read on board each ship comprising the fleet:

HEADQUARTERS, E. C., ST'R ATLANTIC, }
October 25, 1861. }

Special Order, No. 19—

1. This command will sail for its destination in a very few days, under convoy of a naval squadron, commanded by Commander Dupont. The transports will move in three columns, and in rear of the main body of the squadron. The transports belonging to the 1st Brigade will compose the right column; those of the 2d Brigade and Third Rhode Island Regiment the centre; and those of the 3d Brigade and the Battallion of Volunteer Engineers the left column.

2. Each vessel will retain its order in column, and the columns will move in parallel lines equi distant, regulating from the right. The sail vessels and other transports, inadequate to the task of sailing with the fleet, will be towed by such steamers as the Chief Quartermaster may designate. Commander Dupont, in co operation with the land forces, has kindly made such an arrangement of his fleet as will secure the transports from unnecessary diffusion, and all senior officers on transports and masters of vessels will enter into the spirit of, and conform to, those arrangements, a plan of which will be duly given.

The General Commanding announces to the Expeditionary Corps that it is intended to make a descent upon the enemy's coast, and probably under circumstances which will demand the utmost vigilance, coolness and intrepidity, on the part of every officer and man of his command. In consideration of the justness and holiness of our cause, of the ardent patriotism which has prompted the virtuous and industrious citizens of our land to fly to their country's standard in the moment of her peril, he most confidently believes that he will be effectually and efficiently supported in his efforts to overthrow a zealous, active and wily foe, whose cause is unholy and principles untenable.

3. On the approach of the transports to the place of disembarkation, each Brigade Commander will anchor his transports as near each other as practicable, and will, at the proper time, superintend the disembarkation of his brigade. The surf boats, and other means of disembarkation at hand, are believed to be capable of landing at once from three to four thousand men. The surf boats are of different sizes; two of the largest may take the officers and men of a company of 100 men; two of the next size a company of 70 men, and so on in proportion. The other means of transportation may take the remainder of a brigade, with probably one or two sections of field artillery.

4. The disembarkation will be made in three lines. The first line will be the brigade of Gen. Wright, flanked by two sections of Hamilton's Light Battery, accompanied by a squad of Regular Sappers and Miners, and two companies of Serrell's Volunteer Engineers, with a sufficient supply of entrenching tools and sand bags. The second line will be the brigade of Gen. Stevens, and, if necessary, accompanied by a section of Hamilton's Battery and two field pieces, to be manned by a company of the Third Rhode Island Regiment. The reserve will be composed of Gen. Viel's brigade, the remaining portions of Serrell's Volunteer Engineers and the Third Rhode Island Regiment, and will be disposed of according to circumstances.

5. The boats of not only each company, but of each regiment and brigade, will land abreast, as far as practicable, and in order of battle. The utmost effort will be made to effect the landing in that order. Should it be found impracticable to land immediately from the lighters, then the surf-boats, when emptied, will immediately proceed to the rapid landing of the men from the lighters; and as soon as the whole line is landed, all the boats will return and bring forward in like manner the troops of the second line, and so with the reserve.

6. The general officers and commanders of battalions, &c., will be furnished in time with the plan of descent and the particular order of battle. It is probable that the first line will have to conquer the ground on which to establish itself, and if opposed by greatly superior numbers, to manœuvre and probably to momentarily entrench. If not seriously opposed, the first line, after overcoming immediate difficulties, will continue to drive backward the enemy, but will not venture beyond supporting distance from the shore, before the the landing of the General commanding, or without his special order.

7. The commanding officer of the naval squadron has kindly consented to furnish 300 sailors to assist in launching and manning the surf boats, and he appeals to the patriotism of the masters, mates and sailors of the several transports to furnish an additional number of coxswains and oarsmen. Any deficiency of oarsmen in surf-boats will be supplied from the platoons on board of these respectively, so that each boat, when ready, may be rapidly rowed ashore. The soldier oarsmen will land and form with their platoons.

8. General and field officers, with their respective staffs, will endeavor to obtain landing boats for themselves, and the necessary coxswains and oarsmen from the transports and the other hired vessels of the fleet.

9. The senior officer of the troops on board each transport will arrange with the master for voluntary helps of this kind, which may be needed and can be given, and will make a special report to headquarters, as early as practicable, of the assistance thus rendered.

10. As soon as the landing shall have been effected, the surf and other landing boats will revert to the Chief Quartermaster for immediate supplies.

11. The sick and non-effective men will remain on board the several transports, until provision can be made for them on shore. The non-effectives will be specially charged with the care of the sick, under directions to be left by the respective medical officers.

12. Medical officers, excepting one from each brigade, to be designated by the respective brigade commanders, will land with the troops. The three medical officers left afloat will, under the direction of the Medical Director, divide the duty of visiting all the sick on board, including those of the Third Rhode Island Regiment, and the Battalion of Volunteer Engineers. By order of

(Signed,) Brig. Gen. T. W SHERMAN.
LOUIS H. PELOUZE, Captain 15th Infantry, Assistant Adjutant General.

From the Savannah Republican Nov. 6.,

The Situation.

A word upon the present condition of affairs on the coast of Georgia, may not be amiss.

After our evening edition of yesterday went to press, advices were received from below reporting the entire disappearance of the Lincoln fleet from their anchorage off Port Royal. Nothing definite is known, at the time we write, of their direction. Our despatch, announcing the appearance of 41 sail off Stono (about 15 miles south of (Charleston) yesterday morning may throw some light on the subject. And again, they may be the remainder of the fleet that was left behind by the advance squadron, as the expedition is understood to consist of from 80 to 100 vessels.

However this may be, our people should not allow themselves to be seduced into the idea that we shall be overlooked by this infamous band of pirates who have set out to scourge and desolate the Southern coast. They have their work to perform, for to return without an attempt to subdue us would result in a national disgrace. However they shift about, doubtless to deceive us as to the true points of attack, they will be upon us in due time, and we should urge forward every measure necessary for defense. We are pleased to know that this is being done by our military authorities. Every thing is in motion, and our troops so disposed that a very large force can be concentrated at any given point at a few hours' notice. Carolina and Georgia are nobly co operating and making common cause against the enemy. Land where he may, he will have to march over the dead bodies of citizens of both States before he can obtain a foot hold upon our soil.

We learn that Gov. Pickens telegraphed yesterday to our Mayor offering any assistance that may be needed, while our own authorities have tendered fifteen hundred troops to South Carolina in case Charleston or Port Royal should be attacked.

We are rejoiced to see the spirit with which our people, old and young, male and female, contemplate the prospect of an early measuring of arms with the foe. There is no fear, no excitement, but a firm yet quiet resolve to dispute his march even to the last ditch and to the destruction of the last man. They rather rejoice that the time has probably come when Georgians shall have an opportunity for doing their share at home in the great work of Confederate independence. We welcome the enemy to our shores, and shall give them at least "hospitable graves."

Still Later—An Engagement at Port Royal—A Steamer Disabled—Vessel aground and Com. Tattnall Firing into her.

Gen. Lawton returned to the city late last evening, having visited the southern point of Hilton Head during the day, in order to ascertain, as far as possible, the movements of the enemy's fleet. Captain Stewart, whom he saw on the island, says an engagement commenced between seven vessels of the fleet and the fort on Hilton Head, about seven o'clock yesterday morning. It was kept up for a considerable time on both sides, when a large steamer, becoming disabled, was towed out of reach. Another vessel went ashore, and at last accounts Commodore Tattnall was at a convenient distance with his little fleet pouring a heavy fire into her sides.

There seems to be some mistake about the departure of the fleet as reported above. Later and authentic accounts state that thirty one vessels were still in order of battle off Port Royal.

Immediate steps have been taken to furnish all necessary assistance to the garrison at Port Royal. Captain Read, with a portion of his artillery corps, left last night on the Huntrjes, and Colonel Spalding's regiment, 555 strong, will leave on the St. Marys this morning.

Patriotic Example to Young Men.

The following letter from a veteran over 70 years of age, addressed to Colonel Allen, breathes a lofty spirit of chivalry and devotion to country rarely excelled:

WOLFE RIVER, MISS., Oct. 7, 1861.

Lieut. Col. H. W. ALLEN:

Sir—I see in the Democrat your notice to the people of Harrison county, calling on us to be prepared in case of an invasion of our coast. Although I am now over seventy years old, I am, and have been urging this course for the last month upon the citizens living in this neighborhood, and I think they are about to be stirred up. As to myself, I am ready at a moments warning with my musket, ammunition and revolver. I lack a good butcher knife. Although old as I am, I think if the Lord should spare me I could do, or be of some service in case of the enemy's making a landing on our coast. I will further say that in case the enemy does not land on the coast, and makes the attempt to take New Orleans, I will go if I can get there if I have to go by myself. I do think it high time for us to begin to look out and prepare for the coming conflict.

Respectfully yours, &c.,
JOHN HUDDLESTON.

TELEGRAPHIC

Dispatches to the Daily Sun.

INTERESTING WAR NEWS!
IMPORTANT FROM WESTERN VIRGINIA!
LETTER FROM GEN. BEAUREGARD!
&c. &c. &c.

RICHMOND, Nov. 6.—The Richmond Dispatch has intelligence from Cedar Hill that Gen. Floyd commenced cannonading the enemy on Friday last, stopped their transportation, killing a number of their horses and disabling wagons, and killed 29 of the enemy. Floyd controls the road over which the enemy transport their supplies.

It is rumored, but not generally credited, that the Federals crossed the Kanawha river at —— Creek to cut off Col. Jenkins' Cavalry. Col. Jenkins sent word to Floyd that if he would send Infantry reinforcements, he (Jenkins) would cut off the enemy's forces; which was done, and Jenkins killed and captured the entire force, said to number about six hundred.

The morning papers say Gen. Lee left yesterday, charged with the command of the coast defences south of Virginia.

John C. Breckinridge has been appointed a Brigadier General.

RICHMOND, Nov. 7.—The Whig of this morning publishes the following, dated at "Centreville within hearing of the enemy's guns, Nov. 3.

To EDS. WHIG: *Gentlemen*—My attention has just been called to an unfortunate controversy now going on relative to the publication of a synopsis of my report of the battle of Manassas. None can regret more than I do this knowledge.

The President is the sole judge of the time when and what parts of the report of the commanding officer shall be made public. I individually do not object to delaying its publication so long as the War Department shall judge it proper and necessary to the success of our cause. Meanwhile I entreat my friends not to trouble themselves about refuting slanders and calumnies aimed at me.

Alcibiades on a certain occasion resorted to an extraordinary method to occupy the minds of his traducers; let then that synopsis answer the same purpose for me in this instance.

If certain minds cannot understand the difference between patriotism, the highest civic virtue, and office seeking, the lowest civic occupation, I pity them from the bottom of my heart. Suffice it to say, I prefer the respect and esteem of my countrymen to the admiration or envy of the world. I hope, for the sake of our cause and country, to be able, with the assistance of kind Providence, to answer my calumniators with new victories over our national enemies. But I have nothing to ask of the country, government, or my friends, except to afford me all the aid they can in the great struggle we are now engaged. I am not, and never expect or desire to be, a candidate for any civil office in the gift of the people or executive. The aim of my ambition, after having cast my mite in defense of our sacred cause, and assisted to the best of my ability in securing our rights and independence as a nation, is to retire to private life, my means then permitting, never again to leave my home, unless to fight anew the battles of my country.

Most respectfully, your ob't serv't,
G. T. BEAUREGARD.

SAVANNAH, Nov. 7.—The steamer Resolute of the Confederate fleet, came up at 11 o'clock last night for coal, and brought correct particulars of the operations at Port Royal to date. It appears that the report of the disabled steamer and another aground, is incorrect. Monday afternoon, Com. Tattnall with his fleet, went within a mile of the Federal squadron, and engaged them nearly an hour, until they came within the range of the guns at Port Royal, when he retired, and allowed the latter to open on them.

The Commodore again sallied out to a point above three-fourths of a mile from the enemy, when a fierce engagement of orty minutes ensued. The enemy fired rifle shot and shell which fell about in great profusion. Two shots passed thro' the Savannah without serious damage to the vessel. Nobody on board was injured.

Parties at the Fort say, that seven shots from our fleet took effect in the Federal vessels. The latter coming in closer, our fleet retired. Yesterday all was quiet.

The engagement lasted until late in the evening. It is impossible to ascertain the result.

It was reported that the Federals were landing at Hunting Island yesterday.

The firing at Port Royal now heard, commenced at 30 minutes past 7 o'clock. Warm work is anticipated.

Missouri Seceded!

A special dispatch to the Memphis (Tenn.) Avalanche, dated Little Rock, Nov. 3, says that the State Legislature of Missouri has passed the Ordinance of Secession!

THE DAILY SUN.

Friday Morning, Nov. 8, 1681.

For Tax Receiver.

We are authorised to announce the name of WILLIAM A. BOZEMAN as a candidate for Receiver of Tax Returns of Muscogee County at the ensuing election in January next.
Oct8

We are authorized to announce Isaac T. Brooks as a candidate for re-election to the office of Tax Receiver of Muscogee county.

For Tax Collector.

We are authorized to announce Thomas C. Pridgen as a candidate for Tax Collector of Muscogee county at the ensuing election.

The friends of J. J. Roquemore announce him as a candidate for Tax Collector of Muscogee county at the next election.

If elected, Mr. Roquemore will devote one-third of the proceeds of the office to the benefit of the families of soldiers from the county; and if it pays what it does this year will give one-half.

Wo are authorized to announce Jordan L. Howell as a candidate for re-election to the office of Tax Collector of Muscogee county, at the election in January next.

We are authorized to announce JOHN R SANDERS as a candidate for Tax Collector of Muscogee County at the ensuing election.

For Mayor.

We are authorized to announce Dr. JAMES F. BOZEMAN as a candidate for Mayor, at the election in December next. nov7–te

Mayor's Notice

Whereas, His Excellency the President of the Confederate States has appcinted Friday the 15th of November instant, "as a day of fasting, humiliation and prayer," and whereas it is right that every community should reverently observe and respect this just and proper duty. I therefore officially request and invite the citizens of Columbus, to withdraw on that day from the pursuit of their accustomed business, and to assemble in the several churches of the city, to offer up prayer to Almighty God. Let us all acknowledge our dependence upon Him, and solemnly invoke Him to continue to our armies an l to our cause that gracious favor which He has so signally manifested towards us both on land and on sea: and "that He may give us victory over our enemies, preserve our homes and our altars from pollution, and secure to us the restoration of peace and prosperity."

JAMES F. BOZEMAN,
Columbus, Nov. 7, 1861. Mayor pro tem.

The Chewalla.

The steamer Chewalla, J. W. Young Master, will leave for Apalachicola and intermediate landings, at 3 o'clock, this afternoon.

Large Sale.

We invite the attention of planters, stock raisers and others, to the advertisement in another column, of the large estate sale of Daniel Rambo, deceased, on the first Tuesday in December.

Official Vote of Muscogee County.

	Columbus.	Upatoie	Bozeman's	Edwards'	Total
Electors for President.	711	39	29	26	805
For Congress.					
Hines Holt	327	27	8	19	381
M. J. Crawford	378	16	21	7	422
Justices Inf Court.					
H. S. Estes	514	5	6	7	532
John Quin	311	4	26	3	344
J. J. McKendree	310	12	17	3	342

"Columbus Minute Boys."

We are authorized to state that half a dozen more recruits will be received into the ranks of the 'Columbus Minute Boys,' Capt. Hatch Cook. Persons desiring to be enrolled will be required to come supplied with uniforms and blankets. Guns will be furnished them on their arrival. Application may be made to A M. Wollahin, at Cook's Hotel.

This company was mustered into the service of the State on the 1st inst.

More Fine Corn.

We were presented yesterday, by Mr. W. L. Renes, of Green Hill, Stewart county, with three ears of corn, as a specimen of his crop. It is of a mixed variety—of gourd seed and flint. The ears measure eleven to twelve inches in length, and weigh one and a quarter pounds each.

We are pleased to see the spirit of emulation which seems to have taken hold on this branch of agriculture, and trust it will continue until ours shall not only be a corn exporting, but a meat exporting section.

Shinplasters Again!

Eds. Sun: As Shinplasters begin to make their appearance amongst us, allow us to ask one question on the subject. Some time ago a card appeared in your columns, signed by some of our merchants, in which they pledged themselves not to receive any Shinplasters. It is now contended by some, that this card merely referred to Shinplasters issued in other cities, and that the gentlemen who signed their names to said card are at liberty to take change bills issued in this city. But as the card has left a different impression on some minds and every body is more or less interested in it, we should like either you or one of your readers to give us a correct interpretation of it. For if we are again to be doomed to such a currency, the sooner we know it the better.

DIMES.

Columbus, Nov. 7, 1861.

By ELLIS & LIVINGSTON.

AUCTION SALE
—OF—
DRY GOODS, SHOES,
AND
READY MADE CLOTHING!

ON FRIDAY, the 8th of NOVEMBER, at 10 o'clock, we will sell without reserve, at the STORE LATELY OCCUPIED BY MIMS & PERRY their remaining stock of Goods, consisting in part of

LINEN TABLE CLOTHS, NAPKINS;
BIRD'S EYE DIAPER, IRISH LINEN;
HOSIERY, Cotton Undershirts and Drawers;
Gent's and Ladies' HANDKERCHIEFS;
TABLE LINEN, SHIRTS;
PERCUSSION CAPS, POCKET KNIVES;
OIL CLOTH, UMBRELLAS, BOOKS;
LIQUORS, CIGARS, SOAP;
PLATFORM and COUNTER SCALES, &c., &c.
—ALSO,—
17 CASES of SHOES (ASSORTED)
Ready Made Winter Clothing!
Consisting in part of
BEAVER OVERCOATS, CASSIMERE COATS and PANTS—all fresh and of the latest style.
MERCHANTS and TRADERS will do well to be in attendance.
TERMS CASH!
THE STORE WILL BE OPEN THE DAY PREVIOUS TO SALE FOR INSPECTION OF THE GOODS.

nov4-tds ELLIS & LIVINGSTON, Auctioneers.

SPECIAL NOTICES.

Cherokee Cure—*An unfailing cure for Seminal Weakness, Nocturnal Emissions, Impotency, Loss of Power, Pains in the Back, Stone in the Back, Stone in the Bladder, Obstructed and Difficult Menstruation, and all diseases caused by deviating from the path of nature, and indulging in Self Pollution.*—By the use of this "Cure" all improper discharges are removed, the weakened organs of generation speedily cured, and full vigor restored. Either sex, contemplating marriage, should reflect that a sound mind and body are necessary to promote connubial happiness. In the "Cherokee Cure" the poor debilitated, worn down, and despairing devotee of sensual pleasure, will find relief. It is safe and pleasant in taste, but immediate in its action; containing no mineral poison, but is prepared from pure vegetable extracts, in the form of a delicious syrup. Price $2 per bottle, or three bottles for $5, and forwarded by express to all parts of the world.

POTTER & MERWIN, Proprietors, Memphis, Tenn.

For sale by all respectable dealers in Medicines throughout the Southern States.

JOHN WRIGHT & CO., New Orleans, Wholesale Agents.
mh27

STERLING EXCHANGE.

BILLS on LONDON or LIVERPOOL, in sums to suit purchasers, for sale at
June 27–tf BANK OF COLUMBUS.

FALL AND WINTER
READY-MADE
CLOTHING!

ROSETTE & LAWHON
ARE NOW OFFERING
A LARGE ASSORTMENT,
Suitable for the approaching Season,
125 BROAD STREET,
COLUMBUS, GEORGIA.

THE STOCK CONSISTS IN PART as follows:
400 HEAVY OVERCOATS;
300 " CASSIMERE COATS;
500 Pair FANCY " PANTS;
300 HEAVY " VESTS.

BOYS' CLOTHING!

100 SUITS GRAY SATTINETS;
100 Pair MIXED SATTINET PANTS;
100 SATTINET and CASSIMERE PANTS;
100 BLACK and BLUE CLOTH JACKETS;
50 " " " FROCK COATS;

A FULL SUPPLY OF
GENT.'S FURNISHING GOODS!
Under-Shirts and Drawers:
WHITE COTTON;
BROWN COTTON;
WHITE MERINO;
WHITE, all wool;
GRAY, all wool;
RIBBED, all wool;
SHAKER FLANNEL;
CANTON FLANNEL.

LADIES' MERINO VESTS!
Gent.'s Traveling Blankets;
Gent.'s Shawls;
Trunks and Carpet Bags;
500 Umbrellas;
2,000 yards Kerseys.
ROSETTE & LAWHON.
Columbus, Ga., Oct. 10. 6m

Liquors, Wines, Liquors.

AS I AM desirous of closing out entirely my stock of Liquors and Wines of every description, I offer my whole stock (embracing many desirable grades of Rye and Monongahela WHISKEY, Jamaica and N. E RUM, Holland and N Y GIN, Common and Fine BRANDY and Madeira and Port WINE)

At Greatly Reduced Prices, for Cash!

This is an excellent opportunity for dealers to replenish their stocks. To any one taking the whole lot an extraordinary inducement will be offered

Oct 19–tf JNO. N. BIRCH.

CHENEY'S
Anodyne Pectoral Syrup!

FOR the RELIEF and CURE of all diseases of the LUNGS:
Coughs during and after an attack of Cold;
Hoarseness and Difficulty of Breathing;
Bronchitis, Asthma, Whooping Cough;
Coughs following Measles, Pneumonia, Croup, &c., &c.,
Put up in Columbus, Ga. by the Proprietor in person, and every bottle warranted pure as any Cough Remedy now in use.
Sold at the Drug store of PEMBERTON & CARTER, Columbus, Georgia; and at W. G. BOOTHE'S, Butler Taylor county Ga.
Nov. 1–1m JNO L. CHENEY, M D

THE FLORIDA STORE!
Cheap Goods! Cheap Goods!

THE undersigned informs the public that he has removed his Large and Well Assorted Stock of Clothing, Dry Goods, Boots and Shoes, Hats and Caps, &c., &c, from Apalachicola, Fla., to this city, where he will sell at the very lowest rates.

He also desires to call attention to a fine assortment of Wall Paper and Window Shades.

Call and examine before purchasing elsewhere.
A. M. COHEN, No. — Broad st., under Cook's Hotel, at Brook's Old Stand.
Oct12–tf

TO ARRIVE!

10 HHDS. Sugar of various grades; 30 boxes Soap, and many other articles, which will be sold low for cash, at wholesale or retail, by
July 29. M. BIGGERS & CO.

GOOD THINGS!

FRESH Cabbage, Fine Apples, Onions, Irish Potatoes, &c., just received by
Oct 26 J W SAPPINGTON.

COLORED
WOOL YARN
FOR SOLDIERS' SOCKS,
At S. ROTHCHILD & BRO.

200,000 CIGARS!

OF many choice brands, which I will sell to dealers and consumers at very low prices for cash. Orders solicited Good satisfaction guaranteed, by JAS. W. SAPPINGTON,
oct17–tf. No 138 Broad street.

ONION BUTTONS.

10 BUSHELS Onion Buttons just received and for sale by F. M. BIGGERS & CO.

COMMERCIAL.

DAILY SUN OFFICE,
Columbus, Ga., November 4, 1861.

COLUMBUS COTTON STATEMENT.

Stock on hand September 1, 1861		2,334
Received past week	1,634	
Received previously	5,214—	6,848
Total Receipts		9,182
Shipped past week	5	
Shipped previously	945—	950
Stock on hand		8,232

Prices of Breadstuffs.
CORRECTED WEEKLY BY PALACE MILLS.

	Per Bbl.	Half Bbl.	Qr. Bbl
Fine	$7 00	3 50	1 75
Superfine	8 00	4 00	2 00
Extra Family	9 00	4 50	2 25
Double Extra	10 00	5 00	2 50
Bolted Meal and Hominy	$1 10 per bushel.		
Large Hominy from Hom'y Corn.	2 50 per bushel.		
Unbolted Meal and Hominy	1 00 per bushel.		
Bran and Shorts, mixed	1 00 per 100 lbs.		
Rich Shorts	1 25 per 100 lbs.		
Corn	1 00 per bushel.		

WAREHOUSES.

PLANTERS' WAREHOUSE.

THE subscribers, thankful for past patronage, would again offer their services to their friends in all the departments of the

Warehouse and Commission BUSINESS.

The usual accommodations extended to their patrons, and every effort will be made to promote their interest. A liberal patronage for the approaching season is solicited

DILLARD, POWELL & CO.
Columbus, Ga., July 28, 1860. tf

WARNOCK & CO.,
WAREHOUSE
AND
COMMISSION MERCHANTS,
COLUMBUS, GA.,

WILL attend promptly to the storage and sale of Cotton and Commission Business in all its branches. WARNOCK & CO.,
S. B. Warnock, Columbus, Ga.
W. L Salisbury. aug26–tf

HUGHES & HODGES
WILL CONTINUE THE
WAREHOUSE AND
COMMISSION BUSINESS
IN ALL ITS BRANCHES.
Aug. 24–6m WM. H. HUGHES, W. C. HODGES.

FALL STYLE!
HATS CAPS
F. LANDON

WOULD inform his friends and customers generally that he has just returned from New Orleans with a well selected stock of

FALL GOODS!
Embracing HATS of all kinds,
FINE FRENCH HATS!
MILITARY
HATS AND CAPS.
Misses and Children's HATS,
Umbrellas and Walking Canes.

All of which he will be happy to show at his NEW STAND, next door to Redd & Johnson's.

We can supply any quantity of Negro
WOOL HATS.
Columbus, Ga., Oct 10. tf

REMOVAL! REMOVAL!!
J. H. MERRY

HAS removed his CLOTHING STORE to the Building formerly occupied by Messrs. COWDERY & CO., next door to Redd & Johnson's,

NO. 91 BROAD STREET,

Where he will be pleased to offer his customers and the public generally a good stock of

WINTER CLOTHING!

Embracing GENTS' CASS. FROCK and SACK COATS;
GENT'S COL'D and BLACK CLOTH FROCKS;
EAGLE and COLUMBUS FACTORY SUITS;
GENT'S PLAIN AND FANCY CASS. PANTS;
GENT'S PLAIN and FANCY CASS. and SILK VESTS.

GENT'S OVERCOATS!
OF SEALSKIN, BEAVER PILOT AND CLOTH.
Gent's Furnishing Goods:
Heavy Lamb's Wool, Merino, Silk and Cotton UNDERSHIRTS and DRAWERS;
LINEN BOSOM SHIRTS AND COLLARS;
HANDKERCHIEFS TIES, GLOVES, &c
Also, UMBRELLAS, TRUNKS, AND CARPET BAGS. Oct 19–3m

AT REDUCED PRICES!

WE WILL sell all the goods in our stock at REDUCED PRICES. The disadvantages we have to labor under in procuring supplies to keep up our stock renders it desirable to us to close out our entire stock of

Staple and Fancy Dry Goods,
BOOTS AND SHOES,
Hats, Caps, Blankets, Kerseys, &c.
AT REDUCED PRICES!

Merchants wishing to replenish their stocks will find this an excellent opportunity to buy goods that will pay them a good profit, and we invite them to an examination of the goods we are offering.

PLANTERS and HOUSEKEEPERS who buy goods by the piece will also find this an excellent opportunity to buy their supplies GREATLY BELOW THE USUAL PRICES.

We have just received—
100 PIECES OF GEORGIA KERSEYS;
Also, BROWN AND BLACK KERSEYS.
G. W. ATKINSON & CO.
Oct 15 1m

$40.000
WORTH OF
WINTER CLOTHING!

THE greatest inducements of the present time, in providing our Soldiers with Winter Clothing, of almost any variety, can be found at the Store of

JONAS MARCUSE,
139 Broad st., opposite Masonic Hall.

After great trouble and expense I have succeeded in laying in a stock of WINTER CLOTHING unsurpassed in the city, as regards quantity, quality, and style in make—a great proportion of which are suitable for

MILITARY PURPOSES.

I have them now exposed to view in my Store for the purpose of giving military men, and those having friends in the army, a chance of providing soldiers with warm and comfortable Clothing in time to protect them from the early and rigorous winter of Virginia. Already our soldiers in Western Virginia begin to suffer, and the good work of shielding those brave men from the inclemency of that latitude cannot be begun too early.

The remainder of the SUMMER STOCK on hand will be sold at cost.

Staple and Fancy Dry Goods.

I have also on hand a large stock of Staple and Fancy Dry Goods; also, Men's and Boys' Hats and Caps, and Boots and Shoes for Gents, Ladies and Children, which I offer for sale at reasonable prices. Call and see at the store of

JONAS MARCUSE,
aug22 tf No. 139 Broad street.

Glennville Female College.

THE regular exercises of this Institution will be resumed on the **1st Monday in September.**

Confederate Bonds will be received in payment of tuition.

M M GLENN,
aug20-2taw2m Secretary Board Trustees.

FOR SALE,

200 BUSHELS SEED RYE. F. M. BIGGERS & CO.

JAS. A WHITESIDE,
WHOLESALE DRUGGIST,
Store No. 135 Columbus, Georgia,
OFFERS

800 GALLONS KEROSENE or COAL OIL;
400 " 95 per cent. ALCOHOL;
200 Gallons BURNING FLUID;
6,000 Lbs. best White POTASH;
175 " Prime NUTMEGS;
66 doz MUSTANG LINIMENT;
70 " vials assorted VERMIFUGE;
70 " boxes " PILLS;
1,500 lbs. EPSOM SALTS;
1,000 " COPPERAS;
100 bottles SULPHATE QUININE;

The above named articles and quantities constitute a part of my large stock, which I am offering to merchants at satisfactory prices. Those desiring to know my prices will be informed by application in person or by letter; and at retail I am still making a deduction of 12½ to 25 per cent. from the credit prices for Cash. If you wish to save money in buying, patronize the

CASH DRUG STORE!
June 26, 1861 tf

J. H. BRAMHALL,
PRACTICAL WATCHMAKER
—AND—
Manufacturer of Fine Watches,
56 BROAD STREET,
COLUMBUS, GEORGIA.

WATCHES that have been injured by incompetent workmen, put in good sound condition, (if they are worth it,) at a reasonable price

SEWING MACHINES!

Grover & Baker's, Singer's, Wheeler & Wilson's, or any other good Sewing Machine, put in order. Duplicates made were parts are broken or worn out.

Sewing Machine NEEDLES for the following machines for sale: Ladd's, Webster & Co's, Scoville & Goodell's, Keystone State, Quaker City, Watson's, Howe's.

June 21, 1861–1y J H. BRAMHALL.

A. CADMAN,
GUN AND LOCKSMITH,
Crawford St., one door west of Rankin's Corner, Near the Market.
COLUMBUS, GA.

GUNS and Pistols, Shot Pouches and Powder Flasks, repaired. Cabinet, Desk, Trunk and Door Keys of all descriptions made and fitted Trunks, and Patent Trunk and Valise Locks repaired. Bells, all sizes and tones. Fancy Bell Pulls. Patent Bell carriages and wire, with which I will hang Bells and warrant them to keep in order. Andirons and Brass Work, of all sorts repaired. Terms cash on delivery.

May 5, 1861 1y

CHANGE OF SCHEDULE.

Mobile and Girard Rail Road,
Girard, Ala., Oct. 1, 1861.

FROM and after this date, the Mail Train will leave the Girard Depot daily (Sundays excepted) at 2:40 p. m., and arrive at Union Springs at 6:28 p. m.; leave Union Springs daily (Sundays excepted) at 6:35 a. m. and arrive at Girard at 10:15 a. m.

The Freight Train will leave Girard every day, (Sundays excepted,) at 6:00 a. m., and arrive at Union Springs at 12:00 m. Leave Union Springs every day, (Sundays excepted,) at 12:45 p. m., and arrive at Girard at 6:25 p. m.

sept27–tf B. E. WELLS, Sup't.

SUMMER DRESS GOODS!
TWO HUNDRED
French Organdie and Jaconet
MUSLIN DRESSES
AT $2 50 EACH.
LAWNS, BERAGES, GINGHAMS,
AND OTHER SUMMER GOODS,
Will be offered at reduced prices from this date.
JAMES McPHILLIPS,
June 22 Masonic Building.

COTTON BATTING
—FOR—
QUILTS and COMFORTS.

OUR people are called upon to send their Blankets to the Soldiers. Quilts and Comforts are good substitutes. The Eagle Company are now manufacturing the Cotton Batting required in making them.

They also make KNITTING COTTON, SEWING THREAD, &c., &c., all of which can be found at the stores of the merchants in the city.

aug10–dw3m J. RHODES BROWNE, Agt.

Notice to Debtors and Creditors.

ALL persons having claims against Benjamin Y. Martin, deceased, are hereby notified to render them duly authenticated within the time prescribed by law, and those indebted to said deceased are requested to make immediate payment.

In the absence of the executor payments can be made and claims rendered to William H Brannon, Esq. J. J. MARTIN, Ex'r.
October 23. d6tw5t

FOR SALE,

500 LBS. Nonpareil, 500 lbs. Brevier Type, head letter, cases, dash rules, advertising rules, column rules, chases, &c., &c., in fact a complete outfit for a paper 26 by 36. The materials have been used but a short time, and everything is complete and in perfect order. For further particulars apply to

J. J. MARTIN,
oct23-tf Ex'r estate B. Y. Martin.

JUST RECEIVED BY
J. W. PEASE,
THE ONLY COMPLETE SOUTHERN EDITION OF
HARDEE'S TACTICS

With Sixty-Nine Plates, showing every Position in the Manual and every Movement in the Company and Battalion Drill, and containing twenty pages Music, Roll Call, and Reveille, with fifty additional pages of Colt's Revolver Manual, &c. &c. &c.

In two Volumes—Sixty-Nine Plates—Muslin.
Price $3 00
Sent by mail 3 25
A liberal discount on large orders.
july26 J. W. PEASE

Terms Cash.

HAVING to pay Cash entirely for all goods with which to replenish our stock, we are compelled to adopt the Cash system.
Sept. 16 tf. SMITH & DANIEL.

Stocking Yarn,

WOOL and Cotton Mixed, for sale by
Sept. 16-tf. J. H. MULFORD.

ON CONSIGNMENT.

50 BOXES Tobacco, a good article, for sale by
Oct12 WARNOCK & CO.

Yarn for Soldiers Socks.

COLORED Cotton and Wool Yarn at JAMES M'PHILLIPS',
Sept. 16-tf. Masonic Hall Building.

Rye vs. Coffee.

50 BUSHELS choice Seed Rye, also, a cheap and elegant substitute for Coffee. For sale
Sept. 16 tf by JNO N BIRCH.

MILITARY BUTTONS!

A GOOD supply of GILT BUTTONS, large and small sizes. For sale by
July 2–tf T. S. SPEAR.

WAR IN FACT!
LOUIS HAIMAN & BRO.
Manufacture to Order,

OFFICERS and SERGEANT'S SWORDS; CAVALRY SABRES; BAYONETS to Shot Guns and Rifles, of the finest finish;
BRASS BUCKLES and PLATES for Belts and Cartridge Boxes, and MOUNTINGS for Bayonet Scabbards.
TIN and SHEET IRON FURNITURE for Camp Service.
Our prices are reasonable. Call first door south of Dr. Ware's Drug Store, Broad st., Columbus, Georgia. Orders promptly attended to.
July 8, 1861. 1y

SALT, SALT!

1,000 BUSHELS Turk's Island Salt, said to be greatly superior to Liverpool for sale low by
Oct 19 JNO. N. BIRCH.

FALL AND WINTER
DRY GOODS!
JAS. McPHILLIPS
HAS A LARGE STOCK OF
Fancy and Staple Dry Goods
CONSISTING OF
SILK and WORSTED DRESS GOODS;
MERINOES, POPLINS, VELONES, &c.;
CASHMERE SHAWLS;
Long and Square THIBET SHAWLS;
Heavy WOOLEN SHAWLS;
New Styles CALICOES and GINGHAMS;
HOSIERY, GLOVES, EMBROIDERIES and LACES;
BLEACHED HOMESPUNS and SHEETINGS;
IRISH LINENS, TOWELINGS, TABLE CLOTHS, and in fact a
A General Assortment of Goods
suitable for the present season, all of which will be sold at
REASONABLE PRICES!
An early call and inspection of the stock is solicited.
JAMES McPHILLIPS,
Oct. 9, 1861. Masonic Hall Building.

MILITARY WORKS!

A NEW supply of the following Military Books just received and for sale, for cash only, at the Book Store of J. W. PEASE.

HARDEE'S TACTICS, in two volumes, being the only complete Southern edition, with maps and plates. Price, by mail $3 25
THE VOLUNTEER'S HAND-BOOK, containing an abridgment of Hardee's Infantry Tactics. Price, by mail $1 00
GILHAM'S SCHOOL FOR THE SOLDIER, for Infantry and Rifle Drill. Price, by mail...75 cts.
BAYONET EXERCISES AND SKIRMISHERS' DRILL, with suggestions for the soldier in actual service. Price, by mail $1 50
ALSO,
New Pocket Maps of Virginia. Price, by mail $1
" " " " " Seat of War 1
" " " " Confederate States 1
Columbus, Aug. 28, 1861.

BREAD FOR THE ARMY!
CHARLES CRICHTON,
150 Broad st., Columbus,

DESIRES to notify the public generally, that he is prepared to supply Bread and Crackers in sufficient quantity to feed the Confederate States Army.

Dealers and consumers can be supplied with any of the following on short notice:

Pic Nic Crackers,	Water Biscuit,
Butter Crackers,	Abernathy Biscuit,
Sugar Crackers,	Cracknell Biscuit,
Soda Biscuit,	Loaf Bread,
Wine Biscuit,	Pilot Bread.

He is prepared to furnish Parties or Set Suppers in styles to suit the wishes of the public.
A share of patronage is solicited. june18-tf

GROCERIES, &c.

WE have just received, and offer to the trade or by retail, the following goods:
20 bbls. LARD;
25 kegs LARD;
4 bbls LARD OIL;
1 bbl. COPPERAS;
30 bbls. SYRUP;
15 half bbls. SYRUP;
10 bbls. OLD CORN WHISKY, pure;
4 " PEACH BRANDY, three years old;
3 " APPLE " " " "
100 boxes SOAP;
15 " CASTILE SOAP;
10 " SODA;
5 kegs "
20 boxes CANDLES;
2 bags PEPPER;
1 " ALLSPICE;
8 " RACE GINGER;
600 " POTASH;
1000 yards KERSEY.
F. M. BIGGERS & CO.
Columbus, Ga., Sept. 10 tf

Troy Manufacturing Company.

WOODEN WARE, FURNITURE, MATTRESSES, &c., &c., for sale by TROY MANUFACTURING CO.

SPINNING WHEELS,

AT wholesale and retail by TROY MANUFACTURING CO.

CEDAR BUCKETS.

A FINE lot of brass and iron bound, for sale by the TROY MANUFACTURING CO.

CAMP STOOLS.

FOR sale by the TROY MANUFACTURING CO.
Columbus, Ga., Sept. 25.
Papers in which we advertise copy to change.

SOLDIER'S GOODS!

WE HAVE now on hand a large lot of White, Red, Yellow and Grey FLANNELS;
GREY GEORGIA JEANS;
BROWN NORTH CAROLINA JEANS;
BROWN GEORGIA JEANS;
GREY AND WHITE JEANS;
STRIPED WOOL LINSEYS;
HICKORY AND FLANNEL SHIRTS;
WATER-PROOF BOOTS AND SHOES;
WOOL AND BUCKSKIN GLOVES;
KNITTED SHIRTS AND DRAWERS;
MILITARY BUTTONS;
ALL KINDS OF OVERCOATS;
INDIA RUBBER SUITS—Coats, Leggins, and Caps;
WOOLEN and CHENILLE COMFORTERS
In fact everything wanted by our Soldiers in camp. S. ROTHCHILD & BRO.
Columbus, Ga., Sept. 28, 1861 tf

DRY GOODS! DRY GOODS!

WE HAVE paid particular attention to the replenishing of our Dry Goods Stock which, we can assure our customers and the public in general, is as complete and well assorted now as any to be found anywhere, and comprises a large lot of
LADIES' DRESS GOODS;
FANCY AND STAPLE DRY GOODS;
BROWN AND BLEACHED SHEETINGS;
FLANNELS AND LINSEYS;
HOSIERY, GLOVES, HANDKERCHIEFS;
SHOES OF ALL DESCRIPTIONS;
A LARGE lot of GOODS for SOLDIERS' Wear and a good many more articles too numerous to mention. We will sell any of the above goods as low as can be expected at this time, and solicit a share of public patronage, as we expect to spare no pains to please.
S. ROTHCHILD & BRO.
Columbus, Ga., Sept. 28, 1861 tf

TO WHOM IT MAY CONCERN.

IN consequence of my absence to the war, cash will in all cases be required for goods purchased, or for work done, at my establishment; and all parties having unsettled accounts with me will oblige me by settling without delay.
aug15–tf D. B. THOMPSON.

NOTICE.

R. W. MILFORD is authorized to act as my agent in the transaction of any business during my absence from the city.
D. B. THOMPSON.
Columbus, Ga., Aug. 15, 1861. tf

To Farmers and Planters!

THE best Manure now made in the world is the Penn City Manufacturing Co.'s

No. 1 Superphosphate of Lime!

In recommending this Superior Fertilizer to the attention of Farmers and others interested in Agriculture, we claim for it the advantage of being perfectly reliable, much superior to any other article sold under the name of Superphosphate of Lime, and one that the farmer can depend upon as being a No. 1 extra article.
HULL, DUCK & CO.,
Feb. 16–tf Agents for Columbus, Ga.

ROPE AND BAGGING.

150 COILS of Rope and 150 bales of Bagging, for sale by
Oct 19–tf WARNOCK & CO.

FOR RENT AND SALE.

TO RENT,

THE PLANTERS' HOTEL, on Broad street, suited for a private boarding house. For terms, apply to SMITH & DANIEL, occupying a part of the building.
Columbus, Sept. 11. tf

FOR RENT,

THE Store No. 102 Broad street, next to Mr. J. Kyle, now occupied by Mr. Redd.
—ALSO—
No. — Broad street, occupied by Freidenburg & Co. Possession 1st October. Rent moderate.
Also, several Rooms to rent.
T. C. DEMPSEY, Perry House,
sept10-tf or Macon, Ga.

FOR RENT,

THE Rooms over my store, nine in number, well adapted for a Boarding House. To a good tenant an inducement will be offered. E. BARNARD.

For Rent!

A STORE, No. 34 Broad street, next door below "Warren's Arcade." Possession given immediately.
—ALSO—
OFFICES and BEDROOMS
in that desirable location known as "Gunby's Corner." J. RHODES BROWNE.
Columbus, Aug. 7. tf

FOR RENT,

A STORE on Broad street, one door above the Troy Factory Ware Room. Possession on the 1st October. Apply to
August 6–tf S ROTHCHILD & BRO.

FOR RENT.

THE commodious Eating House known as the GEM, under Jones' Building, will be rented low to a good tenant Apply to JOHN A. JONES, or JAMES WARE,
April 18–tf at Hunt & Ware's.

FOR RENT,

A DESIRABLE place in Linnwood two miles from town, containing 15 acres of land in a good state of cultivation; the improvements consist of a comfortable Dwelling containing five rooms, all necessary out buildings, viz: negro house, kitchen, stable, wash house, &c., with a good well of water, pump and spring house. To a good tenant an inducement will be offered. Possession given immediately. Apply to
JOHN McILHENNY, at the Gas Works.
Columbus, Ga, Oct. 31, 1861. 2w

FOR RENT IN LINNWOOD,

THE House, with seven acres of land, now occupied by R. C. Shorter, opposite the residences of Messrs. Patten and Nuckolls. Possession given 1st of October. Apply to
sept14 C. E. DEXTER, Trustee

COLUMBUS CITY BONDS FOR SALE.

BONDS issued by the City of Columbus to the Opelika and Talladega Rail Road, for sale by J. R. SLAUGHTER,
President O. and T. R. R.
Apply to L. G. Bowers, Columbus, Ga.
January 23 1861. tf

MILITARY--MILITARY.

WAR NEWS!

TWENTY able bodied men, of good character, will be received for the "TERRELL FLYING ARTILLERY," now in Virginia

An assurance of immediate duty in the most interesting and effective arm of the service is the inducement held out to all desiring to enlist in defence of their country.

A complete military outfit and transportation free of charge will be furnished by application at the Drug Store of JOHN W. BROOKS.
October 26 tf

COMPANIES WANTED!

Fairfax C. H., Va., October 14, 1861.

TWO additional Companies, numbering one hundred and twenty strong each, is authorized to be received into the 15th Alabama Regiment, to be armed and equipped on arrival.

Apply to EDWARD CROFT, Columbus, Ga., for transportation and orders.
JAMES CANTEY,
oct15-tf Colonel 15th Alabama Reg't.

WAR! WAR! WAR!
COLUMBUS FLYING ARTILLERY!

THE undersigned having authority from the War Department to raise and equip a Company to command a Battery of

FLYING ARTILLERY!

for immediate and active service; and having the Cannon, Horses, &c., already provided, are desirous of enlisting

ONE HUNDRED AND FIFTY MEN

for this purpose. Those wishing to serve their country have now the rare opportunity of entering this most attractive and effective arm of the service.

Men of Good Character Only

will be received, and all such who will report themselves to either of the undersigned, at the earliest possible moment, will be provided with good quarters, uniforms, and all the necessary equipments free of expense.

Your country earnestly appeals to your patriotism and valor, let the brave then rally to the defence of their homes and firesides.
EDWARD CROFT, at Gunby & Croft's Store.
A. I. YOUNG, at Eagle Factory.
oct4-tf

GROCERIES! GROCERIES!

WE HAVE just received and offer to the trade, or by retail, for Cash, the following goods, to wit:
75 small packages of Lard,
25 bbls. and tierces Lard,
1500 lbs. Rock Potash in jars and cans,
40 boxes Star Candles,
2000 Canvass Hams,
40 boxes Soap,
3 chests Tea,
60 boxes Tobacco, of different qualities,
500 bushels Rye,
100 sacks Salt,
Beef Tongues,
Matches, Alspice and Pepper,
And many other goods may be found in our stock. F. M. BIGGERS & CO.
AND TO ARRIVE FROM NEW ORLEANS.
75 bbls. New Syrup,
12 hhds. Sugar,
50 bbls Onions. Oct12

SEWING MACHINE!

A SUPERIOR WHEELER & WILSON SEWING MACHINE, for sale by T. J. HUNT,
oct17-tf at Spear's Jewelry Store.

SUNDRIES! SUNDRIES!

1,000 BUSHELS Turk's Island or Packing SALT;
150 Sacks Liverpool SALT;
85 Bales Heavy Gunny BAGGING;
350 Coils Heavy Machine ROPE;
10 Hhds. Choice New Orleans SUGAR;
50 Barrels New Orleans SYRUP;
5 Tierces Prime RICE;
150 Smoked BEEF TONGUES;
50 Boxes TOBACCO, various brands;
60 Bales (5 lbs. each) Superior SMOKING TOBACCO;
5 Kegs and 10 half kegs POWDER;
30 Quarter Boxes RAISINS;
50 Cases Wolfe's Cognac BRANDY, *pure;*
20 " " Irish and Scotch Whiskey, *pure;*
800 Lbs. Maccoboy SNUFF, in jars and in bulk;
40 Dozen "Eagle Mills" Mustard, ¼ lb. cans;
20 Dozen YEAST POWDERS;
50 Dozen Mason's BLACKING;
6 Baskets and 3 Cases Fine Champagne;
60 Barrels LIQUORS, various kinds and grades;
And many other articles too numerous to mention, which I offer to the trade or at retail at the lowest price for Cash
Oct 19–tf JNO. N. BIRCH.

MILITARY GOODS!
S. ROTHCHILD & BRO.

HAVE now on hand and offer at prices to suit the times:
100 Gray Flannel OVERSHIRTS;
200 Gray and White UNDERSHIRTS;
300 Pairs Cotton and Wool SOCKS;
100 Wool Soldiers' SCARFS;
300 Pounds Black and Slate FLAX THREAD;
100 Gross MILITARY BUTTONS;
FLANNELS and LINSEYS;
GREY GEORGIA CASSIMERES.
Call early and supply yourselves.
nov 2 tf

BREAKFAST BACON.

A SUPERIOR article, just received and for sale by F. M. BIGGERS & CO.

THE CONSTITUTION OF THE STATE OF GEORGIA.

ARTICLE 1.

DECLARATION OF FUNDAMENTAL PRINCIPLES.

1. The fundamental principles of Free Government cannot be too well understood, nor too often recurred to.

2. God has ordained that men shall live under government, but as the forms and administration of civil government are in human, and, therefore, fallible hands, they may be altered, or modified, whenever the safety or happiness of the governed requires it. No governments should be changed for light or transient causes; nor unless upon reasonable assurance that a better will be established.

3. Protection to person or property is the duty of Government; and a Government which, knowingly and persistently denies, or withholds from the governed such protection, when within its power, releases them from the obligation of obedience.

4. No citizen shall be deprived of life, liberty or property, except by due process of law; and of life or liberty, only by the judgment of his peers.

5. The writ of "*habeas corpus*" shall not be suspended, unless, in case of rebellion or invasion, the public safety may require it.

6. The right of the people to keep and bear arms shall not be infringed.

7. No religious test shall be required for the tenure of any office; and no religion shall be established by law, and no citizen shall be deprived of any right or privilege by reason of his religious belief.

8 Freedom of thought and opinion, freedom of speech, and freedom of the press, are inherent elements of political liberty. But while every citizen may freely speak, write, and print, on any subject, he shall be responsible for the abuse of the liberty.

9. The right of the people to appeal to the courts; to petition Government on all matters of legitimate cognizance; and peaceably to assemble for the consideration of any matter of public concern—shall never be impaired.

10. For every right, there should be provided a remedy; and every citizen ought to obtain justice without purchase, without denial, and without delay—conformably to the laws of the land.

11. Every person charged with an offence against the laws of the state shall have the privilege and benefit of counsel:

shall be furnished, on demand, with a copy of the accusation, and with a list of the witnesses against him:

shall have compulsory process to obtain the attendance of his own witnesses:

shall be confronted with the witnesses testifying against him, and

shall have a public and speedy trial by an impartial jury.

12. No person shall be put in jeopardy of life or liberty more than once for the same offence

13 No conviction shall work corruption of blood, or general forfeiture of estate.

14. Excessive bail shall not be required, nor excessive fines imposed, nor cruel and unusual punishments inflicted.

15. The power of the courts to punish for contempt shall be limited by legislative acts.

16. A faithful execution of the laws is essential to good order, and good order in society is essential to liberty.

17 Legislative acts in violation of the fundamental law are void, and the Judiciary shall so declare them

18. *Ex post facto* laws and laws impairing the obligation of contracts, and retro-active legislation injuriously affecting the right of the citizen, are prohibited.

19. Laws should have a general operation; and no general law shall be varied in a particular case by special legislation, except with consent of all persons to be affected thereby.

20. The right of taxation can be granted only by the people, and shall be exercised only to raise revenue for the support of Government, to pay the public debt, to provide for the common defence, and for such other purposes as are specified in the grant of powers.

21. In cases of necessity, private ways, and the right to carry water over-land, for the purpose of mining and draining, may be granted upon compensation being first paid; and with this exception, private property shall not be taken, except for public use, and then only upon just compensation—such compensation, except in cases of pressing necessity, to be first provided and paid

22. The right of the people to be secure in their persons, houses, papers, and effects, against unreasonable searches and seizures, shall not be violated; and no warrant shall issue but upon probable cause, supported by oath or affirmation, and particularly describing the place or places to be searched, and the persons and things to be seized.

23. Martial law shall not be declared, except in cases of extreme necessity.

24. Large standing armies, in time of peace, are dangerous to liberty.

25 No soldier shall, in time of peace, be quartered in any house without the consent of the owner; nor in time of war, but in a manner prescribed by law.

26. The person of a debtor shall not be detained in prison after delivering *bona fide* all his estate for the use of his creditors.

27. The enumeration of rights herein contained shall not be construed to deny to the people any inherent rights which they have hitherto enjoyed

28. This declaration is a part of the Constitution, and shall never be violated on any pretence whatever.

ARTICLE II.

Sec. 1.—1. The Legislative, Executive and Judicial Departments shall be distinct, and each department shall be confided to a separate body of magistracy. No person or collection of persons, being of one department shall exercise any power properly attached to either of the others, except in cases herein expressly provided.

2. The legislative power shall be vested in a General Assembly, which shall consist of a Senate and House of Representatives.

3. The meeting of the General Assembly shall be annual, and on the first Wednesday in November, until such day of meeting shall be altered by law. A majority of each house shall constitute a quorum to transact business, but a smaller number may adjourn from day to day, and compel the attendance of their members in such manner as each house shall prescribe. No session of the General Assembly shall continue for more than forty days, unless the same shall be done by a vote of two thirds of each branch thereof.

4. The compensation of the members and officers of the General Assembly shall be fixed by law, at the first session subsequent to the adoption of this Constitution; and the same shall not be increased so as to affect the compensation of the members or officers of the Assembly by which the increase is adopted.

5. No person holding any military commission or appointment, having any emolument or compensation annexed thereto, under this State or the Confederate States, or either of them (except Justices of the Inferior Court, Justices of the Peace, and officers of the militia), nor any defaulter for public money, or for legal taxes required of him, shall have a seat in either branch of the General Assembly; nor shall any Senator or Representative, after his qualification as such, be elected to any office or appointment by the General Assembly having any emoluments or compensation annexed thereto during the time for which he shall have been elected.

6. No person convicted of any felony, involving any species of the *crimen falsi*, before any court in this State or the Confederate States shall be eligible to any office or appointment of honor profit, or trust, within this State.

7. No person who is a collector or holder of public money, shall be eligible to any office in this State, until the same is accounted for and paid into the Treasury.

Sec 2—1. The Senate shall consist of forty-four members, one to be chosen from each Senatorial District, which district shall be composed of three contiguous counties. If a new county is established, it shall be added to a district which it adjoins, until there shall be another arrangement of the Senatorial Districts The Senatorial Districts shall not be changed, except when a new census shall have been taken.

2. No person shall be a Senator who shall not have attained to the age of twenty five years, and be a citizen of the Confederate States, and have been for three years an inhabitant of this State and for one year a resident of the district from which he is chosen.

3 The presiding officer shall be styled the President of the Senate and shall be elected *viva voce* from their own body.

4 The Senate shall have the sole power to try all impeachments. When sitting for that purpose they shall be on oath or affirmation; and no person shall be convicted without the concurrence of two-thirds of the members present. Judgment, in cases of impeachment, shall not extend further than removal from office and disqualification to hold and enjoy any office of honor, profit or trust within this State; but the party convicted shall, nevertheless, be liable and subject to indictment, trial, judgment, and punishment according to law.

Sec 3.—1. The House of Representatives shall be composed as follows: The thirty-seven counties having the largest representative population shall have two Representatives each. Every other county shall have one Representative. The designation of the counties having two Representatives shall be made by the General Assembly immediately after the taking of each census

2. No person shall be a Representative who shall not have attained to the age of twenty-one years, and be a citizen of the Confederate States, and have been for three years an inhabitant of this State, and for one year a resident of the county which he represents.

3 The presiding officer of the House of Representatives shall be styled the Speaker, and shall be elected *viva voce* from there own body.

4. They shall have the sole power to impeach all persons who have been or may be in office.

5. All bills for raising revenue, or appropriating money, shall originate in the House of Representatives; but the Senate may propose or concur in amendments as in other bills.

Sec. 4—1. Each House shall be the judge of the election returns, and qualifications of its own members; and shall have power to punish them for disorderly behavior or misconduct, by censure, fine, imprisonment, or expulsion; but no member shall be expelled except by a vote of two-thirds of the House from which he is expelled.

2. Each House may punish, by imprisonment not extending beyond the session, any person not a member, who shall be guilty of a contempt, by any disorderly behavior in its presence, or who, during the session, shall threaten injury to the person or estate of any member, for anything said or done in either House, or who shall assault any member therefor, or who shall assault or arrest any witness going to or returning therefrom, or, who shall rescue, or attempt to rescue, any person arrested by order of either House.

3. The members of both Houses shall be free from arrest, during their attendence on the General Assembly, and in going to or returning there from, except for treason, felony, or breach of the peace. And no member shall be liable to answer, in any other place, or anything spoken in debate in either House.

4. Each House shall keep a journal in its proceedings, and publish them immediately after its adjournment. The yeas and nays of the members on any question shall, at the desire of one fifth of the members present, be entered on the journals. The original journals shall be preserved (after publication) in the office of the Secretary of State; but there shall be no other record thereof.

5. Every bill, before it shall pass, shall be read three times, and on three separate and distinct days, in each House, unless in cases of actual invasion or insurrection. Nor shall any law or ordinance pass which refers to more than one subject matter, or contains matter different from that is expressed in the title thereof.

6. All acts shall be signed by the President of the Senate and the Speaker of the House of Representatives; and no bill, ordinance, or resolution intended to have the effect of law, which shall have been rejected by either House, shall be again proposed under the same or any other title, without the consent of two thirds of the House by which the same was rejected.

7. Neither House shall adjourn for more than three days, nor to any other place, without the consent of the other; and in case of disagreement between the Houses on a question of adjournment, the Governor may adjourn them.

8. Every Senator and Representative, before taking his seat, shall take an oath or affirmation to support the Constitution of the Confederate States and of this State; and also that he hath not practised and unlawful means, either directly or indirectly, to procure his election And every person convicted of having given or offered a bribe, shall be disqualified from serving as a member of either House for the term for which he was elected

9. Whenever this Constitution requires an act to be passed by two-thirds of both Houses, the yeas and nays on the passage thereof shall be entered on the journal of each.

Sec. 5.—1 The General Assembly shall have power to make all laws and ordinances, consistent with this Constitution and not repugnant to the Constitution of the Confederate States, which they shall deem necessary and proper for the welfare of the State.

2. They may alter the boundaries of counties, and lay off and establish new counties but every bill to establish a new county shall be passed by at least two thirds of the members present, in both branches of the General Assembly.

3. They shall provide for the taking of a census or enumeration of the people of this State, at regular decades of years, commencing at such times as they may prescribe.

4. The General Assembly shall have power to appropriate money for the promotion of learning and science, and to provide for the education of the people

5. The General Assembly shall have power, by a vote of two-thirds of each branch, to grant pardons in cases of final conviction for treason, or to pardon or commute in cases of final conviction for murder.

Sec. 6.—1. The General Assembly shall have no power to grant corporate powers and privileges to private companies, except to banking, insurance, rail roads, canal, plank road, navigation, mining, express, lumber, and telegraph companies; nor to make or change election precincts; nor to establish bridges and ferries; nor to change names, or legitimate children: but shall by law prescribe the manner in which such power shall be exercised by the courts But no bank charter shall be granted or extended, and no act passed authorising the suspension of specie payment by any chartered bank, except by a voice of two-thirds of each branch of the General Assembly.

2. No money shall be drawn from the Treasury of this State, except by appropriation made by law; and a regular statement and account of the receipt and expenditure of all public money shall be published from time to time.

3 No vote, resolution, law or order shall pass, granting a donation or gratuity in favor of any person, except by the concurrence of two-thirds of each branch of the General Assembly.

4 No law shall be passed by which a citizen shall be compelled, directly or indirectly, to become as stockholder in or contribute to a rail road or other work of internal improvement, without his consent; except the inhabitants of a corporate town or city. This provision shall not be construed to deny the power of taxation for the purpose of making levees or dams to prevent the overflow of rivers.

Sec. 7—1. The importation or introduction of negroes from any foreign country, other than the slaveholding States or Territories of the United States of America, is forever prohibited.

2. The General Assembly may prohibit the introduction of negroes from any State; but they shall have no power to prevent immigrants from bringing their slaves with them.

3 The General Assembly shall have no power to pass laws for the emancipation of slaves.

4. Any person who shall maliciously kill or maim a slave, shall suffer such punishment as would be inflicted in case the like offence had been committed on a free white person.

ARTICLE III.

Sec. 1.—1. The Executive power shall be vested in a Governor, who shall hold his office during the term of two years, and until such time as a successor shall be chosen and qualified. He shall have a competent salary fixed by law, which shall not be increased or diminished during the period for which he shall have been elected; neither shall he receive, within that period, any other emolument from the Confederate States, or either of them, or from any foreign power.

2. The Governor shall be elected by the persons qualified to vote for members of the General Assembly, on the first Wednesday in October, in the year of our Lord 1861; and on the first Wednesday in October in every second year thereafter, until such time be altered by law; which election shall be held at the place of holding general elections, in the several counties of the State, in the manner prescribed for the election of members of the General Assembly. The returns for every election of Governor shall be sealed up by the managers separately from other returns, and directed to the President of the Senate and Speaker of the House of Representatives, and transmitted to the Governor, or the person exercising the duties of Governor for the time being, who shall, without opening the said returns, cause the same to be laid before the Senate, on the day after the two Houses shall have been organised; and they shall be transmitted by the Senate to the House of Representatives. The members of each branch of the General Assembly shall convene in the Representative chamber, and the President of the Senate, and the Speaker of the House of Representatives shall open and publish the returns in presence of the General Assembly; and the person having the majority of the whole number of votes given in, shall be declared duly elected Governor of this State; but if no person have such majority, then from the two persons having the highest number of votes, who shall be in life, and shall not decline an election at the time appointed for the Legislature to elect, the General Assembly shall immediately elect a Governor *viva voce*; and in all cases of election of a Governor by the General Assembly, a majority of the votes of the members present shall be necessary for a choice Contested elections shall be determined by both Houses of the General Assembly, in such manner as shall be prescribed by law.

3. No person shall be eligible to the office of Governor who shall not have been a citizen of the Confederate States twelve years, and an inhabitant of this State six years and who hath not attained the age of thirty years.

4. In case of the death, resignation, or disability of the Governor, the President of the Senate shall exercise the Executive powers of the Government until such disability be removed, or a successor is elected and qualified And in case of the death, resignation, or disability of the President of the Senate the Speaker of the House of Representatives shall exercise the Executive power of the Government until the removal of the disability, or the election and qualification of a Governor.

5 The Governor shall, before he enters on the duties of his office, take the following oath or affirmation: "I do solemnly swear or affirm (as the case may be,) that I will faithfully execute the office of Governor of the State of Georgia; and will, to the best of my abilities, preserve, protect and defend the Constitution thereof."

Sec. 2—1. The Governor shall be Commander-in-Chief of the army and navy of this State, and of the militia thereof.

2. He shall have power to grant reprieves for offences against the State, except in cases of impeachment, and to grant pardons, or to remit any part of a sentence, in all cases after conviction, except for treason or murder in which cases he may respite the execution, and make report thereof to the next General Assembly.

3. He shall issue writs of elections to fill vacancies that happen in the Senate or House of Representatives, and shall have power to convene the General Assembly on extraordinary occasions; and shall give them, from time to time, information of the state of the Republic, and recommend to their consideration such measures as he may deem necessary and expedient.

4. When any officer shall become vacant by death, resignation, or otherwise, the Governor shall have power to fill such vacancy, unless otherwise provided for by law; and persons so appointed shall continue in office until a successor is appointed agreeably to the mode pointed out by this Constitution, or by law in pursuance thereof.

5. A person once rejected by the Senate shall not be re-appointed by the Governor to the same office, during the same session, or the recess thereafter.

6. The Governor shall have the revision of all bills passed by both Houses, before the same shall become laws, but two-thirds of each House may pass a law, notwithstanding his dissent; and if any bill should be returned by the Governor within five days (Sundays excepted) after it has been presented to him, the same shall be a law, unless the General Assembly, by their adjournment, shall prevent its return. He may approve any appropriation and disapprove any other appropriation in the same bill, and the latter shall not be effectual unless passed by two-thirds of each House.

7. Every vote, resolution, or order, to which the concurrence of both Houses may be necessary, except on a question of election or adjournment, shall be presented to the Governor; and before it shall take effect, be approved by him, or being disapproved, shall be re-passed by two-thirds of each House, according to the rules and limitations prescribed in case of a bill.

8. There shall be a Secretary of State, a Comptroller General, a Treasurer, and Surveyor-General, elected by the General Assembly, and they shall hold their officers for the like period as the Governor, and shall have a competent salary which shall not be increased or diminished during the period for which they shall have been elected. The General Assembly may at any time consolidate any two of these officers, and require all the duties to be discharged by one officer.

9. The great seal of the State shall be deposited in the office of the Secretary of State, and shall not be affixed to any instrument of writing, but by order of the Governor or General Assembly; and the General Assembly shall, at their first session, after the rising of this Convention, by law cause the great seal to be altered.

10. The Governor shall have power to appoint his own Secretaries, not exceeding two in number.

ARTICLE IV.

Sec. 1.—1. The Judicial powers of this State shall be vested in a Supreme Court for the correction of errors, Superior, Inferior, Ordinary, and Justices' courts, and in such other courts as have been, or may be established by law.

2 The Supreme Court shall consist of three Judges, who shall be appointed by the Governor, with the advice and consent of two-thirds of the Senate, for such term of years as shall be prescribed by law, and shall continue in office until their successors shall be appointed and qualified, removable by the Governor on the address of two-thirds of each branch of the General Assembly, or by impeachment and conviction thereon.

3 The said court shall have no original jurisdiction, but shall be a court alone for the trial and correction of errors in law and equity from the Superior Courts of the several circuits, and shall sit at least once a year, at a time prescribed by law, in each of one or more judicial districts, designated by the General Assembly for that purpose, at such point in each district, as shall, by the General Assembly, be ordered, for the trial and determination of writs of error from the several Superior Courts included in such judicial districts.

4. The said Court shall dispose of and finally determine every case on the docket of such court at the first or second term after such writ of error brought; and in case the plaintiff in error shall not be prepared at the first term of such court, after error brought, to prosecute the cause, unless precluded by some Providential cause from such prosecution, it shall be stricken from the docket, and the judgment below shall stand affirmed.

Sec 2.—1. The Judges of the Superior Courts shall be appointed in the same manner as Judges of the Supreme Court, from the circuits in which they are to serve, for the term of four years, and shall continue in office until their successors shall be appointed and qualified, removable by the Governor on the address of two thirds of each branch of the General Assembly, or by impeachment and conviction thereon.

2 The Superior Court shall have exclusive jurisdiction in all cases of divorce, both total and partial; but no total divorce shall be granted, except on the concurrent verdicts of two special juries. In each divorce case, the court shall regulate the rights and disabilities of the parties.

3. The Supreme Court shall also have exclusive jurisdiction in all criminal cases, except as relates to people of color, fines for neglect of duty, contempts of Court, violations of road laws, and obstructions of water courses, jurisdiction of which shall be vested in such judicature or tribunal as shall be or may have been pointed out by law; and except in all other minor offences committed by free white persons, and which do not subject the offender or offenders to loss of life, limb, or member, or to confinement in the penitentiary; in all such cases, Corporation Courts, such as now exist, or may hereafter be constituted, in any incorporated city, or town, may be vested with jurisdiction, under such rules and regulations as the Legislature may hereafter by law direct.

4. All criminal cases shall be tried in the county where the crime was committed, except in cases where a jury cannot be obtained.

5. The Supreme Court shall have exclusive jurisdiction in all cases respecting titles to land, which shall be tried in the county where the land lies, and also in all equity causes, which shall be tried in the county where one or more of the defendants reside, against whom substantial relief is prayed.

6. It shall have appellate jurisdiction in all such cases as may be provided by law.

7. It shall have power to correct errors in inferior judicatories by writ of *certiorari*, and to grant new trials in the Superior Court on proper and legal grounds.

8. It shall have power to issue writs of *mandamus*, prohibition, *scire facias*, and all other writs which may be necessary for carrying its powers fully into effect.

9 The Superior and Inferior Courts shall have concurrent jurisdiction in all other civil causes; which shall be tried in the county where the defendant resides.

10. In cases where joint obligors, or joint promissors or copartners, or joint trespassers residing in different counties, the suit may be brought in either county.

11. In cases of a maker and endorser or endorsers of prommissory notes residing in different counties in this State, the same may be used in the county where the maker resides.

12. The Superior and Inferior Courts shall sit in each county twice in every year, at such stated times as have been or may be appointed by the General Assembly.

Sec. 3—1. The judges shall have salaries adequate to their services fixed by law, which shall not be diminished during their continuance in office; but shall not receive any other perquisites or emoluments whatever, from parties or others, on account of any duty required of them.

2. There shall be a State's Attorney and Solicitors appointed in the same manner as the Judges of the Supreme Court, and commissioned by the Governor; who shall hold their offices for the term of four years, or until their successors shall be appointed and qualified, unless removed by sentence or impeachment, or by the Governor, or the address of two thirds of each branch of the General Assembly. They shall have salaries adequate to their services fixed by law, which shall not be diminished during their continuance in office.

3 The Justices of the Inferior Courts shall be elected in each county by the persons entitled to vote for members of the General Assembly.

4 The Justices of the Peace shall be elected in each district by the persons entitled to vote for members of the General Assembly.

5. The powers of a Court of Ordinary and of Probate shall be vested in an Ordinary for each county, from whose decisions there may be an appeal to Superior Court, under regulations prescribed by law. The Ordinary shall be *ex officio* Clerk of said Court, and may appoint a Deputy Clerk. The Ordinary, as Clerk, or his Deputy, may issue citations and great temporary letters of administration to hold until permanent letters are granted; and said Ordinary, as Clerk, or his Deputy, may grant marriage licenses. The Ordinaries in and for the respective counties shall be elected, as other county officers are, on the first Wednesday in January, 1864, and every fourth year thereafter, and shall be commissioned by the Governor for the term of four years In case of any vacancy of said office of Ordinary, from any cause, the same shall be filled by election, as is provided in relation to other county officers, and until the same is filled the Clerk of the Superior Court for the time being shall act as Clerk of Ordinary.

ARTICLE V.

1. The electors of members of the General Assembly shall be free white male citizens of this State, and shall have attained the age of twenty-one years, and have paid all taxes which may have been required of them, and which they have had an opportunity of paying agreeably to law, for the year preceeding the election; and shall have resided six months within the district or county.

2 All elections, by the General Assembly, shall be *viva voce*, and when the Senate and House of Representatives unite for the purpose of electing, they shall meet in the Representative chamber, and the President of the Senate shall in such cases preside, and declare the person or persons elected

3 In all elections by the people, the electors shall vote by ballot, until the General Assembly shall otherwise direct.

4. All civil officers shall continue in the exercise of the duties of their several offices during the periods for which they were appointed, or until they shall be superseded by appointments made in conformity with this Constitution; and all laws now in force shall continue to operate so far as they are compatible with this Constitution, until they shall expire, be altered, or repealed; and it shall be the duty of the General Assembly to pass all necessary laws and regulations for carrying this Constitution into full effect.

5. All militia and county officers shall be elected by the people in such manner as the General Assembly may by law direct.

6. This Constitution shall be amended only by a convention of the people called for that purpose.

7. This Constitution shall not take effect until the same is ratified by the people. And to this end, there shall be an election held at all the places of public election in this State, on the first Tuesday in July, 1861, when all the citizens of this State entitled to vote for Governor, shall cast their ballots either for "ratification" or "no ratification." The election shall be conducted in the same manner as general elections, and the returns shall be made to the Governor. If a majority of the votes cast shall be for ratification, the Governor shall, by proclamation, declare this Constitution adopted by the people. But if for no ratification, that fact shall be proclaimed by the Governor, and this Constitution shall have no effect whatever.

Done in the convention of the delegates of the people of the State of Georgia at Savannah, on the 23d day of March, in the year of our Lord eighteen hundred and sixty-one.

In testimony whereof the President of said convention has hereunto set his hand, and caused the same to be attested by the Secretary thereof.

GEORGE W. CRAWFORD, President.

Attest: A. R. LAMAR, Secretary.

A CARD.

WE, THE UNDERSIGNED MERCHANTS OF CHARLESTON, have received communications from many of our friends in the interior, stating that TREASURY NOTES AND BONDS OF THE CONFEDERATE STATES would be tendered to them in payment of debts, and that their collections would be stimulated were it generally known that these securities could be freely used by the merchants.

In order that all of our customers may be advised as to our course, we have deemed it proper to issue forthwith a general notice that we will cheerfully receive the aforesaid TREASURY NOTES AND BONDS for all CLAIMS due us.

Charleston, July 20, 1861.

JOHNSTON, CREWS & CO.
CRANE, BOYLSTON & CO.
HYATT, McBURNEY & CO.
GILLILAND, HOWELL & CO.
COURTENAY, TENNENT & CO.
F D. FANNING & CO.
JOHN ASHHURST & CO.
HORSEY, AUTEN & CO.
STEVENSON & CO.,
late Haviland, Stevenson & Co
FORCE & MITCHELL.
NELSON CARTER.
BROWN & PALMA.
D. F. FLEMING & CO.
GEO. W. WILLIAMS & CO.
LANNEAU & WHILDEN.
WILMANS & PRICE.
HASTIE, CALHOUN & CO.
FARRAR, BRO. & CO.
J. E. ADGER & CO.
WALDRON, EGLESTON & CO.
T J. & C. H. MOISE & CO.
McCARTER & DAWSON.
CHAMBERLAIN, MILE & CO.
EDWIN BATES & CO.
HARRAL, NICHOLS & CO.
E. B. STODDARD & CO.
D. R. WILLIAMS & CO.
BOWEN, FOSTER & CO.
H. F. STROHECKER.
DEWING, THAYER & CO.
J. & W. KNOX.
DUNHAM, TAFT & CO.
JOHN G. MILNOR & CO.
ALBERT LENGNICK,
per Attorney Alfred Lengnick.
HASELTINE & WALTON.
M. H. NATHAN.
A. CARTER.
BUFF & DOWIE.
MARSHALL, BURGE & CO.
WEBB & SAGE.
jy31-ow2t PIERSON, SMITH & CO.

CONFEDERATE STATES LOAN!

THE undersigned, Commissioners of the Confederate States Loan, in and for the State of Georgia, announce to the public that the books for the subscription to this Loan are re-opened at the following points, namely: Savannah, Augusta, Macon, Columbus, Albany. We will send books &c, to other points if requested to do so, and it be deemed expedient by us.

Five millions only of the fifteen million Loan have been called for, and eleven millions have been responded to—no subscription being at a less rate than par, and some as high as ten per cent premium. The present exigencies of our national crisis call for the balance of this Loan, and we have no doubt that our fellow-citizens will cheerfully respond to that call. Let it be remembered that, in what they thus advance, they are making an investment at 8 per cent. per annum, (which investment is secured by a special sinking fund,) and that subscriptions may be made in any sum from fifty dollars upwards.

We are authorized to say that these subscriptions will be received in this State in current bank notes which are considered at par at the several centres of trade.

An abounding patriotism has carried, and is carrying, our brave brothers and sons in sufficient numbers to the field; we doubt not that the same fervid feeling will support them there, by rapidly filling the remainder of this Loan.

E. STARNES,
J MILLIGAN,
WM. B. JOHNSTON, } Com'ers.

June 24, 1861. 2aw2w

A CARD.

THE undersigned, being about to leave for the seat of war, desires to return to the citizens of Columbus his thanks for the liberal patronage they have heretofore extended to him, and to ask of them during his absence a continuance of the same.

My business will be in charge of my competent and worthy friend, A. F. Hancock.

J. H. SIKES.

Columbus, June 24 1861. tf

COLUMBUS:

Largest City and Country Circulation

Friday Morning, Nov. 8, 1861.

Commissary General.

Jared I. Whitaker, Esq., of the Atlanta Intelligencer, has received from Gov Brown the appointment of Commissary General of Georgia, with the rank of Lieut. Colonel.

Verily Gov. Brown remembers his **friends.**

A Merited Appointment.

Com. G. N. Hollins, C. S. N., has received from the Department of the Confederate States Navy the appointment of Flag Captain on the New Orleans naval station, dating on the day of his successful attack on and dispersal of the United States vessels at the Passes of the Mississippi.

To be Disbanded.

The Nashville Union says reliable information has reached it that on the 4th inst. Gen. Johnston issued orders to disband the Tennessee troops now organizing under the recent call of the Governor of Tennessee. The only intelligent explanation for this step is the want of arms to place in their hands. Further intelligence is necessary before comment ing on an order which seems to be unaccountable.

Large Shipment of Wool.

Gen. Jas. A. Mabry, of Knoxville, Tennessee, has received a dispatch from an agent he has in Texas, to the effect that he has purchased for him 100,000 pounds of wool. It is the intention of the General to have this wool converted into cassimeres, making more than 100,000 yards. All of this, he intends to have manufactured into clothing at Knoxville.

The Lincoln Army and East Tennessee.

Rumors were rife on the streets yesterday, says the Knoxville Register of the 5th, that the enemy were in considerable force at the State line, moving in this direction through Big Creek Gap. We learn from a reliable source that our cavalry scouts were, day before yesterday, thirty miles beyond the Kentucky line, and that only squads of the enemy (and these were driven in) were seen working upon the road ascending the other side of the mountain.

Speculation and Extortion—Tariff on Whisky.

In the Tennessee Legislature, Mr. Jones presented the proceedings of a meeting of a portion of the citizens of Nashville, in regard to the extortions now practised, at which the following resolutions were adopted:

Resolved, That the Legislature of the State of Tennessee, be requested to pass some law that will prevent the ruinous prices now sought to be placed upon the staples of life, even if it shall become necessary to place the same in the hands of the military authorities.

Resolved, That a law or tax be levied upon every gallon of spirituous liquors distilled from wheat, corn, rye, or potatoes, that shall be sufficient to prohibit the same during the present war and blockade, the proceeds thereof to be applied to the support of families with us, of soldiers on the tented field.

This is a movement in the right direction. Let the Georgia Legislature take this subject under consideration.—*Macon Messenger.*

By the President—A Proclamation.

Whereas, It hath pleased Almighty God, the Sovereign Disposer of events, to protect and defend the Confederate States hitherto, in their conflict with their enemies, and to be unto them a shield.

And, whereas, with grateful thanks we recognize His hand and acknowledge that not unto us, but unto him belongeth the victory; and in humble dependence upon His Almighty strength, and trusting in the justness of our cause, we appeal to Him, that he may set at naught the efforts of our enemies, and put them to confusion and shame:

Now therefore, I, Jefferson Davis, President of the Confederate States, in view of the impending conflict, do here by set apart Friday, the 15th day of November, as a day of fasting, humiliation and prayer; and I do hereby invite the Reverend Clergy and the people of these Confederate States to repair on that day to their usual places of public worship and to implore the blessings of Almighty God upon our arms; that He may give us victory over our enemies, preserve our homes and altars from pollution, and secure to us the restoration of peace and prosperity.

Given under my hand and the seal of the Confederate States, at Richmond, thirty first day of October, in the year of our Lord one thousand eight hundred and sixty one.

JEFFERSON DAVIS.

By the President:

R M. T. HUNTER, Secretary of State.

Won't Stand the Charge.

Dr. Parker, of Chattanooga, Tenn, who was in the Leesburg fight, writes to that place an interesting description of it, from which we extract the following:

Some of our men are of the impression that we will have another engagement in a few days. I cannot think that they will again attack us, or give us a chance to make a charge on them; it is impossible for them to stand a charge, and whenever such command is given they take to their heels. Not one of our men that I have seen was shot in the back; more than one-half of the enemy's men were thus shot. The enemy say we will never encounter a force that will fight more desperately, as they were hemmed in by the river and could not retreat—that they would have run sooner, but had no place to run to. I forgot to say that we took all their artillery and most of their guns, which consisted of Enfield and Belgium rifles, muskets, &c.

Gen. Houston.

The death of Gen. Sam. Houston, of Texas, seems to be confirmed. The Bowling Green correspondent of the Nashville Union says M. Lewis, Esq., a nephew of Gen. Houston, has received information to that effect by letter, from Galveston.

A Methodist Regiment.

The New Orleans Delta of Saturday, says: "A few days ago we had the pleasure of a visit from three distinguished and learned divines of the Methodist denomination, two of whom wore uniforms, and the third still retained his clerical habit. These gentlemen were the Rev. Dr. Carter, President of the Methodist Soule University of Texas; the Rev. Mr Boggs, recently a captain in one of the regiments at Manassas; and the Rev. Mr. Gillespie, our cotemporary of the Christian Advocate, and an eloquent and able preacher. Associated with these gentlemen in this enterprise, is the learned and able Dr. Wilkes, of Texas, and several other prominent divines of the same patriotic persuasion. These gentlemen are commissioned to raise a mounted regiment in Texas; and as Methodist preachers in the South are all good horsemen, and are accustomed to field exercise, to the exposure and danger of camp life, this regiment promises to be one of the most formidable and efficient in the Confederate army. The field, and most of the commissioned officers will be composed of the same class of zealous defenders of the cause of the South and of Christianity. Dr. Carter is an experienced scientific soldier, thoroughly versed in the art of war and skilled in the use of all its appliances. Dr. Boggs has already seen much active service, and doubtless many of the one hundred and twenty Methodist preachers who were included in the rolls of the army of the Potomac, will be assigned to command in this regiment. The equipment of the regiment is to be a very complete one.

The men are to be armed with lances, like those of the celebrated Polish lancers, with revolvers and double-barrelled shot guns. As the regiment will be officered by gentlemen of great sobriety, piety and propriety of conduct, and will naturally excite a peculiar interest and elicit the active and earnest aid of the large body of Christians. whose zealous patriotism and devotion it will represent in this noble struggle for liberty and right, we recommend the young men of the country, who are desirous of participating in the exciting drama, to join its ranks."

Letter from Professor Darby.

AUBURN, Nov. 6, 1861.

Ed's Sun: I notice in your issue of today, a letter from a Mr. Haines of Montgomery, called forth by a published extract of a letter from me, to a friend in Charleston. Although it is said to be from Prof. Darby of South Carolina.

The letter was strictly private, and I was astonished at its appearance. I claimed nothing before the public. What I did claim was to make sulphuric acid from pyrites, without the use of leaden chambers or platina retorts. The possibility of making sulphuric acid from pyrites, I did not suppose, any mere student in Chemistry, was ignorant of; and that it was made in Europe twenty years ago, any one much acquainted with the progress of the science, must have known.

But that it was ever manufactured for commercial purposes, without the expensive apparatus alluded to, I do not suppose. The letter was written in compliance with a promise made at the close of a conversation on that point. It was said that a company was about being formed to manufacture sulphuric acid and one of the company was to go to St. Louis, and endeavor to get lead for the chambers and a retort for concentration, and that sulphur was to be first obtained from the pyrites. I replied, that the pyrites might be used directly, and the chambers and retort were not essential, and that I would return home and repeat in a more careful manner experiments often made in the Laboratory. It was after these experiments were made, that the letter was written. I said I had made sulphuric acid from pyrites. I meant of course under the conditions mentioned.

The apparatus for making sulphuric acid in the ordinary manner, costs from 20 000 to 30,000 dollars. If it can be made at home for as many hundred, it is certainly desirable.

I was informed two years ago, by a manufacturer, that his apparatus cost $32 000, and the expense per annum was 20 per cent of the sum for repairs. Sulphuric acid is the great agent directly or indirectly, of nearly all our Chemical productions, and to produce it cheaply from the rocks of our own hills is certainly something gained.

There are a number of blunders and misstatements in Mr. Haines' letter, which I have no disposition to occupy your space in discussing.

Very respectfully,

J. DARBY.

An Important Movement.

The Clarksville (Tenn.) Chronicle is authorized, by Dr. Blackburn, the agent of the Confederate States, to notice the fact that the Government has rented a large slaughtering house in that city, and is ready through its agents, to contract for any number of hogs and beeves during the packing season.

The Chronicle states that the object of the Government in this operation, is to provide supplies of pork and beef for our army, and the plan of purchasing the live stock directly from the producer, and doing their own packing, must commend itself to every one as a most sensible proceeding. The producer will receive the highest market price—in either currency or treasury notes, he may select.

The Sandersville Georgian says that on Wednesday of last week, Col. William Hurst, of Washington county, had the misfortune to have his barn, containing his wheat and rye crop, about twelve hundred bushels of corn, forage, &c., destroyed by fire. The fire is supposed to have been dropped by a negro woman who was at the barn smoking.

TELEGRAPHIC

Dispatches to the Daily Sun.

INTERESTING WAR NEWS!

SAVANNAH, Nov. 7.—Passengers on the St. Marys, report that the Yankee fleet attempted to pass the batteries at Port Royal, at 9½ o'clock, this morning. Seven of the largest steamers succeeded in a few minutes and were lying in the Bay out of range of the batteries. The firing was continuous and heavy from the batteries.

From the position of the St. Marys it was impossible to see if any of the fleet returned the fire of the batteries as they passed. The opinion is they did not fire a gun.

A large steamer supposed to be the first that ran the gauntlet of the batteries, chased and and fired a shot at the Confederate States steamer Savannah, Commodore Tattnall's flag ship, which escaped into a creek.

The St. Marys left for Savannah at 10 o'clock and it was impossible to learn of casualties.

Col. Wm. H. Stiles' regiment arrived at Hilton Head wharf, five miles distant from the batteries, just as the firing commenced, and left for the scene of action in double quick time.

A Yankee steamer of extraordinary speed tried to intercept the Confederate States steamer Savannah, and must have run aground while making a short cut over a shoal place and did not appear around the point to which she was making.

8 O'CLOCK, A. M.—Forty-one vessels are in sight, 27 of which are transports; the balance, 22, are all steamers.

Col De Saussure's regiment 800 or 900 strong, arrived yesterday afternoon, from Summerville, South Carolina.

The St. Marys passed the Gen. Clinch at 10½ o'clock, having on board Gen. Ripley and Staff, bound to Port Royal.

SAVANNAH, Nov. 7.—7:40 p. m.—Seven Federal vessels passed the battery at Bay Point this morning. After getting inside they opened fire on Hilton Head battery. The batteries at Bay Point and Hilton Head returned the fire. Several guns were dismounted on our batteries, but the result to the vessels is unknown. The firing ceased at dark, but it is expected the enemy will attack and try to effect a landing to night when warm work may be expected.

NASHVILLE, Nov. 6.—A dispatch to the New York Times from Washington, the 31st ult., says the Army of the Potomac will not go into Winter quarters within the present lines of entrenchments. No such purpose is entertained by the Government, and no suggestion has been made to Gen. McClellan whose activity continues great.

The New York World's dispatch says Lincoln has assured parties that a forward movement of the army has been determined on.

The Tribune's dispatches says the Navy Department has recently ordered 500 more rifle cannon.

The Tribune admits the rumor of the absconding of Dupont's Secretary, but says it is unfounded and adds it has reason to believe it was put in circulation by the enemies of the Government.

MEMPHIS, Nov. 6.—Electors for President and Vice President received 2545 votes here to-day. Currin's majority is 1597.

Arrival of the Arago.

NEW YORK, Oct. 31.—The steamship Arago has arrived here with 1276 packages of arms, 600 packages of equipments and clothing for Quartermaster General Meigs, comprising a complete set of arms, equipments and clothing for 12,000 men.

Lieut. Col. Palfrey, commanding the 20th Massachusetts Regiment at the battle of Leesburg in his official report to the Governor, says the loss of the Regiment was about 50 per cent of the officers engaged. Of twenty two only nine are safe Of privates engaged 318 were killed and wounded and 147 missing.

Superintendent Kennedy has issued an order to the Police of New York directing every passenger bound outside the country, to be examined, to see if all have passports.

The Surveyor of the port of New York has seized the ship Joseph W. Drier, two-sixteenths of which was owned by Joseph Phillips, of Louisiana.

Special to the Nashville Union and American.

RICHMOND, Nov. 3.—A private letter from London to the Washington Republican says: "Unless the next few days bring over the news of a brilliant and decisive victory of the Federal Government over the Confederates, England will at once try to raise the blockade of the Southern ports."

Lord John Russel says: I will consider the propriety of sending out ships of war to raise the blockade of the Southern ports."

BRILLIANT CHARGE OF GENERAL FREMONT'S BODY-GUARD THROUGH THE TOWN OF SPRINGFIELD, MISSOURI, ON OCTOBER 24, 1861.—[See Page 722.]

The Philadelphia Inquirer.

ESTABLISHED 1829. PHILADELPHIA, SATURDAY, NOVEMBER 23, 1861. PRICE TWO CENTS.

The War Against Rebellion!

THE VERY LATEST NEWS.

A Brave Philadelphia Soldier.

NEW MILITARY HOSPITALS.

Gen. Smith's Division Reviewed.

SEIZURE OF FORAGE--A RECONNOISSANCE.

A REBEL DESERTER.

THE WAR IN MISSOURI.

Burning of Warsaw by the Rebels.

A Regiment of "Franc Fireurs."

ARMY APPOINTMENTS.

Lord Lyons Expresses No Opinion on the Mason-Slidell Capture.

Trade Re-Opened with the Eastern Shore of Virginia.

LATE FROM FORTRESS MONROE.

Attack Upon a Scouting Party.

Arrival of Pennsylvania Regiments at the Fortress.

LATEST FROM WASHINGTON.

Special Despatches to the Inquirer.

WASHINGTON, Nov. 22.

A BRAVE PHILADEPHIA SOLDIER.

BYRON BARTON, of the Fifth Regular Cavalry, a [illegible] Philadelphia [illegible] had a ballet taken [illegible] leg and one from his back. One received at the same time passed through his head. He is doing well. He was wounded in a reconnoissance of Flint Hill, two weeks ago, under command of General MCCLELLAN, and was left as dying, in a Rebel house, in Vienna. Dr. THOMPSON, of the Forty-third New York Volunteers, took eight men and brought him to the hospital of his Regiment. Gen. MCCLELLAN came twice to see him, in admiration for his bravery, he having been the only man offering to mount Flint Hill when General MCCLELLAN called for volunteers

HEALTH OF PENNSYLVANIA RESERVES.

The sick of General MCCALL's Pennsylvania Reserve Division, having previously lain in tents, were last month removed to the house of ex-Lieut. C. W. COOK, of the U S. Navy, now a Captain in the Rebel army, who vacated it at the commencement of the war. The furniture has been packed away by Assistant Surgeon DICKESON, of the Fourth Pennsylvania Regiment, now detailed to take charge. It now contains forty-eight patients, none of whom are seriously sick, except GEORGE HAWKEY, of the Twelfth Regiment, with typhoid fever, but who will recover.

THE PECULIAR INSTITUTION.

Near General MCCALL's Head-quarters is an old Virginian, who liberated his twelve slaves after the war commenced, and now has them contentedly working upon his farm on wages.

HEALTH OF THE VERMONT TROOPS.

The Vermont regiments are the most sickly in the army, owing to the change of climate from their cool and purer air.

The averge of sick through the army during the last month for the following States, was as follows:—

Vermont	144	Massachusetts	50
Wisconsin	76	Illinois	44
Michigan	77	New York	27
Maine	69	Rhode Island	111
Minnesota	58	New Jersey (supposed)	15
Pennsylvania	52		

The whole average being forty-eight to a regiment for last month

THE NEW MILITARY HOSPITALS.

The bids for erecting the New Hospitals were opened yesterday afternoon. For the one on "Stones Farm," the bids were:—

Joseph Coons, Baltimore	$24,000
R J Mahon, Baltimore	24,840
Francis A Gibbons, Washington	26,200
James W Barker, Washington	30,500
Daniel S. Harkness, Washington	30,575
M. & C Carman, Washington	38,970
J. & G. A. Bincer, Washington	45,000
Fox, McManus & Co., Washington	55,000
W H. Allen, Baltimore	57,932
Painter & Mullnoland, Washington	68,000
Jas. P. Hall & Co, Washington	65,000
P. Crowley, Washington	72,000

For the one to be erected on Judiciary Square:—

James Coons, Baltimore	$22,700
R. J Mahon, Baltimore	23,978
Francis A. Gibbons, Washington	24,600
James W Barker, Washington	27,900
Daniel S. Harkness, Washington	30,100
C. E. Edmonston, Washington	35,500
M. and C. Carman, Washington	37,770
Henry F. Dure, Delaware	37,885
A. Binder, Washington	45,000
Fox, McManus & Co, Washington	55,000
W. H. Allen, Baltimore	57,932
James P. Hall & Co, Washington	65,000
Painter & Mulholland, Washington	68,000

The specifications are very close, and there will be good trouble before the buildings are done.

UNCLE SAM'S WARDROBE.

There is now at the large Clothing Depot, in the Art Building of CORCORAN, opposite the War Department, over *two hundred and fifty thousand* suits of clothing. Captain THOMAS, of Philadelphia, is in charge, and yesterday he filled an order in two hours, for pants, for a whole brigade of four thousand men. There are also an immense amount of tents, &c., in store

DEATHS OF PENNSYLVANIA SOLDIERS.

CHARLES H. MAUGER, Fourth Pennsylvania Cavalry, Company M, at the Seminary in Georgetown; GEORGE ROWERS, Twenty-third Pennsylvania, (three months Regiment), Company K, at the Columbian College in Georgetown.

DEATH OF A MICHIGAN VOLUNTEER.

JACOB FILESTER, First Michigan Cavalry, Company L, at Columbian College.

FLOWER SEEDS AT THE NEW PATENT OFFICE—HOW TO GET THEM.

The new and valuable flower seeds have been arranged for distribution, and by applying to the different members of Congress they can be had at once. The following are the kinds and assortment allotted to each member:—

Names	*Papers*	*Names*	*Papers*
Adonis Ostivalis	6	Mimulus punctatus	2
Antirrhinum MajusCoc-		Petunia Striata	2
cineum	2	Petunia, in var	1
Antirrhinum in var	8	Dianthus hybridus	1
Iberis Kermesina	6	Polemonium Cœruleum	5
Clarkia grandiflora	6	Papaver Ranunculæ-	
Clintonia elegans	2	flora	10
Collinsia grandiflora	6	Potintilla Atrosangui-	
Calliopsis elegans	10	nea	2
Echium violaceum	2	Potintilla formosi	2
Mimulus Aurea	2	Reseda erecta	1
Nolana Atriplicifolia	4	Rhodanthe Manglesii	2
Eschscholtzia Cristata	10	Schizanthus Priestii	10
Erysimum Arkasanum	2	Salpiglossis Atropurpu-	
Geum Atrosanguineum	3	rea	3
" Coccineum	3	Phlox Drummondii Vic-	
Godetia rosea alba	10	toria Regina	1
Ipomœa Atropurpurea	12	Lupinus Hartwegii Cæ-	
" Barlowii	12	lestinus	3
Lupinus Hartwegii	10	Gamolepsis tagetes	3
Monolopia grandiflora	2	Sbortia Californica	2
Oxyurea Chrysanthe-		Sphænogyne speciosa	2
moides	2	Eschscholtzia tenuefo-	
Lupinus Hartwegii ro-		lia	2
seus	3	Pentstemon gentia-	
Lupinus Mutabilis	5	noides	2
Lupinus Nanus	10	Perilla Nankinensis	2
Nemesia Compacta	3	Ricinus Sanguineus	1
Nemophila discoidalis		Salvia Horminum	4
marmorata	2	Salvia Horminum pur-	
Œnothera biennis	10	purea	2
Papaver Marshallii	2	Silene Armeria	4
Lathyrus hybridus	10	Silene bipartita	4
Petunia viridicincta	2	Mathiola annua	4
Sanvitalia procumbens	2	Mathiola annua grandi-	
Cheiranthus cheiriflavus	2	flora	2
Viola odorata	1	Mathiola Cocardeau	1
Campanula Carpatica	2	Mathiola Simplicicaulis	3
" pyramidalis	1	Cheiranthus Cheiri	3
" medium	1	Aquilegia Siberica	1
" speculum	3	" glandulosa	
" pentagonia	2	major	1
" trachalium	2	Anemone pulsatilla	3
" Sinensis	2	Anthemis Arabica	3
Iberis Lagascana	5	Solanium Ovigerum al-	
" odorata	3	ba	5
Canna Indica	3	Browallia demissa	3
" bicolor	1	Anchusa Italica	3
" Coccinea vera	1	Loasa lateritia	2
Dianthus deltoides	2	Malope grandiflora alba	4
Dianthus Garnierianus	2	Callirhoe Digitata	2
Helichrysum Micran-		Tropœolum Shillingii	3
thum	3	Cattells dwf. crimson &	
Helichrysum bractea-		nasturtium	5
tum album	3	Tropœolum Duonetta	
Clarkia pulchella mar-		aurea	2
ginata	2	Chrysanthemum venus-	
Gypsophila elegans	3	tum	2
Kaulfussia Amelloides	3	Chrysanthemum Bur-	
Limnanthus grandiflora	5	ridgeanum	2
Malope grandiflora	10		

RESULT OF A FORAGING EXPEDITION.

A foraging expedition yesterday secured nearly one hundred loads of forage, and returned safely last night.

NEW ROAD FROM FLINT HILL TO GERMANTOWN.

To-day, a contraband having reported that a new road was being made by the Rebels from Flint Hill to Germantown, General PORTER sent out two companies of cavalry to reconnoitre. They returned and confirmed the story. The present road is nearly a bee line. It is a matter of much conjecture what they are building it for

REVIEW OF GENERAL SMITH'S DIVISION.

The review of General SMITH's Division passed off finely to-day.

ALL QUIET.

Everything seemed quiet all through the right wing, centre and left column to-night when our reporter left. Our pickets now extend two and a half miles below Mount Vernon. General quietude prevails in that vicinity.

UNION MEETINGS—[illegible] REFUSED TO SIGN.

Union meetings are held every Wednesday night in Alexandria, and are largely attended. A woman came into Colonel MCLEAN's head-quarters to get her husband released to-day. She claimed to be loyal, yet refused to sign an obligation of loyalty. Her impudence was not gratified.

RENTS IN WASHINGTON.

Washington rents are so high, and stores so scarce, that many citizens are crowding to Alexandria, and the Northern element is already encroaching on the old and sleepy fogies of that city.

APPOINTED RECORDER OF GEN. MCCALL'S DIVISION.

Lieut. E. L CHRISMAN has been appointed by Gen. MCCLELLAN, Recorder of the Board of Examiners for Gen. MCCALL's Division. This is a good appointment, as Lieut CHRISMAN was an able editor and will no doubt make a thorough Recorder, only he is competent and deserving of still higher promotion.

THE PATROL.

Since the commencement of the paying off of the troops, the patrol, composed of regulars, have had much trouble. The volunteers, in spite of the stringent regulations, manage to get into the city and get drunk. This afternoon, the patrol, passing up the avenue, had in charge a boisterous "grey," who persisted in crying out, "I tell you I am a Secessionist at heart." He was taken to the guard house.

A REBEL DESERTER.

A Rebel deserter from one of the enemy's reconnoitring parties, came into our camp yesterday. He reports that the Rebels have an abundance of all provisions except groceries. When the news of the landing of our fleet on the coast of South Carolina reached the encampments in Manassas Gap, the South Carolina troops were wild, and wanted to be sent home at once.

THE PENNSYLVANIA NINETY-THIRD.

The Pennsylvania Ninety-third, from Lebanon county, arrived here last evening, and are quartered at Kendall Green. They are under command of Col. J. N. MCCARTER, who served as chaplain in the Fourteenth Pennsylvania three months service, under Col. JOHN W. JOHNSTON, a brother of Ex-Governor JOHNSTON. Col. MCCARTER was formerly pastor of the St. Paul's Methodist Episcopal Curch in Catharine street, Philadelphia, and is well and favorably known in the old district of Southwark. The regiment is ten hundred and forty-seven strong, and was raised by Col. MCCARTER in twenty-eight days. From the time the regiment left Lebanon, on Wednesday morning, the men never left the cars in a body until they reached Washington. JOHN E. JOHNSTON is the Lieutenant-Colonel of the regiment.

RECONNOITRING PARTIES.

Three strong reconnoitring parties started out this morning in the direction of Fairfax. The Rebels, for the past three nights, have been shooting our pickets in the most cold blooded and deliberate manner.

THE LOWER POTOMAC.

Two new Rebel batteries are reported this morning to have been discovered within five miles of Aquia Creek.

REVIEW OF REGULARS.

On Tuesday next, all the regulars in the army of the Potomac will be reviewed near the Capital, by General MCCLELLAN, the President and the Cabinet.

A NORTHEAST STORM.

Rain has set in to-night, and bids fair to render the roads soon impassable for an army.

AMUSEMENTS IN WASHINGTON.

The rush here to places of amusement is almost unparalleled. At the theatre, HERMANN is drawing crowded houses. To night all the foreign legations have secured seats. Miss CARLOTTA PATTI is singing in the South street Baptist Church. KING's Circus has pitched their tent near WILLARD's. FRANK BROWER, of Philadelphia, has opened a concert saloon in Canterbury Hall, and over a dozen more concerts are drawing full houses.

RECRUITS FOR THE PENNSYLVANIA RESERVES.

Lieut. CHEYNEY NIELDS and private D. PARKER will return to Pennsylvania to recruit 150 men for the First Pennsylvania Reserves.

DEATH OF INDIANA VOLUNTEERS.

J. Q. A. MOFFITT, of the Nineteenth Indiana, Company C, at Georgetown Hospital.

MAJOR-GENERAL H. W. HALLECK, U. S. A.

General HENRY WAGER HALLECK, who has been appointed Major-General, commanding the Department of Missouri, is a New Yorker by birth, having been born on Long Island, in the year 1818. He entered the West Point Academy in 1835, was graduated in 1839, ranking second in his class, and entered the army as Brevet Second Lieutenant of Engineers, his commission bearing date July 1st, 1839. He remained at the Military Academy until June of the next year, as Acting Assistant Professor of Engineering; in 1841 he published a work on "Bitumen and its Uses;" he was made First Lieutenant in January, 1845, and published an able work on the "Elements of Military Art and Science," in 1846.

Shortly after the Mexican war broke out Lieutenant HALLECK was sent to California; and in September, 1848, he was breveted captain "for gallant conduct in affairs with the enemy on the 19th and 20th of November, 1847, and meritorious service in California, May 1st, 1847."

In California he was engaged in the military government, as Secretary of State, under General KEARNEY, Colonel MASON and General RILEY, from 1847 to December, 1849. Afterwards he became chief of the staff of Commodore SHUBRICK, in the further united naval and military operations on the Pacific coast. He was also a member of the convention which met in 1849 to frame the Constitution of the State, and was on the committee which drafted the Constitution.

He was made Captain of Engineers in July, 1853, and resigned his commission the following year, August 1, 1854. From that period until the present year, he was engaged in the practice of law in San Francisco, having during the most of that time been a member of the legal firm of HALLECK, PEACHY, PILLINGS & PARKE.

General HALLECK has recently published an important work on 'International Law," the fruit of fifteen years' study.

Since the breaking out of the present war the Government has recalled him to the army, and he now has the commission of a Major-General, dating from the 10th of August last.

THE LATEST FROM WASHINGTON.

[BY ASSOCIATED PRESS.]

WASHINGTON, November 22 1861.

SEIZURE OF FORAGE—A RECONNOISSANCE.

The reconnoitering and foraging party under Gen BROOKES, which went out yesterday from General SMITH's Division, took possession of Flint Hill and the surrounding country, by throwing out the pickets in different directions, to prevent a surprise, while the forage master gathered and brought away seventy loads of hay, having with him not less than ninety wagons. The only evidence of the presence of the enemy were one regiment of infantry, a squadron of cavalry, and one battery, seen from a prominent position between Fairfax Court House and Centreville, in a westerly direction, about eight miles beyond our outposts. The party retreated late last night, having been altogether successful, and met with no casualties whatever. Information was received that the Rebels had constructed an artillery road from Flint Hill to Germantown.

The report that Dr. MULFORD, Surgeon of the Thirty-third New York Regiment, was accidentally killed at the review on Wednesday, is untrue. He was not even hurt. The only one slightly injured was Dr. DICKERSON, Assistant Surgeon of the same regiment.

Colonel TAYLOR, who was arrested under a misapprehension in connection with the running over of a private on Wednesday, has been restored to his command.

REVIEW OF GENERAL SMITH'S DIVISION.

General SMITH's Division, including the brigades of Generals HANCOCK, BROOKS and BRANNON, and MOTT's and BARR's batteries, in connection with Colonel FRIEDMANN's cavalry, was to be have been reviewed this afternoon by General MCCLELLAN, but, as public business prevented him from being present, General SMITH himself reviewed the division. After passing in review, the regiments were drawn up in line of battle, the artillery occupying the prominent points, and Colonel FRIEDMANN's cavalry having been posted in a position to make a charge. The infantry and artillery first opened fire, which was continued by the entire division for nearly an hour. Movements, as in actual battle, being observed.

They imagined the enemy to be in the direction of Lewinsville. AYRES' Battery, which occupied Smoot's Hill, took part in the engagement. The exercises were closed by a charge from FRIEDMANN's Cavalry, on a fancied column of the enemy's infantry. The only accident was that to CHARLES TREUTER, of Philadelphia, who was thrown from his horse and severely injured. Both the review and the sham battle were in the highest degree creditable to General SMITH's division, and showed rapid progress in discipline and efficiency.

THE LOWER POTOMAC.

The *Wyandonk* ran the blockade last night, reaching Indian Head about moonrise, and the Navy Yard this morning. She was not fired at.

The steamer *E. B. Hall* also ran the blockade downward last night, having on board a large quantity of ammunition and ordnance stores generally.

Two schooners, loaded with wood, ran the blockade successfully on Wednesday night.

The enemy is apparently at work on a new battery at Possum Nose, which is far above the others, on Mr. OTTERBACH's land.

THE MASON AND SLIDELL QUESTION.

Much speculation continues to be indulged in relation to the MASON and SLIDELL question. So far as can be ascertained, the Minister of Her Britannic Majesty's Government has taken no action whatever upon the subject, but will probably await instructions. Nor has there been even an informal conversation between him and the proper Department concerning it. Those who are intimately acquainted with Lord LYONS believe that in this, as in other matters, he has observed his usual discretion in refraining from premature expressions of opinion.

GENERAL MEIGS

While some gentlemen of distinction are desirous that General MEIGS shall take the field, it is known that the Government, appreciating his eminent qualification for the discharge of the extensive and very important labors devolved upon him, is not inclined to transfer him from the Quartermaster General's Department to the performance of other public duties.

APPOINTMENT OF CONSUL.

Col. EINSTEIN yesterday took formal leave in this city of the officers of the regiment which he formerly commanded, having been appointed Consul to Nuremburg. He will leave for Europe by the next steamer.

ATTACK UPON A SCOUTING PARTY.

A DELAWARE COMPANY ENGAGED.

Arrival of Pennsylvania Regiments at Fortress Monroe.

From Our Own Reporters.

FORTRESS MONROE, via Baltimore, Nov. 21.

This morning, about ten o'clock, Company A, of the First Delaware Regiment, left Camp Hamilton on a scouting expedition. The corps was under command of Captain WATSON, of Wilmington. They crossed Hampton creek, and when about one and a half miles beyond our outer pickets encountered a considerable body of Rebel cavalry, who were accompanied by two field howitzers, brass rifled pieces, and the first intimation the Delawarians had of the enemy's position on near approach, was the whistling of a projectile through the woods and underbrush.

Captain WATSON then threw up a temporary defence of brushwood and earth, after advancing to an eligible position, and sent back for reinforcements

General MANSFIELD, accompanied by three companies of the New York Twentieth, Colonel MAX WEBER, proceeded to the relief of the brave Delaware boys.

At the time that the boat left Fortress Monroe, neither the Delawarians or the relief had been definitely heard from, although a report was current that the former had suffered a loss of four men.

General WOOL and staff rode out to the vicinity of Hampton about four o'clock this afternoon.

The Forty-fifth Pennsylvania Regiment, Colonel WELSH arrived at Fortress Monroe, this afternoon, on the steamer *Pocahontas*. They came via Harrisburg and Baltimore.

The Seventy-sixth Pennsylvania Regiment, Col POWERS, is now encamped just beyond the Fortress, and on the road to Back River. The men have not yet received their arms, but will do so immediately.

P. & W.

FROM MISSOURI.

A PRISONER OF WAR ASSASSINATED.

ST. LOUIS, Nov. 22.—Judge THOMAS L RICHARDS, who has been confined as a prisoner of war in the hands of Col. MOORE, of the Home Guards, was shot dead while standing at the window of the Court House, in Memphis, Scotland county, on Monday last. Col. MOORE has offered a reward of $1000 for the apprehension of the assassin.

BURNING OF WARSAW BY THE REBELS.

JEFFERSON CITY, Nov. 22.—Passengers by the train from the West, report that the Rebels burnt the town of Warsaw, night before last, in order to prevent it from being used as winter quarters for our troops. The intelligence reached Syracuse just before the train arrived, and is considered reliable.

A quantity of Government stores were destroyed

A train of eighty wagons, with an escort of two hundred men, left Sedalia a few days ago for Leavenworth. A messenger from the train reached Sedalia at twelve o'clock last night, announcing that they had been attacked near Knob Noster, by a force of from five to six hundred Rebels, and the train captured

Refugees continue to arrive here in crowds, many of them being in a most destitute condition.

British Neutrality.

NEW YORK, Nov. 22d.—The *Post* of this evening says English letters state that the British Government refuses to grant clearances from English ports, to vessels having aboard arms for the United States, and shippers will hereafter be compelled to send such goods in vessels from Continental ports.

A Regiment of Franc Fireurs.

ALBANY, Nov. 22.—Captain CONFORT, of the French army, who has served fourteen years in Algeria, has been, at the request of Gen. MCCLELLAN, authorized to raise a regiment of "Franc Fireurs." Their service will be special, and under the immediate command of the General-in-Chief.

Pilot Boats Purchased by the Government.

NEW YORK, Nov 22.—The Government has purchased one of the Sandy Hook pilot boats, and is examining several others with the same view. They are intended to be used as mail or despatch boats.

REOPENING OF TRADE WITH EASTERN VIRGINIA.

Arrival of Vessels with Freight.

Special Despatch to the Inquirer.

BALTIMORE, Nov. 22, 1861.—Intercourse has at length reopened with Eastern Virginia. Several boats have already arrived at this port from Accomac and Northampton counties, with cargoes of grain, oysters, and other provisions.

The loyal Virginians are greatly pleased with the renewed commercial intercourse and the protection of Government. The Union feeling is now almost universal throughout these counties, and those who were hitherto inclined to favor the Rebels have now espoused the Union cause

TRANSPORTATION OF STORES TO WASHINGTON.

Over four hundred freight cars, filled with army stores and merchandise, are forwarded daily from Baltimore to the capital by the Baltimore and Ohio Railroad Company. Within the past week over four million feet of timber have been transported and an immense quantity of coal, besides the army stores.

FROM THE TWENTY-FIRST REGIMENT.

Correspondence of the Inquirer.

TENALLYTOWN, D. C., November 19, 1861.

Our friends complain that they have heard nothing from our regiment since its departure from Philadelphia. The Germans, as a race, are unassuming, but we must not let our modesty throw us so completely in the shade.

At five o'clock, P. M., of the 30th of September last, we arrived in Washington, after a journey of *twenty-six hours* from Philadelphia. We quartered in a Government building convenient to the depot for the night, and the next morning took up our line of march for Kalorama Heights, where a Provisional Brigade had been established, under Col. LOESER, of Pittsburg, to whom we reported. On the 11th ult., through orders, we marched to and went in camp at this place, reporting to General JOHN J. PECK. The following night, at about eleven o'clock, without baggage, we made a forced march to Chain Bridge—had to *bivouac* for the night, and the next morning "marched back again."

General PECK is a native of the State of New York—a perfect gentleman and thorough soldier, and being an old regular officer, we are held to a strict army discipline. The brigade is composed of the Sixty-second (American) and Fifty-fifth (French) New York Regiments, and Thirteenth (American) and Twenty-first (German) Pennsylvania Regiments. So you see the "honors are easy," both with State and country, and I take it, a good combination.

Fort Pennsylvania, near our camp, was erected within the last three months by the Pennsylvania Reserves. It is most judiciously located, commanding all possible approaches.

Through the efficiency of our surgeons the health of our regiment is very good, and the men are all contented and happy. We have just had our first pay-day. From what I can learn they have all sent liberally to their families; and well they should, for the Government supplies them most bountifully—much better than during the three months' service. The business of the Subsistence Department is so exclusive that from necessity it has become thoroughly systematized.

The following is a list of the officers of the Regiment:—Colonel, JOHN F. BALLIER; Lieut.-Colonel, Adolph Mehler; Major, Geo. Wynkoop; Adjutant, L. J. Ladner; Quartermaster, W. Curson; Surgeon, James M. Boisnot; Assistant Surgeon, George P. Oliver; Chaplain, Henry Giual; Sergeant Major, John Presser; Quartermaster's Sergeant, J. Schneipp; Commissary, Mitchell McMurray; Leader of Band, F. Mayer; Drum Major, H. Rodrian; Secretary, Chas. Even.

Co. A, Capt. Beamish; Lieut's, Mullin and Hough.
Co. B, Capt. Meyer; Lieut's, Fisher and Schuster.
Co. C, Capt Geisz; Lieut's, Beiseil and Lautenbacker.
Co. D, Capt. de Crauzat; Lieut's, Bossert and Bauer.
Co. E, Capt Gessler; Lieut's, Schuler and Meyer.
Co. F, Capt. Garson; Lieut's, Becker and Elser.
Co. H, Capt. Sehr; Lieut's, Rein and Reichart.
Co. I, Capt Voltaire; Lieut's, Hohenstein and Brill.
Co. K, Capt. Kohler; Lieut's, Brurein and Griesheimer.

OUR NEW YORK LETTER.

A WORD TO THE WISE—REBEL COMMUNICATIONS TO BE LOOKED AFTER—PASSPORTS—REV H W BEECHER AND THAT EUROPEAN TOUR—DOINGS IN THE COURTS—ST. CECELIA'S DAY—OUR PRISONERS AT RICHMOND—A MASS MEETING CALLED—MAYOR WOOD ACCEPTS THE MOZART NOMINATION, &C

Special Correspondence of the Inquirer.

NEW YORK, Nov 22.

There is reason to believe that the sympathizers with the Rebels, if not Rebels themselves, have been using Uncle Sam's foreign mail facilities rather freely of late, to correspond with their friends in England; and with a view to put a stop to it, without incurring the odium of countenancing a system of espionage, the Post Office authorities here, I have reason to know, have been in correspondence with the State Department and the Postmaster General at Washington. The conclusions arrived at, of course, are not to be divulged, but I think I may, without impropriety, say that if any of the friends or admirers of JEFFERSON DAVIS entertain the expectation that they can continue to use Uncle Sam, as heretofore, they may as well rid themselves of the hallucination at once.

The steamers to sail to-morrow, for Liverpool and Bremen, have a large number of passengers engaged, and to-day there has been quite a rush to the places where the now indispensible passports are to be procured. The confusion incident to postponing non compliance with the requisitions of the Government in this matter until the day of sailing, now induces people to provide themselves with the documents the day previously.

Mr. BEECHER denies, I see, that he is going to Europe to lecture on the war. But he will scarcely deny that he expressed a determination to that effect, not long ago, and under circumstances, too, which warranted the belief that he would have no objections to have the fact made public.

Mayor WOOD graciously deigns to accept the Mozart Hall nomination for Mayor. In response to the address of the committee appointed to inform him of his nomination, to-day, he made a speech, "defining his position," and promising, if elected, "to endeavor to reform the abuses now prevalent in many branches of the city government, provided the State Legislature gives to the office of Mayor that dignity and respect to which it is entitled."

This being St. Cecelia's Day (in the calendar of the Roman Catholic Church), High Mass was celebrated by Rev. Father LAFONT, in the church of St Vincent de Paul, in Twenty-third street. The altar was beautifully decked with flowers. The choir numbered twenty voices, and the anthems were admirably performed. The church was densely thronged with worshippers.

A mass meeting of Irish citizens will be held some time during next week, for the purpose of urging upon the Government the exchange of prisoners of war; or, if this cannot be done, the establishment of some sort of communication by which the friends of the soldiers can convey funds or clothing to them.

Judge NELSON this morning affirmed, upon appeal, the decisions of the Circuit Court in the matter of the prize vessels *Hiawatha* and *Crenshaw*, so that the cases might be brought to the Supreme Court at its next term. It was ordered that the vessels and cargoes should be appraised and bonded, pending the Supreme Court's decision.

HENRY CURTIS, the murderer of officer MARTIN, was found guilty to-day of murder in the second degree. He will probably be sentenced to-morrow.

Acting Marshal THOMPSON sent Midshipman HICKS, of the privateer *Sumter*, to the Tombs to-day, to await instructions from Washington. The prisoner was captured on the [illegible] in the Gulf of Mexico, while endeavoring to run the blockade. He was formerly of the U. S. Navy; but his mother, a wealthy Southern lady, compelled him, under pain of disinheritance, to give up his commission, and accept service on the *Sumter*.

Wall street was very quiet to-day. The only noteworthy events were a decline in stocks, (caused by a desire to "realize,") and a stiffening up in the rates of sterling bills. Things generally will be feverish until we know of the effect of the *Trent* affair in England.

SECOND BOARD.

$1,000 U. S. 6s, '81..reg	93¼	650 sh Hudson Riv	37
$4,000 do	[illegible]	100 do ..s10	37
$11,000 U. S. 6s, '81..cpn	93⅝	100 sh Harlem R Pf	31
$18,000 U. S. 7s, '65	87¾	100 sh Reading R	34⅛
$1,000 Virginia 6s	48	80 sh Panama R	115
$5,000 Missouri 6s	43	50 do ..s10	115
$1,000 Mich S. 6s, '78	82	150 sh Mich. Cent. R	49
$5,000 Ill Cpn. Bds '62	82	500 sh M. S & N. I R	17⅛
$3,000 California 7s	[illegible]	50 sh M So. & N. I. G	35⅛
100 sh P M S. Co	91	50 do ..s30	35⅝
50 do	91¼	50 sh Gal. & Chi. R..s10	70⅝
[illegible] sh N. Y. Cent R	78⅝	150 do	70¾
300 do	78¾	50 do ..s30	70¾
100 do ..s10	78⅝	950 sh Cleve & Tol	34⅜
125 sh Erie Railway	30¾	300 do ..s30	34⅛
100 do ..b5	31	235 sh Chi. & R. I R	53¾
100 sh Erie Railway Pf.	55	50 sh Chi B & Q R	62
100 do ..b30	54	50 do	61¾
150 do	53⅜	50 do	61⅛

The Money market continues steady, with a moderate business doing at 6@6½ ℔ cent. for loans on call. Prime paper is scarce and wanted at 6½@7 ℔ cent; good endorsed is selling at 8@10 ℔ cent. Foreign exchange is more active and firmer; Sterling is selling at 108@108½ for Merchants', and 108½@109 for Bankers' bills. On Paris 5f 25c@5f 21¼c. Stocks are heavy and lower; Michigan Southern has declined ¼; Cleveland & Toledo ⅜; New York Central, Illinois Central and Hudson, ½; Erie and Michigan Southern Guarantied, ⅞.

CLOSING PRICES—*Reported by R. Toland & Son. Exchange Place.*—Erie, 30⅝@30¾; Reading, 34⅛@34¼; New York Central, 78⅝@78¾; Michigan Southern, 17¼@17⅜; Michigan Southern Guarantied, 35⅞@36; Illinois Central 60⅝@60⅞; Canton, 10@10½; Harlem, 12¼@12½; Harlem Preferred, 31@31¼; Hudson, 37@37¼; Cleveland and Toledo, 34⅛@34⅜. Market heavy.

OFFICE OF THE ASSISTANT TREASURER, U. S., New York, Nov 22, 1861:—

Total Receipts	$4,971,821·05
" Payments (including redeemed 6 ℔ cent. notes)	2,871,189·28
" Balance	9,544,472·97
For Customs	57,000·00
For Treasury Notes	3,607,174·11

Army Appointments.

WASHINGTON, Nov. 22.—The following military appointments were made to-day, viz:—

ROBERT SMYTHE, of Iowa, to be an additional Paymaster of Volunteers.

FREDERICK C. OGDEN, of New York, to be Second Lieutenant of the First Regiment of United States Cavalry.

Captain JOHN W. SCHOFIELD, of the First Artillery, United States army, to be a Brigadier General of Volunteers.

Major THOMAS J. LEAN, of Iowa, now an additional Paymaster, to be a Brigadier-General of Volunteers.

Colonel PHILLIP ST GEORGE COOKE, United States army, recently made a Brigadier-General of Volunteers, was promoted to be a Brigadier-General in the Regular service.

The Steamer San Jacinto.

BOSTON, November 22.—The steamer *San Jacinto* left Newport at midnight

NEW BEDFORD, Nov. 22.—The steamer *San Jacinto* was at Holmes' Hole at ten o'clock this morning. No communication was allowed with the shore.

From Fortress Monroe.

BALTIMORE, Nov. 22.—The Old Point boat has arrived, but brings no news. The passengers report that a flag of truce had arrived from Norfolk with several women and children, but no information could be gleaned from them.

The Steamer United Kingdom.

PORTLAND, Nov. 22.—The steamer *United Kingdom* arrived at this port to-day.

PHILADELPHIA AND NEW YORK—A CONTRAST.—We find in the Salem (Mass.) *Register*, the following just tribute to Philadelphia, from one who has partaken of its hospitalities:—

When our Massachusetts volunteers arrive at Philadelphia, on their way to the war, even if it be at two o'clock in the morning, they are supplied with as good a meal of refreshments, and as well cooked, as any one could wish to eat; but at New York, even though they arrive as late as eleven o'clock in the forenoon, they are marched to Park Barracks, and fed on soup, and nothing but soup, though they stay twenty-four hours. At Philadelphia, no parade is made; but at New York, a great parade is got up by the "Sons of Massachusetts," and the officers are feted and feasted at the Astor, while the privates are left to breakfast, dine and sup on soup.

THE SOLDIER'S FRIEND.

THE WHITE MAN.

JOHN DEAVOURS, B. L. RICHEY, Editors & Publishers.

THE SOUTH; OUR HOME—THE FRONTIER AND ITS DEFENSE.

VOL. 2 WEATHERFORD, TEXAS, THURSDAY NOVEMBER, 21 1861 NO. 18

[*Written for the Richmond Dispatch*]

THE FLAG OF SECESSION.

AIR—"*Star Spangled Banner.*"

O, say, can't you see, by the dawn's early light,
What you yesterday held to vaunting mid dreaming—
The Northern men routed, Abe Lincoln in flight,
And the Palmetto flag over the Capitol streaming.
The pumpkins for fare,
And the foul fetted air,
Gave proof through the night that the Yankees were there,
Now, the flag of Secession in triumph doth wave
O'er the land of the freed and the home of the brave.

'Midst the dust that is raised by the fugitive's feet,
His acts of coercion now bitterly ruing
See the rail-splitter running in panting retreat,
And gallant Virginia in laughter pursuing;
Now he catches a beam,
On the bayonet's fierce gleam,
And he hurries away with a jump and a scream,
And the flag of Secession in triumph doth wave
O'er the land of the freed and the home of the brave.

But where is the despot who came to our soil,
In the garb of the soldier his minions disguising,
And shewed from our field and our homes as their spoils?
We only can say that his speed is surprising.
O'er the fences he made.
When that was his trade.
He has left in his form our vision to fade;
And the Flag of Secession in triumph doth wave
O'er the land of the freed and the home of the brave.

Oh! such is the welcome the Southrons bestows
On the despot who strives to make slaves of a nation.
We have a hand for our friends, but the sword for our foes,
And the charge of our soldiers in fierce exultation.
Then again to the fight,
And God to the right!
The Northmen shall shrink from our warriors' might;
And the Flag of Secession in triumph doth wave
O'er the land of the freed and the home of the brave.

SOMETHING RICH AND RACY.

Jim Lane's Speech in Kansas.

The St. Louis Republican publishes the following report of a speech delivered at Leavenworth, Kansas, by Gen. Jim Lane, United States Senator and Brigadier-General. The Republican's correspondent says the speech created a great sensation in Leavenworth:

Gen. Lane, on coming forward, was received with rapturous applause. He began by saying: "I have come here to-night not to make a speech to you, but to have plain talk about Kansas, and matters relating to the best interests of the country. This is a period of history when every man is called upon to act and act cautiously. It is not expected that every man will join the army, but those who remain at home are not to forget that they may be called upon to act for those in the field. I ask every man who is here to give his protection to the Kansas soldier. I am uttering no words for myself—it is for the soldiers who fights your battle.

"Two months ago the Kansas brigade was organized. I was put at the head with the respect, the confidence, aye, the love of every man in that command. Every day since it entered the field it has been actively engaged for the protection of Kansas and the Government. It has not surrendered. Why is it that these creatures at the fort sneer at it? They abuse the Kansas brigade because we have never engaged the enemy without whipping them like the devil.

Go to Nevada where 55 of the Kansas brigade met and defeated 200 rebels; go to Ball's mill, where 130 Kansans whipped 130 traitors; go to Dry Wood, where 400 men under Montgomery for two hours fought 7000 of the enemy and drove them back from your soil; go to Papinsville where 200 of our men conquered 1800 rebels, killed five of their captains and drove them back to their den; go to Morristown, the death bed of our gallant Johnston, where 400 Kansas brigade drove 600 traitors from their entrenchment; go to Osceola, one of the strongest natural points to southern Missouri, where, after eighty miles march, through the enemy's country, we destroyed more than a million dollars worth of property. Go to these fields and tell me why the Kansas brigade is sneered at.

Our sin is, that we never have been whipped. That brigade is conspired against. This last Sabbath was desecrated by a conspiracy at the fort between Robinson and Prince to destroy the Kansas brigade. Chas. Robinson and Capt. Prince conspired to destroy it. They were guilty of treason baser than that of Price. [Great cheering.] I have come here to talk plainly to you. (Cries of 'That's right, let us have it.) What is the charge they make against the Kansas brigade? We are Jayhawkers!

"I stated in Washington that the institution of slavery could not survive the march of the Federal army. That there would be an army of one *color marching in and an army of another color marching out* of the Slave States. I said, further that confiscation must follow treason, as thunder follows the lightning's flash.

Confiscated property goes to the Government and this rule has been adopted by my brigade. If we are Jayhawkers, we are Jayhawking for the Government.

Now if—oh! the dirty puppy—if that creature Prince, or that still dirtier creature Robinson, can find an instance of a violation of this rule in my command, the guilty man shall be hung.

I have commanded seven armies, and I have found that officers succeed when they treat soldiers as men; do that, and they will fight for you. Why, my soldiers would follow me right into the middle of hell. And let me tell you that if I wanted to make a sure job of capturing the old fellow, I'd take the Kansas brigade, and I'd do it, though he had Robinson and Prince to help him. [Terrific cheering.]

Kansas is the jewel of the west. It is all there is between the Missouri and the Rocky Mountains. It is the jewel in the cap of freedom. In a department with its headquarters at St. Louis, Kansas is not as secure as she should be. So difficult is it to convey intelligence across Missouri, that it is not safe for us to receive our orders from St. Louis. The true interest of Kansas demands that she should be in a separate department with Fort Leavenworth as its base. [Cheers. It is a military necessity.

The appointment of Brigadier General was offered to me, and I intended to accept it when the brigade was organized, but I could not be driven to take it. Although not a brigadier, I have been playing it all over and pretty big—betting high on small cards. [Cheers and laughter.]

For all my labor, hardships and expence, I have not received one dime.—Now don't you think Robinson and Prince could have afforded to let me serve my country for nothing?

If the Government will make a separate department here, I will resign my senatorship and accept it. This department ought to be commanded by a Kansas man. Then we can save Kansas, restore the Cherokee country, and a good deal South of it.

Ask the Government to give this army a sufficient supply of artillery. They have lately ordered two thousand five hundred guns. Can't we have six of them? They are needed for service, and nothing gives the soldier more courage in battle than these big guns.

DRUGS, MEDICINES,

CHEMICALS,

Fancy and Toilet Articles,

WINES,

BRANDIES,

Liquors of Every Kind

PAINTS, OILS DYE-STUFFS,

Patent Medicines, Books,

STATIONERY AND

GARDEN SEEDS,

Directly From France;

SHOT GUNS, CLARET WINE, CHEMICALS &c,

Dr H DESMETH in Weatherford. Parker County, has on hand a large and well selected assortment, of everything that can be found in any Drug Store, which he keeps selling at the customary prices, Everything warranted pure and genuine,

QUININE? QUININE! QUININE?

A large quantity on hand

I. R. WORRALL,

CLAIM AGENT,

austin. texas.

SUCCESSOR TO KERBY & MC CORD.

Will collect all demands against the State of Texas for Ranging Service Supplies furnished &c. &c. and remit proceeds promptly. on receipt of powers of attorney from parties interested

Commission from 5 to 10 pr ct, according to amounts received and labor required

---

WEATHERFORD

Livery and Sale Stable,

THE undersigned would most respectfully announce to their friends and the traveling community that they are now prepared to take care of horses, hire hacks and horses; and to attend to all other business in our line. We will keep on hand a plenty of *Provender*; and an attentive and efficient Ostler, and having a commodious Stable, we will be prepared to do ample justice to those who become our patrons. All we want is a liberal patronage, and a fair chance. Give us a call and get your money s worth.

CUMMINS & BALL.

v1-n51-tf

Notice!

Thos who are iddebted to us by note or account can pay us in Wheat at the Market price. If they do not by 1 st Dec. 1861. they may expect to find them in the hands of an officer for collection

SQUYRES & IGLEHART.

Oct. 9th 1861.

NEW ADVERTISEMENTS.

NOTICE. All persons are hereby notified not to purchase any of the notes given for property belonging to the estate of J. L. Edwards deceased—and the makers of said notes are hereby notified not to pay the same to any one except the undersigned Administrators of said estate.

J. B. TURNER,
S H. PURYEAR,
Administrators of estate of J. L. Edwards dec'd
v2n17 6t pf $340

JOHNSON COUNTY ESTRAY. Taken up by A. C Hoyle, and posted before B. G. Turpin, J. P. for said county. One bay stallion two years old last spring, valued at 50 dollars. One Stallion three years old last spring valued at 50 dollars. One red pided ox seven years old, marked crop off the left, valued at 12 dollars.

Jas H. TORBETT, Clk.
By Jas HINER, Deputy.
v2n17.

STRAYED from the undersined, living at Stephensville, Erath County Texas. One bay horse, branded with the letter J with a half ever it, two years old last spring, being a natural pacer, and between 15 and 16 hands high—another between a brown and bay, branded V, being 4 years old last spring, about 14 hands high—both horses branded on the shoulders. I will give ten dollars for the above described horses delived to me at Stephenville, or any reliable information of them.

JOHN A. GIBBS.
v2n17 4t pf 5 dol,

CAMP Cooper Nov 11 1861. The following described horses, were picked up by a scout of Captains Barry and Begges's company of Rangers. One brown horse supposed to be 10 or 12 years old, star in the face, some saddle marks, crippled in the left fore-parter, no brands percievable. One large bay mule 4 years old, some saddle marks, branded T on the left shoulder. One chestnut sorrel horse 3 years old, star in the face, a natural pacer, no brands. Also two horses taken in July 29th in a fight. One a blue roan horse 7 years old, branded with three parallel lines on the left hip no other brands, both ears split, the other a white horse, supposed to be 10 or 11 years old, no brands percievable.

CAMP Cooper Nov 11th 1861- Stray horses taken in a fight, with the Indians on Pecos River. One roan horse supposed to be 7 or 8 years old, blaze face, right fore foot white, both hind feet white, branded thus X on the right shoulder. One sorrel horse supposed to be 12 or 15 years old, hind feet white, saddle marks blaze face, no brands percievable. One small gray mare supposed to be 5 years old Spanish brands on both thighs, a natural pacer. One brown mule, right eye out, supposed to be 10 or 11 years old, Spanish brand—One brown mule supposed to be 12 or 15 years old, Spanish brand on both thighs.

CAMP Cooper Nov 11th 1861—Horses picked up by Barry's men. One brown mule supposed to be 5 or 6 years old, saddle marks on both sides of the back, no brands percievable—One brown horse supposed to be 4 years old, natural pacer, no brands. Also horses picked up by Barry's and Begge's men—One bay horse supposed to be 5 or 6 years old, branded 56 on right shoulder—one brown horse 6 or 7 years old, no brands.

v2n17 3t pf 8 dol

NOW IS THE CHANCE TO PAY YOUR Subscription. Wheat, Corn, Potatoes, Pork, Beef, Chickens, Eggs, Butter, Turkeys. Geese, Ducks, &c., will be taken at this office in payment for subscription to this paper, at the common market rates. Apply at the White Man office, one door East of the Blackwell House.

Nov. 7th, 1861.

A. H. LATIMER,

Attorney at Law and Notary Public,

BELKNAP, YOUNG COUNTY, TEXAS.

WILL give prompt and assiduous attention to the collection of claims and prosecution of suits in the courts of the 20th Judicial Districts; and the adjoining counties of the 11th. Will locate certificates, investigate land titles, procure patents, &c.

Jno 1-1y.

NOTICE. Loving Clifton Administrator of the estate of E. N. Clement deceased having filed a full and complete exhibit of the condition of said estate, together with his administration account both verified by affidavit, also his application in writing for leave to resign. These are therefore to notify all persons interrested in said estate to be and appear at the November term of the Probate Court of Parker county, to be holden at the Court house in the town of Weatherford on the last Monday in November 1861, and contest said account if they see proper.

J. H. PRINCE, Clk. Parker Co.
Oct. 30th 1861, Pub. 20 days,
v2n15 pf$5

ADMINISTRATORS NOTICE. Whereas Letteters of Administration, were granted to the undersigned at the Sept. Term of the Probate Court of Jack county, A. D. 1861. on the Estate of John McHail, Dec'd. Therefore this is to notify all persons, having claims against said estate, to present them duly authenticated as required by law, and those indebted to said estate, are requested to make immediate payment.

J. A. HALL, Adm'r
v2n15 6t pf$3,50

Citation.

To the Sheriff of Erath Co. Greeting:—Whereas. O. T. Taylor has filed his Petition in our District Court of Erath County, against Wm. C. Hartin, alledging among other things, that said Hartin's residence is unknown to the petitioner—that said Hartin is indebted to petioner, in the sum of 418 dollars and 50 cents as evidences by promisory note, filed with the petioner. with interest at 10 per cent, from the 5th day of October, A. D. 1857. Also, in the further sum of 60 dollars as evidenced by a promisory note, filed in said cause, said 60 dollar note having a credit on the back, of the same for 35 dollars and 10 cents, paid 7th day of September, A. D 1858. Said note being due on the 13th day of May 1856. Petioner also averring that said amounts of money after deducting the credit on the back of said last mentioned note are justly due and unpaid, and that the said debtor, Wm. C. Hartin, so secretes himself, that the ordinary process of the law, cannot be served upon him, and the attachment is not sued out for the purpose of injuring the defendant, and praying for a judgement for the amounts of money mentioned, and an attachment, and said petition being sworn to by the Plaintiff.

These are therefore, to command you to summon the said William C. Hartin, by publication in the nearest newspaper, for four seccessive weeks previous, to the return day hereof, to be and appear on the 7th Monday after the first Monday in March, A. D. 1862, at the Court house, in the town of Stephensville, Erath county, then and there to answer said petition.

Due and legal service and return make hereof, how you have executed this citation

Attest: J. A. McNeil, Clk. of the District court of Erath county. Witness my hand and private seal, there being no seal of office at the the town of Stephenville, Erath county. This October. 23d A. D. 1861.

JAS. A. McNEIL, Clk Dist. Ct. E. C

Received in office, this the 23d day of October, 1861, and I order the same published in the White Man the same being the nearest newspaper.

J. R. WALLER. Sheff. E. C. Tex.
v2n14 ft pf $12,50

STOLEN!

FROM the undersigned living 8 miles East of Birdville, Tarrant County; one Negro fellow named Aaron, about 20 years old, is very pert, quick spoken, hair grows low down on his fore-head, has thick lips, his nose rather turns up, is about 5 feet 11 inches high, and when poken to is very apt to laugh.

Said boy was stolen by two Mexicans named Gonzales and Antome. They also took off 6 head of horses, One a bay mare, trim made one a large brown horse, branded P M on the shoulder. They also took off three six-shooters and two rifles. I will give the following rewards for apprehension so I can get them, if taken in the State $200, if taken out of the State $300—to be paid in State scrip.

J. M. GIBBINS.

THE NEW YORK SUN.

Published daily, Sundays excepted, at the Sun Buildings, cor. of Fulton and Nassau sts, and delivered to Subscribers in New York City and vicinity at SIX AND A QUARTER CENTS PER WEEK.

☞ When sent by Mail, four dollars per year.

THE WEEKLY SUN is published at 75 cts. a year; sixteen months, $1; single copies, 2 cts.

Address "The Sun" Establishment, New York.

THE SUN.

NUMBER 9166 — NEW YORK, MONDAY, NOVEMBER 25 1861. — PRICE ONE CENT

THE NEW YORK SUN

MONDAY MORNING, NOV. 25, 1861.

Slave and Free Labor Contrasted.

The London *Spectator*, received by last steamer, reviews a pamphlet lately issued by E. ATKINSON, an American cotton spinner, and strongly recommends its perusal to its readers. It says that it will cease to assert that cotton cannot be cultivated without the negro, and in proof cites information contained in the publication. First addressing it own readers, as to perusal of the work, it says:

They will, we feel certain, commence the task still more readily if we tell them that the pamphlet is a simple business-like production; that it has no allusions to the "glorious eagle of our common country, which soars above the Alleghanies with a thunder bolt in its mouth and an earthquake in its claws; that it contains only one reference to the American constitution, and that one slightly contemptuous; that nothing is said of the inherent superiority of Republican institutions; and that, in short it is as little like an American pamphlet as vigorous common sense, sound judgement and good temper can make it. The writer starts with the belief that the war must end in emancipation, forcible or gradual, and accepts at once the extremest consequences of that grand result. He does not himself believe that the free blacks will cease to work, for they must live, and as the "proportion of colored paupers and criminals to the colored population in Boston and New York is only about half of that of the whites," he naturally does not imagine that they will resort to crime. But he accepts the extremest view that prejudice can suggest, and argues as if all back men were irredeemably lazy, and would, on emancipation, live, like Carlyle's enemies, the black laborer of Jamaica, "up to their ears in squash." And even then cotton will be produced still cheaper than of old.

COST OF SLAVE LABOR.

The cost of each negro to the planter, as things stand, is now, per annum:

Interest on a good field hand, value $1,500, at 8 per cent	$120 00
Insurance 2 per cent	30 00
Food, clothing, medicines and hospital treatment	90 00
	$240 00

This account charges the rate of interest planters actually pay for money, and assumes the highest value for a good slave, but omits all mention of negro houses, repairs to buildings, cost of tools, salaries of overseers, salaries of white men to do the skilled labor, the keep of the young, the maintenance of the old, and the loss of interest on all except able-bodied hands and breeding women. It shows that every able-bodied slave costs twenty dollars a month, or twenty-two shillings a week—an income which would be wealth to the two millions of able-bodied mean trash, or sufficient to attract the unskilled laboring class of the North, or to draw over hosts of emigants; it is, however, not half the rate the planter can afford to pay. By the universal consent of all parties, slaveholders included, one white man, without an overseer, does the work three slaves can accomplish with one. Taking that statement to be only two-thirds true—and it makes no account of the colossal loss sustained through the habitual wastefulness of four millions of slaves—the planter could still pay 44s. a week, and, with cotton at 5d. a pound, still flourish and grow rich. It is useless to argue that the white trash will not work. They will not without pay, or on the wretched soil to which the monopoly of good land by the great planters condemns them; but they work hard enough in the free states. Admitting, however, even that extraordinary libel on the South, there remains the broad fact that the planter can pay wages equal to the ordinary profit of gold-digging and prosper.

WHITE MEN CAN WORK AT THE SOUTH.

But, granting the wages, it is said white men cannot work at the South. The plain answer to that fallacy is, that they do do it; that in the extreme South there are at this hour eight hundred thousand free whites, over fifteen years of age, exclusively engaged in out-of-door agricultural labor. The exact numbers are:—

In Georgia	93,000	Louisiana	25,000
Alabama	75,000	Tennessee	132,000
Mississippi	56,000	Florida	8,000
Texas	48,000	Arkansas	34,000
South Carolina	48,000.		

And they do not die of it. Some of the cities of the South, full of vice and open drains, are indeed fatal to health, but the cotton lands are unsurpassed for salubrity, and the death-rate is lower among whites than blacks. The land required for cotton culture is a light, sandy loam, easily worked, the ploughing being done with a light plough drawn by one or two mules at a quick walk; the cultivation similar to that of corn, and as capable of being carried on by improved machinery instead of the universal hoe now used by the slaves. The space required for each plant varies, according to the richness of the soil, but by July 1st the ground is fully covered. During the period of extreme heat little attention is required, and while northern laborers are sweltering in the hay-field, under a sun as intense as in the South, the cotton-planter merely watches the growth of the plant. The work of picking requires nimble fingers and the close attention of all hands, men, women, and children. It is continued through the cool autumn, and in favorable seasons far into the winter. One of the great drawbacks to slave cultivation is the want of a more dense population, from which to draw an extra force during the picking season, and fields white with unpicked cotton are not seldom ploughed up to make ready for the planting of the new crop. This would not occur under the small allotment system of free labor."

HOW PROFITABLE CROPS CAN BE RAISED.

If, then, the white man can work on cotton lands as safely as a black man, and the planter can afford wages certain to attract free labor, what imperils the cotton? We shall be asked where the planter is to get capital to pay wages, and we answer, just where he gets it now—from the cotton-factor, who now helps him to buy the black, whose cost amounts to fair wages. Mr. Atkinson may well demand the extension of freedom over a soil so attractive to the emigrant population of the North. Take the case of a man—a real case—who recently settled in Texas, and determined to grow cotton for himself. He had two sons, no slaves, no servants, and only a little land, but he "raised" twenty-two bales, or say 10,000 pounds of cotton, value $1,000, besides his food. In other words he made a profit of £250 a year. That is not precisely the prospect at which a keen Yankee laborer or industrious German emigrant is in the smallest degree likely to sneer. And this crop was raised off new land, with no buildings, and only settled just as wheat land is settled, by the emigrants.

We have said nothing whatever of the difference in product to be caused by a better agriculture. The southern planter scarcely uses the plough, and breaks new land to avoid manure. He wastes a third of his crop, the seed, which gives excellent soap and most valuable oil, and of scientific processes he never hears. Mr. Atkinson enters into all these details, but we prefer the broad simple facts which contain in themselves the whole case, viz.: that the planter now pays for slave labor wages which would attract the white, and that the white man could work as safely as the black on the cotton lands.

We must make one more extract from Mr. Atkinson. It is a dry column of figures, but it is nevertheless worth a cursory glance from those who believe slavery to be at worst an evil necessity:

	Sq. miles.	Free negroes in 1860.	Average to sq mile
Delaware	2,120	19,763	9.30
Maryland	11,124	83,718	7.52
	13,244	103.441	7.81

	Sq miles.	Slaves in 1860.	Average to sq. mile.
South Carolina	29,385	402,541	13.76
Georgia	58,000	462,230	7.97
Florida	59,268	61,753	1.04
Alabama	50,722	435,132	8.57
Mississippi	47,156	439,696	9.26
Louisiana	41,255	332,520	8.06
Texas	237,504	180,388	.77
Arkansas	52,198	111,104	5.14
	575,488	2,422,364	4.21
		Free negroes.	
Isl of Barbadoes	166	124,000	7.47

Average value of land in Barbadoes	$500 per acre.
Average product of sugar per hand in do.	Slave..1,043 lbs
	Free..3,660 lbs
Average cost of sugar per hhd	Slave..$50
	Free..$20

AN EFFICENT OFFICER OF

OUR BRAVE AND VICTORIOUS NAVY.

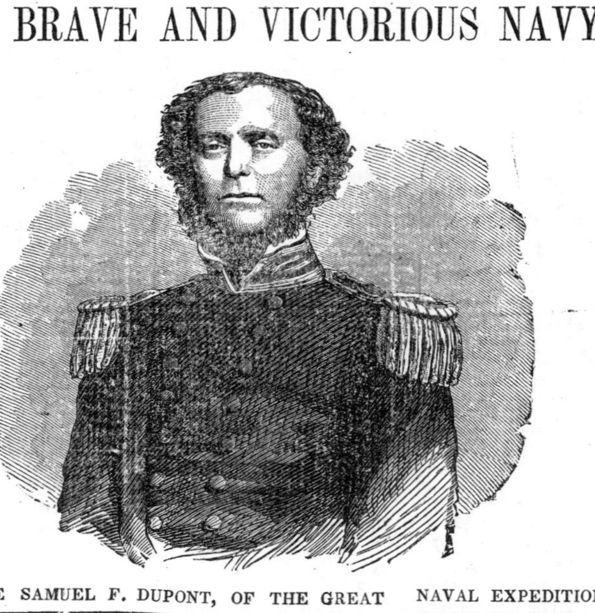

COMMODORE SAMUEL F. DUPONT, OF THE GREAT NAVAL EXPEDITION.

Commodore Dupont, the Gallant Officer of our Navy to whose Good Judgment and Undaunted Heroism, aided by the Bravery of the Federal Forces, is to be Attributed the Brilliant Victory at Port Royal.

The capture of Port Royal has been one of the most memorable events in the Naval history of the United States, and Commodore Dupont will hereafter rank as one of its most efficient commanders. Possessed of excellent judgment and undaunted bravery, he has dared to attempt what has never been attempted by the most formidable naval armaments of Europe—to approach land fortifications of great strength, and deliberately essay their reduction without the aid of a land force, or that of assisting batteries on shore. And, aided by the cool heroism of his marine force alone, he has approached his ships almost within speaking distance of the enemy, and rained upon them for hours such an incessant stream of balls and shells as to dismount many of the heaviest guns of modern times, and to drive away, with murderous slaughter, the rebels who served them.

In connection with the above accurate portrait of the gallant Commodore, we re-publish a brief sketch of his life, which we feel confident will be read with great interest by our many readers.

Commodore Samuel F. Dupont received his first commission on the 19th of December, 1815, being then a citizen of Delaware, though his native state is New Jersey. He has been forty-six years in the United States service, twenty-two of which have been spent at sea, eight on land, and the remainder unemployed. He was last at sea in 1859, having, in May of that year, returned from a three years' cruise. Subsequently, and up to the time when he was ordered to the command of the present fleet, he acted as commandant of the Philadelphia Navy Yard. His present commission bears date September 14, 1855.

The Warren, now used as a storeship stationed at Panama, N. G., was under his command, he being then a Lieutenant, in June, 1836. In that year he was attached to the squadron cruising in the West Indies, under command of Commodore A. J. Dallas.

The United States brig Perry; since commanded by Lieut. Classon, of Brooklyn, and which captured a valuable prize off the Virginia coast, since the breaking out of the rebellion, was under his command, off the coast of Brazil and the West Indies, in 1843.

Commodore Robert F. Stockton, in 1845, flew his broad pennant on the frigate Congress, and by his solicitation Lieut. Dupont was appointed to command her. During this year he carried out Mr. Ten Eyck, U. S. Commissioner to the Sandwich Islands, and also, Mr. Serrill, U. S. Consul to Honolulu.

In 1846 he served in the Pacific squadron, commanded by Commodores Shubrick, and A. C. Jones, being Lieutenant of the sloop-of-war Cyane. Many other important trusts were also committed to his care; and in every instance he has faithfully complied with the requirements of the Government. During the time he was commandant of the Philadelphia Navy Yard he gained the esteem and affection of all who had business relations therein; and when his appointment to the great fleet was there announced, the discrimination evinced by the President therefor was highly commended.

This present command was conferred on him about four weeks previous to the sailing of the fleet, and has met general approval. His flagship is the Wabash, carrying forty guns, lately one of the blockading squadron.

Commodore Dupont is past the prime of life, but still retains his former energy, and we may expect to hear of brilliant acts by the fleet under his command. Time has dealt gently with him. He is yet strong and vigorous, both mentally and physically, and we may confidently anticipate that his forty-seventh anniversary of his service in his country's cause (Dec. 19,1861) will add new and still brighter laurels to those he has already won.

The McManus Obsequies in Ireland.

When the City of Washington approached Cork harbor with the remains of Terrence Bellew McManus, she had her flags at half mast as a signal of mourning. They were met on board by a committee of gentlemen from Queenstown, who presented an address to the American delegation.

On the approach of the steamer to the pier all the vessels in port lowered their flags, and the United States flag over the American Consul's residence ashore, was also at half mast.—An immense crowd was present at the disembarkation of the remains, but owing to the solemn nature of the ceremony, made no demonstration whatever. Here the Cork Committee formally received the American delegation, and mutual addresses were presented.

The public funeral procession took place on Sunday, Nov. 3, the several trades and associations marching in procession and wearing crape and bands, followed by an immense number of citizens walking abreast and bands playing the Dead March in Saul. The day was fine, and for hours before the procession passed, the way was thronged with spectators, and the men stood with uncovered heads as the body was borne along.

In the evening the body was taken to the railway to go by the night mail to Dublin, where it arrived about 4 o'clock on Monday morning, and notwithstanding the early hour, a large crowd was present, and a deputation of the "Brethren of St. Patrick," bearing flambeaux.

Miss M'Manus (the sister of the deceased), and Mrs. Doheny, together with the American deputation, the representatives of the Cork committee, and the members of the Dublin deputation arrived by the train which conveyed the remains.

The Primate, having forbidden the body to be taken to a church, it was conveyed to the Music Hall, which was suitably fitted up for its reception. During the week the building was thronged by a constant succession of visitors all anxious to take a last look of the departed patriot. On Wednesday evening an extraordinary concourse was present, to witness the presentation of an address to the members of the California, Philadelphia, New York and Cork committees, to which an appropriate reply was given. At this ceremony, which was very imposing and affecting, Miss MCMANUS, the sister of the deceased, was present, and a number of distinguirhed persons, including Father Kenyon, Dr. Sigerson and D. O'Sullivan, of Ross.

After lying in state during the week, the body was conveyed on Sunday, Nov. 10th, to its last resting place, in Glasnevin cemetery. All the trades and societies in the city were present, the members wearing insignia of mourning, and the streets thronged by immense crowds, who stood uncovered as the body was borne along. The *De Profundis* was chanted in the old Irish manner when the remains were being conveyed to the toomb, and after the delivery of the oration it was again sung in a most solemn and impressive manner, and the body of the Irish Patriot and English Rebel, TERRENCE BELLEW MCMANUS, was consigned to its final resting place.

In reference to the refusal [illegible] e Primate to permit the body to be taken to [illegible] atholic chapel, a letter on the subject by Fat[illegible] avelle, of Tuam, of which we append so[illegible] extracts, was distributed broadcast throug[illegible] ublin, during the week.

LETTER OF FATHER L[illegible]LE.

"Alas! and alas! that in Irela[illegible] here should be a second sentiment on his cla[illegible] to a national mourning and to national gratit[illegible] He abandoned all for Ireland—wealth, friendsh[illegible] peace, and human happiness.

"Good God! M'Manus denied [illegible] omentary resting place in any church of Irel[illegible], though those whose fathers built those church[illegible] would shed the last drop of their blood to honor [illegible] memory!

"The Whig traitor who sells h[illegible] untry for a daily pound of flesh, the debauchee[illegible] o may die rich are honored with votive praye[illegible] and fragrant incense; yet the portals of the [illegible] mple are closed against the bones of Terence [illegible] w M'Manus, the pure, the noble, the chivalrou[illegible] nd the brave, in the bosom of the land that ga[illegible] im birth, and for which he labored, exiled, sigh[illegible] and died.

"Oh! Ireland! Ireland! is [illegible] s your act? If not, in the name of creed, countr[illegible] d people speak out your sentiment.

"Is patriotism a crime? T[illegible] hen let the patriot Primate of Hungary do penance in sackcloth and ashes.

"And in Poland, where th[illegible] e strong hand of the Czar closes the church agai[illegible] st patriotic priest and people alive; here the Chur[illegible] closes herself agairst the Patriot Dead.

"Dear M'Manus! honored [illegible] e thy memory in every land where freedom still da[illegible] s to breathe. Thou art today ostracised in the hea[illegible] of thy native land; but thy living countrymen hav[illegible] no part in the deed.

Nay, thou art still dearer to them, far and far, from the attempt to dishonor thy name and thy grave, and the principles for which thou hast died, than thou ever would'st have been had the lamp of the sanctuary been permitted to cast its faint and melancholy light on thy precious remains. But thou art enshrined in our hearts a thousand times more than ever; and I, for one, vow never to enter the city in which thou art thus proclaimed on thy bier almost as I am in my parish, without pouring out my soul at thy grave, and vowing a new vow each time of hate and hostility to thy enemy and mine, the enemy of our Creed, our Country, and our Holy Father.

PATRICK LAVELLE.

"To E. J. Ryan, Esq., Secretary to the M'Manus Obsequies Committee."

War Intelligence.

SOUTHERN APPROVAL OF COCHRANE'S SPEECH.

Southern newspapers, published in the border slave states, have expressed their approval of Col. Cochrane's late speech to his regiment at Washington. A late issue of the Frankfort *Commonwealth*, one of the oldest and most influential Journals of Kentucky, says:

"The policy indicated by Mr. Cochrane is exactly right, and in accordance with the usage of civilized warfare. We hope to see it adopted by the Government. It should have been at first. Had it been, many lives of loyal citizens would have been saved that were lost through the anomalous conduct of the Government towards traitors in arms. Since the commencement of this most unnatural war it has been safer to be a rebel than to be loyal to the Government. The extreme punishment of treason has thus far been an 'oath of allegiance,' which a rebel will take with as much *sang froid* as he would a gin cocktail.

"Why should not the slaves of traitors in arms be confiscated to the use of the government? The *Democrat* will not deny that slaves are property, as clearly so as mules. Is it right and proper to confiscate a mule, and put it to hauling transportation? If it is, why is it not equally right and proper to confiscate a slave for a driver of that mule? Both are property, and both are employed by the rebels in their attempt to destroy this government. We believe in 'fighting the devil with fire.' The rebels employ are negroes, armed savages; they resort to all sorts of base means, even to piracy on the high seas. They poison wells, and when they can—as at Guyandotte—they resort to assassination. It is all stuff to talk about fighting such an enemy on 'high points.' The government has been trying the experiment some eight months, with indifferent success. If we meet a rattlesnake in our path, we mash his head if we can. Let this barbarous rebellion be crushed out. We care not how, so it be done quickly."

KENTUCKY AFFAIRS.

The Nolin (Ky.) correspondent of the Cincinnati *Gazette*, under date of Nov. 16th, writes as follows:

The new department created for Gen. Buell excludes the small portion of Kentucky west of the Tennessee river. Leaving out of view, therefore, the posture of affairs at Paducah, Columbus and Hickman, the situation in Kentucky is briefly this: But one rebel army remains in the state. Breckinridge's raw recruits at Prestonburg and Pikeville have been scattered. Zollicoffer has been driven back to the Cumberland Gap, and is reported to be trembling for his safety even there. The only rebel force remaining in his department to engage Gen. Buell's attention, is Buckner's army at Bowling Green—an army which is variously estimated at from eighteen to thirty-five thousand, and which is doubtless much nearer to the smaller of these figures.

Buckner's original plan is known to have been to move directly up the railroad to Louisville. That has probably been abandoned, and it has latterly been supposed that he desires to move across towards Lexington.

Meantime we have four distinct columns of national troops in Gen. Buell's department—those of Gen. Nelson, somewhere on the Big Sandy; Gen. Thomas, at Camp Dick Robinson and beyond; Gen. McCook, at Nolin; and Gen. Crittenden, in the lower Green River Valley. There may, of course, be little skirmishes almost anywhere through the state, where secessionists and Union men become warm enough to prove their faith by their works, but there is no possibility of any important collision in Kentucky, excepting on the Bowling Green line. When that collision shall come would seem, thus far, to rest with our generals to determine.

Such is the condition in which Gen. Buell finds matters in Kentucky. He has plenty of troops to sweep down to Nashville; or plenty to seize the Cumberland Gap, and break the connection on the East Tennessee and Lynchburg railroad; or he may, perhaps, have plenty for simultaneous movements to attain both these desirable ends. Assuredly, he has not enough to keep one column opposite the Bowling Green force, another in extreme Eastern Kentucky, another lying miscellaneously around the country toward Cumberland Gap, another on the Lower Green River Valley, or two or three more at points where the rebels may find it convenient to create diversions. *In other words, the play is up in Kentucky, the game is all in our own hands, if our new General will only concentrate and act.*

Hunting up a Secession Flag.

The correspondent of the Missouri *Republican*, at Camp Herron, Mo., occupied by the 9th Iowa Volunteers, gives an account of the capture of a secession flag that had waved at Manchester, 20 miles from that place, until the successes of the Union troops caused it to disappear.

On the 15th inst., Lieut. Beebe, with 15 men, were detailed, and proceeded part of the way on the cars, and the rest on foot to Manchester, and surrounding Esquire B.'s house, demanded the flag. He protested it was not in his possession with an air of injured innocence.

His lady owned that she had for a time kept it in a box in the garden, but as it was likely to become injured, she took it out, dried it in the sun, when it was taken away by some ladies, whose names she refused to give. Finally, after the lieutenant had placed her husband under arrest, the lady, probably hoping to save her husband, acknowledged that it was taken by a Mrs. S., who resided a mile and a half in the country. Her husband was then sent to Merrimac, escorted by four soldiers, and the remainder started to visit the residence of Mrs. S., who proved to be a very intelligent lady, and was surrounded by a very interesting family. The lady replied to the demand that the lieutenant could search her house, and if he could find anything that looked *like* a flag he was welcome to it.

Accordingly, a thorough search was made, in which the lady and her daughter aided, but no flag was to be found. The lady then thanked the officer for the gentlemanly manner in which the search had been conducted, and added that she trusted he was satisfied. He replied he was quite certain that she had the flag, and that it would have been far better for her to have yielded it; but as she did not, as unpleasant as the task was, he should arrest her and take her to headquarters at Pacific City. Two men were then dispatched for a carriage, and she made preparations to go, but after about an hour had elapsed in waiting for the carriage, the lady again demanded the name of the informants, and when told that it was Mrs. B——, and that Esquire B—— was already under arrest, she then asked whether any indignity would have been offered to her had the flag been found in her possession, to which the courteous Lieutenant replied, "*Certainly not*, madam; our object with Esquire B. was his arrest, and the capture of the flag; but with you, our object was the flag."

"Will you pledge your *honor*," said she, "that if I surrender the flag I shall not be arrested, nor my family disturbed?" When replied to in the affirmative, she added, "I wish you to understand, sir, that no fear of arrest or trouble would ever have made me surrender that flag; but Esquire B.'s family induced me to take that flag to save their family from trouble, saying that it should be a sacred trust, known only to ourselves, and I consequently surrender it."

She then went to a bed that had been fruitlessly searched, took from it a quilt, and with the aid of her daughter proceeded to open the edges of the quilt, and cut the stitches through the body of it and pulled off the top, when behold! there lay the mammoth flag next to the cotton, being carefully stretched twice and nearly half across the quilt. When taken out and spread, it proved to be a *magnificent flag, over twenty-one feet in length and nearly nine feet in width, with fifteen stars to represent the prospective Southern Confederacy.*

"Recollect," said the lady to Lt. Beebe, "that you did not find it yourself, and when you wish detectives you had better employ ladies." She also added, that she gave up the flag unwillingly. The daughter remarked that she had slept under it, and that she *loved* it, and that fifteen stars was not so terribly Disunion, in her estimation, after all.

IN LANCASTER, PENN., almost every family is engaged in the patriotic work of knitting stockings for the soldiers. Several hundred pairs have already been forwarded to the army, and more are being prepared.

RATES OF ADVERTISING.

TERMS CASH, IN ADVANCE.

Advertisements—For every FOUR LINES, thirty-two words, or less, one day, 50 cents; two days, 75 cents; three days, $1; six days, $1 75. All insertions, inside, same price each day.

Marriages and Deaths, 25 cents for each four lines. Monthly advertisements of four lines, inserted at the convenience of the office, $4 for every 24 insertions. Advertisements received until 11 o'clock P. M.

Extraordinary French Trial.

A Paris correspondent writing Saturday Nov. 2nd, gives the following account of a singular murder case that excited great attention in that city:

The principal personages were a *concierge* and his wife, named Lamotte, living in Rue de Genie, who, shortly after their marriage, conceived such a deep hatred to each other that, since 1852, the year after, they agreed not to speak to each other unless when business obliged them to do so, an agreement they strictly kept whenever mutual dislike did not break out in mutual acts of violence. They would have, at that period, sought a separate domicile, had not the Parisian custom of employing none but married people to mind houses, rendered it impossible to find the easy situation of *concierge*, should they have done so. They therefore dragged on life uncomfortably enough, and, when not fighting, kept up a perpetual snarl at one another. This went on in this manner till last Wednesday evening, when the husband entered the lodge in the last stage of intoxication, and, proceeded to tear to pieces his wife's marriage wreath of myrtles and orange blossoms, which, like every other Frenchwoman, she religiously preserved under a glass case upon the chimney piece; a violent discussion took place. Presently one of the tenants, on descending to the spot from whence the cries proceeded, saw Lamotte extended lifeless on the floor, where his wife said he fell, and in falling died, but, on examining the corpse the traces of strangulation were discovered, which gave rise to the suspicion that a murder had been committed. An inquest was accordingly held upon the spot, and steps taken to bring the affair before the law authorities. A *juge d' instruction* proceeded to the house with an eminent surgeon, who at once detected marks of violence, particularly upon the neck. On being submitted to the usual interrogation, the woman Lamotte gave another version of her husband's death. She said that after the quarrel occurred about the wedding-crown of white flowers he went up to a loft overhead, carrying in his hand a leather strap; but that about half-an-hour after she lit a candle to see what had become of him, and on ascending the stairs found him suspended from one of the balusters that surround the landing. She then lost no time in unfastening the strap, and no sooner did so than the corpse tumbled down the steep staircase to the spot where the neighbors found it lying. The magistrates then fastened, with the strap in question, a large bundle to the baluster from which Lamotte was said to have suspended him, and desired the woman to unloose it, as she had done the body of her husband, holding, at the same time, a candle in her hand, but she could not possibly succeed in doing so, and asserted, as her excuse, that a bundle and a man's body were two different things. The body was then put up, but all efforts to unfasten it, as she described having done, proved ineffectual. These circumstances being duly considered, as well as the cross-grained temper of the woman Lamotte, he was arrested.

The Sunday Law.

One of the most prudent and successful enterprises undertaken in this city is thus briefly characterized in the Sabbath Committee's Circular to the clergy, just published, as "The Sabbath and the Public," Document No. 20:—

"Then, (four years ago,) Sunday laws were as obsolete and inoperative in New York as in Vienna: nobody attempted or expected their enforcement. Now, they are as efficiently executed as other statutes, with the cordial approval of our citizens generally. Then, hundreds of newsboys overran the city every Sabbath, disturbing the peace of the whole population; now, the nuisance is abated, and most of our streets are as quiet as those of a country village. Then, more than 5.009 dram shops plied their deadly traffic openly and without hinderance; now, their doors and shutters are generally closed, and if liquors are sold, it is by stealth, and at the hazard of instant arrest for the misdemeanor. Then, a score of theatres made Sunday their chief day of profit and pleasure, with no adequate law to restrain them; now, a stringent law is on our statute book, its constitutionality affirmed, and its penalties inflicted, in spite of the most powerful combinations. Then, the arrests for Sunday crime exceeded the average by 25 per cent.; now, the week-day arrests are 50 per cent more than on Sundays. Then, the secular press ignored the Sunday question as foreign to its objects; since, and now, the entire press of the city, uninterested in Sunday issues—with perhaps a single exception—has been and is earnestly enlisted in support of this reform. Then, the entire German population was claimed to be wedded to Sunday pastimes and opposed to American Sabbath restraints; now, a large and influential body of Germans are avowedly friendly to the due observance of the Lord's Day; and actively hostile to the demoralizing views and customs of the beer-garden classes. In a word, the more offensive forms of Sabbath desecration have been suppressed, in the face of the most virulent opposition of interested parties, by the co-operation of the orderly classes with the public authorities. And a permanent foundation has been laid for all needed further action—legislative, judicial, or executive—for the protection of our civil Sabbath."

Miscellaneous.

THE SUGAR CROP in Louisiana is represented as being below the average this year.

MINISTER DAYTON writes, by the last mails that the feeling in France is growing more and more favorable to this country.

THE GAS WORKS at Palmyra were partially consumed by fire on Tuesday evening. The loss is estimated at $600 to $700.

A SMALL CONGREGATION of one of the churches in Louisville, Ky., observed Jeff. Davis' Fast Day, Nov. 15th, and mourned and prayed for the rebel crew.

A YOUNG GIRL, named Rosa Rose, was found drowned in a cistern, on Sunday evening, in Cincinnati. About a year ago, she formed the acquaintance of a young man, who has since betrayed and deserted her.

THE COLUMBUS, Ohio, *Capital City Fact* suggests that, inasmuch as South Carolina cannot be destroyed by anything short of an earthquake, (an article not among Dupont's stores,) be converted into a contraband colony.

WHEN BYRON CROSSED THE SEA, he sang: "My native land, good night." When Mason and Slidell attempted to cross, they woke up one morning and made the salutation, "My native land, good morning."

MR. HARE, of Casey county, Ky., is the father of seventeen children, and has six sons in Col. Wolford's regiment of cavalry. Such aid to the Government deserves a pension, as the father is quite a poor man.

IN WISCONSIN the whole Republican State ticket is elected, some of the candidates having full 10,000 majority. The Republican candidate for Governor is nearly 4,000 ahead of his opponent.

FIVE OF THE NORTH CAROLINA REGIMENTS, who were enrolled for the war, have been disbanded and surrendered their arms to the state. The Confederate Government gave them neither pay, food, nor clothes, and the Raleigh *Standard* fears that the "other regiments will do likewise, unless their demands are promptly met."

A CINCINNATI POLICEMAN, named John McFarland, on returning home on Tuesday evening, found his wife dead. She had long been ill of a painful chronic disease which at times affected her reason, and, on the evening named, she got out of bed and seizing one of her husband's loaded pistols, placed it at her ear and fired.

AN EXTRAORDINARY RESOLUTION, says the Staten Island *Gazette*, preceded by a preamble on the Quarantine question, is alleged to have been recently adopted by the Board of Supervisors of Richmond County, to the effect that that county should be offered to New Jersey, in exchange for Sandy Hook, as a compensation for allowing a Quarantine to be placed on the latter!

ONE OF THE MOST EXTRAORDINARY salt wells on record, perhaps, is now in operation at Wellsville, Ohio. The well was sunk in anticipation of finding oil, but when at a depth of 480 feet the borers struck a vein of gas, which burst forth with such violence as to eject all the tools used in boring, together with 200 feet of pipe which has been previously introduced. The boring had developed a very strong vein of salt water, which yields a barrel of salt an hour.

LOUISVILLE DAILY COURIER.

NEW SERIES. BOWLING-GREEN, KENTUCKY, TUESDAY, NOVEMBER 26, 1861. NUMBER 38

DAILY COURIER.

BOWLING-GREEN, KY.
Tuesday Evening, Nov. 26, 1861.

Letter from Crab Orchard.

[Special Correspondence Cincinnati Commercial.]

Retreat of the Wildcat Brigade from the Mountains of Kentucky --Disgraceful Culmination and Termination of the Cumberland Gap Expedition.

CRAB ORCHARD, KY., Nov. 17.

My last letter was written from Camp Coburn near Crab Orchard. The Wildcat brigade, or sorrowful fragments of it, had but just staggered into camp after its disastrous retreat from London, and its tattered remains were still straggling up the rugged road miles in the rear, animated by the hope of finally reaching a haven of rest. As that wretched struggle with the elements, over execrable roads, will be remembered by five thousand abused volunteers as long as they retain their faculty of memory, it deserves description.

You will remember that Wednesday afternoon, Nov. 13th, Gen. Schoepf issued an order requiring all the troops to be ready to march at eight o'clock that evening. Commanders of corps were directed to carry with them all their sick, leaving such baggage and stores as could not be transported. Previously there had been rumors of an advance, and when the order to prepare to move was issued to the troops, it was received with exultation. The Tennesseeans were especially delighted, and prepared with alacrity to return to their firesides. It had been currently reported that letters had been received by prominent Tennesseeans from friends at Louisville and Washington, assuring them that the Cumberland Gap expedition would soon be pushed to an issue. This order, therefore, confirmed the report, and I am told that Hon. Andy Johnson, Gen. Carter, Col. Byrd, Col. Spears, and others, were elated at the prospect of an immediate fruition of their hopes. They did not seem to comprehend that the order concerning the sick implied a retrograde movement. But when informed of the fact, they were overwhelmed with sorrow and indignation. Mr. Johnson turned from his informant, and entered his hotel without one word, in utter despair. [illegible] was withheld from the troops until they were moving, when the fact flashed upon them, and they denounced it with the vehemence of disappointed soldiers. Many of the Tennesseeans displayed a strongly mutinous spirit. Some swore they would not recede a foot of the ground which had been conquered; others expressed determination to desert and return to Tennessee at all hazards, and many wept with vexation and despair. Their officers appealed earnestly to their patriotism, announcing to them that Gen. Thomas had ordered them to countermarch in order to meet the rebels, who were reported moving toward Crab Orchard in strong force to cut them off, and that a retrograde movement was necessary to save the expedition. It was also stated by officers of various regiments, that Zollicoffer was reported marching up from Tennessee with a strong column to form a junction with Buckner, to penetrate the Blue Grass country. Such were the facts and statements prior to the hour of marching. The subsequent facts will appear in the following diary:

LONDON, KY., Nov. 13.

Long before 8 o'clock, P. M., most of the troops of the Wild Cat Brigade, with three days' rations in their haversacks, were prepared to march. The sick who could be removed—and there were many too feeble to walk, yet able to ride—were transferred to those wretched instruments of torture to the ill or the healthy—two wheeled ambulances—and to common army wagons, some of which were uncovered, thus exposing suffering men to the raw night air. But many poor bed ridden fellows who were necessarilly left remained confined to the hospitals, a prey to harrowing apprehensions of captivity. Of course surgeons and guards were detailed to minister to their wants and protect them until they should be removed.—But how many men were closely packed in ambulances and wagons I could not learn. Col. Steedman would not leave any, and he had over one hundred stowed away as comfortably as possible. The surgeon of the 33d Indiana, horrified at the order, protested vehemently, but he was informed decisively, the order from Headquarters is that all the sick must be removed, and orders must be obeyed. He still protested that removal would result in the death of some of his patients, and he was told to quarter them with private families at London. But the 33d Indiana brought away one hundred and eighty-nine sick. I did not inquire how many were removed by other regiments, but the number was large. Besides many feeble fellows just discharged from the hospitals, but yet unfit for duty, shouldered their muskets and donned their heavy knapsacks preferring the cruelties of a forced march to the hazards of captivity.

The 14th Ohio had the right of the column. Shortly before 8 o'clock, it marched solemnly by the camp of the 17th Ohio, its band mournfully playing the Dead March—thus expressing the emotions of the troops. It was followed by Standart's and Kenney's batteries, with the baggage trains of each of the foregoing corps. The 17th Ohio fell in their rear, and its sarcastic lads, keenly appreciating the occasion, burst into a satirical paraphrase of their favorite regimental ditty, one strain of which runs somewhat thus:

"Old Zollicoffer can't take us,
Can't take us, can't take us,
On a long summer's day."

It was impromptu at the Wild Cat fight, so was the song as they retreated:

"Old Zollicoffer can't *catch* us.
Can't *catch* us, can't *catch* us,
Cause we're running away."

More forcible than elegant, and more expressive than poetical.

And so each regiment, followed by its baggage train and sad procession of invalids, moved up the road melancholy and mad. Most of the Tennesseeans had fallen in behind the 14th Ohio, and moved on sullen and sorrowful, bitterly expressing their disappointment, and denouncing the frauds with which they had been deluded. Some were imbued with the idea that they were to march up the Somerset road,—about three miles above London—to meet the enemy, and agreed to go that far but not beyond. Upon reaching that point, the head of the column failed to halt. A few Tennesseeans madly broke from the ranks and moved back towards camp. Several threw themselves sullenly on the ground, and refused to march. As we moved forward they continued to leave the ranks in pairs and squads. Then squads multiplied into sections, sections into platoons, and platoons almost into whole companies. A private came back from the front and appealed to an officer to stop the deserters. He said the regiment was disorganized—the men were going back to Tennessee; their officers could do nothing with them. The poor fellows, with despairing exceptions, continued to proclaim their loyalty, but could not stand the disappointment. Occasionally a stout-hearted fellow would proclaim his derminatton to follow the flag wherever orders carried him—"but it's hard on Tennesseeans boys," he would say to the Buckeyes. In a march of four miles we must have passed 200 stragglers. Some were lying prone on the ground, sobbing; some stood by the highway swearing defiantly; others leaned against the fence, sullenly, undetermined whether to move one way or the other. Here was the Adjutant of the regiment addressing a squad, "For God's sake boys move on. Look at the Ohioans. Don't let them beat you. You are fighting for the Union. Let's keep, Tennesseeans, together. Come, boys." "Well, Adjutant," said one, "It will do for you who ride to talk, but we who do nothing but march up and down this infernal road, don't appreciate it." "Get on my horse and I'll walk," said the Adjutant,—and the transfer was made. And so the column trudged onward heavily, and halted for jaded teams to dislodge a wagon from the mire, or pushed ahead, leaving vehicles to be extricated by whomsoever would do it. At midnight there was a long line of straggling Tennesseeans, from the head of their column clean back to their camp. It was marked by the lurid hue of the atmosphere, illumined by their blazing bivouac fires in the forests, around which they huddled in shivering groups.—Hardly a nucleus for the regiment was left in column, though many stout fellows pushed on, determined to follow where orders commanded. But there were pitiful scenes, and heart touching.

Soon after midnight, the 14th Ohio and the artillery men, after scaling Wildcat heights, flung themselves headlong on the ground. None were covered that night—or morning—save by blankets and a veneering of cold, white frost. The sick, too, in the open wagons, lay shuddering and shivering and moaning in the sharp, cutting atmosphere of a November morning. The 17th Ohio halted and bivouacked at two o'clock, in the camp which Zollicoffer's rebels had occupied the night before their repulse. I have told you where the Tennesseeans were, but I know not where was the remainder of the brigade. The Kentucky 3d, (Garrard's) I believe, did not move that night. I know not why. The 38th Ohio and the 33d Indiana pushed forward to the summit of Wildcat, and halted not long before day. The teams were also moving all night long.

The necessity to carry the sick obliged us to leave much stores and ammunition. I am told we left *twenty-two tons* of ammunition at London. And yet, readers, *we were making a forced march to prevent the enemy from cutting us off, or to save Blue Grass.*

Strange that soldiers should leave their ammunition and march to meet the enemy. At Pitman's we met thirteen wagons loaded with commissary stores, *en route* from Camp Dick Robinson for London. These were unloaded immediately, and proceeded to London for patients and stores. Some of the regiments had necessarily left their tents and camp equipage, so that even had fatigue permitted them to pitch tents they could not have enjoyed the luxury.

Nov. 14th—A heavy storm of rain roused the bivouachers from sleep. Their blankets and clothing were saturated with water.—The morning was most dismal. Wildcat Heights crowned with a heavy coronal of mist, frowned in dreary and discouraging altitude before us. The roads were already worked into a tough muck, and the pathway on the edges where the troops walked were slimy and slippery. Beyond was Rockcastle river, swift, and reported unfordable.—But the word was *en avant*. The lads partook of their cold rations and hot coffee, and took up the toilsome march. Every step was laborious to the sturdy, agonizing to the feeble. Knapsacks almost too heavy under fairest auspices, were now doubly burdensome, and the pack horse load was increased by the aggravating weight of water which soaked blankets and heavy army overcoats, and the nasty slime which splashed and plastered each man's breeches as high as his knees in front and rear, and filled his shoes until they overflowed with slush.

During the first mile we passed one baggage wagon capsized in a creek. Its load of commissary stores and baggage were lost. The desolate teamster and jaded horses, bedaubed with mud, gazed at it dismally and hopelessly as we moved forward. Further up the hill a half dozen wagons was stuck, and the poor animals could not move them. A few hundred yards further, barrels of bread were tossed out of wagons and left to destruction in the forests. A stranger to the facts, passing would have said, here is a terrified army fleeing from a pursuing enemy.

Going up the mountain, we pass Tennesseans; some are still pushing on desperately. Yonder is one prone on a bed of leaves. His head is bolstered on a rotten stump.—Exhaustion is graphically pictured on his livid complexion and in his silent form. He is unconscious, while he sleeps the sleep of distress, that the driving rain is beating mercilessly upon him. My comrade startles me—"Is he dead?" Oh, no; he's only an exhausted soldier. He wears no shoulder straps with a silver star on each. But it is yet early in the day. Surely it is not time for soldiers to yield to fatigue. They have marched only one night, and have slept the whole of one or two hours on the damp, frosted soil.

At last the ascent is accomplished by a few. We look back with a sigh of relief, and turn away again with emotions of regret and disgust at the sorrowful and weary file of men, still toiling through the mire, and gazing wistfully to the top. But here is a picture. On the top of a rock on the crest of the hill, there sits a Toledo lad, *writing a letter.* He protects the precious page from the rain with his hat, and the big drops patter on his bare head. He looks care worn and way worn; but his eye is bright, his hand steady. From head to foot he is encased in a thick plastering of clay, and moisture drips from his sleeves.—He replies to my comrade. "No Colonel, I've not given out; I'm a little tired though; I'll make it, Colonel—I'll never give up."

Why in the name of humanity does not the commander send back messengers to halt this column? Is there imminent danger ahead? Cannot these failing men be halted a day for rest? At least let messengers be dispatched to inspire them to march, march, march, to resist the foe. Anything to renew their spirit. But look at these wagon loads of sick soldiers. See them shivering in saturated blankets, seated in pools of water which drip from their clothing as it pours from the clouds. Hear their unceasing, discordant, and harrowing chorus of coughing. Here are candidates for the grave. But the order is stern—"Bring all your sick." "Oh," said one of the Surgeons to me, "that was the cruelest order officer ever give. I protested in vain. I urged that it would kill my patients. But come they must. I shall lose perhaps thirty or forty of my regiment, and it will plant consumption in the lungs of two hundred more."

And here is another picture. We splash along tediously through the mire, and mounted officers encourage their men by kind words of sympathy. Nearly all relieve feeble soldiers by carrying their knapsacks and muskets. Col. Steedman, long racked with chills and fever, and scarce able to sit his horse, rides with his scattered columns. Col. Connell, suffering from illness, bears the burden of a sick soldier's knapsack. Col. Coburn dismounts, and pushes through the mud, while a feeble lad rides his charger. The Captains on foot emulate their superiors, and encouaage them by example.

At Rockcastle river the column is victoriously over Wildcat. The dismal train halts at the ferry, in the mud and rain. The jaded men fall asleep on the sod of a neighboring meadow, waiting the slow process of crossing all that column in one small float. The teamsters stuff their worn out animals with corn. A few, in desperation, plunge into the ford where the water is swift, and some narrowly escape a watery grave. The 14th Ohio loses two wagons and contents including twenty-five or thirty thousand rounds of ammunition. The 17th loses a wagon and 26,000 rounds of ammunition at the ferry. The Tennesseeans lose two wagons and contents with three horses, and the 38th Ohio loses one wagon. How much more was lost I do not know.

This was morning, but the column was long after night in crossing. Afterwards throughout the day the scenes already feebly described, increased and assumed more aggravating forms. The road constantly became more wretched. Men flung away their knapsacks and stalked onward in utter desperation, their officers refusing to see insubordination. Some stumbled and fell by the wayside, where they lay, and slept the sleep of exhaustion. And the sick in the uncovered wagons, and those accursed ambulances, were racked and jounced over rocks and ruts until their weak bones ached, their countenances testifying to their utter wretchedness. And thus, hour after hour, through mud, and slime, and rain, over rocks and rails, and logs, up the roughest and steepest grades, and down the ruggedest descents, our weary, footsore, exhausted soldiers and jaded teams struggled and toiled in pain all that miserable day and far into night; for even at midnight feeble stragglers staggered into Mount Vernon, where the 14th and 17th rested, to find their comrades.

This night the poor lads went to bed supperless, for fatigue was overpowering, and sleep sweeter than meat. Some of them marched fourteen, some sixteen miles that day—thirteen the night and morning before. This day's work was more disastrous than ordinary battles. God knows how many sturdy constitutions it wrecked; how many brave volunteers it will kill.

But I had almost forgot the episode of the day. The few Tennesseeans who had manfully breasted the task with Ohio and Indiana, were mere stragglers. Their officers were scattered as badly as the men. The privates were huddled in shivering groups along the entire route. It seemed as if they never could be collected. A hundred yards or so below a house where I halted for luncheon, there was a party of perhaps a hundred or more. There were two or three with me, bitterly denouncing the countermarch. At that moment an officer rode down the highway, proclaiming joyfully, "Tennesseeans and Kentuckians are ordered back to London!" The hundred below set up a great shout of joy as if they had attained the summit of their desires, and those with me started back almost running bidding a glad good-bye. Alas! poor fellows, you were twenty-four miles from London, exhausted, wet, muddy, almost out of provisions, without tents, and no houses or barns to shelter you from the storm. London will be another charnel house for patriot Tennesseeans. If there was cause for a forced march of the entire brigade from London to Crab Orchard, why order back the Tennesseeans and Kentuckians, before they had approached within fifteen miles of Crab Orchard? If there was no adequate cause for the march, why was not the whole column halted for rest, which it so sorely needed? If there was reason to apprehend that the brigade would be cut off unless it made the forced march, why send the Tennesseeans and Kentuckians back to be sacrificed? Who will answer?

MT. VERNON, Nov. 15.

Thank God, the sun shines to-day. We learn, this morning, that the 38th Ohio encamped five miles below here late last night. During the night, a tree was blown down in the camp, and five men, including three Tennesseeans, were seriously injured. Two have died, and two more are reported fatally hurt.

The 33d Indiana is moving forward slowly in the rear, *somewhere*. The 44th and 17th Ohio lads are bowling ahead cheerily by company, because the sun shines and the roads improve, besides the forced march must end to-day. The brigade can go no further until it gathers its scattered fragments.

An order from Headquarters meets us.—The only one giving relief. The column goes into camp two miles below Crab Orchard.—The lads, inspired, move briskly, and camp is at last in view.

In Camp.—The 17th Ohio, excepting a few feeble stragglers, was first in camp. The 14th followed shortly after, but it had its stragglers, too. Which regiment had not its large share? But Manny Richards, the enterprising teamster of the 17th, pushed in his wagons, and the Fairfield boys pitched their tents merrily. But the prospects for the other regiments was cheerless.—Their wagons were far behind. Officers threatened to move where shelter could be found for the men, but orders must be all obeyed, and they prepared again to bivouack on the cold, cold ground, in the freezing atmosphere of drear November.

But now there is another order fresh from Headquarters at Crab Orchard. Exhausted as they are, soldiers are forbidden to burn rails. They must cut wood for bivouack fires, or sleep in the frosty atmosphere without fires. Orders must be obeyed. Twenty men are detailed to cut wood, and wagons are sent out. Sun set is approaching. Headquarters, who forty hours ago knew the men were coming, knew they were suffering, had not provided axes. Yet the order was *cut wood.* Look at the field adjacent to camp, and see whether rails were burnt.

A member of the Fourteenth, coming in late, reports:—"I saw a dead man of the Fourteenth, lying on the roadside beyond Mount Vernon."—He died of exhaustion. Another says "I saw another dead man on the roadside to-day." He died of exhaustion. A surgeon says:—"I saw two men, yesterday, in the last stage of exhaustion. I gave them whisky to revive them. I could do nothing else. I was compelled to leave them with their comrades, and attend to the sick of my own regiment." They probably died of exhaustion.

Nov. 17th—CRAB ORCHARD.—The 38th Ohio and the 33d Indiana are coming in slowly. The former was more deliberate, but suffered its proportion. The latter are sleeping in the woods without tents. I know not whether the Tennesseeans have got back safely to London.

There is not much beauty, or gaiety in a soldier's life, if it is like this. But the toil, and suffering, and sacrifices, and the manly efforts of brave men obeying orders under circumstances such as I have sketched, are very eloquent. Will soldiers respect, love, and cheerfully fight under officers who abuse them as slaves do brutes?

The amount of physical suffering caused by this march cannot be computed. None can tell how many sturdy frames will bend under disease contracted from this ruthless exposure. The mortality list of the regiments will shortly begin to make a record. Many of the sick who were dragged out of their beds in the London hospitals, to be tortured on the rugged roads, saturated with rain, and chilled with cold, must die. Many of the well must fall ill. Ah, well, there are only 250 sick in the 33d Indiana; only a couple of hundred or so sick in the 14th Ohio; only a hundred or so sick in the 38th Ohio; only several scores sick in the 17th Ohio; only a few hundreds altogether. If they die—recruit the regiments.

The loss of property is nothing. The Government is rich. Only 30 horses belonging to the 17th Ohio were knocked up and rendered unfit for service, and one died; one wagon was lost and 26,000 pounds of ammunition; about the same report is made by the 14th Ohio; so with each of the regiments. But the moral effects of the countermarch is one of its worst features. The mountaineers of Kentucky regard it a retreat, and the prestige of the victory at Wildcat is turned against us. And so ended the great Cumberland Gap Expedition.

But I beg you to wait, readers, for an echo from the Wild Cat Brigade. If I mistake not, there will be a fierce growl ere long from the Tennessee camp, as vehement as the denunciation from "East Tennessee" which you read a day or two ago in the Commercial. And I am inclined to believe that if the indignant letters of the Ohio and Indiana boys are permitted to see the light of public print, none will think I have colored the foregoing picture. W. D. B.

Particulars of Fremont's Removal.

How the Bearer of the Order Reached Fremont.

HOW FREMONT ACTED.

The Difficulty of Getting to See General Hunter.

[Correspondence of the Cincinnati Enquirer.]

ST. LOUIS, Nov. 12, 1861.

On the 29th of October, Gen. Curtis received from the President, per Mr. Swett, a former law partner of Mr. Lincoln, an order from Lieutenant General Winfield Scott, directed to Major General J. C. Fremont, "to turn over the Department of the West to Major General J. Hunter, and to report himself, *by letter*, immediately to headquarters at Washington."

Accompanying this order were instructions from the Executive to General Curtis, viz: "If a decided victory had been won, a substantial battle and not a mere skirmish going on, or if General Fremont was in the immediate presence of the enemy, and about to give battle, then these orders not to be delivered." These orders mean, the one to Fremont announcing his supersedure, and another to General Hunter appointing him to the command.

Gen. Curtis detailed Capt. J. C. McKenny, Adjutant of the 2d Iowa, as the bearer of the dispatches. Captain McKenny was dressed in a secesh uniform, and carried the dispatches and a general pass from General Curtis in the top of his cap. With complete instructions as to his mode of procedure, Capt. McKenny left St. Louis on the morning of the 31st, Thursday, arriving at Rolla at 6 o'clock in the evening. He left Rolla at 11 P. M., and arrived at Springfield on Saturday morning at daylight, going through the lines with the messenger of the Express Company. Capt. McKenny found every thing quiet, and no "laying on" arms, or apprehensions of a fight. He discovered that no battle had taken place, or victory won, nor was any battle going on.—He then made diligent inquiry of a Federal soldier, who, taken prisoner by Price, at Lexington, had been released in exchange, and being the bearer of a flag of truce from Fremont to Price, and had returned from his errand the evening previous. The soldier replied: "The enemy are 40 miles distant from Springfield, below Crane's Creek, toward Cassville." The Captain inquired: 'Do you think Price intends to make a fight?' Answer: "Think he will, but he is going to select his own grounds." The Capt. then inquired of Col. Richardson, in command of the Missouri scouts, and a number of others, all corroborating the statement of the soldier, that the enemy were fully forty miles away. Adjutant McKenny was fully satisfied that Gen. Fremont was "not in the immediate presence of the enemy, about to give battle." He then repaired to Headquarters to deliver his orders. Approaching the sentinels he was informed that all messages, &c., for the Major General must be delived through Col. Eaton, his Adjutant General.

Captain McKenny called on Col. Eaton, who, after a long delay, gave the Captain an audience. Colonel Eaton, inquired: "What is the nature of the information you have for General Fremont?" The Captain replied: "My information is for General Fremont alone." Colonel Eaton went in, and for some time had a conversation with General Fremont, and upon returning demanded of the Captain that the information should be imparted to him, and received the reply: "I tell you, sir, distinctly, that my information is for General Fremont alone." Colonel Eaton returned to the General, and after a brief interview the bearer of dispatches was admitted. It was now about ten o'clock in the morning. The General was standing near the fire place, apparently agitated. After saluting the General, the Captain said: "General Fremont, my name is McKenny. I have dispatches for you." The General made no reply, but seizing the dispatches, hastily tore open the envelope, and with increased agitation read the order, a deep flush crimsoning his face, while his entire frame trembled with nervousness. After reading the order, the General, with much violence, threw the "seal of his destiny" on the table, and with sternness accosted the Captain: "Sir, how did you get admission into these lines?"

Captain McKenny—"General, I came through with the express messenger."

General Fremont—"Did you have a pass, sir?"

Captain McKenny—"None, sir, except a general pass from Gen. Curtis."

Gen. Fremont (pacing the room)—"You can retire, sir, for the present."

Col. Eaton was summoned to the General's presence, and the bearer of dispatches retired. Fearing that Gen. Fremont would not announce his supersedure, the Captain immediately informed Gen Sturgis, Maj. Tatnell, (Surgen) and others of Gen. Fremont's removal, and Gen. Hunter's promotion to the command, adding that he was the bearer of the dispatches. Just as he had concluded, Col. Eaton emerged from the General's room, and taking the Captain aside, said, "On behalf of the Major-General, you are requested not to make known the supersedure of Gen. Fremont for the present, for certain reasons. The Major-General feels hurt at Gen. Curtis for sending the dispatches of such a magnitude by a civilian. The Gen. and myself supposed, from your dress and appearance, that you had important information from the enemy." Capt. McKenney replied, "No, sir; I am an officer of the United States army," and then exhibited Gen. Curtis' pass, in which was given the bearer's rank and title.

The Capt. then remarked to Col. Eaton that he had important dispatches for Gen. Hunter, and must have transportation and pass through the lines.

Col. Eaton replied, "I cannot pass any one through the lines, nor will Gen. Fremont issue a pass to any person. The Gen is greatly surprised that you effected a passage through the pickets when he has given strict and positive orders not to pass any one except on his special orders. I may be able to send a man to pass you out."

Capt. McKenny—"That will do."

It now being evening, Colonel Eaton introduced Captain McKenny to Colonel Wood, who was to furnish transportion. Colonel Wood went to see Colonel Richardson, and did not return until about nine o'clock, when Captain McKenny inquired about the transportation. In a blustering and excited manner Colonel Wood replied: "I did not understand that you wanted it to-night;" and being assured by the Captain that he wanted it immediately, Colonel Eaton, who had been sent for, answered: "We doubt our authority now to issue your transportation, as General Fremont has turned over his command to General Hunter, as you will see by this circular," which the Colonel produced. Colonel Eaton added that he had no information where Hunter was, but supposed he was on the Buffalo road, and that a copy of General Fremont's circular had been already sent to General Hunter, which copy General Hunter never received. After the first appeal to pass through the lines, Colonel Eaton saw General Fremont, and returned with an answer that the General was passing no one through. A second appeal the Captain found equally fruitless, and concluded to try another method.

He called upon Col. Richardson and made known his business, and the efforts being made to prevent him from going through the lines. Col R. furnished the captain two horses and a guide, and the two started at 11 o'clock toward Buffalo. The first guard was passed by means of the countersign, which the captain had overheard Col. Eaton give to an officer. Coming up to the second guard, the captain was overhauled by the corporal of the guard, who demanded to see the pass. Capt. McK. allighted from his horse, and flourishing the pass of Gen. Curtis in front of a blazing fire, remarked that he was in great haste to intercept Gen. Hunter with important dispatches. The corporal passed the captain through the lines, by sending a sentinel along to the outer pickets.

Capt. McKenny rode all night, and arriving at Buffalo, could learn nothing of Gen. Hunter, and leaving word with Major Wright that he had important dispatches for General Hunter, he continued on toward Bolivar. When about ten miles on the road, he was overtaken by the Major, who announced General Hunter's arrival at Buffalo. Capt. McK. returned and delivered his dispatches about 12 M. After dinner, Gen. H., in ambulance, proceeded to Springfield, arriving there about nine o'clock at night. Capt. McK. returned the following morning, when he found all the officers making their calls on the new Commander, and congratulating him upon his promotion. The harmony was general. There was some muttering among the troops, but not the slightest insubordination, no laying on arms through the night, no throwing down of arms on the evening previous or morning after, and not a single officer thretened to resign. General Hunter is esteemed and beloved by the entire army, and the expression is universal that the troops are entirely satisfied with any change the government may deem best for the interests of the service. Up to Monday night, when the Captain left, this good feeling and satisfactory harmony prevailed.

ARREST.—Mr. Geo. P. Buell, the army correspondent of the Cincinnati *Times*, was arrested in this city by Marshal Dent, yesterday. It is understood that Mr. Buell's offence consists in the publication in his paper of information which has been prohibited by the Commanding General. Orders have been issued, we learn, for the arrest of other correspondents in this city.—*Louisville Jour.*, 16th.

Things in Northern Kentucky.

Heavy Reinforcements of the Yankees.

Movements at Louisville and elsewhere unmistakably indicate a speedy advance move of the Yankees in overwhelming numbers.

For some ten days past two or three regiments have arrived at Louisville daily and been sent forward towards Bowling Green.

Gen. Bull Nelson's command has been withdrawn from Prestonsburg to the Mouth of Sandy, whence it was taken to Louisville by steamboats, The Wildcat and Camp Dick Robinson troops seem to be concentrating about Danville and Crab Orchard.

☞ It will be seen by the telegraphic dispatches we copy from Northern papers that the Toronto (Canada) papers are quite severe and pointed against the United States for their seizure of Mason and Slidell from the British steamer.

DAILY COURIER.

ROBERT McKEE, W. N. HALDEMAN, } Editors.

TERMS:

Single Copies..............................Five Cents.
To News Agents and News Boys, ...2½ cents per copy.

OFFICES:

BOWLING GREEN—In the Old Gazette Office.

NASHVILLE—Front Room, second story, in "Union & American Building," corner of Church and Cherry streets.

BOWLING GREEN, KY.

Tuesday Evening, Nov. 26, 1861.

Special Notice to News Dealers.

Hereafter the Courier will be distributed direct by its publishers from their office in Nashville. News dealers and subscribers will therefore address their orders to "Louisville Courier, Nashville, Tenn.

The Courier by Mail.

We yield to the pressing appeals of friends at a distance who wish the DAILY COURIER by mail, in so far as to consent to forward it hereafter to any address desired at the rate of 75 cents per month. $1 will secure it for one and one-third months. All orders for it must be addressed to

W. N. HALDEMAN,
Nashville, Tenn.

Very Particular Notice.

All letters for publication, all correspondence and exchange papers, should, in order to reach us without delay, be addressed to the "Louisville *Courier*, Nashville, Tenn."

To Our Exchanges.

Those friends of the press who receive the COURIER will please send their papers to us addressed, "Louisville Courier, Nashville, Tenn."

The News.

We have through Northern newspapers a budget of information from Yankee land, some of it interesting.

The capture of Messrs. MASON and SLIDELL has caused quite a fluttering amongst the supporters of the shallow-brained Autocrat who rules at Washington. Lord LYONS, the British Minister, it is said, does not attempt to conceal his indignation, regarding the capture as an insult to the British flag, and he even goes so far as to say, the Federal Government must not merely disavow the act, but must release the captives. Canada papers are equally indignant; whilst a representative of Spain declares if the capture had been made on a Spanish ship he would have demanded his passports! The Federal Government, now it has lost the South and its fighting material, is somewhat in the condition of the dead lion, even the Spanish ass presumes to offer it a kick. The old *National Intelligencer* which has outlived its character and usefulness, comes, in company with Messrs. EDWARD EVERETT, E. M. STANTON, and REVERLY JOHNSON, to sustain the act of Com. WILKES, and to save the Government from the shame of disavowing it. We shall soon see what will come of the matter. JOHN BULL is a presumptuous old rip, and when he thinks he can do so with a show of impunity, does not fail to make his power felt.

A year ago, in Texas, there appeared a bold speaker at San Antonio in behalf of the Union. He was as able as he was bold, and eloquent as he was strong. We allude to CHARLES ANDERSON, the brother of SUMTER ANDERSON. He was a resident of Texas, but when the State abandoned the old Union, he adhered to his opinions; and, of course, beame suspected. He attempted, a few weeks ago, to escape, with his family, from the tate, but was arrested. It is now proposed to the Lincoln administration by his friends, to offer to exchange Ex-Gov. MOREHEAD, of Ky., for him. The proposition probably comes too late as the latest advices from Texas announced that his family had gone to Mexico, and that he had escaped, and would probably join them. In his Union harangues he used to vehemently pronounce against "lone stars"—"they are an anomaly in nature," said he—"Stars cluster and constellate." The Anderson stars are clustering and constellating in the Northern firmament. There let them stay. LARY and BOB and CHARLES, great stars, let them give light to the benighted Yankees—the South can spare them.

Dispatches from Rosecrans are announced. He is still on the trail of Floyd. He has not yet won a victory—the phantom is always just ahead, beckening him on, but he cannot grasp it. He is another illustration of the line of the poet—

"Man never *is* but always *to be* blest."

When he gets Floyd in his nets, of course he will announce it.

The Federals appear to be making great preparations still for naval operations on the Southern Coasts. Their exhibitions are noisy and though they accomplish but little, they serve as tubs to the Yankee whale; and make the monied men bleed. Secretary CHASE recently returned to Washington from a short practice of phlebotomy, in Gotham, and regaled a gaping crowd of citizens in Washington with the announcement that they might expect soon to hear something startling from the West. If the battle of Belmont is an indication, we may say, he and they will not be disappointed.

We have little news from the South. The exchange of cannon shots at Fort Pickens seems to have come to a pause on Saturday night, no great damage having been done to either side. What could it have been begun ··?

An interesting correspondence between the Grand Admiral CONSTANTINE, of Russia, and Lieut. Maury, has transpired. We repuplish it from the Richmond *Enquirer*. The gallant Russian invites the Lieutenant to resume his scientific labors under his patronage, but the honest American is constrained to decline the invitation. He prefers to give himself up to the great struggle for Southern Independence. The South is full of men ready to make every sacrifice for her safety. MAURY is one of the noblest of them all.

Gen. PILLOW announces that he can hold Columbus, against any force that may be brought against him; but he wants his rear strengthened. Generals in this age appear to have a delicate regard for their rears, and always wish to have them protected. Our General has succeeded in arousing the people, of Louisiana, Alabama and Tennessee, to the importance of beating back the enemy on the Mississippi river, and they are flocking to the rescue. He tells them, however, they must come organized, and ready to submit to military discipline, or he will not have them. We doubt not he will soon have force enough under his command—we believe he has entire control of things now—and will do something soon to justify Mr. Chase's expectation of startling work in the West.

The telegraph continues to tell us the signs on the Potomac portend a battle. We have ceased to look for anything in that quarter, and do not mind what the telegraph says. The fact is, we begin to suspect that he is a cheat.—*Nashville Patriot.*

A large supply of soap may be extracted from every cornfield at this season of the year. While a thousand pounds of oak wood yield only two and a half pounds of potash, a thousand pounds of corn stalks will yield seventeen pounds of potash, and soap is made out of potash. A thousand pounds of oak leaves burnt to ashes will yield twenty-four pounds of potash, and soap may be made out of potash.

Rev. WM. HOGE, who was associate pastor with Rev. Dr. Spring, in New York city, until a few months past, when he resigned, is now the Pastor of the Presbyterian Church in Charlottesville, Va.

From the Richmond Enquirer.

A High Courtesy from across the Waters.

We have the pleasure of publishing below a very interesting correspondence between the Grand Duke Constantine, Grand Admiral of Russia, and a distinguished citizen of our own State. It will be read with pleasure and pride. Pleasure, that so eminent a person in a distant empire should have paid such homage to science in the person of one of our own philosophers; and pride, that the flattering and generous proffer should have been so nobly responded to.

In the eyes of the wise and good, such respect as the Grand Admiral has thus exhibited for learning, adds a grace to royalty, and sheds lustre upon diadems. But this exhibition, we are informed, is only characteristic of him; for, of all the Princes of Europe, the Grand Duke of Russia is by far the most renowned for enlightened, liberal, and progressive sentiments.

There is, indeed, no government in the world which is doing more for the advancement of science than the Russian Government is at this moment. In everything that relates to the sea, the improvement of navigation or the navy, her Grand Admiral is sure to be found where he ought to be, in the van, taking an enlightened and an active part. His largesses to science are dispensed with a princely munificence.

A private letter has, we understand, been received from a member of his household explaining in detail the exact relations in which he desires Lieut. Maury to be placed towards the Government of Russia. They are those of perfect freedom. The pay and perquisites which he received in Washington are to be repeated in Russia without conditions.—Should he desire to renew there the researches which have been interrupted in Washington, the most ample means and facilities for so doing are to be placed at his disposal; and should he at any time desire to return to America he will be perfectly at liberty to do so. Indeed it is desired that he should occupy very much such a position in Russia as Humboldt did in Prussia.

A most delicate and graceful compliment is this to our fellow-citizen; like that precious quality that is "mightiest in the mightiest," this invitation "blesseth him that gives, and him that takes."

The reply of Lieut. Maury is such as becomes the patriot. His first duty is to his country. When his native State is in danger and calls to him, he recognizes it as no time to seek ease and advantage in a distant land. The wooings even of philosophy are, under such circumstances, less attractive than the thunderings of war. No time for visiting when the invader threatens the homesteads? Liberty and independence secured and peace established, he will appropriately manifest his high appreciation of the courtesy with which he has been honored. Till then he returns his thanks. Such is the spirit which his letter breathes, and it is in harmony with that of the people of his State and of the Confederacy.

Here is the correspondence:

ST. PETERSBURG, 27th July, 1861.
[8th August.]

MY DEAR CAPT MAURY: The news of your having left a service which is so much indebted to your great and successful labors, has made a very painful impression on me and my companions-in arms. Your indefatigable researches have unveiled the great laws which rule the winds and currents of the ocean, and have placed your name amongst those which will be ever mentioned with feelings of gratitude and respect, not only by professional men, but by all those who pride themselves in the great and noble attainment of the human race. That your name is well known in Russia. I need scarcely add, and, though "barbarians," as we are still sometimes called, we have been taught to honor in your person disinterested and eminent services to science and mankind.

Sincerely deploring the inactivity into which the present political whirlpool in your country has plunged you, I deem myself called upon to invite you to take up your residence in this country, where you may in peace continue your favorite and useful occupations.

Your position here will be a perfectly independent one. You will be bound by no conditions or engagements, and you will always be at liberty to steer home across the ocean, in the event of your not preferring to cast anchor in our remote corner of the Baltic.

As regards your material welfare, I beg to assure you that everything will be done by me to make your new home comfortable and agreeable, whilst at the same time the necessary means will be offered you to enable you to continue your scientific pursuits in the way you have been accustomed to.

I shall now be awaiting your reply, hoping to have the pleasure of soon seeing here so distinguished an officer, whose personal acquaintance it has always been my desire to make, and whom Russia will be proud to welcome on her soil.

Believe me, my dear Captain Maury,
Your sincere well-wisher,
CONSTANTINE,
Grand Admiral of Russia.

RICHMOND, VIRGINIA, 29th October, 1861. }

ADMIRAL:—Your letter reached me only a few days ago. It fills me with emotions.

In it I am offered the hospitalities of a great and powerful Empire, with the Grand Admiral of its fleets for patron and friend. Inducements are held out such as none but the most magnanimous of Princes could offer, and such as nothing but a stern sense of duty may withstand.

A home in the bosom of my family on the banks of the Neva, where, in the midst of books, and surrounded by friends, I am, without care for the morrow, to have the most princely means and facilities for prosecuting those studies and continuing those philosophical labors in which I take most delight.—All the advantages that I enjoyed in Washington, are, with a larger discretion, to be offered me in Russia.

Surely a more flattering invitation could not be uttered! Certainly it could not reach a more grateful heart. I have slept upon it. It is becoming that I should be candid, and, in a few words, frankly state the circumstances by which I find myself surrounded.

The State of Virginia gave me birth within her borders; among many friends, the nearest of kin, and troops of excellent neighbors, my children are planting their vine and fig tree; in her green bosom are the graves of my fathers; the political whirlpool from which your kind forethought sought to rescue me has already drawn her into a fierce and bloody war.

In 1778, when this State accepted the Federal Constitution and entered the American Union, she did so with the formal declaration that she reserved to herself the right to withdraw from it for cause, and resume those powers and attributes of sovereignty which she had never *ceded away*, but only "*delegated*," for certain definite and specified purposes.

When the President elect commenced to set at naught the very objects of the Constitution, and without authority of law, proceeded to issue his proclamation of 15th April last, Virginia in the exercise of that reserved right decided that the time had come when her safety, her dignity and honor required her to resume those "delegated" powers and withdraw from the Union. She did so. She then straightway called upon her sons in the Federal service to retire therefrom and come to her relief.

This call found me in the midst of those quiet philosophical researches at Observatory in Washington, which I am now, with so much delicacy of thought and goodness of heart, invited t. resume in Russia. Having been brought-up in the school of State-Rights, where we had for masters the greatest statesmen of America, and among them Mr. Madison, the wisest of them all, I could not, and did not hesitate. I recognized this call, considered it mandatory, and formally renouncing all allegiance to the broken Union, hastened over to the southside of the Potomac; there to renew to fatherland those vows of fealty, service, and devotion which the State of Virginia had permitted me to pledge to the Federal Union, so long only as by serving it, I might serve her.

Thus my sword has been tendered in her cause, and the tender has been accepted. Her soil is invaded, the enemy is actually at her gates, and here I am, contending as the fathers of the Republic did, for the right of self-government and those very principles for the maintenance of which Washington fought when this, his native State, was a colony of Great Britain.

The path of duty and of honor is therefore plain. By following it with the devotion and loyalty of a true sailor, I shall, I am persuaded, have the glorious and proud recompense that is contained in the "well done" of the Grand Admiral of Russia and his noble "companions in arms."

When the invader is expelled, and as soon thereafter as the State will grant me leave, I promise myself the pleasure of a trip across the Atlantic, and shall hasten to Russia, that I may there in person, on the banks of the Neva, have the honor and the pleasure of expressing to her Grand Admiral the sentiments of respect and esteem with which his oft repeated acts of kindness and the generous encouragements that he has afforded me in the pursuits of science has inspired his

Obedient servant,
M. F. MAURY,
Commander C. S. Navy.

To H. I. H. the Grand Duke Constantine, Grand Admiral of Russia, St. Petersburg.

The Fight at Guyandotte.

LYNCHBURG, Nov. 22.

Reliable accounts have been received of the fight at Guyandotte, on the 9th instant. Col. Clarkson's cavalry, of Floyd's Brigade, marched two hundred miles, to Guyandotte, and completely surprised the Yankee troops in the town—numbering two hundred and fifty, under the command of Col. Whaley; a traitor Congressman elected from Western Virginia. Col. Clarkson arrived at the village about eight o'clock in the morning, and took possession of the bridge which cut off the retreat of the enemy. The fight lasted about an hour, the Yankees fighting from houses and places of concealment. Clarkson took ninety-eight prisoners, killed forty, wounded fifty, and caused many to be drowned who attempted to escape by swimming the river. We captured two hundred and fifty Enfield rifles, five thousand dollars' worth of clothing, a number of cavalry horses, and various articles of plunder, valued at $25,000. We lost two killed and five wounded. After our troops left another detachment of the enemy took possession of the town and burned it.

LATEST NORTHERN ADVICES.

We are indebted to Dr. CONWELL, who returned yesterday from a trip North, for late newspapers, from which we make the following extracts.

The Capture of Mason and Slidell—Lord Lyons Belligerent.

WASHINGTON, Nov. 19.—Lord Lyons has not behaved like a diplomatist since the news of the capture of Messrs. Mason and Slidell. Unofficially, he is almost impertinent in his conversation. He assumes that there can be no question between his government and ours, that the United States must yield to the point in controversy, and will disavow the act of Capt. Wikes, and must return Mason and Slidell to the bosom of the only power which seems heartily to desire the dismemberment of this Republic.

Edward Everett, Edward M. Stanton and Reverdy Johnston have expressed the opinion that our right to take and keep Mason and Slidell is unquestionable.

Without waiting to ascertain how far the act of Capt. Wilkes is justified by the acknowledged and established principles of international law, some of the ministers from foreign parts have allowed themselves to be betrayed into expressions exhibiting infinitely more passion and prejudice than judgment and diplomatic intelligence.

The representative of one power openly declared that if Mason and Slidell had been taken from a Spanish ship, he would immediately have demanded his passports. Lord Lyons is said to have assumed a menacing tone, and to have declared that the prisoners must be given up, or ample reparation made for the offense offered to the dignity of the British crown. Nothing of this kind has ever been officially intimated. But in ordinary intercourse these expressions of disapprobation and hostility have been unguardedly made.

TORONTO, Monday, Nov. 18.—The *Globe* and *Leader* newspapers have severe articles to-day on the seizure of Mason and Slidell. The *Globe* says it will add to the strength and dignity of the American Government, if the captives are liberated without remonstrance from Britain. The *Leader* says it is an insult which the meanest Government on earth would not submit to.

WASHINGTON, Monday, Nov. 18.

To the Editor of the Cincinnati Enquirer:

After the exultation, caused by the arrest of Messrs. Slidell and Mason, had subsided, some commenced to see a blunder, but it is now generally believed that if Great Britain should remonstrate, our Government will disavow the act, but refuse to allow the rebel Commissioners to go on their mission. The miscellaneous documents of the would be embassadors were captured, but the confidential instructions were no doubt handed to their friends that went on to Europe.

The *National Intelligencer* has an article, believed to be semi-official, justifying the act of Captain Wilkes, quoting international law, and saying that he had not only a right to arrest Mason and Slidell, but also to seize the vessel, because of the violation of the proclamation of Queen Victoria announcing neutrality, and cites from Wheaton, Phillimore and other writers upon international law, fully establishing these points.

A Desire to Exchange Gov. Morehead for Charles Anderson.

WASHINGTON, Nov. 19.—A strong effort is being made here by prominent Kentuckians to procure an exchange of the Hon. Charles S. Morehead, of Kentucky, now confined at Fort Warren, for Chas. Anderson, of Texas, brother of Brigadier General Robert Anderson, who was seized and imprisoned by the rebels for his adherence to the Union.

Within the last few days immense trains of loaded army wagons, ambulances and artillery wagons have been going to Virginia.

Gen. Porter reports a considerable force two miles from Vienna, whose purpose, according to the rumors which reach him, is to sweep off all the forage beyond Fall's Church.

To-day an engine and cars ran out on the Orange and Alexandria Railroad beyond Springfield, the first time since the Bull Run battle.

A complimentary dinner was given to George D. Prentice, at the residence of Col. Forney. Secretary Cameron made a few remarks.

A Grand Review—The Rebels Impudent.

WASHINGTON, Nov. 20.—The grand review of our troops held to-day at Ball's Cross Roads, has attracted an immense crowd of spectators, and Washington is almost depopulated. Fifty thousand men are under review by Gen. McClellan, and their excellent condition elicits the warmest praise. The soldiers are ready for any service that may be required, and the reception they gave the General shows they have full faith in him as a leader.

Thirteen men of the 14th Brooklyn, New York, who were engaged in the picket fight on Monday, are still missing. It is feared they have fallen into the hands of the enemy. The rebels continue their correspondence with their friends in Washington, and their mail carriers in Virginia still defy the Government, carrying messages to and from Richmond without detention.

A ridiculous report is in circulation here to the effect that the administration has given assurances to the British Government that British vessels shall have access to the cotton ports before the expiration of the winter.

Rosecrans Heard From.

WASHINGTON, Nov. 19.—Dispatches were received to-day from Gen. Rosecrans, that the rebel Floyd, with his entire force, had abandoned his position near Gauley bridge, and had gone towards Richville, where it is understood he intended to make a stand. Gen. Rosecrans was still at Gauley bridge with his entire command. He contemplates making a forward movement as soon as necessary arrangements can be made. The health of the troops is excellent.

From Fortress Monroe—What Lieut. Worden Reports.

FORT MONROE, Nov. 19.—The flag of truce from Norfolk to-day brought down Lieut. Worden, who was taken as bearer of dispatches and imprisoned some time at Montgomery at the breaking out of the rebellion. He has been exchanged for Lieut. Sharp, of the rebels, who was taken at Hatteras Inlet, and has recently been confined on the frigate Congress at Newport News.

Lieut. Worden states that the intelligence of the arrest of Mason and Slidell caused great excitement among the rebels who rejoiced in the prospect of retaliation by England.

Two regiments from Georgia and South Carolina, have abandoned Roancke Island and blown up the battery, and gone home.

The rebel Congress met at Richmond on the 18th inst., without a quorum.

The rebels are strengthening their main battery at Sewall's Point, anticipating an attack.

The Fleet to be Divided—Cotton and Corn—Preparations.

NEW YORK, Nov. 20.—The Times' Port Royal correspondent says the fleet is to be divided, and transports to convey 6,000 troops are to open another port. The transports are now taking in water for fifteen days.

There is sufficient cotton here and on Pope Island unginned to make 3,000 bales. Corn houses are filled with about 10,000 bushels in the ear.

The steamships Delaware, Boston and Cosmopolitan, of the New York S. S. Company, have been chartered by the Government for three months. They will immediately commence coaling. Their destination is said to be Port Royal.

The U. S. transport Atlantic, lying at the foot of Canal street, is now coaling and taking in provisions for Port Royal. She will also carry troops.

The propeller gunboat Oneida, was launched at the Navy Yard this P. M.

The steamer Saxonia, which arrived today from Hamburg, brought as passengers, Prince C. Wrede, of Russia, and the Count de Valentine, of Trieste, who came to offer their services to the Government.

From Baltimore—Seizure of a Hotel.

BALTIMORE, Nov. 20.—Somewhat a sensation was produced this morning in the Western section of the city by the Provost Marshal sending a large force of police to Miller's hotel, and seizing the whole establishment and all its contents, including a large number of horses, the contents of the barroom, safe and vault.

The object of this movement is said to be to prostrate the mail arrangements of the rebel sympathizers here. It is supposed that from this hotel there has been regular communication kept up to West River, and thence to Virginia. The proprietors of the hotel have not been suspected generally, and are regarded as loyal men, but it is supposed that certain employees and lodgers have been receiving and transmitting letters South. A number of letters have been seized, but have not yet been examined.

Two parties, Wm. Hart and John Earl, have been arrested.

What Secretary Chase Says—Something Startling from the West Expected.

WASHINGTON, Nov. 18, 1861.—Secretary Chase returned yesterday. In addressing the bankers at New York on Saturday, he said that the Government saw their way clearly to quell the rebellion; that they had information which warrants them in saying that the public would soon hear glad tidings of success, more startling and more effective in their results than that from Port Royal and the West; that neither the Government nor General McClellan ever had the least idea of placing the army in winter quarters, but, on the contrary, the military plans all contemplate regular, systematic and energetic activity in pushing forward upon the rebels as prudence and judgment dictate; that the Government had ample funds to supply every liability until the 1st of February.

The Seward and Lyons Correspondence in Great Britain.

By the arrival of the steamer *City of Washington*, which left Liverpool on the 6th of November, we have information of how the late correspondence between Secretary Seward and Lord Lyons relative to the arrest of British subjects in this country was received. It made a very unfavorable impression. All the leading London papers assail Mr. Seward and our Government with great bitterness. It is reasonable to conclude that the arrest of Slidell and Mason from a British steamer will not improve the temper of these journals or of the British Government.—*Cin. Enq., 19th.*

THE SALT TRADE.—We learn that Messrs. McDaniel & Irby received orders yesterday for as many as 500 sacks of mountain salt for consumption by the people. They have agreed to furnish the article at $3 50 per sack, while the speculators are holding it at from $7 to $8, and Liverpool salt at $15 to $20. Of course, those who sell salt at more than $3 50 per sack are speculating on the necessities of the people. If one firm can sell at $3 50 all others can, and those who refuse or fail to do it, are grinding the people, in order to fill their pockets with lucre.

Lynchburg Republican.

TO THE LADIES OF

Kentucky and Northern Tennessee.

I have established at Bowling Green, Ky., a GENERAL HOSPITAL for the reception of the sick soldiers of the Central Division (Confederate States Army) of Kentucky. In an enterprise which is so intimately connected with the physical comfort, if not also the life, of the soldier, I feel that you are scarcely less interested than myself. I, therefore, beg to make a few practical suggestions to you, as to the manner in which you may serve those members of the army who are overtaken by accident or disease. A very efficient mode of rendering assistance to the inmates of the hospital is through the agency of RELIEF ASSOCIATIONS, such numbers of which are already in operation in the Confederate States. Can you not organize such Associations wherever they do not exist, and through them forward whatever may be contributed? Where, for any reason, such societies cannot be speedily put in operation, individuals should forward their donations direct to Bowling Green.

Among the articles of daily use in the hospital are the following:—

Bandages—1 inch wide, 1 yard long.
" 2 inches wide, 3 yards long.
" 2½ do do 3 do do
" 3 do do 4 do do
" 3½ do do 5 do do
" 4 do do 6 do do
" 2½ do do 9 do do

A few flannel bandages, two and a half inches wide and nine yards long, will be needed, and lint, scraped and ravelled.

Ring Pads and Cushions.

Cotton Batting and Cotton Wadding; fine Flax and Sponges.

Red Flannel, in the piece.

Bookbinders' Board, for Splints; pieces 18 inches by 14 inches.

Sadlers' Silk for Ligatures, Skeins waxed and wound on cards.

Sewing Needles, assorted, in cases; Linen, Thread, Tape and Scissors.

Adhesive Plaster, Camel Hair Pencils, Oiled Silk, Oiled Muslin, India Rubber and Gutta Percha Cloths, in the piece.

Wrapping Paper.

Cotton Bed Shirts—1½ yards long, 2 breadths of unbleached muslin, 1 yard wide, open one-half yard at the bottom, length of Sleeve three quarters yard, length of Arm Hole 12 inches, length of Collar 20 inches, length of Slit in front 1 yard, fastened with four tapes.

Loose Muslin Drawers—1½ yards long, with a breadth of 1 yard wide muslin in each leg, with a hem and drawing string round the waist and the bottom of each leg; length from waist to crotch on the back 22 inches, and in the front 18 inches, with 3 buttons and button holes.

Bed Sackings of ticking, 1 yard wide and 2 yards long.

Muslin sheets, 4 feet wide and 8 feet long.

Pilllow sacks of ticking, 16 inches wide and 30 inches long.

Pillow cases of muslin, one half yard wide, 1 yard long.

Old linen and cotton cloth, towels, old and new, rough and soft, old sheets, pillow cases, small pillows, old towels, coverlets, old shirts and drawers, old pants, old socks, old handkerchiefs, old jackets, pieces of white domestic, pieces of hickory shirting, country or home made jeans, for fall clothing, wool or woolen yarn, country or home-made blankets and counterpanes; blackberry and raspberry vinegar, crushed sugar, corn starch, sweet oil, can vegetables irish and sweet potatoes, peas and beans, arrowroot sago, tapicca, rice, eggs, chickens, game, brandy, whiskey, tobacco, crackers, biscuits, tea, cocoa, lemon syrup, plum and currant jellies, (small quantities,) oatmeal, flaxseed and flaxseed meal, wheat bran, corn meal, juice of beef, as stock for beef tea, put up in sealed cans, champagne in small bottles for cases of sudden sinking, china feeders of different sizes for administering nourishment where the head cannot be raised; bent glass tubes for similar use; castile soap for washing wounds, common soap, eye shades of green silk with tapes or elastics.

Those of you who live in and around the city of Bowling Green, can render invaluable assistance by acting as nurses at the hospital. The sick chamber is destitute of its chief solace unless graced by the presence of your sex No hand can smooth the sick man's pillow, or sooth his distress, other than your own. Such articles as you prepare should be packed in the most compact form and forwarded to Bowling Green, Ky., marked HOSPITAL STORES.

I am, with sincere respect,

D. W. YANDELL.

Surgeon C. S. A., and Medical Director of Central Division in Kentucky.

BOWLING GREEN, Ky., Sept. 28, 1861.

Recruits for Col. Hunt's Regiment.

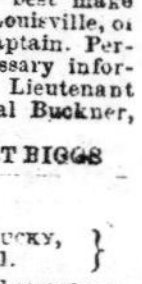

THE undersigned is authorized to raise a company for 12 months, to be attached to the 5th Kentucky Regiment, under command of Col. Thos. H. Hunt, now encamped near Bowling Green. Recruits will be furnished with Rifled Muskets, also with Kentucky blankets, and accouterments of the very best make and belonging to the Citizen Guards of Louisville, of which the undersigned was formerly Captain. Persons desiring to join can obtain the necessary information by applying to Capt. Johnson or Lieutenant Clay, at the Head Quarters of General Buckner, Bowling Green.

Oct. 17–dtf ROBERT BIGGS

NOTICE.

BY authority vested in me by the Commissary Department of the Confederate States of America, I hereby associate with me the firm of E. M. Bruce & Co., as the exclusive and only agents for the purchase of Cattle and Hogs, in the counties of Maury Williamson, Davidson, Robertson, Sumner and Wilson, in the State of Tennessee.

The business will be carried on at Nashville and Clarksville, in the name of E. M. Bruce & Co., for the benefit of said Confederate States.

R. T. WILSON.
Nashville, Nov. 9, 1861.

Nov. 23–2md and w.

RUNAWAY NEGR

IN the Simpson county, Ky., jail, a black fleshy negro, aged about 30 years, represents himself as belonging to Felix Tally, living near Sandersville, Sumner county, Tenn. No particular marks.

W. M. JOHNSON, Jailor.

Nov 18–d1m.

DAILY COURIER.

BOWLING GREEN, KY.

Tuesday Evening, Nov. 26, 1861.

Advertisements.

We do not design to occupy much of our space with advertisements, but will not object to placing one or two columns at the disposal of those friends who may think their interest will be advanced by availing themselves of the advantages of our large circulation.

Notice to Friends.

Those of our friends arriving from the dominions of King Lincoln who may have copies of late Louisville, Cincinnati or Northern papers, will confer a special favor on both ourselves and the public by leaving them at our office, in Nashville, with the least delay possible.

Notice to Correspondents.

We will esteem it a special favor if our friends and correspondents in the various divisions and camps in Kentucky—and especially in Polk's and Zollicoffer's commands—will furnish us with all the gossip and camp news proper to be placed before the public. We wish to make the COURIER both an interesting and welcome visitor to the tent of every soldier fighting our battles for independence. Their letters should be addressed to us at Nashville, Tenn.

Latest Papers.

Persons arriving at Bowling Green with late papers, will please send them to Col. Robert McKee, who may be found near Gen. Buckner's Headquarters.

GEORGE P. BUELL, one of the editors of the Cincinnati *Times*, was recently imprisoned for writing a letter from Louisville revealing movements which Gen. Sherman wished kept secret. He has been released, and writes home that Sherman has been relieved of his command. He adds—

The new commandant finds the troops scattered from one end of the State to the other, and Buell's first business will be to concentrate a powerful army, and move like a tornado upon Tennessee.

Send on your tornado, George! and old fellow, come along with it; but be prepared to remain here.

The Federal General MITCHELL, the "Star Gazer," has been induced to withdraw his resignation, and ordered to report to Gen. Buell. He did so, and was instructed to remain in Porkopolis till called for.

[Special to the Patriot.]

Later from Pensacola.

NO GREAT DAMAGE DONE.

RICHMOND, Nov. 23.—Via New Orleans—The Baltimore Sun of the 20th, reports the arrival of the steamer Norwegian at Portland, with dates of the 8th. No commercial news.

The London Times expresses the emphatic opinion that the reconstruction of the American Union is impossible.

A telegraph dispatch from Barnstown, on the 18th, says the locomotives and machinery belonging to the Baltimore and Ohio Railroad have been removed by the Confederates in the direction of Winchester and the track for twenty miles taken up.

The Washington Star, of the 19th, says the Navy Department expects to hear to-morrow from the Gulf, probably the taking of Pensacola and the Navy Yard by Col. Brown.

Northern journals are jubilant at the arrest of Mason and Slidell. They are to be sent to Boston. The journals consider that Great Britain will not regard their arrest as a matter of any serious consideration.

A gentleman just arrived at Richmond, says the Federal forces in the neighborhood of Alexandria is eighty regiments, many of which are skeletons, with seven Cavalry regiments, also skeletoned, and 19 batteries. He considers that indications favor an early engagement.

PENSACOLA, Nov. 25.—There has been no firing since 4 o'clock Sunday morning. It is now 1 o'clock P. M. and no news; everything is quiet. Two frigates and one sloop of war are outside. We are in momentary expectation of a continuance of the bombardment.

RICHMOND, Nov. 24.—Via New Orleans—The firing on both sides yesterday gradually ceased at night.

Col. Vellipgue was slightly woundad in the arm, but gallantly commanded at hisstpo as commander of Fort McRea

No casualties yesterday. The Navy Yard is but little injured.

The town of Warrington was set on fire by the Federal shells.

The above dispatch is the substance of an official dispatch, dated Pensacola, 6 o'clock yesterday evening.

MOBILE, Nov. 24.—The Advertiser's Pensacola correspondent, yesterday, says the steamer Time escaped and arrived safe.

Our loss up to 1 o'clock was five killed and 12 wounded.

One-half of the cannonade continued tonight presenting a magnificent spectacle. Several bombs exploded over and near Bragg's and Gladdin's staff, injuring none.

Bragg was constantly greeted wherever he went.

Three batteries and the Louisiana Infantry commanded by Capt. Wheat Batchfelder and Lieut. Maeder greatly distinguished themselves, and Capt. Vaubenthuysen's marine battery is entitled to like distinction for great efficiency.

One of the enemy's ships is thought to be severely damaged. She has not fired a gun to-day.

The Niagara was the only vessel engaged to day.

But three frigates are in sight.

Some old buildings were burned by the enemy's hot shot, but the loss amounts to nothing.

Shot passed through the hospital, but injured none, as the sick had been removed.

A number of shells fell in Fort Pickens, it is believed with much effect.

The enemy's land batteries are playing on the navy yard.

Billy Wilson's bullies are taking no part in the fight.

Our loss in killed and wounded is 16.

The Pensacola Press dispatch this morning says the firing ceased at 4 o'clock this morning, and has not been renewed up to 10½ o'clock.

Several buildings in Warrington are burnt.

The Niagara is reported disabled.

Six ships are now outside.

RICHMOND, Nov. 24, 1861.

A dispatch from Pensacola, dated Friday, 9 p. m., says the fight ceased this evening in consequence of darkness and the prevailing rain storm. The casualties to-day, amongst the Confederates, were four killed and ten wounded, mostly at Fort McRae, the enemy's firing resulting in but little damage to our men in the fortifications. We are unable to report the loss or damage done to the enemy.

The following official dispatch has been received:

O'BANNONSVILLE, near Pensacola, Nov. 23, 6 p. m.—The bombardment has just ceased. It continued throughout the day, very deliberately on both sides. We kept the ships at a respectful distance. Fort McRae has suffered, whilst yesterday's damage has been mostly repaired. Col. Villepigue was wounded in the arm by a fragment of shell, but maintained his post manfully in command of Fort McRae.

The town of Warrington is now on fire, caused by the enemy's hot shot.

The navy yard is not much damaged.—There has not been a casualty in it during the day. Our troops are in the highest spirits, and it has been difficult to restrain them.

NEW ORLEANS, Nov. 24, 1861.

Twenty-eight thousand troops were reviewed yesterday by Gov. Moore, Gens. Lovell and Ruggles. The line was seven miles long.

There was one regiment of 1,400 free colored men.

The military display was grand.

One company displayed a black flag.

RICHMOND, Nov. 25.—The bombardment continued all Saturday night, and until 4 o'clock the next morning. The enemy's sand batteries playing on the Navy Yard.

The Niagara is disabled.

Shells were seen to fall in Fort Pickens.

Six Lincoln ships outside.

The last dispatch, dated noon yesterday. Bombardment had not then been renewed.

RICHMOND, Nov. 24, (via New Orleans.)—One universal expression for Gen. Bragg and his glorious forces near Pensacola, for their prudent, gallant and noble conduct Friday and Saturday, in defending our lines and assailing the enemy's post and ships. From the President to the Cabinet, Congressmen, Heads of Departments, all classes of people in all sections, all are eloquent in praises of our noble commander and troops.

ANOTHER TRAGEDY ON ST. CHARLES STREET.—Yesterday afternoon that liveliest of all places in the city, St. Charles street, opposite the Hotel, was again the scene of a bloody drama, which resulted already in the death of one of the two men who participated in it, and will probably cost the other his life. Some time ago Coleman W. Stewart charged Thomas White, who is a steamboat man like himself, with being an Abolitionist. The latter heard of it and said that he would settle that question with Stewart, at the first apportunity. Stewart being informed of White's intention, armed himself with a knife. As for his enemy he provided himself with a revolver to carry on his design.

Yesterday afternoon the two adversaries met, for the first time since a difficulty had sprung between them, on St. Charles street, opposite the hotel. They drew simultaneously. White was stabbed three times and Stewart received three shots in his body.—The former's stabs are in the head, the arm and the side; the two first wounds being dreadful ones. Stewart was shot in the lip, the left breast and the head, and died on the spot, the two first shots being fatal. The body of the dead man and White were carried to the hospital.—*N. O. Picayune.*

The Brave At Home.

The maid who binds her warrior's sash,
And smiling, all her pain dissembles,
And while beneath the drooping lash
One starry tear-drop hangs and trembles—
Though Heaven alone records the tear,
And fame shall never know her story,
Her heart has shed a drop as dear
As ever dewed the field of glory.

The wife who girds her husband's sword,
'Mid little ones who weep and wonder,
And bravely speaks the cheering word,
What tho' her heart be rent asunder—
Doomed nightly in her dreams to hear
The bolts of war around her rattle,
Has shed as sacred blood as e'er
Was poured upon the plain of battle.

The mother who conceals her grief,
While to her breast her son she presses,
Then breathes a few brave words, and brief,
Kissing the patriot's brow she blesses,
With no one but her secret God
To know the pain that weighs upon her,
Sheds holy blood as e'er the sod
Received from Freedom's field of honor!

[From the Lynchburg Republican.]

Cool Impudence.

The subjoined circular, addressed by the parties to the Southern creditors of Devlin, Hudson & Co., New York, is decidedly one of the richest productions which this war has produced. None but these native and adopted Yankees could ever have invented such an astute mode of swindling the Confederacy out of its just rights under the Sequestration act. We are assured by respectable parties in this city, that as late as September last, the United States flag was floating over the house of Devlin, Hudson & Co., that the house was engaged extensively in making up clothing for the Federal army, and that it had made liberal donations towards conquering the South. This house had made a fortune out of the trade of the South, and a large debt was due them from our people.

To save this large indebtedness, the admirable scheme presented below was happily devised by these sharpers. Mr. Charles Hudson and Mr. Richard Robertson have come South, to pocket their Southern claims, while Devlin and Pulliam are to remain North and gather up there the profits of their fat Black Republican jobs! Very handsome arrangement, indeed, if the people of the South were all fools. But as there is some smartness left amongst us, even since our separation from the Yankees, we predict that this scheme to put money into a Black Republican house of the North, will most signally fail; and if Messrs. Hudson & Robertson are not very careful they will be assigned to winter quarters in some commodious tobacco factory in the South for their consummate impudence. They never throught of coming South until the Sequestration act touched their pocket nerves, and they have only come here now to make money out of a section which they have long ago deserted, and whose institutions they have doubtless helped to injure and destroy.

HUNTSVILLE, ALA., Sept. 24.

We beg leave to inform you of the dissolution of the late firm of Devlin, Hudson & Co., of the city of New York, on the 14th day of this present month, September, in which firm we were one-half owners of all the profits and assets, and have sold and transferred to our late partners all of our interest in the stock of goods on hand, and all debts due said firm, except those within the Confederate States, and they (our late partners,) have sold, assigned, and delivered to us all debts and demands of every nature due said firm within the Confederate States.

In consideration of the fact, that we are both native born citizens of Virginia, and having now become permanent residents and citizens of the Confederate States, in due forms of law, we are advised by eminent council that we are entitled to collect and control all debts due our said late firm, and that our interest will in no wise be affected by "Sequestration Act" of the Confederate States Congress, approved the 10th day of August last.

At a proper time we shall call upon you with statement and evidence of your indebtedness to our late firm, and hope until then you will not deem it necessary to report any amounts due the late firms of Devlin, Hudson & Co., Robertson & Hudson, or Robertson, Hudson & Pulliam, to the Receivers for the Confederate States as due to "alien enemies," believing that we shall be able to satisfy you of our right to collect the same before demanding payment.

Very respectfully,
CHARLES C. HUDSON,
RICHARD S. ROBERTSON.

P. S.—Please address for the present Charles C, Hudson, Memphis, Tennessee, or Richard S. Robertson, Huntsville, Alabama, on any business of our late firms.

C. C. H.
R. S. R.

Seizure of a China Vessel as a Privateer.

The following dispatch from San Francisco gives the news of the seizure of the schooner Neva as a privateer:

SAN FRANCISCO, Nov. 12.—The privateer schooner Neva, from China, has been seized here by Captain Peaso, of the revenue cutter Mary.

The reason of the seizure of the Neva by the Mary arose from certain information having been given to the naval officer in the China seas that the former was being fitted out at Shanghai as a privateer.

The American men of war have left that station for home, with the exception of one small vessel, which remains behind at the earnest request of American firms. This vessel has gone suddenly to Shanghai, owing to the purchase there of a schooner for the purpose, it was believed, of being armed as a privateer under the Confederate flag.

Jeff. Davis' Fast-Day in Louisville.

We are informed by a gentleman just from Louisville, that the day set apart by President Davis for fasting and prayer, was quite generally observed by the Southern Rights citizens of Louisville.—Our informant saw a procession of Sunday-school children that day, and he was quite surprised that they were not arrested by the Yankee authorities there. Public service was held in one of the churches at which the Louisville *Democrat* was exceedingly indignant, and gave vent to its rage in the following editorial:

We are credibly informed that on Friday last—Jeff Davis' day set apart for fasting and prayer—one church in our city mustered a small congregation to offer up their prayers in behalf of the traitor and his cause. We have very little inclination to criticise the devotional exercises of any denomination, and much less to envy the heart of those who engage in the religious services asked by Davis, in behalf of his unholy and wicked schemes. It looks like the veriest mockery in view of the rapine and murder committed by Davis' followers, wherever they have obtained power.—When we remember how men have been banished from their homes, or thrown into prison for being loyal to the Government, and obedient to the laws of the country, in the South, is it not a burning shame that there are those in this community, enjoying the protection of the law and the benefits of the Government, who debase their nature, and insult their Maker, by appeals to his throne in behalf of those who are despoiling the land? Their disloyalty is unquestionable. They are in the midst of a peaceable and law-abiding people—hence they are undisturbed.

What would be the fate of a congregation of law-abiding Union men in the extreme South, on a day of national thanksgiving appointed by the President of the United States, who would assemble, and, in prayer, ask Divine interposition in behalf of our bleeding country? They would share the prison cells with the law-abiding people in the South now *in durance vile*—not for breaking the law, but because they would not break it by engaging with them in the damnable treason they are daily practising.

Let them pray, if they can, for the success of those who would burn our city and devastate the country for those who, finding Kentucky ever loyal to the Union, bring battle to her borders, and who desire to make her again "the dark and bloody ground." If they have prayers that can reach the throne in heaven, "Father, forgive them, for they know not what they do."

The Battle at Piketon, Ky.

The Tazewell (Va.) Democrat, of the 16th inst, furnishes the following reliable particulars of the fight at Piketon, Ky:

On the 6th instant (Nov.) Captain John May, in command of some 300 Kentucky militia, set out upon a scouting expedition. Tee confederates had advanced but a few miles when they descried in the distance a large column of United States forces marching in the direction of Piketon. The captain immediately posted his men on a hill-side near the road, and awaited the approach of the enemy in ambush. The confederates occupying a good position permitted the U. S. forces, afterwards ascertained to number 1,500, to approach, when the command "to fire" was given. The first volley from these trusty gentlemen brought every Yankee officer to the ground. The firing was repeated so rapidly that from two to three hundred of the enemy were killed before they could recover from their panic sufficiently to order a flank movement. The confederates now seeing the danger of being surrounded and overpowered by the superior force of the enemy, fell back in good order, the Yankees also retiring in the direction whence they came. It is said that Capt. May kept two men loading for him while he fired at the enemy, and that a Yankee fell at every shot. Another gentleman, posted behind a large rock would, load his gun and mount the rock to fiee; he repeated this manœuvre some 12 or 14 times, when the enemy observing him, demolished his breastwork by a cannon ball, yet he escaped unhurt. This fight took place at Mr. James Lane's a few miles west of Piketon.

The Confederate loss was one or two killed and from ten to fifteen wounded, which forms a striking contrast with the loss of the enemy. We gather the above interesting facts from Kentuckians, now in our village, who participated in the fight.

The Democrat also furnishes the following items:

GEN. HUMPHREY MARSHALL.

This distinguished Kentuckian is now in our village. He will remain a short time to collect men and supplies for a contemplated expedition against the cats-paws of despotism who despoil the fairest portion of his native State.

In addition to Gen. Marshall, there are many refugees here from Kentucky, who have been compelled to leave home in the night or by stealth to avoid being murdered, imprisoned or forced to take the oath of allegiance to the Lincoln Dynasty.

FEDERALS ADVANCING.

There was at last advices a force of about 8,000 Lincolnites in Pike county, Ky. It is easy to divine the cause of their pressing on in the direction of the Pound Gap, and Va. and Ky. Turnpike. The possession of the Saltworks and V and T. Railroad would be to these rapacious cut-throats and robbers, prizes of no ordinary value. While writing a messenger brings the startling news that a band of marauders from this force has invaded Buchanan, Va., and captured and carried off Mr. Denny Coleman and three or four of the Mr. Ratliff's, respectable citizens of that county.

CUMBERLAND GAP EXPEDITION.

[Special correspondence Cincinnati Commercial.]

A Specimen of Sublime Audacity—How it was Snubbed—Cumberland Gap Obstructed and Deserted by the Rebels—Big Creek Gap also Obstructed and Deserted—A Retrograde Movement—We go back to Crab Orchard in Haste.

HEADQUARTERS WILDCAT BRIGADE, London, Ky., Nov. 13, 1861.

The Postmaster at London was offended at my criticism upon the skin-flints of this section, and put on a few atmospheres about it. He had the sublime audacity to refuse to forward any more letters for me by the United States mail, unless they were first submitted for his revision. The mail carrier for the 17th Ohio gave him a gentle admonition about the consequences of tampering with the mails, and my next letter was forwarded. The case was reported at the Headquarters of the 17th Ohio, and the Colonel sent an officer to warn his excellency that any attempt to interfere with the mails would be followed by his consignment to the county jail. The Postmaster really seems to be a very clever fellow, but he lacks discretion. I was not aware, however, that my criticism applied to his particular friends. But I am bound to insist that while there are many hospitable and liberal men here, there are some whose avarice is more promtnently developed than their patriotism, The former denounce the latter more severely thad we do.

WILD CAT AGAIN.

The communication from your Harrodsburg correspondent, to which I alluded in a late letter, caused considerable excitement. I observe by responses that the accounts concerning the number of rebels killed and wounded vary as much as possible upon a limited pattern. I have again endeavored to learn the exact number buried by our troops, and find that my last statement was about correct. The entire number found dead on the field was *eleven*, and *forty-two* wounded received surgical aid at two houses at Laurel Bridge, where Zollicoffer encamped the night after he retreated from Wild Cat. This agrees precisely with the report of a rebel officer which was first published in a Nashville paper, and was subsequently copied by the Commercial. A few others were wounded, but were not considered fit for the hospital. I hope this paragraph will conclude the Wild Cat question, although it is a prolific theme in the midst of profound stagnation.

PROSPECTS.

There is a current rumor in camp that the appeals of prominent Tennesseeans for an immediate movement into East Tennessee is about to be granted by the War Department. Hon. Andy Johnson and Hon! Horace Maynard have been urging this movement vehemently, as essential to the salvation of the Union men of East Tennessee. Readers are supposed to be familiar with their arguments. I will not, therefore, recapitulate. But the rumor of movements caused much enthusiasm among the Tennesseeons, whose anxiety to return to their homes is intense. This desire is paramount. Every other feeling is merged in it.

I place no confidence in the report, because we cannot move. This column is not strong enough to invade Tennessee. To be sure there is no enemy at the Gap, excepting a small garrison, and if we should move forward it is not likely there would be much figting at that point. Our latest information from the Gap,—believed by the General to be perfectly reliable,—is that the rebels have obstructed the Gap with large masses of rock and fallen timber, to an extent which makes it impassable, either by us or by themselves. Advices are also received that they have obstructed Big Creek Gap, below Williamsburg, in a similar manner, and that the main portion of Zollicoffer's forces have moved to some other point not known.

PRESTO.

An order has just been issued ordering every regiment in this brigade to move at 8 o'clock this evening. The object of it is not generally understood. Those to whom it has been explained are surprised and chagrined. The column is ordered to move *back* as rapidly as possible to Crab Orchard, and to transport all the sick who can be removed. The order was predicated upon an order from Gen. Thomas, who forwarded it by express relays from Crab Orchard. It is reported that a heavy column, divested from Buckner's command, is running rapidly forward upon Somerset, to cut us off. Thus, you perceive, a big scare is at the bottom of the retrograde operation. It is not necssary to speculate on the subject. I suspect, however, that this is but a brilliant cover for the ridiculous termination of the Great Cumberland Gap Expedition. It may have been devised, also, as a decent apology for recalling the Tennessee regiments. I have been disposed to think Gen. Thomas was responsible for the failure of this enterprise, but it is now apparent that the late commander of the Department of the Cumberland was the responsible party.

W. D. B.

CAMP NEAR CRAB ORCHARD, KY., Nov. 15, 1861.

After a march of almost unparalleled severity, considering there was no apparent necessity for it, part of the Wildcat Brigade arrived this evening at a point within two miles of Crab Orchard, and went into camp. Many of our poor fellows are still struggling and straggling along the road, painfully striving to reach a harbor of rest. *This march was as disastrous as a battle and defeat.* I have no time now, even if I were not severely fatigued, to depict the wretched picture. I will do it hereafter.

The 14th, 17th, and 38th Ohio will encamp here. The Tennesseeans and 3d Kentucky regiment were ordered back to London, after the advance of the former have reached a point three miles beyond Mt. Vernon. *Many of the Tennesseeans went back before orders were issued to that effect, proclaiming their intention to return home. Our march has temporarily disabled the entire brigade, and large numbers will be in hospital in a day or two.* So ends the "great Cumberland Gap Expedition."

Last night the 38th Ohio encamped five miles south of London. During the night a decayed tree was blown down in camp, and several men were dangerously wounded—one said to be fatally hurt.

W. D. B.

Commercial.

Produce, Grain, Groceries, &c.

CORRECTED BY
B. B. CONNOR & BRO.,
Commission and Produce Merchants,
No. 5 College Street, Nashville.

Nashville Prices Current.

ARTICLES.		PRICES.
ALCOHOL	℔ gal	2 00@
BAGGING—Hemp	℔ yd	.. @ 25
Cotton	℔ yd	.. @ ..
BALE ROPE—Manilla	℔ lb	.. @ ..
Kentucky	℔ lb	.. @ 20
BACON—Shoulders	℔ lb	.. @ 23
Hams	℔ lb	.. @ 25
Sides	℔ lb	.. @ 23
BUTTER—Prime	℔ lb	38 @ 40
Common	℔ lb	.. @ ..
CANDLES—Star	℔ lb	.. @ 50
Sperm	℔ lb	.. @ ..
Parafine	℔ lb	.. @ ..
Tallow	℔ lb	.. @ 34
CHEESE—Western Reserve	℔ lb	.. @ ..
English Dairy	℔ lb	.. @ ..
COFFEE—Java	℔ lb	.. @ ..
Rio	℔ lb	.. @ 90
Laguyra	℔ lb	.. @ ..
COTTON YARNS—700 & 800	℔ doz	.. @ 11
600	℔ doz	.. @ 12
500	℔ doz	.. @ 13
400	℔ doz	.. @ 14
FLOUR—Superfine	℔ bbl	7 25@ ..
Extra	℔ bbl	.. @ 9 25
Sack	℔ 100 lbs	.. @ 4 50
FISH—Mackerel, No. 1	℔ bbl	.. @ 18
" No. 2	℔ bbl	.. @ 16
" No. 3	℔ bbl	.. @ 14 00
GRAIN—Corn	℔ bush	70 @ 75
Oats	℔ bush	.. @ 80
Rye	℔ bush	.. @ 85
Barley	℔ bush	.. @1 25
Wheat, Red	℔ bush	90@1 04
Wheat, White	℔ bush	1 @1 50
GUNNY BAGS—New		.. @ 36
Second Hand		25 @ ..
HIDES—Southern dry salted	℔ lb	16 @ ..
Green	℔ lb	6 @ ..
IRON—Tennessee Bar	℔ lb	6 @ ..
Band	℔ lb	8 @ 8½
Hoop	℔ lb	9½@ 10½
Sheet	℔ lb	.. @ ..
Boiler	℔ lb	8½@ ..
" Pig	℔ ton	80 @ ..
Pittsburg Bar	℔ lb	.. @ ..
LARD—Kegs	℔ lb	.. @ 25
Barrels	℔ lb	.. @ 22
LEATHER—Sole; oak tanned	℔ lb	35 @ ..
Skirting	℔ lb	.. @ ..
Hemlock Sole	℔ lb	.. @ ..
Harness	℔ lb	.. @ 35
MOLASSES—Barrels	℔ gal	33 @ 35
½ Barrels	℔ gal	.. @ ..
NAILS—20d to 4d	℔ lb	8 00@ 10 11
OILS—Linseed	℔ gal	.. @ 2 11
Lard	℔ gal	.. @ 3 12
Tanner's	℔ gal	1 50@ 2 25
RICE—Prime and Choice	℔ lb	4½@ 4¾
SALT—Fine sack	℔ sack	.. @ 12 00
Coarse sack	℔ sack	.. @ 11 50
Barrel	℔ bush	4 00@ ..
SUGAR—New Orleans hhd	℔ lb	5½@ 9
" bbl	℔ lb	6½@ 10
Havana white	℔ lb	.. @ 13
Loaf	℔ lb	20 @ 22
Crushed	℔ lb	20 @ 22
Powdered	℔ lb	18 @ 19
SEEDS—Clover	℔ bush	.. @ $13
Millet	℔ bush	.. @ ..
Timothy	℔ bush	.. @ 5
Herds Grass	℔ bush	1 50@ ..
Orchard	℔ bush	2 00@ ..
Blue Grass, Stripped	℔ bush	1 75@ ..
Blue Grass, Clean	℔ bush	2 00@ ..
Hungarian	℔ bush	1 50@ ..
Flax	℔ bush	.. @ ..
SPIRITS—Whisky—Country	℔ gal	1 25@1 50
Nashville	℔ gal	90 @1 00

Bank Note and Exchange List.

CORRECTED BY THE TRADER'S BANK.

TENNESSEE.

Bank of America	75c dis	Buck's Bank	par
" Chattanooga	par	City "	par
" Commerce	par	Commercial Bank	2 dis
" Knoxville	par	Dandridge "	par
" Memphis	par	Farmers' "	par
" Middle Tenn.	par	Merchants' "	par
" Nashville	par	Northern "	par
" Paris	par	Ocoee Bank	par
" Tennessee	par	Planters "	par
" Tazwell	—	River "	par
" Claiborne	—	Southern "	2 dis
" the Union	par	Sh'lbyv'e "	2 dis
" West Tenn.	par	Traders' "	par
" East	—	Union "	par

BROKEN AND WORTHLESS.

Agricultural Bank, Brownsville.
Central Bak of Tennessee, Nashville.
Farmers' and Mechanics' Bank, Memphis
Mechanics' Bank, Memphis.
Memphis Savings Institution,
Exchange Bank, Murfreesboro'.
Miners' and Manufacturers' Bank, Knoxville
Bank of Trenton.
Bank of Jefferson, Dandridge,

FOREIGN

GEORGIA.		MISSOURI.	
All Old Banks,	½ dis	Missouri Banks	no sale
New Banks	uncertain	ILLINOIS.	
SOUTH CAROLINA.		Illinois Banks	no sale
S. Carolina Banks	½ dis	NORTH CAROLINA.	
LOUISIANA.		N. Carolina Banks	5 dis
N. Orleans Banks	par	VIRGINIA.	
ALABAMA.		Virginia Banks	1 dis
Mobile Banks	2 dis	INDIANA.	
Other Banks	2 dis	State Bank	no sale
KENTUCKY.		OHIO.	
Kentucky Banks	6a8 prem	State Bank	5 dis

Exchange.

	SELLING.
New York Sight very scarce	none selling
Boston "	none selling
Philadelphia "	none selling
Baltimore "	none selling
New Orleans "	1 to 4 prem
Cincinnati "	none
Louisville, "	11 to 17 prem

Specie.

Gold, American 25to26pr | Silver 1gto12pr

Memphis Market.

MEMPHIS, November 22, 1861.

COTTON—40 bales sold to a manufacturer at 7½c. Receipts none. Shipments 68 bales.

TOBACCO—We did not hear of a sale. Prices nominal as quoted below:

MEMPHIS TOBACCO QUOTATIONS.

Inferior Lugs	2½@3½
Good Lugs	4 @4½
Common Admitted	5½@6½
Fair	7 @7½
Fine	8 @9
Choice and Selections	— @—

WHEAT—A good demand again prevailed at unchanged prices. Sales 220 bushels fair red at $1 75, 210 prime, in two lots, at $1 90; 83 fair at $1 95, 66 inferior at $1 45, and 25 do. at $1 60.

FLOUR—The market continues dull, with prices altogether nominal. Small sales only at $10 00@10 50 for extra. Nothing doing in superfine.

RYE—In good demand and firm. Sales 450 bushels at $1 70; 60 choice, sacks returned, at $1 75, and 50 sacks included, at $1 85.

CORN—Market quiet, with small sales at 90@95c for mixed and white. Supplies light.

HAY, OATS AND BRAN—Stocks light. No transactions reported.

POTATOES—300 bushels choice sold at $1 80, and 60 inferior at $1 65.

SUGAR—Demand moderate. Sales 38 hhds at 7½ a 8c for common and centrifugal.

MOLASSES—227 bbls sold in three lots at 22½@23c.

WHISKY—Is in good demand at $1 00 ℔ gallon for rectified.

New Orleans Markets.

NEW ORLEANS, Tuesday, Nov. 19, 1861

COTTON—The sales to-day comprised 60 bales.

TOBACCO—Nothing reported.

SUGAR—The supply is liberal, and the demand is limited at previous prices. About 500 hhds sold at 1@1½ for inferior, 1¾@2¾ for common to good common, 3@3¾ for fair to fully fair, 5½@7½ for clarified yellow, and 6¾@7c for clarified white.

MOLASSES—The receipts are liberal, but with a good demand fuller prices are realized. About 3000 bbls sold at 15@16c for common fermenting and dark, and 17@18c for prime to choice. Also, 300 half bbls at 19@20 and 21c for prime

DAILY COURIER.

BOWLING GREEN, KY.,

Tuesday Evening, Nov. 26, 1861.

The Signing of the "Declaration" at Russellville.

The Convention at Russellville resolved that the Declaration passed by it and the plan of Government adopted should be enrolled on parchment and signed by the members.

Having been enrolled as ordered, it was brought into the Hall in which the Convention assembled, late on the evening of the last day of the session, and spread out on a desk, conveniently placed, for receiving the signatures of the loyal men of whom that body was composed.

It was a solemn hour. The men there met together in solemn council to devise means to preserve the independence of a commonwealth and perpetuate the liberties they had inherited from a past generation, had acted in full view of all the responsibilities they were assuming and of all the perils and possible consequences of the steps they were taking. Resolved not to be slaves, to live as freemen live or die as freemen die, to transmit to their children all the blessings of a constitutional government or dying leave behind them the glorious record of their struggles against despotism, to incite those who shall come after them to glorious deeds in the cause of freedom, these men had met together to pledge to each other "their lives, their fortunes' and their sacred honor" as soldiers in the sacred cause of liberty, and before the world and in the presence of Almighty God to bid defiance to tyranny and usurpation all the powers by which it is sought to establish over them the hateful domination of folly and fanaticism.—They had counted the cost. They had considered the dangers. They had calmly contemplated the magnitude of the contest. As men with stout hearts and strong arms and indomitable will and unconquerable spirit they had thought of the wrongs they had suffered and the injuries they had received and the aggravated evils that must follow submission to these wrongs and injuries, of the duty they owed to themselves, mankind, and posterity, of the inestimable value of liberty and the galling chains of slavery, and with determined purpose and high resolve they had acted, and their action, worthy of such men in a cause, lacked only their signatures to make it complete. As men they had met together—as men they had acted—as men they were about to conclude their labors. If there was a doubting, wavering, timid spirit in the Convention, the sight of that parchment, and the knowledge that the signatures to it would stand forever the record of the part borne by each in the act of emancipation and of the responsibility assumed by each for that act, would cause him to hesitate long before putting his name to the work done by those of whom he had been one. With interest and anxiety we looked around the Hall to see if there was one faint-hearted or recreant man in that assembly of freemen. Thank God! we saw no indication of a desire to evade this test of the sincerity, the faith, and the courage of those who had participated in the proceedings of the Convention. There was no hanging back, no hesitation,—not a halting step, nor the tremor of a muscle. All had been in earnest. Each was ready to make good his pledge of life, liberty, and fortune. Not a man shrank from incurring the penalties of death and confiscation of property proclaimed by a corrupt and factious legislative majority against all who dare to be free.

It was a solemn and impressive scene, at once to make sad the heart of the friend of mankind, and to renew our faith in the capacity of man for self-government,—to bow our heads in sorrow and shame as we think that a Declaration of Independence could be necessary in this age and this country, and to overwhelm us with gratitude, to the Giver of all Good that there is yet enougn of the love of liberty and of fearless, self-sacrificing patriotism left among men to proclaim resistance to tyranny, regardless of consequences. It was a solemn, inspiring, glorious scene, calculated to give mankind a better opinion of itself, to strike terror to the heart of tyranny, to inspire the struggling devotees of freedom with new courage and to nerve their arms for deeds of noble daring, worthy of the descendants of Revolutionary heroes. Men with bowed frames and heads silvered over with the frosts of three quarters of a century, grew erect with conscious power, and their eyes glowed with the fire of youth as they wrote their names with steady hands in bold and regular characters, to the Declaration and Ordinance of Separation, and young men, gathering inspiration from the scene, felt their blood flow faster, and their hopes run higher, and new strength was given to their arms and new courage poured into their hearts, as they enrolled themselves among the few, the immortal ones, whose names were not born to die.

The Declaration of Independence had been passed. The Ordinance of Separation had been adopted. The Plan of the Provisional Government had been agreed to. The work for which the Convention had met was done. One by one the list of counties was gone through with, and as each county was called its members deliberately put their names to the acts of the Convention. It was finished. The Convention adjourned. The members parted, each to go his way, and never again to meet until the Great Day, when the just and unjust shall be gathered together at the bar of the Eternal Jehovah to account for the deeds done in the body.

The Provisional Government—A Subject for its Consideration.

The Provisional Government has been organized in this city under the plan adopted by the Russellville Convention. Governor JOHNSON has taken the oath of office and entered upon the discharge of the very important, very responsible, and very delicate duties of the Chief Executive office of the Commonwealth. The Council have met and organized by the election of WILLIS B. MACHEN as Chairman. By the time this reaches our readers, the Governor's Message will have been delivered, and the Government will be vigorously at work.

To the hands of the Governor and Council the dearest interests of the people and the safety of the Commonwealth are entrusted. Upon their ability, prudence, and zeal very much depends. The responsibilities they will have to assume, the obstacles they must necessarily encounter, the consequences that follow their action are of such a nature as to call out whatever of statesmanship may be possessed by our new rulers. The people of Kentucky know enouno of the men to whom their affairs are now committed to trust them most implicitly, and to the fullest extent, for, with a few exceptions, they have made records that entitle them to the confidence of their fellow citizens.

The Bill of Rights in the Constitution of Kentucky declares "that all power is inherent in the people, and all free governments are founded on their authority, and instituted for their peace, safety, happiness, security, and the protection of property;" and these are the ends to secure which this Government has been organized, and for their advancement all its labors should be, and will be, directed.

The difficulty of accomplishing these objects consists mainly in the fact that a portion of the State is overrun by Abolition armies from Indiana, Ohio, and other Northern States, by which all rights of person and property are disregarded, and many of those entitled to our protection are subjected by the power of force to the grossest indignities and compelled to submit to the greatest outrages and wrongs. Until these vandal hordes shall be driven from our soil, *direct* protection cannot be given to our citizens who are so unfortunate as to be within their lines. The Provisional Government has not the power to arrest and punish those lawless men in Jefferson and McCracken counties, for instance, who violate the laws of the State and rob, plunder, and otherwise maltreat and injure peaceful and law abiding citizens. It cannot cause the arrest and punishment of the men who kidnapped Morehead, Barr, and Durrett, carried them into another State, and incarcerated them in a foreign dungeon.

In those counties overrun by Lincoln's armies, all civil law is suspended by force, and mob law administered according to the caprice or passions of new-fledged military subordinates prevails. In them, the citizen is allowed no redress for wrongs suffered, and has no remedy for evils inflicted upon him. He points in vain to the Constitution and laws of the United States, or of his own State, for the tyrant and usurper whose will is supreme and his word absolute wherever his forces have power to enforce his edict, regards neither one nor the other. He appeals to the courts of justice, but they, corrupted by gold and influence, or intimidated by power, are dumb, and impotent as dumb. His spirit may be as proud and unbroken as that of the wild horse in the deserts of Arabia, his will as unconquerable as that which sustained his fathers in the doubtful conflicts of former ages, but, surrounded by the gleaming banners and glistening bayonets of the oppressor, he is as helpless as the child at its mother's breast; and for the present this government cannot strike from her limbs the manacles which tyranny has riveted on them.

But this Government owes such protection to its citizens all over the State as may be in its power to give them; and we trust and believe its powers will be exerted to the utmost in their behalf.

How protection to any extent may best be given to these unfortunate Kentuckians is a question which we believe the Governor and Council will well, and wisely decide; and to their wisdom and discretion we are content to leave it.—But, as the organ of the people rather than of the Government, we feel at liberty to say, that it is the universal desire that retaliatory measures shall be adopted, through which alone it seems possible to strike at the adherents of LINCOLN'S infernal administration. There are among us many who have sustained that administration and justified all its outrages, claiming to owe allegiance to the government of which it is the head. In defending, excusing, or apologizing for the illegal arests of such citizens as MOREHEAD, STANTON, and others now imprisoned with them, they have put it out of their power to complain if this government should arrest and hold them as hostages for the release or safety of the Kentuckians confined at Forts Warren and Lafayette. Even if they should protest against this government as irregular and revolutionary, and against its acts as illegal, it would not mend their cases, for the arrest and imprisonment of the parties we have referred to was also clearly illegal, there being no warrant for it in the Constitution or the laws. It is possible, aye, probable, that the prompt arrest of a number of these disloyal men equal to that of those heretofore illegally seized by the minions of the usurper in this State, would secure the release of the latter; and a distinct announcement that for every Kentuckian who may hereafter be deprived of his liberty by the Federal authorities without authority of law, one of the adherents of that government in the reach of the Provisional authorities will be arrested, may be the means of giving that protection to the people of the State which the Constitution guarantees and the laws were intended to secure.

This matter is worthy of the early consideration of the Provisional Government, to whose attention we commend it with perfect confidence that their action will be prompt, prudent and wise.

A GENERAL ENGAGEMENT EXPECTED.

LORD LYONS AND MR. SEWARD.

Bombardment Not Renewed.

[*Special dispatch to the Patriot.*]

RICHMOND, Nov. 25, 1861.

I am just telegraphed, by previous arrangement, to come to Centreville. The indications of a general engagement are unmistakable.

A report from Washington states that the relations between Lord Lyons and Mr. Seward are very doubtful.

The bombardment at Fort Pickens has not been renewed to-day.

FROM CAIRO.

The Important part the Gunboats Played in the Belmont Battle—The Appearance of the Battle Field Next Day, &c.

[Special Correspondence of Missouri Democrat.]

CAIRO, ILL., Nov. 12 1861.

THE GUNBOATS.

The gunboats Tyler and Lexington were ordered to drop down to Fort Jefferson on the evening of the 7th. On the morning of the 8th, at 7 o'clock, they dropped down to Lucas Bend with the transports; after landing the men, they took up a position within 1½ miles of the rebel batteries and opened upon them, playing upon them with 6 and 8 inch shell. After firing some thirty rounds of shell they withdrew, as the enemy had got the range, and their missiles were falling thick and fast across our decks and alongside, splashing and dashing in the water, and cutting fantastic *ricochets* through the air; they used upon us then a 94-pound rifled cannon. The Tyler at this time threw a 32-pound shot right near Gen Polk's headquarters, as we have since ascertained from a prisoner.

A NEW SHELL FROM THE ENEMY.

Returning to the transports, we were still within reach of their rifle cannon, and at this time the enemy fired a 94 pound shell, apparently at Gen. Grant and his staff, who were upon the river bank. It passed with a most terrific whiz right over their heads, and buried itself *ten feet* into the solid earth, 100 yards distant. The shell—a perfect curiosity—did not explode, and was dug out the bank and is now on exhibition here. It is 18 inches long, 6 inches in diameter, a sort of bolt of iron, (a cannon within a cannon;) with a brass percussion fuse on the end, that generally explodes on the slightest impression being made upon it. This shell does not answer the description of any known modern or ancient missile of warfare. It is a mongrel between a Hotchkiss shell and some of the English patents. It is said it was made in Memphis. It was fired from a cannon (rifle) 8 tons in weight. The piece on the shell that fits the grooves of the cannon is about 2 inches in depth, and is made of brass and cast to fit the grooves. My informant told me he saw where one of these shells had been thrown over 3 miles, and took effect on a large oak tree twenty inches in diameter, and it fairly cut the tree down as though it had been a sapling.

WE DROP DOWN AGAIN.

About twelve o'clock, by the firing of musketry—of which there was a continuous roar—we knew our troops were having hot work with the enemy, and seeing reinforcement forming on the distant bluffs, we again dropped down the stream and shelled their batteries for three quarters of an hour, with what execution we could not tell, but the shell burst immediately over their heads. The Tyler again succeeded in putting another 32 pound shot near or into General Polk's headquarters, and received in exchange a 24 pound ball through her upper bulwarks, passing diagonally through upper to lower deck, and in its passage took a sailor's head off; fatally wounding another, and after bounding across deck, finished its career by knocking down a large heavy stanchion. This ball is now a trophy.

AGAIN WITH THE TRANSPORTS.

We again withdrew to the transports as one regiment had cut its way through the enemy and was embarking on the transports.

After nearly all had embarked, Gen. Grant ordered the gun boats to drop below the transports, as the enemy were coming upon our rear in large force—and they were plainly visible from the deck of the Lexington. As soon as they discovered we were dropping down they went into the woods, and very soon reappeared abreast of our transports, in a cornfield, and immediately came up to the river bank, six or eight deep, and when within one hundred feet of our transports commenced firing on us. Our men returned the fire and the sound of the musketry was like the explosion of fire crackers on a Fourth of July. The transports then dropped down outside of us towards the Kentucky shore, and there they opened on us again with their rifled guns, shot and shell falling thick and fast all around us. The Tyler and Lexington again opened their broadsides upon the rebels on the banks, throwing shell, canister and grape into their ranks, making terrible havoc. We played on them half an hour, the Tyler throwing some seventy rounds, and the Lexington between thirty and forty—when the smoke from the battle is described as being so thick and black that the sun could not be seen. We then steamed up the river, protecting the transports, and throwing shell back among the rebels until all had *disappeared.* About three miles above, the gun boats hove to, waiting for Col. Buford's Regiment, which was coming into the river above. Having taken it on board the Lexington, and some twenty-eight prisoners, we steamed for Cairo, and here ends the gunboat part of the expedition.

APPEARANCE OF THE BATTLE FIELD NEXT DAY.

After gettitng permission under the flag of truce to go and bury our dead, and relieve the wounded, who had lain upon the field for nearly twenty-four hours, the first thing we saw after landing was two of our dead men lying beside an old house. Three had been thrown into a corn crib near by, and four lay wounded in the house nearly dead. We went on through the woods until we came to a corn field where sixteen of our dead were lying just as they had fallen, and here we also found three of our wounded, who immediately received the attentions of our surgeons. We also saw here large pools of blood from their dead, who had been removed from the field in wagons. Going on half a mile further, we came upon a large party of the enemy burying their dead, which they had collected from the different thickets, about fifty bodies were lying about awaiting burial—none of our killed was among them. Going on further through a clearing we came to the fallen timber where our boys charged and took the enemy's batteries, and where the loss on both sides is represented as frightful. The enemy had buried and removed their own dead, and we found twelve of our men in the position they had fallen. On the river bank we found a number of our dead; and here it was that one of the most heart rending scenes of the whole battle was enacted.

Capt. Brooks, of Buford's regiment, came upon the dead body of his own brother, who was a surgeon in the rebel army; he knew he was a rebel surgeon, but did not know he was in the engagement until he stumbled over his corpse. The scene is described as affecting in the extreme, and it certainly forms one of the most thrilling and horrible incidents in this unholy rebellion. Captain Brooks buried his brother, and put a slab, at the head of his grave.

At this point a great many of the enemy's dead had been thrown off the embankment to escape our notice, but we saw where they had been dragged and pitched off the bank. One of our party looked over, contrary to express orders, and saw, as he supposes, 75 or 100 of bleeding and mangled corpses heaped on heaps among the dismantled rebel artillery. Having buried our dead—some 85 in number—and bring away about 20 of our wounded, we again reached our transports.

APPEARANCE OF THE DEAD AND WOUNDED.

Our dead were mostly lying upon their backs, and everything taken from their bodies that could be of value to the enemy.—The countenances of the dead were mostly expressive of rage. One or two features were expressive of fear. One poor fellow, after he was wounded, bethought himself to take a smoke; he was found in a sitting position against a tree, *dead*, with his pipe in one hand, knife in another, and his tobacco on his breast.

A young lad about 16, was found lying across a log, just as he fell, grasping his musket in both hands.

A wounded man with *both legs* nearly shot off, was found in the woods singing the "Star Spangled Banner;" but for this circumstance, the surgeons say they would not have discovered him.

A captain of one of our regiments to-day was looking at the prisoners we captured at Belmont, and recognized one of them as *his own brother*.

HORATIO.

CAIRO, Nov. 13.

ANOTHER FLAG OF TRUCE—TURNING OVER OF PRISONERS.

I have just returned from meeting a flag of truce from Columbus. We left here at 1 o clock P. M., on the Aleck Scott, Capt. Riley, an old St. Louisan, commanding, and met the rebel steamer Prince ten miles this side of Columbus. Nearing the rebel steamer, we thought they were not sailing under a white flag, which led to the suspicion they were prepared and intended to capture us. Our captain ordered our white flag struck, and we blew our whistle to attract their attention. Rounding to, we observed our mistake; that they had a white flag, displayed, and we immediately rehoisted our flag. We took from here ninety-nine prisoners, and turned them over to the rebels unconditionally.

Among them was a Lieut. A. G. Harris, of the Twelfth Texas Regiment, who used to buy good in St. Louis, and is well acquainted with many of our Main street merchants. He states that he was taken prisoner while attempting to rally a small squad of our men, which he took for his own command. Our men, seeing the "lone star" on his hat, ordered him to surrender. He wonders our men did not shoot him on the spot, and feels very grateful to them in sparing his life.

Lieut. Harris bore a message from Judge Sidney Breese, of Illinois, who accompanied us on the flag, to his old friend Knox Walker, who is colonel of a Tennessee regiment. Walker was private secretary to President Polk, at the same time Judge Breese was in Congress. The Judge wrote on a slip of paper, "Remember the days of auld lang syne," and also requested Lieut. Harris to say to Walker, that if the fate of war ever placed him in our hands, he would go and see him wherever he was.

THE ADIEUS TO THE PRISONERS.

On our way to Columbus we rounded to at Fort Holt and received an additional lot of prisoners. Many of our boys were assembled on the banks, and I was much amused at the adieus to the prisoners. One said, "We hate to give you fellows up, after fighting so hard to get you." "Never mind;, we will be down there again, pretty soon, and then we will show you a *a trick with a hole in it.*" Another said, "We'll whip you every time," &c., &c.

THE REBEL OFFICERS.

I will give you a brief description of a few of the rebel officers, a score or more of whom are crowded upon the Prince's deck. That gentleman sitting beside a lady, who is represented to me as Mrs. Pillow, is Major General Polk. He is fine, fat and sleek, and stands about six feet in his boots; has a smoot face, with hair considerably mixed with grey. He looks as though the priestly toga would much better become him than his uniform, which consists of a suit of blue cloth, with three large gold stars set on either side of his coat collar, and a yellow silk sash bound around his waist, indicating his rank of Major General. On the other side of Mrs Pillow with a pair of crutches across his lap, is her son, Lieut. George Pillow, who was wounded in the late engagement at Belmont.

That gentleman to the left of Pillow, with a fine black moustache and imperial, is Captain Blake, General Polk's Aid-de-Camp. To the right of him clad in a suit of grey, with a heavy moustache and very red face, stands General Cheatham; he looks fierce and *Southern* like an old campaigner just [illegible] from the battle field. At Cheat[illegible] right, in a suit of grey, with long red hair and heavy set whiskers, is General McGowen. Near McGowen stands Capt. Kennerly and his brother, George Kennerly, of St. Louis, who are brothers of Colonel John H. Bowen's wife. I did not make their acquaintance, but learned that Colonel Bowen, with many of our St. Louis "Camp Jackson" rebels, was commanding a brigade, and located a few miles back of Columbus. Bowen's command was not in the Belmont battle.

☞ The household effects of the late Senator Douglas were sold at Washington last week. Many of the articles brought extraordinary prices, as memetoes of the statesman.

Gen. McClellan has ordered six Ohio and two Indiana regiments to Kentucky from Western Virginia. Other Indiana regiments are expected to follow soon.

The Yankees expect to have at least 120,000 troops in Kentucky within the next ten days, and they then expect to "clean out" the Rebels in short order and take possession of Nashville and Memphis. They are making no preparations whatever for winter quarters in Kentucky, that is very certain.

The Editorial we copy in another column from the Cincinnati *Commercial* is deserving of consideration and we ask especial attention to it.

POURING IN.—The St. Louis correspondent of the Cincinnati Enquirer says that troops are pouring in there in large numbers, from Iowa, Wisconsin, Illinois and oterh States, and that Gen. Halleck will soon be ready to start South with 100,000 men.

News from Crab Orchard.

It was reported at Crab Orchard, Ky., on Sunday, that part of the Wildcat Brigade would march to Danville the next day (yesterday.) The alleged object was to prevent any proposed junction between Zollicoffer—who was reported on the Tennessee border, in Scott county, with 10,000 men—from uniting with a column from Buckner's army, said to be marching for Blue Grass *via* Danville. It was also said that part of the column would move towards Columbia. We have but little faith in the rumors about the approach of the enemy in the directions indicated.—*Cin. Com.*, 19*th*.

Serious Affair at Franklin, Ky.

TEN OR TWELVE LINCOLNITES BURNED.

We learn that a squad of twelve men were sent to Franklin, yesterday, to arrest some Lincolnites who were said to be committing depredations in that neighborhood.

They had collected to the number of 12 or 15 at the house of one of their number, one Bell, and defying the party fired upon them, killing one man, said to be Lee, of Louisville, and wounding one or two more.

Our men then charged the house and set fire to it, burning it and all of the men in it, it is believed, but two, who escaped. A detachment of 25 cavalry under Capt. Morgan arrived at Franklin last night to arrest the parties implicated.

The Yankee Retreat from Wildcat.

Much of our space is occupied to-day with the graphic report of the Yankee stampede from Camp Wildcat, but we could give nothing that would prove so interesting to our readers. Their own authorities report it to have been as damaging as a battle and a rout.

Reported Capture of Mobile Steamers in the Gulf.

We are informed on good authority that private dispatches, received in this city last night, from Handsboro', state that the steamer Oregon put in there last evening and reported the capture of the steamers California, of the mail line, the Lewis, the John Briggs, and one other vessel.

We hope the report is not well founded, but fear it is, as the Gulf was known to be filled with Lincoln gunboats. The steamers, except the Lewis, left here yesterday morning.

POSCRIPT—8½ A. M.—The P. C. Wallis arrived this morning from New Orleans, leaving the Carondelet at Grant's Pass. Yesterday, about 1 P. M., at Horn Island, sighted a Lincoln steamer, which had been inside, but was returning towards Ship Island.

The Wallis and Carondelet came though without molestation; the Dick Keys had put back to Mississippi City.

[*Mobile Advertiser*, 24.

☞ Martial law at Knoxville, has been suspended.

E. T. & VA. RAILROAD.—We learn that the bridge over lick creek, recently burned by the Lincoln incendiaries, has been repaired, and that passengers are now going through between this point and Bristol without delay.—*Knoxville Register*.

☞ The Knoxville *Register* says that the fortifications at Cumberland Gap are now completed, and are amply sufficient to defend it from any force from any quarter.

☞ Andy Johnson cried—so says the correspondent of the Cincinnati *Commercial*—because of the utter destruction of all his hopes of reaching East Tennessee by the stamped from Wild-Cat to Crab Orchard.

YANKEE MEANNESS.—A gentleman from General Floyd's camp informs us, says the Lynchburg *Republican*, that, when Colonel Croghon was killed, a *few* days ago, a flag of truce was sent to the enemy, asking the privilege of bearing away the body of the fallen officer. The request was refused, nor would the Hessians give up his horse or his sword.

GEN. BRECKINRIDGE.—We regret to learn that Gen. Breckinridge is quite ill with an attack of jaundice. We pray for his speedy recovery and early resumption of active duties with his magnificent brigade.

☞ Prentice has gone North to hob-nob with his brother nigger-stealers.—The infamous Forney gave him a supper at Philadelphia, at which, it seems, the slavery question was discussed, and the editor was greatly "embarrassed!"—Rich!

GOOD READING.—We have enough good reading, from a budget of late Northern papers in our possession, to last us a week. Some of it is exceedingly rich and racy.

Death of Hon. Henry M. Rust.

We regret to hear that this true and brave man, who was wounded at the battle of Joy Creek, has since died. A more generous, noble and manly soul than his, never beat in human breast. We pray that the lives of a thousand of the Hessian invaders may be made to atone for this.

MARRIED.

In Chattanooga, Tenn., on the 2d inst., by Rev. E. C. W[illegible], JAMES B. COCKE to MISS JULIA, daughter of Ed. Crutchfield, Esq., all of Louisville, Ky.,

In announcing the above auspicious event, we may be permitted to offer our congratulations to the happy refugees, and to most cordially wish them long and prosperous lives.

THE FIRST DIVISION PROCLAMATION.

VOL. I. "TRUST IN THE LORD AND KEEP YOUR POWDER DRY."—CROMWELL. NO. 2.

Published Weekly in Camp of the First Division Department of the West, at OTTERVILLE, MO., DEC. 13, 1861, *By E. F. Chittenden, Co. B, 14th Reg. Ill. Vol.* TERMS: 5 Cents per Copy; 6 for 25 Cents.

The Proclamation:

PUBLISHED WEEKLY IN THE CAMP OF THE
FIRST DIVISION
Department of the West,
BY E. F. CHITTENDEN.

Terms—Five Cents single copy; Six copies Twenty-five Cents—in advance.

A HOME SCENE.

Click, click, click! how the needles go
Through the busy fingers, to and fro—

With no bright colors of Berlin wool,
Delicate hands to-day are full.

Only a yarn of deep, dull blue,
Socks for the feet of the brave and true.

Yet click, click, click how the needles go,
'Tis a power within that nerves them so.

In the sunniest hour of the bright spring,
And still in the night time far away,

Maiden, mother and granddame sit
Earnest and thoughtfull while they knit.

Many the silent prayer they pray,
Many the tear drops they brush away—

While busily on the needles go,
Widen and narrow, heel and toe—

The granddame thinks with a thrill of pride
How *her* mother knit and spun beside,

For that patriot band in olden days
Who died the "Stars and Stripes" to raise.

Now *she* in turn knits for the brave,
Who'd die that glorious flag to save.

She is glad, she says, "the boys" have gone
"'Tis just as their Grandfathers would have done,"

But she heaves a sigh, and the tears will start,
For "the boys" were the pride of granddame's heart.

The mother's look is calm and high,
God only hears her soul's deep cry—

In Freedom's name, at Freedom's call,
She gives her sons—in them her all—

The maiden's cheek wears paler shade,
But the light in her eye is undismayed.

Faith and hope gives strength to her sight,
She sees a red dawn after the night.

Oh, soldiers brave, will it brighten the day,
And shorten the march on the weary way.

To know that at home the loving and true,
Are knitting, hoping and praying for you?

Soft are their voices when speaking your name,
Proud are their glories when hearing your fame.

And the gladdest hour of their lives will be
When they greet you after the victory.

☞Jeff. Thompson reported the whipping he got at Fredericton, Mo., in laconic style: "The enemy came out two to my one, and whipped me, when I left."

THE UNION BOYS:

BY J. H. R., MOWEAQUA, ILLINOIS.

The Sucker Boys are in the field,
Traitors had better scatter,
Or else they'll feel our leaden balls
And so learn "*what's* the matter."
For when you rouse the Sucker blood,
They fear no odds or danger—
Missouri Pukes, or Southern Dukes,
Nor yet the boasting Ranger.

Missouri's Union sons will join
To swell the gallant legion,
To drive the Rebels from the State,
And every other region.
Indiana boys are also there,
To help us make them scatter;
To shell the Rebels out of camp,
And thus to END the matter.

The President the Providential Man.

A gentleman who happens to have looked through the same spectacles as we did—expressing our opinions exactly, as to one or two leading men—has just returned to Boston, after a visit to Washington. The *Transcript* (from which we copy it) describes him as "a gentleman of influence and high financial position," and thus quotes from a private letter of his: "Yes, I have just returned from Washington. I have seen the President, once in committee, once alone, *tete a tete. I like him,* I believe he is the providential man, the PRESIDENT for the occasion. I think him *not only true and sincere, but also sagacious, clear-sighted,* IN-*sighted and wise; firm when his mind is once made up—absolutely immoveable.* Peculiar in the working and unfolding of his mind, he is likely to switch off on a side track when you can see no sufficient reason for his not keeping the main track; but he easily slips back again, with little or no friction or even loss of headway. This troubles and perplexes many. He understands his position and responsibilities. He knows his surroundings. Those who think they are using him are much mistaken. He sees through it all. I feel sure that the committees who have recently conferred with him are willing to leave matters in his hands. Within a week Seward has told a warm friend of his that of all the men he knew, there was no one in the United States so well fitted to carry the country safely through the struggles as Mr. Lincoln. I believe it thoroughly. McClellan is the head of the military practically, He magnetizes the whole army. His influence is felt everywhere. He has great physical endurance and intellectual vigor, and is endowed with military genius, developed by thorough education. Scott is still geeatly respected and much beloved. But the President you may have entire faith in, no matter who doubts.—*Home Journal.*

☞In a speech made by John C. Breckinridge in the United States Senate, on the occasion of moving from the old Senate Chamber to the new one, he said:—"Is "there an American who will deride his "country's laws, pervert her constiiution, "or alienate her people? If there be such "a man, let his memory descend to pos-"terity, laden with the execration of all "mankind."

There is such a man, and his name is John C. Breckinridge, and even as he hath spoken, so be it.

☞Bishop Clark said in his speech at Providence that "it is time the dispensation of hemp commenced."

Major Gen. Henry W. Halleck.

This officer, who is to be the future commander of the Military Department of the West, is one of the ablest and most thoroughly educated military men in the army of the United States. Like the other active Generals now in the field, he is comparatively a young man, being between forty and fifty years of age. He graduated with honor a West Point in 1839, ranking third in his class. He is a native of New York.

In July, 1839, he was promoted Second Lieutenant of the Corps of Engineers, and was the acting Professor of Engineering in the West Point Military Academy from July 6, 1839, to June 28, 1841—and was promoted to a First Lieutenancy 1845.

In 1841, he published a work of high order, entitled "Bitumen, its Varieties, Properties, and Uses," and in 1846 he published a work on "The Elements of Military Art and Science. Was breveted a Captain in 1847 for gallant conduct in affairs with the enemy in Mexico, and for meritorious services in California.

Gen. Halleck (then Captain) was Secretary of State of California, under the Military Government of Generals Harney, Mason, and Riley from its conquest from Mexico, in 1847, to December, 1849.

He was Chief of Staff to Commodore Shubrick during the Naval and Military operations on the Pacific coas; of Mexico, 1847-48, and was a member of the Convention that framed the Constitution under which California was admitted into the Union, and afterwards gave his attention to the law, and was admitted to practice at the bar. For the last dozen years or so he has been the engineer of the Almeden Mining Company, under a salary of $10,000 a year—the richest and most extensive mining interest in California, with the single exception of Fremont's Miraposa. Now he is called into the service of his country, being an experienced officer and a scientific military man—just the man, indeed, to take so important a command as that to be assigned him in the west.

☞The Providence *Journal*, in referring to Gen. McClellan's admirable order on the retirement of Gen. Scott, remarks: "we trust it is not an editorial weaknesss which makes us esteem McClellan all the more highly, that while he has command of our armies he has also command of the English language."

☞Information has been received that the war Department at Washington has shipped, for the use of the Missouri State forces, three thousand stand of arms and five thousand pairs of blankets. More will follow soon.

☞The name of the Captain who marched his Company off the battle-field of Bull Run in regular order, and on the road to Washington, amid the panic rout, was Joseph Hawley, Captain of Rifle Company A, 1st Connecticut Regiment, and formerly editor of *The Hartford Press.* All honor to the journalistic soldier!

☞War is as much better than a tame acquaintance in a permatent separation of the Union as the struggles of suffering life are better than the quiet nothingness of death.—*Louisville Journal.*

☞The current monthly pay, subsistence and allowance of Lieut-General Scott were, and by order of the President continue to be, while he is upon the retired list, as follows:—

Pay, per month	$270
Rations, per month	360
Allowance for servants, per month	90
Allowance for horses, per month	50
Total	$770

—which makes an annual income of $9,240.

In last February Alabama seceded! That, brave old man, Senator Clemens, who had, until then, breasted all the storms of wild fanaticism, and clung to the flag of our Union, yielded to the popular clamor, and unsheathed his sword in a cause he hated, and one he knew could not succeed. He wrote the following to a friend:

"We are out; we have bid adieu to the Stars and Stripes, and abandoned the high privilege of calling ourselves American citizens. I am not ashamed to confess that I could not restrain my tears when the old banner, which I have followed through so many dangers, was torn down, and the flag of Alabama was raised in its place. I cannot restrain them now when I am writing; but the deed is done—a new era has dawned, and all that I can promise is that no effort shall be spared on my part to prevent it from becoming an era of disgrace. If we are not involved in a war we soon will be. *There is no hope of peace; and he is but little better than a madman, who dreams of long exemption from invasion.* I shall meet it when it comes as a soldier should, and fight through it as long as a hope remains. *When every thing is lost, as I fear it may be,* unless wiser counsels shall prevail than those which have heretofore directed us I shall drag my body to the nearest battle field, and lay down a life which has lost its value."

How swiftly has his prediction been verified. Ere the echoes of his voice, pleading to the fanatics to "stop!" had died away, the cry ran out, To arms! A State then prosperous is now bankrupt; all the horrors of war is upon them; business ruined, and in addition to the restless nights they pass for fear of a servile insurrection, *they will wake some morning and hear the roar of Federal cannon at Mobile.* The battle field will be near to the home of Senator Clemens, and unless some unseen hand shields him, his prophecy will be fulfilled *to the letter!*

Circumstances of the Death of John A. Washington.

A correspondent of the *Gazette,* writing from Cheat Mountain, says:

I have the pleasure, and it is indeed a pleasure, to send you the news of the death of John A. Washington, who was killed yesterday afternoon, about seven miles south of Elkwater camp. The circumstances are as follows: In company with three other officers, he was approaching our fortifications with a view of making reconnoisances. Secreted in a bush by the roadside were a number of the Seventeenth Indiana regiment, and as Washington and his companions came up the road, the Indiana boys arose from their place of concealment and fired. Washington fell from his horse on the first round, having received three bullets, two of which passed entirely through the body, entering at the right breast, and one of the quartette was also hit, but the two remaining unhurt manged to get him away by supporting him on his horse. The body of Washington was conveyed to the quarters of Colonel Waggoner. He lived for the space of half an hour, and never spoke save to utter once, "O, my God!" The next day his body was sent to the rebel camp, under a flag of truce. In the pockets of Washington was found one hundred dollars in *United States* gold currency and a splendid gold watch. His dress was new and of a most elegant make, broadcloth coat and pants, and a white satin vest. His shoulder straps denoted him to be a Colonel—one of the Virginia regiments I suppose.

☞The New Albany *Ledger* says that the Indiana boys in Missouri, recently captured a camp of rebel troops, nearly all of whom were suffering with the ague. To use the language of the directions on quack medicines, they were "well shaken before taken."

what the Star-Spangled Banner Signifies;

The following description of the significance of the different parts of the American flag will be interesting to many of our readers. It was written by a member of the Committee of the Continental Congress appointed to design a flag for the young republic, when the matter was before that body, and recently reproduced by A. W. Street, Esq., in a lecture on the battle of Saratoga:

"The stars of the new flag represent the new constellation of States rising in the West. The idea was taken from the constellation of Lyra, which, in the land of Orpheus, signifies harmony. The blue, in the field, was taken from the edges of the Covenanter's banner, in Scotland. significant of the league covenant of the United Colonies against oppression, incidentally involving the virtues of vigilance, perseverance and justice. The stars were disposed in a circle, symbolizing the perpetuity of the Union; the ring, like the circling serpent of the Egyptians, signifying eternity. The thirteen stripes showed, with the stars, the number of the United Colonies, and denoted the subordination of the States to the Union; as well as equality among themselves. The whole was the blending of the various flags, previous to the Union flag, viz: the red flags of the army, and the white ones of the floating batteries. The red color, which in Roman days was the signal of defiance, denoted daring, and the white purity."

DIVISION OFFICERS:

Acting Major-General,
Hon. THOMAS J. TURNER.

Acting Assistant Adjutant,
C. C. CLARK.

Acting Assistant Quarter-Master,
J. CONDIT SMITH.

Acting Division Surgeon,
O. M. BRYAN.

Chief of Commissary,
Captain W. J. BENNER.

Complete List of the
THE OFFICERS AND SOLDIERS
composing the
14th Regiment Ill. Volunteers.

Lieutenant-Colonel,
WILLIAM CAM.

Major,
Jonathan Morris.

Acting Adjutant,
Robert P. McKnight.

Quarter-Master and Acting Ass't Com. Sub.
John F. Nolte.

Surgeon,
F. W. Kersting.

Chaplain,
Rev. Wm. J. Rutledge.

Sergeant Major—Francis W. Fox.
QuarterMaster Sergeant—J H Stewart.
Commissary Sergeant—Henry C. Denison.
Hospital Steward—Homer Wilson.
Drum Major—Wm. Emery.
Fife Major—Theodore S. Shorb.

ARTILLERY COMPANY,

Captain......F. H. CHAPMAN.
Lieutenants:
J. M. JOHNSON, J. M. EIDSON, A. HOYER.
Amos B. Dennison, Orderly Sergeant.

SERGEANTS.

Samuel S. Bunce, | *Alexander Livingston*
Felix Emery,

Wm McLosky, Corp'l | *Philip Snow.*
Wm. Steinmitz,

CANNONEERS:

J W Andrews	Geo Morgan,	D J Solomon,
M Bright,	And. Miller,	C C Scott,
C Brown	J McKenzie,	J W Stubbles,
B Ball,	John Myers,	J Smith,
J Coulter,	J Pray,	E Simon,
J Creamer,	I T Pette,	J B Sanders
H H Durham,	Th Patterson,	J Schillinger,
J H Geiser,	Alex Roland,	E Weinshank,
A C Lovejoy,	Z. Roberts,	A J Whitsell,
E J Livermore	John Spicer,	J B Wolfe.

Co. A, Captain...... ——— ———.
Lieutenants—H. RODECKER, CHAS. OPITZ.
John S. Morgan, Orderly Sergeant.

SERGEANTS.

Charles Nikel, | *Elijah M. Bond,*
Eben. Richardson, | *AugustineA. Snow.*

David Carr, Corp'l, | *Robert Armstrong,*
John Alves, | *L. J. Parmenter,*
Abraham J. Sailor, | *A. Brashears,*
Josiah Williams, | *Joseph Huber.*

Musicians—S. L. Griffin, Joseph Heina.
Wagoner—William Sayles.

L.P.Bourquin	J. N. Harris,	R. McFarland
D. W. Batch-elder,	A. Hatfield,	A.W.McCon-nell,
E. M. Baylor,	Ch. Hatfield,	W. J. Nelson,
L. W. Beals,	John Hess.	A. J. Norton,
Isaac Bell,	Or. Hellings-worth,	Wm Parsons,
Wm Brannan,	C. R. Jones,	H. C. Phelps,
A. W. Buck,	D. Kalliher,	J. H. Plank,
Arch. Boyd,	James P. Karr	R. B. Poole.
A. Buckhart,	Robert Kiug,	J. Randall,
Jos Burnett,	Sol. W. King,	G. M. Rhine-berger,
P. Burnett,	Ed. Knight,	W. J. Roach,
Charles Burns	Alb Krausse,	Ch. Schramm,
A. Christianer	Chris. A. Kuhl	F M. Schaffer
Geo Comming	G. R. Leeds,	Eli Shaw,
H. Clemons,	P. W. Light,	John Steele,
Geo. W. Day,	Chas. Lincoln	O Tisdale,
H. Ducker,	Abner S. Liv-ermore,	Wm Torrey,
Chas. Dunker	D. Loomis,	George Tracy
W. H. Dutch,	W.C. Morrow	Chas Troster.
J. R. Ewing,	Wm. J. Muck	Chas Watson,
D. S. Finney,	C. Mullaine,	Th Webster,
M. Finney,		Ch Williams,
Ed. E. Foster		Wm. Wisby.

B Captain....DUDLEY C. SMITH.
Lieutenants—G. A. POTEET, GEO. WRIGHT.
Jerome J. Hinds, Orderly Sergeant.

James J. Durkee, | *Henry M. Peden,*
Henry Harbaugh, | *George E. Lowe.*

M.H. Copeland, Cor'l, | *William M. Sinclair,*
E. F. Chittenden, | *Samuel Huson,*
Eleazer Slocum; | *Hiram Collins.*
C. S. Woodward.

Musicians—J. W. Bugh, J. D. M. Conrad.

J. Anderson,	W.G.Hopkins	S.N.Richm'nd
D. B. Baker,	Julius Hoppe,	W.S.Richard-son,
G. W. Baker,	J. Krippner,	J. Richardson
W.M.Bradley	John Keisler,	W.W.Robins,
Cass Burrus,	E. F. Knight,	Joseph Reid,
John Beck,	M. C. Kelly,	A. Robnitt,
M. E. Bacon,	C. W. Keiffer,	E.H.Robins'n
Fred. Bechtel	M. H. Karr,	Henry Rob'rts
Chas Clemons	WWLaughlin	Jacob Shields,
H. S. Cowen,	Rich'd Lyons,	Jas H. Shaw,
J. W. Clark,	D.Y. Milligan	Henry Schoen
C. A. Conrad.	B.W.Milligan	A W Sherlock
Thomas Day,	A.W.Munger,	R Underwood
James Dugan,	A. H. Morgan	John M. Un-derwood,
Peter DeKolf,	Jonathn Mars	Henry Unger,
John Dill,	Simon Mars,	J. C. Vander-pool,
John S. Davis	John Murphy	J. Q. Wright,
Jas A. Frost,	Wm. H. Neal	M. Woodling,
Chris. Fegan,	L. H. Parker,	Jas. H. Wells,
Rich'd Fegan,	Geo. O. Peck,	Phil. Weiman
M.HGraham.	W. G. Phelps	Arthur Wils'n
P. Grady,	W.S.Prentice,	Sam'l Waugh
David Hand,	Jno.Quinlivan	Wm. White.
Sam. Harshey	Ch. Rafsnider	
Fred Holton,	Lou. Rhoden-hausler,	
H. Hartman,		
L F. Hadley,		

D Captain; Rev. THOS. J. BRYANT.
Lieutenants—R McKNIGHT, J.E. WILLIAMS
Carlos C. Cox, *Orderly Sergeant.*

G W Bates, *Sergeant* | Robert Walker,
John W Henderson, | R D Bibb,

Thomas A Weisner, | Joseph C Carroll,
Reuben E Weisner, | David Baker,
John H Hogan, | William A Wilson,
Robert Jarvis, | Henry E. Backus.

Musicians—F R Gray, ——— ———.

J W Altum,	Sam'l B Duly.	Thos Pierson,
Jac Bowman,	Al Farmer,	Jos Pierson
Th D Barton,	Rob Fisher	Wm Rath,
I P Barton,	James Gray,	E S Reynolds
Ch H Barton,	Philem'nGaut	Mich'l Ronan
Wm Bloom-camp,	G Hamman,	Sam Sanders
Noah Boyd,	Jonn Hiner,	J Shelburn,
Jas M Boring	H H Jennings	A Shelburn,
Chas Brown,	John Jeffreys,	Thos L Short
John Brown,	James Kelley	Cor Scott
John L Bell,	Thos J Kidd,	Joseph Smith
C B Cash,	Wm A Lakin	P B Sharp,
Daniel Cox,	Mich'lLynch	F M Sharp,
J Cunningham	JN Montgom-ery,	Mark Tracy,
S Culbertson,	B F Mytinger	Sam'l Walker
John Dunn,	FM Mytinger	H Williams
J LDuckw'rth	G McDonald,	G B Wylder
Wm L Duck-worth,	I N Melton.	B Wylder
G H Davidson	Saml Mouder,	Rob Wylder
WHDavidson	Fred Moore,	J Whitworth,
J G Davis,	James Niece,	Thos Whaley
J Dennis	Eilis Niece,	George Wells
	Th Patterson,	AJ Worcester
	Alb Perkins,	Chas Yeoman
		Wm R Love.

E Captain, FREDERICK MEAD.
Lieutenants—J. M. EARLY, E. A. NORTON.
R Haynie, Orderly Sergeant.

A H Corgill, | *Alonzo Gillespie.*
Joseph Ham,

Jas L Garman, | *James Simpson,*
John Murphy, | *Christian Goodman*
Isaac McKay, | *John Clark,*
John Smedley, | *John Goldsmith.*

Musicians—Chas Burgess, G M McNeely.

Wm Andrew,	A Ferguson,	Thomas Neal
Charles Hllen	Wm Geer,	John Pray,
Chas Abbott,	Wm Gibbs,	O Pierce,
Wm Burley,	Geo Gurley,	Ed Potter,
Benj. Boll,	S O Graham,	C Philbrick
Isaac Ball,	A Grugsby,	S Rinehard
A Bickford,	John Fum,	A Rutledge
E Baylor	Arth'r Hutton	Robert Riley,
Jas Brown,	John Hardin,	G Stevenson,
P Brown	D J Hornbeck	Nath'l Stone,
D S Bell,	W Heathcote,	John Sifford
Wm Clark,	B Hopper,	wm Smith,
John Cox,	Sol Hopper,	Samuel Smith,
Alex Carnes,	Wm Hills,	Th Summers,
L Carleton,	Peter Johns	John Stubbs,
Henry Coats,	Chas Jones,	Th Tovera,
Elijah Coydel	John Klmnan,	T J. Turner
L Cummings,	Harvey Linn,	Jos Todd
Wm Cowan,	H Lowry,	W Trent,
P Carroll	Wm Leiper,	W A Trent'
Henry Drake,	Levi Lukins	S W Tryon,
Thos Daily,	P McNulty,	Jos White,
H Dennison,	E McIntyre	JasWaddell
Henry Ewing	J Montgom'ry	Th Wilson,
Chriz Ersman	J Mitchell,	Jos Wasson
Geo Eldridge,	wm Moore,	F Zimmerman
John Evers,	Jno Moore,	
Eph Freeman	Saml Marquis	

F Captain....M. S. LITTLEFIELD.
Lieutenants—T. H. SIMMONS, J. D. MOORE
A. W. Mendenhall, Orderly Sergeant.

Wm. A. Patton, | *T. H. Leonard,*
J. A. Davies. | *I. B. Stafford,*

S.N.Drew, Corp'l, | *J. A. Eberman,*
R. P. Aullabaugh. | *G. R. Pinckard,*
John W. Smith, | *William Catt,*
J. H. Humphreys, | *Brook Stafford.*

G. Arkbauer,	W. A. Hoag,	F C Pollock,
Jas. Austin,	F. Hoag,	Wm. E. Pitt,
Wm. Bartley,	M. J. Hull,	J. V. Parker,
G. R. Buck-master,	John Higgins,	Z. Roberts,
Jos. D. Beck,	G. W. Hilly,	W C. Robert
M. Bright,	F. M. Hilly,	A Rowland,
G.W.Bridges,	John Hogan,	I D Rowden,
J. B. Boyd,	J. Holloran,	Jas Rowden,
E. Brewer,	H. a beri ch,	Ch Rudolph,
Ed. Brewer,	John Haenky,	A C Richards
L. H. Craig,	J.W. Johnisee	L P. Richard,
J.W.F Court	John Keyo,	W F Randle,
Jack'n Davis,	Jos. Leigh,	D P Smutz,
M. Dwyer,	S. Leonard,	S C Smith, *sen*
E.G.Davids'n	. Leighton,	S C Smith, *jun*
W.H.Dawson	Asbury Mott,	John Smith,
W. N. Darr,	C. F. Miner,	Geo D Smith,
Mich'l Daily,	T.S. Milliken,	W W Slaten,
Allen Dennis,	John Monk,	Eph Sanpare,
A. J. Estes,	N. Miller,	G W Taylor,
W. J. Elliott,	M. McMena-min,	G W Thoms'n
M. W. Free,	Wm. Moore,	G W Vinson,
J.G.Freeman,	F. McBain,	W Wilson,
N. Grosjan,	Wm. Noland,	W D Wilson,
D. Gosling,	T. A. Price,	Nath'l Ware,
	S. S. Price,	Seym'r W erts.

G Captain....LOUIS C. REINER,
Lieutenants—A. SCHMIDT, J. RIPPSTEIN
Frederick Steinly, Orderly Sergeant.

Charles Meyer, | *Charles Milde,*
Louis Reichat, | *Charles Schnarr.*

Philip Beil, Corp'l, | *Henry Abt,*
Casper Reisser, | *John Miller,*
G. Reinhardt, | *C. Bellinghausen*
Marx Helmich; | *Balzer Grebe*

F Albert,	R Harder	W Schonthal,
Fr Alexander	J Harrington,	Fred Schwarz
Chales Adler,	Wm Hanson,	Ch Schlutter,
Wm Barthun,	A Hofmeyer,	Adolph Segin,
Adam Best	J Hauenstein,	W Saame
Paul Buck,	F W Jacobi	Ch Straisch
A Barthling,	Jacob Jacke	J Schindler,
John Conzet	G Klett,	Henry Strah,
Fr C Cope,	Chas Kneisel,	A Sanders
Wm Deicken,	Henry Kipp,	F A Simon,
John Distel	Michael Klein	A Spengler,
L Deitschl'r	Carl Koehler,	J Schaefer,
J Dnnker,	John Kraemer	Willi'm Stauf,
D Deever	Oscar Kibele,	J C Schoatler,
Ignatz Deebs,	N Koenig,	W Van Uibert
D Ellwanger,	P Lemmer,	Henry Voege,
John Falk,	A Martin	W H Vickerg
Jac Fischer	H'nry Mayers	G F Weber,
A Gutzmann,	Fr Mayers,	C Wehrend,
A Gottlob,	M Moser	Fr Winters,
W Greiner,	C Meirciss,	H Weiler,
J Gardner,	G Nicolaus,	Nicola's Walk
R Gaynard,	John Preisser	Wm Weise,
Geo Heutter,	H Richberg	J S Weiden-keller,
George Hees,	F Rummel'n	John Zoll.
M Huberty,	A Rosentiel	
W Hespell,	Fred Stuber	

H Captain....ANDREW SIMPSON.
Lieutenants—J.W.HARTLEY, O. P. SQUIER
Z. Payson Shumway, *Orderly Sergeant.*

J. A. Berlin, *Serg't,* | Henry McKenzie,
Charlesw'th Powel | Edward W.Percy,

Austin B. Bostic | Edwin A. Salter,
E. C. Banning, | Jefferson Osborn,
| Leroy L. Key,

Musicians—Joel A. Prior, Morris Ray.

W T Brawley	Wm George	J Miller,
WCBradshaw	Owen Gillon,	D McLaugh-lin,
WWBoldman,	A Hatchett,	J Myers,
J M Bisby,	C K Harnel	E Parish,
C C Bond	BF Hatford	S H Polley,
J D Bankson,	H H Hatfield,	M Persinger
Uriah Boroff,	H H Higbee,	Ch Pohlmnan
W T Blythe,	J Holston,	L M Recker,
A N Behymer	D R Jay,	J S Ruby,
Simon Bartley	F Jouitt,	C Rush,
Ed Branch,	J Kelso,	M Rice,
C WW Clark,	F M Kelly,	G A Rowley,
HCoundif,	S Keton,	J H Rayburn,
Milton Cloud,	La F. George	S B Root,
wConley,	S Logan,	C Shephard,
HHCampbell	A Lovejoy,	J Stewart,
Elmore Carter	L Losier,	N Stout,
Paul Conner,	JMcKenzie,	W O Stephens
R E Dovle.	JMeteer,	A Stine,
David Dwyer,	S McKenzie,	C Selover,
John Durbin.	LM'Cracken,	C Tetrick,
wm Drory,	J M'Cracken	AWestbrook
Isaac Deedr,	E Maloney,	R Westbrook,
wm T Elam,	A Mansfield,	A Thompson
C East,	Cyrus wright	

I Captain......J. W. MEACHAM.
Lieutenants—E. D. WARD, L. W. COE.
Martin V. Wyatt, *Orderly Sergeant.*

James S. Cloud, | Gilb. G Morehouse,
Major E Barger, | Benjam'n H Burch.

John W Luttrell, | Robert Henry,
Jas H Kennedy, | Felix Sims,
Wm L Tuttle | Alex S Erving,
John L arris, | Willlam C oe.

Musicians—B F Church, Jos M Wilson.
W W Standage.... *Wagoner.*

C C Allen,	W C Green,	I N Merwin
G H Barker,	P H Good,	R C Newman,
M Burch,	J *W* Gunn,	W A Neal,
M Burnett,	D Hazzard,	J H Nall,
W Barger,	*W* arper,	F M Runkel
W Barlow,	B M Hughes,	W Sears,
A L Bacon,	C SHowel	E Sperry,
J W Brecken,	M Heffin,	A A Sweet,
C S Barker,	w C Holliday	M V B Slagle
F H Bruce,	G O Harming,	W H Scott,
JO Chapin,	T L Hanly,	R Scott,
J Coffel,	w *H*olmes,	G Scott,
T P Cunning-ham,	C Jones,	H Tenyck,
A S Cunning-ham,	H S Keplinger	I L Thomas,
J L Cole,	*W* P Kimber,	J W Thomas,
W P *W* Cam-ell,	*W* HKay,	D Tindle,
W N Criswell	P Kehoe,	W Taylor,
O S Droke,	J D Lankton,	H C willitt,
C Dix,	J Lillian,	A Vieira,
J *W* Dalton,	C C Lyons,	P *H* Vancleve,
J Dodd,	*W* E Lashmet	T V Welch,
I P H Droke,	MMaloney -	A Wilson,
J Erhart,	M M Meach-am,	J *H* wyatt,
B L Farmer,	J w Meacham	J w Talking-ton,
GHGoldsmith	J Meacham,	DBTalington,
	W Murry,	J Talkington,
	J A Morgan,	

K Captain......HENRY CASE.
Lieutenants—W.N. SHIBLEY, WM. MASON
William W. Strong, *Orderly Sergeant.*

John Alderson, | George W. Ebey.
John Kirkman,

F Ebey, | Daniel Wells.
M P Rollins, | William Haas,
Thos Galloway, | John Asher,
Wm H Thomas. | Frank Wilbur.

B Andrews,	J C Howell,	J M Rowland,
Jno G Bush	C Henly,	J Robinson,
HBurns,	P B Hope,	R H Ridgway,
J J Brant,	D W Haskell,	F P Shuman,
J Beard,	D Hanes,	J Sharp,
E Bland,	T Henesy,	C Stevenson,
L E Brown,	J Johnson,	H Stahl,
J. Chrisinger,	— Jackson,	J Scott,
WJCarpenter,	W R Jennis,	W H Sweeny,
B Curry,	J Knopp,	S S Smith,
L S Cobb,	B Lindall,	G Seaman,
L M Combs,	D Lacy,	J W Toffinder,
J Covington,	M Langley,	W H Prue,
J M Duff,	G Langley,	T Peal,
J N Deweese,	J W Mellon,	J Veaus,
W H H Ed-wards,	W H Moss,	NAWills,
T Eby,	J McCormack	JWarrell,
W *H* Faring-ton,	J H Madden,	J Ward,
N Fulks,	D McArtha,	L H A Wells,
I B Fisher,	T Martin,	D Weaver,
J L Fields,	F North,	J H Wilkins,
J C Gillham	F Peak,	J J west,
J F Harriss,	S Pitman,	J C watt,
	C Peak,	
	J Platner,	

THE ILLUSTRATED LONDON NEWS.

No. 1121.—VOL. XXXIX.] SATURDAY, DECEMBER 14, 1861. [WITH A SUPPLEMENT, FIVEPENCE

OUR CONTROVERSY WITH AMERICA.

THE attitude and bearing of the people of England under the circumstances which have arisen in connection with the seizure of the Confederate Commissioners on board the Trent have been in all respects worthy of the occasion. This is not the verdict of mere self-complacency, but ample testimony has been borne by the press of France to the mingled dignity, moderation, and firmness of purpose which have been displayed by the whole country, and without exception of class. The bitterest satirists on England and the English have failed to find anything in our conduct on which to base even a sneer; while for an accusation no shadow of a foundation has been discovered. If it were necessary we might quote some of the language of writers in Continental journals in which our national spirit, our unanimity of feeling, and our consciousness of being in the right are held up to admiration in no measured terms; but we only refer to these eulogies for the purpose of illustration, and with no desire to make more of a highly creditable state of things than it deserves. It would certainly have been a melancholy thing if a country like this should on the occurrence of an act of aggression have set about to scold and vapour with all the sound and fury of those, whether persons or nations, who are assured neither of their position nor the rights of the matter in dispute; and therefore, while admitting simply and unostentatiously the justice of any commendation which we have received for our conduct in this juncture of our national affairs, we can afford to be almost surprised that any one should have conceived it could have been other than it has been. It is to be observed that, as the time since the intelligence of the Jacinto affair was received has run on, the public mind has taken a calmer view of the situation; but, nevertheless, there has not appeared any abatement of the resolute determination to hold to the honour of England at all hazards which was the first sensation that pervaded the land. If there be any change in the view of this question—and we think there is—it is a growing incredulity with regard to the necessity for a resort to the bloody arbitrement of the sword. Reflection, consideration, examination of the subject in all its bearings, seem to lead to something like a conviction that, if a similar process be applied to the question on the other side of the water, it must result in a peaceable issue. The most recent accounts show that some change has come over the spirit in which most of the Federal so-called organs of public opinions deal with this subject. The tone adopted by these journals is much more serious and practical than that which characterised the delivery of opinions on the first blush of the matter; and something has been done to familiarise the popular mind in America with the surrender of the Confederate Commissioners as a contingency by no means remote. Some of them go so far as to say that the recent event cannot—we suppose because it ought not—be a cause of war; and others have allowed that, if the act of the officers of the Federal navy is not justifiable by the law of nations, it cannot inflict any wound on the national honour to make a suitable apology. The signs of the existence of such a feeling, however feeble they may be, are not without significance, and from them may be drawn auguries of things to come which, we believe, the most sensitive Englishmen would be willing enough to witness. It must be remembered that these indications of a tendency to

CAPTAIN WILKS, OF THE SAN JACINTO.

MR. MASON.

MR. SLIDELL.

THE CONFEDERATE COMMISSIONERS TO ENGLAND AND FRANCE SEIZED ON BOARD THE TRENT.—SEE NEXT PAGE.

FORNEY'S WAR PRESS

VOL. 1. PHILADELPHIA, SATURDAY, DECEMBER 21, 1861. NO. 6

PARSON BROWNLOW, THE UNION PATRIOT OF TENNESSEE.

MAP OF THE DOOMED CITY OF CHARLESTON, S. C.,

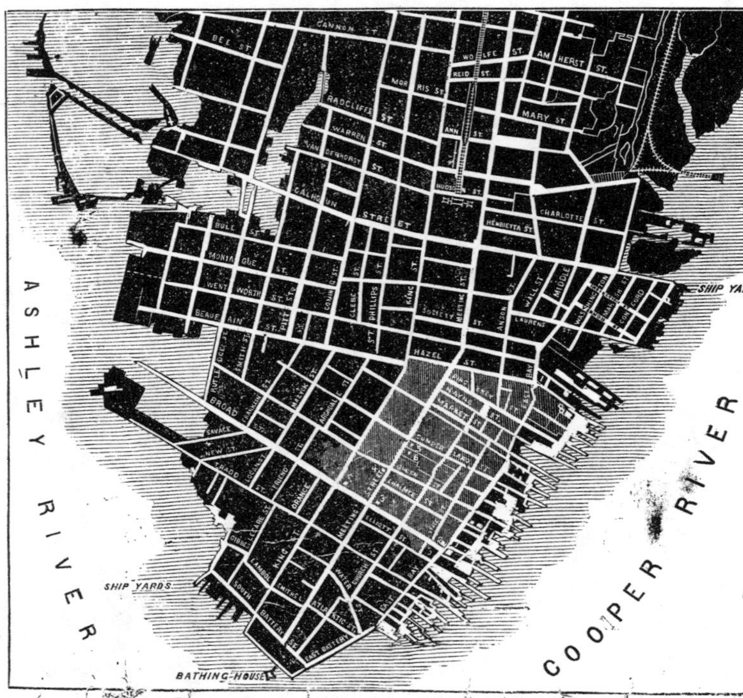

SHOWING THE BURNT DISTRICT, DECEMBER 11 AND 12, 1861.

1. Custom House and Post Office. 2: Mercury Office. 3. Court House. 4. Mills House. 5. Secession Hall. 6. The Market or Circular Church. 7. Cathedral. 8. Russel & Old's Sash and Blind Factory, (where the fire broke out.)

☞ *See Eighth Page.*

A STORY OF THE WAR.

HOW IT WAS THAT MICKEY FREE WENT FOR THREE YEARS.

[Written for the War Press.]

BY FERDINAND L. SARMIENTO.

It was night, and I was stationed on picket duty near the Chain Bridge. It was the early part of autumn, and the air was warm and close. The dark clouds were rolling up in grand and heavy masses toward the zenith, while the fitful glare of the lightning gave every indication of a rapidly approaching storm. Darker and darker it grew—grander and more sublime, till the little stars hid themselves in fear and left the vivid lightning alone, to blinden while it aided sight.

Piled up, pile on pile, the gigantic cloud-throne of the storm-king towered in all the majesty of gloom; and, while the attendant lightning, courtier-like, hinted ever at his sovereign's power and might, the sycophant thunder, like a poet laureate, echoed in long and vibrating peals the fearful greatness of his monarch's court.

Soon the great rain drops came pattering down, and soon a thick watery veil hid the storm-king from our sight, while the parched earth threw out from myriad censors the refreshing frankincense of grateful tribute. Retiring under cover, I prepared to await the passage of the storm. "Here's room, yer. honor," said a tall and good-humored-looking fellow, who was shaking off the rain drops much as a Newfoundland dog would do; indeed, in magnanimity and gentleness of spirit, Mickey Free—for so he was named—bore a striking resemblance to one of those noble creatures. "Here's room, yer honor, and proud to have ye."

Mickey Free had been a porter in my father's store, and was now "Chorporal Free, at yer sarvice." His honesty and good nature had always made me feel an affection for him, which was returned by a devotion that would have been proved by the sacrifice of his life, if needs be. So Mickey and I sat down side by side, to wait, as comfortably as we could, until the rain was over. We had not long to wait, for the storm ceased much sooner than we had expected, or even hoped; so I prepared to stroll out again, with Mickey as my companion.

"It's all over, yer honor," said he; "and the stars are a winkin' and blinkin' in the sky as though the storm had washed their little faces, and some of the soap suds had got in their eyes." True, the storm had passed, and the night, like a beauty that had wept her fancied sorrows out, now was smiling, as at the untoward fancy which had caused her tears. The rich perfume of the herbage, too, arose in voluptuous beats of fragrant soothing freshness, while the little crickets recommenced the song which the storm had only interrupted.

All about the sleeping capital was one immense encampment, and when the moon broke through the scudding clouds, it was to light in myriad snowy heaps the tents of our noble army. From the distance soft strains of music came undefined, like rich perfumes on the senses—then swelling louder and louder as they neared, told the march of many troops. The march—yes, amid the soothing calm of Heaven—the march to battle, honor, death!

Rich and inspiriting the martial music burst upon the ear, while the shouts of the men as they passed the different camps, sent a thrill of enthusiasm and of patriotism through one, that lit up the soul with sublimest fires, the guides to noblest actions. The sweet sounds swell, then die away, fainter and fainter, till, gone altogether, a vacuum rests within the soul that needs a sigh to fill it. And that sigh was there, as I thought of my home in the distant north, where the queen-like forests had already put on their royal robes to greet in sorrowing gorgeousness the conquering winter-king. What is there, methought, to make one desert home and its loved ones, to go forth to battle and to death?

There is a feeling which men call patriotism. It is the *altar* on which we place our idol—home. Yes, *patriotism*, love of country, which exists in every true man's heart, and which, though often contaminated and sunk to the base level of the world's muddy current by contact with the common cares of life, the least storm peal of danger frees it from its sordid load and lets it rise and float to light and purity, to be bleached anew by the warming sun of honor and of duty.

"Begorra, there's many a one here that patriotism has not stirred," interrupted Mickey Free, for involuntarily I had thought aloud. "Sure, there's meself, I'm sorry to say, who never once thought of my country when I went for three years!"

"Why was it, then, Mickey, that you left a good situation, and your old mother? Was it a burning desire for glory, or was it just out of that love for fighting, which I verily believe to be the besetting trait of all your country?"

"It was just neither, sir—sur—sure, sir, it was *love!*"

Love! Well, of all the beings to come under that subtile influence, Mickey Free is the most singular, thought I. Certainly the last one whom I should ever have suspected of dallying with *its* downy thorns, and come bleeding away. Here is a case of "unrequited love," which I must hear, and which assuredly cannot fail to be amusing; for, like the generality of people, I was apt to conclude that, because the exterior of the man was coarse, and his manners rough, that he must necessarily be devoid of those deeper feelings and exquisite sensibilities which we expect to find alone in the man of education and refinement. I had yet to learn that the rough skinned rind oft contained a juice as rich as the most beautiful of God's fruits—that the thorny flower of love pricked as pure a blood from peasant as from earl.

Mickey had ceased his walk, and seated himself upon the turf, his eyes downcast, his expression so sad and thoughtful, that I said, with all my former levity gone, and more of feeling than I can well explain, "Tell me, Mickey, how it was."

"Sure, I will, sir; and maybe it will be a relief to me—not that I care about her, sir—not a bit, not a bit!" though the gulp which accompanied belied his words.

"Not a bit, sir, not a bit," he kept repeating, as though he fain would assure himself of the fact.

"You see, sir, I had a cousin—Rose O'Leary was her name; we called her Rose for short. You see, Rosy's mother died when she was a wee little thing, and we two were always brought up together. I do believe that I loved Rosy from the time we were babies together, for I did use to be putting me arms about her and a smotherin' her with kisses till she would have to set up a squall to get rid of me, and until me poor mother would cry out, 'Mickey, why *do* ye be teasin' the baby? Sure, can't you love it without kissin' it all the time?' Ah! but I loved her, and when she grew up as tall and beautiful as a lily, I felt often like kneeling down to her, so bewildered was I with the perfume of her beauty and goodness. Sure, her every action was grace, and so light was her foot that she could have leaped over the church steeple without so much as saying 'by yer lave.' Indeed, it's often I was afraid she would fly away and be an angel, and leave me desolate and heart-broken. As time went on I loved her more and more, and though I never said a word about it, I knew that she loved me, for there's plenty ways of telling, sir—the step, the look, the very tone of voice—they all speak to the heart that is willing to listen. Now, one evening, soon after the troubles commenced at Fort Sumpter, and everybody was talkin' of the rebellion, I was seated in our little kitchen with me mother and Rosy on either side of me, when we got talkin' of our friends that had gone to the wars. 'Sure, it's Mickey that would make the illegant soger,' says Rosy. Now, whether it was pride or a wish to be agreeable to Rosy, or what not I don't know, but I said, 'Sure, it's what I've been thinkin' of this long time!' The Lord forgive me the lie, for I never once had thought of it before. So, taking down an old musket that belonged to me father, I began to go through the 'drill' just as I had often seen the Home Guards do; and ye ought to have seen Rosy's eyes a glistenin' with love and pride as she looked at me. 'Attention!', says I 'eyes right! eyes left! eyes front!'"

"Och, murder, but it's the genius he has for a soger!" says me mother; "his own poor father over again."

"Genius!—it's inspiration he has," says Rosy.

"Whist, till ye see me go through the motions," says I, for Rosy's blarney and me own conceit, was ateing me up.

"Sh-o-u-l-d-e-r ahrms! Faith I spoke it just like a gineral on parade—the first part long, and the last word short and quick.

"S-h-o-u-l-d-e-r ahrms!—no, it's P-r-e-s-e-n-t ahrms, I mean."

"Oh, isn't it beautiful?" says Rosy; "begorra, it's a gineral he'll be," while her eyes looked up into mine so sweet and lovin' like.

"S-h-o-u-l-d-e-r ahrms! O-h-r-d-e-r ahrms! and with that down it come, right down on me foot, and all the genius and inspiration was knocked clear out of me. Sure, it all come from lookin' at Rosy; and, begorra, me toe—it was *mashed*, for I was so in the heat and earnest, that I brought the old musket down like a steam pile-driver.

"So, takin' me toe in both hands, says I, it's aisy seein' that it isn't worth while tryin' to do anything with sich a musket as this; sure, now, if it was a rigulation musket it wouldn't do the likes of that at all, at all.

"Sure, them old-fashioned muskets do be always dangerous weapons," says Rosy, while the sweet dew-drop of sympathy just moistened her eyes.

"Och, they don't be usin' them at all now," says I.

"The heavens presarve us," exclaimed Rosy; "maybe it will be after going off and killin' some of us."

"How can it, and it not loaded?" says me mother.

"Divil a dependence to be placed on it, loaded or not loaded," says I, for me toe was hurting me like anything, and limping to the settee I prepared to have me toe tied up with laudanum and camphor, while Rosy mixed me somethin' warm to prevent inflammation. After that we had a long talk upon the subject, and it was agreed that the want of good ginerals would make them be glad to get hold of a real military genius, and that I must try for a high position in the ahrmy. And until we went to bed we talked of nothing else but what I'd do when I got to be a gineral. Not that I cared for a gineralship for me own sake; but I thought how nice it would be for Rosy, when we should be married, to have the people call her 'Mrs. Gineral Free, of the United States ahrmy.' But, begorra, I soon found that all the gineralships were filled already, and that I would have to be contented with something lower; so the next morning I went down and listed in the 69th, after hearing that all the positions were filled, and that I would have to wait till the first vacancy before I could be promoted, though the recruitin' sargeant said that I'd certainly be a gineral the first vacancy.

"And how long will that be?" asked Rosy.

"Sure, it can't be very long," says I, "for I hear they are going to choose two corporals next week, and we have marchin' ohrders already."

"Marchin' ohrders! and sure, you won't be after lavin' us?"

"After lavin' yer; and sure, how can I go to the wars and not lave ye?"

"Och ho! och ho!" cries Rosy, "and it's shot ye'll be, and murthered! And it's breakin' me heart I'll be with thinkin' and dreamin' of ye! Och, Mickey, how could ye?—and lave your poor mother and me?"

"Now, may I never see light!—wasn't it yerselves that said, 'What an illegant soger I'd make?'" cries I in a rage.

"But we didn't want you to go way and get kilt," says they; and here they both set up sich a howl, that I was turned almost wild with the noise and the grief. Sure, I wished then I hadn't listed, but it was too late to repine, so I went down to the ahrmary to drill, and there learned that we were to march the very next day.

Ah! that was a sad day when we left. The flags were all a flyin' and the people all a-pushin' forward, with joy and enthusiasm in their features, to see us march by, while our own hearts were sad enough. I had bid me poor mother good-bye at the house, and her last words had been, "Now, Mickey, dear, fight for the blessed country of your adoption like a true son of Erin, and never let it be said that a Free turned his back on the inimy. It's prayin' for ye night and day I'll be, and may it plase the Lord to bring ye safe back again to yer poor old mother. And don't forget yer own prayers, Mickey; it's a consolation they'll be to ye, for it's not skylarkin' yer going, but to fight and die, if needs be, in a just and holy cause."

"Faith, the tears came into me eyes as me poor mother spoke, when I thought what would become of her if I was to be kilt; and I would have desarted that very moment, but I said, no, no, Mickey Free, it's yer own mother would disown ye if ye once thought of doing so.

"Rosy O'Leary was to go down to the ahrmory o see me off, and faith, 'see me off' was the word,

[CONTINUED ON EIGHTH PAGE.]

GENERAL SHERMAN'S HEADQUARTERS, HILTON HEAD, SOUTH CAROLINA.

FRANK LESLIE'S WAR MAPS.

FRANK LESLIE, Publisher. 1862. 19 City Hall Square, N. Y.

INDEX.

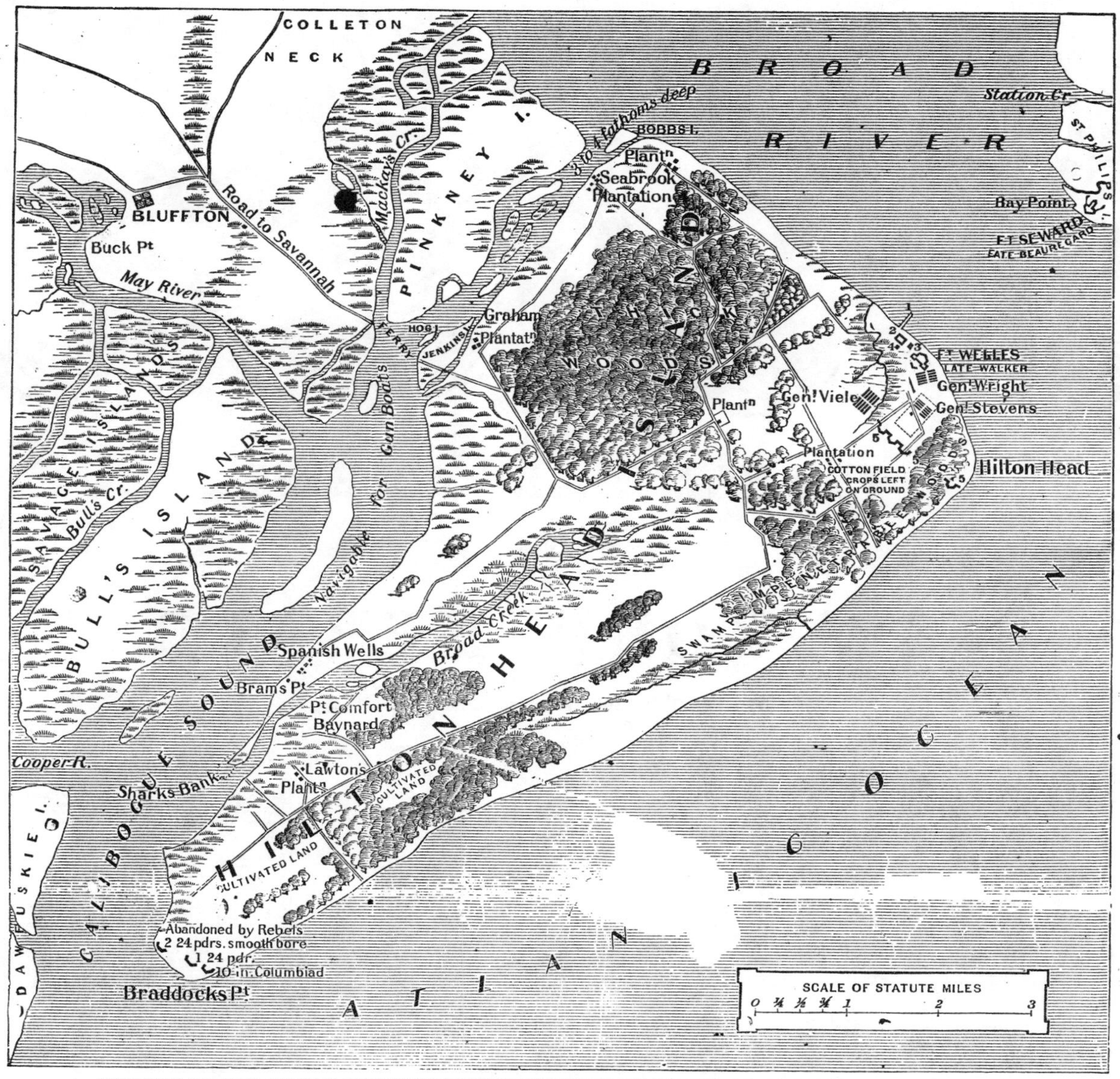

MAP OF HILTON HEAD ISLAND, SHOWING ITS TOPOGRAPHY AND THE VARIOUS WORKS CAPTURED FROM THE REBELS, WITH THE NEW ONES ERECTED BY THE U. S. FORCES.

Our War Chart—Its Utility.

The importance of Maps to the proper comprehension of military operations cannot be over-estimated, and is universally conceded. Descriptions of military movements, as well as of battles, however clear and accurate, leave only a confused impression on the mind, unless accompanied by plans showing the relations of the contending forces, not only as regards strategic centres, but also as regards the natural features of the country, streams, mountains, &c. Hardly a day passes by without the announcement of some change of position on the part of one or the other of the belligerents. Either Gen. Sherman has made some advance in South Carolina, or Gen. Buell some new move in Kentucky. The intelligence, however, as we have said, leaves only the vaguest impression, and gives us no notion of what the movements imply or are intended to accomplish, unless we at once follow them out on the map. Maps, therefore, as well of the general field of operations, whereby the whole plan of the campaign can be taken in at a glance, as also, on a larger scale, of the particular centres of operations, are *indispensable companions of the newspaper*. For our own use and instruction we had put together a series of such maps, illustrating the whole field of the war, complete and in its parts, and finding their utility, we now reproduce them for the benefit of the public, at a price little more than nominal. These maps illustrate not only all that has been done, but will enable the public to follow with eye and pencil every future movement. We may soon expect to hear of active operations at Port Royal and the mouth of the Savannah River; at the mouth of the Mississippi, as well as in Kentucky and Tennessee. With these maps before him, the extent and bearing of these operations will be clear and intelligible to the general reader, who otherwise will only be bewildered by what he reads. We know of no more rational occupation than that of "posting up" the operations of the war, or "checking-off" the movements of the troops, on both sides, on these maps. This can easily be done with differently colored pencils, the *blue* marks indicating the national forces, the *red* the rebel armies. The advance or secession of the respective colors will show, day by day and week by week, the loss or gain of the national arms, and in the end present a real historical picture of the war.

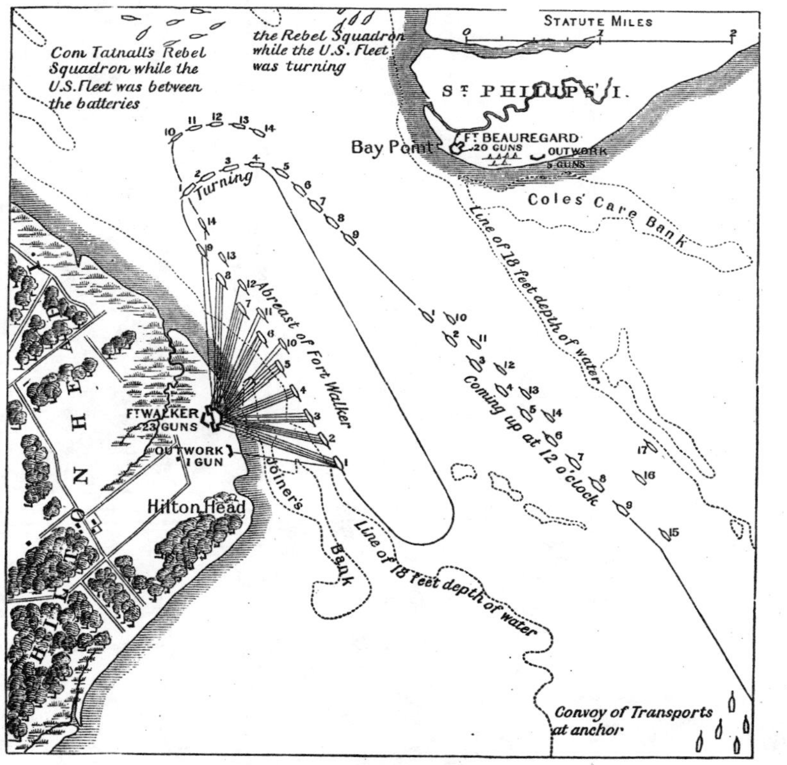

ORDER OF BATTLE IN THE CAPTURE OF PORT ROYAL.

References—1, Flagship Wabash; 2, Susquehanna; 3, Mohican; 4, Seminole; 5, Pawnee; 6, Unadilla; 7, Ottawa; 8, Pembina; 9, Vandalia, towed by Isaac Smith; 10, Bienville; 11, Seneca; 12, Curlew; 13, Penguin; 14, Augusta; 15, Pocahontas; 16, R. B. Forbes, and 17, Mercury, tugboat, came in from outside the bar about 12 o'clock.

Leading Incidents of the War,

DECEMBER, 1860,

20. South Carolina secedes.
25. Major Anderson withdraws from Fort Moultrie to Fort Sumter.

JANUARY, 1861,

2. Fort Pulaski seized by the Rebels.
4. Mobile Arsenal seized by the Rebels.
9. Star of the West fired upon by the Rebels in Charleston.
10. Arsenals and Forts of Louisiana seized by the Rebels.
13. Pensacola Navy Yard seized by the Rebels.

FEBRUARY

25. Gen. Twiggs traitorously surrenders the Forts in Texas to the Rebels.

APRIL

13. Surrender of Major Anderson (Fort Sumter) to the Rebels.
19. The Massachusetts Troops attacked by a Baltimore Mob.
20. Burning of Norfolk and Gosport Navy Yards, to prevent the Vessels and Stores from falling into the hands of the Rebels.

MAY

24. The National Troops take possession of Alexandria—Assassination of Col. Ellsworth.
27. Gen. Butler takes possession of Newport News.
31. Cavalry Skirmish at Fairfax Court-house.

JUNE

2. Battle of Philippi.
10. Battle of Big Bethel.
11. Skirmish at Romney.
17. Battle of Booneville.

JULY

2. Skirmish at Martinsburg.
3. Skirmish at Briar Fork, Mo.
11. Defeat of the Rebels at Rich Mountain.
12. Battle of Corrick's Ford—Gen. Garnett killed.
21. Battle of Bull Run.

AUGUST

7. Hampton burnt by the Rebels.
10. Battle of Wilson Creek—Gen. Lyon killed.
20. Battle of Summersville.
28. Capture of Hatteras by the National Troops.

SEPTEMBER

6. Paducah, Ky., occupied by the National Troops.
10. Battle of Gauley River—Gen. Floyd defeated.
20. Surrender of Col. Mulligan at Lexington.

OCTOBER

5. Battle of Chicamacomico, between the Rebels and the Monticello.
8. Rebels attempt to surprise the Wilson Zouaves on Santa Rosa Island, but are defeated with great slaughter.
21. Battle of Ball's Bluff—Gen. Baker killed—Skirmish at Fredericktown, Mo.
25. Major Zagonyi's Grand Charge at Springfield, Mo.—Capture of Port Royal and Forts Walker and Beauregard.

NOVEMBER

7. Battle of Belmont, Mo.
8. Mason and Slidell captured.
23. Engagement at Pensacola between the Rebels and the National Troops at Fort Pickens.

DECEMBER

4. Ship Island occupied.
5. Occupation of Beaufort.
18. Battle of Dranesville, Va.—Capture of 2,000 Rebels by Gen. Pope at Milford, Ky.
26. Mason and Slidell Surrendered.

Description of Maps.

OCCUPATION OF PORT ROYAL, S. C.

On the 7th November, 1861, by a cleverly conceived naval manœuvre, Commodore Dupont, who commanded the U. S. Naval Expedition to the South, succeeded in bombarding and capturing Forts Walker and Beauregard—the former situated on Hilton Head Island, and the latter on Edding Island—both of them guarding the entrance to Port Royal. After five hours heavy firing, General Drayton, who commanded the rebels at Fort Walker, gave orders to evacuate the place, and Colonel Lee, the commandant of Fort Beauregard, simultaneously retreated from Edding Island, both taking the route to Blufftown, and from thence to Grahamville and Coosawatchee, on the line of railroad between Savannah and Charleston. The loss of the U. S. forces was 8 killed and 27 wounded—that on the part of the rebels supposed to be about 120. The rebels fought with great courage, but their guns were not well handled. There are now about 15,000 national troops at Port Royal. Beaufort was occupied by them on the 5th December. The town was entirely deserted by all the white inhabitants.

FORT PICKENS, SANTA ROSA ISLAND AND PENSACOLA.

Thanks to the courage of Lieutenant Siemmer, Fort Pickens was saved to th[illegible] has since enabled us to keep u[illegible] ma[illegible] ulf coast—a [illegible] est importance on its [illegible] account, saying nothing of the great annoyance the rebel privateers might give our commerce if it were in their possession. Fort Pickens is now held by the U. S. regular troops, under Colonel Harvey Brown, one of our most experienced soldiers. It is situated on the western point of the island of Santa Rosa, which is about forty miles long, and averaging from half a mile to a mile in breadth. This island forms, as it were, a sort of breakwater to Pensacola bay, and is only separated from the mainland of Florida by a strait of about a mile wide. The guns, therefore, of Fort Pickens are in full range of Fort McRae, a rebel fort opposite Fort Pickens. There have been three memorable engagements at this point during the present war—on the 9th October, when a night attack was made by a portion of the rebel forces under General Braxton Bragg upon Wilson's Zouaves, who, with the aid of Colonel Brown's regulars, drove the assailants to their boats with great slaughter; on the 13th November, when Lieutenant John Russell, with a few marines, cut out and burnt the pirate schooner Judith from under the very guns of the dockyard at Pensacola; and thirdly, on the 23d November, when, after two days cannonading between Fort Pickens and Fort McRae, both parties gave up the artillery duel. Opposite to Santa Rosa General Bragg has erected extensive batteries, and established a large camp, where regiments are collected and drilled, previous to being despatched to the seat of war in Virginia.

MAP OF CHARLESTON.

As the place of initiation of the present rebellion the bay of Charleston will be always famous, and we therefore give a map of it as it was on the 12th April, 1861, when the rebel batteries, directed by General Beauregard, opened their fire upon Fort Sumter, then held by Major Robert Anderson and ninety-two men, who, after a desperate resistance of thirty-four hours, surrendered to the enemy, and were despatched to New York in a Federal steamer.

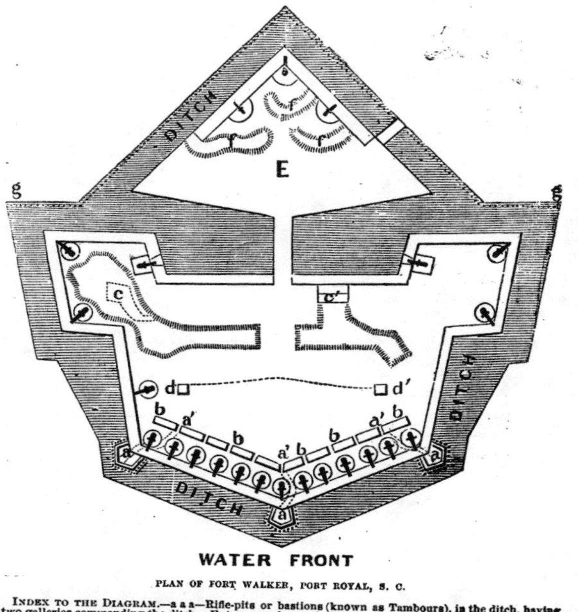

PLAN OF FORT WALKER, PORT ROYAL, S. C.

Index to the Diagram.—a a a—Rifle-pits or bastions (known as Tambours), in the ditch, having two galleries commanding the ditch. Entrance underneath the parapet, coming out at a' a' a'. In many respects this is preferable to a counterscarp gallery, but these were too close to the glacis, and could have been too easily bridged. The approaches for storming would have to have been made from under the cover of the beach; no protection against hand grenades. To have attempted to storm the parapet at once would have been almost impossible.

b b b—Are traverses to protect those serving the guns.

c c'—Are magazines. In c' a quantity of shell, some charged. They are mostly percussion; very few fuses.

d d'—Ovens for heating shot; d' was destroyed by a shot, and then a traverse was thrown up to connect the two.

E—A lunette—not finished—for defence against land attack.

. . . .—Pickets in the ditch—badly driven, and too near the counterscarp. It would be very easy jump over them from the glacis into the ditch. The glacis should have been three feet higher.

f f f—Traverses. g g—Salient points, unprotected.

THE NEW YEAR'S ADDRESS

OF THE

NEWSMEN

OF THE

NEW YORK HERALD,

To its Subscribers and Readers, January 1, 1862.

ONCE, again, in her course
Round the centre and source
Of her life, light and beauty, our planet has run
Her circle of seasons. Again 'tis begun;
Unfailing and true, as through thousands of years,
In that concord sublime of the heavenly spheres.
When human affairs are thus govern'd—ah! then
The millenium will shine on the children of men.
But, hold! 'tis no part of the Newsman's economy
To leave Mother Earth for the realms of astronomy.

THE UNION—live the Union!
With the New Year's dawn we bring
Our tribute to the Union, and
Rejoicing while we sing
Of its unconquerable power,
That it has passed its darkest hour.

THE UNION, 'twas the Union
Which closed our last refrain;
With the Union—*vive la* Union,
We begin our present strain—
As, like a bird upon the wing,
The past year's grand events we sing.

THE UNION—from our Union
What blessings have been given,
Descending upon all alike,
As the gentle dews of Heaven.
Sacred this war, though saints deplore,
Which aims these blessings to restore,
North, South, East, West, forevermore.

How glorious and grand
Our country did stand;
How happy and prosperous our Heaven-favored land,
As it were but yesterday amply possessing
All resources and forces of power, every blessing
Which earth can bestow—with a government proved
The best since our globe out of chaos was moved—
So strong, foreign threats we dismissed in contempt;
So benign, we imagined our Union exempt
From traitors and treason for ages to come—
When the whole land was roused by the roll of the drum
Of a fierce insurrection, the silliest and worst
With which any people have ever been cursed;
A war continental, and, sad the confession,
Inflamed by this will-'o-the-wisp of Secession.
The fruits of a long agitation of slavery,
The work of fanatics, and treason, and knavery—
Secession, rebellion, sword, fire and slaughter,
On mountain and plain, on the land and the water,
Are wasting our country. These things be our theme,
Though strange, wild and dark as the fantastical changes of
some horrible dream.

Ere the first morning sun
Of the year Sixty-One,
This insane rebellion had fairly begun.
Crazy South Carolina had bolted, and raised
Such a fuss, such a muss, that it crackled and blazed
Like a fire o'er the South, while "Old Buck" stood amazed—
Still pouting and doubting,
Or waking to quaking and shaking,
And whining, and pining, and dining, and wining;
While sappers and miners were sapping and mining,
And smoking, and joking, and croaking,
And pledging and hedging;
In promises spacous and gracious,
In performances often fallacious;
Still grumbling, and mumbling, and fumbling,
While the country to ruin was tumbling;
To conspirators wincing and mincing,
Their ways were so very convincing.
Decoyed, still among them he cuddled,
Bamboozled, befogg'd and bemuddled;
Still moaning and groaning,
Beseeching and preaching,
And moping, and groping, and hoping,
Gallivanting, and canting, and soaping,
Till his Cabinet revealings
Of treason and stealings,
Reduced the old man to a poor trembling mouse,
Afraid of his shadow even in the White House;
But, deserted, beleaguered, and weak from old age,
The HERALD stuck by him till drawn from the stage.

As it was, had it not
Been for Old Winfield Scott,
And his vigilant eye on the fire-eaters' plot,
"Old Buck" and "Old Abe" would have fallen a prize
To a Jacobin mob under Skyrocket Wise;
And our National Capital, in their possession,
Would have been the headquarters of rampant secession.

But Scott saved "Old Buck,"
And "Old Abe" had the luck
To be warned in good time, by a whisper from Puck,
Of cutthroats in Baltimore, lying in wait—
So casting aside his official estate,
And rigg'd as a Scotchman, and travelling all night,
By a roundabout road, with the morning's gray light,
"Honest Abe" safe in Washington, caused some surprise,
And some fun at his run and his Highland disguise.

Yet still there were dangers;
But Scott had his rangers
Maintained on the watch, till the crisis was past
Of the inauguration,
Which brought to the nation
The hope that the clouds were dispersing at last.
'Twas a foolish and almost a fatal delusion,
For the rebels were widening their plots of confusion.
Seven States had gone out—
With the Palmetto shout
Of mock independence they went up the spout—
Had set up Jeff. Davis—were hotly employed,
With the cannon and muskets provided by Floyd,
In arming for war, while imploring for peace,
Only asking a full and a final release,
Only calling to us, in an innocent tone,
"We are sinking the Old Ship, pray let us alone."

To "Honest Abe Lincoln,"
A queer fact to think on,
They sent up this olive branch, all the time arming;
But he, not quite ready, was patient and steady,
And his answer delayed, till the case was alarming.
For, under this fooling, secession was cooling—
"They must strike or it dies," so their fiat went forth,
And then Sumter's story, of Anderson's glory,
Aroused like a trumpet the Sons of the North.

With the flames and the smoke,
And the thunders which broke
From the walls of Fort Sumter, our people awoke,
Our proud Empire City still leading the way
To the nation's high cause in her battle array.
By thousands and millions, from Kansas to Maine,
Our people came out, this high cause to maintain;
Lifting high the old flag from the East to the West,
And resolved that its wrongs should be amply redressed.

And the South! Why, God bless ye,
All over Secessia,
Its Jacobin clubs all opposers expelling,
Carousing, and threatening, and arming, and yelling,
Soon reduced every State in revolt to their sway,
And dragg'd in four more to their rebel array—
North Carolina, Virginia, Arkansas, Tennessee—
And how, from an outrageous case, you shall see:—
A club of conspirators, summoned by Wise,
Came down upon Richmond, and took by surprise
A loyal Convention, as robbers sometimes
Take a traveller's watch, and his jewels and dimes.
Like brigands, they forced that Convention to sign,
In secret, their bill of Secession. 'Twas fine
Thus to make of Virginia, with all her old pride,
A mule, yea, a jackass, for Davis to ride.

Thus the people down there in the "Ancient Dominion"
To the Jacobins yielded their right of opinion;
For her traitors declared that you cannot refuse,
With four hundred thousand fat niggers to lose.
Unless you fall in, and before its too late,
We'll take them, and drive you, disgraced, from the State;
Fit only to dwell in that Yankee communion
Which seeks to beguile us with songs of "the Union."
Thus the poor "Old Dominion" succumb'd, it is true,
And thus situated, what else could she do?
But Western Virginia (where the almighty nigger
Is accounted a humbug, and cuts a small figure)
Stood fast by the Union, and still standing fast,
Defies all Secessia, and will to the last.

Old Virginia was cold,
And before we were told
That she had been captured, and shackled, and sold,
In pursuing the plans of Floyd, Letcher and Wise,
Harper's Ferry and Norfolk were seized by surprise—
The one to secure a great arsenal of rifles,
And muskets, and pistols, and other such trifles;
The other to capture a squadron which lay
Asleep in the trap of Elizabeth Bay,
And the Navy Yard there, with its millions of stores
Of warlike materials, and cannon by scores.
But when traitors contrive, and resolve, and conspire,
In plots such as these, they should look out for fire.
Harper's Ferry they seized; but too late at the scene,
A fire had despoiled them of that magazine.
Wise was not half so smart as the madman John Brown,
When with twenty-five followers he captured the town;
And Letcher fell short of his grand speculation
At Norfolk—'twas spoil'd in a grand conflagration.
Best of all, the conspirators had to forego
All their plots for the seizure of Fortress Monroe,
So that still we retained that strong lock and its key,
Which shuts up the State, like a wall, from the sea.
And over the Bay, we have lately brought back
The counties Northampton and old Accomac,
Rendered famous by Wise, and its bountiful dishes
Of ducks, oysters, crabs, and all sorts of choice fishes.

And Maryland next,
By conspirators vex'd,
And caught in their toils, was extremely perplex'd
What to do, where to go, till our soldiers dispers'd
Those Baltimore roughs—of all ruffians the worst—
And her bridge-burning night birds, a dastardly crew,
And warned them to find something better to do.
And thankful that city may be, and with reason,
In losing her bold legislators of treason;
And thankful, in view of her late pranks so dashing,
That she has escaped a most terrible thrashing.
And thanks for the now full and cordial communion
Between the Old State and the North and the Union.

Big Bethel—a blunder;
Vienna—no wonder;
Rich Mountain—a sharp peal of good Union thunder.
'Twas there in his victories McClellan displayed
That genius and skill in war's terrible trade
Which have placed on his shoulders the mantle of Scott,
"*Sans peur, sans reproche,*" without blemish or spot.

Bull Run! 'twas "On to Richmond,"
Cried Greeley and his crew—
"Onward," their hue and cry; so march'd
Our army raw and new.
It went rejoicing in its strength,
And in its grand display;
Bleeding and broken, it return'd
From that disastrous day.
That Sabbath morning brightly dawn'd
Along our glittering lines,
For miles o'er fields of grass and grain,
And groves of oaks and pines;
In the pomp and pride of battle
As on a gay parade,
But ah! how different was the scene
Beneath that evening's shade!
The conflict opened gloriously
Along our fiery track,
And full three miles we still advanced
And drove the rebels back;
From bridge, copse, trench and battery,
Our flag still rising higher,
And through a storm of shot and shell,
Through dust, and smoke, and fire;
Until we thought the day was ours—
When wearied from the fight,
By thousands we sat down to rest—
But 'twas a brief respite:
For the rebel Johnston's squadrons
Had come, and with them, too,
Our fancied day of Austerlitz
Was changed to Waterloo.
Our Grouchy was Old Patterson,
Some sixty miles away,
With five and twenty thousand men,
And thus we lost the day.
And yet while brave men are esteemed
For deeds of glory done,
New York will boast her heroes,
At the battle of Bull run.

With this change in the tide,
Kentucky was tried
By secession, but loyal Kentucky allied
To three strong Union States, looming up at her side,
And cherishing still the wise teachings of Clay,
Found secession a game which she never could play.
Although she betrayed quite a weak partiality
For that wretched secession device of neutrality,
Which means, if you give all we ask, and disown
The Union, and fight it, we'll let you alone.
But this sort of luck was too mean for Kentuck,
And driven to close quarters, she fights like a buck,
And the secession crew may regard themselves lucky,
If with a whole skin they escape from Kentucky.

Unhappy Missouri!
Its most savage fury
This fierce war has brought upon loyal Missouri.
Over her fair fields its march may be traced,
By broad belts of country despoiled and made waste;
Their people like wandering gypsies are found,
Their homes laid in ashes or torn to the ground;
Their women and children, exhausted and falling
In death on the highway—still piteously calling
Upon their protectors, cut down by the fury
Of savage marauders. Unhappy Missouri!
Yet Boonville, and Springfield, and Carthage will stand,
And Lexington, high with the names of our land
Of heroes immortal; and Belmont, in story
And song, will live long in the annals of glory.
But will glory repay the poor mothers and daughters
Made widows and orphans by such dreadful slaughters?
Our country, we answer—whatever the cost,
We must rescue our country, or all will be lost.

And East Tennessee,
Stronghold of the free—
That it should be rescued all good men agree,
And promptly, we hope, Parson Brownlow will hear
The sounds of its coming deliverance near.
And that from those mountains we'll open the gates
To reunion in all the "Confederate States."

Well done! We can boast
On our Southern seacoast—
Our Soldiers and Sailors. Come join in the toast.
Captain Wilkes, 'tis conceded, has done pretty well,
For those lost children, Mason and Johnny Slidell,
Head chiefs of secession, and of it crammed full,
And nabb'd from that kidnapper known as John Bull.
He has heard all about it; and pitching, and rearing,
He calls it an "insult outrageous and daring."
A most diabolical act of aggression,
Which must be atoned for. "Huzzah!" cries Secession.
A shout which informs that now our true plan
Is to keep England quiet as long as we can.
And to give her no cause for a league with Jeff. Davis,
With her much needed stores, and her armies and navies.
The *Times*, call'd the Thunderer, has not deigned to flatter us
And pooh-pooh's that little affair at Cape Hatteras—
That neat operation which broke up some juggling
And a brisk little trade in the business of smuggling.
And at Chicamacomico—mark well the spelling—
Those land crabs for once, got a good Union shelling.

But in South Carolina!
Oh! Cesar! and Dinah!
Where secession is worshipp'd as something divine-ah!
There we brought down their boastings in terror and sorrow.
For as once, it rained fire and brimstone from Heaven—
For sins which could not, by the Lord, be forgiven—
On the vile city Sodom and wicked Gomorrah;
So the sun was obscured by the smoky eclipse,
From that tempest of fire from our circle of ships,
As they moved like a shoal of sea monsters at play,
In that beautiful water of Port Royal Bay.
"It seemed," said a darkie, "You done us so brown,
Dat de earth was gwine up, and de heavens comin' down."

Hark! Louder and higher
Comes that wild cry of "Fire."
From Charleston—wide raging—dome, tower and spire
Are flaming and crackling; and in the wild glow,
The woodlands above and the waters below,
Fort Sumter, the bay, and its isles, and the ocean,
Are illumined as by some volcanic commotion.
A city laid waste, in this dread visitation
To treason, secession and nullification.

Billy Wilson's game chickens,
Down there at Fort Pickens,
Were really beginning to spoil for a fight,
When the rebels surprised them,
And nearly capsized them,
Stealing down on their camp, under cover of night;
But our fellows soon rallied, and then from their slaughter
The rebels, like ducks, scampered off to the water.
Since which, General Brown, these attentions rewarding,
Has quieted Bragg with a wholesome bombarding.

Captain Hollins, the hero
Of Greytown, the Nero,
Has fallen in glory somewhat below zero.
Since that brilliant achievement, in which he essayed
To open our tight Mississippi blockade,
His "Turtle" did wonders; but, as the fact shows,
His "Turtle" did nothing but break his own nose.
"We peppered them well, the Hessian crew, darn 'em."
Oh! Hollins, you humbug, don't tell that to Barnum.
But our chaps? Well, so far as we are enlightened,
Our chaps, though not hurt, were most shamefully frightened.

But, in this rattling fashion,
For days we might dash on,
Yet one moment longer we ask your compassion.
We have a grand army, and what is its score?
Six hundred and sixty-five thousand, and more.
And the line around which this immense army hovers?
Two thousand miles long is the line which it covers,
With our Navy—no longer contemptibly small—
Two hundred and fifty odd vessels in all.
And the men? Some twenty-five thousand. The cost?
Including what's stolen, and squandered, and lost,
And contractors' big swindles, and oysters and toddy,
Bad beef, and bad pork, and bad blankets and shoddy,
Our Army and Navy's expenses and pay
Are not quite two millions of dollars a day.
Mon Dieu!—and no battle—this really is funny.
Is this war, then, reduced to the bluff game of money?
Perhaps; yet why should this excite any wonder?
'Tis the pause in the storm ere it breaks forth in thunder.
Has the Sumter been caught? Yes—that is, she's been found
A half dozen times, though still bobbing around.
And when will they hang those condemned privateers?
Wait a bit—think of brave Col. Corcoran, my dears.
But an exchange of prisoners?—our soldiers demand it.
Very true; but you know, well, we can't understand it.

Good morning! time passes:
Touch lightly your glasses.
Peace, peace to the brave fellows slain at Manassas,
And all o'er the land, in this deadly contention
Of brothers with brothers. And yet we must mention
A thing or two more; for you know that at parting
With friends it requires a good deal of starting.
The Potomac blockade: can't tell what the matter is;
Perhaps we're afraid of those secession batteries;
Or, perhaps, we may think them entitled to no regard
Till McClellan has settled with Toutant de Beauregard.
Whatever the mystery, it seemeth outrageous
That the rebels in that noble river should cage us,
And that we are contented at long range to shell them,
With forces on hand quite enough to expel them.
The Potomac! fair stream of America's pride,
Of Washington's birth—where he grew up and died;
Where the chief and the shrine of Mount Vernon forever
Will brighten the face of the beautiful river—
The Potomac, alas! that its shores should now be,
From its rise in the mountains far down to the sea,
The scene of red slaughter, of scouts, guerrillas,
Camps, armies and batteries, and forts and flotillas.
Shade of Washington! rise, interpose and restore
Our land to thy faith in the Union once more!
And what of Fremont? Why, his case simply teaches
That a man, now and then, gets too big for his breeches.
And our secession peace men—that rascally set?
Inquire at Fort Warren or Fort Lafayette.
And our hot abolition disturbers and screechers—
The Garrisons, Greeleys, and Cheevers and Beechers?
Still scattering their firebrands of discord, and brewing
In Congress their schemes for the nation's undoing.
If they had their deserts they would now be held faster
Than any ass of the class of the Abbe McMaster.
But let "Honest Abe" still maintain his position,
Resisting this rank anti-slavery sedition,
And soon we shall silence its base coalition.

Bon jour! We are sure
That you cannot endure
This long rigmarole. Yet a word in your ear:
With the day's liberalities,
Not to say prodigalities,
The Newsman, you know, has his "Happy New Year."
Shall we summon the shadow of Douglas, who died
Holding up for the Union, and fast by its side?
Or need we recall such as Baker and Lyon,
And Ellsworth and Ward? In the sweet peace of Zion
May they rest. So, good morning! but yet, by the way,
Good luck to George Opdyke, our Mayor to-day.
With "great expectations" he's this day anointed,
And they are not likely to be disappointed,
If we may rely on his friends, who assure us
That if we are sick he's the doctor to cure us.
But we very much fear he will never cry "Land, ho!"
If hampered and worried like Mayor Fernando.
We hope for the best; and we hope very soon
That the *World*, and the *Times*, and the howling *Tribune*
Will find abolition sedition a sell,
And "cease to do evil and learn to do well."
We hope this rebellion will shortly be ended—
That the States in revolt will be soon again blended
With the States still in loyalty true to the Union,
And blended for ages in cordial communion.
In this hope that our skies will again soon be clear,
Dear ladies, to you, and all friends, far and near—
To "Honest Old Abe," and (he's right, never fear),
To our Army and Navy a "A HAPPY NEW YEAR."

VOL. 1. PHILADELPHIA, SATURDAY, JANUARY 11, 1862. NO. 9.

NEW YEAR'S EVE AT THE OUTPOSTS.

A STORY OF THE WAR.

BY ESSEX.

[Written for The War Press.]

It was New Year's eve. Along our lines at every camp, the soldiers were making merry in honor of the ending of the old year. Around the bivouac fires gay groups are singing jolly songs, while up and down the streets of the camp others are dancing with fantastic antics, now coming with uncouth gambols into the red light of the flames, and again leaping away into darkness, until they looked like dusky imps engaged in an unearthly carouse. Ever and anon, above the hubbub, sounded a musical note, the screech of a trumpet, the strike of a banjo, or the deep boom of a drum, as some jolly drummer struck a thunderous accompaniment to the merry discords. But while all appeared so gay, here and there were some sad faces, where men sat apart and alone in their tents thinking of home, or of the last New Year's eve, passed so differently with loved ones far away.

At the outposts it was the same thing there, where the pickets were gathered around their fires; there was the same jollity, although they were so near a wary foe, and each man knew that when he went out to his lonely sentinel duty, he might fall by the bullet of a lurking enemy, and so never return. But, despite this reflection, the men were as carelessly happy as if there had been no such thing as danger, until, as the night advanced, and the cold increased, one by one they sank to sleep—and slept soundly, too, wrapped in their blankets, though with no bed but the hard ground, no tent but the dim heavens far above.

At one station, well out in the open country towards the fatal road of Manassas, Lieutenant Hastings had charge of a picket of twenty-five men. Early in the evening they had built a hut of evergreens to protect them from the cold north wind; before it was their fire, and in this protection they had made merry, calling it their Christmas house, and drinking such mild toasts as they were permitted in its honor. Now, however, they were all asleep, except the sentries on guard, and the young lieutenant, who, wrapped in his cloak, paced slowly back and forth near the glowing fire.

Arthur Hastings was thinking—as where did he not?—of his fair young bride. He was recalling, as he never could help doing when quite alone and free from anxiety about his duties, all the sad history of the past. Once more he thought of the first time he saw Georgia Beaufort at evening parade at West Point, now more than two years ago, when he was a cadet there. He remembered how lovely she looked in that bewitching round hat, and how he was at once enthralled by her delicate Southern beauty. How gaily the time sped during that enchanted time! How he dreamed over the sunny days when he climbed with her the heights of Fort Putnam, or wandered at her side through the dangerous mazes of flirtation walks. And then those nights when he danced with her at the cadet hops, and the hurried walk home across the dim parade ground, with the lingering pressure of the hand at parting. Again, he dwelt on all those happy moments until he came to the time when Georgia was to go away to her Carolina home; and recalled, with a wild thrill, the last evening when he had at last avowed his honest love, and obtained her whispered promise to be his wife.

In his reverie, he skipped the long winter that followed, that was cheered only by her letters and the day of his honorable graduation, and remembered only with lingering fondness the month he had spent with Georgia in the mountains of Virginia as her proud and happy lover. Then came his visit at autumn to the old plantation that was Georgia's home; and his heart beat as he dreamed again over the gay wedding that he thought then had made his love secure forever. There was a week of true Southern festivity, and then he first saw the serpent through the flowers, and he clenched his hands and set his teeth as he remembered how Georgia's brothers had whispered the word "Secession," and dared to offer him honor and office, and even his fair young bride, as a bribe to betray the country that had educated him, and the flag he had sworn to protect A gasping sigh as he thought of the angry words that had followed, and the hurried parting with his pale and weeping wife, who had besought him to go, in mortal dread of his life and hers, and had solemnly sworn to rejoin him very soon.

"And yet," he murmured, coming to the old sad conclusion, "that was more than a year ago!"

For a while, it is true, her letters had helped him to bear the separation, and he had next his heart now the little package that was so precious, but for six months past he had heard no word from her. He saw her brothers' names as high in rank in the rebel army. He knew how bitter was the feeling against the North; might not she, too, have been carried away by it, and be ready to forget and repudiate her Northern husband?

So the night wore on, and still Authur Hastings walked his self-appointed beat. Since this separation, he had never been able to sleep till the night was well nigh spent. His comrades knew him for a silent and reserved man, but his soldiers could have said that no kinder officer ever cared for their wants or sympathized with their wishes.

After a while the red moon, shining dimly through the clouds, threw down a few pale rays on the desolate scene; and the lieutenant, looking up, wondered idly if Georgia, too, was looking at that same chilly lustre. In her Southern home, far away, were they treading some gay scene to see the old year out and the new year in, and was she there forgetful of her deserted husband?

At this moment the sharp crack of a musket shot broke the interval of his dream, and brought Lieut. Hastings back from his own reveries to the stern realities of the present. With a word he had aroused the sleeping soldiers, and hastened in the direction whence the sound proceeded. Before he had gone far, he met two men coming in breathless. They were sentinels falling back to the picket.

"Pete Jones is gone, sir," gasped one of them, as Hastings stopped him; "I saw him fall."

The lieutenant turned back with them, and when they reached again the main body, it was evidently time for action. By the pale moonlight they could catch glimpses of dark figures gliding along the road, and just as Hastings gave the order to take position behind the shelter of some bushes, there was a rattling volley that brought down one of their foremost men, and showed that the rebels must be in considerable force. The soldiers returned the fire with some effect, apparently, for the rebel ranks seemed in some confusion. The lieutenant ordered the men to lay down to reload, and thus the second round passed harmlessly over their heads.

"Now up, boys! and give it to them! Take good aim—steady, fire!" shouted Hastings; and the men responded to their lieutenant's voice gallantly.

Their unbroken front and well-directed shots evidently told, and disconcerted the enemy. They had come out merely for a skirmish or to pick off some lonely sentinels, and did not half like this serious work. Hastings heard the order given,

"Fall back!"

"They are running, men!" he cried; "advance—come on! we'll have some of them yet!" and he sprang forward, followed by his whole command

By this time the rebels were in full retreat. Dispersing, they seemed to disappear among the bushes and behind fences. But the men's blood was up—with excited cries they followed the flying fugitives.

It was wild work, this chasing a vanishing foe over the dangerous paths that led to Manassas. Some of the "Confederates" fled like deer, others stood and returned the soldiers' fire, and were in turn shot down or brought in prisoners. Hastings was cheering his men on, when he saw a man whose dress and hat appeared to indicate a rebel officer hurrying not from them, but towards them. A soldier near levelled his gun.

"Stop!" cried the lieutenant; "take him prisoner; but don't shoot him!"

The man dropped his gun, and at the instant the officer sprang with a cry that seemed almost one of joy towards the lieutenant. He looked very young—slight and boyish in figure, wrapped in a dark heavy cloak, and wearing a broad hat shaded with plumes, and looped on one side with a medallion bearing the rebel letters of the "C. S. A."

He held out his sword to Hastings, but, touched with his extreme youth, the lieutenant said, kindly,

"Keep your sword, sir, and consider yourself under my charge."

The men had gone far enough, and Hastings feeling that there might be danger of falling into an ambush, ordered the recall, and started to return to the camp. The rebel officer walked by his side; but Hastings noticed, after some moments, that he seemed to move so slowly that he paused, and said, courteously—

"This has been a hard night's work; you are tired; you had better take my arm."

The young officer, with muttered thanks, seized the proffered arm, and clung to it convulsively. Then Hastings noticed that he trembled visibly, although he was evidently making a strong effort to control himself Yet, the lieutenant could not despise him—he rather felt the strongest pity.

"Do not be distressed," he urged. "I will protect you entirely, and you shall share my tent tonight. I am alone; the second lieutenant is in Washington."

So they went on until they reached the camp; the soldiers looked sleepily out at the little band of prisoners, and their returned comrades; but Hastings hurried on without pausing to his own tent. Once under its shelter, he threw a fresh log on the dying fire, and lit a candle; then, for the first time, he looked at his captive.

Short and slight in figure, wrapped in a heavy cloak, the wide brimmed hat shading a pale face, out of which a pair of wild, bright eyes shone through a tangled mass of curling hair. He looked very young, and yet a thick black moustache shaded his upper lip.

Hastings regarded him with troubled surprise. Was this some near relative of his lost wife? Those eyes haunted him strangely.

"You must be very weary—let me give you some brandy." And Hastings turned to where his pocket-flask lay. "You will take some, wont you?"

No answer, only the rebel still looked at him with that strange questioning earnestness. His lips moved, but he could not speak. Hastings repeated his question, going a step nearer.

"You had better take some."

Then the young officer raised his hand—a hand small and white, to his head; in an instant the shading hat was off, the moustache had disappeared, and he staggered to his feet.

"Arthur!—my own Arthur!—don't you know me?"

"Georgia! my wife! my wife!"

They were clasped in each other's arms, and the long months of separation were forgotten in that blissful moment.

At first Hastings was too happy even to wonder, but at last, when the first wild moments were passed, while he still held his boy-wife close, lest she should fade away, he asked—

"And how did you escape?"

"I swore I would come," replied Georgia. "I had promised to be yours eternally, and I had sworn to join you. Never for an instant since we parted have I given up that hope, and you see I am here."

Then, with many interruptions, she told the story of the past: how she had waited and waited since the war broke out; how, at first, she had tried entreaties to be permitted to join her husband, and they had been refused; then, how she had bent all her energies to escape; how she had succeeded, after long delays, in reaching Richmond; and how there she had succeeded in obtaining her present disguise, and in it joined the army at Manassas.

"I pretended to be on the staff of General H., and so last night got leave to come out when they went to attack your pickets. I was resolved to be taken prisoner, but I was so afraid you might not be here. When I heard your voice, I knew it at once, and I could hardly help then telling you who I was."

"My poor, poor darling! how you must have suffered!" said Hastings, as he looked at the sweet white face beside him. "But it is all over now; nothing shall ever part us again."

So Lieut. Hastings' sad reveries were ended once and forever. Georgia loved him better than home, or kindred or country; and whereas at evening all had seemed so dark, he could now, with grateful confidence, look forward to a happy New Year.

GENERAL BURNSIDES.

GENERAL BLENKER.

GENERAL HEINTZELMAN.

GENERAL DON CARLOS BUELL.

GENERAL KEYES.

GENERAL W. B. FRANKLIN.

COLONEL WISTAR.

WALTER LE CLARE;

OR, THE VICTIM OF SECESSION.

That scene—they two so young and fair—ah, well might angels weep!—the tempter and the tempted. See—with all a woman's earnestness she is striving to gain her purpose—he wavers—two mighty elements struggle in opposition within his manly bosom; love for her who is about to prove a second Eve, and devotion to his country. Oh, how can he speak those words of refusal; how disappoint the ambition of her whom he loved better than life? But he will speak—she is gazing with her own bright, beautiful eyes into the very depths of his soul-speaking orbs, as though she would read his answer there ere it fell from his lips—they parted; no sound issued; he was almost spellbound. Never, never had she appeared so regally handsome, Walter thought, as she stood before him in her bewitching beauty; and his soul sickened at the thought of what one so queenly would have him do. A moment, and his answer. Slowly it came, and low; yet so distinct that it might have been heard at the farthest corner of that splendid drawing-room.

"Mary, I am true to the Union and my country."

"Then, Walter Le Clare, you have never loved me, or else—"

"Mary," he began—

"You are a contemptible coward!" rang on his tortured ear. He sprang to his feet. 'Twas a fearful sight to see that brave loving man so strongly moved; he stood erect, with his arms tightly folded across his chest; the hot blood, madly leaping, freshly started through his swelling veins, dyed his whole face a burning red; but the passion lasted not long, for the blood receding, left his forehead calm and white as snowy marble; the fire-light of indignation went out from the beautiful eye, and in place of its lurid glow, came back the old love-flame that used to sparkle there, together with a mingled expression of reproach and forgiveness—a single glance—when, bowing low, he turned and was gone.

* * * * * *

And now, for an introduction to the persons, at whose conversation, contrary to the rules of good breeding, we have been uninvited listeners; rather late, perhaps—well, "better late than never."

Mary Langley, at the period of her introduction to you, dear reader, had just entered upon her nineteenth year. She was a tall dark beauty of Georgian birth, with hair black as a raven's wing, and of that peculiar glossiness seen only in the wavy ringlets of Spanish senoritas; her eyes, large, dark and brilliant, seemed to burn you with their very intensity of expression. Her form, delicately rounded and most exquisitely developed, would have been the delight of a modiste; united with those personal charms was a mind well stored with all the current literature of the day, besides many of the works of the old masters; and a taste refined and cultivated. She had been left an orphan at the age of seventeen, and having chosen Mr. Walter Le Clare, senior, guardian of her property, came to reside with him about a year previous to the return of Walter, who was summoned from an unfinished tour on the continent to the bed-side of his aged father. To describe our hero but few words are necessary. He was what now is seldom found—a true Southern gentleman, handsome, cultivated, polished, talented, and possessed of all those qualities which contribute to form nature's nobleman. Arrived at home, he found his father just recovered from a severe attack of typhoid fever, and anxious to have him remain; a task which Walter found by no means difficult, since it was now brightened and beautified by the presence of Mary Langley. Thus brought into association, need we tell the result? It was no matter of surprise to old Mr. Le Clare, when, descending into the breakfast room one fine May morning, he found them hand in hand, waiting his appearance. The opening of the present rebellion saw them happy, and only waiting the completion of some alterations and additions to the Le Clare mansion, before joining hands where hearts were already united. The clamor of secession had in him no advocate, no listener; on the contrary, he wrote, spoke, and labored against it in vain. Because of his superior military knowledge—he having graduated with the highest honors from West Point, and spent some time in observing the defences and fortifications of several places celebrated in the Crimean war—the rebel leaders were anxious to have him take command of a regiment; but finding that he spurned with indignation the commission offered him, they, knowing the influence exerted by a woman over a man that truly loves her, determined to bestir themselves in another direction. In pursuance of this resolve, parties and balls were given and attended by their wives and daughters. Here Mary Langley, the acknowledged belle of Montgomery, and a courted beauty, heard and imbibed the sentiments of her Alabamian sisters, as was intended, together with the same idea held by many at that time, and not yet given up, viz: establishing a monarchical government; and determined to imitate the example set by many of her friends in persuading their lovers and other male friends, to join the Confederate army that they might wreathe their fair brows with fresh laurels of conquest and victory, in the courts of royalty or the halls of nobility. Hence the scene at the opening of this story.

Chagrined at her failure, the traitoress hastily dispatched a note to the "Congress," then in session, the result of which will soon be apparent. When Walter left the drawing-room, he went to the stable, and, as was his custom when irritated, mounted his favorite horse, a gallant little bay, and galloped over to the neighboring plantation on which Charles Grantner, his bosom friend, lived. Having remained over to dinner, he was riding slowly homeward, when he was met by James, the negro valet-de-chambre, in great agitation, and quite out of breath. Coming up to him, he was surprised to see ters in his eyes and marks of distress on his countenance; dismounting, he sat down on a small flat rock near by; and bade James take a seat beside him. The latter obeyed, and essayed to relate the cause of his disturbance in the following manner:

"Oh, marster Walter! You never saw sich doins in your life—nobody ever did. I have been huntin' and huntin' you ever so long. Jeff Davis done gone and sent them 'federate devils to 'fiscate the property, and take all on us niggers to work in the 'trenchments, and dig the fortycations. Oh lord! Mars' Walter, do save us! I learn as how you could." Here he began to wring his hands.

With a hurried "follow me!" Le Clare leaped in his saddle, and was out of sight; putting spurs to his horse he was soon at home. The most dire confusion prevailed—servants were running hither and thither, shrieking and uttering the most vehement lamentations. Entering the parlor, he found two officers, who had come direct from headquarters bearing a commission, and in case of his refusal, a notice of the confiscation of his own and father's estate without reserve.

"Rather beggary and honor"—he was about to say, when the door opened, and Mary Langley entered, her countenance wrought up to an apparent expression of the most intense agony, supporting his father, whose trembling frame could ill brook the evils of poverty.

Stretching his arms towards Walter, the old man cried, "Save me, my son!" and would have fallen at his feet had he not caught him in his arms.

"Say no more, my dearest father—I will."

He paused—the great drops of sweat stood upon his forehead; (what a trial!) but his aged father must not be thrown upon the cold charity of the world by any deed of his—no, no! He fell!—avert his doom, kind Heaven!—and became a *traitor*.

On, on—through the rebel camp, past sentinel and guard, we go, stopping at that large white tent. 'Tis the Colonel's; he is within, writing. Peeping over his shoulder we observe his letter is to "Mary." Skipping, we will read:

"There was some fighting yesterday; the victory is with the Federal troops. To-morrow the din of battle may be renewed. Then Walter Le Clare will go forth a dishonored man, to raise his hand against the flag which has protected him on land and sea; in savage wilds and foreign courts." Passing on to the postscript: "P. S.—A courier brings the news of my father's death. Should I survive the battle, farewell, Mary! God bless thee; for then I go to join the Union army—not that I love thee less, but my country more.

WALTER."

'Tis the evening after the battle of Bull Run. The ground is strewn with the dead and dying. A little to the right of yonder heap of ghastly corses, lies the body of a handsome young officer, clad in the uniform of the Confederate army; one hand is on his heart, the other grasps a small Federal flag, which he got his death wound in wresting from a brave son of the 69th, and which, in his dying hour he had laid under his head, and prayed for with his last breath. Reader, he was Walter Le Clare.

Who First Answered the President's Call

[Correspondence of The Press.]

CAMP GRIFFIN, Va., January 4, 1862.

In your issue of the 31st of December, under the head of "Record of the Rebellion, &c." you assert that the Ringgold Artillery, of Reading, Pa., was the first company of volunteers that responded to the call of the President. In a subsequent issue, a letter from a former member of the Ringgold Artillery goes to prove that the artillery *was not* the first company, but that it arrived at Washington *together with four other companies*—one from Allentown, two from Pottsville, and one from Lewistown. The latter company—the Logan Guards—commanded by Captain John B. Selheimer, if any, were the first to answer the President's call, and it is about time they receive the credit for so doing.

On the morning of the 16th of April, at nine o'clock, the Logan Guards received orders from Governor Curtin to proceed immediately to Harrisburg, and by nine o'clock that night they were ready to leave for that place with one hundred members. Through some mismanagement of the railroad company, they did not get off until the next morning at four o'clock. As a consequence, they arrived in Harrisburg about six o'clock on the morning of the 17th, which was, however, at least *one hour before the arrival of any other company*. After the other companies arrived, they were all sworn in together; and on the morning of the 18th the five companies left Harrisburg for Washington city. During their passage through Baltimore, and their entrance into Washington, *the Logan Guards had the right, and were the first company to report themselves for duty to the Adjutant General*. It is but just, therefore, that the credit should fall on those who deserve it—the gallant Logan Guards, Captain John B. Selheimer, of Lewistown, Mifflin county, Pennsylvania.

ONE WHO KNOWS.

The Weekly Delta.

VOLUME XVII. NEW ORLEANS SATURDAY, JANUARY 11, 1862. NUMBER 14.

WEEKLY DELTA

PUBLISHED EVERY SATURDAY MORNING,
BY THE NEW ORLEANS DELTA NEWSPAPER COMPANY,
No. 94 Camp Street.

Terms of the DELTA, Invariably in Advance.

DAILY DELTA,

(Sunday included) ....$10 per annum.

SEMI-WEEKLY DELTA:

Will be published every Tuesday and Friday morning. The terms will be $5 per annum—for two copies $9 per annum.

WEEKLY DELTA,

Containing all the news of the seven days previous, up to 2 o'clock Saturday morning, $3 per annum; $5 for two years; $2 for six months; 5 copies, to one person, one year, $12; 10 copies, to one person, one year, $20.

Packages of ten and upward, sent to one person, for less than one year, at the rate of 5 cents each, in advance.

SUNDAY DELTA,

Facile Princeps among family journals, $2 per annum mailed; $2 25 delivered in the city; 5 copies, to one person, one year, $7; 10 copies, to one person, one year, $15.

Packages of ten and upward, sent to one person, or less than one year, at the rate of 3 cents each, in advance.

POSTMASTERS

will be allowed a commission of FIFTY CENTS on each subscriber for the Weekly or Semi-Weekly Delta, at the full price, and ten per cent. on subscriptions to the Daily Delta.

All remittances by mail at our risk, provided the parties making the remittance take a receipt from the Postmaster for the same. Remittances of the current money of the States received at par. We are not accountable for any transactions of traveling agents, unless they hold our written authority.

TO SUBSCRIBERS:

Green wrappers signify that your subscription will expire in three weeks.

When you wish your paper changed from one Post-office to another please mention BOTH offices.

A DIPLOMATIC RECORD OF SHAME.

That the diplomatic correspondence in relation to the Trent affair is the most momentous which this century has produced events may have yet to determine, but that to the Government which provoked it it furnishes one of the most disgraceful records of all history is not open to any kind of dispute. It is difficult to say whether moral or intellectual obliquity is more manifest in Seward's voluminous and tortuous letter to Lord Lyons. Though it was too late for him to surrender the Commissioners with grace, since he had failed to offer reparation before a peremptory demand for it was made, he might at least have saved appearances by excluding from his letter that pitiable inconsistency which looks the more contemptible from the cloud of verbal obscurity and technical subtlety which he throws around it.

The willful inconsistency of a wicked mind may be bold; the acknowledged inconsistency of a frank and generous spirit is honorable; but the inconsistency of Seward is as far from that of bold wickedness as from that of honorable frankness—it is the inconsistency of sheer cowardice and meanness.

Mr. Seward maintains that the Commissioners were contraband and liable to capture; that they were captured in a proper manner under justifying circumstances; that the international law authorizing their capture provides no mode of adjudicating the case in an admiralty court; that the only error of Capt Wilkes consisted in releasing the Trent; that if that vessel had been retained and subjected to judicial proceedings, the case would have been decided against her, and against the Commissioners. But a judicial inquiry being lost by the release of the Trent, there was no recourse left but to a diplomatic discussion of the matter between the two Governments. It is not shown upon what maxim of international law Mr. Seward unhesitatingly yielded on a peremptory diplomatic demand a point he was fully satisfied could have been successfully maintained in a judicial trial.

But while Mr. Seward argues that principles of international law and the facts of the case justify the capture, he admits it to have been in conflict with principles which had ever guided American policy. Yet, though Mr. Seward "could not deny the justice of the claim presented" by England, viewed from the stand point of recognized American principles and policy, he distinctly states that "if the safety of the Union" required such a course, he would, as a matter of "right and duty," reject the claim and detain the prisoners. Herein he makes expediency the measure of right and duty, and asserts that a momentary exigency should override the plain requirements of justice. Such an audacious affirmation of the doctrine of the knave and the tyrant that "the end justifies the means" will be duly appreciated by the power to which it is addressed.

M. Thouvenel's letter in relation to the Trent affair is of the utmost significance. His intervention in the discussion is pointed, and the more so that it is gratuitous. Scarcely anything could more forcibly evince the determination of the French Government to make an issue with the Federal Government whenever visible grounds were offered for doing so in conjunction with England, or even without that conjunction should the latter power fail to act.

Seward's letter to Adams threatening all foreign powers with war that may recognize the Confederate States, must be received in Europe with disgust and contempt, when interpreted by the commentary afforded in the surrender of the Commissioners, an act so obviously inspired by a cowardly dread of war. European nations will see clearly enough that the arrogance of the Northern Minister is without firmness, and that his threats are worth as much as his word, which is worth precisely nothing.

One remark in this last document, however, is suggestive of profitable reflection. When Mr. Seward says that "the life of the insurrection is sustained by the hopes of recognition in Great Britain and France," and that "it would perish in ninety days if these hopes should cease," he ejects one of those round falsehoods for which he is remarkable. But while the assertion may show what value he attaches to a recognition, it should warn us not to look to the benefits of a future contingency with an overconfident reliance that may tend to relax our energies instead of stimulating us to vigorous exertion. Hopes that produce languor are absolutely pernicious.

The banks of New York, Philadelphia and Boston suspended specie payments simultaneously on the 30th ult. The movement was by concert. The New York banks give as the reason "the heavy draft upon the banks for coin, caused by their large advances to the Government." The loss of specie in the New York banks during the week ending on the 30th ult. was upwards of seven millions, leaving but little over twenty-three millions in their vaults. The Committee of Ways and Means in the Federal House of Representatives in view of the suspension, have inserted another section in the finance bill providing for the immediate issue of fifty millions of treasury notes, payable on demand, without specifying any particular place of payment, and to be receivable for all Government dues, and be a legal tender in private as well as public business.

FROM ARIZONA.—The Houston Telegraph publishes the following extract from a private letter, dated Mesilla, December 9th:

I learn that the advance guard of Riley's regiment reached Bliss yesterday, having been forty-five days on the way. We came through in thirty, and did not hurry. The small pox has broken out among our troops at Bliss, Fillmore, Dona Ana and Mesilla, and so far has been very fatal.

Stafford's company is still at Las Cruces, and have as yet escaped; but they expect it daily. I have no more news. Weather very cool; but we have plenty of clothes and blankets. Our spies report no movement of the Federals yet.

The reported resignation of Brig. Gen. Pillow is confirmed by the Memphis papers. He took leave of his brigade on Tuesday, and left on the train for Nashville. The cause of his resignation is not stated, but the Appeal says it is supposed he will proceed to Richmond, probably to lay the reasons for his action before the War Department.

The Little Rock Gazette says that Dr. P G. Hooper, of that place, has received from the War Department the appointment of Medical Purveyor and Chief Surgeon for the Indian Territory West.

TELEGRAPHED TO THE DAILY DELTA.

MEMPHIS, Jan. 3.—A dispatch is received here from Little Rock, containing official intelligence from the Northwest, which states that Col. McIntosh's command, comprising four regiments, had a fight with the Indian Chief Opothayoholo, seventy-five miles northwest of Fort Gibson, which lasted four hours, and resulted in a total route of the enemy. The enemy lost 200 killed, wounded and missing, and 100 taken prisoners. The Confederate loss was 12 killed and 20 wounded. Col. McIntosh was still pursuing Opothayoholo, and the latter was fleeing to Kansas. The Confederates captured a large number of wagons and one hundred Indian horses.

MEMPHIS, Jan. 3.—Late advices via New Madrid state that the Federal Congress is split into three factions, a Union party, a slavery exterminating party, and a peace party, headed by Vallandigham. The Cabinet is also split on the Mason and Slidell affair; it is understood that no advance movement will be made till the difficulty is settled.

A gentleman from St. Louis says Halleck is rigorous on the Secessionists; he levies taxes on their property, and they are compelled to pay or be confined in prison. The Confederate prisoners who are brought to St. Louis are treated very roughly.

Eleven gunboats have been sent from St. Louis to Cairo.

RICHMOND, Jan. 3.—The editor of the Petersburg Express has a dispatch stating that a flag of truce has brought late papers to the Norfolk Day Book, of which the following is a summary:

WASHINGTON, Dec. 31.—There is reason to believe that Mason and Slidell will sail January 1st, but the surrender does not come up to the demand of the ultimatum A part of Seward's bargain is that Wilkes shall not be censured.

The London Post says England will have a reckoning as to the stone fleet.

The Boston papers say Lord Lyons has ordered the Niagara to take out Mason and Slidell to England.

McClellan is still very sick, and Ben Ward, of Ohio, is suggested as his successor. The Persia has arrived at Halifax with troops. England's war-like preparations will continue in view of the difficulties arising from the stone blockade. The surrender of Mason and Slidell, it is said, is not the whole of England's demand.

RICHMOND, Jan. 3.—The steamer which Lord Lyons selected to take out Ministers Mason and Slidell, was the English ocean steamer Niagara.

The London Post (Lord Palmerston's organ) says, the harbor of Charleston belongs to the world and cannot be given up to an ineffectual blockade.

The Burnside expedition has not yet sailed. A large number of frigates, transports and schooners are congregating in Hampton Roads.

NASHVILLE, Jan 4.—The Legislative Council of Kentucky on yesterday elected Henry C. Burnett and Wm. E. Simms, Confederate Senators.

BOWLING GREEN, Jan. 4.—It was reported here yesterday that four thousand Federals were at Brownsville, and that their cavalry scouts, numbering about 300 men, had driven in some of the Confederate pickets.

Capt. Eaton, a deserter from the Lincoln army at Calhoun, reached Hopkinsville the night of the 31st ult., and four others on the 1st inst. One of them, Mr. Clark, reports the Federal army at Calhoun as being completely demoralized, desertions occur daily, and threats of mutiny are openly and defiantly made. He also states that great dissatisfaction pervades the army generally, and whenever an opportunity offers itself the soldiers will desert by thousands.

RICHMOND, Jan. 4.—Government has received official intelligence confirming the recent battle between Col. McIntosh and the Indian chief, Opothayoholo.

Judge Hemphill, member of Congress from Texas, died at the Exchange Hotel this morning.

MANASSAS, Jan. 5, 1862.

Gen. Van Dorn was violently thrown from his horse to-day, in attempting to leap a ditch while riding from Gen. Beauregard's headquarters to his own.

He is badly hurt, but it is hoped not dangerously.

An aid, Capt. A. V. Vertner, was also thrown, and had his leg broken.

RICHMOND, Jan. 6.—The New York Herald of the 2d inst. is received. The Herald's Washington correspondent says McClellan is advancing in the drilling and discipline of the army; also in the receiving of supplies. He will soon advance his columns on the Potomac and by sea The cause of his retarded movements has been the delay of the fleets and the difficulties with England.

LOUISVILLE, Dec. 31.—The Northern Bank of Kentucky has suspended. The People's Bank, formerly at Bowling Green, is reorganized at Louisville.

The rumors of engagements in Southern Kentucky are unreliable.

CINCINNATI, Dec. 31.—Buckner's cavalry on yesterday were near the Federal pickets, and it is supposed he intends attacking McCook in force and destroy Green river bridges, then retire.

WASHINGTON, Dec. 31.—Federal reconnoissances show that the Confederates have strong picket guards beyond Dranesville but no troops at Dranesville; further, that the Confederates have moved their outer lines backwards a few miles, indicating that they are going into winter quarters.

The Maryland Legislature has met. H. Winter Davis, Reverdy Johnson and Thomas Swann are competing candidates for the Federal Senate.

BOSTON Jan. 1.—Messrs. Mason and Slidell have left Providencetown. There they will take passage on the steamer Rinaldo for Europe.

RICHMOND, Jan. 6.—The body of Col. Hugh McLeod is in this city, en route for Texas He died at Dumfries, on the 3d inst. Col. McLeod was a native Georgian, and commanded the celebrated Santa Fe expedition under President Lamar.

RICHMOND, Jan. 6.—In Congress to-day eulogies were delivered by Mr. Ochiltree of Texas, Mr. Johnson of Arkansas, Mr. Boyce of South Carolina, Mr. Venable of North Carolina and Mr. Price of Virginia, on the death of Judge Hemphill, of Texas; after which, appropriate resolutions were adopted, and a committee of one from each State appointed to arrange the funeral ceremonies. The funeral ceremonies will take place to-morrow morning, at 11 o'clock.

No other business was transacted. The members of Congress are daily returning from the enjoyment of the holidays.

MEMPHIS, January 6.—Gen. Jeff. Thompson leaves on to-morrow for New Orleans. Gen. Price is reported at Springfield with ten thousand men. Military movements to clean out the Federals in Northern Missouri will be made soon.

RICHMOND, January 6.—In the absence of official facts we give the following: Many extravagant reports have prevailed at Staunton the past two days about Col. Johnson's movements at the Allegheny Mountain and the approach of Federals, but many of them are discredited. This afternoon we have a report of a battle near Romney and our taking 5[illegible] prisoners; also a skirmish near Hanging Rock, between Winchester and Romney, but, like the former reports from the Mountain region, there are portions probably true, but they are confused and unreliable.

PETERSBURG, Jan. 6.—A flag of truce from Old Point brings to the Norfolk Day Book the New York Herald of the 3d inst. The Herald says Mason and Slidell sailed in the Rinaldo from Providencetown, on the 1st of January, in a perfect hurricane.

Gen McClellan is much improved.

Three thousand troops for Butler's expedition sailed on the Constitution on the 3d of January.

Gen. Williams, of Kars, is erecting fortifications to command Detroit.

The Spanish troops entered the city and fort at Vera Cruz, on the 17th of December, without opposition. The Mexicans abandoned their artillery and munitions of war. The French fleet has arrived at Havana

The London Times is terribly indignant at the stone blockade, and calls it an act of hostility to the whole human race.

The French press criticise Lincoln's message unfavorably.

BATON ROUGE, Jan. 6.—In the Senate the Hon. A. M. Gray, on sufficient evidence having been shown of his election, was qualified and took his seat as Senator for the parishes of Avoyelles, Pointe Coupee and West Feliciana.

In the House, the bill incorporating the New Iberia and Sabine Railroad Company was passed.

A joint resolution passed both Houses tendering to Gov. Jackson, of Missouri, now in the city of New Orleans, the hospitalities of the State and inviting him to visit Baton Rouge

After which both Houses adjourned, on account of the death of the Hon. Matt. Brown, a Representative from the parish of Orleans.

RICHMOND, Jan. 7.—R. C. Wayne, the present Adjutant General of the State of Georgia, has been appointed a Brigadier General in the Confederate service.

Some vigorous skirmishing occurred last week above Winchester and toward the Potomac, in which several prisoners were taken, and a few killed and wounded on our side. The Virginia and Arkansas regiments were principally engaged in this skirmish.

It is reported by passengers from Wilmington that Burnside's expedition was seen off Hatteras.

Congress this morning attended Judge Hemphill's funeral. The afternoon session was unimportant.

RICHMOND, Jan. 7.—Intelligence from Camp Allegheny, of the 5th inst., states that apprehensions existed there of the Yankees cutting off our supplies, and reports were current that the Federals were at Huntersville and Monterey, where there are large quantities of Confederate stores. Intelligence is anxiously awaited.

RICHMOND, Jan. 7.—The editor of the Wilmington Journal says so far as he can learn, there is no truth in the Burnside expedition having been seen off Hatteras.

NASHVILLE, Jan. 7.—A gentleman has arrived here direct from Louisville, and states that the Federal army between Louisville and Bowling Green numbers one hundred thousand men, twenty-five thousand of whom are unfit for duty, the larger portion of this number in consequence of sickness.

The Federals are pushing the work on Green River bridge, which will be completed in a few days, when it is probable a movement will be made towards Bowling Green. A gentleman just arrived here from Paducah says it is reported the Federals intend concentrating a force of one hundred thousand men at that place, and it is also reported here this evening that the Federals are crossing Green River in considerable force.

NASHVILLE, Jan. 8.—The Louisville Journal, of the 31 instant, denies the report that the Northern Bank of Kentucky had suspended.

The St. Louis Democrat, of the 31st, says orders from Washington directing the suspension of coin payments on demand for U. S. Treasury Notes have been received by the Sub-Treasury of that city, and are obeyed.

A dispatch from a leading bank in New York to a banking house at St. Louis, dated 30th, says: U. S. Treasury notes are not redeemed. We cannot receive them on deposit until provision is made for payment.

The Cincinnati Commercial of the 30th ult., says it is reported that Gen. Buell writes to Washington, saying his army in Kentucky is an armed mob, and he must have time to work it up before he makes an advance.

MEMPHIS, Jan. 8.—A mercantile firm here has received a letter from a friend in South Kentucky, stating that the Federal Government has made clandestine arrangements and pardoned all the convicts and desperate characters North, and will scatter them through the South, to set fire and burn everything, especially manufactories and machine shops, the Federals paying for all the fires and accessories, believing it to be a good mode for crippling the South. This information is obtained from a party in the employ of the Federal Government, and was communicated to warn the South, by a sympathiser.

Nothing important from Columbus.

Twenty Federal officers resigned at Cairo and have returned home.

RICHMOND, Jan. 8.—The statement published that the Treasury Department have purchased gold at a large premium to pay the January and March interest on the funded debt is unfounded, the gold has been in the Treasury for some time to meet this payment. The Confederate bonds of fifteen millions, the issue of March, are quoted at 102, interest off.

Dispatches from Europe have been recently received by the Department, which were written previous to the reception in England of the news of the capture of Mason and Slidell. They represent the feeling in France and England at that time to have been very favorable to the cause of the Confederate States.

RICHMOND, Jan. 8.—Passengers from the mountains report Huntersville burnt by the Yankees, also that heavy skirmishing continues above Winchester; but nothing official has been received by the Department corroborating these reports.

Wm H. Hurlbut, who has been confined since June last on suspicion of being a spy, has been released by Gov. Letcher.

Louisiana Legislature.

BATON ROUGE, Jan. 9.—In the Senate, the House bill appropriating [illegible],000,000 to arm and equip the State militia, and the House bill withdrawing from sale all the public lands on which saline waters are situated, were both passed.

A bill to amend the act of 1855 relative to elections was passed.

Mr. Buffington offered a bill for the management of the Penitentiary.

Mr. Dupuy offered a bill authorizing the Police Jury of Iberville parish to close the mouth of Bayou Plaquemine.

In the House, the Finance Committee reported a bill for the relief of the State Treasury.

The Naval Committee reported a bill relative to Branch Pilots for the port of New Orleans.

Mr. McDonald offered a bill supplementary to the Soldiers' Relief act, declaring that act is not to be construed as exempting soldiers' property from taxes, which passed.

Mr. Carroll offered a bill providing for the State's surrender of its interest in the New Orleans, Jackson and Great Northern Railroad, which was referred.

Mr. Salomon offered a bill to reorganize the police of New Orleans. Referred.

The special order of the day was the Senate Naval bill appropriating $2,500,000 to build a navy for State defense.

Mr. Tappan offered a substitute providing for the issuance of three million dollars in bonds of the State, the proceeds when realized to be tendered to the Confederate Government to purchase gunboats or other war vessels to be used for the defense of Louisiana, the amount to be refunded to the State by the Confederate Government at some future time. It was debated at length, and no definite action taken.

NASHVILLE, Jan. 9.—Col. Lubbock, of the Texas Rangers, died here this morning. He was yesterday elected Colonel, having previously been a Lieutenant Colonel. His remains left this evening *en route* for Texas.

RICHMOND, Jan. 9.—Intelligence has been received at Norfolk stating that Burnside's expedition was off Hatteras on Tuesday last.

THE ENEMY AT BILOXI.

We are indebted to Mr. Pradat, of Biloxi, for the following statement of what occurred at Biloxi, on the approach of the enemy's vessels and troops before that place:

About 11 o'clock, 31st December, three ships of war entered the pass. Two officers landed under a flag of truce and United States flag, viz.: Gen. Phelps and Capt. Smith. They demanded a surrender of the town from the Mayor, James Fearll. We asked two days for consideration. They replied that they would give an hour, and, if we did not surrender, the town would be shelled at the expiration of one hour. Forty or fifty marines landed and took possession of two guns, which they took on board the steamer Lewis; they captured one schooner, Capt. Spader, loaded with lumber. They said they would take possession of all the adjacent waters and all craft on them. Gen. Butler, Capt. Smith stated, was on Ship Island with a large force, and expected to land immediately. Three ships crowded with soldiers were in front of the town when Phelps and Smith landed, in position to shell the town if it was not surrendered. They said they would protect Union men and their property, and they hoped they would make us all Union men.

Ninety eight soldiers have died since the expedition left Annapolis, October 22; 84 since it landed at Port Royal, November 7. The whole number sick, from its arrival to the end of November, exclusive of the 8th Michigan, was 4282. Of this number there remained at the end of the month 634 requiring hospital treatment. The 5th Michigan, not included in the above, because its returns have been sent back for correction, has suffered more than any other regiment, and would swell the total of sick to nearly 5000. The returns for December are not made up. More than 300 patients are now in hospital; a still larger number [illegible] in quarters for want of hospital tents, and the sick list daily enlarges.

[Port Royal cor. N. Y. Tribune.

FROM THE SEAT OF WAR IN VIRGINIA.

Special Correspondence of the Delta.

RICHMOND, December 29, 1861.

No one who has not tested it can form an idea of the striking and agreeable contrast between the climate of South eastern Virginia and that of the States lying north of the Potomac. While in more septentrionalian regions the streams are ice-bound and the ground covered with snow, in this latitude there has been but little frost, and the fleecy product of the clouds has but once, and that but transiently, whitened the surface of the earth. During a sojourn of two weeks in Norfolk I was greatly surprised to find a winter climate as mild and gentle as that of Italy. During that whole period, the very depth of winter, not a flake of snow visited the lower air; ice was but once or twice to be seen, and then only by those who look earlier than I do upon the sun, and the skies were generally clear and glowing with Southern light. For many days the air was warm and spring-like; thick clothing was discarded, and fires were superfluous. I might, indeed, have imagined my self once more breathing the mild breezes of Louisiana. True, the rich tropical vegetation was lacking; the *embarras* of verdure, which soothes the eye in New Orleans even during the winter months, was absent; yet in Norfolk the indications that we have not wholly lost the influences of a Southern sun, are not entirely wanting. Winter struggles for the mastery with the genial breezes which come from the gulf stream, laden with Floridian warmth, and for many a day is forced to abdicate its throne and sceptre. Even as late as Christmas, vegetation displays a vigor entirely unanticipated by those who have associated the season, in this latitude, with dessicated gardens, snow-covered fields, and ice-ribbed streams. The grass is yet green; and many a blooming rose sheds its perfume on the air. The brilliant foliage of the magnolia, not the magnolia grandiflora, but a species known here as the bay and the laurel, recall, although perhaps faintly, the groves of Feliciana, and an occasional live oak, which would not be misplaced on the banks of the Teche, shows that we are still in a region, which, even as to its climate, is entitled to be called the South.

Norfolk, as no doubt you are aware is situated on the north bank of Elizabeth river, a stream which in its name possesses its only fluvial characteristic. It is nothing more nor less than an arm of the sea penetrating inland from Hampton Roads, and in which the ocean tides ceaselessly ebb and flow. From the city to Hampton Roads the distance is five miles, with water in the channel and at the entrance of the river sufficient for vessels drawing 18 feet. Hampton Roads are the embouchure of James river. At their gates stand Fortress Monroe and the Rip Raps or Fort Calhoun, which forbid the ingress of any vessels except those bearing the U. S. flag. On our side of the roads are several batteries which have already become well known to the public from the attempts at various times made on them by the Federal ships of war. The principal of these batteries are at Sewell's Point and Pig Point. Craney Island, which lies directly in the mouth of Elizabeth river, is strongly fortified. The works at this place have been erected chiefly by Company F, an organization composed of the first young men of Norfolk. These gentlemen volunteered at the first call of the State, and devoted themselves with so much zeal and energy to the task imposed on them that, although entirely unaccustomed to manual labor, they soon succeeded in rendering Craney Island an insuperable barrier to any assault of the enemy. I may mention here, as an illustration of the ardent patriotism of the young men of Norfolk, that there is not one capable of performing military duty that is not in the ranks of the army. A short distance behind Norfolk is Tanner's Creek, which, together with another broad and deep stream, the two being connected by a magnificent work, known as the entrenched camp, constitutes a perfect defense against any advance of the enemy from that direction.

The town or city of Norfolk is one of the oldest in the State. Its natural advantages are unsurpassed. Its harbor, capacious and sheltered on all sides from the fury of the tempest or the wave, is equal to any in the world. Yet, on account of the sectional legislation of the old Government, by which, in the course of time, the capital of the country became concentrated in the Northern cities, Norfolk for a long time languished, and finally abandoned its ineffectual competition with New York and Boston. But, there can be no doubt that the new regime will give a great incentive to the place; will remove the burthens imposed by Northern legislation, and permit Norfolk to assume its proper place as one of the greatest commercial cities of the continent. Even in the last few years a marked improvement has taken place under the influence of the railroad system by which Norfolk is connected with the whole country, and of the effects upon her destinies anticipated as the result of the completion of the James River and Kanawha Canal. At present the city contains about 20,000 inhabitants, who constitute a society which, for elegance, hospitality, and all the social virtues, cannot, I am sure, be excelled in America. Nor have I ever seen, in any one place, of equal size, so many brilliantly beautiful women. While, in most places, beauty is the exception, in Norfolk it is an invariable rule. In fact, the beauty of the Norfolk ladies is phenomenal; and I have been contented to accept and to enjoy its contemplation as a phenomenon, [illegible] people, who persist in searching for material causes to account for abstract and metaphysical truths, declare that the fact to which I have alluded, is attributable to fish diet, the waters in the vicinity of Norfolk being famous for opulence of fish and oysters. And, indeed, one might, from this circumstance, imagine Norfolk to be inhabited by a universally ichthyophagous population. But, if I may judge from my hotel experience, during which I was restricted to the inevitable and insuperable chub, I should say that the Norfolkians, if they eat fish at all, are simply monichthrophagous. I therefore dismiss the theory as unworthy of consideration. The streets of Norfolk are not remarkable for regularity. On the contrary, they indulge in every conceivable variety of angle, except the right angle. Main street—of course there is a Main street—follows a devious and uncertain course of about a mile from Chamberlain's Wharf, on Elizabeth River, to where it runs up against the depot of the N. and P. railroad company. On this street are situated most of the stores; but it is also adorned with a number of elegant residences. Granby, Freeman and Bute streets are handsome avenues, well built, and lined with elegant edifices. Many of these were tastefully built, according to the most approved modern style. But there are in Norfolk many relics of a former generation, when people didn't seem to care particularly about the outside appearance of their houses. Among these are a number of odd-looking buildings, the roofs of which form an angle with the wall so remarkably obtuse that they seem to be a sort of additional story, while through the roofs squint funny little dormer windows, which appear to be stretched open with astonishment at the pretension of their parvenue neighbors.

Norfolk boasts of two hotels—the Atlantic and the National; both kept as well as ordinary hotels in ordinary cities like Norfolk; both under the control, of course, of "accommodating proprietors" and "polite and gentlemanly clerks." Mr. Newton, the proprietor of the Atlantic, is, in truth, a generous man and a public spirited citizen. As an instance of his liberality and energy in the prosecution of beneficent purposes, I may mention that the moment he received intelligence of the Charleston fire, he headed a list for the benefit of the sufferers with a donation of fifty dollars, and undertook himself the labor of extending the subscription, by means of his personal exertions. The sum thus collected amounted in a few days to twelve hundred dollars, which sum was immediately transmitted to Charleston as a testimonial of the generosity and sympathy of the people of Norfolk. Hotels in all places have their peculiarities. The hotels of Norfolk are, at this time, especially idiosyncratical. Hotels generally are cosmopolitan. The hotels of the Confederate States have lost their cosmopolitan character, and have ceased to afford materials for the study of human nature in the aggregate, and present only illustrations of human nature as developed in this Republic. The hotels of Norfolk are an exception. Their parlors constitute the only point in the Confederacy at which the representatives of Northern society and of Southern society are yet permitted to be placed *en rapport*.

In these rooms you may, at any time, observe a congregation of incursive Southerners and excursive Northerners; of Yankees waiting for an opportunity to revisit the glimpses of the boreal moon, and of returned Southerners, overjoyed to find themselves once more upon their natal soil. Those going North are chiefly ladies and children, detained in the Confederacy since the beginning of the war, and now availing themselves of the facilities for escape afforded by the flag of truce. There are, however, many persons of European birth, English, French and German, who are seeking this method of reaching their respective countries; also exchanged or released prisoners. Among those returning are also many children and ladies; and lately there has been a crowd of exchanged prisoners, who have been released on parole by the Northern Government under the agreement with Commodore Stringham. In my last I alluded to the history of these prisoners during the period of their captivity. A few more particulars concerning them may not prove uninteresting. The following is the order under which they were released:

HEADQUARTERS OF THE ARMY,
ADJUTANT GENERAL'S OFFICE,
Washington, Nov. 29, 1861.

SIR—The General-in-Chief directs that the two hundred and fifty prisoners of war named in the list enclosed in your letter of the 13th inst. be sent by sea to Fortress Monroe, Virginia, and thence by flag of truce to Norfolk, on condition that they take oath not to bear arms against the United States, according to the form inclosed herewith. It may be understood, that should any particular officers or men now prisoners in the hands of the enemy, be set free in consequence of this action, a like number of the same grade of the prisoners herein referred to, may be released from their parole.

I am, very respectfully,
Your obedient servant,
L. THOMAS, Adjutant General.

To Col. F. Dimmick, 1st Artillery U. S. A., Fort Warren, Boston, Mass.

The form of oath referred to in the above is as follows:

FORT WARREN, BOSTON, Dec. 13, 1861.

We, the undersigned, commissioned officers, as severally designated, do solemnly swear that we will not take up arms against the United States, or serve in any military capacity whatever, against them, until regularly discharged, according to the usages of war, from this obligation.

(Signed) WILLIAM F. MARTIN, Col 7th Reg., N. C. V.
G. W. JOHNSON, Lieut. Col. " "
J. A. J. BRADFORD, Col. C. S. A.
And others.

The departure of the released captives from Fort Warren was attended with incidents which every one may imagine. The prisoners [illegible]

Mr. Ely was a favorite, received presents of dinners, and bouquets, and a writing desk from a young lady. [illegible]

Breckinridge, Humphrey Marshall, and Preston, of Kentucky visited him in prison. [illegible]

Mr. Ely says there are [illegible] wounded [illegible]

BOSTON, Dec. 28.—The public [illegible] the surrender of Messrs. Mason and Slidell to the British Government [illegible] afternoon. [illegible]

NO TREATY WITH MEXICO.

Minister Corwin has made no treaty with Mexico and the Times' special states that Gen. Miramon is now on his way from New York to Mexico [illegible] to co-operate with the Spanish invaders [illegible] government [illegible] to erect a Spanish monarchy.

THINGS AT WASHINGTON.

Minnesota Row, to be called the Douglas Hospital, will soon be opened [illegible] charge of [illegible]

Gen. McClellan will be out on Monday.

Judge [illegible] here, [illegible] Apaches [illegible] government [illegible] Albert Pike.

Col Co[illegible] Forts Stre[illegible]

Lord Lyons [illegible] of the surrender [illegible] John Bull [illegible]

The government [illegible] sentiment [illegible] manifest [illegible]

There [illegible] praised the [illegible] followed, [illegible] banner.

An order [illegible] once relieved [illegible] His loyalty [illegible]

Commander [illegible] moted to [illegible]

Intelligence [illegible]

A DIPLOMATIC RECORD OF SHAME.

That the diplomatic correspondence in relation to the Trent affair is the most momentous which this century has produced events may have yet to determine, but that to the Government which provoked it it furnishes one of the most disgraceful records of all history is not open to any kind of dispute. It is difficult to say whether moral or intellectual obliquity is more manifest in Seward's voluminous and tortuous letter to Lord Lyons. Though it was too late for him to surrender the Commissioners with grace, since he had failed to offer reparation before a peremptory demand for it was made, he might at least have saved appearances by excluding from his letter that pitiable inconsistency which looks the more contemptible from the cloud of verbal obscurity and technical subtlety which he throws around it.

The willful inconsistency of a wicked mind may be bold; the acknowledged inconsistency of a frank and generous spirit is honorable; but the inconsistency of Seward is as far from that of bold wickedness as from that of honorable frankness—it is the inconsistency of sheer cowardice and meanness.

Mr. Seward maintains that the Commissioners were contraband and liable to capture; that they were captured in a proper manner under justifying circumstances; that the international law authorizing their capture provides no mode of adjudicating the case in an admiralty court; that the only error of Capt Wilkes consisted in releasing the Trent; that if that vessel had been retained and subjected to judicial proceedings, the case would have been decided against her, and against the Commissioners. But a judicial inquiry being lost by the release of the Trent, there was no recourse left but to a diplomatic discussion of the matter between the two Governments. It is not shown upon what maxim of international law Mr. Seward unhesitatingly yielded on a peremptory diplomatic demand a point he was fully satisfied could have been successfully maintained in a judicial trial.

But while Mr. Seward argues that principles of international law and the facts of the case justify the capture, he admits it to have been in conflict with principles which had ever guided American policy. Yet, though Mr. Seward "could not deny the justice of the claim presented" by England, viewed from the stand point of recognized American principles and policy, he distinctly states that "if the safety of the Union" required such a course, he would, as a matter of "right and duty," reject the claim and detain the prisoners. Herein he makes expediency the measure of right and duty, and asserts that a momentary exigency should override the plain requirements of justice. Such an audacious affirmation of the doctrine of the knave and the tyrant that "the end justifies the means" will be duly appreciated by the power to which it is addressed.

M. Thouvenel's letter in relation to the Trent affair is of the utmost significance. His intervention in the discussion is pointed, and the more so that it is gratuitous. Scarcely anything could more forcibly evince the determination of the French Government to make an issue with the Federal Government whenever visible grounds were offered for doing so in conjunction with England, or even without that conjunction should the latter power fail to act.

Seward's letter to Adams threatening all foreign powers with war that may recognize the Confederate States, must be received in Europe with disgust and contempt, when interpreted by the commentary afforded in the surrender of the Commissioners, an act so obviously inspired by a cowardly dread of war. European nations will see clearly enough that the arrogance of the Northern Minister is without firmness, and that his threats are worth as much as his word, which is worth precisely nothing.

One remark in this last document, however, is suggestive of profitable reflection. When Mr. Seward says that "the life of the insurrection is sustained by the hopes of recognition in Great Britain and France," and that "it would perish in ninety days if these hopes should cease," he ejects one of those round falsehoods for which he is remarkable. But while the assertion may show what value he attaches to a recognition, it should warn us not to look to the benefits of a future contingency with an overconfident reliance that may tend to relax our energies instead of stimulating us to vigorous exertion. Hopes that produce languor are absolutely pernicious.

THE LATEST FROM PRICE'S ARMY.—The St. Louis papers have the subjoined telegram from Otterville, Mo., dated the 26th ult.:

Information which is supposed to be reliable has been received here on the retreat of Price southward. The day after the party Gen. Pope sent out to Johnson county drove in Rain's pickets, Price withdrew Rain's division across the river, and the next day marched eight miles southward with his whole force. At last accounts one division of his army was at Neosho, and the main army under Price had just left Humanville on its way to Arkansas.

Price says that his retrograde movement was in obedience to orders from the President of the Confederate States, but his men generally believe that it was in consequence of Gen. Pope's advance, and Price's fear that a force would be thrown forward to cut off his supplies southward, and another advance in front, in which event his supplies would have been exhausted [illegible]d he would have been compelled to [illegible]ng position at Osceola.

[illegible]FLAG.—On the unfurling of the battle [illegible]s of the second corps, Army of the [illegible] General G. W. Smith issued an order, [illegible]:

[illegible]dy hallowed by the hands that made [illegible]torious, be made the banner of your [illegible]nation's prayer will rise for your suc[illegible]g beneath its sacred folds. The en[illegible] have so long desired to attack on the [illegible]e Potomac, again advances with an [illegible] If they dare come here, they will be [illegible] attempt to avoid and pass you, their [illegible]e prepared to act in any emergency. [illegible] determined to destroy our Govern[illegible] our people to submit to theirs. Re[illegible] only alternative for your country is [illegible] submission to Northern despotism.

ESPIONAGE.—We are informed that [illegible]orities have directed that all letters [illegible]deral post offices in Northwestern [illegible] sent to Washington for examination. [illegible]s to get information from the South [illegible]rvice to them, and to implicate par[illegible]ise with the rebels.

[Bowling Green Courier.

[illegible]MONG THE TIGERS.—We understand [illegible]ccurred among some of the members [illegible], at Bristoe Station, near Manassas [illegible]rday last, in which one of them was [illegible] a cut from a bowie knife, and seve[illegible] wounded. The fight was the result [illegible]c. [Lynchburg Republican, 31st.

[C]OMMERCIAL.

[NEW] ORLEANS, Friday Evening, Jan. 10, 1862.

[illegible]—Sugar and Molasses—are the only promi[illegible]rket which have shown any movement of mo[illegible]week, but owing to the difficulty of forward[illegible] railroad, the demand has been more moderate. [illegible] very little has been done. Flour has been [illegible]wn some movement, with prices tending in [illegible]visions have retailed slowly at previous rates. [illegible]n cloudy and rainy.

[illegible]y transactions reported since our last review, [illegible] delivery at 8¼@8½c. for middling, 170 bales [illegible]sier rates, and 100 and 150 bales for future [illegible]

[illegible]ber 1, 1861	bales.	10,118
....	000	
....	1,994 –	1,994
		12,112
....	00	
....	00	00
[illegible] cleared..........		12,112

[illegible] have been further sales of about 60 bhds., [illegible] city consumption, at full prices. We quote, [illegible] follows:

TOBACCO QUOTATIONS.

....	3½@4
....	4 @5½
[illegible]eaf.................	6 @7
....	7¼@8½
....	8½@[illegible]
....	11 @13

[S]TATEMENT OF TOBACCO.

[illegible]ember, 1861	hhds.	15,121
....	00	
....	547—	
		15,667
....	00	
....	00—	00
[illegible]red..........		15,667

[illegible]ly has been more than ample for the demand [illegible]eing checked by the difficulty of forwarding [illegible]ilroad, and prices have tended in favor of [illegible]ave shown no quotable decline. The week's [illegible] hhds., the market closing at the following [illegible]y fully fair, prime and choice were scarce. [illegible] firm prices. The other descriptions were [illegible]

....	1¾@2
[illegible]mon.........	2½@2¾
....	2¾@3[illegible]
....	3[illegible]@4[illegible]
....	6 @[illegible]
....	8 @9

[illegible]8 hhds., 513 bbls.; exports, none.

[illegible]emand has been fair, and with moderate re[illegible]en maintained. The sales of the week com[illegible] 3000 half bbls., the market closing at 17@19c. [illegible]oice fermenting, and 19@20 for prime to [illegible] 21@22c. for fermenting in half bbls., and 22@ [illegible] receipts, 17,776 bbls.; exports, none.

[illegible]pts have been more moderate, but the demand [illegible]changed prices. The sales up to Thursday, [illegible] about 2000 bbls. at $9 for fine, $10 12½@ [illegible] and $11 ℔ bbl. for good and choice extra. [illegible] (in lots) at $10 25 for superfine, and $11 ℔ bbl. [illegible]ceipts, 4914 bbls.; exports, none.

[illegible]ts have been more liberal, and meeting with [illegible]nd, prices have tended in favor of buyers. [illegible] sold up to last evening at 93@95c. and $1 ℔ [illegible] low and mixed. To-day 1900 sacks sold at [illegible]nd mixed. Week's receipts, 15,531 sacks;

[illegible] sales embrace about 100 sacks at $1 10 ℔

[illegible]ales of 400 sacks at $1 25@$1 75 ℔ bushel.

[illegible]pply of rectified is light Old Bourbon and [illegible]en retailing at $1 35@$1 50 and rectified at [illegible]eek's receipts, 113 bbls.; exports, none.

[illegible]ery little left on sale. Mess is retailing at [illegible] the inspection warehouses on the 1st instant [illegible]s. Week's receipts 59 bbls.

[illegible]k is very light. Shoulders are retailing slow[illegible] 1 s 25, clear sides 27@28, plain hams 22@23, [illegible] ℔ lb. Week's receipts, 8 casks; exports, [illegible]

[illegible]et is dull, and prices are tending downward. [illegible] expectation of more liberal receipts. At re[illegible] obtained for kegs, and 26@27c for tierces. [illegible] of sales of 180 tierces at 25@25c. Week's [illegible]d 2 kegs; exports, none.

[illegible]ly is very light. Mess is retailing at irregular [illegible] quality. The stock at the Inspection Ware[illegible] inst. was 00 bbls. Week's receipts, 81 bbls., [illegible], 00 bbls.

[illegible]ly is fair and the sales embrace 2,200 sacks at [illegible] lbs.

[illegible]es embrace 100 sacks red, for future delivery, [illegible] spot at $1 50, 233 at $1 75, 24 at $1 87½, and [illegible]2 ℔ bushel.

[illegible] Southern Hay at $20@$30 ℔ ton. 40 bales Crab [illegible]

[illegible] BALE ROPE—At retail we quote Kentucky [illegible] ℔ yard cash for handloom to the best power[illegible] 1st inst. 1945 pieces. India Bagging may be [illegible] yard. Stock on the 1st inst. 6874 bales. Bale Rope may be quoted at 24@25c. for hand-made and machine made, according to quality. Stock of all kinds on the 1st inst., 11883 coils. Iron Cotton Ties sell at 18@20c. ℔ lb cash.

BUTTER AND CHEESE—The supply of choice Western Butter very light and prices may be quoted at 40@50c. Old Western cheese, none in the market.

RICE—CAROLINA—There has been a limited demand at 5¾@6c. ℔ lb.

SALT—LIVERPOOL—Dealers supply their regular customers at $8 50 for coarse and $9 for fine, and $5 ℔ bag of two bushels of packing Salt. Stock on the 1st inst. of all kinds equal to 52,690 bags Liverpool.

OILS—We quote Lard Oil at $3 ℔ gallon. Coal Oil none in the market. Cotton Seed Oil at $1 50 for crude, $1 65@1 70 for refined and bleached. Rosin Oil at 40c. ℔ gallon for crude or gas, and 75@$1 for tanner's and machinery.

COFFEE—There have been no further sales; the last reported were at 65@70c. ℔ lb for Rio.

GUNNY BAGS—We have heard of no further sales. We quote 30c. for second hand and 35c. for new bags. Stock on the 1st inst., 1400 bales.

HIDES—The receipts have been light, and the demand is limited. We quote Atakapas Hides at 8@10c. for dry-salted and flint, which are very scarce, and 5c. ℔ lb for green-salted. Mexican flint, none in the market.

TALLOW—There is none offering. The last sales were at 14c. for city rendered. We quote prime city rendered nominally at 14@16c. ℔ lb.

LIME—There is no stock of Thomaston and Western. Of Alabama the stock is light, and is retailing at $3 75@$4 ℔ bbl.

CATTLE MARKET.

JEFFERSON CITY, Jan. 11, 1862

Arrived during the week 1533 Texas and 211 Western Beeves, 1622 Hogs, 850 Sheep. 381 Veal and 39 Milch Cows. Amount of stock sold was 1377 Texas and 28 Western Beeves, 679 Hogs, 771 Sheep, 381 Veal and 29 Milch Cows. Stock remaining on sale is 505 Texas and 88 Western Beeves, 1409 Hogs, 460 Sheep, and 13 Milch Cows:

Texas Cattle, first quality, ℔ head	$30 00@40 00
Texas Cattle, second quality	20 00@30 00
Western Beef Cattle, first quality, ℔ head..........	30 00@40 00
Western Beeves, second quality..........	20 00@30 00
Hogs, first quality, gross, ℔ 100 lb..........	10 00@12 50
Hogs, second quality, gross ℔ 100 lb..........	8 00@10 00
Sheep, second quality, ℔ head..........	3 00@ 5 00
[illegible], first quality, ℔ head..........	11 00@13 00
Veal Cattle, second quality, ℔ head..........	8 00@11 00
Milch Cows, ℔ head..........	45 00@60 00

THE TRENT AFFAIR.

The Correspondence in Full.

Mr. Seward to Mr. Adams.

(Extract.)

DEPARTMENT OF STATE,
WASHINGTON, November 30, 1861.

Charles Francis Adams, Esq., &c., &c.:

Sir—Your confidential note of the 15th of November, not marked as a dispatch, has been submitted to the President, and I hasten to reply to it in time for Wednesday's mail.

No Minister ever spoke or acted more wisely, in a crisis which excited deep public solicitude, than you did on the occasion of the Lord Mayor's dinner. We are impressed very favorably by Lord Palmerston's conversation with you. You spoke the simple fact when you told him that the life of this insurrection is sustained by the hopes of recognition in Great Britain and in France. It would perish in ninety days, if these hopes should cease. I have never for a moment believed that such a recognition could take place without producing immediately a war between the United States and all the recognizing powers. I have not supposed it possible that the British Government could fail to see this, and at the same time I have sincerely believed the British Government must, in its inmost heart, be averse to such a war as I know this Government is.

I am sure that this Government has carefully avoided giving any cause of offense or irritation to Great Britain. But it has seemed to me that the British Government has been inattentive to the currents that seemed to be bringing the two countries into collision.

* * * * * * *

I infer from Lord Palmerston's remark that the British Government is now awake to the importance of averting possible conflict, and disposed to confer and act with earnestness to that end. If so, we are disposed to meet them in the same spirit, as a nation, chiefly of British lineage, sentiments and sympathies—a civilized and humane nation, a Christian people.

Since that conversation was held, Capt. Wilkes, in the steamer San Jacinto, has boarded a British colonial steamer and taken from her deck two insurgents, who were proceeding to Europe on an errand of treason against their own country. This is a new incident, unknown and unforeseen, at least in its circumstances, by Lord Palmerston. It is to be met and disposed of by the two Governments, if possible, in the spirit to which I have adverted. Lord Lyons has prudently refrained from opening the subject to me, as, I presume, waiting for instructions from home. We have done nothing on the subject to anticipate the discussion, and we have not furnished you with any explanations. We adhere to that course now because we think it more prudent that the ground taken by the British Government should be first made known to us here, and that the discussion, if there must be one, shall be had here. It is proper, however, that you should know one fact in the case, without indicating that we attach any importance to it, namely, that in the capture of Messrs. Mason and Slidell on board of a British vessel, Capt. Wilkes having acted without any instructions from the Government, the subject is, therefore, free from the embarrassment which might have resulted if the act had been specially directed by us.

I trust that the British Government will consider the subject in a friendly temper, and it may expect the best disposition on the part of this Government.

Although this is a confidential note, I shall not object to your reading it to Earl Russell and Lord Palmerston, if you deem it expedient.

I am sir, your obedient servant,

WILLIAM H. SEWARD.

Earl Russell to Lord Lyons.

FOREIGN OFFICE, Nov. 30, 1861.

The Lord Lyons, K. C. B., &c., &c., &c:

My Lord—Intelligence of a very grave nature has reached Her Majesty's Government.

The intelligence was conveyed officially to the knowledge of the Admiralty by Commander Williams, agent for mails on board the contract steamer Trent.

It appears from the letter of Commander Williams, dated "Royal Mail contract packet Trent, at sea, November 9th," that the Trent left Havana on the 7th inst., with her Majesty's mails for England, having on board numerous passengers. Commander Williams states that shortly after noon, on the 8th, a steamer having the appearance of a man-of-war, but showing no colors, was observed ahead. On nearing her, at 1:15 P. M., she fired a round shot from her pivot gun across the bows of the Trent, and showed American colors. While the Trent was approaching her slowly, the American vessel discharged a shell across the bows of the Trent, exploding half a cable's length ahead of her. The Trent then stopped, and an officer with a large armed guard of marines, boarded her. The officer demanded a list of the passengers, and compliance with this demand being refused, the officer said he had orders to arrest Messrs. Mason, Slidell, McFarlane and Eustis, and that he had sure information of their being passengers in the Trent. While some parley was going on upon this matter, Mr. Slidell stepped forward and told the American officer that the four persons he had named were then standing before him. The commander of the Trent and Commander Williams protested against the act of taking by force, out of the Trent, those four passengers, then under the protection of the British flag. But the San Jacinto was at that time only two hundred yards from the Trent, her ship's company at quarters, her ports open, and tompions out. Resistance was, therefore, out of the question, and the four gentlemen, before named, were forcibly taken out of the ship. A further demand was made that the commander of the Trent should proceed on board the San Jacinto, but he said he would not go, unless forcibly compelled likewise, and this demand was not insisted upon.

It thus appears that certain individuals have been forcibly taken from on board a British vessel, the ship of a neutral power, while such vessel was pursuing a lawful and innocent voyage, an act of violence which was an affront to the British flag, and a violation of international law.

Her Majesty's Government, bearing in mind the friendly relations which have long subsisted between the United States and Great Britain, we are willing to believe that the United States officer who committed the aggression was not acting in compliance with any authority from his Government; or that, if he conceived himself to be so authorized, he greatly misunderstood the instructions which he had received. For the Government of the United States must be fully aware that the British Government could not allow such an affront to the national honor to pass without full reparation, and Her Majesty's Government are unwilling to believe that it could be the deliberate intention of the Government of the United States unnecessarily to force into discussion between the two Governments a question of so grave a character, and with regard to which the whole British nation would be sure to entertain such unanimity of feeling.

Her Majesty's Government trust, therefore, that when this matter shall have been brought under the consideration of the Government of the United States, that Government will, of its own accord, offer to the British Government such redress as alone could satisfy a British nation, namely: the liberation of the four gentlemen, and their delivery to your Lordship, in order that they may again be placed under British protection, and a suitable apology for the aggression which has been committed.

Should these terms not be offered by Mr. Seward, you will propose them to him.

You are at liberty to read this dispatch to the Secretary of State, and if he shall desire it, you will give him a copy of it.

I am, &c., RUSSELL.

Mr. Seward to Lord Lyons.

DEPARTMENT OF STATE,
WASHINGTON, December 26, 1861.

The Right Honorable Lord Lyons, &c., &c.

My Lord—Earl Russell's dispatch, of Nov. 30th, a copy of which you have left with me, at my request, is of the following effect, viz:

That a letter of Commander Williams, dated "Royal Mail contract boat Trent, at sea, Nov. 9th," states that the vessel left Havana on the 7th of November, with her Majesty's mails for England, having on board numerous passengers. Shortly after noon on the 8th of November, the United States war steamer San Jacinto, Capt. Wilkes, not showing colors, was observed ahead. The steamer, upon being neared by the Trent, at 1.15 in the afternoon, fired a round shot from a pivot gun across her bows, and showed American colors. While the Trent was approaching slowly toward the San Jacinto, she discharged a shell across the Trent's bows, which exploded at half a cable's length before her. The Trent then stopped, and an officer, with a large armed guard of marines, boarded her. The officer said he had orders to arrest Messrs. Mason, Slidell, McFarlane and Eustis, and had sure information that they were passengers in the Trent. While some parley was going on upon this matter, Mr. Slidell stepped forward and said to the American officer that the four persons he had named were standing before him. The commander of the Trent and Commander Williams protested against the act of taking those four passengers out of the Trent, they being under the protection of the British flag. But the San Jacinto was at this time only two hundred yards off, her ship's company at quarters, her ports open and tompions out, and so resistance was out of the question. The four persons before named were then forcibly taken out of the ship. A further demand was made, that the commander of the Trent should proceed on board the San Jacinto, but he said he would not go unless forcibly compelled likewise, and this demand was not insisted on.

Upon this statement Earl Russell remarks that it thus appears that certain individuals have been forcibly taken from on board a British vessel, the ship of a neutral power, while the vessel was pursuing a lawful and innocent voyage, an act of violence which was an affront to the British flag and a violation of international law.

Earl Russell next says that Her Majesty's Government, bearing in mind the friendly relations which have long subsisted between Great Britain and the United States, are willing to believe that the naval officer who committed this aggression was not acting in compliance with any authority from his Government, or that if he conceived himself to be so authorized he greatly misunderstood the instructions he had received.

Earl Russell argues that the United States must be fully aware that the British Government could not allow such an affront to the national honor to pass without full reparation, and they are willing to believe that it could not be the deliberate intention of the United States unnecessarily to force into discussion between the two Governments a question of so grave a character, and with regard to which the whole British nation would be sure to entertain such unanimity of feeling.

Earl Russell, resting upon the statement and the argument which I have received, closes with saying that Her Majesty's Government trust that when this matter shall have been brought under the consideration of the Government of the United States, it will, of its own accord, offer the British Government such redress as could alone satisfy the British nation, viz: the liberation of the four prisoners taken from the Trent, and their delivery to your Lordship, in order that they may again be placed under British protection, and a suitable apology for the aggression which has been committed. Earl Russell finally instructs you to propose these terms to me, if I should not first offer them on the part of the Government.

This dispatch has been submitted to the President.

The British Government has rightly conjectured that it is now my duty to state that Capt. Wilkes, in conceiving and executing the proceedings in question, acted upon his own suggestions of duty without any direction or instruction or even foreknowledge of it on the part of this Government. No direction had been given to him or any other naval officer to arrest the four persons named, or any of them, on the Trent or any other British vessel, or on any other neutral vessel, at the place where it occurred, or elsewhere. The British Government will justly infer from these facts that the Government of the United States not only have had no purpose, but even no thought, of forcing into discussion the question which has arisen, or any other, which could affect, in any way, the sensibilities of the British nation.

It is true that a round shot was fired by the San Jacinto from the pivot gun, when the Trent was distantly approaching. But, as the facts have been reported to this Government, the shot was, nevertheless, intentionally fired in a direction so obviously divergent from the course of the Trent, as to be quite as harmless as a blank shot, while it should be regarded as a signal.

So also we learn that the Trent was not approaching the San Jacinto slowly when the shell was fired across her bows, but on the contrary, the Trent was, or seemed to be, moving under a full head of steam, as if with a purpose to pass the San Jacinto.

We are informed, also, that the boarding officer (Lieut. Fairfax) did not board the Trent with a large armed guard, but he left his marines in his boat when he entered the Trent. He showed his instructions from Capt. Wilkes to search for the four prisoners named, in a respectful and courteous, though decided manner, and he asked the captain of the Trent to show his passenger list, which was refused. The lieutenant, as we are informed, did not employ absolute force in transferring the passengers, but he used just so much as was necessary to satisfy the parties concerned that refusal or resistance would be unavailing.

So also we are informed that the captain of the Trent was not at any time or in any way required to go on board the San Jacinto.

These modifications of the case as presented by Commander Williams are based upon our official reports.

I have now to remind your lordship of some facts which doubtless were omitted by Earl Russell, with the very proper and becoming motive of allowing them to be brought into the case on the part of the United States in the way most satisfactory to this Government. These facts are, that at the time the transaction occurred, an insurrection was existing in the United States, which this Government was engaged in suppressing by the employment of land and naval forces; that in regard to this domestic strife, the United States considered Great Britain as a friendly power, while she had assumed for herself the attitude of a neutral, and that Spain was considered in the same light and had assumed the same attitude as Great Britain.

It has been settled by correspondence that the United States and Great Britain mutually recognized as applicable to this local strife these two articles of the declaration made by the Congress of Paris in 1856, viz: that the neutral or friendly flag should cover enemy's goods not contraband of war, and that neutral goods not contraband of war are not liable to capture under an enemy's flag. These exceptions of contraband from favor were a negative acceptance of the parties by the rule hitherto everywhere recognized as a part of the law of nations, that whatever is contraband is liable to capture and confiscation in all cases.

James M. Mason and E. J. McFarlane are citizens of the United States, and residents of Virginia. John Slidell and George Eustis are citizens of the United States, and residents of Louisiana. It was well known in Havana, when these parties embarked in the Trent, that James M. Mason was proceeding to England in the affected character of a Minister Plenipotentiary to the Court of St. James, under a pretended commission from Jefferson Davis, who had assumed to be President of the insurrectionary party in the United States; E. J. McFarlane was going with him in a like unreal character of Secretary of Legation to the pretended mission. John Slidell, in similar circumstances, was going to Paris as a pretended Minister to the Emperor of the French, and George Eustis was the chosen Secretary of Legation for that simulated mission. The fact that these persons had assumed such characters, has been avowed by the same Jefferson Davis in a pretended message to an unlawful and insurrectionary Congress. It was, as we think, rightly presumed, that these Ministers bore pretended credentials and instructions, and such papers are in the law known as dispatches. We are informed by our Consul at Paris, that these dispatches having escaped the search of the Trent, were actually conveyed and delivered to emissaries of the insurrection in England. Although it is not essential, yet it is proper to state, as I do upon information and belief, that the owner and agent and all the officers of the Trent, including Commander Williams, had knowledge of the assumed characters and purposes of the persons named when they embarked on that vessel.

Your Lordship will now perceive that the case before us, instead of presenting a merely flagrant act of violence on the part of Capt. Wilkes, as might well be inferred from the incomplete statement of it that went up to the British Government, was undertaken as a simple, legal and belligerent proceeding of Capt. Wilkes to arrest and capture a neutral vessel engaged in carrying a contraband of war, for the use and benefit of the insurgents.

The question before us is, whether this proceeding was authorized by and conducted according to the law of nations. It involves the following inquiries:

1. Were the persons named and their supposed dispatches contraband of war?

2. Might Capt. Wilkes lawfully stop and search the Trent for these contraband persons and dispatches?

3. Might he exercise that right in a lawful and proper manner?

4. Having found the contraband persons on board and in presumed possession of the contraband dispatches, had he a right to capture the persons?

5. Did he exercise the right of capture in the manner allowed and recognized by the law of nations?

If all these inquiries shall be resolved in the affirmative, the British Government will have no claim for reparation.

I address myself to the first inquiry, namely: Were the four persons mentioned and their supposed dispatches contraband?

Maritime law so generally deals, as its professors say, *in rem*—that is, with property, and so seldom with persons—that it seems a straining of the term contraband to apply it to them. But persons as well as property may become contraband, since the word means broadly "contrary to proclamation, prohibited, illegal, unlawful."

All writers and judges pronounce naval or military persons, in the service of the enemy, contraband. Vattel says, war allows us to cut off from an enemy all his resources, and to hinder him from sending ministers to solicit assistance. And Sir William Scott says you may stop the embassador of your enemy on his passage. Dispatches are not less clearly contraband, and the bearers or couriers, who undertake to carry them, are under the same condemnation.

A subtlety might be raised whether pretended ministers of a usurping power, not recognized as legal by either the belligerent or the neutral, could be held to be contraband. But it would disappear on being subjected to what is the true test in all cases—namely, the spirit of the law. Sir Wm. Scott, speaking of civil magistrates who were arrested and detained as contraband, says:

"It appears to me, on principle, to be but reasonable that when it is of sufficient importance to the enemy that such persons shall be sent out on the public service, at the public expense, it shall afford equal ground of forfeiture against the vessel that may be let out for a purpose so intimately connected with the hostile operations."

I trust that I have shown that the four persons who were taken from the Trent by Capt. Wilkes, and their dispatches, were contraband of war.

The second enquiry is, whether Capt. Wilkes had a right, by the law of nations, to detain and search the Trent?

The Trent, though she carries the mails, was a contract or merchant vessel—a common carrier for hire. Maritime law knows only three classes of vessels—vessels of war, revenue vessels and merchant vessels. The Trent falls within the latter class. Whatever disputes have existed concerning the right of visitation or search in time of peace, none, it is supposed, has existed in modern times about the right of a belligerent in time of war, to capture contraband in neutral and even friendly merchant vessels, and of right of visitation and search, in order to determine whether they are neutral and are documented as such according to the law of nations.

I assume in the present case, what, as I read British authorities, is regarded by Great Britain herself, as true maritime law, that the circumstance that the Trent was proceeding from a neutral port to another neutral port, does not modify the right of the belligerent captor.

The third question is, whether Capt. Wilkes exercised the right of search in a lawful and proper manner?

If any doubt hung over this point as the case was presented in the statement of it adopted by the British Government, I think it must have already passed away before the modifications of that statement which I have already submitted.

I proceed to the fourth inquiry, namely: having found the expected contraband on board the Trent, had Capt. Wilkes a right to capture the same?

Such capture is the chief, if not the only recognized object of the permitted visitation and search. The principle of the law is, that belligerents exposed to danger may prevent the contraband person or things from applying themselves or being applied to the hostile uses or purposes designed. The law is so liberal in this respect that when contraband is found on board a neutral vessel, not only is the contraband forfeited, but the vessel which is the vehicle of its passage or transportation being tainted, also becomes contraband, and is subjected to capture and confiscation.

Only the fifth question remains, namely: Did Capt. Wilkes excercise the right of capturing the contraband in conformity with the law of nations?

It is just here that the difficulty of the case begins; what is the manner which the law of nations prescribes for disposing of the contraband, when you have found and seized it on board of a neutral vessel?

The answer would be easily found, if the question were what you should do with the contraband vessel. You must take or send her into a convenient port, and subject her to a judicial prosecution there in admiralty, which will try and decide the questions of belligerency, neutrality, contraband and capture. So, again, you would promptly find the same answer if the question were: What is the manner of proceeding prescribed by the law of nations in regard to the contraband, if it be property or things of a material or pecuniary value? But the question here concerns the mode of procedure in regard, not to the vessel that was carrying the contraband, nor yet to contraband things which worked the forfeiture of the vessel, but to contraband persons.

The books of law are dumb, yet the question is as important as it is difficult. First, the belligerent captor has a right to prevent the contraband officer, soldier, sailor, minister, messenger, or courier from proceeding in his unlawful voyage and reaching the destined scene of his injurious service. But on the other hand, the person captured may be innocent—this is, he may not be contraband. He therefore has a right to a fair trial of the accusation against him. The neutral State that has taken him under its flag is bound to protect him if he is not contraband, and is therefore entitled to be satisfied upon that important question. The faith of the State is pledged to his safety if innocent, as its justice is pledged to his surrender if he is really contraband. Here are conflicting claims, involving personal liberty, life, honor and duty. Here are conflicting national claims, involving welfare, safety, honor and empire. They require a tribunal and a trial. The captured and the captors are equal; the neutral and belligerent States are equals. While the law authorities are found silent, it was suggested at an early day by this Government that you should take the captured persons into a convenient port, and institute judicial proceedings there to try the controversy. But only Courts of Admiralty have jurisdiction in maritime cases, and these courts have formulas to try only claims to contraband chattels, but none to try claims concerning contraband persons. The courts can entertain no proceeding and render no judgments in favor of or against the alleged contraband men.

It was replied, all this is true; but you can reach in those courts a decision which will have the moral weight of a judicial one by a circuitous proceeding. Convey the suspected men, together with the suspected vessel, into port, and try the question whether the vessel is contraband. You can prove it to be so by proving the suspected men to be contraband. If the men are not contraband, the men will escape condemnation. Still there is no judgment for or against the captured persons. But it was answered, that there would result from the determination of the court, concerning the vessel, a legal certainty concerning the character of the men.

This course of proceeding seemed open to many objections. It elevates the incidental inferior private interest into the proper place of the main paramount public one, and possibly it may make the fortunes, the safety or the existence of a nation depend on the accidents of a merely personal and pecuniary litigation. Moreover, when the judgment of the prize court upon the lawfulness of the capture of the vessel is rendered, it really concludes nothing, and binds neither the belligerent State nor the neutral upon the great questions of the disposition to be made of the captured contraband persons. That question is still to be really determined, if at all, by diplomatic arrangement or by war.

One may well express his surprise when told that the law of nations has prescribed no more reasonable, practical and perfect mode than this of determining questions of such grave import between sovereign powers. The regret we may feel on the occasion is nevertheless modified by the reflection that the difficulty is not altogether anomalous. Similar and equal deficiencies are found in every asylum of municipal law, especially in the asylum which exists in the greater portion of Great Britain and the United States. The title to personal property can hardly ever be resolved by a court without resorting to the fiction that the claimant has lost and the possessor has found it, and the title to real estate is disputed by real litigations under the names of imaginary persons. It must be confessed, however, that while all aggrieved nations demand, and all impartial ones concede, the need of some form of judicial process in determining the character of contraband persons, no other form than the illogical and circuitous one thus described exists; nor has any other yet been suggested. Practically, therefore, the choice is between that judicial remedy or no judicial remedy whatever. If there be no judicial remedy, the result is that the question must be determined by the captor himself, on the deck of the prize vessel. Very grave objections arise against such a course. The captor is armed; the neutral is unarmed. The captor is interested, prejudiced and perhaps violent; the neutral, if truly neutral, is disinterested, subdued and helpless. The tribunal is irresponsible, while its judgment is carried into instant execution. The captured party is compelled to submit, though bound by no legal, moral or treaty obligation to acquiesce. Reparation is distant and problematical, and depends at last on the justice, magnanimity or weakness of the State in whose behalf and by whose authority the capture was made. Out of the disputes reprisals and wars necessarily arise, and these are so frequent and destructive that it may well be doubted whether this form of remedy is not a greater social evil than all that could follow if the belligerent right of search was universally renounced and abolished forever. But carry the case one step farther. What if the State that has made the capture unseasonably refuse to hear the complaint of the neutral or to redress it? In that case the very act of capture would be an act of war, of war begun without notice and possibly without provocation. I think all unprejudiced minds will agree that, imperfect as the existing judicial remedy may be supposed to be, it would be as a general practice, better to follow it than to adopt the summary one of leaving the decision with the captor, and relying upon diplomatic debates to review his decision. Practically, it is a question of choice between law with its imperfections and delays, and war with its evils and desolations. Nor is it ever to be forgotten that neutrality, honestly and justly preserved, is always the harbinger of peace, and, therefore, is the common interest of nations. Which is only saying that it is the interest of humanity itself.

At the same time it is not to be denied that it may sometimes happen that the judicial remedy will become impossible, as by the shipwreck of the prize vessel, or other circumstances which excuse the captor from sending or taking her into port for confiscation. In such a case the right of the captor to the custody of the captured persons and to dispose of them, if they are really contraband, so as to defeat their unlawful purposes, can not reasonably be denied. What rule shall be applied in such a case? Clearly the captor ought to be required to show that the failure of the judicial remedy results from circumstances beyond his control and without his fault, otherwise he would be allowed to derive advantage from a wrongful act of his own.

In the present case, Capt. Wilkes, after capturing the contraband persons and making prize of the Trent, in what seems to us a perfectly lawful manner, instead of sending her into port, released her from the capture and permitted her to proceed with her whole cargo upon her voyage. He thus effectually prevented the judicial examination which might otherwise have occurred.

Now, the capture of the contraband persons and the capture of the contraband vessel are to be regarded, not as two separable or distinct transactions under the law of nations, but as one transaction—one capture only; then it follows that the capture in this case was left unfinished or abandoned. Whether the United States have a right to retain the chief public benefits of it—namely: the custody of the captured persons, on proving them to be contraband—will depend upon the preliminary question, whether the leaving of the transaction unfinished was necessary, and, therefore, voluntary. If it was necessary, Great Britain, as we suppose, must, of course, waive the defect and the consequent failure of the judicial remedy. On the other hand, it is not seen how the United States can insist upon her waiver of that judicial remedy, if the defect of the capture resulted from an act of Capt. Wilkes, which would be a fault on their own side.

Capt. Wilkes has presented to this Government his reasons for releasing the Trent. "I forbore to seize her," he says, "in consequence of my being so reduced in officers and crew, and this derangement would cause innocent persons to suffer, there being a large number of passengers who would have been put to great loss and inconvenience, as well as disappointment from the interruption it would have caused them, in not being able to join the steamer from St. Thomas to Europe. I, therefore, concluded to sacrifice the interest of my officers and crew in the prize, and suffered her to proceed, after the detention necessary to effect the transfer of those Commissioners, considering I had obtained the important end I had in view, and which affected the interest of our country, and interrupted the action of that of the Confederates."

I shall consider first how these reasons ought to affect the action of this Government, and secondly how they ought to be expected to affect the action of Great Britain.

The reasons are satisfactory to this Government, so far as Capt. Wilkes is concerned; it could not desire that the San Jacinto, her officers and crew should be exposed to danger and loss by weakening their number to detach a prize crew to go on board the Trent. Still less could it disavow the humane motive of preventing inconvenient losses and perhaps disasters to the several hundred innocent passengers found on board the prize vessel. Nor could this Government perceive any ground for questioning the fact that these reasons, though apparently incongruous, did operate in the mind of Capt. Wilkes and determined him to release the Trent. Human action generally proceeds from mingled and sometimes conflicting motives. He measured the sacrifices which his decision would cost. It manifestly, however, did not occur to him that beyond the sacrifice of the private interests (as he calls them) of his officers and crew, there might, also, possibly be a sacrifice even of the chief and public object of his capture, namely: The right of his Government to the custody and disposition of the captured persons. This Government can not censure him for this oversight. It confesses that the whole subject came unforeseen upon the Government, as doubtless it came upon him. Its present convictions on the point in question are the result of deliberate examination and deduction now made, and not of any impressions previously formed.

Nevertheless, the question now is, not whether Capt. Wilkes is justified to his Government in what he did, but what is the present view of the Government as to the effect of what he has done? Assuming now, for argument's sake only, that the release of the Trent, if voluntary, involved a waiver of the claim of the Government to hold the captured persons, the United States could, in that case, have no hesitation in saying that the act which has thus already been approved by the Government, must be allowed to draw its legal consequence after it. It is of the very nature of a gift or a charity, that the giver can not, after the exercise of his benevolence is past, recall or modify its benefits.

We are thus brought directly to the question, whether we are entitled to regard the release of the Trent as involuntary, or whether we are obliged to consider that it is voluntary? Clearly the release would have been made solely upon the first ground assigned for it by Capt. Wilkes, namely, a want of sufficient force to send the prize vessel into port for adjudication. It is not the duty of a captor to hazard his own vessel in order to secure a judicial examination to the captured party. No large prize crew, however, is legally necessary, for it is the duty of the captured party to acquiesce and go willingly before the tribunal to whose jurisdiction it appeals. If the captured party indicate purposes to employ means of resistance which the captor can not with probable safety to himself overcome, he may properly leave the vessel to go forward, and neither he nor the State he represents can ever afterwards justly object that the captor deprived her of the judicial remedy to which she was entitled.

For the second reason assigned by Capt. Wilkes for releasing the Trent differs from the first. At best, therefore, it must be held that Capt. Wilkes, as he explains himself, acted from combined sentiments of prudence and generosity, and so that the release of the prize vessel was not strictly necessary or involuntary.

Secondly—How ought we to expect these explanations by Capt. Wilkes of his reasons for leaving the capture incomplete, to affect the action of the British Government?

The observation upon this point which first occurs, is that Capt. Wilkes's explanations were not made known to the authorities of the captured vessel. If made known to them they might have approved and taken the release upon the condition of waiving a judicial investigation of the whole transaction, or they might have refused to accept the release upon that condition.

But the case is not with them, but with the British Government. If we claim that Great Britain ought not to insist that a judicial trial has been lost because we voluntarily released the offending vessel, out of consideration for her innocent passengers, I do not see how she is bound to acquiesce in the decision thus made by us, without necessity on our part, and without knowledge of conditions or consent on her part. The question between Great Britain and ourselves, thus stated, would be a question not of right or of law, but of favor conceded by her to us, in return for favors shown by us to her, of the value of which favors on both sides we ourselves shall be the judge. Of course the United States could have no thought of raising such a question in any case.

I trust that I have shown, to the satisfaction of the British Government, by a very simple and natural statement of the facts and analysis of the law applicable to them, that this Government has neither meditated nor practiced nor approved any deliberate wrong in the transaction to which they have called its attention, and on the contrary, that what has happened has been simply an inadvertency, consisting in a departure by the naval officer, free from any wrongful motive, from a rule uncertainly established, and probably by the several parties concerned, either imperfectly understood or entirely unknown. For this error the British Government has the right to expect the same reparation that we as an independent State should expect from Great Britain, or from any other friendly nation in a similar case.

I have not been unaware that, in examining this question, I have fallen into an argument for what seems to be the British side of it against my own country. But I am relieved from all embarrassment on that subject. I had hardly fallen into that line of argument when I discovered that I was really defending and maintaining not an exclusively British interest, but an old, honored and cherished American cause, not upon British authorities, but upon principles that constitute a large portion of the distinctive policy by which the United States have developed the resources of a continent, and thus becoming a considerable maritime power, have won the respect and confidence of many nations.

These principles were laid down for us in 1804 by James Madison, when Secretary of State, in the Administration of Thomas Jefferson, in instructions given to James Monroe, our Minister to England. Although the case before him concerned a description of persons different from those who are incidentally the subjects of the present discussion, the ground he assumed then was the same I now occupy, and the arguments by which he sustained himself upon it have been an inspiration to me in preparing this reply.

"Whenever," he says, "property found in a neutral vessel is supposed to be liable on any ground to capture and condemnation, the rule in all cases is, that the question shall not be decided by the captor, but be carried before a legal tribunal, where a regular trial may be had, and where the captor himself is liable to damages for an abuse of his power. Can it be reasonable, then, or just, that a belligerent commander, who is thus restricted and thus responsible, in a case of mere property of trivial amount, should be permitted, without recurring to any tribunal whatever, to examine the crew of a neutral vessel, to decide the important question of their respective allegiance, and to carry that decision into execution by forcing every individual he may choose into a service abhorrent to his feelings, cutting him off from his most tender connections, exposing his mind and his person to the most humiliating discipline, and his life itself to the greatest danger? Reason, justice and humanity unite in protesting against so extravagant a proceeding.

If I decide this case in favor of my own Government, I must disavow its most cherished principles, and reverse and forever abandon its essential policy. The country can not afford the sacrifice. If I maintain those principles and adhere to that policy, I must surrender the case itself. It will be seen, therefore, that this Government could not deny the justice of the claim presented to us in this respect upon its merits. We are asked to do the British nation just what we have always insisted all nations ought to do to us.

The claim of the British Government is not made in a discourteous manner. This Government, since its first organization, has never used more guarded language in a similar case.

In coming to my conclusion I have not forgotten that if the safety of this Union required the detention of the captured persons it would be the right and duty of this Government to detain them. But the effectual check and waning proportions of the existing insurrection, as well as the comparative unimportance of the captured persons themselves, when dispassionately weighed, happily forbid me from resorting to that defense.

Nor am I unaware that American citizens are not, in any case, to be unnecessarily surrendered, for any purpose, into the keeping of a foreign State. Only the captured persons, however, or others who are interested in them, could justly raise a question on that ground.

Nor have I been tempted at all by the suggestions that cases might be found in history where Great Britain refused to yield to other nations, and even to ourselves, claims like that which is now before us. Those cases occurred when Great Britain, as well as the United States, was the home of generations which, with all their peculiar interests and passions, have passed away. She could in no other way so effectually disavow any such injury as we think she does by assuming now as her own the ground upon which we then stood. It would tell little for our own claims to the character of a just and magnanimous people, if we should so far consent to be guided by the law of retaliation as to lift up buried injuries from their graves to oppose against what national consistency and the national conscience compel us to regard as a claim intrinsically right.

Putting behind me all suggestions of this kind, I prefer to express my satisfaction that, by the adjustment of the present case upon principles confessedly American, and yet, as I trust, mutually satisfactory to both of the nations concerned, a question is finally and rightfully settled between them, which, heretofore exhausting not only all forms of peaceful discussion, but also the arbitrament of war itself, for more than half a century alienated the two countries from each other and perplexed with fears and apprehensions all other nations.

The four persons in question are now held in military custody at Fort Warren, in the State of Massachusetts. They will be cheerfully liberated. Your Lordship will please indicate a time and place for receiving them.

I avail myself of this occasion to offer to your Lordship a renewed assurance of my very high consideration.

WILLIAM H. SEWARD.

Lord Lyons to Mr. Seward.

WASHINGTON, Dec. 27, 1861.

Hon. Wm. H. Seward, &c.:

Sir—I have this morning received the note which you did me the honor to address to me yesterday, in answer to Earl Russell's dispatch of 30th November last, relative to the removal of Mr. Mason, Mr. Slidell, Mr. Macfarland and Mr. Eustis, from the British mail packet Trent.

I will, without any loss of time, forward to her Majesty's Government a copy of the important communication which you have made to me.

I will, also, without delay, do myself the honor to confer with you personally on the arrangements to be made for delivering the four gentlemen to me, in order that they may again be placed under the protection of the British flag.

I have the honor to be, with the highest consideration, sir, your most obedient, humble servant. LYONS.

M. Thouvenel to M. Mercier.

(Translation.)

ADMINISTRATION OF FOREIGN AFFAIRS,
POLITICAL DEPARTMENT, PARIS, Dec. 8, 1861.

Sir—The arrest of Messieurs Mason and Slidell on board the English packet Trent by an American cruiser, has produced in France, if not the same emotion as in England, at least extreme astonishment and sensation. Public sentiment was at once engrossed with the lawfulness and the consequence of such an act, and the impression which has resulted from this has not been for an instant doubtful.

The fact has appeared so much out of accordance with the ordinary rules of international law, that it has chosen to throw the responsibility for it exclusively on the commander of the San Jacinto. It is not yet given to us to know whether this supposition is well founded, and the Government of the Emperor has, therefore, also had to examine the question raised by the taking away of the two passengers from the Trent. The desire to contribute to prevent a conflict, perhaps imminent, between two powers, for which it is animated by sentiments equally friendly, and the duty to uphold, for the purpose of placing the right of its own flag under shelter from any attack, certain principles essential to the security of neutrals, have, after mature reflection, convinced it that it could not, under the circumstances, remain entirely silent.

If, to our deep regret, the Cabinet at Washington were disposed to approve the conduct of the Commander of the San Jacinto, it would be either by considering Messrs. Mason and Slidell as enemies, or as seeing in them nothing but rebels. In the one as in the other case there would be a forgetfulness, extremely annoying, of principles upon which we have always found the United States in agreement with us.

By what title in effect would the American cruiser, in the first case, have arrested Mason and Slidell? The United States have admitted with us, in the treaties concluded between the two countries, that the freedom of the flag extends itself over the persons found on board, should they be enemies of one of the two parties, unless the question is of military people actually in the service of the enemy. Messrs. Mason and Slidell were, therefore, by virtue of this principle, which we have never found any difficulty in causing to be inserted in our treaties of friendship and commerce, perfectly at liberty under the neutral flag of England.

Doubtless it will not be pretended that they could be considered as contraband of war. That which constitutes contraband of war is not yet, it is true, exactly settled. The limitations are not absolutely the same for all the powers; but in what relates to persons, the special stipulations which are found in the treaties concerning military people define plainly the character of those who only can be seized upon by belligerents; but there is no need to demonstrate that Messrs. Mason and Slidell could not be assimilated to persons in that category. There remains, therefore, to invoke, in explanation of their capture, only the pretext that they were the bearers of official dispatches from the enemy; but this is the moment to recall a circumstance which governs all this affair, and which renders the conduct of the American cruiser unjustifiable.

The Trent was not destined to a point belonging to one of the belligerents. She was carrying to a neutral country her cargo and her passengers, and moreover it was in a neutral port that they were taken. If it were admissible under such conditions, the neutral flag does not completely cover the persons and merchandise it carries, its immunity would be nothing more than an idle world; and any moment the commerce and the navigation of third powers would have to suffer from their innocent and even their indirect relations with the one or the other of the belligerents. These last would no longer find themselves as having only the right to exact from the neutral entire impartiality, and to interdict all intermeddling on his part in acts of hostility. They would impose on his freedom of commerce and navigation restrictions which modern international law has refused to admit as legitimate! And we should, in a word, fall back upon vexatious practices, against which, in other epochs, no power has more earnestly protested than the United States.

If the Cabinet at Washington would look on the two persons arrested as rebels, whom it is always lawful to seize, the question, to place it on other ground, could not be solved, however, in a sense in favor of the commander of the San Jacinto. There would be in such case misapprehensions of the principles which makes a vessel a portion of the territory of the nation whose flag it bears, and violation of that immunity which prohibits a foreign sovereign, by consequence, from the exercise of his jurisdiction. It certainly is not necessary to recall to mind with what energy, under every circumstance, the Government of the United States has maintained this immunity, and the right of asylum which is the consequence of it.

Not wishing to enter upon a more deep discussion of the question raised by the capture of Messrs. Mason and Slidell, I have said enough, I think, to settle the point that the Cabinet at Washington could not, without striking a blow at the principles which all neutral nations are alike interested in holding in respect, nor without taking the attitude of contradiction of its own course up to this time, give its approbation to the proceedings of the commander of the San Jacinto. In this state of things, it evidently should not, according to our views, hesitate about the determination to be taken.

Lord Lyons is already instructed to present the demand for satisfaction, which the English Cabinet is under the necessity of reducing to form, and which consists in the immediate release of the persons taken on board the Trent, and in sending explanations which may take from this act its offensive character towards the British flag.

The Federal Government will be inspired by a just and exalted feeling in deferring these requests. One would search in vain to what end, for what interest, it would hazard or provoke by a different attitude a rupture with Great Britain.

For ourselves, we should see in that fact a deplorable complication in every respect of the difficulties with which the Cabinet at Washington has already to struggle, and a precedent of a nature seriously to disquiet all the powers which continue outside of the existing contest. We believe that we give evidence of loyal friendship for the Cabinet of Washington by not permitting it to remain in ignorance of the condition of things, of our manner of regarding it. I request you, therefore, sir, to seize the first occasion of opening yourself frankly to Mr. Seward, and, if he asks it, send him a copy of this dispatch.

Receive, sir, the assurance of my high consideration.

THOUVENEL

Monsieur Henri Mercier, Minister of the Emperor at Washington.

Mr. Seward to Mr. Mercier.

DEPARTMENT OF STATE,
WASHINGTON, Dec. 27th, 1861.

Sir—I have submitted to the President the copy you were so good as to give me of the dispatch addressed to you on the 31 December, instant, concerning the recent proceedings of Capt. Wilkes, in arresting certain persons on board of the British Contract and Mail Steamer Trent.

Before receiving the paper, however, the President had decided upon the disposition to be made of the subject, which has caused so much anxiety in Europe. That disposition of the subject, as I think, renders unnecessary any discussion of it in reply to the comments of M. Thouvenel. I am permitted, however, to say that M. Thouvenel has not been in error in supposing, first, that the Government of the United States has not acted in any spirit of disregard of the rights or of the sensibilities of the British nation, and that he is equally just in assuming that the United States would consistently vindicate, by their practice on the occasion, the character they have so long maintained, as an advocate of the most liberal principles concerning the rights of neutral States in maritime war.

When the French Government shall come to see at large the views of this Government and those of the Government of Great Britain on the subject now in question, and to compare them with the views expressed by M. Thouvenel on the part of France, it will probably perceive that while it must be admitted that those three powers are equally impressed with the same desire for the establishment of principles favorable to neutral rights, there is at the same time not such an entire argument concerning the application of those principles as is desirable to secure that important object.

The Government of the United States will be happy if the occasion which has elicited this correspondence can be improved so as to secure a more definite agreement upon the whole subject by all maritime powers.

You will assure M. Thouvenel that this Government appreciates as well the frankness of his explanations as the spirit of friendship and good will towards the United States in which they are expressed.

It is a sincere pleasure for the United States to exchange assurances of a friendship which had its origin in associations the most sacred in the history of both countries.

I avail myself of this opportunity to renew to you, sir, the assurance of my high consideration.

WM. H. SEWARD.

Mr. Henry Mercier, &c.

DIED:

On Friday, January 3, at 10 minutes past 11 o'clock, P. M., MARY JANE KEADY, consort of Thomas Freeland, aged 36 years and 3 months.

On Tuesday, December 24, 1861, at Camp Hunt, in Virginia, Lieut. A. B. JONES, of the 5th Louisiana Regiment, aged about 24 years.

On Saturday morning, Jan. 4, at half-past 3 o'clock, OLIVER M. WHITE, aged 45 years, a native of Kennebunk, Maine, and for the last 20 years a resident of this city.

On Saturday morning, the 4th inst., at half-past 6 o'clock, Dr. JAMES C. B. HARVEY, a native of Virginia, in the thirty-sixth year of his age.

Yesterday morning, at 11 o'clock, J. W. WILDER, aged about 40 years.

On Tuesday, December 24, 1861, at Camp Hunt, Va, HENRY S. FORWOOD, aged 26 years, a native of Harford county, Maryland.

On Tuesday morning, the 7th inst., at 3 o'clock, V. J. MARTIN, aged 72 years, a native of France.

On Tuesday, Jan. 7, at 3½ o'clock, J. J. LUGENBUHL.

On Thursday afternoon, 9th inst., Mrs. ELIZA SHEFFIELD WOODNUTT, wife of Sebastian Seiler, formerly editor of the German Gazette and New Orleans Journal of this city.

ST. JOHNS MIRROR.

EXTRA.

JACKSONVILLE, JAN. 17, 1862.—1½ P. M.

☞ As we desire to obtain a sufficient number of subscribers to defray the cost of Telegraphing, those who will take the Extras regularly, are requested to inform the Carrier, or the undersigned.

Single copies five cents.

JOS. F. ROGERO.

By Telegraph.

WILMINGTON, Jan. 16.

All is quiet at the Fort. There is a very heavy sea with thick fog. No shipping in sight yesterday or early this morning.

RICHMOND, Jan. 16.

About one hundred and eighty Yankee prisoners leave here to-morrow for the North. They go by a flag of truce to Newport News. In Congress nothing made public to-day.—Despatches from Norfolk to-night report the troubles in Lincoln's Cabinet as culminating. The announcement of the resignation of Cameron is generally credited. The troubles in the Federal Congress are also increasing.

Financial affairs at the North continue to become more and more embarrasing.

NEW ORLEANS, Jan. 16.

The sloop "Henry" has arrived from Havana, with dates to the 9th. She reports that the French fleet left on the 2d, for Vera Cruz, comprising 9 line-of-battle ships, 3 frigates and 3 propellers. It was reported that Vera Cruz was abandoned on the arrival of the Spanish fleet. The land force is commanded by Gen. Prim. The British fleet has been withdrawn. The steamer Calhoun had arrived at Havana. She makes the one hundred and first Southern vessel that has arrived there during the blockade. Business in Havana exceedingly dull.

NASHVILLE, Jan. 15.

A tobacco house in Henderson, Ky., owned by Kerr & Co., in Liverpool, was burned on the 9th inst , together with $9000 worth of tobasco. The Fire was the work of an incendiary. Gen. Hallock has appointed a new Board of Assessors in St. Lewis, to assess new levies on the 2d inst. No redress is allowed from their decission.

SAVANNAH, Jan. 17.

There were four Federal vessels off the bar yesterday P. M. It is reported that there were thirteen in Warsaw Sound this morning. There is no information of Burnsides' Expedition, but if the above report is true, the presence of so many vessels would indicate the arrival of a portion of that fleet in our waters.

The Philadelphia Inquirer.

ESTABLISHED 1829. PHILADELPHIA, SATURDAY, JANUARY 18, 1862. PRICE TWO CENTS.

War Against Treason!

MR. CAMERON CONFIRMED.

William E. Lehman Keeps His Seat.

THE FORTIFICATION BILL.

IMPORTANT FROM KENTUCKY.

GEN. GRANT'S ARMY NEAR COLUMBUS.

CAPTURE OF TWENTY-THREE REBELS.

Gen. Sigel to Command a Division.

ICE BLOCKADE OF THE MISSISSIPPI.

FROM FORTRESS MONROE

MORE PRISONERS COMING.

REBEL VESSELS CAPTURED IN THE GULF.

Fort Pickens Re-Opening Fire!

THE TOWN OF WARRINGTON IN FLAMES.

A Breach in Fort Barrancas!

GOV. DAWSON ASSAULTED AT SALT LAKE CITY.

Rebel Steamer "Sumter" at Cadiz.

THE LATEST SOUTHERN NEWS.

CONGRESSIONAL AND LEGISLATIVE.

Special Despatches to the Inquirer.

WASHINGTON, January 17, 1862.

General Cameron's Nomination.

The fight in the Executive Session of the Senate, over Mr. CAMERON's nomination, was renewed this morning with fierce energy. Senators TRUMBULL, GRIMES and HALE opened their batteries against him, which were replied to by Senators COWAN and WILMOT. Many Democrats voted in his favor, because they had accepted his hospitality, and were personally intimate with him while he was a Senator. The Republican Senators were afraid of complicating themselves with the corruptions by voting for him, and demanded assurances that future investigations will not make revelations implicating him personally. These were obtained after a fashion, and served as an anodyne.

The President and Cabinet desired his confirmation on account of their past intimate relations. The following was the vote on the nomination of Mr. CAMERON :—

YEAS.—Messrs. Anthony, Browning, Carlile, Chandler, Collamer, Cowan, Dixon, Doolittle, Fessenden, Foote, Harlan, Harris, Howe, King, Lane (Ind.), Lane (Kansas), Latham, Morrill, Pomeroy, Saulsbury, Sherman, Simmons, Sumner, Ten Eyck, Thompson, Wade, Wilmot, Wilson—28.

NAYS.—Messrs. Bright, Clark, Foster, Grimes, Hale, A. Johnson, Kennedy, McDougall, Nesmith, Pearce, Powell, Rice, Trumbull, Wilkinson—14.

ABSENT.—Messrs. Bayard, W. Johnson, Willey—3.

General CAMERON is indignant at the implied condemnation of the vote, and especially at Mr. TRUMBULL, who, he boldly asserts, was made Senator by his influence.

General CAMERON and Secretary STANTON had an interview of long duration, at the War Department, this morning.

The New Secretary of War.

Every train brings in additions to the noble army of martyrs to their country, in the shape of contractors and middle-men, anxious to arrange their little matters before twelve o'clock on Saturday night.

The change at the War Department grows in public favor every hour, or rather the expression of it finds vent when freed from the fetters and shackles that have so long controlled it. Secretary STANTON has no political friends to reward and no political enemies to conciliate.

His administration will be marked by the proper and wholesome encouragement of bravery and good conduct among the troops. He will adopted the system of making individual gallantry, military tact and sagacity, and personal good conduct the means of promotion and advancement. Personally, he combines, in a remarkable degree, moral and physical courage. Military men now feel that they are safe in his hands from the petty assaults of envy and jealousy, while they are devoting themselves to the discharge of their duty in the field.

Nominations of Shields and Meagher.

The nominations of SHIELDS and MEAGHER stick in the Senate, and doubts are raised whether they will pass.

Ordered Off.

Two or three regiments of regulars, which have been stationed here to perform police duty, have been ordered to the other side of the Potomac.

The Bullet Proof Vest.

A board of officers, appointed by the War Department to examine and report on a patented bullet proof vest or steel canvas, covered with cloth, experimented to-day, with favorable results. The commission was composed of Generals MEIGS, PORTER, STONEMAN, and Colonels SIBLEY and KINGSBURY. The experiments were eminently satisfactory, the vest resisting pistol bullets fired at ten paces. Here is another use for Pennsylvania iron, and a field for inventors and artisans. It will be tested with rifles.

Protest against Wilson, of Missouri.

A telegraphic protest has been received from parties in St. Louis, against allowing ROBERT WILSON—to be appointed Senator in place of TRUSTEN POLK, expelled—to take his seat. Mr. WILSON has many friends who insist that he is a strong Union man. The only suspicion taken is his appointment by Governor GAMBLE, who has displayed an inexcusable want of force and energy in driving the Rebels from Missouri.

The Finance Measure.

The finance measure agreed on by Secretary CHASE and the Bankers was before the Finance Committee of the Senate to-day, and met with decided opposition. It was not adapted to present exigencies. It is said that a combination has been formed to test the constitutionality of the income tax—the tax on incomes over eight hundred dollars passed last evening—on the ground that it is a direct tax, and is prohibited by the Constitution.

Naval Matters.

The steamer *King Philip*, Captain WM. MITCHELL, went down to the flotilla yesterday, and returned last night. She reports that the *Anacostia*, yesterday, bombarded the Rebel battery at Cockpit Point, with what result has not been ascertained. The Confederates fired four shells at the steamer, with the usual result—nothing hit and nobody hurt.

The *Stepping Stones*, Captain GRUMLER, returned to the yard yesterday afternoon.

The *Jacob Bell* has been hauled on the ways for repairs.

The Ball's Bluff Blunder.

The Investigating Committee on the conduct of the war, examined Captain F. G. YOUNG, aid to Colonel BAKER, to-day. This gentleman has been a victim to the persecutions of General STONE, so transparent and groundless that the president insisted it should cease. General STONE's conduct is undergoing a searching investigation, and some startling developments may be expected.

Payment of Troops.

The payment of the troops is progressing finely. The Ninth Pennsylvania Reserves, Colonel JACKSON, was paid off yesterday. It was expected the Second Pennsylvania Reserves would be paid off to-day.

Arrest of a Pennsylvania Volunteer.

JOHN BOYLE, a private in the Twenty-third Pennsylvania Regiment, has been arrested on a charge of attempting to kill a regular soldier.

Taking the Oath.

The oath of allegiance was administered today to seven persons who escaped from the Rebel army.

Miscellaneous.

Several peddlars have been arrested during the past few days and fined thirty dollars each for trafficking without a license. They were mostly from Philadelphia.

Several sutlers will give up their business as soon as their regiments are paid off. Some of the regiments are now without sutlers. Under the contemplated law, the profits of sutlers will be cut down from twelve hundred to about one hundred and fifty dollars per month, and probably less.

Some six or eight horse inspectors from Pennsylvania, it is reported, have been ordered to report themselves here immediately.

Election of State Treasurer.

HON. HENRY D. MOORE.

Special Despatch to the Inquirer.

HARRISBURG, Jan. 17.—From present appearances, it is believed that Hon. HENRY D. MOORE will be re-elected State Treasurer. The Union Democrats and Union Republicans will doubtless unite upon him. It is claimed that his administration of the State finances at a most critical period was all that could be desired, and that his success in negotiating the war loan at a time when pecuniary affairs had become embarrassed through the Executive power, was a severe and favorable test of his financial abilities. Mr. MOORE has been a member of Congress, and at one time ran for Mayor of the city of Philadelphia. L.

THE WAR IN MISSOURI.

AN ICE BLOCKADE OR THE MISSISSIPI RIVER.

ST. LOUIS, Jan. 17.—The navigation of the Mississippi river is entirely suspended here, in consequence of the gorging of the ice twenty miles below the city, extending to a point some distance above.

The troops are now being sent to Cairo by railroad, but their advance is materially retarded by the inadequate means of crossing the river, our ferry boats not being able to run, and the ice not sufficiently strong to bear heavy weights. The weather is now moderating again, and the prospects of a speedy opening are fair.

General PRICE, the member elect from the Fifth Congressional District, left for Washington to-day.

No person will hereafter be allowed to leave the city until his baggage be inspected by an officer appointed for that purpose, and his trunks sealed.

Some of our papers are ventilating the antecedents of the newly-appointed Senator from Missouri.

GEN. SIGEL TO COMMAND A DIVISION.

ROLLA, Mo., Jan. 17.—The brigade which has left here for the West, within the last three days, is composed of the Thirty-fifth and Thirty-sixth Illinois, the Ninety-fourth Missouri, and BOCHOFF'S and HOFFMAN'S batteries, under command of General OSTERHAUS. Another brigade, under Gen. SIGEL, will probably leave in a day or two. General SIGEL will doubtless assume the command of the entire division at the proper time.

From Salt Lake City.

OUTRAGEOUS ASSAULT ON GOV. DAWSON.

SALT LALE CITY, Jan. 17.—Governor DAWSON left here December 31st, on account of a personal difficulty. He was pursued, whipped and robbed, twelve miles east. Seven desperadoes, who committed the assault, were arrested, and three of them in endeavoring to escape from the officers, were killed'

The Pirate Sumter.

REPORTED ARRIVAL AT CADIZ, HAVING BURNED THREE VESSELS.

NEW YORK, Jan. 17.—The following is a copy of a despatch received per the *Arabia*, at Halifax :—

"LONDON, via QUEENSTOWN, Jan. 9, 1862.

"HIRAM BARNEY, Collector, New York:—The *Sumter* has arrived at Cadiz, having burned three vessels. C. F. ADAMS, U. S. Minister."

Virginia Legislature.

DEFEAT OF THE PENNSYLVANIA CENTRAL RAILROAD BILL.

WHEELING, Va., Jan. 17.—The bill known as the Pennsylvania Central Railroad bill, was defeated in in the lower House of the Legislature, to-day, by a vote of 24 to 9.

GENERAL DON CARLOS BUELL.

The stirring events that are expected soon to take place in Kentucky naturally excite an eagerness to know something of the young General who has the chief command there. General BUELL is a native of Ohio, but went, in early boyhood, to Indiana and lived with his relatives at Lawrenceburg, whence he was appointed a cadet at West Point. He was remarkable as a boy for his firmness, resolution and invincible pluck. He graduated at West Point in 1841, and became a Second Lieutenant in the Third United States Infantry. He served with great distinction in the Mexican war, and was twice brevetted for conspicuous gallantry in the field.

He was at Palo Alto, Resaca de la Palma and Monterey, and at the great actions on General SCOTT's line, until at Churubusco he received a desperate wound from a bullet, which passed through his body. We have heard it said by an army officer, that he received this wound in mounting a redoubt when others hesitated, to overlook the position of the enemy, and that when he fell, as it was supposed mortally wounded, the officer commanding the division exclaimed: "There has fallen the bravest man in the army." Indeed, among the younger officers, he was familiarly called "the bravest of the brave."

One of the first acts of General MCCLELLAN, after being assigned to the command of the Army of the Potomac, was to get General BUELL, then a Lieutenant-Colonel in the regular army, appointed a Brigadier-General of Volunteers, and ordered from California to take command of a division of the Army of the Potomac.

General BUELL is remarkable for his industry, energy and self-possession. Indeed, his coolness and self-possession are such distinguishing traits of his character, that it is believed that he could think just as calmly, and form his plans as naturally, in a tempest of grape as in the quiet of his tent. In the regular army he is esteemed emphatically a fighting man, and while he will not strike a blow too rashly, the country may be sure that he will fight with a will at the proper time.

He is 43 years of age, about five feet eight inches high, of compact frame and very deep chest, indicating great vital power. He possesses almost herculean strength in his arms, and can lift a weight at arm's length that would seem too much for one of twice his weight and muscle. His hair is light and very thin on top, approaching baldness; his beard, of the same hue, worn full and unshaven, is beginning to be sprinkled with grey. His eyes are blue and firm, yet gentle in their expression; but terribly steady and unmoved in the midst of excitement or danger. His weight is perhaps 165 pounds, his carriage erect, his step measured, his air quiet and easy, and not calculated to provoke attention. In 1852, Gen. BUELL married Mrs. MASON, the widow of Gen. MASON, of the United States Army, so well known for his service in California at the time of the conquest of that country. He has no children.

IMPORTANT FROM KENTUCKY.

General Grant's Army within Twelve Miles of Columbus.

CHICAGO, Jan. 17.—The *Times* has a special, dated "Twelve miles from Columbus, Jan. 16.—An additional force, with General GRANT'S staff, left Cairo yesterday, at 10 o'clock, overtook Generals MCCLERNAND'S, PAINE'S, and COOK'S commands during the afternoon. I am not permitted to state where we are going, or what troops we have. Heavy pickets are placed in all directions. No skirmishing yet."

LOUISVILLE, Jan. 17.—The Munfordsville correspondent of the *Journal* of this city says the Rebels are driving cattle into the ponds and watering places on the route of the advance of the United States Army, and killing them, so as to render the water unfit for drinking.

From Cairo and Paducah.

TWENTY-THREE REBELS CAPTURED — HEAVY CANNONADING UP THE TENNESSEE—A BATTLE IMPENDING.

CAIRO, Jan. 17.—Advices from Cape Girardeau state that the expedition which left here for Dallas and Bloomfield, returned this morning, bringing twenty-three prisoners, and among them Captain DAY, of JEFF. THOMPSON'S army.

Reports from Paducah say that heavy cannonading was heard up the Tennessee river this morning.

Gen. GRANT sent instructions to all the hospitals here to-day, to be in readiness at short notice.

Nothing of importance has been heard from the expedition.

FURTHER FROM WASHINGTON.

[BY ASSOCIATED PRESS.]

ARREST OF A FUGITIVE FROM JUSTICE.

WILLIAM LEE, the Chief of Police, from Elmira, New York, arrested, here, last night, ROBERT TURNER, charged with making a deadly assault on Officer HUNT, a policeman of Elmira. TURNER is one of the four ruffians arrested by LEE, last summer, on suspicion of knocking down and robbing a British marine. LEE left to-day with his prisoner for Elmira.

CITY BRANCH POST OFFICES.

The bill which passed the House to-day, relative to the establishment of Branch Post Offices in cities, authorizes and directs the Postmaster-General, if in his opinion the public interest or convenience may require it, to establish one or more Branch Post Offices, to facilitate the operations of the Post Office in any city or place, which in the opinion of the Postmaster-General may require such additional accommodation for the convenience of the inhabitants; and it shall be deemed the duty of the Postmaster-General to prescribe the rules and regulations for the Branch Post Offices which may be established. The Postmaster-General is also authorized to charge one cent, in addition to the regular postage, for every letter deposited in any Branch Post Office to be forwarded by mail from the principal office, and which shall be prepaid by stamp, and one cent for every letter delivered at such Branch Post Office, to be paid on delivery, provided that no letter shall be sent from the principal office to such branch office for delivery, except by request of the party to whom the same may be addressed, and provided that the expense of such branch service shall not exceed the receipts on account thereof. The tenth section of the act to establish certain post routes, and for other purposes, approved March 3d, 1847, is repealed.

THE NAVY YARD DIFFICULTIES.

The House Committee of Naval Affairs have before them the subject of the employment of workmen and laborers in the several Navy Yards, their pay, etc., and will soon report whether any further legislation is necessary.

THE LOWER POTOMAC—FIGHT AT COCKPIT POINT.

The steamer *King Philip* returned from the Potomac flotilla last night, and reports that the *Anacostia* yesterday bombarded the Rebel battery at Cockpit Point, with what result has not been ascertained. The Rebels fired four shells at the steamer, with the usual result—no damage done.

BRIGADIER-GENERAL MEAGHER.

The Colonels and Officers of the Sixty-ninth and Eighty-eighth New York Regiments, and the Officers of the Batteries attached to them, Major O'NEILL commanding, to-day sent to the Senate Military Committee a memorial heartily and unanimously endorsing the appointment of Colonel MEAGHER as their Brigadier-General. General SHIELDS also has addressed a most cordial letter to Senator WILSON, the Chairman of that Committee, earnestly advocating the confirmation of his friend and countryman.

THE FORTIFICATION BILL.

The Fortification bill, which passed the House today, appropriated an aggregate of $5,960,000, and includes the following items for the year ending 1863 :—

For Fort Montgomery, at the outlet of Lake Champlain	$100,000
" Fort Knox, at Narrows of Penobscot River, Maine	100,000
" Fort on Hog Island Ledge, Portland Harbor	100,000
" Fort Warren, Boston Harbor	75,000
" Fort Winthrop	50,000
" Fort at New Bedford Harbor	100,000
" Fort at Mileto Point, opposite Fort Schuyler, New York	200,000
" Fort on the site of Fort Tompkins, Staten Island, New York	200,000
" Fort at Sandy Hook, New Jersey	300,000
" Fort Delaware, Delaware River	60,000
" Fort Carroll, Baltimore Harbor	200,000
" Fort Calhoun, Hampton Roads, Va	200,000
" Fort Taylor, Key West, Florida	200,000
" Fort Jefferson, Garden Key, Florida	200,000
" Fort at Fort Point, San Francisco Bay, California	200,000
" Fort at Alcatroz Island, San Francisco Bay, California	150,000
" Contingencies of fortifications, including field works	500,000
" Bridge trains and equipage for armies in the field	250,000
" Tool and siege trains for armies in the field	250,000

FOR THE YEAR ENDING JUNE 30, 1862.

For fortifications on the Northern frontier, including the fortifications at Oswego, Niagara, Buffalo, Detroit and Mackinaw	$750,000
" Fort Montgomery, at the outlet of Lake Champlain, N. Y.	50,000
" Fort Knox, Penobscot River, Maine	50,000
" Fort on Hog Island Ledge, Portland Harbor, Maine	50,000
" Fort Winthrop and exterior batteries, Boston Harbor	50,000
" Fort at New Bedford Harbor, Mass	50,000
" Fort Adams, Newport, Rhode Island	50,000
" Fort Schuyler, East River, New York	25,000
" Fort at Willetts' Point, opposite Fort Schuyler, New York	50,000
" Fort Richmond, Staten Island, N. Y	25,000
" Fort on site of Fort Tompkins, Staten Island, New York	50,000
" Commencement of the casemates at the Battery on Staten Island, New York.	100,000
" New Battery at Fort Hamilton, at the Narrows, New York	100,000
" Fort Mifflin, near Philadelphia, Pa	25,000
" A new Fort opposite Fort Delaware, on the Delaware shore	200,000
" Fort Monroe, Hampton Roads, Va	50,000
" Fort Taylor, Key West, Florida	100,000
" Fort Jefferson, Garden Key, Florida	100,000
" An additional Fort at the Tortugas, Fla	200,000
" A Fort at Ship Island, Coast of Mississippi	100,000
" Contingencies of fortifications	100,000
" Bridge trains and equipage	250,000

New York Legislature.

ALBANY, Jan. 17.—Concurrent resolutions were reported in the Assembly to-day in favor of Congress levying a direct tax to defray the interest of the entire indebtedness of the National Government, &c., and that said tax be made permanent, and be increased yearly whenever an increase of the National debt is duly authorized by law; that the people of the State of New York will cheerfully coöperate with her sister loyal States and the United States Government in willing submission to all burdens necessary to be incurred, and that by adopting the policy here indicated, the Government will command the confidence of all persons having money to lend, and be able to obtain all the fiscal means needed for a vigorous prosecution of the war.

Further from Port Royal.

EXPEDITION TO SAVANNAH.

NEW YORK, Jan. 17.—Advices from Port Royal state that the expedition towards Savannah was supposed to be in progress. Reconnoitering parties have proceeded towards Tybee Island with apparatus for removing obstructions from the river and creeks south of the Savannah river.

It is understood that the land force will consist of 10,000 men, and that Warsaw Inlet would be the first destination of the expedition.

A line of railway was progressing across Hilton Head Island.

From General Banks' Column.

FREDERICK, Md., Jan. 17.—Nothing of the least interest has transpired for several days past along the line of the Upper Potomac.

Death of Robert S. Oakley.

NEW YORK, Jan. 17.—ROBERT S. OAKLEY, President of the National Bank Note Company, died yesterday.

CONGRESSIONAL PROCEEDINGS.

WASHINGTON, Jan. 17, 1862.

Senate.

Mr. CHANDLER (Mich.) presented the credentials of Hon. JACOB M. HOWARD, Senator elect from Michigan, in place of Mr. BINGHAM, deceased.

Mr. HOWARD then appeared and took the oath.

Several petitions, in favor of emancipation, were presented.

Mr. TRUMBULL presented a petition for Mr. C. L. SANFORD, who represents himself as a contractor with Messrs. CUMMINGS and TUCKER, on the strength of the information he received from the War Department, that they were authorized to act for the Government; but he is now surprised to learn that CAMERON says the heads of bureaus had made all the contracts. He asks the passage of a law to legalize his contract and prevent loss to honest contractors. Referred.

Mr. WILMOT (Pa.) presented a petition asking that homœopathic physicians be appointed in the army.

Mr. COLLAMER (Vt.), from the Committee on Post Offices, reported back the same bill in relation to the letters of sailors and marines. The bill, which extends the privilege of sending letters not pre-paid to sailors and marines, was then passed by the Senate.

Mr. FESSENDEN (Me.), from the Committee on Finance, reported back the House joint resolution, declaratory of the purpose of Congress to impose a tax.

Mr. CARLILE (Va.) objected to the consideration of the resolution, but subsequently withdrew his objection.

The resolution was then passed—yeas, 39; nays, Mr. POWELL.

Mr. DIXON (Conn.), from the Committee on Contingent Expenses, reported back the resolution to pay Mr. STANTON, the contestant of Mr. LANE'S seat, the usual compensation and mileage.

Mr. HALE said Mr. STANTON had already received one mileage.

Mr. FESSENDEN (Me.) moved to amend the resolution, so as to be exclusive of mileage. Agreed to.

The resolution as amended was then passed.

Mr. FOOTE (Vt.), from the Committee on Public Buildings, reported a resolution ordering the removal of the army bakeries from the Capitol.

Mr. WILSON introduced a bill in relation to volunteer service in any particular State.

Mr. TRUMBULL (Ill.) offered a resolution to pay $1000, out of the Contingent Fund, for the funeral expenses of Senator BAKER. Referred.

Also, a resolution in relation to the pay of the first Senators and Representatives from Minnesota.

Mr. BROWNING (Ill.) introduced a bill for the better organization of the artillery of the army of the United States. Referred.

After an Executive session, the Senate adjourned till Monday.

The following is the bill in relation to sutlers in the army, recently introduced by Senator WILSON, (Mass.)

That the Quartermaster-General and Commissary-General shall furnish for the use of the army, the following articles, viz:—Cheese, tobacco, segars, pipes, matches, blacking, blacking brushes, clothes brushes, tooth brushes, hair brushes, course and fine combs, emery crocus, pocket handkerchiefs, stationery, armor oil, sweet oil, rotten stone, razor straps, razors, shaving soap, soap, suspenders, scissors, shoe strings, needles, thread, knives, pencils, Bristol brick, to be delivered on requisition to the several Quartermasters, for the use of the officers and soldiers of their respective regiments in the army and volunteer service, to be charged to said Quartermaster, respectively, at such price for each article as shall be fixed by said Quartermaster-General and Commissary-General, before delivery. The number and character of said articles; also the price at which they shall be charged to said Quartermasters, may be changed from time to time by said Quartermaster-General and the Commissary-General.

Section 2. *And be it further enacted*, That the several regimental quartermasters shall deliver to the officers and soldiers of their respective regiments such of the articles enumerated in the preceding section as they may desire, not exceeding in amount, in any one month, one-fourth part of the pay of any such officer or soldier for that month, and shall cause the same to be charged to them on delivery at the prices fixed as provided in the preceding section; and the amount so charged shall be a lien upon the pay of such officer or soldier, and shall be deducted from the same by the paymaster before any dues from the United States are paid to him, and the amount so deducted shall be credited to the respective quartermasters, in liquidation of their account with the proper accounting officers.

Section 3. *And be it further enacted*, That the several regimental quartermasters may each elect from their respective regiments a non-commissioned officer or private as a clerk, who shall have the rank and pay of a sergeant of cavalry, and whose duty it shall be to keep true and fair accounts of all receipts, sales and other transactions herein required; and said accounts shall be open at all times to the examination of the Inspector-General, or any persons detailed by him for that purpose.

Section 4. That the price fixed by the Quartermaster-General and Commissary-General, upon the several articles mentioned in the first section of this act, shall in no case fall below nor exceed ten per cent. the actual cost of each article, including transportation and the increased expenses to the place of their delivery to the officers and soldiers of the several regiments.

Section 5. The office of Sutler in the army and volunteer service, except that of Post Sutler in the regular army is hereby abolished, and it shall not be lawful for any person to trade in any manner within the army or volunteer force, with any of the officers or soldiers thereof, without permission of the commanding General of the Army.

Section 6. It shall not be lawful for any regimental quartermaster or other person to receive, directly or indirectly, from any officer or sutler or other person in his behalf, any compensation for either of the articles mentioned in the first section of this act, except the first affixed thereto, as herein provided. And any quartermaster or other person violating any of the provisions of this act shall be dismissed from the service and shall not be eligible to a reappointment therein.

Section 7. That this act shall take effect in thirty days after its passage.

House of Representatives.

Mr. TRAIN (Mass.) introduced a bill transferring the penitentiary buildings of the District of Columbia to the War Department, for the use of the United States Arsenal. Referred.

On motion of Mr. FENTON (N. Y.), over one hundred bills from the Court of Claims were referred to the Committee on Claims.

Mr. DUNN (Md.), from the Committee on Patents, reported a bill authorizing the Commissioner of Patents to examine the application of SAMUEL BENTS, for the renewal of his patent for a process for pulling wheat, the patentee having, by mistake, failed to make the application for that purpose within the time prescribed by law. The patent expires on the 9th of March next. The bill was passed by 24 majority.

Mr. DUNN also reported a bill for the extension of the patent of JOHN G. MERVINE, for an improvement in the manufacture of lamp black. Postponed.

The House then resumed the consideration of the contested election case of BUTLER vs. LEHMAN, in the First Congressional District of Pennsylvania.

A vote was first taken on the substitute reported from the minority of the Committee on Elections, that J. M. BUTLER is not, and Mr. LEHMAN is, entitled to a seat as Representative from the First Congressional District, and it was adopted.

The resolution of the majority, thus amended, was agreed to—yeas, 77; nays, 67.

YEAS.—Messrs. Allen, Alley, Ancona, Baily (Pa.), Biddle, Blair (Va.), Browne (R. I.), Browne (Va.), Buffinton, Cobb, Cooper, Corning, Cox, Cravens, Crisfield, Crittenden, Delano, Dunlap, Dunn, Edwards, English, Fouke, Gooch, Goodwin, Gurley, Haight, Harrison, Hickman, Holman, Hooper, Horton, Johnson, Kellogg, Killinger, Knapp, Law, Lazear, Leary, Logan, Mallory, Maynard, Menzies, Morris, Noble, Noell, Norton, Nugen, Odell, Pendleton, Perry, Rice (Mass.), Richardson, Riddle, Robinson, Rollins (Mo.), Sargeant, Sheffield, Steele (N. Y.), Steele (N. J.), Stratton, Thomas, Train, Trimble, Tipton, Vallandigham, Vibbard, Voorhies, Wadsworth, Ward, Webster, Whaley, White (O.), Wickliffe, Wood, Woodruff, Worcester, Wright—77.

Recapitulation—Democrats, 54; Republicans, 33.

NAYS.—Messrs. Aldrich, Bailey (Mass.), Baker, Baxter, Beaman, Bingham, Blair (Mo.), Blair (Pa.), Blake, Campbell, Chamberlain, Colfax, F. A. Conkling, Roscoe Conkling, Conway, Covode, Cutler, Davis, Dawes, Diven, Duell, Edgerton, Eliot, Fenton, Fessenden, Frank, Granger, Hale, Hauchett, Hutchins, Julian, Kelley, Kellogg, Lansing, Loomis, Lovejoy, McKean, McKnight, McPherson, Marston, Mitchel, Moorhead, Morrell (Me.), Morrell (Vt.), Olin, Patton, Phelps (Cal.), Pike, Pomeroy, Potter, Rice (Me.), Sedgwick, Shanks, Sherman, Sloan, Spaulding, Stevens, Trowbridge, Van Horn, Van Valkenburgh, Van Wyck, Wallace, Walton, Wheeler, White, Wilson.—67. All Republicans.

Mr. LEHMAN, therefore, continues a member of the House.

Mr. ALLEY (Mass.), from the Post Office Committee, reported a bill authorizing the establishment of Branch Post Offices in cities. Passed.

The House concurred in the Senate's amendments to the House bill to promote the efficiency of the Dead Letter Office.

Mr. DELANO (Mass.) made a report from the Committee for the District of Columbia, on a resolution referred to them relative to Marshal LAMON'S jail regulations. They say it was strictly in his official discretion to make rules to remedy existing abuses, and though they can see no necessity for subjecting members of Congress to the idle ceremony of procuring passes signed by the President of the Senate or Speaker of the House, yet there is nothing so palpably oppressive and onerous in the regulations as to call for the special intervention of the House. Hence the Committee ask to be discharged from the further consideration of the subject.

The further consideration of the report was then postponed.

Mr. STEVENS (Pa.), from the Committee on Ways and Means, reported a bill for the support of the West Point Military Academy. On his motion, the Committee obtained leave to sit during the sessions of the House. He took occasion to explain the reason why the appropriation bills were not sooner reported, adding that he had been informed that numerous libelling letter writers and journals had been finding fault with the Committee for not reporting an equitable tax bill. The Committee, however, are gathering facts, and work for hours after attending to their business in this hall. He desired to say that the criticisms and libels of the press would not make them move one minute faster than a due regard to the public interest would permit.

Mr. FENTON (N. Y.), rising to a privileged question, inquired by what rule Marshal LAMON occupied a place on the floor of this House?

The SPEAKER replied that he was not aware of such a rule, and had no doubt the Doorkeeper would enforce the rules.

Mr. VALLANDIGHAM (Ohio.)—Perhaps the Marshal has a warrant for somebody here.

Mr. KELLOGG (Ill.) inquired whether the enforcement of the rules was to operate on the Marshal only? He did not see anybody interfering with the business of the House. Then why should Mr. LAMON be made an exception, when others, who were not members, were also on the floor.

The SPEAKER directed the Doorkeeper to enforce the rules, and expressed the hope that members would not hereafter insist on introducing their friends here.

The Doorkeeper then went to Marshal LAMON, who was standing near the door, and after speaking a few words to him, he turned and left, with a look of disgust at the whole body.

The House resumed the consideration of the Fortification Bill in Committee of the Whole on the State of the Union. During the debate on amendments,

Mr. ARNOLD (Ill.) said it would be better to act on the bill specifically, the items being based on official estimates. It was not to be supposed that this bill embraced all the fortifications necessary to the Atlantic coast and Western lakes; but the Select Committee have the subject under consideration, and will, at an early day, report the result of their deliberations.

DEFENCES OF THE DELAWARE.

Mr. CAMPBELL (Pa.)—This is for the defence of a harbor of refuge in the Delaware. This harbor of refuge is formed by a breakwater, three-fourths of a mile in length, and another about one quarter of a mile long, forming a safe and secure harbor, in which there are often as many as 150 or 170 vessels riding at anchor, secure from all danger from the sea. The general average is, perhaps, thirty or forty. At the present time there is not a single gun in position on this breakwater to protect these vessels from privateers, or to prevent them from running in and destroying the commerce of Philadelphia there, while at the same time, in case of a foreign war, it would form a safe and secure retreat for a foreign foe, whence they can issue and destroy our commerce and connection with the capital. I do not ask this as a matter of interest to the commerce of Philadelphia, but as of interest to the whole Union. Ships now run there, and can communicate with Philadelphia and other ports on the seaboard, and receive their sailing directions by telegraph.

In the last war it was deemed of sufficient importance to erect a small battery at that place. But at this time there is not a single gun. General TOTTEN thinks this place should be protected. I would tell the Committee that we have not adequate protection of the river, and that with the appropriate armament and garrison of the forts we have already, they are not sufficient to protect our channel from the inroads of a hostile fleet. We wish to protect this harbor of refuge, that our ships may have adequate and secure protection. I doubt if there is any such breakwater or any such work made by any foreign Government that is not protected.

The amendment asks for $150,000 for fortifications to protect this harbor of refuge formed by the breakwater at the mouth of the Delaware river. I do not ask this as a matter of interest to Pennsylvania, but as a matter of general interest to the whole country.

Mr. MORRILL (Vt.) did not think it wise for the House to transcend the limits of the bill.

Mr. WRIGHT (Pa.)—There is no city upon the Atlantic coast, or near it, that is in so defenceless a condition as the city of Philadelphia at this time.—The harbor of New York is well fortified. They have upwards of a thousand guns in forts and fortifications for the defence of that position. Boston has four hundred guns in forts and fortifications for the defence of that harbor. The only defences of the city of Philadelphia, is Fort Mifflin, some seven or eight miles below the city, and which is almost in a state of dilapidation, and old Fort Delaware, some fifty miles further down the Delaware River. The capacity of both of these forts, armed to the fullest extent, is about one hundred and twenty-five guns; and, perhaps, there are at this time not more than fifty guns mounted.

These are all the defences which the great City of Philadelphia has against any enemy that may approach it up the Delaware bay and river. The amendment proposed is for the erection of a fortification to protect what is called the harbor of refuge; that is immediately on the inside of the breakwater which was erected some years ago by the Government at that place.

There is a demand, a pressing demand, that this should be done, and done immediately. At this moment there is nothing to prevent a hostile fleet from coming up your river, pass Fort Delaware and Fort Mifflin, for they are entirely inadequate to prevent any invading fleet that might choose to come up the Delaware river. If there ever was a time when something of this kind should be immediately done for the defence of the metropolis of the great State, that time is now.

The Committee on Military Affairs have, it is true, referred to them a general system which is to include all the approaches to the city, but I do not think that the adoption of this amendment would interfere in any way with the actions of that Committee, with regard to the general system of defence. The appropriation here is small, the amount of property that seeks safety in this harbor of refuge, which is immediately inside of the breakwater, is often of a very large amount. I hope the amendment may prevail.

Mr. BIDDLE argued that the fortification, instead of being merely local in its character, was one of immense importance to the whole country.

Mr. KELLEY did not wish the subject to be treated as a local one. It was not a local question. The question is whether the $150.000 shall be appropriated to complete a great national work upon which the Government has already expended millions.

The harbor of refuge at the mouth of the Delaware has cost the Government four millions of dollars, and it lacks only its armaments, and the Chief of Engineers has said it should be done.

Mr. CRITTENDEN (Ky.) suggested that we have not money enough to carry on the war within our borders. To this should all our energies be directed. It was no time to enter into expensive precautionary measures against a foreign war, which he hoped was far distant. Let us defend the Government, and when peace shall ensue to the country, we can provide against the danger of foreign war.

Mr. WRIGHT (Pa.) agreed with Mr. CRITTENDEN. There should be no new works commenced unless there was an absolute necessity for them. He had been informed that the bill appropriated between five and six millions of dollars. In order to afford time for examination into some of the items he ineffectually sought a postponement of its consideration.

All the amendments proposed were voted down.

The Committee then rose, when the bill, as originally reported, was passed by the House.

Mr. HOLMAN (Ind.), from the Committee on Army Contracts, reported a resolution, which was adopted, calling on the Secretary of War to communicate to the Committee a copy of the contracts for the purchase of horses for Colonel WILLIAMS' Regiment of Cavalry, now in Kentucky.

Mr. STEELE (N. J.), of the same Committee, reported a resolution that they inquire into the several orders or contracts—one for 50,000 and another for 25,000 Enfield rifles—whether these contracts have been extended or annulled; whether they have been sold or offers made to sell them, etc.

Without transacting any other business, the House adjourned till Monday.

ARMY PAY.—The reduction in pay per month which the commissioned officers of the Army will be subjected to if the Senate bill passes both houses will be as follows :—

	Present pay.	*Proposed pay.*
Major-General	$469·00	$300
Brigadier-General	323·50	240
Colonel	218·00	200
Lieutenant-Colonel	184·00	180
Major	195·00	150
Captain	118·50	120
First Lieutenant	108·50	100
Second Lieutenant	103·50	80
Surgeon-General	228·33	200
Surgeons, ten years service	223·00	180
Surgeons, less than ten years.	187·00	150
Surgeons, five years service	137·00	120
Surgeons, less than five years.	120·00	100
Paymaster-General	228·33	200
Deputy Paymaster-General	211·00	180
Paymaster	187·00	150
Chaplain	—	80
All military storekeepers	—	120

THE "ELEVENTH OHIO."

VOL. I.] PUBLISHED FOR THE REGIMENT, B' WRIGHT, HOWARD AND LAMBRIGHT. [No. 1

"Death to Traitors."

SINGLE COPIES, POINT PLEASANT, VRGINIA, JANUARY 20, 1862. FIVE CENTS

When General Floyd, from Cotton Hill,
Thought, Yankees, now I'll maul ye,
He threw across an iron pill,
To drive them from the Gauley.

His ragged troops he scattered out
From ferry, falls, to Raleigh,
And bragged he'd make a speedy route
On the other side of Gauley.

Your bully guns you thought could scare.
But Simmons, soon he saw ye,
And sent [illegible]
From the other side of Gauley.

The ferry boat you thought to spa[illegible]
I know it must annoy ye
To see her cross from bank to bank,
And dare you on the Gauley.

The Gipsey* camp you tried to shell.
You thought, now I'll destroy ye,
Much quicker you could go to [illegible]
Than drive them from the Gauley.

But changes come, and soon you found
From your own side they saw ye.
You faced about, and with one bound,
Skiddaddled from the Gauley.

The name [illegible]

THE WOUNDED SOLDIER.

I'm wounded, Effie, and they say, I never can get well;
'Twas in the thickest of the fight that I got hurt and fell.
It seems to me like ages, yet it's but a month to-day
Since you promised that you'd wait for me though I were years away.

Do you remember--oh! how well it all comes back to me!—
Our sitting in the bright moonlight, under the maple tree;
When first I said I loved you, and then told you we must part,
For not e'en you could keep me, when my country had my heart?

But I knew you did not wish it, as, your little hand in mine,
You did not try to stay me by any word or sign;
But trying to keep back the tears, although a few would fall,
You bade me trust in God, your God, whatever might befall.

But all my bright ambitious hopes forever now are fled,
And the sunlight of to morrow will fall upon me dead;
There'll be one soldier less to fight, one less on earth to love,
But there'll be another hand to strike the golden harps above.

I have a mother in the skies; I wonder if she'll know
The little baby that she left so many years ago
But I'm weary, and I cannot think: let this your comfort be,
Your love has been the brightest thing in all the world to me.

On the 25th of April, 1792, Benjamin Ullin left the Stockade, above the mouth of the Kanawha river, (now Point Pleasant, Va.,) and crossing the Kanawha, he followed a path that led up a point to the top of a hill about a mile below the Kanawha, in pursuit of a stray horse. As he approached the hill, he was seen by three Indians, who on the top, who carefully concealed themselves, and lay in ambush, until he reached the top, when two of them who had arms, fired at him. One of their balls passed through his clothes and touched his right hip, but did not bury itself. Finding their fire had been ineffectual, they separated, two of them running and occupying the only passes by which he could descend the hill, in the direction of the Stockade and the other made [illegible] him. Thus surrounded, he [illegible] but to fall into their hands as a prisoner, or leap down a high precipice of rocks on the north side of the hill, fronting the Ohio river. Acquainted with many of the Indians, and knowing their feelings towards him, he was satisfied that if he fell into their hands, that a certain, if not a lingering death awaited him. In this awful predicament, he stood pondering over his melancholy condition, without arms to defend himself, until the Indian had come nearly up to him, when he summoned up resolution, and commenced a rapid retreat towards the brink of the precipice, hotly pursued by the Indian,--arrived there he did not hesitate, but leaped down the precipice, passing through the branches of a small buckeye tree, he jumped SIXTY-FIVE AND A HALF feet before he reached the ground. Recovering as soon as possible, he made three other leaps, the first seventeen, the second seven, and the third eleven feet, which took him nearly to the base of the hill. He then ran to the Ohio river, plunged into the water, and undertook to swim across, but finding the water very cold, and that the Indians had not pursued him, he returned to the beach and [illegible] recrossed the Kanawha in a small canoe and soon arrived at the [illegible] distance of each leap was measured by Col. Lewis, of Virginia and Col. Boone, of Missouri, who were at the Stockade at the time.

From the fall of the leaves in autumn, to their budding in the spring, the precipice can be seen by boatmen descending the Ohio river, from a great distance, and ever since that occurence, it has received from them the appellation of "ULLIN'S LEAP." Notwithstanding the extraordinary efforts he made, after leaping down the precipice, and which enabled him to effect his escape, they were not made without considerable injury for sometime his life was despaired of, but he finally recovered, and lived to a good old age.

After the treaty of 1795, it was ascer[illegible] Indians [illegible] came to this place, and mingled [illegible] whites, that a story had been in vogue among them, and extensively believed in on the authority of those who chased Ullin, "THAT THEY HAD FIRED ON A PALE FACE WHO RAN TO THE EDGE OF THE PRECIPICE, AND TOOK WINGS AND FLEW OFF."

THE INFANT.

A lovely child lay sleeping, the moonbeams kissed its forehead, and in every ray of light an angel sported. No wonder they should leave their Eden home to linger a while on earth to gaze on aught so lovely. Pure as the snow wreath which mantles the Alpine hills, or the lilly with its brow bedecked with pearls, was this infant—sin had ne'er touched it. Its little heart was far from guile as was the seraph's which looked down upon its beauty. Nor were the angels alone gazing, no, no, a fond mother watched it, and as the moonbeams played around its cheek, she thought of the innocence which dwelt within the heart of her cherished infant.

THE members of the 11th are at present comfortably quartered, in houses.

THE NEW YORK CASKET
IS PUBLISHED EVERY
MONDAY, AT THE JOB BUILDINGS,
SPRUCE-STREET, N. Y.
TERMS: One dollar a year, in advance.
J. C. HAWLEY, EDITOR AND PROPRIETOR.
All letters must be addressed, J. C. Hawley, New York City.

THE WEEKLY CASKET.

A Family Paper, Devoted to the Sciences, Arts, General Intelligence, Poetry, &c., &c.

Volume X.] NEW YORK, JANUARY 22, 1862. [No. 9.

THE POET'S CORNER.

A Glorious Land.

Our Country!—'tis a glorious land!
With broad arms stretch'd to every shore;
The proud Pacific chafes her strand,
She hears the dark Atlantic roar.
And nurtured on her ample breast,
How many a goodly prospect lies
In Nature's wildest, grandest dress,
Enameled with her loveliest dyes.

Rich prairies deck'd with flowers of gold,
Like sunlit oceans roll afar;
Broad lakes her azure heavens behold,
Reflecting clear each trembling star;
And mighty rivers mountain born,
Go sweeping onward, dark and deep,
Through forests where the bounding fawn
Beneath their sheltering branches leap.

And cradled 'mid her clustering hills,
Sweet vales in dream-like beauty hide,
Where love the air with music fills,
And calm content and peace abide;
For plenty here her fullness pours,
In rich profusion o'er the land,
And sent to seize her gen'rous store,
There prowls no tryant's hireling band.

Great God! we thank thee for this home—
This bounteous birth-land of the free,
Where wand'rers from afar may come,
And breathe the air of liberty!
Still may her flowers untrampled spring,
Her harvest wave, her cities rise;
And yet, till time shall fold his wing,
Remain earth's loveliest paradise!

A Parody.

Tell me ye winged winds
That round my pathway roar,
Do ye not know some spot
Where women fret no more?
Some lone and pleasant dell,
Some "holler" in the ground,
Where babies never yell,
And cradles are not found?
The loud wind blew the snow into my face,
And snickered as it answered—"Nary place."

Tell me, thou misty deep,
Whose billows round me play,
Knows't thou some favored spot,
Some [illegible]
Where weary man can find
A place to smoke in peace,
Where crinoline is not,
And hoops are out of place?
The loud winds, sounding a perpetual shout,
Stopt for a while and spluttered, "You git out.

And thou, serenest moon,
That with such holy face,
Dost look upon the girls,
Who with their beaux embrace,
Tell me, in all thy round,
Hast thou not seen some spot
Where muslin is not found
And calico is not?
Behind a cloud the moon withdrew in woe,
And a voice sweet, but sad, responded "Poh!"

Tell me, my secret soul—
Oh! tell me, Hope and Faith,
Is there no resting place
From women, girls and death?
Is there no happy spot
Where bachelors are blessed,
Where females never go,
And man may dwell in peace?
Faith, Hope and Truth—best boons to mortals given—
Waved their bright wands, and answered, "Yes, *in Heaven*."

OCTOBER.

The month of the falling leaf and the fading flower; the month in which memory and meditation, poetry and fancy love to revel; the month consecrated by so many beautiful and hallowed associations is with us. We rejoice in it.

To the poetic temperament no month teems with more interest; to the reflective mind, no month is so prolific in food for thought and in lessons of instruction as October. Need we dwell upon its beauty? the brilliancy of its sun-set skies, the gorgeousness of its variegated woods, the vitality that floats in its inspired breezes? Each one who has an eye to see and a soul to feel knows this, and what the painter's pencil has so often failed to delineate and the poet's pen to describe, why should I attempt?

The dying swan is said to concentrate and expend all her powers in her last song, and that song through which her spirit is wafted away, away, I know not where, has in it beauty and melody unequalled before. So methinks the year, ere she wraps around her the cold winding sheet of winter, ere she closes her reign to be entombed in the bosom of the ages, makes a mighty effort, and in its last makes its greatest and best exhibition of power and beauty.

But let this pass; it is ours now to pause amid the glorious wrecks of decaying nature, and read the lessons with which every dying leaf teems, and list to the whispers which that mournful breeze sounds in my ear—for it is vocal, and the mind and the spirit that is rightly allured may catch sounds rich with departing music. How much may be heard and learned in wandering through the woods at this season, and how pleasant are these wanderings, for mind and muscle seem to catch the spirit from expiring nature, and we feel strong to think, to suffer, or to act.

Probably the predominating spirit of the season is that of sadness; but it is a healthful, thoughtful, earnest sadness. Involuntary thoughts will come, as departed friends, of stricken hopes and faded joys, that like crushed flowers, strew our path; involuntarily we linger amid the memories that spectre-like haunt the past. We feel this autumn season is strikingly emblematic. "So flourishes and fades majestic man."—With all his glory and pride and power, "a wind passeth over it and it is gone, and the place thereof knoweth it no more forever." The life of a flower is the mournful epitome of human life; it buds, blossoms and rejoices, fades and dies. Life has its spring and harvest time, and life has its autumn, its autumn of old age, of fading flowers, of forsaking friends, of disease, and grave-mounds and death.

These thoughts may bring sadness, but they ought not to bring gloom, for other thoughts and other truths, precious and bright, lie side by side with these. Is not autumn of all ages richest in beauty and glory and fruits? Is it not the culminating of seed and harvest time, in which we shout the "Harvest Home?" May not old age be so? If the seeds of virtue and usefulness are thickly sown in youth, and the whole life has been well spent, these seeds maturing and spreading, will not the old age be good and honored, and glorious? Are not gray hairs a crown of glory when found in the service of righteousness? May not old age rejoice in the work of her hands and the fruits of her labor? May not the top-stone of declining years be brought with shoutings of 'grace!" "grace!" unto it? May she not gather around her the trophies of affection and memory and thought from the pilgrimage she has made, and as truthfully and as gracefully as the golden wheat all ripened and ready for the garner, bow her head full of years and of honors, and with calm dignity and holy trust descend to the portals of the grave?

How glorious the sunset that crowns such a life—how beautiful the ivy that clings around time so well spent.

Then comes another thought—the death of the plants and flowers is not real, but seeming; their form of existence is but changed; they are resolved into their primal elements. These leaves sinking into the bosom of their mother earth, or becoming gases, fructify and enrich earth and air. *Neither do we die!* The clods may lie cold and heavy above us, and, as from the naked, withered tree, the sap seems all to have departed, so our frozen, palsied limbs seem as if life should ne'er again course its swift strong current through the veins. Yet we are not dead, if by death you mean an eternal sleep. Let us learn a lesson from the leaves that fertilize as they fall; from our death even may volumes of instruction come; and, being dead, we may of it speak, like one of old, whose life was a series of mighty exploits, yet who, it is said, accomplished more in his death than in all his life. Our mission ends not when our lips have spoken the last word, when the pulse has throbbed for the last time. As our souls are immortal, our mission is eternal—our examples may cast a light or shade for many years—the echo of our words may sound and sound and be heard forever through the corridor of ages. As the circle made by the fall of a stone in the water widens and gives rise to another circle, thus circle follows and widens over circle to an imperceptible distance, so each life affects some other life, and that another, and so on forever. How important does life seem when we remember that each step we take on its path, leaves an indelible foot-print bright or black, which may prove a beacon light and a guide, or which may cause many to stumble and stray. Let us aim that, Phœnix-like, from the ashes of our decay may arise a mighty power for good; that after we have died the world may be the better that we have lived. Such is the mission of the leaf—shall our's be less?

But thought follows thought, lesson follows lesson. I travel in mind over a few months—I glance a short way in the future, and in striking contrast rises the aspect of nature. Then, in fancy, I see the plains all covered with verdure, the trees rejoicing in strength and foliage, the gardens gay with flowers. I see all nature alive, and active, and beautiful; she already has had her resurrection. And I think I have in this an answer to the question: If a man die, shall he live again? I hear a voice, gathering strength from every bursting blade of grass, from every opening flower, from the loosened tongue of every gushing rill. Whither is it? List! there is no word so noble, so sweet, so inspiring. Listen—*Immortality!* Then I think of one around whose brow last autumn was twined the orange blossom, and who this autumn has meekly closed her eyes, and folded her hands, and gone to sleep with the flowers, the beautiful flowers of her Western home—she who was fairer than them all, and has left behind her a richer fragrance and a more hallowed memory. And then I think—and I thank God for the thought—that the grave cannot keep forever so much beauty, and grace, and love; but at the touch of the Great Life-Giver, the seal shall be removed, the eternal spring tide shall set in, *she* shall live forever. For do we all fade as a leaf, then as a leaf shall we be revived and renewed. A pleasing, glorious thought that this "corruption shall put on incorruption, this mortal immortality."

Has not autumn many voices? Do not rich treasures lie buried in its leafy bed? Is it not covered, not only with a robe gorgeous with beauty, but written over with thoughts of wisdom and value?

Indians, and their Influence upon our Present War.

The following is the views of an Indian chief in regard to the red man's influence in our national troubles. He says:

The sons of America in the past have dealt unjustly with the red man; and so sure as day follows night, and night follows day, so sure there must be a time of retribution. Each and all must receive their natural allowance; if they do not receive it at one time, they surely must at another.

When your forefathers first planted foot upon American soil, instead of looking up to and obeying the natural God, they obeyed the unnatural God; and there are certain seeds which they planted upon the American continent, that you of to-day reap the fruits of. They came with their souls fully freighted with selfishness and bigotry, and because of this unnatural condition of things, their descendants reap the long hoarded reward of vengeance from those they wronged. They wished to become possessed of the soil upon which they landed as easily as possible, and that, too, without rendering back a just equivalent. "How can we get possession of so much of their land?" was a question often asked among themselves. "How shall we extinguish the red man? How shall we bargain with him? We will give him this toy and that toy, and in the simplicity of his nature, we will receive in return for them something of value. We will take his lands—his broad hunting-grounds, and give for them 'a mere song.'" But they knew not how their injustice to the wild children of the forest was hoarded up in the hearts of that race, to be poured out upon the heads of their children's children in coming time.

The credulity and native honesty of the red man made him an easy prey for the shrewd, designing, calculating pale faces. Their moral and intellectual organs were small, and their weak nature betrayed them. But now the red men have grown strong in spirit-life—have perceived the wrong that their white brothers have done them, and so sure as the day follows the night, so surely will the red man return and take care of that which was his own by God-given right.

If you sin against any atom of life in God's universe, that atom will, *some time or other*, bring back to you your fitting condemnation. Indeed, this is a mighty law which follows you even to the spirit-life. The sins of your fathers in the past are now being visited upon you of this day and generation. The thousands of spirits of the red men whom your fathers wronged, are coming back with all the power of their spiritual existence, to fight against you of the North who are endeavoring to sustain the American Government, for they desire to see it overthrown, because they see its foundation was evil. They see it as the foundation of the seeds of wrong against them, and their whole strength is in consequence leagued with the enemies of the Union. The feeling your ancestors planted in the bosom of the red man, by their selfishness and avarice, will receive its law of compensation, and the result is unavoidable. You cannot change the red man's hatred by outward education. You may cover it over and hide it, but the same power is there, and it always will seek its freedom. It is their guide, and they are as fully governed by it as you are by your God—by your consciousness of right; and the red men, acting naturally through your material mediums in a thousand ways you do not know, upon the faculties of man susceptible of use, are exulting in the coming of the hour when their souls may be sated with revenge.

Severe will be the struggle you must pass through, but when the lesson of war is once learned, and its experiences profited by, you will know that the Great Eternal forever guides all things aright, and his hand is seen in all the affairs of mortality. Then your nation will again enjoy the sunshine of peace and prosperity.

Influence of Song.

Most of us have experienced the luxury of tears when listening to an old man who, having led a long career of vice and crime, was at length banished from the country; and who, while undergoing his period of banishment amidst the wilds and jungles of a distant land, heard in the summer eventide, a sweet voice, singing in his own language the very song which had lulled him to his infant slumber, when he knew crime but by name, and knew it only to abhor. It had been sung, too, by the cradle of an infant sister, one who had died young, and is now in heaven; the mother, too, was no more.

But the song—the old song had not lost its influence over him yet. Back came trooping upon him the old memories which had so long slumbered down there, in the unconsumed depths of the heart; the mother and the father; the household gathering; old books; the old school house; the time worn church, half hidden by the old yew trees, where he had first heard the Bible read, all came back upon him as fresh as if it were yesterday; and, overpowered by his feelings, he gave vent to them in a flood of tears. And then the old man grew calm, and his latter days were his best days; and when the term of his punishment had expired, he came back to his fatherland, and there, in that old village graveyard, amid whose grassy hillocks he had played and gamboled, and where the mother and her little ones were sleeping, he lay down his weary limbs, and sank peacefully away into a common grave.

Eloquent Passage.

For the greatest human intellects there is no exception from the common doom. I have sometimes thought how sublime must have been the emotions of that man whose privilege it was to stand by the coffin of Shakespear and gaze on the sweet and noble face, when death hath called out all the strange beauty which never lives there. It was worth a lifetime to have stood there one minute—to have laid your hand on that broad brow, and started at the cold chill; and so pausing to have called up in memory all the magnificent creations of his genius, and worshipped him there in the silence and the gloom:

But he is dead and gone;
At his head a grass-green turf,
At his heels a stone.

So they all go. Man dies, but nature is eternal. The seasons keep their appointed time; day returns with its golden splendor, and night with its eloquent mystery. The same stars which lit the ghastly battle-field of Troy, rough with the dead bodies of ancient heroes—which shone on the marble streets of imperial Rome, and on the sad eyes of vigil sleepers in the living glow of inspiration—the watch fires of the angels which through centuries of devastation and change have still burned on unceasingly—speak to us as they did to Dante and Shakespeare and Milton, of the divine glory, the omnipotence, the everlasting beauty and love of God.

Working Girls.

Here is a chapter in commendation of working girls, a numerous class of the community, whose useful labors are frequently too little appreciated.

"Happy girls! who cannot love them? with cheeks like roses, bright eyes and elastic step, how cheerfully they go to work. Our reputation for it, such girls will make excellent wives. Blessed indeed will those men be who secure such prizes. Contrast those who do nothing but sigh all day, and live to follow the fashions, who never earn the bread they eat, or the shoes they wear; who are languid and lazy from one week's end to another. Who but a simpleton and popinjay would prefer one of the latter, if he were looking for a companion? Give us the working girls, they are worth their weight in gold. You never see them mincing along, or jump a dozen feet to steer clear of a spider or a fly; they have no affectation or silly airs about them. When they meet you, they speak without putting on a dozen silly airs, and trying to show off to better advantage, and you feel as though you were talking to a human being and not to a painted automaton or a fallen angel.

"If girls knew how sadly they missed while endeavoring to show off their delicate hands, unsoiled skins, and putting on a thousand airs, they would give worlds for the situation of working ladies, who are as far above them in intelligence, in honor, in everything, as the heavens are above the earth.

"Be wise then, you who have made fools of youselves through life. Turn over a new leaf, and begin, though late, to live and act as human beings, as companions to mortal man, and not playthings and dolls. In no other way can you be happy and subserve the designs of your existence."

Transmigration of Souls.

The New York correspondent of a western paper tells the following story for the benefit of some hard cases:

He says he once knew a man by the name of Reed, commonly known as "Old Reed." Reed was [illegible]ous in his way, and his religious belief was that after his death he would reappear in the form of an animal, and that he would be a horse. Now "Old Reed" was a hard man, and was not in the habit of treating his family as a religious man should. One day after his wife had suffered his abuse as long as humanity could endure, she concluded to give him a brief talking to—to touch upon his religious belief. So resolutely seating herself by his side, and looking him in the face, while a tear drop glistened in her eye—for she was serious and thoughtful as if he was correct in his faith—she commenced: "Reed, I wish to have a serious talk with you; I have something to say to you, and you *must hear it*. I have a duty to perform, and I shall do it, and if you are miserable hereafter, it will not be my fault. You believe, Reed, that when you die you will turn into some animal, and you think you will be a horse.

"Now if you keep on in your present course, and continue to neglect and abuse your family, squandering your money for drink and at the gambling table, when you die you will turn into some old *twelve shilling* horse, and some dirty clam pedler will get you, and you will be hard worked and half starved, and I shall see you every day before a ricketty old wagon filled with clams. Such will be your eternity? But now, Reed, it needn't be so; your eternity may be a high and a happy one. If you will reform and turn about and become a better man—be kind and affectionate to your family, and treat them as a christian should, why when you die you will turn into a five hundred dollar horse, and some West End buck will get hold of you, and give you a bushel of oats a day, rub you down with pea straw, and have you docked, and your tail set up!" He says "Old Reed" was straightway converted—was reformed—and is patiently waiting for death to introduce him into his coveted horse heaven—where are only "shell roads" and "two-forty" nags with "pricked" tails.

SLANDER.—Against slander there is no defence. Hell cannot boast of so foul a fiend, nor man deplore so foul a foe. It stabs with a smile. It is a pestilence walking in darkness, spreading contagion far and wide, which the most wary traveler cannot avoid. It is the heart-searching dagger of the assassin. It is the poisoned arrow whose wound is incurable. It is as fatal as the sting of the most deadly asp—murder is its employment, innocence its prey, and ruin its sport.

Governors of New York.

Edwin D. Morgan is the nineteenth person elected Governor since the organization of the State Government in 1777.

George Clinton, the first Governor, held the office twenty-one years, John Jay six years, Daniel D. Tompkins about ten years. He resigned the office Feb. 24, 1816, having been chosen Vice-President of the U. S.

De Witt Clinton held the office of Governor about eight years; he died in office Feb. 11th, 1828. William L. Marcy six years, William H. Seward four years.

Governors Morgan Lewis, Joseph C. Yates, Enos T. Throop, William C. Bouck, Silas Wright, John Young, Hamilton Fish, Washington Hunt, Horatio Seymour and Myron H. Clark, each served one term.

Gov. Lewis was the son of Francis Lewis, a signer of the Declaration of Independence; he was an officer in the Revolutionary army, and was present at the surrender of Gen. Burgoyne, in 1779. He was appointed Attorney-General of New York 1791, Chief Justice of the Supreme Court of the State, 1801. He died April 7, 1844, aged 89 years.

Gov. Tompkins was a member of the Constitutional Convention of 1801. Member of Assembly, Representative in Congress, Justice of the Supreme Court, President of the Constitutional Convention 1821. He was elected Vice-President 1816, and re-elected 1820. He died June 11th, 1825, aged 51 years.

George Clinton, John Jay, Daniel D. Tompkins, De Witt Clinton, William L. Marcy and William H. Seward, are the only persons who have been re-elected to the office of Governor. Daniel D. Tompkins was thirty-three years old when first chosen Governor, and was the youngest person ever elected to that office.

Martin Van Buren was elected Governor Nov. 1828, and resigned March 1829, having been appointed Secretary of State by President Andrew Jackson.

Governors Geo. Clinton, John Jay, and Morgan Lewis were patriots of the Revolutionary era. Geo. Clinton was twice elected Vice-President of the U. S. after his retirement from the gubernatorial chair. He died in office at Washington, April 20th, 1812, aged 73 years.

Gov. Jay was appointed Chief Justice of the Supreme Court of New York 1777, President of Continental Congress 1778, Chief Justice of the U. S. 1789, Minister to England 1794; He died May 17, 1829, aged 83 years.

I Still Live.

Lord Byron once remarked that Glory consists in being shot in battle, and having one's name reported wrong in the dead and wounded list.

We were never more strongly reminded of the truth of this assertion, and how little the great are remembered after their death than on hearing a few days since the following anecdote of an eastern farmer trying to repeat the last words of the "God-like Webster," I still live!

A gentlemon remarked, "Life is very uncertain."

"Ah yes," replied the farmer, "that's true, every word of it; and by the way, Captain, that makes me think of what one of your big Massachusetts men said when he died a spell ago."

"Who was it?" inquired the captain.

"Well I don't jest call his name to mind now, but at any rate he was a big politicianer, and lived near Boston somewhere. My newspaper said that when he died, the Boston folks put his image in their windows and had a funeral for a whole day."

"Perhaps it was Webster," suggested the Captain.

"Yes, that's the name! Webster, General Webster. Strange I couldn't think on it afore. But he got off a good thing just before he died. He riz up in bed, and says he 'I AINT DEAD YET.'"

What Makes the Negro Black.

The following explanation by Dr. Draper, of New York, possesses some interest, chiefly because [illegible] Human [illegible] made up of little cells, containing, am[illegible] elements, hæmatin, a reddish substance, wh[illegible] is largely made up of iron. One of the duties of the liver is the removing of the old blood cells and the forming of new ones, and this duty includes the carrying out from the system of all excess of hæmatin. A hot climate disturbs the normal action of the blood, and also of the liver. Imperfect oxygen attends great heat, and adds to the darkness of the arterial blood, while, by the want of energetic respiration which it involves, there is an over fatness and torpidity of the liver. The hæmatin, therefore, by this inaction of the great cleansing agent, is left in the system, and wandering about, takes refuge in the lower and spherical cells of the cuticle, which it thus bronzes from orange-tawny to negro-black, according to the heat of the climate, the inactivity of the liver, and the amount of hæmatin left as refuse in the system.

Cold checks the action of the liver equally with heat, and, therefore, the complexion of the Esquimaux approaches that of the Mongolian and negro. This is certainly a simple and an intelligible explanation. The tendency of coloring matter to deposit itself in the cuticle is well known. But let it not be thought that this darkening process is the result of a disordered, in the sense of an *unhealthful* action of the liver. In that case it would appear that Providence designed only the temperate zones to be inhabited, and the wealth of the tropics to be lost to mankind. In fact, the health and vigor of the tropical tribes show that *all the earth* is man's intended dwelling place.

Amusing Anecdote.

Daniel Webster had an anecdote of old Father Searl, the minister of his boyhood, which is too good to be lost. It was customary then to wear buck-skin breeches in cool weather. One Sunday morning in the autumn, Father Searl brought his breeches down from the garret, but the wasps had taken possession during the summer, and were having a nice time of it in them. By dint of effort he got out the intruders and dressed for meeting. But, while reading the scriptures to the congregation, he felt a dagger from one of the enraged small waisted fellows, and jumped around the pulpit slapping his thighs. But the more he slapped and danced, the more they stung. The people thought him crazy, but he explained the matter by saying: "Brethren, don't be alarmed; the word of the Lord is in my mouth, but the devil is in my breeches!" Webster always told it with great glee to the ministers.

Curiosities of Water.

Water exists around us to an extent and under conditions which escape the notice of cursory observers. When the dyer buys of the dry salter one hundred pounds each of alum, carbonate of soda, and soap, he obtains in exchange for his money no less than forty-five pounds of water in the first lot, sixty-four pounds in the second, and a variable quantity, sometimes amounting to seventy-three and a half pounds in the third. Even the transparent air we breathe contains, in ordinary weather, about five grains of water diffused through each cubic foot of its bulk, and thus rarified water no more wets the air than the solidified water wets the lime or opal in which it is absorbed. Of a plaster of Paris statue weighing five pounds, more than one good pound is solidified water. Even the precious opal is but a mass of flint and water, combined in the proportion of nine grains of the earthy ingredient to one of the fluid. Of an acre of clay land a foot deep, weighing about one thousand two hundred tons, at least four hundred tons are water; and even of the great mountain chains with which the globe is ribbed, many millions of tons are water solidified into earth.

The Philadelphia Inquirer.

ESTABLISHED 1829. PHILADELPHIA, TUESDAY, JANUARY 28, 1862. PRICE TWO CENTS.

War Against Treason!

The Purchase of Naval Vessels.

Report of the Senate Committee on Naval Affairs.

Western Virginia and Slavery.

DEVELOPMENTS OF TREASON.

The Potter Investigating Committee's Report.

DISLOYAL CLERKS AND ARMY OFFICERS.

Floyd's Treason Abetted by an Ordnance Officer.

CONGRESSIONAL AND LEGISLATIVE

THE WA[illegible] IN MISSOURI.

INTERESTING SOUTHERN NEWS

GEN. SIGEL'S RESIGNATION.

MEXICAN AFFAIRS.

MILITARY MATTERS.

LATEST FROM WASHINGTON.

Special Despatches to the Inquirer.

WASHINGTON, January 27, 1862.

Five Minutes with the New Secretary of War.

To-day was the first day that it was generally understood by the people that any one could get to see the new Secretary of War, without an introduction or having to wait in the lobby a week or two, as suited the convenience of some petulant doorkeeper, or, as a military man would say, the outer pickets. Mr. STANTON occupies the room formerly used by the previous administrations, at the head of the stairs in the second story.

The adjoining room is used by Mr. WATSON, Assistant Secretary. In this room Mr. STANTON receives the crowd; in the centre is a table at which his amanuensis, Mr. MOORE, sits, and in the corner is Mr. WATSON, at his desk. The clock strikes ten, the awaiting crowd rush in as the doors swing open, and being among them, we soon find ourselves in the presence of the Secretary. Now one stands in front of him, and with a smiling countenance he reaches out his hand and takes a hearty grip with a grey haired man. "Well, sir, what is your wish?"

"My name is ———; my son fought at Springfield, and was wounded in the arm, he was on FREMONT'S Staff, but is now without a commission; I want one for him that he may again try his other arm here on the Potomac, or in Missouri." "You shall have it, sir!" replied Mr. STANTON, and turning to his Secretary he ordered him to note the case, "return home, "he added," the papers will be sent you," and as the man attempted to thank him, he stepped to one side to two ladies who had just come in. "Madam, what can I do for you?" "Want a clerkship for my son; his father was killed at the battle of Belmont." Turning again he noted the case, took the address, told the lady to send him a sample of her boy's writing and he would care for him.

The other was connected with a Minnesota Regiment over the river, and had some complaint about the treatment she had received in camp from some of the officers. "Madame, you must go to the head-quarters of Gen. McCLELLAN." "I have been there, sir, and they would not read my papers or listen to my case." "Then give them to me and I'll see why."

A small bright-eyed boy, all alone, was trying to work his way through the crowd, and the Secretary turned to him and asked what he wanted. "I want my father got out, sir; he was taken at Bull Run, and has not come home with the rest." He gave his name and regiment, it was noted, and the Secretary, lifting him up, kissed him upon the forehead, and said:—"Your father should be proud of such a noble boy, and I'll see that he is released."

A man, with a half military dress, says he has been wronged by the examining Board, and has been deprived of the command of his regiment (a Philadelphia Cavalry Regiment). "Sorry, sir, if it is not all right; I cannot go back to investigate the acts of my predecessor." The Colonel insisted that his case was a plain one, if he could be heard. "Well," said the Secretary, "if you will get the officers to reconsider it, I will then listen to it."

An individual has some new invention for firearms; "Go to the ordnance department and get them to investigate it, and if they will recommend it, I will be glad to see it adopted." A *Colonel* with a green uniform on has some passes he wants to read; Are you an army officer?" "Yes, sir." "Then you cannot be heard until to-morrow; come and see me then!"

A large and well dressed man wanted a word in private." What about?" Some little matter about a contract he had for horses. "Cannot interfere, sir; go to General MEIGS: if there is anything wrong he will rectify it" Another succeeds in getting him off to the side of the room, and the conversation is inaudible until the Secretary replied:—"No, sir; on no account will I interfere in any contract, while I am here, for anything from a thimble up. There are men appointed to attend to that department, and I shall hold them to a strict accountability for every action."

Two soldiers wanted to be paid for the time they were in confinement at Richmond, having just been released, and presented a furlough they had received a week ago, and also an order for their pay for time and rations. "Why do you not take this to Maj. BECKWITH and have him to attend to it?" "We did, sir, and he says he has no order that will cover our case, and for want of 'forms' we are afraid we will be kept here until our time is up, and we want to go home and see the folks before going at it again." Turning to his Secretary he ordered him to write to Major BECKWITH, and order him to report forthwith in writing why these men were not paid up, instead of being kept waiting. It was done; he signed it himself and said; "Here take that to him, and bring an answer."

A Western man who said he hailed from the Reserve in Ohio, had about a dozen quires of paper written over two or three times, which he said was an "essay on cheese." The Secretary laughed! "You must go to the Commissary-General; he has charge of the feeding of the army." "I have been at first one and another all summer, and somehow or other, I do not get any farther ahead, and that is why I want you to investigate it;" and he commenced to unroll his papers. "Indeed, sir, I do not know how cheese would agree with the soldiers."

"That's just why I want you to read these papers and examine these certificates." "But I have not time, sir." All hands commenced laughing, but the Ohio man stuck it out bravely. "I assure you that there is not a soldier in the army who does not like crackers and cheese, and I can make it for three cents a pound. Now I tell you what you had better do, go to Senator WILSON and get him to put it in his bill, it will then pass the Senate and become an army regulation to give out cheese rations." "Well, could you not endorse it, and then it would be sure to be passed?" "No, I cannot endorse it, because I know nothing about it." "Oh, well I will leave these papers," and he made for the table, "I will never read them, if you do, until the war is over." With a look of despair, Ohio made for the door, inquiring of every one he met, if they knew where Senator WILSON lived?

Judge WILKINS, of Pittsburg, here came in, received a hearty shake of the hand, and a number of congratulations passed between them. The door-keeper of the little room announced the President, and off the Secretary went to see him. He soon returned, however. In came Major BECKWITH, with the note sent by the returned prisoners. "Why are those men kept waiting?" "Because I have no order for their special case."

"Mr. WILSON, issue an order that will cover all the prisoners that may be released in future, and allow them full pay for every day they are confined in Rebel prisons. Major, I have just learned there are over 150 now waiting for their pay; every man must be paid to-day, and speed them on to their homes." A tall man wants a commission in the regular army. "Have you been in any battle yet, sir?" "I was in the Mexican war." "That won't do; that is too far back." "I was at Great Bethel." "That is better. I will examine your record myself and inform you if you are appointed."

A stout healthy young man wanted a commission or clerkship! "Have you been in any battle?" "No, sir." "Then it will be of no use to apply, for I shall make all my appointments from the list of heroes; those who fight the country's battles must be cared for first."

Another wanted an appointment as quartermaster. "There are my recommendations, sir, and I would be glad if you can read them." "I cannot do it now, I have not time; but I will examine them." "Very well," replied the would be quartermaster, "just read them. If you have any better man, according to those papers, let him have the office; in that case I don't want it."

A gentleman stepped up who appeared to be an intimate friend of the Secretary, "Ah," said the Secretary, "I am glad to see you, I have not seen you since we met at Wheeling, a few years ago." He replied that he had been engaged upon the Northwest Boundary Question, and would like to have some conversation about it. "Ah," said the Secretary, "I will appoint a time to see you and have the whole matter talked over, for I wish to know all about it."

A man in citizen's clothes wanted an appointment in the army. "Well," said the Secretary of War, "What are your claims?" "I was an aid-de-camp of Colonel GEARY at the fight of Bolivar, and I am recommended for the appointment by the President." "All right," said Mr. STANTON, "I will attend to your case." Individual insisted upon having a promise, inasmuch as he "had got the endorsement of the President." "The President, sir, is a very excellent man and would be glad if he had an appointment for every man who applied, which, unfortunately for his good nature, is not the case." "Well, sir, I am from St. Louis, I am a Union man, and I must go home I suppose." Well, if I can do anything for you, I will write to you there."

A soldier, in the uniform of a sergeant, handed in a recommendation for a first lieutenancy in an artillery corps. "Well," said the Secretary, "have you ever smelt powder in battle?" "Not exactly, sir; but I have always been ready. I was in the Mexican war." "Can't help the Mexican war," said Mr. STANTON, "that is too far back. Have you been in any engagement in this war?" "No, sir. All I want is a chance to get in one. You can appoint me, and if you don't like it, I won't charge a cent extra pay, if I can only get the commission." The Secretary laughed, said his case would be considered, and he would be informed if the appointment was made.

Another gentleman, who also appeared to be a friend of the Secretary, came in. Said he, "I want to see you." "Come here to my room, and I will sit an hour when you can come, and we will talk over matters." They disappeared for a few moments, and, as they returned, Ex-Senator CRITTENDEN greeted him. He congratulated Mr. STANTON on the country receiving his services, for which Mr. STANTON thanked him, and said he hoped to be an instrument of aid to his country, but he should look to him and others for counsel in guiding his steps. "Any time, Mr. CRITTENDEN, day or night, any hour I shall be glad to see you. You are always welcome; come and see me."

A young man wants a clerkship. "Sorry, sir, there are no vacancies for the position you wish, and I have had over thirty applications already for it. I can do nothing for you."

An officer, who was on SICKLES' staff, wanted an order or some means that he could get his pay. He said that he had been in service for several months and could draw no pay. "It is inconvenient, no doubt, to be without money," replied Mr. STANTON, "and I will immediately order that your case be attended to."

And so it went on for five hours, in which he saw and heard all who came, pleasantly, and none went away but were pleased with their entertainment, and most of them had their hearts made glad. Over two hundred were listened to in this short time.

Lake Defences.

The Committee on Lake Defences have completed their labors, and now only await some arrangements of details by General TOTTEN, Chief of the United States Engineer Corps, when the work will be pushed rapidly forward to completion.

More Rebel Entrenchments.

The arrival of the *Stepping Stones* from the flotilla, to-day, brings news of large numbers of Rebels being at work near the mouth of the Occoquan, throwing up entrenchments, as though they expected they would have to make a stand there to defend their right wing.

Naval Changes.

The U. S. brig *Perry* will sail at once for Aspinwall to take the place of the brig *Bainbridge*, now there, which is ordered to report at Key West for duty in the Gulf Squadron now blockading the Rebel ports.

New Banking House.

JAY COOKE & Co., of Philadelphia, have taken a building here, at the corner of F street and Pennsylvania avenue, and will open a banking house next Thursday.

Probable Appointment.

Colonel D. B. BIRNEY, of Philadelphia, will probably be appointed a Brigadier-General to-morrow.

HON. EDWIN M. STANTON.

For many of the facts contained within the following sketch, we are indebted to the Illinois *State Journal*:—

The Hon. EDWIN M. STANTON, the recently appointed Secretary of War, is a native of the City of Steubenville, in the State of Ohio. His father was an eminent physician, and born in the State of North Carolina, from which State he emigrated in early life to the fertile Territory of Ohio, then just redeemed from the savage. Mr. STANTON received a good academical education in his native city, and at early age began the study of law in the office of the Hon. BENJAMIN TAPPAN, a distinguished jurist and politician of Ohio, who once filled the office of United States Senator. When young STANTON was admitted to the bar, he was taken as the partner of his legal mentor, who soon after retired from the active duties of his profession and left his student in full practice among the front rank of his associates. It is worthy of remark that Mr. STANTON won his spurs among competitors distinguished for talent and experience. He rose rapidly to the very zenith of his profession. Indeed he never started at the foot of it. By nature he is a man of the front rank. Yea, more more than this—nature moulded him for subjugating every obstacle in the way of attaining what is possible. His preceptor, an extraordinary man, watched his rising star with pride, and rejoiced over his growing fame.

At an early age in his profession he was appointed reporter for the State of Ohio, four of whose reports bear his name. During the session of the Supreme Court he was accustomed to attend at Columbus on duties of his office and profession. This fact has given rise to the report that he once resided there, which he never did. He continued to practice in his native and the adjoining counties, until about the year 1847, when he removed to Pittsburg, Pennsylvania, and formed a partnership with the Hon. CHARLES SHALER and THEO. UMBSTARTTER. The firm was regarded as the first in the city, and equal to any in the State. Mr. STANTON now displayed his usual power, and at once took position among the first men of the bar, then noted for its high character. During his residence in Pittsburg, he appeared for the city in the great case of the Wheeling Bridge Company, reported in twenty-second Howard. It may be proper to add that he was one of the counsel, associated with President LINCOLN, in the Manny & McCormick Reaper case, before the Supreme Court. In the winter of 1857–'8, he was selected by President BUCHANAN to go to California to defend the American grantees against claimants, under Mexican grants. In the spring of 1858 he dissolved his connection with the firm in Pittsburg and removed to Washington, and engaged in the practice of his profession. Our space will not permit us to enter into a sketch of his professional career.

His labors in California were herculean. The results of these labors were shown at the next term of the Supreme Court of the United States, in the exposure of most stupendous frauds and in the saving of many millions of dollars to the country. We believe that the United States Government did not lose, at that term, a single California case before that tribunal. The integrity of Mr. STANTON was also manifested in that business, for the most gigantic sums were at his command, had he been disposed to swerve a hair's breadth from the line of duty.

The history of the man selected for the great labor that we have specified, is bound up in a devotion to his profession. He was never a politician, though possessing definite views of the policy and interests of his country. His political opinions are those of the old JACKSON Democratic school. All the teachings and influence of his boyhood are of that type. How he has maintained his integrity the sequel will show.

When the unfortunate, if not wicked, old man at the head of the Republic, found himself and the country deserted by a band of abandoned traitors, and none but that glorious ray of patriotic light—the gorgeous and faithful HOLT—to uphold the falling pillars of the Government, he called Mr. STANTON to the post of Attorney-General. He then used all his energy and zeal to induce the imbecile President to reinforce and supply the heroic ANDERSON in Fort Sumter. Had his counsels prevailed, the revolution would have been quelled in its infancy. It will be remembered that, with Mr. HOLT, he took that stand when Democrats and Republicans stood paralyzed before the astounding progress of treason. When politicians stood amazed, Mr. STANTON spoke bold, dignified, determined words for his country.

It will be seen that he at once took the position of General CASS and General SCOTT for resistance to the traitorous combination. His early teachings, his subsequent life and conduct, places him on the same platform, that of the Hero of the Hermitage.

The Secretary has won his envied place from his devotion to his profession, his power and integrity. In person, he is about five feet nine inches, of full habits; his head is large and full, powerful intellectual developments, covered with coarse, black, curly hair; neck, short and thick, and carries a flood of blood to his eternally active brain; his muscle is pure, firm and healthful. His mind never ceases to act and his body is never fatigued with executing. The former never rests and the latter never bends beneath its work. The writer, when a boy, used to study in a room under his office, and knows that he was accustomed to work all day and until the small hours of the night began their increase. His industry would astonish ordinary men, and the amount of work which he did could never have been endured by other than a man of iron. When immersed in business and surrounded by a multitude of details he seemed at home—confusion under his energy soon become system. He seemed always posted in his business, he never took up a wrong paper, turned to a wrong page or read a wrong extract. His memory never deserted him, and his judgment never erred.

To his present gigantic labor he brings the experience of half a century, for his age is about fifty years, a mind and body in the full vigor of its power, a will which bends time, men and circumstances to overcome whatever obstacle may lie in the way of achieving his country's glory and peace. Never was there a more stupendous labor, and seldom, if ever, was so fine powers of mind and body called to do the work. Mr. STANTON enters the field posted in all the details and ignorant of nothing, but to yield. He has the prestige of success, and stamped by the hand of nature to conquer. In his hands speculating contractors, the cormorants that are eating the life blood of the nation, will be consigned to the doom they deserve. Let the pulse of the nation beat freely once more, for she has a man faithful and effective at the helm.

We cannot better conclude our sketch of Mr. STANTON than by quoting the language of Hon. JOSEPH HOLT, in a letter to Lieutenant Governor STANTON, of Ohio. Mr. HOLT says:—

The selection of Hon. EDWIN M. STANTON as Secretary of War has occasioned me much unalloyed gratification. It is an immense stride in the direction of the suppression of the Rebellion.

So far as I can gather the popular sentiment, there is everywhere rejoicing over the appointment; but that rejoicing would be far greater, did the people know, as I do, the courage, the loyalty, and the genius of the new Secretary, as displayed in the intensely tragic struggles that marked the closing days of the last Administration. He is a great man intellectually and morally—a patriot of the true Roman stamp, who will grapple with treason as the lion grapples with his prey. We may rest well assured that all that man can do will, in his present position, be done to deliver our poor bleeding country from the bayonets of traitors now lifted against its bosom.

Interesting Southern News.

BALTIMORE, Jan. 27.—The Richmond *Dispatch*, of Friday, shows that the Rebels are much perplexed at the defeat in Kentucky. The *Dispatch* says:—"We regret to state that the report of the Federal victory in Kentucky, conveyed to us from Northern sources, is more than confirmed by intelligence received at the War Department.

"It appears that our defeat was more decisive than even the Northern accounts had led us to believe. The editor says that this disaster in Eastern Kentucky, and the apprehension it has excited for the safety of our connection with the Southwest through Virginia and Tennessee and the East Tennessee and Virginia Railroad, and the possible interruption of our intercourse with the South Virginia, Wilmington and Weldon Railroad by the Burnside Expedition, directs attention to the vital importance of completing the connection between the Richmond, Danville and North Carolina Railroads.

The *Dispatch*, of the 25th inst., says:—We have some further particulars this morning relative to our disaster in Eastern Kentucky. They remove all doubt of the death of General ZOLLICOFFER. The battle was brought on by our forces, who attacked the enemy under the apprehension that his force was greatly less than it really was. Notwithstanding the mistake, our men evidently fought bravely; for besides losing their second in command, their Major-General, four Colonels, two Majors and three Surgeons were wounded.

The retreat, which it appears was well defended, was commanded by Colonel CARROLL. It will be seen that the loss on our side is not so large as the first account on our side represented it to be. The Nothern statement and that last received come more nearly agreeing.

The error made by our commanders is a strange one. To attack a fortified army under the impression that it numbered only 1500, when it was 14,000 strong, is a remarkable error. To underrate the enemy in this manner is singular enough, and to fight under such a misapprehension could not but lead to disaster. The scouts must have performed their duty indifferently.

AUGUSTA, Ga., Jan. 23.—A private letter received from Charleston, this morning, says five stone vessels were sunk in the channel, yesterday.

The Savannah *Republican* of this morning says the statement that the Federal vessels had gone up Broad river is incorrect.

The Richmond *Dispatch* contains a despatch from Norfolk, saying that the Baltimore *South*, a copy of which had been received there, contained a statement that a report had reached Baltimore, of the loss of five of the Burnside fleet in Pamlico Sound, and that a large steamer (probably the *Louisiana*) had been burned. Thus it would seem that this report had no other foundation than this Secession sheet—the Baltimore *South*.

FURTHER FROM WASHINGTON.

Staff Appointments of Gen. McClellan.

The Senate, in Executive session to-day, spent two hours discussing the point whether it was necessary to confirm the Staff appointments of Gen. McCLELLAN. The ground taken by some was, that they were merely temporary appointments, and ended with his death or removal; and it was finally decided that they did not need confirmation.

Mr. Tucker's Nomination.

Mr. TUCKER'S nomination as Assistant Secretary of War will have the unanimous report of the Military Committee, and there is no doubt of his confirmation.

General Butler.

General BENJ. BUTLER is still here.

The Commission to Visit our Prisoners.

Bishop AMES, of the Methodist Episcopal Church, and Hon. HAMILTON FISH, of New York, have been appointed by Secretary STANTON to visit our prisoners in the Rebel jails, under such restrictions as the Rebels may stipulate. They are to report at length of each case.

Erroneous Report.

There is no truth in the report that Colonel BIDDLE BOBERTS, of the Pennsylvania Reserves, has been appointed Provost Marshal of Washington, nor is he expected to be. General PORTER continues to act in that position, and ROBERTS was merely detailed as an attorney for General PORTER, it being thought that he could best be spared out of any of the Divisions without detriment to the service.

Soldiers' Letters.

Mr. VAN WYCK will introduce a bill in the House, giving the Chaplain of each regiment power to frank soldiers' letters home to their friends and relatives, and unless the Senate recedes, and consents to pass the bill entirely abolishing the present franking law, he can no doubt carry it through both houses, as few will dare to vote against it if squarely put, knowing that most of the volunteers may in turn have a chance to vote at no distant day.

Gen. Cameron.

Gen. Cameron was serenaded to-night by the band of Col. WILLIAMS' regiment. He leaves with his family to-morrow for "Lochiel."

Gen. Banks.

Gen. BANKS is here to-night, and will go before the Investigating Committee to-morrow.

Treasury Notes.

The bill for issuing Treasury demand notes will come up in the House to-morrow. Mr. SPALDING will present estimates for our future expenses far larger than those of Secretary CHASE, and endeavor to show that he is right.

Commodore Paulding Endorsed.

The Navy Department has sent a letter to Commodore H. PAULDING, endorsing his action in enlisting into the naval service some deserters, who left some Rebel batteries off South Carolina, and came out in a small boat to his vessel.

Army Telegraph Builders.

General PARK SPRING'S Army Telegraph Builders are to have a grand review and inspection at the Telegraph Camp to-morrow, and it is to end with a grand exercise—climbing poles at double quick—and they will also show their ingenuity in digging holes, &c.

"On to Richmond."

Mr. GURLEY, of Ohio, is preparing a speech for delivery to-morrow, on the "On to Richmond" order.

Official Order.

The following order has been issued by the Secretary of State:—

DEPARTMENT OF STATE, WASHINGTON, Jan. 25, 1862.—The Secretary of State will hereafter receive Members of Congress, on business, on Saturdays, commencing with Saturday, the first of next month.

WILLIAM H. SEWARD.

Railroad Completed.

The Railroad from Washington to Alexandria is now completed, and was to-day inspected by Colonel THOMAS A. SCOTT and Captain MORLEY. Cars will be run over it to-morrow.

Western Virginia and Slavery.

WHEELING, Jan. 27.—In the Convention to-day, Mr. BATTELLE, of Ohio county, offered the following propositions in relation to slavery in the new State:—"No slaves shall be brought into the State for permanent residence after the adoption of this constitution. All children born of slave parents in this State on and after the 4th of July, 1865, shall be free, and the Legislature may provide general laws for the apprenticeship of such children during their minority and for their subsequent colonization."

The above propositions were referred to the Committee on General Provisions, which Committee will probably report some time this week. It is not expected that the Committee will report any provision of the above character, the majority being averse to the consideration of the Slavery question; but whenever that Committee make their report, a proposition embodying the sentiments of the Free State men will be brought forward, and will be, from present indications, fiercely contested.

THE WAR IN MISSOURI.

ROLLA, Mo., Jan. 26.—A prominent citizen of Southwest Missouri has just arrived from Mount Vernon, Lawrence county. He says General RAINS, with about four hundred Rebel troops, stayed all night at Mount Vernon, on Tuesday night, the 14th instant, on his way to Granby, where his soldiers said they were going to work at the lead mines. Threats were made to arrest all men who had been connected with Home Guard Companies and put them at work in the mines, in consequence of which a large number of Union men were leaving the country. On the same night that RAINS stayed at Mount Vernon report said that 170 or 200 Rebels were encamped on the head of Spring river, *en route* for Caseyville.

In regard to the number of troops in Northern Arkansas, the same informant says that he has it from good authority that there are only 500 or 600 at Cross Hollows and Cane Hill, in Benton county; but a body of from 3000 to 5000 were at Tillsworth Bend, about fifty miles below Van Buren, on the Arkansas.

Several Secessionists told him that PRICE'S forces at Springfield did not exceed 10,000. This gentleman met the scouts of the United States army fifty miles beyond Lebanon, and other troops at different points this side.

The Canadian Mails.

PORTLAND, Me., January 27.—The Canadian mail train got off the track three times last night. The train has been off the track at Yarmouth, ten miles from this city, since 12 o'clock last night. The engines from here have reached Yarmouth, where the down engine is capsized. The mail train is expected here by 12 o'clock.

The steamship *Hibernia* will sail on the arrival of the mails for Londonderry and Liverpool. She has been detained since Saturday.

Railroad Accident.

BOSTON, Jan. 27.—Rev. H. G. O. DURFES, Missionary to Turkey, was tee person killed on Saturday, on the Troy and Rutland Railroad. He was on a visit to this country, and has two sons in the Union army.

Movements of Steamers.

HALIFAX, Jan. 27.—The steamer *Europa* sailed for Boston at five o'clock last evening. The steamer *City of New York* sailed on Saturday evening for New York.

Fire at the Fulton Bank, New York.

NEW YORK, Jan. 27.—The entire specie of the Fulton Bank was removed safely.

CONGRESSIONAL PROCEEDINGS.

WASHINGTON, Jan. 27, 1862.

Senate.

Several petitions in favor of emancipation; also, for the appointment of Homœopathic Surgeons in the army, were presented.

Mr. SHERMAN (Ohio) presented a petition of the Mayor and authorities of Springfield, Ohio, relative to the National Armory.

Mr. LANE (Ind.) presented the petition of the Board of Trade, of Annapolis, in relation to the National Armory.

Mr. KING presented a petition against all further traffic in public lands.

Mr. HARRIS (N. Y.) presented the memorial of the Chamber of Commerce and others, in favor of the continuation of the coast survey.

Also, a resolution from one branch of the Assembly of New York, relative to frauds, &c.

Mr. HALE (N. H.), from the Naval Committee, made a report in relation to the answer of the Secretary of the Navy to the resolution in regard to the Morgan contracts.

Mr. WADE (Ohio) offered a joint resolution in order to develope, concentrate and bring into effect the mechanical resources of the United States for the suppression of the rebellion and future defence of the country. The resolution authorizes the Superintendent of the Census to perform such duties under direction of the Secretary of War, and collect such war statistics as in the judgment of the Secretary of War may be right and proper.

Mr. GRIMES (Ia.) opposed putting the Superintendent of the Census under the direction of the Secretary of War.

On motion of Mr. FESSENDEN, the latter part of the resolution was modified so as to read, "The Superintendent of the Census is authorized to furnish the Secretary of the War with such war statistics, from time to time, as the Secretary may deem necessary for the use of the Department.

The resolution as amended was passed.

Mr. HALE (N. H.) offered a resolution that the Secretary of the Navy be requested to inform the Senate what was the cost of the ship-of-the-line *Pennsylvania*, how many cruises she has made, and when the ship *Alabama* was built, at what cost, whether she was fit for a sailing vessel, or can be altered to a steamer, &c. Laid over.

Mr. WILSON (Mass.) introduced a bill for the more effectual suppression of the slave trade. Referred.

Mr. KING (N. Y.) presented a resolution from the Legislature of New York, instructing the Senators from that State to vote for the abolition of the franking privilege. Referred.

Mr. WADE (Ohio) called up the resolution making an addition to the joint rules of both Houses, to wit:—That during the present rebellion, when any member of the House or Senate shall rise in his seat and state that the Executive Department of the Government desires immediate action on any matter pertaining to the suppression of the present rebellion, the House or Senate, as the case may be, shall go into secret session, and proceed to the consideration of the measure proposed, and the debate thereon be limited to five minutes to each speaker, and the vote be taken before the adjournment. Any breach of secrecy (unless the injunction be removed) shall be punishable by expulsion, if by a member, and if by any officer of the House, be punishable as the body in which it occurs shall impose.

Mr. WADE (Ohio) modified the resolution, so as to strike out the limitation of debate to five minutes, though he thought he never learned anything after a person had spoken five minutes.

Mr. SUMNER (Mass.) offered an amendment that the question of secret session shall be submitted to the body in which it is proposed, and if the majority decide in favor, it shall go immediately into secret session without debate.

Mr. FESSENDEN (Me.) said he had no objection to the resolution, and no objection to the amendment of the Senator from Massachusetts, if it referred only to the Senate.

Mr. FOSTER (Conn.) did not believe in what the facetious called a "secret session." He thought that what transpired in secret sessions was reported sooner than what took place in open session. He did not consider secret sessions an element of power. He did not object to the resolution, however.

Mr. TRUMBULL (Illinois) was glad the resolution had been offered. He said for some reason the whole country felt more hopeful in the thought that the army was to be used to put down the Rebellion. There seemed to be more activity and preparation for a movement. He thought the credit for this was due to the War Committee. He did not believe in secret sessions, as the people ought to know all that that is being done; but if the Senate thought it necessary to do certain business in secret session, he would not object. But it was a great power to put in the hands of any single member to compel either body to go into secret session. And as for secrecy being maintained, there is a rule now in existence for the expulsion of any member who may divulge the proceedings of the executive session of the Senate. Yet what do we see now? Nearly everything published the next day, in an exaggerated form. He would rather have a regular report than these garbled accounts.

Mr. CHANDLER (Mich.) urged the necessity for the measure, but was in favor of leaving the form of punishment for divulging the proceedings to the discretion of either body. If there was a traitor in this body who would divulge the secrets of his office, he would hang him.

Mr. HALE (N. H.) wanted to say a single word about the disgrace of having garbled reports of everything done in secret session. He gave notice that in future, if he saw the rule relative to secrecy broken, he would bring the subject to the notice of the Senate, and endeavor to have the offender punished.

Mr. WADE said there were measures which ought to be considered in secret session, and if this rule was established he would move a secret session immediately. If we consider business in open session, the Rebels know all about it in an hour. Senators do not seem to realize that we are in a state of war. Indeed, our war has been so much like peace, that it is no wonder. But the Committee of which he was a member (the Special Committee on the Conduct of the War) had determined that something should be done. We must act with the Executive Department or else force the Executive to take into his own hands the powers which belong to Congress. The resolution had been modified so that when any member makes a motion to go into secret session the doors shall be shut and the member state his reasons and the majority determine whether to continue the secret session.

On motion of Mr. SHERMAN (Ohio) the subject was postponed till to-morrow, and the case of Senator BRIGHT taken up.

Mr. LATHAM (Cal.) proceeded to speak at length in favor of Mr. BRIGHT. He contended that public opinion on the 1st of March, 1861, was different from what it is now. The Senator from Indiana was not to be judged by the opinion now for what he did when opinion was very different. If the letter written by the Senator from Indiana had been read in the Senate on the 2d of March, it would have fallen harmlessly on the ears of Senators.

He referred to and read from the speech of the Senator from Texas (Mr. WIGFALL), delivered on the 2d of March, which was full of treason, yet no notice was taken of it. He also referred to the speech of Mr. TOOMBS, on the 2d of January, declaring that the South had armed themselves; yet these men were allowed to go home. If, from these speeches, the Senator from Indiana knew that war was inevitable, the other Senators must have known it, and they were equally guilty in not having these traitors arrested. But none of these speeches were believed by the people of the country, and none of the Senators who made them were expelled or their names stricken from the roll till July.

He claimed that on the 1st of March there was no war and no one dreamed that war would ensue. Congress did not believe there would be any war, for it adjourned on the 4th of March without even the introduction of any measure calculated for a state of war. He quoted the inaugural of the President and the speeches of MASON, DOUGLAS and FESSENDEN, all made after Mr. BRIGHT'S letter was written, and all asserting that there was to be no war. He also quoted the instructions of the Secretary of State as late as the 10th of April, stating that there was to be no war.

The mails were not stopped till May. He contended that all these facts showed conclusively that no one believed there would be war, and there could have been no disloyal intent in the mind of the Senator from Indiana when he wrote this letter, as early as the 1st of March. Many of the newspapers now howling for the blood of the Senator from Indiana, were then willing to let the Southern States go in peace rather than have war. He read an extract from the New York *Tribune*, of the 8th of November, 1860. The Senator from Kentucky seems to find fault at the Senator from Indiana because he voted for BRECKINRIDGE. He (Mr. LATHAM) also voted for BRECKINRIDGE.

Mr. DAVIS said he complained because the electoral ticket was run in Indiana when the only object was to insure the defeat of DOUGLAS and elect LINCOLN. He asked if the Senator from California subscribed to the doctrine of State Rights as taught by Virginia politicians?

Mr. LATHAM replied that he was not to be diverted by the discussion of party politics. His views on State Rights were well known, but he had always opposed the doctrine of Secession from the first.

Mr. DAVIS was glad to hear it. He thought that the doctrine of State Rights, as entertained by Virginia politicians, had created all the political mischief and debauched the public mind.

Mr. LATHAM continued—He was opposed to the proscription of any man for his political opinions. The bells of time are ringing changes fast, and the old landmarks of the Constitution are fading away.

(Continued on the Eighth Page.)

Daily Democrat

PRINTED AND PUBLISHED BY
HARNEY, HUGHES & CO.

Office--79 Third Street, east side, between Market and Jefferson.

SATURDAY MORNING.........FEBRUARY 1, 1862.

Railroad Matters.

DEPARTURE OF TRAINS.

LOUISVILLE, NEW ALBANY AND CHICAGO RAILROAD.

On and after Tuesday, Dec. 3, passenger trains will leave New Albany as follows:

LEAVE NEW ALBANY.

Chicago and St. Louis Express (daily except Sundays)........ 8:40 A. M.
St. Louis Night Express (daily)........ 9.30 P. M.

ARRIVE AT NEW ALBANY.

St. Louis Express........ 5:55 A. M.
Reaching Louisville........ 8:00 A. M.
St. Louis and Chicago Mail........ 7:20 P. M.
Reaching Louisville........ 8:15 P. M.

JEFFERSONVILLE RAILROAD.

FROM JEFFERSONVILLE.

Cincinnati and Eastern Express........ 3:00 P. M.
Connection Train (at Seymour with O. and M. Railroad) East and West........ 9:00 P. M.

LOUISVILLE AND LEXINGTON R. R.

Passenger Train No. 1........ 5:50 A. M.
Passenger Train No. 2........ 2:00 P. M.
Accommodation Train........ 4:10 P. M.

LOUISVILLE AND NASHVILLE R. R.

Passenger Train for Elizabethtown and Camp Nevin leaves daily at........ 7:50 A. M.
Bardstown (Sunday's excepted)........ 3:00 P. M.

Closing and Arrival of the Mails at the Louisville Postoffice.

Eastern, Western, and Northern closes at 12:00 M., and arrives at 12:00 M.

Southern Kentucky, via L. & N. R. R. (small offices close at 9:00 P. M. the previous evening), closes at 6:30 A. M., and arrives at 5:00 P. M.

Mailboat to Cincinnati, Ohio, closes at 9:00 A. M., and arrives at 6:00 A. M.

L. & F. R. R. closes at 12:00 at night and 1:00 P. M., and arrives at 11:06 A. M., and 6:30 P. M.

Shelbyville closes at 12:00 at night, and arrives at 6:00 A. M.

Lebanon R. R. closes at 12:00 at night, and arrives at 6:00 P. M.

Bardstown R. R. closes at 3:00 P. M., and arrives at 9:30 P. M.

Shawneetown Stage (tri-weekly) closes at 12:00 at night, and arrives at 6:00 P. M.

Henderson and River (tri-weekly) leaves Monday, Wednesday, and Friday, at 1:00 P. M., and arrives at 6:00 A. M.

Taylorsville Stage closes at 8:00 A. M., and arrives at 4:30 P. M.

☞ On routes where the principal mails close at 12:00 at night, the way-mails close at 9:00 P. M.

LOCAL NEWS.

Don't Send us 10-Cent Stamps.

We can not use any stamps of a greater denomination than three cents, and we must therefore caution our friends against sending them. It will only subject us to the necessity of returning them.

☞ A letter from Munfordville, Jan. 30th, says: "The remains of Gen. Zollicoffer and Lieut. Peyton arrived at this place at 12 o'clock to-day. They were escorted to division headquarters by Company E, Forty-ninth Ohio, Captain Bartlette. Gens. McCook, Johnston and staffs accompanied the remains, which were escorted with due honors, and transferred to metallic coffins, sent here for that purpose by Gen. Buell, and were embalmed by Division Surgeon of Gen. McCook's staff and Dr. Goldsmith, of Gen. Wood's brigade. The remains are accompanied by Gen. Zollicoffer's Brigade Surgeon, who is a prisoner. They will start early to-morrow morning for Bell's Tavern, with a flag of truce, under the command of Gen. Johnson and staff. Gen. Zollicoffer's surgeon was very much affected by the kind treatment he received from Gens. McCook and Johnson, and especially with the attention paid to the remains of Gen. Zollicoffer. He said he didn't expect it. He also said peace would be declared in sixty days." He, no doubt, feels it ought to be.

POLICE PROCEEDINGS.—*Friday, Jan.* 31. L. Y. Baily was sworn and admitted to this bar.

Peace warrant by John Fitzpatrick vs. Thos. Cooly; $100 for three months; gone up.

Elizabeth McKee was presented; no one appearing against her, she was discharged.

Jas. McKay was also presented and discharged.

Joseph Bradly, drunk and abusing his family; $200 for six months; gave bail.

Jas. H. Montgomery, killing G. D. Gibbs; $2000 to answer manslaughter.

In our report yesterday we stated that Jack Sandford was sent up in default of $200 bail. This is not so; he gave bail.

☞ The city court was, yesterday, rendered very interesting by the eloquent and powerful arguments of Nat Wolfe, Jas. Speed, and Wm. G. Reasor. Wolfe and Speed, in their arguments, convinced a great many that were present that the killing of John Gibbs by J. H. Montgomery was done in a sudden heat of passion, which, according to law, is manslaughter. Mr. Reasor, however, in turn, showed, by his argument, which was very powerful and ingenious, as also by the law book, Greenleaf on Evidence, that the deed was murder; and if it was not murder, the time was not far distant when there would be no such thing as murder.

GROCERY ESTABLISHMENT.—We take pleasure in directing the attention of city and country dealers to the advertisement of Messrs. Glazebrook, Brother & Co. in our columns this morning. Their establishment is on Main street, between Seventh and Eighth. Their stock is large, and embraces everything in their line. Sutlers and army contractors will find a varied assortment of such things as they daily need. The members of the firm are gentlemen of well known integrity and business character. Give them a call and learn prices.

FINE TOBACCO.—At the Picket warehouse yesterday, a hhd. of tobacco, grown by Robert Calvin, of Taylor county, Ky., was sold at the extraordinary price of $18 per hundred. Mr. W. S. Anderson, one of our most enterprising manufacturers, was the purchaser.

TOBACCO.—Five hogsheads of old tobacco were sold Thursday at the Pickett Warehouse at $15, $15 50, $15, $14 25, and $16. They were grown by Mr. John Highbaugh, of Larue county, Ky., and purchased by Mr. Wm. J. Anderson, one of our largest manufacturers.

☞ Third street is getting no better fast. The fortunate survivors, who have luckily passed through Third, from Market to Jefferson, may well console themselves that they were not born to be drowned or strangled in the mire.

FANCY.—The Cincinnati Gazette of yesterday publishes a letter dated Louisville, January 28th, which has in it more exaggerations and misrepresentations than it contains sentences.

NO BOTTOM.—The sounding along Third street yesterday would have been most satisfactory to boatmen. It was not "water twain," or "water less twain." On the contrary, it was no bottom.

LOST—A pocket book containing a small amount of money. The finder will oblige by leaving it at Dr. Baum's, on Fifth street, between Main and Market streets.

☞ Advertisers will please hand in their favors as early as convenient to-day for our Sunday edition.

COLONEL WOODRUFF.—We have just seen a letter to Mrs. Woodruff from Captain J. W. Speagur, at Huron, Ohio. He writes that he was released from prison at Columbus, S. C., on the 5th of January, and when he left Col. Woodruff was in good health, and in as good spirits as he could be under the circumstances. Capt. S. says that the treatment the prisoners receive at Columbia is much better than it was at Charleston. He is using all his exertions to have Col. W., and the rest of those he "messed" with, exchanged at the earliest possible moment, and has strong hope that an exchange will soon be effected. Capt. S. intends to take the field again in a few days.

☞ The Volunteers' Family Relief Committee are hereby requested to meet at Dr. Bell's office on Monday, the 3d inst., at 7½ o'clock. A full attendance is desired, as business of importance will be brought before the meeting.

THEO. T. TAYLOR, Sec'y.

LOUISVILLE TYPOGRAPHICAL UNION.—A regular meeting of the Typographical Union will be held on Saturday evening, Feb. 1st, at 6½ o'clock, at Temperance Hall.

A R. SMUTZ, Sec

☞ Col. T. T. Crittenden, commander of the 6th Indiana, was well enough to leave home for his command day before yesterday. The regiment is at Munfordsville, Ky.

CELIBACY OF THE CATHOLIC CLERGY IN FRANCE.—A very interesting case, involving the celibacy of the Roman Catholic priesthood, is about to be tried before a provincial tribunal in France. A little time ago, M. Bron de Mausiare, formerly incumbent of the commune of Cendriex, in Perigord, appeared before the Mayor, and requested him to celebrate his marriage. The Mayor refused point blank, on the ground that being in holy orders is a disability for the contraction of matrimony. M. Bron, in reply, requested the Mayor to inform him what law he relied on to justify his refusal, and as the perplexed functionary hunted in vain through the Code Napoleon, informed him that as priests enjoyed the same privileges as other French citizens, there was no reason for supposing that they were to be debarred from marrying, if they thought proper. The Mayor, however, still refused to perform the marriage ceremony. M. Bron is bringing an action against him to compel him to do so. His case is in the hands of Jules Favre.

A REBEL EXPRESS DETECTED.—It has been discovered that the Secessionists have been running an express from Olney, Ill., to Grayville, thence down the Wabash, across the Ohio, and through Kentucky to the rebel lines. The United States Marshal of the Southern District of Illinois arrested, on Tuesday, a number of those who had been engaged in this contraband express business. Their names and occupations are as follows: R. W. Buckels, merchant; John Riggles, grocery keeper; Thomas O'Leary, livery stable keeper; Geo. Mathews, stage driver; W. M. Smith, a loafer. These were of Grayville, Ill, and were trying to send South machinery for the manufacture of paper. There was also a lady arrested, who has been a very active traveler for some months on treasonable business. The prisoners—in charge of Marshal A. L. Phillips and Sergeant Stanley, of the Seventh Regiment of Illinois cavalry—are on the way to Fort Warren.

☞ The Boston Herald records the sad end of a country girl, who had come to Boston to work. Her parents were well off. She fell into bad ways, and was taken sick with the typhoid fever, and, after lingering for a week, died. During her illness she positively refused to have any one write to her parents, or to speak the name of them or of her sisters in her presence. At times, when she probably thought of home, she would cry and sob in great agony; but death put an end to her crime and suffering. The day following her death she was buried; and the mourners who followed this once beautiful girl of twenty summers to her last resting place were four abandoned women. A sad end and a sad warning to our young girls who are continually flirting the streets with those gay deceivers whose only aim is their ruin.

NEW DESIGNS FOR POSTAGE STAMPS.—In advertising new contracts for envelopes and stamps, we are happy to see the Postoffice Department requires new designs for the latter. The change effected last spring was not only offensive to taste—the heads of the Republican fathers being simple caricatures—but so wretched and inartistic was the execution of the engraving, and so faint the printing, as to place imitation within reach of the coarsest hands.

GENERAL MCCLELLAN INSTRUCTING THE COLONELS.—A letter from George Wilkes to his paper of last week says of General McClellan: "His last movement in the scholarship of his field cadets has been to practice the Colonels of regiments in the manœuvering of brigades; and the fact that this has been done recently, despite of the unfavorable weather, is strong evidence that important exigencies are supposed to be at hand."

☞ A London Rag Brigade is about to be established in London, on the model of the shoe black brigade. Homeless and neglected boys are to be provided with trucks and weights and scales, and are to go from door to door asking for rags, and giving a printed memorandum with the weight and price filled in.

LOTTERIES IN DELAWARE.—The bill revoking the lottery grant to R. France, Esq., of Baltimore, passed the House of Representatives of Delaware last week, by a vote of 14 to 7, and it is said it will also pass the Senate.

☞ Ten new craters have appeared on Mount Vesuvius during the present eruption. English photographers are at work taking photographs of the mountain in its excited state.

☞ Spain is about to pay France a certain indemnity which has been owing since 1823. The original debt amounted to some twenty millions of dollars but is now reduced to five millions.

☞ Free trade will be established this year throughout the whole extent of the Danish territory, and the trade-guilds will exist hereafter only as free societies.

Court of Appeals.

FRANKFORT, Jan. 31, 1862.

CAUSES DECIDED.

Warner vs Magowan, Montgomery; affirmed.
Phillips vs McGuire, Owsley;
Nunley et ux et al vs Moss, Scott;
Fisher et al vs Greathous et al, Union; were reversed.

ORDERS.

Grigsby vs Grigsby, Montgomery; petition for rehearing filed.
Key vs Wright, Washington; continued.
Sparks vs steamer Kate French, Lou. Ch'y; opinion delivered.
Markes vs Dickerson, Nelson; argued by Harlan for appellant and submitted.

[Special Dispatch to the St. Louis Republican.]

CAIRO, Jan. 29, 1862.

Your correspondent arrived this morning from the forces which lately went out in pursuit of Thompson. The army, consisting of Colonels Wallace's, Oglesby's, and Purcell's regiments of infantry, one battalion of the Seventh, and two companies of the First cavalry, are now returning. Part of the cavalry reached Bird's Point last night, and most of the infantry came in this morning on the cars from Charleston. The force penetrated to within a mile of Sykeston, without meeting any body of the enemy. A half dozen or more of Thomson's men were captured at different points, having in their pockets considerable quantities of Price's Missouri scrip, in payment for their services; also discharges from Thompson's army.

The force at New Madrid is entirely disbanded and scattered over the country, according to the report of all the people seen and the returning soldiers who were arrested.

About 300 Arkansas men, who formed part of Thompson's mob, have divided into squads and are engaged in plundering both friend and foe, making whole sections subject to a reign of terror. Even prominent Secessionists are leaving and preparing to leave, everything they owned being taken or destroyed. Prisoners are hung, without trial, by these Arkansas desperadoes, and women have lately become their prey also. We passed spots where the bones of half a dozen or more human bodies were laying exposed beneath trees, said to be those of Union men murdered by the prowling gangs. But few farmers, whatever their politics, have a horse or mule left upon their farms. Landholders are compelled by threats to bring a certain quantity of grain to mill, where it is ground and sent to the rebel army. The whole country is a perfect waste, and at least three fourths of the inhabitants were reduced to a state of desperation.

Thompson's men were enlisted, it appears, for six months. Their time has expired, and they will not again enter the service.

The whole of that portion of the country is at present an almost impassable swamp, the by-paths through which are known only by the inhabitants themselves.

The cavalry that left Bird's Point were obliged to pass through lakes of water miles in extent, part of the time swimming their animals.

A force of one regiment of infantry and a company of cavalry will be stationed for the present at Charleston, in order to act as a check upon rebel depredations in that vicinity.

A notorious horse thief and murderer named Dr. Scales was captured by Major Hull, at Birland, and is to be hung at Charleston to-day.

PLAYED OUT.—The rebel war in Missouri is on its last legs. For several weeks it has been of puny proportions, narrowed down to little predatory operations, such as the plundering of unarmed citizens, and the laying waste of unprotected farms and homesteads. And now appearances indicate that all vestiges of the marauding enemy are to be swept away from Missouri, and the whole territory (or its most important portions lately in possession of hostile forces) reclaimed under the flag of the Union.

There can be no doubt, we suppose, that the expeditions now on the way to the Southwest, from Otterville to Rolla, are to operate against the army of Gen. Price, who, at last accounts, was at Springfield, with a force of between ten and fifteen thousand men. We have here placed the highest estimate upon the number of Gen. Price's command, though we shall be surprised if it is found to reach more than eight or nine thousand fighting troops. Stories have been in circulation in reference to large reinforcements, said to be advancing from the South to the assistance of the rebel General, but there has yet been no confirmation of them from reliable sources, and we are induced to think that they have no truthful foundation. All accounts agree that no labor has been performed or pains taken to strengthen the position at Springfield, by throwing up intrenchments or establishing batteries, and the secession soldiers no doubt acknowledge that they are there at all only by sufferance. We have no idea that General Price will make a stand anywhere in Missouri, and give battle to the Federal columns. Upon learning of the approach of our troops, he will pull up stake, strike camp, and, to use a homely but expressive phrase, "skedaddle." The best possible thing he could do for himself and his misguided men, would be to capitulate on demand, and bid a long farewell to any effort looking to the subjugation of the State; but as the General has committed himself so far to the rebellion, we hardly look for such a proceeding. He will probably retreat into Arkansas, and that will be the last we shall hear of Gen. Price in Missouri. He would be ashamed to come back again, for, whatever his faults, he is a man of sensibility, and will hesitate to rush into further dishonor. —*St. Louis Rep.*, *30th.*

Eight Great Blunders.

We give below an article from the columns of the Religious Herald, a Baptist paper of Richmond, Va. It shows so much more coolness of judgment and candor of mind than we are in the habit of finding in our Southern exchanges, that we deem it worthy of special notice. It says the South has made at least eight great blunders, and enumerates them as follows:

1. In firing upon Fort Sumpter.
2. In believing there would be a divided North and an apathetic Federal Government.
3. In believing that they would have the hearty sympathies of Europe.
4. In believing that the bonds of their Confederacy would readily be taken in Europe.
5. In believing that the military power of the North would be directed in a crusade against slavery, rather than employed for the overthrow of treason, and the establishment of the Union and the Constitution.
6. In believing that Northern courage and physique were no match for Southern, or that in battle one Southerner equalled five Yankees.
7. In believing that the flag of the Cotton Oligarchy would wave above the Capitol at Washington, and the roll of slaves be called on Bunker Hill.
8. In believing that the fancied omnipotence of cotton would dominate the commerce of the world.

GOV. CURTIN—PROBABLE IMPEACHMENT. A special Harrisburg dispatch to the Philadelphia Inquirer says:

"It is believed that the House resolution, calling for the investigation of the acts of the last Legislature, looks to the impeachment of Gov. Curtin. The committee will undoubtedly be appointed, and they can compel the attendance of witnesses, and imprison, in the Dauphin county jail, all those who refuse to testify.

"The Senate passed an investigation resolution, which the House rejected, preferring to act upon its own, no doubt having the fact in mind that, as it must originate all impeachments, it should originate the impeachments. It is claimed that witnesses can be summoned before the committee from any part of the commonwealth."

[Special Dispatch to the Cincinnati Gazette.]

INDIANAPOLIS, Jan. 30.

Reliable advices from Cheat Mountain state that two prisoners, who had just been released from prison at Staunton, Va., and conducted to our lines by a flag of truce, report that the rebels estimate their loss in the Allegheny fight at three hundred, and say that Gen. Johnston was destroying his property and preparing to evacuate his camp when Gen. Milroy's forces were withdrawn. They also report that the people all along the line to Staunton are panic-stricken, and are daily expecting to see our forces marching on Staunton. Many persons living along the route have fled, leaving their houses and property unprotected.

AGAIN RUNNING.—The Wheeling Intelligencer says:

We are pleased to be able to announce that the Baltimore and Ohio railroad, as far as Patterson's creek and beyond, is again in tolerably good condition, and trains are running as usual.

AMUSEMENTS.

THEATER.—The character of Ion was beautifully portrayed last night by Miss Ince. We are sorry to know that her engagement has come to an end.

To-night there is a fine bill, consisting of three pieces: The Broken Sword, Toodles, and Beauty and the Beast. The first is the best melo-drama of its kind known to the modern stage, and is admirably performed by the company. Everybody knows how much fun, mirth and laughter can be extracted from Toodles; and to the lovers of music, the burletta of Beauty and the Beast commends itself in the strongest terms.

We are pleased to learn that Miss Julia Daly, the charming comedienne and vocalist, whose recent triumphs in Europe are familiar to theatre goers, is engaged, and will shortly appear. One of her most attractive pieces is a comedy called Our Female American Cousin.

MOZART HALL.—This evening, at Mozart Hall, the minstrels make their last appearance. They have performed for nine or ten nights to very good audiences, considering the tightness of the money market and the inclemency of the weather. We understand that they will perform in New Albany, Monday and Tuesday evenings. As this is the last night, we advise all who would see them to be in attendance early.

BUSINESS NOTICES.

A Word to Newspaper Readers.

The Daily Morning Democrat and Evening News supply all the dispatches, local and general news. Those who wish to keep posted with the stirring events of the times, should be supplied with both editions. The morning edition costs twenty-five (25) cents for every two weeks, and the evening edition fifteen (15) cents for two weeks. This places a paper within the reach of all.

ESPECIAL NOTICE TO SUTLERS AND DEALERS.—We have now in store, and will be receiving daily, a superior article of Western Reserve, Hamburg, and English dairy cheese, dried beef, beef tongue, extra spiced pigs' feet, Bolongna sausage, figs, almonds, filberts, Brazil nuts, sardines, No. 1 roe herring, 500 boxes No. 1 smoked herring, sour krout, white beans, new fall sugar-cured bacon, breakfast bacon, 100 barrels pearl hominy, 50 casks old hams and shoulders, clear and ribbed sides (that will be sold very low), 350 sacks No. 1 Pennsylvania buckwheat flour, potatoes, onions, &c., all of which will be sold low by

CLIFFORD & Co.,
General Commission Merchant,
dec7dtf 226 West Main street.

NOTICE.—We have in store and to arrive a large and fresh supply of groceries, consisting in part of sugar, coffee, molasses, tea, nails, cordage, soda, pepper, spice, indigo, madder, wooden ware, mackerel, white fish, and many other things, which we are selling low for cash, or country produce. We call the attention of sutlers to our large stock of tobacco and cigars, pickles, preserves, pepper sauce, oysters, sardines, &c.

GLAZEBROOK, BRO. & Co.,
Grocers and Commission Merchants.,
fldly Main st., bet Seventh and Eighth.

☞ When the army moves it will be found that an excess of baggage will be a great inconvenience. Officers can avoid this by throwing away their cots and mattrasses and using one of Green & Green's buffalo robes. They fulfill all the purposes of a cot, mattress and blankets. Everything in the military hat and cap line made to order at the shortest notice. Orders for the McClellan cap will receive prompt attention.

ja26 GREEN & GREEN,
At Craig's old stand

☞ At a time when there is great fear that the stock of dry lumber, sash, doors, blinds, &c., will fall short, owing to the vast amount of improvements in Louisville, it will be interesting to the public to know that Alexander, Ellis & Co. have enlarged their factory and have now on hand several million of dry lumber. Call at their office, on Main street, nearly opposite the Galt House, or at their factory, on Fulton, above Preston street.

DR. URBAN'S INEBRIATES' HOPE—*For the Cure of Drunkenness, Delirium Tremens, Neuralgia, and St. Vitus' Dance.*—A most successful and long tried remedy in these dreadful maladies is carefully prepared, with full directions, and sent by mail, post-paid, to any part of the Union, at $1 50 for single packages, or four packages for $5.

RAYMOND & TYLER,
74 Fourth st., near Main.
ja19 deod&weow

WANTED.—A few more men to fill up J. B. Watkins' company in Col. Dent's battalion of Provost Guard. Recruiting office corner of Sixth and Grayson streets. This company is composed of a fine body of men. A few more such, and the company will be complete. ja24 tf

UNCURRENT MONEY.—All depreciated moneys received for subscriptions will be taken only at its current rates by the brokers.

☞ J. N. Collins sells the best of coal at his office, Third street, between Market and Jefferson. Give him your orders. dtf

MARRIED,

On the 29th January, by the Rev. Geo. C. Lorimer, Mr. HARRY W. THOMPSON and Miss MALLIE DICKSON, eldest daughter of A. S. Woodruff, all of this city. *

DIED,

On Thursday evening, January 30, 1862, ANNIE M., daughter of William F. and Fannie Bryan, aged 2 years and 5 months. *

The friends of the family are invited to attend the funeral from the residence of her parents, in Jefferson county, on Saturday morning, February 1, 1862.

VOL. 1. PHILADELPHIA, SATURDAY, FEBRUARY 1, 1862. NO. 12.

A BALL AND A DUEL.

A STORY OF THE WAR.

[Written for The War Press.]

BY ESSEX.

It was the night of a cavalry ball. In the long, low mess room, that had been decked so prettily with flags, were assembled the beauty and fashion of Washington—and that means of our country, for among the fair strangers there assembled, there were representatives of nearly all the loyal States, and even of some disloyal ones, too. Where there were so many lovely women it was hard to make a choice; and yet to Jessie Curtis, I think, would have been generally conceded the palm. She was a delicate blonde, with waving golden curls, that contrasted well with her floating dress of pale blue. Around her hovered perpetually a circle of devoted admirers, and her laugh rang out ever and anon in all the innocent freshness of girlish happiness; for Jessie was very young, this was her first ball, and she enjoyed it with all the careless delight of youth and a light heart. Before the evening was half over, she had partners engaged for enough sets to have kept them dancing from that time through all the next day, and she was asked out by so many, that finally her little head became confused, and she at last rather recklessly resolved to trust to luck for having her engagements come out all right.

This was very well for a while, and as the musi; struck up, each time Jessie found her hand claimed by some gallant young officer; so that she began to think it would all go on well till the end, although she was sure she had forgotten to write down some of the names on her card.

Soon the golden moments of a ball dance themselves away, and so it grew very late, and people were beginning to go home, when the band struck up an inspiring gallop. Jessie had not the faintest idea who her partner was, but gayly awaited her destiny, knowing well enough, if no one appeared then she should have her choice of half a dozen young men who stood around her.

Another minute, and almost simultaneously two officers made their way through the group to her side. One was Major Wentworth, a dashing dragoon, tall and dark and a little flushed just now with the champagne he had been recklessly drinking; the other was Captain Murray, of the artillery, a slight, aristocratic-looking man, with a delicate yellow moustache, shading a firm and rather haughty mouth. He was the first to speak.

"I believe I have the honor of Miss Curtis' hand for this dance."

"Beg your pardon," said Major Wentworth, stepping nearer; "but this is my dance; is it not, Miss Curtis?"

Poor Jessie grew suddenly sober, and looked from one to the other in distress.

"This is the fourth gallop," Capt. Murray went on coolly; "Mis Curtis, don't you remember the fourth gallop you promised me?"

"It is the tenth dance," persisted Major Wentworth, "and you promised me the tenth dance."

"I—I," stammered Jessie; "I don't remember."

"Here is my card," said Capt. Murray, "it may assist your memory."

"And here is mine, Miss Curtis," added Major Wentworth, hurriedly and rather angrily.

By this time the group around Jessie was increased by several idlers, who were attracted by the unusual sounds. Jessie, like a frightened child, stood among the crowd of soldiers, the only woman, fair and fragile.

"I am very sorry," she said, in a low voice.

Without heeding her words, Capt. Murray held out his arm, saying, in a determined tone,

"We are losing this fine music, Miss Curtis; had we not better start?"

"Not while I'm here!" exclaimed Major Wentworth, in excitement.

From the first moment of the dispute, Capt. Murray had not betrayed, by look or motion, the slightest knowledge of Wentworth's presence; and this course had probably done more than anything else to exasperate him. But one who knew Murray well would have seen by his compressed lips, and the heightened color of his usually pale cheek, that he was really by no means as cool as he looked.

Jessie, in great trouble, gave a glance around the group, as if seeking in vain for an escape.

Again Capt. Murray offered his arm.

"Miss Curtis, this is really too bad; you must not waste any more of this capital dance—come."

There was a quiet determination in his voice that carried its weight with Jessie, and at the same time he quietly laid his hand on hers and drew it through his arm

"By G—d, sir!" cried Wentworth, in ungovernable rage, "this is too bad! Miss Curtis, I say this is my dance." And he threw himself before them, his tall figure effectually preventing their exit.

This violence helped to restore Jessie's presence of mind. Without dropping Murray's arm, she looked steadily up, and said, in a voice that trembled a little, but was still quite distinct—

"I am very sorry, gentlemen; I must have made some mistake; but as I am very tired, I will not dance any more to-night. Capt. Murray, I will trouble you to help me find mamma, who must be ready to go home."

With a slight and rather haughty bow she stepped forward, and Wentworth could do no less than let her pass. He drew aside, and then for the first time Murray looked at him. There was something so cool and provokingly triumphant in the clear glance of his gray eyes, that Wentworth, in a towering rage, vowed vengeance as he turned away.

Capt. Wentworth had known Jessie before, and Major Wentworth had been only introduced that evening. It was no wonder, then, that, disgusted with his violence, she had chosen rather an old friend, than a new acquaintance as her escort. But she was so startled and overcome at what had happened, that she scarcely knew how she got through the crowd to her mother, as she hung pale and trembling on his arm Capt. Murray liked that gentle pressure, and was sorry when at last they found Mrs. Curtis, who, still a handsome woman, was chatting pleasantly with some older officers.

On the way to the carriage, Capt. Murray contrived to whisper to Jessie his regret at what had passed, and to ask if he might call the next day to ascertain that no ill effects had followed this agitation. Jessie's reply, with a bright blush and smile, was very favorable, and as the carriage drove away, the captain looked after it full of bright fancies.

GEN. B. F. KELLEY.

MAJ. GER. H. W. HALLECK.

GEN. F W LANDER.

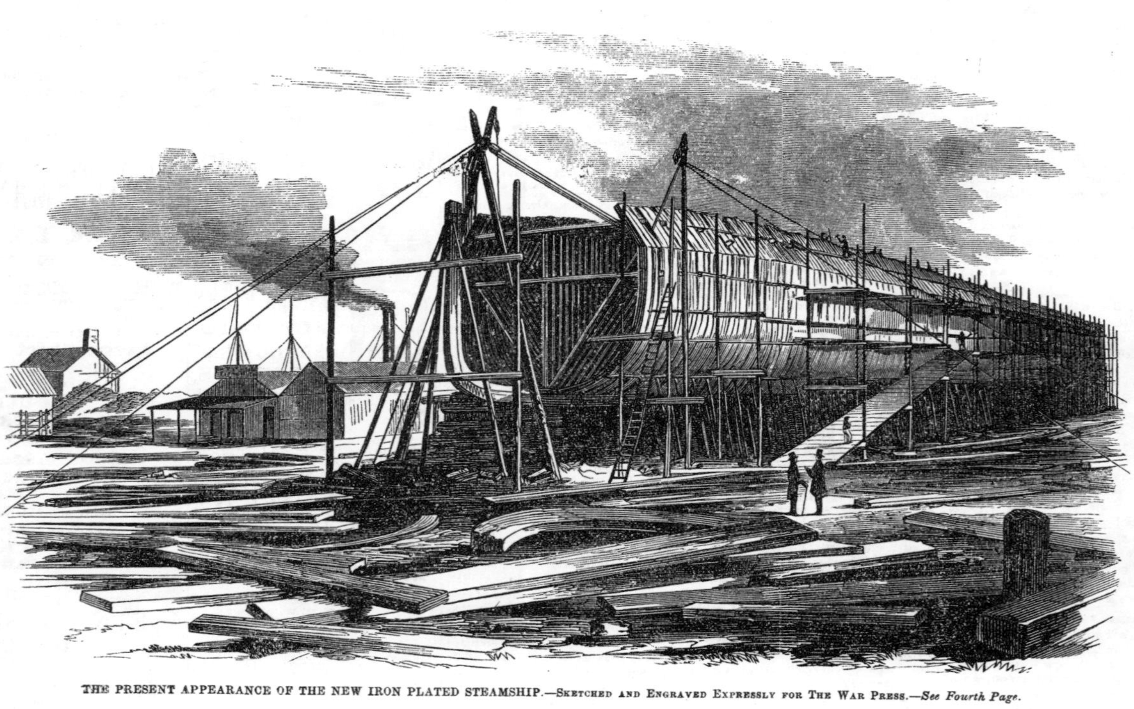

THE PRESENT APPEARANCE OF THE NEW IRON PLATED STEAMSHIP.—Sketched and Engraved Expressly for The War Press.—*See Fourth Page.*

THE NEW IRON PLATED STEAMSHIP AS IT IS TO BE WHEN FINISHED.—Sketched and Engraved Expressly for The War Press.—*See Fourth Page.*

For a second a fair young head crowned with golden curls leaned out in the moonlight, but that was enough. Jessie was thinking of him, and with a last graceful bow, he turned happily away. The smile of joy was yet on his lips, when at the top of the steps a heavy hand was suddenly laid on his shoulder. With a start, he turned and met Major Wentworth's black eyes flashing angry defiance.

"Well, sir!" exclaimed Murray, shaking off the touch, and drawing himself away proudly.

"What apology have you to offer for your conduct?" he demanded, in a voice thick with anger, and perhaps with the influence of the wine.

"Apology!—none, sir!" replied Murray.

"But I insist upon having one, and before those who saw the insult, too."

"Major Wentworth," said Murray, coolly, "I am not aware of having insulted you in any way; I have done nothing for which I can or will apologize.'

"Done nothing?" roared Wentworth. "Did you not carry that girl away from me—"

"Speak more courteously of Miss Curtis, if you please," cried Murray, his eyes gleaming with suppressed excitement.

"I'll speak as I choose of her, or any other woman," Wentworth shouted, "and you shall beg my pardon for this, as well as the other impertinence.

"Major Wentworth," said Murray, calmly, "you are excited now; to-morrow I will hear what you have to say on this subject; you will find me with my battery at Fort R. any time after ten o'clock. Now, will you let me pass?"

"No, I will not;" and Wentworth planted himself squarely in his place.

Murray looked like a slight man, but he was a practised gymnast, and now by a sudden exertion of strength he quietly put out both hands and turned Wentworth's huge frame out of his way; then, without heeding the angry curse he hurled after him, went on, and quietly rejoining a brother officer, went out with him as if nothing had happened.

The next day as Capt. Murray was writing letters in his tent, an orderly looked in and handed him a card.

"Lieutenant Colonel Raymond,—th cavalry!" said Murray; "I don't remember him;" then added to the orderly, "Show him in."

A tall, soldierly man stepped into the tent, and very shortly explained his business. He was the bearer of a challenge from Major Wentworth to Capt. Murray.

It must be confessed this took Murray entirely by surprise. He had regarded the last night's adventure as merely a drunken bravado, and had quite forgotten it in his pleasanter memories of Jessie; but here was a peremptory demand, either for an apology or a fight. Now Murray knew well enough he had nothing to apologize for, and so, after a moment's thought, he told Lieut. Col. Raymond that he would that evening send him his reply, and then went on to turn the conversation into other and pleasanter channels.

When his unwelcome guest was gone, Captain Murray slowly, and lost in thought, walked over to his friend Capt. Fairchild's tent, and to him related the whole story of what had occurred. Long and earnestly the friends discussed this untoward event; but on one point Murray was immovable.

"I must fight, John," he said. "I have never had but one opinion about duels; sometimes they are necessary; in this case one certainly cannot be avoided. That Wentworth is a wretched bully, but I am a pretty good shot, and I think he will be sorry he troubled me." There was a gleam in Murray's eye as he spoke that augured ill for his antagonist.

Before the friends parted, an answer to the challenge was written, and Fairchild had his orders how to settle the preliminaries. But no one would have thought who saw Capt. Murray that evening as he lounged into the parlor at Willard's—so exquisite in dress, so calm in bearing—that he had what might be a desperate duel in prospect for the morning.

Jessie Curtis was there, lovely as a dream, surrounded as usual by a small court. She blushed as she recognized Capt. Murray, but, after the first salutation, he sat quietly at her mother's side until one by one her admirers departed and left him "master of the situation."

Then Capt. Murray drew his chair nearer hers. A moment after, the long swell of the music of a band serenading some notability, stole in through the closed blinds, and with delight Murray seized the opportunity to ask Jessie if she would go into the balcony to hear it better. It was a warm night in early November, the moonlight was lovely, and as he stood there with Jessie at his side, looking fair and fragile as an angel in the soft white shawl she had wrapped around her, it was very hard for Murray to resist the wild inclination he felt to avow his long-cherished passion. But he felt, in view of the uncertainty of his fate, he had no right to ask any woman to link her happiness with his life; only after a while he said—

"Miss Jessie, if I were in hospital wounded, would you come to see me?"

Jessie started visibly at the abrupt inquiry, and answered, "Certainly, Capt. Murray, but why do you ask such a question? There is no talk of an advance, is there?"

"Not at once perhaps, and yet I cannot tell how soon I may see active service. If I am called out, you will think of me?"

"Constantly," Jessie faltered, with drooped head.

It was very hard for Murray to restrain himself; he could not help seizing for even an instant her little hand, and saying hurriedly—

"Miss Jessie, perhaps to-morrow night I can say to you all I must not say now. I may at least tell you that you are dearer to me than anything in the world except my honor, and now remember the promise you just made, and good-by."

The fair girl at his side had so evidently responded to this appeal that he durst not trust himself to linger longer, but as he uttered the last word he tore himself away, and, leaving Jessie lost in delicious amaze, hurried through the crowd and out to his lonely encampment.

The next morning, while the sky was yet gloomy with the lingering dawn, a little party of four horsemen made their way along one of the various roads of Virginia to the shelter of a grove. They rode in couples. In front were Captains Murray and Fairchild; they had been the first to start, but Major Wentworth and Lieut. Col. Raymond followed them closely. Reaching the spot selected, which Raymond and Fairchild had fixed upon as

[CONTINUED ON EIGHTH PAGE.]

GENREAL BUELL'S DEPARTMENT.

THE VICTORY AT MILL SPRINGS.

The Battle—A Detailed Account—The Loyal East Tennessee Troops—Results of the Conflict.

ZOLLICOFFER'S (LATE) ENCAMPMENT, January 20, 1862.

Here I sit, in a cedar log cabin, inside the entrenchments of the wonderful position of old "Zolly," to write you a letter, on contraband paper, with a contraband pen, and contraband ink. Where shall I begin—what shall I write first? There are incidents enough, if all recounted, to fill a volume; things that took place in this, the most complete victory, and most overwhelming, total overthrow the Secession army has yet met with in this rebellion. To begin at the beginning, and tell the story straight:

Just at daybreak on Sunday morning, the 19th of January, sharp firing commenced with the pickets in the same spot where the firing was last Friday night; the long roll beat in the Indiana Tenth, and they formed instantly and marched to the support of their pickets. The Tenth and Kinney's battery were close together, and half a mile in advance of everything. The battery got ready for action on the instant, and awaited orders. By the way, Stannard's battery and Wetmore's four-gun battery were both in park, one on each side of Kinney's battery. The First Tennessee was about a quarter of a mile in the rear of these batteries, in the woods. The Fourth Kentucky, Col. Fry, was the next on the road, half a mile in the rear of the batteries; it was forming as I ran past, getting to my own regiment, (for I slept in Kinney's battery); the Second Tennessee another quarter of a mile in the rear of the Fourth Kentucky. By this time the cavalry were running their horses all over the country in every direction—except towards the firing, which still continued at intervals. The Second was just getting breakfast, and supposing it to be only a picket fight, kept on cooking and eating, though very few had eaten anything when the column of our force appeared coming on in our rear. Lieut. Colonel Trewhit promptly got us into line and double-quickened us into the road ahead of the advancing column; the Fourth Kentucky had gone when we reached their encampment. The firing still continued, and very briskly; we kept on at double-quick, all hoping and believing that we would have a chance to smell burnt powder. But when opposite the encampment of the Tenth Indiana, up rode the Colonel, and halted us for further orders; we all thought—if we didn't say it—d–n further orders.

The Tenth Indiana went into the woods about a quarter of a mile in advance of their tents, to the support of their pickets; and bravely did they support them, too, for over half an hour, against the whole force led against them; and never retreated a step, nor gave an inch of ground, until nearly surrounded by overwhelming numbers; then, to save themselves from being entirely surrounded, they unwillingly gave way. Here was a crisis; and yell on yell went up from the lantern-jawed Secessionists; they thought the day was all their own. But, happily, any disastrous consequence was prevented by the arrival of the Fourth Kentucky and Ninth Ohio to the support of the gallant Tenth. Again our men made a stand; now there was fighting in good earnest, and the Second Minnesota joined in with the Tenth and the Fourth and the Ninth Ohio. Volley after volley rattled in quick succession, and sometimes it seemed as though there was only one continuous volley, interrupted now and then by the growling of the "yellow pups," which had been brought to bear on the enemy; and when they once commenced, they distributed their favors freely in all directions, in the shape f shot and shell; and, gentlemen, excuse me from being the recipient of any such favors. There were only two or three shots from cannon fired by the enemy, and they were either badly aimed or the pieces were out of range, for the shot did not disturb anybody. Once they threw a shell into the air, which burst when some four or five hundred feet high. No damage was done by it, and their artillery seemed to be of no use to them whatever, while, on the contrary, ours seemed to be of immense use to us; and it was most ably and effectively handled. After a little more than two hours of hard fighting, a most tremendous volley of musketry, followed by a ringing shout from our side, seemed to have decided the battle in our favor, for from that time, although firing was kept up at intervals, the Secessionists, whipped and cowed, began their retreat, which, in about twenty minutes more, became a total rout; and from the indications along the road, which we afterwards passed over, the flight appeared to have been a regular race from that point back to their entrenchments, to see who could get there first, and the devil take the hindmost.

All the credit and honor of this battle is due to the 10th Indiana, the 9th Ohio, the 4th Kentucky, and 2d Minnesota, for they did all the fighting, as it were, single-handed, with the exception of what support they received from the artillery They all fought nobly, and judging from the sound of the musketry, they never wavered from a fixed determination to gain the victory. The combatants were so near to each other at one time, that the powder burned their faces in the discharge of their pieces; but the underbrush was so thick that bayonets were of but little use, and a charge could hardly have been made.

The most important event of the day was the death of Zollicoffer. Col. Fry, of the 4th Kentucky, charged up a hill by himself upon a group of mounted officers, and fired at the one he conceived to be the chief among them; he fired two shots; both of them took effect, and Zollicoffer, one of the master spirits of the rebellion, fell off his horse dead. Col. Fry was, luckily, unhurt, but his horse was shot through the body, the bullet entering only a few inches behind the Colonel's leg. This must have been a deadener to all the hopes the Secessionists had for victory, as from this moment began the retreat; and so closely did our forces push upon them that they were obliged to leave their illustrious leader where he fell, by the side of the road

What were the East Tennesseans doing, during all this engagement, with their boasted bravery? The First Regiment I know but little about, except that it marched towards the edge of the woods in which the firing was going on, and disappeared from sight. As a regiment they did not fire a gun; but Lieutenant Colonel Spears, who is a whole team and a horse to let, some way got in ahead of his men, and where the fighting was; he shot a few times with his revolver, and turned round to see where his men were, when he perceived an officer in between him and where his regiment ought to be, evidently trying to cut him off But the officer, who turned out to be Lieutenant Colonel Carter, waked up the wrong passenger when he got after Spears, and the tables were turned; for instead of cutting Colonel Spears off, the colonel took him prisoner and brought him back into the regiment. The Second Tennessee went through various and sundry evolutions; they were marched and counter-marched, right-obliqued and left-obliqued, right-faced and left-faced, and brought up all-standing in a briar-patch.

Well, finally we were formed in a line of battle, out of all harm's way, and remained so until the firing was nearly all over, when we were double-quicked to the edge of the woods, and halted again until the firing receded and died away entirely.

It is needless to comment upon the conduct of the Tennesseans; to say what they could have done, or would have done, under other circumstances. Here is the fact what they did do, and that was simply nothing. As to the rest, the future will decide.

Our course was now steadily forward to the main road that led to Zollicoffer's encampment on the Cumberland. I shall not attempt to describe the battle-field, the dead or the dying. Of course, in all battles, somebody must be killed. and somebody must be wounded; this was no exception to the general rule. I shall mention only one of the dead—that one Zollicoffer. He lay by the side of the road along which we all passed. and all had a fair view of what was once Zollicoffer.

The march was now steadily but cautiously forward. Two pieces of artillery were taken; one was crippled in the woods near the battle ground, and the other was found stuck in the mud about a mile in the rear; also two wagons with ammunition. No incident worth mentioning occurred on the march, which was deliberately but steadily forward, with the artillery well up, until a final halt was made, about half-past four, within a mile of the breastworks of the famous fortifications on the Cumberland, which have been reported impregnable. Here the artillery was again planted, and set to work shelling the wonderful fortifications; and a continuous fire was kept up for nearly an hour Every shell that was thrown we could hear burst distinctly. There was only one cannon that answered us from the breastworks, and that one sounded more like a potato pop-gun than anything else I can liken it to, and did us no damage, as the shot never reached us. This one piece was only fired four times. Night closed in and the firing ceased. We all laid down on the wet ground, in perfect security, to rest our weary limbs, the distance we had come being over ten miles on the direct road, let alone the bushes and underbrush we went through, to say nothing about two or three dress parades of the 2d for somebody's amusement, but not our own, I can assure you. And then the roads and fields were awfully cut up, and mud was plenty, as it had rained a good part of the forenoon. Our men laid down to rest without a mouthful to eat, many of whom had eaten no breakfast; but as Captain Cross said, "the man who could not fast two days over Zollicoffer's scalp, was no man at all;" and there was no grumbling, as there was necessity for it. However, the teams came up in the night with crackers and bacon.

Now here is the summary, so far as I know, up to Sunday night: We are within a mile of Zollicoffer's encampment; Zollicoffer is killed and his forces have been whipped—some two hundred of them being killed and a great many wounded; one of Crittenden's aids, a lieutenant colonel. and three surgeons, are taken prisoners, but how many more I know not; two pieces of artillery and three wagons were left. and the road was strewed with guns, blankets, coats, haversacks, and everything else that impeded flight; on our side from 20 to 30 are killed, and from 80 to 100 wounded, having no prisoners taken that we know of.

On the morning of the 20th, soon after dayli ht, several of the regiments were moved forward toward the breastworks, and a cannon ball or two fired over into them; but no answer was made, all was quiet. The regiments moved steadily on and into their fortifications, it being ascertained that there was no one to oppose them. The enemy having crossed the river during the night, or early in the morning, the rout was complete. It seems as though there was a perfect panic among them, their tents having been left standing, and their blankets, clothes, cooking utensils, letters, papers, etc., all left behind.

The position is a pretty strong one, but not near so much so as we had been led to suppose. Huts were built, nicely chincked with mud, many of them having windows in them for comfortable winter quarters. How much work the devils have done here, and how little it has profited them! I have been wandering around all day, and seeing and hearing what I could. The Cumberland makes one side of the encampment safe, by an abrupt bank 250 feet high. I went down to the river bottom, to which there is a road on our side. Here were all or nearly all of their wagons, some twelve or fifteen hundred horses and mules, harness, saddles, sabres, guns; in fact, everything. It was a complete stampede, and by far the most disastrous defeat the Southern Confederacy has yet met with. Ten pieces of cannon, with caissons, are also here. To all appearances, they seem to have completely lost their senses, having only one object in view, and that was to run somewhere and hide themselves.

Now, to account for the battle taking place as it did. There were eleven rebel regiments here, two being unarmed; and Zollicoffer, who was the presiding devil, although Crittenden had taken the command, thought the Tenth Indiana and Kinney's battery were just two regiments by themselves, and did not know that they were supported by the balance of the division, which was out of sight behind on account of the timber; and he conceived the happy idea of rushing upon and capturing these two regiments to get their arms to supply his own unarmed men. So he took all the available force he had—some 8,000 or 9,000 men—and made the attack—with what result has already been shown. Now this only goes to prove that, in order to put this rebellion down, we must *do something* In this fight four of our regiments whipped and completely routed the great army that was under Zollicoffer, killed the old devil himself, and may be Crittenden too, for he has not been heard of since the battle. The prisoners we have taken estimate our force at 20,000; bah! we can take them any time, and any place, and giving them the odds three to one, whip them every time. Their cause is a bad one; they know it; and the only way their men can be induced to fight at all, is by their leaders getting in the very front rank with them.

The Second Minnesota captured a banner from the Mississippi regiment, which had on it the "Mississippi Butchers." They may be good butchers, at home, but they make a mighty awkward fist at butchering Yankees. They had better go home and tend to their business. Nearly every man has a trophy of this victory; there are plenty to get, certain; and I sit writing this. now, with a Louisiana Zouave head-dress and tassel on my head.

I give you a copy of two or three of the documents found in the camp. The following was found on a table, in one of the cabins:

"COLONEL SPEARS: We fought you bravely and despe ately, but misguidedly. We leave here under pressing circumstances, but do not feel that we are whipped. We will yet succeed, and"——

Here the circumstances became so *pressing* that the writer did not wait to finish the epistle. Col. Spears supposes the writer to be Major John W. Bridgman, of the Tennessee cavalry.

The following was written on a piece of brown paper, with a pencil:

"Jan 19, 1862. FISHING CREEK.

"The great battle at Fishing Creek took place. Our loss was great. Supposed to be eight hundred killed and wounded, and a great many taken prisoners. We will try them again at our breastworks if they come to us."

At the bottom of the paper, upside down, is a name I cannot make out, and then "Polasky."

Here is another paper, which is evidently the result of a council of war, held before this force came across the north side of the Cumberland:

"The result of your crossing the river now will be that you will be repulsed and lose all the artillery taken over.

"Dec. 4, '61, ESTILL."

"Another 'Wild Cat' disaster *is all we* can look forward to. FULKERSON."

"We will cross over and find that the enemy has retired to a place that we will not deem advisable to attack, and then we will return to this encampment. LORING."

Estill is a colonel from Middle Tennessee. Fulkerson is a major, and one of the big heads of the Secession party in Tennessee. It seems that there was oppos tion in the camp to the move on to this side of the river, but old Zollicoffer, the head devil of the army, ruled the roast and did come over. Some of these predictions proved to be strictly true; it did turn out to be a "Wild Cat" disaster, only worse, and they did lose all their artillery; and, more than all, the old he-devil Zollicoffer lost his life. The rout has been complete and total. His whole force is entirely scattered, and if the victory is followed up across the river, they will never rally together again.

It is now nearly three o'clock in the morning while I write, and, with a few reflections. this already long letter—perhaps too long—shall be closed.

What a lucky thing that Zollicoffer was bold enough to attack our force; had he not done so, no battle would have been fought here for a long time. And this victory cannot be credited to the skill of a brigadier general The battle was entirely accidental; the position was entirely a chance position, and the men themselves, led by their colonels, fought the battle and won it. The Tenth Indiana got into the fight supporting their pickets, the Fourth Kentucky and Ninth Ohio rushed in, without orders, to support the Tenth. Whether the Second Minnesota had orders to go in or not, I do not know. And these four regiments did all the fighting that was done, and that was enough to whip the eight regiments Zollicoffer had in the engagement.

The Ninth Ohio, which some way I came very near omitting, deserves especial praise. Colonel McCook rushed his men up just about the time the Tenth Indiana was giving ground. And the Indiana boys say the Ninth fought like tigers, and are just such backers as they would always like to have. FELIX.

Further Particulars.

Col. Green Clay, aid to Gen. Schoepff, reached our city last evening, having left the scene of the late victory on Monday, and from him we gather some additional particulars which give us a better insight into the fight. Prisoners report that Gen. Geo. B. Crittenden had been appointed to the command of the rebel forces, but he had not arrived in camp. Gen. Zollicoffer was killed at very close quarters; he had ridden up to Col. Fry and told him not to shoot at his own men, when Col. Fry replied that he was not doing so. Soon after this the encounter commenced which proved fatal. The regiments engaged in the fight were the Tenth Indiana, Fourth Kentucky, Second Minnesota, and Ninth Ohio, with a portion of Woolford's cavalry and two batteries. The Tenth Indiana was in the advance, and contested the ground nobly, but a bayonet charge being ordered, the Ninth Ohio advanced with the cold steel and soon broke the rebel ranks, when a panic flight ensued, the retreating columns being followed by shells, which did terrible execution, and vollies of musketry were poured in upon them. An order was found in the entrenchments after the final flight, signed by Col Cummings, from which it is evident that he succeeded to the command after Zollicoffer's fall, and gave the order to disperse.

From accounts furnished by records found in camp and by prisoners, the rebel force consisted of about ten thousand infantry, eighteen hundred cavalry, and sixteen pieces of artillery. Two of the latter have not been discovered, and were probably concealed. Zollicoffer was in strong position, and his entrenchments could have been defended against thirty thousand men. It had winter quarters of log huts for fifteen thousand men, and everything was very comfortable. So precipitate was the evacuation, that trunks were left in the huts, as if the owners had gone out to a dress parade; shaving materials were left behind, private correspondence, miniatures, extra clothing, &c. The rebels seem to have been well clothed in jeans, but they were without overcoats. Their discarded knapsacks contained two or three days' rations. They were well supplied with blankets, and had plenty of old army regulation ones, white and black striped, which were unbaled.

The rout of the rebels was pressed until our men reached elevated positions which partially commanded the camp. Our regiments were thrown across the country from White Oak creek to the Cumberland river, while Col. Harlan's regiment was advanced some distance on the top of a hill to prevent the enemy from occupying it during the night. Zollicoffer was evidently under the impression that Gen. Thomas had but two regiments with him, and that the reserves could not come up on account of the swollen streams. He therefore left his entrenchment and marched eight miles in the hope to cut him off. He was correct in a measure, for Gen. Schoepff on Friday sent three regiments, the Twelfth Kentucky and First and Second Tennessee, and a battery, to Gen. Thomas, but they did not arrive in time to participate, and on Sunday he sent the Thirty-first, Thirty-fifth, and Thirty-eight Ohio from Somerset, and they were obliged to cross Fishing creek by means of an overstretched cable, to which they clung, advancing hand over hand, stringing along the rope, such was the swiftness of the current and the depth of the water. When Zollicoffer discovered his mistake, his men fought well, but they could not resist the bayonet charge. Our men shot with great precision; the forest trees through which the enemy retreated were riddled with balls.

It is uncertain whether the steamboat was fired by our shells or destroyed by the rebels. The conflagration was watched from the hills by our men, while "bombs bursting in air" lent a terrible reality to the scene. The body of Gen. Zollicoffer was placed in a tent under a guard of honor, awaiting a flag of truce from the rebels for its delivery, but his men are so demoralized and scattered that it is hardly possible the requisition will be made, unless it comes from Bowling Green. The rebel general had but one wound, the fatal one in his breast, and his features, after he had been washed, were calm and life-like. Colonel Hoskins was ordered to go a few miles above Somerset and obtain twenty coal barges, and it is probable that with these Gen. Thomas crossed the river.—*Louisville Journal.*

Incidents Before and After the Battle.

The Somerset correspondent of the Cincinnati *Gazette* writes as follows:

LISTENING, AT SCHOEPFF'S CAMP, TO THE ROAR OF BATTLE.

Sunday morning came, dark and rainy—a fit day for a Sabbath battle. At six minutes before eight o'clock we heard the first boom of cannon. We had frequently heard what we imagined to be artillery firing before, but always found out that it was distant thunder, or something similar in sound; but there was no doubt as to this. The imagination may mistake other sounds for cannon, but there is little danger of ever mistaking the heavy boom of artillery for anything else. The battle was evidently raging somewhere near General Thomas' camp. Yet it was so unexpected to us that we could scarcely believe the evidence of our own ears. That the enemy should leave his entrenchments to attack us in the open field, seemed almost incredible. Major Coffee, of "Wolford's Cavalry," was the only one who could offer any solution of the mystery. He knows Major General Crittenden personally, and remarked "George is drunk, as usual, and come out for a fight."

The cannonading continued, with but brief pauses, for two hours, and then ceased. We waited in suspense for two hours more, but no news. The wildest rumors began to circulate: The rebels had completely surrounded Thomas, and taken his whole force prisoners; they were about to cross Fishing creek to complete the day's work by demolishing us. The general impression seemed to be that something had gone wrong.

Schoepff Receives News of the Rebel Attack and Repulse.

About noon Lieutenant Colonel Moore and I went over to headquarters to see if we couldn't get some information. We found Lieutenant Munoz, one of the general's aids, busily engaged in examining the bottom of a well. He was the only officer visible, and we approached him. "No news," was his answer to our question, and still he peered with anxious eyes down the well. It is still a wonder to me, what our good friend the lieutenant was looking down there for, though in the dismal condition of external nature, and the general uncertainty which prevailed, it was about a good a thing as a man could do. Probably he was trying to see whether he couldn't get out some of that truth which they say lies hiddan in a well, and which is so rare an article in Southern Kentucky.

Just then we saw coming over a hill opposite, at full speed, Major Lawrence, Captain Hewit, and a third person with the inevitable Wolford's cavalry blunderbus slung over his shoulder. He and his horse looked like an incarnation of the demon who may be presumed to preside over mud. If there was one square inch on their several bodies visible through the surrounding crust of earth and water, my eyes failed to perceive it. But his first words were decidedly those of a man of like passions to other mortals. "Hurrah, Zolly's dead!" He sought the General, while the Major stopped to tell us that the rebels were routed and our men were in full pursuit of them towards the river. In a moment out rushed General Schoepff, bare-headed and jubilant. "Munoz, go and tell the Seventeenth, Thirty-fifth, Thirty-eighth, and Thirty-first Regiments to prepare to march instantly." "Instantly," he repeated in his quick, decisive way. We hurried back to camp. The boys had not eaten their dinners yet. They were tired with Saturday's march. They had no meat for breakfast. There were no crackers, only cornmeal to make bread of, and no time to prepare it. But it made no difference. The only anxiety was lest Thomas should drive the enemy over the river before we could get down. Boys sick in the hospitals hurried out to get their muskets. Our regiment, which could not have brought out three hundred men for dress parade, marched five hundred strong to battle, and one company gone to repair the road to Stanford. It was the same with all the rest of the brigade. Cols. Bradley and Vandevier left their rooms where they had been lying dangerously ill for weeks, to head their regiments. I did not see the latter, but Col. B. looked as the Cid Campeador must have done when the Spaniards placed his corps at their head to lead them once more to victory.

March of Schoepff's Brigade.

We reached Fishing creek in an hour and a half. It was running breast high, and the current very swift. There was no time to bridge it. A rope was stretched across. The men strapped their cartridge-boxes upon their shoulders, and, with one hand holding their gun-locks out of the water, and with the other clinging to the rope to keep themselves from being swept down the stream, they pressed across. All the horses and mules that could be found were put in requisition for ferriage. But it was night before the last man was over. Four miles march brought us to General Thomas' camp. All along the road we had heard the report of Gen. Zollicoffer's death. The country people who have suffered from his lawless soldiery, or feared their ravages, were wild with delight. One old woman on the road exclaimed, "I've got two children in the fight, but I don't trouble myself about them. I'm so glad that Zollicoffer is dead." We had disbelieved the reports, knowing how such rumors spread after a battle, but on arriving at the camp we made inquiry, and found that there was no doubt of the fact.

Appearance of Zollicoffer's Corpse.

Colonel Connell, who had known Gen. Zollicoffer in Washington, asked to be permitted to see the corpse, and I went with him. He lay in a tent, wrapped in an army blanket, his chest and left arm and side exposed. A tall, rather slender man, with thin, brown hair, high forehead, somewhat bald, Roman nose, firm, wide mouth, and clean-shaved face. A pistol ball had struck him in the breast, a little above the heart, killing him instantly. His face bore no expression, such as is usually found on those who fall in battle; no malice, no reckless hate, not even a shadow of physical pain. It was calm, placid, noble. But I have never looked on a countenance so marked with sadness. A deep dejection had settled on it. "The low cares of the mouth" were distinct in the droop at its corners, and the thin cheeks showed the wasting which comes through disappointment and trouble.

"Where, Oh! Where" is George B. Crittenden?

One mystery is still unravelled. Where is Major General George B Crittenden? Nothing was seen of him after the battle turned against him. It appears that he did not get back to his camp, for the order of retreat was signed by "Col. Cummings, acting brigadier general, in command of the troops." Did he put on a "hat, a kerchief, and a muffler, and so escape?" I think that any woman's gown might fit him, since this battle of Cliff creek, without hunting for that of "my aunt, the fat woman of Brentford."

There is a strange rumor floating through the country and in our camps that he was cut off from the main body of his army, and, with two regiments, is still hiding somewhere in the woods this side of the river. Nobody can tell the exact spot, but the forests are wide and wild, abounding in squirrels and woodchucks, and there are still some chickens left on the scattered farms I don't believe any one will ever be able to find the mythical rebels, but I have no doubt that the children in the western part of Pulaski county will, for a long time, be afraid to go out alone at night, or into the woods in daytime, and that they will grow up with the fixed idea, which they will in turn transmit to their descendants, that somewhere upon the hills, on the Cumberland, or among the wild cliffs of Fishing creek, wanders a lost major general, with a sword ten feet long and eyes like balls of fire, and with him two thousand gigantic Tennesseans who live on babies and apple-jack, drink Jeff Davis' health from gourds full of blood, and sing "Dixie". in the tree tops all night long in the full of the moon. F.

Kentucky Speculation about "What Next."

If now Generals Thomas and Schoepff, with Colonel Munson's brigade, will cross the Cumberland, at the earliest possible moment, and push down into Tennessee via Albany, they can take possession of the East Tennessee and Virginia Railroad, and cut off all communication between the forces in Virginia and in West Tennessee, while those now at Columbus and Bowling Green will have all to do they can possibly want to keep their entrenchments. If Boyle's brigade should join the others, they might, after taking the railroad, move west upon Nashville and take it with force enough to hold it against any attack.—*Louisville Democrat.*

A Forward Movement of General Buell's Column Anticipated.

The correspondent of the Cincinnati *Gazette*, writing from Green river under date of January 20, says:

Three cheers, "Hurrah, hurrah, hurrah," "tiger." You must certainly pardon this outburst, as it could not possibly be prevented, and I am confident, if you were here, you would join me. The following order has just been issued, viz:

"Commandants of divisions, brigades, regiments and detachments, will draw and prepare three days' rations immediately." Now, who is there would not get enthusiastic over such an order, when we all know so well what is to follow, and an order we have been waiting patiently for weeks. Everything is now excitement, fresh camp-fires brightening up in every direction, and the rations are fast being prepared.

To-morrow morning, I presume, we will be on our way toward Buckner, and perhaps before you get this we will have had some exciting times.

Incidents of the Battle of Mill Springs.

A gentleman direct from the vicinity of Somerset informs us that there were eleven of the Tenth Indiana killed, ten of the Second Minnesota, eight of the Fourth Kentucky, eight of the Ninth Ohio, and one or two of the Woolford Cavalry. The Michigan Engineer and Mechanic Regiment dug trenches and buried the dead, the funeral service having been appropriately performed on the occasion. Wounded prisoners state that there was no general enthusiasm, but that the growing discontent induced Gen. Zollicoffer to make a speech to his troops the day before he led them to battle, in which he declared with emphasis that "he would take them to Indiana or go to h—l himself!"

After Colonel Fry's horse was shot and disabled, he mounted the splendid gray charger which Zollicoffer had ridden. As the Federal army advances, the Union people creep out of their holes and hiding places, and evince the most frantic delight. They are eager to receive arms, and to be marched against those who have so long terrorized their homes. As plenty of muskets were found in the deserted camp of the rebels, we presume their wishes will be gratified. One man, residing on the Cumberland, had been robbed of six hundred bushels of corn, and he is willing to give the marauders a receipt in full for it if he can only get a few cracks at them. Captain Noah, of the Second Minnesota, informs us that a large number of the dead rebels were shot through the head which shows the precision of the aim of our marksmen. Capt. Kinney's Ohio battery of four rifled and two smooth-bore 6-pounders threw elongated shells charged with shrapnell, which did terrible execution, filing the forest with rebel dead like cord-wood.—*Louisville Journal.*

THE LOSS AT SOMERSET.

LOUISVILLE, Jan. 22.—The entire United States loss in the late fight was 39 killed and 150 wounded.

General Thomas' forces took 14 cannon and 1,400 mules and horses. General Thomas is across the river in pursuit. The steamboat and eight barges used by the rebels were burned. The United States troops used the remaining barges in crossing the river.

LOUISVILLE, Jan. 22.—General Thomas now reports the Federal loss at the recent battle at 39 killed and 127 wounded. Among the wounded are Col. McCook, of the Ninth Ohio, and his aid, Lieut. Burt, of the Eighteenth United States Infantry. Of the rebels Zollicoffer and 114 others were killed, 116 wounded, and 45 taken prisoners.

A prisoner says that Geo. B. Crittenden was the first in command of the rebel forces, and Zollicoffer the second. Crittenden fled to the woods, taking the wrong road, and it is supposed he will be captured.

The Federal forces actively engaged were the Tenth Indiana, Fourth Kentucky, Second Minnesota, and Ninth Ohio—their respective loss being in the order named.

They were reinforced, after the first and severest engagement, by the Twelfth and Eighteenth Kentucky, First and Second Tennessee, Fourteenth, Thirty-first, Thirty-fifth, and Thirty-sixth Ohio Regiments, and Standard's, Whitmore's, and Kenney's batteries.

The rebel forces were estimated at 10,000

Green C. Clay, of Bourbon county, son of Brutus Clay, and aid to Gen. Schoepff, was with General Thomas in the engagement, and has just arrived, bringing a splendid silk rebel flag, bearing the inscription: "Presented to the Mountain Rangers, Captain F. A. Ashford, by Mrs. W. D. Charderoyne."

Col. S. S. Fry, of the Fourth Kentucky Regiment, had his horse shot from under him by one of Zollicoffer's aids, when he turned and shot Zollicoffer through the left breast.

The first breaking of the rebel ranks was effected by Col. R. S. McCook, of the Ninth Ohio, acting brigadier general, who ordered his men to charge bayonets, which put the rebels to immediate flight.

The last order issued to the rebels, which was found in their encampment, was signed by Colonel Cummins, the senior in command, after the death of Zollicoffer and flight of Crittenden, directing the rebels to disperse and save themselves in the best way they could.

The *Journal* says Gen. Thomas, with a large force, has crossed the Cumberland, and is hunting the flying rebels through Wayne county.

The Instructions to Gen. Thomas.

LOUISVILLE, Jan. 23—The Louisville *Journal* says that the instructions of Gen. Buell show that he is fully master of the situation. It was arranged that Gen. Thomas should leave Jamestown and Gen. Schœpff advance from Somerset, thus hemming in Zollicoffer from the west and north.

Some Secession spy carried the intelligence of Gen. Thomas' movements to the rebel camp, and Zollicoffer. making a forced march on Saturday afternoon, reached Gen. Thomas' encampment on Sunday morning.

In the meantime, Major Sheppard, with the Eighteenth regulars, and Colonel Manson's brigade of the Tenth Indiana, Colonel Harcan's Tenth Kentucky, Colonel Fry's Fourth Kentucky, reached General Thomas' camp after a forced march of twenty-five miles, so that he was able to advance upon the rebels and drive them before him until he reached their entrenchments at night.

A private letter from Somerset says that the citizens and soldiers are struggling in loaded with the trophies of battle. Our bullets were sent with unerring aim, and many of the rebels are shot in the forehead, breast and body. The Union people here have flocked to the battle-field in droves and are jubilant at the result.

It is thought that General Crittenden is among the prisoners disguised as a surgeon.

AFFAIRS IN EASTERN KENTUCKY.

The Fruits of Garfield's Victory.

The following proclamation has been issued in Eastern Kentucky:

HEADQUARTERS 18TH BRIGADE, PAINTSVILLE, Ky., Jan. 16, 1862.

CITIZENS OF THE SANDY VALLEY: I have come among you to restore the honor of the Union, and to bring back the Old Banner, which you all once loved, but which, by the machinations of evil men, and by mutual misunderstandings, has been dishonored among you. To those who are in arms against the Federal Government, I offer only the alternative of battle, or unconditional surrender. But to those who have taken no part in this war, who are in no way aiding or abetting the enemies of the Union—even to those who hold sentiments averse to the Union, but yet give no aid and comfort to its enemies—I offer the full protection of the Government, both in their persons and property.

Let those who have been seduced away from the love of their country, to follow after and aid the destroyers of our peace, lay down their arms, return to their homes, bear true allegiance to the Federal Government, and they shall also enjoy like protection. The army of the Union wages no war of plunder, but comes to bring back the prosperity of peace. Let all peace-loving citizens who have fled from their homes return and resume again the pursuits of peace and industry. If citizens have suffered from any outrages by the soldiers under my command, I invite them to make known their complaints to me, and their wrongs shall be redressed and the offenders punished. I expect the friends of the Union in this valley to banish from among them all private feuds, and let a liberal-minded love of country direct thrir conduct towards those who have been so sadly estranged and misguided. Hoping that these days of turbulence may soon be ended, and the better days of the Republic soon return.

J. A. GARFIELD, Col. Commanding Brigade.

A correspondent of the Cleveland (Ohio) *Herald*, writing from Col Garfield's command, says:

The above proclamation was issued by Colonel Garfield, just after his brilliant victory over the rebel forces under Humphrey Marshall, on the 10th of January, at the forks of Middle creek, Floyd county, Ky. Our army, the day after the battle and retreat of the enemy, occupied Prestonburg, two miles from the battle ground, to recruit our wearied men, and take possession of some stores left there by the rebels. The night before the battle the enemy had engaged in hauling away their stores to their camp, two miles distant. Our night march had cut them off suddenly from Prestonburg—coming in between them and their remaining stores. We got some twenty boxes of shoes and knapsacks, twenty-five guns, &c. These we found lying on the bank of the river—some of them lying in the water, evidently thrown there in haste, expecting that they would go down the river from the "Lincolnites," as they call us here! Colonel Garfield's victory grows in magnitude upon our hands, now that the smoke has cleared away.

The report first sent you, made the number of the killed some 50 or 60! But subsequent examinations on the field, and the admissions of the rebel officers, make their killed 125, and as many more wounded! We found 27 left on the field unburied, among whom was one field officer and two captains laid under a shelving rock, covered with leaves. Sixty more they had thrown hastily into a deep ravine on their side of the hill, and covered them with leaves and brush! Three wagons, loaded with the dead, were drawn off during the battle! Three of their wounded died before they had got a mile from the field of battle. The rebel Colonel Trigg, told the family where they left the two dead above mentioned on their retreat, that they had lost 125 killed and a large number wounded, and that they thought they had killed 600 Federals.

Now, the facts are these, as regards our loss: We lost only one man on the field of battle—one brave Kentuckian fell after he had sent two rebels to their final account. We had fourteen wounded, two of whom have since died; the rest are doing well, and most of them but slightly wounded. This is to us perfectly marvellous, but we have established one fact, viz—that a good oak tree is better to fight behind than a rock. The rebels got behind rocks, and when they fired at our men they had to expose their heads and necks, hence the fact that all their dead left on the field were hit in the head, neck, and upper part of the chest. Our men stood erect behind the large trees, and exposed themselves but very little either in loading or firing Major Pardee and Colonel Crane were with the men on the hills and told them not to shoot a gun unless they could see an enemy, and to take fair aim. The boys, after a few shots, were as calm as if they had been shooting at a target. They often talked to each other in this wise: "Now, Jim, do you see that rebel's head above that rock?" "Yes." "Will you try him while I am loading, and if you miss him I will give him a trial." Thus the battle on our side was conducted for five hours. There was but one of our men hit as high up on the body as the cartridge belt. He was hit in the neck and since died.

We all think our youthful commander is brave and competent, and has well sustained himself and the confidence reposed in him by his country.

Old General Marshall said to Union friends on his retreat from his fortifications, and three days before the battle, "that Garfield, the Yankee, had outwitted and outgeneraled him, and there was no use in denying it, and that he was compelled to retreat." Said he, further, "I have intercepted one of his despatches, and he knows all about the roads, hills, streams, fortifications, rifle-pits, number of my guns, their size, &c., and has them all mapped off better than we have them in our own camp; and how the confounded Yankee got the facts I can't tell."

This was all literally true. Colonel Garfield is a hard worker, a close observer, and spends much time, when others are asleep, over his maps.

We are now in Paintsville, a few miles below the battle-ground. Here we have our stores. Marshall was thirty miles from the battle-ground when last heard from, and still going in "double quick."

How Contrabands Enter the Union Camps in Kentucky, and how they are Disposed of.

A Munfordsville correspondent of the *Herald* says: In Camp Wood, from which I write, there are about five hundred blacks, who admit and represent themselves to be slaves of masters living in the part of the State occupied or threatened by the rebels. As a general thing, these men admit that they fled from their homes for fear of being transported and sold by the rebels. Many claim that their masters advised them to seek here the protection which they could no longer grant. Others say their masters are rebels, and were selling their fellow-slaves to more Southern residents, and having no disposition to go "down South," they had fled. Varied and interesting are the details which are given, and often important is the information which they bring. Their usual manner of obtaining admission to the camp, where they are met with so much indifference, is described as follows: A refugee or contraband presents himself to the outposts, who, of course, stop him and demand the pass which he has not in his possession. The slave, of course, proceeds to tell his story. It being none of the guard's business, he compels him to remain where he is until the relief guard comes around. Then he is generally taken to the headquarters of the pickets, and here made to stay until the force on duty is relieved and returns to camp. He is taken along with the force retiring from duty, and his case presented to the brigade commander for adjustment. The brigadier, having no instructions, refuses to listen to the history or complaint, and the slave falls into the hands of the guard to whom he first presented himself, and who, not being entitled to a servant nor having rations to spare, turns him over to his own captain or lieutenant, or to the officers of some other company, who, on next pay day, enter the negro's name on the pay roll as a servant, and get his rations allowed. He thus becomes glad of protection and support, and of an opportunity to make by extra duty a few spare cents, devotes himself to his duties of boot-blacking, clothes brushing, and running of errands. When he sees a fair opportunity for bettering his condition, the slave, who soon comes to understand and appreciate his peculiar *status*, exchanges his master at will. Staff and cavalry officers are particular favorites with the slaves. They enlist in their service with much satisfaction, and, when firmly established in the liking of their masters, look down with contempt upon the lesser lights that revolve about the tents of infantry officers. They make excellent grooms, and take pleasure in attending to horses.

To have excluded the slaves now in this camp would have been to put them into the hands of the rebels, who would have undoubtedly put them to work on their fortifications or sent them farther South. To admit them is not only humane to them, but justice to ourselves. When they are once in they are subject to military restriction, though not to military rule, and cannot leave at will. Becoming the private servants of officers, they are not amenable to military duty, but their temporary masters are answerable for their good conduct. When claimed by masters who are loyal, they are given up on sufficient proof of ownership, unless such masters reside within the lines of the enemy. As the slave may be capable of giving information, and as generally no reliance can be placed on his promises or oaths he is retained. But, loyal or disloyal, a master resident within our own lines finds no difficulty in reclaiming and obtaining his servants. General Buell lately delivered up a servant who ran away over ten years ago, and who had ventured, as the free servant of a cavalry officer, to come into the State. This state of contraband affairs is due, I think, to the faithful execution by General Buell, of the commands of General McClellan. There is no doubt that the results are entirely satisfactory to the most ultra pro-slavery men in the State, and only unsatisfactory to the rabid Secessionists in our midst and the equally rabid Abolitionists in yours.

It is not improbable that the representations of the slaves, as to being advised to leave home by their masters, are in the main true. While visiting the opposite side of the river, a day or two since, I came upon the headquarters of the outposts. The officer in command pointed me out a party of eight negroes who had just been brought in. He also read me a letter which they bore, and which they stated was from their master. It was directed "To any officer commanding at Munsfordsville," and stated that a party of rebels had the day previous taken all the stock and wagons on his farm, and had threatened to return and take his slaves. He had, in consequence, advised them to leave and to go to Munsfordville, where he hoped protection would be granted them. I believe they made their way into camp in the usual way.

I am told by the commissary of this division that on New Year's day he visited the town opposite, and there saw not less than 300 negroes, whose masters had taken them there for the purpose of hiring them for the ensuing year. The owners desired to hire them to officers, who could thus protect them; but it was found impossible to dispose of them at any price.

GENERAL HALLECK'S DEPARTMENT.

A Spicy Correspondence.

A correspondent of the New York *Times*, writing from the United States Gunboat Fleet, at Fort Jefferson, under date of January 18, says:

In order that your readers may form a correct estimate of the authors of the subjoined correspondence, respectively, a brief explanatory statement seems to be necessary. Marsh Miller, the commander of the rebel gunboat *Grampus*, is one of the most desperate, and, at the same time, cowardly men in Secesh. We have driven him before us at least a dozen times, and now he sends us this absurd challenge. The *Grampus* is well known to be a species of spouting-fish, and this particular one frequently runs up the Mississippi to blow, and then runs down again. We are going down the river, to-morrow, to see if his courage is up to the standing point; but we are afraid he will draw a bee-line to Columbus, as he has heretofore always done.

The public well know that Captain Porter is not one of the rose-water heroes, and he will not be expected to waste compliments on men whose treasonable and cowardly conduct he holds in supreme contempt. The following is a verbatim copy of his first despach to the commander of the *Grampus*, written after he had repeatedly driven the craven rebel down under the shelter of the land batteries at Columbus:

PORTER TO MILLER.

Come out here, you cowardly rebels, and show your gunboats. PORTER.

MILLER'S REPLY.

MARINE HEADQUARTERS, COLUMBUS, Ky., Jan. 13, 1862.

Commander PORTER, on United States Gunboat *Essex*:

SIR: The iron-clad steamer *Grampus* will meet the *Essex* at any point and time your Honor may appoint, and show you that the power is in our hands. An early reply will be agreeable to

Your obedient servant, MARSH J. MILLER, Capt Commanding C. S. I. C. steamer *Grampus*.

CAPTAIN PORTER'S REJOINDER.

UNITED STATES GUNBOAT ESSEX. WM. D. PORTER, Commanding, FORT JEFFERSON, Saturday, Jan. 18, 1862.

To the traitor Marsh Miller, commanding a rebel gunboat called the *Grampus*:

Commander Porter has already thrashed your gunboat fleet, shelled and silenced your rebel batteries at the Tod Banks; *chased your miserable and cowardly self down behind Columbus*; but, if you desire to meet the *Essex*, show yourself any morning in Prenlys' Bend, and you shall then meet with a traitor's fate—if you have the courage to stand.

God and our country; "Rebels offend both." PORTER.

Our flag-ship, the *Benton*, has been condemned. Her machinery does not work satisfactorily, but Captain Porter thinks she is fast enough for our purpose. He says we don't contemplate *running*, and for this reason he would rather have them all slow, so that if they get into a tight place they will be obliged to fight their way out. Captain P. only believes in running when the enemy lead the way. SIGNAL.

Movements of the Rebel Price.

[Correspondence of the Chicago Journal.]

ROLLA, Mo., January 20, 1862.

Things at Rolla begin to look like war, decidedly. About 6,000 troops have moved from that post, beside the 3,000 cavalry that had previously gone, and several more regiments have had orders to be ready, so as to march at a very early day, probably next week at the furthest. Among those who will go, the Thirteenth Illinois and Fourth Iowa will have a prominent place; and to the Thirteenth Illinois rough campaigning will not be news, for they have already had some little experience, but are not as well pleased to go that way again, for they somehow had strong hopes of being ordered to service down the river, as that looked more like coming directly at the enemy, and striking more directly at the heart of rebellion. But perhaps as much real progress will be made by striking a telling blow here in Missouri as would be the case if we went to Kentucky, and we will not seem to doubt the strength of their army by hinting that they have any need of our help.

We have heard from Price's army almost every day from gentlemen well known here in Rolla, who have been living in Springfield until now. Yesterday a sergeant of the regular army, and who has remained in Springfield, having been wounded at the battle of Wilson's creek, came to our office and told us many things of interest about Price and his arrangements; and to-day another, whose name I do not feel at liberty to use, gave much more valuable information. These last accounts agree that Price has a very considerable effective force, and that he fully intends to give us battle this time, and has even chosen his ground about seven or eight miles on this side of Springfield. The ground is well covered with bushes and woods. He is said now to have an effective force of 20,000 to 25,000, with plenty of artillery and some excellent gunners. If all this is true. he must have produced a very powerful effect by his late speeches. He has lately been stumping the vicinity of Springfield for the purpose of raising recruits; and it is stated by men who have heard him, that he appealed to the audience with tears to take up arms to save Missouri; that if he was obliged to leave the State now it would be given up to Black Republican rule, for he would never come back to try and save it. But I cannot credit the story that Price has over half the effective force that these last statements figure up, or that he intends to give battle at all, unless he can, as usual, be sure of a great advantage.

Great numbers of the inhabitants of Southern and Southwestern Missouri are coming to Rolla to get salt to use in salting their meat, and as the rebels are mixed up with them all through it is very important to keep it out of their hands, and as they have no source from which to draw it honestly they will take every means to get hold of the salt. Now, this kind of game is not well thought of here; we are willing to *pepper* them, but not to *salt* them. This makes it necessary for the provost marshal to be very strict, and nobody gets any salt except on an order from him.

A German, by the name of Martin Schnieder, came to the marshal's office last Tuesday, and stated that on the previous Sunday (12th) seven rebels, four of them having guns, came to his house, two and a half miles from Lane's Prairie, and ordered him to give up his gun and ammunition, but he told them that he would not, and seized it, it being loaded with twelve buckshot, in each barrel, and a double-barrelled one. They swore that they would have it, and were proceeding to use force, when they were warned that to proceed would be dangerous, but not heeding the decided threat of the Dutchman, the foremost man received the twelve buck-shot in the breast, and fell dead on the floor. Another then cocked his gun to shoot, when he re-

FROM GENERAL SHERMAN'S DIVISION.

From Port Royal.

[Correspondence of The War Press.]

U. S. STEAMER POCAHONTAS,
PORT ROYAL, S. C., Jan. 18, 1862.

My last letter was intended to give some points of information relative to Tybee Island, and operations in that vicinity. Since that time a New York and Connecticut regiment have been landed on the island; various and extensive reconnoissances have been made inland, developing important facts in relation to the numbers and condition of the rebel forces and fortifications about Savannah. The *Fingal* is, in all probability, blocked in effectually; it is impossible for her to pass out of Savannah river, and Warsaw Sound is carefully guarded by several efficient vessels. There is a strong rebel battery in Warsaw Sound to prevent a flank movement on Savannah, but Captain Gillis, of the *Seminole*, has exchanged shots with the battery, and is confident of being able to take it when sufficient force is given him to hold it. But a short time since, a deserter from Fort Pulaski brought the important intelligence that the *Fingal* would attempt to get out of Warsaw Sound at a certain hour that night. Captain Missroon immediately despatched the *Seminole*, *Pembina* and *Henry Andrews* to intercept her. Lights were seen, either from the *Fingal*, or shown as beacons to direct her out. A party of Tatnall's sailors, reconnoitring in a boat, approached rather too near our vessels, and were intercepted by the *Henry Andrews*. They beached the boat, and two of the crew, probably from disaffection, tarried behind and were captured. They confirmed the statement of the deserter from the fort, and thus was the first attempt of the *Fingal* to escape beautifully foiled. We returned to Port Royal to coal about the 17th ult., and when ready for sea, we were detailed to assist in the stone-fleet expedition to Charleston, of which you have long ago received full and accurate accounts. Although sixteen ships were sunk, the main channel only was obstructed. Maffitt's and the North channel will, in all probability, soon share a similar fate, John Bull to the contrary notwithstanding. The object of the expedition having been accomplished, we were ordered to blockade Stono inlet, about ten miles below Charleston.

This place, though of little notoriety, is well worthy of notice. Under favorable circumstances, twelve feet of water can be carried in the channel. It is strongly fortified and garrisoned by about fifteen hundred men, and is a point from which Charleston might be effectually attacked. Several steamers were seen daily inside the inlet, one of which, on a certain occasion, ventured farther out than was exactly prudent, and was honored with a salute from our ten-inch gun.

In answer to this, a shore battery opened on us with rifled guns, throwing their shot with great accuracy. We immediately got under weigh, and engaged the battery for about an hour, but with no definite results, as the shoalness of the water prevented us from getting within effective range. On the 10th inst., four deserters from the rebel army made their escape from the inlet in a small sailboat, and arrived safely on board our ship. They had obtained permission, during our absence for a short time, to use the boat, ostensibly for the purpose of oystering and fishing at the mouth of the inlet, but in reality of making good their escape from the fetters with which they were unwillingly bound. When their intentions were discovered, the most active exertions were made to prevent their escape; the batteries opened on them, and a large and well-manned boat was despatched in pursuit; but, having a stiff breeze in their favor, which they used to their utmost advantage, they baffled their pursuers, and escaped. They were delighted beyond measure at their success, and bring valuable information in regard to the strength of the rebel fortifications, and the numbers of their forces around Stono and Charleston. Their statements correspond with each other, and are clear and intelligent.

They state that nearly all their regiment, a large number of whom are foreigners or Northern men, would hail a similar opportunity with delight, and I have no doubt their good fortune was envied by many a sad and longing heart. They were poorly clad, and had been destitute of nearly all the comforts of life; in fact, life had ceased to be a comfort, and they resolutely determined to escape or die in the attempt. There are at Stono about four batteries, mounting in all about fourteen guns, including two of 10-inch calibre and several rifled. The place is well adapted and the works well arranged for defence, and the importance of the position has evidently been appreciated.

We are now at Port Royal coaling and getting our new mainmast, the old one having been shot through in the engagement at Hilton Head.

We will shortly reappear on the blockade, and may in a short time accumulate sufficient items of interest for another letter.

Reported Abandonment of Fort Pulaski.

A correspondent of the *Tribune*, writing from Hilton Head, under date of January 20, says:

A report just comes that Fort Pulaski has been abandoned by the rebels. Prudence was considered, on their part, the better part of valor. It was only a question of a short time, as the fort was thoroughly invested, and would have been taken in a few days.

A movement will soon be made in another direction, and you will hear enough to satisfy all croakers, so far at least as this (Sherman's) expedition is concerned.

The Emancipated Slaves at Port Royal

The Hilton Head correspondent of the *Advocate and Journal* gives the following description of the manner in which the "contrabands" at Port Royal celebrated Christmas Eve:

Christmas Eve was celebrated by the colored people at Gen. Drayton's plantation. About 11½ o'clock a bell was rung, and precisely at 12 a pine fire was kindled in front of the cabin where the meeting was to be held. They called the festival a serenade to Jesus. One of the leaders, of which there were three, was dressed in a red coat with brass buttons, wearing white gloves. The females wore turbans made of cotton handkerchiefs. All ages were represented, from the child of one year to the old man of ninety.

After singing for some time, a prayer meeting was held. The prayers were fervent and powerful, and when an allusion would be made to the soldiers who had come from their distant homes in the North country to "help and save de poor slave, and, like Jesus, bring dem good tidings of great joy," a shout went up that sent its notes on the still night air to the distant pickets in the surrounding pines. When asked, as they could not read, how they could quote the Scriptures, they replied: "We have ears, massa, and when de preacher gives out his texts, den we remembers and says dem over and over till we never forgets dem; dat's de way, massa, we poor people learns de word of God."

The next exercise consisted of speaking and singing at intervals While one was speaking, another would take a blazing pine torch from the fire and hold it up, so that all might see the speaker. At 2 o'clock a recess was had, and all were invited to partake of coffee, which luxury they can now purchase without any difficulty, as they have plenty of money, obtained of the soldiers for vegetables and poultry.

The first exercise consisted in singing hymns and spiritual songs, among which were those beginning, "Salvation! O the joyful sound;" "The voice of free grace;" "Come, humble sinner, in whose breast;" "O poor sinner! can't stand de fire, can't stand de fire in dat great day;" and a Christmas song containing a medley of everything that the fruitful mind of the leader could suggest, with the refrain, "We'll wait till Jesus comes." One of the leaders lined the hymns, and though none of them could read, it was remarkable with what correctness they gave the words. Their Scripture quotations were also correct and appropriate, not only having the exact words, but naming the chapter and verse where they could be found.

After this came what they called the shouting exercise. It was introduced by the beating of time by three or four with the feet. Soon the whole company formed into a circle, and commenced jumping and singing to the time and tune of

"Say, brothers, will you meet me,
Say, brothers, will you meet me,
Say, brothers, will you meet me,
On Canaan's happy shore."

This was continued until the most fertile imagination was exhausted, embracing an invitation to sisters, soldiers, preachers, &c., to meet them on Canaan's happy shore.

Never did these poor slaves celebrate a Christmas eve under such circumstances before. Whatever may be their future, they are now, "to all intents, purposes, and constructions whatever," free; that they may "choose it rather" is beyond question most certain. As they have not forsaken their masters, but, on the contrary, their masters have forsaken them, all must agree that they are not only entitled to their freedom, but to the produce of their labor; and we opine that no maintenance of the original status of the Government will ever be effectual in reducing them to slavery.

Jan. 4.—The negroes have proved all along our friends. They have been our guides, our spies, our means of information, and have done not a little toward adding luxuries to the fare of the camp. The African is naturally imaginative and an exaggerator. To Sambo a regiment is "tousands ob dem," and a few guns grow marvellously numerous as his tale is oftener told. But, due allowance being made—with some of the most intelligent and observing very little is necessary—the negroes can be, and have been, made a great help to us in our movements.

I am told that one of our most prominent officers has frequently declared that he has relied much on the information brought by our dark-skinned friend, and has not found it at fault with ascertained facts. In this particular expedition to Port Royal Ferry, they saved us, by their warning statements, from an ambush concocted by the rebels, and, besides this, gave other information in regard to the character of the country, the routes, the movements of the enemy, their force, their intentions, which ought to make every officer and soldier grateful to them as useful and reliable friends, for by means of it many lives were saved, and greater precision and boldness were secured to our movements.

I assure you, it is much for an army in a hostile country to have the help of the strong arms and shrewd observation of a large class of the population. While white men have fled before us like foxes, only taking breath to curse and malign us, the black men have staid to be our friends. Surely these poor fellows have earned, in their services to the Union, the right to their freedom. They—the house servants, particularly—have heard their masters' dinner talk, and their apparently dull ears have been quick to catch details of intended movements. So from them, coming with bundle in hand to our lines, we can learn the spirit of the rebel people as well as their devices against us. Surely, we ought to receive them with kindness, and reward their friendship.

The Cotton Gathering at Port Royal.

Col. Reynolds, the Government agent at Port Royal to superintend the gathering, ginning, and transportation of cotton on the sea islands, arrived at Washington on Saturday, and had a long interview with the Secretary of the Treasury. He has already secured more than $1,000,000 worth of cotton. The two or three thousand negroes just freed are industrious and orderly, and do their work well and cheerfully They need clothing and medical attendance. He desires to take back with him an ample supply of the former, and several physicians, who shall devote themselves to these interesting workmen.

Affairs in Savannah, New Orleans, and Columbus.

A Cairo correspondent of the Cincinnati *Gazette*, in a letter dated January 20, says:

A gentleman connected with a well-known leather firm of Boston, arrived here last Friday evening, direct from New Orleans. He went down in the latter part of October, and has since that time till within the last ten days, been in Savannah and New Orleans, endeavoring to sell or in some way realize upon some Southern property. He is a shrewd, intelligent business man, and his accounts of matters in the South differ so essentially in some particulars, from the most pleasing stories we have hitherto had, that it may be well to occupy some space with them.

Militia Called Out in North Carolina.

The Charlotte (N. C.) *Democrat*, of the 21st inst., says: "In anticipation of the invasion of North Carolina, it is contemplated to call out the militia in several of the eastern counties. The call has not yet been made, but the Raleigh *Journal* says that it will embrace thirty-three counties.

"P. S.—We learn that the military have been ordered out since the arrival of the Yankee Burnside Expedition at Hatteras, and it appears from the Raleigh *Register*, of Saturday, that a draft has been made in Wake county. The *Register* says there is quite an excitement there in regard to a draft, which has been made for one-third of the enrolled militia. Substitutes, we expect, will be in demand.

The Rebels Fly the Black Flag.

"Whatever may be said of the truth or the falsity of the report that after the capture of Port Royal the rebels hoisted the black flag at Charleston, their brethren at Pensacola, either imitating their diabolical example, or carrying out the piratical suggestion, actually display a flag with death's head and cross-bones wrought in white on a red ground, over what is probably one of their encampments, in the woods in the rear of and between Barancas and the lighthouse. There is no mistake about this, for I saw it with the aid of a powerful telescope belonging to one of our party. 'Death, and no quarter,' is therefore their motto."

FROM THE SOUTH.

The Defeat in Kentucky Admitted—The Burnside Expedition.

BALTIMORE, Jan. 27.—The Richmond *Dispatch* of Friday says that the rebels are much perplexed at the defeat in Kentucky.

The *Dispatch* says: "We regret to state that the report of the Federal victory in Kentucky, conveyed to us on Wednesday night from Northern sources, is more than confirmed by intelligence received at the War Department.

"It appears that our defeat was more decisive than even the Northern accounts had led us to believe. The editor says that this disaster in Eastern Kentucky, and the apprehension it has excited for the safety of our connection with the Southwest, through Virginia and Tennessee, and the East Tennessee and Virginia Railroad, and the possible interruption of our intercourse with the South Virginia, Wilmington, and Weldon Railroad by the Burnside expedition, directs attention to the vital importance of completing the connection between the Richmond, Danville, and North Carolina Railroads."

AUGUSTA, Ga., Jan. 23.—A private letter received from Charleston, this morning, says five stone vessels were sunk in the channel yesterday

The Savannah *Republican*, of this morning, says the statement that the Federal vessels had gone up Broad river is incorrect.

The War and Blockade Prices Among the Rebels.

An interesting private letter from an intelligent subject of King Jeff Davis states that a great Union reaction is quietly at work all over Secessia, and that the "awful war prices" of everything down there, except beef and bread, are contributing powerfully to dissipate the delusions of a Southern millennium in a Southern confederacy. The writer in question gives the following specimens as the average prices of certain indispensable articles throughout the rebellious South:

Quinine, per ounce. $10.
Opium. per ounce, $3.
Gunpowder, per pound, $3.
Common boots, per pair, $16.

At this rate, with the fall of a single one of the main army props of this rebellion, the whole fabric will come to the ground in a mass of ruins. The skies have cleared up; the ground is hardening. A few days more of such weather will usher in a succession of events that will electrify every loyal heart throughout the Union. This rebellion is bound to come down soon in a general collapse.

Statement of a Refugee from Richmond—The Fears and Troubles of the Secessionists—The Union Sentiment in North Carolina.

A Baltimore correspondent of the *Herald* says that a gentleman arrived there on the 24th inst., from the South, escaping across the Potomac near Port Tobacco, which is in one of the lower counties of this State. He was in Richmond on the 19th, and represents affairs in that city as in a miserable condition. The soldiers rove about that city committing depredations of all kinds against the citizens and their property, becoming intoxicated and doing as they feel disposed. He states that a deep gloom hung over that city when the announcement was made public of the death of ex-President Tyler. Flags hung throughout the city at half-mast, and many public buildings, as well as private ones, were draped, in mourning. In fact, gloom and despondency encircled that doomed city. I learn, too, that only some 5,000 soldiers garrison Richmond, which is only used as a school of instruction, preparing recruits for active service.

General Magruder still commands at Yorktown. Himself and troops much fear an attack from General Wool. It is true that he had applied to Jeff Davis for authority to burn Yorktown, in case he was attacked and unable to hold his position, which had been granted. Magruder was intoxicated nearly all the time, and the men under him complain bitterly of their treatment. My informant states that a few weeks since he saw General Magruder review his command, and the men made a handsome appearance and seemed very proficient in drill. He spoke to them on that occasion, assuring them that they should soon meet the Yankees, and have occasion to achieve a brilliant victory; but, up to the time my informant left, his promise had not been fulfilled.

Much fear and discontent existed throughout the South, in view of an anticipated attack by the Burnside expedition. Its destination was unknown, but many surmises were expressed, most of them taking for granted that Newbern, N C., was the locality. Two regiments, which were withdrawn from the army of the Potomac, had been sent to the North Carolina coast, and passed through Richmond on last Sunday, the 19th, for that point. Newbern had been fortified, presenting, as was represented in Richmond, a formidable appearance, and was garrisoned by about two thousand troops, and was believed to be strong enough to oppose the expedition. Great excitement prevailed throughout the Old North State, the rebels being low-spirited and dejected at affairs as they presented themselves, and those who were suspected of loyalty to the Union Government were elated at the prospect of a speedy release from tyranny and oppression. Many Union men still remain in that State, although they are quiet, and, when occasion offers, they will, as my informant says, fight gallantly for the Union.

The British steamship *Gladiator*, from a Cuban port, had arrived in a Floridian port, bringing a cargo valued, as was estimated, at two millions of dollars. She brought many valuable kinds of medicines, which were needed in the South, as well as a large quantity of cannon, and improved firearms. Her arrival was hailed with joy, and heralded throughout the South as another proof of the inefficiency of the blockade.

Several incendiary fires had occurred in Richmond and Norfolk, which were attributed to Yankee spies; and, again, many believed and said they were produced by the slaves, many of whom, it was whispered, desired the success of the Union forces. Norfolk was being put in a high state of defence, for an attack in any quarter. Guns continued to be mounted, blocks being used for that purpose. General Huger still maintained command in Norfolk, and was using every exertion to render that city able to hold out against any number of men which might be brought against it. The people seemed to place confidence in him, knowing, as they said, his ability as an officer and soldier. He was very popular.

General Beauregard and Ben McCulloch were in Richmond on Sunday. It was rumored that McCulloch was to be court-martialed, at the instance of General Price, for going into winter quarters in Arkansas, and refusing to reinforce him on the eve of a battle in Missouri.

There have been many deaths in the rebel army lately from typhoid fever, which disease prevailed to a fearful extent on the Potomac. Five or six buildings in Richmond have been converted into hospitals, and were crowded with patients. At Winchester, the same state of sickness existed In fact, the mortality of the rebel army was fearfully great.

In reference to the resignation of the rebel leader, Pillow, the *Enquirer* states:

General Pillow's resignation is reported to have been caused by disagreement between him and General Polk as to the proper policy for conducting operations.

A Word About Floyd.

In a letter from Bowling Green, published in the Richmond *Dispatch*, we find the following notice of the Prince of Thieves:,

"Having just gotten here, I shall content myself with a reference to the Virginia troops under Gen. Floyd. His brigade is encamped about three miles west of Bowling Green, and seems ready to measure swords with the foe. Although this gallant command has performed much arduous service, its sanitary condition is good, and the General deserves the thanks of the country for his daring campaign in Western Virginia. The theatre of his operations there was so beset with difficulties, both moral and physical, that he was denied a fair field against the enemy, and it was but an act of justice on the part of Government to send him to an arena where those incumbrances would not be encountered. The Fifty-sixth Virginia Regiment has been assigned for the present to his command, and it is quite probable that this arrangement will be permanent. Its encampment is situated three hundred yards from the General's headquarters, and presents a military and comfortable appearance."

Our Prisoners at Richmond.

Corporal Merrill, of the New York Twenty-seventh regiment, recently released from Richmond, is engaged in writing some interesting sketches of his captivity, for the Rochester *Express*. We copy the following paragraphs:

The Surgeon.

The head surgeon of the establishment was Dr. Peachy, of Richmond. He had a numerous corps of assistants, consisting principally of medical students, who had gladly availed themselves of the opportunity to engage at once in an extensive, if not a successful practice. Dr. Peachy himself is an amiable, kind-hearted gentleman, whose sympathies seemed deeply enlisted in behalf of his unfortunate patients, and was untiring in his professional attentions.

Sisters of Charity.

The Sisters of Charity, of Richmond, had volunteered their services in behalf of the wounded, and many a poor fellow would gladly testify to their kind and unremitting attention.

Visitors and Nurses.

Hardly were the prisoners bestowed in hospital quarters before the place literally swarmed with visitors. The greater portion of them were ladies, who brought us dainties of every description, and in some instances articles of underclothing, which were greatly needed. It is undoubtedly the fact that the benevolence of many of these ladies was prompted by feelings of loyalty to the Federal Government, which in no other way could find a practical expression.

Undoubted Unionism.

Among them was at least one, a lady of the highest social and political connections in Richmond, whose name (which I would gladly publish) I am induced from prudential motives to withhold. On the day of our arrival she visited the hospital, attended by a female companion and a negro servant, bearing baskets generously laden with luxuries of every kind. Her pockets also, were crammed with plug tobacco and cakes of Castile soap, which she clandestinely distributed among the patients. To her kindness and ingenuity I was indebted for the secret conveyance of the first letter which I was enabled to write, and also the first, as I was afterward informed, which left Richmond from the prisoners taken at Bull Run.

The anxiety of this kind lady to more fully relieve the distresses of the wounded prisoners finally overcame her discretion, and her work of benevolence was stopped by a formal investigation. It was argued by the hospital authorities that the Confederate wounded were more properly the subjects for the exercise of Southern benevolence, and that the extravagant charities bestowed upon the "Yankees" were evidence of a "Union" sentiment that should not be tolerated.

The lady in question, as well as others, equally generous, were grossly assailed by the Richmond press, and were afterwards prohibited from administering to our comfort, and finally were refused admission to the hospital. In this connection, I may state that several of our lady visitors informed me that they belonged in the North, but were compelled to remain in Richmond. One lady whose acquaintance I made in the hospital informed me that the stars and stripes were concealed in her house, and she only waited a favorable opportunity to fling them to the breeze!

A Confederate Fraud.

It will be remembered that in Norfolk an order was issued asking all "alien enemies" who desire to return North to report themselves at a given time to the Confederate authorities, and they would be then sent under a flag of truce to Fortress Monroe. As a result, a large number who had succeeded in evading suspicion presented themselves at the place indicated, where their names were registered. But instead of being sent to Fortress Monroe, they were arrested and sent to Richmond. Here, of course, they were subjected to a system of *espionage* established by King Jeff to promote the safety of his Confederate despotism.

Amputation.

The amputating room was in the centre of the building, within easy call of any part of the hospital, and the frightful cries of the unfortunate subjects, while undergoing surgical operations, added a tenfold torture to the pangs of those who were in waiting. Upon the average, as the physicians estimated, but one in ten survived their amputations Consequently, when one of our number was removed to the "amputating table," we felt that we looked upon him for the last time. These operations frequently lasted from one to two hours, the patient being under the influence of chloroform and whisky. Frequently the subject survived several days, but in great suffering.

Mr. Merrill, after relating several cases of surgery, of a very distressing nature, thus describes one of a different sort:

A Bogus Sufferer.

A young man was borne into the hospital who represented that he had seven bullets in his body. His suffering had excited much sympathy at Manassas, and he had to be carried to the cars on a litter. His groans drew tears from even the Confederate guards, and every one who approached him expressed the opinion that it was the most shocking case that had been found. He was handled with exceeding carefulness and placed upon a cot, not, however, without extorting the most terrible groans. Dr. Peachy approached him and inquired as to the nature of his wounds. "Seven bullets," was the response. "But where are they?" continued the Doctor. "One of them went in my ear, and I feel it in my head," was the reply. "But you can't find it, and there's no use of trying"

As to the locality of the other wounds, he professed ignorance, with the exception of one, which he said had shattered his foot. The foot was examined, and the heel of it was found to be slightly contused. Finally, he confessed that this was the extent of his injuries. He had feared that unless dreadfully wounded he would be roughly treated, if not put to death, and had accordingly determined to resort to Yankee tricks. It was highly successful. He was named "Seven Bullets," and is known by no other title among his prison associates to this day.

We find the following in the Southern papers:

General Beauregard to Command at Columbus.

To-day's Richmond *Dispatch* has reliable authority for making the statement that General Beauregard takes command of the army at Columbus, and General Gustavus W. Smith succeeds him in the position he has so long and acceptably occupied. At Columbus, we understand, he is subordinate to no one except General A. Sydney Johnston. This change goes into effect without delay.

Reported Destruction of the Green River Bridge.

NASHVILLE, Jan. 27.—Reports from Bowling Green confirm the washing away of the pontoons and the newly constructed portion of the Green River bridge.

The Death of Zollicoffer.

NEW ORLEANS, Jan. 25.—A large meeting was held at the St. Charles Hotel, last night, to express regret at the death of Gen. Zollicoffer, the distinguished statesman and soldier.

Destructive Fire at New Orleans.

NEW ORLEANS, Jan. 25.—A destructive fire occurred this morning, destroying two stores on Magazine street, occupied by C. C. Gaines & Co. and H. H. Hansell. Loss $150,000. The insurance does not exceed $20,000.

The Rebel Steamer Calhoun Abandoned and Burned.

AUGUSTA, Jan. 25.—The Charleston *Courier* of this morning says that information has been received that the Confederate steamer *Calhoun*, on her way from Havana, with a large and valuable cargo, was chased by a Lincoln cruiser, and abandoned and burned.

The Capture of Cedar Keys—The Town and Five Schooners Burned.

A despatch from Augusta says that the Savannah *News* confirms the reported capture of Cedar Keys. The Federals burned the wharves and five schooners in port; also, fifty bales of cotton, and one hundred and fifty barrels of turpentine.

Enlisting for the War.

The Richmond *Dispatch* has heard that in Wayne county, North Carolina, where it was proposed to draft, the militia to a man instantly volunteered for the war This unexpected response was so universal that contentions resulted upon the question of remaining at home; and those upon whom the lot fell were loud in their expressions of disappointment.

Letter from Hon. Joseph Holt on the Appointment of Secretary of War.

In a letter from Hon. Joseph Holt to Lieutenant Governor Stanton, he uses the following enthusiastic language respecting the appointment of Hon. Edwin M. Stanton as Secretary of War, viz:

ST LOUIS, Jan. 16, 1862.— * * The selection of the Hon. Edwin M. Stanton as Secretary of War has occasioned me unalloyed gratification. It is an immense stride in the direction of the suppression of the rebellion. So far as I can gather the popular sentiment, there is everywhere rejoicing over the appointment; but that rejoicing would be far greater did the people know, as I do, the courage, the loyalty, and the genius of the new Secretary, as displayed in the intensely tragic struggles that marked the closing days of the last Administration. He is a great man intellectually and morally—a patriot of the true Roman stamp, who will grapple with treason as the lion grapples with his prey. We may rest well assured that all that man can do, will in his present position be done to deliver our poor, bleeding country from the bayonets of traitors now lifted against its bosom.

Sincerely yours, J. HOLT.
Hon. B. Stanton, Columbus.

THE AMOUNT EXPENDED.—The Committee on the Relief of the Families of Volunteers paid out during the last week the sum of $13.881.57. During the same period, $3,980.72 was paid out by the Committee on the Safety and Defence of th City.

FROM GEN. HUNTER'S DIVISION.

The Battles Between the Loyal Indians and the Rebels.

A correspondent of the Cincinnati *Gazette*, writing from Fort Leavenworth, under date of January 15, says:

The news from the Indian country is of great interest. On the arrival home of the Indian delegation from Washington, they represented the magnitude of the Federal forces and their vast resources for carrying on the war, to the several tribes, who at once collected a large force and declared themselves in behalf of the Union. This Indian army, numbering nearly four thousand men, was placed under the command of Ho pothe-yo-hola, an aged Creek chieftain who fought under Jackson in the war of 1812, and is at present well known to the national officers. The principal chiefs under him were Yusten-rick-co-chokme, Pascofar, Cho-fo-lop-haigo, Ah-ha-luck, Yuste-migo, and Sua-muckee-micco—mostly of the Seminoles.

This force, armed with common hunting rifles and bows and arrows, and stationed on the Verdigris river, near Coody's Bluffs, was attacked, on Christmas day, by Ben McCullogh's Texan Rangers and a large force of rebel Indians, and, after a desperate conflict, was defeated. Two hundred of the Cherokees stood their ground until every man but one was killed. The Creeks fled before the desperate charge of the Rangers. The Seminoles took advantage of the ground, and acquitted themselves in a manner worthy of the highest praise.

One incident of this battle for freedom we would fain notice, as the historian may fail to chronicle it: to wit, the heroic conduct of Ho-pothe-yo-ho-la, the silver-haired chieftain in command, who, having been driven from his first position by an irresistible charge of the enemy, sought a second one, and declared his intention of dying rather than retreat further; and he was only prevented from carrying out this declaration by being seized by two of his warriors and carried off the field, whilst a dauntless band of his braves covered his retreat by opposing the pursuing foe in the most unflinching and fearless manner. Three hundred Cherokees (commanded by John Ross) were stationed between the mouths of the Verdigris and Grand rivers. The latest intelligence from that quarter is that they were surrounded by the rebels, and it is supposed they have been entirely cut to pieces ere now.

The result of the war in the Indian Territory has proved very destructive to the loyal tribes, who have been compelled to leave their towns to the mercy of an unsparing foe. It is the belief of the principal chiefs that they would have been able to have stood their ground had they not been destitute of ammunition. General Hunter had ordered 4,500 pounds of ammunition to be loaded into wagons, on yesterday, while Mr. Johnson, agent for the Delawares, secured the services of twenty-five warriors to serve as an escort, and the writer was to accompany the expedition; but before the arrival of the time appointed for our departure, intelligence was received of the total rout of the loyal tribes, and their arrival in Southern Kansas, where some thirteen thousand men, women, and children, are now awaiting assistance from the Government—they being destitute, having to leave their homes in such haste as to prevent them from making the necessary preparation for their comfort. And when we consider that these hapless mortals were, in their destitute condition, forced to travel for eight days through an uninhabited country, we may have a faint realization of the amount of suffering which they must have endured. This news was received on yesterday evening, and on this morning General Hunter despatched sixteen wagons, ladened with ammunition, flour and bacon, to the relief of the reported sufferers. E. H. Corruth, the celebrated mediator between the Government and the Indians, will, by order of General Hunter, start to Southern Kansas on to-morrow, for the purpose of taking the census of all the tribes represented, and at the same time will organize the warriors into regiments, which will at once apply for acceptance into the Government service, and will, no doubt, prove efficient auxiliaries, as Mr. Corruth, who has just arrived from their headquarters, reports them filled with revenge, and desirous of at once being led against an enemy who vanquished them, because destitute of the necessary munitions to enable them to make a successful resistance.

THE DEFENCES AT COLUMBUS.

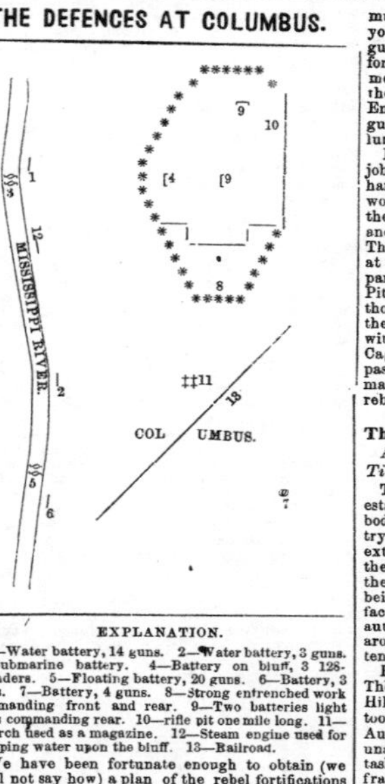

EXPLANATION.

1—Water battery, 14 guns. 2—Water battery, 3 guns. 3—Submarine battery. 4—Battery on bluff, 3 128-pounders. 5—Floating battery, 20 guns. 6—Battery, 3 guns. 7—Battery, 4 guns. 8—Strong entrenched work commanding front and rear. 9—Two batteries light guns commanding rear. 10—rifle pit one mile long. 11—Church used as a magazine. 12—Steam engine used for pumping water upon the bluff. 13—Railroad.

We have been fortunate enough to obtain (we shall not say how) a plan of the rebel fortifications at Columbus The sketch was drawn from memory by one who has been there, and knows all about the place. Of course, it is not drawn with the precision which a practiced engineer would give, but it is sufficiently accurate to present an intelligible idea of the place and its surroundings. Many of our readers have been at Columbus, and will recognize the features at a glance.

Columbus is situated on a bluff, just below a bend of the Mississippi river. The bluff is of limestone, and had an agency in turning the river at this point. It is about seventy-five feet high, and is flanked by a narrow strip of land at its base, overflowed at times by high water. The village is situated on its southern slope. The country in the rear has been heavily timbered, but the rebels have made good use of their axes, and hundreds of acres are leveled to the ground, presenting an abboth as formidable to our troops as that around Washington to the rebels under Beauregard and Johnston. The railroad enters the town through an excavation about fifteen feet deep With this general view of the surrounding topographic features, our readers will readily understand the accompanying sketch.

Commencing up stream, we find at figure 1 a fourteen-gun battery under the bluff When our informant saw it, it was simply a breastwork, but it is now reported that the rebels are casemating it with the timber which was cut out at O'Neil's mill, which was burned by Gen. Paige on the return of the expedition last week.

In the river in front of the battery is a submarine battery or torpedo. Continuing on, we come to a stationary steam engine, (12), used to pump water upon the bluff for the use of the troops Still further along, near the point where the bluff retreats from the river, is a three-gun battery, (2). The Rev. Gen. arch-rebel Bishop Polk's headquarters are there. Continuing on to the lower end of the town, we come to a three-gun battery on shore, near the railroad depot; also, a floating battery of twenty guns, the wharf boats, and some old flats having been used for the purpose.

Back of the depot, overlooking the town, is a circular work of eight guns (7) commanding the river, also the approaches to the town from the rear.

Ascending now the bluff (at figure 4) there is a work containing three guns, which carry projectiles weighing 128 pounds each This battery has a range of the river for four miles.

Immediately south of this there is a strong entrenched work with a breastwork at the edge of the bluff, and a ditch and breastwork at the rear, thus commanding both front and rear. There are also (at 9, 9) two works mounting sixteen guns, designed solely to protect the rear. Still farther towards the rear is a long rifle-pit as breastwork, extending from the edge of the bluff on the north to the railroad excavation on the south An idea of the area may be had when it is considered that this pit is more than a mile long

A church (11) is used for a magazine. Last week Commodore Foote made a reconnoissance of the place with two of his gunboats, whereupon the ammunition was speedily removed further South, beyond the reach of his shells. There are about 80 guns in all, exclusive of field artillery. The rebel force is variously estimated at from 25,000 to 40,000 men, probably 30,000 is a fair estimate. Some of the regiments are well armed with Springfield and Enfield muskets, while some of them have only shotguns. There are not many sixty-days men in Columbus, but mainly troops enlisted for the war.

It will be seen by this sketch that it is no trifling job which Com. Foote and Gen. Grant have on their hands. If an attack is made, there will be serious work. Com. Foote is extremely anxious to obtain the mortars which have been promised him again and again, but none of them have been received. The thirty-eight boats prepared for them are lying at the levee in Cairo. Why cannot the Naval Department send a portion of those now casting at Pittsburg to Cairo? Let it be remembered that those batteries on the bluff will be entirely out of the reach of our gunboats in close action. But with those thirty-eight mortars, Com. Foote and Capt Constable would produce a stampede surpassing that from Hilton Head. Without them, it may be feared that an attack will not dislodge the rebels from their strong position.

The Rebel Fortifications at Centreville.

A Washington correspondent of the Chicago *Times* says:

The headquarters of General Beauregard are established at Centreville, around which the main body of the army is entrenched The whole country, between the Potomac and Occoquan rivers, is extremely hilly; and, while this renders difficult the operations of large bodies of troops, it renders the country easy of defence. General Beauregard, being a scientific officer, took advantage of this fact, and employed the months of the summer and autumn, from August to November, in erecting around Centreville twenty-six forts, which, in extent and strength, rival those southwest of this city.

How could he do this without its being known? The answer is contained in a single word: Munson's Hill. By throwing forward a few regiments, he took possession of Munson's Hill about the end of August, which General McClellan at that time was unable to hold, he having but just commenced the task of *making soldiers* out of the disorganized fragment of the Bull Run rout By making a show of fortifying that hill, he diverted attention from what he was really doing. But there was one man in Washington, and probably only one, who penetrated his designs. General McClellan knew that he was fortifying at Centreville. But to what extent even he was ignorant until apprised by a deserter long after the evacuation of Munson's Hill.

Why has Beauregard thus fortified Centreville? When the Union army of the Potomac moves the reason will become manifest. Centreville is the key of Manassas Junction, and Manassas Junction is the door to Richmond, and, indeed, it may be said, to the whole of Virginia. Examine a military map of the country; trace the roads, the streams, the ranges of hills, and it will be seen that a Union army entering by any other door will be sure to be surrounded, cut off from their base of operations, and destroyed. If the strong lines of Manassas can be forced, and the communication be kept open with this city, a Union army can advance southward, conquering as it advances, and laying the whole country under contribution. Hence the importance of fortifying Centreville.

These twenty-six forts are so situated as to command every possible approach to Centreville, from Arcola, on the Gum Spring road, on the left, to the Occoquan river, two miles below Union Mills, on the right. On the morning of the battle of Bull Run, the Confederate army was posted on the right bank of that stream, from the Stone Bridge to Union Mills. The reconnoissances made by Gen. McDowell on the day previous enabled him to cross a large portion of his force (Gen. Hunter's column) at Sudley's Ford, a mile and a quarter above the Stone Bridge. This disarranged Beauregard's whole plan of battle, and came near defeating him. The hardest fighting of the day, and till 4 o'clock in the afternoon, took place west of Sudley's Ford, and between it and the Warrenton turnpike. The two forts, then, between Arcola and Sudley's Ford, are designed to prevent the ford from being used by the Union troops. The largest and strongest forts are called Fort Beauregard, Fort Davis, and Fort Slidell. They all command roads that must be taken in order to approach Centreville All of the twenty-six forts are mounted with suitable artillery. It was to celebrate the completion of these works that the great review of 70,000 Confederate troops took place early in December, at which Jeff Davis was present, and at which the "battle-flags" were presented to each regiment.

Hon. John Tyler.

We copy the following from Richmond papers of the 20th instant:

The following resolution was adopted in the Virginia Legislature on Saturday, when the announcement of the death of John Tyler was made:

Resolved, "That with the consent of his family, his remains be deposited in the Hollywood Cemetery, in the city of Richmond, near the remains of James Monroe, and that the Governor of this State be authorized to ca[illegible] a suitable monument to be erected to his memory."

Richmond Dispatch.
BY COWARDIN & HAMMERSLEY.
THE DAILY DISPATCH is served to subscribers at TWELVE CENTS PER WEEK, payable to the Carrier weekly. Price for mailing, $5 a year, or $3 for six months, in advance.
THE SEMI-WEEKLY DISPATCH is issued every TUESDAY and FRIDAY at $3, in advance.
THE WEEKLY DISPATCH is issued every FRIDAY, and mailed to subscribers at $2 per an'm.

DAILY DISPATCH.

VOL. XXI---NO 29. RICHMOND, VIRGINIA, MONDAY MORNING, FEBRUARY 3, 1862. PRICE TWO CENTS.

MONDAY MORNING.........FEB. 3, 1862.

FROM NORFOLK.

[OUR OWN CORRESPONDENT.]

The Great Burnside Armada—Its Backbone Broken—The Excitement of the North—Confederate Reconnoisance—Northern Finances—Letters from Correspondents, &c.

NORFOLK, Jan. 31, 1862.

At last we have received some news of the Burnside expedition from a Northern source, and find that it exceeds, in its chapters of disasters, the most exaggerated rumors that have been floating through our streets. The sum total of it is, that the backbone of the armada is broken, and so much damage has been done it by the long storm that reinforcements become necessary before putting the plan of the expedition into execution. Burnside has burnt his fingers in this little project; but he is still valiant, and calls as loudly for more men as King Richard did for "a horse." He has become terribly severe, and will undoubtedly, in a sheer fit of desperation, throw himself upon the North Carolina coast, in the hope of recovering the prestige lost with so many of his ships. The very full telegraphic dispatch sent you yesterday give the main portion of the Northern news, and I need not recapitulate. The most striking points are that Gen. Burnside expected to find plenty and willing pilots to conduct him through the inlet, and found none; that mention of loss of life has been so studiously avoided [illegible] missing, not reported lost, and that many of the gun-boats refused to move from Fortress Monroe—whereupon Burnside attempts to shift the responsibility of the disaster upon contractors. Those items will furnish material for considerable thought and speculation.

Some days ago, when the rumor reached the Yankees, from this city, that the Louisiana was lost, it was very generally discredited, and published in their papers as a "blamed rebel falsehood," in order to keep up the public credit as long as possible. Still there were many misgivings, and many fears that all was not right; and some went so far as to hint at disasters which the Government (*a la* Ball's Bluff) was trying to conceal. On Thursday, however, the startling news burst upon the people, and, of course, was differently received. In New York the excitement was intense. Stocks fell at once; the Bulls and Bears went to gambling furiously; brokers regarded the information as news of the sinking of a vast amount of money; shipowners saw in it new chances for speculation, and a ready sale for more old hulks; contractors saw new bargains in supplies.—But the mass of the people saw the failure of one of their dearest hopes and immense destruction of public property, and its consequent loss of life. See how differently the world looks at disaster!

We now have information from both sides. Burnside arrived at Hatteras on the 15th; some of his vessels ran ashore and were lost; others were missing; a few he got inside, where he now is endeavoring to get the remainder over the bar. Several times his fleet has been seriously annoyed by our little gunboats, although the sea was too high for them to operate with success. On Monday and Tuesday of last week two of our steamers went down Pamlico sound on a reconnoitering expedition. At about 11 o'clock, A. M., as they were nearing Hatteras, three or four Yankee steamers hove in sight. Our vessels pushed on, when the number of the enemy soon increased to twenty-one, and all joined in chasing our two gun-boats. After keeping up the chase for several hours, our vessels being faster than theirs, all dropped astern except four, and at dusk they were still in sight some miles behind. Our gunboats rejoined the fleet. Since, two or three gun-boats have been down at different times and met with the same experience. It was thought that as soon as the sea became calm there would be a fight.

But it is useless for me to speak further of this affair, as the full extracts from Northern papers, which will be sent you, gives the information at greater length than I would be able to do in my short corner of the paper. I hope, however, to go down to the sound tomorrow, and shall, possibly, glean some items of interest for those who choose to follow me in the journey.

Another important item is regarding financial affairs in Yankeedom, which grow no better as rapidly as can be imagined. A vast public debt is accumulating, with no prospect as yet of money to meet it. The probability of a paper currency has caused an increase of price in every quarter, preparatory to its certain depreciation, and thinking men are becoming seriously alarmed. There is strong opposition to the bill I spoke of in my last, to raise money by direct taxation for a series of years, and it is believed that the bill cannot pass the House, owing to the fierce denunciation of it by the Western members. If it fails, what, in the name of wonder, can be done next? What new expedient can be devised?

Since I last wrote, many letters of encouragement have been sent me by unknown persons, some of them so kindly that I beg leave to notice them, promising not to encumber your columns often with private affairs. I would inform "T. M." that I think it impossible to get the back numbers he requires; inquire at the *Dispatch* office. "Tar Forest Nymphs" wish to know if I would object to give them certain information of a personal nature? None in the world, my dear Oreades; but, then, if I tell you here, there is that sly step-dame—the public—who will hear every word. What else can I say except to express gratification at your note? "J." sends me an elegant smoking-cap—so fine indeed that it makes me quite ashamed of my poor little, dingy pipe, with its wooden bowl. I wish I knew "J.'s" address, that I might express my thanks. From "Lillian Clifford" I have a little book of pins and needles. They will prove very useful to me, for my buttons are the most obstinate in existence; they will persist in coming off at the most unwarranted time. "O.," I publish it at your desire. Here it is:

WAITING

All day long beside the window,
Gazing through the mist and rain,
Up and down the street she watches—
Watches closely—but in vain;
And with half a sigh she murmurs,
"Will he never come again?"

All day long beside the window,
In both hope and fear she sate,
And the hopes and fears commingled,
Make her whole frame palpitate—
Fill her beating heart with wonder,
Why it is he comes so late.

And the light grows dim and dimmer,
Night advances on the day,
One by one the street-lamps glimmer
Through the darkness, far away—
Then she says, "I wait no longer,"
And she slowly turns away.

Once again beside the window—
Only dark and rain she sees—
Then she turns from weary waiting,
Softly strikes the ivory keys,
Pouring out her wealth of sadness
In bewailing threnodies.

Gloomy hours of expectation!
By the gas-light's steady glare
Stands she at the parlor mirror,
Folds her dress and smoothes her hair,
Thinking when he stands before her,
If he, too, will call her fair.

But he comes not. In her chamber,
Still depressed by foolish fears,
She throws her face upon the pillow
And relieves her grief in tears,
Sadly weeping, until sleep,
Like some good angel, soft appears.

Night, with all its dreams, is over,
And the morning comes again,
Bringing news of a fierce battle,
Fought upon Manassas plain;
And she reads, with deepest anguish,
His dear name among the slain.

BOHEMIAN.

Things in Washington, Baltimore, Philadelphia, and New York—Condition of the Cities and of the People—Historical Reminiscences—Services of Norfolk Citizens.

[SPECIAL CORRESPONDENCE OF THE DISPATCH.]

NORFOLK, Jan. 31, 1862.

I have very late and reliable intelligence from the Northern cities, and from Washington and Baltimore. The New York of 1862 is far different from the swarming, hive-like, noisy, driving, dashing, thriving Empire City of 1860. You may perambulate about town now without the danger of being knocked down and run over in the hurry of affairs. Business is dull; the people complain bitterly of the continuance of the war. Real estate has fallen in some parts of the city below *zero;* hundreds of stores are closed; fires occur frequently; the people are dissatisfied and restless, and the low rumbling of a storm that will shake the mammoth city to its deep foundations are already heard.

Philadelphia is a slow-looking place, compared to its business-like and cheerful appearance in days of prosperity. Baltimore looks more like going ahead, but judging from the suppressed murmurs that are heard, there may soon be an eruption of the volcanic fires that are struggling for vent. Washington is a muddy place. An armed soldiery is the great feature, while the beautiful public structures of stone form a striking contrast to the modest looking private buildings.—There, the contractors, office-seekers, and all the crowd of scramblers after money, are as busy as ever; but Washington too, presents the sad effects of the war waged by misguided fanatics and unscrupulous demagogues.

If the historic chapters relative to the present stupendous revolution, which are to be read by coming generations, shall present a truthful record of events that marked the commencement of the struggle for liberty in Virginia, some exploits in this section of our noble old State will be recorded as possessing vast importance. There are some names, too, still unwritten upon the scroll of fame, that will descend with those of the heroes of those days, far down the track of time.

There was a time here when men hesitated, waited, reasoned, while the plot was thickening for our subjugation and enslavement. That brief period unimproved, and the tramp of hostile forces would have been heard in our streets; our peaceful homes and altars would now be invaded, and the seaport of Virginia, unless its buildings had again fed the flames as in '76, would have been in the hands and at the mercy of the vandal hordes of the North.

One of the enemy's powerful war ships was so close at hand that the boatswain's whistle could be distinctly heard on shore. Her great guns pointed towards our peaceful dwellings; but her officers knew not of the determined spirit of resistance that fired the hearts of some who were ready and eager to step forth to the hazardous task of duty, just when the deep-toned mutterings from the black storm-cloud of revolt were first heard in the distance.

In the report from the office of Detail and Equipment to the Convention, by Captain Barron, there are allusions to important measures taken here relative to the magazine, &c., and the report may have been necessarily brief. A few additional particulars will not be inappropriate here.

It was decided by one or two bold and daring spirits to remove the vast quantity of powder stored in the Government magazine upon the shore, a mile below the city. And so well devised was the plan, so cautiously was it executed, so eagerly and so rapidly, and yet so quietly, was the work done, that thousands of the citizens knew nothing of the important matter until the labor was accomplished. Shall we particularize with regard to those who so bravely and so carefully toiled in behalf of their country's honor on that night, when the explosion of a single package would have been death and ruin, and revealed the plot by a wide-spread destruction?

At the beginning of active hostilities here many of our volunteer officers and men of the revenue, as well as the navy officers, most gallantly did their duty. This much should be said, too, of that valuable class of men in a seaport, the pilots.

Our esteemed fellow-citizen, Capt. Rich'd Evans and Capt. Osmond Peters, on the op-

The Potter Investigating Committee—The Yankees Overhauling Gen. Floyd—Interesting Particulars.

The committee appointed by the House of Representatives, at the extra session, to investigate the cases of disloyal clerks and other persons in the employment of the Government, have completed their report. The Washington correspondent of the New York *Post*, who seems to have been furnished with a copy of the document, writes as follows:

Charges against more than five hundred persons have been investigated; in many cases the evidence was so unsatisfactory that it was only sent to the proper authorities, to warn them against possible danger, and it has been suppressed in the report. The testimony against the clerks is of a uniform character. They are charged with uttering the most disloyal sentiments, speaking against the war, expressing sympathy for the rebels and their cause. Numerous cases are brought up and considered in the report, and it is unnecessary to quote them.

The most important case in the report is that of Lieut. Colonel Wm. Maynadier.

This officer holds the responsible post of Assistant to the Chief of Ordnance. The principal charges affecting his loyalty are—first, that he was a party to the effort, in December, 1860, of John B. Floyd, then Secretary of War, to transfer cannon to the South, under the pretense of arming fortifications at Galveston and Ship Island, which, in fact, had no existence; but, in reality, to furnish the munitions of war for the intended rebellion; and, second, that he was privy to the sale, by Floyd, of 100,000 or more muskets to A. A. Belknap, and 20,000 to other parties, in violation of law, and to the great detriment of the public service, the object being to disarm the Government and to arm its rebel enemies.

Lieutenant-Colonel Maynadier, in executing, or attempting to execute, the order of Floyd, for the transmission of 141 of the largest cannon from Pittsburg to the Gulf of Mexico, did it with the full knowledge that one of the forts was unfinished, and the other not even begun. It is scarcely less clear that Maynadier must have known or believed that the object of Floyd in giving the order was to disarm the Government, and to arm its rebel enemies. He is conceded to be one of the most intelligent men in the army, and has been in the Ordnance Department as assistant for nearly twenty years.—He speaks with evident pride of the confidence reposed in him by Jefferson Davis and Floyd, of their frequent consultations with him in preference to his superior, Col. Craig, and it is, therefore, not to be believed that he would have withheld an opinion from the Secretary of War in regard to the impropriety of sending cannon to the Gulf coast to arm fortifications which had no existence, from motives of mere modesty. He says that "his duty was obedience; not questioning." On the 17th of September following, Colonel Craig was relieved from duty as head of the Ordnance Bureau, and on the 23d Maynadier was substituted in his place. The day preceding the appointment a proposition was made to Floyd by A. A. Belknap "to purchase of the Department from one to two hundred and fifty thousand of United States flint-locks and altered percussion muskets, and to have the same delivered to me or my agents in New York city." This fact is taken from Belknap's evidence before the Military Committee of the last House of Representatives, report No. 85, which your committee have felt at liberty to use in this connection.

"As originally written," says Belknap, "the proposal was for two dollars per gun, but the words 'and fifteen cents' were interlined before the paper was presented to the War Department."

On the back of said letter is the following endorsement: "The within proposition is accepted to the extent of one hundred thousand muskets, and as many more up to the maximum number as the service will spare. Signed, J. B. Floyd, Secretary of War."

Subsequently Floyd, by a strange freak, professed to discover that the price for which the arms were sold was less than he supposed when he accepted the bid, and said that they should not be delivered for less than $2 50 per musket. Belknap leaves us to infer that the new terms were accepted, and says that "Secretary Holt refuses to give me the guns."

Lieut. Col. Maynadier speaks of this transaction as if he had been a party of Belknap, and declares that "not a single musket has been sold to Belknap at any price." According to the written reports of Col. Craig made to G. H. Lamar on the 24th day of November 1860, 5,000 to the State of Mississippi on the 4th of December, and 5,000 to the State of Louisiana, on the 15th of the same month. All these sales, then, occurred within less than a month after the removal of Colonel Craig and the appointment of Lieut. Col. Maynadier, and immediately under his eye. If he protests against the sale of more small arms.

The enemy's forces, reported by their best informed journals to be 55,000 strong, I had learned from reliable sources, on the night of the 20th, were being concentrated in and around Centreville, and along the Warrenton turnpike road, to Bull Run, near which our respective pickets were in immediate proximity. This fact, with the conviction that, after his signal discomfiture on the 18th of July, before Blackburn's Ford—the centre of my lines—he would not renew the attack in that quarter, induced me at once to look for an attempt on my left flank, resting on the Stone Bridge, which was but weakly guarded by men, as well as but slightly provided with artificial defensive appliances and artillery.

In view of these palpable military conditions, by half-past four A. M., on the 21st July, I had prepared and dispatched orders, directing the whole of the Confederate forces within the lines of Bull Run, including the brigades and regiments of Gen. Johnston, which had arrived at that time, to be held in readiness to march at a moment's notice.

At that hour the following was the disposition of our forces:

Ewell's brigade, constituted as on the 18th of July, remained in position at Union Mills Ford, its left extending along Bull Run, in the direction of McLean's Ford, and supported by Holmes's brigade, 2d Tennessee and 1st Arkansas regiments, a short distance to the rear—that is, at and near Camp Wigfall.

D. R. Jones's brigade—from Ewell's left, in front of McLean's Ford, and along the stream to Longstreet's position. It was unchanged in organization, and was supported by Early's brigade, also unchanged, placed behind a thicket of young pines, a short distance in the rear of McLean's Ford.

Longstreet's brigade held its former ground at Blackburn's Ford, from Jones's left to Bonham's right, at Mitchell's Ford, and was supported by Jackson's brigade, consisting of Colonels James L. Preston's 4th, Harper's 5th, Allen's 2d, the 27th, Lieut. Col. Echoll's, and the 33d, Cumming's Virginia regiments, 2,611 strong, which were posted behind the skirting of pines, to the rear of Blackburn's and Mitchell's Ford, and in rear of this support, was also Barksdale's 13th regiment Mississippi volunteers, which had lately arrived from Lynchburg.

THE BATTLES OF 1861.

OFFICIAL REPORTS.

THE BATTLE OF MANASSAS, July 21, 1861.

REPORT OF GEN. BEAUREGARD.

HDQ'RS 1ST CORPS ARMY OF THE POTOMAC,
MANASSAS, August 26, 1861.

General: * * * * The War Department having been informed by me, by telegraph on the 17th of July, of the movement of Gen. McDowell—Gen. Johnston was immediately ordered to form a junction of his Army Corps with mine, should the movement, in his judgment, be deemed advisable. Gen. Holmes was also directed to push forward with two regiments, a battery, and one company of cavalry.

In view of these propositions, approaching reinforcements modifying my plan of operations, so far as to determine on attacking the enemy at Centreville as soon as I should hear of the near approach of the two reinforcing columns, I sent one of my Aids, Col. Chisholm, of South Carolina, to meet and communicate my plans to Gen. Johnston, and my wish that one portion of his force should march by the way of Aldie, and take the enemy on his right flank and in reverse at Centreville. Difficulties, however, of an insuperable character in connection with means of transportation, and the marching condition of his troops, made this impracticable, and it was determined our forces should be united within the lines of Bull Run, and thence advance to the attack of the enemy.

Gen. Johnston arrived here about noon on the 20th July, and being my senior in rank, he necessarily assumed command of all the forces of the Confederate States, then concentrating at this point. Made acquainted with my plan of operations and dispositions to meet the enemy, he gave them his entire approval, and generously directed their execution under my command.

In consequence of the untoward detention, however, of some five thousand (5,000) of General Johnston's Army Corps, resulting from the inadequate and imperfect means of transportation for so many troops, at the disposition of the Manassas Gap Railroad, it became necessary, on the morning of the 21st, before daylight, to modify the plan accepted to suit the contingency of an immediate attack on our lines by the main force of the enemy, then plainly at hand.

The enemy's forces, reported by their best informed journals to be 55,000 strong, I had learned from reliable sources, on the night of the 20th, were being concentrated in and around Centreville, and along the Warrenton turnpike road, to Bull Run, near which our respective pickets were in immediate proximity. This fact, with the conviction that, after his signal discomfiture on the 18th of July, before Blackburn's Ford—the centre of my lines—he would not renew the attack in that quarter, induced me at once to look for an attempt on my left flank, resting on the Stone Bridge, which was but weakly guarded by men, as well as but slightly provided with artificial defensive appliances and artillery.

In view of these palpable military conditions, by half-past four A. M., on the 21st July, I had prepared and dispatched orders, directing the whole of the Confederate forces within the lines of Bull Run, including the brigades and regiments of Gen. Johnston, which had arrived at that time, to be held in readiness to march at a moment's notice.

At that hour the following was the disposition of our forces:

Ewell's brigade, constituted as on the 18th of July, remained in position at Union Mills Ford, its left extending along Bull Run, in the direction of McLean's Ford, and supported by Holmes's brigade, 2d Tennessee and 1st Arkansas regiments, a short distance to the rear—that is, at and near Camp Wigfall.

D. R. Jones's brigade—from Ewell's left, in front of McLean's Ford, and along the stream to Longstreet's position. It was unchanged in organization, and was supported by Early's brigade, also unchanged, placed behind a thicket of young pines, a short distance in the rear of McLean's Ford.

Longstreet's brigade held its former ground at Blackburn's Ford, from Jones's left to Bonham's right, at Mitchell's Ford, and was supported by Jackson's brigade, consisting of Colonels James L. Preston's 4th, Harper's 5th, Allen's 2d, the 27th, Lieut. Col. Echoll's, and the 33d, Cumming's Virginia regiments, 2,611 strong, which were posted behind the skirting of pines, to the rear of Blackburn's and Mitchell's Ford, and in rear of this support, was also Barksdale's 13th regiment Mississippi volunteers, which had lately arrived from Lynchburg.

Along the edge of a pine thicket, in rear of and equi-distant from McLean's and Blackburn's Fords, ready to support either position, I had also placed all of Bee's and Bartow's brigades that had arrived—namely, two companies of the 11th Mississippi, Lieut. Col Liddell; the 2d Mississippi, Col. Falkner, and the Alabama, with the 7th and 8th Georgia regiments, (Colonels Gartrell and Lieut. Col. Gardner,) in all 2,732 bayonets.

Bonham's brigade, as before, held Mitchell's Ford, its right near Longstreet's left, its left extending in the direction of Cocke's right. It was organized as at the end of the 18th of July, with Jackson's brigade, as before said, as a support.

Cocke's brigade, increased by seven companies of the 8th, Hunton's, three companies of the 49th, Smith's Virginia regiments, two companies of cavalry, and a battery under Rogers of four 6-pounders, occupied the line in front and rear of Bull Run, extending from the direction of Bonham's left, and guarding Island, Ball's and Lewis's Fords, to the right of Evans's demi-brigade, near the Stone Bridge, also under Gen. Cocke's command.

The latter held the Stone Bridge, and its left covered a farm ford about one mile above the bridge.

Stuart's cavalry, some 300 men of the army of the Shenandoah, guarded the level ground extending in rear from Bonham's left to Cocke's right.

Two companies of Radford's Cavalry were held in reserve a short distance in rear of Mitchell's Ford, his left extending in the direction of Stuart's right.

Col. Pendleton's reserve battery of eight pieces was temporarily placed in rear of Bonham's extreme left.

Major Walton's reserve battery of five guns was in position on McLean's farm, in a piece of woods in rear of Bee's right.

Hampton's Legion of six companies of infantry, six hundred strong, having arrived that morning by the cars from Richmond, was subsequently, as soon as it arrived, ordered forward to a position in immediate vicinity of the Lewis House, as a support for any troops engaged in that quarter.

The effective force of all arms of the army of the Potomac on that eventful morning, including the garrison of Camp Pickens, did not exceed 21,833, and 29 guns.

The army of the Shenandoah, ready for action on the field, may be set at 6,000 men and 20 guns.*

The brigade of Gen. Holmes mustered about 1,265 bayonets, 6 guns, and a company of cavalry about 90 strong.

Informed at 5:30 A. M., by Col. Evans, that the enemy had deployed some 1,200 men† with several pieces of artillery, in his immediate front, I at once ordered him, as also Gen. Cocke, if attacked, to maintain their position to the last extremity.

In my opinion, the most effective method of relieving that flank was by a rapid, determined attack, with my right wing and centre on the enemy's flank and rear at Centreville, with due precautions against the advance of his reserves from the direction of Washington. By such a movement, I confidently expected to achieve a complete victory for my country by 12 M.

These new dispositions were submitted to Gen. Johnston, who fully approved them, and the orders for their immediate execution were at once issued.

Brigadier-General Ewell was directed to begin the movement, to be followed and supported successively by Generals D. R. Jones, Longstreet, and Bonham respectively, supported by their several appointed reserves.

The cavalry, under Stuart and Radford, were to be held in hand, subject to future orders and ready for employment as might be required by the exigencies of the battle.

About 8.30 A. M., General Johnston and myself transferred our headquarters to a central position about half a mile in rear of Mitchell's Ford, whence we might watch the course of events.

Previously, as early as 5:30, the Federalists in front of Evans's position—Stone Bridge—had opened with a large 30-pounder Parrot rifle gun, and thirty minutes later, with a moderate, apparently tentative fire from a battery of rifle pieces, directed first in front at Evans's, and then in the direction of Cocke's position, but without drawing a return fire and discovery of our positions, chiefly because in that quarter we had nothing but eight 6-pounder pieces, which could not reach the distant enemy.

As the Federalists had advanced with an extended line of skirmishers in front of Evans, that officer promptly threw forward the two flank companies of the 4th South Carolina regiment, and one company of Wheat's Louisiana battalion, deployed as skirmishers, to cover his small front. An occasional scattering fire resulted, and thus the two armies in that quarter for more than an hour, while the main body of the enemy was marching its dubious way through the "Big Forest" to take our forces in flank and rear.

By 8.30 A. M., Colonel Evans, having become satisfied of the counterfeit character of the movement on his front, and persuaded of an attempt to turn his left flank, decided to change his position to meet the enemy, and for this purpose immediately put in motion to his left and rear six companies of Sloan's 4th South Carolina regiment, Wheat's Louisiana battalion's, five companies, and two six-pounders of Latham's battery, leaving four companies of Sloan's regiment under cover as the sole, immediate defence of the Stone Bridge, but giving information to General Cocke of his change of position and the reasons that impelled it.

Following a road leading by the Old Pittsylvania (Carter) mansion, Colonel Evans formed in line of battle some four hundred yards in rear—as he advanced—of that house, his guns to the front and in position, properly supported, to its immediate right. Finding, however, that the enemy did not appear on that road, which was a branch of one leading by Sudley's Springs Ford to Brentsville and Dumfries, he turned abruptly to the left, and, marching across the fields for three-quarters of a mile, about 9 30 A. M. took a position in line of battle; his left, Sloan's companies, resting on the main Brentsville Road, in a shallow ravine, the Louisiana battalion to the right, in advance some two hundred yards, a rectangular copse of wood separating them—one piece of his artillery, planted on an eminence some seven hundred yards to the rear of Wheat's battalion, and the other on a ridge near and in rear of Sloan's position, commanding a reach of the road just in front of the line of battle. In this order he awaited the coming of the masses of the enemy, now drawing near.

In the meantime, about 7 o'clock A. M., Jackson's brigade, with Imboden's, and five pieces of Walton's battery, had been sent to take up a position along Bull Run to guard the interval between Cocke's right and Bonham's left, with orders to support either in case of need—the character and topographical features of the ground having been shown to General Jackson by Captain D. B. Harris, of the Engineers, of this Army Corps.

So much of Bee's and Bartow's brigades, now united, as had arrived—some 2,800 muskets—had also been sent forward to the support of the position of the Stone Bridge.

The enemy beginning his detour from the turnpike, at a point nearly half-way between Stone Bridge and Centreville, had pursued a tortuous, narrow trace of a rarely used road, through a dense wood, the greater part of his way, until near the Sudley Road. A division under Colonel Hunter, of the Federal regular army, of two strong brigades, was in the advance, followed immediately by another division under Colonel Heintzelman, of three brigades and seven companies of regular cavalry and twenty-four pieces of artillery—eighteen of which were rifle guns. This column, as it crossed Bull Run, numbered over 16,000 men of all arms by their own accounts.

Burnside's brigade, which here, as at Fairfax C. H., led the advance, at about 9 45 A. M. debouched from a wood in sight of Evans's position, some 500 yards distant from Wheat's battalion.

He immediately threw forward his skirmishers in force, and they became engaged with Wheat's command and the 6-pounder gun under Lieutenant Leftwich.

The Federalists at once advanced, as they report officially, the 2d Rhode Island regiment volunteers, with its vaunted battery of six 13-pounder rifle guns. Sloan's companies were then brought into action, having been pushed forward through the woods. The enemy, soon galled and staggered by the fire, and pressed by the determined valor with which Wheat handled his battery until he was desperately wounded, hastened up three other regiments of the brigade and two Dahlgren howitzers, making in all quite 3,500 bayonets and eight pieces of artillery, opposed to less than 800 men and two 6-pounder guns.

Despite this odds, this intrepid command of but eleven weak companies maintained its front to the enemy for quite an hour, and until Gen. Bee came to their aid with his command. The heroic Bee, with a soldier's eye and recognition of the situation, had previously disposed his command with skill—Imboden's battery having been admirably placed between the two brigades under shelter behind the undulations of a hill about 150 yards north of the now famous Henry House, and very near where he subsequently fell mortally wounded, to the great misfortune of his country, but after deeds of deliberate and ever-memorable courage.

Meanwhile, the enemy had pushed forward a battalion of eight companies of regular infantry and one of their best batteries of six pieces, (four rifled,) supported by four companies of marines, to increase the desperate odds against which Evans and his men had maintained their stand with an almost matchless tenacity.

Gen. Bee, now finding Evans sorely pressed under the crushing weight of the masses of the enemy, at the call of Col Evans threw forward his whole force to his aid across a small stream—Young's Branch and Valley—and engaged the Federalists with impetuosity; Imboden's battery at the time playing from his well-chosen position with brilliant effect with spherical case, the enemy having first opened on him from a rifle battery, probably Griffin's, with elongated cylindrical shells, which flew a few feet over the heads of our men, and exploded in the crest of the hill immediately in rear.

As Bee advanced under a severe fire, he placed the 7th and 8th Georgia regiments, under the chivalrous Bartow, at about 11 A. M., in a wood of second-growth pines to the right and front of, and nearly perpendicular to, Evans's line of battle, the 4th Alabama to the left of them, along a fence connecting the position of the Georgia regiments with the rectangular copse in which Sloan's South Carolina companies were engaged, and into which he also threw the 2d Mississippi. A fierce and destructive conflict now ensued—the fire was withering on both sides, while the enemy swept our short, thin lines with their numerous artillery, which, according to their official reports, at this time consisted of at least ten rifle guns and four howitzers. For an hour did the stout-hearted men of the blended command of Bee, Evans, and Bartow, breast an unintermitting battle-storm, animated, surely, by something more than the ordinary courage of even the bravest men under fire; it must have been, indeed, the inspiration of the cause, and consciousness of the great stake at issue, which thus nerved and animated one and all to stand unawed and unshrinking in such extremity.

Two Federal brigades of Heintzleman's division, were now brought into action, led by Ricketts's superb light battery of six ten-pounder rifle guns, which, posted on an eminence to the right of the Sudley Road, opened fire on Imboden's battery—about this time increased by two rifle pieces of the Washington Artillery, under Lieut. Richardson, and already the mark of two batteries, which divided their fire with Imboden, and two guns, under Lieuts. Davidson and Leftwich, of Latham's battery, posted as before mentioned.

At this time, confronting the enemy, we had still but Evans's eleven companies and two guns—Bee's and Bartow's four regiments, the two companies 11th Mississippi, under Lieut. Col. Liddell, and the six pieces under Imboden and Richardson. The enemy had two divisions of four strong brigades, including seventeen companies of regular infantry, cavalry and artillery, four companies of marines, and twenty pieces of artillery.* Against this odds, scarcely credible, our advance position was still for a while maintained, and the enemy's ranks constantly broken and shattered under the scorching fire of our men; but fresh regiments of the Federalists came upon the field; Sherman's and Keye's brigades of Tyler's division, as is stated in their reports, numbering over 6,000 bayonets, which had found a passage across the Run about 800 yards above the Stone Bridge, threatened our right.

Heavy losses had now been sustained on our side, both in numbers and in the personal worth of the slain. The 8th Georgia regiment had suffered heavily, being exposed as it took and maintained its position, to a fire from the enemy, already posted within a hundred yards of their front and right, sheltered by fences and other cover. It was at this time that Lieut.-Col. Gardner was severely wounded, as also several other valuable officers; the Adjutant of the regiment, Lieut. Branch, was killed, and the horse of the regretted Bartow was shot under him. The 4th Alabama also suffered severely from the deadly fire of the thousands of muskets which they so dauntlessly affronted under the immediate leadership of Bee himself. Its brave Colonel, E. J. Jones, was dangerously wounded, and many gallant officers fell, slain or *horse de combat*.

Now, however, with the surging mass of over fourteen thousand Federal infantry, pressing on their front, and under the incessant fire of at least twenty pieces of artillery, with the fresh brigades of Sherman and Keye's approaching—the latter already in musket range—our lines gave back, but under orders from Gen. Bee.

The enemy, maintaining their fire, pressed their swelling masses onward as our shattered battalions retired; the slaughter for the moment was deplorable, and has filled many a Southern home with life long sorrow.

Under this inexorable stress, the retreat continued until arrested by the energy and resolution of Gen. Bee, supported by Bartow and Evans, just in rear of the Robinson House, and Hampton's Legion which had been already advanced, and was in possession near it.

Imboden's battery, which had been handled with marked skill, but whose men were almost exhausted, and the two pieces of Walton's battery under Lieut Richardson, being threatened by the enemy's infantry on the left and front, were also obliged to fall back. Imboden, leaving a disabled piece on the ground, retired until he met Jackson's brigade, while Richardson joined the main body of his battery near the Lewis House.

As our infantry retired from the extreme front, the two 6-pounders of Latham's battery, before mentioned, fell back with excellent judgment to suitable positions in the rear, when an effective fire was maintained upon the still advancing lines of the Federalists, with damaging effect, until their ammunition was nearly exhausted, when they, too, were withdrawn in the near presence of the enemy, and rejoined their captain.

From the point previously indicated, where Gen. Johnston and myself had established our headquarters, we heard the continuous roll of musketry, and the sustained din of the artillery, which announced the serious outbreak of the battle on our left flank, and we anxiously, but confidently, awaited similar sounds of conflict from our front at Centreville, resulting from the prescribed attack in that quarter by our right wing.

At 10½ A. M., however, this expectation was dissipated, from Brigadier-General Ewell informing me, to my profound disappointment, that my orders for his advance had miscarried, but that in consequence of a communication from Gen. D. R. Jones, he had just thrown his brigade across the stream at Union Mills But, in my judgment, it was now too late for the effective execution of the contemplated movement, which must have required quite three hours for the troops to get into position for the attack; therefore, it became immediately necessary to depend on new combinations and other dispositions suited to the now pressing exigency. The movement of the right and centre, already begun by Jones and Longstreet, was at once countermanded with the sanction of General Johnston, and we arranged to meet the enemy on the field upon which he had chosen to give us battle. Under these circumstances our reserves, not already in movement, were immediately ordered up to support our left flank—namely, Holmes's two regiments and battery of artillery, under Captain Lindsey Walker, of six guns, and Earley's brigade. Two regiments from Bonham's brigade, with Kemper's four six-pounders, were also called for, and, with the sanction of General Johnston, Generals Ewell, Jones, (D. R.,) Longstreet and Bonham, were directed to make a demonstration to their several fronts to retain and engross the enemy's reserves and forces on their flank, and at and around Centreville. Previously, our respective Chiefs of Staff—Major Rhett and Colonel Jordan—had been left at my headquarters to hasten up, and give directions to any troops that might arrive at Manassas.

These orders having been duly dispatched by staff officers, at 11.30 A. M. General Johnston and myself set out for the immediate field of action, which we reached in rear of the Robinson and widow Henry's houses, at about 12 meridian, and just as the commands of Bee, Bartow, and Evans, had taken shelter in a wooded ravine behind the former, stoutly held at the time by Hampton with his legion, which had made a stand there after having previously been as far forward as the turnpike, where Lieutenant Colonel Johnson, an officer of brilliant promise, was killed, and other severe losses were sustained.

Before our arrival upon the scene, General Jackson had moved forward with his brigade of five Virginia regiments from his position in reserve, and had judiciously taken post below the brim of the plateau, nearly east of the Henry House, and to the left of the ravine and woods occupied by the mingled remnants of Bee's, Bartow's, and Evans's command, with Imboden's battery, and two of Stanard's pieces placed so as to play upon the on-coming enemy, supported in the immediate rear by Colonel J. L. Preston and Lieut.-Colonel Echolls's regiments, on the right by Harper's and on the left by Allen's and Cumming's regiment.

As soon as General Johnston and myself reached the field, we were occupied with the reorganization of the heroic troops, whose previous stand, with scarce a parallel, has nothing more valiant in all the pages of history, and whose losses fitly tell why, at length, their lines had lost their cohesion. It was now that Gen. Johnston impressively and gallantly charged to the front with the colors of the Fourth Alabama regiment by his side, all the field officers of the regiment having been previously disabled. Shortly afterwards I placed S. R. Gist, Adjutant and Inspector-General of South Carolina, a volunteer Aid-de-Camp of General Bee, in command of this regiment, and who led it again to the front as became its previous behavior, and remained with it for the rest of the day.

As soon as we had thus rallied and disposed our forces, I urged Gen. Johnston to leave the immediate conduct of the field to me, while he, repairing to Portico—the Lewis House—should urge reinforcements forward. At first he was unwilling, but reminded that one of us must do so, and that properly it was his place, he reluctantly, but fortunately, complied; fortunately, because from that position, by his energy and sagacity, his keen perception and anticipation of my needs, he so directed the reserves as to ensure the success of the day.

As Gen. Johnston departed for Portico Col. Bartow reported to me with the remains of the 7th Georgia volunteers, (Gartrell's,) which I ordered him to post on the left of Jackson's line, in the edge of the belt of pines bordering the southeastern rim of the plateau, on which the battle was now to rage so long and so fiercely.

Col. Wm. Smith's battalion of the 49th Virginia volunteers, having also come up by my orders, I placed it on the left of Gartrell's as my extreme left at the time. Repairing then to the right, I placed Hampton's Legion, which had suffered greatly, on that flank somewhat to the rear of Harper's regiment, and also the seven companies of the 8th (Hunton's) Virginia regiment, which, detached from Cocke's brigade by my orders and those of Gen. Johnston, had opportunely reached the ground. These, with Harper's regiment, constituted a reserve, to protect our right flank from an advance of the enemy from the quarter of the Stone Bridge, and served as a support for the line of battle, which was formed on the right by Bee's and Evans's commands, in the centre by four regiments of Jackson's brigade, with Imboden's four six-pounders, Walton's five guns, (two rifled,) two guns (one piece rifled) of Stanard's and two six-pounders of Rogers's batteries, the latter under Lieut. Heaton; and on the left by Gartrell's reduced ranks and Col. Smith's battalion, subsequently reinforced Falkner's Second Mississippi regiment, and by another regiment of the army of Shenandoah, just arrived upon the field, the Sixth (Fisher's) North Carolina. Confronting the enemy at this time, my forces numbered, at most, not more than 6,500 infantry and artillerists, with but thirteen pieces of artillery, and two companies (Carter's and Hoge's) of Stuart's cavalry.

The enemy's force, now bearing hotly and confidently down on our position, regiment after regiment of the best equipped men that ever took the field—according to their own official history of the day—was formed of Colonels Hunter's and Heintzelman's divisions, Colonels Sherman's and Keye's brigades of Tyler's division, and of the formidable batteries of Ricketts, Griffin, and Arnold regulars, and Second Rhode Island, and two Dahlgren howitzers—a force of over 20,000 infantry, seven companies of regular cavalry, and twenty-four pieces of improved artillery. At the same time, perilous, heavy reserves of infantry and artillery hung in the distance around the Stone Bridge, Mitchell's, Blackburn's, and Union Mills Fords, visible ready to fall upon us at any moment; and I was also assured of the existence of other heavy corps at and around Centreville and elsewhere, within convenient supporting distances.

Fully conscious of this portentous disparity of force, as I posted the lines for the encounter I sought to infuse into the hearts of my officers and men the confidence and determined spirit of resistance to this wicked invasion of the homes of a free people which I felt. I informed them that reinforcements would rapidly come to their support, and that we must at all hazards hold our posts until reinforced. I reminded them that we fought for our homes, our firesides, and for the independence of our country. I urged them to the resolution of victory or death on that field. These sentiments were loudly, eagerly cheered, wheresoever proclaimed, and I then felt reassured of the unconquerable spirit of that army, which would enable us to wrench victory from the host then threatening us with destruction.

Oh, my country! I would readily have sacrificed my life, and those of all the brave men around me, to save your honor and to maintain your independence from the degrading yoke which those ruthless invaders had come to impose and render perpetual; and the day's issue has assured me that such emotions must also have animated all under my command.

In the meantime, the enemy had seized upon the plateau on which Robinson's and the Henry houses are situated—the position first occupied in the morning by Gen. Bee, before advancing to the support of Evans.—Ricketts's battery of six rifle guns—the pride of the Federalists, the object of their unstinted expenditure in outfit—and the equally powerful regular light battery of Griffin, were brought forward and placed in immediate action, after having, conjointly with the batteries already mentioned, played from former positions with destructive effect upon our forward batteries.

The topographical features of the plateau, now become the stage of the contending armies, must be described in outline.

A glance at the map will show that it is enclosed on three sides by small water courses, which empty into Bull Run within a few yards of each other, half a mile to the south of the Stone Bridge. Rising to an elevation of quite one hundred feet above the level of Bull Run at the bridge, it falls off on three sides to the level of the enclosing streams in gentle slopes, but which are furrowed by ravines of irregular direction and length, and studded with clumps and patches of young pines and oaks. The general direction of the crest of the plateau is oblique to the course of Bull Run in that quarter and to the Brentsville and turnpike roads, which intersect each other at right angles. Immediately surrounding the two houses before mentioned, are small open fields of irregular outline, and exceeding 150 acres in extent. The houses occupied at the time, the one by the widow Henry, and the other by the free negro Robinson, are small wooden buildings, the latter densely embowered in trees and environed by a double row of fences on two sides. Around the eastern and southern brow of the plateau, an almost unbroken fringe of second-growth pines gave excellent shelter for our marksmen, who availed themselves of it with the most satisfactory skill. To the west, adjoining the fields, a broad belt of oaks extends directly across the crest on both sides of the Sudley Road, in which, during the battle, regiments of both armies met and contended for the mastery.

From the open ground of this plateau the view embraces a wide expanse of woods and gently undulating, open country of broad grass and grain fields in all directions, including the scene of Evans's and Bee's recent encounter with the enemy, some 1,200 yards to the northward.

In reply to the play of the enemy's batteries, our own artillery had not been idle or unskillful. The ground occupied by our guns, on a level with that held by the batteries of the enemy, was an open space of limited extent, behind a low undulation, just at the eastern verge of the plateau, some 500 or 600 yards from the Henry House. Here, as I have said, 13 pieces, mostly six-pounders, were maintained in action. The several batteries of Imboden, Stanard, Pendleton, (Rockbridge Artillery), and Alburtis's, of the army of the Shenandoah, and five guns of Walton's, and Heaton's section of Rogers's battery, of the army of the Potomac, alternating to some extent with each other, and taking part as needed; all from the outset displaying that marvellous capacity of our people as artillerists, which has made them, it would appear, at once the terror and the admiration of the enemy.

As was soon apparent, the Federalists had suffered severely from our artillery, and from the fire of our musketry on the right, and especially from the left flank, placed under cover, within whose galling range they had been advanced. And we are told in their official reports how regiment after regiment, thrown forward to dislodge us, was broken, never to recover its entire organization on that field.

In the meantime, also, two companies of Stuart's cavalry (Carter's and Hoge's) made a dashing charge down the Brentsville and Sudley road upon the Fire Zouaves—then the enemy's right on the plateau—which added to the disorder wrought by our musketry on that flank. But still the press of the enemy was heavy in that quarter of the field, as fresh troops were thrown forward there to outflank us, and some three guns of a battery, in an attempt to obtain a position apparently to enfilade our batteries, were thrown so close to the 33d regiment, Jackson's brigade, that regiment, springing forward, seized them, but with severe loss, and was subsequently driven back by an overwhelming force of Federal musketry.

Now, full time had come for us to assume the offensive and recover the plateau. It was done with a promptness and vigor, and at the same time, Jackson's brigade pierced the enemy's centre with the determination of veterans, and the spirit of men who fight for a sacred cause; but it suffered seriously. With equal spirit the other parts of the line made the onset, and the Federal lines were broken and swept back at all points from the open ground of the plateau. Rallying soon, however, as they were strongly reinforced by fresh regiments, the Federalists returned, and by weight of numbers pressed our lines back, recovered their ground and guns, and renewed the offensive.

By this time, between half-past 2 and 3 o'clock P. M., our reinforcements pushed forward, and, directed by General Johnston to the required quarter, were at hand just as I had ordered forward, to a second effort, for the recovery of the disputed plateau, the whole line, including my reserve, which, at this crisis of the battle, I felt called upon to lead in person. This attack was general, and was shared in by every regiment then in the field, including the 6th, (Fisher's) North Carolina regiment, which had just come up and taken position on the immediate left of the 49th Virginia regiment. The whole open ground was again swept clear of the enemy, and the plateau around the Henry and Robinson houses remained finally in our possession, with the greater part of the Ricketts and Griffin batteries, and a flag of the 1st Michigan regiment, captured by the 27th Virginia regiment, (Lieut. Col. Echols,) of Jackson's brigade. This part of the day was rich with deeds of individual coolness and dauntless conduct, as well as well directed embodied resolution and bravery, but fraught with the loss to the service of the country of lives of inestimable preciousness at this juncture. The brave Bee was mortally wounded at the head of the 4th Alabama and some Mississippians, in the open field near the Henry House; and a few yards distant the promising life of Bartow, while leading the 7th Georgia regiment, was quenched in blood. Col. F. J. Thomas, acting Chief of Ordnance, of Gen. Johnston's staff, after gallant conduct and most efficient service, was also slain. Col. Fisher, 6th North Carolina, likewise fell, after soldierly behavior, at the head of his regiment, with ranks greatly thinned.

Withers's 18th regiment, of Cocke's brigade had come up in time to follow this charge, and in conjunction with Hampton's Legion, captured several rifle pieces which may have fallen previously in possession of some of our troops; but if so, had been recovered by the enemy. These pieces were immediately turned and effectively served on distant masses of the enemy by the hands of some of our officers.

While the enemy had thus been driven back on our right entirely across the turnpike, and beyond Young's branch on our left, the woods yet swarmed with them, when our reinforcements opportunely arrived in quick succession, and took position in that portion of the field. Kershaw's 2d and Cash's 8th South Carolina regiments, which had arrived soon after Withers's, were led through the oaks just east of the Sudley-Brentsville road, brushing some of the enemy before them, and taking an advantageous position along, and west of that road, opened with much skill and effect on bodies of the enemy that had been rallied under cover of a strong Federal brigade posted on a plateau in the southwest angle, formed by intersection of the turnpike with the S. B. road. Among the troops thus engaged, were the Federal regular infantry.

At the same time, Kemper's battery, passing northward by the S. B. road, took position on the open space—under orders of Colonel Kershaw—near where the enemy's battery had been captured, was opened with effective results upon the Federal right, then the mark also of Kershaw and Cash's regiments.

Preston's 28th regiment, of Cocke's brigade, had by that time entered the same body of oaks, and encountered some Michigan troops, capturing their brigade commander, Col. Willcox.

Another important accession to our forces had also occurred about the same time, 3 o'clock P. M. Brigadier General E. K. Smith, with some 1,700 infantry of Elzey's brigade, of the army of the Shenandoah, and Beckham's battery, came upon the field, from Camp Pickens, Manassas, where they had arrived by railroad at noon. Directed in person by Gen. Johnston, to the left, then the mark of the enemy, on reaching a position in rear of the oak woods, south of the Henry House, and immediately east of the Sudley Road, Gen. Smith was disabled by a severe wound, and his valuable services were lost at that critical juncture. But the command devolved upon a meritorious officer of experience, Col. Elzey, who led his infantry at once somewhat further to the left, in the direction of the Chinn House, across the road, through the oaks skirting the west side of the road, and around which he sent the battery under

(Continued on Fourth Page.)

* That is, when the battle began—Smith's brigade and Fisher's North Carolina came up later, and made total of army of Shenandoah engaged of all arms 8,334. Hill's Virginia regiment, 550, also arrived, but was posted as reserve to right flank.

† These were what Colonel Evans saw of General Schenck's brigade of General Tyler's division, and two other heavy brigades, in all over 9,000 men and 13 pieces of artillery—Carlisle's and Ayres's batteries. That is, 900 men and two 6-pounders, confronted by 9,000 men and thirteen pieces of artillery, mostly rifled.

*See Official Reports of Colonels Heintzleman, Porter, &c.

(Continued from First Page.)

Lieut. Beckham. This officer took up a most favorable position near that house, whence, with a clear view of the Federal right and centre, filling the open fields to the west of the Brentsville-Sudley Road, and gently sloping southward, he opened fire with his battery upon them with deadly and damaging effect.

Colonel Early, who, by some mischance, did not receive orders until 2 o'clock, which had been sent him at noon, came on the ground immediately after Elzey, with Kemper's 7th Virginia, Hays's 7th Louisiana, and Barksdale's 13th Mississippi regiments. This brigade, by the personal direction of General Johnston, was marched by the Holkham House, across the fields to the left entirely around the woods through which Elzey had passed, and under a severe fire, into a position in line of battle near Chinn's House, outflanking the enemy's right.

At this time, about 3.30 P. M., the enemy driven back on their left and centre, and brushed from the woods bordering the Sudley Road, south and west of the Henry House, had formed a line of battle of truly formidable proportions of crescent outline, reaching on their left, from vicinity of Pittsylvania, (the old Carter Mansion,) by Matthew's and in rear of Dogan's, across the turnpike near to Chinn's house. The woods and fields were filled with their masses of infantry and their carefully preserved cavalry. It was a truly magnificent, though redoubtable spectacle, as they threw forward in fine style, on the broad gentle slopes of the ridge occupied by their main lines, a cloud of skirmishers, preparatory for another attack.

But as Early formed his line, and Beckham's pieces playing upon the right of the enemy, Elzey's brigade, Gibbon's 10th Virginia, Lieut.-Col. Stuart's 1st Maryland, and Vaughn's 3d Tennessee regiments, and Cash's 8th, and Kershaw's 2d South Carolina, Withers's 18th, and Preston's 28th Virginia, advanced in an irregular line almost simultaneously, with great spirit, from their several positions upon the front and flanks of the enemy in their quarter of the field. At the same time, too, Early resolutely assailed their right flank and rear. Under this combined attack the enemy was soon forced, first over the narrow plateau in the southern angle made by the two roads so often mentioned into a patch of woods on its western slope, thence back over Young's branch and the turnpike into the fields of the Dogan farm, and rearward, in extreme disorder, in all available directions, towards Bull Run. The rout had now become general and complete.

About the time that Elzey and Early were entering into action, a column of the enemy, Keye's brigade of Tyler's division, made its way across the turnpike between Bull Run and the Robinson House, under cover of a wood and brow of the ridges, apparently to turn my right, but was easily repulsed by a few shots from Latham's battery, now united and placed in position by Capt. D. B. Harris, of the Virginia Engineers, whose services during the day became his character as an able, cool and skillful officer, and from Alburtis's battery, opportunely ordered by Gen. Jackson, to a position to the right of Latham, on a hill commanding the line of approach of the enemy, and supported by portions of regiments collected together by the Staff officers of General Johnston and myself.

Early's brigade, meanwhile, joined by the Nineteenth Virginia regiment, Lieut.-Col. Strange, of Cocke's brigade, pursued the now panic-stricken, fugitive enemy. Stuart, with his cavalry, and Beckham, had also taken up the pursuit along the road by which the enemy had come upon the field that morning; but, soon cumbered by prisoners who thronged his way, the former was unable to attack the mass of the fast-fleeing, frantic Federalists. Withers's, R. J. Preston's, Cash's, and Kershaw's regiments, Hampton's Legion, and Kemper's battery also pursued along the Warrenton road by the Stone Bridge, the enemy having opportunely opened a way for them through the heavy abatis which my troops had made on the west side of the bridge several days before. But this pursuit was soon recalled, in consequence of a false report which unfortunately reached us that the enemy's reserves, known to be fresh and of considerable strength, were threatening the position of Union Mills Ford.

Colonel Radford, with six companies Virginia cavalry was also ordered by General Johnston to cross Bull Run and attack the enemy from the direction of Lewis's House; conducted by one of my aids, Colonel Chisholm, by the Lewis ford, to the immediate vicinity of the Suspension Bridge, he charged a battery with great gallantry, took Colonel Corcoran, of the 69th regiment New York volunteers, a prisoner, and captured the Federal colors of that regiment, as well as a number of the enemy. He lost, however, a promising officer of his regiment, Captain Winston Radford.

Lieut.-Colonel Munford also led some companies of cavalry in hot pursuit, and rendered material service in the capture of prisoners and of cannon, horses, ammunition, &c., abandoned by the enemy in their flight.

Captain Lay's company of the Powhatan troops, and Utterback's Rangers, Virginia volunteers, attached to my person, did material service, under Captain Lay, in rallying troops broken for the time by the onset of the enemy's masses.

During the period of the momentous events fraught with the weal of our country, which were passing on the blood-stained plateau along the Sudley and Warrenton roads, other portions of the line of Bull Run had not been void of action, of moment, and of influence upon the general result.

While Colonel Evans and his sturdy band were holding at bay the Federal advance beyond the turnpike, the enemy made repeated demonstrations, with artillery and infantry, upon the line of Cocke's brigade, with the serious intention of forcing the position, as General Schenck admits in his report. They were driven back with severe loss by Latham's (a section) and Rogers's four six-pounders, and were so impressed with the strength of that line as to be held in check and inactive, even after it had been stripped of all its troops but one company of the 19th Virginia regiment, under Captain Duke, a meritorious officer. And it is worthy of notice that, in this encounter of our six-pounder guns, handled by our volunteer artillerists, they had worsted such a notorious adversary as the Ayres's—formerly Sherman's—battery, which quit the contest under the illusion that it had weightier metal than its own to contend with.

The centre brigades—Bonham's and Longstreet's—of the line of Bull Run, if not closely engaged, were, nevertheless exposed for much of the day to an annoying, almost incessant fire of artillery of long range; but, by a steady, veteran-like maintenance of their positions, they held, virtually, paralyzed all day, two strong brigades of the enemy, with their batteries (four) of rifle guns.

As before said, two regiments of Bonham's brigade, 2d and 8th South Carolina volunteers, and Kemper's battery, took a distinguished part in the battle. The remainder, 3d Williams's, 7th Bacon's South Carolina volunteers; 11th (Kirkland's) North Carolina regiment; six companies 8th Louisiana volunteers; Shield's battery, and one section of Walton's battery, under Lieutenant Garnett, whether in holding their post or taking up the pursuit, officers and men discharged their duty with credit and promise.

Longstreet's brigade, pursuant to orders, prescribing his part of the operations of the centre and right wing, was thrown across Bull Run early in the morning, and under a severe fire of artillery, was skillfully disposed for the assault of the enemy's batteries in that quarter, but were withdrawn subsequently, in consequence of the change of plan already mentioned and explained. The troops of this brigade were, 1st, Major Skinner; 11th, Garland's; 24th, Lieut. Col. Hairston's; 17th, Corse's Virginia regiments; 5th N. Carolina, Lieut. Col Jones, and Whitehead's company Virginia cavalry; throughout the day these troops evinced the most soldierly spirit.

After the rout, having been ordered by Gen. Johnston in the direction of Centreville in pursuit, these brigades advanced near to that place, when night and darkness intervening, Gen. Bonham thought it proper to direct his own brigade, and that of Gen. Longstreet, back to Bull Run.

Gen. D. R. Jones early in the day crossed Bull Run with his brigade, pursuant to orders indicating his part in the projected attack by our right wing and centre on the enemy at Centreville, took up a position on the Union Mills and Centreville road, more than a mile in advance of the Run. Ordered back in consequence of miscarriage of the orders to Gen. Ewell, the retrograde movement was necessarily made under a sharp fire of artillery.

At noon this brigade, in obedience to new instructions, was again thrown across Bull Run to make demonstrations. Unsupported by other troops, the advance was gallantly made until within musket range of the enemy's force—Col Davis's brigade in position near Rocky Run and under the concentrated fire of their artillery. In this affair the 5th, Jenkins's South Carolina, and Captain Fontaine's company of the 18th Mississippi regiment, are mentioned by Gen. Jones as having shown conspicuous gallantry, coolness, and discipline under a combined fire of infantry and artillery. Not only did the return fire of the brigade drive to cover the enemy's infantry, but the movement unquestionably spread through the enemy's ranks a sense of insecurity and danger from an attack by that route on their rear at Centreville, which served to augment the extraordinary panic which we know disbanded the entire Federal army for the time. This is evident from the fact that Colonel Davies, the immediate adversary's commander, in his official report, was induced to magnify one small company of our cavalry, which accompanied the brigade, into a force of 2,000 men; and Colonel Miles, the commander of the Federal reserves at Centreville, says the movement "caused painful apprehensions for the left flank" of their army.

General Ewell, occupying for the time the right of the lines at Bull Run, at Union Mills Ford, after the miscarriage of my orders for his advance upon Centreville, in the afternoon was ordered by Gen. Johnston to bring up his brigade into battle then raging on the left flank. Promptly executed as this movement was, the brigade, after a severe march, reached the field too late to share the glories, as they had the labors, of the day. As the important position at the Union Mills had been left with but a slender guard, General Ewell was at once ordered to retrace his steps and resume his position to prevent the possibility of its seizure by any force of the enemy in that quarter.

Brigadier General Holmes—left with his brigade as a support to the same position in the original plan of battle—had also been called to the left, whither he marched with the utmost speed, but not in time to join actively in the battle.

Walker's rifle guns of the brigade, however, came up in time to be fired with precision and decided execution at the retreating enemy, and Scott's cavalry, joining in the pursuit, assisted in the capture of prisoners and war munitions.

This victory, the details of which I have thus sought to chronicle as fully as were fitting an official report, it remains to record, was dearly won by the death of many officers and men of inestimable value belonging to all grades of our society.

In the death of General Barnard E. Bee the Confederacy has sustained an irreparable loss, for with great personal bravery and coolness he possessed the qualities of an accomplished soldier and an able, reliable commander.

Colonels Bartow and Fisher, and Lieutenant-Colonel Johnson, of Hampton's Legion, in the fearless command of their men, gave earnest of great usefulness to the service had they been spared to complete a career so brilliantly begun. Besides the field officers already mentioned as having been wounded while in the gallant discharge of their duties, many others also received severe wounds after equally honorable and distinguished conduct, whether in leading their men forward or in rallying them when overpowered or temporarily shattered by the largely superior force to which we were generally opposed.

The subordinate grades were likewise abundantly conspicuous for zeal and capacity for the leadership of men in arms. To mention all who, fighting well, paid the lavish forfeit of their lives, or at least crippled, mutilated bodies on the field of Manassas, cannot well be done within the compass of this paper, but a grateful country and mourning friends will not suffer their names and services to be forgotten and pass away unhonored.

Nor are those officers and men who were so fortunate as to escape the thick-flying, deadly missiles of the enemy, less worthy of praise for their endurance, firmness, and valor than their brothers-in-arms, whose lives were closed, or bodies maimed, on that memorable day. To mention all who exhibited ability and brilliant courage, were impossible in this report; nor do the reports of brigade and other subordinate commanders, supply full lists of all actually deserving of distinction. I can only mention those whose conduct came immediately under my notice, or the consequence of whose actions happened to be signally important.

It is fit that I should in this way commend to notice the dauntless conduct and imperturbable coolness of Col. Evans, and well indeed was he supported by Col. Sloan, and the officers of the 4th South Carolina regiment, as also Major Wheat, than whom no one displayed more brilliant courage until carried from the field, shot through the lungs, though happily not mortally stricken. But in the desperate, unequal conduct, to which those brave gentlemen were for a time necessarily exposed, the behavior of officers and men generally was worthy of the highest admiration, and assuredly hereafter all those present may proudly say: We were of that band who fought the first hour of the battle of Manassas. Equal honors and credit must also be awarded in the pages of history to the gallant officers and men who, under Bee and Bartow, subsequently marching to their side, saved them from destruction, and relieved them from the brunt of the enemy's attack.

The conduct of Gen. Jackson also requires mention as eminently that of an able, fearless soldier, and sagacious commander, one fit to lead his brigade; his efficient, prompt, timely arrival before the plateau of the Henry House, and his judicious disposition of his troops contributed much to the success of the day. Although painfully wounded in the hand, he remained on the field to the end of the battle, rendering invaluable assistance.

Col. Wm. Smith was as efficient as self-possessed and brave; the influence of his example and his words of encouragement was not confined to his immediate command, the good conduct of which is especially noticeable, inasmuch as it had been embodied but a day or two before the battle.

Colonels Harper, Hunton, and Hampton, commanding regiments of the reserve, attracted my notice by their soldierly ability, as with their gallant commands they restored the fortunes of the day, at a time when the enemy, by a last desperate onset, with heavy odds, had driven our forces from the fiercely contested ground around the Henry and Robinson houses. Veterans could not have behaved better than these well led regiments.

High praise must also be given to Colonels Cocke, Early, and Elzey, brigade commanders; also, to Colonel Kershaw, commanding, for the time, the Second and Eighth South Carolina regiments. Under the instructions of General Johnston, these officers reached the field at an opportune, critical moment, and disposed, handled and fought their respective commands with sagacity, decision, and successful results which have been described in detail.

Col. J. E. B. Stuart likewise deserves mention for his enterprise and ability as a cavalry commander. Through his judicious reconnoissance of the country on our left flank, he acquired information, both of topographical features and the positions of the enemy, of the utmost importance in the subsequent and closing movements of the day on that flank, and his services in the pursuit were highly effective.

Capt. E. P. Alexander, C. S. Engineers, gave me seasonable and material assistance early in the day with his system of signals. Almost the first shot fired by the enemy passed through the tent of his party at the Stone Bridge, where they subsequently firmly maintained their position in the discharge of their duty—the transmission of messages of the enemy's movements—for several hours under fire. Later, Capt Alexander acted as my aid-de-camp in the transmission of orders and in observation of the enemy.

I was most efficiently served throughout the day by my volunteer aids, Cols. Preston, Manning, Chesnut, Miles, Rice, Heyward, and Chisholm, to whom I tender my thanks for their unflagging, intelligent, and fearless discharge of the laborious, responsible duties entrusted to them. To Lt S. W. Ferguson, A. D. C., and Col. Heyward, who were habitually at my side from 12 noon until the close of the battle, my special acknowledgments are due. The horse of the former was killed under him by the same shell that wounded that of the latter. Both were eminently useful to me, and were distinguished for coolness and courage, until the enemy gave way, and fled in wild disorder in every direction—a scene the President of the Confederacy had the high satisfaction of witnessing, as he arrived upon the field at that exultant moment.

I also received, from the time I reached the front, such signal service from H. E. Peyton, at the time a private in the Loudoun cavalry, that I have called him to my personal staff. Similar services were also rendered me, repeatedly during the battle, by T. J. Randolph, a Volunteer Acting A. D. C. to Colonel Cocke.

Captain Clifton H. Smith, of the General Staff, was also present on the field, and rendered efficient service in the transmission of orders.

It must be permitted me here to record my profound sense of my obligations to General Johnston, for his generous permission to carry out my plans, with such modifications as circumstances had required. From his services on the field, as we entered it together, already mentioned, and his subsequent watchful management of the reinforcements as they reached the vicinity of the field, our countrymen may draw the most auspicious auguries.

To Colonel Thomas Jordan, my efficient and zealous Assistant Adjutant-General, much credit is due for his able assistance in the organization of the forces under my command, and for the intelligence and promptness with which he has discharged all the laborious and important duties of his office.

Valuable assistance was given to me by Major Cabell, chief officer of the Quartermaster's Department, in the sphere of his duties—duties environed by far more than the ordinary difficulties and embarrassments attending the operations of a long organized regular establishment.

Col. R. B. Lee, Chief of Subsistence Department, had but just entered upon his duties, but his experience, and long and varied services in his department, made him as efficient as possible.

Capt. W. H. Fowle, whom Col. Lee had relieved, had previously exerted himself to the utmost to carry out orders from these headquarters, to render his department equal to the demands of the service; that it was not entirely so, it is due to justice to say, was certainly not his fault.

Deprived by the sudden severe illness of the Medical Director, Surgeon Thomas H. Williams, his duties were discharged by Surgeon R. L. Brodie, to my entire satisfaction, and it is proper to say that the entire medical corps of the army at present, embracing gentlemen of distinction in the profession, who had quit lucrative private practice, by their services in the field and subsequently, did high honor to their profession.

The vital duties of the Ordnance Department were effectively discharged under the administration of my Chief of Artillery and Ordnance, Colonel S. Jones.

At one time, when reports of evil omen and disaster reached Camp Pickens, with such circumstantiality as to give reasonable grounds of anxiety, its commander, Colonel Terrett, the commander of the entrenched batteries, Captain Sterrett, of the Confederate States Navy, and their officers, made the most efficient possible preparations for the desperate defence of that position in extremity; and in this connection, I regret my inability to mention the names of those patriotic gentlemen of Virginia, by the gratuitous labor of whose slaves the entrenched camp at Manassas had been mainly constructed, relieving the troops from that laborious service, and giving opportunity for their military instruction.

Lieutenant-Colonel Thomas H. Williamson, the engineer of these works, assisted by Captain D. B. Harris, discharged his duties with untiring energy and devotion, as well as satisfactory skill.

Captain W. H. Stevens, Engineer Confederate Army, served with the advanced forces at Fairfax Court-House for some time before the battle; he laid out the works there, in admirable accordance with the purposes for which they were designed, and yet so as to admit of ultimate extension and adaption to more serious uses as means and part of a system of real defence when determined upon. He has shown himself to be an officer of energy and ability.

Major Thomas G. Rhett, after having discharged for several months the laborious duties of Adjutant-General to the commanding officer of Camp Pickens, was detached to join the army of the Shenandoah, just on the eve of the advance of the enemy; but volunteering his services, was ordered to assist on the staff of General Bonham, joining that officer at Centreville on the night of the 17th, before the battle of Bull Run, where he rendered valuable services, until the arrival of General Johnston, on the 20th of July, when he was called to the place of Chief-of-Staff of that officer.

It is also proper to acknowledge the signal services rendered by Colonel B. F. Terry and T. Lubbock, of Texas, who had attached themselves to the staff of General Longstreet. These gentlemen made daring and valuable reconnoissances of the enemy's positions, assisted by Captains Gores and Chichester. They also carried orders to the field, and on the following day, accompanying Captain Whitehead's troop to take possession of Fairfax Court-House, Colonel Terry, with his unerring rifle, severed the halliard, and thus lowered the Federal flag found still floating from the cupalo of the Court-House there. He also secured a large Federal garrison flag, designed, it is said, to be unfurled over our entrenchments at Manassas.

In connection with the unfortunate casualties of the day—that is, the miscarriage of the orders sent by courier to Gens. Holmes and Ewell to attack the enemy in flank and reverse at Centreville, through which the triumph of our arms was prevented from being still more decisive, I regard it in place to say, a divisional organization, with officers in command of divisions, with appropriate rank, as in European services, would greatly reduce the risk of such mishaps, and would advantageously simplify the communications of a General in command of a field with his troops.

While glorious for our people, and of crushing effect upon the *morale* of our hitherto confident and overweening adversary, as were the events of the battle of Manassas, the field was only won by stout fighting, and, as before stated, with much loss, as is precisely exhibited in the papers herewith, marked F, G, and H, and being lists of the killed and wounded. The killed outright numbered 369—the wounded 1,483, making an aggregate of 1,852.

The actual loss of the enemy will never be known, it may now only be conjectured. Their abandoned dead, as they were buried by our people where they fell, unfortunately, were not enumerated, but many parts of the field were thick with their corpses, as but few battle-fields have ever been. The official reports of the enemy are studiously silent on this point, but still afford us data for an approximate estimate. Left almost in the dark in respect to the losses of Hunter's and Heintzleman's divisions—first, longest and most hotly engaged—we are informed that Sherman's brigade—Tyler's division—suffered, in killed, wounded, and missing, 609—that is, about 18 per cent. of the brigade. A regiment of Franklin's brigade—Gorman's—lost 21 per cent. Griffin's (battery) loss was thirty per cent., and that of Keye's brigade, which was so handled by its commander as to be exposed to only occasional volleys from our troops, was at least 10 per cent. To these facts add the repeated references in the reports of the more reticent commanders, to the "murderous" fire to which they were habitually exposed—the 'pistol range' volleys, and galling musketry, of which they speak, as scourging their ranks, and we are warranted in placing the entire loss of the Federalists, at over forty-five hundred in killed, wounded and prisoners. To this may be legitimately added as a casualty of the battle, the thousands of fugitives from the field, who have never rejoined their regiments, and who are as much lost to the enemy's service as if slain or disabled by wounds. These may not be included under the head of "*missing*," because in every instance of such report, we took as many *prisoners* of those brigades or regiments as are reported "*missing*."

A list appended exhibits some 1,460 of their wounded and others who fell into our hands and were sent to Richmond. Some were sent to other points, so that the number of prisoners, including wounded who did not die, may be set down as not less than 1,600. Besides these, a considerable number who could not be removed from the field died at several farm houses and field hospitals within ten days following the battle.

To serve the future historian of this war, I will note the fact that among the captured Federalists are officers and men of *forty seven* regiments of volunteers, besides from some nine different regiments of regular troops, detachments of which were engaged. From their official reports, we learn of a regiment of volunteers engaged, six regiments of Miles's division, and the five regiments of Runyon's brigade, from which we have neither sound or wounded prisoners. Making all allowances for mistakes, we are warranted in saying that the Federal army consisted of at least fifty-five regiments of volunteers, eight companies of regular infantry, four of marines, nine of regular cavalry, and twelve batteries, one hundred and nineteen guns. These regiments, at one time, as will appear from a published list appended, marked "K," numbered in the aggregate 54,140, and average 964 each; from an order of the enemy's commander, however, dated July 13th, we learn that one hundred men from each regiment were ordered to remain in charge of respective camps—some allowance must further be made for the sick and details, which would reduce the average to eight hundred—adding the regular cavalry, infantry, and artillery present, an estimate of their force may be made.

A paper appended, marked "L," exhibits, in part, the ordnance and supplies captured, including some 28 field pieces of the best character of arm, with over 100 rounds of ammunition for each gun, 37 caissons, 6 forges, 4 battery wagons, 64 artillery horses, completely equipped, 500,000 of small-arms ammunition, 4,500 setts rounds of accoutrements, over 500 muskets, some 9 regimental and garrison flags, with a large number of pistols, knapsacks, swords, canteens, blankets, a large store of axes and entrenching tools, wagons, ambulances, horses, camp and garrison equippage, hospital stores, and some subsistence.

Added to these results may rightly be noticed here that by this battle an invading army superbly equipped, within 20 miles of their base of operations, has been converted into one virtually besieged, and exclusively occupied for months in the construction of a stupendous series of fortifications for the protection of its own capital.

I beg to call attention to the reports of the several subordinate commanders for reference to the signal parts played by individuals of their respective commands. Contradictory statements, found in these reports, should not excite surprise when we remember how difficult, if not impossible, it is to reconcile the narrations of bystanders, or participants in even the most inconsiderable affair, much less the shifting, thrilling scenes of a battle-field.

Accompanying are maps showing the positions of the armies on the morning of the 21st July, and of three several stages of the battle; also, of the line of Bull Run north of Blackburn's Ford. These maps, from actual surveys made by Captain D. B. Harrison, assisted by Mr. John Grant, were drawn by the latter with a rare delicacy worthy of high commendation.

In conclusion it is proper, and doubtless expected, that through this report my countrymen should be made acquainted with some of the sufficient causes that prevented the advance of our forces and prolonged, vigorous pursuit of the enemy to and beyond the Potomac. The War Department has been fully advised long since of all of those causes, some of which only are proper to be here communicated. An army which had fought as ours on that day against uncommon odds, under a July sun, most of the time without water and without food except a hastily snatched meal at dawn, was not in condition for the toil of an eager, effective pursuit of an enemy immediately after the battle.

On the following day an unusually heavy and unintermitting fall of rain intervened to obstruct our advance with reasonable prospect of fruitful results. Added to this, the want of a cavalry force of sufficient numbers made an efficient pursuit a military impossibility.

Your obedient servant,
G. T. BEAUREGARD,
General Commanding.

To Gen. S. Cooper,
Adj't and Inspec'r Gen., Richmond, Va.
[Official.] R. H. Chilton, Adj't.

NOTICE.—All persons having claims against the Estate of ALEXANDER STIRLING, deceased, as well as those indebted, will please present the same to Mr. E. B. Cook for settlement.
EMILY J. STIRLING,
Administratrix of the Estate of
ja 23—1m Alexander Stirling, dec'd.

ELECTION CARDS.

THE CONFEDERATE CONGRESS.
MARTIN MEREDITH LIPSCOMB
A CANDIDATE.

To the Voters of the Metropolitan Congressional District:

From an interchange of opinion with many of my fellow-citizens, I find a large majority of them in favor of a *new shuffle* for candidates for the position made vacant by the lamented John Tyler.

Without intending any disparagement to the talents of either Mr. Lyons or Mr. Macfarland, (the defeated candidates at the last election,) I will call attention to the meagre vote received by those gentlemen as an evidence of their strength with the people. With this view of the case, and at the earnest solicitation of many true friends, who have stood by me in good and evil report, I hereby announce myself a candidate for Congress. In this limited space, it will be impossible for me to fully present my views upon the momentous questions and events that now agitate the public mind; expecting, as I do, to present myself to the voters of the district at the various court-houses and camps, I shall content myself at present by briefly stating my position.

Firstly.—I am in favor of an OFFENSIVE WAR, carrying it to the very hearth-stones of our enemies, asking nor giving quarter to none, dealing our blows thick and fast, until the Yankee nation shall cry "*Hold, enough.*"

Secondly.—I shall advocate the passage of a bill which shall make it imperative that all unmarried men shall enlist for *the war*; and any deficiency arising from that source shall be made up from married men without children; and, furthermore, that the monthly pay of the soldiers shall be increased to an amount sufficient to supply them with all the actual necessaries of life.

Thirdly.—I am in favor of all measures tending to develop the manufacturing and agricultural resources of our beloved South; in fact, all measures which separate us for *all time* from that nation of mountebanks residing over the "SUSQUEHANNA."

I am yours, respectfully,
MARTIN MEREDITH LIPSCOMB.
fe 1—tde*

RICHMOND, JANUARY 23, 1862.
TO WM H. MACFARLAND, Esq.—DEAR SIR: A vacancy having occurred in Congress by the death of Mr. TYLER, we respectfully request that you will announce yourself a candidate.

Very truly, yours,
WM. H. MACON, New Kent,
MICHAEL GRETTER,
LEWIS WEBB,
THEO. ROBERTSON,
ORANGE BENNET,
GEORGE W. SMITH,
PEYTON JOHNSTON,
GEO. W. GILLIAM,
P. K. WHITE,
C. J. SINTON,
ED. S. FURNEYHOUGH,
WM. H. BOCOCK,
JAS. P. HEATH,
WM. K. WATTS,
WM. GRAY,
JOHN W. WRIGHT,
A. A. FARLEY,
WM. H. ROBERTS,
of Richmond Howitzers,
P. A. HAXALL,
I. H. WALKE,
WM. SMITH,
MILES TURPIN,
MILES C. EGGLESTON,
ELIJAH BAKER,
WM. L. McMINN,
N. T. PATE,
D. M. ROBERTSON,
JAS. A. SCOTT,
JAS. WALSH,
SAM'L C. DONNAN,
For themselves and others.

RICHMOND, January 28, 1862.
GENTLEMEN: Sincerely grateful for the call which you, and many others of my fellow-citizens, have made upon me, I do not hesitate to announce myself a candidate to represent our District in CONGRESS. My duties in Congress will not permit me to go through the District, as under other circumstances I would gladly do. I content myself with announcing my inextinguishable devotion to our cause, and to eternal separation from the people beyond the Susquehannah.

Your friend and fellow citizen,
ja 3—ts WM. H. MACFARLAND.

FOR CONGRESS.—TO HON. ALEXANDER R. HOLLIDAY: Believing that you are the choice of the people of this District to represent them in Congress, and that your ability and experience would be of the greatest value to the State at this time, we most earnestly invite you, at once, to declare yourself a candidate. You will be voted for by
ja 31—3t* MANY OF THE PEOPLE.

JAMES LYONS, Esq., FOR CONGRESS, From the Richmond District, composed of the cities of Richmond and Williamsburg, the counties of Henrico, Hanover, New Kent, Charles City, Elizabeth City, James City, Warwick, and York.
ja 31—10t*

TO THE VOTERS OF THE CITY OF RICHMOND.—L. M. JUDE, the Clerk of the Night Watch will be voted for as CAPTAIN of the Night Watch, to take the place of the late A. Wilkinson, and will be supported by Many Voters of this city.
ja 29—1m*

RICHMOND, Jan 22, 1862.
JAMES LYONS, ESQ.:—DEAR SIR: A vacancy having occurred in the representation of this district, by the death of our late distinguished Representative, John Tyler, we request you to announce yourself as a candidate to fill it.

Very respectfully, your ob't servants,
Wm. G. Crenshaw, John Ahern,
Thos. W. Doswell, C. Stebbins,
E. T. Winston, Jos. Doerflinger,
Wm. Taylor, and many others.

RICHMOND, Jan. 22, 1862.
To Messrs. Wm. G. Crenshaw, Thomas W. Doswell, E. T. Winston, William Taylor, John Ahern, C. Stebbins, Joseph Doerflinger, and others:
GENTLEMEN: Your note of this date, requesting me to announce myself as a candidate for Congress, has just been received, and, in compliance with your request, with many thanks for your kindness, I now announce myself a candidate.
Most respectfully, yours,
ja 28—2w* JAMES LYONS.

BOARDING.

BOARDING—A few gentlemen can obtain BOARD, with comfortable ROOMS, in a private family, On Clay street, between 4th and 5th. House next to the corner of 4th st., south side.
fe 1—2t*

PERSONAL.

NOTICE TO THE PUBLIC.—The original and only SOUTHERN HARMONEONS in the Confederate States are now playing at Metropolitan Hall, in this city, but will appear in other cities on some future occasion. Any company at present playing in Lynchburg or elsewhere under this name, are imposters. WELLS & CO.
fe 1—2t*

DIRECT IMPORTATION. RUN THE BLOCKADE. Just received per steamer Ella Warley, direct from England, 50,000 yellow Envelopes, business size. Also, 10,000 white do., ladies' size; 5,000 assorted colors do., ladies' size; 20 reams flat unruled white Letter Paper; 250 gross Steel Pens.
W. HARGRAVE WHITE,
fe 1—2t* 173 Main street.

POST-OFFICE, RICHMOND, VA., February 1, 1862.
DROP LETTERS.—The law of Congress requires all letters dropped in the Post-Office to be PRE-PAID, at two cents each. The failure to pre-pay will prevent their being placed in the boxes for delivery.
fe 1—3t THOS. B. BIGGER, P. M.

SELLING OFF TO CLOSE IN SPRING. I still have on hand a lot of single and double Bedsteads; cheap Bureaus; Wardrobes—also, some fine; Spring Chairs, Sofas, parlor Chairs, centre Tables, Sofa Beds, Bookcases, Sideboards, Extension Tables, Cotton, Shuck and Hair Mattresses, all sizes. Also, a lot of Camp Furniture, chest Stools, Chairs, patent Cots, Comforts, Pillows, Bolsters, &c., &c., and many other useful articles, which I cannot name, all of which I will sell low for cash only. Persons wishing to buy will do well to call and see for themselves.
R. GATHRIGHT,
Governor street,
ja 31—1w* bet. Main and Franklin.

SOLDIERS, ATTENTION.—If you want a real good and serviceable KNAPSACK, or WATER-PROOF COAT, CAPE, LEGGINS, GAITERS, HAVERSACK, BLANKET, &c., go to the KNAPSACK DEPOT, corner of Governor and Main streets, over Mr. Spence's Clothing Establishment, where you will find a full assortment, cheap. Sutlers and companies supplied.
ja 31—1m*

SUNDRIES.—Epsom Salts, Coxe's Sparkling Gelatine, Genuine English Perfumery, Hair Dye, Nail Glue, Candle-Wick, Lamp Oil, Virginia Snake-Root, Powdered Gum Arabic, Syringes, Baker's Bitters.
L. WAGNER, Druggist,
ja 31—3t* 6th and Broad streets.

FOR SALE. A SEWING MACHINE, in perfect order, One of Singer's largest size. Address, "W.," at this office. ja 31—3t*

OFFICE OF R. T. FOSTER & CO.,
RICHMOND, Jan. 31, 1862.
WE WILL REDEEM, in bankable funds, the notes of the VIRGINIA SAVINGS BANK, when presented in sums of *five dollars* and upwards.
ja 31—3t R. T. FOSTER & CO.

WANTS.

WANTED.—At Royster Hospital, 25th street, six steady, reliable white MALE NURSES, and six steady, reliable slave MALE NURSES. None need apply without the best recommendations. Apply to Dr. Crenshaw, next door below Spotswood Hotel, or at Hospital from 10½ to 1 o'clock. fe 1—6t

WANTED.—A Gentleman and Lady wishes to obtain BOARD In a private family, somewhere on Shockoe Hill. Address "W. J. E.," Box 76, Richmond Post-Office.
fe 1—3t*

WANTED—1,000 cords STAVE BILLETS, For which a high price, in cash, will be paid on delivery.
HAXALL, CRENSHAW & CO.
fe 1—3t

WANTED.—I wish to get, to-day, ten MEN for an ARTILLERY COMPANY, And will pay them a bounty that will give to each a good outfit.
ROBERT HILL,
Substitute Agent, six doors above
fe 1—3t* City Water Works.

WANTED—A LADY To assist in SEWING In a private family. Address
fe 1—2t* "R.," Dispatch office.

WANTED—SUBSTITUTES. I wish to employ four SUBSTITUTES for the volunteer service during the War. To suitable men liberal compensation will be paid. Apply at my office, Front Building Shockoe Warehouse.
THOS. TINSLEY JOHNSON.
ja 31—3t*

WANTED—A HOUSE and LOT suitable for a small family, and convenient to our place of business. Rent from $300 to $600 will be paid. Apply to
BENNETT & TOLLESON,
ja 31—3t* 159 Main street.

WANTED—A SUBSTITUTE FOR THE WAR—A liberal bonus offered.—Inquire of G. W. Jones, opposite the Express office, between 9th and 10th sts. ja 31—3t*

WANTED—A SUBSTITUTE, To serve in a select Cavalry Company, now in comfortable winter quarters in the army of the Potomac. A good horse and outfit furnished; also, a liberal bonus. Apply to "Box 435," Richmond, Va. ja 30—5t*

WANTED—Immediately, BLACKSMITHS and HELPERS. Also, WOOD-WORKERS, to make light spring wagons. Apply to
JOHN DOES,
Corner 9th and Broad street, or at his shop, on Marshall, above 1st st. ja 30—1w*

WANTED—Several FINISHERS, to work on Engines. High wages paid. Also, one man who understands making Coke from Bituminous Coal.
ja 30—3m ETTENGER & EDMOND.

WANTED—GAS FITTER. A good GAS FITTER will be given liberal wages and steady employment by immediate application to the subscriber.
C. H. LANGLEY,
13th street, between Main and Cary.
ja 29—ts

WANTED.—The subscriber wishes to employ FIVE MEN, who are not liable to militia duty, as SUBSTITUTES, for which a liberal bounty will be given. Apply to-day to the subscriber, at George I. Herring's store, No. 56, Main street, or No. 3, Columbian Hotel.
ja28—6t* JOHN W. CHRISTMAS.

WANTED TO EXCHANGE—City Property for Country Property. Apply to
GODDIN & APPERSON.
ja 17—d17, 18, & 20—w 24 & 31—d 1, 2 & 4 F*

WANTED—A situation as TEACHER, in some Academy or school, by a gentleman competent to teach the classics and sciences; and who is willing to go South. Best testimonials furnished. Address "P. N. M." Gainesville, King William county, Va. ja 27—7t*.

WANTED—TO PURCHASE—A HOUSE, In the city or suburbs, Containing five rooms. Address, stating all particulars, "J. B. S.," Richmond P. O.
ja 27—12t*

WANTED—NOTICE! NOTICE!! NOTICE!!! I wish to employ twenty-five BLACKSMITHS and twenty-five WHEELWRIGHTS, to work for the Army of the Potomac, at or near Manassas station. Liberal wages paid for good workmen.
ALFRED M. BARBOUR,
Chief Quartermaster Potomac District.
Centreville, Jan. 1, 1862. ja 10—eod1m

WANTED—Immediately, to go to Pittsylvania C. H., several good MACHINISTS and GUNSMITHS, to whom constant employment and liberal wages will be given. Apply at once, to
GEO. W. HALL,
At E. H. Stokes's, corner of Franklin street and Locust Alley. ja 25—1m*

WANTED—MULES and NEGROES.—I wish to purchase six young and sound broke MULES, of good sizes. I also desire to purchase three young negro MEN—those from the country preferred, as I want to employ them in the country. For such as will suit I will give the highest market price in cash.
TRUMAN A. PARKER,
ja 24—12t* Corner Cary and 10th sts.

WANTED—3 WHITE BOYS, To learn the Confectionary Business. Apply to A. ANTONI.
None need apply unless they can come well recommended. A. A.
ja 17—ts

WANTED.—I wish to purchase from 5,000 to 20,000 acres of good TAN BARK (timbered) LAND, on, or near, the James River and Kanawha Canal, for the purpose of erecting a tannery. I will pay for such land a fair cash price; or I will exchange a fine farm, on the Rappahannock river, for such land as above mentioned. Apply, at once, to
WM. F. SMOOT, Bowling Green,
ja 20—1m* Caroline county, Va.

WANTED.—Volunteers to form an Artillery Company, nearly full, to man the batteries in and around the city of Richmond, for the period of 12 months, and for no other purpose. Call at Hall, on 10th st., between Main and Cary streets. Those not having any place to stay can remain at the Hall until mustered into service.
R. A. MILLS, Captain.
ja 23—10t* A. TIMBERLAKE.

WANTED—A REGIMENT OF MEN FOR MANNING THE BATTERIES.—The Governor has authorized Messrs. J. PANNILL and WILLIAM P. BURWELL to say that he will receive, for twelve months, a number of companies, to organise a regiment, for the special purpose of manning the Batteries in and around the city of Richmond.

Any companies forming for this special service in the city or counties in which the militia has been ordered to hold itself in readiness, will apply forthwith.

Any persons in the city or country desirous to enlist in Company "A," now forming in this city, can apply, by letter or in person, at
J. PANNILL'S Counting-room,
Shockoe Warehouse, or
WM. P. BURWELL'S Law Office,
ja 15—1m* Bank st.

WANTED—NEGRO LABOR.—The James River and Kanawha Company wants to HIRE negro CARPENTERS and LABORERS, to work on the repairs of the canal during the present year. Liberal wages will be paid, and rations, clothing, and medicine and medical attendance furnished. For further information address the undersigned, in this city, or see the Company's Agents along the line of the canal, who are authorized to hire.
E. L. CHINN, Sup't
ja 15—dts J. R. and K. Canal.

WANTED—1,000 cords PERSIMMON TIMBER, suitable for manufacturing Shoe Lasts, for which the highest cash price will be paid. Also, the public to know that we have on hand and are constantly manufacturing all kinds of Shoe LASTS and Boot and Shoe TREES, at our manufactory, on 13th street, in rear of Shockoe Warehouse.
ja 22—1m* BOYLE, GAMBLE & CO.

WANTED.—A PHYSICIAN wishes to buy a small FARM, of from 100 to 300 acres, within twenty or thirty miles of Richmond, and near the river or one of the railroads. He wants good dwelling and other houses, and would prefer to buy the situation of some practicing physician. He will pay cash, or give Richmond property in exchange. Give particular description and the price, and address, for one month,
ja 21—1m* M. D.

WANTED—Immediately, 10,000 SILLS, Delivered on the line of the road between Richmond and Aquia Creek. Dimensions: 8 feet long, 9 inches diameter at small end, smoothly hewn to a thickness of 6 inches, clear of any defect calculated to impair strength. No sills will be received under size.

TERMS—For white or post oak, 40 cents each, cash, or 43 cents 6 months; for red or chesnut oak 33 cents each, cash, or 35 cents 6 months. For further information, apply to Section Masters, on line of road, or to
WM. N. BRAGG, Sup't Road.
Office R., F. & P. R. R. Co.,
Richmond, Jan. 22, 1862. ja 22—ts

WANTED—TO BUY—A young WOMAN, with or without incumbrance, competent and qualified as a house servant. Apply at corner of 12th and Franklin streets, over Confederate Commissioner's Office.
ja 1—ts

WANTED—Bonds of the Confederate States, of the PRODUCE LOAN, by
ja 8—ts BACON & BASKERVILL.

GROCERIES, LIQUORS, &c.

IN STORE and FOR SALE, A small lot of ADAMANTINE CANDLES.
R. W. PIERCE & CO., Cary st.,
fe 1—6t* Between 13th and 14th.

REMOVAL.—We have removed our Store to the large four-story Warehouse on Cary street, between 13th and 14th streets, four doors below our old stand, and have in store and for sale—
10,000 lbs prime BACON.
200 bushels Black-Eyed PEAS.
200 bushels BEANS.
500 bbls. FLOUR, different grades.
20 bbls. Mountain WHISKEY.
100 bushels TIMOTHY-SEED.
100 bushels CLOVER-SEED.
1,000 lbs. Country SOAP.
200 kegs LARD.
20 bbls. LARD.
20 boxes Adamantine CANDLES.
fe 1—ts R. W. PIERCE & CO.

HONEY AND PEACH BRANDY. Just received, a very superior cask of Old PEACH BRANDY. Also, 100 gallons pure Virginia HONEY, in bottles, put up expressly for family use, and for sale by
R. A. E. DABNEY,
ja 31—3t* Corner Broad and 7th sts.

200 BBLS. COMMON WHISKEY, distilled in the West,
40 bbls. BRANDY, GIN, and RUM,
25 eighth and quarter casks fine BRANDY,
20 bbls. GOLDEN SYRUP,
20 hhds. choice N. O. SUGAR,
50 sacks Virginia fine SALT,
95 " G. A. SALT,
50 bags COFFEE,
50 casks ALE and PORTER,
80 half-chests and small boxes extra quality Gunpowder TEA,
100 bbls. Refined SUGAR, all grades,
40 " Crushed and Powdered SUGAR,
100 half bbls. Family Roe HERRINGS,
50 bbls. N. C. and Halifax Cut HERRINGS, New LARD and BACON,
50 kegs Bicarb. SODA,
50 boxes and 20 bags PEPPER,
100 kegs pure WHITE LEAD,
500 bags Blackeye PEAS,
200,000 CIGARS, various brands,
100 boxes SOAP,
25 baskets OLIVE OIL,
20 cases SARDINES,
60 bbls. Stuart's Mountain WHISKEY,
200 baskets and cases Mumm & Co.'s, Chas. Heidsick's, and other brands of fine CHAMPAGNE WINE,
500 boxes Manufactured TOBACCO,
Starch, Wrapping Paper, Fig Blue, Blacking, Indigo, Matches, Yeast Powders, Flour, all grades; Peach, Cherry, and Blackberry Brandy.
For sale by WM. B. JONES & CO.,
ja 30—12t 15th st., between Main and Cary.

OLD VIRGINIA RYE WHISKEY.
50 bbls. Virginia WHISKEY, of good quality.
10 bbls. very fine old Rye WHISKEY, part five years old.
300 boxes and packages fine Chewing and Smoking TOBACCO.
10 bags Rio Coffee.
New Orleans, Clarified and Crushed SUGAR.
In store and for sale by GEO. I. HERRING,
ja 29—1m* 56 Main street.

C. A. BALDWIN & CO., (*Late of Alexandria,*) Having removed to the three story brick Storehouse on 13th, between Main and Cary streets, a few doors south of the Dispatch office, offer for sale at the lowest market rates
25 hhds. New Orleans and Clarified SUGARS.
175 boxes good to very superior TOBACCOS.
100,000 CIGARS, of various qualities.
50 cases Smoking TOBACCO.
1,000 lbs. CANDLE-WICK.
1,100 pair Soldiers' SHOES,
500 pair BROGANS
To which they will be adding daily such goods as their customers need. They invite country merchants, and particularly their old friends visiting this market, to give them a call.
ja 25—1m

GEO. M. FLECK RO. J. CHRISTIAN.
GEO. M. FLECK & CO., Manufacturers of superior White Wine and Pure Cider VINEGAR, For Pickling, &c. Main street, near 20th. Richmond, Va.
Orders sent by mail promptly attended to.
ja 28—2m*

SUGAR, COFFEE, SPICE, &c.
13 bbls. Crushed SUGAR,
13 hhds. N. O. SUGARS,
5 bags Rio COFFE,
9 bags PEPPER, PIMENTO, and GINGER,
In store and for sale by
DUNLOP, MONCURE, & CO.
ja 28—6t

BRANDY AND CLARET WINE.
5 ½-casks Dark and Pale BRANDY, superior quality,
75 cans St. Julian and Margaux CLARET,
In store and for sale by
DUNLOP, MONCURE, & CO.
ja 28—6t

REMOVAL.—WILLIAM T. KING has removed his stock of GROCERIES to the house vacated by Austin & Gentry, 3 doors west of his old stand.
In addition to the best asortment of Groceries to be obtained during the war, the subscriber will keep on hand a stock of Hay, Corn, Rye, Oats, Mill Feed, Bolted Meal, &c., at lowest cash prices
ja 25—1m WM. T. KING.

RICHMOND COFFEE MILLS, SAM'L YOUNGER & CO., Prop'rs, Coffee Dealers and Tea Merchants.
From and after the 1st February next, and during the blockade, *a first class and beneficial substitute for Coffee* will be provided for the trade and public in 1 lb. and 2 lb. packets, *ground and ready for use*. These will be packed in cases of 20 pounds each and upwards to suit purchasers.—The retail price at the stores will be 25 cents per pound marked on the labels.
Corner of 8th and Main sts.,
Opposite the Spotswood Hotel.
Coffee roasted for the trade in quantities not less than 100 pounds. ja 22—11t*

CONFEDERATE MILLS,
Office 29 Pearl street.
I AM NOW PREPARED to furnish "Confederate Mills" FRESH GROUND COFFEE, an excellent substitute for the pure article. It is put up in pound papers, neatly labelled, and packed in cases of sixty-four pounds each. Price 20 cents, subject to a discount to the trade.
G. W. ROBINSON,
ja 15—1m* Agent for the Manufacturers.

LIQUORS, GROCERIES, &c.
400 bls. Extra 1, Extra 2, and No. 3 Coffee SUGAR,
75 bbls. Crushed and Powdered SUGARS,
50 bags prime Rio COFFEE,
25 eighth and quarter casks fine FRENCH BRANDY,
100 barrels Common and Rye WHISKEY,
20 do. RUM and GIN,
25 do. Peach and Apple BRANDY,
20 do. Sweet Malaga WINE,
50 cases SARDINES,
300,000 CIGARS, assorted brands,
50 bbls. Golden SYRUP,
10 bags PEPPER,
100 bags Soft Shell ALMONDS,
100 boxes Ground PEPPER,
25 bbls. Pecan NUTS,
100 boxes Rhine WINE, very fine,
100 boxes fine CHAMPAGNE,
1000 bags GROUND PEAS,
50 kegs Sup. Carbonate SODA,
50 boxes MUSTARD,
100 boxes TOBACCO,
For sale by
THOMAS JONES, No. 8 Main st.,
ja 13—1m Richmond, Va.

CASTILE SOAP.—140 boxes pure CASTILE SOAP, Of recent importation. Just received and in store.
For sale by
ja 1—ts BACON & BASKERVILL.

J. H. STEVENS & CO., ENVELOPE MANUFACTURERS, CHARLOTTE, N. C.—We are now manufacturing ENVELOPES on an extensive scale by machinery, and are prepared to furnish any amount, on reasonable terms. Cash orders from the trade respectfully solicited and promptly attended to.
J. H. STEVENS,
ja 30—8w* W. H. SCHUTT.

PEG MACHINE FOR SALE.—I have for sale a PEG MACHINE New, and in good running order. One man and a boy can make from 8 to 12 bushels per day. For particulars address H. A. WISWELL, Staunton, Va., or G. W. LAKE, Richmond, Va. ja 29—5t*

CHINA, EARTHEN-WARE, AND GLASS-WARE, at Wholesale and Retail, No. 19 Pearl street.—We have yet on hand a very fine assortment of RETAILING GOODS, of every description.
Also, at Wholesale, a supply of all the articles usually purchased by Country Merchants, Hotels, &c., &c. Please give us a call.
WM. F. PUTLER & SON,
ja 31—6t Importers, 19 Pearl street.

PECAN NUTS.
25 barrels PECAN NUTS,
For sale by G. W. ROBINSON,
ja 29—6t* 29 Pearl st.

I HAVE ESTABLISHED A BROOM MANUFACTORY, And solicit orders, at 29 Pearl street.
ja 15—1m* G. W. ROBINSON

DRIED PEACHES.
125,000 pounds unpeeled DRIED PEACHES, halves quarters, and mixed, packed early in liquor barrels, and in safe keeping order.
For sale by
ROWLAND & BROTHERS,
ja 23—10t* Norfolk, Virginia.

LOST, STRAYED, &c.

LOST OR STRAYED—A BLACK HORSE. He has a blaze in his forehead; his hind feet are white, and a large scar on his front knee. All expenses will be paid and a liberal reward given if returned to
DR. F. DEANE,
fe 1—3t* Cor. of Grace and 7th streets.

LOST—A TRUNK—$25 REWARD.—On the 24th of December last, a large TRUNK, marked F. T. DAVIS, Winchester, was lost somewhere on the Railroad, probably at Manassas Station. Agents and Baggage-Masters will please look out for said Trunk, and if found, write to J. LUCIUS DAVIS,
ja 31—6t* Box 712, Richmond, Va.

LOST—On 30th January, between Col. Baldwin's office, on 7th street, and the office of the Wise Legion, a POCKET-BOOK, containing money to the amount of $500, and some notes on demand. The finder will receive a reward of FIFTY DOLLARS, by leaving the same at this office. ja 31—3t*

LOST—On Thursday morning, a small PEARL BREASTPIN. The finder will be suitably rewarded by leaving it at PURCELL, LADD & CO.'S Drug store.
ja 31—3t*

ESTRAY.—Came to my place, on the Grove road, one and a half miles from town, on the night of the 28th inst., a HORSE with saddle and bridle. The owner is requested to come forward, prove property, pay charges, and take him away
T. E. HAMBLETON, Jr.,
ja 31—3t* 16 Pearl st.

STRAY HORSE.—On Wednesday, the 22d instant, a bright Sorrel HORSE, blaze face, four white feet and nine years old last spring, was taken from the picket ropes near the city reservoir, and has not since been heard of. I will give a reward of $20 for his return to General WINDER, in this city.
WM. J. FIZER, 1st Jr Lieut.,
Capt. McComas's company, Wise Legion.
ja 31—6t*

$10 REWARD.—Strayed from a lot west of the Penitentiary, early in December last, a large bay horse MULE, with a white spot on the right shoulder. The above reward will be paid for her delivery to us, corner of 7th and Canal streets.
ja 31—3t* J. & J. TURNER.

STRAYED AWAY—Monday last, a yellow COW, speckled face and legs, crumpled horns, and white belly. She is heavy with calf, and may have a calf by now. A liberal reward will be paid for her recovery, or any information concerning her, by
JOHN JAISER, Stall No. 11,
ja 31—3t* New Market.

LOST—COUPONS.—Lost in transmission by mail to Charlottesville, Va., the following Coupons of the Orange and Alexandria Railroad Company:

No. 731 to 736 inclusive,	$40	each,	....	$240 00
" 64 to 66	"	20 "	....	60 00
				$300 00

Interest payable in May and November, at New York. All persons are cautioned not to buy or trade for them, as the same will not be paid.
ja 29—ts C. W. PURCELL & CO.

LOST—$25 REWARD—Between the First Market and Brooke Avenue, a BLACK BAG, Containing two Account Books and sundry papers. I will give the above reward for their delivery to me, at
Nos. 17 and 19, First Market.
de 21—ts JOHN LINDSEY.

EDUCATIONAL.

FREDERICKSBURG HIGH SCHOOL, FOR GIRLS. WM. B. JOHNSON, PRINCIPAL.
The next session of this School will commence on the 17th of February next, and continue five months.
The number of BOARDERS is limited to ten; and a full corps of Teachers is employed, all boarding with the Principal.
Circulars will be sent, on application, to Fredericksburg, Va.
fe 1—12t* WM. B. JOHNSON, Principal.

BOARDING AND DAY SCHOOL, FOR YOUNG LADIES, *Franklin street, between 3d and 4th*
The Misses CLOPTON (daughters of the late Judge Clopton) opened School on the 1st of October, 1861.
Circulars of terms, etc., will be sent to those desiring them. ja 23—1m*

SERVANTS FOR HIRE.

FOR HIRE—Five able-bodied Farm Hands; three Boys, accustomed to farm work; three Men, for ordinary work, and three Women, for kitchen and house work.
THOS. J. BAGBY, Agent for
Hiring out Negroes, Renting out Houses,
fe 1—2t No. 8 Wall street.

FOR HIRE—A WOMAN, With two children, one six years and the other two months old. She can be found at Cary street jail. For a good home, the terms will be made satisfactory.
ja 29—eod3t* ELLETT & DREWRY.

NEGROES FOR HIRE.
We have for hire the following description of SERVANTS, viz:
Chambermaids, Washers and Ironers;
Cooks, Washers, and Ironers;
Blacksmiths, Carpenters;
Shoemakers, Bricklayers;
Brick-Yard Hands, Laborers;
Wood-Choppers, Drivers;
Farm Hands, Factory Hands.
Also, several superior Dining-Room Servants.
CLOPTON & LYNE,
Cor. Franklin and Wall sts.,
ja 20—ts Up stairs.

FOR SALE.—A valuable Teamster and Farm hand, about 37 years old. Apply to
ja 18—ts B. A. COCKE.

RUNAWAYS.

RUNAWAY.—$25 REWARD will be paid for the apprehension and delivery in Mr. Grady's Jail of a negro MAN named JOB. It is supposed he is attending in some of the military camps near the city, and at night in Screamersville. He is small of stature; black whiskers; usually wears a blue overcoat and black beaver, or silk hat.
J. L. APPERSON, Adm'r of
fe 1—6t Wm. Jarvis, dec'd.

RUNAWAY.—FIFTY DOLLARS REWARD will be paid for the delivery at our office, or at our Mill in Manchester, of our absconded slave DICK BRYANT. Dick is about five feet eight inches high, light ginger-bread color, and about nineteen years old. Dick had on when he left a brown frock coat, dark pantaloons, and black Russia hat.
ja28—6t DUNLOP, MONCURE & CO.

RANAWAY—From the Carbon Hill Mines, in this county, on 13th inst., HENRY, a brown negro; about 5 feet 7 or 8 inches in height; round face; cheerful countenance; stout figure, and about 24 years of age. Henry was seen, a few days since, on the farm of Mrs. Virginia A. Taylor, in King George county.
TWENTY DOLLARS reward will be paid for his apprehension and delivery, in Jail at Fredericksburg or Richmond.
ja 25—ts JOHN J. WERTH, Agent.

DISSOLUTION.—The firm of WOMBLE & CLAIBORNE is this day dissolved by mutual consent. Either party will sign the name of the firm in liquidation.
JNO. E. WOMBLE,
JNO. H. CLAIBORNE.
Richmond, February 1, 1862.

A CARD.—The undersigned will continue the COMMISSION BUSINESS at the stand recently occupied by Womble & Claiborne, No. 11 Pearl street.
fe 1—d2w JNO. E. WOMBLE.

NOTICE.—Having purchased the interest of G. L. Lownes, deceased, of the late firm of LOWNES & COOK, I will continue the business as heretofore.
All persons indebted to the late firm will please call and settle their accounts; those having claims against the same will present them to me for payment.
I will continue to make all kinds of ORNAMENTAL CASTINGS for Railing and House-Work. Also other Castings and Wrought Iron work done at the shortest notice. Persons wanting work done will please give me a call. Foundry, 8th street near Main. WM. B. COOK.
ja 27—10t*

MILITARY ATTENTION.
BRASS LETTERS, CROSS SABRES, CROSS CANNONS, &c.
The undersigned are manufacturing to order and have always on hand BRASS PRESSED LETTERS, CROSS SABRES, CROSS CANNONS, &c., for MILITARY CAPS. Orders promptly attended to.
LEWIS & KAYTON, Brand Cutters,
13th, bet Main and Cary streets.
Address by mail "Lewis & Kayton," Box 995 Richmond, Va. ja 17—1m*

JUST RECEIVED—100 yards of Crenshaw's best Military GRAY CLOTH. Also, 100 yds. of Crenshaw's Confederate Blue Doeskin CASSIMERE, which the subscriber will sell at a small advance, or MAKE UP in UNIFORMS, at the shortest notice and on reasonable terms.
JOHN HARTZ, Military and Civic Tailor,
fe 1—1m* 8th, bet. Broad and Grace sts.

PATENT AGENCY, RICHMOND, VA., BY JAMES S. FRENCH, Late Examiner in the U. S. Patent-Office.
Patents procured and all business with the Patent-Office promptly attended to.
Office corner of Bank and 11th streets. Address Box 1,017. ja 23—3m*

BOTTLE CORKS, BOTTLE CORKS. BOTTLE CORKS.
50,000 BOTTLE CORKS, for sale by
THOMAS JONES,
ja 27—ts No 8 Main st., Richmond, Va.

Tri-Weekly South Carolinian

Daily Paper $5 per Annum. "BE JUST AND FEAR NOT—LET ALL THE ENDS THOU AIM'ST AT BE THY COUNTRY'S, THY GOD'S, AND TRUTH'S." Tri-Weekly $4 per Annum.

BY R. W. GIBBES. COLUMBIA, S. C., TUESDAY MORNING, FEBRUARY 4, 1862. VOL. XXV.—NO. 15.

BY TELEGRAPH.

Arrival of a French Man-of-War.

NEW ORLEANS, January 31.—It is reported that a French man-of-war is coming up the river. Commodore Hollins has received a despatch to that effect.

From the West.

NASHVILLE, January 30.—The latest advices from Munfordville state that the Yankees have sent back their sick from that place, and are busily engaged bringing up their artillery from Nolin and Bacon Creek. It is said they received marching orders early last week.

Four Yankee Regiments encamped at the bend below Woodsonville, this side of Green River, under cover of their heavy guns on the other side, send out pickets during the day towards Horse Cave, but draw them in at night.

NASHVILLE, January 31.—A private despatch from Bowling Green says that the remains of Zollicoffer and Peyton were received by our out-posts this evening, and will reach here to-day under military escort.

Latest Northern and European Intelligence

RICHMOND, February 1.—The New York *Herald*, of the 30th, says:

There is nothing later from the Burnside fleet. The storms had delayed its operations.

On the 29th, a skirmish occurred near Occoquan, in which nine Texans were killed and one taken prisoner.

The London *Herald*, in urging England to recognize the Southern Confederacy, says that if perfect free trade once be established with the South, England will have a fine market for her manufactured goods.

Lord Derby continues to advocate recognition.

The *Opinione Nationale* says that the Emperor says England will make war on the United States, and warns the French against it.

The French journals severely denounce the stone blockade of Charleston.

Massachusetts is making coast defences.

McClellan is well.

Half a million of dollars has been appropriated by the Federal House for heavy ordnance.

The House Committee has reported adversely to abolishing slavery in the District of Columbia.

Hamilton Fish departs as Commissioner. In Washington, doubts are entertained whether the Commissioners will be permitted to visit the South.

Financial matters continue to agitate Congress and Wall street.

The steamer Philadelphia has arrived at New York with a cavalry company from Fort Pickens.

No later European news.

Washington News.

WASHINGTON, January 23.—Instructions to Gen. Lane have doubtless been carefully elaborated, and are based, substantially, it is believed, upon ideas thrown out in high administration quarters to the following effect: "To let slavery be disposed of by military necessities and the course of events. If slaves come within our lines from the plantations beyond the Federal lines, use them. If they can work on fortifications, &c., use their services, clothe, feed and pay them. If necessary, arm them. If slaves of rebels, free them."

The resignation of Gen. Seigle not having been accepted—his military abilities being highly appreciated—he will not renew it.

Despatches from Nashville and private advices confirm the reported failure of the Federal movement made from Paducah up the Tennessee river and in the rear of Columbus. The enemy has retreated from Mayfield, Murray and all other points in Western Kentucky to which his forces had advanced, and has "crawfished" towards his fortifications at Paducah. It is believed that Halleck will double his forces and try it again as soon as the condition of the roads will permit of the effort.

REBELS IN MONTREAL.—The Louisville *Journal* says there are sixty-seven families at the Donegana House, Montreal, and on the receipt of the first news from England concerning the seizure of Mason and Slidell, so joyful were they that a supper was given by them at the house, costing $1,500.

OBITUARY.

Died, at her residence, in this city, on the 7th of January, after two weeks' illness, of pneumonia, Mrs. MISSOURIE E. D. DREGHORN, wife of Mr. A. J. Dreghorn, and daughter of Mr. Thos. Ligon, of Merriwether County, Ga., in the twenty-first year of her age. But a little more than two years since, she left the paternal roof and her native State to share the fortunes of one with whose life and devotion she had blended her own—having previously, and in the dewy freshness of her youth, consecrated herself to her Saviour, as a member of the Baptist Church. Henceforth the graces of a Christian, enriching and ennobling those of a natural amiability, gave beauty and attraction to her whole life. It was thus that, as a daughter, wife and mother, her pure and gentle virtues awakened the hearty affection of many true friends, whose kindly and constant attentions beguiled the hours of pain, and soothed her passage to the grave. That passage was marked by the calmness, fortitude and trust of the true believer. Conscious and even cheerful to the last, not more than fifteen minutes before she ceased to breathe, she united heartily in the prayers of her pastor, and parted from him with the assurance that her whole desire, as to herself and her loved ones, was that God's will should be done. Without a struggle, and almost imperceptibly, her waiting spirit passed away, leaving to bleeding hearts the sweet impression of her virtue and its persuasive call to that future greeting,

"Where no farewell tear is shed."

J. M. C. B.

TOWN TALK.—Yesterday was a rainy day, and the streets muddy, but that did not prevent gossip circulating and reports spreading. The news from Washington that a battle had been fought at or near Bowling Green, Ky., caused some little excitement, and formed the principal topic of street conversation. Of course, the wish, with every one, was that the Southerners had really gained a decisive victory at that point, and, upon the strength of that very general and patriotic wish, a report was started that Gen. Sydney Johnston had entrapped a large body of Federalists, who had telegraphed to Washington City that unless they were immediately reinforced, they were hopelessly lost; the report had not traveled far before it was enriched and made more acceptable by the addendum that Johnston had cut the Yankees to pieces! To make matters still more gratifying, another report was put in circulation to the effect that Fort Pulaski had opened on the Federal fleet, and sunk three of the enemy's gun-boats!—*Augusta Constitutionalist.*

JONATHAN WON'T FEED SAMBO.—The following is an extract from a letter from a highly respectable and intelligent gentleman in Savannah to his friend in this city. From it, it will be seen that the Yankees are tired of their bargain in "contrabands," and find that the Union sentiment in South Carolina is all a myth:

"The negroes are returning in a very destitute condition to their masters. Sherman sent word to Gen. Lee that the negroes were *starving* and asked for provisions. Gen. Lee replied that if the negroes were returned to their masters, they would be cared for. Two hundred were said to have returned in a body last week. The desertion of Beaufort and the burning of cotton on the sea islands has convinced Dupont and Sherman that there is no Union sentiment here."—*Raleigh Register.*

COUNTING HOUSE CALENDAR—FOR 1862

	SUNDAY.	MONDAY.	TUES.	WEDNES.	THURS.	FRIDAY.	SATUR.		SUNDAY.	MONDAY.	TUES.	WEDNES.	THURS.	FRIDAY.	SATUR.
JANUARY.				1	2	3	4	JULY,			1	2	3	4	5
	5	6	7	8	9	10	11		6	7	8	9	10	11	12
	12	13	14	15	16	17	18		13	14	15	16	17	18	19
	19	20	21	22	23	24	25		20	21	22	23	24	25	26
	26	27	28	29	30	31			27	28	29	30	31		
FEBRUARY							1								
	2	3	4	5	6	7	8	AUGUST,						1	2
	9	10	11	12	13	14	15		3	4	5	6	7	8	9
	16	17	18	19	20	21	22		10	11	12	13	14	15	16
	23	24	25	26	27	28			17	18	19	20	21	22	23
MARCH,							1		24	25	26	27	28	29	30
	2	3	4	5	6	7	8		31						
	9	10	11	12	13	14	15	SEPT.,		1	2	3	4	5	6
	16	17	18	19	20	21	22		7	8	9	10	11	12	13
	23	24	25	26	27	28	29		14	15	16	17	18	19	20
	30	31							21	22	23	24	25	26	27
APRIL,			1	2	3	4	5		28	29	30				
	6	7	8	9	10	11	12					1	2	3	4
	13	14	15	16	17	18	19	OCTOBER,	5	6	7	8	9	10	11
	20	21	22	23	24	25	26		12	13	14	15	16	17	18
	27	28	29	30					19	20	21	22	23	24	25
MAY,									26	27	28	29	30	31	
					1	2	3								1
	4	5	6	7	8	9	10	NOV.	2	3	4	5	6	7	8
	11	12	13	14	15	16	17		9	10	11	12	13	14	15
	18	19	20	21	22	23	24		16	17	18	19	20	21	22
	25	26	27	28	29	30	31		23	24	25	26	27	28	29
JUNE,									30						
	1	2	3	4	5	6	7	DEC.,		1	2	3	4	5	6
	8	9	10	11	12	13	14		7	8	9	10	11	12	13
	15	16	17	18	19	20	21		14	15	16	17	18	19	20
	22	23	24	25	26	27	28		21	22	23	24	25	26	27
	29	30							28	29	30	31			

A List of Letters

REMAINING in the Post Office at Columbia, S. C., February 1, 1862.

Persons calling for letters on this list, will please say "they are advertised:"

Allen, Miss M. & E. J.
Allen, George
Allen, John
Albright, J. W.
Algood, Mr.
Ambuse, Mrs. F.
Ankrum, W. B.
Aveilhe, Capt. P. A.
Barsh, F. H. 2
Barsh, W. P.
Beaufort, Wm.
Belton, Miss Sally
Biggs, Mrs. Sarah 2
Black, Miss Nancy
Bozeman, T. L.
Bradwell, Capt. Jno.
Brennan, Mrs. M.
Briggs, Betsy 2
Brown, Wm.
Burnet, Jourdan
Calhoun, A. P.
Carter, Elleck
Caughman, Miss P. C.
Center, R. T.
Chalmers, Miss Laura
Charles, Mrs. Mary
Chisolm, Lieut. Robt. 2
Chion, Miss E. V.
Cole, P. W.
Colmon, Wm.
Connor, Michael
Coogen, Michael
Craft, James
Craft, Mrs. C. F.
Culbreath, Mrs.
Davis, Ephraim
Dupree, W.
Ellington, R. A.
Fenly, Mrs. D. D.
Fike, C. L.
Funderbunk, G. W.
Gilmer, Mrs. Sarah
Gilliam, Mrs. Susan
Gooden, Mrs. Comfort
Gray, Miss J. C. 2
Graham, N. F.
Green, J. P.
Green, F. D.
Heffron, T. S.
Hertzog, L.
Heyward, Barnwell
Heyward, Miss L. B.
Hicks, Miss S. H.
Hopkins, Gen. J.
Horne, Rev. E. W.
Howell, Joseph
Hunt, Joseph
Hutson, Hon. W. F.
Ivey, Miss L. E.
James, Miss Janie
Jones, A. D.
Jones, Mrs. Jane
Jourdan, Wm.
Kaigler, Miss Sallie
Kennedy, R. A.
Kershaw, Col. J. B.
Keig, Col.
King, J. N.
Kinard Lieut. J. M.
Kirkland, Mrs. R.
Kittrell, J. B.
Leagan, T.
Lester, Mrs. L.
Levingston, J.
Levy, Mrs. Jane
Lowe, Capt. E. M.
Louis, Miss M. A.
Loois, Mrs. S. A.
Mabrie, Miss C. E.
Martin, Josiah 2
Mazyck, Hon. A.
McKinney, M.
McKlemore, George
McLean, Dr. A.
Machean, R.
Meate, R.
Michael, Miss Anna
Middleton, Col. J. A.
Middleton, T. A.
Myers, Miss E. S.
Neely, Miss M. J.
O'Neale, Miss G.
Parrott, Miss J. S.
Patterson, B. J.
Pennington, J. M.
Pike, Mrs. E. A.
Price, Mrs. E.
Rikard, Polly
Rives, R. P.
Rodgers, James
Service, Miss C. E.
Siun, A.
Sloan, Wm.
Stack, Miss A. E.
Stainback, R. P.
Swygert, Mrs. E.
Thompson, Mrs. Jennie
Tindal, J. S.
Tingen, B. S. 2
Tucker, J. H.
Tucker, Miss Fanny
Usher, John
Watson, P. A.
Westmoreland, T. T.
Wildhagen, A.
Williams, Col. J. D.
Williams, L. A.
Wilson, J. E.
Wilson, J. W. 2
Wilson, W. H.
Wilson, Mrs. M. C.
Wood, Miss Anna K.
Woldron, Miss S.
W. Y.

Feb. 2 2 J. B. GLASS, P. M.

SPORTING POWDER, &c.

At the Sign of the Golden Anvil.

WE have just received a small lot of SPORTING POWDER, consisting of Dupont's Rifle, Eagle and Diamond Grain Powder. Also, Hazard's Duck Shooting Powder; which, together with a full assortment of Percussion Caps, Gun Wads and Drop Shot of all sizes, will be sold at a small advance on cost at retail, for cash only.

Jan. 5 FISHER & AGNEW & CO.

(No. 299.)

An Act for the employment of Laundresses in Military Hospitals.

The Congress of the Confederate States of America do enact, That Superintendents of the different Military Hospitals be and they are hereby authorized to employ laundresses for the sick and wounded soldiers, at such rates and in such numbers as may be prescribed by the War Department.

APPROVED December 7, 1861.

(No. 331.)

An Act to authorize the appointment of additional Officers for the Navy.

The Congress of the Confederate States of America do enact, That the President be and he is hereby authorized to appoint the following officers of the Navy, in addition to those heretofore authorized, to wit: two Captains, five Commanders, fifty Lieutenants, ten Assistant Paymasters, and thirty Assistant Surgeons; said appointments to be made from the Navy and from civil life, as the President may see fit, and to terminate at the end of the war.

APPROVED December 24, 1861.

(No. 324.)

An Act to amend an Act entitled "An Act to establish a Uniform Rule of Naturalization for persons enlisted in the Armies of the Confederate States of America.

SEC. 1. *The Congress of the Confederate States of America do enact,* That the provisions of the above recited Act be and the same are hereby extended to all persons, not citizens of one of the Confederate States, who are engaged in the naval service of the Confederate States during the present war with the United States: *Provided,* however, that the oath therein prescribed may be administered by the Captain or other commanding officer of any national ship, to all persons entitled to the benefit of this Act and attached thereto, and that the duties therein imposed upon the Secretary of War in regard to persons in the military service, shall be performed by the Secretary of the Navy in reference to persons in the naval service.

APPRONED December 24, 1861.

(No. 327.)

An Act to provide for the appointment of Chaplains in the Navy.

The Congress of the Confederate States of America do enact, That whenever any vessel of the Confederate States Navy shall be about to depart for any point beyond the limits of the Confederate States, the President may, in his discretion, employ a Chaplain for the voyage, who shall receive the same pay and emoluments as Chaplains in the Army.

APPROVED December 24, 1861.

Charlotte and South Carolina R. R. Co.

COLUMBIA, S. C., JANUARY 21, 1862.

THE ANNUAL MEETING of the stockholders will be held at this place, on WEDNESDAY, fifth of February next, at 10 o'clock a. m.

Stockholders and their immediate families will be passed free coming to and returning from the meeting in reasonble time.

C. BOUKNIGHT, Secretary.

Jan. 12 †12

ANNUAL MEETING OF THE Stockholders of the South Carolina Railroad Company and of the South-western Railroad Bank.

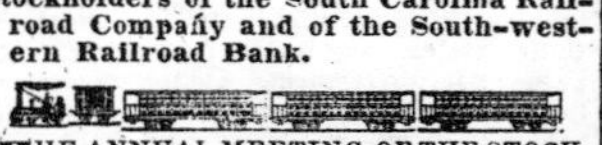

THE ANNUAL MEETING OF THE STOCKHOLDERS of the above institution will be held at the Bank Hall, in Charleston, on the SECOND TUESDAY IN FEBRUARY, it being the 11th day of the month. Hour of convening, 11 o'clock a. m.

On the day following, (Wednesday,) there will be an election held at the same place, between the hours of 9 a. m. and 3 p. m., for fifteen Directors of the Railroad Company and thirteen Directors of the Bank. A committee to verify proxies will attend.

The attention of the Stockholders is called to the following resolution, adopted at the Annual Meeting, in 1854:

Resolved, That every Stockholder who shall have owned his Stock for three months previous to the general Annual Meeting of Stockholders, be permitted to pass on the Road to and from said meeting, free of charge; and that every Stockholder who shall have owned five or more shares for three months previous to the general Annual Meeting of Stockholders, be permitted to pass on the Road, to and from said meeting, with his immediate family, free of charge; and that the resolution of February 12, 1851, upon the subject, be and is hereby rescinded.

Jan. 21 ‡ J. R. EMERY, Secretary.

☞ *Guardian* copy three times a week till day.

New Arrival of Goods!

BROWN'S ESSENCE OF JAMAICA GINGER.
TARRANT'S APERIENT MAGNESIA.
HUSBAND'S MAGNESIA.
CITRATE OF MAGNESIA.
FLOUR OF SULPHUR. CREAM TARTAR.
BURNING FLUID.
SEIDLITZ POWDERS.
WISTAR'S BALSAM OF WILD CHERRY.
LYON'S KATHAIRON.
BARRY'S TRICOPHEROUS.
RED CASTILE SOAP. WHITE BAR SOAP.
CASTOR OIL. For sale only at retail for cash by FISHER & HEINITSH, Druggists.

TANNER'S OIL! TANNER'S OIL!!

At the Sign of the Golden Pad-Lock.

1.000 GALS. TANNER'S OIL. Also a very large assortment of Tanner's and Currier's Tools, of every variety, in store and for sale at very low prices for cash by

Jan. 7 JOHN C. DIAL.

A NEW BOOK.

CAUSE AND CONTRAST, an essay on the American Crisis; by T. W. MacMahon. For sale by TOWNSEND & NORTH.

HOOP IRON.

100 BUNDLES. HOOP IRON, assorted sizes, together with a complete assortment of Rod Iron, Horse Shoe Iron, Band Iron, Oval, Half Round, Round, Square and Flat Iron, for sale by FISHER & AGNEW & CO.

McLean's Strengthening Cordial and Blood Purifier.

A SUPPLY just received at E. SILL'S Drug Store, Opposite Exchange Bank.

Nov. 19

SEED RYE! SEED RYE!!

150 BUSHELS superior SEED RYE, for sale low by JAS. C. KENNETH, Successor to C. H. Baldwin.

Oct. 18

COMMERCIAL.

Columbia Market, for Week ending February 1.

COTTON.—The sales this week amount to 314 bales. Prices of our last fully sustained. We quote 6½@8½c. extremes.

FLOUR.—No change in quotations since our last. We quote $4½ per sack of 98 lbs. Extra family $4¾.

CORN.—In good demand. We quote 90c. per bushel of 56 lbs. in bulk.

PEAS.—90c. per bushel.

HAY.—North Carolina, none in market.

BACON.—Country (hog round) 21c. per 100 lbs.; Western sides, none.

WHEAT BRAN.—None in market.

FODDER.—$1.75 ℔ 100 lbs.

OATS.—We quote 75c.@80c. per bushel.

THE NORFOLK DAY BOOK.

NOW IS THE TIME TO SUBSCRIBE!

TERMS: Daily, one year, $5; Daily, six months, $3; Daily, one month, $1; Weekly, one year, $1.

The DAY BOOK HAS NOW BECOME THE NEWSPAPER OF THE SOUTH. The very latest Northern and European news appears in its columns one, two and three days in advance of all other papers in the Confederacy.

We submit the following extracts from what others have to say of us:

D. T. Bisbie, Esq., who has lately returned from Europe, with important despatches to the Confederate States Government, says in a recent letter: "While in London and Paris, I saw several quotations from the Norfolk *Day Book*, and since my return I have also noticed extracts from the same sprightly journal in the newspapers of New York, Charleston and other cities."

The Wilmington (N. C.) *Daily Journal* says: "The Norfolk *Day Book* has become the most valuable exchange papers we receive, as it contains the very latest news from the Rump Government, as well as foreign news."

Subscribers to the *Day Book* may rely upon having their papers sent promptly by mail.

Address, with amount of subscription enclosed,

JOHN R. HATHAWAY, Editor and Proprietor.

Jan. 21

Blacksmith's Tools.

At the Sign of the Golden Pad-Lock.

A very large supply of BLACKSMITH'S TOOLS, consisting of Bellows, Anvils, Vices, Hammers, Stock and Dies, Screw Plates, Buttresses, Pinchers, Rasps, Files, Farrier's Hammers and Knives, Tongs, Tire Benders, &c., on hand and for sale by

Dec. 5 JOHN C. DIAL.

PAPERS AT THE CAPITAL.

THE SOUTH CAROLINIAN,

Published Daily and Tri-Weekly.

COLUMBIA BANNER,

A Weekly Family Paper.

THIS is the LARGEST FAMILY PAPER IN THE SOUTH, and is offered to the domestic circle for News and Political Intelligence. The Tales and Stories which are offered to the readers of the *Banner* are the efforts of Southern Genius, which it is a pleasure to foster. Original Sketches, Literary and Scientific Essays, and Miscellaneous Selections, regularly make their appearance in its columns.

Subscription—Daily, $6; Tri-Weekly, $4; Weekly, $2 per annum, in advance. Papers stopped when subscription expires.

Jan. 1 R. W. GIBBES, Proprietor.

BOOK BINDING.

South Carolinian and Columbia Banner Office.

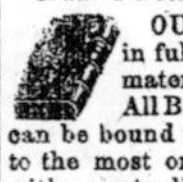

OUR BINDERY is now in full operation, with new materials of every kind. All BOOKS, PAMPHLETS, MUSIC, &c., can be bound in ANY STYLE, from the plainest to the most ornamental, on moderate terms, and with punctuality and despatch.

BLANK BOOKS,

For District Officers, Sheriffs, Clerks, Tax Collectors, &c., &c., as well as for Counting Houses and every other form, will be manufactured to order.

☞ Terms moderate and promptness observed.

January 1 R. W. GIBBES.

South Carolinian Advertising Rates.

SQUARES.	1 mo.	2 mo.	3 mo.	6 mo.	12 mo.
One Square.........	$7	$12	$15	$20	$35
Two Squares........	10	15	20	30	50
Three "	13	18	23	37	60
Four "	16	22	26	45	70
Five "	20	25	29	50	80
Six "	24	28	32	55	90
Seven "	27	31	35	60	100
Eight "	30	34	39	65	110
Nine "	33	37	42	70	120
Half a Column.....	36	40	45	80	130

Tri-Weekly Advertisements, two-thirds above. Professional and Business Cards $20 per an.

Weekly Advertisements 50 cents per square for each Insertion.

Special Notices 50 cents per square for each Insertion, and in no case to be subject to contract. Obituary Notices, Reports, Resolutions or Proceedings of any Society, Association or Corporation, 50 cents per square.

Advertisements not marked on the copy for special time will be inserted until forbid, and payment exacted.

Contract Advertisements payable quarterly; Advertisements from strangers and transient persons payable in advance. All others will be considered due when called for.

Elastic Stockings, Knee Caps, Anklets.

FOR the treatment of varicose veins, weak and swelled joints, &c. A fresh stock just opened at E. SILL'S Drug Store, Opposite Exchange Bank.

March 5

OILS! OILS!! OILS!!!

At the Sign of the Golden Pad-Lock.

3.000 GALS. pure LARD OIL.
2,000 gals. pure COTTON SEED OIL.
1,000 gals. pure COAL OIL.
500 gals. pure LINSEED OIL.
In store and for sale at low prices for cash by

Nov. 7 JOHN C. DIAL.

OLD RYE WHISKEY.

5 BARRELS, of SUPERIOR QUALITY, at E. SILL'S Drug Store, Opposite Exchange Bank.

Aug. 22

State of South Carolina—Richland Dist.

By Jacob Bell, Esq., Ordinary of said District.

WHEREAS Martha Wynn and William H. Jones hath applied to me for Letters of Administration, on all and singular the goods and chattels, rights and credits of Robert T. Wynn, late of the District aforesaid, deceased:

These are, therefore, to cite and admonish all and singular the kindred and creditors of the said deceased, to be and appear before me, at our next Court of Ordinary for the said District, to be holden at Columbia, on Monday, the tenth day of February next, at 10 o'clock a. m., to show cause, if any, why the said Administration should not be granted.

Given under my hand and seal of the Court, this twenty-seventh day of January, in the year of our Lord one thousand eight hundred and sixty-two, and in the eighty-sixth year of the sovereignty and independence of South Carolina. JACOB BELL,

Jan. 28 tu2 Ordinary Richland District.

LAMPBLACK! LAMPBLACK!!

At the Sign of the Golden Anvil.

5 BBLS. LAMPBLACK just received and for sale by FISHER & AGNEW & CO.

Jan. 7

Old Cognac Brandy and Bourbon Whiskey

A SUPPLY, of unsurpassed purity, at E. SILL'S Drug Store, Opposite Exchange Bank

Dec. 2

GENUINE HAVANA SEGARS.

A FEW thousand genuine HAVANA SEGARS, imported on a vessel which has very recently run the blockade, just opened at E. SILL'S Drug Store, Opposite Exchange Bank.

Oct. 31

LIME! LIME!! LIME!!!

At the Sign of the Golden Anvil.

100 BBLS. FRESH LIME, just received and for sale at $1.60 per barrel, in lots of ten barrels and upwards; and $1.65 per barrel in less quantities.

Jan. 28 FISHER & AGNEW & CO.

COLLETON BITTERS.

A SUPPLY at E. SILL'S Drug Store.

Nov. 19

LYRICS AND SKETCHES.

THIS is the title of a new Southern book of poetry and prose, very neatly bound, by William M. Martin, with a brief memoir of the author, by J. W. D. Price—plain, 70 cents; gilt, 85 cents, or 15 cents extra when ordered by mail. Send orders to TOWNSEND & NORTH, Booksellers.

Jan. 5

COXE'S SPARKLING GELATINE.

COOPER'S AMERICAN ISINGLASS, French ISINGLASS, LIQUID RENNET, FLAVORING EXTRACTS, of extra purity and strength, embracing every variety among them, Rose, Vanilla, Peach, Pine Apple, Nectarine, Almond Nutmeg, Lemon, Orange, &c. A large supply just opened at E. SILL'S Drug Store

CHOICE COUNTRY BACON.

2.000 POUNDS CLEAR SIDES.
1,500 pounds SHOULDERS.
1,000 pounds HAMS.
1,000 pounds sugar-sured HAMS.
In store and for sale cheap for cash by

Nov. 5 JAS. C. KENNETH.

FOR SHERIFF.

MR. EDITOR: At the request of many friends, I announce myself a candidate for SHERIFF of Richland District, at the ensuing election.

Oct. 13 E. S. PERCIVAL.

FOR SHERIFF.

THE friends of JESSE E. DENT, Esq., mindful of the prompt and faithful but impartial and forbearing manner in which, for four years, he discharged the responsible duties of Sheriff of Richland District, beg leave respectfully to present his name as a candidate for re-election to that office. He will receive the cordial support of MANY WARM AND ZEALOUS FRIENDS.

Sept. 29

GUANO.

We have on hand a few hundred barrels of PHŒNIX and JOHNSON ISLAND GUANO, of last spring's importation, which we offer to Planters at $42 per ton, cash, or $50, payable in Middling Fair Cotton, at 10 cents per pound.

These Guanos were used very extensively last year in almost all the cotton-growing Counties of this State and South Carolina. Planters who do not use either, can doubtless get satisfactory information from their neighbors. As our stock is very small, and cannot be increased, those who wish to supply themselves will do well to apply early.

DAN. H. WILCOX & CO., Augusta, Ga.

P. S.—We have also a small quantity of AMERICAN and COLUMBIA GUANO.

Jan. 28 ‡2mo* D. H. W. & CO.

IN THE COMMON PLEAS.

Tracey, Irwin & Co., vs. Charles Street.—*Declaration in Attachment.*

WHEREAS the plaintiff in this action did on this day file his declaration against Charles Street, the defendant, who is absent from and without the limits of the State, (as it is said,) and having neither wife or attorney known upon whom a copy of the above declaration, with a rule to plead thereto, may be served: It is, therefore, in pursuance of the Acts of the General Assembly of the State in such cases made and provided, ordered, that the defendant do plead thereto on or before the 12th day of July, 1862, otherwise final and absolute judgment will be then given and awarded against said Charles Street. A. G. BASKIN, Clerk of the Court.

OFFICE OF COMMON PLEAS, July 11, 1861.

July 12 4tq

Bank Books.

CHECKS on the different Banks, bound in book form, can be obtained at the Bindery of the Carolinian Office. They will be found very useful to every merchant January 1

The South Carolinian.

BY R. W. GIBBES.

SUBSCRIPTION.

Daily Paper, per annum........................ 6
Tri-weekly, per annum.............................. 4
Columbia Banner, (Weekly,) per annumu....... 2

Having adopted strictly the Cash System, no paper will be mailed unless paid in advance.

ADVERTISING.

Advertisements will be inserted in the Daily or Tri-weekly Carolinian as follows: One square (ten lines) or less, first insertion, 50 cents; each subsequent insertion 38 cents; and in the Columbia Banner, or once a week in the South Carolinian, 50 cents each insertion.

☞ The number of insertions must be distinctly written by the advertiser on every advertisement, or they will be inserted until ordered out.

General Newspaper Account of the Burnside Expedition.

Fortress Monroe, January 28.—By the arrival of the steamer Eastern State we have the most direct and official intelligence of the arrival of the Burnside expedition at its destination. The Eastern State left Hatteras Inlet last night, and arrived here late this evening.

The recent storms were unusually severe at Hatteras, and consequently delayed and crippled the expedition; but when the Eastern State left everything looked favorable.

The expedition sailed from Hampton Roads on the 11th and 12th instants, and consisted of one hundred and twenty-five vessels, of all classes. They arrived at Hatteras between the 12th and 17th, having been greatly retarded by severe storms and adverse winds, which prevailed about that time. After their arrival, they experienced a series of storms of such unparalleled severity that for two days in succession, on more than one occasion, it was impossible to hold communication between any two vessels of the fleet.

After the first storm, it was discovered that, instead of vessels drawing eight and a half feet being able to go over the swash, or bars, as Gen. Burnside had been informed, no vessel drawing over seven and a quarter feet could pass into Pamlico Sound. No vessel either could pass the outside bar drawing over thirteen feet, unless skillfully piloted; consequently the steamer City of New York struck on the bar, loaded with a cargo valued at $200,000, and consisting of powder, rifles and bombs, and proved a total loss. The captain and crew, after bravely remaining in the rigging for forty hours, were saved.

The gun-boat Zouave dragged her anchors, stove a hole in her bottom, and sunk, proving a total loss. Her crew was saved.

The steamer Pocahontas went ashore near the light-house, and became a total wreck. Ninety valuable horses, belonging to the Rhode Island battery, were on board, and were all drowned, including several valued at five hundred dollars each.

The Grapeshot parted her hawser, by which she was towed, and went down at sea. Her crew were saved.

An unknown schooner, laden with oats, and another schooner, also unknown, were all lost on the beach. Six of the crew of the latter perished.

The steamer Louisiana struck on the bar, where she still remains. The report of her having been burned is entirely incorrect. She may be got off.

The Eastern Queen and also the Voltigeur are ashore. The latter will probably be got off.

The water vessels had not reached their destination when the Eastern State left, and had it not been for the condensers on board of some of the vessels and on shore, terrible sufferings would have occurred. As it was, the water casks were old whiskey, camphine and kerosene oil casks. It is thought that the Union pilots of Hatteras have proved themselves traitors, having intentionally run several vessels ashore.

One of the storms can only be described as terrific. The waters in every direction were covered with foam, the waves dashing with a clear sweep across the Hatteras shore, and completely cutting off the post from all outside communication. The current was rushing at the rate of five miles per hour, and the chop seas prevented Gen. Burnside from answering any of the signals of distress or communication with his generals. At one time, flags would appear Union down on a number of vessels, indicating a want of water, coal or provisions.

Col. J. W. Allen, Ninth New Jersey regiment, and Surgeon F. S. Weller, with a boat's crew, and the second mate of the Ann E. Thompson, when they found that the troops needed water, manned the life-boat in order to reach the General. Unfortunately the boat was swamped, and the colonel, surgeon and mate were drowned. The boat's crew were saved.

Colonel J. W. Allen was born in Burlington, New Jersey, and is forty-five years of age. He is a civil engineer by profession. He was for several years colonel of the New Jersey militia regiments.

Despite all these adverse circumstances, General Burnside has succeeded in getting over the bar one-half of his vessels, all the gun-boats, and seven thousand troops. Everything appeared in a satisfactory condition when the Eastern State left.

The large transports with the troops remained outside of the bar, until the arrival of the S. R. Spaulding, from Port Royal, on the 23d, when Captain Howes volunteered to bring them all inside. This was accomplished yesterday afternoon, the Eastern State passing the last as she left.

A portion of the gun-boats chartered by General Burnside for the expedition refused to proceed further than Fortress Monroe.

Fall weather has now set in, and the schooners are making their appearance with water and coal, and everything looks promising.

The General is confident of ultimate success, and has the respect of every man under his command.

General Burnside left Fortress Monroe on the Picket, but subsequently took possession of the Spaulding, which he will occupy as his flag-ship. She will be used for taking the remaining troops over the bar. The only troops that have been landed are the Twenty-fourth Massachusetts regiment, and the Rhode Island battery. Colonel Hawkins' regiment goes with General Burnside's expedition, and their place will be supplied by the Sixth New Hampshire.

There has been no loss of life except what is above mentioned. Eleven deaths have occurred since the fleet sailed.

Mr. Shelburn comes in the Eastern State, as a bearer of despatches from General Burnside. We are indebted to Dr. A. Rawlings, the only other passenger, who goes North, for the above statement.

Different statements are received at Hatteras from the surrounding population in relation to the disposition and intentions of the enemy. Some who come in say that they are completely frightened and will not make a stand.

Another report is, that large masses of troops will be concentrated in the vicinity; and still another story, confirmed by many, is that their exertions will be directed chiefly to placing obstructions in our progress to Norfolk.

The rebels keep a good lookout for our movements with their gun-boats.

Two of them made their appearance immediately after the storm, but disappeared when chased.

Additional Particulars.—The Baltimore *American*, of the 29th, is indebted to Mr. James L. Aspril, Purser of the Louisiana, who with Mr. Akers, Engineer of the boat, arrived in Baltimore on the previous evening, for the following additional information in reference to the position of affairs at Hatteras Inlet when the steamer Eastern State left there:

The Pocahontas went ashore on Saturday night week, ten miles North of Hatteras. Before she went ashore her wheel chain broke and her boilers were rolled off their legs. The engineer managed to keep steam up until she was beached, about twenty yards from shore. The crew landed, carrying a large hawser ashore, which they made fast to the beach.

The crew and soldiers on board in charge of the horses numbered eighty men. Those left on board escaped to the shore by the hawser. Some of the horses had been previously thrown overboard to lighten the boat. In three-quarters of an hour afterwards the boat broke into three pieces and floated ashore. In the after cabin, when it came ashore, one of the horses was found quietly eating hay. Of the ninety horses on board only twelve came ashore alive. The men built large fires on the beach, and the light from them was probably taken by the rebels for the burning of a steamer. The crew afterwards made their way to the village at Big Kinnekeath, where they were succored by the inhabitants, and afterwards came down the sound to Hatteras. The soldiers marched down the beach. The officers and crew were quartered on board the Louisiana. The officers are—Henry North, Captain; Mr. Cator, First Mate; Josiah Linthicum, Second Mate; Tone Hamilton, Engineer, and others. They will come up by the next arrival.

The Louisiana went ashore on Tuesday night, the 14th, on the inner bar, at Hatteras Inlet. On Thursday, the 23d, the steamer got afloat, but during a gale on the 24th, again went ashore, the steamer New Brunswick having run over and carried away her anchor. The vessels also collided, and considerable damage was done to the upper works of each. The New Brunswick floated off, but the Louisiana still remained ashore. She remained tight, and would be got off at the first high tide. Her position was not considered dangerous. Capt. William H. Phillips was exerting himself to get her afloat, and from the able manner in which he handled her during the storm, it was believed would succeed.

The bark Voltigeur was ashore inside the inlet. All her cargo was safe, but the vessel would not probably be got off.

The gun-boat Zouave, a purchased vessel, bilged on the 15th, inside the inlet, and sunk on the bar. All her guns and stores were taken off.

The City of New York struck on a bar outside the inlet on the 13th. She broke in two and went to pieces on the next day. Nothing was saved from her. Parts of her cargo floated into the inlet. The officers and crew were all saved.

A schooner, loaded with coal, struck on the inner bar on the 15th. Her crew were saved. A barge, name unknown, was lost outside.

The steamship Suwanee was ashore inside the bar, but would be got off.

When the Eastern State left, the last ship outside, the Aracon, was going in, towed by the S. R. Spaulding. Several of the troop ships, drawing too much water, were lying inside the inlet, but could not pass over the inner bar. The troops on board these vessels were landed and transferred to boats inside the bar. There were about one hundred vessels in the sound and the remainder in the inlet.

On the 21st, two rebel gun-boats came down the sound reconnoitering. Several of our gun-boats started after them, and shots were exchanged, but the thick fog prevented any long pursuit.

During the storm, the beach at the inlet was completely overflowed, and the troops had to move further up to higher ground. No damage was, however, done to the forts.

The Vessels Lost and Disabled.—The Louisiana, disabled, is the largest steamer of the fleet, being one of the only two vessels which could carry an entire regiment. She is said to be the largest, finest and fastest steamer ever built at Baltimore, and was only chartered the day before the sailing of the fleet from Annapolis. Her hull is nearly 300 feet in length, of corresponding breadth of beam, with splendid state-rooms, and originally cost, including furniture, tackle, outfit, &c., about $105,000. She was built in 1852, by Mr. Hugh A. Cooper, the machinery made by Mr. Charles Reeder, and has made over twenty miles per hour. For more than three weeks the steamer has been attached to the Burnside expedition. Her principal officers are as follows: Captain, Phillips; First Mate, Jacob Kirwan; Engineers, George W. Akers and Vance Wilson; Clerk, James Aspril. The Sixth New Hampshire Regiment, Col. Nelson Converse, was on board.

The Grape-shot, reported to have parted the hawser by which she was towed and to have gone down at sea, was one of the floating batteries sent with the expedition. She was formerly a canal boat, was almost solid from deck to keel, and was divided into five compartments. She had but one deck. She was under the command of Master's Mate N. B. McKean, and carried two guns.

The Zouave, also sunk, was a propeller gun-boat, carrying four guns—one thirty-pounder Parrot rifled gun, two twelve-pounder Wiard rifled guns, and one twelve-pounder boat howitzer. She was commanded by Capt. Wm. Hunt.

Companies A, B, C, F, G and K, of the Twenty-fifth New York Regiment, were on board the Zouave. This regiment was attached to Gen. Foster's command. His staff was also on board.

The Eastern Queen and the Voltiguer are reported ashore. The Eastern Queen is a side-wheel steamer, under the command of Capt. Collins. The Fourth Rhode Island, Col. J. D. Rodman, attached to Gen. Park's Brigade, was on board. The Voltigeur is a purchased sailing troop-bark, under command of Capt. Wm. Bly. She had on board a portion of the Eleventh Connecticut, Col. T. H. C. Kingsbury.

The City of New York was an African vessel, 574 tons, fifteen feet draught, and with two decks. She was built of white oak, copper and iron fastened, and was launched at Hoboken, in 1852. She has a vertical engine of 300 horse power. She was 170 feet long, with 26 feet beam, and formerly ran on the line between Boston and Philadelphia.

The Pocahontas was an old steamboat, built some twenty years ago, and used to run on the Chesapeake Bay. For some years she has been laid up in ordinary, and was only chartered a few days before the sailing of the expedition.

England and the Blockade.

The surrender of Mason and Slidell, says the Richmond *Examiner*, although it has resulted in a satisfactory adjustment of the Mason-Slidell affair, may, after all, exercise but little influence in securing perfect harmony between Great Britain and the United States. There is a strong party feeling in England antagonistic to the continuance of the Southern blockade, and the Northern press betray great fear lest this party may coerce the Palmerston administration into a recognition of the Southern Confederacy and the re-opening of our ports. The *Herald*, in an article on the subject, says:

Already violent attacks on the stone fleet have appeared in some of the English papers as a preliminary movement. That the efforts of the party will meet with determined opposition from the present Government we well know, but that the question of recognition will be violently agitated in Parliament on its meeting, early in February, is highly probable.

The question is one out of which the tory party will endeavor to make as much political capital as possible, by creating a feeling in favor of the recognition, and urging the Government to its accomplishment. The recognition would only be asked for with a view to the further step of breaking the blockade—an act which would involve the violator in a war with this country. Mere recognition, although unfriendly to the United States, would not be an actual *casus belli*; but the forcible re-opening of our ports would be an act of direct hostility which we could not overlook. England, then, in adopting such a course, would do so with the full knowledge that it would involve her in a great American war. Louis Napoleon, who is strenuously exerting himself to induce England to assume that attitude of hostility towards the United States which would entangle her in a war, very likely tries to blind her to the danger, as well as the consequences, of a conflict between the two nations. See the allusion to the stone fleet in the *Moniteur* in another column. But he must be regarded in so doing not only as the enemy of both, but of the civilized world. His designs are purely selfish. With the English forces engaged in this country, and those of Spain in Mexico, there would remain no insurmountable obstacle to the extension of his power on the continent of Europe; for, while he, aided by Victor Emanuel, made war upon Austria, and dictated terms to the rest of Germany, Russia, in consideration of not opposing him, would take possession of Constantinople, and cut off the overland communication with India. Thus, in Central and Eastern Europe, France and the power of the North would be simultaneously engaged in destroying the balance of power for their own aggrandizement. What could England do at such a time to resist this tide of invasion? Her own greatness would be destroyed, her own existence imperiled. France and Russia would become the dominant powers in Europe, and, with the peace of the world so far destroyed, it is impossible to tell how far the work of conquest would proceed.

For our own part, we do not believe that the Palmerston administration will either yield to party clamor or become a prey to the machinations of the inscrutable of the Tuileries. It will consequently expose itself to the danger of a defeat, in which event will have the option of resigning or of calling for a general election. Probably it will have sufficient faith in the sober thought and good sense of the people at large to prefer the latter; and if it does so, we have little apprehension of the party in favor of war with the United States being installed in power. The Palmerston Government, being thus restored to public and parliamentary confidence, will adhere to its present course of neutrality. It is only in case Palmerston goes out of office that we fear the blockade will be broken. Even if the present administration should be led to acknowledge the Confederacy, we feel sanguine that so long as Palmerston is at the head of affairs he will use every effort to prevent Great Britain committing such a piece of political folly, not to say suicide, as going to war with the United States when there is neither reason nor object for it. The want of cotton cannot be alleged as an excuse for such a course, as the supply in the Lancashire warehouses is still large—larger than it was at this time last year—and, with the diminished demand for the manufactured article, some months must elapse before there can be any outcry for the raw material.

On the whole, therefore, although we anticipate a period of great political agitation in the English Parliament on the blockade question, growing to some extent out of the affair of the Trent and its discussion, we are sanguine, judging from the complexion of the news by the Europa published this morning, of being allowed to put an end to this rebellion in our own way, without any interference on the part of foreign nations.

Provisional Congress.—We learn that there is no immediate prospect of a dissolution of this body, although its term of existence must expire within a very few weeks, *nolens volens*. Among the bills recently passed is one making some changes in the organization and enlistment of the military force, amendatory of the "act to raise an additional military force, to serve during the war." The first section provides that volunteers may be accepted by the President singly, as well as in companies, squadrons, battalions or regiments. The second, that officers shall be chosen in the manner prescribed by the act for the granting of bounties and furloughs; and that vacancies shall be filled by promotion, according to grade and seniority, except in case of disability or other incompetency; the power being reserved to the President to depart from this rule in honor of any person especially distinguished by his Commanding General for extraordinary merit, or some signal act of military skill and gallantry. The third section provides for detailing one officer, one non-commissioned officer, and one or more privates from each company, to recruit men for filling vacancies occurring in such company; the men so recruited to be mustered in at the time of their enrollment, and entitled to transportation and subsistence, or commutation of subsistence, till they join their respective companies, and to fifty dollars bounty, to be paid at the time of joining the same. The fourth section authorizes the President to appoint and commission suitable officers to raise regiments, &c.; but such officers are not to receive pay until their respective commands are fully organized and reported to the Secretary of War.—*Richmond Dispatch.*

COLUMBIA.

TUESDAY MORNING, FEBRUARY 4, 1862.

To Advertisers.

All transient advertisements must be paid for in advance, and contract advertisements monthly.

Resigned.

J. A. Black, Esq., recently elected Comptroller-General of the State, has resigned the office of Magistrate for Richland.

Mr. Carroll's Card.

We have been requested to call attention to the card of Mr. Carroll, correcting certain rumors prejudicial to his character.

The Treasurer of the Young Ladies' Hospital Association gratefully acknowledges the receipt of $211, the proceeds of the late concert. $25 from Mrs. H. Middleton, the proceeds of the raffle of an Affghan. And $15, a donation from an unknown friend.

Death of A. S. Willington, Esq.

The telegraph, on Sunday, announced the death of this venerable and respected gentleman, identified with the Charleston *Courier* from its foundation. We copy from the *Mercury* its tribute to his memory.

From Europe.

The despatches announcing the arrival at New York of the Africa, bring important intelligence. In relation to the probable alliance of European powers to interpose in our war, we await more definite information. Whether such an alliance will not benefit the North more than the Confederate Government, is an important question.

Recognition.

A Paris correspondent of the New Orleans *Picayune* says:

The Emperor thinks it high time the Confederate States should be recognized by France. I told you some time ago he was determined upon it even before the affair of the Trent occurred; a high authority to-day assured me the Emperor had long ago made up his mind on the subject and in favor of the Confederate States. He approves Lord Russell's note to Lord Lyons without restriction, and lauds England's course. The English Minister accredited to the Confederate States will sail from Portsmouth for Charleston on the 5th January, unless the Commissioners be surrendered.

A Scene in the House.

By the following from the Richmond *Dispatch*, it seems that the Bowling Green battle was believed at the seat of Government as well as here:

"A Scene in the House.—On Thursday night, a stranger, wending his way through Capitol Square, encountered a good-natured news-seeker, and informed him that he was going to the President's house with an official despatch of the great battle at Bowling Green, where 700 Federals were killed, 1,000 made prisoners, and the rest driven into the river. This news, he said, was strictly true, and it was his proud office to communicate it in person to the President. The listener rushed into the Capitol, wrote it all down, marked it 'official,' and sent it immediately to the officers of the House of Delegates. It was silently read, then passed from one to another, until finally a member arose and asked that proceedings might be suspended for the purpose of acquainting the House with some highly favorable news. The despatch was then read out, and its 'official' character explained. Instantly the hall resounded with a shout of joy, and the members gave full license to their expressions of congratulation. They were, however, somewhat mortified the next morning, when they found that the much-abused newspapers failed to confirm the story of the great victory at Bowling Green."

A Nut for Abolitionism.

Not long ago, an occurrence took place in this town that might well make the Abolitionists open their eyes in wonder. An old servant, whose son is owned by a gentleman in Louisiana, asked permission of her master to visit that son. As soon as an opportunity of going out with some white person presented itself, the servant's request was granted. About seventy dollars were entrusted to her protector by her master to defray the expenses of the trip, and the sable mother was sent on her way rejoicing to spend *several months* with her son in Louisiana.

Winnsboro, S. C. BUSH.

Not the Sumter.—The Montreal *Advertiser* makes the following statement concerning the rebel privateer at Cadiz: "The Confederate privateer, or rather public armed ship, which has been playing the mischief with American ships off Cadiz, is not the Sumter, which is yet on her old beat, but one of the new vessels for which the Nashville took officers to Europe. Her name and that of her consorts will be known soon enough; in the meantime, there will be weeping and wailing among the underwriters of Federal war risks."

Gen. Anderson and the Flag of Fort Sumter.—The Boston *Traveller* says:

The time is rapidly approaching when an expedition, specially fitted, will, in co-operation probably with land forces at Port Royal, advance upon, and, in the words of President Lincoln's first proclamation last April, "retake possession" of the Government forts and property in the harbor and city of Charleston. We understand that Gen. Anderson has carefully preserved the Union flag which was lowered from Fort Sumter last spring, and he cherishes the hope that he may be enabled to accompany the expedition, and again wave the beloved ensign over the place now disgraced by the flaunting of the rebel standard.

The Mint in Charlotte.—The Wilmington *Journal*, of the 29th ult., speaking of gold and the mints that have suspended operation by order of the Government, says:

"We think the Confederate Government ought to re-start the mint at Charlotte. We believe that by its means four hundred thousand dollars of coined gold could be introduced into our circulation each year. We believe this could be done for about two per cent., and this the gold-miners would willingly pay. Let Charlotte, Dahlonega and New Orleans pour a million of gold dollars a year into the channel of Southern circulation, and it will make an excellent *amalgam*."

Death of A. S. Willington, Esq.

The community of Charleston was startled, on Sunday morning, by the sad news of the death of Aaron Smith Willington, the aged and well known Senior Editor and Proprietor of the *Courier*. He died quite suddenly, about two o'clock on Sunday morning, of a stroke of apoplexy, experienced only a few hours previously.

Mr. Willington was born in East Sudbury, Massachusetts, March 12, 1781, and had therefore nearly completed his 81st year. In early life he was apprenticed, as a printer, in the office of the Boston *Palladium*, and there gained his first insight into the business in which he afterwards became so successful. In 1802, when Mr. Loring Andrews, of Massachusetts, came to Charleston, with the view of publishing a daily newspaper here, Mr. Willington accompanied him, in the capacity of foreman. Early in January of the following year, "*The Charleston Courier*" made its appearance, as "printed by A. S. Willington for Loring Andrews." Thus, although not at first a proprietor, the deceased was identified, both in name and fact, with the *Courier*, from its original issue, and the remainder of his life was closely interwoven with its fortunes. Through all the early years of the existence of that journal, his industry and unflagging energy were mainly instrumental in giving it support. In 1806, he became one of its proprietors, the style of the firm being then "Marchant, Willington & Co." During the troublesome times of 1812, the *Courier* espoused the cause of the Federal party, which bitterly opposed the war against Great Britain. In the days of Nullification, from 1828 to 1833, the *Courier* became the mouth piece of the Union party in its struggles with the States Rights party; and again, in 1850–'51, when the policy of Secession came to be earnestly urged upon the people of the State, the *Courier* was an organ of the "Co-operationists," as opposed to those in favor of "Separate State Action." In the midst, however, of all these trying periods of political excitement, though party feeling ran high, Mr. Willington incurred no personal odium, even amongst those who most strenuously opposed the politics of his paper. Upon the election of President Lincoln, in 1860, all former party lines were, for the time, obliterated, and the South became an unit for resistance. The deceased fully approved and advocated the final step which separated the Southern from the Northern States of the Union.

Mr. Willington was a man of close observation, and of varied and accurate information. He was eminently upright in all his dealings, pure in his life, and faithful in the performance of all the duties of a good citizen. His excellent judgment and admirable business tact are attested by the fact that, in an avocation that rarely makes men rich, he had amassed an independent fortune. In charities of every kind, he bestowed his well-earned wealth with an unstinting hand.

Mr. Willington had occupied, with ability and efficiency, many honorable positions—having served as Alderman, Member of the Legislature, and as Director in Banks and Insurance Companies. In the declining years of his life his eye-sight became seriously impaired, but, with characteristic industry, he maintained, to the last, as far as possible, those habits of close attention to business to which he had become inured. On the afternoon of the very day on which he was stricken down, he paid his usual visit to the *Courier* officr.

Mr. Willington was twice married—first to Anna, daughter of the late venerable Isaac Course, Esq., and afterwards to Sarah T., daughter of John Pratt, Esq., of Boston, Massachusetts. He had one daughter, Harriet E., to whom he was devotedly attached, and who is now the wife of William Young, Esq., Editor of the New York *Albion*.

The funeral of the deceased will take place to-morrow morning, at St. Philip's Church. Many who have had occasion to know and appreciate his unassuming character and blameless life, will sorrowfully follow his remains to the grave.—*Charleston Mercury, 3d.*

Destructive Fires in New York.—There were no less than eight fires in New York on Saturday and Sunday of last week, involving an aggregate loss of about $800,000. The first fire broke out on Saturday afternoon, in a bonded warehouse, of R. H. Wyate, on Bridge street, which resulted in the destruction of $300,000 worth of property. The building was entirely destroyed. When the fire reached the cellar, where a large quantity of Scotch and Irish whiskey was stored, an explosion took place, the effect of which was terrific. Bricks, boards, pieces of barrels, and other fragments, were thrown in all directions. The immense crowd which had gathered to view the conflagration endeavored to withdraw quickly, but a large number were thrown down and trampled upon. At 1 o'clock on Sunday morning, the building adjoining took fire and burned out some $25,000 more.

On Sunday morning, another fire started at the corner of Fulton and Pearl streets, which resulted in the destruction of ten buildings, used for commercial and manufacturing purposes, together with the Fulton Bank building. The loss at this fire is estimated at about $210,000.

English Cotton Trade Report.—Maurice Williams, cotton broker of Liverpool, publishes a statistical report of the Engliih cotton trade for the year 1861, from which we learn that the total import of the past year, of all kinds, amounts to 2,036,930 bales, against 3,366,686 bales in 1860, being a falling off in the year of 329,756 bales. The export has been very large, showing an increase over last year, and including the cotton exported to the Northern States of America. The stock of cotton actually on hand at Liverpool on the last day of the old year was 622,560 bales, consisting of 279,310 American, 9,400 Egyptian, 27,250 Brazil, 370 West Indian, &c., and 306,140 East India, which, compared with the previous estimate, shows an increase of 71,800 in American, 210 in Brazil, and 21,450 in Surats, and decrease of 3,630 in Egyptians, and 40 in West India—making a total increase of 89,790 bales.

Another Chance for a Difficulty with Great Britain.—The Rio Grande is a neutral stream, the boundary between Mexico and the Confederate States. This river, says the New Orleans *Delta*, has been blockaded by the United States navy, and is now closed to the commerce of the world. The ships of foreign nations, bound for Matamoras and other Mexican ports, are forbidden entrance into the river. The first vessel which was ordered off happened to be an English ship with freight for an English house at Matamoras. No better illustration could be given of the forbearance or imbecility of the British Government in relation to this blockade than would be their acquiescence in such an exclusion of their merchant vessels from the port of a nation not engaged in this war.

THE NEW YORK HERALD.

WHOLE NO. 9281. | NEW YORK, SATURDAY, FEBRUARY 8, 1862. | PRICE TWO CENTS.

THE IMPORTANT VICTORY IN TENNESSEE.

The Capture of Fort Henry---Its Important Strategic Position---Seizure of the Railroad Bridge Connecting Columbus with Bowling Green.

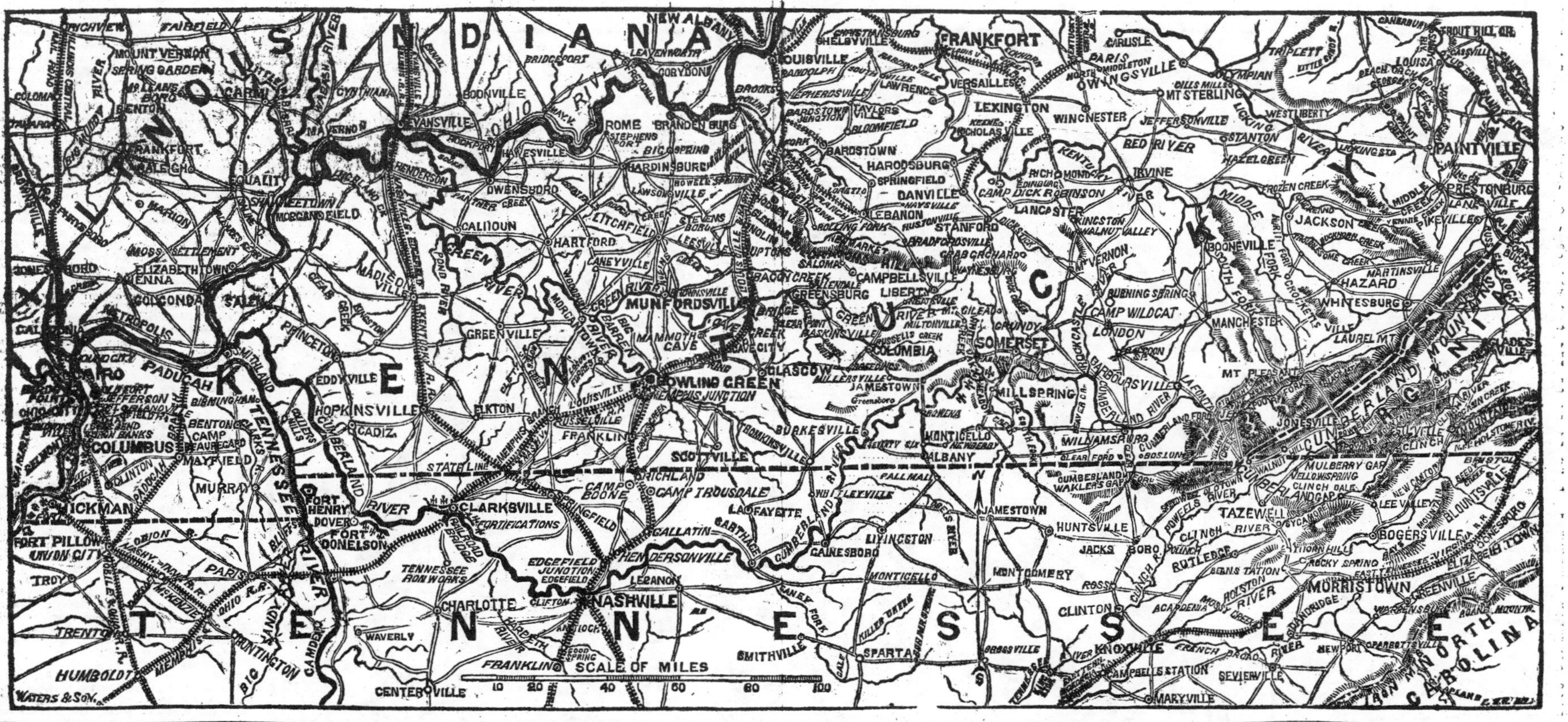

HIGHLY IMPORTANT FROM TENNESSEE.

SPLENDID NAVAL VICTORY.

Surrender of Fort Henry to the Union Gunboats.

Determined Resistance of the Rebels.

THE UNION TROOPS NOT IN THE FIGHT.

Capture of One General, One Colonel, Two Captains and Sixty Privates.

The Memphis and Ohio Railroad Bridge Taken Possession Of.

"Short and Sweet" Official Announcement of Gen. Halleck.

Official Report of Commodore A. H. Foote to the Secretary of the Navy.

Names of the Gunboats Engaged, with the Names of Their Officers and the Calibre of Their Armaments.

SKETCH OF FORT HENRY.

The Key to the Mississippi Valley,

&c., &c., &c.

CAIRO, Ill., Feb. 7, 1862.

We have taken Fort Henry.

It was surrendered to Commodore Foote yesterday at two o'clock in the afternoon, after a most determined resistance.

The fight, which lasted an hour and twenty minutes, was conducted by the gunboats Cincinnati, Essex and St. Louis.

The Cincinnati fired one hundred and twenty-five rounds, and received thirty-four shots from the rebel guns; but only one man was killed.

The St. Louis fired one hundred and ten rounds, but received no damage.

The Essex was disabled after firing ten rounds by a ball striking her boiler. Thirty-two persons on board of her were killed, being scalded to death. Capt. Porter, who commanded her, was badly scalded, but not dangerously so.

One rebel general, one colonel, two captains and one hundred privates were taken prisoners.

The fort mounted twenty guns and seventeen morters.

The land forces did not reach the scene of the action until half an hour after the surrender of the fort.

The Memphis and Ohio Railroad bridge, fifteen miles above the fort, has been taken possession of by our troops.

DETAILS OF THE BATTLE.

CINCINNATI, Feb. 7, 1862.

The *Gazette* and *Commercial's* Cairo correspondence gives the following account of the bombardment and capture of Fort Henry:—

Yesterday, at half-past twelve P. M., the gunboats Cincinnati, St. Louis, Carondelet and Essex, the Tyler, Conestoga and Lexington bringing up the rear, advanced boldly against the rebel works, going to the right of Panther Creek Island, immediately above, where, on the east shore of the river, stands the fortifications, and keeping out of range till at the head of the island and within a mile of the enemy passing the island in full view of the rebel guns. We steadily advanced, every man at quarters, every ear strained to catch the flag officer's signal gun for the commencement of the action. Our line of battle was on the left of the St. Louis, next the Carondelet, next the Cincinnati (for the time being the flagship, having on board Flag Officer Foote) and the next the Essex.

We advanced in line, the Cincinnati a boat's length ahead, when, at half-past eleven, the Cincinnati opened the ball, and immediately the three accompanying boats followed suit.

The enemy was not backward and gave an admirable response, and the fight raged furiously for half an hour. We steadily advanced, receiving and returning the storms of shot and shell, when, getting within three hundred yards of the enemy's works, we came to a stand and poured into him right and left. In the meantime the Essex had been disabled, and drifted away from the scene of action, leaving the Cincinnati, Carondelet and St. Louis alone engaged.

At precisely forty minutes past one o'clock the enemy struck his colors, and such cheering, such wild excitement as seized the throats, arms or caps of the four or five hundred sailors of the gunboats, can be imagined.

After the surrender, which was made to Flag Officer Foote by General Lloyd Tilghman, who defended his fort in a most determined manner, we found that the rebel infantry, encamped outside the fort, numbering four or five thousand, had cut and run, leaving the rebel artillery company in command of the fort.

The fort mounted seventeen guns, most of them thirty-two and thirty-four pounders, one being a magnificent ten inch columbiad. Our shots dismounted two of their guns, driving the enemy into the embrasures. One of their rifled thirty-two pounders burst during the engagement, wounding some of their gunners. The rebels claimed to have but eleven effective guns, worked by fifty-four men—the number all told of our prisoners. They lost five killed and ten badly wounded.

The infantry left everything in their flight. A vast deal of plunder has fallen into our hands, including a large and valuable quantity of ordnance stores.

Gen. Tilghman is disheartened. He thinks it one of the most damaging blows of the war. In surrendering to Flag Officer Foote the rebel General remarked, "I am glad to surrender to so gallant an officer." Flag Officer Foote replied, "You do perfectly right, sir, in surrendering; but you should have blown my boats out of the water before I would have surrendered to you."

In the engagement the Cincinnati was in the lead, and, flying the flag officer's pennant, was the chief mark. Flag Officer Foote and Captain Stembel crowded her defiantly into the teeth of the enemy's guns. She got thirty-one shots, some of them going completely through her. The Essex was badly crippled when about half through the fight, and crowding steadily against the enemy. A ball went into her side forward port, through her heavy bulkhead, and squarely through one of her boilers, the escaping steam scalding and killing several of the crew. Captain Porter, his aid, C. P. Britton, Jr., and Paymaster Lewis were standing in a direct line of the balls passing, Mr. Britton being in the centre of the group. A shot struck Mr. Britton on the top of his head, scattering his brains in every direction. The escaping steam went into the pilot house, instantly killing Messrs. Ford and Bride, pilots. Many of the soldiers at the rush of steam jumped overboard and were drowned.

The Cincinnati had one killed and six wounded. The Essex had six seamen and two officers killed, seventeen men wounded and five missing. There were no casualties on the St. Louis or Carondelet, though the shot and shell fell upon them like rain. The St. Louis was commanded by Leonard Paulding, who stood upon the gunboat and worked the guns to the last.

Not a man flinched, and with cheer upon cheer sent the shot and shell among the enemy.

THE PURSUIT OF THE FLYING ENEMY.

PADUCAH, Ky., Feb. 7, 1862.

Gen. Smith on the west, and Gen. Grant on the east side of the Tennessee river, are pursuing the retreating rebels.

It is reported and credited by some of our officers, that the rebel troops at Fort Henry were not true to the rebel cause, and took advantage of the opportunity offered by an attack to run away from a fight that was distasteful to them.

OFFICIAL REPORTS.

GENERAL HALLECK TO GENERAL M'CLELLAN.

ST. LOUIS, Feb. 7, 1862.

Fort Henry is ours! The flag of the Union is re-established on the soil of Tennessee. It will never be removed.

By command of Major General HALLECK.

W. W. SMITH, Captain and Aid-de-Camp.

COMMODORE FOOTE TO SECRETARY WELLES.

U. S. FLAGSHIP CINCINNATI, OFF FORT HENRY, TENNESSEE RIVER, Feb. 6, 1862.

The gunboats under my command—the Essex, Commander Porter; the Carondelet, Commander Walker; the Cincinnati, Commander Stembel; the St. Louis, Lieutenant commanding Paulding; the Conestoga, Lieutenant commanding Phelps; the Taylor, Lieutenant commanding Gwinn, and the Lexington, Lieutenant commanding Shirk—after a severe and rapid fire of one hour and a quarter, have captured Fort Henry, and have taken General Lloyd Tilghman and his staff, with sixty men, as prisoners.

The surrender to the gunboats was unconditional, as we kept an open fire upon the enemy until their flag was struck.

In half an hour after the surrender I handed the fort and prisoners over to General Grant, commanding the army, on his arrival at the fort in force.

The Essex had a shot in her boilers, after fighting most effectually for two-thirds of the action, and was obliged to drop down the river. I hear that several of her men were scalded to death, including the two pilots.

She, with the other gunboats, officers and men, fought with the greatest gallantry.

The Cincinnati received thirty-one shots, and had one man killed and eight wounded, two seriously.

The fort, with twenty guns and seventeen mortars, was defended by General Tilghman with the most determined gallantry.

I will write as soon as possible.

I have sent Lieutenant commanding Phillips and three gunboats after the rebel gunboats.

A. H. FOOTE, Flag Officer.

THE NEWS OF THE VICTORY IN CONGRESS.

WASHINGTON, Feb. 7, 1862.

Mr. Sedgwick caused the despatch from Flag Officer Foote to Secretary Welles, of the victory at Fort Henry, to be read to the House, and it was received with great demonstrations of applause.

THE NEWS OF THE VICTORY ON THE UPPER POTOMAC.

POOLESVILLE, Feb. 7, 1862.

Official information has been received here to the effect that the rebels have been defeated on the Tennessee river, in Tennessee, with a loss of twenty heavy cannon.

The amount of fighting or the losses on either side in men are not stated, but the rebel General Tilghman and staff, with sixty other prisoners, have fallen into the hands of our victorious troops.

There is great rejoicing over the victory in this division, and General Gorman, commanding here, has ordered a salute of thirty-four guns, one for every State in the Union, South Carolina included.

THE PRELIMINARY DETAILS.

The intelligence received yesterday of the capture of the rebel Fort Henry, on the Tennessee river, following so closely on the Union victory at Mill Spring, naturally created intense excitement in this city and elsewhere. To those remote from the scene of these achievements, and those who pay little attention to the details and immense labor to accomplish these grand results, we will try and elucidate the matter, so that it may be seen that the victory we now chronicle is but the result of a general and well digested plan of our Union military and naval commanders.

First, we will state that the capture of Fort Henry, and the other places which we shall notice hereafter, was not the result of accident, nor were the grounds moved over not thoroughly known to the Union commanders. On the contrary, the ground passed over had been thoroughly reconnoitered, and everything done was accomplished understandingly and with bold determination. The capture of Fort Henry *per se* appears to the superficial reader in the light of a naval victory. Directly it was; but in detail the victory was a combination between the military and naval forces, the latter having the moral support of the former.

From time to time we have published in the HERALD accounts of the movements of the land and naval forces at Cairo; but, as their intended operations were kept quietly in the minds of those by whom they were to be carried into effect, to the outside world they presented a jumbled, mixed state of affairs, with no immediate or ulterior design. The public received the accounts of the apparent inactivity of our forces with no little dissatisfaction; but so far as General Halleck's department is concerned the veil is now drawn, and, presto, appears a record of one of the most brilliant achievements that has yet appeared in the history of the present gigantic rebellion.

The initiatory steps towards the victory which we now record were commenced some time in the early part of January. Like all great military movements, before the great blow is struck it is necessary to make a reconnoissance of the point to be attacked; and as the present one was for no less design than an attempt of the enemy's left flank in Tennessee, where they were in large force, strongly fortified and intrenched, it became necessary, in making a reconnoissance of the enemy's stronghold, to make it in force. In other words, to make it with such a numerical body, in case the enemy forced a battle, as to be in a condition to accommodate them. General Halleck accordingly made such details for this service as the sequel will show have accomplished all he designed, and that highly satisfactory to himself and the country.

Passing from the unnecessary details relative to the preparing troops for a march, we will state that on the 9th of January a large force of Union troops—cavalry, artillery and infantry—under the command of Brigadier General McClernand, left Cairo, Illinois, for a reconnoissance in Southwestern Kentucky, towards the Tennessee border, in the direction of Columbus. This force numbered about 7,000 men. Cotemporaneously with this movement of McClernand's brigade, another force of nearly equal strength, under Brigadier General Paine marched from Bird's Point, opposite Cairo, in the direction of Charleston, Missouri, and thence to the Ohio river, to observe the movements of the rebels at Columbus on the river front. About the same time another brigade, numbering six thousand men, under Brigadier General C. F. Smith, moved from Paducah to Mayfield, Kentucky, and towards Columbus, and another force from Cairo to Smithland, a point on the Ohio river, between the Tennessee and Cumberland rivers. Besides these land forces, and in co-operation with them, several Union gunboats, under the command of Captain Porter, proceeded down the Ohio river and within two miles of Columbus.

The movement of these forces, as before stated, was all for the same object, each having its sphere of action conducing to a common result—the reconnoitering of the enemy's left flank.

The most active part taken in this grand reconnoissance was done under the command of Gen. McClernand, co-operating with his senior and chief of the whole movement, General Grant.

Gen. McClernand's brigade, conveyed in river transports, left Cairo on the 10th ult. for old Fort Jefferson, Ky., about fifteen miles distant. He disembarked his force on the following day and encamped. On the 12th he made a demonstration in the direction of Columbus, with a force of six companies of cavalry and two regiments of infantry, marching for several miles, until they observed the rebel Fort Beauregard. In front of this work was seen a strong abatis of fallen timber, extending over a distance of half a mile, and surrounding the enemy's intrenchments. The rigor of the weather and the non-appearance of any considerable force of the enemy led the Union commander to the belief that the rebels were massed within their intrenchments. The object of the reconnoissance being not to engage the enemy, if it could be avoided, the party returned the same day to Fort Jefferson.

On the 13th another party of Union troops left Fort Jefferson and proceeded to Blandsville, where it selected a strong position for an encampment.

On the 14th the whole of McClernand's force marched to Blandsville. They moved in two columns, with strong guards in advance, so as to command the approaches to Columbus and both bridges across Mayfield creek.

On the 15th an advance was made to Weston, within ten miles of Columbus, going thence to the southwest of the latter to Milburn, taking the town by surprise. Gen. Grant at this point assumed command of the troops. At this place a man came into camp who had just arrived from Columbus. From him was obtained valuable information respecting the condition of the rebels at that place. This refugee stated that the movements of the Union troops had caused much excitement among the rebels, and caused them to withdraw their forces from Fort Beauregard, Jackson, New Madrid and other places.

On the 16th the forces marched to Milburn, and from thence the commander sent a detachment to Mayfield, where it communicated with General Smith's brigade from Paducah.

On the 17th, the object of the expedition having been accomplished, the entire force under McClernand retraced their steps and returned to Cairo in the same order as they came, having travelled a distance of one hundred and forty miles, obtaining the fullest information of the nature of the ground over which they had passed.

MOVEMENTS OF GEN. SMITH'S BRIGADE.

On the 21st of January Brigadier General C. F. Smith's brigade, consisting of 6,000 men, cavalry, artillery and infantry, arrived at Crown Point—a point on the Tennessee river—from Paducah, having marched a distance of one hundred and twenty miles over muddy roads, and crossing numerous swollen water courses. On the 22d ult., the day after the arrival of the brigade at Crown Point, General Smith proceeded on a personal reconnoissance, on the gunboat Lexington, in the direction of Fort Henry. The gunboat proceeded up the west channel of the river, to a point within one mile and a half of the fort. Three rebel steamers were discovered lying off the mouth of the small creek that empties into the Tennessee river just above the fort. A well directed shell was fired from the Lexington, striking one of the rebel craft in the stern. A second shell fell short of its mark just in front of the enemy's works; a third burst in the air, directly over Fort Henry, doubtless doing good execution. The rebels in the fort then brought out a thirty-two-pounder gun to bear on the Lexington, the shot from which fell into the water one-half mile short of its mark. General Smith obtained an excellent view of the rebel fort, camp and garrison, and immediately returned with his brigade to Paducah, having met with the fullest success in the reconnoissance.

THE OCCUPATION OF SMITHLAND.

General Grant ordered the occupation of Smithland, the location of which we have already stated, as that point occupies a central position, and is of considerable strategical value, as a force stationed there would be at all times ready to co-operate with any movement, either on the Tennessee or Cumberland river, as circumstances might require.

Thus it will be seen, from the brief *resume* of the movements of the several brigrades of General Grant's first expedition towards Columbus, it was not, as some supposed, a failure, but, on the contrary, was a decided success in the objects for which it left Cairo.

The second expedition, the result of which we now record, was based upon the information derived from the first, and its grand and glorious result has ere this sent a thrill of gladness throughout the loyal States of the Union. It must be remembered, also, by our readers, that what has now been accomplished has been done by our troops amid great hardships, in marching over muddy roads, amid rain and sleet, with little or no facilities for shielding them from the severity of the unpropitious weather.

IMPORTANCE OF THE SIEZURE OF THE RAILROAD.

The capture of the Memphis and Ohio Railroad bridge, as mentioned in the above despatch, secures an important strategical position, to which others must, in the course of military events, be auxiliary. It in effect turns the enemy's left flank, cuts off the communication between Memphis and Bowling Green, from which the latter is dependent for its supplies, and isolates Columbus from Bowling Green; so that for all military purposes communication is cut off between the rebels at these points. No doubt the federal force will push on until they reach the Nashville and Memphis Railroad, near Camden, Tenn. This point, once in our possession, will cut off Hickman and Memphis from Nashville. This accomplished, then goodbye to Generals Johnston, Beauregard, Buckner and the rebel host. There will be no necessity then to attack Columbus or Bowling Green. Starvation will do the work. The New Orleans *Delta*, in a late edition, says:—"*The safety of the whole South depends on the result of the battle at Columbus. This place once taken, there can be no effectual resistance at other points.*" In military philosophy a position turned and besieged is equal to a place captured. Hence, according to the New Orleans *Delta*, the safety of the whole South is in jeopardy.

DESCRIPTION OF FORT HENRY.

This fort, the only fortification on the Tennessee river of much importance, is situated near the line of Kentucky and Tennessee, on the east bank of the stream. It stands in the bottom, about the high water mark, just below the bend in the river, and at the head of a straight stretch of about two miles. It therefore commands the river for that distance down stream, and very little else. The land around it is a little higher than the fort, and a portion of it is covered with timber. The armament of the fort consists of eight thirty-two-pounders, four twelve-pounders and two six-pounders. The thirty-two and twelve-pounders are heavy guns, and the six-pounders light pieces. On the opposite side of the river are three hills, which completely command the fort. Recently some new fortifications were commenced on these hills, where it was intended to mount some very large guns and three rifled cannon.

The late rebel garrison was composed as follows:—

Brigadier General Lloyd Tilghman, commanding.

STAFF.

Captain Powhatan Ellis, Assistant Adjutant General.
Captain S. C. Morris, Aid-de-Camp.

TROOPS.

Fourth Mississippi regiment.
Seventh Mississippi regiment.
Regiment Louisiana Volunteers.
First Kentucky Volunteers.
One regiment rebel cavalry.

THE TENNESSEE GUNBOAT FLEET.

OFFICERS OF THE FLEET.

Flag Officer..............Andrew H. Foote, U. S. N.
Fleet Captain............Com. A. M. Pennock, U. S. N.
Ordnance Officer.........Lieut. J. P. Sanford, U. S. N.
Ordnance Lieutenant.....Lieut. Byron Wilson.
Flag Lieutenant.........James M. Prickett.
Act. Paymaster, 2d Chief S. Henriques.

The following are the gunboats, with their officers, engaged in the fight:—

GUNBOAT ESSEX, NINE GUNS.

Commander—Wm. D. Porter, United States Navy.
Masters—First, Robert K. Riley; Second, James Lanning; Third, Theodore P. Ferry; Fourth, George W. Walker.
Assistant Surgeon—Thomas Rice.
Acting Paymaster—J. H. Lewis.
Pilots—J. McBride and Marshall H. Ford.
Masters' Mates—James B. Gray and Samuel B. Brittan.
Engineers—Chief, Charles Blaisdell; First Assistant, R. J. Stearns; Second Assistant, George D. Simon; Third Assistant, J. Wetzel.
Gunner—M. B. Snyder.
Armorer— —— Fletcher.
Carpenter—Thomas Steel.

GUNBOAT ST. LOUIS, THIRTEEN GUNS.

Lieutenant Commanding—Leonard Paulding, United States Navy.
Masters—First, Samuel Black; Second, James Y. Clemson; Third, Charles S. Kendrick; Fourth, Alex. Fraser.
Acting Paymaster—Llewellyn Curry.
Surgeon— —— McDill.
Masters' Mates—S. H. McAdams and James P. Paulding.
Pilots—Frank Riley and Robert G. Baldwin.
Gunner— —— Hall.
Engineers—Chief, W. Carswell; First Assistant, T. F. Ackeman; Second Assistant, James L. Smith; Third Assistant, John Wilcoxen.
Carpenter—Robert H. Medill.

GUNBOAT CINCINNATI, THIRTEEN GUNS.

Commander—R. N. Stembel, United States Navy.
Masters—First, vacant; Second, —— Pratt; Third, Charles G. Perkins; Fourth, John Pearce.
Surgeon—Jacob Kinsey.
Paymaster—Baron Proctor.
Pilots—Isaac D. Gaugh and H. Attenborough.
Masters' Mates—Jas. McB. Stembel and Philip Shell.
Gunner— —— Morton.
Carpenter—Thomas B. Gregory.
Engineers—Chief, W. McGarland; First Assistant, S. Lovejoy; Second Assistant, J. Armstrong; Third Assistant, W. J. Sherman.
Armorer—Benj. Marshall.

GUNBOAT CARONDELET, THIRTEEN GUNS.

Commander—Henry Walke, United States Navy.
Masters—First, Richard K. Wade; Second, John Dorety; Third, Charles C. Gray; Fourth, H. A. Walke.
Pilots—William Henton and Daniel Weaver.
Surgeon—James S. McNeely.
Paymaster—George J. W. Nexsen.
Masters' Mates—Theodore L. Gillman and Edward E. Brennard.
Engineers—Chief, W. H. Faulkner; First Assistant, Charles H. Caven; Second Assistant, Samuel S. Brooks; Third Assistant, Augustus F. Crowell.
Carpenter—O. Donaldson.
Gunner—Richard Adams.
Armorer—H. H. Rhodes.

GUNBOAT CONESTOGA, NINE GUNS.

Lieutenant Commanding— —— Phelps, U. S. N.
Masters—First, John A. Duble; Second, Charles P. Noble; Third, Benjamin Sebastian.
Assistant Surgeon—William H. Wilson.
Acting Paymaster—Alfred Phelps.
Engineers—Chief, Thomas Cook, First Assistant, Alex. Magee; Third Assistant, Michael Norton.
Masters' Mates—James Kearney, Richard H. Cuttee.
Gunner—Henry Hamilton.
Carpenter—Andrew Woodlock.
Armorer—James O'Neil.

GUNBOAT TAYLOR, NINE GUNS.

Lieutenant Commanding—W. Gwin, U. S. N.
Masters—First, Edward Shaw; Second, Jason Goudy; Third, James Martin.
Pilots—John Sebastian, David Hiner.
Engineers—Chief, Samuel Goble; First Assistant, D. Edward Weaver; Second Assistant, Edward W. Goble. Third Assistant, Oscar S. Davis.
Armorer—Elihu Stevens.
Acting Paymaster—W. B. Coleman.
Assistant Surgeon—T. H. Kearney.
Carpenter—Thomas Russell.
Gunner—Herman Peters, U. S. N.
Masters' Mates—Ferdinand T. Coleman, Edward D. Brainard.

DESCRIPTION OF THE GUNBOATS.

The gunboats St. Louis, Essex and Cincinnati are about one hundred and seventy-five feet in length, fifty-one feet and a half in breadth, and draw five feet when loaded. The bows and bulwarks consist of about three feet of oak timber, bolted together and sheathed with the best quality of wrought iron plates two and a half inches thick. The sides have the same sheathing, with

[CONTINUED ON EIGHTH PAGE.]

THE NEW YORK HERALD.

WHOLE NO. 9286. NEW YORK, THURSDAY, FEBRUARY 13, 1862. PRICE TWO CENTS.

IMPORTANT NEWS.

The Capture of Roanoke Island Fully Confirmed by the Rebels.

TERRIBLE FIGHTING.

Three Hundred Rebels Killed and One Thousand Wounded.

THE ENTIRE REBEL FLEET DESTROYED

ELIZABETH CITY TAKEN.

The Place Burned by the Rebels.

Two Thousand Rebel Prisoners Taken.

Advance of the Union Troops on Edenton.

OPINIONS OF THE REBEL PRESS, &c., &c., &c.

We learn by the flag of truce which arrived at Fortress Monroe on Sunday of the complete success of the Burnside expedition at Roanoke Island.

The island was taken possession of and Commodore Lynch's fleet completely destroyed. Three hundred rebels were killed and wounded, and two thousand taken prisoners. Scarcely any escaped.

Elizabeth City was attacked on Sunday and evacuated by the inhabitants. The city was previously burned.

The first news of the defeat arrived at Norfolk on Sunday afternoon, and caused great excitement. The previous news was very satisfactory, stating that the Yankees had been allowed to advance for the purpose of driving them into a trap.

The rebel force on the island is supposed to have been only a little over three thousand efficient fighting men.

General Wise was ill at Nag's Head, and was not present during the engagement. When the situation became dangerous he was removed to Norfolk.

All the gunboats but one were taken, and that escaped up a creek, and was probably also destroyed.

One report says that only seventy and another that only twenty-five of the rebels escaped from the island.

General Huger telegraphed to Richmond that only fifty on the island escaped.

There appears to be no bright side of the story for the rebels.

THE REBEL DETAILS.

The following despatches on the subject are taken from the Richmond papers of Tuesday morning:—

NORFOLK, Feb. 10, 1862.

The latest news states that Captain O. Jennings Wise, son of Governor Wise, was shot through the hip and disabled, though his wound was not mortal. Major Lawson and Lieutenant Miller were mortally wounded. *About three hundred confederates were killed. Our wounded number over one thousand.* The number of Yankees wounded is about the same. Midshipman Camm has had an arm shot off. The other casualties are as yet unreported.

A late arrival this morning says that Elizabeth City had been shelled and burned by the Yankees, and that the enemy was pushing on to Edenton.

SECOND DESPATCH.

NORFOLK, Feb. 10, 1862.

A rumor has prevailed that Commodore Lynch's fleet of gunboats had been captured. It is not regarded as true, but *it is believed that all were burned by the confederates to prevent their capture,* with the exception of one, which was endeavoring to make its escape. The fleet went to Elizabeth City from Roanoke Island, and was probably burned at the former point.

THIRD DESPATCH.

NORFOLK, Feb. 10, 1862.

A courier arrived here this afternoon at four o'clock, and brought the intelligence that *Elizabeth City was burned this morning by its inhabitants.* During the conflagration the federals landed a large force. All our gunboats excepting one were captured by the enemy.

General Wise had not yet arrived at Norfolk.

THE VERY LATEST.

The following "very latest" we copy from the Norfolk *Day Book* :—

[From the Norfolk Day Book, Feb. 10.]

It is said that the enemy came up in their boats on the south side of the island, and by means of their boat howitzers *effected a landing in the rear of our batteries,* and that after landing about fifteen thousand on all parts of the island, they marched up and flanked the batteries. It is also reported that, notwithstanding our small force of twenty-one hundred men against about fifteen thousand, on some parts of the island the resistance was of the most desperate nature, and a hand-to-hand contest lasted for a considerable time, showing the most desperate courage. This is said to have been the case particularly with the Richmond Blues, under command of Captain O. Jennings Wise. Captain Wise, we learn, fell bravely urging his men on.

[From the Norfolk Day Book, Feb. 11.]

A courier arrived here yesterday afternoon about three o'clock, from whom we gather the following information :—

The enemy advanced in full force upon Elizabeth City yesterday about seven o'clock, and began an attack upon that place. *The citizens, finding resistance vain, evacuated the place, but before doing so set fire to the town, and when our informant left it was still in flames.*

We have also to record the capture by the enemy of all our little fleet, except the Fanny or Forrest—our informant is not certain which. This eluded the enemy and made up Pasquotank river. She was pursued, however, and fears are entertained that she was captured. It is said that before our boats surrendered they were abandoned, and that their crews succeeded in making their escape. If so, we are at a loss to conjecture why the boats were not fired before they were abandoned.

The disaster to our little fleet is attributed to the fact that, having exhausted their supply of coal and their ammunition, they proceeded to Elizabeth City for the purpose of obtaining a supply. Every effort was made to obtain coal, but without success, and the boats could not, therefore, return to the island and lend any assistance whatever to our forces.

All the details, as published, with reference to the capture of Roanoke Island, are confirmed by the courier, who represents our loss at three hundred killed and wounded, and that of the enemy not less than one thousand killed. Great havoc was made among the enemy while coming up the road leading to the fort. Our forces brought to bear upon them two thirty-two pounders, and at every fire their ranks were terribly thinned. The places of the fallen, however, were quickly filled.

The Pork Point battery was manned by the Richmond Blues, and most nobly did they defend it. During the conflict they were attacked by a whole regiment of Zouaves, and though completely overpowered, they stood their ground. They did not yield a foot until all but seven of them had fallen bleeding to the ground.

There is good reason to believe that had Colonel Henningsen, with his artillery, been on the island, it would not have been forced to surrender. The lack of field pieces was sadly felt, and had they been at hand perhaps the enemy never would have been able to have landed their forces. Colonel Henningsen had orders, we understand, to report at Roanoke Island; but by some misunderstanding he mistook Elizabeth City for his place of destination.

Captain Taylor, of this city, is represented as having distinguishing himself for his coolness and bravery. He fought the enemy like a tiger, and not an inch of ground was yielded by him without its being well disputed.

In addition to the above there are many rumors we might give; but as they are nothing more than rumors we prefer withholding them. Among them, however, is one worthy of notice—that General Wise had been shot while on his way in an ambulance. The statement, so far as we have been able to learn, is untrue. We can only account for it by supposing that the name of the General was confounded with that of his son, who was reported among the killed.

BRILLIANT OPERATIONS AT ROANOKE ISLAND.

Scene of General Burnside and Commodore Goldsborough's Victories—Roanoke Island and Elizabeth City.

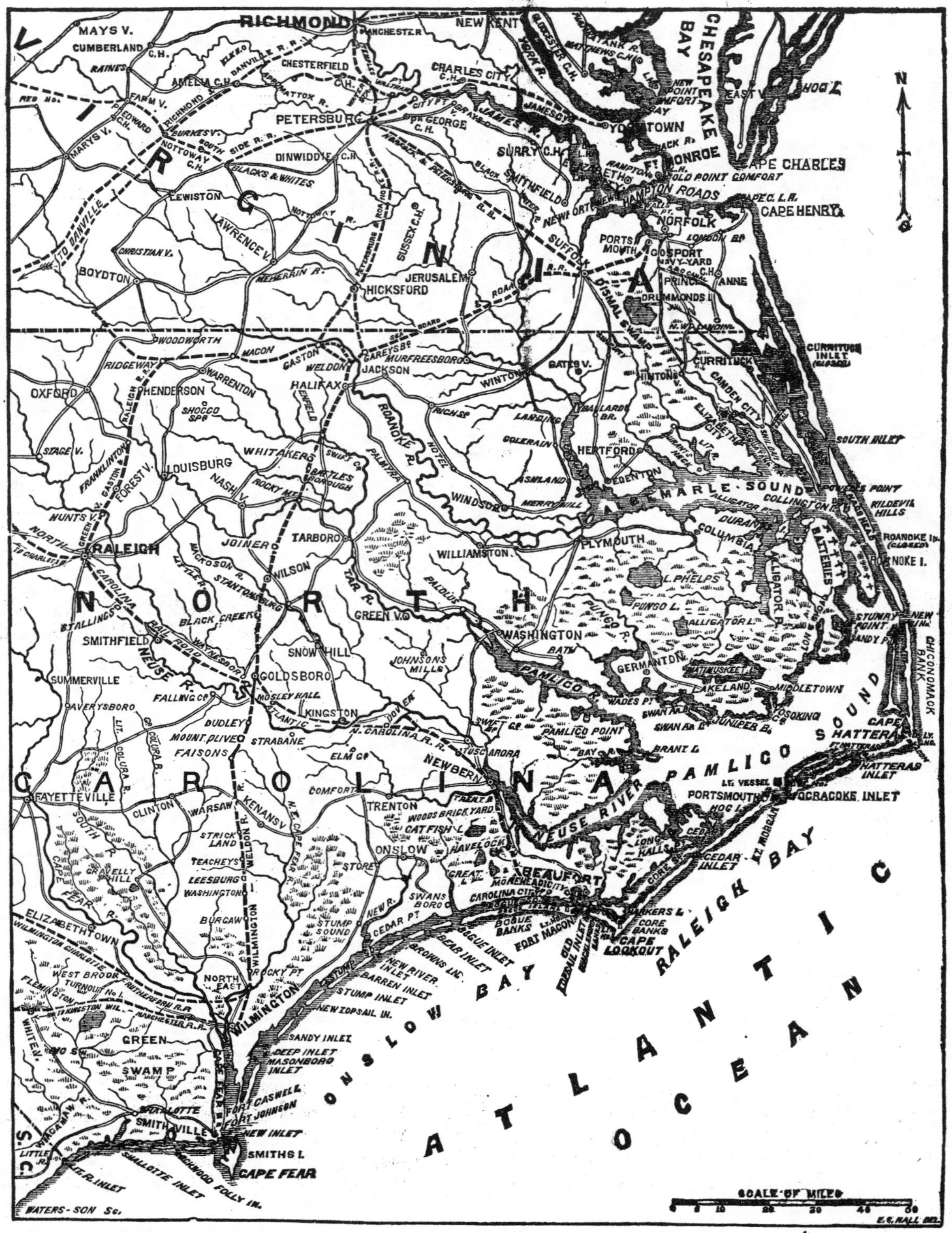

ADDITIONAL PARTICULARS.

[Special correspondence of the Richmond Dispatch.]

NORFOLK, Feb. 10, 1862.

With inexpressible sorrow *I announce the fall of Roanoke Island,* after a spirited and heroic resistance by our brave troops. This occurred between twelve and two o'clock on Saturday, and the news was received here with every indication of regret and indignation. We gather the following particulars from a young man from the Richmond Blues, who participated in the fight, escaped in a small boat and rowed to Nag's Head, where he was taken up by one of our gunboats and brought to this city. He is an intelligent lad, and I believe a son of your Postmaster. The enemy's ships, he says, opened fire on our batteries, at Roanoke Island, about seven o'clock in the morning, and kept up an incessant fire until seven o'clock in the evening, doing, however, but little injury to the island. About nine o'clock the next day (Saturday), the Hessians were allowed to land on a point to the east of Roanoke Island, where they marched upon that point. The booming of heavy cannon in the distance heralded the enemy's approach. Our brave troops prepared to meet them, supposing their numbers to be about 5,000. Gradually the sounds came nearer and nearer, and the shells came thick and fast over our intrenchments. Confident of their own strength, our troops moved rapidly forward, when, in a few minutes, the ball opened and the terrific contest ensued. Bravely did our boys stand up to the overwhelming forces of the enemy, and not till nearly every man was dead or wounded did they leave their stand. Nothing remained but retreat, which our men did, constantly turning and giving them a shot. Finding it useless to hold the island under such overwhelming numbers, the order to retreat from the island was given, and our remaining troops retired, leaving their stronghold in the hands of the enemy.

It will be a pleasure hereafter to record on the page of history the heroic fortitude of our gallant troops. Nobly and well did Captain O. Jennings Wise, of your city, stand up with his men to the fierce encounter, when, suddenly, he was shot through the side and instantly fell. One of his men asking him if he was much hurt—"Not much," said he, "but fight them yet." He was borne from the scene of action in a blanket. *About 300 of our brave boys fell, and nearly all the rest were either wounded or taken prisoners.* The enemy's loss is laid down at 1,000. *Four of their ships were sunk,* they doing but little damage to any of our boats. Commodore Lynch and other parts of our fleet did noble service, his ship being among the first to open fire on the enemy's shipping. At last accounts they were in pursuit of Commodore Lynch.

In the midst of this terrible struggle it will be regretted that General Wise was seriously indisposed at Nag's Head. Both he and his son are expected here to-day. I am sorry to say that but very few escaped from Captain Wise's company. Large quantities of ammunition were saved by our troops. The women, children and a number of negroes are reported now on their way to our city. The enemy will be successfully checked from getting possession of our railroad in that vicinity. Active preparations have been made here regarding this disaster, which it may be imprudent for me to mention. The news fell upon the ears of our citizens with fearful significance. Many would dare shut their eyes against the fact had not dread conviction come so direct. Every man was at his post, and our departments here were engaged in sending despatches to the various encampments. The alacrity with which every officer executed his orders is a theme of public praise, and especial praise is due to the Young Guard, of our city, for their services on the occasion. At a very late hour military movements were going on, and everything is in great excitement.

NORFOLK, Feb. 10, 1862.

The intelligence of the desperate and unequalled contest at Roanoke Island, and its result, have doubtless reached you by telegraph. Of course this is the principal subject of conversation here. Considering all the circumstances attending the fight, a more favorable termination of the affair could scarcely have been expected by those competent to judge. Our force on the island at the time of the attack was but small in comparison with the heavy and numerous force of the enemy. Of the bravery and gallant conduct of our troops too much can scarcely be said in commendation. That they were overpowered by greatly superior numbers, after fighting with a recklessness and desperation never surpassed, is a fact already established, and which will be placed upon the truthful pages of history.

I send you herewith such particulars of the battle as I have been able to gather. A true account cannot be given now. We know enough to cause a deep sigh of grief for the brave men slain, and the gallant sons of the South, who are now captives in this cruel war—of homes rendered desolate, of hearts wrung with anguish, and ties of love and friendship severed. But who believes, except the deluded and revengeful Yankees, that the South will ever yield to them?—that the great cause of Southern liberty, and honor, and humanity is not still onward?

True, the news comes that the hospitable town of Elizabeth City has been shelled and burned, and that the vandal hordes are desolating the pleasant places of the Sound coast. But they cannot go far into the interior, and the day is coming when these Northern minions shall be driven back in disgrace to their inhospitable and barren soil.

General Wise, though still sick, is, I learn, on his way to this city. Captain O. Jennings Wise was dangerously wounded. Major Lawson, Lieutenant Miller and Captain Coles, are reported among the killed. The enemy lost in killed and wounded one thousand; our loss three hundred, *besides more than two thousand prisoners.* We must be nerved for a vigorous resistance, and Providence will assist us as heretofore in this cause of honor, and truth, and human rights.

OPINIONS OF THE REBEL PRESS.

[From the Richmond Examiner, Feb. 11.]

The loss of an entire army on Roanoke Island is certainly the most painful event of the war. The intelligence of yesterday by telegraph is fully confirmed. Twenty-five hundred brave troops on an island in the sea were exposed to all the force of the Burnside fleet. They resisted with the most determined courage; but when fifteen thousand federal troops were landed against them, retreat being cut off by the surrounding element, they were forced to surrender. This is a repetition of the Hatteras affair on a large scale.

It is reported that one regiment from Massachusetts was badly cut up; but it is impossible to ascertain which of the five that were attached to the expedition it was.

All the Southern papers received to-day are unanimous in admitting a complete victory to our troops, and in saying that the loss of the island is a very serious one.

The prisoners captured, numbering at least two thousand, will arrive at Fortress Monroe in a few days.

[From the Richmond Dispatch, Feb. 11.]

THE DISASTER AT ROANOKE ISLAND.

The exciting occurrence at Roanoke Island, resulting in a reverse to our arms, was the theme of conversation yesterday in the city, to the exclusion of almost every other topic. The fact that some of our Richmond companies were engaged in the fight occasioned an intense and painful anxiety, particularly among those who had friends or relatives among them, which could not be well concealed. It is but a short period since the Wise Legion, after an arduous and toilsome campaign in Western Virginia, left here for the coast of North Carolina, and though now defeated in one of the most desperate conflicts of the war, it is at least consoling to know that the men fought with determined bravery, against overwhelming odds, and won for themselves the proud appellation of heroes, of which their present situation cannot deprive them. The Light Infantry Blues (Company A, of the Legion), date their organization as far back as the year 1793, and number among their honorary members many of our oldest and most venerated citizens. The history of the company is so well known that we need not repeat it here. Captain O. Jennings Wise was elected commander a short time before the war broke out, and the corps was one of the first to respond to the call of the country. Captain Wise is reported badly wounded, and Lieutenants Fred. Carter and Charles P. Bigger are taken prisoners, with, it is presumed, a majority of the men. The Jackson Guard and the Light Guard, both attached to the Legion, were enlisted here after the commencement of the war. Captain Hiram B. Dickinson, of the former, and Captain Gus. Wallace, of the latter, reported captured by the enemy, are well known citizens of Richmond. Lieutenant Miller, of the Jackson Guard, is said to be mortally wounded. Major Hugh W. Fry, who is among the prisoners, has many friends here, who regret his misfortune, but who are proud to believe that he sustained himself gallantly in the fight, and the same remark applies to Frank Johnston, of the Blues, as brave a young man as ever shouldered a musket.

The telegraph informs us that our killed and wounded amounts to 300, while that of the enemy reaches 1,000. The reader will find some further particulars of the affair in our Norfolk papers, from which it appears that the infamous scoundrels have shelled and burned the pleasant little town of Elizabeth City, and are threatening Edenton. Their operations in that quarter, however, will be limited; and instead of depressing the spirits of our people, such acts of vandalism will serve to make them more determined, and rouse them to thrice vigorous resistance.

Personally we regret the loss of our accomplished correspondent "Bohemian," whose letters from the Potomac and other points have for some time past adorned the columns of this paper. Dr. Shephordson is well known throughout the South, and in his captivity (which we trust will be brief) he has the sympathy of a vast number of friends.

THE CAMPAIGN IN CAROLINA.

[From the Richmond Dispatch, Feb. 11.]

Until within a day or two past, *the capture of Roanoke Island by Burnside was considered a foregone conclusion.* A fleet of nearly a hundred sail and an army of fifteen or twenty thousand men, with guns and equipments in profusion, were esteemed equal to the capture of any exposed piece of water bound land like the island in question. But the brave resistance offered for nearly two days by our troops, and the hopeful terms in which they spoke of their prospects, led our people to believe that the island might be held. It has, however, been lost, and we are compelled to resign ourselves to the conclusion which a day or two of hope—we confess not strong in our own case—had unsettled.

Burnside has landed, after a hard fight, on a seaboard island, not as advantageously situated, nor encompassed by as rich surroundings of country as Beaufort. His object is supposed by some to be Norfolk; but if we are to believe the recent outgivings of Northern journals, his leading purpose is to make a demonstration against the Weldon and Wilmington Railroad, with a view to cutting our great line of Southern communication. *That thing seems, for the present, to be the especial aim of the enemy in every quarter.* His movements in Western Kentucky and Tennessee seem to have that single object for the present in view; and it has been repeatedly declared by Northern journals that Burnside's primary purpose is a demonstration upon our railroad. It remains to be seen whether such be his real design, and with what success he will prosecute it. The experience of Sherman in a similar undertaking may possibly be his own.

An assault upon Norfolk is the only object next after this railroad enterprise, commensurate in importance with the magnitude of the expedition. In such an undertaking the enemy's vessels could be of little direct use. The water approaches to that city from North Carolina are too narrow, tortuous and easily obstructed to admit the use of vessels; and if the enemy attempts a land attack the chances in our favor of repelling him are two or three to one. The reduction of Norfolk would be the work of months, and could only be effected by a large increase of Burnside's forces, an increase which the Yankee exchequer is not able to afford for an operation stretching through a protracted period. *Nothing at all can save their treasury, and nothing can keep the war on foot but rapid operations and decisive successes.* Yet we do not see wherein the Burnside expedition promises these results more unmistakably than Sherman's did, which landed in November, nearly three months ago.

Measured by its cost to the enemy, not even the capture of Norfolk, if it could be effected, would compensate him for his outlays, and this at last is the true standard by which his successes should be estimated. The South need not expect, and cannot rationally expect, that these huge expeditions, fitted out at immense expense, should fail to effect any achievement. Fifteen or twenty thousand men landed anywhere upon our seaboard must succeed in getting possession. It would be idle to expect otherwise, and imbecile to be discouraged by the fact. The true consideration is, whether such successes repay their cost.

Measured by this standard, the achievements of the Burnside expedition are not likely to be very important. *Its cost cannot have been less, in the first instance, than ten millions of dollars, and its charges every day are at least a quarter of a million.* It has been thirty-one days prosecuting its career to the point of capturing Roanoke Island, a feat which has cost the federal government several millions, independently of the first outlay in the enterprise, and the losses incurred by the storm. If the expedition should succeed in capturing the whole Carolina seaboard, and even a considerable slice of the country besides, together with Norfolk, still the fifteen or twenty millions of federal money laid out in the whole operation would not be reimbursed by half.

We are not of those who suffer discouragement from occasional successes of the enemy. They have far overtaxed the resources of the North in bringing their prodigious forces into the field. The effect may be to damage us considerably, but they are damaging themselves much more. The injury they inflict upon us is local and remediable; that which they bring upon themselves in debt and taxation, is general, universal and enduring. They have chosen a gigantic and expensive programme, which must break down, and which no successes, however great, can compensate the cost of.

THE REBEL ISLAND AND TOWNS.

ROANOKE ISLAND AND ITS ADVANTAGES.

A few days ago we gave a brief description of Roanoke Island, and pointed out the advantages to be derived from its capture and occupation. The news, however, which we lay before our readers this morning, of the brilliant victory of the Union arms under General Burnside and Commodore Goldsborough, is of so much importance that we think it not out of place to give a more detailed account of the island and of the advantages which have fallen into our hands by its capture.

Roanoke Island is twelve miles long and three miles wide, and is about fifty miles up Pamlico Sound. It was said to be fortified by the rebels on the southern, western and eastern shores, and defended with heavy ordnance, and on the 12th January, when the rebels learned of the arrival of Gen. Burnside at Hatteras Inlet, they instantly commenced the construction of a battery about midway of the island. In addition to this they had thrown up five forts, with an intrenched camp in the centre, and had their works garrisoned by some five thousand troops, in order to prevent the passage of our gunboats through the Croatan Sound—the only communication with Albemarle Sound. But the cheering news has now reached us of their being shelled out of their strongholds by the powerful Union expedition which was brought against them, consisting of seventeen gunboats most powerfully armed with rifled artillery, among which were a dozen nine-inch guns, two one hundred-pounder rifled guns, four eighty-pounders, and a large number of eight-inch shell and thirty-two-pounders.

The capture of Roanoke Island is of much importance, inasmuch as it commands all the water communication along the whole North Carolina coast, as well as a portion of Southeastern Virginia. Being in possession of it, we are enabled to cut off all supplies by water from Norfolk, so that hereafter the rebels will be compelled to get their supplies wherever they can, and entirely by land; for Norfolk can also be cut off here, as also from the course across Albemarle Sound northward to the point where the Pasquotank and North rivers empty. There are two routes from this last point to Norfolk—one by Pasquotank river, Dismal Swamp Canal and south branch of Elizabeth river, and the other by the North river of Albemarle and Pamlico Canal, Currituck Sound, the North river of Currituck, the upper cut of the Albemarle and Pamlico Canal, and the Elizabeth river. During the winter months the first is passable for vessels drawing about six feet of water. The Pasquotank river is three miles wide at its mouth, and gradually narrows until at Elizabeth City it is only about three hundred yards wide.

Currituck is about fifty miles long, ten miles wide, and is navigable for vessels drawing ten feet of water. Albe-

[CONTINUED ON EIGHTH PAGE.]

The Philadelphia Inquirer.

ESTABLISHED 1829. | PHILADELPHIA, WEDNESDAY, FEBRUARY 19, 1862. | PRICE TWO CENTS.

FORT DONELSON VICTORY.

PARTICULARS OF THE LAST DAY'S FIGHT.

CLARKSVILLE THE NEXT POINT OF ATTACK.

A CONFLAGRATION AT CLARKSVILLE.

CAPTURE OF SAVANNAH.

Gen. Price Driven from Missouri.

REJECTED ARMY CLOTHING.

THE U. S. NOTE BILL.

Exhibition of Union Feeling in Baltimore.

GREAT REJOICING OVER THE RECENT VICTORIES.

LATER FOREIGN NEWS.

THE NASHVILLE AND TUSCARORA.

THE FORT DONELSON VICTORY!

FURTHER DETAILS.

CHICAGO, Feb. 18.—The *Tribune's* special despatch from Fort Donelson says that the position of the ground occupied by our troops, in the attack upon Fort Donelson, was such that not more than one regiment could operate at the same time, while the Rebels could bring nearly their whole force to bear against us. The first regiment to receive the Rebels was the Eighteenth Illinois, which fought with desperate courage until their ammunition was exhausted, when they were forced to retire. They were replaced by the Eighth Illinois, who were also driven back after firing their last round. Meanwhile the other regiments were lending such feeble assistance as their positions would admit.

General LEW. WALLACE was then ordered to reinforce General MCCLERNAND, and he sent two brigades to the centre. The Thirty-first Illinois, Colonel LOGAN, fought like veterans, defending SWARTZ'S battery, under the most galling fire, until every horse at the battery was killed, together with all the officers who had charge of the guns, as well as the Lieutenant-Colonel, the acting Major, seven Captains, and a number of Lieutenants wounded. The regiment being nearly surrounded, Captain COOKE, who was left in command, drew off what there was left, not, however, until their last round was expended, and they had commenced driving the Rebels before them.

The Second brigade then came up and took the place of the retired one, and fought desperately, losing a great number of killed; but, with the assistance of a portion of WALLACE'S division, the Forty-ninth and Fiftieth Ohio, drove the Rebels back to their entrenchments—gaining a portion of the ground lost. The object of the Rebels was evidently to cut their way through our troops.

The General JOHNSTON taken is BUSHROD JOHNSTON, a Brigadier-General, from Tennessee, and not A. SIDNEY JOHNSTON, as generally supposed.

FURTHER FROM FORT DONELSON.

A FIRE AT CLARKSVILLE — SUPPOSED BURNING OF THE TOWN OR THE REBEL STEAMERS—ARRIVAL OF PRISONERS AT CAIRO.

CAIRO, Feb. 17.—The steamer *Memphis* arrived from Fort Donelson this evening, bringing a Mississippi regiment as prisoners, and 50 or 60 wounded soldiers, who were left at Mound City. Eight or nine other boats are on their way with Rebel prisoners. The Rebels who have escaped, it is supposed, have gone to Nashville or Clarksville, where it is thought they will attempt to make another stand.

This evening a great light was seen for several hours in the direction of Clarksville, and it is supposed that the Rebels have either burned the town, or their steamboats in the river, to prevent them falling into our hands.

The Rebel officers admit that if we take Nashville, the rebellion in Tennessee is gone up.

The prisoners will probably be sent to Camp Douglas, Chicago.

THE GREAT VICTORY.

ANOTHER ACCOUNT OF THE LAST DAY'S FIGHT.

CINCINNATI, Feb. 18.—The following is an account of the fighting on Saturday, at Fort Donelson:—

On Saturday morning the battle was resumed with unusual vigor and determination.

The First, Eighteenth, Twentieth and Thirty-first Illinois Regiments occupied positions above the fort. They were about preparing a little food for the day's sustenance, when the Rebels opened on them a fire of musketry.

A line of battle was at once formed, and the storm of leaden hail returned, perceptibly thinning the Rebel ranks.

The Rebels, from their advantageous positions, showered upon our ranks most murderous volleys of musketry, grape and canister, killing and wounding our men, almost by companies, at every round. Yet every man stood his ground bravely. These four regiments held their ground dealing death, and dying and fighting against appalling odds, and in the face of every disadvantage. The Eighteenth Illinois Regiment seems to have resisted the severest storm. Against their ranks the Rebels directed the heaviest fire; but instead of falling back they advanced to the face of the enemy, and there stood in the very jaws of death, with scarcely a prospect that a single one would escape.

For three hours these regiments, numbering scarcely three thousand men, held their ground against the whole Rebel garrison.

At one time, the Eighteenth, being partially flanked, was exposed to a cross fire of both musketry and artillery, but our right wing soon relieved them. At this critical moment, Colonel LAWLER fell. Captain BUSH, acting Lieutenant-Colonel, then assumed the command, but was soon wounded; Captain CRUSE was shot dead; Captain LAWLER was mortally wounded; Lieutenants MUNSFORD and THOMPSON were killed; Captains DILLON and WILSON, and Lieutenants KELLY and SCANLAN, wounded; so that the daring "Egyptian Regiment" stood before the almost overwhelming force without officers.

They fell in heaps, dead and wounded. Companies were bereft of captains and lieutenants, and captains were almost bereft of companies; the other three regiments did their duty nobly. Colonels OGLESBY, MARSH, and LOGAN dashed along the ranks, waving their hats, and cheering their men on to the conflict. "Suffer death," cried LOGAN, "but disgrace never! Stand firm!" and well they heeded him. Many fell dead and wounded. Among the latter were Colonel LOGAN and Lieutenant-Colonel WHITE.

Colonels OGLESBY and MARSH'S Regiments fought desperately, losing, like the other regiments, an undue proportion of officers.

Colonel OGLESBY displayed a coolness and courage that has elicited the highest praise, and served well in stimulating his men.

Never, perhaps, on the American continent, has a more bloody battle been fought.

An officer who participated, and was wounded in the fight, says the scene beggars description. So thickly was the battle-field strewn with the dead and wounded, that he could have traversed acres of it by taking almost every step upon a prostrate body.

The Rebels fought with desperation, their artillerists using their pieces with the most fearful effect.

On either side could be heard scores of those in command cheering on their men. The four Illinois regiments held their ground full three hours. Nearly one-third had been killed or wounded, and yet the balance stood firm. Finally, reinforcements arrived, and for an hour the slaughter was continued.

About four o'clock our right wing turned the enemy's left, and the Rebels fell back into their fortifications, and our flag was planted upon the position occupied by their left wing—for a time the slaughter then ceased.

DRESSER'S and SCHWARTZ'S batteries were captured during the action, but the Eighteenth Illinois, with clubbed muskets, recovered DRESSER'S battery, while the Thirty-first recovered that of Capt. SCHWARTZ.

STILL ANOTHER ACCOUNT.

ST. LOUIS, Feb. 18.—The Fort Donelson correspondent of the *Republican* gives the following account of the fighting on Saturday:—

"Yesterday (Saturday) morning, just at daylight, a heavy sortie was made by the garrison from the left portion of their works. This attack was made upon the extreme right wing of the Union army, where it was strongest. A part of General MCCLERNAND'S division, under Colonel OGLESBY, consisting of his brigade, was stationed there; also, SCHWARTZ'S and MCALLISTER'S batteries. The point was upon a ridge leading into the right redoubt, and situated just above the main fort. During the previous night the enemy could be heard busily at work, but it was impossible to tell at what, as the thicket and woods encompassed the Union troops on every side, obstructing the view in every direction.

At daylight a large body of the enemy suddenly appeared on the extreme right wing of Colonel OGLESBY'S command, and opened a terrible fire with cannon from their redoubt, playing at the same time upon our forces from the guns which had been placed in position on the night previous.

The camps of the Twenty-ninth and Thirty-first Illinois were most exposed. The whole brigade was at once formed into line as follows:—

The Eighteenth Illinois Regiment held the extreme right; the Eighth Illinois came next; then the Thirtieth Illinois, then the Twenty-ninth Illinois, supporting the right of Captain SCHWARTZ'S artillery, and the Thirty-first Illinois defending the artillery on the left.

From the firing of the first gun until nine o'clock, the battle raged unremittingly and with fearful loss on both sides. Again and again our troops drove the enemy back, but they were often reinforced, while our troops had, owing to the extended lines of the army, and also their position on the extreme right, to fight unassisted.

More gallant fighting never took place than that of the Union troops. Exposed to the terrible firing of triple their number, they stood their ground until, in some regiments, every officer was killed or wounded.

At last, and reluctantly, regiment by regiment, they slowly fell back, leaving SCHWARTZ'S battery and three of MCALLISTER'S guns in the Rebel hands. Retiring a few hundred yards they all then made a stand, and General SMITH arrived with reinforcements, and at once drove the enemy again into their works.

In the first of the battle also, Colonel W. H. L. WALLACE'S Brigade, comprising the Eleventh, Twentieth, Seventeenth and Forty-eighth Regiments, participated; also Colonel MCARTHUR'S Brigade—all of which troops suffered severely. Opposed to these were twelve thousand Rebels, supported by guns that had been carefully placed in proper position.

General GRANT having, in command of the division, driven the enemy back with reinforcements and gained the lost ground, at once ordered an advance by General SMITH on the left.

Charging under a hot fire up the steep hill on which was located the outer redoubt, our troops gained the high breastworks, and with hardly a pause went over them, planting the stars and stripes over the walls under a most galling fire.

They then formed, charged and drove the enemy back until he fell into a new position behind some batteries.

When evening came, the Union troops had been victorious at every point, having gained back the ground lost in the morning, and got within one part of the enemy's works.

Our troops held their position during the night repelling the repeated assaults of the enemy.

The scene within the captured fort after the surrender showed how terribly the Rebel garrison had suffered. Everywhere were lying fragments of shells and round shot, half buried in the earth; tents were torn to pieces, gun-carriages broken, and blood scattered around.

In the left redoubt, where the assault had taken place, the dead bodies lay thickly, and abundant evidence of a stern resistance and gallant attack was visible. On the extreme right, where the desperate sortie was made by the garrison, similar scenes were visible.

The gallantry of the Union troops has been well and severely tested, and they have proved more than equal to the task before them.

As the fleet approached the fort this morning, a salute was fired, and three cheers went up when the American flag was displayed.

No officer in the army had an idea of the extent of the defences of Fort Donelson, until they had been gained and examined.

Sevaral of our men, when out of ammunition, rushed forward, and although exposed to the full fire of the Rebel artillery, gallantly drove their foes back with the bayonet and captured their guns.

The following are the names of some of the Rebel officers captured:—

Colonel GANTT, Colonel VOORHEES, Colonel FORREST, Colonel BROWN, and Colonel ABERNETHY.

LATEST FROM FORT DONELSON.

ST. LOUIS, Feb. 18.—The Fort Donelson correspondent of the *Democrat*, under date of the 17th, says:—"It is impossible to state the precise extent of our captures, everything being in such confusion."

The Fifty-first and Fifty-seventh Virginia, and several Arkansas, Alabama and Texas regiments, were among the forces which left with PILLOW and FLOYD.

The Federal and Rebel officers fraternize with the best feeling, and the views expressed in my despatch of yesterday, respecting the Union sentiment prevailing among the prisoners here, were much strengthened by subsequent intercourse with them. The remark holds specially true of the Tennessee regiments. The best officers among them are those who yielded to popular madness at the eleventh hour. They say they are sick of this unnatural warfare.

Misled by their politicians first, and betrayed by their generals since, they have become most thoroughly disgusted with the bogus Confederacy, and desire to withdraw from it at once.

General GRANT has issued energetic orders for a speedy forward movement to still greater victories.

The Rebel officers assert that Gen. JOHNSTON will concentrate every available soldier in his command at Nashville, and make a desperate attempt to retrieve the misfortunes of the past.

The Rebel surgeons place their loss at between 300 and 400 killed and double that number wounded.

The Relations between Gens. McClellan and Halleck.

ST. LOUIS, Feb. 18.—Several reports having gained currency through the newspapers relative to Generals MCCLELLAN and HALLECK, which are calculated to mislead the public and to create misunderstandings and jealousies, the *Republican* to-day announces, by authority of General HALLECK, that he has at all times received the most hearty co-operation from General MCCLELLAN, and that in all the military operations of this Department he has had the advice and approval of the General-in-Chief. The two Generals are in almost constant communication by telegraph.

Rejoicing at Detroit.

DETROIT, Feb. 17.—The news of the victory at Fort Donelson caused indescribable joy here. A hundred guns were fired on the receipt of the news, and to-night many buildings are illuminated, and the fire department, the military and a large number of citizens are out in a grand procession with banners, torches and rockets to celebrate the great event.

BRIGADIER-GENERAL CHARLES F. SMITH.

General CHARLES FERGUSON SMITH is a native of Pennsylvania, and son of the eminent physician, Dr. SAMUEL B. SMITH. He entered the Military Academy as a cadet in 1821, and graduated in 1825, standing number nineteen in his class. On the 1st of July of that year he was made a second lieutenant of the Second Artillery. In 1829 he was appointed the Assistant Instructor in Infantry Tactics at the Military Academy, which position he retained until September, 1831, when he was promoted to the adjutancy, retaining the same office till April, 1838. During that interval (viz., May 1832) he was made a first lieutenant. On the 1st of April, 1838, he was appointed Instructor in Infantry Tactics and Commandant of Cadets at West Point, which position he filled until September 1, 1842, in the meantime being promoted to the Captaincy, viz., on July 7, 1838. In April, 1847, he was breveted major for gallant conduct in the battles of Palo Alto and Resaca de la Palma, in Texas, his brevet dating from May 9, 1846.

In May 1848 he received another brevet, being that of Lieutenant-Colonel, for gallant conduct in several conflicts at Monterey, Mexico, on the 21st, 22d and 23d of September, 1847, his brevet bearing the last mentioned date. During the following August he received a further brevet (Colonel) for gallant and meritorious conduct in the battles of Contreras and Cherubusco. This brevet dates from August 20, 1847. He was appointed Acting Inspector-General in Mexico during June, 1848. On the 25th of November, 1854, he was promoted to the Majority of the First Artillery, and on the 3d of March, 1855, he was further promoted to the Lieutenant-Colonelcy of the Tenth Infantry. On the 31st of August, 1861, he was made a Brigadier-General of Volunteers, and took charge, under Gen. HALLECK, of the troops at Paducah.

BRIGADIER-GENERAL JOHN A. M'CLERNAND.

Brigadier-General JOHN A. MCCLERNAND was an active leader of the Douglas party in the House of Representatives of 1860, and also in the Charleston and Baltimore Democratic Conventions. He was strongly opposed to BRECKINRIDGE and his party, and as a Douglas man was elected to Congress. He left his seat to take up arms in defence of that Government which he so strongly supported by his speeches in Congress. There is an interesting circumstance in connection with his appointment to the position of Brigadier-General. He had, during the late extra session of Congress, been making, while in his seat, a strongly-worded speech in support of the action of the Government in these troubles, and in the course of some remarks, at the conclusion, he in effect stated that, notwithstanding the thousands of Douglas Democrats who had enlisted in the cause and service of the United States, not one of them had been honored with any high military appointment; other parties had had their appointees, but his party had not, and he thought it somewhat unfair, &c. A leading Republican took up the question after MCCLERNAND had finished, and, complimenting him highly on the patriotic tone of his remarks, intimated that he did not know of a man more entitled to a position than his honored friend from Illinois. Shortly after this discussion in the House, the name of JOHN A. MCCLERNAND appeared on the list of those who were appointed Brigadier-Generals of Volunteers.

In the Belmont fight he manifested that he possessed good military capacity, and during his administration of military affairs at Cairo he secured the good-will of the men under his command. Gen. MCCLERNAND is about forty-four years of age, and rather tall in stature.

LATEST FROM WASHINGTON.

WASHINGTON, Feb. 18, 1862.

Special Despatches to The Inquirer.

General McClellan's Staff.

An editorial article, evidently designed to be malicious, appeared in the *Tribune* of Saturday, which might mislead many who do not know the facts, or who fail to penetrate the designs of that truculent sheet. I have carefully compiled from the *Army Register* the actual staff of General MCCLELLAN as it now exists.

PERSONAL STAFF OF GEN. MCCLELLAN.

General R. B. Marcy, Chief of Staff.
Colonel T. M. Key, Aid.
Colonel T. T. Gantt, (reviewing proceedings of Courts Martial.)
Lieutenant-Colonel N. B. Sweitzer, Aid.
Lieutenant-Colonel E. McK. Hudson, Aid.
Lieutenant-Colonel A. V. Colburn, Aid.
Lieutenant-Colonel P. V. Radowitz, Aid.
Major H. V. Hamerstein, Aid.
Captain E. A. Raymond, Aid.

This is the entire list of the personal staff of General MCCLELLAN who draw pay from the Government, in the double position as Commanding General of the Army and as Commander of the Army of the Potomac.

There have been appointments made of other officers to positions not recognized under existing laws, but to enable them to take a rank in keeping with the responsible duties with which they are charged; they are called Staff Officers. The officers thus situated and the character of their duties are as follows:—

Col. H. J. Hunt, commanding Reserve of Regular Batteries.
Col. D. H. Rucker, Depot and Issuing Quartermaster to the Army of the Potomac.
Lient.-Col. R. Inglalls, purchasing Forage, &c., for the Army of the Potomac.
Col. H. F. Clarke, in charge of the Commissary Department of the Army of the Potomac.
Col. C. P. Kingsbury, in charge of the Ordnance Department of the Army of the Potomac.
Col. C. F. Havelock, Inspector of Volunteer Cavalry for the Army of the Potomac.
Lieut.-Col. J. N. Macomb, in charge of the Topographical Bureau, Collecting Information, Making Maps, &c., for the Army of the Potomac.
Lieutenant-Colonel Wm. Hayes, commanding Light Batteries under Colonel Hunt.
Lieutenant-Colonel G. W. Getty, commanding Light Batteries under Colonel Hunt.
Lieutenant-Colonel B. S. Alexander, commanding brigade of Sappers and Miners.
Lieutenant-Colonel J. A. Hardie, Assistant Adjutant-General Head-quarters Army of the Potomac.
Captain R. B. Irwin, Assistant in Office of Adjutant-General of the Army of the Potomac.
Captain J. Kirkland, Assistant in Office of Adjutant-General of the Army of the Potomac.
Captain A. McClellan, Assistant in Office of Adjutant-General of the Army of the Potomac.
Captain W. P. Mason, Assistant in Office of Adjutant-General of the Army of the Potomac.
Captain W. T. McMahon, Assistant in Office of Adjutant-General of the Army of the Potomac.

The other officers whose names appear in the *Army Register* as being attached to General MCCLELLAN'S staff, either do not draw any pay, or are detached and connected with other commanders.

Veteran Politicians.

Among other gentlemen here in attendance on the Supreme Court, or attending to matters before Congress, one notices REVERDY JOHNSON, of Maryland; TRUMAN SMITH, of Connecticut; JAMES GREEN, of Missouri; GEORGE ASHMAN, of Massachusetts, and HORATIO KING, of Maine. Some of them reap large incomes for their professional services.

Mexican Affairs.

Mr. PLUMB, who brought here the treaty which Mr. CORWIN has negotiated, is said to express his confidence that if our Government will advance a few millions of dollars for the payment of the Mexican bonds held in Europe, the English and French armies will be withdrawn. As for Spain, the Mexicans think that they can take care of her single-handed.

Van Wyck's Report.

The gallant Colonel of the Tenth Legion has aroused a host of enemies by his report, and it is whispered that a reply is being prepared, in which the antecedents of the honorable member will be overhauled. Mr. DAWES, who has done most of the real work of the Committee, is confined to his room by indisposition.

Reduction of Salaries.

A joint resolution has been passed in the Senate providing that the compensation of a Collector of the Customs, Naval Officer, Surveyor of the Port, or any other officer of the Customs, shall not exceed $10,000 per annum. The New York officials have telegraphed an urgent appeal to have this "cutting down" stopped until they come on. Collector THOMAS, of Philadelphia, is already here.

Outlawry.

Senator HARRIS thinks that his proposed plan of "outlawry" will be the only way to punish the chief actors in the present rebellion, as it is very difficult to obtain a conviction for treason.

Order Respecting the Presentation of Rebel Flags.

Secretary STANTON to-day issued the following order:—

WAR DEPARTMENT, WASHINGTON CITY, D. C.
February 18th, 1862.

Ordered, By the President, Commander-in-Chief of the Army and Navy, that on the 22d day of February, in the Hall of the House of Representatives, immediately after the Farewell Address of GEORGE WASHINGTON shall have been read, the Rebel Flags lately captured by the United States forces shall be presented to Congress by the Adjutant-General, to be disposed of as Congress may direct.

By order of the President,
EDWIN M. STANTON, Secretary of War.

The approaching anniversary of the birth of WASHINGTON bids fair to be a grand national day of rejoicing. From all quarters of the land intelligence is being received that it will be kept this year as a day of thanksgiving and congratulation.

The Proposed Reduction of Cavalry.

The House Committee on Military Affairs had under consideration, this morning, a proposition to reduce the Cavalry force of the army to thirty, or at the most forty regiments. The majority of the Committee were of opinion that the present force of seventy-five regiments was not too great in view of the peculiar aspect that the war is beginning to assume. Our Cavalry force, well drilled as it now is, can get over the ground rapidly, and thus shorten the days of the Rebellion.

Homœopathy in the Army.

The Senate Committee on Military Affairs had before them, this morning, a delegation of Homœopathic Physicians and Professors of distinction and character, from the various Atlantic cities, asking the establishment of a Homœopathic Hospital in the District of Columbia. After a patient hearing the Committee intimated an adverse recommendation, assigning the fear of confusion between the two systems.

Reforms in the Navy.

The Sub-Committee of the Joint Committees on Naval Affairs, consisting of the Chairman of each, to whom were referred the recommendations of the Secretary of the Navy in his annual report, have made a report to the Committee. It provides for establishing and regulating the grades of officers in the Navy, making ten separate ranks, from Midshipman up to Commodore or Admiral, and limiting the number of each grade attached to a vessel. It makes an Advisory Board to consult with in regard to promotions. It authorizes the President to appoint Commodores from the present grade of Commanders who may have distinguished themselves by gallant and meritorious conduct during the present war; and, also, for the promotion by two grades of other officers who may distinguish themselves.

The Treasury Note Bill.

A wonderful change has occurred in the condition of the Treasury Note bill since the news of the recent victories. The Committee on Ways and Means are at loggerheads on the Senate amendments, and at the meeting of the committee this morning it looked as if they would all be thrown overboard. The early adjournment to-day was doubtless as much owing to a desire for informal consultation of the business members on the main features of the bill, as for joy at the good news. The sentiment is becoming universal that in the gloomy prospect of two or three weeks ago, Congress passed the legal tender clause and other ticklish provisions which now appear both unwise and unnecessary. A new order of things is about to begin, and Government issues will now need little other propping than the assurance of a vigorous and successful prosecution of the war,

Meritorious Promotions.

The nominations of General GRANT to be a Major-General, and of Colonel GARLAND, who defeated ZOLLICOFFER, to be a Brigadier, sent to the Senate to-day by the President, are an index of his determination to reward good conduct and bravery in the field, wherever it may be found. Secretary STANTON is a strenuous advocate of this system, and lists are now being prepared from the official reports down to the humblest private, so that the nation may do them honor.

Heavy Ordnance.

The Naval Committee of the House will report an appropriation, to-morrow, for the supply of heavy ordnance, as recommended by the Secretary of War. This will enable the iron furnaces and forges of Pennsylvania to furnish guns for the proposed fortifications of the Delaware and other exposed situations on the seaboard. They will also report a bill fixing the taxes on the salaries of officers of the navy towards the expenses of the war.

The Illumination.

It is proposed to have the Capitol illuminated on the night of the 22d with gas. Pipes are to be laid defining the outlines of the edifice, with its dome, which will trace them in lines of fire against the sky.

The Tax Bill.

The tax bill will be reported to the Committee by Saturday from the Sub Committee. Its provisions are so various and manifold, and numerous alterations so inevitable, that it will not be printed until reported to the House. There is the greatest desire to ascertain its main points by speculators and operators.

The Victories.

Salutes were fired last night, this morning, and at noon to-day, at the arsenal and navy yard here, in honor of the successes of our arms.

Confederate Gunnery.

The *Panola*, Lieutenant JACK CROSBY commanding, has made good her passage down the Potomac past the Confederate batteries. She was fired on, but not hit.

The Rebel Flag.

The Navy Department have received—forwarded by Commodore FOOTE—a number of flags taken at Fort Henry; among them the large Confederate flag that was hauled down from the main flag-staff of the post when it surrendered.

Volunteer Cavalry.

Quite a commotion among a certain class of speculators has been caused by the announcement that the Volunteer Cavalry Regiments are to be consolidated, and thus reduced in number. Some of those who have been making a good thing of it by the purchase of horses and uniforms (a per centage going into their own pockets) will now find themselves high and dry.

THE STARS AND STRIPES FLOATING IN ARKANSAS.

Price Driven From Missouri.

GEN. CURTIS IN HOT PURSUIT.

OFFICIAL DESPATCH.

ST. LOUIS, Feb. 18.—The following despatch was sent from head-quarters to-night:—

"*To Major-General McClellan, Washington, D. C.*:—The flag of the Union is floating in Arkansas.

General CURTIS has driven PRICE from Missouri, and is several miles across the Arkansas line, cutting up PRICE'S rear, and hourly capturing prisoners and stores.

The army of the Southwest is doing its duty nobly.

(Signed) H. W. HALLECK, Major-General.

THE REPORTED SURRENDER OF SAVANNAH.

NOT A GUN FIRED.

BALTIMORE, Feb. 18.—It is rumored by passengers by the Fortress Monroe boat, that news had reached Norfolk of the surrender of Savannah without a gun being fired. Our letter from Fortress Monroe makes no mention of the report.

S. S. MILLS, the publisher, and THOMAS S. PIGGOTT, the editor of the notorious secession sheet, *The South*, were this morning arrested and taken to Fort McHenry.

Exhibition of Union Feeling at Baltimore.

BALTIMORE, Feb. 18.—A lecture delivered to-night, at the Maryland Institute, was the occasion of an exciting demonstration of Union feeling. The Rev. Mr. FIEGIT, while delivering a lecture, branched off on political affairs, and alluding to the test oath by the Legislature for clergymen, said that whilst he was a Union man he would suffer martyrdom before he would submit to such an oath, adding, if this be treason, make the most of it. The audience immediately became greatly excited, and all sorts of noises were made; cheers were offered for the Union, and groans for the speaker. The lecturer was compelled to desist, and the audience dispersed.

INTERESTING FROM ST. LOUIS.

RAPID TRANSPORT OF TROOPS—DISPOSAL OF THE WOUNDED AND PRISONERS.

ST. LOUIS, Feb. 18.—Five steamers left for St. Charles, Missouri, to-day, where troops will embark for the Cumberland.

Two regiments arrived from St. Charles to-day, and will immediately proceed South.

The most active and extensive arrangements are being made here for the transportation of troops.

General CULLUM, of General HALLECK'S staff, will go to the Cumberland for the prisoners captured at Fort Donelson, seven thousand of whom will be sent to Chicago, and the balance to Springfield, Illinois, and Indianapolis. Five hundred of the wounded go to Cincinnati, and the balance will be brought here.

The regiments which suffered the most in the battle will be detailed to guard the prisoners in their places of confinement. Some 4000 of these prisoners are now en route from Fort Donelson.

The most extensive preparations are being made to celebrate WASHINGTON'S Birthday.

The United States Note Bill.

REPORT OF THE HOUSE COMMITTEE ON WAYS AND MEANS ON THE SENATE AMENDMENTS.

WASHINGTON, Feb. 10.—The Committee on Ways and Means recommend that the House agree to about two-thirds of the Senate amendments to the U. S. Note bill, and that they disagree to those reducing the number of the U. S. notes authorized to be issued from $150,000,000 to $100,000,000, and to the striking out of the original proviso that fifty millions of the notes shall be in lieu of the demand treasury notes authorized by the act of July last, &c.

The Committee also recommend that the House disagree to the Senate amendment that the July notes shall be receivable in payment of taxes, duties, imports, excises, debts and demands of every kind due to the United States, and of all claims and demands of every kind, except for interest upon bonds and notes, which shall be paid in coin. Also, to disagree to the amendment fixing the redemption of the bonds at the pleasure of the United States after five years, and payable in twenty years from date.

The Committee recommend the retention of the proviso for the exchange of the bonds of the United States bearing interest at 7 per centum, and a disagreement to the Senate amendment authorizing the Secretary of the Treasury to dispose of the bonds at the market value. They recommend a disagreement to the Senate's new section, which pledges the custom duties and the proceeds of the sale of public lands and of property seized and sold under the laws of the United States as the property of Rebels as a special fund for the payment in coin of the interest on the bonds and notes, and for the purchase and payment of one per centum of the entire debt, to be set apart as a sinking fund, the interest on which, in like manner, to be applied to the purchase or payment of the public debt; the residue thereof to be paid into the Treasury.

The Committee recommended the agreement of the House to another new section of the Senate, with an amendment which they propose, namely, authorizing the deposit of notes or coin in exchange for certificates, and instead of five per centum interest on such certificates, to substitute, "at such rates of interest which the Secretary of the Treasury may, from time to time, prescribe, not exceeding six per centum, and any amount of notes or coin so deposited may be withdrawn from deposit at any time after ten days' notice, on the return of the certificates."

The Western Virginia Convention.

WHEELING, Feb. 18, 1862.—The Constitutional Convention adjourned this evening, after fifty-nine days' session.

The Free State measure was defeated. Commissioners were, however, appointed, with powers to reassemble the convention in case the new State was recognized by Congress. This provision is supposed to look to a Free State.

There was great rejoicing here over the Fort Donelson news.

General ROSECRANS ordered a salute to be fired at an early hour this morning.

Rejoicings at Lancaster.

LANCASTER, Feb. 18.—The city is enlivened this evening by the ringing of bells, bonfires, firing of guns, and other demonstrations of joy over the recent Union victories. This demonstration was gotten up by the Association of Patriot Daughters, whose labors in behalf of the volunteers have been unremitting since the issuing of the President's proclamation, in April last. Arrangements are also making for a proper celebration of Washington's birthday in this city.

GENERAL PATTERSON.

PHILADELPHIA, February 17, 1862.

ED. PHILADA. INQUIRER.—DEAR SIR:—Believing you to be a friend to justice and an impartial historian of the events now transpiring in our country, I take the liberty of using your columns for the purpose of refuting, if possible, the effect that might result from the false and ungenerous attack made upon the military fame of our townsman, General PATTERSON, by F. P. BLAIR, in the House of Representatives, on Friday last:—"Mr. BLAIR, in further explanation, said he had never seen any man who would assert that General PATTERSON had yet put himself, in danger or ever would."

The writer of this served in Mexico, in the division commanded by Gen. PATTERSON, and, with his comrades, landed at Vera Cruz on the evening of the 9th of March, 1847. On the 10th we commenced investing the city, marching from its southern end towards the north. Previous to the landing the General had been upon the "sick report," and was so lame as to be compelled to go upon crutches. Yet on the afternoon of the 10th, while the First Pennsylvania Volunteers were receiving the fire of guns from the city, and at the same time an attack from a body of lancers among the sand-hills, I saw him with parts of the heads of flour barrels nailed to the bottom of his crutches (to prevent their sinking in the sand), take the head of our regiment, and lead us into the thickest of the *danger*. For the truth of this I refer to any member of the right wing of the regiment. *We* found no faltering or fear of danger in him at that time; nor, I believe, would any be found now by any but the political renegade, whose new-made friends, by their clamor, caused the loss of the battle of Bull Run.

There are few, I think, who know what our country owes to General PATTERSON for his services at another point in Mexico. I will here quote the words of a writer who was upon the spot, and whose work, "An English Soldier in the United States Army," was published in New York in 1853. After giving a description of the march as far as Plan del Rio, four miles from the afterward famous hill Cerro Gordo, he says:—

"On the evening of the 13th [of April], Gen. TWIGGS, who, during the sickness of Gen. PATTERSON, commanded the forces at Plan del Rio, gave the order for the attack on the enemy's batteries, which we were to take at the point of the bayonet early next morning. The bugles having sounded for the troops to assemble a little before sunset, the captains of companies addressed their men, informing them of the General's intention, and explaining as much of the plan of the meditated attack as would tend to facilitate its execution. They concluded with a hope that all would do their duty gallantly, and requested us to give three cheers, an invitation which was very faintly responded to. The want of enthusiasm displayed by the men arose, I am persuaded, from a want of confidence in the judgment of General TWIGGS, and not from any deficiency of the necessary pluck required for the occasion. But that General, though always admitted to be a brave old cavalry officer, was considered, from his peculiar temperament and previous school of education and discipline, to be totally incapable of successfully directing an operation of such magnitude as the present, which, any person might easily see, required both military talent and skill. Perfectly aware of the enemy's overwhelming force, and the strong nature of his position, and also of the inconsiderate rashness of General TWIGGS and his advisers, we felt that we were in danger of a defeat, or a victory purchased by a lavish and useless expenditure of life. And as we knew that General SCOTT, with a division of the army, was only two days in the rear, no one could perceive the least necessity for either of these alternatives; from either of them, however, we were fortunately saved:

It coming to the ears of General PATTERSON, that an attack was ordered next morning, he immediately resumed the command of the troops by having his name erased from the "sick returns." He then issued an order countermanding that of General TWIGGS, and stating that all active operations against the enemy's position were suspended until the arrival of Gen. SCOTT. This turn of affairs gave universal satisfaction, as General SCOTT deserved and possessed the confidence of both officers and men in the highest degree. We had received apint of flour, each man, for our next day's bread, the biscuit having all been consumed which we had brought with us; and it was considered better to make cakes and toast them on the ashes, than to go without bread all next day. When the news of General PATTERSON's order came, as late as 11 o'clock at night, various groups of anxious-looking faces might be seen by the flickering light of the bivouac-fire, gloomily watching their unleavened ashes and thinking bitterly of the morrow. The announcement produced one of the most sudden illuminations of the human countenance divine among these groups which I ever recollect to have seen; the cakes were either abandoned or carried away half baked, to be finished at some other opportunity, and all retired to sleep, carrying the news to their dreaming comrade, that the attack was deferred until SCOTT came up."—pp. 174-176.

In addition, I would state that this countermanding order of Gen. PATTERSON received the warmest thanks of Gen. SCOTT, and that from that time until the present these two Generals have been warm and intimate friends. In matters military, the opinion of General SCOTT is worth that of thousands of such as BLAIR, "who never set a squadron in the field, nor the divisions of a battle knows, more than a spinster."

In relation to the events immediately preceding the battle of Bull Run, for which General PATTERSON has been so much berated by *political* enemies, only this is to be said at present:—that no one has had the courage to contradict his assertions made recently at the supper of the City Troop; and also, that some developments are likely to be made at the trial of General STONE, which will cover the enemies of our townsman with shame and ignominy.

Yours, VINDEX.

Cotton and Religion "Down" at the South.

Orderly ROBERTS, a Chicago soldier who took part in the Fort Henry battle, sends to the Chicago *Tribune* the following curious letter, picked up in the fort after the surrender; the Rebel writer laments the decline in cotton and religion:—

"BEAR CREEK, MISS., Dec. 16, 1861.

"TO MY BOYS SAMMIE AND THOMAS:—

"After a long silence I will tell you some little news. I told C. D. MOORE to tell you that paper was very scarce in this wooden world. I went to Vaidere to get this, and was glad to get it at fifty cents per quire.

"The health of our country is pretty good. Crops are very short; corn and cotton, especially cotton, not quite half a crop—though it doesn't matter, as we can't get any money for it. For my part, I know not what we are to do; I haven't a red cent. My intention now is to plant only about eight acres in cotton; that will make enough to buy or barter my groceries. I fear, my children, we will not live to see as prosperous a time after this revolution as there was before it.

I often think of the language of our Saviour: "—*Eli, Eli, Lama Sabacthani*—My God, why hast thou forsaken me?" I verily believe all this calamity has come upon us for our wickedness. *Religion is down like cotton*—not worth much—and by the actions of good brethren it might be bought for a mere trifle, though if we were to judge from its sparseness, like salt, it would be worth $40 per sack. Oh, my God, *what will become of us!* Go, if you please, to the churchyard, and you will hear nothing but secular affairs, and war, war.

Dull times everywhere. Money scarce. Pork high—10 to 12½ cents per pound; salt the same; coffee $1·50 per pound, and none to be had at that; calico 30 to 50 cents per yard; domestics, 20 to 25 cents per yard; sugar, 6 to 12½ cents; molasses, 30 to 40 cents; and everything in the same ratio.

I saw your wives not long since; all well, &c. You have heard of MARION's death, I reckon. Poor fellow, he left a bereaved wife and two children. Give my kindest regards to friends, &c. A. HEARN.

LATE FROM THE SOUTH.

We make up the following from late Norfolk and Richmond papers:—

RUNNING THE BLOCKADE.

The Richmond *Dispatch* has a telegram dated New Orleans, Feb. 14, which says:—"The steamer *Victoria* has run the blockade at this port. The blockading steamer fired two hundred shells at her, but she arrived safe. Her cargo consisted of 15,000 stand of arms, a quantity of ammunition, coffee, &c.

A BALTIMOREAN IN TROUBLE.

At the Hustings Court, in Richmond, on Friday, THOMAS J. GOODRICH was tried for an assault upon LEWIS ZIMMER. He was found guilty, and fined $25, and sentenced to six months' imprisonment in the jail. A petition was got up for his release from prison, on account of previous good conduct, and his company being ready to proceed to the seat of war.

THE FEDERAL FLEET NEAR SAVANNAH.

A letter from Savannah, under date of Feb. 10, says:—"The Yankees are still actively engaged in our vicinity. Their gun-boats, to the number of ten, are to be seen in Wall's Cut with a dredging machine, endeavoring to deepen the channel. Nothing has been done to molest them, but Fort Jackson is being strengthened and other batteries finished," &c. The writer appears sanguine of a successful defence of the city.

THE BURNSIDE EXPEDITION.

The Federal troops had all re-embarked at Edenton and gone to some other point. At Elizabeth City about thirty houses and two hotels were consumed. The Federal officers at Edenton had assured the people that they had not come to rob and harrass them; but while the officers were making this assurance and giving orders the soldiers were filling the gun-boats with cotton they found in the cotton-houses.

It was rumored that Elizabeth City had been evacuated by the Federal troops.

FUNERAL OF LIEUT. SELDEN.

The funeral of Lieut. SELDEN, killed at Roanoke Island, took place at Richmond on Friday. The body was conveyed to Christ Church, where a most impressive and appropriate discourse was delivered by Rev. Mr. OKESSON. On the conclusion of the exercises at the church, the remains, followed by a very large procession, composed of naval and military officers, the Mayor and City Council, and citizens generally, were borne to the cemetery.

KILLED AND WOUNDED OF THE CONFEDERATES.

The Norfolk *Day Book* says:—

Our total loss during the Battle of Roanoke Island was eight killed and thirty wounded, as follows:—

Richmond Blues.—Killed—Captain O. JENNINGS WISE, private Wm. H. Bennett. Wounded—Lieutenant Frederick Carter, shoulder; Sergeant George W. Jarvis, side; privates William Ruskell, Frank Johnston, H. Adler and Francis Gamble, each wounded in the leg, not dangerously.

Captain COLES' Company.—Killed—Captain Robert Coles. Wounded—Private Thomas, neck; private Bishop, shoulder, and three others, names not ascertained.

McCulloch Rangers.—Killed—Private Dotson. Wounded—Private Daly, body, and private Collum.

Captain MORRIS' Company.—Wounded—Private Robinson, knee.

Captain SWANN's Company.—Wounded—Lieut. Potier, leg, and two privates, slightly.

Captain DICKINSON's Company.—Wounded—Lieut. Edgar Miller, shoulder.

Captain WISE, at the time he was wounded, was in command of a battalion, composed of the Blues and Green Mountain Guards.

There were two thousand five hundred prisoners of ours taken by the Federals, who are to be paroled for exchange immediately, and will return from Roanoke Island. The Federals confess to a loss of three hundred killed, among them two of their principal colonels and other prominent officers.

REMAINS OF CAPTS. WISE AND COLES.

The remains of Captains WISE and COLES were forwarded by the Petersburg train to their friends in Richmond on Friday. The bodies were in charge of Dr. J. J. SIMPKINS. The funeral of Captain WISE was to be of a very imposing character.

THE HOSTAGES.

Colonel LEE, of Massachusetts, and his brother officers selected by the Confederate States Government as hostages for the good treatment of the captive privateersmen in the North, have been removed from the Richmond jail, in which they were closely imprisoned, to the Confederate States prison, where they are provided with better and more comfortable quarters. This change was induced by the recent action of the Federal Government in placing the privateersmen upon the same footing with prisoners of war.

MOVEMENTS OF GENERALS.

General BRAGG has established his headquarters in Mobile. He reached there on Wednesday last.

Brigadier-General R. H. ANDERSON, who for some months past has been stationed at Pensacola, has been ordered to Virginia.

THE FEDERAL VESSELS.

We learn from a gentleman who arrived from Currituck on Friday, that several of the Federal gun-boats reached the canal on Thursday afternoon, about three o'clock, and commenced a fire of shot and shell on our men, who were engaged in barricading the canal. On Thursday fifty-nine Federal vessels were lying off Roanoke Island, and twenty had gone up the Albemarle Sound.

FROM WESTERN VIRGINIA.

A report has reached us, from a source entitled to confidence (says the Richmond *Dispatch*), that a body of the enemy attacked our cavalry in Mercer county, the latter part of last week. Our cavalry, consisting of not more than two companies (some say one) was surprised and attacked by the enemy, who killed one man and took six prisoners, and captured some of the horses. The Forty-fifth Regiment, Col. HETH, encamped at Pack's Ferry, started to reinforce the cavalry, but fell in with six hundred of the enemy, whom they engaged and repulsed, with what loss is not stated.

MOORFIELDS TAKEN BY THE FEDERALS.

A gentleman arrived from Winchester (says the Richmond *Dispatch*), states that the Federals have taken possession of Moorfields, the county seat of Hardy county. About twenty-five hundred of them (a part of Gen. LANDER's force), marching from Romney, entered the town perhaps on Monday or Tuesday. There was some slight resistance by a small militia force of 700 men, under Colonels MONROE and HARNESS, but they soon retired and the enemy took possession.

The changes in the occupation of that part of Virginia have been very sudden within a few weeks, and with no loss of consequence to the enemy. He withdrew from Romney upon the approach of JACKSON; but as soon as the force under Gen. LORING was ordered away, he returned and mended his hold by extending his line of occupation to Moorfields. Hardy county is one of the richest in the northern portion of the State. The corn crop of that county is immense. Thousands of cattle are in winter driven there to be fattened for market.

FROM GEN. WISE'S COMMAND.

The Richmond *Dispatch* of Saturday says:—On Thursday, at three o'clock, six of the gunboats (side-wheel steamers) of the enemy appeared off the mouth of the Albemarle and Currituck canal, and fired a few cannon shots at the camp of General WISE, then at the bridge a mile or so distant. The General deemed it proper to withdraw towards Currituck Court House, as he had no means of defence against the guns of the boats. This he did. Subsequently he ordered a further withdrawal to Great Bridge, in Norfolk county. A few of the enemy landed at the canal, say two or three hundred, but they did not leave the protection of the boats while observed. Gen. WISE had only some 1200 men. HENNINGSEN's batteries were not with him.

MOVEMENT AND DESIGNS OF THE FEDERALS.

The Wilmington (N. C.) *Journal* of Wednesday says:—

The Federal gun-boats have passed up to Winton, the county seat of Hertford county, on the Chowan river. The Chowan is formed by the confluence of the Meherrin and Nottaway rivers. The main branch of the Nottaway is the Black Water, which is crossed by the Seaboard and Roanoke Railroad, about half way between Weldon and Portsmouth, though rather nearer than the latter place. The Black Water is navigable up the railroad, as a steamer has been running regularly in connection with the railroad trains, although necessarily a small one, owing to the narrowness and crookedness of the stream. The movements of the Lincolnite gun-boats would seem to indicate a desire to force their way up as far as the Portsmouth road, so as either to obtain possession of it, or at least cut off communication by that line.

Although capable of doing much harm to the people resident on the shores of the sounds and the rivers emptying into them, it is evident that there would be no strategic end to be served that would repay the vast outlay of men and money that the Burnside Expedition has occasioned, unless either Norfolk is attacked or possession is obtained of some leading line of railroad, and therefore it is, we take it, that the attention of our authorities will be, or at least ought to be, directed to the protection of the lines of communication, especially of water communication, leading from the navigable waters of Albemarle and Pamlico sounds, in the direction of any of our public works. The Black Water, although deep, is so narrow and crooked that it might be stopped by trees felled across it.

PERSONAL.

Among the arrivals at the Exchange Hotel in Richmond on Friday, were ex-Governor HENRY S. FOOTE, R. J. BRECKINRIDGE, WM. BALLARD PRESTON, Hon. E. S. SPARROW, M. W. CLUSKY, Second Tennessee Regiment, and Captain G. R. GAITHER, of Maryland.

Flags of truce were exchanged on Saturday, at Fort Monroe, for the purpose of sending a few persons South; none came up by the Confederate boat. Several copies of the Norfolk *Day Book*, of Saturday, were received, but they contain very little of interest to the general reader. The leading editorial had for its subject the Federal attack upon Fort Donelson, whilst the news columns are devoted mostly to extracts from Northern and foreign papers. We give the following extracts:—

FUNERAL OBSEQUIES OF LIEUTENANT WILLIAM SELDEN.

On Friday afternoon the funeral obsequies of the late Lieutenant WM. SELDEN took place. The body was borne to Christ Church, and an eloquent and impressive discourse preached by the Rev. Mr. OKESON. Upon the conclusion of the services a large procession was formed, which consisted in part of military officers and escort, the Mayor and City Council and citizens, which followed the remains to the cemetery. The whole scene was sad and impressive, and many eyes unused to weeping dropped the tears of sorrow at the fate of the young patriot, but he died battling nobly for his country.

"VIRGINIA DEFENDERS."

A prominent advertisement is published in the *Day Book*, which calls attention to the fact that thirty or forty men are wanted immediately to fill up the company known as the Virginia Defenders. An eloquent appeal is made on the score of defending the sacred soil of Virginia, and the sum of one hundred dollars bounty in Confederate notes, of course, is guarantied.

THE FIGHT AT ROANOKE ISLAND, ETC.

The *Day Book* appropriates a half column of its leaded matter to further particulars of the fight at Roanoke Island. It states that—

"Pork Point Battery was under the command of Major HILL, and although the enemy directed most of their firing against it, yet, at the end of the first day's fight, only one man was killed and three wounded. During the night the enemy landed a force, estimated at from eight to ten thousand, and at eight o'clock the next morning (Saturday) commenced moving forward, when our artillery stationed on the main road beyond the swamp opened fire with artillery from three pieces, which consisted of one 24-pound howitzer, one 12-pound and one 6-pound field-piece. They were in charge of Lieutenant WILLIAM SELDEN, Lieutenant KENNEY, and a Captain whose name we could not obtain. The guns were managed with great skill and bravery, and nobly poured forth volley after volley for the space of three hours. The Federals brought three of their mountain howitzers to bear upon the work, but the Confederates stood until all their ammunition was gone. In the meantime the vessels of the enemy opened fire with their Dahlgren guns, which, however, did but slight execution. As for the Wier Point Battery, it did not fire more than four shots, as its position was too remote to work effectively. The aggregate killed on the Confederate side was but ten, as follows:—Captain O. JENNINGS WISE, Captain ROBERT COLES, Lieutenant WILLIAM B. SELDEN, and seven privates.

"On Thursday a reconnoissance was made of the enemy's forces off Croatan Island, near Roanoke Island, and the following was the result. They consist as follows:—

"Five side-wheel sea steamers;
"Eight propellers;
"Seven side-wheel river steamers;
"Five steam ferry boats;
"Three canal propellers;
"One stern-wheel steamer;
"Twenty-five transports; making fifty-four in all.

"It is reported that some of the enemy's gunboats have gone up the Albemarle Sound.

"Several of their gun-boats also went up to the canal, and fired shot and shell upon the men who were engaged in barricading the canal.

"General WISE sent a flag of truce to Roanoke Island, which was soon returned with the bodies of the killed, and they were brought up in the steamer *Arrow*.

"We learn from a gentleman who left there on Thursday evening that Elizabeth City had thirty buildings burned, amongst which were two hotels. He says of his own personal knowledge the place was fired by its own citizens.

"The Federals have succeeded in taking twenty-five hundred prisoners. They confess a loss of three hundred killed, amongst whom were two principal colonels, and other prominent officers."

MILITARY APPOINTMENTS.

V. D. GROVER, of Norfolk, has received the appointment of Colonel in the Confederate army, and the *Day Book* appropriates an editorial to his military qualifications and general praise. HOWELL COBB, Colonel of one of the Georgia regiments, has been made a Brigadier-General. Colonel GEORGE W. RANDOLPH, of Virginia, and Colonel JOSEPH L. HOGG, of Texas, have also received commissions of Brigadier-Generals.

LIST OF PASSENGERS RECENTLY ARRIVED FROM THE SOUTH.

As a matter of interest to many, we publish the following list of passengers who have recently reached here from the South under flags of truce from Norfolk to Fortress Monroe:—

Mrs. S. E. Thompson, Miss Susan Bigelow, Mrs. Baggott, Mrs. Milton, Mrs. Woolsey, Mr. John T. James, Miss Virginia James, Miss Emma C. James, Miss Anna James, Master Clement James, Miss Holt, John Henry, Thomas G. Sawyer, John Welsh, H. Fitzgerald, Mrs. Fitzgerald, Peggy Matthews, Miss Laura Dexter, Miss Laura Lacey, Mrs. Rogers, Miss Rogers, Miss Abell, T. S. Cochrane, Mrs. Allen, Patrick Welsh, James Fitzgerald, Mrs. C. M. Norris, Miss Stricker, Mrs. Ellis, Mrs. Sawyer, Mrs. Crawford; Sister M. C. Cullen, Sister M. G. Cullen, Sisters of Mercy; John B. Ryan, William Cuddes, Miss Robinson, Edward Franquer, John Storer, Morris Moriarty and wife, Michael Scanlin, Thomas Ryan, Patrick Flanigan and wife, Daniel Driscoll, Patrick Hanlahan, British subjects; Christian Hemminger, German subject; F. Bellert, A. Bellert, French subjects; Rev. R. S. Wilson, wife and eight children; Joseph Philipps, Prussian subject; Mrs. Lean Guerrier, French subject; Robert Leggett and Edward Brude, British subjects; Captain J. J. Morrill, U. S. steamer *Osceola;* J. B. Kahuwellier, Prussian subject.

The Fort Donelson Victory in Washington

From the Washington Star.

Just as we go to press to-day, Gen. McCLELLAN has received a despatch from the General commanding at Cairo, announcing that on yesterday the two remaining works at Fort Donelson had surrendered to Gen. GRANT.

The total number of prisoners taken is about 15,000. The two principal general officers who surrendered there are General A. SIDNEY JOHNSON and Gen. BUCKNER.

General JOHN B. FLOYD, anticipating the necessity for the surrender, managed to make his escape on Saturday last.

News of this most important event of the war, so far, reached General McCLELLAN an hour before this positive and official despatch, when he was telegraphed of it by Mr. STAGER, Army Superintendent of telegraphs, who announced from Cleveland that Governor YATES had just received this news from Cairo, and that the Stars and Stripes were being raised on the two remaining works (at Donelson) amid salvos from the throats of hundreds of great guns, as the courier left there.

This great victory practically ends the war!

Nashville and Knoxville must both be ours by the end of the week, by which the Rebel army of the Potomac will be entirely isolated from their supports outside of Virginia by the Virginia and Tennessee Railroad line.

That is, from Georgia, Alabama, Kentucky, Tennessee, Louisiana, Arkansas and Texas.

By that time BURNSIDE, too, will have cut their only other line of possible communication south and west, which is through North Carolina by rail.

We are satisfied that our military authorities here anticipate the surrender or evacuation of Columbus ere ten days elapse.

That event will amount to clearing all Kentucky and Tennessee of Rebels in arms, except fugitive bodies of hundreds each, it may be, hiding in mountain fastnesses.

Signally does this great event prove to the world the eminent wisdom and policy of the General-in-Chief, hounded as he has been for months past.

THE NEW CONFEDERATE CONGRESS.

A REBEL BLACK LIST.

Meets in Richmond February 18, 1862.

The Provisional Congress of the Southern Confederacy, which was inaugurated at Montgomery, Alabama, on the 4th of February, 1861, ceased its existence on Monday, and the new Congress met yesterday in the city of Richmond.

It is composed of twenty-six members of the Senate, including two from each of the States of Missouri and Kentucky, and about one hundred and seven Representatives in the House, including also the members from the two States above named. The representation from each State is as follows, compared with the number of members to which those States are entitled in the Federal Congress:—

	Rebel Representation.	Federal Representation.
Virginia	16	13
North Carolina	10	8
South Carolina	6	6
Georgia	10	8
Florida	2	1
Alabama	9	7
Louisiana	6	4
Texas	6	2
Arkansas	4	2
Mississippi	7	5
Tennessee	11	10
Kentucky	11	10
Missouri	9	7
Total	107	83

The Rebel apportionment is based on the ratio of one member for every ninety thousand of population, counting three-fifths for slaves.

The following are the names of the Senators and Representatives elected:—

SENATE.

Those marked with a * were members of the last United States Congress.

ARKANSAS.
Charles B. Mitchell.*
Robert W. Johnson.*
ALABAMA.
William L. Yancey.
Clement C. Clay.*
FLORIDA.
A. E. Maxwell.
James M. Baker.
GEORGIA.
R. H. Hill.
Robert Toombs.*
KENTUCKY.
Henry C. Burnett.*
William E. Sims.*
LOUISIANA.
Edward Sparrow.
T. J. Semmes.
MISSISSIPPI.
Albert Gallatin Brown.*
James Phelan.

MISSOURI.
John B. Clark.*
R. L. Y. Peyton.
NORTH CAROLINA.
George Davis.
William T. Dortch.
SOUTH CAROLINA.
James L. Orr.
Robert Barnwell Rhett.
TEXAS.
Louis T. Wigfall.*
W. S. Oldham.
TENNESSEE.
Langdon C. Haynes.
Gustavus A. Henry.
VIRGINIA.
Robert M. T. Hunter.*
Wm. Ballard Preston.

HOUSE OF REPRESENTATIVES.

Those marked with a * were members of the United States Congress.

Dist. ARKANSAS.
1—Augustus H. Garland†
2—Grandison D. Royston
3—Felix I. Batson.
4—Thomas B. Hanley.
†Cont'd by J. P. Johnson.
ALABAMA.
1—Thomas J. Foster.
2—W. R. Smith.
3—John P. Rawls.
4—Jabez L. M. Curry.*
5—L. F. Lyon.
6—W. P. Chilton.
7—David Clopton.*
8—James L. Pugh.*
9—E. S. Dargan.
FLORIDA.
1—James B. Deskins.
1— —— Hilton.
GEORGIA.
1—Julian Hartridge.
2—David W. Lewis.
3—Hines Holt.
4—A. H. Keenan.
5—C. J. Munnalym.
6—William W. Clark.
7—Robert P. Tripps.
8—Lucien J. Gartrell.*
9—Hardy Strickland.
10—A. R. Wright.
KENTUCKY.
1—Alfred Boyd.
2—John W. Crickett.
3—Henry E. Reed.
4—George W. Ewing.
5—J. S. Chrisman.
6—T. L. Burnett.
7—H. W. Bruce.
8—S. S. Scott.
9—E. M. Bruce.
10—Robt. J. Breckinridge.
11—J. M. Elliott.
LOUISIANA.
1—D. F. Kenners.
2—Charles Villers.
3—John Perkins, Jr.
4—C. W. Conrad.
5—Henry Marshall.
6—Lucien Dupose.
MISSISSIPPI.
1—J. W. Clapp.
2—Reuben Davis.*
3—Israel Welch.
4—H. C. Chambers.
5—Otho R. Singleton.*
6—E. Barksdale.
7—John J. McRea.*
MISSOURI.
T. A. Harris—prisoner.†
Casper W. Bell.†
A. H. Conrow.†

MISSOURI.
Thomas W. Freeman.†
George G. Vest.†
John Hyer.†
Wm. W. Cooke.†
Dist. NORTH CAROLINA.
1—Wm. N. H. Smith.*
2—R. R. Bridgers.
3—Owen R. Keenan.
4—Thos. D. McDowell.
5—A. H. Arrington.
6—J. R. McLean.
7—Thomas S. Ashe.
8—Wm. Lander.
9—B. S. Gaither.
10—A. T. Davidson.
SOUTH CAROLINA.
1—John McQueen.*
2—Wm. Porcher Miles.*
3—L. M. Ayer.
4—Milledge L. Bonham.*
5—James Farrow.
6—W. W. Boyce.*
TENNESSEE.
1—J. B. Heiskell.
2—W. G. Swan.
3—A. G. Welker.
4—E. L. Gardenshire.
5—Henry S. Foote.
6—M. F. Gentry.
7—George W. Jones.
8—Thomas Menees.
9—J. C. A. Atkins.
10—John V. Wright.
11—D. M. Currin.
TEXAS.
1—John A. Wilcox.
2—J. C. Herbert.
3—Peter W. Gregg.
4—F. B. Sexton.
5—Malcolm D. Graham.
6—B. H. Epperson.
VIRGINIA.
1—Muscoe R. H. Garnett.*
2—John R. Chambliss.
3—James Lyons.
4—Roger A. Pryor.*
5—Thomas S. Bocock.*
6—John Goode, Jr.
7—James P. Holcombe.
8—Daniel C. Dejarnette.*
9—Wm. Smith.*
10—Alex. R. Boteler.*
11—John B. Baldwin.
12—Walter R. Staples.
13—Walter Preston.
14—Albert G. Jenkens.*
15—Robert Johnson.
16—Chas. W. Russell.
TERRITORY OF ARIZONA.
C. J. Jones, delegate.

† These men were chosen in a body from General PRICE's Rebel army, and are called commissioners.

The Captured Generals at Fort Donelson.

The Rebel Generals mentioned as captured at Fort Donelson are ALBERT SIDNEY JOHNSTON, PILLOW and BUCKNER. HARDEE appears to have been in Kentucky at the time of the surrender, and FLOYD fled, as he has done before.

ALBERT SIDNEY JOHNSTON is a Major-General in the Rebel army. He has been regarded by many as the finest soldier in the Rebel army; and his military reputation in the Federal army, while he was faithful to the Federal Government, was very high. He is a Kentuckian by birth, and graduated at West Point in 1826. His age is about fifty-five years. He served gallantly in the Black Hawk war, in 1832, and resigned his commission in 1834. He then went to Texas, where he was made successively Adjutant-General of the army, senior Brigadier-General and Secretary of War of the Republic. In 1846 he was made Colonel of the First Texan Rifle Regiment. Afterwards he was acting Inspector-General to Major-General BUTLER, and served in the Battle of Monterey.

In 1849, he was made Paymaster, with the rank of Major. Afterwards he was appointed Colonel of the Second Cavalry, and, under President PIERCE, he was appointed to command the expedition to suppress the Mormon insurrection. For the skill and discretion shown in that appointment, he was breveted a Brigadier-General in 1857. JOHNSTON went over to the Rebel cause last spring, and was at once commissioned as a Major-General. He has had command of "The Armies of the West," and the Rebel Government has relied upon him as one of its main supports.

SIMON BOLIVAR BUCKNER is a Brigadier-General in the Rebel army. He is a Kentuckian, and graduated at West Point in 1844, his age being about 38. He served with distinction as an infantry officer in the war with Mexico, and was wounded at Churubusco. In 1847 he was transferred to the Quartermaster's Department, and in 1852 to the Subsistence Department. In 1855 he resigned his commission. BUCKNER then became somewhat of a speculator, and acquired large property in the free States, chiefly in Chicago. Last Spring he had command of the Kentucky militia, and pretended to be loyal to the Union. But he proved a traitor, and was rewarded by the commission of a Major-General from Jeff. Davis. He is now a prisoner of the Government he has betrayed.

GIDEON J. PILLOW acquired his first distinction, such as it was, in the war with Mexico, where he served as a Major-General. He is a native of Tennessee, and was born June 10th, 1806. He made some sad blunders in Mexico, but his bravery has never been impugned. In catching him, we obtain a prize of less importance than we obtain in JOHNSTON and BUCKNER.

THE SCENE OF THE VICTORY.

THE STRATEGICAL VALUE OF THE FORTIFIED POSITION CAPTURED—THE CUMBERLAND RIVER, CLARKSVILLE, &C.

The capture of Fort Donelson is justly considered of great value. While the repulse of our troops at that point would not have materially affected the general plan of the campaign on our side, its capture will greatly disconcert, cripple and hem in the enemy, and increase their present consternation into a terrible rout on all sides. The taking of this fortified position opens up the Cumberland to Clarksville, about thirty miles distant from Dover, and, after passing that point, to Nashville, about fifty miles further up the river. As our reports state that Commodore FOOTE has gone up the Cumberland to the first named place, a short description of it may not malapropos at the present time.

SKETCH OF CLARKSVILLE.

Clarksville is a thriving post village in Tennessee, and the capital of Montgomery county. It is located on the right or north side of the Cumberland river, at the point where the Red river empties itself into the former stream. It is situated about fifty miles to the northwest of Nashville, the capital of the State. In its prosperous days it had a population of between three and five thousand persons, and had considerable trade. There were at one time two good banks established in the place, and four or five newspaper offices. On the whole, previous to the breaking out of the rebellion, it gave great promise of being a rising place, but at the present time it appears to have greatly retrograded.

DEFENCES, NATURAL AND ARTIFICIAL.

In the neighborhood of Clarksville and for some distance further up the river are a number of bluffs, some of which are precipitous and difficult of access. These have been made use of for the purpose of fortification, and extensive and formidable Rebel works have been in the course of construction there for two or three months. A large number of heavy guns are reported to have been shipped to this point, for the purpose, so it was said, of protecting the railroad bridge and the communication with the capital of the State. It is also reported that ten thousand men left Bowling Green two or three weeks since to reinforce this point, and further, that General HARDEE was in command of the post. The railroad from Louisville, via Bowling Green and Russellville, passes through the village, and it crosses the Cumberland at this point by a valuable bridge. What troops may recently have been at these two last named places have doubtless ere this been sent forward to Clarksville. As Bowling Green is now in the hands of the Union troops, a road is now open to Clarksville, along the railroad, by which it is not at all unlikely our troops may march from General BUELL's department upon the Rebel rear at that place.

THE OTHER IMPORTANT POINTS IN THE MAP.

Bowling Green, sixty-five miles from Clarksville, has recently been taken possession of by the Union forces. A direct railroad connects it with Nashville. This road crosses no important river, and, therefore, cannot be materially injured as a marching road for our troops. Thus not only is Clarksville threatened from this point, by the one railroad, but Nashville is in jeopardy by the other.

Eleven miles south of Bowling Green, along the railroad track, is a small station known by the name of Woodburn. At this point the brigades of Generals BRECKINRIDGE and HINDMAN were located on Thursday last, but have since been reported as having gone to Russellville. They have, doubtless, before this marched to Nashville. It is believed, however, that no Rebel forces exist in Kentucky east of the direct road from Bowling Green, via Franklin, to Nashville. Franklin is nine miles south of Woodburn, and twenty miles from Bowling Green. It is situated on the railroad, as is shown by the map. It is a small post village, and the capital of Simpson county. It is located on Drake's creek, and contains two churches and about four hundred inhabitants.

Nearly due east of Nashville is the city of Knoxville, upon which point General THOMAS is advancing in a Southerly direction, by three routes—from Somerset, Monticello and Cumberland Gap. We mention the fact, but do not deem it politic to point out the roads actually being used as the lines of march.

It is reported that Gen. CRITTENDEN is trying to organize another army at Carthage, on the bank of the Cumberland. This is supposed to be the only Rebel force on the line from General BUELL's department to Nashville. Carthage is a post village of Smith county, Tennessee, and is located opposite to the mouth of Caney Fork. It is fifty miles by land from Nashville, in an easterly direction, and had at one time an academy and one or two churches.

SKETCH OF THE CUMBERLAND RIVER.

As this river will doubtless become one of the important features of the campaign during the next few days, we give a short sketch of it. The Cumberland river is one of the largest affluents of the Ohio. It is very snake-like and circuitous in its course. It rises in the Cumberland Mountains of Kentucky, near the southeastern portion of the State, and, flowing westward and southward, past Somerset and Mill Springs, the recent scene of the defeat and death of ZOLLICOFFER, enters Tennessee between Jackson and Overton counties. After making an extensive circuit through Middle Tennessee, passing in its course Carthage and the city of Nashville, it turns towards the northwest and again enters Kentucky, about ten miles to the east of the Tennessee river. Between Nashville and this point it passes Clarksville and Dover—the former the point to which Commodore FOOTE has gone with his fleet, and the latter the scene of the recent battle and capture of Fort Donelson. Its course, after entering the State of Kentucky, is nearly parallel with that of the Tennessee river, until it enters the Ohio at Smithland. The whole length of the river is estimated at about six hundred miles. During high water large steamboats ascend to Nashville, and small boats about three hundred miles further. About fourteen miles from Williamsburg, in Kentucky, near the Cumberland Mountains, the river has a vertical fall of sixty feet. The area drained by this river is estimated at seventeen thousand square miles.

The Specials at Roanoke.

NEW YORK, Saturday, Feb. 15, 1862.

To the Editor of the New York Times:—

Your Roanoke Island correspondent, in his letter published this morning, speaks of Mr. BENTLEY, of THE PHILADELPHIA INQUIRER, and Mr. SCHELL, of "*Harper's Weekly*," as having entered Fort Huger, after its abandonment by the Rebels, in advance of the army, and hauled down the Rebel flag. Permit me to say that Mr. SCHELL has not been connected with any paper except my own since the commencement of the war, and that his spirited and truthful sketches of the scenes of the glorious victory of Roanoke have been sent to me exclusively, and will duly appear in my *Illustrated Newspaper*

Truly yours, FRANK LESLIE.

THE COMMISSION TO THE SOUTH—GENERAL EXCHANGE OF PRISONERS.—The Hon. HAMILTON FISH and the Rev. Bishop AMES have returned to Washington, and, it is stated, have made a report to the Government respecting their mission to relieve Union prisoners in the South. They repaired to Fortress Monroe, and made known their commission to the Confederate authorities at Norfolk, by whom the matter was referred to Richmond. A reply came refusing to the Commissioners admission to the Confederate territory, but expressing readiness to negotiate for a general exchange of prisoners. Our Commissioners opened negotiation, which resulted in perfect success. An equal exchange was agreed on, but the Confederates had three hundred more prisoners than our Government; but, with commendable magnanimity, they proposed to release those also on parole, if our Government would agree to release three hundred of their men that might hereafter fall into our hands. This noble commission of Secretary STANTON, therefore, has its ample reward. A general "jail delivery" of our soldiers will occur throughout the South, and they will soon be rejoicing in liberty regained. Since the close of this negotiation, with their offer to give liberty to their surplus three hundred Union soldiers, the Confederates have had a reverse, and lost thousands of prisoners at Roanoke Island and Fort Donelson. The question is, shall we be like magnanimous, and give up on parole the large surplus we now have.—*Washington Intelligencer*, 18th.

A SWORD FOR GEN. BURNSIDE.—It was with singular propriety, says the Providence *Journal* that the General Assembly yesterday, while the news of the victory was still coming over the wires, unanimously voted, on the suggestion of Governor SPRAGUE, to present a sword to Gen BURNSIDE.

From General Lander's Division.

GEN. LANDER'S MOVEMENT—WHAT IT HAS DONE, AND WHAT MORE MAY BE EXPECTED—GENERAL UNCERTAINTY.

Special Correspondence of the Cincinnati Gazette.

PAW PAW TUNNEL, VA., Feb. 12.—I have seen and heard enough—without entering into particulars—of the movements completed and in progress in this division of the army of the Potomac, to satisfy me that waiting here for a fight is simply re-enacting the old *role* of Micawber. A fight may turn up within three or four days; there may be no fight at all. Everything is uncertain, dependent on contingencies, and so involved with movements of other Generals, with Rebel indications, the weather, the roads, the transportation, &c., that I am confident General LANDER himself is well nigh as uncertain as the public whether to expect a great battle, or any battle at all, anywhere within the limits of our movements.

THE SITUATION IN LANDER'S DIVISION.

For the present the head-quarters of the division (and a principal portion of the army) are encamped at this point, twenty-six miles east of Cumberland and eighteen in advance of the late position at the mouth of Patterson's Creek.

The Romney movement is over. The place is not permanently occupied—it is scarcely probable that it will be again till we get to Winchester. Whatever strategic importance it may have had, it has lost now.

The whole country between Romney and Hancock is now cleared of Rebel forces. This is the first result of General LANDER's movements.

Nothing now prevents the reopening of the Baltimore and Ohio Railroad clear through to Hancock, fifty-six miles beyond Cumberland, and up to General BANKS' lines. The bridge destroyed by JACKSON, over the Big Cacapon, this side of Hancock, will be completed again to-morrow (Thursday), and trains will at once run through from the Ohio river to Hancock, Maryland. The telegraph is already working, and as I write Hancock is "calling" Paw Paw.

Meantime General WILLIAMS is crossing the Potomac at Hancock (if he has not already completed the work), and is ready to co-operate with LANDER's advance forces in whatever may be further planned.

The Rebels, on the other hand, driven from Hancock and driven from Romney, are massing at Winchester, the great strategic point commanding the left flank of Manassas and the whole extent of the railroad between Hancock and Harper's Ferry.

HOW NEAR THE BALTIMORE AND OHIO RAILROAD IS TO BEING OPEN.

There is no doubt, as has been repeatedly stated before in this correspondence, the chief, if not the only, object of General LANDER's Division, is to reopen the railroad, and thus complete our great Northern base line of operations. Once at Hancock, he has but forty-one miles more to open till he reaches Harper's Ferry, up to within a mile or two of which point cars are now running from Baltimore.

HOW SOON IT CAN BE OPENED.

On this part the rails have been torn up, to complete the Rebel connection from Manassas to Winchester, and five important bridges, including that at Harper's Ferry, have been destroyed. The iron is all ready to relay the track, and most of the work on the bridges is repaired. Clear the road of Rebels, and the managers promise to reopen it in six weeks.

THE PROSPECTS.

What, then, is the prospect of clearing the road of Rebels? There will never be complete security from Rebel outrages till we take Winchester. And it is not probable that we will ever take Winchester till McCLELLAN is ready for his grand advance. LANDER might make a dash on the place, defeat the Rebel army, destroy their stores, and get out of the way again before the Manassas army could get reinforcements up; but the experiment would be a hazardous one, and McCLELLAN is not likely to permit it. LANDER and BANKS have troops enough, if acting in concert, to take Winchester, and make a stand, if the Commander at Manassas saw fit to bring on an engagement there; but LANDER and BANKS have not been doing much in concert, and there is no evidence on BANKS' part that anything of the sort is intended now.

In default of taking Winchester, the railroad may be made reasonably secure by stationing strong forces at Martinsburg and Harper's Ferry, and as a mere speculation on doubtful probabilities it might be suggested that this appears more likely to be the ultimate result of General LANDER's movements than anything else now apparent.

CHANCES FOR MINOR OPERATIONS.

Meantime the General has other reconnoissances in progress, of which no public mention has yet been made, and which may bring about activity in other quarters than those to which attention is now directed. A nice little trap is being set; if the Rebels walk in, all right; if not, no harm is done any way. And there is a hope that JACKSON will be good enough to send out a force to attack the party repairing the Big Cacapon bridge. Nothing would please LANDER better.

For the rest, there is a little force of 1000 Rebel militia encamped only eleven or twelve miles over the mountains, from Paw Paw, that may be unceremoniously gobbled up in a day or two—if they don't run before our men get up, which is by far the most probable result. Our boys entertain a profound contempt for these militia, and declare that "ten will put a hundred to flight" in their case any time.

In brief, so much may be told of the situation and prospects here. Of course there may be changes before this gets into type; there might even be an engagement within a couple of days; but General LANDER himself does not expect much, if any, fighting for some time to come.

The force is trimmed down to fighting trim, the sick and feeble are all sent to the General Hospital, the transportation is put in as efficient shape as possible, and in a word the army is ready for anything, fighting or forced marching, that may be required of it.

The Late Lieutenant-Colonel Viguier de Monteil.

This gallant officer, who lost his life in the battle of Roanoke, was, perhaps, better known to our French than to our native citizens, and we therefore translate from the *feuilleton* of the *Courrier des Etats Unis*, of this date, Mr. MASSERAS' reminiscenses of DE MONTEIL:—

"With his character and military tastes, which he had never abandoned, he could not refrain from taking part in the war. He resolved to do so, notwithstanding the remonstrances of his young and charming wife, now prematurely widowed, and whose future it is to be hoped the Federal Government will secure from want. The D'Epineuil Zouaves were forming; VIGUIER joined them with the grade of Lieutenant-Colonel, and his lively ardor and special aptitude for the work, greatly contributed towards the active organization of the corps. It is said that later he had a serious difficulty with his Colonel; but he left here, nevertheless, with his regiment.

"A peculiar fatality seemed to urge him onward to his death. His regiment, after leaving with the Burnside Expedition, was obliged to return to Annapolis in consequence of the too heavy draught of the steamer on which it was embarked. Instead of leaving with his men, VIGUIER obtained permission to follow the expedition as a volunteer. On the day of the battle he saw the first line of the Hawkins Zouaves hesitate under the fire of the enemy; he seized a gun, rushed to the file and fired as a private. A few moments later an order was sent to take the battery before which the troops were fighting. VIGUIER was the first to advance, crying 'Forward.' A ball struck him as he spoke, entered his mouth and passed through the back of his head. VIGUIER let his gun fall, made a few uncertain gestures with his arms, and fell to rise no more. He died as a true French soldier should."—*N. Y. Post.*

CAPTAIN THEODORE W. DUNHAM.—We visited the quarters of Company F, Eighty-eighth Pennsylvania Volunteers, Captain T. W. DUNHAM, First Lieutenant J. PARKER MARTIN, Second Lieutenant WILLIAM STREET, yesterday, and were entertained in a happy manner. The company is encamped near Fort Ellsworth, and is in a high state of discipline. Captain D. served in the Mexican war, under General NORTH, and was with General PATTERSON in the three months' service. Should opportunity offer, we have no doubt that he and his command will give a good account of themselves, as will the balance of the glorious Eighty-eighth.—*Alexandria Chronicle.*

RICHMOND ENQUIRER.

EXTRA.

PRESIDENT JEFFERSON DAVIS'S INAUGURAL ADDRESS.

Delivered in Richmond, February 22, 1862.

Fellow-Citizens: On this, the birth-day of the man most identified with the establishment of American independence, and beneath the monument erected to commemorate his heroic virtues and those of his compatriots, we have assembled to usher into existence the permanent Government of the Confederate States. Through this instrumentality, under the favor of Divine Providence, we hope to perpetuate the principles of our Revolutionary fathers. The day, the memory and the purpose seem fitly associated.

It is with mingled feelings of humility and pride that I appear to take, in the presence of the people and before high Heaven, the oath prescribed as a qualification for the exalted station to which the unanimous voice of the people has called me. Deeply sensible of all that is implied by this manifestation of the people's confidence, I am yet more profoundly impressed by the vast responsibility of the office, and humbly feel my own unworthiness.

In return for their kindness, I can only offer assurances of the gratitude with which it is received, and can but pledge a zealous devotion of every faculty to the service of those who have chosen me as their Chief Magistrate.

When a long course of class legislation, directed not to the general welfare, but to the aggrandizement of the Northern section of the Union, culminated in a warfare on the domestic institutions of the Southern States—when the dogmas of a sectional party, substituted for the provisions of the constitutional compact, threatened to destroy the sovereign rights of the States, six of those States, withdrawing from the Union, confederated together, to exercise the right and perform the duty of instituting a government which would better secure the liberties, for the preservation of which that Union was established.

Whatever of hope some may have entertained that a returning sense of justice would remove the danger with which our rights were threatened, and render it possible to preserve the Union of the Constitution, must have been dispelled by the malignity and barbarity of the Northern States in the prosecution of the existing war. The confidence of the most hopeful among us must have been destroyed by the disregard they have recently exhibited for all the time-honored bulwarks of civil and religious liberty. Bastiles filled with prisoners, arrested without civil process, or indictment duly found; the writ of *habeas corpus* suspended by Executive mandate; a State Legislature controlled by the imprisonment of members whose avowed principles suggested to the Federal Executive that there might be another added to the list of seceded States; elections held under threats of a military power; civil officers, peaceful citizens, and gentle women incarcerated for opinion's sake, proclaimed the incapacity of our late associates to administer a government as free, liberal and humane as that established for our common use.

For proof of the sincerity of our purpose to maintain our ancient institutions, we may point to the Constitution of the Confederacy and the laws enacted under it, as well as to the fact that through all the necessities of an unequal struggle, there has been no act on our part to impair personal liberty or the freedom of speech, of thought or of the press. The Courts have been open; the judicial functions fully executed, and every right of the peaceful citizen maintained as securely as if a war of invasion had not disturbed the land.

The people of the States now confederated became convinced that the Government of the United States had fallen into the hands of a Sectional Majority who would pervert that most sacred of all trusts to the destruction of the rights which it was pledged to protect. They believed that to remain longer in the Union would subject them to a continuance of a disparaging discrimination, submission to which would be inconsistent with their welfare, and intolerable to a proud people. They therefore determined to sever its bonds, and establish a new Confederacy for themselves. [Cheers.]

The experiment instituted by our revolutionary fathers of a voluntary union of sovereign States for purposes specified in a solemn compact, had been perverted by those, who feeling power and forgetting right, were determined to respect no law but their own will. The Government had ceased to answer the ends for which it was ordained, and established. To save ourselves from a revolution, which in its silent but rapid progress was about to place us under the despotism of numbers, and to preserve in spirit as well as in form, a system of government, we believed to be peculiarly fitted to our condition and full of promise for mankind, we determined to make a new association composed of States homogeneous in interest, in policy and in feeling. [Cheers.]

True to our traditions of peace and our love of justice, we sent commissioners to the United States to propose a fair and amicable settlement of all questions of public debt or property which might be in dispute. But the Government at Washington denying our right to self government, refused even to listen to any proposals for a peaceful separation.—Nothing was then left to us but to prepare for war. [Cheers.]

The first year in our history has been the most eventful in the annals of this Continent. A new government has been established, and its machinery put in operation, over an area exceeding 700,000 square miles. The great principles upon which we have been willing to hazard every thing that is dear to man, have made conquests for us which could never have been achieved by the sword. Our Confederacy has grown from six to thirteen States; and Maryland, already united to us by hallowed memories, and material interests, will, I believe, when able to speak with unstifled voice, connect her destiny with the South. [Great applause.] Our people have rallied with unexampled unanimity to the support of the great principles of Constitutional government, with firm resolve to perpetuate by arms the rights which they could not peacefully secure. A million of men, it is estimated, are now standing in hostile array, and waging war along a frontier of thousands of miles; battles have been fought; seiges have been conducted, and although the contest is not ended, and the tide for the moment is against us, the final result in our favor is not doubtful.

The period is near at hand when our foes must sink under the immense load of debt which they have incurred; a debt which in their effort to subjugate us has already attained such fearful dimensions as will subject them to burthens which must continue to oppress them for generations to come.

We too have had our trials and difficulties That we are to escape them in future is not to be hoped. It was to be expected when we entered upon this war that it would expose our people to sacrifices and cost them much, both of money and blood. But we knew the value of the object for which we struggled, and understood the nature of the war in which we were engaged. Nothing could be so bad as failure, and any sacrifice would be cheap as the price of success in such a contest. [Cheers.]

But the picture has its lights as well as its shadows. This great strife has awakened in the people the highest emotions and qualities of the human soul. It is cultivating feelings of patriotism, virtue and courage. Instances of self-sacrifice, and of generous devotion to the noble cause for which we are contending, are rife throughout the land. Never has a people evinced a more determined spirit than that now animating men, women and children in every part of our country. Upon the first call the men fly to arms; and wives and mothers send their husbands and sons to battle without a murmur of regret.

It was, perhaps, in the ordination of Providence that we were to be taught the value of our liberties by the price which we pay for them.

The recollections of this great contest with all its common traditions of glory, of sacrifice, and of blood will be the bond of harmony and enduring affection amongst the people, producing unity in policy, fraternity in sentiment and joint effort in war.

Nor have the material sacrifices of the past year been made without some corresponding benefits. If the acquiescence of foreign nations in a pretended blockade has deprived us of our commerce with them, it is fast making us a self supporting and an independent people. The blockade, if effectual and permanent, could only serve to divert our industry from the production of articles for export, and employ it in supplying commodities for domestic use.

It is a satisfaction that we have maintained the war by our unaided exertions. We have neither asked nor received assistance from any quarter. Yet the interest involved is not wholly our own. The world at large is concerned in opening our markets to its commerce. When the independence of the Confederate States is recognized by the nations of the earth, and we are free to follow our interests and inclinations by cultivating foreign trade, the Southern States will offer to manufacturing nations the most favorable markets which ever invited their commerce. Cotton, sugar, rice, tobacco, provisions, timber and naval stores will furnish attractive exchanges. Nor would the constancy of these supplies be likely to be disturbed by war. Our Confederate strength will be too great to tempt aggression, and never was there a people whose interests and principles committed them so fully to a peaceful policy as those of the Confederate States. By the character of their productions they are too deeply interested in foreign commerce wantonly to disturb it. War of conquest they cannot wage, because the Constitution of their Confederacy admits of no coerced association. Civil war there cannot be between States held together by their volition only. This rule of voluntary association, which cannot fail to be conservative, by securing just and impartial government at home, does not diminish the security of the obligations by which the Confederate States may be bound to foreign nations. In proof of this it is to be remembered, that at the first moment of asserting their right of secession, these States proposed a settlement on the basis of a common liability for the obligations of the General Government.

Fellow-Citizens: After the struggles of ages had consecrated the right of the Englishman to Constitutional Representative Government, our colonial ancestors were forced to vindicate that birthright by an appeal to arms. Success crowned their efforts, and they provided for their posterity, a peaceful remedy against future aggression.

The tyranny of an unbridled majority, the most odious, and least responsible form of despotism has denied us both the right and the remedy. Therefore, we are in arms to renew such sacrifices as our fathers made to the holy cause of Constitutional liberty. At the darkest hour of our struggle the Provisional gives place to the Permanent Government. After a series of successes and victories, which covered our arms with glory, we have recently met with serious disasters. But in the heart of a people resolved to be free, these disasters tend but to stimulate to increased resistance.

To show ourselves worthy of the inheritance bequeathed to us by the patriots of the Revolution, we must emulate that heroic devotion which made reverse to them but the crucible in which their patriotism was refined.—[Applause.]

With confidence in the wisdom and virtue of those who will share with me the responsibility, and aid me in the conduct of public affairs; securely relying on the patrotism and courage of the people, of which the present war has furnished so many examples, I deeply feel the weight of the responsibilities I now, with unaffected diffidence, am about to assume; and fully realizing the inadequacy of human power to guide and to sustain, my hope is reverently fixed on Him whose favor is ever vouchsafed to the cause which is just. With humble gratitude and adoration, acknowledging the Providence which has so visibly protected the Confederacy during its brief, but eventful career, to Thee, Oh God! I trustingly commit myself, and prayerfully invoke Thy blessing on my country and its cause,

[Continued and enthusiastic cheering]

Evacuation of Nashville.

AUGUSTA, Feb. 22—Private dispatches received here from Chattanooga state that Federal gunboats reached Nashville on Thursday.

SAVANNAH, Feb. 22—General Walker has received despatches which state the Confederates have evacuated Nashville.

THE SUNDAY DELTA

PUBLISHED BY THE NEW ORLEANS DELTA NEWSPAPER COMPANY.

TERMS—PER ANNUM.

DAILY DELTA, (invariably in advance)......$10
WEEKLY DELTA, do. do. 3
SUNDAY DELTA, do. do. 2

For any time less than one year the DAILY DELTA will be delivered to City Subscribers at 20 cents a week.

ADVERTISING RATES

Advertisements $1 a Square for the first insertion. Every subsequent insertion 50 cents.
Advertisements on the Second Page $1 per measured Square each insertion.
Advertisements at intervals $1 a Square each insertion.
Marriage and Funeral Notices $1 each insertion.
A Liberal Discount made to regular Advertisers.

The Semi-Weekly Delta is issued every Tuesday and Friday morning, at $5 per annum.

SUNDAY MORNING, FEBRUARY 23, 1862.

"BRONZE JOHN."

While speculating upon the dispositions of foreign powers for or against intervention in our behalf, we should not overlook a puissance whose exploits are allegorically foreshadowed by one of our gifted poetical contributors. Our recognition by France and England, say European correspondents, followed by the raising of the blockade, is only a question of time. Time is an exceedingly elastic and extensible idea, and this question of time concerning the policy of certain great powers is entirely too indefinite for our needs and purposes. But it is not so with the anticipated services of "Bronze John," the Knight of "the saffron steed and yellow plume." They are a question of but three months. His alliance may be counted upon with perfect confidence. He may come to our aid as invisible as pestilence, but to our foe he will be as mighty as death, and as inexorable as the grave. Wait a little while, ye croakers! before you proclaim that the South has no friends. Hush your screeches, ye sable birds! that come from your nooks and caverns, believing it to be night because a shadow of disaster has fallen on our land. Wait, we say, for "Bronze John." Wait, and he will smite the camp of the invader as the Assyrian host of old were smitten when cold horror came out of the dread stillness of night, and left captain and soldier, rider and horse, stiff and stark upon the plain.

SHARP SHOOTERS.

We are glad to see that a volunteer corps is about to be formed, to serve as sharp shooters in the neighborhood of this city. This body is designed, we understand, to act under the immediate orders of Gen. Lovell, for services of a special character, on occasions requiring skillful and daring reconnoissance. It is to be constituted of capital shots, of experienced woodsmen, practiced hunters, and men ready with the oar of the skiff and the paddle of the canoe, who are able to glide like apparitions through swamps, lagoons and bayous. Such men can not fail to be extremely valuable if the enemy should attempt an approach to the city by land from any place on our coast. They could not only, in that case, reconnoitre, but they could kill or capture the enemy's stragglers, pickets and pioneers. A thousand such men deployed in our swamps as skirmishers might check the advance of ten thousand invaders.

SPECIAL DISPATCHES TO THE DELTA.

From Arkansas and Tennessee.

MEMPHIS, Feb. 22, 1862.

The Appeal has a special dispatch from Clarksville, Arkansas, dated to-day, saying it was reported that Gen. McCulloch was falling back south of Fayetteville, and was being followed by the enemy.

Gen. George Crittenden's command has arrived at Murfreesboro, south of Nashville, from Carthage.

The enemy had not occupied Nashville yesterday. R.

From Richmond.

RICHMOND, Feb. 18, 1862.

Congress has confirmed the nominations of Crittenden and Loring, as Major-Generals.

The free trade bill has been defeated.

We have nothing from Donelson. L. C. D.

FRENCH TROPICAL FEVER AND AGUE MIXTURE.—That this is a discovery destined to supersede every other in the treatment and radical cure of this terrible scourge in wet and exposed latitudes, admits now of no question, as may readily be authenticated by the thousands who have obtained permanent relief. Persons afflicted with this disease should not lose a single moment to procure at Mr. Laplace's well-known pharmaceutical depot, corner of Elysian Fields and Victory streets, opposite the Pontchartrain Railroad depot, a bottle, at least, of this fever and ague antidote. To those who, after faithfully following the printed directions, should feel dissatisfied with the remedy, Mr. Laplace will voluntarily return the cash. A more liberal, and at the same time more convincing, proposition, can not be made.

DIVIDEND.—The directors of the Polk County (Tennessee) Copper Company have declared a dividend of three per cent., payable at the office of the Company, No. 102 Gravier street, on Saturday, March 1. This is the first dividend paid out by the corporation, as the profits heretofore have necessarily been appropriated to increasing the facilities at the mines, and otherwise improving the property of the Company. But for the interruption in transportation, which prevents their getting copper to market, the managers would have been enabled to have divided five per cent. instead of three.

The election of Directors of the New Orleans and Texas Railroad Company, at the St. Charles Hotel last night, resulted in the choice of the following ticket by an average of about 1600 votes, this being a large majority of the stock subscribed and of the votes cast:

L. F. GENERES, J. H. STAUFFER,
J. J. HANNA, B. J. SAGE,
JOHN J. ADAMS, C. M. CONGREVE,
A. M. GENTRY.

This list of names gives earnest of energetic prosecution of the work, and speedy completion of this military necessity, if the public but do its duty in aid of it.

THE IRISH BRIGADE.—We were pleased last evening to shake the hand of our old friend, Capt. Joseph Hanlon, of Company A, Irish Brigade, (now in Virginia.) Capt. Hanlon is here for the purpose of recruiting, and calls upon his countrymen to rally to the support of their adopted flag. Company A has a most worthy representative in the person of Capt. Hanlon, and we hope he may succeed in winning a large number of recruits. We refer to his advertisement.

MUSIC.—L. Grunewald, the publisher, No. 26 Chartres street, has placed before us La Violette—one of ten mazourkas, for the piano, composed by E. Bischoff.

TELEGRAPHED TO THE DAILY DELTA.

From Memphis.

MEMPHIS, Feb. 22.—The latest advices received here state that Nashville was not occupied by the Federals up to Friday night. It is thought that Buell, with a portion of his army, will reach there on Monday next. Gen. Johnston is reported to be at Murfreesboro', where he has been joined by Gen. Geo. B. Crittenden. There is nothing startling this morning.

From Lincolndom, via Richmond.

RICHMOND, Feb. 22.—The Northern papers of the 20th are received.

The Herald says the rebel agents in Paris declare the seceding States will approve a Constitution of monarchy in the South if it can be attended with any prospect of success.

Lincoln Congress.—In the Senate a petition from the citizens of New York was presented, asking that the name of South Carolina be expunged from the list of States; that it be made a territory, and the territory be divided between Georgia and North Carolina.

In the House, resolutions were offered by Hickman, directing the Judiciary Committee to inquire into the allegations against Vallandigham for disloyalty, who vehemently denies the accusations. The resolutions were withdrawn.

The culture of cotton is disappearing from Dutch Guiana.

NEW YORK, Feb. 20.—Cotton market irregular. Sales of middling uplands at 23½ to 25c.

The Herald is delighted with the Queen's speech, and said it extinguished the last glimmering of intervention, and urges the Southern people to rise in general revolution and put down the rebellion.

Washington is to be illuminated on the night of the 22d instant, at the expense of the Yankee Government.

The capture of Gen. Price was announced in the House, causing uproarious applause.

The fire reported on the Cumberland river was caused by the burning of the Tennessee Rolling Mills by the Federals.

The Yankee account says 12 000 stand of arms were taken at Fort Donelson; also 1200 boxes of beef, with other stores. A great number of the dead were unburied on the 18th inst.

ST. LOUIS, Feb. 19.—Capt. Stubbs has captured Gen. Price, Col. Dorsey, Col. Cass and Judge Capt. Budge, of Price's staff. The companies under their command escaped.

The myriads of Northern fanatics who became mad with excitement and joy over the account of the great slaughter of Yankees at Fort Donelson, are slowly recovering their senses.

Stanton recommends the speedy execution of Col. Ansabree, on the charge of cowardice by Gen. Lander, who is sustained.

Lucius H. Chandler is appointed Consul to Matanzas.

The Price reported taken prisoner is not Sterling Price, the great Confederate leader of Missouri.

Five thousand infantry and three batteries of artillery left St. Louis on the 19th. for Cumberland river.

The attacking force of Federals at Savannah is 16,000 strong.

NORFOLK, Feb. 21.—The Federal forces ascended Chowan river again yesterday to Winton, in several gunboats, with a large number of troops. The Confederates opened a heavy fire on them, killing and wounding a number. Some of the Yankees landed and burnt the town, when the Southerners retired. Our loss is said to be two men and two horses. Humbug C. H. Foster is among the Yankees killed.

RICHMOND, Feb. 21.—We have had no Nashville mail for the past seven days, and no dispatches from Nashville for the past two days. It is stated here in telegraphic circles that the telegraph office at Nashville is closed, and the public must draw their own inferences.

RICHMOND, Feb. 22.—Both Houses took a recess this morning to attend the inauguration in the House.

Subsequently Mr. Foote introduced a resolution appointing a committee of one from each State to request the Secretary of War to furnish the fullest minute particulars in reference to the condition of our armies on the field and our seaboard and river defenses, or elsewhere, and report, with a view to enable Congress to pass such measures as will facilitate the establishment of our national independence and a sense of security, peace and safety. The resolution was tabled for the present.

In the Senate the business was unimportant.

President Davis's Inaugural.

Fellow-Citizens—On this the birthday of the man most identified with the establishment of American Independence, and beneath the monument erected to commemorate his heroic virtues and those of his compatriots, we have assembled to usher into existence the Permanent Government of the Confederate States. Through the instrumentality, and under the favor of a Living Providence, we hope to perpetuate the principles of our revolutionary fathers. The day, the memory, and the purpose seem to be fitly associated. It is with mingled feelings of humility and pride I appear to take in the presence of this people and before High Heaven the oath prescribed as a qualification of the exalted station to which the unanimous voice of the people has called me. Deeply sensible of all that is implied by this manifestation of the people's confidence, I am yet more profoundly impressed with the vast responsibility of the office, and humbly feel my own unworthiness. In return for their kindness, I only offer my assurances of the gratitude with which it is received, and can but pledge my zealous devotion of every faculty to the service of those who have chosen me their Chief Magistrate. When through a long course of class legislation, directed not to be for the general welfare, but for aggrandisement in warfare, and against the domestic institutions of the Southern States—when the dogmas of sectional parties, substituted for the provisions of the constitutional compact, threatened to destroy the sovereign rights of those States, six of those States, withdrawing from the Union, confederated together to exercise the right to perform the duty of instituting a Government which would better secure their liberties for the preservation of which that Union was established. Whatever of hope some may have entertained that a returning sense of justice would remove the danger with which our rights were threatened, and render it possible to preserve the Union of the constitution, must have been dispelled by the malignity and barbarity of the Northern States in the prosecution of the existing war. The confidence of the most hopeful among us must have been destroyed by the disregard they have recently exhibited for all time-honored works of civil and religious liberty. Their bastiles are filled with prisoners arrested without civil process or indictment, which they are in duty bound to serve. The writ of habeas corpus was suspended by Executive mandate, and a State Legislature controlled by the imprisonment of its members, whose avowed principles suggested to the Federal Executive there might have been another added to the list of seceded States; elections held under threats of military power; civil officers, peaceful citizens, and gentle women, incarcerated for opinion's sake. We proclaimed, in the capacity of our late associates, to administer the Government as free, liberal and humane as that established for our common use. For the proof of our sincerity of purpose to maintain our ancient institutions, we may point to the Constitution of the Confederacy, or to the laws enacted under it, as well as to the fact that, through all the necessities of an unequal struggle, there has been no act on our part to impair personal liberty or freedom of speech, of thought, or of the press. The courts have been opened, and their judicial functions fully executed, and every right of the peaceful citizen maintained as equally as if the war of invasion had not disturbed our land. The people of the States now Confederate became convinced that the Government of the United States had fallen into the hands of a sectional majority, who would peril that most sacred of all trusts to the destruction of those rights which it was pledged to protect, and they believed that to remain longer in the Union would subject them to a continuance of disparaging discrimination, submission to which would be inconsistent with their welfare, and intolerable to a proud people. They therefore determined to sever its bonds, and establish a new Confederacy for themselves. (Cheers.) The experiment instituted by our revolutionary fathers of a voluntary Union of sovereign States for purposes specified in solemn compact had been perverted by those who feeling they had the power, and forgetting the right were determined to respect no law but their own will, the Government had ceased to answer the ends for which it was ordained and established. To save ourselves from revolution, which in its silent but rapid progress was about to place us under a despotism of numbers, and to preserve in the spirit as well as the form the system of government we believed to be peculiarly fitted to our condition and full of promise for mankind, we determined to make a new association, composed of States homogeneous in interest, policy and feeling. True to our traditions of peace and our love of justice, we sent Commissioners to the United States to propose a fair and amicable settlement of all questions of public debt or property which might be disputed, but the Government at Washington, denying our right to self-government, refused even to listen to any proposals for a peaceful separation. Nothing was then left us but to prepare for war. (Cheers.) The first year of our history has been the most eventful in the annals of this continent. A new government has been established over an area exceeding 700,000 square miles, and the great principles upon which we have been willing to hazard everything dear to man has made conquests for us which could never have been achieved by the sword. Our Confederacy has grown from six to thirteen States, and Maryland, already united to us by hallowed memories and national interests, will, I believe, when able to speak, with united voice connect her destiny with the South. (Great applause.) Our people have rallied with unexampled unanimity to the support of the great principles of constitutional government with a firm resolve to perpetuate by arms the rights they could not peacefully secure. A million, it is estimated, is the standing hostile army, and waging a war along a frontier of thousands of miles. Battles have been fought and sieges conducted, and although the contest has not ended, and did for the moment go against us, the final result in our favor is not doubted. The period is near at hand when our foes must yield under the immense load of debt incurred; a debt which, in their effort to subjugate us, has already attained such fearful dimensions as will subject them to burthens which must continue to oppress them for generations to come. We, too, have had our trials and difficulties, and that we are to escape them in the future is not to be hoped. It was to be expected when we entered upon this war, that it would expose our people to many sacrifices, and cost them much, both in money and blood, but we knew the value of the object for which we have struggled, and understood the nature of the object for which we engaged, and that nothing could be so bad as failure, and any sacrifice will be cheap as the price of success in such a contest. (Cheers.) But the picture has its lights as well as its shades. This great strife has awakened in the people the highest emotions and qualities of the human soul; it is cultivating feelings of patriotism, virtue and courage, and instances of self-sacrifice and generous devotion to the noble cause for which we are contending are rife throughout the land. Never has a people evinced so determined a spirit as that now animating the men, women and children in every part of our country. Upon the first call men fly to arms, and wives and mothers send their husbands and sons to battle without a murmur or regret. It was, perhaps, in the ordination of Providence that we were to be taught the value of our liberties by the price we pay for them. The recollections of this great contest with all its common traditions of glory, sacrifices and of blood, will be a bond of harmony and endearing affection among the people, producing unity in policy, fraternity in sentiment, and joint effort in war. The material sacrifices of the past year have not been made without some corresponding benefits. If the acquiescence of foreign nations in the pretended blockade has deprived us of our commerce with them, it is fast making a self-supporting and independent people. The blockade, if effectual and permanent, could only serve to divest our industry from the production of articles for export and employ it supplying commodities for domestic use. It is satisfaction to know that we have maintained the war by our own unaided exertions. We have neither asked or received assistance from any quarter. The interests involved is not only our own; the world at large is concerned in the opening of our markets to its commerce; and when the Independence of the Confederate States is recognized by the nations of the earth, and we are free to follow our interests and inclinations, by cultivating foreign trade, the Southern States will offer the manufacturing nations the most favorable markets which ever invited their commerce. Cotton, sugar, rice, tobacco, provisions, timber and naval stores, will furnish attractive exchanges. Nor would the constancy of these supplies be likely to be disturbed by war. Our Confederate strength will be too great to attempt aggression, and never was there a people whose interests and principles committed them so fully to a peaceful policy as these Confederate States. By the character of their productions they are too deeply interested in foreign commerce to want a war only to disturb the world, and a war of conquest they can not wage, because the constitution of the Confederacy admits no coerced association. A civil war there can not be between States held together by their volition only, and this rule of voluntary association, which can not fail to be conservative, as by securing a just and impartial government at home it does not diminish the security of obligations by which the Confederate States may be bound to foreign nations. In proof, it is to be remembered that at the first moment of asserting their right to secession, these States proposed a settlement on the basis of common liabilities for the obligations of the General Government. Fellow-citizens, after the struggle of ages had consecrated the right of Englishmen to a constitutional representative government, our colonial ancestors were forced to vindicate that birthright by an appeal to arms. Success crowned their efforts, and they provided for their posterity a peaceful remedy against future aggressions. The tyranny of an unbridled majority, the most odious and least responsible form of despotism has denied us both that right and remedy; therefore, we are in arms to renew such sacrifices as our fathers made to the holy cause of constitutional liberty. At the darkest hour of our struggle, the Provisional gives place to the Permanent Government, and after a series of successes and victories, which covered our arms with glory, we have recently met with serious disasters; but in the heart of that people who are resolved to be free, these disasters tend but to stimulate to increased resistance to show ourselves worthy the inheritance bequeathed us by the patriots of the Revolution. We must emulate the heroic devotion which made severe to them but the crucible in which their patriotism was refined. (Applause.) With confidence in the wisdom and virtue of those who will share with me the responsibility, and aid me in the conduct of public affairs, and securely relying on the patriotism and courage of a people, of which the present war has furnished so many examples, I deeply feel the weight of the responsibilities I now, with unaffected diffidence, am about to assume, and fully realizing the inadequacy of human power to guide and sustain, my hope is reverently fixed on Him whose favor is vouchsafed to the cause which is just, and with humble gratitude and adoration, acknowledging the Providence which has so visibly protected the Confederacy during its brief but eventful career. To Thee Oh God, I trustingly commit myself, and prayerfully invoke Thy blessing on my country and its cause.

Major W. T. Dean, of the 5th Louisiana Regiment, stationed at Yorktown, will leave on Monday evening for his regiment. He will take charge of any letters for any of the Louisiana troops on the Peninsula, if left this day at the store 425 Dryades street.

DIED:

On Saturday morning, 22d inst., at 6 o'clock A. M., CARRIE B., consort of John L. Macaulay, aged 22 years.

The friends of the family, and of her father, John D. Champlin, are invited to attend the funeral on SUNDAY, at 1 o'clock P. M., from No. 199 Canal street.

MARRIED:

On Wednesday, 19th February, by Rev. Father Meredith, Mr. FRED. SEILER to Miss CASSIE VIRGINIA, daughter of Cornelius McCormick, Esq., all of this city.

On Tuesday, the 18th inst., at the residence of the bride's mother, by the Rev. A. D. McCoy, Dr. R. O. RICHARDSON, to Miss PINKIE STOCKMAN, daughter of the late Wm. Stockman, of this city.

By the Rev. Mr. Alexander, JOSEPH L. ROBICHAUX, of the parish of Lafourche, to Miss MARIE FERNANDA BARBA, of this city.

NEW ORLEANS, February 22, 1862.

GENTLEMEN—You are requested to attend a meeting of the Stockholders of the LOUISIANA SALT MANUFACTURING COMPANY, to be held on TUESDAY AFTERNOON, at 2 o'clock, at the store of Abat Generes & Co., No. 54 Royal street, for the purpose of organizing and of electing a President and Board of Directors for the ensuing two years. Respectfully,

feb23 1t2p R. THOMASSY.

A Card.

Certain parties, suspected to be those arrested and tried upon a criminal charge for embezzlement, committed while in the employ of the late Adams Express Company, being unable to circulate their slanders through any portion of the press of this city, have endeavored to injure the Southern Express Company and myself, by publishing, in circular form, serious charges against us. The Southern Express Company, in its services to the Confederacy, needs no defense at my hands, and I can only say, with reference to myself, that during my residence of about five years in the South, I trust my conduct has been such as to need no refutation of the absurd charges contained in the anonymous circulars of slanderers.

J. J. McKEEVER.

New Orleans, Feb 22, 1862. feb22 2p

Notice.

EXECUTIVE OFFICE, NEW ORLEANS, Feb 22, 1862.

In accordance with the provisions of the Act hereto annexed, approved 13th January, 1862, books of subscription will be opened at this office on the 24th inst., to continue open for one week, between the hours of 10 A. M. and 2 P. M. Should more than a million of dollars be subscribed, the excess will be deducted from the largest subscriptions. Payment will not be required until the bonds are ready for delivery.

I take occasion to observe that a loan for so patriotic a purpose should be participated in by the citizens generally, who may thus contribute to the protection of our homes and firesides.

THOS. O. MOORE,
Governor of the State of Louisiana.

[No. 45.]

AN ACT to appropriate One Million of Dollars in Bonds of the State, for the purpose of Arming and Equipping the Volunteers and Militia, for the defense of the State and to repel invasion.

SECTION 1. Be it enacted, &c., That in consequence of the war, and to repel invasion, the Governor be, and he is hereby, authorized and required to issue the coupon bonds of the State for one million of dollars, in sums of fifty, one hundred, five hundred and one thousand dollars, payable in five equal instalments of two hundred thousand dollars each, at eight to twelve years inclusive, to bear interest at the rate of six per cent. per annum, payable annually at the Treasurer's Office.

SEC. 2. Be it further enacted, &c., That the Governor shall invite proposals for the purchase of said bonds by advertisement in two papers published in the city of New Orleans, in both languages, as he may select, reserving the right to reject any or all of said proposals.

SEC. 3. Be it further enacted, &c., That the proceeds of the sale of said bonds shall be placed in the Treasury, to the credit of a fund to be called the Military Fund, and shall be subject to the order of the Governor, for the purpose of purchasing arms and munitions of war and equipments for the Volunteers and Militia of the State.

SEC. 4. Be it further enacted, &c., That this law shall take effect from and after its passage.

(Signed) ADOLPHUS OLIVIER,
Speaker of the House of Representatives.
(Signed) HENRY M. HYAMS,
Lieut. Governor and President of the Senate.
(Signed) THOS. O. MOORE,
Governor of the State of Louisiana.

Approved Jan. 13, 1862. feb23 2ptf

See copy in English and French.

Headquarters of the Surgeon General of the V. and M. of La.

NEW ORLEANS, February 23, 1862.

Official Orders No. 1.

The Headquarters of the Medical Department of the State troops are established at the building on the corner of Common and Baronne streets, where the Surgeons of Brigades will report their appointment in person, and without delay, from 11 A. M. to 12 M., or by letter, where it is impracticable to report in person.

Each Surgeon of Brigade will act as Chief of the Medical Staff of his Brigade; will inform his Regimental Surgeons and Assistant Surgeons that all business to be transacted at these Headquarters must be transacted through him, and that they will be governed by the rules established in the Confederate States' service.

He will proceed at once to organize the Medical Staff of his Brigade, recommending to the Surgeon General for appointment, from the Regimental Surgeons, such officers as Director and Purveyor as may tend to its greater efficiency. He will require the Surgeons and Assistant Surgeons of his command to report to him their names in full, residence, post office, rank, with what regiment serving, what surgical instruments, amputating and pocket cases they have, what medicines, medicine chests, ambulances and litters; as also any such additional information as he may judge desirable. Founded upon these reports, the Brigade Surgeon will forward to the Surgeon General a condensed report of the medical and surgical condition of each regiment of his brigade for field service.

The supply of instruments, medicines and other medical stores is limited; the Surgeons of Brigades should therefore insist that every surgeon furnish himself to the best of his ability before entering upon active service.

By command of WARREN STONE,
Surgeon General of Louisiana.

STANFORD A. CHAILLIE, Asst Surg. Gen. feb23 2pt

Headquarters Fourth Regiment,

THIRD BRIGADE LOUISIANA MILITIA.

Order No 2.

The following is the list of the Field and Staff Officers and Captains of this Regiment:

J. M. MAGEE, Colonel.
Wm. H. Hunt, Lieutenant-Colonel.
John M. Davidson, Major.
L. H. Gardner, Adjutant.
Colin A. Conway, Assistant Quartermaster.
P. C. Boyer, Surgeon.
P. S. Potell, Assistant Surgeon.
S. J. N. Smith, Quartermaster Sergeant.
——— ———, Sergeant Major.

CAPTAINS.

1—Wm. W. Corless, Co. A.
2—Edmund R. Randolph, Co. B.
3—Jas. J. Stewart, Co. C.
4—W. B. Lancaster, Co. D.
5—S. G. Tyler, Co. E.
6—Samuel Myers, Co. F.
7—Geo. McDuffie Burke, Co. G.
8—Robert Dalton, Co. H.

The Company Officers of this Regiment will proceed immediately to enroll and organize their beats, and to give notice to their commands to assemble for further instructions, on TUESDAY NEXT, 25th of February, at 4 o'clock P. M., on Basin street, between Canal and Common streets.

By order of J. M. MAGEE,
Colonel Commanding.

L. H. GARDINER, Adjutant. feb23 1t

Headquarters Chalmette Regiment.

NEW ORLEANS, Feb. 22, 1862.

Orders No. 3.

I—In obedience to the orders from the Headquarters of the Brigade, the Regiment will assemble, fully armed and equipped, on MONDAY, the 24th inst, on Washington Square, at 7¼ A. M.

II—The Captains of Companies will prepare the muster roll of officers and men present in each Company.

By order of Col. IG. SZYMANSKI.

ALF. BOURGES, Adjutant. feb23 1t

Auction Sale

AT H. FRANKO'S,

Corner of Poydras and Carondelet Streets,

E. M. JACOB'S, Auctioneer.

The sale on MONDAY, Feb 24, commences at 10 o'clock A. M., and will consist in different goods only IN LOTS suitable to the trade.

Dealers in Jewelry and the trade are invited to attend the sale.

feb23 2pit

Headquarters

FOURTH REGIMENT LOUISIANA VOLUNTEERS,
BERWICK CITY, February 15, 1862.

All members of the Fourth Regiment absent on furlough will hasten immediately to New Orleans and join the Regiment as it passes to its place of destination.

H. W. ALLEN,
Lt. Col. Comd'g 4th Regt. La. Vol.

feb16

Wanted.

A GOOD CHILD'S NURSE, capable of Washing and Ironing. Apply at the Delta office. feb20 2ptf

C. S. War Tax Assessment.

Second Collection District of New Orleans, between Canal and St. Joseph streets, from the River to the Lake.

Tax Payers are hereby notified that the Assessment Rolls for said District are now subject to inspection in the COLLECTOR'S OFFICE, No. 33 Exchange Alley, (Room No. 12, up stairs,) daily, Sundays excepted, between 10 o'clock A. M. and 2 o'clock P. M., and that any challenge thereof, or appeal therefrom, must be made in writing to the undersigned for FINAL DETERMINATION before the 2d day of March, 1862.

JOHN LAURANS,
C. S. Collector 2d Collection District.

feb7 tmh2

Important to the Deaf.

Dr. W. L. DAVIS,

OCULIST AND AURIST,

Can be found at his office, 217 Canal street, every day, from morning till night, where persons can consult him for the removal of

DEAFNESS AND NOISES IN THE HEAD.

N. B.—All affections of the Ear and eye receive special attention.

feb2 10t2p 3ptf

Auction Sale,

AT H. FRANKO'S,

CORNER OF POYDRAS AND CARONDELET STS.

E. M. JACOBS, Auctioneer.

The following articles will be sold on

Tuesday, Feb. 25, at 10 o'clock A. M.:

Two Fancy Clocks, with flying birds on trees, and music.
One Gold Bracelet, with a small Gold Watch inside.
One Fine Regulator.
One Mysterious Clock, or the Magic Dial; which keeps correct time without any apparent connection between the hands, goes one month, and strikes the hour and half hour.
Two cases of a collection of Butterflies.
One case of a collection of Bugs.
One Aquaria, with Fishes.
Eight Aquarias—empty.
One very fine pair of Scales, with a fine set of weights complete.
One Turning Machine, for a Show Window.
One silver-plated Fireman's Trumpet.
One large Musical Box—plays six choice tunes of operas.
Fifty ounces Quinine.
One Writing Desk.
One fire-proof Iron Safe.
One Mechanical Singing Bird.
Two large Show Cases and Counters.
One Mechanical Clock, with music.
Silver and Silver-plated Ware.
Fine Gold and Silver Watches, and different other goods.

feb23 2p2t

Headquarters Louisiana Militia

ADJUTANT GENERAL'S OFFICE,
NEW ORLEANS, February 22, 1862

Orders No. 126.

Maj. Gen. John L. Lewis, commanding the Militia of the State, will order Brig. Gen. B. Buisson, commanding the First Brigade Volunteer Troops, to report his command prepared for active duty, on MONDAY, the 24th February, 1862, at 9 o'clock A. M.; and will cause commanders of companies to file in the Adjutant General's office a Muster Roll of the names and number of men of their command present for duty. Muster Rolls will be furnished for that purpose.

By order of THOS. O. MOORE,
Governor and Commander-in-Chief.

M. GRIVOT, Adjutant and Inspector General. feb23 1t

Headquarters Louisiana Troops,

MAJOR-GENERAL'S OFFICE,
NEW ORLEANS, Feb. 19, 1862.

General Orders No. 3.

I—The Regimental bounds of the Militia Troops of the late First Division will henceforth be as follows:

FIRST MILITIA BRIGADE—BRIG.-GEN H. C. STORY.

1st Regiment, Col. J. B. Wilkinson commanding, comprises the parish of Plaquemines.

2d Regiment, Col. A. Marrero commanding, comprises the parish of St Bernard.

3d Regiment, Col Geo. Pandely commanding, comprises the 9th Representative District of Orleans.

4th Regiment, Col. G. DeFeriet commanding, comprises the 8th Representative District of Orleans.

SECOND MILITIA BRIGADE—BRIG.-GEN. C. A. LABUZAN.

1st Regiment, Col. W. L. Robertson commanding, comprises the 4th Representative District of Orleans.

2d Regiment, Col. Chas. A. DeArmas commanding, comprises the 5th Representative District of Orleans.

3d Regiment, Col. W. B. Kountz commanding, comprises the 6th Representative District of Orleans.

4th Regiment, Col. Jos. Solomon commanding, comprises the 7th Representative District of Orleans.

THIRD MILITIA BRIGADE—BRIG.-GEN. A. J. POWELL.

1st Regiment, Col. J. M. Putnam commanding, comprises the 1st Representative District of Orleans.

2d Regiment, Col. T. O. Starke commanding, comprises the 2d Representative District of Orleans.

3d Regiment, Col. John Davidson commanding, comprises that portion of the 3d Representative District lying between Julia and Poydras streets, river and swamp.

4th Regiment, Col. J. M. Magee commanding, comprises that portion of the 3d Representative District lying between Canal and Poydras streets, river and swamp.

FOURTH MILITIA BRIGADE—Brig. Gen. L. A. CHARBONNET.

1st Regiment—Col. John M. D. Taylor commanding, comprises that portion lying between Felicity Road, river, Washington street and swamp.

2d Regiment—Col. Wm. Wren commanding, comprises that portion lying between Washington street, river, Toledano street and swamp.

3d Regiment—Col. N. Commandeur commanding, comprises that portion lying between Toledano street, river, upper line of Jefferson and swamp, left bank.

4th Regiment—Col. F. Zaringue commanding, comprises that portion of the parishes of Orleans and Jefferson, right bank.

II—The Colonels of the abovenamed regiments will proceed immediately to divide their regiments into company beats, and will recommend to the Governor suitable persons for captains and lieutenants of their several companies. As soon as their regiments are completely organized, they will report to these Headquarters, giving a full roll of the number of men in each company.

By order of JOHN L. LEWIS,
Major General Commanding.

ERNEST FORSTALL, Aid-de-Camp. feb19 2p

Headquarters Fourth Brigade,

LOUISIANA MILITIA,
NEW ORLEANS, February 22, 1862.

General Orders No. 1.

Having assumed command of the Fourth Brigade of Louisiana Troops, I hereby appoint the following named officers as my staff, viz:

A. B. CHARBONNET, Acting Major and Inspector,
——————, Surgeon of Brigade Staff,
J. G. McLEARN, Brigade Quartermaster,
FELIX VOISIN, Brigade Paymaster,
TOUTANT BEAUREGARD, Aid-de-Camp,
THEOPHILE VILLARS, do.,
AUGUSTE DUGUE, do.

The troops composing this Brigade will recognise, respect and obey them in their respective capacities.

The Headquarters of this Brigade are fixed at No. 53 Carondelet street, where all communications must be sent.

L. A. CHARBONNET, Brig. General,
Comd'g Fourth Brigade L. T.

feb22 3t

Headquarters First Regiment,

CHASSEURS-A-PIED,
NEW ORLEANS, Feb. 22, 1862

Order No. 8.

In obedience to Brigade General Orders No. 3, this Regiment will assemble at the Arsenal, at 7 o'clock A. M., on MONDAY, the 24th inst., fully equipped and prepared for active service—knapsacks filled according to regulation. Captains of companies will furnish muster rolls of the men and officers present, for active service.

By order of J. S. MESILLEUR,
Colonel Commanding.

F. T. GENERELLY, Adjutant. feb23 1t

Headquarters Beauregard Regiment

NEW ORLEANS, Feb. 21, 1862.

General Orders No. 2.

I—The Commanding Officers of the several corps attached to this Regiment will cause the members of their respective Companies to assemble at Company Headquarters, at the times hereafter specified, for inspection:

Glenn Guards, Saturday, Feb. 22, at 7 P. M.
Ed. Thompson Guards, Monday, Feb. 24, at 7 P. M.
Carondelet Light Infantry, Tuesday, Feb. 25, at 7 P. M.
McRee Rangers, Wednesday, Feb 26, at 7 P. M.
Police Guards, A, Thursday, Feb. 27, at 2 P. M.
Police Guards, B, Thursday, Feb. 27, at 7 P. M.
Clay Guard, Thursday, Feb. 27, at 7 P. M.
Reinhart Guards, Saturday, March 1, at 7 P. M.
Belmont Guards, Saturday, March 1, at 7 P. M.

II—Uniformed Companies are requested to be in uniform; ununiformed Companies will appear in citizens' dress.

III—The Orderly Sergeants of the respective Companies will be prepared to hand to the Inspecting Officer the rolls of their Companies, signed under the late Militia law, and a list of members, present and absent.

IV—Lieut. Col. Geo. S. Lacey is hereby detailed for the purpose of inspecting the Companies, under these Orders, and will report to Headquarters.

V—Capt. King, of the Glenn Guards; Capt. Buddecke, of the Ed. Thompson Guards; Capt. DeHart, of the Carondelet Light Infantry; Capt. McRee, of the McRee Rangers; Capt. Reed, of Police Guards, Company A; Capt. Tank, of Police Guards, Company B; Capt. Derickson, of Clay Guard; Capt Scully, of the Reinhart Guards; and Capt. Brown, of the Belmont Guards, are respectively charged with the execution of this order; and are required to have the rolls fully signed and the members of the Company all present.

By order of FRANK A. BARTLETT,
Colonel Commanding Beauregard Regiment.

HARRY H. PRICE, Adjutant. feb22 2p7t

Headquarters Beauregard Regiment

NEW ORLEANS, Feb. 21, 1862.

General Orders No. 3.

I—Companies composing this Regiment will assemble, without arms, for Battalion drill, on FRIDAY, the 28th inst., at Coliseum Square, at 4½ o'clock P. M.

II—Uniformed Companies will appear in full uniform, and ununiformed Companies in citizens' dress.

III—As this drill is called by the Colonel Commanding with the view of commencing a thorough organization of the corps under his command, every member is expected to be present, prompt at the hour specified, and no excuse, except sickness, will be received.

IV—Orderly Sergeants of Companies must be prepared to furnish the Adjutant with reports of men absent and present.

By order of FRANK A. BARTLETT,
Colonel Commanding.

H. H. PRICE, Adjutant. feb22 6t2p

Headquarters Artillery,

FIRST DIVISION, WESTERN DEPARTMENT,
COLUMBUS, KY, Feb. 20, 1862.

All officers, non-commissioned officers and privates belonging to the Heavy Artillery of this Division, actually on furlough or on recruiting service, are ordered to report forthwith to this post for duty.

By order of Brig. Gen. JAMES TRUDEAU, Commanding Artillery, First Division, Western Department, C. S. A.

feb21 2p BARNEY HUGHES, A. A. G.

Proclamation

BY THE

GOVERNOR.

HEADQUARTERS LOUISIANA MILITIA,
NEW ORLEANS, February 14, 1862

The President of the Confederate States having made a requisition upon me to "furnish, from the State of Louisiana, five and a-half regiments of troops for the war," therefore, I, THOMAS O. MOORE, Governor of the State of Louisiana, do hereby proclaim, that volunteers will be received in accordance with the President's proclamation.

Volunteers will be received by companies, battalions or regiments.

Each company will be composed of one captain, one first lieutenant, two second lieutenants, four sergeants, four corporals, and not less than sixty-four privates. Regiments must contain not less than ten companies, and battalions not less than four companies.

Commanding officers will report, as soon as their respective commands are organized, to Adjt. Gen. M. Grivot, New Orleans.

The troops will be mustered into service at convenient camps, and will then be clothed, supplied and armed by the Confederate Government. Each soldier will receive from the Confederate Government a bounty of fifty dollars when his regiment or company is mustered into its service, and will be allowed transportation by it from his home to the place of rendezvous.

It is earnestly desired that the troops now called for be ready by or before the 15th March.

Relying upon the activity and patriotism of my fellow-citizens, I anticipate a response from them as prompt as the emergency demands.

THOS. O. MOORE,
Governor and Commander-in-Chief.

feb15 tmar10

Official.—By the Governor.

HEADQUARTERS LOUISIANA MILITIA,
ADJUTANT GENERAL'S OFFICE,
New Orleans, Feb. 18, 1862.

Orders No. 105.

The Passport Office will be opened daily in the basement story of the building, No. 177 Canal street, between the hours of 9 o'clock A. M. and 3 o'clock P. M. No passports will issue from the Adjutant General's Office, nor will any passports be issued after 3 o'clock P. M.

By order of THOS. O. MOORE,
Governor and Commander-in-Chief.

M. GRIVOT, Adjutant and Inspector General. feb19 2p6t

Meeting of the Foremen of the Fire Department.

NEW ORLEANS FIRE DEPARTMENT,
NEW ORLEANS, Feb. 20, 1862.

At a meeting of the Foremen of the different Companies composing this Department, presided over by the Chief Engineer, the following preamble and resolutions, offered by Mr. James Beggs, Foreman of Washington Engine Company No. 20, were unanimously adopted:

WHEREAS, When we remember the disturbed condition of our country, struggling as it is for liberty and national existence; when we call to mind the fact that a large number of our brothers are absent from us imperilling their lives for that country; when we know that our entire organization at home are enrolled, and cheerfully performing military duty, in order to prepare themselves to do battle, if necessary, in defense of our homes, our firesides, and all that we hold dear upon earth, we can not but arrive at the conclusion that this is no period for a jubilee; therefore be it

Resolved, That the usual celebration of the anniversary of the Fire Department on the 4th of March next, be and the same is hereby postponed to a more appropriate period.

Resolved further, That the Chief Engineer be and he is hereby authorized to have the above preamble and resolution published in the Crescent, Picayune, Delta, True Delta, Bulletin, Bee (French and English) and German Gazette, three times.

DAVID BRADBURY, Chief Engineer.

JAMES DELAMORE, Secretary. feb22 3t

Confederate States Zouaves.

The undersigned calls the public attention to the following card:

WAR DEPARTMENT, January 24, 1862.

To LIEUT. COL. G. COPPENS, Commanding Louisiana Battalion Zouaves:

SIR—In accordance with the above regulations, you are authorized to muster or cause to be mustered into service, Companies of Light Infantry for Three Years' Service, which Companies, when mustered into service, shall be organized by the President into a Regiment or Battalion, as provided in the foregoing regulations.

Respectfully, J. P. BENJAMIN,
Secretary of War.

A BOUNTY OF FIFTY DOLLARS will be paid to each soldier at the time of being mustered into service, and arms, equipments, rations, transportations, etc., will be furnished by the Government as soon as enlisted. The men will have the Zouave uniform.

Organized companies, or parties wishing to organize the same, of one hundred privates, if possible, but not less than sixty-four, in any part of the State, whether armed or not, will have an opportunity of going into active service in Kentucky or Missouri, by sending their muster rolls to the undersigned, at 64 Customhouse street, New Orleans.

GASTON COPPENS,
Lieut. Col. Comd'g La. Zouaves.

feb15 su tu&th tf

Artillery Drivers Wanted.

Thirty able-bodied men, accustomed to the care of horses, are required immediately as DRIVERS for the FIFTH COMPANY WASHINGTON ARTILLERY, for State service.

They will be uniformed and equipped immediately; pay to commence when ordered in the field.

They will rank and be treated as privates in the corps, and will be required to drill once a week, with the battery, while in the city.

They must be sober, and come well recommended, as to character, &c., &c.

An officer will be at the Arsenal daily, from 10 A. M. till 2 P. M., beginning THIS DAY, February 19, to receive recruits and register them. Apply immediately.

Parties so joining will be exempt from serving in the militia or other corps.

W. IRVING HODGSON,
Captain.

feb19 2ptf

Selling Off!

Up to February 16, I will sell the whole contents of my store, consisting of

WATCHES,
JEWELRY,
CLOCKS,
SHOW CASES, &c.,

at wholesale and retail, and after February 16 I will commence to sell at auction all goods left unsold.

Watchmakers and Jewelers will please take notice of it. I am also willing to transfer the lease of my store, with all improvements and fixings of it belonging to me.

H. FRANKO,
Corner of Poydras and Carondelet sts.

Holders of claims, in goods or money, against me, are requested to present the same, and I also request those indebted to me to come forward and settle.

H. FRANKO,
Corner of Poydras and Carondelet sts.

feb9 3taw2p tf

Valuable Squares

AND LOTS OF GROUND IN THE CITY OF JEFFERSON.

The undersigned have various SQUARES and LOTS OF GROUND for sale in Bloomingdale, Hurstville, Rickerville, Faubourg Avart, Bouligny, &c.

These properties are in the vicinity and on the line of the Jefferson City Horse Car Railroad, which will be completed within the next six months, and connects with the upper line of the N. O. City Railroad on Magazine and Prytania street, making this property very desirable for the purposes of either building or speculation.

Apply to H. M. VANSOLINGEN & CO.,
Auctioneers, 29 Commercial Place.

oct27 2dptf

Mrs. C. E. Da Ponte

Respectfully announces that she is prepared to give lessons at the residences of her pupils, or at her own Studio.

DRAWING AND PAINTING

IN OIL OR WATER COLORS,

HEADS, LANDSCAPES AND FLOWERS;

ALSO,

GRECIAN PAINTING, WAX AND PAPER FLOWERS,

197 Camp Street,

Between Julia and St. Joseph streets.

al8 3ptf

Candidate for Mayor,

IRRESPECTIVE OF PARTY.

NEW ORLEANS, January 29, 1862.

To my fellow-citizens of the city and parish of Orleans:

At the reiterated request of many friends and acquaintances, I present myself before you, IRRESPECTIVE OF PARTY, as a Candidate for the office of Mayor; election to take place in June next.

If elected, I shall be governed by this motto: Justice, Law and Order, Improvements, Judicious Economy.

VICTOR WILTZ.

feb21 te*

Gold Laces!

5000 YARDS

of the FINEST QUALITY,

at H. FRANKO'S,

Corner Poydras and Carondelet streets.

feb17 2ptf

Attention!

COLUMBUS, February 17, 1862.

All Officers and Privates of the 13th Louisiana Regiment, 33d Tennessee Regiment, Williams's Light Battery and Depot Battery, detached or on leave, will report at Columbus immediately.

By command of Col. R. L. GIBSON.

BEN KING,
Lieutenant and A. A. A. General.

feb18 2ptf

Wrapping and Envelop Paper.

250 REAMS MANILLA WRAPPING

AND

40 REAMS HEAVY ENVELOP PAPER,

Just received and for sale by

T. FITZWILLIAM,
Stationer, 76 Camp street.

jan21 2ptf

HARPER'S WEEKLY.
A JOURNAL OF CIVILIZATION.

VOL. VI.—No. 270.] NEW YORK, SATURDAY, MARCH 1, 1862. [SINGLE COPIES SIX CENTS. $2 50 PER YEAR IN ADVANCE.

THE SURRENDER OF FORT DONELSON, FEBRUARY 16, 1862.—[SEE NEXT PAGE.]

GALLANT CHARGE OF HAWKINS'S ZOUAVES UPON THE REBEL BATTERIES ON ROANOKE ISLAND.—[See Page 135.]

The Philadelphia Inquirer.

ESTABLISHED 1829. | PHILADELPHIA, SATURDAY, MARCH 1, 1862. | PRICE TWO CENTS.

IMPORTANT WAR NEWS!

Movements of Gen. Banks' Army.

EVACUATION OF COLUMBUS, KY.

THE WAR IN TENNESSEE.

OCCUPATION OF NASHVILLE.

The Rebels Surrounded at Murfreesboro, by Union Troops.

LATE SOUTHERN NEWS.

JEFF. DAVIS' MESSAGE TO THE REBEL CONGRESS.

ARRIVAL OF AN ENGLISH PRIZE SCHOONER.

THE WAR IN ARKANSAS.

Appointment of Officers in Pennsylvania Regiments.

LATE FROM FORTRESS MONROE

THE LATEST FROM WASHINGTON.

Special Despatches to The Inquirer.

WASHINGTON, Feb. 28, 1862.

Expose of the Great Railroad Swindle in Tennessee.

ANOTHER BRIGADIER-GENERAL STONE REFUSED CONFIRMATION BY THE SENATE.

Some time ago the name of AMASA STONE was sent in to the Senate as Brigadier-General, accompanied with the request that he be immediately confirmed. The Senate, on inquiring, found he was to be a "Brigadier-General of Railroads," and detailed to construct a road down through the *mountainous region in Kentucky* and Tennessee, and refused the confirmation. AMASA STONE is a railroad contractor, well-known in Philadelphia. He is of the firm of STONE, QUIGLEY & BURTON, contractors of the Baltimore Central Railroad. He was also in the firm with MALONE, CLARK, GONDER, ISRAEL PAINTER, etc., who had the original contract for building the West Chester Railroad via Media. He has been engaged in a number of other *heavy* contracts.

He is now in Louisville making contracts, for the Government, for the construction of a railroad from Nicholasville, Ky., to Knoxville, Tenn., which is one hundred and eighty miles long. It will take not less than two years to build the road, at a cost of not less *than twelve, fifteen or twenty millions of dollars*. It cannot be completed, or any portion of it, in time for the suppression of the rebellion, and yet STONE is making purchases for the road, of iron, chains, bridges, &c., at an exceedingly loose rate. He has in the last two weeks shipped nearly thirty miles of railroad iron to Nicholasville, Ky., and has a large force at work grading the road, some ten miles of which is already completed.

We conversed with a man yesterday who has just come from there, and he pronounces it an unmitigated swindle upon the Treasury, and that the idea of building it to aid the military Department is a humbug! On making an inquiry as to the authority on which the road is being built, we find that the President, in his last message, recommended the construction of a railroad between these two points, but both houses refused to listen to the project as the Treasury could not stand the drain upon it which would follow. The matter was dropped! Some time afterwards a bill was originated in the Senate to authorize the President to take possession of all railroads and telegraph lines necessary for aid in suppressing the rebellion, but stipulating that the power should end with the war.

WADE, of Ohio, moved an amendment that he be empowered to "extend, repair and complete." The amendment, was carried, and the bill was rushed through the House, as a military measure, without its being read or discussed. It is now found that the bill authorizes the completion of this railroad, without regard to the military necessity for it. The bill, as amended, is what is known as "a snake," and now that it has been exposed, will be repealed or amended, and the power of this second General STONE be taken from him, and the Treasury be saved the leak intended to be opened in it.

If the North must be made to pay for the luxuries and comforts of civilized life for the Rebel crew, let us first reduce them to a state of subjection, and feel assured that the men who furnish the means, by oppressing themselves with burdensome taxes, shall at any time ride over the road with a feeling that their lives are as safe and their rights as fully respected as though they were slaveholders.

The bill of Mr. BLAIR, which was defeated by such a decisive vote this morning, was intended as a feeder to this concern, by raising from twenty to twenty-five thousand more men to be used in grading and building this road.

The Railroad Bridge at Harper's Ferry.

Workmen are rapidly completing the Railroad Bridge at Harper's Ferry. It will be done in about a week, and the road running through to Wheeling in about two or three weeks. No Rebel troops are anywhere on the line of the road now, nor within several miles of Harper's Ferry.

General Stone.

General STONE will not be placed on trial until the Committee on the Conduct of the War have concluded their investigations, and brought all the testimony against him to light. Several more witnesses to-day testified to his conduct at Ball's Bluff, and are making a fearful record against him. Incontrovertible evidence as to his affording Rebels free communication with their friends in Maryland through his lines has been adduced.

More Rebels Arrived.

The notorious ROBERT DRAIN, of Drainsville, and four other Rebels, have arrived here in custody, under escort of Lieut. WOLFF, of Colonel GEARY'S Regiment.

THE ARMY AND NAVY.

MAJOR-GENERAL U. S. GRANT.

Major-General ULYSSES S. GRANT was born at Point Pleasant, Clairmont county, Ohio, April 27, 1822, and entered West Point Military Academy from Ohio in 1839, where he graduated with honors in 1843, and was attached as brevet Second Lieutenant to the Fourth Infantry. He was promoted Second Lieutenant at Corpus Christi, in September, 1845, and served as such through Mexico, under General TAYLOR, at Palo Alto, Resaca de la Palma, and Monterey, and under General SCOTT from Vera Cruz to the city of Mexico, and was twice promoted for his bravery. He was regimental Quartermaster from April 1, 1847, and when he resigned the service, on the 31st of July, 1854, he was a full Captain in the Fourth Infantry of regulars. After his resignation he settled in St. Louis county, Missouri, and moved from there to Galena, Illinois, in 1860. Upon the breaking out of the present war he offered his services to Governor YATES, and was appointed Colonel of the Twenty-first Regiment of Illinois Volunteers, and served with his regiment until promoted a Brigadier-General, with commission and rank from the 17th of May, 1861.

He was engaged as Colonel and acting Brigadier-General in several of the contests in South-eastern Missouri; and his course as commander of the southeast district of Missouri has been thoroughly scrutinized, and among his most praiseworthy acts was the occupation of Paducah, and stoppage of communication and supplies to the Rebels via the Tennessee and Cumberland rivers. The manner in which he conducted the battle of Belmont is still fresh in our readers' minds. The rest of his course as commander there is too well known to be repeated here. After the capture of Fort Henry a new district was created, under the denomination of the District of West Tennessee, and Gen. GRANT was assigned by Gen. HALLECK to the command of it. Gen. GRANT's performance at Fort Henry and Fort Donelson, and his correspondence with the Rebel General BUCKNER are too well known to need description here. He has since been appointed a Major-General by the President, and unanimously confirmed by Congress.

CAPTAIN W. D. PORTER, U. S. N.

We publish herewith a portrait of Captain W. D. PORTER, of the gun-boat *Essex*, who distinguished himself at the battle of Fort Henry, and was scalded by the explosion of a boiler on board the *Essex*.

Captain PORTER is a Louisianian by birth. His father was the famous Commodore PORTER, of the *Essex*, whose fame shines brightly in our naval annals. In 1823 the son entered the navy as a boy on board the United States ship *Franklin*, under command of Commodore STEWART, and received an excellent naval education under Commodores HULL, CHAUNCEY, PATTERSON and RODGERS. He projected and is the founder of the present light-house system; was through the whole Mexican war, where he did noble service; in 1855 was placed on a retired list by a secret Navy Board; four years after was restored to his rank as Commander by President BUCHANAN; was then appointed to the command of the United States ship *St. Marys*, and did important service on the Pacific coast. On the outbreak of the rebellion, he was ordered home from the Pacific; and though he had property in Virginia, which has been confiscated, and many of his family were in the Rebel cause, still he proved faithful to the Government, and, laying aside all personal considerations, tendered his aid in putting down the rebellion, and was assigned to a boat which has been built chiefly under his superintendence. He christened it, after his father's ship, the *Essex*. At the battle of Fort Henry, Captain PORTER ran up within one hundred and fifty yards of the fort, and fought with courage and effect until scalded by the steam issuing from the boiler, the thick plates of which had been penetrated by a ball. The Captain had the presence of mind to close his mouth and eyes, so that his scald is not serious. He says he went into the fight with high colors, and, though disabled, the Stars and Stripes still waved as he floated back.

General Banks' Army.

The *Star*, of this evening, says:—For forty-eight hours this city has been overwhelmed with astonishing rumors concerning the army of General BANKS. One citizen—chronically afflicted with visions of the destruction of Union armies—assured us yesterday afternoon that he had positive information of BANKS' defeat. Another this morning is equally as certain that BANKS is in possession of Winchester; and, still a third, that he certainly has taken seven thousand prisoners. Now, these stories are equally unfounded.

"We have to assure the *Star's* readers that Gen. BANKS' army has seen no enemy of late; certainly not for a week past; and, further, that the enemy is nowhere in force within thirty-five miles of him, and just now nowhere, even with mere picket squads, within twenty miles of him; nor have they been for days past."

The Starke Case.

Having been permitted to take his seat, and to be heard in his own defence, Senator STARKE, of Oregon, has asked for an investigation into the charges of disloyalty against him. Although many believe him loyal and true, yet his opponents will vote for the investigation, and it will probably be made. He is a medium-sized, good-looking gentleman, with a full head, and a pleasant expression of countenance.

All Quiet.

Perhaps it will be a consolation to know that all is quiet along the lines of the army of the Potomac to-night, and no one here expects an advance will be made by the Rebels upon us, at least for a few days.

Senator Powell's Case.

The Senate Judiciary Committee, who have been investigating Senator POWELL's case, have not come to any conclusion. Mr. POWELL made his defence before them.

Emancipation.

Senator CLARK to-day introduced a bill providing for the immediate emancipation of all slaves in the District of Columbia, and allowing loyal owners to seek indemnification in the Courts.

Bounty Money.

Senator WILSON introduced a bill to give every volunteer twenty-five dollars of the hundred dollar bounty money, on their enlisting in the regular army, and allowing them to leave the volunteer forces for that purpose.

Hayti.

The House Committee on Foreign Relations, consisting of Messrs. John J. Crittenden, of Kentucky; Daniel W. Gooch, of Massachusetts; Samuel S. Cox, of Ohio; Albert S. White, of Indiana; Robert McKnight, of Pennsylvania; Alfred A. Burnham, of Connecticut; Francis Thomas, of Maryland; Theodore M. Pomeroy, of New York, and George P. Fisher, of Delaware, have agreed to report against the Senate bill recognizing Hayti. They are preparing a report upon the rights of nations upon the high seas.

Resignation.

Colonel MAXWELL, of the Fifty-seventh Pennsylvania Regiment, has resigned. The vacancy has not yet been filled.

Appointment in the Fifteenth Regiment United States Army.

Second Lieutenant GEORGE BURNS (formerly of the ADAMS' Express Company) has been appointed Quartermaster of the Fifteenth Regiment United States Army.

Gen. Cameron and the Mission to Russia.

General CAMERON is in town, in consultation with the Secretary of State, as to our relations with Russia. He will not receive his final instructions, however, until about the first of April, when he will leave for St. Petersburg.

The Weather.

The high wind to-night, with the thermometer at a low point, is drying up the ground and the roads so rapidly that dust is becoming as much of a nuisance as was mud a few days since.

Lodged in Prison.

The parties arrested in Alexandria, full particulars of which were published in THE INQUIRER yesterday, have been brought to this city, and lodged in the Old Capitol prison.

Promoted.

Colonel JOHN COCHRANE was appointed by the President a Brigadier-General, and his name sent to the Senate to-day.

WAR IN TENNESSEE.

THE REBELS SURROUNDED AT MURFREESBORO'.

Gen. Buell Demands Their Unconditional Surrender! !

Special Despatch to the Chicago Tribune.

CAIRO, Feb. 28.—Advices from the neighborhood of Murfreesboro' state that the Rebels concentrated at that place have been surrounded by General BUELL's forces, so that none could escape.

The Rebels offered to surrender the position to the Federal troops if they would be allowed to march out with the honors of war.

General BUELL refused to allow them these conditions, and demanded their unconditional surrender. He notified them that he would allow two days for consideration, and if the place wat nor surrendered at the expiration of that period he would open fire upon them. The time expired this morning.

The Evacuation of Columbus.

The Rebels to Fall Back on Island No. 10.

THE MEMPHIS AND OHIO RAILROAD TO BE DESTROYED.

ST. LOUIS, Feb. 28.—The Memphis papers of the 19th say that General POLK issued orders on the day previous, directing that the track of the Memphis and Ohio Railroad should be torn up and the bridges destroyed, preparatory to the evacuation of Columbus and demolition of the fortifications.

The Columbus forces are to fall back to Island No. 10, on the Mississippi, about forty miles below Columbus, which, it is said, completely commands the river, and can be fortified with heavy guns and made impregnable against any river attack.

CAIRO, Feb. 28.—We learn from a gentleman who is thoroughly conversant with Kentucky affairs, that the Rebels are dismounting their large guns and columbiads at Columbus, and the work of evacuation is now going on.

Several transports are lying at Columbus to carry off the troops.

Every man coming into Columbus is impressed—even farmers with their teams.

Several hundred negroes were sent to the interior yesterday. This is from a reliable source.

From Harrisburg.

THE APPOINTMENT OF OFFICERS IN PENNSYLVANIA REGIMENTS.

HARRISBURG, Feb. 28.—Heretofore all vacancies occasioned by death, resignation or otherwise, occurring in Pennsylvania Regiments, raised by order of the War Department, have been filled on the part of Governor CURTIN by the appointment of men nominated by their respective Colonels. There is the best authority for asserting that the Governor made no appointments to the California Regiment while commanded by the late Colonel BAKER, and none since but those recommended by Colonel BAKER or Colonel WISTAR, the officer now in command. The late general order on this subject is designed expressly for the protection of subalterns and privates, and will, no doubt, prove effective in securing the promotion of those whose seniority entitles them to it.

Travel to Washington.

BALTIMORE, Feb. 28.—The trains will run regularly to and from Washington after to-day; the cause for the temporary interruption of travel having been removed.

Nashville Occupied by U. S. Troops

THE UNION SOLDIERS CORDIALLY RECEIVED.

GOV. HARRIS FORCED TO LEAVE BY UNION MEN.

REBELS SHOT BY UNION MEN FOR ROBBING THEM.

FLOYD DESTROYS A BRIDGE.

ST. LOUIS, Feb. 28.—The *Democrat's* Clarksville despatch of the 26th says:—General NELSON is in command at Nashville; General BUELL being still on the north side of the river.

The Union sentiment was very strong, and our troops were received with great cordiality.

Great indignation was expressed by the citizens of Nashville against Gov. HARRIS. He was fairly driven away by the Union men—the latter having become bold at the proximity of the Union troops and dared to assert their rights.

The *Democrat's* Clarksville despatch of the 28th says:—The Rebel soldiers before leaving Nashville plundered many dwellings and business houses, and excited great alarm among the people. Several Rebels were shot by the citizens whom they were robbing.

Before leaving, Governor HARRIS made a speech recommending the citizens to burn their private property and calling on the Tenneseeans to rally and meet him at Memphis, but no one paid any attention to him, and it is not thought that he will receive any considerable reinforcements.

General CRITTENDEN's command had joined Gen. JOHNSTON, at Murfreesboro. The railroad bridge at Murfreesboro was destroyed by order of FLOYD, against the urgent entreaties of the citizens, and this wanton act of destruction caused much indignation among them.

CAIRO, Feb. 28.—[*Special to the Chicago Tribune.*]—The Rebel army, in their retreat from Nashville, left behind 1600 of their sick and wounded. They destroyed the bridges and burned all the steamboats lying there but one, which escaped. The Texas soldiers fired the city in many places, but the citizens extinguished the flames.

A great majority of the property owners remained at Nashville to receive the protection of the United States troops. The excitement among them was intense.

Before leaving Nashville, Governor HARRIS made a speech, in which he said he had done all he could, and was going to leave for Memphis, to which place he advised the citizens to follow him.

The Rebel War Department has called on Tennessee for thirty-two more regiments.

An official despatch received from Knoxville says an ample force will advance from Richmond to protect Eeast Tennessee.

Governor HARRIS has taken the field in person.

The story of General BEAUREGARD's illness is unfounded. He left Corinth for Columbus on the 19th.

The Memphis *Avalanche*, of the 24th, says that persons, reported to have left General JOHNSON's command, say he entertains no doubt of his ability to re-enter Nashville whenever he wished to do so.

THE CAPTURE OF NASHVILLE.

CLARKSVILLE, Feb. 24, via Cairo, Feb. 25.—A flag of truce arrived here yesterday from Nashville. The Rebels have destroyed the bridges, pitched their cannon into the river, and evacuated the place. A deputation of prominent citizens asked that private property be respected, and our army take possession. General MITCHELL's Division was then within nine miles of Nashville. General NELSON is up the Cumberland, and will arrive at Nashville to-night.

Major-General GRANT is at Clarksville The Rebels are reported concentrating at some point south or southwest of Nashville.

Northern and Eastern Tennessee are now safe. The weather is delightful for movements, being as warm as May in Ohio, and the roads are rapidly drying up.

ANOTHER ACCOUNT.

We hold Nashville. The citizens sent down a boat, asking the gun-boats to go up, and the gun-boats have gone.

The Rebels evacuated in the greatest haste, leaving guns, transportation, gun-boats and everything. Governor HARRIS left with them, taking away the State records.

The Rebels are reported concentrated at Murfreesboro.

A person just from Nashville describes the Rebels' stampede as a perfect panic. The Mayor made a speech, saying he was still Secession to the backbone. "But," said he, "you see how it is; the game is up, and we must either surrender the town, or have it burned."

When he left they were trying to get away their pork, of which they had large quantities stored there.

The Texan Rangers committed all manner of excesses, on their own friends even, and then left in wild confusion.

FURTHER FROM WASHINGTON.

Contradictions and Explanations of Erroneous Statements.

WASHINGTON, Feb. 28.—In order to correct erroneous statements, it is proper to say:—

First. That permits or licenses for trade in the blockaded ports have not been granted. The only permits are those granted on the recommendation of the War Department for supplies, like sutlers' stores to the troops occupying military positions in the Southern States. This correction is made at the instance of a friendly foreign Minister, who thinks the current statements likely to mislead European merchants and their Governments.

Second. Mr. CAMERON has not received his definite instructions, and is not contemplating an immediate departure on his mission. No new Secretary of Legation has been appointed. GREEN CLAY, who was appointed with Mr. CASSIUS M. CLAY, still retains his place, though he is holding a command in Gen. BUELL's army in Tennessee.

Third. Neither JEFFERSON DAVIS nor any other person has made any communication to the Government concerning terms of submission or compromise. The flag of truce some time ago sent by Gen. JOHNSON to Gen. MCCLELLAN, as also HOWELL COBB's appearance at Fortress Monroe, related to exchanges of prisoners.

The above facts are derived from the best sources of information.

The Better Security of Soldiers' Money Letters.

The following letter has been addressed to all the Generals Commanding Departments, in the expectation that they will cause the information to be communicated to their respective commands:—

POST-OFFICE DEPARTMENT,
APPOINTMENT OFFICE, Feb. 26, 1862.

SIR:—In order to prevent, as far as possible, losses of valuable letters mailed by the soldiers in the various camps, this Department recommend that each Commander of a regiment, or a brigade, shall appoint a trustworthy agent, into whose hands all letters from soldiers containing valuable enclosures shall be placed, with pre-payment by stamps and the registering fee of five cents.

It shall be the duty of said agent to deliver such letters to a convenient Post Office, daily, or as frequently as the mails are sent from such office, with two lists showing the names of the writer, and the address of each letter. One list, with the letters and registering fee, shall be placed in the hands of the Postmaster or Registering Clerk, who shall sign and return one copy, and file the other in his office, with the date when it was received. A failure to register increases the danger of loss. It is respectfully suggested that you take such order upon the proposition as the interest of the soldiers under your command shall require. I have the honor to be, your obedient servant, JOHN A. KASSON,
First Assistant Postmaster-General.

The Western Sanitary Commission.

The Western depots of the Sanitary Commission remain tolerably well supplied with bed clothing and such articles as can be readily provided from household stores. Its treasury, however, is nearly depleted by the recent urgent demands for articles and services of a different character. It is ascertained here that eighty-one severely wounded soldiers were brought to Cincinnati by the steamer *Atta Collyer*, which has of late been employed in the exclusive service of the Commission, and in her trip to Fort Donelson was loaded with hospital stores, and also conveyed thither Dr. NEWBERRY, one of the Secretaries of the Commission, ten surgeons and thirty nurses.

The Army Promotions for Gallant Services

In the late brilliant victories will probably be announced during the next week. They have been delayed until all the official reports have been received.

The Gambling Houses of Washington Closed.

The gambling houses are all closed to-night, the keepers being apprehensive of a visit from the Provost Guard, and alarmed by a recent newspaper publication.

The Returned Prisoners.

About 800 of the returned prisoners are now here. The Pay Department is busy night and day in arranging their accounts, and the furloughs will be prepared at the earliest possible period, in order that they may visit their families and friends.

The Militia of the United States.

It appears from the official returns for 1861, that the grand aggregate of the militia is 3,214,310. The number in Virginia, by the returns for 1861, was 143,000, while those of all the other so-called Confederate States, Virginia included, do not exceed 621,000. These returns, however, are not recent, they date from 1838 to 1859.

Indemnity for a Spanish Vessel.

The House Committee on Foreign affairs have prepared a bill, appropriating nearly $3000 as an indemnity to the owners, officers and seamen of the Spanish barque *Providence*, for her wrongful seizure and detention by the blockading squadron of the United States.

The Post Office following the Army.

First Assistant Postmaster-General KASSON is engaged in sending out instructions and making arrangements for re-establishing post offices and post routes, as our armies advance into the so-called Confederate States.

A. H. Markland is following our forces into Tennessee, and J. J. MILLER, also an agent of the Department in this connection, is operating in the southern part of Kentucky. The post office at Nashville and those in the eastern part of North Carolina will soon be re-opened, the latter State to be supplied with mails by sea.

VERY LATE FROM THE SOUTH.

MESSAGE OF JEFF. DAVIS.

Interesting from Memphis, Nashville, and Fort Donelson.

Proclamation of the Governor of North Carolina Calling for Enlistments.

DRINKING FACILITIES CURTAILED.

The Cotton and Tobacco to be Destroyed.

From the Norfolk *Day Book*, Richmond *Dispatch*, and Raleigh *State Journal*, of Thursday last, we glean the following:—

Message of Jefferson Davis.

The following is the Message of JEFF. DAVIS, delivered to the Rebel Congress:—

Southern Confederacy Attempting too Much.

To the Senate and House of Representatives of the Confederate States:—

In obedience to the provision of the Constitution, requiring the President, from time to time, to give to Congress information of the state of the Confederacy, and recommend to their consideration such measures as he shall judge necessary and expedient, I have to communicate that, since my message at the last session of the Provisional Congress, events have demonstrated that the Government had attempted more than it had power successfully to achieve.

Hence in the effort to protect by our arms the whole territory of the Confederate States, seaboard and inland, we have been so exposed as recently to encounter serious disasters.

Northern "Mudsills" and Mechanics.

When the Confederacy was formed, the States composing it were, in the peculiar character of their pursuits and a misplaced confidence in their former associates, to a great extent destitute of the means for the prosecution of a war on so gigantic a scale as that which it has attained. The workshops and artists were mainly to be found in the Northern States; and one of the first duties which devolved upon this Government was to establish the necessary manufactories, and in the meantime to obtain, by purchase from abroad, as far as practicable, whatever was required for the public defence.

Arms and Navy Wanted.

No effort has been spared to effect both of these ends, and though the results have not equalled our hopes, it is believed that an impartial judgment will, upon full investigation, award the various Departments of the Government credit for having done all which human power and foresight enabled them to accomplish. The valor and devotion of the people have not only sustained the efforts of the Government but have gone far to support its deficiences.—The active state of military preparations among the nations of Europe in April—the date when our agents first went abroad—interposed unavoidable delays in the procurement of arms, and the want of a navy has greatly impeded our efforts to import military supplies of all sorts.

Roanoke and Donelson Not Heard From.

I have hoped for several days to receive official reports in relation to our discomfiture at Roanoke Island and the fall of Fort Donelson. They have not yet reached me, and I am therefore unable to communicate to you such information of past events and the consequences resulting from them as would enable me to make recommendations founded upon the changed condition which they have produced. Enough is known of the surrender at Roanoke Island to make us feel that it was deeply humiliating, however imperfect may have been the preparations for defence.

The hope is still entertained that our reported losses at Fort Donelson have been much exaggerated, inasmuch as I am not only unwilling but unable to believe that a large army of our people have surrendered without a desperate attempt to cut their way through the investing forces, whatever may have been their numbers, and to endeavor to make a junction with the other divisions of the army. But in the absence of that exact information which can be afforded by official reports, it would be premature to pass judgment, and my own is reserved, as I trust yours will be, until that information is received.

Reinforcements Sent Forward.

In the meantime strenuous efforts have been made to throw forward reinforcements to the armies at the positions threatened, and I cannot doubt that the bitter disappointments we have borne, by nerving the people to still greater exertions, will speedily secure results more accordant with our past expectations, and as favorable to our cause as those which marked the earlier periods of the war.

Army and Navy Developing.

The reports of the Secretaries of War and the Navy will exhibit the mass of resources for the conduct of the war which we have been enabled to accumulate, notwithstanding the very serious difficulties against which we have contended. They afford cheering hopes that our resources, limited as they were at the beginning of the contest, will, during its progress, become developed to such an extent as fully to meet our future wants.

Short Enlistments vs. a Long War.

The policy of enlistments for short terms, against which I have steadily contended since the beginning of the war, has, in my judgment, contributed in no immaterial degree to the recent reverses which we have suffered; and, even now, renders it difficult to furnish you an accurate statement of the army.

When the war first broke out, many of our people could with difficulty be persuaded that it would be long or serious. It was not deemed possible that anything so insane as a persistent attempt to subjugate these States could be made—still less that the delusion would so far prevail as to give to the war the vast proportions that it has assumed. The people, incredulous of a long war, were naturally averse to long enlistments, and the early legislation of Congress rendered it impracticable to obtain volunteers for a greater period than twelve months. Now that it has become probable that the war will be continued through a series of years, our high-spirited and gallant soldiers, while generally re-enlisting, are, from the fact of their having entered the service for a short term, compelled, in many instances, to go home to make the necessary arrangements for their families during their prolonged absence.

New Enlistments and the "C. S. A." Army.

The quotas of the new regiments for the war, called for from the different States, are in rapid progress of organization. The whole body of new levies and re-enlisted men will probably be ready and in the ranks within the next thirty days. But in the meantime, it is exceedingly difficult to give an accurate statement of the number of our forces in the field. They may, in general terms, be stated at four hundred regiments of infantry, with a proportionate force of cavalry and artillery, details of which will be shown by the report of the Secretary of War.

I deem it proper to advert to the fact that the process of furloughs and re-enlistments in progress for the last month, has so far disorganized and weakened our forces as to impair our ability for a successful defence; but I heartily congratulate you that this evil, which I had foreseen and was powerless to prevent, may now be said to be substantially at an end, and that we shall not again, during the war, be exposed to seeing our strength diminished by this fruitful cause of disaster—short enlistments.

Our Navy.

The people of the Confederate States being principally engaged in agricultural pursuits, were unprovided, at the commencement of hostilities, with ships, ship-yards, materials for ship building, or skilled mechanics and seamen in sufficient numbers to make the prompt creation of a navy a practical task, even if the required appropriations had been made for the purpose. Notwithstanding our very limited resources, however, the report of the Secretary will exhibit to you a satisfactory proportion in preparation, and certainty of near completion of vessels of a number and class on which we may confidently rely for contesting the vaunted control of the enemy over our waters.

Financial System.

The financial system devised by the wisdom of your predecessors has proved adequate to supplying all the wants of the Government, notwithstanding the unexpected and very large increase of expenditures resulting from the great augmentation in the

(Continued on the Eighth Page.)

THE TRI-WEEKLY TELEGRAPH.

VOL. XXVII—NO. 138. HOUSTON, WEDNESDAY, MARCH 5, 1862 WHOLE NO. 3518

BY SPECIAL EXPRESS!

4 DAYS LATER.

IMPORTANT FROM NASHVILLE.

THE FEDERALS NOT YET IN POSSESSION.

FAYETTEVILLE DESTROYED.

CONFEDERATES AT BOSTON MOUNTAIN.

Battle Imminent at Cumberland Gap.

Enemy's Report of the Fight at Fort Donelson.

Over 5000 Killed and Wounded,

FEDERALS ENTERED NASHVILLE.

ETC., ETC., ETC.

Our special express, Capt. C. A. Turley, arrived at half past 4 this (Monday) afternoon by hand car from Orange, after a most tedious trip, bringing four days later news, much of it of great importance. We give the dispatches in full including the Inaugural and Message of President Davis

MEMPHIS, Feb. 22.—The latest advices received here state that Nashville was not occupied by the Federals up to Friday night. It is thought that Buell, with a portion of his army, will reach there on Monday next, Gen. Johnston is reported to be at Murfreesboro', where he has been joined by Gen. Geo. B. Crittenden. There is nothing startling this morning.

RICHMOND, Feb. 22.—The Northern papers of the 20th are received.

The Herald says the rebel agents in Paris declare the seceding States will approve a Constitution of monarchy in the South if it can be attended with any prospect of success.

LINCOLN CONGRESS.—In the Senate a petition from the citizens of New York was presented, asking that the name of South Carolina be expunged from the list of States; that it be made a territory, and the territory be divided between Georgia and North Carolina.

In the House, resolutions were offered by Hickman directing the Judiciary Committee to inquire into the allegations against Vallandigham for disloyalty, who vehemently denies the accusations. The resolutions were withdrawn.

The culture of cotton is disappearing from Dutch Guinea.

The Herald is delighted with the Queen's speech, and said it extinguished the last glimmering of intervention, and urges the Southern people to rise in general revolution and put down the rebellion.

Washington is to be illuminated on the night of the 22d inst., at the expense of the Yankee Government.

The capture of Gen. Price was announced in the House, causing uproarious applause.

The fire reported on the Cumberland river was caused by the burning of the Tennessee Rolling Mills by the Federals.

The Yankee account says 12000 stand of arms were taken at Fort Donelson; also 1200 boxes of beef, with other stores. A great number of the dead were unburied on the 18th inst.

ST. LOUIS, Feb. 19.—Capt. Stubbs has captured Gen. Price, Col. Dorsey, Col. Cass and Judge Capt. Budge, of Price's staff. The companies under their command escaped.

The myriads of Northern fanatics who became mad with excitement and joy over the [illegible]nt of the great slaughter of Yankees at Fort [illegible]elson, are slowly recovering their senses.

Stanton recommends the speedy execution of Col. Ansabree, on the charge of cowardice by Gen. Lander, who is sustained.

Lucius H. Chandler is appointed Consul to Matansas,

The Price reported taken prisoner is not Sterling Price, the great Confederate leader of Missouri.

Five thousand infantry and three batteries of artillery left St. Louis on the 19th, for Cumberland river.

The attacking force of Federals at Savannah is 16,000 strong.

NORFOLK, Feb. 21.—The Federal forces ascended Chowan river again yesterday to Winton, in several gunboats, with a large number of troops. The Confederates opened a heavy fire on them, killing and wounding a number. Some of the Yankees landed and burnt the town, when the Southerners retired. Our loss is said to be two men and two horses. Humbug C. H. Foster is among the Yankees killed.

RICHMOND, Feb. 21.—We have had no Nashville mail for the past seven days, and no dispatches from Nashville for the past two days. It is stated here in telegraphic circles that the telegraph office at Nashville is closed, and the public must draw their own inferences.

Mr. Foote of Tennessee, introduced a resolution appointing a committee of one from each State to request the Secretary of War to furnish the fullest minute particulars in reference to the condition of our armies on the seaboard and river defenses, or elsewhere, and report, with a view to enable Congress to pass such measures as will facilitate the establishment of our national independence and a sense of security, peace and safety. The resolution was tabled for the present.

NORFOLK, Feb. 23.—The Northern papers of the 22d contain the following intelligence:

WASHINGTON, Feb. 21.—Seventy prisioners of State will be released to-morrow from Forts Warren and Lafayette.

NEW YORK, Feb. 21.—Reinforcements are being sent to Burnside, which will increase his force to 40,000 men.

The prize schooner Major Barbour had arrived at New York.

Gordon, the slave captain, was executed at New York on Friday last. He attempted suicide on Thursday night.

Cotton is unsettled. Sales to-day of 3000 bales, at 22 to 23 cents.

ST. LOUIS, Feb. 21.—Nearly all the Fort Donelson prisoners have arrived here. The officers will be sent to Columbus, Ohio.

PORT ROYAL, Feb. 21.—All quiet. Nothing important from Savannah.

The steamer Nelly Dale and schooner Courier had arrived at Nassau, from Charleston.

The Confederate gunboats attacked the Federal batteries at Venus Point, on the 14th to effect the passage from Fort Pulaski to Savannah, and after an engagement of one hour the gunboats retired.

ST. LOUIS, Feb. 20.—Halleck has telegraphed McClellan that Curtis has taken Bentonville, in Arkansas.

BOSTON, Feb. 21.—Two regiments leave for Ship Island to-day.

ST. LOUIS, Feb. 21.—No preparations have been made for the evacuation. 14 steamers are at the wharf. A General and reinforcements have arrived from the South.

There are four French war steamers in Hampton Roads.

Two more regiments have arrived at Newport News, on the 21st.

It is reported that the exchange of prisoners will be made according to the plan adopted by the U. S. and Great Britain in the war of 1812.

It is rumored that an attempt will shortly be made to go up the Nansemond river to Suffolk.

Gen. Howell Cobb, C. S. A., and General Wool, U. S. A., had a long interview to-day on board of the truce steamer.

A large quantity of arms are expected at Newport News.

The House of Representatives received the Senate amendment to the Treasury note bill on Thursday. The amount is not reduced. The legal tender clause remains, the interest is to be paid in coin.

The Bohemian has arrived with Liverpool dates of the 17th inst.

Lord Derby thinks the assent of the Yankees to the demand for Mason and Slidell ungraceful.

The Nashville started forty hours in advance of the Tuscarora. The officers of the Nashville announced that they would blow her up before they would allow her to be taken.

MEMPHIS, Feb. 24.—The Federals entered the city of Nashville yesterday. They said they would trouble nobody unless interfered with.

LYNCHBURG, Feb. 23.—There have been thirteen land-slides on the Virginia and Tennessee railroad. One culvert has been destroyed, and 150 feet of the crib work gone, in consequence of the recent heavy rains. In three or four days the repairs will be completed.

MEMPHIS, Feb. 25.—The town of Fayetteville, in Arkansas, has been burnt to the ground by order of Gen. McCulloch. The military stores there were first burnt. The Confederate army is at Boston Mountain, preparing for battle. Late advices from Knoxville state that the Confederates at Cumberland Gap have been largely reinforced; also, that the Federals are frequently in sight of our camp, and a fight there is regarded as imminent.

MEMPHIS, Feb. 25—All the steamboats at this city have been ordered to Columbus to-day, it is supposed for military movements, and has given rise to various rumors, but nothing certain.

Gen. Pillow arrived here to-day, and is making a war meeting.

Nothing authentic from Nashville to-night. It is believed the Federals have not entered it yet.

RICHMOND, Feb. 25.—A gentleman captured at Roanoke Island and released, says that 2,440 men were released on parole, and sent to Elizabeth City on steamers. The men made their way to Norfolk in various ways. Portions of them have arrived at Richmond to-day; others are on their route to North Carolina, and some of the troops went across the country to Warrenton.

The result of the battle is as follows: Killed, 13; mortally wounded, who have since died, 3; slightly wounded, 34—all of whom are doing well in the hospital at Elizabeth City, and will soon return home.

Special to the Delta.

MEMPHIS, Feb. 22, 1862.

The Appeal has a special dispatch from Clarksville, Arkansas, dated to-day, saying it was reported that General McCulloch was falling back South of Fayetteville, and was being followed by the enemy.

Gen. Crittenden's command has arrived at Munfreesboro, south of Nashville, from Carthage.

The enemy had not occupied Nashville yesterday.

RICHMOND, Feb. 18, 1862.

Congress has confirmed the nominations of Crittenden and Loring, as Maj. Generals.

The free trade bill has been defeated.

We have nothing from Donelson.

COLUMBUS, KY., Leb. 23, 1862.—We are in possession of information from the enemy. They report their loss in killed, wounded and prisoners at Fort Donelson to be between 5000 and 8000. Gen. Polk has returned from his visit to Gen. Beauregard at Jackson, Tenn. Gen. Beauregard is now nearly recovered and will at once assume command.

Several of the enemy's gunboats are now in sight of this place.

MEMPHIS, Feb. 24.—An attache of the Memphis and Ohio Railroad says that on Friday last a battalion of Confederate cavalry left Paris on a scouting expedition toward the Tennessee river. They hired a man acquainted with the country as a guide, who paoved a traitor, and led the battalion into an ambuscade of the enemy's cavalry, by which three or four of our men were wounded.

The Federals entered Nashville yesterday. They assured the people that no one should be molested, and behaved very civilly.

A gentleman who has arrived from Price's army says the General and his army were South of Fayetteville. McCulloch was at Boston Mountain.

NASHVILLE, Feb. 24.—The Federals in small force appeared at Edgefield (a small town on the opposite side of the river from Nashville) yesterday but retired almost immediately. No Federals are visible this morning. They may come over to-day, and perhaps not for several days.

MEMPHIS, Feb. 24.—The Federals have not occupied Nashville yet. Federal scouts from Buell' army have appeared on the north side of Cumberland river, it is supposed preparatory to an advance of the main column.

Gen. Price and McCulloch are preparing for battle. The former is this side of Fayetteville, and the latter at Boston Mountain with cav lry.

It is reported that nine Federal gunboats, with fifteen transports, were seen Sunday (yesterday) evening near Mayfield Creek, but no immediate attack was expected.

MEMPHIS, Feb. 24.—The Evening Appeal of to day contains a special dispatch from Clarksville, Ark., dated the 23, giving the following intelligence:

"Col. Way's 10th Arkansas Regiment, 850 strong, from Johnson county, left for the field of battle this morning. They are armed with double barrelled guns and rifles.

"A messenger brings news that Gen. Price was this side of Fayetteville, and had with his command all of McCulloch's infantry and Pike's brigade."

The Appeal also says that up to last night Buell's army was not at Nashville. Scouts north of the Cumberland river report that the van of Buell's army had sto[illegible]ait an advance of the main column.

The bridges over the Cumberland at Nashville have been destroyed, by order of Gen. Johnston. The wooden one was burned, and the wire one was cut so as to be useless to the enemy.

An officer who arrived this morning from Columbus, reports that nine gunboats and fifteen transports made their appearance last evening at Mayfield Creek, ten miles above Columbus. No immediate attack is expected however.

The enemy burned the Confederate rolling mill at the Cumberland Iron Works a few days after the fall of Donnelson.

The Northern papers say Hunter's expedition, 35,000 strong, was at Point Sterling.

COLUMBUS, KY., Feb., 24, 1862.

I have before me a St. Louis Republican of this morning. It contains an account of the capitulation at Donelson, the sbustance of which is as follows:

"On the 16th Gen. Buckner proposed on armistice to Gen. Grant and the appointment of Commissioners to arrange terms of capitutation.

MEMPHIS Feb. 25.—The Appeal of this evenin, has a special dispatch dated to-day from Clarksville, stating that the enemy were near at handg and reported to be fifty thousand strong. They were still being reinforced, and moving slowly to await the reinforcements. It would be some time before they would be ready for a more rapid advance. When that takes place the Confederates will also be better prepared than they are at present for the desperate campaign in that section country.

"Gen. Grant replied that he would not negotiate upon terms; that the surrender should be immediate and unconditional. This refused, added Grant, I propose to move on your works forthwith."

Gen. Buckner answered: "The distribution of the forces of my command, incident to an unexpected change of commanders, compel me, notwithstanding the brilliant Confederate victory achieved yesterday to accept your ungenerous and undchivalric terms?"

Halleck telegraphed to McClellan from St. Louis no the 21st inst., that the Federals had taken Bentonville, Arkansas, and captured wagons and baggage.

Gen. Grant's official report of the battle at Fort Donelson says his officers, and particularly the field officers, suffered out of proportion in the casulties. He can not determine, he adds, his loss even approzimately, but admits that it can not fall short of twelve hundred.

Reliable information received here from Paducah is that the Federals would officially report their loss at sixteen hundred, but that in reality it was several thousand.

Mrs. Buckner went up to Columbus to-day, under a flag of truce, to join her husband, the General.

Special to Picayune.

MURFREESBORO', Feb. 21.—I arrived here to-day from Nashville. Gen. Floyd left here yesterday, after seeing the army stores, and the sick and the wounded removed to this place.

In Nashville, the stores, banks, printing offices are closed. Although there have been a great number of removals, a large number of families still remain there.

There was no enemy near Nashzille, or approaching it, when I left that city.

The falling back of our ar my to this place was a preconcerted movement, and was deliberately decided on in a council of war, before leaving Bowling Green.

The panic only prevailed among the citizens of Nashville, many of whom had fled either, but there is none among our troops, who are all in good spirits.

Our army is preparing to meet the enemy on more equal ground, where ne will not have the advantage of navigation.

Governor Harris returned here to-day from Memphis.

The freight trains continue to run still to Nashville.

Let our people keep up their courage and reliance. We will come out all right.

MURFREESBORO', Feb. 24.—The Federal pickets reached Edgefield, opposite Nashville, yesterday at 11 A. M., a force of 6,000 Federals being within eight miles distance.

The Mayor of Nashville went out and surrendered the city.

Col. Forrest's cavalry succeeded, during the last three days, in saving most of the public property in this city.

Our force has greatly augmented here, since the arrival of our army, which is in fine spirits and condition, and are anxious once more to meet the enemy.

Our pickets captured last night, and brought in here, thirty of the enemy.

The damage done to the railroad here will be repaired by Wednesday next.

The whole number of our casualties, killed, wounded and prisoners at Donelson, we learn from reliable sources, was about eight thousand.—*Delta*, 25.

Our agent writing from Hallettsville, Lavaca county, says:

"The news is creating great excitement among us. Captain Preston's company, of this county, leaves for Missouri the 1st of March, about 90 to 100 men, and increasing every day. Capt. Jones' company for Carter's regiment, is now leaving for Hempstead. This takes about 600 men from Lavaca county."

Additional Intelligence.

From the New Orleans and other papers, received by our special hand car express, we compile the following additional items of interest:

The N. O. Bulletin of the 25th says: Yesterday afternoon about 2 o'clock, a fire broke out on Liberty street, between Julia and Girod streets, and destroyed twenty old tenements valued at near $40,000. The cause of the fire is considered to have been entirely accidental, and but for the almost superhuman efforts of the firemen, the fire would have extended all through that section of the city, as the houses were light and mostly of wood.

THE WAR IN ARKANSAS.—We find the following telegram in the Little Rock True Democrat. They are fuller than the dispatches received here.—*Delta*, 26th.

To Major N. B. Pearce, Fort Smith:

Fayetteville, Feb. 17th, 11:30 P. M.,—The General directs that you instruct your trains to stop south of Boston Mountain, on the telegraph road.

(Signed) F. C. ARMSTRONG, Adjutant Gen.

To Col. R. H. Johnson:

Fort Smith Feb. 18th, 10 o'clock, P. M.—Had a fight to-day, at Trott's store, near the Arkansas and Missouri line, on Telegraph road in Benton county. Enemy lost seven hundred. Our loss one hundred. The seventh Iowa completely cut up. Hebert's, McRae's and McNair's, and one Missouri regiment engaged—this comes from Dr. Smith, Missouri army, who was in the fight. N. B. PEARCE,

Major N. B. Pearce, Fort Smith.

FAYETTEVILLE, Feb. 17.—Col Hebert is at Trott's store. The Federals are between him and Keitsville, on the telegraph road, and have been reinforced by a small force from Kansas, making about 20,000 men in all—commissary and amunition teams have been ordered up. Heavy firing heard at this point at two o'clock P. M.

(Signed) M. STODDART.

To able-bodied citizens of Western Arkansas:

FAYETTEVILLE, Feb. 17.—The troops under Generals Price and myself are falling back before a superior force to the Boston mountains. Thousands of Federal hireling are within the lines of your State, while hundreds of men remain at home, notwithstanding their services are needed. Let every man turn out and form companies, and rally to meet the advancing enemy. Rally at once, or it will be too late. BEN MCCULLOCH, Brig. Gen.

To Major G. W. Clarke, Fort Smith:

FAYETTEVILLE, Feb. 17—I am instructed by the General commanding to say that the troops under Gen. Price, of this division, yesterday evening fell back to Cross Hollows, and are continuing to fall back.

This morning, it is probable we may have to abandon this point and make a stand at Boston Mountain.

Urge forward every man to meet the emergency. The enemy received heavy reinforcements yesterday, and are continuing to push down upon us, The Quartermaster here has been directed to move all public property here South of Boston Mountain. Let every man turn out at once.

F. C. ARMSTRONG, A. G.

FROM MEXICO AND THE WEST INDIES.—The Norfolk Day Book quotes from Northern papers the subjoined intelligence from Mexico and the West Indies:

The sickness and death among the allied troops were frightful.

Capt. Maffit, formerly of the Crusader, has taken command of the pirate steamer Cecile.

Talcott, formerly civil engineer of the Mexican Railroad, who left to join the rebels in South Carolina, has returned to Havana in the pirate steamer Kate, and is en route to Vera Cruz, in hopes to obtain his old situation, in which he will be disappointed.

Miramon was arrested on board the steamer Avon, and is confined on board H. B. M. frigate Challenger. He will not be allowed to land.

The British steamer Gladiator is still in Nassau, mounting guns, and she will change her flag and become a rebel privateer.

The allied Commissioners have returned from Mexico.

The Mexican Government insists upon the with drawal of the Spanish forces, and will accept the intervention of England and France.

Gen. Prim has sent on for his family.

The British gunboat Porter has been lost at Alvarado.

Desertions from the Spanish troops at Vera Cruz continue.

NORTHERN INTELLIGENCE.—The following are extracts from the Baltimore Sun, of the 17th:

In reference to the raid up the Tennessee river, the Sun says: "The people of Florence were so delighted to find the stars and stripes once more their protector, that they prepared to give a ball to the officers of the gunboats, but they could not remain to accept the courtesies."

We see it stated by a Northern paper that Fortress Monroe is to be strengthened by heavy Columbiads and Dahlgrens, to be prepared for all emergencies.

The Philadelphia Inquirer says there is no doubt of the departure of Secretary Welles from the Cabinet, and the appointment of Judge Holt, of Ky., in his place.

The Canadian papers complain that the want of arms retards the drill of the numerous volunteer companies that have been formed in the province, in expectation of a Yankee invasion.

Special Dispatch to the New York Tribune.

WASHINGTON, Feb. 13.—Senator Sumner's resolutions on the relations between the United States and the rebel territory, were laid on the table at his motion, where they can be called up whenever he thinks best.

A bill organizing the territory into territorial governments, on the principle of these resolutions, will shortly be reported by the territorial committees of both Houses.

Another bill, establishing a provisional government in South Carolina, has been sanctioned in an important quarter.

No decision has yet, it is believed, been reached by the War Department in the Hunter and Lane matter. Gen. Lane is still waiting at Leavenworth for news from Washington. We have the authority of Mr. Covode for saying that he made the original arrangements with Secretary Cameron by which the Government agreed to furnish Gen. Lane with the troops he wanted, and that throughout the negotiation Gen. Hunter's name was not used, and there was no intimation that any one except Gen. Lane was to have the command.

It is probable that an important command in Texas will be intrusted to Gen. Fremont, and that for reasons of obvious fitness the troops assigned to him will be exclusively Germans.

President Lincoln to-day voluntarily appeared before the House Judiciary Committee and gave testimony in the matter of the premature publication in the Herald of a portion of his last annual message.

Chevalier Wyokoff was then brought before the committee, and answered the questions which he refused yesterday, stating, as is rumored, that the stolen paragraphs was furnished to the Herald by Watts, the President's gardner, who was reported as disloyal by the Potter Committee, and whose nomination to a lieutenancy the Senate so decidedly refused to confirm.

Gen. Sherman, at Beaufort, proposes that the Government shall take charge of the plantations coming into its hands, and shall raise the cotton, employ and pay the negro, keeping the latter under strict but kind discipline of overseers. He also proposes that suitable teachers be provided for the blacks, and religious instructions be given.

THE NEW ORLEANS AND TEXAS R. R.—The election of directors for the New Orleans and Texas Railroad Company, took place in Parlor P., St. Charles Hotel, last night, and resulted in the selection of the following gentlemen: L. F. Generes, I. H. Stauffner, John Q. Adams, A. M. Gentry, B. J. Sage, James J. Hanns, O. M. Congreve.

These gentlemen are pledged to do their utmost to furnish the country with this great military need in the shortest possible time, and it only remains for the capitalists of the country to do their duty in order that the work may be speedily completed. The planters will be called upon, we understand, to contribute their labor, and others whatever aid they can give in the shape of materials, provisions, &c. In short, this must be a joint effort of the people to give us this great military and commercial blessing, more needed at this uncture than any other connected with our city, his State, Texas or the Southwest.—*Picayune*.

A friend writing from Centerville, says: "Since the news of our reverses in Tennessee, the war fever is high. Our District Judge, R. S. Gould has resigned his Judgship, and offers his services as, a soldier to the country. Our War Tax Collector, County Clerk, the District Clerk, and the Postmaster, are all leaving for the wars. There are but ten men left in town. A company is forming for Col. Burnet's regiment, to be commanded by Judge Gould."

PRESIDENT DAVIS'S INAUGURAL.

Fellow-Citizens:—On this, the birthday of the man most identified with the establishment of American Independence, and beneath the monument erected to commemorate his heroic virtues and those of his compatriots, we have assembled to usher into existence the Permanent Government of the Confederate States. Through the instrumentality, and under the favor of a Living Providence, we hope to perpetuate the principles of our revolutionary fathers. The day, the memory, and the purpose seem to be fitly associated.—It is with mingled feelings of humility and pride I appear to take in the presence of this people and before High Heaven the oath prescribed as a qualification of the exalted station to which the unanimous voice of the people has called me. Deeply sensible of all that is implied by this manifestation of the people's confidence, I am yet more proundly impressed with the vast responsibility of the office, and humbly feel my own unworthiness. In return for their kindness, I only offer my assurances of the gratitude with which it is received; and can but pledge my zealous devotion of every faculty to the service of those who have chosen me their Chief Magistrate. When through a long course of class legislation, directed not to be for the general welfare, but for aggrandisement in warfare, and against the domestic institutions of the Southern States—when the dogmas of sectional parties, substituted for the provisions of the constitutional compact, threatened to destroy the sovereign rights of those States, six of those States, withdrawing from the Union, confederated together to exercise the right to perform the duty of instituting a government which would better secure their liberties for the preservation of which that Union was established. Whatever of hope some may have entertained that a returning sense of justice would remove the danger with which our rights were threatened, and render it possible to preserve the Union of the constitution, must have been dispelled by the malignity and barbarity of the Northern States in the prosecution of the existing war. The confidence of the most hopeful among us must have been destroyed by the disregard they have recently exhibited for all time-honored works of civil and religious liberty.—Their bastiles are filled with prisoners, arrested without even civil process or indictment, which they are in duty bound to serve. The writ of habeas corpus was suspended by Executive mandate, and a State Legislature controlled by the imprisonment of its members, whose avowed principles suggested to the Federal Executive there might have been another added to the list of seceded States; elections held under threats of military power; civil officers, peaceful citizens, and gentle women, incarcerated for opinion's sake. We proclaimed, in the capacity of our late associates, to administer the Government as free, liberal and humane as that established for our common use. For the proof of our sincerity of purpose to maintain our ancient institutions, we may point to the Constitution of the Confederacy, or to the laws enacted under it, as well as to the fact that, through all the necessities of an unequal struggle, there has been no act on our part to impair personal liberty or freedom of speech, of thought, or of the press. The courts have been opened, and their judicial functions fully executed, and every right of the peaceful citizen maintained as equally as if the war of invasion had not disturbed our land. The people of the States now Confederate became convinced that the Government of the United States had fallen into the hands of a sectional majority, who would peril that most sacred of all trusts to the destruction of those rights which it was pledged to protect, and they believed that to remain longer in the Union would subject them to a continuance of disparaging discrimination, submission to which would be inconsistent with their welfare, and intolerable to a proud people. They therefore determined to sever its bonds, and establish a new Confederacy for themselves. (Cheers.) The experiment instituted by our revolutionary fathers of a voluntary Union of sovereign States for purposes specified in solemn compact had been perverted by those who feeling they had the power, and forgetting the right were determined to respect no law but their own will, the Government had ceased to answer the ends for which it was ordained and established. To save ourselves from revolution, which in its silent but rapid progress was about to place us under a despotism of numbers, and to perseve in the spirit as well as the form the system of government we believed to be peculiarly fitted to our condition and full of promise for mankind, we determined to make a new association, composed of States homogeneous in interest, policy and feeling. True to our traditions of peace and our love of justice, we sent Commissioners to the United States to propose a fair and amicable settlement of all questions of public debt or property which might be disputed, but the Government at Washington, denying our right to self-government, refused even to listen to any proposals for a peaceful separation. Nothing was then left us but to prepare for war. (Cheers) The first year of our history has been the most eventful in the annals of this continent. A new Government has been established over an area exceeding 700,000 square miles, and the great principle upon which we have been willing to hazard everything dear to man has made conquests for us which could never have been achieved by the sword. Our Confederacy has grown from six to thirteen States, and Maryland, already united to us by hallowed memories, and national interests, will, I believe, when able to speak, with united voice connect her destinies with the South. (Great applause.) Our people have rallied with unexampled unanimity to the support of the great principles of constitutional Government with a firm resolve to perpetuate by arms the rights they could not peacefully secure. A million, it is estimated, is the standing hostile army, and waging a war along a frontier of thousands of miles. Battles have been fought and sieges conducted, and although the contest has not ended, and did for the moment go against us, the final result in our favor is not doubted. The period is near at hand when our foes must yield under the immense load of debt incurred: a debt which, in their effort to subjugate us, has already attained such fearful dimensions as will subject them to burthens which must continue to oppress them for generations to come. We, too, have had our trials and difficulties, and that we are to escape them in the future is not to be hoped. It was to be expected when we entered upon this war, that it would expose our people to many sacrifices, and cost them much both in money and blood, but we knew the value of the object for which we engaged and that nothing could be so bad as a failure, and any sacrifice will be cheap as the price of success in such a contest. (Cheers.) But the picture has its lights as well as its shades. This great strife has awakened in the people the highest emotions and qualities of the human soul; it is cultivating feelings of patriotism, virtue and courage, and instances of self-sacrifice and general devotion to the noble cause for which we are contending are rife throughout the land. Never has a people evinced so determined a spirit as that now animating the men, women and children in every part of our country. Upon the first call men fly to arms, and wives and mothers send their husbands and sons to battle without a murmer or regret. It was, perhaps, in the ordination of Providence that we were to be taught the value of our liberties by the priee we pay for them. The recollections of this great contest with all its common traditions of glory, sacrifices and of blood, will be a bond of harmony and endearing affection among the people, producing unity in policy, fraternity in sentiment, and joint effort in war. The material sacrifices of the past year have not been made without some corresponding benefits. If the acquiescence of foreign nations in the pretended blockade has deprived us of our commerce with them; it is fast making a self-supporting and independent people. The blockade, if effectual and permanent, could only serve to divest our industry from the production of articles for export and employ it in supplying commodities for domestic use. It is satisfaction to know that we have maintained the war by our own unaided exertions. We have neither asked or received assistance from any quarter. The interests involved is not only our own; the world at large is concerned in the opening of our markets to its commerce; and when the Independence of the Confederate States is recognized by the nations of the earth, and we are free to follow our interests and inclinations, by cultivating foreign trade, the Southern States will offer the manufacturing nations the most favorable markets which ever invited their commerce. Cotton, sugar, rice, tobacco, provisions, timber and naval stores, will furnish attractive exchanges. Nor would the consistency of these supplies be likely to be disturbed by war. Our Confederate strength will be too great to attempt aggression, and never was there a people whose interests and principles committed them so fully to a peaceful policy as these Confederate States. By the character of their productions they are too deeply interested in foreign commerce to want a war only to disturb the world, and a war of conquest they cannot wage, because the constitution of the Confederacy admits no coerced association. A civil war there cannot be between States held together by their volition only, and this rule of voluntary association, which cannot fail to be conservative, as by securing a just and impartial government at home it does not diminish the security of obligations by which the Confederate States may be bound to foreign nations. In proof, it is to be remembered that at the first moment of asserting their right to secession, these States proposed a settlement on the basis of common liabilities for the obligations of the General Government. Fellow citizens, after the struggle of ages had consecrated the right of Englishmen to a constitutional representative government our colonial ancestors were forced to vindicate that birthright by an appeal to arms. Success crowned their efforts, and they provided for their posterity a peaceful remedy against future aggressions. The tyranny of an unbridled majority, the most odious and least responsible form of despotism has denied us both that right and remedy; therefore, we are in arms to renew such sacrifices as our fathers made to the holy cause of constitutional liberty.

At the darkest hour of our struggle, the Provisional gives place to the Permanent Government, and after a series of successes and victories, which covered our arms with glory, we have recently met with serious disasters; but in the heart of that people who are resolved to be free, these disasters tend but to stimulate to increased resistance to show ourselves worthy the inheritance bequeathed us by the patriots of the Revolution. We must emulate the heroic devotion which made severe to them but the crucible in which their patriotism was refined. (Applause) With confidence in the wisdom and virtue of those who will share with me the responsibility, and aid me in the conduct of public affairs, and securely relying on the patriotism and courage of a people, of which the present war has furnished so many examples, I deeply feel the weight of the responsibilities I now, with unaffected diffidence, am about to assume, and fully realizing the inadequacy of human power to guide and sustain, my hope is reventiy fixed on Him whose favor is vouchsafed to the cause which is just, and with humble gratitude and adoration, acknowledging the Providence which has so visibly protected the Confederacy during its brief but eventful career. To Thee Oh God, I trustingly commit myself, and prayfully invoke Thy blessing on my country and its cause.

PRESIDENT'S MESSAGE.

Congressional.

RICHMOND, Feb. 25.—The President sent in his message to Congress to-day, in which he says,

Since the delivery of the last message, events have demonstrated that the Government has attempted more than they had the power successfully to achieve. Hence, in the effort to protect the whole territory, both seaboard and inland, we have been so exposed as recently to encounter serious disasters. At the formation of the Government, we were to a great extent destitute of the means for the prosecution of the war on so gigantic a scale as that now attained. The workshops and artisans were mainly found in the North, and one of the first objects for the war was the establishing the necessary manufactories, and the purchase in Europe, as far as practicable, whatever was required for the public defence in April last. But active military preparations in Europe interposed many obstacles to the procurement of arms.

He says he has no official report of the discomfitures at Roanoke and Fort Donelson, but enough is known of the surrender of Roanoke to make us feel deeply humiliated, however imperfect may have been our defence. The hope is still entertained that our report of the loss at Fort Donelson is greatly exaggerated, inasmuch as we are not only unwilling, but unable to believe that a large army of our people would surrender without a desperate effort to cut their way through the investing forces, whatever may have been their numbers, and endeavor to make a junction with other divisions of our army, but the absence of official reports may make premature his judgment. In the meantime strenuous efforts should be made to forward reinforcements to our armies at the positions threatened, and I cannot doubt that the bitter disappointment we have borne, by nerving the people to still greater exertions, will speedily secure results more in accordance with our just expectations, and as favorable to our cause as those which marked the earlier periods of the war.

He says the report of the Secretary of War and Secretary of the Navy exhibit resources for the conduct of the war have accumulated, notwithstanding the serious difficulties against which we have contended, fully equal to meet future wants. He condemns the policy of short enlistments, and considers it has contributed to our recent reverses.

When the war first broke out the general opinion was that it would be short, hence the people were naturally averse to long enlistments, but now as the war will probably continue through a series of years our high spirited and gallant soldiers, while generally reenlisting, are compelled in many instances to go home and make arrangements for their families during a prolonged absence. The quotas of new regiments for the war from all the States are in rapid progress of organization, and the whole body of new levies and reenlistments will probably be ready in thirty days. The number of regiments in the field is four hundred of infantry with a proportional force of cavalry and artillery.

Notwithstanding the great difficulty encountered, the report of the Secretary of the Navy exhibits satisfactory progress in the preparation and early completion of vessels in number and class, on which we may confidently rely for contesting the vaunted control of the enemy over our waters.

The financial system adopted proves adequate for the supply of all the wants of the Government. We have no floating debt, and the credit of the Government is unimpaired. The total expenditure for the year, in round numbers, is $170,000,000.

He says the report of the Postmaster General shows an improving condition, and that it will soon be self sustaining. He recommends the organizing a Supreme Court.

The other business of Congress to-day is unimportant

HOSPITAL, VELASCO, Feb. 27, 1862.

Mr. Cushing—I have the pleasure of acknowledging through your invaluable paper, the receipt of quite a lot of mattresses, pillows, bolsters, pillow and bolster cases, sheets, towels and old linen, from the ladies of Brazoria county—especially San Bernard, Oyster Creek and Gulf Prairie, their names are too numerous to mention. I only mention their location, know that those more remote have not yet had time to send in their contributions to the sick. I also acknowledge the receipt of some valuable contributions of like character, from Mrs. Thompson and Mrs. Hefford, of Matagorda county. I assure you the good people only want to know our wants, and they will lend a helping hand to supply them.

G. M. BAKER, Surgeon, Bates Regiment.

SHINPLASTERS.

Mr. Editor:—Notwithstanding the war made on you for your manly stand against the shinplaster inundation, you may be assured that you are and will be sustained by a very large majority of the people. You are not the first man that has lived among elements of war against a great principle, and at last, those who now so bitterly oppose you will either see and admit their error, or fall before the heavy blows of truth. The waters of the shinplaster freshet are rising higher and higher, and even the whole country is threatened with a tremendous inundation. Our country towns are becoming unsafe, as the waters of the mighty flood are already in the streets, and even the houses of many of them; and the Heavens betoken that the rains will not abate until even there will not be a mountain top to receive the ark of safety.

Soon, very soon, sir, every village and cross-road will have its mighty banker, (?) or perhaps scores of them, until our currency will be literally ruined, distrust be created, and the honest laborers of the land, will find their pockets full of the worthless stuff; and when they look around for the fathers or sponsors for it, lo! very many of them are not to be found, and the very bread needed to support our families during this revolution, cannot be obtained for the want of a safe currency to buy it.

Tell us not that responsible, wealthy men are engaged in this violation of protective laws; for where this is the case it will only be an argument for thousands of men, out of whom a groat cannot be made, to go and do likewise. Why sir, it is even more boldly avowed by some that public opinion will force our Gov. to pardon every man who may be guilty of a violation of the law, even if he be convicted and tried. But let not these violators of law lay this flattering unction to their souls, for public opinion is not made of those of their way of thinking, and we have a Governor who fears not to do his duty.

Let the judges, the grand juries, the district attorneys, petit juries, all do their duty, and we will soon see whether our criminal law is a dead letter.

A VOICE FROM THE COUNTRY.

THE NEW YORK HERALD.

WHOLE NO. 9307. NEW YORK, WEDNESDAY, MARCH 5, 1862.—TRIPLE SHEET. PRICE TWO CENTS.

THE PRESENT AREA OF THE REBELLION.

The Loyal States and Territories of the Union in White, the Disloyal in Black.

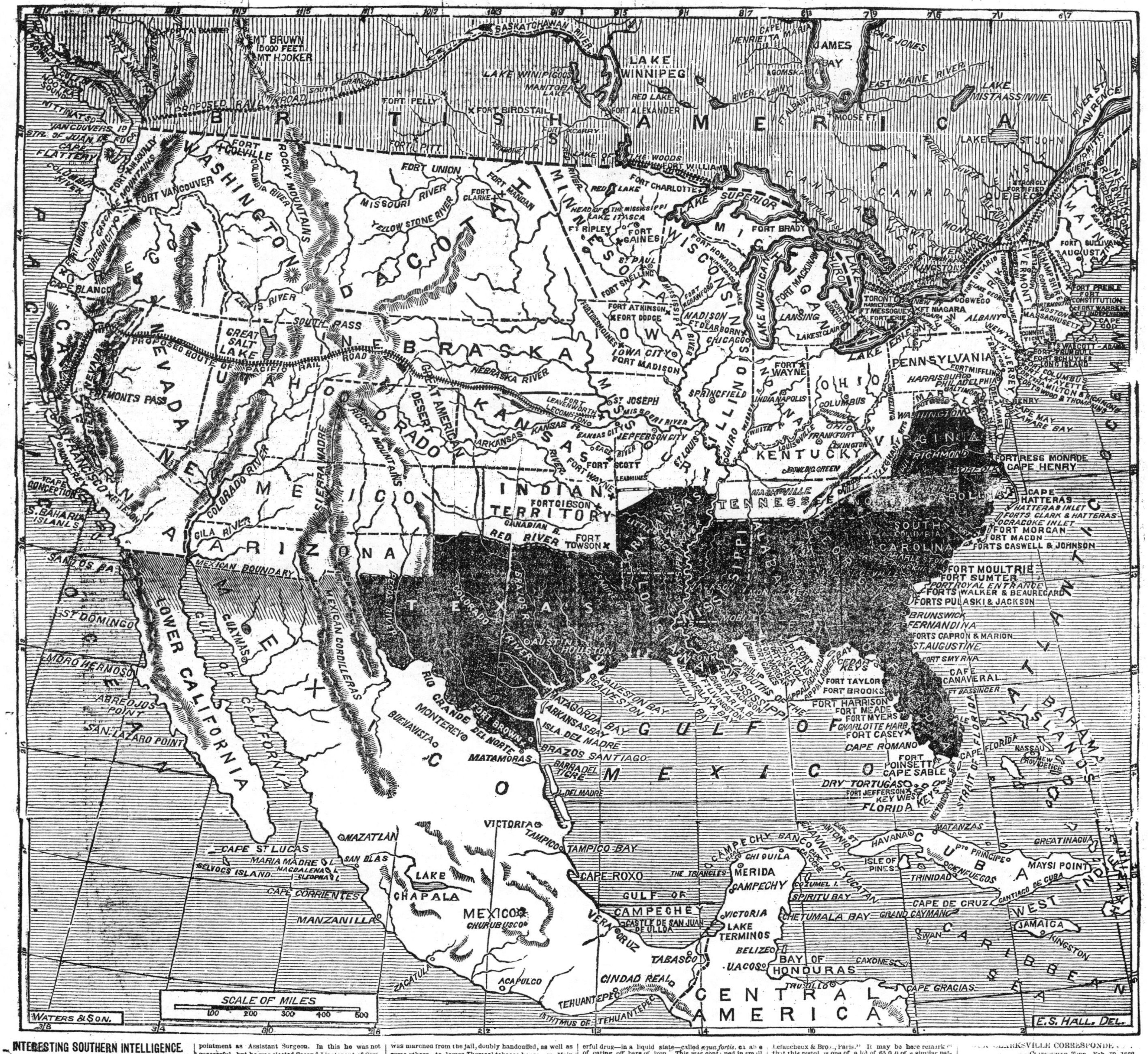

INTERESTING SOUTHERN INTELLIGENCE.

The Retreating Rebels from Columbus, &c., to Make a Stand at Memphis—50,000 Strong.

Particulars of the Escape of Lieut. Briggs, of Ohio.

WHAT THE REBELS SAY IN PRIVATE.

Curious Documents Found in the Rebel Camp.

THE PEOPLE CONDEMNING THEIR RULERS.

THE REBEL CIRCULATING MEDIUM,

&c., &c., &c.,

ESCAPE OF A UNION PRISONER FROM NEW ORLEANS.

ROMANTIC HISTORY OF THE ESCAPE FROM IMPRISONMENT IN NEW ORLEANS OF A UNION PRISONER, AFTER FIVE MONTHS' CONFINEMENT—HIS ADVENTUROUS JOURNEY NORTHWARD, ETC.

Samuel H. Briggs, Second Lieutenant of the First Ohio Regiment, taken prisoner at the battle of Bull run, has just arrived in this city from New Orleans. Lieutenant Briggs is a graduate of the Twenty-third street College of Physicians and Surgeons, New York. He left here at the breaking out of the war for Cincinnati his native place, expecting to obtain an appointment as Assistant Surgeon. In this he was not successful, but he was elected Second Lieutenant of Company K, Captain Burns, and in that capacity entered the battle with his regiment. During the battle Lieutenant Briggs was severely wounded, having his right foot badly maimed by a musket ball. He received other wounds during his captivity and subsequent escape, an account of which will presently appear.

Upon his capture at Bull run Lieut. Briggs was seized by the hair of his head, and pulled about half a mile in that manner. His captors then placed him in a box cart and hauled him to Manassas. At this place he resented some insult from a rebel, who called him "an abolitionist —— ——," when he received a dagger thrust through the fleshy part of the left wrist. From Manassas they took him to Richmond, under a guard oe some twenty-five men, and on arriving at the Broad street railway station an attempt was made to plac- handcuffs upon his wrists, but the Lieutenant resisted, and they did not then succeed in manacling him. His captors now stacked arms, and carried their prisoner to the Richmond jail, where, by the application of chloroform, they succeeded in stupifying the Lieutenant, and finally managed to get the handcuffs upon him. When he awoke he found what had been done, discovered the sponge with which the chloroform had been administered, found that his wound had not been dressed, and, furthermore, ascertained that he had been stripped of his lieutenant's uniform, soiled as it was, and supplied with another, entirely new and of good material. His sword, valued as a presentation from friends, was also taken from him. The Lieutenant describes the jail as a very filthy place, the floor covered with tobacco juice, and the blankets unfit even to stand upon. There were about two hundred and fifty confined in the jail at this time, including a large number of the New York Sixty-ninth prisoners. In his own cell there were twenty-three when they got him there, many of them wounded, and groaning all night. Officers and negroes, with clubs, would come along, and tell them to "Groan, you son of a b——."

On the next morning, the 23d of July, Lieutenant Briggs was marched from the jail, doubly handcuffed, as well as some others, to James Thomas' tobacco house, on Main street, where he obtained a breakfast of corn bread, bull beef well peppered, fried fat pork and rye coffee, without sugar or milk. Breakfast over, Lieutenant Briggs, with two hundred and fifty other prisoners, took the train for Weldon, N. C., *en route* for New Orleans. Among those who shared his captivity at this time were three or four Sixty-ninth troops, the bulk being composed of the Vermont First, Wisconsin Second, Ohio First, Indiana Second and Illinois Third troops. From Weldon the prisoners were hurried over Cape Fear river, under a strong guard, for Wilmington, N. C.; thence to Kingsville, S. C.; Columbia, S. C.; Mifflin, Ga.; Macon, Ga.; Atlanta, Ga.; Griffin, Ga.; Columbus, Ga., to Montgomery, Ala.; thence by James Battle and St. Charles steamers to Mobile, where they took the lake steamers California and Cuba, and reached New Orleans, via Lake Pontchartrain, on the morning of the 28th of July. On their arrival at the end of the lake the prisoners were obliged to walk some nine miles to the city, under an escort of some three or four thousand rebel troops, all heavily armed with French rifles, sabres, huge bowie knives, French navy pistols, &c.

PRISON SCENES IN NEW ORLEANS—THE ESCAPE AND FLIGHT.

On reaching New Orleans Lieutenant Briggs was placed in confinement in the parish prison, the majority of his fellow prisoners being sent to the less comfortable quarters of the city calaboose. From the 28th of July until the period of his escape on the 5th of February—a period of over five months—Lieutenant Briggs was kept in close confinement in the prison. He was naturally restive, and his Buckeye spirit illy brooked this restraint. He was continually under lock and key, and although offered more liberty if he would become more reconciled, he refused all offers of commutation. It being ascertained that he was a gentleman of medical education, he was offered a position in the rebel hospital, but this he also refused.

In the meantime Lieutenant Briggs was meditating schemes of escaping from his hated confinement. He had some friends in the city, who were allowed to visit him and convey him some things for his bodily comfort. Among other things whiskey was not contraband; but in the zinc flasks supposed to contain nothing but whiskey was concealed something better for the interests of a captive than strychnine, and that was a powerful drug—in a liquid state—called *aqua fortis*, capable of eating off bars of iron. This was contained in small three ounce vials, and placed in the whiskey flasks. When the flasks were received the Lieutenant would watch his opportunity, break the flasks, throw away the whiskey, and apply the *aqua fortis* to his prison bars. This was a long, slow, tedious process, occupying, in the intervals during which Lieutenant B. found opportunity to work, some two months. It was executed in this manner:—Taking a string of yarn from his woollen stocking, Lieutenant B. would saturate the yarn with the *aqua fortis*, and proceed noiselessly to saw away at a bar until he had sawed it through. Altogether there were some twelve bars, and some of them required a week's labor to accomplish his purpose, and he was watched almost continually. He succeeded in making an aperture about three feet square, through which himself and three fellow prisoners finally succeeded in making their escape, about one o'clock, on the morning of the 5th of February. His fellow prisoners, who escaped with him, were Charles Tilton, of Boston, Mass., private in Company G, First Ohio; First Lieutenant Charles Blaisdell, of Ohio, also of Company G, same regiment, and Dustin Marshall, of Burlington, private in Company K, same regiment. After making the aperture their escape was not yet secured, as there was a high fence, which enclosed the prison yard, to be scaled. This they finally succeeded in doing, after an hour's time, without attracting attention. All four then made for the shell road, intending to reach Jackson, Miss. After getting out of the city they kept to the woods to avoid detection, and on the first day after their escape they reached a large sugar plantation (Cramer's), about twenty miles from New Orleans. In the rear of this plantation, in a swamp, they remained concealed, and at night again pursued their perilous journey. When within about seven miles of Jackson, Lieut. Briggs and party encountered rebel scouts, who commanded them to halt and give an account of themselves. Having managed to secure some half dozen pistols from drunken soldiers, Briggs' party thought themselves strong enough to fight their way past the scouts of the enemy; but prudence dictated another course. The rebel scouts declared their intention to arrest the whole party as abolitionists, fugitives from prison; whereupon Briggs and his friends started to run. The scouts then fired, and Lieutenant B. received a bullet wound in the right leg, but not sufficiently severe to disable him. He returned the fire, and killed his man, the ball entering about half an inch above the heart. Briggs' party then all fired, and the balance of the rebels—seven in number—took to their heels, leaving on the ground the dead body of their comrade. On examining the body of the dead rebel Lieutenant B. found a splendid French navy revolver, with six barrels, the invention of "[illegible] Lefaucheux & Bro., Paris." It may be here remarked that this pistol is one of a lot of 65,000 of a similar pattern, sent to the Confederates from France by their ambassador, Wm. L. Yancey, and which were received at Savannah in a vessel that succeeded in running the blockade. There was also on the body of the dead rebel a bowie knife, about a foot long and some three inches wide. From lettering upon the cap and on the coat of the rebel, it was ascertained that he had been a member of the Second Alabama regiment, who have won considerable reputation for their daring.

Leaving Jackson, Mississippi, Lieutenant Briggs and party proceeded to a town called Canton, on the Mississippi Central Railroad; thence to Holly Springs, Mississippi; thence to the grand junction of the Memphis and Charleston and the Mississippi Central. From there they went through Jackson, Tennessee, to West Point, Tennessee, and thence to Nashville—all by railway, without intervention.

Lieutenant Briggs was in Nashville on the 16th inst. He remained there one day, stopping at the City Hotel with his party. They were all obliged to take an oath "not to take up arms against the so-called Southern confederacy, nor the State of Tennessee." This oath was administered by Ishman J. Harris, Governor of the State, those who took it being obliged to respond, word for word, kneeling. They then told Lieut. B. that if he was caught with arms in his hands, fighting with the abolitionists of the North against the South, no mercy would be shown him, and that he would be instantly shot down. The rebels offered to purchase the pistols Lieutenant B. and his party had, offering for them eighty dollars each in scrip of the Confederate States, or scrip of the bank of Tennessee. The offer was refused, Lieut. B. stating that the scrip they offered was of no account in the United States. They were then allowed to retain their arms, after an ineffectual attempt to cajole them from them.

Lieutenant Briggs and party were forwarded from Nashville, under a flag of truce, to the lines of the federal forces, under General Buell, at Bacon creek, Kentucky, where they were cordially received and hospitably entertained. They here received the necessary passes from General Buell to proceed on their homeward journey, which they resumed after a short delay. Reaching Louisville, the party were the recipients of a hearty welcome from the Provost Marshal, Colonel Henry Dent, and other public spirited Unionists there. From this point Lieutenant Briggs' friends proceeded homeward, by way of Cincinnati, while he came by way of Pittsburg, arriving in this city yesterday forenoon, his health but little impaired by his adventures and perils in the "land of Dixie." Lieutenant Briggs has a father residing in Massachusetts, whither it is the Lieutenant's purpose to repair immediately.

[illegible] CLARKSVILLE CORRESPONDE[illegible]

CLARKSVILLE, Tenn., Feb 19 1862.

Since my last letter there has been no change in the position of affairs at this place, save the arrival of more troops from St. Louis and the reception of large amounts of supplies, ammunition and stores, that indicate the occupancy of this place as a base of future operations.

The Memphis, Clarksville and Louisville road furnishes railroad communication between Bowling Green and Columbus. The bridge is a beautiful structure, fourteen hundred and seventy feet in length. It is a Howe's truss bridge, having seven spans, resting on stone piers, and furnished with a swing draw at the western end for the passage of steamers. It is approached from the east by a high earth embankment, several hundred feet in length, leading from the high land back of the river. From the west the approach is by heavy trestle work, eleven hundred feet long, crossing the bottom lands that border the river at an elevation of from twenty to twenty-five feet. The bridge itself was not injured by the force from the gunboats, General Halleck having given special instructions for its preservation. Several lengths of the trestle work, however, were destroyed by chopping and burning, so as to necessitate their replacement in order to admit of the further passage of trains. Thi can be accomplished, if it shall ever be desirable for our purposes, in from three to five days. The swing was also thrown open and secured in that position. The telegraph that crosses the river at this point was destroyed.

At the western end of this bridge is the village of Danville, which, in ordinary times, supports a population of from five to six hundred inhabitants. It has now but few male inhabitants, one of whom has his family with him. The rest of the people had fled after the occupation of Fort Henry by the federal forces. Their fear of the Yankee troops is but the natural consequences of the terrible stories that have been carefully circulated throughout the South of the inhumanity and cruelty that characterize our treatment of the people we meet, with which stories the patriotism of the South is fed. The whole South is thus alarmed, and apprehensive only of

THE TRI-WEEKLY TELEGRAPH.

VOL. XXVII—NO. 139 HOUSTON, FRIDAY, MARCH 7, 1862 WHOLE NO. 3519

BY SPECIAL & S. W. EXPRESS.

3 DAYS LATER.

THE ENEMY IN NASHVILLE.

IMPORTANT FROM COLUMBUS.

Enemy Concentrating Etc.

By the New Orleans train which arrived at an early hour this morning, we have at the hands of Capt. Turlay, and by the Southwestern express, three days later intelligence.

A terrible accident occurred on the Jackson and Mississippi road on the 27th, by a passenger train coming in collision, in a dense fog, with a lumber train, killing 25 persons, and wounding many more. The accident occurred below Pontchatoola.

We give the telegraphic dispatches:

MEMPHIS, Feb. 28.—The day has been universally observed here by fast and prayer, and a general suspension of business.

Late advices from Paducah represent that the Federal army has already been concentrated to upwards of 100,000 men, and that they are well armed and equipped.

Nearly all the Federal gunboats were injured in the Fort Donelson fight.

No fighting above yet, but active preparations are still making for the anticipated attack.

Nothing new from Nashville.

RICHMOND Feb. 27.—The President has issued a proclamation declared martial law in Norfolk, Portsmouth and the surrounding country.

It is understood that Congress to-day passed an act authorizing the suspension of the habeas corpus in certain cases.

The Senate has confirmed A. P. Hill and J. J. Pettigrew, both of North Carolina, Brig. Generals.

A resolution was unanimously passed, that the Confederate Government will entertain no peace proposition excluding any portion of the soil of the Confederate States, and declaring that the war will be continued until the enemy is expelled from the Confederacy.

In the House, Mr. Miles, Chairman of the Military Committee, reported a bill creating the office of Commanding General of the Confederate Army during the war. The indications are strong that the bill will be passed. Pending its adoption, the House went into secret session.

CHARLESTON, Feb. 25—Reconnoissances below Savannah reveal the fact that the enemy have erected three batteries of heavy guns, with converging fires, which effectually cuts off the communication between Savannah and Fort Pulaski.

An attack on Savannah is momentarily expected.

There is great activity in military movements here.

A vessel loaded with coffee, medicines and salt, has reached a Confederate port to day.

MURFREESBORO' Feb. 26.—Gentlemen who arrived here this morning from Louisville report that all the prisoners taken by the Federals at Fort Donelson have been thrown into the State Prison of Indiana.

Gen Buckner has been sent to Washington, and it is said, is to be tried as a spy, on a charge of having visited Washington in that capacity.

It is said that when Buckner last visited that city, he was invited to visit the camp of the enemy, but declined doing so.

On Gen. Buckner's arrival at Louisville, he was treated with great indignity.

Gen. Grant's Federal force at Nashville numbers 12,000 men. The flag of the United States was yesterday hoisted on the State capitol, an act which was received by the inhabitants with silent contempt.

Great activity prevails in our army. An early movement is anticipated.

MEMPHIS, Feb. 26.—A passenger from Nashville, who left there on Monday last, says a regiment of Federal cavalry are encamped at Edgefield, opposite Nashville, and on Sunday last Mayor Cheatham formally surrendered the city to the Federal commander, who sent a small detachment to take possession. The Confederate stores were being removed up the river on Sunday. The Federals promise to respect private property.

Gen. Pillow's report of the Fort Donelson fight is published this morning.

The Federals are concentrating in large force near Clarksville, Tennessee, and a desperate fight is anticipated, but it will take some time for the Federals to get ready.

Nothing new from Columbus.

MEMPHIS, Feb. 27.—Passengers from Paris state the Federals were reported advancing upon the town; also that the Confederate cavalry force had left Paris, and the town was at the mercy of the Federals. The people are flying with their slaves, of whom a large number have reached Memphis.

Gen. Johnston told a gentleman on Monday that the Federals had possession of Nashville, and the Federal army was believed to be near

MEMPHIS, Feb. 27.—Buell is at Nashville with 40,000 Federals. A gentleman saw thirteen regiments enter Nashville on yesterday (Wednesday.) They appeared to be well drilled and were fine looking men. Each regiment had a brass band, and all of the bands played "Dixie."

It is reported 20,000 Federals left Commerce for New Madrid on Monday. The roads being bad, they will not get there before to-morrow or next day.

It is also reported the enemy are preparing to leave Paducah for Columbus, and a battle there is imminent. Columbus needs more force there immediately.

It is reported the Federal gunboats went up Tennessee river this morning.

Gen. Johnston has a large army at Murfreesboro, and is preparing vigorously to give the enemy a warm reception.

There was a general stampede of the inhabitants on the approach of the Federals at Paris.

[Southern line still interrupted north of Mobile.—REPORTER.]

Most of the newspaper offices had been removed; also, one-fifth of the Confederate stores.

It is reported Columbus will be attacked very soon. 37 transports were seen at Paducah on Tuesday afternoon, receiving troops.

The enemy are reported to be advancing in the rear of New Madrid in large force.

Preparations are being made to receive the attack on Columbus. All the bridges and houses, and everything that can help the enemy's approach, has been destroyed by our men.

Stirring times are ahead.

MEMPHIS, Feb. 27.—Clarksville has been formally occupied by the Federals.

Com. Foote issues a proclamation promising not to interfere with business or private property, but demands all Confederate property.

Twenty thousand Federal troops, from the Tennessee and Cumberland, have gone back to Paducah. It is surmised their object is to make a flank movement in the attack on Columbus.

The bridges over Mayfield creek have been destroyed to impede their progress. The Federals have a large force in the vicinity of Cumberland Gap. The Confederate forces at the Gap have been reinforced, and the Federals are closely watched.

There has been no quorum of the Tennessee Legislature yet, although a military bill of importance is awaiting action.

Advices from Nashville on Monday afternoon says the Federal officer refused to take possession of Nashville, saying he was not authorized to do so.

Col. Forrest's cavalry were removing the military stores, and no Federal force except that at Edgefield, within thirty miles of the place.

Special to Delta.

MEMPHIS, Feb. 26, 1862.—The Avalanche has the following interesting intelligence from a citizen who left Nashville on Monday morning:

On Sunday a Federal regiment appeared outside of Edgefield, and Mayor Cheatham repaired to it and formally tendered a surrender of the city and public stores to the commander.

The Federals sent fifteen men to take possession of a large amount of bacon and other Confederate stores in this city.

Col. Forrest was at the time engaged in removing the stores out of the city to a place of safety. The Mayor resisted the removal. Col. Forrest told him that he outranked any city officer, and if he was resisted or interrupted he should use force, whether against the Federals or the civil authorities.

A number of low characters about the city commenced depredations upon private property, and the forces under Col. Forrest killed five of them.

The papers of Memphis to-morrow will contain a full report from Gen. Pillow of the battle of Fort Donelson.

MEMPHIS, Feb. 26.—Our scouts at Columbus yesterday reported the enemy twelve thousand strong was moving from Bloomfield, Mo., towards New Madrid, 18 miles distant.

Fifteen thousand troops were at Cairo; thirty thousand in the vicinity of Paducah, and fifty thousand more were expected from other places.

Thirty-nine transports were at Cairo on Wednesday, apparently in readiness to move.

The sick at Columbus are being removed, and some of them have been sent here.

No exit or entrance is allowed at Columbus, except on Government business.

Gen Beauregard is making prompt efforts to repel the attack.

We are to have stirring times, apparently, in a few days.

A large number of troops are enlisting in Tennessee.

It is believed that a grand Confederate army will soon be concentrated in the West, for defensive and offensive movements.

Buell marched into Nashville yesterday with a large army, the band playing Dixie.

Among the whole population, but one one white flag was hung out as the enemy entered.

MEMPHIS, Feb. 27—Passengers who arrived here last night by the midnight train, state that the Federals are advancing on Paris, a Confederate cavalry force having left the scene of action.

Gen. Buckner is at Louisville, indicted for high treason by the Federal Government.

Clarksville has been occupied by Foote's orders. He promised that he would not interfere with business movements in the place, would respect private property, would hold the municipal authorities responsible for good order, and demanded the surrender of Confederate property.

Twenty thousand of the Federal troops recently engaged on the Tennessee and Cumberland rivers have fallen back to Paducah.

Gen. Polk, anticipating the object of their falling back to be for a flank movement on Columbus, has ordered the bridges on the Mayfield road to be destroyed, so as to impede their progress.

MEMPHIS, Feb. 28, 1862.—The Appeal of this morning has information from Nashville to noon on Wednesday last, the 25th, as follows, through a gentleman who left at that hour:

Gen. Buell and Com. Foote had arrived and occupied the city, the former with thirty thousand troops.

Buell crossed over from Edgefield, on the north bank of the Cumberland, twenty-three regiments, and Foote brought up the river, on transports and gunboats, nineteen regiments, numbering 10,000 men, from Fort Donelson. The entire force of the enemy in Nashville, there, consists of forty-two regiments.

The United States flag was immediately raised upon the dome of the capital, and now floats there.

Upon the entrance of the army one Federal flag was exhibited from the shop of a Yankee jeweler named Long, who has long been suspected of disloyalty

Nashville is still strongly Southern. A deep gloom covers the whole community.

The stores are all closed and business is at a perfect stand still. Citizens all avoid any sort of intercourse with the invaders, keeping aloof from them socially.

Special to the Picayune.

It has been ascertained that the whole force of the enemy in the Fort Donelson fight was 83 regiments, numbering 50,000 men.

The Cincinnati Enquirer, of the 13th inst., gives an account of the departure thence of a fleet of thirty steamers, with 1700 mules, and a large shipment of wagons and horses to follow, for Louisville, where they would receive 30,000 troops from Green River, under Gen. McCook. Others are to be tranported to the Cumberland and Tennessee rivers.

These, with those now on the way to the Cumberland and Tennessee from St. Louis, Illinois, Indiana and Ohio, numbering 25,000 men, will increase the enemy's force in that neighborhood over 80,000.

THE BATTLES AT FORT DONELSON!

GENERAL PILLOW'S REPORT.

BATTLE OF TRENCHES, FEB. 11.

Battle with Gunboats, Feb. 13.

Battle of Dover, February 15th.

MEMPHIS, February 25, 1862.

Editors Avalanche:—There is so much anxiety in the public mind to understand the result of the battle of Dover, and the causes which led to the capitulation, and so much excitement among the friends of those surrendered to know their condition, that I deem it not improper to lay before the people my official report of the series of actions occuring at Fort Donelson. This, I am aware, is irregular, and in violation of the usages of the Government; but I feel that the extraordinary circumstances of the case justify a departure from usage so far as to publish the report, not doubting but that the Government will approve of the motive which induces its publication.

GIDEON J. PILLOW, Brig. Gen.

COLUMBIA, TENN., February 16, 1862.

Capt. C. Derrick, Ass. Adjutant General:

On the 8th inst. Gen. A. S. Johnston ordered me to proceed to Fort Donelson and take command of that post. On the 9th inst. I arrived at that place. In detailing the operations of the forces under my command at Fort Donelson, it is proper to state the condition of that work and the forces constituting its garrison. When I arrived I found the work on the river battery unfinished, and wholly too weak to resist the force of heavy artillery. I found a 10-inch columbiad and a 32 pound rifle gun that had not been mounted. Deep gloom was hanging over the command, and the troops were greatly depressed and demoralized by the circumstances attending the surrender of Fort Henry, and the manner of retiring from that place. My first attention was given to the necessity of strengthening this work, and mounting the two heavy guns, and to the construction of the defensive works to protect the rear of the river battery. I imparted to the work all the energy which it was possible to do, working day and night with the whole command. The battery was without a competent number of artillerists, and those that were there were not well instructed in the use of their guns. To provide for this want I placed the artillery companies under active course of instruction in the use of their guns. I detailed Capt. Ross with his company of artillerists to the command of one of the river batteries. These heavy guns being mounted and provision made for working them, and a proper supply of ammunition having been procured by my order from Nashville, I felt myself prepared to test the effect of the fire of the heavy metal against the enemy's gunboats, though the work was much in need of more heavy pieces.

The armament of the batteries consisted of eight 32-pounders, three 32-pound carronades, one 8 inch columbiad, and one rifle gun of 32-pound caliber. The selection of the site for the work was an unfortunate one. While its command of the river was favorable, the site was commanded by the heights above and below on the river, and by a continuous range of hills all around the works to its rear.

A field work of very contracted dimensions had been constructed by the garrison to protect the battery, but this field-work was commanded by the hills already referred to, and lay open to a fire of artillery from every direction, except from the hills below. To guard against the effects of fire of artillery from these heights a line of defensive works consisting of rifle pits and abatis for infantry, detached on our right, but continuous on our left, which defenses for our light artillery, were laid off by Maj. Gilmer, Engineer of Gen. A. S. Johnston's staff, but, on duty with me at the post, around the rear of the battery and on the heights from which artillery could reach our battery and inner field work, enveloping the inner work and the town of Dover, where our principal supplies of quarter and commissary stores were in deposit.

These works, pushed with the utmost possible energy, were not quite completed, nor my troops all in position, though nearly so, when Brig. Gen. Floyd, my senior officer, reached that station. The works were laid off with judgment and skill by Maj. Gilmer, were well executed, and designed for the defense of the rear of the work, the only objection being to the length of the line, which, however, from the surroundings, was unavoidable. The length of the line, and the inadequacy of the force for its defense, was a source of embarrassment throughout the struggle, which subsequently ensued in the defense of the position.

I had placed Brig. Gen. Buckner in command of the right wing, and Brig. Gen. Johnson in command of the left. By extraordinary efforts we had barely got the works in a defensive condition when the enemy made an advance in force around and against the entire line of our outer works.

THE BATTLE OF THE TRENCHES.

The first assault was commenced by the enemy's artillery against the center of our left wing, which was promptly responded to by Capt. Green's battery of field artillery. After several hours of firing between the artillery of the two armies, the enemy's infantry advanced to the conflict all along the line, which was kept up and increased in volume from one end of the line to the other for several hours—when at last the enemy made a vigorous assault against the right of our left wing—the position assaulted being a height commanded by Colonel Heiman, and defended by his brigade, consisting of the 10th Tennessee, under command of Lieut. Col. McGarock, Col. Voorhies's (Tenn.,) Col. Hughes's. (Ala.,) and Col. Head's, (Tenn.,) regiments of Tennessee Volunteers, and Capt. Maney's field battery.

The assault was vigorously made, and the position as vigorously defended, and resulted in the repulse of the enemy here and everywhere around the line. The result of the day's work pretty well tested the strength of our defensive lines, and established, beyond question, the gallantry of our entire command, all of which fought well their part of the line. The loss sustained by our force in this engagement was not large, our men being mostly under the shelter of the rifle pits; but we, nevertheless, had quite a number killed and wounded, but owing to the continued fighting which followed, it was impossible to get any official report of the casualties of the day. On the same day our battery on the river was engaged with one of the enemy's gunboats, which occasioned quite a lively cannonading for more than an hour, in which the gallant Capt. Dixon, of the Engineer Corps, was killed instantly at the battery. This officer had been on duty for some months at the post, and had shown great energy and professional skill; and, by his gallant bearing on that day, while directing the operations of the day under my orders, had justly earned for himself high distinction. His death was a serious loss to the service, and was a source of no little embarrassment in our after operations.

On the 12th we had quiet, but we saw the smoke of a large number of gunboats and steamboats at a short distance below. We also received reliable information of the arrival of a large number of new troops, greatly increasing the strength of the enemy's forces, already said to be from 20,000 to 30,000 strong.

THE BATTLE WITH THE GUNBOATS.

On the 14th these reinforcements were seen advancing to their position in the line of investment, and while this was being done, six of the enemy's iron-cased gunboats were seen advancing up the river, five of which were abreast and in the line of battle, and the sixth was a short distance to the rear. When the gunboats arrived within a mile and a half of the battery, they opened fire upon the batteries. My orders to the officers, Shustep and Stankovitch, who commanded the lower battery, of eight guns, and Capt. Ross, the upper battery, of four guns, were to hold their fire until the enemy's gunboats should come within point blank range of their guns. This they did through the ordeal of holding their fire while the enemy's shot and shell fell thick around their position was a severe restraint upon their patriotic impulses. But, nevertheless, our batteries made no response till their gunboats got within range of their guns. Our entire line of batteries then opened fire. The guns of both parties were well served. The enemy constantly advanced, delivering direct fire against our batteries from his line of gunboats, while the sixth boat, moving up in the rear, kept the air filled with shells, which fell thick and close all around the position of our batteries.

The fight continued, the enemy steadily advancing slowly up the river, and the shot and shell from fifteen heavy rifled guns tearing our parapets and plunging deep into the earth around and over our batteries for nearly two hours, and until his boats had reached within the distance of one hundred and fifty yards of our batteries. Having come in such close conflict, I could distinctly see the effects of our shot upon his iron-cased boats. We had given two or three well directed shots from our heavy guns to one of his boats, when she instantly shrunk back and drifted helpless below the line. Several shots struck another boat, tearing her iron case and making her timbers crack, and splintering them as by a stroke of lightning, when the two fell back. Then a third received several shocks, making her metal ring and timbers crack, when the whole line gave way and fell rapidly back from our fire until they passed out of range.

Thus ended the first severe and close conflict of our heavy guns and the enemy's gunboats, testing their strength and the power of heavy guns to resist them. The hot from our 32-pound guns produced but little effect; they struck and rebounded, apparently doing but little damage; but I am satisfied from close observation that the timbers of the framework did not, and could not, withstand the shock from the 10 inch columbiad or 32-pound rifled guns. The gunboats never renewed the attack. I learn from citizens living on the river below, that one of the injured boats was sunk, and that others had to be towed to Cairo. This information may or may not be true, but it is certain that all of the boats were repulsed and driven back after a most vigorous and determined attack, and that two of the boats were badly damaged, and that a third was more or less injured.

It is difficult to estimate the gallant bearing and heroic conduct of the officers and men of our batteries, who so well and so persistently fought our guns until the enemy's determined advance brought his boats and guns into close and desperate conflict. Where all did their duty so well, it is almost impossible to discriminate. The Captains already named, and their Lieutenants, (whose names, for want of official reports, I cannot give,) all deserve the highest commendation.

Lieut. G. L. Martin, (whose company is now at Columbus, Ky., but who was ordered to that post by Major Gen. Polk,) who commanded one of the guns, particularly attracted my attention by his energy and the judgment with which he fought his gun. The wadding having given out, he pulled off his coat and rammed it down as wadding, and thus kept up the fire till the enemy were finally repulsed.

On the evening of this day we received information of the arrival of additional reinforcements of infantry, cavalry and light artillery, by steamboat, all of which were disembarked a short distance below our position.

THE BATTLE OF DOVER.

On the 14th inst. the enemy was busy throwing his forces of every arm around us, extending his line of investment around our position, and completely enveloping us. On the evening of this day we ascertained that the enemy had received additional reinforcements by steamboat. We were now surrounded by an immense force, said by persons to amount to fifty-two regiments, and every road and possible avenue of departure were cut off, with the certainty that our sources of supply by the river would be cut off by the enemy's batteries placed upon the river above us.

At a meeting of the general officers, called by Gen. Floyd, it was unanimously determined to give the enemy battle next day at daylight, so as to cut open a route of exit for our troops to the interior of the country, and thus to save our army. We had knowledge that the principal portion of the enemy's forces were massed in encampment in front of our extreme left, commanding the two roads leading into the interior, one of which we must take in leaving our position. We knew that he had massed in encampment another large force on the Union ferry road, opposite the centre of our left wing. His fresh arrival of troops which encamped on the bank of the river, two and a half miles below us, from which latter encampment a stream of fresh troops was continually pouring around us on his line of investment, and thus strengthening his general encampment on the extreme right. At each of his encampments, and on each road, he had in his position a battery of field artillery, and twenty-four pound iron guns on siege carriages. Between these encampments on the roads, was a thick undergrowth of brush and black jack, making it impossible to advance or maneuver any considerable body of troops.

The plan of attack agreed upon and directed by Gen. Floyd, to be executed was, that with the main body of the forces of our left wing, I should attack the right wing of the enemy, occupying and resting upon the heights reaching to the bank of the river, accompanied by Col. Forrest's brigade of cavalry; that Brig. Gen. Buckner, with the forces under his command, and defending the right of our line, should strike the enemy's encampment and forces on the Winn's Ferry road; that the forces under Col. Heiman should hold his position, and that each command should leave in the trenches troops to hold the trenches.

In this order of battle it was easy to be seen that if my attack was successful, and the enemy routed, his retreat would be along his line of investment toward the Winn's Ferry road, and thence towards his reserve at the gunboats below. In other words my success would roll the enemy's force in retreat over upon Gen Buckner, when by his attack in flank and rear, we would cut up the enemy and put him completely to rout. Accordingly dispositions were made to attack the enemy, at five o'clock A. M. of the 15th. I moved out of my position to engage the enemy. In less than one half hour our forces were engaged. He was prepared to meet in advance of his encampment, and he did meet me before I had assumed line of battle and while I was moving against him without any formation for the engagement. For the first half of the engagement I was much embarrassed in getting the command in position properly to engage the foe. Having extricated myself from the position and fairly engaged, we fought him for nearly two hours before we made any decided advance upon him. He contested this field most stubbornly. The loss of both armies at this portion of the field was heavy. The enemy's particularly, as I discovered by riding over the field after the battle with Gen. Floyd. The enemy having been forced to yield to this portion of the field, retired slowly toward the Winn's Ferry road, Buckner's point of attack. He did not retreat but fell back fighting us, contesting every inch of ground.

The fight was hotly and stubbornly contested on both sides, and consumed the day till 12 o'clock to drive him as far back as the centre, where Gen. Buckner's command was to flank him. While my command was advancing and slowly driving him, I was anxiously expecting to hear Gen. Buckner's command open fire in his rear, which not taking place, I was apprehensive of some misapprehension of orders, and came from the field of battle within the works to learn what was the matter. I there found the command of Gen. Buckner massed behind the ridge within the works taking shelter from the enemy's artillery on the Winns road, it having been forced to retire before the battery, as I learned from him. My force was still slowly advancing, driving the enemy towards the battery. I directed Gen. Buckner immediately to move his command round to the rear of the battery, turning its left, keeping in the Hollow, and attack and carry it.

Before the movement was executed, my force, forming the attacking party on the right, with Forrest's regiment (cavalry) gallantly charged the battery, supported by a body of infantry, driving it and forcing the battery to retire, taking six pieces of artillery, four brass and two twenty-four pounder iron guns. In pursuing the enemy falling back from this position, Gen. Buckner's forces became united with mine, and engaged the enemy in hot contest of nearly an hour, with large forces of fresh troops that had now met us. This position of the enemy being carried by our joint forces, I called off further pursuit after seven and a half hours of continuous and bloody conflict. After the troops were called off, orders were immediately given to the different commands to form and retire to their original positions in the intrenchments.

The operations of the day had forced the entire command of the enemy around to our right wing and in front of Gen. Buckner's position in the entrenchments, and when his command reached his position he found the enemy rapidly advancing to take possession of this portion of his work. He had a stubborn conflict, lasting one hour and a half, to regain it, and the enemy actually got possession of the extreme right of his position, and he held it so firmly that we could not dislodge him. The position thus gained by the enemy was a most commanding one, being immediately in the rear of our river battery, and field work for its protection. From it he could readily turn the entrenched work occupied by Gen. Buckner, and attack him in reverse or advance under cover of an intervening ridge directly upon our battery and field work. While he held this position, it was manifest we could not hold the main work or battery. Such was the condition of the armies at nightfall, after nine hours of conflict, on the 15th inst., in which our loss was severe, and leaving not less than 5000 of the enemy dead and wounded on the field. We left on the field nearly all his wounded, because we could not remove them. We left his dead unburied, because we could not bury them.

Such conflict and courage have perhaps never before occurred upon this continent. We took about 300 prisoners and large numbers of arms. We had fought this battle to open the way for our army and relieve us from an investment which would necessarily reduce us and the position by famine. We had occupied the whole day to accomplish our object, and before we could prepare to leave, after taking in the wounded and the dead, the enemy had thrown around us again in the night an immense force of fresh troops and reoccupied his original position in the line of investment, thus again cutting off our retreat. We had only about 12,000 troops all told. Of these a large proportion were lost in the three battles. The command had been in the trenches night and day for five days, exposed to the snow, sleet, mud and ice water, without shelter, without adequate covering and without sleep.

In this condition the general officers held a consultation to determine what we should do. Gen. Buckner gave it as his decided opinion that he could not hold his position one half an hour against an assault of the enemy, and said the enemy would attack him next morning at day-light. The proposition was then made by the undersigned to again fight our way through the enemy's line and cut our way out. Gen. Buckner said his command was so worn out and cut to pieces, and demoralized, that he could not make another fight; that it would cost the command three-quarters its present numbers to cut its way through, and it was wrong to sacrifice three-quarters of a command to save a quarter; that no officer had a right to cause such a sacrifice. Gen. Floyd and Major Gilmer I understood to concur in this opinion.

I then expressed the opinion that we could hold out another day, and in that time we could get steamboats and set the command over the river, and probably save a large portion of it. To this Gen. Buckner replied, that the enemy would certainly attack him at daylight, and that he could not hold his position half an hour. The alternative of these propositions was a surrender of their position and command. Gen. Floyd said that he would neither surrender the command, nor would he surrender himself a prisoner. I had taken the same position. Gen. Buckner said he was satisfied nothing else could be done, and that, therefore, he would surrender, if placed in command. General Floyd said that he would turn over the command to him if he would be allowed to withdraw his command; to this Gen. Buckner consented. Thereupon, Gen. Floyd turned the command over to me. I passed it instantly to Gen. Buckner, saying I would neither surrender the command nor myself a prisoner. I directed Col. Forrest to cut his way out. Under these circumstances, Gen. Buckner accepted the command, and sent a flag of truce to the enemy for an armistice of six hours to negotiate for terms of capitulation. Before this flag and communication were delivered, I retired from the garrison.

Before closing my report of the operations of the army at Donelson, I must, in justice to the officers and forces under my immediate command, say that harder fighting or more gallant conduct in officers and men, I have never witnessed. In the absence of official reports of brigade and regimental commanders, (of which I am deprived by the circumstances detailed in this report,) I may not be able to do justice to the different corps; I will say, however, that the forces under my immediate command, bore themselves most gallantly throughout the long and bloody conflict.

I speak with special commendation of the brigades commanded by Cols. Baldwin, Wharton, McCausland, Simenton and Drake, and Capts. Maney and Greene, who fought their guns under the constant and annoying fire of the enemy's sharp shooters and the concentrated fire from his field batteries, from which both commands suffered severely. Capt. Maney himself was wounded, and had several lieutenants and many of his company killed and wounded; so did Capts. Porter and Graves.

If I should hereafter receive the reports of regimental and brigade commanders giving me detailed information of the conduct and bearing of officers and men, I will make a supplemental report. The absence of official reports deprive me of the means of giving lists of the killed and wounded of the different commands. I am satisfied that in such a series of conflicts our loss was heavy. I know the enemy's was, from passing over the battlefield with General Floyd in the evening immediately after the battle. His loss in killed and wounded was terrible, exceeding anything I have ever seen on a battle field. Our force in the field did not exceed ten thousand men, while from what I saw of the enemy's force, and information derived from prisoners, we are sure he had from thirty to forty thousand on the field. I must acknowledge my obligations to Major Gilmer, engineer, for the especial and valuable services rendered me in laying off the works, and the energy displayed by him in erecting their construction, and for his counsel and advice.

I likewise acknowledge my obligations to Col. John J. Burch, my Aid-de-Camp; to Capt. Gus. A. Henry, Major Field, Lieut. Nicholson, Lieut. Chas. F. Martin, and Col. Blandon, my Volunteer Aid-de-Camp; to Major Hays, my Assistant Commissary: Major Jones, my Assistant Quartermaster, for the prompt manner in which they executed my orders, under trying circumstances, throughout the long and continued conflicts, and to Major Gilmer, who accompanied me throughout the entire day. Also to Capt. Parker, of my staff, whom I assigned to the command of Capt. Coss's field battery, with new recruits as gunners, and who fought and served them well.

Col. Brandon was severely wounded early in the action. Col. Baldwin's command constituted the front of the attacking force, sustained immediately by Col. Wharton. These two brigades deserve especial commendation for the manner in which they sustained the first shock of battle, and under circumstances of great embarrassment threw themselves into position and followed up the conflict throughout the day.

Being mostly with the two brigades, I can speak from personal knowledge of their gallant bearing. I must also acknowledge my obligations to Brig. Gen. Johnston, who assisted me in command of the forces with which I attacked the enemy, and who bore himself gallantly throughout the conflict, but having received no official reports from him, I cannot give detailed operations of his command. I have pleasure in being able to say that Col. Forrest—whose command greatly distinguished its commander as a bold and gallant leader, and reflected distinguished honor upon itself—passed safely through the enemy's line of investment, and I trust it will yet win other honors in defense of our rights and the just cause of our country.

GID J. PILLOW, Brig. Gen. C. S. A.

To the Young Men of Arkansas, Texas and Northern Louisiana.

HEADQUARTERS TRANS-MISSISSIPPI DISTRICT,
Department No. 2, Pocahontas, February, 1862.

The question is before us: shall we organize, arm and march to join the army of Missouri, and battle for independence on her soil, where she invites, nay, implores us, to come; or shall we wait to see that gallant and struggling State down-trodden in the dust, manacled and lost—her broad fields and rich granaries opened to supply the tyrant's hordes as they march triumphantly and unopposed to invade our own homes? Shall we strike down the enemy whose gripe is upon our brothers' throat, and who only waits to see HIS last gasp to attack US; or shall we stand by and see our brother perish and meekly await a similar doom? The case is before us for our decision, and it is no dream of the imagination, but a stern reality, and we must decide it. We have VOTED to be free. We must now FIGHT to be free, or present to the world the humiliating spectacle of a nation of braggarts, more contemptible than the tyrants who seek to enslave us.

The flag of our country is waving on the southern borders of Missouri—placed their by my hands under authority from our Chief Magistrate. It represents all that is dear to us in life. Shall it wave there in melancholy loneliness as a fall leaf in our primeval forest, or shall its beautiful field and bright stars flaunt in the breeze over the proud battalions of Arkansas, of Texas and of Louisiana, as they are marshaling to do battle with Missouri for victory, for honor and for independence?

Awake! young men of Arkansas, and arm! Beautiful maidens of Louisiana smile not upon the craven youth who may linger by your hearth when the rude blast of war is sounding in your ear! Texas chivalry, to arms! Hardships and hunger, disease and death are preferable to slavish subjection, and a nation with a bright page in history and a glorious epitaph is better than a vassaled land with honor lost and a people sunk in infamy.

EARL VAN DORN,
Major General.

ITEMS OF INTEREST.

From the Memphis Avalanche, 24.

We have no special list of the killed, wounded and prisoners at Fort Donelson; but there was immense slaughter on both sides. The Federal loss is estimated at 6,000 killed and wounded. Our loss also large—probably, 1,500 killed and wounded. The general opinion seems to number the Confederate loss by surrender about 10,000 of our brave and best men, and at their head Gen. Buckner—one of the best men in our army. He is really a great man. Our prisoners passed Paducah *en route* to Alton, Ill., full of spirit—shouting for Jeff. Davis and the Southern Confederacy! Who does not almost desire to lighten their burdens by dividing them? We almost feel so! Who does not feel willing to fight on in faith and hope as they have done!

The Price reported captured the other day is a son of Gen. Sterling Price, and is a Brigadier General in the Missouri army, appointed in place of Gen. Thos. A. Harris, who was lately elected to Congress.

From the Avalanche, 24th.

The Northern army occupied the city of Nashville yesterday. Whether they arrived there in a large body or a small one, we have not been informed. They made a child's bargain with the citizens who remained; promising to let everybody alone, if everybody would let them alone. Abolitionists are children of the Evil One, and he is the father of liars, and, as a matter of course, the people of Nashville can place as much reliance on the word of one as the other. Vampire like, they will fan them and lull them to sleep with soft words, while they suck their life's blood from them.

Gens. Johnson and Crittenden had formed a junction at Murfreesboro', and are constantly receiving reinforcements, and we shall not be surprised to learn of aggressive movements soon.

Persons reported to have left Johnson's command, say that he entertained no doubt of his ability to reenter Nashville whenever he wished to do. The idea was, that he would try and get Buell between Nashville and the Cumberland.

We learn that some of our citizens are preparing for effective service on the Tennessee river. They will not go in squads of more than five or six. Each man is a practiced shot, with a rifle at long range, and each will go prepared with not less than one hundred rounds. They will take with them nothing but ground coffee, relying upon the citizens and their guns for food. They propose, in these small squads, to guard the Tennessee river. They will take their opportunities from behind trees, logs, and in the narrow bends of the river, to pick off the Lincoln pilots. They can plank a minnie ball in a sheet of foolscap paper, at a distance of six hundred yards; and we venture the assertion, that such a corps of sharp-shooters will be as great a terror to the enemy's boats as our gunboats were at Fort Donelson. Let each county bordering on the Tennessee river, in West Tennessee, send a squad of such men on this duty, and the pilots will soon refuse to ascend a stream where death awaits them behind any big tree. A man may face a known or seen danger; but when he cannot divine how, from what quarter, and at what moment the arrow may be sped, he will shrink from it with an unaccountable dread.

We take the following from the Washington correspondence of the Richmond Examiner:

Lincoln is kept daily informed of everything done in Southland. He knows every gun that is to be casemated, and all the localities where your gunboats are to be built. The number of petticoat spies coming North increases as the tragedy approaches a *denouement*. Until this meretricious intercourse be suppressed by some agency or other, rely upon it your faircity, and the Old Dominion herself, cannot be safe, no! not for a week at a time. You are at any moment liable to be startled by the announcement of the approach of an overwhelming army within three days march of your capitol. It is the Yankee system of espionage which has given rise to the series of expeditions whose blows have not yet been delivered. The mortar expedition soon to be hurled against you may render your uncasemated guns untenable; and there is to be a large fleet of steamers collected in the Potomac below your batteries. These, it is said, will be capable of transporting one hundred thousand men across the river in a day. Some will pronounce this a CASSANDRA cry—let them do so! The time must come when the world will see that your greatest blunder was the policy of permitting so many men, women and children to leave the Confederacy after the breaking out of the war.

* * * * * * * * * *

It is believed here that one hundred and fifty of your regiments will go out of service in April and May, leaving only two hundred and fifty, or one hundred and seventy-five thousand effective men, in the field to contend against five hundred thousand, Then will be an advance, be the consequences what they may.

WASHINGTON, Feb. 12.—The following is Lieut. Commanding Phillips's official report to flag officer Foot, received to-day at the headquarters of the army by telegraph from Cairo.

GUNBOAT CONESTOGA,
Railroad Crossing Tennessee River.
February 10, 1860.

SIR:—We have returned to this point from an entirely successful expedition to Florence, at the foot of the Muscle Shoals in Alabama.

The rebels were forced to leave six steamers, and we captured two others, besides the half-complete gunboat Eastport.

The steamers burned were freighted with rebel military stores.

The Eastport has about 250,000 feet of lumber on board.

We captured two hundred stand of arms and a quantity of clothing and stores, and we destroy the encampment of Col. Crews, at Savannah Tennessee.

We found the Union sentiment strong.

Speculators please read this.

In a letter written in 1779 to Joseph Reed, President of Pennsylvania," General George Washington, in writing of extortioners, who were profiting on the public necessity, said: "It gives me sincere pleasure to find that the Assembly is so well disposed to second your endeavors in bringing those *murderers of our cause*, the monopolizers, forestallers, and engrossers, to condign punishment. It is much to be lamented that each State, long ere this, has not hunted them down as pests to society, and the greatest enomies we have to the happiness of America. I would to God that some one of the more atrocious in each State was hung in gibbets upon a gallows five times as high as the one prepared for HAMAN. No punishment, in my opinion, is too severe for the man who can build his greatness upon his country's ruin."

Condensed Correspondence.

WACO, Feb. 28.—The news of our reverses in Tennessee is arousing our whole population. Capt. Coke's company is about full, other companies are filling up rapidly. Rev. Mr. Daves of the Methodist church has exchanged the pulpit for the army, and is making up a company. Capt. John Stone is also making up a company. We have five full companies and nearly three more from McLennan in for the war.

WEATHERFORD, Feb. 12.—Parker county has one company in Ford's regiment, one in Sibley's Brigade, one in Nelson's regiment, one in Bates' regiment, one in Griffin's regiment, and one other company now ready for the best regiment that offers There are two or three more being raised. Parker has besides this her quota in the frontier regiment. Parker is a frontier county, is liable to Indian raids, and has certainly done as well as any county for the army. We want ammunition very much. With that the old men and boys could fight the Indians while the regular fighting men are in the army. I have four sons in the army, and am over 50 years old, but I could shoot tolerably well yet.

BRENHAM, March 1.—Your suggestion about the Governor moving his office is a good one. If the Governor will establish his headquarters at Houston, infuse some of his own energy into the military and people, establish pony expresses to all important points, he will win the gratitude of his country by securing its defences against invasion.

The Camden Confederate.

VOLUME I. CAMDEN, SO. CA., FRIDAY, MARCH 7, 1862. NUMBER 19.

The Camden Confederate

IS PUBLISHED EVERY FRIDAY BY

J. T. HERSHMAN,

AT TWO DOLLARS A YEAR,

PAYABLE INVARIABLY HALF-YEARLY IN ADVANCE.

Terms for Advertising:

For one Square—fourteen lines or less—ONE DOLLAR for the first, and FIFTY CENTS for each subsequent insertion.

OBITUARY NOTICES, exceeding one Square, charged for at advertising rates.

Transient Advertisements and Job Work MUST BE PAID FOR IN ADVANCE.

No deduction made, except to our regular advertising patrons.

ADVERTISING TERMS PER ANNUM.

One Square, 3 months,	$5
" " 6 "	8
" " 12 "	12
Two Squares, 3 months,	8
" " 6 "	13
" " 12 "	18
Three Squares 3 mos.,	12
" " 6 "	18
" " 12 "	25
Four Squares 3 mos.,	16
" " 6 "	24
" " 12 "	30

☞ Eight dollars per annum for every additional square.

BUSINESS, and PROFESSIONAL CARDS EIGHT DOLLARS a-year. All advertisements for less than three months CASH. If the number of insertions is not specified *in writing advertisements, will be continued till ordered out, and charged accordingly.*

Announcing CANDIDATES, *three months, Five Dollars over that time,* the usual rates will be charged.

No advertisement, however small, will be considered less than a square; and transient rates charged on all for a less time than three months.

TO TRAVELLERS.

—:o:—

SCHEDULE

OF THE

SOUTH CAROLINA RAIL ROAD.

NORTHERN ROUTE.

STATIONS.	DAY TRAINS.	NIGHT TRAINS.
Leave Charleston........	7.00 a m	8.15 p m
Arrive at Kingsville, the Junction of the Wilmington & Manchester R. R..	2,45 p m	3,15 a m
Arrive at Columbia........	4 00 p m	5.0C a m
Arrive at Camden........	4.40 p m	....
Leave Camden...........	5.20 a m	....
Leave Columbia..........	6.15 a m	5.30 p m
Leave Kingsville, the Junction of the Wilmington & Manchester Railroad..	6.45 a m	3.25 p. m
Arrive at Charleston......	3.00 p m	2.30 a. m.

WESTERN ROUTE.

STATIONS.	DAY TRAINS.	NIGHT TRAINS
Leave Charleston.........	7.00 a m	6.30 p m
Arrive at Augusta........	2.45 p m	4.30 p m
Leave Augusta............	8.00 a m	7.30 p m
Arrive at Charleston......	3.30 p m	4.30 a m

THROUGH TRAVEL BETWEEN AUGUSTA AND KINSGVILLE

STATIONS.	DAY TRAINS.	NIGHT TRAINS.
Leave Augusta............	8.00 a m	7.30 p m
Arrive at Kingsville.......	2,45 p m	3.15 a m
Leave Kingsville..........	6.45 a m	3.25 p m
Arrive at Augsta	1.15 p m	11.15 p m

MID-DAY TRAIN BETWEEN CAMDEN AND KINGSVILLE,

MONDAY, WEDNESDAY, AND SATURDAY.

DOWN.	UP.
Leave Camden, 11.40a. m.	Leave Kingsville, 8.5 a. m.
Leave Boykin's, 12.12p. m	Leave Clarkson's 8.20 "
Leave Claremont 1.248 "	Leave Manchester Junction 8.38 a. m.
Leave Middleton 1,10 "	Leave Middleton 8.43
Leave Manchester Junction 1.18, p. m.	Leave Claremont 9.08 "
Leave Clarkson's 1.38 "	Leave Boykin's 9.48 "
Arrive at Kingsville 1.50,	Arrive at Camden, 10.20

Nov. 8—tf H. T. PEAKE, Gen'l Sup't.

Oats and Cow Peas

FOR SALE FOR CASH, AT THE OLD CORNER.

November 1 E. W. BONNEY.

Notice.

I HAVE THIS DAY, OCTOBER 24, SOLD OUT my entire stock of Goods, Wares and Merchandise, in the town of Camden, to J. M. Springer, Esq., who will continue the business at the same stand I have occupied heretofore in the said town. All persons who are in anywise indebted to me, will please make payment of the same to said J. M. Springer, at an early day; and all who have claims against me will present them to him for settlement.

December 13 R. SPRINGER.

STATE OF SOUTH CAROLINA.

EXECUTIVE COUNCIL CHAMBER,
February 20, 1862.

THE FOLLOWING RESOLUTIONS, adopted by the Governor and Council, have been ordered to be published:

Resolved, That the Chiefs of the Treasury be directed to ascertain the amount of gold and silver plate belonging to the citizens of this State, with a view of hereafter taking and melting such portion thereot as may be necessary to constitute the basis of future circulation to provide means for public defence, if such shall be deemed necessary; and to accomplish the object of this resolution, they are hereby authorized to direct the Tax Collector of each District to execute such duties as they may require, with power to administer the usual oaths in receiving tax reurns.

Resolved, That the Mayors and Councils of the cities of Charleston and Columbia shall be and they are hereby authorized to take such steps as are necessary to prevent the selling of spirits to troops in service, and, if necessary for this purpose, to close any or all bar rooms and grog-shops in the said cities, and that the Chief of Justice and Police do give the necessary instructions on the subject.

Resolved, That exemptions to railroad employees shall hereafter be extended only to such persons as are necessary for the business of the roads, and that the Adjutant-General be instructed to respect no exemptions except upon certificate of the Presidents or Superintendants of the roads that the employee is indispensable to the business of the roads, and that the same work cannot be performed by negroes.

Resolved, That fifty thousand dollars be set aside to encourage and force forward the manufacture of salt, and that the Chief of Justice and Police be authorized to execute this in such manner as he may think best for the State.

Extract from minutes of February 19.

Whereas, the enormous and rapid consumption, by distilation, of the grain crop of this State is materially lessening the quantity and enhancing the price of those cereals required for the support of our armies and sustenance of the people: therefore, be it

Resolved, That from and after the tenth day of March next, the distillation of spirits from Indian corn, rye, wheat, barley or other grain shall be and the same is hereby prohibited, during the continuance of the present war, except upon the terms hereinafter provided.

Resolved, That the Governor and Council may, upon the payment of such sums as they may impose in their discretion, grant a license to distill to any person giving bond, with good surety, to be approved by the Clerk of the Court of the District in which he lives, in the penalty of five thousand dollars, conditioned that he will not sell any portion of the spirits distilled to any person other than an authorized agent of the Government of the Confederate States or of this State: *And provided further*, That the person executing said bond shall endorse on the same an affidavit that he will not, in any case, wilfully violate the conditions thereof.

Resolved, That any person distilling without a license as above provided, shall be deemed guilty of a misdemeanor, and shall be liable to a fine not exceeding ten thousand dollars, and imprisonment not exceeding twelve months.

Resolved, That any person licensed to distill, who shall violate the conditions of his license bond, shall, in addition to the forfeiture of the bond, be deemed guilty of a misdemeanor, and subject to the same penalty as above.

Resolved, That in either of the above cases, the distillery itself shall be deemed a nuisance, and subject to be abated.

Extract from the minutes of February 20.

By order of the Governor and Council.

F. J. MOSES, JR., Secretary.

Feb. 21 1

☞ All papers in the State copy twice.

Notice.

THIS IS TO CAUTION ALL PERSONS FROM trading for a Note given to Mr. M. K. Black, for about two hundred and seventy dollars, dated the early part of the present year, and signed by "Sutherland & Lemond and James Dunlap"—the said note having been lost, and since settled, by a new paper. It was given for the hire of *Phil* and *Charles* for the year 1861. E. W. BONNEY.

December 20

From Richmond.

MARTIAL LAW IN RICHMOND—THE WHISKEY QUESTION—ARRIVAL OF THE NASHVILLE.

RICHMOND, March 2.—The President has issued a proclamation declaring martial law in Richmond and in the country for ten miles around the city, and suspending all civil jurisdiction except that of the Mayor of Richmond; also suspending, under authority of Congress, the writ of *habeas corpus*. All distilleries are ordered to be closed, and sales of liquors of any kind are prohibited. The establishments for the sale thereof are to be closed.

The steamer Nashville arrived at Beaufort, N. C., on Sunday morning last. The blockading vessels fired 22 shots at her without effect. She brings about 3,000,000 worth stores, principally for the use the Confederate Departments. She met and destroyed, near the Gulf Stream, a Yankee schooner, bound from Philadelphia to St. Domingo. The Nashville steamed up to the blockading squadron in defiant style, and though at one time within musket shot of the enemy's guns until protected by the guns of Fort Macon, and beyond her chagrined pursuers. Com. Pegram and Paymaster Taylor have arrived in Richmond, and a portion of the Nashville's freight is now being delivered in front of the Treasury Department. Com. Pegram speaks in glowing terms of the hospitalities which he enjoyed in England. He thinks that Belgium will soon recognize the South. The authorities at Bermuda have prohibited the Yankees from coaling there. The Sumter is at Gibralter and at last accounts had captured and destroyed 21 Yankee vessels.

EDWIN DELEON.—Many friends of Edwin DeLeon, in this his native State, will be gratified in reading the following from the New Orleans *Delta*:

"Mr. Edwin DeLeon, late Consul of the old United States in Egypt, and so well remembered throughout the South as one of the ablest champions of our cause, has reached our city after a very adventurous voyage. Mr. DeLeon came in the Victoria, whose narrow escape from one of the blockading squadron off the entrance into Barataria Bay has been already related. It was certainly rather a rough reception of a gentleman on his return to his native country, after nine year's absence, to be greeted by a broadside from a ship-of-war. To make this still more trying, Mr. DeLeon was accompanied by his wife, an English lady, on her first visit to her husband's home. Mr. DeLeon is the bearer of despatches from our commissioners in Europe, and his representation of the sentiment of the people both in England and in France, as strongly in our favor, concurs with the statements of other gentlemen who have had the opportunities of acquainting themselves with the views of those people and Governments.

AUGUSTA.—The *Constitutionalist*, in allusion to the security of Augusta against a gunboat raid, says:

"For the benefit of those who have any apprehensions about Augusta, we will state that Mayor May has been in consultation with the State and military authorities on the subject, and that Gen. Lee has given the necessary orders to have the river obstructed in case of necessity. This can be very easily, readily and effectively done. Besides this, a Yankee gunboat will hardly be able to pass the batteries at Savannah, if they should feel disposed to to make the attempt. Our citizens and our friends abroad, therefore, need have no fears for the safety of Augusta."

An extensive gun factory has been set in operation at Holly Springs Miss. A considerable number of gun-barrels are rolled out every day, and contracts have been entered into to supply the Government with 30,000 guns in a short time.

CONFEDERATE POSTAGE STAMPS.—The five cents stamps hereafter issued will be blue, and the ten cents red, as announced officially.

A Wise Measure.

The Mayor of Charleston has ordered the bar rooms to be closed. The war times demand it, and we hope to see the example followed in our city, and in the cities and towns generally.

The stoppage of the distilleries is a matter of first moment, and we trust a prohibition will be extended to all but those for the Government hospital purposes. The number in our upper districts is astounding. We have the best authority that there are one hundred and fifteen stills running in one of them.

The amount of corn used at each still is twenty bushels a day. No wonder corn should be selling in Charleston at $2. The question is of importance, whether bread or poison is to be distributed to our brave soldiers, whose arms will be strengthened by keeping their heads clear.—*Carolinian.*

THE WAR IN VIRGINIA.—Gen. Johnston has published a very severe but admirable general order, in relation to the conduct of our troops in battle. Before going into battle every captain will call the roll of his company, and coming out of action will again call the roll, and every man missing, who is not dead, wounded or absent on leave, will be court-martialed for cowardice. Carrying the wounded from the field in the midst of an action is also prohibited and every man going to the rear on any pretence whatever will be shot by the file officers. This looks like business.—*Mercury of the 3d instant.*

RETURNED TO THEIR OLD QUARTERS.—Nine of the Federal prisoners who recently escaped from confinement in this city, were returned to their old quarters on Friday—a portion of them were caught in Fairfield District, and the balance in Union. We learn that the citizens of Union are in pursuit of three more. The following are the names of those captured: Fernando Brown, George D. Drury, Ralston Walker, James Huiy, H. Blanchard, C. B. Moore, J. G. Tuttle, T. E. Pomeroy, S. H. Wats.—*Carolinian.*

FROM MANASSAS.—The Lynchburg *Republican* of Thursday says:

A number of ladies—the wives of officers and others in the army—arrived here yesterday evening from Manassas, having left that place in obedience to an order from General Johnston. This, in conjunction with sending off the sick, is conjectured to mean either that an advance of the enemy is anticipated, or our army will make some movement. We are inclined to suppose the latter to be the case.

It is a question deserving and demanding attention and answer whether cravens who have guns, pistols or swords, which they will not use in defence of their wives and homes should be permitted to charge more than three times the original cost, when good citizens and true men offer to purchase. No good merchant or tradesman will become a broker or agent for such cowardly extortioners.—*Charleston Courier.*

A despatch to the Memphis *Avalanche*, from Clarksville, estimates the force of the enemy engaged in the recent attack upon Fort Donelson at 75,000, that of the Confederates at 12,000. Among the killed was Lieut.-Col. Clough, of Texas, and Major Hewitt of the 3d Kentucky regiment. Gen. Buckner, with most of his command, surrendered Sunday morning.

The English seamen who left Norfolk on Thursday in the flag of truce steamer for Old Point, were on Friday sent back to that city by order of Gen. Wool. The cause assigned for this move was, that they were the crew of the Fingall, which run the blockade some time since.

Gen. Beauregard has ordered all the itinerant store keepers away from Columbus, and forbid the selling of liquor within ten miles, or its introduction into camp.

J. T. HERSHMAN, Editor.

FRIDAY, MARCH 7, 1862.

Capt. J. D. Kennedy,

Of the Camden Volunteers, arrived on Wednesday last, from Manassas. He is enjoying fine health, and reports that of his company excellent. The object of his visit is to obtain a few more recruits. We have no doubt he will secure his number in a few days, as those who know him, and for what purpose he is here, will readily respond, if they intend to enter the service at all. He may be seen at McKain's Drug Store, from 10 a. m. to 5 p. m., daily. Those who wish to enroll themselves with him, must make application without delay. A bounty of $50, on entering his list, and commutation for rations allowed until required to leave for the Potomac.

Wayside Hospital, or Soldiers Rest.

We have been informed by several ladies that a Soldier's Wayside Resting Place was in contemplation, but those having the matter in hand have not thought publicity through the paper necessitous, or, perhaps, they have abandoned the idea altogether—we hope not the latter. And we have, too, many good charitable people in our District who have no other means of knowing the wants of our soldiers, except through the press. If it is a private or select matter, we ask pardon for having made reference to it at all. The use of our columns have, long since, been offered for all benevolent purposes.

Why the Nashville Brought no Arms.

Some disappointment was expressed by almost every one, that the Nashville had brought no arms from Europe, for the use of the Government. When, however, it is recollected that the Nashville was tolerated in English waters, and protected from destruction by the neutrality and courtesy of the British Government our readers will at once perceive that to have taken in a cargo of war material such as has been interdicted by the Queen's proclamation, would have been a gross violation not only of hospitality, but of courtesy and the laws of neutrality. The Nashville, it must be remembered, is a Government war ship, and not a merchantman.

Affairs in Tennessee.

We have learned from good authority, says the Savannah *Republican* of the 3d inst., that Johnston left Mufreesboro with his forces some days ago, and fell back on Stephson, where the Nashville and Memphis and Charleston Railroads unite. We feel assured that Johnston is making the very best disposition possible of the forces under his command, and have already learned enough to convince us that no fault lies at his door for any mishap that may have occurred. Perhaps nobody is to blame. We commenced the revolution against a nation three times our number and completely armed, and should not be supprised when the reverses overtake us.

North-western Virginia.—A report was brought down by passengers on the cars yesterday that seventeen Yankee regiments were at Leesburg; that General Jackson has been compelled to fall back upon Winchester, and that General Johnston was moving reinforcements to him at that place. Nothing confirmatory of this report had been received at the War Department; but as it comes by a gentleman who is well known in the city, and was circulated yesterday very generally among some of our public men, we mention it as not an improbable story.—*Richmond Examiner.*

War Upon the Distilleries.—Gov. Brown of Georgia has issued a proclamation commanding every distiller in the State to cease manufacturing ardent spirits after the 15th March instant, under a penalty of seizure of the property thus employed. In case of distillers refusing to obey this order, their stills are to be seized and manufactured into cannon.

Brig. Gen. Bushrod Johnson of Tennessee, who was among the prisoners taken by the Yankees at Fort Donelson, succeded in making his escape and arrived safely at Mufreesboro, on Sunday last. He states that on account of their terrible loss, the enemy was not at all exultant over their victory.

The snow in the Northern section of New York is lying to the depth of five or six feet. Fears are entertained of an inundation along the Hudson and Mohawk.

News from the West.

The following is from the latest Tennessee papers:

THE ENEMY IN NASHVILLE.

Nashville is occupied by the enemy's forces to the number of 8000, commanded by Gen. Buell. The invadors are quartered in the Capitol and all the public buildings of the city, over all of which the stars and stripes are waiving. They are rapidly erecting fortifications—guns, batteries, &c., at every point of approach to the city. The city appears almost literally deserted. Ladies are never seen upon the streets, and the inhabitants keep themselves close. Neil S. Brown and several other prominent citizens have been arrested.

Gen. Buell has entered Nashville, and made a speech to the citizens, in which he disclaimed any purpose of molesting private rights. The U. S. flag was hoisted upon the capitol, amid the cheers of some of the traitors who remained in the city. Buell had issued a proclamation, in which he offers amnesty to all who will take the oath to support the Federal Government.

HOW THE CITY WAS SURRENDERED.

The accounts which we get of the surrender of Nashville are most humiliating. When Mayor Cheatham first offered to surrender the city to the Federal officer in command of the Lincoln cavalry, he declined to accept it, stating as a reason that he was not authorized to accept it. Scouts afterwards went out, in various directions, hunting for a Federal officer with power to act, but after going some twenty or thirty miles they could not find a Federal soldier anywhere.

At last the city was formally surrendered by Mayor Cheatham on Sunday. It is true that the Federals had not previously entered the city, but a regiment of cavalry had encamped in the town of Edgefield, a short distance from Nashville. It was to this point that Mayor Cheatham repaired, and formally tendered the city with all the public stores it contained, to the commander of the Federal forces. The Federals seemed loath to believe that the city had really been surrendered, and accordingly only sent over fifteen men to take possession—and even these seemed to be on the lookout for a surprise of some sort.

There was a large amount of bacon and other army stores in the city of Nashville, and Col. Forrest, of Memphis, was engaged up to Sunday afternoon attending on the saving and transportation of the same. While engaged in this service, Mayor Cheatham opposed, and told him to desist, he having formally given up the same to the Federal officer. Those of us who know Col. Forrest can imagine what his reply would be to such an order. He told the Mayor that he ranked all officers then in the city, that he was a Confederate officer, and that if he did not desist from interference, he would take force. Subsequently, a lot of low flung characters about the city commenced a series of depradations upon private property, and the Mayor being powerless to repress them, it is reported that Col. Forrest took a detachment and meeting them in the public square, killed five of them before they were dispersed.

A Chattanooga correspondent of the Knoxville *Register*, in giving an account of the panic at Nashville, says:

It seems that Gen. Johnston informed the authorities of the city on Sunday last, that he could not hold it, although no enemy was near, or threatened it. Immediately all was consternation and alarm. The Governor and Legislature fled panic-stricken. With this example set them, nothing better could be expected of the citizens! Mr. V. K. Stevenson, Quartermaster-General, and President of the Nashville and Chattanooga Railroad, etc., fled. Early Monday morning he loaded several cars with his personal effects, including his own sacred person, and hastened to this city, where he has ever since remained. By his direction all the rolling stock was hurried to this end of the road, and no effort, or next to none, was made to bring any of the Government property from the doomed city. Nearly a week has elapsed, and no enemy has approached. During this time every pound of bacon and ordnance and quartermaster stores could easily have been removed to Murfresboro, if not further. Instead of this being done, the doors of the storehouses were thrown open, and the people invited to carry off all they wished, and the torch applied to the rest! Was ever such wanton abandonment and destruction of property? The railroad bridge at Nashville and the suspension bridge were both burned.

Clarksville has been formally occupied by Gen. Foote, who has issued an order promising not to interfere with the business movements of the place, and to respect private property, and holding the municipal authorities responsible for the good order of the place. He also requires that all the Confederate property be surrendered up, and that his operations be not interfered with.

At the last acconnts, a force of the enemy was approaching Paris, Tenn., being only seven miles from there. The Confederate cavalry force which has been stationed there since the Fort Henry affair, had left those parts; hence the advance of the Federals upon the town.—That they will take it, there can be little doubt. There is, therefore, another panic at Paris.—The people are fleeing in every direction. A number of families came down upon the train last night, and a car load of negroes.

Major H. W. Fry's P. P. C. to the Yankees at Roanoke.—From Saturday, the day of the surrender of Roanoke, till the following Wednesday, Major Fry was confined in a room in the house of Dr. Ritters, on the island. In this room the Major discovered a portion of a keg of power, the private property of Dr. Riiters. On Wednesday morning, understanding that he was that day to be removed on shipboard, the Major took about twenty pounds of the powder and rolling it in a sheet, made a sort of a cartridge, and rammed it up the pipe of a stove that stood in the room. In the course of an hour after completing this job, the Major was removed, and his mind being otherwise occupied, thought little more of it. From some of our wounded who had been left at Elizabeth City, and who arrived here last night, we are informed that one rainy day last week the Yankees, for the first time, built a fire in the stove. In a few minutes the explosion took place, blowing the house to ruins, and killing and wounding fifteen or twenty Yankees. The accuracy of the above is beyond question.—*Richmond Examiner.*

Nashville News.—A gentleman just from Gen. Critenden's command at Mufresboro' communicates the following items of war news, which we think may be relied upon.

Gen. Buell has entered Nashville, and made a speech to the citizens, in which he disclaimed any purpose of molesting private rights. The United States flag was hoisted upon the capitol, amid the cheers of some of the citizens, who remained in the city. Gen. Buell has issued a proclamation, in which he offers amnesty to all who will take the oath to support the Federal Government. Such proclamations were issued, is will be remembered, in North-Western Virginia, and in the Virginia Peninsula. We know how the vandals kept faith. Can there be Tennesseeans so gullible as to swallow this stale bate?—*Knoxville Register, February 27th.*

Death of Willie Lincoln.—Willie Lincoln, second son of President Lincoln, died on the evening of the 20th. In consequence of this event the public buildings and the private residences of the heads of departments in Washington were not illuminated on the evening of of the 22d ultimo, as previously arranged. The youngest son was dangerously ill and it was feared could not recover.

Arrest of "Union Men" in Richmond.—The *Examiner* says that John Minor Botts, Valentine Heckler, Franklin Stearnes and several other "Union Men" have been arrested in Richmond and confined to jail. Many other arrests will be made in the next twenty-four hours.

Run the Blockade.—The steamer General Miramon, it is stated by the Mobile *Register* has made a successful entry at New Orleans with arms and munitions.

The actual number of prisoners taken at Fort Donelson is 13,300. Among them is Gen. West, who has not previously been mentioned.

Major General Loring has been appointed to take command of all the forces near the North Carolina coast and South of Norfolk.

"I'm getting fat," as a theif said when he was stealing lard.

TEREBENE

LIGHT.

—o—

THE SUBSCRIBERS HAVING INVENTED A

New and Cheap Oil

FOR BURNING,

offers the same for sale in any quantity. It will burn in any kind of Camphine Lamp, without smoke.

The public are invited to call and see the light, and judge for themselves. An ordinary sized Lamp, filled with the Terebene will give more light than ten sperm candles, at a cost of not more than two cents per hour.

HOCOTT & SUTHERLAND.

Camden, S. C., Dec. 13

Notice.

THE UNDERSIGNED INTENDING TO MAKE a change in his business on the first of January next, will dispose of his stock of goods at *exceedingly low prices,* until that time for cash, or to punctual customers. My object is to turn as many goods as possible into cash, giving the purchaser a LIBERAL bargain for his money.
E. W. BONNEY.

Notice.

REQUIRED IN ALL CASES TO PAY CASH for purchases, and the utter impossibility of making collections, I am compelled to inform my customers, that if no special arrangement is made for short credits on or before, I will adopt the cash system exclusively on the first day of January next.

December 6 W. D. McDOWALL.

January 1st, 1862.

HAVING TO PAY CASH FOR ALL MY PURchases, compels me to change my terms of business after this date.

To enable me to replenish my stock, I shall sell in all instances for cash, unless a *special arrangement be made for a short credit.* All goods sold under this arrangement must be considered as *Cash,* when called for.

The reasons which have induced this necessary change, I trust, will be apparent to all. Cash customers solicited.
E. W. BONNEY

January 3.

Cash Store

NO CREDIT

TO ANYBODY

FOR ANYTHING.

500 LBS. EXTRA COUNTRY LEAF LARD; Rice, Salt, Shoes and 200 lbs. Spices;
Extra white Meal and Hominey;
Southern put up Preserved Peaches;
Wax and Sperm Candles;
Crushed, Clarified and Brown Sugar.

All for Cash, and Cash only.

November 29 1y A. T. LATTA.

Bricks, Lumber, &c.

A FEW THOUSAND SECOND-HAND BRICKS seasoned Flooring BOARDS, SHINGLES, &c., for sale at the "Old Corner," for cash only.

November 1 E. W. BONNEY.

Carpets, Rugs, &c.

CARPETS, RUGS & FLOOR CLOTHS ON SALE, at the "Old Corner," by

November 1 E. W. BNNEY.

Winter Clothing and Hats.

A LOT OF PRIME WINTER CLOTHING— also HATS, in a great variety of styles, for sale by E. W. BONNEY.

November 1

Agency

Lynchburg Hose and Fire nsurance Company.

LYNCHBURG, VA.

—o—

Merchants' Insurance Company,

OF RICHMOND, VA.

Policies in the above Companies issued at usua rates.
W. D. McDOWALL,

November 1 Agent.

In Equity—Kershaw District.

BILL FOR PARTITION, CONSTRUCTION OF WILL, &c.

Thomas Lang *vs.* Edward M. Boykin, Mary E. Boykin, Sallie W. Boykin, Harriet Lang, John C. Lang, Edward B. Lang, Theodore Lang, and Samuel W. L. Lang.

It appearing that the above named John C Lang, Edward B Lang, and Theodore Lang, Defendants reside out of and beyond the limits of this State, it is ordered, on motion of Richardson & Gay Complainants Solicitors, that the said John C. Lang, Edward B. Lang Theodore Lang, do plead, answer, or demur to said Bill, within three months from date hereof, or said Bill will be taken *pro confesso* against them.

It is further ordered, that this order be published in the Camden *Confederate,* for three months, once a week.

December 13 3mo WM. R. TAYLOR, C. E. K. D.

Pure Wines,

FOR MEDICINAL PURPOSES, FOR SALE BY

November 15 J. J. McKAIN.

CIRCULAR.

To the Soldiers' Aid Societies of S. C.

In answer to the numerous enquiries which have been made by the different "Aid Societies which have been recently formed throughout the State, I have been intructed by his Excellency Gov. PICKENS, to give the following information.

Depots will be established by the Quartermaster General, both in Charleston and Columbia, for the reception of all donations of clothing; and he is also charged with the duty of forwarding and distributing the same.

The "Department" will receive all donations of clothing, say frock coats and pantaloons, of heavy worsted goods, shirts and drawers, of heavy homespun or flannel, wool, or heavy cotton socks, blankets, new or second hand, also heavy shoes.

The plan upon which the State designs supplying her soldiers with all necessary clothing, is based upon their willingness to surrender to the State the amount of money appropriated by the Confederate Government for this purpose, say forty-two ($42) per annum, this sum not now being sufficient in consequence of the greatly advanced cost of material. It is in view of this fact that these laudable "Associations" of ladies and gentlemen, are cordially welcomed as coadjutors in this noble work, and in proportion to their voluntary contributions of labor and materials, will the absolute cost of clothing for our gallant volunteers be reduced.

In the event that any of the "Associations" should not feel themselves able to furnish both material and labor, the Quartermaster General is instructed by his Excellency the Governor, to re-imburse such Associations the cost of all materials, at a rate not exceeding similar materials purchased by the "Department;" and the quantity allowed for each garment shall be the same as used in our Manufacturing Bureau.

Societies are particularly requested to advise the Quartermaster General of the quantity of work they can do per week, and the amount of donations they will probably send.

To prevent confusion and loss, the following method for marking packages should be strictly observed. All Societies near Charleston, should ship to Charleston and mark thus:

No. 1. TO QUARTERMASTER GENERAL
CHARLESTON, S. C.

From Aid Society at (here insert place.)

Societies near Columbia, should ship and mark thus

No. 1. TO ASSISTANT QUARTERMASTER,
COLUMBIA, S. C.

From Aid Society (here insert name.)

The packages should be marked distinctly, and numbered from one 1) upwards, A correct invoice should accompany each shipment.

All articles shipped at the expense of the State.

November 8 4 S. S. GLOVER, Q. M. G. S. C.

CONFEDERATE STATES OF AMERICA.

DISTRICT OF SOUTH CAROLINA.

THE UNDERSIGNED HAVING BEEN APpointed Receiver by the Hon. A. G. Magrath for the Districts of Fairfield, Kershaw and Sumter, would most respectfully announce to the citizens of the respective districts, that he is now prepared to discharge the duties that devolve upon him by virtue of said office.

I have no doubt that instances may arise where the duties properly discharged may be disagreeable to the parties interested, but relying upon the patriotism and loyalty of our citizens for their assistance in defending the provisions of the law, I shall expect such assistance to be cheerfully tendered, and in all cases that may arise, yield every consideration in my power, the nature of the case may admit of, to such persons as may be affected by its operation; in the mean time I shall endeavor to do my duty to the full extent and letter of the law, and abide the consequences. The Act of Confiscation on the part of the United States deprives our citizens of the property without hope of remuneration; the act of Sequestration based upon principles recognized by the civilized world is intended to reimburse our citizens of the property thus decreed to belong to our enemies.

I would therefore call upon all the citizens of the Districts aforesaid, to aid me by giving such information as they possess of any property, personal or real. that may belong to any citizen who may be recognized as an "Alien Enemy," also all indebtedness in any manner, shape or form, due or payable to citizens of the United States (except Maryland, Kentucky and Missouri) by the citizens of Fairfield, Kershaw and Sumter.

For the information of those who may be interested I would respectfully call attention to the following provisions of the law

1st. It shall be the duty of every citizen to give all the information he may possess to the proper officers of any lands, tenements, hereditaments, goods, chattels, rights and credits within the Confederacy, as held, owned, possessed or enjoyed by any one, for the use and benefit of any "alien enemy" since 21st May, 1861.

2d. It shall be the duty of every Attorney, Agent, Partner or Trustee holding the property referred to, or having any interest therein for an alien enemy, to inform the Receiver of the same, and to render a strict account thereof, and to place the same (as far as practicable) in the hands of the said Receiver, whereupon such person shall be fully acquitted of all responsibility for property so reported

3d. Any person failing to give such information and render such account shall be guilty of a high misdemeaner, and upon indictment and conviction shall be fined in a sum not exceeding $5000, and imprisoned not longer than six months, and shall further be liabl to pay double the value of such property held by him or subject to his control.

NOTE.—All persons who have a domicil within the States with which this Government is at war, no matter whether they be subjects of Great Britain, France, or any neutral nation, or whether they be citizens of the U. S. or not, if they have a domicil or carry on any trade, traffic or business within such boundaries, they are to be recognized as Alien Enemies under the law.

JAS. R. AIKEN Receiver, C. S. A.

mber 22

M'CURRY & HAMMERSLOUGH,

SUCCESSORS TO THE LATE WM. ANDERSON,

South-East Corner of Broad & DeKalb-Streets,

CAMDEN, SOUTH-CAROLINA,

KEEP CONSTANTLY ON HAND

A FULL SUPPLY OF

CLOTHING, HATS & CAPS,

Boots and Shoes, Crockery Ware, Hollow Ware, Tin Ware,
Iron, Nails, Groceries, &c.

November 1 **TERMS CASH.**

MUTUAL

LIFE INSURANCE.

THE SUBSCRIBER HAVING ACCEPTED THE AGENCY OF THE

MUTUAL LIFE INSURANCE COMPANY,

OF RALEIGH, NORTH CAROLINA, AND THE

SOUTHERN MUTUAL LIFE INSURANCE

COMPANY, OF COLUMBIA, SOUTH CAROLINA,

FOR CAMDEN AND VICINITY, is prepared to receive applications for policies of **LIFE INSURANCE,** on the most reasonable terms. The Lives on SLAVES insured at moderate rates.

WILLIAM L. DePASS, Agent

November 1 North Carolina Mutual Life Insurance Company.

WM. L. DePASS,

ATTORNEY AT LAW,

AND

SOLICITOR IN EQUITY,

CAMDEN, S. C.,

Will practice in Kershaw and the surrounding Districts.
November 1

DRAKEFORD & CO.

WE ARE NOW OPENING AT THE Store lately occupied by R. Latta, one door above the "Old Corner," A FRESH ASSORTMENT OF

HEAVY and FANCY GROCERIES.

We have now in Store

BEST BALTIMORE HAMS,

Fine Lard and Bacon Sides,

GOSHEN CHEESE,

White Bread Corn,

FLOUR, RICE, and MOLASSE

ALSO, SIX DIFFERENT KINDS OF FRESH

BOSTON CRACKERS,

Some very Choice Assorted

Pickles, Candies and Spices,

Corn Starch, for Table Use,

Candles, &c.

ALSO,

Rio and Old Java Coffee,

Sugars, Bagging, Rope, &c.

All for sale at the lowest prices for CASH. Call and purchase.

Sept. 18,—tf.

VERY SUPERIOR SEED POTATOES; FINE Dairy Cheese; Figs and Sugar Raisins. Just received at the "Old Corner"

November 7 E. W. BONNEY.

PLOW STEEL.—Also, Plow Iron in all widths. Also, Plow Moulds and Horse Shoe Nails, Traces, Hames, Saddles, &c. Just received at the "Old Corner."

November 7 E. W. BONNEY.

BACON, Sides and Shoulders, of Baltimore curing and very fine for sale at the 'old corner,' by
E. W. BONNEY.

Alabama

Fire, Insurance

COMPANY.

THE Undersigned, as Agent for the above Southern Insurance Company, is prepared to issue policies of Insurance against loss by Fire on all Buildings, &c.

November 1 W. L. DEPASS.

FALL & WINTER

GOODS.

WE INVITE THE ATTENTION of our friends and the public generally to our stock of

FALL AND WINTER

GOODS,

Which is complete in all its various branches.

AND WILL BE SOLD FOR CASH ONLY.

McCURRY & HAMMERSLOUGH.

November 1

Fall Goods.

THE SUBSCRIBER HAS ON HAND OF HIS last Fall purchases:

Super Black Bombazines.
" 5-4 Black all-wool DeLane.
" " " Cashmere and Merino.
" " " Plain and Drilled Alapaccas.
" 4-4 " English Crape.
Colored English Merino.
" Printed DeLanes.
Domestic, Welch and Saxony Flannel.
Merino Vests for children, Misses, ladies, boys & men
" Drawers, for Ladies and Men.
" Union Dresses for Ladies.

Jaconets, Cambrics, Checks, Swiss Parlaton Muslins, White Brilliantes and Dimity Embroideries. Edgings and Insertings, Laces, Linen Cambric Handkerchiefs, Plain, Hemstitch and Embroidered. A good stock of English Cotton Hose and Half Hose, with a fair stock of other goods suitable for families' Fall use.
W. D. McDOWALL.

November 1

Good Servants to Hire.

A GOOD COOK, WASHER and IRONER.

ALSO,

A No. 1 Bricklayer and Plasterer. Also, a good House boy and Farmer. All of whom can be hired to approved persons, by making early application to this office, or Mr. I. B. ALEXANDER.

December 6

STATE OF SOUTH CAROLINA.

HEADQUARTERS, March 5, 1861.

THE PRESIDENT OF THE CONFEDERate States, through the Secretary of War, has called on me, as Governor of South Carolina, to furnish five more regiments for and during the war.

Now, then, under this requisition, I do hereby call for men to come forward as volunteers, individually and separately, or by companies now formed of not less than sixty-eight aggregate to the principles laid down in the resolutions of the Council hereunto attached. Tenders of service will be made in writing to the Adjutant General's office in Columbia. Those volunteering as individuals will be formed into companies as soon as possible, the officers to be appointed by the Governor and Council.

The Secretary of War, in his requisition, says, that "each soldier will receive a bounty of fifty dollars when the Regiment or Company is mustered into service, and will be allowed transportation from his home to the place of rendezvous," and will also be clothed, supplied and armed at the expense of the Confederate States. No man liable to duty will be allowed to enter any other company now in service for any term until this requisition for five infantry regiments be complied with. If these Regiments are not formed by volunteers by the 20th instant, then a conscription will be made to meet the balance of the requisition, upon principles which will be announced in general orders of detail issued by the Chief of the Military Department, in connection with the Adjutant and Inspector-General.

I need not make an appeal to the people to meet this requisition. The country is in danger. We have met with reverses. There is no alternative. We must fight for our homes and our altars. No people are fit to be free unless they are willing to march through the perils of severe conflict and battle. This State was the cradle of the revolution. Let her sons now hang out their battle flags from every home. Let us make the State one entrenched camp, and, if we are to fall, let every freeman find, at least, a soldier's grave. Let all come to their country's call. If we are brave and true, there is no permanent danger. Without difficulty and peril, independence itself would not be valued. No people were ever free without dangers and struggles. Our true safety is to meet every danger with more indomitable courage, and to rise higher with any and every disaster. In the war of our first revolution, South Carolina passed through far more desperate trials. Under the guide of the God of Battles, we must rise to our destiny, and from our very defeats gather renewed strength in the defence of our firesides and of our homes.

Given under my hand and the seal of the State at Columbia, this the 5th day of March, in the year of our Lord one thousand eight hundred and sixty-two, and of the independenre of the State of South Carolina the eighty-sixth. [L.S.]

F. W. PICKENS.

Resolved, by the Governor and Council, That in view of the great requisition for troops for the war by the Confederate Government, no person not now under orders, subject to military duty in South Carolina, shall be permitted to enter Confederate service for a less time than for the war.

Resolved, That the Chief of the Military Department, together with the Adjutant-General, proceed at once to devise a scheme by which all the arms-bearing white male inhabitants of South Carolina, between the ages of eighteen and forty-five, shall be enrolled, as well as those now in service for a less period than the war, as those not in service, from which roll the troops raised shall be subject, by lot, except such volunteers as shall come in as hereinafter provided.

Resolved, That the individual volunteers, for infantry service, will be received until the 20th of March instant, who shall be organized into companies, battalions and regiments—all officers to be appointed and assigned by the Governor and Council, and the troops so organized shall be mustered immediately into Confederate service.

Resolved, That infantry companies already formed, in accordance with the Confederate regulations, volunteering for the war, will be received with their own company officers—the field officers to be appointed by the Governor and Council.

Extract from the minutes of March 3d.

F. J. MOSES, JR., Secretary.

☞ All papers in the State will publish the above proclamation and resolutions until the 20th of March instant, the daily papers publishing every other day.

March 7 7

Muslins, Lawns, &c.,

FOR LADIES' DRESSES, ON SALE, AT THE "Old Corner." E. W. BONNEY.

March 7

Starch! Starch!!

A SMALL LOT OF FINE PURE PEARL STARCH, for sale low, at the "Old Brick Corner," by T. S. MYERS.

March 7 3

Flour Jars,

IN ANY SIZE, JUST OPENED, AT THE "OLD Corner," by E. W. BONNEY.

March 7

STATE OF SOUTH CAROLINA.

EXECUTIVE COUNCIL CHAMBER, March 4, 1862.

THE FOLLOWING RESOLUTION, aopted by the Governor and Council, has been ordered to be published:

Resolved, That the seventh section of an Act entitled "An Act to amend and suspend certain portions of the Militia and Patrol Laws of this State," passed 7th of December, 1861, be altered and amended to read as follows: "That all persons required to perform ordinary militia duty shall be called out for company muster and drill at least once in each month, except those belonging to Beat Companies within the corporate limits of any cities of this State, or within the corporate limits of any town or village containing not less than five hundred inhabitants, including slaves and free persons of color; and all persons in such cities, towns and villages required to perform ordinary militia duty shall be called out for company muster and drill at least once in every two weeks; and in case of default, in either case, to be liable to the same fines and forfeitures now provided by law."

Extract from minutes of March 4th.

By order of the Governor and Council.

F. J. MOSES, Jr., Secretary.

March 7 1

☞ All papers in the State copy once.

STATE OF SOUTH CAROLINA.

ADJUTANT & INSPECTOR GENL'S OFFICE, CHARLESTON, S. C., February 27, 1862.

GENERAL ORDER No. 5.

I. COMPANIES, BATTALLIONS AND Regiments will be accepted to serve "for and during the present war." *No ad'ition ! troops will be received for a shorter term.*

II. Accepted Companies only will be permitted to recruit for twelve months' service until they have the required number.

III. Persons exempted from active service are required to forihwith enroll themselves in Reserve Companies.

IV. No person between the age of 18 and 45 will be permitted to join the Reserves, unless his exemption has been endorsed and approved at this office, or by the Surgeon-General of the State.

By command: S. R. GIST,

Adj. and Inspector-Gen. of S. C.

March 7 1.

Notice.

ALL GUARDIANS, TRUSTEES, &c, WHO are, by law, required to account annually to the Court of Equity for Kershaw District, S. C., will please file their returns with the Commissioner of said Court, on or before the 10th day of March next. Rules will be issued against all defaulters, immediately WM. R. TAYLOR, C. E. K. D.

Commissioner's Office, Feb. 13, 1862.

Februory 21

Apple Brandy.

SEVERAL BARRELS EXTRA FINE APPLE BRANDY, five years old. in store and for sale low for cash, at the "Old Brick Corner"

January 31 3mo T. S. MYERS.

Notice.

ON AND AFTER THE FIRST DAY OF JANUary, I will sell no goods on credit. Cash sales only—and invite all those indebted to me to make immediate payment, or failing to do so will find their notes and accounts in the hands of an attorney for collection. Immediate attention to the above is required. T. S. MYERS.

January 3 3mo

Crockery and Glassware.

A GOOD ASSORTMENT OF CROCKERY AND Glassware on hand, and for sale low at the "Old Corner," by E. W. BONNEY.

February 14

Blanket Shawls

ALL WOOL BLANKET SHAWLS, SUITABLE for Soldier's Shirts, for sale at the "Old Corner," by E. W. BONNEY.

February 14

NOTICE.

RECRUITS WANTED.—ALL PERSONS WHO are desirous of enlisting in my company, now serving in Virginia, are requested to come forward and enroll their names. Congress allows a bounty of fifty dollars to each persons who enlists.

February 21 E. B. CANTEY, Captain.

The Cash System

HAS BEEN FORCED UPON US BY OUR inability to obtain the means of continuing our business from any other source. Our customers will therefore please take notice that we will henceforth fill no orders (unaccompanied by cash) whether for goods from our store or for work from our shop, unless under *previous special arrangements, distinctly made with us.* J. J. WORKMAN & CO.

January 10

Notice.

WE WILL SELL GOODS DURING 1862 FOR cash only. No books or memorandums will be will be kept. No goods will be allowed to leave the store until fully settled for. No orders will be filled unless accompanied by the cash. This notice is intended for one and all; and we very much hope that no one will ask us to depart from this rule, as we are determined to adhere to it without respect of persons.

Dec 20 3m MARONEY, BOSWELL & BRO.

WORSTED DRY GOODS.

ALSO RICH SILK DRESSES, WITH A LARGE quantity of Embroideries, &c., for sale at cost, for cash, at the "Old Corner" E. W. BONNEY.

January 24

Notice.

WE HAVING DISCONTINUED THE CREDIT system entirely, all orders must be accompanied with the cash, or its equivalent. Special agreements, or those we are indebted to, accepted.

December 27 KOOPMANN & SOMMERS.

Notice.

CREDIT SALES, AS HERETOFORE, WILL BE discontinued on and after the 1st of January next. Special arrangements only accepted

December 20 DRAKEFORD & CO.

Final Notice

THOSE WHO ARE INDEBTED TO JOSEPH M. GAYLE, and JOS. M GAYLE & CO., are again notified that the notes and accounts of the said firms are in the hands of W. L DePASS, attorney at law, for collection and unless settled by Return Day, they will be positively put in suit.

November 15

Coperas.

THREE HUNDRED LBS. OF GOOD COPERAS, for sale at a low price, at the "Old Brick Corner"

January 31 3mo T. S. MYERS.

To Rent.

A LOT, WITH A NEW BLACKSMITH SHOP, situated on the corner of Broad and York-street, will be rented for the present year.

January 31 E W. BONNEY.

NOTICE.

THE UNDERSIGNED HAS JUST RECEIVED A good article of HOLLAND GIN, and an excellent article of N. E. RUM A lot of good Rye WHISKEY; also, a few barrels of North Carolina Extra, at the "Old Brick Corner." T. S. MYERS.

January 31 3mo

Wide Iron,

PLOUGH STEEL, SOCKET SPADES, HOES, &c., just received by E. W. BONNEY.

February 7

South-Carolina—Kershaw District.

BY WM. M. BULLOCK, ESQUIRE, ORDINARY.

WHEREAS, JOHN KIRKPATRICK and JAS. D. KIRKPATRICK applied to me for Letters of Administration on all and singular the goods and chattels, rights and credits of Paul F. Villepigue, late of the District aforesaid, deceased:

These are, therefore, to cite and admonish all, and singular, the kindred and creditors of the said deceased to be and appear before me at our next Ordinary's Court for the said District, to be holden at Kershaw Court House on the third day of March next, to show cause, if any, why the said administration should not be granted.

Given under my Hand and Seal, this 12th day of February, in the year of our Lord one thousand eight hundred and sixty-two and in the eighty-seventh year of the Independence and Sovereignty of the State of South Carolina.

February 14 3 WM. M. BULLOCK, O. K. D.

Cough Syrup.

A POSITIVE CURE FOR COUGHS, COLDS, Asthma, Consumption, and all diseases of the Chest and Lungs. Prepared by

December 20 J. J. McKAIN.

PRODUCE.

THE UNDERSIGNED WILL TAKE IN PAYment of debts, all kinds of country produce at the highest market price, at the time of delivery. Anxious to close up his old business, as far as possible, and at the same time accommodate the farmer and planter, he solicits such payments.

January 24 E. W. BONNEY.

Liquid Rennet

BLAIR & WEYTH'S LIQUID RENNET, FOR making, in a few moments, the most delicious desert. For sale by J. J. McKAIN.

December 20

NOTICE.

MR JOS. M. GAYLE IS MY AUTHORIZED Agent during my absence in the service.

January 3 2mo E. A. YOUNG.

HARDWARE,

CARPETS, RUGS and CRUMB CLOTHS, for sale at the "Old Corner." E. W. BONNEY.

January 24

Fine North Carolina Hams.

A SMALL QUANTITY OF NO. CA. HAMS in store and for sale low, at the "Old Brick Corner," by T. S. MYERS.

February 21 6

NOTICE.

ALL PERSONS INDEBTED TO THE ESTATE of JESSE F. YOUNG, deceased, either by note or account, will please call on the Administrator and settle the same, by cash or note, as I wish to get the business closed up in some shape or form, at an early day. J. M. GAYLE, Adm r.

February 14 4

MANSION HOUSE,

CORNER BROAD AND DEKALB STREETS, CAMDEN, SO. CA.

Where Comfort, Cleanliness, Attention and a Good Table, combined, will always be found.

E. G. ROBINSON, Proprietor,

February 7 ly

STATE OF SOUTH CAROLINA.

EXECUTIVE COUNCIL CHAMBER, COLUMBIA, February 25, 1862.

NOTICE is hereby given that all persons having any arms suited for public service, or any lead, powder, saltpetre or sulphur, are earnestly requested to report the same to the Chief of the Military Department, or to agents appointed by him, and that fair prices will be given for them for the use of the State

By order of the Governor and Council.

F J. MOSES, jr., Secretary.

☞ All papers in the State copy three times.

February 28 3

South-Carolina---Kershaw District.

BY WM. M. BULLOCK, ESRUIRE, ORDINARY.

WHEREAS, THOMAS L. BOYKIN APPLIED to me for Letters or Administration on all and singular the goods and chattels rights and credits of Burwell Boykin, jr., late of the District aforesaid, deceased:

These are, therefore, to cite and admonish all, and singular, the kindred and creditors of the said deceased to be and appear before me at our next Ordinary's Court or the said District, to be holden at Kershaw Court House on the seventeenth day of March next, to show cause, if any, why the said administration should not be granted

Given under my Hand and Seal, this twentieth day of February in the year of our Lord one thousand eight hundred and sixty-two, and in the eighty-sixth year of the Independence and Sovereignty of the State of South Carolina.

February 28 2 WM M. BULLOCK, O. K. D.

Commissioners of Roads.

THE COMMISSIONERS OF ROADS FOR KERshaw District will meet in Camden on the 3d Monday in March, at 11 o'clock.

COLIN MACRA,

February 28 3 Clerk of the Board.

Guano.

TWO TONS PERUVIAN GUANO. ALSO A small lot of Patagonian Guano, for sale by

February 28 E. W BONNEY.

Seed Oats.

SEED OATS FOR SALE AT THE "OLD CORner," by E. W. BONNEY.

February 28

Extra Fine Family Flour.

100 BAGS EXTRA FINE FAMILY FLOUR, in store and for sale low, at the "Old Brick Corner," by T. S. MYERS.

February 21 3mo

Save the Pieces.

SPAULDING'S LIQUID GLUE is invaluable to every household. Will mend Wood, China, Glass and Metal. One small bottle will save ten times its cost. For sale by JOHN J. McKAIN.

SANCHEZ SPECIFIC

CAN be sent by mail and will effect a cure sooner than any other medicine, is safe, pleasant and reliable. Sold by J. J. McKAIN.

THE

Anderson Zouave.

SUB HOC SIGNO VINCES.

NO. I. TENLYTOWN, D. C., MARCH 8, 1862. VOL. I.

THE SWEET LITTLE MAN.

DEDICATED TO THE STAY-AT-HOME RANGERS.

Now while our soldiers are fighting our battles,
Each at his post to do all that he can,
Down among rebels and contraband chattels,
What are you doing, my sweet little man?

All the brave boys under canvas are sleeping,
All of them dressing to march with the van,
Far from the home where their sweethearts are weeping.
What are you waiting for, sweet little man?

You with the terrible warlike moustaches,
Fit for a colonel or chief of a clan,
You with the waist made for sword-belts and sashes,
Where are your shoulder-straps, sweet little man?

Bring him the buttonless garment of woman!
Cover his face lest its freckle and tan,
Muster the Apron-string Guards on the Common,
[illegible] is the [illegible] for the sweet little [illegible]

Give him for escort a file of young misses,
Each of them armed with a deadly rattan,
They shall defend him from laughter and hisses,
Aimed by low boys at the sweet little man.

All the fair maidens about him shall cluster,
Pluck the white feathers from bonnet and fan,
Make him a plume like a turkey wing duster,—
That is the crest of the sweet little man!

O, but the Apron-string Guards are the fellows
Drilling each day since our troubles began—
"Handle your walking-sticks!" "Shoulder umbrellas!"
That is the style for the sweet little man!

Have we a nation to save? In the first place—
Saving ourselves is the sensible plan—
Surely the spot where there's shooting's the worst place
Where I can stand, says the sweet [illegible] man.

[illegible] my person [illegible] stranger!
Think how the cowardly Bull Runners ran!
In the brigade of the Stay-at-home Rangers!
Marches my corps, says the sweet little, man.

Such was the stuff of the Malakoff-takers,
Such were the soldiers that scaled the Redan;
Truculent house-maids and blood-thirsty Quakers
Brave not the wrath of the sweet little man!

Yield him the sidewalk, ye nursery maidens!
Sauve qui peut! Bridget, and right about! Ann,—
Fierce as a shark in a school of menhadens,
See him advancing, the sweet little man!

When the red flails of the battle-field threshers
Beat out the continent's wheat from its bran,
While the wind scatters the chaffy seceshers,
What will become of our sweet little man?

When the brown soldiers come back from the borders,
How will he look while his features they scan?
How will he feel when he gets marching orders,
Signed by his lady love? sweet little man!

Fear not for him, though the rebels expel him—
Life is too precious to shorten its span;
Woman her broomstick shall raise to protect him,
Will she not fight for the sweet little man?

Now then, nine cheers for the Stay-at-home Ranger!
Blow the great fish-horn and beat the big pan!
First in the field that is farthest from danger,
Take your white feather plume, sweet little man!

LOVE AND DUTY.

Aveline March was sitting beside the light doorway that divided the room from a conservatory beyond, where the green shadows came and went, and strange, Oriental flowers flamed like torches of vivid color, but she neither saw their brightness, nor heard the musical chirp of the fountain under the acacia trees. No, she sat and pondered with her lily hands clasped tightly together, and the long dark eyelashes drooping low over her pale cheek.

"Only two more days left, and then I shall stand as his bride before God's altar. *His* bride—and Herbert is far away! Alas, I did not know the full extent of my weakness; I thought I had learned to bear my fate—but, oh! there is such a dull, deadly pain at my heart!"

She pressed her hands over her breast convulsively, but started up with a deep [illegible] on her cheek as the door opened.

"Aveline! is that you in the shadow of the arch?"

"Alice!" and Aveline came forward to meet the slight figure that glided in.

"News, Aveline—such news! Guess what it is! No, there's no use, you couldn't dream of it, if you guessed on until midnight!"

The little fairy danced around, clapping her jeweled hands until the diamonds sparkled like stray bits of fire, and the brown curls escaped from their comb, and made a glory round her dimpled face.

"Tell me, Alice," said Aveline, smiling, "have you got a new bracelet? or a new lover? or has your pet kitten caught a mouse?"

"Nonsense!" said Alice, pausing. "Can't you hazard any more sensible guesses? Well, now, I'll tell you—Herbert Arnott is come home—I saw him this very morning—he returned in the last ship from China."

Aveline grew pale as a ghost; even the red light that gleamed through the satin drapery could not illume that ashy whiteness.

"Does—does he know——"

"That you are to marry his white-haired uncle? Yes, he knows it. But, oh! Aveline, you surely, surely will not——"

She stopped abruptly, checked by the lofty glance of Aveline's eye.

"Alice, not a word farther. My word is pledged; Colonel Jefferson has released my father from his pecuniary difficulties—he has behaved in the noblest manner toward us all. In two day's time I shall redeem my promise at the altar."

"But, Aveline, you have not ceased to love Herbert?"

"God knows I have not," said Aveline, a [illegible] perceptible shudder through her slender frame. "Nevertheless, Alice, it is worse than folly to speak of this. Henceforth my whole heart shall be devoted to the noble man, who upheld us in the hour of adversity. He is worthy of the dearest love I have to give—and it shall be his."

"It's a shame!" pouted Alice, "to sacrafice yourself to a rash promise given by your father—to be that gray-haired old man's wife."

Aveline did not answer; she only bent quietly over the flower she was turning round her finger.

"And what is to become of poor Herbert?" pleaded Alice, in a softer accent.

"Let us talk of something else, dear Alice," said Aveline, gently. "There is a protecting Heaven above us all, and Herbert trusts in it as well as myself."

The two young girls vanished into the ensanguined shadows of the curtain folds; the birds chirped and twittered on, and the fountain murmured silver syllables to the soft acacia plumes; and they never knew that bird and fountain had not been the only auditor of their half-whispered words.

Ralph Jefferson leaned against the window-mullions, just where the sunshine struck against a noble pomegranate tree and shivered into lustrous arrows of gold upon his silver locks. Silent and motionless as a statue, he stood with lips closely compressed and eyes full of grave purpose.

"She is a noble girl!" he murmured, "a noble, noble creature. Well, it isn't very agreeable to hear one's self styled a gray-haired old man—but I'm very glad I overheard the conversation—*very* glad! I wonder where nephew Herbert may be?"

The twilight had long since faded into night; the gas-lights shone brilliantly throughout the vast, restless city, and nowhere more cheerily than in the office of

[*Continued on fourth page.*]

THE ANDERSON ZOUAVE
Is Published at CAMP ANDERSON,
EVERY SATURDAY,
BY THE
ANDERSON ZOUAVE 62nd N. Y. S. VOLUNTEERS.

CAMP ANDERSON, MARCH 8, 1862.

GREETING.

Hail to the light! Existence's hail! We breathe, we move, we live. Friends, we greet you with an infantile greeting, on this our birthday! Treat us tenderly, for we are inexperienced. Give us your confidence for we are yet faultless. And as we grow in years make due allowance for our faults of omission and commission. Brethren of the Press,—we extend to you all our hand, and offer you our friendship. We start at peace with all the world except "Secesh," and we hope to form treaties of amity with the rest of the human family. Don't be hard on us brother typos, say all that is true, "nothing extenuate," set nought in malice, for we are all *cantankerous* when abused, but you'll find us mighty nice chaps when well treated. But we won't anticipate anything unpleasant, and hope our good fortune will steer us clear of the shoals and quick-sands of difficulty as we are borne down the river of time. But friends, perhaps you would like to know what right we have to be born, and being born, what we intend to do? Well, necessity, the mother of invention, may claim us as her offspring, for a newspaper has become a necessity to us, and we know of no way to get one regularly except to rely upon our own efforts; so we were forced to be born—by necessity. Now that we are we intend to call on you every Saturday morning, with a clean face, clean conscience, and *summit* that's worth reading.

WHAT WE DO IT FOR.

The idea of a camp newspaper is not a novelty. During the Mexican campaign, and in the Crimean war, some of the more enterprising made this a vehicle of recreation and information to charm away the dull monotony of camp life.

It will readily be perceived how useful, as well as recreatory, an organ of this kind can be made, combining the *utile et dulce:* and if so to those immediately connected with our regiment, how much more so with the dear friends who are anxiously awaiting our return, or who burn with eager expectancy, wishing to hear of some glorious achievement, or even of some brilliant little skirmish or reconnoisance on our part. Such incidents of camp life are soon, we trust, to be allotted us, and a printed medium of this kind will then be more fully appreciated.

As a means of description of those deserving, and for obituary notices of the officer and the soldier, our little paper will prove invaluable to those, who far away in their quiet homes are still ever on the alert to catch the slightest whisper of our fame, or of our ill luck.

It is a part of our design to make our "A. Z." an instructor for officer and soldier alike. To carry out our plan we shall from time to time cull largely from the military works which we have at hand, and in our "*School of the Soldier,*" illustrate and define that which it is most necessary practically to enforce.

Thus do we launch our little sheet, not upon the sea of public favor nor of animadversion, but, secure in our own integrity we court not the one, nor can we well deserve the other.

SANITARY.

A few remarks, in this, our first number, on sanitary rules and regulations, will not be out of place, and may, we hope, be productive of some good to our regiment, although our past and present healthy condition has been far above the general average, still it behooves us to use our utmost endeavors to continue as we have been, one of the healthiest regiments in the division.

The attention of the men is called to the necessity of cleanliness in their persons and clothing. They should wash their bodies once a week, and when circumstances occur to prevent this, their feet should at least be washed. Their clothes should be aired frequently, their underclothes at all times kept clean; their blankets and the interior of their tents exposed to the sun and air on every available opportunity. Light and ventilation are the two great preventatives of disease, and fully within the reach of all. Let every man bear this in mind and he will have but little cause to call for medical agents to preserve him against the diseases so prevalent in our camps. THE DOCTOR.

LOCAL ITEMS.

On Monday the 24th ult. a violent gale assumed command, struck the tents *instanter,* turned out the regiment by a long roll of the bass drum, which was not arrested until it had passed entirely through the camp, and a stump had passed through one of its heads. Wagons were overturned, flags torn to ribbons,—in fact we were visited by a succession of *blows* which continued with unabated fury until our *retreat* was beaten—and even then it came in fitful gusts until "daylight did appear."

Coffee, when imbibed, has always been considered a great *solace,* but the *kernel* introduced lately as a smoker, has become "all the rage" among the Zou Zous.

Tuesday the 25th ult., was a delightful day. The brigade drill-ground was, owing to the gale and frost of the previous 24 hours, in excellent condition, which was taken advantage of by General Peck to order out the A. Z.'s 62d N. Y. S. V., 93d, 98th and 102d Penn. Vols.,) for drill. Our boys felt finely, "were handsomely on deck every pop'," and did excellently well. All felt grateful for the opportunity thus afforded for exercise and improvement in evolutions of the line.

We have to announce the arrival of two new regiments within the limits of our brigade, the 93d Pa. Vols., Col. J. B. McCarter; and the 59th N. Y. S. Vols., Col. W. Linn Tidball. The 59th Regt., we understand, is to be permanently garrisoned at the several forts in the immediate vicinity of Tennallytown.

Sergeant ANDREW CUSACK, of Co. G. 62d N. Y. S. Vols., has been promoted to the rank of Second Lieutenant, *vice* James F. Holmes, resigned.

DIED.

Private WILLIAM SHERWOOD, Co. B. 62d Regt., N. Y. S. Vols., of bleeding of the lungs, at Camp Tennally, on Feb. 20th 1862.

Private FRANCIS NEDDO, Co. B., 62d N. Y. S. Vols., of typhoid fever, at Camp Tennally, Feb. 24th 1862.

On Sunday, March 3d, JAMES CAFFREY, hospital nurse, in the 62d year of his age, from debility. In his death the sick have met an irreparable loss, and the regiment a faithful soldier.

At Georgetown Hospital, on March 1st, of confluent small-pox, private JACKSON SMITH, Co. E. 62d N. Y. S. Vols.

A TERRIBLE ENGINE OF WAR.

Among the terrible engines of war now being constructed for the government, is an iron-clad gunboat, which is being built by the celebrated engineer Ericsson, in New York city. The boat is 72 feet long and 41 feet beam. She will carry six hundred tons, Custom-house measurement. Her armament will consist of two 11-inch Dahlgren guns, placed on a revolving turret on deck. The turret will be 22 feet in diameter, 9 feet high, and 8 inches thick. The entire deck is 8 inches thick, to be covered with solid wrought iron 1 inch in thickness. The deck rests on solid oak beams 10 inches in diameter, placed three feet apart between centres, each beam to be supported by two wrought-iron columns 3 inches in diameter, and heavy wrought-iron diagonal braces.

The turret is revolved by machinery at the will of the officer in command of the guns. The men who load and fire are not required to take aim, that being the duty of the officer controlling the guns, and by means of a lever, works his death-dealing Dahlgrens at pleasure. The men occupying the turrets are in no way exposed to the fire of the enemy; in fact, the only exposure is that of the muzzle of the guns, and that at the precise moment of their discharge. The rudder, the screw propeller, and the anchor, when up, are entirely out of reach of even those elongated shot which do not *ricochet,* but continue their course under water in the direct line of flight The pilot who steers the vessel is protected by a conical-shaped wrought iron casting six inches thick, which rises five feet above the deck.

Attached to the propeller there are two engines and two boilers of four hundred indicated horse power, which will give a space at sea of six knots an hour. Every

The Philadelphia Inquirer.

ESTABLISHED 1829. | PHILADELPHIA, MONDAY, MARCH 10, 1862. | PRICE TWO CENTS.

HIGHLY IMPORTANT NEWS!

OUR FLEET AT FORTRESS MONROE ATTACKED BY THE REBEL STEAMERS ! !

The U. S. Sloop Cumberland Sunk and Congress Burned!

Our Loss from One Hundred to Two Hundred and Fifty.

STILL LATER NEWS!

Iron-clad Steamer "Monitor" Attacked by the "Merrimac."

THE REBEL FLEET DRIVEN OFF.

THE MERRIMAC IN A SINKING CONDITION.

OPENING OF THE TELEGRAPH TO FORTRESS MONROE.

OFFICIAL DESPATCH.

Special Despatches to The Inquirer.

WASHINGTON, March 9, 1862.

The Union Fleet Attacked by Rebel Steamers Merrimac, Jamestown and Yorktown.

WASHINGTON, March 9.—The Government has received information from Fortress Monroe, that, yesterday, the iron-clad steamer *Merrimac* and the gun-boats *Jamestown* and *Yorktown* attacked our fleet, and sunk the U. S. sloop-of-war *Cumberland*, and took the *Congress* The U. S. steamer *Minnesota* was aground when the Fortress Monroe boat left.

DETAILS OF THE DISASTER.

FORTRESS MONROE, March 8.—The dullness of Old Point was startled, at 10 o'clock to-day, by the announcement that a mysterious vessel, supposed to be the Rebel steamer *Merrimac*, and looking like a submerged house, with the roof only above water, was moving down from Norfolk by the channel in front of Sewall's Point. Signal guns were also fired by the United States sloop-of-war *Cumberland* and the frigate *Congress*, to notify the *Minnesota*, *St. Lawrence* and *Roanoke* of the approaching danger, and all was excitement in and about Fortress Monroe.

There was nothing protruding above the water but the flag-staff, flying the Rebel flag, and a short smoke-stack. She moved along slowly, and turning into the channel leading to Newport News, steamed direct for the *Cumberland* and *Congress*, which were lying at the mouth of the James River. As soon as the *Merrimac* came within range of the *Cumberland*, the latter opened on her with her heavy guns, but the balls struck and glanced off, having no more effect on her than peas from a pop-gun. Her ports were all closed, and she moved on in silence, but with a full head of steam.

In the meantime, as the *Merrimac* was approaching the two frigates on the one side, the iron-clad steamers *Yorktown* and *Jamestown* came down the James river and engaged our frigates on the other side.—The batteries at Newport News also opened on the *Jamestown* and *Yorktown* and did all in their power to assist the *Cumberland* and *Congress*, which, being sailing vessels, were at the mercy of the approaching steamers.

The *Merrimac* in the meantime kept steadily on her course, and slowly approached the *Cumberland*, when the latter, as well as the *Congress*, at the distance of one hundred yards, rained full broadsides on the iron-clad monster. The shots took no effect, glancing upwards and flying off, having only the effect of checking her progress for a moment.

After receiving the first broadsides of the two frigates she ran into the *Cumberland*, striking her about midships and literally laying open her side. She then drew off, fired a broadside into the disabled ship, and again dashed against her with her iron-clad prow, and knocking in her side left her to sink, while she engaged the *Congress*, which laid abont a quarter of a mile distant.

The *Congress* had, in the meantime, kept up a sharp engagement with the *Yorktown* and *Jamestown*, and having no regular crew on borrd of her, and seeing the helplessness of resisting the iron-clad steamers, at once struck her colors. Her crew had been discharged several days since, and three Companies of the Naval Brigade had been put on board temporarily until she could be relieved by the *St. Lawrence*, which was to have gone up on Monday to take her position as one of the blockading vessels at the James River.

On the *Congress* striking her colors the *Jamestown* approached and took from on board all the officers as prisoners, but allowed the crew to escape in the boats. The vessel being thus cleared it was fired by the Rebels, when the *Merrimac* and her two iron-clad companions opened with shell and shot on the Newport News batteries. The firing was briskly returned.

Various reports have been received, principally from frightened Sutler's clerks. Some of them represented that the garrison had been compelled to retreat from the batteries to the woods. Another report is, that the two smaller Rebel steamers had been compelled to retreat from the guns of the batteries.

In the meantime, the steam frigate *Minnesota* having partly got up steam, was being towed up to the relief of the two frigates, but did not get up until too late to assist them. She was also followed by the frigate *St. Lawrence*, which was taken in tow by several of the small harbor steamers. It is, however, rumored that neither of these vessels had pilots on board them, and after a short engagement, both seemed to be, in the opinion of the pilots, on the point, aground.

The *Minnesota*, either intentionally or from necessity, engaged the three Rebel steamers at about a mile distance, with only her two bow guns. The *St. Lawrence* also poured in shot from all her guns she could bring to bear, and it was the impression of the most experienced naval officers on the point that both had been considerably damaged.

These statements, it must be borne in mind, are all based on what could be seen by the glass at a distance of nearly eight miles, and by a few panic-stricken non-combatants, who fled at nearly the first gun from Newport News. In the meantime darkness approached, though the moon shone out brightly, and nothing but the occasional flashing of guns could be seen.

The *Merrimac* was also believed to be aground, as she remained stationary at the distance of about a mile from the *Minnesota*, making no attempt to attack or molest her. Previous to the departure of the steamer from Old Point for Baltimore, no guns had been fired for half an hour, the last one being fired from the *Minnesota*. Some persons declared that immediately after the last gun was fired, a dense volume of vapor was seen to rise from the *Merrimac*, indicating an explosion of her boilers. Whether this is so or not cannot be known, but it was the universal opinion that the Rebel monster was hard aground.

Fears were of course entertained for the safety of the *Minnesota* and *St. Lawrence* in such an unequal contest, but if the *Merrimac* was really ashore, she could do no further harm to them. It was the intention of the *Minnesota*, with her picked and gallant crew, to have run into close quarters with the *Merrimac*, avoid her iron prow, and board her.—This the *Merrimac* seemed not inclined to give her an opportunity to do, being afraid to approach her at close quarters when aground.

At eight o'clock, when the Baltimore boat left, a fleet of steam tugs were being sent up to the relief of the *Minnesota* and *St. Lawrence*, and an endeavor was to be made to draw them off from the bar on which they had grounded. The firing had been suspended, whether from mutual consent or necessity could not be ascertained.

The Rebel battery at Pig's Point was also enabled to join in the combined attack on the *Minnesota*, and several guns were fired at her from Sewall's Point, as she went up; none of them, however, struck her, but one or two passed over her.

Arrival of the Iron-Clad Ericsson Steamer Monitor.

BALTIMORE, March 9.—The Old Point boat left at eight o'clock last night. About half an hour after she left the wharf the iron-clad Ericsson steamer *Monitor* passed her, going in, towed by a large steamer. The *Monitor* reached Fortress Monroe by nine o'clock, and may have immediately gone into service. If not, she would be ready to take a hand early on Sunday morning.

The details furnished in the despatch from Fortress Monroe are all the facts, as far as can be ascertained, and are probably the worst possible version of the affair.

THE VESSELS AND SCENE OF CONFLICT IN HAMPTON ROADS.

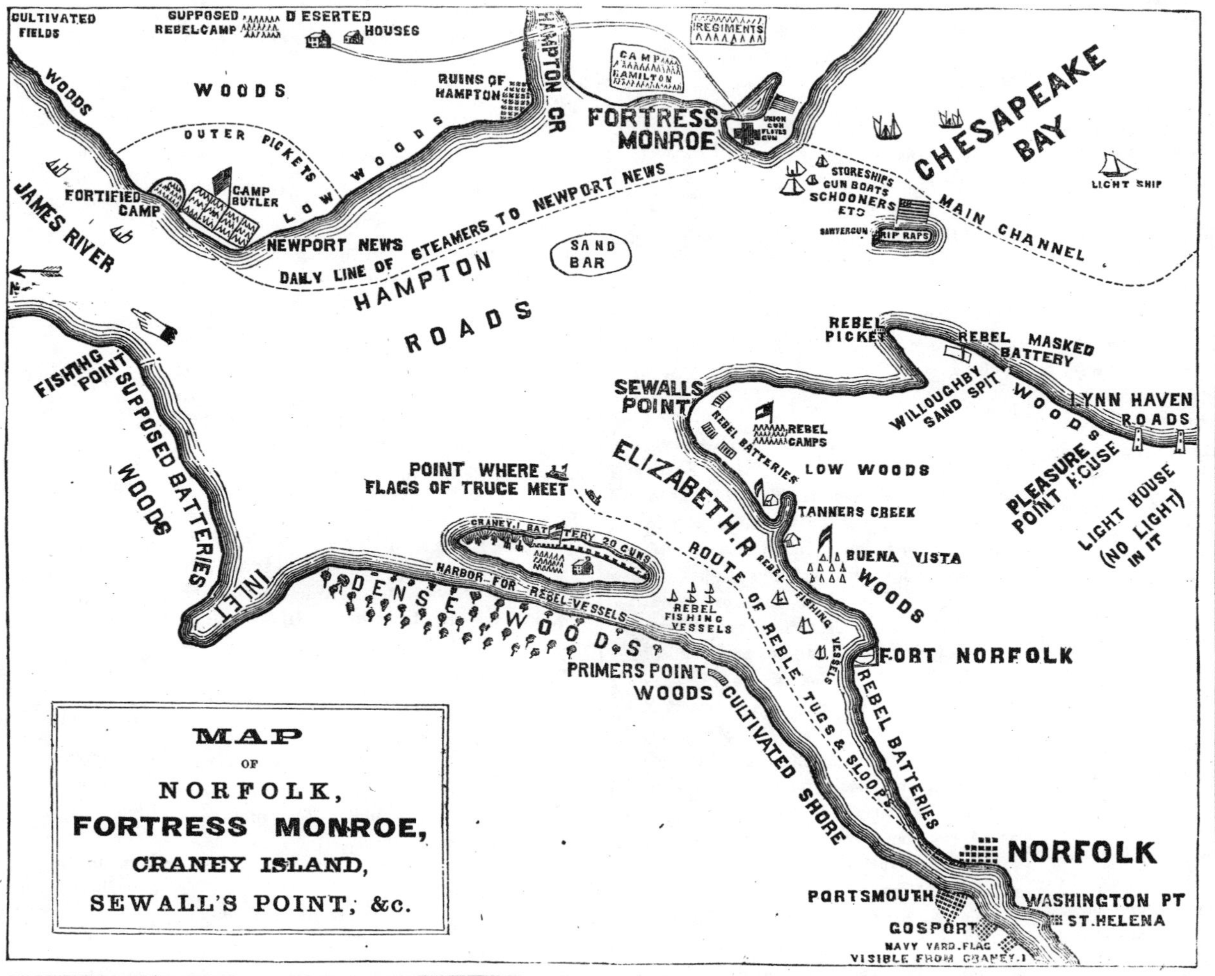

MAP OF NORFOLK, FORTRESS MONROE, CRANEY ISLAND, SEWALL'S POINT, &c.

THE MERRIMAC.

The *Merrimac* was built at Charlestown, Mass., in 1855, was one of the finest steam frigates in the United States Navy, thirty-two hundred tons burden, and carrying forty large guns.

She was partially burned and sunk at the time of the destruction of the Gosport Navy Yard. The Rebels having succeeded in raising the vessel, cut down her hull to within three feet of her light water mark, and built a bomb-proof house of wrought iron plates, three inches thick, on her gun deck.

She is iron-plated, and her bow and stern steel-clad, with a projecting angle of iron for the purpose of piercing a vessel. She has no masts, and there is nothing to be seen over her gun deck, with the exception of her pilot-house and smoke-stack.

Her armament consists of four 11-inch navy guns on each side, and two 100-pounder Armstrong guns at the bow and stern.

THE JAMESTOWN.

The *Jamestown* is furnished with a heavy, clumsy and ridiculous looking iron prow in front, the *point* of which barely projects above the water.

To all appearance the ship is not razeed at all, iron plated or pierced for broadside guns. Her batteries seemed to consist of a 32-pounder rifled gun, fore and aft. They are similar to the Parrot gun. The question was once asked of the Rebel officer, "Are those Parrot guns ?" to which a negative answer was given.

THE YORKTOWN.

The Rebel steamer *Yorktown* was formerly used on the New York and Virginia line of steamers, She is a side-wheel steamer of 1400 tons burden. was built in New York in 1859, and her size is as follows:—Length, 251 feet; breadth, 34 feet; depth, 18 feet. She has been completely fitted out at Norfolk, her sides having been plated with iron, and other means taken to strengthen her and to render her formidable.

THE MONITOR, OR, ERICSSON BATTERY.

This vessel is sharp at both ends, and consists of a lower and upper hull, the sides of the former inclining to an angle of fifty-one degrees, and coming to a point at each end at an angle of eighty degrees. The lower hull is iron-plated. The upper section is five feet high, with perpendicular sides and the same sharp ends, and is forty-one feet four inches wide, jutting over the lower hull three feet and seven inches on each side. The sides of this upper section are a little over three feet in thickness. First, there is an inner guard of six inch plate iron, and upon this a section of white-oak timber, thirty inches thick, and covered with an armor six inches thick, formed of six one-inch iron plates, lapped and firmly riveted together.

The deck or top of the battery is even with the top of the hull, and is covered with two thicknesses of inch plate-iron, fastened to eight-inch oak plank and ten-inch oak timber, but twenty-six inches apart. There is no railing or other obstruction on the top of the battery except a round tower or turret, twenty feet in diameter and nine feet high, and eight inches thick, made of plate iron.

The turret has two port holes, each two feet in diameter, for two eleventh inch columbiads, and is also pierced for musketry. The turret is of immense weight, but made to revolve by machinery from below, so as to bring the guns in any desired range, and to remove the ports from the enemy's guns while loading.

To support, protect and give efficiency to this turret is the whole object of the battery, although its immense weight and power would sink any vessel with which it should come in contact.

The battery is steered from the front, the wheelhouse standing before the turret. The wheelhouse is strongly built of iron, and can be lowered into the hold like a bale of dry goods. When lowered, the top, which is bomb-proof, is level with and forms a part of the deck. The joints are water-tight. The house is pierced for sharpshooters.

The ends of the upper vessel project over the propellor, rudder and anchor. The propellor is, of course, at the stern, and the equipoise rudder behind that, and they are so protected by the upper vessel that they cannot be struck by a ball. The ancher is in front, and is short but very heavy. It is hoisted by a chain running into the hold, up into a place fitted for it, outside of the lower hull, but within the impregnable walls of the upper hull. The entrance to the hold is by small hatchways, which, when closed, form a part of the deck, and are equally secured.

The interior of the battery presents a novel and interesting study. In the bow are the cable and anchor chambers; next the cabin and quarters of the officers and men, and amidships the cook-room, and overhead the small engine which is to furnish ventilation and work the turret. Just abaft are the furnaces, and in the stern the engine working the propeller. The bunkers for wood coal and ammunition, and the water-tanks, occupy every conceivable vacancy. The cabin is neatly but substantially fitted up, and shows that it is meant for use more than pleasure. Taken altogether, it would be impossible to imagine more material, and that more substantial and serviceable, and at the same time more perfect, in a smaller space, than is embodied within this formidable engine of warfare.

Of the efficiency of the battery great hopes are expressed. It has no vulnerable part save the port-holes, which are exposed only for about half a minute in firing. Its shape and massive iron prow will enable it to sink any ordinary vessel with perfect ease. In case it is boarded, no harm is done. The only entrance is at the top of the turret, which cannot easily be scaled, and even then but one man at a time can descend. There are no places in the deck where an entrance can be forced, so that the boarding party may stand until the sea washes them off, or the sharp-shooters assist their departure. It is claimed that it can steam into any port, deliver its effective broadside, and retire in safety.

The battery is now about four feet above water, and weighs 1,400,000 pounds. With the addition of her armament, coal, water and provisions for a thirty day's cruise, she will be but eighteen inches above water and her entire weight will be nine hundred tons. Her two columbiads will carry round balls weighing each one hundred and eighty-three pounds, or conical balls of three hundred and fifty pounds.

THE FLAG-SHIP MINNESOTA.

The *Minnesota* is one of our largest screw steam frigates, 3200 tons burden, rates 40 guns, and was built in 1855 at Washington. She is what is termed an auxiliary propeller, and her engines are 450 horse power. She left Boston as the flag-ship of the blockading fleet, and has been in that service up to the time of the departure of this expedition from Fortress Monroe.

Her guns are very heavy and most effective, as has been proved in the last engagement; two of them are of eleven-inch calibre, capable of throwing balls of one hundred and sixty pounds weight She has made but one regular cruise previous to her present position; that was in the East Indies, from which place she returned in 1858.

THE CUMBERLAND.

The sloop-of-war *Cumberland* is 1726 tons burden, rated twenty-four guns, was built in 1842 at the Charlestown Navy Yard. She is a sailing vessel of good substantial build. She has been the flag-ship of the Home Squadron, sailing under the flag of Commodore PRENDERGAST.

THE CONGRESS.

The frigate *Congress* carries fifty guns. She was built at Kittery in 1841, and measures 1867 tons. She had recently arrived from the coast of Brazil.

THE ST. LAWRENCE.

The *St. Lawrence* also mounts fifty guns, and measures 1726 tons. She was built at the Gosport Navy Yard in 1847.

POSITION OF THE VESSELS WHEN ATTACKED.

The two vessels opposite Camp Butler represent the position of the *Cumberland* and *Congress*, stationed there to watch the James river. The *Minnesota* was aground on the point marked Sand Bar, midway between Sewall's Point and Hampton. The *Merrimac* pursued a course down Elizabeth river.

STILL LATER!

The Iron-Clad Steamer Monitor Attacked by the Three Rebel Steamers.

THE ASSAILANTS DRIVEN OFF.

The Merrimac in a Sinking Condition.

WASHINGTON, March 9—7 o'clock, P. M.—The telegraph line to Fortress Monroe has been completed, and the following despatch has been received direct from that point:—

"The Ericsson iron-clad steamer *Monitor*, arrived at Fortress Monroe last night, and early this morning she was attacked by the three Rebel steamers, the *Merrimac*, *Jamestown* and *Yorktown*. After a contest of five hours, they were driven off, the *Merrimac* in a sinking condition.

Official Despatches from Fortress Monroe.

WASHINGTON, March 9.—The following despatch was to-night received by Major-General McCLELLAN from General WOOL:—

FORTRESS MONROE, March 9—6 o'clock, P. M.—Two hours after my telegraphic despatch to the Secretary of War, last evening, the steamer *Monitor* arrived. She immediately went to the assistance of the *Minnesota*, which was aground, and continued so until a few minutes since. Early this morning she was attacked by the *Merrimac*, *Jamestown* and *Yorktown*.

After a five hours contest, they were driven off, and the *Merrimac* in a sinking condition. She was towed by the *Jamestown*, *Yorktown*, and several smaller boats, towards Norfolk, no doubt for the purpose, if possible, to get her in the dry dock for repairs.

The *Minnesota* is afloat and being towed towards Fortress Monroe.

Despatch to the Secretary of the Navy.

FORTRESS MONROE, March 9—6·45 P. M.—To G. WELLES, Secretary of the Navy:—The steamer *Monitor* arrived at 10 o'clock last night, and went immediately to the protection of the *Minnesota*, lying aground just below Newport News. At seven o'clock A. M., the *Merrimac*, accompanied by two wooden steamers and several tugs, stood out towards the *Minnesota* and opened fire.

The *Monitor* met them at once, and opened her fire, when all the enemy's vessels retired excepting the *Merrimac*. These two iron-clad vessels fought part of the time touching each other, from eight o'clock A. M. till noon, when the *Merrimac* retired. Whether she is injured or not it is impossible to say. Lieutenant J. S. WORDEN, who commanded the *Monitor*, handled her with great skill, assisted by Chief Engineer STEMERS. Lieutenant WORDEN was injured by the cement from the pilot-house beieg driven into his eyes, but I trust not seriously. The *Minnesota* kept up a continnous fire, and is herself somewhat injured. She was moved considerably to-day, and will probably be off to-night. The *Monitor* is uninjured, and ready at any moment to repel another attack.

(Signed) G. V. FOX,
Assistant Secretary of the Navy.

CREW OF THE CUMBERLAND.

REPORTS OF THE LOSS OF LIFE.

NEW YORK, March 9.—A special despatch from Fortress Monroe to the *Tribune* states that the *Cumberland* had a crew of five hundred men, nearly half of whom went down with her, but a negro states that some of the crew who swam ashore gave the number lost at one hundred. The guns of the *Congress* after her capture, were turned on our batteries at Newport News.

General WOOL sent two regiments of infantry, six companies of cavalry, and the Mounted Rifles, by land to Newport News to support General MANSFIELD, in case of an attack.

The Excitement at Washington.

WASHINGTON, March 9.—The excitement at the hotels, and elsewhere, all day, has been intense, consequent on the news from Fortress Monroe.

THE WAR IN VIRGINIA.

OPERATIONS OF GEN. BURNSIDE

Winton, North Carolina, Occupied in Force!

The Stars and Stripes Waving Over the Rebel Battery at Cockpit Point.

THE STEAMER "PAGE" BURNED.

The Rebel Batteries on the Potomac Evacuated.

THE POTOMAC ARMY TO BE DIVIDED INTO FIVE CORPS D'ARMEE.

Indians of Kansas and Nebraska.

FROM GEN. BANKS' COMMAND.

LEESBURG OCCUPIED BY COL. GEARY.

Forts Beauregard, Johnson and Evans in Possession of Geary.

THE REBELS RETREATING.

CHARLESTOWN, Va., March 8.—To-day a Mr. CARTER, member of BAYLIE's Cavalry, together with three valuable horses, carriage and other articles, was captured and turned over to the custody of the Quartermaster. A considerable amount of Rebel scrip was also seized.

Private WHITNEY, of the Michigan Cavalry, who was accidentally wounded on Friday night, died to-day.

Colonel BRODHEAD, of the Michigan Cavalry, has been appointed Chief of the Cavalry for this Division.

During the visit to the residence of Col. LEWIS WASHINGTON, near Hallston, your correspondent was informed that subsequent to the departure of the proprietor in August last, the Rebels paid a visit to the establishment and appropriated a large collection of the portraits of Gen. WASHINGTON and his family, being probably the only collection of the kind extant.

It is to be regretted that previous to the order of General BANKS some wanton depredations were committed on private property in this vicinity, but it is probable that the perpetrators will be detected and severely punished.

LEESBURG, March 8.—Colonel GEARY has taken Leesburg and driven General HILL, with his whole command, from the town and surrounding forts. The Stars and Stripes now wave over all the hills.

The Rebels fell back towards Middlebury, last night. Colonel GEARY left Lovettsville, with his command, and marched through Wheatland and Waterford, taking prisoners at both places, and putting the scattered forces of the enemy to flight.

Shortly after sunrise, this morning, he took possession of Fort Johnson, which was rechristened by the officers Fort Geary. He then entered the camp, with flags flying and bayonets fixed.

The Rebel troops, who had considered this as one of their greatest strongholds, could be discerned through a glass in full retreat.

The command took many prisoners and a quantity of army stores, and are in possession of the Bank, Post Office and public buildings.

Forts Beauregard and Evans are also in our possession.

This achievement, accomplished by a skillful manouvre, is of vast importance. The command is well and in good spirits.

A detachment of the First Michigan Cavalry did much service, under the direction of Col. GEARY, in this movement.

POOLESVILLE, March 8.—To Brigadier-General S. WILLIAMS:—

Leesburg was entirely evacuated yesterday morning. The reports are that Colonel GEARY's advance is there. N. J. T. DANA, Brigadier-General.

THE OCCUPATION OF LEESBURG CONFIRMED.

CHARLESTOWN, Va., March 9.—The report of last night that the United States troops had occupied Leesburg, is officially confirmed. The Rebels evacuated the town on Friday morning, taking all their baggage and supplies to Middlesburg, but it is not known whether the troops retired thither or started toward Winchester. Colonel GEARY occupied the town unresisted yesterday morning, capturing considerable property belonging to the Rebel army.

All was quiet on our frontier last night.

A Scout within Four Miles of Winchester —Skirmishes with the Rebels.

CHARLESTOWN, Va., March 9.—Yesterday, for the first time since our arrival, the country carriages came into town, and the occupants held social intercourse with our officers and soldiers. Suits of secession grey are gradually giving way to other hues, and the ladies are beginning to frequent the streets on business and pleasure.

Dr. WM. ALEXANDER, an eminent physician and unflinching Unionist, died at his residence, in this vicinity, last month. His son, yesterday, returned home from the Charlottesville College, deeply im-

The First Minnesota.

PUBLISHED BY DETACHMENT OF THE

TYPOGRAPHICAL FRATERNITY OF THE FIRST MINNESOTA REGIMENT.

The First Minnesota.

Published in the office of the now defunct "Berryville Conservator," by

ED. A. STEVENS, THOS. H. PRESSNELL, O. NELSON, CHAS. S. DRAKE. FRANK J. MEAD, JULIAN J. KENDALL, HENRY W. LINDERGREEN.

"A chiel's amang ye takin' notes,
An' faith he'll prent 'em."

BERRYVILLE, VA., - - - - - - MARCH 11, 1862.

To our Friends.

It is not without considerable embarrassment that we present to an appreciative public this number of the FIRST MINNESOTA. In the first place the circumstances under which we have assumed the responsibility of its publication, are not of a character to recommend us to the favorable notice of the citizens of Berryville, who have long been accustomed to the semi-occasional perusal of the (to them) highly edifying columns of the Berryville Conservator, and secondly we (the printers of the MINNESOTA FIRST) have always borne the reputation of being very modest men. But remembering the old maxim "when in Rome do as Romans do," and judging from appearances that a paper HAD been published [illegible] we have overcome to a certain extent our "native [illegible]" and herewith present to all creation and [illegible] mankind" Vol. I. No. 1, of the Fi[illegible]

To suc[illegible] our readers who are so fortunate as to wear the livery of our much respected Uncle Samuel, we are constrained to apologize, for being caught, like poor Tray, in bad company; and if we are any judge our company is much worse than that which Tray was so severely punished for being found in, and were it not that we, like Caesars wife are "beyond suspicion," we would not blame our friends of the blouse and jacket for turning the cold shoulder and refusing us our regular rations of the much-coveted "hard bread." Our only apology for making our appearance in "secesh" company is, that the employees of Mr. Gregg hearing, doubtless, that we Vandal Yankees had crossed the Potomac and were on their way to the pleasant little village of Berryville, were kind enough to "set up" and "work off" the first side of the paper.

To our friends in the Northwest we send greeting, and promise them that so long as we drive a pen and shoulder a musket on the "sacred soil," though we may "fire the southern heart" they can rest assured the Union will be safe, even should "somebody have to be hurt!"

If our present calculations hold good, it is probable that the next issue of the FIRST MINNESOTA will be published in Winchester, as Berryville is a small place and we are ambitious, VERY.

With an apology for our impudence we drop ourselves upon the charity of our readers.

AN APOLOGY.

Our short residence in Berryville, and the sudden absquatulation of the local editor, is our apology for the meagre variety in the local column. Our enterprising and progressive nature forbids that this state of things shall long be suffered to exist, and as soon as we can find a young man of satisfactory qualifications, we promise our readers a Local Department—instructive, entertaining, and a faithful mirror of "men and things" in and around Berryville.

CORRECTION.—We announced in our last issue "that the number of our men (Rebels) taken prisoners at Fort Donelson was about 7000." We have since learned from undoubted Union authority that the number of prisoners taken by the victorious Federal Army was at least double. It came to us from Rebel sources, who find it policy to reduce the figures and tinge their saddest reverses with the color of success.

WE are under weighty obligations to Gen. Willis A. Gorman for many favors, not the east of which is a free pass into this office.

The Stars and Stripes in Berryville again!!!

Yesterday afternoon the First Michigan Cavalry entered our town, following closely on the heels of about 100 "Secesh" Cavalry who made an inglorious exit about five minutes previously, acting, no doubt, on the [illegible] honored maxim that

"He who fights and runs away
Will live to fight another day."

A white flag waving from the L[illegible] with the letters "C. S." was tak[illegible] the "invaders" simultaneously w[illegible]ing of the "Stars and Stripes," no[illegible] in the breeze from the Court H[illegible] flag was one belonging to the vet[illegible] from Minnesota—the gift of the fair ladies of *L' etoile du Nord*, to the gallant so[illegible] of [illegible] State.

RUN AWAY EDITOR.

"Lost, strayed, or stolen"—H. [illegible] late editor and proprietor of the "Con[illegible]tor." was last seen yesterday, when he slo[illegible] at the appearance of the Union cavalry in the place. Poor fellow! once he was re[illegible] but now, alas, "how art the mighty [illegible] No description is given, because [illegible] kn[illegible] none, and those wh[illegible] need not wish to. He formerly [illegible] here, and at this desk where [illegible] writing, with the same pen [illegible] we had almost said the same [illegible] God, the paper has never been pollut[illegible] by [illegible] foul touch—and sent forth column after column in vile abuse of the best government [illegible] world has ever known—the government [illegible] towered above all others, and on whose banners might be written "PEERLESS." This Gregg was "lost" to all true principles of manhood, has "strayed" from the tuition of his youth, has "stolen" what?—the true impulses of many, perhaps nearly all of his readers, and—we pause to think how to palliate in some measure his conduct, but confess ourselves unequal to the task—we give it up. "Depart, ye cursed."

AT HOME.

After the varying vicissitudes of camp life, of nearly a twelve months duration, the typos of the First Minnesota Regiment feel again "at home" amid the hurrying scenes of a printing office—getting out the only paper published in Berryville. How jovially we run over the nomenclature of a printing establishment. Reader would you like to listen to the conversation of the typos after taking possession of the office of the Conservator?—"Here is a full case!—Editor, give us fat copy." "Ah! here is a double-leaded item." "Charlie, hurry up that 'Apology.'" "Where is the devil?" He skiddaddled at 3 P. M., armed with the shooting-stick." "The dead matter of the Conservator is not well justified." "The cases in this office are dreadfully dirty." "Ed., finish up 'That Yankee.'" "D—n you, why are you so careless as to pi 'The Runaway Editor.'"

A STANDING ITEM.

"BERRYVILLE is quite lively again, having a large number of soldiers quartered in it." * * Butter and milk and all delicacies will be thankfully received from those in the country having them to spare."

The above extract is from the previous issue of the "Conservator," and we think the times and circumstances compel us to make it a "standing item."

A SPECIMEN BRICK.

Lieut. Sam Raguet, of the First Minnesota —he can "chaw a sea biscuit," and "ride a horse with ease and safety."

I. O. Q. D.

Will meet at "The Swamp" at the appointed time. "Things are working."

Increase of Circulation.

We have the pleasure to announce to our readers that with this issue of the *Conservator* we have largely increased our circulation; and we do not hesitate to announce that our importance as a journal will in the immediate future be second to none in the Union. In addition to our previous circulation among the "Secesh" of Berryville and its vicinity, the boys of the First Minnesota have ordered 10,000 copies for circulation among their friends in the great Northwest.

☞ We learn that Rev. Mr. MEREDITH, Rector of Christ Church, Winchester, has resigned his charge and entered the C. S. Army as a private.

The above was in type before we took charge of the office, and we would add, *on dit*, that he has since been appointed Chaplain, and we trust he will in some degree be successful in improving the morality of the Rebel camp.

TOO BAD.

"Please don't handle the type," are the words posted on the wall. We are sorry, Mr. Gregg, that we must disregard your injunction, but these are troublesome times, and really we couldn't help it. You make an e-Gregg-ious error.

A RELIC.

An old flint lock musket, minus the barrel, was found in the office. It is a perfect type of the condition in which the Southern Confederacy will be found in the immediate future—without an army.

CHANGE.

"A new and beautiful flag was yesterday run up on the Secession pole in this place."—Conservator.

And yesterday a white flag was seen in its place, it soon came down though.

THANKS.

The former editor will accept our thanks for a lot of candles. Did you suppose they would "throw light on the subject," while we were advocating "Liberty and Union—one and inseperable."

WHY IS IT?

"We repeat the question asked before—Why is it that the thievish Yankees can cross the Potomac when they please, and where they please?"—Conservator.

Simply because we know how.

VISIT.

Col. E. L. Sproat, of the Minnesota Militia, now a Volunteer Aid on the staff of Gen. Gorman, paid us a visit last evening. Call again, Colonel.

JUST SO.

"The remarkably fine and pleasant weather we have had of late, illy fits us for the sudden change that has taken place."—*Conservator*.

How do you like the change, Gregg—as far as you've got?

THAT TRADE.

JAP, we sympathize with you in that trade. We are free to admit that "a white man is as good as a nigger—except on horse trades.—But then "you can't always tell.

A TRUISM.

For sometime past Secesh has gone the whole hog in this section of the State. Now we propose to have a little *Gormandizing* on our own hook.

ON DIT.

The men of the Minnesota First are principally *Millerites*. They believe in an early ascension—for Jeff.

NOTICE.

Shinplasters will not be taken in payment for our sheet. Please bear this in mind.

CONFED. NOTES.

"The genuine Confederate Notes are all numbered with RED ink. As there are some counterfeits in Richmond (numbered with BLACK ink), it would be well to observe this particularly."—Conservator.

Genuine in red ink—what more symbolical of the red-handed outrages of Jeff. and his advisers. Red—with what? The blood of Virginians.

THINK IT OVER.

"Our wood-paying subscribers will please send it in as soon as possible, as we are now in much need of the article."—Conservator.

What do you want it for? You ought not to run away, and expect your readers to "send it." By-the-by, have many of your readers paid in advance?

LITTLE RHODY.

Rhode Island has furnished many good batteries, and second to none stands the gallant Battery A, (formerly the 2d), Capt. J. A. Tompkins. This battery threw two shells into the borders of the town yesterday—two were sufficient.

OH, YES.

We would return our thanks to the "devil" for the good order in which he kept the materials of this office, or if Gregg "kept things to rights" we thank him. "Give the devil his due."

A FALLEN STAR

"Another star has made its appearance in the Southern constellation. Missouri has applied and been admitted into the Southern Confederacy, and the President has approved and signed the bill.—*Conservator*.

And now she's out again—almost without money and without Price.

PHENOMENON.

Of course we mean the transfer of *Banks* from the virgin soil of Maryland to the sacred soil of Virginia. Wonder if it hurt much? It is said the Potomac was not at all riled, although it has kicked up a dust on this side.

SHIFTING.

It is rumored that Jeff. Davis is about to relinquish his "big thing" of bottling Northern suckers, and will for the future, devote his energies to sucking the bottle.

☞ The first Union flag which has met the public gaze in this town since the commencement of this rebellion was borne by Sergeant Shepard of Co. B. 1st Minn.

☞ The infantry skirmishers in the advance yesterday were companies B. F. and K. They didn't sweat a bit—secesh did.

☞ This sheet was gotten up in a few hours. Readers will therefore be lenient with us.

☞ A few advertisements appear on our last page. We were in a hurry and had to do it.

☞ Single copies of this paper for sale.—Price 5 cents.

DOWNIE says "we are going to Win-Winchester." We should say so, my dear boy.

☞ To-morrow polls will be opened to take the vote on the Amended Constitution, and will be kept open for three days. As a large portion of the territory of Virginia is now occupied by the Federal army, and the voters therein will be deprived of holding an election, every man in those sections where polls can be opened should vote against any amendment of the Constitution at this time. In justice to the people of the whole State, the matter should be indefinitely postponed.

We think so.

THE MARKETS.

For the information of those who may wish to purchase in a Southern market, we append here to a summary of the Richmond prices. It was prepared by the ex-editor, who we presume has gone down that way to lay in a supply. Mr. Gregg, please save some for us—we will call soon.

FLOUR—Family $8a$8.50, Extra $7.50, Super $7—by the dray load.
GRAIN—Red WHEAT 115a120c, white do. 125a130c. CORN 80c. RYE 90a110c. OATS 85c, and scarce.
GROCERIES—Rio COFFEE 75c. Brown SUGAR 22c, coffee do. 24a25c. N. O. MOLASSES $1.25, Syrups $1a$1.10. Fine SALT $37.50a$40 per sack, Ground Alum do. $25.
WOOL—Arrivals light at 90a95c. per pound.
PROVISIONS—BACON 23a25c, hog round. Choice BUTTER 42c, fair to good 33 to 37c.

THE NORFOLK DAY BOOK.

The very latest Northern and European Intelligence.

NOW IS THE TIME TO SUBSCRIBE.

Terms	Daily, one year	$5 00
	Daily, six months	3 00
	Daily, one month	1 00
	Weekly, one year	1 00

The *Day Book* has now become THE newspaper of the South. The very latest Northern and European News appears in its columns, one, two and three days in advance of all other papers in the Confederacy. We submit the following extracts from what others have to say of us:

D. T. BISBIE, Esq., who has lately returned from Europe, with important dispatches to the Confederate States Government, says in a recent letter:

"While in London and Paris, I saw several quotations from the Norfolk *Day Book*, and since my return I have also noticed extracts from the same sprightly journal in the newspapers of New York, Charleston and other cities."

The Suffolk (Va.) *Christian Sun* says:

"The Norfolk *Day Book*, which is so fast gaining popularity throughout the Southern Confederacy, comes to us greatly enlarged and improved, and gives us Northern and Foreign News in advance of any of our other exchanges, and is, therefore, perused with avidity."

The Wilmington (N. C.) *Daily Journal* says:

"The Norfolk *Day Book* has become the most valuable exchange paper we receive, as it contains the very latest news from the Rump Government, as well as Foreign News."

The Fredericksburg (Va.) *Herald* says:

"The Norfolk *Day Book* contains the latest news from the North, and its editorials are always of an interesting character."

Subscribers to the *Day Book* may rely upon having their papers sent promptly by mail. Address, with amount of subscription enclosed,

JOHN R. HATHAWAY,
February 5, 1862—3m *Editor and Proprietor.*

SEQUESTRATION NOTICE.

I have been appointed RECEIVER, under the Sequestration Act of the Confederate Congress, for the Counties of Jefferson, Berkeley, Morgan, Clarke, Frederick and Hampshire, in Virginia; and I hereby notify every Attorney, Agent, former Partner, Trustee, or other person, holding or controlling any lands, tenements or hereditaments, goods or chattels, rights or credits, or any interest therein, within the said Counties, of or for any Alien Enemy of the Confederate States of America, or of or for any resident of any of the United States at War with the said Confederacy, speedily to inform me, the said RECEIVER, of the same; and to render me an account thereof, and, so far as practicable, to place the same in my hands. Any such person wilfully failing to do so, will be guilty of a high misdemeanor, and liable to be prosecuted and punished as provided by Law. I also notify each and every citizen of the Confederate States, speedily to give information to me (*as he is required by Law to do*) of any and every lands, tenements and hereditaments, goods and chattels, rights and credits, within the said Counties, and of every right and interest therein held, owned, possessed or enjoyed by or for any such Alien Enemy, or resident aforesaid.

☞My Office is in Winchester, adjoining those of my late partners, BARTON & WILLIAMS.

T. T. FAUNTLEROY, JR.,
October 30, 1861—tf *Receiver C. S. A.*

$100 REWARD.

Ran away from the subscriber, in the months of August and October last, TWO SLAVES; one a GIRL, about 18 years old, bright mulatto, tall and slender, hair quite straight, teeth little decayed in front, no mark remembered save a mole quite conspicuous near the right eye. She calls herself MARY RANDOLPH. She ran away the 2d of August, taking with her a quantity of clothing, among it several fancy dresses. The other, a BOY of 15 years, bright mulatto, about 5½ feet high, with low forehead, hair growing closely around it, not very intelligent, and stammers slightly in talking. He is a brother of the girl, calls himself FREDERICK RANDOLPH, and ran off in October, wearing a coarse leghorn hat, brown pants with stripes down the sides, and a dark sack coat.

I will give $50 apiece if they are taken in Clarke, $60 apiece in Frederick, and what the law allows if taken in any of the border Counties, or out of the State.

A. L. P. LARUE.
December 18, 1861—6m

TULEYRIES FOR RENT.

I wish to rent this elegant MANSION HOUSE and GARDEN to a gentleman who has a family, until I can sell the whole estate. The Tuleyries is the healthiest and most beautiful residence in the Southern Confederacy.

Early application is desired, and will not be rented to any one unless binding themselves to take good care of the House, &c. One room will be reserved for myself, as it is necessary for me to be on the farm several times during the year.

JOS. T. MITCHELL,
Agent and Attorney in fact for the heirs of
July 26, 1861—tf *Col. Jos. Tuley, dec'd.*

$100 REWARD.

—The above reward will be given for the apprehension of NEGRO MAN, JAMES JOHNSON, belonging to the estate of Jacob Isler, dec'd. Said Negro is about 5 feet 4 inches high, of copper color, and about 20 years old. Fifty Dollars reward will be given if taken out of the County of Clarke, in this State, and $100 if taken in Maryland or any of the Free States. Said Negro to be delivered in the jail of Clarke or Jefferson.

WM. A. CASTLEMAN,
August 8, 1861—tf *Adm'r of Jacob Isler, dec'd.*

WILLIAM R. DENNY,

(SUCCESSOR TO J. H. CRUM & CO.,)

Dealer in Books and Stationery, Dry Goods and Notions,

Will continue the sale of the same style of Goods heretofore sold at the old stand, ☞ one door South of Taylor Hotel, ☞ and will continue to sell Goods at the small profits for which this Store has been famous. [Winchester, September 25, 1861

FROM WINCHESTER TO LEESBURG.

LLOYD & BYRD are now running a *Tri-Weekly Line of Stages* between Winchester and Leesburg. Leaves Winchester every Tuesday, Thursday and Saturday morning. Leaves Leesburg every Monday, Wednesday and Friday morning. [July 12, 1861

SADDLE AND HARNESS MAKING IN WINCHESTER.

I would respectfully inform my old customers and the public generally, that I have commenced business again at my old stand, on Main Street, a few doors North of the Taylor Hotel, where I am fully prepared to accommodate them with everything in my line. I will constantly keep on hand all such articles as pertain to my line of business, viz: *Saddles, Bridles, Harness, Collars, Whips, Trunks of all kinds, Valices, and all kinds of Saddle and Harness Hardware.* All in need of any such articles are invited to give me a call, as I will furnish as good and cheap wares as any similar establishment in the Valley.

Thankful for the liberal patronage bestowed upon me heretofore, I would respectfully solicit a continuance of the same. F. W. KOHLHOUSEN

☞I will keep for sale WINE, of my own making—an excellent article. The *Sparkling Catawba* and the *Clinton*, which have been pronounced by good judges to be first-rate. As they are pure they are very useful in sickness, or for persons having Dyspepsia. I will sell by the bottle, by the dozen, or by the gallon.

Also, GRAPE and CIDER VINEGAR for sale. F. W. KOHLHOUSEN.
Winchester, October 2, 1861—tf

SADDLES! SADDLES!! ENCOURAGE HOME ENTERPRISE!

The undersigned respectfully informs his friends and the public that he has on hand a large assortment of all the various kinds of *Saddles and Harness*, a few doors North of KOHLHOUSEN'S old stand, Winchester, Va. He will also keep on hand an assortment of *Saddle and Harness Hardware* of the best quality, such as Bridle-Bits, Stirrups, &c. Also, an excellent assortment of Whips of all kinds, Bridles and Collars. And also an assortment of *Trunks* of all kinds, including fine French Trunks for Ladies; Valices, &c.;—all of which he will sell on the lowest and most accommodating terms. Having a practical knowledge of the business, he hopes to be able to give general satisfaction. He invites a call and a trial from the public.

January 1, 1861 W. C. COOPER.

BOOT AND SHOE ESTABLISHMENT AT RIPPON, JEFFERSON CO., VA.

The undersigned, at the solicitation of many friends and customers, has removed his Shop to *Rippon, Jefferson County, Va.*, where he intends to prosecute his business with all the energy and skill which he may possess. He will manufacture to order, of the best material, and in the latest style and in the most substantial manner, any and every description of work in his line, for Ladies, Gentlemen, Misses and Servants. *Repairing* done at the shortest notice, and on reasonable terms.

Thankful to the friends of Clarke and Jefferson who have so liberally patronized him in the past, he hopes to receive their orders for the future, as, from contiguity of position, and enlarged preparations for the accommodation of the public, he is sure he will be prepared to give general satisfaction.

☞His material being *all cash*, he will be thankful to his friends to bear him in remembrance in this respect. *Country Trade* will be received in exchange for work at fair market prices.

April 16, 1861 JOHN AVIS.

NEW SHOE ESTABLISHMENT.

I have again commenced the Shoemaking business on my own account at Wickliffe, and have procured the best workmen in the State of Virginia, and the best selection of materials that could be had. I would return my sincere thanks for the patronage I received when in business before, and hope for a liberal share for the future. I ask you to come and look at my work, ask my prices, and you will surely deal. I will keep constantly on hand a good assortment of *ready-made Boots and Shoes*, to which I would invite the attention of the public.

☞I will also repair all kinds of *HARNESS*, and will pay the highest market price for *HIDES*.

January 15, 1861 M. L. SINCLAIR.

HO! FOR THE TOBACCO AND CIGAR STORE!

Another wagon-load of Tobacco, Cigars, Snuff, &c., &c., just received, and purchased for the cash. Returning my thanks to my customers and the public generally for the liberal patronage extended to me, I would inform them that I can sell Tobacco and Cigars at *greatly reduced prices*, having bought another large and well-selected stock at surprisingly low prices. *Tobacco worth 37½ and 50 cents, selling at 20 and 25 cents per pound!* My stock embraces the finest and best brands of Tobacco and Cigars manufactured, which I am selling at nearly *one-half* of regular prices. ☞Don't forget the sign of "Pompey," opposite the Post-Office.

Berryville, April 9, 1861 Z. GRAY.

NOTICE.

—All persons indebted to JOHN H. CRUM & Co., will as speedily as possible settle their accounts, at the old stand, to myself or FRANK G. WALTER. This is necessary because of the death of MR. CRUM, whose business his Administrator desires to settle speedily. All persons having claims against JOHN H. CRUM & Co., will please at once present them for payment.

WILLIAM R. DENNY,
Winchester, Sept. 25, 1861 Surviving Partner.

MORE GOODS!

I have this day (September 26th) bought the entire *STOCK OF GOODS* of the house of J. P. HEIRONIMUS & Co., for cash, amounting to about $10,000, and will be sold at low figures for *cash*.

Winchester, Oct. 2, 1861 C. B. ROUSS.

WILLIAM R. DENNY,

ONE DOOR SOUTH OF TAYLOR HOTEL,

Has on hand a lot of good quality of *Ladies' Home-Made Morocco Shoes*, which will be sold at the *old* prices. [Winchester, September 25, 1861

NAILS.

—250 kegs best Wheeling Nails, for sale by BAKER & BRO.
Winchester Depot, January 8, 1861

OILS, PAINTS AND GLASS

—In large quantities and great variety, for sale by
Winchester, April 17 BAKER & BROS.

NEW HARDWARE STORE.

The undersigned has just returned from the East, having made large additions to his stock of Hardware, by purchases made exclusively for cash, direct from first hands in New York and Philadelphia, is enabled to exhibit one of the largest and best assortments of Goods in his line ever offered in this market, consisting in part of the following articles:

HOUSEKEEPING GOODS of every description; Table Cutlery, in great variety; Pocket Cutlery, a large assortment of the best makes and most approved styles. Also, Scissors, Shears, Razors, Butcher Knives, Metal Sifters, Skimmers and Ladles, Coffee Mills, Japaned Ware, Brittannia Ware, Tea Scales, Table Castors, Stair Rods, Waiters, Candlesticks, Snuffers, Tea Kettles, Bake and Frying Pans, Tea and Tablespoons, Coal Hods and Shovels, a full stock of Iron Spoons, Enameled Ware, Preserving Kettles, Hand Bells, Fenders, Shovels and Tongs, a large assortment of Plated Tea and Tablespoons, Knife Cleaners, &c.

BUILDING HARDWARE of every description; Farmers' and Mechanics' Tools of all kinds; a very large assortment of Looking-Glasses, at unusually low prices. Also, all sizes Looking-Glass Plates; Gilt Moulding for Picture and Looking-Glass Frames, all widths and different styles.

Also, Shot and Lead; a general variety of Shoe Findings and Ambrotype Stock;—all of which will be sold at low prices for cash, and by so doing hope to receive a continuance of the favors shown the old house. Call and examine stock and prices and judge for yourself. GEORGE W. KELLER,
Successor of Charles L. Crum.

☞Sign of the Big Anvil, 2d door South of the Court-House, Winchester. [April 16, 1861

TO THE BRAVE SOLDIERS OF THE SOUTH.

There seems to be some discontent among the troops, from the fact that they cannot get a fight from the Abolitionists, but the Hessians are sharp—they know our soldiers by reputation, and consequently won't toe the mark.

Old Lincoln, "they say," only wanted to immortalize his name in some way, for fear it might be forgotten. To say he has succeeded, would be a lame expression. His name will be handed down through all eternity—doubtless he will hold some office under the devil. He has done more harm than any other man since the creation. He has, with a fiendish malignity, unsurpassed by the savage or barbarian, brought a calamity upon a happy country and a mighty people, amounting to universal destruction. Talk of Arnold or Judas; why they were white men compared to this scoundrel and his satellites, Scott, Seward, Greeley, Butler & Co.

We take this occasion to renew the offer of $20,000 for the head of Lincoln, or $1,000 for either of his pet Kangaroos. Also, to say that we are selling

GOODS

very cheap, and expect a little lot this week from the Abolition Devils. C. B. ROUSS.
Winchester, July 12, 1861

Z. GRAY, TOBACCONIST, BERRYVILLE, VA.,

Having opened a store on Main Street, opposite the Post-Office, in the room recently occupied by E. V. Kercheval as a Tailor Shop, will keep constantly on hand all kinds of *Tobacco, Segars, Snuffs, &c.*, which he offers to the citizens of Berryville and vicinity at as low prices as similar articles can be had at any other place. By close attention to business, and an endeavor to accommodate, he hopes to receive a liberal share of public patronage. In proportion as his business increases, he will enlarge his stock and give it a greater variety. In returning his thanks for favors already extended to him, he would also solicit the further patronage of his old friends and customers. ☞Look for the Sign—"Pompey"—opposite the Post-Office. [December 18, 1860

PUMP MAKING, PIPE BORING, &c.

T. J. BRAGG respectfully announces to the citizens of Clarke and adjoining Counties, that he is always prepared to make and repair *Pumps, Bore Pipes*, and lay them properly, at the shortest notice, at low prices and on accommodating terms. All work guaranteed, and unless satisfaction is given no charge will be made. Those wanting anything done in the above line, will please inform him by letter or otherwise. His Post-Office is Berryville, Clarke County, Virginia. [April 2, 1861—y

TO WAGON-MAKERS

—*Thimble Skeins and Pipe Boxes, for Carriages, Buggies, Light and Heavy Wagons.*—This improved Box will be found to combine all that is desirable in a wagon-box; running easier than any other description in the market, and for durability, fully equal to the iron axle; while, being *lighter and cheaper*, they are decidedly better. Also, a first-rate article of Blacksmith Drill;—for sale at the HARDWARE STORE of
Winchester, Sep. 28 L. E. SWARTZWELDER.

DRY GOODS, COTTON YARN, &c.

—We have just received a large assortment of unbleached and bleach'd Sheetings and Shirtings; plain, twilled and col'd Osnaburgs, for servants; children's wear; Prints; plaid Cottons; Cotton Yarn, colored and white; Carpet Chain; Wrapping Cotton; Candlewick and Batting, all lengths;—for cash, and at very low prices. BAKER & BROTHERS.
Winchester, April 16, 1861

MACKEREL AND HERRING.

—We have in store and for sale at low prices, No. 2 and 3 Mackerel; new Eastern Herrings; old do., very cheap; old Potomac do. BAKER & BRO.
Winchester Depot, April 16, 1861

RICH JEWELRY.

—The *latest styles* of best quality and most durable workmanship, just received by J. MEREDITH & SON.
Winchester, November 17, 1860

BROWN SHEETINGS.

—5 bales heavy yard wide brown Cottons, just received and for sale by BAKER & BROS.
Winchester, July 5, 1861

FINE WATCHES.

—The largest stock of *Watches* in the Valley. Come and see.
Winchester, Nov. 27 J. MEREDITH & SON.

BOOTS, SHOES, HATS AND CAPS

—A full assortment for sale by
Winchester, Jan'y 8 BAKER & BROS.

CABINET-MAKING, UPHOLSTERY, AND GILT FRAME ESTABLISHMENT.

I respectfully inform the public that I continue at my old stand, on Loudoun Street, Winchester opposite WOLFE & MILLER'S Store, and nearly opposite the Bank of Winchester, where I keep on hand and manufacture to order, all kinds of Cabinet Work, (whether fancy or plain,) Gilt, Rosewood and Mahogany Frames, either with or without glasses. Also, Oval Frames, suitable for Photographs, and any size Frame with or without Looking-Glasses. [These Frames can be washed without injury to them.] Window or Curtain Cornices—all of which will be manufactured and sold on the lowest terms.

I also keep on hand and manufacture to order all kinds of COFFINS, from the plainest to the richest and most elaborately worked Mahogany Coffins, mounted and trimmed in the most appropriate and tasty style. Also, covered with black cloth, &c. I have lately had made an elegant and neat HEARSE, which will enable me to attend promptly to calls in the Undertaking line not only from this but the surrounding country. And my charges will be unusually low either for Coffins or for use of Hearse.

Upholstery, &c.—All kinds of Mattresses (hair, shuck, &c.,) kept on hand and made to order; Looking-Glass Plates for Mirrors or for Parlors, on hand, at wholesale and retail; Trimmings for Frames of all kinds, such as Tassels, Cords, &c. Also, all kinds of Carved Work executed according to any pattern; Chairs of various kinds, including cane-bottom, rocking, &c.

☞Furniture repaired at the shortest notice.

References—Thomas McCormick, Col. T. Smith, Dr. William Hay, Beverly Randolph, George Carter Blakemore, Dr Benjamin Harrison, John Page, Jr., Dr. S. S. Neill, and other citizens of Clarke and adjoining Counties.

April 16, 1861 JOHN VILWIG.

CUMMINGS' HAY, STRAW AND FODDER CUTTER.

Economy is Wealth.

Using a Fodder Cutter of the Cummings variety is economy—ergo, it is wealth; and that is what most of us are seeking industriously. Twice in Clarke County, with the Machine before the eyes of the parties concerned, have I been offered $10 difference between my $30 Cutter and Baltimore Cutters that had just cost $40. As often as the "law allows," have I received the Premium of the Valley Agricultural Society—and always in other places; in Richmond it took three premiums at once. It may be used for hand or horse power without alteration.

CORN SHELLERS of the most approved kind, always on hand. The farmers of Clarke will find it to their interest to examine my make of WAGONS and PLOWS before purchasing. Every thing guaranteed to be as represented.

☞Refer to EDW'D MCCORMICK, THO'S MCCORMICK, P. H. POWERS, DR. W'M D. MCGUIRE, CHAMP SHEPHERD, and numerous others in Clarke who have used my manufactures. T. H. KERN,
Winchester, December 18, 1860 Depot.

WATCHES, JEWELRY, &C., IN WINCHESTER.

The undersigned, grateful for past encouragement, asks the continued attention of his friends and the public generally to the fact that he keeps on hand a good assortment of all articles in his line of business, viz: Gold and Silver Lever, Ancre and Lepine Watches; one-day, eight-day and thirty-day Clocks; Breast-Pins, Ear-Drops, Chains, Seals, Keys, Spectacles of every kind, Thimbles, Shields, &c. Additions to his stock of the latest styles are constantly being made. Time-Pieces of every description *repaired with great care.* Jewelry also repaired at the shortest notice. CHARLES TRIBBY,
Nearly opposite the Taylor Hotel, Winchester.
September 21, 1859

FINE WATCHES, JEWELRY, SILVER AND PLATED WARE, &c.

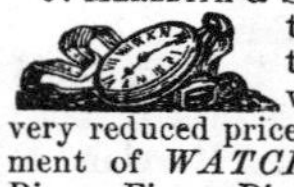

J. MEREDITH & SON, *Winchester, Va.*, have added to their stock a fine selection of the latest styles of *JEWELRY*, which they are determined to sell at very reduced prices. In addition to a choice assortment of *WATCHES*, they name: Broaches, Ear-Rings, Finger Rings, Bracelets, Gold Chains, Miniature Lockets, Thimbles, Cuff Pins, Signet Rings, Gold Pens and Pencils, Bosom and Sleeve Buttons, Gold and Silver Spectacles, superior quality Cake, Fruit and Card Baskets, Castors, &c.; which they offer at very reduced prices. Watches, Clocks and Jewelry *repaired in the best manner.* [Oct. 26, 1859

BERRYVILLE DRUG STORE.

W. R. HELVESTINE

Keeps constantly on hand all kinds of DRUGS AND MEDICINES, PAINTS, OILS, FANCY ARTICLES, &c.; and every article pertaining to the Drug Business. A call is solicited from his old friends and customers. He feels confident that he can accommodate and please all who are in want of anything in his line of business. ☞Store on the corner three doors East of the Union Hotel.

SUGAR, MOLASSES AND COFFEE.

We have recently added to our stock 10 hhds. of very good Porto Rico Sugar; 10 do New Orleans do; 5 do Cuba do; 10 do Sugar-Molasses; 15 do common Philadelphia Syrup; 50 bbls. white Sugars, various qualities; 60 bags Rio Coffee; 15 do Old Government Java do; 10 do Jamaica do; 10 do white Laguayra do; 10 gross Hummell's Extract of Coffee. BAKER & BROS.
Winchester, April 16, 1861

THE AUCTION GALLERY! ROOMS ALWAYS OPEN.

Elegant Pictures from 12½ cents up.

Call up and examine specimens—and every Picture must give entire satisfaction, or no charge. A splendid assortment of Cases now on hand.

Winchester, September 28 C. B. ROUSS.

SILVER AND PLATED WARE.

—Silver Ware of our own make always on hand. Also, a large stock of *Albata Plated Ware*, to which constant additions of the most elegant designs are made.
Winchester, Nov. 27 J. MEREDITH & SON

BERRYVILLE CONSERVATOR.

Vol. III. BERRYVILLE, VA., WEDNESDAY, MARCH 12, 1862. No. 26.

Official Report of the Battle of Manassas.

REPORT OF JOS. E. JOHNSTON, GENERAL COMMANDING.

Headquarters Army of the Potomac,
Fairfax C. H., October 14, 1861.

To the Adjutant and Inspector General, Confederate States Army:

Sir: I have the honor to submit to the honorable Secretary of War a report of the operations of the troops under my command which terminated in the battle of Manassas.

I assumed command at Harper's-Ferry on the 23d of May. The forces at that point then consisted of nine regiments and two battalions of infantry, four companies of artillery with sixteen pieces without caissons, harness or horse, and about three hundred cavalry. They were, of course, undisciplined, several regiments without accoutrements and with an entirely inadequate supply of ammunition.

I lost no time in making a complete reconnoisance of the place and its environs, in which the Chief Engineer, Major (now Brigadier-General) Whiting ably assisted. The results confirmed my preconceived ideas.

The position is untenable by any force not strong enough to take the field against an invading army and to hold both sides of the Potomac. It is a triangle, two sides being formed by the Potomac and the Shenandoah, and the third by Furnace Ridge. The plateau thus enclosed, and the end of Furnace Ridge itself, the only defensible position, which, however, required for its adequate occupation double our numbers, was exposed to enfilade and reverse fires of artillery from heights on the Maryland side of the river. Within that line the ground was more favorable to an attacking than to a defending force. The Potomac can be easily crossed at many points above and below, so that it is easily turned. It is twenty miles from the great route into the Valley of Virginia from Pennsylvania and Maryland, by which Gen. Patterson's approach was expected. Its garrison was thus out of position to defend that Valley, or to prevent Gen. McClellan's junction with Gen. Patterson. These were the obvious and important objects to be kept in view. Besides being in position for them, it was necessary to be able, on emergency, to join Gen. Beauregard.

The occupation of Harper's-Ferry by our army perfectly suited the enemy's views. We were bound to a fixed point. His movements were unrestricted. These views were submitted to the military authorities. The continued occupation of the place was, however, deemed by them indispensable. I determined to hold it until the great objects of the Government required its abandonment.

The practicable roads from the West and Northwest as well as from Manassas meet the route from Pennsylvania and Maryland at Winchester. That point, was therefore, in my opinion, our best position.

The distinguished commander of the army of the Potomac was convinced, like myself, of our dependence upon each other, and promised to co-operate with me in case of need. To guard against surprise, and to impose upon the enemy, Major Whiting was directed to mount a few heavy guns upon Furnace Ridge and otherwise strengthen the position.

I was employed, until the 13th of June, in continuing what had been begun by my predecessor, Col. (now Major-General) Jackson, the organization, instruction, and equipment of the troops, and providing means of transportation and artillery horses. The river was observed from the Point of Rocks to the western part of the county of Berkeley—the most distant portions by the indefatigable Stuart, with his cavalry. Gen. Patterson's troops were within a few hours of Williamsport, and Gen. McClellan's, in Western Virginia, were supposed to be approaching to effect a junction with Patterson, whose force was reported, by well-informed persons, to be 18,000 men.

On the morning of the 13th of June, information was received from Winchester, that Romney was occupied by 2,000 Federal troops, supposed to be the van-guard of McClellan's army.

Col. A. P. Hill, with his own (13th) and Col. Gibson's (10th) Virginia regiments, was dispatched by rail-way to Winchester. He was directed to move thence towards Romney to take the best position and best measures to check the advance of the enemy. He was to add to his command the Third Tennessee Regiment, which had just arrived at Winchester.

During that day and the next, the heavy baggage and remaining public property were sent to Winchester by the rail-way, and the bridges on the Potomac destroyed. On the morning of the 15th, the army left Harper's-Ferry for Winchester, (the force had been increased by these regiments since the 1st of June,) and bivouacked four miles beyond Charlestown. On the morning of the 16th, intelligence was received that Gen. Patterson's army had crossed the Potomac at Williamsport, also that the United States force at Romney had fallen back. A courier from Richmond brought a dispatch authorizing me to evacuate Harper's-Ferry at my discretion.

The army was ordered to gain the Martinsburg Turnpike by a flank movement to Bunker's Hill in order to place itself between Winchester and the expected advance of Patterson. On hearing of this, the enemy recrossed the river precipitately. Resuming my first discretion and plan, I proceeded to Winchester. There the army was in position to oppose either McClellan from the west or Patterson from the north-east, and to form a junction with Gen. Beauregard when necessary.

Lieutenant-Colonel George Stewart, with his Maryland Battalion, was sent to Harper's-Ferry to bring off some public property said to have been left. As McClellan was moving south-westward from Grafton, Col. Hill's command was withdrawn from Romney. The defence of that region of country was entrusted to Col. McDonald's regiment of cavalry. Intelligence from Maryland indicating another movement by Patterson, Col. Jackson, with his brigade, was sent to the neighborhood of Martinsburg to support Col. Stuart. The latter officer had been placed in observation on the line of the Potomac with his cavalry. His increasing vigilance and activity was relied on to repress small incursions of the enemy, to give intelligence of invasion by them, and to watch, harass, and circumscribe their every movement. Col. Jackson was instructed to destroy such of the rolling stock of the Baltimore and Ohio Rail-Road as could not be brought off, and to have so much of it as could be made available to our service brought to Winchester.

Maj. Whiting was ordered to plan defensive works, and to have some heavy guns on navy carriages mounted. About twenty-five hundred militia, under Brig. Gen. Carson, were called out from Frederick and the neighboring counties to man them.

On the 2d of July, Gen. Patterson again crossed the Potomac. Col. Jackson, pursuant to instructions, fell back before him. In retiring he gave him a severe lesson in the affair at Falling Waters. With a battalion of the 5th Virginia regiment (Harper's) and Pendleton's Battery of Field Artillery, he engaged the enemy's advance. Skillfully taking a position where the smallness of his force was concealed, he engaged them for a considerable time, inflicted a heavy loss, and retired when about to be outflanked, scarcely losing a man, but bringing off forty-five prisoners.

Upon this intelligence the army, strengthened by the arrival of Gen. Bee and Col. Elzey, and the 9th Georgia regiment, was ordered forward to the support of Jackson. It met him at Darkesville, six miles from Martinsburg, where it took up a position for action, as Gen. Patterson, it was supposed, was closely following Col. Jackson. We waited for him in this position four days, hoping to be attacked by an adversary at least double our number, but unwilling to attack him in a town so defensible as Martinsburg, with its solid buildings and enclosures of masonry. Convinced at length that he would not approach us, I returned to Winchester, much to the disappointment of our troops, who were eager for battle with the invaders. Col. Stuart, with his cavalry, as usual, remained near the enemy.

Before the 15th of July, the enemy's force, according to the best intelligence to be obtained, amounted to about 32,000. Ours had been increased by eight Southern regiments. On the 15th of July, Col. Stuart reported the advance of Gen. Patterson from Martinsburg. He halted, however, at Bunker's Hill, nine miles from Winchester, where he remained on the 16th. On the 17th he moved to his left, to Smithfield. This created the impression that he intended to attack us on the south, or was merely holding us in check, while Gen. Beauregard should be attacked at Manassas by Gen. Scott.

About one o'clock on the morning of July 18th, I received from the Government a telegraphic dispatch, informing me that the Northern army was advancing upon Manassas, then held by Gen. Beauregard, and directing me, if practicable, to go to that officer's assistance, sending my sick to Culpeper Court-House.

In the exercise of the discretion conferred by the terms of the order, I at once determined to march to join Gen. Beauregard. The best service which the army of the Shenandoah could render was to prevent the defeat of that of the Potomac. To be able to do this, it was necessary, in the first instance, to defeat Gen. Patterson or to elude him. The latter course was the most speedy and certain and was, therefore, adopted. Our sick, nearly seventeen hundred in number, were provided for in Winchester. For the defence of that place the militia of Gens. Carson and Meem seemed ample; for I thought it certain that Gen. Patterson would follow my movement as soon as he discerned it. Evading him by the disposition made of the advance guard under Col. Stuart, the army moved through Ashby's Gap to Piedmont, a station of the Manassas Gap Rail-Road. Hence the infantry were to be transported by the railway, while the cavalry and artillery were ordered to continue their march. I reached Manassas about noon on the 20th, preceded by the 7th and 8th Georgia regiments, and by Jackson's brigade, consisting of the 2d, 4th, 5th, 27th, and 33d Virginia regiments. I was accompanied by Gen. Bee, with the 4th Alabama, the 2d and two companies of the 11th Mississippi. The President of the rail-road company had assured me that the remaining troops should arrive during the day.

I found Gen. Beauregard's position too extensive, and the ground too densely wooded and intricate to be learned in the brief time at my disposal, and therefore determined to rely upon his knowledge of it and of the enemy's positions. This I did readily, from full confidence in his capacity.

His troops were divided into eight brigades, occupying the defensive line of Bull Run. Brig. Gen. Ewell's was posted at the Union Mills Ford; Brig. Gen. D. R. Jones' at McLean's Ford; Brig. Gen. Longstreet's at Blackburn's Ford; Brig. Gen. Bonham's at Mitchell's Ford; Col. Cocke's at Ball's Ford, some three miles above; and Col. Evans, with a regiment and battalion, formed the extensive left at the Stone Bridge. The brigades of Brig. Gen. Holmes and Col. Early were in reserve in rear of the right. I regarded the arrival of the remainder of the army of the Shenandoah during the night as certain, and Patterson's, with the Grand Army, on the 22d, as probable. During the evening it was determined, instead of remaining in the defensive positions then occupied, to assume the offensive, and attack the enemy before such a junction.

Gen. Beauregard proposed a plan of battle, which I approved without hesitation. He drew up the necessary order during the night, which was approved formally by me at half-past four o'clock on the morning of the 21st. The early movements of the enemy on that morning, and the non-arrival of the expected troops, prevented its execution. Gen. Beauregard afterwards proposed a modification of the abandoned plan—to attack with our right, while the left stood on the defensive. This, too, became impracticable, and a battle ensued, different in place and circumstance from any previous plan on our side.

Soon after sun-rise, on the morning of the 21st, a light cannonade was opened upon Col. Evan's position; a similar demonstration was made against the centre soon after, and strong forces were observed in front of it and of the right. About 8 o'clock, Gen. Beauregard and I placed ourselves on a commanding hill in rear of Gen. Bonham's left—near 9 o'clock the signal officer, Capt. Alexander, reported that a large body of troops was crossing the valley of Bull Run, some two miles above the bridge. Gen. Bee, who had been placed near Col. Cocke's position, Col. Hampton, with his legion, and Col. Jackson, from a point near Gen. Bonham's left, were ordered to hasten to the left flank.

The signal officer soon called our attention to a heavy cloud of dust to the north-west, and about ten miles off, such as the march of an army would raise. This excited apprehension of Gen. Patterson's approach.

The enemy, under cover of a strong demonstration on our right, made a long detour through the woods on his right, crossed Bull Run two miles above our left, and threw himself upon the flank and rear of position. This movement was fortunately discovered in time for us to check its progress, and ultimately to form a new line of battle nearly at right angles with the defensive line of Bull Run.

On discovering that the enemy had crossed the stream above him, Col. Evans moved to his left with eleven companies and two field-pieces, to oppose his advance, and disposed his little force under cover of the woods near the intersection of the Warrenton Turnpike and the Sudley Road. Here he was attacked by the enemy in immensely superior numbers, against which he maintained himself with skill and unshrinking courage. Gen. Bee, moving towards the enemy, guided by the firing, had, with a soldier's eye, selected the position near the Henry House, and formed his troops upon it. They were the 7th and 8th Georgia, 4th Alabama, 2d Mississippi, and two companies of the 11th Mississippi regiment, with Imboden's battery. Being compelled, however, to sustain Col. Evans, he crossed the valley and formed on the right and somewhat in advance of his position. Here the joint force, little exceeding five regiments, with six field-pieces, held the ground against about fifteen thousand United States troops for an hour, until, finding themselves outflanked by the continually arriving troops of the enemy, they fell back to Gen. Bee's first position, upon the line of which Jackson, just arriving, formed his brigade and Standard's battery. Col. Hampton, who had by this time advanced with his legion as far as the turnpike, rendered efficient service in maintaining the orderly character of the retreat from that point; and here fell the gallant Lieut. Col. Johnston, his second in command.

In the meantime, I awaited with Gen. Beauregard, near the centre, the full development of the enemy's designs. About 11 o'clock, the violence of the firing on the left indicated a battle, and the march of a large body from the enemy's centre towards the conflict was shown by clouds of dust. I was thus convinced that his great effort was to be made with his right. I stated that conviction to Gen. Beauregard, and the absolute necessity of immediately strengthening our left as much as possible. Orders were accordingly at once sent Gen. Holmes and Col. Early to move with all speed to the sound of the firing, and to Gen. Bonham to send up two of his regiments, and a battery. Gen. Beauregard and I then hurried at a rapid gallop to the scene of action about four miles off. On the way I directed my chief of artillery, Col. Pendleton, to follow with his own and Alburtis' batteries. We came not a moment too soon. The long contest against five-fold odds and heavy losses, especially of field officers, had greatly discouraged the troops of Gen. Bee and Col. Evans. Our presence with them under fire, and some example, had the happiest effect on the spirit of the troops. Order was soon restored, and the battle re-established, to which the firmness of Jackson's brigade greatly contributed. Then, in a brief and rapid conference, Gen. Beauregard was assigned to the command of the left, which, as the younger officer, he claimed, while I returned to that of the whole field. The aspect of affairs was artificial, but I had full confidence in the skill and indomitable courage of Gen. Beauregard, the high soldierly qualities of Gens. Bee and Jackson, and Col. Evans, and the devoted patriotism of their troops. Orders were first dispatched to hasten the march of Gen. Holmes', Col. Early's and Gen. Bonham's regiments. Gen. Ewell was also directed to follow with all speed. Many of the broken troops, fragments of companies and individual stragglers, were re-formed and brought into action with the aid of my staff and a portion of Gen. Beauregard's. Col. (Governor) Smith, with his battalion, and Col. Hampton, with his regiment, were ordered up to reinforce the right. I have since learned that Gen. Beauregard had previously ordered them into the battle. They belonged to his corps. Col. Smith's cheerful courage had a fine influence, not only on the spirit of his own men, but upon the stragglers from the troops engaged. The largest body of these, equal to about four companies, having no competent field officer, I placed under command of one of my staff, Col. F. J. Thomas, who fell while gallantly leading it against the enemy. These reinforcements were all sent to the right to re-establish more perfectly that part of our line. Having attended to these pressing duties, at the immediate scene of conflict, my eye was next directed to Col. Cocke's brigade, the nearest at hand. Hastening to his position, I desired him to lead his troops into action. He informed me, however, that a large body of the enemy's troops beyond the stream and below the bridge threatened us from that quarter. He was, therefore left in his position.

My headquarters were now established near the Lewis House. From this commanding elevation my view embraced the position of the enemy beyond the stream and the approaches to the Stone Bridge, a point of especial importance. I could also see the advance of our troops far down the valley in the direction of Manassas, and observe the progress of the action and the manœuvres of the enemy.

We had now sixteen guns and two hundred and sixty cavalry and a little above nine regiments of the army of the Shenandoah, and six guns and less than the strength of three regiments of that of the Potomac, engaged with about thirty five thousand United States troops, amongst whom were full three thousand men of the old regular army. Yet this admirable artillery and brave infantry and cavalry lost no foot of ground. For nearly three hours they maintained their position repelling five successive assaults by the heavy masses of the enemy, whose numbers enabled him continually to bring up fresh troops as their preceeding columns were driven back. Col. Stuart contributed to one of these repulses by a well timed and vigorous change on the enemy's right flank with two companies of his cavalry. The efficiency of our infantry and cavalry might have been expected from a patriotic people accustomed, like ours, to the management of arms and horses, but that of the artillery was little less than wonderful. They were opposed to batteries far superior in the number, range and equipment of their guns, with educated officers and thoroughly instructed soldiers. We had but one educated artillerist, Col. Pendleton, that model of a Christian soldier, yet they exhibited as much superiority to the enemy in skill as in courage. Their fire was superior both in rapidity and precision.

About two o'clock an officer of Gen. Beauregard's Adjutant General's office galloped from Manassas to report to me that a United States army had reached the line of the Manassas Gap Rail-Road, was marching towards us, and then but three or four miles from our left flank.

The expected reinforcements appeared soon after. Col. Cocke was then desired to lead his brigade into action to support the right of the troops engaged, which he did with alacrity and effect. Within a half hour the two regiments of Gen. Bonham's brigade (Cash's and Kershaw's) came up, and were directed against the enemy's right, which he seemed to be strengthening. Fisher's No. h Carolina regiment was soon after sent in the same direction. About 3 o'clock, while the enemy seemed to be striving to outflank and drive back our left and thus separate us from Manassas, Gen. E. K. Smith arrived with three regiments of Elzey's brigade. He was instructed to attack the right flank of the enemy now exposed to us. Before the movement was completed he fell, severely wounded. Col. Elzey at once taking command, executed it with great promptitude and vigor. Gen. Beauregard rapidly seized the opportunity thus afforded him, and threw forward his whole line. The enemy was driven back from the long contested hill and victory was no longer doubtful. He made yet another attempt to retrive the day. He again extended his right with a still wider sweep to turn our left. Just as he re-formed to renew the battle, Col. Early's three regiments came upon the field. The enemy's new formation exposed his right flank more even than the previous one. Col. Early was, therefore, ordered to throw himself directly upon it, supported by Col. Stuart's cavalry and Beckham's battery. He executed this attack bravely and well, while a simultaneous charge was made by Gen. Beauregard in front. The enemy was broken by this combined attack. He lost all the artillery which he had advanced to the scene of the conflict; he had no more fresh troops to rally on, and a general route ensued.

Instructions were instantly sent to Gen. Bonham to march by the quickest route to the turnpike, to intercept the fugitives, and to Gen. Longstreet, to follow as closely as possible upon the right. Their progress was ckecked by the enemy's reserve, and by night at Centreville.

Shenck's brigade made a slight demonstration towards Lewis's Ford, which was quickly ckecked by Holme's brigade, which had just arrived from the right. His artillery under Capt. Walker, was used with great skill.

Col. Stuart pressed the pursuit of the enemy's principal line of retreat, the Sudley road. Four companies of cavalry, under Col. Bradford and Lieut. Col. Munford, which I had held in reserve, were ordered to cross the stream at Ball's Ford, to reach the turnpike, the line of retreat of the enemy's left. Our cavalry found the roads encumbered with dead and wounded, (many of whom seemed to have been thrown from wagons,) arms, accoutrements, and clothing.

A report came to me from the right that a strong body of United States troops were advancing upon Manassas. Gen. Holmes, who had just reached the field, and Gen. Ewell on his way to it, were ordered to meet this unexpected attack. They found no foe, however.

Our victory was as complete oa one gained by infantry and artillery can be. An adequate force of cavalry would have made it decisive.

It is due, under Almighty God, to the skill and resolution of Gen Beauregard, the admirable conduct of Gens. Bee, E. K. Smith and Jackson, and of Colonels (commanding brigades) Evans, Cocke, Earley and Elzey, and the courage and unyielding firmness of our patriotic volunteers. The admirable character of our troops is incontestibly proved by the result of this battle; especially when it is remembered that little more than six thousand men of the army of the Shenandoah, with sixteen guns, and less than two thousand of that of the Potomac, with six guns, for full five hours successfully resisted thirty-five thousand United States troops, with a powerful artillery and a superior force of regular cavalry. Our forces engaged, gradually increasing during the contest, amounted to but—men at the close of the battle. The brunt of this hard-fought engagement fell upon the troops who held their ground so long with such heroic resolution. The unfading honor with which they won was dearly bought with the blood of our best and bravest. Their loss was far heavier, in proportion, than that of the troops coming later into acion.

Every regiment annd battery engaged performed its part well. The commanders of brigades have been already mentioned mentioned. I refer you to Gen. Beauregard's report for the names of the officers of the army of the Potomac who distinguished themselves most. I cannot enumerate all of the army of the Shenandoah who deserve distinction, and will confine myself to those of high rank. Cols. Bartow and Fisher, (killed,) Jones, (mortally wounded,) Harper, J. F. Preston, Cummings, Falkner, Gartrell, and Vaughan; J. E. B. Stuart of the cavalry, and Pendleton of the artillery. Lieut. Col. Echols, Lightfoot, Lackland, G. H. Stewart, and Gardner. The last named gallant officer was severely wounded.

* * * * * * *

108 killed, 510 wounded, 12 missing. That of the army of the Shenandoah was 270 killed, 979 wounded, 18 missing.

That of the enemy could not be ascertained. It must have been between 4,000 and 5,000. Twenty-eight pieces of artillery, about 5,000 muskets, and nearly 500,000 cartridges; a garrison flag and 10 colors were captured on the field, or in the pursuit. Besides these, we captured 64 artillery horses, with their harness, 26 wagons, and much camp equipage, clothing, and other property abandoned in their flight.

[The above is all that was in type of the report, and the copy could not be found—more's the pity.—Eds. First Minnesota.]

STANDING COMMITTEES IN C. S. CONGRESS.

HOUSE COMMITTEES.

On Elections—Messrs. Smith of N. C., Vest of Mo., Staples of Va., Crockett of Ky., Gardenhire of Tenn., Curry of Ala., Clapp of Miss., Dawkins of Fla., and Tripp of Geo.

Ways and Means—Messrs. Kenner of La., Jones of Tenn., Bonham of S. C., Garnett of Va., McRae of Miss., Lyon of Ala., Machen of Ky., Holt of Geo., and Graham of Texas.

Military Affairs—Messrs. Miles of S. C., Kenan of Geo., Pugh of Ala., Davis of Miss., Harris of Mo., Swann of Tenn., Bridges of N. C., Batson of Ark., and R. A. Pryor, of Va.

Foreign Affairs—Messrs. Foote of Tenn., Perkins of La., Smith of Ala., Dejarnette of Va., Barksdale of Miss., McQueen of S. C., Breckinridge of Ky., Preston of Va., and McLean of N. C.

Naval Affairs—Messrs. Conrad of La., Boyce of S. C., Wright of Geo., Clopton of Ala., Currin of Tenn., Smith of Va., Gaither of N. C., Dawkins of Fla., and Chambliss of Va.

Judiciary—Messrs. Gartrell of Geo., Russell of Va., Dargan of Ala., Moore of Ky., Garland of Ark., Heiskell of Tenn., Gray of Tex., Ashe of N. C., and Holcombe of Va.

Commerce—Messrs. Curry of Ala., Trippe of Geo., Cooke of Mo., McDowell of N. C., Lyons of Va., Sexton of Tex., Villere of La., F. W. Bruce of Ky., and Chambliss of Miss.

Post-Offices and Post-Roads—Messrs. Chilton of Ala., Conrow of Mo., Royston of Ark., Johnson of Va., Clark of Geo., Davidson of N. C., Welch of Miss., Hilton of Fla., and Herbert of Texas.

Territories and Public Lands—Messrs. Wilcox of Tex., Marshall of La., Jenkins of Va., Freeman of Mo., Foster of Ala., Batson of Ark., Lewis of Geo., Ewing of Ky., and Meneese of Tenn.

Indian Affairs—Messrs. Singleton of Miss., Elliott of Ky., Hanley of Ark., Dupre of La., Goode of Va., Tibbs of Tenn., Wright of Tex., Arrington of N. C., and Ralls of Ala.

Patents—Messrs. Bell of Mo., Lander of N. C., Read of Ky., Chilton of Ala., Staples of Va., Marshall of La., Hilton of Fla., Strickland of Geo., and Wright of Texas.

Claims—Messrs. Smith of Va., Clopton of Ala., Burnett of Ky., Villere of La., Clapp of Miss., McLane of N. C., Munnerlyn of Geo., Farrow of S. C., and Gardenhire of Tenn.

Accounts—Messrs. McQueen of S. C., Foster of Ala., Keenan of N. C., Strickland of Geo., Hanley of Ark.

Rules and Officers of House—Messrs. Jones of Ten., Perkins of La., Boteler of Va., Lewis of Ga., and Smith of N. C.

Pay and Mileage—Messrs. Burnett of Ky., Singleton of Miss., and Bridgers of N. C.

Enrolled Bills—Messrs. Elliott of Ky., Chambers of Miss., and Tibbs of Tenn.

Flag and Seal—Messrs. Boteler of Va., Smith of Ala., and Gray of Texas.

SENATE COMMITTEES.

Foreign Affairs—Messrs. Orr of S. C., Yancey of Ala., Wigfall of Tex., Clark of Mo., Preston of Va.

Finance—Messrs. Barnwell of S. C., Hunter of Va., Davis of N. C., Semmes of La., and Henry of Tenn.

Commerce—Messrs. Clay of Ala., Maxwell of Fla., Dortch of N. C., Peyton of Mo., and Burnett of Ky.

Military Affairs—Messrs. Sparrow of La., Preston of Va., Johnson of Ark., Wigfall of Texas, and Henry of Tenn.

Naval Affairs—Messrs. Brown of Miss., Oldham of Tex., Baker of Fla., Simms of Ky., Dortch of N. C.

Judiciary—Messrs. Hill of Ga., Haynes of Tenn., Phelan of Miss., Semmes of La., and Burnett of Ky.

Indian Affairs—Messrs. Johnson of Ark., Clay of Ala., Oldham of Tex., Peyton of Mo., Simms of Ky.

Post-Offices and Post-Roads—Messrs. Oldham of Texas, Mitchell of Ark., and Baker of Fla.

Public Lands—Messrs. Clark of Mo., Baker of Fla., and Yancey of Ala.

Patents—Messrs. Maxwell of Fla., Haynes of Tennessee, and Hill of Geo.

Claims—Messrs. Davis of N. C., Burnett of Ky., and Peyton of Mo.

Territories—Messrs. Wigfall of Texas, Brown of Miss., and Yancey of Ala.

Accounts—Messrs. Mitchell of Ark., Dortch of N. C., and Simms of Ky.

Printing—Messrs. Phelan of Miss., Hill of Geo., and Clark of Mo.

Enrollment—Messrs. Phelan of Miss., Maxwell of Fla., and Mitchell of Ark.

[The first mentioned member of each Committee is constituted the Chairman thereof.]

THE NEW SOUTH.

Vol. 1. No. 1. Port Royal, S. C., March 15, 1862. Price Five Cents

THE WAR.

TENNESSEE AND KENTUCKY.

The latest news from the war is quite as welcome as any that has preceded it. The occupation of Nashville by the government forces is placed beyond a doubt. Gen. Buell at the head of a portion of his command entered the city on the 2d inst. The rebel troops, after committing all manner of depredations on public property, destroying railroad bridges, &c., fell back on Murfreesboro, on the Nashville and Chattanooga Railroad, thirty-two miles southeast of the capital. It is thought they will avail themselves of the mountain passes in that neighborhood, and oppose the advance of our army into Northern Alabama. Gen. Buell had with him in his advance from Bowling Green to Nashville, portions of McCook's and Mitchell's divisions, but, soon after his arrival at the latter place, was joined by Crittenden's and Nelson's commands, who went up the Cumberland by steamer. His force, allowing for garrisons at Bowling Green and other points occupied, can not be less than forty thousand troops. As our troops progress in Tennessee, we hear the most gratifying evidences of the revival of Union feeling among the people. The left wing of Buell's army, under Gen. Thomas, by this time must be in the vicinity of Knoxville.

The bearers of the rebel flag of truce, who met Commodore Foote and General Cullom, near Columbus, on the 23d inst., made a proposition for the evacuation of Columbus. This was referred to General Halleck. But the terms proposed were rejected by that officer, and the answer despatched by the flag of truce which went down from Cairo on the 24th.

But since then Columbus has really been abandoned. The following dispatch received from Commodore Foote, dated Cairo, March 1, settles the matter:

"Lieut. Commanding Phelps, sent with a flag of truce to-day to Columbus, has this moment returned, and reports that Columbus is being evacuated. He saw the Rebels burning their winter quarters, and removing their heavy guns on the bluffs. But the guns in the water batteries remain intact. He also saw a large force of cavalry drawn up ostentatiously on the bluffs, but no infantry was to be seen, as heretofore. The encampment seen in our armed reconnoisance a few days since has been removed. Large fires were visible in the town of Columbus, and upon the river banks below, indicating the destruction of the town, military stores, and equipments,

A. H. FOOTE, Flag Officer."

It was believed that our forces would occupy the place on March 2d. The rebels were to fall back on Island No. 10 in the Mississippi River.

Gen. Buell has also telegraphed that Murfreesboro had been abandoned by the rebels, who were retreating along the Nashville and Chattanooga Railroad, tearing up the rails as they proceeded, thus rendering pursuit difficult.

A great change is found to have occurred already in the political feeling in Tennessee, and the War Department feels itself warranted in taking measures immediately to raise and arm volunteer troops in that State. The important announcement is also made by authority, that the Tennessee and Cumberland Rivers will be opened this week to free and unrestricted commerce, under the order of the Secretary of the Treasury. This will prove a just measure of relief to the loyal people of Tennessee, who have been subjected to the greatest deprivations during the rebel occupation of the State.

More than this, business messages have been received in New York by telegraph from Nashville for the first time since early last summer; the Post Office is taken possession of by the government; and the President has designated the Hon. Andrew Johnson to be a Brigadier General, and he proceeds to Tennessee immediately, to open a military provisional government of Tennessee until the civil government shall be reconstructed.

The rebel forces under Albert S. Johnston are being steadily pressed backward by Gen. Buell. Cotton to the value of $100,000 has fallen into our hands at Nashville, and the Treasury Department has taken measures to have it brought to New York. So the work goes bravely on.

The Rebel army, in their retreat from Nashville, left behind 1600 of their sick and wounded. They destroyed the bridges and burned all the steamboats lying there but one, which escaped. The Texas soldiers fired the city in many places, but the citizens extinguished the flames.

A great majority of the property owners remained at Nashville to receive the protection of the United States troops. The excitement among them was intense.

Before leaving Nashville, Gov. Harris made a speech, in which he said he had done all he could, and was going to leave for Memphis, to which place he advised the citizens to follow him.

The Union sentiment was very strong, and our troops were received with great cordiality.

Great indignation was expressed by the citizens of Nashville against Gov. Harris. He was fairly driven away by the Union men—the latter having become bold at the proximity of the Union troops, and dared to assert their rights.

The Mayor made a speech, saying he was still Secession to the backbone. "But," said he, "you see how it is; the game is up and we must either surrender the tow[illegible] it burned."

Lieut Gro[illegible] sends a dispatch to Flag Officer Foote, from which we make the following extracts:

U. S. GUNBOAT TAYLOR, CAIRO, Feb. 23, 1862.

"SIR: I have returned to this place, after having gone up the Tennessee river as high as *Eastport, Miss.* I am happy to state that I have met with an *increased* Union sentiment in South Tennessee and North Alabama. I saw few Mississippians. In Hardin, McNary, Wayne, Decatur, and a portion of Hardiman, all of which border upon the river, the Union sentiment is strong, and those who do not express themselves openly loyal, are only prevented by the fears of the military tyranny and coercion which is practiced by marauding bands of guerilla companies of cavalry.

The glorious successes of our arms at Forts Henry and Donelson have been most beneficial to the Union cause throughout south and west Tennessee and Alabama. Union men can now begin to express their loyal sentiments without fear of being mobbed, especially along the banks of the river. I have enlisted seventeen men and brought down fourteen refugees."

From the direction of Murfreesboro advices state that the rebels concentrated at that place have been surrounded by Gen. Buell's forces, so that none could escape.

The Rebels offered to surrender the position to the Federal troops if they would be allowed to march out with the honors of war.

General Buell refused to allow them these conditions, and demanded their unconditional surrender. He notified them that he would allow two days for consideration, and if the place was not surrendered at the expiration of that period he would open fire upon them.

ARKANSAS.

In this State General Curtis seems to be doing a good deal of work that was hoped and promised from Gen. Lane and Gen. Hunter. He has got the start of those officers, and is now only waiting for supplies to push on more rapidly and energetically than ever. He first routed Price at Sugar Creek, in Benton county; then drove him from Bentonville; then pursued him to Cross Hollows, where he had resolved to make a stand. Price, reinforced by McCulloch, appears, however, to have thought better of it, and made a run instead of a stand. Curtis followed him to Fayetteville; but Price and his men, after setting fire to the town, fled, and Curtis's forces marched in among the smoking ruins.

Curtis is now forty miles beyond the Missouri line, and not more than forty from the Arkansas River. The Boston Mountains, near him, are said to be full of Union people, and John Ross with the Cherokees, is only waiting for a chance to declare in favor of the Union.

NORTH CAROLINA.

A dispatch fram Com. Goldsborough to Secretary Welles, dated U. S. Steamer Philadelphia, off Roanoke Island, Feb. 23, says:

"The reconnoitering party sent up the Chowan River, has returned. It did not go beyond Winton. There the enemy, in considerable force, opened a heavy fire upon the vessel in advance, the Delaware, with a battery of artillery and musketry, which induced our force to attack it in return, both by landing the New York Ninth Zouaves, and with the guns of the vessels that could be brought to bear on the enemy. The enemy soon took to flight and the houses he occupied as quarters were burned. Not a man on our side, of either arm, was injured.

The Raleigh Register says all the prisoners taken at Roanoke Island have been released on parole.

THE POTOMAC.

Gen. Banks has made an advance on the Upper Potomac, crossing on the night of the 23d from Sandy Hook to Harper's Ferry. Strong reinforcements went over on the 25th and occupied Bolivar, Charlestown and both banks of the Shenandoah. Martinsburg is also occupied by our troops. Whether any peculiar significance is to be attached to this advance is unknown; it is surmised, however, that this is the premonitory symptom of a general movement. The sentiment among the people is said to be strongly in favor of the Union; and there is more reason to credit this, because of the Union speech lately made at Martinsburg by Mr. Faulkner, ex-Minister to France, and occupant of Fort Lafayette. That gentleman, known as a political trimmer, has openly announced that the secession game is played out, and that all the people on the Upper Potomac agree with him in the sentiment. The rats are leaving the sinking ship.

Gen. Lander died on the 2d inst., at Paw Paw, in Western Virginia. His death at this juncture is a disaster. He was a native of Massachusetts and had been by profession an engineer. He served as a colonel under McClellan in the brilliant campaign which first made known to the world the superlative abilities of the Commander-in-Chief, and was made a Brigadier in July. He received his death wound at Edward's Ferry; but refused at first to succumb to its influences. Gen. Shields succeeds to his command. Gen. Lander was recently married to the distinguished actress, Miss Jane Davenport.

News from Rebel Sources.

The Rebel newspapers are gloomy in the extreme. They acknowledge the extent of their disasters, abuse Jeff Davis, say his inauguration is a mockery and his government a failure, but they still att[illegible] of desperation. The inaugural splurge of Jeff Davis is one of the most remarkable documents that ever emanated from what purported to be a government. He says in his opening sentence "events have demonstrated that the (Rebel) government has attempted more than it has power successfully to achieve"; he says that the Rebels "were destitute of the means for the prosecution of a war on so gigantic a scale as that which it has attained; calls the surrender at Roanoke Island "deeply humiliating however imperfect may have been the preparations for defence"; and in regard to Fort Donelson, hopes that "our losses have been exaggerated." He speaks bitterly of the enlistment plan and thinks it probable that the war will continue through a series of years. The only hope he has is that the Federal Government will not be able to support its extravagant expenditure.

REBEL STATEMENT OF THE DONELSON AFFAIR.

"Our loss at the Fort Donelson fight of four days is put down at 1600. The Yankee loss was 4000.

Fort Donelson was surrendered on Sunday, the 16th, in accordance with the decision of a council of war held the previous night. Gen. Buckner was left to make it known to Gen. Pillow and staff. Gen. Floyd and eight hundred of his brigade went to Clarksville on Sunday morning. Buckner remained. This statement seems confused. We can't understand how a council of war was held in Pillow's absence, or when Gen. Buckner was *left* to make known to him the intention to capitulate.

Our army of twelve thousand, says the dispatch, capitulated on Sunday morning.

It is believed that Nashville has been evacuated and the army has fallen back, but to what point is unknown."

NEWS FROM SAVANNAH.

AUGUSTA, Feb. 26, 1862.

The Savannah Republican of this morning says that communication with Fort Pulaski has been effectually closed by the federals, who have erected three batteries for heavy guns.

THE POST OFFICE FOLLOWING THE ARMY. First Assistant Postmaster General Kasson is engaged in sending out instructions and making arrangements for re-establishing post offices and post routes, as our armies advance into the the so-called Confederate States.

A. H. Markland is following our forces into Tennessee, and J. J. Miller, also an agent of the Department in this connection, is operating in the southern part of Kentucky. The post office at Nashville and those in the eastern part of North Carolina will soon be open.

THE NEW SOUTH.

PORT ROYAL, SATURDAY, MARCH, 15, 1862.

THE NEW SOUTH.

Issued weekly from "THE NEW SOUTH" printing office—Union Square, Port Royal, S. C. Price five cents per copy.

Advertisements one dollar a line, each insertion.

Terms, invariably cash.

ADAM BADEAU....................EDITOR.

JOS. H. SEARS....................PUBLISHER.

INAUGURAL.

Not often has a newspaper occupied so singular a position as that filled to-day by "The New South."—Issued in a military command, addressed mostly to soldiers at the seat of war, its audience is yet not purely military, but in part naval, in part civil; it is possible that some portion may be found at the North, it is not impossible that we may occassionally reach the ear of Southerners, debarred now for a twelvemonth from learning what the sentiments and intentions and power of the nation really are.

In acting as spokesman both to and for this varied population we shall have several aims in view: first of all to support, so far as we are able, the national government. In order to do this more effectually we shall abstain from the discussion of exciting political topics, believing that the business of our most immediate readers is now military, not political, and that it is the province of the true patriot at this juncture, to do nothing to divide the national forces, or to distract their energies from the one great object of us all, the suppression of the Rebellion. Here is a common ground where all can meet, and on that we mean to plant ourselves. It shall be our endeavor to strengthen the hands of the government and those who represent it, to incite the courage and fortify the endurance of its defenders, not to sow the seeds of discord among those who are themselves battling against the results of discord. Next we desire to furnish news of interest and importance to our readers; for the life and basis of a newspaper are its reliability in this regard.—Information concerning public matters at the North, the movements of the national armies and affairs abroad, will be presented in a condensed form, it is true, but still we trust a correct view of all important affairs will be afforded. The doings within this military command will of course receive a due share of attention; Port Royal, Beaufort, Tybee and Otter Islands, and other places occupied by our forces will not be neglected, and proceedings of every nature fit for publication will be chronicled; but none of our loyal readers will complain if we with hold any thing that could by any chance prove of service to the enemy. The news of the fleet, however, the daily li e in camp, the health of the command, and a thousand other details will at once suggest themselves as proper subjects for report. These matters it is hoped, will prove of sufficient interest to the country at large for us to rely on a support from other quarters not altogether insignificant.

And if an occasional copy of a Union paper should [illegible] deluded and [illegible] people with [illegible] the hopelessness of their effort may be afforded them. When they discover that the Unionists are so firmly established here as to issue and support newspapers, they will admit that we have no idea of returning; they will conclude that our occupation is not purely a military one; they will perhaps see how desperate is their own condition, and submit more readily to the government which has never wished to do more than bring them back to their allegiance, but which is determined to do that at every cost and at every hazard, and if need arises by the employment of every means.

Newspapers receiving the present number of "*The New South*," and wishing to exchange, will please commence forwarding their issues at once.

Our next number will contain a complete list of the deaths in this command, since the sailing of the Expeditionary Corps, in October last.

The Situation.

Our contemporaries at the North are in the habit of announcing in their daily issues the situation of military affairs, sure that nothing else can have so great an interest for their readers. We can not promise to be equally explicit in our developments, though perhaps we might be equally accurate without occasioning much harm; but instead of attempting to tell all that we know and a great deal more that we guess in regard to operations in this vicinity, it has occurred to us that a synopsis of what has already been accomplished here since the 7th of last November, may well supply the place of an article on the "Situation."

Since the capture of Port Royal and the landing of the Expeditionary Corps, events have not been laggard. A great harbor, previously almost unknown to the world, has been opened; light ships and buoys established; the results of the coast survey verified; piers have been built for the landing of stores, and as many as seventy or eighty vessels may be constantly seen in the bay—men-of-war, transports, merchant ships, steam tugs, schooners, sloops, &c. Since the battle of Hilton Head the Navy has reconnoitered the entire coast between Fernandina on the South and Stono Inlet on the North; has penetrated into other bays and inlets often as far as ten or twenty miles; taken the first possession of Tybee Island and North Edisto; driven the enemy out of the town of Rockville; assisted in the dash made upon Port Royal Ferry on the 1st of January; sunk the stone fleet in Charleston Harbor; supervised the colony of Negroes at North Edisto, and played its part in the movements at Fernandina.

Since the 7th of November, a town has sprung up on Hilton Head, where at least a thousand civilians must be now employed, in one capacity or another,—teamsters, carpenters, machinists, laborers, newspaper reporters, sutlers, post masters and editors; and, of late even women and children have been seen within the limits of the command. Long lines of hospitals, stables and store houses for quartermasters and commissaries' use, b[illegible]ries, negro quarters [illegible] other buildings have been erected, quite transforming the appearance of the spot. Negroes have been set to work at varions tasks and become entirely accustomed to their new condition, cotton to the value of hundreds of thousands of dollars has been obtained from the Sea Islands, the blacks laboring vigorously and willingly, collecting, ginning and baling.

Since the 7th of November, long lines of fortifications have been thrown up on this island, and lined with armament which defies any attack; Beaufort—the "Newport" of South Carolina, has been occupied by federal troops, Tybee Island has been held and put into a position of defence; Otter Point has been seized; Bay Point occupied and strongly fortified; troops have been thrown upon nearly every one of these famous "Sea Islands" and the entire coast definitely abandoned by Rebel forces.

Since the date of our arrival here, there has occurred one brisk little engagement with the enemy at Port Royal Ferry, in which the National forces, both Army and Navy manifested pluck and coolness—the most desirable qualities in soldiers or sailors. The nerve of officers was equally apparent. The result proposed was completely accomplished and the enemy driven back from an annoying position, his battery destroyed and his impertinence chastised.

More important however than any purely military movement made here since the 7th of November, has been the blockading of the Savannah River; effected by the erection of two forts on Jones and Bird islands, within eight miles of the city of Savannah; works erected under infinite difficulties and amid great danger on spots hitherto supposed to be absolutely untenable if not inaccessible; and which have already proved their efficiency by driving off the Rebel fleet and forcing Tatnall to acknowledge that "he could not have remained ten minutes longer within their range without being smashed to pieces."

The Situation then is one upon which those who have contributed to accomplish it, may honestly congratulate themselves and that may well prove an auspicious augury for the events which are to follow.

The Western Victories.

The successes which have attended our arms at the West, continue, and the results are even greater than the successes themselves. Fort Henry, Fort Donelson, Mill Spring have demonstrated beyond a shadow of doubt, two things which the rebels proclaimed were not demonstrable—the bravery of Northerners and the existence of a Union spirit in the slave states. The question of relative manhood is set at rest forever, after the gallant bayonet charge of the Ohio regiment at Somerset, and the desperate valor with which the troops from Southern Illinois held their own, through the weary hours of Saturday, the 15th of February. In neither of these instances was it preponderanee of force which decided the result at that particular spot; and in neither of these instances did the Rebels hesitate when once they discovered they were fairly whipped—to yield. Let us hear no more then of the superior bravery of the Southerner. Indeed the Richmond papers have already learnt the lesson of the day, and acknowledge that they "have relied too much upon the cowardice of the enemy."

The other result accomplished by the battles in Kentucky and Tennessee, is that the population of these states is really waiting to come back to its allegiance. And not only of those states; the revulsion extends over into Alabama—and by the very latest dates we learn—to Mississippi. If a reaction begins in Jeff Davis's own state, it is fair to presume that it is destined to be universal. The patriotic spirit that would not be smothered in Eastern Tennessee when things looked darker, now breaks out clearly in the light of our successes; and volunteers are received by the government; while a second gunboat expedition up the Tennessee River was as brilliant in its discoveries as its predecessor, that so stirred the country. Nashville and Columbus are now in our hands. The Tennessee and Cumberland rivers are open to free and unrestricted commerce, trade has begun again between Nashville and New York, and every proof of loyalty is given by the people who we have so long heard were unanimous in favor of the rebellion.

The beginning of the end is surely evident; for the alacrity with which our generals advanced and followed up these victories affords the best possible presage of still more glorious achievements and still more happy re-unions.

The Reviews.

The Review of troops at Hilton Head on Monday, March 3, was unanimously pronounced by old army officers, one of the finest they had seen. More than one regiment of volunteers extorted from the regular officers, this praise.

The inspection at Beaufort on the 6th was equally satisfactory; the three arms of the service seemed to vie with each other; artillery, cavalry and infantry manifesting the most gratifying improvement in drill and discipline. It has always been said that volunteers were the best material in the world for soldiers; it has already been proven that the material required working up; what results can be attained when it is worked up have been shown the world within the last month at the West. The fact that the process of working goes on here, was evidenced by these reviews. When the time comes for the army here to act on a scale and in events commensurate with those that have attracted the attention of the country elsewhere, the army here will be ready.

A CONTRAST. Brig. Generals Grant and Buell have both been made Major Generals since the result of their brilliant movements at the West has reached the government; and have besides made their names familiar in the mouths and hearts of their countrymen, as household words. The latest news from North Carolina is that Brig. Gen. Huger has been placed under arrest. While the *Raleigh Reporter* thinks "this news too good too good to be true," the Memphis journals announce Floyd as a traitor and scoundrel; he is even twitted with the thefts which he perpetrated on the National Government in order to recommend himself to the rebels.

OTTER ISLAND. An unfortunate circumstance occurred yesterday morning at Otter Island. Two small parties of the 45th Pennsylvania regiment went out to surround a number of Rebels, supposed to be lurking in the vicinity. They were led along different routes by negro guides, but the guides were stupid, and in the grey of morning, the two detachments came upon each other, when one party fired; two were killed on the spot, Captain E. Y. Rambo, and a corporal, whose name we have not yet been able to learn; two were severely wounded in the lungs, and are unlikely to recover, and several others were slightly wounded.

News of this Command.

THE FALL OF FERNANDINA.

Our account of the capture of Fernandina is necessarily incomplete; no military details can be furnished in these columns, of any recent movement.

On the 1st of March the combined national force appeared off Fernandina. The entrance to the harbor lies between two islands, Amelia and Cumberland; at this point is situated Fort Clinch, an unfinished casemated work, with one tier of guns which had never been mounted when the place was seized by the Rebels a year ago. Two or three miles further in, on the southern side of Cumberland Sound, is Fernandina; on the same side but nearer to Fort Clinch, lies Old Fernandina; the population of both places together does not amount to more than ten or twelve hundred.

Batteries had been erected by the Rebels all along the Sound, and in various other positions commanding the approach. On the 2d of March, the field batteries were found to be completely abandoned, while at nearly the same time it was discovered that even Fort Clinch had been evacuated. The enemy had fled without firing a gun. Fourteen heavy pieces were left behind, all of them spiked, and numerous others seemed to have been carried off; probably as many as forty or fifty; the number is by some even estimated as high as eighty or ninety. The whole garrison, calculated to be 5000 strong, had also decamped, and the population of the town was hurrying off in railroad cars; a few shells stopped the train; some of the passengers took to the woods, and escaped; among them, it is said, was Senator *Yulee;* most of them, however, were brought back. They were principally women and children, and returned to their homes; some were unwilling, but many expressed no dissatisfaction.

The population that remains represents that the Rebels had fled on the day subsequent to the appearance of our fleet, and that the town was to be burnt within the next twenty-four hours. They declare that the place was evacuated under orders from Richmond, it having been determined to abandon the entire coast. They also assert that our arrival there has been anticipated since last December.

The prompt flight without the shadow of an attempt at resistance, indicates any thing but the chivalric and desperate behavior we have been taught to expect; and none of the unwillingness to receive the old National authority, which has been lately inculcated by the so called government of the Rebels. If the victory was bloodless it was none the less important, and affords a sure indication that one of two circumstances exists; either a revulsion in the Southern feeling, originating in the recent National successes at the West; or an extension of the panic which has begun there even to this the opposite side of the continent.

PORT ROYAL.

The steamer Mississippi, from Fortress Monroe, with Gen. Butler aboard and a body of reinforcements for his command, got aground on Frying Pan Shoals, on Friday morning, the 28th inst., in sight of Cape Fear. Her anchor was immediately cast and she struck on it, knocking such a hole in her bottom as to cause a serious injury. Accordingly she put into this port on the 2nd inst., having been obliged to keep men at her pumps constantly after the accident. She went direct to Seabrook, where the troops under Gen. Butler were encamped. On the 11th she was so far repaired as to be got off, but ran aground again within a few hundred yards of Seabrook Landing. The Captain is named Fulton, and a Southerner by birth; he has been placed under arrest. Gen. Butler, his staff and a portion of his force proceeds to their destination on the Matanzas, loaned for that purpose, by Gen. Sherman. The Mississippi, which has been again got off, conveys the remainder of her original complement. Colonels Neal Dow, Dudley and Gooding are with Gen. Butler; Mrs. Butler also accompanies the General. The health of the forces is good.

The Delaware was the last steamer for New York; she carried no mail, as there were doubts of her seaworthiness. The first news of the fall of Fernandina was conveyed North by her, other than that contained in Com. Dupont's despatches direct by the Alabama, which left on the 4th inst.

The Atlantic arrived at this port on the 7th inst., bringing a mail and New York papers up to the 3d inst. Among her passengers was Mrs. General Stevens. The Atlantic will probably return on the 17th, carrying a mail. This favorite vessel is of as much importance to the service as if employed in the more technical departments of the army or navy, and if strictly attached to either arm, could hardly be more efficiently worked.

Col. Fellows, now in command of this post, has his head quarters in the long line of buildings recently put up for officers' quarters immediately to the rear of Gen. Sherman's staff camp. The adjutant of the post will transact all his official business at that place.

Since the 1st of January over 300,000 letters have been received or sent from the Port Royal post office.

A General Court Martial has been sitting for several days past at Hilton Head, of which Col. R. Williams, of the 1st Massachusetts Cavalry, is president, and Capt. L. H. Pelouze, A. A. Adjutant General, is judge advocate. Several important cases were tried before it; one was that of an infantry captain advising a sick private to desert; and another the heinous offense of a sentinel sleeping on post; both punishable with death. The decision of the court is not yet announced.

LATER FROM CHARLESTON.

The Rebel schooner Shamrock was captured on the 10th in the Dawho River, near Edisto; a Charleston Courier of the 5th was aboard, from which we learn the following items:

The mayor proclaims that no person is allowed to leave the city without a pass.

The Governor (Brown) of Georgia recommends cotton growers to plant no cotton this year.

The British vessel Rinaldo communicated with Fort Sumter on the 4th inst., sending despatches to Bunce, the consul.

An advertisement announces no freight received at the railroad depot for the Nashville and Chattanooga Railroad.

The Rebel steamer Nashville ran the blockade off Beaufort, N. C., on the 28th of February, at day-break, the stars and stripes at her peak and the old private signal at her main; when she got close enough to lay her course for the channel, the National flag was hauled down, and the stars and bars hoisted fore and aft. The blockader fired twenty-one shots, but all fell short. The Nashville ran in under Fort Macon, at the rate of fourteen knots.

The Nashville brought no arms, greatly to the dissatisfaction of the rebels.

The following is the account, in the Savannah Republican, of the fall of Fernandina:

"A dispatch received here yesterday, states that the enemy has landed on Cumberland Island, and sent a detachment to occupy the town of Fernandina. Most of the citizens abandoned the place some weeks ago, and the military was withdrawn from Amelia Island, on which Fernandina is situated, about two days since; consequently no resistance was offered. If the enemy should not burn the place, they are welcome to it, as they will reap but little benefit from its possession."

TYBEE.

Gen. Gilmore is now in command of the troops on Tybee Island.

A daily line of communication is established between Hilton Head and Tybee. Capt. Fuller, Assistant Quartermaster on Gen. Sherman's staff, has been recently detailed for duty at Tybee.

EDISTO.

A daily express line now connects North Edisto and Otter Point with Hilton Head.

BEAUFORT.

At the review, last week, General Sherman and his staff were present, Gen. Stevens, in command at Beaufort, with his staff, of course receiving the reviewing officer. Quite a number of civilians, clerks and others, were present, and one or two ladies even looked on the unusual sight of Federal troops reviewed on the soil of South Carolina. Some of the officers of Gen. Butler's staff were also among the spectators; while in the background the negroes congregated, staring in wonder and admiration at the show. The day was favorable, and the troops acquitted themselves more than creditably at this, the first formal review which has occurred at the Newport of the South, since Gen. Drayton left it for Hilton Head, about the 1st of last November.

Mr. Pierce and the Rev. Mr. French, the two gentlemen to whom the care of the negroes in this command has been committed, arrived at Hilton Head by the Atlantic, bringing with them a party of instructors and agents to assist in the performance of the novel and various duties about to be assumed. Twelve of the teachers are young ladies. The whole party left immediately for Beaufort, where their head quarters will be established. Mr. Pierce is to supervise the general management of the blacks in their ordinary labors, and Mr. French, the educational and religious instruction to be imparted.

DAWFUSKIE.

Notwithstanding the extraordinary hardships and exposures to which they have been subjected, the troops at Dawfuskie, under Gen. Viele's command are in a good state of health. Any thing more difficult than dragging heavy guns through the mud and mire of these swampy islands, has not been attempted during the war. The danger of interruption from the enemy was of course great, and the labor had all to be done by night. The work was really an achievement and deserves to be so noted. The Rebels admit that it secured the blockade of the Savannah; but they will not acknowledge the batteries to be any thing but floating ones. It would not be politic to tell their own people what difficulties were trampled upon by the Yankees so close to Savannah and Pulaski. It would be manifestly improper to state the forces at these places; Major Beard of the 48th New York, commands Battery Hamilton, on Bird Island, and Lieut. Col. Barton of the same regiment, is in command of Fort Vulcan.

Capt. Collins of the Unadilla, is in command of the naval force in that quarter.

THE VERY LATEST.

New York papers of the 5th and 6th, brought by the Flora, contain the official reports of the occupation of Columbus by our forces. Great quantities of guns, amunition and other stores, fell into our hands; the Rebels are said to have withdrawn to Island No. 10 in the Mississippi River, about fifty miles further down. Previous to evacuating Columbus they made every attempt to destroy the works and stores, but were unable to complete the devastation. They set fire to the town.

Despatches from Richmond, via Norfolk, as well as news we get through the loyal newspapers inform us that the capital of the Rebel dominion has been placed under martial law; the Hon. John M. Botts and twenty other influential and wealthy citizens have been arrested for treason, (which means loyalty), and riotous demonstrations of Union sentiment continue. All over the walls of houses are placarded announcements that "The Day of Deliverance is at Hand," "Wait a Little Longer," and similar significant expressions.

The Charleston Courier of the 10th reports an important engagement in Hampton Roads. According to this Rebel authority, the Merrimac was gotten out of Norfolk harbor, and ventured out in the teeth of the Minnesota and one or two gunboats lying near Fortress Monroe. The Minnesota of course resisted the attempted passage, and a general fight began. The batteries at Newport News and on Sewall's Point all opened fire, several gunboats came out from Norfolk, and the Ericsson floating battery was called into play. The Rebels call the action a brilliant one, and speak of riddling the Minnesota; but we all know what their boasting means, and how important it is to them at this juncture to infuse a little confidence into their unreliable masses. The gist of the matter is this; the Merrimac was driven back according to their own story, after two days fighting. We have no account of the matter as yet from loyal sources. The occurrence took place on the 8th and 9th inst. Capt. Van Brunt, of Massachusetts, commands the Minnesota.

The Flower of Liberty.

BY OLIVER WENDELL HOLMES.

What flower is this that greets the morn,
Its hues from Heaven so freshly born?
With burning star and flaming brand
It kindles all the sunset land;
O, tell us what its name may be!
Is this the Flower of Liberty?
    It is the banner of the free,
    The starry Flower of Liberty!

In savage nature's far abode
Its tender seed our fathers sowed;
The storm-winds rocked its swelling bud,
Its opening leaves were streaked with blood,
Till, lo! earth's tyrants shook to see
The fullblown Flower of Liberty!
    Then hail the banner of the free,
    The starry Flower of Liberty!

Behold its streaming rays unite
One mingling flood of braided light—
The red that fires the Southern rose,
With spotless white from Northern snows,
And, spangled o'er its azure, see
The sister Stars of Liberty!
    Then hail the banner of the free,
    The starry Flower of Liberty!

The blades of heroes fence it round;
Where'er it springs is holy ground;
From tower and dome its glories spread;
It waves where lonely sentries tread;
It makes the land as ocean free,
And plants an empire on the sea!
    Then hail the banner of the free,
    The starry Flower of Liberty!

Thy sacred leaves, fair freedom's flower,
Shall ever float on dome and tower,
To all their heavenly colors true,
In blackening frost or crimson dew;
And God love us as we love thee,
Thrice holy Flower of Liberty!
    Then hail the banner of the free,
    The starry Flower of Liberty!

Warlike Wit.

The Confeds have come to the conclusion that Donelson is not their forte.

An army generally has but two wings, but that of Gen. Price flew as if it had at least twenty.

Jeff Davis in the attitude of prayer, at the conclusion of his inaugural, and the poor fist he makes at it, reminds one of the two boys under the tree, in a thunder storm, where one in the danger of his position, remarked in terror-stricken tones, to his companion, "Jim, can you pray?" and meeting with a negative response, exclaimed, wildly, "Well, I can't, but by G—d something has got to be done!" As Artemas Ward says, "The moril is obvis."

Prentice says that since Floyd stole himself away from Fort Donelson, he will have nothing more to steal, unless he undertakes the desperate task of outwitting the devil, who has a claim upon him to be hereafter settled.

Warranted to "carry" every thing before him—Our gallant Porter.

The rebels are fleet of foot, but they couldn't escape Foote's fleet.

Business motto of Generals Curtis and Sigel—one Price—and no deviation.

What is the Pillow of the rebellion composed of? White feathers.

It is said that the more fiery of the secessionists of Nashville are gnashing their teeth ferociously. The Louisville Journal suggests that the name of the town be written Gnashville.

Mr. Cameron, we see, is on the point of leaving for Russia. His fitness as a minister has been questioned, but that he will *make a good figure* wherever he is, can not be doubted.

In the 3d Wisconsin volunteers, it is a rule that no soldier can leave the camp without a pass. The chaplain one day was distributing tracts; among them was one headed: "Come sinners, come!" Soon after the tract was picked up in camp, and under the heading was penciled, "Can't do it! Col. Rogers won't sign my pass."

New Cap for the Southern Army—Capitulation.

What style of goods do the Southern Rebels remind us of?—Worsted.

Safe against Drowning—Davis and Beauregard.

Prevailing Religion down South—Quakerism.

Personal.

Brigadier General Edwin Price, "son of the old man," has left St. Louis behind him. The young gentleman named, whose career, military and otherwise, has not been very brilliant, so far, was forwarded a few days ago to the Alton Penitentiary, in company with three colonels who were bagged at the same time.

Among those present at the funeral of the President's son were the members of the Cabinet, Foreign Ministers, Members of Congress, officers of the Army and Navy and other friends of the family.

A number of the sons of New England gave to Col. Lee, a Ball's Bluff prisoner, a brilliant entertainment at Willard's.

REWARDS FOR GALLANTRY. The President will nominate as Major Generals, Brigadier Generals Smith, McClernard and Wallace, who commanded divisions at the battle of Fort Donelson, and as Brigadier Generals, the colonels comanding brigades there. Subordinate officers will also receive proper promotion. The President, through the Secretary of War, will, in his order of the day accompanying the announcement of these deserved rewards of valor, strive to pay a just tribute to every man, high or low in rank, who contributed to the glorious result. Flag Officer Foote and his brave sailors will doubtless not be forgotten.

Among the rebel prisoners captured at Fort Donelson, and now at Evansville, Ind., is Col. J. B. Clay, grandson of the great Henry Clay. He is said to have been one of the Staff of Gen. Buckner.

In these days, when it is so fashionable in some quarters to despise West Pointers, it may be well to remember that McClellan, Halleck, Buell, Curtis, Grant, Smith, Burnside, Pope, Sturgis, and Thomas are all West Pointers. The gallant Lyon, the first distinguished victim of the war, was a West Pointer, too.

In this command, Gen's Sherman, Viele, Stevens, Wright and Gilmore are all graduates of this Military Academy, as well as ten members of Gen. Sherman's staff—Captains Hamilton, Saxton, Pelouze Morgan and Hascall, and Lieutenants Shunk, Porter, Wilson, Tardy and O'Rorke.

Gen. Stone's friends are urging Gen. McClellan to bring that officer forthwith to a court martial. As the Joint War Committee has not yet terminated its investigation into the crime or blunder at Ball's Bluff, this court will not be ordered at present.

A Philadelphia paper says: We notice the arrival in this city, of Rev. Mr. Wilson, of Beaufort, South Carolina. He has always remained a strong Union man, although surrounded with serious difficulties. He may be expected to preach on next Sabbath morning and evening at the Spring Garden Baptist Church.

The President got out of bed one night lately to read a St. Louis dispatch stating that Columbus was evacuated by the rebels. He was called up at two o'clock the same night to read another denying the first.

POST OFFICE CIRCULAR.

Port Royal, S. C., March 1, 1862.

OFFICE HOURS FROM 8 A. M. UNTIL DARK.
ON SUNDAYS FROM 8 TO 9 A. M.

The P. O. Department of the U. S. having established a regular office here, all persons, not soldiers, marines, or Navy sailors, will be required to pre-pay their postage. Soldiers' letters, not prepaid, "must be certified by a field or staff officer of the Regiment to which the soldier belongs," thus

> SOLDIER'S LETTER.
> *A. B. WATSON.—Major 8th Mich. Vols.*
>
> JAMES M. BEEBE, Esq.,
> BOSTON, MASS.

Marines' or Navy Sailors' letters must be certified by a commander or lieutenant on board the vessel to which the marine or sailor is attached, thus

> NAVAL LETTER.
> *THOS. G. CORBIN.—1st. Lt. U. S. S. Wabash.*
>
> MESSRS. C. W. FIELD & Co.,
> NEW YORK.

Commissioned officers will prepay their postage as heretofore.

It is better for ALL to *prepay* their postage as the amount must be collected of the friends to whom letters are sent.

We are prepared to register letters and to give the official receipts therefor, the extra fee for which is ½ dime per letter. "Registering" is not a government insurance on letters. It makes it more certain that they will be delivered only to the persons to whom they are addressed.

Letters will not be delivered from this office to officers, privates, or sailors not fully authorized by their chief commanding officer to receive them. Soldiers will receive their letters only from their regimental post master, and sailors from some officer of the ship to which they belong.

Civilians in Government employ are requested to have their letters come directed to the care of the person under whose particular charge they are—Surfmen or Boatmen to care of Harbor Master, Teamsters, Carpenters, Blacksmiths, Bakers Laborers, &c. &c. to care of their Overseer. This will aid all in getting their letters promptly and save much time for Government and themselves.

Stamps of the various denominations and stamped envelopes are always for sale at this office.

By a recent order of the Chief Quartermaster of this division all vessels before leaving Port Royal, will report at the Post Office for mails—no matter how short a distance they are to go.

JOS. H. SEARS, P. M.

SAILING DIRECTIONS
FOR ENTERING
The Harbor of Port Royal, S. C.

GENERAL DIRECTIONS.

A Light Ship has been moored in eight fathoms, off Martin's Industry Shoal, at the entrance of the Harbor. She is painted Red, with the name "RELIEF" in white letters on each side. She carries two WHITE LIGHTS at a height of 42 feet above the water, and will be visible 13 miles in clear weather from a vessel's deck. She is in

NORTH LATITUDE, 32deg. 05min. 57sec.
LONG. W. from GREENWICH 80deg. 33min. 22sec.

BEARINGS.

From the Light Ship, Large House on West end of Bay Point (East side Port Royal Harbor,) bears N. N. W. ½ W., distant 10½ miles.

Tybee Light House W. by S. ¾ S. distant 15 miles.
Entering Buoy, South channel, W. by S. ¾ S. distant 2½ miles.
Entering Buoy South East channel, N. N. E. ½ E., distant 2⅝ miles.
Large Black Buoy on S. E. end of Gaskin Bank, S. W. by W. ¾ W. distant 3⅓ miles.

All the Bar Buoys are on the Martin's Industry side of the channels. There are four RED buoys in the South channel, to be left on the *starboard hand entering*, and two BLACK buoys in the South East channel, to be left on the *port hand entering*. The best sailing line for steamers is about a vessel's length from the buoys, on the side indicated by their color.

A large black buoy has been placed on the South East side of the Gaskin Bank, in 5 fathoms of water. Vessels coming from or going to the Southward should not cross the shoal to the Westward of this buoy.

Nineteen and a half feet at mean low water may be found in the South channel, and twenty-one feet in the South East channel. Mean rise and fall of tide six and a half feet.

The *Entering Buoys* in both channels are painted in perpendicular stripes—black and white. That at the entrance of the South East channel has a staff and cross with letters S. E. upon it to distinguish it in thick weather from the other which has neither staff nor cross.

To Enter Port Royal Harbor by the South Channel.

COURSES AND DISTANCES.

1. From Light Ship to Entering Buoy W. by S. ¾ S. 2½ miles.
2. From Entering Buoy to first Red Buoy N. W. by N. 1 mile.
3. From 1st Red Buoy to 3d Red Buoy N. by E. 2¼ miles, passing 2nd Red Buoy midway on the course.
4. From 3d Red Buoy to 4th or upper Red Buoy North 1¾ miles to point of junction of South and South East channels.
5. From upper Red Buoy to Black Buoy on S. E. end Fishing Rip, N. N. W. ½ W.

This course will bring the Light Ship over the stern, and the large house with platform on the roof, at West end of Bay Point, ahead.

6. If bound into Beaufort River, steer from Fishing Rip buoy N. W. ½ N. 3 miles, until house on Bay Point bears E. N. E., after which the chart will be the best guide up the river.
7. If bound to Hilton Head steer N. W. by W. from Fishing Rip buoy 3 miles, and anchor off the piers now erecting there.

To Enter Port Royal Harbor by the South East Channel.

Vessels coming from the Northward and steering for the Light Ship will make the Entering Buoy of this channel on the starboard hand, two and a half miles before coming up with the Light Ship. On seeing the Buoy steer for it, passing it on either hand; thence steer W. by N. ½ N. 2½ miles to the second or inner black buoy, passing the first black buoy midway on this course.

From the inner black buoy steer N. N. W. ¼ W. 5 miles to Fishing Rip buoy, having the Light Ship astern, and the house on Bay Point ahead, and passing the upper red buoy of the South channel at the junction of the two channels, 2 miles on the course.

From Fishing Rip follow the directions given for the South channel.

* One of the buoys in the South channel is on this range, but is *not* to be steered for after coming up with the second or inner black buoy, where the course is changed as above directed.

NOTE. All bearings here given are magnetic. The distances are in nautical miles. Magnetic Variation at Port Royal in Jan. 1862—3deg. East.

PORT ROYAL HARBOR, S. C., Jan. 12, 1862.

The above proposed sailing directions are respectfully submitted to the Flag Officer for his examination and approval by

CHAS. O. BOUTELLE, } ASSISTANT U. S.
Com'g Surv'g Steamer Bibb. } COAST SURVEY.

Examined and approved.

S. F. DUPONT, Flag Officer,
Commanding South Atlantic Block'g Squadron.

The Philadelphia Inquirer.

ESTABLISHED 1829. | PHILADELPHIA, SATURDAY, MARCH 15, 1862. | PRICE TWO CENTS.

THE LATEST NEWS.

THE REBEL PANIC EXTENDING

THE MONITOR AND THE MERRIMAC.

NEW CONFISCATION BILL.

THE CONDEMNED CLOTHING CONTRACTORS.

The Rebels Firing on Our Vessels at Aquia Creek.

FROM FORTRESS MONROE

A VISIT TO THE MONITOR.

THE WAR IN THE WEST.

NEW MADRID IS OURS!

THE LATEST FROM WASHINGTON.

WASHINGTON, March 14.

Special Despatch to the Inquirer.

Capture of New Madrid.

President LINCOLN received a despatch, to-night, that the glorious banner of the Union waves over New Madrid, Missouri.

Military Appointments.

The President has sent to the Senate the following appointments for Brigadier-Generalships:—LEONARD F. ROSS, ABRAHAM PIATT, JAMES CRAIG, JAMES STEDMAN, H. C. DE AHNA and JAMES B. RICKETTS; for Inspector-General, ROBERT C. BUCHANAN. The Senate confirmed, to-day, the appointment of Major-General MCDOWELL. Assistant Secretaries of War THOMAS A. SCOTT and JOHN TUCKER arrived here to-day.

Mr. Mercier and Stevens' Battery.

The French Minister, Mr. MERCIER, made an application, through Secretary SEWARD, for permission to examine the models and plans of the STEVENS' Battery. It resulted in a cordial invitation from Mr. STEVENS to a minute inspection of all the details of the marvelous invention. Accordingly, the distinguished representative of the most progressive nation of Europe, spent nearly two hours in Mr. STEVENS' apartments, this evening, and made a laborious and searching scrutiny of every part of the far-famed battery, expressing unqualified delight and satisfaction at every part.

Mr. MERCIER is both practical and intelligent, and his questions evinced great knowledge of the entire subject. Every detail was accurately explained, and he went away delighted. The Naval Committees of both Houses are ready to report in favor of the immediate completion of the battery. The Committee propose to visit Fortress Monroe to-morrow, in order to inspect the "Monitor."

The Rebel Panic Extending.

From unquestionable evidence received to-day by the highest official circles, there is no doubt that the panic and consternation which originated among the Rebels at Manassas have extended all through the Rebel communities which are now threatened by our troops.

The leaders are desperate and hopeless, and have resorted to an entire draft of the people of Virginia, a measure which they never dared to adopt until now, when even such an arbitrary act cannot avail them. The result is that the people are already openly canvassing the question of clinging to their sinking scheme, with death and defeat in certain prospect, or of saving their lives and property by a return to an allegiance which they only deserted under compulsion, and through the machinations of a fraudulent and deceptive sham election.

The Monitor and Merrimac.

The most distinguished naval officers are by no means sanguine that the "Merrimac" is so badly hurt that she cannot again come out and attack our fleet. But such a plan of operations has been adopted as will result in her complete discomfiture when she shall make the attempt. We are not at liberty to disclose the plans adopted, but those wiseacres who insist that the "Merrimac" can grapple the "Monitor" and tow her into Norfolk harbor with the ease that a giant Baldwin locomotive could drag a milk train, will surely be disappointed. The little David, in her anointed strength, will smite the monster and utterly destroy her. So let your merchants and underwriters possess their souls in peace.

Captain Worden, of the "Monitor."

Captain WORDEN is at the house of Lieut. WISE, under the most skillful medical treatment and faithful nursing. It is not yet known whether the sight of one eye is entirely destroyed. When a gentleman told Secretary STANTON, to-day, that it was feared that the gallant sailor would lose the sight of one of his eyes, he exclaimed, "Then we will fill the other with diamonds."

A New Confiscation Bill.

Senator HARRIS presented a Confiscation bill this morning, differing in many of its leading provisions from those already offered. It proposes the confiscation of all property belonging to those engaged in rebellion after the passage of the act, the proceeds to go into the Treasury; the President at any time to have power to suspend the operations of the law.

Affairs at Alexandria and Fairfax.

The Provost Marshal at Alexandria to-day closed all the drinking houses and all the stores of sutlers who had been selling liquors.

A number of itinerant speculators went to Fairfax Court House yesterday, and took possession of the vacant stores to commence business. The Provost Marshal, however, promptly ejected them.

Return of the War Committee.

Messrs. COVODE, JULIAN and ODELL, a Sub-Committee on investigating the Conduct of the War, visited Centreville and Manassas to-day, and returned stored with valuable information.

Captain Shultz.

The many friends of Captain SHULTZ, who was the victim of some poisoned food in New York, will be glad to learn that he has entirely recovered.

Dwellings Burned at Centreville.

Yesterday evening, a number of dwellings in Centreville were wantonly burned by some of our soldiers.

Return of the Assistant Secretary of War.

The Assistant Secretary of War, Mr. SCOTT, returned from the West to-night.

Harbor Defences.

Commodore STEVENS has obtained permission from the War Department to place the large Rodman gun now on the Rip Raps at Fortress Monroe on board of the strongly-built steamer "Naugatuck," to be used as a defence in the harbor of New York, in the event of the "Merrimac" escaping past Fortress Monroe. Arrangements are being made to obstruct the channel of the Delaware in such event, so that the good people of Philadelphia may sleep soundly in their beds, without fear of the iron monster.

Iron-Clad Ships.

Senator HALE presented a bill this morning, which passed two readings, containing important provisions in reference to the construction of iron-clad ships and batteries. The first section appropriates one million of dollars for the immediate construction of an iron-plated ram, of six thousand tons burden, on the best and most scientific model.

The second appropriates five hundred thousand for the purchase and erection of suitable machinery at the Washington Navy Yard, for forging iron-plates to be used for protecting the sides of ships-of-war.

The third section appropriates seven hundred and fifty thousand dollars to complete the Stevens battery.

The fourth section appropriates fifteen millions of dollars to construct iron-clad sloops-of-war.

The entire bill is comprehensive and elaborate, and is just what the country actually needs at the present time.

The Condemned Clothing and Swindling Contractors.

The Commission appointed to investigate the immense swindle in clothing is holding daily sessions at the office of Captain DANIEL G. THOMAS, Military Storekeeper.

The following persons, connected with the Philadelphia Arsenal, are here undergoing examination:—Colonel CROSSMAN, Captain ALLEGOOD, Inspectors KERN, KELLEY, KING, YATES and PERKINS. The Investigating Board consists of Colonel SACKETT, Inspector-General; Colonel CHAPMAN and Captain BLANCHARD.

The condemned clothing fills four large warehouses fronting on an entire square, and covering almost as much ground as the Pennsylvania Railroad depot. It comprises over forty thousand infantry coats, over fifty thousand great coats, over fifteen thousand pairs of boots, and almost every other article of clothing, reaching in value about a million of dollars. Nearly all of it was furnished from Philadelphia, and your good city owes it to her fair fame to have the stain removed and the swindlers punished.

The Rebels Firing on our Vessels again at Aquia.

The Rebel batteries at Aquia Creek opened upon our vessels again yesterday, firing six shots at the *Achilles*, a Government transport, on its way to Washington. None of them took effect.

Post Office Regulations.

POST OFFICE DEPARTMENT, APPOINTMENT OFFICE, March 13, 1862.—Postmasters who make up packages for members of Congress direct, under the order of December 3d, 1861, and mail them direct to Washington, should write distinctly on each package "Congress," embracing therein only matter for Senators and Representatives. This will enable any distributing office through which they may pass to place them without delay in the Congress bag.

(Signed) JOHN A. HASSON,
First Assistant Postmaster-General.

Lecture by Wendell Phillips.

WENDELL PHILLIPS lectured to a dense auditory to-night, at the Smithsonian Institute.

OUR ADVANCE COLUMN.

The Entry of the Third Regiment New Jersey Volunteers into Manassas.

Correspondence of the Inquirer.

FAIRFAX COURT HOUSE, VA., March 12, 1862.

Yesterday the Third Regiment of New Jersey Volunteers, under Colonel GEORGE W. TAYLOR, leading the advance of the Grand Army of the Potomac, entered the great stronghold of the traitors in Virginia, and planted in its place the glorious old flag of the Union.

The Morning March.

Long before the dawn the regiment was in line at the outpost where they had been picketing, three miles beyond Fairfax Station, on the Alexandria and Orange Railroad, and, in the best spirits, and with the utmost alacrity, commenced their march. The morning was clear, and the weather just right for pleasant marching. Following the railroad, we made good time, reaching the far-famed Bull Run at sunrise. We found the stream about sixty feet wide, and much swollen by the recent rains.

The massive stone bridge of the railroad had been blown up, but we made a short detour and crossed on the ruins of the wagon road bridge, which was still smoking, having been fired by the Rebels but a few hours before. The opposite banks were precipitous and were one long line of rifle pits, commanding the approaches from the low bottom-lands on the north, from which a most harrassing fire could have been poured upon advancing troops, especially while scaling the immediate banks.

The View From the Hill-top.

A short distance from the stream, the hills rose to the height of one hundred and fifty feet, and reaching their acclivities we had a comprehensive view of the surrounding country for many miles. These acclivities were also entrenched. From them we saw in the distance to the north, the town of Centreville, with its extensive fortifications and deserted Rebel quarters, and nearer to the stream, the battle grounds of the battles of the 18th and 21st of July. To the south before us were earthworks of every description, from the rifle pits to the more formidable battlements for heavy guns, and a vast array of deserted quarters, extending to and beyond the Junction several miles distant.

Over all the vast range, desolation and loneliness reigned supreme. The hosts of the enemy, who so lately marshaled there, had gone. The farm-houses like mournful mementoes in the midst of the desolation, were entirely stript of their former surroundings. Fences, barns, shade-trees—everything, indeed, available for the construction of quarters and for fuel—were entirely swept away. Not a vestige of them remained, as far as the eye could reach. It seemed as if pestilence and fire had scourged the whole land. There was not a living thing—horse, cow or hog—to be seen. All had been swept away by the consuming army. Deep wagon ways ran in every direction, almost covering all the hills and valleys, telling a solemn story of the recent life and battle.

The Entry into the Fort.

At 10 o'clock A. M., after three miles of double quick from Bull Run, we entered the main fortress at the Junction, and immediately the old flag of the Union was hoisted on the Rebel flag-staff, and as its glorious folds caught the fresh morning breeze, it was greeted with three rounds of deafening cheers. A few moments after, our brave General KEARNEY dashed in on his white charger, and drew up in front of our line, and as he lifted his cap under the stars and stripes, three more rounds of applause welcomed the hero of Chepultepec.

The order to stack was given, ranks were broken, and in a twinkling the boys were deployed in every direction to take an inventory of the effects of the departed. The smoke was still rising from the black ruins of the numerous quarters and store-houses recently fired. Some of the quarters had not been fired. They were filled with articles of value which time had not permitted their owners to carry away. The haste had been great. Fear and panic had come upon the enemy, and so precipitate was their flight that they were glad to get off without taking anything with them but their frightened selves. Stores of every description, provisions of every kind, and in great profusion, lay scattered over the whole area of the fort, as things of no value.

All the guns had been taken, and all their shot and shell, but they had left rifles, pistols and a great number of their huge sword knives. There were provisions enough to last our regiment for weeks, and of good quality. Beef, pork, flour, rice, tea, beans, molasses, whisky and tobacco lay every where around, and there seemed no end to supplies of clothing. The boys were not slow to appropriate what lay before them. In an hour every one of them had a change of clean shirts and drawers, besides a store in his knapsack, and all who were in the habit of indulging were merry on old rye.

After the first general inventory was taken, it was amusing to see them disposed about in groups, partaking of the good things they had found and chatting merrily over the adventures of the day. Among other things found were barrels of eggs, already cooked by the fire. These, and plenty of good beef and ham, were very acceptable after the long and tiresome march of the morning. In the midst of the feasting and merriment, General MCCLELLAN came up, followed by several regiments of cavalry, and soon after, our regiment marched to Centreville, reaching there at dusk, after a march of nearly thirty miles during the day. Here we found good quarters, and remained during the night to rest before proceeding to Fairfax Court House.

THE NEW IRON-CLAD WAR STEAMER, NOW BUILDING IN PHILADELPHIA.

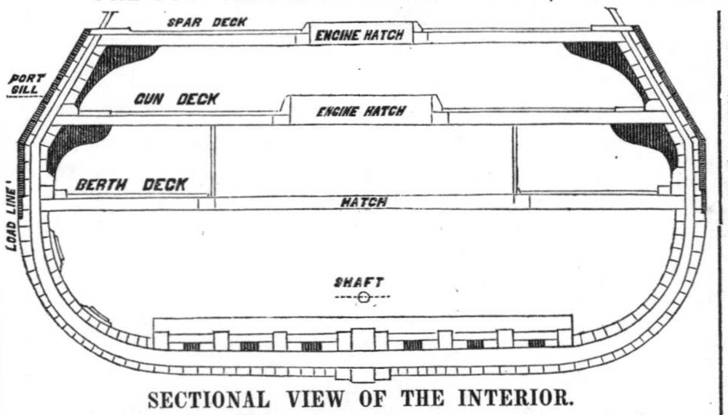

SECTIONAL VIEW OF THE INTERIOR.

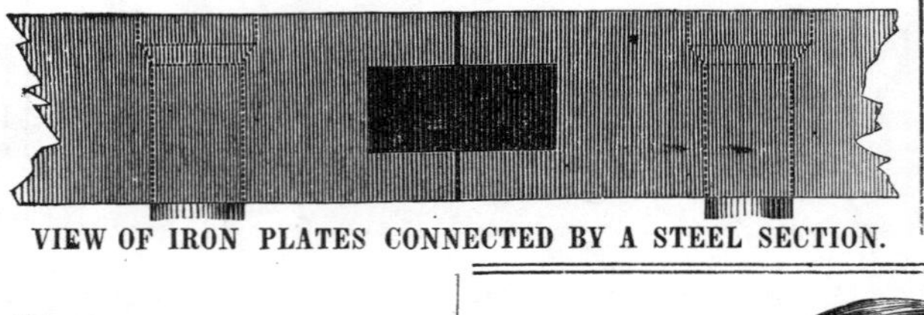

VIEW OF IRON PLATES CONNECTED BY A STEEL SECTION.

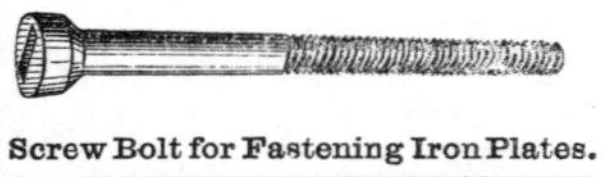

Screw Bolt for Fastening Iron Plates.

We present to-day cuts descriptive of the iron-clad war steamer, now building in Kensington, at the yard of Messrs. CRAMP & SON. The whole frame, which is entirely solid, is in position, and rapid advance is being made towards the planking. The build is quite peculiar, being exceeding flat-bottomed, and having the stern rounded in the style of two hundred years ago. Her whole appearance indicates great strength. Even now, before being iron-clad, she is apparently twice as strong as any vessel ever built. The plates intended to be used in the casing of the frigate are of superior manufacture, and altogether weigh seven hundred and fifty tons. The Bristol Works, near our city, have contracted to furnish one-half of the plates, and BAILEY, BROWN & Co., of Pittsburg, the other half.

The heaviest plate yet prepared weighs six thousand nine hundred and eighty-eight pounds; the lightest six thousand two hundred and forty-eight. These plates are connected by a steel section, and fastened to the timber of the vessel by heavy screw bolts. The ship has two floor timbers to each frame, each forty feet long, eighteen inches deep, and thirteen inches thick. The balance of the frame is ten inches thick, and tapers from seventeen-and-a-half inches at the floor-head to seven inches at the plank-sheer.

The spar deck will be covered fore and aft with one inch iron-plates before the deck plank is put on. She will be provided with an extra steering apparatus, so arranged that she can work without the rudder, if necessary. The weight of the hull of this vessel will be 1970 tons, and the iron plating 820 tons, making a total of 3830 tons. Her draught of water will be fifteen feet. When completed, she will be two hundred and forty-five feet long, fifty-seven feet six inches beam and twenty-five feet depth of hold. Her machinery is being constructed by the Messrs MERRICK, of Southwark.

ANOTHER VICTORY.

"NEW MADRID IS OURS."

THE U. S. FORCES IN POSSESSION.

WASHINGTON, March 14, 11 o'clock, P. M.—President LINCOLN has just received a telegraphic message from Brigadier-General STRONG, briefly announcing that

"NEW MADRID IS OURS."

New Madrid and Its Importance.

New Madrid is the capital of New Madrid county, Missouri; is situated on the Mississippi River about twenty-seven miles south-southwest from Columbus, Kentucky, in an air line, but much farther by the winding course of the river. It is two hundred and eighty miles southeast of Jefferson City, and before the outbreak of the Rebellion did a large business in shipping corn, lumber and cattle for Southern markets.

Its importance grows out of the fact that it has been occupied by the Rebels ever since they first moved on Columbus last summer. It was the base of the operations of JEFF. THOMPSON and others, northward and westward into Missouri, which, it will be remembered, gave the Federal officers much trouble. The town was greatly injured by an earthquake in 1811, and, on account of the frequency of these disturbances, and its liability to them, the houses are mostly built of wood. It was founded in 1780.

Passes to Fortress Monroe Suspended.

Special Despatch to The Inquirer.

BALTIMORE, March 14.—All passes, except to persons in Government service, have been suspended between Baltimore and Old Point, until otherwise ordered. Civilians and others at Old Point not in Government employ are being sent to Baltimore.

English Opinion on the American War.

NEW YORK, March 13.—A letter from London, dated the 1st of March, to the *Commercial*, says:—On the whole there is an obvious growth of the impression in England that the struggle in America will be terminated this spring. American securities have consequently been buoyant.

Major-General Fremont's Movements.

General FREMONT is expected to arrive here to-day. Already a new German regiment is partially raised in New York, it is said here, to accompany him to East Tennessee and Georgia.

CAPTAIN JOHN LORIMER WORDEN.

Captain (formerly Lieutenant) JOHN LORIMER WORDEN, the hero of the great naval battle at Hampton Roads, and who commanded the gallant little *Monitor* in her engagement with the *Merrimac*, is a native and citizen of New York, from which State he received his appointment to the navy in 1834. His entry, as a midshipman, into the service, bears date the 10th of January in that year, his commission as Lieutenant, the 30th of November, 1846. During this time he has seen nearly sixteen years of sea service. His shore and other duty amounted, at the end of 1860, to nearly seven years. Since his appointment he has been only three years unemployed. His total length of service up to the present time exceeds twenty-eight years.

He was last at sea in November, 1860, on board the sloop *Savannah*, twenty-two guns, on the blockading squadron, and was granted a short leave of absence on his return. After this he was sent as a special messenger to Fort Pickens, with despatches to Captain ADAMS, of the *Sabine*. ADAMS was in command of the fleet which, carrying two companies of artillery, had been sent to Fort Pickens for the purpose of its reinforcement. Leaving Washington with despatches which conveyed orders to that effect, on the 7th of April, Lieutenant WORDEN, journeying by way of Richmond and Montgomery, arrived at Pensacola on the 11th. Fearing an arrest and search, owing to the excited state of the country, he tore up his despatches after committing them to memory. As he anticipated, he was arrested at Montgomery, Alabama, and as no papers were found on his person, he was allowed to pass.

On his arrival at Pensacola he obtained a pass from the Rebel General BRAGG permitting him to carry a verbal message from Secretary CAMERON to Captain ADAMS. He went to him and repeated from memory his despatches. The fort was reinforced by Captain VODGES that night; Lieutenant WORDEN took the cars at 8 P. M., on the 12th, on his return, and on the 13th, when within about five miles of Montgomery, he was arrested by five Rebel army officers, under the pretence of having broken his parole, but the main object was to obtain his despatches to the Government, if he should have had any in his possession. He was sent to Montgomery, where he was kept for some time as a prisoner of war. There was an intense excitement against him, as the Rebel General BRAGG had collected a force of 1000 men and intended to attack Fort Pickens the very night it was reinforced. This he subsequently learned. Lieutenant WORDEN was kept in confinement until the middle of November last, when he was exchanged and went to Fortress Monroe where he joined the *Minnesota*. He was afterward detached from that vessel and appointed to the command of the *Monitor*. His gallant performance at the battle of Hampton Roads is recorded in every heart. Under Providence he saved our navy.

FROM FORTRESS MONROE.

A VISIT TO THE "MONITOR."

The Interior and Exterior Described

EFFECT OF BALLS OF THE "MERRIMAC."

Visit to the Minnesota, the Rip Raps, Wrecks of the Cumberland and Congress, Newport News, &c.

Visit to the Monitor.

I had the pleasure to-day of accompanying Lieut. WM. M. JEFFERS when he proceeded, under orders from Commodore GOLDSBOROUGH, to take command of the "Monitor," and relieve Lieutenant SELFRIDGE of the "Cumberland," who had been appointed temporarily in the absence of Lieutenant WORDEN. As we approached this novel naval wonder I was struck with the pertness of the Norfolk description of her as "*a Yankee cheese box on a raft.*" It gives a better idea of her appearance than any of the engravings or descriptions in the New York papers.

They all fail to afford a correct idea of the general appearance of the vessel, and especially when she is in action. She is oval shaped, 172 feet long and 41 feet in width at the centre. Her hull rises perpendicularly out of the water, as straight all round as the sides of a stone wall, and as flat on top as a table, without any rail or guards around her. She has two square smoke-stacks, about seven feet in height; but in time of action these are removed, and the smoke and steam comes through grates in the deck, the iron of which is about eight inches thick. Nothing remains on her deck but the pilot-house, which is a square iron statue, about three feet high, about the size of an ordinary dry goods box.

When walking her deck, although anchored at the end of Hampton Bar, where the sea is quite rough, not the slightest motion of the waves could be felt. Her deck is as firm and steady as a rock. This position, half way between Newport News and Soller's Point, has been chosen in order to keep watch and ward over the "Merrimac" should she attempt to make another visit to the Roads. Steam is all the time kept up, and a man on the lookout with a glass keeps a constant watch from the top of the tower.

The tower rises about nine feet high from the deck, and looks, when close to it, like a large iron gasometer, or gas holder. On closely examining it, however, you find that its sides and top are about one foot thick, whilst the whole tower is 22 feet in diameter, and that it has two oval shaped portholes, close together on one side, not more than two feet apart, and not more than three feet above the deck.—The interior of the tower exhibits still stronger the superior strength of the vessel.

There is a solidity about it that makes the thought of any earthly power disturbing its movements or penetrating its interior seem simply ridiculous. An examination of this part of the vessel explains the confidence which her officers and men have in her entire and complete invulnerability. They say, "we fear nothing on land or water, and are ready, whenever the order is given, to proceed direct to Norfolk or Richmond."

INTERIOR OF THE TOWER.

The guns set side and side in the centre of the tower, and are intended to be fired simultaneously, the close proximity of the muzzles of the two guns enabling the two balls to strike the sides of the enemy in similar proximity to each other. The moment the guns are fired two immense pillars of steel, on the inside, about six feet long, two feet in width, and one foot in thickness, slide before the portholes, completely closing them and protecting the gunners from the balls of the enemy.

EFFECTS OF THE SHOT.

There are marks on the tower and hull of about twenty balls, and some of them seem to have struck the tower fair and square, with no more apparent effect than could be produced by the blow of a sledge hammer. The paint is rubbed off, and if repainted it would be difficult to discover where most of the shots struck. The gunners of the enemy seem, however, to have early abandoned the attempt to damage the tower, though most of their balls even there were aimed at the port-holes, three striking in close proximity. Two of the six or seven marks on the tower are said to have been accidental shots from the guns of the "Minnesota."

The greater part of the shot marks are on the edge of the hull, which, it should be remembered, does not rise more than twelve inches out of the water. They seem to have been under the impression that there must be a weak spot underneath the water line, and they hammered away all round, but here, too, the invulnerability of the "Monitor" was equally great, and the indentations are only to the extent of a fraction of an inch. There is a small fracture of the edge of the iron at one point, which only seems to show its great strength at a point which might be supposed to be weakest.

The shot that struck the square pilot-house did little more than knock the cement out. Had the pilot-house been round instead of square, as it is now proposed to make it, the ball would have glanced and lost half of its force, and failed to injure the eyes of the gallant commander. He is, however, I am pleased to learn, rapidly recovering. The retiring of the "Merrimac" from the contest with her insignificant antagonist is not to be wondered at, when the exercise of all the power she possessed, for five hours, had done little more than deface her paint.

The attempt of the "Merrimac" to run her down left no mark on the iron, except some splinters from her timbers, which are sticking to a nut and screw on her hull. She struck her precisely amidships, directly opposite the centre of the tower, and this experiment having so entirely failed, it was evident that no hopes could be entertained from its repetition.

WHAT THE GUNNERS SAY.

I had a conversation with the gunners, and they are thoroughly satisfied that at least three of their balls passed through the iron roof of the monster, and they think that if they had used the wrought iron balls they could have sunk the monster Rebel. They had positive orders from Captain DALHGREN not to use them until they were first experimented with, and none were used, the impression being that they would be liable to burst the guns.

THE NEW COMMANDER.

Lieutenant JEFFERS took command shortly after coming on board, when the whole crew were called upon deck, numbering about fifty all told, and the order of Commodore GOLDSBOROUGH relieving Lieutenant SELFRIDGE, and highly complimenting him, was read to them. They gave three hearty cheers for their new commander, and three for the retiring commander, which must have been heard way over in Dixie, at Sewall's Point camp.

Lieutenant JEFFERS has been for a long time a resident of Annapolis, and considers himself half a Marylander, whilst two of the Third Assistant Engineers, Messrs. HANDS and SUNSTROM, are Baltimoreans. There are also two other Baltimoreans among her crew. Lieutenant JEFFERS had command of the gun-boat "Underwriter" at the taking of Roanoke Island and the taking of Elizabeth City, evincing great gallantry and seamanship, and but returned yesterday from the Burnside Expedition, with Commodore GOLDSBOROUGH, on board the steamer "Spaulding," when he was immediately appointed to the "Monitor," and has the utmost confidence in the entire invulnerability of his noble craft.

If the "Merrimac" again comes out he will work hard for the honor of sinking or capturing her. She will have a clear field, all the wooden vessels being out of the way, and her commander will not be hampered by the duty of protecting the "Minnesota" as was Commander WORDEN, his manœuvring being mainly directed to that object by keeping the "Merrimac" from running into her as she lay helpless on the bar.

BENEATH DECK.

Beneath deck the "Monitor" is as neat and compact as above deck, and has been fitted up with a great deal of taste for the comfort and convenience of her officers and crew. The ward-room is very pleasant, and the state-rooms quite comfortable. The engine-rooms are large and well ventilated. As to her propeller and rudder it is difficult to find them when inside of the vessel or outside of it, and I should judge, from the general silence on the subject, that the peculiar character and locality of these important adjuncts of locomotion are not to be made public at present.

Suffice it to say that they are not visible outside of the vessel, nor is it discernable which is her stem or which her stern, as she moves with equal facility both ways, and I was assured that she can move at better speed than her monster antagonist.

She has an immense flag flying from her stern, and with steam always puffing away, stands prepared for another encounter at any moment.

THE SPEED OF THE MONITOR.

The information has gained ground that the "Merrimac is superior in speed to the "Monitor," and that if the former chose she could run past her and go out to sea. This, I was assured, is an entire mistake. The speed of the "Merrimac" is not over five knots an hour, whilst that of the "Monitor" is about seven. On putting the question to one of her gunners as to their relative speed, and the abi.

(Continued on the Eighth Page.)

VOL. 1. PHILADELPHIA, SATURDAY, MARCH 22, 1862. NO. 19.

THE ARMY OF THE POTOMAC.

The Pennsylvania Reserves.

Washington Before the late Forward Movement.

Washington having for months been the nucleus o a vast collection of troops, it bears the appearance, so far as a display of military strength and power can produce that effect, of a great European capital. Within a short distance, more than a quarter of a million of the most active, patriotic, and ambitious citizens of this great republic have been gathered together. Engaging with all the ardor and energy that characterize the American people in their varied military and civil pursuits, nowhere else can be found an equal display of restlessness and superhuman mental activity Even Paris, when occupied by the armies of the Allied Powers of Europe, could not have presented a much more animated scene.

We have long boasted that our Government was so beneficent in its nature, and so universally popular, that no aid from armed soldiery was required to maintain and support the civil powers in the execution of their duties. And we once fondly dwelt on the fact that our highest officers of State needed no guard to secure their safety, and that our political metropolis needed the presence of no soldiers to preserve its tranquillity. The rebellion has changed all this; and though our hearts may be saddened by the thought that a stern necessity has arisen for the employment of an immense army to enforce the authority of the noble free Government which was once cheerfully obeyed throughout the length and breadth of our land; yet, no patriot can repress a feeling of honest pride in the mighty proofs of strength and stability which the dangers that lately threatened our national integrity have produced, and in the noble army which sprung into existence with magical rapidity at the first summons of danger.

Mounted patrols guard all the street corners of the capital, and though their services are rarely called into active requisition, their presence serves as a constant check upon turbulent spirits, and as an admonition to all disorderly or disaffected persons, of the nearness of a strong hand ready to crush and punish any riotous or disorderly demonstration.

THE PASSES ISSUED BY THE PROVOST MARSHAL.

The first step necessary to commence a safe journey to any camp south of the Potomac is a pass from the Provost Marshal, at whose office a number of clerks detailed from the ranks of the regulars are constantly employed, under the direction of General Andrew Porter and his aid-de-camp, C. D. Mehaffy, in issuing these necessary permits to those who show sufficient cause for receiving them. They read as follows:

TO ALL WHOM IT MAY CONCERN.

No. ——

HEADQUARTERS CITY GUARD,
PROVOST MARSHAL'S OFFICE, WASHINGTON.

Know ye that the bearer —— has permission to pass over any bridge or ferry to Virginia, and within the lines and back, for the purpose of ——, being subject to the inspection of guards or patrols.

By command of
A. PORTER, Brig, Gen'l U. S. A.,
Provost Marshal.
C. D. MEHAFFY, Aid-de-Camp.
(This pass will expire ——.)

In availing myself of the benefits of the above pass, I do solemnly affirm that I am a true and loyal citizen of the United States, and that I will not give aid, comfort, or information to the enemies of the United States' Government in any manner whatsoever. (Signed) —— ——.
(This pass to be taken up at its expiration.)

VISIT TO CAMP PIERPONT.

Armed with this permission, we promptly departed on the road to Langley's, for the purpose of visiting the Pennsylvania Reserves. Soon after the commencement of the journey, an opportunity was afforded of obtaining practical information of the shocking condition of the roads along the Potomac. Although they had been, as we were told, much improved by a few days of comparatively fine weather, it was not easy to imagine how, at any time, they could have been in a much worse condition. At some points, for a long distance the bed of the road was covered with liquid mud from twelve to eighteen inches deep. At others, holes three or four feet deep had been made in the very centre of the roadway; and at others, masses of thick and comparatively solid clay had been formed in ruts from two to three feet deep.

Not far above Georgetown, we discovered a terrible breach in the Ohio and Chesapeake Canal, which had entirely checked navigation to that city, and thus seriously increased the difficulties of the Government in furnishing supplies from Washington. It was generally supposed that some of the Secession miscreants of that vicinity had purposely opened this leak to render indirect but valuable "aid and comfort" to the enemy.

THE CHAIN BRIDGE.

The next point of interest was the Chain Bridge, a structure that will forever possess a historic interest. On a high bluff in its rear a battery was planted previous to the passage of our troops over it into Virginia, that shelled and virtually destroyed a mill on the south bank of the Potomac, in which some of the enemy had taken refuge. Amusing scenes frequently occur between the guard stationed at the entrance to the bridge and the drivers of wagons who attempt to smuggle supplies of whisky into the camps. Very ingenious devices are resorted to. Sometimes the contraband luxury is concealed in a barrel of onions; sometimes in a cask of butter; sometimes in loaves of bread; but as the soldiers do not scruple to send their sharp bayonets through any suspicious packages, these schemes generally prove unsuccessful.

The southern bank of the Potomac for some distance above the Chain Bridge, and for several miles below, is formed by an almost perpendicular mass of rocks, from fifty to a hundred feet high, and, at most places, it is nearly as difficult to ascend without ladders these massive natural walls as it would be to climb the smooth surface of a high brick house.

A short distance beyond the Chain Bridge a new military road leading to the left was constructed some months ago, and a new bridge was erected by our soldiers over a beautiful mountain stream, which supplied the water-power of the ruined mill referred to above. It is a very substantial structure, and although made chiefly of logs, will evidently prove very durable and serviceable.

FORT MARCY.

The next point of interest was Fort Marcy, which contains five or six cannon, mounted on gun-carriages. It is surrounded by an abattis formed of the limb of trees with their thickest ends deeply imbedded in the earth; and behind this a trench some four or five feet wide and about five feet deep is dug, which was designed to serve as a rifle-pit in case of an attack by the enemy.

SOLDIERS' GRAVE-YARD.

A short distance east of Camp Pierpont, at a point about a quarter of a mile south of the turnpike, is an unenclosed soldiers' cemetery, which contained about twelve or fifteen newly-made graves. At the head of each was what appeared to be a marble tombstone, and we afterwards learned that it was the custom of our soldiers of the army of the Potomac to always mark in this way the final homes of their brave companions. The teams plying between Washington and the camps not unfrequently contained these memorials. Before one of the tents of the regiment under the command of Col John Taggart, of your city, I noticed a newly-arrived tombstone with this inscription:

"Ould Mac—by the [illegible]h
Regiment, P. R. V. C."

This affectionate and unpretending tablet will doubtless mark the resting place of a true, brave, and manly spirit.

Passing Langley's, where a new building, erected as a tavern stand, with the appropriate sign of a painted spread-eagle, was occupied as General McCall's headquarters, we saw on the right a small frame church, which was used as a hospital, and, a short distance beyond, a small cluster of unpretending tents, close to the roadside, was pointed out to us as the headquarters of General Ord, the hero of the fight at Dranesville—a victory for which, by the way, the Reserves never received as much credit as they deserved. The rebel account of the battle bestowed, by implication, more praise upon them than the accounts which originally appeared in the North.

THE ENCAMPMENT.

A few hundred yards beyond this tent is located, on the right, the encampment of the Third Regiment, under command of Colonel Sickel, and, in close proximity, are the other regiments composing the division. The scene was a very lively and animated one. The soldiers were in excellent health and spirits, and looking as happy as schoolboys on their play-grounds. Most of them enjoy their present life, which has its peculiar charms, and they would consider it more of a sacrifice to be obliged to remain at home than to serve their country on the tented field. The presence of so large a force; the military exercises in which they engage; the glorious successes of the Union arms, and the mighty evidences of the power of the Republic by which they are daily surrounded, have banished every thought of fear from their hearts, and, in ordinary times, there are fewer men quaking with terror in the camps than among the same number engaged in quiet, civil pursuits, far away from the scene of hostilities.

HOW WASHINGTON IS DEFENDED.

It is only by riding to the outskirts of our camps that a clear idea of the mighty cordon of defences thrown around the capital can be obtained. There has been, first, a large force kept within the boundaries or in the rear of the city, consisting of a number of infantry, cavalry, and artillery regiments. Second, a complete line of forts on the south bank of the Potomac, stretching for miles along the river and commanding the whole country for a vast distance. Third, the camps extending from Gen. McCall's division on the right to a point below Alexandria, in an almost uninterrupted line, and consisting of a band of soldiers more numerous than the whole adult male population of any of our largest cities Beyond this line, at a distance of about two miles, were thrown the infantry pickets who kept watchful guard over the whole line entrusted to their care, and beyond their line again the cavalry pickets were constantly scouting through the country for a distance of from three to twelve or fifteen miles, regulated by their position and by the exigencies of the service.

THE DESOLATION OF WAR.

For miles around our encampments the whole country has been entirely stripped of the fences which once enclosed it. A considerable number of houses have been burned down, but in most instances by the rebel soldiers, who never hesitated a moment about applying the torch to the dwellings of Union men. Only those houses which were deserted were injured by our troops, and such desertion was considered prima facie evidence that the former occupants had joined the rebels' forces. Many fine forests have been entirely felled to the earth, with not a stump left as a vestige of their former existence, and many a fine field has been entirely cut up by the numberless teams that constantly ply in every direction.

THE CONTRABANDS.

While the whole country is intensely excited about the slavery question, there is comparatively little feeling in relation to it in the army. Absorbed in military duties, it has little disposition to enter into bitter discussions of political affairs. A terrible blow has been struck at slavery along the whole line occupied by our army. Of the active slaves, a large portion are carried South, and kept in the rear of the enemy's lines, and a considerable number of those not thus disposed of escape to the North, or seek shelter within our lines. Few but the old and infirm, and the young and helpless, are left lingering around the old homesteads where they have passed their lives. The characteristically happy disposition of the race, however, makes them comparatively well contented with their lot, whatever it may be.

THE FORWARD MOVEMENT.

On Monday, the 10th inst., the forward movement of the whole army of the Potomac commenced, and, leaving their old tents undisturbed, under the protection of a strong guard, they set forth to face whatever new perils they may be called upon to encounter in the mighty conflict which is now impending.

A RATHER PLEASANT INCIDENT.—A few days ago, as General Buell was riding on horseback through the streets of Nashville, an aristocratic lady, a Mrs. W., living in a fine, large house, stood at an open door or window, waved a rebel flag toward him, and cried, "Hurrah for Jeff Davis and the Southern Confederacy!" The General reined in his horse, turned toward the lady, touched his hat with all the courtesy and suavity for which he is remarkable, and, surveying the fine house from top to bottom with the eye of a connoisseur, quietly remarked, "An excellent house for a hospital." In less than two hours every room was full of sick soldiers, and Mrs. W. was politely requested to take kind care of them. We heartily congratulate her upon her blessed privilege of ministering to the needs of suffering patriots.—*ousville Journal*.

THE NAVAL BATTLE IN HAMPTON ROADS BETWEEN THE MONITOR AND THE MERRIMAC.—SKETCHED AND ENGRAVED FOR THE WAR PRESS.

THE SOUTHERN SECTION OF THE CHAIN BRIDGE ABOVE GEORGETOWN, D. C.—SKETCHED BY G. B. P. RINGWALT, AND ENGRAVED FOR THE WAR PRESS.

FORT MARCY, NEAR THE CHAIN BRIDGE.—SKETCHED BY G. B. P. RINGWALT, AND ENGRAVED FOR THE WAR PRESS.

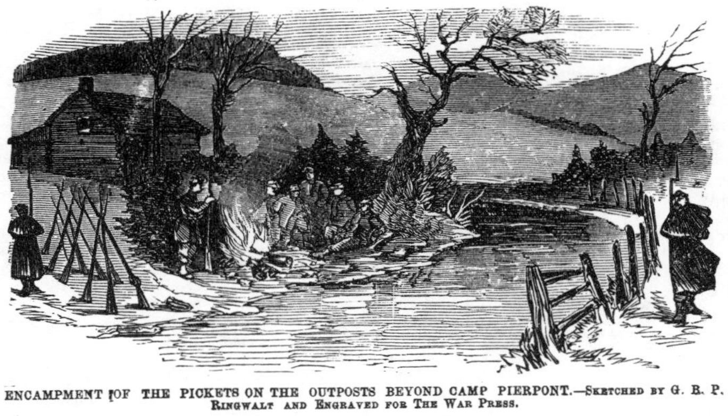

ENCAMPMENT OF THE PICKETS ON THE OUTPOSTS BEYOND CAMP PIERPONT.—SKETCHED BY G. B. P. RINGWALT AND ENGRAVED FOR THE WAR PRESS.

LOCAL AND STATE NEWS.

THE BATTLE NEAR WINCHESTER.—In addition to the particulars published in the Examiner and Dispatch of yesterday, we have later and reliable intelligence from the Valley, derived from gentlemen who arrived on the Orange and Alexandria train last night, from Staunton.

Yesterday morning, about 8 o'clock a courier arrived at that place and came on the Central Railroad, with dispatches to Gen. Johnston. He reports Gen. Jackson's loss at 500 killed and wounded. The enemy captured two of our guns from the Rockbridge and Augusta artillery.

The forces on both sides withdrew from the battle field after the engagement. The enemy have since advanced to Woodstock, Shenandoah county. The forces under Gen. Jackson fell back in good order and their rear was protected by Ashby's Cavalry. It was the intention of Gen. Jackson to renew the battle.

Dr. McGuire, of Winchester, who visited the battle field on Monday, after the forces on both sides had withdrawn, says that he walked over about one acre of the ground that the enemy occupied and that their loss was very heavy.

We have ascertained that there are thirty odd-licensed dram shops in this city besides the other rum holes, where that article it is sold clandestinely, or given in barter to negroes for stolen goods.

What cesspools of corruption!—Enough to poison the atmosphere and send forth a foul malaria for miles around. And what is the duty of the conservators of the peace, those into whose hands the best interests of the community are entrusted at this fearful crisis? It is the duty first, of the Court, to withhold the sanction of law to the traffic; then of the Council to pass ordinances that will reach all cases, and punish severely by confiscation and fine, such as defy the law. Then we should have a Mayor and police that would be vigilant, energetic, enterprising, and possessed of the nerve required to execute the laws. If those now in office—we make no exception—cannot be brought up to this point, they must be compelled to give place to others. The public interests must not be subordinate to private considerations. We owe it to our city; to the thousands of soldiers that are casually amongst us; to the cause of law, order, and good government, that we be careful in the selection of our officers for the ensuing year; and especially, that the fruitful source of disorder be removed out of the way. Now, more than ever, the obligation is upon us to maintain the laws against all offenders, and to use a wise forecast in selecting the men who will be most likely to subserve our purposes. Let us depose every man whose chief strength heretofore has been with the worst classes of society; and if we see the whiskey drinkers and sellers, the gamblers, harlots, and loafers, electioneering for their favorites, let us take our cue therefrom, and vote in solid phalanx against them.

Surely, the better element, in such a struggle, would predominate. We urgently call upon every good citizen to do his duty, and we shall then be able to have a city government that will be a terror to evil doers.

FOREIGN RESIDENTS.—We are informed that a large number of foreign residents who have been here for years, now claim that they are citizens of another country, and will not take up arms to defend this; and some of them even refuse to take the oath of allegiance. They are domiciled amongst us; their interests are here; they make their money and hold their property here, whilst our laws protect them in person and property. And yet, they refuse to give their services to protect the State, when she calls upon them.

Something ought to be done with these people. They should be compelled to naturalize at once and become citizens, or be invited to depart from amongst us.—We want none amongst now whose sympathies are not with us.

We are requested to call attention to the fact that there will be a meeting of the ladies, held at the Hall of the Young Men's Christian Association, at ten o'clock this morning, for the purpose of getting up an interest upon the subject of that important arm of our defence, gunboats. A full attendance is desirable.

LITHOGRAPHIC STONES.—We are requested by Col. Blanton Duncan, of Richmond, to enquire whether any of our tobacconists have lithographic stones, a supply of which he wants for the use of the Government.

COLLISION ON THE SOUTH SIDE ROAD.—We hear that there was a collision on the South Side road near the Junction, yesterday. The extent of the disaster was not ascertained.

The cars with the Richmond mails, due at noon, reached here at 7 o'clock last evening.

LADIES' MEETING.—In pursuance of previous call, a large number of the ladies of Lynchburg assembled in Masonic Hall, to consider the propriety of raising a fund with which to assist the Ladies of Richmond and of Virginia, to build an iron-clad vessel for the defence of our waters from the invasion of the enemy.

On motion of Mr. ——, Mrs. Chaplin was called to the Chair.

Mr. Speed then, by special request, addressed the meeting in an eloquent and forcible manner, explaining the object of the meeting, and the noble and patriotic character of the undertaking. At the conclusion of his remarks, he moved the appointment of a committee of five to report resolutions to be acted on at an adjourned meeting of the ladies, whereupon the President appointed the following committee:

Mrs. J. R. McDaniel, Mrs. Ro. L. Owens, Mrs. Dr. J. H Patterson, Mrs. J. M. Speed, and Mrs. Gen. E. Kirby Smith.

On motion of Mr. Speed, the editors of the city papers were requested to publish notice of adjourned meeting, and urge a full attendance of the ladies.

Judge Wilson appearing in the Hall, arose and made some very appropriate and stirring remarks favorable to the enterprise.

On motion, the meeting adjourned to 10 o'clock Thursday morning (to-day.)

MARRIED,

On Wednesday morning, March 26th, at the Court Street Methodist Episcopal Church, by the Rev. J. [illegible] Edwards, Mr. EDMOND W. JONES to Miss ALICE SANFORD WILLIAMS, all of this city.

OBITUARY.

The death of Gen. DAVID RHODES, which occurred at his residence, on the — of February, has already been announced; yet, the death of so good and useful a man, obviously demands a more extended notice. The greater part of his life was spent in this city, and had he lived until the first of this month, he would have been 67 years old. At the age of 18, he volunteered his services in the late war with Great Britain, and served in the army until the conclusion of peace. He was the first Captain of the first Artillery Company ever formed in this place, and was afterwards Brigade Inspector of this brigade; and, at a later period, was elected Brigadier General, and acted as such, until the condition of his health and of his private affairs made it a duty to resign. For many years, he was Clerk of the Circuit Court of Law and Chancery of this city, Clerk of the Common Council of this city, and also, Clerk of the District Court held here. The duties of all these offices he performed most faithfully and well; for he was a man of uncommon industry, and capable of performing a large amount of labor, and was exact and methodical in all that he did. He was prompt and accommodating, and ever at his post.

But, we do not feel at liberty to indulge in high-wrought panegyric, though the character of the subject of this notice might justify it. The best eulogy we could pronounce, would be to portray his virtues, as he practiced them. And, as the exhibition of these virtues, while living, was without ostentation, any marked notice of them, now, would be inconsistent with his character; and so far, unjust to his reputation. We would speak of him only as he really was, a "true Virginia gentleman of the old school." Cordial in manners, warm in heart, and sincere in friendship; whilst his domestic affections were deep and enduring. In a word, he was a virtuous and estimable citizen; and, we trust, an humble christian—whose faith in the Lord Jesus exercised a transforming power upon his heart and life. For twelve years past, he has been a devout member of the second Presbyterian Church. About six years since, he was smitten by paralysis, and has been mostly confined to his house until his death. The disease slowly advanced upon him, until quite recently, when the paralysis affected nearly his whole frame. Until now, he had indulged some hope of returning health, and life had charms for him—tender and numerous were the cords of endearment that bound him to earth. But to "the will of God" he submitted with the docility of a little child; and when failing powers indicated that his "time to die" was approaching, he was enabled to commit his loved wife and children, his absent sons and daughters, and himself, into the hands of a faithful and covenant-keeping God.—Death had no terror to him; for he felt that the Great Shepherd was near. When almost gone, in answer to a question, he replied: "*Jesus is with me, I know*," and thus he departed, to be, we trust, ever present with the Lord. May those dearest to him on earth, who so deeply revere his character, imitate his piety and practice his virtues.

M.

LATEST NEWS BY THE MAILS.

Battle Near Winchester.

GEN. JACKSON REPULSED.

The Enemy Advancing.

Dispatches were received last night in official quarters, stating that a battle had taken place between Gen. Stonewall Jackson's command and a large force of the enemy, about five miles from Winchester, and that we had sustained a reverse, our forces having been compelled to fall back in the direction of Strasburg. The force under Gen. Jackson is stated to have been about 5,000 men, while the enemy is said to have been some 17 or 18,000 strong.—Our loss in officers is said to have been very large. We annex a copy of one of the official dispatches, which we were enabled to obtain at a late hour last night:

AN OFFICIAL ACCOUNT.

Gen. Jackson engaged the enemy, 18,000 strong, at Barton's Mills, five miles this side of Winchester. The fight occurred on Sunday, about 4.30 P. M. After a severe contest, Gen. Jackson was compelled to retreat, with a heavy loss of men and officers.

Capt. Antium was wounded, and was taken prisoner.

Lieuts. Dale and Wilson, of the Fifth Va. regiment were killed.

Capt. Buford is missing. Maj. Jackson and Lieut. Williams are missing, and supposed to be killed.

Our loss is estimated to be about 200.

Gen Jackson retreated to Cedar creek. The baggage is reported to be all safe in his rear.

The enemy is advancing.—*R. Exam.*

In addition to the above, the Dispatch of yesterday contains the following:

The news from the Valley is not near so encouraging as that published in our yesterday's issue, and in some degree less hopeful for our cause. We see nothing in the news received, however, to discourage us, or to cause a feeling of gloom to ensue. That our army has been repulsed, from the information before us, we are disposed to believe, but the confidence we feel in Gen Jackson, and his gallant troops, leaves abundant room to hope that his withdrawal from the field of conflict on Sunday, was as successful as his evacuation of Winchester two weeks ago.

Our news is predicated upon a telegram received at the Governor's office, yesterday, from Major Harman, at Staunton.—The dispatch states that Gen. Jackson engaged the enemy within a few miles of Winchester, at half-past four on Sunday afternoon, and that the fighting continued until nightfall, when our troops fell back to Cedar Creek, about two miles from Strasburg. Our loss is known to be about 200, a heavy proportion of which is company officers. Among the killed or missing the names of Capt Antrim, Lieut. Dale, Major Jackson, and Lieut. Williams, are given.

It is difficult to understand the circumstances connected with this engagement, particularly as previous information seemed to leave little doubt of the evacuation of the town of Winchester by the enemy. This was doubtless the impression of Gen. Jackson, or he would hardly have marched his men forty miles to engage a largely superior force. The withdrawal of their force was no doubt a ruse to entrap him, and has too nearly succeeded, not to admit the question of a want of caution somewhere.

The telegram also state that the enemy were in pursuit of our forces; and if so, it is not at all improbable that a second engagement has taken place ere this.

Up to 11 o'clock last night, no later intelligence was received.

The Little Rock (Ark.) *True Democrat*, of the 13th, contains some items concerning the great three day's fight, which had not before reached us:

THE BATTLE IN THE WEST.

Clarksville, the point from which our telegraphic despatches are sent, is but a little over half way from the city of Van Buren, so that a courier has to ride fifty miles before the dispatch can be telegraphed. This will account for the intervals in the dispatches, and the difficulty of getting full information.

We have very little to add to the information contained in the dispatches to be found in another column. The fact is certain, that a bloody battle has been fought with immense loss of life The battle field extends over ten miles, and on every mile of the route are a thousand dead men.—The battle was the most desperately contested of any fought during the war. Our loss in officers is reported as terrible. McCulloch, McIntosh, McRae, Slack and others, have fallen. Braver and nobler men never died for freedom.

Our forces at Boston Mountain were supposed to be in the neighborhood of 30,000, opposed to 34,000 Federals. The latter were western men and regulars. Among the forces of the enemy was one regiment of cavalry armed with revolving rifles and two extra cylinders, so that they could fire 18,000 shots without reloading. They also had Sturgis's battery manned by regulars, and said to be the best drilled and disciplined body on the continent. If, as we are led to believe, the Federals were reinforced by the column from Kansas, the odds against us were as two to one.

Our troops fought for three days and nights, and more desperate fighting was never done. We await the particulars with anxiety, and shall issue bulletins as fast as dispatches are received.

BY TELEGRAPH.

Congressional.

Richmond, March 26.—The President has appointed to the Territory of Arizona, and the Senate confirmed the following officers for that Territory. John R. Baylor, Governor; Robert Jocelyn, Secretary; Alex. M Jackson, Chief Justice; Columbus Upton, Associate Justice; Russell Howard. District Attorney; Samuel J. Jones, Marshal.

The Hon. W. L. Yancey arrived and took his seat in the Senate this morning.

SECOND DISPATCH.

OFFICIAL DISPATCH FROM GENERAL JACKSON.

Retreat of Federals to Winchester.

ISLAND NO. TEN IMPREGNABLE.

FIGHTING CONTINUES.

Capture of 100 Federal Artillery Horses near Corinth, &c &c.

Richmond, 26th March.—President Davis has received a letter from Stonewall Jackson which says he had a fight at Winchester on Sunday with 18,000 federals, which lasted from four o'clock in the evening until night; firing on both sides then ceased. Jackson then fell back to a better position at Cedar Creek, leaving Ashby on the field, where he stayed until morning.—The enemy moved also in the night, pushing his retreat towards Winchester. Our loss is considerable in officers and men.—The loss of the enemy is enormous.

Four Yankee prisoners, captured at Evansport, arrived here to-day. One from Sickles' brigade said he deserted, and three others from Massachusetts. Reported all quiet on the Potomac.

Late Northern papers received, say: The Yankee Senate refused to confirm the appointment of Sickles as Brigadier General. The prisoners say he is very unpopular with his Brigade.

The remains of Col. Cameron have been disinterred at Manassas, and sent North by the Yankees.

Three Yankee drummer boys were brought up from Yorktown.

A large force is said to be landing at Old Point.

The Savannah Republican of this morning, says: The Yankees are in full possession of Johnston's River, Florida.

About 2,500 Yankees are at Jacksonville. They have torn up the Railroad, and are using the iron for the defence of the city.

A special dispatch to the Savannah Republican, from Baldwin, says: A small detachment of Confederates stole on the Yankee picket guard at Jacksonville, killing four and capturing three. Lieut. Strange, of the Confederates, was wounded; and, it is feared, mortally.

Information from Island No. 10 received last night says there was heavy cannonading on Sunday last. Two of the enemies gunboats have been destroyed. One was sunk below Hickman and the other sunk within sight of the Island.

The soldiers on the Island are in good spirits and declare they can hold it against the world.

The enemies land forces at New Madrid are estimated at forty thousand; sixty of them came down in small boats through the swamp to Gayoso, and captured seven citizens, formerly of Gen. Thompson's army.

Yesterday the Confederate scouts at Corinth captured one hundred artillery horses belonging to the Yankees and were compelled to leave the guns as the enemy were close at hand.

3D DISPATCH

LATER FROM THE NORTH.

News from Island No. 10 was received at Chicago, March 24th.

A special dispatch to the Tribune, dated 9 o'clock, Sunday night, Off Island No. 10, says: Firing has been conducted slowly, day and night, at intervals of half an hour. The fire was mostly concentrated upon the upper battery, which is now falling to pieces. The battery has not replied for two days. Only one gun can be seen in position, and that is quiet.

The batteries on land are mysteriously silent. The encampments are growing smaller and smaller every day. Transports still continue flying about, apparently carrying away troops. The river is still rising, and everything is overflowed. The rebels are fairly drowned out of some of the batteries. They have been attempting the erection of new ones, but the well directed fire of our mertars prevents them.

A special dispatch to the Times, at Cairo, says:

The steamer Lake Erie, which left Island No. 10 at 11 o'clock last night saw the light of a large fire near the Kentucky shore which kept increasing as they got up the river. It is supposed to be one of the rebel transports set on fire by the bursting of some of our shells.

Another dispatch to the Tribune Saturday night says: The gunboat Mound City fired twenty shot in the middle of the batteries and had considerable effect.

Our officers with the aid of their glasses counted five rebels killed. The shot on Sunday, the mortars fired, owing to the weather, we could not ascertain the effect.

St. Louis, March 24th.—A dispatch to the Sec'y of War from Gen. Halleck says: A detachment of the first Cavalry sent out from Jefferson City, under Gen Totten against a guerrilla party, had a skirmish with the enemy, killing two, wounding one, and taking 75 prisoners, over 20 horses, 48 kegs of powder, and a quantity of arms captured. Our loss 400,

Post-Master General Blair has issued instructions to all publishers, not to publish anything that will give information to the rebels, under penalty of exclusion from the mails.

Cincinnati, March 24.—Wendall Phillips the notorious abolition agitator attempted to lecture in the Opera House to-night but met with rather an unexpected demonstration He avowed himself an abolitionist and disunionist, whereupon he was egged and stoned. He was taken away by friends.

Washington, March 24th.—A dispatch from the Surgeon of Gen. Shields' army to the Surgeon General at Washington says in relation to the battle on Sunday: Our loss is from 75 to 100 in killed, and 250 wounded. I have seen 225 of the enemy dead.

Winchester, March 24th.—The rebels have been driven back to Strawsburg with heavy loss. One French officer came up to-day. All quiet here.

FROM EUROPE.

NORFOLK, March 26.—The steamer Hansa arrived at New York with dates to the 20th inst.

In the House of Lords, Lord Campbell called attention to the inefficiency of the blockade of the Confederate ports, and moved for a correspondence on the subject.

Lord Russell replied to the proof advanced by Lord Campbell, of the inefficiency of the blockade, and recounted the efforts made by the North to render it effective. He considered that the want of cotton in the English market was the best test that the blockade was not an empty one. He added that the removal of the old feeling between the North and South was impossible, and he hoped the North would consent to a peaceful separation of the States, and trusted that within three months the war would close, leaving emancipation possible to be effected by gradual peaceful means. He said no formal communication had been made by the French government in regard to the inefficiency of the blockade.

The Annie Childs, a screw steamer, arrived at Queenstown, from Wilmington, N. C., recently.

The ship Maria arrived at Liverpool from Bombay. She fell in with the brig Esperior, from London, bound for New York, with their crew in a starving condition. They supplied them.

Two hundred thousand pounds sterling in Australian gold recently arrived in England.

The latest via Queenstown, March 10th reports American securities firm.

The Asia arrived to-day with commercial news of the Liverpool Cotton Market.

Cotton closed dull.

Sales Monday and Tuesday of 8000 bale—3000 to speculators and exporters.

Prices unchanged.

Breadstuffs dull.

4th DISPATCH.

LATEST FROM JACKSON'S ARMY.

Enemy's Loss Immense.

OUR WOUNDED BROUGHT TO STAUN TON, &c., &c.

RICHMOND, March 26.

Gov. Letcher has received the followin dispatch from Staunton, dated March 26

Gen Jackson's army is between Mou Jackson and Woodstock, in good conditio

Captains Robertson and Howard we wounded and taken prisoners. Lt. Junk (instead of Maj. Jackson) is missing.

One hundred and fifty wounded arrive here this morning The Yankees fired our flag of truce, and refused to permit to bury our dead.

The enemy's loss is very heavy. Th were repulsed and driven from the fie twice.

Latest from Yankeedom.

FORT MACON BLOWN UP.

Steamer Nashville Burnt, &c., &

RICHMOND, March 26.

A dispatch from Fortress Monroe, dat March 23d, says, that the steamer Chanc lor Livingston arrived from Hatteras, l Friday, and brings intelligence that, imm diately after the occupation of Newbern, t expedition to Beaufort started. The pla was found to have been evacuated bef our troops approached.

Fort Macon was blown up by the rebe and the rebel steamer Nashville was bu to-day.

Gen. Burnside occupied Newbern.

It has been ascertained that 16, troops are on the road from Goldsboro', reinforce the rebels at Newbern.

The steamer Swance sailed for Hatte March 23d, with mails and passengers.

A 2d dispatch from Washington, da March 24th, says:

Col. Segar, the representative from Accomac district, arrived here this mo ing, and confirms the intelligence of destruction of the privateer Nashville Fort Macon by the rebels.

LATEST FROM MISSOURI

From a private source we learn that Baltimore Argus of Saturday evening p lished from the Cincinnati Enquirer Price had captured and cut to pieces 5, Yankees under Siegel, (?) and was sup ed to be marching on St. Louis We b it is true.—*Fred News of the 22d.*

THE BATTLE OF PEA RIDGE, ARKANSAS—THE FINAL ADVANCE OF OUR TROOPS, MARCH 8, 1862.—[See Page 202.]

LOCAL AND STATE NEWS.

We are gratified to learn that at the meeting held on Thursday, by the ladies, interested in the gun boat enterprise, the sum of $461 was subscribed for the purpose. It is very important that the quantity of iron should be increased, to enable the Government to construct a sufficient number of these boats; and to this end, all persons who have old iron lying about their premises should gather it up and place it at the disposal of the Government agents. The foundry of Mr. Deane, located here, could, we are informed, turn out twice the quantity of Government work it is doing, if iron could be had. The demand for shot and shell, as every body must know, is very great, and all the iron that is lying waste about the country should be gathered up to be converted into missiles with which to greet the invader, or iron-clad vessels to protect our cities.

We hope that our readers will act upon these suggestions which are derived from the ladies.

We understand that the jail birds are having a lively time at the hotel de Wade. They have taken down "the middle wall of partition" and have all things in common, circulating from one apartment to another. It may be necessary to deprive these unruly fellows of their liberty.

Mr. Editor:—I see by your paper that "Many Citizens" have called upon Alderman Saunders to declare himself a candidate for the Mayoralty of our city at the approaching municipal election. The writer has been aware, for some time, that *many* of our *citizens* have become tired of paying more than five thousand dollars a year for the support of an establishment that has proved wholly incapable of administering the laws or of supporting the dignity of the city. Yet, "many citizens" have, from personal considerations, heretofore voted against their honest convictions. Will they again do so in the approaching election? Do the offices of this city belong, in perpetuity, to a special few, or do they belong to the loyal citizens, to be by them bestowed upon the most competent and worthy—upon men who will not seek the support of that class who are most obnoxious to the law; but upon men who, rising to the dignity of the office, will disdain to place themselves under obligations to those who are most likely to be the first offenders? Our citizens are not more intractable than other people. They want an uniform and impartial enforcement of the law and will cheerfully acquiese in any regulation that they know will be equally enforced against others; but the feeble, hesitating, and uncertain policy which has governed in the administration of our laws has disgusted *many citizens* with the laws, instead of with the administrators of the laws. Will the people give us a chief magistrate not wholly devoted to his ease—one that will have the energy to sometimes go out of his daily path to take a view of the city and its condition; and, above all, one who will see that his subalterns neither sleep on their posts, nor eat the bread of idleness at the expense of the

TAX PAYER.

Mr. Editor:—There is a notice in your paper, of "a meeting of some of the ladies of Lynchburg, to consider the propriety of raising a fund with which to assist the ladies of Richmond, and Virginia, to build an iron-clad vessel for the defence of our waters from the invasion of the enemy." But, must the noble hearted women of Virginia turn their attention from the care of our sick and wounded soldiers, and from raising money to help to clothe them, and working to make their clothes, and, best of all, from administering in various ways to their spiritual good, to a purpose most praiseworthy in itself, but not belonging to us, as women, to perform? It is the duty of men. We cannot do everything; and, in in the things enumerated above, we have a wide field of usefulness before us, and one that cannot be performed by men. Let us not leave the place our Creator seems to have assigned us. If we do our duty in it, we can really do more good to our country than in any other way. The cry of distress is going up all around us, and our part is almost as important as that of the other sex. We have read with disgust of the meetings held in some parts of the North, to advocate *woman's rights*, in which (mistaking their mission upon earth) they purpose to bear an equal part with the other sex in all their occupations and pursuits. Let us not imitate them in this great error, but believe, that God has given to each sex its appropriate sphere of action, and let us thank Him that our part is nearer to the precepts and practice of our blessed Saviour.

A LADY.

Metal.—In response to Gen. Beauregard's call for bells, we understand that the Catholic Archbishop and clergy of this diocese have agreed to contribute their church bells whenever it shall be decided they are necessary. Father Mullen, of St. Patrick's church, has already written on to Gen. Beauregard, offering him the heavy bell of that church whenever he desires to have it. Of course, church bells should be called for only in the last resort. Whenever the supply of other metal is exhausted, then let the churches give up the loud voiced monitors with which they call the faithful to prayers, and change them to guardians of those faithful called to the bloody prayer of a fearful duty.

[*N. O Crescent.*

The Legislature.—In the Senate, on Thursday, a joint resolution was adopted, instructing our Senators and Representatives in Congress to endeavor to procure the passage of such laws as will confirm the assurances given by ordinances of the Convention, to Virginians in the Army and Navy of the United States at the commencement of the present difficulties. A joint resolution to rectify the inequality of Virginia's contribution of men and means to the present war, was laid on the table.

The bill generally known as the "Stay Law," was passed. It differs from the Ordinance of the Convention in that it authorizes trials by juries of actions of detinue and unlawful entry, and entry and detainer, and in contests about wills; and provides for sales under decrees of courts of estates of decedents for distribution; also, authorizes the trials of suits when a security gives notice to the creditors to institute a suit, and provides for the collection of the annual interest on debts.

The Salt bill was passed, providing for the purchase and equitable distribution of 400 000 bushels of salt, the same to be distributed by agents appointed by the Governor, at a maximum salary of $800i

The Small Note bill, in the form of a substitute offered by Mr. Armstrong, was passed. This gives authority to the Banks to issue notes of a less denomination than $5, and not less than one dollar, to an amount not exceeding ten per cent of their capital; and any Banks failing to issue such notes, shall pay sums less than $5 in specie. It also authorizes the city of Richmond to issue notes of a less denomination than one dollar, to an amount not exceeding $500,000, and all other towns with a population of 2,000, and the towns of Leesburg, Lewisburg, and Warrenton, to an amount equal to double the annual State tax on the real and personal property within their corporate limits.

The House of Delegates, yesterday, passed Senate bills providing for annual sessions of the General Assembly; and to authorize vacancies to be filled *pro tempore* in certain offices after the ratification of the amended Constitution; also a joint resolution requiring the Auditor and other State officers and corporations to make annual reports in the event of the ratification of the amended Constitution; also a House bill exempting certain parties from military duty upon religious grounds. The parties exempted are Friends and Tunkards. Exemptions are granted them upon condition that they pay $500 each into the Treasury and two per cent. tax on all their property.

A communication was read from Judge Pitts, denying the charges against him for disloyalty. It was laid on the table.

The House passed the "Stay Law" from the Senate.

A variety of unimportant bills were considered, rejected and laid over.—*Whig.*

RELIGIOUS NOTICE.

The Rev. Wm. V. Wilson will preach at the Second Presbyterian Church on Sabbath morning at 11 o'clock A. M.

MILITARY NOTICES.

ATTENTION RECRUITS.

WANTED immediately, recruits to fill up my company to the maximum number. I have a fine prospect of getting a Field Piece as soon as I have the requisite number of men. A bounty of $50 will be paid to each recruit upon his reception. None but able bodied sound men will be received. As it is almost a certainty that my present company which has been in the service since the war, will be changed into Artillery, I wish to get it filled out as soon as possible, that it may the more quickly be drilled and ready for the field. I can be found at the Exchange Bank for the present.

SAM'L V. REID,
Captain and Recruiting officer C. S. A.

mar 14-ts

Cavalry Recruits Wanted.

Head'qrs. Co. B, 2d Va., Cavalry,
Leesburg, Feb. 19, 1862.

FOR the purpose of filling my company to the maximum number and with a view to ultimate re-organization, I desire a number of recruits.—Able bodied men with good characters and good horses, are earnestly requested to join us instead of subjecting themselves to a draft. For information apply to Camillus Christian at the Exchange Bank, or direct to me at Leesburg, Va.

C. M. BLACKFORD, Captain.

☞ Persons now in service wishing to join this company at the expiration of their term will please let me know.

feb 20-d&ts C. M. B.

Recruits.

WANTED from 50 to 75 able-bodied men to fill the ranks of an Artillery Company now in the field. This company is attached to the Reserve Corps of Artillery, commanded by that gallant officer, Col Wm. N. Pendleton. Fifty dollars bounty will be paid to each recruit as soon as he reaches camp.

The draft will soon be upon you. Do not wait to be forced into the service, but come forward willingly and volunteer for the defence of your country.

Clothing, transportation, &c., furnished free.—Call at the recruiting office, nearly opposite the Virginian Office, in the room formerly occupied by A. M. Trible, Esq., up stairs.

LIEUT. EDMUND TAYLOR.
feb25-3tawts C. S. Army, Recruiting Officer.

Recruits Wanted.

Headquarters, Company I,
2nd Regiment Virginia Cavalry,
Leesburg, Va, Feb. 27, 1862.

THE subscriber, commanding the above named company, wishes 150 men to enlist for the war, either as Cavalry or Flying Artillery, as a majority of the company may determine. He wants none but able bodied fighting men. Men who will shrink from no duty, either picket or any other. Having been in the service since June last, he has seen enough to satisfy himself that this is no place for "FANCY MISS NANCIES," and he wants none of them. All men wishing to join will report to me at Leesburg; J. M. Cobbs, Lynchburg; Jno. Pannill, Green Hill; or Sergeant Wm. E. Franklin, Leesville.

Transportation and all things needful furnished.

JOHN D. ALEXANDER,
Captain of Com. I, 2nd Reg. Va Cavalry,

mar 4-1m

Wanted

THREE GOOD COOPERS, qualified to put up tight work, for which good wages will be paid by job or year. Address

J. C. DEYERLE,
Big Spring Depot,
sept8-cts Montgomery Co., Va.

LATEST NEWS BY THE MAILS.

FROM THE NORTH.

The Fight near Winchester—Gen Shields Loses an Arm—Colonel Murray Killed—Fourteen Captains and Lieutenants Dead.

The Norfolk Day Book is in possession of the Baltimore American of the 26th, from which the following is extracted:

Despatches from Winchester confirm the defeat of the Rebel army under Gen. Jackson in the battle of Sunday. The Rebels have been driven back to Strasburg with heavy loss, and more than one thousand of their small arms have been captured. The fighting yesterday was confined to skirmishing, in which we had ten killed and wounded. An official despatch from a surgeon in General Shield's division states that our loss in the battle of Sunday was from seventy-five to one hundred killed and about two hundred and fifty wounded. He also states that he saw on the field "two hundred and twenty-five of the enemy dead."

Winchester, March 24, 11 o'clock p. m. In consequence of the forward movement of our forces, the reports of the killed, wounded and missing, cannot be accurately ascertained, but it is estimated that our loss was 80 to 100 killed, among them were one Colonel and fourteen captains and lieutenants.

During the fight at Winchester on Sunday, the Federal General Shields was struck by the fragment of a shell on his left arm, shattering the bone, and rendering amputation necessary.

An official dispatch received at Washington last night from Winchester says that Gen. Banks was then at Cedar Creek, two miles from Strasburg, which place he intend to take to-day.

The Pennsylvania Legislature yesterday adjourned as a mark of respect for the memory of Col. Murray, of the 84th Pennsylvania regiment, who was killed in the battle near Winchester on Sunday.

The Secretary of War has ordered a special Court Martial for the trial of sundry newspaper proprietors who have "violated the articles of war" by the publication of movements of the army. The Washington Star says that the cases of the publishers of the Boston Courier and New York Journal of Commerce are the two first to be brought to the Court Martial's attention.

The mortar fleet has left Key West for Lake Pontchartrain, to attack New Orleans. It consisted of 21 mortar vessels, 8 steamers, and 1 storeship, in three divisions under the command of Commander David D. Porter, U. S. Navy.

The Washington correspondent of the Philadelphia Press, "Occasional," states that Bailie Peyton has announced his adhesion to the National Government, and that G. A. P. Nicholson, who has been quiet during all the troubles, will probably follow his example.

It is thought that Emerson Etheridge will be returned as Senator from the State of Tennessee, as colleague of Andrew Johnson, who, of course, will resume his seat after a loyal State government is organized.

The report of the capture of Wm. L. Yancey proves as we anticipated, incorrect.

In the U. S. Senate, yesterday, a communication was received from the Secretary of Navy in relation to the Stevens iron plated battery. The joint resolution from the House proposing pecuniary aid to the States undertaking the emancipation of slaves was discussed during the morning hour. The bill for the abolition of slavery in the District of Columbia was then taken up.

In the House of Representatives yesterday, the certificate of election of Mr. Segar from the First District of Virginia was presented and referred. A resolution of thanks to Gen. Burnside and his officers and men under his command was passed.

Mr. Morehead, of Pa, introduced a resolution inquiring why Col. Corcoran has not been released by the rebels, and declaring that there ought to be no further release of prisoners until he is delivered up. The Tax bill was then taken up.

In the Senate, on Monday, Mr. Ten Eyck presented the joint resolution of the Legislature of New Jersey, asking Congress to take immediate action for the defence of the coasts of New Jersey, Pennsylvania and Delaware.

Mr. Sherman presented the resolutions of the Legislature of Ohio against any propositions for the settlement of the rebellion, except an unconditional surrender and the condign punishment of traitors.

Mr. Morrill presented the resolutions of the Legislature of Maine, endorsing the Administration, and in favor of the confiscation of the property of the rebels.

On motion of Mr. Stevens, the House resolved itself into Committee of the whole, and took up the Tax bill.

Mr. Clemens, of Tennessee, offered an amendment, which was adopted, that Tennessee might have until the first of December next to assume payment of her portion of the tax.

The Sumter was still at Gibraltar on the seventh, and the Tuscarora watching her.

THE FIGHT IN THE VALLEY.

We have received some few additional particulars of the fight near Winchester on Sunday last. As stated in our issue of yesterday, our force in the engagement scarcely exceeded 3,500. One regiment was held as a reserve, and from 1,300 to 1,800 of our troops failed to arrive in time to participate in the engagement.

We append a list of the wounded in company A, of this city, which has been furnished us by a gentleman who left Woodstock on Tuesday night: Sergeant Tucker Randolph; Privates Grey, Picot, Annally, Kenny or Renwig, Danforth, O. Taylor and E. Taylor. Most of these were only slightly wounded. There were none of the members of this corps killed.

Among the killed and wounded in the 23d regiment we have the following names: Lieut. E. C. Crump, of Company H, (Richmond Sharp Shooters.) wounded, but not dangerously. Lieut. Crump is from this city, and was an occasional correspondent for this paper, over the signature of "Ned."

H. L. Francisco, company G, killed. He was from Louisa county.

Serg't Venable, company I, killed. From Prince Edward co.

Capt. J. T. Walton, company H, wounded in the arm. From Charlotte county.—Privates John O. Pettus, of same company, killed, and P. G. Eubank, mortally wounded. John H. Pettus wounded and missing.

Lieut. Curtis, of company F, slightly wounded.

Second Lieut. Jack Heth, of the Irish battalion, was killed in the action. If we are not mistaken, Lieut. Heth was a stepson of Frederick Boyden, formerly proprietor of the Exchange Hotel, in this city, and is doubtless remembered by many of our citizens.

A gentleman who was engaged in the fight arrived in this city yesterday evening and from him we obtain some fuller particulars. On Saturday morning a brush fight took place between the commands of Col Ashby and Chew's Artillery, and the advance guard of the enemy's forces. It is alleged that it was in this fight that Gen Shields was wounded. He was wounded in the arm, which was amputated after his return to Winchester.

General Banks had his horse shot under him.

After the fight on Sunday the enemy retired to Winchester, and information from citizens who came out the next day states that they were engaged all night in bringing their killed and wounded, which they admit to be not less than 1,500. Some even put it as high as 8,000.

General Jackson in person headed five different charges, each time driving the enemy back upon his reserves.

In one of the gallant charges made, a portion of Col. Fulkerson's regiment was surrounded and made prisoners. The loss of this regiment is about 150, a number of whom no doubt are in the hands of the enemy as prisoners.

Matches! Matches! Matches!

I WOULD respectfully inform my friends and the public, that I am engaged in the Manufacture of FRICTION MATCHES of a quality equal to any made, and at prices as moderate as the times will justify.

Orders solicited, promptly filled and satisfaction guaranteed. Factory on the Canal just below the Langhorne Foundry. Samples may be seen at J. L. Winston's Furniture Store, opposite the Norvell House.

J. H. C. WINSTON.

jan 9-ts

To Officers Raising new Companies.

THERE seems to be a misapprehension on the part of many persons, in supposing that no new companies will be received, until old companies are filled. I am authorized by the Secretary of War to receive ten new companies, and their bounty and pay will commence from date of their muster.

By authority of Secretary of War.

THOS. A. HARRIS,
mar 11-ts Mustering officer.

NEW LONDON ACADEMY.

THE exercises of this School will be resumed the 1st day of April.

☞ Address the Principal at Forest Depot.

JNO. H. WINSTON,
mar 27-d&c8t Principal.

Wanted.

TO work on the repairs of the James River and Kanawha Canal a number of ABLE-BODIED NEGRO MEN, to whom good wages will be allowed and their hire paid promptly at the end of the year.

DUNCAN GRANT.
Galt's Mills,
mar 24 d&c2w Amherst co., Va.

VIRGINIA to wit:—At rules held in the Clerk's office of the Franklin County Court, the 5th day of March, 1862:

Thomas B. Greer and Celestia his wife, and Whitmell P. Taliaferro, Plaintiffs.

Against

James Patterson, Administrator of Richard M. Taliaferro, dec'd, and Ferdinand L. Claiborne and Emily his wife Henry Taliaferro, Tazewell Taliaferro, Susan Taliaferro, Richard H. W. Dillard, Charles T. Dillard, William C. B. Dillard, Thomas C. Dillard, Anne Rosella Dillard, Martin P. Dillard, Mary Dillard, Hugh Nelson and Lucy A. his wife and Richard M. Taliaferro. Defendants.

IN CHANCERY.

(The object of this suit is for an account to be taken of advancements made by the said Richard M. Taliaferro, dec'd, to his children in his life time.)

It appearing by an affidavit filed that the Defendants, Ferdinand L. Claiborne and Emily his wife, Susan Taliaferro, Henry Taliaferro, Tazewell Taliaferro and Thomas C. Dillard, are not residents of the State of Virginia, it is ordered that they do appear here within one month after the due publication of this order and do what is necessary to protect their interest in this suit; and that a copy of this order be forthwith published in some newspaper printed in the city of Lynchburg, once a week for four successive weeks, and posted at the front door of the Court House of this county on the first day of this next County Court.

A copy—teste,
RO. A. SCOTT, D. C.
Gilmer, P. Q. mar 12 w4w

VIRGINIA.—At rules held in the Clerk's office of the Circuit Court of Montgomery, in the month of February, 1862:

William Thomas, Plaintiff.

Against

William Argabright and James M. Evans, Administrator, with the will annexed of Wm. Argabright, deceased. Defendants.

IN CHANCERY.

The object of this suit is to attach the estate and effects of the Defendant, William Argabright, who is a non-resident, in the hands of the Defendant, James M. Evans, Administrator, with the will annexed of William Argabright, dec'd, or which may hereafter come into his hands, (the said estate of the said Wm. Argabright, being his interest in the estate of the late Wm. Argabright, deceased.) so that the same may be held subject to the claim of the Plaintiff, and to enjoin the Defendant, Wm. Argabright, and all others concerned from disposing of the same, and it appearing from affidavit, that William Argabright is not a resident of this State, it is ordered that he appear here within one month after due publication of this order, and do what is necessary to protect his interest, and that a copy of this order be published once a week for four successive weeks in the "Lynchburg Virginian," a paper published in the city of Lynchburg, and posted on the front door of the Court House of said county on the first day of the next Court.

A copy—teste,
mar 19-w4w WM. M. BAINETZ, D. C.

BY TELEGRAPH.

Richmond, March 28.

House of Representatives.—A resolution was adopted, adjourning the body on the first Monday in April.

Senate—A bill was passed allowing the President four additional Aids on his staff. The debate was of such a tenor as not to warrant the conclusion that the President intends taking command.

Recruits Wanted for the Heavy Artillery Service.

I AM authorized by the Secretary of War to raise a company of Heavy Artillery for the war.

This is the most pleasant branch of the service, as it is free from the tedious marches, and most of the drudgery attendant on camp life. $50 bounty will be paid. I have authorized Jehu Williams to receive the names of recruits.

Persons wishing to enlist will please call as speedily as possible, at his store, where they will find an enlisting roll.

WILLIAM KING,
mar 7 Lieut. in Latham's Battery.

$50 Reward.

FOR FLAM, a dark brown boy, 15 years old very sprightly and quick spoken. Had on when he left, about the 1st March, a drab fulled cloth coat, pale blue pants and cap. Last time he was seen was with the 1st Georgia Regiment. I will pay the above reward if taken without the State, or 10 Dollars if taken within the State and confined so I get him again.

GEO D. DAVIS,
Administrator of Pleasant Preston, dec'd.

mar 21 d2tw&cts

Law Notice.

ARRANGEMENTS have been made by the surviving partners of the law, firm of Garland, Slaughter & Co, to have the assistance of older counsel in conducting their litigated cases, without additional expense to their clients. At the earliest moment after the termination of the war, S. Garland, Jr., expects to resume the active duties of his profession.

J. F. SLAUGHTER,
S. GARLAND, Jr.

feb 18 ts

SAL ERATUS AND SODA.—Sal Eratus for sale by

STABLER & JONES,
jan 21 Druggists.

---

200 KEGS OLD DOMINION NAILS—assorted

LEE, ROCKE & TAYLOR,
jan 30 105 Main street.

---

10 BBLS. OLD PEACH BRANDY, for sale by

BOCOCK & PARRISH,
feb 19-ts No. 9, Bridge street.

DRUMHEAD CABBAGE SEED.
SALSAFY SEED, for sale by

mar 21 W. A. STROTHER & CO.

VIRGINIA to wit:—At rules held in the Clerk's office of Franklin County Court, the 5th day of March, 1862:

George D. Davis and John T. Davis, late merchants and partners, trading under the firm and style of Davis & Brothers, Plaintiffs.

Against,

James Patterson, Administrator of Richard M. Taliaferro, dec'd., and Henry Taliaferro, Defts.

IN CHANCERY.

(The object of this suit is to subject the interest of the Defendant, Henry Taliaferro, in the estate of the said Richard M. Taliaferro, dec'd, to the payment of the Plaintiff's demand against him.)

It appearing by an affidavit filed that the said Henry Taliaferro is not a resident of the State of Virginia it is ordered that he do appear here within 1 month after the due publication of this order, and do what is necessary to protect his interest in this suit; and that a copy of this order be forthwith published in some newspaper printed in the city of Lynchburg, once a week for four successive weeks, and posted at the front door of the Court House of this county, on the first day of the next County Court.

A copy—teste,
RO. A. SCOTT, Clerk.
Dillard, P. Q. mar 12-w4w

VIRGINIA to wit:—At rules held in the Clerk's office of the Franklin County Court, the 5th day of March, 1862:

George D. Davis and John T. Davis, late merchants and partners, trading under the firm and style of Davis & Brother.

Against

James Patterson, Administrator of Richard M. Taliaferro, dec'd, and Tazewell Taliaferro, Defendants.

IN CHANCERY.

(The object of this suit is to subject the interest of the Defendant, Tazewell Taliaferro, in the estate of Richard M. Taliaferro dec'd, to the payment of the Plaintiff' demand against him.)

It appearing by an affidavit filed that the Defendant, Tazewell Taliaferro, is not a resident of the State of Virginia it is ordered that he do appear here within one month after due publication of this order, and do what is necessary to protect his interest in this suit and that a copy of this order be forthwith published in some newspaper printed in the city of Lynchburg, once a week for four successive weeks, and posted at the front door of the Court House of this county, on the first day of the next County Court.

A copy—teste,
RO. A. SCOTT, Clerk.
Dillard, P. Q. mar 12 w4w

VIRGINIA to wit:—At rules held in the Clerk's office of the Franklin County Court, the 5th day of March, 1862:

Henry L. Muse, trustee of James W. Eubank, who sues for the benefit of Mitchell M. Woody and Lucinda Hutcherson, Administrators of William Hutcherson, dec'd, Plaintiffs.

Against

James Patterson, Administrator of Richard M. Taliaferro, dec'd., and Henry Taliaferro, Defts.

IN CHANCERY.

(The object of this suit is to subject the interest of the said Henry Taliaferro in the estate of the said Richard M. Taliaferro dec'd, to the payment of the Plaintiff's demand against him.)

It appearing by an affidavit filed that the Defendant, Henry Taliaferro, is not a resident of the State of Virginia, it is ordered that he do appear here within one month after due publication of this order and do what is necessary to protect his interest in this suit, and that a copy of this order be forthwith published in some newspaper printed in the city of Lynchburg, once a week for four successive weeks, and posted at the front door of the Court House of this county on the first day of the next County Court.

A copy—teste,
RO. A. SCOTT, Clerk.
Dillard, P. Q. mar 12-w4w

VIRGINIA to wit:—At rules held in the Clerk's office of the Franklin County Court, on the 5th day of March, 1862:

Benjamin F. Cooper and Richard P. Williamson, Administrators of Lawson Williamson, dec'd, Plaintiffs.

Against

Sterling L. Cooper and Anne E. his wife, Thomas D. Hunt and Sally his wife, Julia G. Williamson, Susan M. Williamson and William F. Williamson, Defendants.

IN CHANCERY.

(The object of this suit is for a sale of the estate real and personal, of Lawson Williamson, dec'd, and a distribution of the proceeds among those entitled thereto.)

It appearing by an affidavit filed that the Defendants, Sterling L. Cooper and Anne E. his wife are not resident of this State, it is ordered that they do appear here within one month after due publication of this order, and do what is necessary to protect their interest in this suit and that a copy of this order be forthwith published in some newspaper printed in the city of Lynchburg, once a week for four successive weeks, and posted at the front door of the Court House of this county, on the first day of the next County Court.

A copy—teste,
RO. A. SCOTT, Clerk.
Dillard, P. Q. mar 12-w4w

The Philadelphia Inquirer.

ESTABLISHED 1829. PHILADELPHIA, SATURDAY, MARCH 29, 1862. PRICE TWO CENTS.

The Devastating Rebellion.

LATEST FROM WASHINGTON.

GEN. CADWALADER APPOINTED MAJOR-GENERAL.

BAYARD TAYLOR TO BE SECRETARY OF LEGATION.

THE TAX BILL.

SECRETARY SEWARD GONE TO WINCHESTER.

LATE FROM THE LOWER POTOMAC.

REBEL PROPERTY SECURED AT SHIPPING POINT.

The Rebels Along the Rappahannock.

Special Despatches to the Inquirer.

WASHINGTON, March 28, 1862.

The Army of the Potomac—Cavalry Skimish near Dumfries.

Two squadrons of the First New Jersey Cavalry, under command of Colonel WINDHAM, yesterday surrounded a company of Rebel Texas Rangers, near Dumfries, twelve miles below the Occoquan. A few shots were fired on both sides without injury, excepting that one of our men was slightly wounded in the wrist. Ten prisoners were taken and brought to Washington. Our troops have captured a number of wagons loaded with wheat, but owing to a want of horses, were enabled to bring off only four of them to their camp.

General Cadwalader a Major-General.

General CADWALADER was to-day appointed by the President Major-General of Volunteers, and is earnestly desirous of at once taking the field. His claims have been strangely overlooked until now, while the brave hero of so many hard-fought battles in Mexico was willing to serve in any capacity rather than let his sword swing idly in its scabbard. This new appointment will not interfere with his commission in the regular army, but is intended to give him at once the command of a Division. A number of his old officers are desirous of serving under him, and a responsible position will no doubt at once be given him.

Fire in Alexandria.

A fire broke out in an empty store-house near the Government dock at Alexandria, last night, about eight o'clock. The building was a frame one and very light, causing a great glare, and many thought that an extensive conflagration was raging. The miserable fire apparatus of the municipality were on the ground promptly, and worked by volunteers, but did but little good, owing to their inadequacy. Fortunately the air was calm, and the flames were confined to the building in which they originated.

Pardoned by the President.

JAMES GILL and WILLIAM WITHERILT, who were convicted in Florida, and sent to the Penitentiary here for seven years, for resisting and preventing the master and pilot of an American vessel in the free and lawful exercise of their authority and command on board thereof, were yesterday pardoned by the President. They were both subjects of Great Britain, had been in the Penitentiary about three years, and were pardoned through the intercession of the British Minister.

A Correction.

A statement which appeared in some of the New York papers, stating that Mr. RIGGS, the well known banker of this city, had been engaging in whisky speculations, is incorrect, and arose from a confusion of names with another party. Mr. RIGGS has never been engaged in any operations connected with whisky, and has never bought or sold it, except the proper quantity which a generous gentleman might keep to dispense at his hospitable mansion. We may here mention that to-day he advanced the entire sum necessary to pay off a regiment of District Volunteers without any discount whatever, although from five to ten per cent. is the rate on the streets. The amount is several thousand dollars, and the funds will not be forthcoming from the Treasury for some time.

The Tax Bill.

The House hammered all day on the ponderous tax bill. The principal discussion was on the excise on whisky and distilled spirits, which were the subject of an immense fluctuation. Coal oils were also experimented on to see what they would bear.

Much to the surprise of every one the House passed a tax of three per cent. on paper, with little opposition.

The Pay Rolls of Officers.

Some outside speculators have been doing a thriving business by discounting the pay rolls of officers, at ten per cent. This coming to the knowledge of some of the Pennsylvania paymasters, they raised the sum of two hundred thousand dollars, and cashed in full the pay rolls of officers as they were presented, thus saving them the ten per cent. discount. The pay rolls which the brokers and speculators have cashed will not probably be paid for some months to come. This, it is hoped, will put an end to any future speculation of the kind.

The Iron-Clad Ships.

The Senate galleries were crowded to-day to hear the speeches on the appropriations for iron-clad ships, including the Stevens battery. After a long debate, the appropriation for the Stevens battery was passed with an amendment, providing that it shall be satisfactory to the Navy Department.

Flag to be Presented.

Secretary SEWARD has had made to order a magnificent silk flag, which will be presented by him to-morrow, through Mr. MORRIS, of the State Department, to the One-hundred-and-third New York Regiment, commanded by Baron EGLOFSTEIN.

Errand of Mercy.

Secretary SEWARD went to Winchester in a special train, this morning, accompanied by several leading physicians of this city, to visit and relieve our wounded soldiers there, taking with them a quantity of articles for their comfort and cure.

The Bull Run Affair.

Mr. ODELL, of the Committee on the Conduct of the War, has gone to New York to confer with General SCOTT in relation to the military movements which preceded the battle of Bull Run.

Falling in Price.

Since the blockade of the Potomac has been removed, articles of general consumption have greatly fallen in price, both manufactured goods and provisions. This depreciation of prices continues now from other, but unmentionable, causes.

Carl Shurz.

The report that CARL SHURZ had been confirmed by the Senate as Brigadier General, is not true. His name is before the Senate, but his nomination *has not* yet been acted on.

Secretary of Legation.

BAYARD TAYLOR has been appointed by Secretary CAMERON his Secretary of Legation to Russia, and he has accepted.

Secretary of Legation.

General CAMERON has tendered to BAYARD TAYLOR the post of Secretary of the Russian Legation. It is as yet uncertain whether he will accept.

Bodies of Deceased Soldiers.

The bodies of the following named soldiers were embalmed this morning, and forwarded to their destination:—

H. BENNETT, Co. H., Sixth Maine, died with spasms, aged twenty years; belongs to Dexter, Maine.

R. W. ROBERTS, Co. A., Third Indiana Cavalry, died of pneumonia, aged forty-five years; belongs to Gray's Plains, Ripley county, Indiana.

J. R. SMITH, One-hundred-and-third Pennsylvania Volunteers, Co. C., died of pneumonia, aged twenty-five years; belongs to Armstrong county, Pennsylvania.

One Hundred and Third Pennsylvania.

The One Hundred and Third Pennsylvania Regiment was paid off by Major WILEY, of Lancaster, Pa. He disbursed amongst the officers and men $70,000, of which $52,000 was sent home to their families, in Armstrong, Butler, Clarion and Venango counties.

Shutting up the Restaurants.

The new Provost Guard have gone to work with much earnestness. Last night several restaurants and low groggeries were closed for violating the regulations. One of them (the Atlantic Garden, a lager beer saloon,) was closed this morning, and draped in mourning by the proprietors.

Sick Soldiers Sent Home.

This morning about four hundred sick and convalescent soldiers were brought up by the Alexandria boat. They are to be sent to the hospitals in Philadelphia.

Abolishing Sinecures.

A number of Government offices, which are a little more than sinecures, are to be abolished at an early day. Retrenchment is now the order of the day.

The Railroad to Manassas.

The cars are now running to Manassas, and the road is open for miles beyond.

The Minister to Russia.

General CAMERON has signified his intention of leaving for Russia about the middle of next month.

THE BATTLE NEAR WINCHESTER, VA.

THE KILLED AND WOUNDED.

The Bombardment of Island No. 10.

EXCITEMENT AT BURLINGTON. N. J.

REV. SAMUEL AARON PELTED WITH ROTTEN EGGS.

The Latest from Fortress Monroe.

FROM THE LOWER POTOMAC.

THE BATTLE NEAR WINCHESTER.

LIST OF KILLED AND WOUNDED.

WINCHESTER, March 28.—The following is a more complete list of the killed and wounded in the battle of last Sunday:—

EIGHTY-FOURTH PENNSYLVANIA.

The following is the Sugeon's return of killed and wounded in the Eighty-fourth Pennsylvania Regiment:—

KILLED.—Colonel William G. Murray, Captain Patrick Gallagher, Second Lieutenant Charles Keen, Privates Paul McLaing, Job Miller, John Gilmore, Aaron B. Wayght, James Myers, Leo Keech, Wm. Fowler, John Kelly, Jeremiah Gates, Thomas Hancoff, Simon Kerscher, John McClaren, Jacob Wainwright, James Graham, David G. Smith.

WOUNDED.—Privates Wm. S. Davis (mortally), Thomas Ravenhill, Danl. McLane, Peter Muller, Saml. Burk, Adam Frank (slightly), James Burn (mortally), Michael Forney (severely); First Lieut. Saml. Byron; Corporals Peter Lines, John Shadden, Alfred Crague, Chas. Parker, F. S. Simmons, Mack Saxton, Alex. Warn (slightly); Privates Reuben Killiam, James Kurtz, Torrence Kinney, Isaac Johnson, Abram Hertzler, Jacob Spidle, John Jennings; First Lieutenant B. Morrow (slightly); Sergeants Henry Funk (seriously); Corporals James M. Price, Charles Mummy, T. C. Fowler (slightly), Privates C. D. Bowers, Wm. Prosser, J. G. Teeter, J. S. Wheeler, Gay Holcomb (slightly); Sergeant Philip Smith (slightly), Corporal Emmanuel Brubaker (seriously), Alexander Taylor, James Gallagher (slightly); Privates P. P. Hawkin, Thomas Gorman (slightly); Corporal Shurcaker (slightly); Privates John Folbert (seriously), Daniel Bettler, Sergeant Sanford Johnson, William E Stead (slightly), Sergeant Franklin Houston; Privates Henry Strickler (slightly), William Cassidy (mortally), Christopher Smith (seriously), John Dacree, Abraham Hertzler (slightly).

SIXTY-SEVENTH OHIO REGIMENT.

KILLED.—Sergeant David Brecker, Corporal J. A. Lantz, Privates L. P. Smith, McMaster, Henry Cowels, Edwin Mercer, Captain H. G. Ford, Sergeant Wiggins, Privates Robert Norris, John Fox, Nicholas Gersler, Robert Feare, John H. Greene, Adam Sutton, P. Gallagher.

WOUNDED.—Private Wm. Gray, John Conley, Wm. Miller.

FOURTEENTH INDIANA.

KILLED—Corporals, Jacob Fust, L. W. Keller; privates, Edward Nerlit, Peter Shaffer.

WOUNDED—Captains, J. H. Martin, J. H. Kelly; Lieutenants, Negge, Mayhoff, Dalzel, J. M. Mitchell, Thomas Kidd; Corporals, G. W. Smith, Weisner, J. F. Mull, Alex. Putnam; privates, Chas. C. Warren, Frastina Brown, John A. Marks, Edward J. Waldron, James Quillian, W. Kapper, Henry Harier, Frank Feldman, Henry Harter, Jacob Ottinger, Wm. Ottinger, James Jolly, J. E. Spaker, Howard Jespakes, Howard Lenor, Peter Malloy, Mike Prater, Wm. Neice, Mike Mutville, John G. Conley, T. H. Burnett, Harrison Anderman, Jefferson Thomas, Wallace Hooker, Cornelius Obeam, C W. Mears, Drummer, Elijah Barret, Severn S. Crump, Wm. Miller, J. H. Rosser Howard, Laner Keggs, J. Rober, P. F. Barret, A. Wesler, T. Wilbert, Wm. Miller.

SEVENTH INDIANA.

KILLED.—Privates Michael McGee, Charles Gill.

WOUNDED.—Second Lieutenant S. S. Lyun, Sergeant S. H. Davis, Privates Henry Owenson, John W. Jones, George K. Lovert, George Holmes, Matthew R. Porter, N. Ridgeway, Charles Montague, Albert Williamson, Henry Thompson, James McKnight, James Hunt.

TWENTY-EIGHTH NEW YORK.

WOUNDED.—Private W. Sterling.

EIGHTEENTH OHIO BATTERY.

WOUNDED.—Private Andrew Sharp.

TWENTY-NINTH PENNSYLVANIA.

WOUNDED.—Private Wm. Williams.

FIFTH CONNECTICUT.

WOUNDED.—Privates H. Welles, Patrick Cummins.

THIRD WISCONSIN.

WOUNDED—Private A. S. Tracy.

FIRST VIRGINIA VOLUNTEERS, U. S.

WOUNDED—Sergeant George Trust. Corporal W. H. Hitchcock, privates Joseph Simmons, J. McFarland, Wm. Murphy, J. M. Fordice, Chas. Potsten, David Reed, George W. Stakeman, H. McCormick, S. J. Martin, Chas. Rawlings, Lawson Drews, F. Robinson, Samuel Burnet, Jas. Brown, Thornton Crow.

ONE-HUNDRED-AND-TENTH PENNSYLVANIA.

Wounded—Wm. A. Callahan, Sergeant-Major M. Cunningham, Jacob Swartz, James French, Alfred Brown, Corporal Charles Wheatley, Wm. P. Ramsey, Joseph Cooper, John Dawson, Thomas M. Sloan, J. W. College and W. H. Stull.

EIGHTH OHIO.

KILLED.—Tobias M. Edwards.

WOUNDED.—Sergeant A. S. Brown; Corporals Purce, Isaac Hinkley; Privates Stephen Lillis, George C. Flander, James Emerson; Lieutenant Craig; Privates J. Parson, A. E. Brown, A Fry, D. R. Parker.

THIRTEENTH INDIANA.

WOUNDED.—Sergeant F Cowan; Corporals J. T. Graham, H. Hardin; Privates, George W. Baker, Wm. Mallory, F. H. Weller.

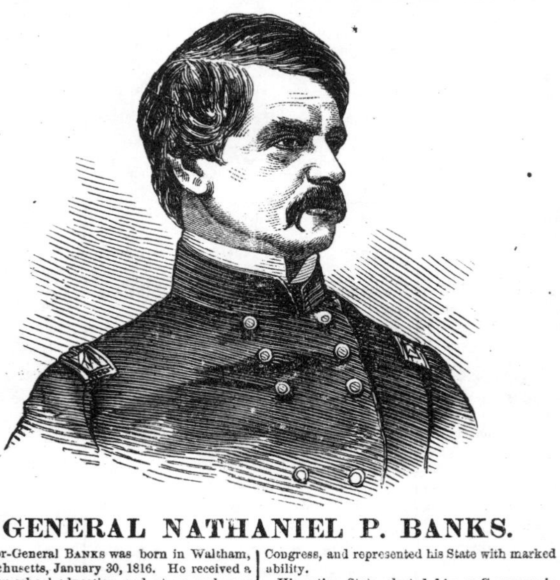

GENERAL NATHANIEL P. BANKS.

Major-General BANKS was born in Waltham, Massachusetts, January 30, 1816. He received a common school education, and at an early age worked in a cotton factory, of which his father was overseer. He afterwards learned the trade of a machinist. Being decidedly literary in his tastes he soon became the editor of a paper in his native village. Under President POLK's Administration he received an appointment in the Boston Custom House. Exerting a powerful influence in the Democratic party, he was elected in 1849 to the Massachusetts House of Representatives. His name appears on the rolls as a "machinist." In 1850 he commenced the practice of the law. In 1851 he was re-elected and chosen as Speaker of the House. He was again elected to the same body in 1852. In 1853 he received an election to the ensuing Congress. During this year he was President of the convention called to revise the Constitution of Massachusetts. He was re-elected to Congress in 1854, and chosen as Speaker of the House after an exciting contest of more than two months. In 1855 he received a re-election to Congress, and represented his State with marked ability.

His native State elected him as Governor, in 1857, and, under his able management, a military system was inaugurated which has since proved itself of great value in preparing that State for the present crisis. Possessing great administrative talent and executive ability, after his term of office had expired he was elected President of one of the leading New England railroads. Subsequently he became the acting manager of the Illinois Central Railroad, representing not only the New England but the foreign interests in that organization. Upon the outbreak of the present Rebellion his efficient services were soon desired by the Government, and he received the appointment of Major-General, May 30th, 1861, and has proved himself a faithful and efficient officer.

For several months past he has had command of a division of the army upon the Upper Potomac, and, even while we pen this sketch, is triumphantly leading his victorious army up the valley of the Shenandoah.

DEATHS OF THE WOUNDED.

The following, who were wounded on Sunday, died last night, and were interred to-day by Captain J. H. VANDEMAN, of the Sixty-Sixth Ohio, who was appointed by General SHIELDS to perform that duty

Sergeant John Kelly, of Co. I., Seventh Ohio; Corporal Hare, of Co. H., Fifth Ohio; Privates Thornton J. Crow, Co. D., First Virginia; Mark L. Hellen, Co. E., Thirteenth Indiana; Lawrence Wenzer, Co. A., Sixty-seventh Ohio.

The body of Sergeant-Major JAS. D. WEBB, of the Seventh Ohio, who died last night, will be retained till the arrival of his friends.

Lieut. WILLIAMS, of the Twenty-ninth Ohio, and one of Col. TYLER's staff, who was killed on the battle-field, were buried yesterday.

GENERAL NEWS FROM THE SEAT OF WAR.

Four prisoners were brought in to-day. They were taken at their homes, their term of service in the Rebel army having expired.

The officers in charge speak in high terms of the attentions of Dr. MILLER, a resident physician to our wounded.

The officers of the Baltimore and Ohio Railroad speak confidently of establishing through connections to Cumberland by Sunday.

General SHIELDS is in comfortable condition, his wounds rapidly healing.

There is no news of importance from Strasburg to-day.

The list of killed and wounded come in slowly. It is hoped that they will be completed by Monday. The bulk of the casualties, as sent, are achieved to be nearly correct.

An official report, just received from the One-hundred-and-tenth Pennsylvania, sums up as follows:—Killed in action, 8; wounded, commissioned officers, 3; non-commissioned and privates, 43.

The Latest from Strasburg.

STRASBURG, March 28.—The Rebel ASHBY, with four guns, appeared near Strasburg, yesterdays and threw several shells into our camp, killing or wounding one of our men. His position was such as to prevent any attempts to cut him off, but our guns drove him away. Gen. BANKS reconnoitred all the positions within several miles of the camp, returning after dark. JACKSON is supposed to be keeping very quiet below Edinburg. Most of the people of Strasburg have been Unionists throughout the war, and are so still. An agent of the Manassas Railway Company, who has been hiding in the mountains for weeks, to avoid JACKSON, has returned and given much valuable aid to Gen. BANKS. Many of the inhabitants have been remaining for weeks in the mountains and caves. All is quiet to-day.

Edinburg is five miles southwest of Woodstock, and is a small but flourishing village of Shenandoah county. It was formerly called Stony Creek, from the stream on which it is situated. It is connected by a turnpike with Staunton.

THE WAR ON THE MISSISSIPPI.

Important from the Mississippi.

ST. LOUIS, March 28.—A Cairo despatch says that heavy firing and rapid cannonading at Point Pleasant was heard at the fleet, night before last.

Point Pleasant is on the Missouri side of the Mississippi, about seven miles below New Madrid. It is occupied by Gen. POPE, who has erected batteries for the purpose of preventing the Rebel transports and gun-boats from passing to and from Island No. 10.

Captain MAYNADIER and Colonel BUFORD, who accompanied Professor STEINER in his balloon reconnoissance on Tuesday, discovered that the shells from our mortars have generally fallen beyond the enemy's batteries.

The elevation of the mortars and the charge of powder have both been too great. This will be remedied immediately, and greater execution may be expected hereafter.

The Bombardment of Island No. 10.

CAIRO, March 28.—(Special to the Chicago *Times.*)—An arrival from Island No. 10 yesterday, reported the effect of our fire on the Rebel batteries was very serious, and the upper battery was entirely silenced. Sixty-one men have been killed, and twenty or thirty were killed on the Island.

The Rebels continue to fortify.

Steamers can be seen continually running up and down between the Island and main land. There have been no tidings from Gen. POPE.

Correspondence Cincinnati Commercial.

U. S. FLAG SHIP "BENTON," March 25, 12 M., 1862, three miles above Island No. 10, Mississippi River.—From army officers who visited the *Benton* we learn that our mortar shells have, in several instances, proved very disastrous to the enemy. One shell fired from a mortar moored low down on the Missouri Point, yesterday afternoon, was seen to burst directly over one of their camps on the main (Kentucky) shore. Limbs of the dead and wounded could be seen flying in the air, while the enemy carried off several of these unfortunates. During last night they likewise removed many of their tents further back from the shore, evidently to get out of the range of our mortar shells, if possible. A little more elevation, however, will reach their new quarters.

The enemy nightly send scouts or pickets to the sunken steamer *Winchester*, lying in the point chute, on the Missouri shore, to observe our movements and to give the alarm in case our gun-boats attempt to run the blockade.

From 6 to 8 o'clock P. M., yesterday, lights in the east and from camps on Island No. 10 indicate that the enemy were communicating. From 12 to 4. A. M., to-day, the firing of great guns, in the direction of Point Pleasant, was distinctly heard. The enemy were again, evidently, trying to run our battery at Point Pleasant with their gun-boats.

The mortars have been paying their respects to the enemy at intervals all day—a number of the shells, apparently, doing execution.

FROM THE LOWER POTOMAC.

LANDING AT SHIPPING POINT.

SPOILS SECURED.

MORE DESERTERS.

THE REBELS AT THE RAPPAHANNOCK.

WASHINGTON, March 28.—The steamer *Yankee* arrived at the Navy Yard last night, from an expedition down the Potomac.

She reports that on Monday morning two boats' crews of the *Yankee* landed at Shipping Point, to remove the guns left by the Rebels; but while they were so engaged, a squadron of Rebel cavalry, said to be the Dumfries Cavalry, numbering fifteen hundred, made their appearance on the hill. Our men immediately pulled off, after securing two guns—one a 9-inch Dahlgren, and the other a long 32-pounder, both being smooth bore—which were brought up to the yard, and found to be double-shotted.

The *Yankee* fell out into the stream at the appearance of the enemy, and had trained her guns, but the cavalry retired and kept out of range. The *Yankee* brought up, in addition to the two Rebel guns, one hundred and sixty nine-inch shells, loaded, and four hundred six-inch shells, unloaded, which were taken from the Rebel batteries. She also brought off a handsomely made cot, on which is painted the name of Colonel J. J. PETIGREW, of the Twelfth North Carolina Volunteers. The cot is made of Brussels carpet, and has about it pockets for the reception of pistols. All the sutlers' stores, which consisted of several bags of peanuts, boxes of segars and tobacco, were brought off. Numerous bottles and jugs were found labeled "old rye," &c., but not a drop was found in them.

Two deserters came from Aquia Creek, a few days since, and stated that they were from Captain ELDELIN'S ("LUM COOPERS") Company, of the First Maryland Regiment, which they escaped from at Fredericksburg. They state that "LUM" had got a furlough for his company for one month, to visit Richmond on account of some meritorious service himself and company had performed, but what service it was they could not tell. They say that large numbers of troops are congregating along the banks of the Rappahannock, where they (the Rebels) say that they will make a stand. One of the deserters gave his name as BROWN, but the other's name we were unable to ascertain. They are both Baltimoreans, and were sent over to the military authorities.

Every now and then a refugee finds his way to some vessel of the flotilla. Among the last who escaped is a Dr. EASTMAN, a New Yorker by birth, but who has resided near Dumfries for several years past. He states that the Rebels had cleaned him out, stripping his farm of everything. The last horse he had was confiscated by Brigadier-General BAYLY, last week, for his own use.

These refugees are sent up to this city, and at the present time quite a number are here.

ASSISTANT SECRETARY WATSON.

Assistant Secretary of War, P. H. WATSON, Esq., left Washington on the evening before last for a brief trip to Fortress Monroe, where it is hoped that he will rapidly recruit his health and strength, so impaired of late by over-labor in the discharge of his official duties.

GENERAL SPECIAL PERMITS

for trading have recently been granted by the Treasury Department, for trading between Nashville and intermediate points. The intercourse is strictly confined to loyal men.

At Evansport the Rebels have left the saw mill untouched, and there is sufficient lumber at the mill to make quarters for several thousand men.

Two deserters came off from Aquia Creek a few days since, who state that large numbers of Rebel troops are congregating at Rappahannock, where they will make a stand.

Contrabands are coming daily to the flotilla. Thirty-seven arrived in one day, lately, from the vicinity of Dumfries, and were sent over to the Maryland shore.

White refugees also find their way to the flotilla from day to day. Among the latter is Dr. EASTMAN, a New Yorker by birth, but who has resided near Dumfries for several years past.

INTERESTING WASHINGTON NEWS.

Matters at the National Capital.

WASHINGTON, March 28.—The Hon. Mr. STANTON, of Kansas, served notice to-day on the parties interested, to the effect that he intended to contest the Senatorial seat of General LANE.

Nothing has as yet been heard of any offensive movement of the Rebel iron-clad steamer *Merrimac.*

General CAMERON visited the Senate this morning.

The Treasury Department to-day received from the engravers nearly a million dollars' worth of the new legal-tender notes.

In the Senate, to-day, Mr. WRIGHT, of Indiana, introduced a compromise bill on the question of the abolition of slavery in the District.

The following letter, from Secretary WELLES to Lieut. WORDEN, is published by authority:—

NAVY DEPARTMENT, March 15, 1862.

SIR:—The naval action which took place on the 10th instant, between the *Monitor* and the *Merrimac*, at Hampton Roads, when your vessel, with two guns, engaged a powerful, armored steamer, of at least eight guns, and after a few hours' conflict repulsed her formidable antagonist, has excited general admiration, and received the applause of the whole country. The President directs me, while earnestly and deeply sympathizing with you in the injuries which you have sustained, but which, it is believed, are but temporary, to thank you and your command for the heroism you have displayed and the great service you have rendered.

The action of the 10th, and the performance, power and capabilities of the *Monitor* must effect a radical change in naval warfare. Flag Officer GOLDSBOROUGH, in your absence, will be furnished by the Department with a copy of this letter of thanks, and instructed to cause it to be read to the officers and crew of the *Monitor.*

I am, respectfully, your obedient servant,

GIDEON WELLES.

Lieutenant JOHN L. WORDEN, United States Navy, commanding United States steamer *Monitor*, Washington.

The Secretary of the Treasury has recently issued special licenses for commercial intercourse, under the act of July last, which prohibits shipments from those ports of the United States heretofore declared by the President to be in insurrection, without a written permit.

The licenses do not now extend further than Nashville and intermediate points. Nothing shipped under them are to be disposed of to persons in arms against the United States, or to others furnishing them aid and comfort.

It is expected that the new legal tender notes will be paid out by the Treasury about the 1st of April.

An order has been issued for the restoration of the mail service between Boonville, Missouri, and Independence, which was suspended in December last, in consequence of the Secession war. This important service runs along the south side of the Missouri river, through Lexington, &c.

Steam Communication between Washington and Fortress Monroe.

Arrangements are nearly completed for establishing a line of steamers between Washington and Fortress Monroe, so as to secure a daily arrival—the trip to be made in nine hours. The proprietor will extend the facilities for carrying the mails, and it is more than probable that the Post Office and War Departments will encourage the enterprise.

The Proposed Tax on Crude Oils, &c.

At the suggestion and urgent solicitation of Representatives MCKNIGHT and PATTEN, of Pennsylvania, and FENTON, of New York, who represent mostly the petroleum or rock oil region, the Committee on Ways and Means has consented to the striking out of the proposed tax on crude oil and rock oils, leaving the tax of eight cents per gallon on the refined article, with a drawback when entered for exportation.

The Tenth Legion of New York.

This afternoon a splendid flag was presented to the Tenth Legion (the Fifty-sixth Regiment of New York Volunteers), by Major MORTON, of New York, who referred to the great issue of the present struggle, and to the patriotism of the section of country from which the Legion came—the birthplace of DEWITT CLINTON, WM. H. SEWARD, and the headquarters of WASHINGTON during the Revolution.—Colonel VAN WYCK, in response, assured him, in the name of his regiment, that the banner should never be trailed in dishonor. They might fail, but falter, never! The determination, for all time, of a Republican Government, was now staked as the wager of the battle. Better perish the whole army of the Union than imperil the freedom of mankind and the principles of constitutional government. The army was invincible, because they realized the great issues at stake, and were panting for the conflict.

Release of State Prisoners.

The following named prisoners were to-day released by the Commission relating to State prisoners:—O. NORRIS BRYAN, A. J. MICHAEL and WM B. BRYAN, on giving their written parole. F. P. ELLIS was discharged on taking the oath of allegiance. E. P. BRYAN, H. A. STEWART, P. W. COOPER and W. J. RAISIN were recommitted.

The Re-establishment of Southwestern Trade.

Secretary CHASE means to carry out the principle he announced some time ago, that commerce shall follow the flag and has accordingly issued instructions to the Treasury agents, collectors and surveyors on the Ohio and Mississippi, dispensing with applications to the Secretary for licenses to trade, and authorizing the shipment of all goods not intended for the aid of the Rebellion, to all places occupied by our troops in the Valley States. Applications for permits can be made henceforth to the collectors or surveyors of the different ports.

THE WAR IN TENNESSEE.

CHICAGO, March 28.—A special despatch to the *Tribune* from Cairo says:—A gentleman from Pittsburg and Savanna, Tenn., arrived here this morning, and furnishes the following intelligence.

On Monday last, a reconnoissance in force was made at Pea Ridge, on the Mobile and Ohio Railroad, where the Rebels were said to be fortifying, but no enemy was found.

Our forces are continually augmenting by the arrival of fresh troops.

The latest advices from the Rebel camps at Corinth, Miss., gives the strength of the force there at 70,000.

On Sunday last a force of United States troops was sent to Nicholas Landing, sixty miles south of Savanna, which seized 15,000 pounds of fresh pork and 49,000 pounds of cured hams and shoulders. For a long time this has been the mart for the pork business of the C. S. A.

Within the last two weeks large quantities have been sent southward by teams.

On Monday an engagement occurred between the gun-boats *Tyler* and *Lexington* and a masked battery, in the vicinity of Eastport.

The gun-boats fired fifty shot. The *Tyler's* smoke-stack was struck once. The effect on the enemy's works was not ascertained.

Captains BEDARDEN and CARSON returned to Savanna from Nashville on Tuesday night, overland.

Excitement at Burlington, N. J.

BURLINGTON, N. J., March 28.—The Rev. SAMUEL AARON, a Baptist preacher of Mount Holly, New Jersey, attempted to deliver an abolition lecture, at the City Hall, last evening. He commenced by denouncing the Administration, and avowing himself opposed to the manner in which the war was conducted, whereupon the crowd commenced hissing and storming him with eggs. This produced much excitement, especially among the ladies in the audience. Several of them jumped out of the windows. In the meanwhile the crowd was crying "kill him," "tar and feather him." The Mayor of the city was present, and endeavored to stop the confusion, but did not succeed. Finally Mr. AARON withdrew, and was taken away by his friends. No one was hurt, so far as is known.

From Fortress Monroe.

FORTRESS MONROE, March 27.—The work on the artesian well inside of the Fortress has been recommenced for the season. It has now reached a depth of 385 feet, the last 100 feet of which have been through fine tough clay. The steamer *Atlantic* arrived from New York this morning, on her way to Port Royal. The arrival of several paymasters this morning is the occasion of much joy to the soldiers. A flag of truce was sent out to-day, but no news was received from the South.

The Mass. Legislature and Gen. Stone.

BOSTON, March 28.—A resolution instructing the Committee on Federal Relations to petition the President to cause General STONE to be immediately tried was almost unanimously voted down in the House to-day, as being an uncalled-for interference with the military authorities.

A Prisoner Murders his Keeper.

HARTFORD, Conn., March 28.—DANIEL WEBSTER, the Warden of the State Prison at Wethersfield, was murdered by a refractory prisoner, who had managed to secrete a knife about his person, with which he committed the deed.

Naval Items.

BOSTON, March 28.—The United States steam sloop-of-war *Canandaigua* was launched to-day. The gun-boats *Genesee* and *Tioga* will be launched next week.

PENNSYLVANIA LEGISLATURE.

HARRISBURG, March 28, 1862.

Senate.

The Senate was called to order at 11 o'clock by the Speaker.

Prayer by Rev. Mr. MARTZ, of Harrisburg.

PETITIONS.

Mr. CONNELL, a petition from 234 citizens of Frankford, for the incorporation of the Frankford Railway Company.

Messrs. NICHOLS and DONOVANN each presented remonstrances against the passage of House bill No. 557, supplement to the Philadelphia and Delaware River Railroad Company.

Mr. DONOVANN, a petition in favor of House bill 143, to prevent the fraudulent use of castings.

Mr. CLYMER, a remonstrance against the North Philadelphia Plank Road Company.

BILLS INTRODUCED.

Mr. BENSON, a supplement to the Fall Brook Railroad Company.

Mr. McCLURE, joint resolutions relative to tonnage duties.

Mr. SMITH (Philadelphia), a bill to promote the efficiency of the military of the city of Philadelphia.

BILLS CONSIDERED, &c.

Mr. LOWRY, Chairman of the Select Committee to investigate the affairs of the Bank of Commerce at Erie, reported a bill of expenses amounting to $885·96.

On motion of Mr. CONNELL, the supplement to the act incorporating the city of Philadelphia, relative to recording ordinances, was taken up and passed.

On motion of Mr. SMITH (Philadelphia), the bill relative to agencies of foreign insurance companies, was considered and postponed.

On motion of Mr. CLYMER, the bill granting the Supreme Court jurisdiction of a Court of Chancery, in all cases of mortgages, &c., was taken up.

On motion of Mr. BOUGHTER, the supplement to the act incorporating the city of Harrisburg, was taken up and passed.

On motion of Mr. CONNELL, the bill granting a pension to HENRY STUART, a disabled soldier, was considered and passed.

The bill to incorporate the Chesnut Hill Cemetery Association was considered and passed.

On motion of Mr. STINE, the supplement to the Catasauqua and Fogelsville Railroad Company was taken up and passed.

On motion of Mr. CONNELL, the supplemnt to the Philadelphia and Cresson Navigation Company was taken up and passed to third reading, when it was laid over. Adjourned.

House of Representatives.

The House was called to order at 10 A. M. by the Speaker.

Prayer by Rev. Mr. CATTELL.

The Appropriation Bill was received from the Senate with amendments. It was referred to the Committee of Ways and Means of the House; ordered to be printed and to be reported not before Wednesday next.

ADVERTISING DELINQUENT TAY PAYERS.

Mr. WILDEY asked that the Clerk read an editorial from THE INQUIRER in relation to the bill requiring the payment of mercantile taxes to the Receiver of Taxes instead of to the City Treasurer. The article denounced the proposed change.

Mr. SMITH (Philadelphia) read an extract from the *Bulletin*, favoring the change.

The bill, as it passed the two Houses, and was signed by the Governor, is as follows:—

Be it enacted, &c., That from and after January 1st, 1863, the charge for advertising delinquent tax payers of the city of Philadelphia shall not exceed fifteen cents for all advertising of each name in any one Ward, which shall be payable by the person or persons liable for the tax; nor shall the same be inserted in more than two newspapers, and if the name of any person shall be so advertised, after having paid their tax, the Receiver shall pay the expenses thereof.

Section 2. It shall be the duty of the Mercantile Appraisers of Philadelphia, in making their returns of mercantile assessments to the Receiver of Taxes of said city, to make the said returns on or before April 1st, 1862, and each and every year thereafter; and the said Receiver be and he is hereby directed and authorized, in and for the collection of this and all State taxes, to make, under oath, weekly returns thereof to the State Treasurer.

Any and all delinquents of mercantile taxes to be proceeded against by said Receiver, in the same manner, and within the time prescribed by existing laws, under a penalty of fifty dollars for any neglect by said Receiver; and the said Receiver shall be allowed and shall receive for the collection of said taxes the compensation now allowed by the law.

Any act or acts hereby altered or supplied, or that are inconsistent with this, be and the same are hereby repealed.

Mr. HOPKINS declared that the act had passed the House without due reflection—that it placed an important trust in the hands of an irresponsible officer, and that the second section, while it provides that the Receiver shall make weekly *returns*, does not require that he shall make weekly *payments* to the State Treasurer.

Mr. DENNIS was glad to find an opportunity to express his hearty disapproval of the act which it was proposed to repeal. He believed that every office holder, during good behavior, should receive all the emoluments to which he was justly entitled, and would never vote, no matter to which party the incumbent belonged, to take one dollar of such emoluments. Considered as a law, the bill was most pernicious, and he trusted that there would be no hesitation upon the part of the members on either side of the House in voting for its repeal. No city member was cognizant of the exact manner in which it had been passed.

Mr. ABBOTT said that the second section was certainly objectionable.

An act repealing the above bill was presented by Mr. WILDEY, and passed unanimously.

CONGRESSIONAL APPORTIONMENT.

It was decided that the Congressional apportionment bill should be considered on Wednesday next.

EXTRA SESSION OF 1861.

An act was passed relative to the tax imposed for the payment of the expenses of the extra session of 1861. The act provides that the special tax of one half mill on the dollar shall be levied and collected only on such real and personal property as was liable to pay 2½ mills on May 16th, 1861.

PUBLIC BILLS DEFEATED.

An act giving Justices of the Peace power to try cases of incendiarism.

An act to authorize the settlement of military supplies irregularly ordered.

An act to pay the officers and men of Col. J. W. MCLANE and Captain DICK.

SUNBURY AND ERIE RAILROAD.

A short but exciting controversy took place upon the bill to repeal the Sunbury and Erie act of 1861. It was considered in Committee of the Whole, and the Committee rose, reported progress, and asked leave to sit again. The question was put by the Speaker—"When shall the Committee have leave to sit again?" The Fourth of July was named; also April 16th and April 11th. All these propositions were lost, and Wednesday next was fixed upon.

REPORTS OF COMMITTEES.

The following bills were reported favorably by the various committees:—

An act regulating water companies; relieving the widow of JOHN HANEY; granting additional powers to the Courts of Common Pleas in the Tenth District; an act relative to the Pennsylvania Canal; for the relief of GEO. S KEY; confirming the revised grade regulations of the 1st and 2d sections of West Philadelphia; relating to the Shamokin Valley Railroad Company; to incorporate the Easton and Iron Hill Railroad; for the relief of the Chester Valley Railroad Company.

The House then adjourned until 3 o'clock P. M. on Monday next.

The Baltimore and Ohio Railroad.

BALTIMORE, March 28.—We are at length able to make the following reliable announcement, which will be received with interest by mercantile classes East and West:—

The engineers and tract layers report that their forces engaged in restoring the tract of the Baltimore and Ohio Railroad, have finished their work with the exception of three miles only, about midway between Martinsburg and Harper's Ferry.

All the numerous bridges, large and small, are thoroughly completed, and the last rail necessary to re-connect Baltimore, Washington, Wheeling, Parkersburg, &c., will positively be laid on Sunday morning, the 30th inst.

Large quantities of freight, for the Government and on private account, from East and West, are loaded, and have been pushed forward to Harper's Ferry on the one side, and Martinsburg on the other, to go through on Sunday and Monday, as soon as the track is ready. The first through passenger trains will leave Baltimore, Wheeling and Parkersburg on Wednesday, April 2d, at the latest.

The restoration of this great line of communication will certainly be permanent and effectual, as the country south of it is fully occupied and possessed by Government troops in the Departments of Generals MCCLELLAN, DIX and FREMONT respectively.

Renewed life and energy is inspired in the business community of Baltimore by this happy result.

Opening of Navigation.

DUNKIRK, N. Y., March 28.—Navigation on Lake Erie is now open to Toledo.

Weekly Courier

Tuesday, April 8th, 1862.

☞ The Ladies of the Military Aid Society have a large quantity of work on hand to be done immediately, for the Hospital, and request those in the city and country who are members of this Society, will please send in for it.

☞ Reference is made to the advertisement of Theodore V. W. Wensel, calling for volunteers in the Natchez Light Artillery Company. This is one of the first companies formed in Adams county, the command has been twice under severe fire at Pensacola, and having re-enlisted for the war or two years, they now desire a few recruits to fill up their ranks. The company has excellent officers.

☞ We learn from a private dispatch received from Jackson yesterday, that the Natchez squad of the "Nightingale Brigade," were to leave at once for Corinth, Miss. God prosper their efforts with the sick and wounded at this important crisis!

☞ A dispatch to the N. O. Delta, dated Bay St. Louis, April 5, says that 2000 yankees landed at Pass Christian last Friday. Our troops retired after exchanging a few shots. A launch, also, with 100 men came into Bay St. Louis, captured a schooner and cut the telegraph cable.

☞ We had quite a shower of hail in Natchez last Saturday night. Things have again assumed the usual appearance of Summer since that time.

☞ We tender our thanks to Messrs. Cavanagh & Miller, for the promptness with which they furnished private dispatches of the battle at Corinth. In the absence of press dispatches, they satisfied the public mind in a great measure, and gave a breathing spell to many agitated and interested friends of our absent volunteers.

Plant a Provision Crop. Those who anticipated a Cotton crop with which to pay their debts, should reason with themselves, that it is more profitable to plant a provision than a cotton crop. Corn can be as easily shelled and packed in bags for market, as Cotton can be ginned and packed in bales for the same purpose. The cash will command one as readily as the other, and while cotton will become a drug upon the market, corn will prove remunerative.

☞ Our Hospital Committee are putting the Marine Hospital in the best of trim for patients. Their industry, and that of the ladies in charge, are unceasing. Let our country people at once second these efforts, by furnishing hospital supplies and money. Every room may be wanted for the wounded in the great battles of the Mississippi Valley. Let us spare neither exertions or means to give quiet and health to the painstricken Volunteer.

Dr. Woolfson.

This gentleman, an Optician and Oculist of high order, favored us with a visit yesterday. His design is to open an office in Natchez for the benefit of persons suffering from any disease of the eye or impairment of sight. The letters and recommendations shown us by Dr. Woolfson, from gentlemen of the highest respectability and worth, are a sufficient guarantee of his position as a gentleman and of skill and superiority in his profession. The press throughout the South commend him highly. Says the Baton Rouge Advocate:

Dr. Woolfson. This gentleman has been sojourning in our midst for the past two weeks and leaves to-morrow morning for Natchez. The Doc[illegible] is not only an Optician and Oculist of the [illegible] enthusiastic lover of the South. At the commencement of the war he left his property in Washington City and went to Richmond and cast his fortunes with the South.

Notice will be given of the time and place of the Doctor's opening his office.

The Military Tax.

On the 26th January, 1861, the Convention of Mississippi authorised the Governor to borrow money to the amount of $1,000,000, on the credit of the State, and issue notes therefor payable on the 1st June, 1862, '63, '64.

The State was without credit, and the Convention; by way of offering an inducement to capitalists to invest, gave two very important considerations:

1st. They offered the highest rate of interest ever given by any government.

2d. They provided the revenue to meet the debt.

They went further and declared "that the faith of the State is hereby pledged for the redemption of the 'Treasury notes,' and no law shall be passed to impair their validity and obligation." In §1 of the Ordinance they prescribed the duties of Tax Collectors to collect the Tax in the manner now provided by law for the collecting of other taxes, and in §7 of the same Ordinance they order Tax Collectors to collect in the manner county taxes are collected the special tax of 50 per cent., &c., on the State tax, and "the amount of such special tax shall constitute a special fund for the redemption of the principal and interest of the Treasury notes, and said tax shall be irrepealable by the Legislature until said notes shall be paid or satisfied, at which time the collection of said tax shall cease.

The manner in which county taxes are collected is prescribed in the Code.

At the time of the above Ordinance the Confederate States were not in being. State taxes were receivable in 1st, current coins of the United States, and 2d, State warrants. County taxes were receivable in current coins and county warrants.

The reason why the military tax is only payable in specie or Treasury notes themselves is obvious. The contract of the State with the note holder of '62, is: present your note at the Treasury on the 1st June, 1862, and I will pay you in specie the note with interest at 10 per cent.

This contract is fixed and irrepealable. It is beyond the power of legislation, or even of a Convention. But the cry is we cannot get specie nor can we buy the notes.

We would earnestly appeal to every patriot throughout the State, if he has any specie to sell it, or any of these Treasury notes, to dispose of them to their neighbors for this especial purpose.

We are daily making greater sacrifices; let us all stand by and uphold the credit of the State.

But suppose it to be true that we cannot raise the coin, we have yet another alternative. We can sacrifice our household silver. Let it be melted into bullion and be placed in the vaults of the Treasury. The expedient may appear ridiculous or monstrous, but it is a matter of paramount importance just now to sustain our credit by a full liquidation of that debt. If we do so, the $333,333⅓ of notes due in 1853, and the like amount due in 1864, become at once a good currency. But, in addition to this, our State has authorized the issue of cotton loan notes to the amount of $5,000,000, if called for, and the issuance of $2,500,000 treasury notes for military purposes. This last is to pay our soldiers—to pay our merchants and mechanics for their equipment. It requires no prophet to say that the value of the present and prospective issues depend in a great measure on the fate of the notes which fall due in the ensuing June.

To sum up what we have said in a small compass: the State had just seceded from the Union; she anticipated the necessity of a military equipment; she had no money in her treasury, and was without foreign credit; she was forced by her peculiar situation to offer a high premium for a loan and levy a tax to redeem it when due.

Times have changed—specie has disappeared—distresses of all kinds are upon us—the contract is upon us and we cannot avoid its responsibility. If you cannot do better—if you cannot pay your tax in any other way, sacrifice your spoons and save your State. The Sheriffs are bound to go forward. It is better to give up your silver than to have property distressed and sold for God knows we have *distress* enough without that. A distress and sale of property now would be like milking a dry cow.

We are sending bells and kettles for cannon. If we can do no other way we must give in our spoons for the credit of the State. The amount of notes and interest due on the 1st June is, say in round numbers, $340,000. It is probable that one-half may be absorbed in the payment of the tax, leaving $170,000 still in the hands of holders. It is earnestly to be hoped that the holders of these notes will distribute them through the country to tax payers, if possible, at their par value.

Courier Dispatches.

Naval Fight near Bay St. Louis

Federal Vessel Disabled.

A CONFEDERATE PILOT WOUNDED.

Bay St. Louis, April 4....It is reported here that our gunboats Oregon, Carondelet and Pamlico met the Yankee boats New London, Calhoun, and one high pressure steamer, this morning at three o'clock.

They fought until daylight and at a short distance.

The high pressure Yankee boat is reported disabled.

A ball went through the pilot house of the Oregon, wounding the pilot.

From Saturday morning's Extra Courier.

Charleston, April 4....Northern papers of March 31, contain European news of the 19th of March.

In a discussion in Parliament on the subject of the arrest of a Lieutenant of the steamer Sumter, it was stated that the Lieutenant has not been [illegible] to America as a politi-

The London News predicts an almost endless war, and thinks that the rebellion will end in a military dictatorship.

On the 18th funds had an upward tendency.

Sales of cotton on the 18th and 19th, were 12,000 bales, of which speculators and exporters took 3500.

Consols 93⅞.

Northern papers report that the bombardment of Island No. 10 was continued on Friday, the rebels firing with great spirit and preparing for a protracted defence. They are mounting additional heavy guns.

Owners of slaves in the District of Columbia are rapidly removing them.

A dispatch from Fortress Monroe dated the 9th, says that Burnside occupies Beaufort.

No resistance was offered by the inhabitants.

The Confederates, 500 strong, garrison Fort Macon, and refuse to surrender.

A British man-of-war anchored in Hampton Roads on the 1st inst.

Richmond, April 3....Yesterday, the Senate passed a bill increasing the number of depositories in the C. S. Treasury, to be located by Secretaries.

The House passed a bill to admit duty free all imports, except from the United States.

There is nothing more of interest to-day in either House. All quiet here.

There is nothing new from the Valley of the Potomac or Peninsular. The enemy is not advancing.

Richmond, April 4....Capt. Morgan arrived here last night. Senator Gwinn of California arrived yesterday.

Reports from Washington say that McClellan is very unpopular with the Yankees. When the army reached Centerville and found fortifications evacuated, demoralization ensued without parallel since the great defeat of July last.

The army became mutinous for want of provisions and returned to the Potomac.

Victory at Corinth.

General Johnston Killed!!

☞ We have been politely furnished the following dispatch to Messrs. Cavanaugh and Sullivan, received this morning:

Mobile, April 6....We have won a most glorious victory.

We have captured Gen. Prentiss and a large number of officers.

Gen. A. Sidney Johnston fell at half-past two p. m., yesterday, in the arms of victory. Thank God, he has rescued his character.

This is from the battle field, written on yesterday, on Yankee paper. L'Hommidieu.

Jackson, April 7....To Messrs. Cavanaugh & Miller:

We have now a glorious victory.

We have entirely routed the enemy, and captured a large number of prisoners, including Gen. Prentiss and many officers, and are now in hot pursuit.

Gen Johnston was killed yesterday at half-past two, by a minnie ball entering his body and a piece of a bomb shell shattering his thigh. He fell leading the charge.

We have captured nearly all their artillery and thousands of prisoners.

Gen. Beauregard is in command and says he can capture or exterminate the whole Yankee command.

Give three cheers. Taney,
Operator at Jackson. Miss.

OFFICAL REPORT.

Richmond, March 5....Reports that they are fighting near Yorktown have been current all day.

The report is generally credited that the enemy attacked our lines at half-past two, aided by gunboats.

The fighting continued until twelve o'clock, when the enemy ceased firing.

Our troops maintained their position.

An official dispatch was received at 3 o'clock this afternoon saying that there has been no general engagement.

The armies are very near each other.

Another battle is impending.

The News Confirmed!

Beauregard's Official Dispatch.

The Battle of Shiloh!

Richmond, April 7....To S. Cooper, Adjutant General:

The battle of Shiloh began April 6th.

This morning we attacked the enemy in a strong position in front of Pittsburg, and after a battle of ten hours, thanks be to the Almighty, gained a complete victory, driving the enemy from every position.

The loss on both sides is heavy—including the loss of the Commander-in-Chief, Gen. A. Sidney Johnston, who fell gallantly leading his troops into the thickest of the fight.

(Signed) G. T. BEAUREGARD.
General Command'g.

The above is the official dispatch received this morning.

Memphis, April 7....The latest reports from Gov. Harris at Corinth, state that we have had a hard fought battle. Our victory is complete.

The relative loss is not known it is heavy on both sides.

Unfortunately Gen. Johnston fell at half past 2 o'clock, P. M.

We have taken large numbers of prisoners, among them Gen. Prentiss certain.

Several other Generals are reported taken.

The land fight has closed, but there is heavy firing from gunboats.

We have captured all the enemy's tents, stores and large amount of artillery, a large number of muskets. Two thousand prisoners have already been sent to the rear.

Corinth, April 6......The great battle commenced at daylight this morning.

The Yankees were driven back two miles.

Our columns are still advancing.

The First Louisiana regiment have taken a Federal battery. Several others were captured.

Gen. Gladden, of La., had an arm shot off.

Col. Williams, of Memphis, was killed.

Battle Field, April 6—6½ p. m....The battle of Shiloh has been fought and resulted in victory for the Confederate army.

Gen. A. S. Johnston was killed at while leading a charge. He was struck by a ball and a piece of a shell.

Gen Prentiss was captured. He says they had 35,000 men in the field [illegible] batteries engaged which were mostly captured.

Gen. Buell had a portion of his forces at Duck river.

We have taken the enemy's camp with all their ammunition, stores, &c.

The battle was very severe, the loss is very severe on both sides.

Fighting is going on yet. Gen. Polk is in advance, and fighting.

Gens. Prentiss, Grant, Sherman, McClernand, Wallace and Smith commanded the Federals.

Gen. Smith is sick, and 2000 prisoners were taken and sent to our rear.

It is reported here that our forces are fighting Buell, to-day.

Gen. Clark and Col. Brown of Mississippi, and Col. Richards of Missouri, are wounded.

The Federals were driven to the river, and are attempting to cross on transports.

Many prisoners are still being brought in.

Card.

The recruits to Capt Bisland's Company—"Natchez Rifles"—desire to tender their most grateful acknowledgements to the Ladies of the Sewing Societies of Natchez, for their kindness in preparing their outfit for the service, and for their generosity in providing them with everything that solicitude for a soldier's comfort could suggest. They would also return thanks to the Military Aid Committee for assistance received from them.

Camp Hope, Isle of Hope, Ga., March 21, 1862.

OBITUARY.

Died, near Washington, Miss., on the 25th inst., Mrs. VIRGINIA BRANCH, wife of Hon. L. W. Bryan, in the thirty-first year of her age.

The sprightly, beautiful child approached womanhood, combining so many of the lovely elements of character that she attracted the admiration and esteem of all who knew her.

The duties and cares of mistress, wife and mother, while they tempered the romantic charms of young life, served only to give additional lustre to her character.

She possessed sprightliness without levity—grace without affectation—gentleness without being weak, and dignity without reserve. For months she had been in close proximity to death, assured by her physicians that she could live but a little while, and might, from the nature of her disease, die at any moment.

Convictions of religious truth and duty had grown with her growth, and ripening into their full proportions, intelligently and earnestly she sought and obtained a clear sense of pardon and acceptance through Jesus Christ. Abating nothing from the ties of friendship, the devotion of a wife, or the tenderness of a mother, she calmly resigned all, and cheerfully waited, with the repose which faith in God inspires, until her change came.

A light has been extinguished, and desolate is the once happy home. But virtue does not die, nor can death retain its dominion over those who sleep in Jesus.

Sunnyside, March 28, 1862.

MARRIED.

On the 20th ult., by John D. Thomasson, Esq., at the residence of the bride, on Bœuff River, Mr. F. R. MARSCHALK, of Wilkinson county, to Mrs. M. A. THERREL, of Franklin Parish, La.

DIED.

At "Glenwood," on the 3d inst., MARTHA WILLIS, fourth child of Albert W. and Matilda B. Dunbar, aged nine months and eighteen days.

For Colonel.

We are authorized to announce LEMUEL P. CONNER, Esq., as a candidate for Colonel of the Adams County Militia.

To-Day's Notices.

"A Little More Grape, Capt. Bragg."

THE RECENT GLORIOUS NEWS FROM our gallant army, should stimulate every citizen to co-operate with it the most effectively in his power. Now that the tide has turned, is the moment to strike with effect. The ruffian hordes who threatened our firesides and loved ones, at the last advices, were flying before our victorious Beauregard and Bragg. To this position they must be held, and to effectually secure this no man must linger at home who can be effective in the field.

ARTILLERY is the great right arm of our defence. A Company is now well advanced in Natchez, with every assurance that A SPLENDID BATTERY will be furnished whenever the gallant sons of old Adams announce themselves "Ready."

Our fellow citizens of Natchez and Adams County are invited to attend a meeting for the purpose of facilitating this movement on

FRIDAY, the 11th inst.,

at 11 o'clock A. M., at the Court House. Come all. Come with a will. Come prepared to aid in dealing out a little more of that "grape" with which our gallant Beauregard and Bragg are now driving back our fell invaders.

Natchez, April 8. 1862.—d:wtd

Attention Volunteers.

THE UNDERSIGNED has been authorized to receive recruits for
NATCHEZ LIGHT ARTILLERY COMPANY,
Captain R T English

For particulars, call at the office of A Perrault, Main street.

ap8—d10w2 THEODORE V. W. WENSEL

Attention Artillery.

THERE IS AN ARTILLERY COMPANY now forming in this County—more men are wanted.

The Rolls will be found at the offices of Mr James A Steele, Circuit Clerk, and Mr. A. C. Ferguson, on Main street.

There are assurances that the Battery will be completed and ready for delivery to the Company as soon as formed. Come forward men and sign your names. mar19-dtf

To the Citizens of Adams Co'y.

NOTIFICATION HAVING BEEN GIVEN that in a few days two hundred of our sick soldiers will arrive in Natchez upon the assurance that hospital accommodations will be provided for them, and in order that proper arrangements may be made for their reception, the following gentlemen have consented to serve as a Hospital Aid Committee:

GEO. W. KOONTZ,
E. B. BAKER,
JAS. N. STOCKMAN,
A. K. FARRAR,
LEM. P. CONNER.

The Committee, co-operating with the Physicians of the County, respectfully notify the citizens of the County, that the Marine and State Hospitals are now being cleansed and prepared for the purpose in view: but that they are deficient in many of the articles necessary to the comfort and convenience of patients; and that it is necessary that the citizens of the county with as little delay as possible, send in as many of the following articles as they can contribute, namely:

- Cots or single Bedsteads,
- Matresses and Pillows; Sheets and Pillow Slips,
- Napkins and Towels; Blankets and Comforters,
- Dry Moss for Matresses,
- Mosquito Bars and material for same,
- India Bagging and Lowells for Cots,
- Wash Bowls, Basins, Tumblers and Pitchers,
- Bathing Tubs, and Bed Pans.

The dimensions of Cots to be made by persons who can and are willing to make them—should be 7 feet in length by forty inches in width. They must also be provided with head and foot boards, and rods for mosquitoe bars. It is earnestly desired that the above or any other donations of Hospital Stores, or supplies of any kind, be sent to the store of E. B. Baker, where they will be taken charge of by the above-named Committee, who will distribute the articles as the necessities of the various Hospitals may require. This course is deemed indispensable in order that the supplies may be equitably distributed.

Cash contributions are very necessary, and may be paid to Geo. W. Koontz.

The necessities of the occasion make it necessary for the Committee to urge upon the citizens a prompt and liberal action. ap3—d:wtf

SPRING AND SUMMER

CLOTHING.

VIT & COULSON,
MAIN STREET, NATCHEZ.

We are prepared to furnish our old patrons and the public generally, with a superior article of Spring and Summer Clothing.

Call soon and secure an outfit for the season.

April 5th, 1862.—tf

Light. Light!! Light!!!

Blockade or No Blockade!

THE GREATEST INVENTION OF THE AGE.
Confederate Illuminating Oil,
for burning in Coal Oil Lamps. The greatest Illuminator in the Southern Confederacy!

It can be burned in all kinds of Coal Oil Lamps by a simple patent attachment applied to the wick tube, at the trifling expense of fifty cents, which can be attached or removed at pleasure. The Oil can be used with perfect safety, as it cannot be exploded, and produces as brilliant, soft and beautiful light as the best article of Coal Oil. One gallon of it will afford as much light as one gallon and a half of the best Coal Oil, or four gallons of Cotton Seed Oil, or 18 pounds of Sperm Candles.

J. S. Murphy & Co, New Orleans, are the manufacturers of the Oil; and proprietors of the patent attachment for burning it in Coal Oil Lamps. Agents wanted in all the principal cities of the Southern Confederacy.

An unlimited supply of Oil and Lamps for sale at the Drug Store of **W. H. FOX, Sole Agent,**
ap4—d4w1 Main street, Natchez, Miss.

One Thousand Dollars Reward!

THE MAYOR AND SELECTMEN OF THE City of Natchez, in Common Council convened, have authorized, and hereby

Offer a Reward of

ONE THOUSAND DOLLARS

for the discovery and apprehension of the person or persons by whom STEPHEN ODELL was brutally murdered, while asleep in his own home, in this city, on the night of the 16th of March last.

All communications on the subject, addressed to the undersigned, will receive prompt attention.

JOHN HUNTER, Mayor.
Natchez, April 2, 1862. ap3-d5

One Thousand Dollars Reward.

I WILL PAY THE SUM OF

$1,000 DOLLARS

for the detection and conviction of the person or persons who murdered, or procured the murder of, the late STEPHEN ODELL, who was barbarously assassinated, at his own home and in his own bed, in Natchez, on the night of March 16th, 1862. In view of the atrocity of the crime, all good citizens are interested, and requested to aid in its detection.

A. F. ODELL.
April 4th, 1862. ap5—d:w1m

Notice to Tax Payers.

PLANTERS AND OTHERS who have Cotton can obtain advances of money on it from the State, which money is good for all State and County Taxes, except the Military Tax, which must be paid on or before the 1st day of April, 1862, in gold or silver, or State Treasury notes due June 1st, 1862.

Acts of the last Legislature extending the time for the payment of Taxes do not apply to the Military Tax; the law as it now stands requires a distress and sale for the collection of it after the 1st of April.

mar28—dtf O. METCALFE, Sheriff.

C. S. War Tax.

ALL PERSONS OWING C. S. WAR TAX, are hereby notified that the same must be paid between the 1st and 20th days of May next.

For the purpose of receiving said Taxes, I will attend at the Sheriff's office, at the Courthouse in Natchez, it being the most convenient for all Tax-payers in the District of Adams county, daily, from the 1st to the 20th day of May next.

Nothing but coin or Confederate States Treasury Notes, will be received in payment of this Tax.

The time in which the tax is to be collected being short, all persons are therefore cautioned to ascertain before hand the amount of their Taxes and come prepared to pay it, that they may not incur the penalty of the law by neglect.

O. METCALFE,
Collector for said District.
Natchez, April 8, 1862–d15w3

Notice.

THE Board of Police of Adams County, Mississippi, will, on the Second Monday in April, it being the 14th instant, receive Sealed Proposals from any competent person or persons, stating the amount such person or persons are willing to receive as an annual salary for the discharge of the duties of

Superintendent of Roads and Bridges,

In said county, as provided in the act in relation to the same; which Sealed Proposals shall be accompanied by the name of such person or persons as the party bidding shall propose to give as security on his bond, required by the provisions of said act. WM. CANNON,
Natchez, April 2, 1862—d&w:tm Pres't.

Rally by Companies---Rally!

LIEUT. CAMPBELL MARSH is duly empowered to recruit for the Battalion to be raised under the auspices of Col. Wm. H. Tayler Lt. Col. F. M. Blackburn and Major M. B Harris, by authority of the War Department, as soon thereafter as practicable on the expiration of the Twelfth Miss Volunteers, in May ensuing.

A year's experience in actual service as second in command of the Natchez Fencibles—added to nine years' civic association as an officer of the same—is an assurance of his capability.

To the young men of Adams, Wilkinson, Franklin and Jefferson counties, and the parishes of Louisiana adjacent, an earnest invitation is extended to enlist. They may be assured that the *morale* of this Battalion will be unsurpassed, and though all will be subject to strict military discipline, the etiquette of gentlemanly association will be strictly observed, and if need be, enforced.

Notice of the time and place of the opening of the Recruiting Office will be made known in due time.

mar18–d1ew&wtf

☞ Concordia Intelligencer copy tf

An Experienced Lady

TEACHER, competent to give instruction in Music on the Piano; French to speak fluently, as well as drawing and the English branches, desires a situation in a Seminary, or family in the country, on low terms.

References given by addressing
jan16—d1wtf MRS. M. D. SHAW, Natchez.

Supplies for Hospital.

I AM an authorized agent to collect supplies for the Hospitals of Mississippi at Corinth, Oxford, and Vicksburg. I wish cotton or linen cloth of any kind for bandages, dressing wounds, &c. Sheets, old or new; Single Matresses; Pillows; Pillow Slips; Comfort; any kind of Second-hand Clothing that will do for a change on the sick bed; Towels; Socks; Brandy or Whisky; home made Wine; Pickles; Jellies; Preserves; and any other comforts individuals may contribute.

Direct the boxes to me, Jackson, Miss., or Vicksburg. I will take them to their destination. Beef, Mutton and Poultry are much needed. It is earnestly wished they be contributed. Any one wishing to give these, will write me at Vicksburg, Miss. I will arrange by letter how and when to ship them. They will only be needed as used. I request that every one sending a box will write me a list of all the articles contained in it, and by whom contributed. I wish to publish a list of all that is subscribed.

At the Hospitals at Oxford and Vicksburg, negro servants are wanted, both men and women. Any one wishing to contribute their services will please write me. A supply of all these articles is needed immediately. I hope those who appreciate its importance will not await. Troops are rapidly accumulating upon our line of defence, and great battles will soon be fought.

mb25—w4 C. J. HESTER.

Legal Notice.

STATE OF MISSISSIPPI,
ADAMS COUNTY.

In the Circuit Court of said county—to May term thereof, A. D., 1862.

State of Mississippi, vs. Blackwell & Murphy. — Attachment for $243 75.

THE WRIT OF ATTACHMENT in the above stated cause having been executed, and the said Blackwell & Murphy, defendants, not being found, or summoned: Notice is hereby given that a writ of attachment was lately issued from the office of Chas. F. Merrick, Esq., a Justice of the Peace in and for said county and State aforesaid, at the suit of the State of Mississippi, against the estate of Armistead Blackwell and Felix G. Murphy, partners under the firm name and style of Blackwell and Murphy, for the sum of $243 75, and that the same is pending in the Circuit Court of the County of Adams, State of Mississippi, and that unless the defendants appear on the first day of the next term of said Court, being the first Monday of May next and plead to said action, judgment will be entered against defendants and garnishee, the property attached will be sold, and the effects in the hands of the garnishee disposed of according to law.

SEAL — Witness, James A. Steele, Clerk of the Circuit Court of said county, and seal of office, the 15th day of March, 1862. JAS. A. STEELE, Clerk.

Stanley O. Thomas, District Attorney.
Natchez, March 18, 1862–w4

Attachment Notice.

STATE OF MISSISSIPPI,
ADAMS COUNTY.

In the Circuit Court of said County, to May Term, A. D. 1862.

AUGUSTUS T. WELCH vs. MARY M. MORRISON.

Attachment for $1703 59, and 8 per cent. interest from March 16, 1859, less the following credits, to-wit:

January 5, 1860	$400 00
March 10, 1860	137 75
May 19, 1860	40 00

NOTICE IS HEREBY GIVEN to Defendant in the above stated cause, that an attachment was issued from the office of Charles F. Merrick, Justice of the Peace in and for said County, on the 1st day of March, A. D. 1862, at the suit of the Plaintiff and for the amount stated above, against the estate of the above Defendant, and unless Defendant appear on the 1st day of the next Term of the Court aforesaid, to be holden at the Courthouse in said County, on the sixth Monday after the fourth Monday of March, 1862, and plead to said action, judgment will be entered against said Defendant, and such other steps taken as by the statute in such cases made and provided are required.

SEAL — Witness my hand and seal, this 1st day of March, A. D., 1862.

CHARLES F. MERRICK, J. P.
Carson & Shields, Attorneys for Plaintiff.
Natchez, March 25, 1862.—w4

Thomas Griswold & Co.

(FORMERLY HYDE & GOODRICH.)
Corner of Canal and Royal streets, N. O.

MANUFACTURERS OF JEWELRY, SILVER WARE, Swords and Military Acccoutrements, and importers of Watches, Diamonds, Clocks, Bronzes, Porcelaine, Plated Ware, Guns, Cutlery and Fancy Goods.

The subscribers, Wm. M. Goodrich, Henry Thomas, Jr., and A. B. Griswold, call attention to the change in the style of this firm, which is still conducted by the same partners who have managed its affairs for the last fifteen years. With the same capital and business facilities as formerly, we shall have always on hand, the largest and best selected stock of goods in our line, in the Confederacy tates. aug 29—w1y THOS. GRISWOLD & CO.

HEMP BALING TWINE, for sale by
oct9 T. O. POLLOCK.

The Daily Delta.

VOL. XVII. NEW ORLEANS, TUESDAY, APRIL 8, 1862. NO. 111.

THE DAILY DELTA

FROM OUR EVENING EDITION OF YESTERDAY.

GEN. A. S. JOHNSTON.—The report of the death of Gen. A. S. Johnston, in the midst of the great victory gained by him and his army over the invaders of our country, sent a thrill of sorrow to the heart of our population. The fall of this noble chieftain on the field of his glory, will sadden the nation's joy for the triumph of our arms.

LIEUT. VERTNER.—Lieut. Vertner, reported to have been killed in the recent battle on the Tennessee river, was Aaron V. Vertner, a nephew of Gen. Van Dorn, and was one of that General's aids for some time in Virginia. He subsequently became aid to Gen. Hindman, and was acting as such when killed.

GLORIOUS VICTORY IN TENNESSEE.

The news from Corinth and Memphis received last night, indicates that the Confederate army has achieved a brilliant and decisive victory over the Federal forces. The facts as stated are, that our army attacked the enemy at 5 o'clock yesterday morning, taking them completely by surprise. At the last accounts it was stated that the Federal forces had been driven back a considerable distance, with the loss of eight batteries of artillery and a very large number of men. The operator at Corinth states that it was asserted there that the total defeat of the Federal army was considered certain.

Gen. Hardee's brigade commanced the action. The brigades of Gen. Breckinridge and Gen. Hindman covered themselves with imperishable glory.

Gen. Beauregard commanded the right wing, and had advanced as far as the Tennessee river, driving the enemy before him. The enemy's force is estimated at 125,000 men.

We know that Gen. Prentiss and 6000 prisoners have fallen into our hands.

Although we have not yet received intelligence of the final result of the battle, there is every reason to believe that the Confederate army has gained a brilliant and decisive triumph, and that, within a few days, the whole of Tennessee will be liberated from the invader.

We expect to receive during the day full particulars of the battle from our attentive correspondent.

THE BATTLE OF SHILOH.

Our information this morning confirms last night's presages of a glorious victory over the Federal army on the banks of the Tennessee river. It appears that the success is complete. The invading force was not only defeated, but broken and routed. Such as were not captured were forced to escape with so much precipitancy that all their cannon and camp equipage, and a vast amount of stores fell into the hands of our troops.

But let us not delude ourselves with the idea that this triumph, glorious and complete though it may be, is necessarily decisive of the fate of the war, or even of the campaign. It was not the whole of the enemy's army, that was defeated. The reports transmitted to this city, of the immense force accumulated by the enemy in the neighborhood of Savannah, on the Tennessee river, were evidently exaggerated. The army, which landed there, consisted, according to Gen. Prentiss's statement, of six divisions, his own consisting of 7000 men. But the statement of the correspondent of the Cincinnati Gazette, published in another column, says that six divisions came down with the main expeditions, and found, already arrived, enough men to form two more divisions. Even if no reinforcements were subsequently received, the Federal force must have amounted to 50,000 men—probably to more than 60,000. Gen. Buell had not effected a junction with this column. The object of the attack was to prevent this junction, and overwhelm the nearer army, before Buell could come to its relief. The brilliantly successful consummation of this purpose affords a shining commentary on the genius which conceived, the skill which conducted, and the heroic courage which executed the movement.

It is impossible at this moment to speculate with any reasonable confidence on the results which ought to flow from the victory. If it has been so decided as to involve the destruction of the entire Federal force engaged, and if our army is in a condition to follow it up with vigor, the legitimate military consequence would be the immediate retreat of Buell and the evacuation of Nashville; followed by the recovery of Forts Henry and Donelson. But, in the absence of definite information we must accept the triumph simply for its present glories, and the assurance it conveys of the skill of our Generals, the courage of our soldiers, and the strength of our cause.

WHAT THE MORNING JOURNALS SAY.

The *Crescent* shows from Northern journals that in spite of the boasted but superficial successes of the Yankees, the more reflecting among them are becoming alarmed for the future. The New York Commercial Advertiser is afraid that the cotton crop of 1862 will go by the board unless the Yankees speedily get possession of the cotton region of the South. The beginning of April was fixed for the fulfillment of this condition. The time is at hand, and the condition is absent. The present month decides the extent of the cotton crop of the year. The Yankees have nothing to expect from that crop, or the crop of 1861. The one will not be enough to offer a valuable booty, the other will vanish in smoke before the hand of Northern rapacity can grasp it. The New York Evening Post is alarmed on another score. "Almost any other people would have been driven to an extremity of despair by such a series of overwhelming reverses. Nevertheless," adds the Post, alluding to the spirit recently displayed by the Southern people, "they continue the contest, and their journals give out ominous hints of great recoveries which they soon expect to accomplish." To this the Crescent subjoins:

Precisely so. We shall "continue the contest" until victory crowns our efforts. Such a feeling as "despair" is not known in the South. It never will be known; and if the enemy should succeed in what they are now after particularly—the control of the Valley of the Mississippi, and the capture of our seaport towns and cities—the war would be further from a termination than ever, and an unalterable resolve to conquer or die, instead of "despair," would animate all Southern hearts. We would still have four or five hundred thousand square miles of territory inaccessible to ships and gunboats in which to fight the battle for freedom, and there we would fight it until we won it.

The *Bulletin* notes the delay of the enemy in attacking New Orleans—a delay that must prove fatal to his hope of an invasion of the Mississippi Valley, if prolonged until the weather shall become somewhat warmer. The Bulletin conceives that this delay results from the fact that an advance against the city from below was made dependent upon the descent from above by means of gunboats and mortar flats. Hence, being disconcerted at Island No. 10, he is perplexed at the mouth of the river. Should he at last make the attack from below, the Bulletin is confident of his signal failure, saying:

It would not be politic for us to state the reasons for this opinion, and we shall not, therefore, do so. Our defenses are in good hands, and we believe they are equal to the emergency. If the enemy make the attack, we think he will be baffled. At the same time we cannot be too vigilant, and should leave nothing undone which can conduce to the safety of this great emporium. Its possession would give the enemy more joy than all of his other victories put together.

The *Bee* has some fitting observations on the revival of the "ninety day" delusion of the Yankees with regard to the duration of the war. Many of their journals assert that the war can not last longer than June. With the refined New York Tribune, they "spit on a later period." If the Yankees think the North can not hold out beyond that time, very well; but as for the South, we are prepared to eternize the war, if the enemy is not disposed to stop short of eternity.

LETTER FROM MEMPHIS.

Special Correspondence of the Delta.

MEMPHIS, April 4, 1862.

Have you heard of the wooden guns at Centreville? Upon this subject I must ask you to print in the Delta the following choice thing from the Washington National Republican of March 15th:

Human history contains no parallel to the military perfomance on the Potomac, of which the *finale* is the bill pending in the House, to impose an annual internal tax upon the people of this country, estimated to produce one hundred millions of dollars. When the facts are all brought out and established by such evidence as is necessary to inspire belief in what is apparently so incredible, it is not merely America which will be amazed. Blundering so stupendous will receive, as it deserves, the attention of the world.

We obtained yesterday, from a most careful and reliable gentleman, for many years a member of Congress, who had just arrived here from a thorough personal inspection of Centreville and Manassas, the following accounts:

The fortifications at Centreville, (distinguished by the letters of the alphabet.) have the number of embrasures and of wooden guns pointing terrifically through them, as stated below:

Batteries.	Embrasures.	Wooden Guns.
A	7	7
B	7	6
C	3	1
D	7	3
E	5	1
F	9	2
G	6	7
H	6	5
I	4	..

Number of embrasures......54
Number of wooden guns......31

The guns were pine logs, charred black, with muzzles delineated with chalk, and properly protruded from the embrasures.

No real guns had ever been mounted. This was the representation made by the negroes, and the appearance inside of the work proves this representation to be correct.

A negro, who had been kept at work for months by the Confederates, reports them as having said that these pine logs would answer just as well to "skeer the enemy."

The Republican concludes this interesting fiction with these energetic words:

It was for the nineteenth century and for this new world that these performances on the Potomac were reserved. The old world was too much exhausted, and former centuries had not the necessary science and money, even if they had the genius. An army nearly double that with which Louis Napoleon fought the battle of Solferino held at bay, for nobody can tell how many weeks, by thirty-one wooden guns, is something which mankind never saw before and may never see again. Let us of the cotemporary generation rejoice that it has been our pre eminent fortune to witness it.

I will not comment; I leave that to your editorial pen. But I waft you a full and hearty laugh.

There is no news from Island 10; that is, nothing new. I am informed by officers recently from that place, that the apprehension entertained by many persons that the Federals would or might cut a channel around the Island, is groundless, as such a work, if practicable at all, could scarcely be accomplished within six months' time. The distance across the bend is one mile and a half, and the forest is so dense that it would be necessary to tear it up by the roots. Nothing has been accomplished there since I last wrote you, and I perceive from the tone of the Federal papers that they are despairing of being able to capture the place. They state truly that it is being constantly strengthened.

That affair at Union City, (the facts of which seem so difficult to obtain) as an aromatic, is not taking the people's noses by storm. The latest version of the affair reduces the captures down to a much lower figure than that stated at first. There is a report in circulation, (and I mention it only as a report) that an order for an investigation of the affair has been issued at headquarters.

The Confederate Army about Corinth is huge in numbers, and increasing every moment. Van Dorn and his staff arrived here a few days since, and the General has since returned to his command in Arkansas. But it is well understood that his army is to be brought to Corinth immediately. Boats left here the early part of the week for that purpose.

Martial law increases rather than diminishes in vigor here. Many persons heretofore addicted to the "beverage," find it impossible to "run the blockade," and must, from necessity, become sober men. The druggists have a monopoly of the liquor trade, being the only persons allowed to sell, upon a prescription by a physician. This is rather hard upon men who have grown gray in Memphis in the wholesale business. I hear many persons say that a purer article can be obtained from a regular liquor house than can be easily found in a drug store. I think myself that the monopoly is wrong.

Whatever fear of our city falling into the hands of the enemy may have animated us heretofore, is now dissipated, and we feel the pleasure of security wrap us like a garment. The feeling is, that Island No. 10 can not be taken, having been reinforced, as the Federals inform us, to 15,000 men, and that Johnston, Beauregard and Bragg will destroy the Federal army on the Tennessee.

It is announced that the Virginia is ready for another cruise in search of Lincoln's blockaders. We shall have a good account of her, no doubt, and that speedily. B.

The Directors of the Virginia Central Railroad have passed a resolution allowing the Rev. A. E. Dickinson, General Superintendent of Army Colportage, to travel free over the road.

TELEGRAPHED TO THE DAILY DELTA.

General Engagement at Monterey, on the Tennessee River.

Enemy Defeated with Heavy Loss.

A large number of Prisoners and Eight Batteries taken.

Gen. Grant commanding the Federals.

Fighting Terrific.

Gen. Prentiss & 6000 Federals Taken.

MEMPHIS, April 6.—Last Friday night one of the enemy's gunboats succeeded in passing Island No. 10, is now at Madrid.

Fighting commenced this morning at 5 o'clock near Monterey, on the Tennessee river. It was a general engagement. Gen. Hardee engaged the enemy at first, the other divisions taking part during the day, until the enemy were defeated. A large number of prisoners were taken, together with eight batteries. Gen. Grant commanded the Federals. The fight was terrific.

So far, we know of the capture of Gen. Prentiss and 6000 Federals by our forces. There is no doubt we have gained a glorious victory.

SPECIAL DISPATCHES TO THE DELTA

FURTHER FROM THE GREAT BATTLE ON THE TENNESSEE RIVER.

Our Victory Complete.

Loss Heavy on Both Sides.

GEN. JOHNSTON REPORTED KILLED.

Prentiss and other Federal Generals Captured.

Also, All the Enemy's Tents, Stores &c.

Together with a large Number of Cannon and Muskets.

An Immense Number of Federal Prisoners.

MEMPHIS, April 7, 1862.

Gov. Harris telegraphed yesterday evening to the Memphis Avalanche from Corinth in regard to the great battle which commenced yesterday morning, about fifteen miles from Corinth, near the Tennessee river.

He reports our victory to be of a most decisive character. The relative loss was not known, but was great on both sides.

Gen. A. S. Johnston fell at half-past 2 o'clock P. M.

The fight between the land forces was supposed to have closed, but heavy firing had commenced between our forces and the enemy's gunboats on the Tennessee river.

It is impossible to know the precise number of prisoners captured from the enemy. But it was immense. Five thousand had already been brought to the rear, and the work of capturing the routed Federals, scattered and flying in all directions, was going on.

Gen. Prentiss, who was long in command at Cairo, was among the prisoners. Several other Federal Generals are reported to be also in our hands.

We have captured all the enemy's tents and camp stores, a large amount of ammunition and small arms.

Out of twenty or twenty-five batteries of artillery possessed by the enemy, it is believed that he has saved but an insignificant portion.

It is not known whether Buell effected a junction with Grant; but nothing reported from the battle field indicates that such was the case. It is believed that only Grant's column of fifty or sixty thousand, were engaged, and that our Generals will turn their attention to Buell at once.

Dispatch from Gen. Beauregard.

GEN. BEAUREGARD TO HIS BROTHER.

APRIL 6.

Dear Brother—We have won a glorious victory. I am unhurt.

G. T. BEAUREGARD.

LATEST FROM RICHMOND.

RICHMOND, April 6.—Reports of a heavy skirmish near Yorktown yesterday, is confirmed by an official dispatch. The general opinion is fighting will be renewed to-day. Nothing later received this morning. There was a collision on the Central Road last night. Three killed and thirty wounded. Particulars not yet received.

FATAL AFFRAY.—A difficulty took place at Mrs. McDougal's, Fredericksburg, Va., on Monday last, between Thomas Ryan and Michael Russell, which resulted in the former drawing a pistol and shooting Russell, killing him instantly. Ryan is in jail. Both were members of the 2d North Carolina regiment.

NORTHERN ACCOUNT OF THE LOSS IN THE NAVAL BATTLE.

The following official report embraces a full and correct exhibit of the casualties on the frigate Congress in the action of the 8th inst., at Newport News, namely:

Philadelphia, March 19.—*Sir*—I very respectfully submit the following report of the casualties which occurred on board the United States frigate Congress in the action of the 8th inst., at Newport News, namely:

Total number of officers and men on board........484
Number accounted for........298

Killed, wounded and missing........136
Wounded taken on shore........26

Killed and missing........110
Wounded, since dead........10

Killed, missing and died on shore........120

I regret exceedingly to record the death of Master's Mate Peter Hargous. He was a good, brave and promising young officer, and is universally regretted.

I have the honor to be, very respectfully, your obedient servant,

AUSTIN PENDERGAST, Lieut. U. S. N.

Note.—Young Hargous was probably killed by the same shell that killed the gallant Lieut. Jos. B Smith. Immediately after its explosion, inquiry being made for Lieut. Smith, the old gunner of the ship, pointing, answered, "There he lays, sir," and beside him lay the remains of poor young Hargous.

A WORTHY AND DISTINGUISHED MAN OVERWHELMED WITH CALAMITY.—The subjoined letter records a new calamity, which has befallen our distinguished Southern champion and worthy fellow-citizen, William Gilmore Simms, Esq., which will doubtless enlist the sympathy of the entire State. He has, indeed, been sorely tried, most sadly beset by family afflictions and pecuniary losses. He has buried nine of fourteen children, one or more of them recently; within the past two years he lost his dwelling house in this city, by fire, and was entirely uninsured; and now a fire of unknown origin has consumed his noble and hospitable homestead, with many valuables, and he is rendered homeless and houseless. This happened, too, while he was benevolently sheltering two families besides his own. He was insured in the Fireman's Insurance Company; and he will scarcely receive the full amount of his policy, in consequence of the heavy losses of that company, by the late disastrous conflagrations; but we have reason to believe that he will realize more than he and his neighbor friends anticipate.

Our friend, writing us just before the recent disaster, said:

"You have heard, I take it, of our continued losses. We have buried nine of fourteen children. For myself, further, I need not tell you that my copyrights and plates are all confiscated and lost—some $25 000—the whole earnings of my life, save my library. I realized annually from my copyrights, from $1200 to $1800 "Othello's occupation's gone!" and cotton is not to be sold. But I do not regret the loss—present or to come—or the privation, if I can bestow upon my children the more prescious inheritance of independence."

What an effecting portraiture! What manly fortitude? What noble and disinterrested patriotism! What an appeal to public sympathy—to Southern hearts and Southern purses—an appeal, not made by the sufferer, but by the heart-rending facts of the case. Let it call forth a noble, patriotic and generous response. [Charleston Courier.

SEIZURE OF MORE RICE BOATS.—By a letter received in this city on Sunday, we learn of the capture in Bull's Bay of four more rice boats. The vessels captured are the George Washington, Capt. Finegan, Lydia and Mary, Capt. Leonard, Julia Warden, Capt. Kroeg, and Doar's sloop.

The officers and crews of the captured vessels, with the exception of the Lydia and Mary, are believed to have been made prisoners.

The George Washington and Lydia and Mary belonged to our fellow townsman, Mr. James Vidal.

Capt Leonard, of the Lydia and Mary, writes on Friday to Mr. Vidal as follows: "The Yankees have taken the George Washington, Capt. Finegan and crew; also the Julia Warden, Capt. Kroeg. They burned Mr. Doar's sloop near the lighthouse on Cape Romain I have run the Lydia and Mary in toward Oyster Bay, and will endeavor to get assistance from Major Manigault's battalion to keep off the enemy until I can get her into Santee." On the envelop, dated Saturday morning, Capt. Leonard says: "The Yankees have taken the vessel and are now carrying her out." [Charleston Courier.

THE VIRGINIA READY FOR ACTION.—The annexed paragraph, from the Norfolk Day Book, of the 13th, would indicate that the Virginia is "all right" again. It will be seen that she has undergone some improvements that will render her even more formidable than she was at her first introduction to the Federal fleet. Says the Day Book:

"The Virginia, it is intimated, while up here, has changed her forward and aft pivot guns for two of the celebrated Armstrong guns, which lately found their way into this vicinity. She is now 'cocked and primed,' as the saying is, to do any little job of work our folks may conclude to put her at, with as much ease, facility and dispatch, as she did her admirable job of destroying those three first class Yankee men-of-war on Saturday and Sunday last. Long may she wave!"

DESERVED PROMOTION.—We are pleased to learn that Dr. Sam Bard has been commissioned captain to raise a company for Col. Harmon's regiment. His success heretofore in obtaining recruits for this command gives assurance that he will soon be at the head of a gallant corps. The other officers will be chosen as soon as the command is made up. A private donation of $1000 has already been made to aid in equipping the force, which, in addition to the provision made by Government, will insure a complete outfit. Capt. Bard is also appointed general agent for the regiment, and is authorized to receive and receipt for all contributions of money, cotton, blankets, etc., that may be made. He can be found daily until 12 o'clock, at Col. Harmon's headquarters, in the Walker Block, on Main street. [Memphis Appeal, April 1st, 1862.

Dr. Shepardson, the lively and genial "Bohemian" of the Dispatch, who was taken prisoner at Roanoke Island, and has since been liberated on parole, is about to bring out a fine collection of the Lyrics of the War.

THE CITY.

INCENDIARISM.—This morning at about 10 o'clock a fire occurred in a two-story frame dwelling, corner of Third and Laurel streets, belonging to Mr. Good. It was unoccupied at the time and had evidently been set on fire on the lower floor near the door, as the key was in the door and there was a quantity of kindling wood inside of it when the fire took place. The flames were extinguished, however, before the engines reached the place, without effecting any material damage. Suspicion attaches to a negro woman who was seen to leave the house with a basket five minutes before the alarm was given.

LETTERS FOR THE SEAT OF WAR.—Dr. Mercier leaves to-morrow morning for the seat of war near the Tennessee river, and will take any letters for the army left with him this afternoon. They should be sent to his office, 198 Canal street, and it must be remembered that he can take nothing but letters.

SAD ACCIDENT.—We learn from Mr. McVea, clerk of the Vicksburg steamer Louis d'Or, that the daughter of A. Sidney Robertson was drowned on Saturday, near Port Hudson, by the sliding in of a portion of the river bank on which she was standing. The deceased was thirteen years of age, and an only child.

HIGH SCHOOL EXAMINATION.—This highly interesting exercise takes place in the Fourth District to morrow and the two succeeding days, Wednesday and Thursday, and will be concluded with the distribution of diplomas.

THE DAILY DELTA

PUBLISHED BY THE NEW ORLEANS DELTA NEWSPAPER COMPANY.

TERMS—PER ANNUM.

DAILY DELTA, (invariably in advance)......$10
WEEKLY DELTA, do. do. 3
SUNDAY DELTA, do. do. 2

For any time less than one year the DAILY DELTA will be delivered to City Subscribers at 20 cents a week.

ADVERTISING RATES

Advertisements $1 a Square for the first insertion. Every subsequent insertion 50 cents.
Advertisements on the Second Page $1 per measured Square each insertion.
Advertisements at intervals $1 a Square each insertion.
Marriage and Funeral Notices $1 each insertion.
A Liberal Discount made to regular Advertisers.

The SEMI-WEEKLY DELTA is published every Tuesday and Friday morning, at $5 per annum.

TUESDAY MORNING, APRIL 8, 1862.

We have been kindly furnished with the following private dispatch from Capt. A. F. Haynes, of the Crescent Rifles, Crescent Regiment:

CORINTH, April 6.—No commissioned officer in our company hurt. Sergeant John Laurens and privates R. J. Camm killed. Privates E. Carter, Jr., and Benj. D. Wall wounded.

THE ENEMY IN THE RIVER BELOW.—Reliable information from below represents the enemy to be towing up his mortar boats to the proximity of the forts. His vessels in all are not les than thirty-seven, and among them there are not less than thirteeen steamers, but of what class and dimensions we are not apprised. It would seem that an attack is intended at an early moment. Gen. Lovell and his subordinate officers are unremitting in the preparations for defense.

We are requested by Mr. DeBow, General Agent of the Produce Loan, to state that he is ready to deliver Confederate bonds to all subscribers to whom he has issued receipts, and that he has now the assurance of being able to do the same promptly for all future receipts The Register of the Treasury writes: "There will be no delay in this office."

The intense heat of the weather should admonish our citizens to be very guarded in the cleanliness of their premises, and the public authorities should look well to the condition of the streets, and do everything to promote the general hygiene. The large number of strangers now in this city renders this an imperative duty. In the defense of New Orleans an important point will be to secure the health of the troops who are congregated here, and it is not too soon, as the records of the Board of Health and Charity Hospital show, if consulted for a great many years, to engender in our climate pestilence from imprudence and exposure at almost any moment.

AFTER VICTORY.

The hour of victory is scarcely less trying than the hour of defeat. If the losses and difficulties of the one put fortitude and skill to the severest test, the opportunities and gains of the other put prudence and energy to the highest proof. To know when to bring on a battle, to know how to conduct a battle when begun, to know what use to make of victory—these are three essential attributes of a consummate general. The last is the crowning quality. The others are inconsequential without it. The victorious column remains a fragment which can be fitted to no grand, symmetrical and enduring superstructure.

We have fought and won a great battle on the Tennessee river. In the language of Gen. Beauregard, our victory was complete. The details, such as have been received by telegraph, are sufficient to show that, with respect to the enemy's forces engaged, the result was decisive. Driven back upon the river, with immense slaughter and the loss, apparently, of nearly all his artillery, stores and camp equipage, there would seem to have been but one hope of refuge for his beaten, broken, and scattered column, and that was in the facilities of retreat that might be afforded by his gunboats and transports. The flying troops of Grant, Prentiss, McClernand, and others were wildly seeking escape upon the transports under cover of the gunboats. But numbers of them, it would appear, were cut off from this chance. Thousands of them must have been slaughtered and captured in their confused and panic efforts to avail themselves of the transports and gunboats to cross the river. The effect of the battle, then, would be the virtual annihilation of the Federal army engaged, unless such a result were prevented by the interposition of some circumstance not now definitely ascertained.

The appearance of Buell's army, or a large portion of it, to act as a reserve and a cover for the remnant of the defeated forces, might save it and check, perhaps, for a time the operations of our victorious troops. We can not believe that the arrest would be more than temporary. Gen. Beauregard would doubtless immediately proceed to devise another plan of attack, the result of which may be readily anticipated.

Supposing, however, that Buell failed to effect a junction with the routed Federal army, and that he remained on the upper side of the Tennessee river, we can hardly doubt that Gen. Beauregard would, as soon as possible, cross the river and proceed to attack him. But first he would have to be sure that the enemy's army on this side the river was effectually disposed of and could not recover and menace his rear. As for the Federal gunboats and transports, they could not molest him seriously without an accompanying land force. Nor is it probable that Federal reinforcements could be speedily sent up that river from Cairo and Paducah. The enemy's whole disposable forces at those places were no doubt in the expedition which has just been defeated. If Gen. Pope's army at New Madrid are not detained there by Gen. Van Dorn, the latter would be able, no doubt, to reach the Tennessee river quite as soon as that army could ascend it.

These remarks presume that the enemy will not at once evacuate Tennessee, but will renew his attempt to penetrate the lower Mississippi Valley from the base of the Tennessee river. However this may be, the situation, viewed in any aspect, is one to call for the very highest exhibition of sagacious and vigorous generalship, in order that the fruits of the recent victory may be plucked when ripe, and not left to ripen until they are withered.

It is profoundly sad, in contemplating this splendid triumph, to know that the able and gallant officer, the noble spirit and bright intelligence, who presided in organizing the battle, did not live to drink the music of the final shout of victory resounding from the field of his glory. Like Wolf, he fell "leading his troops"—according to the generous testimony of Gen. Beauregard—"into the thickest of the fight." Let us devoutly pray that, like Wolf, he died in the rapturous consciousness that the path of duty he trod so nobly was also the path of victory. The laurels that would have wreathed his brow must now wreathe his tomb. A nation's tears will bedew them, a nation's gratitude will keep them fresh; history will be proud to exhibit, poetry will fondly interweave them in lofty song, for all future time.

SPECIAL DISPATCHES TO DAILY DELTA.

FURTHER DETAILS OF THE BATTLE.

The Victory Complete.

Gen. A. S. Johnston Killed by a Minie Ball.

Gen. Bushrod Johnson wounded

Reported Abandonment by the Enemy of their Transports and Gunboats.

GEN. BEAUREGARD'S OFFICIAL DISPATCH.

MEMPHIS, April 7.

The following dispatches were received here this morning:

CORINTH, April 6, 2 o'clock.

A great battle commenced this morning at daylight. Our forces have driven the enemy back two miles, and our victorious columns are still advancing. The First Louisiana (Regulars) has taken a battery. Several other batteries have been captured. Gen. Gladden, of New Orleans, had an arm shot off. It was reported that the left wing of our army had reached the Tennessee river, below the enemy's right. The loss is very heavy and the battle is still furiously going on. It is stated that Gen. Buell had crossed the river. Col. Kit Williams is reported among the killed.

We have the enemy's camp, all his ammunition, stores, etc. The battle was very severe, and the loss heavy on both sides. Fighting is still going on near the river, the enemy having retired to their rifle pits. Gen. Polk is advancing and fighting. Gens. Prentiss, Grant, Sherman, McClernand, Wallace and Smith commanded the Federal forces. Gen. Smith was sick. It has been a glorious day for us. Report says that among the slain on our side were Col. Bote of Nashville, and Col. Brown of Mississippi. Gen. Hindman's horse was killed by a shell. The fall injured the General's leg.

A dispatch sent by a General high in authority announces as his opinion that the entire Federal force, gunboats and transports, are in the power of the Confederates. R.

CORINTH, April 6, 3½ P. M.

The battle is still raging fiercely. Gen. Bushrod Johnston was wounded in the side. We have already captured four batteries. The enemy is still back.

BATTLE FIELD, April 6, 6½ P. M.

The battle of Shiloh has been fought and resulted in a glorious victory of the Confederate arms. The enemy have been driven to the river, and are now trying to cross in transports under cover of a heavy fire from their gunboats.

Gen. A. S. Johnston was killed while leading a charge.

Gen. Prentiss has been captured. He says that the enemy had 35,000 men in the field, and that only his division and Gen. Sherman's were engaged. They had 18 batteries engaged, which were almost all captured by us.

MEMPHIS, April 7.

The latest from the field confirms our previous reports. At 6:30 P. M. the enemy were in full retreat down the river banks, the Confederates pressing them gallantly, led by Gen. Polk.

Gen. Johnston was killed instantly by a Minie ball in his body, and a fragment of a shell chattering his leg.

The slaughter on both sides was tremendous.

Great havoc was made among the Federal officers.

Gen. Beauregard is now in command of the whole army. He pronounces the victory equal to that of Manassas.

It is reported that the Federals have abandoned their transports. R.

Official Report of the Battle.

RICHMOND, March 7.—The following official dispatch was received here this morning:

To Gen. S. Cooper, Adjutant General:

The battle commenced on the 6th of April. We attacked the enemy in a strong position in front of Pittsburg, and after a severe battle of ten hours duration, thanks be to the Almighty, we gained a complete victory, driving the enemy from every position. The loss on both sides is heavy, including the Commander-in-Chief, Gen. A. S. Johnston, who fell gallantly leading his troops into the thickest of the fight.

G. T. BEAUREGARD,
General Commanding.

Further Particulars.

MEMPHIS, April 7, 1862.

Rev. Mr. Rogers has just arrived from Corinth, bringing two prisoners captured by himself. He states that the battle commenced on the right, and extended thence to the center and the left. The fighting was desperate all along the line.

The Confederates drove the Federals back to the river, when they rallied and advanced upon our lines again, but were driven back a second time.

Heavy firing was heard to-day, but it is supposed that there was no general battle.

Buell, with his column of 40,000 men, did not arrive in time to take part in the battle.

The body of Gen. Johnston arrived at Corinth at 12 o'clock to-day. It is supposed that Buell arrived today, and a terrible battle may be expected to-morrow. A vast number of Federal prisoners was taken—at least 4000. The Federal loss in killed and wounded is between 3500 and 4500; that of the Confederates from 1500 to 2500. R.

The attention of housekeepers and others is called to the large sale of fine furniture, elegant piano forte, beautiful plated china and glassware, curtains, shades, &c; also, fine barouches and buggies.

TELEGRAPHED TO THE DAILY DELTA.

The Battle of Shiloh.

MEMPHIS, April 7.—The great battle of Shiloh commenced at daylight yesterday morning. The Yankees were driven back two miles. Our victorious columns are still advancing.

The 1st Louisiana Regiment took a Federal battery, and several others have been captured.

Gen. Gladden, of the 1st Louisiana, had an arm shot off.

Col. Williams, of Memphis, was killed.

BATTLE FIELD, April 6, 6:30 P. M.—The battle of Shiloh has been fought, and resulted in a great victory for the Confederate arms.

Gen. A. S. Johnston was killed at 2 o'clock, while leading a charge. He was struck by a ball and a piece of shell.

Gen. Prentiss has been captured.

He says they had 35,000 men in the field. They had eighteen batteries engaged, the most of which were captured.

Gen. Buell had a portion of his force at Duck River.

We have captured the enemy's camp, all their ammunition, stores, &c.

The battle was very severe. The loss heavy on both sides. Fighting is going on yet.

Gens. Prentiss, Grant, Sherman, McClernand, Wallace, and Smith, commanded the Federals. Gen. Smith was sick. 2000 prisoners have been taken and sent to our rear.

It is reported here that our forces are fighting Buell to-day.

Gen. Clark and Col. Brown of Mississippi, and Col. Rich of Missouri, are wounded.

The Federals have been driven to the river and are attempting to cross on transports. Many prisoners are being brought in.

The latest report from Gov. Harris, at Corinth, says: "We have a had a hard fought battle. Our victory complete. Relative loss not known, but very heavy on both sides. Unfortunately Gen. Johnston fell at half-past 2 o'clock, P M

"We have taken a large number of prisoners, among them Gen. Prentiss, certain. Several other generals reported. Land fight closed but heavy firing from gunboats.

"We have captured all the enemy's tents, stores, and a large amount of artillery. A large number of muskets and 2000 prisoners already sent to the rear."

We have been kindly favored with the following extract from a letter from an officer in New Mexico. It confirms our previous news:

NEAR FORT CRAIG, Feb. 22, 1862.

We had a glorious fight yesterday, lasting from 9 A M. until dark, and heavy firing all the time. We defeated them with only some thirty killed on our side. It was a perfect rain of cannon and rifle balls continually. About sundown our men, some 900 strong, charged a heavy battery and some 23 or 2400 troops, routing them completely and taking some ten pieces of artillery, composed of 6, 8, 12 and 24-pounders. The field this morning is covered with their dead, and they have already carried off eight wagon loads. We are encamped on the field of battle. Major Lockridge was killed. My men fought like tigers, and our first fire killed fifteen of the enemy. I will write at length to-morrow. New Mexico is ours.

FROM FORT PILLOW AND ISLAND TEN.—The storm of Tuesday night was very severe at Fort Pillow and Island 10. At the former place several trees were blown down within our lines, and a number of tents capsized. No lives were lost, however.

At Island 10 the Kanawha Valley was driven from her moorings to the Tennessee shore toward the Island. She was capsized in the river, when her boilers rolled overboard and her cabin parted from the hull. The officers and crew, thirty in number, with Lieut. Sanders, of Rucker's battery, succeeded in reaching the floating wreck, which floated down the river, until within three or four miles of New Madrid. One of the crew swam ashore and notified the officers of the Grampus, who got up steam, rescued the whole party, and towed the cabin ashore. The crew lost their entire baggage. The De Soto was also blown ashore and lost her rudder, but she was enabled to render some assistance to the wrecked crew. The latter reached the city on the Scotland, which arrived last evening.

With the aid of glasses it was seen that the smoke-stacks of one of the enemy's gunboats, and also one of their transports, had been blown down during the gale.

The enemy continued to shell the Island at long range, and with considerable intervals between their fires. The bombardment continued without results. It is known that the enemy continued to occupy their batteries on the Missouri shore. Their force was not known, nor was anything ascertained of their movements on land. [Memphis Appeal.

CHURCH BELLS NOT EXPECTED.—The subjoined correspondence explains itself:

MEMPHIS, March 22, 1862.

Gen. G. T. Beauregard, Jackson, Tenn.:

My Dear Sir—I am directed by the First Baptist Church of this city to tender to you, for the Confederate States, the bell of our church—with the prayer that God may give you wisdom to direct our army, that you may be able to drive the invader from our soil, and that peace and prosperity may speedily be restored to our entire Confederacy.

Will you direct me what to do with the bell?

Accept our best wishes for your health and prosperity. Your ob't serv't. J. G. FLOURNOY.

HEADQUARTERS ARMY OF THE MISSISSIPPI,
Corinth, March 30, 1862.

My Dear Sir—Your letter of the 22d inst., offering me, for the use of the Confederate States, the bell of the First Baptist Church, has been received.

I have the assurance from a number of persons that the planters will all furnish me their bells; and, relying upon this promise, I have declined the offer of many churches to furnish me theirs also.

With my kindest thanks for your wishes for our common cause, and my health and prosperity. I remain yours, very respectfully, G. T. BEAUREGARD,
General Commanding.

To J. G. FLOURNOY, Esq., Memphis

FEDERAL LOSS AT FORT DONELSON.—The Nashville Times (Federal) says: "The heaviest loss to any one of the Federal regiments at Fort Donelson was the 11th Illinois, which went into the fight with five hundred men and officers, and came out with one hundred and seventy. Two companies in this regiment, company K, Capt. Carter, of LaSalle, went into action with sixty two men, and came out with nine. Company H, Capt. Coates, of Peru, went in with fifty-one men, and came out with ten. This will give an idea of the hard fighting and terrible loss sustained."

CITY INTELLIGENCE

THE NEWS.—Our streets yesterday morning presented an animated scene as the news of the great victory gradually unfolded itself to the public gaze. Thousands of persons were abroad, many of them in groups, listening to the reading of the dispatches. The excitement was evidently a pleasant one, to judge from the expression of faces, but there was no noise, no buzzing or throwing up of hats, such as we read of as occurring in the U. S. Congress, at the news of a Spartan band having ceased to ship their huge army at Donelson, when broken down by exhaustion. Southerners take victories as matter of course. When the bunting was thrown to the breeze, however, from our office and in other localities, the news boys gave vent to their feelings by a continued round of cheering, considerably interspersed with throwing up hats. They had this advantage in discretion, though, over the Yankee Senators, that each one threw up some body else's hat—not his own.

TOO INDUSTRIOUS.—The following places have been reported for breaches of the 8 o'clock regulation, viz: a grocery on Dryades between Poydras and Lafayette streets; another on the corner of Bienville and Franklin streets; a coffeehouse on the corner of Chartres and Toulouse streets, kept by Mr. Brunet; two shoe stores, one of Mr. A. Beach, 184 Bourbon street, the other, of F. de Vresse, 159 Royal street.

FIRE.—At half-past 1 o'clock, yesterday afternoon, a fire occurred in the premises of Mr. W. E. Strange, corner of Pacanier and Orange streets. I caught in the kitchen, from the stovepipe, and was extinguished with slight damage.

THE SUREST, QUICKEST AND MOST PLEASANT WAY FOR CHILDREN TO LEARN FRENCH.—

By practice.
By an elightened practice.
By mostly cultivating the ears.
By a good habit.
By agreeable conversational exercises in relation with their capacities.
By a great deal of tact and nice discernment on the part of the teachers.

N. B.—Parents wishing their children to board at the establishment, where they will hear and speak nothing but French, should apply immediately, at Prof. Brette's, 13 St. Charles street.

THE BEST, MOST AGREEABLE AND ONLY WAY TO LEARN THE FRENCH, COMBINED WITH A SPLENDID TABLE. A few genteel persons will be accepted as boarders at Prof. Brette's, 13 St. Charles street, by applying early this week.

A large number of accomplished young French ladies are affording the boarders the fairest chance of acquiring the true daily spoken French, in all its purity and excellence.

No English allowed to be heard and spoken after the first week.

N. B. The terms for the present are within the means of everybody.

In times like these, all home manufactories should be earnestly encouraged. Our enterprising citizens are investing their capital liberally for the public benefit, and it would be unjust and impolitic to fail to appreciate their efforts. Among the most enterprising of this class are Messrs. L. W. Lyons & Co., the well-known clothing merchants, whose emporium is on the corner of St. Charles and Common streets. They employ in their home manufactory 140 hands, and have invested in this branch of their business alone over $70,000.

A COUNCIL OF WAR IN WASHINGTON.—The New York Times, of the 21st ultimo, says:

The statement, published last week, that a council of war in Washington decided, eight to four, that the army of the Potomac should not be moved against the enemy at present, is entirely untrue. The generals were unanimous that an advance was possible and proper. The only difference was as to the plan of the proposed attack.

To which the Washington Republican, the organ of President Lincoln, replies:

The "statement" referred to was made by us, upon authority much better than that of the Times, and is true. Four generals believed that an immediate advance should be made. Eight opposed it. The President sided with the four, and therefore, by order of March 8, constituted the Potomac army into four divisions, to be commanded by them.

GEN. SHIELDS—*Prophesy Fulfilled.*—The Columbia Guardian says Gen. Shields commanded the Palmetto Regiment in Mexico. After the campaign he paid a visit to Columbia, and was feted and feasted. In the course of a speech he made from the portico of one of our hotels, after applauding the daring and heroic deeds of their regiment, he said in substance that he hoped, if ever he drew his sword against South Carolinians, his arm might be severed from his body. The prophesy or self-malediction has been literally fulfilled. Recreant as he has proved himself to be to his most solemn asseverations, the only regret felt here is that the shell only fulfilled the malediction he invoked upon his body.

A correspondent on one of the Federal gunboats above Island 10, writes to the St Louis Republican as follows: "Capt. Sanford has 1,700 tons of shot and shell, including 50,000 rounds for gunboats, and 11,000 rounds for the mortars, and averages of 500 rounds for each piece of ordnance in the squadron."

To the Christian Public.

Our arms have been crowned with a glorious victory. With you we are profoundly grateful to God. We suggest that our Mid-day Prayer Meeting, held TO-DAY, at the church on Lafayette Square, be generally attended, to express our gratitude to God for this signal instance of his favor.

B. M. PALMER,
ap8 1t. J. B. WALKER.

Headquarters Department No. 1.

NEW ORLEANS, April 7, 1862.

Special Orders No. 78.

XXXI—All persons employed at the C. S. Arsenal as mechanics and laborers, having exemptions from military duty signed by Capt. Richard Lambert, C. S. A., commanding Arsenal, are hereby exempt from such service

* * * * * * *

By command of MAJOR GEN. LOVELL.
J. G. PICKETT, Asst. Adjt. General. ap8 1w

New Orleans and Texas Railroad Company.

This Company is now prepared to receive Proposals for the GRADING, BRIDGING and SUPERSTRUCTURE of their entire Road, from New Iberia, on the Bayou Teche, to Orange, on the Sabine river, one hundred and seventeen miles.

The road passes through the prairies of Calcasieu, a region of country perfectly healthy and abundantly supplied with provisions, being adjacent to the great stock and grain growing region of Texas; and safe from invasion, the coast of the Gulf being lined by an impassable marsh.

It is the only link wanting to connect New Orleans with the railroad system of Texas, and thus opening to our whole country one of the most productive regions on the continent

This Company will be prepared to contract, with one or more individuals, for the construction of the whole or a part of their road or to hire from one to two thousand Negroes.

Payments will be made in money, and such proportions of stock as is usual for each class of work.

Transportation, provisions and clothing for all Negroes brought on this work will be furnished, if desired.

There will be about one million and a half cubic yards of Excavation and Embankment, and about thirty thousand lineal feet of Bridging.

The wants of our community require the completion of this Road in the shortest possible time, and it will be done. All interested parties will keep this in mind.

Communications must be addressed to

COL. A. M. GENTRY, President,
or to E. L. HERIOT, Chief Engineer.
mar29 1m3taw 90 Common street, N. O.

Confederate States Zouaves.

The undersigned calls the public attention to the following card:

WAR DEPARTMENT, January 24, 1862.

To LIEUT. COL. G. COPPENS, Commanding Louisiana Battalion Zouaves:

Sir—In accordance with the above regulations, you are authorized to muster or cause to be mustered into service, Companies of Light Infantry for Three Years' Service, which Companies, when mustered into service, shall be organized by the President into a Regiment or Battalion, as provided in the foregoing regulations.

Respectfully, J. P. BENJAMIN,
Secretary of War.

A BOUNTY OF FIFTY DOLLARS will be paid to each soldier at the time of being mustered into service, and arms, equipments, rations, transportations, etc., will be furnished by the Government as soon as enlisted. The men will have the Zouave uniform.

Organized companies, or parties wishing to organize the same, of one hundred privates, if possible, but not less than sixty-four, in any part of the State, whether armed or not, will have an opportunity of going into active service in Kentucky or Missouri, by sending their muster rolls to the undersigned, at 64 Customhouse street, New Orleans.

GASTON COPPENS,
feb15 su tu&th tf Lieut. Col. Comd'g La. Zouaves.

Valuable Squares AND LOTS OF GROUND IN THE CITY OF JEFFERSON.

The undersigned have various SQUARES and LOTS OF GROUND for sale in Bloomingdale, Hurstville, Rickerville, Faubourg Avart, Bouligny, &c.

These properties are in the vicinity and on the line of the Jefferson City Horse Car Railroad, which will be completed within the next six months, and connects with the upper line of the N. O. City Railroad on Magazine and Prytania street, making this property very desirable for the purposes of either building or speculation.

Apply to H. M VANSOLINGEN & CO,
oct27 2dptf Auctioneers. 29 Commercial Place.

Empty Flour Bags Needed.

The Committee of Supplies want to purchase Five Thousand Bags, suitable for Flour.

By order of Committee:
ap4 1w2p H. T. LONSDALE, 89 Gravier street.

Battle Flags

Made to order, at

DETER'S WORSTED STORE,
mar30 2ptf Canal street, near Dauphine.

Notice.

The Provost Marshal's Office in the First District of New Orleans is removed from the City Hall to the southwest corner of Carondelet and Common streets. H. M. SPOFFORD,
mar28 tf Provost Marshal.

Notice.

Any person having a copy of Gurwood's Orders of Wellington, will confer a great favor on one of our Generals, commanding in the field, by making the fact known to D., at this office. mar11 tp

Southern Clothing Establishment.

HOME MANUFACTORY.

MILITARY UNIFORMS.

We are prepared to uniform as viz:

2 Regiments in heavy French BLUE COTTONADE.
1 .. .. BROWN KERSEY.
1 Battalion in superior heavy Black CLOTHS and DOESKINS.
1 .. .. Black CORDUROY and VELVETINE.
4 Companies in DRAB LINSEYS, Woolen.
3 .. GRAY CLOTH, ..
2 .. MIXED, ..
1 .. BLUE JEANS, ..
1 .. BROWN JEANS, ..
5 .. CAMBLET JEANS, ..
2 .. Heavy Dark Mixed COTTONADE.

The above we can manufacture to order into Uniforms with dispatch, in the most durable manner and approved styles, as may be desired, trimmed with Orange, Mazarine Blue, Carmine Red, Dark Green or Black.

1,000 Grey Flannel CAMPAIGN SHIRTS, with pockets.
1,000 Linen Check .. .. ..
1,000 Cotton .. ..
1,000 Canton Flannel UNDERSHIRTS.
1,000 .. .. DRAWERS.
2,000 pairs BUCKSKIN GLOVES.
Officers Uniforms made to order.
Officers Dragoon Long OVERCOATS, with Capes.
Waterproof Overcoats, Leggins, Caps, and Blankets.

L. W. LYONS & CO.,
26, 28 and 30 St. Charles street,
ap6 2t2p corner of Common street.

To the Friends of Gen. Sterling Price.

Having the authority from Major Gen. PRICE, endorsed by Gov. JACKSON of Missouri, and being encouraged by Gen. LOVELL, I appeal to the friends of Gen. Price, and most earnestly entreat the brave men of New Orleans, and others who may be in this city, to raise and organize immediately two companies of Flying Artillery, and for that purpose I have opened two offices—at 151 Camp street, opposite St. Patrick's Church, and 220 Tchoupitoulas street, opposite St. Mary's Market—where soldiers may apply for bounty money and all information required. JOHN P. McMILLIN.

REFERENCES:
Hon. CHAS. DERBIGNY,
Hon. CHRISTIAN ROSELIUS,
Hon. ISAAC E. MORSE,
Major Gen. LEWIS,
Gen. GRIVOT.

N. B.—I have appointed for the Hannibal Light Artillery Company the following officers:

Captain—H. H. HERON.
1st Lieutenant—GEO. O. BEARES.
2d Lieutenant—WILLIAM BRADLEY.
3d Lieutenant—D. CRONAN, JR.
4th Lieutenant—SAMUEL T. PALMER. apr3 tf

Headquarters Department No. 1.

NEW ORLEANS, March 31, 1862

General Orders No. 17.

It is ordered that Tobacco be added to the list of articles mentioned in General Orders No. 13, current series, as necessary to be reported by owners or agents to the Provost Marshals. It will be reported within the next five days, or be subject to seizure.

By command of MAJOR GEN. LOVELL.
ED. A. PALFREY, Major and A. A. General. apl 2w

Headquarters Department No. 1.

Confederate States of America,
New Orleans, La, March 20, 1862.

Special Orders No. 63.

XII—All process from any court of law or equity in the parishes of Orleans and Jefferson, for the ejection of the families of soldiers now in the service of the Government, either on land or water for rent past due, is hereby suspended, and no such collections shall be forced until further orders.

* * * * * * *

By command of MAJOR GEN. LOVELL.
J. G. PICKETT, Asst. Adjt. Gen. mar21 1m

Headquarters Department No. 1.

CONFEDERATE STATES OF AMERICA,
New Orleans, March 29, 1862.

Special Orders No. 71.

* * * * * * *

XXXIV—Officers of the regular service are hereby ordered not to visit any of the Camps in the vicinity of this city for the purpose of enlisting soldiers into their companies, who have been transferred to the command of this Department by the Executive of Louisiana. Any officer violating this order will have his recruiting orders immediately revoked,

* * * * * * *

By command of MAJ. GEN. LOVELL.
J. G. PICKETT. Assistant Adjutant General. mar30 2w

Headquarters Chalmette Regiment.

CAMP CHALMETTE, April 6, 1862.

Orders No. —.

1—This Regiment having received marching orders, all absentees from Camp without leave are hereby commanded to report immediately at these Headquarters.

II—Absentees neglecting to comply with the above will subject themselves to having their names published as Deserters in the public prints of the city. Squads will be detached for the purpose of arresting them, and the aid of the different Provost Marshals is solicited in the consummation of this order.

By order of Col. IG. SZYMANSKI,
Commanding Chalmette Regiment.
ALFRED BOURGES, Adjutant. apr6 3t

The Safety Committee

Give notice that they have made arrangements with the following houses, who have kindly offered to sell for the Committee their Breadstuffs, etc., at tariff prices, in small quantities, as the poor may need:

AVET & BRO., corner Old Levee and Bienville streets.
W. A. VIOLETT & CO., 49, 51, 53 and 55 New Levee streets.

They will sell at Tariff prices, except in small quantities, when a small additional price must be put on to cover cost:

Say Rice .... ℔ tierce, 7¼c.
.. .. by retail, 7¾c.
Flour.. ℔ sack, $7 50
Peas .... ℔ bushel, $1 75

By order of Supply Committee:
mar26 H. T. LONSDALE.

Committee of Public Safety.

NEW ORLEANS, March 22, 1862.

Notice is hereby given to Planters and other citizens wishing to donate old Iron Copper, Brass, Lead, or Bells, to our Government, that the steamer Sallie Robinson, Capt. Jos. Saliba, has been chartered by this Committee to bring such donations to the city. Neither the Confederate nor State Government have any agents whatever in the country to purchase such articles.

mar23 12t2p GEO. C. LAWRASON, Sec'y.

Committee on Public Safety.

NEW ORLEANS, April 5, 1862.

Notice is hereby given that F. H. HATCH, Esq, Collector of the Port, will hereafter receive and acknowledge the receipt of all Bells and valuable Metals; and Capt. H. J. RAPHAEL, of the Ordnance Department, all the Old Iron contributed by planters and other citizens for the use of our Government.

ap6 2plm GEO. C. LAWRASON, Secretary.

Committee of Public Safety

NEW ORLEANS, March 30, 1862.

Notice is hereby given to planters and other persons donating old Iron to the Government, that the BOTTOMS of old sugar kettles, GRATE BARS, and all iron that has been badly burnt, being worthless, should not be sent to the city.

mh30 2dp m GEO. C. LAWRASON, Secretary.

Committee of Public Safety.

NEW ORLEANS, March 30, 1862.

Notice is hereby given to Steamboat Captains that only Four (4) Dollars per ton freight will be allowed by this Committee for old Iron brought to the city.

mar30 2plm GEO. C. LAWRASON, Secretary.

Scott's Cavalry Regiment.

NEW ORLEANS, March 29, 1862.

Capt. KOSCIUSCO R. HYAMS is authorized to raise a Company of Mounted Men to be attached to my Regiment. I will supply arms and all equipments, except horses. He will report to me with his company on Elk river, Middle Tennessee, or at Gen A. S Johnston's Headquarters. J. S. SCOTT,
Colonel 1st Regiment La. Cavalry.

Under the above authorization I am now raising a Company. Until mustered into service members received will rendezvous at Blue Cane Plantation, Back River, Parish of Catahoula. Communications addressed to me there will be promptly forwarded, if left at the Adjutant General's office, New Orleans, or at No. 123 Common street.

apr2 3taw2w K. R. HYAMS.

Come One! Come All!

COAL OIL! COAL OIL!

We have just received from Havana twenty barrels of genuine

KEROSINE OIL,

which we will sell by the gallon or barrel.

BOSTICK & SEYMOUR,
apr3 tf 36 Fulton street.

Spy Glasses for the Army.

Twenty-four ordinary Marine Spy Glasses are urgently needed for the military signal service. None to be purchased in the market.

I appeal to the public spirit of the citizens in the vicinity of New Orleans, Mobile, Memphis and Jackson, Miss., to send the Spy Glasses in their possession, not indispensably employed, to the Ordnance Officers or Quartermasters at these points, to be paid for at a fair valuation, and sent to the Headquarters of Gen. Beauregard.

E H. CUMMINS,
ap6 2p1w Captain C. S. A., Signal Officer.

Volunteers Relief Committee.

CITY HALL, ROOM No. 13,
NEW ORLEANS, April 5, 1862.

At the last meeting of the Common Council this Committee was authorized to extend its enrollment of the families of volunteers so as to include all "who shall have been mustered into the service of the State and in camp," and to "place on the pay-rolls the names of the mothers and sisters of volunteers mustered into active service, wherever they shall have good proof that said parties were dependent on said volunteers for their support, and are in needy circumstances."

Parties interested must make application to the Committee in the ward in which they reside, as follows:

FIRST WARD—At 391 Nayades street, from 8 to 12 o'clock. Committee—E. Cox, S. A. Kingsland, M. Gordon, Jr.

SECOND WARD—At F. Aicklin's, 312 Apollo street, from 12 to 4 o'clock. Committee—J. M. Laborde, F. Aicklin, Thompson Greenfield.

THIRD WARD—City Hall, Room No. 13, from 10 to 12 o'clock. Committee—Gerard Stith, T. W. Bothick, Wilhelmus Bogart.

FOURTH WARD—At Jules Benit's, 84 Bourbon street, from 10 to 2 o'clock. Committee—Jules Benit, Dr. Chas. Delery, Aug. Delassus.

FIFTH WARD—At Oscar Robin's, corner Villere and St. Anne streets, from 10 to 3 o'clock. Committee—Dr. O. Robin, Lafayette Guyol, Jules Cassard.

SIXTH WARD—At J. A. D'Hemecourt's, 297 Royal street, from 10 to 3 o'clock. Committee—L. E. Forstall, Francois Correjolles, J. A. D'Hemecourt.

SEVENTH WARD—Committee—Frejus Seichsnaydre, Alexis Robert, W. C. C. Claiborne.

EIGHTH WARD—At the office of the Branch of the Merchants' Insurance Company, corner of Casacalvo and Elysian Fields streets, from 12 to 4 o'clock. Committee—S. P. Delabarre, B. L. Robertson, Judge T. H. Kennedy.

NINTH WARD—At 55 Louisia street, from 7 to 9 o'clock. Committee—J. Magioni, Emile Tabary, G. de Feriet.

TENTH WARD—At the office of the Seventh Justice of the Peace, Magazine street, between St. Andrew and Josephine streets, from 12 to 3 o'clock. Committee—Chas. Mensman, E. A. Patterson, A. D. Kelly.

ELEVENTH WARD—At D. T. Glenn's, corner Washington and Bacchus streets, from 12 to 2 o'clock. Committee—Jas. H. Huckins, D. T. Glenn, E. Macpherson.

GERARD STITH, President.
J. C. DELAVINE, Secretary. apr6 3t

Amended Tariff BY THE PROVOST MARSHALS.

The following is the amended Tariff by which is to be regulated, from the date hereof, until otherwise ordered, the sale of the articles therein mentioned:

BEEF—ON FOOT.	
First quality, not to exceed	12 cents per pound.
Second quality,	10 cents per pound.
Third quality,	8 cents per pound.
BEEF—BY RETAIL.	
First class, comprising loins and ribs, not to exceed	20 cents per pound.
Second class, round, rump and chuck, not to exceed	12½ cts per pound.
Third class, neck, shoulder and cheeks, not to exceed	8 cents per pound.
PORK.	
On foot, gross, not to exceed	11 cents per pound.
By retail,	20 cents per pound.
Green Meat, hog round, at wholesale, not to exceed	24 cents per pound.
Green Meat, hog round, at retail, not to exceed	26 cents per pound.
BACON.	
Hams and Sides, at wholesale, not to exceed	28 cents per pound.
Hams and Sides, at retail,	30 cents per pound.
Shoulders, at wholesale,	24 cents per pound.
Shoulders, by retail,	27 cents per pound.
Lard, in tierces,	23 cents per pound.
Lard, in kegs,	28 cents per pound.
FLOUR.	
Extra Double, at wholesale, not to exceed	$17 per barrel.
Extra Double, by the barrel,	$18 per barrel.
Superfine, at wholesale,	$14 per barrel.
Superfine, by the barrel,	$ 5 per barrel.
Fine, at wholesale,	$11 per barrel.
Fine, by the barrel,	$12 per barrel.
BREAD.	
First quality	7 ounces, per loaf of 5 cents.
First quality	14 ounces, per loaf of 10 cents.
Second quality	8 ounces, per loaf of 5 cents.
Second quality	16 ounces, per loaf of 10 cents.
RICE.	
At wholesale, not to exceed	7½ cents per pound.
By retail	8 cents per pound.
CORN.	
At wholesale not to exceed	$1 20 per bushel.
By retail,	1 50 per bushel.
CORN MEAL.	
Not to exceed	$1 80 per bushel.
PEAS.	
At wholesale, not to exceed	
By retail,	
HAY, OATS AND WHEAT.	
Western Hay, not to exceed	$65 per ton.
Crab Grass,	$45 per ton.
Oats,	$1 25 per bushel.
Wheat,	$2 50 per bushel.
SALT.	
Liverpool fine, wholesale, not to exceed	$5 per 100 weight.
Liverpool fine, retail,	7 cents per pound.
Liverpool coarse, wholesale,	$4 per 100 weight.
Liverpool coarse, retail,	6 cents per pound.
Packing salt, wholesale,	$3 per 100 weight.
Packing salt, retail,	5 cents per pound.

Small retailers in Lard are allowed an advance not to exceed 25 per cent.; and small retailers in Flour 15 per cent.

P. SOULE,
H. M. SPOFFORD,
CYPRIEN DUFOUR,
H. D. OGDEN,
N. TREPAGNIER.

New Orleans, March 30, 1862. apl 2ptf

Notice to Steamboats.

NEW ORLEANS, April 2, 1862.

All Steamers and other vessels leaving the port of New Orleans, via the Mississippi river, are hereby notified that Lieut. W. McILREEVY, in the First District, and Sergeant J. E. HOLLAND, in the Second District, are appointed Inspectors of River Passports. The inspection will be made at the wharf, or in the stream, at the option of the Inspector, immediately before the departure of each boat.

Captains of Steamers, and others who take away passengers from New Orleans, without an approval of their passports by an Inspector, or who violate any other order of the Provost Marshals, will be dealt with summarily. H. M. SPOFFORD,
Provost Marshal, First District.
CYPRIEN DUFOUR,
ap3 2ptf Provost Marshal, Second District.

Board of Provost Marshals.

All Masters of Steamboats engaged in trade are hereby inhibited from taking white men as deck hands, and are required to discharge at once such as may now be employed by them.

The Captains, Clerks, Mates, Carpenters, Pilots and Engineers are the only white men to be employed on such boats

N. TREPAGNIER.
P. SOULE.
C. DUFOUR.
H. M. SPOFFORD,
V. BURTHE,
GEO. GARR.
apr1 H. D. OGDEN.

Board of Provost Marshals.

All traffic in paper currency tending to create distrust in the public mind, or otherwise to produce embarrassment, shall be held as acts of hostility against the Government, and will be dealt with summarily.

P. SOULE,
GEO. GARR,
V. BURTHE,
C. DUFOUR,
H. M. SPOFFORD,
H. D. OGDEN,
apr1 N. TREPAGNIER.

Board of Provost Marshals.

NEW ORLEANS, March 27, 1862.

The Traffic in Gold and Silver against the Notes of the Confederate States of America is hereby expressly prohibited.

Delinquents will be visited by prompt and severe punishment.

By order of the Board:

N. TREPAGNIER,
H. D. OGDEN,
H. M. SPOFFORD,
VICTOR BURTHE,
CYPRIEN DUFOUR,
mar28 2dptf PIERRE SOULE.

The office of the Provost Marshal for the Fourth District, (Rousseau street, between Jackson and Philip streets,) will be open for business daily, (Sundays excepted,) from 8 A. M. to 6 P. M.

mar21 2p H. D. OGDEN, Provost Marshal.

Candidate for Mayor, IRRESPECTIVE OF PARTY.

NEW ORLEANS, January 29, 1862.

To my fellow-citizens of the city and parish of Orleans:

At the reiterated request of many friends and acquaintances, present myself before you, IRRESPECTIVE OF PARTY, as a Candidate for the office of Mayor; election to take place in June next.

If elected, I shall be governed by this motto: Justice, Law and Order, Improvements, Judicious Economy.

feb21 te* VICTOR WILTZ.

Mrs. C. E. Da Ponte

Respectfully announces that she is prepared to give lessons, at the residences of her pupils, or at her own Studio, in

DRAWING AND PAINTING, (Oil or Water Colors,)

HEADS, LANDSCAPES AND FLOWERS.

Also:

GRECIAN PAINTING, WAX AND PAPER FLOWERS.

Residence 197 Camp street, between Julia and St. Joseph streets.

THE NEW YORK HERALD.

WHOLE NO. 9344. NEW YORK, THURSDAY, APRIL 10, 1862.—TRIPLE SHEET. PRICE TWO CENTS.

THE BATTLE FIELD AT PITTSBURG LANDING.

Scene of the Great Conflict at Pittsburg Landing on Sunday and Monday, April 6 and 7, 1862—The Seat of War from Nashville to Corinth and from Island No. 10 to Memphis.

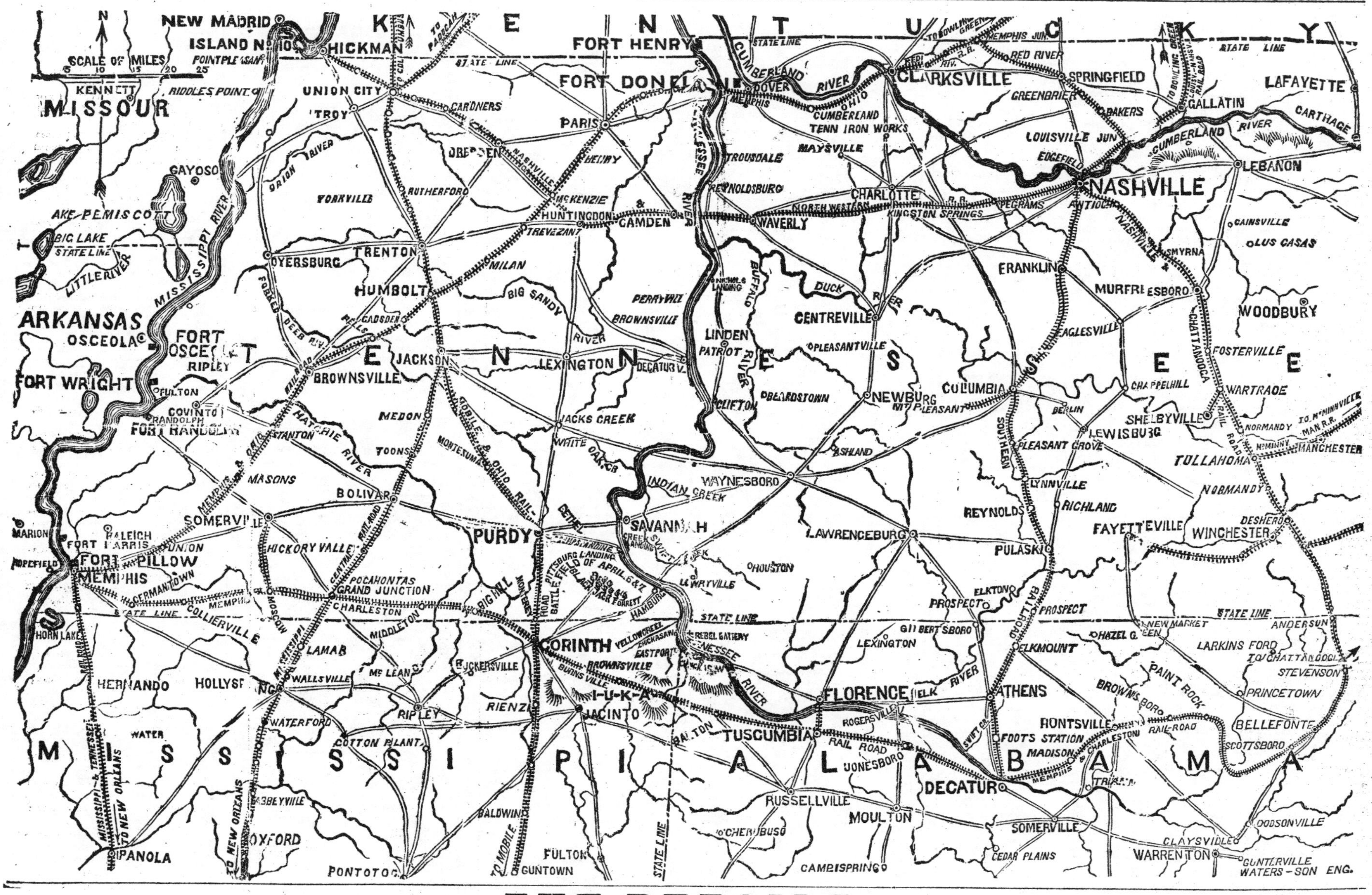

THE DETAILS.

See Second and Third Pages for the Particulars of this Great Battle.

The Daily Delta.

VOL. XVII. NEW ORLEANS, THURSDAY, APRIL 10, 1862. NO. 113.

THE DAILY DELTA

FROM OUR EVENING EDITION OF YESTERDAY

NOT KILLED.—The friends of Lieut. Blaize Cenas will rejoice to learn that he was not killed, as reported previously.

The numerous friends of Col. Adams, of the 1st Louisiana Regulars, will be glad to learn that the report of his death is unfounded. He is, however, badly wounded.

GEN. VAN DORN.—We learn from authority which we consider reliable, that Gen. Van Dorn, with six thousand of his command, has arrived at Memphis on his way to Corinth.

We learn from the proper authority that the enemy have left Pass Christian, Biloxi and the Gulf coast, and that the telegraph line to Mobile will probably be open for the transmission of messages to-day.

CAPT C. C. CAMPBELL, SUMTER RIFLES, CRESCENT REGIMENT.—A private dispatch received this morning, numbers this fine officer and estimable gentleman among the killed in the second day's fight on the Tennessee river.

Judge Voorhies kindly sends us a dispatch from his brother, by which we learn that he returned to camp without accident, and that his company, Orleans Guards Co. D., was in reserve on the 6th, and in the battle on the 7th.

THE GREAT BATTLE.—We publish an interesting account of the battle of Shiloh, by a correspondent of the Memphis Avalanche, who was a participant in the action. It contains a partial list of the killed and wounded.

RUMORED DEATH OF GENS. BUELL AND SHERMAN.—The telegraphic operator at Memphis mentions an extensively circulated report to the effect that Gen. Sherman had been killed by Morgan's cavalry, and that Gen. Buell was killed in the battle of Monday.

We are delighted to learn that Major Avegno, of the 13th Regiment, is not killed. We still, however, have to regret that he is severely, perhaps dangerously, wounded. Let us hope that he may live to serve his country on other fields, and return to his native city covered with well-won honors.

We are sorry to learn that Major T. B. Monroe, of Kentucky, was wounded in the recent battle. He filled the distinguished position of Secretary of State up to the time when he joined Gen. Breckinridge's Brigade. This brigade was in the first day's battle and probably the second. It was badly cut up, and doubtless did good service.

GEN. JOHNSTON'S BODY.—Just before going to press we learn that the body of the lamented Gen. Johnston has arrived, escorted by his brother-in-law, Gen. Wm. Preston, Col. Dudley, Major Munford, Col. Wickliffe, Capt. Jack, and others of Gen. Johnston's staff. The body was received at the depot, by the civil and military authorities, who will make arrangements to pay due honors to his memory.

ISLAND NO. TEN.—A report has been circulated this morning, to the effect that Island No. Ten had fallen into the hands of the enemy. The following dispatch, received by Major Z. Trudeau, shows that the report must be unfounded. The dispatch is dated at Memphis, at 10 o'clock last night:

"Your brother arrived from Corinth to-day; *was ordered to Island Ten*—is slightly wounded in the leg by a shell."

We may state, in addition, that the operator at the telegraph office here has received a dispatch from the operator at Memphis, saying that the report is unfounded.

AVOYELLES.—We believe that no parish in the State has contributed more men to the war, in proportion to its population, than the parish of Avoyelles. In addition to several companies, sent early in the war, the steamer Dr. Beatty last evening brought down *five* new companies from this parish—the Mansura Guards, Capt. E. Joffrin, numbering 83 men; the Marksville Guards, Capt. L. Barbin, 79 men; the Avoyelles Fencibles, Capt. H. W. Verstille, 78 men; the Chasseurs a Pied, Capt. Leon Phillipson, 70 men; and the Creole Rebels, Capt. J. J. Ducote, 79 men.

We are indebted to Mr. R. P. McMaster for the following private dispatch:

CORINTH, April 8, 1862.

I am safe. Cullen killed. All the rest well.

SAML. ALLSTON,
Twiggs Guards.

CORINTH, April 8, 1862.

Was in the fight; all right. Macbeth, (of the house of Judson & Co.,) killed; Fowler, (proprietor of the foundry) badly wounded. T. A. ENDERLE,
[illegible] Co. H, Orleans Cadets, Crescent Regiment.

To Burkette, 93 Camp street.

Mr. R. D. Brown has politely furnished us with the following private dispatch:

CORINTH, April 8, 1862.

Your men are safe and well. We have driven the enemy to the river. Battle over. E. H. HYDE,
Beauregard Rangers.

ORLEANS CADETS, COMPANY D, ALL SAFE.—The following dispatch announces the safety of Company H, Crescent Regiment, formerly Company D, Orleans Cadets:

CORINTH, April 8, 1862.

Henry Perry, Sr.:
In the fight yesterday. I am safe; so is my company. HENRY PERRY, JR.,
First Lieutenant, Company H, Crescent Regiment.

We are indebted to Messrs. Warren & Crawford for the following dispatch from their clerk, Mr. F. B. Fleetas, who arrived with the Leeds' Light Horse, too late for the battle:

CORINTH, April 8, 1862.

George Crawford, Washington Artillery; Louis Cucullu and P. J. Lefebvre, of the Orleans Guard, are safe; Jean Lefebvre, Orleans Guard, slightly wounded.
F. B. FLEETAS.

Mr. B. Biscoe has kindly placed the following private dispatch at our disposal:

CORINTH, April 8, 1862.

The following members of Company D, Confederate Response, are safe in camp: Clark, Hardie, Pollard, McTyre, Vandegriff, Page, Houston, Clabb, Duggan, Beard, Euricht, Collins, Minford, Miller, Brisbin, Adams, Porter, Chandler, Clark, Keane, Hopkins, Rouch, Winfree, two Watsons, Patton, F. Bennett, Roberts, Kakenot, Thomas, Jas. Bogart, Kingsbury, Huges, J. P. Butler, Sinclair, St. Clair, Stehle, Coste, Finnie, Kelleher, Florence, J. S. Rivers and Heron. Some of them are slightly wounded. Others are coming in. Some of the wounded are probably prisoners. McMurdo, Hyatt, Bonner, Goodwyn, Bryant, and Daniels are on their way in.

A. MONHEIMER.

1ST LOUISIANA INFANTRY.—We are indebted to the politeness of our neighbor of the Crescent for the following important dispatch:

CORINTH, April 8.—The following officers of the 1st Louisiana Infantry are killed: Capt. Wheat, Lieut. Bond and Lieut. Levy.

Col. Adams is badly wounded.

Wounded—Capts. Kent, West, Trezevant and Preston; 1st Lieuts. Sparks, Benton, Reed, Butler and Stringfellow; 2d Lieuts. Behan, Gladden, Mader, Kibby, Grivot and Kennedy.

The other officers safe. A. KENT.

WHAT THE MORNING JOURNALS SAY.

The *Bee* considers that the next thirty or sixty days will be fraught with events of unspeakable magnitude to the South. To support his desperate finances the enemy must make desperate efforts to speedily achieve some signal advantages. With respect to his expeditions by land and sea aimed at the heart of the South, there is another reason to compel him to make the most of the next sixty days. The deadly heat of our summer would shower upon him the missiles of an invisible artillery; "Bronze John" would wave his magic lance in front of his columns, and they would wilt like leaves touched by the arid kiss of the Simoom. The Bee remarks in conclusion:

We must not only expect, but prepare to offer a desperate defense to a desperate attack. If the Confederate armies can successfully resist the power of the Yankees for a month or six weeks, we shall have every reason to hope for a respite, since they will be unable to stand the climate. We must baffle the schemes of the enemy, and we can do so by exerting all our energies. Whatever numerical force may become requisite to insure this paramount object must be raised, either voluntarily or by conscription. Whatever means of annoyance or destruction to the foe can be devised must be placed in requisition. Whatever increase of strength may be needed to our batteries and fortifications must be added without delay. We must all be willing to give our share of time and money, and personal effort, and danger to defeat the designs of the insolvent invader, and if we are unanimous and fully resolved never to yield, but to fight with desperation to the last extremity, we shall, with the blessings of Providence keep back the Yankees till the fervent heats of a Southern sun warn them of approaching disease and death.

The Bee takes a sensible view of the situation at Corinth, observing:

The dispatches from the seat of war in the West relative to the second day's fight are, thus far, exceedingly meager. That from Gen. Beauregard himself, however, shows pretty clearly the state of the case. Our troops won a glorious victory on Sunday, and struck a telling blow at the enemy. Gen. Beauregard's object was to defeat and demoralize Grant's division, not to engage all the Federal forces in Tennessee. His object was accomplished; but when Gen. Buell brought up [illegible] reinforcements, threatening by sheer numerical superiority to overwhelm our comparatively feeble troops, exhausted by hard fighting, like a judicious and prudent commander, the gallant Louisianian held them in check till evening, and then fell back in good order to Corinth.

The *Picayune* has a well considered and happily worded article on the battle of Shiloh, where, it says, were reaped the first fruits of the grand Southern rally, from which an era in this war is to date for both belligerents. We copy the following reflection:

It is the first example of bold aggressive advance, and whatever be the future of the next, it is a brilliant success, and an auspicious omen; and it teaches new lessons of the nature of this war. It is a blow to the overweening confidence of the enemy, which will be a heavy discouragement to the advance movements which he thought to be so easy. It has already forced him to a huge effort, under a disastrous reverse, to retrieve losses and reunite the broken links of his extended plans; perhaps, in the event of a repeated defeat, to make him change it altogether and remodel it, at the cost of delays that may be full of peril. A succession of such blows would break the back of the anaconda which has been coiled about us with so much powerful and costly effort. The serpent's head is in this Northwestern expedition. If we can wound it fatally there, the extremities can only show the contortions of coming dissolution. They will be paralyzed and die. Victories, battles, even incessant attempts planned with skill and executed with daring, will disjoint the whole cumbrous plan, and make it drag a weary length slowly and heavily in the effort to move forward.

The *Crescent* comments fittingly on the programme of extermination avowed by the gentle McCook, one of Lincoln's military pets, to the Rev. Geo. C. Harris, of Nashville. The execution of the programme would be Cook's commentary on Lincoln's text. Lincoln has said that "all indispensable means" to put an end to the rebellion must be employed. McCook says he is ready, as military butcher, to "make it a war of extermination," unless the "rebels" will confess themselves subdued and ask for mercy. McCook promises to try the virtue of ropes. The rope has two ends. McCook may yet experience its benefits, but at that end which contains the noose.

The *Bulletin* counsels a dignified course towards the great European powers, avoiding flunkyism on the one hand, and petulance and spleen on the other.

We learn from the Louisville Journal of the 22d that Alexander Cassedy, of that city, Adjutant General to Gen. Buckner, who was taken prisoner at Fort Donelson, died on the 21st ult. at Camp Chase, near Columbus, Ohio. Mr. Cassedy was a brave man, and was universally beloved by a large circle of friends in Kentucky and elsewhere. Even the Journal is compelled to acknowledge that "he was a great favorite with all who knew him."

CUTE.—We gave yesterday an instance of "cuteness" on the part of a fellow to get himself exempted from militia duty, and to day a friend furnishes us with an instance of much more cleverness shown by a member of an Exemption Board in a neighboring county. The subject was a man who claimed exemption on the ground of the loss of an eye. When brought before the Board, one of the members pertinently asked the claimant "if he did not always shut one eye in taking aim to shoot?" On an answer being given in the affirmative, the member instantly decided that the loss of the eye was no just ground for exemption, "for," said he, "Mr. ——, you should be thankful for the loss, because it will save you the trouble of shutting your eye when you go to shoot." In this view he was sustained by his brother members, and the applicant was ordered to take his place in the militia.

Commodore Samuel Mercer, of the U. S. Navy, died in Philadelphia, on Thursday, the 8th of March, in the sixty-fourth year of his age. The deceased was a native of Maryland, and was appointed from that State on March 4, 1815. He was educated in the Orphan House.

THE GREAT BATTLE.

From the Memphis Avalanche of the 8th.

I hasten to comply with your request, and to fulfill my promise, but am too thoroughly "used up" to do more than give you a brief outline of the battle of Monterey, and sketch some incidents and scenes which may gratify your readers.

Allow me to speak of myself only to connect the story with what I saw, and excuse the seeming egotism.

I procured a map at Corinth, (herewith furnished to you for lithograph, if you please,) which portrays the positions of all the forces, roads, river towns, etc. It represents Gens. Polk, Breckinridge, Crittenden, Loring, Wood, Slaughter and Hardee on the right wing, about twenty miles east of Corinth, and four miles north of the Memphis and Charleston Railroad; Gens. Johnston, Cheatham, Bowen and Clark on the left wing at Bethel, say twenty miles north of Corinth; while our center is at Monterey, northeast of Corinth, commanded by Gens. Withers, Gladden, Ruggles, Chalmers and Hindman.

Buell is advancing rapidly from some point west of Duck river, and promised to form a junction by Tuesday with Gen. Grant whose left wing rests on the Tennessee, his center five miles northeast of Monterey, and his right extended nearly to Bethel.

Our Generals hold a council of war, and determine on one of the most hazardous enterprises ever undertaken—yet sanctified of course by success—to cross innumerable swamps, over which retreat would be impossible. Under powerful combinations, they are to fall upon the foe and crush his columns before Buell can reach the field.

Cheatham, Clark, Bowen, and A. S. Johnston move at 2 o'clock P. M., at double quick, and ordered to flank the enemy's right, if found practicable. The right wing had moved a few hours before. The center, already in advance, is the only force dreamed of by the enemy in reach of them.

They are gloating over the prospect of annihilating this command by overwhelming numbers, as they had the forces of the only man like Marshal Ney, "the bravest of the brave," at Donelson.

Behold a mighty army has fallen like magic upon him, and Austrians in Italy, who thought Napoleon had fallen from the clouds, were not more surprised than Gen. Grant. On his left are 20.000 men exclaiming in an unknown tongue, "we come to Beanra."

"We fight Yankees" "*Liberte ou mort!*" Hear their shouts and songs on the winding Tennessee, whose crystal waters mirrored the beauties of the Court of Maria Antoinnette, when countless exiles settled a little to the South and braved the forest and the plague, rather than submit to the haughty Bourbons.

Their songs still live. March on! march on! is echoed by the hills. The thunder of the cannon, and pealing muskets, the flashing of the bayonets and clashing swords, startle the confident foe, and ere he dreams the danger nigh, his forces are torn as forests by the whirlwind which once disolated this very scene. His center struggles against a different race, but not less heroic. The gallant Hindman is charging every point, his forces weakening, and his ammunition well nigh exhausted. The gallant Billy Govan bears dispatches to the left wing. Never did I meet so calm a man in such a storm. He halted at my request, and was dividing his crayon with me when one of the shells, which went shrieking over our heads like storm fiends, fell near and exploded. Another topped a tree over our heads, and Billy, while my nerves were quaking, seemed disdainful of the messenger.

I moved to the left, where Gen. Beauregard sat on a stump "moving the whole scene." "Bring up that artillery, and we will soon break their lines," he exclaimed. Feeling that his words were words of doom, I asked Col. Tate the hour. It was just one minute after ten. The artillery opens. I could but pity the poor fellows as they bowed their heads, sank suddenly, or leaped up into the air, and our poor fellows were falling meanwhile all around me, one exclaiming "My God!" another, "Help me!" another, "My poor wife!" and others heedless of all but freedom, cheering their comrades in the very death struggle.

Hindman receives his ammunition—the foe flies before him, a shell bursts in his horse and hurls him in the air! From my position the enemy is falling back. [illegible] the field, and night closes on [illegible] brother from [illegible]

Killed and Wounded.

J W Thompson, 13th Tenn, wounded; J B Eslin, do; Sam Cole, killed; E O Chambers, do; Capt W D Bethel, 22d Tenn, wounded; Lieut J T Hines, 5th Tenn, wounded; Gen Clark, do; K Maddin, 13th Tenn, do; Jno Gibson, 5th Tenn, do; W R Mattews, Clark's Battalion, do; M Pointer, Holly Springs, do; Lieut Abbott, 22d Tenn, killed; J M Jones, do, John Wells, 3d Miss bat, do; Lieut E C Holmes, 4th La, do; Sam M Miles, do, arm off; Patrick Lacey, 3d La, wounded; Timothy Boothe, 5th La, do; J W Yates, do; Lieut Cooper, do; Srgt Major Brown, 11th La, do; Thos Waelfer, 154 Tenn, do; W A King, do; J Hutchinson, 13th Tenn, do; W B Duke, do; J Dallis, 7th Louisiana, do; W P Vandevort, 13th Tennessee, do; Jacob Baugh, 55th Tenn, do; S H Palmer, do; E R Hele, 154th Tenn, do; Corp P B Bobbin, 3th La, do; Octave Dupre, do; J A Wharton, 13th Tenn, do; O Centine, 4th La, do; T J Quintard, 154th Tenn, do; Geo. Bosh, 12th Tenn, do; T. Anderson, 3d Miss Bat, do; Murrel, 5th Tenn, killed; L Lead, 27th Tenn, wounded; W B Jones, do; Brown, 13th Tenn, do; Adjutant 13th Tenn, do; Capt Wilkins, do; Harvey Walker, do; John Savage and Capt Morgan, Shelby county, do; Lieut Bell, do; Capt W Crawford, 1st Ark, do; Maj Doak, killed; J J Maggins, 8th Ark, wounded; R C Tyler, do; Maj B Lowry, 6th Miss, wounded; Lieut Col Stewart, do; Mike Daffee, 8th Ark, wounded, McMinn, 16th Ala, do; Capt Pitman, 13th Tenn, do; A J Radkin, 44th, do, do; Lieut DeAbbott, 154th, do; Perriman, 9th Ark, shot in the head; S M Armstrong, 13th Tenn, wounded; Capt Tye, (Bates Regiment,) do; W D Franks, 9th Ark, do; J A Drown, 5th Tenn, do; Major Henry, do; Capt Sutherland, killed; M V Morris, 13th Tenn, wounded; Lieuts Rice and Dyer, 13th Tenn, do; Geo Wood reported killed; Jimmy McMannus, (our Jimmy) wounded slightly; Capt Chairs, 154th, killed; J H McConly, do, wounded; E W Bradford, 155th, do; Leroy Reese, do, do; Fred Wekell, 154th, in the mouth; R F Maclay, 4th La, wounded; R H Wells, 3d Miss, do; J S Mays, 12th Tenn, do; Peter Duffee, 8th Ark, do; Jacob Oldham, 4th La, do; Gay Bridges, do; S Green, do; Wm Smith, 4th La, wounded; Lieut Miller and younger brother, La. regiment, wounded; Col Kit Williams, killed; Kilpatrick, Marshall county, Miss, wounded; Capt Johns, 6th Tenn, killed; Gen. Hindman, shell exploded in horse, and wounded by concussion; P Lawlor, 4th La, wounded; Jas McDonald, 4th La, wounded; D J Robichaux, 4th La, do; A J Thompson, 4th La, wounded; J P Muse, 4th La, wounded; T J Andrews, 4th La, wounded; Lt Col Tyler, 4th La, wounded; —— Grisson, John Black, two Scarboros, Ren Lique, Adj't Howell, 13th Tenn, wounded; W L McWhiter, 27th Tenn, wounded; Joshua Phillips, 55th Tenn, grape shot in eye; J Moore 27th Tenn, wounded; C J. White, 27th Tenn, wounded; A C Christian, 1st Florida Battalion, wounded; Capt Fowler, Confederate Battalion, wounded; Capt H A Rogers, 9th Tenn, wounded.

RESULT OF THE BATTLE.

A gentleman of distinction who arrived in the city last night, upon the very best official authority, estimates the Federal loss in the battle of the 6th, as follows: Killed and wounded, 12 000 to 15 000; prisoners, 2000 to 3000; field artillery, about 100 pieces; small arms, 20,000; together with all their tents, baggage wagons, ammunition, camp equipage, etc. Our troops occupied the quarters of the enemy the night after the battle, using their hospitals for our wounded.

The Confederate loss in killed, wounded and missing, is estimated at five thousand. Of these Memphis has furnished her full share, and our citizens are looking for the details with the greatest anxiety. It is to be hoped there will be no unnecessary delay in spreading them before the public at the earliest moment. A certainty, even should it be contrary to our wishes, is preferable to continued suspense.

FROM KEY WEST.—The Key West correspondent of the Boston Journal, under date of the 6th, writes as follows:

Obstructions in the Mississippi.—I have conversed with some prisoners recently taken in reference to the obstructions placed across the Mississippi by the rebels, to prevent the passage of the Union men-of-war. From them I learn there is an immense raft of logs, containing eighty thousand feet, stretched across the river at a place called "The Jump." The raft is secured to the banks of the river on either side by heavy chains, which are dropped when any of the Confederate steamers pass. This formidable obstruction is commanded by a strong battery.

RESIGNATION OF THE REV. DR. HAWKS.—The Rev. Dr. Hawks, who in consequence of his secession proclivities, fell into great disfavor with his congregation, has resigned his pastoral charge over Calvary Church in New York.

W. A. Lord, transportation agent on the Mobile and Ohio Railroad, died recently in consequence of an injury received on the road.

CLIPPINGS FROM THE LOUISVILLE JOURNAL.

To such extent does the Examiner carry its horror of panic makers in the present excited state of the Secession nerves, that it opposes, on military principles, and at the suggestions of an "ingenious army officer," the dissemination of religious tracts having alarming titles. On this subject it says:

"One of our ingenious military friends thinks the colporteurs are doing great harm in our army by circulating terrible tracts in the camp, and on the eve of expected battles confronting our men with little pamphlets, entitled 'Are you Ready to Die?' 'Sinner, you are soon to be d—d,' &c."

Floyd says that before determining to make a fight at Fort Donelson, he carefully weighed the chances of success. His was evidently a bad weigh.

Perhaps the scales have fallen from your eyes at Beauregard's way.

THE MAN WHO SAT ON THE POWDER.—Can any one read the report of Com. Goldsborough of the brave sailor, John Davis, who covered a barrel of gunpowder in a magazine with his person, while the flames kindled by an exploded shell were burning around him, without a thrill of emotion? Such deeds of daring redeem and dignify war. History never tires of celebrating the brave Dutch officer who, at the siege of Antwerp, rather than surrender the place, fired the magazine and perished in the explosion. Davis's act was one of equal spirit and courage, and the people will remember him. [New York Evening Post.

The greatest scandal to our troops in Tennessee seems to be that they can't catch Col John Morgan, the very active and mischievous rebel marauder. How long before this scandal will be wiped out?

Jack has just commenced an A B C class. He is preparing a "school for scandal."

The rebel Government at Richmond doesn't know what amount of paper currency it has issued. Probably it couldn't guess within two hundred bushels.

About two hundred bushels less than the Yankee Government—we guess.

Let our soldiers wear beards. Else how can they beard the rebels?

They got a pretty rough shave the other day.

When Slidell was arrested on the Trent, he made what seemed a desperate effort to throw himself into the sea through a hole not half so large as his body. But perhaps he felt small enough to crawl through any hole.

Seward was more fortunate than Mr. Slidell. He crawled through a hole no bigger than a man's hand or the little end of a horn—John Bull's for example.

CASUALTIES IN THE VALLEY FIGHT.—We have seen a letter from the gallant Capt. Thom, of the 1st battalion of Virginia regulars, who was slightly wounded. He received a Minie ball through the pocket Testament in his side pocket, which so checked its force that it merely bruised the skin and bruised the chest slightly. He also received a slight wound in the right hand, from which some temporary inconvenience may result. Capt. T. speaks in the highest terms of praise of the officers and men of his company. They went into the fight with thirty-six muskets, and of this number lost one killed and nine wounded. Lieuts. Randolph and Howard, the letter states, is uninjured.

We have been informed by private source of the fall of Capt. Wm. Bayliss Rector, of Campbell county, who commanded a company in the 42d Regiment. He behaved most gallantly, and when shot was standing on a stump, waving his sword and cheering on his men. The orderly sergeant of the same company, Mr. Walter Brown, son of Rev. Richard Brown, of Campbell, was also killed. There were four others wounded and four missing.

At a late hour last night we had an interview with Capt. Thom, who had just arrived from Staunton.

The statements which he gave us fully confirm the previous accounts of the heroism of our troops. He exhibited the perforation in the left breast of his coat, made by a Minie ball, which struck a Testament in his pocket and glanced off upon his vest. His escape is miraculous.

We regret to learn that Capt. J. Z. Jones, commanding, was shot down during the battle. It is to be hoped that his wound did not prove fatal.

From all accounts that we have received, the Irish battalion must have fought with heroic desperation. The fact that so many of the officers were wounded, is a proof of the assertion. Our last news from Gen Jackson encourages us in the belief that, should the enemy give him another opportunity for a fight, he will add fresh glory to the Southern arms.

The number of our wounded in the hospital at Staunton is about 180. Philip Williams, Esq., Rev. B. F. Brooks, and other citizens of Winchester, were permitted, two or three days after the fight, to come out from Winchester and bury our dead, and report that there were 83 found upon the field in all. When we consider the small number of prisoners taken by the enemy, we have a full confirmation of previous accounts that our loss was by no means so great as that of the Federals.

Other persons who left Winchester after the fight report that the consternation of the Yankees was intense; that they were fully aware of the fact that they had encountered a "stone wall" whose strength was really impregnable.

Lieut. Jack Heth, heretofore reported among the killed, was buried in the M. E. churchyard at Newtown. [Richmond Dispatch, April 1.

THE DOINGS OF THE ENEMY OF THE POTOMAC. From the Fredericksburg Recorder, of the 1st inst., we copy the following:

Rumors have been floating around for several days past, in regard to the doings of the enemy in their advance from Manassas toward our lines. It is said they have burned and destroyed a large number of farm houses and barns, besides stealing all the provisions they could find.

It seems to be pretty well authenticated that our men have burnt the railroad bridge over the Rappahannock river of the Orange and Alexandria road. There is a good deal of speculation as to the intention of the enemy in advancing. Some believe they will cross the river at one of the fords, and march by land to attack our columns. Our own opinion is, they will repair the railroad preliminary to a move, and that this large force, which is spoken of, has been thrown forward merely to protect those engaged in this work.

It was rumored here on Saturday that John T. Kelley's flour mill, with 6000 bushels of wheat, had been destroyed. We have, however, heard nothing confirmatory of this. A gentleman who was in a skirmish with a detachment of cavalry on Friday last, as one of a party of scouts, estimates the enemy's force at 35,000 strong.

It is said by persons from the Potomac that large quantities of troops still continue to pass down daily.

The heavy firing heard here on Friday last is said to have proceeded from the advance guard of the enemy near Bealton Station. They are said to have fired their artillery at regular intervals as they moved along, in order to be certain that there were no rebels about. One of the prisoners captured by our scouts on Friday last, a drummer in one of the Yankee regiments, says that McClellan has told the men that they will have Richmond without fail in less than sixty days.

It was reported in town yesterday that McClellan had gone to the Peninsula.

THE GALLOWS IN RICHMOND.—*Two Spies to be Hung.* We learn that the sentence of a court martial has been given in this city for the execution, on the gallows, of two Federal spies, who are now in jail here. Their names are John Scully and Price Lewis. They were arrested in this city some weeks ago, and, we believe, claim to be Englishmen. It is said that they will be hung to-morrow, although the finding of the court is subject to the President's review. The proofs against these men are said to be damning, they having been identified by some of the victims of their own brutality, as parties who had been instrumental in the arrest of a number of Southern ladies in Washington, and had made a practice of insulting and maltreating females whose "loyalty" to Lincoln was suspected.
[Richmond Examiner, 3d.

LATER FROM FLORIDA.—We are informed that the steamer St. Mary's and the yacht American, after the occupation of Jacksonville by the Yankees, were run up to Dun's lake and sunk by the Confederates.

The Yankees dispatched in pursuit the steamer Darlington and a gunboat, and while these vessels were in the lake, endeavoring to raise the sunken vessels, some good citizens obstructed Dun's creek, a narrow channel connecting Dun's lake with the St. John's river, by felling trees. At our latest reports, preparations were made to give the Yankee crews that went up a good reception with rifles. We commend the example to all who are near the banks of rivers, occupied by the Yankees. [Charleston Courier.

Joseph Mayo has been re-elected Mayor of Richmond, Va.

BEAUFORT, FORT MACON, &c.—From a reliable source we learn that up to the 21st instant Fort Macon was not attacked, but that a Yankee regiment was at Sheppardsville on the night of the 21st. Sheppardsville is in Carteret county, about fourteen miles from Beaufort and sixteen miles from Fort Macon. The captain of the advanced company of this regiment stated to a gentleman who conversed with him, that at the same time he left Newbern for Beaufort or the vicinity, some boats had left for Swansborough. [It is since ascertained that they have taken possession of Swansborough, which is a small port at the end of Bogue Sound, about sixty miles from Wilmington.] Not half a dozen persons had left Beaufort, their means of egress having been cut off. The Carolina City Hotel had been burnt by order, it is said, of Col. White, the commandant at Fort Macon, for what reasons we cannot imagine. Fort Macon is fully furnished for six months, which will serve for eight or ten months if carefully preserved. There are five North Carolina companies there, having probably about three hundred effective men. These companies are Capt. Cogdell's (formerly Andrew's) from Wayne, Capt. Pool's and Capt. Manney's, from Carteret, and Capt. Guion's from Newbern. These have no higher officer than a Captain, and Col. White of the Confederate army of Mississippi is in command. He is a graduate of West Point, about 28 years of age, and had been in the U. S. Army. He has the reputation of being as brave a man as ever lived. [Fayetteville (N. C.) Observer, 31st ult.

RUNNING THE BLOCKADE.—We are happy in being able to state that Mr. T. Hernandez, pilot, who was captured some time since in attempting to run the blockade, has finally succeeded in bringing safely into a Confederate port, on Sunday last, a brig laden with a valuable assorted cargo. [Savannah News, 2d inst.

The enemy now confess that the prisoners they took at Fort Donelson number less than six thousand—a wonderful falling off from their first boasts of twenty thousand and fifteen thousand. And even for the number they got paid very dearly!

THE CITY.

MORE TROOPS.—The steamer Dr. Batey arrived this morning from Gordon's Landing, bringing down from Avoyelles Parish the following troops:

Mansura Guards, 82 men rank and file, under the command of Capt. E Joffroin.

Creole Rebels, 81 men, under the command of Capt. J. J. Decota.

Avoyelles Fencibles, 78 men, commanded by Capt. H. W. Verstile.

Marksville Guards, 80 men, Capt. L. Barbin.

Marksville Chasseurs-a-Pied, 80 men, Capt. L. Phillippon.

Also Lieut. J. C. Jeffrion, recruiting officer Company G, Scott's Cavalry, with 16 men.

The Philadelphia Inquirer.

ESTABLISHED 1829. PHILADELPHIA, FRIDAY, APRIL 11, 1862. PRICE TWO CENTS.

LATEST WAR NEWS!

THE GREAT BATTLE NEAR CORINTH.

ANOTHER ACCOUNT OF THE TERRIBLE CONFLICT.

PROCLAMATION OF THE PRESIDENT.

THE VERY LATEST FROM FORTRESS MONROE.

THE REBELS GATHERING A LARGE FORCE AT YORKTOWN.

ANOTHER DESPERATE FIGHT PROBABLE.

THE TEXANS EVACUATING NEW MEXICO.

PROCEEDINGS OF CONGRESS.

DOINGS AT HARRISBURG, PA.

LATEST FROM WASHINGTON.

THE GREAT BATTLE NEAR CORINTH.

ANOTHER ACCOUNT.

HOW THE BATTLE COMMENCED.

CINCINNATI, April 10.—The correspondent of the Cincinnati *Times* gives the following account of the Pittsburg battle:—

"Our forces were stationed in the form of a semi-circle, the right resting on a point north of Crump's Landing, our centre being in front of the main road to Corinth, and our left extending to the river in the direction of Hamburg, four miles north of Pittsburg Landing.

At 2 o'clock on the morning of the 6th, 400 men from General PRENTISS' Division were attacked by the enemy, half a mile in advance of our lines. Our men fell back on the Twenty-fifth Missouri, swiftly pursued by the enemy.

The advance of the Rebels reached Colonel PEABODY's brigade just as the long roll was sounded and the men were falling into line. The resistance was but short and they retreated under a galling fire until they reached the Second Division.

At six o'clock the attack has become general along the entire front of our lines. The enemy, in large force, drove in the pickets of Gen. SHERMAN's division, and fell on the Forty-eighth, Seventieth and Seventy-second Ohio regiments. These troops had never before been in action, and being so unexpectedly attacked, made as able a resistance as possible, but were, in common with the forces of Gen. PRENTISS, compelled to seek support on the troops immediately in their rear.

At one o'clock the entire line of both sides was fully engaged. The roar of cannon and musketry was without intermission from the main centre to a point extending half way down the left wing.

The Rebels made a desperate charge on the Fourteenth Ohio Battery, and not being sufficiently sustained by infantry, it fell into their hands. Another severe fight occurred for the possession of the Fifth Ohio Battery, and three of its guns were taken by the enemy.

By eleven o'clock commanders of regiments had fallen, and in some cases not a single field officer remained; yet the fighting continued with an earnestness which showed that the contest on both sides was for "death or victory!" Foot by foot the ground was contested, and finding it impossible to drive back our centre, the enemy slackened their fire and made a vigorous effort on our left wing, endeavoring to outflank and drive it to the river bank. This wing was under General HURLBURT, and was composed of the Fourteenth, Thirty-second, Forty-fourth and Fifty-seventh Indiana, Eighth, Eighteenth and Twenty-first Illinois. Fronting its line, however, were the Fifty-fourth, Fifty-seventh and Seventy-seventh Ohio, and Fifth Ohio Cavalry, of SHERMAN's division.

For nearly two hours a sheet of fire blazed from both columns, the Rebels fighting with a valor that was only equalled by those contending with them. While the contest raged the hottest, the gun-boat *Tylor* passed up the river to a point opposite the enemy and poured in broadsides from her immense guns, greatly aiding in forcing the enemy back. Up to three o'clock, the battle raged with a fury that defies description. The Rebels had found their attempts to break our lines unavailing. They had striven to drive in our main column, and finding that impossible, had turned all their strength upon our left. Foiled in that quarter, they now made another attack on our centre, and made every effort to rout our forces before the reinforcements which had been sent for should come up.

At five o'clock there was a short cessation in the firing of the enemy, their lines falling back for nearly half a mile. They then suddenly wheeled, and again threw their entire force upon our left wing, determined to make a final struggle in that quarter; but the gun-boats *Tylor* and *Lexington* poured in their shot thick and fast with terrible effect.

In the meantime General LEW. WALLACE, who had taken a circuitous route for Crump's Landing, appeared suddenly on the enemy's right wing. In the face of this combination of circumstances, the Rebels felt that their enterprise that day was a failure, and as night was approaching, fell back until they reached an advantageous position somewhat in the rear of, yet occupying, the main road to Corinth.

The gun-boats continued to send their shell after them until they got out of range.

After a weary watch of several hours of intense anxiety, the advance regiment of General BUELL's army appeared on the opposite bank of the river, and the work of crossing the river began, the Thirty-sixth Indiana and Sixty-eighth Ohio being the first to cross, followed by the main portion of NELSON's and BRUCE's divisions.

Cheer after cheer greeted their arrival, and they were immediately sent to the advance where they rested on their arms.

All night long steamers were engaged in ferrying General BUELL's forces across. When daylight broke it was evident that the Rebels, too, had been stronly reinforced.

The Second Day's Fight.

The battle was opened by the Rebels at 7 o'clock, from the Corinth road, and in half an hour extended along the whole line.

At nine o'clock the sound of artillery and musketry fully equalled that of the previous day. The enemy was met by the reinforcements and the still unwearied soldiers of yesterday with an energy they certainly could not have expected. It became evident that they were avoiding the extreme of our left wing, and endeavoring with perseverance and determination to find some weak points by which to turn our forces. They left one point, but returned to it immediately, and then as suddenly, by some masterly stroke of Generalship, directed a most vigorous attack upon some division where they fancied they would not be expected; but the fire of our lines was as steady as clock work, and it soon became evident that the enemy considered the task he had undertaken a hopeless one.

Further reinforcements now began to arrive, and they were posted on the right of the main centre, under WALLACE. Gens. GRANT, BUELL, NELSON, SHERMAN and CRITTENDEN were everywhere present, directing the movements for a new stroke on the enemy. Suddenly both wings of our army were turned upon the enemy, with the intention of driving them into an extensive ravine. At the same time a powerful battery was stationed in the open field, and poured volley after volley of cannister into the Rebel ranks.

At 11½ o'clock the roar of the battle shook the earth. The Union guns were fired with all the energy that the prospect of the enemy's defeat inspired, while the Rebels' fire was not so vigorous, and they evinced a desire to withdraw. They finally fell slowly back, keeping up a fire from their artillery and musketry along their whole column, as they retreated. They moved in excellent order, battling at every advantageous point, and delivering their fire with considerable effect. But from all the divisions of our army they were closely pursued, a galling fire being kept upon their rear.

The enemy had now been driven beyond our former lines, and were in full retreat for Corinth, pursued by our cavalry.

The forces engaged on both sides, in this day's battle, are estimated at about seventy thousand each.

FURTHER DETAILS.

CAIRO, April 10.—An arrival from Pittsburg says the enemy, in making the first attack on Sunday morning, carried the Stars and Stripes and wore the Union uniforms. Gen. BRAGG is reported killed.

Provisional Governor JOHNSON, of Kentucky, is wounded and a prisoner.

It is stated that General PRENTISS escaped in the confusion of the enemy's retreat on the second day of the fight. Our total loss is about seven thousand. This is the estimate of military commanders who were in the engagement. Of these about two thousand were taken prisoners, and the balance killed and wounded in the usual proportions.

General WALLACE of Illinois, was reported dead, as it was thought impossible that he could live. He was, however, living on Wednesday, and improving. He was shot back of the ear, the bullet coming out at the nose.

General HALLECK passed Cairo to-day, *en route* for Pittsburg.

Five thousand prisoners are expected to-night from Island No. 10.

Every preparation is being made here for the reception of our wounded at Pittsburg.

CHICAGO, April 10.—We are beginning to get some reliable details from the great battle at Pittsburg from several gentlemen who were on the field after the fight. From their statements we gather the following:—

General PRENTISS' brigade, consisting of the Sixty-first Illinois, Seventeenth Wisconsin, Twenty-fourth Indiana and Seventy-first Ohio, were attacked while eating their breakfast, by what seemed to be the entire Rebel force. PRENTISS had no artillery. His Brigade was cut to pieces and forced to retire, and General PRENTISS and many of his troops were taken prisoners.

At 12 o'clock the entire line was fiercely engaged, but in full retreat. At 4 o'clock P. M. the enemy had taken SCHWARTZ's battery of six guns, DRESDEN's battery of four guns, WATERHOUSE's battery and also two Ohio batteries, the names of which are not given.

Thousands of our troops had taken refuge under the bank of the river, and utterly refused to fight; in fact, they could not, as the officers and men were mixed in inextricable confusion. The army at this time seemed utterly defeated.

At this juncture, the gun-boats *Lexington* and *Tylor* opened a tremendous fire of shot and shell upon the enemy, and kept it up every half hour.

JUST BEFORE THE BATTLE.

Special Correspondence of the Inquirer.

FIVE MILES INLAND FROM PITTSBURG LANDING, Tenn., on the Road to Corinth, Miss., Saturday, April 5, 1862.

Yesterday afternoon, about four o'clock, two regiments of the enemy made a reconnoissance on our right (General SHERMAN'S Division), and succeeded in capturing five of our men—one major, one lieutenant and three privates—who were on picket duty. A brigade was immediately ordered out, as it was believed that the Rebels were in force, and, after moving one mile beyond our picket line, came up to a masked battery, but found it out in time to fall back to a safe position, in the meantime firing upon the Rebels, who endeavored to cut them off.

We obtained a position in the edge of a wood, and, in about two hours, drove them down the Corinth road, they taking their guns along. Subsequent observation showed twelve Rebels lying dead, and three wounded, the latter being captured. Night coming on, nothing has been done since, except a general distribution of cartridges, etc., and last night an order to sleep on our arms, which was done. We are anticipating a renewal of the scene this afternoon, and I have no doubt but that the ball is just now commencing in earnest.

Affairs here are of so entirely a military character that I cannot find an opportunity to lay hold of anything except it concerns the movements of troops, etc.; and aside from that, the system of espionage lately established prohibits me from saying what I feel it my duty to say with reference to many matters. I bide my time, hoping that a few days longer may produce results that will repay me for the risk and anxiety I experience here in these gloomy forests. Sickness in camp continues to increase, and it is to be hoped that some excitement will be afforded the men, for it would benefit them a thousand fold more than all the physic and tonics that could be administered in the form of drugs and medicines. We buried three from our regiment, Twenty-fifth Missouri, yesterday.

H. B.

FROM NEAR YORKTOWN.

NEAR YORKTOWN, April 9th, 1·20 P. M.

To the Associated Press:—The weather still continues unfavorable for military operations. It has been raining for two days. The creeks are much swollen, and the low ground covered with water, making the road almost impassable for empty wagons.

Information received shows that the Rebels have a force of sixty thousand, which is rapidly being added to by troops from the neighborhood of Richmond, which is one day from Yorktown by railroad and river. They have four steamers and sixteen transports in use, and, by the time the roads are in condition for the Union army to move, the Rebels may be able to meet them with one hundred thousand men—the flower of their army, with their best arms Besides, they are in a strongly entrenched position.

Previous to our troops occupying their present position, the military authorities had mo means of ascertaining the extent of the Rebel works. Information obtained through deserters, contrabands and other sources, show that the enemy have nearly five hundred guns, some of them of the largest calibre.

The Rebel General, JOHNSTON, with some of his forces, has arrived and taken command in person, showing that they intend making a desperate resistance to the advance of our troops at every point.

The entrenchments extend entirely across the peninsula from James to York river.

The cheering news from the Western Department arrived here to-day, and our troops are wild with enthusiasm over the result, and are anxious to be led to action, that they may perform similar deeds of valor.

THE HEROES OF THE RECENT GLORIOUS UNION VICTORY AT PITTSBURG LANDING.

MAJOR-GENERAL GRANT.

Major-General ULYSSES S. GRANT was born at Point Pleasant, Clairmont county, Ohio, April 27th, 1822, and entered West Point Military Academy, from Ohio, in 1839, where he graduated with honors in 1843, and was attached, as brevet second lieutenant, to the Fourth Infantry. He was promoted second lieutenant at Corpus Christi, in September, 1845, and served as such through Mexico, under General TAYLOR at Palo Alto, Resaca de la Palma and Monterey; and under General SCOTT from Vera Cruz to the city of Mexico, and was twice promoted for his bravery. He was regimental Quartermaster from April 1, 1847, and when he resigned the service on the 31st of July, 1854, he was a full captain in the Fourth Infantry of Regulars. After his resignation he settled in St. Louis county, Missouri, and moved from there to Galena, Illinois, in 1860.

Upon the breaking out of the present war he offered his services to Governor YATES, and was appointed Colonel of the Twenty-first Regiment of Illinois Volunteers, and served with his regiment until promoted a Brigadier-General, with commission and rank from the seventeenth of May, 1861. He was engaged as colonel and acting brigadier-general in several of the contests in Southeastern Missouri, and his course as commander of the Southeast district of Missouri has been thoroughly scrutinized; and among his most praiseworthy acts was the occupation of Paducah and stoppage of communication and supplies to the Rebels via the Tennessee and Cumberland rivers. The manner in which he conducted the battle of Belmont is still fresh in our readers' minds. The rest of his course, as commander there, is too well known to be repeated here, and certain it is that his action in every instance has been applauded both by his superior officers and the people. After the capture of Fort Henry a new district was created, under the denomination of the District of West Tennessee, and General GRANT was assigned by General HALLECK to the command of it.

He was in command of the Union forces at Fort Donelson, and his noted correspondence with General BUCKNER gained him the soubriquet of Unconditional-Surrender GRANT, answering to his initials of U. S. GRANT. For the success of that action he was created a Major-General; but, being unavoidably absent from the field during the early portion of the fight, it was reported that he was temporarily deprived of his command until the matter could be investigated. After a few days he was, however, again ordered into the field, and the manner in which he has conducted the present action will remove from him all the remains of his former discomfiture. General GRANT is a noble, brave and efficient soldier, as his actions have plainly proved throughout the present contest, and, in fact, throughout the whole of the Western war.

MAJOR-GENERAL BUELL.

General DON CARLOS BUELL, the commander af the District of Ohio troops in the field, is a native of Ohio, and is about forty years of age. He entered the Military Academy at West Point as a cadet in the year 1837, and was breveted second lieutenant of the Third Infantry July 1, 1841. In June, 1846, he was appointed first lieutenant, and was breveted captain September 23, 1846, for gallant and meritorious conduct during the several conflicts at Monterey, Mexico. During 1847 and 1848, he acted as adjutant of his regiment, and was particularly distinguished in the battle of Cerro Gordo. On the 20th of August, 1847, he was breveted major of the army for gallant and meritorious conduct in the battles of Contreras and Cherubusco, and was severely wounded in the latter. He was appointed in January, 1848, Assistant Adjutant-General, with the rank of captain, still holding his brevet rank of major. He relinquished his rank in the line during March, 1851.

At the commencement of the present troubles he was still holding the position of Assistant Adjutant-General. On the 11th of May, 1861, he was promoted to a Lieutenant-Colonelcy in the Adjutant-General's department, and by Congress he was created a Brigadier-General of volunteers, his commission bearing date May 17, 1861. With that rank he took charge of the Department of the Ohio, and under his direction the advance of the Union forces to Bowling Green and Nashville was conducted. At about the 20th of March, 1862, he was confirmed by Congress as Major-General of volunteers, and took command of the army in the field. The advance along the railroad from Nashville to Columbia, and from thence by turnpike roads to Savannah, has been performed with marked rapidity, and the junction with General GRANT's forces took place not a moment too soon.

THE REBEL FLOATING BATTERY AT ISLAND NO. 10.

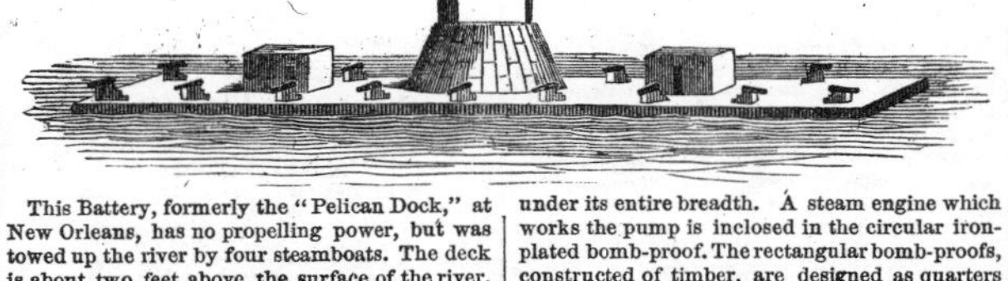

This Battery, formerly the "Pelican Dock," at New Orleans, has no propelling power, but was towed up the river by four steamboats. The deck is about two feet above the surface of the river, but can be lowered or elevated by letting in or pumping out the water from the hollow space under its entire breadth. A steam engine which works the pump is inclosed in the circular iron-plated bomb-proof. The rectangular bomb-proofs, constructed of timber, are designed as quarters for the men. The guns are mounted *en barbette*, and none of them are smaller than 32-pounders.

LATE WASHINGTON NEWS.

A GIGANTIC RAILROAD SCHEME.

THE STEVENS' BATTERY.

Pennsylvania Reserves Out West.

A REBEL GENERAL.

SENTENCED TO BE HUNG.

Nominated a Brigadier-General.

Special Correspondence of the Inquirer.

WASHINGTON, April 10.

A Gigantic Speculation—Grand Railroad Scheme.

Mr. WRIGHT reported a bill into the House this morning, from the Committee on Military Affairs, entitled "An Act to facilitate the transportation of troops, munitions, stores and mails of the United States, between the cities of Washington, Baltimore, Philadelphia and New York." Its provisions will be found in the following brief synopsis:—

Section 1. The Secretary of the Treazury is authorized to guarantee the bonds of the Metropolitan Railroad Company to the amount of two millions of dollars, payable in thirty years at six per cent., to be issued when the said company shall execute a mortgage on their road, rolling stock and property, and also conditioned for two per cent. per annum for a sinking fund for the redemption of the bonds. The Company shall immediately construct a railroad to Gaithersburg, Md., and from there connect with the Philadelphia, Wilmington and Baltimore Railroad at such point, near Baltimore, as the Secretary of War may direct; also, to connect with the Northern Central or such other roads as now exist or may hereafter be finished or constructed running into Pennsylvania or New York, and to make extensions in any direction, and towards any point of the compass. In consideration of these inordinate and tremendous privileges, the said Company is to carry freight at four cents per ton per mile, and soldiers and sailors at two cents per mile.

Section 2 provides, that when the Company shall bring evidence of its owners or engineers that it has expended fifty thousand dollars, he shall deliver that amount of bonds.

Section 3. The Company is authorized to lay tracks through any of the streets of Washington and Georgetown.

Section 4 provides for the sale of the road in default of its interest, and its purchase by the United States.

Section 5. The Company is authorized to construct a double track upon the line of any railway, when the Secretary of War shall so direct, and authorizes the Secretary of the Treasury to issue bonds to an indefinite amount for such construction upon the demands of the owners of the road.

Section 6. The rate of fare to be two and a half cents per mile for through passengers, and three cents per mile for way passengers. *Provided*, That for better accommodations than are now afforded, the company shall have the right to charge an additional rate of one cent per mile.

Altogether, this bill designs to aid one of the most magnificent projects of the day, and confers upon a half dozen individuals privileges which are worth fifty millions of dollars. It completely tramples upon the clearest rights of five States, and aims to reduce to bankruptcy some of the most loyal corporations in the land. It is an instance of national ingratitude that ignores the services of the existing lines by whose labors the National Capital was saved exactly one year ago, merely to enable a handful of speculators to fasten a huge job upon Congress, while the shrieks of dying soldiers and sorrow-stricken families echo over the land.

It is evident that the Committee cannot have given the subject a thorough investigation, and there can be no doubt that it was hurried through in the immense press of business which has weighed so heavily upon the most laborious and hard working committee in the House. If this bill shall become a law it will establish a precedent for future bogus railroad grants and aid to flimsy corporations from a heavily taxed and depressed people, who, while willing to spend their last dollar for the public defence, will never consent to be taxed to enrich a hungry band of railroad jobbers and speculators.

Nominated to a Brigadier-Generalship.

The President yesterday sent to the Senate the nomination to a Brigadier-Generalship of Major SAMUEL W. CRAWFORD, of the Thirteenth Regular Infantry, Inspector-General of Gen. ROSENCRANS' division. Major CRAWFORD is a native of Philadelphia. He entered the army in 1851 as a Surgeon, at the head of his class. He was at once sent to the frontier, where he remained for several years. In 1857 he traveled throughout Mexico, and made a daring and successful ascent of the volcano Popocateptl. For his researches he was honored by the Geographical Society of Mexico with membership. He was subsequently made Bearer of Despatches to the State Department. In 1858 he was assigned again to duty on the frontier, with the late lamented General LYON, and he continued the warm friend and correspondent of that patriot until his death.

In 1860 Major CRAWFORD was ordered to Fort Sumter. During the long imprisonment of that brave band, and in the final bombardment, he bore a conspicuous part, and commanded for hours the battery exposed to the fire of Fort Moultrie and Sullivan's Island. After the fall of Sumter he was assigned to duty with General ROSECRANS' command, and took an active part in driving FLOYD from Western Virginia. So valuable have been his services in that section that the delegation from Virginia waited upon the President and requested his nomination to a General of Brigade. Philadelphia cannot but be gratified at the well-merited reward thus bestowed upon one of her sons.

The Stevens Battery.

The appropriation for the completion of this immense iron-clad frigate passed the House by the decisive vote of eighty-two to forty-one. The bill goes back to the Senate by reason of non-concurrence in some of the Senate amendments, but there is no doubt that it will be a law within the next week. The Secretary of the Navy, who has displayed commendable zeal and energy on the subject of constructing iron-clad ships, it is believed will cordially co-operate with Mr. STEVENS in making his renowned battery a credit to the nation.

Competent scientific and nautical men say that, when finished, she will surpass the *Warrior* or *La Gloire* as much as either of them excel an ordinary wooden ship. The Navy Department need desire no prouder monument of its efficiency than the completion of this single impregnable and destructive battle-ship.

Pennsylvania Reserves Out West.

It will be gratifying to Pennsylvanians to know that the Union gun-boat *Carondelet*, which recently made the gallant dash of running the blockade by the Rebel batteries at Island No. 10, on the Mississippi, getting safely into her desired position under a fire of forty shots, is manned entirely by volunteers from the Pennsylvania Reserve Corps, MCCALL's Division. The quota of volunteers from the Division, for the gun-boat service, was sixty men, ten from each regiment, and they left General MCCALL's Head-quarters here, after inspection of the detachment by the General himself, on Monday morning, the 17th of February. They are a fine body of men, and nobly are they sustaining the reputation of Pennsylvania. They left under charge of Sergeant H. S. FISHER, Fifth Regiment.

A Rebel General.

Considerable curiosity has been excited here to know something of a Rebel officer who figures in the reports.

General W. W. MAKALL, captured at Island No. 10, is a native of Virginia, and was formerly Assistant Adjutant-General in our army. No longer since than last June he came home from California at the expense of the Government, drew his pay, and resigned. For two or three weeks he hung around Elkton, Maryland, to the intense disgust of loyal men there, and suddenly disappearing, now turns up a "General." His whole family have lived on the Government all their lives.

List of Prisoners from the United States Ship "Congress."

The following has been received at the Navy Department:—

The subscriber, PETER J. HARGOUS, is, of course, included among the prisoners.

TOBACCO WAREHOUSE, RICHMOND, VA., April 3, 1862.

SIR:—The following is a correct list of the men taken prisoners from the United States ship *Congress*, on the 8th of March last, at Newport News, viz:—William Robinson, seaman; James A. Wicks, second master; Jeremiah O'Connor, captain of the hold; Arthur Clegg, do.; David Sherry, boatswain's mate; Amos Gatupe, carpenter's mate; Peter Barker, colored, cook; Charles Costello, seaman; Thomas C. Jones, do.; Samuel Kelly, do.; Michael Quinn, ordinary seaman; Jno. Tonsen, do.; W. H. Williams, do.; Benjamin F. Wing, landsman; Math. Kenny, do.; Edward Morrissey, do.; Daniel Barton, colored, do.; James McCauley, do.; John Beard, ordinary seamen; John Williams, landsman; John O'Malley, marine; Wm. Baldwin, coast guard, Ninety-ninth Regiment N. Y. S. V.; John Blackwood, do.; Richard Thomas, do.; Miller Delane, do.; Archibald McClain, do.; John Peterson, do.; Francis Kenny, do.; James Goodwin, do.

In the hospital at Portsmouth, Va., John Collins, quarter gunner, slightly wounded; Thomas Forward, landsman, badly burned; Flynn, do., left leg ampntated.

I am, sir, very respectfully, your obedient servant,

PETER J. HARGOUS,
Master's Mate, United States Navy.

To Hon. GIDEON WELLES, Secretary of the Navy.

Sentenced to be Hung.

In the course of the past summer Mr. SAMUEL P. CARUSI, a native of this city, and son of our fellow citizen Mr. SAMUEL CARUSI, was arrested by the military authorities here on some charge implicating his loyalty. He was, however, promptly discharged on taking the oath of allegiante to the United States, and returned to his home in Westmoreland county, Virginia.

The Union prisoners last arrived in this city bring to his parents here the distressing intelligence that some time since he and two others were arrested by the Rebel authorities on a charge of being Union spies, and that he has been tried in Richmond, where he is now imprisoned under sentence of death. His father is endeavoring to enlist the influence of the Government here in his behalf; it is sincerely to be hoped with success.

The War in New Mexico.

WASHINGTON, April 10.—The following was received to-day by the Secretary of War:—

"KANSAS CITY, April 10.—The Santa Fe mail has arrived.

"The Texans, one hundred and fifty strong, had evacuated Santa Fe, and were marching along the river. It is reported that General CANBY had intercepted an express with orders commanding the Texan forces to evacuate the territory and return to Texas.

"Colonel SLOUGH had left for Union City with one thousand four hundred men, to make a junction with General CANBY.

"The Texans were exacting contributions and forced loans from the inhabitants, and clothing and provisions were being taken from the merchants without regard to their politics or circumstances."

FORT UNION, New Mexico, March 23.—[Correspondence of the Missouri *Republican*.]—Our column, under command of Colonel SLOUGH, is breaking up camp for a forward movement south towards the Rebel forces. The Texan army occupies a strong position in the vicinity of Albuquerque, 175 miles south of this depot, about midway between this fort and Fort Craig, where General CANBY was at last accounts.

The Texans have taken up this as the strategic point, doubtless intending to march upon either column as they leave their stronghold—Fort Union or Fort Craig—and by their superior force (which is estimated at 2400 strong and twenty-one pieces of artillery) whip one, face about and assault the other column before they can form a junction, and cut us up in detail.

It would seem that Col. SLOUGH and Gen. CANBY, the commanders of the two depots, are not acting in concert, and sound men of the army fear that this movement—one of the most difficult of military combinations—may prove successful, and render our depot at Fort Union—the only supply left us—comparatively defenceless. I sincerely believe Col. SLOUGH will march beyond supporting distance of the depot. The Texans are occupying Santa Fe, a hundred miles south of this, with from a hundred to two hundred troops.

From Fortress Monroe and the Peninsula.

BALTIMORE, April 10.—The Old Point boat has arrived. The news of the capture of Island No. 10 caused great enthusiasm and rejoicing. The storm still continued, but had somewhat abated last evening.

The accounts from the Peninsula report our troops meeting the storm with characteristic ingenuity in the way of improvised shelters. Their enthusiasm and confidence in General MCCLELLAN is unabated.

Though the storm at this time is unfortunate, the time has not been lost, and the retreat of the Rebel MAGRUDER and his forces, or their defeat, is about as certain as any possible future event. The prospect of a clear-up in the weather is looked for with great anxiety at Old Point, from a belief that the sunshine and the *Merrimac* will come together. All seem confident that she will be captured or sunk if she comes out.

LATEST.

WASHINGTON, April 10.—The latest news received from Cherrystone reports everything quiet in the vicinity. A strong wind was blowing, and the sea was running very high.

The Baltimore and Ohio Railroad.

BALTIMORE, April 10.—The Directors of the Baltimore and Ohio Railroad have passed the following:—

Whereas, Publications have been made in some of the journals of the Northern and Western States, alleging disloyalty on the part of officers and employees of this Company, and assigning this as a reason why the Government of the United States have not, at an earlier period, assisted the Company in opening the road to its Western termini;

And whereas, The officers of this Company have the entire confidence of the Government, as is well known to this Board, and the delay by the Government in furnishing any assistance to enable the Company to open its road has not been owing to the cause alleged;

And whereas, This Board, in accordance with our views, are opposed to the employment of any persons by the Company who are known to be disloyal; therefore,

Resolved, That the employment, in any capacity whatever, of any person known to be disloyal to the Government, will meet with the unqualified disapprobation of the Board, and if any persons, now in the employ of the company, shall be discovered to be disloyal to the Government, the removal of such persons be imperatively demanded.

Resolved, That no person shall be appointed to any position, or employed in any capacity, by the officers of this company, except loyal citizens of the United States.

The Occupation of Corinth, Miss.

WASHINGTON, April 10.—Despatches have been received here to-day, confirming the report of the occupation of Corinth, Mississippi, by the troops under Gen. BUELL.

General Banks' Command.

EDENBURG, Va., April 10.—All is quiet in this Division.

The enemy's pickets have not been seen during the severe storm which has prevailed for the past two days.

Auction Sale of Wool at Boston.

BOSTON, April 10.—At the auction sale to-day 600,000 pounds of wool were sold at 43@48c., the bidding closing firm. Average price 45c.

Among the purchasers were BULLOCK & Sons and ROBINSON & Co., of Philadelphia. The lots were all sold.

THE NEW YORK HERALD.

WHOLE NO. 9345. NEW YORK, FRIDAY, APRIL 11, 1862. PRICE TWO CENTS.

THE GREAT VICTORIES.

Important Details of the Battle at Pittsburg, Tenn.

Heroic Conduct of the Troops Engaged in the Conflict.

Graphic Description of the Grand Coup de Grace of the Union Army.

One Hundred and Forty Thousand Men in the Battle.

The Rebel General Bragg Reported Killed.

Names of Some of the Officers Engaged.

Important News from Island No. Ten.

One Major General, Three Brigadiers and Five Thousand Soldiers Taken Prisoners.

An Immense Quantity of Munitions of War Captured.

PROCLAMATION BY THE PRESIDENT.

Thanks for the Glorious Victories and Prayers for the Restoration of Peace,

&c., &c., &c.

CINCINNATI, April 10, 1862.

The Cincinnati *Times* gives the following additional particulars of the Pittsburg battle:—

Our forces were staioned in the form of a semicircle, the right resing on a point north of Crump's Landing our centre being in front of the main road to Corinth, and our left extending to the river in the direction of Hamburg, four miles north of Pittsburg Landing. At two o'clock on the morning of the 6th 400 men of Gen. Prentiss' division were attacked by the enemy half a mile in advance of our lines. Our men fell back on the 25th Missouri, swiftly pursued by the enemy. The advance of the rebels reached Col. Peabody's brigade just as the long roll was sounded and the men were falling into line. Resistance was but short, and they retreated under a galling fire until they reached the lines of the Second division.

At six o'clock the attack had become general along our whole front. The enemy in large numbers drove in the [illegible] of General Sherman's division, and fell on the Eighth, Fiftieth and Seventy-second Ohio regiments. These troops were never before in action, and being so unexpectedly attacked, made as able a resistance as possible, but were, in common with the forces of General Prentiss, forced to seek support of the troops immediately in their rear. At one o'clock the entire line on both sides was fully engaged. The roar of cannon and musketry was without intermission from the main centre to a point extending half way down the left wing. The rebels made a desperate change on the Fourteenth Ohio battery, which, not being sufficiently supported by infantry, fell into their hands. Another severe fight occurred for possession of the Fifth Ohio battery, and three of its guns were taken by the enemy.

By eleven o'clock a number of commanders of regiments had fallen, and in some cases not a single field officer remained; yet the fighting continued with an earnestness which showed that the contest on both sides was for death or victory. Foot by foot the ground was contested, and finding it impossible to drive back our centre, the enemy slackened their fire, and made vigorous efforts on our left wing, endeavoring to outflank, and driving it to the river bank. This wing was under Gen. Hurlburt, and was composed of the Fourteenth, Thirty-second, Forty-fourth and Fifty-seventh Indiana; Eighth, Eighteenth and Twenty-first Illinois. [The Fourteenth Indiana regiment was not there. It is serving under General Shields in Virginia.—ED.] Fronting its line, however, was the Fourteenth, Fifty-seventh and Seventy-seventh Ohio, and Fifth Ohio cavalry, of General Sherman's division For nearly two hours a sheet of fire blazed from both columns, the rebels fighting with a vigor that was only equalled by those contending with them. While the contest raged the hottest the gunboat Tyler passed up the river to a point opposite the enemy and poured in broadsides from her immense guns, greatly aiding in forcing the enemy back. Up to three o'clock the battle raged with a fury that defies description. The rebels had found every attempt to break our lines unavailing. They had striven to drive in our main column, and finding that impossible had turned all their strength upon our left. Foiled in that quarter, they now made another attempt at our centre, and made every effort to rout our forces before the reinforcement, which had been sent for should come up.

At five o'clock there was a short cessation in the fire of the enemy, their lines falling back for nearly half a mile, when they suddenly wheeled and again threw their entire forces upon our left wing, determined to make a final struggle in that quarter; but the gunboats Tyler and Lexington poured in their shot thick and fast with terrible effect. Meanwhile General Wallace, who had taken a circuitous route from Crump's Landing, appeared suddenly on the enemy's right wing. In the face of this combination of circumstances the rebels felt that their enterprise for the day was a failure, and as night was approaching fell back until they reached an advantageous position somewhat in the rear, yet occupying the main road to Corinth.

The gunboats continued to throw shell after them until out of range. After a wearied watching of several hours of intense anxiety, the advance regiments of General Buell appeared on the opposite bank of the river. The work of passing the river began, the Thirty-sixth Indiana and Sixty-eighth Ohio being the first to cross, followed by the main portions of Generals Nelson and Bruce's divisions. Cheer after cheer greeted their arrival, and they were immediately sent to the advance, where they rested on their arms for the night. All night long steamers were engaged ferrying General Buell's force across, *and when daylight broke it was evident the rebels too had been strongly reinforced.*

The battle on Monday was opened by the rebels at seven o'clock from the Corinth road, and in half an hour extended along the whole line. At nine o'clock the sound of artillery and musketry fully equalled that of the previous day. The enemy was met by our reinforcements and the still unwearied soldiers of the previous day with an energy they certainly could not have expected. It became evident they were avoiding the extreme of our left wing, and endeavoring, with perseverance and determination, to find some weak point by which to turn our force. They left one point but to return to it immediately, and then as suddenly would, by some masterly stroke of generalship, direct a most vigorous attack upon some division where they fancied they would not be expected; *but the fire of our lines was as steady as clock work,* and it soon became evident that the enemy considered the task they had undertaken a hopeless one. Further reinforcements now began to arrive, and took position on the right of the main centre, under General Wallace.

Generals Grant, Buell, McClernand, Nelson, Sherman and Crittenden, were everywhere present, directing movements for a new stroke on the enemy. *Suddenly both wings of our army were turned upon the enemy, with the intention of driving them into an extensive ravine;* at the same time a powerful battery, stationed in the open field, poured volley after volley of canister into the rebel ranks. At half-past eleven the roar of the battle shook the earth. The Union guns were fired with all the energy that the prospect of the enemy's defeat inspired, while the rebels' fire was not so vigorous, and they evinced a desire to withdraw. They finally fell slowly back, keeping up a fire from their artillery and musketry along their whole column as they retreated. They went in excellent order, battling at every advantageous point, and delivering their fire with considerable effect; but from all the divisions of our lines they were closely pursued, a galling fire being kept upon their rear.

The enemy had now been driven beyond our former lines, and were in full retreat for Corinth, pursued by our cavalry.

The forces engaged on both sides in this day's battle are estimated at about seventy thousand each—an entire force of one hundred and forty thousand men.

CAIRO, April 10, 1862.

An arrival from Pittsburg Landing says that the rebels, in making the first attack on Sunday morning, carried the Stars and Stripes and wore the federal uniform.

General Bragg is reported to have been killed. Provisional Governor Johnson, of Kentucky, is wounded and was taken prisoner.

It is stated that General Prentiss escaped in the confusion of the rebels' retreat on the second day's fight.

Our total loss is about 7,000. This is the estimate of the military commanders who were in the engagement. Of this number about 2,000 were taken prisoners, the balance are killed and wounded in the usual proportions.

General Wallace, of Illinois, was reported dead, as it was thought impossible that he could live; he was, however, living on Wednesday, and improving. He was shot in the back of the ear, the bullet coming out of his nose.

CHICAGO, April 10, 1862.

A special despatch to the Chicago *Tribune* from Cairo says—

From several gentlemen who were on the field after the fight the following is gathered:—

General Prentiss' brigade, consisting of the Sixty-first Illinois, Seventeenth Wisconsin, Twenty-fouth Indiana and Seventy-first Ohio, were attacked while eating their breakfast by what seemed to be the entire rebel force. General Prentiss had no artillery, and his brigade was nearly cut to pieces and forced to retire. General Prentiss and many of his men were taken prisoners.

At twelve o'clock the entire line was engaged, but soon in full retreat.

At four o'clock the enemy had taken Schwartz's battery of six guns, Dresden's battery of four guns, and Waterhause's battery; also two Ohio batteries, name not known.

Thousands of our soldiers who had taken refuge under the bank of the river urterly refused to fight, and, in fact, they could not, as officers and men were mixed in inextricable confusion.

The army at this time seemed to be utterly defeated. At this juncture, the gunboats Lexington and Tyler opened a tremendous fire of shot and shell upon the enemy, and kept it up every half hour during the night. Some of the shells set the woods on fire and many dead rebels were burned.

At seven in the evening the firing had generally ceased. About midnight the rebels attempted to plant a battery within three hundred yards of our siege guns, but were driven away by the gunboats and siege guns, supported by three regiments of Gen. Mitchell's division, which had arrived and crossed the river about six in the evening.

Our informants persist in estimating our lass on Sunday at 3,000 killed and 5,000 wounded as being a low figure.

During the night the rebels were reinforced by Generals Van Dorn and Price, from Arkansas, with a very large force.

General Lewis Wallace came up with the Eleventh and Twenty-third Indiana, Forty-fourth Illinois and Eighth Missouri and Millard's battery, and in the morning fiercely attacked the enemy's left wing. They went into the fight at the double quick with tremendous shouts, and did horrible execution. By ten o'clock they had driven the rebels back two miles. At about ten o'clock the rebels were reinforced, and for a few minutes our men were forced to yield.

The other divisions of General Buell's army now appeared, and at once became fully engaged. For two hours all the destructive elements of the earth seemed to be striving for the mastery on this fatal field, but at last the Southern chivalry broke and fled in all directions.

General Buell followed the flying foe with 12,000 troops, mostly cavalry, smiting without mercy those who would not surrender.

He was reported to have taken Corinth, with all its immense stores of arms and ammunition.

The rebel troops were mostly from Texas, Mississippi and Louisiana, with many from Georgia and Alabama.

Our informants say that they could ride through the battle field where our forces were posted, but the dead were so thick in the enemy's lines that they could not do it there. They assure us that the rebels occupied our camps on Sunday night and took care of our sick and wounded, destroying nothing—expecting confidently to have our entire army the next day. They thought the battle already fought and won.

On Monday General McClernand cut his way through the enemy that hat had surrounded him. Most of his troops behaved with great gallantry; but the Fiftieth Ohio were ordered to the rear in disgrace, for refusing to fight.

Our infoamants state that John C. Breckinridge is taken prisoner. They say they saw him pass to the general headquarters.

THE TROOPS ENGAGED.

List of the Officers of Those Regiments Especially Mentioned by the Correspondents.

We have given the names of the field officers of those regiments specially mentioned by the correspondents as having been actively engaged in the fight. Of course this does not constitute the force under General Grant. There appears to be a mistake about the Fourteenth Indiana regiment, which was acting under Gen. Shields at Winchester, and is still in the same command.

GEN. GRANT'S STAFF.

Chief of Staff.........} Col. J. D. Webster.
Chief of Engineers.......}
Assistant Adjutant General...Captain John A. Rawlings.
Aid.............Captain Clark B. Lagow.
Aid.............Captain Wm. S. Hillyer.
Volunteer Aid.........Major John Riggin, Jr.
Chief Quartermaster.........Captain R. B. Hatch.
Chief Commissary.........Captain W. W. Leland.
Ordnance Officer.........Captain W. F. Brink.
Medical Director.........Sur. James Simons, U. S. A.
Medical Purveyor.........Asst. Sur. J. P. Taggart, U.S.A.
Paymaster.........Major I. N. Cook.
Aid and Special Scout.........Capt. Irving W. Carson, killed.
Commissary of Subsistence.........Captain Du Barry.
Aid*.........Captain R. L. Shelly.
Aid*.........Captain Wm. O'Donnell.

* These officers were sent specially from General McClellan's staff to join that of General Grant.

Nearly every one of the above officers left the position around the General Commanding, and headed some portion of the forces during the heaviest part of the battle.

ILLINOIS TROOPS.

EIGHTH ILLINOIS VOLUNTEERS.
Colonel.........Frank L. Rhodes.
Lieutenant Colonel.........John P. Post.
Major.........G. M. Bruce.
Adjutant.........Wm. C. Clark.

ELEVENTH ILLINOIS VOLUNTEERS.
Colonel (Brig. Gen.).........W. H. L. Wallace, killed.
Lieut. Col., commanding.........T. E. G. Ransom.*
Major.........Garrett Nevins, wounded.
Adjutant.........C. E. Dickey.

* Lieut. Col. Ransom was wounded at Fort Donelson, where the regiment was so severely cut up.

FIFTEENTH ILLINOIS VOLUNTEERS.
Colonel.........T. J. Turner.
Lieutenant Colonel.........E. F. Welles.
Major.........Wm. R. Goddard, killed.
Adjutant.........C. C. Clark.

EIGHTEENTH ILLINOIS VOLUNTEERS.
Colonel.........M. K. Lawler.*
Lieutenant Colonel.........Thomas H. Burgers.*
Major (Acting Colonel).........S. Eaton, fatally wounded.
Adjutant.........——

* These officers were wounded at Fort Donelson, and were not present on this occasion.

TWENTY-FIRST ILLINOIS VOLUNTEERS.
Colonel.........J. W. S. Alexander.
Lieutenant Colonel.........George W. Peck.
Major.........Warren E. McMakin.
Adjutant.........C. B. Steele.

This regiment was originally commanded by General Grant when he was simply a Volunteer Colonel.

THIRTY-SECOND ILLINOIS VOLUNTEERS.
Colonel.........J. Logan,* severely wounded.
Lieutenant Colonel.........J. W. Ress.
Major.........William Hunter, killed.
Adjutant.........James F. Dresh.

* The Colonel of this regiment is from Macoupin county, Illinois, and is not the John A. Logan, member of Congress.

FORTY-SIXTH ILLINOIS VOLUNTEERS.
Colonel.........John A. Davis, mortally wounded.
Lieutenant Colonel.........John J. Jones.
Major.........Benjamin Dornblasser.
Adjutant.........T. S. Rutherford.

FORTY-EIGHTH ILLINOIS VOLUNTEERS.
Colonel.........Hon. I. N. Haynie, M. C., wounded.
Lieutenant Colonel.........William W. Sandford.
Major.........M. Mayfield.
Adjutant.........William Prescott.

This regiment suffered somewhat at Fort Donelson, where they lost their former Lieutenant Colonel.

FIFTY-SECOND ILLINOIS VOLUNTEERS.
Colonel (Acting Brig. Gen.).........T. W. Sweeney, wounded.
Lieutenant Colonel.........J. S. Willson.
Major.........Henry Stark.
Adjutant.........E. J. Allen.

FIFTY-FIFTH ILLINOIS VOLUNTEERS.
Colonel (Acting Brig. Gen.).........Davis Stuart, wounded.
Lieutenant Colonel.........—— ——
Major.........—— ——
Adjutant.........—— ——

FIFTY-SEVENTH ILLINOIS VOLUNTEERS.
Colonel.........S. D. Baldwin.
Lieutenant Colonel.........F. J. Hurlburt.
Major.........N. B. Page, (killed.)
Adjutant.........N. E. Hahn.

OHIO VOLUNTEERS.

FOURTEENTH OHIO VOLUNTEERS.
Colonel.........James B. Stedman.
Lieutenant Colonel.........G. P. Este.
Major.........Paul Edwards.
Adjutant.........E. D. Brapley.

These officers were also under Gen. McClellan in Virginia.

FORTY-EIGHTH OHIO VOLUNTEERS.
Colonel.........Peter J. Sullivan.
Lieutenant Colonel.........Job Reeder Parker.
Major.........James Wise.
Adjutant.........Robert McGill.

FIFTIETH OHIO VOLUNTEERS.
Colonel.........Stephen McGroarty.
Lieutenant Colonel.........Michael P. Noland.
Major.........—— ——
Adjutant.........—— ——

FIFTY-SEVENTH OHIO VOLUNTEERS.
Colonel.........William Mungen.
Lieutenant Colonel.........J. N. Hathaway.
Major.........S. B. Walker.
Adjutant.........O. S. Price.

SIXTY-EIGHTH OHIO VOLUNTEERS.
Colonel.........Samuel H. Steedman.
Lieutenant Colonel.........R. K. Scott.
Major.........John S. Snook.
Adjutant.........George E. Welles.

SEVENTY-FIRST OHIO VOLUNTEERS.
Colonel.........Rodney Mason, wounded.
Lieutenant Colonel.........—— Kyle, mortally w'nded
Major.........George W. Anderson.
Adjutant.........—— ——

SEVENTY-SECOND OHIO VOLUNTEERS.
Colonel.........R. P. Buckland.
Lieutenant Colonel.........Leroy Crockett.
Major.........—— ——
Adjutant.........Eugene A. Rawson.

SEVENTY-SEVENTH OHIO VOLUNTEERS.
Colonel.........J. Hildebrand.
Lieutenant Colonel.........—— ——
Major.........Ben. D. Fearing.
Adjutant.........Thos. J. Cochran.

FIFTH OHIO CAVALRY.
Colonel.........Wm. H. H. Taylor.
Lieutenant Colonel.........Thomas T. Heath.
First Major.........Frederick Scherer.
Second Major.........—— ——
Third Major.........—— ——
Regimental Adjutant.........Spencer Franklin.

FIFTH OHIO BATTERY.
Captain.........A. Hickenlooper.
First Lieutenant.........William P. Chapman.
Second Lieutenant.........Conrad Gansevoort.

FOURTEENTH OHIO BATTERY.
Captain.........J. B. Burrows.
First Lieutenant.........—— ——
Second Lieutenant.........—— ——

INDIANA TROOPS.

TWENTY-FIFTH INDIANA VOLUNTEERS.
Colonel.........James C. Veatch.
Lieutenant Colonel.........Wm. H. Morgan, sev'ly w'd.
Major.........John W. Foster.
Adjutant.........Wm. H. Walker, Jr.

THIRTY-FIRST INDIANA VOLUNTEERS.
Colonel (Act. Brig. Gen.).........Chas. Cruft, wounded.
Lieutenant Colonel.........Fred'k Aru.
Major.........—— ——
Adjutant.........—— ——

THIRTY-SECOND INDIANA VOLUNTEERS.
Colonel.........Augustus Willich.
Lieutenant Colonel.........Hy. Von Debra.
Major.........F. W. Schnakenburg.
Adjutant.........Carl Schmidtt.

This is the gallant German regiment that fought so bravely at Munfordsville, Ky.

THIRTY-SIXTH INDIANA VOLUNTEERS.
Colonel.........Wm. Grose.
Lieutenant Colonel.........O. H. P. Carey.
Major.........Thos. W. Bennett.
Adjutant.........—— ——

FORTY-FOURTH INDIANA VOLUNTEERS.
Colonel.........H. B. Reed.
Lieutenant Colonel.........S. J. Stoughton.
Major.........—— ——
Adjutant.........Hon. Chas. Case, M. C.

FIFTY-SEVENTH INDIANA VOLUNTEERS.
Colonel.........Cyrus L. Hindes.
Lieutenant Colonel.........F. A. Hardin.
Major.........—— ——
Adjutant.........—— ——

KENTUCKY TROOPS.

SEVENTEENTH KENTUCKY VOLUNTEERS.
Colonel.........J. H. McHenry, Jr., wounded.
Lieutenant Colonel.........A. M. Stout, wounded.
Major.........J. Calhoun.
Adjutant.........E. L. Starling.

The Officers of the Gunboats.

No one should overlook the services of the gunboats Tyler and Lexington in this memorable battle. We give the names of the gallant officers of the Tyler, but are unable to give those of the Lexington at present.

GUNBOAT TYLER—NINE GUNS.
Lieutenant Commanding—W. Gwin, U. S. N.
Masters—First, Edward Shaw; Second, Jason Goudy; Third, James Martin.
Pilots—John Sebastian, David Hiner.
Engineers—Chief, Samuel Goble; First Assistant, D. Edward Weaver; Second Assistant, Edward W. Goble; Third Assistant, Oscar S. Davis.
Armorer—Elihu Stevens.
Acting Paymaster—W. B. Coleman.
Assistant Surgeon—T. H. Kearney.
Carpenter—Thomas Russell.
Gunner—Herman Peters, U. S. N.
Master's Mates—Ferdinand T. Coleman, Edward D. Brainard.

Help for the Wounded Soldiers of the West.

Mr. James A. Roosevelt, of No. 94 Maiden lane, has received a despatch from the Western Sanitary Commission, asking for shirts, drawers, sheets, &c., for the army of the West. The following is the despatch:—

WESTERN SANITARY COMMISSION, } ST. LOUIS, April 9, 1862. }
JAS. A. ROOSEVELT, 94 Maiden lane, New York:—
Send us shirts, drawers and sheets; all you can. Great battle. Sending four hospital steamers to Gen. Grant.
J. E. YEATMAN, President.

The charitably disposed are thus given a fine opportunity to display their benevolence by sending goods or money in accordance with the above appeal. Mr. Roosevelt will forward to the West anything that may be left at his place, No. 94 Maiden lane.

Or may be sent direct to Joseph E. Yeatman, President Western Sanitary Committee, St. Louis, per Adams' Express.

Supplies for the Wounded.

ST. LOUIS, April 10, 1862.

Two steamers, fitted up as floating hospitals, left here yesterday for the Tennessee river, and large contributions of all kinds of supplies are being made to-day to furnish two more, which will leave this evening. The Western Sanitary Commission is moving earnestly and with energy in this matter, and every effort will be made for the speedy relief of our wounded soldiers at Pittsburg Landing.

Colonel Kelton, Assistant Adjutant General, and General Ketchum are in charge here while General Halleck is in the field.

CHICAGO, April 10, 1862.

Every preparation is being made here for the reception of our wounded from Pittsburg.

Five thousand prisoners are expected to arrive here to-night from Island No 10.

LOUISVILLE, April 10, 1862.

Forty physicians and nurses arrived from Frankfort this evening, and will immediately leave on the steamer Autocrat for Fort Donelson and Pittsburg Landing. Several other boats, with similar aid, are passing down the river from this city and elsewhere.

BOSTON, April 10, 1862.

The Board of Brokers to-day voted $500 in aid of the wounded at Pittsburg Landing.

IMPORTANT FROM ISLAND NO. 10.

One Major General, Three Brigadiers and Five Thousand Soldiers Taken Prisoners—An Immense Quantity of Military Stores Captured.

ST. LOUIS, April 10, 1862.

A special despatch to the *Republican*, from Island No. 10, says that two hundred hogsheads of sugar and several hundred barrels of molsses, eighty cannon, four hundred wagons, one hundred and twenty-six horses, sixty mules, five thousand stand of arms, thirty pieces of light artillery, and great quantities of blankets, clothing, &c., have fallen into our hands.

The total number of prisoners captured is five thousand, with one Major General (Makall), and three Brigadier Generals (Gault, Walker and Schaum). The prisoners are being embarked as rapidly as possible for Illinois.

We also took about fifty-six thousand solid shot, and immense quantities of ammunition.

CAIRO, April 10, 1862.

With a few exceptions the whole rebel force around Island No. 10 are now prisoners. An attempt was made by them to cross Lake Redfoot on rafts, but they were surrounded and compelled to surrender.

Thirteen guns were taken instead of the number previously reported.

The prisoners say that seventy were killed on the Island by our mortars.

PROCLAMATION BY THE PRESIDENT.

Thanks for the Victories and Prayers for the Restoration of Peace.

WASHINGTON, April 10, 1862.

It has pleased Almighty God to vouchsafe signal victories to the land and naval forces engaged in suppressing an internal rebellion, and at the same time to avert from our country the dangers of foreign intervention and invasion.

It is therefore recommended to the people of the United States that, at their next weekly assemblages in their accustomed places of public worship, which shall occur after the notice of this Proclamation shall have been received, they especially acknowledge and render thanks to our Heavenly Father for these inestimable blessings; that they then and there implore spiritual consolation in behalf of all those who have been brought into affliction by the casualties and calamities of sedition and civil war, and that they reverently invoke the Divine guidance for our national counsels, to the end that they may speedily result in the restoration of peace, harmony and unity throughout our borders, and hasten the estalishment of fraternal relations among all the countries of the earth.

In witness whereof I have hereunto set my hand and caused the seal of the United States to be affixed.

Done at the city of Washington, this tenth day of April, in the year of our Lord one thousand eight hundred and sixty-two, and of the independence of the United States the eighty-sixth.

ABRAHAM LINCOLN.

By the President—WM. H. SEWARD, Secretary of State.

Te Deum in Honor of the Victories.

BOSTON, April 10, 1862.

Resolutions were unanimously adopted in both branches of the Legislature to-day, in furtherance of the suggestions of the Secretary of War, inviting the citizens of the Commonwealth to join, on Sunday next, in a general *Te Deum* in honor of our recent victories, and congratulating the Western States upon the valiant deeds of their soldiers in the Valley of the Mississippi.

Governor Andrew has ordered a salute of one hundred guns to be fired to-morrow at noon in honor of the recent victories.

National Salute in Honor of the Victory.

PROVIDENCE, April 10, 1862.

By order of Lieutenant Governor Arnold a national salute was fired here this afternoon, in honor of the great victory in Tennessee.

The Reported Occupation of Corinth Not Confirmed.

WASHINGTON, April 10, 1862.

Up to four o'clock this afternoon the government had received no official despatch confirmatory of the occupation of Corinth by our troops.

Movements of General Halleck.

CHICAGO, April 10, 1862.

General Halleck passed Cairo to-day, *en route* for Pittsburg Landing.

Telegraphic Communication Opened Between Louisville and Savannah, Tenn.

LOUISVILLE, April 10, 1862.

Telegraphic communication was opened between Savannah, Tenn., and this city this afternoon.

Irishmen in Charleston.

The Charleston papers publish the names of the officers of the St. Patrick's and Hibernian Societies of that city, just elected at the annual meetings. It appears that the Irish organizations still exist, notwithstanding the war. The St. Patrick's Society elected the following officers:—M. F. Moloney, President. T. L. Quackenbush, first Vice President. Thos. Maher, second Vice President. Dr. Leslie Owens, Treasurer. Daniel F. Twohill, Secretary. Finance Committee—P. O'Donnell, John O'Mara, Michael Gannon, B. Rodlin and John Burke, Jr. Relief Committee—Garret Byrne, John Barry, Timothy Meenahan, Michael Kennedy, Thomas Murphy, William Eldrd. On Letters—John D. Kennedy, James Wallace, Michael Feehan.

The new officers of the Hibernian Society are as follows:—

S. K. Robinson, President. W. H. Gilliland, Vice President. W. P. O'Hara, Treasurer. A. A. Allernong, Secretary. John J. Ferrall, Keeper of Hall. Committee on Finance—J. W. Caldwell, J. L. Patterson, A. McKensie, E. P. Milliken, J. W. Brownfield. Committe on Relief—W. H. Gilliland, W. H. Houston, W. McBurney, E. M. Carey, John F. O'Neill. Committee on Ground—Thomas Ryan, C. H. Symonton, Andrew Cunningham.

Postal Affairs.

[From Holbrook's United States Mail.]

ABUSE OF THE MAILS.—But few persons are aware of the extent to which the mail and post office facilities afforded by the government are employed to answer the ends of swindlers, and for immoral and vicious purposes. One of the latest dodges of these rogues is the publication of advertisements in country papers, signed by names somewhat similar to those of well known and respectable New York firms, promising, on the receipt of a certain sum, to send by mail some article, such as a gold watch, books, &c., worth four times the amount. Of course the goods are never sent, and the luckless victims either never hear anything further of their investments, or the sharpers answer their complaints by a lying letter, asserting that the remittance never reached them. Other scoundrels make use of the post office for the circulation of obscene books and prints, and flood the country with their circulars, offering their filthy wares for sale. We understand that a quietus will ere long be given to the disgusting traffic of these latter gentry, by the passing of a law authorizing postmasters to exclude these corrupt publications from the mails.

MAILS FOR CALIFORNIA, OREGON AND WASHINGTON TERRITORY.—The editor of this paper and the Postmaster of New York are in the daily receipt of letters asking how the mails are sent to California, &c., how often it is despatched, the dates of the departure of steamers, &c., &c. It seems that, notwithstanding the overland mail has been in operation since last June, and Congress has expressly forbidden the transmission of the above mails otherwise than across the continent, people generally, and even New York merchants engaged in the California trade, suppose that their letters are still sent by steamer. To all such we wish to state, in the plainest terms, that the mails to the Pacific States are sent overland, that they are despatched twice each day from the New York office, and six times a week from St. Joseph, Mo.

COUNTERFEITS.—Last evening counterfeit fives on the Merchant's Bank of Albany made their appearance Through the efficiency of the telegraphic operator at the police headquarters. Mr. Chapin, the police were notified and the merchants throughout the city put on their guard. But few were passed.

LARGE DEMAND FOR LOBBYING.—The Rochester *Democrat* says that Simon B. Jewett, of that city, has brought a suit for $100,000 against the New York Central Railroad for services rendered during the effort to carry through the consolidation act, and has retained as his counsel Hon. H. R. Selden and Hon. S. E. Church.

NEWS FROM THE RAPPAHANNOCK.

Health of the Troops—Reception of the News of the Recent Victories—Brentsville Occupied by Our Forces—Movements of the Rebels, &c., &c.

MANASSAS, April 10, 1862.

Notwithstanding the terrible storm of the last three days, the health of the troops in the Department of the Rappahannock is unusually good. A few are suffering from colds, but otherwise none have been afflicted.

The news of the capture of Island No. 10, and the victory at Pittsburg was read to the several brigades, exciting intense enthusiasm, particularly in the brigade composed principally of Western men.

The country between Manassas and Warrenton has been effectually cleared of rebel scouts, rendering foraging much less hazardous. A great amount of hay, grain and straw has been found through Prince William county, which the army is taking possession of, receipting for the same in due form.

Brentsville is occupied by our forces. Many of the inhabitants remain, but appear indifferent to the advance of the Union army.

The rebels are reported to be intrenching themselves on the south bank of the Rappahannock.

News from General Banks' Department.

EDENBURG, Va., April 10, 1862.

All is quiet. The enemy's pickets have not been seen during the severe storm of the past two days.

MOVEMENTS OF GENERAL FREMONT.

The Union Troops in Possession of Monterey and Crabbolton—The Enemy Driven Back.

WHEELING, April 10, 1862.

Hon. E. M. STANTON, Secretary of War:—

General Milroy is in possession of Monterey and Crabbolton. The enemy's mounted scouts are still in sight of Monterey. Their rear guard was driven back by our troops. They are reported fortifying themselves east of the Shenandoah Mountains. J. C. FREMONT, Major General Commanding.

IMPORTANT FROM NEW MEXICO.

Santa Fe Evacuated by the Rebels—Reported Order to the Rebels to Abandon the Territory—Forced Contributions Exacted by the Enemy, &c.

WASHINGTON, April 10, 1862.

The following was received to-day by the Secretary of War:—

KANSAS CITY, April 10, 1862.

The Santa Fe mail has arrived. The Texans, one hundred and fifty strong, had evacuated Santa Fe and were marching up the river.

It was reported that Colonel Canby had intercepted an express with orders to the commander of the Texan forces to evacuate the Territory and return to Texas.

Colonel Slough had left for Fort Union with fourteen hundred men to make a junction with Colonel Canby.

The Texans were exacting contributions and forced loans from the inhabitants. Clothing was being taken from the merchants without regard to politics or circumstances.

[Correspondence of the Missouri Republican.]

FORT UNION, March 23, 1862.

Our column, under command of Colonel Hough, is breaking up camp for a forward movement south towards the rebel forces. The Texan army occupies a strong position in the vicinity of Albuquerque, seventeen miles south of this depot, about midway between this and Fort Craig, where Colonel Canby was at last accounts. The Texans have taken up this as a strategical point, doubtless intending to march upon either column as they leave their stronghold of Forts Union or Craig, and by their superior force, which is estimated at 2,400 men and twenty-one pieces of artillery, whip one, and face about and assault the other column before they can form a junction.

It would seem that Colonel Hough and [illegible] Canby, the department commander, are [illegible], and sound men fear that this movement, one of the most difficult of military combinations, may not prove successful, and render our depot at Fort Union, which is the only supply depot left us, comparatively defenceless. I can scarcely believe, however, that Colonel Hough will march beyond supporting distance of this depot. The Texans are occupying Sante Fe, one hundred miles south of here, with from one hundred to two hundred troops.

Return of a Released Union Prisoner from Richmond.

CONDITION OF OUR SOLDIERS IN THAT CITY—NEWS OF COLONEL CORCORAN, ETC.

Colonel W. E. Woodruff, who commanded the Second regiment of Kentucky Volunteers previous to the battle of Bull run, and who was taken prisoner four days before that memorable contest, arrived in this city direct from Richmond last evening. Colonel Woodward brings intelligence of the condition of our prisoners among the rebels, and describes their treatment as most barbarous and inhuman. Colonel Corcoran is still in Richmond, and no signs of a speedy release are at all in prospect. He also brings a letter from Lieutenant John W. Dempsey, addressed to Lieutenant Connolly, of the Sixty-ninth, who has but recently returned from a lengthy incarceration. The following is the letter:—

FRIEND CONNOLLY—I expected a letter from you, but suppose you have been kept busy ever since your arrival. I wish you to call on Mrs. W. D. and tell her to have a fatigue cap made for me, two rows of buttons taken off my coat, and have a blue cord put along the outer seam of my black trowsers, and keep them until I telegraph from Fortress Monroe, and then she will meet me with them at Washington; but when that time may be I cannot tell. Can anything be done for us poor unfortunates? Yours truly. JOHN W. DEMPSEY.

The letter has been written on the back of one of Colonel Corcoran's cards, which has also been sent to Lieutenant Connolly by that gallant soldier, and which reads as follows:—

Compliments of Colonel Michael Corcoran, Sixty-ninth regiment, N. Y. S. M., who feels like a lion.

The rumor that Colonel Corcoran has been detained a prisoner longer than was expected, from the fact of a number of maps and charts having been found in his pocket, Colonel Woodruff states to be a wicked falsehood. The Union prisoners at Richmond are now confined in a dilapidated bacon house, and undergoing much hardship.

Mr. T. G. Hargous, Master's Mate, and thirty-six men, all of the frigate Congress, had arrived in Richmond.

The following Union officers have also recently arrived at the rebel capital:—

Major Steinhauser, Sixty-eighth New York.
Captain Botecher, Sixty-eighth New York.
Lieut. L. G. Camp, Sixty-eighth New York.
Lieut. Neustadter, Eighth New York.
Dr. A. C. Williams, First New York artillery.
Lieut. C. W. Tilletson, Ninety-seventh New York.

Provisions are described as exceedingly high at Richmond; coffee $1 per lb., peck of potatoes 75 cents, one dozen of eggs 40 cents, &c.

Col. Woodruff was met on his arrival in this city by Capt. Kirker, Lieut. Connolly, and other officers of the Sixty-ninth regiment, and escorted to the St. Nicholas Hotel, where he will be pleased to see any of the friends or relatives of the prisoners who have been confined with him, and give them such information as he may possess. It is the intention of the Colonel to recount his experience among the rebels in a lecture.

Coroners' Inquests.

FATAL ACCIDENT AT THE HOUSE OF REFUGE.—An inquest was held yesterday at the House of Refuge upon the body of one of the inmates, named James Verner, who was accidentally killed by falling down a flight of stairs. Deceased, it appears, was endeavoring to slide down the bannisters, when he missed his hold and fell headlong to the floor below, killing himself almost instantly. Verdict in accordance with the above facts.

A SHIP CARPENTER KILLED.—As a ship carpenter named Samuel Riley was engaged at work upon the Italian frigate in Webb's yard, at the foot of Fifth street, yesterday morning, he fell from a stage, and was so severely injured that he died in a few minutes afterwards. The Coroner was notified to hold an inquest upon the body.

SUICIDE OF A FEMALE.—Early last evening a female named Ann Robertson, aged twenty-five years, committed suicide at 157 Ludlow street, by taking laudanum. No cause could be ascertained for committing so rash an act. The coroner was notified.

Superior Court—Part First.

Before Hon. Judge White.

Caleb Marshall vs. William Koblenk.—This was an action on a note of hand, and the jury returned a verdict for plaintiff for $1,030.

IMPORTANT FROM YORKTOWN.

One Hundred Thousand Rebels Concentrated on the Peninsula.

The Enemy's Position Defended by Nearly Five Hundred Cannon.

General Joe Johnston and Jeff. Davis in Command of the Rebels.

Reception of the News of the Victories in the Southwest.

Intense Enthusiasm Among the Union Troops.

Gen. McClellan's Army Eager to Meet the Foe,

&c., &c., &c.

NEAR YORKTOWN, April 9—1:20 P. M.

The weather still continues unfavorable for military operations. It has been raining for nearly two days. The creeks are very much swollen, and the low grounds covered with water, making the roads almost impassable for empty wagons.

Information received shows that the rebels have a force of sixty thousand, which is rapidly being added to by troops from the neighborhood of Richmond, which is one day from Yorktown by railroad and river, *they having four steamers and sixteen transports in use, and by the time the roads are in condition for the Union army to move the rebels may be able to meet them with one hundred thousand men.*

The flower of their army, with the best arms, are in a strongly intrenched position. Previous to our troops occupying the present position, the military authorities had no means of ascertaining the extent of the rebel works.

Information obtained through deserting contrabands and other sources show that *the enemy have nearly five hundred guns,* some of them of the largest calibre. The rebel General Johnston, with some of his forces, has arrived, and taken command in person, showing that they intend making a desperate resistance to the advance of our troops at every point. *Their intrenchments extend entirely across the peninsula from the James to the York river.*

The cheering news from the Western Department arrived here to-day, and our troops are wild with enthusiasm over the result, and are anxious to be led to active similar deeds of valor.

Our Baltimore Correspondence.

BALTIMORE, April 9, 1862.

The Rebels at Richmond Fully Aware of the Movements of General McClellan Before Richmond—The Measures which They have Taken to Arrest His March—General Jos. E. Johnston in Command at Yorktown, with One Hundred Thousand Men—[illegible]—the Defences of Yorktown, &c.

The accounts of the progress of affairs at Yorktown which have reached this city through channels believed to be reliable, differ materially from the accounts furnished by the government. It was known at Richmond when the bulk of the Union army of the Potomac moved from Manassas to Washington; it was known there when the *corps d'armee* had landed and were assembled at Fortress Monroe; it was known there when General McClellan and his staff arrived at the Fortress; and it was known there when the march on Yorktown commenced, and what number of troops General McClellan had wherewith to make the attack. These facts convinced the Confederate government at Richmond that their hour was come, unless they took instant measures to arrest the march of General McClellan. The fortifications of Yorktown, which I have minutely described in former letters, were all that could be desired, both as to strength and armament. But Gen. Magruder had as yet only 35,000 troops. The withdrawal of such a large number of Union troops from Manassas rendered it unnecessary to keep the main body of the army of the Rappahannock along that stream, and from that army accordingly Gen. Magruder has been largely reinforced Troops have been arriving at Yorktown from Richmond and Gordonsville every day for the last week. It is believed that Gen. Jos. E. Johnston and Jeff. Davis are both at Yorktown, and that General Johnston is in command. The number of rebel troops there cannot be less than 100,000.

NEWS FROM FORTRESS MONROE.

BALTIMORE, April 10, 1862.

The Old Point boat has arrived.

The news of the capture of Island No. 10 caused great rejoicing and enthusiasm.

The storm still continued, but had somewhat abated toward evening.

Reports from the army represent our brave forces facing exposure undauntedly, and meeting it with characteristic ingenuity in the way of improvised shelter. The enthusiasm and anxiety to meet the enemy were unabated, and confidence in General McClellan was unbounded. Though the storm at this time is unfortunate, the time has not been lost, and the retreat of Magruder and his forces, or their defeat, is about as certain as any possible future event.

The prospect of clearing up is looked for with anxiety at Old Point, in the belief that sunshine and the Merrimac will come together. All seem confident that she will be captured or sunk if she comes out.

WASHINGTON, April 10, 1862.

The latest news received from Cherrystone reports everything quiet in the vicinity of Fortress Monroe. A strong wind was blowing and the sea running very high.

Snow at Philadelphia.

PHILADELPHIA, April 10, 1862.

Twelve inches of snow fell last night, but is rapidly disappearing under sunshine.

Court of Appeals.

ALBANY, April 10, 1862.

The following is the calendar of the Court of Appeals for Friday, April 11:—66, 68, 69, 70, 71, 72, 73, 74, 75, 76, 77.

Drill of the Eleventh Regiment N. Y. S. M.

The following regimental order explains itself:—

REGIMENTAL ORDER—NO. 4.

HEADQUARTERS ELEVENTH REGIMENT N. Y. S. M., } WASHINGTON RIFLES, NEW YORK, April 4, 1862. }

This regiment will parade in fatigue dress, fully armed and equipped, with knapsacks and overcoats rolled on, with one day's rations for battalion drill at East New York, on Thursday, the 17th instant.

Regimental line will be formed at the regimental armory, at eight o'clock A. M precisely.

Field music and non-commissed staff will report to the Adjutant fifteen minutes before formation.

Field and staff officers will report to the Colonel, mounted, at the same time and place.

Officers and non-commissioned officers of this regiment will assemble in fatigue dress, with side arms, at the regimental armory, at eight o'clock P. M., on Thursday, the 10th, and Monday, the 14th instant, for general instruction and military improvement. By order of

F. VILMAR, Adjutant. J. MAIDHOF, Colonel.

THE NEW YORK HERALD.

WHOLE NO. 9349. — NEW YORK, TUESDAY, APRIL 15, 1862.—TRIPLE SHEET — PRICE TWO CENTS.

SITUATIONS WANTED—FEMALES.

For Other Wants See Eighth Page.

A YOUNG GIRL DESIRES A SITUATION AS NURSE and seamstress, or would instruct children in the preparatory branches of an English education; is willing to make herself generally useful, and has no objection to the country. Apply at 19 State st., New York.

A RESPECTABLE YOUNG GERMAN GIRL WISHES a situation in a private family going to California, as a seamstress; can speak German, English and French; can bring good city reference. Inquire of Miss Hoffman, 135 Pitt st., N. Y.

A SITUATION WANTED—BY A RESPECTABLE WOMAN, as first class cook; she thoroughly understands her business in all its branches; can give the best of city reference. Apply until engaged at 491 6th av.

A PROTESTANT GIRL WANTS A SITUATION, AS nurse or seamstress; was three years in her last place; has good city reference. Apply for two days at No. 109 West 25th st.

A RESPECTABLE YOUNG GIRL WISHES A SITUATION as waitress; the best of city reference from her last place. Can be seen for two days at 109 East 19th st., corner 3d av.

A SITUATION WANTED IN HOBOKEN—OR A SHORT distance in the country, by a respectable young woman, as laundress and chambermaid; do general housework if wanted, in a small family; the best of reference from her last place. Call at No. 8 Willow st., third house from the riding school, first floor, Hoboken, for two days.

A SITUATION WANTED—BY A YOUNG WOMAN, AS chambermaid and waitress, or waitress alone. Can be seen at 42 West 30th st., near Broadway; has good city reference.

A SITUATION WANTED—BY A YOUNG WOMAN, TO cook, wash and iron, or to do general housework. Good city reference. Call for two days at 14 Clarkson st., first floor, front room.

A PROTESTANT GIRL WANTS A SITUATION AS laundress, or as chambermaid and laundress; understands all kinds of fine washing and ironing and fluting; best city reference. Can be seen at 38 West 13th st., between 5th and 6th avs., for two days.

A SITUATION WANTED—BY A RESPECTABLE WOMAN, as first class cook; understands her business in all its branches; best city reference. Can be seen for two days at 87 3d st., second floor, corner of Lexington and 3d av.

A SITUATION WANTED—BY A HIGHLY RESPECTABLE and well recommended young woman, as first class cook in a hotel, boarding house or respectable restaurant; understands all kinds of jellies, game, &c.; is an excellent pastry cook; no objection to go to the country. Call at 237 Elizabeth st., first floor, in the rear.

A SITUATION WANTED—BY A RESPECTABLE GIRL, as chambermaid and waitress or to take care of children; best city reference can be furnished from her last place. Call for two days at 159 av. C, corner of 10th st., second floor.

A RESPECTABLE WOMAN WANTS A SITUATION; is a good cook, and willing to make herself useful; would assist in the washing. City reference. Call for two days at 82 West 20th st., between 6th and 7th aves., front basement.

A SITUATION WANTED—BY A MIDDLE AGED woman, to do general housework or go out by the day in a small family; a good home preferred to high wages. City reference. Call for three days at 87 28th st., between 6th and 7th avs., in the rear, top floor.

A STEADY, INDUSTRIOUS YOUNG WOMAN DESIRES a situation as cook, washer and ironer, or to do general housework; understands her duties thoroughly. Best of city reference. Call for two days at 469 4th st., rear.

A RESPECTABLE WOMAN WANTS A SITUATION TO do general housework in a small private family. The best of city reference can be given. Call for two days at 154 Norfolk st., first floor, in the rear.

A SITUATION WANTED—BY A YOUNG GIRL, AS chambermaid and waiter. Has the best of city reference. Can be seen for two days at 126 26th st., between 7th and 8th avs., top floor, back room.

A SITUATION WANTED—BY A YOUNG WOMAN, AS first class cook; understands all kinds of pastry, jellies, &c. Seven years' city reference. Can be seen at 164 East 9th st.

A YOUNG WOMAN WISHES A SITUATION AS FIRST class laundress; understands the doing of all kinds of fine washing and French fluting in the neatest style; has no objection to go to the country with a family; has the best of city reference. Can be seen for two days at 115 West 15th st., near 6th av.

A SITUATION WANTED—BY A NEAT, TIDY YOUNG girl, as chambermaid and to take care of children, or would do waiting; is willing to make herself useful; good reference. Call for two days at 96 West 20th st.

A SITUATION WANTED—BY A RESPECTABLE WOMAN, to cook, wash and iron in a private family; she is an excellent washer and ironer and a first rate baker; she thoroughly understands her business in all its branches; has no objection to go a short distance in the country; has the best of city reference. Call for two days at 139 29th st., between 2d and 3d avs.

A SITUATION WANTED—BY A RESPECTABLE young girl, to do housework in a small private family; is willing and obliging; is a first rate washer and ironer and a good plain cook; would have no objection to go to the country for the summer; has the best of city reference from her last place. Can be seen for two days at 437 7th av.

A RESPECTABLE GIRL WANTS A SITUATION TO DO chamberwork and waiting or housework in a small private family. Has good reference from her last place. Call for two days at 132 West 33d st., near 7th av.

A YOUNG WOMAN WANTS A SITUATION TO DO the housework of a small private family or would go as nurse. Can give good city reference. Can be seen for two days at 23 Carroll st., first floor, Brooklyn.

A SITUATION WANTED—BY A YOUNG PROTESTANT girl, as good plain cook, washer and ironer or as chambermaid and waiter. Can be seen for two days at 69 Prospect st., Brooklyn.

A SITUATION WANTED—BY A RESPECTABLE GIRL, as chambermaid and to do fine washing and ironing; would do housework for a small family. Has no objection to go in the country. Good city reference. Can be seen for two days at 211 West 16th st., between 7th and 8th avs.

A RESPECTABLE COLORED WOMAN WANTS A situation as laundress. Can give good city reference. Can be seen for two days, at 78 East Thirty-second st., between Fourth and Lexington aves.

A RESPECTABLE GIRL WISHES A SITUATION TO do general housework or as laundress. No objection to go a short distance in the country. Can be seen for two days at 253 7th av., between 26th and 27th sts.

A SITUATION WANTED—AS LAUNDRESS AND chambermaid, by a young woman who has lived in that capacity in one of the first families in this city, from whom she can furnish unexceptionable reference. Can be seen at 109 West 20th st., between 6th and 7th avenues.

A YOUNG WOMAN WISHES A SITUATION AS CHILDREN'S nurse and plain sewer, or would do chamberwork and assist in washing and ironing; has no objections to the country for the summer. Has the best of city reference. Call at 130 West 20th st., between 7th and 8th avs.

A RESPECTABLE GIRL WANTS A SITUATION IN A private family as cook and good washer and ironer; is willing and very obliging. Call at 21 West 12th st., in the store, for two days.

A SITUATION WANTED—BY A RESPECTABLE young girl, as chambermaid and waitress. City reference if required. Call at 294 West 17th st., between 9th and 10th avs.

A RESPECTABLE YOUNG WOMAN WANTS A SITUATION as chambermaid and laundress; can do French fluting; understands her business. Has no objection to the country. Good city reference. Call at 126 East 39th st., near 3d ave.

A RESPECTABLE GIRL WISHES A SITUATION TO do general housework in a small private family. Good city references. Call at 167 Smith st., Brooklyn.

A SITUATION WANTED—BY A RESPECTABLE young girl, lately arrived from Europe, to do general housework in a small family; has no objection to go a short distance in the country. Call at 360 2d ave., near 23d st., for two days.

A SITUATION WANTED—BY A FIRST CLASS COOK; understands cooking in all its branches, jelly, pastry and all kinds of soups and game; lived in the best families; either first class family or boarding house. Best of references. Call for two days at 59 East Houston st., in the dry goods store.

A RESPECTABLE YOUNG GIRL WANTS A SITUATION as chambermaid and fine washer and ironer, or as waitress, or would do the general housework in a small family; best city reference from her last place. Call for two days at 163 30th st, first floor, front room.

A YOUNG WOMAN WHO IS A FIRST RATE WASHER and ironer, wishes the washing of a few gentleman or of a small family, at her own house; best reference given, if required. Call at 115 East 37th st., top floor, front room.

A SITUATION WANTED—BY A RESPECTABLE MARried woman, as wet nurse; good city reference. Call for two days at 283 6th st., near Lewis st.

A SITUATION WANTED—BY A RESPECTABLE girl, as good plain cook; is a most excellent washer and ironer, and a good bread, biscuit, pie and cake baker; would do the work of a small private family; country and city reference. Call at 95 West 19th st., between 6th and 7th avs.

A SITUATION WANTED—BY A YOUNG WOMAN; IS a good cook, washer and ironer; best city reference given; also a chambermaid and waiter. Call for two days at 89 West 19th st., in the basement.

A SITUATION WANTED—BY A YOUNG WOMAN, AS first rate cook and excellent washer and ironer in a small private family; no objection to the country; two years' reference. Can be seen for two days at 240 1st av., between 14th and 15th sts., first floor.

A RESPECTABLE GIRL WANTS A SITUATION AS wet nurse; has the best city reference. Can be seen for two days at 60 West Washington place, first floor.

A RESPECTABLE YOUNG GIRL WANTS A SITUation to do general housework; no objection to go a short distance in the country; the best of city reference can be given. Call for two days at 213 East 23d st., top floor, front room.

A RESPECTABLE YOUNG WOMAN WISHES A situation as nurse and seamstress, or chambermaid and seamstress. Can give good city reference. Has no objection to the country. Can be seen for two days at 444 East 4th st., in the rear.

A SITUATION WANTED—BY A RESPECTABLE young girl, to cook, wash and iron or to do general housework in a small private family. The best of city reference can be given. Can be seen for two days by calling at 27 Desbrosses st.

A RESPECTABLE GIRL WISHES A SITUATION AS laundress; has no objection to do fine washing, ironing and chamberwork. Has the best of city reference. Can be seen for two days at 21 Washington square.

THE IMPORTANT OPERATIONS ON THE MISSISSIPPI.

Appearance of Island No. 10—The Gunboats, Transports, Land Batteries, &c., at the Time of the Surrender.

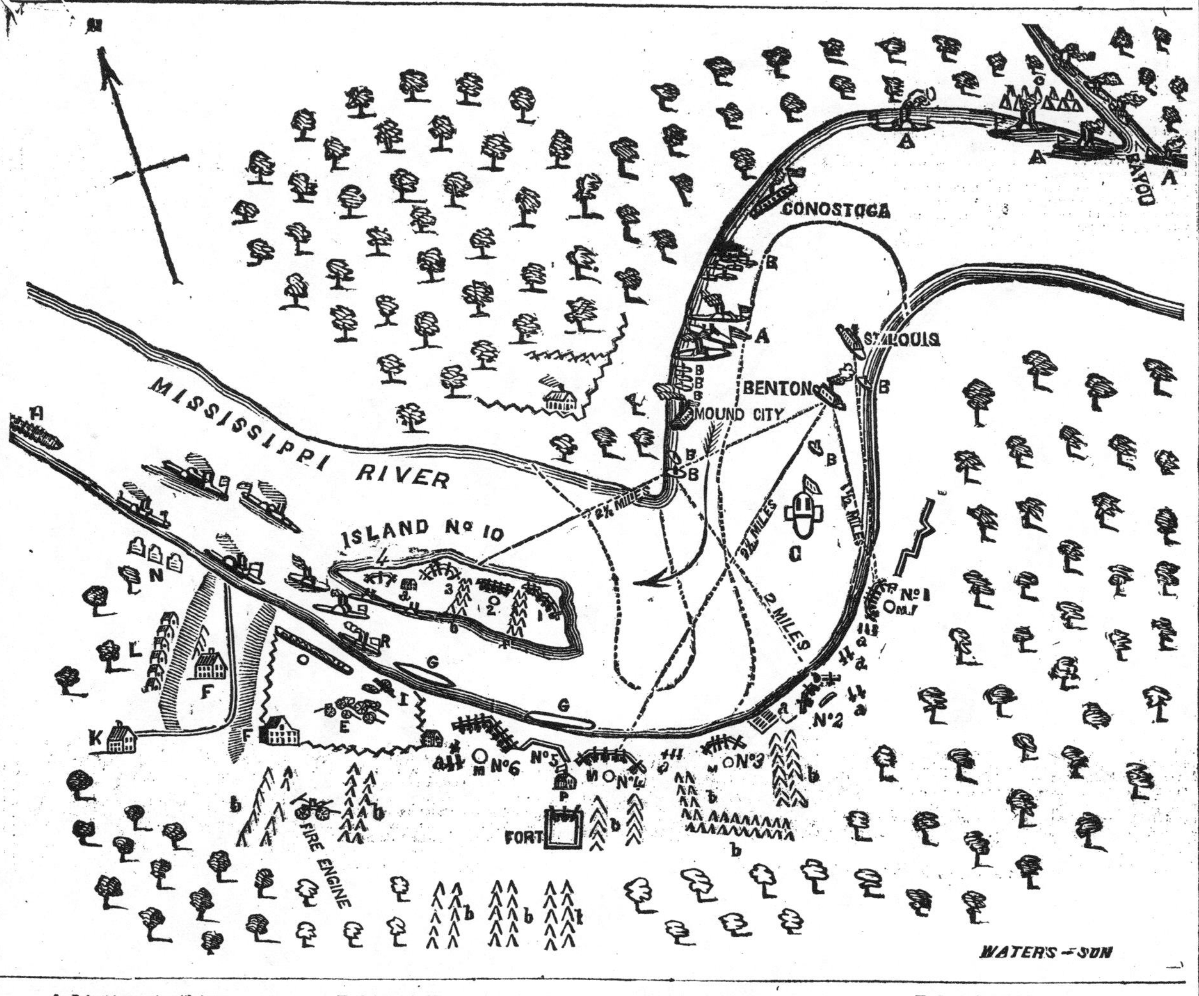

A—Federal transports, with troops.
B—Mortar boats.
C—Rebel steamer De Soto, with flag of truce.
D—Tug going to truce boat.
E—Deserted caissons.
F—Ordnance buildings.
G—Wharf boats.
H—Floating battery.
I—Shattered field piece.
K—Crudup's house.
L—Crudup's negro shanties.
M—Magazines.
a—Guns not mounted.
b—Rebel encampments.
c—Federal encampments.
N—Group of grave stones.
O—Piles of commissary stores.
P—Rebel headquarters.
R—Steamer Grampus, since sunk.

SITUATIONS WANTED—FEMALES.

A PROTESTANT GIRL WANTS A PLACE IN A SMALL family. Inquire at 89 Ridge street.

A SIUATION WANTED—BY A YOUNG WOMAN, TO cook, wash and iron. Good city reference, Call for one day at 129 Court st., near Wyckoff, Brooklyn, second floor, back room.

A RESPECTABLE YOUNG WOMAN WISHES A SITUATION as cook, washer and ironer. Good city reference can be given. Call for two days at 119 Court st., Brrooklyn.

A SITUATION WANTED—BY A GERMAN WOMAN, who speaks English, with some American family, Protestant, to do chamberwork and up stairs work. City reference. Call at 314 5th st., near av. A.

A YOUNG WOMAN WISHES A SITUATION AS STEWardess; is accustomed to the sea; would travel. Good reference given. Can be seen for three days at 43 Hamilton st.

A RESPECTABLE YOUNG WOMAN WANTS A SITUAtion in a private family to do general housework; is a good plain cook and an excellent washer and ironer. The best of city reference can be given from her last place. Call for two days at 110 Warren st., between Hoyt and Bond, Brooklyn, first floor, back room.

A RESPECTABLE MARRIED WOMAN WISHES A situation as wet nurse. City reference given. Can be seen at 55 3d ave.

A RESPECTABLE YOUNG WOMAN WISHES A SITUAtion as cook, or to do general housework in a small family. The best of city reference given from her last place, where she has lived two years. Call at 225 Gold st., Brooklyn, for two days.

A RESPECTABLE YOUNG GIRL WANTS A SITUAtion as nurse; is accustomed to children; is a good plain sewer. Satisfactory references given. Call at 289 Hicks st. first door from Atlantic, Brooklyn, second floor, room No. 5.

A RESPECTABLE WOMAN WOULD LIKE TO GO OUT by the day to do cleaning; thoroughly understands her business. Apply at 52 Sheriff st., second floor, front room.

AS NURSE.—A RESPECTABLE YOUNG WOMAN wishes a situation as nurse in a private family; can take care of a baby from its birth; is a good sewer; has long and satisfactory city references; can produce ten years' references from her last two places. Can be seen for two days at 343 2d ave., second floor.

AS COOK.—THOROUGHLY UNDERSTANDS HER business; would have no objection to assist with the washing; would go a short distance in the country; has got the best of city reference. Can be seen for two days at 39 West 30th st.

A SITUATION WANTED—BY A RESPECTABLE WOman, as good plain cook; is willing to assist in the washing and ironing; no objection to go a short distance in the country; good reference. Call at 77 West 19th st., between 6th and 7th aves., front basement.

A SITUATION WANTED—BY A RESPECTABLE GIRL, as chambermaid, or to take care of children and do plain sewing; can do all kinds of embroidery; is willing to assist in washing and ironing; has lived six years in her last place; best city references. Apply for two days at 122 East 22d st., between 2d and 3d aves.

A RESPECTABLE MIDDLE AGED ENGLISH PROtestant woman wishes a situation as seamstress and to do light chamberwork, or seamstress and nurse. City reference. Can be seen at 1,284 Broadway.

A RESPECTABLE PERSON WISHES A SITUATION as seamstress and to take care of grown children; understands cutting and fitting children's clothing and all kinds of family sewing. Best of city reference from where she has lived five years. Can be seen for one day at 65 West 30th st., between 6th and 7th aves.

A RESPECTABLE GIRL WANTS A SITUATION AS chambermaid and waitress, or to assist with the fine washing and ironing, or take charge of children; is a neat sewer; would do general housework in a small private family; is a good baker; no objection to go to the country. Best of city reference from last place. Can be seen for two days at 309 Hicks st., between Amity and Pacific, Brooklyn, second floor, back room.

A YOUNG GIRL WISHES A SITUATION AS CHAMbermaid and waitress, or to take care of children and do sewing; no objection to go a short distance in the country; good reference. Call at 114 11th st., between 5th and 6th avs.

A SITUATION WANTED—AS NURSE AND PLAIN sewer. Call for three days at 149 Grand st., second floor, front room.

A SITUATION WANTED—BY A PROTESTANT GIRL, to cook, wash and iron; good two years' reference from her last place. Call at 250 Bridge st., Brooklyn.

A RESPECTABLE MARRIED WOMAN WHO HAS lost a baby, five weeks old, would like to take a baby to wet nurse at her own residence. No objection a to baby from its birth. Apply at 169 East 22d st., third floor, front, room No. 12.

A SITUATION WANTED—BY A RESPECTABLE GIRL, as nurse and chambermaid or to do plain sewing. Best of city references given. Can be seen for two days at 462 6th av., corner 28th st., room No. 5.

A YOUNG GIRL WANTS A SITUATION TO SEW WITH a dressmaker or tailoress, where she could board with the family; would sew for a small compensation. Call on or address Mary, 106 2d st., Williamsburg.

SITUATIONS WANTED—FEMALES.

A SITUATION WANTED—BY A YOUNG WOMAN; IS A good plain cook, good washer and ironer. Good city reference. Can be seen for two days at 380 1st av., between 22d and 23d sts.

A RESPECTABLE GIRL WISHES A SITUATION AS chambermaid and waitress; is willing to assist in washing and ironing. Good city reference can be given. Inquire for two days at 484 7th ave., between 39th and 40th sts.

A RESPECTABLE YOUNG WOMAN WANTS A SITUAtion as chambermaid or nurse; is a good plain sewer and an excellent washer and ironer; no objection to the country. Call at 204 21st st., between 1st and 2d avs., top floor, front room.

A RESPECTABLE GERMAN GIRL WISHES A SITUation to do chamberwork, fine sewing and ironing; good references given. Call at 410 7th avenue, near 35th st.

A RESPECTABLE WOMAN WISHES A SITUATION, AS cook and to assist in washing and ironing, in a private family; has the best of city reference; no objection to the country. Apply for two days at 177 East 28th st., between 1st and 2d avs., first floor, back room.

A MOST RESPECTABLE PROTESTANT YOUNG GIRL wants a situation to take care of children and to do light chamberwork or wait on table, in a small private family, where she can make herself generally useful. Apply for two days at 326 West 16th st.

AS COOK—WANTED, A SITUATION, BY A YOUNG woman, as first class cook; she thoroughly understands her business in all its branches; has no objection to go a short distance in the country for the summer months; best of city reference from her last place. Apply for two days at No. 5 6th st., second floor, back room.

A SITUATION WANTED—BY A YOUNG AMERICAN girl, to do plain cooking, washing and ironing, or to do general housework in a small family. Has the best of city reference from her last place. Call at 576 8th av., corner 41st st., third floor, back room.

A SITUATION WANTED—BY A RESPECTABLE GIRL, as good plain cook, excellent bread and biscuit baker and first class laundress; is not afraid of work. Best of city and country reference. Apply at 115 East 13th st., corner of 3d av., over the store, for two days.

A SITUATION WANTED—BY A YOUNG WOMAN, who is a good plain cook, an excellent baker and a good washer and ironer. Good city reference can be had from her last place, where she has lived near two years. Call at 86 West 17th st., between 6th and 7th avs. Call at the front basement.

A SITUATION WANTED—BY A RESPECTABLE young woman, as nurse and plain sewer, or chambermaid and waitress. Good city reference. Can be seen at 99 West 19th st.

A SITUATION WANTED—BY A COMPETENT YOUNG woman, as chambermaid and waitress. Has two years' reference from her last place. Can be seen at No. 1 Harrison st., room No. 3.

A SITUATION WANTED—TO DO CHAMBERWORK and waiting, or general housework; has city reference. Can be seen for two days at 181 West 31st st.

A HIGHLY RESPECTABLE GIRL WANTS A SITUAtion; is a good cook, washer and ironer, or would do general housework. Has good city reference. Can be seen for two days at 196 27th st., second floor, next the store.

A YOUNG WOMAN WISHES A SITUATION AS NURSE and seamstress; is capable of taking care of children; understands working on Wheeler & Wilson's sewing machine, or would like to travel with a family. The best of city reference from her last place, 94 40th st., between Broadway and 6th av.

A YOUNG WOMAN WISHES A SITUATION AS chambermaid and waitress, or as chambermaid and to do sewing, or as waitress alone. Can give the best of reference from her last place. Call for two days at No. 6 East 31st st.

A RESPECTABLE MARRIED WOMAN, WITH A fresh breast of milk, wishes a situation as wet nurse. Can be seen at 180 Prospect st., Brooklyn.

A RESPECTABLE GIRL WISHES A SITUATION AS good cook; is willing to assist with the washing and ironing in a nice private family. Can give good city reference. Call at 292 10th ave., between 28th and 29th sts.

A RESPECTABLE YOUNG GIRL WANTS A SITUAtion to do chamberwork or general housework. The best of city reference can be given. Apply at 402 Hudson ave., Brooklyn.

A SITUATION WANTED—BY A RESPECTABLE young woman, as chambermaid and waiter, or to assist with washing and ironing; can give two years' reference from her last place. Can be seen at 118 West 27th st., near 7th av.

A SITUATION WANTED—BY A YOUNG WOMAN, TO do chamberwork and waiting and assist in washing and ironing, or would do light housework; no objection to go a short distance in the country; has the best city reference. Call at 191 West 20th st.

A SITUATION WANTED—BY A YOUNG GIRL, TO DO chamberwork and sewing, or would assist in washing; is neat and tidy; would go a short distance in the country. Call Tuesday and Wednesday at No. 2 East 30th st.

A SITUATION WANTED—BY A RESPECTABLE young girl, as chambermaid and to assist in the washing and ironing, or to cook wash and iron for a small family; has the best of city reference from her last place. Call at No. 126 West 37th st., near 7th ave., first floor.

SITUATIONS WANTED—FEMALES.

A SITUATION WANTED—BY A RESPECTABLE young girl to do chamberwork and waiting, or to do chamberwork and to assist with the washing; is capable of doing both; is a neat and tidy girl, and is obliging and willing; has the best of city reference from her last place. Call at 437 7th ave. until suited.

WANTED—A SITUATION, BY A RESPECTABLE GIRL, as chambermaid or nurse; would take charge of a baby from its birth. Can give good city reference. Can be seen for one day at 103 Smith st., corner Pacific st., Brooklyn.

WANTED—A SITUATION AS LAUNDRESS, OR would assist at chamberwork, or do the fine washing. Call at 111 15th st. Can give good reference. Can be seen for two days in the basement.

WANTED—A SITUATION AS NURSE AND SEAMstress, by an experienced girl, with good references. Call on W. T. Hatch, Esq., 77 Clark st., Brooklyn.

WANTED—A SITUATION, BY AN HONEST, INDUStrious girl, to do general housework; is a good washer and ironer; can give the best of reference from her present employer, at 113 Varick st.

WANTED—A SITUATION AS CHAMBERMAID AND seamstress; understands sewing on Wheeler & Wilson's sewing machine; has good city reference. Call for two days at 191 East 12th st.

WANTED—A SITUATION, BY A RESPECTABLE woman, as cook and chambermaid; good city reference given. Apply at 474 8th av. for three days.

WANTED—A SITUATION, BY A RESPECTABLE young woman, as waitress or chambermaid and waitress; the most respectable city reference can be given. Can be seen for two days at 154 West 27th st., between 7th and 8th avs.

WANTED—A SITUATION, BY A YOUNG WOMAN, as seamstress, or to do chamberwork or take care of children; no objection to go in the country. Can be seen for two days at 152 East 32d st., back room.

WANTED—A SITUATION, BY A HIGHLY RESPECTable woman, as nurse; is capable of taking care of children from their birth; can sew, or would do chamberwork if required; is trustworthy and obliging; best of city reference from her last place. Call at No. 3 West 24th st.

WANTED—BY A RESPECTABLE PROTESTANT girl, a situation as chambermaid and to assist in washing and ironing, or to do plain sewing; good city reference can be given. Call for two days at 131 East 22d st.

WANTED—BY TWO RESPECTABLE GIRLS, SITUAtions in a respectable family, one as cook and the other as chambermaid; have good city references; the cook has lived five years in her last situation. Apply for two days at 281 Hudson street.

WANTED—A SITUATION, BY A RESPECTABLE young girl, as chambermaid and nurse; is a good plain sewer; has no objection to the country; good city reference can be had. Apply at 274 Gold st., between Willoughby st. and Myrtle ave., Brooklyn.

WANTED—A SITUATION, BY A YOUNG WOMAN, TO do chamberwork and sew or chamberwork and fine washing; has the best of recommendations; has no objection to go a short distance in the country. Can be seen for two days at 434 4th ave., between 30th an 31st sts., second floor, back room.

WANTED—A SITUATION, BY A YOUNG WOMAN, AS good plain cook, washer and ironer; has the best of city reference; is willing to go a short distance in the country. Can be seen for one day at 434 4th ave., between 30th and 31st sts., second floor, back room.

WANTED—A SITUATION, BY A RESPECTABLE young woman, to do up stairs work, as waitress, or to do housework in a small private family; can give good city reference from her last place. Call for two days at 214 West 21st st., between 8th and 9th aves.

WANTED—A SITUATION, BY A RESPECTABLE GIRL; is a first rate cook, washer and ironer; also a good baker of bread and pies; understands all kinds of family cooking; has the best of city reference. Call for two days at 131 West 31st st., near 8th ave.

WANTED—BY A RESPECTABLE YOUNG WOMAN, a situation to do chamberwork and waiting; has good city reference. Call for two days at 431 7th ave., near 36th street.

WANTED—BY A RESPECTABLE PROTESTANT WOman, a situation as cook; understands all kinds of pastry and baking; can take charge of a small dairy; has no objection to go in the country; city and country references. Can be seen for two days at 285 1st av., corner of 17th st., third floor, back room.

WANTED—BY A RESPECTABLE AMERICAN WOman, a situation as wet nurse. Apply at 765 3d ave., top floor. Best of city reference.

WANTED—A SITUATION AS CHAMBERMAID, BY A girl who can come well recommended; is willing to take care of children and assist in washing and ironing. Call at or address 39 Strong place, South Brooklyn.

WANTED—BY A RESPECTABLE GIRL, A SITUAtion as chambermaid and waitress; can do fine washing and ironing. Apply at her present place, 55 Laight st., for three days.

WANTED—BY A RESPECTABLE MARRIED WOMAN, a child to wet nurse at her own residence, where it will have a mother's care. Address 10½ Grove st. in the rear, for three days.

SITUATIONS WANTED—FEMALES.

WANTED—A SITUATION, BY A RESPECTABLE young girl, as chambermaid and waitress, or to take care of children, or to do plain sewing; is willing and obliging. Has two years' city reference. Call for two days at 175 West 20th st., in the rear, third floor.

WANTED—A SITUATION, BY A RESPECTABLE girl, as nurse and seamstress. Best references from her last place, where she has lived two years. Call at 81 Butler st., between Hoyt and Smith, Brooklyn.

WANTED—A SITUATION, BY A YOUNG WOMAN, TO do the general housework of a small private family. Can be seen for two days, until suited, at 151 West 26th st., between 7th and 8th avs., in the rear, second floor, back room.

WANTED—A SITUATION AS SEAMSTRESS AND chambermaid by a young woman who can cut and fit ladies' and children's dresses; can give good city reference. Inquire at 161 East 24th st.

WANTED—BY A YOUNG WOMAN, A SITUATION IN a private family as cook, washer and ironer; is a good plain cook and first rate laundress. Call for two days at 155 West 37th st., second floor, front room.

WANTED—A SITUATION, BY A RESPECTABLE young girl, as chambermaid and waitress; has no objection to do housework in a private family; the best city reference can be given. Inquire at 241 Elizabeth st. for two days.

WANTED—BY A VERY RESPECTABLE YOUNG woman, a situation as chambermaid and to do plain sewing, or to assist in the washing and ironing. Best of city reference. Call at 105 East 10th st. for two days.

WANTED—BY A RESPECTABLE YOUNG GIRL, A situation as chambermaid, or chambermaid and seamstress. Best city reference given. Can be seen for two days at 130 East 25th st., top floor, front room.

WANTED—BY A RESPECTABLE PROTESTANT WOman, a situation as first class laundress; understands French fluting. Good city reference given. Call at 81 West 19th st., near 6th av.

WANTED—BY A RESPECTABLE YOUNG WOMAN, A situation as laundress or chambermaid; would also do the fine washing and ironing; has the best of city reference. Can be seen for two days at 175 West 32d st.

WANTED—BY A RESPECTABLE YOUNG WOMAN, a situation as chambermaid and to assist in washing and ironing; has lived in her last situation five years, and can have the best of reference in the city. Apply at M. A. Emerson's fancy store, 290 3d av.

WANTED—A SITUATION, BY A RESPECTABLE young girl, as nurse and seamstress, or as chambermaid and to assist with the washing and ironing. Call at 15 Woodhull st., Brooklyn.

WANTED—BY A RESPECTABLE YOUNG WOMAN, A situation as first rate cook; is a good baker of bread and biscuit, understands all kinds of pastry and desserts; no objection to the country; would assist in the washing. Can be seen for two days at 150 East 37th st., between 2d and 3d avs. Best reference.

WANTED—BY A SMART AND TIDY YOUNG WOMAN a situation as nurse and seamstress or waitress. Can give the best of city reference. Can be seen for two days at 124 West 32d st., top floor, front room.

WANTED—A SITUATION, BY A RESPECTABLE young woman, as chambermaid and waitress in a small private family; is a competent person and fully understands her business; is very willing and obliging and kind to children. The best city reference. Call at 82 West 33d st.

WANTED—A SITUATION, BY A RESPECTABLE girl, as chambermaid and to do the fine washing, or to assist in the washing and ironing; the best references. Can be seen for two days at 260 East 15th st. None but for the country need apply.

WANTED—BY A YOUNG GIRL, A SITUATION AS nurse and to do plain sewing in a respectable family; has lived over five years in her last place. The best city references. Call for two days at 307 1st av.

WANTED—BY A RESPECTABLE YOUNG GIRL, A situation as plain cook, washer and ironer, or as laundress; best of city reference given. Call at 40 East 32d st.

WANTED—BY A RESPECTABLE YOUNG WOMAN, a situation to take care of children, do embroidery and plain sewing; has good reference. Call at 261 West Houston st.

WANTED—A SITUATION, BY A RESPECTABLE young woman, as chambermaid or waitress; is willing to assist in the washing and ironing; has the best of city reference from her last place. Call at 44 Schermerhorn st., near Court, Brooklyn.

WANTED—BY A RESPECTABLE WOMAN, A SITUAtion as cook; is a good baker; good city reference from her last place. Call for two days, if not engaged, at 196 7th ave.

WANTED—BY A RESPECTABLE WOMAN, A SITUAtion to do general housework, or to take care of children and do chamberwork; good reference given. Call at 150½ West 28th st., near 7th ave.

WANTED—A SITUATION, FOR A COMPETENT GIRL, as waitress and chambermaid, or as seamstress and to do chamberwork; can be well recommended by her present employer, at 43 West 24th st.

For Other Wants See Eighth Page.

OPERATIONS ON THE MISSISSIPPI

Interesting Details of the Surrender of the Rebels at Island No. 10 and New Madrid.

Map of the Island and Its Surroundings.

The Military Canal from Island No. 9 to New Madrid.

THE WAY IT WAS OPENED.

Invitation of General Pope to Six Thousand Rebels to March Into His Camp.

The Steamers, Land and Floating Batteries, Guns, Generals, Inferior Officers, Regiments and Small Arms Taken.

Topography of the Rebel Positions on the Peninsula.

Doubts, Division and Distrust of the Rebels of Their Cause.

Despairing Letter from a Rebel Colonel to A. M. Gentry, of Texas.

Secession Poetry and the Stimulant of Southern War Songs.

Important Communication from an Arkansas Officer, &c., &c., &c.

Our Mississippi River Correspondence.

ON BOARD THE GUNBOAT CARONDELET,
NEAR ISLAND NO. 10, April 8, 1862.

The Gunboat Carondelet Running Past the Rebel Batteries—A Remarkable Incident—Impossibility of Dislodging the Enemy by Gunboats—Commodore Foote, Colonel Bissell and General Pope Arrange to Land a Force in Their Rear—Exploration of Colonel Bissell in Canoes—The Results Favorable—Preparation and Sailing of the Diminutive Fleet—Impediments and Hardships Through the Sag—They Finally Emerge—A Masked Battery on the Tennessee Shore Opens on Them—Colonel Bissell Apprises Commodore Foote—He Sends the Carondelet to His Assistance—A Terrific Storm Prevails as She Passes the Batteries—The Rebels Open Fire—Safe Arrival and Enthusiasm of the Crew—The Signal—The Excitement on Their Arrival at New Madrid—The Plans of Commodore Foote—Doings for the Week, &c., &c.

The most brilliant exploit performed since the war commenced, or at least the most brilliant one that it has been my lot to chronicle, was consummated last night by the iron-clad gunboat Carondelet, under command of Captain Walke, in running past the rebel batteries below us, and going to the support of General Pope at New Madrid. You are aware that for several days past Colonel Bissell, of the Engineer regiment, has been engaged in the arduous task of transporting steamers overland from this point to New Madrid. I say overland; but perhaps I should explain what I mean by the word. I would not have the public infer that the crafts were taken over, as the children of Israel were, from one side of the Red Sea to the other, "dry shod," or that they were taken any part of the way except by water; but I will say that if any reader of the HERALD has a desire to perpetrate a feat of which to boast in his old age, and will come to this place before our troops have masticated all the cereals upon the neighboring plantations, I will take him to an old Union farmer who will treat him to "corn dodger," the derivative of which was raised last year upon ground over which the boats were taken.

But let me take a shorter cut to get at the facts. After the first day's fight with the rebels here it became obvious to every one that the enemy could never be dislodged by gunboats and mortars alone, and that our only hope of success lay in getting a land force in the rear of them. Accordingly Commodore Foote conferred by letter with General Pope, who had just succeeded in driving the rebels out of Southeast Missouri, and asked his co-operation. General Pope signified his willingness to lend the aid of his brave infantry; but how to cross his troops over the swift torrent of the Mississippi was the question. There was not a single craft propelled by steam in the hands of Union men below our own fleet, nor could we send one of ours to him, except by the rebels, in order to "press it into service." To attempt to run one past the rebel batteries would be to send her to sure destruction, and to hope to cross without the aid of steam, or in any other way, was sheer chimera. But where there is a will there is a way, it is said, and here is a proof of the correctness of the saying. Colonel Bissell was called into council, and when told what was wanted promised to have the needed transports at the New Madrid levee inside of two weeks. That night the Colonel, with a party of picked men, started in canoes to explore the country lying in the bend of the river between General Pope's forces and Commodore Foote's flotilla. About half a mile above New Madrid, Chepousa creek, a small "bayou," empties into the Mississippi river, up which the Colonel and his party went some four miles, to a locality known as "the Sag." This "Sag" is a sort of prolonged indentation in the earth, caused by the earthquake of 1811, and reached from Chepousa creek to Dry Bayou, a distance of over five miles. Dry Bayou unites with the Mississippi just at the foot of No. 8 Island, about four miles above where we are now at anchor. The Colonel's party went through "the Sag," having to cut a pathway for their boats through the tangled floodwood that had been deposited there during the last half century—emerged into Dry Bayou, down which they came to the river and to the fleet in safety, arriving at the flagship after thirty-six hours of uninterrupted labor. It would do you "a heap of good," (as they say out West) to see the old Commodore's eyes glisten when the Colonel reported to him his success and unyielding belief in the feasibility of his project. An order was given to lend every aid possible. Details of men and boats, and axes, and ropes and spades and pikes, and every other thing needed, were made. The "light draught and fast sailing stern wheel steamer W. B. Terry," (I quote from one of her advertisements,) was placed at his disposal, and on Thursday, March 20, the little fleet entered Dry Bayou on its return trip. From that time until to-day the toil of getting through has been incessant. Thousands of trees have had to be cut and dragged away from the banks of the narrow creeks in order to allow the high chimneys and upper works to pass through; stumps and floodwood without limit have had to be removed; the channel of "the Sag" has had to be deepened in many places, and obstacles almost insurmountable have been met and overcome, such as would have discouraged any one but a Yankee of the Bissell school, or the daring and unflinching Western boys whom he commanded. Wednesday afternoon the Terry emerged from "the Sag" into Chepousa creek, and, with all hands on board,

New-York Daily Tribune.

VOL. XXII....No. 6,562. NEW-YORK, WEDNESDAY, APRIL 16, 1862. PRICE TWO CENTS.

THE FALL OF FORT PULASKI—APPROACHES TO SAVANNAH.

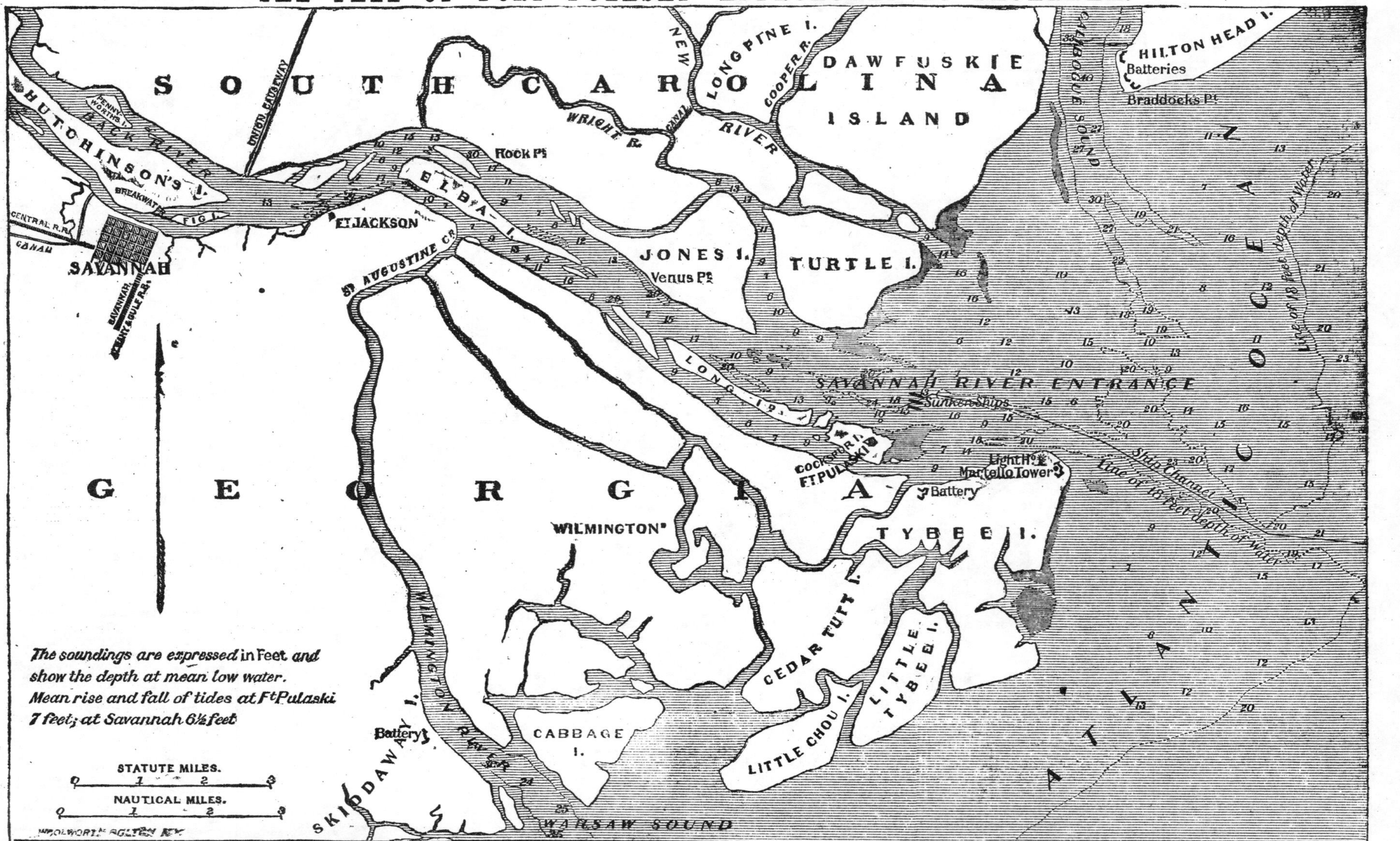

THE FALL OF FORT PULASKI

DETAILS OF THE BOMBARDMENT.

The Fort Surrendered on Friday Afternoon

THE WALLS BREACHED

THE FORT RIDDLED BY THE PARROTT SHOT.

Over 1,000 Shells Exploded Within It.

ONLY FOUR OF THE ENEMY WOUNDED.

FORTRESS MONROE, Monday, April 14, 1862.

A flag of truce went up to Craney Island this afternoon, and brought back two Norfolk papers. They were taken to headquarters, and, although containing the important information of the unconditional surrender of Fort Pulaski, an effort was made, in accordance with the policy that prevails here, to keep even good news from the representatives of the press. I am, however, able to give you the substance of the glorious news, as published in *The Savannah Republican*.

The Republican says, substantially, that it learns with deep regret that after a gallant defense against guns most superior, Fort Pulaski surrendered at 2 p. m. yesterday, the 11th. Corporal Law of the Pulaski Guards, who did not leave for Thunderbolt until after the flag was hauled down, brings the intelligence of the sorrowful event. The surrender was unconditional. Seven large breaches were made in the south wall by the Federal battery of eight Parrott guns at King's Landing. All the barbette guns on that side were dismounted, and also three of the casemate guns, leaving but one gun bearing on that point. Three balls entered the magazine, and a clean breach was made in it.

The balls used were conical, and were propelled with such force that they went clear through the walls at nearly every fire.

Col. Olmstead, who was in command, telegraphed on the previous evening that no human being could stand upon the ramparts for even a single moment, and that over 1,000 large shells had exploded within the fort.

The Republican pubishes the above as a postscript to a part of its edition, and makes no comments, nor gives any particulars as to the number of men and officers in the fort at the time of the surrender. It says, however, that none of its defenders were killed, and but four wounded.

SKETCH OF FORT PULASKI.

We reproduce Dr. Russell's description of Fort Pulaski, which he visited on the 1st of May, 1861:

It is said that "fools build houses for wise men to live in." Be that true or not, it is certain that "Uncle Sam" has built strong places for his enemies to occupy. To-day I visited Fort Pulaski, which defends the mouth of the Savannah River and the approaches to the city. It was left to take care of itself, and the Georgians quietly stepped into it, and have been busied in completing its defenses, so that it is now capable of stopping a fleet very effectually. Pulaski was a Pole who fell in the defense of Savannah against the British, and whose memory is perpetuated in the name of the fort, which is now under the Confederate flag, and garrisoned by bitter foes of the United States. Among our party were Commodore Tatnall, whose name will be familiar to English ears in connection with the attack on the Peiho Forts, where the gallant American showed the world that "blood was thicker than water;" Brigadier-General Lawton, in command of the forces of Georgia, and a number of naval and military officers, of whom many had belonged to the United States regular services. It was strange to look at such a man as the Commodore, who for 49 long years had served under the Stars and Stripes, quietly preparing to meet his old comrades and friends, if needs be, in the battle-field—his allegiance to the country and to the flag renounced, his long service flung away, his old ties and connections severed—and all this in defense of the sacred right of rebellion on the part of "his State." He is not now, nor has he been for years, a slaveowner; all his family and familiar associations connect him with the North. There are no naval stations on the Southern coasts, except one at Pensacola, and he knows almost no one in the South. He has no fortune whatever, his fleet consists of two small river or coasting steamers, without guns, and as he said, in talking over the resources of the South, "My bones will be bleached many a long year before the Confederate States can hope to have a navy." "State Rights!" To us the question is simply inexplicable or absurd. And yet thousands of Americans sacrifice all for it. The river at Savannah is broad as the Thames at Gravesend, and resembles that stream very much in the color of its waters and the level natures of its shores. Rice-fields bound it on either side, as far down as the influence of the fresh water extends, and the eye wanders over a flat expense of mud and water and green oziers and rushes, till its search is arrested on the horizon by the unfailing line of forest. In the fields here and there are the whitewashed, square wooden huts, in which the slaves dwell, looking very like the beginnings of the camp in the Crimea. At one point a small fort, covering a creek by which gunboats could get up behind Savannah [Fort Jackson], displayed its "garrison" on the walls, and lowered its flag to salute the small blue ensign at the fore which proclaimed the presence of the Commodore of the naval forces of Georgia on board our steamer. The guns on the parapet were mostly field-pieces, mounted on frameworks of wood instead of regular carriages. There is no mistake about the spirit of these people. They seize upon every spot of vantage ground and prepare it for defense. After steaming down the river about 12 miles the sea opened out to the sight, and on a long, marshy, narrow island near the bar, which was marked by the yellowish surf, Fort Pulaski threw out the Confederate flag to the air of the Georgian 1st of May. The water was too shallow to permit the steamer to go up to the jetty, and the party landed at the wharf in boats. A guard was on duty at the landing—tall, stout young fellows, in various uniforms, or in rude mufti, in which the Garibaldian red shirt and felt slouched hats predominated. They were armed with smooth-bore muskets (date 1851), quite new, and their bayonets, barrels, and locks were bright and clean. The officer on duty was dressed in the blue frock-coat dear to the British Linesman in days gone by, with brass buttons, emblazoned with the arms of the State, a red silk sash, and glazed kepi, and straw-colored gauntlets. Several wooden huts, with flower-gardens in front, were occupied by the officers of the garrison; others were used as hospitals, and were full of men suffering from measles of a mild type. A few minutes' walk led us to the fort, which is an irregular pentagon, with the base line or curtain face inland and the other faces casemated and bearing on the approaches. The curtain, which is simply crenellated, is covered by a Redan surrounded by a deep ditch, inside the parapet of which are granite platforms ready for the reception of guns. The parapet is thick, and the scarp and counterscarp are faced with solid masonry. A drawbridge affords access the interior of the Redan, whence the gate of the fort is approached across a deep and broad moat, which is crossed by another drawbridge. As the Commodore entered the Redan, the guns of the fort broke out into a long salute, and the band at the gate struck up almost as noisy a welcome. Inside, the parade presented a scene of life and animation very unlike the silence of the city we had left. Men were busy clearing out the casemates, rolling away stores and casks of ammunition and provisions; others were at work at the gin and shears; others building sand-bag traverses to guard the magazine doors, as though expecting an immediate attack. Many officers were strolling under the shade of an open gallery at the side of the curtain which contained their quarters in the lofty bomb-proof casemates. Some of them had seen service in Mexican or border warfare; some had traveled over Italian and Crimean battle-fields; others were West Point graduates of the regular army; others young planters, clerks, or civilians, who rushed with ardor into the 1st Georgia Regiment. The garrison of the fort is some 650 men, and fully that number were in and about the work, their tents being pitched inside the Redan or on the terreplein of the parapets. The walls are exceedingly solid and well built of gray brick, strong as iron, and upward of six feet in thickness, the casemates and bombproofs being lofty, airy, and capacious as any I have ever seen, though there is not quite depth enough between the walls at the salient and the gun-carriages. The work is intended for 128 guns, of which about one-fourth are mounted on the casemates. They are long 32's, with a few 42's and columbiads. The armaments will be exceedingly heavy when all the guns are mounted, and they are fast getting 10-inch columbiads into position *en barbette*. Everything which could be required, except mortars, was in abundance—the platforms and gun-carriages are solid and well made, the embrasures of the casemates are admirably constructed, and the ventilation of the bombproof carefully provided for. There are three furnaces for heating red-hot shot. Nor is discipline neglected, and the officers with whom I went round the works were as sharp in tone and manner to their men as volunteers well could be, though the latter often are enlisted for only three years by the State of Georgia. An excellent lunch was spread in the casemated bombproof which served as the Colonel's quarters, and before sunset the party were steaming toward Savannah through a tideway full of leaping sturgeon and porpoises, leaving the garrison intent on the approach of a large ship, which had her sails aback off the bar, and hoisted the Stars and Stripes, but which turned out to be nothing more formidable than a Liverpool cotton ship. It will take some hard blows before Georgia is driven to let go her grip of Fort Pulaski. The channel is very narrow and passes close to the guns of the fort. The means of completing the armament have been furnished by the stores of Norfolk Navy-Yard, where between 700 and 800 guns have fallen into the hands of the Confederates; and, if there are no columbiads among them, the Merrimac and other ships, which have been raised, as we hear, with guns uninjured, will yield up their Dahlgrens to turn their muzzles against their old masters.

MAP SHOWING THE UNION BATTERIES.

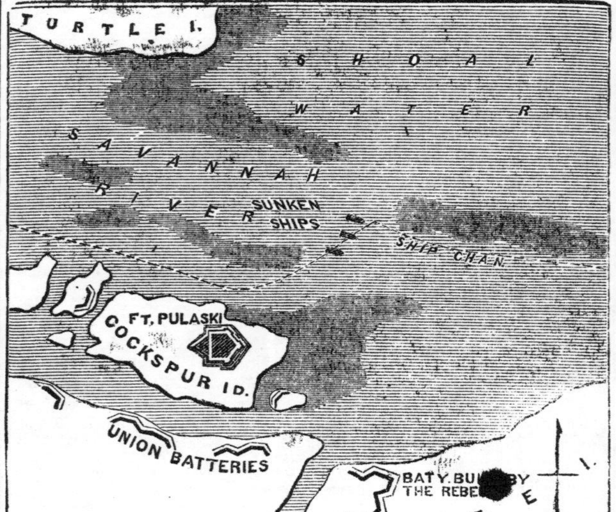

Tybee Island is in our possession, having been captured last Winter by Com. Dupont. The Battery shown in the smaller Map was built by the Rebels. The Union Batteries were constructed on the long marsh south of the Fort, and on the little Island between Cockspur and Long Islands, heavy timber foundations being requisite to keep the guns from sinking out of sight.

The following is compiled from the latest information in regard to the fort and its armament:

FORT PULASKI.

Fort Pulaski guards the city on its sea approaches. It is built on Cockspur Island, 14 miles from Savannah, at the mouth of Savannah River. The site of the fortification was selected by Major Babcock of the United States Engineer Corps, about 26 years ago, but it was not till 1831 that the work of erecting the present massive masonry fortification was commenced in earnest. In that year Captain (now General) Mansfield took charge of its construction. The fort was finished a few years ago, at a cost of $963,000. The fort is of pentagonal form, covering several acres. Its walls are 40 feet high, and present two falls on the sea approach, with ranges of fire fire radiating at opposite angles. The fort is embrasured on the front and channel side for one row of guns, under bomb-proof casemates, with an additional tier of guns open or *en barbette*.

The salient points and flanking approaches on the rear of the work have no embrasures for heavy cannon, but are thoroughly covered by enfilading musketry loop-holes, which renders a landing or escalading extremely hazardous to an enemy. The full armament of the fort consists, in the lower tier, of sixty-five 32-pounders (iron pieces), and the upper tier of fifty-three 24-pounders, four 10-pounder flanking howitzers, one 13-inch mortar, twelve 8-inch columbiads, and seven 10-inch mortars—in all one hundred and fifty guns. The columbiads are heavy and very destructive weapons of long range, and adapted to use spherical shot or shell. They are capable of an elevation of one hundred and eighty degrees, and a vertical fire of five degrees, depressed to thirty-six degrees elevation.

The interior of the fort is well supplied with massive furnaces for heating shot, officers' quarters, soldiers' barracks, and an immense supply of shot, powder, and muskets. A wide ditch surrounds the work, which, when dry, can be used by the sharpshooters, or could, if necessary, at the approach of an enemy, be easily flooded. Beyond the ditch is a glacis or inclined bank, which is enfiladed by the guns from the lower or casemate row of the fortification. The full war garrison of the fort is 800 men, but one-half that number could hold it successfully against a very large force. Vessels of any considerable size, in beating up the channel to Savannah, are obliged to approach within 70 yards of the fort, and at this point many guns of large caliber can be made to concentrate their fire.

It covers a larger area than Fort Sumter, but has one tier of guns less.

The capture of the fort will undoubtedly soon be followed by the capitulation of Savannah. The only obstacle to our advance is

FORT JACKSON.

This is a small work, built on a low marsh, four miles from Savannah, on a site near the bend of the river, and commands important points on the channel, on the interior line of fortifications. It is built of heavy brick masonry. Its armament consists of ten 24-pounders (iron guns), three field-pieces, five 8-inch howitzers, one 10-inch mortar, and one 8-inch mortar. It cost the Government $80,000.

On Jan. 3, 1861, two weeks prior to the passage of the Ordinance of Secession by the Convention of Georgia, Forts Jackson and Pulaski were seized by the State troops, by order of the Governor.

SAVANNAH.

The excellent Map of Savannah and its approaches, which we publish above, is from *Frank Leslie's Illustrated Newspaper*, engraved by G. Woolworth Colton.

Savannah is the largest city, and the chief commercial port Georgia. It is situated on the right bank of the Savannah River, 18 miles from its mouth, 90 miles W. S. W. of Charleston, and 188 miles E. S. E. from Milledgeville. The site of the city is a sandy plain, elevated about forty feet above low water mark. It is regularly laid out, with wide but unpaved streets. At every other corner there is a public square, usually circular or oval in shape, planted with the Pride of India tree.

Among the public buildings are the City Exchange, Theater, Court-House, State Arsenal, Artillery Armory, Lyceum, Oglethorpe Hall, St. Andrew's Hall, and Custom-House.

The city has fourteen Protestant and two Catholic churches, one synagogue, five banks, and a public library. A monument has been erected in Johnson square to the memory of Gen. Green, and another to the memory of Pulaski. Savannah is the center of a very extensive system of railroads, to wit:

The Central, connecting Macon with Savannah, 192 miles; the Waynesborough and Augusta, 53; the Milledgeville and Eaton, 39; the South-Western, 50; the Muscogee, extending from Columbus to the South-Western, 71; the Macon and Western, 101; the Western and Atlantic, 140; the Georgia, 170; the Athens Branch of the Georgia, 40; the Washington Branch of the Georgia, 17; the Rome Branch of the Western and Atlantic, 20; the Atlantic and Lagrange, 80; the East Tennessee and Georgia, 82—making the total length of these railroads 1,055 miles.

The harbor of Savannah is one of the finest on the Southern coast, and the river is navigable by steamboats to Augusta, about 230 miles from its mouth. Vessels of fourteen feet draught can go up to the wharves, and those of larger size to Five Fathom Hole, three miles below the city. The city has hitherto communicated daily by steamers with Charleston, and twice every week with Augusta, excepting a few months in the dry season.

Savannah now enjoys a better reputation for salubrity than formerly—a result which may be ascribed partly to the improved method employed in cultivating the rice lands in its vicinity.

The population of Savannah in 1860 was 22,292.

The Philadelphia Inquirer.

ESTABLISHED 1829. | PHILADELPHIA, THURSDAY, APRIL 17, 1862. | PRICE TWO CENTS.

THE LATEST NEWS.

THE BATTLE OF SHILOH.

Official Despatches of Gen. Grant.

COM. FOOTE ON HIS TRAVELS.

HE ATTACKS FORT PILLOW.

Slavery Abolished in the Capital of the Nation!

THE EMANCIPATION BILL SIGNED BY THE PRESIDENT.

INTERESTING FROM FORT PULASKI.

Gallantry of Our Soldiers at the Capture of the Fort.

LATEST FROM NEW MEXICO.

The Rebel Report of the Surrender of Fort Craig False.

CAPTURE OF A PORTION OF ASHBY'S CAVALRY.

The Latest News from Europe.

FROM HAVANA AND MEXICO.

THE LATEST FROM WASHINGTON.

WASHINGTON, April 16th, 1862.

Special Despatches to the Inquirer.

Ericsson Batteries for the Western Waters

The Navy Department has invited, proposals by mail or telegraph, to the 30th inst. at noon, with general specifications and plans for the construction of one or more, up to four, iron gun-boats for the Mississippi and Gulf service with two turrets, on the plan of the Ericsson turrets, for eleven-inch guns; the thickness of the iron to be eight inches, the sides to be plated with iron of three inches in thickness, in one or two layers, to extend two and a half feet below the load line; the vessels not to be less than two hundred and twenty feet in length and fifty-six in breadth, and not to draw over six feet of water when loaded and ready for service; to be propelled by screws, to insure a speed of nine knots or sea miles through the water per hour. Applicants will state the time in which the vessel or vessels can be built, and the price.

General McClellan's Staff.

Major Lecomte, of the Swiss army, who was attached to General McClellan's Staff, has been called home by his Government, to the regret of the latter gentleman, as expressed in a complimentary letter.

The Certificates of Indebtedness—Twenty Per Cent. to be Redeemed.

The Secretary of the Treasury has decided, it is said, to redeem twenty per cent. in cash of the certificates of indebtedness issued before the 7th inst. It is thought that he will receive forty per cent. additional of these certificates in payment of the bonds he may thereafter sell.

Resignation Withdrawn.

Senator Hale, this morning, withdrew his resignation as Chairman of the Senate Committee of Naval Affairs. This affords much satisfaction, as the Senator from New Hampshire, ever since occupying that position, has displayed a zealous devotion to the national interests and an untiring industry in raising our Navy to its present point of efficiency.

Postal Matters.

Utah is not, under official construction, on the Pacific coast; therefore, letters from the East to and from that Territory, are chargeable with the three cent rate of postage only.

The Post Office Department now supplies mails to Waterford and Leesburg, Virginia, from the Point of Rocks, Maryland, and has re-established post offices at both these towns. Banks' division is supplied with mails by military messengers.

Affairs at the Navy Yard.

The *Wyandank* is lying at the wharf, having her machinery overhauled. The *Cœur de Lion* has just come off of the ways, where her hull has been put in complete order. She has had a new wheelhouse put on, and this morning the new smoke-stack was being put in place. The *Leslie* is being painted, and is having new boilers put in. A number of other boats are also being repaired.

The carpenters, under Master Carpenter Talbott, are busily engaged in getting out the framework for an experimental iron-clad battery which has been designed by Constructor Pook at the instance of Captain Dahlgren. The battery will consist of heavy timbers, eighteen inches square, firmly braced together, which will be covered with wrought-iron plates four and a half inches thick. It will be erected about two hundred yards from the shore, and, when finished, its qualities will be fully tested by the heavy guns in the battery on the wharf.

Experiments with Cannon.

Some interesting experiments were tried with steel cannon at the Arsenal this morning.

Hotel Thieves.

An arrest was made to-day of several colored servants at Willard's Hotel, on the charge of robbery. Their operations were not against the guests, but were exceedingly damaging to the proprietors.

Found Dead.

Private Humphreys, of the Ninety-first Pennsylvania regiment, was found dead last evening, opposite the south gate of the Capitol. He was killed by stumbling and striking his head against an iron casting, thereby fracturing his skull. His body was taken in charge by his comrades.

Personal.

Collector Thomas and Navy Agent Chambers are here in consultation with the respective departments to which they are subordinate.

National Cannon Foundry.

Hon. Thos. M. Williams, member of the Pennsylvania Legislature, is here, and had an interview with Secretary Stanton and President Lincoln this morning, in reference to the establishment of a National Cannon Foundry, in Pittsburg, and other matters in which he has taken an earnest interest.

Operations of Secretary Chase's Little Navy.

The credit of the late naval operations on the Western shore of Virginia, belongs to the Revenue Cutter service, under the control of Secretary Chase. During the last summer, the steamers *Reliance*, *Hercules* and *Tiger* were purchased by Mr. Chase, with which and two sailing cutters, under his direction, the Rebel mails and communications have been entirely prevented. These vessels also rendered most efficient service in the capture of the two Eastern counties of Virginia, and have given other evidence of the growing efficiency of an important arm of the public service, heretofore grossly neglected.

The Emancipation Bill.

The President's message, returning the bill for the abolition of slavery, is a law, the President having sent it into the House this morning, with a message recommending the passage of a supplementary act to exclude minors and lunatics from the provision requiring all claims to be filed within ninety days from the passage of the bill. This is so manifestly just that there is no doubt of the early passage of such a resolution.

The Pennsylvania Reserves.

It will be gratifying to the friends of the Pennsylvania Reserves, to learn that this brave and gallant body of men, by some changes which have taken place, have been placed in active service. The arrangements have been made for the Reserves to depart for their new scene of action.

Conspirators at Washington.

It is very evident, from circumstances which have come to light, that there is a band of conspirators in this city and Baltimore, who, by some unknown means, furnish the Rebels at Richmond, almost daily, with valuable information.

The Secesh report of the death of General Buell is flatly contradicted at the War Department.

Business Delays.

A number of gentlemen who have recently been confirmed by the Senate for important military positions, complain of the circumlocution through which they are subjected to obtain their commissions. Northern impatience must submit with a good grace to the slow mode of doing business in Washington.

Congressman Sedgwick.

Much sympathy is expressed for Congressman Sedgwick, who to-day received the intelligence of the death of his youngest son, by drowning, at Syracuse.

Resignations in the Cabinet.

The streets have been filled with rumors to-night, of the resignations of several members of the Cabinet, but there is no foundation whatever for such reports.

Visit to Manassas.

A party of railroad Presidents, about a dozen in number, visited Manassas to-day.

SLAVERY ABOLISHED IN THE DISTRICT OF COLUMBIA.

MESSAGE OF THE PRESIDENT APPROVING THE ACT.

WASHINGTON, April 16.—The following Message was received by the House of Representatives, to-day, from the President:—

Fellow citizens of the Senate and House of Representatives:—The act entitled "An act for the release of certain persons held to service or labor in the District of Columbia," has this day been approved and signed.

I have never doubted the Constitutional authority of Congress to abolish slavery in this District, and I have ever desired to see the National Capital freed from the institution in some satisfactory way. Hence, there has never been in my mind any question upon the subject except the one of expediency, arising in view of all the circumstances. If there be matters within and about this act which might have taken a course or shape more satisfactory to my judgment, I do not attempt to specify them.

I am gratified that the two principles of compensation and colonization are both recognized and practically applied in the act. In the matter of compensation it is provided that claims may be presented within ninety days from the passage of the act, but not thereafter; and there is no saving for minors, *femmes covert*, insane or absent persons. I presume that this is an omission by mere oversight, and I recommend that it be supplied by an amendatory or supplemental act. ABRAHAM LINCOLN.

April 16th, 1862.

The President to day nominated to the Senate James G. Bennett, Ex-Mayor of Washington; Hon. Samuel F. Vinton, of Ohio, and Daniel R. Goodloe, formerly of North Carolina, Commissioners, under the act abolishing slavery from the District of Columbia, to investigate and determine the validity and value of the claims presented.

COM. FOOTE AGAIN AT WORK.

ATTACK ON FORT PILLOW.

WASHINGTON, April 16.—The Secretary of the Navy has received the following despatch:—

CAIRO, Ill., April 15.—The Western flotilla has been within three quarters of a mile of Fort Pillow, and then returning, took up a position two miles further up.

The Rebel gun-boats escaped below the fort.

Ten mortar and gun-boats had opened fire on the fort.

This is up to six o'clock last evening.

General Pope's command has occupied the Arkansas side of the river.

Fort Pillow.

It is situated on the first Chickasaw Bluff, about eighty miles above Memphis by the course of the river, which gradually rises from a low bank to a shelving bluff a hundred and fifty feet in height. The position is not unlike that of Columbus on the land side, with the exception that the bluffs are not so steep, and the river makes a more decided curve under the bluffs. It may be considered a strong position, not, however, very much stronger or much weaker than Columbus and Island No. 10. It is vastly stronger from the land approaches, great care having been taken to guard against an attack from the land.

The fortifications consist, first, of a line of water batteries extending, as at Island No. 10, around the shore at the bend for a mile and a half. These are mounted by about forty heavy guns; only one of which is a ten inch, similar to the Lady Polk—the rest being rifled sixty-fours and thirty-twos. The up stream battery was at last accounts under water.

On the land, the Rebels have constructed a line of breastworks, made to run as at Donelson, so as to occupy the ridges of a series of hills. They have field and siege pieces stationed at the most salient points, amounting to about thirty in all. Their camps are situated in the hollows in the rear of the batteries. Capacious magazines have been dug in the sides of the hills, which are stowed full of ammunition.

The Hatchie river falls into the Mississippi nine miles below the fort, between which lie a long line of high bluffs. The current of the river sets strongly in to the shore batteries. Another favorable feature is found in the nature of the ground. The bluff is gravelly, and the sides of the hill so slanting that the mortars can land their shells into the water batteries with the greatest ease. The number of guns is about eighty in all. The works at Fort Harris have been abandoned, and all the guns sent to Fort Pillow.

The Commander of Fort Pillow.

General Villipigue is a Creole, a native of Louisiana, and, like Pierre Toutant, now known as Beauregard, had a Spanish mother and a French father. He is said to be an excellent officer, a fine engineer and artillerist. The Louisiana journals declare him fully equal to Beauregard, and regret Villipigue has had no opportunity thus far to employ his great military genius. They say he will prove his ability beyond question at the earliest opportunity, and teach the Yankees a terrible lesson, should they ever venture to attack Pillow, which is now styled the key of the Mississippi, as Columbus and Island No. 10 were, until they were lost to the enemy.

INTERESTING FROM FORT PULASKI.

THE FEDERAL BATTERIES.

AN IMPORTANT CAPTURE.

Special Correspondence of the Inquirer.

TYBEE ISLAND, April 9th.

The Federal battery on King's Landing, directly opposite to Fort Pulaski, mounts ten 13-inch mortars, two columbiads and four rifled cannon, throwing either shot or shell. This battery will be by far the most effective in the coming bombardment, which may open now at any time.

Another battery, situated a mile farther south, and within a mile of the old Spanish fort on this island, mounts two 13-inch mortars, a rifled cannon and a columbiad.

The magazines which our forces have built to support these two batteries contains twenty-two thousand pounds of powder, twenty thousand 10-inch and 13-inch shells, and thirty thousand solid shot.

The old Spanish fort, or, as it is now called, the Martello Tower, situate on the southeastern extremity of Tybee island, was repaired and mounted with an effective armament by our troops of thirty-two and sixty-four pounders.

Breastworks, a mile in circumference, have also been built, entirely surrounding the fort.

The battery on King's Landing was entirely built by our troops during the night, the work upon it commencing at sundown and ending at sunrise.

The mortars with which it was mounted, each weighing ten tons, were drawn from the beach, a distance of two miles, by the soldiers.

It was a difficult but necessary mode of transportation. Roads had to be made and trees felled in order to accomplish this end. It required three hundred men to haul the massive mortars with any degree of progress. Ammunition has been prepared by our troops for a ten days' bombardment. The troops upon Tybee island, a week ago, did not exceed two thousand. Shells have been thrown from the parapet of Fort Pulaski which struck inside of the breastworks of the Spanish fort. Owing to some defect, none of them exploded, and thus failed to do any damage.

A day or two since, our troops captured a white man and two negroes in a boat, who were carrying a mail and provisions to the Rebels in the fort. They were stealthily rowing through a creek, and were taken within four hundred yards of the fort.

The time occupied by this unfortunate trip from Savannah was thirty-six hours. Our troops were very much refreshed by this accession to their commissary department, and upon the Rebel mail being overhauled valuable information was gained.

The captured white man is a native of Connecticut, and had resided in Savannah for nine years, being engaged in the fishing business. Upon being brought into the Union camp, he recognized among our soldiers an old companion, who had sold him a boat but a little over a year ago.

He, therefore, became very communicative on many subjects of interest to the commandant of the post.

Upon being asked why he, a Northern man, should be engaged in aiding the Rebels, he said that he did it for the sake of money. He received fifty dollars for every trip to the fort; the negroes and boat where provided for him by the inhabitants of Savannah. He said the fishing business had become very dull, and it was necessary that he should do something for a living.

Our troops, using the negroes as guides, have explored all the creeks leading from the mainland to the fort, and placed pickets in their vicinity in order to prevent any further attempts to relieve the garrison in a similar manner. D.

Gallantry at Fort Pulaski.

It appears by an official report to the Secretary of War, that the large guns for the batteries at Fort Pulaski were hauled by the men with their own hands a considerable distance through a deep swamp, that being the only mode by which they could be transported and placed in position. A report of the 7th of April stated that the fire would be opened on the 8th. The Fort was captured on—according to the rebel accounts—the 11th.

THE BATTLE OF SHILOH, TENNESSEE.

General Grant's Official Report.

WASHINGTON, April 16.—The following is Major-General Grant's official report of the battle of Pittsburg Landing:—

The Official Report of the Battle of Pittsburg Landing.

HEAD-QUARTERS DISTRICT OF TENNESSEE, PITTSBURG, April 9.

To Captain N. H. McLane, A. A. General, Department of Mississippi, St. Louis:—

CAPTAIN:—It becomes my duty again to report another battle, fought between two great armies; one contending for the maintenance of the best Government ever devised, and the other for its destruction. It is pleasant to record the success of the army contending for the former principle.

On Sunday morning our pickets were attacked and driven in by the enemy. Immediately the five divisions stationed at this place were drawn up in line of battle to meet them. The battle soon waxed warm on the left and centre, varying, at times, to all parts of the line.

The most continuous firing of musketry and artillery ever heard on this continent was kept up until nightfall, the enemy having forced the entire line to fall back nearly half way from their camps to the Landing.

At a late hour in the afternoon a desperate effort was made by the enemy to turn our left, and get possession of the landing, transports, &c. This point was guarded by the gun-boats *Tyler* and *Lexington*, Captains Gwin and Shirk, United States Navy, commanding, with four twenty-pounder Parrott guns and a battery of rifled guns. As there is a deep and impassable ravine for artillery or cavalry, and very difficult for infantry at this point, no troops were stationed except the necessary artillerists and a small infantry force for their support. Just at this moment the advance of Major-General Buell's column (a part of the division of General Nelson) arrived, and the two Generals named both being present, an advance was immediately made upon the point of attack, and the enemy was soon driven back. In this repulse much is due to the presence of the gun-boats *Tyler* and *Lexington*, and their able commanders, Captains Gwin and Shirk, United States Navy.

During the night, the divisions under Generals Crittenden and McCook arrived. General Lew. Wallace, at Crump's landing, six miles below, was ordered at an early hour in the morning to hold his division in readiness to be moved in any direction to which it might be ordered.

At about 11 o'clock, an order was delivered to move it up to Pittsburg, but owing to its being led by a circuitous route, it did not arrive in time to take part in Sunday's action. During the night all was quiet, and feeling that a great moral advantage would be gained by becoming the attacking party, an advance was ordered as soon as day dawned. The result was a gradual repulse of the enemy at all points of the line, from nine o'clock until probably five in the afternoon, when it became evident the enemy was retreating, before the close of the action.

The advance of Gen. F. J. Wood's Division arrived in time to take part in the action. My force was too much fatigued from two days' hard fighting and exposure in the open air to a drenching rain during the intervening night, to pursue immediately. The night closed in cloudy and with heavy rain, making the roads impracticable for artillery by the next morning. Gen. Sherman, however, followed the enemy, finding that the main part of the army had retreated in good order. The hospitals of the enemy, filled with wounded, were found all along the road as far as the pursuit was made. Dead bodies of the enemy and many graves were also found. I enclose herewith the report of Gen. Sherman, which will explain more fully the result of the pursuit and of the part taken by each separate command.

I cannot take special notice in this report, but will do so more fully when the reports of division commanders are handed in. Major-General Buell, commanding in the field with a distinct army corps under his command, and which did such efficient service commanded by himself in person, will be much better able to notice those of his command who particularly distinguished themselves, than I can. I feel it a duty, however, to a gallant and able officer, Brigadier-General W. T. Sherman, to make special mention that he not only was with the command during the entire of two days' action, but displayed great judgment and skill in the management of his men. Although he was severely wounded in the hand on the first day, his place was never vacant. He was again wounded, and had three horses killed under him.

In making this mention of a gallant officer, no disparagement is intended to the other Division Commanders, Major Generals John A. McClernand and Lew. Wallace, and Brigadier-Generals S. A. Hurlbut, B. M. Prentiss and W. H. L. Wallace—all of whom maintained their places with great credit to themselves and the cause. General Prentiss was taken prisoner in the first day's action, and Gen. W. H. L. Wallace was severely and probably mortally wounded. His Assistant Adjutant General, Capt. Wm. McMichael, is missing, and was probably taken prisoner.

My personal staff are all deserving of particular mention, they having been engaged during the entire two days in carrying orders to every part of the field. It consists of Colonel J. D. Webster, Chief of Staff; Lieut.-Colonel J. B. McPherson, Chief of Engineers, assisted by W. L. B. Jeremy and Wm. Rassac, Captain J. A. Rawlings, Adjutant-General; W. S. Hillyer, W. R. Rawley and C. B. Lagow, aids-de-camps; Colonel G. Bride, volunteer aid, and Captain J. H. Hawkins, Chief of the Commissary, who accompanied me upon the field.

The Medical Department, under the direction of Surgeon Hewitt, Medical Director, showed great energy in providing for the wounded, and in getting them from the field, regardless of danger.

Colonel Webster was placed in special charge of all the artillery, and was constantly upon the field. He displayed, as he always has heretofore, both skill and bravery, and at last in one instance he was the means of placing an entire regiment in a position for doing the most valuable service, and where it would not have been but for his exertions.

Lieutenant-Colonel McPherson, attached to my staff as Chief of Engineers, deserves more than a passing notice for his activity and courage. All the ground beyond our camps for miles has been reconnoitred by him, and plans have been carefully prepared under his supervision, giving accurate information of the nature of the approaches to our lines.

During the two days' battle he was constantly in the saddle, leading the troops as they arrived to points where their services were required. During the engagement he had one horse shot under him.

The country will have to mourn the loss of many brave men, who fell at the battle of Pittsburg, or Shiloh, more properly. The exact loss in killed and wounded will be known in a day or two. At present I can only give it approximately at 1500 killed and 3500 wounded. The loss of artillery was great, many pieces being disabled by the enemy's shot, and some losing all their horses and many men. Not less than 200 horses were killed. The loss of the enemy in killed and left upon the field was greater than ours. In wounded, the estimate cannot be made, as many of them must have been sent to Corinth and other points. The enemy suffered terribly from demoralization and desertion. A flag of truce was sent in to-day from Gen. Beauregard.

I enclose herewith a copy of the correspondence.

Your obedient servant,

U. S. GRANT,
Major-General Commanding.

Letter from General Beauregard.

HEAD-QUARTERS OF THE DEPARTMENT OF THE MISSISSIPPI, MONTEREY, April 8.—Sir:—At the close of the conflict of yesterday, my forces being exhausted by the extraordinary length of time during which they were engaged with the guns on that and the preceding day, and it being apparent that you had received and were still receiving reinforcements, I felt it my duty to withdraw my troops from the immediate scene of the conflict.

Under these circumstances, in accordance with the usages of war, I shall transmit this under a flag of truce, to ask permission to send a mounted party to the battle-field of Shiloh, for the purpose of giving a decent interment to my dead.

Certain gentlemen wishing to avail themselves of this opportunity to remove the remains of sons and friends, I must request for them the privilege of accompanying the burial party; and, in this connection, I deem it proper to say that I am asking only what I have extended to your own countrymen under similar circumstances.

Respectfully, General, Your obedient serv't,

P. T. BEAUREGARD.

General Grant's Reply.

HEAD-QUARTERS OF THE ARMY, IN THE FIELD, PITTSBURG, April 9.

Gen. P. T. Beauregard, Commanding the Confederate Army of Mississippi, Monterey, Tenn.

Your despatch of yesterday is just received. Owing to the warmth of the weather I deemed it advisable to have all the dead of both parties buried immediately. Heavy details were made for this purpose and it is now accomplished. There cannot, therefore, be any necessity of admitting within our lines the parties you designed to send, on the grounds asked.

I shall always be glad to extend any courtesy consistent with duty, and especially so, when dictated by humanity. I am, General, respectfully,

Your obedient servant, U. S. GRANT,
Major-General Commanding.

Sherman's Pursuit of the Rebels.

HEAD-QUARTERS, FIFTH DIVISION.

Major-General Grant, Commanding the Army in the Field—Sir:—With the cavalry placed at my command and two brigades of my fatigued troops, I went, this morning, out on the Corinth road. One or another of the abandoned camps of the enemy lined the roads, with hospital flags for their protection. At all we found more or less wounded or dead. At the forks of the road I found the head of Gen. Wood's Division. At that point I ordered the cavalry to examine both roads, and found the enemy's cavalry. Colonel Dickey, of the Illinois Cavalry, asked for reinforcements. I ordered Gen. Wood to advance to the head of his column, cautiously, on the left hand of the road, whilst I conducted the head of the Third Brigade of the Fifth Division up the right hand road.

About half a mile from the forks there was a clear field through which the road passed, and immediately beyond a space of two hundred yards of fallen timber, and beyond an extensive camp. The enemy's cavalry could be seen in this camp, and after a reconnoissance I ordered the two advance companies of the Ohio Seventy-seventh, Col. Hildebrand, to deploy as skirmishers, and the regiment itself forward into line with an interval of one hundred yards. In this order I advanced cautiously, until the skirmishers were engaged. Taking it for granted that this disposition would clear the camp, I held Col. Dickey's Fourth Illinois Cavalry ready to charge.

The enemy's cavalry came down boldly to the charge, breaking through the line of skirmishers, when the regiment of infantry, without cause, threw away their guns and fled. The ground was admirably adapted to a defence of infantry against cavalry, the ground being miry and covered with fallen timber. As the regiments of infantry broke, Dickey's Cavalry began to charge their carbines and fell into disorder. I instantly sent orders to the rear for the brigade to form in line of battle, which was promptly executed. The broken infantry and cavalry rallied on this line, and as the enemy's cavalry came to it our cavalry in turn charged and drove them from the field.

I advanced with the entire brigade upon the same ground, and sent Colonel Dickey's cavalry a mile further on the road. On examining the ground which had been occupied by the Seventy-Seventh Ohio, we found fifteen dead, and about twenty-five wounded. I sent for wagons, and had all the wounded carried back to camp, and the dead buried; also, caused the whole camp to be destroyed. Here we found much ammunition for field pieces, which we destroyed; also two caissons, and a general hospital with about 289 Rebel wounded, and about 50 of our own. Not having the means of bringing them off, Colonel Dickey, by my order, took a surrender signed by the Medical Director Lyle, and all the attending Surgeons, and a pledge to report themselves to you as prisoners of war; also a pledge that our wounded would be carefully attended to and surrendered to us to-morrow as soon the ambulances could go out.

I enclose within the document, and request you to cause to be sent out wagons and ambulances for the wounded of ours to-morrow, also that wagons be sent out to bring in the many tents belonging to us, which are pitched all along the roads for miles. I did not destroy them, as I knew the enemy could not move them. The roads are very bad, and they are strewn with abandoned wagons, ambulances and limber boxes. The enemy has succeeded in carrying off the guns, but has crippled his batteries by abandoning the hind limber boxes of at least twenty guns. I am satisfied that the enemy's infantry and cavalry passed Lick Creek this morning, traveling all last night, and that he left behind all his cavalry, which has protected his retreat, but the signs of confusion and disorder mark the whole road.

The check sustained by us at the fallen timbers delayed our advance, so that night came on before the wounded were provided for and the dead buried. Our troops being fagged out by those three days of hard fighting, exposure and privation, I ordered them back to camp, where all are now.

I have the honor to be your obedient servant,

Brigadier-General W. T. SHERMAN,
Commanding Division.

LATER FROM EUROPE

THE CANADA AT HALIFAX.

HALIFAX, April 16.—The Royal mail steamship *Canada*, from Liverpool, on the 5th instant, via Southampton, on the 6th, arrived at this port to-day.

The English House of Commons, on Friday, debated the question relative to the value of fortifications and floating batteries, and resolutions were adopted providing for the suspension of the works at Spithead. The House will also soon consider the expediency of empowering the Government to use the money already voted for the forts in the construction of iron-sheathed vessels.

The Continental news is generally important.

The ship *Yorktown*, from London for New York, was burned by a Rebel pirate.

The *Canada* has 38 passengers for Boston, for which point she sailed at eleven o'clock this morning.

The French and Continental, as well as the English press, discuss the great importance of the experience gained by the engagement between the *Merrimac* and *Monitor*. It is generally admitted that maritime warfare has undergone a change, and that the *Monitor* is a solution of the question between wooden vessels and iron ones.

PETERSBURG, April 5th.—The *Academy Gazette* states that the Minister of the Interior has officially announced that the Government intends preserving the censorship over all periodicals, but to do away with it gradually by judicial proceedings.

PARIS, April 6th.—The question of the Society of St. Vincent de Paul is definitely settled. The conferences of the society will henceforth be separate and independent of the Central tie.

MADRID, April 6th.—It is officially declared that the Spanish Government has most resolutely determined not to attempt to infringe on the sovereignty and independence of the Mexicans.

BERLIN, April 6th.—A confidential letter from the Minister of Finance to the Minister of War is published, urgently requesting the reduction of the military budget by two and a-half millions, in order to remove the present additional taxes.

GENERAL NEWS.

The steamship *Hammonia*, from New York, reached Southampton on the night of the 3d inst.

The steamship *Great Eastern* is advertised to leave Milford for New York, on the 6th of May.

In the House of Lords, on the 3d inst., the Duke of Somerset said that in the course of the present year England will have ten effective armor-plated vessels afloat, and in the course of next year five or six more.

In the House of Commons, on the same evening, Mr. Fitzgerald gave notice that he would soon call attention to the relations of England with Mexico.

Lord Palmerston announced that Parliament would adjourn for the Easter recess from the 1st to the 28th of April.

Mr. Gladstone made his financial report. He stated that the actual expenditure of the Government, during the past year, was £70,868,000, and the revenue £69,674,479, showing a deficit of £1,160,000. He estimated the revenue next year at £70,190,000, and the expenditures at £70,040,000, thus showing a small surplus. As regards changes in duties and taxes, the only alteration of consequence is a commutation of the hop duty, the amount of which is to be got in the future from beer, at the rate of 3d. per barrel, instead of from the material. The duty on playing cards is reduced from one shilling to three pence. Foreign bonds and loans, of all descriptions, are to pay one eighth per cent. The other changes are merely modifications of sundry licenses and the wine dealers. The 15th of September is the day fixed for the repeal of the hop duty.

Mr. Gladstone, in the course of his speech, adverted to the great drawbacks arising from the American crisis, which had turned out worse than was anticipated. The cotton crisis was a most serious feature to England. A blockade had of course been expected, but it had proved far more vigorous, and extended over a greater line of coast than had been anticipated, and its effect had been nearly to double the price of cotton. The loss on the American trade was great, the exports having fallen from nearly twenty-two millions sterling in 1860 to only nine millions in 1861. Trade with America, according to recent returns, was however improving.

In the House of Lords, on the 4th inst., the Marquis of Normanby again recurred to the Italian grievances, and Lord Kinnaird adverted to the acts of Russian violence to Poland.

Earl Russell gave some explanations, but declined going into the general question of the two countries.

In the House, Mr. Layard said that the Government had received official information that a convention had been entered into between the Commissioners of the Allied Powers and the Government of Mexico, and it was true that the British forces had been withdrawn from Mexico, except a small body of men; that it was not the intention of the Government that they should take any part in the expedition into the interior, and they would all be brought home, except about one hundred, who would be left there for the performance of ordinary duties. Although Her Majesty's Government did not entirely approve of all the articles of the convention, they approved of it generally.

Mr. Denman called attention to the Polish question.

Lord Palmerston, in response, renewed the question of Poland, and expressed sympathy with the Poles, but recommended them to wait patiently, and he believed that the kindly feelings of the Emperor of Russia, would ultimately grant their desires.—The subject was one in which England could not wisely interfere.

Mr. Osborne moved the resolution that it is expedient to suspend the construction of the proposed forts at Spithead until the value of iron roofed gunboats for defence shall have been fully considered. He referred to the exploits of the *Merrimac* and *Monitor*, and claimed that the invention of the principle of the *Monitor* belonged to Captain Coles, whose plans were long since submitted to the Admiralty and reported favorably upon, and then shelved. He opposed permanent fortifications, and hoped the Government would not plunge the country into useless expenditure on them. Sir Morton Peto seconded the resolution.

Lord Palmerston admitted the great importance of the question, and rejoiced that it was not brought forward in a party spirit. The question had occupied the earnest attention of the Government. He did not deny that the action of the *Merrimac* and *Monitor* had taught a lesson, but whilst it had done that in one direction, it had also given a warning in another, as showing what they could not do as well as what they could do. He pointed out the drawbacks of the *Monitor*, and what England was doing with iron ships, and said that tenders had been sent out for the construction of a ship on Captain Coles' principle.

He questioned the expediency of entirely neglecting the fortifications, and favored both forts and floating batteries. He said the Government was not averse to suspending the works at Spithead for a time. The Defence Committee had been instructed to reconsider the subject, and after Easter he would bring the whole subject again before the House.

After some further debate the resolution was amended, to the effect that the House will at an early day empower the Government to expend the money voted for fortifications, etc., on iron-sheathed vessels, and was then agreed to.

Preparations had been commenced for cutting down the *Royal Sovereign*, one of the finest ships in the English navy, from a 131 screw three-decker to a 12-gun ship, on Captain Coles' plan. The *Bulwark*, 91 guns, was also to be converted into an armor-plated frigate.

A prospectus is issued of a British Columbia Overland Transit Company, whose object is to establish a regular transport system for mails and passengers, by carts and relays of horses, through the British territory.

The *Army and Navy Gazette* observes that there is more than the usual element of uncertainty about the issue of the civil war in America, owing to the ignorance of the real capacity of the South to resist, and of the capacity of the North to move. The Federals will have to prove, by getting to Richmond, that they have a Quartermaster-General's Department, a good Commissariat and military train.

The budget is generally very favorably received, and although some of the conservative and ultra liberal journals express some dissatisfaction, the general conviction was that no serious opposition will be shown to it. It is almost universally admitted that the existing circumstances would not justify any remission of taxes.

The London *Globe*, the ministerial organ, remarks that Mexican politics have got into a more perplexed entanglement than ever, but that so far as the English Government is concerned, there is no reason to believe that its views have undergone the slightest change. England will not mix herself in any recondite schemes affecting the future of Mexico.

VERY LATEST.

The Paris correspondent of the London *Daily News* says the difference between England and France in Mexican affairs is very ticklish. It continues to be given out that Spain agrees with France and will disavow the Convention.

It is rumored that King Victor Emmanuel is expected in Paris on a visit to Napoleon.

The Paris journals assert that King Victor Emmanuel will go to Naples at the end of April, accompanied by Ratazzi and Popoti.

The Paris *Moniteur* announces that the sum to be paid by any person desiring exemption from military service is fixed for this year at 2500 francs, and the bounty for re-enlistment for seven years is fixed at 2200 francs.

The Calcutta, China and Australian mails left Alexandria, April 4th, for Marseilles.

The ship *Yorktown*, a regular packet from London to New York, has been captured on her voyage by a Rebel privateer.

FRANCE.

The *Moniteur* announces that, in order to lighten the burdens of the treasury, and enter forthwith into the economy promised in the budget, the Emperor has ordered a reduction of 32,000 men in the effective strength of the army. The disbanding of the One-hundred-and-first and One-hundred-and-second Infantry Regiments, and sale of 2200 horses, is also ordered.

General Goyon's return from Rome was regarded as almost certain.

The Paris Bourse was firm at 70f. 15c. for the Rentes.

ITALY.

It is asserted that detachments of the French troops have received orders to traverse the frontiers to prevent the passage of brigands from the Pontifical States into Italy, and arrest such persons, even should they be found unarmed.

The French troops have also been instructed to arrest any Pontifical gend'armes who may aid the brigands.

SPAIN.

It was asserted that Spain, although wishing to receive explanations relative to the doubtful articles of the treaty recently concluded between the Juarez Government and the representatives of the Allies, has no intention of making a new treaty.

INDIA.

A private telegram from Calcutta, of March 15th, quotes freights to London at 62s. 6d. per ton, being 2s. 6d. decline. Produce is quiet. Imports show a strong market.

LONDON MONEY MARKET.—The Funds were steady on the 4th inst., but closed rather weak and the market inactive. The demand for discount was again more active and only good short paper was taken at 2¾ ℔ cent. The applications at the Bank were rather large. The Egyptian loan introduced into London is for £1,811,000 in 7 ℔ cent. bonds issued at 82½.

Commercial per Canada.

(The weekly Cotton market was received per *Norwegian*.)

TRADE REPORT.—The Manchester market is steady and firmer.

LIVERPOOL BREADSTUFFS MARKET.—The market is generally quiet and steady, except for Flour, which is still declining. The various circulars report:—Flour downward, and declined 6d @1s.; quotations range 24s.@29s. Wheat is quiet and steady; red Western 11s. 3d.@11s. 2d.; red Southern, 11s. 4d.@11s. 6d.; white Western, 11s. 9d.@12s.; white Southern, 12s @12s. 6d Corn quiet; mixed 27s. 6d.@28s.; white 33s @34s 6d

LIVERPOOL PROVISION MARKET.—The Provision market is generally quiet and steady. Bigland, Athya & Co. and others report Beef steady; Pork firm; Bacon easier; Lard heavy and declined 2d.; quoted 41@42s.; Tallow steady at 45@46s.

LIVERPOOL PRODUCE MARKET.—Ashes quiet; Pots 32s. 9d.; Pearls, 32s.; Rosin, common, dull at 14s.; Spirits of Turpentine inactive at 68@70s.; Sugar dull and declined 6d.; Coffee firm; Rice still declining; Cod Oil quiet and steady; Linseed Oil still advancing; quoted 37s. 6d @38s.

LONDON MARKETS.—[BARING'S.]—Breadstuffs dull. Iron dull. Scotch Pig 51s. 6d. Sugar quiet. Tea firm. Coffee buoyant. Rice quiet. Tallow inactive at 46s. Spirits Turpentine nominal. Cod Oil inactive at £39. Sperm Oil dull at £93. Linseed Oil downward at 37s.@37s. 3d.

LONDON MONEY MARKET.—Consols closed Friday night at 93¾@93⅞ for money.

American securities were quiet and firm. Sales of New York Central at 72½; Erie 34; Illinois Central 44 discount.

THE LATEST.

(Via Queenstown.)

LIVERPOOL COTTON MARKET.—The sales of Cotton on Saturday reached 7000 bales, including 2000 bales to speculators and exporters. The market closed upward, but quotations remained unchanged.

Breadstuffs. Flour steady. Wheat quiet and easier. Corn inactive.

Provisions.—The market closed quiet and steady. Bacon has a declining tendency.

LONDON, Saturday evening.—The Sugar market is firmer.

LONDON MONEY MARKET.—Consols closed on Saturday at 93⅞@94 for money.

AMERICAN SECURITIES.—The latest sales were:—Illinois Central, 43¾@43¼ discount; Erie, 34@34¼.

HAVRE COTTON MARKET.—The sales of Cotton for the week foot up 2250 bales; Orleans *tres ordinaire*, 156f.; *bas*, 146f. The market is dull, but quotations firm. The total stock in port is 77,000 bales

PARIS, Saturday evening.—The Bourse closed firm; Rentes, 70f.

From Fortress Monroe.

FORTRESS MONROE, April 15.—The French Minister at Washington, M. Mercier, arrived here, from Annapolis, this morning. He was saluted by the French steamer *Gassendi*, and subsequently landing, to pay a visit to General Wool, he received a salute from the water battery of the Fortress.

This afternoon the *Gassendi* steamed up to Norfolk, with the French Minister on board.

The steamboat *Nelly Baker*, Capt. Colden, formerly plying between Boston and Nahant, has been placed on the line between here and Ship Point. She will make a daily trip each way with mails and passengers.

The Union and Lincoln guns were each fired to-day to try their range. The shot from the former fell a short distance off Sewall's Point.

The flag of truce from Norfolk, to-day, brought down two ladies, and also the sword of the Captain of the French war vessel, the *Proney*, which was wrecked on the North Carolina coast some time since.

A report was brought from Norfolk, which was current there, that General Buell had been killed.

BALTIMORE, April 16.—The *American's* special correspondent says, speaking of the visit of the French steamer, with the French Minister, to Norfolk:—"Some speculation was entertained here in naval circles, as to what course the French Minister and the commander of the steamer will pursue at Norfolk. Will he salute the Rebel flag, and will the Rebel guns salute the French flag? It is a nice point of national etiquette. No guns have yet been heard in the direction of Norfolk, and the French steamer must have reached Norfolk long before the time of closing this.

"The flag of truce boat reports that the *Merrimac* was not in sight, and has evidently returned to Norfolk. The hands on board the flag of truce boat had some talk, but disclosed nothing as to the movements of the *Merrimac*. Some of the Rebels bantered our men on the subject, saying that there was no use in wasting coal; that she could come into the Roads whenever she chose to do so, that our vessels were afraid to come from under the guns of the Fort and meet her."

Thanks of the Navy Department to the Officers of the Gun-boats "Carondelet" and "Pittsburg."

The following letter of thanks has been issued from the Navy Department, addressed to Flag Officer Foote:—

NAVY DEPARTMENT, April 12th, 1862.

SIR:—The Department desires you to convey to Commander Henry Walke and the officers and men of the *Carondelet*; also to Acting First Master Hoel, of the *Cincinnati*, who volunteered for the occasion, its thanks for the gallant and successful service rendered in running the *Carondelet* past the Rebel batteries on the night of the 4th inst. It was a daring and heroic act, well executed and deserving of special recognition.

Commendation is also to be extended to the officers and crew of the *Pittsburg*, who, in like manner, on the night of the 7th inst., performed a similar service. These fearless acts dismayed the enemy, enabled the army under General Pope to cross the Mississippi and eventuated in the surrender to yourself of Island No. 10, and finally, to the capture, by General Pope, of the fort on the Tennessee shore and the retreating Rebels under General Makall.

I would also, in this connection, convey the acknowledgments which are justly due the officers and crews of the several boats, who, in conjunction with a detachment of the Forty-second Illinois Regiment, under Colonel Roberts, captured the first Rebel battery and spiked the guns, on Island No. 10, on the night of the 1st inst.

Such services are duly appreciated by the Department, which extends to all who participated in the achievement.

I am, respectfully, your obedient servant,

GIDEON G. WELLES, Secretary of the Navy.

From California.

SAN FRANCISCO, April 11.—Arrived, ship *Lucy Ann*, from Newport; barque *Constance*, from New Zealand.

The steamer *St. Louis* sailed for Panama to-day, taking but few passengers and $615,000 in treasure for New York, and $209,000 for England.

APRIL 12.—The Mexican Mill, situated on a part of the Comstock Silver Lead, was burned yesterday. The loss amounted to about $150,000.

The Ice on the Newfoundland Coast.

HALIFAX, April 16.—The steamship *John Bell*, from Liverpool for New York, arrived here last night. She reports having encountered considerable ice on the Newfoundland coast. The mail schooner hence had to put back, being unable to land.

Gen. Makall at Fort Warren.

BOSTON, April 16.—Gen. Makall and five other Rebel officers, captured at Island No. 10, were taken to Fort Warren to-day.

New-York Weekly Caucasian.

"I hold that this Government was made on the WHITE BASIS, by WHITE MEN, for the Benefit of WHITE MEN and THEIR POSTERITY FOREVER."—[*S. A. Douglas.*

VOL. I. NEW YORK, SATURDAY, APRIL 19, 1862. NO. 29.

THE FREEDOM OF THE PRESS.

"Every citizen may freely speak, write, and publish his sentiments on all subjects, being responsible for the abuse of that right; and no law shall be passed *to restrain or abridge the liberty of speech or of the press.*"—[*Constitution of the State of New York, Art. I, Sec. 8.*

"Were it left to me to decide whether we should have *a government without newspapers, or newspapers without government, I should not hesitate a moment to prefer the latter.* But I should mean that every man should receive those papers and be capable of reading them."—*Jefferson*

"UNDER NO POSSIBLE EMERGENCY, NOT EVEN IN INSURRECTION, OR AMID THE THROES OF CIVIL WAR, *can this Government justify official interference with the freedom of speech or of the press*, ANY MORE THAN IT CAN WITH THE FREEDOM OF THE BALLOT. The licentiousness of the tongue and of the pen is A MINOR EVIL COMPARED WITH THE LICENTIOUSNESS OF ARBITRARY POWER."—*F. P. Blair, senior*

THE NEW YORK WEEKLY CAUCASIAN

Is published EVERY FRIDAY MORNING, at No. 162 NASSAU STREET, and can be obtained, by out of town dealers, through all City News Agents. It is for sale at the principal News Stands in New York and Brooklyn.

It will also be served by carriers in New York and Brooklyn for THREE CENTS per week, by sending address to the office, or at $1 50 per year, payable in advance.

☞ Subscribers in the country, where they receive their papers per express or otherwise, at their own expense, will be furnished at the rate of $1 per copy.

SINGLE COPIES, 3 CTS.

FREE NEGROISM:

OR THE

Results of Emancipation

IN THE NORTH AND THE

WEST INDIA ISLANDS.

WITH

Statistics of the Decay of Commerce,

IDLENESS OF THE NEGRO,

HIS RETURN TO SAVAGISM,

&c., &c., &c.

JAMAICA.

Jamaica is about 150 miles long by about 50 in width. Its area is about 6,400 square miles, or 4,000,000 of acres. It is the largest and most valuable of the British West India Islands. The last census taken was in 1844, when the population stood as follows:—Whites, 15,776; negroes, 293,128; mulattoes, 68,529. By the census of 1861, the only one taken since, the population is stated as follows:—Whites, 13,816; mulattoes, 81,065; negroes, 346,374. The whole number of persons who can read is set down at 80,724, and 50,726 as able to read and write. It will be seen from this that over 300,000 can neither read nor write. The education is evidently confined to the whites and mulattoes, leaving the negroes in their natural ignorance, where they have neither oral nor any other instruction. Of course "educated," negroes are simply monstrosities, but as some people seem to suppose that "freedom" will develop such "white crows," we have cited these statistics to show that Jamaica has not yet produced them, after a twenty-five years' trial. The white population, it will also be seen, is gradually decreasing—dying out—through the blood of the negro.

The productions of Jamaica are similar to those of the other West India Islands. The soil is deep and fertile, and one of the best in the world for the production of sugar, coffee, pimento and ginger. It is also rich in minerals, cabinet woods, &c., and the low grounds yield abundantly the plantain, banana, yam, sweet potatoes, pine apples, oranges, pomegranates, &c, &c. Jamaica has been in possession of England ever since the days of Oliver Cromwell, and at the time of the prohibition of the importation of negroes from Africa in 1807, was in a most flourishing condition. Her history, since then, has been one of gradual but sure decay. The restriction upon her supply of labor produced some decrease in her productions, and the abolition of "slavery" in 1833 hastened the final destruction of the Island. The negroes freed in 1833 were to serve five years as apprentices, and on the 1st of August, 1838, to have their unconditional liberty. For this injury to the negro and crime towards the white man, the planters were allowed about $30,000,000, the whole sum expended in all the Islands, by the British government, being about $100,000,000. And what is the result? Facts speak louder than words, and to them we appeal. The value of the exports of Jamaica (we quote from the Cyclopedia of Commerce, published by Harper & Brothers, of this city,) before and after the emancipation, will illustrate what we say:—

Years.	Value of Exports.
1809	£3,033,234
1810	2,303,579
1853	837,276
1854	932,316

The largest productions of Jamaica were before the restrictions upon the importation of negroes. The largest sugar crop was in 1805, when it was 150,352 hogsheads. In 1855 it was only 28,177 hogsheads. In 1859 it was only about 20,000. The largest coffee crop was in 1813, when it was 34,045,585 pounds. The average crop for the past ten years has not been over 5,000,000 pounds. The only crop that has increased is that of pimento, which, instead of being an evidence of the industry of the negro, is a direct proof of his idleness. The pimento tree grows wild in Jamaica, and rapidly spreads over land formerly under cultivation. The rapidity with which estates have been abandoned in Jamaica and the decrease in the taxable property of the Island, is astounding. The movable and immovable property of Jamaica was once estimated at £50,000,000, or nearly $250,000,000. In 1850 the assessed valuation had fallen to £11,500,000. In 1851 it was reduced £2,000,000 and Mr. Westmoreland, in a speech in the Jamaica House of Assembly, stated it was believed, that the falling off would be £2,000,000 more in 1852. From a report made to the House of Assembly of the number and extent of the plantations abandoned during the years 1848, '49, '50, '51 and '52, we gather the following facts:—

Sugar estates abandoned	128
" partially "	71
Coffee plantations abandoned	96
" partially "	66

The total number of acres thus thrown out of cultivation in five years was 391,187! This is only a sample, for the same process has been going on ever since emancipation. In the five years immediately succeeding emnacipation, the abandoned estates stood as follows:—

Sugar estates 140	168,032 acres.
Coffee plantations 465	188,400 acres.

These plantations employed 49,383 laborers, whose industry was, therefore, at once lost to the world, and the articles they had raised were just so much subtracted from consumption. The price of these articles, sugar and coffee, was increased on account of the diminished production, and that increased cost represented the tax which the world paid for the privilege of allowing Sambo to loll in idleness. The Cyclopedia of Commerce says:—

"The negro, on whom the cultivation of the islands depends, has gradually retired from labor, and retrograded in the social scale.* The Jamaica negro can earn enough on a sugar plantation in a few weeks to buy a small patch of freehold land. The wood upon it forms his cottage; the vegetables, which grow almost spontaneously, support him. When his little property does not require his care, he works from time to time for hire; but, as plantation after plantation is abandoned, and the country returns to its primeval forest, he is confined more and more to the society of his own race, and though not more addicted to crime, *is rapidly receding into a savage state.* During slavery the dissenting ministers possessed great influence over him; he now prefers the established church because it costs him nothing; but he cares little for either. Not feeling the want of education, he does not seek it for his children, whom he prefers employing in his own service. Hence, churches nor schools are wanted in Jamaica, but congregations and scholars. These observations are observed by the last returns, which fix the diminution of children in schools, in 1854, as compared with the previous year, at 2,000, and show this decrease to be less conspicuous in those belonging to the established church of England and Scotland, than in those of the Baptists and Independents. We can scarcely blame the negro for following the bent of his inclination; but it is evident that, under these circumstances, unless there is a large and immediate supply of immigrants, to meet the supply of whose introduction, averaging at least £10 per head, there are no available funds, *all society will come to a speedy end*, and the island become a second Hayti. Already the enormous depreciation of property has caused the ruin of so many, that the name of Jamaica proprietor, once used proverbially to indicate [illegible] with poverty and distress."

Such, then, is the condition of Jamaica, as stated in an impartial work. Let us hear now what the London *Times* candidly owns up to. It says:

"There is *no blinking the truth.* Years of bitter experience, years of hope deferred, of self-devotion unrequited, of prayers unanswered, of sufferings derided, of insults unresented, of contumely patiently endured, have convinced us of the truth. It must be spoken out loudly and energetically, despite the wild mockings of 'howling cant.' *The freed West India slave will not till the soil for wages;* the free son of the ex-slave is as obstinate as his sire. He will not cultivate lands which he has not bought for his own. Yams, mangoes and plantains—these satisfy his wants; he cares not for yours. Cotton, sugar, coffee and tobacco he cares but little for. And what matters it to him that the Englishman has sunk his thousands and tens of thousands on mills, machinery and plants, which now totter on the languishing estate, that for years has only returned him beggary and debt. He eats his yams and sniggers at 'Buckra.' We know not why this should be, but so it is. The negro has been bought with a price—the price of English *taxation* and English *toil.* He has been redeemed from bondage *by the sweat and travail of some millions of hard-working Englishmen.* Twenty millions of pounds sterling—one hundred millions of dollars—have been *distilled from the brains and muscles of the free English laborer*, of every degree, to fashion the West India negro into a 'free, independent laborer.' 'Free and independent' enough he has become, God knows, but laborer he *is not;* and, so far as we can see, *never will be.* He will sing hymns and quote texts, but honest, steady industry he not only detests but *despises.*"

Such is the testimony of the London *Times*—such the universal evidence of every candid individual. How different is this picture from that predicted by the Abolitionists! The Rev. Dr. Channing made the following prophecy as the result of emancipation:—

"The planters, in general, would suffer little, if at all, from emancipation. This change would make them *richer* rather than poorer. One would think, indeed, from the common language on the subject, that the negroes were to be annihilated by being set free; that the whole labor of the South was to be destroyed by a single blow. But the colored man, when freed, will not vanish from the soil. He will stand there with the same muscles as before, only strung anew by liberty; with the same limbs to toil, and with *stronger motives* to toil than before. He will work from *hope*, not fear; will work for himself, not for others; and unless all the principles of human nature are reversed under a black skin, he will work *better than before.* We believe that agriculture will revive, our worn-out soils will be renewed, and the whole country assume a brighter aspect under *free labor.*"

Well, "the principles of human nature are reversed under a black skin"—that is, of *white* human nature, and it was from a total misconception of the negro that Dr. Channing fell into his grand mistake. Mr. Anthony Trollope, an Englishman, and an anti-slavery man, who has written a book on Jamaica, seems to know rather more of the negro than Dr. Channing did. Hear him:

"A servile race, peculiarly fitted by nature for the hardest physical work in a burning climate. The negro has no desire for property strong enough to induce him to labor with sustained power. He lives from hand to mouth. In order that he may have his dinner, and some small finery, he will work a little, but after that he is content to *lie in the sun.* This, in Jamaica, he can very easily do, for emancipation and free trade have combined to throw enormous tracts of land out of cultivation, and on these the negro squats, getting all that he wants with very little trouble, and sinking, in he most resolute fashion, to the savage state. Lying under his cotton-tree, he refuses to work after ten o'clock in the morning. 'No, tankee, massa, me tired now; me no want more money.' Or, by the way of variety, he may say:—'No, workee no more; money no nuff; workee no pay.' And so the planter must see his canes foul with weeds, because he cannot prevail on Sambo to earn a second shilling by going into the cane fields. He calls him a lazy nigger, and threatens him with starvation. His answer is: 'No, massa; no starve now; God send plenty yam.' These yams, be it observed, on which Sambo lives, and on the strength of which he declines to work, are grown on the planter's own ground, and probably planted at his own expense.

"There lies the shiny, oily, odorous negro, under his mango-tree, eating the luscious fruit in the sun. He sends his black urchin up for a bread-fruit, and, behold, the family table is spread. He pierces a cocoa-nut, and lo! there is his beverage. He lies on the ground, surrounded by oranges, bananas, and pine-apples. Why should he work? Let Sambo himself reply: 'No, massa, me weak in me belly; me no workee to-day; me no like workee just um little moment.'"

This is a graphic description of the negro character, where the climate gives him a chance to show out his real nature. The same author says that "one-half of the sugar estates, and *more than* one-half of the coffee plantations have gone back *into a state of bush.*"

The idea of working for pay never entered in black nature. As long ago as Mungo Park traveled in Africa, he discovered that "paid servants, persons of free conditon, voluntarily working for pay, *are unknown here.*" No traveler in Africa, down to Dr. Livingston, has reversed that judgment.

In Lewis's West Indies, written 17 years before emancipation, it is remarked: "As to free blacks, they are unfortunately lazy and improvident; most of them half starved, and only anxious to live from hand to mouth." Even those who profess to be tailors, carpenters, or coopers, are, for the most part, careless, drunken and dissipated, and never take pains sufficient to attain to any dexterity in their trades! *As for a free negro hiring himself out for plantation labor, no instance of such a thing was ever known in Jamaica.*" Earl Grey said, in the House of Lords, on June 10, 1852, "that it was established by statistical facts that the negroes were *idle, and falling back in civilization;* that, relieved from the coercion to which they were formerly subjected, and a couple of days' labor giving them enough food for a fortnight, the climate rendering clothing and fuel not ne- [illegible] give a greater amount of service than for mere subsistence." Sir H. Light and Gov. Barkley have both shown, also, that the majority of the free negroes of the West Indies are living in idleness, and the French colonies, according to a work from M. Vacherot, published a few years ago at Paris, demonstrate the same ruinous result under their emancipation act.

In a memorial addressed to Queen Victoria, in February, 1852, by the Council and Assembly of Jamaica, after alluding to the distressed condition of the island, and the probable complete abandonment of the sugar culture throughout the British Antilles, unless a remedy were provided, the moral deterioration of the island is thus noticed:—"Convinced that in granting freedom to the British slave it was never intended to allow him to sink into a state of barbarism and uncivilization, we still feel it our duty to assure your majesty that the *downward progress of the agricultural resources of the colony has been already accompanied by a retrogression in morals on the part of the lower classes.*"

Captain Hamilton, on his examination as a witness, before a select committee of Parliament, stated that "*Jamaica, without any exaggeration, had become a desert.*"

In 1850 Mr. John Bigelow, then one of the editors of the New York *Evening Post*, paid a visit to Jamaica, and wrote a book thereon. As the testimony of an anti-slavery man, his statements are given. Mr. Bigelow says that the land of that island is as prolific as any in the world. It can be bought for $5 to $10 per acre, and five acres confer the right of voting and eligibility to public offices. Planters offer $1 50 per day for labor; 16 days' labor will enable a negro to buy land enough to make him a voter, and the market of Kingston offers a great demand for vegetables at all times. These facts, said Mr. Bigelow, place independence within the reach of every black. But what are the results? There has been no increrse in voters in 20 years. Lands run wild. Kingston gets its vegetables from the United States.

After describing the immense sources of wealth to be found in Jamaica, Mr. Bigelow says:

"Such are some of the natural resources of this dilapidated and poverty-stricken country. Capable as it is of producing almost everything, and actually producing nothing which might not become a staple with a proper application of capital and skill, its inhabitants are miserably poor, and daily sinking deeper into ihe utter helplessness of abject want.

'Magnas inter opes inops.'

"Shipping has deserted her ports; her magnificent plantations of sugar and coffee are returning to weeds; her private dwellings are falling to decay; the comforts and luxuries which belong to industrial prosperity have been cut off, one by one, from her inhabitants, and the day, I think, is at hand when there will be none left to represent the wealth, intelligence and prosperity for which the Jamaica planter was once distinguished."

But we will accumulate proof—pile it up, if needed. Mr. Robert Baird, who is an enthusiastic advocate of "the glorious Act of British Emancipation," on visiting the West Indies for his health, could not fail to be struck with the desolate appearance there.

"Hope," says Mr. Baird, "delights to brighten the prospects of the future; and thus it is that the British West India planter goes on from year to year, struggling against his downward progress, and still hoping that something may turn up to relieve his ruined fortunes. But all do not struggle on. Many have given in, and many more can, and will, confirm the statement of a venerable friend of my own—a gentleman high in office in one of the islands above mentioned—who, when showing me his own estate and sugar works, assured me that for above a quarter of a century they had yielded him nearly £2000 per annum; and that now, despite all his efforts and improvements, (which were many) he could scarcely manage to make the cultivation pay itself.

"Instances of this kind might be multiplied till the reader was tired and even heart sick at such details. But what need of such? Is it not notorious? Has it not been proved by the numerous failures that have taken place of late years among our most extensive West Indian merchants?"*

Again he says:—"That the West Indians are always grumbling is an observation often heard, and, no doubt, it is very true that they are so. But let any one who thinks that the extent and clamor of the complaint exceeds the magnitude of the distress which has called it forth, go to the West Indies and judge for himself. Let him see with his own eyes THE NEGLECTED AND ABANDONED ESTATES—THE UNCULTIVATED FIELDS, FAST HURRYING BACK INTO A STATE OF NATURE, WITH ALL THE SPEED OF TROPICAL LUXURIANCE—THE DISMANTLED AND SILENT MACHINERY, THE CRUMBLING WALLS, AND DESERTED MANSIONS, WHICH ARE FAMILIAR SIGHTS IN MOST OF THE BRITISH WEST INDIAN COLONIES.—Let him then transport himself to the Spanish islands of Porto Rico and Cuba, and witness the life and activity which in these slave colonies prevail. Let him observe for himself the activity of the slaves—the improvements daily making in the cultivation of the fields and in the processes carried on at the Ingenois or sugar mills—and *the general, indescribable air of thriving and prosperity which surrounds the whole*—and then let him come back to England and say, if he honestly can, that the British West Indian planters and proprietors are grumblers, who complain without adequate cause."

*"The West Indies and North America," by Robert Baird, A. M.

We might fill a volume with such quotations, showing the steady decline of the Island. But it is well to note the moral condition of the negro. The *American Missionary Association* is the strongest kind of Abolition testimony in regard to the moral condition of the negroes.—The *American Missionary*, a monthly paper, and organ of the Association for July, 1855, has the following quotation from the letters of one of the missionaries:—

"From the number of churches and chapels in the Island, Jamaica ought certainly to be called a Christian land. The people may be called a church-going people. There are chapels and places of worship enough, at least in this part of the Island, to supply the people, if every station of our mission were given up. And there is no lack of ministers and preachers. As far as I am acquainted, almost the entire adult population profess to have a hope of eternal [illegible] with churches. In view of such facts, some have been led to say, 'The spiritual condition of the population is very satisfactory.' But there is another class of facts that is perfectly astounding. With all this array of the externals of religion, one broad, deep wave of moral death rolls ever the land. *A man may be a drunkard, a liar, a Sabbath-breaker, a profane man, a fornicator, an adulterer, and such like—and be known to be such—and go to chapel and hold up his head there, and feel no disgrace from these things*, because they are *so common* as to create a public sentiment in his favor. He may go to the communion table and cherish a hope of heaven, and not have his hope disturbed. I might tell of persons, guilty of some, if not all of these things, ministering in holy things."

The Report of the American and Foreign Anti-Slavery Society, for 1853, p. 170, says of the negroes:

"Their moral condition is very far from being what it ought to be. It is exceedingly dark and distressing. *Licentiousness prevails to a most alarming extent among the people.* * * * * The almost universal prevalence of intemperance is another prolific source of the moral darkness and degradation of the people. The great mass among all classes of the inhabitants, from the governor in his palace to the peasant in his hut—from the bishop in his gown to the beggar in his his rags—are *all slaves to their cups.*"

So much for "freedom" elevating the blacks. It is complained that the marriage relation is not always regarded where "slavery" exists, but it would seem, from this statement, that "slavery" had done more for the moral improvement of the negro, in this respect, than he was at all disposed to do for himself.

Sewell, in his work on the "Ordeal of Free Labor," in which he defends emancipation, and pleads for still more extended privileges to the blacks, says of Kingston:

"There is not a house in decent repair; not a wharf in good order; no pavement, no sidewalk, no drainages, and scanty water; no light, [illegible] nothing like work done. wreck and ruin, destitution and neglect. The inhabitants, taken *en masse*, are steeped to the eyelids in immorality. The population shews unnatural decrease. Illegitimacy exceeds legitimacy. Nothing is replaced that time destroys. If a brick tumbles from a house to the street, it remains there. If a spout is loosened by the wind, it hangs by a thread till it falls; if furniture is accidentally broken, the idea of having it mended is not entertained. A God-forsaken place, without life or energy, old, dilapidated, sickly, filthy, cast away from the anchorage of sound morality, of reason and of common sense. Yet this wretched hulk is the capital of an island the most fertile in the world. It is blessed with a climate the most glorious; it lies rotting in the shadow of mountains that can be cultivated from summit to base with every product of tropic and temperate region. It is the mistress of a harbor wherein a thousand line-of-battle ships can ride safely at anchor."

A most important witness as to the condition of Jamaica is Mr. E. B. Underhill, a gentleman sent out by the Baptist Missionary Society of London, to investigate the moral and religious condition of the people. Mr. U. tries to put the very best face upon matters, and is an enthusiastic Abolitionist. Of Jamaica he says:

"There were very few disposed to take a hopeful view of the prospects of the country. The newspapers, with scarcely an exception, represent things in the darkest light; and if we may believe the statements unceasingly made, Jamaica is hopelessly ruined. In the usual course of things, the inhabitants of a country are proud of their native land, are disposed to hide her faults, and to apologize for weaknesses. In Jamaica it is not so. Planters, officials, clergymen, merchants, shopkeepers, seem to take delight in exposing the worst features of its social life, in declaiming against the lower classes of the people, in representing everything as gone to utter decay, and in depreciating the prospects before them. Nothing is right. The Government is extravagant and bad. The officers are venal. The legislature is governed by class interests, and addicted to 'log rolling.' The planters are poor, their estates worthless, and their cultivation thriftless and unskillful. The people are idle, vain, improvident, unchaste. Their religion is hypocrisy. Their social condition is one of African barbarism and dark superstition. In short, the island is in a state of irretrievable decay. Such is the picture which is held up to a stranger, and no little pains are taken to make him believe it to be a faithful representation. *There is much in the appearance of Kingston to corroborate this view.* Its wharves are comparatively silent. The large stores and warehouses which follow the line of the harbor are but partially occupied, and betray but few signs of active business. Some are tenantless. Here, forty years ago, *the commerce of Central and Southern America had its entrepot.* It was the mart where the production of the tropical countries of the West were exchanged for the manufactures of Europe."

Mr. Underhill endorses the stories "of the crowds of bastard children" in the Island, and says it is "too true." "Outside the nonconformist communities," he says, "neglect of marriage *is almost universal.* One clergyman informed me that of seventeen infants brought to his church for baptism, *fifteen*, at least, would be of illegitimate origin." In fact, from all the admissions made, it does not appear that there is any more marriage in Jamaica than in Africa. The churches, Mr. Underhill allows, are less attended than formerly, and there is evidently little of the religious training of the whites left among the people. The negro, however, has all the advantages of "impartial freedom," and "the highest offices of the State are open to colored men. They are found," says Mr. U., "in the Assembly, in the executive, on the bench and at the bar. All colors mix freely." This would be the paradise for Seward, Phillips and Greeley. Mr. Underhill estimates the annual loss of wages to the people, from the decay of estates and plantations, cannot be less than £300,000, or nearly $1,500,000! Negroes who work at all, cannot be prevailed upon to do so, generally, more than four days in the week, and rarely five. Mr. U. also states that it has been officially ascertained that *two-thirds* of the persons employed on sugar estates are *women and children.* Yet, notwithstanding all these facts, the anti-slaveryite still adheres to his favorite hobby. He has excuses and palliatives for his friend, the negro. True, Jamaica is ruined, but still emancipation is a success. The sea- [illegible] planters have not treated the blacks kindly, and they have bought patches of ground of their own rather than labor for others. Such are some of the excuses of the friends of Sambo. But the facts still stand out in bold relief, despite the assertion of "negro missionaries," who are interested in keeping up the delusion. The *facts* they do admit. They cannot deny or controvert them. This is all we ask—we need none of their excuses. In order to relieve themselves of the odium of having ruined the fairest Island of the Antilles, they would naturally look for reasons not chargable to them. But figures do not lie. The exports of Jamaica have been gradually decreasing ever since "slavery" in that Island was interfered with, until they have dwindled down to insignificance, and, as the London *Times* says, "there is no blinking the truth." The negroes will not work for wages, and hence the tropics are going back to jungle and bush, while white men are taxed double the price they ought to be for all tropical products.

[To be concluded next week.]

LETTERS FROM MAJOR JACK DOWNING.

NUMBER SIX.

WASHINGTON, April 15th, 1862.

To the Editers of the Cawcashin:

SURS: I've ben kinder sick sence I writ you last. The truth is, this clymate in the spring is raly very weeknin to the constitushin. Linkin, too, has been terribully anxus about war noose, and the nigh approach of hot weather. But the great subjeck which the Kernel and I have been considerin, is the "contrybands." What is to be done with 'em? That's the questshin, and Linkin ses he'd like to see the feller that can tell him. One night Linkin got a big map, an he sot down, and "Now," ses he, "Majer, let's take a look at all creashin, an see ef ther aint sum place whar we kin send these pesky kinky heds, and git red of 'em." "Wal," ses I, "Kernel, I'm agreed." So we went at it. First Linkin put his finger on Haty. "Now," [illegible] ger constitushin. Suppose they go thar?" "But," ses I, "Kernel, they won't go, an ef they did, they wouldn't do nothin." "Wal," ses he, "no matter, ef they won't trouble us here enny longer." "But," ses I, "ther's one more resin. The iland aint large enuff to hold all the niggers—four millions or thereabouts." "Wal," ses he, "ther's Centril Ameriky—what do you think of that spot?" "Wal," ses I, "Kernel, that's a fine country, naterally. The Creator fixed it up on a grand skale, but you can't make a treaty with it, enny more than you can count the spots on a little pig, when he keeps runin about the hull time. The truth is, you can't tell who'll be President of it from one mornin to the next, and the niggers you send there might all git their throats cut jest as soon as they landed." "Wal," ses Linkin, "that's a *slight* objecshin. But let's turn over to Afriky. There's Libery, how would that do, Majer?" "Wal," ses I, "Kernel, that country is about the biggest humbug of the hull lot. Fust off, sum raly good peeple thought it was goin to amount to sumthin, but after forty years of spendin money on it, ther aint enny more chanst of civilizin Afriky in that way than ther is of makin a rifled cannon out of a bass wood log. A few dominys, who can't git enny boddy willin to hear 'em preach, hev got hold of it, an are makin a good thing out of it. As for sendin our niggers ther, why it would take all the shippin of the world, and more money than Chase could print by steam in a year." "Wal," ses Linkin, "where on arth kin we send 'em?" "Now," ses I, "Kernel, I've got an idee of my own about that matter. I think they are best off where they are and jest as they are, but ef you must git red ef 'em, I would send 'em all to Massa-chews-its! Peepul who are so anxus to have other folks overrun with free niggers, ought to be willin to share sum of the blessins themselves. So let all that are here in Washington be sent rite off to Boston." "Yes, that might do," ses Linkin, "but then, ef they are entitled to their freedom, they orter be allowed to go where they are a mind to." "But," ses I, sum States won't have 'em at all, an they can't go there. So what's to be done?" "Wal," ses Linkin, "I tell you what it is, Majer, this is an almighty tuff subjeck I know somethin about splittin rails, and what hard work is ginerally, but this nigger questshin has puzzled me more than enny thing I ever got hold of before." "Wal," ses I, "Kernel, I kin explain the resin why." Ses he, "Let's hear you, Majer." "Wal," ses I, "Kernel, where do you carry your pocket book?" Ses he "What on arth has that to do with the subjeck?" Ses I, "Hold on, you'll see." "Wal," ses he, "I always carry it rite there in my left hand trowsers pocket." Ses I, "Didn't you ever have a hole in that pocket for a day or two, and had to put your pocket book in sum other?" Ses he, "Majer I have." Ses I, "What did you do with it then?" "Wal," ses he, "I put it in my right hand pocket, but it kinder chafed my leg there, cause it warn't used to it, and it also felt mity onhandy. So I put it in my side coat pocket, but every time I stooped over, it would drop out. Then I put it in my coat tail pocket, but I was kept all the time on the *qui vivers*, afeerd sum pickpocket would steal it. At last, in order to make it safe, and sure, I put it in the top of my hat, under sum papers, but the hat was too top heavy, and over it went, spilling everything. I tell you I was glad when my pocket was fixed, and I got it back in the old spot."

"Now," ses I, "Kernel, that's jest the case with the niggers. The minnit you get 'em out of ther place, you don't know what on arth to do with 'em. Now, we've been here all the evenin sarchin over the map to see ef we can't find sum place to put 'em. But it is all no manner of use. Yourve got to do with 'em jest as you did with your pocket-book. Put 'em whar they belong, an then you won't have any more trubbil."

Linkin didn't see eggaztly how I was gwin to apply the story, an wen he did, he looked kinder struck up. Wen I saw that I hed made a hit on him, I follered it up. Ses I, "Kernel, this goverment ain't out of order, as Seward an Chase kontend. They are only tryin to run it *the rong way*—that's what makes all the trubbil. I once hed a thrashin machine, an I sold it to old Jim Dumbutter, an after he got it he sed it warn't good for nothin—that it wouldn't run, &c. So I went over to see it, an I vow ef he didn't have the machine all rong eend foremist. I went to work at it, an, after a leetle wile, it went off like grease, jest as slick as a whistle. You see, old Dumbutter didn't understand the [illegible] Now, ses I, Kernel, our Constitushin is a Dimmycratic machine, an its got to be run as a Dimmycratic machine, or it *won't run at all!* Now, you see, Seward is tryin to run it on his 'higher law' principle, but it warn't made for that, an the consekence is, the thing is pretty nigh smashed up."

Wal, ses Linkin, "things do look kinder dark. I don't know whar we will come out, but I guess I'll issoo a proclamashin for the ministers to pray for us. Perhaps they will do sum good." Ses I, "Kernel, that reminds me of old Elder Doolittle, who cum along the road one day rite by whar old Sol Hopkins, a very wicked old sinner, was hoein corn. The season was late, an the corn was mity slim. Ses the Elder:—'Mister Hopkins, your corn is not very forrard this year.' 'No, its monstrus poor,' ses Hopkins, 'an I guess I shan't have half a crop.' Wal, ses the Elder, 'Mister Hopkins, you ought to pray to the Lord for good crops, perhaps he will hear you.' 'Wal, perhaps He will, an perhaps he won't,' ses old Sol, 'but I'll be darned ef I don't beleave that this corn needs *manure* a tarnel sight more than it does prayin for.' Now, ses I, Linkin, I think this country is somethin like old Hopkinses corn. *It needs statesmanship a good deal more than prayin for.*" Linkin didn't seem to like that observashin of mine much, for he turned the subjick, an he ain't axed me what it was best to do with the niggers sence.

The other day the Kernel got off a good joke on Seward. You know what a solem looking chap he is naterally. Wal, since he has got to be Chief Clark of the President, he seems to look solemer than ever. He cum into Linkin's room, an the Kernel ses, "Have you heerd the news, Boss?" "No," ses Seward, "what is it?" Wal, ses Linkin, "the Giascutis is loose." "What's that?" ses Seward. Why, ses Linkin, "ain't you never heerd the story of the Giascutis?" Seward sed he never had. Wal, ses the Kernel, "I must tell you. Several years ago, a couple of Yankees were travelin out West, an they got out of money. So they koncluded to "raise the wind" as follers:—They were to go into a village, an announce a show, pretendin had jest captured on the Rocky Mountains a bran new beast such as was never seen before. The name was the 'Giascutis.' It was to be shown in a room, an one of the fellers was to play Giascutis. He was put behind a screen, an had sum chains to shake, an he also contrived to growl or howl as no critter ever did before. Wal, the peeple of the village all cum to see the Giascutis, an, after the room was filled, his companion began to explain to the audience what a terribul beast he had, how he killed ten men, two boys an five hosses in ketchin him, an now how he had got him, at 'enormous expense,' to show him. Jest as everybody was gapin an starin, thar was, all at once, a most terrific growlin, and howlin, an rattlin of chains, an, in the excitement, the showman, almost breathless, yelled out, at the top of his voice, 'the Giascutis is loose. Run! run! run!' An away went the people down stairs, heels over head, losin all they had paid, an seein nothin." Now, ses Linkin, "'the Merrymac is out,' an wen I read about the vessels, an tug-boats, an steamers, all scamperin off as soon as she was seen, I thought she was the 'Giascutis,' sure, only I'm afraid she is a real Giascutis, an no mistake." Since then, Linkin calls the Merrymac the Giascutis all the time. Your friend,

MAJER JACK DOWNING.

A Voice from Michigan.

The Pontiac (Mich.) *Jacksonian* says:—"By Tuesday's mail we learn that among the State prisoners released from Fort La Fayette are Guy J. Hopkins, David C. Wattles and Isaiah Butler, the Lapeer "traitors." Now, were we either of these men, the first business we should have in hand after our arrival home, would be to procure the arrest *in a legal manner*, of every man who had by word or deed been instrumental in our captivity. And we would give neither rest to our feet or sleep to our eyelids, until each and every one of them had either proved the charges against us or paid the full penalty of the law for their infamous and atrocious outrages. Thus has this most shameful innovation upon the rights of freemen terminated. Stand up, base libeler of the *Advertiser*, and dare to justify your foul charges.—Stand up, insignificant echo of the *Gazette*, and receive the flogging that you richly merit. Were all men like you two, the Goddess of Liberty, yea, the very name of liberty, would become a fable, and the only security to life and property would lie in stout arms and keen blades. Shame! shame! In a Christian land, boasting of its civil and religious liberty—the freedom of speech and of the press—a press is tolerated, supported, in urging the people to overthrow all law and institute anarchy in its stead. But a day of reckoning is at hand, and we trust the really guilty, whether in Fort La Fayette or in Pontiac, may meet with the justice their acts deserve."

THE CONTRABANDS AT FORTRESS MONROE.—An intelligent correspondent of the Buffalo *Courier*, writing from Fortress Monroe, says: "Among the troublesome subjects growing out of this war is the contraband question. I visited their quarters yesterday, and, to tell you the truth, I was disgusted; and you know my nasal organs are not over sensitive. There are about forty families here, which means about two hundred persons. They are a nasty, lazy, shiftless set. As for work, they cannot get enough out of them for healthy exercise; but I noticed three or four long-faced, white-neckties, severely-pious-looking Abolitionists here on a kind of missionary duty, and I suppose that they will make the matter all right. A friend of mine offered to give twenty-five dollars towards ducking one of the fools."

THE DAILY DELTA

SATURDAY MORNING, APRIL 19, 1862.

CONTRABAND INTELLIGENCE.—Our Memphis correspondent alludes to certain contraband intelligence which somehow crept into one of our city papers. The public will hardly understand the significance of that allusion, nor will it perhaps appreciate as it should the difference between the Delta, which scrupulously refuses to publish information that might be of any advantage to the enemy, and other journals which, reckless of every consideration but their own immediate interest, jump at every opportunity to give important news of our own or the enemy's movements, and thus enable the enemy to concert his operations to the best advantage. It is very probable that the attack upon our forts below was hastened by just such disloyal intelligence.

BOMBARDMENT OF FORT JACKSON.—A furious bombardment of this fort commenced yesterday morning and continued, it is understood, without sensible abatement or intermission, all day. The enemy had advanced his ships and mortar boats from their former place behind the headland and forest, and come within view of the two forts, when they were put in position for bombardment by tying them to piles driven for that purpose. Their shells reached easily, and fell with uncomfortable frequency around, and within Fort Jackson. It is said, indeed, that these projectiles were hurled upon the fort at the rate of eight in a minute, or upwards of five thousand in a day of twelve hours. The fort had replied to the bombardment with spirit, and, as we are advised, not without effect, striking several of the enemy's gunboats, sinking two, and setting a frigate on fire. We have reason to believe that reinforcements were sent to the forts yesterday evening.

LOOK TO OUR RIVER DEFENSES.

These columns have not been noted in this war for uttering the language of mere sensation. They have not been devoted to the office of the alarmist. On the other hand, they have not teemed with the extravaganzas of an exuberant and irrational confidence. They have not croaked amidst the sunshine nor despaired in the shade. But there were times when the cause of the country could not be better served than by creating in the public mind a wholesome alarm for its safety, and at such times this journal has not been silent in regard either to the reality or the magnitude of the danger. For a like reason it would be grossly delinquent in our press to attempt to disguise that the enemy is making tremendous exertions with extremely formidable appliances to get possession of the Mississippi river, and that in consequence of these efforts, New Orleans is in serious peril. It is well for our citizens to know these facts and to look at them squarely—to face them like men, earnest, sensible, resolute, calm and courageous men, and not to seek refuge from solicitude and from work in idle dreams and vain speculations. The defense of the river should at this conjuncture be the paramount object of their concern. Upon its defense hangs the fate of New Orleans and the Valley of the Mississippi. What are they do- objects, is preeminently and peculiarly their war. Are they contributing all their capabilities, individual and collective, moral and physical, to the defense of the river, the defense of New Orleans, the defense of the Valley of the Mississippi? Are those who have wealth, and those who have influence, and those who have skill and science, and those who are capable of vigorous activity, doing all that can be done in the circumstances to push the work of river defense by the employment of every appliance for destroying the enemy's ships and gunboats or preventing his further progress? If they are not doing this, they are fearfully delinquent, and their indolence is suicidal. Is there any important work which could be expedited by the timely use of money? There is plenty of money—plenty of currency—plenty of gold and silver, if need be—which might be thus applied. Let it be forthcoming at once, in the name of all that is precious and sacred to the heart and in the esteem of every loyal Orleanian. Is more skilled and unskilled labor wanting to forward expedients of defense? Let proper committees be appointed to search the whole city over, the entire country around, to ransack every village and every plantation for mechanics and laborers, until the present number employed upon our defensive preparations shall be doubled, trebled, or quadrupled, as the occasion may require. History is eloquent in testifying to the prodigious achievements which great cities may accomplish when their people are united and aroused. Athens, Carthage, Venice, Florence, often concentrated within their narrow limits the might of extensive kingdoms. Many a time the feudal monarchs were humbled before the free cities of Europe. It was a few Dutch cities that defeated at last the military power of Spain, and secured their independence by bringing skill against skill, work against work, and unconquerable perseverance against obstinate schemes of conquest. Let not history look back with scorn upon the puny efforts of New Orleans to defend herself from invaders more rapacious and despotic than the Persians of Xerxes, slaughtered and dispersed by the cities of Greece, and more intolerant and cruel than the Spaniards by the cities of the Netherlands. The name of New Orleans has never once been coupled with defeat and surrender. She has been crowned with the prestige of victory. Shall she be uncrowned and loaded with the humiliation of conquest by the most hated and loathsome of foes?

Those in want of fine horses of every description, a fine stallion, barouches, buggies, &c., are called to the large sale of fine stock this day, at 12 o'clock, at the Tattersall's stables, 164 Gravier street, by R. Montgomery & Bro. For particulars see advertisement.

DRAINING.—Proposals are asked for digging a draining canal.

HEAVY ARTILLERY.—Wanted, more men. See advertisement.

THE BATTLE OF SHILOH.

The Battle and the Victory.

The death of Gladden devolved the command of the Pensacola Brigade on Colonel Daniel W. Adams, who still moved forward on the right, with Cleybourne, Hindman and Chalmers's brigades, cut down to mere regiments, carrying other batteries and sweeping from their camps large bodies of infantry, who kept up, however, even in their retreat, a cruel fire of Minies. Finally driven to their fifth camp, the enemy gained a position on a ridge from which the ground sloped into a hollow, where our men were collected in a crowded mass. Then they had us at great advantage, their flanks being covered by undergrowth which swarmed with sharpshooters, and their batteries admirably posted to play upon our advancing lines. The eagle eye of Hindman saw the desperate nature of our position. He could only recover himself by charging their batteries at every risk. Adams's brigade was pressing their left, but it would be in vain, if Hindman did not clear the large mass that still clung to the ridge, with their frowning batteries. Resting his men for a few minutes, riding down their ranks and addressing to them words of cheer and encouragement, he formed them and ordered the charge.

It was done with a rush and yell; but the terrific fire of the batteries and of their infantry supports swept the men down in such numbers as to cause them to recoil. Again resting his men in the undergrowth and collecting all the stragglers from the other commands, he ordered another charge, with the same disastrous results and recoiling effect. It was now evident that Hindman's force was too weak to carry this position. Looking around for help, he perceived several bodies of our men advancing on his left. He rode towards them and soon met the fine brigade of Col. Gibson, of Louisiana, of Ruggles's division, composed of the 4th and 13th Louisiana, 1st Texas, and a Tennessee regiment, with a strong battery. Uniting these forces and advancing the battery of the Jefferson Mississippi Artillery, the whole line rushed upon the enemy's strong position, delivering their fire and charging with a terrible whoop. This onset was irresistible, but fearful was the loss it produced in our ranks. Our two regiments, the 4th and 13th, were shivered at if by thunderbolts. At least one fifth of each of them were cut down, killed or wounded. The gallant and accomplished acting brigadier had his horse shot under him; the clothes of the intrepid and chivalric Col. Allen were riddled with balls, one of which struck him in the face, inflicting a painful but slight wound; the youthful Major Avegno, of the 13th, had his horse shot under him; and that gallant son of Erin, Capt. Stephen O'Leary, of the 13th, received two bullets in his body, while scores of the officers and men strewed the ground or dragged themselves to the rear. But the point was gained, the batteries of the enemy were in our possession, and the ridge afforded a fine position for our cannon to play with much destruction upon their retreating masses.

It was as the batteries were thus playing upon the affrightened enemy that the undaunted Hindman, ever in the front, and whose escape thus far had been one of the marvels of the day, was seen on the crest of the hill waving his cap in triumph. Almost at the same moment his charger was observed to leap high into the air, and falling with great violence, rolled over and over, apparently crushing the noble rider beneath his huge corse. A large shell had struck him in the breast and torn his whole forequarters into shreds. The soldiers, to whom their commander had so endeared himself by his splendid valor, held their breaths with deep anxiety, and men who had faced the enemy's batteries so many times unmoved and unblanched, grew pale with terror at the fearful spectacle of the fall of their beloved chief. Inexpressible was the relief, unbounded the joy of the brave men of Arkansas, Texas and Tennessee, as they saw the frail body of their gallant leader disentangled from the crushed remains of his charger, and standing erect, feebly cheering and waving his hat. Then uprose from our whole line the loudest cheer of the day. No victory yet won caused such joy and enthusiasm. Still, the noble General had been terribly contused. This, and his great exhaustion, had placed him *hors du combat*, and his friends bore him to the rear.

scribed, were all witnessed by the Commander-in-Chief of our Army, who, from the beginning of the fight, had occupied a position near all the critical points. His cool sagacity comprehended every movement and its consequences, and with infinite self possession amid a continual shower of shot, shell and Minie balls, he issued his orders to the various corps and divisions to move to the several positions where they were most needed. After the storming of the fifth camp he discovered the shattered condition of Hardee's division, and consulting with Gen. Bragg, the Chief of the Staff, the order was quickly determined on to bring up the reserves—Polk on the left and Breckinridge on the right, while Ruggles, with his several brigades, was to move against the center. "This thing must be done with the bayonet," he shouted along the lines. "Every man must be brought into the fight." Bragg galloped towards the center to direct these movements. This gallant and energetic officer had also, from the beginning, been in the midst of the fiercest of the fight. Two horses had been killed under him. Never were orders more quickly executed than those for the advance of our reserves. They had already pressed forward to the front, and were near at hand to fill the gaps created by the incessant combat of the morning. Breckinridge's strong column came up compactly and steadily, taking the place of Hardee's division, the fragments of which, however, still unsated and unexhausted, marched with the Kentuckians, in a noble rivalry to share in every triumph of the day. Polk, too, as ardent and enthusiastic as a young soldier in his first skirmish, pushed forward his brave Tennesseeans, with his splendid batteries, Bankhead's, Smith's and Polk's leading. A nobly appearing chief, so full of vigor and life, he dashed along the lines, inspiring his men by his brave and self-possessed bearing. Clark led the First Division, the chivalric Planter-General of Mississippi, among the first to abandon the ease and comfort of a luxurious home, to engage in the perilous conflict for Southern independence. Conspicuous on his staff we observed the noble form and dauntless front of that gallant champion of Southern rights on another field, Major W. H. McCardle, of Vicksburg. Clark's fine division needs no appeals or incentive. It overflows with ardor and impatience for the conflict. The Tennesseeans burning to avenge the wrongs and insults of their State—the Mississippians shouting "Donaldson" as their new battle-cry—the "bloody Louisiana," Eleventh, with the cool and intrepid veteran Marks to lead them, as he led them to victory and glory at Belmont, responded with a shout to the command to forward.

Meantime, the Chief of the Staff, Bragg, having explained to Ruggles, in the center, the order of the advance—gallopping in front of the several brigades, and delivering to each a few words of encouragement, next proceeded to the right, and held a brief consultation with Breckinridge. And now the whole army advanced, Cheatham's, the last division, forming close on Clark's, ready to leap into the first opening in the front lines. The fight now became universal. Each line poured forward, and encountering every hundred yards or so a battery strongly supported by infantry, with the same unvarying result. Often our lines would recoil and falter under the iron tempests from these terrible batteries, but their indomitable chiefs would re-collect and re-form the men and return to the charge. It was in one of these charges that the noble and patriotic Commander-in-Chief received the wound which produced his lamented death. The enemy maintained his position with unusual firmness. Three several times did our brave fellows throw themselves upon it, and were hurled back, as if by a resistless and superhuman power. The brigade and regimental officers gallopped along the lines calling loudly for another charge. The lines halted—the men seemed transfixed with horror or stupified with dismay—they neither advanced nor receded, but glaring at the frightful row of big-mouthed cannon which appeared to cover their whole front, and then, at the ground before them, covered with their killed and wounded comrades, they paused, faltered, and seemed to be fast verging towards dismay and panic. It was a critical point in the drama. Unless that battery was forced and its supports driven in, the enemy would have us at great disadvantage. Johnston perceived this—Johnston, whose actions throughout the day had so changed the ideas of those who had so falsely interpreted his wise and masterly retreat from Bowling Green into proofs of over-caution and lack of daring and energy—who, in his plan and execution of this battle, had evinced a boldness approaching to audacity—an audacity that proved to be the highest wisdom and skill. The sagacious Kentuckian saw and appreciated the imminence of this peril to the army, if the strong position now held by the enemy was retained. He determined to throw himself into the breach—not in a spirit of bravado, of a mere vain-glorious desire of parading his heroism—least of all, from any such petty and ignoble weakness, as that imagined by small minds—a feeling of chagrin and conscious injustice on account of the criticisms and censure that had been so heedlessly indulged towards him by the thoughtless and uninformed—but from a high and lofty spirit of patriotism and self-sacrifice, that looked only at the danger to his country and his cause, which confronted him. Seeing the inability of the other commanders to reform the broken and dismayed line, he rode forward, with the ever cool and undaunted Breckinridge, and, seizing a musket, presented it at a charge bayonet, and called on the men to follow. The grand figure of the Commander-in-Chief, mounted on a large bay horse, looming up from the foreground, (so conspicuous a target for the enemy's sharp shooters,) seemed to expand to gigantic proportions, as he beckoned his men on to the charge. The gallant Kentuckians were the first to follow—Tennesseeans, Mississippians and Arkansians caught the heroic contagion, and now the line moved steadily forward at double quick, and then, with a wild rush, receiving the deadly iron blast as it swept along the slopes, and pouring over the batteries, they scattered the heavy masses of the infantry in the wildest confusion. This was perhaps the mightiest effort of physical force and courage of the day, and when it was performed the tall figure of Breckinridge could be seen on the crest of the hill, waving his cap in triumph, whilst the shouts of his men echoed far off like the roar of many waters. As soon as Gen. Johnston perceived the success of his appeal, and that his men had caught the spirit which he sought to infuse into them, and were moving forward with the requisite vigor and resolution, he rode from the front, and returned to his original commanding position, a little in the rear and on the right, and waited the result of the assault. It was only when its success was evident and the enemy was in retreat, that one of his aids, perceiving blood on his clothes, anxiously asked if he was not wounded. He replied, "Only a scratch!" adding in entire unconsciousness of self, "Was not that splendidly done; glorious fellows; we have got them now." There was a pause and a few minutes of observation and consultation, when evident symptoms of weakness manifesting themselves, the aids of the General insisted that he should dismount and have his wound examined. He did so in a careless and unconcerned manner. His boot being pulled off, it was discovered to be full of blood, and that the purple current was still flowing rapidly from a small wound under the knee. It proved, on examination, to be what Dr. Choppin pronounced the smallest wound that he ever knew to produce death in a hale and vigorous man. But an artery had been severed. Though much blood had been lost, the presence of a surgeon, or the application of a proper ligature by any one familiar with the location of the artery, would have saved his precious life. But the humanity and generosity of Johnston had deprived him of the aid of his accomplished surgeon. He was the victim of his own philanthropy. In passing through the enemy's camp, he had observed some of the wounded of the enemy suffering grievously from their wounds and crying aloud for help. "Stop, Doctor, and help these poor fellows," he said to Dr. Yandell of his staff, who promptly dismounted and was engaged in dressing their wounds, when Johnston and his staff were riding forward to engage in the active scene of the terrible struggle in front. The surgeon was therefore absent when the wounded General dismounted and fell exhausted on the ground, surrounded by his grief stricken staff. He grew ra- ... a few words of kindness to his friends, and of joyful exultation at the victory already won, only escaped him, when in fifteen minutes after he received the wound he departed this life gently and with a smile irradiating his grave and serious countenance. So sudden and mournful an incident in the very midst of victory seemed to palsy the gallant gentlemen of his staff. Personally devoted to him by ties and sympathies of the strongest nature, by his pure and unselfish traits, his entire freedom from all petty jealousy, his lofty moral courage and fearless personal bearing, they were unnerved by the great calamity which had fallen upon them, the army, and the country. Mournfully they bore his remains to the rear, where they were placed in an ambulance and sent to Corinth.

Thus fell Albert Sidney Johnston, the second General in the Confederate army. A native of Kentucky, a cadet from Louisiana, a long resident of Texas, these States may claim to share in the honor of contributing so noble and brave a patriot and soldier to the cause of Southern independence. A soldier of the Texan war of independence—a successful and brilliant chief in the Mexican war, he had appropriately closed his noble career in a great battle for the rights and independence of the South. His name and virtues, and his heroic sacrifice, will ever be held in warm recollection and affection by his grateful countrymen. The melancholy intelligence of Johnston's death was quickly communicated to Gen. Beauregard, who occupied a prominent position near the center of the army, where he was actively engaged in superintending the formation and advancing of troops. "This is sad news, indeed," he exclaimed to his aids with a deep sigh. "Gentlemen, to your horses, we must go to the front;" and quickly the staff were all mounted, and escorted by the fine troop of the Louisiana Jefferson Mounted Guard, Capt. Guy Dreux, the General-in-Chief now proceeded rapidly towards the front. Meantime the whole army had been set in motion, chiefly under the direction of the ubiquitous and indomitable Bragg. Every division, every brigade, every regiment was brought into requisition, and in turn was hurled against the enemy's lines and batteries. Clark, on the left, had led his division far into their camps, making many desperate charges. In one of these, Ruggles's brigade, in which was our fighting "Louisiana," Col. F. Marks, was brought suddenly under a terribly destructive fire. The brigade faltered at first, in some confusion. More than a hundred of the 11th had been cut down. But again they came back, and were again shivered like a wave against a rocky shore. Finally, however, their indomitable fortitude conquered, and the enemy were routed and fell back under a terrible fire from Bankhead's, Polk's and Smith's batteries. The casualities of these assaults were terrible. The gallant Marks had been badly shot, and his youthful Major cut down with a severe wound, and now the Lieutenant Colonel, Barrow, and the heroic Captain, Ed. Austin, of the Cannon Guards, set to work vigorously to restore order and confidence to the mutilated remnant of that once strong regiment. Stewart's brigade, of the same division, shared a like fortune and like triumphs. The gallant Polk, of the Polk battery, in bringing his guns into position, fell severely wounded. Many others, officers and men, of these brigades, were in like manner placed *hors du combat*. A shade of grief and distress darkened the calm and serene countenance of the gallant General of the corps, the patriotic Polk, as riding down the lines he observed the fearful gaps which had been made in his corps.

Cheatham's division had got fairly in on the extreme left and was actively at work. Our whole line began now to assume a firm order and continuity which it had not before had. Bragg took charge of the right, and center, and Polk of the left, and both pressed the enemy with unbroken steadiness and vigor. The enemy gave way slowly, retiring towards his camp, fighting whenever the ground afforded a favorable position for a battery, and for their legion of sharp shooters. Ruggles, near the center, had held his division chiefly in reserve, throwing forward his brigades to support and aid those engaged in assailing the batteries. Anderson had already stormed and carried several of them. Gibson's had performed like service near our right, and Pond's Third Brigade was ordered on like duty, but by some mistake the brigade was not held well together, and when ordered to charge, Col. Mouton, of the gallant and steady 18th, found the whole burden of the charge thrown upon his small regiment, which gallantly obeyed, but was fearfully cut up. In all that army there was no gallanter or abler regimental commander than our Creole Colonel, not one who bore himself so like a veteran. Wounded in the face, his clothes riddled with balls, he maintained his position in front, keeping his men well together, and driving them ahead with resistless might. The confusion incident to so extensive a formation, under such a terrible fire, with so many inexperienced officers, led to sad mistakes, by which several of our regiments suffered at the hands of their own friends. The Orleans Guards, wearing a uniform resembling that of the enemy, were frequently fired upon by our own troops. The gallant Creoles, however, never faltered or shrunk, but though embarrassed by their isolated position, cut off from the rest of the brigade, they marched forward, charging and routing several bodies of the enemy. This battalion, and our noble Crescent Regiment, were left pretty much, as orphans, to take care of themselves. They groped their way through the forest, hunting for the enemy, and throwing themselves on every side where they were needed. The Crescent, after marching through the enemy's camp, proceeded in the direction of the river, to dislodge a strong force of the enemy, which was firing with great effect from the cover of some cotton bales and a hedge in an old field. Col. Smith, leading his boys gallantly into the field, gave the order to charge, and it was done with steadiness and vigor, the enemy flying from their cover through the hedge, which the Crescent occupied, and from an old log house opened upon the enemy, who had halted a short distance off. This drew a heavy fire of musketry upon the Crescents, from which they suffered some casualties. In the meantime the enemy having established a battery to sweep the field, Col. Smith, with great sagacity, moved his regiment off under cover of the woods. There he fell in with a strong force, which had been formed by Gen. Polk, to surround a large encampment of the enemy.

The Crescents arrived in time to participate in this, one of the most glorious events of the day. The troops were quickly formed, the most dangerous and prominent position being assigned to the Crescent. The order was to encompass the camp on all sides, and open upon it a heavy fire. A force of cavalry were ordered up to cut off the retreat. Unfortunately it did not arrive in time, but the infantry regiments quickly gained their position, the Crescent leading. It was a large encampment, evidently of two or more brigades. A short resistance was made, a few volleys fired, but the Crescent and several other regiments poured a heavy fire into the camp from across a ravine, and then filing around were about to charge, when the enemy ceased firing, and several white handkerchiefs were seen waving from muskets. The troops ceased firing, and an officer of the enemy, who turned out to be Adj. Gen. Morton, came forward to Col. Smith and offered to surrender the whole force. Gen. Polk now rode up, and presently Gen. Prentiss, commanding one of the divisions of the enemy, came out of a tent, stepped forward and surrendered. The officers of the command generally remained clustered around the General, and the men collected in groups through the camp, having stacked their arms. The absence of the cavalry, however, enabled a large number of the prisoners to escape towards the Tennessee river, and we only succeeded in capturing about 2700, including three Colonels, four Lieut. Colonels and about forty Captains. They were all of the division of Gen. Prentiss, and belonged to Missouri, Illinois, Ohio and Iowa regiments. They had arrived but a few days before and declared that they were completely surprised, and had no idea we were near when the attack was commenced. The prisoners were sent to the rear, and Gen. Prentiss and staff were escorted to Beauregard's headquarters, which were now established near the center of the enemy's camp.

The whole army had now passed through and beyond the enemy's camps. What remained of his force had been driven now three quarters of a mile beyond, and was heavily massed towards the river, under the plunging and vertical fire of shells from the gunboats, the commanders of which, knowing the relative positions of the two armies, could now throw their dangerous and destructive projectiles so as to inflict no damage upon their own men, and to produce great confusion in our ranks. In this they achieved no little success. Our regiments were frequently thrown into confusion by the bursting of shells in their midst and around them. The Crescent, which had moved very near the river, came in for a large share of these terrifying missiles. The more dangerous Minie balls produced no such terror. The enemy being unseen added to the nervousness of our men.

Our infantry was now utterly worn out. The men fell down in the ranks from sheer exhaustion. They had fought for twelve hours, an incessant and unparalleled fight, charging fearful batteries, routing and pursuing large bodies of infantry, and performing such prodigies of valor as, if fully related, would fill a large volume. The infantry are now no longer available, even if the enemy were within reach, save to hold him in his present exposed position until the cannon can all be brought up to play upon him. Our regiments are severely cut up, many of them disorganized, broken into detachments that wander around seeking their commanders. There is no demoralization, no fear—not all the horrors and dangers of the terrible and uninterrupted conflict have affected their unconquerable spirits. The woods for miles are full of the wounded, and the hospitals are crowded. Every species of vehicle is employed to conduct them to the rear. Hundreds are borne on litter or on blankets. The surgeons are now busy in their terrible labors. Large details, too, to attend the wounded, have further reduced the army. And now the whole army is collected in advance of the enemy's camps, with the fragments of brigades and regiments consolidated with little reference to their original formation. But Breckinridge, now some distance in advance, holds what remains of his division well together, and Cheatham is not far off defending our left. Both these officers have performed wonderful exploits of gallantry, endurance and fortitude. The high soldierly qualities of Breckinridge filled all beholders with amazement. The oldest regular officers of the army bestowed the warmest eulogies upon him. Not alone his personal heroism, but his amazing self-possession—his infinite patience and tact, his quick sagacity and unerring judgment—were themes of universal admiration. Wisely now was he assigned the position of guarding the enemy, and holding the advance of the army.

It was in the last assaults, as the enemy fell back through his camps, now stretching along an open country—on his large parade grounds—on one of which a spacious square had been carefully cleared and leveled, where Grant intended to hold a grand review on Monday, the 7th April—it was here that his greatest losses had been incurred. His dead lay in heaps and thickly strewn in every direction.

The artillery were all hurried forward to complete the work. Thirty six of our best guns were now brought into position on a ridge at a distance of three-fourths of a mile from the enemy's main body. There was the Watson heavy battery, of Breckinridge's Division, among the first to take its place, under the fearless and skillful Beltzhoover, who had already performed several brilliant feats in aid of Cheatham's movement. In this battery the liberal and patriotic gentleman after whom it was named, who had been instrumental in putting it into the field with his own means, worked at the guns as an artillerist. There, too, was the battery of the still unwearied Robinson, of Mobile, whose guns were the handiwork of one of our own foundries, Leeds & Co.—and splendid guns they were—which had been incessantly engaged all day, performing, among other notable exploits, that of silencing and capturing a large battery of the enemy without the necessity of an infantry support. There were Bankhead's, powerful pieces, which had been hard at work during the day; Polk's, Smith's, the Jefferson county (Miss.) battery, and Girardey's Washington Artillery, of Augusta, the only representatives of Georgia on the field; and last, though far from least, our own Washington Artillery, which, too, had had no pause during the day in its gigantic labors and constant progress over all obstacles, utterly reckless of the enemy's stronger batteries or of his swarms of sharpshooters. These guns took up position and opened their fire. They had filled their exhausted caissons from the enemy's magazines; vigorously they set to work to finish off the victory of the day. Such firing was never perhaps before heard on this continent. The gunners emulated each other in the celerity of their loading and priming. For two hours were these incessant volleys continued, mingling in one horrid roar that shook the earth for miles around and filled the heavens with sulphurous vapor and odor. Every description of projectile was called into use. Shell, canister, round hot, percussion shells, James' shells, were poured upon the enemy with relentless fury. He replied from some of his remaining batteries and from some field works, established near the river to protect his retreat, whilst the gunboats unceasingly threw their large shells in every direction over the camps and fields occupied by our troops. These shells, thrown with reckless uncertainty and wide range, were excessively annoying and inflicted much damage, wounding and killing many of our men. But the other practice of the enemy produced little effect upon our batteries or our troops. A vast amount of ammunition was consumed in the prolonged exchange of fires between the batteries; but from the position of the enemy, selected in an exposed and open locality, crowding towards the river, our fire must have inflicted a heavy loss. But the shades of evening began to darken over the scene. The curtain of night was about to fall on the bloodiest tragedy ever enacted on this continent. As long as there was a streak of light by which a gun could be aimed, our indefatigable artillerists would make use of it. But now the darkness comes to the relief of the distracted and persecuted foe, with undeserved mercy draws over him a shield, and affords him the respite and security for which, throughout that long day, he had doubtless so fervently prayed. What relief must have been this kindly interposition of nature! Nothing more can now be done. Our batteries are limbered up; some remain in their position; others return to the camp, that the men and horses may be refreshed and the caissons refilled. One of these was our Fifth Company. In the highest joy and exaltation over their triumph and the gallant deeds those chivalric young men merrily returned to the camp of the enemy. And then occurred a scene which gave a suitable and appropriate conclusion to the services of the day. The men formed in line, the Captain thanked them for their gallant and efficient conduct, and then Mr. F. N. Thayer, a well known and greatly esteemed citizen, in the name of his comrades, proposed that they should all kneel and offer up a prayer to Almighty God for their safety and their triumph. A prayer was read by Mr. Thayer, in his peculiarly impressive style, from the Common Prayer Book. Sergeant Bakewell added a few words of eloquent thankfulness, and the whole company uttered a solemn "Amen." Rarely has there been exhibited so sublime a display of natural piety as that of those gallant young men, who had been all day engaged in the wildest scenes of mortal destruction and reckless daring—who had not had a moment for reflection or thought, for any gentle or tender emotion now kneeling in the midst of an enemy's camp, surrounded by the dead and dying, and all the desolating consequences of a deadly and remorseless conflict, and offering up fervent prayers to Almighty God for his care, protection and aid in the hour of danger and trial.

TELEGRAPHED TO THE DAILY DELTA.

From Wilmington.

WILMINGTON, April 18.—A private letter of the 17th from Fort Macon, says the enemy attacked the fort last Saturday and have been fighting two days. Col. White sent out part of his men on the beach and found there 300 Yankees. They killed 15 of our men. We then retreated to the fort. Col. White opened fire upon them with canister, killing a large number. The enemy have built a battery two miles from the fort on the beach and planted mortars and large size siege guns. There are 11 large ships outside. The enemy have ... gunboats to operate in the Sound. They are committing every imaginable outrage in Carteret and Onslow counties. The fort had not been taken on Wednesday.

From Richmond.

RICHMOND, April 18.—The enemy have occupied Falmouth, opposite Fredericksburg, this morning. The Confederates burnt the bridges across the Rappahannock and evacuated the city.

From Knoxville.

KNOXVILLE, April 18.—The Register has a dispatch dated Bridgeport, April 18, which states that neither Decatur or Decatur bridge has been taken, and that there are only 3000 Yankees at Huntsville, the balance having fallen back. There are none on this side.

The steamer Lookout was not taken, but is at Guntersville, with 2000 sacks of Government corn and saltpeter untouched.

A man just from Nashville says the enemy are removing their stores, sick and wounded, also their cannon over the river, to Edgefield.

A gentleman from War Trace says Col. Stearns killed 75 of the enemy in the late fight, and wounded a large number.

Only two bridges have been burnt on the Charleston Railroad.

Our pickets went to Bellefonte last night, but saw no enemy. From the best information the enemy had gone back to Huntsville.

From Richmond.

RICHMOND, April 18.—There is a report, seemingly reliable, brought by the Orange train this evening, that Stonewall Jackson had a fight with the enemy yesterday morning; but the enemy being overpowering Jackson fell back, and was in full retreat towards Staunton. No statement of the loss on either side, further than that forty Confederates were taken prisoners. It was supposed Jackson would not make a stand until he reached Waynesboro'.

Col. McKinney, who was killed on the Peninsula Wednesday, was buried here this evening. There was a large turn-out.

SAVANNAH, April 18.—There was a skirmish on White Marsh Island on Wednesday, between some companies of the 13th Georgia Regiment and a Michigan regiment. The latter were repulsed with a loss of about twenty.

The Confederate loss in killed and missing 5, and slightly wounded 7.

There was an accident on the Atlantic and West Point Railroad yesterday. The train had soldiers on it. Greene, of Tennessee was killed, and about 26 others slightly wounded.

Congressional.

RICHMOND, April 18.—The Senate passed the bill increasing the postage to ten cents on single letters. Also, the House bill prohibiting the sale of cotton, sugar and tobacco to the enemy.

The House passed a bill to raise bands of partisan rangers.

Van Dorn's report of the battle in Arkansas was presented to-day.

At 4 o'clock in the afternoon of Thursday, the Yankees appeared six miles from Falmouth. Our pickets were driven in and several wounded. The infantry and cavalry were sent out but were twice repulsed by the enemy, who being in large force, advanced. Our troops fell back to Fredericksburg, set fire to three bridges across the river; also burnt three steamboats and twenty-two vessels, loaded with 100,000 bushels of corn, and 100 bales cotton at the depot. The panic among the inhabitants was tremendous. Our troops evacuated the city, and the enemy sent a shell after them which struck a cotton factory, doing much damage. All the rolling stock of the railroad company was saved, with the exception of eight cars.

The following letters, from Corinth, have been left at this office for distribution:

Mr. Geo. Schneider, Miss E. Doyle.

AUTHORIZATION.—Capt. H. B. Knox and B. E. Chaney give notice elsewhere that they are duly authorized by Col. Alex. Smith to raise companies for his regiment.

FROM THE SEAT OF WAR IN THE WEST.

Special Correspondence of the Delta.

MEMPHIS, April 16, 1862.

It has been in vain that I attempted during the past half dozen days to telegraph you. Intelligence in regard to many army movements and other important facts, have been declared contraband by the military authorities. They are not allowed to be published here by the papers. I see some things in the Picayune that got through, though not from this point. I state these facts to acquit myself in your eyes of a reasonable charge of neglect of duty.

I suppose that you have learned in some way or other that Gen. Price is here, and has been for quite a week. His army is also coming. At least twelve thousand of these have already arrived, and others on the way will probably swell the numbers to twenty thousand. Van Dorn has not yet arrived, remaining behind to bring up the rear. Only the cavalry of the Missouri army remain to keep up appearances and harass the enemy in the mountains of the West. Van Dorn, it is said, is to take command at Fort Pillow, with a part of his force, while Price, with the remainder, goes to Beauregard. This distribution of that force has already, in fact, been made. Price has created great enthusiasm here, and has been feasting and holding crowded levees since his arrival. No one can look upon him and not be impressed with the conviction that he is a great man. In height he is 6 feet 2 inches, erect and splendidly proportioned. His head is of the noblest mould, and every feature stamps him a man of mark. His hair is white, and flows over a face full of roses. I learn that he never indulges in the use of ardent spirits, and I guess that such is the fact in a good degree with his army, for I have not yet seen one of them drunk. Mark it, that whenever he gets to Corinth, or wherever our army shall be, he will infuse new fire into the bosoms of our troops. He is to-day the most popular man in the army, and, I think, deservedly so.

The report is here that the Federals have left the Tennessee, but it is not well established; and it is also reported that a column of thirty thousand have landed at Forked Deer river, with the purpose of assailing Fort Pillow in the rear. I am inclined to credit this, for it seems a probable move, and one likely to give us trouble. Their purpose most likely is to plant batteries below the fort and cut off all communication with it. But I suppose Beauregard knows what is afloat, and is prepared to checkmate. An opinion is expressed that the Federals, despairing of conquering our army at Corinth, have divided theirs—one wing moving up the Tennessee to hold the railroad, while the other moves down to threaten Memphis by way of the river. This movement would make a corresponding one on the part of the Confederates inevitable, at least in my opinion. I have no thought that they will attempt again to fight our concentrated forces. Defeat they know awaits them whenever and wherever they do.

Since writing the foregoing, it is ascertained to be true that the Federals are moving away from their late position on the Tennessee. The Federals have driven in our pickets on both sides of the river at Fort Pillow. It is said by men who came down to-day that the Federals are cutting a trench on the Arkansas side across the bend of the river to enable them to take advantage of the high stage of water and leave the fort in the rear. A gentleman who surveyed the river at that place last summer has shown me a rough diagram of the river. I cannot draw myself, but will probably be able to make you understand that, as the ground is very low on the Arkansas side, and the water very high, such a feat might be performed.

I hear it asserted, within the last hour, that Beauregard is moving his army to Jackson to meet the Federal army, who are supposed to be marching in that direction. Gen. Price has been to Corinth and has just returned. His forces now here are going into encampment at Fort Pickering, two miles below the city. A report came into town, from Corinth, that Gen. Bragg is dead. It is not confirmed, and I trust will not be.

Federal authorities report Buell mortally wounded. There is no denial of the report of the death of Gens. Sherman, Wallace and Crittenden. It is quite likely that they were killed. The guard who accompanied the prisoners to Mobile have just returned, and report the conduct of Gen. Prentiss as very shabby. He attempted to make a Union speech to a crowd at Grenada, and narrowly escaped rough treatment. He is evidently attempting to provoke stringent measures for some purpose; either for martyrdom or retaliation on Buckner.

Y.

Persons wishing to send letters to their friends in the Washington Artillery, in Virginia, can send them by Lieut. Ed. Owen, on Sunday morning, by leaving them at Messrs. Geo. Connolly & Co.'s, 56 Carondelet street.

DIED:

At the residence of John Watt, Esq., in this city, on the 15th inst., at 1 40 A. M., of wounds received at the battle of Shiloh, on the 6th inst., Capt. HENRY HUNTINGTON, of the 18th Louisiana Regiment, a native of Adams county, Miss., in the 42d year of his age.

Natchez papers please copy.

The Tri-Weekly Mercury.

DAILY PAPER—TEN DOLLARS PER ANNUM, PAYABLE HALF-YEARLY IN ADVANCE.

VINDICE NULLO
SPONTE SUA SINE LEGE FIDES RECTUMQUE COLENTUR.

COUNTRY PAPER—THRICE A WEEK—FIVE DOLLARS PER ANNUM, IN ADVANCE.

VOLUME LXXX. | CHARLESTON, S. C., TUESDAY, APRIL 22, 1862. | NUMBER 11,427

NEWS BY TELEGRAPH.

NEWS FROM RICHMOND.

RICHMOND, April 20.—Official despatches received here state that the mortar fleet of the enemy is bombarding the works just below the city of New Orleans. The bombardment has continued for three days. If the forts should be reduced, the iron-clad boat, the *Louisiana*, which is said to be superior to the *Virginia*, is expected to contribute to the defence of the city.

Fredericksburg has been occupied by a column under the command of McDOWELL, and our forces there, which consisted only of three regiments, two of infantry and one of cavalry, retired, having first burned the three bridges over the Rappahannock, the *St. Nicholas* and steamer *Virginia*, and eight or more vessels laden with corn, also one hundred and twenty-five bales of cotton, what little tobacco there was in the warehouse, and such commissary stores as could not be transported.

We have a report that Stonewall JACKSON had another fight with the enemy on Thursday morning, but, being overwhelmed by numbers, was compelled to fall back towards Staunton. This, however, is discredited by the War Department, as it conflicts with the official accounts.

The Senate has passed the House bill appropriating $1,500,000 for the construction of a railroad between Galveston and New Orleans. Also, the House bill authorizing the organization of bands of partizan rangers. The Senate refused to concur in a House resolution rescinding the resolution of adjournment fixed for Monday, the 21st. In both Houses the report of the Committee on the Flag and Seal was presented. The House postponed the consideration of the report, for the present, by yeas 39, nays 21.

ATTACK ON FORT MACON.

WILMINGTON, N. C., April 19.—On Saturday or Sunday last fighting commenced at Fort Macon, Col. WHITE had sent out a part of his force on the beach to attack the enemy's pickets. The Yankees turned out three hundred men against them, killing fifteen of our men. The balance retreated to the Fort, and Col. WHITE fired canister at the enemy, killing large numbers of them. The enemy has built a battery on the beach within two miles of the Fort and planted mortars and large siege pieces. He has thirteen large vessels outside. He has also sent to Newbern for gunboats to operate in the Sound. They say that as soon as they take the Fort they are going to Swansboro'. The enemy are committing the most unheard of outrages in Onslow and Carteret counties.

RICHMOND NEWS AND GOSSIP.

(FROM OUR OWN CORRESPONDENT.)

RICHMOND, Wednesday, April 16.

Yankee Account of Shiloh—Funny Features—Visit of the French Minister—Balloon, Frogs or Tobacco—Floyd's Report of the Defences at Donelson—Troops Passing, &c., &c.

As usual, we are indebted to the Yankees for the first "reliable" account of the battle of Shiloh, or Shilosh, as it is now spelled. Our own official report may be confidently looked for about the 4th of next July. To thank the Lord for a loss of 20,000 killed, wounded and missing, and to reverse the facts in regard to the captured guns and generals, is a proceeding truly Yankeefied and very wonderful, if it had not occurred so uniformly. We may always guage the enemy's loss by his report of our own. Confessing to 20,000 at Shiloh, they put down the rebel loss at 35,000 to 40,000; we may rest satisfied, therefore, with this last statement as an accurate account of the damage they received. Verily, Johnston and Beauregard hit them a heavy blow. Another funny feature in the Yankee news of this morning is the assertion that the object of the Merrimac was to engage the Monitor while the Patrick Henry and the Jamestown ran the blockade; and yet the "Merrimac affects the stock market unfavorably," although she is "no match for the Monitor."

Conjecture busies itself about the visit of the French Minister to this city. Wags say that he comes to look after his compatriot who was captured in the balloon the other day, or else to lay in a summer supply of the peculiar and high flavored frogs which grow only on the banks of the James River and Kanawha Canal—a luxury of which he has long been deprived. Reasonable folks say that he comes to look after the tobacco owned by the Emperor, which is stored in our warehouses, and is in danger of being burned in the face of McClellan as he advances to the capture of "the rebel Capital, rebel President, and rebel Congress." It is certain that our Secretary of State did not look look as smiling this morning as the bright weather warranted; and the determination of Congress to "make tracks" on Monday next reminds one of the Pennsylvania regiments who marched from the field of Manassas "to the sound of the enemy's cannon."

Floyd's account of the defences at Donelson will increase the admiration of the country for the devoted and heroic men who sacrificed themselves for the cause in that wretched man-trap. He tells us that the fort mounted only thirteen guns, of which but three were of any use whatever against iron gunboats, and that the entrenchments and rifle pits were hastily thrown up, in the face of the enemy, after the fight had commenced. Yet the telegraph reported Donelson as "impregnable," and I well recollect the phrase, "our lines are entrenched all around; Donelson can't be taken." The Whig is hardly too severe when it characterizes the concocters of such dispatches as "fools or knaves."

Infantry and cavalry in large numbers passed through this morning. The men were mostly Virginians, not at all showy or imposing in their dress and physique, but serviceable for all that. I believe the Virginians have fought well wherever they have been tried. A large body of artillery have also passed through. HERMES.

RICHMOND, Thursday, April 17.

Lee's Mill—Virginia and South Carolina Regiments Distinguish Themselves—Heavy Sand-Bag Business—Big Battle near this City—Mercier's Designs Unknown, &c., &c.

Owning the Yorktown telegraph, the Government keeps back all despatches from that quarter. But it is known that on yesterday our troops took Lee's Mill at the point of the bayonet, and that the fight raged from 3 to 7, p. m., and when night closed our men "held their own." A Virginia regiment (the 15th), and one from South Carolina (the 6th, I believe), especially distinguished themselves—the latter wading breast deep in mud and water to get at the enemy.

It is plain that McClellan is waiting the arrival of the Stevens Battery, which will give the Virginia all she can do. The Monitor will then be carried to York River, run past the Yorktown batteries, enfilade them, and drive our men off.—The transports will then follow in the Monitor's wake, land troops in Magruder's rear and on his right flank, and cause him to fall back. This can be repeated. Meantime the dirt flies in mountains. Ten thousand spades, and half as many picks, have been sent down; 8000 more spades are called for, and to-day every woman in Richmond is at work upon a little matter of 150,000 sand bags. Richmond may, therefore, be regarded as in a state of siege. There are reasons for believing that the great battle will be fought, not on the Peninsula, but within ten or twenty miles of the city. It is said that our generals want to draw the enemy as far as possible from his big fort and his gunboats. But McClellan is under a cloud, and the pressure of public opinion at the North may compel him to fight sooner than we expect. He promised to be here by the 20th or 25th of this month. Another good sign is seen in the active movements of Magruder, like that at Lee's Mill. A few heavy blows will help to demoralize the grand army; and it is hoped they will be kept up, maugre the sand bags.

Our boys continue to press down toward the scene of action. Two regiments went by this morning with palmetto in their caps.

Count Mercier's design is still a matter of mere conjecture. The Examiner of this morning tells him plainly that mediation is worse than useless, but that active intervention will result in almost any commercial privilege he may ask. We await the upshot of his visit with no feigned indifference. We have other matters to think about. We are rather weary of man-traps, and we are impatient to hear from Beauregard. News comes slowly from Corinth.

Our papers are counting too much, I fear, on the effects of the Southern sun upon the Yankees. I have no objection to the sun's assistance, but there is no good ground to believe that it will seriously impair the fibrous integuments of our codfish friends. Bullets and bayonets are the only reliable anti-Yankee remedies yet discovered. The Committee on the Roanoke Island affair publish a long report, exculpating General Wise. Individual shin-plasters have been suppressed by Gen. Winder—a good egg. The Yankees did little but steal chickens and rifle private houses at and near Tappahannock. Negros ran away from them. HERMES.

TRI-WEEKLY MERCURY.

TUESDAY, APRIL 22, 1862.

Interview between General Beauregard and his Prisoner, Gen. Prentiss.

Prentiss.—You have met and overcome to-day the best troops we have.

Beauregard.—I am glad to hear it, and trust that the result of this day's work may bring your Government to a frame of mind more favorable to peace.

Prentiss.—That can hardly be, sir. If your army had pushed on after the battle of Manassas, it might have taken Washington, and overrun the North, and brought us to peace. We had an insufficient supply of arms then, and were not prepared. The muskets purchased in Belgium by Fremont were of but little account; you could turn your thumb in the muzzle, the bore was so large. We also procured from England the old arms that have been stored away as useless in London Tower ever since the war with Napoleon in 1815. They are of no value whatever. It is only within the last sixty days that we have become thoroughly and efficiently armed. Our supply is now ample, and we cannot be overcome. Your Government has made two mistakes—first, in not availing itself of the fruits of the battle of Manassas; and secondly, in waiting until we had become well armed and organized. We have now 250,000 men in camps of instruction, who will be brought upon the field as they may be needed.—We do not doubt the final result.

Beauregard.—Nor do we. Our cause is just, and God will yet give us the victory.

(*From the Accounts of the Battle.*)

The Mississippians, Tennesseeans and Louisianians suffered terribly. All the troops behaved most gallantly. Never did men fight better; and yet many of them were *raw troops, fresh from their homes.* The 21st Alabama Regiment took two batteries, and the First Louisiana a section of artillery; other regiments did equally well.

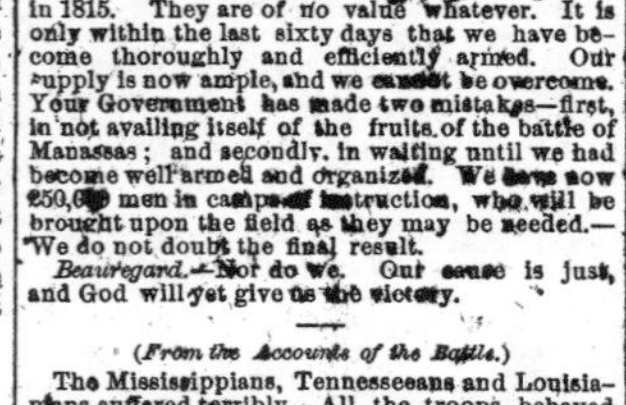

The New Flag of the Confederacy.

The Committee appointed by Congress to choose a suitable flag for the Confederate States, has at last closed its labors, and recommended for adoption the design given above. The flag is thus described in the terms of English heraldry:

On a field *gules* (red); a saltier *argent* (white); a Norman shield *azure* (blue), charged with a sun *or* (yellow).

The new ensign is certainly rich, brilliant, and easily distinguishable. The Sun has been very frequently urged as the proper emblem for the South, and the rays, which are to be alternately long and short, will suffice to represent the separate sovereignty of the States. Many would have preferred a more simple arrangement, to consist of two colors only; but, inasmuch as the Committee's device in no wise resembles the flag of the Yankees, we suppose that it will be generally well relished by the people. The new flag, however, has yet to receive the sanction of Congress, and may be rejected altogether by that body.

The Conscription Law.

The new and important Conscription measure recently adopted by Congress, will be found in our columns this morning. An incorrect version of the law appeared some days ago in both the papers of this city; but, inasmuch as the matters regulated by the Act are those which most intimately concern the great body of the people, we republish it, in its corrected and official form.

PERSONAL.—Col. ST. LEGER GRENFELL, Capt. GRIFFIN and Mr. KINEBROUGH, lately reached this city from abroad.

Hon. R. Kidder Meade, of Petersburg, late United States Minister to Brazil, is dead. He died at his residence in that city on Wednesday night, of an attack of gout on the stomach of not more than twenty-four hours' duration.

The New York Herald, of 14th, says: "Later intelligence from Port Royal indicates that the operations of Gen. Hunter's department are progressing favorably, but to enable him to carry out to the fullest extent his programme, and facilitate matters on the coast, it is necessary that he should be speedily reinforced with fresh troops, and we presume the War Department is not blind to the necessity."

The papers of the enemy contain Com modore Foote's official account of his occupation of Island No. 10, on the 8th instant. From this it appears that General Pope had succeeded in crossing the Mississippi below the Island, whereupon our forces evacuated the Island and the works on the neighboring Tennessee shore. Seventeen of our officers and 368 privates, besides some sick soldiers and employees, were taken by the enemy. Also 70 pieces of cannon and 4 steamers.

Governor Shorter of Alabama, has issued a sharp proclamation on the subject of planting cotton at this juncture. He concludes by "giving notice" as follows: "I shall urge upon the next session of the General Assembly the duty and sound policy of taxing all cotton beyond what may be needed for home consumption and the supply of seed for another year, to the full extent of its value, and I think it every way probable that persons who will persist in planting the usual crop of cotton, or more than one acre to the hand, will not be allowed to enjoy the fruits of such a selfish and unpatriotic course."

THE CONFEDERATE CONGRESS.

Our Richmond exchanges, received since our last issue, brings the detailed reports of three days' proceedings. On Wednesday no action of importance was taken in either House.

THURSDAY'S PROCEEDINGS.

In the Senate on Thursday a bill was passed; making provision for the coinage of the Confederate States. The bill established mints at Charlotte, North Carolina; Dahlonega, Georgia; New Orleans, Louisiana. A bill was also passed to compel disbursing officers or agents of the Government in the army to make speedy returns. The Senate then went into secret session.

The House, after some time spent in secret session, took up a bill to provide for the safe and expeditious transportation of troops and munitions of war by railroad. The bill provides for the appointment by the President of a "military chief of railroad transportation," who shall have the rank of a lieutenant-colonel, and receive compensation of five thousand dollars per annum, payable quarterly, and who shall be selected from the railroad officers in the Confederate States, with a special view to his judgment, skill and experience in the practical details of railroad operations and machinery. It also provides for the appointment of a district military superintendent, who shall have the rank of major, with the annual salary of sixteen hundred dollars.

The bill, after a sharp discussion, was passed—yeas 38, nays 33.

Mr. Wright, of Georgia, signified the intention of the delegation from that State to enter a protest against the bill, as they had a railroad which was pouring a million of dollars annually into the treasury of the State.

Mr. Miles, from the Committee on Military Affairs, reported a bill to amend "An Act for the increase of the military establishments of the Confederacy, and for the establishment and organization of the army of the Confederate States of America." Passed.

The House then again went into secret session.

FRIDAY'S PROCEEDINGS.

In the Senate, Mr. Clay, of Alabama, from the Committee on Commerce, reported back a House bill prohibiting all persons from selling cotton, sugar, tobacco, syrups, &c., and its transportation to or from any port, or place, in the possession of the enemy. Concurred in.

The bill increasing the rate of postage on single letters for any distance to ten cents was taken up and passed.

In the House of Representatives Mr. Miles said: The Military Committee had under consideration "A bill to raise bands of partizan rangers." The Committee have instructed me to report the same back, and ask to be discharged from its further consideration, and report a substitute for the bill. The original bill provides for the payment of a premium of five dollars per head on every one of the enemy killed. The substitute provides for the purchase, by the government, of all arms and munitions of war captured by the partizan bands from the enemy. It provides, further, that the number of persons in a band shall be unlimited; and they may be received for a short or long time, at the discretion of the President. The service is independent of the main army. The bill was passed.

A bill was passed, providing for the enlistment of one baker in each regiment of the army, when practicable.

A communication was received from the President, transmitting the official report of Gen. Van Dorn.

REPORT OF GEN. VAN DORN.

"HEADQUARTERS TRANS-MISSISSIPPI DISTRICT,
"JACKSONPORT, ARKS., March 27, 1862.

"GENERAL: I have have the honor to report, that while at Pocahontas, I received dispatches on the 22d February, informing me that Gen. Price had rapidly fallen back from Springfield, before a superior force of the enemy, and was endeavoring to form a junction with the division of Gen. McCulloch at Boston Mountain.

"For reasons which seemed to me imperative, I resolved to go in person to take command of the combined forces of Price and McCulloch. I reached their headquarters on the 3d of March, and being satisfied that the enemy, who had halted on Sugar Creek, fifty-five miles distant, was only awaiting large reinforcements before he would advance, I resolved to attack him at once. Accordingly I sent for General Pike to join me near Elm Springs, with the forces under his command, and on the morning of the 4th of March moved with divisions of Price and McCulloch by way of Fayetteville and Bentonville to attack the enemy's camp on Sugar Creek. The whole force under my command was about 16,000 men.

"On the 6th we left Elm Springs for Bentonville, and from prisoners captured by our scouting parties on the 5th, I became convinced that, up to that time, no suspicion was entertained of our advance, and that there was strong hopes of our effecting a complete surprise, and attacking the enemy before the large detachments encamped at various points in the surrounding country could join the main body. I therefore endeavored to reach Bentonville, eleven miles distant, by a rapid march, but the troops moved so very slowly that it was 11 a. m., before the head of the leading division (Price's) reached the village; and we had the mortification to see Seigel's division, seven thousand strong, leaving it as we entered. Had we been an hour sooner we should have cut him off with his whole force, and certainly have beaten the enemy next day.

"We followed him, our advance skirmishing with his rear guard, which was admirably handled, until we had gained a point on Sugar Creek, about seven miles beyond Bentonville, and within one or two miles of the strongly entrenched camp of the enemy.

"In conference with Generals McCulloch and McIntosh, who had an accurate knowledge of the country, I had ascertained that by making a detour of eight miles I could reach the Telegraph Road leading from Springfield to Fayetteville, and be immediately in rear of the enemy and his entrenchments.

"I had resolved to adopt this route, and therefore halted the head of my column near the point where the road by which I proposed to move diverges, threw out my pickets, and bivouacked as if for the night. But soon after dark, I marched again, moving with Price's division in advance, and taking the road by which I hoped before daylight to reach the rear of the enemy.

"Some obstructions, which the enemy had hastily thrown in the way, so impeded our march that we did not gain the Telegraph Road until near 10 o'clock, a. m., of the 7th.

"From prisoners with forage wagons, whom our cavalry pickets brought in, we were assured that we were not expected in that quarter, and that the promise was fair for a complete surprise. I at once made disposition for attack, and, directing Gen. Price to move forward cautiously, soon drew the fire of a few skirmishers, who were rapidly reinforced, so that before 11 o'clock we were fairly engaged, the enemy holding very good positions and maintaining a heavy fire of artillery and small arms upon the constantly advancing columns who were being pressed upon him.

"I had directed Gen. McCulloch to attack with his forces the enemy's left, and before 2 o'clock it was evident that if his division could advance, or even maintain its ground, I could at once throw forward Price's left advance over the whole line, and end the battle. I sent him a despatch to this effect, but it was never received by him. Before it was penned, his brave spirit had winged its flight, and one of the most gallant leaders of the Confederacy had fought his last battle.

"About 3 o'clock, p. m., I received by aid-de-camps the information that Generals McCulloch, McIntosh, and Col. Hebert were killed, and that the division was without any head. I, nevertheless, pressed forward with the attack, and at sunset the enemy were flying before our victorious troops at every point in our front, and when night fell we had driven them entirely from the field of battle. Our troops slept upon their arms nearly a mile beyond the point at which he made his last stand; and my headquarters for the night were at the Elk Horn Tavern. We had taken, during the day, seven cannon and about two hundred prisoners.

"In the course of the night I ascertained that the ammunition was almost exhausted, and the officer in charge of the ordnance supplies could not find his wagons, which, with the subsistence train, had been sent to Bentonville. Most of the troops had been without any food since the morning of the 6th, and the artillery horses were beaten out. It was, therefore, with no little anxiety that I watched the dawn of day. When it came, it revealed to me the enemy in a new and strong position offering battle. I made my dispositions at once to accept the gauge, and by seven o'clock the cannonading was as heavy as on the previous day. On the side of the enemy the fire was much better sustained, for, being freed from the attack of my right wing, he could now concentrate his whole artillery force. Finding that my right wing was so much disorganized, and that the batteries were, one after all other, retiring from the field with every shot expended, I resolved to withdraw the army; and at once placed the ambulances with all of the wounded they would bear, upon the Huntsville road, and a portion of McCulloch's division, who had joined me during the night, in position to follow, while I so disposed of my remaining force as best to deceive the enemy as to my intention, and to hold him in check while executing it. About ten o'clock I gave the order for the column to march, and soon afterward for the troops engaged to fall back and cover the rear of the army. This was done very steadily. The attempt was made by the enemy to follow us, and we encamped about 3 p. m., about six miles from the field of battle. Soon demonstrations were made by his cavalry upon my baggage train, and the batteries of artillery were turned by different routes from that taken by the army, but they were instantly checked, and thanks to the skill and courage of Colonel Stone and Major Wade, all of the artillery and baggage joined the army in safety.

"So far as I can ascertain, our losses amount to six hundred killed and wounded, and two hundred prisoners, and one cannon, which, having become disabled, I ordered to be thrown into a ravine.

"The best information I can procure places the enemy's killed at more than seven hundred, with at least an equal number wounded. We brought away about three hundred prisoners (so that his total loss is about three thousand), four cannon, three baggage wagons, and one burnt upon the field. Three cannon taken by McIntosh in his brilliant charge, the horses having been killed, could not be brought away.

"The force with which I went into action was less than fourteen thousand men; that of the enemy is variously estimated at from seventeen to twenty-four thousand.

"During the whole of this engagement I was with the Missourians under Price, and I have never seen better fighters than these Missouri troops, or more gallant leaders than Gen. Price and his officers. From the first to the last shot they continually rushed on, and never yielded an inch they had won; and, when at last they received orders to fall back, they retired steadily and with cheers. Gen. Price received a severe wound in the action, but would neither retire from the field nor cease to expose his life to danger.

"No success can repair the loss of the gallant dead who fell on the well-fought field. McCulloch was the first to fall. I have found him, in the frequent conferences I had with him, a sagacious, prudent counsellor, and a bolder soldier never died for his country.

"McIntosh had been very much distinguished all through the operations which have taken place in this region; and, during my advance from Boston Mountain, I placed him in command of the cavalry brigade and in charge of the pickets. He was alert, daring, and devoted to his duty.—His kindness of disposition, with his reckless bravery, had attached the troops strongly to him, so that, after McCulloch fell, had he remained to lead them, all would have been well with my right wing; but, after leading a brilliant charge of cavalry, and carrying the enemy's battery, he rushed into the thickest of the fight again at the head of his old regiment, and was shot through the heart. The value of these two officers was best proven by the effect of their fall on the troops.

"So long as brave deeds are admired by our people, the names of McCulloch and McIntosh will be remembered and loved.

"General Slack, after gallantly maintaining a long, continued and successful attack, was shot through the body, but I hope his distinguished services will be restored to his country.

"A noble boy, Churchill Clarke, commanded a battery of artillery, and during the fierce artillery action of the 7th and 8th was conspicuous for the daring and skill which he exhibited. He fell at the very close of the action. Colonel Reeves fell mortally wounded about the same time, and was a great loss to us. On a field where were many gallant gentlemen, I remember him as one of the most energetic and devoted of them all."

General Van Dorn refers for farther particulars to the reports of other officers who were in the engagement.

On motion the House adjourned.

THE REPORT OF THE COMMITTEE ON THE AFFAIR OF ROANOKE ISLAND.

The committee has published a report, which satisfactorily establishes the fact that the disaster at Roanoke was the unavoidable consequence of the action and orders of the Government at Richmond. The following paragraph presents the conclusion of the Committee:

General Wise, finding that his written appeals for aid in the defences of the island to headquarters at Norfolk and to the Department at Richmond were neglected and treated with indifference, repaired in person to Richmond, and called upon the Secretary of War, and urged in the most importunate manner the absolute necessity of strengthening the defences upon that island with additional men, armament and ammunition. The Secretary of War replied verbally to his appeals for reinforcements, that he had not the men to spare for his command. General Wise urged upon the Secretary that General Huger had about 15,000 men in front of Norfolk, lying idle in camp for eight months, and that a considerable portion of them could be spared for the defence of the rear of Norfolk, and especially as his (General Wise's) district supplied Norfolk and his army with nearly or quite all of his corn, pork and forage, that reinforcements at Roanoke Island were as absolutely necessary to the defence at Norfolk as forces in its front, and that particular or special posts should not be allowed to monopolize nearly all the men, powder and supplies. In reply to all his urgent appeals for the means of defence, General Wise, on the 22d of January, received the following military order, No. 17:

"Brigadier-General Henry A. Wise, Provisional Army, will immediately proceed to Roanoke Island, North Carolina, and assume command of the Confederate States troops at that place.

"By command of the Secretary of War:
[Signed] "JOHN WITHERS,
"Assistant Adjutant-General."

It is apparent to the committee, from the correspondence on file of General Wise with the Secretary of War, General Huger, his superior officer, the Governor of North Carolina, and other persons, that he was fully alive to the importance of Roanoke Island, and has devoted his whole time and energies and means to the defences of that position; and that he is no way responsible for the unfortunate disaster which befel our forces on that island on the 7th and 8th of February. But the committee cannot say the same in reference to the efforts of the Secretary of War and the commanding officer at Norfolk, General Huger.

It is apparent that the island of Roanoke was important for the defence of Norfolk, and that General Huger had under his command at that point upwards of fifteen thousand men, a large supply of armament and ammunition, and could have thrown in a few hours, a large reinforcement upon Roanoke Island, and that himself and the Secretary of War had timely notice of the entire inadequacy of the defences, the want of men and munitions of war, and the threatening attitude of the enemy. But General Huger and the Secretary of War paid no practical attention to those urgent appeals of General Wise, sent forward none of his important requisitions, and permitted General Wise and his inconsiderable force to remain to meet at least fifteen thousand men, well armed and equipped.

If the Secretary of War and the commanding general at Norfolk had not the means to reinforce General Wise, why was he not ordered to abandon his position and save his command? but, upon the contrary, he was required to remain and sacrifice his command, with no means in his isolated position to make his escape in case of defeat. The committee, from the testimony, are therefore constrained to report that, whatever of blame and responsibility is justly attributable to any one for the defeat of our troops at Roanoke Island, on the 8th of February, 1862, should attach to Major-General B. Huger and the late Secretary of War—J. P. Benjamin.

All of which is respectfully submitted.

B. S. GAITHER, Chairman.

BATTLE OF SHILOH—THE SECOND DAY'S FIGHTING.

(*Correspondence of the Mobile Advertiser.*)

BATTLE FIELD OF SHILOH,
Monday Night, April 7.

We have had another day of battle and blood. The fight was renewed this morning at eight o'clock by the enemy, who had been reinforced during the night; and with the exception of short breathing spells, it raged with tremendous violence and fury until night separated the combatants. The apprehensions expressed in my letter of last night have been realized. Buell did come up this morning, and with him came large reinforcements. But I am anticipating the events of the day. Let me resume the narrative where my last letter left it, and rehearse the varying fortunes of the day in the order of their occurrence. This is necessary to a proper understanding of the battle; and until this general sketch or outline is drawn, it will be impossible to enter into those minor details which constitute an interesting feature in the picture. Night alone prevented us from reaping the fruits of our brilliant victory of yesterday. It was quite dark when we chased the foe back to Pittsburg Landing, where he sought protection from his gunboats and river works.—Had Beauregard possessed the power of Joshua to command the sun to stand still in the heavens for the space of an hour our victory would have been as complete as that of the great Hebrew warrior. As it was, we expected to be able to capture so much of the Federal army this morning as could not be transferred to the other bank of the river last night, unless large reinforcements should come to their relief.

The enemy received the most important aid from his gunboats. Indeed, he is indebted to these gunboats for his escape from certain destruction. They, together with his river works, answered the valuable purpose of fortifications, to which he could retire when beaten on the field. With only our light field pieces, it was impossible to operate at night with any hope of success against these works and boats, or to prosecute during the heavy storm that followed, the work of completing the victory. Our forces had reached the river in one or two places as night came on, and in this way had gained some knowledge of the ground and the nature and position of the enemy's defences. With this knowledge, and the enemy driven into close quarters and caught between our lines and the river, there was every reason to believe we would be able to capture the larger part of his forces this morning, provided they were not reinforced during the night or transferred to the other bank of the river.

The boats kept up a constant fire during the night from their heavy guns. It appears that the enemy did not seek to recross the river. Knowing that large reinforcements were at hand, he held his position on the river bank until this morning. Gen. Beauregard knew there was a division of 7,000 men at Crump's Landing, a few miles below Pittsburg, and he gave orders last night to proceed against them this morning, and to capture them. This division succeeded, however, in forming a junction with the forces at Pittsburg, and at 8 o'clock this morning the Federals, thus reinforced, moved out from the river and offered us battle. They must have known that other reinforcements were at hand, and that they would arrive upon the field at an early hour. The fight was renewed about a mile and a half from the river, or midway between the river and the Federal encampment. The enemy came up to the work with great spirit and resolution. Appeals had doubtless been made to the men during the night, and the re-possession of their camp represented to them as a point of honor from which there could be no escape. The attack was directed against our centre; and though vigorous and spirited, and not expected, it was repulsed, and the enemy driven back with great slaughter. He rallied again, however, and this time he moved with an increased force upon our right wing. Here, too, he was repulsed and forced to retire. His next attempt was directed against our left wing, his attacks growing more vigorous and his forces increasing with each succeeding movement. Indeed it was now evident that he had received large accessions to his ranks, and that we had fresh troops and heavy odds to contend against. But the Confederates nobly did their duty, and the attack on the left was also repulsed. The enemy again retired, but only for a time; for Buell's forces had now come up, and the attack was renewed all along our lines, on the right, centre and left. Simultaneously with this, an attempt was made to turn both our wings.

The battle now raged with indescribable fury. I have never heard or imagined anything like the roar of the artillery, and the incessant rattle of the small arms. The deep thunder bass of the one, and the sharp, shrill tenor of the other, intermingled with the shrieks of bursting shells and the whizzing of cleaving rifled cannon balls, were grand beyond description. It was the awful Hymn of Battle, rolling upward to the skies and literally shaking the earth beneath. It was a solemn anthem, the notes of which were traced in blood, and uttered from brazen throats, that might have satisfied Mars himself.

The Confederates stood their ground against the furious onset, and for the fourth time the enemy was compelled to retire. It was now one o'clock. Our men were greatly exhausted; they had fought eighteen hours, and withal had slept but little, having been engaged much of the preceding night in searching out and taking care of the wounded. It was evident, too, that the enemy had been largely reinforced, and that each succeeding attack was made by fresh troops and overwhelming numbers. In view of these facts, and in order to rest his men, and to prevent an unnecessary loss of life, Gen. Beauregard availed himself of the falling back of the Federals to withdraw his troops to the enemy's line of encampment, where we rested last night. This was about a mile and a half from the point where the fight commenced this morning.

The enemy hesitated for some time, but finally came up and renewed the conflict. He was met with undiminished courage and resolution by the Confederates, who displayed the greatest possible gallantry. The battle raged on, and night alone separated the combatants. At length the enemy fell back, and so did the Confederates, both sides badly worsted and severely punished.

Having said thus much, I feel it to be my duty as a faithful chronicler of the times, to refer to a matter here which had a controlling influence upon the fortunes of the day.

Our attack yesterday was so sudden and successful, that the enemy found it impossible to remove his quartermaster and commissary stores, or even to save the baggage of the men. The temptation thus presented was too great for our troops to resist. Sunday night large numbers of them, supposing there would be no more fighting, set to work to gather up such spoils as the Federal encampment contained. There were arms, overcoats, caps, shoes, coffee, sugar, provisions, trunks, blankets, liquors, private letters, and numberless other things which the enemy had been compelled to abandon. Such of our troops as were engaged in searching out the wounded and dead, or were not restrained by a sense of duty, wandered from their respective camps, and spent much of the night in plundering. Orders had been issued by Gen. Beauregard positively prohibiting anything of the kind, but many of the troops are raw, and officers and men were alike elated at our success; and, consequently, the necessary steps were not taken to enforce the orders of the Commander-in-Chief. At an early hour this morning, the men renewed their search after the spoils of victory, and many of them were separated from their commanders when the enemy renewed the battle. Some of them had even started back to their camps, loaded with such articles as they had been able to find. After deducting the killed and wounded, and those who were engaged in removing the wounded, it would be no exaggeration to say five thousand sound and able bodied men had thus wandered out of the line, and took no part whatever in the battle to-day. On the other hand, the enemy had been largely reinforced. Thus, with a diminished force on our part, we had to meet fresh troops and a more numerous army than that we encountered yesterday. And thus, too, the spoils have prevented us from again driving the enemy back into the Tennessee, notwithstanding the great odds in his favor. It was well enough, while the conflict lasted, that our troops should exchange their smooth-bored muskets and shot guns for the splendid arms thrown away by the retreating foe; but there can be no excuse for the disgraceful proceedings to which I have alluded. The spoils of victory are not less demoralizing than defeat and disaster. Such is the lesson taught by history in all ages of the world, from the time when Achan was reduced by "the wedge of gold," down to the present day.—It is hoped that the experience of this day will not be thrown away either by our officers or soldiers.

COMMUNICATIONS.

HEADQUARTERS,
SULLIVAN'S ISLAND, 9th April, 1862.

To the Editor of the Mercury:

DEAR SIR: You will please publish the following communications, in justice to myself and regiment, and oblige. Respectfully,
Your obedient servant,
J. FOSTER MARSHALL,
Col. Comd'g Forces on Sullivan's Isl'd.

HEADQUARTERS, SULLIVAN'S ISLAND.
18th April, 1862.

GEN'L: I am in possession of the fact that there is in circulation a rumor to the effect "that you tendered to my regiment the position of being one of the So. Ca. regiments to go to Corinth, that I refused to accept the offer, and that another regiment had to be ordered to take my place."

I respectfully ask you to say whether you ever offered the place to my regiment? Whether or not, when you informed me that you had ordered two So. Ca. regiments (Cols. Manigault's and Lythgoe's) that I did not ask the favor for my regiment to go in the place of Col. Lythgoe's, or as an additional regiment? Whether or not, as soon as the news came that a part of Col. Lythgoe's regiment had deserted at Augusta, did I not again tender you my regiment to take the place of Col. Lythgoe's? And, lastly, your reasons for keeping my regiment on the island?

An answer to the above is solicited at your earliest convenience. Respectfully,
Your obedient servant,
J. FOSTER MARSHALL,
Col. Comd'g Forces on Sullivan's Island.

To Brig. Gen. RIPLEY,
Comd'g 2d Mil. D., S. C.

HEADQUARTERS,
2D MILITARY DISTRICT, 19th April.

COLONEL: The report mentioned in your letter is untrue. You were not offered a choice.—Your regiment was retained here because it was indispensable. When the news arrived of certain men from the 19th regiment having deserted from Augusta, you applied at once to have your regiment sent to Corinth, in order to do away with what you, in my opinion, properly considered a disgrace to the State. I did not order your regiment, because I could not spare or *replace* it.
Respectfully,
R. S. RIPLEY,
Brig. Gen. Comd'g.

To Col. J. FOSTER MARSHALL,
Comd'g Forces on Sullivan's Island.

CAMP PILLOW, HEADQUARTERS,
JOHN'S AND WADMALAW ISLANDS,
April 15.

To the Editor of the Mercury: Some week or two ago I noticed in your paper a very liberal subscription from the Edgefield and Barnwell Rangers, Capt. Twiggs, for building an iron-clad gunboat. Thinking that the example was worthy of imitation, a subscription was set on foot in my own regiment and the other companies constituting my command on these islands. I send you below the result of the effort. The amount subscribed would have been much larger but for the absence of many of the officers and soldiers from sickness. When they return the amount will probably be much more.

The object of this communication is to propose to the officers and soldiers now in service from this State to join us in this enterprise, and when a sufficient amount is raised, to have a committee, consisting of one from each command, to meet in Charleston or some other convenient place, to devise measures for its speedy completion. The boat is, of course, to be the joint property of the subscribers, but to be volunteered "for the war" to the Confederate States. The speedy co-operation of the other commands in this important measure is cordially and respectfully solicited.
J. H. MEANS, Col. Comd'g
John's and Wadmalaw Islands.

SUBSCRIPTION OF THE 17TH REGIMENT, S. C. V. (COL. MEANS.)

Field and Staff	$415.00
Company A, Capt. Culp	74.00
" B, Capt. Meacham	125.00
" C, Capt. Wilson	408.00
" D, Capt. Caskey	54.00
" E, Capt. Sadler	250.00
" F, Capt. Rice	240.00
" G, Capt. Coleman	165.00
" H, Capt. Witherspoon	256.00
" J, Capt. Kearse	241.50
" K, Capt. Beatty	210.00
	$2503.50

SUBSCRIPTION OF CAVALRY, S. C. V. C. (PORTION OF COL. BLACK'S BATTALION.)

Edgefield and Barnwell Rangers, Capt. Twiggs	$745.00
Chester Troop, Capt. Walker	717.00
Abbeville Troop, Capt. Owens	775.00
Spartanburg and Laurens Troop, Capt. Nesbit	244.00
Stono Scouts, Capt. Walpole	90.00
	$2,578.00
	$2,503.50
Total	$5081.50

To the Editor of the Charleston Mercury:—I send you the money subscribed by the Holcombe Legion for the building of a gunboat for the defence of Charleston harbor. The amount sent is somewhat more than at first promised. You are at liberty to appropriate it to whatever gunboat you may choose, but I hope it may be an iron-clad vessel. I understand there is great difficulty in procuring iron. Cannot something be done with the Spartanburg Iron Works? I am no advocate for the Government taking charge of works of internal improvement, but as it is charged with the public defence, I think the State Government or the Confederate Government might, with perfect propriety, take charge of those works, and develop them sufficiently to meet our most urgent wants, provided the present Company does not choose to do so of its own accord. Respectfully,
P. F. STEVENS,
Colonel Holcombe Legion, S. C. V.

SUBSCRIPTION OF THE HOLCOMBE LEGION TO GUNBOAT FUND.

Field and Staff	$255.00
Cavalry.	
Company A, Captain Walsh	376.25
" B, Captain Taylor	508.00
" C, Captain Spearman	163.85
" D, Captain McKissick	100.75
	[illegible]
Infantry.	
Company A, Captain Smith	$104.25
" B, Captain Sloan	99.25
" C, Captain Bomar	68.75
" D, Captain Crawley	185.25
" E, Captain Robuck	92.25
" F, Captain Zeigler	276.00
" G, Captain Heller	88.75
" H, Captain Maffitt	140.25
" I, Captain Bishop	59.00
	$1045.75
Total subscription	$2544.60

It is an established fact that great numbers of the Yankees at the battle of Shiloh were iron-clad. Many of the new "patent" breastplates were taken from the bodies of the enemy's killed. One of them had eight indentations. The ninth shot, however, struck the man in the head and he fell dead. There were eight shots thrown away.

The Macon Telegraph, of the 12th inst., says: "J. N. Neuffer, an individual well known in Charleston and at Nashville, was on yesterday examined before Judge Myers at Marietta, on charges affecting his loyalty to the South, and was committed to jail there until bail for his appearance at Court should be given."

A destructive smash-up occurred on the Atlanta & West Point Railroad, four miles south of Newnan, Ga., on the 15th instant. A number of soldiers were on board, *en route* for Corinth, one of whom was killed (a Tennesseean), and some twenty-five wounded, but not dangerously. Nine of the front cars were completely wrecked.

THE NEWS OF THE WAR.

THE GREAT BATTLE OF SHILOH—WHAT HAPPENED AFTER THE FIGHT.

Yesterday we received a large number of our Southwestern exchanges, filled with interesting details of the great battle of Shiloh, but we are compelled, by want of space, to be brief in our selections. We make room for an interesting letter from the Corinth correspondent of the Mobile *Advertiser*:

CORINTH, April 10.

The railway lines leading from this place are much occupied just now in removing the wounded, and in performing such other labor as the military authorities require of them. The wounded are being removed principally to Memphis and Oxford. Unfortunately some were left on the battle field, and have not been recovered. There is reason to hope, however, that they will be humanely treated by the enemy. In this connection let me call the attention of the country to the following correspondence between General Beauregard and Gen. Grant:

GEN. BEAUREGARD TO GEN. GRANT.

HEADQUARTERS ARMY OF THE MISSISSIPPI, MONTEREY, April 8th, 1862.

SIR: At the close of the conflict of yesterday, my forces being exhausted by the extraordinary length of time during which they were engaged with yours on that and on the preceding day, and it being apparent that you had received, and were still receiving reinforcements, I felt it my duty to withdraw my troops from the immediate scene of conflict.

Under these circumstances, in accordance with usages of war, I shall transmit this under a flag of truce, to ask permission to send a mounted party to the battle field of Shiloh, for the purpose of giving decent interment to my dead.

Certain gentlemen wishing to avail themselves of this opportunity to remove the remains of their sons and friends, I must request for them the privilege of accompanying the burial party; and in this connection, I deem it proper to say, that I am asking only what I have extended to your own countrymen under similar circumstances.

Respectfully, General,
Your obedient servant,
[Signed] G. T. BEAUREGARD, Gen. Com'g.
To Maj. Gen. U. S. Grant, U. S. A.,
Com'g U. S. Forces near Pittsburg, Tennessee.

REPLY OF GEN. GRANT.

HEADQUARTERS ARMY IN THE FIELD, PITTSBURG, TENN., April 9, 1862.

Gen. G. T. Beauregard, Commanding Confederate Army of the Mississippi, Monterey, Tenn.:

SIR: Your despatch of yesterday is just received. Owing to the warmth of the weather, I deemed it advisable to have all the dead of both parties buried immediately. Heavy details were made for this purpose, and it is now accomplished.

There cannot, therefore, be any necessity of admitting within our lines the parties you desire to send, on the ground asked.

I shall always be glad to extend any courtesy consistent with duty, and especially when dictated by humanity.

I am, General, very respectfully, your obedient servant, U. S. GRANT, Major General.

Gen. Grant has doubtless had our dead buried, but the judgment of mankind will not approve of his refusal to allow the parents and friends of the slain the privilege of recovering the remains of their loved ones, or of designating the places where they have been interred. He declines to do unto Gen. Beauregard as Gen. B. has done unto Federal commanders on a former occasion.

The extent of our casualties has not yet been ascertained, the regimental and brigade reports not having been sent in. It is believed, however, that our loss is much less than it was first supposed to be, especially in killed. The battle was fought for the most in the woods, and the timber protected our men in a measure from the enemy's fire. For the same reason, many of the wounds inflicted—a large majority of them—were comparatively slight. A great many were shot in the hands and arms. It would be no exaggeration to say that I saw myself at least 100 who had been thus wounded. Many had been shot in the mouth, or had their faces slightly marked. One poor fellow had six teeth carried away by a ball, but received no other injury. Another had his entire chin shot away, yet he continued to fire at the enemy until he literally bled to death!

Our killed will hardly exceed 600—some say 400. There is a similar difference in the estimates of the wounded—some putting it at 2000, others as high as 3000. It is probable that 2500 will cover our entire loss in killed, wounded and missing. Monday night it was believed to have been much heavier. A considerable portion of our forces are still on active duty, and in close proximity to the enemy, and hence the difficulty of procuring exact results.

We can only offer conjectures as to the casualties of the enemy. Officers who had better opportunities than I of forming a correct opinion, think that 4000 will cover their killed and wounded, and that the same number will cover their loss in prisoners, including some 200 officers. This would make their entire loss about 8000.

One of the greatest curiosities found on the battle field is the steel breastplate worn by the enemy. Several of them were picked up, one of which I have seen myself. It is made in two pieces, which are sewed in the front part of the vest, and extend from the waist to the neck. It covers the entire breast, and is about as thick as the plantation cross cut saw. Whether these breast plates are worn by the Northern soldiers generally, or only by their sharp shooters, I cannot say; but by whomsoever worn, they can only be considered by all brave men as badges of cowardice.

Below I hand you a list of the killed and wounded in the Twenty-Second, Twenty-Fifth and Twenty-Sixth Alabama regiments. You have already been furnished with the casualties in the Twenty-First regiment. The Seventeenth, Eighteenth and Nineteenth regiments have been ordered to ———, in the immediate vicinity of the enemy, and I have been enabled to procure lists of their losses.

CAPTURE OF TORIES IN TENNESSEE.

The Knoxville *Register*, of the 17th inst., says:

The streets were full of rumors on yesterday, some of them of a very extravagant nature, in regard to the results of Capt. Ashby's encounter with the gang of "Stampeders," whose departure we noticed a day or two ago. The following are the facts in the case:

As soon as the fact of their having started for Kentucky was brought to the notice of the authorities here, Capt. Ashby, with a detachment of men, consisting of his and Capt. Bradley's companies of cavalry, were started in pursuit. Having placed Capt. Bradley to guard a gap below, he pushed forward and came up with the tories about eight miles about Fincastle, in Campbell county, giving them immediate battle, killing thirty, wounding the same number, and capturing four hundred and twenty-one prisoners, with a loss to himself of five wounded, all of whom, it is feared, mortally. We regret to learn that Lieut. Gibbs, of Capt. Ashby's company, was among the wounded on our side. We had only seventy men in the attack.

AFFAIRS BELOW SAVANNAH.

The Savannah *Republican* of yesterday says:

On the banks of the Savannah all seems quiet. The enemy, few in numbers, are still lying in our lower river, and, so far as seen, no reinforcements have reached them. They have not a force equal to an attack on the city, and its augmentation would seem inconsistent with the pressing demands from other points at the present time. Meanwhile we are not idle. The military authority here are using all means in their power to strengthen our defences and make them impregnable. Come in what numbers he may, the enemy will have his hands full in his march upon Savannah. A gunboat came up Freeborn's Cut yesterday forenoon, to within about two miles of our battery at Causton's Bluff, but no gun was fired on either side. A Federal propeller also came up the river yesterday and fired a shot in the direction of Mackey's Point, but it fell far short of the mark.

THE FIGHT ON THE PENINSULA.

From various sources of information we gather the following account of the fight for the Peninsula:

The fight occurred on Wednesday at Lee's Mill, and was commenced by the invaders, who attempted to drive our forces from that position. They have long desired to obtain possession of this mill, as it is not only a strong position, but the mill itself furnishes provisions to a considerable extent of our troops.

It is stated that the Fifteenth North Carolina had been in line of battle for three or four hours during the day, momentarily expecting an attack, but the enemy not appearing, they were ordered to stack arms and prepare for dinner. While enjoying their repast, a couple of Yankee companies waded Warwick river, a very narrow stream, which was believed to be unfordable, and, thus eluding our pickets, came suddenly upon the camp. The long roll was sounded immediately, and the men rushed to their arms, driving the enemy back into the creek, killing all of both companies except eight, who surrendered and were taken prisoners. The enemy, hearing the firing, appeared in large numbers on the opposite bank of the river, and the fighting became general. The fight lasted from three p. m. until seven. Gen. Howell Cobb commanded, and it is stated the troops under his command were handled with great skill. One report says that the enemy must have had an entire brigade engaged, and that the river and the hill beyond were literally covered with the dead and wounded. We took several prisoners, who made various statements as to their numbers, etc. The Fifteenth North Carolina regiment was engaged, and the colonel of that regiment, Robert M. McKinney, was killed while bravely leading his men into the fray. Colonel McKinney was a young gentleman of thorough military attainments, having graduated with distinction at the Virginia Military Institute. He was a native of Lynchburg, Virginia, where his parents still reside. Colonel McKinney was only twenty-five years of age.

YANKEE ACCOUNTS FROM YORKTOWN.

A despatch from Washington, in the New York papers of the 12th, says of affairs at Yorktown:

Parties come up from the army report no special change in affairs. Continued skirmishing going on, and a brilliant little affair occurred yesterday morning, in which Griffin's battery participated with marked effect, killing and wounding twenty-seven rebels. The rebel position extends across the Peninsula, from Yorktown to Warwick, near James river, a short distance above Mulberry Point. The conformation of the land, and the making in of the creek from James river, shortens their line of defence, and enables them to command, with their fortifications, all the Peninsula. Generals Lee and Joseph E. Johnston are both reported to be with the rebel forces here—one commanding at Yorktown and the other at Warwick, Magruder holding a subordinate command at Williamsburg. Rebel forces reported at fifty thousand. General McClellan has ordered several siege pieces to the Peninsula.

LOCAL MATTERS.

A SKIRMISH occurred early last Saturday morning on John's Island, in which one of our men, Mr. JOHN B. WHALEY, a member of Captain NESBIT'S mounted corps, was seriously, if not mortally wounded. It appears that three companies of the enemy attempted a landing with two pieces of artillery. They were fired upon by twelve of our men who were posted as pickets in the neighborhood. The fire was returned, and as our men fell back, Mr. WHALEY received a ball through his body. Up to one o'clock on Saturday he still survived, but fears were entertained that his wound would result fatally.

FATAL RAILROAD ACCIDENT.—As the down train of the South Carolina Railroad had reached within thirty-three miles of Charleston, between two and three o'clock on Sunday morning, the engine and one of the passenger cars were thrown from the track, in consequence of the switch not being properly adjusted. Two of the cars were badly smashed, and Mr. JOHN AHRENS, Mr. JOHN SPAIN, and Mr. MAT. SHEA, were so badly injured as to cause their death almost immediately. Some other passengers were slightly wounded.

SUBSCRIPTIONS FOR THE GUNBOAT.—Besides the munificent military subscriptions, of which notice will be found in another part of this paper, we have received the following:

From Mrs. G. VARN, Broxton's Bridge, $10.
From Miss M. C. M., Broxton's Bridge, $5.
From Miss S. E. DELOACH, Prince William, $3.
From Mrs. W. R. TUTEY, Prince William, $2.
From Mrs. A. M. PEEPLES, Prince William, $2.
From Mrs. C. MIXSON, Prince William, $1.
From C. M. W., Georgia, $1.
Also, a crochet lady's collar.

From the ladies of St. Matthew's Parish, through J. B. Welling, Esq., $205, contributed as follows: Mrs. David Houser, $20; Mrs. J. J. Wannamaker, $10; Mrs. Dr. W. L. Pou, $10; Mrs. Thos. K. Zimmerman, $10; Mrs. B. H. Zimmerman, $10; Mrs. Mary Gates, $10; "A Friend," $10; "A Friend," $10; "A Friend," $10; Ladies of Mr. Farnum's family, $10; Mrs. John Sellers, $5; Miss Frances Sellers, $5; Mrs. Dr. W. C. Whetstone, $5; Mrs. B. E. Gates, $5; Mrs. W. Houser, $10; Mrs. A. V. Hennon, $5; Miss M. A. Riley, $5; Mrs. Sarah Felker, $5; Miss Anna Smoke, $5; Miss H. C. Cummings, $5; "A Friend," $5; "A Friend," $5; Mrs. Mary Cuther, $2; Mrs. Nathan Walling, $2; Mrs. S. J. Josey, $2; Mrs. M. A. Carroll, $2; Mrs. Julia Darden, $2; Mrs. Melcha Holman, $1; Mrs. P. A. Buyck, $1; Miss J. Buyck, $1; Mrs. L. Myers, $1; Miss Lizzie Fraeser, $1; "A Friend," $2; "A Friend," $1; Miss E. M. Rumph, $5; Mrs. J. W. Zeigler, $5; "A Friend," $2. Total, $205.

From Mrs. James McCown, Florence, $10.

The contributions sent by Mrs. M. HAWKINSON were received, and acknowledged in our issue of the 10th instant.

TRACTS FOR SOLDIERS.—We refer our readers to the list of "Tracts for Soldiers" which will be found in another column of this morning's paper. The titles indicate variety, and an adaptation to the wants of the soldier. Those who are interested for the spiritual well being of the army, may obtain here the means of accomplishing great good. These tracts are published by the Colportage Board, of which Rev. W. D. RICE is the General Superintendent.

HAVANA MARKET.—Through the attention of a gentleman, lately arrived, we have been placed in possession of the Havana Mercantile Report of April 12. We make the following extracts:

Sugars—Clayed.—Sales for the week had taken place to a fair extent at 6½@6¾ rials per arrobe, basis No. 12, although 7 rials had been paid in some exceptional cases. The stock of Clayed Sugars at Havana and Matanzas was estimated at 350,000 boxes, against 323,000 in 1861, 250,000 in 1860, and 270,000 in 1859.

Muscovadoes.—Considerable sales have been made at outports at 5@5½ rials for ordinary refining qualities, and 6@6½ rials for good Centrifugal.

Molasses.—About 1000 hhds. clayed have found buyers during the week, at 1½ rials per keg. No transactions in Muscovadoes.

Coffee.—105 bags Santiago de Cuba sold at $17½, and 150 at $18 per quintal.

Cotton.—No sales or exports during the week. The cargo of the Austin, from New Orleans (1150 bales), was being transhipped.

Hay.—The market was overstocked with ordinary descriptions, selling at 20 to 22 rials per bale.

Beef and Pork.—American Mess Beef was selling at $18 per barrel. Pork selling at $9¾@16 per barrel.

Rice.—Sales about 8000 bags during the week. Java and India Rice had sold at 10¾@14¼ rials per arrobe. Spanish from 10¼@13 rials.

Salt.—A cargo from Liverpool had been sold for a market in the Confederate States at $4 per 200 pounds.

DROWNED.—We regret to learn that Mr. LESLIE D. OWENS, a member of the Washington Artillery, and a young gentleman highly esteemed by all who knew him, was drowned on Sunday morning, while bathing near the camp of his company at Adams' Run. His body was recovered, and will be brought to Charleston to-day.

DESERTERS.—A report has reached this city that five persons—four men and a boy—came ashore in a boat on Saturday night, from the enemy's fleet and landed on Sullivan's Island, where they are now held as prisoners.

A SMALL SCHOONER and a pilot boat were seen in company with the fleet on Sunday, off this Bar, and are supposed by some to be prizes. The blockaders off Charleston generally number six or seven vessels, mostly steamers.

OBSEQUIES OF GEN. GLADDEN.—The remains of Gen. A. H. GLADDEN were solemnly interred at Mobile on the 12th inst. The funeral sermon was preached before an immense concourse by the Rev. Mr. BURGET, at the Government street Presbyterian Church. The corpse was escorted to the grave by Maj. Gen. T. J. MCCOY and staff, Brig. Gen. T. J. BUTLER and staff, a number of other officers and the soldiery.

W. H. H. DERWORT, Broker and Auctioneer, No. 51 Broad-street, sold on Friday last, at private sale, for cash, a boy 14 years old for $800.

NEWS BY TELEGRAPH.

FIGHTING IN NORTH CAROLINA.

NORFOLK, April 20.—There was heavy cannonading yesterday at the Rip Raps, from which place thirty-one shells were thrown at Sewell's Point, but without doing any damage. Heavy discharges of musketry, continuing for several hours, were heard on Friday.

On Saturday, a force of the enemy, supposed to number about 5000, landed on the Pasquotank River, in Camden County, North Carolina, and near Elizabeth City. They were attacked at one o'clock, p. m., by Col. WRIGHT, with the Third Georgia Regiment, and Capt. FERRIBEE'S Militia Company. The battle lasted five hours, and our little force fought with the greatest bravery. The enemy's loss was heavy. Our loss was six killed (including Captain MCCOMAS, of Henningsen's Battery, Wise Legion, and Lieut. WILSON, of the Third Georgia Regiment) sixteen wounded, and fifteen missing. At midnight, Col. WRIGHT'S force retired from the field, and fell back to the Half Way House, on the Dismal Swamp Canal—a very strong position. Reinforcements have been sent down.

Our wounded—most of whom are but slightly injured—have arrived here, and been placed in the hospital. The body of Capt. MCCOMAS has also arrived.

LATEST FROM WILMINGTON.

WILMINGTON, N. C., April 20.—Nothing further from Fort Macon. It is generally believed that communication with the fort has been cut off. The blockaders captured a schooner on Friday last, off Cape Fear Bar. The schooner was, at the time, trying to make her way in. All quiet here.

THE WAR IN THE WEST.

MEMPHIS, April 18.—*Despatch to Savannah Republican.*—The enemy commenced the bombardment of Fort Pillow on Sunday, the 13th inst., and renewed it next day, but without results. Five gunboats and three mortar-boats are engaged in the siege. The Federals have landed a considerable force above the Fort on Forky-deer River.

At Shiloh, as at Manassas, we did not know the real extent of our victory, and consequently failed to improve it, as under different circumstances we might have done. All accounts from the North and West show an immense Federal loss. Nine boat loads of wounded have passed Paducah, and private accounts put the actual loss of the enemy at 18,000, including 4,000 prisoners. They claim 800 Confederate prisoners. A gentleman just from Paducah says the enemy is greatly disconcerted, and has already got enough of BEAUREGARD and Corinth. It is believed that the Federals are falling down the river, with the view of marching across and joining the forces from the Mississippi, and then marching on Memphis. Northern news of the 14th states that the wounded continue to arrive, and great grief and despondency fill the country. Huntsville has not been retaken.

THE BOMBARDMENT OF THE FORTS BELOW NEW ORLEANS.

NEW ORLEANS, April 21.—The *Delta* has the following special despatch:

Fort Jackson, April 20, 8.30 p. m.—The enemy's fire has very much slackened. He has already consumed in the bombardment 370,000 pounds of powder, and over 1,000 tons of iron. History records no bombardment equal in severity to that to which we have been exposed. Our loss, so far, 5 killed and 10 wounded. The firing is now very slow. The mortar boats are out of sight, behind a point of woods. We sunk two of the mortar boats yesterday and disabled a steamer.

FROM RICHMOND—ADJOURNMENT OF CONGRESS.

RICHMOND, April 21.— In the Senate, to-day, Mr. SEMMES, of Louisiana, moved to take up the House bill repealing the Tariff; negatived. Mr. HUNTER, of Virginia, was re-elected President *pro tem.* of the Senate. The bill increasing the postage rate to ten cents, was taken up and passed. The open session was of brief duration.

In the House, Mr. DAVIS, of Mississippi, moved a suspension of the Rules to allow him to introduce a resolution requesting the President to order Gen. J. JOHNSTON to make an immediate attack upon the enemy on the Peninsula. Lost: yea 1 (Mr. DAVIS), nays 57. At 3 p. m., both Houses adjourned, to meet on the 3d Monday in August.

There is no news here. It has been raining all day.

LADIES' GUNBOAT FAIR.—A meeting of the ladies who intend to take part in the Ladies' Gunboat Fair, and of the gentlemen senior and junior managers, was held at the Depository, Chalmers-street, on Saturday last, at 5 o'clock, p. m. On motion of the Hon. WM. ALSTON PRINGLE, RICHARD YEADON, Esq., was called to the chair, and W. D. H. KIRKWOOD, Esq., was appointed Secretary. Mr. YEADON addressed the meeting at considerable length, explaining the objects of the meeting, enlarging on various topics appropriate to the existing period of ruthless war and vandal invasion, and lauding the ladies for their patriotic efforts to give Charleston the means of naval defence, by the construction of gunboats. He stated in the course of his remarks that the only way in which the ladies could accomplish their ardent wish and settled purpose, to give an iron-clad gunboat, or war steamer, was to contribute their present and future donations to the construction of the first iron-clad war steamer, now being constructed under the direction of Capt. INGRAHAM, the hero of the Koszta exploit, and the destined victor, under the Confederate flag, in our own waters—that in an interview that morning with that distinguished officer, he learned that it would cost at least $250,000 to construct a single iron-clad war steamer, the iron alone being estimated to cost $72,000—that it was visionary to suppose that the ladies could raise such a sum, if at all, in time to have any practical effect in defending our city, or raising its blockade—that he had therefore submitted to Captain INGRAHAM a proposal (subject to the ratification of the lady donors of the Gunboat Fund), that the ladies would contribute at least $50,000 to aid the Confederate Government in constructing the first iron-clad steamer for the defence of Charleston, provided the Government would constitute the steamer "The Ladies' Gunboat," or "The Ladies' War Steamer," and confer on it the time-honored and laurelled name of "The Palmetto State"—that Captain INGRAHAM approved of the project, and undertook promptly to submit it to the proper authorities at Richmond. Mr. YEADON then put the proposal to the vote of the ladies present at the meeting, and it met their unanimous concurrence; whereupon he stated that, unless objected to by a majority of the lady donors throughout the State, such would be the order of proceeding, if the Confederate Government should sanction the scheme.

The following programme of action, or order of proceeding for the Fair, on suggestion of Mr. Y., was then unanimously adopted by the ladies present:

1. The Fair to be held on the first Tuesday in May next.

2. The Military Hall, in Wentworth-street, to be the *locus in quo* of the Fair.

3. A grand raffle to take place, on the last day of the Fair, of all the valuable articles of jewelry, plate, embroidery, etc., etc., etc., contributed for the benefit of the Gunboat Fund—the whole to be embraced in one grand scheme, after the model of the late New Orleans raffle for a similar object; the chances to be at $1 each—the prizes, of course, to be as numerous as the articles contributed, and the number of chances to be, in some measure, regulated by the value of those articles.

4. The Junior Managers to meet as soon as practicable, and make all necessary arrangements for the Fair; and their Chairman authorized to have printed, immediately, 10,000 tickets of admission to the Fair, to be sold at a suitable price.

It was also understood that the Junior Managers would arrange the scheme of the raffle and issue tickets for chances. All persons who have already taken chances at raffles, previously advertised, where the chances are at $1, to be considered as having paid for chances in the grand raffle, unless they shall recall their subscriptions.

On motion of Judge PRINGLE, the meeting then adjourned.

The Junior Managers are respectfully solicited to meet at once, and proceed in the discharge of the duties assigned them.

The ladies who are to take or to serve tables, are also respectfully and earnestly solicited to work up to the appointed time.

LADIES' CHRISTIAN ASSOCIATION.—The inclemency of the weather having prevented the regular weekly meeting of this Society, we make the following acknowledgments, that our friends may know their donations have been received:

From Mrs. Wm. Laidler, 1 basket of eggs.
Mrs. and Miss Carson, of Midway, 1 dozen pair socks.
Miss C. R., 6 pair socks.
Blackville Soldiers' Relief Association, 1 bale containing mattrasses, comforts, blankets, and other bedding; also, 2 boxes, containing books, socks, clothing, sage, red pepper, flaxseed, wine, jelly, medicine, &c.
From the Beech Island "Volunteers Aid Society," 2 bales, containing 104 pair socks, 12 comforts, 20 shirts, 20 pair drawers, 2 pair pantaloons, 2 gloves, and 2 scarfs.

We have given to the Rikersville Hospital—8 bottles of wine, 1 basket eggs, red pepper, 1 bottle pickles. Citadel Square Hospital—3 dozen eggs, 2 bottles wine. To Dr. Smith—paregoric, camphor, laudanum, cholera syrup, salts, 6 bottles blackberry cordial, and 7 bottles mustard. To some soldiers who left for Tennessee in haste, we gave 15 shirts, 22 pair drawers, 11 pants, 13 pair socks. Individual application for sick soldiers—2 bottles blackberry cordial, 2 bottles brandy, 1 bottle mustard, ½ lb. of tea, 2 musquito nets.

Mrs. L. CHAPIN, President.

ACKNOWLEDGEMENT.—I return the warmest thanks to J. K. SASS, Esq., for the donation of a large bundle of *Tracts* for the soldiers in Atlanta. God will surely bless such efforts to extend His "name and influence" among His dispersed children.

A. F. FREEMAN,
President St. Philip's H. A. S., Atlanta, Ga.

Tribute of Respect.

At a regular meeting of the Ætna Fire Engine Company, held at Mills House Hall, on the evening of the 14th inst., the following Preamble and Resolutions were adopted:

Again are we called upon, through the mysterious dispensation of Divine Providence, to mourn the removal from among us of another one of our members. DRAYTON CANTWELL, who though but lately connected with us, yet, by the modesty of his demeanor, and the deep interest which he took in the affairs of this Company, won our regard and esteem, and whose absence will long be retained in our memory. For some time had our deceased comrade been sorely afflicted; but it has pleased the Great Disposer of good and evil to release him from those sufferings; and while we cannot but lament his loss to us, yet are we convinced that our loss is his gain, and that he has departed for that rest where pain and disease and death shall trouble him no more forever. Our deceased friend was possessed of many of the good qualities which should characterise the man. Upright and strictly honest in all his dealings with his fellows, prompt in the discharge of all the duties allotted to him, and ever ready to assist in carrying out any project for the advancement of the interests of this Company, or the good of its members. In all the social relations of life we find him exemplifying his outward conduct—as a son, dutiful and affectionate; as a brother, tender and solicitous for the welfare of those whom he considered as needing his special brotherly care and protection. With these recollections of our deceased friend pressing upon us, therefore, be it

1. *Resolved*, That in the death of DRAYTON CANTWELL the Ætna Fire Engine Company has sustained the loss of an honored and highly esteemed member, whose absence from our midst we deeply lament.

2. *Resolved*, That as a token of our respect for the memory of the deceased, this Company wear the usual badge of mourning for the space of thirty days.

3. *Resolved*, That a blank page in our Minute Book be inscribed to his memory.

4. *Resolved*, That a copy of this preamble and these resolutions be transmitted to the relatives of the deceased, with our sincere sympathy of condolence in their sad bereavement.

5. *Resolved*, That this preamble and these resolutions be published in the daily papers of the city.

From the Minutes. JOS. A. THOURON, Secretary.

OBITUARY.

DIED, suddenly, at Aiken, on the 30th ult., WILLIAM JOHNSON HAGOOD, in the 55th year of his age.
"Blessed are the pure in heart, for they shall see God."

OBITUARY.

It becomes our melancholy duty to record the death of our friend, Mr. JOHN H. ASHBY, who died on Pawley's Island, in this State, on Tuesday, the 2d instant. At the time of his demise he was in camp at that place as a private in the cavalry corps of Captain JOHN H. TUCKER, in which Company he had made many friends during the brief time he had been with them. His disease was typhoid pneumonia, which led on to rapid consumption, that terminated fatally at the time stated. In 1856 our friend, then in the prime of manhood, when the South was asking the aid of her people to protect our claims to the Territory of Kansas, was among the first of our young men to join a heroic band of gentlemen from the city of Charleston, to defend our Southern citizens, and protect their property in that distant land. But all our efforts proved unavailing against the tyrannical march of the invading horde from the North; and, after being in several engagements with the vandals, in which he conducted himself with credit, he was forced to return home, not, however, until he had contracted the disease which has just ripened into maturity, and closed his existence. He was a native of the State of Virginia, but of late years a resident of this town. Though feeble and in very delicate health, he could not be restrained from joining a military company in defence of his home. The hardships, privations, exposure and sufferings of camp life he endured willingly and without a murmur, and when called to pay the debt of nature, and part with kindred and friends, he was calm and composed, and his spirit took its flight as if in a dream of peacefulness and contentment. Friends were satisfied his waning health would not stand the fatigue and duties of a soldier's life, particularly on a bleak island shore, and they remonstrated with him to abandon his intentions, and remain within his quiet home; but no! his spirit was aroused, his purpose fixed to meet the enemy and drive him back from the soil of his love and enjoyment, when the messenger of death came, and he fell a victim in a righteous cause in the defence of his oppressed country.

Before his death he seemed to realize his approaching dissolution, and requested a friend to bring to his assistance the wife of his love. His wish was immediately complied with, and the writer of this feeble tribute to departed worth, had the pleasure of witnessing a most affecting interview between a devoted wife and dying husband. Her kind words and presence seemed to cheer and rekindle within him hopes of recovery, but alas! when hope was brightening fast, the cherished object of his heart was called away from him in the sudden illness of their youngest child, when he bid her go and return; but it was their last meeting in life.

Mr. A. was in his 32d year; possessed of a noble disposition, patient, exact and upright, and discharged his obligations with probity and fidelity as husband, father and friend.

On the Sunday night following the death of the subject of the above notice, his youngest child, SARAH VIRGINIA LEAPARE, after much suffering, died, aged two years one month and eight days. Medical aid was useless, and the little sufferer, in all her purity and innocence, took her flight to regions beyond our view, and to-day is with the angels in that paradise of eternal glory—heaven. Oh! SALLIE! thou art now swelling the notes of praise to the Saviour of the blessed, and in His keeping we will confide our trust. Mourners! weep not for her; but as you think of her happy life and peaceful close, endeavor to meet her in that land of rest where blossoms never fade. Let us hope that God will purify and comfort the heart of the bereaved widow and mother, now suffering under the stroke of this severe chastening, and bless and protect her two remaining fatherless children in their journey through this cold-hearted and friendless world. A FRIEND.

GEORGETOWN, S. C., April 17, 1862.

—o—

DIED, at Knoxville, Tennessee, (Confederate Hospital), J. J. SLATER, of Clarke County, Alabama, formerly of Bamberg, S. C., in the 26th year of his age.

—o—

DIED, in McPhersonville, on the 13th instant, in the seventh year of his age, JAMES GREGORIE ELLIOTT, only son of WILLIAM WAIGHT and ELIZABETH M. ELLIOTT.

COMMERCIAL.

Latest Dates.

HAVANA	March 1
HAVRE	March 22
LIVERPOOL	March 23

Consignees per South Carolina Railroad, April 21.

670 bushels Corn, 128 bushels Oats, 42 bushels Meal, 225 bushels Rice Flour, 9 bales Fodder, Mdze, Cattle, &c. To Fraser & Dill, H C Nichols, G W Williams & Co, G M Fairlee, J T Henery, A H Abrahams & Son, F Rielly, Ingraham & Webb, Chamberlain, Miller & Co, W G Bancroft & Co, J G Milnor & Co, H W Kinsman, Ravenel, Huger & Milliken, J & J D Kirkpatrick, Major H Lee, T O Lowndes, D N Ingraham, G W Steffins & Co, H Cobia & Co, Capt F L Childs, Mowry & Co, E L Kerrison, Gilliland, Howell & Co, Johnson, Crews & Co, Hyatt, McBurney & Co, J D Kennedy, D F Armstrong, Blakeley, Williams & Co, Simons & Bros, L A Edmonston, J J Cohen, P C Gaillard & Co, Jno Fraser & Co, Nayler, Smith & Co, Cadow, McKensie & Co, Mathiessen, O'Hara & Co, Farnum & Dotterer, and Order.

—o—

Consignees per Charleston and Savannah Railroad, April 21.

300 bushels Corn, 310 bushels Rough Rice, 10 bales Hides, Furniture, Stock, Mdse, &c. To Capt F L Childs, Coffin & Pringle, Deveaux & Heyward, O'Hear, Roper & Stoney, J G Bucker, Legare, Colcock & Co, G Reeder, Cochran, W M Smith, C T Lowndes, Miss C E Bishoff, W L Sims, Jas D Taylor, W C Bee & Co, W H Heyward, Mrs M A Reynolds, J Bonnell, Mrs F A Jones, Robertson, Blacklock & Co, Dr Prince, Dr T E Hertz, P Ezekial, N O Tilton, T G Brown, and Order.

MARINE NEWS.

Charleston.—Lat. 32.47 N. Lon. 79.27 W.

SUN RISES 5H. 28M. SETS 6H. 32M.—HIGH WATER, 2H. 29M.

WIND—W.

ARRIVED.

April 21.

Sloop Amelia, Cooper River. 500 bushels Rough Rice, and 80 bales Straw. To T G Simons & Sons.

EXTRA DE LA RENAISSANCE LOUISIANAISE.

NOUVELLE-ORLEANS, MERCREDI SOIR, 23 AVRIL 1862.

LES FORTS.

Du milieu de la foule des rumeurs qui circulent à toute heure et du chaos des rapports sans nombre qu'on prétendait toujours arriver directement des forts, il nous est possible enfin de distinguer la vérité et de la placer tout entière sous les yeux de nos lecteurs.

Cette vérité que nous cherchions si assidûment nous l'avons trouvée dans la correspondance officielle suivante, entre le Major Général Lovell et le Brig. Gén. Duncan qui commande aux forts attaqués. Rien ne saurait être plus complet, plus certain; aussi traduisons nous littéralement, comme suit:

DEPECHE OFFICIELLE DU MAJOR GEN. LOVELL AU BRIG. GEN. DUNCAN.

N lle-Orléans, 21 Avril. 1862.

Au Gen. Duncan, Fort Jackson.

Dites à vos officiers et à leurs hommes que leur constance héroïque à supporter un des plus terribles bombardements qui aient jamais eu lieu, que leur courage et l'adresse avec lesquels ils repoussent l'ennemi toutes les fois qu'il ose sortir de son abri font l'admiration générale et seront consignés dans l'histoire comme de magnifiques exemples aux patriotes et aux soldats. Des familles anxieuses, mais pleines de confiance, de nombreux amis suivent leurs actions avec un ferme espoir basé sur l'indomptable courage et l'habilité militaire qu'ils ont si vaillamment déployés. L'ennemi continuera de mettre à l'épreuve votre patience, mais nous espérons qu'il n'obtiendra pas de plus grands résultats qu'il ne l'a fait jusqu'à présent, toutes les fois qu'il a osé se montrer à découvert.

M. LOVELL,
Maj. Gén. Comdt.

REPONSE DU GENERAL DUNCAN A LA DEPECHE DU GEN. LOVELL.

Fort Jackson, 22 avril, A. M.

Au Major-Général Lovell,

Je n'ai pas de nouveau rapport à vous adresser ce matin. Le bombardement continue avec furie. L'ennemi le poursuit vigoureusement en relevant tour à tour ses divisions. Une des canonnières à trois mâts, peinte en gris, s'est montrée à la pointe ce matin, mais a été bientôt touchée et s'est retirée. Nous sommes tous pleins de confiance, en bonnes dispositions, et pleins d'ardeur. Je ne puis parler en termes assez élogieux des officiers et des soldats. Je n'ai pas de nouvelles pertes à vous annoncer. J'apprends que certains journaux de la ville ont publié des rapports alarmants qu'ils prétendent venir d'ici. Je désire qu'il soit bien connu que toutes les dépêches officielles sont envoyées par moi-même. J'examine les dépêches particulières. Que le peuple ait donc confiance et courage et nous ne démériterons pas de la patrie.

J. K. DUNCAN, Brig.-Général.

Plus de commentaires inutiles donc, plus de terreurs sans fondement. Les nouvelles importantes en bien ou en mal, sont adressées par le Général Duncan lui-même au général Lovell et quand elles mériteront la publicité, elles seront publiées par ce dernier.

Le *Louisiana* a dû prendre part à la fête aujourd'hui. Nous en aurons sans doute bientôt des nouvelles.

☞ *Pas de dépêches de la Presse Associée.*

LETTRE DE CORINTH.

—o—

Correspondance particulière de la Renaissance.

Barbarie des Fédéraux—Monstruosité commise sur le corps du jeune Daron—La cavalerie de Dreux—Terrible accident de chemin de fer—Urgence de corps d'Infirmiers—Dévouement de dames de la Nlle.-Orleans—Insolence des prisonniers Yankees—Irrégularités de la poste.

CORINTH, MISS. CAMP BUISSON.
Jeudi, 17 avril 1862.

Messieurs les Editeurs de la RENAISSANCE.

On n'est pas encore fixé—et on ne le sera sans doute pas de longtemps—sur nos pertes et celles des Yankees. On dit que ces dernières atteindront le chiffre de 25,000 tués ou blessés.

On répète que des scènes, dignes d'un autre âge, se sont passées sur le champ de bataille—que des mutilations barbares ont été lâchement commises sur nos blessés. On cite—entre autres monstruosités—le cas du jeune Daron qui, laissé quelques heures sur le terrain, aurait été revu la tête séparée du tronc.

D'après l'inventaire fait par nos troupes dans les camps yankees, qu'ils ont pris un à un le dimanche, les soldats fédéraux devaient mener grande et joyeuse vie. Sûrs de leur triomphe, ils entonnaient déjà le fameux *Nunc est bibendum!* d'Horace. C'est, ivres de rhum et de whiskey sans doute, qu'ils se sont livrés aux indignités que je rappelle ici. Triste vengeance d'hommes qui lâchent pied devant toutes les charges; qui reculent quand les murs de bayonnettes se hérissent et marchent sur eux—qui retraitent dès qu'ils entrevoient le combat corps à corps.

J'ignore si le fait suivant vous a été transmis—il est assez important pour le consigner ici. Le 7, Beauregard fit demander au gén. Grant la permission de relever nos morts et nos blessés. A cette ouverture le chef fédéral répondit qu'il ne pouvait permettre aux nôtres de franchir ses lignes—mais que déjà, nos morts étaient enterrés, et qu'il serait pris soin de nos blessés comme des siens. La suscription de cette lettre portait: "*Au général Beauregard, commandant les forces des Etats Confédérés du Mississipi.*" C'est, je crois, la première admission de notre existence nationale, politique venue de l'autre camp, et Grant signait "*Général COMMANDANT les forces des Etats-Unis.*" Ceci semble confirmer le bruit de la mort de Buell, qui était lui, le véritable commandant en chef.

Quelle est la vérité à cet endroit, je l'ignore, mais un officier yankee prisonnier nous a affirmé que Buell était tombé sur le champ de bataille de Shiloh pour ne plus se relever. On tenait, ajoutait-il, à cacher cette perte à l'armée—perte qui serait lourde, car Buell a toujours été mis, comme talent, à côté du gén. McClellan.

Je vous ai dit que la cavalerie Dreux forme l'escorte de Beauregard. Fait providentiel, elle était au milieu même de la fournaise, chargée de transmettre les ordres, et cependant, pas un de ses membres n'a été atteint. Comme si Dieu avait étendu sa droite sur ces patriotes qui se sont ralliés au nom du jeune officier, mort si malheureusement, si prématurément....

Dans ma lettre précédente je vous ai parlé d'un accident survenu sur le chemin de fer de Memphis, à deux milles en deçà du Grand Junction. Le bris d'un essieu a causé le déraillement; et les wagons, lancés à toute vitesse, se sont fracassés en s'escaladant les uns les autres. Ils étaient remplis de pauvres blessés retournant au foyer, et plusieurs d'entre eux, échappés à mille dangers, ont trouvé là une fin horrible. Ce sinistre spectacle sera longtemps devant mes yeux. J'ai vu l'un d'eux couché sur le sol, la cuisse droite broyée et prise sous deux wagons énormes, dont il supportait tout le poids. Rien ne saurait exprimer le martyre de cet infortuné—pourtant pas un cri ne s'échappait de sa poitrine, pas une larme de ses yeux. Il attendait avec une résignation indicible qu'on le délivrât de cette épouvantable machine de bois et de fer qui l'étreignait, pulvérisait ses os. Je ne croyais pas vraiment que la créature pût arriver à ce degré de courage. Après de longs efforts, cet homme a été enfin dégagé, et on espérait le sauver, quand nous avons laissé Grand Junction. Pendant toute la durée de son supplice, il ne nous a adressé que ces mots: combien de temps faudra-t-il pour me tirer de là? A vrai dire, les blessés—et il y avait là des plaies hideuses—enduraient tous leurs tortures avec une énergie surhumaine—l'un d'eux, ayant à peine l'usage de ses jambes, persistait toujours à se charger d'un drapeau yankee qu'il rapportait en trophée chez lui: c'était sa seule préoccupation. En les conduisant, je pensais qu'on peut et qu'on doit accomplir de grandes choses avec de tels lutteurs.

Dans la malheureuse guerre qui se poursuit tout a été improvisé. Il n'est donc pas étonnant que des vices se rencontrent fréquemment quelle que soit la sollicitude du gouvernement central, il ne saurait tout realiser dès le début. Cependant, il est un detail sur lequel j'appelle l'attention de la presse, les ambulances. Elles sont déplorables, et cette négligence nous vaut des pertes énormes. On doit mieux aux soldats de notre indépendance. Corps d'infirmiers, voitures, cacolets, civières, tout cela est d'une urgence qu'on ne saurait exagérer. Si cette vérité avait été bien comprise, nous aurions sur le champ de bataille de Shiloh, enlevé bien des proies à la mort, bien des victimes aux outrages des Yankees.

On affirme que l'uniforme bleu des Gardes d'Orléans leur a valu plusieurs blessés. Chose bien triste à relater, ils ont été dans la mêlée, pris pour des yankees—dont l'uniforme se rapproche beaucoup du leur—et nos propres troupes ont fait feu sur eux. Pareille confusion avait eu lieu déjà, vous vous en souvenez, à Manassas, à cause de la similitude trompeuse, qui de loin, existe entre notre drapeau et celui des Etats-Unis. Deux graves inconvénients auxquels il devrait être remédié sans retard.

Corinth est plein d'animation. Il y a quelque chose dans l'air qui semble annoncer qu'un grand drame se passera là. On n'y voit que tentes, bivouacs, on n'y entend que tambours, clairons, musique militaire. La discipline y est très stricte—l'autre jour, deux soldats appartenant à je ne sais quels corps, y ont été fusillés pour cause de désertion.

Nous avons ici un hôpital de la Louisiane, où les blessés reçoivent d'excellents soins grâce à des femmes dévouées, venues de tous les points de la Confédération. Trente dames de la Nouvelle-Orléans nous sont arrivées il y a trois jours—Anges de charité.

Nous jouissons tous d'une excellente santé, mais nous regrettons la Grande Junction, matériellement parlant. Là bas, du moins, nous pouvions acheter bien des vivres: mais ici, où toute une armée a ses quartiers, c'est une chose impossible. La privation est d'autant plus sensible, que nous sommes à la demi-ration. Nous nous consolons en regardant nos chevaux pour lesquels le fourrage et le maïs manquent absolument. Or, comme ils ne sont pas cosaques, je plains les pauvres bêtes. C'est surtout aux chevaux que l'on peut appliquer le mot de Mr Scribe à propos de la gloire:

"Aux estomacs à jeûn elle ne suffit pas."

Le capitaine Morgan, que l'on serait parfois tenté de prendre pour un personnage légendaire, est à Corinth. Il existe bien réellement en chair, en os, et ceux qui en douteraient pourraient s'assurer du fait en prenant des renseignements auprès d'un bon nombre de prisonniers yankees, dont le terrible capitaine s'est emparé, dans la journée du 6, la trique à la main.

Les prisonniers ont défilé, par milliers sous nos yeux, vous savez qu'on les a faits par regiments entiers. Parmi eux se trouvait le général Prentiss qui, rencontrant notre capitaine à la Grande Jonction, lui a tendu la main en ajoutant: "Vous pourrez dire, Monsieur, que vous avez serré la main du général Prentiss." Sa tenue était encore pleine d'arrogance et ses compagnons de captivité, qui savent que chez nous on respecte l'infortune même quand elle est indigne, ses compagnons hurlaient le "Hail Columbia."

Deux des prisonniers yankees, l'un du Missouri, l'autre de la Virginie, étaient dernièrement sous la garde d'un ministre protestant, du nom de Rogers, qui s'en était emparé sur le champ de bataille, et avait demandé le privilége de les conduire seul à Memphis. Armé d'un assez piètre mousquet, revêtu du costume sévère de ses fonctions, il faisait bonne garde, je vous l'assure, et avait la rage dans l'âme. Son fils unique—drame sinistre—était tombé à ses côtés en combattant pour notre cause.

Le général Prentiss, qui reconnaissait la valeur de l'avantage remporté par nous le 6, représentait la journée du 7, comme une revanche pour les Fédéraux, une défaite pour nous. Cette assertion n'a rien de vrai. Avec des troupes qui venaient de gagner pouce à pouce un terrain considérable, que les rigueurs de cette route sanglante avaient haussées, c'eut été folie à Beauregard de livrer encore bataille à une armée sans cesse renouvelée, appuyée par des canonnières agissant, sans risques, à une portée formidable. Pour garder tous les trésors enlevés à l'ennemi—hommes, chevaux, armes, 30 ou 40 canons, munitions, vivres—pour éviter les coups d'une flotte contre laquelle nous étions impuissants—pour nous sauver d'un coûteux revers, il ne nous restait que le moyen de la retraite. Ainsi, le sang n'était plus versé inutilement, et si l'ennemi osait nous poursuivre, il lui fallait renoncer à l'abri de ses chaloupes protectrices. Cette retraite a été—tous semblent le croire—admirable d'ordre, d'harmonie—l'œuvre d'un officier froid, consommé. Elle s'est opérée sous les yeux de Beauregard, avec ce calme qui caractérise tous ses actes. Des derniers, notre général en chef a quitté le lieu du combat.

Parmi les officiers chargés de couvrir ce dernier mouvement, je dois citer le lieutenant-colonel C[illegible]ard, arrivé quelques instants auparavant. Charge lui a été donnée d'une demi-brigade où figuraient le capitaine Morgan et ses fantastiques cavaliers. La nature se répète parfois—ces gaillards là semblent reproduire dans notre siècle les anciens cavaliers numides. Homme et cheval ne font qu'un. Vrais centaures.

La poste se complaît toujours dans son irrégularité chronique. J'ai reçu, aujourd'hui, 15, des lettres du 7. Quant aux journaux, pas un depuis longtemps. Même reproche à l'adresse de la compagnie du rail-road. Grâce à son incurie, une multitude d'objets s'égarent ou sont volés journellement. On assure que des colis—pour une valeur de $200,000 ont déjà disparu du dépôt à Corinth. Dans le département civil comme dans le département militaire, vous le voyez, à chaque pas les traces d'une déplorable administration. Fasse le ciel qu'elle ne conduise pas à la démoralisation de l'armée.

Quatre de nos membres nous ont quittés pour cause de maladie. La nostalgie a aussi son influence sur le physique. Les froids ont fait place à une chaleur excessive, et je crains bien que sous peu notre pesant uniforme ne soit plus tolérable. La pensée seule m'en préoccupe si, comme cela est probable, nous sommes appelés à faire des marches forcées.

Les Gardes d'Orléans sont toujours à la Grande Jonction. Ils s'y reposent de leurs fatigues. Leur état de souffrance n'étonnera personne quand on saura que le 6 et le 7 on leur distribuait pour toute nourriture un demi buiscuit par homme.

On m'assure que les gentilles laitières, dont j'ai parlé dans ma première lettre ont éveillé plus d'une jalousie à la Nlle-Orléans. J'en ai dit mon *mea culpâ*. Mais qu'on ne s'en inquiète plus. Désormais nous sommes loin de Lagrange et leur lait n'enivrera plus personne. La femme est un mythe à Corinth. On se rappelle bien avoir vu une ou ou deux de-ci de-là, mais on n'en a conservé qu'une idée très confuse.

Puisque j'ai écrit le nom de Lagrange, permettez moi de rectifier un correspondant de l'Abeille qui a pretendu que, pour les heures passées là par quelques uns de nous, nous avions été condamnés au trou.—C'est l'appellation pittoresque que l'on donne ici à la salle de police—peut-être parce que l'eau y séjourne. Le trop rigide correspondant s'est trompé—il n'a jamais été question pour nous de la punition que sa plume nous a infligée, à ma vive humiliation, je vous l'avoue.

L. PLACIDE CANONGE.

PRIX EXORBITANTS.

Les marchands de Corinth auraient bien besoin que des prévôts-maréchaux missent un frein à leurs spéculations exorbitantes en soumettant la vente des articles à un tarif comme celui qui régit le marche de la Nouvelle-Orléans.

Le prix de quelques articles, indiqués dans une correspondance, semblent presque incroyables.

Ainsi le tabac se vend 50 cents le plug; le papier 50 cents le cahier; les enveloppes 50 cents la douzaine et l'encre se cède à 25 cents l'encrier.

Les Bananes.

Nous voyons par le *Planter's Banner* que la culture du bananier fait de rapides progrès dans quelques unes des paroisses de la Louisiane et principalement dans celle de Ste-Marie. Deux habitans de cette paroisse, MM. G. L. Fesuelier et Washington Smith, ont particulièrement bien reussi dans cette culture. Le premier possède une souche de cette belle plante qui contient environ 200 fruits. Les plants de bananiers que l'on cultive dans la paroisse Ste-Marie ont été apportés de Tehuantepec par M. Fuselier.

Evening Delta.

PUBLISHED AT 1 P. M. NEW ORLEANS, FRIDAY, APRIL 24, 1862. OFFICE--94 CAMP STREET.

THE EVENING DELTA.

Important Notice.—See in another column a highly important notice to cotton planters and owners of cotton and lessees of cotton presses.

WHAT THE MORNING JOURNALS SAY.

The *Bulletin* commends to the consideration of the bold and ingenious the heavy rewards offered by the Committee of Public Safety for the destruction of the enemy's invading vessels by private enterprise. It also urges the importance of night work upon certain objects by a system of relief. It also speaks with gratification of the "inspiring" news from the forts below, received yesterday.

The *Bee* refers to the deep impression made on the public mind of England by the exploits of the Virginia, and the revolution made in naval warfare which is marked by those exploits. A similar revolution, it urges, must follow in seashore fortifications, which must be sheathed in iron in order to resist the assault of an iron-clad fleet.

The *Crescent* has some fitting reflections upon Mr. Russell's testimony to "the constancy and unshaken faith" exhibited by the South in this war; and Talk on 'Change has the following about a personage who has been giving us some trouble below the city:

The commander of the mortar squadron now investing the forts below is David D. Porter. He was born in this city, at least so traditional history informs us. His father, David Porter, commanded on this station previous to the war of 1812. Of course, history gives us to understand who Com Porter, of the Essex of 1812, was. He left the service of the old United States under the sentence of a six months' suspension during the administration of John Quincy Adams. He entered the service of the Mexican States in 1826. In the summer of 1827 he visited New Orleans for the purpose of recruiting and aiding the Mexican Navy. One of his sons accompanied him. Whether it was the one in command of the squadron now investing the forts below New Orleans, or the one who was wounded in the attack on Fort Henry, we cannot say; but this much we can assert, that in the month of August, 1827, the citizens of New Orleans gave something of a public reception to Com. David Porter, then Commander-in-Chief of the Mexican Navy. A public dinner was given him at the old Planters' and Merchants' Hotel, on Canal street, at which one of these Porters, then a midshipman in the Mexican Navy, was present, and made a speech or a talk.

The *Picayune* dwells upon the sterling moral characteristics displayed by our men at Shiloh, and remarks;

There is one notable feature of this admirable conduct of our men which has come to our knowledge through the medium of private and authentic information. We have been told that among those of them who stood firmest, fought bravest, and suffered most, were the most exemplary in personal private character. There is said to have been a most marked seriousness in the conduct and deportment of those young volunteers, on entering into the contest and throughout its continuance. We can readily conceive of this; for the cause in which they were engaged, and to which, with impulsive ardor, they had devoted themselves, was one of high principle, of deep, religious significance. Its elements were the noblest and holiest that constitute a motive of action, and it is not to be wondered at that they should have had their influence upon the minds and upon the conduct of such men as those who fought and won at Shiloh.

THE BATTLE AT WINCHESTER.

The Northern papers are filled with narratives and incidents of the late battle near Winchester. Some of them are very interesting. The correspondent of the New York Post gives a vivid description of the battlefield and his visit to the sick and wounded, from which we take some passages:

The light was so dim that it was not easy to make out how the battle was fought, or count the dead then lying there. The field was even then quite stripped of everything in the shape of relics, and soldiers were searching for something to carry away as mementoes of the fight.

Near the field where the rebel battery had been posted there were terrible evidences of the conflict. Here and there, at long intervals, lay a Federal soldier, stark and stiff; just on the edge of the woods lay two heaps of them, five or six in each, their hats over their faces concealing ghastly wounds. Back in the woods and fields to the right, where the flank movement was accomplished, other dead Federals lay, with here and there a rebel. But farther on in the thickets the sight was sickening and saddening in the extreme. Dead rebels, with most horrible wounds, lay thickly strewn over the ground. Most of them had fallen backwards and with pale, ghastly faces, clotted with blood, were a sight I shall not soon forget. Dangling from a tree hung a naked human foot—taken completely off above the ankle by a round shot—a ghastly spectacle. Close together lay a horse and rebel, beast and man in death reduced to equality.

Preparations were made for the burial of the killed. Under the direction of the Mayor of Winchester some fifty citizens collected the dead, dug a great pit on the battle-field, and gently laid the poor fellows in their last resting place. It was a sad sight, and sadder still to see women looking carefully at every corpse to try to identify the bodies of their friends. Scarcely a family in the county but had a relative there, and what torture of anxiety must have been suffered, knowing only that their friends were in the fight, and ignorant whether they were prisoners at Baltimore, suffering in the hospitals, or lying unburied on the sand. But their suffering did not mollify these secession women. Every womanly, even human feeling seems to have been extinguished in their intense hatred of "the Yankees." They would say, "You may bring the whole force of the North here, but you can never conquer us; we will shed our last drop of blood," &c., &c.

The courthouse, Union Hotel, and a large store were at once converted into hospitals. There was little or no bedding, and the men were laid down on the floor with blankets, or any covering which could be found, over them, and the surgeons of the division set at work. There were some very sad sights in the hospital. At the Union Hotel lay a rebel badly wounded in the lungs, who positively refused all medical treatment. One young, fair, blue eyed fellow—a rebel—was very anxious to take the oath of allegiance. He thought if he could only take that he should get well. But the wound was mortal.

As one of our officers was passing through the large room of the hotel, thickly crowded with wounded, one of them called out to him. Stooping down he recognized in the face, blackened by powder and dirt, the well known features of a college classmate, George Washington. He had entered Harvard in the class of 1801; was beloved and respected by all his class. For sometime he resisted his father's request to come home, but at last yielded to parental authority; and when once in Virginia, it was but a short step to join the army. He entered, with his brother, Jackson's army as a private, and was shot in the lungs on Sunday. The wound is probably mortal. A sad meeting this for college classmates who had parted only six months before at a convivial supper given by Washington.

"Great Events Are at Hand."—The New York Herald thinks great events are at hand. From preparations now being made by the armies of the Union on one side and by the rebel hosts on the other, and from various signs and indications, the public mind, says the New York Herald, may be prepared for a series of tremendous events within the next fortnight. The Herald proceeds:

A number of desperate battles, some of them of great magnitude, will be fought throughout the South, probably beginning with Virginia and followed up in other States with great rapidity. Johnston and Smith were by last accounts on the line of the Rappahannock, with their late Army of the Potomac, their center being at Gordonsville, their right extending to Fredericksburg and Yorktown, and their left to the mountains. Whether they have since fallen further back, or even totally abandoned Virginia, we have no means of knowing. But whether they make a stand or retreat they will have to fight at last.

There is another rebel army in Southwestern Tennessee and Alabama, Beauregard commanding the first corps, Bragg the second, and General Albert Sidney Johnston, the defeated General, commanding the wreck of the army which evacuated Bowling Green, and has recruited in its retreat. In all, perhaps these different corps number from sixty thousand to seventy thousand men, and are in process of being reinforced daily from the farther South. They must soon come into collision with the armies led by Halleck and Buell, which have already penetrated Tennessee and Alabama. Albert Sidney Johnston was, by latest intelligence, at Decatur, Alabama; and Beauregard was at Corinth, in Mississippi, where the State borders both Alabama and Tennessee.

The army of Joe Johnston, in Virginia, will have soon to fight, be captured, or run away; and even flight may not save it. The chances are that the whole of that army and its Generals, together with the rebel President, rebel Cabinet, and rebel Congress, will be bagged.

The Great Yankee Army which was Used Up on Sunday.—A correspondent of the St. Louis Republican, writing under date of March 27, gives us some interesting particulars regarding the great Yankee army which has just been cut to pieces and scattered broadcast by the gallant Confederates near Corinth:

Few rivers (Tennessee) have ever had as imposing a sight on their banks. Sixty thousand men and miles of horses, wagons, cannons, and so forth, are there; although everything is bustle and preparation, there is no confusion. The law of order was never better illustrated. It is vast military machinery, where men are the springs and wheels all moving regularly, surely on in the great work of preparation. Wagons are loaded before they seem hardly to have reached the goods, and tents are moved in a fraction of the usual time. There is no lounging or anxiety to shirk, but universal cheerfulness and confidence. The tone of the Western army is completely changed. It is no longer "If we capture such a place," but "When we capture it." The soldiers there think of nothing but victory. They have confidence in themselves, and the haunting, terrified apprehension has fled. They believe now that as they march forward it is to conquer. This peculiarity, so different from the gloom produced by reverses and inactivity, at once strikes the stranger.

A happier, healthier, more efficient army than that now at Savannah and Pittsburg never, probably, went to war. Each regiment is burning to win laurels to wear with their companions who got fame and scars at Fort Donelson. Opposed to this noble army is a rebel force of forty-five thousand, lying in wait behind their works, eighteen miles distant. Corinth is a position naturally strong, and formidable defenses have been erected there. Rifle-pits, redoubts, abattis and other means of strength, from behind which to hurl destruction upon an assailant force, have been constructed. The very best rebel military talent, embracing Beauregard, Bragg and others, is concentrated there, and at Corinth will be fought the great decisive battle of the Western campaign. Forty heavy guns and a great number of field pieces are possessed by the enemy, and immense stores of provisions are gathered in. The flower of the South are congregated there to offer battle, and they cannot retreat except by sacrificing everything.

The road between the Union camps and Corinth is a long and excellent turnpike, and the distance can be easily traversed in a day. Gen. Grant has his headquarters at Savannah, while the bulk of his army is at Pittsburg. Parade grounds and spots for comfortable quarters are being cleared, and everything gives token of a week's longer stay there. During that time Gen Buell is expected to reach a point from which he can carry out successfully the part assigned him.

Whilst at Savannah, word reached there that Gen Wallace, with fifteen thousand men, having taken a circuitous route, had penetrated to Florence and destroyed rebel railroad communication in that direction with the South.

SPECIAL DISPATCHES TO THE DELTA

THE LATEST FROM THE FORTS.

Several of the Enemy's Gunboats passed the Forts.

THEY ARE BEING RESISTED.

Steamer Star Burnt and Several others Burning.

The Steamer Doubloon Safe.

THE ENEMY'S OPERATIONS IN THE RIVER.

The following dispatch was received this morning by the Governor. It indicates a desperate attempt on the part of the enemy to capture the city by avoiding the forts. At the Major-General's office we are assured that there is no serious cause for alarm:

Quarantine Station, April 24—A. M.

Several of the enemy's gunboats have passed the Forts, and are being resisted.

Two steamers have already passed this point, and are scanning every place.

The Star has been burnt, but do not know of any other damage.

Two or three vessels are now burning.

The Doubloon has got up safe.

(Signed) A. E. Tulda, Operator.

THE ENEMY AT THE QUARANTINE.

Seven of Our Boats Fired.

FURTHER PARTICULARS.

Pointe-a-la-Hache, April 24, 1862.

The enemy with strong force are up to Quarantine.

I left my station at Quarantine when the enemy got within a quarter of a mile of me and shot through me.

I regret to say that seven of our vessels were fired when they were overpowered, and I believe everything belonging to us has fallen into their hands.

I am on my way up to the city.

F. B. Renshaw, C. S. Navy.

To Com'r Whittle, C. S. Navy, New Orleans.

Gen. Lovell.—We learn authoritatively that Gen. Lovell was, at 12 o'clock at Sugar-house Point, six miles below the city, on the other side. He is expected to arrive momentarily.

The operator at Point-a-la-Hache telegraphs that Capt. Grant, when passing that station, reported that he believed one of the enemy's vessels were coming up the river, but was not certain.

THE CITY.

The following letters from Corinth are left at this office for distribution:

Mrs C T Holmes,	A D Curry,
Mrs D A Fisher,	Adolphus Hamilton,
Mrs S E Winter,	Jas F Pendergrast,
Miss Mary Mead,	Fred Suller.

The Alarm.—It is singular on what a small basis a kind of panic can build itself up among the timid. Many persons seem quite alarmed at the supposition that the enemy will soon be up the river, when they have positive assurance from headquarters that there is no serious danger. It is pleasant, though, to see the alacrity, the almost joy, with which our fighting population spring to arms. They seem actually to be glad of a prospective chance to meet the enemy. If some of them should manage to elude our gunboats and get past the fortifications, we could still anchor out the Mississippi and give them more than they bargained for.

The Roll of the Drum.—The Roll of the Drum is generally supposed to be a sound replete with warlike significance. It is the music of the soldier, the melody of battle. But of all the rolls of the drum, that which, to our mind, expresses the greatest nonchalance, the most supreme indifference to danger and coolness in the midst of peril, is the roll of the auctioneer's drum, calling housekeepers together to buy old mattresses and pillows, when they are frightened to death with the idea that an insatiable enemy is about to take all their new ones. We think the auctioneer is right, however. Keep cool! till you can see through the smoke. He's the man for dangerous times.

COMMERCIAL.

Delta Office, Wednesday, April 24, 1862.

COTTON—Nothing reported yet.

SUGAR—There is more demand in a small way, by parties anxious to invest, and holders have consequently asked fuller prices, but the sales do not exceed 400 hhds.

MOLASSES—There is very little on sale, and the sales have been confined to a few small lots at yesterday's prices.

Nothing else reported.

EVENING DELTA

FRIDAY EVENING, APRIL 24, 1862.

DEATH OF CAPT. LEEDS.—We deeply regret to learn that Capt. Thomas Leeds, of the Orleans Light Horse, died yesterday at Jackson, Miss., on his way home. He had been quite ill before starting, and was by no means recovered at the time of leaving, and the great fatigue and exposure to which he was subjected, immediately on his arriving at Corinth, proved too much for his enfeebled health. His remains will arrive by the 11 o'clock train this morning.

CAPTAIN FAYSSOUX.—It has been a genera ground of complaint and surprise that one of the most experienced and skilful naval officers in this city has not been employed in some position where his great talents and daring might prove of great service to our cause. We refer to Capt. Fayssoux, formerly of the Texan and more recently of the Nicaraguan navy; an officer whose exploits during the wars of Gen. Walker were the themes of so much praise. Capt. Fayssoux is in the prime of life, full of vigor and spirit, and can fight a ship as well as any man in the Confederate States. By all means let his services be secured by the commanders of our army and navy.

THE ORLEANS GUARDS.—In justice to a gallant officer and gentleman, we would supply an omission in our correspondent's narrative of the transactions of this noble batt lion in the fight of Shiloh, by stating that, af er Major Queyrouze was wounded the command of the battalion fell upon the senior Captain, Charles Roman, of Company A, who ably supplied the place of the Major, and gallantly led the battalion through all the subsequent events of the contest. Capt. Roman showed himself to be a most efficient and reliable officer, and an excellent commander. His conduct equaled that of his heroic brother, who, as Lieutenant Colonel, so nobly supported the vigorous and daring conduct of the intrepid Mouton, of the 18th Louisiana.

COL. POND AND HIS BRIGADE.

In the sketch of the battle of the 6th, by A W., he adopted an error, which was a very prevalent one, in representing the charge made by the 18th Louisiana and Orleans Guards on a strong battery of the enemy, supported by a large force of infantry—which resulted in such fearful loss—as having been made by order of Col. Pond, who commanded the brigade. The facts we have since learned more correctly. The following description of this affair, which was communicated to the True Witness, is, in the main, correct, except in the censure of Col. Pond, who, we learn, gave the order to charge, which had been sent to him by Gen. Hardee, after protesting against it as a murderous and impracticable attempt to carry the battery:

We pushed on until we emerged from the thick woods into a large open field. Here we saw a regiment of Federals retreating on our right through one of their camps, and received the order to charge them; we did so, and received a volley which wounded one of our company, but with the 18th Regiment, we drove them through the camp, taking some prisoners. Passing beyond this camp, we went on through more thickets and woods until we reached a point beyond which we could not advance. The retreating Federals leaving camp after camp, had concentrated upon the hills bordering the river and were there making a desperate attempt to stop our advance. It was at the foot of one of these hills that we paused. There was a battery of artillery upon its summit, but removed from sight over the edge of the hill, and several regiments were ambushed in the dense wood that covered the eminence, pouring a storm of bullets and grape about us that threatened to annihilate us. Just then we discovered another Yankee camp on our left, with a regiment drawn up in battle to assail us. The situation was desperate. Gen. Pond ordered the battery to be taken. The 16th and 18th Regiments were ordered to defile round its right and we around the left of the hill, until fairly abreast of the cannon, and then make a combined attack at the point of the bayonet. Unfortunately for the success of the movement, the distance we had to march around the base of the hill added to the obstructions of the way, delayed us until the 16th and 18th Regiments had formed in line, and we arrived at our position just as they charged up the hill, shouting with enthusiasm. It was too late to help them and we saw them disappear with misgiving and doubt. Soon came the deafening roar of artillery and whistling of rifle balls. The ground shook under our feet; the very air seeming alive with hissing serpents, and the crash of trees and branches marked the passage of the missiles from the enemy. In a few seconds we received in our ranks the remnants of the two regiments that had just braved so nobly their own destruction. We were ordered to fall back out of the reach of fire and rally for another charge. In the meantime, Gen. Pond, as if he wished to see how many men he could sacrifice without benefit, ordered our battalion to charge the battery. It was a criminal blunder. We were but 350 men, without a reserve, unassisted by artillery, and he threw us against a force of 500 men and a battery of guns, which were protected by woods, while we marched up in full sight within fifty yards of their position. Again the storm of shot and shell and grape came upon us with terrible effect, and the melting ranks soon proved, what we all knew before, that we could not take the battery alone. The order was given to fall back, and we had to leave behind several of our friends who had advanced too near the enemy and fallen on the field. In the movement of falling back, part of the battalion was separated from the rest, and from that time until yesterday we did not know what had become of many of them. I will add here that later in the evening the 16th, 18th, and another regiment, assisted by a battery of artillery, made another charge against our ambushed enemy, and succeeded in capturing the guns that had made such havoc in our ranks, and driving the enemy from the camp.

We have the best authority for saying that Col. Pond was not responsible for this destructive charge—that he remonstrated against it—that he sought to have the aid of his battery, (Ketchum's) with which he could have dismounted and driven off the enemy; but his battery had been ordered to another part of the field by a superior commander. He made and led the charge, believing that he was required to sacrifice his command in obedience to the orders of his superior. His brigade had been previously reduced by the detaching of the Crescent Regiment and the 38th Tennessee for operations in another part of the field. This was done by a superior officer.

ROUGH NOTES

From the Diary of one of Gen. A. S. Johnston's Aids—Major D. M. Hayden—giving an account of what occurred under his personal observation in the battle of Shiloh, on Sunday, April 6th, 1862.

On the morning of April 6th I left Corinth and arrived at Monterey about 1 o'clock, and here witnessed the most painful sight that a soldier is called upon to see—a deserter was shot by order of Gen. Bragg.

While lunching, Clanton's Alabama cavalry company brought in as prisoner a Major and two Lieutenants, one of them belonging to the staff of a Federal General. The prisoners were all handsomely mounted. A few minutes after ten or fifteen more arrived, who said they were surprised.

Gen. Breckinridge arrived at sundown, and a council of officers, consisting of Gens. Johnston, Beauregard, Bragg and Breckinridge, was held. Gen. Johnston ordered the grand attack to be made on Saturday, the 5th. But at 12 o'clock at night a dispatch was received from Breckinridge stating that his artillery was stuck in the mud and had stopped his train. To which Johnston replied, "Cut a new road for your column."

The rain was constant until 5 o'clock, and of course we could not get much sleep.

At 6 o'clock we took a cup of coffee and started for the battle-field, some four miles distant, being joined by Gens. Bragg and Beauregard. By 7 o'clock it had cleared off, but as yet nothing was heard of Breckinridge's Brigade, which was composed of the Kentuckians Carroll's and Crittenden's commands. Gen. Hardee met us upon the field and reported skirmishes with the enemy that morning.

Another conference was held, and it was decided to await the arrival of the Breckinridge brigade. At 12 o'clock Gen. Johnston, followed by his staff, reviewed the right division of his army. When they began to cheer his approach he checked them, because it would call the attention of the enemy to their position. His advice to his men was brief and characteristic; it was, "Look along your guns and fire low."

At 1 o'clock, in company with Gen. Beauregard, he reviewed the left wing, which was under command of Gen. Bragg.

In the afternoon Gens. Polk and Hardee were summoned, and another council of officers was held at the cross roads, within a few hundred yards of the spot where we all bivouacked the night before the battle. The question was—as we have lost a day shall we fight? It was decided to strike.

At 8 o'clock we bivouacked by fires. The General slept in an ambulance in which were brought our blankets from our single tent at Monterey. Preston, Wickliffe and myself slept by the same fire. Gen. Hardee came to our fire at 12 o'clock and said his men were out of provisions. As Gen. Johnston had spent the night before without sleep, I did not wish to awaken him, and directed Gen. Hardee to Col. Jordan, chief of Beauregard's staff.

The General had ordered his horse at 5 o'clock, April 6, Sunday morning. We all got off in fine spirits, our pickets having announced by 5½ o'clock that the ball was opened. By 6½ firing was heard nearly all along the line. The Generals separated, and the General commanding made his way where the firing was heaviest.

Col. Hindman charged the enemy and routed them taking a large camp and se[illegible] brass guns, and driving them towards their center. Judging from the number of our wounded that I passed over I think our loss was heavy here, for we met the combined fire of their gunboats, artillery and Minie rifles, which was truly terrific.

Gen. Gladden's brigade were the only troops of Bragg's division on the right. Gen. Johnston ordered this brigade to "charge bayonet," but the order was countermanded on learning from one of Gen. Gladden's aids that he was severely wounded. Col. Preston then carried the order to Hindman's brigade, who made a splendid and victorious charge. As an evidence of the accuracy of the shooting on both sides, I will state that I saw a small tree with thirteen distinct shots—seven of the enemy's and six of ours—within a range of four feet.

We found the Federal camps to be very fine, and their equipments in clothing complete.

A member of the staff, in jest, brought out a lot of overcoats, and said, "Here, gentlemen, are overcoats for the whole staff." The General quietly rebuked him with, "None of that, sir; remember we do not come here to plunder."

It was while under this fire that Capt. Brewster expostulated with Gen. Johnston against his personally exposing himself. I was not near enough to hear his reply, but it had no effect, for he smilingly rode to the brow of the hill, where we could distinctly see the enemy retreating.

Gen. Withers joined us here, and the enemy's gunboats got such a good range of us that one of their balls fell within ten steps of me.

Heavy firing from the upper camp, Gen. Johnston proceeded to the spot, where he remained a time, calmly marshaling his forces and bringing his troops into proper position. It was here I met Capt. Inge, of the Southrons. Young Bennet, with face all blackened, stepped up and asked if I knew where his company was, that he had got separated from them. I pointed to where they were and he rushed off to meet them.

As soon as Gen. Johnston ascertained that we were under the fire of the enemy, he ordered a Texan regiment to charge the camp on the opposite sid e of the hollow. In descending the hollow, the nature of the ground somewhat disordered their lines, but they again formed at the base of the hill and routed the camp in fine style.

I was then sent for Gen. Chalmers, who received orders to push up the road and sweep down the river to where we heard heavy firing—supported by part of Wirt Adams' regiment.

At this moment Major Smith, of Gen. Johnston's staff, called for reinforcements for Gen. Cheatham, who had a hard fight on hand near the center of the encampments. Two messengers were sent to Breckinridge to reinforce Cheatham. Fortunately he arrived in time at a great cost of life; for although Gen. Bowen was ordered up at a double quick, Breckinridge had shelled the camp and routed the enemy before he reached the place.

Gov. Harris led the East Tennesseeans himself in this part of the conflict.

Gen. Johnston, elated with the entire success of the day, took his position before the brigades of Bowen and Breckinridge, and gave the order, "fix bayonets." The last moment I saw him, before his fall, he was haranguing his troops. The charge was made with a shout, and the enemy fled in confusion. I was by the side of Bowen, and the Minie balls flew so close that they clipped his hair. I started to the right to see what had become of Chalmers, when I met Col. O'Hara, who announced that Gen. Johnston was wounded. We followed him down into the ravine, where we found him reclining in the lap of Gov. Harris, who had gently lifted him from his horse.

I was told that the only and last words he ever spoke were, some minutes after he was shot, "Governor, I believe I am seriously wounded." Col. Preston, in an agony of grief, threw his arms around him, and called aloud and asked if he knew him.

I caught hold of his hand and saw that he was still breathing. We administered a little stimulant, but he was totally unconscious, and quietly breathed his last at 30 minutes past 2.

We prudently concealed his death.

Thus fell one of the greatest Generals of the age. He fell where heroes like to fall, in the arms of victory, upon the battle-field. It is a mistake to suppose that the censure of ignorant men, about his recent maneuvers, drove him to a rash exposure of his person. In this battle he was elated from the very beginning; he knew that victory was certain, and his countenance gleamed with the enthusiasm of a great man, who was conscious that he was achieving a great success that was to carry his name down to the latest syllable of recorded time.

His body was borne from the field by myself and three others of the staff.

Breckinride's reserve composed a division of seven or eight thousand men, his own brigade of gallant Kentuckians, and Crittenden's and Carroll's commands, who were placed under him a few days before the battle.

All of our Generals were conspicuous for bravery and gallantry; but you must excuse a Kentuckian who was an eye witness, for saying that Gen. Breckinridge's conduct on that day was perfectly glorious, equaling in every respect the daring of Murat, united with the coolness of Wellington.

I was near Major Tom. Hawkins, who was wounded in the chin by a grape shot, and saw Col. Hodge dismounted by a Minie ball passing through the neck of his beautiful mare—both of Gen. B.'s staff.

RIVER INTELLIGENCE.

NEW ORLEANS, Thursday, April 24, 1862.

On the levee business is decidedly dull. The John Walsh was unable to get off on Tuesday evening. She left yesterday in the forenoon.

The departures yesterday were the Acadia for Bayou Sara, Anna Perrett for Opelousas, Twilight for Camden, and John Walsh for Memphis.

The arrivals were the Texas from Jefferson, Newsboy from Attakapas, Sallie Robinson from the Coast, Morgan Nelson from Sabine River, and Red Chief No. 1 from Bayou Bartholomew.

Passengers for Red River will find the fine steamers Gen. Hodges and Texas ready to leave this evening for Shreveport and Jefferson.

The Attakapas packet Newsboy will positively leave this evening at 3 o'clock for Berwick's Bay and all landings on the Teche.

The Red Chief No. 1 came in from Bayou Bartholomew, Bœuf River and Lower Tensas, with a good trip. She is ready to receive for the above streams, to leave on Saturday evening. Shippers should remember that the Red Chief is the only boat running in Bayou Bartholomew.

BOATS LEAVING.

THURSDAY PACKET FOR FORT ADAMS.—The large and fast passenger packet Laurel Hill, Capt. S. Heno, with Mr. Alcee Grass, clerk, will leave for Baton Rouge, Bayou Sara, Fort Adams, and all way landings, at 5 o'clock this evening.

NEWSBOY FOR ATTAKAPAS VIA PLAQUEMINE.—The regular passenger packet Newsboy, Capt. Allen Fowler, will leave this evening at 3 o'clock for St. Marcinsville, Berwick's Bay, and all landings on the Teche. Mr. R. W. Allen is her clerk.

GEN. HODGES FOR RED RIVER.—The splendid pasenger packet Gen. Hodges, commanded by Capt. R. Steade, one of the most competent and gentlemanly officers on the river, leaves this evening for Jefferson, Shreveport, and all landings on Red River. Mr. W. S. Steade has charge of the office.

TEXAS FOR JEFFERSON AND SHREVEPORT.—The fine very light draught passenger steamer Texas, Capt. Chas. W. Stinde, will leave this evening at 5 o'clock for Jefferson, Shreveport and all way landings on Red River. Mr. D. A. Orvis is in the office.

MARINE INTELLIGENCE

PORT OF NEW ORLEANS.

OFFICE OF THE DAILY DELTA
Thursday Evening, April 24 1862.

CLEARED THIS MORNING.

No clearances this morning.

ARRIVED THIS MORNING.

STEAMBOATS.

Laurel Hill, Heno, from Bayou Sara.
J M Sharp, Dye, from Fort Adams.
Empire Parish, Bayhi, from Donaldsonville.
Arkansaw, Bennett, from Arkansas River.
Drover, Glasscock, from Bayou de Glaze.

RECEIPTS FROM THE INTERIOR.

FORT ADAMS—Per steamer J M Sharp—16 bbls molasses E M Ross—50 do A G Marrionneaux—30 do A Miltenberger &co—40 do Lauve & LeBlanc—155 hf do John Watt &co—6 hhds sugar J Perkins—50 do Roman, Olivier &co—46 do J W Burbridge &co—40 do V Allain—20 do Braud & Landry—12 do Harrington, Britton &co—10 do R Tramontana—6 do J Mezzi—234 bales cotton Levy & Deiter sundries to order—Total, 234 bales cotton 220 hhds sugar 155 hf and 136 bbls molasses.

BAYOU DE GLAZE—Per steamer Drover—30 hhds sugar and 427 sks corn Hawkins & Norwood—44 bbls molasses Bellocq, Noblom &co—30 sks corn and sundries to order.

DONALDSONVILLE—Per steamer Empire Parish—30 hhds sugar C H Kernion—89 do Darby & Tremoulet—6 do R Brugier—68 do Roman, Olivier &co—20 do A D Kelly &co—5 do J Labatut—50 do P Lanaux—27 do do 16 bbls molasses J M Putnam—20 do P Maspero—261 do do and 18 tcs do M L Bringier &co—128 bales cotton to Pothier & Faucheux—Total, 128 bales cotton 521 hhds sugar 18 tcs 467 bbls molasses.

BAYOU SARA—Per steamer Laurel Hill—19 hhds sugar and 68 bbls molasses E Durrive &co—274 do Menard & Vignaud—50 do do R Nugent &co—98 do Braud & Landry—31 do Augustin & Thibaut—10 do A Miltenberger &co—58 do M Gordon, 33 tcs do and 58 hhds sugar Lapice, Bros &co—32 do J S Wallis—15 do V Allain—16 do A J DaSilva & Gerard—39 do A G Marrionneaux—Total, 179 hhds sugar 23 tcs 680 bbls molasses.

FORT SMITH—Per steamer Arkansaw—25 hhds sugar E Durrive &co—25 do Stuart & James—260 sks cotton seed Battle, Noble &co and sundries to order.

THE TRIWEEKLY TELEGRAPH.

VOL. XXVIII—NO. 17. HOUSTON, FRIDAY, APRIL 25, 1862 WHOLE NO. 3512

BY SPECIAL EXPRESS,

Important from Richmond.

FREDRICKSBURG EVACUATED.

Bombardment of Fort Macon.

Bombardment of Fort Jackson.

CONFLICTING ACCOUNTS.

Etc., Etc., Etc.

The N. O. train arrived Wednesday night at 10 o'clock, bringing the N. O. papers of the 19th and 20th, from which we take the following intelligence:

WILMITGTON, April 18.—A private letter of the 17th from Fort Macon, says the enemy attacked the fort last Saturday and have been fighting two days. Col. White sent out part of his men on the beach and found there 800 Yankees. They killed 15 of our men. We then retreated to the fort. Col. White opened fire upon them with canister, killing a large number. The enemy have built a battery two miles from the fort on the beach and planted mortars and large size siege guns. There are 11 large ships outside. The enemy have sent to Newbern for their gunboats to operate in the Sound. They are committing every imaginable outrage in Carteret and Onslow counties. The fort had not been taken on Wednesday.

RICHMOND, April 18.—The enemy have occupied Falmouth, opposite Fredericksburg, this morning. The Confederates burnt the bridges across the Rappahannock and evacuated the city.

KNOXVILLE, April 18.—The Register has a dispatch dated Bridgeport, April 18, which states that neither Decatur or Decatur bridge has been taken, and that there are only 3000 Yankees at Huntsville, the balance having fallen back. There are none on this side.

The steamer Lookout was not taken, but is at Guntersville, with 2000 sacks of Government corn and saltpetre untouched.

A man just from Nashville says the enemy are removing their stores, sick and wounded, also their cannon over the river, to Edgefield.

A gentleman from War Trace says Col. Stearns killed 75 of the enemy in the late fight, and wounded a large number.

Only two bridges have been burnt on the Charleston Railroad.

Our pickets went to Bellefonte last night, but saw no enemy. From the best information the enemy had gone back to Huntsville.

RICHMOND, April 18.—there is a report, seemingly reliable, brought by the Orange train this evening, that Stonewall Jackson had a fight with the enemy yesterday morning; but the enemy being overpowering Jackson fell back, and was in full retreat towarss Staunton. No statement of the loss on either side, fureher than that forty Confederates were taken prisoners. It was not supposed Jackson would meke a stand until he reached Waynesboro'.

Col. McKinney, who was killed on the Peninsula Wednesday, was buried during the evening. There was a large turn-out.

SAVANNAH, April 18.—There was a skirmish on White Marsh Island on Wednesday, between some companies of the 13th Georgia Regiment and a Michigan regiment. The latter were repulsed with a loss of about twenty.

The Confederate loss in killed and missing 5, and slightly wounded 7.

There was an accident on the Atlantic and West Point railroad yesterday. The train had soldiers on it. Greene, of Tennesse, was killed, and about 25 others slightly wounded.

RICHMOND, April 18.—The Senate passed the bill increasing the postage to ten cents on single letters. Also, the House bill prohibiting the sale of cotton, sugar and tobacco to the enemy.

The House passed a bill to raise bands of partisan rangers.

Van Dorn's report of the battle in Arkansas was presented to-day.

At 4 o'clock in the afternoon of Thursday, the Yankees appeared six miles from Falmouth. Our pickets were driven in and several wounded. The infantry and cavalry were sent out but were twice repulsed by the enemy, who being in large force, advanced. Our troops fell back to Fredericksburg, set fire to three bridges across the river; also burnt three steamboats and twenty-two vessels, loaded with 100,000 bushels of corn, and 100 bales cotton at the depot. The panic among the inhabitants was tremendous. Our troops evacuated the city, and the enemy sent a shell after them which struck a cotton factory, doing much damage. All the rolling stock of the railroad company was saved, with the exception of eight cars.

MEMPHIS, April 18.—News from the North to Monday last states that the dead and wounded continued to come in, and that the people were despondent. As at Manassas, so at Shiloh; they did not know the extent of our victory. H. P.

CORINTH, April 19.—A letter from Gen. D. C. Buell, dated, Headquarters of the Army of the Ohio, to Gen. Beauregard, commanding the Army of the Mississippi, was received to day, ratifying the exchange of wounded prisoners, as arranged by Breckinridge. The letter says that information regarding certain missing Louisiana officers and privates will be communicated as soon as obtained

Col. Jacob Thompson leaves to-morrow for Richmond, with a large number of the enemy's flags—trophies of the battle of Shiloh.

From the Delta, 19th.

BOMBARDMENT OF FORT JACKSON.—A furious bombardment of this Fort commenced yesterday morning and continued, it is understood, without sensible abatement or intermission, all day. The enemy had advanced his ships and mortar boats from their former place behind the headland and forest, and come within view of the two forts, when they were put in position for bombardment by tying them to piles driven for that purpose.

Their shells reached edasily, and fell with uncomfortable frequency around, and within Fort Jackson. It is said, indeed, that these projectiles were hurled upon the fort at the rate of eight in a minute, or upwards of five thousand in a day of twelve hours. The fort had replied to the bombardment with spirit, and we were advised, not without effect, striking several of the enemy's gunboats, sinking two, and setting a frigate on fire. We have reason to believe that reinforcements were sent to the fort yesterday evening.

From the True Delta, 20th.

THE FORTS BELOW.—We are in possession of information from Forts Jackson and St. Phillip, which we deem neither prudent nor adviseable to give publicity to. We will, however, say this much, that our authorities—nay, every man in the city, who professes to have a heart or a soul within him—should prepare to meet the coming issue with unblenched faces.

The hour is rapidly approaching when the question will be solved whether or not New Orleans will be a conquered city.—The issue is now to DO OR DIE. Who will be so craven as to falter?

Special to Delta.

MEMPHIS, April 18.—The Confederates have cut the levees on the Arkansas side of the river, above Fort Pillow, thus flooding the country. This is done to prevent the enemy advancing on that side. On the Tennessee side the Fort is so well protected as to be considered invulnerable. R.

From the Delta of the 20th.

AFFAIRS AT THE FORTS.—No material change occurred yesterday, as far as ascertained, at the forts as respects the activity and precision of the enemy's shelling It is understood, however, that his ships were unable to bear our fire this side of the point, and retired behind it. The number of shells he had thrown up to about 2 o'clock, is said to have been about 4000.

MEMPHIS, April 18.—Latest advices from Paducah say that the Federals have only two hundred prisoners, taken on both days of the late battle.

A Federal transport reached Paducah on Friday last, filled with wounded.

Gen. Buell was not among the wounded.

His reinforcements on Monday, the 7th, were fully 35,000.

The enemy confess a great defeat and loss, and it is rrported that he will withdraw from before Corinth, Beauregard's position and his army being too strong to be resisted with success.

It was believed that an attempt would be made to reunite the shattered columns of the enemy somewhere on the Mississippi river.

Troops were to be taken down the Tennessee and the Mississippi, but none had arrived at Paducah on Friday night.

The enemy is horribly cut up, shattered and disorganized. Great excitement and consternation prevail among them; everything is doubt and confusion, and they are mourning and despondent.

Nothing new on the Mississippi above.

The Confederate army is reorganized, reinforced, ready for another fight, and confident of victory, if the shattered enemy ever recover sufficiently to make another. H. P.

CORINTH, April 18, 1862.—It is almost impossible to get through mail or express matter, on account of the irregularity of the trains.

There was a collision last night at Pocahontas, a few miles below Corinth, which has blocked up the road.

A Nashville corespondent writes:

Ladies who make mouths and cast vituperation from their pretty lips, will have to learn to behave themselves or keep in doors. These insults are of various styles, and one which appears to be very studied is said to have been offerd to Gen. T. L. Crittenden. The story is told that as Crittenden was standing on the sidewalk near the Post Office, two splendidly dressed ladies followed by a dirty, slovenly black negro wench approached him. As they passed they put their handkerchiefs to their noses and gracefully drew their skirts aside from contact with his suit of "Lincoln" blue. The negro wench followed the example, and passed by, leaving the astonished General looking after the party with amazement. The ladies give a great deal of trouble here.

A TENDER REPROOF.—A little boy had one day done wrong, and was sent, after maternal correction, to ask in secret the forgiveness of his Heavenly Father. His offence had been passion. Anxious to hear what he would say, his mother followed him to the door of his room In lisping accents, she heard him ask to be made better, and then, with childish simplicity, he added, "*Lord, make ma's temper better, too!*"

THE BATTLE OF SHILOH.

Notes Upon the Battle Ground.

SECOND DAY.

Special Correpondence of the Picayune.

CORINTH, Miss., April 10, 1862.

Night had closed the battle of the 6ths leaving us in possession of all the enemy', positions, their batteries and camps, except that of the Federal General, C. F. Smith, on the Tennessee river, at Pittsburg. After fourteen hours' continuous fighting, in which we had driven the superior forces of the enemy back for nearly six miles, achieving a splendid and triumphant victory, our men, totally exhausted, occupied the enemy's tents on that bloody field of human carnage, and slept upon their arms. During the night a furious thunderstorm followed, and the rain fell in torrents, accompanied by hail.

Day dawned on the morning of the 7th, (Monday) disclosing a cloudy, murky sky. The order of battle was nearly as follows: Gen. Beauregard, with Gen. Hardee's command, consisting of Hindman's and Wood's brigades, on the right; Gen. Breckenridge, with Stathem's and Bowen's brigades, on the left of Hardee; Gen. Bragg, with Ruggles's division and Anderson's brigade, formed the left; and Gen. Polk, with Gen. Cheatham's division, composed of Bushrod Johnson's brigade, with Cols. Stephens's and Douglas's and Preston Smith's Tennessee regiments supporting the centre and right as reserves.

The enemy having been largely reinforced with fresh troops late on the preceding night, by Gen. Buell's forces coming up, a furious assault was made at sunrise on our extreme right, and then commenced another battle; a more desperate, more deadly, and more stubborn conflict than the day before, and considering the worn and jaded, wet and hungry condition of our men, and the superior numbers of the enemy, it was another Thermopylæ, where the Federal Xerxes found another Leonidas.

The attack was commenced half a mile from the river by the enemy, with a tremendous roar of musketry, Hardee sustaining the shock with his command, who returned the volley in gallant style, and opened on the enemy's concealed position with our artillery with great effect. The conflict raged with great fury, and the roar of musketry and artillery was incessant and deafening, Capt. Rutledge's Tennessee battery greatly aiding to hold the enemy in check. Hardee had now engaged the enemy up to half past 8 A. M., who continued to press forward, and succeeded in capturing two of our guns, belonging to the 5th Company of Washington Artillery, which were afterwards recaptured by the gallant First Missouri, Col. Rich, himself wounded, when fell the lamented Capt. Sprague. At this time Major Jno. H. Kelly, commanding battalion of McCarver's Arkansas regiment, of Wood's brigade, greatly distinguished himself by rallying his men on every occasion, and acting with great gallantry throughout the day, having had two horses killed under him. The enemy having increased their forces, their fire of artillery was now tremendous, Hardee replying with his batteries, when Gen. Breckenridge was ordered to charge. Cool and self-possessed, and ever looking the chieftain on the field, he led his column with great bravery, hurling destruction on the foe, recapturing our battery, and staggered the enemy back.

In this charge Col. Hill's Tennessee, a battalion under Capt. Lockhart of the Engineers, placed in command by Gen. Beauregard, with Major Brent of his staff on the right, and Col. Richard's Louisiana regiment gallantly advanced in the face of the enemy's fire. Capt Lockhart had his horse shot under him, and Col. Chisolm, of Gen. Beauregard's staff, had his horse wounded.

In the meanwhile our whole line had become engaged, Gen. Bragg having driven the enemy back half a mile on his left wing, but the enemy flanking him by large reinforcements drove him back to his former position. The enemy then advanced on our centre, when a most furious conflict ensued. Burn's Mississippi and Ketchum's Alabama batteries doing terrible execution. The enemy reeling under our fire attempted to flank Burn's battery, which mowed them down like grass, forcing them to fall back. It was at this time that the enemy changed his heavy forces to the right, and General Bragg's attention having been directed by the tremendous heavy fire in that quarter, with his masterly military sagacity and generalship, sent over Ruggles's command and Burn's battery to the relief, which Gen. Beauregard immediately ordered forward to the support of Breckinridge and Hardee. General Anderson's brigade, with the 11th Louisiana, under the gallant Captain Austin, and a portion of the Confederate Response now marched out to an open field to take one of the enemy's batteries, but fell back under a galling fire to a thicket. One of our batteries now opened fire on the enemy's left, driving them back, while we captured two pieces of the enemy's artillery, the horses all being killed.

Col. Russell's brigade now came up and engaged the enemy, who was ambuscaded in a thicket, while all our forces became generally engaged, our troops disputing the ground with desperation, and the enemy forced to reel back notwithstanding they were being reinforced by fresh regiments. This may be said to have been the bloodiest contest of the battle field; the whole earth seemed to shake with the roar of musketry and the booming of artillery. It was here that the gallant Russell, of Tennessee, lost more men of his command in twenty minutes than during the rest of the two days' fight. It was here the chivalrous Col. Kit Williams of Tennessee, was killed, and that the Brave Col. Blythe, of the Mississippi battalion, fell mortally wounded; here that Colonel Preston, of Tennessee, on the staff of Gen. Stewart, and scores of our brave countrymen, were slain. Here, too, Maj. George Williams had his horse shot under him, and Col. Richmond, both of General Polk's staff, had two horses killed under him in less than twenty minutes. The gallant Col. Alfred Mouton, of the 18th Louisiana, was also wounded, while leading a charge, and three pieces of Stamford's Mississippi battery were retaken in a desperate charge by the brave Alabamians of the 14th regiment.

It was now about 12 noon. Gen. Cheatham's division, of Gen. Polk's corps, which had moved towards the centre, and had supported Hardee and Breckinridge, driving the enemy for three-quarters of a mile in front of a peach orchard on the right, now discovered the enemy marching around by the left to flank us, when he immediately changed his position to meet them Passing in the rear of Bankhead's battery in a ravine, he charged the enemy with Cols. Stephens's, Douglas's, and Preston Smith's Tennessee regiments at the distance of 300 yards over a hill, under a frightful fire, driving them back with immense slaughter. This charge was made under the eye of Gen. Beauregard, who pronounced it one of the most desperate and gallant charges made during the day. Gen. Cheatham now occupying the enemy's position on the top of the hill, opened a raking fire with two pieces of artillery on his right, and two on his left, and with our battle flag in his hand, rode up and down the lines cheering our men. The conflict at this moment was terrible, the enemy advancing to within 300 yards of our lines, and disputing the ground inch by inch, with their immensely superior numbers. Capt. Melancthon Smith's Mississippi battery here did great execution, and rendered distinguished services throughout the battle, having had 43 horses killed, and never lost a gun. It was during this storm of battle, when the columns of the enemy went down in bloody rolling waves, as our artillery swept over them, that the brave Cheatham, dismounting from his horse, served a gun of one of our batteries with appalling effect.

Bragg, Beauregard, Hardee, Breckinridge, Polk and Cheatham, were now all driving the enemy before them, and performing deeds of valor never exceeded in the brightest days of chivalry. It was about 2 P. M. that Gen. Beauregard, perceiving our lines wavering under a raking covered fire of the enemy, dashed forward on his horse, and seizing the colors of the battalion of Orleans Guards, cried out, "charge—charge them, my braves!" and leading the column in person, soon routed the covered foe from their position. The gallant Col. Augustin then took his colors from his brave chief, now much exhausted, and continued to advance amid the wild shout and battle cry of our men.

Gen. Bragg, who had sustained our left flank with unparalleled heroism, was now left with only Ketchum's battery, Looney's Tennessee regiment, and one of Arkansas and Mississippi. These regiments had again and again driven back the enemy, but were at last flanked by such great odds as to compel them to resume their original position. The firing had now ceased on the right, the enemy, appalled by the terrible slaughter of their men, having refused to make another advance. We now occupied Shiloh Church, and the whole ground between Owl and Lick creeks. Our troops were also completely exhausted, and from the nature of the extened grounds, had straggled and scattered very much. From the late rains, the fields and roads had become trampled into horrid mire by our artillery and cavalry, and as yet was common report by the prisoners that the enemy had been hourly receiving reinforcements, Gen. Beauregard, at half-past 3 P. M., determined to withdraw from the field. Col. Thos. Jordan, Adjt. Gen. of Beauregard, was accordingly instructed to prepare a position to fall back, which he did, about a mile in the rear. Our troops now retired in perfect order, as if coming from a drill. Gen. Bragg, to cover the retrograde movement of his three regiments from the field, kept up a brisk fire from Ketchum's battery until it was accomplished. The battery then withdrew, and the din of battle ceased.

General Bragg and staff were the last to leave the ground, though he was frequently urged before to retire, saying that he would never leave the battle field so long as one of his soldiers remained before him. His heroic valor and generalship throughout the battle has won for him imperishable fame. Our army had reformed in line of battle with perfect coolness and regularity, and the enemy making no demonstrations, the order was given to fall back to Corinth. Breckinridge with his command being left on the field where we first engaged the enemy, as a rear guard. All things considered, the movement was executed with a decorum and order highly creditable to our troops, and which might well excite the admiration of veterans. To fully appreciate this, but let the reader turn to the campaign of Sir John Moore, who with his highly disciplined veteral regular troops, fell back before the superior forces of Soult, in 1803, and witness the terrible irregularities, demoralizaton and outrages committed by them on their retrograde march. It was worthy of remark, also, that on both days of the battle we were fighting a covered enemy, who concealed themselves most of the time in ambush until driven out, and that notwithstanding their vestcoats of steel mail and superior numbers, we whipped them with their own arms and ammunition, captured on the battle field.

On Monday morning, while a brigade was moving into the hottest of the fight on the centre, Gen. Beauregard rode up, when Col. Jacob Thompson cried out three cheers for Beauregard, which were heartily given. While thus standing, a private said, "General, you are in direct range of the cannon." The General replied, "Never mind, my good fellow, you do your duty, and I will attend to mine."—The private retorted, saying, "Well, then General, it is not your duty to sacrifice your life, while it is mine." The General smiled, thanked the private, and moved down the line.

It was about the turning point of the battle on Monday, about 2 o'clock, when private John Williams, of company C, 10th Mississippi, was returning to the field with a message for General Bragg, in a double-quick trot, when a straggler asked him what was the matter, "The mather," said Pat, "begora, I'm afraid they'll kill all the Yankees before I get back—come on now, if ye's want to get the last shot."—Williams got to the field, "went in," and came out with a standard of colors which he took in a charge.

I must not close without speaking of the hospital scenes at Mickey's House, on the last night of the battle, for it is impossible for me at this time to descri e them. The house and surrounding tents were filled with our own, and the enemy's wounded, who had been taken prisoners. Arms, legs, hands and feet, just amputated, lay scattered around—the groans of the wounded and the dying mingled together. The vigilant, scientfic, and unceasing attention of our Surgeon George W. Lawrence, and Dr. Chas. E. Michel, Inspector of Hospitals, of Hardee's corps, their skill in operating, the humanity manifested, and their general administration, richly deserve to be made public.

I would like also to describe the enemy's camps, in which were found every article that a soldier could desire, from the commonest article to that of costly luxuries. Besides their arms, steel-plated vests, many of which were left by the Yankees in their hurry, were quantities of port-folios filled with every sort of design of letter paper and envelopes, all impressing on the Yankee mind that they are fighting for "Union and the constitution," (!) and not for Abe Lincoln's free niggers. There were also numbers of obscene love letters, Testaments, Bibles, prayer books, boots and shoes, clothing of every kind, gloves, shirts, splendid camp equipage, writing desks, magnificent blanket shawls, beds, stoves, wine, brandies and liquors of all kinds, tobacco, coffee, sugar, rice, beans, and in short everything that the most wholesale extravagance could supply an army with in every particular

It must be confessed that the capture of these tents tended to demoralize our men very much, as hundreds left the ranks to pillage the enemy's camps. The most of them however, were afterwards burned, with much of their contents.

And in closing I must pay a deserved tribute of fame to our glorious cavalry corps, especially those of Col. Forrest, Col. Wirt Adams, Col. John Morgan, Col. Bennett's, and others whom I cannot recall, whose deeds of chivalry and gallantry were never exceeded by the knights of old in the days of Richard Cœur de Lion.

SPARTA.

VALVERDE PLANTATION, COLUMBIA, April 21, 1862.

ED. TELEGRAPH.—You have done well, inculcating through your editorials and published correspondence the planting of a large breadth of land in corn, so that our people and armies may have cheap food, which is the great element of national strength. This course has been generally pursued by our planters, and with anything of a favorable season the corn crop of this vicinity will be very much greater than last year.

But something more than planting is needed to raise corn. It must be attended to, cultivated and gathered. To do this our servants must be kept in good health. Nothing conduces more to this than sufficient and proper clothing, and here is the point where the shoe pinches the planter in his efforts to make food cheap, and our nation strong. You have told us that Gov. Moore of Louisiana has so arranged the penitentiary manufactory of that State, that cloth is exchanged *pro rata* for cotton. Cannot the sale of cloth by our penitentiary be in some way so arranged? As now practised planters can get the penitentiary cloth only through speculators, who have time to travel over the country to buy up wool to exchange for the products of the looms, if indeed they can obtain it by that means.

We are told that the army requires all the cloth the penitentiary can make; but cannot a portion of it be devoted to the necessities of the producers of corn? Considered in a proper light, they too contribute to our defence, and to the success of our righteous cause. With corn at 25 cents a bushel we can carry on the war for an almost interminable period; but two dollars a bushel for the staff of life will conquer us in a very short time. I would respectfully submit these views to the early consideration of Gov. Lubbock. Yours,

J. S. THRASHER.

☞ It is intimated in the True Delta of the 20th, that the N. O. city banks have determined to resume specie payments. The Delta quotes city bills at 25@30 per cent. premium. Mobile do, 5@8c. Other Southern banks, 3@5 per cent. premium.

FORNEY'S WAR PRESS

VOL. 1. PHILADELPHIA, SATURDAY, APRIL 26, 1862. NO. 24.

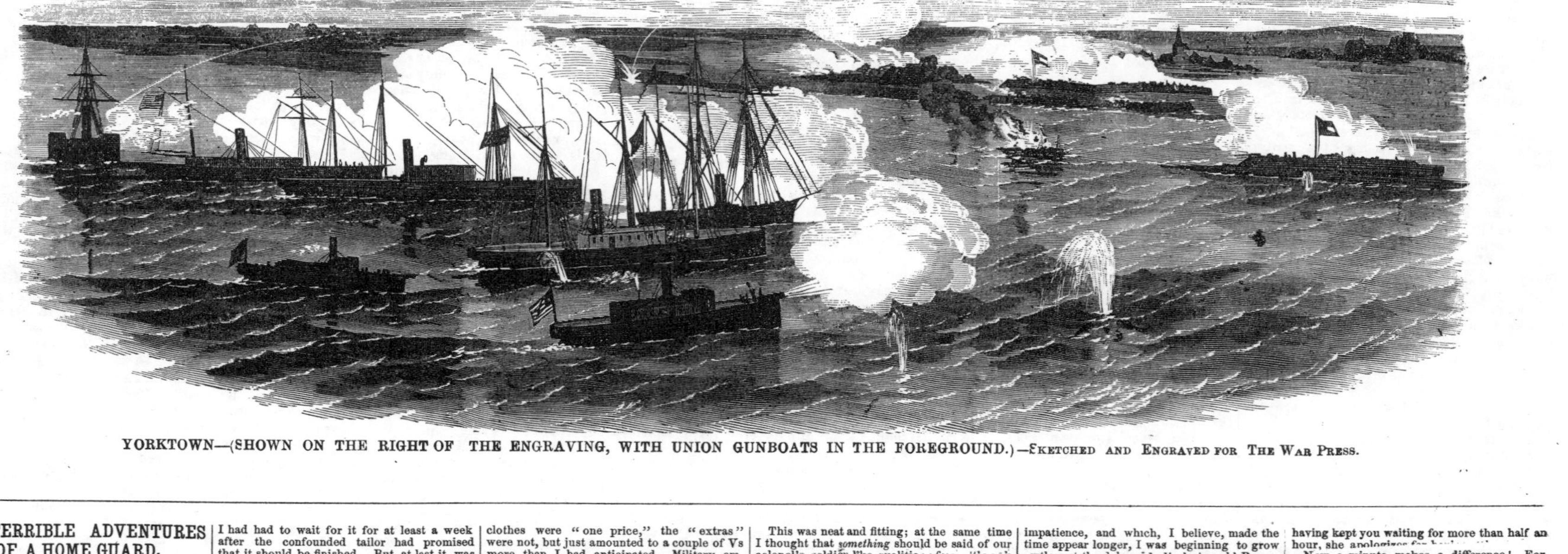

YORKTOWN—(SHOWN ON THE RIGHT OF THE ENGRAVING, WITH UNION GUNBOATS IN THE FOREGROUND.)—SKETCHED AND ENGRAVED FOR THE WAR PRESS.

YE TERRIBLE ADVENTURES OF A HOME GUARD.

BY FERDINAND L. SARMIENTO.

[For The War Press.]

I was elected a captain in the Home Guards about the 1st of May last, and upon that auspicious (and, for me, *proud*) occasion, took vows which, I am sincerely happy to say, the rebels have never yet given me an opportunity to break. I swore to defend my country and my flag! and I also swore—which oath has been religiously kept—to parade whenever I could before the door of my beloved Eliza Jane.

I was always what you might term "a good looking fellow"—straight up and down—with just the least bit of a military walk; but when I got my *uniform* on—by Jove, I was splendid! and if the large pier-glass in which I surveyed myself had been the liquid sheet of water which it resembled, I doubt not but I should have incurred the dread fate of the beauteous Narcissus and have fallen in love with myself, to fall, in turn, intoxicated with delight, into its glassy depths. As it was, I managed to exist; and determined now to punish the fair sex in general, and *one* in particalar, for the neglect which had hitherto been shown to my merits.

Strange to say, however, (and this I must say as a nota bene,) the women did not regard me in quite the favorable light which I had anticipated! I could only account for this in one way, and that was by concluding that the statement laid down by a profound philosopher—a friend of mine and a bachelor—was correct—viz: That women never value anything that they possess. "All their joys," so argues my friend, "are in anticipation. They see a 'love of a bonnet,' and no sooner do they buy it and get it home than it changes to 'a perfect fright of a thing.' They see something wonderfully cheap, 'selling off below cost,' and are crazy until they invest; when, presto, change, they discover that 'it is not worth while ever to buy cheap articles; they don't pay for the trouble of making up!'" So it is; and thus they treat us who have valiantly sworn to defend their homes to the last. They treat us exactly like they do the "love of a bonnet," after they have it safe home. They know they have us, and tire in consequence immediately. Yes, and under the influence of this feeling, too, totally ignore us, even glittering with gold-lace and tinsel show, as we are, and prefer some sturdy "private," who is bound for the South, and whose shoulders, they insist, in their foolish fashion of anticipating, will be hidden by a colonel's insignia, at least, when he returns. So they go on anticipating, until, at last, in this dreamy, romantic sort of a way, they fall in love with some poor devil, who, perhaps, is gone never to return, while our merits—the merits of the very ones who *stay* at home to protect them—are passed over with a slighting smile of sarcasm, or a caustic remark about being "Invincible in peace and invisible in war!" Invisible, indeed! Ain't we visible every fair day? Ain't we to be seen at the theatres, at the Germania—every where? What do they expect of us? Do they expect us to go and take Richmond and guard our own city too? or do they expect us to risk our lives and sell things "below cost" at the same time?

But to return to my uniform, which was the all-engrossing subject with me. I had had to wait for it for at least a week after the confounded tailor had promised that it should be finished. But at last it was to be done—positively finished at last—when I should be enabled to exhibit to the world the vast amount of patriotism which had been so long hidden within me. Imagine, then, my disappointment, my anguish, when upon the day appointed, Simms (that's my man) came to inform me that Botts, Snooks, & Co., "the celebrated never-lying one-priced tailors," had said, in answer to his demand for the clothes, that they were very sorry, but that it would be impossible to let me have them before next Saturday. "Saturday! I almost shrieked—Saturday! what do the fellows mean? Saturday! why do they expect my regiment to wait?" [N. B.—I forgot in my fury that our regiment was not to march—that, on the contrary, we were quietly to settle down and mind the cradles of our little ones, or, if we were unmarried men, the cradles of some other persons' little ones.] But these things never occur to a man when he is in a flurry, so I continued to storm away at the inexcusable remissness of my tailors, and vowed that they shouldn't have the uniform in their hands another moment. But what could I do? I was completely at their mercy. I had bought my own cloth, and the rascally fellows had it cut up, probably, by this time—or even if they had not, would swear they had, so there was nothing for it but to grin and bear it. I could understand now how it was that young ladies felt so disappointed when their new cloaks happened not to be finished in time for church; and how they could go into hysterics, get attacks of sick headache, etc., etc. I could sympathize with them now; I could feel for them, and ah! how I longed to weep with them; but all the weeping in the world would not have hastened things a whit. Tears avail not against stern fate, and every man knows that these tailors are the living representatives of fate in this world, ever ready, with their huge shears, to clip piece by piece our hopes, and cut our figures all awry. So there was nothing for it but to wait.

But at last the eventful day arrived, and my uniform was really finished. I'm sure I don't see how it was that Botts, Snooks, & Co., "never-lying one-price" men, managed to keep their word even now! It was a happy day—a day of pure and unqualified pleasure. Unqualified, did I say? If so, I'm wrong—the *bill* came with the clothes, and though the clothes were "one price," the "extras" were not, but just amounted to a couple of Vs more than I had anticipated. Military embroidery had gone up, so I was informed; shoulder straps cost enormously now; it was all Mr. Horstman's fault, no doubt. But I was satisfied; I had learned, even by living the quiet life of a favored citizen of the city of Brotherly Love, that if one wanted a gratification one must pay for it.

This was no time, however, for philosophizing—to which, by-the-by, I am a little prone. It was Saturday afternoon, when, as all the world knows, Chestnut street is crowded with specimens of female beauty to be found nowhere else, so I must hasten and complete a little business matter to which I had been attending, and then sally forth to carry out my contemplated vengeance upon the members of the fair sex in general, and *one* in particular.

Our colonel was to be presented with a sword, as a testimonial, I believe, of the respect and regard of the men and officers under him. This was the business to which I refer, inasmuch as the responsible duty of getting the thing up, and also of delivering the usual "presentation speech," had devolved upon me. The sword, as may be supposed, was to be a tasteful and magnificent one—[N. B.—I had expended all my well-known taste in arranging its details.] In short, it was to bespeak at once our liberality as well as the high regard which we entertained for our commanding officer. Ahem! I believe the colonel himself was the first one to suggest the thing; and, if I mistake not, paid almost the whole amount out of his own pocket. Such is, however, the usual course, as I have since understood; and this was not an isolated case. The sword was now finished; indeed, lacked but one thing, a suitable inscription, for which a blank space had been left. Now, this inscription had puzzled me greatly, inasmuch as it was most desirable to have a fitting and appropriate one, as well as one which would not cost too much to engrave; for so much had the "meetings" and *accompaniments* on the subject of the great sword presentation cost, that little of the original sum remained. It was, therefore, peculiarly difficult to hit upon the exact thing—viz: a legend composed of a few words, so as to not cost much in the engraving, and one at the same time *appropriate*; but at last I got one to suit. It ran thus:

To Col. —— ——, Commanding — Regiment]
Philadelphia Home Guards,
As a Testimonial of our Deep Respect.

This was neat and fitting; at the same time I thought that *something* should be said of our colonel's soldi[illegible] he had been a shoemaker all his life, and had probably never seen a camp or heard a gun fired during the whole of that time, I thought a little flattery might not be amiss, so I added to the above—in my directions to the engraver—"and (*provided it don't cost any more*) of our perfect confidence in his high military qualities."

This business over, I issued forth for a promenade on our most crowded thoroughfare. I must say I felt a little sheepish at first; felt too tight; felt red in the face; imagined everybody was looking at me; altogether, was glad to escape into the classic halls of the "Continental." Once there, though, out of the range of the many brilliant eyes of the Germania-bent damsels that crowded the street, I felt relieved.

In the sombre halls of the "Continental," then, I soon gained renewed courage, and whilst I supped my brandy and water [N. B.—Nothing looks more military than brandy and water], I began to cogitate upon the late confusion into which the fair enemy had just thrown me. Why, thought I, should not a man who has nobly resolved to die, if necessary, for his own dear home, don a uniform, and show to the world the great resolves that are within him? What difference is there, after all, between a volunteer for the war and a Home Guard—between one who goes away to die for his home, and one who stays at home to die for it? No great difference, as I can see. And is one, because he chooses to remain inactive—the hardest duty of a soldier—is he, I ask all reasonable people, is he to be scoffed at and jeered at because he wears a uniform? If so, I will none of it, and the Home Guard may go to——"Halt, there!" cries conscience; "you came very near breaking Article XXXIV of the rules and regulations of the 'Stay-at-home Guards,' and which expressly forbids all swearing. A pretty example for an officer to set!"

Deeply exercised at my near approach to a *lapsus linguæ*, I inadvertently stuck a cracker in my pocket and started up the street to delight with my new trappings the eyes of beloved Eliza Jane, who, I doubted not, would be in ecstasy over her soldier lover.

As it was now dark, I succeeded admirably in passing for a regular officer, and soon stood before the stately mansion of my adorable.

Stamping the door-step with true military impatience, and which, I believe, made the time appear longer, I was beginning to grow when the door opened, disclosing old Pomp. Now, Pomp was an old family servant, having been born in the family, and he assumed all the liberty towards his master's friends that a favorite darkey in the South would do. Old Pomp, then, seeing an officer all glittering with gold lace, did not know what to make of it at first, but soon recognizing me, he exclaimed: "Why, Lord-a-massy, massa! why, is you goin' to de wars? I allers said you's de gemman for a soldier. Lord! Lord! so you's gwan to de wars?"

"Why, no, Pomp," I answered, in my most condescending manner; "not quite, yet; in fact—in fact"—

"But you expects for to go soon?"

"Well, no, Pomp. In fact, I've—I've only joined the Home Guards."

"De Home Guards! Ki, ki, ki! Is *dat* all? Lord-a-massy! if I didn't tink you's gwan to be a *soldier*," cried the old rascal, with a grin on him that showed all his ivories.

Umph! that comes from having servants who are too free. But I would put a stop to all that if ever I became a leader in that establishment; that I was determined on. "He'll not venture his freedom on me then!" I muttered, as he showed me, with the grin still on his features, into the elegant drawing-room of my intended, and where he left me whilst he went to inform that beloved being of my arrival.

Now, if there is one thing that I hate, it is to wait for a lady that "will be down in a minute." I would like exceedingly to know how many seconds young ladies generally estimate to a minute, and how it is that the fashionable schools instruct the two sexes so differently on so important a point? How many seconds make a minute according to young ladies? I would really like to know. When *I* went to school, sixty seconds only were estimated to a minute, and a minute, though often long, was sure to pass eventually. Thus boys are taught; but young ladies, bless my soul! have such an opposite computation of time, that *our* seconds may prolong to minutes, and minutes may dissolve into hours, and yet it comes under their appellation of a "minute." If you are inclined to doubt this, reader, just call upon any of your lady friends, or, better still, just "wait a minute" for her while she puts on her bonnet; and having kept you waiting for more than half an hour, she apologizes [illegible]

Now, a minute makes a difference! For instance, a husband comes home to dinner. "Dinner is not ready, but will be served in a minute," says the cook. Husband innocently supposes that with women, as with men, a minute is conceded to consist of sixty seconds. Hapless mortal! Sixty seconds pass—no dinner. Sixty more seconds elapse—still no dinner!

"How many seconds are there in a minute?" asks the husband, in a furious rage.

"Now, my dear, *do* have patience for only *one minute*," implores the wife.

"A minute, madam; how long is a minute? How long *is* a minute, madame, I ask?"

"Now don't be preposterous, Edward," retorts the wife, bridling up.

"Preposterous, madame! The"—(ah! take care of Article XXXIV of the rules and regulations!) and, at last, out of the house bounces the husband, mad and furious, dinnerless and breathless, with perhaps a new and sterling reason for buying a new dinner-set.

It is all the affair of a *minute*, you see. A minute—but of how many *seconds?*

In my case, this "waiting for a minute" was particularly annoying. Pomp, I knew, would hasten to inform his mistress of my very military appearance, and once in a while I could even hear "snickering" on the staircase, and in the hall outside; but, at last, after sundry low laughs, and whisperings of "you go first;" "no, you go in," &c., my adorable Eliza Jane entered the room, accompanied by the most roguish of cousins, whilst both of their faces showed plainly that it was with the greatest difficulty that they could keep from roaring right out.

My evening was not particularly pleasant. I felt stiffened, contracted, while the disposition on the part of the girls to laugh seemed every moment on the increase; and I really do believe that they dropped their handkerchiefs for no other reason than to see me try to stoop and pick them up. Altogether, I approve of the German fashion of treating young ladies. We Americans are entirely too polite. They are just as able to stoop and pick up their own handkerchiefs as we are; indeed, what with our tight coats, neckties, and unmentionables, much more so.

Soon, however, the old gentleman came in, (don't be frightened, reader, I don't mean the "gentleman in black," but Eliza Jayne's father.) He had just been reading his evening paper, and, mark the nonchalant air with which, after of course, having just got a new load of ideas therefrom, was dying to fire them off at some one, which is very entertaining, no doubt, if you happen to be a subscriber to an opposition paper; but where you have already read the *same* paper, it is an unmitigated bore. It happened, this evening, that the editor of the paper aforesaid had shown very conclusively, and with his accustomed wise foresight, that the rebels must be starved out in a month, if not in less time, and the father of my adored one grew eloquent over the fact. So strongly did he put the "points" at me, that I grew quite heated, and drew forth my pocket-handkerchief with a flourish, while I enlarged upon the points brought to bear, as a military man should; but, as fate would have it, in drawing forth my handkerchief, the ill-starred cracker, which I had thrust into my pocket at the "Continental," dropped out,

[CONTINUED ON EIGHTH PAGE.]

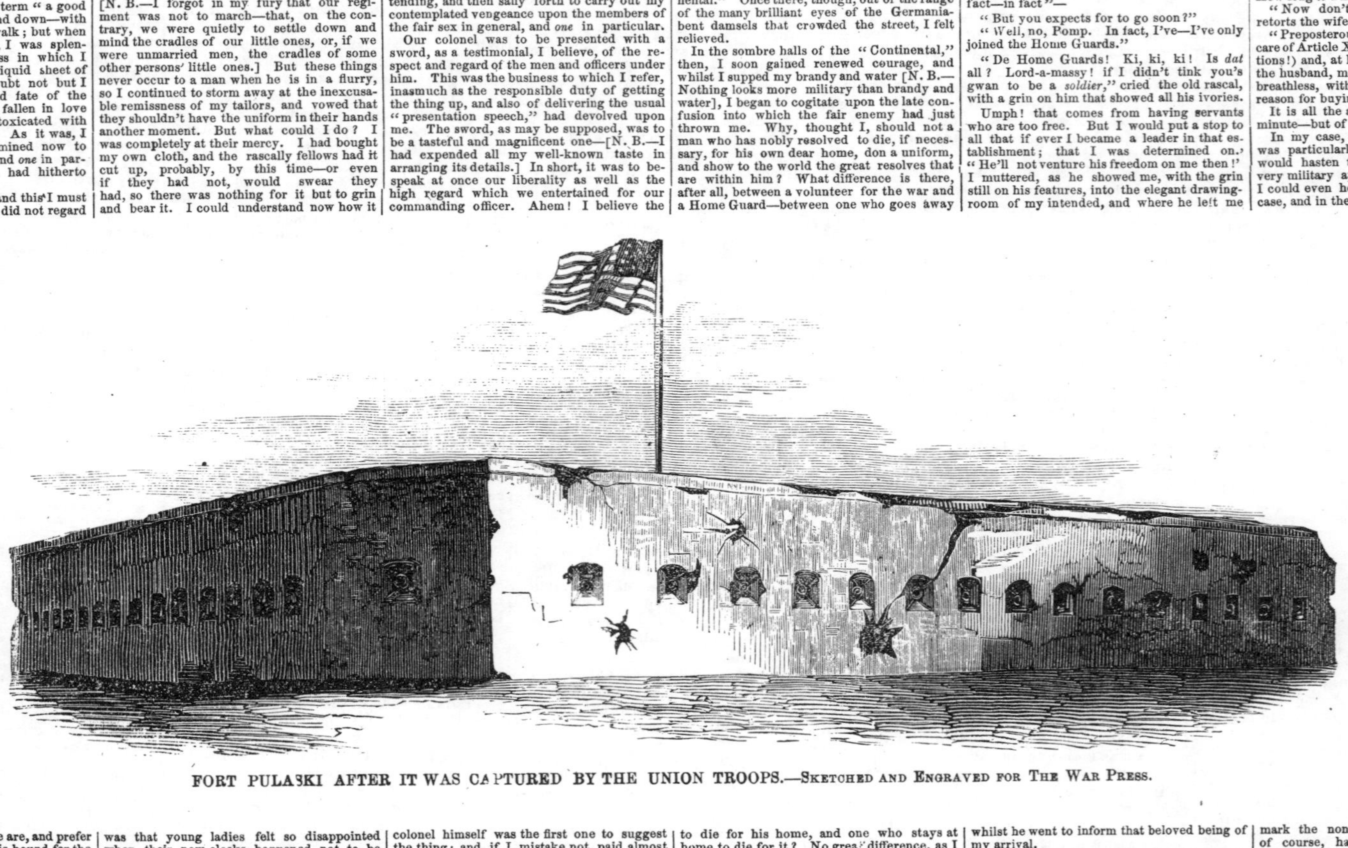

FORT PULASKI AFTER IT WAS CAPTURED BY THE UNION TROOPS.—SKETCHED AND ENGRAVED FOR THE WAR PRESS.

New-York Daily Tribune.

VOL. XXII.....No. 6,572. NEW-YORK, MONDAY, APRIL 28, 1862. PRICE TWO CENTS.

FROM GEN. BANKS'S DIVISION.

Jackson Retreated to Gordonsville.

HIS CRUELTY TO PRISONERS

HIS MILITIA DESERTING.

CAMP NEAR SPARTA, Va., Friday, April 25, 1862.

Several deserters and refugees corroborate previous reports that Jackson, after flying from our advancing column on Friday last, pushed forward to a point one mile north of Harrisonburg, where a turnpike branches to the left, passing Magaugheystown on the south fork of the Shenandoah and the Blue Ridge, and running thence to Gordonsville.

Jackson's wagon train had been pushed toward Staunton, but hearing that that town was in possession of the Union troops, he remanded it to Harrisonburg. At an early hour on Saturday morning, Jackson, with his whole force and train, took the Gordonsville pike, and at latest accounts had reached Magaugheystown.

On Saturday night a squadron of the 1st Vermont Cavalry, while scouting the Luray road beyond Massanetten Mountain, fell in with a body of the enemy's cavalry. A skirmish ensued, resulting in the capture of seven of the enemy and eleven of their horses. None of our men were hurt; but a Lieutenant had his horse shot under him.

The Paymaster of the Vermont Cavalry arrived at camp yesterday, to the great delight of the Green Mountain Boys.

A train, containing shoes, stockings, &c., for Gen. Williams's division, reached Mount Jackson on Friday. They will be distributed to-day. The stone turnpikes of this region are very destructive to shoes.

The weather since Friday has been very inclement, owing to a prevailing north-easter, the dampness penetrating tents and clothing, and chilling the bodies of the men. There are loud calls for the restoration of the whisky ration.

The inhabitants of this lovely and fertile valley, although they gave an almost unanimous vote for Secession, now sincerely regret it, and appear well pleased in the belief that the war in Virginia is nearly at an end. Fresh meats and breadstuffs abound in this section, and the owners are not disposed to conceal or spirit them away beyond our reach.

The Rebel Jackson's retreat from this place had a beneficial effect on the volunteers and drafted men from Rockingham and the surrounding counties. Large numbers of them daily come into our lines and deliver themselves up. It is stated that hundreds of them are now in the Massametten Mountains, hiding from Ashby's scouts, only awaiting an opportunity to escape and claim protection from Gen. Banks. One who came in yesterday reported that he found a cave a few miles hence, where were concealed sixteen refugees and deserters, who will probably come into town to-day.

A portion of Ashby's cavalry are scouting both sides of the mountain near Harrisonburg, watching our movements, and endeavoring to catch deserters. The main body, however, are believed to have gone with Jackson, wherever he may be.

The refugees and deserters are turned over to Lieut.-Col. Batchelder's (Provost Marshal) department, and examined by Col. Clark, of Gen. Banks's staff.

Dr. Baxter, late Assistant Surgeon of the Wisconsin 3d, has been appointed Medical Purveyor for this Department, and is temporarily stationed at Strasburg.

It is a fact worthy of notice that the Rebel hospitals are models of comfort, convenience, and cleanliness. At Mount Jackson three large two story frame buildings have been recently constructed on the most approved plan, being lathed and plastered and divided into appropriate wards. The ceilings are high, and the ventilation perfect. They are sufficient to accommodate six hundred patients, and will be occupied by our sick.

Wagons are actively collecting forage and other supplies, which are more abundant here than they were in Shenandoah and Frederick Counties.

A Union hostage, who escaped from Jackson on Saturday morning, reports his force at that time six miles east of Harrisonburg, which place he left in a perfect panic.

The Union hostages taken by Jackson from Winchester and the valley—many of whom are sixty years old and upward, sick and crippled—were barbarously compelled to march on foot behind the train, up hill and down, through mud and creeks, in some cases falling down from sheer exhaustion. This act has caused great indignation in our army, and loud cries are made for retaliation upon prominent Secessionists hereabout.

HARRISONBURG, Friday, April 25, 1862.

Last night a strong reconnoissance was made from Newmarket toward Staunton. On reaching Mount Crawford, eight miles south of the town, the bridge over a branch of the south fork of the Shenandoah was found burnt, and the stream too deep and rapid to cross. A bridge over another branch of the same stream was also burnt. This was done last Tuesday evening, not by the Rebels, but by the citizens, as stated by persons in the neighborhood.

It was ascertained from citizens, that yesterday a body of mounted Rebels came to the river, intending to cross, but the current was too deep and strong to hazard the attempt. They stated that *our troops were in possession of Staunton*. To-day, one of our brigades passed through the town and took possession of one of the principal avenues leading from here.

Since our first entrance into the town, no effort has been made by the rebel forces to reenter.

As usual in all the towns of this Valley, but few males remain.

It is reported that Jackson is in front, and rumor says he has been reinforced, but has burnt bridges over the Shenandoah, which prevents the possibility of any night attack.

The roads, with the exception of the stone turnpikes are almost impassable. We have a strong picket in front to-night.

HARRISONBURG, Va., Saturday, April 29, 1862.

Nothing worthy of notice transpired last night. Deserters from Jackson's militia report him making very slow progress toward Gordonsville, and that 800 militia have deserted since his escapade. The Shenandoah bridge has not yet been burned, but pickets are stationed there ready to apply the torch on our first approach.

HARRISONBURG, Va., Saturday, April 26—P. M.

Jackson is resting on the east side of the Shenandoah, with his whole force, about sixteen miles hence. His scouts frequently make a dash on our pickets. One of the latter was killed this afternoon. The spongy nature of the soil prevents an advance at present. The weather is clear and pleasant.

FROM SHIP ISLAND.

BOSTON, Saturday, April 26, 1862.

Arrived, ship Black Prince, from Ship Island on the 6th, via Havana on the 15th inst.

Left at Ship Island, ships Great Republic, from Portland; Parliament, from Boston, and Western Empire, from do. Both the latter ships landed their cargoes, consisting of horses, in good order.

Also, left at Ship Island, the ships Eliza and Ella, from Boston; bark Wild Gazelle, from Boston.

Also, in port, ships Idaho, Ocean Pearl, E. W. Farley, Undaunted, and North America (uncertain).

NEW-ORLEANS CAPTURED

Our Gunboats Pass Fort Jackson.

GREAT EXCITEMENT AT NEW-ORLEANS.

THEIR ARRIVAL BEFORE THE CITY

PANIC AMONG THE CITIZENS.

Immense Destruction of Property.

THE REBELS BURN THEIR COTTON AND STEAMBOATS.

REBEL REPORT OF THE AFFAIR.

FORTRESS MONROE, April 27, 1862.

Hon. E. M. STANTON, Secretary of War.

A fugitive black, just arrived from Portsmouth, brings *The Petersburg Express* of yesterday, which contains the following dispatch:

MOBILE, Friday, April 25, 1862.

The enemy passed Fort Jackson at 4 o'clock yesterday morning. When the news reached New-Orleans the excitement was boundless. Martial law was put in full force, and business was completely suspended.

All the cotton and steamboats, excepting such as were necessary to transport coin, ammunition, &c., were destroyed.

At 1 o'clock to-day the operator bade us good by, saying that the enemy had appeared before the city.

This is the last we know regarding the fall. Will send particulars as soon as they can be had.

The negro bringing the above, reports that the Rebels have two iron-clad steamers nearly completed, and that it is believed that the Merrimac will be out to-morrow. JOHN E. WOOL.

HEADQUARTERS OF THE DEPARTMENT OF THE RAPPAHANNOCK, April 27, 1862.

Hon. E. M. STANTON, Secretary of War:

I have just returned from the camp opposite Fredericksburg. I was told *The Richmond Examiner* of the 26th had been received in town, announcing as follows:

"New-Orleans taken. Great destruction of property, cotton, and steamboats. Steamboats enough saved to take away the ammunition. Great consternation of the inhabitants."

IRVIN McDOWELL, Major-General.

BOSTON, Saturday, April 26, 1862.

A Ship Island letter of the 6th inst. states that Gen. Williams's Brigade left there on the 2d inst. for New-Orleans.

MAP OF NEW-ORLEANS AND THE MISSISSIPPI DELTA.

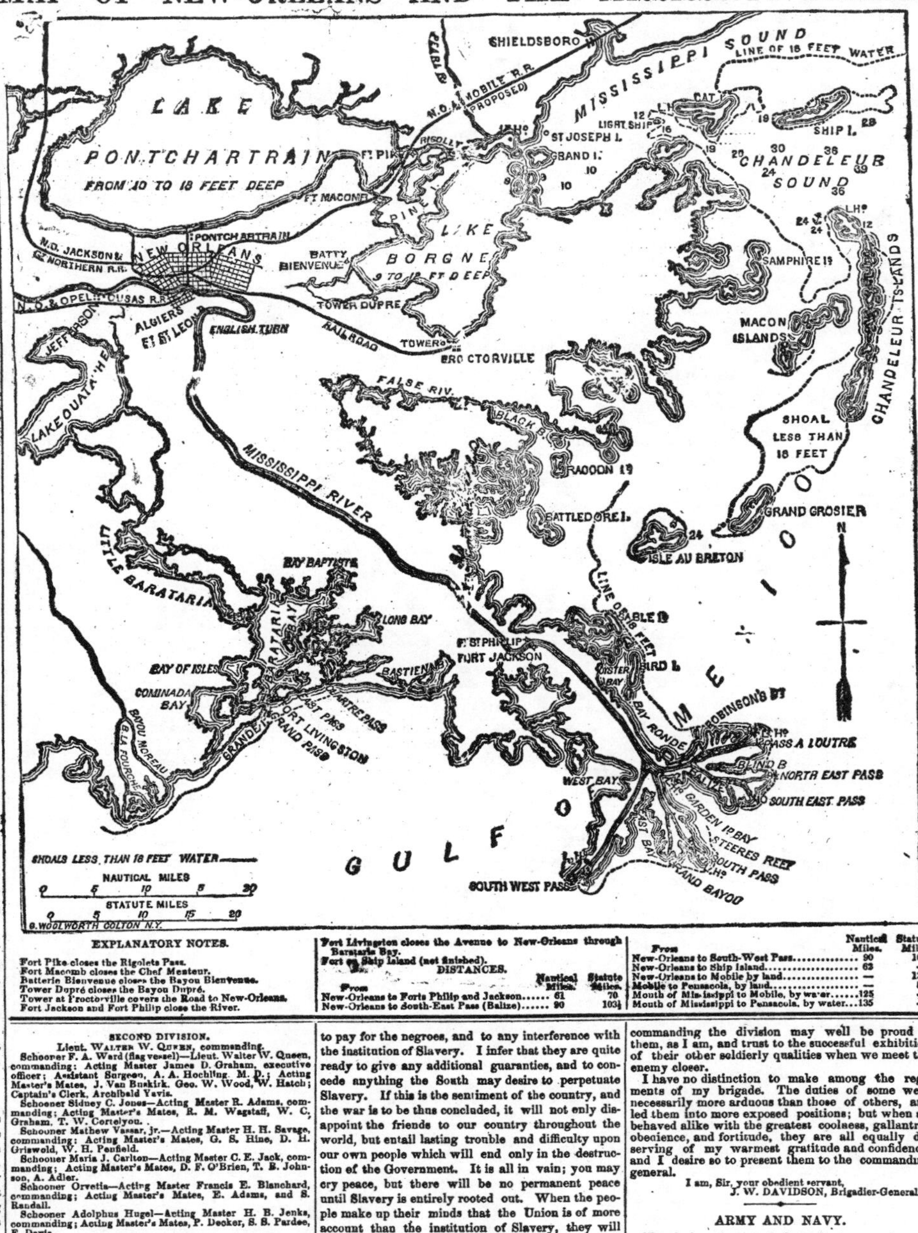

EXPLANATORY NOTES.

Fort Pike closes the Rigolets Pass.
Fort Macomb closes the Chef Menteur.
Batterie Bienvenue closes the Bayou Bienvenue.
Tower Dupré closes the Bayou Dupré.
Tower at Proctorville covers the Road to New-Orleans.
Fort Jackson and Fort Philip close the River.
Fort Livingston closes the Avenue to New-Orleans through Barataria Bay.
Fort on Ship Island (not finished).

DISTANCES.

From	Nautical Miles.	Statute Miles.
New-Orleans to Forts Philip and Jackson	61	70
New-Orleans to South-East Pass (Balize)	90	103¼
New-Orleans to South-West Pass	90	103¼
New-Orleans to Ship Island	62	—
New-Orleans to Mobile by land	—	135
Mobile to Pensacola, by land	—	59
Mouth of Mississippi to Mobile by water	125	—
Mouth of Mississippi to Pensacola, by water	135	—

MANSFIELD LOVELL.

The Major-General in command of the Rebel forces at New-Orleans is Mansfield Lovell, who, it may be remembered, was Deputy Street Commissioner in this city previous to the breaking out of the rebellion. He was born in the District of Columbia, and is now about 43 years of age. He graduated at West Point Military Academy on the 30th of June, 1842, having entered as a Cadet in 1838. Several of his classmates are now Generals in the Union army; and two of them, Rains and G. W. Smith (formerly Street-Commissioner in this city), are now in the Rebel army. He was promoted to a Second Lieutenancy of the 4th Artillery in July, 1842, and to a First Lieutenancy in the same regiment in February, 1847. In 1847 and 1848 he served in the capacity of Aid to Gen. Quitman, in the Mexican war, and was wounded in the assault of Chepultepec in September, 1847, for which he was breveted Captain in July, 1848. He was also wounded in the attack on the De Belea Gate. On the 18th of December, 1854, he resigned his connection with the U. S. Army to join the expedition got up for the purpose of revolutionizing the Island of Cuba, under Gen. Quitman. Gustavus W. Smith was with him in this project, and when the plans fell through, by becoming public and proving unpopular, Mr. Lovell came to New-York, and procured for himself the position of Deputy in the Street Commissioner's office. While here, he organized and commanded what was known as the City Guard of New-York—a company of the 9th Regiment, N. Y. S. M. When the rebellion broke out Gen. Sanford offered the services of the First Division to the Governor for the purpose of aiding to put down the Secession movement. At this Lovell was disgusted, and at once resigned his commission, after which he remained in the city for some time, preparing himself for the exit which he subsequently made to Rebeldom. He left the city very quietly, his departure having been covered by the movements of his superior in office, G. W. Smith, who soon followed, *his* departure having been aided by some of our City officials, who kept the matter in silence for weeks after the Rebel Street Commissioners had left the city. The next that was heard of them, was that they were serving the Rebel cause as Generals. G. W. Smith is now in Virginia, where he is likely to fall into the hands of our army; and it is not improbable that Lovell is already captured at New-Orleans.

THE FLEET BEFORE NEW-ORLEANS.

The following is a list of the officers and vessels of Flag-Officer Porter's flotilla, as made up at the Brooklyn Navy-Yard. Some changes were made, however, at Key West, and it has been corrected accordingly:

FIRST DIVISION.

Lieut. WATSON SMITH, Commanding.

Schooner Norfolk Packet (flag vessel)—Lieut. Watson Smith, U. S. N., commanding; Acting Master, Edgar C. Merriam; Executive Officer, Assistant-Surgeon A. B. Judson, M. D.; Acting Master's Mates, W. E. Fentress, W. Collins; Captain's Clerks, John Roby, W. Ferguson.

Schooner Oliver H. Lee—Acting Master Washington Godfrey, commanding; Acting Master's Mates, E. A. Howell, A. J. Parsons, J. A. Chadwick.

Schooner Para—Acting Master G. N. Hood, commanding; Acting Master's Mates, W. W. Hughes, J. C. McDonough, E. Ryan.

Schooner C. P. Williams—Acting Master, A. R. Langthorne, commanding; Acting Master's Mates, J. R. Fegan, W. Cowlings, G. O. Penfield.

Schooner Arletta—Acting Master Thomas E. Smith, commanding; Acting Master's Mates, Israel S. Bunce, S. W. Fitchette, Thomas Devine.

Schooner W. Bacon—Acting Master W. P. Rogers, commanding; Acting Master's Mates, G. W. Lane, L. Bartholomew, E. W. Pelton.

SECOND DIVISION.

Lieut. WALTER W. QUEEN, commanding.

Schooner T. A. Ward (flag vessel)—Lieut. Walter W. Queen, commanding; Acting Master James D. Graham, executive officer; Assistant Surgeon, A. A. Hoehling, M. D.; Acting Master's Mates, J. Van Buskirk, Geo. W. Wood, W. Hatch; Captain's Clerk, Archibald Yavis.

Schooner Sidney C. Jones—Acting Master R. Adams, commanding; Acting Master's Mates, R. M. Wagstaff, W. C. Graham, T. W. Cortelyou.

Schooner Mathew Vassar, jr.—Acting Master H. H. Savage, commanding; Acting Master's Mates, G. S. Hine, D. H. Griswold, W. H. Penfield.

Schooner Maria J. Carlton—Acting Master C. E. Jack, commanding; Acting Master's Mates, D. F. O'Brien, T. B. Johnson, A. Adler.

Schooner Orvetta—Acting Master Francis E. Blanchard, commanding; Acting Master's Mates, E. Adams, and S. Randall.

Schooner Adolphus Hugel—Acting Master H. B. Jenks, commanding; Acting Master's Mates, P. Decker, S. S. Pardee, F. Davis.

Schooner Geo. Mangham—Acting Master John Collins, commanding; Acting Master's Mates, J. M. Richards, S. A. O'Brien, W. Dade.

THIRD DIVISION.

Lieut. K. RANDOLPH BREESE, commanding.

Barkentine Horace Beals (flag vessel)—Lieut. K. Randolph Breese, U. S. N., commanding. Acting Master, Geo. W. Sumner, Executive Officer; Assistant Surgeon, Robert T. Edes, M. D.; Acting Master's Mates, T. H. Lavensaler, E. Booth, R. M. Clark; Captain's Clerk, Albert W. Bacon.

Schooner John Griffith—Acting Master, H. Brown, commanding; Acting Master's Mates, S. Rowland, J. S. Hyde.

Schooner Sarah Bruin—Acting Master Abraham Christian, commanding.

Schooner Racer—Acting Master, A. Phinney, commanding; Acting Master's Mates, E. S. Wanter, H. C. Whitmore, D. B. Carey.

Brig Sea Foam—Acting Master, H. E. Williams, commanding; Acting Master's Mates, J. L. Perkins, Joseph Moss, Ambrose Felix.

Schooner Henry Janes—Acting Master, Lewis Pennington, commanding; Acting Master's Mates, R. N. Spate, A. Soper, Z. Predmore.

Schooner Dan Smith—Acting Master, G. W. Brown, commanding; Acting Master's Mates, W. Brown, Erick Gabrielson, R. Somers.

RESERVE DIVISION OF STEAMERS.

Steamer Octorara, flag-ship of Commander Porter, Lieut. Geo. Brown commanding.
Steamer Harriet Lane, Lieut. J. D. Wainright commanding.
Steamer Owaska, Lieut. John Guest commanding.
Steamer Westfield, Commander Wm. B. Renshaw commanding.
Steamer Clifton, Lieut. J. H. Baldwin commanding.
Steamer Miami, A. D. Harrell commanding.
Steamer Jackson, Lieut. Samuel Woodworth commanding.
Steamer R. B. Forbes, Acting Master —— Fly commanding.

All these vessels carry a 13-inch mortar weighing about 17,000 pounds. The fleet left Key West on the 6th of April.

FROM ALABAMA.

THE LATE BRIDGE-BURNING EXPEDITION.

WASHINGTON, Saturday, April 26, 1862.

The Navy Department has received dispatches from Com. Foote inclosing a report from Lieut. Commanding Gwin, dated the 14th inst., in which he says:

"The Tyler and Lexington convoyed two transports, containing 2,000 troops, infantry and cavalry, under command of Gen. Sherman, to Chikasaw, Ala., where they disembarked, and proceeded rapidly to Bear Creek Bridge, at the crossing of the Memphis and Charleston Railroad, for the purpose of destroying it, and as much of the trestle work as they could find.

"The expedition was entirely successful; the bridge, consisting of two spans of 110 feet each, was completely destroyed—that is, the superstructure, together with some 500 feet of trestle work, and half a mile of telegraph line. The Rebels made a feeble resistance to our cavalry, 120 in number, but soon hastily retreated, losing four killed. Our loss none."

The Navy Department is desirous of learning the address of Mr. Birney, the inventor of the combustion shell.

WHAT IS THOUGHT IN EUROPE.

Extract from a private letter dated

LIVERPOOL, April 12, 1862.

I hope I may be disappointed, but it looks to me as if we were going to fulfill the predictions of Mr. Spence in his work on the American Union, page 158, an extract from which I inclose you. This book has been very generally read in England. It has undergone four editions.

All the merchants I see from New-York tell me they are opposed to the President's recommendation to pay for the negroes, and to any interference with the institution of Slavery. I infer that they are quite ready to give any additional guaranties, and to concede anything the South may desire to perpetuate Slavery. If this is the sentiment of the country, and the war is to be thus concluded, it will not only disappoint the friends to our country throughout the world, but entail lasting trouble and difficulty upon our own people which will end only in the destruction of the Government. It is all in vain; you may cry peace, but there will be no permanent peace until Slavery is entirely rooted out. When the people make up their minds that the Union is of more account than the institution of Slavery, they will settle the question, and not until then.

THE ADVANCE TO YOUNG'S MILL.

GEN. DAVIDSON'S OFFICIAL REPORT.

HEADQUARTER'S THIRD BRIGADE SMITH'S DIVISION, Camp near Lee's Mill, Warwick River, Va., April 12, 1862.

Capt. L. D. CARNE, Assistant Adjutant General:

SIR: Having been directed by the General commanding the division to furnish a report of the operations of my brigade from the 5th inst. to the present time, I respectfully state as follows:

The advance of the division from Young's Mill was formed by my brigade, the 7th Maine, Col. Mason commanding, being deployed as a line of skirmishers in front, with a section of Kennedy's battery, Lieut. Cowan, following the road. The 33d New-York, Col. B. F. Taylor, 77th New-York Volunteers, Col. McKean, and the 49th New-York, Lieut.-Col. Alberger, in the order named, moving in rear of this advance in column.

About four miles from Young's Mill, at 11 a. m., the enemy's pickets were driven in, exchanging occasional shots with our skirmishers, and a mile further on, through dense woods, we came in sight of an open space of the position of the enemy's line of earthworks in our front. The 7th Maine, as skirmishers, were halted in the edge of the woods, about 950 yards from the works, the section of artillery placed in battery, and the 33d, 77th, and 49th New-York State Volunteers formed rapidly in line under the fire of the enemy's shell and canister. The left of the 7th Maine were in an exposed position, being about 500 yards from the smaller work, but partly concealed by the woods. Wheeler's battery, which followed my brigade, came into position on the right and left of our road, and opened on the enemy. My aid-de-camp, Lieut. Long of the 33d New-York, who had climbed a tree for observation upon our left, reporting to me that two regiments were moving down upon our left flank, Lieut.-Col. Alberger, 49th New-York, was thrown back at obtuse angle with the rest of my line to meet their intentions. With these disposals we awaited the arrival and reconnoissance of Gen. Smith.

The troops of my brigade maintained their position as above stated until 7 o'clock of the evening of the 7th, when they were withdrawn about one mile further in the rear.

My casualties are as follows:

APRIL 5.—One private of the 7th Maine and one of the 49th New-York killed, and two privates of the 7th Maine and one of 49th New-York wounded.

APRIL 6.—Three privates of the 49th New-York wounded severely; one officer, Lieut. George Gale of the 33d New-York, seriously wounded; one of the 77th seriously wounded.

APRIL 7.—One private of the 7th Maine seriously wounded; one of the 77th seriously wounded.

APRIL 8.—One private wounded, 33d New-York Volunteers.

APRIL 11.—One corporal, 7th Maine, killed, and one private wounded.

The 49th Regiment and a company of the 33d New-York, the latter under command of Lieut.-Col. Corning, were much exposed to the fire of the enemy's rifle-pits while we lay in position.

I regret to state that Lieut. Swan, Company A, and Bugler Brown, Company D, 7th Maine Volunteers, were captured by the enemy on the 5th inst., being separated from their command by a swamp while skirmishing.

I desire to bring specially to the notice of the General the cheerfulness, obedience, and fortitude of the regiments of my brigade, lying, as they did, for fifty-four hours under the close artillery fire of the enemy, two nights exposed to a violent storm, without an opportunity of exchanging a shot, except from light field-pieces, and bearing—some regiments of it—thirty-six hours duty as skirmishers to the front, and willing for more. I think the general commanding the division may well be proud of them, as I am, and trust to the successful exhibition of their other soldierly qualities when we meet the enemy closer.

I have no distinction to make among the regiments of my brigade. The duties of some were necessarily more arduous than those of others, and led them into more exposed positions; but when all behaved alike with the greatest coolness, gallantry, obedience, and fortitude, they are all equally deserving of my warmest gratitude and confidence, and I desire so to present them to the commanding general.

I am, Sir, your obedient servant,
J. W. DAVIDSON, Brigadier-General.

ARMY AND NAVY.

The closing of most of the volunteer rendezvous has had a stimulating effect upon recruiting for the regular army. The various offices in this city booked upward of 30 men last week, which is more than double the weekly average of the last three months; and, in addition to this, the applicants generally were of a better class than those who usually present themselves for enlistment. The country stations are beginning to send more men in, both to Governor's Island and to the two regiments (the 8th and 12th Infantry) at Fort Hamilton. Company A of the 8th has been full some time, and its Captain, Col. M. Coggswell, of the Tammany regiment, is very anxious to lead it to the field, if he cannot go back to the Tammany. The Colonel is still on parole, and there does not appear to be any immediate likelihood of his being exchanged. Lieut. S. P. Ferris, of this regiment, has taken charge of the rendezvous in Eighth avenue.

The death of Major-Gen. Charles F. Smith, Colonel 3d United States Infantry, will lead to the following promotions:

Lieut.-Col. William Hoffman, 8th Infantry, to be Colonel of the 3d, vice Smith deceased; Major Wm. Chapman, 2d Infantry, to be Lieut.-Colonel of the 3d, vice Hoffman promoted; Capt. Charles D. Jordan, 8th Infantry, to be Major of the 2d, vice Chapman promoted; First Lieut. James J. Van Horn, to be Captain 8th Infantry (Company D) vice Jordon promoted.

Col. Hoffman is a native of this State and has been in the service since July 1, 1829; having been appointed from the West Point graduates of that year, to a Brevet Second Lieutenancy in the 6th Infantry. He was twice brevetted for gallant and meritorious conduct during the Mexican war.

Affairs at the Brooklyn Navy-Yard remain the same as last reported, with the exception that the frigate Sabine, supply steamer Massachusetts, storeship Release, and gunboat Dawn have left the yard.

Another Monitor has been commenced at the Continental Iron Works, Greenpoint, where there are now three Monitors in the course of construction. Two others will be commenced at an early date. These vessels will have two turrets each.

A Sergeant's guard of marines will leave the Flushing-avenue Barracks to-day for the new gunboat Itaska, at the Philadelphia Navy-Yard.

Naval recruiting has not been very brisk lately. The number of men shipped last week did not exceed 91, many of whom have previously served in the navy. There is a good chance now for seamen and ordinary seamen, who are particularly needed for the new gunboats and other vessels going into commission here and at the other Navy-Yards.

Recruiting for the marine corps is not so satisfactory as it has been. The office in the city does very little business, and but four or five men per week are enlisted at the Barracks.

WAS IT A PRIVATEER?—The schooner Castor, Capt. Hooper, from Sierra Leone, (Africa,) March 24, palm oil, hides and nuts, to Bierwith & Rochell, arrived here yesterday, and reports, 12th inst., lat. 22°, lon. 53°, was chased, for 6 hours, by a small schooner of about 100 tons. On finding she could not catch us, she stood to southward. She was painted black, with a white streak, and had a large number of men on deck. Showed no colors.

FROM FORTRESS MONROE.

Details of the Skirmish Under Gen. Reno.

NAMES OF THE WOUNDED.

FORTRESS MONROE, Friday, April 25, Via BALTIMORE, Staurday, April 26, 1862.

The steamer Thomas Morgan did not arrive here till noon to-day.

A schooner was overhauled at 8 o'clock this morning, by the steam gunboat Cohasset, on suspicion of an attempt to run the blockade and enter Elizabeth City. The captain was taken on board the Minnesota, and stated that he was bound for Hatteras Inlet. He had a cargo of beef and pork, etc. His papers were taken from him.

A flag of truce to-day returned with the schooner Mississippi, which brought down from Norfolk, yesterday, 17 Union prisoners wounded at the battle of South Mills, the location of the engagement of last Saturday, previously reported.

The Union troops consisted of parts of five regiments, the 21st Massachusetts, the 51st Pennsylvania, the 9th New-York, the 89th New-York, and the 6th New-Hampshire, under the command of Gen. Reno, numbering five or six hundred men. They landed below Elizabeth City, and marched up to the canal without opposition. The object of the movement was to break up the locks. The engagement took place during the afternoon, and the Rebels were driven from the field. Late in the evening it was known that the Rebels were receiving re-enforcements, and Gen. Reno retired during the night.

No transportation having been provided for the wounded, they were left in a temporary hospital, and Assistant Surgeon Warren of the 21st Massachusetts was detailed to remain with them.

Several others, who were only slightly wounded, left with the other troops, among them Col. Hawkins, wounded in the left breast or shoulders.

The wounded men, on their arrival here, were taken to the General Hospital, and properly cared for.

They complain that while they were in the hands of the enemy they did not have enough to eat, but were otherwise properly taken care of.

The following are the names of the wounded:

Lieut. Lewis Hallman, 51st Pennsylvania, Co. D; in the left thigh.
John Dunn, 21st Massachusetts, Company B; in the left leg.
E. E. Barker, 21st Massachusetts, Company C; in the right shoulder.
W. W. Done, 21st Massachusetts, Company C; in the forehead.
Jas. B. Brown, 21st Massachusetts, Company G; in the right thigh.
Chas. H. Walter, 9th New-York, Company A; in the right thigh.
Wm. Cortelyou, 9th New-York, Company B; in the right leg (amputated).
John Curtin, 9th New-York, Compay B; in the left arm (amputated).
J. T. Kelly, 9th New-York, Company E; in the right side.
G. W. Wilcox, 9th New-York, Company F; in the face.
Alexander Denney, 9th New-York, Company H; in the left arm.
Avril Harris, 89th New-York, Company A; in the right wrist.
Jacob Laning, 51st Pennsylvania, Company A; in the lower jaw.
Jos. H. Searfrass, 51st Pennsylvania, Company A; in the right ankle.
Benj. Hively, 51st Pennsylvania, Company B; in the right side.
Abraham Custor, 51st Pennsylvania, Company C; in the stomach.
Jacob S. Buskirk, 51st Pennsylvania, Company H; in the left arm.

Assistant Surgeon Warren of the 21st Massachusetts, detailed to attend the wounded, accompanied the party.

Capt. W. M. Bartlett, Acting Lieutenant-Colonel of the 20th Massachusetts Regiment, was shot before Yorktown on Wednesday, and has had his left leg amputated. He came to Baltimore this morning, and is doing well.

FORTRESS MONROE, Saturday, April 26, 1862.

Harper's Weekly, on its arrival here this morning, was seized by Major Jones, on account of objectionable editorials and a map of the vicinity of Yorktown.

A flag of truce to Craney Island to-day took up a number of letters for prisoners and others at the South, and also the Secretary of the Spanish Legation at Washington.

The weather is disagreeable. Wind N. E.

All the yards and lower masts of the Galena have been taken out, and nothing can be seen above decks but the smoke-stack.

WOUNDED FROM PITTSBURG LANDING.

PITTSBURGH, Pa., April 27, 1862.

The steamer Marengo and Hailman, sent from this city to Pittsburg Landing, returned to-day with 70 wounded, who were placed in the Marine Hospital. The boats started with nearly 500, all of whom were left at points on the river near their homes. Among the wounded are two Rebel prisoners.

FROM McDOWELL'S ADVANCE.

LETTER FROM A SOLDIER.

FALMOUTH, opp. Fredericksburg, on the Rappahannock, CAMP PROSPECT, April 18, 1862.

DEAR BROTHER: Your letter and map found me in this place this afternoon. We got here this morning after a long and weary march. We left Camp Progress on last Tuesday afternoon, at 5 o'clock, and marched to Cattlett's Station, a distance of ten miles, on the railroad track. It was a very rough march. In fact, it is the roughest kind of walking on the sleepers of a railroad. We stayed there until Thursday morning, when we took up our line of march at 6¼ o'clock. The 2d Berdan Sharp-shooters had the right. I am wrong; they were not on the advance. There were two companies of Bayard's Cavalry on the right. After them came two companies of skirmishers; then came the Harris Light Cavalry; after them the Berdans; then came the gallant 14th. After us came the rest of the brigade, making in all two batteries of artillery, two regiments of cavalry, and five regiments of infantry. We had marched about eighteen miles when we heard firing ahead. The cavalry were then driving in the enemy's pickets. We then halted, and Gen. Angus went ahead to reconnoiter, and coming back soon after, called on us, and we gathered ourselves. Being an almighty hot day, and being almost ready to drop, we threw our knapsacks on the side of the road, and washed the sweat and dust off our faces, got some food, water in our canteens, and then we were ready. We expected a brush before we went a mile. The General got up a plan both to deceive the enemy and rest us. He brought up Bayard's cavalry, and each of the cavalry men took one of our muskets, and we walked alongside holding on to the stirrups. That was done to make the enemy think that they were Secession cavalry bringing in prisoners. We got on to the horses after walking a short distance, and had ridden about a mile (in single file) when we heard firing ahead, and we dismounted, and the cavalry got on, and off they went at a two-forty gait. It was the pickets again, and our cavalry went after them as fast as they could go. In short, the cavalry had three skirmishes with the enemy's pickets before we halted. There was one lieutenant of cavalry killed, and one man had his arm broken. The cavalry cleared one of the Secession camps, and we stayed there that night. We got there about 9½ o'clock p. m., and dark as pitch, after marching 27 miles; and, oh, how hot!

That night we were aroused twice by the firing ahead. The two regiments of cavalry were sent out that night on the representation of a man they brought in. He said he could take them by a road so as to get in the rear of the Rebel cavalry. So they went with him, and got out about a mile and a half, when they found themselves in a mud hole, and the road was barricaded. The Rebels opened fire on them from the front and flanks, killing six men. So they had to come back in confusion. It being dark, of course they could not see. We started this morning at about 4 o'clock, and with such slow marching and frequent stoppages, it took us four hours to march four miles, we came in sight of Fredericksburg about 8 o'clock a. m. We saw a large force of the Rebels in full retreat. We fired six shells at them. The first shell scattered the cavalry in all directions. We marched through Falmouth with flying colors, to the tune of *Vive l'America*, on April 19. They burned the three bridges, and they have surrendered the city. The Mayor was over here this afternoon. The General has given him two days to build a bridge in.

Newbern Daily Progress.

VOLUME 4. NEWBERN, N. C., MONDAY EVENING, APRIL 28, 1862. NUMBER 176.

The Newbern Progress,

Is published Daily and Weekly by

E. L. DAVENPORT & CO.,

From the Progress Buildings, Craven Street.

E. L. DAVENPORT. GEO. MILLS JOY.

TERMS OF PAPER.

DAILY PROGRESS, one year	$6 00
" " 6 months	3 00
" " 3 months	1 50
" " 1 month	50
WEEKLY PROGRESS, one year	2 00
" " 6 months	1 00

All subscriptions to be paid in advance.

ADVERTISING RATES.

The following rates will be charged for all advertisements inserted in the "Daily Progress" after this date:

ONE SQUARE OF TWELVE LINES, OR LESS.

One day	$ 75	Two weeks	$3 50
Two days	1 00	One month	5 00
Three days	1 37	Two months	8 50
Four days	1 75	Three months	12 50
Five days	2 00	Six months	20 00
One week	2 50	One year	30 00

Twelve lines or less will be in all cases counted as a square and additional squares will be charged the same.

RATES IN THE WEEKLY.

One square, one insertion, $1.00, and 25 cents for every subsequent insertion.

No attention will be paid to advertisements sent by letter, unless a remittance in money accompany them.

JOB PRINTING,

Of every description, neatly and promptly executed at this office.

Declaration of Independence.

IN CONGRESS, JULY 4, 1776.

THE UNANIMOUS DECLARATION OF THE THIRTEEN UNITED STATES OF AMERICA.

WHEN, in the course of human events, it becomes necessary for one people to dissolve the political bands which have connected them with another, and to assume, among the powers of the earth, the separate and equal station to which the laws of nature and nature's God entitle them, a decent respect to the opinions of mankind requires, that they should declare the causes which impel them to the separation.

We hold these truths to be self-evident:—that all men are created equal; that they are endowed by their Creator with certain unalienable rights; that among these are life, liberty, and the pursuit of happiness. That to secure these rights, governments are instituted among men, deriving their just powers from the consent of the governed; that whenever any form of government becomes destructive of these ends, it is the right of the people to alter or abolish it, and to institute a new government, laying its foundation on such principles, and organizing its powers in such form as to them shall seem most likely to effect their safety and happiness. Prudence, indeed, will dictate, that government long established should not be changed for light and transient causes; and accordingly all experience hath shown, that mankind are more disposed to suffer, while evils are sufferable, than to right themselves, by abolishing the forms to which they are accustomed. But when a long train of abuses and usurpations, pursuing invariably the same object, evinces a design to reduce them under absolute despotism, it is their right, it is their duty, to throw off such government, and to provide new guards for their future security. Such has been the patient sufferance of these colonies, and such is now the necessity which constrains them to alter their former systems of government. The history of the present king of Great Britain is a history of repeated injuries and usurpations, all having in direct object the establishment of an absolute tyranny over these States. To prove this, let facts be submitted to a candid world.

He has refused his assent to laws the most wholesome and necessary for the public good.

He has forbidden his governors to pass laws of immediate and pressing importance, unless suspended in their operation, till his assent should be obtained; and when so suspended, he has utterly neglected to attend to them. He has refused to pass other laws for the accomodation of large districts of people, unless those people would relinquish the right of representation in the legislature—a right inestimable to them, and formidable to tyrants only.

He has called together legislative bodies at places unusual, uncomfortable, and distant from the repository of their public records, for the sole purpose of fatiguing them into a compliance with his measures.

He has dissolved Representative Houses repeatedly, for opposing, with manly firmness, his invasions on the rights of the people.

He has refused, for a long time after such dissolutions, to cause others to be elected; whereby the legislative powers, incapable of annihilation, have returned to the people at large for their exercise, the State remaining, in the mean time, exposed to all the dangers of invasion from without, and convulsions within.

He has endeavored to prevent the population of these States; for that purpose obstructing the laws of naturalization of foreigners; refusing to pass others to encourage their migration hither, and raising the conditions of new appropriations of lands.

He has obstructed the administration of justice, by refusing his assent to laws for establishing judiciary powers.

He has made judges dependent on his will alone, for the tenure of their offices, and the amount and payment of their salaries.

He has erected a multitude of new offices, and sent hither swarms of officers, to harass our people, and eat out their substance.

He has kept among us, in times of peace, standing armies, without the consent of our legislatures.

He has affected to render the military, independent of, and superior to the civil power.

He has combined with others to subject us to a jurisdiction foreign to our Constitution, and unacknowledged by our laws; giving his assent to their acts of pretended legislation:

For quartering large bodies of armed troops among us:

For protecting them, by a mock trial, from punishment for any murders which they should commit on the inhabitants of these States:

For cutting off our trade with all parts of the world:

For imposing taxes on us without our consent:

For depriving us, in many cases, of the benefits of trial by jury:

For transporting us beyond seas to be tried for pretended offences:

For abolishing the free system of English laws in a neighbouring province, establishing therein an arbitrary government, and enlarging its boundaries, so as to render it at once an example and fit instrument for introducing the same absolute rule into these colonies.

For taking away our charters, abolishing our most valuable laws, and altering, fundamentally, the forms of our governments:

For suspending our own legislatures, and declaring themselves invested with power to legislate for us in all cases whatsoever.

He has abdicated government here, by declaring us out of his protection, and waging war against us.

He has plundered our seas, ravaged our coasts, burnt our towns, and destroyed the lives of our people.

He is at this time transporting large armies of foreign mercenaries to complete the works of death, desolation, and tyranny, already began with circumstances of cruelty and perfidy, scarcely paralleled in the most barbarous ages, and totally unworthy the head of a civilized nation.

He has constrained our fellow-citizens, taken captive on the high seas, to bear arms against their country, to become the executioners of their friends and brethren, or to fall themselves by their hands.

He has excited domestic insurrections amongst us, and has endeavoured to bring on the inhabitants of our frontiers the merciless Indian savages, whose known rule of warfare is an undistinguished destruction of all ages, sexes, and conditions.

In every stage of these oppressions we have petitioned for redress in the most humble terms: our repeated petitions have been answered only by repeated injury. A prince, whose character is thus marked by every act which may define a tyrant, is unfit to be the ruler of a free people.

Nor have we been wanting in attentions to our British brethren. We have warned them, from time to time, of attempts by their legislature to extend an unwarrantable jurisdiction over us. We have reminded them of the circumstances of our emigration and settlement here. We have appealed to their native justice and magnanimity, and we have conjured them by the ties of our common kindred to disavow these usurpations, which would inevitably interrupt our connexions and correspondence. They too have been deaf to the voice of justice and consanguinity. We must, therefore acquiesce in the necessity which denounces our separation, and hold them, as we hold the rest of mankind—enemies in war, in peace friends.

We, therefore, the representatives of the United States of America, in General Congress assembled, appealing to the Supreme Judge of the world, for the rectitude of our intentions, do, in the name and by authority of the good people of these colonies, solemnly publish and declare, that these United Colonies are, and of right ought to be, free and independent States; that they are absolved from all allegiance to the British crown, and that all political connexion between them and the State of Great Britain is, and ought to be, totally dissolved; and that, as free and independent States, they have full power to levy war, conclude peace, contract alliances, establish commerce, and to do all other acts and things which independent States may of right do. And for the support of this declaration, with a firm reliance on the protection of Divine Providence, we mutually pledge to each other our lives, our fortunes, and our sacred honour.

JOHN HANCOCK.

SIGNED BY

John Hancock,	Jas. Smith,
Sam'l Adams,	Geo. Taylor,
John Adams,	James Wilson,
Rob't Trent Paine,	Gro. Ross,
Elbridge Gerry,	Cæsar Rodney,
Josiah Bartlett,	Geo. Read,
Wm. Whipple,	Thos. M'Kean,
Mathew Thornton,	Samuel Chase,
Step. Hopkins,	Wm. Paca,
William Ellery,	Thos. Stone,
Roger Sherman,	Charles Corroll,
Sam'l Huntington,	George Wythe,
Wm. Williams,	Richard Henry Lee,
Oliver Wolcott,	Th. Jefferson,
Wm. Floyd,	Benj. Harrison,
Chal. Livingston,	Thos. Nelson, jr.
Fran's. Lewis,	Fran. Lightfoot Lee,
Lewis Morris,	Carter Braxton,
Rich'd Stockton,	Wm. Hooper,
Jro. Witherspoon,	Joseph Hewes,
Fras. Hopkinson,	John Penn,
John Hart,	Edward Rutledge,
Abra. Clark,	Thos. Heyward, jun.
Rob. Morris,	Thos. Lynch, jun.
Benjamin Rush,	Arthur Middleton,
Benja. Franklin,	Button Gwinnett,
John Morton,	Lyman Hall,
Geo. Clymer,	Geo. Walton.

From the Wide World.

INEZ;

— OR —

The Quadroon Bride.

A TALE OF GEORGIA.

BY ELLA GORDON.

CHAPTER I.

[*Continued from yesterdays paper.*]

It was not long ere the ardent and warm-hearted Frenchman surprised Imogene with an avowal of affection The handsome impulsive Victor, was no common lover, and with a beating heart and flushed cheek, Imogene placed her hand in his, and yielded to the entrancing dream of happiness without a thought of the future.

Mrs. Sumner's health had now become so far reestablished that she was desirous of passing the winter in Rome, greatly to Imogene's delight. And to Rome, imperial Rome—the city of seven hills, once the mistress of the world, whose cathedrals, temples, ruins and fountains, are still the glory of Europe—Mrs. Sumner and Imogene proceeded.

Imogene was scarcely seventeen, excessively beautiful in face and figure, which, added to her reputation as an heiress of one of the largest plantations in Georgia, immediately won for her crowds of admirers and suitors. As soon as she was seen on the *Corso*, or at an occasional *conversazione*, the enthusiastic Italians became lavish in their praises of her beauty. In her mother's *palazzi*, gathered the wealthiest and handsomest men of the *noblese*. Poets sang her loveliness; artists portrayed it on the glowing canvas, and cardinals, nobles and ambassadors thronged around her carriage as she drove at sunset on the *Corso*, or through the grounds of the Villa Borghese.

Confiding in her truth and constancy, Victor mingled his unobtrusive attentions with the brilliant throng that hovered around her; yet at times he felt depressed and melancholy; the sudden transition from retirement to the abandonment of gayety, was distasteful and often he would leave some brilliant party for the solitude of his own apartment. Wishing to divert him from his moody fancies, of which his misfortunes, Imogene saw with regret were the cause, she proposed to visit St. Peter's to witness the exhibition of the illuminated cross.

As she entered the building, the profound solemnity and vast grandeur of the matchless Structure filled her with blended awe and admiration. The immense dome, the work of the illustrious Michael Angelo, with its Mosaic pictures, the high altar, with its magnificent canopy of bronze, the gilded roof, the statues, monuments and Mosaic ceilings, impressed her powerfully; and when the hundred lamps burning over the supposed tomb of St. Peter were suddenly extinguished, and a stupendous cross appeared suspended from the dome, midway beneath the altar and the nave, shedding through the edifice a soft, bright light, then as if by magic, fading away, the lamps burning anew in brilliancy, and the *misere* swelling through the lofty edifice, her eyes filled with tears, a dizziness overcame her and she clung convulsively to Victor's arm.

"You are so excitable, Genie,' he murmered, tenderly; "look up—it is over; the town is dispersing, let us return home."

"You think me weak, Victor" replied Imogene, half-smiling through her tears; "but this scene is so imposing, so grand! Can anything be equal to St. Peter's!"

The crowd was dense, and passing into the vestibule, they were compelled to wait the ebb and flow of the great living tide. The sudden glare of a lamp near by revealed to Imogene a gentleman who was regarding her with an earnest, scrutinizing gaze. Too well she remembered that never to be forgotten face, seen last by her father's death bed—that of Roscoe Marchmont! Averting her face she hurriedly passed on and entered her carriage.

Victor had also noticed the stranger's gaze, and Imogene's evident agitation. For the first time a doubt stole into his heart; his warm nature was chilled by the rapid change of Imogene's manner; dark thoughts swept through his mind, and he leaned back in the farther end of the carriage, silent and constrained. As he handed Imogene out, she said gently:

"Come to me to-morrow, dear Victor, at ten; I have something I wish to say to you"

Up the wide staircases of the sombre, gloomy *palazzi*, Imogene glided, and straightway sought her mother's presence, and walking up to her, said, quietly:

"He has come, mother—he has come at last!"

Mrs. Sumner looked at the brilliant eyes and scarlet cheeks of her daughter with astonishment.

"Who has come, Imogene. I do not understand."

"Colonel Marchmont has come for his bride; and I—oh, I cannot, cannot meet him! I love another—I am already the promised wife of one who is dearer to me than life!"

"Imogene, my child, you distress me! To whom have you pledged yourself? Who could have demanded a promise from you, knowing that you were already plighted to another?"

"To Victor, mother; but he was, still is, ignorant of this miserable engagement."

Mrs. Sumner sighed.

"And you are sure, Imogene, that you love this young man—Victor?"

"Love him—love Victor! Yes, mother. dearly—dearly!" and Imogene hid hid her blushing face on her mother's shoulder.

"He has many noble qualities; I know of no one to whom I would sooner entrust my child. He is not rich, I think?"

"No, he has nothing beyond his profession; but I—I am wealthy, I have enough for both."

"I will think of this, and talk with Colonel Marchmont on the subject.—Leave me now, Imogene, I am greatly fatigued, and need rest. I am too weary scarcely to think."

"Forgive me, I have been selfish and forgetful;" and with a light kiss, Imogene left her mother and sought her own apartment.

She was too excited to slumber, and seating herself by the window, she gazed out upon the now quiet city. Capitoline hill—that high place, that rock of triumph, where Rome was wont to embrace her conquering heroes, was bathed in silvery light; the soft starlight floated on the river and trembled through the dark ruins where once had trod earth's proudest princes; whose walls had rung alike with the eloquence of orators, statesmen and imperators—but now forever hushed and voiceless. Rome, destroyed by quarrels of faction, and intestine troubles, was Rome no longer, save in memory and name! Suddenly the dark shadow of a man falling upon the pavement, recalled her wondering thoughts; he paused opposite the dwelling, and gazed earnestly up at the casement; the pure moonlight shone full upon his broad, white brow, revealing the features of Victor. Taking a boquet from a flower-vase which stood near, Imogene cast it upon the pavement, then dropping the snowy curtain, was soon wrapped in slumber.

CHAPTER II.

"The ring you gave, the kiss you gave,
The curl of raven hair,
Pledges of truth, and gifts of love,
Where are they now, oh! where?
The ring is broken, and by whom?
The kiss has been profaned;
And many, many bitter tears
That shining curl have stained.'—L. E. L.

In the *Cafe Royale* sat a party of gentlemen. The gay jest, bacchanalian song and convivial toast went round with unrestrained freedom; wines of every description, from the sparkling Champagne to the choice Canary flowed freely, until at last the gay banquiters grew uproarious.

"Come, Marchmont," exclaimed one, "you are dull to-night; rouse yourself, man, and drink a bumper to the fair Immogene—*la belle Americaine.*"

Scarcely had the words passed his lips when a swift blow from Marchmont's arm caused the speaker to reel backwards. The blood gushed from his nostrils, and with a tiger-like bound, he sprang towards Marchmont and clenched his throat.

"Shame—shame Marchmont! Villiers! stand back!" cried several voices, and with severe struggles the combatants were parted.

"Villiers, if you are a man, meet me on the Campagna, to-morrow, at sunrise, or apologize for the insult offered Miss Sumner, my intended wife!"

Glances of astonishment passed from one to the other, as Marchmont ceased speaking, and the next moment Harry Villiers came forward, extending his hand towards Marchmont, saying, frankly:

"I apologize, certainly; though, hang it! I'd as lief fight as not."

Colonel Marchmont bowed, professed himself satisfied, and the banquet proceeded.

To be Continued.

☞ The preternatural desire of the Rebel chivalry to die "in the last ditch," has divided itself between "prospecting" for said ditch, and the procurement of substitutes to do their dying when the ditch is found. From $500 to $1500 is offered for substitutes for those who have vowed and sworn, time and time again, that their greatest happiness could only be the meeting of the Yankees "foot to foot and eye to eye."

☞ Pat said the fiddle was the shape of a turkey and the size of a goose. He turned it over on its back and rubbed its belly with a stick; and och! St. Patrick how it did squale!

LIST OF LETTERS

Remaining in the Newbern Post Office uncalled for, up to April 17.

A

Arnold, Jas H
Allen, Jesse H
Anderson, George
Applegate, Lewis
Amsbry, C H
Adams, George S
Allen, George E
Adams, Corp Wm E
Ames, M B
Adland, Corporal
Alesamcle, Otis
Arvedson, Wm
Aumick, Wm
Averill, Jos
Abbott, John H
Arthur, J B
Adams, Daniel H
Adams, Henry

B

Bradley, Hudson H
Brooks, Steven
Brown, Westley
Breed, Lieut Chas A
Bigelow, George W
Brownell, Sergt Robt S
Budd, Captain
O'Bryan, Pat
Bassett, Darius
Bible, Adjt Daniel P
Brown, Geo S
Bray, Josiah C
Burns, L
Brown, Capt Joel W
Boyd, P er
Burn Ra om S
Brunley, Silas
Butter, Wm
Bailey, Ira C
Buffington, Charles
Bidele, Lieut James C
Birley, R
Bailey, David I
Barr, Henry E
Burgess, James K
Buel, Howard
Bowman, John
Broodeur, Joseph
Bennett, Herbert
Brimhall, Alvin
Brown, Capt. Joel W
Berniger, Josiah
Beld, Seargt L W
Bezworth, Levi
Bidwell, M S
Bradley, Philo P
Blackwell, Clayton E
Busdick, Stephen M
Billings, Chas M
Bruon, Joshua
Buckle, Edward
Bailey, Joseph
Banning, Richmond
Brown, Robert
Bettwood, Edmond
Bush, Hiram H
Barnes, Capt Wm

C

Copeland, John
Chase, Philip S
Corbey, John
Crawford, Henry
Chamlin, Albert B
Childs, George E
Cavenaugh, Luke
Critchett Chas E
Crowningshield, Geo F
Curtis, Capt Chas A
Cobb, Lewis H
Cheney, Capt E H
Clemence, Geo B
Castle, Matthew
Carter, Durur
Carpenter, George
Collum, Andrew J
Carrington, Lieut
Corbey, John W
Cushing, Patrick
Crummett, Joseph
Chandler, John
Conner, John O
Clarke, George P
Crown, Henry
Carwell, Wm W
Crowninsshield, Caleb 2
Clark, Andrew
Connell, Patrick
Crocker, Ferdinand
Cummings, Lieut P C
Cutting, Warren J
Coggeshall, Capt Geo
Carp, Chas D

D

Dyer, Reuben
Dawley, Benj H
Denham, Wm Sherman
Doane, Reswell L
Demary, James L
Dow, Dr Hiram
Dewell, Capt J H
Dolan, Felix
Daniels, Austin
Dey, Richard
Daffee, John
Daly, John
Dechant, John
Derby, Wm P
Daniels H Austin
Disbrow, David or H
Dillon, Robt
Dyer, Reuben
Dray, Wm
Donelly, Francis
Douglass George L
Dunham, Serg Jas M
Dean, Geo B
Davis, John J

E

Evans, John A
Eastly, J
Eckert, Joseph
Edwards, Wm H
Emson, Wm L G
Elliott, H H

F

Fisk, Chas
Foster, John
Ford, W N
French, Isaac
Fuller, Daniel
Francis, Thomas
Fullum, Geo E
Flim, Jas S
Farrell, Wm
Farnham, Geo H
Ford, Chas M
Folsem, Lieut Chas M
Frippo, John
Farnham Geo H
Fenton, Wm H
Fitch, John
Fowler, W
Fay, Dennis
Francis, Lieut H W
Field, John A
Fay, Edward

G

Gross, Joshua F 2
Gerring, Albert H
Goodnough, George H
Gaven, Jas A
Glover, Chas F
Galvin, Michael A
Gray, Sarg't Wm B
Gove, W Augustus
Gleason, Michael
Gaffney, Andrew J
Gifford, Henry C
Grace, Levi C
Gross Samuel A
Goldsmith, Joseph C

H

Hall, Samuel
Hayden Loring
Howard, Michael

H

Holbrook, Chas W
Howell, Marshall
Huntington, Wm
Hentage, Richard
Harris, Albert
Holmes, Lyman N
Hart, Julien A
Henery, Peter
Harris, John
Higgins, John C
Hale, Frank S
Hulse, Joel

I

Irvin, Morgan

J

Jacobs, Zebalee
Jones, Julius
Jenks, Albert J
Jellson, G W
Jones, B D
Johnson, Thos
Jones, Nicholas L
Johnson, Isaac
Jonston, Thomas
Jarves Lieut H D 2
Jameson, Edward 2
Jolly, Wm H
Judkins, Oliver P D
Jordan, Robert

K

King, Julius
Kearney, Jas
Kille, David 2
Keough John
Kelt, John
Keeler, Silas P
Kerbey, J S 2
Knowlton, Martin W
Keney, Wm
Killey, Thos
Kennedy, Thos
Kelly, George R
Kelly, Thos

L

Livermore, Henry N
Lewis, George
Longley, Edmund
Little, Stephen D
Lippincott, Chas
Lyman, L F 2
Lawton, Benj
Lard, Almon
Lippincott, Wm
Leach, Henry B
Lochers, Mr
Loper, Henry
Lyman, Levi Francis
Leiser, Chas S
Lewis, Harry
Lee, Jas C
Lyon, Lieut Jas W
Linscott, Wm C
Lydig, Lieut
Lord, Hiram L

M

Murphy, Barnard 2
Magoin, Calvin S
Mathers M
Meniman, Capt Richard 4
McCarter, John G
Manley, E W 2
Mendenhall, John
Mathews, John S
Merrivin, Daniel
Mather, Jas
Mantor Alfred L
Metcalf, Prescott
Mansfield, Geo S
Munroe, Chas H
Miller, Seth B
McKissick, Hugh
Merriam, John S
McDonnell, Pat
Marks, C M D
McDevitt, Wm
Mount, Caleb H
Morgan, Joseph
Macdonald, Lieut Henry J
Marshal, Thos
Manning, J A
Munsick, David
March, Frederick A
Mack, Isaac
Manley, E W

N

Nate, Asa B
Nelson, John W
Neal, Hanah or Rue
Neal, Nathan O
Newton, Isaac R
Newbery, S C Capt

O

O'Bryan, Terance
O'Conner, Courneleous
Orr, Alex J
Orcutt, Wm L

P

Parker, S E
Palmer, George E
Poole, Frank
Purdy, Davius
Palmer, George E
Penny, Capt Joseph
Pike, Elbridge
Pierce, Samuel
Pavey, Nathan B
Pierce, Capt D E
Pike, Chas W
Parker, Thos
Patter, R K
Purdy, Davius
Pattes, John A
Parker, George W
Putnam, Capt John W

R

Roads, Chas L
Raw, John
Remont, Joseph
Reicher Philip
Ruoklin, Jas S P
Ricketts, Thos
Roach, Wm
2Richardson, Warren
4Roberts, George W
Richmond, S E & E O
Rodman, Col J P
Richardson, Frank
Roberts, George W
Randolph, J
Reed, Edwin R
Rogers, Wm
Rollins, George
Reed, Andrew J

S

Stewart, Capt C S
Sassaman, Emanuel
Sassaman, George
Soul, Rev George 2
Sayre, Samuel A
Spaulding, Lieut M H
Shiedan, Patrick
Stephens, Somers
Smith, Mathew
Simpkins, Thos
Sasseir, Robert
Shaw, Chas H
Shea, Patrick
Slorven, Wm M
Simpson Wm H
Stevens, Irving
Simmons, Lord
Schock, Theodore
Smith, Chas M 2
Sherry, Peter
Stephens, Edward
Sxott, Francis F
Sulivan, Michael
Stevens, Jas M
Smith, Chas 2
Stillman, Henry W 3
Sechen, Wm H
Somers, Capt Henry
Stedson, Coast Guard
Southwick, Ed L
Shepard, Jas M
Smith, George H
Swasey, Thos jr
Smith, Fred W
Sanborn, L B
Strong, Wm
Silver, Chas N
Smith, Mathew
Shea, J
Stone, Clovin
Smith, Fred W
Sparks, Wm H
Smith, Lieut C S
Sims, Capt Sam'l H
Saywer, Capt C Westley
Sparks, Chas M

T

Taylor, George W
Thomas Hauson A
Thurber John H
Taney, Albert A
Traver, Jonas
Tillinghast, Henry M
Turnbull, Leander L
Tucker, Albert O
Taft, John A
Thompson, Silas
Turkey, Peter
Tilden, Lt C Linger

V

Vandine, Seargt M
Vottage, Corp George E
Vaile, Jeffery
Vance, Robert
Valentine, Erasmus
Vaille, Luther P
Vaster, Andrew
Vantuken, Daniel
Van Winkle, Francis

W

Waldren, Col
Wilkinson, Elbert R
Weisley, Jestus
Walbery, George W
Wolfe, Jas H
Whitcomb, Alonso D
Wenty, Jacob,
Willber, Stephen
Williams, Joseph
Wheeler, Jared
Weaser, Wm
Wait, Lieut Marvin
Winslow, George A
Wood Wm
Weeks, Reuben
Whitney, Daniel
Worrall, Alex
Wentworth Lieut Eli
Woodward, Westly
Worden, Thos A
Wilcox, Edward
Watts, Wm B
Wilson, Robert
Winslow, George A
Wood Hiram L
Wanbold, Martin A
Wilson, G W Corp
Wild, Serg't Alfred
Weeland, John S
Whitney, Daniel
Weir, George D
Warren, Dr O

Y

Young, Wm

Persons calling for these letters, will please say they are advertised.

JOHN B. REED,
apr 19 Post Master.

JEROME TAYLOR,

SUTLER TO 17TH MASS. REGT

DEALER IN

Groceries, Fruits, Tobacco, Segars, Snuff, Butter, Cheese, and an endless variety of Sutler's Goods, which he will sell as low as the lowest.

Craven St., 3 doors South of Pollock St., *NEWBERN, N. C.*

Newbern, April 24, 1862. *1m173

RICE, KENDALL, & CO.,

WHOLESALE

Paper Warehouse.

IMPORTERS OF

Paper Manufacturers Materials,

FELTS, WIRES, &C.,

20 & 22 Water St.,---Simmons Block,

BOSTON.

Information Wanted.

OF the Captain and crew of the Schooner Robert Gilfillan, of Wilmington, Delaware, which was burned by the Steamer Nashville on her voyage to Beaufort, N. C., February 26, 1862. Captain's name, Frank Smith; Mate's name, J. Willets.—Their friends, and the owners of the vessel have heard nothing from them since she was burned, and are very anxious to know where they are.—Any information from them may be communicated through the office of this paper, and will be thankfully received. 172tf

---

BEST

Family Groceries ! !

THE SUBSCRIBERS,

Sutlers for the 23d Reg't, Mass. Vol.,

Beg leave to call the attention of citizens, officers and commissaries of regiments to their stock of Groceries, which they will sell at the

LOWEST MARKET PRICES.

FARIS & RICHARDSON.

Cor. Pollock and Craven Streets,

(*Opposite* Bank of North Carolina.)

N. B.—Highest market prices paid for Eggs, Poultry and Country Produce generally.

Newbern, N. C., *April* 19, 1862. 171

ADAMS'

Army Express,

Will convey packages to and from Newbern, within all points of the United States at

REASONABLE RATES.

All Orders will be Promptly and Faithfully Executed.

MONEY AND

ARTICLES OF VALUE.

Will be transported carefully and promptly. The ability and standing of this Company for years past, are a sufficient guarantee for their

FAITHFUL PERFORMANCE

of all business entrusted to their charge.

Office in

HARRISONS' BRICK BLOCK,

Pollock St. 3 doors South of Bank of Commerce.

Newbern, March 29, 1862 10t165

G. L. JUDD,

Dealer in

Army and Navy

EQUIPMENTS!

—AND—

OFFICER'S

FURNISHING GOODS!!

At Adams' Express Office,

Pollock Street, Newbern, N. C.

(*Three doors South of Bank of Commerce.*)

Officers can rely on obtaining the best quality of Equipments and Furnishing Goods, at moderate prices. Orders by express and mail promptly attended to.

Orders will be taken for UNIFORM CLOTHING, from the celebrated establishment of Devlin & Co. New York Undress Uniform clothing kept constantly on hand.

Newbern, April 2, 1862. 166tf

P. C. CUMMINGS,

Sutler 11th Reg. C. V.,

Has opened a store on the

Cor. Craven and South Front St.,

And also

A Tent at the Camp of his Regiment,

Where can be had the usual assortment of SUTLER GOODS, at regular prices.

CALL AND SEE.

RESTAURANT!

Gentlemen can be accommodated with

MEALS AT ALL HOURS,

ALSO BY THE WEEK,

At the Restaurant adjoining the Gaston House.

April 26, 1860. 175tf

SMITH'S

Bullet-Proof

VEST,

(OR JACKET,) Made by

G. & D. COOK & CO.,

NEW HAVEN, CONN.,

And sold by

H. H. & C. W. ELLIOTT,

231 Broadway, New York.

Sold in Newbern by

BARTLETT & MANN,

Agents for Manufacturers,

Pollock Street, Opposite the Post Office.

Newbern, March 19, 1862. 4t165

NEW STOCK.

Dry Goods, Clothing,

GROCERIES, FRUITS, &C.,

—FOR SALE BY—

C. B. Dibble,

Near the Gaston House.

Consisting of Calicoes, Lawns, Brilliants, Sheetings, Shirting, Towelling, Mens Clothing and Furnishing Goods, Boots, Shoes &c.

Sugar, Butter, Cheese, Lard, Coffee, Tea, Spices, Segars, Tobacco, Snuff, Starch, Salt, Oranges, Apples, Lemons, Raisins, Figs, Dates, Nuts, Pie Fruits, Peaches, Plums, Cherries, Pine Apples, Fresh Tomatoes, Sardines, Sausage Meat, Lobster, and a variety of other Can Goods, Yeast Powder, Saleratus; Soap, etc, etc, etc., &c.

Newberne March 22d, 1862 163tf

ATTENTION!

WILLIAM BERKELE

Has opened a store,

Directly opposite the Post Office,

And offers for sale a choice lot of

ORANGES,

Figs, Apples, Segars, Tobacco, Snuff, Coffee, Tea, Sugar, Spices, Fresh Tomatoes and Peaches, Preserved Fruits, Crackers, Cheese, Butter, Hams, Boots, Shoes, Calicoes, Soda, Starch, Confectionery, Beer,

Together with a variety of articles usually kept in such places. We are the first to open mercantile business in Newbern after its capture, and will sell as cheap as any one else, and of as good quality. Call and examine.

WILLIAM BERKELE.

Newbern, March 22 1862 165

C. W. SMITH,

Sutler of 51st Reg. N. Y. V.

Can be found by his old friends at the Store, in **Craven St., 3d door from Pollock St.,** Nearly opposite the Post Office,

Where can be found his usual assortment of all goods that can be found in the market.

COME ONE, COME ALL

1860-61.

GEO. ALLEN,

Dealer in

FANCY and STAPLE

DRY GOODS,

22, Pollock Street,

NEWBERN, N. C.,

Has in Store a large Stock of assorted *FALL and WINTER*

DRESS GOODS,

LINSEYS,

NORTH CAROLINA

CHAMBRAYS,

PLAIDS, CHECKS, BLACK and Colored Cloths and *Cassimers,* *Satinets,*

North Carolina and Virginia

TWEEDS and KERSEYS,

Osnaburgs and Sheetings,

MERINO and LINEN SHIRTS,

FRONTING LINEN, HOSIERY,

Gloves, Trimmings,

Cotton, Needles, Thread, Silk, &c., &c.

ALSO A GOOD ASSORTMENT OF

BLACK and COLORED HATS and CLOTH CAPS, BOOTS, GAITERS and SHOES.

All of which will be sold on reasonable terms.

Sept. 21 1861, daw ly

HOTELS.

GRANGER HOUSE,

WEST SIDE OF RAILROADS;

Goldsboro', N. C.

Right Hand Side Going South.

Left Hand Side Going North.

MEALS READY ON ARRIVAL OF THE CARS.

BAGGAGE TAKEN TO AND FROM R. R. FREE OF CHARGE.

ATTACHED,

One of the best Barber Shops.

The public may expect

GOOD FARE,

Attentive Servants, accommodating officers, with every other comfort found in a SOUTHERN HOTEL!

T. A. GRANGER,

(Late of the Atlantic House, Beaufort, N. C.,)

Jan. 16 *Proprietor.*

THE ECONOMIST

COOKING STOVE,

FOR WOOD OR COAL,

WITH A SAND OVEN.

This is the most valuable improvement that has been made in Cooking Stoves during the past twenty years.

THE SAND OVEN

Equalizes the heat on the same principle as the Brick Oven of ancient renown.

THE SAND OVEN

Retains the heat long after the fire has gone out.

THE ECONOMIST

Without the Sand Oven, is ahead of all competitors.

THE ECONOMIST

With the Sand Oven, is out of reach of them.

THE ECONOMIST

Is the most economical and durable Stove in the world.

THE ECONOMIST

Has a most perfect arrangement for Broiling.

THE ECONOMIST

Heats water for the Bathing Room, &c., as quickly as any Range, and at half the cost for fuel.

THE ECONOMIST

Will do more Baking, Boiling and Broiling, with a given quantity of fuel, than any other Stove or Range.

THE ECONOMIST

Is the Stove.

Household Words,

Conducted by Chas. Dickens,

Author of "Pickwick Papers." Nicholas Nickleby, Dombey & Son,' etc.

RE-published monthly by the subscribers from advance sheets, under the sanction of the London publishers, and by special arrangement with them. Each monthly number contains

TALES, STORIES AND OTHER ARTICLES

BY CHAS. DICKENS, WILLIAM HOWITT, LEIGH HUNT, BARRY CORNWALL, WILKIE COLLINS,

And almost every conspicuous English writer thus rendering it by far the most interesting, varied, and decidedly the *Best Literary Periodical* in the English Language. No work of the kind contributes so successfully and so much to the floating literature of the day; its sharp, crisp, genial articles, and its admirable stories are more extensively copied by contemporary publications than those of any other work whatsoever.

TERMS WITHOUT PREMIUM.

25 *Cents per number*, $3 00 *a Year.*

A prompt remittance of $3 00 will secure regular delivery, post paid.

TERMS TO CLUBS.

Two copies for one year,	$5 00
Five " " "	10 00
Eleven " " "	30 00

Clergymen and Teachers supplied at Two Dollars a year.

The volumes of Household Words commence with the September and March Numbers, but subscriptions may begin with any number desired.

Sets of Household Words, 18 volumes, can now be had, bound in cloth, at $1 75 per volume.

Sent free, by express or mail, on the receipt of price. Back numbers of Household Words can be furnished at the office of publication, price 25 cents each. Address,

FREDERICK A. BAKER,
No. 26 Nassau St., New York.

THE DISCIPLES' ADVOCATE.

AT the late Session of the General Conference of the Disciples of Christ in North Carolina, it was resolved to establish a Monthly Periodical of the above name. The "Advocate" belongs to, and is the organ of the Disciples of Christ in this State. The editorial management of the "Advocate," for the present Conference year, has been committed to my hands and, in accordance with the duty of my office, this Prospectus is issued. As the paper belongs to the Disciples, and not to the Editor, it is to be hoped that they will make a united and a strong effort to sustain it. Let each Disciple feel that he or she, as the case may be, has a personal interest in the "Advacate," and work for it accordingly. All the profits arising from the publication, after paying the Printer and the Editor, will be appropriated to the support of the Evangelists.

This Periodical will be devoted to the advocacy of Primitive Christianity, the union of Christians, and the conversion of sinners; and whatever else may tend to the promulgation of the truth, and the edification of the saints. And as the Editor is elected to serve from one Conference to another, it is deemed best to issue the first number at once, so that the volume may begin and end with the *Conference year.*

TERMS:—The "Disciples' Advocate" will be issued monthly, in the same style of the "Christian Preacher," at $1 per annum.

All letters on business, communications for publication, pledges and subscriptions, should be addressed to the Editor, Dr. Jno. T. Walsh, Kinston N. C.

JNO. T. WALSH, ED. D. A.,
Kinston, N. C.

HERZOG'S PROTESTANT THEOLOGICAL ENCYCLOPEDIA.

Part Fourth now ready

THE ENCYCLOPEDIA OF PROTESTANT THEOLOGICAL AND ECCLESIASTICAL LITERATURE—Being a Condensed Translation of Herzog's real Encyclopedia, with additions from other sources. By the Rev. J. H. A. Bomberger, D. D., assisted by distinguished Theologians of various denominations. It is based upon "Herzog's Real Encyclopedia for Protestantische Theologien Kirche," published in Germany, and will embrace all subjects belonging properly to the Literature of the Protestant Catholic Religion and Church, furnishing the most reliable results of recent study, research and discoveries in the various departments of science in its relation to Christianity, including the several branches of

1 BIBLICAL LITERATURE.—Biblical Philology, Geography, History, Botany, Geology, Natural History, Antiquities, Criticism, and Hermeneutics.

2 SYSTEMATIC LITERATURE.—Apologetic, Dogmatic, Moral Sciences, Polemical and Pastoral Theology, Homiletics, Liturgical Church Polity and Church Arts.

3. HISTORICAL LITERATURE.—Church History and Antiquities, History, Theology of Sects and Heresies, Patriotic History, Biography &c.

4. HISTORICAL SYMBOLISM; or a Representation of the Comparative Position and Relation of the various Evangelical Denominations, and their respective Doctrinal and other Characteristics.

The work of Herzog numbers more than *one hundred contributors*, including the *ripest scholars* and most *evangelical theologians* of Germany, and the articles are the results of their best judgment and most careful research.

PLANS AND TERMS OF PUBLICATION.

It will be issued in 16 parts of 128 double column pages, at Fifty Cents each, and will form, when complete, two super royal octavo volumes.

The numbers will be sent by mail to subscribers, free of postage, upon the receipt of the subscription price in advance

☞ Agents are wanted to canvass for subscribers to the Work, either in numbers or complete, to whom liberal discounts will be given.

LINDSAY & BLAKISTON,
Publishers, Philadelphia.

☞ Subscriptions received by Rev. J. D. Lawyer, Agent, Auburn, N. Y.

The Water-Cure Journal.

DEVOTED TO PHYSIOLOGY, HYDROPATHY, and the Laws of Life and Health, with Engravings illustrating the Human System—a Guide to Health and Longevity. Published monthly at *One Dollar* a year.

Good Health is our Great Want. We can obtain it only by a knowledge of the Laws of Life and the causes of Disease, which are clearly presented in the Water Cure Journal. Particular directions are given for the treatment of ordinary cases at home, so that all may apply it. Believing Health to be the basis of happiness, we rely on the friends of good health to place a copy of the Water Cure Journal in every family. Now is the time to subscribe,

---

Albany House!

BY WM. WALTER COOK,

Craven Street,

NEWBERN, N. C.

A FIRST CLASS

EATING SALOON,

where may be found Oysters, Ale, and all the delicacies of the season. 168

LEATHER!

THE NEWBERN STEAM TANNERY

WM. P. MOORE, Jr., Proprietor

CAN furnish at short notice and on good terms the following, viz:

HARNESS Leather;

SOLE LEATHER;

RIGGING LEATHER;

Upper Leather;

Tanned Calf Skins;

Cartridge Box and Haversack Leather;

Leather suitable for Pistol Holsters

Leather for Sword and Bayonet Scabbards, Gun Covers, &c.;

Prepared Sheep Skins for Cannon Swabs;

Kettle and Bass Drum Heads;

PLASTERERS HAIR;

The highest cash prices paid for Green and Dry Hides

Sheep Skins;

BEAR SKINS;

DEER SKINS, &c. &c.,

Newbern, une 21 d&wtf

☞ Petersburg Express and State Journal times

IRON! IRON!

SWEDES AND ENGLISH

AT AUTION,

By S. M. WEST, Auctioneer.

ON Wednesday, March 5th, we will sell at public auction at our store, at 11 o'clock, A. M., FIFTY TONS SWEDES AND ENGLISH IRON, assorted sizes, from one to ten inches wide.

Also fifty bags choice Cuba Coffee.

O. G. PARSLY & CO.,
[Feb 19, d2w] Wilmington, N C.

A NEW LAW BOOK.

Cantwell's Practice at Law.

JUST PUBLISHED, a treatise upon the Practice at Law in North Carolina, by Edward Cantwell, LL. B., author of the N. C. Justice, etc.

CONTENTS.

Of Legislative Power in General; Legislative Powers in North Carolina; Legislative Powers of Justices of the Peace; County Boundaries—Deeds, etc., County Revenue and Charges; Court Houses, Prisons, &c.; County Trustee; Jury Trials; Fairs and Public Sales; General Assembly; Inspections; Public Landings, &c; Poor Houses and Hospitals; Registers and Clerks; Rivers and Creeks, Gates, Ferries and Bridges; Weights and Measures; Idiots and Lunatics; Retailers; Neuse River; Public Roads and Cartways; Public Landings and Inspections; Mills and Millers; Ordinaries and Constables; Patrol; Wardens of the Poor; Prison Bounds; Roads, Ferries and Bridges; Poll Tax Exemptions; Executive Power in General; Executive power in North Carolina; Executive Power of the Courts. Chief Justice and Clerk; Attorneys at Law; Attorney General; Reporter and Marshal; Clerks and Solicitor; Counsel for Paupers; Guardians; County Attorney; Auctioneers, County Court Clerks; Coroners; Boundary Commissioners; Committee of Finance, County Trustee; County Treasurers Special Court; Commissioners of Fairs; Inspectors, Superintendents of Schools Commissioners of Navigation; Wardens of the Poor; Registers; Commissioners of Rivers and Creeks Sheriffs; Constables; Rangers; Standard Keepers; Retailers, Administrators; Chairman of Special Court; Commissioners of Deeds and Conveyances; Commissioners of Low Lands; Entry Takers and Surveyors; Superintendants of Elections; Guardians and Receivers; Inspectors; Commissioners of Internal Improvements; Partition; Patrol Committees; Processioners; Tax Listers and Boards of Valuation, Overseers of Roads and Rivers; Commissioners of Wrecks; Tobacco Pickers and Coopers.

The Appendix contains forms of Deeds and Conveyances, as follows:

Agreements, Assignments, Awrads, Bills of Sale, Bills of Exchange and Lading, Bonds, Miscellaneous Bonds, Contracts, Deeds, Marriage Settlements, Mortgages, Copartnership Articles, Notes, Releases, &c.

This Book contains 556 pages, is gotten up in superior style, and bound in Law Calf. Price, single copy, $5,00.

EDWARD CANTWELE,
Corner of Davie and Wilmington Sts.,
Raleigh, N. C.

Jan. 23, 1861.

PROSPECTUS

OF THE

SCIENTIFIC AMERICAN.

IT IS an Illustrated Periodical, devoted to the promulgation of information relating to the various Mechanical and Chemical Arts, Manufactures, Mill Work, and all interests which the light of practical science is calculated to advance.

All the most valuable patented discoveries are delineated and described in its issues, so that, as respects inventions, it may be justly regarded as an *Illustrated Repertory*, where the Inventor may learn what has been done before him in the same field which he is exploring, and where he may publish to the world a knowledge of his own achievements.

Reports of American Patents granted are also published every week, including official copies of all the Patent Claims. These Patent Claims are furnished from the Patent Office Records expressly for this paper, and published in the Scientific American *in advance of all other publications.*

Mechanics, Inventors, Engineers, Chemists, Manufacturers, Agriculturalists, and people in every profession of life, will find the Scientific American to be of great value in their respective callings—It counsels and suggestions will save them hundreds of dollars annually, besides affording them a continual source of knowledge, the value of which is beyond pecuniary estimate.

Terms of Subscription:—Two Dollars a year, One Dollar for six months.

CLUB RATES.

Five Copies, for Six Months............$4.
Ten Copies, for Six Months..............$8.
Ten Copies, for Twelve Months........$15.
Fifteen Copies, for Twelve Months....$22.
Twenty Copies, for Twelve Months....$28.

Southern, Western, and Canadian money or Post-office stamps, taken at par for subscriptions. Canadian subscribers will please remit twenty-six cts. extra on each year's subscription, to pre-pay postage.

For all clubs of twenty and over, the yearly subscription is only $1 40. Names can be sent in at different times and from different Post Offices. Specimen copies will be sent gratis to any part of the country

MUNN & CO., Publishers and Patent Agents,
No. 128 Fulton Street, New York.

THE WAY OF THE WORLD.

A DOLLAR NEWSPAPER. To be published weekly in Greensborough, N C.; by James Albright. Terms—Twelve months, One Dollar; six months, fifty cents; single copies, five cents.

Having been in the printing and publishing business for the last ten years, we have long since become disgusted with long and dashy prospectures, and will simply say that we expect to publish as good a paper as possible for the price and hard times. We will be entirely independent in every thing. And while we will adhere closely to virtue, truth, and justice, we will take no pains to please a world.

"Where honest thoughts are a reproach to man,
Where knaves look great, and groaning virtue starves,
A world of madness, falsehood, and injustice"

We shall endeavor to make the paper what its title indicates—a truthful shadow of *The Way of the World!*—its virtues, its vices, its realities and fancies; yet we are frank to admit

"Tis a very good world that we live in,
To lend, or to spend, or to give in;
But to borrow, or beg, or get a man's own,
'Tis the very worst world that ever was known!"

We desire the paper to speak for itself

Please do not trouble us with letters unless you send the money, for they will in *no case* be attended to.

FOR SALE.—A house and lot at a pleasant village on N C. R R. For further information apply to Editor of Progress. Feb. 28, 1862 d&w.

AHEAD OF ALL COMPETITION.

JOB PRINTING

Of Every Description

DONE AT THE

Progress Office

IN THE BEST STYLE of the ART

AND WITH THE

GREATEST POSSIBLE DISPATCH

Having made large accessions to our Establishment in the way of

New Presses, Type, Paper, Cards, &c.

and having in our employ good workmen, we are better prepared than ever to serve our patrons and the public.

WE PRINT

Business and Professional Cards at $2 50 to $5 00 per thousand—according to size.

WE PRINT

Hand-Bills at $3 00 to $10 00 a thousand—according to size.

WE PRINT

Bill-Heads,	**Labels,**
Circulars,	**Bills of Lading**

Bank Checks, Wedding and Visiting Cards,

Catalogues, **Legal Blanks,**

and in fact every description of work for less than it can be done elsewhere.

Especial attention given to Book and Pamphlet Work.

Call at or send your orders to the

PROGRESS BUILDINGS,

Craven street, Newbern, N. C.

☞ Prices moderate and work executed with the neatest accuracy and punctuality.

SPECIAL NOTICES.

SYLVESTER TAYLOR,

BREAD CAKE AND CRACKER BAKER,

ALSO

Wholesale and Retail dealer in

Confectionaries, Foreign and Domestic Fruit, Nuts, Segars, &c.

AT BANK'S OLD STAND,

POLLOK STREET,

Newbern, N. C.

Sept. 3 dly

SARAH J. JONES,

Pollock Street,

(House next to the corner of Muddy,) solicits

SEWING

From the officers and soldiers. 168

SOUTHERN MANUFACTURES.

PROFESSOR DOHERTY having been long engaged in studying and teaching the theory and practice of Modern Chemistry in its application to the useful arts, and the improved methods of manipulation in the manufacture of many of those important and necessary articles of universal consumption, so much requied at present in the Confederate States, is now prepared to enter into partnership with reliable associates; who can command sufficient capital, and can give their time to works of useful and profitable industry.

Professor Doherty is occupied with his school—Newbern Academy—and can spare but one whole day in the week, but mornings and evenings are also at his command, and he could direct and superintend various important and lucrative manufactures; for example: Soda, Soap—Rosin Soap, Refined Soap; Candles—tallow and adamantine; Lime powder, Starch, Ink, &c. Professor Doherty also desires to sell shares in a new patent Water Filter, and in the patent right of his approved Conical Bullet for smooth bore guns.

N. B. Where personal superintendence and instruction are inconvenient or impossible, full and explicitly written instructions can be furnished at reasonable rates. Apply to

PROF. W. H. DOHERTY, A. M.
Dec 3, 1861—d&w1m Newbern, N. C.

☞ **LAW NOTICE.**

THE SUBSCRIBER HAS removed his LAW OFFICE to the office adjoining his residence on the east side of East Front Street, two square, South of Mr. Wm C. Whitford's store.

ALEX JUSTICE.

jan 6 dtf.

MILITARY BOOKS, PAPER, PENS INK, SEALING WAX, RED TAPE, WAFERS, INVELOPES,

Just received at Mrs Stanly's Book Store. Military Books Including, Hardee's Tactics; Gilham's Manuals; Army Requisitions; Laws of the Army and Navy; Southern Military Manuals; Science of War; Roberts Hand Books of Artillery; Troopers Manuals; Ordnance do, Southern Flag Songsters, &c.

Any persons needing any of the above articles will please call immediately for them as Mrs Stanly designs leaving town in a day or two. All persons owing her by note or account will please call and settle immediately

feb 18 dtf.

N O T I C E.

THOSE persons who have open accounts with me will please close them by note if the cash is not convenient, which notes will be held until the war is over. Cash is prefered as I wish to keep up a good supply of provisions.

sept 5 JNO. E. FORD.

"BURNETT'S Preparations."—KALLISTON Cocoaine, Oriental Tooth Wash; Whitcomb's Asthma Remedy, and Flavoring Extracts of Lemon, Orange, Nutmeg, Vanilla, Peach, Rose, Almond, Cinnamon, Clover, Celery and Nectarine. Just received and for sale by

April 21 JAS W CARRER, Druggist.

J. W. WATSON has just received a fresh supply of Photograph and Ambrotype materials, plain and fancy, cases of every description, frames, &c. He is prepared to make Photographic views, Stereoscope pictures, &c., &c., &c.—Don't forget the place, Craven Street.

July 10 dtf J. W. W.

The Tri-Weekly Mercury.

DAILY PAPER—TEN DOLLARS PER ANNUM, PAYABLE HALF-YEARLY IN ADVANCE.

VINDICE NULLO
SPONTE SUA SINE LEGE FIDES RECTUMQUE COLENTUR.

COUNTRY PAPER—THRICE A WEEK—FIVE DOLLARS PER ANNUM, IN ADVANCE.

VOLUME LXXX. CHARLESTON, S. C., TUESDAY, APRIL 29, 1862. NUMBER 11,433

NEWS BY TELEGRAPH.

LATEST REPORTS FROM NEW ORLEANS.

MOBILE, April 26.—A despatch, just received from Jackson, Mississippi, says: "Thirteen of the enemy's gunboats have anchored in the river opposite the city of New Orleans. A proposition made by the Confederates to evacuate the place is now pending. Various exciting rumors are afloat. The foregoing, however, is reliable." As telegraphic communication with New Orleans is closed, the above information must have been brought to Jackson by railroad.

(*Later and Official.*)

RICHMOND, April 27.—Official despatches received this morning, state that the enemy's fleet had approached New Orleans, and demanded the surrender of the city. General LOVELL refused to surrender, but evacuated the city with his forces, falling back to Camp Moore, on the New Orleans, Great Northern and Jackson Railroad. Before leaving, however, he destroyed the cotton and all the public property which he was unable to remove, while the boats were coming up to the city. The new and powerful iron-clad steamer *Mississippi* (unfinished), was burned to prevent her from falling into the hands of the enemy. The despatches make no mention of the iron-clad steamer *Louisiana*.

[In the above despatches, our readers have all the intelligence of the fall of New Orleans that the Government, in pursuance of its uniform policy of reticence in regard to our disasters, has suffered to reach us over the wires. We have gathered, however, from other sources than the telegraph, some information of an interesting character, concerning the recent events below the Crescent City, and we give this information as we have obtained it, without vouching for its accuracy:

On Saturday evening Commodore HOLLINS passed through Columbia *en route* for Richmond. We are informed that he expressed amazement at the news from New Orleans. He stated that there were 100 heavy guns in position on the levee, or river bank, between Fort Jackson and the city; that the *Louisiana* was ready, waiting to encounter any gunboats that might pass the forts and batteries; that numerous "boarding parties," composed of the most active and resolute men, were organized to board and take the enemy's vessels at all hazards; and that the *Mississippi*—the consort of the *Virginia*—although still unfinished, could, if necessary, be brought into action. In view of all these circumstances, we are told that Commodore HOLLINS could not understand, or credit the statement that the city had succumbed.

For ourselves, without being able to explain all the circumstances of this sudden reverse, we fear that the news is too true. The Richmond papers give the official statement that the *Louisiana* went down the river on Monday last. It is certain that private despatches have been received in Richmond to the effect that she had encountered some of the enemy's gunboats, armed with heavy rifled guns, and that, after a brief contest, she was *sunk*. This is probably the key to the mystery. The *Louisiana*, we believe, was a merchant steamer, converted into a war steamer, and it is likely that her timbers were unable to support her iron armor in withstanding the shock of rifled artillery. It seems impossible that the enemy's gunboats could have gained the mastery of the river unless the *Louisiana* was first either disabled, captured or destroyed. And we think that she was destroyed.]—MERCURY.

FROM MEMPHIS.

MEMPHIS, April 25.—(*Despatch to the Savannah Republican.*)—The Louisville *Journal*, of the 17th inst., says the Federal Congress has ordered an investigation into the surprise of the Federal forces at Shiloh. The indignation of the people at the unnecessary and heavy loss of life, through the surprise, is said to be great throughout the North. It is reported, says the *Journal*, that Mr. STANTON, the Federal Secretary of War, has resigned, owing to political differences with the administration.

Matters at Corinth and the neighborhood remain as they were. There is no immediate prospect of a renewal of the fight. The Federals seem to have taken a second thought at Fort Pillow. Accounts just received from the fort report all as quiet.

FATAL RAILROAD ACCIDENT.

MOBILE, April 25.—The up train, which left here yesterday for Corinth, ran off the track a few miles above Enterprise, Miss., killing six men, among them five soldiers of the 19th South Carolina Regiment. About twenty were wounded.

FROM EAST TENNESSEE.

KNOXVILLE, TENNESSEE, April 26.—A prisoner, escaped from Lexington, Ky., says that ten thousand of the enemy are concentrating at that place to make a descent on Cumberland Gap. The Nashville *Banner* has been suppressed by order of ANDY JOHNSON. The enemy are fortifying Huntsville, Ala. The Southern cause is daily gaining ground in Kentucky, owing to the Yankee War Tax and Emancipation scheme.

LATEST FROM THE NORTH.

NORFOLK, April 27.—We have received Northern papers of Friday, the 25th inst.

The Chicago *Times*, of the 24th, contains a despatch stating that Gen. MITCHELL's division of the Federal army had arrived at Tuscaloosa, and held possession of 200 miles of the Memphis and Charleston Railroad. [The announcement that the enemy have reached Tuscaloosa is doubtless an error—Tuscumbia is the place meant.]

Heavy reinforcements for HALLECK's army reached Pittsburg Landing, on the 22d instant, and everything was being made ready for another great battle near Corinth. General GRANGER, in command of 500 cavalry, had a skirmish with the rebels, on the 23d instant, near Pittsburg. The fight lasted an hour, but the loss on both sides was inconsiderable. The general aspect of affairs was unchanged. The country between Cairo and Mound City was inundated on the 23d, and a large portion of the Cairo and Fulton Railroad was washed away.

Despatches from the Peninsula, dated the 24th, received in Baltimore, state that preparations are rapidly progressing for an attack upon Yorktown. The iron-clad screw gunboat *Galena* arrived in Hampton Roads on Wednesday.

From Washington we have news that the ratifications of a SEWARD-LYONS treaty "for the suppression of the slave trade" will soon be exchanged. The main features of the treaty are the mutual concession of the right of search, and provisions for the summary punishing of those found engaged in the trade. SHERMAN's amendment to the Confiscation Bill, naming certain classes as subject to the penalties of the bill, has been adopted. The French Minister, after his return from Richmond, had a long interview with SEWARD. He had also sent despatches to New York, where a steamer is waiting to take them to France.

Advices from Nassau, N. P., state that the steamer *Nashville* had returned to that place, after making an unsuccessful effort to run the blockade at Charleston. One of her paddle-boards was badly damaged. She has a full cargo of guns and ammunition, brought out from England by the *Gladiator*. The Havana *Diairo* states that persons from New Orleans reported that Forts Jackson and St. Philip had been abandoned, and that the Federal fleet can easily ascend the river to the city.

The latest advices from Vera Cruz state that the French had resolved that their division of the expeditionary forces alone should advance against the Capital without delay, assuming all the consequences. The Spanish and English Plenipotentiaries had, therefore, resolved to withdraw their forces and to march back to Vera Cruz.—The French division had begun its march upon the City of Mexico.

The sales of cotton at Liverpool on the 13th inst., were 7,000 bales—3,000 to speculators. Market buoyant. In Havre on the 10th, the sales of the week amounted to 6,000 bales. Orleans *Tres Ordinaire* 158f.; *Bas* 151f. Stock 91,000 bales. The Bombay steamer carried out £450,000 in specie for the purchase of cotton. The Bourse closed firm at 70f. 10c. Consols at London closed at 93¾ to 93⅞.

In New York on the 24th cotton was quiet. Sales 700 bales at 29½c. Pork firm at $12. Rosin $8.

TRI-WEEKLY MERCURY.

TUESDAY, APRIL 29, 1862.

The Fall of New Orleans.

New Orleans has fallen—the great iron-clad steamer, the *Mississippi*, is destroyed—her companion, the *Louisiana*, is supposed to be at the bottom of the river—and the *Manassas Ram* has disappeared from public vision. This is the news of this morning; and this, the last feature of the War. With it, we suppose our last struggle for the command of the waters has terminated. By July, the iron-clad steamers of the enemy are to ride in triumph on river and sea. The fate of Memphis is no longer doubtful, and the whole Valley of the Mississippi must be at the mercy of the enemy.

To this point the military policy and administration of Mr. JEFFERSON DAVIS has reduced the fortunes of the Confederate States.

What is in store for us in the future, it is impossible to predict. But one thing is certain. Without improvement in the conduct of our affairs, the same fate must follow us still—on land, as on water; ~~and Nashville, Huntsville and~~ New Orleans cannot be the last of our disasters.

But our disasters are not vital. We have two magnificent armies still in the field. We have a people in earnest, inhabiting an immense country, which cannot be held down, even if overrun. Much remains for hope, and much to cheer. Let energy give life to our counsels and actions, and we fear not the result.

A brave and great People can bear, and have borne, much of disaster, peril and suffering at the hands of one man—incompetent, perverse. But there is an end to endurance, and the People of the South cannot afford to be destroyed. And they *will* not. There are strong arms, and stout hearts, and means enough in the land, to achieve our Independence beyond peradventure. But we must rise to the times. The wisdom and strength and energy of the country must be brought into play. All obstacles that stand in our path must be mastered or swept aside, without hesitation, fear or remorse. The administration of our affairs MUST be reformed and energised. The end must be achieved. And nothing can be allowed to interpose, or to balk our fortunes as a People.

Slavery in the District of Columbia.

The bill for the abolition of slavery in the District of Columbia was returned to Congress by President Lincoln with the following message:

Fellow-Citizens of the Senate and House of Representatives: The act entitled "An Act for the release of certain persons held to service or labor in the District of Columbia" has this day been approved and signed. I have never doubted the constitutional authority of Congress to abolish slavery in this District, and *I have ever desired to see the National Capital freed from the institution* in some satisfactory way. Hence there has never been, in my mind, any question upon the subject, except the one of expediency arising in view of all the circumstances. If there be matters within and about this act which might have taken a course or shape more satisfactory to my judgment, I do not attempt to specify them. I am gratified that the two principles of compensation and colonization are both recognized and practically applied in the act.

In the matter of compensation it is provided that claims may be presented within ninety days from the passage of the act, but "not thereafter," as there is no saving for minors, femmes covert, insane or absent persons. I presume this is an omission by mere oversight, and I recommend that it be supplied by an amendatory or supplemental act.

April 16, 1862. ABRAHAM LINCOLN.

Lincoln, on the same day, recommended to the Senate JAMES G. BERRET, ex-mayor of Washington; Hon. SAMUEL F. VINTON, of Ohio, and DANIEL R. GOODLOE, formerly of North Carolina, commissioners under this act, whose duty it shall be to investigate and determine the validity and value of the claims presented by the owners of slaves.

AWFUL CATASTROPHE IN MEXICO.—The Mexican village of San Andres Calchicomula, not far from Orizaba, was, during the first week of last month, the scene of an awful catastrophe—either a powder store explosion or an earthquake. According to official accounts, 1039 men, either soldiers or officers, were killed, and 225 women, children, and men, more or less dangerously wounded. It is said, in a letter from Orizaba, that the total of the victims of this terrible accident amounts to 2300, of whom 2000 were killed and 300 wounded. "There is not," says the letter, "a single pane of glass, nor one article of glassware, left unbroken in the dwelling houses. Buildings were generally damaged in the town as well as the neighborhood. The political chief of Orizaba returned his thanks to the French and Spanish officers for the voluntary assistance they gave the victims."

THE LATEST NORTHERN NEWS.

Our news this morning is very interesting. We have Northern papers up the 24th instant, from which we get the detailed account of the fall of Fort Pulaski, Gen. GRANT's official report of the battle of Shiloh, and other intelligence of an important character. We present a summary:

"HIGHLY IMPORTANT -A VALUABLE DESPATCH FROM GEN. BEAUREGARD INTERCEPTED."

Under this heading, the New Yord *Herald* publishes the following despatch from Nashville, under date of 15th instant:

Later information from the South is of the utmost importance. Beauregard's army has been terribly demoralized, and, according to his own confession, he has now only 35,000 men. The following telegram has been intercepted by Gen. Mitchell, and is a full confession of the hopelessness of the rebel cause in the West. I append it *verbatim*, leaving you to comment on its importance.

CORINTH, April 9.

To Gen. Samuel Cooper, Richmond, Va.—

All present probabilities are that whenever the enemy move on this position, he will do so with an overwhelming force of not less than 85,000 men. We can now muster only about 35,000 effectives. Van Dorn may possibly join us in a few days with about 15,000 more. Can we not be reinforced from Pemberton's army? If defeated here we lose the Missisippi Valley, and probably our cause. Whereas, we could even afford to lose, for a while, Charleston and Savannah, for the purpose of defeating Buell's army, which would not only insure us the Valley of the Mississippi, but our independence. G. T. BEAUREGARD.

THE FALL OF FORT PULASKI—FULL AND INTERESTING PARTICULARS.

The New York *Herald* has a long account of the bombardment and capture of Fort Pulaski. After describing minutely the vast array of guns and mortars in the *eleven* batteries which bore upon the fort, it gives the following correspondence:

HEADQUARTERS, DEPARTMENT OF SOUTH, TYBEE ISLAND, Ga., April 10, 1862.

To the Commanding Officer, Fort Pulaski:

SIR: I hereby demand of you the immediate surrender and restoration of Fort Pulaski to the authority and possession of the United States.

This demand is made with a view to avoiding, if possible, the effusion of blood, which must result from the bombardment and attack now in readiness to be opened.

The number, calibre and completeness of the batteries surrounding you, leave no doubt as to what must result in case of refusal; and as the defence, however obstinate, must eventually succumb to the assailing force at my disposal, it is hoped you will see fit to avert the useless waste of life.

This communication will be carried to you under a flag of truce by Lieut. J. H. Wilson, United States Army, who is authorized to wait any period not exceeding thirty minutes from delivery for your answer.

I have the honor to be, sir, your most obedient servant, DAVID HUNTER, Major General Commanding.

REPLY.

HEADQUARTERS, FORT PULASKI, April 10, 1862.

Major-General David Hunter, Commanding on Tybee Island:

SIR: I have to acknowledge the receipt of your communication of this date, demanding the unconditional surrender of Fort Pulaski.

In reply, I can only say that I am here to defend the fort—not to surrender it.

I have the honor to be, very respectfully, your obedient servant, CHAS. H. OLMSTEAD, Colonel First Volunteer Regiment of Georgia, commanding post.

Lieutenant Wilson was received at the wharf, and his despatch conveyed to Colonel Olmstead. He remained in the boat until the reply was received, about fifteen minutes after, when he immediately returned to Tybee, and delivered it to General Hunter. Upon its contents—so laconic and soldierly—becoming known, signal was made for the first gun to be fired. General Hunter, General Benham, General Gilmore, Captain Rogers and others, immediately hurried out to the batteries, where a good view could be obtained.

THE BOMBARDMENT.

On Thursday morning, at 23 minutes of eight, the fire was opened by a discharge of a thirteen inch mortar from Battery Halleck, fired by Lieut. Horace Porter, of the Ordnance Department, the shell exploding in the air; and this was succeeded by a thirteen inch shell from Battery Stanton, which exploded short. In a moment or two several of the mortars were discharged from the other batteries; but none of the shell were effective, the firing being two wild and the fuses too short. Three minutes after the first fire Fort Pulaski reponded from a ten inch barbette gun, the shell exploding harmlessly over Tybee Island. The fire soon became general on both sides, little damage being done by either for some time, as we had not attained the correct range, and the enemy were not quite sure of the position of our battery. Soon, however, we observed the dust begin to fly from the pancope, between the south and southeast faces, and we were satisfied that the breaching batteries (Halleck, Scott, Siegel, McClellan and Totten), on Goat Point, were in full play, sending their rifled balls, solid ten inch shot and heavy shell, with terrible effect against the brick walls. Unfortunately, through some weakness of the iron carriages of the ten-inch columbiads, two of the columbiads which were throwing solid ten-inch shell were dismounted by recoil, jumping backwards directly off their carriage. The rifled guns were served rapidly and with skill, and in an hour or so but one gun on the barbette was in play, and that fired only occasionally. The fire was evidently too hot for the rebels, as they did not stick to their guns very closely. They played at our different batteries from their thirty-twos and forty-twos in casemate; but finding their range too short to reach the mortar batteries, they concentrated their fire upon the Goat Point batteries, occasionally giving Battery Burnside a few moments attention, when Sergeant Wilson, of the Sappers and Miners, who commanded it, had got his range, and was annoying the fort with thirteen inch shells, which burst in and over it. No damage was done. At twenty minutes past eleven the flag on Pulaski came down, the lanyards having been cut by a fragment of shell from mortar No. 2, Battery Stanton, worked by Corporal Trumbull, Seventh Connecticut Volunteers. The result was hailed with loud cheers, that extended from battery to battery along the line. The flag was down twenty minutes or more, and then appeared again, on a temporary flag staff, and floated gayly in the breeze. The bombardment went on all day, the fire from our batteries being more effective every minute. The enemy, finding that our thirteen-inch shells were not so destructive as they expected, began to work their barbette guns with great energy, and give us some trouble. Our parrott guns were brought to bear upon them, and a hot fire was poured upon their guns, and one or two of them dismounted. The fire from the breaching batteries became more and more disastrous to the enemy as the day advanced. The pancope began to assume a mottled aspect. It appeared to have the small-pox, blotches appearing all over it. These after a while ran together, and deep holes in the face of the wall of the pancope were discovered, which became deeper and deeper, and finally assumed the form of a breach. The breach at dusk, at which time the fire was temporarily suspended on both sides, was not entirely through the wall, except at one small point, through which a gleam of sunlight was caught, about sunset. During the night an occasional shell was thrown from batteries Burnside and Halleck, and from the rifled guns of Battery Siegel. The enemy made no reply, but seemed to be engaged in repairing damages. We had lost not a man during the day, and sustained no damage of consequence to our batteries.

Such as were injured were repaired by the engineers during the night, and were made ready by daylight for another day's operations. At daylight on Friday fire was again opened by our batteries and quickly responded to by the enemy—who had got their barbette guns in position during the night—with great rapidity and some precision, as I can testify to myself, if a lame wrist, obtained in a rapid movement in dodging a shell, may be considered good authority.

A ten-inch shell entered one of the embrasures

Slavery in the District of Columbia.

The bill for the abolition of slavery in the District of Columbia was returned to Congress by President Lincoln with the following message:

Fellow-Citizens of the Senate and House of Representatives: The act entitled "An Act for the release of certain persons held to service or labor in the District of Columbia" has this day been approved and signed. I have never doubted the constitutional authority of Congress to abolish slavery in this District, and *I have ever desired to see the National Capital freed from the institution* in some satisfactory way. Hence there has never been, in my mind, any question upon the subject, except the one of expediency arising in view of all the circumstances. If there be matters within and about this act which might have taken a course or shape more satisfactory to my judgment, I do not attempt to specify them. I am gratified that the two principles of compensation and colonization are both recognized and practically applied in the act.

In the matter of compensation it is provided that claims may be presented within ninety days from the passage of the act, but "not thereafter," as there is no saving for minors, femmes covert, insane or absent persons. I presume this is an omission by mere oversight, and I recommend that it be supplied by an amendatory or supplemental act.

April 16, 1862. ABRAHAM LINCOLN.

Lincoln, on the same day, recommended to the Senate JAMES G. BERRET, ex-mayor of Washington; Hon. SAMUEL F. VINTON, of Ohio, and DANIEL R. GOODLOE, formerly of North Carolina, commissioners under this act, whose duty it shall be to investigate and determine the validity and value of the claims presented by the owners of slaves.

General H. A. Benham, Commanding Northern District, Department of the South, Tybee Island, Ga.

SIR: I have the honor to transmit herewith the terms of capitulation for the surrender to the United States of Fort Pulaski, Ga., signed by me this 11th day of April, 1862.

I trust these terms will receive your approval, they being substantially those authorised by you as commander of the district.

The fort hoisted the white flag at a quarter before two o'clock this afternoon, after a resistance since eight o'clock yesterday morning, to the continuous fire of our batteries.

A practicable breach in the walls was made in eighteen and a half hour's firing by daylight.

I have the honor to be, very respectfully, Your most obedient servant, Q. A. GILLMORE, Brigadier General Volunteers, commanding United States Forces on Tybee Island, Georgia.

We captured with the fort three hundred and sixty prisoners, including the commander, staff and line officers. Their names are as follows:

Colonel Charles H. Olmstead, commanding post; Major John Foley, Adjutant M. H. Hopkins, Quartermaster Robert Irwin, Commissaries Robt. D. Walker, J. T. McFarland, Sergeant Major Robert H. Lewis, Quartermaster Sergeant Wm. C. Crawford, Ordnance Sergeant Harvey Sims.

Officers of the Montgomery Guard, Savannah, Georgia.—Captain, L. J. Gilmartin; First Lieutenant, John J. Symons; Senior Second Lieutenant, Christopher Hussey; Junior Second Lieutenant, C. M. Murphy.

German Volunteers, Savannah.—Captain, John H. Stiegen; Senior Second Lieutenant, Henry Warner; Junior Second Lieutenant, Charles Umbach.

Oglethorpe Light Infantry, Savannah.—Captain, T. W. Sims; First Lieutenant, H. C. Truman; Junior Second Lieutenant, James Ackerman.

Wise Guard, Macon County, Ga.—Captain, M. J. McMullin: First Lieutenant, T. W. Montford Senior Second Lieutenant, J. D. N. Lullow; Junior Second Lieutenant, John Blow.

Washington Volunteers, Savannah.—Captain, John McMahon; First Lieutenant, Francis Blair; Senior Second Lieutenant, J. C. Rowland; Junior Second Lieutenant, A. J. McArthur.

The balance of the three hundred and sixty are privates and non-commissioned officers. With the fort we took forty-seven guns, ten inch and eight inch, two rifled, but mostly casemate thirty-twos and forty-twos. Also seven thousand shot and shell, and in the magazine we found about forty thousand pounds of powder of various qualities. About three months' supply of provisions was taken, and will be well used by our troops.

The fort has been badly used by our shot and shell. The interior presents a melancholy aspect. The barricades or splinter proofs are torn to pieces in many places; pieces of brick, timber, stone, cannon balls, unexploded projectiles and shells, fragments of shell, etc., strew the parade ground in the interior of the work. At the angle of the breach, the arches have been torn out, guns dismounted, and debris of brick and timber, broken gun carriages, muskets, etc., fill up the casemates. And in one or two places where shell entered the embrasures and burst inside, you can trace the flight of each fragment as it ripped up the woodwork and shattered the brick work in the casemates. The officers' quarters were badly shattered. The breach being very large, several rifle balls passed through it, over the terra plain, and began to batter the magazine on the northwest corner in a manner that carried terror to the hearts of the enemy. From their experience they knew that it was possible for a rifle shell to pass entirely through the walls of the magazine and blow it up, and with it the fort and all its occupants. This induced a surrender, and the white flag went up. It will cost $50,000 to put the fort into the same condition of defence that it was before we opened fire. The walls are greatly shaken, and all believe had the bombardment continued half a day longer the entire wall of the pancope would have fallen into the ditch a mass of ruins. The men could feel the walls of the fort tremble and quake when a solid ten-inch shot struck it, and from that fact you can get a tolerably correct idea of the immense force with which they strike. It was terrific. Out of fifteen guns and mortars *en barbette* but four of them were serviceable. The balance were dismounted, or otherwise rendered incapable of use.

wounded in the hand on the first day, his place was never vacant. He was again wounded, and had three horses killed under him. In making this mention of a gallant officer no disparagement is intended to the other division commanders—Major-Generals John A. McClernand and Lew. Wallace, and Brigadier-Generals S. A. Hurlbut, B. M. Prentiss, and W. H. L. Wallace—all of whom maintained their places with credit to themselves and the cause. General Prentiss was taken prisoner in the first day's action, and Gen. W. H. L. Wallace was severely and probably mortally wounded. His Assistant Adjutant General, Capt. William McMichael, is missing, and was probably taken prisoner. [Here follows a notice of the officers of his staff.]

The country will have to mourn the loss of many brave men who fell at the battle of Pittsburg, or Shiloh, more properly. The exact loss in killed and wounded will be known in a day or two; at present I can only give it approximately at 1,500 killed and 3,500 wounded. The loss of artillery was great—many pieces being disabled by the enemy's shot, and some losing all their horses and many men. There were probably not less than two hundred horses killed.

The loss of the enemy in killed and left upon the field was greater than ours. In wounded an estimate cannot be made, as many of them must have been sent to Corinth and other points. The enemy suffered terribly from demoralization and desertion.

A flag of truce was sent to-day from General Beauregard. I enclose a copy of correspondence. I am, respectfully,

Your obd't servant, U. S. GRANT, Major General Commanding.

FROM THE VALLEY OF VIRGINIA.

The following despatches from Gen. BANKS to LINCOLN's Secretary of War would seem to confirm the report of the falling back of "Stonewall JACKSON:"

NEW MARKET, April 19.

Hon. E. M. Stanton, Secretary of War:

To-day I have been to the bridges on the south fork of the Shenandoah, in the Massanutten valley, with a force of cavalry, infantry and artillery, to protect the two important bridges that cross the river. We were within sight of Suray, at the south bridge. A sharp skirmish occurred with the rebels, in which they lost several men taken prisoners. Their object was the destruction of the bridges. One of the prisoners left the camp on the bank of the Rappahannock on Tuesday morning. There were no fortifications there up to that time. Other reports indicate a strong force at Gordonsville, and a contest there, the whole resulting in a belief that they are concentrating at Yorktown. I believe Jackson left this valley yesterday. He is reported to have left Harrisonburg yesterday for Gordonsville, by the mountain road. He encamped last night at McGaugeytown, eleven miles from Harrisonburg. N. P. BANKS, Major General Commanding.

NEWMARKET, April 20—9 a. m.

To Hon. E. M. Stanton, Secretary of War:

The flight of Jackson from the Valley, by way of the mountains, from Harrisonburg towards Stannardsvills and Orange C. H., on Gordonsville, is confirmed this morning by our scouts and prisoners. N. P. BANKS, Major General Commanding.

MISCELLANEOUS.

The water in the Tennessee river is fast falling.

Lincoln has nominated General Shields for Major General.

Tar is selling in Philadelphia at $5.75 per barrel, and rosin at $7.25 in gold.

The Federals claim to have taken 200 Confederate prisoners at Shiloh.

The 3d Alabama regiment has donated $1,000 towards building a gunboat for the defence of Alabama.

The elections in the Northwest are resulting in heavy Democratic or anti-war victories. Springfield, Ill., Lincoln's own town, has gone against him.

Col. John H. Forney, of the 10th Alabama, has been promoted Brigadier, and assigned to duty on the coast.

Mrs. Fremont has lined with silk and otherwise renovated the old flag her husband hoisted on the highest peak of the Rocky Mountains in 1841.

Three more of Erricsson's batteries are being constructed at Greenpoint, New York, on the plan of the Monitor, to be ready in three months.

The New York Herald of Wednesday says that the iron-clad steamer Galena left that port on Tuesday morning; place of destination not mentioned.

The remains of Major Robert B. Armistead, of the 22d Alabama Regiment, who fell at Shiloh, were interred at Montgomery, on the 8th instant.

The gallant Col. Jno. Echols, of the Twenty-seventh Virginia Regiment, who was severely wounded at the battle of Kernstown, has been promoted to the rank of Brigadier General.

Gen. McClellan has a sister (Mrs. English) living in Alabama, the wife of a wealthy planter.—Young English, a nephew of McClellan, has gone up to Corinth, the Mobile papers say, to fight for the South.

The storm of the 3d inst. did a large amount of damage at Paducah. The Methodist Church, several business houses, and a great many private dwellings, were unroofed, and otherwise injured.

One of the New York papers has a representation of the armor which is in use by some of the enemy. This, it is supposed, is the same as that which was found on the dead in the battle of Shiloh. Price, $5 for privates, and $7 for officers.

A note from Knoxville says that on the 21st inst. Mrs Maynard and Mrs. Brownlow received notice to be ready in thirty-six hours to pass by escort beyond the lines of the Confederate Government.

The female prisoners, Greenhow, Baxley, and Mrs. Morris, still linger in the old Capitol prison. Mrs. Morris has not yet completed her preparations for departure to Dixie. The others are ready and willing to go.

Commodore Vanderbilt has made Mr. Lincoln a present of his steamship Vanderbilt, now lying at Hampton Roads, and has offered to sell his next best steamer to the Government, iron-clad, at a price to be fixed by its own appraisers.

The naval battle in Hampton Roads, between the Monitor and Merrimac, is the absorbing topic throughout Europe. The Emperor Napoleon has been heard to say that it is now settled that there is no navy in the world that could make head against iron-clad steamers.

The New York Herald surmises that the object of the visit of the French Minister to Richmond was to persuade President Davis to give up the struggle on condition of a liberal amnesty. It says he was closeted with Mr. Seward for two hours before leaving Washington.

A number of "secesh women" in St. Louis have been restricted in their movements, and their limits for locomotion curtailed by a military order. They have been in the habit of cheering in the streets the rebel prisoners as they passed along. The women are all in high standing in good society.

The Houston Telegraph has from the western part of the State, dreadful accounts of the drouth now prevailing, and its effects upon the cattle. Thousands upon thousands of them are dying for want of water. If it does not rain soon there will be hard times in Western Texas before the year is out.

A leader in the St. Louis Republican, of the 10th, expresses the utmost horror in view of the terrible carnage in what it calls "this unholy rebellion," and pleads earnestly for a termination of "this wicked assault upon the nation's life," and upon a "government which never did the South any willful harm."

The canal cut across the peninsula at New Madrid, Missouri, through which the Yankee steamers and several barges were taken, is twelve miles long, through heavy timber which had to be sawed off by hand four feet under water. The idea of this laborious undertaking originated with General Schuyler Hamilton, and the work was performed by Colonel Bissell's Missouri Engineering Regiment.

Thomas T. Tansall, late United States Consul at Tangiers, and Mr. Myers, Purser of the Sumter, arrested at Algeciras, Morocco, arrived at Boston on the 18th, in the bark Harvest Home. The prisoners were in irons, which were removed by order of Marshal Keyes, and they were sent to Fort Warren, to await instructions from the government.

The Yankee Congress is getting ready a new confiscation bill "providing for confiscating the slaves and property of all persons actually in arms against our Government, or officially connected with the bogus Rebel Government. The provisions are also to include the conductors of Secession newspapers. The bill will also provide that none of the parties named shall hereafter hold any office of trust, honor or profit under the Government of the United States."

The 14th Mississippi regiment, whose term of enlistment had expired some days before the late battle on the Tennessee, anxious to strike a blow for their native land, decided to remain until after the battle; and most gloriously did they uphold the flag of their gallant State. Having done their duty, as well to themselves as to their country, they will now return home on a short visit, and then re-enter the service for the war. Their noble example should not be lost upon other six and twelve months' troops.

The editor of the Nashville Republican Banner has been arrested and imprisoned by order of "Hon. Andrew Johnson, Military Governor of Tennessee." The cause of the arrest is that the general tone of the paper is inimical to the Government of the United States. In consequence of the arrest the Banner has been suspended.—The Banner was one of the oldest papers in Tennessee, having been in existence over half a century.

It has been definitely settled to re-arrange the Yankee Cabinet, by transferring Secretary Welles to the Mission to Spain, made vacant by the appointment of Carl Shurz as Brigadier General, and the appointment of a new Secretary of the Navy. Several names are mentioned for the latter post, among whom are Gen. Banke, Governor Sprague, Gen. Walbridge, and Senators Hale and Wilson. Other changes are rumored.

The Richmond Enquirer says: It is a fact that there is a pretty fair supply of United States Treasury Notes in this city. It is a fact that they are sold and greedily bought up at fifty cents on the dollar, and it is also a fact that a certain class of traitorous individuals are exceedingly anxious to enter largely into the trade. Now these are significant facts; and the first question that occurs is, where do the notes come from, and why are the shavers so eager to enter into the trade?

Miss Narcissa Sanders is the stepdaughter of Hon. A. V. Brown, who left a princely residence in the beautiful hills which encircle Nashville. She is young, beautiful, witty, and was a noted belle at the Capitol at Washington. The Federal commander, McCook, having known her formerly, upon taking possession of the city, called to pay his respects, and sent up his card from the door. Her reply was: "Tell him to please excuse me; I am in mourning for my country, and can see no one."

On account of the scarcity of forage, Gen. Van Dorn has ordered all the cavalry enlisted for twelve months to be temporarily dismounted and serve as infantry. The horses will be taken care of by the government while the cavalry is acting as infantry, but while serving as such they will be entitled to all the privileges and pay of cavalry. This order of General Van Dorn evinces the high spirit of justice by which he is actuated. The men have the privilege of selling their horses, or sending them to other than government depots, if they desire.

On Saturday week Gen. Humphrey Marshall's camp was made to resound with gladsome shouts and huzzas at the arrival of a squad of gallant and true Kentuckians from Covington and its vicinity. They enrolled themselves as soldiers for the war. They represent that thousands are ready to follow their example should Gen. Marshall make another forward movement into Kentucky. No Lincoln troops are in Eastern Kentucky except some 800 at Pikeville. These are there as a blind to prevent the forward movement of our troops.

The Memphis papers state that the Eleventh Louisiana regiment went into the battle of Corinth about six hundred strong, and the loss in killed and wounded was one hundred and seventy—a ratio of over twenty-eight per cent. This heavy loss is accounted for by the fact that the regiment was ordered to take a battery, which was hidden from them by tents. After charging through the camp they found themselves still some two or three hundred yards from the battery, *supported by three rifle regiments*. The regiment, therefore, had to fall back and take another route, but in the meantime lost a great many. On the next charge they were partially supported by another regiment, and took the battery. The enemy fled before the bayonets reached them.

THE DAILY TRUE DELTA.

JOHN MAGINNIS, Proprietor. OFFICE--18 ST. CHARLES STREET. TERMS--TEN DOLLARS PER ANNUM.

VOLUME XXV. NEW ORLEANS, WEDNESDAY MORNING, APRIL 30, 1862. NUMBER 137

The Daily True Delta

[FROM OUR YESTERDAY'S AFTERNOON EDITION.]

THE LATEST AGONY.

The inquiries addressed to us by at least a thousand tongues as to whether the city is really to be bombarded at noon to-morrow, and what families should do, and what we ourselves intend to do, and what every body else should do, exceed in number our powers of enumeration. If it be any gratification to any body to know exactly how we do feel in regard to this matter, we shall cheerfully unbosom ourself to him. In the first place, then, we would premise that unless Commodore Farragut desires a pretext, and parties in the city are anxious to afford one to him, to bombard the place, it is very unlikely to occur; although so extraordinary are the daily events of these strange times that it is unsafe to predict anything. Our position as a city is one of complete helplessness. The general charged with its defence abandoned it as untenable; and although there is a numerous class still here — hitherto unnoticed as fighting patriots — who now maintain this opinion to be incorrect, we incline to the Lovell side of the question rather than theirs. It was always understood among men who knew anything, that our city must fall when the fleet of the Federals forced the river or silenced our forts. The latter have been skilfully and resolutely defended, and it is affirmed that they failed in ability to arrest the passage of the enemy only because of the perfidy, or something else, of a Mr. Fairfield, who was appointed by Commodore Mitchell as signal-man below the forts on the night that the achievement was accomplished. Whether this person was unfaithful, incapable or negligent, is not shown; the harshest judgment has been passed on his conduct, and if he be in this vicinity, it will be necessary for him to offer an explanation. Be this, however, as it may, the forts were passed, our gunboats, or such of them as were fit for service, made a good fight of it, and stood up to their work while they could float. Our farcial defenses at Chalmette made a show of resistance, and our city fell helpless before the vessels of the invader. The sequel sensible people would not look for in a conflagrated city or a destroyed population; but, as we have said, these are times when the most unusual and eccentric occurrences may be looked for, and the bombardment hypothetically threatened by Commodore Farragut may actually occur. The intimation that officer gives to Mr. Mayor Monroe to have the women and children removed within forty-eight hours shall not be complied with by the writer hereof, for two good reasons; the first being, that we have no suitable place to remove them to, and the second being our determination to cluster them about ourself so that the shell which kills one shall kill all. We have lived in a Thug-hell for six or seven years past, and bomb-shells cannot be much less merciful.

We hope this explanation will be the means of satisfying every one who is curious to know our opinions on the absorbing topic of the day; at the same time we cannot help adding the expression of our humble belief, that if the burly fellows innocent of camp life who are so eager to have the city reduced to ashes, would transfer themselves to Corinth, they can there find a suitable field for the expenditure of their surplus valor unstimulated and uninspired by other motive than uncalculating devotion to their country, right or wrong.

THE NEW CUNARDERS.

The most successful navigation company in the world is the Cunard, and it has been so simply and solely because it has kept pace with the spirit of the age, and although accused of a too obstinate adherence to model, it has never allowed itself to be surpassed in the great requisites of ocean voyaging, viz: speed and safety. It has recently been adding new wonders to its line, one of which, the China, a propeller, made the voyage from Queenstown, Ireland, to New York in nine days four hours, running time. She is thus spoken of by a New York paper:

The China is really a magnificent vessel. She has been built and engined by Robert Napier & Sons, of Glasgow, and her launch, trial trip and ocean performance prove that she has been constructed in a manner worthy of the reputation of that firm. The dimensions of the China are: Length, 326 feet; breadth, 40 feet 6 inches; depth, 27 feet 6 inches; gross tonnage, 2529.01; allowance for propelling power, 989 40; register tonnage, 1539.61. The China has two beautifully formed engines, of the collective power of 550 horses, of the oscilating geared description.

The British Board of Trade has certified, according to the act of parliament, that the China can accommodate 1039 passengers, arranged in the following divisions, namely: First class, aft, 268 passengers; second class, forward, 771 passengers. The China is suited for either passenger or goods traffic. She is fitted, like the ordinary mail steamers of the Cunard line, with a dining saloon on deck—the after part for the first cabin, the rest for the fore cabin passengers. The panels and ceilings of the saloon are handsomely painted, but without any pretension to profuse decoration, and are replete with every requisite for elegance and comfort.

Everything about the vessel speaks of strength and security, and yet on her trial trip, recently made in Scotland, she showed a greater rate of speed, with the relative amount of power to tonnage, than had been obtained from any vessel constructed in the Clyde. On that occasion the China ran to the lights between the Cloch and Cumbrae under the following conditions: First, from Cloch to Cumbrae, against a strong flood tide and strong south-west wind, in sixty minutes and four seconds; second, from Cumbrae to Cloch, with a light drain of tide in the ship's favor, in fifty-five minutes and thirty seconds—the latter giving a speed of 14.9 knots, equal to seventeen and a quarter statute miles per hour. On her trial trip the pressure of steam was eighteen pounds. She went round to the Mersey with only twelve pounds pressure.

The government shipwright surveyor of England measured the China as to her capacity for the transport of troops previous to her departure from England, and reported that she could carry 1500 men with her after cabins standing. As the ships belonging to this company have more than once been taken up by the government in the time of its need, and at the shortest notice, it is worthy of mention that the cabin and other fittings of the China can be removed, without injury, at a moment's notice, and they can be readily replaced when the "special service" for which the ship has been employed has been fulfilled.

The same company have also ready for their line, the Scotia, which the London Times thus noticed on her arrival at Liverpool from the Clyde:

The new steamship Scotia, built under special survey expressly for the British and North America Royal mail service, arrived in Liverpool from the Clyde, where she was built, on Thursday afternoon, having made the run from the Cloch lighthouse on the Clyde to the Bell buoy at the mouth of the Mersey, in twelve hours and four minutes. The machinery worked admirably, and in proof that the vessel is perfectly manageable, she was easily moved round in the Mersey within her own length. A person who was on board during the trip to Liverpool states that she is "as stiff as a church." The trial trip on Wednesday, before the Scotia left the Clyde for Liverpool, was highly satisfactory, notwithstanding the unpropitious state of the weather.

The distance was performed under the following conditions:

Against a strong flood tide, and also against a double-reefed topsail breeze of wind, from the Cloch to Cumbrae Light in fifty-nine minutes; after passing the Little Cumbrae, the Scotia was brought round with great ease, and performed the upward run between the Cumbrae and Cloch Lights—but on this occasion with wind and tide in her favor, in forty-nine minutes, mean time fifty-four minutes. The rate of speed will be understood by the following:

59 minutes=13.893 knots, or 16.010 miles per hour.
49 minutes=16.734 knots, or 19.277 miles per hour.
30.632 35.287

Mean speed, 15.316 knots, or 17.643 miles.

It is anticipated that under ordinary circumstances the maximum speed of the Scotia will be about nineteen miles an hour. The trial referred to was made to test the efficiency and speed of the vessel for the mail service, which was done under the superintendence of Mr. John Dinnen, inspector of machinery, and Mr. James Luke, master shipwright of the admiralty, Whitehall; the Board of Trade being locally represented by Mr. Geo. Barber, shipwright surveyor, and Mr. H. R. Robson, inspector of machinery for the Clyde.

From these samples of what one British company is doing, it will be seen how rapidly ocean steaming is attaining perfection; and it will convey painful impressions also to many here who have so often deplored the fatuity which has left this country so destitute in this important arm. John Bull is something of a patriot, even if he does not make a great noise about it.

Mexico--An Important Movement.

Mexico, the theater of countless revolutions and unstable governments, is about to launch the Ship of State, preparatory to another voyage of governmental discovery. The indications are that those at the helm will continue their cruise this time until the Monarchical system is discovered.

[From the Brownsville Flag, April 3.]

MOMENTOUS REVOLUTION IN MEXICO.—The condition of Mexican nationality is undergoing a profound and comprehensive revolution; and the disruption of the United States will make the change easy and somewhat acceptable. Mexico must soon become a consolidated government, and we incline to the belief that she will adopt the monarchical system. It is evident to us that she must consolidate, and the movements of Vidaurri and Comonfort, under the direction of Doblado, reveal the threads of centralization. In 1859 the present Mexican Secretary of State, Manuel Doblado, then the active and sagacious Governor of Guanajuato, passed through Minatitlan, and in an interview with several foreigners at the American Consulate, he deplored the condition of his country, admitted her failure to be a constitutional republic, and confessed his intention to seek a change in her political status. At that time he favored the introduction of an American force into the State, with which the civil war could be suppressed, and a permanent government established, with ten thousand foreign troops to assert its supremacy over local outbreaks. Minister McLane was approached on the subject, but that gentleman discountenanced the plan because he did not believe our form of government admitted of our assuming a quasi protectorate over neighboring nations, for Doblado insisted that the foreign army, for its own bettter discipline, and for the safety of Mexico, should be officered, governed and paid by the United States, Mexico furnishing the money. Volunteers were all that Mr. McLane could propose, and these Gov. Doblado declined to consider. What our government could not furnish, the Mexican secretary has found, or probably will find, in Europe. The negotiation at Orizaba, in our opinion, will result in the realization of Doblado's plan, but whether it will terminate in a monarchy under Maximilian I, or in a dictatorship under Juarez, Doblado, Comonfort or Vidaurri, is a matter at present apparently undetermined. The Mexican Government, under Doblado's masterly guidance, is evidently in movement towards some change, and probably the president himself does not know the extent of the changes which his secretary of state proposes. The division of the nation has been surreptitiously abolished by the erection of military districts consisting of several States, wherein martial law has been proclaimed, and the civil authorities superseded. In Tamaulipas, the office of governor has been virtually abolished, for there is no such authority acknowledged by the general government as existing in the State. Vidaurri is absolute from the Rio Grande to San Luis Potosi, and he is warily drawing the lines so that he may maintain the power he has so curiously and so opportunely attained, both by the invitation of a party in the State and by the appointment of the government. The same clandestine revolution has been achieved in all the frontier States, until at present Mexico may congratulate herself on being a compact centralization of five or six military districts instead of twenty-five distracted and refractory principalities, at war with themselves, with each other, and with the nation. As a matter of course, this condition of affairs cannot continue except by the installation of a firm and terrible central power, which will have the means to suppress all symptoms of disorder and revolution. A national force of Mexicans cannot be depended on to do this, for it is too liable to be seduced into pronunciamentos. Such was the opinion of Santa Anna, and such, we have reason to believe, is the conclusion of the Juarez cabinet. In lieu of native soldiers, foreign mercenaries will not do, for they would imitate the Byzantine Janizaries, who, from hired defenders soon raised themselves to be the despotic rulers of the state. The only feasible plan, therefore, is the one proposed by Doblado, that Mexico shall borrow an organized and subordinate army from some foreign state, and that that force shall be strong enough to maintain peace, and enforce order and authority in the country until the people become satisfied to live without revolutions. To do this the State organizations will have to be abolished and disarmed, the government will have to be consolidated, and the officers subjected to a stricter supervision. This we believe to be the programme under consideration at Orizaba, and if it is successfully presented by Doblado, and then successfully carried out, Mexico will have undergone a most momentous and a highly beneficial revolution. The dissolution of the United States will facilitate the change, too, for we no longer offer them that example of prosperity, greatness and peace which they have vainly striven to imitate during the last forty years. The Republic of Washington and the Utopia of Rosseau are alike inimitable by the Mexicans except in their failure.

Home Department.

Action of the City Authorities.

The Mayor's Message to the Common Council—Action of that Body—Mayor's Reply to Commodore Farragut's Renewed Demand—His Letter Announcing the Surrender of the Forts.

The following is the Mayor's message to the Council, accompanying Flag-Officer Farragut's communication, received yesterday:

MAYORALTY OF NEW ORLEANS,
City Hall, April 28, 1862.

Gentlemen of the Common Council:

I herewith transmit to you a communication from Flag-Officer Farragut, commanding the United States fleet now lying in front of this city. I have informed the officer bearing the communication that I would lay it before you, and return such answer as the city authorities might deem proper to be made.

In the meantime, permit me to suggest that Flag-Officer Farragut appears to have misunderstood the City of New Orleans. He has been distinctly informed that, at this moment, the city has no power to impede the exercise of such acts of forcible authority as the commander of the United States naval forces may choose to exercise; and that, therefore, no resistance could be offered to the occupation of the city by the United States forces. If it is deemed necessary to remove the flag now floating from this building, or to raise United States flags on others, the power which threatens the destruction of our city is certainly capable of performing those acts. New Orleans is not now a military post; there is no military commander within its limits; it is like an unoccupied fortress, of which an assailant may at any moment take possession. But I do not believe that the constituency represented by you or by me embraces one loyal citizen who would be willing to incur the odium of tearing down the symbol representing the State authority to which New Orleans owes her municipal existence. I am deeply sensible of the distress which would be brought upon our community by a consummation of the inhuman threat of the United States commander; but I cannot conceive that those who so recently declared themselves to be animated by a Christian spirit, and by a regard for the rights of private property, would venture to incur for themselves and the government they represent, the universal execration of the civilized world, by attempting to achieve, through a wanton destruction of life and property, that which they can accomplish without bloodshed, and without a resort to those hostile measures which the law of nations condemns and execrates, when employed upon the defenseless women and children of an unresisting city.

Very respectfully,
JOHN T. MONROE, Mayor.

The following is the resolution of the City Council, after receiving the Mayor's message:

Resolved, That the views communicated by his Honor the Mayor to the Common Council, respecting the answer which it behooves the city of New Orleans to return to the ultimatum of Flag-Officer Farragut, meet the unreserved approbation of this Council, and embody their own views and sentiments, and the Mayor is therefore respectfully requested to act accordingly.

S. P. DELABARRE,
President pro tem. of Board of Ald.
J. MAGIONI,
President Board Asst. Aldermen.

Approved April 28, 1862.
JOHN T. MONROE, Mayor.

A true copy:
M. A. BAKER, Secretary to Mayor.

The following is the Mayor's reply to the communication of Flag-Officer Farragut, received yesterday:

CITY HALL, NEW ORLEANS, April 29, 1862.

To Flag-Officer D. G. Farragut,
U. S. Flag-ship Hartford:

Sir—Your communication is the first intimation I ever had that it was by "your strict orders" that the United States flag was attempted to be hoisted upon certain of our public edifices, by officers sent on shore to communicate with the authorities. The officers who approached me, in your name, disclosed no such order, and intimated no such design, on your part; nor could I have for a moment entertained the remotest suspicion that they could have been invested with such powers to enter on such an errand, while the negotiation for a surrender between you and the city authorities were still pending. The interference of any one, under your command, as long as these negotiations were not brought to a close, could not be viewed by me otherwise than as a flagrant violation of those courtesies, if not the absolute rights, which prevail between belligerents under such circumstances. My views and my sentiments, with reference to such conduct, remain unchanged.

You now renew the demand, made in your former communication, and you insist on their being complied with, unconditionally, under a threat of bombardment within forty-eight hours; and you notify me to remove the women and children from the city that they may be protected from your shells.

Sir, you cannot but know, that there is no possible exit from this city for a population which still exceeds, in number, one hundred and forty thousand, and you must, therefore, be aware of the utter inanity of such a notification. Our women and children cannot escape from your shells, if it be your pleasure to murder them on a mere question of etiquette. But, if they could, there are but few among them who would consent to desert their families and their homes, and the graves of their relatives in so awful a moment; they would bravely stand the sight of your shells, rolling over the bones of those who were once dear to them, and would deem that they died not ingloriously by the side of the tombs erected by their piety to the memory of departed relatives.

You are not satisfied with the peaceable possession of an undefended city, opposing no resistance to your guns, because of its bearing its doom with some manliness and dignity; and you wish to humble and disgrace us by the performance of an act against which our nature rebels. This satisfaction you cannot expect to obtain at our hands.

We will stand your bombardment, unarmed and undefended as we are. The civil world will consign to indelible infamy the heart that will conceive the deed and the hand that will dare to consummate it.

Respectfully,
JOHN T. MONROE, Mayor.

The following letter was received by the Mayor this morning from Flag-Officer Farragut:

U. S. FLAG-SHIP HARTFORD,
At Anchor off the City of New Orleans,
April 29, 1862.

To His Honor the Mayor and City Council of the City of New Orleans:

Gentlemen—The Forts St. Philip and Jackson having surrendered, and all the military defenses of the city being either capitulated or abandoned, you are required, as the sole representative of any supposed authority in the city, to haul down and suppress every ensign and symbol of government whether State or Confederate, except that of the United States. I am now about to raise the flag of the United States upon the Custom-house, and you will see that it is respected with all the civil power of the city.

I have the honor to be, very respectfully, your obedient servant,

D. G. FARRAGUT,
Flag-Officer Western Gulf Blockading Squadron.

Capture of a Confederate Steamer.

AN EXCITING CHASE.

The capture of the steamer Magnolia, as a prize, with a thousand bales of cotton aboard, by two United States steamers engaged in the blockade off the mouth of the Mississippi, has been briefly noticed. The vessel was taken into Key West, where she was condemned, and then sent to New York. The Herald gives the following account of her capture:

At half-past six o'clock, A.M., of February 19, it then being foggy, the Magnolia made her escape through Pass-a-l'Outre, Mississippi river. The fog lifted just as she was passing the United States steamer Brooklyn, which vessel was then engaged in the blockade of that pass, and the latter immediately slipped her cable and started in chase. The Mercedita also gave chase. The Magnolia had got a start of three or four miles before the Brooklyn could get up sufficient steam to go at any speed, and made every endeavor to get to windward of the latter. Captain Craven, however, managed his vessel (the Brooklyn) admirably, and the Magnolia, soon seeing that dodge wouldn't work, changed her course and ran for Mobile.

About ten o'clock A. M. the Brooklyn had gained sufficiently to open fire from her guns, and the shot were from that time to the moment of the capture flying thick and close about the Magnolia. Capt. Shannon, of the latter, with a pertinacity worthy of a better cause, refused to surrender, being determined not to give up, as he afterwards said, so long as his vessel was untouched, or a hope of escape remained. It is perfectly wonderful that so many shots were fired without any of them taking effect; and the fact that the Brooklyn's crew were nearly all men who had hardly ever before fired a gun, furnishes the sole explanation. She had been in commission but a few weeks.

At half-past two, P. M., the blockading vessels off Mobile—the steamers South Carolina, Huntsville and gunboat Hesca—discovered the flying vessel, and soon afterwards the Brooklyn in chase. They all got under way, and were observed by the Magnolia. The South Carolina was blockading the entrance to Mobile bay, to the westward of Sand Island Lighthouse; the other two vessels there to the eastward. As the chance of escaping two vessels was not so good as that of escaping one, Captain Shannon changed the course of the Magnolia to the northwest, hoping to run by the South Carolina and get his vessel on shore. The South Carolina, though broken down and almost disabled, had still enough of Alden's energy in her to block the game, and, opening her fire, the Magnolia soon found her shots coming so close to her that, to use Captain Shannon's words, "it was no use a tryin' any longer;" and so, according to the plan arranged before leaving New Orleans, they attempted to destroy her.

Blowing up the boilers was not a part of the original plan. Some of her pumps had been plugged up before she sailed; and her water pipes were cut, and the appliances for closing them broken off, and other measures that it was thought would inevitably sink her were taken. She was set on fire in several places in her fire room and amongst her cotton, and cans of turpentine were found on some bales and barrels of rosin broken amongst others. Just as these preparations were made, the second engineer, a Mr. Wilde, proposed to Capt. Shannon to blow up the boilers. The latter assented, and the explosion was soon heard. All hands then deserted her, and, in a drenching rain, pulled in the boats to the South Carolina, and surrendered themselves as prisoners. On the way to the latter, Capt. Shannon observed that the vessel was not sinking, and tried to induce his men to return, that they might complete the work of destruction. They refused to go back.

By this time a party of men, headed by Lieut. James Parker, of the South Carolina, had got on board. He was the first person on board, and the first object that met his view was the miserable man who had proposed the explosion, scalded, perfectly white, delirious and dying.

The Magnolia was soon put to rights; the leaks stopped and the fire put out, and that night the South Carolina towed her to Ship Island, where she was repaired and sent to Key West. By decree of the Prize Court there she has been condemned, and sent here for sale. At the time of her capture she had on board about one thousand and fifty bales of cotton, which she brought here also for sale.

She left Key West on Tuesday, 25th ult., and though she has but one boiler that can be used, she made the trip in six days. Since leaving Hatteras she has encountered heavy north-east gales, and has behaved well throughout the passage. Her engine was built at the Atlantic Works in 1857, and works splendidly in all respects. Her draught is very light and speed great, and, when both boilers are in order, will prove, if the government takes her, admirably fitted for service in the shallow bayous of the Gulf States as a gunboat.

Her cargo of cotton will be disposed of by Mr. J. C. Clepp, United States Marshal at Key West, who came to this city on board of the vessel. Yesterday afternoon the steam tug Active went alongside, in order to take off some of her cotton, which will at once be sold at auction—the proceeds, of course, to go into the coffers of our national treasury.

SPECIAL NOTICES.

NOTICE IS HEREBY GIVEN to all persons who purchased goods at our sale on the 23d instant, that the goods purchased by them are now, and have been ready for delivery since the 24th instant, and that payment for the same will be received in Confederate money, and Notes of the State of Louisiana and the City of New Orleans, provided the same be made this day.
All goods not called for will be stored at the risk and sold for account of the purchaser.
ap20 1t McCERREN & LANDRY.

NOTICE—The holder of a certain Note, dated January 25th, 1862, at three months from date, drawn by T. R. BRADY, and payable at Bank of New Orleans, for seven hundred and sixty-five dollars and sixty-four cents ($765 64) received by Mr. William Titterton, will please present the same for payment to the undersigned, as no interest will be allowed on same.
T. R. BRADY & CO.,
Lumber Yard, corner Julia and New Levee streets.
ap30 3t

NOTICE—CONFEDERATE AND CITY NOTES will be received in redemption for all PLEDGES remaining in the LOUISIANA LOAN & DEPOSIT OFFICE, as soon as business is resumed.
J. HART,
ap28 6t¶ 104 Gravier street.

NOTICE TO PASSENGERS ON THE N. O. CITY RAILROAD CARS.—Passengers losing articles in any of the N. O. City Railroad Cars are particularly requested to apply for them at the office of the Company, No. 4 Royal street, when, if they have been found by the drivers, they will be restored to the owners.
Several articles, embracing Ladies' Parasols, Purses, &c., that have been found by drivers of cars and left at the office, have not been called for, which the owners can obtain on application at the office.
ap24 10t WM. P. SINNOTT, Secretary.

GRAND SECRETARY'S OFFICE—Odd Fellows' Hall, New Orleans, April 16th, 1862.
I. O. O. F.—NOTICE TO STOCKHOLDERS IN ODD FELLOWS' HALL—An election for Ten Directors of Odd Fellows' Hall Association will be held in the office of the Grand Secretary, in Odd Fellows' Hall, on MONDAY, 5th May. Polls open from 10 o'clock A. M. to 4 P. M.
ap16td HENRY BIER, Secretary.

REMOVAL—DR. HOWARD SMITH has removed to the north-west corner of Carondelet and St. Joseph streets. ap7 1m*¶

OFFICE COMMISSIONERS SECOND DRAINING DISTRICT—Room No. 22 City Hall—New Orleans, April 5, 1862.
ALL OWNERS OF LANDS lying within the Second Draining District which is bounded below by Julia street and the New Canal, and above by the Jefferson Railroad, and extending from the Mississippi river to Lake Pontchartrain, are hereby notified that the Second Instalment of the assessment for the cost of draining said District is now due, and payable at this office. All bills not paid by the First of July next will be subject to proceedings according to law.
ap6 tjy1 L. H. PLACE, President.

OFFICE N. O. J. AND G. N. RAILROAD—New Orleans, Dec. 14, 1861.—On and after Sunday, the 15th inst., the passenger trains on this road will leave New Orleans at 7 A. M. and 5 P. M. The morning train connects with the Mississippi Central Road, and the evening train with the Southern Road for Mobile.
T. S. WILLIAMS,
de14 General Superintendent.

PELICAN LODGE, CHAPTER AND COUNCIL, No. 15, F.·. A.·. S.·. M.·., will hold its regular Meetings every First and Third SUNDAY of each month, at 11 o'clock A. M., at the Scotch Masonic Temple, Odd Fellows' Hall, corner of Camp and Lafayette streets. All members are requested to be punctual, and visiting B.·. are respectfully invited to attend.
Officers for 1862—Gustavus Devron, T.·. P.·. G.·. M.·.; Wm. R. Miller, 1st Lieut.; J. B. McLin, 2d Lieut.; Michael Hahn, G.·. Orator; Edwin Firth, G.·. Secretary; John Purcell, G.·. Treasurer; Geo. E. Pitcher, G.·. M.·. E.; Placide Bienvenu, G.·. M.·. C.·.; J. W. May, Capt.·. of the Guards.
de24 1y EDWIN FIRTH, Grand Secretary.

UNION LODGE NO. 6, F.·. S.·. M.·., working under the jurisdiction of the Supreme Council of the Sovereign and Independent State of La., meets EVERY TUESDAY EVENING, at 7 o'clock, at their Room, Odd Fellows' Hall.
Officers for the ensuing year—S. H. Brown, V.·. M.·.; F. J. Rice, First Surveill.·.; D. R. Hughes, Second Surveill.·.; Louis Dufau, Orator; Charles Assenheimer, Secretary; F. Sallean, Treasurer; Ph. Helm, M.·. E.·.; Jotham Potter, M.·. of C.·.; Wm. Moales, I.·. G.·.
ja6 CHAS. ASSENHEIMER, Secretary.

CRESCENT LODGE NO. 8, I. O. O. F., Odd Fellows' Hall, Room No. 1.—At a regular meeting of the above Lodge, held on Thursday, July 7, 1859, the following officers were duly installed, to serve during the ensuing term: S. L. Butler, N. G.; George T. Sears, V. G.; Peter Williams, Secretary; O. E. Wilcox, Treasurer.
ju16[Signed] PETER WILLIAMS, Secretary.

DELTA LODGE NO. 15, I. O. O. F.—New Orleans, January 6, 1862.
At a regular meeting of this Lodge, held on the above date the following officers were duly installed to serve for the ensuing term:
A. Muir, N. G.; C. C. Bridges, V. G.; P. C. Carey, Secretary; T. W. Bothick, Treasurer.
ja11 6m P. C. CAREY, Secretary.

F. A. M.—MOUNT MORIAH LODGE, NO. 59, meets EVERY TUESDAY EVENING at 7 o'clock, in the Lodge Room, corner Camp and Lafayette streets. Officers for the year 1862:
John Booth, W. M.; F. W. Delesdernier, S. W.; Wm. D. Bedford, J. W.; Wm. McCulloch, Treas.; Jas. Furneaux, Sec'y; Wm. Ewing, S. D.; J. H. Eckert, J. D.; E. W. Barnes, M. C.; J. G. Dunlap, Chaplain; P. Monson, Tyler; A. Wang and J. McLaughlin, Stewards.
ja11 1y JAS. FURNEAUX, Secretary.

TO PLANTERS.

We are compelled to give notice that we cannot at present receive further orders for goods. The orders received and registered up to this time, accompanied with cotton, cash or drafts, will require all the goods we can make up to the first of September. Planters are hereby notified that we cannot receive any more cotton or orders. Public notice will be given in due time when present engagements will be completed.
ap23 20t S. M. HART & CO.

Wrapping Paper, Twine and Sealing Wax.

POSTOFFICE DEPARTMENT,
Richmond, March 22, 1862.

SEALED PROPOSALS will be received at this Department, until the 10th of May next, at 12 M., for furnishing WRAPPING PAPER, TWINE and SEALING WAX, for the use of the Postoffice Department of the Confederate States, for one year, from and after the date of the execution of the contract. The said articles are to be delivered free of expense, as required, at this Department. The estimated quantity of each article, and the quality thereof, required yearly, is as follows:
2200 Reams Manilla or Sized Wrapping Paper, 20 by 25 inches, and to weigh not less than 24 pounds to the ream, and each ream to contain 20 perfect quires; 10 reams of the same kind of paper, 26 by 32 inches in size and to weigh not less than 34 pounds to the ream.
3000 pounds Cotton Twine, 4 strands, hard twisted, and in balls to weigh 1 pound each; 500 pounds of the same kind of Twine, in spools, each spool to weigh from ½ to 2 pounds.
2000 pounds coarse Hemp Twine, about one-eighth of an inch in diameter, well twisted, and in balls or hanks weighing from 1½ to 2 pounds each.
150 pounds of Scarlet Sealing Wax, of a good quality for ordinary use.
Proposals will be received for each article separately, or for the whole. The contract will be awarded to the lowest and best bidder, the best bid to be determined after a careful examination for the purpose of ascertaining which bid will, in its practical results, be most advantageous to the Department. The Postmaster-General reserves to himself the right to reject any bid where it is apparent that a part of the articles are bid for at a very low and a part at a very high rate, without proper regard to portion each, for the purpose of affecting the aggregate of the bids under the estimate contained in the advertisement.
Samples of each article required must accompany the proposals, and each bidder must furnish with his proposal evidence of his ability to comply with his bid.
Two sufficient sureties will be required to a contract. Failures to furnish the articles contracted for promptly, or furnishing articles inferior to those contracted for, will be considered a sufficient cause for the forfeiture of the contract and the enforcement of the penalty.
Bidders will state the earliest period at which they will be able to furnish supplies of the articles bid for, in the event of the contract being awarded to them, as it will have an important bearing upon the awards. No bids will be considered which fixes a period beyond the 30th of June for the delivery of supplies.
Proposals must be marked on the outside of the envelope, with the name of the article or articles proposed for, and the package containing the proposals addressed to the "Chief of the Appointment Bureau," Richmond, Va.
JOHN H. REAGAN,
ap2 1tw4w Postmaster-General.

The Best Remedy for a Diseased Liver.

DR. THOMAS BLAKE'S AROMATIC BITTERS may be relied on as the most agreeable and efficacious remedy for a Diseased Liver that has ever been discovered. And as there is no complaint that "flesh is heir to" so common as this—which affects every other part of the system—it follows, as a matter of course, that BLAKE'S BITTERS must be the most valuable and popular medicine in the world. Every day certificates are voluntarily sent the Doctor, bearing the most grateful testimony to the excellence and efficacy of these PURELY VEGETABLE BITTERS.
For sale in New Orleans, wholesale and retail, at proprietor's prices, by
J. WRIGHT & CO.,
de11 1y 21 151 and Chartres

MISCELLANEOUS.

THEATRICALS—Wanted, Ten or Twelve YOUNG LADIES, between 9 and 14 years of age, to make up a BALLET CORPS. None need apply unless willing to travel with a company. They will be well cared for, and every pains will be taken to make them comfortable.
For further particulars apply to Mrs. CREED, corner of Common and Dryades streets, entrance 48 Dryades street. ap30 6t*

ALL ABSENT MEMBERS from the SUMTER REGIMENT are expected to report immediately to the Colonel. Transportation can now be obtained on application to the proper quarters.
By order. COL. G. A. BREAUX.
JOHN H. ILSLEY, Adjutant. ap29 1t

HEADQUARTERS EUROPEAN BRIGADE, No. 42 Old Levee street, between Customhouse and Bienville.—New Orleans, 27th April, 1862—11 o'clock A. M.—By order of his Honor Mayor J. T. MONROE, dated this day, I hereby assume the command of all the Foreign Troops.
I call upon all good citizens to give me what aid and assistance they can to preserve order and tranquility in the City, and they are requested to assemble forthwith at a central point in each of their respective Districts, and report immediately to these Headquarters. PAUL JUGE, JR.,
ap28¶ tf General Commanding.

HOOP IRON—14,000 pounds ⅞ inch HOOP IRON, a superior article, in quantities to suit customers. For sale by
F. M. FISK,
ap20 6t No. 135 New Levee street.

SUNDRIES! SUNDRIES! SUNDRIES!
200 Bags Extra FLOUR.
200 Bags Superfine FLOUR.
1000 Bushels WHITE CORN MEAL.
1000 Bushels YELLOW MEAL.
500 Bushels WHITE GRITS.
500 Bushels YELLOW GRITS.
500 Bags RYE FLOUR.
100 Bags UNBOLTED FLOUR.
100 Bags RICE FLOUR.
100 Bags RYE MEAL.
00 Sacks BUCKWHEAT.
500 Bags CORN.
Families supplied. Stuff delivered to all parts of the city free of charge. Prices in conformity to General Order No. 15.
ROBINSON & BRO.,
Eagle Mills, 136 Poydras street,
ma27 0t Between St. Charles and Carondelet.

PRINTERS INK!

SOUTHERN INK MANUFACTURING COMPANY, AMITE, LOUISIANA.
THOS. H. SHIELDS & CO., SOLE AGENTS.
We have just received a large shipment from the manufactory, and are prepared to receive orders. This Ink is warranted equal to any yet made. In all cases orders must be accompanied with the cash.
PRICES—News 25c. to 30c.; Book from 50c. to $2 per pound oc6 1y

THOS. H. SHIELDS & CO.,

Manufacturers and Dealers in
TYPE, PRESSES, INKS;
NEWS, BOOK, WRAPPING AND PRINTING PAPERS;
Envelopes, Cards, Card Boards, Foreign and Domestic Stationery.
59 Gravier street and 10 Bank Place, New Orleans. oc6 1y

WANTS--LOST--FOUND

LOST OR MISLAID, on Tuesday, 29th instant, TWO RINGS, one a plain Cornelian and the other a Blue Enameled Ring, tied up in a handkerchief; also one Ear-Ring. The finder will be liberally rewarded by returning them to No. 188 Fulton street, corner of St. Joseph.
ap30 C. B. SULLIVAN & BRO.

STOLEN FROM THE LEVEE—4 boxes Copper, 28 sacks Wool, 300 sacks Peas, 400 sacks Corn, and Lard and Bacon, to be delivered to the steamer B. L. HODGE.
ap26 3t¶ JOHNSON, Clerk.

WANTED—A Person well acquainted with the manufacture of Star or Stearine Candles. Apply to A. D. GRIEFF & CO.,
ap17 tf Nos. 48, 50 and 52 Old Levee street.

LOST OR STOLEN—On the 21st of January, 1862, a little BOY, named JOHN MITCHELL SULLIVAN, aged 5 years; fair complexion, light brown hair and hazel eyes. Any person giving information to the undersigned of his whereabouts will be liberally rewarded. W. J. SULLIVAN,
ap7 tmy1*¶ McDonoughville.

WANTED—Good BRASS MOULDERS and BRASS FINISHERS. Apply at the Southern Brass Foundry, corner of Fulton and St. Joseph streets.
ma8 tf C. B. SULLIVAN & BRO.

WANTED—THREE good MOULDERS, to whom good wages and steady employment will be given. Apply at
ARMSTRONG'S FOUNDERY,
ma24 tf¶ Cor. New Levee and Erato sts.

$20 REWARD—My GRIFF BOY, DAN, 16 years of age, left about two weeks since. Had on blue cottonade pants and black felt hat. Talks quick and has a scar on his forehead. The above reward will be paid for his arrest.
ARMSTRONG'S FOUNDRY,
ma11 tf Cor. New Levee and Erato sts.

$100 Reward!

RAN AWAY from the undersigned, in February last, the griff boy EDWARD, aged about 33 years, a carpenter by trade and very intelligent, about 5 feet 9 or 10 inches in height, mild spoken and can read and write. Was purchased from Mr. Wharton, De Soto Parish.
I will give the above reward if lodged in any jail in the State, or returned to me at 250 Baronne st.
ja8 tf SAMUEL JAMISON.

MANUFACTURES.

John Armstrong's

FOUNDRY AND BOILER MANUFACTORY,
Corner of Erato and New Levee Streets,
New Orleans, La.

MANUFACTURER of Vertical and Horizontal STEAM ENGINES, SUGAR MILL, Draining Machines, Saw Mills, Cotton Screws and Gearing.
Iron Columns and Fronts of Buildings, Furnace Mouths, Grate Bars, Bone Black, Revivifiers, Gas Retorts, Railroad Frogs, &c. Low Pressure, Locomotives, Flued and Cylinder Boilers of all kinds, Filters, Juice Boxes and Clarifiers, &c. mar2

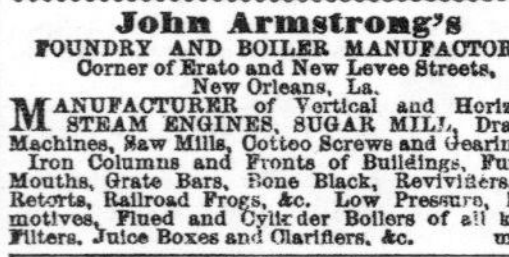

B. ANTOGNINI & E. RICHARD,
15..........Conti Street..........15
MANUFACTURERS OF

Slate-Bed Billiard Tables.

HAVING obtained from M. Berger a certificate, establishing the superiority of their BILLIARD TABLES over those of the other manufactures, and also the privilege of using in future the name of this celebrated professor, deem it their duty to communicate the fact to amateurs. M. Berger, being furthermore desirous of testifying his high appreciation of Messrs. Antognini & Richard's Tables, has ordered, for his private use, a Slate-bed Billiard Table, which he is now using in Havana, and upon which he practiced in this city, at the White Hall, on St. Louis street. Amateurs can call and see certificate.
Will be found in the same establishment a splendid selection of Satin, Oak, Mahogany and Rosewood BILLIARD TABLES, with Slate, Marble or Wood Beds, furnished with the Mechanical Cushions.
Being in connection with European and Northern houses, they offer a complete assortment of French and American Billiard Table Goods—such as Cloths, Balls, Cues, Cue-Cutters, Cue-Leathers, Pool Baskets and Balls, &c., &c.
Also on hand, second-hand Tables, Keno Boxes and Cards, Ten-Pin Balls and Pins, Bagatelles, Pigeon Holes and DOUBLE-WHEEL ROULETTES.
Prices very moderate.
We constantly repair Billiard Cushions of northern factory. no12 1y

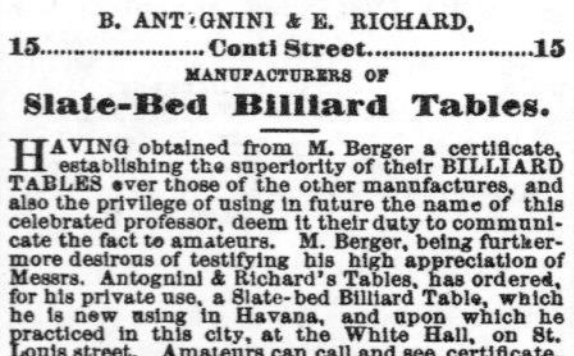

PELICAN

Wagon and Cart Repository.

THE subscribers have on hand, and are constantly receiving from their Manufactory at Pittsburg, Penn., Plantation and Road Wagons, for horses and oxen. Cane Wagons and Carts, Drays, Ox and Timber Wheels, with and without axles; Warehouse and Steamboat Trucks; Jersey and Baggage Wagons, Baggage and other Carts, for horses and oxen; Handcarts, Wheelbarrows of every description, and all other articles in the wheelright line, made of the best seasoned materials, and warranted to be superior to any other manufacture, which will be sold at reduced prices, and lower than any other establishment in the Southern country. Purchasers will find it to their interest to call and examine our stock before purchasing elsewhere. We use none but Black Locust Hubs, with White Oak Spokes and Fellees. All work made by us warranted. Apply to
PHELPS, PARK & CO.,
40, 42 and 44 Perdido street.
N. B.—We keep constantly on hand a large assortment of PLOWS and PLOW POINTS, from the celebrated manufactory of Hall & Speer and R. Hall & Co.

Notice.

ALL Newspapers in the South advertising for us will please change our advertisements, as to location, from St. Louis to 175 Main street, Memphis, Tenn., as we have removed our establishment to the latter place; and all papers heretofore mailed to us at St. Louis, should be mailed to our present address at Memphis. All papers in which we are advertising are requested to notice this.
m POTTER & MERWIN.

HEALTH IS MAN'S CHIEF BLESSING!

"Oh Happiness, how far we flee
From thy own paths in search of thee!
From Health, thy own pure fount, we stray,
Nor God-given instincts e'er obey;
Too proud from Nature's self to learn—
Nature's own remedies we spurn."

WRIGHT'S
SOUTHERN
INDIAN VEGETABLE

PILLS

ARE OFFERED TO THE PEOPLE OF THE
CONFEDERATE STATES OF AMERICA
AS A
PURE, HARMLESS, SIMPLE
AND
NATURAL ALTERATIVE AND BLOOD PURIFIER,
FOR THE
Toning and Fortifying of the System against Diseases, either Occasional or Epidemic; and for the cure of all Ailments having the name of
Intermittent, Remittent, Nervous, Inflammatory and Putrid Fevers; Measles, Small Pox and Erysipelas; Inflammation of the Brain, Throat, Stomach, Lungs, Liver, Intestines, Kidneys and Bladder; Pains in the Stomach, Back and Side; Consumption; Dropsy of the Head, of the Chest, of the Abdomen and of the Limbs; Scrofula, Scurvy and Syphilis; Cancer, Gravel, Loss of Appetite; Sick Headache; Spitting of Blood; Rheumatism, both Acute and Chronic; Diarrhœa, Dysentery and Colics; Syncope, Apoplexy and Paralysis; Dyspepsia, Hypochondriasis, Tetanus, Epilepsy, Whooping Cough, Palpitation of the Heart, Ulcers and Sores of every description; Hysterics, Weak Nerves and Lowness of Spirits; Suppression, and other delicate Female Complaints.

WHAT ARE THESE PILLS?

Composed of the simple extracts of four plants, common to most of the woods in Central Alabama and Mississippi, these pills combine in a remarkable degree the four great curative powers known to modern science, assisting Nature to expell all disease from the system without crushing its elasticity or poisoning its courses by the introduction of nauseous drugs or mineral agents.
There is not a remedy used by the medical profession or known to the scope of science, that combines, in such perfection and with such harmonious results, the four great agencies of health—the *Sudorific* the *Diuretic*, the *Expectorant* and the *Cathartic*.
This is *not a "patent medecine."* These pills have been used for many years, they have been analysed by chemists, they have received the fullest endorsement from the most eminent medical practioners, and *they have never failed of success*.
No pretentions of originality are made in their favor; no assertions of astounding discoveries in some impossible manner are set forth; no effort is made to delude or humbug any one. All that is claimed is, that these pills have been proven to be a remarkable remedy, operating with certainty upon the whole system, prompt in their effect, agreeable in their nature and as harmless for evil as bread and water.

HOW THEY ARE MADE.

Wright's Southern Indian Vegetable Pills have been hitherto solely and are now mainly prepared to fill special orders from physicians, druggists, planters, and other regular customers, who use them altogether on account of their knowledge that they are made of pure, simple and efficacious ingredients; and because of their confidence in Dr. Wright, as being free from the imputation of offering anything to the trade that is not pure and genuine. The new process of distilling the plants and purifying the essential elements from all foreign matter, (which was mainly the discovery of that great chemist, Dr. Torrey,) has alone enabled him to make these pills at a cost sufficiently reasonable to place them before the public as a general remedy. The following certificate from the well-known analytic chemist, Dr. Preston, is a sufficient guarantee of their purity:
DR. JOHN WRIGHT: *Sir*—At your request I have subjected to the test of analysis a quantity of your Southern Indian Vegetable Pills, selected at random, and take great pleasure in certifying that I found them to contain nothing deleterious to the human system, but on the contrary, they possess the Sudorific, Diuretic, Expectorant and Cathartic properties in a remarkably harmonious combination, and my opinion is that they are the greatest universal remedy known to the world. Respectfully,
A. D. PRESTON, M. D.

THEIR USE BY THE PROFESSION.

If the indorsement of their virtues by every leading physician who has tried them, and their general use among their practice, can be a recommendation to the public, then Wright's Southern Indian Vegetable Pills have a claim upon the popular confidence which can be set up for no others that we know of. On this subject we are induced to insert the following extract of a private letter from the venerable Dr. Henshaw, one of the ablest and most experienced leaders of his profession in the whole South:
"It may be said that I am injuring the prestige of my profession by acknowledging how much its services can be dispensed with, but I permit no narrow prejudices of that nature to sway my conscientious sense of duty toward those who have placed their bodily well-being so much in my keeping. I might easily have told them these pills were of my own preparation, but that I adhere to the good old principle: 'Give unto Cæsar the things that are Cæsar's.' My advice to all who are within the range of my practice is, to keep your pills by them, and at the first warning which disease gives them, commence taking them according to the directions, and keep up their use until they are certain they have driven off the enemy. In nine cases out of ten where I am afterwards called in, I only reiterate the same instructions, and my patients recover their health in spite of themselves, and greatly to the annoyance and astonishment of those who firmly believe they cannot be cured of any ailment without swallowing an immense quantity of nauseous and disgusting drugs."

TESTIMONY OF A MINISTER.

In this respect we think it worth while to publish two letters received from gentlemen whose high standing renders their testimony of no little weight with people of common sense. One is from the Rev. J. S. Barret, so widely known and loved throughout Arkansas, and more lately called to a new field of labor in Northern Texas, who wrote to Dr. John Wright, under date of the 20th of September, 1858, as follows:
"You little know the good which has been accomplished already by those few boxes of pills you recomended to me at that visit. They have been a blessing to many an unfortunate member of my little flock and in all this neighborhood they are hailed as the harbinger of health. I am satisfied now, my dear friend, that you even under-estimated their value at the time you explained their effects to me. Such a sure and pleasant remedy was never before given to helpless man by his merciful Author."
The other is from a wealthy and successful planter of Alabama, which we insert entire.

LETTER FROM A PLANTER.

ROSEVALE, ALA., November 4, 1860.
MESSRS. JOHN WRIGHT, & Co., New Orleans, La.
Gents—Inclosed please find my check No. 791, at three days sight, on Mobile, for $149 50, in settlement of account to date. You will please forward to me three dozen boxes more of Wright's Southern Indian Vegetable Pills. They are the greatest thing I ever came across, and save me a heavy medical bill yearly on my place. The directions are so plain and so easily understood that my overseer finds no difficulty in treating every case of sickness that comes to his knowledge, with promptness and perfect success. My negroes are healthier and stronger than those of any plantation I know, and I candidly confess it to be my opinion, and that of my overseer, that this agreeable fact is solely due to the care which is taken of them at the first complaint of sickness, and their being treated by a course of these pills. I use them altogether in my own family, and would not be without a full supply for a small fortune. This may seem high praise to you, but I assure you it is nothing more nor less than the plain, matter-of fact truth. Please forward the pills at once, and by the same route as before. Yours, truly,
THOS. C. HENDERSON.

LIVER COMPLAINT.

From Dr. Humphries, of Charleston, S. C., we have received the following honest letter, written to him by a poor but worthy man who is now a strong and stalwart soldier in the army of Southern independence:
DR. HUMPHRIES: *Dear Sir*—I don't know what to say to make you know how grateful I feel for those boxes of Wright's Southern Indian Vegetable Pills you gave me. After having suffered for so many years, and thought I never was going to get my health or be worth one good day's work, I am now as strong and hearty as I ever was in my life, and that, too, after having tried everything else I ever heard of, and getting all kinds of doctors, who could tell me it was an affection of the liver but could not cure it, although God knows I took enough of their prescriptions. If the prayers of a poor man like me will help you any, doctor, you have mine.
Yours, gratefully and truly,
JOHN W. SIMMONS.

Send for a circular of these pills. It contains full and interesting facts, with important suggestions to the sick and suffering, complete directions for the use of the pills, and a special card to females which every one of the sex ought to read.

WRIGHT'S
Southern Indian Vegetable Pills
Are manufactured expressly for use in the
CONFEDERATE STATES OF AMERICA,
Under the personal direction of Dr. John Wright, in his Pharmaceutical Laboratory, New Orleans.
J. WRIGHT & CO.,
Sole Proprietors,
de1 No. 21 Chartres street, New Orlean

I. O. O. F.

Grand Lodge of Louisiana.

THE R. W. GRAND LODGE OF LOUISIANA, I. O. O. F., meets semi-annually on the Fourth TUESDAYS in January and July, 1862, in Grand Lodge Room, Odd Fellows' Hall, corner of Camp and Lafayette streets, New Orleans:
Officers for the present year—Gardner Smith, of Commercial Lodge, No. 12, M. W. Grand Master; Luther Homes, of Delta Lodge, No. 15, R. W. D. Grand Master; J. F. Caldwell, of Hope Lodge No. 14, R. W. Grand Warden; Henry Bier, of Hope Lodge No. 14, R. W. Grand Secretary; F. W. Delesdiniere, of Southwestern Lodge, No. 40, R. W. Grand Treasurer; H. G. Stetson, of Southwestern Lodge, No. 40, and F. A. Dentzel, of Louisiana Lodge No. 1, Grand Representatives; Rev. J. R. Gutheim, of Howard Lodge, No. 13, W. Grand Chaplain; R. L. Bruce, of Orleans Lodge No. 11, W. Grand Marshal; J. A. Sylvester, of Crescent Lodge, No. 8, W. G. Conductor; G. Tiemann, of Hermann Lodge, No. 39, W. Grand Guardian; John Frankford, of Crescent Lodge No. 8, W. G. Herald.
District Deputy Grand Masters.—John P. Barnett, of Covenant Lodge, No. 17, District No. 2, New Orleans, comprising Washington No. 2, Covenant No. 17, and Columbus No. 24; J. T. Barrett, of Jefferson Lodge, No. 9, District No. 3, New Orleans—Jefferson No. 9 and Pacific No. 33; V. Richard, of Excelsior Lodge, No. 34, District No. 4, Excelsior No. 34; C. N. Ealer, of St. Landry Lodge, No. 25, District No. 6, St. Landry No. 25; J. N. Collins, of De Soto Lodge, No. 7, District No. 7, DeSoto No. 7; John Moore, of New Iberia Lodge, No. 36, District No. 11, New Iberia No. 36; J. C. Loye, of Claiborne Lodge, No. 45, District No. 12—Neith No. 21 and Claiborne No. 45; A. Millspaugh, of Prairie Lodge, No. 37, District No. 13, Prairie No. 37; S. E. Hunter, of Clinton Lodge, No. 27, District No. 14, Clinton No. 27; G. M. Zinser, of Germania Lodge, No. 29, District No. 1—Teutonia No. 10 Independence No. 23 Germania No. 29, Hermann No. 39 and Helvetia No. 44; F. W. Pike, of Assumption Lodge, No. 43, District No. 17, Assumption No. 43.
Standing Committees—State of the Order—P. G. M. Ed. Pilsbury, Templar Lodge No. 16; P. G. M. Richard Swain, of Crescent Lodge, No. 8; and P. G. S. Newberger, of Jefferson Lodge, No. 9. Judicial—P. G.s, James Furneaux, of Southwestern Lodge, No. 40; P. G. Thos. Cripps, of Hope Lodge, No. 14; and Jos. West, of Louisiana Lodge, No. 1. Petition and Appeals—P. G. M., J. G. Dunlap, of Howard Lodge No. 13, P. G., L. F. Tower, of Commercial Lodge No. 12; P. G., D. C. Byerly, of Templar Lodge, No. 16. Legislative—P. D. G. M. Thos. N. Blake, of Commercial Lodge No. 12; P. G., J. H. Gennisson, of Louisiana Lodge, No. 1; P. G., Robt. Pitkin, of Orleans Lodge, No. 8. Finance—P. G. M., H. G. Stetson, of Southwestern Lodge, No. 40; P. G., George Dirmeyer, of Magnolia Lodge, No. 22; P. G., A. Porteous, of Howard Lodge, No. 13. Constitution and By-Laws—P. G. M., Howard Millspaugh, of Covenant Lodge, No. 17; P. G., H. L. Kelsey, Southwestern Lodge, No. 40; P. G., J. M. Winslow, of Washington Lodge, No. 3. Credentials—P. G., F. A. Dentzel, Louisiana Lodge, No. 1; P. G., Josiah Folger, of Union Lodge, No. 6; P. G., J. N. Otto of Independence Lodge, No. 23.
All communications to the R. W. Grand Master or Grand Secretary, should be forwarded to the office of the Grand Secretary, in Odd Fellows' Hall.
HENRY BIER, Grand Secretary.

Subordinate Lodges.

LOUISIANA LODGE No. 1 meets every Friday evening in room No. 5, Odd Fellows' Hall. Officers—W. McConeghey, N. G.; P. P. Walsh, V. G.; Thos. Phillips, Secretary; Joseph West, Treasurer.
WASHINGTON LODGE No. 3 meets every Thursday evening in Marigny Buildings, Third District. Officers—E. H. Garland, N. G.; E. Bezenote, V. G.; Chas. Stanmyer, Secretary; J. M. Winslow, Perm. Secretary; John E. Tallon, Treasurer.
UNION LODGE No. 6 meets every Monday evening in room No. 5, Odd Fellows' Hall. Officers—J. I. Baringer, N. G.; J. C. Cooper, V. G.; Jos. Folger, Secretary; Jno. B. Heno, Treasurer.
CRESCENT LODGE No. 8 meets every Thursday evening in room No. 1, Odd Fellows' Hall. Officers—Mose Mitchell, N. G.; Henry Leith, V. G.; Thos. Moran, Secretary; L. N. Jahan, Per. Secretary; M. H. Meyer, Treasurer.
JEFFERSON LODGE No. 9 meets every Thursday evening in Jefferson Hall, Fourth District. Officers—E. M. Rusha, N. G.; W. Woodson, V. G.; J. W. Allen, Secretary; M. M. Wootan, Per. Secretary; W. Wink, Treasurer.
TEUTONIA LODGE No. 10 meets every Tuesday evening in room No. 2, Odd Fellows' Hall. Officers—S. Gugenheim, N. G.; C. Beddeges, V. G.; F. Heer, Secretary; J. E. Reuter, Per. Secretary; H. C. Finke, Treasurer.
ORLEANS LODGE No. 11 meets every Tuesday evening in room No. 1, Odd Fellows' Hall. Officers—E. L. Bercier, N. G.; John Burrows, V. G.; Newell Guild, Secretary; J. H. Tenney, Treasurer.
COMMERCIAL LODGE No. 12 meets every Wednesday evening, in room No. 5, Odd Fellows' Hall. Officers—J. L. Abright, N. G.; E. Jacobs, V. G.; Geo. Hews, Secretary; L. F. Tower, Per. Secretary; Geo. Graham, Treasurer.
HOWARD LODGE No. 13 meets every Thursday evening in room No. 5, Odd Fellows' Hall. Officers—J. F. Read, N. G.; Michael Woods, V. G.; J. W. Sheerer, Secretary; B. DaSilva, Perm. Secretary; A. DeSola, Treasurer.
HOPE LODGE No. 14 meets every Wednesday evening in room No. 1, Odd Fellows' Hall. Officers—W. F. Sylvester, N. G.; G. W. Roper, V. G.; Jos. Murphy, Secretary; S. M. Todd, Treasurer.
DELTA LODGE No. 15 meets every Monday evening in room No. 1, Odd Fellows' Hall. Officers—A. Muir, N. G.; C. C. Bridges, V. G.; P. C. Carey, Secretary; Luther Homes, Treasurer.
TEMPLAR LODGE No. 16 meets every Friday evening in room No. 1, Odd Fellows' Hall. Officers—J. R. Alexander, N. G.; G. G. Pomet, V. G.; C. G. Warner, Per. Secretary; G. De Castro, Treasurer.
COVENANT LODGE No. 17 meets every Tuesday evening in Marigney Buildings, Third District. Officers—J. P. Baker, N. G.; E. Goldman, V. G.; L. C. Duran, Secretary; John S. Maunsell, Per. Secretary; Howard Millspaugh, Treasurer.
POLAR STAR LODGE No. 19 meets every Wednesday evening in Polar Star room, St. Louis street. Officers—Jules Girard, N. G.; C. Antognini, V. G.; L. Pasquier, Secretary; J. Brussard, Per. Secretary; A. Dudoussat, Treasurer.
MAGNOLIA LODGE No. 22 meets every Tuesday evening in room No. 5, Odd Fellows' Hall. Officers—C. Florat, N. G.; J. Crellin, V. G.; M. Morrison, Secretary; S. Boullemet, Treasurer.
INDEPENDENCE LODGE No. 23 meets every Wednesday evening in room No. 2, Odd Fellows' Hall. Officers—L. Lohmullar, N. G.; G. F. Mathes, V. G.; A. Ernst, Secretary; H. Pressler, Per. Secretary; F. Barthel, Treasurer.
COLUMBUS LODGE No. 24 meets every Wednesday evening in Algiers. Officers—L. Johnson, N. G.; T. F. Nelson, V. G.; J. W. Fitz Henry, Secretary; R. M. Aikeman, Treasurer.
GERMANIA LODGE No. 29 meets every Tuesday evening in Lone Star Hall, Fourth District. Officers—Wm. Sander, N. G.; P. Kettenring, V. G.; Chris. Noesser, Secretary; Chas. F. Burner, Per. Secretary; Wm. Nolting, Treasurer.
PACIFIC LODGE No. 33 meets every Wednesday evening in Pacific Hall, Jefferson City. Officers—Jos. L. Henry, N. G.; Wm. McAree, V. G.; Thomas Booth, Secretary; D. J. Fleury, Treasurer.
HERMANN LODGE No. 39 meets every Wednesday evening in Marigny Buildings, Third District. Officers—Wm. Kraft, N. G.; J. F. Huff, V. G.; J. Kiefer, Secretary; W. Weisheimer, Treasurer.
SOUTHWESTERN LODGE No. 40 meets every Friday evening in room No. 2, Odd Fellows' Hall. Officers—Jotham Potter, N. G.; C. H. Hanna, V. G.; Jas. Furneaux, Secretary; F. W. Delesdernier, Treasurer.
MERCHANTS' LODGE No. 42 meets every Monday evening in room No. 2, Odd Fellows' Hall. Officers—Wm. W. C. King, N. G.; R. A. Howard, V. G.; W. H. Lindo, Secretary; George H. Grieff, Treasurer.
HELVETIA LODGE No. 44 meets every Thursday evening, in Helvetia Hall, Jefferson City. Officers—Peter Siren, N. G.; Fred. Erz, V. G.; George Springer, Secretary; Daniel Weidner, Per. Secretary; H. Rau, Treasurer.

Interior Lodges.

DE SOTO LODGE No. 7 meets at Baton Rouge on Thursday evenings. Officers—No returns.
NEITH LODGE No. 21 meets at Shreveport on Wednesday evenings. Officers—N. Seligman, N. G.; H. Linman, V. G.; F. W. Spieker, Secretary; A. Shaffner, Treasurer.
ST. LANDRY LODGE No. 25 meets at Opelousas every Saturday evening. Officers—Omer Poiret, N. G.; C. H. Potier, V. G.; S. P. Clark, Secretary, C. Ealer, Treasurer.
CLINTON LODGE No. 27 meets at Clinton on Wednesday evenings. Officers—No returns.
EXCELSIOR LODGE No. 34 meets at Thibodaux on Saturday evenings. Officers—A. Robichaud, N. G.; H. Hoffmann, V. G.; C. P. Binnings, Secretary; V. Sancon, Per. Secretary; H. Cazenavette, Treasurer.
NEW IBERIA LODGE No. 36 meets at New Iberia on Saturday evenings. Officers—Wm. A. Robert, N. G.; W. G. Daunt, V. G.; L. Siegel, Secretary; John Moore, Treasurer.
PRAIRIE LODGE No. 37 meets at Washington on Saturday evenings. Officers—No report.
ASSUMPTION LODGE No. 43 meets at Napoleonville on Saturday evenings. Officers—No returns.
CLAIBORNE LODGE No. 45 meets at Minden on Thursday evenings. Officers—J. C. Loye, N. G.; M. C. Smith, V. G.; R. A. Johnson, Secretary; J. G. Lewis, Treasurer.
HENRY BIER, Grand Secretary.

"Odd Fellows' Rest."

BOARD OF DIRECTORS FOR 1861—Officers—Gardner Smith, President; S. Boullemet, Treasurer; Henry Bier, Secretary; Daniel Merritt, Sexton. Cemetery Committee—Henry Bier, B. DaSilva, J. A. Sylvester. Finance Committee—Jos. West, J. M. Winslow, James Furneaux. Members—James Furneaux, R. W. Grand Lodge; Jos. West, Louisiana Lodge No. 1; J. M. Winslow, Washington Lodge No. 3; A. W. Hyatt, Union Lodge No. 6; J. A. Sylvester, Crescent Lodge No. 8; J. H. Tenny, Orleans Lodge No. 11; Gardner Smith, Commercial Lodge No. 12; B. DaSilva, Howard Lodge No. 13; Henry Bier, Hope Lodge No. 14; T. W. Bothick, Delta Lodge No. 15; T. F. Bragg, Templar Lodge No. 16; A. Caillier, Polar Star Lodge No. 19.
VAULTS, and the opening of the same, must be applied for at the office of the Secretary, Odd Fellows' Hall, corner Camp and Lafayette streets.
Price of Lots and Vaults—Regular lots, 10 ft. square, $150; ditto, 7 by 9 feet, $75. Vaults, (double) to Stockholding Lodges, $55; ditto, to all others, $60; single, to Stockholding Lodges, $45; to others, $50.
Vaults cannot be opened unless a certificate of ownership be first obtained from the Secretary.
Information relative to the purchase of lots, etc., can be had on application to
HENRY BIER, Secretary O. F. Rest.

General Relief Committee I. O. O. F

This body meets on the First Friday of each month, at the office of the Grand Secretary, Odd Fellows' Hall, at 7 o'clock P. M.
D. C. BYERLY, President.
HENRY BIER, Secretary and Treasurer.

FOR SALE----TO RENT.

A DESIRABLE LOT within half a block of the City Railroad for Sale, for Confederate Notes. The above Lot is on Music street, near the corner of Love street, Third District. It is well filled and fenced with plank boards. The banquette is paved and paid for. There are shade trees planted on the banquette and in the rear of the lot; and it is in a very quiet neighborhood. Most of the residents living around are small property owners.
Apply to Mr. JAS. O'HANLON, grocer, corner of Love and Music streets. ap27 7t

FOR SALE OR RENT, in Covington, La., a COTTAGE-HOUSE, situated right in front of the Stone Spring; all newly finished. The plan of the House can be seen by calling at Mr. A. HERBEZ'S, No. 187 St. Peter street, between Marais and Tremé.
ap16 12t*

TO RENT—A SUIT OF ROOMS fronting on St. Charles street, opposite Lafayette Square. Will be rented together or singly, to gentlemen or families. Attached to the above is a fine bath-room. Apply to 153 St. Charles street. ma4

For Sale.

300 Barrels First Quality CEMENT.
10 Kegs PRESSED SPIKES—7 Inches.
Apply to DENNIS CRONAN,
de10 tf¶ Mechanics' Exchange.

LEGAL NOTICES.

Succession of Ramon Farias.

SECOND DISTRICT COURT OF NEW ORLEANS. No. 11,233.
BY McCERREN & LANDRY—G. W. McCerren, Auctioneer—Office and Salesroom, Masonic Hall, St. Charles st.—Will be sold at the Merchants and Auctioneers' Exchange, on SATURDAY, May 10, at 12 o'clock, by virtue of and in pursuance to an order from the Hon. J. Bermudez, Judge of the Second District Court of New Orleans, rendered in the matter of the above succession, dated New Orleans, April 4th, 1862—
The following described LOT OF GROUND in the First District, in the square bounded by Gravier, Liberty, (late St. Paul,) Howard, (late Gironde,) and Perdido streets, measuring 18 feet front on Gravier, by 100 feet on the division line next to Liberty street, thence running in the rear on a straight line towards Howard, (late Gironde,) thence 38 feet 5 inches and 3 lines, thence to the front 10 feet 11 inches, thence running in an oblique line in the rear of the lot next to Howard street 21 feet, and thence to the place of beginning on the division line of the lot next to Howard street 100 feet—all American measure.
All as per plan exhibited at the Merchants and Auctioneers' Exchange.
Act of sale before M. Hahn, notary public, at the expense of the purchaser.
Terms—Cash.

Succession de Ramon Farias.

DEUXIEME COUR DE DISTRICT DE LA NOUVELLE-Orléans—No. 14 233.
PAR McCERREN & LANDRY—G. W. McCerren, encanteur—Bureau et salle de ventes à l'Hôtel des Franc-Maçons, rue St.-Charles—En vertu d'un ordre émané de l'Hon. J. Bermudez, Juge de la Deuxième Cour de District de la Nouvelle-Orléans, rendu dans l'affaire de la dite succession, daté Nouvelle-Orléans, le 4 avril 1862, il sera vendu à la Bourse des Négociants et Encanteurs, SAMEDI, le 10 mai 1862, à midi la propriété suivante:
UN TERRAIN situé dans le Premier District, dans l'îlet borné par les rues Gravier, Liberté, (anciennement St. Paul,) Howard, (anciennement Gironde,) et Perdido, mesurant 18 pieds de face à la rue Gravier, sur 100 pieds de profondeur sur la ligne de division après la rue Liberté de là courant sur une ligne droite dans le fond du côté de la rue Howard, (anciennement Gironde,) de là 38 pieds 5 pouces et 3 lignes, de là à la façade 10 pieds 11 pouces, de là courant sur une ligne oblique dans le fond du terrain après la rue Howard 21 pieds, et de là au point de départ sur la ligne de division du terrain après la rue Howard 100 pieds—le tout mesure américaine.
Le tout d'après plan exposé à la Bourse des Négociants et Encanteurs.
Acte de vente pardevant M. Hahn, notaire public, aux frais de l'acquéreur.
Conditions—Comptant. ap8 13 my4 9 10

HOFFMAN & MARKS,

(James Hoffman, Auctioneer,)
No. 63 CHARTRES STREET, NEW ORLEANS,
having opened a general Auction business, are ready to receive Goods on consignment, and will give their punctual attention to in and out-door sales.
ap5 1mo

Pure Lard Oil and Stearine,

MANUFACTURED AND
FOR SALE BY A. D. GRIEFF & CO.,
Nos. 48, 50 and 52 Old Levee st.,
ap13 tf New Orleans.

SEED RICE
AND
COW PEAS! COW PEAS,
In Lots to suit Purchasers,
FOR SALE BY
CUCULLU & JULIAN,
ma30 1m 30 Poydras street.

HOMINY! HOMINY!
50 bbls. CREOLE HOMINY, for sale by
ROBINSON & BRO.,
EAGLE MILLS,
136 Poydras street, between St. Charles and Carondelet streets. ma6 60t

CRACKED CORN! CRACKED CORN!

500 Bags CRACKED CORN, for sale by
ROBINSON & BRO.,
EAGLE MILLS,
136 POYDRAS STREET.
Corn Cracked to order. ja31 90t

THE OLD ESTABLISHED JOHN TOOLE REMITTANCE OFFICE.
THE undersigned continue the usual facilities this long established office has for many years afforded.
Remittance to England, Ireland and Scotland, in sums to suit; passengers having careful attention and comfort; claims collected on accommodating terms, in either country.
Letters from a distance, post-paid, will have prompt attention.
ROBINSON & OLIVER, Agents.
ja22 6md&1tW 28 Bank Place.

Fruit, Shade and Ornamental Trees.

EVERY description of Fruit, Shade and Ornamental TREES, SHRUBBERY and Greenhouse PLANTS, Fine ROSES, &c., of his own growth, can be obtained at the establishment of
JOHN M. NELSON, Camp street,
Opposite Lafayette Square, New Orleans.
All Plants warranted free of Coco. fe8 3m

To Jewelers, Dentists, Gilders and Platers

F. WALLACH, GOLD AND SILVER REFINER, Assayer and Sweep Smelter.
Notifies that he buys all sweepings, clippings and ashes; also, old Gold and Silver.
Office, 97 Canal street; Refinery, 117 Circus street. Persons residing in the country can address him care of S. MARX, No. 97 Canal street, Importer and Dealer in Watches, Jewelry, &c. ma12 3m¶

Notice to those Afflicted.

DR. MULLEN has removed from No. 86 Customhouse street to No. 95 EXCHANGE PLACE. The reputation of the writer is so well established that all that is necessary to say to those who have contracted any of those dreadful diseases known and called SECRET DISEASES, in any part of their various forms, is that the writer, after a most successful practice of twenty-six years, confined strictly to Venereal Diseases and Diseases of the Blood, (having created and relieved many who were past all hope, many of whom had been under the treatment of eminent physicians, without receiving any benefit whatever,) is enabled to offer you positively a safe, certain and speedy cure. Should any of the unfortunately afflicted see this short advertisement, they will do well to call at No. 95 Exchange Place before applying elsewhere, and avail themselves of the subscriber's long and successful experience.
B. F. MULLEN, No. 95 Exchange Place,
my20 between Bienville and Conti streets.

T. W. Bothick, Undertaker,

LAFAYETTE STREET, between Liberty and Howard sts., New Orleans.
Metallic, Mahogany Black Walnut and Oak COFFINS always on hand.
Hearses, Carriages and Cabs for hire. Funerals attended to in person by the proprietor; and he hopes, by strict attention, to obtain a share of public patronage. se18 59 y

DR. MULLEN has removed from No. 86 Customhouse street to No. 95 EXCHANGE PLACE. Strangers in the city see Dr. Mullen's advertisement in the other columns of this paper. He is one of the very best in his profession now in the United States. All that stand in need would do well to give him a call. No. 95 Exchange Place.

JOHN TURPIN, 129 Common street, Importer of Wines, Brandies, &c., &c. Sole Agent for Jeffrey's Edinburgh Ales, &c. Nathaniel Johnston & Son's Clarets in casks and cases; Hennessy Brandy, in half and quarter pipes; Old Port, Blackburn, Madeira and Sherry Wines; Scotch and Irish Whisky, Jamaica and Santa Cruz Rums, London Cordial Gin, Boker's Bitters, &c.; Champagne, Piper Heidsick, Sparkling Hock, Moselle, Bass' London Porter, India Pale Ale, &c., quarts and pints. ap13 1y

A. D. DONOVAN, COTTON FACTOR, Commission and Forwarding Merchant, No. 51 Carondelet street, (Union Row,) New Orleans. y29 1y

The Daily True Delta
Home Department.

Common Council.

The two Boards met last evening, and adjourned to meet to-day at twelve o'clock.

The Great Agony Over.

The Mayor did not haul down the flag of Louisiana, which floated from the dome of the City Hall, the women and children were not removed from the city, and Capt. Farragut did not execute his threat to bombard it. But the captain did send two hundred armed marines ashore, yesterday, with two howitzers, to protect the individuals who were to perform the feat of hauling down our State flag and hoisting the Federal flag over the Customhouse. We were in error in stating that the Federal flag was to be raised over the City Hall, which error arose from the fact that a flag of that description was taken into the City Hall. Neither was the Federal flag raised over the Mint, which was understood to be part of the programme.

Sun-Struck.

It was rumored quite currently last evening that three of the Federal marines sent ashore yesterday to aid in hauling down our State flag from the City Hall and hoisting the Federal flag over the Custom-house, were sun-struck as they were returning to their vessels, while on the levee—one of them very severely. We were not on the levee, consequently cannot vouch for the truthfulness of the report. But we do know that the sun does have a very serious effect upon the unacclimated.

Police Items.

Notwithstanding the intense excitement of the last few days, the police reports have furnished us but very few items. There have been a considerable number of arrests, but they have been mostly for petty offenses, such as getting drunk, lying on the banquet or in the streets, or disturbing the peace. There have been several arrested as dangerous and suspicious characters. This state of things is attributable in no small degree to the closing of the coffee-houses and the efficient service rendered the police by the European Brigade.

Európean Brigade.

Our citizens owe a deep debt of gratitude to the European Brigade for the prompt and efficient aid it has rendered during the last few days of excitement, in preserving the order and quiet of the city, and protecting the lives and property of our citizens. And yesterday, when it was understood that the brigade was about to disband, some of our citizens waited upon the officers and requested them to continue their valuable services a few days longer, the command readily responded to the request, for which they deserve much credit and the lasting thanks of every lover of peace and good order.

Keep Cool.

That our citizens have had cause for the most intense excitement for the last four or five days, there is no denying. But uncertainty has resolved itself into certainty; we have all been grievously disappointed, if not grossly deceived, and we may as well accommodate ourselves to a state of things we cannot now avoid or easily change. Keeping up the excitement will do no good, but may result in much harm. The warm and unhealthy season is rapidly approaching, which should warn us to beware of undue excitement and unnecessary exposure to the sun. We have noticed many upon the streets and levee led there by the existing excitement, exposing themselves to the scorching rays of the noonday sun, who, we know, are unused to such exposure. The result of this will be unfavorable to health. This season has been more backward than usual, and the heat of summer is coming upon us all of a sudden, which will be very apt to produce disease, let us be ever so careful of our persons.

Sudden Death.

Yesterday afternoon, about four o'clock, a man died very suddenly at Greenwood Cemetery. The Coroner was notified of the fact late last evening. We have had a greater number of sudden deaths this season than we remember having occurred any previous year.

The Sinking of the McRae.

The officers and men of the Confederate steamer McRae feel much chagrined at the imputation cast on them by Commodore Farragut—that of sinking their vessel in port while she was under a flag of truce. The officers and men of the McRae may make themselves easy in this matter, as no one of common sense would suppose them guilty of such a foolish act. The boat, from the injuries received by her in the naval conflict above the forts, could no longer float.

Burning the Cotton on the Coast Plantations.

We learn from a gentleman who arrived in this city yesterday from Baton Rouge, having made the trip in a skiff, that Gov. Moore issued a proclamation on Saturday last, requesting the cotton planters of the State to burn all the cotton. Our informant states that the recommendation seemed to be universally complied with, as the river banks between here and Baton Rouge presented one sheet of flame as he passed along.

HENRY McGUINN,
DEALER IN
OAK, ASH AND PINE WOOD,
SAND, SHELLS, &c.
Office, corner Magnolia and Julia streets, (opposite the Bridge.)
All orders left at the Mechanics' and Dealer, Exchange, Box No. 16, will be promptly attended to—wishing his portion of the public patronage, and that of his former friends and acquaintances.
ja tf

SOUTHERN BRASS FOUNDRY.
NOS. 2, 4 AND 6 ST. JOSEPH STREET, AND No. 188 FULTON STREET.
At the SOUTHERN BRASS FOUNDRY all kinds of Brass work necessary for Gas, Steam, or Water Fixtures is manufactured.
Also, Plumbers' Brass work, of all descriptions, including Globe, Valve, Gauge, Cylinder, Bib and Stop Cocks, &c.
Also, Military Brass and Iron work, of all kinds, done with dispatch and at the lowest possible rates.
Brass Castings made at the shortest notice.
ma8 tf C. B. SULLIVAN & BRO.

Gas Fixtures.

THE undersigned begs leave to call the attention of his patrons and the public in general to his large and well assorted stock of Gas Fixtures of the newest and most elegant designs, such as Chandeliers, Pendants, Brackets, &c. Also, a choice selection of Globes, of every pattern and shape.
Chandeliers repaired and bronzed.
WM. SOMMER, Gas Fitter,
82 and 84 Baronne street,
between Union and Perdido streets.
N. B.—Dwellings, Stores, Offices, &c., fitted up at the shortest notice and at moderate rates. ap7 tf

For Gonorrhœa, Gleet, Weakness, Pains in the Back Stricture, and all Urinary Affections.
THE GREAT ENGLISH REMEDY, SPECIFIC SOLUTION.—This world-renowned preparation cures all affections of the generative organs, whether recent or chronic. Physicians of England, of France, and of America, acknowledge its efficacy. Thousands of sufferers have been relieved by it. Purely vegetable in composition, it is as harmless as it is efficacious. The system becomes invigorated, and the debilitated body and depressed mind are restored energy.
Sole Agent for the United States,
B. ABRAMS, Apothecary,
14 Camp st., corner Gravier.

CONERY, E., Wholesale Grocer, No. 2 Front street, opposite Canal street Ferry Landing, has constantly on hand a large and complete assortment of Groceries, for sale at the lowest cash prices and on the most reasonable terms. se9 1y

DR. S. B. LEFEBVRE, No. 249 Common street. Office hours—from 7 to A. M., 12 to 1 P. M., and to 7 P. M.

The Daily Delta.

VOL. XVII. NEW ORLEANS, THURSDAY, MAY 1, 1862. NO. 128.

Shinplasters and Confederate paper will be received in payment for board and tuition, at Prof. Brett's, 13 St. Charles street.

Citizens of New Orleans.

The Common Council have passed the following resolutions:

Resolved, That the Mayor be, and is hereby, authorized to organize, outside of the regular police of the city of New Orleans, a Citizens' Police in each Precinct, and for that purpose to summon and compel service in the respective precinct of any resident.

Resolved, That every citizen is bound to comply with the orders he may receive from his Honor the Mayor to perform special duty on the police.

Resolved, That the Special Police so appointed shall wear a badge and carry such arms as the Mayor may determine.

S. P. DELABARRE,
President pro tem. Board of Aldermen.
J. MAGIONI,
President Board of Assistant Aldermen.

I hereby notify all good citizens to report to Paul Juge fils, General Commanding European Brigades, who is invested by me with full authority to act for the preservation of the public peace. Gen. Juge is authorized in my name to disperse all assemblies composed of more than six persons.

JOHN T. MONROE,
Mayor of the City of New Orleans.

Approved April 30, 1862. myl 2p1f

To All Good Citizens.

You are hereby requested, in compliance with the Mayor's Proclamation, issued yesterday, to repair to the places hereinafter mentioned, at 9 o'clock precisely THIS MORNING, to aid and assist me in preserving peace and order:

At least 100 citizens of the Second District, at Gen. Maignan's Headquarters, Rampart street, between Main and St. Philip.

At least 50 citizens of the First District, at the Headquarters of Col. de la Valle, No. 5 Front Levee.

At least 50 citizens of the First District, at the Headquarters of Col. Fogo, No. 89 Gravier street.

At least 100 citizens of the Second District, at Col. Manint's Headquarters, Customhouse street, between Royal and Bourbon.

At least 50 citizens of the Second District, at the Headquarters of Col. Ferrier, Hospital street, between Royal and Bourbon.

At least 50 citizens of the Third District at Col. Avendano's Headquarters, corner of Elysian Fields and Greatmen streets.

At least 50 citizens of the Fourth District, at Col. Artigue's Headquarters, corner of Chippewa and Louisiana avenue.

It is important that all good citizens should be punctual to this call.

PAUL JUGE FILS,
General Commanding Foreign Brigades.

myl 2p

Notice by the Mayor.

MAYORALTY OF NEW ORLEANS,
City Hall, April 29, 1862.

The public are hereby notified that the European Brigade, Paul Juge fils, General Commanding, have been requested and have consented to continue patrolling the city, in conjunction with the ordinary police, for the purpose of preserving peace and order. It is hoped that all good citizens will contribute their assistance in this effort to maintain the tranquility of the city.

apr30 5t2dp JOHN T. MONROE Mayor.

Proclamation by the Mayor.

MAYORALTY OF NEW ORLEANS,
City Hall, April 29, 1862.

It is requested that all citizens retire to their homes during the performance by the United States forces of those acts of authority which it would be folly to resist. Any violence or disorder would be productive of the most serious disasters, and entail danger and suffering on the unresisting population of the city.

Fellow-citizens, the honor and dignity of New Orleans have been maintained. The flag of Louisiana is not to be removed from this building by any act of your authorities, but by those who have the power and the will to exercise it.

You are enjoined to preserve order, and that silence, more eloquent than words, which befits so solemn an occasion.

apr29 2p JOHN T. MONROE, Mayor.

Proclamation by the Mayor.

MAYORALTY OF NEW ORLEANS,
City Hall, April 26, 1862.

To the Keepers of Grocery and of Provision Stores:

The city authorities request that all keepers of Grocery Stores and other establishments where Provisions are sold, immediately open their respective places of business, and not force the authorities to measures they would wish to avoid. It is also recommended that the ordinary currency continue to be received. It is as good now as it ever has been, and there is no reason to reject it. Those who refuse to receive it must share the evils and inconveniences they thus participate in inflicting on the community. It is hoped that a spirit of accommodation will now be evinced by all persons. Those individuals who hold Confederate money, and wish to part with it, can have it exchanged for City Bills by applying to the Committee of Public Safety.

For the better preservation of public order, it is particularly desired that all citizens be at home by 9 P. M., and that ladies and children remain within doors as much as possible.

ap27 2p5t JOHN T. MONROE, Mayor.

Proclamation by the Mayor.

MAYORALTY OF NEW ORLEANS,
City Hall, April 26, 1862.

The sad and melancholy circumstances through which we are passing require the utmost wisdom and forbearance on the part of our citizens. They should not suffer themselves to be carried away by too keen a sense of the difficulties by which they are surrounded, but ought, on the contrary, to aid the Municipal Authority in maintaining order in the city. To facilitate my duties as the constituted Chief of the Police, I have called to my assistance the services of the European Brigade, and they have been invested by me with the duty of watching over the public tranquillity. Patrols, under the direction of the commanding officer of said Brigade, should be treated with respect and obeyed.

JOHN T. MONROE, Mayor.

Approved April 26, 1862.
WM. FREER, Chairman Safety Committee.

Committee of Public Safety.

NEW ORLEANS, April 28, 1862.

Resolved, That the Committee of Public Safety will receive, until further notice, the following individual and other small Notes circulated as money in this community, and that they believe our citizens may rely on this currency.

Resolved, That this Committee will add to this list such other names as they may deem worthy of the confidence of the community.

State Treasury Notes.
Confederate Notes.
Magee & George.
J. & J. C. Davidson.
Leeds & Co.
Henderson & Gaines.
Thomas, Griswold & Co.
Thos. C. Payan.
Jackson Railroad Company.
H. Fassman & Co.
City of Baton Rouge.
City of New Orleans.
C. W. Cammack.
McDonel & Magraw.
Geo. W. Gregor & Co.
Dan Edwards & Son.
Joseph Santini.
Jacob Zolly.
Smith & Hine, or Stuart & James.
H. E. Lawrence, or P. Cazenave.
D. M. Hildreth & Co.
Cresap & McMillan.
Sam'l Bell.
Picayune Office.
D. H. Holmes.
J. Hockersmith & Co.
Britton & Co.

A true extract from the minutes.

ap29 2ptf GEO. C. LAWRASON, Secretary.

Fire Department.

OFFICE CHIEF ENGINEER FIRE DEPARTMENT,
New Orleans, April 29, 1862.

The members of the Fire Department are hereby notified that on the alarm of ten taps of the fire alarm bells they are to immediately assemble at their different Engine and Hook and Ladder Houses.

At the alarm of one tap repeated three times the Assistant Engineers and commanding officers of companies will immediately proceed to the office of the Chief Engineer to receive orders.

In case the alarm is given for any of the regular Fire Districts, the companies performing duty in the district for which the alarm is given, will immediately proceed to the location of the alarm.

All companies are hereby notified to continue to perform their duty as heretofore, and use all their exertions in the preservation of life and property.

apr29 DAVID BRADBURY, Chief Engineer.

Headquarters European Brigade.

NEW ORLEANS, April 27, 1862—11 o'clock A. M.

By order of his Honor Mayor J. T. MONROE, dated this day, I hereby assume command of all the Foreign Troops.

I call upon all good citizens to give me what aid and assistance they can to preserve order and tranquility in the city, and they are requested to assemble forthwith at a central point in each of their respective Districts and report immediately to these Headquarters, No. 42 Old Levee street, between Bienville and Customhouse.

PAUL JUGE FILS,
General Commanding.

ap28 2ptf

Fifty Dollars Reward.

LOST, on the evening of the 27th of April, between the hours of 6 and 9 o'clock, in the Third District, one pair of diamond Ear-rings, four diamonds in each; one pair of emerald Ear-rings, one large diamond Ring, one diamond Ring, enameled, with the inscription "Bob to Rite" inside, and one diamond Ring set in the center of a small black stone. They were all locked together in one of the ear-rings. The finder will receive the above reward by leaving them at the office of the Delta with the cashier. apr28 2ptf

Notice.

NEW ORLEANS, April 28, 1862.

It having been found impracticable to distribute provisions through the Free Market, as advertised in yesterday's papers, in addition to those already having tickets, other arrangements will be made as soon as practicable, and due notice will be given thereof through the newspapers.

JOHN T. MONROE, Mayor.

City papers copy. apr28 3t2p

THE DAILY DELTA

GEN. LOVELL'S LETTER.—The letter written by Gen. Lovell, and published in yesterday's Delta, was intended to be addressed to the editors of this paper, and should have appeared in that form in our columns.

THE SURRENDER OF THE FORTS.

The circumstances which led to the surrender of Fort Jackson, after its gallant defense, are most melancholy and mortifying. We can well appreciate and sympathize with the feeling of indignation and disgust with which the senior officers refer to those circumstances. The first of these causes of our defeat was the want of command, organization and energy in our squadron. The commanders refused or failed to watch and defend the chains and other obstructions below the forts; they would not, even under the protection of the guns of the fort, perform this duty, and the enemy actually succeeded in cutting away these obstructions, which they could not have done if the gunboats had taken the places they were directed to take in order to guard the chains. The Louisiana, with its powerful battery, was rendered of no use by the refusal of the commander in charge of her to place her in a position where she might have been effective, and where she would have materially aided the forts, and, in the opinion of experienced officers in the forts, would have prevented the passage of the United States ships. The next delinquency of the gunboats was in failing to keep the river lighted. As long as this duty was confided to the fort it was promptly and regularly done, but when the ships undertook it, it was grossly neglected. On the night (Thursday) when the enemy effected his passage, it was entirely omitted, though it was perceived by the commandant of Fort Jackson that the enemy was preparing to force a passage. There was no light by which the ships could be seen until they were near the fort, and the smoke from the first discharge of the guns of the fort obscured the view so that but little time was allowed to play upon them. There was from the beginning a lamentable want of system, organization and discipline in the squadron, which, under proper command, it is believed might have been arrested by our squadron alone. Under these circumstances we are not astonished that the men in the fort became dispirited. But there was nothing to justify their open and violent mutiny. For this they merit universal denunciation and execration. It was true some of the enemy's ships had passed the fort, but it was still in good fighting condition, and if the men had stood by their officers, the remainder of the squadron would have been kept from passing, and the ships which had passed would have been left in an isolated and perilous position. The enemy had already offered honorable terms of surrender, which Col. Higgins declined. Capt. Porter, commanding the mortar fleet, had written a letter, acknowledging the heroism and stubborness of the defense, and soliciting a termination of a conflict, the result of which was only a question of time. This demand, the second made by him, showed the enemy's anxiety to bring the fight to a close. There was no difficulty in interpreting its meaning and motive. It was rejected, and the commander of the fort set to work to repair damages for a renewal of the combat. In expectation of such renewal, Gen. Duncan issued an address complimenting the garrison for its heroic perseverance, thanking them for their patience, fortitude and resolution, and urging them to further efforts and sacrifices, and the result would be a glorious victory. By some traitorous means it had been communicated to the men that the city had surrendered, that further resistance would be unavailing, and that if the conflict was continued, and the garrison captured, they would all be put to the sword.

Under these influences the men arose at midnight, spiked some of the guns, dismounted others, and openly resisted and defied the authority of the officers. There was one honorable exception to this disgraceful and shameful conduct. The St. Mary's Cannoneers, a country volunteer company, took no part in these mutinous proceedings, and were faithful to the last. Every officer of the garrison stood bravely to his post. They were all filled with mortification at the conduct of the men, who, during a bombardment of eight days and nights, had behaved so bravely and manfully. A most noble and heroic defense was thus sullied by the most shameful abandonment of duty on the part of the men. Their conduct, however, only serves to brighten by contrast the luster of the courageous devotion of the gallant commander and his officers. All honor, then, to the heroic Duncan, Higgins, and their associates, in one of the most brilliant actions of this war!

THE STATUS OF OUR CITY.

We presume the forces of the United States will land in the course of the day and take military possession of the city. We repeat what we have before said, that their landing should not only be unopposed, but that it would be unbecoming and improper for the people to indulge in any expressions of a hostile or insulting character towards them. There is nothing submissive or cringing in such a course. It is due to the victor that when a virtual surrender is made, he should not be interrupted in the exercise of the rights of conquest by those who have been included in the surrender. This is not only the legal course, but it is that which policy and our own interests and those of our country demand. By placing ourselves in the position of a defeated people, which is our true and only status, we come under the protection of the laws of nations and of war, which prescribe the power and duties of the victor and the vanquished. The security of personal and private property, an immunity from military violence, and the investment of the victor with all the duties and responsibilities of the police and government of the city, are some of the consequences and incidents of this relation. The moment the city is occupied by the enemy the powers and functions of all other magistrates cease, or become dependent on his will. The whole care and responsibility of the government are devolved upon the victor.

It is barely possible the U. S. authorities may assume the position that this is a rebellion and that all the people who directly or indirectly have sanctioned the resistance to the domination of the United States are to be treated as rebels. Untenable as this position may be, it can have no sanction or authority in law, reason or fact, and we doubt if it will be insisted upon, if our whole people *are true to themselves, their oaths, their consciences and their duty.* But if any give way, if ever so small a number submit to the demand that they should declare their allegiance to the conqueror, they will stimulate and encourage the U. S. authorities to persecute and outrage those who can not in conscience and honor make such submission.

If we are unanimous, if the whole people stand together, if one sentiment and will prevail, there is little danger of the United States achieving anything valuable or encouraging by its military occupation of the city. It was thus the people of Moscow and of Madrid bore themselves when their cities were occupied by two hundred thousand French soldiers. Napoleon said he could "conquer their armies, but not their affections." The consequences of any attempt to divide the people—to create factions, to excite animosities among citizens—would be deplorable indeed. Whatever may be the issue of our present unfortunate condition, nothing could so add to its horrors as any such division among our own people.

When the United States authorities take possession, the regulations they prescribe, so far as they do not violate conscience or the laws of nations, should be conformed to. The attempts of small and unauthorized parties to resist such regulations ought to be discountenanced. The citizens are then on their parole to remain quiet, moderate and orderly. This, so far from being submission, is the course of true manhood—of the dignity and fortitude that become freemen.

THE CITY.

The people of New Orleans have set, within the past few days, an example of patience and propriety under most painful and aggravating circumstances. We were prepared for outbursts of feeling and collisions with those who had come to deprive us of our rights and liberty, which, in a people who love independence of thought and action, would have been natural, if not justifiable. The control over themselves which our people have exhibited is creditable to their good judgment, and largely due to the prudent and judicious conduct of our municipal authorities; and we trust such restraint may characterise their deportment under the still deeper provocations that may await them. The commander of the enemy's fleet, now threatening with his guns our destruction, has not on all occasions avoided offending the sensibilities of our proud population, although we must admit he has exercised a degree of prudence for which we were not prepared.

For the information of our country readers and our absent citizens, it may be well to state that the telegraph offices have been closed for several days to all general business, and we believe are now closed entirely.

The Post Office remains open, but is guarded by marines from the United States fleet. No mails, however, from the North via the Jackson Railroad have arrived since Friday last. We understand they have been stopped at some station on the railroad by competent authority. We trust that some arrangement may be made by which our people may be enabled to keep up communication with their absent friends. The trains on the Jackson road have ceased to run with any regularity, but we are informed those on the Opelousas road run as before. The river travel and business are entirely stopped. With these exceptions, locomotion goes on as it always did. So far Commander Farragut has not interfered with the liberties of any of our citizens, and the only United States troops to be seen in our streets are the few marines guarding the Custom House. The land forces are understood to be on the way up the river, under command of Gen. B. F. Butler, and may be looked for at any moment.

Our streets are remarkably quiet. Most of the stores have been closed since Friday last, and remain closed, with a few exceptions. The principal hotels are closed, and there is some difficulty among those who have been in the habit of making these establishments their homes in effecting other arrangements. The bar rooms have all been closed since Friday last. For some days there was great difficulty in passing the miserable currency we are cursed with, but, thanks to the judicious measures taken by the authorities, confidence in it has been partially restored. The markets are still very meagerly furnished, and, to provide regular supplies of food for this large population, will require all the wisdom of those who have our welfare in their keeping, for the ordinary intercourse between the city and country must, to a considerable extent, continue broken up. Still we do not think our people will advantage themselves by leaving the city with their families. They will find more comforts here than they can possibly find in the country, and we have not been surprised that many of our citizens who had left have returned. Those who intend serving in the army will, of course, make their way to some point where they can strike a blow for their loved home. The Mayor and Council have not abdicated their functions, but will continue their exercise until superseded by the military power which is about to come into our midst. This they intend doing in the interest of their constituents.

U. S. officers, who have come ashore on business, have been subjected to insults by rabbles of boys and thoughtless persons. This is very reprehensible and ought to be prevented. We think Capt. Farragut takes a very erroneous view of his duties, when he sends officers ashore, on any mission, without asking of the Mayor the protection of a police escort or supplying such escort himself. He assumes that the city authorities are responsible for such tumultuary violence, and that he would have the right to punish the city for the violences of a few reckless persons.

It would almost seem that the United States commander sought a pretext for inflicting unnecessary and wanton wrong and injury on the city. He claims that the city is in the occupation of the United States, and yet keeps his whole force on his ships, and neglects to send ashore any troops to protect, guard and enforce his authority. This is all wrong. If officers come ashore, in the present condition of affairs, the police authorities ought to be notified, and requested to secure them protection and escort. Such a course would prevent the exciting and discreditable scenes that have been exhibited in our streets.

We learn that there are several steamers up the river, loaded with provisions for this city, which will not come into our port unless assurances are given by the commander of the United States squadron that they will not be seized or interrupted in their business. Such assurances have become necessary, since it is stated that several steamers—the private property of citizens—have already been detained by the United States vessels in port. We do not understand upon what grounds those seizures were made, especially as Commodore Farragut, in his first message to the Mayor, pledged himself to protect private property. The free passage of steamers to the city from the up-river is absolutely necessary to the sustenance of this population, and we hope that Com. Farragut does not intend to add the threat of starvation to the other menaces which he has launched against this city.

THE FRENCH CONSUL'S PROTEST.—We have been shown a copy of what purports to be the protest of the Commandant of l'Aviso a vapeur de Milan, the French sloop now in our port, addressed to Commodore Farragut, of the United States squadron, against the threat of bombardment of this city. It is in the following terms:

Commander of the United States Squadron, now in the port of New Orleans:

Sir—Sent by my Government to protect the persons and property of its citizens, who are here to the number of thirty thousand, I regret to learn at this moment that you have accorded a delay of forty-eight hours for the evacuation of the city by the women and children. I venture to observe to you that this short delay is ridiculous, and, in the name of my Government, I oppose it. If it is your resolution to bombard the city do it; but I wish to state that you will have to account for this barbarous act to the power which I represent. In any event, I demand sixty days for the evacuation.

DE CLOUET,
Commandant of the steamer Milan, opposite the City of New Orleans.

Our citizens should not receive and credit the various rumors in circulation, calculated to inflame our people and to beget a feeling of hostility against individuals. Some of these rumors implicate citizens in acts of sympathy and collusion with the United States authorities. Names are now mentioned of citizens who are reported to have gone to the United States squadron. In the cases named, we have found on inquiry that the rumors were unfounded. Such rumors ought not to be circulated. They involve charges too serious to be made on light and unsubstantial authority.

FORT ST. PHILIP.—Our paragraph referring to the conduct of the garrisons of the forts below the city, who mutinied and refused to continue the fight, though not intended for the command at Fort St. Philip, might be considered as applying to that garrison. We take great pleasure in correcting such an impression. Fort St. Philip was under the command of Capt. Squires, and the whole garrison remained true and faithful to the last, not the slightest manifestation of a mutinous spirit being exhibited by them. This completes the honorable military record of this heroic garrison.

INTELLIGENCE FROM THE PENINSULA.—We have been favored with the following brief letter, received here from a member of the 1st Louisiana (Dreux's) Battalion:

OUTPOST ARMY OF PENINSULA,
WARWICK RIVER, April 9, 1862.

My Dear Parents—I have just time to say that skirmishing commenced along the entire line on the morning of the 5th inst. An engagement is momentarily expected. Sergeants Bartoly and Jenkins are killed. **

ARRIVALS FROM FORT JACKSON.—The following officers of the heroic garrison of Fort Jackson, arrived at the Brooks House this morning: H. W. Fowler, 1st Lieutenant; W. C. Ettis, 1st Lieutenant; Capt. J. C. Lamon and 1st Lieut. L. B. Taylor, all of the 1st Louisiana Regiment of Artillery.

THE COMMON COUNCIL.

BOARD OF ALDERMEN.—This Board met at 12 o'clock yesterday, pursuant to adjournment, Mr. Delabarre in the chair.

Mr. Stith presented the following resolutions, which were unanimously adopted:

Resolved, That the Common Council of the city of New Orleans has witnessed the gallantry and heroism with which Gen. Duncan has conducted the defense of Forts Jackson and St. Philip, with feelings of unbounded admiration and respect; and that they look upon his efforts to vindicate the honor of our flag and the sacredness of our cause, as upon titles that will endure in the memory of all patriotic and high minded citizens, as long as there will be any reverence shown among us to noble deeds performed with a mighty courage and the most unselfish devotion.

Resolved, That Gen. Duncan has well merited of his country, and that this city and this State plead for him before the Government of the country the highest rewards that can be offered to bravery and patriotism.

Mr. Stith also presented the following resolutions, which were unanimously adopted:

Resolved, That this Council, in its own name and in behalf of the city of New Orleans, returns its thanks to Gen Paul Juge and the brigades under his command for their prompt and spirited compliance with the various requests addressed to them by the municipal authorities, and for the zeal and devotion with which they have performed the duties devolved upon them whilst in charge of the good order and tranquility of the city. Their services have protected the lives and the property of our citizens in the transit of a crisis which was so likely to put them in danger.

Resolved, That the Mayor of New Orleans be respectfully requested to transmit to Gen. Paul Juge a copy of these resolutions, with the proper manifestations of our gratitude and respect.

Mr. Delabarre presented a resolution requesting Gen. Paul Juge to continue the services of the European and French Brigades in connection with the police, under the direction of the Mayor, was concurred in.

Mr. Delabarre also presented a resolution authorizing the Mayor to organize a citizens' police outside the regular police force, and to compel citizens to serve therein in their respective districts, which was adopted.

The amendment by the Board of Assistant Aldermen to the ordinance to construct a double track railroad from Canal street to New Levee, down to Delery street, in the Third District, so as to require the approval of the City Council to the sale of the contract, was concurred in.

A resolution, adopted by the Board of Assistant Aldermen, authorizing Gen. Paul Juge to furnish supplies to his command at the expense of the city, was concurred in.

Mr. Stith presented the following resolution, which was unanimously adopted:

Resolved, That the Finance Committee be, and they are hereby, authorized to warrant on the Comptroller for the payment by the Treasurer of such sums as may be necessary to pay the expenses of the nurses now engaged in attendance on the sick and wounded soldiers in our hospitals.

BOARD OF ASSISTANT ALDERMEN.—All the resolutions adopted by the Board of Aldermen were concurred in.

The portion of the Mayor's message in relation to making provision for the increase of the police force, was referred to the Finance Committee.

A resolution was adopted authorizing Gen. Juge to furnish supplies to his command at the expense of the city.

The Board then adjourned.

WHAT THE MORNING JOURNALS SAY.

From our Edition of Yesterday Evening.

The *Bulletin* expresses its satisfaction with the manner in which our municipal authorities upheld the honor of the city, in the negotiations with the enemy touching the demand to lower the State flag, and applauds the firmness of authorities and people in maintaining the point of honor made, until the enemy, by hauling down the flag with his own hands, conceded the point to us. In this connection, the Bulletin correctly remarks that New Orleans could only have been held by us through the success of the Confederate fleet and the forts below, and pays a just tribute to the heroic defense made by our gallant sailors and soldiers—a defense which procured from the enemy terms of capitulation as favorable as is ever granted to the vanquished.

The *Crescent*, referring to the landing of the Federalists and the hauling down of our State flag, gives the following eloquent and graphic description of the circumstances attending the memorable event:

A parley was held in the Mayor's apartments, the tenor or result of which we did not learn, but in the course of fifteen minutes an officer and marine were seen on the topmost height of the building to rapidly approach the flag—the emblem of the State, which has flattered amid sunshine and storm, through victory and defeat, almost from the time our troubles began. In a minute that flag was lowered and fell to the roof—in a second the eyes of the Southern multitude dropped to the ground, and the mind, heart and soul of the mighty concourse there assembled were filled with sensations which no pen can possibly portray. Old, grey-haired men wept tears of anguish; mothers, with babes in their arms, bedewed their offspring with great drops of affliction; the middle aged and the young of both sexes were lost in deepest woe, and the solemn silence of the scene over all gave the melancholy picture an air of sublime grandeur to which our "young experience can find no parallel."

As if arousing from a dreadful reverie, all eyes were again uplifted, expecting to behold in the place of the chosen emblem of our State sovereignty the vaunted "flag of the free." For no act thereafter could have surprised our people, no greater affliction could be visited upon them—their misery was complete. But they were spared the sight. Probably through protest, or from the fact that this edifice was exclusively municipal, the stars and stripes were not raised, and the soldiers and marines, bearing with them their trophy, filed away in the distance and were soon lost to the detested sight.

As if to relieve the burdened heart, the manly form of Gen. Duncan was seen upon the portico, and then arose such loud and earnest huzzas as made the air reverberate and seemingly the very earth to shake. The multitude were then addressed by the Mayor and probably other citizens of prominence, but, sick and weary at heart, we betook ourselves in quiet away to mourn the saddest day in all our chequered existence.

The Crescent manfully concludes:

Despair not, a righteous cause will eventually triumph, and the invincible spirit that animates the Southern heart will yet spread, like the wildfire of Rhoderic Dhu, throughout the length and breadth of the land, and millions yet unborn will reap the glorious harvest of our toils and melancholy privations.

In another article the Crescent earnestly counsels the people to respect law and order, counsel which every good citizen will regard as peculiarly becoming to us in our present circumstances.

The *Bee* likewise urges the maintenance of order, and justly praises the conduct of the Foreign Brigade, under Gen. Paul Juge, fils, and Gen. Maignan.

The Bee, referring to the disaster which has befallen us, observes:

We have lost all but our honor, and that this remains to us is our only consolation. The city has not been surrendered; it has been captured. We have done all that men could do to meet this calamity, and it now behooves us to bear it with the unshaken fortitude of the truly brave. Every one will now feel the necessity of abstaining from any misplaced or hostile demonstration. Not only would this be in bad taste, and unworthy a chivalrous and gallant people, but it might afford a pretext for reprisals which we are in no condition to resist. Let us maintain our dignity, and we shall win the respect and esteem of the Federals. No nobler spectacle can be witnessed than that of brave men accepting calamity with serene resignation, when it is absolutely irremediable. The events of the past few days will constitute a memorable chapter in the future history of our country.

The *Picayune* on the same subject, remarks:

The State flag was struck by no son of Louisiana, or citizen of New Orleans. It was taken away as the trophy of an enemy, and the bare pole stands to remind us that, with the consent of our adversaries, we have no longer a State of Louisiana. Over the public buildings reclaimed as the property of the United States, the Federal flag flies, because protected by the guns of the Federal squadron. But the city of New Orleans has sustained her dignity in her fall. The flag of the Government of her choice no longer flies over the people who love it, but it was only lowered when superior numbers came and force overthrew right. A flag waves over it which they have again and again repudiated as alien to their affections, and now look at as a token of the presence of an enemy, but no act or word of theirs has given sign of assent to the claim of right with which power unfurls it above them. They see in it the symbol of conquest, which reduces them from the rank of citizens in a commonwealth based on the consent of the governed, to be vassals of a victorious invader; but they have struggled gallantly to avert that fate; they have lavished priceless blood and unlimited treasure to uphold the cause they believe to be holy; and, in its adversity, they have shown fearlessly in the face of the world that they do not love it less, and that they have no regrets for what has been done and suffered, except for what has been unavailing.

It is a melancholy position, but it has its duties to be met with firmness. We can not tell what may be designed for us by those who have our lives and fortunes in their hands, but we do know that nothing can be gained for the credit or success of our cause, nothing for the immense and varied interests embraced within the limits of this vast city, by acts of violence or disorder. It should be the first duty of every man to keep the peace, and to maintain the security of persons and property, both of which are likely to be endangered during the unsettled and tumultuous days which follow a change of authority. There is great danger, amidst the distresses which necessarily prevail, and the passions they are so well calculated to provoke, that great efforts and great concert of effort may be required to quiet the popular excitement, and more especially to relieve the impending wants of a large part of the unemployed poor. Notwithstanding the presence of the enemy, this is the great social duty of every man within the city, and it must be attended to at once, cheerfully and effectually. It is sufficient to point out, without enlarging upon this source of peril, to call the earnest attention of the authorities and of every citizen to the pressing nature of this emergency.

MAYOR'S MESSAGE.

The Council held a meeting at noon yesterday, when the following message from the Mayor was received and read:

Since your last meeting events have occurred which will occupy a conspicuous place in the history of the country and of the age. It is unneccessary for me more than briefly to recapitulate them. They are sufficiently well known from the publicity which has attended them and the reports of the public press. It is enough for me to state that yesterday morning the answer you had agreed upon to flag officer Farragut's demand of the day before was transmitted to him, through the hands of my Secretary, Mr. Baker, who was accompanied by Messrs. Soule and McClelland. The result of the interview of Mr. Baker with the United States Commander was that the latter abandoned his purpose of bombarding the city, and signified his intention of removing the flag from this building by means of his own forces.

Accordingly at 12 o'clock, Capt. Bell, accompanied by an escort of United States marines, with two cannon, came to the City Hall, and the flag was then taken down by the United States officers. Thus the position assumed by New Orleans has been fully sustained. I am glad to say that the peace of the city has been preserved during the excitement of the last few days, as far as it was in my power to effect that object. The violations of public order have been few in number and slight in character. This is owing to the valuable services rendered by the European Brigades, Paul Juge, fils, General Commanding, and the zeal and energy of the ordinary police force. It is still, and will be for some days, necessary to continue these efforts for the preservation of public tranquillity, and I would therefore request you to authorize or suggest some arrangement by which the services of the European Brigades may be for the present retained.

I have been compelled to increase the number of police in order to meet the demands made upon me within the last few days, and such increase I am confident ought to be maintained. I hope you will make some provision for the excess of expenditures over the amount provided for in the budget thus demanded by the public necissities. I would likewise suggest that such action as may seem expedient be taken for the relief of those of our population who are now in a suffering condition for want of the ordinary necessaries of life.

JOHN T. MONROE, Mayor.

THE SUCCESSION TO THE THRONE OF GREECE.—A telegraphic dispatch of four lines in our impression of Saturday, though probably not one in a thousand of our readers noticed it, settles the fate of a kingdom. The arrival of a Bavarian Prince and his two young sons at Athens would be to the general public an event no more extraordinary than the record of the travels of any other distinguished foreigner. The telegraph, however, informs us that the elder of the two boys whom Prince Luitpold of Bavaria accompanies to Athens has been named "successor to the throne of Greece," and this announcement indicates the settlement of a long standing European difficulty. King Otho, though married (1836) to Maria Frederica Amelia, daughter of the late, and sister of the present Grand Duke of Oldenburgh, has no issue, and for many years past the succession has been, as it were, a bone of contention in the Bavarian family from which the King springs. It is understood that the next brother of King Otho, Prince Luitpold Charles Joseph William Louis, of Bavaria, "a lieutenant-general of Bavaria, commander of the 1st division of the army, proprietor of the 1st Regiment of Bavarian Artillery, and of the 7th Regiment of Austrian Artillery," whose arrival at Athens we chronicled on Saturday, declined to accept the reversion of the crown of Greece some years ago, on the plea of repugnance to quit the religion of Rome for that of Greece—a condition made indispensable by the 38th article of the constitution adopted by King Otho after the bloodless revolt of September, 1843: "Every successor to the throne of Greece must profess the orthodox faith." It would seem that matters are now settled, so far as anything can be settled in Greece, by the nomination to the throne, in reversion, of the elder son of Prince Luitpold, who, though personally averse to exchange one faith for another, has no objection to his son doing so. Prince Louis Leopold Joseph Marie Alois Alfred, the King of Greece in prospective, was born on January 7, 1845, and is the eldest son of Prince Luitpold by the Archduchess Augusta Ferdinanda Louise Marie Jeanne Josephe, daughter of Leopold II, Grand Duke of Tuscany. [Morning Post.

MAIL AT CAMP MOORE.—A through mail arrived on Tuesday at Camp Moore.

To the Planters.

We are compelled to give notice that we can not at present receive any further orders for Goods. The orders received and registered up to this time, accompanied with cotton, cash or drafts, will require all the goods we can make up to the 1st of September.

Planters are hereby notified that we can not receive any more cotton or orders. Public notice will be given in due time when present engagements will be completed.

apr22 2p20t S. M. HART & CO.

MISSISSIPPI RIVER PLANTATION FOR SALE—I offer for sale my Plantation, on the Mississippi river, known as BONHAMPTON, containing about One Thousand Acres, five hundred of which are cleared. The place is highly improved, with every building that a purchaser would desire—two Brick Dwellings, Steam Gin and Saw Mill, Frame Quarters and Barn—in fact, everything that could be desired to make it one of the most desirable places on the river.

I will sell this place with or without TWENTY or TWENTY-FIVE NEGROES, as the purchaser may desire.

For particulars, inquire of A. J. RUGELEY & CO., or to the undersigned, on the premises.

dec18 tf jan19Wtf D. W. C. BONHAM.

FOR SALE OR TO RENT FOR THE SUMMER.

BYRNE'S PROPERTY, situated nearly a mile to the west o the town of Biloxi, Miss., on the Gulf coast. The dwelling contains seven rooms furnished, and on the place there is a good vegetable garden and orchard, abundance of poultry and milk; stable, kitchen and servants' rooms detached from the main building; with a splendid wharf and bath-house. For terms, &c., which will be moderate, apply to

BYRNE, VANCE & CO.,
No. 3 Carondelet st

mv24Wtf

JAMES F. MUSE,
COMMISSION AND FORWARDING MERCHANT
CORNER OF COMMON AND FRONT STS.

sep17-1y sep26W

Seventh Brigade Journal.

VOL. I. COLUMBIA, TENN., FRIDAY, MAY 2, 1862. NO 8.

Seventh Brigade Journal.

FRIDAY EVENING, MAY 2, 1862.

PRINTERS OF THE SEVENTH BRIGADE JOURNAL:

Foreman:

Serg't Thos. Bryant, Co. K, 1st Wis. Reg.

CORP. J. A. KELLER, CO. B, 79TH PENN. REG

" C. W. WILEY, " " "

HOMER G. LEONARD, CO. K, 1ST WIS. REG.

H. M. GEITER, CO. I, 79TH PENN. REG.

WM. K. WISE, CO. D, " "

Important to Citizens of Tennessee

General Order from Gen. Buell!

HEAD-QUARTERS, DEPART. OF THE OHIO, Nashville Tenn., February 26, '62.

GENERAL ORDERS, No. 13

The General commaning congratulates his troops that it has been their privilege to restore the national banner to the Capital of Tennessee. He believes that thousands of hearts in every part of the State will swell with joy to see that honored flag reinstated in a position from which it was removed in the excitement and folly of an evil hour; that the voice of her own people will soon proclaim its welcome, and that their manhood and patriotism will protect and perpetuate it.

The General does not deem it necessary, though the occasion is a fit one, to remind his troops of the rule of conduct they have hitherto observed and are still to pursue. We are in arms not for the purpose of invading the rights of our fellow countrymen anywhere, but to maintain the integrity of the Union, and protect the Constitution under which its people have been prosperous and happy. We cannot therefore look with indifference on any conduct which is designed to give aid and comfort to those who are endeavoring to defeat these objects; but the action to be taken in such cases rests with certain authorized persons, and is not to be assumed by individual officers or soldiers. Peaceable citizens are not to be molested in their persons or property. Any wrongs to either are to be promptly corrected and the offenders brought to punishment. To this end all persons are desired to make complaint to the immediate commander of officers or soldiers so offending, and if justice is not done promptly, then to the next commander, and so on until the wrong is redressed. If the necessities of the public service should require the use of private property for public purposes, fair compensation is to be allowed. No such appropriation of private property is to be made except by the authority of the highest commander present, and any other officer or soldier who shall presume to exercise such privilege shall be brought to trial—Soldiers are forbidden to enter the residences or grounds of citizens on any plea without authority.

No arrests are to be made without the authority of the Commanding General, except in case of actual offence against the authority of the Government; and in all such cases the fact and circumstances will immediately be reported in writidg to Head Quarters through the intermediate commanders.

The General reminds his officers that the most frequent depredations are those which are committed by worthless characters who straggle from the ranks on the plea of being unable to march, and where the inability really exists, it will be found in most instances that the soldier has overloaded himself with useless and unauthorized articles. The orders already published on this subject must be enforced.

The condition and behaviour of a corps are sure indications of the efficiency and fitness of its officers. If any shall be found to disregard the propriety of conduct which belongs to soldiers as well as citizens, they must not expect to occupy the posts of honor, but may rest assured that they will be placed in positions where they cannot bring shame on their comrades and the cause they are engaged in. The Government supplies with liberality all the wants of the soldier. The occasional deprivations and hardships incident to rapid marches must be borne with patience and fortitude.—Any officer who neglects to provide properly for his troops or separates himself from them to seek his own comfor, will be held to a rigid accountability.

By command of GENERAL BUELL.

JAMES B. FRY, A. A. G. Chief of Staff.

Official J. M. WRIGHT.

General Order of Gen. Negley.

HEAD QUARTERS, 7TH BRIGADE, Columbia, April 3, 1862.

GENERAL ORDER NO. 22.

I. This Camp will be known as Camp Morehead, in honor of General I. K. Morehead, M. C. of Pennsylvania.

II. The commanding General expects a continuance of the strict discipline and gentlemanly conduct which has already earned an enviable reputation for this Brigade. While your conduct towards peaceable citizens should be marked with kindness and propriety, do not forget your high responsibility, or cease for a moment to be vigilant, prudent and determined against the enemies of your country.

By command of GEN. NEGLEY,

Commanding Post.

JAMES A. LOWRIE, A. A. General.

———o———

Incidents of the Battle.

I am so everwhelmed with incidents of the battle that it puzzles me to select the most interesting. I will give you a few by way of variety:

A member of Gen. Buell's staff had a shell pass so close to him that it took off one half of the skirt of his coat, and the head of a soldier in the rear. Yet he was uninjured.

Gen. Buell had a horse shot from under him and several shells exploded near him and Gen. McCook without injuring either.

The color-sergeant of one of the regiments was shot down receiving five balls in less than a minute. The standard was immediately seized by a youth about nineteen years of age, who amid a perfect shower of balls, rushed about eighty yards ahead of the regiment, and waved the flag defiantly at the rebels. His clothes were torn with bullitts, but he escaped unhurt. I endeavored to get his name and failed, but I learn he will be mentioned in the official reports.

One company in an Illinois regiment had every officer, commissioned and non-commissioned, shot down. By consent, a private assumed command, and conducted them handsomely through the fight.

Among the wounded Rebels was a youth from Alabama. Both of his legs were shattered.—During the battle he asked for water and was supplied. He then said:

"This is my mother's fault, I did not want to fight against the Union, but she called me a coward and forced me to enlist."

He gave the National soldier a ring and requested him to send it to his mother, and to say to her that he died a brave boy, but regretting that he had taken up arms against his country. What will be the pangs of that mother's heart when she receives this message?

There were few Colonels who were not struck with balls. One of the most remarkable escapes was that of Col Mimgen, of Ohio. His horse's mane was nearly cut away with bullets, and several passed through his clothing, but he was not even scratched. The Rebel sharpshooters aimed constantly at our officers of all ranks. Some of the regiments, have scarcely an officer on duty, but have plenty of good material in the ranks to fill all vacancies.

A National and a Rebel soldier were found dead, side by side with hands clasped. It is supposed, that they fell near each other, mortally wounded, and making friends died in peace.

The killed and wounded in the Second Kentucky were all shot within five minutes. The experience of the regiment in Western Virginia enabled them to dodge balls, shell and bullets, while for several hours they were protectidg a battery, and during that time not a man was wounded. They charged, however, in the face of a heavy fire, and it was during that charge they suffered. Its a bully regiment.

One young Ohio volunteer who had been recently wounded, and died before picked up, was found with the minature of a young lady friend to his lips. His comrades state that he an idea he would be killed, and was several times seen looking the daguerreotype while the regiment was in reserve.

BRECKENRIDGE AND ROSSEAU.—The officer's freely denounced Breckenridge as a coward They stated that the whole army was disgusted with him. His brigade was in Monday's battle, and at no time would Breckinridge venture within range of our guns, but, keeping at a safe distance, dispatched all his commands by his aids. By a singular chance, too, his whole brigade was pitted against the Louisville Legion, the first corps of Union troops formed in Kentucky and a portion of Rosseau's brigade. It will be remembered that when Kentucky was wavering in her position the gallant Rosseau commenced recruiting soldiers for the Union in Louisville.

Breckinridge was then playing the sneaking traitor in the Senate of the United States, and he was bitterly denunciatory of Rosseau. Both have expressed a desire to meet each other on the field, and the only earthly wish of Breckinridge's brigade was to meet the gallant Louisville Legion. Their desire was gratified Monday, and the long looked for contest came off. The contrast between the two Generals was striking—Rosseau, the soul of honor and chivalry, rode down his line, amid showers of bullets and balls urging his brave boys to follow him to victory or death. His tall, soldierly form was a splendid target, but the roar of the battle and the conflict of arms nerved his gallant soul to the highest pitch of heroism.

In the hottest of the fight appeared Rosseau, waving his sword, and crying. "On my gallant lads." But Breckinridge, the Rebel, sent forward his command, and coward and traitor as he is, quailed and trembled before the roar of artillery. The contest between the brigade of Breckinridge and the Louisville Legion was short. The Legion advanced steadily, and three times drove their opponents to new positions, thinning their ranks by every fire.—Running out of ammunition their place was supplied, and when they again returned to the contest Breckinridge's brigade was *non est.*

BARBARITY OF THE REBELS TOWARD THE WOUNDED.

There are some shocking incidents relative to the wounded. The rebels, it will be remembered, took possession of a portion of the Federal camp on Sunday—actually sleeping on Sunday night in the the tents of several of our regiments. Most of our wounded who fell outside of the line occupied by them on Sunday night, fell into their hands. They allowed the helpless to lie there—not even allowing the National surgeons taken prisoners to attend to them. Our poor fellows lay there until the ground was retaken on Monday. Some were found who had crawled to water, and there died. Some inhuman barbarities were also practiced upon the dead, some of whom were stripped, and, in one instance at least, the body was mutilated in the most vulgar and blackguard style! Many were found on which the huge Mississippi bowie-knives had been used after death.

Many of the wounded secessionists died before they were found after the battle. One party of some forty men were found in a ravine, where they had crawled to obtain water, and some died with their heads in the brooks. Another party was found close to the Corinth road partially consumed by fire. It seems that they had been placed probably for shelter, in a pile of brush, and then deserted. Our shells set fire to the brush heap, and two days after the battle their crisped bodies were found.

THE SHILOH CHURCH.

I visited to-day the Shiloh Church, from which the battle takes its name. It is an unfinished log structure with a shingle roof. The good people of this locality about a year ago, took a notion to serve God and keep the Sabbath, but before sufficient money was raised to complete the rustic temple of worship, they changed their notion. The house, which is a very small one, was roofed but not "chinked," and only partially floored, but in warm weather meetings were held in it. The exterior of the building is now adorned with numerous bullet marks, some of which penetrate deep into the logs.

The building was used, after the battle, as a hospital for the wounded rebels. When I was there, all had been removed to the steamboats but two. One of these, a Tennessean, was wounded in the leg, and was quite talkative.—He said he came up with the reinforcements on Sunday night, and was wounded early on Monday. He was of the opinion that the rebel cause had "gone up."

The other prisoner had received a bullet in the back of his head, and was insensible. He was quite young, and ere this is dead.

So much for Shilohn Church, which small and rude as it is, will hereafter be looked upon with interest.

———o———

THE Norfolk Day Book is very much elated at Beauregard,s exaggerated account of his success at Shiloh, and magnanimously asks: "Is it not a favorable time for the Confederate Government to propose to the Government at Washington a cessation of the fierce and unnatural strife? Not until every rebel arm is laid down, we can tell the Day Book. There can be no terms made within treason.—*Louisville Jour.*

Rich Extracts from Rebel Papers.

From a rebel mail-bag captured at Lebanon, we have a large lot of Dixie papers, which we will give extracts from to our readers from time to time.

The Southern Confederacy, published at Atlanta, Ga., dated Feb. 19, 1861, has an article which is worthy of notice. It makes this striking confession of the awful delusion which the Southern people have been laboring under:

We are in need of a sound public opinion now. We are a people of extremes. Under the lead of men who ought to know better, the South was induced to believe that war would not follow the disruption of the Federal Government. War did come; a few victories created the opinion ... the forces *then* in the field. Recent disasters have carried us to the other extreme, and if these disasters should be repeated, it is to be feared that a state of despondency will follow. Let it be our part to show that there is, and can be, no real cause for despondency. Federal successes have not yet been as great as any reasonable man might have expected from the beginning. They will enter and ravage some of our territory. The Empire State cannot hope for exemption. Let us look this danger in the face.

Here is another confession which ought to startle our people like a thunder clap:

THE WICKEDNESS OF OUR SOLDIERS.

It has been the lot of the writer to see something of the soldiers of other countries. It pains him to say that he has not seen in others an approximation to the wickedness which is unblushingly exhibited by large bodies of our soldiers. Let any one travel in a railroad car with a body of our troops—let *him hear their oaths, their obscenity; let him observe their indifference to the presence of ladies,* and as a Georgian he will be pained beyond measure. *In no other country would such things be tolerated. Yet they are borne in silence.*

He tells also a tale which we commend to the especial notice of the poor—the men whom a rich rebel Confederate Senator called the "mud sills of society."

MEN WHO OUGHT TO GO INTO THE ARMY.

Public sentiment has not yet viewed with a sufficient stern frown, the able bodied men of some degree of intelligence and fortune, who are taking no part in the public defence. There are thousands of such in the State. *Our privates are mostly very young men or poor men. The class referred to will not serve without office.* It is true that *the associations of a private in some of our companies would be disagreeable to men of education and refinement.*

———o———

Unionism in North Carolina—The Union Home Guards Wide Awake.

A Newbern correspondent of the New York *Tribune* writes that the Stars and Stripes are flying in the Western counties of North Carolina. All through the mountain region the old flag can be seen, where brave men have collected together to defend its honor.

Soon after Newbern was captured, an important engagement took place in the Western part of the State, between a large Rebel force and the Union Home Guards, resulting in a complete rout of the former, who it appears, lost all the guns belonging to one battery, all the camp equippage, wagons, and supplies of all kinds belonging to the rebel force, with three companies of cavalry which were entirely cut off, and obliged to surrender, or in other words "were retained." The Raleigh *Standard* called it a "most disgraceful riot," which is truly a very polite term for a defeat. It appears that the Union men in the mountains had been hanging a notorious rebel character, one Colonel Dodge, who had charge of the militia, and had resorted to a sweeping impressment; hence the difficulty.

The Union men are strongly in the ascendency all through the western counties of this State, are well armed, and have a complete organization, under competent leaders. The *Standard* says they have threatened to take Raleigh, and suggests the importance of fortifying the city in every direction, and a general fall back of their rebel forces in the State to that point.

———o———

Beauregard's Speech.

On the Commodore Perry, which went to Cincinnati with a load of wounded, was a Rebel Major, (we did not learn his name,) who had been wounded. He states that before the fight Beauregard made a speech to his men to the following effect:

The engagement now before them was to be the decisive battle of this contest; if they lost, it was all lost; if they gained it, the prospect was bright. They had not had any pay, and if they failed in this battle, would not get any, for their money would not be worth a cent; if they gained a victory, each man should have $1,000. This promise it was, says the Major, which nerved the rebel forces with such desperation and determination. But it was all of no avail, and they have fled not to be coaxed into another fight.—*Louisville Journal.*

Seventh Brigade Journal.

FRIDAY EVENING, MAY 2, 1862.

The Tyranny of Secessionism.

We have heard a great deal said by the people of the South since the Federal Army have came into the States that endeavored to get out of the Union about the tyranny and oppression exercised by our men. All through the South the people have been taught to hate the Northrn people and especially the Union Army by the foul misrepresentation made by the rebel leaders and Generals as to the object our army had in coming down here. From the first uprising of the people of the North, on April last, o quell the rebellion, the instigators and abettors of the secession movement have on every possible occasion, sought to poison the minds of the people, and make them believe that the sole object of our Army was to coerce and subdue them. [illegible] possession of any of the Seceding States, they would burn their cities, destroy their property, and spread ruin and desolation wherever they went. As our Army have advanced, the deluded people of the Seceded States, have changed their minds. They see that they have been deceived, since that instead of destroying property, the Federal Army protects it, and the citizens themselves are safer within our lines, than they were before the rebel Army was driven out.

What a striking contrast between the course pursued by the United States Government and the Union Army, and the usurping Government of Jeff. Davis and the rebel Generals. Citizens in the States under Secession rule, are no longer safe. They cannot tell at what moment they may be torn away from home and family, and forced into the rebel army. If they say ought against its injustice and resist the enforcement of the odious and tyrannical conscript act, they are dragged off to prison or shot down. He who dares express the least Union sentiment endangers his life. To bolster up a worthless currency, vigilance committees threaten with severe punishment all who refuse to take the Confederates Notes, which are not worth the white paper upon which they are printed. The following paragraph from a Virginia paper will serve to show what desperate means are being resorted to, to prop up this wicked rebellion:

"The militia are gathering at their different places of rendezvous in goodly number.—One of the recusant ones, who utterly refused to go, and swore he would die before he would go, drew a knife upon the guard who went for him, when the guard fired upon him, breaking his leg about the knee joint. His leg will have to be amputated—a sad warning to all others of his disposition. Our court met yesterday to transact business in connection with the proclamation of the President to establish martial law in this county. We hope that when this law is carried out the Union men will be hunted up and treated as they deserve."

Yet, after all the facts are known, there are those in Tennessee and other Southern States who prate about the tyranny of our government. None are so blind as those who will not see.

—o—

TENNESSEE POST-OFFICES RE ESTABLISHED.—The Nashville Union learns from the post-master of that city that the following post-offices have been re-opened by the United States authority, and the following postmasters appointed:—Murfreesboro, H. S. Pugh; Springfield, Mr Bugg; Lebanon, G. H. Glenn; Watertown, Wilson county, W. L. Wallace; Liberty, DeKalb county, Mr. Waters; and Smithfield, same county, G. Beckwick. Wherever the Federal flag follows the flying rebels, the blessings of law and the diffusion of intelligence follow. Long sundered friends and acquaintances may now correspond directly with the localities above indicated.

—o—

MORE DEVELOPMENTS.—This war is making extraordinay developments. The siege and capture of Fort Pulaski have demonstrated the great power of Parrot guns. The projectiles sent out by this formidable weapon penetrate stone and brick walls, and carry everything before them. This war has demonstrated that "wooden walls" and stone barricades are but board partitions when Parrot guns are around.

—o—

CLOSE SHAVE.—Lieut. Colton, had his life sayed in the battle of Winchester by a pair of scissors in his vest pocket, which the bullet struck and glanced off.

Voice from Tennessee.

We need not say anything to deepen the interest of the following letter (says the Cincinnati *Enquirer*,) received by yesterday's mail from one of the most respectable houses in the interior of Tennessee. If aught were wanting to infuse new strength and vigor into the efforts of the Government and people to crush out this unholy rebellion, it is the disclosure of such facts and feelings as are here exhibited. Who will consent to leave the true men in the seceded States unprotected by the strong arm of the Union, to which their best wishes and hope, have clung through the dark days of rebel dominion;

——, TENNESSEE, April 9, 1862.

Dear Friend:—After so long a time, having passed through the most awful reign of terror that a free people were ever made to suffer, we are permitted to open a correspondence with you. We can partially breathe free again. It is useless to try to give you a faint idea of the tyranny which has been exercised over the many (although you may have been led to believe they were few) men in Tennessee whose only crime was that they loved their country, and would not raise their arms against a Government which had always protected them and cost them nothing.

We say we begin to breathe again the air of freedom, from the fact that one division of the Union army has passed by and South of us, and which we trust will not return until the rebellion is put down, and God grant that it soon may be. This wish, publicly expressed two months since, would have cost a man his life. We are happy to say that many are beginning to see and feel that the one real object now is to put down the rebellion.

The worst feature, and most to be lamented over, is that there are so many of our poor boys in the rebel army against their will, being pressed into the service. No longer back than November, Tennessee had but 25,000 men in the field. A requisition was then made for 30,000 more, and in order to get them out, our Governor, King Harris, ordered a draft to be made; and may we never behold such a time again.—Noble hearted young men, with tears in their eyes, would say to those who had families,—"You stay and take care of your wife and little ones, and we will go, asking God to forgive the crime of fighting against principle. "We often asked ourselves, How can such a thing be proper?

—o—

☞ To show our citizens the difference in the South, between Confederate notes and provisions, we quote from the *Opelonsis* (La.) *Courier*, April 5th:

We read in the *Patriot*, our neighbor, of the 29th:

"We are not to have any more meat. Our butchers tell us they cannot buy beeves for Confederate money, and the owners thereof will not receive any thing but gold and silver for them. That's patriotic! To depreciate the currency of the country is a hundred fold worse than to fall in the ranks of the Yankees and fight for subjugation of the South.

Undoubtedly, those who have beeves and other necessaries of life for sale, and who refuse Confederate State notes at par in payment thereof, lack that patriotism without which we cannot acquire our independence, and their names should be recollected for a time which may not far off. If every one of us do not aid by all the means in our power, the government of our country, we might as well fold our arms on our breast and wait for the Yankees to come and put the yoke on our necks. Then, those who have beeves and other property, will see the enemy take the same in exchange of—nothing.

This is not the time for those who possess to enrich themselves at the expense of the poor or af those who are making an honest living.

We might relate, as a collary to the above an anecdote which was related to us the other day:

"An old Jew, rich as Crœsus, who made an immense fortune in New Orleans, lately refused to take Confederate State bills in exchange for his goods. The Governor sent for him, and intimated the incompreptibility of his conduct with that of the entire population of New Orleans.

The Jew insisted, and continued to sell his goods for nothing else than gold or silver.—General Lovell then sent for him, but Crœsus was inaccessible to any good sentiment, and he emphatically refused to sell his goods for anything else than gold or silver.

"Then," said the General, "I give you twenty days to settle your business and leave the country." And the General left, leaving to martial law to do the rest.

—o—

Worthy his Name.

Charles Carroll, of Carrollton, grandson of the famous signer of the Declaration of Independence, is, with one or two exceptions, the largest slaveholder in Maryland. Kind as a parent to his three hundred negroes, he hails the President's plan of emancipation with gladness. He has told his slaves not to leave him, because the time would come when they would be free on their native soil, and that then he would employ them as free laborers at good wages.

Col. M'Tavish, another grandson of the signers, owns fifty slaves, and is heartily in favor of emancipation. But then he is a Republican in politics, believes in the Chicago platform, and spoke, acted, and voted for Abraham Lincoln.—*Chicago Tribune.*

Who are qualified Voters.

The Nashville *Union and American*, recently the great rebel organ of this State, conducted under the eye of Isham Harris, contained the following editorial, on Tuesday, July 30, 1861:

WHO ARE QUALIFIED VOTERS.

This question has been suggested to us by the following communication from a friend in this county. Can a man, who does not acquiesce in the action of his State and obstinately refuses to acknowledge allegiance to the Confederate States, legally vote at the election on Thursday? We think not. As long as Tennessee was one of the United States, no man was entitled to a vote who was not a citizen of the same. Now that she is a lawful member of the Confederate States, no one ought to be entitled to a vote who was not a citizen of the same, and is ready to declare his allegiance, when challenged.—Otherwise rebels against her authority, and traitors against the Government, may exercise the great franchise of voting. Let the inspectors of elections see to this important point.—The following is the communication referred to:

A COUNTER REVOLUTION.

"An enthusiastic William H. Polk man, writing from this city to a man in the country, seems anxious to get up a counter revolution against Governor Harris. He says, in his letter: "Out of the fullness of the heart the mouth speaketh, but I feel such an interest in the election for Governor, that I cannot remain silent. If my views do not accord with your own, burn this sheet and excuse me. I write in sincerity, have no ends to accomplish but the good of my country. I feel sure, if you were to see what I see, and hear what I hear, it would astound you. In my opinion, we are on the verge of despotism. I look for an inquisition to be set up in the event that Harris is elected at the August election.

* * * *

Col. Polk will not have time to visit—— during the canvass, he is now in the field. If you can think as I do, I pray you to do all you can to promote his election. He is worthy. If East Tennessee will give Col. Polk their usual majority, I have no doubt of his success in the election, and we have the best assurances that East Tennessee will be almost a unit for Polk."

If the writer of the foregoing letter will only reflect that Union banners were allowed to fly in the city, after the withdrawal of Tennessee from the Union, he will be satisfied that he has done Gov. Harris a wrong, and that no "despotism" or "inquisition" would ever be dreamed of in Tennessee, unless the followers of Abe Lincoln should succeed in their darling wish of reinstating that ruthless tyrant in power, whose mercenaries murder women and children, burn towns and pillage and murder the population, as they have advanced into the country. It is to effectually checkmate despotism, and the inquisitorial dynasty, which has robbed the telegraph offices of private despatches, and seized the papers of private citizens, without warrant of law, that Governor Harris has effectually labored. He has but poor thanks for his patriotism, and if any considerable number of citizens agree with the gentleman whose letter we have quoted. But this cannot be. Gov. Harris has his reward in the grateful appreciation of his countrymen, as will be demonstrated by the overwhelming majority he will receive on Thursday next.

They will say, "we want no better man than this; "well done, thou good and faithful servant." Whatever may be the merits of Mr. Polk, the people will say, we have one that we have tried in a great emergency, we know him to be true, and we will not exchange him now, especially as we have invited him to serve us again, because we know that the State is safe under his guidance. East Tennessee may do as she pleases; we do not wish to control her people. But Middle and West Tennessee will stand by the man who has sustained them and their brave volunteers in the great crisis through which we are passing.

Consider this calmly, reader. Here is a proposition, seriously urged, to deprive a man of the right of voting—a Tennesseean—an old citizen of Nashville. And what provokes this proposition? Why, an old man writes a letter to a friend, and the letter is broken open at the Nashville Post Office, probably, and it is found that this old man, who had been voting as he pleased for half a century here, had actually said that he thought Col. Polk was worthier of the Governor's office than Gov. Harris. This was the "head and front of his offending." He a gray-haired Tennesseean, dared to question the fitness of King Harris to rule the people! Wonderful audacity! And who was this old man? Col. R. H. McEwen. Presumptuous old man, not to bow your honored head in the dust before the awful majesty of King Isham! And now let us hear some insolvent rebel open his mouth to plead against the tyranny of Abe Lincoln, and for the mild and liberal sway of Jeff. Davis. Speak out, rebels!

—o—

DEATH OF GEN. CHARLES F. SMITH.—The nation will profoundly regret the death of this gallant officer, which occurred at Savannah, Tenn., on Friday. He was a Pennsylvanian by birth, a graduate of West Point, and must ever be regarded as the real captor of Fort Donelson.

The Brooklyn Navy Yard—Our Next Iron Clad Monitor.

Since the commencement of the war, upwards of one hundred and thirty vessels have been repaired and refitted, comprising sloops of war, gunboats, transports and storeships; three new vessels—the *Oneida*, *Octorora* and *Adirondack*—have been built, and two—the *Lackawanna* and *Ticonderoga*—are in progress of erection. Beside the ship building, refitting and repairing done here, this yard manufactures all the oakum used in the Navy. Should it become necessary to work at night, gas pipes have been laid around the dry dock, with gutta pipes attached, so that lights can be carried to any portion of a vessel in the dock. Lanterns are also fixed in the adjoining sheds, so that the entire place could be illuminated in a manner that would afford as much facility for the operatives to work as by day. The present force of operatives numbers 3,000, all of whom are considered masters of their respective trades.

The iron-clad steam sloop-of-war *Galena* will be towed to the yard to-morrow. She was to have arrived there last week, but, owing to some slight alterations, she will not be ready until then. She is to be armed and equipped forthwith. The *Galena* is one of the three iron clad vessels contracted for by the Secretary of the Navy, under authority of the act of Congress approved August 3d, 1861. The other two are the *Monitor* and *Keasington*. Of the *Monitor* it is not necessary to say more than that the public are by this time pretty well acquainted with her. The *Galena* has also been described several times, but the following particulars will bear repetition.

She was designed by Mr. Julius Patterson, and constructed at Mystic, Conn., by Maxon, Fish & Co., the builders of the gunboat *Owasco*, now in active service. Naval Constructor Rook was charged with the superintendence of the work. As soon as possible after being launched, in February, she was sent to the Continental Iron Works, at Greenpoint, Long Island, to receive her armor, which consists of iron plates, 25 feet long, 4 inches wide, and 3 1-2 inches thick, overlapping each other, and extending four feet below the water line. Her dimensions are: length over all 208 feet: breadth of beam, 36 ft.; depth of hold, 12 1-2 feet; burden, 1,000 tons. She is not at all like the *Monitor*, being simply an iron-plated screw steamer of great strength, and modeled with a view to speed. She is pierced for 18 guns, but will carry six only, viz: 4 Dahlgreen and 2 Parrott guns. Her rigging is made of copper wire.

—o—

GEN. PRESTON KILLED.—A despatch has been received in Washington, stating that Gen. Wm. Preston, a Confederate officer, was killed on the 7th. Gen. Preston was Minister to Spain during the Buchanan administration. As a whig, he voted for Gen. Scott at the Presidential election in 1852. But in Congress, during the Pierce administration, he was very influential in carrying the Kansas-Nebraska bill. Subsequently he was a Buchanan elector. In the Mexican war he served as Lieutenant Colonel of Kentucky volunteers. He was a man of remarkably fine personal appearance, and some oratorical powers.

Seventh Brigade Journal.

FRIDAY EVENING, MAY 2, 1862.

The Seventh Brigade Journal

Will be regularly issued semi-weekly, during the occupation of Columbia by the Brigade.—Persons wishing the *Journal* will please leave their address at the office.—50 cts. per month in advance. Advertisors can leave their advertisements at the same place. Newsboys can be supplied in future at 3 o'clock on Tuesday, and Friday afternoons.

—o—

Post Commandant.

Brigadier Gen. JAS. S. NEGLEY has been appointed by Gen. BUELL Post Commander at Columbia. His Head Quarters are in the Sibley tent on the lawn of the Columbia Athenæum, entrance on Main Street.

—o—

Provost Marshal.

Gen. JAMES S. NEGLEY has appointed Capt. Thomas H Green, Provost Marshall of the City. Captain Green's Co.—Co. K, 1st Wisconsin and Co. A, 79th Pennsylvania Volunteer Infantry, the Provost Guard. The Head-Quarters of Capt. Green are in front of the new Episcopal Church, on Main Street. It is necessary for those leaving the City to obtain passes from Captain Green.

—o—

Medical Director.

Maj. F. H. Gross, Medical Director can be found at Gen. Negley's headquarters on Main Street in the lawn of the Columbia Athenæum.

—o—

Post Commissary.

The office of Capt. Wm. J. Kane, Post Commissary in this City, is on the South-East corner of Main street and the Public Square.

—o—

Post Quartermaster.

In the absence of Captain R. Stein, Lieut. Starkweather is acting as Post Quartermaster. His office is on the North-West corner of Main street and the Public Square.

—o—

WE are under obligations to the gentlemanly agent of Adams Express Co. in this city, for late Cincinnati, Philadelphia and New York papers.

—o—

It would be the part of wisdom for the young man who wrote that slanderous and insulting notice a short time since, and for the lack of bravery posted it up in the darkness of night;—fit time for such a nefarious deed—to attend an institution of learning and study the primary branch of spelling before he undertakes to write anything more for the public eye. And now young man, as we are giving advice, we will further suggest that it is not policy for you in a financial point of view, to run down the "Green Back," as you call it, for don't you readily give six dollars Tennessee money for five of the former? Young man are you not aware that for you to slander and insult your neighbors, merly because they are true to the Union, and not traitors as you are, proves that you are not a gentleman, and that you do not possess the traits of either manhood, honor or chivalry.

—o—

ARRESTED.—The Provost Marshall, on Tuesday last, arrested Mr. Rye, Cashier of the Branch Bank of Nashville, which is located in this city. He was arrested on the charge of treason, and was sent to Nashville.

—o—

REPORTED CAPTURE.

There was quite an alarm created last night by a report which came in town that there was quite a force of Cavalry out about fifteen miles. The troops in town were put in readines to receive them should they make an attack. This cavalry force, it is said, captured Capt. Kendrick of Company A, Seventy-ninth Penna. Regiment, and his party, which were putting in repair the telegraph line between here and Pulaski. The Cavalry came on them by suprise.—They fought bravely for a short time, but were overcome by the superior number of the enemy. We have no further particulars. A force has been sent out in pursuit of the enemy.

—o—

SINGULAR.—At Yorktown a soldier, named Corporal Tucker, was injured under remarkable circumstances. The shot, in passing, did not strike him, but the violence of the missle raised a swelling on his breast and bereft the poor man of speech. The doctors think that he will regain his utterance.

Glorious News from North Carolina.

FORT MACON TAKEN BY GEN. BURNSIDE.

We have received news from a reliable source that Gen. Burnside has succeeded in taking Fort Macon. No particulars.

—o—

Heavy Capture of Heavy Guns.

Since the 1st of January the Union forces have captured from the rebels five hundred and ninety siege guns and field pieces. This artillery would equip a grand army, and when it is remembered what pains the rebels have had to procure these guns, the severity of the loss will be fully apparent. Many of these guns have been brought, at a great expense, from England, having been procured by special agents, shipped on special vessels, and run all the risks of capture from our blockading fleet. Others have been cast in rebel founderies at Richmond and Norfolk, after great trouble in procuring iron and workmen. Now, with all these guns captured, the rebels have to fall back upon their bell metal, for their money has pretty well given out, and it is not safe to risk the blockade now-a-days.

—o—

CAIRO, April 28.

The steamer Estilla, from Pittsburg Landing has arrived.

The army is still gradually advancing, but everything is quiet.

There is no news of importance from Fort Pillow. The mortars still fire occasionally.

Refugees from Memphis report a strong Union feeling existing there. The majority of the people are anxiously awaiting the arrival of our forces to take possession.

It was believed that the city would not be burned, but that all the cotton, sugar, and molasses would be des royed.

Van Dorn, Price, and Jeff. Thompson were at Memphis with about 6,000 miserably clad troops. They remain there to awe the people into submission to the conscription act, which is being enforced. Hundreds of the inhabitants are leaving daily to avoid impressment. Most of the twelve months' men, whose time of service is about to expire, refuse to re-enlist under any circumstances. They are deserting in large numbers.

Refugees report General Villidque still in command at Fort Wright. He has a force of six or eight thousand men. Guns from Fort Randolph have been taken there. A large number of negroes were constantly at work strengthening the fortifications.

There is a report there, which is deemed reliable, that a rebel gunboat fleet is coming up the river to attack our flotilla, and then make a bold stroke for the possession of the Mississippi. On the reception of this report, a steamer was immediately dispatched to Island No. 10, having on board sufficient gunners to man the batteries there.

Refugees report a desperate censorship exercised at all points South over the public prints, which dared utter nothing derogatory to the cause of the rebellion. They say the Union men there are firm and loyal as ever, rejoicing at the near approach of the Federal army. Union clubs in Memphis are nightly holding correspondence with similar clubs in nearly every large city in the South.

General Printiss and other Federal prisoners had been in Memphis, and were received with marked attention from the Union people. They were taken to Tuscaloosa.

Fort Paris, just above Memphis, had been overflowed by a crevasse, which caused also much damage to the surrounding country.

—o—

PITTSBURG LANDING, April 29.—A very intelligent sailor, of Boston, deserted from the rebes this side of Corinth, reports that the capture of New Orleans was known in the rebel camp on the morning of the 27th; also states that on the 18th, the time of two Louisiana regiments, enlisted for 12 months expired, but by the new conscript law they were required to serve two years longer. On being so informed they laid down their arms and refused to fight, when Beauregard detached four regiments to guard them as prisoners.

—o—

The Richmond *Dispatch* says that several stores in that city are closed, and the following card posted on the doors: "Gone with the militia—will return when the war is at an end. By order of John Letcher." The suspension appeared to be general among the druggests. Among the excuses offered for exemption from draft, are some extremely ludicrous.

—o—

THE IRISH FAMINE.—The persisng necessities of our own people during this period of domestic war, cannot wholly repress contributions for the relief of foreign sufferers. Among the manifestations of benevolence in this way, is a contributions taken last week in all the Catholic churches in the diocese of Chicago out of which $1,000 have been already sent to Archbishop McHale, and $500 to the Central Committee in Dublin.

The statement of the Irish Archbishop seemto many to be scarcely warranted by the facts. Close attention to the subject satisfied us that the actual deficiencies of the Irish corps were not exaggerated though the peasantry seem in rather better condition to meet the calamity than they were in the famine of 1847.

Fifteen Battles in Less than Three Months.

Within the last ninety days the following battles were fought and won by the Federal forces:

Battle of Somerset, General Thomas commanding.
Mill Spring, Gen. Garfield.
Roanoke Island, Gen. Burnside.
Newbern, Gen. Burnside,
Fort Henry, Gen. Grant.
Fort Donelson, Gen. Grant.
Pea Ridge, Gen'ls. Curtis and Sigel.
Winchester, Gen. Shields.
Yorktown, Gen. McClellan.
Corinth, Gen. Grant.
Fort Craig, New Mexico, Col. Canby.
Island No. 10, Commodore Foote and General Pope.
Pittsburg Landing, April, 6 and 7th.
Bombardment of Fort Pickens, Colonel Brown.
Hampton Roads, between the Federal navy and the Merrimac.

In addition to the above the enemy have been compelled to evacuate Manassas, Bowling Green and Columbus.

There is no instance in the history of any other rebellion where so many battles of the magnitude of the above were fought in so short a space of time.

The line of battle reaches from Kansas to Fortress Monroe, a distance of 1,500 miles. This is the longest line of battle the world ever saw.

—o—

AFFAIRS AT MEMPHIS.—A letter from Cairo says that, on Wednesday succeeding the battle of Pittsburg Landing, Gen. Prentiss and two thousand three hundred and eighty-six Union prisoners passed through Memphis. The men were in good spirits, and kindly treated by the inhabitants, particularly the Irish and German women. The citizens contented themselves with waving handkerchiefs and looking the interest they dare not openly express. Prentiss made a Union speech to his men, and the citizens cheered him. Provost Marshall E. D. McKissock bade him remain silent. Prentiss told him that he had four to one more friends in Memphis that he (McKissock), and said to the citizens, "Keek quiet for a few weeks, and you will have an opportunity to cheer the old flag to your hearts content." Our soldiers sang "The Star-Spangled Banner," "Red, White, and Blue," "Happy Land of Canaan," and "Old John Brown," as they were starting on the cars for Tuscaloosa, Alabama, where they are at present confined.—There were one hundred and fourteen Union officers among the prisoners. Beauregard claims to have taken 3,000 prisoners. There are 5,000 bales of cotton, 7,000 hogsheads sugar, and 20,000 barrels molasses now lying upon the levee, of which the cotton will be burned, and the sugar and molasses rolled into the river on the approach of the Federal forces. The citizens and newspapers are opposed to burning the city, but soldiers and country people favor it.

—o—

A correspondent writing from Cairo says that the greatest calamity from below is the entire inundation of the Lower Mississippi, which is over its banks on both shores on the levees from Memphis to Natchez. All along from Natchez to Grand Gulf, and Vicksburg, up to Memphis, the cattle are standing in the water, and perishing, while steamers can only land passengers and freight at the points named, unless flatboats are brought alongside of the steamers. The destruction of property is immense, incalculable. The overflow is attributed to the breaking and in many places to the cutting of the levees. Plantation after plantation is submerged, and all the stock drowned or swept off by the flood, and the products destroyed. It is really a distressing state of affairs.

The De Sota, which arrived at Cairo on Thursday from the flotilla, in front of Fort Pillow, brought thirty bales of cotton for a Union citizen below Osceola upon her up trip. The steamer came across a flatboat, upon which were three families, driven from their homes by the flood. The boat was leaking badly and on the point of sinking with all on board when discovered. They were left at Hickman. Owing to the darkness of the night she was compelled to tie up to the trees along the shore, and while there her men picked up a machinist named Wm. Roberts, formerly of Philadelphia, who, to avoid impressment, left Memphis in December last, and took to the swamps, where he has since resided. The flood had driven him from his hiding place, and when discovered he was almost reduced to starvation. The De Soto carried him to Hickman. She also ran into a skiff filled with negroes escaping from some plantation, all but one of whom were drowned.

—o—

LIEUT. WORDEN.—Monday forenoon the President received the magnificent gold snuff box, appropriately engraved and embossed, which he is to present to Lieut. Worden, U. S. N., the commander of the Monitor, from the citizens of Buffalo, New York—ex-President Fillmore being among the subscribers to it. Lieut. Worden has been removed to the Washington Observatory for change of air. He is slowly improving. He can see imperfectly, when the bandages, which are kept on most of the time, are removed.

GEN. HALLECK.—A Western letter-writer gives the following pen sketch of the commander of our armies in the Southwest:

"To those who have never seen Gen. Halleck, it may be interesting to know that the steel engraving of him is a very correct likeness. I suppose there is but one, as I never have seen or heard of more. It gives, however, the idea of a large man, while he is below the medium hight, straight, active and well formed, and has a brisk, energetic gait, significant of his firm and decisive character. His nose is delicate and well formed, his torehead ample, his mouth by no means devoid of humor, and his eye the most remarkable I ever saw in any man, except Professor Agassiz. It is of a hazel color, clear as the morning star, and of a most intense brilliancy. When he looks at a man it seems as though he were literally to read him through and through. No amount of oly duplicity, no brazen effrontery, no studied concealment, could avail anything before that keen, penetrating glance. It is an eye to make all rogues tremble, and even honest men look about them to be sure they have not been up to some mischief.—The profound and implicit confidence of all who have had dealings with him, is no mystery after seeing what manner of man he is."

—

REBEL LOSS IN CANNON.—Since the commencement of the present year the rebels have lost an aggregate of nearly six hundred large sized guns and artillery pieces, at the following places:

Mill Spring,	10	Evansport,	7
Fort Henry,	17	Newbern,	10
Roanoke Island,	42	Fort Marion,	5
Elizabeth City,	5	Winchester	2
Bowling Green,	49	Island No. 10,	83
Fort Donelson,	65	By Gen. Pope,	124
Bird's Point, Mo.,	5	Fort Pulaski,	47
Columbus,	15	On vessels,	10
Fort clinch,	15	Miscellaneous,	15
Pea Ridge,	13	New Madrid	36
Shipping Point,	6		
Total,			585

The compiler of the list has omitted some one hundred heavy guns captured at the Hatteras and Port Royal forts, and other place.

—o—

R. E. THOMPSON, a candidate for the Confederate Congress in Sept. 1861, said, in the Nashville *Union and American*, that, rather than see Tennessee stay in the Union, he would see the Omnipotent wave the hand of desolation and utter war over our happy land, and sink it beneath lakes of devouring flame!" Mr. Thompson has seen "desolation" over the fair face of Tennessee and 'famine shrieking in the empty cornfields; he has witnessed "utter war" over that once happy state; he has read of, for we don't believe he has had the courage to witness the "devouring flame" which reddened Forts Henry and Donelson, Pittsburg Landing and the Field of Shiloh, but still Tennessee will say in the Union! Neither famine nor war, nor the lava that flows from the belching volcanoes of "mortal engines, whose rude throats the immortal Jove's dread clamors counterfeit," have been able to swerve her patriotic sons from their duty. The truth was for a time "crushed to earth" beneath the iron heel of the most terrible and relentless despotism the world ever knew, but Phœnix like, it has arisen from the ashes of desolation, war, and devouring flame, and now soars proudly and triumphantly over nearly all the States, and its majestic flight will soon be winged over every green vally and every sky-kissing hill throughout the length and breadth of Tennessee.—*Louisville Journal.*

—o—

A ROMANTIC STORY.—A few days since a young man named Smith died at Wolcottville, Conn., from wounds contracted in the battle at Newbern. He was in three battles, and was wounded at Newbern by a shot through the arm, which, for want of attention, caused his death. In the battle at Newbern he was providentially saved by a woman who accompanied her husband into the army. Finding her husband was determined to go, she said: "I go with you to take care of you and help you fight the battles." She dressed herself in the true Bloomer costume, and with Minie rifle in hand she went into the fight, and was in three battles—the last at Newbern. When finding her husband missing, she went in pursuit, and in her travels found young Smith lying in low ground, apparently dead, but on turning him over found that he had life. She gave him some cordials, he revived, and she sent for an ambulance and carried him to the hospital, where if he had remained longer, he would probably have lived.

—o—

AFFAIRS AT FORT WARREN.—Fort Warren, says the Boston *Herald*, is kept so close that it is almost as difficult to get news from there as from Yorktown. We understand, however, by one who has been there, that the health of the garrison is very good, only three or four men being sick. Buckner and Tilghman, who have been in close confinement for some weeks, have been allowed, since last Sunday, an hour each day to walk by themselves on the parapet over the sallyport. Mayor Brown, late of Baltimore was visited one day this week by his brother.

—

The Mobile Tribune says that the cotton in Giles and Murray counties, Northern Alabama, has been and is being burnt as the Union troops approach. Scott's Louisiana cavalry do the work, in the most cases with the hearty consent of the owners. The Charleston Christian Advocate says the Florida planters are also moving their cotton into the open fields so as to be able to burn it in case of necessity.

—o—

Seventh Brigade Journal.

FRIDAY EVENING, MAY 2, 1862.

BROWSING AROUND.—A party of gentlemen, among whom was a Doctor of Divinity of great comeliness of manner and eligance of address, some months since called at the White House to pay their respects to the President. On inquiring for that dignitary the servant informed them the President was at dinner, but he would present their cards. The doctor demurred to this, saying they would not disturb Mr. Lincoln, but would call again. Michael persisted, in assuring them it would make no difference with the President, and bolted in with the cards.—In a few minutes the President walked into the room with a kindly salution, and a request that the friends would take seats. The doctor expressed his regret that their visit was so ill-timed, and that his Excellency was disturbed while at dinner. "Oh! no consequence at all," said the good natured, Mr. Lincoln; "Mrs. Lincoln is absent at present, and when she is away I generally browse round."—*New Bedford Mercury.*

—0—

The wife of the poet Dryden complained that he passed all his time in reading, and never devoted a thought to her. "I wish I were a book," she cried, "and then, at least, you would look at me occasionally." "A book," exclaimed the poet. "I wish you were! That is, I would have you an almanac, 'which changes every year!'"

—0—

Lord Bacon well said: "You may take sarza to open the liver, prepared steel to open the spleen, flowers of sulphur for the lungs, castor for the brain; but there is no opening medicine found for the obstructions of the heart, beside a faithful friend, to whom you may impart griefs, joys, fears, hopes, suspicions, cares, counsels, and in short, whatsoever lies on the heart, and the seal, as it were, of a civil confession.

THOMAS A. DODSON and others *VS.* MASTIN FITZGERALD and others.—*Order of Publication*

IT appearing to me from complainant's bill filed in this cause, that Marian Dodson, Madison Johnson, Francis Johnson, Nelson Johnson, Louisa Johnson, John Church and wife Unity, Robert Lindsey and wife Lydia, Jackson Fitzgerald, Martin Church, Gideon Petty and wife Elizabeth, Louiza Petty, Parthena Petty, Washington Petty, Allen Petty, Carroll Petty, William Church, Thomas Church, Pinkey Dodson, defendants in this cause, are non-residents of the State of Tennessee, so that the ordinary process of law cannot be served on them; it is therefore ordered by me that publication be made in the Columbia Herald, a newspaper published in the twon of Columbia, Tennessee, for four weeks, the last of which shall be at least five days before the setting of the next term of the Chancery Court to be held for the county of Maury, at the Court House in the twon of Columbia, Tennessee, on the third Monday in March next, requiring the said Marion Dodson, Madison Johnson, Francis Johnson, Nelson Johnson, Louisa Johnson, John Church and wife Unity, Robert Lindsey and wife Lydia, Jackson Fitzgerald, Martin Church, Gideon Petty and wife Elizabeth, Louiza Petty, Parthena Petty, Washington Petty, Allen Petty, Carroll Petty, William Church, Thomas Church and Pinkey Dodson, defendants, to appear, and plead, answer or demur to the complainant's bill—or the same will be taken for confessed as to them, and set for hearing exparte.

feb. 8-4t. A. M. WINGFIELD, C. & M.

WM. GALLOWA[Y] VS. WM. PERRY, JR., ET ALS.—ORDER OF PUBLICATION.

IT appearing to me from Complainant's bill, that John S. Abernathy is a defendant and non-resident of the State of Tennessee, so that the ordinary process of law cannot be served on him. It is therefore ordered by me that publication be made in the Columbia Herald, a newspaper published in Columbia, Tenn., for four weeks, the last of which shall be at least five days before the next setting of the Chancery Court for Maury county, Tenn., to be held at the Court House in Columbia, on the 3d Monday in March next, requiring the said John S. Abernathy to appear and plead, answer or demur to Complainant's bill, or the same will be taken for confessed as to him and set for hearing ex parte. A. M. WINGFIELD, C. & M.

jan 20-4w

J. O. YORK VS. JAMES K. P. CAMPBELL, ET AL.—ORDER OF PUBLICATION.

IT appearing to me from Complainant's bill, that J. K. P. Campbell, one of the defendants, is a non-resident of the State of Tennessee, so that the ordinary process of law cannot be served on him. It is therefore ordered by me that publication be made in the Columbia Herald, a newspaper published in Columbia, Tenn., for four weeks, the last of which shall be at least five days before the next setting of the Chancery Court for Maury county, to be held at the Court House in Columbia, Tenn., on the 3d Monday in March next, requiring the said Campbell to appear and plead, answer or demur to Complainant's bill, or the same will be taken for confessed as to him and set for hearing ex parte.

A. M. WINGFIELD C. & M.

SHIELDS VS. A. M. WINGFIELD, C. & M., ET ALS.—ORDER OF PUBLICATION.

IT appearing to me from Complainant's bill, that Lewis Rowe and wife Lucy B., and Elijah M. Lancaster and wife Clarinda D., and John Abbott and wife Betsy B., and John O. Wing and Leathy N. Weston and Eliza P. Cummings, are defendants and are non-residents of the State of Tennessee, so that the ordinary process of law cannot be served on them. It is therefore ordered by me that publication be made in the Columbia Herald, a newspaper published in the town of Columbia, for four weeks, the last publication to be at least five days before the next setting of the Chancery Court for Maury county, Tenn., to be held at the Court House in Columbia, Tennessee, on the 3d Monday in March next, requiring the said non-residents to appear and plead, answer or demur to Complainant's bill, or the same will be taken for confessed as to them and set for hearing ex parte.

A. M. WINGFIELD, C. & M.

jan 20-4w

R. H. HILL ET AL. VS. J. K. P. CAMPBELL ET AL.—ORDER OF PUBLICATION

IT appearing to me from Complainant's bill, that J. K. P. Campbell is one of the defendants to said suit and is a non-resident of the State of Tennessee, so that the ordinary process of law cannot be served on him. It is therefore ordered by me that publication be made in the Columbia Herald, a newspaper published in Columbia, Tenn., for four weeks, the last publication to be at least five days before the next setting of the Chancery Court for Maury county, Tenn., to be held at the Court House in Columbia, on the 3d Monday in March next, requiring the said Campbell to appear and plead, answer or demur to Complainant's bill, or the same will be taken for confessed as to him and set for hearing ex parte.

A. M. WINGFIELD, C. & M.

jan 20-4w

JAMES M. PANNELL VS. JAMES K. P. CAMPBELL ET AL.—ORDER OF PUBLICATION.

IT appearing to me from Complainant's bill, that James K. P. Campbell is a defendant and non-resident of the State of Tennessee, so that, the ordinary process of law cannot be served on him. It is therefore ordered by me that publication be made in the Columbia Herald, a newspaper published in Columbia, Tenn., for four weeks, the last publication to be at least five days before the next setting of the Chancery Court for Maury county, to be held at the Court House in Columbia, on the 3d Monday in March next, requiring said Campbell to appear and plead, answer or demur to Complainant's bill, or the same will be taken for confessed as to him and set for hearing ex parte.

A. M. WINGFIELD, C. & M.

jan. 20-4w

Family Groceries.

REMARKABLY CHEAP!

DAVID A. DUGGER,

HAS opened a Commission, Wholesale and Retail House in the new Towler block on the East side of the Public square. His

FAMILY GROCERIES,

Embracing almost everything in the Grocery line that can be procured in our young Republic. His sugars and molasses consists of a great variety of qualities, which were purchased in New Orleans in large quantities for wholesale and retail purposes. Many of these Groceries have already arrived, and others are expected by every train, which enables him to accommodate families by the barrel or in larger or smaller quantities, as may be desired, at prices that cannot be under-sold by any.

It is his intention to keep constantly on hand a good supply of flour and meal, and other produce from the country.

SHERIFF SALE.

BY virtue of an execution to me directed from the Circuit Court of Maury county at the January term 1862, in favor of Ewing, McCrory & Co., against Jared O. Church and James M. Harwell, I will proceed to sell for cash to the highest bidder, at the Market House in the town of Columbia, on Monday the 10th day of March next, all the right, title, claim and interest of said Church & Harwell, in and to two Lots of ground with the improvements thereon, situated in the town of Columbia and bounded as follows: One lot is bounded on the North by the Female College lot—South by W. H. Pillow's lot—East by Glade street—West by Embargo street, containing 2¾ acres.

The other lot is bounded on the North by Hodge & Shelton's lots—South by McCrory's lots—East by Glade street, and West by Embargo street, known as the Columbia Tennessee Female College lot. Levied on as the property of J. O. Church,

feb. 15, pr.'s fee $5. THOS. J. CROSBY, Shff

NOTICE.

THE Provost Marshal's Office is for, the present in the Sibley Tent, in front of the Episcopal Church, where persons desiring can procure passes.

NATHAN VAUGHT VS. S. L. LONG.—ORDER OF PUBLICATION.

IT appearing to me from Complainant's bill, that S. L. Long, the defendant, is a non-resident of the State of Tennessee, so that the ordinary process of law cannot be served on him. It is therefore ordered by me that publication be made in the Columbia Herald, a newspaper published in Columbia, for four weeks, the last of which shall be at least five days before the next setting of the Chancery Court for Maury county, Tenn., to be held at the Court House in Columbia, on the 3d Monday in March next, requiring the said Long to appear and plead, answer or demur to Complainant's bill, or the same will be taken for confessed as to him and set for hearing ex parte.

jan. 20-4w A. M. WINGFIELD, C. & M.

L. P. KIRBY VS. SUSAN KIRBY.—ORDER OF PUBLICATION.

IT appearing to me from Complainant's bill, that Susan Borders, now Susan Kirby, the defendant, is a non-resident of the State of Tennessee, so that the ordinary process of law cannot be served on her. It is therefore ordered by me that publication be made in the Columbia Herald, a newspaper published in Columbia, Tenn., for four weeks, the last of which shall be at least five days before the next setting of the Chancery Court for Maury county, Tenn., to be held at the Court House in Columbia, on the 3d Monday in March next, requiring the said Susan Kirby to appear and plead, answer or demur to Complainant's bill, or the same will be taken for confessed as to her and set for hearing ex parte.

A. M. WINGFIELD, C. & M.

jan. 20-4w

WM. A. ALEXANDER VS. THOMAS J. COLEBURN ET AL.—ORDER OF PUBLICATION.

IT appearing to me from Complainant's bill, that Thomas J. Coleburn, one of the defendants is now absent from the State of Tennessee, so that the ordinary process of law cannot be served on him. It is therefore ordered by me that publication be made in the Columbia Herald, a newspaper published in Columbia, Tenn, for four weeks, the last of which shall be at least five days before the next setting of the Chancery Court for Maury county, Tenn., to be held at the Court House in Columbia, on the 3d Monday in March next, requiring the said Coleburn to appear and plead, answer or demur to Complainant's bill, or the same will be taken for confessed as to him and set for hearing ex parte. A. M. WINGFIELD, C. & M.

jan. 20-4w

P. D. FRANKLIN VS E. C. OVERTON ET AL.—ORDER OF PUBLICATION.

IT appearing to me from Complainant's bill, that James K. P. Campbell is a defendant and non-resident of the State of Tennessee, so that the ordinary process of law cannot be served on him. It is therefore ordered by me that publication be made in the Columbia Herald, a newspaper published in the town of Columbia, for four weeks, the last publication to be at least five days before the next setting of the Chancery Court for Maury county, Tenn., to be held on the 3d Monday in March next, requiring said Campbell to appear and plead, answer or demur to Complainant's bill, or the same will be taken for confessed as to him and set for hearing ex parte.

jan 20-4w A. M. WINGFIELD, C. & M.

JACOB HOOFMAN VS. JAMES S. BINGHAM ET AL.—ORDER OF PUBLICATION.

IT appearing to me from Complainant's cross bill filed, that John T. Fike is a defendant and a non-resident of the State of Tennessee, so that the ordinary process of law cannot be served on him. It is therefore ordered by me that publication be made in the Columbia Herald, a newspaper published in the town of Columbia for four weeks, the last publication to be at least five days before the next setting of the Chancery Court for Maury county, Tenn., to be held at the Court House in Columbia, Tenn., on the 3d Monday in March next, requiring the said Fike to appear and plead, answer or demurr to Complainant's cross bill, or the same will be taken for confessed as to him and set for hearing ex parte.

jan 20-4w A. M. WINGFIELD, C. & M.

ELIAS RUMBO VS. ABRAHAM LINCOLN, ET AL.—ORDER OF PUBLICATION.

IT appearing to me from Complainant's bill, that Abraham Lincoln, President of the United States, is a non-resident of the State of Tennessee, so that the ordinary process of law cannot be served on him. It is therefore ordered by me that publication be made in the Columbia Herald, a newspaper published in the town of Columbia, Tenn., for four weeks, the last publication to be at least five days before the next setting of the Chancery Court for Maury county, Tenn., to be held at the Court House in Columbia, on the 3d Monday in March next, requiring the said Lincoln to appear and plead, answer or demur to Complainant's bill, or the same will be taken for confessed as to him and set for hearing ex parte.

A. M. WINGFIELD, C. & M.

jan 20-4w

EDWARD WILLIAMS ET AL. VS. WM PERRY, JR., ET AL.—ORDER OF PUBLICATION.

IT appearing to me from Complainant's bill, that John S. Abernathy is a defendant and non-resident of the State of Tennessee, so that the ordinary process of law cannot be served on him. It is therefore ordered by me that publication be made in the Columbia Herald a newspaper published in Columbia, Tenn., for four weeks, the last of which shall be at least five days before the next setting of the Chancery Court for Maury county, Tenn., to be held on the 3d Monday in March next, at the Court House in Columbia, requiring said Abernathy to appear and plead, answer or demur to Complainant's bill, or the same will be taken for confessed as to him and set for hearing ex parte.

A. M. WINGFIELD C. & M.

jan. 20-4w

JAMES R. HANNAH VS. THOMAS J. COLEBURN ET AL.—ORDER OF PUBLICATION.

IT appearing to me from Complainant's bill, that Thomas J. Coleburn and Abraham M. Loony are defendants and are absent from the State of Tennessee, so that the ordinary process of law cannot be served on them. It is therefore ordered by me that publication be made in the Columbia Herald, a newspaper published in Columbia, Tenn., for four weeks, the last of which shall be at least five days before the next setting of the Chancery Court for Maury county, Tenn., to be held at the Court House in Columbia, on the 3d Monday in March next, requiring the said Coleburn and Loony to appear and plead, answer or demur to Complainant's bill, or the same will be taken for confessed as to them and set for hearing ex parte.

A. M. WINGFIELD, C. & M.

jan. 20-4w

W. J. DALE & GEO. W. CAMPBELL EXR'S. VS J. K. P. CAMPBELL.—ORDER OF PUBLICATION.

IT appearing to me from Complainant's bill, that James K. P. Campbell, the defendant in this case, is a non-resident of the State of Tennessee, so that the ordinary process of law cannot be served on him. It is therefore ordered by me that publication be made in the Columbia Herald, a newspaper published in the town of Columbia, for four weeks, the last publication to be at least five days before the next setting of the Chancery Court at Columbia, Tenn., to be held on the 3d Monday in March next, at the Court House in Columbia, requiring the said J. K. P. Campbell to appear and plead, answer or demur to Complainant's bill, or the same will be taken for confessed as to him and set for hearing ex parte.

A. M. WINGFIELD, C. & M.

jan 20-4w

JOHN B. JOHNSON ADM'R &C, VS. E. C. OVERTON ADM'R & J. K. P. CAMPBELL.—ORDER OF PUBLICATION.

IT appearing to me from Complainant's bill, that James K. P. Campbell, one of the defendants, is a non-resident of the State of Tennessee, so that the ordinary process of law cannot be served on him. It is therefore ordered by me that publication be made in the Columbia Herald, a newspaper published in Columbia, Tenn., for four weeks, the last of which shall be at least five days before the next setting of the Chancery Court for Maury county, to be held at the Court House in Columbia, on the 3d Monday in March next, requiring the said Campbell to appear and plead, answer or demur to Complainant's bill, or the same will be taken for confessed as to him and set for hearing ex parte.

A. M. WINGFIELD, C. & M.

jan. 20-4w.

SEWING MACHINES FOR SAIF,

1door West of Hugh's Gallery,

NASHVILLE, TENNESSEE.

The Daily Delta.

VOL. XVII. NEW ORLEANS, FRIDAY, MAY 2, 1862. NO. 129

Notice.

Holders of Checks drawn on me by J. N. Bradford & Co., are notified that they will be paid on presentation.

R. F. HARBISON,
40 St. Charles street.

may1 3t*

A Card.

NEW ORLEANS, May 1, 1862.

There are a great many of the non-commissioned officers and soldiers from Forts Jackson and St. Philip now in the city, who are reviled and jeered at by the people as the traitors who betrayed the forts. All these are true men, who stood to their work gallantly and heroically, through good and bad report, and they deserve well of the citizens of New Orleans. The traitors are mostly all in the hands of the enemy, and none of them are in the city. It is only necessary for the people to be aware of these facts to do the men ample justice.

J. K. DUNCAN,
Brigadier General.

my1

A Card.

To the Editors of the Delta:

I have been deeply pained and mortified by learning that for the last three days reports have been widely circulated through the city that I had gone on board the Yankee fleet now opposite the city. I have been at home since last Saturday, quite ill the most of the time, and under the treatment of my physician. So far from going on board of the fleet of the enemies of that Government in which I was born and all my children raised, and to whose Constitution I have sworn a willing allegiance, such a thought never entered my mind, and I beg of the public, and particularly of my friends, to give no credence to the reports thus injuriously circulated against me.

Yours, truly,
A. P. FIELD.

may1 2p1t

Allen Guards.

FORT JACKSON, April 28, 1862.

I hereby certify that the following members of the company of Allen Guards, under my command, bravely remained at their posts when the remainder of the company, and other troops at Fort Jackson, basely deserted during the past night of the 28th inst:

Sergeant J. Laviston,	Privates A. McChin,
Sergeant J. List,	A. Mayers,
Corporal R. Coolidge,	Denis Magner,
Corporal J. Thrall,	Ed Roach,
Corporal J. Chadwick,	Denis Ryan,
Privates Thos. Allen,	J. P. Simpson,
F. Austin,	Geo. D. Stephens,
J. Brennan,	R. H Taylor,
H. G. Brunete,	Lewis Vassil,
Thos. Coyne,	Mat. Wild,
Geo Drew,	Thos. Wright,
Sam. Edwards,	Henry Williams,
John Geary,	John McNeil,
R. D. Holmes,	Wm. Maxwell,
F. G. Hennessey,	Geo. O'Brien,
Geo. Kountz,	Denis O'Brien,
Thos Keely,	Brgn O'Neil,
Pat Lane,	J. A. Shinn,
Wm La temore,	Wm. Coles,
Mike McMahan.	

S. JONES,
Captain of Allen Guards.

my1 2dp

Headquarters European Brigade.

NEW ORLEANS, May 1, 1862.

General Orders No. 61.

I—All orders relating to requisitions for Provisions are hereby revoked.

II—All requisitions for Provisions must in future be approved at these Headquarters

III—No bills for Provisions will be paid by the City Council unless these orders are complied with

By order of PAUL JUGE FILS,
General Commanding.

MARK QUAYLE, Brigade Major.

my1 tf

Dissolution.

NEW ORLEANS, May 1, 1862.

I this day withdraw from the firm of A. H. MAY & CO., having disposed of my interest in it to the remaining partners. They are authorized to continue the business without changing the style of the firm.

CHAS. T. PICTON,
per pro THOS. C. HERNDON.

my2 1m

Citizens of New Orleans.

The Common Council have passed the following resolutions:

Resolved, That the Mayor be, and is hereby, authorized to organize, outside of the regular police of the city of New Orleans a Citizens' Police in each Precinct, and for that purpose to summon and compel service in the respective precinct of any resident.

Resolved, That every citizen is bound to comply with the orders he may receive from his Honor the Mayor to perform special duty on the police.

Resolved, That the Special Police so appointed shall wear a badge and carry such arms as the Mayor may determine.

S P. DELABARRE,
President pro tem. Board of Aldermen.
J. MAGIONI,
President Board of Assistant Aldermen.

I hereby notify all good citizens to report to Paul Juge fils, General Commanding European Brigades, who is invested by me with full authority to act for the preservation of the public peace. Gen. Juge is authorized in my name to disperse all assemblies composed of more than six persons.

JOHN T. MONROE,
Mayor of the City of New Orleans.

Approved April 30, 1862.

my1 2ptf

Proclamation by the Mayor.

MAYORALTY OF NEW ORLEANS,
City Hall, April 26, 1862

To the Keepers of Grocery and of Provision Stores:

The city authorities request that all keepers of Grocery Stores and other establishments where Provisions are sold, immediately open their respective places of business, and not force the authorities to measures they would wish to avoid. It is also recommended that the ordinary currency continue to be received. It is as good now as it ever has been, and there is no reason to reject it. Those who refuse to receive it must share the evils and inconvenience they thus participate in inflicting on the community. It is hoped that a spirit of accommodation will now be evinced by all persons. Those individuals who hold Confederate money, and wish to part with it, can have it exchanged for City Bills by applying to the Committee of Public Safety.

For the better preservation of public order, it is particularly desired that all citizens be at home by 9 P. M., and that ladies and children remain within doors as much as possible.

JOHN T. MONROE, Mayor.

ap27 2p5t

Proclamation by the Mayor.

MAYORALTY OF NEW ORLEANS,
City Hall, April 26, 1862

The sad and melancholy circumstances through which we are passing require the utmost wisdom and forbearance on the part of our citizens. They should not suffer themselves to be carried away by too keen a sense of the difficulties by which they are surrounded, but ought, on the contrary, to aid the Municipal authority in maintaining order in the city. To facilitate my duties as the constituted Chief of the Police, I have called to my assistance the services of the European Brigade, and they have been invested by me with the duty of watching over the public tranquillity. Patrols, under the direction of the commanding officer of said Brigade, should be treated with respect and obeyed.

JOHN T. MONROE, Mayor.

Approved April 26, 1862.
WM. FRERET, Chairman Safety Committee.

Proclamation by the Mayor.

MAYORALTY OF NEW ORLEANS,
City Hall, April 29, 1862.

It is requested that all citizens retire to their homes during the performance by the United States forces of those acts of authority which it would be folly to resist. Any violence or disorder would be productive of the most serious disasters, and entail danger and suffering on the unresisting population of the city.

Fellow-citizens, the honor and dignity of New Orleans have been maintained. The flag of Louisiana is not to be removed from this building by any act of your authorities, but by those who have the power and the will to exercise it.

You are enjoined to preserve order, and that silence, more eloquent than words, which befits so solemn an occasion.

JOHN T. MONROE, Mayor.

ap 29 2p

Headquarters European Brigade.

NEW ORLEANS, April 27, 1862—11 o'clock A. M.

By order of his Honor Mayor J. T. MONROE dated this day, I hereby assume command of all the Foreign Troops.

I call upon all good citizens to give me what aid and assistance they can to preserve order and tranquility in the city, and they are requested to assemble forthwith at a central point in each of their respective Districts and report immediately to these Headquarters, No. 42 Old Levee street, between Bienville and Customhouse.

PAUL JUGE FILS,
General Commanding.

ap28 2ptf

Notice by the Mayor.

MAYORALTY OF NEW ORLEANS,
City Hall, April 29, 1862.

The public are hereby notified that the European Brigade, Paul Juge fils, General Commanding, have been requested and have consented to continue patrolling the city, in conjunction with the ordinary police, for the purpose of preserving peace and order. It is hoped that all good citizens will contribute their assistance in this effort to maintain the tranquility of the city.

JOHN T. MONROE Mayor.

apr30 5t2dp

To the Planters.

We are compelled to give notice that we can not at present receive any further orders for Goods. The orders received and registered up to this time, accompanied with cotton, cash or drafts, will require all the goods we can make up to the 1st of September.

Planters are hereby notified that we can not receive any more cotton or orders. Public notice will be given in due time when present engagements will be completed.

S. M. HART & CO.

apr22 2p2m

Fifty Dollars Reward.

LOST, on the evening of the 27th of April, between the hours of 6 and 9 o'clock, in the Third District, one pair of diamond Ear-rings, four diamonds in each; one pair of emerald Ear-rings, one large diamond Ring and one diamond Ring set in the center of a small black stone. The finder will receive the above reward by leaving them at the office of the Delta with the cashier.

apr28 2ptf

THE DAILY DELTA

THE UNITED STATES MILITARY COMMANDER.

B. F. Butler, the General of the United States who is to command the forces that will occupy this city, is a lawyer of prominence in Lowell, Mass., who has also figured conspicuously as a politician under the old organization of parties in the United States. Previous to the present revolution, he had been conspicuous in New England politics for his vigorous and constant hostility to the anti-slavery parties in New England, and for his general concurrence with the Southern or national wing of the Democratic party. He was also regarded as an earnest State Rights Democrat of the Jeffersonian and Jacksonian shool. In the National Democratic Conventions his course was considered as national and in accordance with the views maintained by the Southern branch of the party. In the convention of 1856, he was a warm supporter of Franklin Pierce for the Presidency, and in the Charleston Convention he voted to the very last for Jefferson Davis. Mr. Davis held then the views upon which the Southern States have based their rights to secede from the Union. Gen. Butler was regarded as of the same school of politics as Gen. Pierce and Caleb Cushing. Early in the beginning of this war he astonished his old party associates by offering his services to maintain the Government of Abraham Lincoln, whose politics and party he had so long and so bitterly opposed, and has been very active and prominent in giving his aid to prosecute this war. We state these facts of his career, which are matters of history. Our readers must make their own conclusions and form their own opinions, as to the probable course and bearing of their new Governor.

As important facts in the history of the events of the last five or six days we would state that the occupation of this city, now momentarily expected by the United States forces, secures to them the control of the lives and property of one hundred and fifty thousand inhabitants, nearly all them non-combatants. The property remaining in the city is altogether of the description known all over the world as private property. Of other property, which has been recognized in all other countries, and in other wars but these as private, and not subject to seizure in war—that which forms the commerce of our people, and which has contributed mainly to the vast trade of our city—there is little or none left in our port. The cotton, which the United States authorities have in other places seized and appropriated, without authority of any law of nations, as recognized by civilized communities, was all consumed the moment the announcement was made that the Federalists had passed the forts.

This was done by order of the Governor of Louisiana and of the military commander of the Confederate States. Fifteen thousand bales were consumed, the value of which would have been about a million and a half of dollars. The tobacco now stored here, being all held by foreign residents or on foreign account, was not destroyed. The specie of the banks, to the amount of twelve or fifteen millions, was removed from the city and placed in a secure place; so of nearly all the stores and other property of the Confederate States. The records of the Court and of all the offices of the Confederate States were in like manner disposed of. There remain the public buildings, the Customhouse, the Post Office and the Mint. Of provisions of every kind, there is a scant supply, barely sufficient for the wants of the people. Of ships and steamers, which ordinarily at this period of the year crowd our wharves, as far as the eye can reach, there is not a single one left. The only ships in our port are the armed ships of the United States. They lie at the head of our principal streets, commanding them with their powerful batteries. The prospects of any arrival of cotton are poor. By order of the Governor, the cotton on the banks of all the streams has been everywhere set on fire. Not a bale could be picked up by the most diligent and enterprising search. The whole valley of the Mississippi is now being illuminated by the conflagration of this most valuable article of commerce. The execution of this order of the Government, though not prompted by any motive of the sort, will send grief and misery to the great manufacturing communities of the old world. The Confederate Government and the people aver that they have been forced to this great sacrifice by the enemy's threat and the performance of it, on a small scale, to confiscate this valuable product to their own use. It is a heavy loss to our own people, but they claim no commiseration or sympathy for such sacrifice. They can live without the proceeds of their cotton, and for the present the Southern people are, and will be content, with a bare subsistence. They have planted large crops of cereals, and will soon be quite independent of all other communities for the means of comfortable subsistence.

Such is historically our situation, and in the presence of a hostile military force, virtually occupying the city, our functions as public journalist become those of the chronicler of facts, the mere historian of the condition of this city and of the Southwestern Valley of the Mississippi.

We are happy to publish the card of Col A. P. Field. It furnishes an illustration of the propriety of the recommendation in our morning edition, that our people should discountenance the rumors put in circulation implicating the fidelity of citizens.

CORRESPONDENCE BETWEEN THE MAYOR AND CAPT. FARRAGUT.

The following letters conclude the correspondence which has been going on for several days between the U. S. Flag-officer and the Mayor of this city. It will be seen from the letter of Capt. Farragut that he seeks to vindicate himself from the conclusion that he intended to threaten the city in a certain event. We would further add, in justification of the construction placed by the Mayor and the people—and we may say of the foreign Consuls—on Flag-officer Farragut's letter, that when Commander Bell delivered the last letter to the Mayor the following conversation occurred:

Mayor Monroe. "As I consider this a threat to bombard the city, and as it is a matter about which the notice should be clear and specific, I desire to know when the forty-eight hours began to run?"

Commander Bell. "It begins from the time you receive this notice."

The Mayor then drew his watch and showing it to Commander Bell said: "Then you see it is fifteen minutes past 12 o'clock."

The Commander recognized the correctness of the time and made some remarks, which were understood by all present to convey distinctly the threat, that if the flag was not hauled down in forty-eight hours the city would be shelled.

The letters below were laid before the Council by the Mayor, but the Council did not see any necessity for any action on them:

MAYORALTY OF NEW ORLEANS
City Hall, May 1, 1862.

To the Common Council, in Joint Session:

Gentlemen—I herewith lay before you a copy of a communication received yesterday from Flag Officer Farragut. You will observe that the note intimates a misinterpretation, on the part of the city authorities of Flag Officer Farragut's previous communication.. I venture to say, gentlemen, that no reasoning mind can fail to place on the note of Monday, the 28th instant, the interpretation attached to it by the people of this city. The notification to remove our women and children within forty-eight hours, in case we adhered to our resolution not to haul down our flag, can be construed in no other way then as a threat to bombard the city. The meaning was plain not only to us, but to the consuls of the foreign nations residing here. But in so clear a case argument is superfluous

Flag Officer Farragut informs us that, in consequence of the offensive nature of our answer to his threat, he declines further communication with us, and shall, on the arrival of Gen. Butler, hand the city over to his charge. He certainly should be conscious that the city of New Orleans sought no communication with him, or his forces, and that the cessation of intercourse, while it depended entirely on his will, could not fail to be quite as agreeable to us as to him. It would add still further to our gratification should Gen. Butler find it equally unpleasant to hold communication with the city.

Respectfully,
(Signed) JOHN T. MONROE, Mayor.

U S FLAG SHIP HARTFORD,
At Anchor off the City of New Orleans,
April 30, 1862.

To his Honor the Mayor and City Council of New Orleans:

Gentlemen—I informed you in my communication of 28th of April, that your determination as I understood it, was not to haul down the flag of Louisiana on the City Hall, and that my officers and men were treated with insult and rudeness when they landed, even with a flag of truce, to communicate with the authorities, &c, and that if such was to be the determined course of the people, the fire of the vessels might at any moment be drawn upon the city.

This you have thought proper to construe into a determination on my part to murder your women and children, and made your letter so offensive, that it will terminate our intercourse, and so soon as Gen. Butler arrives with his forces, I shall turn over the charge of the city to him, and resume my naval duties.

Very respectfully, your obedient servant,
(Signed) D. G. FARRAGUT,
Flag Officer Western Gulf Blockading Squadron.

Some of our citizens have been unjustly charged with infidelity to the Government, and, on mere rumors, or utterly insufficient grounds, subjected to mortification and insult. We have heard of several instances of such conduct on the part of the reckless and thoughtless that are shameful and outrageous. There seems to be a proneness on the part of certain violent, excitable and heedless people, to create and foster the very suspicion, which all good citizens should desire to see discountenanced, that there exist traitors and bad citizens in our midst. Nothing is more necessary for our safety, our peace and our future, than that our people should present themselves as a unit in the present condition of our affairs

The man who seeks to divide us now is truly a great enemy of our city. The man who encourages broils and personal disputes is a bad and dangerous man, whose crime and baseness will never be forgotten by our people. There is no reward or favor that will ever compensate him for the curses and hate which will pursue him throughout life. Let us, then, exercise charity, forbearance and confidence towards our own people, crediting no charges of bad conduct against any one which do not rest upon good and substantial grounds, upon satisfactory evidence. Let us abstain from circulating idle rumors and scandals, implicating our fellow-citizens, or from asking questions which frequently give rise to these scandals.

LANDING OF U. S. TROOPS.—Three regiments of U. S. troops and several cannon were landed last evening from the transports, at the foot of St. Joseph street, and forming into column marched up St. Joseph into St. Charles, and thence to Canal, and down Canal to the Levee. The regiments were preceded by their bands, which played Yankee Doodle and other airs that have not been heard in these streets for a long time. There was not a very large crowd of people on the sidewalk, and no demonstrations were made by the spectators nor the troops.

Shinplasters and Confederate paper will be received in payment for board and tuition, at Prof. Brette's, 13 St. Charles street.

The resolutions of thanks of the Councils to Gen. Duncan are richly deserved by the gallant General, but they are quite faulty in the omission to recognize the other officers and the men who were faithful in that heroic defense. From all we can learn, all the officers, including conspicuously the indomitable, skillful and brave Col. Higgins, the commander of Fort Jackson, upon whom fell the chief brunt of the combat, nobly did their duty, and are entitled to the warmest gratitude and applause of the people. Some mention, too, should be made of the officers of our gunboats who were equal to the occasion and their duty. The conduct of Capts. McIntosh and Grant, of Lieuts. Huger and Kennon, was worthy of the highest eulogy. Two of them, McIntosh and Huger, are dreadfully wounded. It would be a consolation in their afflictions to them and their families to receive some token of the public admiration and gratitude.

We are requested and authorized to state that the men of the gunners of the Forts Jackson and St. Philip, who are now in the city, are of those who were true and faithful, and did not desert their officers. The mutineers have not yet appeared among us. It would be a great wrong to offer any insult to the brave fellows who were true to their duty, because of the misconduct of the faithless. Our citizens should take care that the faithful men are not only protected, but rewarded and befriended.

We expressly disclaimed any belief in or any responsibility for the authenticity of the document published in the Delta of yesterday, as the protest of the French commander of the steamship of war now in our port, addressed to the Commodore of the United States fleet. It was handed to us by a highly respectable French gentleman, who believed in its genuineness, though he did not vouch for it. We hasten to state that it is repudiated by the parties in whose name it purports to be addressed.

WHAT THE MORNING JOURNALS SAY.

From Yesterday's Evening Edition.

The *Picayune* emphatically censures the conduct of Com. Farrigut in raising his flag over the Confederate Government buildings in the city without landing a force adequate to the protection of his colors. The wrong thus done by Com. Farrigut is clearly and ably set forth in the subjoined extract from the Picayune's article:

The city and its inhabitants are in the power of the public enemy, but he has only taken formal possession, and that in a manner to produce mischief without compensating advantage to any of his own proper and lawful objects as a conqueror. We yielded because he was too strong, and resistance would be unavailing and calamitous. He landed a small force, sufficient to take down the flag of Louisiana from one place, and to put up the emblem of the authority under which he invades us at another. But he provided no force to supply the moral power of civil obligation which he took away, and left his flag under a feeble guard, with the extraordinary charge to the authorities of the subjected city "that they shall see that it is respected."

The flag has since been so displayed, and is a prolific source of disquietude to those reflecting persons who are desirous that the inevitable change of government shall be effected with as little disturbance as possible, and that nothing may occur to aggravate the terms of antagonism which must necessarily exist between the victors and the vanquished. It is not a condition, which by any of the laws of war an occupying force has the right to make, that captives shall be the guardians of the standard of their conquerers. To have left that flag, after the main object was accomplished of receiving the proof of the absence of all public purpose to resist, and to command the municipal authorities to give it especial protection, under implied threats of vengeance for failure, was a wanton aggravation of the difficulties of their position, which Capt. Farragut has no right to make.

It was putting up a provocation to disorder in the midst of a numerous and excitable population, stung with the mortifications of recent defeats, and likely, as popular masses always are, to vent their feelings in forms dangerous to the public peace, and leading to acts of unreasoning and perhaps uncontrollable violence. A humane and considerate man would have reflected well on these things before assuming a show of authority and setting up its symbols without providing an adequate force of his own to maintain it against the irregular exhibitions of hostility he knew to be inevitable.

It was not to be doubted that the public authorities would, as guardians of the peace and property of the citizens, so long as they were left in possession of any power, do all they could to suppress all unruliness of conduct tending to a breach of order, and that they would be for their own sakes equally vigilant, although they might individually share in the feeling of repugnance to the flag, while they deplore and oppose the intemperance and disorder to which it gives rise among the unreflecting and the turbulent. But if from any cause they should be unable to control these exhibitions, and the popular resentments should be too strong for reasoning and authority, the responsibility, to humanity at least, for all the consequences will incontestibly attach to those who sent this irritating symbol without adequate support from its own friends, and without any warrant of usage in war, or public advantage, among a heated multitude.

If a riot should occur too strong for the control of the civil powers, and acts should be committed contrary to the moral sentiment of the city, against the Federal flag or its supporters, such as Commodore Farragut hinted at, in his communication of the 28th, as likely "to draw the fire of the fleet" upon the city, the bloodshed, the disorder and the crimes which would follow, will be justly chargeable to the perverseness with which he insists on an imperfect occupation of the city, and inflicts upon its authorities distasteful, and, it might be, impossible duties

The *Bulletin* deprecates the disorders committed in this city, by men and boys, during the period that has elapsed since the advent of the enemy's fleet before the city, and admonishes every good citizen to aid the authorities in suppressing those disorders and arresting the disposition to pillage, which has occasionally manifested itself. Says the Bulletin, referring to the disorderly:

Many of these persons are mere boys in years, though adults in mischief. Others are of mature age, and ought to be in the ranks of the army—serving their country in the tented field, instead of remaining at home and disgracing the city by their ruffianism and gasconading.

The *Crescent* shows how causeless the food panic at present pervading the city is. Many of those most panic-stricken on this subject, have already in their houses food for weeks, and the Crescent is confident that before the present stock is exhausted abundance from abroad will be pouring into us.

The Crescent reiterates the advice to the people to deport themselves with calmness, patience and dignity.

The *Bee*, reviewing the condition of affairs in our city, observes the quietness that pervaded throughout Wednesday, and urges that so long as crowds gather about Federal sentinels, to sneer at and abuse them, there is danger of disorder and tumult. The Bee, noticing the services of the foreign brigade in preserving order, says:

The foreign population in our midst have a clear title to our warm and lasting remembrance. It will scarcely be believed, and yet we assert the fact upon the authority of officers of the French brigade, that because in the exercise of their duty these military companies were occasionally compelled to disperse groups of excited men they were assailed with the reproach of being aiders and abettors of the Lincolnites.

Several of the members of the brigades were so indignant at these calumnious imputations, that they threw down their muskets and refused to perform further duty. All that can be said in extenuation of the vile slander is that it was uttered by a class of men who only flourish amidst turbulence and mischief.

The Bee insists that as one of the means of preserving the quiet of the city, the grocery and provision stores must be opened in order that the people may procure food, and to prevent congregations of idlers, pertinently adding:

The confusion which at first prevailed with respect to the currency is rapidly disappearing. Confederate notes, State and City notes, and the individual notes of parties believed to be responsible, are freely circulated, received and paid out. The resumption of business habits by the community in general would tend materially to the restoration of confidence in the currency.

There is no likelihood of any interference whatever in the ordinary pursuits by which the citizens gain their livelihood. On the contrary, close attention to our own concerns will do much to ensure tranquillity and good order. An ancient proverb says that the idle man's brain is the Devil's workshop.

FROM BATON ROUGE.—*The Governor's Proclamation.*—We have intelligence, says the Picayune, from Baton Rouge as late as Monday morning. A gentleman who left there on that morning, and came down the river in a skiff, arriving here at 12 M., on Tuesday, gives us the following facts:

The passing of the Federal fleet above our forts was announced at the capital on Thursday morning, and immediately thereupon preparations were made for the removal of the State archives, and for the destruction of cotton and sugar. The archives have been removed to a place in the interior where the enemy is by no means likely to find them, and all the cotton at Baton Rouge and along the river is now a mass of smouldering fire. All the sugar, too, has either been carried to a place of security, or destroyed. Our informant did not visit the arsenal, and armory and other Confederate buildings, and therefore cannot speak positively on the point, but his impression is that all the Government stores, machinery, ammunition, &c., have either been removed, or left in such a condition as to be valueless to the enemy.

Immediately upon his arrival at the capital, Gov Moore issued a proclamation, announcing the great disaster to our arms, and counseling the people in patriotic language as to their duty in this their hour of adversity. The Governor does not attempt to deprecate the enemy's success, but at the same time he calls upon all citizens of the State to do all in their power to render that success as fruitless and as short lived as possible. With this view, he enjoins the destruction of cotton, sugar and other property liable to seizure and appropriation by the enemy. Colonels of militia are enjoined to see to the execution of this order.

There was quite a ferment among the people of Baton Rouge when it was announced that the enemy's fleet had passed the forts. Preparations were made for a general departure to the interior, and though all excitement had passed away when our informant left, still, numbers continued to leave, both by land and water, in anticipation of a visit from the fleet, no portion of which, we are assured, contrary to city reports, had visited the capital.

Our informant is positive that none of the fleet have been higher up than Carrollton. He saw none on Monday on his way down. Nor could they have passed him during the night unobserved, as he was awake every hour. We conclude, then, that up to noon Tuesday, Baton Rouge had not been occupied, nor had the Federal flag been hoisted on the Capitol, notwithstanding the averment of all the "Reliables" in the city.

ADDRESS OF A SPANISH BEGGAR.—"Gentlemen, consider, with a little commiseration, that, if you were in my place, and I in yours, I should give you, with good heart and good will, whatever you might have need of to continue your journey, and to succor you in your necessity." To this the address of another Spanish beggar may be added: "Night has exceedingly favored me by making me meet such brave Frenchmen as you, in order that I might supplicate you to have pity on me, poor and distressed as I am; for during the day I could not, for all the treasures of the earth, have revealed my wretchedness to the world; therefore, I fervently implore you, gentlemen, graciously to bestow upon me some liberality worthy of French generosity." [L'Esprit des Espagnols.

We call attention to the advertisement elsewhere of lost jewelry. It is known that a portion of this jewelry was picked up by a colored woman, and she is notified to return it and receive the reward, or suffer the legal consequences.

THE CITY.

MYSTERIOUS CIRCUMSTANCE.—A few days ago a man hailing from New York took board with a Creole family in the First District. He gave his name, but such was its peculiar euphony, or rather lack of it, that the Gallic family with whom he lodged declared their inability to pronounce it. Hence, whatever may have been his patronymic, the spelling thereof must remain a mystery to this reporter. It was remarked that his favorite diet was pork and the semi-liquid extract of cane juice; and this fact gave rise to the suspicion that he had not correctly given the latitude of his alleged residence. It was supposed in fact that he came from "down East," and his particular brevity of pantaloon, combined with other peculiarities, strengthened this opinion. He drank inordinate quantities of Mississippi water, and abhorred all other kinds, as if he labored under a suspicion that they might be tinctured with "rat bait."

In brief he "sickened," and yesterday complained of pains at the back of the neck and violent fever. Last night when the cold norther blew up, he grew sensibly worse and was taken with violent vomiting. The ejections from his stomach have the appearance of coffee grounds. His skin has somewhat of a saffron hue. But what all these symptoms indicate, we are not sufficiently posted to say. The patient is at this moment as ill as ever he was, and what his fate may be, we are unable to devine.

We are no alarmists, and hope our citizens may not infer from what we have said that "Yellow Jack" has made his appearance.

UNITED STATES FORCES.—Several United States vessels arrived last evening, crowded with troops. Among them we recognized the Empire City, formerly running between this port and New York, and the Mississippi, of Boston.

About 6 o'clock three regiments disembarked, and marching down the levee to Poydras street, thence to St. Charles, and along Canal, were in part quartered in the Customhouse. The remainder returned in the direction of their vessels. We are not aware that any demonstration was made by the populace during the march of these regiments. There are probably from five to six thousand United States soldiers now in the city, and more are expected.

COTTON DESTROYED.—It is reported that a large quantity of cotton on plantation, near the river, has been burnt, and that Gov. Moore has issued a proclamation requesting the owners of plantations remote from navigation not to destroy any more of the staple.

ARRESTS.—R. Solomon was arrested in the First District, charged with improperly detaining property belonging to the Committee of Public Safety. His side of the question is yet to be heard.

There were a few unimportant arrests for drunkenness and breach of the peace, and two persons were arrested for attempting to set fire to the Marine Hospital.

The following letters were left at this office for distribution:

Miss Jane O'Connor, Camp street,	Mrs R B Wingfield,
Mrs G E McLay,	Mrs J C Harris,
Peter Markey,	Mrs Lovelaird,
Robt Hackney.	M A Waterron,

CITY COUNCIL.—The city fathers held a meeting yesterday, but their proceedings were in secret and have not transpired.

LEVEE BROKEN.—Officer A. Levy reports that the levee, at the foot of Nunn street, has broken loose, and the water is flowing in rapidly.

FIRE ALARM.—There was a false alarm of fire in the Fifth District about 7 o'clock.

CATTLE MARKET.

JEFFERSON CITY, May 1. 1862.

Arrived yesterday, 16 Veal. Amount of stock sold was 50 Veal. Stock remaining on sale is 16 Veal:

Texas Cattle first quality, ₩ lb net	15	@	00
Texas Cattle, second quality, ₩ lb net	12	@	00
Texas Cattle, third quality, ₩ lb net	10	@	00
Texas Cattle, lower grades, ₩ head	$20 00	@	$40
Hogs, first quality, gross ₩ 100 lb	15 00	@	00 00
Hogs, second quality, gross ₩ 100 lb	12 00	@	0 00
Sheep, first quality, ₩ head	5 00	@	8 00
Sheep, second quality, ₩ head	0 00	@	0 00
Veal Cattle, first quality, ₩ head	12 00	@	15 00
Veal Cattle, second quality, ₩ head	—	@	9 00
Milch Cows, first quality, ₩ head	60 00	@	75 00
Milch Cows, second quality, ₩ head	45 00	@	50 00

Candidate for Mayor,

IRRESPECTIVE OF PARTY.

NEW ORLEANS, January 29, 1862.

To my fellow-citizens of the city and parish of Orleans:

At the reiterated request of many friends and acquaintances, I present myself before you, IRRESPECTIVE OF PARTY, as a Candidate for the office of Mayor; election to take place in June next.

If elected, I shall be governed by this motto: Justice, Law and Order, Improvements, Judicious Economy.

VICTOR WILTZ.

feb21 te*

The Daily Delta.

VOL. XVII. NEW ORLEANS, TUESDAY MAY 6, 1862. NO. 131.

DIED:

Yesterd y morning, 5th inst, Mme MARIE CEPHIN PISEROS, aged 30 years.

The friends and acquaintances of the Piseros and Holliday families are requested, without further notice, to attend the funeral, to take place 'h's Day at 4 o'clock, P. M., at the Red Church, Parish of St. Charles The funeral will leave her mother's residence in Carrollton, at 11 o'clock, A. M.

On Sunday night, the 4th of May, at 11 o'clock, in the 47th year of his age, Dr A. C. HENSLEY, a nat ve of Frankfort, Ky., and since 1847 a resident of this city.

Headquarters Dep't of the Gulf.

NEW ORLEANS, May 5, 1862.

General Orders No. 22.

The Commanding General of the Department having been informed that rebelious, lying, and desperate men have represented, and are now representing, to the honest Planters, and the good people of the State of Louisiana, that the United States Government by its forces have come here to confiscate and destroy their crops of Cotton and Sugar: It is hereby ordered to be made known, by publication in all the newspapers of this city, that all cargoes of Cotton and Sugar shall receive the safe conduct of the forces of the United States, and the boats bringing them from beyond the lines of the United States forces may be allowed to return in safety after a reasonable delay, if their owners shall so desire. Provided, they bring no passengers, except the owners and managers of said boats, and of the property so conveyed, and no other merchandise except provisions, of which such boats are requested to bring a full supply for the benefit of the suffering poor of the city.

By command of Major General BUTLER.
GEO. C. STRONG, A. A. G., Chief of Staff. may6

HEADQUARTERS DEPARTMENT OF THE GULF,
New Orleans, May 2, 1862.

General Orders No. 16.

I—Major J. M. BELL, Volunteer Aid de-Camp of the Staff Division, is hereby appointed Provost Judge of the City of New Orleans, and wi l be obeyed and respected accordingly.

II—Capt. J. H. FRENCH, Aid-de-Camp and Acting Inspector General, is hereby appointed Provost Marshal of the City of New Orleans, and Capt. S. K. STAFFORD, Aid-de-Camp, Deputy Provost Marshal They will be obeyed and respected accordingly.

By command of MAJOR GEN. BUTLER.
GEO. C. STRONG, A. A. General, Chief of Staff.

Under the foregoing order the undersigned this day assumes the position of Provost Marshal, for the purpose of carrying out such of the provisions of the Proclamation of the General Commanding within this Department as were not left to Municipal action; and insuring life, property and tranquility to all peaceably disposed citizens. He informs the public that, until further notice, his office will be in the United States Custom House on Canal street.

Particularly does he call attention to the prohibition against assemblages of persons in the streets; the sale of liquor to soldiers; the necessity for a license upon the part of keepers of public houses, coffee-houses and drinking saloons; to the posting of placards about the streets giving information concerning the action or movements of Rebel troops, and the publishing in the newspapers of notices or resolutions laudatory of the enemies of the United States.

The soldiers of this command are subject, upon the part of some low-minded persons, to insult. This must stop. Repetition will lead to instant arrest and punishment.

In the performance of his duties the undersigned will in no degree trench upon the regularly established police of the city, but will confine himself simply to the performance of such acts as were to be assumed by the military authorities of the United States; and in such action he hopes to meet with the ready co-operation of all who have the welfare of the city at heart.

JONAS H. FRENCH,
may6 e&m Aid-de-Camp and Provost Marshal, New Orleans.

THE DAILY DELTA

The decision of Gen. Butler, as communicated to the conductors of the press in this city, subjects the newspapers to the alternative of the publication of his advertisements and orders, or the suspension of the paper declining them, and the seizure of the office and material, to be used by his own agents for their own purposes or those of the United States. Under this decision, we do not feel at liberty to decline the publication of said orders.

There are a great number of men in our city who were recently employed on the gunboats engaged in the defense of the city who are suffering greatly for the want of means to supply themselves and families. They are worthy objects of public kindness and liberality, and we think it the obvious duty of our citizens to contribute to relieve them. These men have suffered grievously in a cause in which the whole people were interested, and their claim for relief is of the first character.

The City Council has acted promptly in the matter of procuring provisions for the city. By agreement with Gen. Butler the cars of the Opelousas Railroad, under the direction of P. S. Wiltz, will be allowed to run for the purpose of bringing supplies to the city. Steamboats, for similar purposes, will be allowed to ply between this port and Red River, under charge of A. D. Grieff, and between this city and Mobile under Moses Greenwood. In this manner we think an abundant supply of provisions may be obtained for the use of our people.

OUR MARKETS.—There was quite an improvement in the markets yesterday and the day before. Ever since the occupation of the city by the United States forces the stalls have presented a most desolate aspect—no meats, no fish, no eggs, few vegetables, and a very scant supply of bread. But during the last two days there has been quite an improvement. Fish has been quite plentiful, vegetables in remarkable supply, and meat, though still lamentably scant and of very indifferent qualty, is certainly beginning to improve. Prices are still frightfully high and the difficulty of making change very annoying. It is hoped that the gentlemen who have taken charge of the transportation of provisions will hurry up their boats and relieve us of the present pressure and scarcity.

OUR SITUATION.

Our readers will perceive, by reference to the resolutions of the Council, published in another column, that the city authorities will continue to administer the government of the city, "with the understanding that they shall not be interfered with in all matters of police proper, unless disturbances should occur calculated to endanger the relations created by the existing state of things between the city and the invading army." This resolution having been communicated to the Commanding General of the United States forces, that officer has agreed to the same, and signified in writing his ratification of a convention in the words quoted above, entered into between the city authorities and himself, "believing the action of the City Council to be within the terms and spirit of the proclamation."

Gen. Butler has also signified his consent that the present currency of the city remain undisturbed and to the organization of a citizen patrol to aid the ordinary police force in maintaining order.

The city authorities having pledged themselves in behalf of our citizens for the safety of the officers and soldiers of the United States army when moving through our streets, and that our people would refrain from molesting or insulting them, Gen. Butler has also signified his intention to remove his men, with the exception of a guard, to the environs of the city. We think we may promise, on behalf of the people of New Orleans, that they will redeem the pledge thus given by the Mayor and Council.

Regarding the measures taken to bring in adequate supplies of food, Gen. Butler has consented that communication be opened with Mobile, for the purpose of procuring a boat load of flour in that market for the use of our people; also, that the Opelousas Railroad may transport hither provisions of all kinds, and that communication be had with the mouth of Red River by means of steamboats, so that the live stock and provisions there accumulated may be transported to New Orleans.

It will be seen by the resolutions of the City Council that agents have been appointed to superintend the purchase and transportation of supplies, according to the above arrangement, and that they are authorized by the general orders of the commanding officer of the Federal forces to take the necessary measures to carry out forthwith the wishes of the Council.

For the successful result of this treaty with Gen. Butler, our people are largely indebted, as has already been recorded in these columns, to the good offices of Hon. Pierre Soule, who readily consented to lend the aid of his great talents and valuable services to the City Council in the conduct of these delicate and difficult negotiations.

A meed of praise should also be awarded to the courage and firmness of Mayor Monroe, and to the discretion and wisdom of the City Council, during the trying crisis through which we have passed. We think we may assure our readers that our relations with the invading army are now, under these circumstances, on as satisfactory a basis as could be expected.

H. M. SUMMERS.

Two officers whom, from their uniform, we presumed to be officers of the U. S. Navy, brought us yesterday the communication which follows, from H. M. Summers, relative to the report of the trial of Col. Danl. Edwards, for offering an insult to Summers, which appeared in the Delta of the 4th inst. The report which this letter aims to correct was furnished us by a gentleman who was present, and is in the main confirmed by Col. Edwards. We publish Summers's written statement, and leave our readers to determine which to believe. There is, however, one part of Mr. Summers's letter which has no relation to the matter at issue between him and Col. Edwards, upon which we desire to make a remark. This is the allusion "to the questions which now divide the people in this unhappy city." Mr. Summers has not been, we understand, for some time, a resident of this city, and it may be through ignorance that he has used this language. Lest, however, it may deceive his present associates, we deem it our duty to say that there is no division among the people of this city on the questions referred to. There is perfect union and harmony among our people. If Mr. Summers considers himself one of the people of New Orleans, he is thus far the only dissentient from the course and sentiments which this city has exhibited and still maintains. There is another portion of his letter upon which we desire to remark. He asserts that "his opinions have been too freely expressed to be now called in question—they have never been disguised." We have never thought Mr. Summers's opinions upon any question of sufficient importance to inquire into, but when we perceived that he had become the object of popular odium from his supposed hostility to the unanimous sentiment of the people of New Orleans, we took some trouble to inquire into the facts, and from the assurances of several credible persons, were gratified to learn that great injustice had been done him; that when charged with disloyalty to the South, he had several times appeared before the Provost Marshals who were in power here before the occupation by the United States, and that on the very last occasion of such appearance, the very day, we believe, the United States ships were announced as having passed the forts, he declared to a prominent and reliable citizen that he felt deeply mortified that his loyalty to the Confederate States should be questioned; that he had contributed his blood and treasure to aid the cause, though at the commencement of the agitation he was not a Secessionist, but a co-operationist; that he had a son and son-in-law in the army of the Confederate States, and that he had gone with his native State, Tennessee. We desire to do injustice to no man. But when a man places himself in Mr. Summers's position, and seeks to compromise the whole body of his fellow-citizens, by a sudden change of his position and views, we owe it to our people, and even to the authorities of the United States, to state facts which can be established by competent testimony. The right of Mr. Summers to think for himself on the question which divides the United States and the Confederate States—to retain his Union sentiments, and to join the United States in the present controversy, we do not call in question; but that he did not to the very last moment declare different opinions, and was not an aider and abettor of the revolution, which he has now associated himself with the United States to suppress and punish, is the particular point which it concerns his reputation to justify and make clear:

LETTER FROM H. M. SUMMERS.

To the Editors of the Daily Delta:

Gentlemen—In your edition of the 4th inst. I find an entire misrepresentation of the facts of the case connected with the arrest and release of Dan'l Edwards. On Friday evening last I was sent from the St. Charles Hotel to the Customhouse, guarded by a company of United States troops to protect me from a mob. On the way down I was jeered at, and the word traitor was freely used toward me by many in the crowd. Several arrests were made by the soldiers. Among them was Edwards. On our arrival at the Customhouse the Commanding Officer asked me if I knew Edwards, and what kind of a man he was. I informed him I had known Edwards for a number of years; I had always esteemed him a gentleman, and that I thought him incapable of lending himself to aid in giving countenance to such outrages as were perpetrated by the mob on that evening, and asked the Commanding Officer, if not incompatible with his duty, to allow Edwards to be released.

Edwards sent for me, and most emphatically disclaimed ever having used the word traitor on the occasion. He said the only remark made by him when I passed was, "Halloo, Summers;" and that only as a term of recognition, and not opprobium. I heard that expression, and it was all I heard from him.

On Saturday morning Edwards and myself were brought before Gen. Butler, at the St. Charles Hotel, when Edwards made a statement to this effect: That he was on his way from his dinner to his place of business when he was intercepted by the crowd, and seeing me surrounded by soldiers was very much surprised, which caused him to make use of the expression mentioned above. Upon this statement, with a disclaimer of all intention of committing any disorder, and ample apology for the expression, being vouched for by a gentleman of this city as a peaceable citizen, well disposed to good order, who had never taken any active part in this rebellion, he was released.

That portion of the report which Edwards excuses himself for using the word traitor toward me because we had heretofore co-operated together in the Southern cause, is false; for I never exchanged one word on opinion pro or con with him upon the questions which now divide the people in this unhappy city.

My opinions have been too freely expressed to be now called in question. They have never been disguised. I ask, sirs, you give this a place in your paper.

Respectfully, yours,
H. M. SUMMERS.

New Orleans, May 5, 1862.

R. M. Montgomery & Bros. will sell this day, at 11 o'clock, at the Old Auction Mart, 87 Camp street, a large assortment of household furniture, removed for convenience of sale.

OUR FIRST SUNDAY UNDER UNITED STATES DOMINATION.

Yesterday was a remarkably peaceful and quiet day. The weather was delightfully balmy and vernal. Our people came forth in great numbers, to enjoy the delicious atmosphere, to learn the news, and to view the strange soldiers, who are to be seen in every direction, promenading the streets and regarding with characteristic curiosity the many peculiarities of our city. There was in the deportment of our people a manifest reaction from the deep sorrow, gloom and mortification which for several days after the capture of the city darkened the minds and countenances of all. Indeed, there was a perceptible vivacity and buoyancy in the demeanor of all classes. This was due to several causes, among which we may mention the existence of and general credit by our people of very exhilarating news, but, more than all, it was due to the consciousness of the proud, manly, dignified and harmonious state of popular opinion, feeling and purpose in this city. History has no similar instance of so united and unanimous a population as that of New Orleans in the present emergency. It is this knowledge which has suppressed all tumult and violence—which enables the soldiers of the United States, a little while ago regarded with such intense hate and enmity, to walk our streets in perfect security from insult and annoyance. It is true, there is not the slightest intercourse between either officers and soldiers and our citizens, except of an official character. Our people submit to military rule, but with not the slightest sacrifice of their honest convictions, and with a unanimous protest against the political authority of the United States within this city and State. They are of one will, one feeling, one determination on this point. They offer no resistance to Gen. Butler's military authority, but they say calmly, resolutely, and earnestly, it is not of their will, desire or consent, but by their coercion and subjugation that they so submit. In good faith they will observe both obligations, abstaining from every effort to insult, annoy, or harass the military occupants of our city on the one hand; and on the other, preserving their independence, their conscience, and their right to determine for themselves the political institutions and authority under which they prefer to live. Gen. Butler has the power to enforce the observance of the former: God Almighty alone can control the latter obligation.

POLICE.—The attention of the city police is called to the recent violations of the ordinances against lewd women parading our principal thoroughfares, at times when respectable people are abroad. Also, to several instances of officers wearing uniforms, not those of the Confederate States, escorting, in public thoroughfares, these disreputable characters. If such improprieties are permitted, our decent citizens will be excluded from the use of the streets. We think it would be wise and proper in Gen. Butler to issue some military order against such practices by U. S. officers; and whether he does or not, it is the duty of our city authorities to see that such nuisance is abated, and such improprieties promptly punished.

WHAT THE MORNING JOURNALS SAY!

From our Edition of Yesterday Evening.

The *Crescent* urges the necessity of prompt and immediate arrangements for supplying the city with fresh meat, and of some provision to improve the sanitary condition of the city by cleansing the streets, gutters, &c., referring to the unusually large number of unacclimated persons now in our city. These subjects are of very pressing importance, and demand immediate attention. One has already been attended to, but the sanitary precautions are still neglected.

The *Bulletin* has the following just and sensible views on a very important subject:

CONFEDERATE NOTES.—We are surprised to notice so few advertisements by parties wishing to sell their goods or property for Confederate notes. We are aware this may be ascribed to its not being deemed necessary, since it is well understood everywhere that no other currency is expected in payment. But still offers through the advertising columns of the press to deal for Confederate paper would lead to many a trade which might not otherwise be made. Such advertisements would have the good effect of inspiring increased confidence as well as of promoting business We advise our friends, whatever they have to sell for Confederate notes, whether slaves, lands or merchandise, by all means to advertise.

RESOLUTIONS OF THE CITY COUNCIL.

The City Council, at a meeting held on Saturday last, passed the following resolutions:

Resolved, That the municipal authorities will continue their normal functions, with the understanding that they shall not be interfered with in all matters of police proper, unless disturbances should occur calculated to endanger the relations created by the existing state of things between the city and the invading army.

The necessities of the people require that the circulation created by the city authorities in the name of the city remain undisturbed.

The city authorities should have power to organize citizen patrols in lieu of an additional force of policemen, that they may be enabled to maintain and protect the public tranquillity.

It is expected that immediate provision will be made to procure those articles of subsistence most needed, and that such measures will be taken as will secure safe means of transporting them from the place where they may be had to the city of New Orleans.

The City Council would remind the Commanding General of the promise he made to Mr. Soule to remove the guard from the avenues of the City Hall, upon the pledge taken by Mr. Soule and ratified by the Council, that the public archives shall remain intact.

Resolved, That a copy of these resolutions be transmitted by the Secretaries of the Common Council, to the Commanding General of the U. S. Army, in possession of the city, and that the same be offered as an embodiment of the answer of the municipal authorities to the suggestions discussed in the conference had between the General and said authorities

GERARD STITH,
President pro. tem. Board of Aldermen.
J. MAGIONI,
President Board of Assistant Aldermen.
Approved May 3, 1862.
JOHN T. MONROE, Mayor.

HEADQUARTERS DEPARTMENT OF THE GULF,
New Orleans, May 3, 1862.

The Commanding General believes the action contemplated by these resolutions to be substantially European Brigade having been relieved from duty, a patrol of citizens armed with sabers or revolvers, or both, may be added to the police, not to exceed two hundred and fifty.

The General has already taken such measures to aid the city authorities in procuring food, in the extremity of suffering, as, in his judgment and upon consultation with the committee of the citizens, have been deemed sufficient, and has transmitted copies of the accompanying orders.

By command of MAJOR GEN. BUTLER.
GEO. C. STRONG, A. A. G.

The above indorsement having been made by Gen. Butler, on the action of the Council, that body met yesterday (Sunday) and passed the resolutions below:

Resolved, That in accordance with General Order No. 19, issued by Major Gen. Butler, with regard to the importation from the city of Mobile to the city of New Orleans of a boat load of flour for the use of the citizens of New Orleans, Mr. Moses Greenwood be and within the terms and spirit of his proclamation. Ibe he is hereby appointed the agent of the city of New Orleans to attend to the shipment of said cargo of flour, and that he is also authorized to take all the necessary steps to carry this resolution into effect.

S. P. DELABARRE,
President pro tem. Board of Aldermen.
J. MAGIONI,
President Board of Assistant Aldermen.
Approved May 4, 1862.
JOHN T. MONROE, Mayor.

Resolved, That in accordance with general order No. 20, issued by Major General Butler, with regard to the provisions of all sorts to be imported to the city by Opelousas Railroad, Mr. P. S. Wiltz be and he is hereby appointed the agent of the city of New Orleans to attend to the transportation of said provisions and live stock, and that he is also authorized to take all the necessary steps to carry this resolution into effect.

S. P. DELABARRE,
President pro tem. Board of Aldermen.
J. MAGIONI,
President Board of Assistant Aldermen.
Approved May 4, 1862.
JOHN T. MONROE, Mayor.

Resolved, That in accordance with general order No. 21, issued by Major General Butler, with regard to the provisions, live stock and flour, now at the junction of the Red and Mississippi rivers, A. D. Grieff, Esq., be and he is hereby appointed the agent of the city of New Orleans to attend to the transportation of said provisions, live stock and flour, and that he is also authorized to take all the necessary steps to carry this resolution into effect.

S. P. DELABARRE,
President pro tem. Board of Aldermen.
J. MAGIONI,
President Board of Assistant Aldermen.
Approved May 4, 1862.
JOHN T. MONROE, Mayor.

The following are the General Orders issued from Gen. Butler's Headquarters, permitting the introduction of supplies of food:

HEADQUARTERS DEPARTMENT OF THE GULF,
New Orleans, May 3, 1862.

GENERAL ORDERS No 19

The Commanding General of this Department has been informed that there is now at Mobile a stock of flour, purchased by the city of New Orleans for the subsistence of its citizens. The suffering condition of the poor of this city for want of this flour appeals to the humanity of those having authority upon either side.

For the purpose of the safe transmission of this flour to this city, the Commanding General orders and directs that a safe conduct be afforded to a steamboat, to be laden with the same, to this place.

This safe conduct shall extend to the entire protection of the boat in coming, reasonable delay for discharge and return to Mobile.

The boat will take no passengers save the owners and keepers of the flour, and will be subject to the strict inspection of the harbormaster detailed from these Headquarters, to whom its master will report its arrival.

The faith of the city is pledged for the faithful performance of the requirements of this order, on the part of the agent of the city authorities, who will be allowed to pass each way with the boat, giving no intelligence to the Confederates.

By command of Major Gen. BUTLER.
GEO. C. STRONG, A. A. G.

HEADQUARTERS DEPARTMENT OF THE GULF,
New Orleans, May 3, 1862.

GENERAL ORDERS No. 20.

The President, Directors and Company of the Opelousas Railroad are authorized and required to run their cars over their road for the purpose of bringing to the city of New Orleans all materials for provisions, marketing and supplies of food, which may be offered, in order to supply the wants of the city.

No passengers, other than those having the care of such supplies, as owners and keepers, are to be permitted to come into the city, and none other are to leave the city. All other supplies are prohibited transport over the road, either way, except cotton and sugar, which may be safely brought over the road, and will be purchased at their fair market value by the United States, in specie.

The transmission of live stock is specially enjoined. An agent of the city Government will be permitted to pass over the road, either way, stopping at all points, on the faith of a pledge of such Government that he transmits no intelligence and affords no aid to the Confederates.

The officer commanding the post having the terminus of such road within his pickets, will cause a thorough inspection of the cars and boats for the purpose of furthering this order, and will offer no other hindrance so long as this order is in good faith complied with.

By command of Major Gen. BUTLER.
GEO. C. STRONG, A. A. G., Chief of Staff.

HEADQUARTERS DEPARTMENT OF THE GULF,
New Orleans, May 3, 1862.

GENERAL ORDERS No. 21.

The Commanding General of the Department of the Gulf has been informed that live stock, flour and provisions, purchased for subsistence of the inhabitants of the city of New Orleans, are now at the junction of the Red and Mississippi rivers.

The suffering condition of the poor of the city, for want of these supplies, appeals to the humanity of those having authority on either side.

For the purpose, therefore, of the safe transmission of these supplies to the city, the Commanding General orders and directs that a safe conduct be afforded for two steamers, to be loaded with provisions, cattle and supplies of food, either alive or slaughtered, each day, if so many choose to come.

This safe conduct shall extend to their entire protection by the forces of the United States during their coming—reasonable delay for discharge, not exceeding six days, unless in case of accident to their machinery, and in returning to or near the junction of the Red and Mississippi rivers.

And safe conduct is further granted to boats laden, as before stated, with provisions for New Orleans, from any point above the junction of such rivers, if at any time during which these supplies are needed the forces of the United States should be at or above such junction.

The boats will take no passengers save the owners and keepers of the freight aforesaid, and will be subject to strict inspection of the Harbor Master, detailed from these Headquarters, to whom they will report their arrival.

The faith of the city is pledged for the faithful execution of the requirements of this order, on the part of the agent of the city authorities, who will be allowed to pass with the boats, either way, he giving no intelligence or aid to the Confederates.

By command of Major Gen. BUTLER.
GEO. C. STRONG, A. A. G.

THE CITY.

THE SHUNAMITISH WOMAN.

It came to pass that on the 5th day of the month, which was yesterday, in the Third District of the beleaguered city, that a man of war of the tribe of the strangers that are at our gates, journeyed forth into the innermost recesses of the city as a seeker of rights.

And he buckled on his armor and put scrip into his purse—and rejoiced exceedingly in his heart, saying: Now, verily, am I strong, both in pistol and purse, and no man shall make me afraid.

And he came to pass the house of a publican, where beer is vended for sheckles of silver, but he passed it not, but went in. And the publican, who was of the tribe of the Teutons, straightway arose and said unto the man of war, verily, friend, you have journeyed far and the sun beateth sore upon thy head and upon thy loins, and surely thou art athirst? And the man of war replied, yea, verily.

And the Teuton brought forth a vessel of abomination, which is called a jug, and said unto the man of war, Drink thee, friend, and rejoice exceedingly. And the man of war drank until he thirsted no longer, and having paid his reckoning, went on his way rejoicing.

And as he journeyed into the recesses of the city, it appeared unto him that the houses whirled round about, and the trees danced jigs; and he sat him down upon a door step, in a street which is called Craps, to commune within himself what next to do.

And while he was sitting there, a damsel of fair proportions and beautiful to look upon came out at the gate, and spake unto him, saying: Valiant man of war, surely thou art weary and heavy laden, and would needs have rest. Now, therefore, I pray thee come in unto me and abide until morning, for my mother is a serving woman in the house of a task master, and my father tendeth sheep in the fields afar off, and it grieveth me to be alone. Then the heart of the man of war yearned towards the damsel, and he entered in and took possession. And the damsel spread him a couch of fine linen and of the fleece of lambs, and made him drink of the juice of the poppy—but he knew not of what he drank. And he slept a sleep that was exceeding sound, and knew not what the damsel did in his sleep.

In the third hour of the morning he awoke from his slumbers, and his tongue clove to the roof of his mouth, so that he could not call unto the damsel for drink for which his soul thirsted. Then he cast about him to see the fair virgin, but she had departed thence, no one knew whither. Whereupon he was exceeding wroth, and he lifted up his voice and swore aloud, for his anger had loosened his tongue. And betaking himself again to the house of the publican, he would fain have drowned his sorrows by draining of the wine skin that maketh drunk, but lo! the damsel had despoiled him of his scrip, and the publican knew him not any longer. For the rest, is it not written in the records of the Recorder for the District which is called the Third?

DISTRESSING OCCURRENCE.—A most melancholy and distressing event occurred on Saturday evening, which has deprived this community of a most excellent citizen and diffused general sorrow through a large circle. Dr Hensley, who had long resided here and was greatly esteemed for his many amiable traits, being engaged in one of the clubs on Canal streets in the discussion of some military question relative to the defenses of the city, with several gentlemen, all of whom were intimate friends, some hasty and violent words arose between him and Judge John W. Price, of the Fourth District Court, which resulted in Judge Price stabbing Dr. Hensley with a pen-knife. After receiving the wound Dr. Hensley exclaimed that he was dying, and proceeded to dress his own wound, and to give directions as to the manner in which he should be disposed. Judge Price, seized with remorse or with the consciousness of the rash deed he had committed, rushed to him to beg his forgiveness, declaring that he knew not what he was doing. It was, we learn, a most affecting scene, in which the unfortunate homicide displayed far more grief and misery than his victim. No young man in this community was more respected, more universally esteemed for amiability and peacefulness than Judge Price. It is scarcely possible to conceive that such an act could have been committed by him while in the possession of his faculties and his moral sense. Dr. Hensley died last night.

THE STREETS.—There were crowds of people congregated on the streets this morning—some to witness the marching of the United States soldiers, who are constantly busy moving about the city, and some to inquire the news, of which there is great abundance, but of a very indirect and unreliable character. We observed that there was some addition to the number of stores opened, although the great majority still remain closed. For the enlightenment of those who still keep their establishments hermetically sealed, with the vain hope of exacting higher prices from the necessities of the people, when it shall please the proprietors to throw open their doors, we would state, that the blockade is now open, and if all signs do not fail, we may soon be flooded with all kinds of produce, and at prices far below the figures ruling at present. We would suggest that all dealers open their doors and get clear of their stock before the glut comes.

MARINE HOSPITAL.—At this institution, situated on Common street, a number of sick and wounded have been quartered, and it is understood are suffering for many little delicacies and comforts that it is not in the power of the institution to furnish them. They are attended by many ladies of the city who have volunteered for the purpose, and who are unremitting in their attention. Those of our citizens who can spare from their superfluities, either in the way of money, linen, clothing, or little home delicacies, will find in the sufferers referred to, fitting objects of their bounty.

POLICE.—There was the usual routine before Recorder Emerson this morning. Several cases of assault and battery were tried, and some for riot and disorder. One man, tried for biting off the end of another's nose, was put under bonds to keep the *piece;* but as the piece had fallen into the gutter, he found it impossible to comply with the judgment of the court.

BELLIGERENT SOLDIER.—George, a United States soldier, was arrested by officers Terrade and Lafferrandrie, on Royal street, for being drunk and committing several assaults and batteries upon the persons of peaceable citizens passing in the street. He was sent to the Chief of Police, to be dealt with by the military authorities.

BREAK IN THE LEVEE.—At the foot of St. Anne street the river has risen above the levee, and the water is flowing over quite freely. The levee is paved at this point with round stones, and there being no washing away of the embankment, no serious damage can occur.

DROWNED.—The dead body of a man, supposed to have been drowned, was yesterday found in the river, at the foot of Poydras street.

EXCITED ETHIOPIANS.—Several disorderly assemblages of the long heeled emigrants from the spicy land of Ethiopia, were yesterday broken up by the police.

TROOPS.—The regiments encamped on Lafayette Square this morning struck their tents and removed to other quarters—we can not say where.

POLICE.—John Keating was arrested in the First District, charged with disturbing the peace, carrying concealed weapons, to wit: a bowie knife, and endangering the lives of his fellow citizens.

Wm. Ryan was arrested for dangerously wounding a man named Charles Parish, on Gravier street. The assaulter had the skin of his eyebrow peeled completely off by the blow which he received, and the blood flowed profusely.

Fire Department.

OFFICE CHIEF ENGINEER FIRE DEPARTMENT,
New Orleans, April 29, 1862.

The members of the Fire Department are hereby notified that on the alarm of ten taps of the fire alarm bells they are to immediately assemble at their different Engine and Hook and Ladder Houses.

At the alarm of one tap repeated three times the Assistant Engineers and commanding officers of companies will immediately proceed to the office of the Chief Engineer to receive orders.

In case the alarm is given for any of the regular Fire Districts, the companies performing duty in the district for which the alarm is given, will immediately proceed to the location of the alarm.

All companies are hereby notified to continue to perform their duty as heretofore, and use all their exertions in the preservation of life and property.

apr29 DAVID BRADBURY, Chief Engineer.

THE CAMP KETTLE.

We know only our Country.

VOL. 1. BEAUFORT, S. C. MAY. 15, 1862. NO. 12.

The Camp Kettle
Is published every opportunity by the 100th. PENN'A. (ROUNDHEAD) REG'T, COL. LEASURE, COMMANDING.

FUNERAL OBSEQUIES OF THE DEAD OF THE 8th MICHIGAN REGIMENT.

On the receipt of the news of the battle on Wilmington Island, in which the Michigan 8th was engaged, much excitement and sympathy were awakened in the Brigade, and at the same time the Honduras arrived having on board the dead bodies, and immediate measures were taken by General Stevens to have them consigned to the grave with suitable honors. On the following morning, the 18th, the ten soldiers were consigned to their last bivouac, with all the funeral honors due men who had fallen in the war for the Union. The firing party, escort and pall bearers were from the 100th Penna. (Roundhead) Regiment, and the bodies were followed by a vast concourse of officers and soldiers. General Stevens and Staff, with the Colonels and commanding officers of the 2nd Brigade were in the procession, and the Regimental Band of the 79th N. Y. Vols. (Highlanders) led the funeral cortege with the solemn wail of the Dirge, and the Chaplain of the 8th Michigan, Rev. Mr. Mahan, assisted by the Chaplain of the 100th Penna. Regiment of volunteers, the Rev.R. A. Browne, conducted the solemn services of the burial.

In the afternoon Adjutant Pratt was buried with the same solemnity, the firing party and escort being furnished by 50th Penna. Regiment, and the music by the band of 100th Penna. Regiment On the following day, in like manner, the remains of Lieut. Badger were consigned to the keeping of a soldier's grave, and in the after noon the troops present turned out to receive the Regiment on its return, and congratulatory addresses were made to the Michigan 8th. by General Stevens, Col. Leasure, of the 100th and Col. Christ, of the 50th Penna. Volunteers.

ON PICKET.

After all, picket duty has its pleasure For instance, in the morning we are on duty at the Ferry, and our mess mates have just sent us some hot coffee to wash down the "cooked rations," and we have sat down to enjoy our breakfast, keeping our faces "Dixie"ward, to watch the motions of Pickie on the other side. There goes a flash and here comes a shell over our heads, and lights in the mud where it explodes and sends the "free soil" of South Carolina all over us, and muddies our coffee and good government trowsers. There comes another, that falls short, but kicks up a dust among the dry sand,and if we were inked before, we are sanded now, and for "fear of accidents" we gather up the fragments of our breakfast,and postpone our appetite till we have tried the effect of a "minnie"conical on the gunners "over the water," with the effect of convincing their better reason into a "suspension of hostilities," and anon, comes the relief, and we deploy into an old cotton field, and go to gathering blackberries for our dinner, none the less demanded on account of our interrupted breakfast. Sometimes, too, our neighbors over the water, talk "Bull Run" at us, and we reply by refering them to Pea Ridge, Ft. Henry, F. Donalson, Island No. 10, Corinth, Hatteras, Newberne, Hilton Head and Pulaski, whereat they become wrathy, and we regret to say, profane and terribly given to "humors," that are far from healthy. Natheless," we rather like them for the fun they afford us, and wish they had better "small clothes."

Stevens House.

This new hotel has recently been opened in Beaufort by H. G. Ely, and is doing a good business. we are informed that the accommodations are good, and that the Host is a "host in himself." The Hotel is on Bay street, near the wharf, and is a fine building, and most pleasantly located for business and comfort. We wish success to the "Stevens House."

Pork Rations,

We would advise the soldiers to save up their pork rations, and sell them back to the Commissary, and thus save up a company fund, with which to buy eggs, vegetables and such other articles of food as are more suitable to this climate. The ration, as issued, is far more than the soldier can eat, both in pork and other articles, and all should be drawn, and resold, and the proceeds put into the company fund to purchase other and more suitable food, or, at least to give variety to the ordinary rations.

Progress.

General Hunter, pursuant to instructions from the War Department, has resolved to organize two Regiments of contrabands for the purpose of releiving the Union soldiers from many duties that can be quite as well performed by the blacks as by the northern troops, with the effect if preserving many lives to the army for more responsible duties. If the Rebels use the blacks against us, the rule may work in the other direction as well, and just possibly, better. We shall see. Who was it said "the world dident move?"

Thanks.

The undersigned desires to express on behalf of the 100th Regiment Penna. (Roundhead) Vols., his heartfealt thanks to the patriotic Ladies and citizens of Lawrence, Mercer and Washington counties, Pennsylvania, for their liberal contributions to the Hospital Stores of the Regiment. Long before the tape officials looked after the interests of our sick,these home contributions met every want, and supplied all our necessities. May the choicest blessings fall upon all those who have remembered us.

DANIEL LEASURE, Colonel
Commanding 100th Regiment Pennsylvania (Roundhead) Vols.

News.

Our distant friends ask why, we do not publish more news in relation to the doings of the troops in the "Department of the South." In reply we merely state that such information could be used by a present enemy, long before it would gratify the curiosity of distant friends It is sufficient to say that, the "Department of the South" is doing its duty, and that in any event it will continue to do its duty Entire confidence in those in command here, and a very high standard of discipline, are hopeful omens of future success, as well as present safety, and with this meagre item of military news, our friends must for the present content themselves, relying upon letter writers for more extensive information.

Free Labor.

The trial of free labor in Sonth Carolina is progressing steadily and satisfactorily. Many of the deserted plantations are showing signs of a new civilization. Under the benign rule of General Hunter the slave falls very naturally into a free man, and the ex-slaves themselves say that, twelve "free niggers" do more work for pay, than twenty slaves did under the lash. Northern enterprise under the supervision of competent men, is giving intelligent direction to the dark mind of the servile race of this hotbed of rebeldom, and it would seem as if a just retributive Providence was about to demonstrate on the soil of South Carolina the greatest problem of the age, viz: That slavery is not necessary to the production of cotton even in South Carolina.

Special Orders.

The following order explains itself, and we may add, meets the hearty approbation of all, except those personally interested in selling or drinking:

HEAD QUARTERS:—2nd Brigade,
Northern District, Deparment of the South,
Beaufort, S. C., May 9th, 1862.
Special Orders No. 24.

The sale of all intoxicating drinks, whether spiritous or fermented, is from this date absolutely prohibin the town of Beaufort and within the limits of this command All persons found violating this order, will be immediately sent beyond the limits of this command and their goods confiscated.

By Order of Brig. Gen. STEVENS,
HAZARD STEVENS,
Capt and Asst. Adj. General.

Detailed,

The following named non commissioned officers and privates of the 100th Regiment Penne. vols. have tendered their services to Gen. Hunter, to drill the contrabands, and on Monday last reported themselves at Hilton Head to enter upon their duties. They will be commissioned as Captains and Lieutenants as soon as they prove their competency, by the President or Congress. Two full regiments of ex-slaves are to be formed immediately, and officered by well drilled men from the troops here, viz:

William J Randolph, Sergt comp. F.
William James, Sergt. comp. C.
Robert Hamilton, Sergt. comp. D.
R W. Weller, Sergt, comp F.
S. Scott Veon, corporal comp K.
R. M. Gaston, corporal comp F.
J. F. Johnson, corporal comp G.
John H. Grace, corporal comp G.
Robert G. Christy, corporal comp H.
Alex Heasly corporal comp B.
Edward F. Oliver, corporal comp B.
James Pomeroy, corporal comp B.
John Klotzbucher, private comp A.
John Harvey, private comp D.
William Pearson, private comp D.
Thos. C Randolph, private comp F.
Stewart Alford, private comp F.
John O.Kerr. private comp F.

Promotions in the 100th Regt. Pa, Roundhead, Vols. Since its Organization.

James Armstrong, Capt. company A, to be Lieut. Col

David A Leckey, Capt. company M, to be Major.

Wm. F. Templeton, 1st Lieut. of company A, to be Captain vice Armstrong pronmoted.

Joseph H. Penticost, 2nd Lieut. company A, to be 1st, Lieut. vice Templeton promoted.

William Ocker, sergt. company A to be 2nd Lieut. vice Pentecost promoted.

David Critchlow, Segt. Major, to be 2nd Lieut. company C, vice Powers promoted to be Adjutant

1st Lieut Thomas J. Hamilton, company D, to be Captain, vice Shurlock resigned

1st Segt. James Calhoun, company D, to be 1st. Lieut. vice Hamilton promoted.

Sergt Daniel Frazier, company D, to be 2nd Lieut. vice Caughey resigned.

2nd Lieut. Samuel J. Book company E, to be 1st Lieut. vice Nelson resigned.

Sergt Norman Maxwell company E,to be 2nd Lieut. vice Book promoted

Sergt. David Patton company F, to be 2nd Lieut. vice Banks deceased.

2nd Lieut. Thos. H. Curt company G, to be 1st Lieut. vice Grace resigned

Sergt. John Cochran company G, to be 2nd Lieut. vice Curt promoted.

Sergt John S. Pomeroy company I, to be 2nd Lieut. vice Tidball resigned.

Sergt. Samuel J. Morrow, company I, to be 2nd Lieut. vice Pomeroy resigned.

2nd Lieut Anson B. Campbell company M, to be Capt. vice Leckey promoted.

Segrt. James S M'Feeters, company M, to be 2nd Lieut. vice Campbell promoted.

1st Sergt. Jefferson Justice, company H,to be Regimental Quartermaster, vice Leslie reassigned, at his own request to his company.

The following extract of a letter from Capt. Baker of the 9th Maine Regiment, at Fernandina, will explain the facts in relation to the death of young Chase, alluded to in our last.

He was shot through the heart while on guard at Judge O'Neal's plantation, near Fernandina.Flat. At the time of the surprise he was in an out building cooking his supper. We have been informed that he saw the enemy when within a few rods of him, and ran through the back door of the cook house, and went into the main house where the remainder of the guard were assembled, caught up his musket, and opened the front door to get a shot at them. Not being able to get a good chance to fire, he closed the door perhaps five seconds, and opened it again, when a Sergt. named Brock, fired at him, killing him dead. He fell back without uttering a word. The remainder of the Picket, six, in number, were taken prisoners.

There is no one of our regiment who regrets the loss of Mr. Chase, more than I do. He was a faithful soldier. and an upright, honest man, He was much beloved by all who knew him, more especially by our own company.

Most Respectifully Your obt. Servt.
S. D. BAKER,
Capt. comp I, 9th Regiment Maine Vols.

Drill.

The troops here drill early in the morning and in the evening after 4 o'clock and at those times the atmosphere is very pleasant. The balance of the day is devoted to all sorts of rest and recreation Gymnastics occupy a large portion of the time, and quite an amount of ingenuity is shewn in the various apparatus under the cool shade of the magfiificent live oaks amongst the various camps In one company of 100th Regt. we notice a bathing establishment, under the charge of one of the members, formerly attached to a "water cure." It is very nicely and ingeniously gotton up, and we are pleased see liberally patronized. Altogether, with easy drills, and gymnastics, the troops here are doing very finely.

HEALTH OF THE TROOPS.

Notwithstanding many fears and many prophecies, the health of the troops here is improving instead of deteriorating. All the hospitals are about empty, except a few cases of chronic disease of no special account. The morning report of the 100th Regiment Penna. (Roundhead,) Vols. only shows seven men in the hospital, not one of whom is not able to walk about the beautiful hospital grounds during even the hottest part of the day, and as it is by much the largest regiment in the Brigade, it may be infered the rates of the others are about the same. Indeed we know the other hospitals might as well shut up, for all the custom they get. Of course there are always some men on the sick list that are not very sick. One man is excused for a sore toe, another for a felon on his finger, a third for a head ache, a fourth for a sort of general "ornariness," and so it goes. In a regiment of a thousand and odd men twenty five are excused from duty, being reported on the sick list temporarily, and yet not one of the whole twenty-five declines his rations. In this service, we only know well men and sick ones, and if a man is not exactly well, he is excused from duty, and put for that day at lesat, on the "sick list." Thus, at all times, the number on the sick list, seems larger than it really is. The truth is, the troops here are acclimated, and moreover, are under officers who are men of age, and large experience, and who make it a matter conscience to preserve their men from sickness. The most minute matters are looked after with a supervision that under other circumstances would prove a serious annoyance, but here is absolutely necessary to the general welfare. As to heat, about which such exaggerated rumors are afloat in the North, it amounts to just nothing at all. The thermometer does not range as high as on a June day North, and the heat only lasts from ten till two o'clock, the balance of the day and night being the most delicions temperament in the world, and the sea breeze sweeping across the orange orchards, and groves of spices as it comes inland, is laden with perfumes of the Orient. With proper care on the part of the men,and watchfulness on the part of the officers, there need be no more sickness here than in the North, and the sick returns show that in the same number of men the northern troops are far more healthy than the southern troops, even in the climate to which the latter are bred and born.—There is no doubt a physiological reason for this, in the greater power of resistance to exciting causes of diseases on the part of northern born men, but this only proves that, physiology, as well as everything else, is "down on" this rebellion, and "bound to" see the Union through.

DIED.

At Beaufort, S. C. on Saturday, May 3rd, Second Lieut. James L. Banks, of company F, 100th (Roundhead) Regiment of Pennsylvania Volunteers, of congestive fever, after an illness of two days.

As an officer, and a gentleman, Lieut. Banks was very highly esteemed, and his loss will long leave a void in the Regiment. Of the void left at home, we dare not trust ourselves to speak, but those who miss and mourn him there, have our warmest sympathies.

One day last week a colony of bees "swarmed" upon a bush beside one of our picket posts, and a couple of the boys seeing they were "secesh," captured them, and "swore them in"-to an empty keg, and gave them to the Colonel, who has them located on the upper piazza of his quarters, under the folds of the "old flag," and the little Repulicans seem to thrive very well under "Yankee" rule in "Dixie."

THE WEATHER.

The weather here is delightful, with but little rain, and although the middle of the day brings the mercury to eighty or ninety in the shade, the seabreeze compensates for it, and comes up the bay as cool and grateful as an "ice cold lemonade." We have just tried the last named article and can recommend it.

THE PEOPLE'S PRESS.

VOL. XII. SALEM, NORTH CAROLINA, FRIDAY MORNING, MAY 16, 1862. NO. 3.

The People's Press,

PUBLISHED WEEKLY

BY L. V. BLUM,

EDITOR AND PROPRIETOR.

PRICE.---Two Dollars a Year,

PAYABLE IN ADVANCE.

☞ No paper will be discontinued until all arrearages are paid, except at the option of the Editor.

Any person procuring FIVE new subscribers and remitting Ten Dollars, will be entitled to a sixth copy gratis.

TERMS OF ADVERTISING.

One square, (fifteen lines or less,) first insertion, One Dollar; and twenty-five cents for every subsequent insertion. Deductions made in favor of standing advertisements, for a square, as follows:

For three months, - - - -	$3 50
For six months, - - - -	$5 00
For twelve months, - - -	$8 00

Professional or Business Cards, not exceeding five lines in length, Five Dollars a year;---longer ones in proportion.

Miscellaneous.

LAURA;

—OR—

"THE SNOW FLAKE."

BY ANNA M. BATES.

It was a wild, stormy evening in March. The wind dashed fitful gusts of sleet and rain against the windows of the room where Captain Leslie and his wife were sitting. The conversation in which they had hitherto been engaged had lapsed into a silence, only broken by the fierce rush of the storm without. A cheery fire glowed in the grate and diffused a rosy lustre over the whole apartment, that wore a pleasant and homely aspect. The golden hands of the clock were pointing to the hour of twelve, when suddenly there was a sharp ring at the door, and then the sound of retreating footsteps. Captain Leslie was a brave man, but as he rose to go forth into the hall his wife clung to him in an infirmity of fear.

"Stay, my husband," she besought him; "surely no honest person would be abroad at this dead hour of the night."

But he wrenched away his arm from her grasp, and proceeded to open the door.—Nothing was visible in the thick darkness; but presently they heard the faint, feeble wailing of a child, and procuring a light, they found a large basket in the porch.—With some curiosity they bore it in the warm lighted parlor, and folding back the wrapping in which it was enveloped, the form of a beautiful infant appeared. Its little eyes were closed in softest slumber, and a smile that told of angel visions, rested upon its velvet lips. A dainty robe of white, richly embroidered, and a cloak of soft rose colored satin protected the little form; and from its neck, encircled by a chain of gold, hung a small locket of antique workmanship.

The warm, motherly feelings of a woman rose in Mrs. Leslie's breast. Very tenderly she lifted the little fondling from its bed and bore it to the fire, whose warmth brought back the life of its purple limbs. In vain they sought for word of explanation accompanying the child thus strangely thrown upon their protection.

"Well, let us keep it," said Mrs. Leslie, "we have no children of our own and this one may live to be the comfort of our old age. It is evidently no common child, and my heart is strangely warmed toward it." Perhaps the thought of her own unblessed infancy—for she never had a childhood—rose before the speaker's mental vision. Early orphaned, her marriage with Captain Leslie had relieved her from the drudgery and bondage heaped upon her by a maiden aunt; and so no wonder she pitied the desolate.

"If you are willing to adopt the babe," replied her husband, "I have certainly no objection. She shall be our daughter, and we will call her Laura, or the *Snow-Flake*, for was she not wafted to us in the midst of the storm?"

Months, years went by like phantoms in that quiet home; and what changes did Time bring! The roses that decked the bridal of the year were not fairer than those that blushed on Laura's cheek; and the stars were not brighter than her eyes; nor the winds sweeter than her voice. She had grown dear as life itself to her adopted parents, and Mrs. Leslie found great delight in cultivating her young mind.—When she was seven years of age, as near as they could judge, a great change came. A relative of Capt. Leslie died, bequeathing him a large fortune. Previously he had been far from rich; but had managed to live upon half pay and small annuity. Now their style of living was necessarily greatly changed. They left their quiet home and went to reside in the costly mansion of the deceased relative.

Pomp, splendor, and magnificence were now their attendants. Servants came and went to do their bidding; they were surrounded by gorgeous furniture, rich old pictures, fair statues, and costly services of gold and silver, that made life seem like a fairy tale—a round of pleasure and gay entertainment. More years went on and Laura was a woman, a belle, a beauty, the admired of all admirers. Jewels that might have won a prince's ransom, encircled her fair, round arms, and flashed out in her night-black hair. She was the acknowledged heiress of Capt. Leslie's vast wealth; no wish was ungratified; friends surrounded her and she was happy. Happy as the world goes, for the deep fountains of her nature were yet sealed.

Was it not natural that many should seek to win the beautiful girl? Caleb Ruthven was a young man of much wealth his exterior was polished, his face and figure handsome. Captain and Mrs. Leslie admired him, Laura could not plead indifference, so she had promised, and a few more months would make her his wife. Did they juge rightly in that they called Caleb Ruthven all that was good and noble? Let us see.

Suddenly Captain Leslie grew abstracted and sad. He was frequently absent from home; he tarried long over the golden goblet to "look not on the wine when it was red," and at night, long after the family had retired, his restless feet were heard pacing the library floor until the gray dawn broke.

The blow came at last! they were penniless! They who had grown accustomed to personal habits of noble expenditure; who had deemed their wealth as exhaustless as the sea, must now leave the elevations of grandeur for the humbler walks of life.

Captain Leslie had in an evil hour been lured to the gaming table and forgotten in the accursed excitement of the play, his home, his friends, his God. Madly and recklessly he staked the bulk of his princely fortune and lost. Nor was this all, for his three richly laden ships, that were freighted with precious things, sunk at sea. He bent beneath these strokes of misfortune like "a reed bendeth to the tempest."

It was now the native strength of Laura's character shone forth. She comforted and soothed Mrs. Leslie and her husband, and with uncommon foresight began to make plans for the future. They had still the same annuity previously devoted to charitable purposes and barely sufficient to maintain them in the cheapest possible way. A small cottage was taken in the suburbs of the town and Laura proposed to take music scholars and execute embroidery for the shops of the city.

It was the night before their removal.—Laura sat alone in the splendid drawing room busied in bitter thoughts. It was a sweet summer eve and the moonlight swept peacefully over the graceful trees that grew beside the balcony, and laid its white hands upon the dewy, fragrant flowers, that glistened like stars among the soft, green leaves. But Laura heeded not the beauty of the hour. She was musing with bitter intensity over the falsehood and inconstancy of those summer friends who surrounded her in the day of prosperity but now had left her to feel the coldness of desertion, while a dark night of trial hung over her head. Caleb Ruthven, her own affianced husband, had left her in her fallen fortune; at least, he had not called since the news of Capt. Leslie's poverty became known. Oh! could it be that he was like the rest? She heard the sound of a familiar footstep upon the marble stair of the balcony. She rose and went out in the moonlight, as she had often done before, to meet her lover. It was he. Yes, as she sprang forward, eager to greet him, the cold reserved expression of his face, struck like the chill of death to her heart. She drew herself up with a woman's pride and silently motioned him to enter the room she had just left. He seated himself, and commenced a confused apology for not calling on her before. She interrupted him with an impatient jesture. Upon her fair white hand glistened the ring of their engagement. As he gazed upon it his face flushed, his voice faltered, but he said: "Deeply as I regret it, Miss Leslie, I fear it will not be convenient for me to consummate our engagement that was to be sealed at the altar next month. The embarrassed condition of your father's affairs and my own present want of ample means for his maintenance, compel me to ask an idefinite postponement of the affair, or perhaps the dissolving of the bond altogether."

Her face grew perfectly white with excitement, and her dark eyes flashed with scorn. "Here is your answer," she said proudly; she tore the ring from her finger as if it had been a viper, and flung it on the ground and trampled on it, exclaiming, "Mercenary man! thus I abhor and despise you! Henceforth and forever we are strangers!" He looked back to gaze upon her as he left the room. She stood there as a superb animated statue in the attitude ot queenly scorn. Caleb Ruthven never forgot her look; it haunted him for many a day and hour. The night was but a little older when the fair round moon looked with a beaming glance through the tall windows of the room where Laura lay asleep, woreout with the warfare of contending thought. A few tears glistened on her cheeks. Suddenly she awoke with a half sigh. Wonder not, as the terrible realities of the situation flashed full upon her that she shrunk back appalled. Nurtured in luxury it was bitter to know that poverty must be hers; that she must go forth and struggle with the wild waves with no strong arm to lean on; for *he* was false, FALSE! She said the word over to herself many times to accustom her heart to the sound.

"Oh, Heavenly Father," she murmered, kneeling reverently, "let thy strength be given me."

She rose with composure, and going to the mirror adjusted her disordered hair, then passed with a firm step into the room of her parents. Briefly she related to them the incidents of her meeting with Ruthven.

"My poor lamb," said Capt. Leslie, as she concluded—he opened his fatherly arms, and she wept upon his breast, forgetful that his rash acts had brought all their sorrow. As they grew more composed, they discussed together plans for their future. The next day commenced their removal to their new home. All the rich furniture, pictures, and statuary, with Laura's costly harp, were left behind to be sold with the house and grounds. Her piano she retained for its usefulness, and with no servant and but few relics of former grandeur they commenced life once more.

To a stranger, their cottage home had a lovely look. A few graceful trees threw their shadows in front of the little garden, blooming with summer flowers; within, the small rooms were fresh and clean and filled with evidences of refinement and taste. As weeks went by in the samesweet calm quiet, the tone of mind in this unfortunate family grew more peaceful and resigned. Yet it was with no uncommon pang they learned that their dear old home had passed into the hands of an utter stranger, an elderly care-worn man, who had just come from a distant land over the sea, in the reputed possession of great wealth; yet without kindred or family. As the summer went on, Laura, humbling all pride to suit their fallen fortunes busied herself in embroidering delicate muslins and laces for the shops of the city.

She used to carry them home herself when the weather was fine, and the walk, though long, seemed to invigorate her.—For many times she had met and passed by a dark, elderly stranger, who never failed to regard her intently as long as she was in sight, and once she heard him say: "she is very like Therese, but it cannot be." One fine winter's day as she was walking leisurely along to the shop of her employer, she felt the clasp of the chain on her neck give way. It slipped down upon the sidewalk, but ere she could stoop to pick it up, the dark stranger who stood near reached down for it and handed it to her gracefully. She thanked him politely.

"Madam," said he in an agitated voice, "will you step aside with me and allow me to examine the trinket attached to this chain?"

"Certainly," said she, acceding to his request and handing him the locket. He took it and touching a secret spring, which she had not known, it flew open and disclosed two pictures; one, the very counterpart of Laura herself; the other, a dark, stately man, and around the rim of gold that encircled these two faces was engraved in the finest Spanish: Therese and Carlos Mercedes."

"Fair lady," said the stranger, "how came you by this locket that once belonged to my wife?"

"I know not," she replied, "it has been on my neck ever since I could remember, and my parents never told me why."

"You have parents then?"

"Yes, sir, I am the only child of Captain Leslie."

"Leslie," he repeated in a musing tone. "why, he was the former owner of my present mansion here, and now he lives at"—

"Vine Cottage No. 5, Elmwood Place, on the road to Newbury," she returned.

He took out his tablets and wrote the direction saying—"I shall do myself the pleasure of calling on your father soon, perhaps to night." He handed her his card, and they parted after he had begged Laura to forgive his rudeness in questioning her.

"I hope," he said, "to find a friend among you."

When she returned home she told all to her friends; they repaid her confidence by imparting in return the story of her early life that had thus far been sedulously kept from her, and expressed the thought she might find her real parent in Signor Mercedes. What a blow was this to Laura! She had no claims upon the Leslies then! She was not the daughter, then, of the gentle woman who had nurtured her infant years so tenderly; she was only the child of their adoption and a *foundling!* As the sunset hues grew brighter in the West and quivered in the crystalized branches of the garden trees, making them gorgeous with rich prismatic hues, she sat eagerly gazing down the road that led to the city. Her watching was soon rewarded by the dark outline of a horse and rider in the distance, and as he approached and drew rein beside the gate, her heart beat high as she recognized Signor Mercedes. He entered, and after the usual salutations commenced abruptly. "The strong resemblance of your daughter to my dead wife and strange possession of the locket containing both our portraits, have called me hither to-night to ask an explanation. Mrs. Leslie, is she your daughter?"

"She is not," replied the lady with tears gathering in her eyes, "save by adoption, by duty and mutual love," and she fondly kissed the fair brow of Laura who sat by her side.

"Then she is mine by all that is holy," he exclaimed. "Look on her and upon this picture," and he displayed the soft dark eyes and queenly brow of the lady's portrait, then called them to note the striking resemblance between himself and the features of the gentleman. It was all the same save a few deep lines Time had left upon his brow.

"I will tell you my story," he resumed, "and Laura may receive or reject me."

"I am of Spanish descent, but traveling at an early age in Hungary, became acquainted with and married the fair Therese Vaninsky and settled with her near the home of her parents, but I was unjustly accused of forming a conspiracy against the government. My estates were confiscated, and only by flight I escaped the prison for which they designed. We fled to these shores in the first friendly vessel, and here for three years fortune and peace smiled upon us. At the end of that time I received an intimation that a noted conspirator had, in dying confessed my entire innocence of the nefarious designs laid to my charge, and that if I were living and would return, my property would be restored to me. You were very young then, my daughter, but your mother being anxious to accompany me, exerted all her feeble strength in embroidering rich robes and a cloak of soft rose-hued satin for you to wear. I think she overworked herself, for the day previous to that appointed for our departure she was stricken down with the fever."

"You shall not wait for me," she said "Go, I shall soon be well, and then you come for me."

"I did go. I kissed you my little daughter, as you lay asleep; I gave Therese a last embrace, and we parted—forever. I left all the funds I could spare, and as I thought a trusty servant, but as it proved, my confidence was misplaced. I was delayed a long time in transacting my business affairs I wrote constantly, but my letters were unanswered. As soon as possible I returned and went to the place where I had left her. She was not there, but some old residents in the neighborhood told me she died a short time after my departure, and went with me to her grave. They added that the faithless serving woman had secured all my wife's valuables and journeyed away with our child. I sought for her in vain; I returned to my own land; wealth flowed in upon me, but I was alone. I came back to die on Therese's grave, and I have found you. Oh my daughter!"

She sprung up into his arms, "Father! MY Father!" it was all she said.

Without a word Mrs. Leslie left the room but presently returned bringing an infant's white robe richly wrought, yet of a by gone pattern, and a little satin cloak with its rose hue changed by time. She laid them on Signor Mercede's knee, he kissed them and they all wept. The Market town of R. where he had left Therese was but ten miles distant from the former country residence of Captain Leslie. It was plain the unprincipled serving woman had grown weary of her charge and left the babe at Captain Leslie's door It was a sweet re union. I cannot stop to tell you how they all went back to the dear old home with its pictures, its statues and murmuring fountains; how their lives were all made bright in the sunshine of happy love.

Again, LAURA, as the daughter of Signor Mercedes, resumed her former proud position in society. Once more throngs of flatterers surrounded her, and among them Caleb Ruthven hastened to "bow the knee" to the divinity he pretended to adore, but he had proved how false and hollow were his protestations. Laura's lessons of adversity had not been in vain. The poor learned to love and bless her, and the years, as they rolled away, only left her dearer to the heart of her parent and to the declining years of Captain and Mrs Leslie, whose closing days were made bright with plenty in the luxurious home of the Snow Flake.

"Cast thy bread upon the waters, and thou shalt find it after many days!"

THE FALL OF NEW ORLEANS.

FURTHER PARTICULARS.

The New Orleans Delta, of Saturday, April 26th, the day after the Federal fleet arrived in front of the city, gives the following particulars of the fall of New Orleans:

OUR GREAT DISASTER AND HUMILIATION.

Yesterday New Orleans was subjected to the most terrible humiliation and degradation which have ever fallen upon a brave and true people After a valiant defence by our forts below the city—after exhausting all our resources and skill—the greater resources on water of the enemy enabled them to pass our exterior fortifications with their large fleet, and they approached the city with a squadron of fifteen of their largest vessels, all steamships, gunboats or mortar vessels. There was a large force of land troops in the city; but of what avail were they against the ships and gunboats of the enemy? At the moment it was announced that the ships had passed the forts, it became evident to all reflecting persons that the city was defenceless. Steps were then taken to render it a barren conquest. By order of the Governor and military authorities, all the Government munitions and stores were sent away. Such material of war as could not be removed was destroyed. Orders were also issued to destroy all the cotton in this city. This was also done.—The troops under the command of Gen Lovell were marched to the interior lines of the city—a few miles below, these lines would have been formidable against any army advancing by land; but the batteries near the river were quite weak and ineffective against the ships—especially in the present stage of the river—the high surface of the water enabling them to completely command the surrounding country. In the condition of affairs it was quite obvious that the enemy's fleet would meet with no serious obstacle in passing up the river. Accordingly it was announce at an early hour that they were coming. Their vessels came up slowly, as if feeling their way —the Hartford, the flag-ship of Commodore Farragut, leading. Then followed the Brooklyn, the Richmond, and nine other ships, big and little. As these ships approached the batteries, about six or seven miles below the city, our artillerists opened upon them from both sides of the river, but, as the guns were only 24s, they produced but little effect. The ships replied with several broadsides, which showed that they completely commanded our batteries The batteries, though manned by unpracticed gunners, kept up the fire for some time, but with no effect, and under such discouraging circumstances as to render it an obvious policy to withdraw the gunners and the troops. The batteries were accordingly abandoned, and the troops were marched to the Jackson railroad In the meantime the hostile squadron steamed up the river. A terrible and melancholy spectacle was presented to the victorious ships. The whole levee, for miles, was wrapt in smoke, from the burning cotton and gun carriages, which the authorities had ordered to be consumed. In the river were many hulls of burning ships, the debris of our fleet and of the merchant vessels and steamers which contained cotton.

The squadron proceeding up the river, the great multitude clustered on the levee looking on in disgust and horror at the dismal spectacle. As they passed, a few shots were fired by some of our soldiers, but without orders. The ships did not reply, but proceeded slowly along our levee. A feeble cheer was raised on board of one of the ships, which was responded to by something like a cheer from a few persons in the crowd. The cheers, whether intended as such or not, drew upon the parties who were suspected of giving them some dozen or so of pistol shots, by which several persons were wounded.—The squadron being advanced, the for-most ship, as far as the Fourth District, came to an anchor—the ships to the number of thirteen taking up positions in front of the city, so as to command the several streets. After remaining in this position for a half an hour, a boat came ashore with two officers, one Captain Bayleis, second in command of the squadron, Capt Farragut being flag officer, and a Lieutenant. These officers were greeted on touching the shore with the most uproarious hozzas for "Jeff. Davis and the South," and with the most threatening demonstrations They had neglected to bring a flag of truce, and it was a proof of the good sense of even an infuriated mul-itude that they were allowed to land. They, however, proceeded under the protection of some gentlemen, who undertook to conduct them to the Mayor's office in a drenching rain, followed by a furious and excited mob. Though no violence was offered to the officers, certain persons who were suspected of favoring their flag and cause, were set upon with great fury, and roughly handled. On arriving at the City Hall, it required the intervention of several citizens to prevent violence being offered to the rash embassador of an execrated dynasty and Government.

The Mayor received the Federal officers in his office, with proper dignity. Capt. Bayleis stated the purport of his mission. He had been sent by Capt. Farragut to demand the surrender of the city and the elevation of the flag of the United States over the Custom House, the Post-office, the Mint and the City Hall. The Mayor replied that he was not the military commander of the city, that he had no authority to surrender it, and would not do so, but that there was a military commander now in the city, and he would send for him, to receive and reply to the demand.

A messenger was despatched for General Lovell. In the interval a number of citizens who were present, got into conversation with the United States naval officers. The Lieutenant seemed to be a courteous, well behaved gentleman, who bore testimony with apparent earnestness to the vigor and valor of the defence of our forts, and was quite communicative. The senior officer was more reserved, but still made large professions of peaceful intents. It was difficult, however, for him to conceal the bitter sectional hate of a Massachusetts man against a true Southern community. In the course of the conversation, however, this officer remarked that Captain Farragut deeply regretted to see the spirit of incendiarism which prevailed in the city in the destruction of cotton and other things. The Mayor remarked that he differed from him; that the destruction was of our own property, and did not concern outsiders. Capt. Bayleis replied that it looked like biting off one's nose to spite his face. The Mayor replied that we had judged differently.

After awhile, Gen. Lovell arrived in front of the City Hall, and was greeted with loud cheers by the crowd outside. On entering the Mayor's office, Capt. Bayleis introduced himself as second in command of the U. S. squadron in front of the city. Gen. Lovell replied, "I am Gen. Lovell, of the army of the Confederate States, commanding this Department" The officers then shook hands, and Capt. Bayleis stated his mission to demand the surrender of the city and the elevation of the U. S. flag over the Custom House, Mint, and Post Office—adding that he was instructed by Capt. Farragut to state that he came to protect private property and personal rights; that he had no design to interfere with any private rights, and especially not with the negro property.

Gen Lovell replied that he would not surrender the city, nor allow it to be surrendered; that he was overpowered on the water by their superior squadron, but that he intended to fight them on land as long as he could muster a soldier; that he had marched all of his armed men out of the city; that he had evacuated it; and if they desired to shell the town, destroying women and children, they could do so. That it was to avoid this he had marched his troops beyond the city limits, but that a large number even of the women of the city had begged him to remain and defend the city even against shelling. He did not think he would be justified in doing so. He would, therefore, retire and leave the city authorities to pursue what course they should think proper. Capt. Bayleis said that no such purpose was entertained by Capt. Farragut, reiterating the expression of his regret at the destruction of cotton. Gen. Lovell interrupted him by saying that it was done by his authority. Capt. Bayleis said that he had no doubt Gen. Lovell had done his duty and they were doing theirs. It was then concluded that Capt. Bayleis and the other officers would return to their ships, and the Mayor would call the Council, and lay before it the demand of Capt. Farragut. The officers requested to be protected in their return to their ships, and Gen. Lovell directed Col. Lovell and Major James to accompany them. The officers accordingly proceeded to the rear of the City Hall, where they took a cab and proceeded to the wharf.

During the interview an immense and excited crowd of people had congregated about the City Hall, who alternately hurrahed for Jeff Davis, for Gen. Lovell, and most vigorously groaned for "Lincoln and his squadron."

To calm this multitude, Pierre Soule addressed them in a few eloquent and effective words, counselling moderation, self possession, fortitude, and confidence in their cause, declaring that the honor of the Government and city was in safe hands, and that General Lovell's answer to the demand to surrender was worthy of the commander of a brave people.

Gen. Lovell, on appearing on the steps, was also loudly cheered. He addressed the multitude in a short speech, declaring his purpose not to surrender the city, but to retire with his army and fight the Lincolnites, whom they could always whip on land. He briefly sketched his course in the preparation of the defence of the city. That he had done all he could do with the means at his disposal. That he came here six months too late, and that it was beyond his resources to contend successfully against the enemy's power on water.

He advised the citizens to bear themselves manfully, never to stoop or submit to the Lincoln domination, and to wait with patient fortitude for the deliverance from bondage which must soon come to them. The General then mounted his horse, and accompanied by his staff, rode to the Jackson railroad, where he took the last car, having already sent his army ahead of him.

Further from New Orleans.

We have some further accounts of the capture of New Orleans. The gunboats of the enemy suffered terribly in their attempt to pass Forts Jackson and St. Phillip. The Confederate gunboat Gen. Quitman ran into one of them, and both sunk in a very few minutes, with all on board. The McRae also went down, firing her last broadside just as she was sinking beneath the waters. The Yankee boats which succeeded in getting up to the city bore honorable testimony of the spirit of our men and the accuracy of their aim. Some of them were completely riddled by our shot, and all were more or less damaged. They were not iron-clad, or did not appear to be. As the boats were coming up the river a crowd was collected on the levee, among whom was a small knot of traitors, who hurrahed for the Union. An immediate response to this demonstration was given by revolvers in the hands of the citizens, who fired into them, killing three and wounding six. The statement by Commodore Farragut, that women and children were shot and killed, is a base fabrication.—When the officer bearing the demand for the surrender of the city landed on the levee, he was greeted with a welcome and shake of the hand from a solitary individual. The officer passed on, but his friend soon after paid the penalty of his treason with his life.

The Yankee flag placed over the Mint was torn down on Saturday evening, 26th ult., by some spirited citizens. The Crescent says:

The men engaged in this gallant enterprise, we learn, were Vincent Hoffernan, W. B. Mumford, N. Holmes, John Burns and James Reed They tore the flag into shreds, and each with a piece in his hand marched up town in triumph.

The shots fired by the Federal vessel came very near demolishing several houses in the vicinity of the Mint, and a shell lodged in the roof of the dwelling of Mr. J. A. Lacour, corner of Victory and Frenchmen streets; but luckily, not exploding, inflicted no serious damage. Mr. Lacour got the shell out from his roof, and brought it up town. We could not have believed that a civilized people could have so forgotten their dignity as to have permitted themselves to have endangered the lives of unoffending women and children, in thus wantonly firing into a city; but the fact is patent—the deed was done.

Under the caption of "Talk on 'Change," the Crescent says:

There were no gatherings on the flags of Carondelet street. In and about the City Hall and on Camp street, the throng of citizens were immense. We were astounded at the large numbers of women and children that promenaded the several streets, having their termination on Canal street. Of course, there was nothing of a business nature thought of, the chief attraction was in and about the City Hall. The proceedings of the City Council will be found elsewhere. A number of the Federal vessels proceeded up the river on Saturday evening, but returned yesterday forenoon.

The flags of the different Consulates, or the representatives of the European Governments, are all displayed from their respective offices, excepting in two or three instances. The Consulate of Bremen has no flag, and two or three other nations have no representatives here. Several private citizens, foreign subjects, have hoisted their country's emblem over ther residences.

The destruction of property has been immense; much more so than necessary. True, all the cotton was expected to have been burnt; but why the sugar and molasses on the levee was sacrificed in the manner it was, that is, carried off by pilferers and the rabble, we cannot say. A part of a cargo of provisions, just landed from Red river, was also stolen. If the agrarians had made an equal division, it might have been of more benefit, but some parties, not satisfied with baskets and bags of sugar rolled away hogsheads, others barrels of sugar; in fact never was such a scene of pilfering heard of before, nor such scenes as occurred last Friday in this heretofore peaceable city. Measures, it will be observed, have been taken by the authorities to put a stop to these disgraceful doings.

The telegraph has informed us that the enemy fired upon a crowd of women and children. We find the following account of the disgraceful affair in the Crescent:

On Saturday, about noon, a party of men, who have recently returned from Beauregard's army, went down on the levee with a band of music and a Confederate flag, to give vent to their feeling in face of the Federals. The levee was densely crowded with people, among whom were a great number of women and children; but this did not deter the sharpshooters on board the vessel nearest the shore from opening fire upon the men engaged in the hamless exhibition of patriotism, which resulted in the death of an innocent bystander and the wounding of two others. We do not commend the action of the young men who provoked the unforfortunate affair, but we cannot refrain from condemning the cruelty of the parties who could level their guns at a crowd for the fault of two or three.

THE CITY OF NEW ORLEANS.

New Orleans is so well known, and has been so frequently visited by our people in every section of the Confederacy, that a description of the place may be deemed superfluous, but as there are doubtless many who have never seen it, to these a brief description will not prove uninteresting.

The place is built around a bend in the river, from which circumstance it has been denominated the "Crescent City." The site inclines gently from the margin of the Mississippi towards the marshy ground in the rear, and is from 2 to 5 feet below the level of the river at the usual spring freshets. To prevent inundations, an embankment or levee about 15 feet wide and 6 feet high, has been raised, extending 120 miles above the city, and to Port Plaquemine, 43 miles below it. This forms a delightful promenade. The city now extends from 6 to 7 miles along the river, and 5 miles to Lake Pontchartrain.

The streets are of convenient breadth, well paved and usually intersect each other at right angles. Canal street is the broadest, being 190½ feet in width, with a grass plot in the middle about 25 feet wide, extending throughout its entire length. Most of the buildings are constructed of brick, and are generally low except in the business portion, where they are usually five or six stories high. The dwellings in the suburbs, many of them, particularly in Lafayette, are surrounded with spacious yards, beautifully decorated with the orange, lemon, magnolia and other ornamental trees. A basement about 6 feet high constitutes the only cellar, as none are sunk below the surface on account of the marshy character of the ground. In different sections of the city are several public squares, among which may be mentioned Jackson square, formerly Place d'Armes. It is ornamented with shell walks, shrubbery, statuetts, etc., and is much frequented for recreation. Lafayette Square, in the Second District, is finely laid out, and adorned with a proportion of shade-trees. Congo Square, in the rear of the city, is also a handsome enclosure.

The public buildings of New Orleans are splendid specimens of architecture. The Custom House is probably the largest building in the Confederacy, covering an area of 87,333 superficial feet. Its dimensions are—Canal street front, 334 feet; Custom House street, 252 feet; New Levee street, 310; Old Levee street, 297 feet; height, 82 feet. The general business room is 116 feet by 90, and has 50 windows. The Mint in New Orleans is near the river. It is a massive structure, 282 feet long, 108 feet deep, 3 stories high, with two wings, each 81 feet by 29. The Municipal Hall, opposite Lafayette square, is a beautiful marble edifice in the Grecian style of architecture. The Odd Fellows' Hall erected in 1852, and the Merchant's Exchange, are both extensive buildings.

Many of the churches are large and costly structures. There are 35 in the city, 12 of which are Roman Catholic, 7 Episcopl, 6 Presbyterian, 5 Methodist, 3 Lutheran, 2 Baptist, and 3 Jewish Synagogues.

The hotels of New Orleans are conducted upon a scale of magnitude scarcely equalled in any city on the Continent. The St. Charles was completed in the autumn of 1852, at a cost of nearly $600,000. It rented for $40,000 per annum, and the rent of the basement alone, is estimated at $16,000. The St. Louis and Verandah Hotels, are also constly establishments. The city contains 4 or 5 theatres, the principal of which are the St. Charles, the Orleans and the American. The first of these is 132 feet long by 170 deep, and cost $350,000. Among the most remarkable bank edifices may be mentioned the City Bank, Canal Bank and Bank of Louisiana. The market houses and cotton presses of New Orleans, are also deserving notice. The centre building of the New Orleans cotton press is 3 stories high, and surmounted by a dome, the summit of which commands a fine view of the city. Not less than 150,000 bales of cotton, on an average, are annually pressed at this establishment.

The benevolent, literary and educational institutions, are among the most extensive and best conducted in the country. There are over 40 school houses in the city, and the average annual attendance is 20,000 pupils.

New Orleans is distinguished for the ability displayed in the management of its public journals. About 20 newspapers are published in the city, 9 or 10 of which are dailies. Several are printed in the French Language.

New Orleans was named in honor of the Duke of Orleans, regent of France during the minority of Louis XV. Its population a few years since, as ascertained by a local census, was 146,448, of whom 29,174 were slaves and colored. During the business season the population is estimated at 175,000. The assessed value of real and property is about $75,000,000.

LATE FROM NEW ORLEANS.

The New Orleans Delta of Saturday evening, May 5, has the following interesting intelligence of affairs in the Crescent City:

GEN. BUTLER AND THE CITY AUTHORITIES.—Negotiations between Gen. Butler and the city authorities are still pending.—Last night the Mayor and Council, accompanied by their adviser, Hon. Pierre Soule, had an interview with the commanding officer of the United States forces, now occupying this city, at his headquarters, at the St. Charles Hotel. Gen. Butler read to the Mayor and Council the proclamation, substantially as it has been published and circulated among our citizens. Mr. Soule on the part of the city authorities, communicated to Gen. Butler their views as to the civil government of the city and the administration of its municipal affairs in this crisis, stated distinctly that the Mayor and Council would continue in the exercise of their official functions, if left entirely free in the performance of their duties, but would, if at all interfered with by the military power of the United States authorities, yield to the latter the entire control and management of the city. After some discussion it was agreed upon that the Mayor and Council should continue to minister the government of the city in all respects as before, with the exception of taking cognizance of political offences or interferences with the military power of the United States, which Gen. Butler reserves to be dealt with by his own Provost Marshal.

With respect to our citizens being treated as "rebels," Gen. Butler distinctly stated that no person who "preserved quiet and order" and refrained from giving aid and comfort to the enemies of his Government "will be disturbed either in person or property."

Nothing was said as to tendering an oath of allegiance to the United States to any citizen.

The question of food was brought up and Gen. Butler recognized it as one of paramount importance. He stated he would not offer any opposition to the introduction of supplies of food by the ordinary means of transportation. Steamboats and railroad cars to run as usual, he reserving to himself to say who should come into and who should go out of the city.

We believe these were the principal points discussed in the interview. Details were left to be arranged to-day at another conference which is now being held.

PEOPLE'S. PRESS.

SALEM, N. C.

FRIDAY, MAY 16, 1862,

WANTED, at this office, an apprentice to the printing business.

NEW ARRANGEMENT.

Owing to the advanced price of everything (except newspapers) the *Press* will not be sent to subscribers, after their term expires, at club rates, in the future.

The *Press* will be conducted strictly, hereafter, upon the CASH system; and persons will please bear in mind that, when they order the *Press*, to remit any amount, not less than 50 cents, and their favors will receive prompt attention.

Terms.

One year,	$2.00.
Six months,	1.00.
Three months,	50.

☞ See interesting account of the fall of New Orleans, and the evacuation of Norfolk. Also somewhat detailed accounts of the battles in Virginia.

☞ The Petersburg Express states that Gen. Wool sent a flag of truce into Norfolk Saturday morning, informing the citizens that they would be allowed 48 hours to take the oath of allegiance to the Lincoln Government. In the event of refusal, they were informed that they would be treated as prisoners of war.

The Express also says that the lady and family of President Davis passed through Petersburg on Saturday last, *en route* for the South.

SALT.—Wagons are passing through this place daily on their way to the Virginia Salt Works. One of the wagoners informed us he paid one dollar per bushel, and was only allowed at the rates of ten bushels (500 lbs.) for a two-horse wagon.

COMMON SCHOOLS.—The following extract from Rev. C. H. Wiley's address, (Superintendent of Common Schools for the State at large) to the Chairman of the Board of County Superintendents, will be interesting to a number of our readers.—We learn that the Spring distribution for 1861 and the Spring distribution for 1862 still remain unpaid. The Literary fund was set apart for the benefit of Common Schools, and we hope that in the end, our Common School system will not suffer on account of the troubles now upon us:

"GENTLEMEN: On the first and second days of this month the President and Directors of the Literary Fund held their annual Spring meeting, at which I was present.

At this meeting it was ordered that the Fall distribution for 1861, due and payable by a previous order, on the first of this month, be paid out to the persons entitled to draw the same; and you will thus perceive that all doubts on this subject are now at an end. As it is probable that most of the boys of the State, who are of sufficient size will be needed in the fields and shops during the Summer, no special order was made by the Literary Board for another distribution from the School Fund before the Fall; but it is desired, if possible, and under all circumstances, to have Winter schools.

You will, therefore, endeavor to infuse into the public mind a spirit of quiet assurance and of confidence in the future, and to preserve in as perfect order as possible the whole machinery of our great and hopeful system of schools."

COL. VANCE.—The rumor that Col. Z. B. Vance had been appointed Brigadier General, is unfounded. Col. Vance was in Richmond completing the arrangements for his Legion. Forty companies have tendered their services to join his Legion.

SHIN-PLASTERS.—We learn from the Salisbury Watchman, that the most important case before Rowan Court during last week, "was five indictments against Jack Hall for the issuance of shin-plasters.—He submitted and was fined $10 and costs in each case."

At last accounts there were only about 100 Yankee troops at Washington, in this State.

OUR COAST.—Accounts from Wilmington state that the Yankees had effected a landing at Swansboro' in Onslow County.

N. C. STOCKS.—North Carolina Bonds are selling in Richmond at 115.

DIVIDEND.—The Bank of North Carolina has declared a dividend of 3 per cent.

RICHMOND, May 7.—Hon. Robt. E. Scott, of Fauquier, one of the most distinguished jurists of Virginia, and a prominent member of the late State Convention, was killed on Saturday by a marauding party of Yankees in Fauquier county.

The Governorship.

It is with deep regret that we learn, from a communication from W. A. Graham, which we copy, that he declines to be a candidate for the office of Governor.

We are sorry to announce this fact, and we believe that a large majority of the people of North Carolina will be very much disappointed. Mr. Graham could have been elected by an overwhelming majority, as we believe no man in the State enjoys the confidence of the people in a greater degree.

There are still other gentlemen in the State—good and true men—whom we vastly prefer to Wm. Johnson, of Mecklenburg. And there will, no doubt, be two candidates in the field, to make the election interesting!

THE LOSSES AT SHILOH.—The Memphis Argus puts down the killed, wounded and missing, in 39 Regiments of our army at Shiloh, at 927 killed, 4,471 wounded, 331 missing. Total 5,798. The regiments not yet heard from officially will probably swell the list to 7,000. It is estimated that one in fifty of the wounded have died or will die. The Argus says that our forces at the commencement of the battle could not have exceeded 30,000, so that nearly one-fourth were killed and wounded.

Gen. Beauregard's official report states that "our loss in the two day's killed outright was 1,728, wounded 8,012, missing 958—making an aggregate of casualities 10,698. This sad list tells in simple language of the stout fight made by our countrymen in front of the rude log chapel of Shiloh, especially when it is known that on Monday, from exhaustion and other causes, not 20,000 men on our side could be brought into action. Of the losses of the enemy I have no exact knowledge.—Their newspapers report it as very heavy. Unquestionably it was greater even, in proportion, than our own, on both days, for it was apparent to all that their dead left on the field outnumbered ours two to one.—Their casualties, therefore, cannot have fallen many short of 20,000 in killed, wounded, prisoners and missing."

Gen. Beauregard states the enemy's force on Sunday at 45,000. On Monday 20,000 of these who remained were reinforced by 33,000 fresh troops, making 53,000 in all, who were gloriously resisted by the 20,000 gallant spirits who fought on the second day.

Reorganization.

The 21st Regiment has been reorganized and is now in Ewell's Division of Gen. Jackson' Army.

We have received a letter from Camp, dated Swift Run Gap, Rockingham County, Va, May 5, 1862, from which we make the following extract, showing the present organization of the Regiment:

The 21st Regiment has been reorganized. It formerly contained 12 companies; but the recent act of Congress establishes the number of Companies in a Regiment at 10. So the "Yadkin Grey Eagles" and the "Forsyth Greys" have been detached and formed into a battalion of Sharp-shooters.

The officers of "Wharton's Special Battalion" are, R. W. Wharton, Major.

Co. A. N. G. Hunt, Captain; R. E. Wilson 1st Lieut.; Richard Woodruff, 2d Lieut.; David Osborne, Brevet 2d Lieut.

Co. B. P. D. Headly, Captain; John Cooper, 1st Lieut.; Cornelius Shults, 2d Lieut.; Larkin Owen, Brevet 2d Lieut.

The officers of the 21st Reg't. N. C. T. are: Thomas Settle, Colonel; R. K. Pepper, Lieut. Col.; Dr. Saunders Fulton, Major.

COMPANIES.

Davidson Guards—J. C. Hedgcock Captain; J. F. Beal, 1st Lieutenant; J. H. Miller 2nd Lieutenant; J. P. Oaks, Brev. 2d Lt.

Townfork Invincibles.—(Stokes—formerly Capt. Westmoreland,) H. S. Liegham, Capt.; V. W. Hazlip, 1st Lieutenant; T. B. Gentry, 2nd, and V. M. Tuttle, Brevet second Lieut.

Rockingham Invincibles.—(formerly Capt. Boyd.) W. J. Pfohl, Captain; S. C. James 1st Lieutenant; E. M. Matthews 2nd, and John G. Martin, Brevet 2nd Lieutenant.

Mountain Tigers.—(Surry, formerly Capt. Waugh;) A. P. Shore, Captain; Henderson Jones 1st Lieutenant; Wm. Martin 2nd and Jasper Cockerham, Brevet 2nd Lieutenant.

Mountain Boys.—Stokes—(formerly Capt. Pepper.) W. S. King, Captain; Wilburn Shaub, 1st Lieutenant; S. M. Jessup 2nd, and A. J. Nunn, Brevet 2nd Lieutenant.

Surry Marksmen.—(formerly Capt. Gilmer) ———, Captain; M. L. Patterson, 1st Lieutenant; Joseph A. Hill 2nd, and R. P. Raleigh, Brevet 2d Lieutenant.

Forsyth Southrons—F. P. Miller, Captain; J. L. Pratt, 1st Lieutenant; S. D. Newsom 2d, and Calvin Crews, Brevet 2nd Lieutenant.

Forsyth Rifles—(formerly Capt. Belo,) Alexander Miller, Captain; D. P. Jackson 1st Lieutenant; G. T. Clayton 2nd, and John W. Miller, Brevet 2nd Lieutenant.

Guilford Dixie Boys.—William A. Rankin, Captain; Eli Gilmer, 1st Lieutenant; J. S. Dick, 2nd, and J. F. Stewart Brevet 2nd Lieut.

Blue Ridge Riflemen.—Surry—B. Y. Graves, Captain; Bird Snow, 1st Lieutenant; L. T. Whitlock 2nd, and S. T. Scott, Brev. 2d Lieut.

DIED.

In this place, on Tuesday May the 13th, Mrs. ELIZA LOUISE LASH, wife of H. M. Lash, Esq, of this place, aged 28 years, 9 months and 13 days.

"'For ever with the Lord!'
Amen, so let it be;
Life from the dead is in that word,
'Tis immortality."

In this county, on the 4th inst., HUGH PATTERSON, aged about 70 years.

In Stokes county, on the 26th of April, EDMUND L. MARTIN, Esq., aged 58 years.

The News.

It appears that there has not been anything like a battle on the Peninsula, since that which took place near Williamsburg, on Monday, the 5th inst., an account of which appears elsewhere. There was a small skirmish a day or two after at West Point; but little loss occurred on either side. It is ascertained that the 4th and 5th N. C. State Troops, and the 13th and 14th N. C. Vols., were in the fight and behaved nobly. Col. McRae's and Col. Scales' Regiments were badly cut up. It is rumored that McRae lost half his men.

An account of the evacuation of Norfolk will be found in this issue. Norfolk and Portsmouth are now occupied by from five to twelve thousand of the enemy. Public property worth nearly forty million was destroyed by the Confederates before evacuating.

THE VIRGINIA MERRIMAC DESTROYED.—The Virginia was destroyed by order of Commodore Tatnall. He ascertained Saturday that Norfolk had been evacuated by our troops, and was in possession of the enemy. The pilots aboard advised against going round to York river. The crew then proceeded to lighten her in order to take her into James river. The coal and pig iron were thrown overboard until, it is said, the wood work of her hull was exposed. Finding it still impracticable to ascend the river, it was determined to abandon her and burn her, which was accordingly done.

THE STATE CONVENTION.

This body adjourned on Tuesday morning last, the 13th instant.

The Spirit of the Age says: "The Convention has been chiefly engaged, since our last, in considering propositions for constitutional amendments. An ordinance relative to the legislative department of the State, embraces the following amendments to the Constitution: 1st, requiring payment of tax immediately preceding the act of voting; 2d, restricting the right of suffrage to free white citizens of the Confederate States; 3d, excluding paupers from voting: 4th, for holding biennial elections, but annual sessions of the Legislature, to be limited to 50 days; 5th, prescribing qualification of members of the Legislature, &c. Most or all of the amendments, we believe, were adopted, except the one excluding paupers from voting.

The ordinance to punish "sedition" has been indefinitely postponed. Mr. Graham's proposition to remove all restraint from the liberty of the press and of speech, except when abused as in the case of slander, was voted down by a large majority.

A letter to the Convention from the Adjutant General to the Convention, stated that North Carolina has now 54 Regiments in or ready for service, with 15 companies unattached.

A motion to change the basis of representation was rejected by a vote of 17 for, to 62 against. An ordinance concerning salt has been passed, but we do not know its provisions. Also one to provide for the collection of taxes. Also one authorising the Miners and Planters Bank to establish an Agency east of the Blue Ridge."

The Standard of Wednesday, says:

"On Monday, among other things, an ordinance reported by Mr. Gilmer from the finance committee, was passed, to issue two millions of dollars in treasury notes, to meet the liabilities of the State. Also, an ordinance to charter a Railroad from Fayetteville to Florence, South Carolina; also, an ordinance exempting members of the Society of Friends from military duty in the war, on their paying in each case $100; also, an ordinance to secure to citizens driven from their homes by the enemy, the right to vote for Governor in any County in the State. The ordinance to establish the office of Lieutenant Governor was taken up, debated, amended, and then laid upon the table."

From the Standard.

My name having been mentioned in several of the newspapers of the State, in the number of those from whom a Governor shall be chosen at the ensuing election, and recommended by a public meeting recently held in the County of Wake, I esteem it proper publicly to announce, that I must decline to be considered a candidate for that office. The reasons for this conclusion, arising out of the situation of my family and private affairs, have been freely assigned to all with whom I have communicated in conversation or by correspondence, and need not be repeated. I offer my unfeigned thanks to those kind friends, and the conductors of public journals, who have been pleased to render me this assurance of their confidence, and my cordial co-operation in whatever may tend to the safety, independence and good government of the country.

W. A. GRAHAM.

May 9, 1862.

SIX REGIMENTS RUNNING.—The correspondent of the Chicago Times says that in the battle of Shiloh the 77th Ohio regiment fled without firing a gun; and the 53d, 57th and 71st fired one or two rounds and then fled.—Also that the 18th Wisconsin and 17th Iowa fled after firing two or three rounds.

DESTRUCTIVE CONFLAGRATION.

AUGUSTA, May 12.—There was a destructive fire at Atlanta yesterday. A large amount of bacon and salt was destroyed.

[SECOND DESPATCH.]

AUGUSTA, May 12.—There was a destructive fire at Atlanta on the 11th, in Wallace's Warehouse, containing 800 bales cotton, 200 tierces rice, 25,000 lbs. government bacon, other government stores; 200 bbls. sugar, a quantity of oil and hides Nearly 10,000 lbs. was destroyed together with the warehouse, and the adjoining buildings were badly damaged. Total loss $100,000; insurance $35,000. The Augusta Insurance and Banking Company lose about $16,000. Two men were seriously injured, one of them it is supposed mortally.

REJECTED.—The people of Virginia have refused to ratify their new Constitution by a small majority—678. It is supposed that the war interfered seriously with fair expression of the popular will.—The Convention was several months engaged in elaborating the Constitution, which has just been rejected, at a cost of several hundred thousand dollars.

LATEST NEWS.

Startling News!

From the Charlotte Daily Bulletin.

RICHMOND, May 14.

Four Yankee gunboats are coming up the James River.

The flag of truce steamer which took prisoners to Newport News, returned this afternoon, and passed 4 gunboats, including the Monitor, this side of City Point. [Twelve miles from Petersburg.

Much uneasiness prevails. The Northern newspapers are said to be filled with extravagant exultations at the present aspect of affairs.

MOBILE, May 13.

On the 9th inst, near Corinth, Col. Wood ward with the 1st Kentucky Cavalry and a detachment of Texas Rangers attacked the Federals at Elk River, killing several and captured two Captains, two Lieutenants and forty-three privates and eight negroes. The Confederate loss was five killed, including Capt. Harris of the Texas Rangers. Seven were wounded. The above is official.

FURTHER DETAILS.

AUGUSTA, GA., May 12th, 1862.—All is quiet at Corinth to-day. It is believed the enemy is slowly advancing on our lines by three routes.

Jeff. Thompson has taken command of the Confederate gunboats on the Mississippi river. He attacked the Federal gunboats above Fort Pillow to day (10th inst.,) destroying one mortar vessel, and damaging two others. Confederate loss four killed and eight wounded.

The Montgomery Advertiser says that the Navy Yard at Pensacola has been blown up and burned by the Confederates.

ANOTHER BATTLE!
From Gen. Jackson's Command.

RICHMOND, May 9.—A dispatch from Staunton this morning says Gen. Jackson's advanced force engaged the enemy near McDowell's, at 5 p. m. yesterday. After four hours fighting, the Confederates succeeded in driving the enemy back. Our loss is said to be 300. General Edward Johnson was wounded in the ankle; Col. M. G. Harman and Capt. Dabney, of the 52d regiment, were wounded in the arm. Col. Gibbons of the 10th Virginia regiment was killed. A big fight is expected to-day. The Richmond Examiner of this morning says (on the authority of Capt. Hill of the steamer Shultz,) that our batteries at Day's Point, (Isle of Wight county,) was attacked by three gunboats yesterday and silenced one vessel and an iron clad Galena. Three hundred and twenty Hessians captured at Williamsburg on Monday, arrived here last evening. The city is greatly excited in consequence of reports received that more fighting has occurred on the Peninsula.

GENERAL JACKSON'S VICTORY!

RICHMOND, May 10.—The following official dispatch was received this morning from T. J. Jackson, addressed to Adjutant General Cooper, dated Valley District, May 9, via Staunton, May 10.

"*To Gen.* S. COOPER, *Adj't. Gen'l:*

"God has blessed our arms with victory at McDowell's, yesterday."

(Signed,) T. J. JACKSON,
Major General.

DISPATCH FROM GOV. LETCHER.

RICHMOND, May 10.—A Telegram from Gov. Letcher, received this morning, from Staunton, states that General Jackson dispatches "We have gained a brilliant victory. The enemy is in full flight, hotly pursued by our forces. Our loss is forty killed and two hundred wounded. The enemy's loss is heavy. They left all of their dead and wounded upon the field."

The Monday morning 2d edition of the Bulletin states that Jackson had found about 500 dead and wounded on the field, and that he was in hot pursuit of the retreating yankee army.

FURTHER FROM THE MCDOWELL FIGHT.

From passengers by the Central train Sunday afternoon, the Richmond *Dispatch* has some further particulars of the fight at McDowell on Thusday the 8th inst. Up to Saturday evening, the enemy were still retreating. and Gen. Jackson pursuing them, but with not much prospect of coming up with them. They had taken the Franklin road through the county of Pendleton, which is the most direct road to Cumberland, Md. Prisoners captured represent that Gen. Fremont was expected to reinforce Milroy on the day the fight occurred.

Our loss in the fight was 300 killed and wounded, principally in the Twelfth Georgia regiment, which suffered severely. We captured in the engagement about one hundred boxes of fixed ammunition, from 400 to 500 Enfield rifles and Minie muskets, 60 to 75 cavalry saddles, and from 160 to 200 head of cattle. These latter were afterwards claimed by citizens of the county of Highland, from whom they had been stolen by the enemy. Citizens of the neighborhood state that the loss of the enemy in the fight of Thursday was very heavy, and believed to be from 1,800 to 1,800.

Glorious News from the Western Army!

ANOTHER ENGAGEMENT—THE ENEMY ROUTED—PRICE AND VAN DORN IN PURSUIT—THE YANKEES RUNNING LIKE SHEEP—CONFEDERATE LOSS SLIGHT.

RICHMOND, May 10.—The following is a copy of an official dispatch from Gen. Beauregard, addressed to Adjutant General Cooper, dated

CORINTH, May 9, via Mobile.

We attacked the enemy to day and drove him from his position.

(Signed,) G. T. BEAUREGARD.

SECOND DISPATCH.

AUGUSTA, May 10—The Corinth correspondent of the Mobile Advertiser, telegraphs: "I have just returned from the rout. The enemy has been driven across Seven Mile Creek, running like sheep. It appears Pope's Division of the Federal Army alone occupied Farmington, Halleck, with the main body, is still on the River. The Confederate loss is slight. The Federals retreated so rapidly that we were unable to capture many prisoners. Price and Van Dorn led the attack. We captured a Telegraph Office at Farmington, and then returned to Corinth. It is reported that the confederate forces operating down the Tennessee have captured a large number of prisoners and a large amount of property at Paris and Paducah."

From the Peninsula.

A couple of gentlemen from the army of the Peninsula, who reached Richmond Monday afternoon, state that McClellan's army was just this side of New Kent Court House on the morning of that day, and Gen Johnston's forces were but three miles ahead, hotly pressed by the Yankees. It was thought that Gen. Johnston was endeavoring to reach a point on the Chickahominy, known as Buttom's Bridge, but nine miles distant, where he would make a stand. If the supposition be correct, the great trial of strength between the two armies, cannot be deferred much longer.

Buttom's Bridge in New Kent County, is on the main stage road between Williamsburg and Richmond, and but fifteen miles from the latter city. The country in the immediate vicinity is admirably adapted for a battle-field, and one in which cavalry and artillery can be used most advantageously. It is also in easy marching distance of Richmond, and our army can be reinforced from the capital as rapidly as may be required by any emergency which may occur. But should the uncertainties of battle throw the scale against the Confederates at Buttom's Bridge, another advantageous position is presented at Boar Swamp, in Henrico county, six miles east of the Bridge, and nine from Richmond. The latter is possibly the best position, and while a show of fight may be made at Buttom's Bridge it is not unlikely the great struggle will occur at the Swamp.

Petersburg Express.

THE BATTLE AT WILLIAMSBURG.
TERRIBLE SLAUGHTER OF YANKEES —CAPTURE OF PRISONERS AND CANNON.

PETERSBURG, Va. 7, 1½ A. M.—A bearer of special dispatches from Gen. Magruder, arrived here this evening on his way through to Richmond, conveying highly important and gratifying intelligence in reference to the engagement at Williamsburg, Va., on Monday last. We learn that on Monday the enemy appeared in front of our fortifications at Williamsburg, in large force, and at 2 o'clock, p. m., a battle commenced, which raged furiously until dark closed the scene, when the enemy were in full retreat, and Gen. Stuart's cavalry brigade in hot pursuit. The battle is said to have been one of the fiercest of the war while it lasted, and resulted in a glorious victory to the Confederate cause. Although our troops fought a portion of the engagement behind entrenchments, our loss is represented as having been 500 in killed and wounded. Among our losses we regret to hear, that there were nineteen officers, the gallant Col. Ward, of Florida, falling while bravely leading his men to the fray. The enemy's loss is known to have been fearful, but we could gather no particulars as to precise numbers. We captured 900 prisoners and 12 splendid field-pieces. Only a portion of our forces were engaged, the great bulk of the Confederates being several miles in rear of Williamsburg. The charge of Stuart's cavalry brigade is said to have been fearful, mowing the Hessians down by the score, and securing prisoners in large numbers. It is not positively known who commanded the Federalists, but it is thought that McClellan was about. He captured no "lunette" for this time.

The above information we get from a source entitled to the most implicit confidence, and we know that it has been confirmed by reliable despatches which have already gone to Richmond. The bearer of this pleasing intelligence was despatched to City Point by Gen. Magruder, but the telegraphic station at that locality having been abolished, an engine was pressed into service at the Point, and the glad tidings sent over the wires from Petersburg. It is a matter for rejoicing, that the "On to Richmond" by the way of the Peninsular, has met with a very decided check at Williamsburg.

ADDITIONAL.

Some five or six soldiers, who were wounded in the fight on Monday, reached Petersburg last evening. Among the number is Joseph Delano, son of Mr. Charles A. Delano, of Petersburg. Mr. D. was severely wounded in the hand, losing a thumb and fore-finger. These soldiers were wounded early in the engagement, and could not give any detailed account of the fight. They state that the battle was long and bloody, beginning about eleven o'clock and continuing until dark. Nearly the whole of Gen. Longstreet's brigade was engaged, although Gen. Johnston commanded in person.—Our force is said to have been some eight or ten thousand, and that of the enemy is estimated to have been at least twice as much. They were reinforced rapidly, while the main body of our army was ten or fifteen miles distant and reinforcements did not reach us, until five o'clock, p. m.

We repulsed the enemy, driving them back at least two miles, killing and wounding over one thousand, and taking several hundred prisoners. One account says that the cannon we took from the enemy, for want of transportation, was spiked and left upon the field, but this statement needs confirmation. We regret to learn that Gen. Richard H. Anderson of S. C., was killed, also one of his aids, but we could not ascertain the name of the latter. Gen. Jubel A. Early, of Franklin, was badly wounded. Several of the yankee officers were killed, and many of them taken prisoners. The Thirteenth N. C. Regiment was engaged, and among those seriously wounded, is Capt. Irving, Company B. One of the wounded soldiers, who arrived last evening states that the enemy landed in his transports on York river, near Williamsburg, and in this way brought his artillery to the scene of action without trouble. It is also stated that we fought entirely without artillery, but we think this must be a mistake.—The enemy are said to be again preparing for an advance, and another fight is hourly expected, if indeed it has not already taken place.

LATER.

We met with a participant in the battle late last night, who informed us that the 13th Virginia Regiment, Col. Samuel Garland, suffered very much in the engagement. Col. Garland was badly wounded in the arm, but had his wound dressed and returned to the field, where he exchanged his sword for a musket, and aided in peppering the enemy whenever he could see him. The North Carolina Thirteenth, Col. Scales, was also badly cut up. Capt. Bailey, of Company B. was severely wounded and left on the field. In Company B, out of 53 men but 25 effective men were brought out.—Capt. Irving was seriously wounded, and Lieutenants Alexander and Thompson, shared the same fate. There is but one commissioned officer left unhurt. Col. Mott, of Alabama, is dangerously wounded. [Express.

Cartridges picked up on the battle field of Shiloh consisted of five buckshots, kept together in a copper wire net, in shape like the little vials containing homeopathic medicines. No doubt the copper used in the making of those new-fangled missills may account for the incurableness of many a wound received by our soldiers at the last battles.

The Evacuation of Norfolk.

From the Petersburg Express.

Just as we expected, the traitor Byers, who stole the Confederate steamtug *A. J. White*, and went over to the enemy on Thursday, communicated such information to General Wool, as to precipitate the occupancy of Norfolk by the Yankees and hasten its abandonment by our troops. On Friday, the enemy landed a heavy body of troops, variously estimated at from five to ten thousand, at Ocean View, some eight or ten miles in the rear of Norfolk, and commenced a march upon the city. The forces consisted of infantry, artillery and cavalry, and the latter came near cutting off a large portion of Col. Chambliss' regiment which had been stationed near Sewell's Point. Our forces, among them the Confederate Cadets of this city, tribble-quicked towards the old borough, and made a very narrow escape. It is said that when we burnt Indian Poll Creek Bridge, across Tanner's Creek, the Yankee cavalry were at one end of it, and would have seriously interfered with our operations, but for the Beauregard Artillery, of Lynchburg, who by a few well directed shots, sent the Yankee horsemen flying beyond the reach of our guns.

It is believed that all of our troops, arms, and ammunition, quartermaster's and commissary's stores were safely removed. But we regret to hear that the Confederate loss at the Gosport Navy Yard, has been immense. An employee in the yard ever since the war commenced, estimates the loss there at six millions or more. A large quantity of very valuable machinery, and some $200,000 worth of copper have been left to the enemy! All the buildings that could be destroyed, were fired and consumed. Some of them being fireproof, could not be so destroyed.—The Dry Dock, one of the most costly and perfect establishments of its kind, probably in the world, was blown up.—This Dock is said to have cost $5,000,000 and required several years for its construction.

It is a matter of universal regret, that two gunboats, which had just been completed, and received their armament and stores, were burnt. These could easily have been carried to Richmond, passing to the mouth of James River under the protection of the Merrimac. Four other gunboats, on the stocks, and unfinished, were also consigned to the flames. The splendid transport Wm. Selden and a number of smaller steamers, tugs, etc., were all burnt. These two, it is stated, could have been carried to Richmond without risk. But we presume the Confederate government has more money than it knows what to do with, and desires to give employment to artizans in building new vessels.

The Twelfth Virginia Regiment was the last to leave Norfolk. They crossed the river to Portsmouth, and from there marched a distance of 26 miles to Suffolk.

The troops on Crany Island are supposed to be safe, but we have been unable to hear from them. There were two companies in that garrison from this place.

It is generally believed by the few civillians who did get off, that not more than one hundred males outside the army, have left Norfolk. Many females have left since it became known that the city was to be abandoned to the tender mercies of the Lincolnites, and a large number who desired to leave, still remain because of their inability to get away. Soldiers inform us that when they passed through Norfolk, Saturday morning, they were everywhere met by groups of ladies, who with tears in their eyes, implored their protection.

Strange to say, our authorities decided very suddenly to evacuate the place, but gave the people no information of the fact; and stranger still, they first sent the greater portion of the troops away and then commenced to move the valuables. Common sense would have suggested that our troops be retained to hold and defend the place until every article of value had been removed. "West Point" thought differently, however, and hence the brilliant but very precipitate departure.

BURYING SOLDIERS PREMATURELY.

Most, if not all, of the soldiers who die in the various hospitals located in this city, are interred at Oakwood Cemetery, in the eastern suburbs. It cannot be supposed that when so many men are to be attended to, that all can have that care and attention bestowed on them that they would get at home or here under more favorable auspices, consequently many become food for worms that might otherwise be living. It does seem, however, eminently proper that when, to all appearance, the poor volunteer has shuffled off this mortal coil, his body should be retained a sufficient length of time to put the truth beyond doubt. We fear this is not always done. Anxiety for the living swallows up respect for the dead, and the remains of the latter are often hurried too precipitately to the place of interment. It would seem that there should be attached to each hospital a place for the temporary deposit of those who die or are supposed to have died from disease. We are led to make these suggestions from having heard that on two occasions recently parties who were about being subject to the rites of burial in Oakwood Cemetery had signified their disapprobation of the proceeding while on their way thither. The driver of the hearse in one instance, as we hear, was horrified at the vigorous manifestations of the supposed defunct, and quickly carried him to a place where he could be released from his unpleasant predicament. In another instance, as we learn Mr. Radford, keeper of the cemetery, having undoubted assurance, from the knocking and exclamations of the subject, opened the coffin and sent the supposed dead man back for further medical treatment. While attaching no blame to any one, the matter is mentioned in the hope that it will induce a caution that experience has abundantly shown to be necessary.—*Rich. Dispatch.*

EXTRAORDINARY ADVENTURE.

Yesterday evening Capt J. T. Montgomery arrived here from Corinth, whither he had gone when the wires first flashed the news of Sunday's great fight. After staying there till he desired to return, he left on the Memphis & Charleston Railroad Wednesday night, the 9th, and arrived at Huntsville next morning, no one on board dreaming that the Yankees were in the place. He was in the hindmost car, and as the train stopped, he heard some one say, "The Yankees have got us," and looking out, he saw them thick as bees around the engine and coming down along the train. He quickly stepped out, took a back street and was soon out of sight. Near the outskirts of the town, he entered a house, exchanged his uniform for citizens clothes, came back into town, hired a horse and buggy and negro driver at a livery stable, and started for the Tennessee river at the nearest point. He had proceeded but a little ways until a couple of mounted Federal officers having got scent of him from finding his name on his trunk in the cars, came up and accosted him as a Captain Montgomery. He repudiated the name—said his name was Johnston, and said that he was going to his home from town. They told him they knew better; that he was Capt. Montgomery of the rebel army, and their prisoner, and must go with them. Quietly remarking that they must know more about his business than he did himself, he turned and started with them

They stopped on the roadside to chat with some negroes they found in a field. (Yankees will take no negroes.) They were both very near the Captain. Catching the proper moment when their attention was directed to the negroes, he drew a pistol, from his pocket, and instantly put a ball through the heart of one, who fell down dead. Another moment and he had put a ball through the other, who reeled and clung to his horse a few moments. Meantime the Captain was speeding his way back towards the river. Looking back as he got nearly out of sight, he saw the 'Yankee' fall from his horse sprawling on the ground. He reached the river safely, turned the negro driver back with the horse and buggy, and got himself ferried across, just as fifty well armed and mounted men approached the bank, and could find no means to cross after him. They discharged their guns at him without effect. He took to the mountains, made his way to Chattanooga, and reached here last evening.

The Captain has been raising a regiment of Mounted Artillery. This is the kind of an officer his men will have to serve under.

Atlanta (Ga.) Confederacy, April 16.

DISTANCES ON THE MISSISSIPPI.

As the eye of the public is now turned to the Mississippi Valley, the following table will be found of interest, as showing the distance between the towns along the river from St. Louis to New Orleans:

	Miles.
St. Genevieve,	60
St Mary's Landing,	12
Chester,	8
Liberty,	10
Wilkinson's,	10
Cape Girardeau,	50
Commerce,	15
Cairo,	35
Columbus,	20
Hickman,	17
Island No. 10,	28
New Madrid,	10
Point Pleasant,	12
Tiptonville,	8
Island No. 14,	12
Gayoso,	8
Caruthersville,	2
Fort Pillow,	45
Memphis,	78
Mouth of St. Francis,	80
Helena,	10
Mouth of White,	84
Napoleon,	21
Columbia,	65
Princeton,	50
Lake Providence,	25
Vicksburg,	75
Grand Gulf,	50
Rodney,	20
Mouth of Red river,	65
Bayou Sarah,	30
Port Hudson,	12
Baton Rouge,	28
Plaquemine,	20
Donaldsonville,	35
New Orleans,	78

Pikes and Lances.—Alison, the historian of the great French wars, tells us that in all the charges made, in all the battles between the French and English, from 1793 to 1815, from Toulon to Waterloo inclusive, the bayonets never crossed but on one occasion, viz: at the combat of Fuentes d'Onoro, in the Peninsula. One side or the other, he says, invariably gives way before the weapons come in contact.

A report of the British Adjutant-General was published a few years ago, from which we learn that the British army 50,000 strong, fired at the battle of Vittoria, 1,600,000 musket and rifle shot. They had a large body of cavalry and 150 pieces of artillery. The cavalry, the artillery, and the bayonet, were all in active requisition. The whole number of French killed, wounded, and prisoners, fell short of 8,000.

These are significant facts, in connection with the pike. They show that there is not half the danger from musket firing that raw soldiers are apt to imagine. They show also that it is in the power of pikemen, brave and well disciplined, to break the of ranks the infantry nine times out of ten, by a resolute charge from a proper distance, and they will suffer comparatively very little from the shot of the infantry in making it. Cromwell's men used to cut the pike inhalf when they mounted a parapet or stormed a breach, and they were never known to fail.

The lance is nothing more than the pike used by horsemen. It is one of the most formidable weapons in the world, when thus used, and is superior to all others in breaking squares of infantry. We wonder, in Virginia, where there are so many fine hores, and where every body is a good rider, it has not been brought into general use. It would render great service, we have no doubt. We hope the pike, at least, is in a fair way to be estimated at its proper value —*Dispatch.*

HON. JOHN J. CRITTENDEN AND SECRETARY SEWARD.

The New York correspondent of the Syracuse (N. Y.) Union says:

Speaking of Secessionists, leads me to remember Ex-Governor Morehead, of Kentucky, who has recently been liberated from Fort Warren, on condition of his not returning home, but remaining in the "Free States" during the war. An anecdote is current as to how the Governor got his release, wich I am assured is well founded. It seems that Ex Senator Crittenden demanded it, and was assured by President Lincoln that Morehead should be let out. A week went by, and nothing more was done. A second visit to the White House gave the information to Mr. Crittenden that Seward had been promptly ordered by the President to release the Prisoner, but, for some reason of his own had declined to obey, and a second written request was then and there made out, signed by the Presidential hand, and dispatched to the State Department. Mr Seward quietly consigned it to the flames, however, and Mr. Morehead remained in the casemates a fortnight or three weeks longer.

Again the indefatigable Kentucky loyalist called on the President, and a third and equally ineffectual message was the result; the prisoner still lingered in the Boston Harbor. At last Crittenden called on Seward himself—six weeks had elapsed since his first interference. He demanded to know why his old friend was not discharged. Seward faltered and equivocated; Crittenden lost his temper—the old lion was aroused, and in the plainest possible Anglo-Saxon, he vented his opinion of "the first officer under the Government." "I always knew," he roared "that you were a liar and a dirty dog, and you have proved it now more clearly than ever." Mr. Seward, in the most Christian manner, meekly declined a retort; but handed Mr. Crittenden the order for the release of Mr Morehead, and so he got his liberty.

THE CONSCRIPTION.

Many persons desire information on the operation of this law. We have published the law itself, the bill on exemptions, the regulations adopted by the Secretary of War, and to-day we publish the letter of the Secretary to Gov. Clark, elucidating several points in its operation.

To relieve further anxiety and to prevent unnecessary trouble, either to the people or to the Military Department here, in seeking information, we will say, that as yet, no arrangement has been made between the Governor or Adjutant General of the State and Secretary of War, in regard to the Conscription, that we know of. Officers have not yet been appointed to enrol the conscripts or to draft them. When this is done the public will be advised of it. In the meantime we make the following suggestions:

1. Let the people remain at home who do not intend to volunteer, and quietly pursue their business.

2. Until the 17th inst., every man between the ages of 18 and 35—may volunteer and join a new company which can be filled up by that time or one already in service from this State as a recruit.

3. Read the exemption law and see if you belong to either of the classes therein exempted, and if you do, make yourself easy, and answer to your name when you are called.

4. When the names of all those who have not volunteered between 18 and 35 are enrolled, then the conscription will begin. We presume that those who are necessary to fill up the companies already formed to 125 for infantry, 150 for artillery, and 80 for cavalry, will be selected by draft and sent at once to recruit the companies; and that those who are not drafted will be sent into camps of instruction or suffered to remain at home until called for.

5. Those who intend to hire substitutes need not be in haste, as it is understood to be the purpose of the Secretary of War to release every man in the army over 35 years of age. Many who are released will doubtless wish to return, and can readily be employed as substitutes.

6. Whether the Secretary of War designs to release those persons under 18 and over 35 years who are *substitutes* for the war, has not yet been decided we believe. Our impression, however, is, that persons wo are *substiiutes* for those who are over 18 and under 35, will be retained in the service, but substitutes for men over 35 may be released. [Standard.

GUBERNATORIAL.

It's a humbug, it's a farce, it's all stuff, to say no party feeling exists in North Carolina. That man is humbugged, badly humbugged, who supposes that No-party will not run a candidate for Governor.—They will do it—mark what we say. It is their determined policy to keep in office one of the same click that now rules or rather that misrules the destiny of North Carolina. We have no confidence in their professions of love and good will to all men. Didn't they make the same like professions in November last? And at the same time persistently refuse to vote for any electoral ticket that did not endorse the jagged, crooked Military-Board-Gubernatorial Administration? "If they will do so in the green tree, what will they do in the dry?" Why do they not come out and let the world—the people, know that they do not intend to vote for any man who was not a Secessionist before Lincoln's infamous proclamation? Why endeavor to keep dark their true purpose? Very obviously, because the true people, learning their real party intentions, would indignantly disdain to entertain for one moment, the conniving trickery to which some would and are resorting, for the purpose of getting into office. The Winston Sentinel, for example, pretends to be ever so very anxious to get the people united It pretends to care naught for the past parties; and to show its no party feeling, suggests the names of *five original Secessionists*, and ONE original Union man, as its preference for the position of Governor. The Sentinel manifests a preference for Hon. John M. Morehead. No wonder the Sentinel claims such a preference. Gov. Morehead, from his extreme age, has lost, to some extent, his once powerful energy, and is consequently not an available man, certainly will not be a candidate. We are greatly inclined to doubt the sincerity of the Sentinel in its devotion to Gov. Morehead. We suspect the Sentinel only used the name of Morehead to afford a clue or an excuse for presenting the claims of its pets, Messrs. Avery, Johnston, Craig, Reid and Clingman. Why is the Sentinel unwilling to support W. A. Graham? "a man of gigantic intellect, a man that can rise superior to the difficulties that surround us, and inspire by the magic of his intellect, and the wisdom of his acts, the confidence of the whole people?" We repeat: Why not support Mr. Graham? But, if the Sentinel is partial to a Western man, why does it forget the name of the intrepid Vance?—the hero of Newbern, whose name has been strongly pressed throughout the State for that position? Evidently because the brave Vance is available, and if elected, would say to the vampires, who live on public plunder: "Take your bed and walk."

Henderson Times.

AN INGENIOUS COUNTERFEIT.—We were shown a counterfeit 50 cents bill, last week, purporting to be of the printed issues of the State of North Carolina, but executed with a pen. The different varieties of type with which the genuine are printed, are all well imitated, and the quality of the paper about the same. The counterfeit bore the signature of Henry Hardie and was well executed. The bill would deceive a casual observer or ignorant person This one was detected at the store of Wallace & Elias, in this place.

We learn that the "Five Cents" State issues are being raised to 50 cents. Look out.

Iredell Express

John Baxter, Esq., formerly of this State, but now of Knoxville, Tenn., was lately arrested on a visit to Memphis, upon frequent representations of suspicions of his loyalty by persons about Knoxville to Gen. Kirby Smith. The death of Gen. Johnston caused him to be under arrest for 16 days, but on examination he was at once released.

For the People's Press.

PUBLICATIONS OF THE GENERAL TRACT AGENCY.

No. 1.	A Voice from Heaven,	4	pages.
" 2.	Don't Put It Off,	4	"
" 3.	Self-Dedication to God,	4	"
" 4.	Private Devotion,	4	"
" 5.	The All-Sufficiency of Christ,	4	"
" 6.	The Act of Faith,	4	"
" 7.	Motives to Early Piety,	4	"
" 8.	The Sentinel,	4	"
" 9.	Come to Jesus, by N. Hall,	32	"
" 10.	Casting Our Burden on the Lord, by Rev. Joseph M. Atkinson,	8	"
" 11.	Are You Prepared?	4	"
" 12.	Prepare to Meet Thy God,	4	"
" 13	An Appeal to the Young, by Rev. Jas McGready,	4	"
" 14.	Come and Rest, by Rev. J. C. Ryle,	4	"
" 15.	The Soldier,	8	"
" 16.	Your Soul—Is It Safe?	16	"
" 17.	The New Year,	4	"
" 18.	A Mother's Parting Words to her Soldier Boy,	8	"
" 19.	The Great Gathering,	4	"
" 20.	Lovest Thou Me?	4	"
" 21.	Individual Effort,	8	"
" 22.	The French Soldier,	4	"
" 23.	Call to Prayer, by Rev. J. C. Ryle,	16	"
" 4.	Christ in You, by Rev. C. F. Deems, D. D,	8	"
" 5	Christ's Gracious Invitation,	8	"
" 6.	Are You Ready?	4	"
" 7.	The Life Preserver,	4.	"
" 8.	The Precious Blood of Christ, or How a Soldier was Saved,	4	"
" 9.	"My Spirit Shall Not Always Strive," by Rev. J. H. Fowles, of S. C.,	4	"
" 30.	Why Will Ye Die? by Rev. A. M. Poindexter, D. D., of Va.,	8	"
" 31.	The Improvident Traveler, by Rev. W. J. Hodge, D. D.,	4	"
" 23.	Don't Swear, by Rev. J. B. Jeter, D. D.,	8	"
" 33.	Soldiers, Conquer Your Great Enemy, by Prof. W. H. Owen,	4	"
" 34.	Where are the Christians in the Army, by a Lady of N. C.,	4	"
" 35.	"Who will Show us Any Good," by Rev. W. J. Hoge, D. D.,	4	"
" 36.	What wilt thou that I should do unto thee," by Rev. W. J. Hoge, D. D.,	4	"
	"Hymns for the Camp,"	128	"

Since June 1st, 1861, we have published of the above tracts over five million of pages, over half of which we have given away, mostly to the soldiers, and the other we sold at about the cost of getting them out, 1,500 pages for One Dollar; Come to Jesus, Call to Prayer, Your Soul—Is it Safe, 3 cents each, which is as cheap as we heretofore got them from the North. Hymns for the Camp, 12 and 15 cents a copy.

Each publication is approved by all the Pasors of this city.

W. J. W. CROWDER, Agent.
Raleigh, N. C.

Executive Department N. Carolina.

ADJUTANT GENERAL'S OFFICE,
Raleigh, April 28, 1862.

General Order No. 6.

ALL COMPANIES AUTHORIZED BY THE GOVERNOR to be raised prior to the passage of the law known as the "Conscription Bill," must come to Camp Mangum, near this City, before the 17th day of May, otherwise they will not be received. All those not in by that time will be subject to the War Department under that law, and had better remain at home till ordered by that Department.

By order of Gov. CLARK:
J. G. MARTIN, Adjutant Gen.

SCHOOL COMMITTEEMEN, 1862

DIST.	COMMITTEEMEN.
1.	N Thornburg, P W Raper, William Idol.
2	J H Harmon, Allen Watson, J A Young.
3	Stephen Hester, John Lowry, A Dwiggins.
4	Shepperd Preston, Joel Fulton, F J Fulp.
5	Smith Linville, W J Pegram, David Linville.
6	Wm Gibbins, Pinkney Stafford, Jno. Shields
7	John Hasten, Henry Sapp, Levi Matthews.
8	Israel Robinson, G W Wilson, J W Shelton.
9	C B Ogburn, S F Dean, J R Jones.
10	John E Clayton, Tyre Carter and Rob't Moir.
11	Alex. Martin, Amos Stuart, E J Hine.
12	A G Thomas, Jacob Sink, Benjamin Spach.
13	Henry Clinard, Henry Reed, J M Charles.
14	John L Steward, J W Hester, W U Lomax.
15	A H Cristman, W W Phillips, H D Swaim.
16	A M Kinnamon, H Albertson, A Nicholson
17	J P Crews, John Beeson, David Robinson.
18	Rob't Marshall, Willis Marshall W Hampton.
19	J E Matthews, T M Marshall, Michael Reed.
20	J M Stafford, Sam'l Laugenour, W L Swaim.
21	Jesse Mock, A T Spach, W W Thornton.
22	George Burke, Andrew Burke, Wm Ebert.
23	R Gray, H A Holder, A J Stafford.
24	Alex Bevil, Peter Fetter, G H Renegar.
25	Chas Miller, Robert Walker, James Ogburn.
26	Tandy Marshall, Wm McMillan, M J Crews.
27	J Guthrie, E Perril, Edward Marshall.
28	John Boyer, Solomon Vogler, John Harper.
29	John Miller, James Crews, Lewis Thomas.
30	Thomas Spaugh, Nath. Ketner, E W Griffith.
31	C H Hauser, D B Butner, N T Fetter.
32	William Flynt, Wm. Shouse, Sam'l Styers.
33	Allen Flynt, Israel Moser, Wm F Clayton
34	Alex Ridings, John Blackburn, Thos Craft.
35	John L. Conrad, Nath. Pfaff, Jesse Conrad.
36	Josiah Leinbach, Wm. Leinbach, E P Pfaff.
37	T C Johnson, Beverly Jones, B Hendricks.
38	A P Styers, John Null, H G Anderson.
39	Henry Hart, Wiley Hauser, Wm Griffith.
40	Wm B Stype, J H. Pledger, L C Laugenour.
41	Wm. Goslin, Philip Mock, H R Lehman.
42	E Doub, Thos Poindexter, Thomas Long.
43	Benton Brinkley, Wm. Spainhower, I Sides.
44	W Payne, Samuel Kinnamon, Henry Long.
45	Wm B Doub, E L Strupe, Wm Spainhower.
46	R Leinbach, H Beckle, James Crim.
47	T F Keehln, J L Fulkerson, George Swink.
48	James L. Crews, J H Moser, N F Sullivan.
49	Wm A Boljack, B A Carmichael, G A Banner.
50	John Grubbs, D Baily, Henry Fogle.
51	Isaac Morris, Wm Campbell, Wm H Swaim.
52	Jesse Mock, A. Sink, (the other from Davidson.)

☞ Committeemen will please call at the office of the Western Sentinel and get the blanks upon which they are required by law to make the return of the number of children in their respective district.

J. W. ALSPAUGH,
april 25–52–4t. C. B. S. C. S.

Executive Department of North Carolina.

ADJUTANT GENERAL'S OFFICE.
RALEIGH, March 22nd, 1862.

General Order, No. 5.

ALL NEW COMPANIES OF NORTH Carolina Volunteers must be tendered directly to the State, otherwise the bounty authorized by the ordinance of the Convention to raise North Carolina's quota of troops will not be paid to them, as the law does not allow it. The Companies so tendered will be organized into regiments by the State. the Commissioned officers will elect their field officers. The bounty will be paid each Company as soon as possible after their arrival in Camp.

II. No organization of Regiments or Battalions will be recognized unless the same is done by authority of the State and in compliance with its laws.

III. These Troops being raised for immediate field service should have no more baggage than each man can carry in his knapsack. It is desirable that each man bring a blanket (if he can furnish it,) any additional articles must necessarily be lost if brought.

IV. All communications on military matters must be sent to this Office. In no other way will they receive immediate attention.

By order of Governor CLARK, [48–4t
J. G. MARTIN, Adjutant General.

☞ All papers in the State copy four times.

MAIL ARRANGEMENTS.

Northern Mail, via High Point, arrives daily by 7 o'clock, a. m.
Closes daily, at 5 p. m.

Southern Mail, via High Point, arrives daily, by 7 a. m.
Closes daily, at 5, p. m.

Jefferson Mail, (Western,) arrives Tuesday, Thursday and Saturday, by 6 p. m.
Closes, Sunday, Tuesday and Thursday at 9 p. m.

Wytheville (Va.) Mail (Western,) arrives Wednesday, Friday and Sunday by 4 p. m.
Closes, Monday, Wednesday & Friday at 9 p. m.

Reidsville Mail, arrives Tuesday, Thursday, and Saturday by 6 p. m.
Closes, Sunday Tuesday and Thursday at 9 p. m.

Greensborough Mail, (via Kernersville,) arrives Tuesday and Friday by 4 p. m.
Closes, Wednesday and Saturday at 6 a. m.

Walnut Cove Mail, (via Walkertown and White Road, arrives every Sunday by 9 a. m.
Closes every Saturday at 6 a. m.

Winston Mail arrives daily, except Sunday, at 7, p. m.
Closes daily, except Sunday, at 7½ p. m.

Office Hours:—From 7 to 11½, a. m.
From 1 to 5 p. m.

C. A. KEEHLN, P. M.

The Daily Delta.

VOL. XVII. NEW ORLEANS, FRIDAY, MAY 16, 1862. NO. 139.

NEW ADVERTISEMENTS.

Notice.

The Delta will publish this letter, taken fr m t e bod, o a spy—H. H. Zacharie.

B. F. BUTLER,
Maj r-General Commanding.

NEW ORLEANS, May 8th, 1862.

[DEAR] ELLEN—Knowing you would be anxious to hear as to my whereabouts, and how I was coming on, I have determined to write this, and trust to the kindress of Giffen Smedes as to its reaching you. I called upon them to-day, and I was told, if they could, they would send it the first opportunity.

The day after I reached the city I called on Mrs. Gracey, and learned from her the trouble you had in getting away; but I was glad to hear you had succeeded at last, and I trust you got through your journey without difficulty.

How and what shall I say as to the events that have happened since I saw you last? You were here during the most momentous time—that is, when the city was threatened with bombardment—and of course need no news from me on that point; but I can tell you, thanks to the talents of P. Soule, we have been granted more privileges than we expected. The Mayor is allowed to carry on the city affairs as usual, and the Yankees are to be kept outside of the city limits; though, to tell the truth, I believe they will be more rejoiced than ourselves when they leave, as they must have learned by this that they are really in an enemy's country, as they have been made to feel it in every way. The way they are snubbed on every side is awful. Let me give an instance: Last Sunday two two officers marched into Dr. Palmer's Church, and coolly seated themselves in a pew where a lady was sitting; but as soon as they had settled themselves, she stood up, and, drawing her dress close to her, she left the pew to themselves and their reflections. Well done, was it not?

I have been some days in the city, the regiment having been disbanded at Camp Moore a week after we left the city, by order of General Lovell, he giving us back to State service.

The city is full of rumors of all kinds, denied to-day and confirmed to-morrow, so that it is impossible to credit anything. We are told the Confederate flag floats over the Capitol at Washington and that Beauregard has whipped Buell at Monterey. And so w.ge.

I forgot to mention that Gracey had not got back, but as the boats can come to the city, I look for him daily.

How is Ned coming on? I suppose he enjoys himself with the boys. Tell him I hope he will do everything as you tell him, as that is the way he can please me most.

Give my regard to Joe. Tell her I send this to her care, and do not forget me to Mrs. Cade and your pupils.

I shall not write again till I hear from you, as it is impossible in these exciting times to calculate from one day to another; but believe me, I shall avail myself of the first chance of doing so. Till then,

Believe me always,
BRO. JOHN.

P. S.—I have written this in the library, for the privilege of which I am indebted to the gentlemanly librarian, Mr. Kerr, who begs to be remembered to you and Joe.

may16 BRO. JOHN.

Notice.

HEADQUARTERS DEPARTMENT OF THE GULF,
NEW ORLEANS, May 15, 1862.

General Orders No. 28.

As the officers and soldiers of the United States have been subject to repeated insults from the women (calling themselves ladies) of New Orleans, in return for the most scrupulous non-interference and courtesy on our part, it is ordered that hereafter when any female shall, by word, gesture or movement, insult or show contempt for any officer or soldier of the United States, she shall be regarded and held liable to be treated as a woman of the town plying her avocation.

By command of MAJOR GENERAL BUTLER.
GEO. C STRONG, A. A. G., Chief of Staff. may16 3t

Important Notice.

The ADAMS EXPRESS COMPANY having re-established their Agency in this city, are prepared to forward, with accuracy and dispatch, Freight, Money and Valuable Packages to all Loyal States.

The first Express will leave per U. S. steam transport Matanzas, during the present week.

Office in the Custom House—entrance on Canal street, near Fulton.

may14 2p6t ASA S. BLAKE, Agent.

TO RENT—A Parlor, Dining Room, 4 Bed Rooms and Kitchen, furnished or unfurnished. The house is lighted by gas, and is located in the lower part of the Fourth District, between Nayades and Prytania streets. Address B B. B., Delta office. may16

Leaves on Friday, May 16, at 12 M.

FOR UPPER COAST AND RED RIVER—The light draught passenger steamer A. W. QUARRIER, F. A. Blossat master, will leave as above from the foot of Common street. For freight or passage, apply on board.

Passengers and shippers will have to procure passports and permits from the proper authorities. may16 1t*

FIFTY DOLLARS REWARD — Lost or Stolen from Jackson Railroad cars or depot, on April 24th or 25th, Two Trunks, one half barrel and one box marked R. Spence, Amite, and containing Sheets, Pillow Cases, Towels, Table Linen, Ladies, Gents' and Children's Clothing and Shoes; also, Indigo Starch, Candles, Soap, etc., etc. The above reward will be paid for the recovery of the above property, or in proportion for any part of the same, by delivering same to

may15 1w POST & MEL, 78 Poydras street.

Notice.

NEW ORLEANS, May 8, 1862.

The undersigned hereby gives notice to the public and parties interested that he has been appointed by the Agent of the City Council for the purchase and transportation of provisions for the city by way of the Mississippi river, (A. D. Grieff, Esq.) Inspector of Passports of parties proceeding to the interior for the above purpose, and of invoices of goods, and manifests of boats, arriving in the city under the arrangement between the Commanding Officer of the United States forces and the City Council.

All persons having the Passport of the United States authorities, and proceeding up the river; also, all parties bringing provisions and supplies into the city by way of the river, are instructed hereby to report at my office, 100 Gravier street.

may9 tf BENJ. S. HARRISSON.

Fire Department.

OFFICE CHIEF ENGINEER FIRE DEPARTMENT,
New Orleans, April 19, 1862.

The members of the Fire Department are hereby notified that on the alarm of ten taps of the fire alarm bells they are to immediately assemble at their different Engine and Hook and Ladder Houses

At the alarm of one tap repeated three times the Assistant Engineers and commanding officers of companies will immediately proceed to the office of the Chief Engineer to receive orders.

In case the alarm is given for any of the regular Fire Districts, the companies performing duty in the district for which the alarm is given, will immediately proceed to the location of the alarm.

All companies are hereby notified to continue to perform their duty as heretofore, and use all their exertions in the preservation of life and property.

apr29 DAVID BRADBURY, Chief Engineer.

Come One! Come All!

COAL OIL! COAL OIL!

We have just received from Havana twenty barrels of genuine

KEROSINE OIL,

which we will sell by the gallon or barrel.

BOSTICK & SEYMOUR,
apr3 tf 36 Fulton street.

Valuable Squares

AND LOTS OF GROUND IN THE CITY OF JEFFERSON.

The undersigned have various SQUARES and LOTS OF GROUND for sale in Bloomingdale, Hurstville, Rickerville, Faubourg Avart, Bouligny, &c.

These properties are in the vicinity and on the line of the Jefferson City Horse Car Railroad, which will be completed within the next six months, and connects with the upper line of the N. O. City Railroad on Magazine and Prytania street, making this property very desirable for the purposes of either building or speculation.

Apply to B. M. VANSOLINGEN & CO.,
oct27 2dptf Auctioneers, Commercial Place.

First Draining District.

OFFICE COMMISSIONER FIRST DRAINING DISTRICT,
No. 20 City Hall, New Orleans, May 12, 1862.

All owners of lands lying within the First Draining District, which is bounded by the river Mississippi in front, Julia street and the New Canal above, Lake Pontchartrain in the rear, and Bayou St. John, Canal Carondelet and St. Peter street below, are hereby notified that the first installment of the assessment for the cost of draining said district is now due and payable at this office. All bills not paid by the 12th of July next will be subject to proceedings according to law.

may11 2p2m N. E. BAILEY, President.

Confederate Notes

AND OTHER SMALL BILLS TAKEN AT

THE QUEEN OF THE SOUTH.

A large assortment of Black Lace Points, Shawls, Mantillas, Veils, Mitts, and wide Flouncery Lace, which will be sold at the same price as in times of peace.

161 CANAL STREET,
may11 2p8t* between Bourbon and Dauphin.

Dissolution.

NEW ORLEANS, May 1, 1862.

I this day withdraw from the firm of A. H. MAY & CO., having disposed of my interest in it to the remaining partners. They are authorized to continue the business without changing the style of the firm.

CHAS. T. PICTON,
may2 1m per pro THOS. C. HERNDON.

Fifty Dollars Reward.

LOST, on the evening of the 27th of April, between the hours of and 9 o'clock, in the Third District, one pair of diamond Ear-rings, four diamonds in each; one pair of emerald Ear-rings, one large diamond Ring, and one diamond Ring set in the center of a small black stone. The finder will receive the above reward by leaving them at the office of the Delta with the cashier. apr28 2ptf

THE DAILY DELTA

In giving publicity to order No. 28, from Gen. Butler, we have little apprehension that our readers will suspect that we do so with any other feelings but those which pervade this whole community. Such publicity may not be unproductive of good results.

Relative to a statement which appeared a few days ago in regard to 400 bales of cotton, brought to the city since it was occupied by the United States troops, by Mr. Lanfear, we are requested by that gentleman to say that this cotton was purchased with English dividends on English account, and is to be sent to the English owners, and that Mr. Lanfear asked Gen. Butler to protect it as threats had been made to burn it.

New Orleans, at present, is without a hotel. The St. Charles is occupied exclusively by General Butler and staff. Sentinels march in front and around it—heavy connon are placed on the banquette before it. The City and St. Louis Hotels are closed, and the St. James is a hospital for Federal soldiers. The Customhouse is occupied by a regiment of Federal soldiers. Lafayette Square is an encampment for another regiment, and the Mint is similarly occupied.

HAVANA FRUIT, &c.—We noticed quite a good supply of fresh tropical fruit and other products of Cuba, in various places in the city yesterday. Luscious bananas and fragrant pine-apples were quite plenty. But oh! what prices—one dollar and seventy-five cents for pine-apples, twenty-five cents for bananas, &c. There is also a supply of those convenient articles (found so useful in tropical climes for keeping water cool) called monkeys. These are jars in which water may be kept nearly as cool as ice, by suspending them in a draught.

Another steamboat arrived at our wharf yesterday, bringing a large amount of provisions—flour, corn, live cattle and salt meats. There are other boats expected, and the prospects of a good supply of provisions are quite encouraging. The markets begin already to exhibit quite an improvement upon their bare, destitute aspect for some days past. The supply of fish, especially, is encouraging. If our people would determine to imitate the conduct of the most prudent and judicious of our old residents, and confine themselves chiefly to fish diet, they would not only have better health, but would soon reduce the prices of meats to more reasonable rates.

WHAT THE MORNING JOURNALS SAY.

The *Bulletin* discusses the issues between the Northern Unionists, or conservatives, and the Abolition disunionists, and seems to think that the latter are the most consistent. The former, discarding the old doctrine of State Rights, takes position on the old Federal platform, seeking to establish a government of a majority disregarding the rights of the States; the latter see little value in the Union or the Government, unless they be used to effect the abolition of slavery.

The *Bee* administers a severe lesson to those pretentious critics who reprove and condemn the acts and plans of military chiefs, in ignorance of the science of war, and of the circumstances which surround those who conduct the operations of our armies.

The *Picayune* dwells upon the duties of the times, in the exercise of an enlarged and earnest charity.

The New York Herald, referring to the capture of this city, says:

What old England failed to do with all her power, has been handsomely accomplished by New England. The manner in which the success at Forts Jackson and St. Philip was followed up, is highly commended. In thirty hours our brave men consummated their victory, and appeared before the great city of the Southwest to receive its submission.

We do not know what share England had to do with capturing this city. The United States fleet, under the command of Captain Farragut, a Tennesseean by birth, assisted by commander Bell, a North Carolinian, and by commander Harrison, a Virginian, brought their powerful squadron, through the fire of the forts, and anchored in front of the city, every portion of which was commanded by their batteries. In this position they demanded its surrender. No surrender was ever made. Gen. Lovell evacuated it with his troops, and after several days of dilly-dallying, Commander Farragut landed his marines and sailors, and raised the United States flag over certain public buildings. Three or four days after this had been done, when there was not a soldier in the city nor a cannon mounted, Gen. Butler arrived with several regiments of troops and occupied the city. This and a good deal more that will be written hereafter, is the history of the transaction. Without disparagement to either Commander Farragut or Gen. Butler, we think impartial history will assign the "honor" of effecting the reduction of this city to some other commanders, who have not yet had full justice done them.

Mr. Sanford Jones, who was wounded on the hand car by a picket of United States soldiers, near Kennerville, died yesterday at the St. Louis Hotel. This is the third person who has lost his life in this unhappy affair. We have not yet heard that any investigation has been had, or any explanation made of the circumstances of the killing of three of our citizens, who were entirely unconscious of violating any orders or doing anything wrong.

NO COTTON.—We learn from a passenger who came down from Red River on the steamer Quarrier, that while the corn crops in that region were abundant and promising, he did not see a single cotton stalk.

DISTRESS IN ENGLAND.

The London Times of the 16th says:

Deep is the distress and small the means to obviate it. The town of Blackburn contains sixty-three thousand people, nearly one-fourth of whom are now suffering privation from the scarcity of food, clothing, bedding and fuel. When the mills are in full operation, twenty thousand three hundred and fifty persons are employed; but at the present time upwards of one-third, or nearly seven thousand, are wholly unemployed, at a cost to the workers alone of about £6,000 a week in wages.

And this is only the beginning of the distress which in a few weeks will extend through all the dense manufacturing communities of Europe. At the last accounts from England there was still a good supply of raw cotton, which was growing "small by degress but beautifully less."

In the season before the last all the cotton raised in the South was hurried forward, in apprehension of the war. On the 1st of September, 1861, the amount of cotton on hand in this city was but ten thousand bales. The large supply in Europe enabled the man turers to keep up through the past winter is true the price of the raw staple n doubled in value, and a corresponding add was made to the price of the manufact goods. Thus the capitalists were enabl sustain themselves, just as our sugar pla make as much out of a large crop, at prices, as from a full crop at small pr But the consumers of sugar are not so satisfied. They are taxed by the incre rates or compelled to reduce their cons tion. So with the laborers in the cotto tories. They have received no higher w from the incressed cost of material, they had less employment, and now it is ver rapidly to a condition when two-thirds of will have no employment at all. The mon June has been indicated by the sagacious a telligent as the period when the distress al beginning to manifest itself will become versal. It will be perhaps then the p time to begin the discussion of the que whether "Cotton is King." When the s of American cotton is exhausted, full ju may be done to this question. The w world is interested in its solution. Sho be determined, as we confidently belie will be, that this product is the real ba the commerce and manufacturing indus the great commercial and manufacturing na of the world, it may open the eyes of who have so steadily pursued and soug annihilation of the source of this great w this chief agency of modern civilization commerce.

The Southern States are greatly interested in testing and determining this question. They can afford to dispense with the profits of one or two crops, to afford full opportunity to those who think they can do without our products, or can supply the want of them from other countries, of proving the soundness of their theories and the justice of their estimates The grain and provisions raised during the present and the next season, will abund supply our whole population with the n of comfortable subsistence. As long as can live thus comfortably on their planta they may well dispense with foreign lux and abate those extravagances by which greatly weakened themselves and incr the wealth and power of those who against their institutions and interests.

THE TRAITOR MAURY.

HE EXTOLS JOHN TYLER AND DISCOURSES OF THE NAVY.

Under this caption the New York Evening P. the following reference to a letter which it repr from a gentleman who a few months ago enj world-wide reputation for all the virtues and in tual gifts that can enoble a man:

Among the rebel documents found on board of the vessels of Lynch's fleet at Roanoke Isla the following letter from Matthew F. Maury, lat mander in our navy, and Superintendent of t tional Observatory at Washington. It will b that Maury laments the loss of John Tyler's se and entertains great hopes of the rebel navy:

SPECIAL SERVICE, NAVY DEPART
January 19, 1862

Dear Lynch—In my judgment, the greatest us since the war occurred yesterday, when Mr. Tyler died. It is to him that we are mainly indebted for these new sinews to our naval arm. Your own letter was appropos; it helped the cause along. I am very solicitous that the enemy should not be aware as to the extent of our preparations, for there is no necessity of letting contractors or any one else, except the few persons engaged with this armament as a whole, know the extent of it. More is already publicly known of it than I could wish, and I fear the keeping of it to ourselves is out of the question. Still, the best secrecy is *celerity*, and we must drive ahead. Minor has the guns in hand, most of the engines and boilers are provided for, and by the end of this week I hope to be able to say that in ninety days or less all the hulls will be ready for the machinery. I should have said the *last* hull. These difficulties being overcome, then the great one—that of providing officers and men for one hundred steam launches—commences.

Pray, take the matter up, think over it, and let me have the benefit of your thoughts Here is where we are at present: A call has been made upon the army for a transfer to us of all the sailors in the State, and a law has been passed offering a bounty of fifty dollars to all who will ship for the war; also, a law for the appointment of fifty lieutenants and masters during the war. The crew of each boat will be about forty, all told. These, both officers and men, have to be trained and drilled. Indeed, it may be said that the whole force nearly has to be created, for the most of the officers have to be made and educated; still, with proper encouragement and facilities, that, you will agree with me, is not an impossibility.

We want one hundred lieutenants to command these boats; where are they to come from? Judging from the way things look at present, we shall not, I fear, be able to get more than twenty from those now in the navy. The new law for fifty will, I suppose, give us, say thirty, who were formerly in the old navy, and who, resigning before secession commenced, have not been admitted into the Confederate navy. Where are the rest to come from? My own thoughts suggest as a source of supply the educated youth of the land—young men of the best blood, between the ages of eighteen and twenty-five, who have pride, ancestral renown, and family reputation to encourage them and to be sustained. The choice lies between these and merchant captains, pilots and watermen generally.

Then there are wanting one hundred 2d lieutenants, to be rated as such, or as masters or mates. The rating is immaterial; they are to be second in command, and are also to aim the guns. Some of these will come from the navy, and some from those who resigned more than a year ago from the old navy. For the rest, as in the other case, I would draw upon the blood of the land. By blood I mean, as you are aware, no particular condition in life, but all, however humble their condition, whose hearts glow with patriotism, and who, in such a cause, have the spirit to dare and to do. These are the bloods for me.

Some of the boats are already in a state of forwardness; and as soon as they are ready, convert them into school and training and practice ships. Send these young aspirants, of both grades, to them for drill and training. As more are launched, send out the cleverest of these to help as drill masters; receive on board, also, the engineers and crew; have a receiving ship near, and draw from her every hour or so, from sunrise to sunset, a fresh set, to be drilled and "put through" with all the motions. All of which is to be done under the eyes of regularly qualified officers of the service.

Now, considering our means and resources, that all the vessels are steamers of the same model, and that they are intended for bay and river navigation only, I think that we can manufacture a pretty good set of officers and capital guns' crews.

Nevertheless, my friend, we shall in this have among our brother officers, I fear, old notions and professional prejudices to contend with: "What, make a man a lieutenant who has never been at sea, and then give him the command of a gunboat!"

It is to you, and such men as you are, my friend, who are capable of viewing such things by the lights of an unbiassed mind and judgment, that I look for support and encouragement in this scheme. If you can chalk out a better, pray let me have it. But if no better plan suggests itself, pray assist me with your influence in gaining countenance and support for this. The whole expedition is to be sub divided into divisions of five or ten boats each, under the general charge each of a regular navy officer; so that, as a rule, the boats will

THE EVACUATION OF YORKTOWN.—The following from the Richmond correspondence of the Charleston Mercury will serve to explain the necessity which induced the evacuation of Yorktown by Gen. Johnston. Under date of April 30th it clearly foreshadows the event:

The evacuation of Yorktown may be looked for at an early day. In the first place, the Yankee gunboats in York river are throwing 120 pound conical shell at our shore batteries from a distance of three and a half miles—far beyond the reach of any cannon we have—three of our best guns having burst during the last week. Another gun was received on Monday, from which results were expected. My informant says that seven of these great shells were fired into the battery while he was present; five exploded, killing only one man, a Georgia soldier, who was standing in the door of his tent some distance in the rear of our batteries. Of the two that did not explode, one buried itself nine and the other twelve feet in the earth.

In the next place, the Yankees have been permitted to throw up breastworks a mile long within twelve hundred yards of the village of Yorktown. Given the gunboats and the intrenchments, with their long range ordnance, and the evacuation of Yorktown follows by necessity. The Enquirer of this morning confirms the conclusions drawn from the statements made to me last evening by a gentleman just from the Peninsula, and which have just been narrated. Our soldiers have

posed to be her unknown but handsome cavalier) proceeded to develop himself by pulling off his disguise. Her astonishment was great! and the old gentleman, falling on his knees, proceeded to beg pardon in the most plaintive manner, promising his fair captive everything that taste could devise or money purchase, if she would consent to become his, and his only, That dodge wouldn't do, and he then threatened her with the disgrace that would attend the publication of the circumstances.

But she was a bold girl, and not to be taken in after that fashion. All her Castilian and Gallic blood at once mounted to her cheek, and drawing from her girdle a rather formidable gold-hilted and jewelled stilletto, she looked the old brute hard in the eyes; and waving the flashing instrument thrice over her head in glittering circles, she exclaimed: "Look here, driver! bring that ar carriage to the door immejuntly! And you, you blasted old thief of the earth, you stand back, or I'll let your gizzards out in less than no time!"

There was no arguing the point. The young lady was in the carriage in a twinkling, and in a few minutes more stood under the roof of her anxious parents, who were none the wiser of the night's adventures. And to this hour none know of this strange romance but the fat old victim of his own superior folly, the young lady, the "duenna sage," and the driver of the carriage, who told the inditer hereof under a pledge of secrecy as to names and localities.

FARTHINGALES.—It is hinted that a project will shortly be set on foot in the City Council for widening the sidewalks, for the laudable purpose of giving room to the unrestricted spread of crinoline in our now too narrow streets. The banquettes are only about wide enough to admit the passage of two fashionable ladies abreast, and it is proposed to enlarge them, so that at least three can pass without serious derangement of their trailing dimity.

It may be a subject of curious study to the dashing *demoisselles* who constitute such a lovable border to

Notice.

HEADQUARTERS DEPARTMENT OF THE GULF,
NEW ORLEANS, May 15, 1862.

General Orders No. 28.

As the officers and soldiers of the United States have been subject to repeated insults from the women (calling themselves ladies) of New Orleans, in return for the most scrupulous non-interference and courtesy on our part, it is ordered that hereafter when any female shall, by word, gesture or movement, insult or show contempt for any officer or soldier of the United States, she shall be regarded and held liable to be treated as a woman of the town plying her avocation.

By command of MAJOR GENERAL BUTLER.
GEO. C STRONG, A. A. G., Chief of Staff. may16 3t

of which the war and the blockade have for the time being deprived the people of the South, and the want of which is felt, as is reasonable it should be felt, but not so unreasonable as that for their sake any thought of submission should be entertained. There are other things upon which the blockade is put, and we trust may stay put—we mean especially patent medicines and intoxicating beverages, and we don't know which has done the greater amount of harm. They are about equal, but there is some fun and sociability in "she sperits," but none at all in the abominable decoctions out of which sundry quacks build up colossal fortunes, and out of the fortunes build up "palatial" residences

We wish to remind our readers that the great sale by R. M. Montgomery & Bro., of elegant furniture from the St. James Hotel, and pianofortes, will be continued this day, at 10½ o'clock, in the Armory Hall, up stairs. The furniture to be sold this day comprises the larger portion of the finest and richest articles in the hotel, among which are some rich rosewood parlor and chamber sets, and one elegant bridal suite. Most of the carpets unsold are of the finest quality, and little soiled. The pianos are all of excellent tone and finish, three of which are unsurpassed, and can chal-

W. J. Kearney was charged with committing a nuisance.

The other arrests were unimportant, being principally of negroes, some of whom claim to be free, but can show no free papers.

FIRE.—About 6 o'clock last evening a fire broke out in the tower of the Cathedral, fronting on Jackson Square, but the fire brigade was promptly on the spot and soon extinguished the flames. The fire originated from lighting the gas in the illuminating clock facing

In giving publicity to order No. 28, from Gen. Butler, we have little apprehension that our readers will suspect that we do so with any other feelings but those which pervade this whole community. Such publicity may not be unproductive of good results.

without producing much pain. But, pshaw! cobblers, slings, and so forth! What are cobblers good for but to save our "soles," or slings except to throw pepples at the Northern Goliahs. And mint! What is any sort of mint good for when there is nothing to cool?

And the gout—there is a great cure for the gout all around—a homœpathic cure for the gout. A cure by very small doses. *Similia similibus, curantur.* Every man with sore toes treads on every other man's sore toes, and between this curative process and the enforced virtue of abstinence the thing works all right.

Corns! Who would have corns? Corns are the result of tight shoes—high heeled French boots, and other fashionable abominations. We shall soon get clear of effects, now that we are pretty near through with the cause. We shall wear moccasins, or perhaps what has been felicitously and philosophically described as "a footless stocking without a leg." Some obtuse persons might think we meant by that last remark to go barefooted. We can't keep people from thinking. We want them to think with us, that it is better to bear all trifling privations good humoredly, as though bearing them not. It is not only the best plan, but even in a selfish point of view it is much the wisest.

A NORTHERN VIEW OF THE SITUATION AT CORINTH.—We find in a late Memphis paper the following extract from a letter from the Federal camp on the Tennessee river. The extract is quoted from a Northern paper:

Before another week closes Corinth will probably be won or lost, the two great armies of the South and West again meet together, and Halleck conquer Beauregard or Beauregard conquer Halleck. These two generals, who, so far, have proved themselves the best on their respective sides, will, in a few days, meet where merit is best tested—on the field of conflict. The coming contest will be one of terrible interest. The Union army is in a position from which it cannot retreat. Opposed to our army is the best talent and the finest soldiers in the Confederate service. They are well disciplined and thoroughly armed, facts which the late engagement abundantly proved. Their leaders are Beauregard, Hardee, Bragg, Polk, Boyd and Breckinridge, the four former military strategists of the first order.

Preparations go steadily forward here and the troops daily advance. Some of the divisions now are posted within a mile of the rebel pickets. Numbers of new batteries and fresh soldiers have arrived, and evidently before another week the fate of Corinth will be decided.

THE RIVER.—The Memphis Appeal, of the 11th, says "the river is slowly falling."

daunted, the gay old sinner called to his aid a sage duenna, of the Ethiopian stock, who in the likeness of a vendor of bouquets, found admittance to the presence of the young lady. She (the duenna) the old gent plied with huge sums of money, and thus won her, body and soul, to his designs. Representations were made to the young lady that she was not the object of the old gent's passion, but of a nephew of his, who was represented to be a remarkably fine looking young, dashing and wealthy cavalier—and to confirm the impression as to good looks, a picture of the supposed young man was exhibited to the lady, borrowed, mayhap, from some daguerrean artist for the purpose. As to the evidence of the wealth of the supposed lover, the valuable presents showered through the hands of the "duenna sage" was proof enough. By dint of this sort of wheedling, the young lady was induced to agree to an elopement with the handsome young man, and everything was arranged for their flight.

The old gent referred to, so largely afflicted with white cravat and scented gloves as aforesaid, rejoiced exceedingly at the success of his plans, and straightway set about preparing "the needful" for a journey across the waters, perhaps to Cuba, with his fair and blushing prize. For some days he was observed quietly and unobtrusively *bogueing* about among the shops of money changers and exchange brokers, and it was ascertained that he had purchased considerable amounts of exchange on different cities in Europe, summing up many thousands of dollars. The old chap appeared too to have recently assumed a self-satisfied air, not at all usual with him, and there was a singular watering of the corners of his libidinous mouth, and a strange glimmering of his eye—of his two eyes—that showed he had something very dainty in anticipation, either in the way of eatables or othewise.

All things being arranged, the young lady a few nights ago effulged from the protecting roof of the paternal mansion. A carriage was in waiting, and being assisted by the duenna she got in and was rapidly whirled away, as she had been led to believe, towards the lake, for the purpose of taking passage in a gay yacht which was to convey her and her Lothario to Cuba, or some other delightful island. But, to her great astonishment, the carriage stopped at a rather grand but antiquated dwelling in the extreme outskirts of the city, and the old gent (whom she sup-

Sheep:

Texas Cattle, first quality, ℔ net	— —@— 25
Veal Cattle, first quality, ℔ head	22 00@— —
Veal Cattle, second quality, ℔ head	— —@— —
Milch Cows, first quality, ℔ head	— —@— —
Milch Cows, second quality, ℔ head	— —@— —
Texas Cattle, second quality, ℔ net	— —@— —
Texas Cattle, third quality, ℔ net	— —@— —
Texas Cattle, lower grades, ℔ head	— —@— —
Hogs, first quality, gross ℔ 100 ℔	— —@— —
Hogs, second quality, gross ℔ 100 ℔	— —@— —
Sheep, first quality, ℔ head	— —@— —
Sheep, second quality, ℔ head	— —@—

Clothing for Confederate Notes.

We are offering our LARGE and FASHIONABLE assortment of MEN'S, YOUTHS', BOYS' and CHILDREN'S CLOTHING, SHIRTS and FURNISHING GOODS at reasonable prices, and will receive CONFEDERATE NOTES and Notes approved by the Committee of Public Safety.

L. W. LYONS & CO.,
26, 28 and 30 St. Charles street,
may10 3t2p corner of Common street.

Candidate for Mayor,

IRRESPECTIVE OF PARTY.

NEW ORLEANS, January 29, 1862.

To my fellow-citizens of the city and parish of Orleans:

At the reiterated request of many friends and acquaintances, I present myself before you, IRRESPECTIVE OF PARTY, as a Candidate for the office of Mayor; election to take place in June next.

If elected, I shall be governed by this motto: Justice, Law and Order, Improvements, Judicious Economy.

feb21 te* VICTOR WILTZ.

Corn Meal.

A Corn Meal Mill has been established in the building recently occupied by Cook & Brother, corner of South Market and Levee streets, for the accommodation of the poor. Sold in small quantities only, at the rate of $1 80 per bushel, until further notice.

JAS. BEGGS,
JAMES DAVIS,
may5 e&mtf Committee.

To the Planters.

We are compelled to give notice that we can not at present receive any further orders for Goods. All orders received and registered up to this time, accompanied with cotton, cash or drafts, will require all the goods we can make up to the 1st of September.

Planters are hereby notified that we can not receive any more cotton or orders. Public notice will be given in due time when present engagements will be completed.

apr22 S. M. HART & CO.

THOMAS FORISTER, BRICK LAYER, has for sale, at all times, Fire Bricks, Tiles and Clay. Also, Red Brick, Sand, Lime and Cement. Office Canal street Ferry House. may2 3t* JAS. R. KANE, Agent.

WAR SUPPLEMENT. FRANK LESLIE'S ILLUSTRATED NEWSPAPER

Entered according to the Act of Congress in the year 1862, by FRANK LESLIE, in the Clerk's Office of the District Court for the Southern District of New York.

No. 343—VOL. XIV.] NEW YORK, MAY 17, 1862. [SUPPLEMENT WITH PAPER No. 342. PRICE 12 CENTS.

THE GREAT BATTLE OF PITTSBURG LANDING.

THIS great battle, extending over the 6th and 7th of April, the greatest as far as numbers are concerned, and the bloodiest ever fought on this continent, is very fully illustrated in our present issue, by our Special Artist, Mr. Henri Lovie, who also furnishes us with a very clear and impartial account of the action both of Sunday and Monday, which we subjoin:

The Battle of Sunday.

Before the enclosed sketches can reach their destination, you will undoubtedly be in possession of carefully compiled and elaborate accounts of the numerous engagements constituting the great battle of Pittsburg. I shall therefore confine myself to a mere outline of the battle, and such details only as will be necessary to explain the sketches and maps enclosed. These sketches I selected from a large number of notes, made in every part of the extensive territory over which the battle raged, with a view of not only putting before your readers the most prominent actions but also of illustrating most effectually the varied characteristics of the fight. I have been laboriously careful in getting the scenery, locality and actions accurate, believing that future events will place this battle amongst the most prominent of the war.

The map of the roads and positions of our camps will greatly facilitate a clear understanding of the events, and a few topographical explanations will be sufficient to acquaint the reader with the battle-grounds. The entire country,

THE WAR IN TENNESSEE—BATTLE OF PITTSBURG LANDING—GATHERING THE WOUNDED IN BLANKETS AFTER THE BATTLE.—FROM A SKETCH BY OUR SPECIAL ARTIST, MR. H. LOVIE.

THE BATTLE OF PITTSBURG LANDING—LEFT WING—THE WOODS ON FIRE DURING THE ENGAGEMENT OF SUNDAY, APRIL 6, 44TH REGIMENT INDIANA VOLUNTEERS ENGAGED.—FROM A SKETCH BY OUR SPECIAL ARTIST, MR. H. LOVIE.

Camp of Gen. Oglesby's Brigade. 18th Illinois. 8th Indiana. McClernand's Headquarters. Rebel Batteries in play. 49th Ill. 17th Ill. 45th Ill. 48th Ill. 20th Ill. 11th Ill. Sutler's House. 11th Iowa

THE BATTLE OF PITTSBURG LANDING—CENTRE—DESPERATE DEFENCE OF GEN. McCLERNAND'S SECOND LINE, BY THE NATIONAL TROOPS, SUNDAY MORNING, APRIL 6.—From a Sketch by our Special Artist, Mr. H. Lovie.

THE BATTLE OF PITTSBURG LANDING—RETREAT OF DRESSER'S BATTERY, CAPT. TIMONY, CENTRE OF NATIONAL POSITION, SUNDAY MORNING, APRIL 6—FIVE MEN AND 48 HORSES KILLED.—Sketched by our Special Artist, Mr. H. Lovie.

The Courier

Volume X. NATCHEZ, WEDNESDAY, MAY 21, 1862. Number 115.

Official Paper for the City and County.

TO THE PATRONS OF THE COURIER.

Mr. R. M. Spurgeon is now Clerk of the Courier Office, and is authorized to collect and receipt for all monies due the establishment, as also, to do all other business pertaining to his department.

The Natchez Daily Courier.

Natchez, Mississippi:

Wednesday, May 21, 1862.

FEDERAL GUNBOATS. The Natchez and Vidalia coast was clear of these pests, all day yesterday. We only heard of one boat passing up, and that apparently one of the old Balize tugs. We are unable to speak advisedly, but presume they are concentrating their force on Vicksburg. A day or two passed by, and their whole movements will probably transpire.

Selling Off.

In order to clear his store for any business emergency, Mr. S. Schatz, under the hill, offers a portion or all of his valuable stock of goods for sale, for Confederate money. Our old friend has full confidence in the Confederacy, and he is disposed to show it by his acts. It is to be understood, however, that he will not refuse any other notes, but will cheerfully sell for them, likewise. Read his advertisement, in this morning's issue.

Foraging.

The system of foraging, by the enemy, on our river places, has commenced in earnest. We understand that one of their boats stopped at Quitman's Landing, sent out foraging parties, and took away what pork and sheep they saw fit.

We have stood on the defensive in this war so far, but a few hundred thousand hungry men marched to the enemy's country, would at least arouse the Federals to the consequences of their conduct.

SUNDAY UNDER FEDERAL UNITED STATES DOMINATION. Yesterday was a remarkably peaceful and quiet day. The weather was delightfully balmy and vernal. Our people came forth in great numbers, to enjoy the delicious atmosphere, to learn the news, and to view the strange soldiers, who are to be seen in every direction, promenading the streets and regarding with characteristic curiosity the many peculiarities of our city. There was in the deportment of our people a manifest reaction from the deep sorrow, gloom and mortification which for several days after the capture of the city darkened the minds and countenances of all. Indeed, there was a perceptible vivacity and buoyancy in the demeanor of all classes. This was due to several causes, among which we may mention the existence of and general credit of our people of every exhilerating news, but more than all, it was due to the consciousness of the proud, manly, dignified and harmonious state of popular opinion, feeling and purpose in this city. History has no similar instance of so united and unanimous a population as that of New Orleans in the present emergency. It is this knowledge which has suppressed all tumult and violence—which enables the soldiers of the United States, a little while ago regarded with such intense hate and enmity, to walk our streets, in perfect security from insult and annoyance. It is true there is not the slightest intercourse between either officers and soldiers and our citizens, except of an official character. Our people submit to military rule, but with not the slightest sacrifice of their honest convictions, and with a unanimous protest against the authority of the United States within this city and State. They are of one will, one feeling, one determination on this point. They offer no resistance to Gen. Butler's military authority, but they say calmly, resolutely, and earnestly, it is not of their will, desire or consent, but by their coercion and subjugation that they so submit. In good faith they will observe both obligations, abstaining from every effort to insult, annoy, or harrass the military occupants on the one hand; and, on the other, preserving their independence, their conscience, and their right to determine for themselves the political institutions and authority under which they prefer to live. General Butler has the power to enforce the observance of the former; God Almighty alone can control the latter obligation.

[*N. O. Delta.*

TRIAL TRIP OF A NEW FRIGATE. The Paris correspondence (April 8) of the London Times, says:

A letter from Lorient, of the 3d inst., says that the trial trip of the iron-plated frigate Couronne has been eminently successful. She is by far the most perfect frigate of that class yet built in France. She goes through the water as well under sail as by steam, and she answers her helm admirably.

THE BATTLE OF GLORIETTA.

Our gallant Bill Scurry, with his "ragged Texians," has gained another victory over the Federals in New Mexico. The importance of this victory will be understood when the strategy that led to it is explained.

Glorietta is the name of a canon about 23 miles East of Santa Fe, on what is called the old Fort Union road. Fort Union lies a little North of the St. Louis and Santa Fe trading road and is about 70 miles from Santa Fe. From the East of the mountains there are two passes, one through this canon and one at Galistoe. Fort Union, the strongest Fort in New Mexico, has been heavily garrisoned, not only with regulars but with a powerful detachment of Pike's Peak volunteers. It is to be observed that Pike's Peak is about 200 miles North of Santa Fe, and the population is made up of adventurous men from the North-western States. They are naturally Abolitionists, and being without the ties of family, have volunteered *en masse* in answer of Canby's call for help against the Texians. There was a regiment of them at Val Verde, and they were driven from the field.

After the battle of Val Verde, Sibley pushed on and occupied Northern New Mexico including Santa Fe. He took Santa Fe on the 15th of March, and since that has established his headquarters there. On taking possession he raised the Confederate flag, made of a captured U. S. flag, on the Federal flagstaff, had a salute fired from a captured Federal Battery, and Dixie played on the instruments of a captured U. S. band.

On the night of the 23rd, Sibley, then at Albuquerque, learned that the enemy, 2200 strong, had left Fort Union on the 22d. This is the same we have heard via St. Louis. Pyrom was in command of 150 Texians at Santa Fe. Gen. Sibley at once sent Major Shropshire forward to reinforce him, with orders to hold Canon Glorietta at all hazards. He also sent Col. Scurry to Galisteo, to guard the other pass, with orders to repair to Pyrom's support in case he was attacked. The object was to guard both canons, and by whichever the enemy approached to concentrate both forces and attack him. These points are but 13 miles apart.

On the evening of the 26th, Pyrom's advance guard reached Johnson's Rancho at the mouth of the Canon Glorietta. Soon after, a picket of thirty men started to explore the canon. They found the enemy in ambush who at once attacked them and took the whole picket, but one, prisoners, and sent them at once to Fort Union. This gave Pyrom the alarm, and he at once placed his cannon in battery to command the mouth of the canon and opened fire on the enemy, holding them at bay the whole evening.

Meanwhile he sent a dispatch to Scurry for help. The messenger did not reach Scurry's camp till midnight. Scurry at once put his command in motion and reached Pyrom in two hours, and took command of the whole force, which then embraced 1,100 men. These men embraced detachments from all the regiments and two section's of Teel's battery. It should be mentioned that Pyrom had agreed upon an armistice to bury the dead and remove the wounded till 8 in the morning.

On the expiration of the armistice, Scurry opened the ball with the discharge of four guns in the mouth of the canon. The enemy replied at once with rifles, their cannon being in the rear. This was kept up for half or three-quarters of an hour, when Scurry ordered a charge. Our boys drove them from their position, and then followed them through the canon, a distance of five miles. The fighting here was most desperate. The enemy had the aid of their mountain howitzers, after the first mile. There were four gallant charges made by our boys, and three by the regulars of the enemy. We should have stated that the enemy's was two regiments of Pike's Peakers and 600 regulars, the latter being all old regular U. S. dragoons, commanded by Capt. Howland, of the old U. S. mounted rifles. Their conduct was itself equal to their reputation. For six full hours the battle raged in the canon when the enemy was driven from the same end they went in at. Scurry now charged them again, and put them to utter rout, following them ten miles, when his men were too exhausted to go further, and the chase was discontinued.

The enemy left 500 men killed and wounded in the canon, and lost 200 besides. Our loss was 68 killed and wounded, including the brave Major Raguet and Capt. Charley Buckholts (of Austin,) of the 4th Regiment; and Major Shropshire of Colorado, of the 5th.

Scurry's conduct was most gallant. He never flagged, and was always the same Bill Scurry, full of humor, we all know so well. He always carries the same laugh on the battle field he does everywhere. He was wounded in both cheeks by minie balls. Pyrom had his horse blown from under him by a shell. Rev. L. H. Jones, Chaplain of Reily's regiment, was wounded. He was, at the time, holding a white flag over the body of a dying man and administering to him the comforts of religion. He was severely wounded by a minie ball, but we trust not mortally.

During the fight, the enemy sent a small flanking force and got possession of Scurry's wagons, 4 miles distant, and burned them.

We have no list of the killed and wounded further than the above.

Gen. Sibley is fully alive to his situation. With a small force of fighting men under his command, he has about 3,000 men to fight, but he has all the important points, the passes, and an army of scouts, and is determined to cut his army up in detail. Having routed this force at Canon Glorietta, on its way to reinforce Canby at Fort Craig, he has set his forces to watching for Canby.

It was Canby's plan to meet his reinforcements, form a junction with them, and attack Sibley, but Sibley never waits to be attacked. At the time of the battle of Glorietta, Canby was already on his way up. Sibley set out to meet them and our informant believes, that by the 7th or 8th of April he must have met him and had another fight. Canby's force was about 2800, made up of 800 regulars and 2000 New Mexican volunteers. Sibley was moving against him with his whole force. If he did meet him there is no doubt he whipped him again, and is now in possession of all west of Fort Union. Fort Craig is abandoned and blown up. Canby had but two guns, when Sibley had a full battalion of 14 guns, under Teel.

We expect to hear a good account of our boys there yet, though we should be glad to see some heavy reinforcements going to their help. We believe Sibley will be able to maintain himself in the territory. If he does, the importance of his conquest cannot be over estimated.

[*Houston (Texas) Telegraph, 5th inst.*

How they Took a Fort!

New Mexican Items.

The Galveston (Texas) Telegraph, gives us a few items of news from New Mexico, which are of interest, and some of them quite amusing:

During the fight of Glorietta, New Mexico, Tom Green was watching Canby, Sibley was at Albuquerque, and Steele was at Dona Ana.

Since then Steele has gone up to reinforce Sibley. Our men have captured three months supplies.

On one occasion three of our men under Dr. Cavanaugh, went up to fort Cubero, 60 miles west of Albuquerque, and demanded the unconditional surrender of the fort, with all its contents, and the garrison of 48 armed men, as prisoners of war. The Doctor gave them ten minutes to decide whether they would surrender or be put to the sword! At the end of ten minutes, the garrison marched out and stacked their arms and surrendered as prisoners of war! They were paroled by the Doctor and sent off. He captured at this point, $150,000 worth of supplies, all of which were safely transferred to Albuquerque. Dr. Kavanaugh's report is exceedingly rich. He divides his force of three men, (Gardenhire, Gillespie and Thompson,) into three divisions,—right wing, centre and left wing. He describes the movements of his investing army with all the grandeur of a large army, and signs the report as Commander-in-chief of the Confederate forces in the District of Cubero!

Major Tom Ochiltree, who has been promoted to the office of A. A. G., had two horses shot under him at the battle of Valverde.

Bill Scurry's charge, at Valverde, was characteristic of him. He gave the order, which was repeated by the other officers, when he jumped in ahead, crying out, "Come on my ragged —— Texians. Now is your chance. Give it to them," at the same time jumping up and laughing. His good humor inspirited the boys, and at it they went, and swept everything before them.

Capt. Shropshire charged a regiment of Pike's Peakers with his company and put them to flight. He was promoted for his gallantry.

SPLENDID DOGS. The following, copied from a late New York paper, will interest all fanciers of the canine race:

Mr Francis Butler has shown us two of the largest and most powerful dogs we have ever seen. These noble animals, leonine in size and strength, which he calls Prince and Bruno, were bred by him, on his place at Bushwick, Long Island. Prince, the Siberian bloodhound, is nephew to the renowned Giant Prince, with whom Mr. B. was introduced to the Queen at Windsor Castle, when Her Majesty was pleased to entitle him the King of Dogs. Yet his successor, the subject of the present sketch, although but ten months old, promises fair to outstrip him in beauty and muscular proportions. Even now he trots carelessly along with a boy of fourteen upon his back. He is already over seven feet in length, thirty-four inches in height, and weighs about one hundred and sixty-pounds; color, black and white spotted; short hair. Bruno's color is black and tan, with long flowing hair. He looks something like an overgrown domesticated bear, with the exception of his fine, open, intelligent countenance. In size he nearly equals Prince, although in outward appearance they form a perfect contrast. Mr. B. has taken great pains in producing this breed, and as far as we can judge, with perfect success. Bruno's weight is about one hundred and forty pounds; his height thirty-three inches. They are perfectly trained and docile—lambs with their masters, yet lions on guard.

☞ The Paris Mercury, a secession sheet published at Paris, Monroe county, in this State, has been suppressed by the orders of Provost Marshal General Farrar.—*St. Louis Democrat.*

TELEGRAPHIC

Rather Tight on the Press!

What Chance Have We?

Major-General Butler's Gag-Laws.

[From the N. O. True Delta, May 18.

Special Orders Number. 39—

FIRST. The New Orleans Bee newspaper, having published an elaborate though covert argument in favor of the cotton burning mob, is hereby suppressed. No publication of any description will issue from that office until further orders.

SECOND. The New Orleans Delta newspaper, having, in an article of to-day's issue, discussed the cotton question in a manner which violates the terms of the proclamation of first of May, instant, from these headquarters, the office of that paper will be taken possession of and its business conducted, under direction of the United States authorities.

General Orders Number 29—

FIRST. It is hereby ordered that neither the city of New Orleans, nor the Banks thereof, exchange their notes, bills or obligations for Confederate notes, bills or bonds; nor issue any bill, note or obligation payable in Confederate notes.

SECOND. On the 27th day of May, instant, all circulation of, or trade in Confederate notes, and bills, will cease within this department; and all sales or transfers of property made on or after that day, in consideration of such notes or bills directly or indirectly, will be void and the property confiscated to the United States—one-fourth thereof to go to the informers.

From Vicksburg.

There was no fighting at Vicksburg, up to 4:30 P. M., yesterday.

From Corinth.

CORINTH, May 15....All is quiet here. The weather and roads are in good condition, but the enemy hesitates to advance.

Six paroled prisoners were sent off to-day. The escort found the enemy's pickets four miles distant.

Col. Morgan has not been captured as was reported.—*Mississippian.*

Interesting Matter on next page.

THE MONITOR. A correspondent of the Liverpool Mercury submits the following plan for overcoming the Monitor:

"Surely nothing can be more easily mastered by the good and British plan of boarding; only let the borders carry with them sacks of some deleterious substance well known to chemists, and pour the contents down the grating through which the smoke and steam pass in time of action. The rats will thus be suffocated in their hole, for an unventilated hole her lower decks appear to be."

BIRTH.

On the 9th of April, 1862, Mrs. GEORGIE CHANDLER, of a daughter.—*Memphis Argus.*

The Natchez Daily Courier.

"A Word Unspoken."

There is a word unspoken oft,—
  Yet why, 'tis strange to tell—
One single syllable so soft
  Can work a sovereign spell.

It has a home in human heart,
  Nor spurns its native ground,
And still, as if by magic art,
  It roams the wide world round.

Though sages say the way is plain,
  To prove its humble birth;
They oft confess their logic vain—
  "Alas! 'tis not of earth!"

It moves in every walk of life,—
  It breathes on every gale,—
Subdues the thoughts of hate and strife,
  And soothes affliction's wail:—

It brightest seems in sorrow's hour,
  Like star of summer night,
That shimmer's on, though clouds may lower
  To quell its liquid light.

It cheers through life,—inspires in death;—
  An Angel, from above,
It wings its way o'er earth and saith—
  My only name is LOVE!*

REV. HENRY G. PERRY.

* 1 John, 4: 16.

Courtship in Church.

A young gentleman happening to sit at church in a pew adjoining one in which sat a young lady for whom he conceived a violent passion, was desirous of entering into courtship upon the spot; but the place not suiting a formal declaration, the exigency of the case suggested the following plan: He politely handed his fair neighbor a bible open, with a pin stuck in the following text—Second Epistle of John, verse fifth—"And now I beseech thee not as though I wrote a new commandment unto thee, but that which we had from the beginning—that we love one another."

She returned it, pointing to the second chapter of Ruth, verse tenth: "Then she fell on her face, and bowed herself to the ground, and said unto him, why have I found grace in thine eyes, that thou shouldst take knowledge of me, seeing that I am a stranger?"

He returned the book, pointing to the twelfth verse of the third Epistle of John: "Having many things to write unto you, I would not write with paper and ink, but I trust to come unto you, and speak face to face, that our joy may be full."

From the above interview a marriage took place the ensuing week.

A Memory.

There is a compound, a sort of beverage, on top of which we dimly remember to have seen strawberries floating, their pleasant fragrance mixing sweetly with the more pungent aroma of a vegetable production somewhat of the color of grass; the whole blended and amalgamated into a perfect *bouquet*, by the flavor of a liquid said to have been imported from France, where it is put up by sundry eminent chemists, among others by that celebrated *savant*, M. Otard, of Bordeaux. The compound had a pleasant gurgling sound, produced by small and transparent lumps of ice, causing a delightful coolness, blandified by a saccharine infusion. Drawn into the mouth by moderate suction applied to a straw, one end of which should be firmly but gently held between the lips, while the other is inserted into the glass vessel known as a tumbler, in which the ingredients are usually mixed, we have known people to swallow a considerable quantity without any very marked expressions of repugnance.

But this was long ago. The compound is said to have been a sinful compound, and martial law has been declared against it, and there has been a blockade placed upon it, and the places that used to know it, know it no more, but not forever, for the natural man is strong, and the old Adam that *would* eat the apple still survives in his descendants, who, in times long away after this, when we shall have passed from the stage—when our bones are dust, and our swords are rust, and our souls are with the saints, we trust, will not only make, but will take mint juleps, not only by sucking, but by sipping, drinking, gulping and swallowing, for man is weak and juleps are powerful.—*Wilmington Journal.*

TEXAS. It is said that nearly the whole of her population capable of camp duty, have entered the public service. She has, it is said, 78,000 men now in the Confederate service.

SEXTON'S REPORT.

Of Deaths in the City of Natchez for the Week ending the **19th of May, 1862.**

May 14—Mrs. Susan B. Smith, heart disease, age about 28 years.
" 15—Negro Child, pneumonia, age 18 mo's.
" 16—Man at S. H., name not reported, dropsy.
" 17—Fanny Tillman, scarlet fever, age 7 yr's.
" 17—Ida Weeks, scarlet fever, age 3½ years.
" 17—E. Irvine Weeks, scarlet fever, age 15 months.
" 19—Catharine Tirnay, inflammation of Toncils.

A true copy from Sexton's Report.
C. F. MERRICK, City Clerk.

Weights and Measures.

BUSHEL.	POUNDS.	BUSHEL.	POUNDS.
Wheat,	60	Blue Grass Seed,	14
Shelled Corn,	56	Buckwheat,	52
Corn in the ear,	70	Dried Peaches,	33
Rye,	56	Dried Apples,	24
Oats,	32	Onions,	57
Barley,	47	Salt,	70
Irish Potatoes,	60	Stone Coal,	80
Sweet Potatoes,	55	Malt,	33
White Beans,	60	Bran,	20
Castor Beans,	40	Turnips,	55
Clover Seed,	60	Plastering Hair,	8
Timothy Seed,	45	Unslacked Lime,	80
Flax Seed,	56	Corn Meal,	48
Hemp Seed,	44	Fine Salt,	55

A box 24 by 16 inches, 22 deep, contains 1 barrel.
" 16 by 16½ " 8 " " 1 bushel.
" 8 by 8⅓ " 8 " " 1 peck.
" 7 by 4 " 4⅘ " " ½ gallon.
" 4 by 4 " 2⅓ " " 1 quart.
Ten Gallons Pickled Onions,............83 pounds.
" " Sour Krout,............81 "

Committee of Public Safety.

NEW ORLEANS, April 28, 1862.

RESOLVED, That the Committee of Public Safety will receive, until further notice, the following individual and other small notes circulated as money in this community, and that they believe our citizens may rely on this currency.

RESOLVED, That this Committee, will add to this list such other names as they may deem worthy of the confidence of the community.

State Treasury Notes.	Dan. Edwards & Son.
Confederate Notes.	Joseph Santini.
J. & J. C. Davidson.	Jacob Zoelly
Leeds & Co.	Smith&Hi e or Stuart&James.
Henderson & Gaines.	H. E. Lawrence or P. Cazendoe.
Magee & George.	D. M. Hildreth & Co.
Thomas, Griswold & Co.	Cresap & McMillan.
Thomas C. Payan.	Samuel Bell.
Jackson Railroad Company.	Picayune Office.
H. Fassman & Co.	D. H. Holmes.
City of Baton Rouge.	J. Hockersmith & Co.
City of New Orleans.	Britton & Co.
C. W. Cammack.	Ben. Miller.
McDonel & Magraw.	Adam Wagner.
Geo. W. Gregor & Co.	G. W. H. Lehde.

A true extract from the minutes:
GEO. C LAWRASON, Secretary.

County and City Officers.

County Government.

HIRAM CASSIDY, Judge of Circuit Court.
JAMES A. STEELE, Clerk
REUBEN BULLOCK, Judge of Probate.
RO. S. WOOD, Clerk
OREN METCALFE, Sheriff of Adams co'y.
A. D. PICKENS, County Assessor.
JOHN B. DICKS, County Treasurer.
WM. G. FOULES, Surveyor.
FORD HOLMES, Overseer of Roads.
JAS. C. BRANDON, County Physician.
H. LAZARUS, Overseer of the Poor.
T. N. STRICKLAND, Ranger.
JOHN MCDOWELL, Jailor.

Board of Police.

WILLIAM CANNON. President.
MEMBERS,
FOUNTAIN W. FORD, | GEORGE W. BAYNARD,
LEWIS W. BRYAN, | THOS. C. POLLOCK.
RO. S. WOOD, Clerk.

Natchez City Government.

JOHN HUNTER, MAYOR,
JAS. N. STOCKMAN, JAS. CURRY, ROBERT WALKER, } Selectm'n { J. P. WALWORTH, H. M. BALDWIN, WM. DIX.
HENRY PATTERSON, Collector.
SAM'L A. PATTERSON, Treasurer.
J. HEWETT, Solicitor.
CHAS. F. MERRICK, City Clerk.
HUGH LYLE, Health Officer.
GILES M. HILLYER, Printer.
C. M. BENDROOK, Clerk of the Market.
L. M. PATTERSON, City Marshal.
H. B. COZZENS, City Surveyor.
Messrs. BALDWIN, DIX and STOCKMAN, Commissioners of Health.

Standing Committees for 1862:
On Roads.—Messrs. Curry, Baldwin and Walker.
On Finance.—Messrs Walworth, Baldwin and Stockman.
On Accounts.—Messrs. Baldwin, Stockman and Walworth.
On Gas.—Messrs. Stockman, Walker and Dix.
On Public Property.—Messrs. Walker, Baldwin and Walworth.
On Propositions and Grievances.—Messrs. Dix, Walker and Curry.
On Safety.—Messrs. Dix, Curry and Walker.
On Landing.—Messrs. Curry, Stockman and Dix.
On Enrolled Bills.—Messrs. Walworth, Stockman and Dix.

To-Day's Notices.

To-Day's Notices.

Our subscribers, who have heretofore received their paper from the Postoffice, will hereafter find them at the Courier Office. Our country and city friends can get them as early as 6 o'clock, A. M.

All those who have quit sending for their papers, for fear of the invader or other reasons, will have the generosity to call and pay up arrears, or they will be considered our debtor until they order their papers stopped.

Free Market.

Donations to the Free Market can be made to either Jas. N. Stockman, Jas. A. Steele, Chas. M. Benbrook, Miller M. Stewart or T. J. R. Keenan, the Committee, who have charge of the Market.

To-Day's Notices.

Notice to Tax Payers.

PLANTERS AND OTHERS who have Cotton can obtain advances of money on it from the State, which money is good for all State and County Taxes, except the Military Tax, which must be paid on or before the 1st day of April, 1862, in gold or silver, or State Treasury notes due June 1st, 1862.

Acts of the last Legislature extending the time for the payment of Taxes do not apply to the Military Tax; the law as it now stands requires a distress and sale for the collection of it after the 1st of April.

mar28—dtf O. METCALFE, Sheriff.

Dissolution.

THE Co-partnership heretofore existing between Charles Green and the undersigned, under the name of Charles Green & Co., has been dissolved. The business of the firm will be settled by Andrew L. Wilson, one of the undersigned.

A. L. WILSON,
JOHN SMYTH,
ap23—30ds MARY E. LACOSTE.

C. S. War Tax.

ALL PERSONS OWING C. S. WAR TAX, are hereby notified that the same must be paid between the 1st and 20th days of May next.

For the purpose of receiving said Taxes, I will attend at the Sheriff's office, at the Courthouse in Natchez, it being the most convenient for all Tax-payers in the District of Adams county, daily, from the 1st to the 20th day of May next.

Nothing but coin or Confederate States Treasury Notes, will be received in payment of this Tax.

The fractional amounts due from each person must be paid in coin. I am held responsible by the C. S. Treasurer for specie, for all fractional amounts, and all other sums collected in specie.

The time in which the tax is to be collected being short, all persons are therefore cautioned to ascertain before-hand the amount of their Taxes and come prepared to pay it, that they may not incur the penalty of the law by neglect.

O. METCALFE,
Collector for said District.
Natchez, April 8, 1862–d15w3

Richmond. Hartford. Cayuga. St. Patrick's. Odd Fellows Hall. Brooklyn. City Hall. St. Charles Hotel. Mississi

THE WAR IN THE SOUTH-WEST—THE VICTORIOUS NATIONAL FLEET, FLAG-OFFICER FARRAGUT, COMING TO ANCHOR BEFORE

Katahdin. St. Louis Hotel. Pinola. Cathedral. Mississippi. Pensacola

S, AND COMMANDING ITS SURRENDER.—FROM A SKETCH BY OUR SPECIAL ARTIST, MR. WM. WAUD, ON BOARD THE MISSISSIPPI.—SEE PAGE 102.

"ON TO RICHMOND"—GREAT BATTLE OF WILLIAMSBURG, VA., ON THE PENINSULA BETWEEN YORK AND JAMES RIVERS, MAY 6.—FROM A SKETCH BY OUR SPECIAL ARTIST WITH GEN. MCCLELLAN'S ARMY.—SEE PAGE 103.

Lynchb'g Virginian.

Tuesday..................May 27, 1862.

Effect of the War upon the Northern Politicians.

The North is far from being a unit upon the war question in all its phases. It is the Black Republican's war, and the Democrats and Whigs—we mean those of them who did not go over to Lincoln—whilst they have been swept into the current, and have been compelled to give their countenance to the effort to "vindicate the flag and restore the Union,"—thereby presenting the appearance of a thorough obliteration of old party lines North—feel that if they had been successful the war would not have been forced upon the country. They support the war while it is popular, but no longer. If a series of severe reverses should come, and the current of Northern sentiment begin to turn, it would be found that many of the men who now give their countenance to the war, would seek to put themselves at the head of an anti-war party, and join issue with the Republicans. The latter have embarked all their political capital in the struggle, and if it fails they are undone. Of this, the shrewd politicians on the other side are fully aware, and but for the extraordinary and unexpected series of successes that have attended the Yankee arms in the last few months, such a party would have been organized North ere this. Let the armies now confronting ours near Richmond, and those that face Beauregard at Corinth be defeated, and we shall see a peace party spring up with wonderful activity in the North. The Republicans know this, and hence the amazing energy they display in prosecuting the war to a successful issue. If it fails, wo be to the Seward's, the Lincoln's, the Hale's, and the hosts of these fanatical leaders who have been disturbing the public peace for years, succeeding at last in bringing upon their country all the calamities of civil war. They will be held to a fearful account.

The loss of Southern trade, the sacrifice of thousands upon thousands of lives, and the accumulation of a debt that will involve the whole North in bankruptcy, will be charged to the account of these plotters of mischief, and systematic agitators who are now sustained, because they are in power, by thousands of their fellow-citizens who have really no sympathy with their views, and will be glad to avail themselves of the opportunity that will be afforded of driving them into political exile and disgrace.

Already there are signs of serious dissensions in Congress. The radical abolitionists, such as Lovejoy, Sumner, Wilson, and the like, who see nothing beyond the prospect of gratifying their long-cherished hatred of Southern slaveholders, are led on to the adoption of such extravagant and reckless legislation as is well calculated to alarm their cooler and more sagacious associates. The recoil seems to have commenced, and when the fruits of the mad legislation of the abolition Congress shall have been seen, in the desperate resistance of the Confederates, the still deeper alienation of our people from the Yankees, and the declining prospect of ever winning them back to the Union, the Whigs, Democrats, and the more conservative Republicans will repudiate the present leaders, and as a peace offering to the justly incensed South, with a view of making favorable terms with us out of the Union, will place these miserable wretches under the ban. That time is coming, and as before intimated, the two great and decisive battles—decisive for the party in power—go against them, it will be almost at hand.

Let them enjoy their brief day of power; but if the Southern people be united, and true to themselves, they will not only soon see the whole North at their feet, but the miserable miscreants who have been the chief authors of their wrongs, driven, by their own people, in disgrace from the high places they have polluted, content if they may escape with their lives. The jealousy of the politicians out of power will dictate the favorable moment to inaugurate this opposition. In this view, the pronunciamento recently put forth by the Democratic Congressmen, though amounting to nothing in itself, is not without significance.

Nous verrons, as Father Ritchie was wont to say.

Lincoln has repudiated Gen. Hunter's proclamation, and that officer, it is said, will probably resign.

Correspondence of the Virginian.

CAMP NEAR RICHMOND,
May 23d, 1862.

Editor Virginian:—I have nothing of importance to chronicle since I last wrote you, save a considerable skirmish on yesterday between the forces under Gen. Magruder and the advance guard of the enemy.

The damage to our forces was inconsiderable, while that of the enemy, though unknown to us, is believed to have been heavy, as he fell back in disorder.

Heavy firing is going on in the same direction to-day, and as general orders have been issued for cooking three days rations, and for having five roll calls per day, we may safely conjecture that a general engagement is momentarily expected. We remark, in passing, that there is wretched mismanagement in the commissary department of our army, and, notwithstanding the order above referred to, we are and have been for some days past, only able to draw half rations daily. We were instructed to-day not to rely entirely upon the Commissariat but to furnish ourselves as best we could with the necessary subsistence. We were at first somewhat puzzled to interpret this order. A witty friend, however, came to our relief, by telling us that the General meant it as a modest hint to slay any stray hog, beef or mutton that might stray into our lines, and that he had loaded his gun accordingly.

The weather here is excessively warm, and must necessarily increase sickness, which already prevails to an alarming extent, produced, I suppose, in a great measure, by the fatigue and exposure incident to our retreat.

The soldier's life, though a hard one, full of trials, hardships, and privations, is not without some bright spots—oases, I suppose I may call them. Man may learn much of his fellows, and has before him, at all times, a wide field for the performance of kindly acts, in aiding the needy, and in alleviating the condition of the suffering. Besides these, nature's panorama is ever before him, and he who loves all that is in her handiwork—he who derives his chief pleasure in the contemplation of grasses and springing flowers, who listens with "rapt ear" to the whispers of leaf stirring breezes or the roar of the tempest, the voice of waters, and the dash of ocean's surge—looking thus from "Nature up to Nature's God" has ample opportunity to hold.

"Converse with Nature's charms, and view
her stores unrolled."

What will your gentle readers think when I tell you that there are several women, who followed our armies. Not *vivandrous*, but loving affectionate wives, who have followed their husband's fortunes through all their trials. The devotedness of woman—her fortitude, has been the theme of poet and philosopher, from the day when her gentle foot first pressed the flowering sod of Eden. There are not a few whose names are immortalized upon the deathless page of history, and in our own day of outrage and wrong, there are spirits whose devotion is no less deathless than was Gertrude Vandewater's; whose love is as changeless as was that of Arabella Stuart. May their husbands be spared to them.

Gen. Wise is having another brigade assigned him, and will at once enter the field of operations with his command. He attended our brigade drill evening before last, and, while his "eagle eye" has lost none of its fire, his head is much whiter, and he shows, in soldier's parlance, that he has "seen service."

I am still of the opinion expressed in a former letter, that the first heavy fighting here will be on the road from Old Church, Hanover county. This is the best road for the enemy's artillery to advance, and recent information at these headquarters, indicate that he is availing himself of it. But the roll sounds and I must "to horse."

***.

CAMP NEAR RICHMOND,
May 24th 1862.

Editor Virginian:—From the crack of dawn this morning, up to the present hour, 2 o'clock P. M. the roar of cannon, and the rattle of musketry has been continuous, in the direction of Mechanicsville turnpike, and directly east of Richmond, on the road up which we marched to our present encampment. Every thing points to an approaching general engagement. Coming events are casting their shadows before them. We know not what an hour may bring forth. The great battle of this war, is now about to be fought. The result of it will probably decide the fate of the South.

The battle will doubtless be one of the fiercest and bloodiest on record. The flower of both armies are marshalled for the fight. The prize for which the North contends is the Capital of the South. That for which we contend is not alone the safety of Richmond—but for our honor—the priceless boon of liberty—the safety and honor of our families—our altars and the graves of our sires. The contest is an unequal one, in more respects than one, but we have buckled on our armour, and girded ourselves for the fight, relying upon the justice of our cause, the Providence of that God who rules the free, and who does not always give the battle to the strong or the race to the swift.

I am writing within twenty feet of where our Battallion is drawn up in line of battle. Our line extends from some point on or near the Central Rail Road in a southwesterly direction across to James River. The gallant Magruder, whose very name is yet a terror to the Yankees, is on our left, and has been the first to engage the enemy here. Longstreet is on our right, and in our front is one who has won for himself and command imperishable honors. Let our people keep calm. I trust the day of deliverance is near at hand.

History is full of instances where nations have been delivered from threatened subjugation, by great battles before the very gates of their Capitals.

Several prominent citizens of King and Queen, and Gloucester counties, have been arrested by the Federals and carried before Gen. McClellan. They were told at first they would be required to take the oath of allegiance, to the Lincoln Government. This they refused to do, and were finally released. One of them a Dr. Tabb, visited our camp yesterday. He gave us an amusing account of his arrest, by a Captain, and a company of Dutch, not one of whom could speak intelligent English. The only intelligent remark he could make out was "you musht git your *deum and go mit me to de Gineral." Such are the people we are fighting. But I must close. When I shall trouble you again "this deponent saith not."

In haste, yours truly,

***

*meaning horse.

THE ARMIES AT CORINTH—THE SITUATION.

The correspondent of the Memphis Appeal writes very encouragingly of affairs at Corinth. Speaking of the two armies, he says:

From all the information we have at hand, Halleck has not yet moved any considerable portion of his Union army from the river. The expedition to Farmington and in the direction of our right, was only a reconnoissance in force. It consisted of 20,000 men—the whole of Pope's command at New Madrid—and was put forward for the purpose of becoming acquainted with the country and obtaining knowledge of our position and forces.

"But what is Halleck about all this time?" He is daily receiving reinforcements and organizing his artillery. The two days battle at Shiloh made dreadful havoc with his command, far greater than has yet been supposed. By his own confession, if we are to believe the so called official figures, he lost nearly five thousand killed on the field and mortally wounded. From the manner in which the "three thousand mortally wounded" are spoken of, indeed, we are left to infer that they might as well have been counted among the "killed on the field." They died before they could be removed. The great number of the wounded proper, therefore, can well be imagined. It could not have been less than twenty thousand, which would make at least twenty-five thousand put *hors du combat* on that memorable field.

Halleck's muster-rolls called for 61,000 men in the original expedition up the river. Of these, after deducting the missing, the sick, and such as were detailed on other duty, he was able to bring 45,000 upon the field. To these is to be added Buell's command of 25,000 put *hors du combat*, and Halleck has left to start a new with an army of 45,000 men, all told, and making no allowance for sickness. To these he has since added Pope's command of 20,000 which brings his number up again to 65,000 men, and no more. For whatever reinforcements he may have received, in small detachments from other sources, have been more than outnumbered by the sick.

From all we can hear, the rotton limestone water of the country in which they are encamped has proved very unwelcome, and made many whole regiments are now unfit for duty. Add to this the demoralization of the whole army, resulting from the great disaster at Shiloh and the no less disgraceful surprise and fight at Farmington, and the reader can well imagine what, condition the invading army is in. What with mingling of shattered regiments in one, the dismissals and re-organization made necessary by the disgraceful cowardice at Shiloh, and the bringing up of necessary artillery, Halleck may have enough to do for days to come.

In the meantime, the dry season, in the opinion of the country people, has at last set in. The tributaries of the Tennessee have all dried up, and that river itself is reported to have fallen nine feet three days ago, since which time the heats have been even more oppressive, and the drought, of course, still more severe. It is the general belief, indeed, that if the enemy do not move within the next week, and this weather continues, they will find themselves in an awkward place. In the meantime, our armies moving towards the Ohio on their right, and through Tennessee and Kentucky on their left, are well calculated to give them some uneasiness.

As to our own army, it is daily strengthening our works and taking new positions corresponding with the movements of the enemy. This gives ample employment for their hands, while their spirits continue the very best. Every man knows and continually bears in mind that Halleck has been re-inforced by every man fit for service in the West, and that if we beat his army here, completely cut it up and destroy it, as we can, the gates of the whole West and Northwest are opened to us.

FROM THE NORTH.

Special Correspondence of the Philadelphia Press.

From Washington.

THE HOMESTEAD BILL—FINAL PASSAGE OF THE ACT—THE PRESIDENT WILL SIGN THE BILL.

A committee of conference agreed this morning on the Homestead bill, and both houses have adopted their report, thus securing the passage of the bill. It provides that any person who "is the head of a family, or who has arrived at the age of twenty-one, and is a citizen of the United States, or who shall have filed his declaration of his intention to become a citizen, and who has never borne arms against the United States, or given aid and comfort to the enemy, shall, after January 1, 1863, be entitled to enter one quarter section (160 acres) of the unappropriated public lands, upon which said person may have filed a preemption claim. It is also provided that all commissioned, non-commissioned officers, musicians, privates, &c., in the military or naval service of the United States, during the present war, shall be entitled to the right of homestead secured by the act, without any limitation.

The other features of the act simply relate to the legal course to be pursued in entering the land. There is no doubt that the President will sign this bill.

FROM GEN. HALLECK'S ARMY.

NEAR CORINTH, VIA CAIRO. May 15th.—A special field order has just been issued, which says that guards will be immediately placed along the line of Chambers' creek, and no officers or soldiers will be permitted to pass to the rear, and no citizens to the front, of the line without special authority. Commanders of army corps and divisions will see that their camps are cleared of all unauthorized hangers-on, and any one attempting to evade this will be compelled to work in entrenchments, batteries or in the construction of roads.

His order is understood to apply to all persons, correspondents included.

Fifty-seven privates, three corporals and one sergeant, captured at Dresden, Tennessee, came this morning under a flag of truce. The equal number will be sent to-morrow in exchange. Col. Jacob Thompson, of Beauregard's Staff, formerly Secretary of the Interior, accompanied the flag. He admitted the fall of Norfolk, New Orleans and Pensacola, but denies the fall of Richmond.

Deserters are coming in by squads daily. All agree that the Rebels are still at Corinth fortifying. Picket skirmishes have been going on all day, with a half dozen wounded on our side.

OUR PRISONERS IN THE NORTH.

The Yankee papers advocate putting all the "rebel prisoners" they have to work. The Philadelphia *Press* says:

Put them to work. Employ them to retribute, in some degree, the destruction and devastation they have been the instruments in perpetrating. Set them to work in constructing new fortifications in places sufficiently remote from their late fellow-conspirators to be secure from recapture or escape. It is no objection that quarrying, walling or digging are foreign to their avocations at home. They worked with a will, or under constraint, to destroy bridges, to tear up railroads, to obstruct common highways, to burn houses, to dig ditches, to throw up earthworks and embankments, whence to slaughter their faithful fellow-countrymen, and now, neither they, nor any others, can complain at their being employed in similar works of construction, not of ruin, for the benefit of those whom they have done so much to injure. Nor can they complain at being employed in labours which would have to be done by our soldiers or citizens, every man of whom is the equal, at least, of the best of them—a voter, one of the sovereign people from whom emanates the government. Employing the prisoners on public works would somewhat compensate the expense of maintaining them.

From the New York World, May 15.

THE COMING FIGHT AT CORINTH.

The country will learn with profound astonishment that the correspondents of newspapers will not be permitted to telegraph an account of the coming battle at Corinth after it has taken place until the report is first revised by a military censor at Cairo. Mr. Stanton is evidently determined to doctor the news before it is given to the country, but why he should want to do so is a mystery that passes comprehension. If we are beaten, the fact must come out. It cannot be concealed. If we are victorious, the sooner it is known the better. There is no ground for saying that reports of the newspaper correspondents will not be correct. They have notoriously been so in every instance hitherto. If they have differed from the official reports, so much the worse has it been for the official reports, for when the truth regarding past battles has all come out, it has been the former, not the latter, which were confirmed. The poor excuse that these reports might give aid and comfort to the enemy is too obviously absurd to be for a moment entertained. What the effect of such an order as this upon the stock market must be is apparent. It is to be presumed that Mr. Stanton contemplated that painful contingency before issuing it. If not, he has less shrewdness than his admirers suspect him of.

COMMERCIAL.

LYNCHBURG MARKETS,
REPORTED BY
A. B. RUCKER,
PRODUCE BROKER,
183 MAIN STREET.

☞ These quotations, it will be understood, represent wholesale prices generally.

APPLES.—Green—none offering.

BACON.—Continues to arrive slowly, with sales 33 to 35c.

BEESWAX.—Receipts continue light, with sales 30 @ 32c.

BUTTER.—Choice for table scarce and sells readily in packages suited for shipping at 55 @ 62½c Cooking 40 @ 50c.

CORN MEAL.—Stock light—$1.00 to 1.05

CORN.—Receipts light. Last sales at $1.00.

CLOVER SEED.—$12 to 12.50.

FRUIT.—Dried Apples $1.50 to $1.75 per bushel—28 pounds; Unpealed Peaches $2.50 to $2.75 per bushel—33 pounds; Pealed Peaches $4.50 to $5 per bushel—40 pounds.

FLOUR.—With light receipts. Superfine $7 to 7.25; Extra $7.50 to 7.75; Family $8 to 8.25.

FLAXSEED.—The demand for sowing has increased the demand. Sales $1.75 to 1.80.

FEATHERS.—Dull and plenty—34 to 37 cents.

GRASS SEED—The large receipts of Clover has caused a considerable decline. I notice sales at $12 to $15; Timothy $4 to $4.50; Orchard $1.75 to $2.00; Evergreen $1.75 to $2.00; Randal $1.75 to $2.00; Herds $1.50.

HAY—Baled $1.40 to $1.50; per wagon load $1.25 to 1.35.

LIME—Mountain $2 to $2.25.

IRON—With increased demand, I notice sales $175 to 185 per ton.

LARD—Demand good—21 @ 22c.

ONIONS—Stock light—$2.75 to $3 per bushel.

OATS—Sheaf $1.40 to 1.50 ꟑ wagon load; Shelled—70c. for White; 75 cts. for Black per bushel 33 pounds.

TOBACCO—Sales continue light, but prices are well maintained. Lugs $2 to $4.50; Leaf $5 to 8.50 for good shipping; Manufacturing $8 to $15.

WHEAT.—$1.60 to 1.35 for Red; $1.30 to 1.40 for ole q White.

To all Whom it may Concern.

NOTICE is hereby given to all absentees from the 2nd Va. Cavalry, whether on sick leave or otherwise, without proper authority, that, unless they report to their respective companies on or before the 25th day of May, they will be published as deserters.

The Sheriffs and Constables of the counties of Albemarle, Amherst, Appomattox, Bedford, Botetourt, Campbell, Franklin and the city of Lynchburg, are earnestly requested to *apprehend* any man they may find in these counties after the 25th of May. A reward of $25 will be paid for each man delivered at my camp.

I am instructed by Major Gen. Ewell, commanding 3d Division, to say that he will allow absentees to be transferred into Infantry and their places supplied by the drafted men, who are anxious to furnish their own horses.

I regret to announce publicly that there are over 100 men absent from this Regiment, most of whom are perfectly well. Mothers, sisters and sweet hearts, remember that the gallant loved ones now in the field are doing double duty—that the reason they are never had a furlough is because these laggards are away. Your noble boys can't be spared and they are too generous and brave to shrink from duty.

The military authorities at Lynchburg are earnestly requested to drive such men back to camp.

THOMAS T. MUNFORD,
Colonel 2nd Va. Cavalry.

may 24-5t

LOCAL AND STATE AFFAIRS.

Dr. S. D. Hopkins, of Fincastle, is authorized to receive subscribers for the Virginian.

The article in yesterday's paper, concerning the participation of the companies of Capts. Pierce and Patterson in the affair at Drury's Bluff should have been credited to the Richmond *Dispatch*.

ENGAGEMENT AT LEWISBURG.—A fight took place on Saturday in the streets of Lewisburg, between some 1800 of our troops under Gen. Heth, and a force of the enemy, supposed to be about 4,000. Deceived as to the numbers of the enemy, our forces made the attack, and drove the Hessians through the streets, when a reserve of the enemy falling upon the unfortunate 45th Virginia, the latter broke and fled, thus losing to us all the advantage we had gained. It is said that this running regiment was assaulted by double its own numbers. From the information we have at this writing, it is believed that our loss was about two hundred, though this is mere speculation. We had captured 170 of the enemy and sent them to the rear — an officer who was in the engagement counted sixty-five dead Hessians on the field, though what their whole loss was is not known.

Capt. G. G. Otey, commander of the Otey Battery of Richmond, was severely wounded, and reached his friends in this city on Sunday evening.

LATER.

By an officer who arrived here last night from Fincastle, we were informed that an official dispatch had been received by Gen. Loring, from Gen. Heath, stating that he was upon the eve of victory when an unaccountable panic seized a portion of his men, and he was compelled to fall back with a loss of thirty killed wounded and missing, and two pieces of artillery.

The gentleman from whom we received his information read the dispatch, and we are induced to believe that it is perfectly reliable. He says that the artillery reported captured was one from Capt. Otey's and one from the Greenbrier Artillery, the horses of which were killed.

We captured 75 prisoners, 40 of whom were cavalry and 35 infantry, including some of the pickets who were sleeping on their post.

Among the casualities reported on our side is Major Finney killed, Major Edgar and Capt. G. G. Otey wounded. The enemy's loss is supposed heavy.

From the above, it would not appear that the defeat was so disastrous as at first reported, but merely a slight reverse.

We understand that Gen. Heath is severely censured for the movement which brought on the engagement, but whether there are just grounds or not for the censure we are unaware.

SEVERE HAIL STORM IN BEDFORD CO.—We understand there was a very disastrous hail storm passed over a portion of Bedford county on Friday last, totally destroying the crops in the neighborhood.

OIL MANUFACTORY.—Messrs. Scott and Wade are manufacturing Lard Oil in this city, and turn out an article which, for lubricating purposes is equal to the best sperm oil we have ever used.

The residuum, or refined lard which is left after extracting the oil, is excellent for pastry; and, from our observation we should say makes better and lighter pastry than the lard which has undergone no such process.

It can be bought cheaper than the market price of lard. We wish these deserving gentleman great success.

LATEST BY THE MAILS.

OUR LINES ABOUT RICHMOND.

There was some action on our lines in the neighbourhood of Richmond on Saturday.

From such reliable particulars as we have, it appears that the enemy made a demonstration in the neighbourhood of New Bridge and Mechanicsville on Saturday.

At New Bridge two companies of the Fifth Louisiana regiment were surprised, the enemy having captured the only cavalry picket that was out. We learn that our loss in this engagement was about sixteen killed and thirty wounded.

On Saturday afternoon the enemy took posession of Mechanicsville, which is about four miles from the city boundary, on the road which extends from eighteenth street. Three pieces of the Washington Artillery were placed across the Chickahominy, but our forces were directed to fall back to the other bank of the stream, which they did after a sharp cannonading. Captain ROSSER was wounded in the arm by a fragment of a shell. On occupying Mechanicsville Saturday afternoon the cheers of the Yankee army were vociferous and might have been heard for miles.

Yesterday, there was an entire quiet on our lines, and not a shot exchanged on any portion of them as far as we could learn. In the neighbourhood of Mechanicsville, the two armies are distinctly confronted on opposite ranges of hills not more than a mile apart. The enemy's pickets, extend to the bridge over the Chickahominy, and our picket lines are not more than six hundred yards apart, a cavalry picket of the enemy being posted directly in the turnpike on the other side of the Bridge.

Yesterday the enemy were throwing up entrenchments about Mechanicsville, and planting batteries to command the bridge and turnpike.

About two or three miles to the north the enemy have posession of the Central railroad, at what is known as Atlee's Station. The situation is such as keeps the public in constant and daily expectation of a general engagement —*Examiner*

FOREIGN INTERVENTION IN AMERICAN AFFAIRS.

The rumor that France and England purpose to interfere in American affairs continue to excite considerable speculation in the North. The Washington correspondent of the Philadelphia *American*, writing on the subject, says:

Letters received by the last steamer from Paris point most unmistakeably to an intervention of some kind in our affairs. One of these, from a former member of the British Parliament, states, in the clearest and most unhesitating manner, that Louis Napoleon is pressing the ministry hard to join him in the movement, and the published letters by the last steamer assert that instructions of the same nature have been forwarded to both the French and British ambassadors at Washington. The cause of this renewed interest in our affairs was mainly to be traced to the immense increase in the number of poor thrown upon the public charity, and the fact that although a year had elapsed none of the staple articles of the South, so greatly needed in England and France, had been received, while the supply of these already on hand was dwindling rapidly away.

From the tenor of these letters the probable meaning of Count Mercier's visit to Richmond is pretty clearly manifest—it was doubtless to feel the pulse of the rebel government upon the question of the war, and report the same, as the Count is known to have done, immediately on his return to his government. Neither is it difficult to surmise what the answer of Jefferson Davis and his Cabinet was to the interrogatories of the minister. With their usual bravado, they probably informed him that "the South would fight to the last man, woman and child; that it wanted no compromises with the North; and all that it desired from the Northern people was to be let alone."

Count Mercier is known to have repeated his visit once to the rebels after this interview; but whether Lord Lyons, or a representative from him, ever went on the same errand, is not definitely known, although remarks about his going were, a few weeks since, prevalent. According to the foreign dispatches, the "instructions" of the ministers at Washington are "identical," and if Lord Lyons did not have a direct interview with the rebel government Count Mercier probably acted as spokesman for both.

DESTRUCTION OF COTTON IN THE SOUTH.

The following is a copy of a dispatch, dated Camp Moore, La., May 8th, received in Richmond May 9th;

Hon. J. P. Benjamin:

The Governor of Louisiana directs me to inform you that all the cotton on the Mississippi river up to the mouth of Red river, has been burnt, and all on its tributaries is ready for the torch. He issued a proclamation ordering its destruction in the event it could not be removed into the interior; but the spontaneous action of the people anticipated his order. We have traveled in the Red and Ouachita rivers since the fall of New Orleans, and find the sentiments of the people unanimous to destroy the whole crop rather than permit a pound to fall into the hands of the enemy. The capital is fixed temporarily at Opelousas.

Publish this, if necessary, for the information of the people.

T. O. MANNING, A. D. C.

Alonzo Church, D. D., for many years President of the Georgia State University died at his residence near Athens, Ga., on Sunday night, after a painful and lingering illness.

ANOTHER FEATURE OF YANKEEISM—NEGROES PLACED ON THE SAME FOOTING WITH WHITES.

In the Senate of the United States the bill proivding for the education of coloured children in the District of Columbia was taken up and anended so as to put the coloured population on the same footing with the whites in all trials and punishments, AND IT WAS PASSED—YEARS 20, NAYS 7.

The extreme abolition measures of Yankee Congress had aroused a deep feeling among the conversatve classes of Washington city. A meeting had been held in the south ward of the "Union Democrats and Union Whigs, and other conservative voters who adhere to the principles of the Constitution and the Union." Resolutions were adopted declaring in favour of "all constitutional efforts to maintain the honour and integrity and the existence of the national Union," and also the following:

"*Resolved*, That in affirming our devotion to the Union as against the disorganizing and revolutionary principles of abolitionists and their aiders and abettors, whatever name they may assume to cloak their unholy and unpatriotic designs, and to declare our uncompromising opposition to all their efforts to elevate the negro by force of legislation to a position in this District for which he is unprepared, and all of which efforts tend to the injury and oppression of the white race, by encouraging the emigration to this city of an indolent and worthless population from the adjacent slaveholding States; and we also declare an uncompromising opposition to the effort which is now in progress to impose upon this city the odious task of schooling negro children."

THE KILLING OF HON. RO. E. SCOTT—THE YANKEE VERSION OF THE AFFAIR.

In the Yankee House of Representatives a communication had been received from the Secretary of War, in answer to a resolution, enclosing a report from General Geary, in relation to the murder of Hon. Robert E. Scott and Mr. Matthews, who were killed between Warrenton and Salem, Va.

A Northern paper gives the following summary of the report:

The report states that an armed party, headed by Mr. Scott and a Mr. Matthews, went to arrest two soldiers of the Seventh Wisconsin Regiment, who were reported to be marauding in the neighborhood, and on their attempting to enter the farm-house in which the soldiers were, they were resisted, and in the affray Messrs. Scott and Matthews were killed, and one of the soldiers wounded—the other making his escape.—The wounded soldier stated that they both belonged to the Seventh Wisconsin regiment, and had been taken prisoners by the rebels, from whom they escaped, and at the time of the affray they were looking for their regiment. They had, however, been committing depredations through the section of country through which they passed.

General Geary before the affray, having heard of their depredations, had sent out a squad of cavalry to capture them.

THE EDUCATIONAL SYSTEM IN VOGUE AT PORT ROYAL.

Major Pangborne, of the army, who has just returned from Port Royal, states that the educational system that has been improvised for the benefit of contrabands does not work well, but that some two thousand acres of land are in cultivation by them, under the supervision of suitable business persons. Major P. states that hundreds of the army intend to locate themselves upon the "Sea Islands" after the close of the was. Amid regions of swamps are found large and fertile plantations, which are as blooming gardens of fruits and flowers.—The grand old mansions have been deserted by their owners, but one has been protected by the military on account of its being the property of descendants of General Green, of Revolutionary fame. The land on which it is located was granted to him by the State of South Carolina, for his great service in freeing the South from the controls of the British forces.

GERMAN SOLDIERS.

The following is from the "Lounger's" department of Harper's Weekly, of May 3rd:

LOUISVILLE, KENTUCKY.

"DEAR LOUNGER;—I am angry with you, but you must not resent it until you hear the reason and decide the merits of the cause. I am jealous of the praise you bestow upon the brave troops of every State of the Union, without ever as much as mentioning my countrymen, the Germans; or giving them credit for a single brave action and you know the latter are not few. Let me state to you a few facts. In the first place, we come here to better our condition, and to be free; and, I think, you will acknowledge that a more law abiding and patriotic element is not found in our country.

"When this rebellion broke out we volunteered our full quota to the ranks.—Just take, as example, the State of Missouri. In St. Louis, out of a population of 160,000, 60,000 are Germans. These have furnished three-fourths of all troops raised in Missouri. Two-thirds of the principal men in St. Louis (Germans excepted) are Secessionists; but they were kept at bay by the Germans under the old flag. And through hard trials these patriots have gone. Three times were the Home Guards of St. Louis attacked by the mob, but stood their ground well. For a time no soldier in uniform could go single through the streets of the city without danger of assassination. One by one did the first Volunteers go to the Arsenal to fill the regiments that were recruited there by Seigel, Blair, Boernstein, Osterhaus, and others, under our lamented Lyon. Nobly have they done their duty everywhere.—Hardly an engagement but the Germans have had their representatives there. Do you remember Carthage—how General Siegle, *with 1500 Germans, whipped* 8000, *rebels?* Have you forgotten Max Weber at Hatteras Inlet, Willich at Rowlets Station, or the Ninth Ohio at Mill Spring, or Blenker's Division at Bull Run, and the crowning victory at Pea Ridge, which was so largely due to our own Siegel? I think it is not right to ignore so entirely the services of an adopted population of about seven and a-half millions of our twenty-three millions. I am your constant reader, and hold your views of this war as correct and most prophetic. I do sincerely believe the end will be according to your predictions; for they are just and right. If a man kicks up a fuss let him bear the consequences.

BY TELEGRAPH.

Glorious Success of Stonewall Jackson.

RICHMOND, May 26.—Authentic information has been received here of another victory by Stonewall Jackson at Front Royal, Warren county.

The enemy were routed and a number of prisoners and arms captured.

[2ND DISPATCH.

RICHMOND, May 26th.—The Examiner has received the following special dispatch:

Jackson and Ewell have taken Front Royall and Winchester, and gained a complete victory.

Four thousand prisoners were captured, and they are still coming in.

All the enemy's stores were taken at Winchester.

Our loss is one hundred killed and wounded.

3D DISPATCH.

Official Account of Jackson's Success.

RICHMOND, May 26.

The following official dispatch was received from Staunton this morning.

"Our forces entered Winchester on the 25th (Sunday,) capturing all the enemy's commissary and ordinance stores.

"They tried to burn the town, but were too closely pursued.

"We took the 1st Maryland Regiment and the 1st Vermont Cavalry at Front Royal, and two thousand prisoners at Winchester.

"Our loss was one hundred killed and wounded.

"Our forces are still in pursuit and the enemy completely routed."

[4TH DISPATCH.]

LATER FROM VICKSBURG AND CORINTH.

MORE OF PICAYUNE BUTLER'S TYRANNY.

AUGUSTA, May 26th.

The Jackson Mississippian has a dispatch from Vicksburg, dated the 20th, which says all was quiet.

The enemy's mortar boats and transports were at Bayou Sara, on Monday, the 21st.

The Federals ordered the women and children to leave the city in 24 hours. The Mayor asked till Friday morning.

The Mobile Register has a dispatch from Corinth, dated the 22nd, which says Halleck failed to make an attack to-day.

There was considerable skirmishing on the Monterey road towards evening.

Hindman's artillery shelled the enemy from a house on the Farmington road.

Our pickets now occupy Farmington, the enemy being driven back.

Picayune Butler has suppressed the New Orleans Delta and Bee for styling the burning of cotton "patriotism."

He also issued a proclamation declaring that after the 27th of May, Confederate money must cease to be the medium of trade in New Orleans.

The Memphis Appeal, of the 20th, says all was quiet at Fort Pillow. There has been no firing for several days.

The Savannah Republican says forty or fifty Federals landed and went up from Pilaka to Welaka, and were fired upon by the Confederates. Twelve of the enemy were killed.

Tuesday, a barge with twenty one Federals approached St. Mark, and were ambuscaded and seventeen killed.

5TH DISPATCH.

RICHMOND, May 26.

There has been no skirmishing in this vicinity.

The city is quiet, and the community generally confident of success.

Gen. Jackson's victory has produced cheerful feelings.

True Democrat Bulletin.

Telegraphs by the Memphis and Little Rock Line.

LITTLE ROCK, : : : : : May 27, 1862.

Special to the Memphis Appeal.

RICHMOND, May 26th, p. m.—General Jackson won two great victories at Front Royal and Winchester, on Friday and Saturday, the 22d and 23d. Banks' army has been completely routed, with the loss of all his ordnance, commissary and quartermaster stores and four thousand prisoners. The first Maryland regiment and first Vermont cavalry were taken entire. The enemy was hotly pursued beyond Winchester, and in their retreat they unsuccessfully attempted to fire the town.—We lost but three officers. Capt. Sheels, Fletcher and Paxton, and only one hundrad killed and wounded,

Signed, DIXIE.

VICKSBURG, May 26, p. m.—The federal gun boats fired about fifteen shots at our batteries this evening. We returned the fire when they retired. All is quiet now.

MEMPHIS, May 27.—A Pittsburg correspondent of the Chicaga Post, telegraphs under date of the 18th, to that paper, as follows:

"From the most reliable information we can gather from deserters from the rebel army, they have now not less than 150,000 men under arms at Corinth. Our army has been in sight of the enemy's pickets for the last ten days, and the whole army is in a position to attack at any moment, and yet we are not ready, and nobody knows why not."

The Weekly Courier.

Vol. XXXIII. NATCHEZ, MISS., WEDNESDAY, MAY 28, 1862. No. 23.

Weekly Courier

FEDERAL GUNBOATS. The Natchez and Vidalia coast was clear of these pests, all day yesterday. We only heard of one boat passing up, and that apparently one of the old Balize tugs. We are unable to speak advisedly, but presume they are concentrating their force on Vicksburg. A day or two passed by, and their whole movements will probably transpire.

Foraging.

The system of foraging, by the enemy, on our river places, has commenced in earnest. We understand that one of their boats stopped at Quitman's Landing, sent out foraging parties, and took away what pork and sheep they saw fit.

We have stood on the defensive in this war so far, but a few hundred thousand hungry men marched to the enemy's country, would at least arouse the Federals to the consequences of their conduct.

How they Took a Fort!

New Mexican Items.

The Galveston (Texas) Telegraph, gives us a few items of news from New Mexico, which are of interest, and some of them quite amusing:

During the fight of Glorietta, New Mexico, Tom Green was watching Canby, Sibley was at Albuquerque, and Steele was at Dona Ana.

Since then Steele has gone up to reinforce Sibley. Our men have captured three months supplies.

On one occasion three of our men under Dr. Cavanaugh, went up to fort Cubero, 60 miles west of Albuquerque, and demanded the unconditional surrender of the fort, with all its contents, and the garrison of 48 armed men, as prisoners of war. The Doctor gave them ten minutes to decide whether they would surrender or be put to the sword! At the end of ten minutes, the garrison marched out and stacked their arms and surrendered as prisoners of war! They were paroled by the Doctor and sent off. He captured at this point, $150,000 worth of supplies, all of which were safely transferred to Albuquerque. Dr. Kavanaugh's report is exceedingly rich. He divides his force of three men, (Gardenhire, Gillespie and Thompson,) into three divisions,—right wing, centre and left wing. He describes the movements of his investing army with all the grandeur of a large army, and signs the report as Commander-in-chief of the Confederate forces in the District of Cubero!

Major Tom Ochiltree, who has been promoted to the office of A. A. G., had two horses shot under him at the battle of Valverde.

Bill Scurry's charge, at Valverde, was characteristic of him. He gave the order, which was repeated by the other officers, when he jumped in ahead, crying out, "Come on my ragged —— Texians. Now is your chance. Give it to them," at the same time jumping up and laughing. His good humor inspirited the boys, and at it they went, and swept everything before them.

Capt. Shropshire charged a regiment of Pike's Peakers with his company and put them to flight. He was promoted for his gallantry.

TELEGRAPHIC.

Rather Tight on the Press!

Major-General Butler's Gag-Laws.

[From the N. O. True Delta, May 18.

Special Orders Number. 39—

FIRST. The New Orleans Bee newspaper, having published an elaborate though covert argument in favor of the cotton burning mob, is hereby suppressed. No publication of any description will issue from that office until further orders.

SECOND. The New Orleans Delta newspaper, having in an article of to-day's issue, discussed the cotton question in a manner which violates the terms of the proclamation of first of May, instant, from these headquarters, the office of that paper will be taken possession of and its business conducted, under direction of the United States authorities.

General Orders Number 29—

FIRST. It is hereby ordered that neither the city of New Orleans, nor the Banks thereof, exchange their notes, bills or obligations for Confederate notes, bills or bonds; nor issue any bill, note or obligation payable in Confederate notes.

SECOND. On the 27th day of May, instant, all circulation of, or trade in Confederate notes, and bills, will cease within this department; and all sales or transfers of property made on or after that day, in consideration of such notes or bills, directly or indirectly, will be void and the property confiscated to the United States—one-fourth thereof to go to the informers.

The Battle of Williamsburg.

We have been politely furnished by a respected fellow-citizen, the following additional casualties at the late Williamsburg battle:

Among the notable Federal miscreants who fell on the field, is the notorious General, Dan. Sickles. He was mortally wounded.

Of the Confederates, Lieut. Col. Zebulon York, of the 11th La. Regiment, was wounded. He is now at the Medical College, in the city of Williamsburg.

☞ We learn that Gen. Dahlgren, Commandant of the counties of Adams, Jefferson, Claiborne, Franklin and Wilkinson, has decided to make our village the depot for arms, provisions and forage, for the troops which are to be speedily raised for the protection of the river counties. The planters of this neighborhood will soon be called upon to furnish the latter named articles.

[*Fayette Gazette, May 17,*

From Corinth.

Special to the Memphis Appeal.

CORINTH, May 16.....Two Federal prisoners, captured by our pickets to-day, on the Purdy road, state that Halleck is waiting for us to make the attack.

The prospects of a general engagement seem to grow distant.

This has been observed as a day of fasting and prayer by our army, so far as was consistent with military duties. Rev. Dr. Palmer delivered most stirring and eloquent sermons to our troops—in the morning in Gen. Hindman's division, and in that of Gen. Hardee in the evening.

The heated term and drouth have set in.

The Tennessee is falling fast.

Repulse of the Federal Gunboats.

RICHMOND, May 15....The enemy attacked our batteries, on Wilder's and Drary's Bluffs, James river, this morning at eight o'clock.

The Monitor and Galena opened the fire at five hundred yards distance, with great rapidity and violence. Our batteries replied deliberately.

At one o'clock P. M., the Gelena was set on fire. The other gunboats have retreated down the river.

Our loss is four killed and eight wounded. Our troops are in high spirits, and confident of success.

Richmond to be Defended to the last Extremity.

RICHMOND, May 15....The following proclamation was issued to-day, by the Governor of Virginia:

"The General Assembly of this Commonwealth having resolved that the Capitol of the State shall be defended to the last extremity, if such defense be in accordance with the views of the President of the Confederate Sates; and having declared that whatever destruction or loss of property, either State or individual, shall result thereby, will be cheerfully submitted to;—and this action being warmly approved and seconded by the Executive; therefore, I do hereby request that all officers who are out of service from any cause, and all others who may be willing to unite in defending the Capital of the State, to assemble this evening at the City Hall at 5 o'clock, and proceed forthwith to organize force, &c. Prompt, efficient and resolute action is necessary. We have a gallant army in the field upon whom we fully and confidently rely; but no effort should be spared which can contribute to this noble object. The Capital of Virginia must not be surrendered. Virginians must rally to the rescue.

Given under my hand and under the seal of the commonwealth of Virginia, this 15th day of May, 1862, and 86th year of the Commonwealth.

JOHN LETCHER.

In accordance with this proclamation, a large assemblage gathered in the City Hall. Fine spirits prevailed. Brief addresses by Gov. Letcher and Mayor Mayo, were made. Both declared they would never surrender the city. The announcement was received by loud cheering.

Resolutions were adopted for organizing a regiment of volunteers to defend the city.

The latest report from the river states that the Monitor and Galena are steaming down the river.

LATER.

RICHMOND, May 16....The city is very quiet today. Business is suspended in accordance with the President's proclamation. The Federal gunboats have gone down James River below City Point.

ALIEN RESIDENTS—*The Conscription Act.* The following dispatch announcing a decision upon a point of considerable interest, has been placed at our disposal:—*Jackson Mississippian.*

RICHMOND, May 13.

Honorable E. Barksdale:

The Attorney General of the Confederate States, has decided that aliens permanently residing in the Confederacy, are subject to Conscription.

G. W. RANDOLPH,
Secretary of War.

☞ Mr. Joseph Arrighi of Natchez, in company with some seven or eight philanthropic ladies, who are on their way to some of the hospitals in the Confederacy, to assist in nursing our sick and wounded soldiers, passed through our village on Thursday last.—*Fayette Gazette, May 17.*

FROM FORT PILLOW. The Victoria is the latest arrival from Fort Pillow. Her officers inform us that the Yankee gunboats have gone up the river, fearing that Commodore Montgomery would attack them again.—*Memphis Daily Argus, May 17.*

Punishing the Traitors.

It is said that nine hundred of the citizens of Nashville have been arrested and will be tried for treason. The punishment for what the Yankees call treason is death, and this is the fate which these tyrants will really execute upon all in the South who practically maintain that doctrine of the sovereignty of the States in which they were educated from childhood, and which no one, either in the North or South has ever disputed up to the present war. The whole programme of the invaders is worthy the dark ages. The scaffold is to groan with victims, and the whole property of the Southern people to be taken from them. It is well that they have permitted the cloven foot to be seen thus early. It is well that they have given the Southern people this unmistakable indication of what is in store for them. They have convinced the most incredulous that it is as idle as it is unmanly to expect compassion or clemency at their hands. When they entered Nashville, they were gentle and bland in their professions, till they had almost lulled the suspicious into security. But the threat of McCook that they would deal with the rebellion with gloves off, is already found to be something more than an empty menace. There is no hope whatever for the South except in such resistance as men make to outlaws and pirates.

[*Richmond Dispatch, May 9th.*

☞ The Louisville Journal says:

"In fact there is no earthly truth more certain, more indisputable, than that, however desolating the war may be, there can never be peace in this country until what was one country shall be again one country. It may be a republic, it may be a kingdom, it may be a despotism, it must and will be one. The whole people, North and South, may as well make up their minds at once."

In other words, they must have the South, though constitutional liberty should perish. They see that a despotism is inevitable, and are educating the people to it by degrees. The admission, from such a source, that "it may be a kingdom, it may be a despotism, it must and will be one," is very significant.—*Daily Avalanche.*

☞ Type will go estray sometimes. A rapt lover once addressed some verses to his "mistress' eyebrows," commencing—

"My Mary is the rarest rose,"

but what was his consternation when he saw it in print—

"My Mary has the reddest nose."

Friday, May 23d, 1862.

Probate Court.

Judge Bullock is still confined to his bed from the dangerous and almost fatal wound received by him last week, from the goring of a vicious bull, that should long since have been confined or killed. Though the Judge is slowly improving, he will not be able, it is thought, to hold the regular May term of the Probate Court of this county, which is designated by law to be held next Monday.

Clerk, Robert S. Wood, of this Court, a member of the "Natchez Southrons," returned home last week from Corinth an invalid, and has been confined to his bed ever since, with a violent attack of typhoid fever. He was pronounced convalescent yesterday, but it is apprehended that the disease, with previous infirmities from fatigue, exposure, &c., in battle, camp and on the march, has so much shattered his system as to require weeks yet for his restoration to health.

In the meantime, however, persons having deeds, mortgages, &c., for record in the Probate Clerk's office, can have immediate and prompt attention, on application to the Deputy having charge of the office, at the usual hours. Should the enemy quarter among us, the opportunity now offered for having deeds, &c., recorded, may not continue.

An Insolent and Low Order.

The following New Orleans order of General Butler is strictly *picayuneish.* He has evidently discovered that the men of the South are not alone his enemies—but the women have manifested their disapprobation of his presence, and that of his army, among them. We look upon the order as beneath the dignity of a man, much less a General who would pride himself upon his fine feathers and virtues. To our construction of the wording of the order, it appears insolent and low:

[Copy] "NEW ORLEANS, May 15, 1862.

"General Orders, No. 28.

"As the officers and soldiers of the United States have been subject to repeated insults from the women (calling themselves ladies) of New Orleans, in return for the most scrupulous non-interference and courtesy on our part: It is ordered, that hereafter, when any female shall, by word, gesture, or movement, insult or show contempt for any officer or soldier of the U. States, she shall be regarded and held liable to be treated as a woman of the town plying her avocation.

(Signed) MAJOR-GEN. BUTLER," &c.

Putting the most favorable construction on the words of this Order, and we then have the most insignificant position for an honorable officer and true soldier. Probably the ladies point at the General, and otherwise manifest their displeasure at his presence! So did the little boys in the streets of Baltimore, when it took two soldiers to mount him on his horse! Ah, General! the way of the subjugator will be harder and harder, unto the bitter end.

RICHMOND GOSSIP. The Richmond correspondent of the Charleston Mercury, writes under date of the 6th inst:

"Doubtless the Confederate government had good reasons for permitting the important movement, now in progress, to get into the mouths of everybody in the streets. I commit no imprudence, therefore, when, without entering into particulars, I state that the President has finally consented to give up the war against gunboats, and to concentrate our armies in the interior, preparatory to striking a blow, which, if successful, is to be followed up—even though the Yankees should suffer and become enraged in consequence. What the issue of the new policy may be, depends on troops and arms and generals. Commenced last year, our advantages would have been great. Its success now might reasonably have been calculated upon, if common discretion had marked its initiation and execution.

Proclamation!

EXECUTIVE OFFICE,
Jackson, Miss., May 16, 1862.

Whereas, by the blockading of our ports, and the invasion of our soil by the enemy, the present crop of cotton has been excluded from market, and it would be unwise in our planters by planting a full crop to diminish the value of the one now in store. Moreover, the inundation of the valley of the Mississippi, and the partial interruption of agricultural operations by volunteering to serve in the army, will diminish the production of grain in the State, while the necessity of subsisting our population and the army which defends our liberties, calls for a greatly increased production. Patriotism, has doubtless, prompted many persons to suspend the cultivation of cotton for the present, in order to meet the necessities of war, but in order to be effectual, the policy should be general. Therefore, I, John J. Pettus, Governor of the State of Mississippi, do issue this proclamation, enjoining all planters to plant not more than one acre to the hand in cotton, and the remainder of their arable land in grain.

By the Governor, JOHN J. PETTUS.
C. A. BROUGHER, Secretary of State.
May 17, 1862.

COTTON BURNED. If 22,000 bales of cotton were burned at New Orleans and Baton Rouge, it will go very far to heal the force of the great blow inflicted by the loss of the former city. Seward had no doubt assured England and France that the cotton trade would be re-opened with the reduction of the Southern ports. Now if the French vessels see the smoke and ashes of the burned cotton, they will be assured that our defence is in earnest, and that the success of the enemy will bring ruin upon the manufacturing interests of Europe. When Europe adds to the destitution of the last year, the cessation of the present year, a gap will be made in her manufactures that cannot be bridged by economy, nor filled up by Indian culture. Europe will see that if we are to fall, we pull down the pillars of commerce with us; and that if civilization will not sympathize with, it shall participate in our misfortunes.

[*Richmond Whig, 6th.*

☞ Lieut. S. D. Stockman, of the Natchez Southrons, has received the appointment of Commissary of the 10th Mississippi Regiment, with the rank of Captain.

A FEW PLAIN WORDS.

As previously stated, arrangements were made to publish the Daily and Weekly Courier during the coming Summer, or to the end of the War. This was done, thinking that we had a civilized foe to deal with, and not a fiend in human shape. The war upon the press at New Orleans, however, admonishes us in vivid characters, too plain to be misunderstood, that in the end we have nothing to hope for but the bitterness of an enslaved mind, and not one ray of freedom of expression of opinion on paper or otherwise. The Federal edicts must be law, and this law we must be the means of promulgating, if we publish a paper. Such has been the decision in New Orleans, and such, doubtless, would be their position in Natchez. The removal of an office of the size and cost of the Natchez Daily and Weekly Courier, would involve us in an expense which we cannot now incur; it is as much the fixture of a city as a gin-house and quarters are to a plantation; in the city's general welfare it is as much connected, and amid adversity it falls with the business of the place in which it is located. Such is our situation now. *When a garrison of Federal Soldiers is in Natchez, we cannot print a paper,* however much we may desire to keep the record perfect for a long series of years.

Our reasons for coming to this conclusion, are in a *few plain words,* as follows:

The Federals would not allow us an expression of an opinion.

They would force us to a publication of their infamous orders, or subjection of the property of the office to confiscation to the United States.

They would forbid us advocating, in any particular, the cause of the Southern Confederacy.

Having the mail facilities in their own hands, for news of any kind we should be subjected entirely to the misrepresentations of their venal Federal press.

Although not present at the meeting of citizens of Adams county and Parish of Concordia, which passed the following resolutions, yet we feel it a duty we owe the public as well as ourselves, to adhere as strictly as possible to their injunctions—and for these reasons, if for no other, we could not print a paper under Federal rule. We give the resolutions as a reminder of their pledge then made for the future conduct of our people:

Resolved, That whatever line of conduct, is adopted by this meeting, in view of the impending danger, should be uniformly and without exception, adhered to by every citizen of county, and parish of Concordia, remaining within the same.

Resolved, That for the mutual support and safety of the citizens of the county, and adjoining parish, remaining therein, each of them should solemnly pledge to the other his word and his honor that he will take no oath or do no act incompatible with his allegiance to the Confederate States of America.

Resolved, That every citizen of the said county and parish who is unwilling to make the foregoing pledge, ought to remove forthwith, and that the honor and safety of the others demand a prompt compliance with, and rigid enforcement of this resolution.

For these and other equally strong reasons, we now say what we do. We do not want to see one of the Federals here—they have no right on this soil in the business of *invasion* and *subjugation.* We hate the very sight of them in this wicked capacity; and trust that they may meet the same feeling wherever they go in the South. However we may have felt, in years long past, inclined to respect them in times of peace, all falls to the ground when they come to our doors with the oily tongue of *professed good,* with the *stiletto in their belt,* ready to *strike to the heart our kindred and our friends.*

We repeat, *we cannot publish a newspaper in Natchez, if garrisoned by the Federalists;* NOR WILL WE.

One more injunction, and we have done with our *few plain words.* Let every planter live firmly up to the following Act of Congress, and the enemy will have little hope from garrisoning any Southern city:

(Confederate Act, passed April 19, 1862.)

SECTION 1. The Congress of the Confederate States of America do enact, that it shall be unlawful for any person, by himself, his agent, or in any manner whatever, transport to any port or place in the Confederate States, which may be at the time in the possession of the enemy, or to sell therein any cotton, tobacco, sugar, rice, molasses, syrup or naval stores.

SEC. 2. Imposes heavy penalties.

We close by saying, that we have full faith in the final triumph of Southern Institutions. That, although at times our cause may look dark and disheartening, yet we look forward to a bright and glorious future. The science of war is fully understood by those we have in the tented field; they are such officers and soldiers as "NEVER SAY FAIL," and they will bring our proud Republic in good time to an honorable haven of Peace and Safety.

Our patrons will therefore, without further notice, know when our paper will be stopped.

Ventured Too Far.

Four of the enemy's crews, last Wednesday, ventured too far from their gunboats, for their own comfort. A short distance from Quitman's Landing, they were "snapped up" by some wiley conscripts afloat in that section, and when last heard from, had taken passage for the interior with two dark-looking pilots aboard. They are in a safe port ere this, and firm at anchor.

AMUSING. While the corps of prisoners from Col. Morgan's command, were taking a steamer from the enemy, on which they were being transported as prisoners of war, to St. Louis, and coming to Clarksville on their own account, he, (the Colonel, and the rest of his men,) were near the centre of Kentucky, taking the railroad cars, on which he supposed they were to be conducted. The account is highly amusing, as well as interesting, notwithstanding it is from a Federal source. It will be found in to-day's paper.

RETURNED. We were gratified to meet in our office last Saturday, our former friend and associate in office business, Wm. W. Duncan. For several months he has been with the Natchez Fencibles in Virginia, until the 12th Mississippi regiment was ordered as a re-enforcement at the battle of Williamsburg. In this march he became, with others, overdone by fatigue, when he was taken prisoner and marched by the enemy to Fortress Monroe. Here, a large number of Federals arrived the same day under a flag of truce, to be exchanged, when, among others, he was permitted to return to Richmond by the Confederate transports, on his parole. Mr. Duncan is in excellent health, (and reports the same of the corps of Fencibles.) though looking somewhat fatigued from his long, round-about journey home.

Great Overflow of Water.

Our friends at Vidalia, opposite Natchez, are suffering terribly from the back-water out of lake Concordia. The overflow of that lake has covered nearly every plantation this side, on the river front. For miles, the country now presents one great sea of water, with an occasional building and a few trees above the flood. Our planters in Concordia parish are suffering terribly.

There is a decided fall in the water reported at Memphis, but its effects will not reach here for many days—not in time, as we had ardently hoped, to save much distress from the flood.

Col. John Morgan in Kentucky.

Another Daring Adventure—A Railroad Train Captured and Destroyed—Large Haul of Money, and Prentice, of the Louisville Journal, 'shaking in his shoes.'

The Memphis Avalanche obtains the following account of John Morgan's last exploit in Kentucky, from the Louisville Journal of the 13th. Although a Federal account, it is very interesting:

Yesterday, at about half-past twelve or one o'clock, when the cars from this city for Nashville had got to Woodland, two miles this side of Cave City, they were stopped by Col. John Morgan and his men, numbering about two hundred.

Major Coffee and an Irishman fired at the rebels, whereupon a considerable number of shots were fired, chiefly by the rebels, who seemed to be aiming principally at the engineer, but nobody was killed or hurt. Morgan took possession of the train, which passed on to Cave City, where about forty-five freight cars, three passenger cars, and one locomotive were destroyed. One passenger car and the express car were permitted to return to Louisville. Major Coffee and Major Helveti were captured and carried off, and eight or ten thousand dollars taken from the express agent. [The Memphis Appeal says $50,000.]

The special object of Morgan was to re-capture the one hundred and eighty-three men, including his brother, who were taken the other day by Gen. Dumont. The prisoners, however, were not on board, being still detained in Nashville. Morgan swore to some gentlemen on the cars that he would have the prisoners at all hazards—that by Saturday next he would, if necessary, have four thousand men together for that purpose.

We are told, that, but for the earnest interposition of Mr. Moses R. Morrison, the route agent, and our fellow-citizen, Dr. Bush, both of whom have been fellow townsmen and intimate acquaintances of John Morgan, the remaining locomotive, passenger car, and express car, would have been destroyed. The mails were spared, and this forbearance, we have no doubt, was due to Mr. Morrison's influence. Mr. M. speaks of Morgan's deportment in very favorable terms. The rebels didn't fire till after Major Coffee had fired, and even then, as M. stated, without his order.

Morgan's intended raid, we are told, was known at Elizabethtown yesterday morning. A citizen at that place was about starting on the cars for Nashville, but a friend or acquaintance warned him not to go, as, if he did, he would be captured. Morgan informed the railroad passengers that Gen. O. M. Mitchell had been cut off by the rebels. He, and his Pathfinder Ferguson, sent to us their kindest regards, and the former vowed that he would yet make us his prisoner, but we hope and trust that this was another mistake.

When the passengers returned from Cave City, Morgan was there on the look-out for the train from Nashville, but our informant was able to send a dispatch to Bowling Green, and thus prevent the cars coming this side of that place.

Now for Prentice's Lament!

How much longer are these raids of Morgan to be continued? Can no way be devised to put an end to them? Must all communication between Louisville be broken up by them? If this bold partisan leader can come with two hundred men from Corinth almost to the bank of Green river, what is to prevent his gathering two thousand men, cutting the telegraph wires, and making a dash some night into Louisville?

Letter from a Passenger on the Train.

We have received the following statement from a passenger on the train captured by Morgan:

To the Editors of the Louisville Journal:

MAY 11....When the morning express train of the Louisville and Nashville line got opposite to Woodland, quite a commotion was produced among the passengers upon seeing a company of ladies and children running towards the train, hallooing at the top of their voices and making motions for us to stop.

When the train stopped amid the din of confusion, we could hear the words, "run back, for Morgan and his men will fire upon you." We could see ahead of us smoke and flame, as if Cave City was on fire, and the cars immediately took the back track, but had not proceeded far before obstruction upon the track stopped them. Here were several moments of anxious suspense, not knowing what our fate was to be. We were much relieved when Morgan's men emerged from the bushes and took possession of the train. When we got there we found the village untouched, but a train of cars on fire.

The train was variously reported at from thirty-three to forty-one cars and a locomotive. Our train was then parted, and three of the passenger cars subjected to the torch likewise. After taking from the express agent a large package of money—the amount was not known—Colonel Morgan magnanimously permitted the balance of the train and passengers to return to Louisville. When we got back as far as Woodland, we found six more cars in flames. Most of the cars, I think, were loaded.

Morgan's ostensible object in thus paying Kentucky this unexpected visit, was to rescue his men taken by the Federals some days ago. We do not know whether he succeeded or not. He was anxiously looking for the Nashville train when we left. The number of his men is variously reported at from two hundred to one thousand. We did not see over forty or fifty.

At the first of the excitement we heard several pistol reports at the head of the train, but no one was hurt, and no individual or private property was molested. The Federal soldiers were taken prisoners, but such was the confusion that I could not learn how many. I think, however, there were only five or six on the train, and one of that number was permitted to return in virtue of the pleading of his wife, who happened to be on board. Among the number taken I heard the names of Major Coffee and Major Helveti. Col. Morgan spared the mails for the sake of an old friend, the carrier, Mr. Morrison.

T. R. LINE,
Of Gordonsville, Ky., on board train.

Vicksburg and the Enemy.

It is pretty generally believed, and not without some show of sound reasoning, that the Federals will not attack the fortifications below Vicksburg without the assistance of their mortar boats. It is also believed that these boats were sent round to Mobile, to make an attempt to take that city. Whether they will be re-called is yet a matter of uncertainty.

Notwithstanding these speculations, we heard heavy cannonading north of us yesterday; but whether it was at Vicksburg, or where, has not transpired.

Weekly Courier

"A Word Unspoken."

There is a word unspoken oft,—
Yet why, 'tis strange to tell—
One single syllable so soft
Can work a sovereign spell.

It has a home in human heart,
Nor spurns its native ground,
And still, as if by magic art,
It roams the wide world round.

Though sages say the way is plain,
To prove its humble birth;
They oft confess their logic vain—
"Alas! 'tis not of earth!"

It moves in every walk of life,—
It breathes on every gale,—
Subdues the thoughts of hate and strife,
And soothes affliction's wail:—

It brightest seems in sorrow's hour,
Like star of summer night,
That shimmer's on, though clouds may lower
To quell its liquid light.

It cheers through life,—inspires in death;—
An Angel, from above,
It wings its way o'er earth and saith—
My only name is LOVE!*

REV. HENRY G. PERRY.

* 1 John, 4: 16.

TELEGRAPHIC.

Affairs in Virginia.

PETERSBURG, May 19......Eighteen of the Monitor's crew came ashore at three o'clock this evening at City point. They were surprised at the landing by confederate pickets, and ordered to surrender.

Nine of them, including four officers, laid down their pistols and cutlasses. The others rushed to their small boat and pulled for the Monitor. Eight were killed and the remaining one lost an arm.

The Monitor opened with heavy guns and prevented the rescue of the boat and survivor. The men captured reached here at half-past six o'clock and marched through Sycamore street to Huger's headquarters.

They were surrounded by a large crowd. One of the officers was a paymaster, the others midshipmen.

None of the Confederate soldiers were hurt.

Late Northern papers report the sinking of the Mound City and Cincinnati gunboats by Jeff. Thompson and the cotton fleet. The Benton was badly damaged.

They acknowledged a loss of one thousand killed and twenty-five hundred wounded, and six hundred prisoners in the Williamsburg fight.

Special Dispatches to the Mississippian.

Later from Vicksburg.

VICKSBURG, May 20....All is very quiet here now. There is no prospect of a fight until the mortar boats and transports arrive. They were at Bayou Sara on Sunday. C. McLAURIN.

Our private advices are to Thursday morning. There was a unanimous determination to resist the invaders to the last extremity.—ED. COURIER.

THE EUROPEAN INTERVENTION.

RICHMOND, May 20......The Enquirer of this morning has extracts from Northern papers of the 16th, bringing English dates of the 3d.

The prominent subjects of discussion is the rumored English and French intervention in American affairs. The Paris correspondent of the New York Herald, April 29th, says that notes have been passing between the Governments within the last week, in relation to this matter. "There is no doubt," says the Enquirer, editorially, "that our extracts from the latest European intelligence received at the North, indicates on the part of England and France a disposition to intervene for the resteration of peace on this continent. The feeling exhibited is altogether in favor of acknowldging the pretensions of the Confederate States."

Lincoln has issued a proclamation declaring that the blockade of the ports of Buford, Port Royal, and New Orleans, shall so far cease as he may determine by the first of June, that commercial intercourse with these ports, except as to persons, things and information contraband of war, may from that time be carried on, subject to the laws of the United States.

Five Thousand Yankees Hemmed In.

800 Prisoners Taken.

RICHMOND, May 20......The Lynchburg Virginian to-day says, abont 5000 of the enemy were caught between the forces of Generals Heath and Marshall, near the Narrows of New River in Giles county. The enemy seeing their predicament broke and fled, without making an attempt to fight. Eight hundred prisoners were captured, who surrendered their arms and were paroled.

It is believed that this news is confirmed by official dispatches received this afternoon.

MORGAN'S CAPTURED MEN.

MONTGOMERY, May 20....Lt. Colonel Wood, with seventy of Morgan's men, who were captured at Lebanon, escaped by overpowering the Yankee crew on the boat which was conveying them to St. Louis. They took the boat down to Clarksville where they all landed safely.

Col. Morgan arrived here to-day, en route for Corinth, and left on a boat this evening.

☞ The following is the correspondence between the "Authorities of Vicksburg" and the Federal Naval Officer. We copy from the Whig:

MAYOR'S OFFICE, VICKSBURG, MISS.,
May 18, 1862.

To S. Phillip Lee, Commanding Advance Naval Division:

Your communication of this date, addressed "To the Authorities at Vicksburg," has been delivered to me. In reply, I will state to you, that so far as the municipal authorities are concerned, we have erected no defenses, and none are within the corporate limits of the city.

But, sir, in further reply, I will state that neither the municipal authorities nor the citizens will ever consent to a surrender of the city. Respectfully,

L. LINDSEY, Mayor.

VICKSBURG, MISS., May 18, 1862.

S. P. Lee, Com. Advance Naval Division, U. S. N.:

SIR—As your communication of this date is addressed to the "Authorities of Vicksburg," and that you may have a full reply to said communication, I have to state that Mississippians don't know, and refuse to learn, how to surrender to an enemy. If Com. Farragut, or Major-General Butler can teach them, let them come and try. As to the defenses of Vicksburg, I respectfully refer you to the reply of Brig. Gen. Smith, Commanding forces at Vicksburg, herewith enclosed. Respectfully,

JAS. L. AUTRY,
Military Governor, and Commandant Post.

HEADQUARTERS DEFENCES VICKSBURG,
May 18, 1862.

S. P. Lee, U. S. N., Commanding Advance Division:

SIR—Your communication of this date, addressed to the "Authorities of Vicksburg," demanding the surrender of the city and its defenses, has been received. In regard to the surrender of the defenses, I have to reply, that, having been ordered here to hold these defenses, it is my intention to do so as long as it is in my power.

M. L. SMITH,
Brigadier General Commanding.

Their Work Commenced.

We learn that men from one of the enemy's gunboats, seized four persons on their way from Waterproof to Natchez last Sunday, and after catechising them, permitted them to pass on giving their parole. This is but the commencement of the dirty work they are sent South to perform.

GOOD RIVER NEWS.

MEMPHIS, Tuesday Evening, May 20.

The river is going down rapidly—falling at the rate of an inch in two hours.—[Argus.

BATTLE OF SHILOH.

Gen. Beauregard's Official Report.

HEADQ'RS ARMY OF THE MISSISSIPPI,
CORINTH, MISS., April 11, 1861.

General: On the 2d ultimo, having ascertained conclusively, from the movements of the enemy on the Tennessee river, and from reliable information, that his aim would be to cut off my communications in West Tennessee with the Eastern and Southern States, by operating from the Tennessee river, between Crumps Landing and Eastport, as a base, I determined to foil his designs by concentrating all my available forces at and around Corinth.

Meanwhile, having called on the Governors of the States of Tennessee, Mississippi, Alabama, and Louisiana, to furnish additional troops, some of them, chiefly regiments from Louisiana, soon reached this vicinity, and with two divisions of General Polk's command from Columbus, and a fine corps of troops from Mobile and Pensacola, under Maj. Gen. Bragg, constituted the army of the Mississippi. At the same time Gen. Johnston being at Murfreesboro', on the march to form a junction of his forces with mine, was called on to send at least a brigade by railroad, so that we might fall on and crush the enemy should he attempt an advance from under his gunboats. The call on General Johnston was promptly complied with. His entire force was also hastened in this direction, and by the 1st of April our united forces were concentrated along the Mobile and Ohio Railroad from Bethel to Corinth, and on the Memphis and Charleston Railroad from Corinth to Iuka.

It was then determined to assume the offensive and strike a sudden blow at the enemy in position under General Grant, on the west bank of the Tennessee, at Pittsburg and in the direction of Savannah, before he was reinforced under General Buell, then known to be advancing for that purpose by rapid marches from Nashville via Columbia. About the same time, General Johnston was advised that such an operation conformed to the expectations of the President.

By a rapid and vigorous attack on General Grant, it was expected he would be beaten back into his transports and the river, or captured, in time to enable us to profit by the victory and remove to the rear all the stores and ammunitions that would fall into our hands in such an event, before the arrival of General Buell's army on the scene. It was never contemplated, however, to retain the position thus gained, and abandon Corinth, the strategic point of the campaign.

Want of general officers, needful for the proper organization of divisions and brigades of an army brought thus suddenly together, and other difficulties in the way of an effective organization, delayed the movements until the night of the 3d inst., when it was heard from a reliable quarter that the junction of the enemies armies was near at hand; it was then, at a late hour, determined that the attack should be attempted at once, incomplete and imperfect as were our preparations for such a grave and momentous adventure. Accordingly, that night, at 1 o'clock A. M., the preliminary orders to the commanders of corps were issued for the movement.

On the following morning the detailed orders of movement, a copy of which is herewith marked "A," were issued, and the movement, after some delay, commenced, the troops being in admirable spirits. It was expected we should be able to reach the enemy's lines in time to attack them early on the 5th inst. The men, however, for the most part, were unused to marching, the roads narrow, and traversing a densely wooded country, became almost impassable after a severe rain storm on the night of the 4th, which drenched the troops in bivouac; hence our forces did not reach the intersection of the roads from Pittsburg and Hamburg, in the immediate vicinity of the enemy, until late Saturday afternoon.

It was decided that the attack should be made on the next morning, at the earliest hour practicable, in accordance with the orders of movement—that is, in three lines of battle: the first and second extending from Owl creek, on the left to Lick creek on the right, a distance of about three miles, supported by the third and the reserve. The first line, under Major General Hardee, was constituted of his corps, augmented on his right by Gladden's brigade, of Major General Bragg's corps, deployed in line of battle, with their respective artillery, following immediately by the main road to Pittsburg, and the cavalry in rear of the wings. The second line, composed of the other corps of Bragg's corps followed the first at a distance of five hundred yards, in the same order as the first. The army corps under General Polk following the second line, at the distance of about eight hundred yards, in lines of brigades, deployed with their batteries in rear of each brigade, moving by the Pittsburg road, the left wing supported by cavalry; the reserve, under Brigadier General Breckinridge, followed closely the third line, in the same order, its right wing supported by cavalry.

These two corps constituted the reserve, and were to support the front lines of battle, by being deployed when required on the right and left of the Pittsburg road, or otherwise act, according to the exigencies of the battle.

At 5 A. M., on the 6th instant, a reconnoitering party of the enemy having become engaged with our advanced pickets, the commander of the forces gave orders to begin the movement and attack as determined upon, except that Trabue's brigade, of Breckinridge's Division, was detached and advanced to support the left of Bragg's corps and line of battle, when menaced by the enemy, and the other two brigades were directed to advance by the road to Hamburg, to support Bragg's right; and at the same time, Mancy's regiment, of Polk's corps, was advanced by the same road to reinforce the regiment of cavalry and battery of four pieces, already thrown forward to watch and guard Grier's, Banner's and Borlan's Fords of Lick creek.

Thirty minutes after 5 o'clock A. M., our lines and columns were in motion, all animated evidently by a prompting spirit. The front line was engaged at once, but advanced steadily, followed in due order with equal resolution and steadiness by the other lines, which were brought successively into action with rare skill, judgment and gallantry, by the several corps commanders, as the enemy made a stand, with his masses rallied for the struggle for his encampments. Like an Alpine avalanche our troops moved forward, despite the determined resistance of the enemy, until after 6 o'clock P. M., when we were in possession of all his encampments between Owl and Lick creeks but one. Nearly all of his field artillery, about thirty (30) flags, colors and standards, over 3,000 prisoners, including a division commander (General Prentiss) and several Brigade commanders, thousands of small arms, an immense supply of subsistance, forage and munitions of war, and a large amount of means of transportation—all the substantial fruits of a complete victory—such, indeed, as rarely have followed the most successful battles; for never was an army so well provisioned as that of our enemy.

The remnant of his army had been driven in utter disorder to the immediate vicinity of Pittsburg, under the shelter of the heavy guns of his iron-clad gunboats, and we remained undisputed masters of the well selected, admirably provided cantonments, after over twelve hours of obstinate conflict with his forces, who had been beaten from them and the contiguous covert, but only by a sustained onset of all the men we could bring into action.

Our loss was heavy, as will appear from the accompanying return marked "B." Our Commander-in-Chief, Gen. A. S. Johnston, fell mortally wounded and died on the field at 2:30 P. M., after having shown the highest qualities of the commander, and a personal intrepitity that inspired all around him, and gave resistless impulsion to his columns at critical moments.

The chief command then devolved upon me, hough at the time I was greatly prostrated and suffering from the prolonged sickness with which I had been afflicted since early in February. The responsibility was one which in my physical condition I would have gladly avoided, though cast upon me when our forces were successfully pushing the enemy back upon the Tennessee river, and though supported on the immediate field by such corps commanders as Major General Polk, Bragg and Hardee, and Brigadier General Breckinridge commanding the reserve.

It was after 6 o'clock P. M., as before said, when the enemy's last position was carried, and his forces finally broke and sought refuge behind a commanding eminence, covering the Pittsburg landing, not more than half a mile distant, and under the guns of the gunboats, which opened on our eager columns a fierce and annoying fire with shot and shell of the heaviest description. Darkness was close at hand. Officers and men were exhausted by a combat of over twelve hours without food, and jaded by the march of the preceding day through mud and water, it was therefore impossible to collect the rich and opportune spoils of war scattered broadcast on the field left in our possession, and impracticable to make any effective dispositions for their removal to the rear.

I accordingly established my headquarters at the Church of Shiloh, in the enemy's encampment, with Major General Bragg, and directed our troops to sleep on their arms, in such positions in advance and rear as corps commanders should determine, hoping from news received by a special dispatch that delays had been encountered by Gen. Buell in his march from Columbia, and that his main force, therefore, could not reach the field of battle in time to save Gen. Grant's shattered fugitive forces from capture or destruction on the following day.

During the night the rain fell in torrents, adding to the discomfort and harrassed condition of the men. The enemy, moreover, had broken their rest by a discharge, at measured intervals, of heavy shells thrown from the gunboats, therefore, on the following morning the troops under my command were not in condition to cope with an equal force of fresh troops, armed and equipped like our adversary, in the immediate possession of his depots, and shattered by such an auxiliary as the enemy's gunboats.

About 6 o'clock on the morning of the 7th of April, however a hot fire of musketry and artillery, opened from the enemy's quarter, on our advanced line, assured me of the junction of his forces, and soon the battle raged with a fury which satisfied me I was attacked by a largely superior force. But from the onset our troops notwithstanding their fatigue and losses from the battle of the day before, exhibited the most cheering, veteran-like steadiness. On the right and centre the enemy was repulsed in every attempt he made with his heavy column in that quarter of the field; on the left, however, and nearest to the point of arrival of his reinforcements, he drove forward line after line of his fresh troops, which were met with a resolution and courage of which our country may be proudly hopeful. Again and again our troops were brought to the charge, invariably to win the position at issue, invariably to drive back their foe. But hour by hour thus opposed to an enemy constantly reinforced, our ranks were perceptably thinned under the unceasing fire of the enemy, and by 12 meridian, eighteen hours of hard fighting had sensibly exhausted a large number, my last reserves had necessarily been disposed of, and the enemy was evidently receiving fresh reinforcements after each repulse; accordingly, about 1 P. M., I determined to withdraw from so unequal a conflict, securing such of the results of the victory of the day before as was then practicable.

Officers of my staff were immediately dispatched with the necessary orders to make the best dispositions for a deliberate, orderly withdrawal from the field, and to collect and post a reserve to meet the enemy, should he attempt to push after us. In this connection I will mention particularly my Adjutant General, Col. Jordan, who was of much assistance to me on this occasion, as he had already been on the field of battle on that and the preceding day.

At two o'clock P. M., the lines in advance, which had repulsed the enemy in their last fierce assault on our left and centre, received the orders to retire; this was done with uncommon steadiness, and the enemy made no attempt to follow.

The line of troops established to cover this movement had been disposed on a favorable ridge commanding the ground of Shiloh Church; from this position our artillery played upon the woods beyond for a while, but upon no visible enemy and without reply. Soon satisfied that no serious pursuit would be attempted this last line was withdrawn, and never did troops leave a battle-field in better order; even the stragglers fell into the ranks and marched off with those who had stood more steadily by their colors. A second strong position was taken up about a mile in rear, where the approach of the enemy was waited for nearly an hour; but no effort to follow was made, and only a small detachment of horsemen could be seen at a distance from this last position warily observing our movements.

Arranging, through my staff officers, for the completion of the movements thus begun, Brigadier General Breckinridge was left with his command as a rear guard to hold the ground we had occupied the night preceding the first battle, just in front of the intersection of the Pittsburg and Hamburg roads, about four miles from the former place, while the rest of the army passed to the rear in excellent order.

On the following day General Breckinridge fell back about three miles to Mickey's, which position we continued to hold, with our cavalry thrown considerably forward in immediate proximity to the battle-field.

Unfortunately, towards night of the 7th instant it began to rain heavily; this continued throughout the night; the roads became almost impassable in many places, and much hardship and suffering now ensued before all the regiments reached their encampments. But despite the heavy casualties of the two eventful days of the 6th and 7th of April, this army is more confident of ultimate success than before its encounter with the enemy.

To Major-Generals Polk, Bragg, and Hardee, commanding corps, and to Brig-Gen. Breckinridge, commanding the reserve, the country is greatly indebted for the zeal, intelligence, and energy with which all orders were executed—for the foresight and military ability they displayed in the absence of instructions in the many exigencies of the battle, on a field so densely wooded and broken, and for their fearless deportment as they repeatedly led their commands personally to the onset upon their powerful adversary. It was under these circumstances that General Bragg had two horses shot under him, that Major-General Hardee was slightly wounded, his coat rent by balls and his horse disabled, and that Major-General Breckinridge was twice struck by spent balls.

For the services of their gallant subordinate commanders, and of other officers, as well as for the details of the battle-field, I must refer to the reports of corps, division and brigade commanders, which shall be forwarded as soon as received.

To give more in detail the operations of the two battles resulting from the movement on Pittsburg than now attempted, must have delayed this report for weeks and interfered materially with the important duties of my position; but I may be permitted to say, that not only did the obstinate conflict for 12 hours, on Sunday, leave the Confederate army masters of the battle-field, and our adversary beaten, but we left that field on the next day only after eight hours' incessant battle with a superior army of fresh troops, whom we had repulsed in every attack on our lines—so repulsed and crippled, indeed, as to leave it unable to take the field for the campaign for which it was collected and equipped at such enormous expense, and with such profusion of all the appliances of war. These successful results were not achieved, however, as before said, without severe loss, a loss not to be measured by the number of the slain or wounded, but by the high social and personal worth of so large a number of those who were killed or disabled, including the commander of the forces, whose high qualities will be greatly missed in the momentous campaign impending.

I deeply regret to record, also, the death of the Hon. George M. Johnson, Provisional Governor of Kentucky, who went into action with the Kentucky troops and continually inspired them by his words and example. Having his horse shot under him on Sunday, he entered the ranks of a Kentucky regiment on Monday, and fell mortally wounded towards the close of the day. Not his State alone, but the whole Confederacy, has sustained a great loss in the death of this brave, upright, and able man.

Another gallant and able soldier and Captain was lost to the service of the country, when Brigadier General Gladden, commanding 1st Brigade, Withers's Division, 3rd Army corps, died from a severe wound received on the 5th instant, after having been conspicuous to his whole corps and the army for courage and capacity.

Major General Cheatham, commanding 1st Division, 1st corps, was slightly wounded, and had three horses shot under him.

Brigadier General Clark, commanding 2d Division of the 1st corps, received a severe wound, also on the 1st day, which will deprive the army of his valuable services for some time.

Brigadier General Hindman, engaged in the outset of the battle, was conspicuous for a cool courage, efficiently employed in leading his men ever into the thickest of the fray, until his horse was shot under him, and he was unfortunately so severely injured by the fall that the army was deprived, on the following day, of his chivalrous example.

Brigadier Generals B. R. Johnston and Bowen, most meritorious officers, were also severely wounded in the first combat, but it is hoped will soon be able to return to duty with their brigades.

To mention the many field officers who died or were wounded while gallantly leading their commands into action, and the many brilliant instances of individual courage displayed by officers and men in the twenty hours of battle, is impossible at this time; but their names will be duly made known to their countrymen.

The immediate staff of the lamented Commander-in-Chief, who accompanied him to the field, rendered efficient service, and either by his side or in carrying his orders shared his exposure to the casualties of a well contested battle-field. I beg to commend their names to the notice of the War Department, namely: of Capts. H. P. Brewster and N. Wickliffe, of the Adjutant and Inspector General's Department.

Capt. Thos. O'Hara, Acting Inspector-General.

Lieuts. Geo. Baylor and Thos. M. Jack, Aids-de-Camp.

Volunteer Aids-de-Camp, Col. William Preston, Major D. M. Hayden, E. W. Munford, and Calhoun Benham.

Major Albert J. Smith and Captain Wickham, Quartermaster's Department.

To these gentlemen was assigned the last sad duty of accompanying the remains of their lamented chief from the field, except Capts. Brewster and Wickliffe, who remained, and rendered valuable services as staff officers, on the 7th of April.

Governor Isham G. Harris, of Tennessee, went upon the field with Gen. Johnston, was by his side when he was shot, aided him from his horse, and received him in his arms when he died; subsequently the Governor joined my staff and remained with me throughout the next day, except when carrying orders or engaged in encouraging the troops of his own State, to whom he gave a conspicuous example of coolness, zeal and intrepidity.

I am also under many obligations to my own general, personal and volunteer staff, many of whom have been so long associated with me. I append a list of those present on the field on both days, and whose duties carried them constantly under fire, namely:

Col. Thos. Jordan, Capt. Clifton H. Smith and Lieut. John M. Otey, Adjutant General's Department.

Major George W. Brent, Acting Inspector General; Col. R. B. Lee, Chief of Subsistence, whose horse was wounded; Lieut. Col. F. W. Ferguson, and Lieut. A. R. Chisolm, Aid-de-Camp.

Volunteer Aids-de-Camp, Col. Jacob Thompson and Major Numa Hughelin.

Major H. E. Peyton.

Capt. Albert Ferry.

Capt. B. B. Waddell.

Capt. W. W. Porter, of Major-General Crittenden's Staff, also reported for duty, and shared the duties of my volunteer staff on Monday.

Brigadier Gen. Tradeau, of Louisiana Volunteers, also, for a part of the first day's conflict, was with me as a volunteer aid.

Capt. E. H. Cunnings, Signal Officer, also was actively employed as a staff officer on both days.

Nor must I fail to mention that Private W. E. Goldsby, 11th regiment Virginia Volunteers, Orderly to my Headquarters since last June, repeatedly employed to carry my verbal orders to the field, discharged the duty with great zeal and intelligence.

Other members of my staff were necessarily absent from the immediate field of battle, entrusted with responsible duties at these headquarters; namely: Capt. F. H. Jordan, Assistant Adjutant-General in charge of General Headquarters.

Major Eugene E. McLean, Chief Quartermaster; Captain E. Deslonde, Quartermaster's Department.

Lieut. Col. Ferguson, A. D. C., early on Monday was assigned to command and direct the movements of a brigade of the 2d corps.

Lieut. Col. Gilmer, Chief Engineer, after having performed the important and various duties of his place with distinction to himself and material benefit to his country, was wounded late on Monday. I trust, however, I shall not long be deprived of his essential services.

Captain Lockett, Engineer Corps, Chief Assistant to Col. Gilmer, after having been employed in the duties of his corps on Sunday, was placed by me on Monday in command of a battalion without field officers. Capt. Fremeaux, Provisional Engineers, and Lieuts. Steel and Helm, also rendered material and ever dangerous service in the line of their duty.

Major-General (now General) Braxton Bragg, in addition to his duties of Chief of Staff, as has been before stated, commanded his corps—much the largest in the field—on both days with signal capacity and soldiership.

Surgeon Foard, Medical Director, Surgeons R. L. Brodie and S. Choppin, Medical Inspectors, and Surgeon D. W. Yandell, Medical Director of the Western Department with General Johnston, were present in the discharge of their arduous and high duties, which they performed with honor to their profession.

Capt. Tom Saunders, Messrs. Scales and Metcalf, and Mr. Tully, of New Orleans, were of material aid on both days, ready to give news of the enemy's positions and movements regardless of exposure.

While thus partially making mention of some of those who rendered brilliant, gallant or meritorious service in the field, I have aimed merely to notice those whose position would most probably exclude the record of their services from the reports of corps or subordinate commanders.

From this agreeable duty I turn to one in the highest degree unpleasant—one due, however, to the brave men under me, as a contrast to the behavior of most of the army who fought so heroically. I allude to the fact that some officers, non-commissioned officers, and men, abandoned their colors early on the first day to pillage the captured encampments; others retired shamefully from the field on both days, while the thunder of cannon and the roar and rattle of musketry told them that their brothers were being slaughtered by the fresh legions of the enemy. I have ordered the names of the most conspicuous on this roll of laggards and cowards to be published in orders.

It remains to state that our loss in the two days in killed outright was 1,728, wounded 8,012, missing 959—making an aggregate of casualties of 10,099.

This sad list tells in simple language of the stout fight made by our countrymen in front of the rude log chapel of Shiloh, especially when it is known that on Monday, from exhaustion and other causes, not twenty thousand men on our side could be brought into action.

Of the losses of the enemy I have no exact knowledge. Their newspapers report it as very heavy. Unquestionably it was greater, even in proportion, than our own, on both days, for it was apparent to all that their dead left on the field outnumbered ours two to one.

Their casualties, therefore, cannot have fallen many short of 20,000 in killed, wounded, prisoners and missing.

Through information derived from many sources, including the newspapers of the enemy, we engaged on Sunday the Divisions of Generals Prentiss, Sherman, Hurlbut, McClernand, and Smith, of 9,000 men each, or at least 45,000 men. This force was reinforced on Sunday night by the Divisions of Generals Nelson, McCook, Crittenden and Thomas, of Major-General Buell's army, some 25,000 strong, including all arms. Also, General L. Wallace's Division of General Grant's army, making at least 33,000 fresh troops, which, added to the remnant of General Grant's forces—on Monday morning amounting to over 30,000—made an aggregate force of some 53,000 men, at least, arrayed against us on that day.

In connection with the results of the battle, I should state that the most of our men who had inferior arms exchanged them for the improved arms of the enemy. Also, that most of the property, public and personal, in the camp from which the enemy was driven on Sunday, was rendered useless or greatly damaged, except some of the tents.

With this are transmitted certain papers, to-wit:

Order of movements marked "A."

A list of the killed and wounded marked "B."

A list of captured flags marked "C," and a map of the field of battle marked "D."

All of which is respectfully submitted through my volunteer Aid-de-Camp, Col. Jacob Thompson, of Mississippi, who has in charge the flags, standards, and colors, captured from the enemy.

I have the honor to be, General,

Your obedient servant,

G. T. BEAUREGARD,
General Commanding.

To General S. COOPER,
Adj't and Insp'r Gen'l, C. S. Army,
Richmond, Virginia.

[From the Jackson Mississippian.

Picayune Butler's Last.

We learn from gentlemen direct from New Orleans, that this monster, the mention of whose name is nauseous, has consummated his infamy in an order just issued by him. We regret that we could obtain no copy for publication. Its character, is so marked and infamous as to leave but little room for misapprehension. We may, therefore, safely trust the memory of our intelligent informant as to its contents. He states that in return for the *courtesy* and *clemency* shown by the Federal officers to the citizens of New Orleans, the *women* of the city, calling themselves *ladies*, have taken special pleasure in exhibiting their contempt for those officers in various forms; that such conduct, on their part, exposes them to the suspicion of being *women of the town*, engaged in their occupation, and, if so treated by the Federal officers, will have no one to blame but themselves. He further gives notice, that in future any indignity offered to the Federal officials, by word, look, sign, or gesture, will be severely punished.

We knew that the vile sentiment was festering in his heart, but did not suppose he would dare to express it. Is it possible that he can breathe the atmosphere of New Orleans an hour after the issuance of such an order? Is there no Jackson amongst her brave and chivalric sons who will offer himself a martyr in defense of the chastity of the mothers, wives and daughters of the city, and gladly give up his own to take the life of the ruffian and the outlaw, who dares to breathe suspicion against their angelic purity? Is all manhood lost, that such a wretch is allowed to live, move and have his being amongst us? We will not believe it. On the contrary, we shall soon expect to hear that the insult to the fair daughters of New Orleans has been wiped out in the blood of their cowardly slanderer. And when it is done, let the occasion be propitious—not in his orisons, but "when he is drunk, asleep, or in the incestuous pleasures of his bed—then trip him, that his heels may kick at Heaven, and that his soul may be as damned and black as hell whereto it goes."

"Such is Life!"

Two of the enemy's frigates have been anchored several days past, near Quitman's Landing, a few miles above Natchez. Various have been the speculations why they should tarry there, unless they are supply ships or have sickness on board. We are informed, that there have been several burials on shore; over one of the graves, on a neat little head-board, painted in black letters, is the following inscription:

"WILLIAM PRESTON,
Quartermaster U. S. Ship Hartford,
Died May 19th, 1862........Aged 63 years."

This record is ominious. It is but the commencement of the bitter end of those who seek our subjugation for their own aggrandizement. The heat of summer is upon them; sickness and death is overtaking them in their presumptuous aggressions; and the newly turned earth marks their progress through a land of freemen. How sad to contemplate the fate of man so fallen! They seek the bubble fame at our expense; but the delta of the South is their last resting place.

From Corinth.

CORINTH, May 15....All is quiet here. The weather and roads are in good condition, but the enemy hesitates to advance.

Six paroled prisoners were sent off to-day. The escort found the enemy's pickets four miles distant.

Col. Morgan has not been captured as was reported.—*Mississippian.*

BIRTH.

On the 9th of April, 1862, Mrs. GEORGIE CHANDLER, of a daughter.—*Memphis Argus.*

DIED:

At "Forrest Home" near Summit, Miss., May 12th, 1862 from the effects of a wound received at the battle of Shiloh, April 7th, 1862, 1st Sergeant RIALDO JAMES V. DOWNER, of the McNair Rifles, 3rd Battalion Miss. Infantry, aged 26 years and 5 months. R. B. D.

☞ New Orleans papers, please copy.

SEXTON'S REPORT.

Of Deaths in the City of Natchez for the Week ending the **19th of May, 1862.**

May 14—Mrs. Susan B. Smith, heart disease, age about 28 years.
" 15—Negro Child, pneumonia, age 18 mo's.
" 16—Man at S. H., name not reported, dropsy.
" 17—Fanny Tillman, scarlet fever, age 7 yr's.
" 17—Ida Weeks, scarlet fever, age 3½ years.
" 17—E. Irvine Weeks, scarlet fever, age 15 months.
" 19—Catharine Tirnay, inflammation of Toncils.

A true copy from Sexton's Report.

C. F. MERRICK, City Clerk.

Lynchb'g Virginian.

Wednesday, ...May 28, 1862

Destruction of Private Property in War.

It is deemed by some persons a very great hardship that private property should be seized and destroyed by the Government, to prevent its falling into the hands of the enemy. We have heard men say that their tobacco and cotton should not thus be seized and committed to the flames. Such men take a very superficial view of things, and do not seem to understand the obligations of patriotism. If, in a spirit of mere wantonness, the Government should lay violent hands upon, and destroy the property of its citizens, or should appropriate such property to its own use, without offering compensation to the owners, their conduct would be most reprehensible. But the dread exigencies of war frequently require that the Government, in mercy to its citizens, and to strip the enemy of the means of furnishing his army and of protracting war, should apply the torch, and burn what cannot be removed out of the reach of the foe. It may be a hard necessity, but a necessity, nevertheless.

No man ever impeached the integrity, humanity, or unselfish patriotism of the Father of his Country. He, who, for seven weary years, gave up all the comforts of an abounding home—giving his services to his country gratuitously all that time, did not scruple to recommend this policy to his countrymen, and to act upon it himself.

Immediately after the disastrous affair on Long Island and the evacuation of New York, when Washington, in conjunction with Green, Putnam, Lee, Heath, and others, was executing those military movements in the neighborhood of the city which served so greatly to embarrass the enemy, he gave orders that all the stock, hay, grain, &c., that could not or would not be removed out of the way of the enemy, by their owners, should be destroyed. In a letter to Green he thus stated his reasons therefor: "Experience has shown," said he, "that a contrary conduct is not of the least advantage to the poor inhabitants, from whom all their effects of every kind are taken without distinction and without the least satisfaction."

This reasoning was conclusive. If he had failed to destroy such property, it would have been seized and appropriated by the enemy. By depriving them of its use, the owners were not worsted, whilst the cause for which the patriots struggled was benefitted.

According to the examples of the present war, can our readers cite a single instance in which the Yankee marauders have paid the rightful owners, or any body else, one cent for all the cotton that rewarded their freebooting expeditions to the South? There has been no such instance. The enemy expected to be reimbursed for the heavy expense of those piratical expeditions to the Southern coast, by appropriating the large supplies of cotton known to have been retained there. How much better would it have been if the people had [illegible] earlier in the war the same course [illegible] pursuing now? In that event, thousands of bales of cotton that were taken to Northern ports as the trophies and spoils of war, would have been ending, by their ashes, the soil upon which the great staple will be grown hereafter, whilst Northern looms would have been sooner stopped, and the Yankee manufacturers all the earlier reached that beggary to which we hope to see them reduced.

With this experience before us, we hope no man will hereafter hesitate to fire his cotton and tobacco upon the approach of the enemy; but if he should, he may have the satisfaction, if it be any, of seeing his products contribute to the means employed to crush the liberties of his country.

The Great Struggle.

The battle which, above all others is to have most important bearing upon the [illegible] may be joined at any moment, and the Capital of the Confederacy shake in the near approach of armed men, or [illegible] with the thunder of the enemy's [illegible]. Never had men more to inspire them to perform great and heroic deeds.—[illegible] side, the early achievement of our [illegible], and the fate of the most beautiful city in the whole South, are the issues. Thousands upon thousands of the fair daughters of Virginia, within sound of the enemy's guns, will listen with attentive ears and eager hearts for the couriers who shall bring tidings of the progress of the battle.

Oh, what agonising suspense will be there! Will Heaven bless the arms of our brave men, that the fate of the women of New Orleans may not await those of the proud Capital of Virginia!

Who can tell what a brutal enemy, flushed with success after the termination of such a battle as that must be, will do? Or rather, what would he not do? The heart sickens at the thought of any thing short of a signal victory for our army.

Upon the other hand; see what the enemy has to goad him on. For more than twelve months his legions have been marshalled for this fight. The capture of Richmond has been their theme by day and by night. Their President, Cabinet officers, Congressmen and Generals have descanted in their hearing, upon the success of the great achievement committed to their arms. The eyes of the civilized world are upon them, and if they fail, the great booty is lost, and the brilliant scheme of subjugation is a failure. An indignant and outraged people will rise up in their wrath to smite and destroy the desolaters of their homes, and the destroyers of their peace. This is the fate that awaits the hired mercenaries who now pollute our soil; and that they will be impelled to fight with desperation, no man can doubt.

We have indicated the motives that must animate the contending hosts. Which should be the stronger, and prevail?—the love of home, of liberty, of our women and children and all our sacred rights; or the spirit of adventure and the lust of booty which predominate in the breasts of our mercenary invaders? Suppose they even outnumber us? What of that?—Said Antigonus to his army under similar circumstances, "but, my soldiers, how many do you reckon me for?"

Must not the soldiers of liberty, their patriotic leaders and holy cause, be accounted something? If it was a crime for a Roman soldier to fear while Cæsar lived, how can our soldiers fear with such leaders as Johnston and the host of brave, wise, and true men who stand in front of them, whilst the women of Richmond are breathing out prayers and good wishes for their success.

With these sources of inspiration, and trusting in that Being who defends the right, how can our gallant soldiers fail?

"Hurrah for Jackson!"

This, in other days, was the shibboleth of a great party; and it bids fair to be revived with even more than its former witchery. All over the land we may now hear "hurrah for Jackson!" the brave, indomitable "stone wall" Jackson. If the gallant Virginian were not in the prime of life—only thirty-nine, with the promise of many years of usefulness before him—we should feel inclined to cry hurrah for old "Stone wall." Jackson is the man for the times, and if a kind Providence will watch over and preserve his valuable life, his name alone, will be worth fifty thousand soldiers.

All honor to Jackson! and may a grateful country have him and his matchless troops embalmed in its affections. Long may the dashing knights of the Shenandoah Valley live in story and in song.

The reader is referred to Jackson's account of himself in our telegraphic column to-day.

LATEST FROM THE NORTH.

THE ATTACK ON DREWRY'S BLUFF—WHOLESALE LYING—FROM NORFOLK, ETC

Northern papers of the 20th inst. contain the first Northern account of the affair at Drewry's Bluff (15th inst.) which has reached us. We published a synopsis of the report under the telegraphic head, in Saturday's paper. From the numerous statements in the account, which we know to be false, it is fair to infer that the Yankee writer at Fortress Monroe has not given the full extent of the damage to the Yankee flotilla. He says:

The great anxiety which has prevailed here for a week past to hear from the expedition up James river, has at last been gratified.

This afternoon the little Naugatuck was descried coming down the Roads, and immediately the anxious ones hurried to the beach to ask whether "the Monitor was shelling Richmond?"

Having conversed with one of the officers of the Naugatuck, I am enabled to give you the following interesting particulars:

Last Sunday morning the Monitor, Galena and Naugatuck started for the rebel capital via James river. They were immediately followed by the Aroostook and Port Royal.

They silenced several of the batteries which lined the shore, and passed some with the most contemptuous silence. [All a lie.]

The Captain of the Monitor stood upon the turret and waved his cap to a battery which he considered unworthy of the notice of his pet, although three balls struck the Monitor's turret with considerable force.

The progress of the fleet was a continued success *until* they arrived to within about seven miles of Richmond. Here the river takes a sharp turn around a precipitous bluff fully one hundred and fifty feet in height. [Another Munchausenism.]

Upon the top of this bluff the rebels have erected a most *scientific and formidable battery*, mounting many guns of superior range and calibre. This battery commands the river in the most effective manner, and it soon became evident to our fleet that an engagement of no ordinary character was imminent.

On last Thursday morning, at seven o'clock, our fleet formed their line of battle and commenced the reduction of the rebel stronghold.

From the unusual elevation of the battery, and the difficulty our men experienced in getting the proper range, they were for a time unable to do any execution. In the meantime the battery poured an *incessant fire of shell and ball* down upon the decks of our vessels and did a *fearful work!*

The Naugatuck, after several brilliant shots, burst her one-hundred pound rifled Parrott gun killing the gunner and wounding several others. Having no other armament except two boarding howitzers, and being thus disabled, she withdrew from the engagement.

The Galena suffered severely—the rebel shots riddling her deck with great ease, and several of the balls entering her side. Fourteen of her crew were killed and thirteen wounded; the majority of the latter, however, will recover. Those who were killed were terribly cut and mangled—none beyond the hope of recognition. For one hour the Galena was exposed to the entire fire of the rebel battery. On account of the narrowness of the channel, she could not "spring" or turn so as to work to advantage.

The Monitor, however, maintained her superior strength and invulnerability.—The balls glanced harmless from her tower of strength and fell into the placid waters of the river. For sometime she labored under the greatest difficulty in acquiring the requisite elevation for her guns. But having once obtained it she poured her missiles with fearful effect upon the battery, and thus encouraging her associates the fleet belched forth such iron hail that the battery was silenced for three quarters of an hour. At this juncture our vessel *ran short of ammunition*, and retired from action, while the rebels re-manned their guns and again commenced the conflict.—A portion of the fleet came down the river to Jamestown Island, near Williamsburg. The Monitor and Galena remained in order to keep the rebels awake, the Monitor firing regularly once in two minutes, (it is stated above that the ammunition gave out—liars should have good memories,) fully sustaining the reputation of the "chese box" The Aroostook and Port Royal were not materially injured. The action lasted four hours and a-half, constituting one of the most brilliant of the war.

About a quarter of a mile further up the river the rebels have made a strong barricade to the further progress of a hostile fleet. They have sunk the Yorktown and Jamestown in the channel, and driven immense piles from one side of the river to the other, forming a stockade similar to that in the entrance to Norfolk harbor.

The guns of the battery are said to be manned by the remnants of the crews of The Merrimac, Yorktown and Jamestown the firing was excellent, showing a great deal of skill.

The Naugatuck escaped serious injury by having her pilot house and deck protected by iron rails laid transversely.

ANOTHER AND MORE TRUTHFUL ACCOUNT.

A letter dated Baltimore, 19th inst., says

The Old Point boat arrived this morning at the usual hour.

A gentleman who was at Fortress Monroe and Norfolk yesterday, furnishes the following information:

The repulse of the gunboats at Fort Darling, seven or eight miles below Richmond, was generally regarded as *a very serious affair*, though no full account of it has been made public.

On board the Naugatuck *eighteen men* were reported killed by the explosion of a big gun. The boat was, of course, made useless in the fight, and was withdrawn.

The Galena was riddled by the shots from the Rebel batteries, having been perforated" as in the despatch said, no less than eighteen times. The loss of life on board was not stated, but it was thought to be heavy.

The Monitor was struck repeatedly, but was said to be uninjured. She, however, could do nothing offensive, as the batteries are on so high a bluff that it was impossible to give her guns sufficient elevation for the proper range.

EFFECT OF THE NEWS.

The repulse of the gunboats had a depressing effect at Philadelphia and New York. The Philadelphia Inquirer says "our people have acquired such voracious appetites for victory, that nothing short of complete and instant triumph in every undertaking will now satisfy them. Hence the news of the temporary check to the James river squadron, on Thursday last, threw a film of shadow over the broad countenances of the people.

A letter from New York, dated May 10, says: "The town was in a very bad humor all the morning The unsatisfactory telegram about the mishap to our gunboats up the James river, was productive of a very general diffusion of 'blues.' That class of people who always prefer the gloomy side of a picture were certain that the affair was a regular 'skedaddle,' and that the prestige of the Monitor was gone."

COMMERCIAL.

LYNCHBURG MARKETS.

REPORTED BY

A. B. RUCKER,

PRODUCE BROKER,

138 MAIN STREET.

☞ These quotations, it will be understood, represent wholesale prices generally.

APPLES.—Green—none offering.

BACON.—Continues to arrive slowly, with sales 28 to 30c.

BEESWAX.—Receipts continue light, with sales 30 @32c.

BUTTER.—Choice for table scarce and sells readily in packages suited for shipping at 55@62½c Cooking 40@50c.

CORN MEAL.—Stock light—$1.00 to 1.05

CORN.—Receipts light. Last sales at $1.00.

CLOVER SEED.—$12 to 12.50.

FRUIT.—Dried Apples $1 50 to $1.75 per bushel—28 pounds; Unpealed Peaches $2.40 to $2.75 per bushel—33 pounds; Pealed Peaches $4.50 to $5 per bushel—40 pounds.

FLOUR.—With light receipts. Superfine $7 to 7.25; Extra $7.30 to 7.75; Family $8 to 8.25.

FLAXSEED.—The demand for sewing has increased the demand. Sales $1.75 to 1.80.

FEATHERS.—Dull at 37 cents.

GRASS SEED.—The large receipts of Clover has caused a considerable decline. I notice sales at $14 to $15; Timothy $4 to $4.50; Orchard $1.75 to $2.00; Evergreen $1.75 to $2.00; Randal $1.75 to $2.00; Herds $1.50.

HAY—Baled $1.40 to $1.50; per wagon load $1.25 to 1.35.

LIME—Mountain $2 to $2.25.

IRON—With increased demand, I notice sales $175 to 185 per ton.

LARD—Demand good—21@22c.

ONIONS—Stock light—$2.75 to $3 per bushel.

OATS—Sheaf $1.40 to 1.50 ☞ wagon load; Shelled—70c. for White; 75 cts. for Black per bushel 33 pounds.

TOBACCO—Sales continue light, but prices are well maintained. Lugs $2 to $4.50; Leaf $5 to 8.50 for good shipping; Manufacturing $8 to $15.

WHEAT.—$1.30 to 1.35 for Red; $1.35 to 1.40 for oice White.

LOCAL AND STATE AFFAIRS.

Dr. S. D. Hopkins, of Fincastle, is authorized to receive subscribers for the Virginian.

All day yesterday and the day before, our people were joyous at the intelligence from the Valley, and honor to Jackson and his gallant men was freely accorded.

We have never seen the people of the city more jubilant, though no extravagance was manifested in their demonstrations.

We lost only three officers, Capts. Sheet, Fletcher and Paxton. We expect to get Banks and his army.

Such is the substance of a telegram to the Governor respecting the battle at Winchester.

TRIBUTE OF RESPECT.—At a meeting of Co. A (Rifle Greys) 11th Regt. Va. Vols. held around the Bivouac fires, on Chickahominy River, Monday evening, May 13th 1862 Lieut. J. A. Kennedy was requested to preside. Sergt. Wm. H. Taylor was appointed Secretary. The following preamble and resolutions were offered and unanimously adopted:

Whereas, It has pleased our Heavenly Father, to take from our ranks and society, our gallant, daring, and cherished comrades, Jno. R. Raine, John F. Gooldy, S. P. Stewart, John H. Slagle and Wm. H. Torrence, while nobly fighting for freedom, against tyranny, invasion, and oppression on the battle field of Williamsburg, fought May 5th 1862.

Be it resolved 1st. That by the deaths of our above named companions, our country has lost five brave, loyal, and patriotic defenders; ourselves five accomplished true and manly friends.

2nd, That whilst we miss their gay laugh, merry wit, and dry joke, around our fires at night, and feel saddened that they should be taken from amongst us, in the bloom of youth, and usefulness, we rejoice that we can answer proudly to all interrogatories, "dead on the field of honor."

3rd. That a non-commissioned officer be appointed to answer for them at every Roll-Call, so as to keep forever green in our memory, their numerous chivalrous deeds, and that the company were the usual badge of mourning for 30 days.

4th. *Resolved*, That a copy of these resolutions be sent to the bereaved Parents or friends of the heroic dead, and that our Captain be requested to communicate the unutterable sorrow which oppresses us, in a letter of condolence to the same.

5th *Resolved*, That the proceedings of this meeting be published in the Lynchburg papers.

LIEUT. JOS. A. KENNEDY, President.
SERGT. WM. H. TAYLOR, Secretary.

MARRIED,

On Monday, May 26th, by Rev. Wm. H. Kinckle, Mr JOHN F. MITCHELL and Miss NANNIE TOMPKINS, daughter of Henry Hall all of this city.

At the residence of the bride's father, A. T. Blanks, Esq, in the county of Halifax, on the 13th inst., Miss KATE BLANKS, to Maj. A. G Pendleton, jr., of the 4th Regiment Virginia Volunteers.

☞ Richmond papers copy.

At Union Station church, on Thursday, the 22d, by the Rev. MR CHRISTIAN, JAMES H. COGHILL to Miss ADDIE KELLY, third daughter of Nelson Kelly, Esq., all of Henrico county.

OBITUARY.

DIED, of typhoid pneumonia, on Tuesday, the 29th ult., at his late residence in Campbell county, Va., about 4 miles east of the village of Leesville, BEVERLY ARNOLD, consort of Susan G. Arnold, at the ripe age of 64 years, 11 months and 9 days.

The deceased had been in feeble health for many years, but the illness of which he died was of but one week's duration. He was conscious for several days preceeding his death, that the hour of dissolution was rapidly approaching; and though fully persuaded that his days were numbered, he was calm to the last, and breathed his last without a struggle, just as the King of Day sank beneath the horizon. He leaves a widow and two sons to mourn their loss. Although there is no remarkable event in his history for us to record, yet we would fail to do him justice should we omit to notice some prominent traits in his character of sterling value. Industry, economy, fidelity, veracity, integrity, temperance, love of order and peace and obedience to the "power that be," characterized him throughout his life. We might truthfully and appropriately inscribe on his tombstone, Hic jacet vis probes. He was an affectionate husband, a kind and indulgent father and lenient master.

He and his companion lived together peacefully, harmoniously and happily for nearly two score years embracing the palmiest days of our once glorious Republic, enjoying many of the blessings attendant upon national prosperity; but scarcely had the sun of our national glory set, and the last lingering ray of twilight faded, and the night—the dark and stormy night of adversity—drawn its mouth over our national sky, ere the faithful and affectionate wife was called to relinquish her claim upon him, who had so long and so faithfully loved, honored, protected and supported her, and pursue the remainder of her journey through this "wilderness of woe," solitary and alone, amid the "darkness and gloominess and thick clouds," that hang like a pall over our beloved land. May He who has promised to be a husband to the widow and father to the fatherless, fulfil that promise to this bereaved family. May they bow submissively to this afflictive dispensation, and lean confidingly upon the arm of our Heavenly Father; and so will it redound to their spiritual good unto edification.

May the presence of the Lord be the widow's comfort and solace; and may the sons take warning and "set their houses in order," and "prepare to meet their God."

S.

Col. BENJAMIN T. PRESTON, of Franklin county, Va., is dead. He died at his residence on the 18th day of the present month (May,) in the 38th year of his age. His disease was consumption.

Col. Preston was an upright man, and highly esteemed by all who knew him. He was kind as a husband, father, neighbor and master.

He had for several years been a member of the Baptist Church. As such, he was consistent and useful. He died in full assurance of faith. He leaves a devoted companion and a large circle of relations and friends to mourn their loss, but they sorrow not as those without hope.

P.

Died, on Tuesday morning the 27th inst., KINKLE, son of John and Mary Jane Henry. The funeral will take place this morning at the residence of Mr. Henry, and the remains will be carried thence to Friend's Burying Ground for interment. The friends and acquaintances of the family are invited to attend.

FUNERAL NOTICES.

The funeral of BENJAMIN MATHEWS KYLE will be preached on Sunday, June 1st, 1862, by the Rev. H. P. Mitchell, of Lynchburg.

The friends of the deceased, as well as the friends of Capt. Jno. S. Kyle, are invited to attend.
may 28-c3t

The Funeral Services of MORRIS CONSTANTINE, son of T. C. S. and A. H. Ferguson, will take place at his Father's residence this evening at 4 o'clock.

The friends and acquaintances of the family, are invited to attend.

VIRGINIA:—At rules held in the Clerk's office of the Circuit Court of Campbell County, on Monday, the 5th day of May, 1862:

Richard G. Brown, surviving partner of himself and Henry W. Brown, late merchants and partners trading under the style and firm of R. G. Brown & Son, Plaintiff.

Against.

James W. Pendleton, surviving partner of himself and William Bayliss Rector, late merchants and partners trading under the style and firm of James W. Pendleton & Co. Defendant.

IN CHANCERY.

The object of this suit is to recover against the defendant $212 90, with legal interest thereon from the 22d day of December, 1861, until paid, and the costs attending such recovery; and to attach the estate of the defendant, consisting of a tract of land near Concord Depot, in said county, containing 8 acres and 5⅛ poles, and to subject the same to the payment of the plaintiff's demand and it appearing by proper affidavit filed that the defendant is not a resident of this State, it is ordered that he appear here within one month after due publication hereof, and do what is necessary to protect his interests.

A copy—Teste,
JNO D. ALEXANDER, Clerk.
JNO. C. MURRILL, P. Q.
may 10-w4w

LATEST BY THE MAILS.

THE POSITION OF THE FEDERAL FORCES IN THE VALLEY.

The movements of the Yankee forces in the Valley and Western Virginia have of late been so intricate and erratic that it has been difficult to keep up with their different geographical positions. But by a very late arrival from General JACKSON'S headquarters, we have been placed in posession of their supposed locations and forces up to Friday night last. The successes of General JACKSON since that time have, of course, affected their positons materially, but we give the intelligence for what it is worth. General WILLIAMSON, with a brigade, had gone to reinforce MILROY, after his defeat, who was in the vicinity of Franklin, in Western Virginia, on the Romney road. Shields had given the Confederate forces the slip, and had crossed the ridge with about 10,000 men, and, as report says, had effected a junction with McDowell at Fredricksburg. Blenker, with between ten thousand and twelve thousand Dutch, was at or near Front Royal, on the Shenandoah, and his division is the one that Jackson found and defeated previous to his descent upon Winchester.

BANKS was at and between Newtown and Winchester with about twelve thousand men, and Jackson in his rear, between Front Royal and Winchester, eighteen miles distant from the latter place General Hatch and Schenck are with Banks, holding subordinate commands. Williamson, after reinforcing Milroy, would, it was known, in the event of the capture of Winchester, be compelled to move back towards Cumberland, Maryland. Cheat Mountain was in possession of two thousand Confederate guerrillas, and his retreat in that direction would be checked. The mountain position was taken immediately after the battle of McDowell.—*Examiner*.

PRAYER CONTRABAND.—It appears that Picayune Butler intends to regulate the religion of the people of New Orleans Apprehending that they might do some obnoxious praying on last Friday, he issued the following order. Butler, by his brutal orders, is doing good service in the Southern cause:

NOTICE.

HEADQ'RS DEPARTMENT OF THE GULF
New Orleans, May 13, 1862.

General Orders, No. 27.

It having come to the knowledge of the Commanding General that Friday next is proposed to be observed as a day of fasting and prayer, in obedience to some supposed proclamation of one Jefferson Davis, in the several churches of the city, it is ordered that no such observances be had.

"Churches and religious houses are to be kept open, as in times of profound peace." but no religious exercises are to be had upon the supposed authority above mentioned.

By command of Major Gen. BUTLER.
Geo. C Strong, A. A General.

THE WAR IN THE SOUTHWEST.

A letter to the Memphis *Appeal*, from Corinth, dated May 15, says:

We have at last reached that stage of the war, however, when the final issue must be met. The decisive conflict cannot be avoided much longer. A fight, then, must be here, or near here, soon, that will go far towards deciding the great struggle, whether we are to be bondsmen, hewers of wood and drawers of water to those we hate, or whether we are to be free. All the available resources of the West and Northwest, both of men and money, are concentrated before us. Defeat would be utter destruction. Retreat, worse. For it would involve all alike in irremediable ruin and disgrace. Fight, then, they must and that before the summer solstice is over. And on the result of that fight it depends whether we are to overrun their country or they overrun ours. The issue is a great one. It involves the end of the war. Everything depends upon it. Hence Halleck's hesitation of his Government. If he is whipped here, as he doubtless will be all the country north of us will be open to our victorious army. but from all the land will go up such a howl of despair as has never been heard from any people.

THE PRISONERS TO BE PAROLED.

Orders were received from Gen. Beauregard, says the Macon *Telegraph*, to put the Northern prisoners at Camp Oglethorpe upon parole. As soon thereafter as descriptive rolls can be made out and they are sworn not to bear arms in this war until regularly exchanged, they will be sent up to the Federal lines beyond Chattanooga, and there turned loose to seek their homes, which we hope they will enjoy so much as to avoid assailing those of other people.—The prisoners were highly edified with the tidings yesterday.

PROMOTIONS.

Colonel Samuel Garland of the 11th Va. Regiment, has been appointed Brigadier General, and assigned to the Brigade lately commanded by Gen. Early. He has won his distinction by faithful service, and the exhibition of high military talent.

Lieut. Col. David Funsten is thus promoted to the rank of Colonel and the command of the Regiment. The Regiment, although regretting to lose Col. Garland, could not have been better pleased with any sucessor than Colonel Funsten. Major Morris Langhorne becomes Lieutenant Colonel, and Capt. Clement takes rank as Major.—*Enquirer*

WHAT THE YANKEES ARE DOING.—In pursuance of their "on to Richmond" idea, the Yankees have transported rolling stock up the Pamunkey river to the White House, and are now running trains from that point nearly up to Dispatch station, on the York River Railroad. A telegraph line has been constructed, and is now working, from McClellan's headquarters at New Kent Court House, to Washington city.—*Dispatch.*

A CONFEDERATE SHIP RESCUED FROM HER CAPTORS.

The Mobile *Advertiser*, of the 20th, publishes a telegram from Charleston, which we have no recollection of having seen in any other quarter. It states that the captain and crew of the Charleston ship Emily St Pierre, captured some time ago by the blockaders off Charleston harbor, rose on their captors, who were taking the vessel to New York, overpowered the Yankee prize crew who had been placed in charge of her, and carried the vessel back to Liverpool.

Mr. Adams, the United States Minister to England, on learning of her arrival, demanded from the British Government the restoration of the vessel.

The accuracy of the statement above made, we have no means of determining, but hope it may be correct. We have observed nothing with reference to it in any Northern news that has reached us.

To all Whom it may Concern.

NOTICE is hereby given to all absentees from the 2nd Va. Cavalry, whether on sick leave or otherwise, without proper authority, that, unless they report to their respective companies on or before the 25th day of May, they will be published as deserters.

The Sheriffs and Constables of the counties of Albemarle, Amherst, Appomattox, Bedford, Botetourt, Campbell, Franklin and the city of Lynchburg, are earnestly requested to *apprehend* any man they may find in these counties after the 25th of May. A reward of $25 will be paid for each man delivered at my camp.

I am instructed by Major Gen. Ewell, commanding 3d Division, to say that he will allow absentees to be transferred into Infantry and their places supplied by the drafted men, who are anxious to furnish their own horses

I regret to announce publicly that there are over 100 men absent from this Regiment, most of whom are perfectly well. Mothers, sisters and sweet hearts, remember that the gallant loved ones now in the field are doing double duty—that the reason they are never had a furlough is because these laggards are away. Your noble boys can't be spared and they are too generous and brave to shrink from duty.

The military authorities at Lynchburg are earnestly requested to drive such men back to camp.

THOMAS T. MUNFORD,
Colonel 2nd Va. Cavalry.
may 24-5t

VIRGINIA: At Rules held in the Clerk's office of the County Court of Bedford County on Monday, the 5th day of May, 1862:

Jesse L. Quarles and John R. Steptoe, late partners and tavern keepers, who sue for the benefit of John R. Steptoe, Plaintiffs.

Against

Samuel H. Gwatkin, Edmund W. Horsley in his own right, and as administrator of Mary Gwatkin, dec'd, and Lucy his wife William A. Hardy and Catharine his wife, John W. Otey and Francis his wife, James Gwatkin, George Johnson and Eliza his wife, ——— Flant and Mary his wife, Defendants.

IN CHANCERY.

The object of this suit is to subject the interest of the defendant, Samuel H. Gwatkin, in the estate of Mary Gwatkin, dec'd, to the payment of the sum of $351 51 as of the 25th day of April, 1862, the amount of the plaintiff's demand.

And it appearing by affidavit filed, that the defendants Samuel H. Gwatkin, James Gwatkin, George Johnson and Eliza his wife, ——— Flant and Mary his wife, are not inhabitants of this State it is ordered that they do appear here within one month after due publication hereof, and do what is necessary to protect their interests, and that a copy of this order be published for four weeks successively in the Lynchburg Virginian, a newspaper published in the city of Lynchburg, and posted at the front door of the Courthouse of this County, on the first day of the next term of this Court.

A copy—teste,
A. A. ARTHUR, Clerk.
WM. L. GOGGIN, P. Q.
may 8-w4w

BY TELEGRAPH.

Further from Gen. Jackson's Victory.

Richmond, May 27.—The following dispatch was received by Gov. Letcher this morning:

STAUNTON, May 27.

Banks' army is routed completely. He is still flying in utter consternation; worse than Bull Run.

Cannon, stores, and provisions are still being captured by our forces.

Official From Gen. Jackson.

WINCHESTER, May 26.

To GEN. S. COOPER, Adj't. Gen:

During the last three days, God has blessed our arms with brilliant success.

On Friday, the Federals at Front Royal were routed, and one section of their artillery, in addition to many prisoners, were captured.

On Saturday, Banks' main column, while retreating from Strasburg to Winchester, was pierced in the rear, part retreating towards Strasburg.

Sunday, the other part was routed at this place.

At last accounts, Brig.-Gen. George W. Stewart was pressing them with cavalry and artillery and capturing fugitives.

A large amount of medical ordnance, and other stores have fallen into our hands.

[Signed] T. J. JACKSON,
Major-General Commanding.

The Enemy About Vicksburg.

VICKSBURG, May 26.

Two vessels arrived at the fleet to-day. They are supposed to be Yankees waiting an attack.

All quiet here to-day.

Battle Anticipated at Richmond.

RICHMOND, May 27th.—There was heavy skirmishing from 1 to 7 o'clock this afternoon in direction of Hanover C. H., and is believed to be in that vicinity. The cannonading was heard here.

No particulars have yet been received. This skirmish is believed here to be the prelude to a general engagement.

2D DISPATCH.

PARTICULARS OF THE FIGHT AT HANOVER, C. H.

Yankee Loss 180—Confederate's 6.

RICHMOND May 27th.—In the skirmish this afternoon at Hanover C. H., the twenty-fifth New York and the twenty-eight North Carolina Regiments were principally engaged. Eighty Federals were killed and sixty captured. The prisoners have arrived here. The confederate loss is 6 or 8.

Nothing has yet been heard from the skirmish at Atlee's Station.

THE PHILADELPHIA INQUIRER.

FRIDAY, MAY 30. 1862.

The Latest News!

From McClellan's Army.

Jackson's Communication with Richmond Cut off!

Retreat of Gen. Banks!

List of Killed & Wounded

Letter from Norfolk, Va.

Origin and Result of a Riot there.

The Battle of Shiloh!

Beauregard's Report-Rebel Loss 10699

Late from New Orleans.

General Butler restoring Order.

From Fortress Monroe!

FORNEY'S WAR PRESS

VOL. 1. PHILADELPHIA, SATURDAY, MAY 31, 1862. NO. 29.

RICHMOND THE CAPITAL OF REBELDOM.—SKETCHED AND ENGRAVED FOR THE WAR PRESS.—See fourth page.

THE CASKET OF LETTERS.

A STORY OF THE WAR.

BY ESSEX.

Susie Carroll was a handsome Kentucky girl, full of spirit and daring, and not afraid of anything when she knew she was in the right. She was engaged to Raymond Belmont, a fine young fellow, one of those noble specimens of manly beauty that we find nowhere in greater perfection than in the fair State of Kentucky. This engagement no one suspected, except Susie's elder sister Agatha, a quiet, gentle lady. The sisters were orphans. They lived with their uncle, Judge Benton, and as they had lost their parents in early childhood it had drawn the bonds of affection very strongly between them.

There was little sympathy between the girls and their uncle. He was a stern, cold man—a strong Secessionist—his only son in the rebel army, and the Misses Carroll were devoted to the Union. Young Belmont, too, was heart and soul with the cause of his country, though he durst not openly avow his sentiments, as the community in which they lived was outwardly devoted to the rebel cause, and around the town "Confederate" camps lay thick and strong. Only when quite alone did these three dare to whisper to each other their real sentiments, and try to contrive a means of escape from the home they had once loved, but which now seemed like a prison.

Of course, Susie's beauty attracted to her side many of the rebel officers, and while secretly hating the cause in which they were engaged, she yet sometimes, with pardonable coquetry, found amusement in their society, and a mischievous pleasure in tormenting them. So it happened that one mild summer evening—for we are writing of events that happened some time ago, before Kentucky was ours—that Susie sat in the parlor playing chess with Capt. Johnston, a rebel Zouave officer. The games had gone on to Susie's success, and she had won, on the first, candy, on the second, gloves.

"Now," cried the Captain, "just one more game, Miss Susie; I don't like to go off defeated entirely. What will you bet?"

"Nothing," said Susie; "let's play for fun."

"Oh, no! I won't do that; it is not exciting enough. Come, I'll make you a tempting offer. I'll bet my diamond ring against your casket;" and he pointed to a small inlaid box that stood at Susie's side.

She started and turned pale. That box contained Raymond's letters to her. There was in it what Captain Johnston would have called "treason" enough to ruin them both. She was so fearful that some accident might happen to it, that she had recently been in the habit of often carrying it about with her when she could not leave it in Agatha's charge, and her solicitude regarding it had awakened Captain Johnston's curiosity, perhaps his suspicions.

Now, she hastily protested that she did not care for the ring, and would rather play for nothing. But the Captain insisted; and, suddenly fearing that her persistence might arouse his suspicions, she consented, believing that she should certainly win.

"Well," she said, "I consent on one condition.

"What is that?"

"That you will give me the countersign for to-night."

It was the Captain's turn to hesitate—but after a moment, with a laugh and a muttered "I don't see what good it can do you," he gave it "*Manassas.*"

Only half satisfied was Susie. Confident in her superior ability, she allowed the game to begin. But whether her great desire to win this time made her less clear-headed, or whether the Captain had concealed his real powers until now, at the end of half an hour she found herself checkmated, and Johnston in possession of her casket. Greatly distressed, poor Susie yet durst not remonstrate, and, as if he feared some opposition, the Captain rose at once, and taking a hasty farewell, walked off in triumph with the box under his arm.

As soon as he was gone, Susie rushed up stairs to Agatha, who had been out early in the evening, and now sat alone in her room.

"Oh, sister! dear sister!" she cried, "that horrid Johnston has got my casket!"

"What!" exclaimed Agatha, starting up, pale and trembling, for she knew what that announcement implied only too well. "Why, how came he to get it. Oh, Susie! Susie! this comes of your coquetry, and now we shall all be ruined!" And sinking down, she buried her face in her hands, while Susie, in rapid words, told all that had happened.

"Oh! what shall we do? what shall we do?" moaned Agatha; "if they read those papers they will kill Raymond and put us in prison."

Susie was very pale, but she said resolutely, "Agatha, Captain Johnston shall never read those papers; I will have them back to-night."

"Why, Susie! what do you mean?"

"I mean what I say," replied Susie resolutely. "My culpable self-confidence has done the mischief. I never dreamed he would be able to beat me at chess. I would not have taken his ring, but I never thought to risk my casket; yet I had no right to be so reckless; now I must undo what I have done."

"And how can you get them?"

"From his tent."

"You in Captain Johnston's tent!" gasped Agatha, "Susie, are you crazy?"

"I never was more calm. I have the countersign, and I can get into camp; the Captain sleeps alone, and I think I shall succeed."

The horror on Agatha's face was something amazing to see. "Susie," she cried, starting forward, "what do I hear you say? Why, they will not let a woman inside the camp even with the countersign."

It was Susie's turn to look surprised. "Why, you dear simpleton," she said, "you don't suppose I intend to go in my present dress?"

"How then?" asked Agatha, half relieved, half distressed.

"I am going to steal John's Zouave dress; I know where he keeps it. I am about the height of the Captain's orderly. I noticed him when we were in camp; he is a short, good-looking boy. I have no doubt I can succeed in deceiving him; so come, now, get your wits about you, and help me to dress, that's a good girl."

It took Agatha some time to comprehend all, still longer to give her consent to her sister's starting on this wild expedition; but Susie had so much courage and energy, and the crisis seemed so imminent, that at last she consented to give what help her shaky fingers were capable of affording.

It was now quite late, and all the house was asleep, as they stole softly up stairs to the entry wardrobe, where hung the Zouave uniform young Benton had worn when the war first began, and which he had since exchanged for a cavalry dress. In essential points it was like the uniform worn by the regiment to which Capt. Johnston belonged, and from its baggy make, formed an admirable disguise for the figure and walk. Dressed in it, Susie looked like a very promising young recruit; but all was not yet done, and seizing a scissors before Agatha could prevent her, she began to cut off her splendid hair. Agatha fairly cried as the raven masses fell in a lustrous black heap into the snowy towel, and when her sister was gone, she carefully put away those splendid tresses as a memento of those dark hours of the rebellion.

Some brown paint from her box of water-colors dyed her fair cheeks till they looked as if they might have been long exposed to the Southern sun; and then hiding a sharp knife and a tiny pistol, that Raymond had given her, in her belt, and giving her sister one farewell kiss, Susie was ready for her adventurous expedition.

Fortunately, it was a dark and moonless night, and Susie stole unobserved down the yard and out of the gate. Then she paused a moment to still the beating of her heart—for, to tell the truth, she was very nervous—but, remembering all that was at stake on her courage, she tried to grow more calm, and was soon able to go on with steady steps. Trying to assume an air of indifference, she walked boldly on down the street. Once or twice the patrol challenged her; but her steady replies disarmed suspicion, and so she passed on until she reached the lines of Captain Johnston's camp. The sentry on duty there brought his piece to bear, with a sharp cry of "Halt!" as he caught a glimpse of Susie's boyish-looking figure. She stopped, with her heart again beating painfully.

"Advance and give the countersign."

With a great effort Susie mastered an emotion and stepped out. "Manassas," she said in a firm voice.

"All right;" and the frightful musket was lowered as the sentry resumed his march, while Susie glided past him into the camp.

It was all still and quiet there. The men had long since gone to sleep, and only the loud snoring of some stentorian slumberer sounded on the quiet air. There were no lights to be seen except in the guard-house and one or two of the officers' tents, and Susie stole on, congratulating herself on her security, when at a turn in the canvas straet she came on the officer of the guard going the "the grand rounds."

"Helloa," he cried, stopping short, and laying his hand on Susie's shoulder, "what are you out for?"

Susie was ready to drop. The young man was one she knew very well and recognition seemed inevitable; but the very imminence of the danger gave her courage.

"Captain's orderly, if you please, sir," she said, drawing gently away.

"What captain's?"

Here was an awful dilemma, but she answered, finally, "Captain Johnston, Company I."

"Oh! little Tom; to be sure, I remember; but what brought you out so late?"

"Captain sent me in town."

"The deuce he did! he's a pretty fellow. I shall report him for improper conduct in letting his orderly out so late."

Susie did not care to remonstrate, but with a military salute, very creditably given, hurried away towards Johnston's tent.

Her courage almost failed her. What if he were already reading those fatal letters? As she came in view of it she saw that the light was burning, and her breath almost ceased. How could she find out if she was too late? Very cautiously she stole to the side of the tent, and peeped in between the flaps. Her casket stood on the table, and Johnston, seated near, was drawing off his boots. As he kicked them out of the way he laid his hand on the box, and involuntarily Susie's slight fingers crept to the handle of her pistol.

"No, by Jove!" he muttered, suddenly drawing his hand away, and starting up. "It seems too bad to break open the little thing's casket. I won't do it without consulting the colonel; though, if she is a d—d Abolitionist, she deserves anything."

"Kentucky chivalry!" Susie ground the words between her teeth, and wondered with intense astonishment what had made him suspect her.

Meantime she kept a sharp watch on Johnston, who took up the cabinet and set it carefully on a shelf that ran across the tent; then seizing a pencil, wrote a few words hastily on a slip of paper, and went to the door of his tent.

"Tom!"

Susie shrank away, fearing the orderly would appear, but there was no reply.

"Tom!" he shouted, again adding below his breath—"Confound the boy, how he sleeps."

Susie gave one hasty glance towards the orderly's tent; there were no signs of life, and thinking it better to play the part herself, than that he should be roused, she stepped forward.

"Oh, here you are, Tom. What a while you were coming! You must be quicker than this if you ever hear the long roll at midnight. Here, take this note to the colonel the first thing in the morning."

"Yes, sir;" and Susie took the note and pretended to hurry off, but she went only just beyond the tent and there watched till she had the satisfaction of seeing the light put out in Johnston's tent. Then, crouching down in the shadow, she waited patiently till he should be asleep. Once, she was startled by the approach of the officer of the guard, and narrowly escaped a second discovery, which would inevitably have sent her to the guard-house, by dodging behind the tent. At last the heavy breathing of the tired captain assured her that all was safe, and she stole softly to the entrance of the tent. The cords were tied on the inside, but with the sharp knife she had concealed they were soon severed, and she stood within the tent. Only guided by the recollection of where she had seen the box deposited, she noiselessly stepped towards the shelf, and in a moment the casket was safe in her hands. As she turned to go out, being not so cautious as when she entered, she jostled the captain's sword, and it fell clattering on the floor.

The Captain started up. "What the d—— Tom," he cried, "What are you after." But there was no one there, and thinking he must have knocked it off himself, the dreamy Captain resumed his slumbers.

For Susie, almost frightened out of her wits, had waited for no reply, but fled hastily away until she came once more in sight of the sentries. Here her instincts of prudence made her resume a more quiet gait, though she still went on as if in haste, saying as she approached the guard:

"Manassas! don't stop me—urgent business," and so hurrying past the surprised sentinel, went with all the speed she dared towards her home.

Arrived at her uncle's, she quietly opened the gate, and stole beneath Agatha's window, picking up a piece of gravel to toss against the glass, which had been the preconcerted signal that her sister might let her in. She did not succeed the first time, and was stooping to find another small stone, when she was suddenly and rudely seized by the collar, and a man hissed in her ear:

"How dare you come here?"

Intensely amazed, and at last fairly overcome, Susie, pale and trembling, turned upon her antagonist.

"Let me go, or I will shoot you!"

"Never," he cried, shaking her violently, "Till you tell me why you are prowling under a lady's window?"

Something in the tone in which these words were uttered startled Susie, and she looked her captor full in the face. It was enough, and with a surprised cry, she breathed the word

"Raymond!"

"Susie!" he gasped, letting her go in utter amaze. "Is it possible? but what is the meaning of this disguise? I swear, I thought you were a rival!"

A few hasty words had told him all, but he, too, had a story to relate. That night his papers had been seized; he feared for his life, and had come to say good bye, while he made one desperate effort of flight.

"But you shall not go alone!" cried Susie, "Agatha and I will go with you. After what has happened to-night we dare not stay."

Raymond was overcome with this devotion, but when Agatha had joined them, as she did in reply to their summons, she agreed that it was their only safety. There was a hasty packing of a few valuables, a farewell note written to their uncle, and by means of the countersign, before morning the little party were beyond the rebel lines.

Once arrived in the free North, Susie and Raymond were married, and she had the satisfaction of seeing him wear the Union uniform—while those left behind were greatly amazed at the flight; and Captain Johnston, more bewildered than any one else, to this day cannot satisfactorily account for the sudden disappearance of the Casket of Letters.

MY HOSPITAL EXPERIENCE.

[From the Cincinnati Commercial.]

"What shall I do to pass my time away pleasantly and usefully?" was the question I put to myself after the last "good-bye" had been spoken, the last kiss exchanged, and the parting words of my husband had died out of the now desolate room, leaving a lingering echo in my heart which sounded like Desolation. "It will never do to sit down here idly, and brood in vain regret during his absence; and surely, if *he* thought I should do nothing but pine and grieve for him, it would add a heavier weight than now rests upon his mind, for then two sore causes of trouble would rest upon him. It is enough to feel that our dear country calls for him in her affliction, and God go with him in her cause. I should blush for him if he held aloof now, nor offered himself in the full vigor and pride of his young life, as a shield against the arrows of destruction which threaten her, and which have already severed some of the brightest links which united our beloved nation, and while he has gone forth, brave in defence of right and truth, shall I sit down and cry like a miserable, selfish child, because it cannot have the toy it loves best always in its hands? No, no. That will never do! I should never claim to be a daughter of my proud, beautiful mother, America, could I for one moment be guilty of such selfish weakness."

So ran my thoughts as I stood beside the window, listening to the last clang and clatter of the bell on the boat which bore him away.

Slowly it put off from the wharf, and then up to God went as deep and fervent a prayer as ever wife breathed, for guidance and safety. His last kiss was still warm upon my lips—his last words ringing in my ears—and soon, perhaps, that voice, with its loving tones, might be forever hushed, and the warm lips cold and mute, under the icy seal of death! Yet not for one moment would I have recalled him, even while I grew sick at heart, and a heavy dread strove to creep into my brain, driving away its usually hopeful and pleasing fancies.

"It is right and just," I murmured, as I turned away, "and God will go with him. I know what I shall do. I shall go and take care of the poor sick boys up at the hospital."

To think, with me, is to act. In a moment my bonnet and cloak were donned, and I was on my way with a light heart. Are there any wives, mothers, or sisters, who will wonder how I could feel light-hearted when I had just sent my husband away to battle—perhaps never to look upon his dear face again? I will tell you why. *I trusted in God, and was yielding to an impulse to good deeds.* I say good, because I was animated solely by the desire to render assistance and relieve suffering, and not for what other people might think or say of me.

On entering the hospital, I found the attending physician, Dr. L——, there, and introduced myself.

"I have nothing to do," I said, "and want you to employ me. Can I render assistance in any way?"

"Yes, madam," was his prompt response. "If you will come in sometimes and prepare something nourishing, and talk to them, to keep them in good spirits, we shall be very glad."

"I shall certainly do so. I am glad if I can be of use."

I laid aside bonnet and cloak, without further ceremony, and went to the sickest man I saw.

"How do you feel?" I asked, bending over him.

"Weak, ill—nigh to death," he replied, in a tone so pitiful and full of despair that I felt the tears spring to my eyes. I sent them back to their source, however, and spoke in a full, firm, yet kind tone.

"Oh, no; you are not near death. You are ill, but you will not die. Uncle Sam has use for you yet, and in a few days you'll be up and ready to shoulder your musket again. Don't you think so?"

His eyes sparkled in their deep sockets, and a momentary flush rose to his pale cheek.

"Oh, if I could only think so! But the time drags so slowly, and here I lie useless, helpless, keeping those who could fight away to take care of me."

"Oh, well, you needed a little rest any way," I said cheerfully. "Now, I want to do something to cure you. Dou you want your face bathed?"

"Yes, if it is not too much trouble," he said eagerly.

"Not a bit. Now be easy, and I'll soon have you feeling nicely."

I got a basin of water, combs, brushes, sponge, and soap, and came back to him. His large dark eyes rested with child-like pleasure on my face, as I carefully bathed his face and hands. He had grown so feeble that he could scarcely connect a sentence without pausing, and lay panting on his elbow from the slightest exertion. After bathing his face, I took the comb and straightened out the snarled masses of long black hair that grew thickly over his brow. I soon found that illness had made him childish, though I at first started at his childlike bluntness.

"You're mighty purty," he said suddenly, and for a moment I did not know what to say, but then, I thought, "I may seem so to him, poor fellow," and only smiled in reply.

"What's your name?" he next asked.

"S——," I replied.

"You ain't married, are you?"

"Yes, and my husband's gone to fight as you did at Fort Donelson."

"Oh, dear," he said fretfully, "I'm so sorry. What did you get married for? Never mind, I'll put a spider in his dumpling when I get well."

With the last words, a mischievous light broke over his face, and his black eyes twinkled. I laughed merrily at him, and he seemed to enjoy it hugely. Poor fellow! little enough amusement he had. If he could amuse himself at my expense, I would have no objections.

My next patient was an orphan boy, sixteen years of age. Frank B—— belonged to Birge's Sharpshooters, and a braver heart never beat in the bosom of mortal than that which throbbed in his.

While bathing his face, I asked him what induced him to leave his home and friends in Nebraska to come away and peril his life at such an early age. His reply is worthy to be written by that of the noble Nathaniel Hale, who regretted having but "one life to offer to his country."

He said: "I joined the army because I was young and strong. I have but one life, and that would be worth nothing to me if not offered to my country."

Noble boy! How many more like him have fallen willing sacrifices!

The next day I carried a basket of apples, oranges, pies, tea, &c., to the hospital. As I went in, several of the men lifted their heads, and nodded pleasantly.

"I'm glad you have come back," said one, and another thought, "it looked so much like home to see a woman amongst them."

My "admirer" with the black eyes clasped my hand when I offered him an orange, and kissed it gratefully.

"If I live," he said, "I'll always pray God to bless you. If I die, I'll watch over you from Heaven."

Poor fellow! I wonder if from that Heaven, to which his spirit has flown, he is watching over me to-night as I pen these lines?

Frank's blue eyes greeted me with a glad smile before I was near enough to speak to him. When I bent over and asked him how he felt, he answered me cheerfully, saying he hoped to be able soon to return to his regiment.

I bathed his face, gave him a cup of hot tea, with some toast, and left him sleeping sweetly.

Those who have never visited the hospital cannot conceive of the wretched condition in which the men are brought into them. That day twenty-eight were brought from Donelson and Savannah, and such objects I never saw. Their faces and hands were stiff with coal-dust, and burning with fever. Their hair long and matted—beard uncut and full of dirt.

It was a serious task to attempt rendering them comfortable, but I did not shrink from it. On the contrary, I felt grieved at my inability to serve more than one at a time. Oh, how I longed for the power then to stir some of my own sex, who in that town passed their days in thoughtless idleness, to action, if only for an hour, to assist in bringing those poor sufferers to a comfortable condition.

From morning till noon I toiled faithfully, glad from my heart, and thankful for the impulse that had sent me there. I went home and dined, and feeling tired, wanted to lie down and rest. But then I remembered I had promised to bring some fruits to the boys in the afternoon, and I could not feel satisfied till I had done so, knowing that I could rest at any time, while they lay tossing and restless with fever and pain, perhaps longing for a cooling draught they could not get.

It was four o'clock before I got away again, and then I was really tired. So days merged into weeks, and it became a regular routine. From eight till ten or eleven, and from half past one till four, I took pleasure amongst them, even while pain stirred my heart to see their sufferings. One by one I could see them fading. No care or skill could save them. They had offered their lives to our country, and she accepted the sacrifice.

Poor little Frank B—— daily grew weaker. Nothing could tempt him to eat, and his cough grew worse, while his face became thin and pale. He never lost his joyous spirit, but always seemed hopeful, even when too ill to rise from his berth.

One afternoon I was startled on entering, by the most piteous cries, and found that they came from my little favorite, generally so brave and patient.

"Why, Frankie, what is the matter?" I asked, bending over him.

"Oh, you have come. I did wish for you so much. Oh, I shall die, and I wanted somebody by who seemed to care for me a little. You do like me, don't you, dear Mrs. S——? You've been so kind to me. Oh, this pain! I can't stand it long!"

His hand grasped mine nervously, and every fibre of his frame quivered with pain. I saw that the dews of death were standing thickly already on the broad, beautiful forehead over which the fair hair clustered so prettily, and my eyes filled with tears of sorrow deeper than words could express. I stooped to kiss him, and a glad cry escaped the poor blue lips of the dying boy.

"Oh, kiss me again, wont't you? That is like my sister. Do kiss me once more, I feel better. Oh, I wouldn't mind to die if my sisters were here to tell me they loved me. You do love me a little, don't you?"

"Yes, a great deal, Frankie; as much as if I were your sister. Don't you think so? I'm sure you'r a good boy, and I'm sorry to see you suffer so."

He drew me down to him, and pressed his face close to my arms. I could endure no more. The poor boy's mute appeal for tenderness and sympathy in his dying hour, far from home, breathing out his young life amid strangers, unnerved me. I drew that young bright head to my bosom, and my tears fell fast upon its sunny curls.

Did the gentle sisters he loved have one thought of the scene that was transpiring on that night, while perchance they sat and talked of him, their only and petted brother, in their far-off home in Nebraska?

"You will stay with me to-night, won't you!" he pleaded again. "Oh, you won't leave me to die alone!"

"No, Frankie, I'll stay with you."

He was comforted, and became more quiet, as I clasped his hands and tried to soothe him. Gradually a purple hue overspread his face. Now his lips became whiter and the large clear eyes grew restless. When he could no longer speak, those eyes plead for some tokens of endearment, and each time that I pressed a kiss upon his forehead, a look of deep and earnest gratitude softened the suffering expression of his face.

About nine o'clock he breathed his last, and now every time I look down at my hand, and see the little ring of mine he wore before he died, I seem to see the parting look of his great sad eyes ere they fixed in death. How sad the task to brush back the damp locks from the cold brow, and compose the blue limbs in their last repose! That night I wept and prayed for the sisters as I had never wept and prayed for myself, for he was all they had.

A few days after this another of my patients, who was fast recovering, I thought, had a relapse, and was again confined to his berth. There had been a storm that dashed in the windows, and he got wet.

[CONTINUED ON EIGHTH PAGE.]

THE PHILADELPHIA INQUIRER.

TUESDAY, JUNE 3, 1862.

From Gen. McClellan!

The Great Victory at Richmond--The Anaconda Coiling himself closer Around the City!

From Halleck's Army!

The Rebels Completely Demoralized

Weekly Courier

Friday, May 30th, 1862.

Our readers, we know, will thank us, for the spirited Parody, in our second page. It has been kindly placed at our disposal, by a friend, to whom we are indebted for hitherto favors. He would not give us the name of the author,—but only told us that it was the production, in a leisure moment, of an accomplished and patriotic lady of Natchez. How it makes the blood course, like quick-silver, through the veins! Heaven grant, the prediction in stanza third, may speedily become history! But if that should be denied us, then let it be said, that "disdaining to yield," our courage was equalled only by our fortitude.

THE ANACONDA,

With his back broken at Winchester, Va., and his tail cut off at the battle of Glorietta, New Mexico.
WASHINGTON CITY.
(Head of Anaconda.)

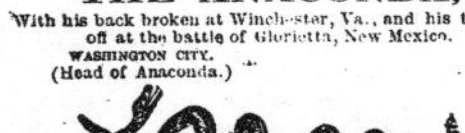

Back Broken by "STONEWALL" JACKSON.
Tail Cut Off AT NEW MEXICO.

In a few days, the bowels will be taken out at Corinth, and the head crushed at Washington City.

Various have been the speculations relative to the Federal gunboats all leaving these parts, Vicksburg, Grand Gulf, Rodney, &c. towards New Orleans. When we recall to mind the fact, that a Mayor and other City Officers are to be elected at New Orleans next Monday, it will not appear at all strange that the whole Federal force should again be summoned before that city. The ideas of freedom with Picayune Butler now, associate only gunboats and bayonets before the ballot-box. At all hazards, he must have Lincoln city officers, or the destruction of the rights of the people and the city.

Subjugation Abroad.

The London Times maintains the late Federal successes only bring the enemies of the South face to face with their greatest perils. It holds that so long as the people of the Confederate States are firm and in earnest in resistance and endurance, their subjugation is an impossibility. In a leader of the 10th of April, referring to Federal gains in Tennessee and on the seaboard the times uses this language:

What must naturally occur to any European who has read a single page of military history is, that the progress of a hundred thousand men, ever so well equipped and commanded, into a country which reckons is distance by hundreds of miles, may be very likely fighting the air or lashing the waves. From Nashville, east, south and west, for at least five hundred miles, all is Southern interest and feeling. There is no divided allegiance or treachery there. But the condition of the country makes invasion at once uneasy and ineffective.

The population is sparse, indeed, compared with European nations. There are wildernesses to be traversed, forests to be penetrated, swamps to be waded through, and even Indian settlements to be crossed, before the country can be conquered in any sense of the word; and the only result must be, that for every man of the conquering army there will still be half a dozen ready to defend the soil. The invading army may conquer where it stands; and go where it will; but when it begins to break up, to occupy, to reap the fruits of the conquest, and to put itself in the place of the original proprietor, then it seems to disappear in the immensity of its own task. In other words, the conquest of such a country, in any real sense of that word, seems an impossibility, so long as the occupants are animated by the feelings which nobody denies to the South.

The incidents of the war bring this out, even while they expose the difficulties of the Southern cause. The troops which for these ten months have baffled the immense numbers and wealth of the North, are ill-clothed, ill-fed, ill-armed, ill-housed and ill-appointed in every way. Through all this winter they have slept on the bare ground, with few and scanty meals, unable to afford stimulants, and with the oldest muskets and fowling pieces. Yet they fight bravely, by the admission of their foes, even when, as at Fort Donelson and on the coast, it was under a shower of shells which they could not return.

When such is the spirit, what is the hope of their conquest, and can the North really expect to subjugate them and reduce them to a virtual dependency? They have only to hold out and they know they must beat the North at the game of obstinacy. They stand on their own soil and defend their own homes. They can do this cheaply enough, but a war which is cheap to them will be ruinous to the invader, who brings his men and his material over a thousand miles, as we found to our cost in the war of Independence, and again in the unfortunate quarrel of 1813-'14.

A Souvenir of Gen. Magruder.

Little events after all make up the best part of a man's life. They are numberless, have immemorial dates, and though not scattered over with the roses of immortality, cluster together in a garland, equally, perhaps, as sweet, even if there are wild flowers (and wild oats,) in the midst. When Gen. Magruder, then a Colonel, was in command of the forces at San Diego, he met with his first and only defeat. He essayed a serenade, in honor of the several ladies who were on a visit to Newton, with particular preference to one in whose future welfare he nourished a remote interest. Accordingly all of the officers of the mess, who could sing, blow, or beat time, were pressed into service, and the knightly party left the mission about midnight, in a spring wagon, plentifully laden with every imaginable variety of musical instruments. There was a jovial young surgeon, of fine good nature and exuberant spirits along, who had installed himself on the rear seat with his instrument, which happened to be a bottle of whiskey, in his arms; and upon which he played with such effect during the ride, that he became thoroughly inspired with the genius of music. In those days there was a Bowery song, quite popular, the chorus of which ran into the following rhyme:

"O, my name is Jake Keyser, I was born in [illegible] Garden, [illegible]
But its no use a blowing, for I am a hard one,
And I am bound to be a butcher, by heaven or die!

This unfortunate song somehow occurred to the Doctor, and he could no more get it out of his head than perpetrate a surgical operation on a shadow. The consequence was, he could not help singing it, and when the whole party was duly arranged under the favorite window, in fond anticipation of a shower of bouquets and bon-bons, with flutes, fiddles and voices upraised in the plaintive legend—

"Oft in the stilly night,"

Far louder than all the music, broke out the chant,

"O, my name is Jake Keyser!"

The party was panic stricken, but the gallant Colonel soon recovered his mental equilibrium, turned fiercely upon the delinquent Æsculapius and commanded him to desist from the interruption and hold his peace. With admirable strategy the Doctor backed himself against an adjacent fence, where he could deliver himself safely, and with the most intense dignity responded:

"Col. Magruder, I'm officer of the army—army; when I'm at th' mission, I'm under your orders; consider self so, and obey 'em. But when I'm down serenadin'—serenadin', I say Col.

"I'm bound to be a butcher, by Heaven, or die!

Then moving off into a waltz of a frantic description, he executed about one-half of his favorite opera, and tumbled over on the turf. In the meantime a night cap and a shot gun emerged from one of the upper windows of the house, and a pack of hounds and a bull terrier set up a desperate bulla bulloo underneath. The Col. ordered a retreat immediately, which was affected in tolerable good order, with the loss of the Doctor, who was taken prisoner by the night cap, and sent back to camp before day next morning.

The story is vouched for by Lieut. D——, formerly of the U. S. Army, who related it with fine effect, a few evening ago in the parlor of the Spotswood.

THE MISSISSIPPI.

A Parody on, "The King Shall Have His Own Again."

They've laid it low our kingly stream,
With mockery and insult ta'en;
For us it flowed, for us it gleamed,
For us it nourished all,—in vain.
But loyal hearts are yet not dead,
And the South shall have her own again.

Ho! for a brighter day! what Ho!
Our River must be ours again.
Wipe out the days of pain and woe!
And strike for Liberty amain!
One glorious hour, one conquering blow,—
And the South shall have her own again.

Perchance, before to-morrow's sun
Shall set beneath the western main,
The foeman's hour-glass shall have run,
And Justice come in Victory's train.
Forward, strong hearts! the day is won;
And the South shall have her own again.

But let us win, or let us lose,
What heart to yield shall not disdain,
'Till God, in His good time shall choose
To free our River from its chain.
And far and wide shall spread the news,
The South has got her own again.

Further from Grand Gulf.

Gen. Banks' Division Routed.

4,000 Prisoners Taken by Gen. "Stonewall" Jackson.

The Federal Division Entirely Broken and Confederates in Pursuit.

Skirmishing Continues at Corinth.

BROOKHAVEN, May 27, 1862.

To Mr. Wm. A. L'Hommedieu:

Yesterday, our artillery at Grand Gulf, fired into the enemy's boats and disabled three, that floated back down the river.

On Friday last, Gen. Jackson, at Winchester, Va., captured the Federal army and all the stores that they had; took 2000 prisoners.

Our boys were still after them.

Prisoners are still coming in.

We have completely routed their whole force.

There is still skirmishing going on at Corinth.

Everything is quiet at Vicksburg.

C. HARVEY.

Further Particulars.

We are indebted to our esteemed fellow-citizen Mr. ROUDEBUSH, just from Jackson, for the following further particulars received there by telegraph as he was leaving for home:

Gen. Jackson's forces entered Winchester on the 25th, capturing all the enemy's commissary and ordnance stores.

The Federals tried to burn the town but were too closely pursued by our forces.

We took the first Maryland regiment and the first Vermont Cavalry regiment, at Front Royal, and 2000 more prisoners at Winchester.

Our forces are still in pursuit.

The enemy was completely routed.

From Savannah.

Twenty-nine Federals had been killed in a skirmish, near Savannah, Ga.

Later from Baton Rouge.

BATON ROUGE, May 29, 11 A. M.......Yesterday the Federals attempted to land a garrison, when our guerrillas fired on them, killing five. They then commenced throwing shot and shell. One passed through the Harney House (Hotel.) Several other houses were also struck.

They have now 10 vessels and two transports, and are landing troops.

RUSSELL, Operator.

[From Special Dispatches to Daily Mississippian.]

Enemy Within Seven Miles of Richmond.

RICHMOND, May 23....There was sharp skirmishing about seven miles northeast of the city this afternoon. The particulars are not yet ascertained except that the enemy was attacked and repulsed with loss.

The prevailing opinion is that a general engagement will soon take place.

RICHMOND, May 24.....Heavy cannonading was heard this morning in the direction of the skirmishing yesterday. It commenced about daybreak, and still continues. No report has been received yet. It is now raining fast.

RICHMOND, May 24....Sharp skirmishing this morning at New Bridge, some distance from the locality of the last skirmish by the 5th Louisiana on picket duty. The point was attacked by a large force of Yankees. The firing continued several hours. About forty Confederates were wounded. None killed.

RICHMOND, May 24....In the skirmish yesterday afternoon, the enemy had four pieces of artillery and the Confederates one. The enemy threw a large number of shells without damage. A regiment of Federal Cavalry charged our battery, but a few shells thrown in their midst reversed their course, and they and their artillery fled precipitately.

Northern Intelligence.

RICHMOND, May 24....Late Northern papers received at the Daily Express office. The repulse of the gunboats on James River had a depressing effect in New York and Philadelphia, and was regarded as a very serious affair at Old Point, but no full accounts allowed to be made public.

Seventeen men were killed on the Nangatuck by explosion of a one hundred-pound parrot gun. The boat was rendered useless, and withdrawn from the fight.

The Galena was riddled by shot from the rebel batteries. Eighteen went through her deck and sides. Fourteen of the crew were killed and thirteen wounded. The killed terribly cut and mangled; many beyond hope of recognition. The Monitor maintained superior strength and invulnerability. The balls glanced harmless from her tower. Aristook and Port Royal not materially injured.

The unusual elevation of the rebel batteries, and the difficulty of the gunboats getting in the proper range, prevented for a time any execution. Meantime the rebel batteries poured incessant fire, shot and shell, upon the decks of the gunboats, and did a fearful work. The body of M. Barnum, gunner of the Galena, was carried to Fortress Monroe for interment.

Seward and Wells visited Norfolk on Friday. Col. Brown, of the 20th Indiana Regiment, stationed at Portsmouth, went out of town to take a ride. An hour afterwards, the horse returned riderless. He is supposed to have been killed by the rebels.

Nothing important from Halleck or McClellan, and not a word of Milroy and Cox.

Over five hundred vessels are to sail for southern ports by the first of June. Two hundred clearances of vessels with ice have been made for Chagres.

The following statement of the question of Grain vs. Cotton, is made by a practical farmer, who draws his conclusions from a series of close and detailed calculations:

Every bale of Cotton made causes forty bushels of corn less to be produced.

Every ten bales requires labor that, if directed into proper channels, would add one soldier to the army.

The farmer who plants his whole farm in grain, though he may sell at the highest market price and give nothing, does more for his country than he that plants a third or a fourth of a Cotton crop and gives all his surplus provisions to the cause of the war.

YANKEE PRISONERS. Fifteen Yankee prisoners captured in skirmishes at Corinth, arrived in our city yesterday evening.—[*Jackson Mississippian.*

Saturday, May 31st, 1862.

Public attention is directed to the notice of Sheriff Metcalfe, in to-day's paper.

About the last of the enemy's gunboats and transports passed down the river yesterday. They have made a quick trip to Memphis and Fort Pillow! Something remarkable! they didn't leave any Memphis papers containing a description of their adventures by flood and field.

ARMY NEWS. We heard of a case of recruiting for the Confederate army, on last Thursday, rarely equalled, but seldom excelled in any part of the world. Natchez and its vicinity has ever proved prolific in many things, but in this instance far outstrips all previous calculations in this war. Without mentioning names, we learn that the wife of a volunteer, now in the Virginia army, has recruited his squad at home with three boys, at one birth. What chance have the Federalists, in a country like this?

It is not cities, or towns, or rivers, says the "Mississippian"—it is not broad acres—waving with the yellow and golden harvest, or white with that product whose sceptre, though now disputed, will yet be triumphant—which constitute the Southern Confederacy. It has its capitol not in cities or towns, but in the brave and virtuous hearts of its citizens. We may be exterminated, but we cannot be conquered.

HOSPITAL STORES, &c.

The increased number of our sick seems to be bringing out the resources of the country. Hospitals are now being established at all points upon the railroads, and kind hands are employed in ministering to the necessities of our disabled soldiers. The people of this county, ever ready for good works, have contributed largely to the establishment of Hospitals here and elsewhere, and stand ready to do more. Some of the ladies of this city have been for weeks in charge of a Hospital at Corinth. They are now *en route* for Brookhaven, to establish themselves there. Besides this, we have another band at Jackson, Miss. To enable these ladies to render all the service in their power, all the hospital stores, now in the city and county, are to be sent to Jackson and Brookhaven. Persons wishing to make contributions for these Hospitals, are requested to send them before 4 o'clock this afternoon, to the State Hospital.

For the Natchez Daily Courier.

A Card.

At a meeting of the "Young Ladies' Matrimonial Society," the following resolution passed without opposition:

"In consequence of our unprotected, unfortunate, and lonely situation, the members of this band, do hereby resolve to receive from all respectable single gentlemen, between the ages of thirty-five and ninety, any and all attentions which they may deem proper to bestow,—provided they do not forget to propose. We therefore think it wise to notify the gentlemen of our determination, as affairs are very uncertain regarding our sweethearts in the war."

For further particulars, address "Desdemona," President of the Young Ladies' Matrimonial Society.

We advise those wishing young and interesting wives to apply soon.

Offers from juveniles (those under thirty-five) will not be accepted. DESDEMONA.

We exceedingly regret that fair "Desdemona" re-considered her resolution, directing all communications to be left at the Daily Courier office. We had almost fancied that she was about to place us in possession of something rich and racy, for an evening's entertainment. Being *fully* thirty-six, hale, hearty and saucy, our fair friend may yet secure our services as Private Secretary. Who knows! EDITOR.

The following noble compliment, nobly won, was conferred on a private in his army, by Gen. Beauregard. Mr. Jones is a native of Fairfax county, but a resident of Warrenton, Va., and his town, county and State will do well to be proud of the young hero, who has won such uncommon honors. The order which follows was read at the head of every regiment in Beauregard's whole army. All praise to the General who thus honors merit even in the ranks:

HEADQUARTERS ARMY OF THE MISSISSIPPI,
CORINTH, Miss., April 12, 1862.

[GENERAL ORDERS No. 14.]

The Commander of the forces desires to call the special attention of the army to the intrepid behavior of Private Elcon Jones, Company K, Seventeenth Regiment Virginia Volunteers, while on detached service in the Signal Corps, during the bombardment of the upper or Rucker's Battery at Madrid Bend; when the signal flag having been twice shot from his hand, was, nevertheless, promptly recovered by him, and messages accurately transmitted without interruption.

Preferring the post of danger and of duty to the relief proffered by his commanding officer, Private Jones remained at his perilous position for six days and nights, affording an example of patriotic devotion and personal valor eminently worthy of the emulation of his young countrymen in arms.

By command of General BEAUREGARD.
(Signed) F. H. JORDAN,
Assist. Adjutant-General.

The London Standard says: "*By recognizing this blockade of the Southern coast, we are condemning thousands of Englishmen to starvation, and are giving a most unfair assistance to the Federal Government.* The fleet which it ought to employ in the blockade is devoted to predatory incursions on the enemy's territory. We are aiding to protract a barbarous war, and putting ourselves forward to pay its costs. The law of blockade is one which must be construed strictly. A nation which avails itself of a measure so injurious to neutrals must fulfill every one of the conditions under which its exercise is permitted. If it makes default in one, its right is lost. The Federal Government has made default in the most important requisite of a blockade. The default amounts, in the language of a great Federal authority, to an 'entire defeasance to the measure.' It should be understood in Lancashire that the distress which prevails, and the starvation which threatens, have no other cause than Earl Russell's sympathy with the North."

SICKNESS. We are informed that there is an immense amount of sickness among the Federal troops on the transports. It appears that they have run short of medicines, and a party of them made a visit to a drug store in Warrenton and sacked it of all its contents. One boat is said to be filled entirely with their sick.

CAPTURED. The Federal fleet in front of Warrenton is committing all sorts of depredations upon the people along the shore. Two citizens of Warrenton, Mr. Walker and Mr. Gardner, have been captured and carried off to their boats.

It is the general impression that the enemy has landed the troops from the transports at some point below this city. We do most ardently hope this may be so. But few of them will ever get home again to tell the fate of their companions, if they venture upon the soil of old Warren.—*Vicksburg Citizen.*

ST. CHARLES HOTEL, NEW ORLEANS. The subscriber flattering himself that, he can keep a hotel, has taken this extensive and favorite establishment. He would be happy to *take in* his numerous friends and the public generally.

N. B. The best of liquors at the bar. All guests are requested to deposit their valuables with the undersigned. B. F. BUTLER.

THE BATTLE OF ARMAGEDDON. The war correspondent of the Mobile Register writing in reference to disaffection among the Kentuckians and Tennesseeans at Nashville, says:

The discontent among the Kentuckians was increased by a sermon preached in Nashville by the Rev. Mr. Baldwin, the author of "Armageddon, or the United States in Prophecy." You may remember the work, and that the author's study of the Prophecies led him to the conclusion that the great battle of "Armageddon," spoken of in Revelations, would be fought about this time in the Valley of the Mississippi. He referred to the same subject in his sermon in Nashville, and told his hearers that the battle would take place by the 20th of June—that the Federal host would be overthrown and dispersed—and that their dead carcasses would make "all the land to stink." An effort was made by officers present to stop him, but the soldiers, who were deeply interested, would not allow it to be done.

Col. Morgan in Tennessee.

His Narrow Escape from Capture.

The Knoxville Register, of Wednesday, has an interesting letter from its army correspondent, giving an account of Col. Morgan's expedition from Corinth into Tennessee, which we transfer to our columns. It will be seen that the gallant Morgan came near being captured by an overwhelming force of the enemy:

SPARTA, TENN., May 8th, 1862.

We left Corinth on the 20th of April, and crossed the Tennessee river on the 26th and 27th, arrived at Lawrenceburg on the 31st, learned the Federals were in possession of Pulaski, and on "May day" we had a frolic with them, in which we took 290, and 24 officers, including Gen. Mitchell's son, killed 13, and lost none. The country had become alarmed, and troops were sent to the Tennessee river to cut us off. We continued on the next morning, and encamped 13 miles from Shelbyville that night. Marched the 3d and encamped within 6 miles of Murfreesboro' at night.

At dawn on the 4th our pickets and the Federal pickets had an engagement. We passed around the place and crossed the Nashville and Murfreesboro' pike to Smyrna, where we tore up the railroad track and cut the telegraph wire, attacked a battery and received a dispetch that was being transmitted to Col. S. Mathews, commanding at Nashville, relative to our being in the vicinity, and the cavalry that had been sent in pursuit of us. Col Morgan answered it in Col. Matthews' name, and ordered the cavalry to Shelbyville, saying that it was about to be attacked by Gen. Price. We arrived at Lebanon at night on the 4th, the men and horses being greatly fatigued, and considered that we had eluded pursuit for the present.

At dawn, on the 5th, our pickets were driven in, and before our men could get to horse, the enemy was upon us in overwhelming numbers. Col. Morgan and Lieut. Col. Wood, (of W. Adam's regiment,) after most desperate efforts, succeeded in getting the men collected and the most desperate fighting ensued that is on record, but all of no avail. Our small force of 350 men, though the bravest of the brave, were surrounded by legions, estimated and since known to be 4,000 strong. Col. Morgan charged through them with about 100 men, and took the road leading to Carthage, which is on the Cumberland river 20 miles distant. Col. Wood and men were driven to the College where they fought until 12 o'clock, refusing to surrender, although they were well aware that they were cut off from all the passes of escape, and that artillery would be brought to bear on them in a short time, until their ammunition gave out, and the citizens had begged them to give up for the Federals were about to burn the town.

Col. Morgan arrived at this place with 40 men the next day. I arrived some four hours later with 31. Our men have been coming in at all hours since. We have now here something over 100, and are expecting more.

Gen. Dumont, Col. Woolford, and a Pennsylvania Colonel were taken prisoners early in the action in town, and as soon as they made known their rank, their swords were restored to them again by our gallant colonel M.

The fight was kept up the whole distance from Lebanon to Carthage, and a volley of 50 guns were fired at Colonel Morgan as he climbed the bank after crossing the river.

The account is necessarily very imperfect in its most interesting details for the time that was allotted for writing before the leaving of the gentleman who is to be the bearer is so short that it excludes all of a particular character.

In haste, GORDON E. NILES,
Refugee, Editor and Publisher of the Lockport, N. Y., Daily Adv. and Dem.

P. S. Col. Morgan and men are in good health and spirits, but greatly fatigued, and it will not be but a short time before the Yankees will hear from us again.

ESCAPED. Capt. Aston Madeira, of the 2d Kentucky Regiment who, with his entire company was taken prisoner at Fort Donelson, has escaped from Columbus, Ohio, and is now safe in Canada, where he was kindly received, and whence he writes that he will soon find his way back to his duties in the South. He states that he has more friends and money than he ever had in his life.

[*Jackson Mississippian.*

The Rev. Nathan Bangs, D. D., one of the fathers of American Methodism, died at his residence, in New York, on the 3d of May. He was 84 years old, and had been a minister upwards sixty years.

Tuesday, June 3d, 1862.

All letters for Corinth will be taken by J. C. Boyd, if left at the store of E. Boyd, by Wednesday, 10 o'clock.

SUBJUGATION IMPOSSIBLE. The capture of some of our principal cities, seaport and fortifications may serve to depress some portion of the Southern people, and cause them to look to the issue of the war with apprehension. If there be any disposed to despond, we advise them to refresh their memory concerning the events of the old revolution by reading the following extract from an article in the London Times. That paper expresses the belief that if the people of the South are in earnest, the subjugation of them by the North is a thing impossible:

Let it be remembered that we took all these cities, and Boston and New York besides, during the War of Independence. We marched three armies into the country, winning every battle, and taking every city, until the scanty population closed behind us and cut off our communications. We had nothing to conquer but the Atlantic coast, and nothing to meet but raw volunteer levies and peasants in arms; and our generals, although we condemn them by the event, were experienced soldiers of good reputation in Europe. We found, after a fair trial, that the achievement was impossible. It was not so much these volunteers or the French as the country which beat us.

Interesting Matter on next page.

The New York Tribune has openly declared that McClellan's great victory at Williamsburg was in truth a disastrous defeat. The Tribune does not like McClellan, and hence is moved to utter the truth.

Old Lawrence Forever.

Capt. James A. Hoskins was stationed with his famous artillery company from Lawrence county, on the heights near Grand Gulf. A day or so ago, the enemy's transports attempted to pass. Capt. Hoskins planted his battery in a favorable position and poured a volley into them, completely disabling one of them and turning the course of them all. Three cheers for Lawrence! Three cheers for Capt. Hoskins and his gallant men!

It is reported that the enemy will attempt to land at Grand Gulf with the view of penetrating the interior of our State by way of Port Gibson. If this is his intention, Capt. Hoskins and his men will have ample opportunity to win a name for themselves, and they are the men to contest every inch of ground, and make themselves a perfect terror to the dastards. We predict a brilliant career for this artillery company.

Jackson Mississippian, May 28.

Mr. J. J. Gregg, Treasurer of the Graniteville Manufacturing Company, says: "After testing all kinds of oil, we have settled on the Peanut, as the best lubricator to be had anywhere in quantity in the Confederacy."

Army Correspondence.

CAMP SMITH, NEAR CORINTH,
May 25, 1862.

DEAR COURIER: After "a time" I have at length found leisure to send you a few lines, by reason of my being in the hands of the surgeon, and, of course, "I've nothing else to do."

I shall pass over the incidents of my trip to this place, by merely saying that at Vicksburg more activity was displayed, if possible, in sending cotton, sugar and molasses, and everything else which could, in any way, be of service to the Yankees, than in Natchez—that corn, instead of cotton, covers the ground on both sides of the railroad from Jackson *via* Meridian to Corinth; that soldiers, in trains of one-fourth of a mile in length, were hurrying to the seat of war, and that I arrived here Tuesday afternoon at 3 o'clock, just fifty hours from Natchez.

Everything here is in a constant state of activity. Advance posts, picket duty, guarding the trenches and drilling, occupies almost all the time of the brigade to which I am attached—Gen. Chalmers'—and the brave, gallant *little* Tenth regiment is, in consequence, always on the alert, without a word of complaint or murmur from its men or officers. One, and the paramount, reason of this is, every man connected therewith has every confidence in the judgment and ability of its commanding officer, Col. R. A. Smith. He is one in a thousand, always where the danger is greatest; by word and deed inspiriting his men to deeds of noble daring, and endearing them to him by his care and kindness. One instance: at the close of the battle of Shiloh, one of the "Southron's" was found by him on the battle field sick, when, with an entire abnegation of self, he immediately dismounted from his horse and placed the sick man in his place, and ordered him to Monterey, thus probably saving a life and the service of an excellent soldier.

The ranks of the Southrons are beginning to fill up again with furloughed soldiers, who were wounded at Shiloh, or have again regained their health after severe sickness. This company is in every way peculiarly fortunate—fortunate in having such kind friends at home to supply their wants, and fortunate in its officers.

Capt. Inge is every way peculiarly fitted for his office—calm, cool and courageous, with the confidence of the entire company in his wisdom and prudence. He is emphatically a worker, and a hard one, and the wonder is how he has been able to stand so much fatigue.

Butler's proclamations have, in the army, raised a feeling of indignation it would be difficult to express on paper. Every man grasps his weapon firmer, and a sternness wrinkles the countenances of all heretofore wreathed with smiles.

Rev. Dr. Palmer, of New Orleans, is now preaching to the regiment at the Colonel's tent, and I will close for the purpose of listening to him.

More anon, J. E. P.

CITY COUNCIL.

At a called m[illegible]
this day at 5 o'c[illegible]
Esq., Mayor, M[illegible]
worth.

The Mayor st[illegible]
ing to transact [illegible]
before the regu[illegible]
failed for want [illegible]

The Sexton r[illegible]
ending 26th ins[illegible]
19th inst.

Mr. Walworth [illegible]
which was rece[illegible]
To the Mayor a[illegible]

Gents. The [illegible]
referred the re[illegible]
beg leave to re[illegible]
same and find [illegible]
on hand. on G[illegible]
Grave Yard A[illegible]
dent scholars [illegible]
due Treasurer [illegible]
and having can[illegible]
fied, present th[illegible]
Re[illegible]

The Superint[illegible]
report, with a[illegible]
were received [illegible]

The bonds an[illegible]
were received [illegible]

The following [illegible]
ally allowed an[illegible]
their respective [illegible]
Natchez Institu[illegible]
and janitor, f[illegible]
J. D. Baker—1 [illegible]
contract to 3[illegible]

C. Green & Co.—220 bbls. coal for Institute	220 00
L. M. Patterson—1 mo's salary as Marshal and removing nuisances	50 85
P. H. Farley—1 mo's salary as Superintendent of Engines to 24th inst.	50 00
L. H. Cory & Co.—Removing nuisances into river to 1st inst.	50 00
L. H. Cory & Co.—lumber furnished	16 60
J. C. Brown—gunny bags for city corn	16 0fi
J. D. Baker—salary in full as extra police officer	22 50
Walter Sterns—storing coal for Institute	3 30

On motion of Mr. Walworth, it was

Resolved, That the Mayor be authorized and requested to make a new contract with a reliable person to remove nuisances into the river.

On motion of Mr. Baldwin, it was

Resolved, That for the purpose of further supplying the demand for change, the Mayor and City Clerk are hereby authorized to issue the notes of the city, in sums of *one dollar, fifty cents, twenty-five cents* and *ten cents*, to the amount of *four thousand dollars*, redeemable in Confederate Notes, and place them in the hands of the City Treasurer to be exchanged for notes of the Confederate States.

On motion, the Board adjourned to Tuesday, June 10th, at 5 o'clock P. M.

C. F. MERRICK. City Clerk.

THE RIVER. The highest water of the seasons, and the highest ever known here, was Saturday night, 24th inst., being then about sixteen inches above the water of 1859. But on Sunday morning a fall of several inches was reported, which increased the further down we went, thereby indicating a break in the levee below. We have heard since that the break occurred near Vidalia. Up to Thursday morning the fall here exceeded a foot, but we do not think that it was caused by that break alone, for there is certainly a natural fall in the river. We heard sometime ago that, at Memphis, the fall exceeded four feet; three days ago we heard of a fall of over five feet at Napoleon, and of eighteen inches at Vicksburg; so we may safely presume that the river will not reach again its former height, but that the water will recede and our planters soon be enabled to put in their crops. Crops means, of course, *grain*, as there will hardly anybody think of planting a seed of cotton.

[*Tensas* (*St. Joseph, La.*) *Gazette, May 30.*

EPISCOPAL CONVENTION. The Forty-sixth Annual Convention of the Episcopal Church in North Carolina was held in Chapel Hill last week, meeting on Wednesday morning and adjourning on Saturday morning. The attendance was not large, though sufficient to form a quorum for the transaction of business, which was not the case at Morgantown last year.

The Constitution of the General Council of the Church in the Confederate States was ratified; and resolutions were adopted to appropriate to the present condition of the country.

The London Herald announces the departure of another powerful French squadron, ostensibly for Vera Cruz, but in reality (it thinks) for New Orleans.

Dispatches to Courier.

Late from Richmond.

Violent Storm - - - Richmond Flooded.

More Heavy Skirmishing.

RICHMOND, May 31....We had a violent thunder and rain storm here last evening, continuing several hours.

About nine o'clock at night, the Richmond Gas Works were completely flooded by water, throwing the whole city into total darkness.

There was more skirmishing going on yesterday on the Williamsburg road. Capt. Scarborough, of North Carolina, was killed.

The fight is again progressing, (this morning,) on the Williamsburg road, near the Chickahominy river. This river was much swollen by the rain last evening. No reports of the engagement have yet been received.

From a portion of Saturday Evening's Extra.

Skirmishing Below Mobile.

MOBILE, May 31....A special dispatch to the Mobile Tribune, dated at Pallard, May 30th, says a skirmish occured there day before yesterday.

The Simpson Rangers drove off the Federal guard from O'Bannonville bridge and burned the bridge.

Our loss was one man and three horses. The enemy's loss is unknown.

Three citizens of Oakfield were taken prisoners and conveyed to Pensacola.

The Federals are not advancing.

"Hurrah for Jackson!"

[From the Jackson Mississippian's Special Dispatches.

"Stonewall" Jackson's Great Victory.

Further Particulars.

Official Dispatch from Stonewall.

RICHMOND, May 27, via Mobile....The following is the dispatch received yesterday from Stonewall Sackson:

WINCHESTER, May 26, 1862....Gen. S. Cooper, Adjutant General: During the last three days God has blessed our arms with brilliant success. On Friday the Federals at Front Royal were routed and one section of Artillery, in addition to many prisoners captured. On Saturday Bank's main column whilst retreating from Strasburg to Winchester was pierced in the rear—part retreating towards Strasburg. On Sunday the other part was routed at this place. At last accounts Brig. Gen. George H. Stewart was pursuing the Cavalry and Artillery, and capturing fugitives. Large amounts of Medical, Ordnance and other stores have fallen into our hands.

(Signed) T. J. JACKSON,
Maj. Gen. Comd'g.

STILL LATER!

Banks' Army Flying in utter Consternation.

RICHMOND, May 28, via Mobile....The following dispatch was received this morning by Governor Letcher:

about seven o'clock, but were repulsed by Whiting's division.

RICHMOND, May 31....Latest reliable reports from the battle field represent, that the enemy were driven a mile and a half from their position. Our forces are now occupying their camps. We captured three batteries after most desperate fighting—the enemy being protected by entrenchments and woods. Several hundred prisoners were taken.

RICHMOND, May 31....The heavy rain of last night caused a flood in the Chickahominy; several bridges are washed away. Three divisions of the enemy were caught this side of the river, and ambulances sent down to bring in their wounded. More firing of artillery and musketry distinctly heard here to-day. No couriers yet arrived.

RICHMOND, May 31....Northern papers of the 29th, brought from the battle field, state that McClellan telegraphed to the Secretary of War that the battle of Hanover Court House resulted in a complete route of the enemy, with a loss of one thousand (a lie). Federal loss three hundred and seventy-nine killed, wounded and missing. The confiscation bill has passed the House of Representatives. The Philadelphia Enquirer says that Jackson's success has aroused the North. Volunteers are pouring in. Geo. F. Shipley, of Maine, has been appointed military commander of New Orleans, in the absence of Gen. Butler.

AUGUSTA, May 31....The Richmond Dispatch of the 30th, says the Federal army is falling back. Gen. Smith's brigade pursuing them. It is reported in Richmond that Stonewall Jackson crossed the Potomac river, and is now at Williamsport, Md., or Fredericktown turnpike. This movement is thought to have caused the Federals to retrograde from Richmond.

The Richmond Examiner says that Gen. Branch, in Tuesday's fight, at New Hanover, succeeded in getting off his entire command.

The town of Ashland is still in our lines.

ONE DAY LATER.

RICHMOND, June 1....The battle of yesterday took place in the vicinity of Boar Swamp, between the Railroad and Williamsburg road, about seven miles from the city. All accounts sent yesterday are correct in the main.

Some cannonading is heard this morning.

RICHMOND, June 1—(Sunday)....The fight is progressing furiously to-day—chiefly musketry. No definite reports from the field of battle. The general tenor of the statements of wounded soldiers, indicate that the Confederates are following up their success of yesterday.

Prisoners are constantly coming in.

Gen. Buel was not present. Gen. McClellan is commanding in person.

It is now believed that the larger portion of the Federal army is on this side of Chickahominy Creek.

Gen. Hatton, of Tenn., was killed yesterday.

RICHMOND, June 1....No definite accounts received of result of the battle of to-day, but all this evening. Fleet laying before point. All quiet.

THE ANACONDA,

With his back broken at Winchester, Va., and his tail cut off at the battle of Glorietta, New Mexico.

WASHINGTON CITY.
(Head of Anaconda.)

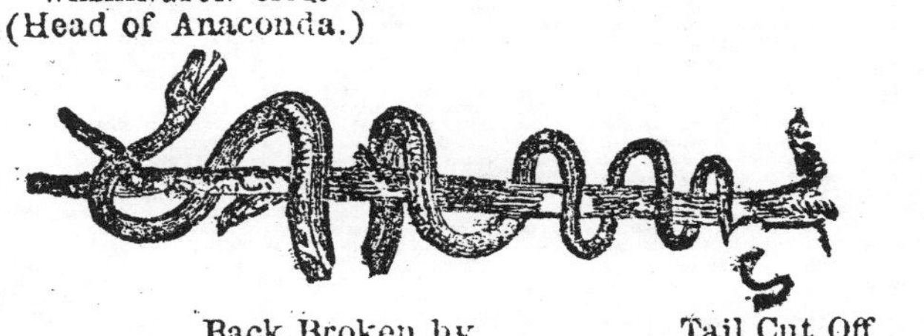

Back Broken by "STONEWALL" JACKSON.
Tail Cut Off AT NEW MEXICO.

In a few days, the bowels will be taken out at Corinth, and the head crushed at Washington City.

Late from Corinth.

We have seen a gentleman direct from Corinth. He corrects the impression that prevailed to some extent that the enemy had fallen back. Our line advanced about a half mile on the right.

Gen. Beauregard has issued an order requiring the burning of all extra tents—officers are allowed only sixteen pounds of baggage. He declared that the Confederate army had assumed the offensive, and that he did not wish it to be encumbered with unnecessary baggage or tents.

Gen. Beauregard has also issued an order excluding all correspondents from the lines—making it a penalty of death if improper news be transmitted. This fact accounts for the failure of our special correspondent at Corinth to supply us with late dispatches from that interesting locality.

Skirmishing is going on daily with slight casualities on both sides.—*Mississippian, May 28.*

BATTLE of RICHMOND.

RICHMOND, May 31....A battle has been progressing all day, near Chickahominy, about 7 miles from Richmond; all reports from the field are favorable. The engagement is very severe and the losses on both sides are heavy. Our wounded have been coming in for several hours. It is believed the fight will be renewed to-morrow.

The community is in good spirits, confident of a victory.

RICHMOND, May 31....Gen. Hill's division commenced the fight this morning. Rhodes and Garland's brigades bore the brunt of the battle for some time. Rain's and Anderson's brigades also bore conspicuous parts until our reinforcements arrived. The enemy was also reinforced and the fighting continued with great desperation on both sides, but the enemy were finally driven from their redoubts and their own batteries were taken and fired at them.

Prisoners taken say Gen. Buell is in command.

President Davis and Gen. Lee, were at the field and their presence greatly increased the enthusiasm of our troops.

All accounts agree that the Confederates displayed great bravery.

The Yankees stubbornly contested every inch, whilst giving away before the impetuous charges of our troops. No reliable estimate of the casualities has yet been made. A large number of Confederates are wounded in the arm and hand.

Gen. Rhodes was slightly wounded. No other General officers on our side, are hurt, so far as known.

The enemy tried to make a flank movement

New-York Daily Tribune.

VOL. XXII....No. 6,605. NEW-YORK, THURSDAY, JUNE 5, 1862. PRICE TWO CENTS.

THE BATTLE OF SEVEN PINES.

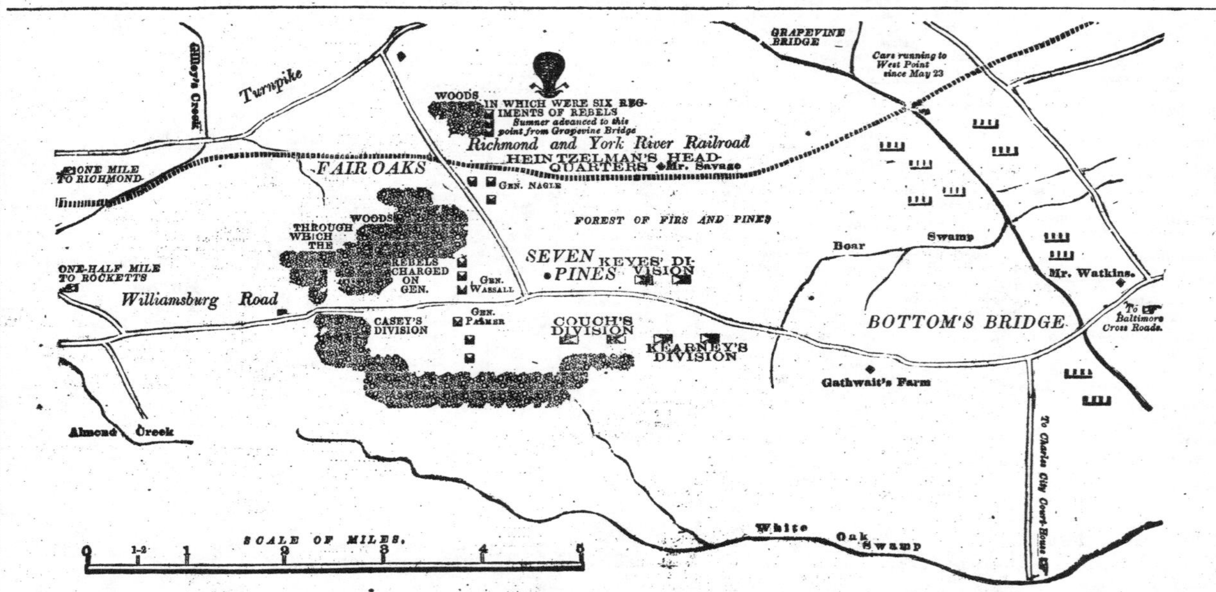

The basis of the sketch of the Battle of Seven Pines, which we give above, is a drawing specially brought to us from the battle field. The positions of our troops, which are represented by ▣ and ▭, are given as they were at the time of the Rebel attack, except those of the three regiments behind the woods to the north of Fair Oaks, which are the positions they assumed when ordered up in support of Naglee's right. The three regiments were the 1st Minnesota on the right, John Cochrane's in the center, and another on the left. Between them and Naglee came up the 69th and 88th New-York regiments, regiments which, not having seen fight before, fired rather wild, but which found their element in the use of the bayonet. Grapevine Bridge is one of the bridges thrown across the Chickahominy by Gen. McClellan. Another, between the Railroad Bridge and Bottom's Bridge, was carried away by the storm. The balloon, from which Prof. Lowe telegraphed the movements of the enemy, was anchored to the ground by a cable.

HIGHLY IMPORTANT FROM CORINTH.

BEAUREGARD'S ARMY DISPERSED

Pope Thirty Miles Below Corinth.

TEN THOUSAND PRISONERS TAKEN

15,000 Stand of Arms Captured.

Beauregard Tells His Men to Save Themselves.

THE ENEMY'S LOCOMOTIVES CAPTURED.

General Demoralization of the Rebels.

WASHINGTON, Wednesday, June 4, 1862.

The following dispatch was received this afternoon at the War Department:

HALLECK'S HEADQUARTERS, Wednesday, June 4, 1862.

Hon. E. M. STANTON, *Secretary of War:*

Gen. Pope, with 40,000 men, is thirty miles south of Corinth, pushing the enemy hard.

He already reports 10,000 prisoners, and deserters from the army, and 15,000 stand of arms captured.

Thousands of the enemy are throwing away their arms.

A farmer says that when Beauregard learned that Col. Elliott had cut the railway on the line of retreat, he became frantic, and told his men to save themselves the best they could.

We have captured nine locomotives and a number of cars. One of the former is already repaired and is running to-day. Several more will be in running order in two or three days. The result is all I can possibly desire.

H. W. HALLECK, Major-General Commanding.

The Siege and Occupation of Corinth.

From Our Special Correspondent.

CORINTH, Friday Evening, May 30, 1862.

PRELIMINARY OPERATIONS.

It was in the last days of last month—that is, three weeks after the battle—that the army had sufficiently recovered from the fearful shock of the memorable 6th and 7th of April, and repaired its great numerical losses by battle and disease with re-enforcements from the North, to make the first forward move from the scene of action in the direction of Corinth. Its lines at that time extended from in front of Hamburg Landing in a north-westerly direction to Shiloh Chapel—a distance of four miles—and some two miles beyond. Gen. Pope's army of the Mississippi then formed the left, Gen. Buell's army of the Ohio the center, and Gen. Grant's army of the Tennessee the right.

Before commencing the advance upon Corinth a reorganization of the army took place, by which Gen. Grant was made second in command; the First Division of the army of the Ohio was transferred to the army of the Tennessee, and its commander, Major-General Thomas, placed in command of the whole right, and two divisions of the army of the Tennessee, respectively commanded by Major-General Wallace and Brigadier-General Judah, constituted into a reserve under Major-General McClernand. Each of the two wings, as well as the center, also had a special reserve consisting of one division. Thus organized for aggressive movements, the gradual approaches to the enemy's position began.

NATURE OF THE COUNTRY.

The character of the country between the field of Shiloh and the vicinity of Corinth is undulating throughout. The elevations are neither of considerable altitude nor very abrupt, although the roads make some steep ascents. Here and there some broad ridges and depressions extend, affording room for farms, the poor improvements of which, however, indicate but scanty rewards of the husbandman's labors upon the thin soil. Fine forests of full-grown timber, free from underbrush, upon the hills, cover the whole ground and make up somewhat for the absence of other attractions. But few small streams are found, the principal of which are Lick and Chamber's Creeks—the former following a north-easterly course between Pittsburg Landing and Monterey, and the latter an easterly between Monterey and Corinth. Extensive bottoms border each. In the dry season, hardly any water remains in either of them. The population is sparse and mostly in a pitiful state of poverty and ignorance.

HOW OUR ARMY ADVANCED.

Since the first advance until the occupation of the line of encampments held by the army yesterday, the several divisions have each struck and pitched their tents seven times. The distance from Shiloh and Hamburg—the respective starting points—being about eighteen miles, the successive moves averaged but 2½ miles, with intervening halts of from one to four days. Over four weeks having been thus consumed, celerity of movement could not well be claimed for the great Union army of the West. It is true, in the early part of this month, an expeditious advance was difficult, owing to the bad condition of the roads, and the necessity of much preparatory labor upon them—especially in the Lick and Chamber's Creeks bottoms, which had been reduced to extensive swamps by the continued rains of April.

But the sunshine of the last three weeks had removed the natural obstructions, and since the middle of the month better progress might have been made, and the problem that has so long perplexed the army no less than the whole North, viz—whether the enemy would venture a battle at Corinth—solved many days before this. This is no captious criticism, but the opinion of many of the Generals commanding under Gen. Halleck. The only plausible explanation of this trying dilatoriness is furnished by the supposition that the Commander-in-Chief deemed the greatest caution necessary in view of the entire want of trustworthy information as to the numerical strength and defensive preparations of the enemy.

It is certain beyond doubt that up to the 9th inst., even the question, whether the enemy was at all in force at Corinth, was not affirmatively answered in the minds of our generals. Up to that time, the belief that the Rebels would not await our appearance in front of Corinth was almost universal. A series of collisions between our outposts and reconnoitering parties and more or less strong bodies of the enemy, together with the statements of deserters, exchanged prisoners, and other direct and indirect evidence soon after, however, left no doubt that the whole of the hostile army was still massed at the point against which the Union operations were directed. Yet it was apparent, from the fact that no attempt was made to oppose our advance across the swamps along Lick and Chambers Creeks, that, if serious opposition lay within the plans of Gen. Beauregard, it would be reconnoitered only in close proximity to Corinth.

FIELD WORKS CONSTRUCTED.

As our lines were pushed forward they became by degrees contracted, so that when, on the 18th, the left rested at Farmington the front was but about four miles long. At first they formed a sort of semi-circle, the right and left out-reaching the center, but on the stated day the front presented a nearly straight line. Corinth being then approached within four miles, and the enemy showing himself in greater numbers and simultaneously at more points than heretofore, the presumption of his continued presence in full strength was natural, and hence our advance became attended with better guaranties against sudden attacks in the shape of field-works. Double lines of elaborate breastworks were constructed in front of the right and left and a single one in that of the center, and the several batteries of siege guns so placed as to sweep every road leading out from Corinth and completely protect the fortifications.

A strong *point d'appui* and safe retreat in case of repulse being thus secured to each portion of the army, forward movements were again resumed. The advance henceforth was more laborious. Heavy timbers, varied only in few places by farms, with a thick undergrowth, impenetrable to infrantry as well as cavalry and artillery, encompassed our whole line. Roads had to be cut and clearings made in these Mississippi jungles. So great was the difficulty of working through them, that during the last week scarcely a few hundred yards were daily gained upon the enemy. Previous to advancing from point to point, the woods in front were regularly shelled along the line. At times, the Rebels replied with a few rounds from undefinable positions, but most of our firing remained unreturned.

GENERAL ADVANCE ACROSS TWO-MILE CREEK.

On the 27th our lines were carried forward to within a short distance of Two-Mile Creek, a water-course forming an arc from the Corinth and Purdy road to the Memphis and Charleston Railroad, running almost parallel to and about half a mile north of the Rebel breastworks, and crossing the Farmington and Corinth Road about two miles north of Corinth, from which its name is derived. It is bridged at this crossing, and it was generally supposed that its passage would be hotly contested, and that an attempt to cross it would certainly bring on a general engagement. On the morning of the 28th, three strong columns of infantry—one from each wing, and one from the center—with powerful complements of artillery, moved toward the creek. The purpose of those from the left and center was to reconnoiter, and, if practicable, secure the crossing. The column starting from the right was intended to occupy the attention of the enemy in that direction while the demonstrations to the left were being made.

As conjectured, their approach to the creek was severally opposed by large bodies of the enemy, and an action of some duration ensued, conducted on both sides principally with artillery, and resulting in the retreat of the Rebels behind the works, and the occupation of the crossing by the force from Gen. Pope's corps. The loss of his column was some thirty killed and wounded, but that of the two other columns trifling.

During the night severel brigades threw up a new line of breastworks along the creek, for protection from the fire of the enemy's artillery, which was now presumed to be in close range from behind his works. The reserves of the several divisions, the main one under Gen. McClernand, were also moved up, and the whole army got in readiness for the battle, which was surely expected for the following day.

THE LAST DAY OF THE SIEGE.

The enemy failing to open the ball on yesterday morning, Gen. Pope commenced shelling his battery near the bridge. After a few minutes, he replied, and continued a brisk fire for half an hour, when he ceased, and withdrew his battery beyond our range.

During the day a lively shelling of the woods in front was kept up at intervals along the line. Skirmishers were also sent to within easy range of the Rebel breastworks. The Rebels made but a slight show of resistance. This gave rise to a wide-spread apprehension that the enemy, if at all disposed to fight, would at least not accept battle this side of Corinth.

Our entire front was now so close to the enemy's works that the next step had to be an effort to carry them by assault. This seems to have been, indeed, Gen. Halleck's purpose, as orders were given in the course of the evening for a general advance on the coming morning. The long-delayed battle would thus have come off this day, had it not been for the strange developments of the forenoon.

The whole of Wednesday night and of yesterday the cars were heard running south of Corinth. Some believed that the enemy was leaving; others that he was being re-enforced. The latter opinion was strengthened by the stories of deserters that came into our lines on Thursday morning and claimed that Gen. Lovell had arrived with his army from the interior of Mississippi—statements now proved absolute falsehoods, but in full keeping with the improbabilities heretofore palmed off upon our generals by the same class of individuals.

FIRST NEWS OF THE EVACUATION—THE ENEMY BLOWING UP HIS MAGAZINES.

Between 2 and 3 o'clock this morning more fugitives from the Rebel army found their way to the pickets of the various divisions. Upon being interrogated, they made the startling statement that the rear guard of the enemy had commenced marching out of Corinth in a southerly direction, and that there was not now a Confederate soldier in the town. Offering to answer with their lives for the correctness of what they asserted, they obtained credence, and their intelligence at once communicated to headquarters. At about the same time several explosions were heard in rapid succession, which the deserters professed to believe to be caused by ammunition stored in storehouses fired by the Rebels before they retreated from the place.

GEN. POPE MARCHES INTO CORINTH—THE TOWN SURRENDERS.

With daybreak rumors of the evacuation were already circulating through the army. A general eagerness to ascertain the truth in the premises became manifest. Gen. Pope's corps being somewhat nearer to the breastworks than the other portions of the army, was the first to solve the question. His avant guard moved upon the Rebel breastworks at about 6 o'clock, and shortly afterward entered them unresisted. Being now satisfied that the enemy had really abandoned Corinth, the whole corps pushed on in quick step, and the head of the column, the 39th Ohio, entered the town a little after 7.

The divisions moving upon the town from the center and left over the Hamburg and Corinth, Pittsburg and Corinth, Corinth and Purdy roads severally, reached the outskirts of the place between 8 and 10 o'clock, when they were halted, and afterward returned to their encampments.

Gen. Nelson was met a short distance from town, while advancing over the Hamburg Road, by the Mayor, who came to surrender the town, and ask the protection of private property—a request, the fulfillment of which was, of course, promised.

The few representatives of the Press remaining near Gen. Halleck's army subsequent to the enforcement of the order prohibiting the stay of civilians within its lines, deeming it dictated by discretion to keep in the rear, did not succeed in making their way to Corinth until this afternoon.

WEAKNESS OF THE REBEL FORTIFICATIONS.

The roads to the place are in the best possible condition, and were in no way obstructed by the Rebels. A good deal had been said about a formidable swamp in front of the enemy's fortifications, but nothing of the kind was noticed. The "fortifications" hardly deserved the name. They were the simplest description of breastworks, hardly affording protection for infantry from musketry, not to speak of artillery. They are not half as strong as those constructed by our troops in a single night. Their appearance indicated that they were hastily thrown up some time since—probably after the retreat of the Rebels from the battle-field of Shiloh as a means of defense against an immediate attack by our forces—and could not have possibly been expected to prove a serious impediment to us. At several commanding points the ground had been seemingly prepared for heavy artillery, but there were no positive indications of such ever having been placed in position. There were, however, embrasures for light pieces near the roads, and such seemed to have been put to use to cover the former. On the whole, the "fortifications" afford the best possible evidence that Beauregard had no idea of running the risk of battle before Corinth.

The breastworks run over a succession of hills from a point near the Memphis and Charleston Railroad east of Corinth to near the Purdy and Corinth road about a mile north of the town. Their entire length is said to be five miles.

APPEARANCE OF THE TOWN—THE POPULATION.

From the ridges upon which the breastworks extend there is a steady decline for a mile and a half to the town, which is situated upon a slightly undulating ground, almost like a plain. Corinth is built regularly, the streets intersecting each other at rectangle. It contains quite a number of fine edifices, both for purposes of business and residence, and is altogether the best-appearing town of its size the Army of the West has seen since its invasion of Southern soil. There are, perhaps, three hundred buildings, which must have been inhabited in ordinary times by some two thousand inhabitants. The houses were standing, with the exception of the depot and two or three storehouses burned by the Rebels. But the population—a more general exodus has probably not occurred in this war. All that remains of it are not over a hundred old men, women, and children of both colors.

The main street of the town runs from the west to the east, parallel to the track of the Memphis and Charleston Railroad. Of the numerous stores, but two or three remained open.

STATEMENTS OF THE PEOPLE ABOUT THE REBEL ARMY.

One of these is occupied by a druggist, whose stock, however, had dwindled down to almost invisible proportions. He claims to be a Unionist, and freely communicated all he knew about the situation of matters previous to and during the evacuation. His account was consistent and intelligent, and certainly seemed worthy of credit. He stated that a worse, more shattered, and demoralized army than that of the Confederates after their retreat from Shiloh was never seen. It was only a week after the battle that it had all returned to the vicinity of the town, and weeks elapsed subsequently before anything like order was re-established among it.

After the battle it did not number 30,000 fighting men, and at no time after it—so he asserted positively—were there ever over 60,000 men under command of Gen. Beauregard. Generals Hardee, Van Dorn, Bragg, and Polk commanded the four corps into which the army was divided. The removal of the sick, wounded, and stores continued twelve days. The main body of the army was sent off by rail toward Memphis between Saturday and Wednesday last, and was supposed to have disembarked at Grand Junction. Only about one-third of the army remained after Wednesday under the immediate direction of Beauregard. The greater part of these were constantly on duty in our front; and it was understood that they were to keep up a show of resistance until there was danger of being surrounded or cut off from retreat. Their camping equipage was removed on Wednesday and Thursday. About midnight on Thursday they commenced their retreat through the town, and at 3 o'clock the last of them were gone. They marched in a southward direction, the rolling stock on the Mobile and Ohio Railroad having previously been sent South.

His statement in regard to the time the evacuation began is borne out by the fact that the Rebels left absolutely nothing behind them beyond a few barrels of flour, the contents of which were scattered upon the streets in various places. Even their hospitals were completely emptied. Everything had likewise been removed from the Post-Office and the houses occupied as headquarters. Beauregard's staff occupied the principal hotel—the Teshamingo House, which is also completely deserted.

Immediately after the first of our troops entered the town the Stars and Stripes were raised over the Court-House. During the first hours of the occupation many houses were broken open by stragglers from the ranks, who loaded themselves with plunder, but toward noon guards were stationed all over town, and the wanton interference with private property stopped.

DESERTERS COMING IN.

As soon as cavalry and artillery could be brought up, pursuit was made of the retreating enemy for a distance of five miles. Nothing was, however, seen of him. While going and returning, Rebel soldiers came out of the woods lining the roads, singly and in squads, to the number of over 100, and gave themselves up, claiming to be treated as deserters.

FREMONT'S PURSUIT OF JACKSON.

AN ENGAGEMENT BEYOND STRASBURG.

THE REBELS RESUME THEIR RETREAT.

Smith and Longstreet in the Valley with 15,000 Rebel Troops.

MARTINSBURG, Wednesday, May 4, 1862.

Trustworthy statements from Strasburg say that Jackson's whole force, with his train and prisoners, succeeded in passing through toward Newmarket.

The firing on Monday was an attack by Gen. Milroy on Jackson's rear guard at Fisher's Hill, a strong strategic point a mile and a half from Strasburg.

From the best information obtainable, the enemy held their ground, and resumed their retreat during the night.

It is reported that Jackson's advance guard were in Newmarket on Monday night. The Rebel Gens. Smith and Longstreet were in the Valley with 15,000 men, but their exact position was unknown.

The Number of Prisoners Taken by Jackson—Reoccupation of Winchester—The Baltimore and Ohio Railroad.

Special Dispatch to The N. Y. Tribune.

HARPER'S FERRY, Wednesday, June 4, 1862.

Mr. Eicheleger, formerly of New-York, but recently engaged in business at Winchester, reached here to-day. Himself and partner were taken prisoners by the Rebels, but he managed to escape, and walked to this place. The Rebels took 2,100 prisoners, 40 of whom were officers and 60 civilians. They were taken to Lynchburg. Our forces hold Martinsburg, and by this time are at Winchester. Col. Kenly of the 1st Maryland left Martinsburg, on parole, for Baltimore, by way of Frederick, this morning. Nine deserters from Jackson's army were sent to Baltimore this afternoon. Mr. Smith, Master of Transportation of the Baltimore and Ohio Railroad, has gone to Martinsburg. He thinks that all the damage done to the railroad by the Rebels may be repaired without difficulty, and the road put in order by Saturday.

MOVEMENTS OF WOUNDED.

PHILADELPHIA, Wednesday, June 4, 1862.

The steamer Whildin arrived at 1 o'clock this morning from James River, having on board 400 wounded Pennsylvania soldiers from the late battle on the Chickahominy.

BOSTON, Wednesday, June 4, 1862.

A private dispatch states that the steamer Daniel Webster left the White House last night with 242 wounded New-England soldiers, including Brig.-Gen. Devens and Col. Briggs, for Boston.

MRS. GREENHOW'S REPORTED LEVEE.

BALTIMORE, Wednesday, June 4, 1862.

The statement telegraphed from here that Mrs. Greenhow, Mrs. Baxley, and Mrs. Morris were permitted to hold a levee while here waiting for the departure of the Old Point boat, proves to have been based on exaggerated statements. A number of female Secessionists visited the hotel, but it is said they were denied admission, Gen. Dix having given special orders to allow them no communication with any one whatever. Some may have succeeded in greeting them as they were about leaving for the boat.

THE BATTLE OF THE SEVEN PINES.

Bloody Check Sustained by the Union Advance.

McCLELLAN ON THE GROUND.

THE CAUSES OF OUR DEFEAT.

LIST OF KILLED AND WOUNDED.

Correspondence of The N. Y. Tribune.

SAVAGE'S STATION, York River and Richmond R. R., May 31, 1862.

At 1 o'clock this afternoon a musketry fire in front of the left wing and upon Casey's Division, told us that the enemy had commenced the fight, which policy and necessity had suspended on our part. The storm of last night was the most furious fall of rain and explosion of lightning I ever saw. Not a regiment, not a company, scarcely an officer was exempt from its chilling and exhausting effects. The Rebels seized upon it as an element of military advantage, and, having fully prepared themselves, fell suddenly on our pickets, scattered them inwards, and held Casey's regiments in actual battle while their pots and kettles were yet on the fires, and many of the men were drying their wet clothes. I cannot tell in the confusion, which now reigns supreme, how the small earthwork and the rifle-pit at the front were so quickly taken out of our possession. The number and the quality of the guns in the fort I am ignorant of. But pits, fort, and guns, whether siege or field, changed owners suddenly.

Now I face the first truth in the history of the Union Disgrace at the Seven Pines—and I shall not dodge it. The important place of danger, the front, was committed to a General whose division composed of raw troops marched down Fourteenth street, in Washington, in the last week of February, 13,000 strong—and has been so neglected and so allowed to go undisciplined, that 7,000 of them could not by any possibility have been gathered together this morning—a division so left to itself to luck, and the devil, that it has lost, literally lost, 700 men and upward since it left Williamsburg—a division whose commander has long been conspicuous as searching, miles ahead of his marching columns, for comfortable quarters. Upon this division, out of place in the front, the shock of battle fell—and knocked it into disorder and ruin faster than I conceived it possible for Anglo-Saxon troops to be moved by any power less than God's thunderbolts. Oh! how much I have learned to-day, and how much I have unlearned!

Gen. Peck's military family were at their rice and coffee in the open air at a quarter before 1 o'clock in the afternoon. The unmistakable rattle of musketry fired by companies and by column in front brought the graduate of every battle-field in Mexico right to his feet. He mounted instantly and ordered his brigade under arms. In the short space of time consumed by me in rolling up my blankets and overcoat, and saddling a restless horse, and riding twenty rods toward the front—not twenty minutes—the current of straggling and skulking had fully set in, and was sweeping in a great shameful flow down the Williamsburg road. It was the most astonishing of spectacles. Great, healthy, vigorous men, who had volunteered to fight the battles of Freedom, walking rapidly back from the first touch of the foe, with boxes full of cartridges and muskets in their hands, sound in wind and limb, but, thank God! looking mean as sheep-thieves when they encountered the stare of brave men, and simulating lameness and every form of sickness when cavaliers, not combatants by profession, damned them in their fury for cowards, and endeavored to breast them backward with their horses into the fight—great hulking poltroons, falling into every possible variety of limp out of rapid, strong walking; depressing at pleasure either shoulder with terrible wounds; quickly gathering into their bosoms mutilated arms, wholly untouched with bullets; going through the whole disgusting pantomime of sickness of the stomach in reply to fierce questions as to where they were going, and why the devil they were not fighting; with false speech and falser looks asserting every conceivable acute attack of disabling disease as a justification for going to the rear, and letting the cause they had sworn to defend go to the devil. It was amazing. It was a new revelation! But a moment's reflection, and a sharp observation of the numbers on the caps of the streaming cowards, explained the phenomenon, as it appeared to a civilian. The brass figures 100, 101, 103, 104, told of enlistments as late as January and February, and conclusively proved the greenness and inexperience of troops who had been taught nothing save how to march and to camp, and who deteriorated daily under the command of a General who had neither youth, enthusiasm, pride, or combativeness. To these, the sight of falling comrades, and the shrieking of the wounded, and the groaning of the dying, instead of being the food of a fierce fury, served only to open the veins of manhood, and let all courage out. Down the road they came—over the fields on either side of the road they straggled fast—through the safer woods they skulked away, and sought the rear. Most were muddy, showing that they had lain down to avoid the shell and shot—very many were without arms and accouterments. The crowd grew thicker. The Provost Guard formed across the road to stem its dastardly flow. Before 3 o'clock, Gen. Keyes found that Casey's entire division was gone! He sent to Heintzelman for instant help. The brave Pennsylvanian was already on his way to the place where he was wanted. He came on the ground about a quarter after 3, and gathering as rapidly as he could all the elements of the situation in the strange woods and unknown swamps, took command, and infused his indomitable spirit into the failing fight. He sent back for Kearney, and Jamieson, and Birney, and Berry—he who so timely brought salvation upon his bayonet points to us at Williamsburg. While they were coming up, I went ahead once more to see the 55th go into fire. Their movement in response to the order "Forward!" was not impulsive from front to rear. It hitched, in sections, like the drawing out of the joints of a field glass. Omen of evil! In thirty minutes red-capped and red-trousered men, mostly without their muskets, were under the fire of the scorn and the jeering of the New-York 62d—a fire more galling and insupportable, as it seemed to me, than any that ever spouted from muskets. "Mounsheer, the muss is the other way!" "Hello, youngsters! we are Union men; we ain't Rebels. What are you running at *us* for?" "The 62d is good shelter; fall in behind!" Not a wrathful reply was made. The bursting of the Rebel shells over head, the screaming of their solid long shot, and the cutting off of the tree-tops, made the place and the time totally unsuited for repartee or discussion. The 62d opened its laughing ranks, and the gory-colored, but unbloody, passed through and passed on.

About 4 o'clock, Couch and Peck came from the left, and passed through the line of fire and went at right angles over to the railroad, to repel a movement in a similar direction made by the Rebels away beyond the scene of Casey's disappearance. The conflict they sustained in the woods was bloody and unequal. Peck's horse was shot through the neck, shot again in the flank, and soon had both his hind legs cut off by a cannon ball. Re-enforcements were called for, and Heintzelman intercepted a regiment moving to the front, and ordered it over to the railroad. He subsequently ordered Birney's Brigade to march right up the track and save the fight. The brigade did not get into action, and Birney is under arrest. McClellan, before this, at his headquarters, twelve miles off, roused by the cannonade and by the telegraph, got out of his sick bed and put a portion of Sumner's Corps into motion up the railroad. Kearney, too, had come up the Williamsburg road, and Jamieson had gone eagerly forward into the hell of shell and shot and smoke, as did Berry at the head of his Michigan men. A ball tore off his hat, and his manly fight was fought bareheaded. The line of battle at this time was nearly a mile wide, and almost wholly in the woods. The enemy, in overwhelming numbers, had forced us back at least a mile, and were piling up troops on our right toward the railroad. The firing at this point at about 5 o'clock was a marvel to me. It is claimed that that at Williamsburg was heavier twice or thrice during the day, but that is not my judgment. I can compare this to nothing but the roar of Niagara. It had no spaces—no cracks. It was solid, continuous, deafening. Over it the incessant bursting of shells and screaming of solid conical shot ribbed the racket with great seams of noise, which compelled men touching each other in opposite saddles to shout when they talked. The straggling set in briskly from before this fire. Superhuman efforts, headed by Heintzelman, and aided by his Surgeon, Milhau, and Colonel Adams, and others, stopped a full regiment for awhile, and rallied them around their colors, but could not long hold them against the storm of whistling bullets and case-shot. The crowd rolled off the field, carrying away some who meant to stay. To my dying day I shall have in my ears the wailing shriek of a private of the 1st Long Island, shot dead beside my horse with a percussion musket-ball, whose explosion within its wound I distinctly heard, and which must have overwhelmed him morally more than it did physically. Not running, nor terrified—only unwilling to stay—this crowd straggled partly in the road, mostly in the woods, back, back, to the line of the rifle-pits Couch had made a week ago. On the way Hooker's Brigade was met, and met with the hurrahs of applause due to brave men.

Darkness left Sedgwick on the railroad, master of the ground occupied in the afternoon by the Rebel forces, and from which he had gallantly driven them. Our extreme right is now beyond the advance of yesterday. We are probably behind the morning position of our center three-quarters of a mile, and a full mile behind our morning's position on the left. The loss of property and material is awful, embracing eight guns and the contents of at least four camps. The loss in killed, wounded, and missing is more awful.

Among the dead is Casey's Commander of Artillery, Col. Bailey, and Col. Howell of the 85th Michigan. The wounded include Gens. Wessels, Devens, Cols. Campbell, Champlin, Briggs, Morris and a large number of Captains and minor officers. Up to 9 o'clock in the evening, 100 wounded, operated on, had been sent off by rail to West Point or the nearest landing. 'Tis but a tithe of the whole. The surgeons are yet at work.

Heintzelman's horse was shot, as was Peck's and Jamieson's; Keyes was wounded, and numerous staff officers were dismounted.

It is now 2 o'clock in the morning, and McClellan is here, and the best troops in the army are within his short reach, and the sun will set to-morrow upon a great Union victory, or upon the bloodiest defeat that Rebellion ever gave to Constitutional Government and its armed defenders.

The Second Day—Good News!

Correspondence of the N. Y. Tribune.

SAVAGE'S STATION, Sunday morning—7½ o'clock.

While waiting to make up from the Surgeons' memoranda a list of the killed and wounded in the battle of the Seven Pines, I listen to the furious musketry which this morning renews the fight upon the ground where the combatants separated last night. It is about a mile off only, and the white smoke rising through the dark pines and oaks marks accurately the altar on which Slavery and rebellion

See Eighth Page.

Daily Mississippian.

COOPER & KIMBALL,

PROPRIETORS.

$5000 will be Given by One Man for BUTLER'S Head!

COLUMBUS, Miss., June 2, 1862.

Editor Mississippian: I like the suggestion of your correspondent in offering a reward for the head of the infamous General commanding the Yankee forces in N. O., BUTLER. I will be good for $5000. Let the money go to the family of the party who succeeds in the undertaking, if he should forfeit his life in so doing. B.

THE THREE DEGREES.—It has been said that the stages of a Yankee's progress are, first to get on; next to get honor; and last to get honest.

☞ We see it stated in an exchange, that the Bank of France was lately robbed of 150,000f. by one of its attachees.

MR. SOULE.—The Delta, of late date, learns that Mr. Soule "has been arrested on a high political charge, and that he will probably go North in the course of a few days."

FRANCE AND JAPAN.—We read that it is currently believed in Paris that the Japanese Embassy have concluded a treaty with the Emperor, in virtue of which he undertakes to send to Japan eighty millions of francs worth of machinery and metalic goods, and is to receive in return wool, cotton, and textiles to a like value.

PARSON BROWNLOW INVITED TO BOSTON.—The Ancient and Honorable Artillery Company have invited the celebrated Parson Brownlow, of Knoxville, Tennessee, to deliver the annual election sermon before that body on the next Monday in June, in Boston. The Parson is just now quite the lion of the North.

☞ A correspondent of the Montgomery Advertiser gives the following list of gentlemen that the Lincolnites have in prison in Huntsville:

Dr. Thomas Fearn, Ex-Gov. R. Chapman, Bishop H. C. Lay, George P. Beirne, Esq., William Acklen, Samuel Cruse, Wm. McDowell, A. J. Withers, G. L. Mastin. J. G. Wilson, Willis Harris, Wm. H. Moore, Thos. J. McCalley.

EAST TENNESSEE.—The Knoxville Register of the 20th ult. says: We learn that the Conscript Act is to be suspended in East Tennessee, and the official announcement of the fact will probably be made shortly. We trust that this will have the effect to entirely allay the stampeding of that class of citizens who are averse to military duty, and they will now apply themselves quietly to their respective avocations, especially the agricultural portion of them.

☞ In the following, the Delta describes the reason why the Mayor was sent to Fort Jackson:

STATE OF LA., MAYORALTY OF NEW ORLEANS, CITY HALL, May 16th, 1862.

Maj. Gen. Benj. F. Butler, Commanding U. S. Forces:

SIR—Your general order No. 28, of date of 15th inst., is of a character so extraordinary and astounding, that I cannot, holding the office of Chief Magistrate of this city, chargeable with its peace and dignity, suffer it to be promulgated in our presence without protesting against the threat it contains, which has already roused the passions of our people, and must exasperate them to a degree beyond control. Your officerr and soldiers are permitted by the terms of this order to place any construction they may please upon the conduct of our wives and daughters, and upon such construction to offer them atrocious insults.

The peace of the city and the safety of your officers and soldiers from harm or insult have, I affirm, been successfully secured to an extent enabling them to move through our streets almost unnoticed, according to the understanding and agreement entered into between yourself and the city authorities. I did not, however, anticipate a war upon women and children, who so far as I am aware, have only manifested their displeasure at the occupation of their city by those whom they believe to be their enemies.

"I will never undertake to be responsible for the peace of New Orleans while such an edict which infuriates our citizens, remains in force.

To give a license to the officers and soldiers of your command to commit outrages such as are indicated in your order, upon defenceless women, is, in my judgement, a reproach to the civilization, not to say to the Christianity of the age, in whose name I make this protest.

I am, sir, your ob't servant,
JOHN T. MONROE, Mayor.

Immediately upon the receipt of this epistle the Provost Marshal brought the Mayor before Gen. Butler. The Mayor was then told that the language of the letter would not be tolerated, and that if he believed that he could no longer control the "aroused passions of the people," he would be relieved of any responsibility for the tranquillity of the city and sent to a place of safety himself, to wit: Fort Jackson. The Mayor said that he only desired to vindicate the honor of the virtuous women of the city. He was informed that there was no vindication needed, because the order did not contemplate any virtuous woman, for the General did not believe that such person, by word, gesture or movement, meant to insult any one of his officers or soldiers. And the order implied to no others, save those that had insulted the troops.

The Mayor said with this explanation he was satisfied, and would withdraw his letter. He therefore signed the following written apology, and left for his home:

General Butler:

This communication having been sent under a mistake of fact, and being improper in language, I desire to apologize for the same and to withdraw it.

JOHN T. MONROE, Mayor.

May 16, 1862.

Now the matter touching Order No. 28 was supposed to have been ended.

But this course did not suit the keepers of John T. Monroe, and on the evening of the same day Gen. Butler received the following letter:

MAYORALTY OF NEW ORLEANS,
City Hall, May 16, 1862.

Major-General Butler:

SIR—Having misunderstood you yesterday in relation to your General Order No. 28, I wish to withdraw the endorsement I made on the letter addressed to you yesterday. Please deliver the letter to my Secretary, Mr. Duncan, who will hand you this note.

Your obedient servant,
JOHN T. MONROE,
Mayor.

To this General Butler returned the following answer:

HEADQUARTERS DEPARTMENT OF THE GULF,
New Orleans, May 16, 1862.

SIR:—There can be, there has been, no room for misunderstanding of General Order No. 28.

No lady will take any notice of a strange gentleman, and *a fortiori* of a stranger simply in such form as to attract attention. Common women do.

Therfore, whenever, woman, lady or mistress, gentle or simple, who, by gesture, look or word, insults, shows contempt for, thus attracting to herself the notice of my officers and soldiers, will be deemed to act as becomes her vocation as a common woman, and will be liable to be treated accordingly. This was most fully explained to you at my office.

I shall not, as I have not, abate a single word of that order, it was well considered; and if obeyed, will protect the true and modest women from all possible insult. The others will take care of themselves.

You can publish your letter, if you publish this note and your apology.

Respectfully, BENJ. F. BUTLER,
Major-General Commanding.

JOHN T. MONROE, Mayor of New Orleans.

A true copy.
P. AD FORTIER, Clerk to Mayor.

Land Batteries and Gunboats.

The subjoined article—which we clip from a late number of the Richmond Whig, has a striking applicability to this latitude, as well as that of Mobile and Richmond. We commend it to the attention of those commanding our batteries at Vicksburg:

From the Richmond Whig.

The repulse of the Yankee fleet below this city Thursday morning, by the incomplete and unprotected batteries at Drewry's Bluff, is a hopeful prelude to the conflict soon to occur at that point. The successful resistance by Fort Wright to the passage of the enemies' boats down the Mississippi, protracted as it is, is another encouraging circumstance. History abounds with signal illustrations of the superiority of shore batteries over naval armaments. Some of these we find referred to in a late issue of the Mobile Register, and as the question is one of paramount interest just at this time to the citizens of Richmond, we avail ourselves of the Register's citations. They are well calculated to encourage us in a resolute and unyielding defence of our city. If it be said that naval armaments are greatly improved since the occurrence of the events alluded to, let it be remembered that the means of resistance and defence are equally improved.

In 1794, two British ships, a 74 and a 32, attacked a small town in the bay of Martello, Corsica, which was armed with one gun in barbette and a garrison of 30 men. After a bombardment of two and a half hours, these ships were forced to haul off with considerable damage and loss of life. The little tower received no injury and its garrison was unharmed. Here *one* gun ashore was successful against 106 afloat.

In 1797, Nelson attacked the little inefficient batteries of Santa Cruz, with eight ships and four hundred guns. He was repulsed with a loss of 250 men, while the garrison received no damage. A single ball from the land sunk one of his ships with every soul on board.

In 1798, a French flotilla of 52 brigs and gunboats, manned with 7000 men, attacked a small English redoubt on the Island of Marcou, which was armed with 10 guns, the largest 32's and the smallest 4 pounders, and garrisoned with 250 men. The result was a retreat of the French fleet with great loss of life—seven of their vessels sunk and one captured.

In 1802, Admiral Samaurez, with an English fleet carrying 502 guns, attacked the Spanish and French defenses of Algesiras. The French land battery mounted only 12 guns, the disparity was reduced by a French force afloat, to 196 English guns on shipboard against 12 on shore. Notwithstanding the superiority of nearly 17 to 1, the battery compelled the English to retreat with great loss. Shortly after this the French and Spanish fleets attacked the *same* English squadron with a force of *three* to *one*, but met with a signal defeat. Yet a land battery of 12 guns had whipped the same victorious fleet.

In 1803, an English garrison near Port Royal Bay, with 100 men and 15 guns, repelled a French squadron of two 74-gun ships, a frigate and a brig, assisted by a land attack of 200 men. The redoubt did not lose a man, and the French lost fifty men.

In 1806, a French battery of only two guns and twenty-five men resisted two British 80-gun ships and two frigates. The carriage of one of the land guns failed on the second fire, so that the action was fought with only one gun. Here was a single piece of ordnance and twenty-five men against a naval force of one hundred and fifty guns and thirteen hundred men. The assailants lost thirty-seven men, the eighty gun ship was disabled, while the garrison was unharmed. In 1808, a French land battery of *three* guns drove off an English seventy-four and a bomb vessel.

In 1814, when the English advanced against Antwerp, they established a battery of two guns in a bend of the Polder Dyke—the armament was a long 18 pounder and one 5½ inch howitzer. The French determined to dislodge the English, and dropped down with the tide an eighty gun ship and anchored her off the Flanders shore, six hundred yards from the battery. Only the eighteen pounder could be brought to bear upon the ship. The garrison had to leave their gun at every broadside, but whenever the fire slackened for a moment they sprang to their gun and managed to give at least one shot for eighty. This strange combat lasted for five hours, when the ship had to give up the fight with forty killed and wounded, her commander among the latter. The redoubt lost one killed and two wounded.

Our limited space admonishes us that we must stop with the record before we have fairly begun it. The whole history of gunnery shows that land batteries are invincible by ship batteries. The attack on Copenhagen in 1801, the passage of the Dardanelles in 1807, and the attack on Algiers in 1815, are noted feats of the English navy; but they are not even exceptions to prove the rule. Copenhagen was not conquered by the fleet of Nelson, but by his diplomacy when he was on the verge of ruin. Lord Exmouth, at Algiers, was indebted to a lucky land breeze, which enabled him to escape destruction at a lucky moment; while the case of Admiral Luckworth in the passage of the Dardanelles is only one of wonderful escape, favored by a strong current and fair wind. Out of eleven sail only two escaped. The rest were terribly cut up by the shore batteries. If the latter had been properly prepared and manned, Gen. Jomini says the expedition would have cost the English their whole squadron.

Surely, examples like these should give us confidence in our ability to defend this beautiful capital, so shut in and hedged round by natural muniments, and so worthy of the most heroic struggle.

It has been deliberately resolved and openly proclaimed that Richmond is to be defended to the last. Let it be a defense that will shine in history by the side of Leyden and Saragossa.

$5000 will be Given by One Man for BUTLER'S Head!

COLUMBUS, Miss., June 2, 1862.

Editor Mississippian: I like the suggestion of your correspondent in offering a reward for the head of the infamous General commanding the Yankee forces in N. O., BUTLER. I will be good for $5000. Let the money go to the family of the party who succeeds in the undertaking, if he should forfeit his life in so doing. B.

THE NEW-YORK TRIBUNE.

THE NEW-YORK DAILY TRIBUNE
IS PUBLISHED EVERY MORNING AND EVENING
(SUNDAYS EXCEPTED)
BY THE TRIBUNE ASSOCIATION,
IN THE TRIBUNE BUILDINGS, CORNER OF NASSAU AND SPRUCE STREETS, OPPOSITE THE CITY HALL,
And delivered to City Subscribers at 12½ cents per week. Mail Subscribers $6 per annum in advance; $3 for 6 months.

THE NEW-YORK TRIBUNE
FOR EUROPEAN CIRCULATION
is published on the departure of each Mail Steamer for Liverpool at $5 per annum, postage included. Single Copies Five Cents. Address THE TRIBUNE ASSOCIATION,
No. 154 Nassau-st., N. Y.

New-York Daily Tribune.

THE NEW-YORK TRIBUNE.

THE NEW-YORK WEEKLY TRIBUNE,
A VERY LARGE PAPER FOR THE COUNTRY,
is published every SATURDAY MORNING at the low price of $2 per annum, in advance. Three copies for $5; Five Copies for $8; Ten Copies for $12; Twenty Copies to one address (and any larger number at the rate of $1 per annum), $20; Twenty Copies to address of each subscriber (and any larger number at the rate of $1 20 each), $24. Any person sending us a club of twenty or more will be entitled to an extra copy. Subscriptions to commence at any time.
Advertisements in THE WEEKLY TRIBUNE cost ONE DOLLAR A LINE for each insertion. Nothing inserted for less than $5.

THE SEMI-WEEKLY TRIBUNE
is published every TUESDAY and FRIDAY MORNING. Price $3 per annum: Two Copies for $5; Five Copies for $11 25.

VOL. XXII.....No. 6,607. NEW-YORK, SATURDAY, JUNE 7, 1862. PRICE TWO CENTS.

THE CITY OF MEMPHIS.

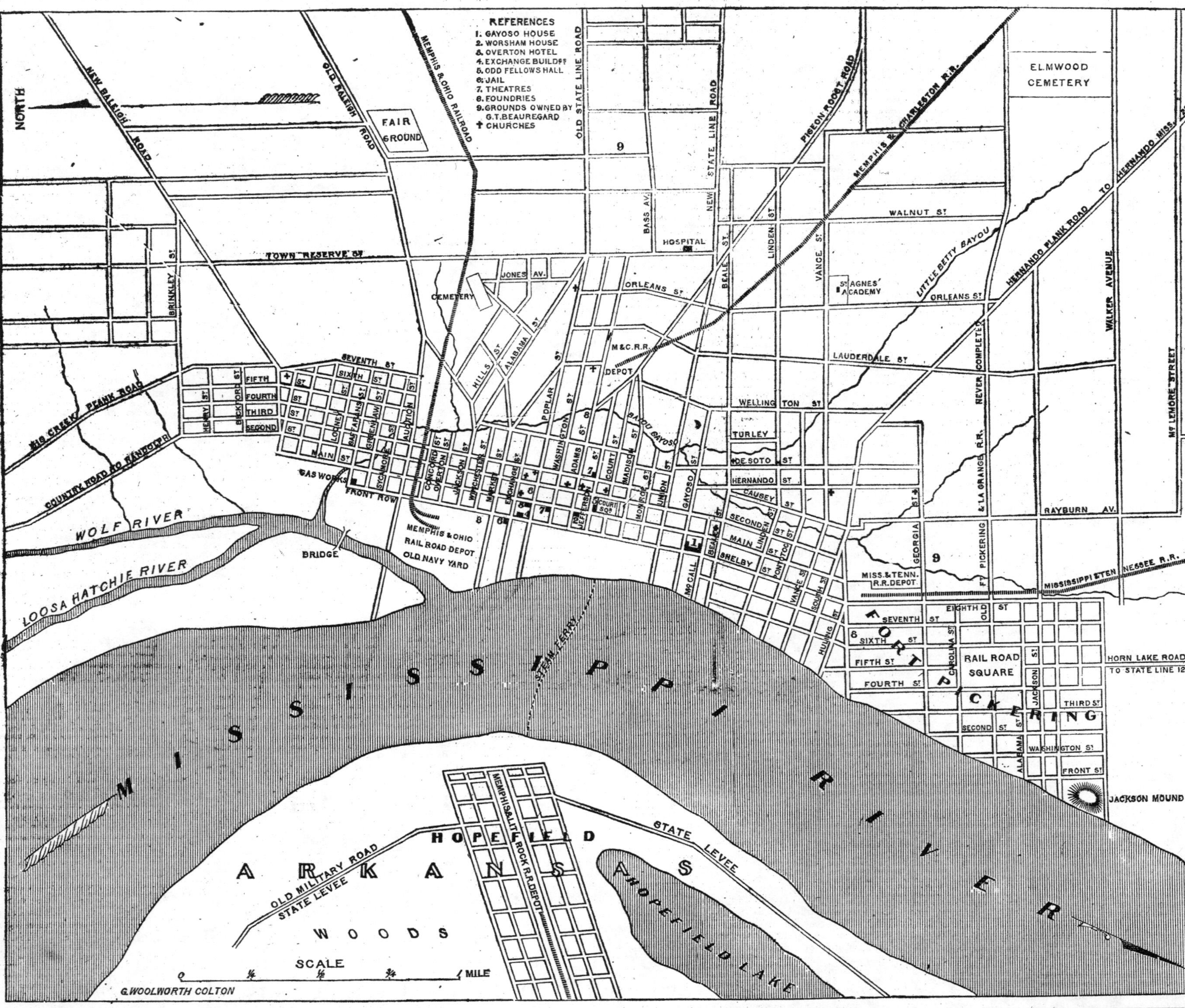

FORT PILLOW EVACUATED.

FORT RANDOLPH DESERTED

OUR TROOPS IN POSSESSION.

The Flotilla on the Way to Memphis.

CHICAGO, Friday, June 6, 1862.

Cairo dispatches state that the steamer Shinghies has arrived from the fleet, and reports that at the time she left the flames were breaking out in the barracks of the fort, and the gunboats had dropped down the river.

CAIRO, Friday, June 6, 1862.

Fort Wright is evacuated, and we are now in possession. The flotilla has passed Fort Randolph en route to Memphis.

CAIRO, Friday, June 6, 1862.

There is yet some doubt that our fleet has passed Fort Randolph, where the Rebels are said to have taken the guns which they removed from the fort above. They left only five or six guns. Before leaving, they destroyed the barracks, camp equipage, gun carriages, and such stores as could not be transported. They also burned the cotton, of which the breastworks were constructed.

The flotilla cast off at 5 o'clock yesterday morning, and were followed by the transports carrying the 46th Indiana, Col. Fitch, who now occupy the works, which are said to be of great strength, and if properly manned, could have successfully resisted a large force. The Rebels, after leaving the fort, destroyed the pontoon bridge which they had constructed some weeks since over the Hatchie River.

When the De Soto, which last arrived from the fleet, left, the gunboats had passed the Fort, and gone down the river. It is reported that the Rebels have evacuated Fort Randolph. If this is the case, nothing can prevent the fleet from arriving at Memphis to-day.

WASHINGTON, Friday, June 6, 1862.

The following dispatch has just been received at the War Department:

CAIRO, Friday, June 6, 1862.

The De Soto has arrived direct from Fort Pillow. Our forces occupy the fort. The enemy burned everything. A number of guns were found. The large mortars had been destroyed.

The gunboats have passed Fort Randolph.

WASHINGTON, Friday, June 6, 1862.

The following was also received to-day at the Navy Department:

CAIRO, Friday, June 6, 1862.

To the Hon. GIDEON WELLES, *Secretary of the Navy.*

The dispatch boat of last night reports the evacuation of Fort Pillow and its occupation by our troops. Most of the flotilla had passed below Randolph.

A. M. PENNOCK, Commander, &c.

FROM GEN. HALLECK'S ARMY.

Further Details of the Evacuation of Corinth—Pursuit of the Rebels—A Brilliant Cavalry Demonstration in the Rear of the Enemy—Demoralization of the Rebel Army—Movements of the Army, &c.

From Our Special Correspondent.

CORINTH, May 31, 1862.

From the statements of the remaining citizens of Corinth, it can be safely inferred that the rumors of great sufferings in the Rebel army from sickness and want of food and water, must have had some foundation in fact. They seemed to have had an abundance of flour, but were on short rations of everything else. That the scarcity of water must have been great, the dry condition of all the streams in the neighborhood of the town and the fewness of wells amply proves. It was daily growing more oppressive with the advance of the hot season, and would have alone eventually compelled the Rebels to evacuate.

The cavalry sent in pursuit of the retreating Rebels under command of General Jackson report that they found all the roads leading South strewn with arms, blankets, knapsacks, coats, etc. This indicates that the retreat of the rear-guard was very precipitate. The presumption is that it was made so by the appearance in their rear of a mounted force dispatched over a circuitous road on Wednesday last by General Pope in the direction of Booneville, some thirty odd miles south of Corinth, with orders to destroy the bridge on the Mobile and Ohio Railroad in that vicinity. That this expedition was successful is inferred from the fact that the last Rebel column marched overland.

Closer investigation on yesterday and to-day revealed that the destruction of property by the Rebels was very great. A number of wagons and large quantities of barreled beef beside flour were comprised in the destruction.

The appearance of the ground lately occupied by the Rebel encampments shows that their camp-police must have been miserable. Disgusting filth characterized them all, and at some points an overwhelming stench prevailed.

Sickness is reported to have ravaged fearfully among the new conscripts hurried up from Louisiana, Alabama and Mississippi; no adequate provisions for either quartering or feeding them have been made. A regular sick train left Corinth for the interior of Mississippi every morning.

The reported withdrawal of the greater part of the Rebel army in the direction of the Grand Junction seems to have given rise to apprehensions of demonstrations on our right flank or rear with Gen. Halleck. The work of the breastworks along the Purdy and Corinth, constructed by the reserve for the protection of the right, was discontinued upon the news of the evacuation, but suddenly ordered to be resumed with a double force yesterday afternoon. Gen. Wallace's division was also sent out upon a reconnoissance in the direction of Purdy to prevent any possible menace of our rear.

Deserters still come in, and are picked up by the cavalry in considerable numbers.

SUNDAY, June 1, 1862.

The demonstration by a mounted force in the rear of the enemy, alluded to in my last, has proved an entire success. The expedition, consisting of the 2d Iowa Cavalry under command of Col. Elliott, returned this evening. What it achieved during its absence of four days certainly deserves to be classed among the most memorable exploits of this war. They started out with the break of day on the 28th, and after a forced march, continued night and day, over circuitous roads, which none of the regiment had ever seen before, across numerous streams, and through a country every inhabitant of which was an enemy, they struck the Mobile and Ohio Railroad on Friday morning, on Cypress Creek, close to Booneville, nearly forty miles south of Corinth. To their astonishment they found the bridge they had come to destroy already burned, and what was a matter of still greater surprise, they found a train of twenty-six freight-cars, drawn by two locomotives, and loaded with provisions, forage, ammunition, several thousand muskets and shot-guns, three pieces of artillery, clothing, and miscellaneous baggage, standing abandoned on the track.

As was afterward ascertained, the bridge had been prematurely set on fire by frightened pickets, that mistook the Rebel rear guard for the Union advance. While a portion of the regiment rudely surrendered the train and contents to flames with the aid of combustibles brought along, the remainder dashed through the town, for the depot and engine-house, which was also soon in flames. Four locomotives were burned with the latter, and large quantities of Rebel stores with the former. They next destroyed the track for several hundred yards, disabled the switches, and rendered a culvert impassable. All this work of destruction was accomplished in a few hours. Their appearance in the place was telegraphed to the next station before they could cut the wires, and when they had nearly finished their job, a platform train carrying a battery and a large body of infantry approached the town, as far as the destruction of the track allowed. Before they could effect their disembarkation, however, the Union cavalry was collected and managed to retreat unattacked.

In the town they found nearly two thousand sick. Both on the way to Booneville and back to Corinth, they met more or less numerous detachments (some pickets and other stragglers) of Rebel cavalry and infantry; upon which they swooped, disarmed and dismounted, and being unable to bring them along, let loose, after paroling them. Between 600 and 700 of the enemy were thus disposed of. They reached this camp without losing a man or a horse, loaded with every description of booty. They had altogether made over 160 miles. Startingu ot with but three days' rations, which were consumed at the end of the second, the men subsisted for two days solely on the meat of cattle, and the animals on the forage they managed to pick up along the road.

This achievement was bold and graceful enough to immortalize the regiment. It is the same daring body that made the gallant charge on the Rebel battery in the skirmish near Farmington on the 8th, in which they lost a considerable number of killed and wounded, and no less than 108 horses.

We have hourly augmenting evidences of the utter demoralization that must have of late pervaded the Rebel ranks. The number of deserters that have entered our lines or given themselves up to our cavalry cannot now be less than 1,500. Nearly the whole of the 13th Louisiana has deserted the Rebel standard, and the greater portion of the 20th, from the same State, has followed their example. These two regiments are almost wholly composed of foreigners—principally Germans—whom either absolute want or outright force drove into the Rebel army. Nearly all express a willingness to enter the Union ranks.

The whereabouts of the different fragments of the Rebel army have not yet been definitely ascertained; but the expression seems now to prevail at headquarters that the greater part has gone South and not West. At least the measures taken by Gen. Halleck indicate such a belief. Gen. Pope's whole corps has received orders to prepare for a march South, and will start in the morning. During the whole "siege," the Army of the Mississippi, so renowned for its enterprise in the operations against Island No. 10, distinguished itself by remarkable activity and pluck, and it may well be said to constitute the flower of Gen. Halleck's army.

ARRESTED FOR TREASON.

LOUISVILLE, Thursday, June 5, 1862.

James Trabue, one of our principal dry-goods merchants, who has been South for five months, and who returned yesterday, was arrested to-day by the military authorities. He refused to take the oath of allegiance, and was committed to the military prison.

FROM GENERAL M'CLELLAN'S ARMY.

The Rebel General Johnston Mortally Wounded.

REBEL LOSS ESTIMATED AT 10,000

Terrible Confusion at Richmond.

ALL THE TROOPS OUTSIDE THE CITY

Preparations for a Determined Resistance.

A FLAG OF TRUCE FOR REBEL BODIES.

MCCLELLAN'S HEADQUARTERS, Friday, June 6, 1862.

Two deserters who came in this morning state that Gen. Jo. Johnston was seriously if not mortally wounded through the groin by a Minie ball during the late battle. Gen. G. W. Smith is now in command. Other information received goes to corroborate the statement.

These deserters state that the rebel loss is estimated at 10,000 men in killed, wounded, and missing. No material change has taken place in the position of the enemy.

A contraband has arrived who left Richmond yesterday. He represents things there as in a terrible state of confusion and uncertainty. No troops are in

See Eighth Page.

Continued from First Page.

the city excepting those doing guard duty, and tending the sick and wounded, all being compelled to remain outside. There were no signs of evacuation, but on the contrary everything goes to show a determined resistance on the part of the Rebels.

The contraband states that during the fight of Sunday, the house tops and all elevated positions were covered with people to witness the battle, every one expecting to see our troops driven into the Chickahominy; but when they saw the Rebels running toward the city, the greatest consternation prevailed. Many of the inhabitants have crossed the James River, expecting the city to be occupied by our troops soon.

It is rumored that Gen. Magruder is going to resign, having become disgusted with the Rebel military administration.

We are informed that there are no troops between the Rappahannock and the army of the Potomac under command of Gen. McClellan.

Everything has been very quiet to-day.

A flag of truce came in to-day from Gen. Huger, asking for the bodies of Gen. Pettigrew, and Cols. Davis, Lightfoot, Long, and Britton, who were supposed to have been killed in the late battle. Col. Davis was the only one killed. Lightfoot and Long are prisoners, and Britton was wounded, as also Gen. Pettigrew. Col. Davis's body will be returned.

The Battle of Seven Oaks.

From An Occasional Correspondent.

HEINTZELMAN'S HEADQUARTERS, Monday, June 2, 1862.

Saturday night closed upon the battle-field of that day with the enemy in full force in front. Our troops were under arms all night along the entire line of action, prepared for the renewal of the fight the next morning. During the night the enemy had advanced fully up to the furthest point made by them the day before, and were strongly posted on both sides of the railroad. Gen. Sedgwick's division had arrived on the right on Saturday evening, too late to take part in the action of that day, but fresh and eager for that approaching. During the night, Birney's brigade had been posted at better advantage of position than had been the fortune of our troops occupying that and the adjacent grounds of the day before; and with the determination to redeem the losses of Saturday inspiriting our entire line, the action commenced. The regiments to which the brunt of the battle fell were those which had not suffered much in the contest of the day before, although all of Heintzelman's corps, or Hooker's and Kearney's divisions, and Keyes's corps, were represented in it. I cannot say that any organized body from Casey's division participated in Sunday's work. The affair is yet too recent to admit of a description in full that would do justice to all the parties deserving especial mention, and to mention a part might do injustice to others. Two brigades, however, whose spheres of action were within the field of my personal observation, I do not hesitate to mention, although others may be equally deserving. There can be no question that Sickles's brigade in Hooker's, and Birney's in Kearney's division, covered themselves with glory in their several charges, each against a force much their superior in numbers. Unfortunately for himself, Gen. Birney was ordered under arrest early in the morning for some infraction of orders, and the command of his brigade devolved on Col. J. H. Hobart Ward of the 38th New-York. Under this gallant officer, this brigade, consisting of the 38th and 40th New-York and the 3d and 4th Maine, and to which the 7th Massachusetts had been temporarily attached, drove a much stronger force of the enemy, through a heavy wooded swamp, out of the woods into an open field, where two regiments of the brigade were posted so as to give them a galling fire that soon compelled them to fall back; and when Col. Ward ordered the bayonet charge, the entire brigade gave them the point, and drove them for nearly a mile in a perfect rout. Sickles's brigade also gave the enemy a taste of the bayonet, and drove them with great slaughter out of the rifle-pits from which they were dealing death to our troops. These successes, followed up with courage and promptness, and sustained by the hard fighting in Sedgwick's division, settled the fortune of the day, and changed what had been the closest contested and severest engagement east of the Alleghanies into a substantial triumph of our arms. The Rebels fell back all afternoon, and a reconnoissance to-day discovers none within a distance of three miles of our position of Saturday.

The conduct of the Rebels in the engagements of yesterday and the day before was worthy of a better cause. General officers speak of some of their charges on Saturday as splendid; but they were in strong force, the attacking party, and had the choice of ground—three points in their favor; and if they had any good fight in them, it should come out under such circumstances. They outnumbered our troops about five to one, according to the best reconnoissance that could be made—five distinct lines of battle, lying in order, supporting each other. Their loss must be greater than our own in killed—perhaps not so great in wounded. They used a cartridge of one ball and three buckshot—most effective in short ranges, and more destructive than the most prized rifle-ball, as they wound more than they kill.

From prisoners taken yesterday I hear of one Alabama regiment that went into the engagement over 1,300 strong on Saturday morning. Sunday morning it reported only 150. Col. Bratton of the 1st South Carolina, taken prisoner by Birney's Brigade, confirms that statement, and gives similar reports of other cases. His own regiment had more than fifty killed by one fire of one of our regiments, armed with the Austrian rifle.

But our own loss was very heavy, particularly in wounded, and fully up to the day before. Birney's Brigade suffered in killed and wounded less than 200, mostly in the 3d Maine and 40th New-York. The latter has not yet been able to ascertain the names of the killed and wounded. The 38th New-York suffered some, but not to the extent of either of the others named; while the 4th Maine, being posted near the railroad track, and using it for a breastwork, lost but very few, and all of its wounded being slightly.

But in Sedgwick's Division the loss was very severe, the number of wounded reported being near 1,000. These are now being brought over for removal by cars to White House, all of the wounded in Heintzelman's corps having been sent on. The cars move but slowly, and while waiting for return trains, the ground around headquarters is covered with the wounded—hundreds of them without shelter; and to add to the horrors of their situation, we have had severe thunder-storms for two nights in succession, to which these wretched sufferers are exposed.

MOVEMENTS IN FRONT.

To-night the divisions on the left took position in advance, yet not as far as Casey's occupied before being routed on Saturday. The camps are full of rumors that Richmond is evacuated, but whether or not there is truth in the rumor it is impossible to determine here, although so near. It is certain, however, that our troops furthest advanced can see no Rebel camps at this part of the line, and the theory that the fight of Saturday was to cover some movement in the rear of it may be correct. If they have not evacuated Richmond, and do not immediately do so, there can be no question that we are on the eve of the most terrible battle of the war. Guns were heard this afternoon in the direction of James River, and there is a rumor that the gunboats have passed the obstructions, but is hardly believed. If true, then the great struggle cannot much longer be delayed.

The following additions to the list of casualties of Saturday's engagement are all that can be obtained to-night. The Pennsylvania regiments in Gen. Kearney's division all suffered severely, particularly in the loss of officers, and it will be sometime before the confusion and disorganization into which they have thus been thrown will be settled into a state of order permitting them to know who are their killed and wounded. Large numbers have been sent off to the hospitals below, whose names and regiments have not been ascertained, and many of the killed are already past identification.

Gen. Howard, Maine, lost right arm.

ONE-HUNDREDTH NEW-YORK.

KILLED.—John Jordan, Company B; Albert Pervorst, Company B.

WOUNDED.—Lieut. Wm. Brown; Cristopher Scharbel, Company A; Mark Myers, Company K; John Chrisman, Company C; P. Shumaker; Henry Dressing, Company C; John Starke, Company A; Geo. Newland, Company K.

THIRD MICHIGAN.

WOUNDED—Isaac Shekel, Co. B; George Gardner, Co. H; George Kibby, Co. B; Oster Swinson, Co. H.

ONE-HUNDRED-AND-FIRST PENNSYLVANIA.

KILLED—Col. Wilson.

WOUNDED—Duncan McAllister, Wm. H. Beikerstoff.

ONE-HUNDRED-AND-SECOND PENNSYLVANIA.

WOUNDED—D. Hainey, Co. A; John H. Randolph, Co. H.

ONE-HUNDRED-AND-THIRD PENNSYLVANIA.

WOUNDED—J. H. Scott, Co. E.

ONE-HUNDRED-AND-FOURTH PENNSYLVANIA.

WOUNDED—Fenton Lowder, Co. G; Chas. Keizer, Co. D; Christian Sherman, Co. K; Quartermaster J. K. Hendrick; Levi M. Brickers, Co. I; Levi Rodney, Co. H; Corp. Thomas Harnie, Co. K; Augustus Hampton, Co. I; Wm. Seily, Co. I; James Betty, Co. B; Christian Bitterman, Co. B.; Wm. Borlear, Co. G; Wm. Frankenfield, Co. G.; Jacob R. Brinker, Co. B; Daniel Crader, Co. D; Wm. Carmel, Co. I; John Holmes, Co. B; Samuel Taylor, Co. C; Charles King, Co. G; Adam J. Kuhn, Co. G; Wm. Staple, Co. K; Frank Garret, Co. K; Sampson Rice, Co. K; Edward B. Johnson, Co. B; Geo. S. Connor, Co. G; Amasa H. Deits, Co. I; Henry Detweiter, Co. K; Martin Hofford, Co. G.

ONE HUNDRED AND FIFTH PENNSYLVANIA.

KILLED.—Wm. H. Suisher, Co. A.

WOUNDED.—Joseph Means, Co. A.

FIFTY-SEVENTH PENNSYLVANIA.

WOUNDED.—Geo. Bell, Co. E; Myron McDonald, Co. A.

SIXTY-SEVENTH PENNSYLVANIA.

WOUNDED.—Wm. Tompkins, Co. B; Jesse Shiber, Co. D; Israel Spencer, Co. A; Corporal Casey Atherton, Co. D; J. A. Espy, Co. K; Isidor Stenordorp, Co. K.

SIXTY-THIRD PENNSYLVANIA.

WOUNDED.—David Mehaffey, Co. E.

FIFTH PENNSYLVANIA.

WOUNDED.—John Patterson, Co. A.

SIXTY-SEVENTH NEW-YORK.

WOUNDED.—Capt. Van Ness, Sergeant-Major Martin Allen, Solomon G. Painter, Co. E; James C. Dewitt.

FIRST NEW-YORK BATTERY.

WOUNDED.—H. Remington, Co. H.

NINETY-EIGHTH NEW-YORK.

WOUNDED.—Joseph Dufries, Co. E; George H. Williams, Co. E.

FIFTY-SIXTH NEW-YORK.

WOUNDED.—Valentine Caseboum, Co. E.

EIGHTY-SEVENTH NEW-YORK.

WOUNDED.—Addison Huntington, Co. A.

SECOND MICHIGAN.

WOUNDED.—Byron W. Long, Co. E.

ELEVENTH MAINE.

WOUNDED.—Edwin Haysuck, Co. E; G. H. Hennister, Co. F.

TENTH MASSACHUSETTS.

KILLED.—Capt. Smart, Capt. Day, Lieut. Leland.

WOUNDED.—Harry Ultey, Co. H; M. Borden, Co. K; Corporal H. G. Herman, Co. F.

The following are a portion of the casualties of the battle of Sunday, June 1:

FOURTH MAINE.

KILLED—Augustus Packer, Co. K; Dennis Knowles, Co. I.

WOUNDED—Sanford Colson, Co. I; George Steel, Co. H; Simon Higgins, Co. H; John C. Currier, Co. K; Seth C. Young, seriously, Co. K.

THIRD MAINE.

KILLED—Wm. Heath, Co. C; I. Dalton, Co. C; A. C. Bray, Co. F; W. F. Meader, Co. F; J. H. Gerdener, Co. F; H. K. Maye, Co. F; John F. Cole, Co. I.

WOUNDED—Capt. Richmond, Co. K; Lieut. Worcester, Co. C; Lieut. Haskell, Co. K, fatal; Lieut. A. L. Merril, Co. D; Sergt. R. M. Bryant, Co. H; Sergt. B. H. Hall, Co. F; Sergt. Chas. Bradbury, Co. K; Sergt. Wm. L. Dunlap, Co. F; Sergt. Briggs, Co. B; Sergt. O. P. Morrill, Co. B; David Freeman, Co. K; W. H. Lyon, Co. B; Franklin Thompson, Co. B; Joseph Evans, Co. I; G. R. Packard, Co. F; H. Webbur, Co. B; I. W. Murphy, Co. B; R. Hyde, Co. B; H. N. Leighton, Co. B; E. Thompson, Co. F; Sergt. Samuel L. Gilman, Co. F; G. S. Wing, Co. F; C. F. Morris, Co. B; H. G. Smith, Co. C; H. Babb, Co. C; Wm. Horn, Co. C; Ornis Weeks, Co. C; Chas. Welch, Co. C; Jas. Williams, Co. C; Chas. C. Co. C; J. W. Philbrook, Co. K; J. F. Caslin, Co. K; Henry Penman, Co. K; A. J. Woodbury, Co. K; N. C. Moor, Co. A; J. W. Elwell, Co. A; J. B. Watson, Co. A; E. P. Shaw, Co. A; C. A. Coombes, Co. A; H. F. Francis, Co. A; R. Dixon, Co. D; T. B. Merry, Co. D; B. F. Brooklands, Co. D; L. M. Higgins, Co. D; H. K. Dunton, Co. D; N. F. Hennerson, Co. D; A. B. H. Wood, Co. K; H. G. Newell, Co. K; H. Johnson, Co. K; J. C. Hanson, Co. K; B. W. Smart, Co. K; George Gardner, Co. I.

FREMONT'S PURSUIT OF JACKSON.

Great Rise in the Shenandoah—Check to the Pursuit—Construction of a Pontoon Bridge—400 Prisoners Captured.

FREMONT'S HEADQUARTERS, MOUNT JACKSON, Va., Friday, June 6, 1862.

Further pursuit of Jackson has been impossible to-day, owing to the sudden rise of the Shenandoah River. A pontoon bridge, replacing the bridge burnt by the Rebels, was completed, and part of Gen. Fremont's force crossed this morning. It rained hard all night and day, and the river began to rise very rapidly, and rose 12 feet in four hours, bringing down great quantities of drift-wood and heavy timber, which finally parted the bridge in the middle. The material was all saved, and no accidents occurred. Four hundred prisoners have been taken.

FROM FRONT ROYAL.

SEIZURE OF GRAIN AND FLOUR.

Special Dispatch to The N. Y. Tribune.

FRONT ROYAL, Friday, June 6, 1862.

Capt. Sanderson, Chief Commissary, has taken possession of all the flour mills in the valley, together with the grain and flour on hand.

Safe guards have been granted by the Commanding General to all families who request them, without respect to their loyalty or disloyalty, and the soldier who violates them will do so under the penalty of being immediately shot.

The weather is still unsettled, and the roads almost impassable. Both branches of the Shenandoah are still rising.

THE EFFORT TO EXCHANGE COL. CORCORAN.

Another Breach of Faith on the part of the Rebels.

FORTRESS MONROE, Friday, June 6—5:30 p. m.

The Massachusetts, which went up James River on Sunday night last with privateers to be exchanged for Col. Corcoran and others, held as their hostages, returned this morning, bringing back the privateers with her. Gen. Huger promised, on behalf of his Government, that the hostages would be exchanged for the privateers. Acting upon this intimation, the privateers were sent up, and on their arrival at City Point, trains of cars came down from Petersburg with a flag of truce to receive them.

The expected hostages not being on board, however, the privateers were not given up, but a communication was sent to the Rebel Government asking an explanation. Answer came back to the effect that Gen. Huger exceeded his authority, and that further conference would be necessary before the exchange could be completed. It was immediately replied by the flag of truce boat that they would remain at City Point a reasonable time in order for the proposed further conference.

This was sent to the War Department at Richmond, and immediate answer promised the Massachusetts. The M. waited till the next day without receiving any further communication, when, after sending a boat ashore, and learning that nothing was expected from Richmond, she started on her return down the river. During her stay at City Point, some of the privateers were very indignant at the delay which they were obliged to submit to, and the intention was secretly expressed to seize the boat on the passage down. Necessary precautions were taken, however, by Col. Whipple, who was in command of the flag, and no trouble arose.

FROM FORTRESS MONROE.

BALTIMORE, Friday, June 6, 1862.

The steamer Mystic arrived this morning with 241 prisoners recently captured by General McClellan, including eleven officers.

The British sloop-of-war Racer sailed this morning.

The hulks used as store and hospital ships, which were towed down outside of the Point when fears of the Merrimac were uppermost in the minds of our naval commanders here, were towed up again to-day, and resumed their old anchorage-ground in the Roads.

Newport News has been abandoned as a military post, and the ordnance stores are being removed to the fortress.

THE WAR IN THE SOUTH-WEST.

ROLLA, Mo., Thursday, June 5, 1862.

Cols. White and Vanaling of the Rebel army, and James Massey, Secretary of State under Claib. Jackson, with about twenty ordinary Rebels, were captured at Cassville a few days since.

Advices from Gen. Curtis's army in Arkansas say that scouting parties from Gens. Carr and Osterhaus's Divisions, in front of Little Red River, and from Gen. Steel's on the left and rear, have been very successful lately in breaking up Rebel camps, and running down guerrillas. Lieut.-Col. Lewis of the 1st Missouri fell in with a party west of Searcy, and charged on them, killing four, and wounding about twenty, and scattering the rest.

Near West Point, a party was routed by Major Hawkins of the 6th Missouri, and a Rebel lieutenant taken prisoner. Lieut. Rickets of the 9th Illinois Cavalry attacked a party at Caiche River, killing four, wounding four, taking two prisoners, and driving the rest into the swamps. Major Bowen, commanding a detachment of his own battalion and the 3d Iowa Cavalry, at 9 p. m. on the 8th of May, fell upon a Rebel camp at Kickapoo Bottom, which is west of Batesville about 55 miles, killing three, and scattering the Rebels in every direction, capturing a large amount of camp and garrison equipage, 22 prisoners, 25 horses, 54 guns, 30 or 40 bowie-knives, and 30 revolvers. This was a daring attack, the men leaving their horses and charging in the swamps with their carbines. Our troops can take the Rebels on their own ground of guerrilla warfare, and show superior arms and braver conduct.

PADUCAH, Friday, June 6, 1862.

Col. Noble, commanding at this post, with nearly his entire command, are under marching orders for down the river, and will leave to-morrow.

ST. LOUIS, June 5, 1862.

A general order from Gen. Halleck says that the State of Missouri, except the Counties of Mississippi, New-Madrid and Pemiscate, will hereafter constitute the Military Department of Missouri, to be commanded by Brigadier-Gen. Scofield. The forces in South-West Missouri will be subject to the order of Major-Gen. Curtis, Commander and Military Governor of Arkansas. The County of Mississippi will belong to the District of Cairo, under Gen. Strong, and the Counties of Pemiscate and New-Madrid to the District of Columbus, under Gen. Quimby.

FROM THE MISSISSIPPI FLOTILLA.

Continued Improvement in our Mortar-Practice—Another Narrow Escape of Gen. Villipigue—Firing of the Rebels—Shadows of Death—Desperate Characters on the Mortar Fleet—A Fearless Scapegrace—Deplorable Condition of Arkansas—The Evacuation of Corinth—The Effect of the Movement—Its Influence on Pillow.

From Our Special Correspondent.

MISSISSIPPI FLOTILLA, NEAR FORT PILLOW, 75 MILES ABOVE MEMPHIS, Saturday, Midnight, May 31, 1862.

During the past three or four days the firing of our mortars has been quite regular, and Plum Point Bend has, to a certain degree, presented the appearance of carrying on a siege.

CONTINUED IMPROVEMENT IN OUR MORTAR FIRING.

Our mortars are much better managed than they were, and as the gunners are apprised by signals from boats lying off Craighead Point of the bearing and range of the shells, our bombs, for the most part, explode where they are liable to do damage.

The angle at which our mortars are now discharging, is generally forty-five degrees, and the quantity of powder used averages twenty pounds; seven pounds being the charge of the bombs, which of themselves weigh 215 pounds. After various experiments, this elevation and amount of powder appears the best calculated to throw shells directly into the enemy's works.

A number of bombs have been placed there within the past two days, and from the manner in which the earth has been thrown up, it is fair to suppose some injury to the enemy has been wrought.

ANOTHER NARROW ESCAPE OF GEN. VILLIPIGUE.

An intelligent deserter from the Fort says one of our bombs burst, on Thursday, over the camp occupied by the managers of the water-batteries, and that a large fragment fell into Villipigue's tent, while he was smoking and reading a work on Artillery Practice; the mischievous metal burying itself in the earth at a distance of not more than four feet from the Creole chief.

The General instinctively jumped to the other side of the tent, and a number of soldiers outside who saw the shell burst, and the huge rent it had made in the canvas, ran into the officer's headquarters, expecting to find him killed, or at least severely wounded. They supposed their fears were realized when they beheld Villipigue, or "little pig," as many of his men who cannot pronounce his French name, call him—covered with dust, and lying in a corner where his sudden and extraordinary saltation had thrown him.

The Confederate corypheus looked dull enough when he rose, remarking that those d——d Yankee bombs appeared to have a particular animosity against him, as this was the third time they had come so near him that he could smell the sulphur of h—l.

Villipigue *has* had several narrow escapes, and though a Rebel, seems to entertain a just idea of his future state—if the Calvinistic creed be correct—however defective his comprehension may be of the present crisis and its results.

FIRING OF THE REBELS—SHADOWS OF DEATH.

The Rebels use their mortars almost altogether in firing at us, and usually the shots are well made. Their shells have burst again and again over and near our mortar-boats without injuring any one.

A quarter of a second more occupied in the burning of the fuse, or the variation of the melted fraction of an inch in the elevation, would have sometimes transferred more than one of our brave fellows to a less troublous state of existence.

Though but very few lives have been lost at Plum Point Bend during this siege of nearly seven weeks, the narrow escapes have been innumerable; some of them almost sufficient to convince one of the truth of Necessitarianism.

Those who have not witnessed battles would be astonished to perceive how much lead and iron and steel is required to kill a man. In an engagement where, perhaps, not more than twenty are lost, hundreds escape by what is popularly called a miracle. Death is a poor marksman with all his cruelty. He throws a thousand darts before he can strike his victim once.

DESPERATE CHARACTERS ON THE MORTAR FLEET.

The officers of the mortar fleet have had a great deal of difficulty with their men, composed of the worst and most desperate characters from the army of the Potomac, since the flotilla left Island No. 10.

The men are brave as Belisarius and reckless as Don Carlos, and, when sober, can generally be managed; but, under the influence of liquor, they are capable of any excess or crime, and are fairly demonized.

They have, according to report, committed various outrages at different times, and a party of them in one instance actually drove off the crew of a transport and took possession of the boat. They have had quarrels, fights, and rows without number, and many of them are constantly under arrest. Their officers are rarely among them without being armed, and they say they often apprehend assassination, and go prepared for any desperate emergency.

Pickets are stationed in the woods on Craighead Point to prevent any of the Rebels from stealing up to the mortar-boats, and, a few nights ago, some of the mortar-men fired upon several privates of the 46th Indiana, and killed two, under the impression, they allege, that they were enemies.

Probably the mortar men were mistaken, but they have obtained such a reputation for recklessness that the regiment feels greatly embittered against them, and does not hesitate to declare their companions-in-arms were slain from mere wantonness or to gratify some private malice.

Some of the mortar-men, the Indianians declare, would as soon kill an innocent person as drink a glass of whisky, and would regard the shooting down of two soldiers as a capital joke. This is not true, probably, but it shows the kind of reputation the mortar men have acquired.

A FEARLESS SCAPEGRACE.

One of these notorious men was on the Point the other day, acting as picket, and as he had manifested some symptoms of ebriety before he went there, Lieut. Wheelock concluded to look after the scamp. He walked to the spot where the picket was posted, and found the fellow seated under a tree brushing away the musketoes very listlessly, and cursing the Rebels, who were throwing shells from their mortars across the river. Just as the Lieutenant was approaching, a bomb fell within five feet of the picket, who saw the fuse still burning, and knew it must explode.

The mortar man looked at it very coolly and never stirred, but apostrophised the shell thus: "D——n you! who cares for you? Burst and be d——d; nobody's afraid, you d——d old Rebel."

The fearless scapegrace had hardly finished his speech, when the bomb burst, tearing up the ground and covering him with dirt, but doing him no injury. "Bah! I knew you couldn't hurt nobody, you d——d old Rebel," remarked the mortar man, and continued to brush away the musketoes with the most imperturbable sang froid.

DEPLORABLE CONDITION OF ARKANSAS.

Fifteen refugees reached the flotilla yesterday from Crittenden County, Ark., on their way to the North, having left Secessia on account of the conscription act, and the general disorder and distress prevailing in their State. They report the condition of affairs there as deplorable in the extreme. The people, in many parts of Arkansas, are suffering for the common necessaries of life. They are in constant dread of servile insurrection: their cotton has been entirely destroyed in many parts of the State: they fear "invasion" from the North: business is not only stagnant, but without prospect of improvement. They have no confidence in their leaders, and the message of Gov. Rector, advising them to secesh from Secessia, has distracted and bewildered them to an extraordinary degree. They have few soldiers, and in the existing condition of things they know not where to look for aid, or where to turn for comfort.

They have left the United States, and are ordered to withdraw from the Confederacy. They have no protection North or South. They want everything, and have nothing. They are despoiled and desperate in the present, and the future offers no hope of amelioration. Ruin seems to stare the citizens of Arkansas in the face, and the general feeling of the people, not wedded to the sinful sham of Secession—and even of many of them—is to fly to the land of liberty, where they can at least enjoy what they may acquire without fear of robbery or molestation.

Hundreds of persons would abandon Arkansas for ever if they had the means of getting away, say the refugees, and the sight of the old flag would be hailed with delight, as the precursor of the establishment of protection, law, and order.

THE EVACUATION OF CORINTH.

Intelligence reached here this morning that Beauregard's army had evacuated Corinth, and retreated to Columbus, Miss.—a movement I mentioned as probable in a recent letter, and which was reported to have occurred some weeks ago, when I referred to the location and character of the town. I should not be surprised if, indeed I expect to learn that, the evacuation of Corinth began at the time I stated, and has been progressing ever since. It is reasonable to suppose the evacuation of Corinth may increase the probability of a similar course by the enemy at Fort Pillow.

FROM CAIRO.

Renewed Activity at the Flotilla—Captain Stembel—Arrivals from the Tennessee—the Censorship.

From Our Special Correspondent.

CAIRO, Ill., Wednesday, June 4, 1862.

ACTIVITY AT THE FLOTILLA.

There are many indications of an early movement at the National Flotilla. Absent officers are hastening back to their posts on the gunboats. The Cincinnati, here to repair damages received during the onslaught of the Rebel rams three weeks ago, is again ready for action, and will go down the river this evening. In the absence of Capt. Stembel, she is commanded by Mr. D. R. Hoell, her former First Master, who was appointed Lieutenant in the navy for his skill and daring in running the blockade of the Rebel batteries at Island No. 10, with the St. Louis. The Union rams are also with the Flotilla, their commander anxiously awaiting leave to run past Fort Pillow and pay his compliments to the Rebel gunboats below. It is believed that permission will soon be accorded, and ere many days the Mississippi once more be open from Cairo to the Gulf.

CAPT. STEMBEL OF THE CINCINNATI

is still at home, recovering from his wound. The selection of naval officers for the West has been extremely fortunate; we have no truer or more gallant men, upon sea or land, fighting the battles of nationality and freedom. Among them all there is none abler or worthier than Capt. Stembel. His services have been eminent ever since he took command of one of the wooden gunboats early last season. At Fort Henry he commanded the flagship, which was struck by thirty-one balls, and his coolness and courage received special commendation in the report of Commodore Foote. In the late brief but desperate encounter with the Rebel rams, where he was wounded, and his boat bore the brunt of the conflict, his deportment won universal praise. The hope is expressed that he may be made a flag-officer—a promotion that has been fairly earned, and would be fitly bestowed.

TROOPS TURNED BACK.

During the last two days several regiments of Kansas and North-Western troops from the arrested New-Mexican expedition have arrived here, on their way to Pittsburg Landing. Gen. Halleck, since discovering that his grand army was in no imminent danger from the empty breastworks of Corinth, orders them to turn back, and they will probably be sent in another direction. The Kansas 1st had already gone up the Tennessee when the order arrived here.

A. D. R.

THE LATE STORM.

Terrible Disasters in Pennsylvania—A Whole Town Swept Away—Great Loss of Life—Immense Destruction of Property.

EASTON, Pa., Friday, June 6, 1862.

Fearful accounts of damages have been received from Mauch Chunk and vicinity. The dam there, as well as at two other places, was swept away. Many houses were washed off. The railroad bridge is also gone. Canal navigation is stopped for the season. The Lehigh Valley Railroad will not be in running order for several weeks. The whole town of Weissport is washed away. There are but three houses left out of about 300. The loss of life has been terrible. Weissport is in Carbon County, Pa., on the Lehigh River.

12 m.—The Delaware and Lehigh are falling rapidly. They have already receded twelve feet. The Lehigh Valley Railroad is very badly torn up. The Belvidere Delaware Railroad will be repaired in a few days. The Delaware, Lackawanna and Western Railroad will be running in about a week. A part of the basin of the Delaware Canal here has been washed out, and two breaks are reported in the first level. The lower portions of the outlet lock are gone. The damage at Glendon is very great. The furnaces are all chilled. The lumber men are heavy losers. Millions of feet of sawed lumber, and thousands of logs, have been carried away. The number of persons drowned is not ascertained. The list will be fearful.

XXXVIITH CONGRESS.

FIRST SESSION.

SENATE......WASHINGTON, June 6, 1862.

The VICE-PRESIDENT presented a resolution of the citizens of New-York, in favor of the establishment of a mint in that city.

A Committee of Conference was appointed on the Indian Appropriation bill, which was returned from the House with amendments.

A communication from the Secretary of the Navy, transmitting the official reports of operations on the Lower Mississippi, the capture of New-Orleans, &c., was received.

Mr. HALE (Rep., N. H.) offered a resolution calling on the Secretary of the Treasury to inform the Senate how much of $72,672, paid to Marshals in the District of Columbia for the year ending June 30, was for personal service, and how much on other accounts, and the details of the accounts. He said there had been paid to Marshal Lamon, who was appointed in March, $22,054, and to Marshal Selden, before him, $50,000.

Mr. POWELL (Dem., Ky.) offered a resolution that the Secretary of War inform the Senate whether Major-General Hunter has been authorized by the Department to muster a regiment of negroes or persons of African descent into the service of the United States, if a Colonel and other officers have been appointed, and whether they have been clothed and armed at the expense of the United States. Laid over.

Mr. SUMNER (Rep., Mass.) offered the following:

Whereas, Edward Stanly, assuming to act under a letter from the Secretary of War, appointing him Military Governor of North Carolina, a post unknown to the Constitution and laws, has undertaken, by virtue of such military authority, to surrender fugitive slaves contrary to the intent and meaning of the act of Congress recently adopted; also, to banish an American citizen in violation of the personal right secured by the Constitution; also, to close schools maintained by the charity of good men for the education of colored children, in defiance of every principle of morals and religion, and degrading to our National character; therefore,

Resolved, That any such letter assuming to create any person Military Governor of any State is without sanction in the Constitution and laws, and that its effect is to subordinate the civil to the military authority; that it is contrary to the spirit of our institutions and is in derogation of the powers of Congress, which, where a State Government fails into the hands of traitors can be the only authority except martial law.

Objected to, and laid over.

Mr. SUMNER also offered another resolution that such office of Military Governor is contrary to the Constitution and laws, destructive to the civil authority, and contrary to the spirit of all our institutions. Laid over.

Mr. SUMNER moved to take up the resolution for the expulsion of the Senator from Oregon (Stark). Rejected—Yeas 16, Nays 21.

At 1 o'clock the Tax bill was taken up.

Mr. ANTHONY (Rep., R. I.) moved to reconsider the vote laying a tax on slaves. He said he did it at the request of others, and should vote against it.

Mr. SUMNER (Rep., Mass.) hoped it would not be reconsidered. He referred to the proceedings of North Carolina, taxing slaves, and he said there certainly was no constitutional objection against it.

Mr. DOOLITTLE (Rep., Wis.) thought the question's constitutionality was not settled, though the Senator from Massachusetts declared there was no constitutional objection.

Mr. SUMNER said if it was a capitation or poll-tax, he should regard it as unconstitutional, but as it was not a poll-tax, he regarded it equally conceded that it was constitutional.

Mr. DOOLITTLE thought such decidedly contrary to the Constitution, and regarded it unwise at present, because in fact it will principally fall on your friends.

Mr. HALE (Rep., N. H.) contended that practically this was a tax on slaves, though perhaps called by another name, and no phraseology can cover it up from the common sense of the people. He quoted from Judge Story in regard to the capitation tax, and said he would not, even to reach his cherished object, violate the Constitution. He entirely repudiated any idea that property could be held in man. He feared that the treatment of Anti-Slavery men in this country had made them resentful, but such feelings should be laid aside in legislating for the country.

Mr. WILMOT (Rep., Pa.) contended that this tax was perfectly constitutional. It was not a capitation tax, but it proposes to tax the claims a master has to the services of slaves.

Mr. HARLAN (Rep. Iowa) thought it could not be denied that there was a right of property in slaves in some States, in a qualified sense at least. There was no doubt as to that, and also as to the constitutional right of taxation. He would willingly give the benefit of the doubt to the country and to the Treasury, though he had no doubt as to the constitutional right to lay the tax.

Mr. BROWNING spoke against laying such a tax, as being a mere capitation tax and unconstitutional.

Mr. COWAN (Rep., Pa.) claimed that a fair construction of the Constitution was clearly against the proposed tax. It was perfectly evident that the framers of the Constitution intended to prohibit just such a tax as is now proposed to be laid, and, second, no true Union man would try to avoid the spirit and intent of the Constitution. The very men who propose to lay this tax on slaves, would, with their other hand free all the slaves of Rebels, and thus destroy the very source of revenue which they propose to collect. But he was sorry to say he was obliged to come to the conclusion that $2 per head was not the real reason for this measure. It might be said he was reproaching the Senate. Well, he intended to do so. It might be said he intended to lecture the Senate if he thought they deserved it by passing acts which were calculated to trample on the Constitution. It might be said he was dogmatic. Well, he intended to be dogmatic.

Mr. WADE (Rep., Ohio) (in his seat)—All but the 'matic."

Mr. COWAN—When that Senator settles a little account which he has with his colleague in the other House, I presume it will be time enough for me to pay attention to that kind of remark. Till then, he must excuse me. When he said he intended to be dogmatic, he meant that he intended to express his own opinion firmly, as he had a right to.

M. WADE, (Rep., Ohio)—I see no necessity for Senators rising here and making special protestations of their devotion to the Union, and I do not like this continual assumption of devotion to the Constitution. I am willing to hear arguments, but I will allow no man to get up here and, by implication, reproach me with perjury. And especially I do not like this lecturing by one of whom I don't know where he earned the authority to lecture this Senate. How long has he been here, Sir, and where did he come from? Who ever heard of him before he came here, and what right had he to come into this Senate with the authority and presumption to be its guardian? I had rather be lectured by any other member of this House. I was going on to say, Sir, that I am very patient in being argued with from a respectable source, and to have even my course in this Senate criticised, but I am very anxious that that criticism shall come from a source of some authority. And when a man comes in here and undertakes to scold this body for not doing what he imagines to be right, I insist that he shall come with some authority as a man of talent and a gentleman who has acquired some authority to lecture his fellow-men. I do not deny that a man has a right to take a seat on this floor, and if he sees fit to do it, he may become the mere advocate and watch-dog of traitors in the field, he may vote for them, argue for them, and he may scold for them, if he pleases, and I will not undertake to correct him. But let not such a one rise here to criticise my course, much less to reproach the Senate of the United States. Putting on airs here as though a gentleman from the wilds of Pennsylvania in the middle of his first session had the right to reproach the Senate for the course they have taken. I wonder the Senate did not tremble under such a reproach. What argument has that Senator ever made, what vote has he given, what position has he occupied upon any question arising here between traitors and the Government, that he has not acted as their advocate on all occasions? He had the right to do it if he chose, but let not such a one rise here to be overseer and guardian in the Senate. It is very easy for a man to get up here and quote Don Quixote, and quote him as authority on the Constitution. The authority is like the advocate, and one is about as good as the other. What right has he to criticise? I don't know, Sir, but he is the very founder of the Constitution, but I never happened to hear of it. Mr. Wade then contended that the proposition before the Senate was to tax the owners of slaves for a certain species of valuable property which they claimed, not that he admitted any such right of property. On the contrary he believed, under the Law of God, the slave had just as much right to the master's service as the master had to his, but the moment anything is proposed which touches Slavery, then constitutional arguments are made, and the Senator from Pennsylvania especially bristles all over like a porcupine. Can you tax cotton? "Oh, no!" Can you confiscate property of Rebels? "Oh, no, that is horrible." If any man chooses to be the watch-dog of Slavery, let him; but he should be content with the position, and not undertake to scold the Senate. We are told these measures will irritate the Rebels. Can we irritate those who dig up our soldiers' bones and make drinking cups out of their skulls? Neither will this irritate the Border States. The loyal men of the Border States are not slaveholders—not one in twenty. He had always supported this measure, and should continue to do so.

Mr. COWAN (Rep., Penn.)—No doubt but I am the humblest of individuals, and entirely unknown; and no doubt but this is the first office I ever held in my life. It is true I am here, and that I am unknown, but, Sir, I stand upon this floor as the representative of Pennsylvania, and of nearly three millions of people. I shall not undertake to apologize for my people. I know that when this Administration came into power, with its worthy President, whom I have sustained, and with whom I am proud to agree, all eyes were turned to the State I represent, and all people admitted that upon her decision depended the issue; and when this Rebellion broke out all eyes were again turned to that State, and all people seemed to feel that upon her depended the issue of the contest. Pennsylvania responded, and her troops came first to the rescue of the Capitol. She has a greater number of troops in the field than any other State, and her dead are lying on most every battle-field of the Union. I am not here to apologize for the position I hold as the Representative of Pennsylvania. I am not here to apologize either for my youth or my inexperience. I have never understood that it was necessary to send a man here for years in order to apprentice him to his duty in this body. I have never understood that age or length of service would sanctify folly, or that it would give character to Billingsgate which might well be learned from a fish woman. I have understood that Senators on this floor were equal. I have lectured nobody, reproached nobody, nor been dogmatic against any body. I have assailed no man's person, but I did mean to say that all this talk about Senators lecturing each other, and being dogmatic, was, in my humble judgment, mere idle badinage. I leave the attack which has been made upon me and upon my past history; and if the Senator who has chosen to make this unwarrantable, unjust and ungraceful attack on one so humble and so little known, can reconcile it to his sense of duty and propriety, I am perfectly content to let it pass. I will not advert to his distinguished career, but leave them all to the results of his own calm reflection. I made an argument—whether strong or not, convincing or not, no matter, I made it; and the Senator from Ohio introduced a rude, vulgar, low ejaculation, which I know upon reflection he would not have made. That argument he has a right to answer. Has he? If I, with my insignificance, lectured, reproached, and was dogmatic, how much more was he with his great past fame and long experience when he condescended to indulge in a tirade of half an hour, charging me with being the watch-dog of Slavery, and a hundred other things equally unjust, and equally improper. It is very easy to make that charge, and useless to attempt to repel it. But while I am a representative of Pennsylvania, I am sent here by that State to preserve the Constitution and restore the Union, and in the exercise of that duty I feel myself as much in the line of it when I am defending the South from what I believe to be an unwarrantable attack, and when I am standing up between Slavery and those who would unconstitutionally overthrow it, as if I was defending the interest of the little village where I was born, and far more so. I have resisted projects which I considered mischievous and wrong and unconstitutional, and I have nothing to regret on that subject. With the approval of my own conscience, I am perfectly willing to be adjudged for what I shall say or do.

After further discussion, a vote was taken on the reconsideration of the vote taxing slaves, which was carried, as follows:

YEAS—Messrs. Bayard, Browning, Carlile, Cowan, Davis, Dixon, Doolittle, Foster, Hale, Harris, Kennedy, Lane (Ind.), Latham, McDougall, Nesmith, Powell, Rice, Saulsbury, Starke, Ten Eyck, Willey, Wright—22.

NAYS—Messrs. Anthony, Chandler, Clark, Fessenden, Foot, Grimes, Harlan, Howard, Howe, King, Morrill, Pomeroy, Simmons, Sumner, Trumbull, Wade, Wilkinson, Wilmot—18.

The question then recurred on the adoption of the amendment proposing a tax on persons claiming the service or labor of slaves of $2 each for every person so claimed.

Mr. HOWE moved to amend so as to except those under 10 years, and over 65. Adopted.

The amendment was then rejected as follows:

YEAS—Messrs. Anthony, Chandler, Clark, Fessenden, Foot, Grimes, Harlan, Howard, Howe, King, Morrill, Simmons, Sumner, Trumbull, Wade, Wilkinson, Wilmot—17.

NAYS—Messrs. Bayard, Browning, Carlisle, Cowan, Davis, Dixon, Doolittle, Foster, Hale, Harris, Kennedy, Lane (Ind.), Latham, McDougall, Nesmith, Powell, Rice, Saulsbury, Stark, Ten Eyck, Willey, Wilson (Mass.), Wright—23.

Mr. FESSENDEN (Rep., Me.), spoke at some length in favor of the passage of the tax bill. He would not pretend it was perfect in all its provisions, but this was a new subject in this country, and we have no experience in these matters. This bill was the result of a vast deal of labor and research, and the imperfections which it undoubtedly has should be borne charitably. In referring to the necessity of a tax bill, he estimated the debt of the Government as $700,000,000 at the end of the fiscal year, and that the yearly regular expenses must be greatly increased hereafter, as we must have a larger standing army, and a larger navy.

The tax-bill was passed.

YEAS—Messrs. Anthony, Browning, Carlile, Chandler, Clark, Collamer, Cowan, Davis, Dixon, Doolittle, Fessenden, Foot, Foster, Grimes, Hale, Harlan, Harris, Howard, Howe, King, Lane (Ind.), Latham, McDougall, Nesmith, Pomeroy, Rice, Simmons, Stark, Sumner, Ten Eyck, Trumbull, Wade, Willey, Wilmot, Wilson (Mass.), Wright—37.

NAY—Mr. Powell.

ABSENT—Messrs. Bayard, Henderson, Kennedy, Lane (Kansas), Pearce, Saulsbury, Sherman, Thomson, Wilkinson, and Wilson (Mo).

On motion of Mr. WILSON (Mass.) the Senate went into Executive Session, and subsequently adjourned till Monday.

HOUSE OF REPRESENTATIVES.

The House went into Committee on private bills.

Mr. MORRILL (Rep., Vt.) spoke on donating lands to the several States for establishing agricultural colleges. He appealed to gentlemen to vote upon the merits of the bill heretofore introduced by him. Its passage would have the effect of strengthening the Republic, wronging nobody, and proving a blessing to the entire people for ages to come. Among the branches of education proposed, is military instruction. He showed, at length, the advantages of the system, which would afford an opportunity for education accompanied by a love for useful labor.

Mr. COX (Dem., Ohio), in the course of his speech, said while he was anxious to believe the President right he was against an ambiguous policy as to those who control this House; they have the activity of destruction but not the genius to build up. Salvation is not in their line. The danger was from an alliance between the Republicans and Abolitionists, whose war on Slavery in defiance of the Constitution becomes a crime. He condemned at length the emancipation and confiscation of slaves, remarking that the only safety to the country is in moderate, and not in vindictive counsels.

Mr. NOBLE (Dem., O.) argued that the National Government, being of limited and defined power, conferred upon it by the individual States, has no right to interfere with their local institutions, Slavery included. There was no way under the Constitution of dispensing with it. That was left with the States in which it existed. He insisted that a departure from these principles had always engendered sectional strife. Adjourned till Monday.

Parson Brownlow's Movements.

PHILADELPHIA, Friday, June 6, 1862.

Parson Brownlow, in accordance with the request of the most prominent citizens, will address them at the Academy of Music next Friday evening.

Earthquake at Cairo.

CAIRO, Friday, June 6, 1862.

There were three distinct shocks of earthquake here to-day. They were also felt at several points north as far as Urbana. No damage was done so far as ascertained.

From Kansas.

LEAVENWORTH, Thursday, June 6, 1862.

The Kansas State Senate is engaged as a Court of Impeachment in the case of Gov. Robinson and other State officers. Twenty-two Senators are present. The time so far has been principally occupied on questions in regard to the locality of the Court. But little interest is manifested in the proceedings.

Gen. Blunt has issued an order changing the name of Fort Wise to Fort Lyon.

Receipts of Produce.

JUNE 6.—22,858 bbls. Flour, 100 bbls. Corn Meal, 1,247 bags do., 885 bbls. Whisky, 77,415 bush. Wheat, 117,337 bush. Corn, 12,273 bush. Oats, 11,914 bush. Rye, 4,651 bush. Malt. 2,773 pkgs. Provisions, 456 pkgs. Lard, 201 kegs do.

Passengers Arrived

In bark James Welsh from Minatitlan—R. Goodell, Edward Hatton, Albert Mitchelbury, Edward Wright.

Disasters, &c.

SQUAN VILLAGE, June 5.—The brig Quango of Sidney, with a cargo of coal for New-York, is ashore seven miles south of Squan Inlet. She lays on Outer Bar, anchor ahead and tight.

LOCAL AND STATE AFFAIRS.

SALE OF REAL ESTATE.—The sale of Mr Wm. Crumpton's property, advertised in another column, will be continued to-day.—See advertisement.

ARRIVAL OF YANKEE PRISONERS.—Thirty-seven Federal officers taken by Jackson in the Valley, arrived here by the Orange train yesterday. Col. Murphy, of a Philadelphia Regiment, some officers of the 1st Maryland, and a brother of the late Elisha Kent Kane, were amongst the number.—They were, for the most part, good looking men, and seemed to be cheerful.

We were glad to perceive that there was no disposition manifested by our people to treat them with rudeness or offer them insult. They left via the South Side for North Carolina this morning. The privates will be on to-day.

Gen. Rodes arrived in this city last evening.

LEE MALLORY'S WAR ILLUSTRATIONS.—This interesting exhibition of art continues to attract large and crowded audiences to witness the representations of the naval victory in Hampton Roads, together with the affecting and life-like automatic of the Warrior Steed, which alone is worth the price of admission. This latter figure is the most touching incident of the representations of the battle-field that we have witnessed, and one that has brought the tears to many an eye. The emotions of pain and the attachment the wounded steed displays for his dying master, who lies mortally wounded at his feet, and who in vain attempts to extricate himself from the spot where he has fallen are very touching; indeed the movements of both master and steed, are depicted with great skill. The conclusion of the scene is described by the poetess thus:

"One moment now—the trembling steed again began to reel,
His quivering side was cleft in twain by shafts of random steel;
And low beside his master's head he slowly stretched his form,
Nor heeds the soldier or his steed the shock of battle-storm."

This exhibition continues nightly and will be removed, in a few evenings, to make room for other illustrations.

The Ladies of the "Relief Hospital" return their grateful thanks to Mr. Lee Mallory for his generous contribution for the benefit of the sick and wounded soldiers under their charge. The whole of the proceeds of the first night's exhibition of the "War Illustrations," without any deduction for expenses, has been given them.

Mrs. J. M. SPEED,
Treasurer of Ladies Hospital.

LATEST BY THE MAILS.

We have been favored, says the Petersburg Express, with the New York Herald of Saturday last, from which we copy a few extracts:

NEWS FROM EUROPE—FOUR DAYS LATER.

CAPE RACE, June 6.—The steamship City of Washington, from Liverpool May 28, via Queenstown, was boarded at 5 p. m., off this point.

The steamers Southwick and Gladiator from Nassau with cotton, turpentine etc., had arrived at Liverpool.

The Sumter continued at Gibraltar.

THE AMERICAN CRISIS.

The London Morning Post understands that the demand for the restitution of the Emily St Pierre cannot be complied with, as municipal laws take no cognizance of the act of the three men who captured her as an offence, or recognize it as an injury suffered by the belligerents. Had an American cruiser fallen in with the ship she might have seized her, but there is no municipal law which can warrant the English government in giving her up, and it is therefore bound to refuse compliance with the request.

The London Times in an editorial on the surrender of Norfolk, the destruction of the Merrimac, says the conquest of the South, so far as the water is concerned, seems almost complete. On land, however, the Times says it is premature to say the rebel power is altogether broken. It sees no signs of the end, and no indications as to what that end will be. The Southerners may be beaten in battle, but they have immense territories for retreat. The contest is virtually the whole world against the South, as the North is open to the ships of the world, while the South is completely shut out. The surprise is not that the Confederates retreat, but that they make front at all.

The London Times thinks that General Butler's rule at New Orleans is exceedingly severe and harsh, and calculated to make the raising of the blockade there valueless.

The London Morning Post is very bitter on General Butler's proclamation, and says that not even the Austrians or Russians ever issued more severe decrees.

The Post says if Davis and Beauregard can inflict defeat on the Federals the independence of the South will be achieved. If they are overcome the South may be considered vanquished.

The London Daily News regards the abandonment of Norfolk and the destruction of the Merrimac as of great importance, and that it proves the resignation by the Confederates of the contest at sea.

Two ships are up for New Orleans at Liverpool.

Sir L. "Packegoile" had given notice in the Commons that he would call attention to the destruction of cotton at New Orleans, and the effect it might have on English manufactures. At the same time he would ask if the government intends to take steps for mediation.

Mr. Berkely brought forward his annual motion in favor of the ballot, which was carried by 83 to 50, amidst loud cheers. Leave was given to bring in a bill on the subject.

FROM CORINTH.

The Mobile *Register*, of the 31st ult says:

It is rumored that on Wednesday evening, Gen. Hardee's division was engaged for several hours, a little to the right of Farmington, first driving the enemy back, but being afterwards driven back in turn to their rifle pits. The cannonading is said to have been heavy, ceasing about 6 o'clock.

We have authentic intelligence of important movements among our forces at Corinth, which will be made public in due time.

Under the head "Falling Back," the Mobile *Tribune*, of the 1st instant says:

We learn that our army has evacuated Corinth, and fallen back on the line of the railroad—it is said to Reinzi, twelve and a quarter miles this side of that place.

This movement has no connection with the skirmish which took place last Wednesday; and is considered one of the best in stragetic skill. Our army will be in a healthier position, farther from the Tennessee river, and making almost useless the formidable entrenchments of the enemy, while, at the same time, it is just now as necessary for him to keep his men massed as it was before. So that he loses and we gain by the movement.

REPORTED EVACUATION OF NORFOLK AND PORTSMOUTH BY THE FEDERAL FORCES.

We have learned from what we consider reliable authority that, since the late battles before Richmond, the Yankee forces have been evacuating Norfolk and Portsmouth, and destroying the public property and works at those places, with a view of reinforcing McCLELLAN'S army on the Chickahominy. The dry-dock at the navy-yard had been completely destroyed, and the government work-shops razed to the ground. The fortifications on Craney Island, Sewell's Point and Pig's Point were all blown up and levelled with the earth. We learn further that the track of the Norfolk and Petersburg railroad was torn up sixteen miles south of Suffolk, and the iron carried off. The troops at Norfolk and Portsmouth are said to number between eight and ten thousand, and supposed to have embarked ere this on transports for their destination.

Our informant states that the occupation of Richmond by McCLELLAN was read out four times on dress parade to the troops, who began to inquire how many Richmonds there are in the Confederacy. RICHARD THE THIRD in the battle scene of Bosworth field exclaims, "Methinks there are six RICHMONDS in the field. Five have I already slain! &c.

McCLELLAN has demolished more with his pen than RICHARD claimed to have done with his sword.—*Examiner.*

Halleck's Roorback.

The Petersburg Express of yesterday has a late copy of the New York Herald and says:

We have seen the Herald of last Saturday, two days later. As it contains not the slightest reference to Gen. Beauregards' reported disaster, we are bound to infer that Halleck's telegram of the 4th is an unmitigated lie—manufactured out of the whole cloth—and of a character with the whopper he told about Island No. 10, and its 6,000 prisoners a month or two since.

THE EVACUATION OF CORINTH.

The Atlanta Confederacy regards General Beauregard's evacuation of Corinth, as a master-piece of Generalship, and says "it is equal to a victory over the Yankees, and time will show it." The fact is that Beauregard has not fallen back so far, but that the Federal force is obliged to remain massed at Corinth, where the effects of the climate are telling fearfully upon them.

Dr. J. C. Not, an eminent physician of Mobile, now a Surgeon in Beauregard's army, in a letter to the Mobile Advertiser, gives the following as the main reasons for the evacuation of Corinth.

1st. Water is very scarce and bad, and our army is suffering greatly from sickness.

2d. The enemy are more advantageously posted in point of health, and have received very large reinforcements.

3d. If we should be defeated, it would be the destruction of the army of the Mississippi.

4th. If we were to win a battle, it would be after such a desperate struggle that it would cost us far more than we can now afford. Our army would be so cut to pieces that we should have nothing left to operate against the enemy's troops on the Gulf and the Mississippi river.

5th.—There is nothing at Corinth to fight for. The railroad to the East is cut off from us. The enemy can take Fort Pillow whenever they choose to take the matter seriously in hand. The whole country for fifty miles around is foraged out by our army, and the enemy can find nothing but disease and starvation in our rear. They cannot possibly advance into the interior in any direction where they would not be surrounded by enemies.

If we can keep such an army as we have now, we can, in the course of the summer, cut up in detail any army they may attempt to send out of reach of their gunboats.

The Fabian policy is certainly the best for us in our present condition. The United States Government is wasting away under its millions of expense a day, and we can certainly defend our firesides longer than they can keep up such a war a thousand miles from their resources. Every hundred miles they come increases their expenses in geometrical ratio.

Our generals will no doubt take every means of impeding their progress and annoying them, and if they will keep a few hundred men scattered along the railroads they can render them worthless to the enemy.

FROM NORFOLK.

Late advices from Norfolk represent the Federals in that section as greatly alarmed at the recent movements of Gen. Jackson, and the terrible slaughter of McClellan's army in the battles of Saturday and Sunday, May 31st, and June 1. But three thousand troops now occupy Portsmouth and Norfolk, and these it is said, are being rapidly sent off in other directions. The Federals have torn up the Norfolk and Petersburg railroad sixteen miles this side of Suffolk, and sent the iron off to the North. It is also said that they have blown up all the fortifications around Norfolk, and the rumor was that they contemplated an evacuation of the place. Our informant states that ten valuable negroes were shot down in the streets of Norfolk last week because they refused to leave their owners, and that the Yankees say they have long since ceased to regard the negroes of the South as anything else but a most intolerable nuisance, and one which they intend to abate by the sword, if necessary. We have rumors also that the yellow fever has made its appearance in Norfolk, but we think this incorrect. The withdrawal of the military forces about Norfolk and Portsmouth we think correct, as it is very probable that McClellan needs reinforcements, and that the Yankee capital has been considered greatly endangered by the recent movements of Gen. Jackson. There are other ways to reach that "sink of iniquity," than crossing the Potomac at Williamsport.—*Petersburg Express.*

"FUSS AND FEATHERS'" LAST.

A Yankee paper states that in conversation with a distinguished clergyman from Albany, who was at Gen. Scott's residence last week, the General said: "I think Davis will not be caught. He will probably escape through Texas into Mexico. To the more prominent traitors that may be taken it would mete out a system of judicious but liberal hanging."

BY TELEGRAPH.

More Glorious News from Jackson.

JACKSON AGAIN VICTORIOUS.

Shields Routed with Immense Loss.

OUR LOSS HEAVY.

Fremont Retreating and Blocking His Way.

STAUNTON, June 9.

To Gov. Letcher:

General Jackson has given Shields an awful whipping, capturing one regiment and his artillery, and driven him four miles down the Shenandoah.

Fremont appeared on the opposite bank of the North and Shenandoah Rivers.

Our victory to-day over Shields is complete. If Gen. Jackson had reinforcements he would save all. Our loss is very heavy, but the enemy's was tremendous. The cavalry is still in pursuit. Fremont has crossed the North River, with small force, at Rockland Mills.

SECOND DISPATCH.

STAUNTON, June 9.

General Ashby was killed last Friday.—Our loss yesterday was about two hundred; to-day much heavier. Will give you any news additional that comes to hand.—Great victory over Shields to-day.

THIRD DISPATCH.

STAUNTON, June 9.

Freemont is falling back and blockading the road. Jackson pressing Shields.—Urge forward the reinforcements so that he may follow up his successes.

A. W. H.

Official from General Jackson.

RICHMOND, June 10.

The following dispatch was received this morning by Adjutant General Cooper, from Gen. Jackson, dated near Port Republic, June 9th, via Staunton the 10th.

"Through God's blessing, the enemy near Port Republic was this day routed with a loss of six pieces of artillery.

[Signed] T. J. JACKSON,
Major-General Commanding.

Later from Chattanooga and Vicksburg.

AUGUSTA, GA., June 10th.

A dispatch from Atlanta to the Augusta papers, dated 9th says:

The enemy had retired from shelling distance of Chattanooga. Their loss was 8 killed. The numbers wounded unknown. The Federal gunboats appeared before Shell Mound, and was fired into by our scouts. Three of the enemy were killed. Several citizens were taken prisoners by the Yankees from across the river.

The Savannah Republican's special dispatch says:

Mitchell is said to be with his force opposite Shell Mound. A number of contraband negroes and several discharged Confederates were captured by the enemy on Friday last. Their supposed destination is Chattanooga, but it may be to cover some other movements. All is quiet.—Several spies have been captured.

The Jackson Mississippian has a dispatch from Vicksburg, dated June fifth, which says:

The Federal gunboats and sloop-of-war opened yesterday morning on our batteries and the city. The shot fell thick. One Federal vessel was struck by our shot and left.

The Kennebec, which attacked our battery a week ago, was disabled, and now lies at the bar below the city.

The Houston (Texas) Telegraph of the 17th, contains a demand on the 7th of May, from Capt. Eagle, of the U. S. Frigate Santo, for the surrender of the city of Galveston, saying that in a few days the Federal naval and land force would appear before the city. Gen. Herbert instructed Col. Cooke to say that he would reply when the forces appeared.

The Foreign Consuls on the 22d May communicated with the Frigate Santo, with a view to fixing some point to be respected in bombardment as a refuge for foreign subjects.

Eagles replied that it was not in his power to give any assurance of security, as he could not tell where the shot would fall.

Northern News.

RICHMOND, June 10.

The Herald of the 9th has been received. It gives the names of eleven officers who, with 230 privates, it says, were made prisoners of war at the late battle.

The officers above the rank of Lieutenant are:

Col. Lightfoot, of the 22d North Carolina, Lieutenant Col. Longson and Major Gybal of the 28th Georgia, Major Hubbard of the 8th Ala., and Capt. Mays of South Carolina.

A dispatch to Secretary Welles dated the 6th, announces the occupation of Fort Pillow by the Federal troops.

Dispatches from Paducah, dated 6th inst., say that Col. Noble, with nearly his entire command, are under marching orders for Duck River, and will leave next day.

[Here follows some foreign news taken from the Herald of the 7th which will be found elsewhere.—ED. VIRGINIAN.]

Later from Chattanooga.

ATLANTA, June 10.

Passengers by the State train report that the enemy, variously estimated at from three to seven thousand, left the river opposite Chattanooga, and divided his force, part going down the river.

It is believed he will attempt to cross from the Junction this side to attack the city.

Gens. Kirby Smith, Leadbetter, and Reynolds are there with plenty of troops, determined to meet and repel the enemy.

The people of Chattanooga are calm and free from alarm.

From Richmond.

RICHMOND, June 10.

All quiet to-day in and near Richmond. No fighting yesterday or to-day. Rain continued to fall all day, with slight intermission, until 8 o'clock.

MEMPHIS ABANDONED—THE COTTON AND SUPPLIES BURNED.

The evacuation of Corinth necessarily gives to the enemy possession of a portion of the Memphis and Charleston railroad, and closes to us Memphis and the Valley of the Mississippi. In anticipation of the enemy's occupation of Memphis all the cotton has been destroyed. The latest Memphis *Appeal* says:

Last night, the hour of midnight, when all nature was wrapped in the embrace of Morpheus, or "any other man," a faint representation of the "lake that burneth with fire" was seen painted upon the heavens in the southern part of the city. Tongues asked what it meant. The fiat had gone forth—orders had been given for the large lot of cotton in Pickering to be destroyed, and the home battalion was executing them. As the blaze ascended to the heavens it impressed upon all minds clearly the importance of such action. The cotton has been destroyed, and should the enemy, in the course of human events, get possession of Memphis, he will find no cotton to boast of.

WE have had the opportunity of seeing a letter from the Eastern part of the State, giving details of matters and things going on in Newbern, Washington, and vicinity, since the arrival of "Governor Stanly," who was to have spoken, and we suppose did speak, in Washington on Wednesday, upon which occasion invitations were tried to be put out to get the people to come in to hear him, the Yankee authorities granting passes to go and return. Stanly has with him as his private secretary, a man named Midyett, formerly a merchant in Washington, but who went to California and returned thence with the "Governor." Midyett is said to be a Hyde county man.

By all accounts Stanly is greatly disappointed in not finding the Union feeling that he had expected. He is dissatisfied, and wishes he had staid where he was. One of the first things he met in Newbern, is said to have been the skull of the first Governor Spaight, upon a pole, the Yankee soldiers having violated the graves and vaults, and taken all the iron burial cases they could find to send home dead Lincolnites in. When Mr. Stanly spoke to Burnside about it, he treated it lightly—said "that was nothing."

Mr. Alfred Stanly has been released, and is more bitter against the Lincolnites than ever, and even Ed. Stanly is said not to quite like the programme, but makes any number of promises of redress and reformation, none of which will be carried out. He has not the power, even if he had the best will in the world.

The lawless outrages of the Yankee soldiers still continue, and even grow worse. But a few days since a highly respectable gentleman riding along the road was ordered by a party of soldiers to dismount. He said he was on urgent business, whereupon the officer in command cut him over the head with his sword, inflicting a serious wound.

Robbery of houses and farms, hogs and cattle, and all manner of depredations, and these without redress are the order of the day, and are bound to give the lie to Mr. Stanly's honied professsions.

Wilmington (N. C.) Journal.

CANDID.—A letter, written by the Rev. A. A. Haines, pastor of a church in the interior of New York, to a soldier in the Federal army, was picked up on the battle field. We copy a single paragraph:

The war news just now is very uninteresting. I fear our Generals are not qualified to make much headway, and with all our great army and navy, the South is as strong as ever. The English and French will perhaps take the part of the South in a few months, and then our poor country may be crushed before the combined efforts of her numerous foes. But God is our trust, and let us hope and pray we may have peace soon again, and all our dark apprehensions dissipated.

THE CHRISTIAN BANNER.

VOL. I.] FREDERICKSBURG, VA., JUNE 11, 1862. [NUMBER 6.

Christian Banner.

J. W. HUNNICUTT,---PROPRIETOR.

OFFICE.—In the North wing of the Old Town Hall, one door South from the corner of Princess Ann and Commerce Streets.

SOUTHERN NEWS.

The Vicksburg (Miss.) Citizen, of Friday last has the following:

DESTRUCTION OF PRESIDENT DAVIS' PROPERTY.

We learn that the vandals have come off their boats, and battered down and utterly destroyed the residence of Jeff. Davis, and also that of Joe Davis. Their acts of destruction and vandalism in that neighborhood were complete, leaving nothing but bleak and desolate track behind them.

THE GUNBOATS.

Since the last communication by flag of truce yesterday morning, no change has been made in the fleet. They still maintain their old position out of reach of our guns. Several shots have been fired by the gunboats at our men on the shore between the lower batteries and Warrenton, but no one has has been hurt by them. One heavy shell that did not explode lies in the Warrenton road, and is an object of much curiosity to all who pass that way.

CAPTURED.

The Federal fleet in front of Warrenton is committing all sorts of depredations upon the people along the shore. Two citizens of Warrenton, Mr. Walker and Mr. Gardner, have been captured and carried off to their boats.

SICKNESS IN THE BOATS.

We are informed that there is an immense amount of sickness among the Federal troops on the transports. It appears that they have run short of medicines, and a party of them made a visit to a drug store in Warrenton and sacked it of all its contents. One boat is said to be filled entirely with their sick.

It is the general impression that the enemy has landed the troops from the transports at some point below this city. We do most ardently hope this may be so. But few of them will ever reach home again to tell the tale of their companions, if they venture upon the soil of old Warren.

OUR PROSPECTS.

Whatever doubts we have had as to the merits of our defences here are now rapidly disappearing, and we are assured by the most competent and experienced military judges that our works are of such a character as to bid defiance to the enemy. Every day is adding to our strength.

SCOUTING PARTIES.

Our scouting parties have thus far effected but very little in harrassing the enemy. In a little skirmish on Monday they succeeded in wounding five Yankees but we also had one of our best men seriously wounded. So far the Yankees have had their own way having taken one of our cavalry prisoner, captured several citizens of Warrenton, killed Mr. Johnson, destroyed Jeff. Davis' and Joe. Davis' farms and committing depredations *ad libitum* everywhere. Why is it that our scouts cannot cut off these vandal parties?

BURNING OF THE DE SOTO DEPOT.

This building, located immediately opposite Vicksburg, on the Louisiana shore, was set on fire last night and entirely consumed. No attention was paid the fire, every one thinking that the conflagration was ordered by our military authorities, as a beacon light by which to watch the movements of the enemy. The story now runs that the Yankee scouts came up through the swamp surprised the guard on watch, and set fire to the building. The guard escaped to the point of the river above, and made their way over to the city this morning.

BATTERY ISLAND SHELLED.

The Charlstown Mercury of May 23d, contains the following:

On Wednesday three of the enemy's gunboats shelled the pickets on Battery Island, six of whom, mistaking their orders took refuge in a bombproof, where they were captured by a large party. Coles' and Battery islands were evacuated, everything moveable being carried off and the bar racks on the latter Island burned. In the afternoon the enemy passed through the unfinished piling to a point above Battery Island. At night one Sergeant Wilson was caught by the Confederate pickets in the act of deserting to the enemy. It is said that two heavy guns were abandoned on our outer lines of defence. The enemy are vigilantly observed and all their movements reported; but the general opinion is that half a dozen heavy guns on Coles' Island could have kept them out of the river. Their presence has occasioned the removal of a large force of negroes, and the loss of the crops and stock on several plantations.

By the possession of Stone, only James' Island intervenes between the enemy and the city of Charleston, from which they are distant eight miles as the crow flies.

SOUTHERN NEWS.

From Memphis and Vicksburg—Rebel Accounts of the Battle Near Richmond.

CAIRO, June 5.—A party of engineers and firemen escaped from Memphis with three locomotives, which they succeeded in firing up secretly, and ran them as far as the Obion river.

Having burned the bridges after them in their flight, they left the locomotives at the river, and hastening on foot to Columbus, arrived here today. Our troops will immediately secure the engines. The refugees report a sad condition of affairs in Memphis. They bring with them papers of the 2d of June.

An intelligent and apparently truthful prisoner just from Fort Pillow, says our flotilla can undoubtedly take Forts Pillow and Randolph, and Memphis, whenever it attacks them. Colonel Ellet, commanding the Union ram, is impatient for permission to commence the attack, being entirely confident of success.

The rebel commander at Fort Pillow calls for 50,000 more men.

A despatch from Grand Junction, dated June 2, states that there are no Union troops between Grand Junction and Corinth.

The Little Rock Democrat, of May 29th, publishes a hostile correspondence between Governor Rector and the editor of the Democrat, who denounced Rector for running away from the capital, leaving the State without any Government.

General Curtis is still at Batesville. He had 6,000 troops between the White and Red rivers.

The Vicksburg Evening Citizen, of Saturday, says: Eleven gunboats have gone back, down the river, owing, it is supposed, to insubordination and mutiny. Several remained, and on Friday evening shelled the shore for several hours. The rebel batteries are being strengthened by having additional guns mounted.

The Memphis papers of the 2d contain despatches from Richmond dated the 1st instant, of which the following is the substance:

General Hill's division commenced the fight, on Saturday morning, Generals Rhodes', Garland's, Rains', and Anderson's brigades bearing the brunt, until the arrival of their reinforcements.

The Federals were driven from their redoubts, and their batteries were turned on them.

General Lee and President Davis were on the field. Their presence increased the enthusiasm of our troops. The Yankees stubbornly contested every inch of ground, while they gave way to the impetuous charges of our soldiers. Large numbers of the Confederate soldiers are wounded in the arms and legs.

General Rhodes was slightly wounded.

The enemy tried to make a flank movement about 7 o'clock in the evening, but were repulsed.

On Sunday the battle was renewed, chiefly with musketry. Prisoners are constantly coming in. Gen. Hatton, of Tennessee, was killed. The carnage on both sides was dreadful, the Yankees losing two to our one. About 500 prisoners have already been taken.

The latest intelligence from the battle-field represents that the enemy has been driven back a mile and a half from his position. Our forces occupy his camps.

We captured three batteries after the most desperate fighting. The enemy were protected by the woods and their entrenchments.

LATEST FROM GEN. McCLELLAN.

McCLELLAN'S HEADQUARTERS,
June 5—Evening.

The rebels opened with artillery this morning from five different points, opposite New Bridge, with a view of preventing its reconstruction.—Three of our batteries opened on them, causing them to retreat after a hot fire of two hours.—Our loss was one killed and two wounded.

No further interference took place during the day.

Reconnoissances made to-day show no material change in the enemy's position.

Further information shows that our troops on Saturday and Sunday engaged six divisions instead of four, making a force of seventy-five thousand rebels.

General Birney, of Philadelphia, was relieved of his command on the battle-field by General Heintzelman, he having failed to bring his brigade into action when ordered on Saturday.

A contraband who left Richmond on Tuesday night states that all the carts, furniture cars, omnibusses and carriages to be found, were impressed into the service for the carrying of the dead and wounded from the battle-field, and that the Spottswood and Exchange hotels, together with a number of public and private buildings, were turned into hospitals. All the information shows that the enemy suffered terribly.

The severe storm which set in Tuesday afternoon lasted during the whole of yesterday. The water in the Chickahominy rose to an unprecedented height. The railroad trains from White House to the late battle-field were detained several hours, and the telegraph line was down in many places.

A heavy shower, that set in about dark, had the effect of again raising the water in the Chickahominy.

☞ Let no man be too proud to work.—Let no man be ashamed of a hard fist or a sun burt countenance. Let him be ashamed only of ignorance and sloth. Let no man be ashamed of poverty. Let him only be ashamed of dishonesty and idleness.

SOUTHERN ACCOUNTS OF THE BATTLE.

CAIRO, June 5, 1862.

Memphis papers of the 2d contain despatches from Richmond of the 1st, of which the following is the substance:—

General Hill's division commenced the fight on Saturday morning, Rhodes', Garland's, Rains' and Anderson's brigades bearing the brunt of the battle. Until the arrival of their reinforcements the federals were driven from their redoubts, and their batteries turned on them. General Lee and President Davis were on the field. Their presence increased the enthusiasm of our troops.

The Yankees stubbornly contested every inch of ground; but were compelled to give way before the impetuous charges of our soldiers. A large number of Confederate soldiers are wounded in the arms and legs. General Rhodes is slightly wounded.

The enemy tried to make a flank movement about seven in the evening, but were repulsed.

On Sunday the battle was resumed, chiefly with musketry.

Prisoners are constantly coming in.

General Hatton, of Tennessee, is killed. The carnage on both sides is dreadful, the Yankees losing two to our one.

About 500 prisoners are already taken.

The last despatch, sent on the 1st. says the latest intelligence from the battle-field represents the enemy to be driven back a mile and a half from his position. Our forces now occupy his camps. We captured three batteries after the most desperate fighting. The enemy were protected by woods and entrenchments.

THE WORK OF LIFE.

As on a sun shiny day flying clouds cast their shadows over the fields, one moment at our feet, the next moment gone from our sight, leaving no trace of their passage, so do we come and go from earth, leaving no trace of our course. Though there is a path marked out for us only, along which are joys and sorrows for us alone and, in which we may individually work out the great task of life, given us by our Maker; yet we turn aside, and losing ourselves in the multitude of travelers, journey as "strangers in a strange land" to an unknown city.

We must leave foot-prints behind us—records of lives well spent; writing each day in the heart of our fellow-men, lessons of self-denial, love, truth, and obedience, so that the "mile-stones" of our route shall not speak of Divine counsel slighted, privileges abused, vows broken, and sin triumphant, telling the passerby that here pride made us stumble, and there sloth took us captive, but shall speak of holy purposes realized, noble deeds performed, self-sacrifices enjoyed, temptations overcome, and grace victorious—telling the passerby, that here our faith was strengthened, and there our courage was renewed.

We live only in the present. The past is gone forever, and the future is not ours.—Day by day we are writing our own biography, to be read by coming generations; not in a "new and revised edition" with an "arrata," but in the same old books; with its sad mistakes, foul blots and false teachings. May we keep the page clean the style clear, and the thoughts pure. Let us cast ourselves a "live sacrifice" upon the altar of God, and the incense thereof shall reach Heaven and bless the world,

Where the Corinth Rebels Are.

A correspondent of the Chicago Post writes: "A temporary stand will be made on the Mobile and Ohio road until the main body of the army can complete the fortification of Columbus. At this point they have concentrated and are still gathering all the supplies to be found in the Cotton States. It will be the last ditch. If attacked soon, they will fight until their provisions are exhausted; if not attacked, they can remain in position at most but a few weeks. In either event they will break up into guerilla bands, and prolong the war after the manner of their more Southern neighbors, the Mexicans. A gentleman who has just arrived here conversed with a telegraph operator who was impressed into the rebel service, and has been stationed at Corinth. He made his escape about ten days ago, and says that the day he left a message was sent to Mobile to hold that place at all hazards, as it would be the base of future operations. Large reinforcements were sent there the same day."

☞ When I contemplate the excellent wisdom which made the heavens, attunes all their motions, how am I abashed at that mixture of arrogance and folly, which has at times inclined me to murmur at thy dispensation, O Lord."—*Harvey*.

☞ A good man who has seen much of the world and is now tired of it, says "The grand essentials to happiness in this life are something to do, something to love, and something to hope for."

SECOND TENNESSEE REGIMENT.—J. T. E. McLean of the Western Military Institute, and a native of Tennessee, has been appointed by Governor Johnson to organize the Second Tennessee Regiment. The work is progressing finely.

It is estimated that at least 60,000 militia can be brought into service before the 10th inst., thus setting free for active duty the very large force now engaged in guarding cities, forts and railroads.

SUBMISSION.

This word *submission*, has, for the last two years, produced a greater terror over the Southern people, than any word to be found in any language in the world. *Submission!* Submission to, what? "Submission to old Abe Lincoln! Submission to Black Republican *rule*. Submission to the Lincoln government!" Argue rationally, logically, philosophically, and according to the plainest rules of common sense with secessionists and the best, and profoundest argument we have ever heard them advance to justify them in their reckless course of ruin, is simply this; "What! submit to old Abe Lincon! Submit to Black Republican rule!" This was an irrefragible argument. No one in all the schools of common sense philosophy, could be found wise enough to confute it. Who had to submit to Lincoln? What Government had Lincoln? What power had he, more than was guaranteed to him by the Constitution, being Chief Magistrate of the United States? None whatever! If all the States had remained quietly, and peaceably in the Union, Lincoln could not have inaugurated a civil war upon the South. This was a Constitutional impossibility. The Federal Government never inaugurated war upon the South. South Carolina inaugurated civil war upon the Federal Government. This is a fact which will go down in history to the latest generation of American citizens.

But let us examine and see who are the submissionists. The *people* of South Carolina submitted to Messrs. Rhett, Keitt, Boyce & Co.; Mississippi submitted to South Carolina; Alabama submitted to South Carolina and Mississippi; and Georgia and Florida submitted to these three; Louisiana and Texas submitted to these five cotton States, making seven, and these seven cotton States seceded, not by the votes of the people, but by Conventions, and these several Conventions appointed delegates to meet at Montgomery, Alabama, for the purpose of forming a Provisional Government, and this Convention nominated and elected Jeff. Davis, of Mississippi, as President, and Mr. Stephens of Georgia, as Vice President.—They then mutilated the Constitution of the United States, and with their *improvements*, amendments, and mutilations called it the Constitution of the Confederate States of America. Then this Montgomery Convention, empowered the Conventions of the seven cotton States to appoint members to form a Congress for the purpose of enacting laws, by which to move the grand machinery of this new order of things. All this was done independently of the popular voice of the people of these States. There was no *submission* in all this, was there? Were there no Union men in all these seven cotton States while these things were being acted out? What did they do? What could they do, but submit to the arbitrary will, and yield submission to the Military power of this self-constituted body?

Has not Virginia yielded in humble *submission* through the intrigue of her leaders, to the seven Cotton States Confederacy? Yes, through the treachery of her Legislature and State Convention, Virginia was forced out of the Union on the 18th of April 1861 (as they say,) and was immediately tied on to the Seven Confederate Cotton States, and Richmond was determined on as the Capital of the Confederate States of America, and Jeff. Davis and his Army were urged to hasten on to Richmond and Virginia, to act as a kind of terror to the "*Union Shriekers*," "*Submissionists*," "*Black Republicans*," &c., on the day of election, which took place on the 23d of May, 1861—more than one month from the passage of the ordinance of Secession. And on the day of the election, as we have stated in our editorial in a former number of the Banner, all the principal cities and towns in Virginia were litterally filled with soldiers.—And not only so, but Civil war was inaugurated in Virginia before the election. Gosport Navy Yard was seized, and the Arsenal at Harpers' Ferry was burned before the election. All this was planned and executed for the purpose of forcing Virginia into *submiision* to Secession rule, intrigue, and treachery. So that, at least, seventy thousand majority of the voters in Virginia, had at last to bow at the point of the bayonet in humble submission, to the will, purpose, and determination of a few leaders in the Cotton States, "away down South in Dixey."

This is submission with a tyrant's rod and a vengeance. And all who were opposed to secession, have been forced to *submit*, because a Military despotism has been hanging over them ever since. and this is freedom—Independence!

Submission! Are not the very men who indignantly spurned the idea of submission to the Constituted Authorities of their country, now submiting to the greatest, imaginable indignities from their own servants? Masters have set the ungodly example of non-submission to the "higher powers." and servants have caught the *cue*, and swear, that they will no longer *submit* to their masters. Why do masters submit to the reckless insubordination of their slaves? For the same reason that Union men twelve months ago, had to submit to the will and dictations of secessionists; simply, because, they can't help themselvs:, and, hence anarchy reigns rampant everywhere and among all classes, all over the country! Great God, to what a *queer* state of affairs our country is reduced! Secessionists won't submit to be governed by the Constitution of the United States; and Union men, won't submit to be governed by the Constitution of the Confederate States of America; and servants won't be governed by the legal authority of their masters. This is, indeed, a terrible state of insubordination—We knew from the beginning, that secession would inevitbly produce this state of things, and, threfore, we opposed it. And becaus we did and do oppose it, we are branded as an enemy to the South—How blindly, how wickedly false

In proof that the people of Virginia were forced out of the Union by the actions of the Civil and Military leaders of secession, needs no stronger evidence, than the suppression of the publication of the popular vote of Virginia. Who can tell the number of votes actually polled by *citizens* of Virginia for the ordinance of secession? This is a question of grave importance, which we submit to the leading secessionsts of Virginia. And still the people must submit. This is *submission*.

Nor is this all, when the people of Virginia were called upon this spring to go into a *mock-election* for a President of the Southern Confederacy, they were told, that it would be bad policy to have two candidetes in this early stage of our government, and that war times was no time to be discussing politics; and, therefore, all the citizens voters of Virginia ought to go to the polls and vote for Jeff. Davis. What was the number of votes polled? Who can tell? The people of Virginia ought to know this. We were urged to go to the polls and vote, but we did not. Why should we? Had there been but ten votes cast in the whole state, Jeff Davis would still have remained Prsident of the Southern Confederacy. Virginians have to submit to all this, and that in silence, or be threatened with a drawn halter around their necks. This is submission. Secessionists won't submit to the constituted authorities of their country, but pompously, and arrogantly dictate to others, and unless all others bow in humble submission to them, they are to be hung, shot, banished from their country. Good Lord deliver us!

Once more, when the Malitia were called out this spring, it is well known that they were unwilling to go into service, and government fearing the consequences, Congress passed the act of *conscription*, by which they were all *forced* into service, excepet a few, who so managed their cards, as to *elude* the clutches of the military bands, that were sent through the contry to catch them up and hurry them into the Army. There was no submission in all this, was there? Yes, submission of the most oppressive and aggravating character! Submission, to a military despotism. *Submission*, not to the Constitution of the FederalGovernment,but *submission to secesion* Is it not strange, that men will croak, and croak about submission, and the degredation of submission, while they themselves are trying to browbeat, and force all others, to submit to their lordly dictations? We say that Virginians have submitted long enough to the oppresion and tyranny of petty despots, and it is now time for men who wish to be free, to rise up and assert and maintain their rights.

If the *citizens* of Virginia, were unanimously in favor of secession, why do they go into the army with so much reluctance? If every Southern man is to be left dead on the battle field, unless the South obtain her independence, why is it, that so many Southern men had to be forced into service by an act of conscription? These are questions and facts, which should be duly considered by the people of Virginia. And, finally, suppose the South should gain her independence—what will become of the poor, old, desolated Dominion—Virginia—Her sons gone, her territory desolated, and all left in one common wreck and ruin! We would beseech and entreat our fellow-citizens, to think on this terribly black picture, before all, is lost, and lost forever.

THE CORTESIES OF LIFE.—William Wirt's letter to his daughter on the "small, sweet courtesies of life," contains a passage from which a deal of happiness might be learned:

"I want to tell you a secret. The way to make yourself pleasing to others, is to show them that you care for them. The whole world is like the miller at Mansfield, 'who cared for nobody—no, not he; because nobody cared for him.' And the whole world would serve you so, if you give them the cause. Let every one therefore see that you do care for them, by showing them what Sterne so happily calls the small courtesies in which there is no parade, whose voice is too still to tease and which manifest themselves by tender and affectionate looks, and little kind acts of attention, giving others the preference in every little enjoyment, at the table, in the field, walking, sitting, or standing,"

Virginia the Battle Field.

Is it not strange, that Virginians are so totally blinded to their own interests, and should have suffered themselves to be imposed upon as they have been, by the shrewd political leaders of the Gulf States? Before this war commenced, we predicted that Virginia would be the great battle field of this wicked revolution, and repeatedly said, that if the Gulf States had been geographically located as Virginia was, they would never have seceded. The people of the Gulf States knew that Virginia and all the *border* States would be a *bastion*, a mighty bulwark of defence between themselves and the enemy. They had never supposed that the war would be carri[illegible] into their own territories. No, this was not their calculation.

When the Southern soldiers came into Virginia and to Fredericksburg last Spring twelve months ago, they said that they had come to defend the soil of Virginia. This we regarded as an insult to the intelligence of Virginians—a solemn mockery. They came to meet the enemy on Virginia soil, to keep him off of their own soil, and out of their own territories. This we knew, and the leaders of this revolution in the cotton and sugar States knew the same thing; and yet, it was considered treasonable for any one openly to express such an opinion. Let any one now, take a calm survey of the territorial boundaries of Virginia.

At least two thirds of her beautiful territory, are in the actual possession of the Federal Government while the small portion of Eastern Virginia, which is not yet invaded, and in the centre of which, stand the capital of the State and the capital of the Confederate States, is completely environed, pent up between two powerful, advancing armies, and still, there are those in our midst, professing to be wise, who say "we'll whip them off of every inch of Virginia soil, and make them rue the day they ever set their feet upon it."

If there were the shade of the shadow of a reason for such a conclusion as this, then men might talk, and be listened to, and respected by men of common sense. But when we take into consideration the fact, that the whole of the border of eastern Virginia from the mountains to the Chesapeake bay and round to Suffolk, including the towns and cities of Alexandria, Fredericksburg, Fortress Monroe, Hampton, Yorktown, Williamsburg, Norfolk, Portsmouth, and Suffolk, to say nothing of Winchester, and the whole territory of North Western and the mountain regions of Virginia, are all in the actual possession of the Federal Army, what foundation is there upon which any *sane* man can possibly build the shadow of a hope for the re-taking, holding, and re-possessing "every inch of Virginia territory?"

It was confidently affirmed by the professedly *knowing ones* in our community, until within a few ~~weeks past, that the Federal Army *never* would,~~ nor could get into Fredericksburg, and if men dared to express a contrary opinion, they were ruled out of *loyal* and *decent* society, as traitors, abolitionists, and black-hearted submissionists.

We have always argued, that it is much easier to keep an armed enemy out of our house, than to give him possession, and afterwards to whip him out, and keep him out. Twelve months ago, the Confederate Army was fresh and buoyant with the hope of driving *submissionists* and Yankees out of Virginia, and of keeping them off of her territory. If the Southern Army with Beaureguard, Lee, Johnson, Floyd, Wise, and a host of others to lead it on, with all their munitions of war, Commissary stores, strong fortifications, railroads, &c., &c., were not able to keep the enemy from advancing into the interior of our State, how can they expect, or hope now, since they have destroyed railroads, burnt railroad bridges, demolished towns, committed to the flames millions of dollars worth of Commissary stores, spiked and abandoned hundreds of their best and largest cannons, evacuated and forsaken their strong fortifications, committed to the flames millions of dollars worth of cotton, and well nigh all their navy, and finally with an army of *conscript* soldiers, to drive the Federal Army off of every inch of Virginia territory, re-take, re-possess, and re-hold it? The idea is absurd in thought! And when we try to get our fellow-citizens to reason on the subject, and lay facts before them, which are as plain as Heaven's own light, we are insulted and treated with the utmost indignity and contempt.

With what heart can men fight, who have been *forced*, literally *dragged* from their business, their homes, their wives and children, their fathers and mothers, their brothers and sisters, their friends and all that's dear to them, to go away down South to fight and to defend, the negroes, cotton, and sugar plantations of those wicked politicians, who have forced this common ruin upon us all, while th[illegible] are living at their ease, rolling in [illegible] living in luxury at home, and would co[illegible]emselves degraded to associate with the poor soldier with his knapsack on his back and his musket on his shoulder, and would scorn to permit him to sit and eat at their elegantly furnished and sumptuous tables?

Think of the many precious lives, that have been lost in Western Virginia, on the plains of Manassas, at Yorktown, at Williamsburg, of the bloody battle that is to be fought near Richmond, together with the great anticipated battle that is to take place in a few days at some point between Fredericksburg and Richmond. How many precious, undying souls are to be dashed in a moment into eternity, and perhaps without any preparation to meet their final Judge. And still, preachers, communicants at the altar of the peaceful Jesus, parents, fathers and mothers, wives, brothers and sisters, condemn the man who dares to expose the wickedness of the leaders, and save their husbands and sons from ruin. The Lord have mercy upon the wicked stupidity of mortals.

'Tis strange that things are *so*, but *so* they are, and it seems that there are certain clicks and parties who are determined that things shall thus go on, until our whole State is desolated, our children and friends all killed and murdered out.—Look at the desolation of all the counties between the Rappahannock, and Potomac rivers, at the condition of the country from Hampton to Richmond city, and what will the condition of the country from Fredericksburg to Richmond be, when this war shall have closed? Desolation and ruin meet the eye of the beholder at every point. Nevertheless, there are those who talk, and enter into wild speculation as to the future course to be pursued, and what *must* be done, and what *shall* be done, and unless all others submit to their dictations and mandates, they are ruled out, as traitors, abolitionists, *submissionists*, and are marked, spotted, proscribed, ostracised, and ought to be, and will be driven out of the country or hung when the time comes.

In conclusion, we venture the prediction, *That every foot of territory embraced within the boundary lines of Virginia, when she seceded, will again be brought back into the Union."*

This is only a question of time. Mark, the prediction.

☞ When we closed our office twelve months ago we had on hand a very small lot of paper, all of which we worked off last week, with the exception of enough for [illegible]t two hundred copies. If by any possibility we can obtain means to purchase paper and ink, we shall continure the publication of the Banner, otherwise, we shall be compeled to close our office, and suspend its publication, We simply make this statem ent, that the public may know the reason, should we not be able to continue the publication of the Banner.

☞ For want of advertisements, and to save labor, we republish our editorials of last week, on the forth page of this weeks paper. It is not te be expected, that the whole paper can be filled with solid matter every week. We hope as soon as we get fairly on the way, to obtain a quantity of advertisements. Will not all, who are friendly to our cause, do all they can to advance the Banner?

☞ Every cause must and will produce its legitimate effect; if, therefore, persons do not wish to be insulted, they must not provoke insults.—We make this [illegible]ark by way of a friendly hint to all those, who are seeking notoriety [illegible] offering insults to others, thereby rendering themselves supremely ridiculous in the estim[illegible]n of all wise and prudent persons both male and female.

GUERRILLA WARFARE.—This is a kind of ~~irregular mode of~~ carrying on war, by the constant attacks of independent bands. It was adopted in the north of Spain during the peninsular war. In a word, Guerrilla warfare, is nothing more nor less than a legalized system of plundering, highway robery, murder, and assassination and none but humans *demonized* would inaugerate a mode of warfare so revolting to humanity, civilization, christianity, and the honorable modes of warfare.

☞ The colored population of Fredericksburg, for the most part are strolling about town, looking on at the wonders of creation, careless and indifferent as to the future, and seem to be perfectly happy. We learn that some of them who have left their owners, have rented rooms, and set up for themselves. Being set free as they think, they are going to get rich and grow *fat*. Deplorable state of anarchy and confusion.

What a contrast between the feelings of the colored and white population of Fredericksburg—The former to all outward, human appearance perfectly happy—The latter with painful, bleeding hearts, with all the anxiety and deep-toned feelings that can possibly press upon the hearts of parents, wives, children, brothers, sisters, relatives, and friends, crushed to earth. Terrible thought. Our country ruined, our children, relatives, and friends, butchered up and slaughtered worse than beeves in a slaughter pen, and all on account of the negroes! This is a fact! God Almighty knows, and the world knows it. Can it be possible, that men will sacrifice their country, their children and all earthly happiness for the negro!

☞ We would call attention to the advertisement of Mr. S. Kleinberger, Optician who is associated with the Optical Establishment of Franklin & Co. Washington, D. C., who has the best assortment of Spectacles, mounted in Gold, Silver, Steel, Shell, and Military Field Glasses.

If certain characters could be bought for their legitimate worth, and sold for their own imaginary worth, Heavens! what a grand speculation could be made. What do you think of that reader?

Arrests.

On Thursday, Lieut. John A. Wagner arrested five negro men in the neighborhood of Sandy Bottom for gambling. The parties had staked a shinplaster and a ten cent piece and were going it strong for a fortune. Lieut. Wagner conducted them to the guard house, and on condition of good behaviour in future finally discharged them.

☞ How brightly do little joys beam upon a soul which stands on a ground darkened by clouds of sorrow! So do stars come forth from the empty sky, when we look up to them from a deep well.

☞ Take the seed of thought and immerse it in the waters of Christianity till it germinates, and you have the young twig of happiness, which may grow and blossom on earth, and will bear fruit in eternity.

The Crisis on Us!

Fools belch out nonsense and play the part of furious braggarts, spurning the admonitions of the wise and prudent, the maddening storm gathers blackness and darkness—and the deafening thunders burst over their heads, and the vivid lightnings play at their feet, before they can see and feel the danger, or admit the propriety, or necessity of seeking a place of refuge and security. Thus it is with thousands of poor deluded souls at the present time. The storm has been gathering for more than twelve long months, and the cry has constantly been, "there is no danger," yet when men dared to say, that danger threatened them in the future, they were *spotted*, regarded as traitor and *eyed* as *suspicious characters*, who ought to be reported to the Military authorities, arrested, and sent to Richmond to be tried, condemned, and executed for treason against the *Southern Confederacy*. The leaders in this terrible revolution have cried peace and safety, when sudden destruction was at our very doors. If the *leaders* in this awful *tragedy* have, knowingly and wilfully, deceived the people, then they merit the unmitigated *anathamas* of all Heaven and earth, throughout all time and eternity; if they have done it ignorantly, then they should be held up as brainless objects of pity, scorn, and contempt to the whole civilized world, as blazing beacons to all stupid, unprincipled, political adventurers, through all coming time.

Who is so skeptcail, or stultified, as to deny any longer the fact, that the terribly, awful, anticipated crisis is actually upon us.' Politicians *swindled* the people out of their *rights*—made *slaves* of them, and then promised to lead them to *independence, freedom, prosperity, glory, honor,* and *immortality. Have they done it?* The wide world answers *No!* Where is our independence? Freedom? Prosperity? Glory? Honor? National immorality? Aye, where are the brave, heroic leaders themselves? Politicians turned Generals, and Generals turned cowards, or have proven themselves totally incompetent to accomplish the mighty work they promised to perform.

Not a single promise that the politicians made to the people has been met. In the science of political manœuvering and swindling, they were accomplished proficients, but when they girded on the sword and went out to battle, they proved themselves the veriest of dolts. With but few exceptions what have, they done? They have fallen back from place, to place, and made so many surrenders that there are now but few more important points in the whole Souther[illegible] Confederacy to yield.

When our Army fell back from Centreville and Fairfax Court House, to Manassas junction, this was a "strategic move, indicating great military skill, to draw the enemy from his strong hold."—And when, subsequently it fell back from Manassa to Rappahannock Station this was another grand device of military strategy, "our generals know what they are doing, all is safe in their hands." Again, when our Army fell back from Evan's Port and the whole line of the Potomac to Fredericksburg, this was another move of brilliant Military strategy; [illegible] a bold stand was to be made, and Fredericksburg was to be defended to the very last, and at all hazards. And, finally, on the ever memorable morning of the 18th of April [illegible] by military authority our bridges were burned, and the vessels of poor *seamen* were wrapped in flames, and the *brave, heroic General* fled for his life, carrying with him his whole Army, leaving helpless citizens, unarmed men, defenceless women and children to an unknown and uncared for destiny, this was another magnificently grand, Military strategic move.

Great God! Are *men* to be always deluded in this manner, forever following an *ignisfatuus* to be-dragged into the vortex of irretrievable ruin, and as they plung headlong into the black whirlpool of destruction, unless they shout hosannas to the *demon phantom*, which caused their runin, a thousand voices exclaim, they are traitors, mad-men, fools and ought to be damned! Our Generals have fled, and carried the Army with them. By this act, they declare, that they could not protect us. If they could, why did they not stay and do it? They have left us to our own fate, and it now becomes us as wise and prudent men, to act the part of *freemen*, and take care of ourselves as best we can.

Heart-Rending Thought!

Hundreds of wives and thousands of children, whose husbands and fathers have been forced into the war, are left wholly dependent on their own exertions for the scanty means of a wretched existence. What must be the mental agonies of those husbands and fathers, when they reflect on the helpless and unknown condition of their affectionate wives and dear little children, who are far away and no possible chances of seeing them, it may be, until the war shall have ended, and, perhaps, never again in this life. And what must be the painful reflections of these wives and mothers when they think of their dear husbands and with sorrowing hearts and weeping eyes gaze on their poor little children, the whole responsibility of whose subsistence depends upon them! Wives are left worse than widows, and children worse than orphans. Who but fathers and mothers can feel the deep, heart-felt afflictions of those parents who have sons far from home, in the Army, and poor boys, it may be, are actually suffering for food and raiment, and may be wounded, sick, dying, or dead, and no affectionate hand to administer relief, in a dying hour, and not even a *slab* to tell the stranger, who they were, nor where they lie. And all this affliction and sorrow, pain and death produced, to gratify the unhallowed and wicked ambition of unprincipled, aspiring demagogues!

SECESSION LIKE THE DEVIL.

It is said, that the Devil was a liar from the beginning. If he were a liar from the beginning, he was a liar in the days of Jesus Christ—is a liar still, and will continue to be, till the end of time. He lied to Eve in Paradise, and she influenced by his falsehood, sinned, and ruined the world. If the lies were all written in a book, which the Devil has told, the world itself, would hardly be able to contain it. To say nothing more at present of the old Devil, the father of lies, let us scan a few of the lies of the *Secession Devil*.

1, That the Federal Government could be broken up, the Union dissolved, the old United States divided, and two separate Governments formed out of them, without war, and bloodshed.

2, That if by any possible chance, war should happen, it would commence between the Black Republicans and Conservative men of the North, and would probably end there.

3, That New York, Pennsylvania, Rhode Island, and Delaware, would certainly unite their destinies with the South.

4, That Maryland, Virginia, Kentucky, Tennessee, and Missouri, were all bound to secede, and would certainly go with the Gulf States. This was a *fixed fact*.

5, That in the event, by any possible contingency, there should be war, the South had men, munitions, and ample means of all kinds to prosecute it to a successful and glorious issue.

6, That the North had neither fighting men, money, nor means, to commence, and prosecute a war.

7, That Cotton was King—his throne was in the Gulf States—his empire the world—that all the *little* kings and queens of the earth, were bound to fall down and worship *Him*.

8, That the vexed question of African slavery would be hushed into eternal silence, and the institution of slavery settled upon a firm and immovable basis.

9, That slave territory would be enlarged, and slave property advance one hundred per cent.

10, That England, France, and, consequently, all other civilized nations of the world, would certainly acknowledge the Independence of the Provisional Government. This was a fixed fact, bound to be done of necessity.

11, That England and France, would certainly raise the blockade—their interest would compel them to do it.

12, That the Southern, would be the greatest Government in the world, and the citizens the most free, independent, wealthy, prosperous, and happy people on earth. All these, and many others, are the promises secession made to the Southern people. That they are all false, needs no argument—developed facts prove them so. By these fair promises the people of the South were deceived—they were swindled out of all their rights, as the sequel of this mournful tragedy will prove. Yes, for less than one mess of pottage, the whole South has become bankrupt, and the people plunged into a sea of sorrow, affliction, and death, the breadth, and depth of which none but the all-penetrating eye of omniscience can ever fathom. And yet, because we will not fall down and worship this *demon phantom*, we must be *spotted*, and by ignorant, bigoted partizans branded as an enemy and traitor to the South. We are no *enemy* to the South—we are no *traitor* to the South. No, we love the South, and always have loved her, and because we do, and always have loved the South, we always have, and do despise secession. We have always known, and ever maintained, that the only security the South and Southern institutions had, was contained in the provisions of the Federal Cnstitution. We are no traitor to the South. We indignantly spurn the base imputation, and pronounce it an unmitigated, secession falsehood.

The traitors and enemies of the South, are the secession leaders of the South. Where are the men, who *fired up the Southern heart; and precipitated* this once glorious, independent, prosperous, and happy country into the present terrible revolution? Yes, where are they? Are they in the camp, with their knapsacks on their backs and muskets on their shoulders? Are they found lying side by side with the poor privates on the cold, wet ground? Are they performing the duties of the poor private soldier, exposed to all the dangers of camp life, for the pitiful sum of eleven dollars per month? No, their patriotism never pointed in that direction, With all their boasted patriotism and love of the South, they never intended to make such sacrifices to save her. When, are they? We answer, in Legislative, Congress and Senate Halls, decreeing conscription acts, by which to force and drag men from their homes, their wives and children into camp, to fight and die, while they themselves are living in magnificent splendor, enjoying all the luxuries of life, and wreathing their own brows with laurels which they vainly imagine will be as imperishable as the records of eternity. Those men, who despise traitors and are so very suspicious of the loyalty of others, take special good care to secure to themselves, their children, their *dear* friends, and *near* relations all the fat offices and honorable positions both in the State and in the army. They are so patriotic, and love themselves so well, that they wish to monopolize the whole, lest in the scuffle for the spoils, others should get a part.—is is the mathematical measu ement, the length, breadth, depth, and height of the patriotism of thousands who are so vociferous in exclaiming against the disloyalty of *true patriots, gentlemen,* and *christians*.

Unprincipled politicians, and ignorant, fanatical religionists, North and South have caused all the sorrows, affliction, and troubles of war, that now fill the country. In the abolitionists of the North, and the fire eaters of the South, extremes have met, and the work of ruin is done. Abolitionism and secession combined to effect the overthrow of our Government—the downfall of our country.—Great God! What a fearful retribution awaits them in the awful future!

Predictions of the Christian Banner, January 31st, 1861.

1. Divide the Union—break up the Federal Government, and will not the same proximity still exist between the slave and free States that exist now?

2. Divide the Union, and the same morbid, moral sentiment will still remain in the hearts of abolitionists, which drives them on to daring deeds of madness now.

3. Divide the Union, and a thousand new causes of hate and eternal animosity will spring up among all parties.

4. Divide the Union—break up the Federal Government in advance of terms and treaties of separation between the North and South, and the door for any subsequent, equitable separation is forever closed and the key lost in eternity's depths.

5. Divide the Union, and the flood-gate is hoisted, through which a concentration of curses will flow, that baffles all human thought.

6. Divide the Union—break up the Federal Government, and Civil war begins, which will only end in the domination of the South over the North, or the North over the South.

7. Dissolve the Union, and Military and ecclesiastical despotism, or absolute monarchies will supplant the tree of liberty and all the blessings of freedom.

8. Dissolve the Union—break up the Federal Government, and the liberty of conscience, liberty of speech, liberty of action, liberty of the press, and the liberty of a once free, independent, prosperous and happy people, is gone, and gone forever.

9. Dissolve the Federal Government, and the reign of terror begins.

10. Dissolve the Union, and an era more to be dreaded than the dark ages commences.

11. Dissolve the Union, and the *guillotine* will take the place of the Star Spangled Banner, and whoever dare to speak a word against despots and tyrants, off goes his head.

12. Dissolve the Union, and then the *many*, the *dear* people, the hard working yeomanry, will all become the vassals of the few.

13- Dissolve the Union, and all the poor become the veriest menials of the lords and rulers of the people.

Are Virginians prepared for all these things? If so dissolve the Union—break up the Federal Government, and the work of death and dessolation is done.

14- Virginia's action of secesion, is virtually Virginia's action, for the abolition of all her slave property. *Secession* is virtually *abolition—Secession, is submission.*

15- If Virginia secede from the Federal Government, she will certainly lose all her negro property.

16- She will lose thousands of her noblest sons and fairest daughters.

17- She will lose her money and credit, and wind up in bankruptcy and ruin.

18. She will lose her horses and stock, corn and meat, silver-ware, and valuble house-hold furniture, by midnight assassins, plunderers, and highway robbers—Banditti will prowl, and swarm through the country worse than Egyptian locusts.

19- She will lose many of her fine residences, beautiful villages, and thriving towns.

20- She will lose all her peace, quiet, and happiness, during the whole period of a long, protracted, civil war.

21- She will lose many of her sanctuaries, and her undisturbed public worship of Almighty God.

22- She will lose the kind feeling, friendship, affection, and love, which now exist among friends, neighbors, citizens, and relatives

23- She will lose her schools, and colleges, and all facilities of educating her youth.

24-She will lose all she has gained in agricultural improvements, prosperity, and thrift—Her territory will become a common battle field, and her soil be saturated with the blood of the wounded, dead, and dying—In a word, she will lose all that she now holds near, dear, and sacred, and her history, honor, and glory will end in seas of blood, when the din and strife of the battle-field, and the thunders of civil war shall have passed away. Is Virginia prepare for all these things? If she be, then let her secede, and the sooner the better.

Christian Banner.

May 9th 1861, is the date of the last number of the Christian Banner, up to the present time, To day, May 9th 1862, just one year ago to a day, we again unfurl its sheet to the breeze.—When we closed our office twelve months ago, the *secession flag*—the emblem of *all folly*, was waveing over our city—to-day, the *American Flag*—the Stars and *Stripes*—the proud emblem of a nation's greatness—the Flag, which our fathers won through blood and death—the Flag, which our fathers loved—the Flag which all nations honor—the Flag under which we were born and have lived forty-five years, save one, now floats proudly over us, Long may it wave over the land of the free and the home of the brave—may it wave over *us*, *our* children, *our* grand children, and great-great grand-children, down to the latest posterity, till Gabriel's trump shall sound, and *old* time shall end—then good-bye *old time honored flag*, Heaven is a better place than America.

We resume the publication of the Christian Banner, because we feel it our duty to do all the possible good we can for our country, and fellow-citizens. If we can only accomplish a single *mite* of good, our reward will be sure. We resume its publication, because there is no other paper now published in our town, nor all the surrounding country. Washington city, and Richmond city, are the nearest points to us, where any paper is published. The community needs a paper—whether the people will patronize the Banner or not, we cannot tell. As we used to do in olden times, so shall we continue to do in the future, and that is, to write just as nearly what we please as circumstances will allow. One thing is *certain* and *unmistakable*, and that is, we shall exert our undivided and untiring influence and efforts to get our fellow-citizens to become reconciled and return to the Union. This is our *only* hope of any peace, or happiness in the future.

Reflections.

When we retrospect the pleasures of past years, with warm-hearted friends, the many high and holy privileges we have enjoyed, and now think of the present condition of things around us, and then look into the future at the dark prospects ahead, our phylosophy is well nigh overcome, and we feel that we could weep tears of blood, could tears save our country from endless ruin.

We can scarcely realize the fact, that a whole nation of civilized, Christian people, are straining every nerve and making every possible effort, to cut each others throats, and tear out one anothers hearts. Can it be possible, that a nation so enlightened, so refined, and so *religious*, is engaged in a work so diabolical. Shame! Shame! upon the boasted wisdom, civilization, phylosophy, philanthrophy, patriotism, and Christianity of the American people.

It is an easy matter for a few leaders to get a whole country into difficulties, but a very hard matter to get themselves and their country out of them. A child can fire a house, while a whole community of men may not be able to rescue it from the flames. Such is the present deplorable state and fate of our once happy, and prosperous country.

A few ambitious leaders have brought ruin upon us all, and still the people tamely submit, afraid even to say they execrate the evil, or that their souls are their own. After all that has been said of man, god-like man—what is he but a compound of stupidity, ignorance, and cowardice, which compose the theological pill of total Depravity.

☞ Why is it that men will suffer passion and prejudice to dethrone reason? Let us consider for a moment our present deplorable condition. Our Generals and Army have left us to the mercy of chance, Congress has broken up in a state of terrified confusion, and have gone to seek their safety far from the seat of war, on their cotton, sugar, and rice plantations; the citizens of Richmond have become panic stricken and are leaving, the authorities are making preparations to burn the tobacco and public stores of the Army, that cannot and have not been sent away. These are facts, we presume, that are questioned by no one.

Why is it, that at this important crisis, when the lives of our dear sons and so many of our fellow-citizens are trembling on the very brink of eternity, that the very men, the leaders in this awful tragedy, fly before the advancing enemy? Why do they not stand and face the danger?—Because, conscience has made cowards of them.—They feel the guilt, they dread the penalty, and fly to save their own worthless carcases from being captured; and yet our dear children, neighbors, and friends must stay and fight, and die to protect the pers[illegible] and property of the guilty leaders, who [illegible]red up the Southern heart, and inveigled [illegible] into ruin. Are parents willing to see their own dear children butchered and slaughtered like wild beast, to gratify the unhallowed ambition of cowards, tyrants, and traitors? Can freemen submit to such an outrage? No. Then, let us demand our children—let us call them home, and let Jeff. Davis and his Click go to the devil, where they ought to have been long ago.

☞ Since the surrender of the town of Fredericksburg to the Federal Authorities, hundreds of servants have left their masters, and gone to seek the blessings of freedom! Thousands of them may find when it is too late, that the anticipated blessings of freedom, will result like the anticipated glories of secession. The one idea with them is, freedom, all other blessings will follow as a matter of course. So it was with secession—just secede, and jump into paradise.

☞ Terms for the Banner, advertising, and job work cash in advance. Positively no credit.

THE PENNSYLVANIA RESERVE.

DEVOTED TO LIFE IN THE CAMP, AND THE ENTERTAINMENT OF THE READER.

Published **EDWARD K. MULL, EDITOR AND PUBLISHER.** *Semi-Occasionally.*

VOL. I.] CAMP NEAR FREDERICKSBURG, VA., SATURDAY, JUNE 14, 1862. [NO. 1.

Choice Poetry.

ON THE SHORES OF TENNESSEE.

"Move my arm-chair, faithful Pompey,
In the sunshine bright and strong,
For this world is fading, Pompey—
Massa won't be with you long;
And I fain would hear the South wind
Bring once more the sound to me,
Of the wavelets softly breaking
On the shores of Tennessee.

"Mournful though the ripples murmur,
As they still the story tell,
How no vessels float the banner
That I've loved so long and well.
I shall listen to their music,
Dreaming that again I see
Stars and Stripes on sloop and shallop,
Sailing up the Tennessee.

"And, Pompey, while old Massa's waiting
For death's last despatch to come,
If that exiled starry banner
Should come proudly sailing home,
You shall greet it slave no longer—
Voice and hand shall both be free,
That shout and point to Union colors
On the waves of Tennessee."

"Massa's bery kind to Pompey;
But ole darkey's happy here,
Where he's tended corn and cotton,
For dese many a long gone year.
Over yonder Missis' sleeping—
No one tends her grave like me;
Mebbe she'd miss de flowers
She used to love in Tennessee.

"'Pears like she was watching Massa—
If Pompey should beside him stay,
Mebbe she'd remember better
How for him she used to pray;
Telling him that way up yonder
White as snow his soul would be,
If he served the Lord of Heaven
While he lived in Tennessee."

Silently the tears were rolling
Down the poor old dusky face,
As he stepped behind his master,
In his long accustomed place.
Then a silence fell around them,
As they gazed on rock and tree—
Pictured in the placid waters
Of the rolling Tennessee.

Master, dreaming of the battle
Where he fought by Marion's side,
When he bade the haughty Tarleton,
Stoop his lordly crest of pride.
Man, remembering how yon sleeper,
Once he held upon his knee,
Ere she loved the gallant soldier,
Ralph Vervair, of Tennessee.

Still the South wind fondly lingers
'Mid the veteran's silver hair;
Still the bondman, close beside him,
Stands behind the old arm-chair.
With his dark-hued hand uplifted,
Shading eyes, he bends to see
Where the woodland, boldly jutting,
Turns aside the Tennessee.

Thus he watches cloud-born shadows
Glide from tree to mountain crest,
Softly creeping, aye, and ever,
To the river's yielding breast.
Ha! above the foliage yonder,
Something flutters wild and free!
"Massa! Massa! Hallelujah!
The flag's come back to Tennessee!"

"Pompey, hold me on your shoulder,
Help me stand on foot once more,
That I may salute the colors
As they pass my cabin door:
Here's the paper signed that frees you—
Give a freeman's shout with me—
'God and Union!' be our watchword,
Evermore in Tennessee."

Then the trembling voice grew fainter,
And the limbs refused to stand;
One prayer to Jesus—and the soldier
Glided to that better land.
When the flag went down the river,
Man and master both were free,
While the ring-dove's note was mingled
With the rippling Tennessee!

ONLY HIS PICTURE LEFT.

I've nothing but his picture left—
His shadow—all the rest has fled;
I know not whether now he lives,
Or if he sleeps among the dead:
For many a year has passed away,
Since last I gazed upon his face;
While all that's left me now—I may
The shadow of his features trace.

I've nothing but his picture left:
Ah! nothing—all the rest is gone
Like dew drops that are passed away,
Or silver clouds at early morn.
That voice, whose slightest tone but breathed
To waken raptures in my heart,
Has gone—O! where?—gone like the stars
That at the light of morn depart.

I've nothing but his picture left—
His breath that floated on my cheek,
And hands' warm clasp that thrilled my soul
With fonder bliss than words can speak;
The arm that was my pillow then,
Those soft, warm lips that pressed my own,
And silky curls of chestnut hair
Are, where?—not here—like dreams have flown.

I've nothing but his picture left—
His smile—O! how it thrills me yet—
And sooner than forget that smile,
Ay, sooner must I life forget;
Those speaking eyes, where I could read
The language that his lips did tell,
Were mirrored from his gentle heart—
But time hath chased the silver spell.

I've nothing but his picture left—
O! cold, unfeeling words to speak—
No language have his silent lips,
No gentle warmth is on his cheek,
No sound can penetrate that ear
E'en though *my* voice should whisper low—
And though my lips should press his own
Could not his heart the pressure know.

I've nothing but his picture left—
His proud, sweet eyes still on me gaze,
But not with that soft, changeful light,
Which charmed them so in other days;
The silent lips still on me smile,
Not with the varying smile of yore—
This changes not when mine replies—
It answers back love's smile no more.

I've nothing but his picture left—
Sweet shadow, source of grief and bliss,
What thronging memories swift go by
Whene'er I turn my eyes on this!
Sweet memories of bright former days
When he fond lingered by my side,
And whispered charmed words of love
At Summer's holy eventide.

I've nothing but his picture left—
Sometimes I softly touch his cheek,
And then, almost half-hoping, wait
The dear response my soul would seek;
Then turn with sickened heart away,
At my own folly wild, to weep—
How passing strange a picture can
My captive heart thus spell-bound keep!

I've nothing but his picture left—
His voice, his smile, his lips have fled,
As summer sunbeams glide away
Ere half their golden light is shed.
O! what a world of cloud and blight,
When heart of heart is thus bereft;
But many a lip this tale hath told—
I've nothing but his picture left.

Miscellaneous.

A YOUNG LADY'S LETTER,

ON THE JOY OF SEEING THE AMERICAN FLAG IN NASHVILLE.

[The following letter was written with no thought of publication, but we are sure that our readers will be glad "to rejoice with them that rejoice."]

Rejoice with me, dear Grandma! The glorious Star Spangled Banner of the United States is again floating above us! Oh, how we have hoped for, longed for, prayed for this joyous day! I am wild, crazed almost, with delight. I am still fearful that I shall awake and find our deliverance, our freedom, is all a dream. I cannot believe that is a positive fact, it has come upon so unexpectedly, this successful move of the Union army. Grandma, I cannot write connectedly at all. Forgive me all faults of composition, for I can see the Stars and Stripes of my own ever-loved flag floating from the State House, the first time my eyes have been gladdened by such a sight for nearly a year. So great is my ecstacy I cannot sit still—I cannot keep my eyes on the paper—indeed, I cannot do anything but sing, whistle, or hum "Yankee Doodle," "Hail Columbia," "The Star Spangled Banner," and feast my eyes on those victorious colors.

Oh, Grandma, you cannot imagine our happiness at this sudden change in the aspect of public affairs. The morning that Fort Donelson surrendered, there seemed to be such an intense feeling of bitterness here against the Union men! The papers (how little did they imagine that *that* would be their last issue) came out on that Sunday morning with maledictions and threats the most inhuman against them, saying that if any such *fiendish villain* yet remained in our midst he must and should be dealt with instantly as a traitor of the deepest dye.

We have had so much to bear since I wrote you! My father and brother have been taunted, sneered, and hissed at, threatened by every one, until endurance was becoming impossible. But *nothing*—(I am *so* proud to say it, and I thank God for it)—nothing could make them play the hypocrite. They believed the Federal cause was just and right, and they would, in spite of *our* prayers and tears, express their opinions openly, and denounce secession boldly. We have been warned, since Zollicoffer's death, that there was imminent danger here for them; and the hatred toward Union men was becoming so intense that both Ma and I have been in an agony of suspense. We could not leave home, as we never did, without being insulted. I have had to sit quietly by and hear my father and my brothers denounced as traitors. My temper is quick, and the curb that I have been obliged to keep upon it has been a galling one—indeed, sometimes I have thought all that was gentle and womanly in me was turned into bitterness and hate.

For my idolized brother I have felt more keenly than for anything else. He is naturally sensitive, and of such delicacy of feeling that he has suffered deeply. Being drafted, he procured a substitute; and though displaying so much moral courage, he has been hissed at as a coward ever since, until he would vow to escape and join the Federal army, and several times endeavored to do so; but Pa, discovering his plans, prevented him from it by showing him the ruin he would bring upon us all by such a step. The cloud was lowering over us, growing darker day by day, and I thought the silver lining never would appear; but *it is here!*—even now beaming upon us so brightly that we scarce can credit the reality!

Can you wonder that, in the state of feeling I was in that Sunday morning, dear Grandma, when Tom knocked at the door and called out to me that Fort Donelson was surrendered, and the Federal army would soon be in Nashville, I became perfectly frantic with joy?

I ran screaming over the house, knocking down chairs and tables, clapping my hands and shouting for the "Union" until the children were terrified and Pa and Ma thought I was [illegible]! I rushed into the parlor and thundered "Yankee Doodle" on the piano in such a manner as I had never done before. I caught little Johnny up in my arms, and held him over the porch railing up stairs, until he hurrahed for the Star-Spangled Banner, Seward, Lincoln, and McClellan! The little fellow thought his sister was going to kill him, she looked so wild, and would not come near me again for several days.

Just in the midst of these rejoicings intelligence came that Johnson's army from Bowling Green had evacuated that place, and was even then passing on the turnpike to Nashville. Could it be possible? Yes, indeed! There they were, retreating most valiantly. Grandma, you never saw such a frightened looking set of men! They could not get over the river fast enough! I never bade the Southern army "God speed" but that once; and then I did it with my whole heart. May their present advance be successful even to the Gulf of Mexico itself!

If you could have seen Breckinridge! the meanest, most downfallen looking specimen of humanity imaginable. The army did not stop in Nashville *one day*, but went on as swiftly as possible. The citizens here were mortified and exasperated to the quick by this surrender. Floyd remained in Nashville a few days after his *brave* escape from Fort Donelson. After the army had gone, and the city had sent commissioners to surrender, he had both bridges destroyed, though he could give no reason for it, and though it was against the prayers and protestations of the citizens. He is a wicked wretch. Is it wrong to wish that he may soon meet the fate he deserves?

It was not until a week after Donelson's fall that the Federals came in. We, whose *all* depended upon their speedy arrival, had begun to think that they were not coming after all, and *our* freedom was not yet at hand, but on a Sunday afternoon, my brother came in the picture of happiness, with the intelligence that Buell would be here in a few days; that he had ridden up and met his advanced guard, and that *now* at last we could rejoice. Buell came in at night. The troops were in perfect discipline, and completely amazed the poor duped people here by their orderly behavior. For the people really believed that the soldiers would not stop till they had *murdered all the women, and eaten the children*; but when it was seen that they took nothing *without pay*, the people were rejoiced to *sell*, for money of any kind has long been a marvellous sight here.

But oh, Grandma, I have not told you what did *me* more good than anything else—the *panic* here on the 16th. Away flew the citizens without stopping for anything! The brave city regiments who, on the 15th, took their stand on the square, with Andrew Ewing at their head, and vowed to die there, fighting even against myriads of the "barbarians," should they ever reach Nashville, heard at 12 o'clock on the 16th of the surrender of Donelson, and at 8 o'clock in the evening of that same day, not *one* of the gallant determined braves was to be found within miles of Nashville! Didn't I clap my hands and shriek for joy when it was told on Monday, the 17th, that not one editor remained in our city! that their wicked threats had been published for the last time here!

The town is almost deserted, so many families have left their homes, and fled, panic-stricken, away. It is so distressing to think of the sufferings they have brought upon themselves so needlessly. The Federals have interfered with no one whatever, and have behaved much better than the rebel army. The Governor and the Legislature left the very day Donelson surrendered. May they never return!

Grandma, you will think me a heartless girl to write thus, and I know it is wrong, but you would excuse me if you knew what we had to contend with. I speak the truth when I say that, notwithstanding our former social position and popularity, there is not now one family of all our friends who would cross our threshold, or bid us welcome to theirs. My noble uncle is always an exception. He and Pa have stood firmly together, enduring the tempest, and nothing now should ever divide us. Mr. ——, too, has never faltered in his allegiance. When the death of his only son was told him, his exclamation was, "Would to God he had died in a nobler cause!"

But I tremble when I think of the possibility of a reverse—that the Confederates should ever get back here. Then *our* doom is spoken—either flight—beggary—or, remaining, death.

Oh, that the United States troops would push onward rapidly, and make an end to the rebellion, while the Confederates are quaking with fear and dismay. Give them no time to rally.

Now that the railroad and telegraph will soon be opened, we will be again in a civilized country, and surely we have cause to rejoice, for we have been living in utter darkness a long weary time. If you could see my father it would do you good. He looks happy again! The gloomy, sad brow of two weeks ago is once more smoothed with content. Three cheers for the sight of the old banner!

Your affectionate
GRANDDAUGHTER.

———o———

MRS. PARTINGTON ON PICKETS.—"As for sleeping on pickets," said Mrs. Partington to a volunteer who had dropped in to see her, "I don't see how they can do it without hurting 'em. Sleeping on a post would be a great deal more sensible, unless there's a nail in it, which might be prejudicious to the uniform. Every one to his taste, and such things as where a man shall sleep is at his own auction; but nobody can help thinking that either a picket or post is a very uncomfortable thing to sleep on. At any rate, there isn't much room for any more than one in a bed, and—"

The man interposed to tell her the nature of pickets and posts in military parlance, to which she listened very attentively, while Ike was trying experiments in Prestidigitation, by essaying to rub the cat and the soldier's little brown dog into one.

———o———

Who would not believe an Almanac? The Confederate Almanac for 1862, published by the Rev. Dr. Summers, at the Southern Methodist Publishing House, announced "An eclipse visible over the Confederate States!" To this the Nashville *Union* added, "That about the same time there will be a total eclipse of the Confederate States, visible over all creation."

THE SONS OF ERIN.—The Irish race, in the present awful crisis, have displayed a constancy and a courage that ought never to be forgotten by the American people. The German and the Frenchman come here animated by an undying attachment to their fatherlands, and while they, too, have manifested heroic devotion to the cause of their adopted country, it is the Irishman alone who becomes a thorough American. British rapacity, British insolence, and British aristocracy have made him so much a subject in Ireland, that he longs to be a freeman in America, and when he reaches our soil, his first and constant thought is to gather around him the relatives and friends that he has left at home. When England strikes at the American Union, without provocation, and in the face of the concessions of this Government, is there an Irishman anywhere, here, in Canada, in Australia, or in Ireland itself, that will not feel that this new evidence of the audacity of England is Ireland's opportunity?

———o———

TRUE PATRIOTISM.—The following item has been sent to the Harrisburg Union by a lady, and its authenticity may be relied upon:

"A patriotic boy, whose mother wrote and asked him if he did not want to return home, replied: 'I enlisted for three years, and shall not come home until my time expires, unless I am sent in my coffin.' This patriotic boy is but twelve years old, and is a drummer in one of the Pennsylvania regiments. He is the youngest son of General John W. Geary. When such sentiments as these animate even our boys, we cannot wonder that victory greets our triumphant arms in every battle."

———o———

☞ The Louisville Journal says: A letter from the Tennessee river, containing contraband information, and which we therefore suppress, contains the following paragraph about the loyalists who have appeared on the Tennessee river:

"This invaluable class is composed—according to a careful analysis, made by an eminent chemist on the spot—of ten parts of unadulterated Andy Johnson Union men, ten of good lord good devil-ites, five of spies, and seventy-five of scallowags, too lazy to run, therefore disqualified for service in the Secesh army, and too cowardly to steal on their own responsibility, but willing to be enrolled as "Home Guards," so as to plunder their neighbors under the Union flag."

———o———

A MATCH RACE FOR REBEL ARROGANCE.—A good anecdote is told of one of the Connecticut boys. While in conversation with a rebel, after the capture of Fort Pulaski, the latter said: "At least, with all our faults, we never made wooden nutmegs." The Yankee, a very demure-looking specimen, innocently replied: "We do not make them of wood any longer," and pointing to one big projectile lying near, which had breached the fort, added quietly: "We make them now of iron."

———o———

☞ Henry O'Connor, of Muscatine, Iowa, district attorney, and reputed to be one of the best lawyers in the State, joined the first company that was raised in that place after the war broke out, as a private. He was with the 1st Iowa at the battle of Wilson's Creek, and fought like a Turk. On returning home, he was offered a commission—any he might choose in a regiment. But his reply was, 'D——n your commission; all I want is a gun.'

———o———

A SERIOUS BUSINESS.—The rebels at Richmond, fully expecting McClellan to take possession of that capital, have removed their valuables and public records, and among others, the marriage license forms; so that "no authorized permits to commit matrimony are to be had" for the present. This will be a terrible punishment to the secesh women of that city. All the Union ladies, we hope, had already been provided for, who were in that line, before the disappearance of the "documents."

———o———

THERE is but one Bull Run, but the rebels have made a good many bully runs.

THE PENNSYLVANIA RESERVE.

"In Dixie's land we'll take our stand,
And live and thrive in Dixie."

EDWARD K. MULL, Editor.

FOR THE
Week ending Saturday, June 14, 1862.

☞ Single copies of the "*Pennsylvania Reserve*" can be had by calling on the Editor at his quarters, Company F, 3d Regiment, P. R. C.

☞ Persons at a distance wishing to subscribe for the "*Pennsylvania Reserve*" can do so by remitting us *twenty-five cents*, which will entitle them to the paper for two months—*five numbers*.

The best plan will be for four or more persons to club together.

We do not wish to receive subscriptions for a longer period than two months.

All letters addressed as follows will be sure to reach us: EDWARD K. MULL, *Company F, 3d Reg., P. R. C., McCall's Division, Washington, D. C.*

To the Reader.

The belief that a paper devoted entirely to life in the camp will be acceptable alike to the soldiers, to the dear ones at home, and to those who desire to preserve for future reference a true and faithful *Mirror of Life in the Camp*, has induced me to commence the publication of the *Pennsylvania Reserve*. I will not pretend to publish a *newspaper*; but a paper that will amuse my comrades in arms, and help to lessen the tedium of the long and monotonous hours of camp life. To this end I shall, from time to time, serve up the incidents which transpire in the camp or on the march.

It will also be my aim to make the *Reserve* a welcome visitor to our relatives and friends at home; nothing shall be admitted into its columns that may not be read with propriety by the most fastidious.

It is not my desire to follow in the beaten track of newspaper editors by making many promises in the outset, which are never carried out. The main feature of the paper I have stated above. If I succeed in making the *Reserve* sufficiently interesting to merit your approbation and encouragement, my object will be attained.

If the *Reserve* meets with the proper encouragement, its publication will be continued as long as circumstances will permit.

I can assure you, dear reader, that I shall at least *try* to please you, and give you your money's worth. "*I can't," never accomplished anything—"I'll try," has done wonders.*

EDWARD K. MULL, *Editor.*

Apologetical.

The *Reserve* was got up in great haste, and under many disadvantages. We hope, therefore, our readers will overlook all shortcomings in the present number. We are obliged to attend to our daily routine of duties, and the publication of the *Reserve* dare not, in the least, interfere with those duties. It will, therefore, be apparent to all connected with the army that we have very little time to devote to our paper. However, all our leisure hours shall be devoted to make the *Reserve* a welcome and entertaining companion to our readers, and no pains shall be spared to gain this end. Most of our articles are written after "taps," by the dim light of an attenuated tallow "dip." But we agree with the celebrated Sam Patch, that "some things can be done as well as others."

Soldiers' Letters.

We are aware that many letters intended for men in the Reserve Corps are miscarried, in consequence of their address not being written proper. To avoid mistakes being made by the post office clerks, the address should be written very plain—the letter of the company, number of the regiment, and name of the colonel commanding, should always be given. The following form will serve as a guide for our friends at home:

CORPORAL JOHN SMITH,
Comp. A, 3d Regiment, P. R. C.,
Care of Col. H. G. Sickel,
McCALL'S DIVISION,
Washington, D. C.

Attention!

Our friends in the different regiments will greatly oblige us if they will send us information of incidents and events that may happen in their regiments. Send us the facts, no matter in what shape, if time or circumstanees will not admit of your writing them out, and we will put them into shape.

LOGIC.—The other other day Corporal Swipes was invited to take dinner with a friend in the 4th regiment. While he was "stuffing" himself with the "good things," he let himself loose as follows:

"All human things are hollow. I'm a human thing; therefore, I'm hollow. It is contemptible to be hollow, therefore, I'll stuff myself as full as I'm able."

Religious Services in Camp.

It is no insignificant comment upon the Christian spirit of the age, that the civil war now going on in this country is being made a medium of missionary effort; for, while it is true that the various religious denominations are largely represented among the thousands that have volunteered in their country's service, it is no less true that many in regiments accompanied by *faithful* chaplains, have listened to the story of the Cross with a regularity and interest since the commencement of the war, to which they had not before been accustomed. It would, of course, be impossible to estimate the fruits of these labors among the soldiers; but that they belong to the category of *blessings* arising from the war no one ought to doubt. And what a category that will be! The harvest of war is not a universal blight. The tillage which it employs does not foster the "thorn and the brier of vice" without also developing the "fir and the myrtle of virtue." Already our present conflict has wrought incalculable good. And who can doubt that when the storm of battle is over, and our strong field-hardened legions return to the peaceful pursuits of home, a hardier generation will be the issue? And, some, it may be hoped, will honor the labors of the army chaplain by the concession that listening to the Gospel on the tented field first taught them that "the fear of the Lord *is* the beginning of wisdom."

An Amusing Scene.

The following amusing incident happened when our brigade was marching through Fauquier county:

The brigade was halted in a large field by the road side, for the purpose of resting the men, and giving them an opportunity of eating dinner. A crowd of from fifty to seventy colored individuals were soon assembled to get a sight of "Massa Linkum's soldiers." Men, women, and children, of all ages, sizes, shapes, and colors, were out in full force. Many rich and amnsing remarks were passed between them. While they were discussing the prospects ob de war in gineral, and de fate ob nigga-drivers in particular, one of the brass bands struck up a lively air. The motley crowd became fairly crazy with delight and excitement as the *sole* stirring sounds fell upon their enraptured ears. Involuntarily their feet began to move—said feet resembling Western hams, with bean poles stuck in their middles. Unable to contain themselves any longer, they all, old and young, joined in a regular Virginia "break down."

Those danced who never danced before,
Those who danced now danced the more.

Such a combination of shouts and yells, from soldiers and niggers, as went up from that field was never heard before by mortal man. Had the rebel army been within hearing distance, we have no doubt they would have "skedadled," thinking that the army was after them at a charge bayonet, on the double-quick.

The ludicrous performances of the cullud folks were greatly enjoyed by all present, and even created a smile on the sedate countenance of our General. We doubt whether a happier set of niggers ever existed than those were, for the time being. We also doubt whether there was one in the party that ever had the satisfaction of listening to a brass band before.

Dear reader, have you ever in your life honored a nigger camp meeting with your presence? If so, you may perhaps be able to form a faint idea of the scene we have *attempted* to describe.

Contrabands.

We noticed but very few white people along our route from Catlett's station to this place, many having gone to Richmond. Those who do remain are ashamed to show their faces. We noticed several of the F. F. V's peeping at us from behind doors and shutters as we passed by their houses. A large number of darkies are, however, left behind to the mercy of the "Yankees." How and where these poor people obtain the necessaries of life, is a mystery to us. Many of them have scarcely clothes enough to cover their nakedness. Our men relieved the hunger of many of these poor creatures by supplying them with an abundance of crackers from their well-filled haversacks. Many a "may de Lord bress yer, honey," fell from the lips of the half-starved negroes.

The darkies soon became convinced that we are not the blood-thirsty savages we were represented to be by their masters, who even persuaded them to believe that "de Yankees would burn all the old niggers to death, and sell all the young 'uns away down Souf." The old darkies are very talkative, but, with a few exceptions, as ignorant as brutes. We asked one of them whether his master was a Secessionist or a Unionist? "No, massa," he replied, "he am neider one of them." Well, what is he then, if he is neither? "Why, massa, he hab been a Methodist dese twenty-fibe years!"

The Reliable Gentleman.

The reliable gentleman is an important personage in times of excitement. He is always on hand to satisfy the anxious, and he is never slow in fulfilling the general desire. When there is a universal desire that a certain object shall be accomplished, the Reliable Gentleman turns up to accommodate the dissatisfied. It was the Reliable Gentleman who informed the public on several occasions that Beauregard was killed, and his death concealed in order not to dispirit the rebel soldiers. It was the Reliable Gentleman who had the news that Baltimore had been shelled from Fort McHenry, on the terrible Sunday which succeeded the 19th of April last year, and the number of houses that were burned, and the number of Secessionists killed, were, according to his testimony, tremendous.

About the beginning of September last, the Reliable Gentleman saw Jeff. Davis "kick the bucket" at Richmond, and he spread the news with the utmost assiduity. The Reliable Gentleman also assured the public sometime in September, that the Pennsylvania Reserves were "terribly cut up." The Reliable Gentleman was present at the death of Ben. McCulloch, at the battle of Wilson's Creek, and not being believed at that time, he returned to the contest, and killed poor Ben again. The Reliable Gentleman was also present at the battle of Drainsville, and saw Col. Kane fall from his horse *three times* with not less than half a peck of secesh bullets in his head. He also saw the gallant colonel jump up each time, and again mount his horse. Poor Tom Taylor was litterally shot to pieces by the blood-thirsty Reliable Gentleman. A few weeks ago the Reliable Gentleman informed the Philadelphia *Inquirer* that the rebels were to make an attack on General McCall's division, and the *Inquirer* was green enough to believe the lie. For the New York *Herald*, the Reliable Gentleman is a constant and invaluable correspondent, and he furnishes that unusually active journal with its regular weekly lie, which is of an exceedingly startling character, and is denied by the *Herald* within a few days afterwards. The Reliable Gentleman is, in fact, a perfect angel to sensation newspapers, and keeps them posted far in advance of fact or probability, to the manifest benefit of their third and fourth editions.

But important as are the services of the Reliable Gentleman at the *North*, they are but trifling to the exploits of his cousin and namesake at the *South*. In that region the Reliable Gentleman sets on foot the most tremendous stories, and swears to them as solemnly as a witness in a court of justice. It is in the details of victories which never occurred that the chivalric Reliable Gentleman is most proficient. He is constantly giving accounts of battles, skirmishes, and captures, which are never reported at head-quarters. Sometimes he takes a Pennsylvania regiment prisoners without the loss of a single soldier—a fact which Governor Curtin learns of from no other source. It was the Reliable Gentleman who informed the Richmond papers that three thousand Confederates had to contend against fifteen thousand Pennsylvanians at the battle of Drainsville. He will shortly report the capture of Washington, and give the only reliable report of the speech of Jeff. Davis at Independence Hall, Philadelphia.

The Reliable Gentleman is, therefore, an important assistant to the movements of either army. He is worth a dozen telegraphs, and is never so happy as when relating some striking circumstance which no other person has heard. He generally brings good news; and if what he tells never did happen, it is usually true that those who hear his stories strongly desire that they should be true.

NO GO.—We are told that there are numerous semi-military gentlemen in the habit of sporting undress uniform in Washington, who frequently find themselves in trouble. The patrols ask all such for their passes. When they answer that "they do not belong to the army," the officer of the guard tells them that if they don't want to be put in the guard-house they had better take off that uniform.

How to Make Wrappers.

Of course you all wish to send a copy of the *Reserve* to your friends at home, and as wrapping paper and paste are scarce articles in camp, we will tell you how to make a neat and convenient wrapper. Take a common adhesive letter envelope, seal it by wetting the gum, then cut both ends open, slip the paper in, leaving the ends open.

☞ At what point do armies generally enter hostile cities? Corporal Swipes thinks, at the point of the bayonet.

☞ It is reported by a Baltimore paper that a man in that city thinks so much of Jeff. Davis that he has named his dog in his honor. Hard on the dog, that!

Obituary.

We have a task to perform which almost overwhelms us with grief and sorrow. We find ourselves called upon to write the obituary of one of our comrades. Grim-visaged Death has stalked into our midst, and cut down one of our number, and we bow our heads and smite our breasts. But a few days ago he was in the full bloom of life and vigor, but now, alas! he sleeps beneath the "sacred soil" of Virginia.

We deeply mourn the premature death of our late companion; we would be unjust to him did we not pay that tribute to his memory which the dignity of a fallen associate demands. What makes the sad occasion doubly mournful, is the fact that he fell before the fire of a musket in the hands of one of our own men, and what is still worse, he died an ignominious death!

He was shot down like a *dog* while in the act of deserting, by one of Col. Magilton's camp guards. Thus, instead of dying upon the field of honor like a true patriot, he has paid the penalty of his cowardly act by sacrificing his worthless life upon the altar of shame and infamy. His name was "Jeff.," and was the same old *bull dog* formerly owned by the notorious Mrs. J——, the mother of the villain who murdered the noble young Ellsworth at Alexandria.

Soon after the arrival of the Reserves at Langley, the "unlucky dog" was persuaded by private Zeitz, of Captain Richards' company, to forsake his mistress. Jeff. was brought to the camp, and showing his strong attachment to (beef steak) the Union, was persuaded to join the company, of which he was a member up to the time of his death, drawing his rations the same as the other do—"boys."

The *caput mortuum* of poor "Jeff." were interred by a detachment of the "awkward squad," with military dis-honors. "*De mortuis nil nisi bonum.*" A shingle with the following lead-pencil epitaph upon it marks his dishonored grave:

Beneath this sod poor Jeffy lies,
Shot by a Reserve, dot rat his eyes.

"Who is Your Father?"

The woman of the United States are truly a credit to the American eagle, and a great expense to their husbands and fathers, but they don't exactly understand the most pressing wants of the soldier. For instance, a young girl of Philadelphia, about seventy-five years of age, has been sending thousands of piano tracts to the different regiments, and the consequence is, that the camp grounds are literally covered with paper balls. These tracts the boys think, are very good for dying sinners and other southerners. The wicked scamps say they would sooner have the "History of the Four Kings" for general use. A fellow by the name of Boger—the boys call him "Fatty," for short—got one of these tracts the other day. It was headed, "Who is your Father?" "Fatty" read the question over two or three times, and then dashed the tract to the ground, and took a "jaw" of tobacco to check his emotions. We saw that "Fatty" didn't understand what the tract really meant, and so we explained to him that it was intended to signify that God was his father. The gifted young soldier looked at us for a moment, and then says he: "Look here, Mully, Bill Boger was my daddy, and if you come round here to speak disrespectful of my mother, I'll punch your d—d innards out of you, mind that!" After the delivery of this terrible declaration by the promising young disciple of Mars, it suddenly occurred to us that we had some very important business to attend to in some other part of the camp, so we left in "double-quick."

WOULDN'T STAY DOWN.—One of Colonel Jackson's "boys" reported himself sick to the doctor a few weeks ago. The doctor told him that he must give him an emetic. "It's no use," said the patient, "I have tried it twice before, and it wouldn't stay on my stomach five minutes."

OBEYING ORDERS.—Captain BRINER, of Company D, says he has one of the most obedient boys in his company the world ever saw. He tells him to do as he pleases, and he does it without murmuring.

Y. M. C. A.—What has become of the Young Men's Christian Association which was in such a flourishing condition at Camp Pierpont? We are sorry that the Association should be "played out" so soon.

A GOOD HIT.—A volunteer and some citizens were talking about the war, at Elmira, a few days since, when, a difference having arisen, some person proposed to settle it by taking a drink. "No! no!" said the volunteer, "that is no way to talk. You and all other men, who can possibly leave home, should agree to enlist. This war must be fought out and settled with all possible despatch. Drinking won't settle it; for if it would, our officers would have settled it long ago!"

WARLIKE NEWS FROM HAMBURG, PA.

CHILDREN IN ARMS!

Great excitement in Camp among the Hamburg Volunteers!

THEY FEAR THEIR HOMES WILL BE MADE DESOLATE BY THE REBELLIOUS INFANT-RY.

The following warlike news we copy from the Hamburg *Schnellpost*. It is the "wind up" of an advertisement for a "grand concert" by Professor Shollenberger:

"*Front seats reserved for the ladies; children in arms not admitted.*"

The children in arms! Goodness gracious, what does all this mean? Are the children in rebellion against their dads and mams, or are they up in arms to oppose the election of *Ike Heckman* to the justiceship? Professor, oh, most worthy and musically-inclined Professor, we pray you, nay, we beseech you, in behalf of the Hamburg volunteers, do not keep us in suspense, but let us know post haste, are our dear homes in danger of being made desolate by the rebellious *infant*-ry? Is the great one horse village of *Kerchersteltel* really on the eve of civil war? If so, we will immediately set the facts before Old Abe, and urge him to detach half a dozen regiments from the Reserve Corps for immediate operations in Hamburg.

An Hour at the Railroad Bridge.

The other day we spent a curious hour at the railroad bridge which spans the Rappahanock at Fredericksburg. There was that spirit of lassitude which seems to belong to the life of a soldier. A sentinel or two passed up and down the bridge examining the travelers and looking at every pass with that degree of dignity and sternness which belongs to your true-bred military man. We don't know why true-bred military men should be dignified and stern, but, as they nearly all possess these qualities, we suppose it is according to the "articles of war." A corporal was leaning up against a post, as if the post had been erected expressly for corporals to lean against, and half a dozen privates were smoking, talking, and dozing under a shed, and looking as if they had joined the army to get rid of the trouble of taking care of themselves. We also saw a couple of fancy lieutenants a short distance below the bridge playing "Bob and Pete." They evidently mistook us for a brigadier, and skedadled.

Corporal Swipes in a Fix.

While the Reservss were encamped at Langley last winter, Corporal Swipes was present at a meeting of the Young Men's Christian ASSociation one evening. The performance not being of sufficient interest to keep him awake, he was soon in the embrace of Morpheus, and having a large chew of tobacco in his mouth at the time, he accidentally swallowed it, which, of course, created somewhat of a rumpus in his bread basket. One of the "brethren," who was on the lookout for stray souls, noticing the unfortunate Swipes wriggle in his seat, the tears flowing from his eyes, stepped up to him, and affectionately inquired, "How is it with you, my friend?" The Corporal looked up, and answered: "Oh! very bad, and I want to go out. I have swallowed a thundering big jaw of tobaccer, and my innards is kicking up a h—l of a revolution. If ever I go to sleep again with tobaccer in my mouth, I hope I may be d—d!"

Dreary.

The other day, while the rain was drizzling, we had occasion to go to the Sutler, and as we passed down the muddy parade ground, we could not help but pity the members of the band as they stood and piped away under the black canopy, with an extremely discontented flag floating over them. We can't think what the tune was, but it was something very dreary from "Norma," with a vain attempt at "Annie Laurie," and a desperate struggle with the drums and noisy instruments followed. A couple of officers stood under a brush-covered shed, evidently lamenting the impossibility of wearing their *very* ugly and unbecoming "regulation hats"—poor fellows, we couldn't help "heaving" a sigh for them. Colonel Sickle's marque loomed up gloomily, and gave an appriate finish to the scene. The rain, and the dreary music swelting, with all the associations and reflections connected with the drenched flag, made the day to us sad and long.

PLEASANT DELUSION.—A fellow in the 6th regiment says, when he had the "yaller janders," last winter, a dime looked like a quarter eagle. Quite a pleasant delusion, indeed.

Corporal Swipes says it wouldn't be bad if all the Sutlers had the "janders."

WASHINGTON HEADQUARTERS
FOR

STATIONERY
AND
BLANK BOOKS,
WHOLESALE AND RETAIL.

SUTLERS AND PEDLERS

Supplied at New York prices. Cheap Letter Paper, Note Paper, Envelopes, Union Papers and Envelopes.
Blank Books, Portfolios,
Buck Purses, Playing Cards,
Military Works, Newspapers, Periodicals,
Gold Pens, Pencils, Inks, &c., at
tf SHEPHERD'S, cor. 7th and D sts.

WALL, STEPHENS & CO.,
MILITARY AND NAVAL

MERCHANT TAILORS,
AND DEALERS IN
SWORDS, SASHES, BELTS, EPAULETS, SHOULDER STRAPS, GAUNTLETS, GLOVES, &c.,

AND EVERY VARIETY OF
READY-MADE CLOTHING,
AT REASONABLE PRICES.

WALL, STEPHENS & CO.,
322 Pennsylvania Avenue,
tf Bet. 9th and 10th streets.

STEWART, STEVENS, CLARK & CO.,
SOLICITORS FOR

MILITARY CLAIMS,
No. 450 Pennsylvania Avenue,
WASHINGTON, D. C.

JOSEPH B. STEWART, HESTOR L. STEVENS, EDWARD CLARK, OSCAR A. STEVENS, WILLIS E. GAYLORD.

All disabled Soldiers, and Widows, Minor Children, or other heirs of deceased soldiers,

Are Entitled to Pensions.

All Soldiers who serve two years, or during the war, if it sooner closes, will be

ENTITLED TO $100 BOUNTY.

The Widows and other legal heirs of deceased Volunteers, are entitled to

Pensions and the $100 Bounty.

We shall devote ourselves to the procurement of these Pensions and Bounties, and the payment of war claims and claims for indemnity.

☞ Our charges will be TEN DOLLARS FOR OFFICERS and FIVE DOLLARS FOR PRIVATES, for each Pension or Bounty and Back Pay obtained, and ten per cent. on amount of Claims for MILITARY SUPPLIES or CLAIMS FOR INDEMNITY.

Stewart, Stevens, Clark & Co.,
450 Pennsylvania Avenue,
WASHINGTON, D. C.

SAMUEL V. NILES,
(Late of the General Land Office,)

General Military and Naval AGENCY,
Office and Residence, 202 I Street,
Between 20th & 21st sts., Washington City, D.C.

Having had the exclusive charge of the "*Revolutionary and War of 1812 Bounty Land Bureau*," *General Land Office*, for several years, and being familiar with the business of the various branches of that department, and of the Bureau of the "*Commissioner of Pensions*," offers his services to the public as an ATTORNEY AND SOLICITOR in the adjustment and collection of

Demands and Claims against the Government,

In all departments, especially claims growing out of the present war.

PARTICULAR ATTENTION GIVEN TO PENSIONS due to OFFICERS, SOLDIERS, and SEAMEN of the ARMY and NAVY of the United States, their widows or minor children.

CLAIMS for INDEMNITY, HORSES, (lost, died, or killed while in the service,) and for the EXTRA PAY, and ARREARS OF PAY, due soldiers of the United States.

Any other business requiring the services of an attorney at Washington, will meet with prompt attention.

VICTOR B. BELL. CHARLES E. GREEN.

BELL & GREEN,

Attorneys for Claimants,
AND SOLICITORS OF

American and Foreign Patents,
No. 15 FEDERAL BLOCK,
Washington, D. C.

Army and Navy Pensions Procured,
Bounty, Arrears of Pay, Accounts for Recruiting Service, Pay for Horses lost in Military Service, and

Every Description of Claims against the Government
COLLECTED.

Quartermaster's & Commissary's Accounts
SETTLED.

Business with the General Land Office promptly attended to.

Particular attention paid to

Procuring Patents for Inventors

REFERENCES:

Hon. A. G. Curtin, Governor of Pennsylvania.
Hon. Richard Yates, Governor of Illinois.
Hon. O. M. Hatch, Secretary of State of Ill.
Hon. Lewis Clephane, P.M., Washington, D.C.
Hon. David Tod, Governor of Ohio.
Hon. Jesse K. Dubois, Auditor of Illinois.
Hon. Wm. Butler, Treasurer of Illinois.
Hon. W. W. Seaton, Editor Nat. Intelligencer.

PRISON LIFE
IN THE

Tobacco Warehouse,
AT RICHMOND.

BY A BALL'S BLUFF PRISONER,
Lieutenant WM. C. HARRIS,
OF COL. BAKER'S CALIFORNIA REGIMENT.

CONTENTS.

PREFACE.

These sketches were written to lessen the tedium of my lengthy imprisonment; and if they serve to recall to my prison-companions the scenes enacted in the old Warehouse, and enlist the interest and sympathies of the reader, they will have accomplished all that is desired by the publication of them.

With the exception of "Homeward Bound," they were all written within prison walls and brought to the North sewn securely in the lining of an overcoat.

I confidently trust to my brother-officers for their testimony as to the fidelity of description of our "domestic economy," and the accuracy of detail in the varied incidents in our prison-life in the Tobacco Warehouse.

W. C. H.

PHILADELPHIA, *March* 25, 1862.

☞ Complete in one volume, price 50 cents, or handsomely bound in cloth, 75 cents.

Sent free by mail on receipt of price.

Published by

GEORGE W. CHILDS,
Nos. 628 and 630 Chestnut Street,
tf PHILADELPHIA.

IMPERIAL FIRE ARMS
MANUFACTORY.

D. D. CONE,
GENERAL AGENT U. S. ARMY,

HEAD-QUARTERS, 410 WEST SIXTH STREET,
WASHINGTON, D. C.

☞ Revolvers, Drums, Rifles, Sword Trappings, Bowie Knives, Passants and Military Goods generally.

THE MERRILL CARBINE,

A favorite with officers generally, at manufacturers' prices. The Imperial Revolver is a universal favorite in the Grand U. S. Army, strong, light, durable, and forcible. Good for a Rebel at 150 yards.

THE FINEST SWORDS,

In Gold, Silver, and Steel Scabbards manufactured to order.
tf.

CARD PHOTOGRAPHS.

—:o:—

JAMES S. EARLE & SON,
816 Chestnut Street,
PHILADELPHIA,
Have an immense assortment of

CARD PHOTOGRAPHS,
Comprising Portraits of all the great United States

Generals,
Authors,
Statesmen,
Musical Celebrities,
Divines, &c., &c.

All of which are contained in a Catalogue—which will be furnished *gratis* on application.

PHOTOGRAPH ALBUMS of all sizes and prices from 75 cents to $20.

Send for a Catalogue.

EARLE'S GALLERIES,
tf PHILADELPHIA.

WE OFFER TO MILITARY MEN A large assortment of GRAY and BLUE FLANNEL OVERSHIRTS, WHITE SHIRTS, DRAWERS, CAMP BLANKETS, HALF-HOSE, &c., &c., which we invite all cash purchasers to examine before making their selections.

WALL, STEPHENS & CO.,
322 Pennsylvania Avenue,
tf Bet. 9th and 10th street.

SWORDS! SWORDS!!

—o—

OFFICERS' PRESENTATION
AND

Regulation Swords,
OF OUR OWN MANUFACTURE.

BLADES WARRANTED OF SUPERIOR TEMPER,

Also SASHES, BELTS, FIELD GLASSES, TELEMETERS, etc.

Any description of SWORDS made to order.

☞ DESIGNS SENT BY MAIL.

BAILEY & CO.,
No. 819 Chestnut Street.
PHILADELPHIA.

NOTICE.

ADAMS' EXPRESS COMPANY.

This Company offers to the public "Unequalled Advantages" for the Safe and Quick Dispatch of Heavy Freights, Packages, Valuables, Money, &c., &c., to all parts of the United States.

Expresses to and from the North and West depart from and arrive in Washington twice daily.

All Expresses are in charge of *experienced and reliable* Messengers.

All packages for the Soldiers carried at "ONE-HALF" our usual rates.

All Goods for the so-called "Confederate States," and all Articles "Contraband of War," will be REFUSED.

Our Expresses leave New York at 1.5 and 6 p. m. arriving in Washington at 6 a. m., and 5.30 p. m.

Expresses leave Philadelphia at 8.30 a. m. and 11 p. m., arriving in Washington at 5.30 p. m., and 6 a. m.

Expresses leave Baltimore at 4.20 a. m. and 3 p. m, arriving in Washington at 6 a. m. and 5.30 p. m.

Expresses for all points North and West leave Washington at 7.30 a. m. and 2.30 p. m., daily.

Special Contracts for large quantities of Freight can be made on application at this office.

All Goods called for and delivered *free* of extra charges.

W. PARSON,
Superintendent Adams' Express Company.
Washington, August 23, 1861. tf

Victor Hugo's Great Novel.
LES MISERABLES.

The American copyright translation is published and for sale this morning, in two styles, viz:

Large octavo, paper covers, price 50 cents, and on superior paper, elegant cloth binding, $1.

It is almost unnecessary for the publisher of this magnificent work to say anything in its favor.

The French *feuilletonists* and critics have exhausted every adjective in its praise.

The fabulous amount of $80,000 is reported as having been paid to the author for the copyright.

Machinery of the most gigantic character has been set at work in Europe to enhance its sale there.

Its appearance has been followed by a *furore* unparalleled in the literary world. Two enormous editions of ten thousand copies each were swept off within the week of its publication, and telegraphic orders arriving from all parts of Europe remained unfilled.

It is the acknowledged literary event of the century. In the way of a novel, there's nothing grander in all literature.

*** Sold by booksellers everywhere, and sent by mail FREE, on receipt of price, by

CARLETON, Publisher,
(Late Rudd & Carleton,)
No. 413 Broadway, cor. Lispenard st.,
tf New York.

Artemus Ward His Book.

AN ENORMOUS SUCCESS.

More than 4,000 Copies sold already.

A New Edition Ready THIS MORNING.

ARTEMUS WARD HIS BOOK.

A volume, containing all the rich, humorous writings of the great Showman. Superly illustrated with plenty of comic drawings, and elegantly bound in cloth. Price, $1.

"No volume, so full of rich fun was ever before published. * * There are more laughs between these covers than were ever before collected. * * There isn't a dull paragraph in the book. * * In the field of broad wit, Artemus Ward is without a rival; he is unprecedented and overpowering."

*** Sold by booksellers everywhere, and sent by mail FREE, on receipt of price, by

CARLETON, Publisher,
(Late Rudd & Carleton,)
No. 413 Broadway, cor. Lispenard st.,
tf New York.

WHY PAUL FERROLL KILLED HIS WIFE.

A capital New Novel, by the Author of "PAUL FERROLL."

Paper covers. Price 50 cents; Cloth bound, $1.

Already has a THIRD EDITION of this strange and interesting novel been called for.

"It could only have been written by a woman profoundly conversant with the worst characteristics of her sex, and equally so with all that is charming in the female character."—*Boston Courier.*

CARLETON, Publisher,
tf New York.

WALL, STEPHENS & CO.,
322 Penna. Avenue,

MILITARY AND NAVAL
MERCHANT TAILORS,

And Ready-Made Clothiers, and extensive dealers in Gentlemen's Furnishing Goods.
tf

THE

OFFICIAL WAR MAP.

HAZARD'S RAIL ROAD AND MILITARY MAP
Of the Southern States.

FROM THE MOST AUTHENTIC Sources, and the Coast Survey, engraved in the Finest Style of Map Making. It gives so recent and such valuable facts concerning all the Railroads, that the War Department immediately authorized its publication, and distributed ONE THOUSAND COPIES among the Generals and Colonels of the Army.

As it is THE ONLY MAP that is authorized as OFFICIAL, it is the most Reliable and Authentic, and from its large size—32 by 55 inches—shows at a glance the Principal Places, and all the Strategic Points. GEN. MCCLELLAN has acknowledged the great importance of it to his movements.

BEAUTIFULLY COLORED, PRICE ONLY ONE DOLLAR, to compete with inferior maps. In Cloth Case, $1 50. Dissected and Mounted on Muslin, $2 50. Mounted on Muslin, with Rollers, and varnished, $2 50. Sent Free by Mail on receipt of Price.

WILLIS P. HAZARD,
No. 724 Chestnut Street, Philadelphia.

☞ As every intelligent man wants THE BEST and ONLY OFFICIAL MAP, Agents can make money rapidly by selling this.

☞ NEWSPAPERS inserting this three times shall receive a copy by Mail. tf

---

THOMAS E. LLOYD,

Attorney for Claimants,
AND AGENT FOR PROCURING

Bounty Lands, Pensions, Arrears of Pay, Extra Pay, &c.,
WASHINGTON, D. C.,

Will give prompt and efficient attention to the prosecution of Claims of every description against the Government, and make no charge unless successful.

Both *references* and *charges* for services will be made satisfactory.

☞ Pensions secured for soldiers wounded or diseased during the existing war; also, for the widows and orphans of soldiers who have died from wounds or disease incurred while in the United States service: also *Bounty Money* for the heirs-at-law of soldiers deceased during the existing war.

Fees divided with attorneys or other persons forwarding business.

The highest prices paid for Land Warrants.

Address

THOMAS E. LLOYD,
Attorney for Claimants,
No. 476 Seventh street,
Washington, D. C.

N. B. Editors of papers publishing the above card will be entitled to my services to the amount of their charges. T. E. L. tf

---

MILITARY BOUNTY, BACK PAY, PENSIONS, &c.—Particular and prompt attention given to the claims of widows and heirs of Regulars and Volunteers of Army and Navy, as also those disabled in the service.

Being located at the Capital, we have peculiar facilities for adjusting all claims committed to our care. We have appointed agents through the States to transmit the testimony to us for immediate attention, and will warrant speedy settlement, until which, no fees required. Address, in person or by mail, our agents, MOODY & BALLINGER, 144 South FOURTH Street, Philadelphia.

BARROWS & REED,
Washington, D. C.

REFER TO

Hon. J. W. Grimes, U. S. Senate.
Hon. James Harlan, U. S. Senate.
Hon. M. S. Wilkinson, U. S. Senate.
Hon. Preston King, U. S. Senate.
Hon. C. B. Sedgwick, House of Represen's.
Hon. A. B. Olin, House of Representatives.
Hon. I. N. Arnold, House of Represen's.
Hon. C. Delano, House of Representatives.
Hon. S. G. Daily House of Representatives.
Hon. J. A. Kasson, First Ass't P. M. Gen.
Wm. M. Swain, Philadelphia. tf

PENSIONS,
BOUNTIES,
LAND WARRANTS,
AND ARREARS OF PAY,

Secured for Soldiers, or their legal representatives at low rates, by the subscribers.

Also, claims of citizens of the United States against Costa Rica, under treaty of July 2, 1860, and claims of any description necessary to be presented at the Departments of Government, in this city.

CLARK & GAYLORD,
No. 450 Pennsylvania Avenue,
tf Washington, D. C.

PATENT OFFICE BUSINESS.

Soldiers' Pensions & Bounties.

SOMES & ALEXANDER.

The undersigned have entered into a copartnership, as ATTORNEYS and SOLICITORS for the procuring of PATENTS, and all other kinds of business at the Patent Office.

Especial attention will be given to rejected applications, to extensions and opposition to extensions, and to taking and preparing evidence and arguments in interference cases.

The undersigned will also attend to obtaining PENSIONS and BOUNTIES for Soldiers serving during the present and previous wars, and to the prosecution generally of all similar classes of business with the Government.

Office, corner of Seventh and F streets, opposite Patent Office.

DANIEL E. SOMES,
C. M. ALEXANDER.
tf

BUY YOUR BLANK BOOKS at SHEPHERD'S, corner 7th and D streets.

FORNEY'S

"WAR PRESS."

The intense interest everywhere felt in the mighty contest in which the Armies and Fleets of the Nation are engaged,

ON THE POTOMAC,
IN WESTERN VIRGINIA,
IN KENTUCKY,
IN MISSOURI,
ON THE SEA COAST,

and elsewhere, and the existing demand for a Weekly Journal that will furnish a full and accurate account of the thrilling events of this exciting and ever-memorable period, acceptable alike to Soldiers in Camp, to Peaceful Firesides, to those who wish to obtain the latest war news, and to those who desire to preserve, in a convenient form, for future reference, a *correct History of the Great Rebellion*, has induced me to commence the publication of a GREAT WAR PAPER, (in lieu of the present issue of the *Weekly Press*,) to be called "FORNEY'S WAR PRESS." It will be printed in superior style, on a large quarto sheet of eight pages, and each number will present the following ATTRACTIVE FEATURES, viz:

A BEAUTIFUL ENGRAVING,

illustrating an event of the War, or a MAP of some locality where important operations are in contemplation.

A RECORD OF THE LATEST WAR NEWS

from all parts of the country, received during each week by Mail and by Telegraph, from numerous SPECIAL CORRESPONDENTS, and all other reliable sources of information;

THE LETTERS OF "OCCASIONAL,"

whose epistles from Washington during the last three years have been singularly correct in their statements and predictions, and whose comments upon public affairs have been copied and read with deep interest throughout the whole country.

A THRILLING SKETCH OR TALE,

illustrative of the romantic incidents connected with the War; GLEANINGS FROM THE RICH TREASURES OF WAR-WIT AND WAR-POETRY, that are elicited by the mighty events now transpiring.

ABLE EDITORIALS ON THE GREAT QUESTIONS OF THE DAY;

THE LATEST LOCAL AND GENERAL NEWS;

A SUMMARY OF RELIGIOUS INTELLIGENCE, interesting to all Denominations;

IMPORTANT ARTICLES FROM FIRST-CLASS WRITERS;

ACCURATE MARKET REPORTS,

Including the Cattle Markets of Philadelphia, New York, and other places, the Money Market, and Reports of the Prices of Produce and Merchandise.

Efforts will constantly be made to introduce such new features as will render the "WAR PRESS" one of the most popular and attractive Journals of the country. If, contrary to general expectations, the war should be suddenly brought to a close, its columns will be filled with articles that will prove deeply interesting to its readers.

TERMS:

One copy, one year	$2 00
Three copies, one year	5 00
Five copies, one year	8 00
Ten copies, one year	12 00

Larger Clubs will be charged at the same rate, thus 20 copies will cost $24; 50 copies will cost $60; and 100 copies, $120.

To every Subscriber remitting us $2 we will forward by mail a first-rate, new, large COLORED MAP of the Southern States, which gives the most useful and comprehensive view of the Seat of War, and descriptions of the important localities of the South, that has yet been published. Its retail price is fifty cents, and it is well worth double that sum.

We will also forward one copy of this Map to any person who sends us a club of three, of five, or of ten subscribers.

Any person sending us a club of twenty subscribers, accompanied with $24, will be entitled to an extra copy (for the getter up of the club,) and also to a copy of the above-mentioned Map.

ALL POSTMASTERS,

and other loyal citizens, are earnestly solicited to assist in extending the circulation of the "WAR PRESS." They may rest assured that they will thereby not only secure to subscribers a first-rate journal, but one which will be an earnest champion of the vigorous prosecution of the war and the restoration of the Union.

SPECIMEN COPIES will be furnished to those who request them.

Subscriptions may commence at any time. Terms ALWAYS CASH, in advance.

All Letters to be addressed to

JOHN W. FORNEY,
"PRESS," Office, 111 SOUTH FOURTH ST.,
tf PHILADELPHIA.

NEWS FROM THE WAR.—[DRAWN

[Special Artist, Mr. Winslow Homer.]

VOL. 1. PHILADELPHIA, SATURDAY, JUNE 14, 1862. NO. 31.

[Written for The War Press.]

A DUEL FOR A FLIRT.

A STORY OF THE WAR.—BY ESSEX.

Kate Downing was the handsomest and liveliest girl in the town of L. Her witty sayings were quoted everywhere, her flirtations formed the theme of perpetual gossip. Last winter every one thought that Charlie Warren would certainly be the favored one, and Miss Kate's coquetries would surely end in marriage this time, and I rather think Mr. Charlie thought so himself. He knew he was a good match—I fancy he knew he was good-looking, too—and beyond a doubt he knew how many encouraging whispers he had received, how many sly favors had been his. So, when the war broke out, and Charlie resolved to march with his regiment, he was quite sure that before he went he should have her promise to be his bride the very first furlough he should have. Full of this thought, he put on his lieutenant's uniform one evening, and made his way to Mr. Downing's handsome residence.

He found in the parlor the victorious Kate surrounded by three admirers, with each of whom she was alternately coquetting. Charlie waited patiently until they were gone, devoting himself to Mrs. Downing until he had outstaid every one. He had noticed with pain that Kate paid not the slightest heed to his new dress, and when they were at last alone, he saw with sudden anguish how cold was the light of her clear black eyes.

"Kate," he said, drawing his chair near her, "I am going to Washington with my regiment."

"So I have heard, Mr. Warren," replied Kate, in a tone of ice.

"But before I go, dearest Kate," persisted Charlie, trying not to notice her coldness, "I must beg you once more to give me your promise. You know well how long I have loved you. Now, that I am going away to danger, will you not let me take with me the consolation of knowing that you will certainly be one day mine?"

Kate patted her little foot on the floor for a moment in silence; then she said abruptly, "If you really loved me as much as you profess you would not go away."

"What!" cried Charlie in amaze, "Do you think I ought to stay at home in a time like this, when our country needs the support of every honest man?"

Kate made no answer.

"If my regiment had marched without me would you not have been ashamed to call me even friend?" he went on impetuously.

"Yes," faltered Kate, "but I do not see how you can bear to go."

"I can hardly endure the thought of separation," said Charlie, earnestly, "you cannot tell how much pain that thought has cost me; but, my dear Kate," he added, tenderly, taking her hand, "the memory of you will give me courage, the hope of seeing you again will enable me to bear the long waiting."

Kate shook her head. "You don't love me, Charlie," she reiterated, mournfully.

Charlie was so delighted at her return to the old friendly address, that he seized both her hands in his, and poured out all his tender affection. Kate listened patiently, but all the time there was a shade of reserve. She would make no promise, either then or at any future interview, and when at last Charlie marched away with his regiment, he had no better consolation than a half assurance that at least she would form no other engaement, a permission to write to her, and a little piece of blue ribbon that he carried next his heart, and that he swore should never be disgraced. If he could have looked into her pretty boudoir an hour after his regiment had started, he would have been secure that he would not easily be forgotten. Kate had gone with a gay party to see them off, and her laugh was as merry as any there as she waved her handkerchief, and kissed her hand to the departing heroes, but once alone, her indifference melted away in a long and passionate burst of tears.

I am afraid Kate was an ingrain coquette, for before poor Charlie had been gone a month she was flirting desperately with George Hudson, a young lawyer in L., giving it as her reason for preferring him that she was sure he would not be such a goose as to leave a good practice and go off to the war. So, all summer they were riding, and walking, and boating together, until, by-and-by, the good gossips of L. began to think that this time it certainly must be an engagement.

What it might have resulted in, there is no telling, but just after the battle of Bull Run a battery of artillery was got up in L., and Hudson, who, in the intervals of his work, had been all summer studying military books, was offered the post of lieutenant.

Kate's disgust may be imagined when she found her new lover about to desert her. However, after the first outburst of indignation, she resolved, like a true coquette, not wholly to lose her agreeable captive, and so dissembled her disappointment far enough not to quarrel with him, and on the very evening before he left she went with him to a party. She looked very lovely that night in a white dress, trimmed with bows of rose-colored ribbon. To do her justice, I don't think she meant to go beyond a flirtation with Hudson; but when he parted with her in the moonlight at her own door, his accents were so pleading, he looked so very sad, that she could not refuse his humble request to be allowed to take with him one little pink-knot that had come loose from her dress.

"Thank you! thank you, Miss Kate!" he cried, enthusiastically. "I shall wear this ribbon in my first battle, and I swear to you it shall go to victory or it shall be soaked in my blood."

Kate shuddered, and at the same moment a thought of Charlie came over her that made her half regret the gift. "Mr. Hudson," she said, giving him her hand kindly, "I have no doubt you will always be in the front of battle, but I earnestly hope you will return in safety."

Hudson pressed the little hand to his lips, and, full of happiness in these words, left her, with the fond belief that she would certainly yet be his. Kate shed no tears over his departure. She was saddened, perhaps, and she missed his devoted attentions, but there was no more than a pensive regret in thinking of his absence.

The papers informed her that both her lovers were near Washington, and the weeks rolled away in quiet inaction, while they had little to do but dream of her. Meantime, Kate found L. uncommonly dull. Every one was saddened; all the "beaux" were gone to the war; there was no more fun there, so by and by she went to New York to make a visit.

October there was pleasant enough. There is always something going on in the metropolis. But after a while she had an opportunity of going to a gayer city still. Her friend Mrs. Banks was going to join her husband, Col. Banks, in Washington, and asked Kate to accompany her. Of course, Kate was wild with light, wrote home for leave, and got by return of mail permission to go from her indulgent father, and a nice sum to spend on her outfit. A fortnight later, and one fine November morning Kate and her friends arrived in the capital.

Two little notes which she was careful to send on two different days, informed her two admirers of her arrival, and brought them on two successive evenings to pay her their court. She was really delighted to see them both again; though there is no doubt that Warren had a warmer greeting than Hudson. For a while all went on very well. Kate continued to flirt with both, as well as with numerous others who were captivated by her sweet face and winning ways; and accident so far befriended her that the two rivals scarcely ever met. At last, however, fate ordained that this sunshine should be terminated by a final storm.

It was the night of a military ball. The long, low mess-room was prettily draped with flags, and wreathed with evergreens, and an excellent band discoursed most inspiring music. Kate drove to the ball with Colonel and Mrs. Banks, and was met almost simultaneously at the door by the two lieutenants. Then for the first time they seemed to see in each other antagonists for Kate's favor. They had been acquainted in L., and had met with cordiality wherever they had been thrown together; but to night, as their eyes encountered, there was a gleam of mutual distrust in the glances they exchanged.

Kate was as beautiful as a young queen, and seemed to enjoy tormenting every one. As she leaned on Hudson's arm on the way to the dance, she took a wicked pleasure in noticing that Warren was watching them intensely, and on that very account threw all the devotion possible into her manner, answering Hudson's tender speeches so favorably that he was quite happy, and absolutely certain that she had very nearly given him the right to call her his own. Yet a little later when it was Warren's turn, and she was holding his hand in a waltz, there could be no doubt that he alone was the favored one; at least, he was convinced of that, and all the momentary jealousy he had felt of Hudson vanished in his abounding happiness.

Meanwhile Hudson, in his turn, was enduring the torments of distrust, and his black eyes flashed ominously as he watched those two so careless of him.

So time ran on till supper was announced. Kate had made no engagement for it, and saw with dismay both her admirers approaching at once. They both looked so terribly in earnest that she durst not trifle with either, but with a laugh, that was rather forced, took an arm of each and so went in to supper. There was a great crowd and, as the evening advanced, a good deal of noise. There was no wine on the table, but, in some of the officers' quarters near, certain privileged guests could get something much stronger. So it happened that, just as Kate was getting desperately uncomfortable under the double devotion of her two attendants, a rowdy, half-tipsy officer, who disgraced the uniform he wore, staggered very rudely against her, and then, with an oath, attempted an apology that was almost an insult.

As by one movement, Warren and Hudson seized him and pushed him away, and Warren said, rather stiffly:

"Thank you for your assistance, Mr. Hudson, but I believe it is my place to chastise this insolent puppy."

"Excuse me," retorted Hudson, "but anything that troubles Miss Denning is my concern."

"Really," sneered Warren, "I think you are quite mistaken in interesting yourself in that young lady's affairs."

"By G—! sir," cried Hudson, in ungovernable rage, "Do you mean to insult me? I repeat what I said before, and unless you can prove that you have a better right than I, you must apologize."

"Never!" exclaimed Warren, angrily. Then, after a pause, he added: "but let us waive our own dispute for the present, and first get what satisfaction we can from this impertinent fellow."

At the first words of this angry colloquy Kate had disappeared. Casting one terrified glance at the belligerents, she had accepted the offered arm of Captain Curtis, who quietly led her back to the ball-room. This Captain Curtis was a very old friend of Kate's; he had known her from childhood, and having a very sweet wife of his own had taken only an unusual interest in her flirtations for the last few seasons. To-night, however, he had been really pained; he had seen that her coquetry was really very wrong, and had scarcely wondered that it had finally led to a violent outburst. As he watched her pale and agitated face, he mentally reflected that it was no more than right she should be frightened; so he stood by her side in silence, not caring, even if he could, to draw her thoughts into any less melancholy channel.

Meantime, both Warren and Hudson felt that that was not the time to settle their dispute, and, waivin their own grievances, insisted first upon an apology from the offender. This was given at once in a shambling way, which was all that could be expected under the circumstances, and, after a hearty shake, Warren released him. This matter settled, both the young men, without exchanging any further conversation, went in search of Kate. They found her still standing beside Captain Curtis. She looked up with a sigh of relief as they approached, and her eyes sought Warren's anxiously. Hudson noted this, and set his teeth tight as he vowed revenge.

Poor Kate was so terribly afraid of still further complicating matters that she did not dare to accept the escort of either of the young men, but in her hurry and excitement nervously bade them both so cold a farewell that neither of them felt very amiable after it. She was sincerely alarmed this time. She had heard men say they would kill themselves when she had been cruel, or swear they would shoot a rival in a moment of jealousy, but she had never seen such earnest hate in any one's looks before; and after she got to her own room she had a hearty cry, and vowed earnestly that if Charlie Warren would only ask her once more, she would take him and give up flirting forever.

The next day she was nervous and anxious, starting every time there was a knock at the door, and refusing to go out lest she should miss a visit she so much longed for. But the whole day passed without her seeing either of her admirers, and all the evening, while listening to the gay talk of some other officers, she was thinking only of Warren; and when, after ten o'clock, Capt. Curtis came up to her, just as the last visitor had taken his leave, and asked for a few moments' talk with her she was anything but reassured by his grim, stern manner.

Now, to tell the truth, the Captain was very much saddened by the events of the past twenty-four hours. After Kate left the night before there had been very angry words between Warren and Hudson. They had resulted in a challenge from the latter to the former. As soon as he received it, Warren had gone to Captain Curtis to act as his second. The Captain was intensely shocked at this request, and had spent a good portion of the day in vainly endeavoring to persuade him not to accept it.

"I must," Warren had said over and over again. "You know how long and how truly I have loved Kate. I never thought her capable of so much coquetry; but although I have given up all hopes of her now, I must not be disgraced in her eyes."

His reiterations at last convinced the Captain that further remonstrances were useless; and determined to stand by his friend to the last, he had consented to act as his second. All the preliminaries of the duel were now arranged. They were to meet in a wood near Washington, and in order to shield as far as possible all parties from the severe consequences of detection, the expedition was to be made to appear as got up for the purpose of practising at a mark.

Capt. Curtis had left Warren writing in his tent the few letters that in the event of a fatal result would be his last words to relatives and friends, and had come to Kate resolved to tell her enough of the truth to give her a severe fright, and cure her of her dangerous coquetry. But as soon as they were alone she seized his arm with such a pale, frightened face that he half relented.

"What is it, Capt. Curtis? Oh! please speak quick?"

"It is no bad news from home, Kate," he said. "You need not look so distressed."

"I know," faltered Kate. "I am not afraid of that, but—but—Charlie—Charlie Warren."

"He is well," replied the Captain stoically.

"Why has he not been here?"

"My dear Kate," replied the Captain, touched by her honest interest, "I will not deceive you. Warren is too busy to-night to come up, the quarrel between him and Hudson is not yet settled." And then the Captain went on to tell Kate something of what had occurred. He did not tell her the whole state of affairs, but he did not spare her as to what Warren had said of her flirting, and he told her enough to make her very anxious. Yet, man-like, as soon as he had inflicted the pain, he was sorry. She was so sincerely wretched, so lovely in her grief, that when at last she bowed her fair head in her hands and wept convulsively, he began to think he was a brute after all, and to attempt such consolation as was possible, ending by promising that he would do all in his power to bring Warren to see her early the next morning.

"Tell him anything you choose, Captain," she faltered, "only don't let them fight."

That was a dreadful night for poor Kate; worse than the last one. She had never known before that she could lie awake long hours and be so wretched. But she would have been a thousand times more miserable if she had known the danger that threatened honest Charlie Warren, as he stood in the dim sunrise, with Hudson's unerring pistol pointed at his breast.

The morning crawled away. Kate took her breakfast in her room, and then, dressed in tasteful *negligée*, sat alone in the parlor, awaiting the coming of her lover. But she had a long time of suspense to endure before she heard a rapid stride along the entry, and, without waiting for an answer to his knock, Captain Curtis entered, very pale, his hair tossed, his dress disordered, and splashed with mud.

"What has happened?" gasped Kate, starting up.

"They have met; Hudson has shot Warren. I pitied you last night, Kate Denning, but not this morning, when Hudson gaily left the field, with a knot of pink ribbon in his button-hole, and I took this from Charlie's breast." And, as he spoke, he tossed to Kate the little blue bow she remembered so well, only that now it was crumpled and torn, and stained deep with fresh blood.

She had listened in horror-struck silence until that last act; but when she saw this dreadful corroboration of all she feared, her strength forsook her, and she sank fainting on the floor. Captain Curtis was sorry again, as he raised her and dashed some of the ice-water, that stood near, into her white face. She recovered in an instant, with a long groan.

"And I have killed him."

"No, no, Kate—no!" cried the Captain; "he is not dead, though he is hard hit."

"Not dead!" And Kate started up, looking almost happy at the revulsion of feeling. "Then take me to him—oh! Captain Curtis, for God's sake take me to him. I will nurse him so tenderly, for, oh!—I don't care now who knows it—I love him with all my heart."

"You are a noble girl, after all," said the Captain, taking her hand. "Forgive me if I have inflicted pain."

"No, I deserved it all," replied Kate. "I will forgive everything if you will only take me to him."

So it was settled. Mrs. Banks was out. Captain Curtis was certainly a suitable escort, and in half an hour they were driving to the camp. Warren had been conveyed after his hurt to his own tent. No one suspected what had really happened. It was supposed he had been accidentally shot, and had concealed the name of the person who had wounded him from a proper delicacy. The surgeon had dressed his injury, and pronounced it, though serious, not very dangerous; and he lay alone in a high fever that followed the first exhaustion when Captain Curtis looked into his tent.

"Ah, Charlie! how are you? Well enough to see a visitor?"

"Yes, gladly, I am so lonely here."

Captain Curtis adjusted his couch a little and said, "it is a lady."

"A lady! who—what do you mean? not my mother, surely."

"No, it is Kate Denning."

And in a moment Kate had stolen in, the Captain had disappeared, and they two were alone together. Kate knelt beside the couch as she took the hot hand Warren put forth.

"Charlie, can you forgive me?"

"Last night I thought I never could," said Charlie, honestly, "but now I can."

"Yes! yes! Charlie, you must forgive me. Indeed, I never meant to flirt so much. I—I—always loved you."

"My own Kate."

At that sweet confession Charlie tried to draw her towards him, and Kate yielded to the feeble pressure, and so all doubt or distrust between those two was over forever.

Kate could not stay long there; it was not best; but the next day Charlie was removed to the hospital, and there Kate was his faithful nurse during many days. Whether love helped or not I cannot tell, but certainly his recovery was very rapid. Kate was proud of her engagement now, and Charlie could afford to smile; when one day she received from Lieut. Hudson a polite note, returning the knot of rose-colored ribbon that had so nearly given him a fatal victory.

"Oh," said Kate, "If I could have guessed into what sort of battle he would wear it, I would have died rather than he should have it."

"Never mind, darling," whispered Charlie, "I can bear that he should have won the duel, as I have won you."

DESPERATE BAYONET CHARGE OF THE TWENTY-THIRD PENNSYLVANIANS, AT THE BATTLE OF FAIR OAKS.

[SKETCHED AND ENGRAVED FOR THE WAR PRESS.]

THE above engraving is a correct representation of the gallant and successful charge of the Twenty-third Pennsylvania regiment, Col. Neill commanding, at the recent great battle in front of Richmond, as sent to us by one of our special correspondents. The regiment [illegible] was attached to Couch's division, and was posted in the advance, on the extreme right. The rebels came on, anticipating an easy victory, and in obedience to orders, the men of the Twenty-third did not fire a shot until the rebels [illegible] gave them one volley, and then, under the lead of their gallant Colonel, charged with the bayonet upon the rebel ranks, fighting desperately; but overpowered by numbers, they were compelled to fall back a short distance, when the [illegible] was again formed, and again they dashed at the foe. The fight by this time had become general along the line, yet few regiments, if any, did better work than the Twenty-third Pennsylvania. For full particulars of the engagement, and a list of the killed and wounded, see our other pages.

[For The War Press.]

THE SOLDIER'S DREAM.

BY JOHN W. MORRISON.

'Tis midnight, and dead silence reigns
Around our lovely camp;
No sounds are heard, save the song of the bird,
And the sentinel's ceaseless tramp.

Fair Luna, with her silvery sheen,
Comes forth to grace the night;
And the gentle breeze stirs the leaves on the trees
That are clothed in the soft moonlight.

Within a tent, in whose open door
The moon is sweetly gleaming,
On the cold damp ground, wrapped in slumbers profound,
Lies a soldier quietly dreaming.

What happy thought has caused that smile
O'er his parted lips to roam?
He is back once more to the well-known door
Of his native Northern home.

Once more he sees his father's form,
His sister's smiling face,
His dearly-loved mother, and kind-hearted brother,
All are clasped in a warm embrace.

Once more by evening's crimson light,
He wanders down the vale,
To the foot of the hill where the murmuring rill
Heard many a tender tale.

His heart beats quickly, and his steps
He hastens as he spies,
Beneath an oak's shade, a most beautiful maid,
With the love-light in her eyes.

A moment more and the yielding form
Is in his strong arms twined,
And the still, solemn grove heard a tale of deep love
That was wafted by evening's light wind.

How loth was our patriot-soldier boy
From his beautiful dream to waken,
To take a rude seat his good breakfast to eat
Of luscious white beans and bacon!

Beaufort, S. C., May 30, 1862.

[Written for the Boston Journal]

THE BURIED VOLUNTEER.

BY MRS. J. H. HANAFORD.

Not where his fathers rest, beside the sea,
But far away upon Potomac's shore,
Or in the distant West his grave may be
Who comes to his New England home no more.

Fond hearts are aching in their silent grief,
Within the cot which love a palace made;
While patriot pride and Christian hope, relief
Offers to those who mourn their cherished dead.

Comfort will come but only, Lord! from thee—
In thee, Oh Christ! alone the heart is glad;
Whose earthly hopes like shadows seem to flee,
Whose loss uncounted makes each moment sad.

When to the din of battle he, the brave!
Rushed like a hero, at his country's call,
He thought to win a garland or the grave—
To live a conqu'ror or a martyr fall.

Now angels chant their pæans o'er his head;
The land he loved—the land for which he died—
Counts him amid her dear and honored dead,
And writes his name on History's page with pride.

O, buried Volunteer! thy praise shall sound
Sweet in thy children's ears in days to be,
And when blest Freedom circles earth around,
God, with Truth's champions, will remember thee.

BEVERLY, Mass., April 4, 1862.

A CORRESPONDENT asks whether the Federal anaconda "belongs to the army or the navy?" They own him in common. He is a joint-snake.

RICHMOND ENQUIRER----EXTRA.

SUNDAY MORNING, June 29th, 1862.

THE BATTLES ON FRIDAY AND SATURDAY.

VICTORY ON THE NORTH OF CHICKAHOMINY.

HALF OF McCLELLAN'S ARMY BEATEN AND DRIVEN FROM THEIR STRONGHOLDS.

IMMENSE SLAUGHTER.

Over Five Thousand Prisoners Taken---The Bucktails in Misery---The Battle on Saturday---An Armistice Agreed Upon---Incidents, &c., &c.

The right wing of the enemy having been driven from its advanced positions, near Mechanicsville, on Friday morning, fell back upon its stronger works in the direction of the centre. Gen. "Stonewall" Jackson was bearing down upon them with invincible energy, supported in front by Gen. A. P. Hill's Division, when Longstreet's Division was ordered, about four o'clock in the afternoon, down the north bank of the Chickahominy, to follow up the advance of Hill's Division on the main batteries of the enemy at the mill beyond Gaines' cross roads. The Division (Longstreet's,) halted by the Chickahominy, and Gen. Pickett's Brigade was detached as an advance to support Gen. Hill's assault, the latter being then engaged in a terrific fight in front of the works in view. Upon reaching the scene, Pickett's Brigade was ordered to support a battery which was then playing upon the enemy, who were returning a hot fire upon Gen. Hill's left. The brigade was then ordered to charge, which being accomplished, resulted in the repulse of the enemy. An Alabama and a Mississippi regiment came up to the support of the brigade, when the latter were ordered to fall; the Alabamians and Mississippians then charged over them upon the enemy, and the brigade arose again and followed.

The charge now became desperate, and never were such harassing difficulties encountered and successfully overcome. Our men found themselves suddenly charging upon the enemy in a dense wood, forming a portion of an extensive swamp, which presented somewhat the appearance of the pit of a theatre, surrounded by a ditch five feet wide by five feet deep, while on the opposite side, the mud of the marsh was knee deep, over which arose the hill, upon which the enemy's batteries were placed. At the foot of the hill the enemy had erected a parterre of infantry works, and another at the top, overlooking it, and also one on the edge of a ravine on the left of the brow of the hill. A battery was stationed in the ravine, while three others, in two tiers, ribbed the front of the hill, the whole presenting a fire upon our forces which told with terrible effect.

But our troops rushed on, crossed the swamp, the field officers having dismounted from their horses, it being impossible to carry them on, and charged upon the foremost batteries. In the first essay, the brigade and its support were repulsed; in the second they paused and laid down. The 4th Texas, and several North and South Carolina regiments came up; the rest of Hill's Division was pressing on, and Longstreet's was rapidly approaching the scene of conflict. The third charge was made, and the battery was taken. The number engaged in this charge was not more than 4,500, while that of the enemy on the ground numbered about 10,000, comprising General Porter's Division. Our supports now came up, and secured the possession of the hill, capturing many prisoners. The enemy's cavalry made an attempt to retake the position, but were repulsed, and fled precipitately. As our troops gained the brow of the hill General Jackson appeared on our left, about four hundred yards off, just completing his irresistible storm on the enemy's right flank, and siding materially in securing the position then in the possession of our forces.

The General engagement, closing with this brilliant finale, brought into the field 40,000 Confederates and 50,000 Federals.

The enemy was pursued for some distance out, when they finally disappeared, it being now eight o'clock at night, and our men, commended by their officers for their gallantry, and flushed with victory, were content to stop upon the field of their success and rest for the night. We regret to learn that our loss was very severe. It is estimated that in killed and wounded, Gen. Pickett's Brigade lost from 40 to 50 per cent. Such daring, such sacrifices, were never before made before the altar of liberty.

Among the lost of Pickett's Brigade, were Col. Withers, of the 18th Virginia, mortally wounded in the breast; Gen. Pickett was wounded in the arm, severely, but not dangerously; Maj. Wilson, of the 28th Va., was wounded in the leg and side; Capt. Speesard, of the 28th Va., disabled; Capt. Robertson, of the same, in the breast, but not seriously; Capt. Nelson, also of the 28th, reported killed, but believed to be a mistake. The total loss of the 28th Virginia alone amounted to about sixty per cent. of its whole force engaged.

We have been unable to gather the full particulars of our loss, nor that of the enemy, except so far as we learn from our prisoners, who represent their loss as very severe.

Two regiments, captured during the day, the 11th Pennsylvania and the 4th New Jersey, about six hundred in all, together with their officers, reached the city about ten o'clock, Saturday morning, and were quartered in the Libby and Greaner's Prisons.

Portions of several Federal Brigades were also captured on various parts of the field, and among them were large numbers of field and company officers. There arrived in the city at an early hour on Saturday, Maj. Gen. John F. Reynolds, of Illinois; Brig. Gen. Rankin, of Pennsylvania, (Philadelphia,) and Capt. C. Kingsbury, Jr., aid to Gen. Reynolds. Several Colonels also arrived at the same time. The whole number of prisoners taken in the four days' fighting sums up, in round numbers, FIVE THOUSAND.

Twenty-three hundred and fifty privates and ninety-three officers, have already been brought to Richmond.

Our Generals, accompanied by staff and regimental officers, rode over the battle field of Friday, on Saturday afternoon, and estimated the number of Federals left dead on the field, at one thousand. A large number of their wounded also fell into our hands. Their total loss in the several engagements, is estimated at about TEN THOUSAND, in killed, wounded and prisoners. Our loss, all told, does not exceed twenty-five hundred. The fighting on the Confederate side exhibited a degree of coolness and undaunted heroism which have never been excelled in the history of nations. The work of our men was rendered brilliant by the number, style and irresistibility of their bayonet charges, which carried every thing before them, and so completely eclipsed the "bayonet charges," which McClellan pictured up for the popular mind of the North, on the occasion of the battle of the "Seven Pines," that not even the shadow of a respectable hand to hand resistance was offered them.

In our combined assault upon this last and strongest series of works on the right wing of the enemy, our forces increased to upwards of forty thousand men, while the enemy presented a force of about fifty thousand strong, consisting of the whole of Gen. Fitz John Porter's *corps d'armée*, a division from Franklin's and a division of McCall's *corps d'armee*. The enemy was thus driven back upon his centre, and his entire plans disconcerted. He was busily fortifying his position on the north on Saturday, in order to resist attack from the rear.

The plan of attack in this day's battle may be summed up as follows: General Jackson made his way around the entire rear of the enemy, and pitched into their left driving, or rather "huddling" them all up on their centre. He then passed around their rear and came up on their left, which Gen. A. P. Hill's corps was pursuing down upon the right of their centre, while General Longstreet and General D. H. Hill were driving back their front in the same direction. It must be understood that the battle was fought between one portion of our forces and one-half of the enemy, the other half being on this (South) side of the Chickahominy, where no fighting of importance occurred at all.

Gen. McClellan, though immediately near, and expected to command his forces in person, did not appear on the field. The prisoners taken by us manifested a strong feeling in consequence of this circumstance, and stated that the entire army engaged was similarly influenced.

THE BATTLE ON SATURDAY ON THE SOUTH SIDE OF THE CHICKAHOMINY.

No fighting occurred on the north side of the Chickahominy, on Saturday. At an early hour, Gen. Magruder, whose forces threaten the front of the enemy's forces on the southside, sent forward a portion of Gen. Toombs' brigade, to capture a battery on the Nine Mile road. Our men were elated with the idea of at length joining in the fray which had so long been in progress, and moving on marched upon and charged the battery and captured it. The enemy, however, had a strong battery of howitzers in the rear, with which they played upon our men incessantly, so that at length they were compelled to abandon the work. Our loss in this charge was about two hundred, killed and wounded. Most of our killed and wounded in this engagement, including Col. Lamar, of Georgia, who was severely wounded in the leg, were left in the hands of the enemy.

No more fighting occurred along the lines during the rest of the day. An armistice was agreed upon in the afternoon, for the exchange of the wounded and the burial of the dead, and thus closed the events of the day and week, the field, for the most part, in our possession, and the mantle of victory covering our dead.

THE POSITION.

Our Generals having disconcerted the enemy's centre, and the latter seeing no earthly chance for themselves, so completely were they hemmed in, it is said, immediately made for their gunboats on the Pamunkey, but, to their utter surprise and horror, found themselves outflanked by the indomitable Jackson and his brave army. They then re-crossed the swamp in the wildest confusion, and fled towards their gunboats on the James River, closely followed by Jackson, Hill and Longstreet, who expected to overtake McClellan and his half of the army Saturday night or early Sunday morning.

The other half of the Federal army is represented as completely surrounded by our troops. Magruder in front, Holmes on their right, and "Bethel" Hill and other Generals in their rear. It was expected that all of these Generals would move against the enemy at an early hour Sunday morning, while those of our troops in their rear will probably advance upon the enemy towards Richmond. The enemy was, on Saturday, busily employed in strengthening his fortifications, both in front and rear, so as to resist, if possible, the combined assaults of our forces—their rear being at the time totally unprepared to meet any vigorous attack.

We have thus given in as concise a manner as possible the position of the two armies before Richmond, as explained to us by a gentleman of known intelligence and reliability.—The reader will thus perceive that the skies are indeed "bright and brightening." Let the people of the Confederacy place implicit confidence in the skill of our officers and the valor of our troops, and with the aid of a just God we will yet annihilate or capture the entire army of George B. McClellan, "General commanding the army of the Potomac."

ARRIVAL OF PRISONERS.

All day Saturday prisoners were being sent to the rear, and, as fast as circumstances would permit, were sent to the city. About two thousand had arrived here Saturday afternoon, among whom are many officers. We have obtained the following partial list of the officers captured:

Thos. O'Niell, Major 2d Battalion N. York Artillery.

Thos. Chapman, 2d Lieut. company E, 95th Penn.

E. W. Whittemore, 2d Lieut. company E, 1st Battalion 17th U. S. Infantry.

Geo. C. Davenport, 1st Lieut. company B, 3d Penn.

John Eckbinger, Captain company F, 8th Penn.

A. E. Miles, Captain company E, 1st Penn. Rifles.

P. G. McNaughten, 1st Lieut. company D, 1st Penn. Rifles.

T. B. Lewis, 2d Lieut. company B, 1st Penn. Rifles.

C. A. Bayard, 1st Lieut. company K, 1st Penn. Rifles.

S. M. Wells, Jr., Porter's Staff.

L. B. Watts, company F, 8th Penn.

R. D. Hall, company B, 1st Penn. Rifles.

THE CRENSHAW BATTERY.

The casualties in this Battery, which behaved with distinguished gallantry, on Thursday last, before the enemy, were as follows: Killed, 2—R. N. Hines and Sydney Strother; Wounded—B. F. Graves and Daniel Lancaster—legs amputated; W. B. Allen, in the thigh; T. S. Rider, in the breast; Thomas J. Mallory in the neck; Marion Knowles, in the knee; Geo. S. Young, in the neck. Twenty-one horses belonging to the battery were shot, and two pieces of artillery disabled.

The above Battery reported for duty Saturday morning with three pieces, with crippled and jaded horses; but Gens. Gregg and Hill seeing their condition, made a brief speech to them—complimented them highly for their gallantry—said they had richly won a respite, and they were therefore permitted to come to the city last night. They will remain here until their guns are repaired and then report again for duty. The members of the company will, to-day, attend in a body the funerals of their deceased comrades, Hines and Strother, who will be interred with military honors.

"A HARD ROAD TO TRAVEL."

A sparkling little *jeu d'esprit* was fulminated by a young gentleman, at one of the hotels on Saturday. Some one asked if it was possible for McClellan's army ever to get to Richmond. The *Pun-ic* joker responded, "If he does, he will have to level two Hills, wade through a Longstreet, pass a pretty strong Pickett, travel over a considerable number of Rhodes, and then batter down a "Stonewall." Certainly a hard road to travel.

"ON TO RICHMOND."

Gen. Reynolds, of Illinois, captured on the battle field of Friday, and brought to this city on Saturday, met an officer in the Confederate service, with whom in "old times" he had been a *bon compagnon*. In that pleasant conversation which ensued, the Confederate officer said "Well, General, you have got to Richmond at last." "Just as I predicted," replied the General. "When do you suppose McClellan will be here," jocosely asked the Confederate officer. "I wouldn't be surprised to hear of his arrival to-night," responded the General with a smile, dashed with an interesting spark of bitterness.

READING THE LOVE LETTERS FROM YANKEE LAND.

During the engagement in front of Richmond, on Friday evening last, Gen. Lee, accompanied by his Staff, came upon a deserted camp on the field from which the Yankees had just been driven. A large number of Yankee knapsacks were piled up and strewed around, and amidst them, in a recumbent posture, with his boots magnificently elevated, was discovered a stalwart Confederate soldier, reading a letter taken from a mass of similar documents which the knapsacks contained. A humorous grin was playing over his features when the General and his Staff came up. "What are you doing here?" Gen. Lee inquired. "Reading—don't you see?" replied the soldier, scarcely observing them.—The General deeming his easy manner, and easy position by no means becoming a Confederate soldier, when the roaring of the battle was thundering around, informed the literary hero who he was, which caused him to jump up about three feet from the ground, "scared half to death," and commenced bowing, blushing and apologizing in the most amusing style imaginable. The General then asked him what he was doing there, to which he answered, that he was placed in charge of the knapsacks; but when asked who placed him there, he was covered with confusion, and finally stammered out that "he didn't know the officer's name." He was then ordered to take care of the useful things, not mind reading the letters, and to report to the first Quartermaster, after which he would rejoin his regiment as speedily as possible.

A YANKEE BALLOONIST MAKES A SHORT TRIP.

A body of our infantry, under cover of a dense thicket intervening, passed around, on Thursday last, to the flank of a number of Yankees, who were evidently the "Balloon Guard," and was rapidly approaching in musket shot of them, just as one of their "Professors" was about to make an ascension. They halted in order to give the aerial voyager time to get up. The balloon was soon under weigh, and the windlass unwound, but as the observant Professor attained a height of about two hundred feet, he perceived, to his horror and consternation, our infantry marching upon his "base of operations." Giving a shout, he ordered those below to haul him in, which was obeyed; but the operation being too slow, he leaped out of the car, grasped the rope and slided down with a speed which would have done credit to the expertness of a Gorilla. The balloon soon followed, was bursted up, put in a cart, and "Professor," balloon, guard and all mizzled, just in time to save themselves from capture.

"WE OUGHT TO HAVE HAD A NAVY."

In conversation with some of the prisoners who arrived on Saturday, a citizen, addressing an officer, remarked, "If we'd have had a Navy, this war would have been ended six months ago." The officer, with an emphasis that indicated earnestness, replied, "I wish to God, you had had a navy, then, six months ago!" Nearly all of the prisoners seem to entertain similar sentiments as to the folly of carrying on the war.

TWO ENTIRE REGIMENTS TAKEN.

The 11th Pennsylvania Reserve Corps, commanded by Colonel Gallaher, and the 4th New Jersey, were taken prisoners on Friday. The entire regiments, with their officers, except those killed, were brought to this city Saturday.

THREW DOWN THEIR ARMS.

We are told that several regiments of Yankees, seeing no possible chance of escape, deliberately threw down their arms and surrendered unconditionally.

YANKEE OFFICERS' QUARTERS.

A large number of the quarters of the Yankee officers on the Chickahominy, which are now in possession of our brave men, were filled with the choicest edibles, brandies, whisky, wines, &c., all of which were, of course, confiscated.

LIEUT. COL. SAM. B. PAUL.

This gallant officer, formerly Provost Marshal at Manassas, and Lieut. Col. of the 28th Virginia, during the campaign on Manassas Plains last year, but who had since resigned both positions, was requested by his old regiment to resume his position of command, on the occasion of the battle of Friday, in the absence of his successor. The same compliment was extended to and accepted by him on the occasion of the battle of the "Seven Pines," in which he acted with characteristic gallantry and received distinguished mention in the report of the commanding General. On this occasion he again accepted and bore himself with even more ardor and intrepidity than before, as the exigency called for a greater degree of impetuosity and daring. Dismounting from his horse, as his brigade (Pickett's,) made their ever to be remembered charge through swamp and wood upon the batteries of the enemy, he gave it and his sword in charge of a courier, and with pistol in hand, charged on with his men, and went with them to victory.

A PRISONER ACCIDENTALLY SHOT.

On Saturday last a crowd around the captives in front of the Libby prison pressed upon the guards to such an inconvenient extent that it was impossible for a time for them to turn around. In the midst of the confusion the gun of one of the guard, which was slung over his shoulder, became entangled, or was struck on the trigger by some of the crowd, and exploded, a part of the contents penetrating the foot of one of the prisoners.

WHAT WE HAVE GAINED.

In the first place we have driven the enemy from all his strongest original positions on the North of the Chickahominy. We have the glory on our side of a daily succession of victories, which has completely disconcerted the plans of the enemy. We have re-opened the communication on the Fredericksburg and Central Railroads, cut off the enemy from his principal avenues of supply and escape, destroyed his telegraphic communication, and taken possession of the York River Railroad, besides capturing the latest Baltimore mails sent up that route.

THE BUCKTAILS PLAYED OUT.

The Regiment of Bucktail Rifles, of Fremont's command, whose watch word was, "We never Surrender!" adorned the streets on yesterday, with their bucktail plumes on their way to the Confederate States prison. Nearly every one of them was either killed or captured.

COLORS BROUGHT IN.

About 10 o'clock this (Sunday) morning the regimental colors of the 4th New Jersey, the 11th Pennsylvania Reserve, and Stockton's Bucktail Rifles, arrived, with another batch of Yankee prisoners. They were all splendidly made flags, one being the "stars and stripes," and the others made of green silk, with State arms and mottoes emblazoned.

☞ For later and additional details see "Enquirer" of to-morrow morning.

DESPATCH FROM GENERAL LEE TO PRESIDENT DAVIS.

The following despatch was received by the President, at a late hour last night, from Gen. Lee:

HEADQUARTERS, &c.,
June 27, 1862.

His Excellency President Davis:

MR. PRESIDENT.—Profoundly grateful to Almighty God for the signal victory granted to us, it is my pleasing task to announce to you the success achieved by this Army to-day.

The enemy was this morning driven from his strong position behind Beaver Dam Creek, pursued to that behind Powhite Creek, and finally, after a severe contest of five hours, entirely repulsed from the field. Night put an end to the contest. I grieve to state that our loss in officers and men is great. We sleep on the field and shall renew the contest in the morning.

I have the honor to be, very respectfully,
(Signed) R. E. LEE, General.

Lynchb'g Virginian.

Tuesday,..............July 1st, 1862.

The Prospect.

The defeat of McClellan, the Yankee tax bill just passed, and the news from abroad, must tend powerfully to strengthen the hands of the Peace party of the North.—In like manner it should encourage the hearts, and nerve the arms of our people. These events, all transpiring simultaneously, will have an unhappy effect on Wall Street, and tend to depress the Northern stock market. Yankee bills of credit will not rule high to-day. Their promises to pay will go a begging. Upon the other hand, Confederate funds should be worth more now than they have been at any time during the war. The lack of confidence which some persons have manifested in them and more have *felt*—and which has been one cause, if not the chief cause, of the enormous prices which all articles of commerce have attained—should be felt no longer. Prices, exorbitant beyond all comparison, and consequent chiefly upon apprehensions of a depreciated paper currency, should come down, and people who buy tobacco and other articles at any price that may be asked rather than retain in their possession Confederate money—should show their patriotism, and secure a good interest upon their investments too, by buying Government bonds.

We should rejoice above all things if the vultures who have been buying up sugar, and other necessaries, and holding them for fabulous prices, should be caught by an early peace, and an opening of our ports.

There are such in this as in all other communities, and they will neither have nor deserve to have the sympathy of the people. Let them look out for the collapse that is coming.

"I Shall Press the Rebels to the Wall."

So wrote more than a month ago, the boastful and arrogant commander of the Yankee expedition to Richmond. He did not even intimate the existence of a lingering doubt of the complete success of his plans. Previously, he told his legions that "they had met their *last* reverse they had seen their *last* retreat," and the credulous soldiers of fortune who hung their prospect of pillaging Richmond on the skill and transcendent abilities of the "young Napoleon," believed him. How have these several pledges to his government and to his soldiers been fulfilled?—Instead of "pressing the rebels to the wall" McClellan has encountered a "wall," even Stonewall Jackson; and now so far from pressing towards the "wall" he is running away from it, and taking to the water.—Was ever humiliation greater? Did Divine Providence ever so chasten the pride of man? "Let not him who girdeth on the harness boast himself as he that putteth it off."

It would have been well for McClellan had he remembered the occasion of this utterance, and the fate of the man who having prepared horses and chariots, and armies innumerable, supposed that he could control issues, which are only with the Lord of Hosts. On the Peninsula he has made his grave, and hereafter beside the waters of the Chickahominy may be written *hic jacet* McClellan!

Suspension of Beauregard.

A silly sensation rumor has been put in circulation, to the effect that this universal favorite of the army, and the most fortunate of all our Generals, has been suspended from his command. With what show of reason the authors of such a statement could commend it to the public credulity, we are at a loss to conceive.

It would be a most flagitious act that could justify, in the eyes of the people, the deposition of the hero of Manassas and Shiloh, and the public has heard of nothing of the kind alleged to Beauregard. Even if the statement were true, we should doubt the policy of publishing it at this time. But, there is not a word of truth in it.

By permission of the Secretary of War, Rev. William A. Crocker has established in Richmond that much needed thing an Army Intelligence Depot, where the friends of soldiers can, on application, learn their whereabouts after battle, whether living, wounded, or dead. Mr Crocker will, after each engagement, require a number of assistants to gather up the data on which to furnish the information which it is his duty to give. The clerical force needed is to be in the shape of soldiers unable to perform regular duty in the field. We hope the enterprise may be fruitful of good results.—*Dispatch.*

The March of the Vandals.

The Rockingham *Register* of Friday last gives the following account of Fremont's march in the Valley and the devastation consequence thereon. It says:

We had not the opportunity, last week, to refer particularly and fully, to the numerous outrages perpetrated upon our people by the Lincoln Army, under Fremont, during their very brief stay in Rockingham. They staid but 6 days in the county, yet in that short period the thieving, robbing villians were very busy, and carried off and destroyed hundreds and thousands of dollars worth of property of all kinds. Wherever they went, they were like a dreadful curse that had fallen suddenly upon the country. Their main object in coming to the upper Valley was to "*catch Jackson.*" Hence they pursued a pretty straight line in the wake of our army, which in good order retired before the superior numbers of the lawless, half-civilized horde. Fremont's Army was evidently in a destitute, if not suffering condition, which added to the rapacity of the naturally bad and vicious elements of which it is was mainly composed. The Army under Banks has been represented as "Angels," compared with the Army commanded by Fremont, and, indeed, the comparison is not an inapt and untruthful one. Whatever may be said of the Army under Banks; yet it was admitted that there was some sort of control exercised over their movements, and the majority of their officers seemed to be gentlemen desirous to make a good impression upon our people. But Fremont's Army seemed to care nothing for nobody, and evidently felt at liberty to rob and plunder defenceless end unprotected people at will. Their pathways was everywhere marked with desolation. Indeed, we had no idea that in the short space of six days so much harm could have been done, so many thefts and robberies committed, as signalized the coming in and going out of this last instalment of the Federal Army. A large portion of it was composed of unnaturalized Dutch, many of whom could not speak a word of English. They came like a dreadful swarm of pestiferous blood seeking vampyres, and carried consternation and terror wherever they went.

They came up the line of the McAdamized turnpike from Mt. Jackson, in Shenandoah, and reached Harrisonburg on Friday about 11 o'clock, A. M. Portions of the Army passed through the same evening, and on Sunday morning the main body of the "Grand Army" started to "catch Jackson." The desolated fields on both sides of the road between Harrisonburg and Port Republic look as if the "angle of destruction" had smitten them, whilst the quiet inoffensive country people living on the line of their march all have their tales to tell of the wanton wrongs and robberies perpetrated by this lawless band of half-famished villians.

We have been trying to get a full and accurate statement of the losses sustained by each and all of our fellow citizens; but we have found it impossible to do so. We will commence the list, and continue its publication from week to week until completed.

The most of the robberies in Harrisonburg would properly come under the head of petty larcenies, and were mainly the stealing of something to eat, although we have heard cases in which they stole tools of various kinds, cooking utensils, &c., &c. The most prominent, bare faced and outrageous of their robberies here was the robbery of our new Masonic Hall of its emblems, jewels, character, &c., &c. They broke in, stole whatever of value they could lay their hands on, and slept all night in the hall. Gen. Fremont is or was, we learn, a Mason; yet we heard of no condemnation from his lips of this act of villainy which ought to consign its perpetrators to the State prison.

The *Register* then devotes more than three columns to a minute recital of the thefts and robberies of these scoundrels, giving the names of the parties, including defenceless widows, who were plundered of their beds, plate, linen, and everything that the Hessians could lay their hands upon. The *Register* concludes:

But time and space would fail us to recount all the thefts and robberies committed by them during their stay in Rockingham. They never even offered their worthless receipts for the property they took. They took almost everything, and wantonly destroyed what they could not use or carry away with them. Persons tell us that they could perceive but little difference between officers and privates; they seemed all to be upon a regularly organized plundering expedition in the name of the government and under the protection of the flag of the late United States.

GEN. SHIELDS "KICKED OVERBOARD."

The Washington despatch in the Herald of the 24th, says:

The nomination of Gen. Shields, as Major General, was rejected by the Senate to-day in executive session. It is said there was not a vote in his favor. The testimony adduced before the committee on the conduct of the war, in regard to the battle of Port Republic showed, in the estimation of Senators, that General Shields was either insane or totally incompetent. It is said that many of the officers, medical and military, nearest to the person of General Shields for some time past, have been ready to bear testimony to his insanity. Some Senators call it by a different name, but it was sufficient to cause his rejection as a Major General, and will probably deprive him of any military command whatever.

Debate in the British Parliament on Picayune Butler's Brutal Order.

The following is the debate referred to in the article from the New York *Herald* which was published in our last. It will be seen that in the Lords, Commons, and Press of England, the order is denounced as degrading to the civilization of the age. The English Premier did not hesitate to call it "infamous," which declaration drew cheers from his auditors. Whether the wish expressed by the Ministry, that the Federal Government would disavow the act of Butler, shall be heeded or not, it will not alter the fact that that government has refrained up to this time, from any public disavowal of an act that has provoked the reprobation of the civilized world. Its action will have no more merit than that of the surrender of Mason and Slidell, which was dictated, not by a sense of right, but wrung from them by the force of circumstances, the full effect of which they were not prepared to accept. We append the report of the debate.

In the House of Lords on the 13th of June, Earl Caernavon called attention to General Butler's proclamation relative to the ladies of New Orleans, but condemned it in severe terms, as without precedent in the annals of war, and asked if the government had information of its authenticity, and if it had protested against it. He also asked if there was any truth in the rumors of the mediation of France and England. The success of such policy would depend greatly upon the manner in which, and the time at which it was offered; but trusted the government was in a position to give the subject favourable consideration.

Earl Russell said that, from Lord Lyons' dispatches the government believed the proclamation was authentic; with respect to any action of the United States Government in the way of approval or disapproval they had no information. Lord Lyons had made no representations to the American Government on the subject, and he did not appear to have any official information concerning the proclamation upon which he could do so. For his own part, he (Earl Russell) hoped the American Government would, for its own sake, refuse its sanction to it, and disavow it. The proclamation was important to the whole world. The usages of war should not be aggravated by proclamations of this character. He thought that such proclamation, addressed to a force that had just captured a hostile city, was likely to lead to great brutality. He thought there was no defence for this proclamation, and he sincerely hoped the American Government would disavow it.

In the House of Commons Sir J Walsh made enquiry as to the authenticity of General Butler's proclamation, which he denounced as repugnant to the feelings of the nineteenth century, and moved for any correspondence on the subject.

The London *Post* of June 11 denounces, in the strongest terms, the proclamation of General Butler relative to the ladies of New Orleans. It regards it as the greatest insult that could be offered to the Federal army, and thinks the government is bound to recall General Butler and have him court martialed. Such an act as that of Butler's, says the *Post*, if not promptly disavowed, would soon turn the scale, finally and decisively, in favor of the Confederate cause.

Lord Palmerston thought that no man could read the proclamation without feelings of the deepest indignation. [Cheers] It was a proclamation to which he did not scruple to attach the epithet of infamous. [Cheers.] An Englishman must blush to think such an act had been committed by a man belonging to the Anglo-Saxon race—If it had sprung from some barbarous people not within the pale of civilization one might have regretted it, but would not have been surprised. But that such an order should have been issued by a soldier—by a man who had raised himself to the rank of a general—was a subject not less of astonishment than pain. He could not bring himself to believe that the Government of the United States would not, as soon as they had notice of the order, have stamped it with their censure and condemnation. Her Majesty's Government received a dispatch yesterday from Lord Lyons enclosing a copy of the proclamation of General Beauregard, in which allusion was made to the order of General Butler.—There was no objection to lay the dispatch on the table. With regard to the course that the government might think fit to take, that is a matter for their discussion; but he was persuaded that there was no man in England who would not show the feeling so well expressed by Sir James Walsh and Mr. Gregory

Just Received at Henry J. Abrahams & Bro's,

10 BALES Grenitville 4-4 Sheetings.
15 " Rock Fish 4-4 Sheetings.
15 " Beaver Creek Sheetings.
23 " Georgia Osnaburgs.
12 " Ocmulgee Ducks.
12 " Palmetto Ducks.
7 " Georgia Jeans.
1 Case Organdies.
1 " Jaconet Lawns.
15 Pieces Black Alpaccas.
50 " Berages (for Veils.)
3000 Blocks Yarns.
1000 Doz. Alexander's Spool Thread.
July 1

MADDER, Sup. Car. Soda, Castile Soap, Camphor, Matches, Washing Soap, Porter, Washing Soda, for sale by
july 1 J. H. THOMPSON.

Sulphur.
JUST to hand and for sale by
july 1 J. H. THOMPSON.

More of their Villainy.

A friend, for the truth of whose statements we will vouch, writing to us from Surry C. H., gives the following account of the depredations of the enemy in that section. Truly, the people of Virginia will have cause to remember for many a long year to come, the army of marauders whom Lincoln has sent amongst them for the purpose of winning them back to the Union. How we shall be able to tolerate a Yankee amongst us when the war comes to a close, it is difficult to imagine now. Let our people remember their wrongs and never more dream of resuming intercourse of any kind with them. Our friend says:

The general feature in this section, connecting us with the war, is the stampede of negroes. From some farms, especially about Suffolk, and Smithfield, all the hands have gone. I am informed that Maj. Wm. Allen on Jas. River has lost 300. Much grain has to be lost, I fear for want of hands to reap it. In some instances farmer's after losing some hands have removed the rest leaving their harvest to perish. Negroes in some instances who have refused to go voluntarily have been forced off. I know a gentleman whose negro man was carried at the point of the bayonet after having had the bayonet put beneath his skin. I have heard of several well authenticated cases of force. This is at present a greatly afflicted section; it is so mostly on account of the depredations of marauding parties consisting of white men and negroes both, armed and making their visits at night. A man lies down at night with the prospect of a living, but wakes up in the morning to find his slaves all off and none to work his crop. Even the free negroes go off. Some rascal put a report into very general circulation among the negroes, that Gov. Letcher had ordered all the blacks both slaves and free to be handcuffed and carried South. We have reason to believe that this caused not a few of both free and slave to go off.

THE SICK FROM THE YANKEE ARMY

There is an immense deal of sickness in McClellan's army. It is so great, indeed, that the North is alarmed at it. The following paragraph, from the Washington correspondence of a Northern paper, shows that the Yankee heart even, has been touched by the distressing and harrowing scene:

The hospitals are everywhere crowded with the sick and wounded of our own intrepid soldiers. Ambulances are are slowly driving from the wharves to the hospitals, filled with brave fellows, whose emaciated and sorrowful appearances, as they are seen reclining on their hard couches, call forth from every heard capable of feeling a most intense anxiety for their restoration to health, and a sincere prayer that soon the Almighty God will stretch His hand over the devastating horrors of the battle field, and proclaim "peace and good will" throughout the length and breadth of our unhappy land.

Just Received at H. J. ABRAHAMS & BRO.,

50 PIECES Plain Swiss Muslins.
100 Dresses Embroidered Muslins.
40 Pieces Esmarelda Muslins.
4 " Plain Black Silk.
80 Dresses Fancy Silks.
2000 Yards Cambric and Swiss.
Edgings and Insertings.
500 Fans, all of which will be sold exceedingly cheap for the times.
July 1

Porter.
300 DOZ. HIBBARD'S BEST LONDON PORTER for invalids. For sale by
July 1 J. H. THOMPSON.

Castor Oil.
JUST to hand and for sale by
J. H. THOMPSON,
July 1 Druggist.

Madder.
A SMALL lot of MADDER for sale by
J. H. THOMPSON.
July 1

LABORERS WANTED.
CONFEDERATE STATES OF AMERICA, WAR DEP'T ENGINEER BUREAU, Richmond, Va., June 24, 1862.
THE prompt repair of the injury done to the James River and Kanawha Canal by the late freshet being a matter of great public importance, the Government of the Confederate States wishes to employ
FIVE HUNDRED HANDS
to work upon the Canal near Lynchburg, for which the highest price will be paid in cash.
Persons having hands to hire will send them to the agents of the James River and Kanawha Company at Lynchburg or Richmond.
Albert Michaels, Elias L Chinn and James M. Harris are authorized to hire hands in the name of the Government, and any contracts made by them, or either of them, will be fulfilled.
By order of the Secretary of War.
A. L. RIVES,
Acting Chief Engineer Bureau C. S. A.
The undersigned earnestly appeals to all who feel an interest in the Canal to aid in accomplishing the object indicated by the above advertisement. If farmers and others will hire their hands even for a few days, they will render a valuable service to the public at this time; and they may confidently rely upon the work being finished to return them on any particular day they may name.
THOMAS H. ELLIS,
President of the J. R. & K. Co.
June 27-dec1w

MILITARY NOTICE.
ALL the men within the bounds of the 91st Regiment, between the ages of thirty five and forty-five, including those who have been exempt, and also those who have furnished substitutes, are required to assemble at Watkin's Shop, on the 3d day of July, 1862, for the purpose of being organized into companies.
By command of Wm. H. Richardson, Adj't Gen.
RO. W. CALLAWAY,
Major Commanding 91st Reg't.
P. S.—All persons between the ages of eighteen and thirty-five are required to meet at the same place and time above mentioned. By command.
RO. W. CALLAWAY,
Major Commanding 91st Reg't.
je 21-d3july
Republican copy.

40 HHDS. PRIME TO CHOICE N. O. SUGAR on consignment and for sale by
LEE, ROCKE & TAYLOR,
june 18 105, Main st.

AUCTION SALES.
THIS DAY.
By B. AKERS, AUCTIONEER.

Negroes at Auction.
I WILL sell on Tuesday morning, July 1st, at half-past 9 o'clock, a NEGRO MAN about twenty-eight years old, also a GIRL about sixteen
Terms cash. B. AKERS, Auct'r.
July 1-1t

FUTURE DAY.

Valuable Real Estate AT AUCTION.
AS Executor of D. Staples, dec'd, I will sell to the highest bidder, on Wednesday, the 2nd July, 1862, the real estate of said decedent, consisting of the Store House now occupied by Messrs. Bocock & Parrish, in Lynchburg, a farm of 80 acres land, with good dwelling, (late residence of dec'd.) near the city where place (now occupied by Col. H. Rucker,) adjoining the farm, containing 4 acres land.
Sale to commence at 4 o'clock, P. M.
Sale to take place in front of Bocock and Parrish, Bridge street.
Terms liberal and made known on day of sale. D. S. STAPLES, Executor.
B. AKERS, Auctioneer.
je 26 tds

LONGSTREET'S DIVISION, RIGHT WING, HEADQUARTERS 1ST BRIGADE, June 20th, 1862.
WAR DEPARTMENT, ADJ'T AND INSP. GEN'S OFFICE, Richmond, June 18, 1862.
GENERAL ORDERS No. 43.
I. WITH the consent and approbation of his Excellency Governor Letcher, all Sheriffs, Deputy Sheriffs and Constables of the State of Virginia are authorized and requested to apprehend deserters from the army, wherever they may be found, and to deliver them to the officer of the army at the most convenient post or station, or to lodge them in jail and report their names and Regiments to General S COOPER, Adjutant and Inspector General, Richmond.
Thirty dollars will be paid for each deserter delivered to an officer, and fifteen dollars for each deserter lodged in jail. No allowance will be made for expenses of apprehension or transportation.
All jailors receiving deserters are requested to detain them. The usual allowance for the support of prisoners will be made.
II. Transfers from the line to Partizan corps will not be permitted, and if any officer of Partizan corps knowingly enlist men from the line, the authority to raise the Partizan corps will be revoked, in addition to such punishment as a Court Martial may inflict.
By command of the Secretary of War.
(Signed) S. COOPER,
je 25-1w Adj't and Inspt Gen'l.
The attention of all absentees from the 11th Virginia Regiment is called to the above advertisement of one week. All absentees will report immediately to Lieut William S. Thayer, Co. H, 11th Virginia Regiment. A list of the wounded has been furnished. Those claiming to be sick will be required to furnish a Surgeon's certificate to the date they report to Lieutenant Thayer. Those failing so to do or failing to report to Lieutenant Thayer at John B. Shaner's, will be published and dealt with according to law.
K. OTEY, Capt., Commanding 11th Va. Reg't.
J. L. KEMPER, Brig. Gen. Commanding, 1st Brigade. Je 25-1w

LEE, ROCKE & TAYLOR,
WHOLESALE AND RETAIL
Grocers, Commission and Forwarding Merchants,
(At the Old Stand of Lee, Rocke & Co.)
No. 105 Main Street, Lynchburg, Virginia
WILL pay particular and prompt attention to the sale of Tobacco, Wheat, Corn, Bacon, Lard, Butter, Feathers and Country Produce generally; make liberal advances on produce or merchandise in hand for sale; guarantee and cash time sales when required; attend promptly to goods consigned to be forwarded; have always on hand a large and well selected stock of Groceries Imported and Domestic Liquors, Wines, &c., &c.
Grain Bags furnished at the usual rent when produce is consigned to us.

ALLEGHANY SPRINGS, MONTGOMERY CO., VA.
THE great number of applications for board has induced the Proprietors to open this place.—It will be kept in as good style as the circumstances of the country will admit.
Passengers will leave the train at Shawsville Station—omnibuses will be in waiting to convey them 3½ miles to the Springs.
Visitors will be received from this date.
Board per week for 4 weeks and over........$12 50
" under 4 weeks and over.......... 14 00
je12-1m BOOTH, COLHOUN & CO.

GENERAL NEWSPAPER ADVERTISING AGENCY.
THE SUBSCRIBER still continues his *Advertising Agency* at the VIRGINIAN OFFICE, where he may be found at all times, ready and willing to wait on his friends and the public. I am Agent for all the newspapers on the Railroad from Lynchburg, Va., to Chattanooga, Tenn., and will receive and forward advertisements to any paper in the *Southern Confederacy* with the utmost dispatch.
Dull times is the time for advertising, in order to keep up a brisk business.
A. WADDILL, Foreman Virginian Office.

Lost.
ON the 2nd of June, in the battle at Port Republic, my FREE PAPERS, issued by the County Court of Campbell about May 1856, at which time I was employed at the factory of Mr. P. Preston, dec'd I am hired by Capt. Terry, of the 7th Louisiana Regiment, and will pay a liberal reward for their recovery.
je 24-4w4 WILLIAM GEORGE.

Surgeon's Instruments Lost.
LOST on Monday evening last, between the Norvell House and the Claytor Hospital, a CASE OF SURGICAL INSTRUMENTS, marked P. J. H. The finder will be suitably rewarded by leaving them at the Virginian Office.
P. J. HALE, Ass't Surgeon Claytor Hospital.
June 18-dts

For Sale.
A FAMILY OF VALUABLE NEGROES. Apply to JAS. A. STIGLER,
je 25 dts No. 100, ... street.

Farm for Rent on James River.
I OFFER for rent the TRACT OF LAND in Amherst County, now occupied by Hiram Kyle. This tract of land lies on James River, about 14 miles below Lynchburg.
Je 26 d4t&3t G. W. WARWICK.

$5.00 REWARD.
ESCAPED from its cage, on Saturday, a DARK COLORED CANARY BIRD. The above reward will be paid for its delivery at this office.
Je 24 ts

ALL members of the Latham Battery who are absent without leave, or whose furloughs have expired, are required to meet me forthwith at S. B. Thurman's store, 120 Main street, Lynchburg, Va., or they will be published as deserters.
By order of Capt. Dearing.
June 20-ts Lt. JOS. L. THOMPSON.

50 BAGS PRIME CUBA COFFEE on consignment.
apr 15 LEE, ROCKE & TAYLOR.

LOCAL AND STATE NEWS.

Some fifty or sixty Yankee prisoners were brought to this place from the West yesterday.

COL. ROBERT E. WITHERS.—We rejoice to hear that this gentleman who though wounded in the arm, stomach, and thigh severely, may recover. We saw a dispatch yesterday from Mr. Gwatkin, with whom he is staying, says the Surgeons have strong hopes of him. Mrs. Withers is with him.

FOURTH OF JULY.—Taking it for granted that we of the South, who only, are true to the doctrines of the father's of the Revolution, and maintain the right of every people to choose their own form of government, will observe "Independence Day" in all future time—we cannot think of a better means to signalize the coming anniversary than to open our Churches in the morning, and gathering there, humbly and devoutly return thanks to Almighty God for the great deliverance he has recently vouchsafed us. What say the christian people of Lynchburg?

THE LATE COL. J. G. SEYMOUR.—The remains of this lamented officer who fell in the engagement of Friday last, will be here for temporary interment, in Spring Hill Cemetary, this afternoon. The remains will be carried from the cars immediately to the grave.

We knew Col. Seymour. He was an accomplished gentleman and a man of great moral worth. A Georgian by birth, he lived in New Orleans and conducted the *Commercial Bulletin* for many years, indeed up to the time he went into the service as commander of the 6th Louisiana Regiment

Col. Seymour served his country in the Florida and Mexican wars; was far advanced in life; of venerable appearance, and, we always thought, bore a strong resemblance to the late President Taylor.

We trust that our citizens will pay the respect due to his exalted worth.

OBITUARY.

It is indeed sad, day after day, to see friends, claiming space in your columns to say to the world, *another* brave one gone; another loved one snatched from a fond family to the cold embrace of death. How much more fully than ever do we feel the force of those touching lines—

"Friend after friend departs,
Who hath not lost a friend?"

And who indeed has been spared in this general wrecking of hopes, and breaking up of home circles? Can we not look around and receive our answers from sad pale faces and sable garments? This community has been called upon to pass through deep waters. A McKinney, a Meem and many other gallant spirits, who, from childhood, have been in our midst, have fallen—their lives a sacrifice to their country. And while memory wanders over the names of the departed brave, the heart dwells fondly on that of Lieut. John H Didlake.

He was born in Lynchburg, Oct. 24th, 1834, where he lived, was loved and respected, until September, 1859, when he left friends and home to seek his fortune in the city of New Orleans. There, by his skill and attention, he was rapidly rising in business, when the tocsin of war called him to the defence of his mother State. Nobly and quickly did he respond. Not ambitious of office, he entered the service as a private, but for gallantry was readily promoted to the rank of 1st Lieutenant. As a soldier and officer he had no superior: strict in his attention to duty, ever at his post.

On the 9th of June he roused himself from his sick bed to rush into battle, and the missile of death that laid him with the early dead, found him hat and sword in hand cheering his men, bidding them "never give up—conquer or die." He was a respectful, obedient son, devoted brother, warm, unchanging friend. His bright, quick mind, peculiarly delicate sense of honor, and social generous disposition rendered him a favorite with all who knew him. His manly face was a true index of his heart, and spoke at a glance of truth, sincerity, gentleness and unsurpassed courage. How painful to feel that such a heart lies still and cold, never more to throb tenderly with love for friends and home on earth, high with solemn and proud hope at the sound of battle. "He being dead yet speaketh" in clarion tones, urging his comrades to deeds of daring. His memory shall live, loved and cherished in the hearts of sisters, brothers and friends, until another call shall summon all, not to war, but to peace, there to meet our heroes where the din of battle shall no more be heard, telling of shattered hopes and bleeding hearts. A.

BY TELEGRAPH.

LATEST FROM THE GREAT BATTLE.

Immense Number of Stores Destroyed!

3,000 ADDITIONAL PRISONERS CAPTURED.

THE BATTLE YET RAGING!

The Yankee Gunboats Defeated.

&c., &c., &c.

Richmond, June 29.—Only a few brigades of the attacking column of Confederate army were engaged yesterday. Magruder's and Hugers Divisions were still held in reserve on the west side of the Chickahominy, where it was understood that McClellan was yesterday massing large bodies of troops.

A renewal of the conflict was expected this morning.

Two regiments of Magruders Division, the 7th and 8th Georgia, suffered severely yesterday in attempting to take a battery near Seven Pines, defended by at least two brigades of yankees.

Col. Lamar of the 8th was wounded and taken prisoner.

Lieut. Col. White of the 7th wounded in the neck.

The casualties of the two regiments was about 200.

There seems to be no doubt that McClellan's communication with his source of supplies is effectually cut off.

SECOND DISPATCH.

RICHMOND, June 29.

From the latest reports there has been no fighting to-day up to 11 o'clock.

Our army was then in line of battle, and it was expected would soon advance upon the enemy.

The anxiety to hear from the battle field is intense, though everybody is confident of a decisive victory

The citizens are rigidly excluded from the lines, and reliable information of the progress of events is very difficult to obtain.

THIRD DISPATCH.

SUNDAY NIGHT, 29th.

The remnant of McClellan's army is now on this side of the Chickahominy.

The bridges were destroyed to prevent pursuit from the Confederates on the North.

It is believed here that McClellan is retreating towards the Jim River, where his troops may embark in gunboats under protection of their gunboats.

All the latest reports from the lines give this information, and state that our army was pursuing the enemy and hope to capture many of them before night.

FOURTH DISPATCH.

RICHMOND, June 30.

Yesterday afternoon McClellan destroyed immense quantities of stores of every description, abandoned all his fortifications preparatory to retreat towards James River, which was commenced last night through White Oak Swamp.

The Yankees have been closely followed by our troops, and hundreds of prisoners have been taken

It is confidently expected that the greater portion of the fugitives will be intercepted and captured before night.

Stuart's cavalry captured three thousand Yankees yesterday, who were trying to escape to York River.

FIFTH DISPATCH.

RICHMOND, June 30.

The attack upon the Yankee fortifications at Ellyson's Mills, on Friday, was made by the 44th and 48th Georgia and 2d and 3d North Carolina.

The 44th and 3d suffered extremely.

The 19th Mississippi went into the fight with 521, had 31 killed and 150 wounded, the 2d Miss. Battalion had 30 killed and wounded, 2d Miss regiment 19 killed and 71 wounded, the 11th Miss. 16 killed, 144 wounded, 7 missing, the 6th N. C 4 killed 43 wounded, 4th Alabama 23 killed, 104 wounded, 8 missing.

SIXTH DISPATCH.

RICHMOND, June 30.

Reports from the lines are somewhat conflicting. A majority of the sentiment today is that our army had hemmed the Yankees in and that the greater portion of them would be captured before night.—The dearth of information from the lines to-day has been remarkable and no news whatever could be obtained from the War Department.

Several hundred prisoners, captured by Gen. Stuart, passed through the city this evening.

SEVENTH DISPATCH.

RICHMOND, June 35.

A courier arrived from Bermuda Hundreds this afternoon at 6 o'clock and reported that a portion of the Federals have been driven to the river where, under cover of their gunboats they are endeavoring to embark.

Four transports have passed down the river heavily loaded. Our field pieces on the Chesterfield side engaged their gunboats and poured a galling fire into them. Their gunboats dropped down to Turkey Island and were followed by our field pieces.

The enemy are fleeing down the river bank hotly pursued by our troops and were falling thick and fast,

At last accounts the firing was incessant.

Yankee Fleet Approaching Vicksburg.

&c., &c.

AUGUSTA, June 28.

The Mobile Evening News of the 26th has a dispatch dated Vicksburg 25th which says:

All Farragut's Fleet are in sight below, also twelve transports of the Davis fleet from above are visible near the mouth of Yazoo River.

A fight occurred yesterday between Grand Gulf and Port Gibson, 20 yankees were killed.

No casualties on our side.

British Steamer in Charleston Harbor.

&c., &c.

CHARLESTON, June 28.

The British Steamship Racer instead of lying outside the bar as usual when she comes here, this evening entered the harbor and now lies anchored at the wharves.

It is reported that a French War Steamer is also expected.

The community are much mistified at this unusual feat.

Latest Northern News.

RICHMOND, June 31.

The New York Herald of the 26th has been received.

In the fight of *Wednesday* Hookers division with Hentzlemans corps, supported by Gen. Keys were engaged.

McClellan in his dispatches to Stanton says:

It was not a battle but that the advantage sought was fully attained with little loss though the enemy resisted stubbornly.

The Herald says the feud in the Republican party of New York state is daily increasing in extent and bitterness.

Gold advanced to 108½. The demand for gold from Bankers who are remitting to Europe proceeds of American stock sold for European account—is in excess of supply. Cotton market excited, with an advance of 2½ to 3 cents per pound.

From Mississippi.

GRENEDA, Miss., June 27.—A courier from Gen. Villepigue's camp, who arrived to night, reports that Jackson's Cavalry made a dash yesterday, on the Memphis and Charleston Railroad, burnt the bridge, eleven miles from Memphis, and captured seventeen cars laden with commissary and quartermaster's stores, and over forty officers connected with those departments.

The Great Battle.

The *Enquirer* says:

Our Generals having disconcerted the enemy's centre, and the latter seeing no earthly chance for themselves, so completely were they hemmed in, it is said, immediately made for their gunboats on the Pamunkey, but, to their utter surprise and horror, found themselves outflanked by the indomitable Jackson and his brave army. They then re-crossed the swamp in the wildest confusion, and fled towards their gunboats on the James River, closely followed by Jackson, Hill and Longstreet, who expected to overtake McClellan and his half of the army Saturday night or early Sunday morning.

The other half of the Federal army is reported as completely surrounded by our troops. Magruder in front, Holmes on their right, and "Bethel" Hill and other Generals in their rear. It was expected that all of these Generals would move against the enemy at an early hour Sunday morning, while those of our troops in their rear will probably advance upon the enemy towards Richmond. The enemy was, on Saturday, busily employed in strengthening his fortifications, both in front and rear, so as to resist, if possible, the combined assaults of our forces—their rear being at the time totally unprepared to meet any vigorous attack.

Important From Europe.

The Arabia has arrived at Halifax with later and highly interesting news from Europe. The Paris correspondent of the London Daily "News" says it is affirmed that France has determined to ask England to join in meditation, which would be refused just at this juncture.

Other correspondents speak as if France was already assured of the co-operation of England in her schemes for intervention. It says that after two discussions in the French ministerial councils, one of which was held yesterday, within a few hour's of the Emperor's department for Fontainbleau, meditation was resolved upon, and that simultaneous propositions should be made by England and France at Richmond and Washington, and that in case of their refusal, either by the North or South the two Powers will impose peace upon the belligerents by force of arms.

COMMERCIAL.

LYNCHBURG MARKETS,

REPORTED BY

A. B. RUCKER, PRODUCE BROKER.

133 MAIN STREET.

These quotations, it will be understood. represent wholesale prices generally.

APPLES.—Green—none offering.

BACON.—Continues to arrive slowly, with sales 28 to 30c.

BEESWAX.—Receipts continue light, with sales 30 @32c.

BUTTER.—Choice for table scarce and sells readily in packages suited for shipping at 55@62½c Cooking 40@50c.

CORN MEAL—Stock light——$1.00 to 1.05

CORN—Receipts light. Last sales at $1.00.

CLOVER SEED.—$12 to 12.50.

FRUIT—Dried Apples $1 50 to $1.75 per bushel—28 pounds; Unpealed Peaches $2.40 to $2.75 per bushel—33 pounds; Pealed Peaches $4.50 to $5 per bushel—40 pounds.

FLOUR.—With light receipts. Superfine $7 to 7.25; Extra $7.30 to 7 75; Family $8 to 8.25.

FLAXSEED.—The demand for sewing has increased the demand. Sales $1.75 to 1.80.

FEATHERS.—Dull and plenty—34 to 37 cents.

GRASS SEED—The large receipts of Clover has caused a considerable decline. I notice sales at $14 to $15; Timothy $4 to $4 50; Orchard $1.75 to $2.00; Evergreen $1.75 to $2.00; Randal $1.75 to $2.00; Herds $1.50.

HAY—Baled $1.40 to $1.50; per wagon load $1.25 to 1.35.

LIME—Mountain $2 to $2.25.

IRON—With increased demand, I notice sales $175 to 185 per ton.

LARD—Demand good—21@22c.

ONIONS—Stock light—$2.75 to $3 per bushel.

OATS—Sheaf $1.40 to 1.50 ℔ wagon load; Shelled—70c. for White; 75 cts. for Black per bushel 33 pounds.

TOBACCO—Sales continue light, but prices are well maintained. Lugs $2 to $4.50; Leaf $5 to 8.50 for good shipping; Manufacturing $8 to $15.

WHEAT.—$1.30 to 1.35 for Red; $1.35 to 1.40 for choice White.

Lynchb'g Virginian.

Thursday,....................July 3, 1862.

The Price of our Liberties.

We cannot hear of the progress of our victorious troops; of the valor and prowess displayed in charging heavy batteries, and in dashing upon the serried columns of the enemy, without thinking of the cost in blood and carnage to ourselves. And these reflections repress that exultation we should otherwise feel. If none but the invaders of our soil, the men who come here for the purpose of fastening upon us a tyranny which we despise; or for the still more ignoble purpose of plundering our people, should be made to bite the dust, we might feel none other than emotions of delight. We should feel that they had rushed upon a fate which was well merited, and were not deserving of our sympathy. But the case is different, for the pathway of our noble troops as they press on to victory, is through the blood of their own brave comrades. Every proud achievement of theirs carries sorrow to many a Southern household, and points a spear that must anguish in stricken hearts till this generation shall have passed away. The wise, the noble, the true, the brave, the good,—the young men, who are the hope of the country, are the price, the costly price of our victories.

The monarch of Israel rejoices that his throne is established by the overthrow of its enemies, but the heart of the parent mourns even an erring son, by whose death the peace of his kingdom is secured. Nature will be true to herself, and we cannot help feeling sad when we reflect upon the loss to the country and to families, of so much that is manly and excellent. This tempers our joy with grief, and should prompt us to mingle our tears with those who are now being so sorely bereaved.

A wail of anguish is going up all over this land from those who have given their best beloved ones to the country, to be slain in the most unjust war that was ever waged upon any people. Over their gory remains let us vow that the people who have brought this evil upon us, can never again sustain to us any other relations than those of alien enemies.

Old Abe Makes a Speech.

We alluded yesterday to the fact that Lincoln had gone on a "tower" to General Scott. It appears that when he visited the hoary old Virginia traitor, he acknowledged that he had come to have "a confab." In the speech which he made on his return to Jersey City, he assured his devoted admirers that he was not intent upon "making or unmaking any generals now in the army." He had not however then heard of McClellan's failure before Richmond, and that unexpected result may require a new arrangements of the commands. We are little concerned to know Abraham's pleasure in the premises, and only publish the speech that others may see how "the animal is viewed through a fog." That such a speech as this could have called forth plaudits from a Northern audience, only indicates the extent to which the national taste has been vitiated and debased, by the coarse jester and buffoon who essays to offer his pointless wit and vulgar nonsense to the people.

The Yankees Reinforced.

From the Petersburg *Express* of yesterday we have positive information that the enemy were reinforced yesterday from below. We know not the extent of the reinforcements, but the "Vanderbilt," a very large transport, was certainly in the lower James yesterday, crowded with troops.—More reinforcements were probably carried up last night. The immense train of wagons seen yesterday at Berkley, are to be used, no doubt, for the purpose of carrying ammunition and provisions to the now much discomfitted foe. It is gratifying to know that we are prepared to meet these reinforcements with fresh troops, man for man.

From the N. O. Picayune.

HOW GEN BUTLER MAKES MEN CONVICT THEMSELVES.

Gen. Butler learned the other night of a conspiracy between six men, French and Spanish creoles, to take his life. Next morning four of them were arrested and brought before Gen. Butler. They protested their innocence; but they were ordered to be chained together until they should conclude to divulge the secrets of the conspiracy.

REJECTED RECRUITS.

At a late inspection of a camp at Lynfield, Massachusetts, two fifth of the recruits were rejected as being disqualified by their youthfulness or age, small size, or want of powers of endurance for the service.

The Late Operations.

From the Richmond Enquirer of Tuesday:

The complex character of the movements of Confederate army, for three days preceding the great victory of last Friday, renders a discription very difficult for readers not familiar with the country embraced. We shall attempt to describe them as clearly as we can. On Thursday at three o'clock Major General Jackson took up his line of march from Ashland, and proceeding down the country between the Chickahominy and Pamunkey rivers, he uncovered the front of Brig. Gen. Branch by driving off the enemy collected on the North bank of the Chickahominy river, at the point where it is crossed by the Brook Turnpike; General Branch, who was on the South bank, then crossed the river and wheeled to the right, down its Northern bank. Proceeding in that direction, General Branch, in like manner, uncovered, at Meadow Bridge, the front of Maj. Gen. A. P. Hill, who immediately crossed. The three columns now protected *en echelon*—Gen Jackson in advance, and on the extreme left, Brig. Gen. Branch (who was now merged with Gen. A. P. Hill on the right, immediately on the river, Jackson, bearing away from the Chickahominy in this part of the march, so as to gain ground towards the Pamunkey, marched to the left of Mechanicsville, while Gen. Hill, keeping well to the Chickahominy, approached that village and engaged the enemy there. The military talent exhibited by Gen. Hill in this approach and assault, is worthy of great commendation, and has won imperishable honors for that gallant young officer, while the courage, ardor, and firmness of his officers and men in the assault of the enemy's earth works at Elleyson's Mill, have reflected the greatest glory upon the Confederate army. Driven from the immediate locality of Mechanicsville, the enemy retreated during the night down the river to Powhite Swamp, and night closed the operations of Thursday.

As soon as General Hill cleared the road at Mechanicsville, General Longstreet's *corps d'armee*, consisting of his veteran division of the Old Guard of the Army of the Potomac, and General D. H. Hill's division, debouched from the woods on the South side of the Chickahominy, and crossed the river at Mechanicsville. The position of our army on Friday night may be described as forming, with the Chickahominy, an acute angle; our left still in advance under General Jackson, lying over towards the Pamunkey; General Hill occupying Mechanicsville and the centre, and General Longstreet with General D H Hill, composing our right, lying immediately along the Chickahominy.

Tuesday morning the general advance *en schelon* again began; General Jackson in advance and far to the left, gradually converging to the Chickahominy again; General A. P. Hill in the centre, and bearing towards new Coal Harbor; General Longstreet and Gen. D. H. Hill, coming down the Chickahominy to New Bridge. Arrived at Hogan's House, near New Bridge, Gen. Lee awaited the consummation of his magnificent strategy—courier after courier arrived informing him of the approach of each division. As soon as Jackson's arrival at Coal Harbor was announced Gen. Lee and Gen. Longstreet, accompanied by their respective staffs, rode by Gaines' Mill and halted at New Coal Harbor—here they joined Gen. A. P. Hill. Soon the welcome sound of Jackson's guns announced his arrival and that he had begun.

The enemy now occupied a singular position; one portion of his army on the outside of the Chickahominy, fronted Richmond, and was confronted by Gen. Magruder—the other portion on the north side had turned their backs on Richmond, and fronted destruction in the persons of Lee, Longstreet, Jackson and the Hill's.

These last were therefore advancing on Richmond with their backs to the city, such was the position in to which General Lee had forced McClellan. The position which the latter here occupied, however, was one of great strength.

The operations of our army since Sunday morning have been principally on the Richmond side of the Chickahominy; on Sunday, however, Jackson commanded Bottom's Bridge and though unable to cross it because it was under range of the guns of the enemy, he prevented its use by the enemy while he built himself another a mile above, where he crossed his army to the South side on Sunday evening, leaving General Stuart's cavalry on the North side.

The retreat which began from the North side on Friday night, on yesterday changed into a flight; and the *foot races* of the armies of the Potomac are now being run down towards the James River, through Charles City. The position of the armies at the time of writing this, owing to McClellan's "rapid movements and brilliant strategy" may be designated as decidedly shifting; indeed "dissolving views" are the principal parts of the flying Federal panorama.

The result of the conflict thus far is a splendid tribute to the capacity of our Commanding General Robert E. Lee. Henceforth his name is as immortal as history can make a man. The facts when analyzed, as we hope soon to be better able to do, will display a combination of strategy, prudence, vigor and sagacity in planning the attack, that have rarely been equalled in the history of military operation. We are proud of the pure patriot and modest general who has thus unhorsed the boasted "Young Napoleon."

Jackson having begun the contest, it was taken up by General A. P. Hill in the center and by D. H. Hill on the left; Longstreet in reserve, supported immediately the centre under General A. P. Hill. From the beginning of the conflict Jackson pressed up and D. H. Hill down the Chickahominy. Our wings were thus approaching each other, while our centre was driving the enemy back upon the river. From 4 o'clock until eight the battle raged with a display of the utmost daring and intrepidity on the part of the Confederate army. The enemy's lines were finally broken and his strong positions all carried, and night covered the retreat of McClellan's broken and routed colums to the south side of the Chickahominy. This retreat to the Richmond side of the river was continued through Friday night, and the morning of Saturday. Closely watched and pressed by our army, he held his fortified camp on the south side of the Chickahominy during Saturday, but evacuated it during the night, and resumed his retreat, taking direction towards James River.

Lincoln's Speech at Jersey City.

My warm Union loving friends of New Jersey:

It is not the first time I have been honored with your cordial welcome in this very place; and I have only to warmly thank you for your present recognition of me, although I had hoped that I should have passed unnoticed. (Loud cheers.) I admire not only your generosity as citizens, and your strong attachment to the Union, but I also notice with much pleasure the gallantry and daring bravery of your noble troops on the battle field, both officers and men: (Great applause.)—When animals and birds are viewed through a fog they cannot be seen to advantage. You may all feel anxious to know about my flying visit to West Point to see General Scott; but I am sure you will feel satisfied when I tell you that it was not to make or unmake any generals now in the army. (Great cheering.) The Secretary of War has put an injunction on the press, lest it might tell more than is requisite, and if I were to give you too much information he might bear a tight rain on myself. (Great laughter and cheers.) My time is nessessarily limited, and as I see the cars in readiness, I hope you will permit me to conclude for the present by again thanking you for the reception I have received in your city. (Bursts of applause)

Three cheers having been called for Gen. Scott, who was present, they were warmly accorded, and the veteran bowed his acknowledgments.

FUNERAL NOTICES.

The funeral services of the late J. Kirk Seabury will take place from the 2nd Presbyterian Church this afternoon at 3 o'clock. The Rev. R. B. Thompson, D. D. will officiate.

The friends of the family are invited to attend.

The funeral of Orderly Sergeant John F. Mitchell, late of Co, A. 11th Va. Regiment, will take place from the residence of his father, (corner of Madison and 5th sts,) this morning at 9 o'clock.

Members of the Rifle Grays in the city are earnestly invited, as also the friends and acquaintances of the family.

The funeral of the late Col. L. G. Seymour will take place this morning at 11 o'clock, from the Va. & Tenn., Railroad Depot. The remains will be interred in Spring Hill Cemetary.

The Funeral Services of Hamy James infant son of Major S. T. Peters, will take place this morning, at the residence of his Father on Harrison Street, at 10 o'clock A. M. The friends and acquaintances are invited to attend.

THE NEWS.

MOVEMENTS BEFORE RICHMOND.

A DESPERATE BATTLE ON MONDAY EVENING AND YESTERDAY.

THE FEDERAL ARMY DEMORALIZED.

McCLELLAN'S SPEECH TO HIS ARMY.

Latest from the Lines of the Enemy's Retreat.

Dispatch from President Davis.

News from the line of operations, now 12 miles from the city, came up early yesterday morning, giving accounts of a desperate battle near White Oak swamp, on Monday evening, between Longstreet's command and the enemy. The latter, having found themselves hemmed in on all sides, and being provided with but a limited supply of stores and ammunition, attempted the hazardous expedient of fighting their way through. The battle raged fearfully for some hours, and the losses on both sides were very heavy. Among the killed, was Lieut. Col. Joseph V. Scott, of the 3d Va. Regiment, whose remains were brought to the city on yesterday, to be sent to Petersburg, the late home of the gallant officer, to-day. Many others fell in the engagement, but the enemy was finally driven back. Many prisoners were taken, and among them Maj. Gen. McCall Two other Generals were also captured, according to the account of a courier from the scene of operations.

Yesterday morning, the enemy made another desperate attempt to escape by way of the Quaker Road to James River, but were signally defeated. Officers who arrived yesterday afternoon, and reported the progress of affairs at headquarters brought information of the utter demoralization of the Federal army, adding that "it has gone to pieces," also that a large number of prisoners had been and were being taken at the time of their departure. To secure the *debris* of the army was the work then in progress.

This intelligence gives, in brief, a view of the events which transpired on yesterday. Details of the battle reached us in a disconnected form, all, however, tending to substantiate the above, and recounting a number of splendid movements, which add laurels to the chaplets already won by our invincible troops.

President Davis was on the field during the day, and made a narrow escape, we understand, from injury, which might possibly have proven fatal. He had taken position in a house near the scene, when word was sent him by Gen. Lee to leave it at once, as it was threatened with danger. He had scarcely complied with the advice before the house was literally riddled with shell from the enemy's batteries.

Prisoners state that on Monday evening McClellan addressed his troops in an animated strain, conjuring them, "for God's sake and the sake of their country and the old flag around which so many fond recollections clustered, to join in one more last struggle to reach our gunboats on the James river. I have been frustrated in all my plans against Richmond. We must cut our way to the river, and then I shall await reinforcements. I do not give up the hope of yet capturing Richmond." Their fighting subsequently showed that his words were not without effect, though eventually to little purpose.

Late yesterday evening, the enemy's gunboats opened in the direction of our position, but without any material results. Heavy firing occurred in the vicinity of Drury's Bluff and gave rise to many foolish rumors.

STILL LATER.

A severe battle took place yesterday afternoon, about sixteen miles from Richmond, and one mile to the right of the Charles City road. The artillery practice was very brisk for some hours, commencing at an early hour in the afternoon. A little before seven o'clock the infantry opened in full volley, and a wide-extended and terrific fire, mingled with the roar of artillery, raged until nine o'clock. A very heavy battle has obviously been fought—About nine o'clock a large conflagration lit up the horizon in the direction of the battle field. We regard this as the sign of victory to our side, for the enemy have invariably destroyed their stores when compelled to retreat. We understand that Huger's division had an important position in the fight, though he was supported by many other troops.

The *bulk* of McClellan's army is evidently in the position indicated by the battle of yesterday afternoon. We think, therefore, there is every probability of our capturing a very large portion of it. The country is one of the worst in the world for military operations, being almost all of it in dense wood, and a large part of it in swamp—The chief trouble is to *find* the enemy, and the larger part of several days has been consumed in the hunt. We must therefore be patient. A prisoner taken yesterday says the soldiers regard themselves as "bagged." We think they are not far from the truth.—*Enquirer of yesterday.*

It appears from such information as we were able to obtain at a late hour last night that our forces leading in the pursuit—Jackson's and Huger's divisions—came up with the retreating columns of the enemy about 8 o'clock yesterday morning. Jackson's forces attacked the left flank of McClellan on the road leading along the west bank of the Chickahominy from Bottom Bridge to the Long Bridge, at a point seventeen miles from Richmond, while Magruder and Huger, later in the day, fell upon his right flank. Fighting was reported to be still going on up to nine o'clock last night, the enemy endeavoring to make his exit to the river through our lines, which had again enveloped him. Brigadier-General Fitz St. John Porter is reported to be among the number of prisoners taken by us.

Last evening very heavy though distant firing could be heard, in the direction of James river, and was naturally supposed to come from the enemy's gunboats covering the retreat of McClellan's army. The details of information from the river is doubtful; but there appears to be no doubt that the enemy's gunboats have been engaged during yesterday with Holmes' brigade, and that a number of Federal transports are in the river with reinforcements, which are possibly a portion of Burnside's command. There has been no attempt to reinforce McClellan from the transports which seem to corroborate the conclusion that that commander is sensible that the fortunes of the contest have been lost, and that his only anxiety now is to effect his retreat.

A dispatch was received from the lines last night from President Davis stating that the condition in which affairs were then standing was all that the country could desire.—*Examiner of yesterday.*

LONGSTREET'S DIVISION, RIGHT WING,
HEADQUARTERS 1ST BRIGADE,
June 20th, 1862.

WAR DEPARTMENT,
ADJ'T AND INSP. GEN'S OFFICE,
Richmond, June 18, 1862.

GENERAL ORDERS
No. 43.

I. WITH the consent and approbation of his Excellency Governor Letcher, all Sheriffs, Deputy Sheriffs and Constables of the State of Virginia are authorized and requested to apprehend deserters from the army, wherever they may be found, and to deliver them to the officer of the army at the most convenient post or station, or to lodge them in jail and report their names and Regiments to General S COOPER, Adjutant and Inspector General, Richmond.

Thirty dollars will be paid for each deserter delivered to an officer, and fifteen dollars for each deserter lodged in jail. No allowance will be made for expenses of apprehension or transportation.

All jailors receiving deserters are requested to detain them. The usual allowance for the support of prisoners will be made.

II. Transfers from the line to Partizan corps will not be permitted, and if any officer of Partizan corps knowingly enlist men from the line, the authority to raise the Partizan corps will be revoked, in addition to such punishment as a Court Martial may inflict.

By command of the Secretary of War.
(Signed) S. COOPER,
je 25-1w Adj't and Inspt Gen'l.

The attention of all absentees from the 11th Virginia Regiment is called to the above advertisement of one week. All absentees will report immediately to Lient. William S. Thayer, Co. H, 11th Virginia Regiment. A list of the wounded has been furnished. Those claiming to be sick will be required to furnish a Surgeon's certificate to the date they report to Lieutenant Thayer. Those failing so to do or failing to report to Lieutenant Thayer at John B. Shaner's, will be published and dealt with according to law.

K. OTEY, Capt.,
Commanding 11th Va. Reg't.

J. L. KEMPER:
Brig. Gen. Commanding,
1st Brigade. je 25-1w

LOCAL AND STATE AFFAIRS.

There is hope says the Richmond *Whig*, of Col. Withers' probable recovery. Capt. Wall, of Prince Edward, who succeeded him in command, has had his leg amputated, and is getting on quite well, under the circumstances. He is at the American Hotel.

MORE VICTIMS.—Three bodies were brought up yesterday, of those who fell in the bloody fight of Monday last. Col. Seymour, of the 6th La. Regiment, Serg't Major J. Kirk Seabury and Orderly Serg't John F. Mitchell, the two last natives of this city and members of the 11th Va. Regiment. They will be buried to-day, as will be seen by notices in another column.

The following list of casualties in the 11th Va. Regiment, and the Lynchburg Beauregards, is taken from the Richmond *Whig* of yesterday:

In the severe engagement of Monday evening, between Longstreet's and Huger's Divisions on our right, near the river, and the enemy, the following casualties occurred in the 11th Virginia Regiment, Major Otey commanding.

Killed—Lieut W R Abbot, Lieut Dix, Sergeant Major J Kirk Seabury, Caplain Rev J C Granbury (supposed), Privates John Mitchell, James Lavinder, Thomas Jones, E Fox, Wm C Jacobs, G W Hanna. (Some of these, it is hoped, may yet be living.)

Wounded—Wm Elder, A G Akers, G W Borden, W Garnet, Wm R Haymaker, Jno Hite, S Shelton, G W West, J W Miles, J Gardner, John Blanks, J Perdue, Field Cunningham, J E Reynolds, B W Stringfellow, Wm S Perter, A J Bythes, E M Hobson, J W Hendricks, J Pucket, Wm Browne, Wm Everett, Wm K Trigg, W Winston, J R Holcombe, Wm Early, W H Taylor, C C Harvey.

THE LYNCHBURG BEAUREGARD ARTILLERY.

Among the exciting incidents of Monday's operations was a fierce encounter on the Charles City road, between the Beauregard Artillery of Lynchburg and a Federal battery, which was covering the retreat of the retiring Yankees. The engagement lasted about two hours and was exceedingly hot. The Beauregards stood to their posts like heroes, under a constant shower of shell and shot, and poured a deadly fire into the enemy's battery.

The casualties on our side were as follows:

Killed—Private Charles Kulchke.

Wounded—Lieut J J Shoemaker, in the leg, not dangerous, Serg't A F Stratton, neck and leg severely. Serg't R C Burkholder, very slightly in the head, and private Wm S Reid, on the finger.

One horse was killed, and two or three others wounded.

Our Killed and Wounded.

We wish that it were in our pewer to publish all the names of the gallant heroes who have been killed, or wounded, in the battles before Richmond. But our limited space forbids, and we can therefore only insert the names of such as our own readers are most interested in.

The gallant 28th Va., Regiment which greatly distinguished itself in the recent battle, is made up, for the most part, from the neighboring counties, and we avail ourselves of the first opportunity to acquaint our friends of the casualties therein:

List of casualties in the 28th Va. Reg't., Col. R. C. Allen, Commanding in the battle of the 27th instant:

Field—Major W C Wilson, badly wounded in thigh.

Company A, Lieut. Jas D Fink, Commanding, killed. Wounded—Serg't Joel B Walker, leg broken, and amputated below knee, Privates Philip T Burger, in hand, J G Haves, in thigh, severe, Jno W Camper, in leg, slight, E O Simmons, leg broken, W Obenchain, in neck.

Killed 1, Wounded 6.

Company B, Lieut. Goode, Commanding wounded in thigh, slight. Wounded—Privates W H Jones, in thigh, slight, Hugh M Hall, in shoulder, slight, John Abbott, in shoulder, slight, J J Eakin, in shoulder, slight.

Killed None, Wounded 5.

Company C, Capt. Sheppard, Commanding wounded in head slight. Killed—Lieutenant. James H Reynolds, Corp'l Geo L Kintzley, privates John W Givens, Philip J Williams. Wounded—1st Serg't Wm E Reynolds, Privates B M Kerr, Jno T Driver Jas R McPherson, Geo L Reynolds nature of wounds not known.

Killed 4 Wounded 6. Aggregate loss 10

Company D Lieut. Stewart, Commanding.—Killed—Corp'l A Overstreet, Col. Corp'l Jno W Beard. Wounded—1st Serg't Jno P Wairound, Privates A L Blankenship Harry Barton Thos D Carroll, Joel M Franklin, Josiah Dooley, Jno S Tuttle Felding Sutile, Jno T Payne, character of wounds not known.

Company E, Lieut Minor, Commanding. Wounded—Serg'ts Kelley, J J Ester, Corp'l Patterson; Privates Alex. Farriss, Jas G Richardson, Wm J Simpson, character of wounds unknown

Missing—Private E W Martin.

Killed none, Wounded 6, Missing 1. Aggregate loss 7.

Company F, Capt. Hugh Nelson, Commanding.—Wounded—1st Sergt M M Lowry, in hand, slight, Serg't J H Ellis, in arm, slight, Serg't Jno C Rucker, in hand, slight, Corp'l M V Shelton, in groin, severe, Privates Thos Puckett, in thigh, severe, Thos Monroe, in groin, severe, J B Tanner, in right breast, severe, Jno R Wilson, in thigh, L B Wright, in side, A R Wright, in hand, W H Mitchell, in thigh, Chas Padget, in thigh, M B Clayton, in leg, slight, W P Wright, in neck and shoulder, severe, Jno R Ellis, in shoulder, severe.

Killed, none, Wounded 15. Total 15.

Company G, Lieut. Holland Commd'g.—Wounded—Lieut. Holland, in both thighs, severe flesh wound, Privates Stephen Chaffin, in leg, O V B Dearing, in arm, broken, R A Foster, in abdomen, mortal, R M Johnson, in arm and leg, R Mitchell, in groin, J D Williams, in arm, W A Walker, in leg and body, W C Creasey, missing.

Killed, none; wounded, 8; missing, 1. Aggregate loss 9.

Company I, Lieut A H Hoge Commd'g. Wounded—Lieut. A H Hoge, in shoulder. Killed—privates R S Phillips and Jas Murray. Wounded—Serg't A Lewis in hand and arm, Corp'l A Ramsey, in arm, fractured, Corp'l W L Williamson, in arm and leg, both fractured, Corp'l P W Loyd, in side, slight, Privates Sam'l M Brown, in hand, slight, David Collins, in body, Jno W Hix, in shoulder, slight, Jos P Lemon, in hand, A J Moseley, in thigh, slight, W W Meador, in foot, severely, Jno H persinger, in leg, severely, Chas H Settle, in hand, severely, Wm Schoonover, in hand, slightly, J B Thompson, in thigh, severely H S Trout, in knee, slightly, J W Whitesell, in hand, severe, Jno R Hardy, in thigh John W Carroll, in leg.

Killed, 2; wounded, 19. Aggregate loss 21.

Company K, Capt. Robertson commanding. Wounded—Capt Robertson, in leg, severe. Killed—Corporal W A Peters and private A S Richardson. Wounded, Serg't G W Shaver, in arm, Serg't W D Woodson, in groin, severe. Privates L B Cundiff, slightly, B Painter, slightly, Wm Slack, in arm and head, Wm H Tyler, in face, severe, Wm H Turner, in arm, slight.

Killed, 2; wounded 8. Aggregate loss, 10.

Killed	11
Wounded,	83
Missing,	2
Aggregate	96

WM. C. LEFTWICH, Adj't.

BY TELEGRAPH.

From Mobile.

MOBILE, July 1.

A special dispatch to the "Tribune," dated Grenada, Miss., 30th, states that Northern papers of the 25th inst., says:

Buell is advancing on Chattanooga, and Morgan simultaneously advancing on Knoxville, for the relief of East Tennessee.

A dispatch to the Chicago "Tribune," says:

Hindman's Confederate army in Arkansas number from 25 to 30 thousand. The Yankee General Curtis is being reinforced.

Jackson's Tennessee cavalry burnt 1,500 bales of cotton, within 11½ miles of Memphis.

The vote for the Municipal election at Memphis was small. No responsible candidate for office.

The London "Times" regards Bank's defeat in the Valley by Ewell as a most important affair for the Confederates—on account of the lesson which it teaches the North in showing them that they must make efforts greater than any they have put forth, in order to restore a single border State to the Union. It also says the subjugation of the South is more and more impossible.

Encouraging News From Arkansas.

MOBILE, July 1.

A special dispatch to the "Advertiser" dated Jackson 30th says;

Gen. Chalmers has taken possession of Bolivar, Tenn.

Col. Tappen, of our Arkansas forces says:

Gen. Hindman with 30,000 men has Curtis completely cornered.

The State is blazing with excitement.

The battery at Narals Bluff commanding White River is supported by 5000 Confederates.

The people along the river refuse to trade with the Yankees.

From Tennessee.

KNOXVILLE, June 30.

Buell's army is rapidly crossing the Tennessee River at Florence and concentrating their forces at Bridgeport thirty miles from Chattanooga.

The enemy crossed with artillery over Battle Creek yesterday.

General Harry Heath has been assigned to the command at Chattanooga.

All quiet towards Cumberland Gap.

(The above dispatches were received early yesterday morning, since which time the telegraph lines have been down, consequently we are without any information of the movement of the army, near Richmond yesterday —ED. VIRGINIAN.)

ALMANAC.

1862.	Sunday.	Monday.	Tuesday.	Wen'day.	Thursday	Friday.	Saturday
AN'Y	...	...	...	1	2	3	4
	5	6	7	8	9	10	11
	12	13	14	15	16	17	18
	19	20	21	22	23	24	25
	26	27	28	29	30	31	..
'Y	..	..	..	..	..	...	1
	2	3	4	5	6	7	8
	9	10	11	12	13	14	15
	16	17	18	19	20	21	22
	23	24	25	26	27	28	..
MAR..	..	..	..	..	..	..	1
	2	3	4	5	6	7	8
	9	10	11	12	13	14	15
	16	17	18	19	20	21	22
	23	24	25	26	27	28	29
	30	31	..	..	..	..	...
APRIL	..	..	1	2	3	4	5
	6	7	8	9	10	11	12
	13	14	15	16	17	18	19
	20	21	22	23	24	25	26
	27	28	29	30	..	..	..
MAY..	..	..	..	..	1	2	3
	4	5	6	7	8	9	10
	11	12	13	14	15	16	17
	18	19	20	21	22	23	24
	25	26	27	28	29	30	31
JUNE.	1	2	3	4	5	6	7
	8	9	10	11	12	13	14
	15	16	17	18	19	20	21
	22	23	24	25	26	27	28
	29	30	..	..	..	..	..

1862.	Sunday.	Monday.	Tuesday.	Wedn'day	Thursday	Friday.	Saturday
JULY.		..	1	2	3	4	5
	6	7	8	9	10	11	12
	13	14	15	16	17	18	19
	20	21	22	23	24	25	26
	27	28	29	30	31	..	..
AUG'T	..	..	..	..	..	1	..
	3	4	5	6	7	8	2
	10	11	12	13	14	15	9
	17	18	19	20	21	22	16
	24	25	26	27	28	29	23
	31	..	..	..	..	..	30
SEPT.	..	1	2	3	4	5	6
	7	8	9	10	11	12	13
	14	15	16	17	18	19	20
	21	22	23	24	25	26	27
	28	29	30	..	..	..	..
OCTO.	..	..	...	1	2	3	4
	5	6	7	8	9	10	11
	12	13	14	15	16	17	18
	19	20	21	22	23	24	25
	26	27	28	29	30	31	..
NOV'R	..	..	..	..	...	..	1
	2	3	4	5	6	7	8
	9	10	11	12	13	14	15
	16	17	18	19	20	21	22
	23	24	25	26	27	28	29
	30	..	..	..	..	..	..
DEC'R	..	1	2	3	4	5	6
	7	8	9	10	11	12	13
	14	15	16	17	18	19	20
	21	22	23	24	25	26	27
	28	29	30	31	..	..	..

COMMERCIAL

LYNCHBURG MARKETS.

REPORTED BY

A. B. RUCKER,
PRODUCE BROKER,
183 MAIN STREET.

☞ These quotations, it will be understood, represent wholesale prices generally.

APPLES.—Green—none offering.

BACON.—Scarce and in demand. Last sales 45 to 47. The Government cleared the market last week at 35c. Since then no receipts.

BEESWAX.—35 to 37½c.

BUTTER.—Receipts increasing with sales 50 to 60 for table; 50 to 55c for cooking.

CORN—$1.20 to 1.25.

CORN MEAL—Very scarce, ready sale $1.75 to 1.80 for city consumption.

CLOVER SEED.—$12 to 12.50.

FRUIT—Dried Apples $2.00 to $2.50 per bushel—28 pounds; Unpealed Peaches $2.50 to $3.00 per bushel—33 pounds; no Pealed Peaches offering.

FLOUR.—Receipts light. Last sales $10 for Superfine; $11 for Extra; $12 for Family. The Government having cleared the market during the past week at $8.50, has detered owners from sending forward supplies. Under existing circumstances the citizens who have no supply must do without.

ONIONS—Stock light—$2.75 to $3 per bushel.

FLAXSEED.—$1.90 to $2 per bushel of 56 pounds.

FEATHERS.—The market has been cleared at 45c. I quote at 45 to 47c.

GRASS SEED.—Nominal—nothing doing.

HAY—Baled $1.50 to $1.60; per wagon load $1.30 to 1.40.

LIME—Mountain $3 to $3.50.

IRON—Demand good at $1.80 to $2.00 ℔ ton.

LARD—30 to 32 cents in firkins.

OATS—Sheaf $1.50 to 1.75 ℔ wagon load; Shelled 85 to 90c per bushel 33 pounds.

TOBACCO—Sales increasing with rapidly advancing prices. Lugs $6.50 to $9; Leaf $7.50 to $12; Shipping $12 to $20; Manufacturing $14 to $35—the latter for bright wrappers.

WHEAT—Receipts very light. Sales $1.45 to 1 50. None of the city mills are grinding at the present time.

AUCTION SALES.

THIS DAY.

BY B. AKERS, AUCTIONEER.

THE WAR FOR THE UN

—A CAVALRY CHARGE.

THE NEW YORK HERALD.

WHOLE NO. 9439. NEW YORK, WEDNESDAY, JULY 16, 1862.–TRIPLE SHEET. PRICE TWO CENTS.

THE CENTRE OF THE REBELLION.

The Seat of War Around Richmond----Scene of the Seven Days Battles----McClellan's New Base of Operations.

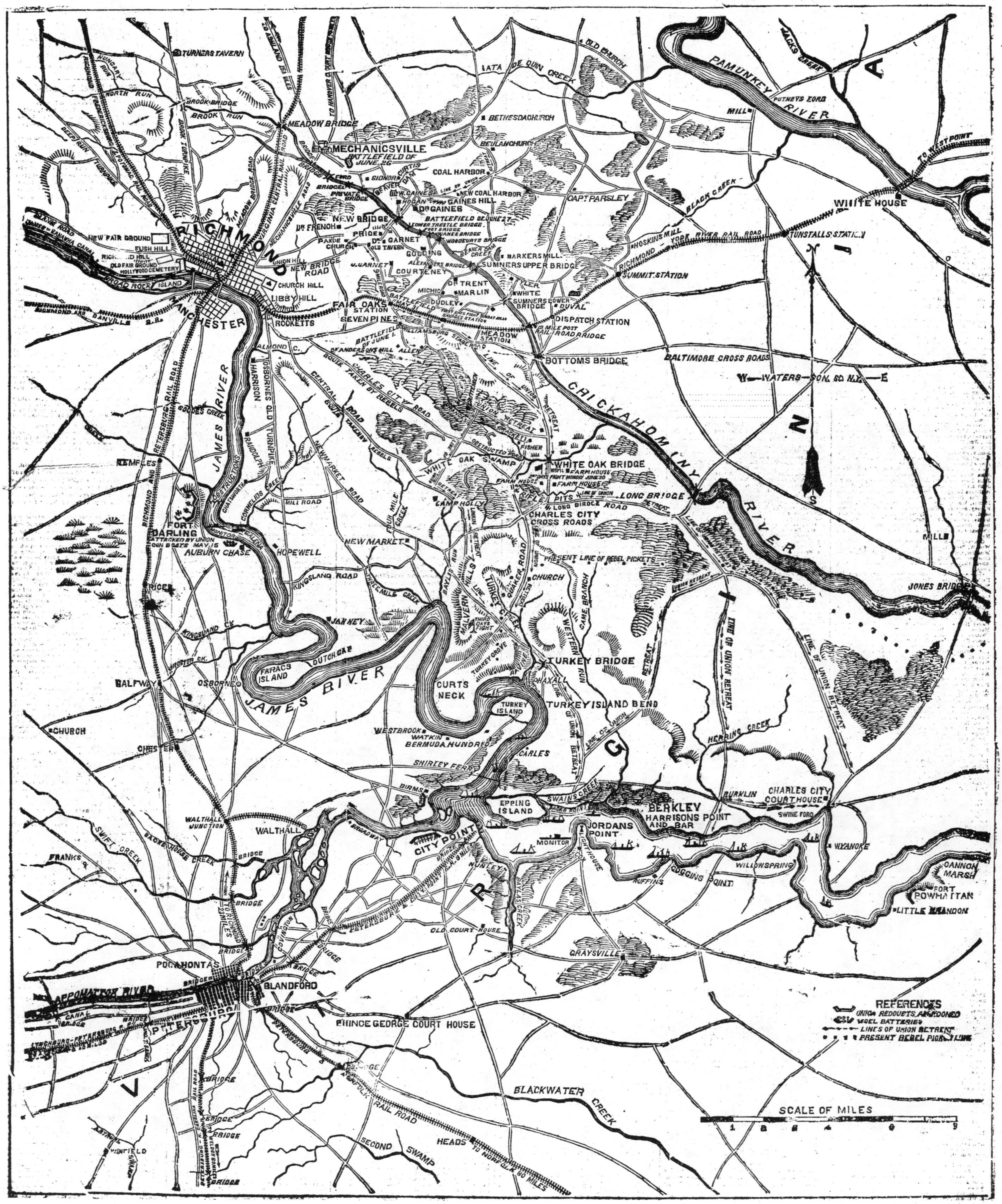

The Tri-Weekly Mercury.

DAILY PAPER—TEN DOLLARS PER ANNUM, PAYABLE HALF-YEARLY IN ADVANCE.

—VINDICE NULLO
SPONTE SUA SINE LEGE FIDES RECTUMQUE COLENTUR.

COUNTRY PAPER—THRICE A WEEK—FIVE DOLLARS PER ANNUM, IN ADVANCE.

VOLUME LXXXI. | CHARLESTON, S. C., SATURDAY, JULY 26, 1862. | NUMBER 11,510

THE BATTLE OF THE SEVEN PINES—GEN. JOHNSTON'S OFFICIAL REPORT.

RICHMOND, June 24, 1862.

Gen. S. Cooper, Adj't and Insp'r Gen'l:

SIR—Before the 30th May, I had ascertained from trusty scouts, that Keyes' corps was encamped on this side of the Chickahominy, near the Williamsburg road. On that day Maj. Gen. D. H. Hill reported a strong body immediately in his front. On receiving this report, I determined to attack them next morning—hoping to be able to defeat Keye's corps completely in its more advanced position before it could be reinforced.—Written orders were despatched to Major Generals Hill, Huger, and G. W. Smith. General Longstreet, being near my headquarters, received verbal instructions. The receipt of the orders was acknowledged. General Hill, supported by the division of General Longstreet (who had the direction of operations on the right), was to advance by the Williamsburg road to attack the enemy in front; General Huger, with his division, was to move down the Charles City road, in order to attack in flank the troops who might be engaged with Hill and Longstreet, unless he found in his front force enough to occupy his division. General Smith was to march to the junction of the New Bridge road and the Nine Mile road, to be in readiness either to fall on Keyes' right flank or to cover Longstreet's left. They were to move at daybreak. Heavy and protracted rains during the afternoon and night, by swelling the stream of the Chickahominy, increased the probability of our having to deal with no other troops than those of Keyes. The same cause prevented the prompt and punctual movement of the troops.—Those of Smith, Hill, and Longstreet were in position early enough, however, to commence operations by 8 o'clock, a. m.

Major General Longstreet, unwilling to make a partial attack, instead of the combined movement which had been planned, waited from hour to hour for Gen. Huger's division. At length, at 2 o'clock, p. m., he determined to attack without those troops. He accordingly commenced his advance at that hour, opening the engagement with artillery and skirmishers. By 3 o'clock it became close and heavy.

In the meantime, I had placed myself on the left of the force employed in this attack, with the division of Gen. Smith, that I might be on a part of the field where I could observe, and be ready to meet, any counter movements which the enemy's General might make against our centre or left. Owing to some peculiar condition of the atmosphere, the sound of the musketry did not reach us. I, consequently, deferred giving the signal for Gen. Smith's advance till about 4 o'clock, at which time Major Jasper Whiting, of Gen. Smith's staff, whom I had sent to learn the state of affairs with Gen. Longstreet's column, returned, reporting that it was pressing on with vigor. Smith's troops were at once moved forward.

The principal attack was made by Major General Longstreet, with his own and Major General D. H. Hill's division—the latter mostly in advance. Hill's brave troops, admirably commanded and most gallantly led, forced their way through the abattis which formed the enemy's external defences, and stormed their entrenchments by a determined and irresistible rush. Such was the manner in which the enemy's first line was carried. The operation was repeated with the same gallantry and success as our troops pursued their victorious career through the enemy's successive camps and entrenchments. At each new position they encountered fresh troops belonging to it, and reinforcements brought on from the rear. Thus they had to repel repeated efforts to retake works which they had carried, but their advance was never successfully resisted.

Their onward movement was only stayed by the coming of night. By nightfall they had forced their way to the "Seven Pines," having driven the enemy back more than two miles, through their own camps, and from a series of entrenchments; and repelled every attempt to recapture them with great slaughter. The skill, vigor, and decision with which these operations were conducted by Gen. Longstreet are worthy of the highest praise. He was worthily seconded by Major General Hill, of whose conduct and courage he speaks in the highest terms.

Major General Smith's division moved forward at four o'clock—Whiting's three brigades leading. Their progress was impeded by the enemy's skirmishers, which, with their supports, were driven back to the railroad. At this point, Whiting's own, and Pettigrew's brigade, engaged a superior force of the enemy. Hood's, by my order, moved on to co-operate with Longstreet. General Smith was desired to hasten up with all the troops within reach. He brought up Hampton's and Hatton's brigades in a few minutes.

The strength of the enemy's position, however, enabled him to hold it until dark.

About sunset, being struck from my horse, severely wounded by a fragment of a shell, I was carried from the field, and Major General G. W. Smith succeeded to the command.

He was prevented from resuming his attack on the enemy's position next morning by the discovery of strong entrenchments, not seen on the previous evening. His division bivouacked, on the night of the 31st, within musket shot of the entrenchments which they were attacking, when darkness stayed the conflict. The skill, energy, and resolution with which Maj. Gen. Smith directed the attack, would have secured success if it could have been made an hour earlier.

The troops of Longstreet and Hill passed the night of the 31st on the ground which they had won. The enemy were strongly reinforced from the north side of the Chickahominy on the evening and night of the 31st. The troops engaged by Gen. Smith were undoubtedly from the other side of the river.

On the morning of the 1st of June, the enemy attacked the brigade of Gen. Pickett, which was supported by that of Gen. Pryor. The attack was vigorously repelled by these two brigades, the brunt of the action falling on Gen. Pickett. This was the last demonstration made by the enemy.

Our troops employed the residue of the day in securing and bearing off the captured artillery, small arms, and other property; and in the evening quietly returned to their own camps.

We took ten pieces of artillery, six thousand (6,000) muskets, one garrison flag, and four regimental colors, besides a large quantity of tents and camp equipage.

Major General Longstreet reports the loss in his command as being about................3,000
Maj. Gen. G. W. Smith reports his loss at....1,283

Total..4,283

That of the enemy is stated in their own newspapers to have exceeded ten thousand—an estimate which is, no doubt, short of the truth.

Had Major General Huger's division been in position and ready for action, when those of Smith, Longstreet and Hill moved, I am satisfied that Keyes' corps would have been destroyed, instead of being merely defeated.* Had it gone into action even at 4 o'clock, the victory would have been much more complete.

Major Generals Smith and Longstreet speak in high terms of the conduct of their superior and staff officers.

I beg leave to ask the attention of the Government especially to the manner in which Brigadier Gens. Whiting and R. H. Anderson, and Cols. Jenkins and Kemper and Hampton, exercising commands above their grades, and Brig. General Rhodes, are mentioned.

This, and the captured colors, will be delivered by Major A. H. Cole, of my staff.

I have been prevented, by feebleness, from making this report sooner, and am still too weak to make any but a very imperfect one.

Several hundred prisoners were taken, but I have received no report of the number.

Your obedient servant,
(Signed) J. E. JOHNSTON, General.

*See Longstreet's report.

DISTRESSING CASUALTIES.—Mr. Philip M. Ouzts was almost instantly killed on the 16th inst., at Mrs. R. M. Fuller's Mill in this neighborhood. He was caught by the saw and terribly mutilated before he could be assisted.

Young Edward Talbert, son of Captain B. M. Talbert of this district, was drowned in the Savannah river one day last week. With a number of youthful companions, he was bathing in the stream, and happening to be drifted into very deep water he unfortunately failed to stem the current, and sunk beyond the reach of aid.—*Edgefield Advertiser.*

TRI-WEEKLY MERCURY.

SATURDAY, JULY 26, 1862.

Secret Sessions in Congress.

Military authority and military discipline have always been supposed to be adverse to public liberty. The reason is obvious. Military authority and discipline establish a despotism. To command on the one side, and to obey on the other, are its principles. Public liberty, on the contrary, can exist only in the atmosphere of free enquiry. A free press, and free debate in all assemblages of the people, are the two grand instrumentalities of public liberty. Hence, one of the first things the Government of President LINCOLN did, when it determined to establish a military despotism over the North, was to abolish the freedom of the press. The other instrumentality of liberty, freedom of speech and debate, they also abolished in the primary assemblages of the people, *by mob violence;* but they did not, because we presume they dared not, attempt to suppress free debate *in the Congress* of the United States. Free debate, with open sessions, without which free debate is useless, because it cannot reach the people, has been retained by the Representatives of the people in the Congress of the United States.

In the Confederate States, the press has been kept free, not without, however, very decided indications, on the part of the military authority, of a desire to suppress it; but open sessions, with free debate, have been suppressed. The Congress of the Confederate States, in spite of the plain mandates of the Constitution requiring publicity of their proceedings, has been little else than a secret Executive Council. What measures have been proposed in Congress to promote the welfare of the people, and by whom proposed, and the votes of their Representatives upon them—the people know nothing. What course the Executive has pursued—what measures have been recommended, and what defeated by the Executive, are kept from the people. It is only after a measure has been ripened into Executive approval, that it is published and known. Free debate is, therefore, practically abolished, because it does not reach the people, whilst the responsibility of the Representative to the constituent is also abolished.

Now we know very well that this strange disregard of the first principles of liberty, in a struggle to obtain it for ourselves and our posterity, can be defended by very plausible sophisms. It is argued that our differences, if known to our enemies, would weaken our cause; and especially ought all collisions with the Executive to be suppressed, because his folly must be most dangerous. A want of confidence in him must weaken the energies of the people. Therefore, they should be deceived into the belief, that Congress is unanimous in the policy of the Government, and that the Executive has its confidence.

It is very difficult to persuade an honest man that deception can at any time be good policy; but when it is systematically practiced to the practical overthrow of the principles of the government itself, it is a declaration that the government is an evil, and ought to be abolished. If, in a representative free government, it is expedient that the people should know nothing of the speeches or conduct of their representatives, then representation ought to be abolished, and free debate be suppressed. In other words, the government is a nuisance, to be circumvented and put aside, and ought to be overthrown.

But further still: Do not secret sessions produce the very evil it is intended to prevent? Does it not exasperate differences, and upset the equilibrium of the Constitution? An Executive in power for six years, with the vast patronage a war produces, will surely grow insolent and aggressive by the irresponsibility which secret sessions produce. Every member of Congress has the right and the duty of laying before the Executive the claims of his constituents to office and place under the government. If he is compliant to Executive dictation, his recommendations will be regarded; if not, they will be registered to be proscribed from office. Will not this tend to exasperate the independent representative, whilst it commands the adherence of the sycophant? The same result may attend measures. A measure not recommended by the Executive, or intended to rectify its abuses, if supported by a representative, draws upon him Executive proscription. Will this harmonize differences and strengthen the government in its legitimate operations? On the contrary, shielded from any responsibility to the people by secret sessions, will not the Executive grow more aggressive, and more presumptuous, until at last he shall look upon Congress as a mere registering office, where his desires may be recorded? He may soon consider himself, like LOUIS XIV., as "the State," and all who may oppose his will, as mischievous agents or traitors. In the meantime, that cardinal principle of all free governments, the independence of the Legislative of the Executive department, will have been practically abolished; and the government shall become free only in name. Secret sessions in Congress cannot co-exist with a free government. One of two things ought to be done—discontinue the secret sessions in Congress, or abolish the government of the Confederate States in form as well as in fact.

ABOUT FRICTION MATCHES.—The value of the friction or lucifer match will never be realized by the coming generation, for they will know nothing of the difficulties of obtaining and preserving fire previous to their invention. So rapidly do we move on, that persons that remember the tinder-box are getting old. Then matches made by hand were valuable and carefully preserved; now they are as abundant as dew-drops of an autumn morning, and almost as cheap. An English writer says that one firm, Messrs. Dixon, of London, constantly employ four hundred workmen in making matches, and make twenty-two hundred millions in a year. The average consumption in England is two hundred and fifty millions a day, or eight to each individual in the Kingdom. It is as large or larger in the United States. There are two manufactories in Austria and Bohemia that turn out forty-five thousand million in a year. The friction match is therefore one of the institutions of modern times, and one that, having once known and employed, we could no more do without and move on at the rapid rate we are doing, than we could live without air or water.

CONSCRIPTS IN COLUMBIA.—The *Guardian* of yesterday says: "Our streets have been crowded with conscripts and volunteers for the past few days. They are all fine looking soldiers, and all appear cheerful and eager to enter upon active duty."

THE EXCHANGE OF PRISONERS is proceeding as rapidly as circumstances will allow, a large number of Yankee sick and wounded having been sent to City Point on Saturday, and others will be sent off by different routes.

THE PROGRESS OF THE WAR.

LATEST FROM THE NORTH—MORGAN'S ADVANCE IN KENTUCKY—THE SIEGE OF VICKSBURG ABANDONED—HALLECK'S MYSTERIOUS VISIT TO WASHINGTON—NEWS FROM M'CLELLAN'S ARMY—POPE'S NEW ORDERS—GENERAL SUMMARY.

Our dates from the North are one day later, including Baltimore papers of July 19, from which we gather the following news summary:

THE SIEGE OF VICKSBURG ABANDONED.

The Baltimore *Sun*, of the 19th inst., contains the following:

Advices from before Vicksburg to the 10th instant represent that the siege would be temporarily abandoned, and that some of the vessels would return South, probably to New Orleans. On account of the low water in the river, the proposed new channel will prove a failure.

MORGAN'S ADVANCE TOWARD CINCINNATI.

A despatch dated Cincinnati July 18, says:—The town of Cynthia, 66 miles from here, surrendered at five o'clock yesterday to the rebels after a half hour's fight. Morgan's force numbers about 2,500. A soldier who also came into Boyd's says that Morgan's men fired two rounds after the surrender of the town, and that Captain Anthony's company from Newport are all killed or made prisoners.

The excitement at Newport and Covington is very high, and increasing. The citizens are organizing rapidly for the defence of Newport, and the provost marshal arrests all sympathizers to-day.

A despatch from Lexington, Kentucky, to the Cincinnati Gazette, states that Morgan encamped close to Versailles, Kentucky, on Monday evening last. His men had taken possession of a large number of valuable horses belonging to persons in that neighborhood. Another band of guerillas, two hundred in number, were within six miles of Lexington on Tuesday morning, and the trains which left the latter city for Frankfort, during the afternoon of the same day, were compelled to return in consequence of the railway track being torn up at Midway, and of preparations having been made to blow up the bridge in the vicinity on the arrival of the train. The banks at Lebanon, Danville, Frankfort, and other inland towns, have sent their funds to Louisville for safekeeping. Two of the religious weeklies, the True Presbyterian and the Baptist Recorder, have been suppressed at Louisville, and several preachers are under arrest, among them the Rev. Stuart Robinson.

HALLECK'S VISIT TO WASHINGTON.

A despatch from Corinth, dated July 17, says:

General Halleck has given up the command of the army of the Southwest. He has issued a general order, saying that in giving up the immediate command of the troops constituting the army of the Southwest he desires to express his high appreciation of the endurance, behavior and soldierly conduct which they exhibited on all occasions, and to express to the commanders of army corps and their subordinates the warmest thanks for their cordial co-operation. He says the soldiers who have so nobly done their duty have accomplished much towards crushing this wicked rebellion, and if they continue to exhibit the same vigilance, courage and perseverance, will, it is believed, soon bring the war to a close.

The Philadelphia Inquirer says: Gen. Halleck was some time ago invited to visit Washington to confer with the President upon the various military operations in progress in the several sections. The position of affairs in the Southwest will now allow his absence. It is understood that on his arrival at Washington he will be assigned to the position of general commanding the armies of the United States, both in the Southwest and in Virginia. He will consequently remain in Washington, and be in constant intercourse with the President and War Department.

Gen. McClellan will continue in command of the army of the Potomac, and Gen. Pope of the army of the Rappahannock, the confidence of the President being unabated in both of these gallant officers.

The New York Post says: Gen. Halleck goes to Washington to assume command of all the troops in Virginia, not as an active commander in the field, but as the consulting General of the President. The President admits that it is fully time that one mind should direct all the loyal forces in Virginia, and that the "army of the Potomac" and the "army of Virginia" should act in concert. To enable this to be done, it is asserted that Gen. Halleck will be put in command, with the understanding that he will remain in Washington.

The Washington Star says: We have reason to believe there is truth in the report that General Halleck is now on his way to this city, sommoned here by the Government. It is not so certain, we apprehend, that the Government has determined to retain him at this point as military adviser, as alleged.

CHARGES AGAINST GEN. MITCHELL.

The Washington *Star* says:

We learn that Col. Norton, recently in the service under Gen. Mitchell, having reached here some days ago, bearing the formal charges against Gen. Mitchell, was yesterday examined at length before the Committee on the Conduct of the War with reference to them.

It is said to-day that these charges allege that he refused to take any notice whatever of rapes committed on negro women by his men (of Turchin's brigade) in the presence of respectable white females, or of indiscriminate, atrocious, and persistent plundering of and outrages upon Union citizens by the same brigade. The charges are said further to allege that he has used Government transportation for cotton bought by parties in whose speculations he was personally pecuniarily interested. It is further understood that the Hon. Geo. S. Houston, of Alabama (former Chairman of the Committee of Ways and Means, United States House of Representatives), is expected to be the main prosecutor of Gen. M., Mr. H. having maintained his *status* as a Unionist.

Some time since Gen. M. tendered his resignation to the President, but it has not yet been accepted. The charges against him will doubtless be promptly disposed of by the Government.

THE CONFISCATION BILL A LAW.

The following message has been received in the Federal Congress:

Fellow-Citizens of the Senate and House of Representatives:

Considering the bill for "an act to suppress insurrection, to punish treason and rebellion, to seize and confiscate the property of rebels, and for other purposes," and the joint resolution explanatory of said act, as being substantially one, I have approved and signed both.

Before I was informed of the resolution, I had prepared the draft of a message, stating objections to the bill becoming a law, a copy of which draft is herewith transmitted.

ABRAHAM LINCOLN.

July 17th, 1862.

This is the "explanatory" resolution alluded to:

Resolved, By the Senate and House of Representatives, etc., That the provisions of the third clause of the fifth section of an act to suppress insurrection, to punish treason and rebellion, to seize and confiscate the property of rebels, and for other purposes, shall be so construed as not to apply to any act or acts done prior to the passage thereof, nor to include any member of a State Legislature or Judge of any State Court who has not, in accepting or entering upon his office, taken an oath to support the Constitution of the so-called Confederate States of America; nor shall any punishment or proceedings under the said act be so construed as to work a forfeiture of the real estate of the offender beyond his natural life.

THE WAR IN THE VIRGINIA VALLEY—PLAN OF GEN. POPE'S CAMPAIGN.

The Northern papers publish several general orders of Major General POPE, who has assumed command in the Valley, indicating the manner in which he intends to conduct the campaign in the country through which his army moves. We have not room to publish these orders in full, but we give the most striking features of them in the following extracts. General POPE inaugurates a system of tyranny and despotism worse even than that of Austria:

The troops of this command will subsist upon the country in which their operations are carried on. Vouchers will be given to the owners, stating on their face that they will be payable at the conclusion of the war, upon sufficient testimony being furnished that such owners have been loyal citizens of the United States since the date of the vouchers.

In any operations of the cavalry forces in this command no supply or baggage trains of any description will be used, unless so stated specially in the order for the movement. Two days' cooked rations will be carried on the persons of the men, and all villages and neighborhoods through which they pass will be laid under contribution for the subsistence of men and horses.

The people of the Valley of the Shenandoah, and throughout the region of operations of this army, living along the lines of railroad and telegraph, and along the routes of travel in the rear of the United States forces, are notified that they will be held responsible for any injury done to the track, line or road, or for any attack upon trains or straggling soldiers by bands of guerillas in their neighborhood.

It is, therefore, ordered that whenever a railroad, wagon road or telegraph is injured by parties of guerillas, the citizens living within five miles of the spot shall be turned out in mass to repair the damage, and shall, beside, pay to the United States in money or in property, to be levied by military force, the full amount of the pay and subsistence of the whole force necessary to coerce the performance of the work during the time occupied in completing it.

If a soldier or legitimate follower of the army be fired upon from any house, the house shall be razed to the ground and the inhabitants sent prisoners to the headquarters of this army. If such an outrage occur at any place distant from settlements, the people within five miles around shall be held accountable and made to pay an indemnity sufficient for the case.

Any persons detected in such outrages, either during the act or at any time afterward, shall be shot without awaiting civil process.

ESCAPE OF CONFEDERATE PRISONERS FROM FORT DELAWARE.

A despatch dated Philadelphia, July 16, says: More than two hundred rebel prisoners effected their escape last night from Fort Delaware and made tracks for Dixie. Upon the arrival of the mail train at Perryville, this forenoon, five of them were found on board, and were arrested and placed under guard.

M'CLELLAN'S ARMY—DOCTORS WILL DIFFER.

The New York *Post's* Washington correspondent writes as follows:

It is thought here (Washington) that there is nothing to prevent a speedy advance of the army of the Potomac upon Richmond, if its leader is so disposed. The fact that the Confederates have fallen back upon Richmond is thought to indicate a new plan of operations.

The army correspondent of the same paper thinks differently, and says:

I see that the papers are trying to make a good case out of our retreat, and call it "strategy." We know better here. The only redeeming feature about it is the invincible valor with which our troops fought against great odds, whipping the enemy in every engagement. Cover it up as you may, it was a disastrous necessity, which was very near resulting in the annihilation of our army. Who is responsible?

The same writer continues:

"I tell you this army is exhausted, and cannot recover from the physical effects of that retreat in one month! It is disheartened, and lacks confidence in somebody, although it does not know whom. An advance now, without heavy reinforcements, would be inevitable defeat.

THE TOTAL LOSS IN THE BATTLES BEFORE RICHMOND.

The New York Times says that the following statement, which comes from an official source, may be relied upon as a perfectly correct enumeration of the Yankee losses during the six days' battles before Richmond:

Corps.	Killed.	Wounded.	Missing.	Total.
Franklin............	245	1318	1179	2737
Sumner............	170	1068	848	2086
Keyes............	62	507	201	777
Heintzelman............	189	1051	833	2073
Porter............	873	3700	2779	7353
Cavalry............	19	60	97	176
Engineers............	—	2	21	23
Total............	1565	7701	5958	15,224

THE CURRENCY OF THE NORTH.

The Yankee Congress has adjourned. Among its last acts was one authorizing the issue of postage and other government stamps as currency. The act goes into operation on the 1st of August. The New York *World* (Republican) strongly condemns the act authorizing the issue of this currency, and says:

Mr. Chase has thus the exclusive honor of being the first financial agent of any government that ever ventured to issue legal tender money of the denomination of "one cent." This bill is the final, crowning act of insanity that consummates this iniquitous paper money system of Mr. Chase. Too much paper money has caused gold to advance to nineteen per cent. premium, or rather has reduced the value of Mr. Chase's legal-tender dollar to eighty-one cents, and Mr. Chase's remedy for this is like unto that of Rehoboam for the evil of the children of Israel—he decreases our paper money by adding about forty to sixty millions of dollars in this proposed supply of postage stamps.

Gold is at nineteen per cent. premium from the use of about $70,000,000 legal tender notes. What, then, will be its price when the politician's and speculator's paper scheme is carried out to its full extent? Any one can make the calculation. The injury to commerce from this act is incalculable. The discount of nineteen per cent. is on every daily and hourly transaction. The British and other foreigners gain this per centage of nineteen per cent. on all they buy from us, and we lose it. The paper system of Mr. Chase is sapping the vitals of the people, and must end in national bankruptcy and ruin. The poor will become poorer, and the rich richer, owing to Mr. Chase's paper system, and the interests of the millions and laboring classes will be sacrificed to those of the rich and favored few.

THE SOUTHERN CONFEDERACY DEMANDS RECOGNITION OF ENGLAND AND FRANCE.

We find the following among the Washington despatches to the New York *World:*

Jefferson Davis has sent a special messenger to the Emperor of France and to the Queen of England with despatches of a private nature demanding the immediate recognition of the Southern Confederacy. The demand is said to be followed by a voluminous bundle of documents, including letters written by the English and French Consuls at Richmond, testifying to the unanimity manifested by the inhabitants of that city in forming a separate government and of their ability to maintain it. Another document, merely devoted to the military operations of the Confederates, states that nearly all the battles fought in Virginia, from Bull Run down to the seven days' fight before Richmond, including the battle of Fair Oaks, and the operations in the Shenandoah Valley, were as many victories won by the South against an enemy vastly superior in men, in material of war, in money, and in resources of all kinds. In a private note addressed by Jeff. Davis to Louis Napoleon himself, the rebel President reminds his Majesty of the fact that nine months ago several cabinet councils were held in Paris with the special object of discussing the propriety of recognizing the Confederate States, who were then thought deserving their recognition, and that the thing was given up only when the reverses of Port Royal and Fort Donelson made the French Cabinet fear that the South would not be able to stand against the North and maintain its independence. The notes end by stating that all fears of that kind ought to be abandoned now, and the series of brilliant victories won by the Confederates, as well as the rapid exhaustion of the resources of the North, ought to satisfy the Emperor of the unanimity of sentiment existing in the South concerning its separation from the North, and of the resources it possesses for the building up of a strong, respected, prosperous and independent nationality.

THE MERRIMAC NO. TWO.

A correspondent of the New York *Tribune* writes from Fortress Monroe the following, which is "news" in Charleston as well as New York:

A few days previous to the evacuation of Norfolk by the rebels, "Merrimac No. 2" was towed from the navy yard in that city up James River to Richmond, where a large number of mechanics have since been engaged in plating her with iron and preparing her for service. Her armor is in plates instead of bars, her sides of wood, and six feet thick; and she will have all the improvements suggested by the career of the Merrimac. In the haste of the evacuation her boilers were left behind on the dock at Norfolk; but she has since been supplied with others at Richmond, which circumstance has occasioned a delay in her coming out. She has received the engines of the Arctic, commanded by Captain Hartstein in his Northern exploration. These engines were taken out of the vessel at Norfolk, soon after her return from her memorable voyage. The name of the new steamer or ram has been changed to the Richmond, is about two-thirds the size of the Merrimac (or Virginia), will draw about ten feet, and is represented as being altogether more formidable than the slayer of the Cumberland and Congress. Deserters, escaped prisoners, and others, represent that she is nearly ready to make her appearance in James River, and the slaughter of any number of our gunboats is confidently counted on. It is said that the obstructions at Fort Darling have been so contrived as to let her drop through, as did the Teazer the other day.

THE "GRADUAL EMANCIPATION" SCHEME.

On Saturday last, the Representatives and Senators of the Border Slaveholding States having, by special invitation of President Lincoln, been convened at the Executive Mansion, he made them a good bye overture in favor of his "gradual emancipation scheme" in view of the fact that Congress would adjourn, and leave him alone in his glory. He urged upon them the policy and importance of the scheme, as the only measure which could reduce the rebellion more quickly than bombs and bayonets, and begged them when they went back to their people to recommend its adoption among them.

The Border State Senators and Representatives returned to their lodgings, held a meeting, and twenty of them agreed to disagree with the President, being unable to see how interfering with private property could bring the war to a close with any more rapidity than the very plausible argument already employed, termed "coercion." Among other reasons presented by them against the policy recommended was the very important one that the "gradual emancipation kick" would cost the Government just a fraction over four hundred and seventy-eight millions of dollars. They could not, therefore, conscientiously circulate the documents in favor of the scheme when they got home.

The minority, consisting of seven members, made a milk and water report, in which they "could not reconcile it with their sense of duty, in this trying hour, to respond in a spirit of fault-finding," and believing that His Excellency meant everything for the best, they couldn't resist his appeal. So they went in for it, body and soul.

OUR VICTORY AT MURFREESBORO.

The Knoxville *Register* furnishes the following particulars of Col. FORREST's brilliant little victory at Murfreesboro:

The number of Yankees killed and wounded was about 125, prisoners captured about 1,250—of the 3d Minnesota regiment, 600; 9th Michigan, 500; 7th Pennsylvania Cavalry, 150; Hewett's Kentucky Battery of 4 guns, 2 brass and 2 steel; 300 horses and mules; 60 wagons; several ambulances, and 2,000 stand of arms. The Federal camps, with all their contents, embracing a large lot of new clothing, were burned, as was also the depot at Murfreesboro, containing near half a million of dollars worth of Quartermaster's and Commissary stores. Several railroad bridges near Murfreesboro were also burnt. The Confederate force engaged 1,300 to 1,600. The Confederate loss in killed and wounded was about 46.

Brigadier General Duffield was badly wounded and paroled; Gen. T. T. Crittenden, of Indiana, with some fifty officers, including Colonels, Lt. Colonels and Majors, were sent, prisoners of war, to Madison, Ga.

MORGAN AT HIS OLD TRICKS.

From the same paper we get the following:

We have information, deemed reliable, that Col. Morgan has cut off a Federal supply train, this side of Richmond, Ky., on its way to Cumberland Gap, and that Col. Spears' Regiment had been sent from Cumberland Gap to intercept him, supposing, we presume, that Morgan's exploit was only a sudden raid into Kentucky, to be followed by a sudden retreat to East Tennessee. It appears, however, if Spears intercepts Morgan, he will have to get in between him and the Ohio River, towards which, we hear, Morgan is dashing, having already burnt the bridge at Richmond, Ky., and spreading consternation amongst the Union tories and joy amongst the friends of the South in his triumph.

INTERESTING FROM THE VALLEY OF VIRGINIA.

The Richmond *Dispatch* publishes the following extract from a letter written by a trustworthy officer of our army in the Valley of Virginia:

"The Yankees are leaving the Valley rapidly. They have a considerable amount of supplies at Winchester yet, and we will either capture or destroy some of them. Our presence, too, induces many to desert, and they flock to us rapidly. Fifteen in one gang came up to Powell's Fort day before yesterday, and five in another. Four hundred deserted from one regiment at Front Royal the past week, leaving nothing but officers. There is great dissatisfaction and demoralization in the Yankee army here, and if their men at home have no greater inclination to fight this war through than their hirlings here, Old Abe will have a sorry time of it in getting his 300,000 additional troops. General Robertson paroles all who voluntarily come into our lines.

"The army of the Valley were turned from their march through Manassas Gap by a few guerillas. They then went up the Page Valley. There was great panic in the whole army. Thirty men turned the course of more than 2500."

MISCELLANEOUS.

The Northern papers report Stonewall Jackson as marching on Winchester, with a large force.

The Baltimore Sun, in speaking of the circulation of postage stamps, denominates it the "sticking plaster currency."

Edwin H. Webster, Yankee Representative from Maryland, has been nominated by Lincoln as a brigadier general of volunteers.

The Washington Star says that a portion of the army of Gen. Pope entered Gordonsville, Virginia, unopposed, and destroyed all the railroad paraphernalia at that point.

Tar is burned daily, as a fumigator, in all the hospitals in Richmond where Yankees are under treatment for wounds. It acts most beneficially as a fumigator.

The Baltimore Sun of the 18th inst. states that Ellis V. McCleese was arrested there the day before by Gen. Wool, and sent to Fort McHenry, upon the charge of having been in Richmond.

The Yankee Congress has adjourned. It is stated that during the recent session there were appropriated about eight hundred millions of dollars, including upwards of five hundred and sixty millions for the army, and somewhat less than one hundred millions for the navy.

The New York Herald says that Butler has sent from New Orleans, as trophies, to the Government at Washington, a complete set of plates, from which the notes of the Confederate States were printed. They are of the denominations of five, ten, twenty, fifty and one hundred dollars.

In view of the daily increasing difficulty of providing for the thousands of contrabands, it is urged that the President should be authorized to purchase lands in Central America for the colonization of the emancipated negros. The proposition is known to be in accordance with the views of the Executive, and finds much favor in Congress.

The Yankees, while operating on the line of the Pamunkey and Chickahominy rivers, received much assistance and information from the Indian tribe in King William, who are familiar with every inch of the country, and therefore expert guides. They still occupy their old settlement, and have not been called to account for their proceedings.

Major Trumbull, of the First Connecticut Artillery, states that that corps had charge of all the siege guns of the army during McClellan's masterly retreat, and saved every one of them. The guns were placed in position on five different occasions during the retreat, and the advancing columns of the enemy thereby held in check, until the positions which the Commanding General designed to secure were gained.

The New York Herald says that the three gunboats of the Monitor model which were ordered by the government some time since are advancing towards completion with commendable speed at Greenpoint. Their length is three hundred and two feet over all, with a breadth of beam of forty-one feet, and a depth of hold of twelve feet. Their armor will be six inches in thickness, and each boat will have two revolving shot-proof turrets.

Mr. A. H. H. Dawson, of Mobile, announces his intention to dedicate to the people of Alabama a volume of memoirs, which shall embrace the history of every Alabamian who has fallen or may fall in this war, either in action, or from disease contracted while in the service of the Confederacy. He requests the relatives and friends of the fallen to assist him in the work by furnishing him with all the information in their power.

The Yankee force at Suffolk, Va., is about 8,000. Gen. Mansfield is in command, aided by two Provosts—Paul de Kay and Van Webber.—The Episcopal Church is used as a negro church by a Yankee from Massachusetts, who officiates every Sunday. During the week the vestry is made a secret bar room, where the "blockade" is run at so much a glass. Mansfield has seized the residence of Nathaniel Riddick, and supplies his table from Mr. R.'s farm.

WAITING TILL AFTER THE WAR.

[*From the Montgomery Advertiser, July 23.*]

In the old Union the South was always beset by a class of time-serving politicians who urged the postponement of every issue of principle with the North as an excuse for their truckling subserviency to unauthorized power. There can be no doubt that these temporizers did more to encourage the North in its aggression, and to conceal from the South the dangerous innovations upon the Constitution, than all other influences together. The people of the South must to-day admit that the only hope there ever was to maintain the United States Government in its original purity was yielded up when they assented from time to time to forego their right to hold their authorities to instant responsibility for every surrender of the spirit of the compact. This is a lesson which ought to be invaluable to the people of the Confederate States in dealing with the officials of their new Government; for, unfortunately, the tendency of human nature toward usurpation and tyranny has been the same everywhere. The Southern people should never forget that they have many of the seeds of error in their system, which, if they would destroy, they must lose no opportunity to nip in the bud. Time will enable these seeds of error to take a rank growth which may finally poison the whole body politic.

These general suggestions have occurred to us in connection with that specious argument so often put forth against the free expression of opinion in regard to public men and measures during the war. The editor or apologist for an obnoxious state of things, who cannot combat you with reason, is sure to resort to the time-server's plea of waiting until after the war to discuss these things. This pretext is asserted as persistently as if it was thought overwhelming. These men must either be very easy to satisfy themselves, or think that the people are a great set of dupes to be satisfied with such clap-trap; but let us assure them that the Southern people have grown a little wiser by their experience, if the time-servers have not. The people can see that the time-servers, while professing harmony in the old Union, did nothing but breed discord, and that the factionists so called, were the wise friends of the South; they can see that, since the beginning of this war, had the views of independent military critics been followed instead of those who professed to believe the President and our Generals all-wise and sufficient, the North would to-day have been occupied by the Southern armies, and our people would not have been overrun at so many points by the Yankees; they can see that if all criticism upon the errors of the war is withheld until after the war, there will then be but little if any virtue in criticism, inasmuch as the abuses of which we complain may be permanently fastened upon the country, or, at any rate, cannot be recalled. There can be no more reason why abuse of power should go unrebuked now than in time of peace; indeed, the reason is not so strong in the former case, because the plea of "military necessity" is so convenient as to make it exceedingly dangerous. But military law, no more than civil law, justifies any infringement of a man's rights. Justice is the end to be sought under each rule, and if it is not administered through all the forms which law and custom have thrown around it, then somebody is responsible, and if the press exposes the outrage, and the Government vindicates its rightful authority, a remedy will be provided. What must be the calm judgment of the country upon those who in the great struggle for Southern independence would stifle the voice of public criticism? Would they have the South waste all this blood and treasure merely to establish another Union of inequality and corruption, to feed one portion at the expense of the other? Is the boasted "harmony" of which we have heard so much in the old Government to be in the new, the synonym of impurity and imbecility? No; thanks to the intelligent patriotism of our people, they are not children to be fed on the "pap" of sucklings. They are fighting for the principles of equality and justice which were denied them, by a course of submission, in the old Government, and they have established a government of their own, the main safeguard of which is, the "eternal vigilance" of the press and the people.

THE MONITOR AND GALENA.

The *Scientific American*, in speaking of the damage done to the above named vessels in the recent engagement at Drury's Bluff, says:

The severest blow we have yet received on the turret was at Fort Darling. It was from a solid ten-inch shot fired from a very heavy charge of powder, from a distance of about eight hundred yards. It struck the turret very nearly perpendicular with its side, making an indentation of three and a quarter inches, but without any visible fracture of the plates. On the inside, opposite the indentation, the plates were somewhat fractured.

The iron-clad Galena was severely handled in this fight, the fire from the batteries being mostly concentrated upon her on finding that their shells were penerating her sides. I am not positive that any shot passed entirely through both sides, but saw where a ten-inch shot had gone through her port-quarter, where her plating is two and a half inches thick with six inches of wood backing, and, after passing over her gun deck, had gone through the wood backing on the starboard quarter and crowded off the iron plating.

Shells penetrated her side where it was of the thickness I have stated above, and exploded on her gun-deck, making terrible havoc among her crew. In two or three places where her spar-deck was struck by ricochet shot, the entire substance of the deck, both wood and iron, for the distance of three feet and the width of the shell, was scooped out, leaving a clear opening through to the space below. This deck, however, is ridiculously light, being made of two-inch plank, covered over with two ¼-inch iron plates. As far as resistance to shot is concerned, she is a miserable failure.

A wild man was captured in the woods of Jackson county, Georgia, a few days since. All efforts to obtain his name and parentage have proved unavailing.

The British astronomical staff who went to Spain in 1860, to observe the total solar eclipse, have not yet completed their report.

VOL. 1. PHILADELPHIA, SATURDAY, AUGUST 2, 1862. NO. 38.

MORGAN, THE GUERILLA LEADER.

[ENGRAVED FOR THE PRESS, FROM A PHOTOGRAPH BY JENNINGS, LOUISVILLE, KY.—SEE PAGE 8]

[Written for The War Press.]

QUARTERING ON THE ENEMY.

A TALE OF POPE'S ARMY.—BY FERDINAND L. SARMIENTO.

The new orders had come, and, with them, new life and vigor to the Army of the Shenandoah. "Onward!" had long been the supplicating cry of the soldiers; but it remained for the energetic Pope to give the word. It was, therefore, with light hearts that our detachment marched out from the little village of N—— in pursuance of the newly-inaugurated policy of our trusty general.

We had but two days' rations on starting out, and, as it was now the morning of the *third* day, we began to call to mind the "order" which warranted us in quartering on the enemy.

It was early morn, and the fine gray mists of the awakening day covered everything as with a protecting veil. The inhabitants of the little hamlets in the distant valleys were still asleep, and the whole landscape was infused with a calm, holy, Sabbath-like quiet. I had seldom witnessed a more beautiful scene than now opened before us, even in this valley, so celebrated for its natural beauties—in no other country had I seen anything to compare to it. One hill rising gently over the other, studded all over with little snowy cottages—charming little valleys with trickling streams, winding like silver ribbons through their ferny depths, with noble groves of dark-leaved chestnuts and graceful cedars filling up their magnificent vistas—these were the objects that were presented in ever-varying pictures to the eyes of the way-farer—while the sweet feeling of peace that rested over all, added, if possible, to the charm. Peace! but why prate of peace? when, before night, our hands may be imbrued in human blood, our swords dripping with the red current of a hundred lives? How little of peace was there really in that scene!

Behind that wall yonder a slight smoke issues, followed by the sharp report of a rifle. One of our saddles is emptied, and, with loud oaths, three or four of our men dash away in the direction of the shot, to punish the contumacious enemy. It is a "bushwhacker," one of those pirates of the land who defy all honorable rules of warfare, and carry on a terrible and exhausting war of blood for blood.

See! the men have returned—they have failed in their search for the assassin. They *did* find a spot trodden and stamped, the fresh green, dewy, leaves still bending crushed and mangled; but of human forms they had seen nothing—thus the cowardly murderer had escaped.

In the meantime the rest of us had crowded around our fallen comrade. The ball had passed right through his heart. He had died almost instantly, without a word, and simply throwing up his arms in agony, had fallen dead from his horse.

It is a sad scene! Ten minutes before, he was as full of life as any of us—his heart swelled with as bright anticipations, his future was crowned with as glittering hopes, and now, now he is dead!

With the mutability of all human things thus brought in one vivid picture before our eyes, we clustered about him. Soldiers are much more affected at the sight of death than many imagine. There is ever a feeling when a comrade falls that brings death right home to the heart—that whispers "*it may be my turn next*," and which lends an awe to the dread approach of the king of terrors that no other circumstances could give.

In the battle-field, I grant, a mad enthusiasm may for the moment make one callous to all the sights of blood and suffering—but in the hospital, or "on picket", or in this horrid species of warfare, I have ever found that soldiers are more impressed even than civilians by such sights. With heads bowed down, then, and in silence our little party took up their course again; the corpse of their murdered comrade in their midst.

Our fallen comrade, Allan Risley, though but a private in our ranks, had won, by his good conduct and gentle manners, the love of both officers and men. I speak the word *love* advisedly, for, surrounded by dangers as we always were—dangers that needed mutual reliance to ward them off—our little troop became almost like brothers; one impulse moved us, one enthusiasm thrilled us all, and the bond of comradeship supplied the place of every other tie.

The only thing of importance that had been found on the body of the murdered soldier was a green morocco case, which contained the miniature of a young man of about his own age—some friend, no doubt—and which was handed to me, as the only officer in the party, for safe-keeping. Inside, it contained the words and date, "Harvard, September 25th, 1859," and as I called to mind the dead soldier, his gentle culture, and warm, sympathetic heart, my grief for his loss returned with redoubled poignancy.

As I have said, it was the morning of the third day of our setting out, and as we must now be in the neighborhood of a large body of the enemy, I determined, in pursuance of orders, to look about for proper quarters, where we might await the approach of our van-guard, which was pressing fast behind us. A large house, standing some distance from the main road, seemed most available for this purpose, and as it seemed to possess ample accommodation for a large number of persons, we turned our horses' heads that way, at the same time indulging in visions of corn-bread, or "Indian pome," as it is called, and a nice slice of bacon, which is, indeed, the principal food of the people of the South. With coffee at two dollars a pound, we did not, of course, anticipate such a treat as that, nor, indeed, was it necessary, for with the trooper

"Good digestion waits on appetite,
And health on both."

On approaching the house we found it a first-class tenement; finely shaded, and a splendid specimen of a Virginia gentleman's mansion. Of the inmates we saw none but the servants, from whom we learned that all the white *male* members of the family had left, and that but the mistress and her daughter remained. Placing poor Allan's corpse in a room, and stationing a guard over it, to await the arrival of our regimental chaplain, we proceeded to distribute ourselves about the house which was ample to accommodate us all. To me had been assigned the "young massa's room," as the grinning "dark" informed me "de best room in de whole house;" and towards midnight I betook myself to it, having been occupied until this late hour in writing letters home.

The heat throughout the day had been extreme, and as night approached, what little air there was died out and left the atmosphere close and sultry. Fearing then that sleep would fail to visit me, to gild with its heaven-born dreams my soldier pillow, I strolled restlessly about the room, looking at the little articles of *virtu* and the pictures on the wall. Of these last there were a number, all of which evinced most excellent taste on the part of their selector or possessor. But *one* struck me particularly. Yes, I could not be mistaken! There was the same broad brow—the same deep, earnest eyes! It was the portrait of our murdered comrade—it was Allan Risley!

I cannot tell the effect this discovery made upon me. At first I could not believe my senses. I was thunderstruck. To think of his cold body being beneath this roof, and *his picture* in my room! This family, then, must have known him—must have been intimate with him.

If I was restless before I was now thoroughly awake, and I threw myself into a chair by the open window, my head on my hand, in deep thought over the strange coincidence.

While thus lost in thought, a light footstep attracted my attention. I looked down. A woman clad in some light, fluttering material was stealing stealthily along, evidently endeavoring to gain the neighboring woods. The *manner* more than the *fact* attracted me, and made me suspect that she was bent on some treasonable errand. Being as yet dressed, I seized a limb of an overhanging tree, and before I knew well what I was doing had swung myself noiselessly to the ground, and was quietly following the waving outline of her figure. From the stately walk and elegant contour of the lady, I at once came to the conclusion that it was the fair daughter of the owner of our quarters. Now, as the whole family were known to partake of strong Secession principles, this midnight jaunt of the young lady might mean us mischief, so I determined to see it out.

On reaching the wood, she at first hesitated; then, seeming to gain courage, she drew a small silver whistle from her bosom, and blew a low, soft strain upon it. It was not long before it was answered, when, reassured, she advanced until met by the tall figure of a man.

Brother and sister—for such they were—had not met for several days, it seemed, as, through information from rebel scouts, the young man had known perfectly well of our approach, and had, in consequence, thought it prudent to absent himself from his home. There was, therefore, a multiplicity of questions of a private character, with which I had naught to do, and I had almost regretted my position as eaves-dropper, when the name of a notorious guerilla chief at once aroused all my attention. From the familiar manner in which his name was spoken, it seemed palpable to me that the young man must have a thorough knowledge both of the man and his movements. Perhaps, even, he was one of his band; but no, that could not be; a young man of apparently such gentle manners, and of such a high position in society, could not belong to a band of murderers. And yet it was well known that some of the highest and wealthiest young men in the Southern country were engaged in this horrid species of warfare. So, thinking, perhaps, to terrify the young man into a confession of the whereabouts of the celebrated assassin of whom he seemed to know so much, I determined to arrest him. I had not forgotten Allan's death, and was bent upon avenging it by the capture and just punishment of his murderer.

I had crept quietly up among the bushes, so near, that I had but to extend my arm, and my hand rested upon the young man's shoulder. Grasping him firmly with the one hand, while in the other I held my ever-ready revolver—"You are my prisoner," I exclaimed.

"Nay," I continued, as I saw him fumbling in his belt for his pistol. "Nay, any resistance, and this ball goes crashing through your brain." And, seeing that I would be true to my word, the young man was fain to drop his pistol, which he had at last drawn from his belt, and surrender himself my prisoner.

His sister, almost terrified to death, at this unexpected interruption of their interview, and fearful of the consequences to her brother, begged me in every conceivable term to liberate him; but, of course, my ideas of duty were much too strenuous to admit of my heeding the tears of the beautiful girl, much as they pierced and lacerated my heart. He might be able to furnish us with information the most valuable in relation to that terrible rebel chief, who, with his satellites, had already brought sorrow to so many of our Northern homes; and to whom, no doubt, we also now owed our loved companion's death. So, assuring him that no harm should befal him, I determined to hold on to him, until, at least, I had drawn whatever information he might possess, from him.

We had reached an open space now, and as the moonlight fell upon the pale features of my captive, I had almost let go my hold upon him, so great was my astonishment. He was the fac simile—the very counterpart of the picture found on my murdered comrade—Allan Risley!

Of this discovery—tallying so strangely with the picture in my bed room—I said nothing. A terrible suspicion had crossed my mind. The bush-whacker! Could it be possible that this young man was the assassin of the morning, and that he had, though unknowingly, killed his friend? I determined to try him.

On reaching the house I turned him over to some of my men, who gazed wonderingly at my unexpected appearance thus in the dead of night and with a prisoner. All being asleep but the small guard placed over poor Allen's remains, I determined to make the same guard answer for my prisoner, whom I ordered to be confined in a small room adjoining. This plan, too, furthered my purpose.

On entering the room where the corpse was laid out, covered with a white sheet, the young man started, and, I thought, turned a little pale, but regaining his composure, a half-bitter smile of triumph lighted his features and curved with a scornful arch his mouth, as he took his seat in the little room allotted for him, alongside of his sister, who had insisted in sharing his captivity.

For a long, long time, I sat talking and endeavoring to discover whether he had any knowledge of the guerilla band existing in the neighborhood—for, although convinced in my own mind that he was acquainted with their doings and whereabouts, I still had no proof against him.

In all his answers he was very guarded—letting no word fall that might be brought against him, and denying any knowledge whatever of even the existence of any such association. But at last, by dexterous management I succeeded in getting him to speak of the murdered form in the next room, and while I dilated at length upon the attendant circumstances of his death, watched his face closely. A man's eyes never lie—and right into his eyes I now looked. He was pale and nervous beneath my fixed gaze; but when I spoke of our unavailing pursuit of the bush-whacker, and the crafty manner in which he had eluded us, all other sentiments seemed to give way to pride, and I again noticed the same scornful and exultant smile of which I have spoken. Still, fear of detection soon grew paramount above all other feelings, I could see, and finding that he became more and more confused every moment, I determined to push him to the wall, and discover at once whether or not he was the real culprit.

I had been describing the whole event of the morning and had detailed it so vividly that even the prisoner bowed his head as though repentant. Among other things, I mentioned the green morocco case and the miniature through which the fatal bullet had passed. This aroused him. At the word miniature, a new and terrible light seemed to break upon him, and he looked up as though blinded in my face. Then, as though reassured, he asked lightly:

"This picture—this picture that the young man carried next his heart; it was doubtlessly the fair face of some mistress?"

"You shall judge for yourself," at the same time drawing forth the blood-stained case—"Behold it!" At sight of the green morocco case he almost fainted with emotion; and bursting it open sat gazing stupidly upon it, as though the terrible shock had bereft him of reason.

Seizing him by the arm, I led him rapidly into the adjoining room, and drawing near the corpse threw back its linen covering. Almost as white as the pale form before him, he gave but one look towards it, when, with a cry of anguish that froze every heart present, he threw himself upon his friend's remains, and with a sob that seemed to let out life itself, exclaimed—"Allan! Allan! *'Twas I that murdered thee!*"

The scene that followed is too horrible to detail. At the words of her brother the young girl had approached the spot where we were standing, and on beholding the pale corpse of our slain comrade, had fallen fainting to the floor. Allan, the dream of her earliest days—the bosom friend of her brother—Allan, her *lover*, was dead!

Oh, the deep anguish of that scene. I shall never forget it! We stood horror-struck, while naught but the low sobs of the unfortunate man could be heard. All at once these, too, ceased; we took hold of him gently and raised him up, but he burst madly from us, and, with a bitter laugh, stood tauntingly and defiantly. *He had become a raving maniac!*

THE REBEL RAM ARKANSAS.

THE FIGHT AT THE MOUTH OF THE YAZOO AND THE DASH DOWN THE MISSISSIPPI.

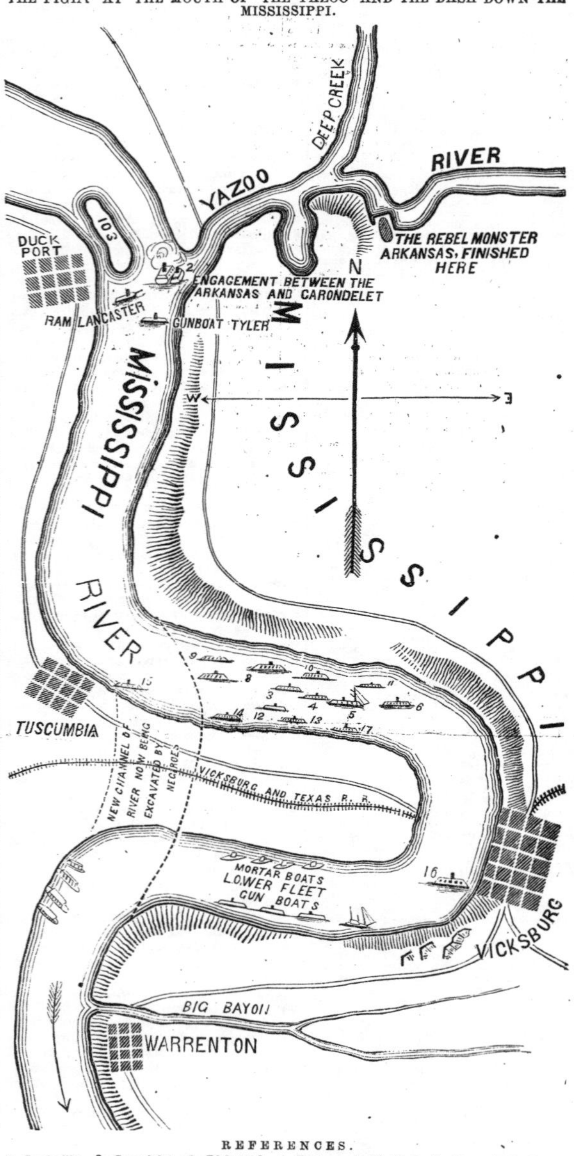

REFERENCES.

1—Louisville. 2—Carondelet. 3—Richmond. 4—Benton. 5—Hartford. 6.—Iroquois. 7—Bragg. 8—Cincinnati. 9—Queen of the West. 10—Sumter. 11—Essex. 12—Oneida. 13—John H. Dickey. 14—Monarch. 15. Caspian. 16—Arkansas, after action.

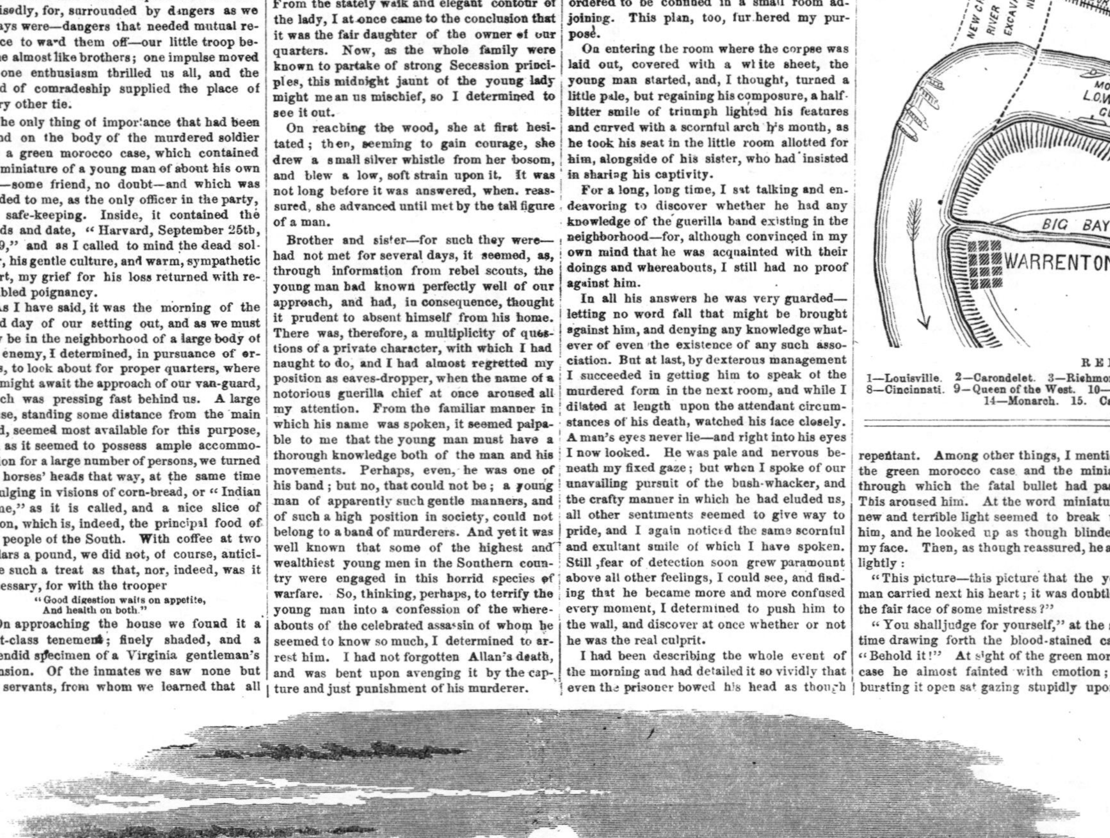

VIEW OF THE BEACH AT ATLANTIC CITY, NEW JERSEY.

A THRENODY

IN MEMORY OF MY SISTER ANNIE.

[For The War Press.]

With steps sad and lonely, full often I tread
The pathway which leads to the place of the dead,
When night's sable curtain is falling around,
Or dews of the morning besprinkle the ground,
To weep o'er a sister; yet why should I mourn,
Since I would not, if able, here bid her return?—
Recall her again from yon regions sublime,
To endure with me here the temptations of time.
No, Annie, dear Annie, tho' now we must part,
Thy image shall never remove from my heart,
While cypress and ivy shall garland thy tomb,
And roses and lilies there shed their perfume.
Like the bow in the heavens, which sweetly appears
When storms have just raged, and the earth is in tears,
Thy spirit will be, when over my soul
The waves of affliction unsparingly roll.
And when my probation on earth shall be o'er,
"When places which know me, shall know me no more,"
By angels upborne may I joyously rise,
To mingle with thee in the bliss of the skies.

ELIOR.

MORGAN, THE GUERILLA.

[See first page.]

Perhaps of all the rebel leaders who have distinguished themselves in this unholy rebellion, none has built up for himself a more extended or during fame than Col. John Morgan. Before attaching his fortunes to the Southern Confederacy, Morgan was a resident of Cincinnati, where he is very well known. He was what some call a "sporting man," but his fellow-citizens called him by the more appropriate names of blackleg and gambler. He married an estimable lady, some years since, but she died eighteen months ago, of grief, over the crimes of her husband. For two or three years, she was an utterly broken-hearted woman, and finally sunk into the grave, about six weeks before Morgan took the last step in the direction of infamy, by joining the Southern Confederacy.

The guerilla chief formerly had an interest in a faro bank in Cincinnati. He was engaged in picking up "seeds," as verdant people who accompanied him to the gambling house were familiarly called. He had no social position in Lexington, save among men of his own class. Honest men always despised him, and none more so than many who are now his admirers.

Col. Morgan himself is courteous and polite. He stands about six feet in height, is slightly round-shouldered, and his dress is distinguished by nothing except a silver crescent, which holds up one side of his wide-brimmed, low-crowned, black felt hat. His face is rather dark-complexioned, with features sharp. He is idolized by his men, who think he is Kentucky's Messiah. He possesses a nervous, energetic temperament, and to be satisfied must always be in motion. He is almost constantly in the saddle, and ever on the alert, both in a precautionary and aggressive sense.

To give the reader an adequate idea of his marauding talents, we take the following from a recent issue of the New York *World*: "Every body's prophecy is fulfilled. The guerillas are awake and abroad. Morgan, the chief of them, is on Northern soil. He crosses two States, and enters a third. He captures Harredsburg, Lawrenceburg, Versailles, and Henderson, Kentucky; rips up the track and burns Elkhorn bridge, of the Louisville and Lexington railroad: burns another bridge on the Kentucky Central, thus severing the communication of Lexington with the North and West; blockades the Ohio river, impresses hundreds of horses, and enlists riders for them all, and halts to get breath in the town of Newberg, Indiana."

The designs of Morgan in making these movements, are variously understood. It is very evident, however, that they embrace more than the seizure, confiscation, and destruction of property belonging to Unionists. It has been alleged, (and the annexed incident forms the supposition) that he did not design to fight with his present force, but only to present to the malcontents a nucleus around which they could rally.

While at Versailles, he was waited upon by a body of rebels, who urged him to leave the State, telling him that his movement was premature, and would ruin the prospects of his friends at the August election, and that a partisan war would be inaugurated by his presence, which would ultimately result in the imprisonment, banishment or death of every Southern sympathizer in the State. The guerilla captain listened attentively to the deputation until they had closed, when he flew into a rage, cursed them, and denominated them as cowards and traitors to the cause of "Southern rights." He declared that he had received at least two thousand letters from Kentuckians, urging him to enter the State, and pledging him an almost unlimited number of recruits exceedingly anxious to lay down their lives in the Southern cause; not only had he been deceived as to the number who would join him, but those who came were generally unarmed and on foot, which rendered it necessary that horses should be stolen to supply them; but that which was the worst of all, he declared, was the invitation to leave the State. He had been deceived, and now he was slighted. He then produced a letter from Capt. Buford, one of the committee then present, in which he was solicited, in the strongest terms, to make the raid. Flinging the document contemptuously at the author, he exclaimed, "There, you d—d hypocrite," and then dismissed the delegation.

Nevertheless, his calculations have not been altogether incorrect. He went into Kentucky with a force inadequate to accomplish what has actually been accomplished; but now his force is large. He has recruited an army of five thousand men, fully, and in many cases splendidly, armed and equipped. He knows, from numerous spies in each and every position held by us, the exact force of the Union arms. His movements show how well he is acquainted with our own. To prevent the reinforcement of Lexington by soldiers from Louisville or Frankfort, he made a demonstration at Midway, and tore up the track. Hence, Cincinnati reinforced Lexington, a strong force being sent there—in fact, all the infantry Cincinnati could spare. No sooner had this been done than he appears north of Lexington, destroys the railroad to Cincinnati, and attacks Cynthiana. Here the hastily reinforced garrison is overpowered, and a Cincinnati artillery company killed or captured. To increase the trouble, a small force of guerillas appears at Falmouth, and reports are heard of an advance on Covington. And it is now apparent that Morgan could have gone to Covington and shelled Cincinnati had not he feared for his retreat.

Morgan is ubiquitous in more senses than one. We feel his power east and west. His force, divided, has appeared in the Blue Grass region, and in the tobacco fields in the Green river valley. He travels with speed. His operations are rapid and vigorous. In a decent cause they would deserve success. Even in this vile cause they meet with unprecedented success, and would stamp the rascal who plans them as a man of ability, if we did not know that he was only a gambler and faro dealer.

WANTED 300,000 MEN.

Three hundred thousand men
Are wanted now to fight;
All earnest, brave, and strong,
To crush the foulest Wrong
That ever smote the Right.

Our valiant ranks are thinned;
Who ever knew before
So few so many meet,
And conquer in retreat?
They must retreat no more!

Fill up their shattered ranks,
Come, fathers, brothers, sons;
The hour is big with Fate,
Ye must no longer wait,
But to the field at once!

Your glorious sires of old
Left in the ground the plough;
They dropped their sickles then,
To reap their fellow-men—
So must their children now!

Come from your country homes,
Ye tillers of the soil,
Whose ruddy cheeks and hands
The fiery summer brands—
All brown with honest toil!

Come from the crowded streets,
The busy city's roar;
East, West, North—far and near,
If Freedom still is dear.
Come, strike for her once more!

Three hundred thousand men
Must hurry to the fight,
So fierce the foe, and strong—
Shall he do more for Wrong,
Than we, brave boys, for Right?

THE LOBSTER.

As a young lobster roamed about,
Itself and mother being out,
Their eyes at the same moment fell
On a boiled lobster's scarlet shell.
"Look," said the younger, "is it true,
That we might wear so bright a hue?
No coral, if I trust my eye,
Can with its brilliance vie;
While you and I must be content
A dingy aspect to present."
"Proud, heedless fool," the parent cried,
"Know you the penalty of pride?
The tawdry finery you wish,
Has ruined this unhappy fish;
The hue so much by you desired,
By his destruction was acquired;
So be contented with your lot,
Nor seek to change by going to pot."

ILLINOIS SECESH.—Jim Clarkson, formerly editor and proprietor of the *State Democrat*, published at Springfield, in that State, has been taken prisoner by the Federal troops in Arkansas. The Illinois *Journal* advises that he be sworn and let go, as the Secesh at Camp Butler don't wish any such fellows sent there.

THE DRUMMER OF COMPANY C.

Here, sergeant! hail me yon ambulance; this boy is one of our corps;
He must not be left till the cart returns, for the night is cold and raw.
Gently! turn his face to the moon, it will soon be from under the cloud.
By Jove! he has chosen a glorious couch, where the ground is newly ploughed.
Loosen his jacket, and slide your hand till you feel the beats of his heart,
Then lift him quietly out of the rut and carry him on to the cart.

Poor fellow! his drum is a total wreck; hold, sergeant; there is the moon!
Ah, lad! it is well we came as we did, for we came not a bit too soon.
That ugly minnie has scored his breast like the gash of a jagged knife,
And the thirsty ground has swallowed his blood, perhaps the blood of his life.
Great Heavens! why, men, it is Jimmy McGraw, the drummer of Company C.
The bravest and best of the lot of our boys, and the stoutest of drummers is he.

"Ah, doctor! I'm gladdened to think that you've come, for I dreamed just now I was dead,
And that hurrying men and maddened beasts went crashing over my head.
I dreamed that I never cared a pin if I was dead or no,
But I hated to know that the men of my corps were flying away from the foe.
I'm glad that you came, for now I shall know whether the fight is won,
And whether the men of Company C were the bravest under the sun.

"They'll tell ye I stood at the right of the line, and gave them the double quick,
And that never a beat of their hearts was lost I could echo with my stick.
For, doctor, dear, the sight was grand when their bayonets flashed in the sun,
And with one grand charge from Company C the enemy broke and run.
I remember the parting volley they gave, there's some of it here in my breast,
But after that it was cold and dark, and I have forgotten the rest.

"It was quite too bad that I should fall so early in the fight,
And should miss the flinging of our flag from the enemy's strongest height.
I can see it float in the moon's soft light, with a wave like an angel's wing,
And I hear on the heights, like an angel's song, their shouts of triumph ring.
Oh, doctor, hasten the cart along! I fear that my life will flee
Before I've a chance to be in their midst and cheer with Company C.

"It was only this noon that a letter from home was put in my eager hand,
And you that have left the loved behind will easily understand
The joy of my heart when I laid it away on my beating breast, unread,
And ran at the call of Company C to place myself at their head.
'Tis here with its seal unbroken yet, 'tis here with my life-blood damp;
But I'll live till you read it me, doctor dear, after we reach the camp."

Steadily! steadily, men, with your load; let him lie here in my tent;
We must keep the life in the boy awhile, for the letter his mother has sent.
Do you mark his eyes, how they follow my hand with an anxious greedy stare;
Never a line but a mother's line could awaken that eager air.
Quietly, lad! by the light of the moon I will read your mother's hymn;
God grant it may put new life in your heart, and strength in your every limb.

"To Jimmy McGraw, of Company C, the Lord betwixt him and harm:
May He lighten his heart and brighten his eye and strengthen the work of his arm.
Ye were always kind to your mother, my boy, and her heart has grown weary and sore,
Since the day when she pressed your cheek to her breast, and ye left her to go to the war.
And yet she is proud that her fatherless boy is fighting the fight of the free,
And prays that the Lord may quicken the hands of the men of Company C.

"The neighbors are asking me every day for news from the lad of their choice,
And many's the tear that I mark in their eyes, and many's the trembling voice.
It is little they have to send to my boy, but if all they had were a charm,
How quick they would send it, with all their hearts, to keep him away from harm!
They tell me that drummers must never be shot; please God that the telling be true,
And that He who can guide the murderous balls will ward them away from you.

"There's never a minute of all the long day that my thought is not faithful and warm,
And never a thing that I see in my walks but your face is a part of its form.
Ye must mind the least word of your captain, my boy, and be true to your duty and name;
The McGraws were always both honest and true, and my boy can't be less than that same.
Never fear for the end if your conscience is right, for the Lord loves the lone widow's son,
And ye'll always be hailed as a hero, my boy, when the war and the fighting is done.

"And think of your mother through every hour, who is praying at home for the day
When the angel of peace shall alight on the land, and the battle cloud vanish away,
When my boy shall return that his mother may lean alike on his heart and his arm,
And never know more of that sickening fear, from the news of a battle's alarm
God bless ye, and save ye, my fatherless boy, make ye able to do and to dare,
Make ye true to your flag, and true to yourself, is the whole of your mother's prayer."

Steadily! steadily, men, with your load, the boy was as honest as brave;
He deserves the flag for his winding sheet, and a volley over his grave.
The letter shall lie on his silent heart; his pillow his broken drum,
For many a time will you hear its beat, long after its voice is dumb.
The boy was a soldier, good and true; may I die as calm as he,
And be shrined in the hearts of a hundred men as brave as Company C.

J. W. WATSON.

VANITY-FAIRISMS.

RAM AWAY!—The daily papers announce, in large capitals, "Another Ram at Savannah;" but what we want to hear about is Another Ram at Richmond, and one well rammed home at that.

MOTTO FOR THE WATERING-PLACE BELLES AND BEAUX.—"Hop" deferred maketh the heart sick.

THE DESPOTISM OF GENERAL BUTLER.—It appears that Gen. Butler, not satisfied with having extracted the sting from the New Orleans *Bee*, has lately commissioned T. B. Therpe, so well known as the "Bee Hunter," to look after the sanitary arrangements of that city—a duty which embraces, of course, the suppression of nuisances, and of all troublesome insects that Bee.

GOOD SHOOTING.—The following dialogue is reported to have recently taken place between a rebel and a Federal picket:

Rebel. "I say, can you fellows shoot?"

Federal. "Waal, I reckon we can some."

Rebel. "Down in Mississippi we can knock a bumble-bee off a thistle blow at three hundred yards."

Federal. "Oh, that aint nothin' to the way we shoot in Varmount. I belonged to a company there, and we went out for practice every week. The captain draws us up in file, and sets a cider barrel rolling down hill, and each takes his shot at the bung-hole as it turns up. It is afterwards examined, and if there was a shot that didn't go in the bung-hole, the member who missed it was expelled. I belonged to the company ten years, and there ain't been nobody expelled."

THE RECONCILIATION.

Blue coat, trimmings of flashing red,
Gilded shoulders, and feathered cap,
An eagle gleaming above your heart—
A bullet may shatter it, mayhap—
Straight, slim form, and elastic tread,
A face that is cheerful, almost gay,
Full of resolve, and courage, and hope,
How brave you are looking, DOUG, to-day.
I saw you last Christmas, at Barron's Hall;
I hated you in your suit of black,
With your glossy collar and smell of musk,
And your neck-tie knotted with such a knack,
Talking your nothings with silly belles,
Obedient servant to kerchief and fan,
Elegant, jovial, "a catch," to be sure,
But to-day you seem to me more of a MAN.
You know, last spring, when we went one night
To the garden, to hear the German band,
You grew sentimental beneath the moon,
And made me an offer of heart and hand.
Well, I—I—think that I answered "no!"
But I was—hasty—and—so—you—see—
Well, take my first kiss! God bless and bring
My hero—my—lover back to me.

A MOAN OVER AMERICA.

[From the London Times, July 8, 1862.]

The news from America is such as a sick old soldier in a thirty-years' war might dream in a nightmare of incessant, aimless, endless, purposeless fighting. Everywhere there is a dead-lock of arms; everywhere one sees armies encamped in morasses, or toiling through mud, under a burning sun, to some point, where, after an even balance of mutual slaughter, they will shortly find themselves as they were, only reduced in numbers, encumbered with sick and wounded, and condemned to many weeks of inaction. The noblest heroism is wasted in the attempt to gain positions, which are either not won, or only won to be found useless. As two desperate wrestlers pass and repass the identical spot over and over again, armies acquire ground only to lose it, and lose it to regain it, and regain it to stand in daily apprehension of a more signal reverse than the last. Far away from the basis of operations, under the burning sun of Charleston, and within four miles of that city, the New York "Highlanders" have been marched up to earthworks, where, after three charges, the last with empty muskets, they left the trenches filled with their dead. The only result is mutual terror and a common determination not to yield. McClellan stands and still stands before Richmond with his eighty thousand men. Between him and the city are seven miles of mud, an equal protection to both armies. He demands reinforcements, which are needed elsewhere, and for the sake of which the right wing of the Northern line has been sadly denuded. Should he be defeated in the battle now imminent his retreat will be disastrous. General Banks, with two other generals of name, has only recovered his position on the Shenandoah to be assured that he will not reap without molestation the plentiful harvest fast ripening about him. The possession of New Orleans leaves the city a desert. No vessel comes up the river. The warehouse gates are all closed. Every commercial transaction is regarded only as bearing on finances or the currency. General Butler is engaged in quarrels with women, with merchants, and with the consuls of all nations, and is hanging men who defy his authority by hauling down the Federal flag, or pretend his authority for the purpose of plunder. In the Mississippi and its tributaries expeditions conducted with much courage and skill end in the possession of earthworks, useless when gained, and costing in one case the horrible death of a whole ship's crew, a hostile shot having penetrated its steam drum. Meanwhile the cry is for more men. A hundred thousand men are wanted, and with doubled bounties and pay, it is said, they will come. Great, indeed, must be their zeal or their cupidity if they join a war which only sends back shiploads of sick and wounded, who would all perish, it is said, in the holds of the "floating hospitals" but for the kindly aid of good women.

The eye wearies itself as it attempts to pierce through this confusion in search of the beginning of the end. On neither side is there any relaxing or relenting. They must have suffered hardships familiar enough to the soldiers of the populous and ill-fed regions in this Old World, but very new to the inhabitants of a land flowing with milk and honey. Yet they endure, and do, and die, with all the spirit worthy of a greater and more intelligible cause. Many thousands of Irishmen have expiated the follies of Repeal by dying to enforce Union; and as many Germans, cast out by their own fatherland, have perished in other men's quarrels. Yet there is no prospect of the war flagging for want of men, and we are compelled to look forward to the possible time when the process of mutual destruction may at least reduce the South to an utter disproportion of force. Is it possible that this is the goal of Northern ambition, and that, like the tyrant of old, they hope to make a solitude and call it a Federal Union? It is at best a dangerous game, for the invaders are neither so much at home in the climate, nor so well under cover, as the inhabitants of the South, nor so able to avail themselves of the resources of the country. But let us suppose the hideous consummation; let us grant that it may be possible to sacrifice man against man, and by dint of money to procure a perpetual succession of American or foreign recruits to supply the exhaustion. What will be the value of a territory from off which the men have been destroyed? Will it be a conquest when the soil alone survives with a miserable burden of women, children, and slaves, the sick, the aged, and the maimed? If this be what the Americans seriously contemplate, then may we well ask which are the best and truest friends to America—we, who have advised them over and over again to divide quietly into two friendly federations, or the men who advise Boston and New York not to draw the rein, or abate the spread of war, till there remains not a man to pull down the Stripes and Stars on the soil of the United States?

The intelligence swells in its range and in its horrors, as the war flows round the whole Union, settles in the deep inlets, fortifies itself in peninsulas, and becomes chronic in vast plains. The long weary columns of slaughter we give to-day can only be considered as an earnest of the worse that may be expected should the defenders of Richmond retreat to the mountains in their rear, and all the other armies now at bay fall back on their supplies and resources in the interior. The mutual charges of inhumanity show how intense is the bitterness already implanted by less than two years' war. Only last year it was a matter of pride and gratification to both sides that Fort Sumpter had fallen without the loss of a man on either side, and it was predicted that the Americans would fight a bloodless war. It is far otherwise now. The greatest brutalities are committed or ascribed, it matters not which; for, if ascribed, they will be retaliated. If scalded sailors leap into the sea, the Confederates are charged with firing canister shot at the boats sent to save the drowning wretches. Elsewhere, the Confederates are charged with massacring housefuls of sleeping "contrabands." These are rumors, and may, or may not, be true. A private authority always needs corroboration or checking. The same doubt cannot be admitted in favor of the authorities at whose mercy lies the hapless city of New Orleans. Its story is to be read in the proclamations and the correspondence of its military masters, and never did conquerors assume such a tone. They have, indeed, conquered the city, its inhabitants, and all its valuable contents, though the latter be paid for by English money, be stored in English names, and only wait for the convenience of a passage to this country. The Americans will one day find that such tyranny recoils back on the heads of those who countenance it, and that they are sanctioning against themselves the principles which they permit towards others. This is the retribution of a policy which looks only to conquest and power. It raises dictators, conquerors, and tyrants, only to bear their yoke when there is no one else to bear it.

ANOTHER TIRADE ON AMERICA.

[From the London Times, July 16.]

We sadly want a Homer for this American Troy. The accounts we have of these battles before Richmond are still very hazy. All that we can safely extract from them is, that the Federals have suffered a severe defeat, and that they have attempted, by frantic boasts and impudent falsehoods, to palm it upon the world as a victory. It is one of the most remarkable circumstances connected with this savage civil war that it seems to have destroyed, in a common ruin, all the finer feelings of those who have taken part in it. We judge only from the universal and uncontradicted testimony of the Government, the Congress, and the press, when we note that pecuniary honesty was the first quality to go. When General Butler became a popular hero the Federal States formally renounced the reputation they had ostentatiously cultivated for gallantry towards women. After the letter from General Beauregard which we published yesterday, we are obliged to withdraw all confidence in the veracity of the highest military officers in the Federal service. There used to be pecuniary honor, manly gallantry, and candid veracity among Americans. What is become of them since this war commenced? Even previous to General Beauregard's letter there had been sufficient evidence of the carelessness or recklessness with which the Federal generals made their official reports. After General McClellan, for instance, had officially described several brilliant bayonet charges, it was tardily discovered that there was only one man on the field who had died of a bayonet thrust. But that two generals should positively and officially announce in a despatch to their Government the capture of 10,000 prisoners and 15,000 stand of arms, and that the fact so solemnly announced should turn out to be an utter falsehood, is, we believe, altogether unprecedented in Europe, and even in America. General Beauregard not only denies the whole story, characterizing it as a lamentable disrespect for truth, but he asserts that the whole of the losses suffered in his masterly retreat were 500 damaged muskets, overlooked in the camp, one or two hundred stragglers, and four sick soldiers, barbarously burnt by Colonel Elliot in a railway station. That General Beauregard has given the correct version of the affair is evident from this, that Generals Halleck and Pope might have readily confuted him by producing the prisoners and the arms. But it is not suggested that any one has ever seen either the one or the other. After the despatch had produced its effect no more was said about this exceedingly important capture of a Confederate army. After this experience, we must have some testimony other than the official report of an American general before we can place confidence in the result, or even belief in the existence of any operation he may describe.

But if the Federal generals sometimes boast of what they never did, the office of the Secretary of War seems to be nothing more than a workshop for falsifications of the clumsiest kind. Commanding all the telegraphic communications of the country, absolutely prohibiting the publication of any independent accounts of military events, Mr. Stanton seems to have adopted it as a rule of official routine, that no first report of a battle shall go forth to the American public which is not intrinsically false, and that even falsehood shall not pass, unless it be exactly cut to the official pattern. The condition of the men who are so mean and spiritless as to continue to conduct newspapers under such a thraldom is necessarily miserable and degrading. The public saw yesterday in our columns an account written by Mr. Charles C. Fulton, "agent to the Associated Press," and purporting to be a description of the events which had happened before Richmond. It bore its own character upon it. It was a romance written to order. Its text was, "We have the grandest military triumph over the enemy, and Richmond must fall." The dissertation was worthy of the text, and the whole performance bore an artificial and untruthful air. As we gather from the published correspondence, Mr. Fulton—who it seems was then in the Federal camp—had been sent for by special train to communicate with the President and the Secretary of War, and had drawn up under their instructions this voluminous piece of false intelligence. He had, in fact, given to a story of a fictitious victory a little *couleur locale*, and had settled in consultation the only intelligence which was to be allowed to go forth. Forthwith, Mr. Fulton printed the victory in the *Baltimore American*, and, to his intense astonishment, he, a few hours afterwards, found himself arrested and on his road to Fort Henry.

Expostulating against this strange reward, for having published the Secretary of War's own romance of victory, Mr. Fulton is told that he is not punished for publishing the statement, but because he had been discovered in betraying to a private friend, in a private telegram, that he had got his news from Washington. The President and the War Department had resented this as an outrageous breach of confidence, and sent Mr. Fulton to Fort Henry accordingly. Perhaps they were right. If Mr. Fulton betrayed a confidence reposed, no one will pity him for his temporary incarceration. We mention the facts, however, not for Mr. Fulton's sake, but in order to show the condition of the American press under the iron hand of the American Government, and the systematic manner in which contemporary history is falsified by men whose conspicuous position ought to make them tenacious of truth.

Under these circumstances, it is reasonable to take every statement telegraphed from the Federal side as strongly as possible against the Federal interest. With this rule of interpretation, it is clear that up to the 7th of this month, General McClellan had made no successful effort to retrieve his fortune, and that Richmond, which was to have fallen on the 4th, is still as far from being taken as ever. But, according to our reading of these telegrams, it is not clear that General McClellan has not met with a subsequent defeat; for when the Federals report "another skirmish, which has resulted in the Confederates being forced to retreat," we have an admission which is quite as strong as that which described the terrible battles of the last week in June. It is possible that in a few days this "skirmish" also may assume a different complexion and a hostile importance. Gradually, also, the facts of General McClellan's great strategic victories will ooze out, and gradually the facts of that victory of the 27th are now oozing out—for even the American Government cannot destroy truth for ever, and must be content with the advantages they can gain by putting out a first false impression. Somebody used to say that a lie had done its work if it could live for 48 hours. In this instance the falsehood has died a very gentle death. On the 2d of July, then, General McClellan was telegraphed by the American Government to have stated that he had lost but one gun and one wagon, and even this admission was eased off by a false report put about that General "Stonewall" Jackson had been killed before Richmond. Just, however, to prepare the way for the future, it was admitted that the Federal army had retreated 17 miles. On the 5th of July the old story is still repeated, and it is re-asserted with obstinate persistency that "the Federal forces were not beaten in any conflict." It is, however, on this date admitted, as a fact which it was impossible any longer to conceal, that General McClellan's division was at first overwhelmed, and that twenty-five pieces of artillery fell into the hands of the Confederates. Two days later a little more is permitted to creep into publicity in New York, and the newspapers are allowed to say, as a Southern version of the Richmond battles, that the Confederates had captured 12,000 prisoners, had got possession of all McClellan's siege guns, and had taken from him supplies sufficient to last the Confederate army three months. If we compare this last report with the first, we probably see the full effect of the official coloring. This is a good example of the way in which a great defeat may be cleverly toned down, and the tidings so gently broken as not to shock an impatient people. It is plain now to the meanest comprehension that McClellan was so thoroughly beaten on the 27th, with loss of guns and baggage, that he would have been driven into the river if his gunboats had not been there to protect him. The Government succeeded in falsifying this fact for a short time, and by so doing hoisted the stupid populace over this difficulty into another fools' paradise. But it is only with the scum of the Atlantic cities these tricks can now avail. They could not avert the panic of the New York Stock Exchange, or stay the shiploads of dollars which took flight for Europe, or delay the departure of the Orleanist Princes, deserting a no longer victorious cause, or prevent the people who are running together to make demonstrations against the means by which the war is conducted, or check the increasing sentiment that there is neither plunder nor glory to be obtained by the invading army in the Federal service, and that all who go South are doomed to melt away through pestilence or fall by the sword. Even in America—credulous and simple as we may there seem to be when we say so—truth and honesty would, we believe, be the best policy. It is coming rapidly to this, that the greater the victory announced, the more terrible will be the defeat believed in; and the President and his War Minister may succeed at last in so mystifying the American public, that if they really should gain a great victory, the announcement of it will put New York into mourning, and ruin all the speculators for a rise in Government stock.

PHILADELPHIA CATTLE MARKET.

JULY 28.

The receipts of Beef Cattle are larger this week than usual, reaching about 1,800 head. The market is not as active as last week, but prices are unchanged, ordinary Western Cattle ranging at from $7 to $8, and Chester county and good Western at from $8@8.75 ₩ 100 lbs, according to quality. As the stock on sale is larger than the demand, the market closed very dull, and prices declined 25c the 100 lbs, and most of the holders being anxious to sell at even lowest figures. In consequence of the large receipts this week 300@400 head will be left over.

The receipts to-day are from the following States: 780 head from Ohio, 673 head from Illinois, and 279 head from Chester county.

J. Abrahams, 48 Illinois steers, selling at from $8 @8.25

E. Scott, 16 Illinois steers, selling at $8.

Kimble & Kirk, 44 Illinois steers, selling at from $7.50 @8.50.

Busby, 85 Chester county steers, selling at $8@8.50.

B. C. Baldwin, 32 Chester county steers, selling at from $8@8.50.

James McFillen, Jr., 75 Western steers, selling at from $8@8.25.

P. Hathaway, 80 Ohio steers, selling at from $7.50@8.50.

P. McFillen, 75 Illinois steers, selling at from $7.50@8.50

Cochran & McCall, 100 Illinois steers, selling at from $8@8.50.

J. Seldomridge, 80 Illinois steers, selling at from $8@8.75.

Mooney & Smith, 190 Western steers, selling at from $8@8.75.

Ullman & Co, 36 Illinois steers, selling at from $7@8.

Fellhimer & Co., 167 Ohio steers, selling at from $7.50 @8.50.

H. Chain, 32 Illinois steers, selling at from $7.50@8.

M. Carson, 25 Chester county steers, selling at from $7.50@8 50.

J. Chaine, 20 Ohio steers, selling at from $8@8.50.

Fuller & Brothers, 68 Illinois steers, selling at $8@8.60.

Chandler & Co., 35 Chester county steers, selling at from $7.50@8 75.

McClese, 34 Chester county steers, selling at from $7@8.

E. McFillen 30 Ohio steers, selling at from $8@8.50.

Smith & Moony, 40 Ohio steers, selling at from $7@8.50.

Frank & Co., 37 Ohio steers, selling at from $7@8.

S. Storm, 32 Ohio steers, selling at from $7@8.

J. McChinson, 47 Illinois steers, selling at from $7@$8 50.

B Hood, 30 Chester county steers, selling at $7 50@8.

A. Kimble, 38 Chester-county steers, selling at from $7@8.50.

Rice & Smith, 101 Ohio steers, selling at from $8@8.75.

Crouse, 66 Ohio steers, selling at from $7.50@8.50.

Airsman, 55 Ohio steers, selling at from $7@8 25.

J. Shelby, 15 Ohio steers, selling at from $7@7.50.

COWS AND CALVES.

The receipts of Cows continue small, reaching about 160 head. There is very little doing, most buyers holding off for lower prices. Springers are selling at $15@28, and $20@35 per head for Cow and Calf, as to quality.

There is very little doing in Calves, and very few offering; 1st quality selling at 4@4¼c, and 2d quality at 3@3½c ₩ lb, according to quality.

THE SHEEP MARKET.

The receipts and sales of Sheep are very large this week, reaching about 8,000 head. The market is not so active, and prices are rather lower, ranging at from $2.50 to $4 ₩ head for Sheep, and $2.50@3 ₩ head for Lambs, as to condition and quality.

THE HOG MARKET.

The receipts and sales of Hogs at Phillip's Avenue Drove Yard reached 500 head this week, selling at from $5@5.50 ₩ 100 lbs net.

The arrivals of Fat Hogs at H. G Imhoff's Union Drove Yard reached 1.862 head this week, selling at from $4.25@4.75 for still-fed; and from $5@5.50 ₩ 100 lbs for corn-fed hogs, according to quality.

The following are the particulars of the receipts:

STILL-FED.

101 J. Colbach, Berks county, Pa.
155 W. Leeds, Carlisle, Pa
95 R. Seidle, Berks county, Pa.
120 J. Colbach, Berks county, Pa.
252 L. W. Washington, Circleville, Ohio.
116 Martin Grube, Lancaster county, Pa.
291 Catral & Hustin, Troy, Ohio.
358 J. Harbine, Green county, Ohio.

CORN-FED.

26 J. Goshring, Fayette county, Pa.
51 R. Hezelt, Fayette county, Pa.
282 J. Gilchrist, Pittsburg, Pa.

Harrisburg Live Stock Market.

HARRISBURG, July 26, 1862.

Total receipts of Live Stock of all kinds for the week, at the Harrisburg Stock Yards: 1,271 Beef Cattle, 2,009 Sheep, 174 Hogs, and 621 Horses. The sales of Beef Cattle were:

Jacob Seldomridge sold 113 head at $4.10 ₩ 100 lbs, gross.

Myers & Bro., 37 head at $4 20.
West & McIntyre 95 head at $4.25.
J. Modderwell, 32 head at $4 10
B. Redd, 15 head at $4.10.
Peter Carper, 118 head at $4.20.
Geo. Myers. 4 head at $4 25.

One lot of Sheep, 191 head, sold at $3.50 ₩ head.

Total sales of Beef Cattle 414 head, at an average of $4.17 ₩ 100 lbs gross.

The following are the droves of Beef Cattle in market this week:

Geo. Lehman	28 head.	Redd & Shannon	30 head.
J. Seldomridge	113 "	M. Semdiz	16 "
West & McIntyre	95 "	J. Modderwell	32 "
Marks & Trueman	35 "	Thos. Glass	64 "
Myers & Bro	56 "	Ward & Porter	48 "
Jas. McCallister	92 "	Holmes & Pfeiffer	85 "
Thos. Mooney	49 "	James Stephens	79 "
Owen Scully	31 "	Phil. Carper	118 "
H. Thompson	41 "	Owen Smith	102 "
J. Driesbach	15 "	E. Williams	155 "

PHILADELPHIA MARKETS.

July 25, 1862

Business generally has been more active this week, and the markets for most of the leading articles of Produce are better. Bark has declined. Breadstuffs move off more freely, and command full prices. Coal and Iron are firm, but not very active. Cotton is quiet at the advance. Fish and Fruit are dull, and prices about the same. Groceries—there is more doing and prices are better. Provisions move off slowly, and quotations are unchanged. Naval Stores are scarce and on the advance. Oils are looking up. Rice has improved. Salt continues firm. Seeds are more active. Tobacco is firm, but inactive. Wool is in request and prices tending upward.

The Dry Goods trade is active, and the prices of Cotton fabrics have advanced considerably this week, but the high views of holders limits operations. Woolens are also better, with a good business doing in the way of sales.

The Breadstuffs market is better, and the demand for most kinds more active this week at an improvement on last week's prices. The sales of Flour comprise about 25,000 bbls, mostly taken for shipment, at $4.75@5.12½ for superfine, $5.12½@5 50 for extra, and $5 50@6 for extra family, the latter for fancy brands, including about 4,000 bbls city mills on terms kept private. The sales to the trade have been to a fair extent at the above figures for superfine and extras, and $6.50@7 ₩ bbl for high grade fancies as to quality. Rye Flour is better, selling in a small way at $3.25 ₩ bbl. Corn Meal is better, and about 250 bbls Pennsylvania sold at $2.87½. Brandywine is held at $3.30 ₩ bbl.

WHEAT.—There is a good demand both for shipment and milling; sales of 40,000 bus fair and prime Pennsylvania and Southern red at 125@132c ₩ bus, including some choice new at the latter figure, and white at 137@143c ₩ bus; a lot of new Kentucky white, the first of the season, has just been received, and was sold at the latter figures. Rye—About 2,500 bus Pennsylvania sold at 70c ₩ bus. Corn is scarce, and prime yellow in demand, with sales of 10,000 bus at 60@62c. Oats are also better, and selling more freely at 42@43c for Pennsylvania, and 41c for Delaware. Barley and Malt are not inquired for.

PROVISIONS.—There is very little demand for barrelled meats, with sales of 500 bbls Western and city-packed Mess Pork at $10 50@11.50 Prime is nominal at $8 75@9. Western Mess Beef is selling at $12, and city packed at $13@15 ₩ bbl. Bacon—There is very little demand, except for Hams, which are wanted, with sales of 450 casks plain and fancy-cured at 7½@9¼c; sides at 5@5¼c for Western and 6c for fine city-smoked, and shoulders 3¾@4¼c. Green Meats—The stock is very much reduced; 400 bbls and tierces Pickled Hams sold at 5¾@7c, the latter for fancy do.; some in salt at 5@5¼c; sides at 5c, and shoulders at 3½@3¾c, cash and 60 days. Lard is held higher; sales of 1,000 bbls and tierces at 9c, now held at 9¼c, and kegs at 9¼@9¾c, cash and short time. Butter—There is some inquiry for solid-packed; sales of 500 packages at 10@12½c, and 300 kegs Western at 14c. Cheese is lower; sales of New York at 8@8¼c. Eggs are selling at 11@12c ₩ doz.

METALS.—There is a firm feeling in the market for Pig Iron; sales of 3,500 tons Anthracite at $24, 6 mos., for No. 1; $23 cash, and $20 for White Iron; Scotch Pig is firm at $25. In Blooms there is very little doing; 2d quality charcoal sold at $50, 4 months; prices of Bar and Boiler plates are steady with a fair trade doing.

LEAD.—A lot of 1,700 Pigs Galena sold in New York, to come here, at $6 80 cash; and 1,500 Pigs here at 7c, holders are firm at the latter rate.

COPPER is unchanged and dull; we quote Yellow Metal at 22c, 6 months.

BARK.—There is a steady demand for Quercitrion at the decline noted last week; sales of 100 hhds 1st No. 1, at $33; for Tanners' Bark there is a steady inquiry at previous rates.

BEESWAX is scarce, with small sales of prime Yellow at 35c, cash.

COAL.—There is more activity in the market, chiefly for the supply of the Government. The damage to the Lehigh Canal and the other transportation companies, by the late freshet, will cause a reduction of nearly one million tons in the annual supply. Holders are firm in their demands, and prices close very firm, the tendency being upward for most kinds.

CANDLES.—Sperm are dull. Adamantine are selling in lots at 16@17½c. Tallow Candles are held higher, in consequence of the advance in the price of Tallow.

COFFEE.—There is a firm feeling in the market, and some holders are asking a further advance of ½c; sales of 1,800 bags, including Rio, at 21½@22¾c; Laguayra 22½@23c; and Cuba 23c, cash and time. There is very little arriving.

COTTON.—The stock here is nearly exhausted, and it meets a moderate inquiry at the late advance. Sales of 300 bales in lots, including Middling and good Middling Uplands, and Orleans, at 48@51c ₩ lb cash.

DRUGS AND DYES.—There is more doing; Alum is in demand, and selling at 2¼@2⅜; Soda Ash 2¾@3c; Sal-Soda firmer; Quinine $2.75, and some Nitrate of Silver also sold on terms kept private.

FISH.—The stock of Mackerel is increasing, but there is very little demand and prices are nearly nominal. Sales from store at $8.25 for No. 1; $6.25 for No. 2, and $6 for new No. 3. A sale of the latter was made from the wharf at $5 50 per bbl. Pickled Herring range from $1.50 to $3.50 for old and new.

FRUIT.—A cargo of St. Barts and one of Bahama Pine Apples have arrived, which is about the only description on the market, and sales are making on private terms. Green Apples sell at $1.50 ₩ bbl; Dried Apples 3@6c, as in quality. There is very little doing in Dried Peaches and prices are nominal.

FREIGHTS.—To Liverpool the tendency is upward; we quote Flour at 3s 6d@3s 9d. Grain at 12@14d; and heavy goods at 35@40s. Vessels suitable for the West Indies are more plenty. Several charters were made at 40@42c for Sugar, and $3@3 75 for Molasses, from Cuba. To Boston the rates are steady at 25c for Flour; 6c for Grain; and 5@6c for measurement Goods. Colliers are getting full rates.

FEATHERS are rather dull; sales of good Southern and Western at 37@42c ₩ lb

GINSENG is scarce, and no sales have come under our notice.

GUANO is dull, as usual at this season of the year; the sales are light, and prices steady.

HIDES are firmer, but without sales to note; City Slaughter are worth 6¼@8c. Two cargoes of Brazil have arrived.

HEMP is quiet, with sales of rough American Dew at $100 ₩ ton, cash.

HOPS are firmly held, with sales of first sorts Eastern and Western at 16@20c.

LUMBER.—There is a fair business doing in all kinds without change in prices. A cargo of Laths sold at $1.25 ₩ M.

MOLASSES.—There is a firmer feeling in the market, and prices are better, without much inquiry; sales of clayed Cuba at 25c., and Muscovado at 27@33c., on usual terms.

NAVAL STORES.—The stock of Rosin is exhausted; sales of common and No. 2 at $12@13. Wilmington Tar is wanted, but there is none here. Pennsylvania and Jersey is selling in a small way at $18@20. Pitch is held at $15. Spirits Turpentine is quiet; sales, in lots, at $1.80@1.85, cash.

OILS.—Fish Oils are steady, with a fair demand; sales of crude whale at 58@60c, four months. Linseed Oil is selling at 90@94c cash Lard Oil is higher, sales of winter at 65@68c. 3,000 bbls Petroleum sold for export on private terms.

PLASTER is arriving freely; a cargo of soft sold at $2.50 ₩ ton

RICE.—The stock is nearly exhausted; sales of East India at 6@6½c.

SEEDS.—There is more demand for Cloverseed, and prices have advanced; small lots sold at $5.50@5.75 ₩ bushel, and 500 sacks, from second hands, at 8¼@9c ₩ lb, now held higher. Timothy is worth $2, and Flaxseed $2.25 ₩ bushel, and scarce.

SALT is held firmly; three imports of 10,787 sacks Liverpool fine and ground have arrived, of which 4,037 sacks of the latter was previously contracted for on private terms. A cargo of Turks Island also sold private.

SPIRITS continue firm and on the advance, with very little Brandy and Gin selling. N. E. Rum is worth 47@50c. Whisky is rather quiet at the advance; sales of Ohio bbls at 33@34c; Penn'a do at 32@32c, and drudge at 31@32c ₩ gallon.

SUGAR.—There is a firm feeling in the market, with sales of 2,500 hhds Cuba at 7¾@9c; Porto Rico at 9¼@9¾c and Havana at 8¾c ₩ lb, on the usual credit. Refined Sugars are higher.

TALLOW has advanced, and is held at 10⅛@10¼c for city; no country here.

TOBACCO.—The stock of manufactured is nearly exhausted and the tendency of prices is higher; for Leaf there is not much demand, but Pennsylvania is coming in rather more freely.

WOOL.—The demand for the new clip continues good, and holders have realized better rates; sales of 200,000 lbs, in lots, at 53@55c, cash, for common to fine fleece, closing at the latter rate for tub.

JULY 28—Evening.

There is no quotable change in Flour; the market is firm, but very quiet to-day with a small business doing, mostly to supply the trade, at $5 for superfine; $5.50@5 62½ for extras; $5.75@6 for family; and $6.50@7 for fancy brands, as to quality. There is very little inquiry for export, and the stock on sale is light. Rye Flour and Corn Meal are scarce and wanted, at fully former rates; the former is worth $3.25, and the latter $2.87½ ₩ bbl for Pennsylvania Meal.

WHEAT continues firm and in good demand at previous quotations; sales include about 6,000 bushels at 130@133c, mostly at the latter rate for prime Jersey and Delaware red, and 140@145c for white, the latter for Kentucky. Rye is scarce, and about 500 bushels Pennsylvania sold at 75c. Corn meets with a good demand at previous prices, and about 5 000 bushels yellow sold at 64c, chiefly afloat. Oats are firm, with further sales of Pennsylvania at 44c, in store. Southern are worth 42c ₩ bushel.

BARK is firm; first No. 1 Quercitron is in request at $33 ₩ ton.

COTTON is unsettled and lower, and no sales are reported to-day to establish a quotation.

GROCERIES AND PROVISIONS are firm, with a good demand for the former at full rates.

WHISKY continues unsettled and dull; bbls are held at 30@31c, and drudge at 30c ₩ gallon.

THE MONEY MARKET.

PHILADELPHIA, July 28, 1862.

There was less demand on the street for Gold to-day. The rate fluctuated from 116¼, at the opening, to 117, falling, at the close, to 116, with an extremely weak market. The tendency was decidedly downward, and a still further decline may be looked for. Old demands were dull, and the ruling figure was 106 for buyers. Silver was inactive at 110, with the demand decidedly short. A fuller business at the Stock Board notes some slight changes in prices. United States one-year certificates advanced ⅛, selling at 98¼. The blank seven thirties were firm at 103, no change; 99 was bid for the 6s of 1881, being a decline of ¼. Pennsylvania fives sold well at 86—Saturday's figure; the Coupon fives declined ¼. City sixes, old, sold well at 98; the new declined ¼. Pennsylvania Railroad first mortgage bonds were firm at 103; second do. 99—both having no change. Philadelphia and Erie sixes brought 93. North Pennsylvania sixes 75—an advance of ½; 98 was bid for the tens. Schuylkill Navigation sixes, 1882, advanced ¼. Reading sixes, 1844, extended, declined ¼. Sunbury and Erie sevens advanced ¼. Lehigh Navigation shares brought 48¼—an advance of ¼. Northern Liberty Gas 30¼. Lehigh Zinc 1?¼. Miners' Bank of Pottsville 40. Wilmington Railroad loan 102. Susquehanna Canal scrip 32. Susquehanna Canal shares rose ¼. Schuylkill Navigation preferred shares 14¼, firm. North Pennsylvania Railroad shared opened at 9, declined ¼ at the second board. Pennsylvania sold at 47, no change. Harrisburg rose ⅛. Norristown declined ¼. Reading was inactive, one lot being sold at 28, which is a decline of ½ on last sales. Catawissa preferred brought 10¼. In local bank shares there was nothing done. Passenger railways were inactive. Race and Vine brought 11½. Bids for the others generally fell off and the market closed dull; about $80,000 in bonds changed hands, and 900 shares. There is only continued ease to note in the money market. Commercial paper is very scarce and commands the lightest figures.

MONEY LIST.

Foreign and Domestic Exchange—Government Securities—Specie and Land Warrants.

CORRECTED WEEKLY BY DREXEL & CO., BANKERS, NO. 34 SOUTH THIRD STREET.

Notes at Par in Philadelphia.

PENNSYLVANIA COUNTRY BANKS.

NAMES OF BANKS.	WHERE REDEEMED.
Allentown Bank, Allentown	Man. & Mech. Bank.
Bank of Catasauqua	Far. & Mech. Bank.
Bank of Chester County	Philadelphia Bank.
Bank of Delaware County	Bank of North Amer.
Bank of Germantown	Farm. & Mech Bank.
Bank of Montgomery County	Western Bank.
Doylestown Bank, Doylestown	Philadelphia Bank.
Easton Bank Easton	Bank of N. America.
Farm. Bank of Bucks Co, Bristol	Farm. & Mech. Bank.
Farm. & Mech. Bank, Easton	Girard Bank.
Farmers' Bank, Lancaster	Mechanics' Bank.
Lancaster County Bank	Western Bank.
Mauch Chunk Bank	Girard Bank.
Miners' Bank, Pottsville	Bank of N. America.
NEW JERSEY—(5s and up).	
Bordentown Banking Company	Western Bank.
Burlington Bank	Philadelphia Bank.
Burlington Co. Bank Medford	Bank of N. America.
Cumberland Bank, Bridgeton	Farm & Mech. B'k.
Farmers' Bank, Mt. Holly	Commercial Bank.
Farm. & Mech. Bank, Camden	Girard Bank.
Gloucester Co. Bank, Woodbury	Farm. & Mech. B'k.
Lambertville Bank	Consolidation Bank.
Mechanics' Bank of Burlington	Bank of N. America.
Mech. & Manuf. Bank, Trenton	Bank of N. America.
Millville Bank, Millville	Philadelphia Bank.
Mount Holly Bank, Mt. Holly	Girard Bank.
Princeton Bank. Princeton	Mechanics' Bank.
Salem Banking Company, Salem	Commercial Bank.
State Bank, Camden	Bank of N. America.
State Bank, New Brunswick	Farm. & Mech. B'k.
State Bank, Newark	Farm & Mech. B'k.
Trenton Banking Co., Trenton	Philadelphia Bank.
Union Bank of Frenchtown	Bank N. Liberties.
DELAWARE—(5s and up).	
Bank of Delaware, Wilmington	Bank of N. America.
Bank of Newark, Newark	Philadelphia Bank.
Bank of Smyrna, Smyrna	Girard Bank.
B'k of Wilmington & Brandywine	Philadelphia Bank.
Citizens' Bank, Middletown	Corn Exchange B'k.
Delaware City Bank, Del. City	Bank of N. Liberties.
Farmers' Bank of Dover	Philadelphia Bank.
Branch at Wilmington	Philadelphia Bank.
Branch at Newcastle	Southwark Bank.
Branch at Georgetown	Philadelphia Bank.
Farm. & Mech. Bank, Milford	Bank of N. America.
Mechanics' Bank, Wilmington	Philadelphia Bank.
New Castle County Bank	Philadelphia Bank.
Real Estate Bank, Newport	Consolidation Bank.
Union Bank, Wilmington	Farm. & Mech. Bank.

PENNSYLVANIA COUNTRY BANK NOTES AT DISCOUNT IN PHILADELPHIA.

Allegheny Bank	½	Iron City B'k, Pittsb.	pre.5
Anthracite B'k, Tamaqua	½	Jersey Shore Bank	¼
Bank of Beaver Co	½	Kittanning Bank	¼
Bank of Chambersburg	¼	Lewisburg Bank	¼
Bank of Chester Valley, Coatesville	¼	Lebanon Bank, Lebanon	¼
Bank of Crawford Co., Meadville	1	Lebanon Val. B'k, Leb.	¼
Bank of Danville	½	Lock Haven Bank	¼
Bank of Fayette Co	½	Mech. B'k. Pittsb.	prem.5
Bank of Gettysburg	¼	Mechanicsburg Bank, Mechanicsburg	¼
Bank of Lawrence Co	1	Merchants' & Manufacturers' Bank, Pittsb.	¼
Bank of Middletown	½	Mifflin County Bank, Lewistown	½
Bank of Newcastle	1	Milton Bank, Milton	¼
Bank of Northumberl'd	½	Monongahela Bank, Brownsville	¼
Bank of Phœnixville	¼	Mount Joy Bank	¼
Bank of Pittsb'g	prem.5	Northumberland County Bank, Shamokin	¼
Bank of Pottstown	¼	Octarora Bank. Oxford	¼
Citizens Bank. Pittsburg	¼	Pittston Bank, Pittston	¼
Clearfield Co. Bank	¼	Stroudsburg Bank	¼
Columbia Bank, Columbia	½	Tioga County Bank	1
Downingtown Bank	½	Union Bank, Reading	½
Exchange Bank, Pittsb'g	½	West Branch Bank, Williamsport	¼
Farmers' Bank, Pottsv'e	½	Wyoming Bank, Wilkesbarre	¼
Farmers' Bank, Reading	¼	York Bank, York	¼
Farmers' & Drovers' Bank, Waynesburg	½	York Co. Bank, York	¼
Franklin Bank, Washington	½		
Harrisburg Bank	½		
Honesdale Bank	½		

DOMESTIC EXCHANGE.

	Discount		Discount.
Boston	par @1-10 prm.	St. Louis	½@¼
New York	par @1-10 prm.	Louisville	2@..
Albany	¼@½	Cincinnati	¼@¼
Baltimore	½@ par.	Cleveland	¼@¼
Washington	¼@¼	Chicago	¼@ par.
Pittsburg	⅜@½	Dubuque, Iowa.	1@..
Detroit, Mich.	⅜@½	Davenport, Ia.	1@..
Lexington, Ky.	2@..	St. Paul, Min.	1@..
Milwaukee, Wis.	¼@¼	Montreal, Can.	@15 prm.

LAND WARRANTS.

	Buying.	Selling.
40-acre Warrants	65	75
80 " "	60	70
120 " "	40	50
160 " "	40	50

Market dull.

CITY WARRANTS.

New.............. 4 dis. | Old.............. 3 dis.

FOREIGN EXCHANGE.

London, 60 days sight	29	@..
Do 3 days	29¼	@30
Paris, 60 days sight	4f25	@4f35
Do 3 days	4f22½	@4f32½
Antwerp, 60 days sight	4f..	@..
Bremen, 60 days sight	92¼	@93
Hamburg, 60 days sight	43	@43½
Cologne, Leipsic, Berlin, 60 days	86½	@87
Amsterdam, 60 days sight	48¼	@49¼
Frankfort, 60 days sight	49	@49¼

Market steady.

GOVERNMENT SECURITIES.

	New York	Prices.
U. S. 6s, due 1881, Registered	99	101
U. S. 7.30 Treasury Notes	103	104
One-year 6 per cent. Certificates	98¼	par.
U. S Demand Notes, old issue	6 to	8 pr.
U. S. Legal-Tender Notes	par.	

Market firm.

SPECIE QUOTATIONS.

BANKABLE CURRENCY THE STANDARD.

GOLD.		SILVER.	
American	15@16 prm	American, prior to 1852	$1.10@1.12
Do (dated prior to 1834)	20@21 prm	Do Quart's	1.06@1.08
Sov'ns, Victoria*	5 50@5.70	Do Dimes and Half Dimes.	1.04@....
Sovereigns, old	5 45@5.65	Do Halves and Qrt's (new)	1.06@1.08
Napoleons (20 frs)	4 40@4 50	Dollars, Am. and Mexican	1.10@1.12
25 Francs	5.40@5.50	Do Sp., perfect	1.12@1.14
10 do	2.25@2.30	Do do Carolus.	1.12@1.14
Prussian Double Fred'k D'ors	8.40@8 50	Do S. American.	1.12@1.12
Doubloons, Sp.	17 50@18 00	Do Norwegian	....@....
Do Mexican	16 50@17 00	Five Francs	1.01@1.03
Do Costa Rica	15.25@15.50	Francs	19
Bars 900 fine	15@16 prm	Guilders	38
California $50 & $20 pieces	4@5 prm	Prussian Thalers	72
California $10 & $5 pieces	4@5	German Crowns.	1.15@....
10-Guilder pieces	4.60@4.70	French do	1.15@....
Ten Thalers	8.40@8.50	Eng Silver ₩ £	5.00@5.10
20 Mille Reis, Brazil	11.00@11 25	Spanish and Mex. sm. silver ₩ oz.	1.22
		Bars, U S assay, ₩ oz.	1.22

* A heavy sovereign weighs 5 dwts. 2¼ grains.

UNCURRENT MONEY QUOTATIONS.

	Discount.		Discount.
New England	¼	Wheeling	2¼
New York city	⅛	Ohio	¼
New York State	¼	Indiana	¼
Jersey—large	par	Indiana—Free	1¼
Jersey—small	⅜	Kentucky	¼
Pennsylvania currency.	¼	Tennessee	40 to 50
Delaware	par	Missouri	2 to 10
Do. small	½	Illinois	1 to 60
Baltimore	¼	Wisconsin	1 to 60
Maryland	¼ to 1¼	Michigan	1¼
District of Columbia	¼	Iowa	1
Virginia	35 to 60	Canada	prm. 10

The Philadelphia Inquirer.

CIRCULATION OVER 65,000. | PHILADELPHIA, SATURDAY, AUGUST 2, 1862. | PRICE TWO CENTS.

LATEST WAR NEWS!

IMPORTANT FROM THE ARMY OF THE POTOMAC.

A Midnight Artillery Skirmish.

"ANOTHER RICHMOND IN THE FIELD."

The Rebel Rams "Richmond" and "Young America" Coming Down the River.

THE FLEET READY FOR A FIGHT.

FROM GEN. POPE'S ARMY.

Enrollment of the State Militia.

AFFAIRS AT THE FEDERAL CAPITAL

AFFAIRS IN KENTUCKY.

Plans of the Secessionists in Kentucky—Interview with the President and General Halleck.

Special Despatch to the Philadelphia Inquirer.

WASHINGTON, August 1.—Ex-Governor DENNISON, Representative GURLEY, LARZ ANDERSON and General BATES, are here as a committee, in behalf of Governor TOD, to represent to the President and General HALLECK the situation along the Kentucky border, and the imminent danger in Kentucky itself. It is understood that the Secessionists are likely to make an effort to overawe Union men, and control elections for county officers in as many localities as possible throughout the State, next Monday.

It is also feared that they may endeavor to bring outside pressure to bear on the Legislature just called to meet in extra session by Governor MAGOFFIN. Ex-Governor DENNISON and the rest have had interviews with the President and General HALLECK, and are closeted with the President again to-night. It is understood that their representations are receiving most careful attention, and that every effort will be made to meet the emergency.

Later.

It is understood that the Ohio Committee have been promised a General from BUELL'S Department to be located at Cincinnati, to have an ample force at his disposal for the protection of the Kentucky border and preservation of order in Kentucky.

FROM THE ARMY OF THE POTOMAC.

A Midnight Artillery Skirmish.

HEAD-QUARTERS OF THE ARMY OF THE POTOMAC, August 1.—About 12 o'clock last night the Rebels opened from the opposite side of the river with two batteries of light artillery.

Their fire was principally directed to the mail boat landing, at the head-quarters of Col. INGALLS, and the shipping and encampments at Westover.

Their pieces were handled well and fired with great rapidity. Four men were killed and some five or six wounded. Several horses also were killed.

The enemy had it all their own way for some time, as our troops were not anticipating an attack. But the thirty-two pounders stationed close to Colonel INGALLS' head-quarters soon silenced their guns. After they opened a few of the vessels were struck, but no serious damage was sustained by any of them.

With this exception nothing has occurred worth mentioning.

Army of the Potomac—Re-arrangement of Various Corps.

WAR DEPARTMENT, ADJUTANT-GENERAL'S OFFICE, WASHINGTON, July 22, 1862.—The designation in "General Orders," No. 225, from the "Head-quarters Army of the Potomac," of the forces commanded by Brigadier-Generals PORTER and FRANKLIN, as the Fifth and Sixth Army Corps, is hereby confirmed. The forces under Major-General DIX will constitute the Seventh, those under Major-General WOOL the Eighth, and those under Major-General BURNSIDE, belonging to the Department of North Carolina, the Ninth Army Corps, respectively.

By order of the Secretary of War.

L. THOMAS, Adjutant-General.

PREPARATIONS FOR DRAFTING.

The Enrollment of the State Militia.

HARRISBURG, Aug. 1.—The following important circular has this day been issued, from which it would appear that the authorities here are actively preparing for any emergency that may arise:—

HEAD-QUARTERS PENNSYLVANIA MILITIA, ADJUTANT-GENERAL'S DEPARTMENT, HARRISBURG, August 1, 1862.—To the County Commissioners:—All County Commissioners who have not complied with the circular issued from these head-quarters, dated July 12th, 1862, are hereby required to complete and return to these head-quarters the enrollments of their respective counties before the 10th day of August. Very respectfully, &c.,

A. L. RUSSELL,
Adjutant-General Pennsylvania.

LATE REBEL NEWS.

Running the Mobile Blockade—The Occupation of Grand Junction by the Rebels.

CAIRO, August 1.—The Grenada *Appeal*, of the 28th ult., contains Mobile despatches announcing that the steamer *Cuba* ran the blockade of that port on the 25th, bringing a full cargo of arms, ammunition, medicines and blankets.

The same paper, in an editorial, announces the occupation of Grand Junction by the Rebel forces on the 25th.

A despatch from Chattanooga, Tenn., says the Federals are evincing great activity, and are evidently preparing for some movement. Trains of cars have arrived at Bridgeport with shells and ammunition.

The Jackson *Mississippian*, says it is authorized to state that a sufficient force will be sent to the Mississippi river, to protect the people of the river counties from invaders.

The Columbus (Ga.) *Times* learns that General TOOMBS has resigned.

The Mobile *News* says one division of LOVELL'S army has been ordered eastward, and are expected in Mobile soon.

War Meeting at Toledo, Ohio.

TOLEDO, Ohio, August 1.—A large and enthusiastic war meeting was held in this city to-day. Business was almost entirely suspended after noon. Speeches were delivered by Hon. H. B. PRINE, T. BACKUS and others.

Arrival from Hilton Head.

NEW YORK, August 1.—The steamer *McClellan*, from Hilton Head, has arrived. Gen. WRIGHT is among her passengers.

OUR FORTRESS MONROE LETTER.

A REBEL ALMANAC.

AFFAIRS IN NORFOLK.

LOYALTY vs. TREASON.

STEAMERS FOR NORTH CAROLINA.

NORFOLK AND SUFFOLK RAILROAD.

THE NEW MERRIMAC OUT.

OUR GUN-BOATS PREPARED FOR HER

Special Correspondence of the Inquirer.

FORTRESS MONROE, VA., July 31, 1862.

I have been placed in possession of a genuine Southern production, in the shape of an almanac for 1862. It is entitled "COTTOMS' edition RICHARDSON'S Almanac, 1862, being the second after bissextile or leap year, eighty-sixth of American Independence and the first of the Southern Confederacy." Then comes a wood cut attempting the coat of arms of Virginia, with the motto *Sic Semper Tyrannus* in capitals. "DAVID RICHARDSON, of Louisa county," is the calculator, tidal recorder, eclipse-foreteller, clerk of the weather, pig doctor and horticultural adviser on the production of squashes and cabbage heads. After giving the old plate of the "Anatomy of man's body as governed by the twelve constellations," Mr. RICHARDSON amuses his searchers after "signs" and truth with the thread-bare story about "two in a bed."

Then he naturally turns aside to a subject more congenial to the Southern taste—*Brimstone*—and informs his readers that it is an excellent thing to "keep vermin out of the head and off the body." The first "axiom" one comes across is a hard hit at the Southern Confederacy, and FLOYD in particular. It runs in this wise:—"*Thieves are as liberal as honest men; but then it is with other people's property.*" That Almanac ought to be suppressed at once; such truths are impolitic just now in the South.

Friday, 18th of July, 1862, is remarkable as the anniversary of "Bull Run;" Monday, 21st, of "Battle of Manassas." But it is equally remarkable that DAVID RICHARDSON has failed to find a single other battle to note for 1861. He does not even immortalize South Carolina by placing the date of her secession in his pages, or the brilliant victory of her 7000 knights over the 70 Unionists of Sumter. There certainly is a little spice of jealousy in the matter.

Here is another apt quotation—couldn't be more appropriate—for the footpads and public scoundrels composing the Rebel Government:—

"*It was odd enough of the thieves who robbed the landlord, to tax him with dishonesty for concealing a part of his money.*"

That *is* good, Mr. RICHARDSON; hit them again! A full and complete list of these precious thieves is given for the warning of honest men, beginning with JEFF. DAVIS, and ending with REAGAN and his Post Office rascals. JOHN LETCHER, the drunkard Governor of Virginia, heads the State officials. North Carolina is honored with a niche for her functionaries; and "*Maryland! My Maryland!*" occupies a page with her Court of Appeals and Circuit Courts; while, on the opposite side,

The Late American Union

Furnishes a table of the dates when the different States were settled and admitted into the Union.

A Cure for Botts

Is given, but it says nothing of the cure JEFF. DAVIS invented when he thought the safest mode of ridding Virginia of a BOTTS that was infecting her with a disorder likely to interfere with his own personal welfare, was to banish it from her borders.

A New Book.

"The Mock Auction. *Ossawatomie Sold.* A mock heroic poem, 10 plates, price 75 cents," is "for sale by all booksellers."

Military Works.—"Hand-book for Active Service, by EGBERT L. VIELE, late United States Army," and "A Manual for Light and Heavy Artillery, with plates," by the same officer. Dismissing this valuable addition to Southern literature and science, we would remark that it is "illegintly" printed on pokeberry-colored wrapping paper, and with all kinds and sizes of worn-out type, the leaves being held together by one stitch of coarse twine. Take it for all in all, it is a wonderful specimen of erudition—weather-wise—and assuredly proves that the "Northern invaders" fib extensively when they intimate that the South can't publish an almanac.

Matters in Norfolk.

Yesterday Captain REDMAN and Captain CORRY, of the Fifty-eighth Pennsylvania, went out with a detachment of men from their companies, to examine the premises of a Rebel, some eight miles from Portsmouth, who was represented to have arms concealed in his house. On arriving there they commenced an examination, which resulted in finding two small field pieces, thirty muskets, two Sharpe's rifles and six or eight swords. The captains then seized a couple of wagons and a half dozen mules, and brought the "contraband articles of war" into camp.

When the affair was reported to head-quarters in Norfolk, great indignation was expressed, and Colonel RICHTER JONES was threatened with a "cashier," and the entire regiment with incarceration in the Rip Raps. It was an outrage on private citizens to take away from them two cannon, thirty muskets, and a-half dozen swords! It could not be allowed, and soldiers and officers are not to judge of a man's loyalty, when he is found hiding arms for transportation into the enemy's lines. He may be a good Union man in the opinion of certain officials, but his Union affinities assuredly are on the side of a *Southern Union*, after the ideas of JEFF. DAVIS. Now the question comes down to this:—

Does the United States Government design to make an exception in its policy toward Rebellion in the Department about Norfolk, or does it desire to have its authority enforced and its dignity maintained in that locality? If the first, things are working along smoothly and decidedly to the advantage of treason; if the latter, then there must be a radical change effected in the machinery now operating with such feeble, nay, imbecile power. Union men are actually heart-sick, and are losing all faith in the Government's readiness to assist them. They see Secessionists favored day by day; they see Rebels depart for their lines with papers from which the words, "taken the oath," are erased; they witness the shipping of peaches, &c., &c., by avowed traitors, while they are refused the privilege. In a word, to be a hater of the American flag, seems to be, in Norfolk and vicinity, the surest passport to favor with some of the officials who sit in the shadow of that banner.

We do know that the Union citizens of Norfolk and Portsmouth are disheartened and indignant at their treatment. A Union man living out of town has a peach crop which is worth $3000, but he is refused permission to boat it to Norfolk, and is compelled to wagon them nine miles around. He says he won't be able to realize $500 on his crop.

The Rebels Grow Insolent

Under this state of affairs, and insult the Unionists with impunity. The two spies arrested a few days since are not yet tried, nor will they be, if procrastination will save their necks.

Only a night or two since, Rebel scouts came down close to the city, and stole ten small boats, which were afterward recaptured. The citizens faithful to our flag are uneasy, and fear a sudden irruption of HUGER'S hordes upon them, without a moment's warning.

A Daily Line of Steamers

Will soon run to Currituck, there connecting with a similar line to Newbern, North Carolina, so that Norfolk will be in close communication with the "Old North State."

The Norfolk and Suffolk Railroad

Has been put in complete repair, and yesterday forenoon the "United States Government" engine thundered along Wide Water street, to the astonishment of everybody.

The *Dirigo*, under contract for the Government, leaves Norfolk soon, via the Albemarle and Chesapeake Canal, for Hatteras Inlet, where Captain PRATT expects to raise the locomotives and other valuable effects lost by General BURNSIDE'S Expedition during the terrific storm which threatened its entire destruction.

The Old Philadelphia Boat "Pioneer," Captain Mitchell,

runs regularly between Fortress Monroe and Norfolk, and is fast becoming as much of a favorite on the Elizabeth as she was on the Delaware river.

Captain MITCHELL is a noble specimen of the man, and bears within his bosom a brave and humane heart, as we well know. This morning the *Pioneer* brought over eleven Rebel prisoners from the Portsmouth Hospital. Sergeant BOSWELL, of the Thirty-first Pennsylvania, was on board, accompanied by his wife, who succeeded in getting his discharge from the hospital, when all others had failed. They are on the *Georgianna*, and expect to reach Philadelphia by the Delaware and Chesapeake Canal.

Four Hundred Union Wounded,

From Richmond, are on board the *Louisiana* at City Point. She is expected here to-night or to-morrow.

One-hundred-and-Fifth Pennsylvania Volunteers.

There are strong probabilities of the One-hundred-and-fifth Pennsylvania Regiment being recalled by the Government, for the purpose of filling up its ranks, so much weakened in the late battles on the Peninsula. From what can be learned concerning this regiment, it has done valuable service to the country. Attached to the First Brigade of General KEARNEY'S Division, it has participated in all the battles before Richmond in which the left wing was engaged. It has lost, in action, three hundred and seventy men. This number, with the usual proportion disabled by disease, has reduced its numbers very much. Two hundred men are all that it now musters for duty. It also lost eighteen out of thirty line officers. In the action of Charles City Cross Roads, this regiment fired one hundred and fifty rounds.

Appearance of the "Merrimac."

5 P. M.—Captain CONE, of the *John A. Warner*, just in, reports that the *new Merrimac made her appearance yesterday, about noon, in company with five other vessels*. Our gun-boats were all ordered up the river above the fleet of two hundred and fifty sail which blocks up the stream at Harrison's Landing. The gun-boats were formed into line of battle, but the Rebel declined combat. If the *Merrimac* passes the fleet, she will do immense damage among our transports; but it is believed Commodore WILKES will sink or capture her. Great excitement prevailed among the transport men, the sutlers and few civilians at the Landing.

Baltimore City Election.

Special Despatch to the Inquirer.

BALTIMORE, August 1.—The whole vote at the special election held to-day was forty-eight hundred and thirty, all Union, and much larger than was expected, as there was no opposing ticket, and not a quarter of the Union voters turned out. Many mechanics and laborers were away in Washington and elsewhere, besides over four thousand in the army. It is a great Union triumph, as it indicates a positive Secession weakness in the city.

OUR PENINSULAR LETTER.

AFFAIRS IN THE ARMY

THE BURNING OF A SCHOONER.

A Grand Balloon Reconnoissance.

THE NEW REBEL RAMS COMING DOWN THE RIVER.

OUR FLEET IN LINE OF BATTLE

A WARM RECEPTION READY.

Special Correspondence of the Inquirer.

HARRISON'S LANDING, VA., July 31, 1862.

For the past three weeks we have been daily reporting the same state of affairs as existing in the Army of the Potomac. So often have we used the term *All Quiet*, that it now seems so much like a stereotype phrase that we hesitate to use it, nor would we do so could we find language which would more briefly and more explicitly convey a true idea of our present position, and, I might add, our prospects for at least a month to come.

Rumors of every kind and character, some of them startling in the extreme, and decidedly on the sensational order, are at all times crowding the market. While *facts* are scarce and not to be had at any price, an active and constant search fails to discover a single item, much to the regret of those you have stationed here to report such facts, and without doubt as much regretted by the *sixty thousand readers* of THE PHILADELPHIA INQUIRER.

The "Inquirer" in the Army.

Speaking of THE PHILADELPHIA INQUIRER, we can state one fact in relation thereto that cannot and doubtless will not be disputed. It is, that no paper which comes among us is more sought after, more frequently quoted, more beloved and respected for its patriotic course, more justly esteemed for its straight-forward, truth-telling editorials, its full, faithful and correct telegraphic news, the general reliableness of its correspondence, and its many local items; nor is there a paper which comes among us more generally read than is that same PHILADELPHIA INQUIRER. For a proof of this fact, we can state, from actual observations, that in point of numbers, none that daily arrive at our mail wharf exceeds that of THE INQUIRER.

The Burned Schooner.

In your telegraph column, in Monday's paper, you have a despatch dated from this place, that the schooner *Reeves*, which was burned in our harbor a few nights since, was set on fire by the Rebels. We do not desire to be at variance with the enterprising and reliable agent of the Associated Press, stationed at this point. Yet we are assured by an officer connected with one of our gun-boats, which at the time was lying near the schooner, it then being the said officer's watch, that the night was so calm, still and quiet, that the slightest noise could be heard at least a mile off, and hence he is sure that no boat could approach the schooner without being heard. He is of the same opinion as ourself, that the vessel was fired by some one on board; and as a proof of this the captain has not been seen or heard of since the night of the fire, while the crew are retained here to await further action. Other facts not necessary to state, warrant us in holding to our original statement, that the vessel was fired by some party attached to it, but for what reason future events must determine.

Balloon Reconnoissance.

Yesterday morning, by order of Commodore WILKES, the balloon corps, under command of the faithful and experienced æronaut, Captain JAMES ALLEN, assisted by Captain JOHN H. STEINER, started down the river on a reconnoitring expedition, the whole being under the command of Captain JENKINS, of the flag-ship *Wachusett*.

During the night previous, and under the immediate supervision of the energetic Captain ALLEN, the balloon *Intrepid*, with its entire working apparatus, was safely and snugly placed on board the barge especially appropriated for such purposes, while all and everything was arranged and in proper order for immediate use.

Towards 5 o'clock, P. M., the steamer *Stepping Stones* took in tow the barge having on board the balloon, working apparatus and a body of men detailed for the purpose of assisting in raising and lowering the balloon, and keeping it in proper position. They proceeded down the river until reaching Fort Powhatan, when they came to anchor. At this point they met the gun-boats *Port Royal*, *Delaware*, and another, whose name we did not learn. There two ascensions were made. After the party for whose especial benefit this reconnoissance was ordered was satisfied with what he had there seen, accompanied by the gun-boats found here, the barge was towed further down the river some ten miles, where another ascension was made. Of the nature and extent of these observations we are not informed, as the parties giving us our information were not among those who made the ascensions, yet did we know we would be unwilling to tell at present.

While the reconnoissance at this latter point was in progress, the little steamer that runs about here as a sort of Orderly, carrying despatches from one point to another, came down with all steam on, having on board Commodore WILKES. He at once ordered the balloon operations to cease, and that all and every gun-boat thereabouts must make all haste up the river to near City Point, eight miles above us, and await further orders.

The steamer *Stepping Stones* then took the balloon barge in tow, and arrived here safely at 2 o'clock P. M.

As we before stated, the extent of the observations are unknown to us, but all and every one with whom we have spoken, and who accompanied the expedition, are unanimous in the assertion that, taking into view the high wind prevailing at the time, it was among the most successful balloon observations ever made, and that what was seen and learned upon that occasion will be of immense advantage to the cause of the Union.

Another Richmond in the Field.

Occasionally, during the morning of yesterda heavy firing could be heard, as if coming from some distance up the river. The cause for it none knew definitely. We all knew that the *Monitor* and *Galena* had taken their usual morning excursion in that direction, and attributed the firing to the fact that a masked battery had been discovered, and which was being silenced.

About one o'clock both vessels were discovered making all haste down the river. The *Galena* immediately reported to Flag Officer Commodore WILKES, on board the flag-ship *Wachusett*, that the new Rebel rams, the *Richmond* and *Young America*, were lying just below Fort Darling, and apparently preparing to come down. The cause for the previously noticed unusual activity among the gun-boats, as well as the hasty ending of the balloon reconnoissance, was then apparent.

Soon after three o'clock, the flag-ship *Wachusett* was seen making her way up the river, and in her wake were some three or four other gun-boats of less calibre. They proceeded up the river some three miles above here, to a point just below where the light-house, called City Point Light, is stationed. Here they found the *Monitor*, and some three or four others. At a given signal they all stationed themselves in line of battle, and are anxiously awaiting an opportunity to give the "distinguished visitor" a cordial reception.

During the night they were joined by some six others, some falling into the line of battle, while the others are in the reserve. We cannot now learn the names of the gun-boats so stationed, but we recognize the "cheese-box" in the advance, the *Wachusett* in the centre, and the *Jacob Bell* in the reserve. Whether the *Richmond* and its *confrere*, *Young America*, will to-day pay us a visit or not remains to be seen. But we feel confident of speaking the truth when we assert that they will not be allowed to return to their "anxious parients."

The reason for the heavy firing heard during the morning was, that previous to the meeting with the Rebel rams the *Monitor* and *Galena* amused themselves by shelling the woods and "playing ball" with some two or three masked batteries.

Honoring the Dead.

At noon yesterday a salute was fired in respect to the memory of the late ex-President MARTIN VAN BUREN.

APPROACHING RICHMOND.

Sanitary Condition of the Army.

ARRIVAL OF DESERTERS.

AN ATTACK BY THE REBELS.

A MYSTERIOUS BOAT CREW.

EXPORTATION OF COWARDS.

DEPARTURE OF GENERAL BERRY.

Special Correspondence of the Inquirer.

WESTOVER LANDING, July 30th, 1862.

The quiet of this place was a little broken to-day, with the rumor that six smoke stacks were seen up the James river, and it was soon bruited forth that the enemy's gun-boats were coming down for the purpose of engaging our gun-boats. Our troops along the shore have been on the *qui vive* all day, anxious to see a naval fight. Our men-of-war are ready, and the jolly jack tars will give a good account of themselves. There is no discount on our sailors; they know how to fight, and will fight; this fact has been well established during the war; the Rebels know full well what is in store for them.

The sanitary condition of Harrison's Landing, vicinity, and the various camps is first-class. No dirt or filth is allowed to remain around; even loose hay is gathered together and burned. In several cavalry regiments, sheds have been erected to screen the horses from the sun's rays. Some of the Generals have complimented camp officials as regards the cleanliness of their camps. This is very encouraging, especially to young officers. The following is an extract issued by the Brigade officer of the day, of the First Cavalry Brigade, on the 25th ultimo:—

"Third Pennsylvania Cavalry—Camp in excellent condition, both as regards its police and order. The arms, horse equipments, &c., show that they are kept in condition worthy of older soldiers, and which reflects credit upon them as a body of men. The cook tents were in good condition. I noticed several sick horses at the picket lines; the general appearance of the horses was good. The sinks were in good condition and well screened with brush. The guard and sentinels were very attentive to their duties and well instructed.—*Official extract furnished to Lieut.-Col. S. W. OWEN, for his information.*"

In the infantry and artillery camps the same good order prevails. The men seem to use every exertion in their power to keep the camps clean and sweet. The improved condition of the men is the result of all this cleanliness.

The rush of officers and men home has decreased wonderfully. Those going are either on recruiting service, or are very sick, the change of climate being really necessary for their health. This is a good sign.

Two more Rebel cavalry deserters came into our lines yesterday, and gave themselves up to the First New York Cavalry. One is from Philadelphia, and the other is from New York. They state that they had been pressed into the Confederate service.

The disease among the horses still continues, although somewhat abated. I was conversing with a Rebel officer at City Point, the other day, who stated that the Virginia farmers about this latitude never work a Northern horse the first summer; they invariably die if they do.

A great many exaggerated camp rumors floating around are published by correspondents from Baltimore and Fortress Monroe, gotten by them from parties *en route* for home, as truth. The capture of a lot of our cattle, and the burning of a schooner by the Rebels opposite this point, is all bosh. There have been no cattle captured, and the fire on board the schooner no doubt was the work of an incendiary.

This evening, after dark, a number of Rebels on the shore opposite Harrison's Landing, fired three or more volleys of musketry into the transports anchored in the stream. For a time there was some considerable consternation among the river craft; lights could be observed dancing from one vessel to another, men hallooing, &c., but a gun-boat soon got in among them; and in a short time all was restored to quietness. I could not learn this evening whether any one was struck or not. I have been expecting an attack of this kind for a long time. The enemy have a wholesome dread of our gun-boats, and have kept at a respectable distance. It was too dark for the enemy to have fired with any accuracy.

JULY 31ST.—The firing that occurred last night, between eleven and twelve o'clock, was from on board the steamboat *Achilles*. Most of the vessels in the harbor are armed with small arms.

The watch on the deck of the steamer saw a small boat approaching, and becoming alarmed, opened on the boat. The men in the boat set up a cry of "don't fire on us; we're the Provost Guard," and all the time kept pulling away.

One of the Provost officers got on the track of two boats, one a black one and the other white, and followed them down the river. The two boats had been hailed by various vessels as they rowed down, and answered that they were Provost Guard boats, Nos. 1 and 2. They escaped in the darkness, and the Assistant Provost did not deem it safe to go on shore, as his force was not of sufficient strength.

Many officers here say that there was no enemy at all. There seemed to be a period of fifteen minutes between the firing. There seemed to be about a dozen discharges at each round of muskets, intermingled with a few pistol shots.

There is no doubt some of the crews of the boats in the harbor go to bed at night really expecting an attack before morning. They get dreaming of attacks and fights, and many times the nightmare has more to do with attacks than anything else.

Very few people believe there was any enemy whatever. If there was they made a very narrow escape. Our Provost is indefatigable, and this affair last night will have a tendency to make him untiring in his exertions to keep the peace of the post, the Rebels to the contrary notwithstanding.

We are prepared to meet any emergency at this point, no matter what the force. We are anxious to meet the reported Rebel fleet.

A number of convalescent officers returned to their regiments last evening.

From the appearance of the heavens, we are about to have a rain storm. It has been threatening for several days.

Two soldiers, prisoners, of the Twelfth Regulars went down in the mail boat this morning. Their heads had been shaved for cowardice in action. They were in charge of the Fifth New York (Zouaves). The army is no place for cowards, and the sooner such fellows are out of it, the better will it be for all hands here.

The body of Quartermaster ALFRED A. SWALLOW, First Regiment Massachusetts Volunteers, has been embalmed, and was sent home this morning.

General BERRY, who has been ill for a long time and who has been battling against it, has been compelled to leave for home in the *State of Maine*. His Brigade will miss him greatly.

The True Policy of Pun\shment.

From the New York Times of last Friday.

One remarkable peculiarity was noticed by all in the grand Union-square meeting, and is an evidence, no doubt, of general popular feeling, and that was, that all demands for the most unsparing punishment of the rebels, and for the most vigorous measures toward them, were met with the greatest applause. From every quarter we receive, ourselves, communications urging the most extreme penalties of the law on the treasonable States and communities. A universal confiscation of real estate, so that loyal settlers may occupy the deserted properties, the wasting of rebel fields and harvests, the armed occupation of their houses, and the appropriation of all property, are some of the mildest of the penal remedies recommended. In the meeting before referred to, one of our most benevolent and excellent citizens, calmly advised sending all the rebel inhabitants further South, and occupying their houses with our soldiers. All these strongly expressed feelings are good signs in one respect—they show that the people demand vigorous action, and wil sustain the Government in it. They prove that the popular instinct feels what has been thus far our mistake—the not striking at our enemy's weakest points. Still, the time has come when sound statesmanship and practical Christianity should indicate some distinctions and limitations in this cry for punishment and revenge. It might as well be understood now as hereafter, that there are some things which the American people can do, and some which it cannot. Whatever be our wrongs received from the South—and their number is infinite—we cannot exterminate or make houseless and landless the whole five or six million whites implicated in this rebellion. The thing is simply impossible. If we begin an indiscriminate, universal policy of destroying rebel property, confiscating it, and "sending women and children South," and the like, we merely excite every man, woman and child to a pitch of fury which would lead them to take to the mountains and swamps rather than submit, and which would call out a storm of wrath to which the rage of Europe, under Napoleon's exactions, was feeble. We must remember, ourselves, how many years it needed before the ashes over our burnt homesteads, in the war of 1812, cooled again. Not all the British victories or insults ever sowed such dragon teeth of hatred as did their destruction of the public buildings of Washington and other towns. To let an army plunder buildings, or even occupy them—to permit every soldier to grasp and get as he likes—is simply to demoralize our army, and enrage the enemy past any possibility of submission.

Our policy is simply this. *This war is a class war.* It is a war of the aristocracy of the South, nominally, against the people—the working people of the North, but really against the whole people, and against Democracy itself. The politicians have hoodwinked the Southern masses or bound them down under the chains of a military despotism. Our great object should be to insert a wedge between the aristocrats and the masses. We can never subjugate the South or hold it, without doing this. We must show the working classes in every way, that we aim at their benefit and are against their proud and oppressive masters. In this view, we think that some portions of Gen Butler's measures in New Orleans, to conciliate the masses and hold down the aristocracy, have been very wise and statesmanlike. With this policy we should strike without favor, at the higher classes. We should free their slaves, not merely from military necessity, but because the emancipation of the negroes tends to depress the traitorous aristocracy, who hate the Union and Democracy, and always will hate them. We should confiscate their estates, and divide them, not merely among our soldiers, but sell them cheaply to, or bestow them on the poor white men of the South. The ruling class, the office-holders and disloyal planters of the rebel States, should be nearly destroyed. No poor man, no mechanic, or laborer, or small farmer, should be injured. The blow should fall on the rich. Then, as our armies advance, they should, of course, to a certain degree, feed on the enemy's country; but this should be done with perfect system and under military law. Plundering, and any occupation without guards of houses, should be strictly punished. There need be no fear that our army will not sufficiently desolate the rebel territory. An army, even to its friends, is like a flock of locusts. Its track, with the best of intentions, over Virginia would be like that of a tempest.

But there are other aspects to this question, which it is the duty of our religious teachers now to present, and yet which, we fear, are not sufficiently presented. If Christianity has any reality, and is not a myth to the Northern people, it is time that its power were felt in this hour of our wrath and distress. Revenge does not belong to nations any more than to individuals. Vindictiveness is not merely a mark af unwise statesmanship, but it is something ogainst which we utter daily prayers. If our holy faith has still a power in the land, it will control those most natural, but bitter cries of a wronged nation for revengeful punishment and evil on its enemies. Justice, legal punishment we must have, but not lawless revenge.

An Important Confession.

A writer in the Grenada *Appeal*, who has recently traveled through Mississippi, makes the following confession:

To my sorrow, I found numbers of men, and even some of our noble southern women, who were discouraged, disheartened, saying, "We're whipped; we're whipped;" and some going so far as to intimate that it would be best, upon the whole, to submit to Yankee rule. This class of croakers," continues the writer, "is rapidly on the increase. Our President and leading Generals are censured, and our civil and military leaders are blamed for not accomplishing what is, in the very nature of the case, impossible."

A Rebel Operator Reads General Halleck's Dispatches for Four Days.

MEMPHIS, July 23.—The telegraph line between Memphis and Corinth is exceedingly important. General Halleck's messages to Commodore Davis, General Curtis and the commandant of this post have all passed over it. Little of the line is guarded, but of late the rebels have refrained from cutting the wires. Their unusual amiability is now explained—they found a better use for it!

For a week the Memphis operators have detected something wrong in the working of the instruments and surmised that some outsider was sharing their telegraphic secrets. They communicated this suspicion to the superintendent at Corinth, who promised to keep a sharp look out.

Yesterday, they discovered that their uninvited confidant could talk as well as listen. The transmission of a message was suddenly interrupted by the ejaculation, "O pshaw!" A moment after it was again broken with "Hurrah for Jeff Davis!"

Individuality shows itself as well in telegraphing as in the footstep or in handwriting. Mr. Hall, one of the Memphis operators, instantly recognized the performer, not by his tune, but his time, as a young man formerly in Buffalo and other Northern offices, but now employed by the Confederates. Mr. Hall surprised him by replying promptly, "Ed. Saville, if you don't want to be hung you had better leave! Our cavalry is closing in on both sides of you!"

There was a little pause, and then the reply: "How in the world did you know me? However, I've been here four days, and learned all we want to know. As this is becoming rather a tight place, I think I *will* leave. You'll see me again when you least expect it. Good bye, boys!"

The rebel operator made good his escape. He had cut the wire, inserted a piece of his own, and by a pocket instrument been reading our official dispatches. Some of the utmost importance, giving the very information most desired by the rebels, were passing, and as they were not in cipher, he must have received them. One from Gen. Hovey, Commandant of this post, in reply to a question from Gen. Halleck, stated the precise number of our available men in Memphis, (only about 3,000,) and their exact location.

The ill effect of this exposure of our weakness has been guarded against as far as possible. General W. T. Sherman has already started for Memphis with two of the three divisions under his command, and will arrive today. So we are in no special danger of a rebel dash.

This brilliant and audacious telegraphic feat was performed between here and Moscow, only twenty-two miles distant, and probably within fifteen miles of Memphis! We are at a loss here to understand why, after the enemy has disappeared, the magnificent army with which General Halleck threatened Corinth is unable to guard 200 miles of railroad and telegraph, or to furnish fifteen or twenty thousand men for the capture of Vicksburg. We hope that our brilliant successes in the West are not to be followed by an era of *how not to do it.*

Nashville News.

From the Nashville Union of the 23d.

PICKETS CAPTURED — RAILROAD BRIDGES BURNED—GREAT EXCITEMENT.

Six of our pickets, who were stationed on the Lebanon road, were attacked yesterday afternoon by a party of twenty guerillas, belonging to Forrest's troop, and all but one captured; one of these subsequently escaped. We learn that the pickets were strolling in an orchard at the time.

Later in the afternoon three bridges on the Chattanooga Railroad were burned down, the nearest seven and the furthest eight miles from the city.

Scouts report Colonel Forrest with a force of from twelve hundred to two thousand within five miles of this place. At the time of writing this paragraph the troops are under arms prepared for an attack, and much excitement exists.

Mr. Powell, of Colonel Wynkoop's cavalry, had a narrow escape the other day. He had been detailed with a few others on secret service near Lebanon, and was captured near that place. He was condemned to be hung, but being exceedingly vigilant gave his captors the slip, and is now safe.

From the Nashville Union, July 24th.

GREAT SKEDADDLE BY FORREST.

On Tuesday night Colonel Haggard's Fifth Kentucky cavalry, who had been in pursuit of the guerillas for several days, came within one mile of Forrest's banditti, on the Murfreesboro' road, thirteen miles from this city, when the whole gang of rebel horse-thieves, chicken-stealers, house-breakers and assassins cut and ran like quarter horses. The last seen of them Forrest was leaning over his horse's neck, whipping for dear life, while his men were dropping pistols, shot guns, canteens, corn dodgers, green apples and stolen chickens along the road. When last seen they were within ten miles of devildom, and still running.

Enlisting in New York State.

The following, from the New York *Commercial Advertiser*, we doubt not, is reliable. It is significant that the new call by the Government will be speedily met:

The activity in enlistments all over this State has settled the drafting question. From every quarter of the State reports are daily received at the general office in Walker street, giving sure promise of an early filling up of the New York quota. Chemung county has already made up her complement of one regiment, and General Arthur is at present engaged in responding to her requisition for clothing, uniforms and equipments. The regiment is quartered at Elmira, and will be mustered into the United States service on Saturday of this week. The counties of Erie, Oneida, Madison, Broome, Schoharie and Albany are rapidly obtaining their respective numbers of troops, and before the lapse of many days will send their regiments into the field. Recruiting in the central and western counties of the State is more active than in the southeastern and northwestern counties, although in every section large numbers of names are added every day to the enlistment rolls.

Battle of Malvern Hill--Rebel Account.

Special Correspondence of the Grenada Appeal.

RICHMOND, July 7, 1862.

I have been upon the battle-field of the 30th of June and the 1st of July, but have no power to describe to you the condition of the country, or the evidences presented to the eye of the terrible conflict that raged there. For five miles along the road pursued by the two armies, the surface of the earth is strewn with tattered blue coats, knapsacks cut to pieces, broken canteens, empty cartridge boxes, and dirty military caps; the fences are down; the trees, riven and blasted by the shells of the artillery, impede the way with their fallen branches; the houses are riddled in weatherboards and shingle roof; here a broken caisson stands in the middle of the road, there the festering carcass of a dead horse poisons the atmosphere with its exhalations, while on every hand the blighted crops of clover, corn, oats and wheat, tell of the ravage which twenty-four hours of warfare accomplished. Perhaps the most awful struggle of the whole war was that of Tuesday, the 1st of July, of which I wrote you so hurried and inaccurate an account that I desire to recur to, the engagement at this time to make even the imperfect and unsatisfactory outline of events presented in this correspondence somewhat more full and truthful with regard to it.

The enemy, flying before our victorious troops, had reached, on Tuesday afternoon, an elevated plateau of land, some sixteen miles from Richmond, and not more than two miles from the James River, where they availed themselves of a strong natural position to make a stand. Between them and the pursuing Confederate column lay, immediately in their front, an open space, nearly level, about twelve hundred yards across, planted in corn, which was scarcely more than ankle high, and edged by a deep, dense wood, out of which the Confederates must necessarily advance. Four powerful batteries, of six guns each, were at once placed so as to sweep the entire plain. About half-past five o'clock a regiment of General Magruder's Division, thrown out as skirmishers, coming upon the open ground, met the heavy fire of the enemy, and fell back to their main body.

This force was drawn up in the woods, ready at the proper moment to charge the enemy's batteries. The Purcell battery had already been ordered to take its position in front of the wood, and had opened a brisk cannonade, when a column of not more than five hundred men rushed forward from their place of concealment at double quick across the corn-field and reached a point probably about 150 yards distant from the guns of the Yankees on our extreme right. The fire had now become terrific. A perfect tempest of iron broke over the field, and to add to the horrors of the scene, immense projectiles from the enemy's gunboats on the river began to fall around the combatants.

It is remarkable that not one of these explosives did our troops any injury, and not more than half a dozen of them burst at all. Just behind the Yankee batteries was a handsome mansion which will be known in the official reports as "Crew's House." Here one of the largest shells thrown by the gunboats exploded, with the most fatal consequences to the Yankees, killing seven men instantly and tearing a gun carriage, and even the brass piece itself to pieces. I saw a shell, doubtless of the same size as this disastrous missile, lying unexploded on field, which measured twenty-two inches in length and ten inches in diameter.

Meanwhile the infantry column having been thinned out to a mere handful, by the withering fire of the enemy's field pieces, were compelled to fall back in disorder, and the Purcell battery having lost more than sixty men killed and wounded and nearly all its horses, was withdrawn, and the Letcher artillery ordered to replace it. The cannonade was still continuous and desolating. A second and larger body of infantry now marched foeward on the outer edge of the plateau to the left of our position and after gaining the very crest of the gentle summit occupied by the Yankees, was driven back with heavy loss.

The Letcher artillery at this moment bore the brunt of the destructive fire of twenty-four pieces of the Yankees, and every moment suffered some loss. A gallant lieutenant was killed at his gun. Two of the men were so mutilated as to be scarcely recognizable in death, and nineteen others were wounded. When it became apparent that this company could no longer maintain its position without immediate support, the third attack was made in heavy column from the centre, the men moving forward in great steadiness, but only to be repulsed as before. Night was now coming on and a flank movement having been made by Jackson on the enemy's right, with great havoc to their ranks, they withdrew with their batteries and retreated in the darkness. Thus was brought to a close the memorable fight of Tuesday, the first of July. It differed from the sanguinary battle of Gaines' Mill in this, that it was fought principally at long range, with artillery, whereas the encounter at the mill was between the infantry, hand to hand, and under the breastworks of the foe.

During the whole of this tremendous cannonade of Tuesday, Gen. Lee's headquarters were at a small house on the road side within range. Several of the enemy's case shots burst in the yard, and upon the day of my visit the fragments of shells could be picked up all around the building.

Continuing my ride beyond the battle field of Tuesday, about a mile and a half I came to the Malvern Hill mansion, which is occupied as a Federal hospital, and there I saw two hundred and fifty of the wounded Yankees, in all conditions of horrible mutilation, many minus a leg or an arm, others with wounds in the head, others again shot in the body, all requiring the utmost care of the surgeons, and yet McClellan had left but three in charge of this and several other hospitals in the neighborhood. One of the wounded men told me their loss in the fight of Tuesday far exceeded, for the number engaged, that of the Seven Pines; another said that had the first attacking column been 3,000 strong, the day would have ended at once in a rout, for the cannoniers of one battery had left their guns, and the infantry supporting it had fled in confusion before the Confederates had proceeded two thirds the way across the field; and a third confessed that McClellan had proclaimed it in a general order, that all the United States soldiers who should fall into the hands of the rebels would be put to death!

The house at Malvern Hill is a quaint old structure of the last century, built of red brick, and stands on a lofty hill, a thousand yards from James river, of whose meanderings, for several miles, it commands a beautiful view. The house was standing in Tarleton's time, and is marked down on the map accompanying the early English edition of his campaigns. A fine grove of ancient elms embowers the lawn in a grateful shade, affording numberless vistas of far off wheat fields, and little gleaming brooks of water, with the dark blue fringe of the primitive pines on the horizon. It seemed a bitter satire on the wickedness of man, this peaceful, serene, harmonious aspect of nature, and I turned from the joyous and quiet landscape to the mutilated victims around me, with something very like a malediction upon Seward and Lincoln and their participants in the crime of bringing on this accursed war.

The Indiana Rebels Killed at Newburg.

We learned yesterday some particulars of the killing of Carney and Mefford, two of the traitors who guided and assisted the rebel guerillas in their attack on Newburg, which have not yet been published. While the rebels were carrying off the plunder they had taken from the hospital and such private houses as they had robbed, and just before they started with the second boat load to the Kentucky shore, these two villains went to a coffee-house and took a drink, remarking to the barkeeper that it was the last drink they ever intended to take in the town, a prophesy which was speedily fulfilled, in a manner very different from what they expected. As they came out they were seen by a young countryman, who had hurried into the town, with a few others, to defend it, when the news of the attack got abroad, and he said they should never leave the town alive. He was armed with an old fashioned large bore rifle commonly called a "yager," and as the traitors were making their way toward the boat, he drew a bead on Mefford and shot him, the ball passing through his hips. The traitor fell mortally wounded, but not dead.

Carney made a dash for the boat when he saw his fellow traitor fall, but he had run only a few feet when a door opened on the street and a citizen, armed with a rusty old musket and bayonet, stepped out and fired at him. The ball struck him in the breast, killing him instantly. The man then walked up to Mefford, who was lying close by, and stabbed him with the bayonet two or three times, but not fatally. Mefford was taken to his house and left there for some time, but the citizens were so perfectly enraged that to prevent his being hung, wounded as he was, Colonel Bates, of the Warrick Legion, determined to take him to Evansville. He was placed on a wagon or dray, for that purpose, and while he was lying there a voice in the crowd cried "Give him air." As the crowd opened a gun was fired through the break and the ball struck Mefford in the neck, breaking it and killing him instantly. Thus perished two traitors, who had guided the enemy to their own town, and assisted them in attacking and plundering their own fellow townsmen. It is a bloody, but a just retribution. We cannot approve the bayoneting and shooting of the wounded traitor, richly as he deserved it, but before it be too harshly censured, let the censor imagine how he would feel if he had been subjected to the same outrages that these people of Newburg were.—*Indianapolis Journal, 26th.*

Gen. Nelson and the Niggers

From the Nashville Union, 25th.

THE RIGHT STEP.

We learn on good authority that Gen Nelson has ordered five hundred negroes' belonging to rebel masters to be sent to him for the purpose of putting them to work for the benefit of the army. We are not informed as to the work they will be required to do, but suppose they will be made to aid in rebuilding the bridges destroyed by the rebels and to construct fortifications. It might be a good plan to fortify Murfreesboro. Gen. Nelson has done exactly right in this case, and we hope his example will be extensively followed by our officers. Why don't our authorities here find work for a few hundred? They might be usefully employed, for ourselves, while at the same time they were kept from aiding the Confederate Government. We hope the matter will be attended to promptly. General Nelson has given strict orders, we learn, that no loyal man's slaves shall be taken, and the same rule would of course be observed here. This is the policy. Weaken the enemy while you strengthen yourself, and make his resources serve your own necessities.

When the Tax Bill Goes Into Effect.

TREASURY DEPARTMENT, July 23, 1862.—By authority of a joint resolution of the Congress of the United States, approved on the 17th day of July inst., notice is hereby given that the 1st day of September next is fixed and determined upon as the day on which the "act to provide internal revenue to support the government and to pay interest on the public debt" shall be put into practical operation; and any act or thing which in said act is required to be done on or before the 1st day of July or August, in the year 1862, shall be done on or before the 1st day of September, 1862; and all parts of said act having reference to said dates of the 1st days of July and August, 1862, shall be taken and construed as having reference to the 1st day of September, 1862.

Collectors and Assessors will be appointed, and whatever other things may be necessary to put the act into practical operation will be done, before the date fixed by this notice.

Personal Habits of Great Men.

Several paragraphs have been going the rounds in relation to the habits of great men which paragraphs, as usual, are all wrong, inasmuch as we have had the pleasure of dining and hobnobbing with all the great men of this and every other country on the face of the globe. A few illustrations will prove this to the satisfaction of everybody.

Mr. Seward generally rises from his bed in the morning about the time he gets up. He rarely if ever eats his breakfast before he gets it. He is not particular what kind of food he has, if he is provided with what he calls for. In his dress he is plain—never appearing in public without his pantaloons. He never wears his vest outside of his coat. He speaks his native dialect without a foreign accent, and uses his tongue in all that he utters. When he walks he uses his feet, which are encased in boots or shoes. As an evidence of the methodical precision with which he attends to business, it is only necessary to allude to the fact that he invariably draws his salary the moment it is due. His memory in this respect is prodigious. He generally writes his letters on paper, and uses a pen, which at intervals he dips into a stand of ink, that he keeps upon his table.

Horace Greeley is said to be the beau ideal of a man of style. He dresses neatly and elegantly. His linen is faultless.—Sometime since he shaved, which has materially altered his appearance. His walk is firm and dignified, like that of a soldier. From the fact that all through his life he has kept his arms well shouldered, it is possible that nature intended him for the infantry. His voice is peculiarly sweet, and when he whispers, one would almost imagine his words were the echoes of an Æolian harp. Somewhat inclined to obesity of late years, he still maintains his reputation as a beau. He reads from right to left contrary to the practice of his friend, Mr. Bennett, who, owing to a visual obliquity, reads from left to right—down the middle, change hands. Mr. Greeley dines on vegetable soup and table beer. He never drinks porter. His hearty Sunday dinners are of crackers and cheese. He retires to bed at an early hour, and almost immediately composes himself to sleep with a copy of the *Tribune*. Sometimes when at a loss for a subject, he varies the monotony of his editorials upon Bennett, by writing a pleasant and exhilarating novelty, involving personal and friendly allusions to the almighty nigger. His editorials are invariably short, (never exceeding four columns each,) pithy and devoid of verbiage.

General McClellan will, should he increase in flesh, be more inclined to corpulency. His age is at present somewhat greater in years than when he graduated at West Point. In disposition he is jocular, when in a joking humor, and exceedingly reticent when he says nothing, which latter fact is amply proved by the brevity and unsatisfactory nature of his dispatches after they have passed through the War Office. As a General he is cautious—particularly so when he is careful. He makes all his advances by going forward, but never adopting the same method in retreating. In his diet he is particularly abstemious when there is nothing to eat, and *vice versa*. He is extremely approbchable when you get near him, otherwise you will be apt to keep your distance. He does not exercise his troops with a two inch drill, nor does he bore his friends in conversation with an auger.—*N. Y. Monitor.*

Death of Capt. Gold T. Curtis.

From the Stillwater Messenger.

A dispatch received from the wife of Capt. Gold T. Curtis on yesterday, announced the death of that officer at St. Louis on Saturday. Although somewhat prepared for such an event,—it being known that he was dangerously ill for a week past,—the announcement of the event cast a universal gloom among all classes of our citizens. Capt. Curtis relinquished a lucrative law practice in the early part of last winter, and devoted his entire energies to the recruiting of a company for the Fifth regiment, of which he was chosen Captain at the organization of the company. His regiment moved early in the spring for Corinth, and although new and undisciplined, it will be remembered participated in the terrible battle of Shiloh, in which Capt. Curtis conducted himself with marked skill and bravery. Always possessed of a delicate constitution, it is not surprising that he could not resist the attacks of disease incident to arduous camp life, and the change of habits and climate. His disease was dysentery, of which he died soon after being removed to St. Louis. His wife hastened to him as soon as advised of his condition some days since, and no doubt reached him in time to minister to his wants.

Capt. Curtis was born in Madison county, New York, in 1819, and was consequently in his 43d year. He was admitted to the bar when but nineteen years of age, since which, until entering the military service, he has devoted his entire attention to the practice of his profession. He located in this city some seven or eight years since, and for two years was Judge of Probate of Washington county. He was also a member of the convention which framed our State Constitution.

The death of Capt. Curtis will create a vacancy in our community which wi l be severely felt. He leaves a most interesting family, who will receive the entire sympathies of our whole community.

—Isaac Curran, a well known and determined Democrat of Springfield, has been appointed consul to the Grand Duchy of Baden, to reside at Carlsrue.

—The immense number of horses and mules sent to the army of Virginia will attract attention. It shows that cavalry is to be relied upon to hunt down guerillas and detached parties who have heretofore so annoyed our armies on their march. We have heretofore relied too little on this arm of the service, as we now find to our great cost. From this time forth, when an army occupies a section of country, there will be no armed parties left in the rear or allowed to hang upon its flanks.—*New York World.*

FROM KENTUCKY.

MORE ABOUT GUERILLAS.

PROCLAMATION OF GOV. MAGOFFIN.

LOUISVILLE, July 29.—It is reported that a band of guerillas, under Gol. Gano, of Morgan notoriety, took Russelville this forenoon, killing one or two of our Lieutenants, and badly wounding Captain Morrow, of the Kentucky volunteers. Other reports say that a collission between the Home Guards at Russelville took place, either from a mistake or otherwise. A few hours after the rebel capture of Russelville, a portion of the Federal regiment was due there, and has probably arrived and reinstated matters.

The line is working south to Nashville, but we can get nothing further from Russelville, which is on a branch line. To-night the theory here is that the rebels took away the operator before the arrival of our forces.

Gov. Magoffin's proclamation of yesterday, calling together the Kentucky Legislature on August 14th, after remarking that "The Military Board still claims the paramount military authority of the Commonwealth, evinces an unwillingness to resign the powers heretofore exercised by them, or to permit their exercise by me," continues, "civil conflict is impending over us. I am without a soldier or a dollar to protect the lives, property, and liberties of the people, or to enforce the laws. Daily appeals are being made to me, as Governor of the State, to protect our citizens from marauding bands, and in the peaceable enjoyment of their property and rights under the Constitution. I am without the means and power to afford relief, and I am left no alternative but to appeal to you, their representatives, in the hope that it will not be in vain. Any attempt upon my part to organize a force for that purpose will certainly but precipitate the evil, and I therefore not unwillingly convene the General Assembly that they may themselves determine the extent of the authority granted by them, and, looking to the policy adopted in the State, and the late action of Congress and the President touching the question of slavery, provide for the safety of our institutions and the peace and tranquility of the Commonwealth."

The New Orders of the War Department--Enthusiasm Among the Soldiers.

Correspondence of the New York Times.

OLD POINT, July 24, 1862.

The new Executive orders, respecting using the property of rebels for military purposes, and also employing contrabands in our army, is hailed with delight among all loyal classes here, civil and military. People pull a long breath, and feel as if we had started afresh—this time on the right road. It is true the order comes rather late, and after we could have prevented the loss of thousands of brave lives and millions of treasure, could we have sooner managed to get the country out of its coils of red tape; but still let bygones be bygones. Let us be happy that matters—bad as they are—are no worse; and like honest Sancho Panza, bid God bless the giver, and not look the gift-horse too closely in the mouth.

There are people in the North who, no doubt, look upon this movement as a sort of semi-abolition one; who think it "unconstitutional" to save the bones and sinews of our Northern white men, by employing the property of Southern rebels in digging our trenches, &c., while our soldiers rest for fighting, and who would make many a Northern fool believe that the army would lay down their arms in disgust if one word was mentioned in their hearing about the negro. I wish to heaven that one of these people had been at my side this morning, to hear what I did from the lips of poor bed ridden fellows, with mutilated limbs, halting, limping, suffering, many dying, on board the S. R. Spaulding. He would have been convinced that, whatever political writers may choose to think of the necessity of having our men murdered by thousands while protecting rebel property, or dying like rotten sheep in swamps, to save the sleek negroes of armed traitors, soldiers who have to undergo those hardships have no sympathies that way.

And let the public be assured that this official order came not one moment too soon, and that the army is going to permit no tampering with it now that it has been promulgated. A cloud—a short time since no larger than the prophet's hand—had made its appearance, and was rapidly swelling into portentous dimensions. That which had hitherto been passing from lip to lip, in timid murmurs, would have soon burst into a roar of thunder so loud that the deafest among us would have been bound to hear. The army will die to a man defending our country, but will not fight for protecting traitors. A broad and distinct line has to be drawn—and that immediately—between those who are for the Union and those who are against it; the former to be encouraged, the latter to be overcome by any and every means known to civilized warfare, and all side issues, be it slavery or anything else, must and will be thrown overboard.

—In the last number of the Danville (Ky.) *Review* Rev. Dr. Breckinridge thus expresses his opinion of his nephew, John C. Breckinridge:

The conquest of his own State by arms was one of the points in this atrocious scheme, to the defense of which the Kentucky Senator lent himself at Washington, in his vehement opposition to the Federal Administration; and in the support of which, on his return to that State in August, 1861, the conspirator became a refugee and the refugee a general in the army of the traitors, and the general an invader of the land to whose defense he owed every drop of his blood. His expulsion, as a traitor to the nation, from the Senate of the United States, a few months later, was the just and natural result. He had not even the poor excuse that he was loyal to Kentucky. He was traitor to her also, and that with a treason aggravated almost beyond historic example, and destitute of every pretext ever plead by traitor before.

THE NEW YORK HERALD.

WHO.ˡE NO. 9467. NEW YORK, WEDNESDAY, AUGUST 13, 1862. PRICE TWO CENTS.

THE BATTLE OF CEDAR MOUNTAIN.

Brilliant Conduct of the Union Troops.

INTERESTING PARTICULARS OF THE FIGHT.

Only Two Divisions of General Banks' Army Engaged.

Over Twenty Thousand Rebels in the Action.

Generals Pope, Banks and McDowell in the Field.

Desperate Charges by the Union Forces.

Heroism of Crawford's and Williams' Brigades.

The Retreat of the Rebels and Our Cavalry in Pursuit.

TOPOGRAPHY OF THE COUNTRY.

Our Troops Before the Fight and the Order of Advance.

GEN. PRINCE A PRISONER IN RICHMOND.

INCIDENTS AND SCENES ON THE BATTLE FIELD.

THE BURIAL OF THE DEAD, &c., &c., &c.

Our Special Army Correspondence.

HEADQUARTERS, ARMY OF VIRGINIA, CULPEPPER COURT HOUSE, Va., August 11, 1862.

I telegraphed you yesterday such facts as came under my own observation pertaining to the battle of Cedar Mountain, especially such as were most important. But there were many matters transpiring during the two days' fighting which must not be lost to history, and which will not be truly chronicled except in the HERALD.

THE FIRST SKIRMISHING

occurred on Friday, August 8, between the cavalry under General Bayard and the rebels under General Wood. General Bayard's brigade consisted of the First Maine, First Rhode Island, First Connecticut, Second Pennsylvania, First Vermont and First New Jersey regiments of cavalry, of General McDowell's corps, and was thrown forward to the Rapidan to reconnoitre and to protect the details engaged in repairing the bridges on the Orange and Alexandria Railroad over Robinson's creek and the Rapidan river.

DISCOVERY OF THE ENEMY.

Early in the forenoon the enemy were discovered crossing the Rapidan some two miles above the turnpike, at a place known as Robinson's ferry, and immediately the First New Jersey was sent off to watch their movements. The Jersey regiment had not proceeded far when two companies detoured to the right and proceeded in the direction of Robinson's mill, further up the creek. Shortly after the two companies had left the balance of the regiment proceeded toward the river, but had not gone far when they came upon the enemy's pickets.

THE FIRST FIRING.

Then a fire was given and returned, which created some little confusion among our forces. However, by order of Gen. Banks and request of Gen. Bayard, the confusion was promptly arrested. The rest of Gen. Bayard's command behaved admirably, and kept the enemy in check during the entire day, retiring at night to the vicinity of Cedar creek.

ARRIVAL OF GENERAL POPE AT CULPEPPER.

General Pope arrived at Culpepper at noon on Friday and ordered his headquarters located at Mr. George's, a mile south of Culpepper Court House; but by some mistake the teams, on coming into town, drove to Mrs. Green's, a mile south of the village, and by one o'clock had the tents nearly all pitched. The teamsters and a few staff officers who directed them suddenly discovered, in consequence of rumors of trouble, the difference between George and Green, and concluded that, under the present circumstances, George was the preferable name, and the General's canvass village was soon packed into the wagons, ready for a grand skedaddle. There was some excitement in the town when the troops and General's headquarters passed back; but at four o'clock McDowell's corps was ordered out on the road four miles from the town, when all became calm again.

GENERAL BANKS REPORTS IN PERSON TO GENERAL POPE.

About dark on Friday evening General Banks reported in person to General Pope, his corps having arrived and gone into camp about a mile west of the village. General Banks' army had encamped the night before at Hazel river, eight miles northwest from Culpepper; but when it became known that the rebels were advancing in force General Pope ordered him into closer position, and General Sigel was ordered to break camp at Sperryville, and come down to General Banks' old camp at Hazel river bridge.

THE POSITIONS ON FRIDAY EVENING AND SATURDAY MORNING.

This was the position, then, on the evening of Friday. General McDowell was four miles south of the town, General Banks was at the town, and General Sigel was at Hazel river bridge, only eight miles away. On Saturday morning General Banks' army took the advance, with orders to proceed cautiously in the direction of Robinson's ferry, on the Rapidan; General Sigel was ordered into town, and General McDowell to remain in *statu quo.*

TOPOGRAPHY OF THE FIELD.

In order to fully understand the position of the two armies, a description of the country in the vicinity of Cedar Mountain will be necessary. South from Culpepper the road leading to Gordonsville runs through some of the finest farms to be found in the Old Dominion. Woods and fields, shallow valleys and gentle acclivities alternate continuously, and everywhere the rank growth of cereals and the substantial farmhouses evidence a degree of thrift and comfort which shows in strange contrast with the desolation which the rebellion has brought upon the land. About six miles from Culpepper a small stream, known as Spring creek, makes across the pike, and empties into Cedar creek about two miles farther down. In going from Culpepper, however, just before reaching Spring creek, a belt of heavy timber, perhaps fifty rods in width, stretches across the road, and this again is prefaced by clover fields and meadows of several hundred acres in extent, beyond which, and half a mile to the right of the turnpike, stands a fine mansion house, now used as a hospital. Just at the southern side of the above mentioned timber the road to Madison Court House leaves the Gordonsville pike, and, pursuing a southwesterly course, crosses Spring, Cedar and Robinson's creeks, and Crooked river, all within a distance of about four miles. These streams all run in a southeasterly course, and empty into the Rapidan some miles below. Immediately beyond Spring creek, on the Madison Court House road, rises a small hill, or, more properly, knoll (No. 1 on the map), some twenty feet in height, and perhaps a quarter of a mile in length. This knoll is cleared and cultivated at its northwestern extremity; but upon its opposing end it is covered with a thin growth of timber. Descending the southwestern side of this rise, we cross the insignificant stream known on the map as Codar creek, a good sized watering stream for a small farm, beyond which rises another moundlike eminence (No. 2), at the southeastern end of which rises

THE BATTLE OF CEDAR MOUNTAIN.

The Position of the Union and Rebel Forces on Cedar, Spring, Robinson's and Crooked Runs, Saturday, August 9, 1862.

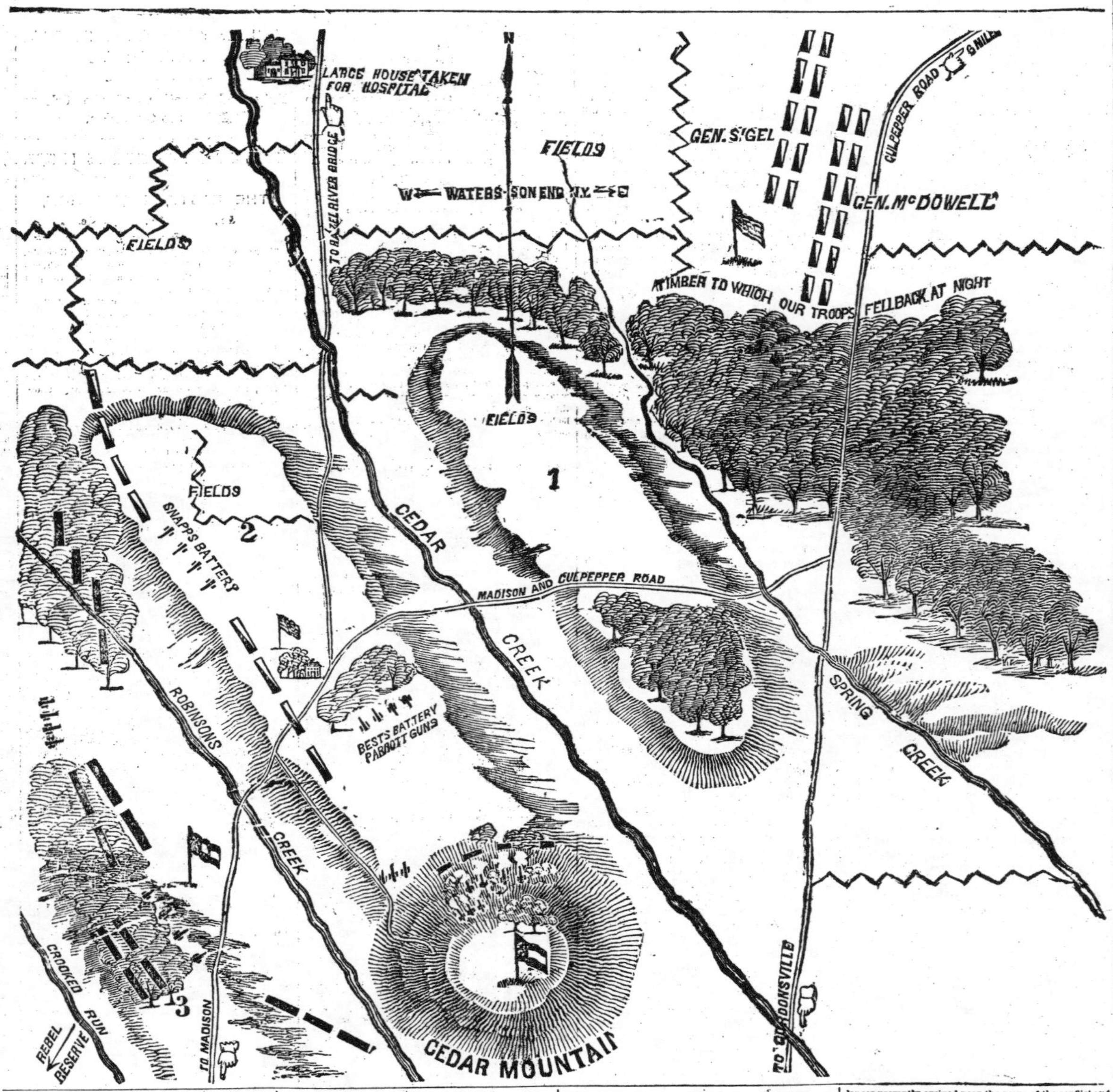

suddenly, like a pimple upon a baby's face,

CEDAR MOUNTAIN,

upon which were planted the enemy's heavy guns. This mountain is one of remarkable beauty. At a distance of four or five miles from its base it seems to rise a perfect cone from the plain below, and from its base to its summit scarcely a deflection is to be observed in its outline form—a perfectly straight line, as if nature had formed it in the same manner that schoolboys form sand hills. The sides of Cedar Mountain are covered with a heavy growth of timber, and its summit is only reached by a poor road leading from the farm on the summit of the second hill. The northern side of Cedar Mountain commands the roads and valleys along its base, and is admirably adapted to defensive operations. The height of the summit is perhaps eight hundred feet above the creeks.

ROBINSON'S CREEK,

which formed the dividing line between the two armies, is scarcely so large as Cedar creek, though the difference between them is scarcely perceptible. The valley through which the creek runs is perhaps a third of a mile wide where the Madison road crosses it, but is narrower above, where the Union right and rebel left flanks faced each other. Beyond this is another rise, shown in diagram as No. 3. This is but a slight eminence, scarcely as high as either of the others, and partially covered with thick timber, in and behind which the enemy were posted in strength. Beyond this last eminence, distant about half a mile, is Crooked river, or, as it is more familiarly known, Crooked run. Cedar creek and Spring creek run down on the east, and Robinson's creek and Crooked run flow past on the west side of Cedar Mountain.

Having thus the topography of the country, together with the diagram of the field, your readers will have no difficulty in understanding readily the plan of

THE BATTLE OF CEDAR MOUNTAIN,

which, by the way, was, for the numbers engaged, the most desperately fought engagement of the war, and terminated in a victory as signal as it was bloody.

EARLY IN THE MORNING

General Pope had sent General Banks' command to the front, and the divisions of Generals Augur and Williams were placed in position about a mile and a half this side the ground which had been the scene of the skirmish of the previous day.

SUBSEQUENTLY, IN THE AFTERNOON,

Crawford's brigade, of General Williams' division, composed of the Forty-sixth Pennsylvania, Tenth Maine, Fifth Connecticut and Twenty-eighth New York regiments, with Best's battery of regulars, moved forward and occupied a piece of high ground lying between Cedar creek and Crooked river, some four miles north of the point where the Culpepper and Gordonsville turnpike crosses the Rapidan river. About three-fourths of a mile south of this point rises the Cedar Mountain, a spur of the great Thoroughfare range. It was from the slope of this eminence that the enemy first opened their fire upon the Union troops.

THE FIRST INTIMATION OF THE ENEMY.

The first intimation our advance received of the presence of the enemy was at the moment when, after emerging from the timber on the north, it began to cross Spring creek. At once a battery of heavy guns, posted in the thick timber half way up the mountain side, belched upon the troops both shot and shell, while another battery of smaller guns at the foot of the mountain gave them a similar reception from the cover of some timber about three-eighths of a mile to the westward.

OUR REPLY.

Preparations were at once made to reply to these civilities, and Best's battery of Parrott guns was immediately planted on the crest of the rising ground we occupied and began replying to the two batteries of the enemy. In the meantime the infantry were posted in line of battle (as shown in the diagram) on the right of the battery, and cheerfully awaited the order which would bring them more actively into the deadly conflict!

THE PERSISTENT FIRING OF THE REBELS.

For half an hour at least the enemy maintained a continuous fire from both their batteries, replied to in rapid succession by Captain Best's, when there opened simultaneously three other rebel batteries, posted in as many different localities, opposite our front and right.

THE REBEL INFANTRY APPEAR.

For some time this contest of shot and shell was kept up; but at five o'clock the rebel infantry were discovered in strong force upon our right and in front, supporting the rebel batteries. The fact was at once communicated, by rapid couriers, to the main body of our troops. Immediately the division of Gen. Augur, with the remainder of Gen. Williams' division, were thrown forward with prompt despatch, and posted advantageously upon the right of Gen. Crawford, and directly fronting the dense timber where the rebel infantry, in strong force, were plainly visible.

GENERAL BANKS NOW RODE ON TO THE FIELD

and directed the operations, the best possible disposition being made for the continuation of the fight now inevitable, and each moment developing in proportions. The manner in which he handled his troops and provided for every emergency, together with the personal gallantry he displayed, being constantly under fire, are subjects of general commendation with officers and men.

GENERAL GEARY IN ADVANCE—BRAVERY OF THE COMMAND.

Gen. Geary's brigade, of Gen. Augur's division, had the advance, which through the brunt of the first part of the day's fight it maintained with skill and courage. This gallant brigade consisted of the Fifth Ohio, Seventh Ohio, Twenty-ninth Ohio, Twenty-eighth Pennsylvania and Snapp's battery. No sooner had these troops formed in order of battle than the rebels opened musketry fire upon them from two sides and in front, while the rebel batteries also directed their death-dealing missiles among the brave fellows, that on the mountain being very destructive in its effects. Notwithstanding this terrible concentrated fire, the troops, under their courageous General (Geary), never faltered or winced.

THE BATTLE BECOMES GENERAL.

It was not till half-past five that the battle became general. Then artillery replied to artillery, musketry to musketry, while infantry met infantry in repeated shocks of deadly strife. Reckless valor and desperation marked the progress of the fight, which continued without pause or lull, with terrible cannonading, until darkness put a stop to the carnage. I have witnessed many battles during this war; but I have seen none where the tenacious obstinacy of the American character was so fully displayed.

THE DETERMINATION OF OUR TROOPS.

Our troops fought with the coolness and valor of veterans, standing up to the fight unfalteringly and unblenchingly in the teeth of a raking and destructive fire of cannon and musketry. No sooner did a volley of musketry or a discharge of artillery mow down the ranks of a regiment than the wide gaps were filled up and new fronts presented.

OUR ARTILLERY PLAY WITH EFFECT.

Once informed of the position of the enemy in force, our artillery opened with terrible effect upon them, compelling regiment after regiment to break and fall back out of range, within the shelter of the dense timber.

DEATH OF THE REBEL GENERALS WINDER AND TRIMBLE.

As regiments thus fell back fresh troops were in quick succession brought up to confront the deadly storm of iron hail from the Union guns, and it was while leading up some of these fresh regiments that Generals Winder and Trimble were killed.

THE REBEL ARTILLERY—CHARGES AND CAPTURE OF REBEL GUNS.

The rebel artillery was served with deadly effect, and at one time it was determined to take one battery that gave the greatest annoyance by the bayonet. A portion of the District of Columbia troops charged most gallantly one of these batteries, and succeeded in taking two of the rebel guns, with but little loss to our brave men. Portions of Augur's and Williams' divisions, including Crawford's and Gordon's brigades, made three dashing bayonet charges upon the rebel artillery. Each time the brave fellows were repulsed with loss, the enemy's overpowering infantry support being too much for our troops to cope with; but uncowed and undauntedly they returned to the charge with increased desperation and renewed vigor. The terrible and continuous infantry fire from the woods with which they were met each time demonstrated unmistakeably that our forces were greatly outnumbered by the foe.

THE EIGHTH AND TWELFTH REGULARS,

attached to General Banks' corps, commanded by Capt. Pitcher, did excellent service. Capt. Pitcher was wounded severely, though not dangerously, in the knee, by a musket shot; but he nevertheless kept the field at the head of his men until the close of the conflict.

THE INFANTRY CEASE FIRING.

With the setting in of night the musketry firing ceased; but the artillery on the mountain kept up an intermittent firing until near midnight. At twilight our troops withdrew to a small copse of wood, about half mile to the rear of their first position, where they were joined soon after by the corps of Generals McDowell and Sigel, who formed on their rear. It was then that the hungry and wearied troops of Gen. Banks were relieved by portions of these fresh troops. The former fell back a half mile, where, in a pleasant clover field, they rested on their arms from the fatigues of the day.

A BRILLIANT NIGHT.

The night was unusually lustrous, a bright moon shedding its radiance all around, and causing all prominent objects to be as plainly distinguishable as in the day. In the west loomed up Thoroughfare Mountain, from whose peak flashed at intervals a rebel signal light, indicative of the presence of the enemy, and to us, at the time, an assurance that the conflict of the past day would be resumed on even a larger scale, and with casualties and losses proportionate to the increased numbers to be engaged.

THE REBEL SIGNAL LIGHTS

engaged the attention of our forces, and the long, dense columns, standing by their muskets, stretching away along the fields, on the plain and the slopes of hills and hollows, were plainly or dimly, according to the distance, descried in the moonlight, with their faces turned towards the enemy. At such a moment, with the experiences of the past day fresh upon them; with the recollection of comrades fallen, of the hairbreadth escapes from imminent death, with the consciousness that all the terrible scenes of the day just passed would be revived in tenfold horrors on the approaching morrow, thoughts alien to that scene and time and place must have passed through the minds of that armed host.

A HASTY BIVOUAC.

At last Crawford's brigade, which had borne the brunt of the fight, threw their exhausted frames upon the moist grass, some to talk over the adventures of the day, others to seek needful repose to meet the toils and dangers of the morrow.

THE NIGHT ATTACK AND CAUSE.

It was here that some of the men incautiously lighted fires, which, revealing their position to the enemy, the result was that the latter commenced shelling them. The firing on this occasion was, on the whole, pretty accurate—so much so, indeed, that their shells burst in the midst of wagon trains, ambulances and horses, a contiguity so dangerous that the men were compelled to move back out of range towards Culpepper. The men, not deeming themselves under particular orders at the time, stood not upon the order of their going, but went quickly.

THE WOUNDED MOVE TO THE REAR.

The slightly wounded, in considerable numbers, covered the roads leading to Culpepper, while numerous ambulances promptly arrived near the scene of the conflict and carried off all who were unable to walk.

THE NEXT MORNING.

The morning's light revealed a scene at which the mind shuddered, but which was composed of those concomitants only which render all battle fields, after the excitement of the conflict has passed away, so terrible and revolting to the unimpassioned beholder. In the fight near Culpepper the loss of field and line officers was very remarkable. Most of our wounded have received their injuries on the lower limbs.

GEN. POPE ON THE FIELD.

During the progress of the fight, when, indeed, it was raging with most fury, Gen. Pope and staff rode on to the field. The General was greeted by his troops with the most vociferous cheering as he rode to the front and took a position in the thickest of the fight. While here intensely occupied in marking the phases of the conflict and revolving the advantages of different positions, he came near falling into a rebel ambuscade, only discovering his danger in barely sufficient time to en[illegible] him to avoid it.

SEVERAL REBEL PRISONE[illegible] FELL INTO OUR HANDS,

from whom I re[illegible]ceived some particulars attending the fight, [illegible] some incidents connected therewith. It is certain, from what I have learned, that Gen. Winder was killed in the fight.

General Jackson is wounded slightly in the hand. General Saxton is mortally wounded. The rebel force engaged in the battle was from forty to fifty thousand.

General Augur's wound is not dangerous. It is a flesh wound in the hip. General Geary is severely wounded in the arm. General Banks had his horse killed under him, as did also the chief of General Pope's staff, Colonel Ruggles. Culpepper is one vast hospital, though most of the wounded will be sent on to Washington for treatment.

WHY OUR TROOPS SUFFERED SEVERELY.

One cause of the amount of casualties falling upon us arose from the necessity which compelled us to cross open ground, for a considerable distance, raked by the fire of the rebels, who were under cover of the woods. Jackson put his usual strategy in proof upon this occasion. He concealed his strength for hours during the day, fighting with cannon planted advantageously, and in his own time unmasking his real strength, and throwing forward massed troops suddenly upon our lines. But here he was checkmated, and his strategy rendered abortive by the watchfulness of our generals and the unswerving gallantry of the brave troops they led.

MAJOR PELOUZE.

Major Pelouze, General Banks' Adjutant, took command of a hesitating regiment and bravely led it through a galling fire. He received two shots, and is severely but not dangerously wounded in the side.

The following is a partial list of our officers killed and wounded:—

Lieut. Col. Crale, 3d Wisconsin, supposed killed.
Major Scott, same regiment, wounded.
Col. Donnelly, 28th New York, wounded.
Major Gray, 109th Pennsylvania, wounded.
Capt. Slyman, 102d New York, wounded.
Capt. Clayton, same regiment, wounded.
Capt. Spring, same regiment, killed.
Capt. Tuttle, same regiment, wounded.
Lieut. Mead, same regiment, wounded.
Capt. McDonald, 1st Pennsylvania cavalry.
Capt. Taylor, same regiment, wounded.
Capt. Hawley, 3d Wisconsin, wounded.
Lieut. Haskell, on Gen. Prince's staff, slightly wounded.
Lieut. Long, 28th New York, wounded.
Joseph M. Gadder, of Gen. Pope's body guard, was killed while Gen. Pope was examining the battle ground.

THE BATTLE A VICTORY, AND WHY.

The victory has been complete, though I am aware that many newspaper writers here look upon the issue of the Saturday's fight as a disastrous defeat, simply because, at the setting in of darkness, our forces retired a half mile to the rear. But the enemy did precisely the same thing. On Sunday morning, however, we advanced again, took up our position upon the field and commenced burying our own and the rebel dead. Nothing but rebel pickets were to be seen in the vicinity all day Sunday; no batteries opened upon us, and in the course of the day General Jackson sent in a flag of truce to ask permission to bury his dead—a favor not generally asked by a victor of his vanquished foe. It is true, also, that when our troops retired from the wood to escape the enemy's shells, which their camp fires had invited, they did so in some haste; but it was not a panic or anything of such a nature. The enemy's guns were posted high above our own, and out of our reach; and to remain in such a position would have been suicide. Consequently they retired individually, but not in disorder. As to our losing a couple of pieces of artillery, the story is all the purest fiction. We captured two from the enemy.

THE BATTLE HAS BEEN A TERRIBLE ONE,

both in regard to the number killed and wounded, on both sides. The terrible ordeal of arms, together with the oppressive heat of the day, rendered *hors du combat* an unusual number of the combatants.

Of individual instances of bravery there were hosts. I could write a book of them, and then have occasion for an appendix. Never did men fight more bravely than did the divisions of Generals Augur and Williams, and I only mention these because they bore the brunt of the affair. There were individual regiments which deserve especial notice; but, where all behaved so well, discrimination or comparison would be invidious.

GENERAL SIGEL'S TROOPS.

Many will probably ask why the corps of Generals Sigel and McDowell did not come up in time to reinforce General Banks. The question is easily answered. General Banks only encountered the enemy at about four o'clock P. M., and it was not until five o'clock that it was known that there was more than a few regiments of rebels—a mere advance guard, similar to Banks' own force—upon our front. Gen. Banks thought himself to be, and, as the sequel proved, was, able to maintain his position, and only sent back for reinforcements when he found the enemy were being greatly reinforced and were massing troops upon him. As soon as General McDowell, who was five miles away on the Culpepper road, found that he was needed, his army corps was pushed forward, arriving upon the ground just as the firing on both sides ceased. It must be remembered that the day was an oppressively hot one, perhaps the hottest of the season, and no troops in the world, under the circumstances, could have reached the field sooner. Experience will teach any one that there is a vast difference between "double quicking" four or five miles over a dusty road, with the thermometer at 98 in the shade, and performing the same feat in January, when he has to agitate his limbs nimbly to keep his blood from congealing. McDowell's forces came up in good time to cover our exhausted troops as they rested for the night, and that was all that could be expected of them. Sigel had to march eight miles to reach the same.

INCIDENTS OF THE FIGHT—A SPUNKY PRIVATE.

Just after the firing of musketry became interesting I noticed a private soldier coming off the field, and, thinking perhaps he was running away to avoid danger, I rode up to him, when I found he had two fingers of his left hand shot away and a third dreadfully lacerated. I saw at once that he had at least a hand in the fight. I assisted him to dress his wound as well as my limited knowledge of surgery would permit, he in the meantime propping up my pluck by his quaint remarks. Said he, "I don't keer a durn for that third finger; for it wan't of no 'count no how; but the 'pinter' and t'other one were right good ones, and I hate to loose 'em. I shouldn't have come to the rear if I had been able to load my gun; but I wasn't." After I had dressed his hand, he looked over in the direction of the firing and stood a moment. Turning to me, and said:—"Stranger, I wish you would jist load up my shooting iron for me; I want to have a little satisfaction out of them cusses for spiling my fore paw." I loaded his gun for him, and he started back for the top of the hill at a double quick in quest of "satisfaction." His name was Lappin, or Lapham, of the Ohio Seventh.

A BRAVE CAPTAIN.

Captain Pitcher, of the Eighth regulars, was wounded severely in the knee; but he kept the field until nearly dark, and only left then through inability to remain any longer. I rode with him to Spring creek, where we found a parcel of cowards running from the field in disorder. Knowing what effect such men would have upon others, the Captain drew his sabre, and, weak as he was, threatened to cut down the first man who should attempt to run away. He afterwards organized the cravens into a provost guard, and planted them across the road to prevent others of the same sort from absconding. The friends of the Captain will be glad to learn that he is doing well.

GENERAL ROBERTS.

This veteran officer seemed almost omnipresent on the field. He is, as you are aware, chief of cavalry on General Pope's staff, and in that capacity was in the thickest of the carnage. When I saw him last he was riding along the road trying to cheer the wounded troops along, and to shame the cowardly ones into a sense of duty.

CEDAR CREEK, August 11—6 P. M.

The HERALD's special correspondent assigned to General Banks' command has obtained a minute account of the origin, disposition and result of the bloody battle of Saturday, August 9, denominated by the enemy "Cedar Creek," and by the Unionists "Slaughter's Mountain." As comprehensive statements have already appeared in your columns, I reserve to the end a history of the earlier features of the fight, and refer in the beginning to facts as yet unrecorded, but highly interesting.

SLAUGHTER'S (CEDAR) MOUNTAIN.

About seven miles from the little town of Culpepper, in a southwesterly direction, and to the left of the high road that leads to Barnett's ford of the Rapidan river, a woody knob or mountain rises and commands from crest a view of all the surrounding country. It is [illegible] a mountain in elevation, but so hi[illegible] scarcely clouds often envelope its crest. [illegible] that the [illegible]ings up its sides, which co[illegible]ners are clearings [illegible] Rev. Mr. Slaughter, a P[illegible] constitute the farm of [illegible] Presbyterian clergyman; and at its base, near[illegible] to Culpepper, lies the pleasant "Elm Farm" of a Mrs. Crittenden. Directly behind Mrs. Crittenden's house a valley or bottom opens out to the south, and by a road that follows the windings of the valley it is believed that most of the rebel army was advanced. The position was a powerful, not to say an impregnable one, for batteries could readily be dragged up the hillsides, and our infantry had often marched up steeper eminences. But an opposing army scattered about the slopes and fields below would find its several components exposed to shot and shell discharges from batteries two hundred or even five hundred feet above them. The country is open and uneven around the front of Slaughter's Mountain; but across the main road referred to there is a deep woods, admirably adapted for the concealment of infantry, the covering of skirmishers or the masking of batteries. In front of the woods lies an old wheatfield, spotted with stone heaps, that could capitally protect sharpshooters, and across the road there is a cornfield, perhaps a hundred acres in area. A shallow run waters both wheatfield and cornfield, trickling obliquely across the road and tributary to

CEDAR CREEK,

a large but insignificant rivulet, which flows over pebbles, pools and miniature cataracts, towards the distant Rapidan. A bottom of soggy grass environs Cedar creek, but the ground developes into a good grazing field directly, which latter ascends toward a fine piece of timber. From the timber grove to Culpepper—still coming north—cannot be more than six miles, and the intervening land is of that rolling, often rugged nature, which has earned for this part of Virginia the popular name of "Piedmont." It was by these quiet creek sides, and at the foot of this picturesque mountain, that the freak of fate or the madness of man located a frightful scene of carnage and despair.

FAMILIARITY WITH THE COUNTRY.

We might possibly have taken position upon Slaughter's knob, and thus have forestalled the enemy; for some of General McDowell's brigades lay back of Culpepper, and our cavalry went regularly far beyond the knob to the margin of the Rapidan. The First and Second Pennsylvania, First New Jersey and Rhode Island regiments had picketed the mountain and beyond it at a time when the enemy's cavalry lay quietly back at Orange Court House. As the main body of our troops had not yet come up from Little Washington, Sperryville, Waterloo and Warrenton, we were compelled to lie quietly at Culpepper and concentrate for a general advance. The enemy, aware of the importance of the mountain and of our incomplete preparations, and being also heavily reinforced, determined to make a bold march across the Rapidan, take possession of the high country and assume the offensive. This he accomplished with the usual promptness of Stonewall Jackson, and so, instead of waiting to be attacked at Gordonsville, menaced us in

[CONTINUED FROM EIGHTH PAGE.]

TELEGRAPHIC.

GREAT SALT LAKE CITY, MONDAY, AUG. 18, 1862. No. 156.

Memphis, 15th.

Reports from White river say that General Hovey's division had a fight on Monday last near Clarendon, Arkansas. The Federal force consisted of six regiments of infantry, the rebel force of eight regiments of cavalry, with a part of Hindman's brigade. The battle raged furiously for some time with destructive effect on both sides, resulting in the defeat and rout of the rebels. Seven hundred prisoners were taken. No further particulars are given.

The Grenada *Appeal* says the rebels destroyed over one million of dollars worth of Federal property at Baton Rouge before they were repulsed.

Fortress Monroe, 16th.

Several transports arrived during the night from Harrison's Landing with sick and wounded soldiers aboard.

A hundred rebel cavalry drove in the Union pickets at Suffolk last night. Some little excitement prevails there to-day on that account.

The Union troops evacuated Harrison's Landing at 8 o'clock this morning. About the same hour, McClellan's advance arrived at Williamsburg. The public property was all removed. "All is quiet."

Washington, 16th.

Col. Corcoran and Col. Wilcox reached Fortress Monroe, this afternoon; and are expected to start at once for Washington. Three hundred and twenty officers have been exchanged; among them is Lieut. Kane.

Culpepper, 16th.

Gen. Sigel, who occupies the advance near Rapidan reports, this mornidg, that the enemy made a feint or an attempt to cross the river, but he drove them back.

Chicago, 17th.

From the Peninsula correspondence of the New York *Times*, we learn that Gen. McClellan was engaged, during the past week, in withdrawing his army from Harrison's Landing; a large body was moving by land towards Williamsburg; the remainder are going down James river, on transports. The place of destination, of course, is not known; tho' conjecture mentions Acquia creek, Fredericksburg and Urbana—points on York river.

St. Louis, 17th.

A fight is reported to have taken place at Muscle park,* Chariton county, on the 14th, between Guitar and Poindexter. The former fought the latter for eighteen miles running. Poindexter's troops were scattered in all directions. A letter dated at Glasgow, Howard county, on the 15th, says—from two to three hundred of their men were killed and wounded.

A good many guerrillas are returning home and have sent word asking on what condition they can remain there.

Washington, 17th.

The Navy department has received the particulars of the capture of the steamer Columbia, by the Santiago de Cuba, seventy-five miles from Abaco. She left Nassau the day previous, under British colors, but no register, and was loaded with munitions of war.—She is an iron propeller, probably intended for a Confederate gunboat. She had on board Charleston, Savannah and Bahama Pilots.

A costruction train was sent yesterday to repair the tunnel at Gallatin. All the hands were captured near that place, but the engineer escaped with the locomotive. It is rumored that the houses of several Union men have been burned at Gallatin.

A camp of instruction for fifty thousand men has been established here. Over three hundred army officers have been stricken from the rolls under the late stringent order.

Culpepper, 17th.

There was a general advance towards the Rapidan, to-day. If the enemy intend to dispute the possession of Orange, they will endeavor to drive us back. Nothing has been heard from them so far.

Col. Fifield went, yesterday, with a construction train as far as Rapidan station, but, learning that a considerable body of the enemy were within gunshot of the river on the other side, it was thought inexpedient to begin repairing the bridge until Gen. Pope's forces, now on their march, should reach the river. Col. Fifield found near the road a lot of flour stored for confederate use, which he seized.

Contrabands from Gordonsville report the continuous arrival of troops from Richmond.

We now occupy the line of the Rapidan from Raccoonboro, on the east to Cove's ford, on the left with pickets and scouting parties beyond these points.

Trenton, Tenn., 17th.

Capt. Fullerton's co., 2d Illinois cavalry, came up with a rebel force of one hundred and fifty strong at Merryweather's ford, Dyer county, a day or two since, and completely routed and drove them into the river. The fight lasted thirty minutes. Captain Fullerton's force consisted of sixty-three men. The enemy's loss in killed, wounded and drowned was large. Ten prisoners, forty horses, a large number of arms and a quantity of ammunition were taken. Our loss, Lieuts. Terry and Goodheart and one private killed and six wounded. Several companies of cavalry from Kentucky have tried to get South, but this is the first company that has crossed the line.

Louisville, Ky., 17th.

Beriah Magoffin has resigned his governorship, and James Robinson, Speaker of the Senate — a strong Union man, becomes Governor defacto for the un-expired term.

Cairo, 17th.

The Grenada *Appeal* of the 11th contains a long account of the Baton Rouge fight, in which it acknowledges the severe repulse of Breckinridge, with a loss of three hundred men. A partial list of the rebel killed and wounded shows that there were six field and company officers killed and thirteen wounded. Among the killed were Gen. Charles Clark of Mississippi, Col. Allen, and Capt. Alexander Todd, Mrs. Lincoln's brother.

Nashville, 17th.

Two bridges on the Kentucky and Edgfield railroad over Red river were burned to-day by the rebels. It is also reported that the track has been torn up, this side of Tullahama.

Two Federal couriers were captured by the Guerillas, nine miles south of this city last night, the dispatches were taken from them, and they were then released, they report a large rebel force under Stearns this side of Murfreesburo.

An armed reconnoisance towards Gallatin last night ascertained that Morgan had decamped in the direction of Huntsville. All railroad communication with this city has been cut off. Telegraphic communication is yet uninterrupted.

New York, 18th.

A letter from Baton Rouge says, the ram Arkansas grounded at a distance of six miles from the city on the 6th. She was engaged with the Essex in a fair, stand-up fight. Porter, commander of the Essex, lay three hundred yards distant from the Arkansas, pouring solid nine inch shot into her until a breach was made, when an incendiary shell exploded in the breach, setting her on fire. The rebel crew then left. She shortly afterwards exploded.

A wounded rebels says, Gen. Ruggles was killed and states that their loss was eight hundred.

Secessionists in Baton Rouge firied on our wounded, as they were being brought in, consequently their houses were pulled down.

Gen. Williams' funeral took place in New Orleans, on the 8th, with very impressive ceremonies.

Among the prisoners taken by the Federals at Baton Rouge was Gen. Allen, of Mississippi, mortally wounded.

Gen. Butler issued a general order announcing in eloquent language the death of Gen. Williams.

The *Tribune* correspondent from Culpepper on the 16th says the enemy appeared in force upon the south bank of the Rapidan yesterday. This morning, at sunrise, they drove in our pickets to within half a mile of Sigel's headquarters. Major Kreps, who occupies the front, advanced with two guns to meet the enemy, who fell back precipitately to the south bank of the Rapidan., where he was supported by infantry and artillery. As Major Kreps approached the river, the enemy opened an artillery fire on him, killing one lieutenant and five privates. It is thought the passage of the Rapidan will be obstinately contested.

The North Star and Roanoke from New Orleans on the 10th, have arrived.

A letter from Baton Rouge, in speaking of the recent rebel attack, says: Rim's battery trice repulsed the foe with great slaughter. Breckenridge lost his right arm by a cannon shot. We captured a large number of prisoners; we also took three guns. The enemy's loss must be severe, as our men charged and recharged on them. The battle was fought on the edge of town, as Gen. Williams was unwilling to expose the women and children. Gen. Williams was killed by a rifle ball.

Another account says, the rebels were estimated at five or six thousand. The combat was obstinate. Our loss was two hundred and fifty killed, including a large proportion of officers. The rebel loss, according to prisoners' statements, was immense. The fight lasted four hours.

The official report of the affair says, our forces were forced to retire about a quarter of a mile from their original position, and the enemy temporarily occupied the camps of three of our regiments, and destroyed much of the baggage and camp equipage. They were, however, driven out, but our men being much exhausted and our numbers lessened by sickness, it was deemed expedient not to pursue. Tee enemy retired several miles and are still retreating. Reinforcements have arrived. Our force engaged was less than twenty-five hundred. The enemy had at least five thousand, with twelve or fourteen field pieces and some cavalry. Breckenridge, on the 6th, asked permission to bury his dead.

A passenger from Baton Rouge says our loss was seventy killed and two hundred and fifteen wounded.

Gen. Williams had three horses shot under him before he was killed.

Washington, 18th.

Cassius M. Clay will be assigned a very important command in West Mississippi.

The troops under the last call are already reaching their destination at the rate of five thousand per day. Within the present week the daily number will be largely increased.

Col. Corcoran, who has arrived, says that Gen. Prince, taken prisoner at the recent battle beyond Culpepper, is kept in prison over a dead house, and that all other officers captured from Pope's command, are shamefully and tyranically treated.

Thurlow Weed sails for Europe to-morrow on important government service.

Private correspondence from London says that Slidell had arrived in that city, and had already had several interviews with Mason for the purpose of deciding on the best step to hasten the recognition of the Southern Confederacy, which seems to have been of late an object of great indifference to the English cabinet

THE NEW YORK HERALD.

WHOLE NO. 9472. NEW YORK, TUESDAY, AUGUST 19, 1862. PRICE TWO CENTS.

THE BATTLE OF BATON ROUGE.

ARRIVAL OF THE NORTH STAR.

Additional Particulars of the Affair.

BRILLIANT UNION VICTORY.

The Rebel Army Under Breckinridge Routed.

Two Thousand Five Hundred Yankees Flog Seven Thousand Rebels.

The Way Brigadier General Williams Was Killed.

The Rebel Generals Lovell and Ruggles Reported Wounded.

The Rebel General Charles Clarke Wounded and a Prisoner.

HEROIC CONDUCT OF THE UNION TROOPS.

The Destruction of the Ram Arkansas by the Gunboat Essex.

HOW IT WAS ACCOMPLISHED.

Official Report of Commander W. D. Porter, of the Essex.

THE REPORT OF OUR SPECIAL CORRESPONDENTS, &c., &c., &c.

The steamships North Star and Roanoke arrived at this port yesterday morning from New Orleans, whence they both sailed on the 10th instant. The news by these arrivals is four days later, and is highly interesting. We have received full particulars of the battle of Baton Rouge from our special correspondents, which we publish below.

Our Baton Rouge Correspondence.

Baton Rouge, La., August 7, 1862.

PARTICULARS OF THE LATE BATTLE.

On the receipt of the intelligence at New Orleans of the battle of Baton Rouge, on the 5th instant, it was determined between your regular correspondent at the first named city and myself that I should proceed at once to Baton Rouge, for the purpose of gleaning all the particulars of the fight, and, in the event of the rebels renewing the attack, to send on by the Roanoke full details to the latest moment. Accordingly, armed with the necessary pass, your special correspondent took passage on the steam transport Empire Parish, Captain Thompson, to whom he is indebted for many courtesies, and arrived at Baton Rouge between eight and nine o'clock this morning. It was rather a difficult matter to get the necessary information, in consequence of the hurry and bustle consequent on the getting up of the necessary official documents for transmission to headquarters at New Orleans, and the sending down the river of the accumulated sick and wounded: but, by dint of patient waiting and perseverance, I obtained from officers engaged in the battle the following interesting facts:—

THE ENEMY RECONNOITERED.

General Williams received information as early as Monday, the 28th ult., that the rebels had started from Camp Moore, for the purpose of making an attack on Baton Rouge. On the receipt of this intelligence he sent out a reconnoitering party to Baton's ferry, on the Amite river, sixteen miles from this place. They returned, reporting that they had not fallen in with the enemy, with the exception of a few pickets on the banks of the river. It seems, however, that the rebels had received information of the reconnoissance, and sent out a force to cut off the expedition party on their return. Our men got scent of this, and by the quickness of their movements escaped falling into the hands of the enemy.

APPROACH OF THE REBELS.

About two o'clock on the afternoon of the 4th information was received from some negroes that the rebels were approaching in force from the Greenwell Springs road, upon which the troops were got under arms, ready for the menaced attack. At half-past three o'clock on the following morning the reveille was beaten, and, the troops having formed, they were marched out to meet the enemy. About a mile out of town our little army was drawn up in line of battle, awaiting the expected attack.

HOW THE BATTLE COMMENCED.

The engagement was brought on by one of the companies of the Twenty-first Indiana, which was on picket duty about a mile back of the camp, being driven in by the rebels. As soon as the firing was heard General Williams sent the other companies of the Twenty-first Indiana to the support of the pickets. On reaching the scene of action they found that the enemy was in too great force to contend with successfully, upon which they fell back to the front of their tents, followed by the enemy. There they made a stand and engaged the entire brigade of General Clarke, consisting of two Mississippi regiments, and a third regiment, composed partially of men from Mississippi, the rest being from Arkansas. The fighting at that place was very severe. The Indiana boys performed prodigies of valor, and kept the enemy in check for a considerable time. General Williams, finding, however, that they were too far advanced to receive support from the other regiments, ordered them to fall back, which was done to the distance of from two hundred to two hundred and fifty yards.

THE STRUGGLE ON THE RIGHT AND LEFT WINGS.

Just about this time the right wing of the Union army was engaged by Colonel Allen's brigade. This wing consisted of the Sixth Michigan and Nims' battery. Simultaneous with this movement our left was attacked by Ruggles' brigade. Attached to the left wing was the Fourteenth Maine and Everett's battery. The fighting at this point was excessively severe, and the roar of battle was heard all along the line from left to right. This lasted for about twenty minutes, during which time the rebels kept their troops masked under the cover of the woods as much as possible, while the Union soldiers were exposed to their fire in the open field. Considerable inconvenience was experienced by our troops, too, in consequence of their facing to the east, which caused the morning sun to shine in their faces, rendering their operations exceedingly difficult. Still our brave troops flinched not, but manfully bore the shock of overwhelming numbers, in the face of every difficulty.

The Thirtieth Massachusetts was now ordered to advance and support the Michigan troops; but while they were getting into position it was found that their aid was not necessary, as the Michigan boys had already repulsed their opponents. The Ninth Connecticut and the Fourth Wisconsin, which were held in reserve, were ordered about the same time to advance in support of the other regiments; but as they were going on the field the enemy retired. At one period of the fight the enemy got into the camp of the Twenty-first Indiana and burned it, upon which this regiment, from the cover of the woods, poured a most terrific volley into them, doing fearful execution, and causing them to retire precipitately. They met a similar fate from the Twentieth Maine, into whose camp they had forced an entrance, though they succeeded in burning this camp too.

BRILLIANT EXPLOIT OF THE SIXTH MICHIGAN.

While the fight was raging three companies of the Sixth Michigan Volunteers were in peril of being cut off by the Fourth and Thirtieth Louisiana regiments, commanded by Colonel Allen, acting as brigadier general. These two regiments suddenly emerged from the woods and marched towards the three companies, with the view of turning their right flank. They had succeeded in capturing two guns belonging to Nims' battery, and a well known rebel officer, named Henderson, was seen to wave a flag in triumph over the guns. Some say it was a black flag; but doubts have been expressed in regard to the correctness of the statement. The two guns were brought to bear on the gallant Michigan boys; but they were too nimble for the rebels. Lying flat on the ground, the rebel balls flew over them, upon which they started to their feet and poured so well directed a volley into the enemy's ranks as to completely astonish him. This was handsomely seconded by the remaining guns of Nims' battery, which, making a detour along the road, so severely galled the Louisiana regiments by a well timed cross fire that when the two companies of the Michigan Sixth came to the bayonet charge the rebels were driven back to the cover of the woods, leaving the two guns they had captured behind them. Nims' battery thus got their own again. The rebel Colonel Allen was mortally wounded in the encounter, and General Williams, the brave Union commander, was killed by a rifle bullet, which pierced his breast. Captain Cordon, of Company F, Sixth Michigan, took the flag of one of the Louisiana regiments. A black flag was also captured—probably the identical one that the rebel officer, Henderson, so defiantly waved over the trophies he was so soon to lose.

INDIANA AND MAINE DISTINGUISH THEMSELVES.

The hardest part of the fighting was in the centre, where the Fourteenth Maine fought with distinguished bravery. The Twenty-first Indiana also fought like tigers, and it is said that a rebel general paid them the handsome compliment of saying that, but for those damned Indianians, Baton Rouge would have been captured, though there are Union soldiers who do not see it exactly in that light.

WHAT THE GUNBOATS DID.

When the long roll was beaten the gunboats Essex, Sumter, Kineo and Katahdin took up their positions, the two former to protect our left and the two latter our right flank. The Essex and the Sumter opened fire in the woods, their shells screaming through the trees, tearing them into shreds and scattering an iron hail around. Signal officer Davis, of the Kineo, stationed himself on the tower of the State House, from which elevation he had an excellent view of the field, and could signal to the vessels where to throw in their shells. After the battle had raged for some time the Union troops began to fall back on the Penitentiary, when several well directed shots from the eleven-inch guns of the boats kept the rebels in check. Shortly after this the firing ceased.

At half-past three P. M. firing was reopened, the gunboats Kineo and Katahdin shelling the woods in different directions where the enemy were, doing great execution. It has been stated that one shell from the Kineo killed from forty to sixty rebels. Towards evening the firing again ceased; but the gunboats continued to send in a shell every half hour in different parts of the woods during the whole night, with the view of keeping the rebels at bay; but they had already fled, the gallant charge of the Sixth Michigan having completed their discomfiture.

BRECKINRIDGE'S SWORD TAKEN.

The rebels were led by Major General John C. Breckinridge, who scampered off in such haste that he left his sword behind. It was picked up on the field, and is retained as a trophy. Perhaps it was this circumstance that gave rise to the report that the traitor lost his right arm. There can be no mistake as to whom the sword belonged, for Breckinridge's name is engraved on it. There were two other Generals on the field, namely, Clarke and Ruggles, and one Acting Brigadier, Allen. General Clarke was taken prisoner, and is now at Baton Rouge, in charge of a personal friend. The rebel troops have been variously estimated at from five to eight thousand, while the Unionists did not exceed two thousand five hundred in number. For the number of killed and wounded I must refer the readers of the Herald to the official accounts, which will accompany this. The principal documents were lost, however, on the Whiteman, when she sunk, of which catastrophe a full account will be given in another part of this letter.

Thus ended the battle of Baton Rouge, by no means the greatest, but certainly the best fought and most stubbornly contested of any during the present war. It would have dispersed to the four winds of Heaven, had that not been done already, the wretched delusion that Southerners are superior in valor to those whom they contemptuously term "Yankees."

DESTRUCTION OF THE REBEL RAM ARKANSAS.

While the firing was going on smoke was seen up the river behind a bend. It was ascertained that it proceeded from the rebel ram Arkansas, in pursuance of the programme laid down for her to attack the Union vessels while their land forces were dealing with our troops. It seems, however, that the commander of the Arkansas thought better of the matter, and did not venture down; for there was the Union ram Essex, as well as the other gunboats, ready to give her a warm reception, and at night the officers of the Union vessels wondered where the Arkansas was. Their curiosity being stimulated by the continued absence of the nondescript, or "What Is It," as Barnum would term it, it was determined that, as the mountain would not go to Mahomet, Mahomet would go to the mountain, and go he did, being represented by the Essex leading, closely followed by the Sumter, Kineo and the Katahdin. On turning the elbow, beyond which her smoke had been seen on the previous day, the monster was discovered to be on fire, close into the bank. The rebel gunboats Webb and Music were by her, but they prudently retired on seeing our boats. It seems that the Arkansas was worked by two engines on one wheel, and that both must be in working order or neither will act. One of the engines got out of order, and the other would not work without its fellow, in consequence of which she got under the bank. It is probable that the Webb and the Music were there to tow her off, but that, on seeing our boats approaching, she was set on fire.

As the Union gunboats approached several shots were fired at the Essex from the Arkansas, one or two of them taking effect, but without doing any damage. In consequence of the immovable position of the Arkansas she could not bring more than one of her two guns to bear, or she might have given the Essex a great deal of trouble, as the latter vessel is quite unmanageable. The Essex ran past the Arkansas to a part of the river where there is a reach of some length, and opened on her formidable antagonist at five hundred yards with three guns loaded with solid shot. One of these took effect right under the port in the starboard bow of the Arkansas, and split in two from the force of the concussion. Commander Porter then ordered the same gun to be loaded with an incendiary shell of his own invention, and, without moving the gun to take a new aim, the shell was fired, entering just where the solid shot had struck. Immediately a jet of flame was shooting upwards from the Arkansas, and in a short time the entire vessel was on fire. It is supposed that the condensed cotton with which the Arkansas is packed caught fire from the shell, and communicating thence to the woodwork soon wrapped the monster in flames. After burning till all her upper works were destroyed she swung off into the stream, where she blew up with a terrific explosion.

The Arkansas was plated with railroad iron on the outside, over a planking of six-inch oak; inside that was six inches of condensed cotton on another six inches of oak. The destruction of the ram caused a feeling of exultation to pervade the whole fleet. Admiral Farragut expressed his deep satisfaction at the event, which was slightly alloyed with a feeling of disappointment that the job on which he had set his mind had not been performed by himself. He, however, gives Capt. Porter all the credit to which so brilliant an achievement entitles him.

THE REBEL'S DREAD OF OUR GUNBOATS.

Two deserters from the Arkansas, who joined the Union navy, say that the commander of that redoubtable craft expressed himself as standing in far more wholesome dread of our gunboats than of iron rams.

NARROW ESCAPE OF SIGNAL OFFICER DAVIS.

While Mr. Davis was on the State House tower a shell from the Kineo, fired over the tower, exploded prematurely, and a fragment passed unpleasantly near to the signal officer.

GUERILLA DOINGS.

Last night as the transport Sallie Robinson was coming up from New Orleans, on getting abreast of Donaldsonville, about midway between the city and this place, she was fired into by a field battery, but without any further damage than a shot through the smokestack. The flagship Hartford had already passed, but the Brooklyn was somewhat astern of the Sallie Robinson. As soon as the Brooklyn arrived at the place a volley of musketry was fired into her without effect. She fired several shots in return, but it could not be ascertained if any one was hit.

WILL THE ATTACK BE RENEWED?

It is impossible to say with anything like certainty whether the rebels will renew the attack on this place. That they cannot do so without strong reinforcements is pretty evident, and the opinion among military men seems to be that, with our strong fleet of gunboats now commanding the river front, they will not dare to attack the place under any circumstances, for it is now an established fact that if there is any thing they dread rather more than they do the author of evil it is a gunboat.

I send you a plan of the battle ground, with the river in front, showing the several positions of the Arkansas and the position of the Essex and the other gunboats.

THE BATTLE AT BATON ROUGE, TUESDAY, AUGUST 5, 1862.

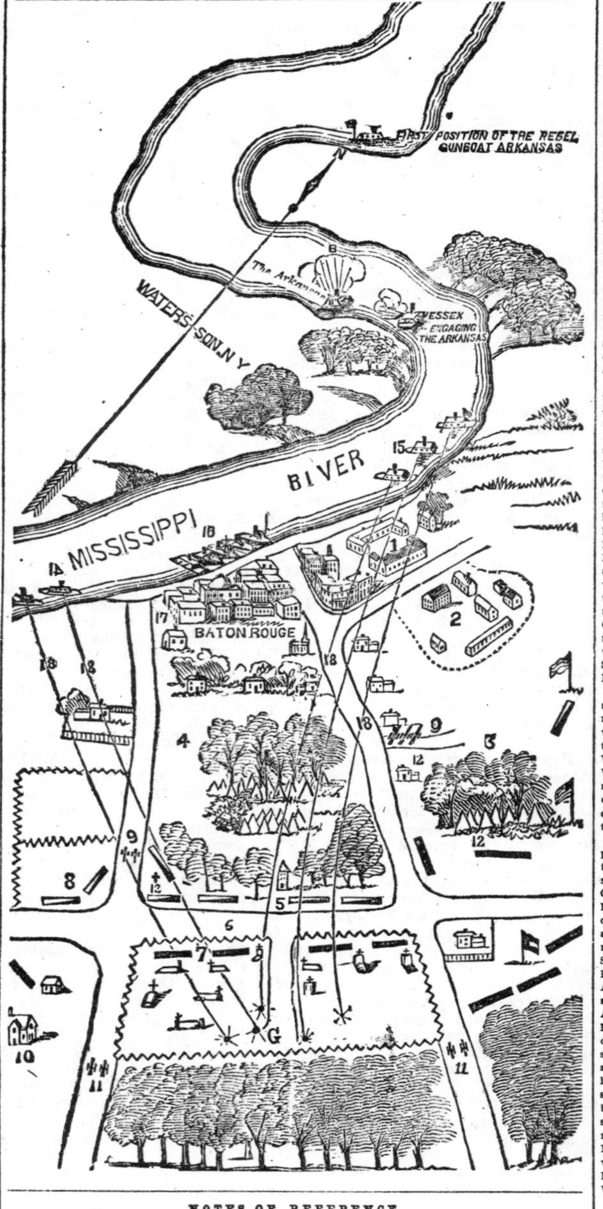

NOTES OF REFERENCE.

1—United States Army Barracks.
2—United States Arsenal.
3—Camp of Maine regiment, burnt by the rebels.
4—Camp of Indiana regiment.
5—Indian and other federal troops repulsing the rebels.
6—High road over which the rebels tried in vain to cross.
7—Graveyard where the rebel centre made the attack.
8—Michigan regiment.
9—United States Artillery.
10—House filled with rebel wounded.
11—Rebel Artillery.
12—Rebel right wing.
12—House that the rebels succeeded in gaining, but could not hold.
13—Where General Williams, United States Army, was killed, leading a charge.
14—Gunboats Katahdin and Kineo.
15—Gunboats Cayuga, Sumter and Essex.
16—Army steamers.
17—Baton Rouge.
18—Line of gunboats' fire.
B—Second position of the rebel ram Arkansas, where she was destroyed and blown up by the Essex, William D. Porter commanding.

Our New Orleans Correspondence.

New Orleans, August 10, 1862.

The Victory of the 5th Instant—Our Forces Engaged—Magnanimous Conduct of the Late General Williams—The Fight in Open Field—The Enemy Outnumber Our Forces Three to One—The Rebel Defeat and Rout—Our Loss in Killed and Wounded—Brilliant Conduct of Our Officers and Men—Death of Colonel Roberts, of the Seventh Vermont Regiment—The Loss of the Enemy—The News Among the Secessionists of New Orleans—Disposition of the Body of General Williams—The Funeral—The Cortege and Religious Ceremonies—The Body En Route for New York, &c., &c.

There has been hardly anything thought of or talked about here for the last two or three days but our glorious victory at Baton Rouge on the 5th inst. As particulars begin to come in, almost every hour shows fresh evidence of the contest having been one of the—if not bloodiest—fairest, most chivalric and gallant actions of the war. Our forces, weakened terribly by the sickness contracted opposite Vicksburg, mustered only twenty-five hundred engaged in the fight, and a large proportion of these leaped from their beds in the hospital to claim a hand in the battle. General Williams, too noble and generous to bring disaster upon the people of the city, disposed his forces a mile outside the limits of the town. There were no breastworks or earthworks of any kind, but a broad, open plain, on which the combatants had to face each other's fire, without any shelter other than occasional trees. The enemy outnumbered our forces three to one, by their own confession; and yet, with all the above disadvantages, and the additional fact that hardly any of our men had ever seen a gun fired in earnest before, and that before the contest was decided their only general officer was killed before their eyes, still they repulsed the foe again and again, and finally routed him completely with terrible slaughter. Thus, in a battle of six hours' duration, with only eight thousand five hundred men engaged, very nearly fifteen hundred were killed and wounded.

Have there been more than three engagements in the course of the war where the fighting was attended with such fearful results? I think not. A naval commander who arrived from the scene of action on Friday said he was satisfied that it was the most desperately fought and splendid battle of the war.

Our loss, as near as we can estimate it at present, is ninety killed and two hundred and fifty wounded. The enemy must have lost at least a thousand in killed and wounded. Over three hundred of them were buried by our soldiers on the field of battle, and if General Williams had survived this, his triumphal climax of a most brilliant life, he would undoubtedly have either captured or destroyed the entire command of the rebels; and that is saying nothing disparaging of Colonel Cahill, who commanded after General Williams' death, for his courage and management were only equalled by the modesty of his despatches. In consummating the brilliant success which Williams commenced, Col. Cahill only met the expectations of those who knew him well. Of the dashing heroism of Colonel Dudley, of the Thirtieth Massachusetts ("Mad Anthony" he is called in the army); Lieutenant Colonel Keith, of the Twenty-first Indiana; Lieutenant Colonel Beene, of the Fourth Wisconsin; Col. Roberts, of the Seventh Vermont, and the others in command of various corps, I cannot speak at length, as the despatches containing details were lost on the steamer Whiteman; but by the next mail I hope to do them that justice which their gallantry deserves. As yet General Butler has not received the list of killed and wounded, owing to the fact that several of the corps engaged are out on scouting duty. I will send it by next mail. Most of the wounded, including quite a large number of the rebels, have been brought to this city, and are now being cared for at the St. James and Charity hospitals.

Besides General Williams, we have to mourn the loss of Colonel George Roberts, of the Seventh Vermont, who fell mortally wounded on the field and died soon after. He was a brave officer and a true-hearted patriot, and was one of the first to answer to his country's call. Capt. Eugene Kelty of the Thirtieth Massachusetts, also yielded up his young life as a sacrifice on the altar of patriotism. It was my good fortune to know the "Little Captain" (as his boys affectionately called him) intimately, and I feel a melancholy pleasure in bearing witness to his gallantry, with hundreds of others who felt a peculiar affection for him. He was only about twenty-five years old, and was for a number of years a resident of New York, and was the brother of the well known upholsterer in Broadway. His knowledge of military tactics was acquired in that finest of all military schools, the second company of our own Seventh, and the effectiveness of his command was the worthiest commentary on the proficiency he gained in the ranks of the National Guard. When, some two months since he marched at the head of his company past the St. Charles (then the residence of General Butler), as his regiment was *en route* to Vicksburg, his superb bearing and thorough air *militaire* was the subject of remark by the gazers from the balcony of the hotel. I little thought then that I had seen for the last time his happy face and felt the latest pressure of his friendly grasp. When it was announced that the enemy were approaching Baton Rouge, although unable to walk, owing to an accidental wound in his thigh from his own sword, he insisted upon leading his men into the field, and was placed on a horse for that purpose. His company (a Zouave corps) was ordered to the advance, with instructions to move only thirty rods forward; but, with that imprudence which seems an almost inevitable accompaniment of youthful bravery, he advanced about a quarter of a mile, and almost immediately received a rifle ball in his side. He fell from his horse, and in an hour expired, being almost the earliest victim of the battle. He was married just before the war to a young and beautiful lady in Boston, where she is now left to mourn her irreparable loss.

> And they who for their country die
> Shall fill an honored grave;
> For glory lights the soldier's tomb,
> And beauty weeps the brave.

The enemy suffered severely in the loss of officers. Brigadier General Clarke was mortally wounded, and is now, with one of his aids, a prisoner in this city. Colonel Allen, of the Fourth Louisiana, Acting Brigadier General, was killed. Brigadier General Helme, of Kentucky, was wounded—probably fatally—and Brigadier General Ruggles is said to have been killed. It was reported that Breckinridge had lost his right arm, but nothing positive is known about it. The fact, however, that his sword, with his name on it, was found on the field, is strong corroborative proof that the story is true.

The news of our glorious success at Baton Rouge has caused the most enthusiastic elation among all who have even a latent spark of patriotism, while to the secesh sympathizers it is as gall and wormwood to the palate. They are awfully down in the mouth, though they impose upon their own credulity to an extent perfectly marvellous. This peculiarity of the rebels in New Orleans I have had occasion to remark before.

It is currently believed among them that the boat destroyed on the 6th was not the Arkansas, but some other boat. There are a great many of them, also, who are firmly impressed with the idea that Breckinridge is in possession of Baton Rouge and has captured our garrison, and that the wounded soldiers whom we have been receiving are prisoners, paroled by the rebel general on account of their condition.

The body of General Williams, which was recovered by the Pinola after it had floated on a piece of the wreck just wide enough to hold the coffin twelve miles, was taken to the City Hall on Thursday evening, where it was laid in state in the Mayor's parlor, and entrusted for the night to the care of a guard of honor from the Thirteenth Connecticut regiment. At ten o'clock the next morning Major General Butler and staff arrived at the City Hall, and at half-past ten the funeral march was taken up from Christ church, on Canal street, in the following order:—The Thirteenth Connecticut regiment, followed by the Second Company Massachusetts cavalry, Lieutenant Perkins commanding, and one section of the First Maine battery, under command of Lieutenant Haley, as the escort. Then some fifty carriages, containing a very large number of naval officers, in the splendor of their very handsome full dress uniform; officers of various regiments; the staff of General Butler, and the General himself, as chief mourner, and a number of the municipal officers of the city, prominent among whom were Col. T. B. Thorpe, formerly of New York, now City Surveyor of New Orleans; Mr. Duvell, Chairman of the Board of Finance, and Mr. Flanders, City Treasurer.

To guard against the possibility of a repetition of the scenes enacted at the church on the occasion of the funeral of Lieutenant De Kay, the First Massachusetts cavalry, Captain S. T. Read, were formed in line in front of the church, under the direction of Lieutenant W. H. Weigel, Aid-de-Camp to General Butler. Lieutenant Weigel was instructed to act with promptness and severity on the first approach of anything like insult to the dead; and the best evidence of the good behavior of the crowd is, that none of them got their heads cracked with the sabres of the cavalry men.

Arrived at the church, the body was followed in by a procession of the military and naval officers, who nearly filled the pews in the centre aisle. Among them I observed Captain Morris, of the Pensacola (senior officer); Captain Palmer, of the Iroquois; Captain Smith, of the Mississippi; Captain Crosby, of the Pinola; Captain Buchanan, of the Gray Cloud; Capt. Fontaine, of the marines, and a host of other gallant officers of the navy. Of the military there were, besides General Butler, Colonels Shaffer and Turner, Major (Judge) Bell, Provost Marshal French and his Deputy, Captain Stafford; Captains Davis, A. A. A. G., Clark and Kensel, and Lieutenants Weigel and Puffer, all of the division staff; Lieutenant Bowles, A. D. C. to Governor Shepley; Colonels Thomas and Brown, of the Eighth Vermont; Lieutenant Colonel Whelden, Thirty-first Massachusetts; Major Sawtelle, Twenty-sixth Massachusetts, and a large number of other officers anxious to pay their last respects to the departed hero. The services in the church were very simple, consisting only in the reading of the burial service by the rector, Dr. Leacock, and the singing of a hymn by the choir. The procession then moved in the same order as before, down to the steamer North Star, where the remains were deposited, to be conveyed to New York. They will be accompanied by Capt. Hoffman, Acting Adjutant General to the late General Williams.

General Butler and his staff then left the carriages, and, mounting their horses, rode home.

The escort was under command of Col. Birge, of the Thirteenth Connecticut. Gen. Phelps was invited to command, but declined on the plea of illness.

The arrangements for the funeral were made by Capt. Kensel, Chief of Artillery, and Capt. Clark, Post Commissary, and formerly of General Williams' staff. While the procession was moving from the church to the steamer Lieutenants Hubbard's and Bradbury's section of the First Maine battery, under command of Capt. Thompson, fired minute guns from the levee. In the streets through which the cortege passed the sidewalks were thronged with people, all of whom behaved thoroughly well, not an instance of insult occurring. General Butler was in town. The shipping in the river displayed their flags at half mast. At the British Consulate, when the procession first passed, the flag was flying from the top of the staff, but at a decided hint from General Butler it was soon lowered to the half.

Thus have the last sad honors been paid to one who was considered in the regular army as having no superior in all soldierly qualities, and who, in social life, elicited an admiration from his friends amounting almost to devotion. His manners were of the most courtly school, refined almost to fastidiousness, and his intelligence was of a broad and high-toned order. Of a playful disposition, he was one of the most cheerful and genial of companions, and his patriotism was of that kind that would have stopped at nothing necessary to restore the Union to its former glory.

His death was of precisely the character that he coveted—to fall at the head of his victorious command.

General Butler's eloquent orders Nos. 56 and 57, which are sent you, are noble tributes of respect to the memory of departed worth and to the splendid valor of our troops.

The Official Reports.

The following are the official reports of the battle that have come to hand:—

HEADQUARTERS, SECOND REGIMENT,
BATON ROUGE, August 6, 1862.

CAPTAIN—I have the honor to report that an attack was made early yesterday morning by a Confederate force of about ten regiments, under command of Major General J. C. Breckinridge, and that after a fight of four hours duration and of great severity the enemy were repulsed.

I regret to state that Brigadier General Williams was killed on the field by a rifle ball through the chest.

During the battle our forces were obliged to retire about a quarter of a mile from our original position, and the enemy were thus able to occupy temporarily the camps of the Twenty-first Indiana, Seventh Vermont and Fourteenth Maine regiments, and to destroy much of the baggage and camp equipage. They were, however, driven out; but, our numbers being much lessened by sickness, and the men on the field being much exhausted by fatigue and heat, it was deemed inexpedient to pursue.

I am unable as yet to give a report of our casualties, which, I am sorry to say, are considerable.

The enemy have retired several miles, and, from all I can learn, are still retiring. I am expecting it possible they may receive reinforcements, and am disposing my troops in the strongest positions. Our force engaged numbered less than 2,500; the enemy had at least 5,000, with twelve or fourteen field pieces, and some cavalry.

The ram Arkansas approached with the intention of engaging our gunboats, but grounded above the point, at a distance of about six miles, and to-day was engaged by the iron-clad Essex and destroyed.

Enclosed are copies of a communication received by flag of truce from Major General J. C. Breckinridge and my reply thereto. You will see by the latter that Brigadier General Clarke and his aid-de-camp have delivered themselves up as prisoners of war.

I have also fully seventy wounded prisoners who were left on the field, also about thirty captured. I would like instructions as to the disposition you wish made of them. Some express a wish to be paroled.

Very respectfully, your obedient servant,
THOS. W. CAHILL, Colonel Commanding Post.

Captain R. S. Davis, Assistant Adjutant General, Headquarters, Department of the Gulf.

The following is the communication of General Breckinridge to Col. Cahill:—

HEADQUARTERS, CONFEDERATE FORCES IN THE FIELD,
NEAR BATON ROUGE, August 6, 1862.

TO THE COMMANDING OFFICER OF THE UNITED STATES FORCES, BATON ROUGE, LA.:—

I have sent Major De Baner with a flag of truce, with the request that he will be allowed to attend to the burial of our dead, who may have been left within your lines. Major Haynes, accompanying, desires to communicate with Brigadier General Charles Clark, that he may supply him with money and clothing, and such articles as may contribute to his comfort. Respectfully, sir, your obedient servant,

JOHN C. BRECKINRIDGE,
Major General Commanding.

Colonel Cahill replied as follows:—

HEADQUARTERS, UNITED STATES FORCES,
BATON ROUGE, La., August 6, 1862.

GENERAL—In reply to your communication of this morning, under a flag of truce, I have the honor to say that we are now engaged in the burial of your dead within our lines, and that we shall soon finish the now nearly accomplished work. General Clarke and his aid-de-camp, Lieutenant Yerger, have surrendered themselves as prisoners of war, and are being cared for by our surgeons. A friend of General Clarke, from this city, will attend to his pecuniary wants. Respectfully, your obedient servant,

THOMAS W. CAHILL,
Colonel Commanding.

Major General J. C. BRECKINRIDGE, Commanding Confederate forces.

Lieutenant Weitzel visited Baton Rouge on the 6th inst. The following is his report of the engagement:—

HEADQUARTERS, BATON ROUGE, August 7, 1862.

GENERAL—I have the honor to acknowledge the receipt of your favor of yesterday.

Your troops at this place have won a glorious victory. I do not consider that there is the least danger of an attack for the present, because one of the several reconnoitering parties sent out this morning, and which has returned, reports five abandoned caissons on the Greenwell Springs road. We have sent out to bring them in. This indicates a hasty retreat on the part of the enemy. Our forces could not pursue.

One-half of the men who left the hospitals to fight could not march a mile. The conduct of these men was magnificently glorious. The attack was undoubtedly made upon representations of rebels within our lines that our troops were nearly all sick and demoralized, and General Breckinridge undoubtedly expected, in conjunction with the ram Arkansas, to make a successful dash. It was a complete failure. The ram is blown up. Their troops were repulsed.

General Williams disposed his forces as follows, viz:—The Fourth Wisconsin on the extreme left, on the right bank of Bayou Gross, with two pieces of Manning's battery in the arsenal grounds on the left bank of Bayou Gross, to sweep the grounds on the left of the Wisconsin Fourth. The Ninth Connecticut was posted on the right of the Fourth Wisconsin, with two pieces in rear of centre, and two pieces in rear of the right. All of these pieces were of Manning's battery, and were posted on either side of the knoll in the Government Cemetery.

Next came the Fourteenth Maine, posted in rear of the Bayou Sara road, and to the left of Greenwell Springs road.

Next came the Twenty-first Indiana, posted in the woods in rear of Magnolia Cemetery, with four pieces of Everett's battery, (under the command of Lieut. Carruth.) on their left on the Greenwell Springs road. The Indiana battery of two pieces came up to the support of these pieces after the battle commenced. Next came the Sixth Michigan, posted across the country road on right of the Magnolia Cemetery and across the Clay Cut road, their left supporting two pieces of Everett's battery, posted on the road on the right of the Magnolia Cemetery.

The Seventh Vermont was posted in rear of the Twenty-first Indiana and Sixth Michigan, on the right of the Catholic Cemetery. The Thirtieth Massachusetts came next, forming the right, and posted about one-half a mile in rear of the State House, supporting Nims' battery.

This disposition of the forces was made with the supposition that the enemy would attack our left flank, under the cover of the ram Arkansas. The right flank depended upon gunboat support. The only fault of disposition—perhaps rendered unavoidable by the formations of the ground—was that the camps of the Fourteenth Maine and Twenty-first Indiana were pitched in front of their position, in line of battle, and consequently came into the possession of the enemy for a short time.

The enemy formed line of battle on the open grounds, bordering on the Greenwell Springs road, and attempted to draw our forces out. Failing in this, they advanced rapidly on the ground between the Clinton and Clay Cut roads. The whole brunt of the attack, consequently, fell upon the Fourteenth Maine, Twenty-first Indiana and Sixth Michigan.

As soon as it became apparent that this was the real point of attack, General Williams ordered up the Ninth Connecticut, Fourth Wisconsin, and one section of Manning's battery, to support the left, and the Thirteenth Massachusetts and two sections of Nims' battery to support the right.

You will therefore see that the disposition (with the slight exception hinted at) and the manœuvering were faultless.

The conduct of our troops was excellent. The Twenty-first Indiana particularly distinguished itself. I saw a number of the dead of the enemy to-day in front of the ground they occupied; but, not content with the check they gave the enemy, this regiment pursued him quite a distance, strewing the ground with his dead.

The brave General Williams fell in front of the Sixth Michigan towards the end of the conflict, while giving his men a noble example of reckless and daring bravery. He was killed by a rifle ball in the chest.

The enemy's forces consisted of two Louisiana regiments (the Fourth and Thirtieth), two Mississippi, the Third, Fourth, Fifth, Sixth, Seventh and Eighth Kentucky, two Tennessee, one Alabama regiment, and thirteen guns and a large guerilla force. Their attacking force numbered fully 6,000 men.

Our actual force engaged was not over 2,000.

Three companies of the Sixth Michigan covered themselves with glory in recovering from a large force two guns posted on the right of the Magnolia Cemetery, which temporarily were left by our forces. These same three companies captured the colors of the Fourth Louisiana, but only after they had shot down four successive color bearers.

The exact loss on our side is not yet reported; but certain it is that it must be less than that of the enemy. I am, sir, very respectfully, your obedient servant,

G. WEITZEL,
Lieutenant United States Engineers and Chief Engineer, Department of the Gulf.

Major General B. F. BUTLER, Commanding Department of the Gulf, New Orleans, La.

Statement of a Union Soldier and Eye Witness.

The following is an extract from a letter written by a Union surgeon who was present on the battle field, and saw eighty-three dead rebels in a cornfield:—

From 5,000 to 10,000 rebels, under General Breckinridge, attacked about 3,000 Union soldiers, stationed on the outskirts of Baton Rouge, at four A. M. on Tuesday, August 5.

The fight lasted until ten, when the rebels were badly repulsed, and retreated in a rou

General Williams was shot through the heart while rallying his right wing, which was being driven in by superior numbers.

The Vermont regiment behaved badly, except its officers. The colonel was killed. The Twenty-first Indiana, Thirtieth Massachusetts, Ninth Connecticut and Fourth Wisconsin did most of the fighting, and nobly, too.

Lieutenant Colonel Keith, Twenty-first Indiana, was wounded through the right shoulder. Adjutant House, Thirtieth Massachusetts, was shot through both legs, and may have to lose one by amputation.

Lieutenant Norcross, from Lowell, of the Thirtieth Massachusetts, arose from his sick bed, joined his company in the thickest of the fight, and with his own hands saved one field piece, about to be taken by the rebels.

Many of our officers are wounded, and our total loss in killed, wounded and missing (as yet not accurately known) is probably about three hundred.

The rebel loss is very great, as witnessed by myself.

The rebel wounded report Gen. Breckinridge with loss of right arm, Gen. Ruggles killed, Gen. Clarke taken prisoner and wounded, Col. Allen prisoner and fatally wounded, also Capt. Chan.

General Lovell is reported killed; but it is probably his brother, as the General is thought to be in Richmond. One rebel told me, as I was amputating his leg, that the rebels lost nearly eight hundred men, which I think is nearly correct.

Breckinridge sent a flag of truce for permission to bury his dead.

Nims' battery saved the day, when two-thirds of its members were on the sick list.

The gunboats Essex, Cayuga, Kineo and Katahdin attacked the ram Arkansas on the morning of the 6th, when she skedaddled into the banks. Her officers and crew ran, and in a few moments after she blew up. The secesh in Baton Rouge fired from their houses on our wounded as they were being brought in. Consequently their houses were pulled down.

Breckinridge made a speech to his men the morning of the fight, and promised to have his band playing in the State House by nine A. M.

Dr. Buffington, a rebel surgeon, told his nigger "Jack" that if they got separated during the fight to go directly to the State House; for he would surely be there by nine o'clock. The "dark" kept the appointment; but the doctor did not.

The Death of General Williams.

GENERAL ORDERS—NO. 56.

HEADQUARTERS, DEPARTMENT OF THE GULF,
NEW ORLEANS, August 7, 1862.

The Commanding General announces to the Army of the Gulf the sad event of the death of Brigadier General Thomas Williams, commanding Second brigade, in camp, at Baton Rouge.

The victorious achievement—the repulse of the division of Major General Breckinridge by the troops led by General Williams, and the destruction of the mailclad Arkansas by Captain Porter of the Navy—is made sorrowful by the fall of our brave, gallant and successful fellow soldier.

General Williams graduated at West Point in 1837; at once joined the Fourth artillery, in Florida, where he served with distinction and was thrice brevetted for gallant and meritorious services in Mexico, as a member of General Scott's staff. His life was that of a soldier, devoted to his country's service. His country mourns in sympathy with his wife and children, now that country's care and precious charge.

We, his companions in arms, who had learned to love him, weep the true friend, the gallant gentleman, the brave soldier, the accomplished officer, the pure patriot and victorious hero and the devoted Christian. All and more went out when Williams died. By a singular felicity the manner of his death illustrated each of these generous qualities.

The chivalric American gentleman, he gave up the vantage of the cover of the houses of the city—forming his lines in the open field—lest the women and children of his enemies should be hurt in the fight.

A good general, he had made his dispositions and prepared for battle at the break of day, when he met his foe.

A brave soldier, he received the death shot leading his men.

A patriot hero, he was fighting the battle of his country, and died as went up the cheer of victory.

A Christian, he sleeps in the hope of the blessed Redeemer.

His virtues we cannot exceed—his example we may

[CONTINUED ON EIGHTH PAGE.]

Respects General Jno. H. Morgan

THE VIDETTE.

EXTRA.

THE VIDETTE.
EXTRA.
IS PRINTED & PUBLISHED SEMI-OCCASIONALLY,
BY "MORGAN'S BRIGADE."
Gordon E. Niles, Editor & Publisher.
HARTSVILLE TENN., August 19, 1862.

The North,

The success which followed the Northern standard in its insolent march of invasion, but a short time since so uniform, seems at last exhausted. The role of victory which they boasted would never end until the rebellion was crushed, and the South utterly subjugated—is played out—and superior numbers, vast expenditure, and careful preparation, so far from securing to the Federal Government a triumphant conclusion of the war, have but the more clearly proven the futility of all its efforts. Never in the history of all the wars that have devastated the earth, has there occurred so sudden and so complete a reversion from conquest and victory, to hopeless defeat, ruin, and bankruptcy, as the Northern Government. Another brilliant victory by Stonewall Jackson, at the Culpepper Court House, or Rapidan, and the swallowing up of the entire Federal army at Cumberland Gap, strikes joy to the millions of concordant hearts that beat in unison with the pulse of liberty.

Outrages Committed at Gallatin

We learn from Mrs. ——, a highly respectable lady, residing in Gallatin, that the Federals advent into that place, the morning following our evacuation, was distinguished by scenes of brutality, indiscriminate robbery and pillage. Indeed, it is known that they came there, not for the purpose of finding the enemy, but for plundor. The house of Mrs. Glover was entered, and upon Mrs. G's. requesting a THING in the Federal uniform with "bars" of a Captainu pon his shoulders, to protect her house which was then being sacked, she was insultingly told to mind her own business, and that if she saved herself she might deem it fortunate.

This is but a single instance of the atrocities they committed, for it is also known that our two men which were killed, were shot after they had thrown up their hands and surrendered, their assassins exclaiming no quarters to Morgan's men. This and similar atrocities has become of such common occurrence that it has necessitated a retaliatory proclamation from Gen. Morgan.

The foregoing facts are but minute atoms in the wrongs which corrupt Northern agents and its base hireling press heap upon Col. Morgan and the troops under his command.

Four hundred and sixty Federal prisoners were paroled by Col. Morgan at Cynthiana, Ky. Each one was sworn not only not to serve against the Confederate cause but became responsible that he would protect the wounded that were obliged to be left behind to the utmost of his power, and return them safe on recovery within the Confederate lines. How has this promise been kept? by sending all the sick and wounded to Camp Chase, thus returning rigor for clemency, insult for good usage. Private friends of Col. Morgan are openly taunted as such and made responsible in a pecuniary manner for being so by heavy fines and threats of confiscation, and imprisonment. These acts of tyranny can only be restrained by retaliation, and to this course Col. Morgan is impelled, however adverse to hard means, by the virulence of his foes.

PROCLAMATION.

HEADQUARTERS MORGAN'S BRIGADE,
HARTSVILLE, TENN.

Having noticed in the Cincinnati Daily Gazette, of the 15th inst., an article dated "Paris, Ky., 14th August, 1862," whereby it appears that the agents of the Federal Government are (to use their own words) forcing Morgan's "friends to pay for the acts of their favorite chieftan," and thus violating all laws hitherto respected and acknowledged by civilized nations, forgetting and wilfully closing their eyes to the fact that I, in my justifiable attacks on Federal troops and Federal property, have always respected the private property and persons of Union men, I do hereby declare that, to protect Southern citizens and their rights, I will henceforth put the law of retaliation into full force, and act upon it with vigor. For every dollar exacted from my fellow-citizens, I will have two from all men of known Union sentiments, and will make their persons and property responsible for this payment. God knows it was my earnest wish to have conducted this war according to the dictates of my heart, and consonant to those feelings which actuate every honorable mind, but forced by the vindictive and iniquitous proceedings of our Northern foes to follow their example, in order to induce them to return to more humane conduct, I will, for the future, imitate them in their exactions, retaliate upon them and theirs the cruelties and oppression with which my friends are visited, and continue this course until our enemies consent to make war according to the law of nations.

Signed by me this 18th day of August, A. D. 1862.

JOHN H. MORGAN,
Col. Commanding Brigade.

Communicated.

CAPT. NILES—Editor &c:—Permit me in your paper to speak of the gallant leader, Gen. MORGAN, now in our midst. I have mingled much in life, have lived where talent, worth and bravery are appreciated. My age would warrant any criticism I might make. I have no favors to ask—no friends but those who are above need. Hence, my eulogy on the distinguished MORGAN and his gallant band is without hope of fee or reward. Unbought, as my efforts in his praise are, they are but the gushing of a heart tuned to the melody of praise for all that is gallant, brave and generous. MORGAN is every inch a MAN with the brightest stamp of pure nobility on his manly face. He moves amongst us the very beau ideal of all that is worthy and valuable. Generous to a fault—just, as Solon—wise, as Lycurgus, and fierce in battle as Ceasar.—In the midst of victory he is ever merciful. Remembering the fact that no brave man takes revenge on his conquered enemy, no foul stain pollutes the escutcheon of his bravery. His heart is ever open to the appeal of the brave or the "fair." Woman's melting eye moulds his warrior heart. The appeal for mercy from lips of woman never fall in vain on his ear.—He has no private revenge to gratify, his every act is for his country's good; his every impulse is that she may be free. Long may he live. The pride of the South, the wonder of the world!

TENNESEAN.

Missouri Patriots in Arms—30,000 in the field.

The St. Louis Republican of the 4th says the rebel gucrillas have taken complete possession of Missouri, and are daily growing into a vast army. Nearly thirty thousand of them have crossed the Missouri river, under protection of Jeff. Thompson, clearing Home guards and militia out as they progress. They are raising a large number of recruits for the Confederate army.

Gamble finds it impossible, under the circumstances, to get the militia to respond to his calls, and has issued an importunate appeal to them to rally, complaining of their apathy in the Federal cause.

MILITARY COLUMN.

HEADQUARTERS,
HARTSVILLE, TENN., Aug. 17th, '62.

BRIGADE ORDERS.

No. 1. The erroneous idea having spread itself amongst the men of this Brigade, that officers and privates have a right to trade or sell the horses they ride, the General in command wishes to explain the same to the troops.

No officer or private can sell or exchange his horse. On entering the service, should a soldier furnish his own horse, it is with the condition that he receives 40 cents per diem for so doing. The horse is therefore virtually hired of him by the Government, and cannot be sold or exchanged except by an express order from the Quartermaster, signed by the Col. Commanding. If, on the contrary, a soldier is supplied with a horse by his Quartermaster, that horse is the property of the Government, and no trading, swapping or selling can be allowed, unless duly authorized by the Quartermaster in writing. The horse thus taken in lieu of the first one is still the property of the Government, and the soldier is bound to produce him when required so to do.

The General Commanding wishing to put a stop to this improper traffic, acquaints the whole command that no horse can, in future, be either exchanged or sold, without an express order, in writing, from his Quartermaster, signed by his own authorization.

2. Adjutants of Regiments or detachments of Regiments, are requested to send in daily to the Adj't General, a detailed account or morning statement of the troops under their command, and Surgeons of Regiments will report to the Adjutant the number of men absent from duty on sick leave, in order that they may be inserted in the morning report.

3. With reference to Brigade Orders No.'s 1 and 2, of the 14th inst, the General in command desires that every recruit should immediately report himself either to these Head Quarters, or if in camp, to Lieut.-Col. Duke, or Major Gano, in order to be attached to their respective companies, and no one will be allowed to remain in camp or to march with the command who is not duly attached.

4. Commanding officers of Companies will inspect arms and amunition, and see that everything is ready for service.

5. The Brigade will hold itself prepared to march at the earliest moment.

Field Officer of the Day,
LIEUT. COL. B. W. DUKE.

Captain of the Day,
LIEUT. N. W. LEA.

By order.
G. ST. LEGER GRENFELL,
Col. and Adj't. Gen'l.

The Kentucky Battle Song.

Cheer, boys, cheer, we'll march away to battle,
Cheer, boys, cheer, for sweethearts and your wives,
Cheer, boys, cheer, we'll nobly do our duty,
And give Kentucky, our hearts, our arms, our lives.

Bring forth the flag, Kentucky's noble standard,
wave it on high 'till the wind shakes each fold out,
Nobly it waves, proudly floating in the vanguard,
Then cheer up, boys, cheer up, with a lusty loud bold shout.

Chorus—Cheer, boys, cheer, &c.

As we slowly march, with heads all lowly bending,
Let us implore a blessing from on high—
Our cause is just, the right from wrong defending,
And the God of battles will listen to our cry.

Chorus—Cheer, boys, cheer, &c.

Though to our homes we never may return,
Ne'er press again our loved ones in our arms,
O'er our lone graves some faithful hearts may mourn.
But cheer up, boys, cheer up, such death hath no alarm.

Chorus—Cheer, boys, cheer, &c.

QUEER—

This is a very good world we live in—
To lend, to spend, or to give in,
But to beg, or to borrow, or to get a man's own,
'Tis the queerest world that ever was known.

LOCAL AND GENERAL.

HARTSVILLE DIRECTORY.

CORPORATION.

JAS. S. DYRD, Mayor.
R. M. POTTS,
JAS. GUINN,
P. J. AVERETT
P. LIPSCOMB,
R. G. HARRIS,
H. S. CETTES.
} Aldermen.

Notice! Notice!

To the Citizens of Hartsville & vicinity.

All kinds of Liqnors are hereby forbid to be sold to the soldiers or citizens, except by an order countersigned by myself or the Gen. Commanding.

GORDON E. NILES.
Capt., & Provost Marshal.

Quarter Master's Department.
Lock's Hotel, August 19, 1862.

All persons having claims against the Quartermaster, are notified to present them for settlement immediately.

D. H. LLEWELLYN,
Quarter Master of Brigade.

The Federal Mothers Lullaby.

BY W. R. S. (a Texan Ranger.)

Hush! baby; hush! my darling,
And still thy wonted cry;
For if Morgan should hear thee,
Then wilt thou surely die.
For he, the naughty Morgan,
Will send thee to thy bier;
Then, oh! what will console me,
When I shall miss my dear?

Hark! baby, hear'st the clatter,
Of hoofs adown the street;
Why, surely, 'tis the Morgan,
Him whom I would not greet.
For there's that in his glances
That make my heart-strings thrill,
So darling, hush thy wailing,
And be for mother still.

Then will the Fed'ral angels
Drive Morgan from the far;
While I shall still be with thee,
And naught thy slumbers mar.
And thou may'st dream of Heaven,
And all its glorious band;
Where you and I forever
May safely hope to land.

Hartsville, August 18 1862.

☞ The VIDETTE is distributed gratuitously.

OBLIGATIONS.—We return our thanks for the abundance of musk mellons, water mellons, peaches, grapes, &c., that *have not* been sent to our sanctum sanctorum.

The Nashville "Dispatch."

Our most royal appology is due the "Dispatch" for confounding it with the "Union" in our yesterday's extra. An insult most damning to any paper that has any pretentions to respectability, and for which reason we are induced to make the amende honorable. The article referred to was headed "Acknowledgements." We regret that the editor of the "Dispatch" did not give us a fraternal call when he was in this place, and we shall be obliged to pay back the slight, by taking up our headquarters at the "Union" sanctum, when we make our visit to the city of Nashville, which we contemplate doing in a few days.

We take the following from the Northern Journals:

NEW YORK, Aug. 14.—Advices from Port Royal state that the negro brigade has proved a failure, and has been disbanded.

HARTSVILLE, Aug. 18.—Advices from Richmond state that the restoration of the Union "has proved a failure.' And is abandoned.

From the Cincinnati Gazette, August 15th.

Footing the Bills.

Captain Glass returned from Kentucky last evening, bringing with him the following interesting document:

PARIS, Ky., Aug. 14, 1862.

$1,800 00.

DEPOSIT BANK OF PARIS,

Pay to George Hatch, Mayor of Cincinnati, or order, eighteen hundred dollars, in full for eight horses and harness that were captured by Morgan's men at Cynthiana, in the battle of 17th July last.

LEONIDAS METCALFE.

That "speaks for itself." But the public will be pleased to know that the claims, one of which is thus discharged, are paid by the Secessionists. Colonel Metcalfe has a large sum on deposit in the bank at Paris, which he has drawn from the sympathizers in that part of Kentucky. He quietly selects his men, makes the assessment, and gives the Secessionists the choice of paying up or making a visit to Camp Chase.

God bless the Ladies of Hartsville, and vicinity, will always be the prayer of the 'soldier printers.'

THE WEEKLY Pioneer AND Democrat.

VOL. XIV.—NO. 10. SAINT PAUL, FRIDAY, AUGUST 22, 1862. NEW SERIES—NO. 454

A BRILLIANT GEM.

The following is from a late number of the London *Athenæum* :

SUMMER.

Lo! lazy Summer, swarthy, in the sun
  Lies panting, with bare breasts, upon the hills,
Swathing her limbs in hazes warm and dun,
Where splendors into dusky splendors run,
  And sultry glory all the heaven o'erfills.

Not a white dimple stirs amid the corn,
  Not a low ripple shivers through the leaves;
Since, wrapped in gold and crimson gleams unshorn,
Came flashing through the east the regal morn,
  No throated twitterings gurgle round the eaves.

Flooded in sunny silence sleep the kine;
  In languid murmurs brooklets float and flow;
The quaint farm gables in the rich light shine,
And round them jasmined honeysuckles twine,
  And close beside them sunflowers burn and blow.

Amid the growing heat I lay me down.
  And into visions swarms the moted air:
Gleams up before me many a famous town,
Pillared and fested with a regal crown,
  Outshimmering in an orient purple glare;

Lo! lowly Tadmor, burning it its sands—
  Baalbeck and Babylon—I see slow streams
Gliding by mosque and minaret—see the gleams
Of seas in sunset—slips of strands,
  And drowsy Bagdad buried deep in dreams;

See swarthy monarchs flushed in purple rings
  Of silken courtiers;—through half-open doors
Catch the spice odors, and the cool of springs
Leaping forever in a maze of wings,
  See light forms dancing over pearly floors!

Sleeping seraglios, spire, and tremulous dome
  Winking and drowsy splendor all the day,—
See forest haunts where thick the lions roam,—
See thirsty panthers splashed in bloody foam
  Leap terribly as lightnings on their prey;

Or stand with Cortez on a mountain peak
  Above the Aztec city—see unrolled
Gem-threaded shores of Montezuma weak;
See the white temples swarming thick and sleek
  And sunny streets stretch up by towers of gold;

See silken sails float by, ambrosial,
  Laden with spices, up a persian glen;
Or stand on Lebanon, 'mid the cedars tall,
Or hear the soft and silver fall
  Of water down a jut of Darien.

But lo! a waking shiver in the trees,
  And voices 'mid the hay-cocks in the glen;
The sun is sitting; and the crimson sears
Are shaken into splendor by the breeze,
  And all the busy world is up again!

Visiting a Secessionist Family.

The correspondent of the Cincinnati *Gazette*, from Huntsville, after a humorous allusion to General Buell's order that the army go on half rations, thus describes an interview with the secessionist woman:

Speaking of the country reminds me of a call I made at the house of a wealthy planter within six miles of this place, recently, when I learned more of the effects of the rose-water policy of some of our great men than I did how to sell tin ware to this dear people. I called where I had some previous acquaintance, and of course was disappointed in finding that the old gentleman was in town, and only the lady of the house with the servants at home.

THE LADY DOES NOT LIKE GEN. MITCHELL.

She delpored the present condition of affairs; hoped that compromise could soon settle our troubles; thinks the Cincinnati *Enquirer* is a most excellent and ably edited paper; would much like that the western states would separate from the eastern, and join the Southern Confederacy; don't see why the *Enquirer* and Mr. Vallandigham do not say more about that, for the South would willingly accept a union with the West. Her husband did not like General Mitchell; he was kind enough to place a guard at their house for four weeks to keep the soldiers from annoying, but then his policy of making the people take the oath who never had been to war was very bad, especially those who have conscientious scruples on the subject.

HER OPINION OF GENERAL BUELL.

"We are delighted with him. He is not so fearful that we are all enemies as General Mitchell was. In fact, we regard him as a most excellent General. Mr. ——— says he heard General Beauregard say that Buell was a model gentleman, if there was one in the North, and our people have great confidence in General Beauregard, and believe any statement he would make."

KISSING A LITTLE BOY.

Just about that time a beautiful little boy of about seven years came near me, whose features were moulded in symmetry, and whose bright eyes looked from beneath a well shaped forehead, that was itself overhung by beautiful auburn locks. Casting the war policy and the war conversation to the dogs, I remarked on the beauty of her little boy, and as I had not kissed a baby "or any other man" for ten fortnights, you may guess that the pulse had told but few beats before I played the country politician most completely.

"Why," said the lady, "that's the child of one of our servants."

"Oh for a lodge in some vast wilderness," was, of course, immediately impressed on my mind.

My lady, however, took the affair mirthfully, and said that the mistake was often made.

You may be sure that I did not ask about the father of that child; nor could I, just then, have come to any other conclusion than that the system of slavery was one that, in practice, overleaped the bounds of domestic virtues and invaded the domains of most infamous harlotry and amalgamation. All this, too, the spirit of noble wives must bear, and with bleeding hearts yet smile, though a beautiful slave entices unwittingly the heart, or, at least, passions, of her husband. Southern wives would have no reason to deplore it if the necessities of war should grind to powder the whole system of slavery, with its attendant vices, provided they held martial obligations as sacred as did the Roman matron.

After the above incident I left, not fully determined whether the joke was on myself or the pretty boy.

Bitter Regrets.

From the National Intelligencer.

Among the correspondence recently found on board of a captured rebel vessel was a letter from a prominent citizen of a Southern State to his wife, who is sojourning at a distance from home. The writer of the letter had just returned from a vist of a week or two at Richmond, and was writing his wife what he saw there. The bitterness with which he condemns the rebellion and bewails the misery and desolation of his once happy and prosperous section of the Union is poured out with all the fervor of sincerity, and we doubt not that he expresses the feelings and hopes of thousands of others who, like him, dare not speak openly. The letter is dated the 30th ultimo. He says:

"This accursed attempt of one section to set up an independent government must, sooner or later *fail*, and *fail ignominiously*. I am bound in duty to share in the burdens, and to do what I may to alleviate the sufferings which the attempt has brought upon those among whom I was born, but I will take no office in it—the highest would be no inducement—nor will I share in the terrible responsibility. No words can depict the horrors which I witnessed both at Richmond and upon my journey there and back. The deaths then occurring at Richmond were fully equal to one hundred and fifty a day. More than seventeen thousand sick and wounded are now in the Richmond hospitals. The recent seeming success of our arms will only serve to accelerate the downfall of our short-lived Confederacy."

Thieving in Washington.

The Washington correspondent of the Springfield *Republican* is responsible for the following statement:

A few days since I chanced to discover that a newspaper man who stood high had been trading in the influence of some of the present members of Congress—and had made his thousands. The M. C.'s probably know nothing of his work, but his relations with them were such that he could promise their votes with a show of probability. Looking over the accounts of the Senate the other day, I found that to one Senator $1,368 had been paid for a clerk to his committee, when in fact he has had no clerk and drew the money in the name of an imaginary character. Another committee did not meet twice, but the clerk, who did not enter the committee room half a dozen times during the session, drew $1,368, or $6 per day. What wonder that white-washing is the order of the day when such outrages upon common honesty were rife? The war and the monstrous debt will drive this kind of respectable villainy from high place because the people won't endure them much longer. It was only the other day that I heard of the latest and most amusing bit of knavery in the capital. A gentleman came here and quietly gave out in a few circles that he was part proprietor and associate editor of a well known New York newspaper. He was careful *where* he went, but he used the argument and with several high functionaries of the government, the President among the rest, to obtain an office. He finally got a capital office on the strength of the falsehood that he was connected with the office in question, and it was not exploded till the stories of his fabrication reached the ears of the genuine proprietors and editors, when they sent word to Washington, "Mr. So and-So has no connection whatever with our journal—if he says so, he lies." Nevertheless the man got his office, and keeps it!

—Speaking of the convincing and conclusive defence of General McClellan, published in the New York *World*, the Springfield *Republican* says "it will be valuable for future reference and may induce some who are wavering to give a heartier support to our young General. We have no hopes of converting Senator Chandler. Had he been a man he would have died of shame before this. He has given more aid and comfort to the enemy than almost any other Northern man, and we are confident he will get his reward in the future. It is well to hold him up to public execration and expose the falsehoods he has told about Gen. McClellan and the army of the Potomac."

THE BATTLE OF CULPEPPER.

FULL AND PERSPICACIOUS ACCOUNT.

REBELS DECIDEDLY WORSTED.

The editor of the Washington *Star*, who was on a visit to his family at Culpepper Court House at the time of the battle on Saturday week, gives the following account of it, containing items of interest not mentioned in other accounts:

On Friday morning last, Gen. Pope, staff and escort, reached Culpepper Court House from his last encampment, near Washington, the county seat of Rappahannock, having put the *corps d'armee* of General Banks, encamped there, in motion in the direction of Culpepper, and passing the encampment of Gen. Sigel, at Sperryville, twenty miles from Culpepper Court House, by the way. At Culpepper Court House General Pope found Brigadier General Crawford, with his brigade of Banks' *corps d'armee* (previously Gen. Hatch's) and Gen. Bayard's brigade of McDowell's cavalry, the extreme advance of his army of Virginia; also, Brigadier General Rickett's division of Major General McDowell's *corps d'armee*, that had arrived two days before from Waterloo and Warrenton, McDowell himself being present and in command of all the forces then there.

At noon on Friday Generals Pope and McDowell received intelligence from the gallant Bayard—who with the two regiments of his cavalry command doing duty immediately under him, a New Jersey and a Pennsylvania regiment had been in the saddle night and day, guarding the Rapidan for a week, from the Raccoon ford down to a point fourteen miles below and south of the railroad—that the enemy at daybreak had crossed the river, with two regiments of Louisiana infantry, two pieces of light artillery, and three small regiments of cavalry, and driven in his pickets. Bayard retired slowly before them, his force of eight hundred tired out cavalry only, not being sufficient to hold the ground in front of such a foe. He, however, disputed it inch by inch with the enemy, and succeeded in capturing about thirty rebel prisoners, including a major, a captain, and two lieutenants on his retreat. His own loss was not over three men. He retired to the north and east side of Robinson river, about eight miles from Culpepper Court House, and there awaited a supporting force to arrive from the immediate vicinity of that point.

At noon of the same day General Pope, on learning these facts, instantly ordered General Crawford to march his brigade to that end. In half an hour after receiving this order Crawford was on the march. As his brigade—the 28th New York, 10th Maine, 46th Pennsylvania, 5th Connecticut, and ten pieces of artillery—filed rapidly through the village of Culpepper Court House to the gay music of its four splendid bands, its appearance was the theme of admiration of the many experienced officers of the staffs of Generals Pope and McDowell, who went over from their encampments near by to see it start out. Crawford proceeded rapidly to the front, and occupied a position about seven miles from Culpepper Court House, immediately in rear of the line of Bayard's cavalry.

Shortly after ordering Crawford, Gen. Pope also ordered the rest of Banks' corps to move rapidly from Hazel river bridge, near Gaiffinsburg, nine miles from Culpepper Court House, where it had arrived the night before, to the scene of expected conflict.

By eight o clock P. M. the heap of Gen. Banks' column was descried marching around the village to its destination, which it reached before midnight. That point was immediately in the rear of Crawford. Major General Sigel was also at the same time ordered up from Sperryville, and by a forced march of twenty miles his advance reached the village by daylight.

Throughout Friday night and Saturday forenoon Bayard continued skirmishing with the enemy's advance, until the latter, at 2 o'clock P. M. had progressed to within long range of Crawford's artillery. At 4 P. M. the enemy developed a heavy increase of artillery, when that of General Banks came up, and went into the action, there not being room enough in the position our forces occupied for bringing the whole of it into play. The contending forces at the opening of the battle were apparently about a mile or more apart, the rebels showing their front upon Slaughter's Mountain, a sugar loaf eminence, situated two miles to the left of the Orange and Alexandria railroad at Mitchel's Station. Our front was on much lower ground, with Cedar run in our rear and a small wooded ridge in the rear of that.

Gradually, from four to six, P. M., the rebels opened new batteries from the woods surrounding the basin or plain laying between the fronts of the two contending forces, each succeeding one being nearer to our position than the former. Thus they played a cross fire from both sides, as well as a direct front one, upon our troops, including the most of General Banks' infantry, that had been put in line for the conflict. So annoying was this fire that attempts were made to take the batteries nearest at hand by charges. Thus Bayard's cavalry, in a gallant charge, is said to have succeeded in taking two of the rebel guns, with no loss to speak of. Subsequently, at 6 P. M., in pursuance of orders, portions of Augur's and Williams' divisions of infantry, including Crawford's and Gordon's brigades, made three most desperate bayonet charges upon the rebel artillery. They were, however, each time received by a very heavy artillery fire, slaughtering them fearfully. That they should have perserved to make three successive charges in the face of such a deadly fire from so superior numbers, concealed in woods, is really the wonder of the war. These charges developed the fact that the enemy actually engaged greatly outnumbered our forces, about seven thousand, in action

Being thus informed of the location of the main body of the rebel infantry, our artillery played havoc with them, driving decimated regiment after regiment back into the shelter of the dense forest, to have their places instantly occupied by fresh regiments to be decimated in the same way. Among others this fire killed the rebel Generals Winder and Trimble. The arm of the former was torn off by a shell and he died very shortly afterwards from the flow of blood, and Trimble was knocked dead from his horse by the explosion of a shell.

Having put the forces of McDowell and Sigel in rapid motion for the field of action, Gen. Pope, with his staff, accompanied by McDowell and his staff, immediately proceeded together from their headquarters in the front. As they passed Ricketts' division, and the head of Sigel's army corps, that lined the road for the whole six miles, each regiment halted for the instant, wheeled into line, and gave Gen. Pope three cheers and a tiger, and then wheeling again into marching column, pushed forward with signal eagerness for the fray.

At seven o'clock, P. M., Generals Pope and McDowell reached the thickest of the fight, and the advanced guard of Ricketts', coming up at the same time, took position immediately in the rear of that occupied by Gen. Banks' corps.

There being no room on the field for deploying more troops of ours than were under Banks, those of Ricketts' could not get into actual action before night came on, which for some hours prevented further fighting. In the course of the engagement our forces engaged had retired perhaps a mile from the position in which they commenced the battle at four o'clock, P. M., the rebels advancing slowly as we receded before them. This movement on the part of Gen. Banks, notwithstanding his heavy loss and the overwhelming force opposed to him, was as regularly conducted as though he was executing an evolution of a dress parade. Not a man of his corps—or, indeed, of any other—showed the white feather, nor did a man ever straggle to the rear to the distance of more than half a mile, where stood a provost guard of Ricketts' corps, bayonet in hand, to check any, if there should be, disposed to skulk off the field. Hundreds of our wounded passed up, limping or being carried to the hospitals established in the rear, and in not one of them retaining consciousness did we discover aught but the most undaunted eagerness to prosecute the engagement.

We left the field at eight o'clock for the night. At midnight a discharge from one of our batteries brought on a renewal of the engagement for two hours, in the course of which each side is believed to have lost two or three hundred more in killed or wounded. By a cavalry charge, after midnight, of the enemy, Generals Pope and McDowell and their respective staffs, were within an inch of being killed or ridden down. They had dismounted in the front to rest a few minutes from the saddle, when the enemy's cavalry made so sudden a dash upon them that they had barely time to mount and get quickly out of the way. In so doing they were mistaken by a company of their own men for charging rebels, and received their fire, killing a few of their horses only.

We hear, after leaving the field, that two of General Pope's staff were killed by rebel fire during the latter part of the engagement, but were then without any means of verifying the fact.

Our loss of regimental and company officers was very heavy. Among those killed were Colonel Crane, of the Third Wisconsin; Major Savage, and Captains Abbott, Russell and Gooding, and Lieutenant Browning, of the Second Massachusetts, Col. Donnelly of the forty-sixth Pennsylvania, was, we fear, mortally wounded. Colonel Creighton and Adjutant Mulyneau, of the Seventh Ohio, are also very badly wounded. Capt. Robert W. Clarke, of the First District regiment, received a wound in the foot. Gen. Augur receiced a Minie ball in his back, as he was in front of his division turning in his saddle to cheer it on. General Geary is wounded in the arm so that he will likely lose it, and General Price is slightly wounded.

Both sides made some hundreds of prisoners in the course of the engagement, and it was from prisoners that it is made certain that rebel loss is equal to ours if not greater. We estimate our killed and wounded at one thousand five hundred, after striving to inform ourselves as correctly as possible upon the subject.

Both armies rested Saturday night upon their arms, in the positions in which the close of the battle found them. Generals Pope, McDowell and their staffs being unremittingly engaged until daybreak in getting theirs into the positions for the expected conflict of yesterday assigned to them.

At daybreak yesterday morning the sharpshooters of the enemy were found precisely where their front was at the close of Saturday's battle, and skirmishing with ours immediately commenced. Their forces had, however, disappeared from sight. At sunrise a rebel brigade, supported by artillery, emerged from the woods in the front, and just as they got into line of battle, Gen. Milroy opened on them with his battery of Wiard guns, which seemed to sweep off an entire company or two, the rest instantly taking to their heels for the cover of the woods. Shortly afterwards General Bayard, who continued, as before, in the extreme front, scouting to the right and left with his cavalry, reported them filing in force in both these directions, as though aiming to flank us on both sides. General Pope immediately dispatched Tower's division of Mc Dowell's corps to follow, watch and confront them on the right, and a division of Sigel's *corps d'armee* to do the same thing for those moving on the left. Gen. Bayard, with two regiments of his cavalry brigade, was thrown in advance of Tower, and the gallant and efficient Colonel Duffie, of Bayard's command, with his own Rhode Island and the First Maine cavalry, was thrown in the advance of our division of observation on the left.

At eleven A. M., it was definitely ascertained from reports from these forces, that the purpose of the enemy could hardly be flank movements. Ere 2 P. M. the impression became general at General Pope's headquarters on the field, that instead of seeking thus to renew the engagement, the rebels were either seeking a new position in the rear or skedaddling.

Since we reached Washington, General Pope has telegraphed here that the engagement was not renewed yesterday afternoon; that the enemy had retired to a position two miles back, and that he advanced his own this morning to that lately held by the enemy.

We omitted to say above that the prisoners say that the rebels commenced the fight with ten thousand men, Gen. Ewell in command, who were received by Jackson with five thousand more before six o'clock P. M., the balance of Jackson's army getting up early in the night. They claim their combined force to be from fifty to sixty thousand strong.

By a break in the telegraph, the reception of General Pope's order to Gen. King to join him with his admirable division was delayed twenty-four hours. He however started his advance from the vicinity of Fredericksburg at four o'clock P. M. of Saturday, and at eight o'clock yesterday morning reached Elk run ford, so he is doubtless up with the main body of the army by this time. From our own knowledge of the situation, we feel sure that the reception of this important edition to his fine army, has already been taken advantage of by Major General Pope, and that he is again in motion towards Gordonsville. His men all believe him irresistible, and feel certain that signal victory will attend his movement at their head, as on all previous occasions when at the head of his western army.

P. S.—We lost a single piece of artillery, one of Best's. It upset in a ditch, and as it could not be righted by those who had it in charge, it was abandoned.

—A Southern subscriber has an excellent communication in the *National Intelligencer* relative to the loyal Union men in the Southern States, and denies with earnestness the position that there is no loyal Union men South. He says:

There are very many men in all parts of the South who are at this moment, as they have ever been, loyal and true to the Union, but they dare not manifest it until they are assured of permanent protection. They have seen repeated instances in which Union men who have shown their colors when the United States forces advanced in their neighborhoods, have been utterly sacrified by the withdrawal of those forces. They are not forgetful of the fate of certain Unionists in the Valley of Virginia, and in parts of Missouri and Tennessee. The people of the South never have been, are not, and never can be, a unit in resisting the supreme law of the land—the Constitution. They may be kept down by an armed minority in their respective States until, by the aid of the United States Government, they can help themselves, but they can be kept down no longer.

—Returns from the North Carolina election show that Vance, conservative, is probably elected over Johnston, rabid secesh, by 25,000 majority. The Petersburg *Express* says: "VANCE carries Clarke by 1,750 majority, Guilford by 1,950, Davidson by 1,200, Alamance by 760, Wayne by 240, and Chatham, Orange, and Johnson by large majorities. Nothing has been heard from the mountains, but his vote there is no doubt nearly unanimous. He is elected by 25,000 majority. A conservative legislature is also elected."

Our Country's Call.

BY WILLIAM CULLEN BRYANT.

Lay down the axe; fling by the spade;
  Leave in its track the toiling plow;
The rifle and the bayonet-blade
  For arms like yours were fitter now.
And let the hands that ply the pen
  Quit the light desk, and learn to wield
The horseman's crooked brand, and rein
  The charger on the battle-field.

Our country calls: away! away!
  To where the blood stream blots the green.
Strike to defend the gentlest sway
  That time in all his course has seen.
See, from a thousand coverts—see
  Spring the armed foes that haunt her track;
They rush to smite her down, and we
  Must beat the banded traitors back.

Ho! sturdy as the oaks ye cleave,
  And moved as soon to fear and flight,
Men of the glade and forest! leave
  Your woodcraft for the field of fight.
The arms that wield the axe must pour
  An iron tempest on the foe;
His serried ranks shall reel before
  The arm that lays the panther low.

And ye who breast the mountain storm,
  In grassy steep or Highland lake,
Come for the land ye love to form
  A bulwark that no foe can break.
Stand, like your own gray cliffs that mock
  The whirlwind; stand in her defence;
The blast as soon shall move the rock
  As rushing squadrons bear ye thence.

And ye whose homes are by her grand
  Swift rivers, rising far away,
Come from the depth of her green land
  As mighty in your march as they;
As terrible as when the rains
  Have swelled them over bank and bourne,
With sudden floods to drown the plains,
  And sweep along the woods uptorn.

And ye who throng, beside the deep,
  Her ports and hamlets of the strand
In number like the waves that leap
  On his long murmuring marge of sand.
Come, like that deep, when o'er his brim
  He rises, all his floods to pour,
And flings the proudest barks that swim
  A helpless wreck against his shore.

Few, few were they whose swords of old
  Won the fair land in which we dwell;
But we are many, we who hold
  The grim resolve to guard it well.
Strike for that broad and goodly land,
  Blow after blow, till men shall see
That Might and Right move hand in hand,
  And glorious must their triumph be.

The Last Illness of Cavour.

"Le Comte de Cavour, Recits et Souvenirs," by M. William de la Rive, now in the press at Paris, is a work which will be eagerly welcomed by every friend of Italian liberty. It contains numerous unpublished facts in the history of the great statesman, and also an interesting narrative of Cavour's last illness, from the pen of his niece, the Countess Alfieri. From this narrative we take the following passage:

CAVOUR'S LAST WORDS ON ITALY AND GARIBALDI.

As soon as the King was gone the Count began talking again.

"Northern Italy is made; there are now no longer Lombards, nor Piedmontese, nor Tuscans, nor Romagnols; we are all Italians; but there are still Neapolitans. Oh, there is much corruption in their country. It is not their fault, poor people; they have been so badly governed. It is the work of that scoundrel, Ferdinand. No, no, a government so corrupt as that can never be restored; Providence cannot permit it. The thing to be done is to moralize the country, to educate the children and young men, to build houses of refuge, to found military colleges; but it is not by reviling the Neapolitans that we shall improve them. They are always asking me for employments, decorations, and advancement; they must work, they must be honest, and then I will give them all these things; but above all, no misconduct must be passed over: the employee should be above suspicion. I would have no state of siege; none of those means which absolute governments resort to. Anybody can govern with the state of siege. I would govern them with liberty, and I would show what ten years of liberty could do for that beautiful country. In twenty years they will be the richest provinces of Italy. No, no state of siege, I beg of you."

"Garibaldi," he continued, "is an honest man. I wish him no harm. He wants Rome and Venice, and so do I; nobody is more anxious about that than we are. As to Istria and the Tyrol, that is another matter. That must be left to another generation. We have done enough for one set of men, for we have made Italy. *Si, l' Italia e, la cosa va.* And then that Germanic Confederation is an anomaly; it will be dissolved, and German unity will be founded; but there is no modifying the house of Hapsburg. What will the Prussians do—they are always so slow to decide? They will take fifty years to do what we have done in three."

"And now while the fever of unity is working in Europe, what a curious thing it is that America has taken it into her head to divide. Can you understand anything of these intestine quarrels of the United States? For my part, I was in my youth an ardent admirer of the Americans, but I have very much changed my opinion of them, and I confess that what is now going on beyond the Atlantic is a perfect riddle to me."

THE EXCHANGE OF PRISONERS.

BUCKNER, TILGHMAN, GANTT, MACKALL AND THE REST FROM ISLAND TEN AND FORT DONELSON.

THEIR ARRIVAL AND RECEPTION IN DIXIE.

INFAMOUS TREACHERY BY THE REBELS.

A correspondent of the Philadelphia *Press* contrived by some surreptitious means to accompany the expedition from Fortress Monroe, which carried up James river some 3,000 rebel prisoners to be exchanged for an equal number of federal prisoners from Richmond. The exchange was expected to take place at City Point, but the rebels being engaged in the erection of batteries there did not want our men to see them, and accordingly selected Akin's Landing, seven miles further up.

It was my lot to be on board the Knickerbocker, and here were the 210 Fort Warren prisoners, included among whom was the rebel Generals Buckner, Tilghman, Mackall, Pettigrew and Gantt, with Commodore Barron, Captains Mitchell and Kennon, and a host of inferior officers of both navy and army. The sixty privates in this batch were chiefly educated men, and associated on terms of entire equality with their officers, occupying the same cabin and the same deck. The private soldiers on the other steamers were in an exceedingly filthy state, which aggravated in appearance by the brown and gray color of their clothes, and their long, uncombed hair. The greasy odor that pervaded them permeated every portion of the vessel. They were very quiet under the many delays they experienced in reaching the terminus of their voyage, knowing well that they would not see their homes, but merely be transferred immediately to the ranks.—Their time was spent in eating and sleeping. gazing vacantly upon the surrounding scenery, and scratching. This last was an absorbing occupation, and was varied by their taking off their shirts and studiously examining the inner side. Fifty Union soldiers guarded each other. A dozen sick rebels died on the way up, having long been previously ill with diarrhea and typhoid. As a matter of trifling import, I will advert to the personal appearance of a few rebels on the Knickerbocker. Buckner is a man of two or three and forty, with a flattened nose, dark complexion and heavy chin. He wore his long, prematurely gray hair pushed behind his ears, and his face shaven, with the exception of the lip and chin. His dress was a plain sack and pantaloons of dark blue cloth, a gray waist coat, and a high gray scull-cap, of indescribable shape, banded by black Scotch checks. His form is moderately thick set. His face is conceded to lack high polish, but his manners are cordial and attractive. As he passes each Union sentinel on landing, he bade him adieu and shook hands with him, much to the sentinel's gratification He is a politician. Hand-shaking is cheap and frequent with him. Every man who takes his hand may one day be of use. The countenance and general air of Tilghman and Barron both bear the impress of high breeding, and both are gentlemen, in the most elegant, if not the highest sense. Tilghman wore a dark blue sack, and pantaloons of most unexceptional cut. The latter were corded with yellow. Upon the turned-up flap of his cream-colored, golden corded, felt hat, were three gold stars, indicating his rank of brigadier general. His face is florid, his features regular and handsome, and his age not over forty. His curly hair is long and brushed back, and prematurely touched with gray, as are also his beard and moustache. His height is say five feet nine. Mackall is a crusty looking old chap of fifty—short and thick set; and Gantt is—goodness knows and nobody cares. We have had enough of the pack.

They inspected silently and with great interest the different gunboats that we passed, and more especially the Monitor and Galena. As a chance shot screamed from one over the hills, their excitement to catch a possible glance of their own forces in the distance was great. Each new feature on shore, as they supposed themselves within their own lines, was eagerly scanned. "There are some of our people," said one, as he saw several Union cavalry officers approach the shore to water their horses. "No, those are Yanks," said another; "don't you see their uniform?" "Why didn't they land us at City Point?" said a third, "there is a railroad there to take us up." "We are fortifying around there," said a fourth. On a first view of negroes, one cried out: "Here are some intelligent contrabands!" A general laugh ensued at this frequent term used by northern papers. Presently the sight offered itself of negro women, whom they knew to be slaves, and their gratulations were lively. The old south was really reached at last. On they came from their distant houses, trooping to the landing, and were received with waving of handkerchiefs and screeches of delight. Ganerals vied with their subordinates in these demonstrations, to which the negro women heartily responded, "Dem's our folks; glad to see you, massa! Dey'r waitin' for you up dar," were severally heard among their shouts of welcome; and one old woman, who led the rest, was profound in her curtisies and gesticulations. "Did you see her throw her arms up and then fold them on her breast? hey?" said a delighted colonel; "G—d d—n her old heart!"

Similar novel expressions of sentiment were made use of on other occasions of that kind that offered themselves; but on a first sight of secesh white women, enthusiasm became boundless. They flung open the blinds and waved their handkerchiefs with a will. No cheers were given in return, but screech followed upon screech and yell upon yell. Many danced. "Sweet as peaches! I know they're pretty," said an excited youth. "Bless 'em, God bless 'em!" said another. "I'd wave 'em my handkerchief if it was not so dirty," said a third; "but never mind, I'll give 'em my hat," and again hats were waived and cries renewed. Soon landing was attained and all descended to go on shore. The army officers were required to go first in order of rank; then the navy officers and privateers, afterwards the privates and finally the sailors. There was no enthusiasm. Not a cheer was given as their feet touched shore, nor was any welcome offered them. Not a wagon was sent from Richmond for the conveyance of officers or baggage,nor was a solitary member of the rebel army present beyond the exchange officer, Major Ould, and two young captains, who, later in the afternoon took a pleasure excursion to the landing in a buggy. Every one slowly ascended to the summit of the gradually sloping bank, and either sat down or stood in groups conversing, in evident expectation of wagons.

Finally, the baggage being placed in Aiken's warehouse, many privates and a few officers concluded to walk, leaving the rest fondly awaiting conveyances. By eight o'clock all had departed—3,013 in number —and an equal amount of noble Union soldiers, who had arrived at two in the morning from Richmond, marched on board. They had received no food since breakfast on Tuesday morning, until their arrival near the landing during the night. Rations were then sent them from our steamers, which they devoured ravenously, and received the officers, who distributed them, with extravagant cheers and congratulations. They complained much of the scanty fare the rebels had given them, but looked well and hearty, notwithstanding. Their march the previous day had been through an intense heat, and several had fallen prostrate on the way. One of these was told to rise by a rebel guard, and on expressing inability, received a blow on the head from the butt of a musket, which drew a stream of blood. Another man, in a similar situation, received a bayonet thrust, which gave him much pain. As our men marched past Libby's tobacco warehouse from their prison on Bell Island, they recognized Gen. McCall sitting at a window, who, on being cheered, said he was glad to see them going back, and bade them farewell.

Newspaper writers often speak of the wild cheering given by our returned prisoners when once they stand again beneath the stars and stripes. I can safely say that not a cheer was given as these men filed on board their several steamers. Their sentiments were absorbed by approaching dinner as they viewed barrels of beef and onions and piles of loaves on the fore deck. When all had left shore the battalion of ragged, coatless rebel soldiers, acting as guard, who had during the embarkation lounged or slept on the adjoining bank, walked off without exchanging adieus.

Down the river the Monitor, Galena and other gunboats each came in for vigorous cheers, and after lying at anchor for several hours off Harrison's Landing, they were marched on shore at dusk, and distributed by the provost marshal to their several regiments. Those few who belonged to Pope's or Burnside's armies will spuedily be sent to them. All that were in good health left Richmond, leaving about 1,500 sick and wounded yet behind.

REBEL TREACHERY.

The officers to be exchanged did not leave Richmond with the privates, and were expected last evening at Aiken's Landing. News finally came to Adjutant General Thomas, that they would not return at present, the Confederate government having concluded to detain them! And thus, after General Thomas had confidingly liberated all their officers, and tenderly sent a number of their sick to City Point, by the Georgia, that they might be taken to Richmond on cars. On the return of this boat to Aiken's Landing, the guard on board, under Lieut. Miller, 10th New Jersey Regiment, were indignant in the extreme, and had they not been restrained by Lieut Miller, would have retaliated by setting fire to Aiken's house and all his out buildings. If any reason had been given for his treachery to General Thomas, he did not communicate it to his subordinates. It was generally considered by them as a retaliation for Pope's recent orders. The indignation of the country on receipt of this news will be great. It will hasten enlistments.

The Rebel Retaliatory Order.

LETTER FROM JEFF. DAVIS TO GEN. LEE.

The following is a letter from Jeff. Davis to Gen. Lee, instructing him to communicate to the Commander-in-Chief of the Federal armies a copy of the order for reretaliatory measures recently issued by the rebel War Department, and which was published in our issue of Sunday last:

RICHMOND, Va., July 31.

SIR—On the 23d of this month a cartel fr a general exchange of prisoners of war was signed between Major General D. H. Hill, in behalf of the Confederate States, and Major General John A. Dix, in behalf of the United States. By the terms of that cartel it is stipulated that all prisoners of war hereafter taken shall be discharged on parole till exchanged. Scarcely had that cartel been signed when the military authorities of the United States, commenced a practice of changing the character of the war from such as becomes civilized nations into a campaign of indiscriminate robberies and murders. The general order issued by the Secretary of War of the United States in the city of Washington, on the very day that the cartel was signed in Virginia, directs military commanders of the United States to take the private property of our people for the convenience and use of their armies without compensation.

The general order issued by Major Gen. Pope on the 22d of July, the day after the signing of the cartel, directs the muder of our peaceful inhabitants as spies if found quietly tilling their farms in his rear, even outside of his lines; and one ot his Brigadier Generals, Steinwehr, has seized upon innocent and peaceful citizens to be held as hostages, to the end that they may be murdered in cold blood if any of his soldiers are killed by some unknown persons whom he designaees as "bushwhackers." Under this state of facts, this government has issued the inclosed general order, recognizing General Pope and his commissioned officers to be in the position which they have chosen for themselves, that of robbers and murderers, and not that of public enemies, entitled, if captured, to be considered as prisoners of war. We find ourselves driven by our enemies by steady progress towards a practice which we abhor, and which we are vainly struggling to avoid. Some of the military authorities of the United States seem to suppose that better success will attend a savage war, in which no quarter is to be given, and no age or sex to be spared, than has hitherto been secured by such hostilities as are alone recognized to be lawful by civilized men in modern times.

For the present we renounce our right of retaliation on the innocent, and shall continue to treat the private enlisted soldiers of Gen. Pope's army as prisoners of war; but, if, after notice to the government at Washington of our confining retaliative measures to the punishment only of commissioned officers who are willing participants in these crimes, the savage practices are continued, we shall reluctantly be forced to the last resort of accepting the war on the terms chosen by our foes, until the outraged voice of a common humanity forces a respect for the recognized rules of war. While these facts would justify our refusal to execute the generous cartel by which we have consented to liberate an excess of thousands of prisoners held by us beyond the number held by the enemy, a sacred regard for private faith, shrinking from the mere semblance of breaking a promise prevents our resort to this extremity.

Nor do we desire to extend to any other forces of the enemy the punishment meted above to General Pope, and such commissioned officers as choose to participate in the execution of his infamous orders.

You are therefore instructed to communicate to the Commander in-Chief of the armies of the United States the contents of this letter, and a copy of the inclosed general order, to the end that he may be notified of our intention not to consider any officers hereafter captured from Gen. Pope's army as prisoners of war.

Very respectfully yours, &c.,
JEFF. DAVIS.
Gen. R. E. LEE, commanding, &c.

LEAVES OF ABSENCE.

IMPORTANT TO OFFICERS AT HOME.

Official War Bulletin.

WAR DEP'T, ADJ'T GEN'LS OFFICE,
WASHINGTON, August 9, 1862.
GENERAL ORDER NO. 1.

First. So much of General Order No. 62, current series, as relates to the extension of sick leaves of absences is hereby revoked, and no applications for such extension need hereafter be made. The order of the President, dated July 31st, General Order No. 92, explains what may be considered as good cause for the absence. Surgeon's certificates of disability required by existing orders and regulations must be forwarded not only to the adjutant general of the army, but also to the commander of the regiment, or, in case of a staff officer to the commanding general.

Second. Officers absent from duty without leave, or beyond their leaves, will not be allowed to draw their pay until a court of commission, which will be ordered on their return to their post or command, shall determine whether there was sufficient cause for their absence. They will accordingly provide themselves with a full description of the nature and cause of their disability, certified by the proper medical authority as required by existing orders and regulations.

Third. Officers of volunteers who are absent from duty on account of disease contracted before they entered the service will be immediately mustered out. Those who have been absent more than sixty days on account of wounds or disease contracted in line of their duty, will be reported to the adjutant general of the army, to discharge, in order that their places may be filled by others for field service. For this class of officers Congress has provided pensions.

Fourth. Applications for pensions must be made to the commissioner of pensions, who is judge of the sufficiency of the evidence in support of such claims, and who furnishes the forms and regulations relating thereto.

Fifth. When an officer returns to his command, after having overstaid his leave of absence, he may be tried by a court martial for this as a military offense, or a commission may be appointed by the commanding officer of his division, army corps or army, as the case may be, to investigate his case and to determine whether or not he was absent from proper cause, and if there should be found to be such proper cause, he will be entitled to pay during such absence.

Sixth. Where troops are serving in an army corps or army, no leaves of absence will be granted on the certificate of a regimental or brigade surgeon till the same has been approved by the medical director of such army corps or army, and no medical director will endorse any certificate until he has made a personal examination of the applicant or received a verbal report from a medical officer appointed by him to make such personal examination. When, after such personal examination it shall be found that the certificate of disability was given without proper cause, the name of the medical officer giving it will be reported to the adjutant general of the army in order that he may be dismissed from the service.

Seventh. Where officers in a division, among corps or separate armies, applications for leave may be made to the adjutant general of the army, but except in very extraordinary cases, no leave of absence will be granted, unless the application be accompanied by a certificate of the same character, as that described in General Order 61.

Eighth. In all cases of personal application for leaves of absence, made to the War Department, the applicant will be examined by a medical officer assigned to that duty in this city.

By order of the Secretary of War.
E. D. TOWNSEND, Adj't Gen.

Assassination of General McCook.

PARTICULARS OF THE AFFAIR.

Correspondence of the Cincinnati Commercial.

LOUISVILLE, August 8.—The remains of the late Bobert L. McCook reached here this evening in charge of Captains Burt and Fuchshulter and eleven of the 9th Ohio. They were received at the Nashville depot by Captain Dillard's Provost Guards and escorted to the Galt House. They leave by train in the morning and will arrive at Cincinnati at noon tomorrow.

I have from Captain Burt the particulars of the death. The brigade left a point fourteen miles below the Tennessee State line for Decherd on the 5th. On the road General McCook, who was unwell, took the advance in a spring wagon, about a mile in advance of the brigade. Suddenly a courier dashed back to the brigade and said the wagon, in which General McCook was riding, had been fired upon by bushwhackers. Immediately Colonel Vandever, of the 35th Ohio, sent Captain Earhart's company forward on double quick to the rescue, loading as they ran. They met stragglers from McCook's body guard retreating, pursued by rebel cavalry. Shots were exchanged and the rebel cavalry retreated. The federal infantry were too slow in pursuit, when Captain Burt, of the 18th Infantry, Lieut. Harris, Captains Fuchshultzer, Stangel, and Captain Thangel, of the 9th Ohio, dashed forward in pursuit of the retreating rebel cavalry. General McCook was then lying on the piazza, at Petty's farm, four miles from New Market, and a half mile from the Tennessee State line. They inquired at the farm house for information of McCook, but the people would or could not give information, fearing if his body was found their buildings and property would be destroyed. McCook hearing the inquiries, told them to open the house to his friends. Dr. Gordon of the 35th Ohio, and Dr. Boyle of the 9th Ohio, came up and examined the wound, pronouncing it fatal. The wound was in the bowels, a single ball entering the left side and coming out between the 9th and 10th ribs. When the physician arrived Gen. McCook was vomiting blood. He was cool and calm to the last, but suffered greatly, giving Capt. Burt and others an account of the assassination. While on the road Gen. McCook met a man in the ravine, and asked him if he knew a good place to encamp. The man told him there was plenty of water on the hill beyond, and seemed anxious to hurry him on.

Arriving at the top of the hill, a shot was fired without effect. As soon as Gen. McCook heard the shot, he told John (his colored servant) to turn back the wagon; that the bushwhackers were upon them. They started back in full speed, Gen. McCook leaning on his knees, and assisting the driver. In the flight a number of shots were fired. Eleven holes were found in the wagon, McCook receiving a single ball. Before the fatal shot was fired, a rebel cavalryman ordered the wagon to halt, leveling a pistol across the horn of his saddle. General McCook told the driver to stop, which the driver was in the act of doing, when the cavalryman ordered a halt the second time, accompanying the order with a discharge of the pistol, the ball piercing the General's side. Captain Brooke, of McCook's staff, implored the cavalryman not to shoot, assuring him the wagon was occupied by a sick man. Another bushwhacker rode up with a cocked pistol, but McCook told him that it was no use to shoot; that he was fatally wounded already.

Captain Brooke then conveyed McCook to Petty's house. The negro, John, escaped to a corn field, as the bushwhackers retreated to kill the negro.

The residents proposed to hide Gen. McCook's body away in the negro quarters, fearing, as they said, if the Yankee should die on their hands their premises would be burned; but he was permitted to die at the farm house.

Recovering from his paroxysm, General McCook said to Captain Burt: "Andy, the problem of life will soon be solved for me." In reply to Father Betty, if he had any message for his brother, Alexander, he said: "Tell him and the rest I have tried to live as a man, and die attempting to do my duty."

To Captain Burt he said: "My good boy, may your life be longer and to a better purpose than mine." Father Betty, the brigade wagon master, was with him in his last moments. Clasping his hands in the death struggle, he said to him: "I am done with life; yes, this ends it all. You and I part now, but the loss of 10,000 such lives as yours and mine would be nothing, if their sacrifice would but save such a government as ours."

Before his death General McCook sent for Colonel Vandever, who drew up his will. In his will he directed that two favorite horses should be given to his brothers, Aleck and Daniel, and the remainder of his property to his mother.

It is known to Capt. Burt and others of McCook's staff, that the General was deliberately assassinated. The sutler of the 9th Ohio heard the bushwhackers arrange a plan for the assassination, but had no opportunity to communicate information to McCook or staff.

—At a recent sale of negroes in Kentucky two likely young negro men brought less than $300 each. Eighteen months ago they would probably have brought over $1,200, and now they sell for little more than good hands hired for two years ago. Here is a striking illustration of the effect of the rebellion upon slavery.

—Governor Johnson of Tennessee has appointed Ex-Governor Campbell of that State an agent to visit the various prisons in the North where Tennesseeans are confined, and should any of them desire to take the oath of allegiance and return to their homes, they will be allowed to do so. All the other prisoners will be exchanged immediately.

FROM POPE'S ARMY.

POPE'S REPORT OF THE BATTLE.

Gallantry of Gen. Banks.

Enemy Across the Rapidan.

HEROISM OF A UNION SOLDIER.

Force of Jackson 60,000.

WASHINGTON, August 15.—Gen. Pope's official report of the battle of Cedar Mountains says:

Thursday the enemy crossed the Rapidan in heavy force. Early on Friday it became apparent that a move on Madison Court House was a feint to drive General Sigel at Sperryville, and the main attack would be on Culpepper, to which place I had thrown forward Banks' and McDowell's troops.

The artillery of the enemy opened early in the afternoon, but he made no advance until five o'clock, and General Banks advanced to the attack. The engagement did not fairly open until six o'clock, but for an hour and a half was furious and unceasing throughout.

I had continued to receive reports from Gen. Banks that no attack was apprehended, and that no considerable infantry force of the enemy had come forward. Yet towards evening the increase in the artillery firing having satisfied me an engagement might be at hand, though the lateness of the hour rendered it unlikely. I ordered Gen. McDowell to advance to Rickett's division to support Banks, and directed Gen. Sigel to bring his men on the ground as soon as possible.

I arrived personally on the field at seven o'clock, and found the action raging furiously. I found General Banks holding the position he took early in the morning. His losses were heavy.

Richett's division was pushed forward and occupied the advance of Gen. Banks. Our troops rested on their arms during the night, and in line of battle. Heavy shelling was kept up on both sides till midnight.

In the morning at daylight the enemy fell back two miles from our front. Our pickets at once advanced and occupied their ground.

The fatigue of the troops, from long marches and excessive heat, made it impossible for either side to resume action on Sunday. The men were therefore allowed to rest.

On Monday night the enemy fled from the field leaving many of his dead unburied.

General Buford, with a cavalry force, was immediately thrown forward in pursuit, and followed the enemy to the Rapidan.

The behaviour of General Banks' corps during this action was very fine. No greater gallantry and daring could be exhibited by any troops. I cannot speak too highly of the coolness and intrepidity of General Banks himself during the whole of the engagement. He was in the front and exposed as much as any man in the command. His example was of the greatest benefit. He merits and should receive the commendation of his government.

Generals Williams, Augur, Gordon, Crawford, Prince, Green and Geary behaved with conspicuous gallantry. Augur and Geary were severely wounded. I desire publicly to express my appreciation of the prompt and skillful manner in which Generals McDowell and Sigel brought forward their respective commands, and established them on the field.

Brigadier General Roberts, chief of cavalry, was with the advance on Friday and Saturday, and was conspicuous for his gallantry, as well as for the valuable aid he rendered. Our loss is about 1500, in killed, wounded and missing.

JOHN POPE,
Major General Commanding.

SIGEL'S HEADQUARTES,
Rapidan, Aug. 14.

The enemy is still reported to be retreating beyond the Rapidan river, although they have a force on the other side, with guns in position, and a large body of cavalry covering the retreat of the main body.

General Milroy is in the advance, with General Bayard's cavalry and some artillery. The river is easily forded at many points.

It is stated that Stonewall Jackson's army numbers at least 60,000 men. He has managed to move them all off safely, excepting a few stragglers. Some of the latter came into our camp last night and said that almost all the Virginia soldiers would desert, and thought they would be well treated.

A Union soldier was found in the woods on Wednesday, with his musket barrel grasped in both hands. The stock was broken off, and eleven dead rebels were lying around him, some with their heads smashed, and others in various ways, all dead. This shows with what desperation the Union hero had fought for his life, but without avail.

Dispatch from Charleston.

BELIEF OF McCLELLAN'S EVACUATION.

NEW YORK, Aug. 15.—The following dispatch appears in the Charleston *Courier* of August 1st:—

RICHMOND, July 29.—The opinion gains ground here that General McClellan is gradually evacuating his position at Berkeley and is reinforcing General Pope with the bulk of his army.

The number of Yankee transports in the James river is immense and great activity is observable among them.

BATTLE IN EAST TENNESSEE

NEAR CUMBERLAND GAP.

A DESPERATE FIGHT.

Union Forces Surrounded.

AND COMPELLED TO SURRENDER.

Rebels in Possession of East Tennessee.

Rebel General Caswell Killed.

NEXT MOVE ON BUELL.

CHICAGO, Aug. 15.—[*Time's* special from Memphis 13.]—The battle commenced on the 7th at Tazewell, seven miles from Cumberland Gap, between the confederate forces under Stevenson, numbering from 12,000 to 15,000, and the federals at that place, numbering 3,000.

The movement was made in front by Stevenson, while Gen. Burton gained the rear by forced marches, and surrounded the federal force.

A desperate fight of four hours ensued, terminating in the surrender of the Federals.

They were driven by superior numbers in front, and when in full retreat were assailed by a flanking force.

The rebels are thus in possession of East Tennessee again.

The next move will be on Buell with an overwhelming force.

Beauregard is at Chattenooga county, operating with Bragg. Their combined fore is not less than 70,000.

The rebel General Caswell, was killed near his residence in Knoxville on the 6th.

A schooner from Havana ran the block at Mobile on the 7th with a cargo of ammunition, salt, and cavalry equipments.

A Vicksburg letter says the streets are beginning to assume former lively appearance. Refugees return opening their places of business. All damages to the city by Federal shells will be repaired within a month.

NEWS FROM WASHINGTON.

WASHINGTON, Aug. 14.—The Navy Department advertised proposals for construction of iron vessels for river and harbor defence.

Lieuts. Frank C. Goodrich, Geo. A. Rawley, Charles R. Noggle, and T. S. Wright, of the regular army, were cashiered for misdemeanor before the enemy, and Captain Carboy, 12th infantry, for drunkenness. Sentences confirmed by Gen. McClellan.

A Washington dispatch to the *Times* says Secretary Seward stated last evening that the current stories published in some of the papers and generally believed here for the last three or days, that General McClellan's army had left the Peninsula, were untrue. Reasons are known here independent of Mr. Seward's statement which leads to the same belief. What may come in future of course remains uncertain. Military matters therefors assume a profoundly mixed appearance. Secessionists have rumors of disaster to McClellan's army—loss of artillery, loss of shipping, etc., but in a very vague form and not regarded credible.

The Richmond *Examiner* of the 12th, contains the following:—Among the prisoners who reached the city on Saturday and Sunday was Brigadier General Prince and thirty-four officers, including one major, one colonel, and other commissioned officers. They are all at the Libby Prison.

The officers from General Pope's command are kept in solitary confinement, in conformity with instructions, and the rule as enforced will not be departed from under any consideration.

About 300 prisoners have arrived at the Libby Prison from Pope's army.

The *Herald's* Harrison's Landing correspondent of the 13th, says that early this morning one of the truce boats arrived here with 147 of our released prisoners from Richmond. Among them are Generals McCall and Reynolds, Colonel Simpson, Major Binney of 4th New Jersey regiment; Colonel Stockton of 16th Michigan: Lieut. Colonel Sweitzer of 62nd Pennsylvania, and other officers captured in the battles on the Peninsula. Officers of high rank state that they have been treated with marked indignity by the rebel authorities.

After twelve o'clock today these returned prisoners will be free to join their several command.

Rebel troops in considerable numbers were seen last evening and this morning on the south side of James River.

Some of our returned prisoners state that on Sunday night over a hundred pieces of artillery passed their prison in Richmond, on their way to reinforce Jackson in front of Pope.

WASHINGTON, August 14.—The following additional regulations for the enrolling of the militia for draft, were issued today:

8. Ordered, That, in filling all requisitions for militia, the quotas of the several States will be apportioned by the Governors among the several counties, and, when practicable, among the subdivisions of counties; so that allowance shall be made to such counties, and subdivisions of counties, for all volunteers heretofore furnished by them and msutered into the service of the United States, whose stipulated term of service shall not have expired.

(Signed) EDWIN M. STANTON,
Secretary of War.

Pioneer & Democrat.

SAINT PAUL.

Saint Paul, Friday, August 22, 1862.

The Disfranchisement of the Citizen-Soldier.

The hardships of War are not confined to the field. The volunteer not only subjects himself to the wearying march, the wasting of disease, and the dangerous chances of battle, but, as our custom has been, he temporarily deprives himself of all rights of citizenship; or, at least, of that right which is prized most highly, inasmuch as it is his peculiar boon, protection, and pride—the right of choosing his own rulers and of making his own laws.

When the regiments now in progress shall have been formed, and the old regiments brought up to their maximum, at least twelve thousand men will have gone into the field from Minnesota. Of this number, ten thousand are legal voters; entitled to a voice in the selection of officers to administer the laws at home, and to represent the people in the National Congress, by virtue of their citizenship; and doubly entitled to that privilege by the fact that, in making a voluntary offering of their lives for their country, they are showing themselves worthy of their citizenship. Twelve thousand comprise at least one-half of all the strictly able-bodied men of the State; and ten thousand are a full third of its legal voters. These men are not absent from the State upon their private business, or under circumstances which show them to be careless of their rights, or indifferent to the exercise of them. On the contrary, the fact of their enlistment shows their appreciation of their rights and duties to be superior to that of their fellows, who have remained behind; while the fact of their absence, so far from curtailing their privileges, should operate to enlarge them, inasmuch as such absence is not voluntary but compulsory—by command of the Government and for its protection. If any citizen is entitled to say what shall be the character of the laws, and the nature of the policies of his State and Nation, and who shall be chosen to frame both, it is the volunteer, who bears not only his full proportion of all common burdens, but who patriotically tenders his life to the general sacrifice.

There ought to be some means devised by which the volunteer can have his rights saved to him, and the free and full enjoyment of them guaranteed. The act of enlistment, which marks him a hero, ought not, also, to brand him as inferior to the meanest coward who ties himself to apron strings that he may not be spirited away from the safe seclusion of home. The volunteer should be a voter; and none the less that he is a brave man and a patriot.

We have not examined the laws to see whether provision is made, in this respect, for the anomalous condition in which our people are placed, on account of the civil war which is upon us. More than likely, no special warrant will be found for taking the votes of citizens outside the precincts in which they reside. But it is a case in which the justice is so clear, that we hope such authority may be found. And, profoundly impressed, as we are, with the rights and wrongs involved in this question, to the thousands of brave volunteers who have gone, and will soon go, beyond our borders, to preserve our own security, and the unity and honor of the Nation, we earnestly commend it to the attention of the State authorities, for their earnest and prompt consideration.

The Telegraphic News.

By an arrival at New York from New Orleans we have an account of the battle at Baton Rouge. Our forces, numbering about 2,500, defeated 5,000 rebels under Generals Lovell and Breckinridge. It is stated that Lovell was killed, and that Breckinridge lost an arm. The commander of the National forces, General Williams, was killed.

The same arrival brings the gratifying news that the Ram Arkansas grounded, and was destroyed by the gunboat Essex.

The news from Cumberland Gap is most gratifying. Instead of being defeated, the Union forces achieved success in a sharp engagement. There has been no fight at Big Creek Gap, as reported, nor any other engagement in the vicinity of Tazewell.

—At the prorogation of Parliament, the Queen avowed her intention of continuing neutral in the American contest.

—Rev. George W. Dunmore, the late lamented chaplain of the 1st Wisconsin cavalry regiment, who fell bravely fighting in the recent assault made on a corps of that regiment by 600 Texans, near Helena, Arkansas, at the time of the breaking out of the rebellion was a missionary in Turkey, in Asia, under the patronage of the A. B. C. F. M., in whose service he had been ten years. On learning of his country's troubles and dangers, he hastened home and entered its service.

SERIOUS OUTBREAK OF THE SIOUX INDIANS.

SEVERAL PERSONS MURDERED.

From the Daily Pioneer of Wednesday, 20th.

The city was considerably excited yesterday and last evening by reports of murders committed by the Indians in Meeker county and at the Agency on the Minnesota river. We have diligently traced these reports, and give the following as the substance of every thing that has come in a reliable form up to alate hour.

MURDERS IN MEEKER COUNTY.

The first news of the Indian raid was brought to the Governor by Mr. George C. Whitcomb, who resides at Greenleaf, Meeker county, about thirty-five miles from Hutchinson. Mr. Whitcomb is the County Treasurer, and well known as a gentleman of truth.

He states that about one o'clock on Sunday last, seven or eight Indians came to the house of Mr. Robinson Jones, in the town of Acton, thirty miles North-west of Forrest City. Mr. Jones soon discovered that their disposition was anything but friendly, and fearing for the safety of his family, he locked the doors of his house, and with his wife, went to the house of Mr. Howard Baker, about a mile distant, and was followed by the Indians.

The Sioux, on arriving at the door of Mr. Baker's house, proposed to the inmates to go out a short distance, and shoot at a mark. An assent was given to the proposition, and the Indians led the way. When they were a short distance from the house, a signal was given, and the Indians turned and fired at Mr. Robinson Jones, who was just outside the door. Howard Baker, Mrs. Jones, and a Mr. Webster, who were inside the door, fell mortally wounded. The Indian who fired at Mr. Jones missed, and fired again, the second shot taking effect. Mr. Baker told his wife, who was unhurt, to go down cellar with her child. She started to go, but when at the head of the stairs she fell down, and was insensible for some time. When she revived the Indians were gone. She got a pillow and put under her husband's head, who was still alive. He directed her to leave him and go to a neighbor's about a mile distant, and give the alarm, which she did.

The people turned out and went to Baker's house, and found four persons dead—Mr. and Mrs. Jones, Howard Baker, and Mr. Webster. The child of Mrs. Baker was found in the house unhurt. It was an infant, only two years old.

When Mr. Jones locked up his house to go to Mr. Baker's, he left a young girl, an adopted child, and the neighbors found, on going to Jones' house, that the Indians had returned and murdered her.

Mr. Whitcomb, who gives us these particulars, was engaged raising a company for one of our new regiments, and was at Forest City. He sent men out to the scene of the murders, who returned and verified the statements we have given. The settlers were rushing to Forest city in great numbers, but nobody had seen any other bands of Indians, than those who committed the murders, and it is not known that any others were in the neighborhood.

MURDERS AT THE AGENCY—A COMPANY FROM FORT RIDGLEY BADLY CUT UP.

Governor Ramsey received, yesterday afternoon, the following dispatch from Lieut. Gere, of the Fifth Regiment, stationed at Fort Ridgley:

FROM LIEUTENANT GERE.

Headquarters Fort Ridgley, August 18, 8 P. M.

Commanding Officer at Fort Snelling:

Captain Marsh left this post at 10½ this morning to prevent Indian depredations at the Lower Agency. Some of the men have returned. I learn from them that Capt. Marsh is killed and only thirteen of his company are remaining.

The Indians are killing the settlers and plundering the country. Send reinforcements without delay. Respectfully,

THOMAS P. GERE,
2d Lieut. Co. B., 5th Reg't Minn. Vol.

P. S.—Please hand this to Gov. Ramsey.

FROM LIEUT. CULVER.

St. Peter, 4 P. M. Aug. 19, 1862.

Governor—

Sir; A second dispatch has arrived from the Fort. Captain Marsh, on hearing of the fight at Red Wood, went with fifty of our company. Only thirteen came back. The Captain was wounded and drowned.

The messenger is at the door, and I close I leave in half an hour for the Fort, with fifty armed men.

N. K. CULVER,
1st Lieutenant 5th Min. Vols.

P. S. Five hundred men are needed.

FURTHER PARTICULARS.

On Friday morning, Major Galbraith left the Agency, with W. H. Shelly, Esq., and about fifty men, volunteers, for Fort Snelling, to be mustered into the service of the United States. On Monday afternoon they arrived at St. Peter, and were overtaken by Mr. Dickinson, a messenger from Red Wood, who informed Major Galbraith that the Indians had commenced an attack on the people of Red Wood, on Monday morning, at six o'clock, and that when he left six men had been shot. Their names were James W. Lynde, formerly State Senator, John Lamb, teamster, —— Wagner, the farmer, and three Germans, whose names were not given. Mr. Dickinson brought one of the wounded Germans to Fort Ridgley, twelve miles distant, and Dr. Muller pronounced him mortally wounded. When Mr. Dickinson got across the river from Redwood, he saw the Indians firing into the trader's stores, and other buildings. About forty men fired into Merrick's store at once. Mr. Dickinson estimated the number of Indians engaged in the firing at about one hundred and fifty.

Major Galbraith, when he learned what had taken place, turned back from St. Peter, and with his men started for Red Wood, and Mr. Shelly came down with the dispatches of Lieuts. Culver and Gere. When Major Galbraith left the Agency, everything was quiet. The Indians had received their annuity goods, and had all disappeared, apparently satisfied with the promise of the Major to send for them as soon as the money arrived to pay off their annuities. It is thought that the Indians were induced to commit these outrages by Indians from Missouri, and secession traders from that State. Mrs. Galbraith and children, as well as the families of the employees, are at the Yellow Medicine Agency.

THE LATEST ACCOUNTS.

Capt. Nelson Roberts, who returned last evening from New Ulm, reports that the people were packing up in that town and all along the frontier and leaving for St. Peter. Captain Marsh's company were fired upon at the Ferry, opposite Red Wood, and it was reported by those who escaped that thirty-seven were killed and wounded. Captain Marsh was reported killed, but these reports had not been confirmed. Capt. N. Robetrs started from New Ulm, with teams for Red Wood, and a short distance out met his brother Louis, coming down from the Agency. The teamsters say they saw one man shot down in a field and another in the road, between Red Wood and New Ulm. Great fears were felt for the safety of the whites at the Upper and Lower Agency. George Gleason and Dr. Humphrey were at Red Wood when Mr. Roberts left. The messengers, with the money to pay off the Indians, were at Fort Ridgley.

MEASURES TAKEN FOR THE PROTECTION OF THE FRONTIER.

As soon as the news of the Indian troubles reached the city, Gov. Ramsey went to Fort Snelling, and orders were given for four companies to be ready to start at once for the scene of the disturbances. The command of the expedition was given to Ex-Governor Sibley. The whole matter was confided to his discretion, and from his knowledge of the country and of Indian character, there can be little doubt of his success in preventing further outrages. We doubt, however, whether he will be able to find a single Indian, when he arrives at the reservation. If he had one or two companies of cavalry, they might possibly be overtaken. The miscreants deserve such a measure of vengeance, as they have never yet received, and we hope it will be administered in the style of Gen. Harney, if they are ever caught.

Are the Loyal States Growing Weary of the War?

The London *Times* argues in a long article that the Loyal States are growing weary of the war for national life and integrity. Such is not the fact. On the contrary, the people of the Loyal States are proving, day by day, their determination to stand by the Government at all hazards, in the prosecution of the war for the purposes solemnly announced by Congress in the Crittenden resolution. Though disappointed at the slow progress of the war, they are not disheartened. They believe that if the rebels are beaten at Richmond, the military power of the rebellion will be destroyed, and it will be impossible for the leaders, under any circumstances, to call together a large army in any part of the seceded States. Then, with a powerful force still in the field, we may look for a reaction in the South against the traitors, and the revival of the Union feeling.

Appointments for the Sixth Regiment.

The Governor has appointed as Colonel of the Sixth Regiment, Captain A. D. Nelson, of the regular Army, who is now on duty in this State.

H. L. Carver, of St. Paul, has been appointed Quartermaster of the Sixth Regiment.

—At Brighton, Iowa, on the 11th, a man named A. Landebaugh was taken in hand by the citizens for disturbing a meeting to raise volunteers, and for cheering for Jeff. Davis and the Southean Confederacy, and a great deal of other disloyal language. The rebel sympathizers pitched in and rescued the man, when the Home Guards turned out and arrested five of the rescuers and sent them under the charge of the sheriff to Davenport. It is getting to be dangerous to be a traitor and live North.

An Enormous Fraud upon Government Suspected.

Senator Wilson, Chairman of the Senate Military Committee on the 28th of March last, while Mc'Clellan's army was embarking for the Peninsula, made a speech in favor of stopping enlistments and reducing the army. Among other things he said:

> I believe we have to day one hundred and fifty thousand more men under the pay of the government than we need or can well use. I have not a doubt of it; and I think it ought to be checked. I think the War Department ought to issue peremptory orders forbidding the enlistment of another soldier into the volunteer force of the United States until the time shall come when we need them. We can obtain them any time when we need them.

In an unhappy hour the Senator made a speech at Newton, Massachusetts, denying *in toto* that he had ever used such language, and said that he had "*always* maintained that the government wanted more men." From the predicament he has thus placed himself in he endeavors to escape by a letter of exculpation. His opinion and action were based, he says, "upon the report of Secretary Cameron, the assurances of Paymaster General Larned, and the estimates of Quartermaster-General Meigs, that we had from seven hundred to eight hundred regiments and *seven hundred thousand men.*" This assertion, coming from the chairman of so important a Committee, arouses a suspicion that the country as well as Mr. Wilson has been cruelly deceived, and that a stupendous fraud has been perpetrated upon the government. The New York *Times* says on this subject:

> Senator Wilson says that he was deceived by three high officers of the government, by the Secretary of War, Cameron, by Paymaster General Larned, and by Quartermaster General Meigs. We stick a pin here, for there is a gravity in this matter that will require it to be probed to the bottom. We will not undertake to do it now, but it must be done hereafter. We merely wish to fix attention now on this point. There has long been a suspicion that a stupendous conspiracy for defrauding the government was covered up in fictitious muster rolls, filed in the War Department, but to the names on which no men ever answered in the field. Senator Wilson says he had "the assurances" of Paymaster Larned (Paymaster-General of the United States,) that 700,000 men were under pay of the government as soldiers. Now, Paymaster Larned deals with figures which are frequently said not to lie. Certainly we might lay something of Cameron's boast of 700,000 men to cabinet gasconade, but when it comes to alloting the money to pay off soldiers enrolled, there should be an approximation to certainty in the "assurances" of the officer performing that duty. Will Senator Wilson and Paymaster Larned anticipate the public demand, and explain the discrepancy that is so manifest and so startling?
>
> The difference in cost to the government, between the numbers reported and those actually in the field, was about $30,000,000 a month, and this margin is too wide to have escaped honest observation for a day, much less for months.

News of Our Own State.

Mrs. Swisshelm says the letter from which she acted in withdrawing Colonel Miller's name from the Congressional canvass, was a base forgery. Mrs. S. seems to be out of humor with everybody, since the prospects of her friend, the Colonel, were darkened. She copies Stanton's order about discouraging enlistments, and adds:

> Under this order, we trust that Mr. Stanton will at once proceed to arrest and imprison Abraham Lincoln, who, for the just punishment of our national crimes, is now President of these disunited States. No man breathing is doing so much as he to discourage volunteer enlistments. By act, speech and writing he is constantly discouraging enlistments. There is no end to the assertions about the unconquerable firmness of honest old Abe; but wherein his firmness consists we are unable to see, unless it is the unalterable fixedness with which he contradicts, today, all that he said yesterday, and the mulish determination with which he stultifies himself every time his Kentucky masters command him.

A son of Lieut. Col. Miller, of the First Minnesota, has enlisted in the Hickory Guards, Minneapolis, Captain Merriman, for the Sixth regiment. He is a graduate of Dickinson College, Pennsylvania' besides being a very clever fellow.

We learn from the Assessor of the town of Champlin that there is but fourteen men left in that town subject to militia duty. Hurrah for Champlin. Quite a number from that town have enlisted in the Anoka company.—*Minneapolis Advertiser.*

A paper numerously signed by citizens of Stearns and adjoining Counties has been sent to Governor Ramsey asking the appointment of Hon. George W. Sweet, of Benton County, as Major in the Seventh Regiment to be raised in this State.

The St. Cloud *Democrat* publishes the following extract from one of the captive officers of the Third Regiment. The author, we presume, is Capt. C. C. Andrews, of St. Cloud. It gives the facts already known of the surrender at Murfreesboro, and says:

> A majority of officers voted to surrender at 2½ o'clock P. M, before the regiment had a chance to fire at once. We had four pieces of artillery to support us. Lieutenant Colonel Griggs, Captain Forest, Captain Holt, Lieutenant Taylor, commanding company H, and myself were the only ones in favor of fighting. At the ballot however only three votes were cast against surrendering—Captain Foster and Lieutenant Taylor being for the minute absent. The men wanted to fight, and are grieved and indignant that they were not allowed to. The men actually shed tears on account of the surrender. So far we are politely treated. The forces in whose hands we are, men as well as officers, are gentlemen in behavior.

Winter Wheat.—Mr. Little, of Lime, has threshed his winter wheat, which yielded forty-seven bushels to the acre. The berry is unusually large and plump, and weighed sixty-seven pounds to the measured bushel. Persons desiring seed wheat can be supplied by Mr. Little.

Messrs. Robert and Theodore Heinze has left with us a sample of their winter wheat, equally as fine as Mr. Little's, and which yielded fifty-eight bushels to the acre. These gentlemen raised seven acres of this wheat, which at present prices will realize for them about $264.—*Mankato Record.*

News and Other Items.

—By the following dispatch of the Governor of Wisconsin it will be seen that all persons who have voted at our elections are subject to military duty:

> Madison, August 13.
>
> To E. H. Brodhead, or Lieutenant Colonel Page, Milwaukee:
>
> The Secretary of War says that all foreigners who have voted at our elections are regarded as having exercised a franchise that subjects them to military duty. A man who votes must bear arms.
>
> E. SALOMON,
> Governor of Wisconsin.

—The bearing and skill of Major General Banks in the battle of Saturday are mentioned with applause by the telegraph. "Banks," say the dispatches, "was on the field throughout the action and constantly under fire. His handling of his troops and personal gallantry are highly praised by his officers." The praise does not surprise us. Banks is no humbug. He is a genuine man. He is a successful man. He has succeeded excellently and eminently in everything he has ever undertaken. He is a strong, brave, quick, sagacious, live man. We have faith in him.—*Louisville Journal.*

—Exceedingly rich new diggings of lead have just been opened eight miles above Galena, by Mr. Wise. S. Hughlett bought one-half these diggings, paying therefor $5,000 in gold.

—The new gunboat made from the Star of the West has come out of the Yazoo, and is ready to take her place by the side of the Arkansas. She is called the Richmond. She is a formidable craft, mounted with a heavy armament and plated with eight-inch iron. She was a sea going steamer, captured by Van Dorn off the Texas coast in the beginning of the war.

—W. B. Allison, of Dubuque, Iowa, has been nominated by the Republicans in the district composed of the northeastern counties.

—Thurlow W. Seward, a son of Secretary Seward, who enlisted as a private a few weeks ago, has been honorably discharged from the service, to enable him to raise a company.

—Morrow B. Lowry, Senator from the Erie district (Pa.,) was indicted at General Sessions at Erie, for perjury. A Washington, D. C., firm of brokers are the prosecutors, and the offence is charged as having been committed in May last, in the form of an affidavit filed in court by Lowry, in a case wherein Messrs. David Paul Brown, of Philadelphia, and E. F. Collyer, of Pittsburgh, two of the best criminal lawyers in the country, appear for the prosecution.

—The Israelites of Chicago, in barely thirty-six hours' time, enlisted a company reaching beyond the maximum, of gallant strong-armed, stout-hearted men, who will make themselves felt in this war. The ladies have set an enduring example by their contributions, their earnest work and their hearty encouragement of recruits. In two days the Israelites have paid in over $11,000; in a day and a half have raised more than a full company and mustered it in; in one day the ladies have subscribed for and made a beautiful flag. Can any town, city or State in the North show an equally good two days' work? The Concordia Guards have our best wishes.

—The correspondent of the Philadelphia *Press* notices the conduct of the 9th Ohio regiment on learning of the murder of Gen. McCook, their old Colonel:

> They fired the dwellings and about twenty out-houses, and destroyed everything upon the grounds. Making complete work of this place, they destroyed all the dwellings in that section of the country, and hung thirteen residents of the neighborhood. I am informed that the scene was most fearful indeed. This regiment is celebrated for its uniform good conduct, and is composed wholly of Germans, who were illustriously instrumental in deciding the battle of Mill Spring. They were devoted in their love and regard for their gallant Colonel, many of whom wept bitterly at the sad termination of his life.

—The steamer Empire Parish, of New Orleans, was lately sent with a load of provisions for the starving inhabitants along the river. On arriving at Landry's plantation, the boat was fired on by rebels from the shore with a howitzer and small field pieces. This is a fair illustration of the manner in which rebels betray their affections for the hand that feeds them.

—As there are many persons who wish to communicate with the different bureaus of the War Department, a memorandum of the proper persons to address may be useful to our readers:

> All letters relating to pay of soldiers on furlough or in hospitals should be addressed to General B. F. Larned, Paymaster General.
>
> Applications for the back pay and the $100 bounty of deceased soldiers should be addressed to Hon. E. B. French, Second Auditor.
>
> Applications for pay of teamsters, employees of Quartermaster's Department, or for horses killed in service, should be addressed to Hon. R. I. Atkinson, Third Auditor.
>
> Applications relating to pay and bounty in the marine or naval services should be addressed to Hon. Hobart Berrian, Fourth Auditor.
>
> Letters concerning soldiers in the army should be addressed to Adjutant General Lorenzo Thomas.

—A private dispatch from Culpepper says that General Geary did not lose his arm in the late battle of Slaughter Mountain, as was reported.

—Senator Joseph A. Wright is stumping Indiana on the war question, and probably with a slight leaning towards the Union State ticket. His appointments run through the month of August.

—The race for the Goodwood, English, cup was won in a canter by Lord W. Powlett's horse "Tim Whiffler." The second horse was Zetland, about a dozen lengths behind the winner, and the Wizard was third. There were only seven runners, and Mr. TenBrock's American horse "Umpire" was about the last in the race.

THE NEW ENDEMIC.

To be rated "unsound"
Showeth wisdom profound,
But our *invalids* puzzle the craft;
For the common disease,
Incidental to these,
Is—an *ague fit*, caused by a *draft.*
—*N. Y. Sunday Times.*

—The correspondent of the New York *World* writes: "Gen. Banks made a desperate fight against fearful odds. An officer of the regular army, who was in frequent intercourse with him during the day, tells me he was always as cool and calm as when in the Speaker's chair, while shells or bullets were whizzing around him. Major Pelouze, of his staff, was wounded.

—A contemporary says the eyes of the loyal North are turned to the negroes of Rhode Island. The whites of them he means, we suppose.

—A correspondent of the *Traveller* suggests that in some way, by proclamation from the President or otherwise, all civil actions in law against those who enlist or are drafted in the army or navy, be suspended for one year or the war, and also all debts now due and the accumulation of interest on all debts, so that all, both creditors and debtors, may fare alike in sacrifices made for their country, then will there be one grand rush for the war.

—It is asserted that not less than eight iron-clad ships, most of them Monitors, are now in hand in New York city and vicinity alone. Two of these are very large vessels, and will not be ready for some time; but one of the new Monitors will be ready in a few days; one is promised by the 1st of September, and another in Captain Ericsson's hands, is to be ready in thirty days. On all these ships the work is going on night and day alike. On one four hundred men are constantly employed; one set of four hundred working by day and another all night. The work is pressed on as fast as possible.

—They say now in Washington that if one asks Mr. Stanton what is going to be done with McClellan's army he exclaims, "I am not General-in-Chief—I know nothing of such matters—ask Halleck!" If you ask the President a similar question, he replies, "You forget we have a General who commands all the armies, and makes all the plans to suit himself—ask him!" And then if you know Halleck and ask him you'll get the reply, "When you see a movement believe in it, and not before!"

—Surgeon—What's the matter with you?

Would-be-Exempt—Weak back, sir; very weak back.

S.—Weak knees, you mean.

W.—Yes, sir, weak knees; very weak knees; can't march.

S.—Yes, I'll give you a certificate—(writes:)

"Upon honor I hereby certify that the bearer, ———, is weak in the knees, a great coward, who shrinks from defending his country. Hope he will be put in the front ranks where he can't run away.

———, Surgeon," &c.

W.—(Handing the surgeon a quarter,) thank you, sir. I knew I was entitled to a certificate. This rebellion, so wicked and monstrous, must be put down. It has done my heart good to see the energy of the President in ordering a draft.

[Here reads the certificate and faints.]—*Hartford Times.*

—A recent census of lawyers in Connecticut gives 321 as the number. The Winsted *Herald* thinks they ought to enlist in a cavalry regiment, they are so good at charging.

—A New York paper says it knows of one young man, robust, vigorous and supposed to be of average respectability, who cut off the forefinger of his right hand to escape the draft. To escape the consequences of this cowardly act, says the New Bedford *Mercurg*, he will have to cut off the forefinger of everyone else.

—The new drafts will give the government one million of men, who can be placed in the field, if the civil officers of the loyal States do their duty, in time for the Fall campaign, fully armed and equipped. To understand the immensity of such a force, it would be necessary to see them drawn up in array. A line marching in single file, allowing two feet for each soldier, would stretch nearly three hundred and eighty miles, and marching at the rate of thirty miles per day, would occupy nearly two weeks in passing a given point; marching in sections of four, with the necessary room for baggage trains and cavalry, at the rate of thirty miles per day, they would extend one hundred and fifty miles, and the head of the column leaving a given point on Monday morning, the rear guard would not reach the same point till Friday night. One million of men on paper is easily expressed; to arm, equip, and feed such a host has never yet been essayed by a civilized people. So says an exchange.

—Some of the strongest Republican papers at the East are demanding the arrest of Wendell Phillips, for discouraging enlistments.

Local Affairs.

FEMALE PATRIOTISM.—The spirit which actuated our Revolutionary mothers, has been happily revived in the person of a beautiful German girl, of this city, under the following circumstances:

Previous to the present call of the President for more volunteers, our fair patriot was betrothed to a young German, of this city, and was to have been married on Monday last. When waited upon by her lover, she informed him that no closer intimacy could exist between them until he enlisted in the service of his country, as she had determined to either marry a soldier patriot or remain single. The result was the enlistment of the young German in the Siegel Guards yesterday, and the consummation of the nuptials of the happy pair, immediately afterwards, making their marriage tour to the country on a furlough. All honor to the brave German girl; and why may we not believe that she, like those we honor in the past, may receive her just dues in the future.

PRINTERS IN THE WAR.—From the subjoined list of names, taken from the muster-rolls of the several companies forming in this city, it will be seen that no class of artisans are so well represented as the printers. At the time of the Mexican war, they turned out to such an extent as to cause the suspension for a time of many of the leading journals of the country; and, at this time, the result will be the same. It has already seriously interfered with the proper transactions of the business in this city, as well as elsewhere. The printers who have enlisted here are all known to us, and they will unquestionably prove themselves as efficient in arms as they have been in the more quiet walks of civil life. Many on the list have been editors of newspapers in different sections of the country, and as a whole they are worthy and intelligent citizens, whose loss will be felt in the community. We wish them "God speed" in their patriotic movements. We give the names of those who have enlisted in this city under the six hundred thousand call: J. B. Bell, A. W. Delany, E. S. Lightbourn, M. B. Field, S. J. Weiting, A. P. Connelly, Aug. Erickson, O. P. Lane, Peter Exel, Peter Litner, Wm. Hill, E. Richards, Frank Moore, Charles Stewart, Wm. Defoe, Lee Davis, Michael Pendergast, Stephen Miller, Le Vinne P. Plummer, Erank E. Daggett, and Henry Jarvis. We will add thet, in addition to these, there are not less than twenty-five from this city in the other regiments now in the field.

MILITARY.—Yesterday our streets were thronged during the whole day with soldiers passing through on their way to the Fort to join the several regiments for which they were enlisted. We will not attempt to enumerate the various companies, for it was impossible to ascertain them correctly.

The steamer Canada arrived early in the morning, having on board Captain McLaren's company from Red Wing, consisting of 95 men; also, Lieutenant Philtrom's company from the same place, consisting of 83 men; and Lieutenant Hackett's company of Wabashaw county, consisting of 71 men. The boat proceeded to Fort Snelling and the three companies disembarked and and went into quarters. They were all fine looking men and will no doubt add to the honor which Minnesota's soldiers now have acquired.

The War Eagle arrived with 108 men from Red Wing, in command of Captain Bank; Captain Woodward also brought up 61 men from Houston county, all of whom went to the Fort yesterday forenoon.

The Union Guards, Captain Grant, went to the Fort yesterday morning and took up quarters. The company went into an election for Lieutenants in the afternoon; some dissatisfaction, however, arose among the members, so that they only proceeded to elect a First Lieutenant, when Henry Gillam was the unanimous choice.

The Winona company, Captain Curtis, arrived yesterday morning and went to the Fort soon after on the steamer Pomeroy. They paraded through our streets early in the morning and were cheered on every corner and square for their fine soldierlike appearance. Captain Curtis may be proud of such a company.

The Halleck Guards, Lieut. Gilfillan, last evening numbered ninety-four men. They were united with a part of a company from Sibley county.—*Daily of Tuesday.*

PRESENTED.—Lieut. Matthias Hall, of the Sigel Guards, was happily surprised Monday afternoon, on being presented with a splendid regulation sword, sash and belt, by Messrs. Borup & Champlin and Borup & Oakes. Lieut. H. had been in the employ of Messrs. B. & C. for a number of years, previous to joining the Guards, and he was very highly regarded by them. The sword was given as a token of respect. A note accompanied the sword, requesting him to use it, if possible, for the preservation of the Union. We know he will do it.

COMMISSIONED.—The following commissions have been issued by the Adjutant General since the 16th inst., for the 6th, 7th, 9th, 10th, and 11th Regiments:

Sixth Regiment.—Dana White, 1st Lieutenant Co. C—McClellan Guards.

H. P. Grant, Captain Co. A—Union Guards, St. Paul.

Henry A. Partridge, 2d Lieutenant Co. B—Hickory Guard.

Shephard H. King, 1st Lieut. Co. B.

E. E. Hughson, 1st Lieut. of Grenadiers.

Joseph C. Whitney, Captain Co. D.

D. Albaugh, 2d Lieutenant Co. D.

Orlando C. Merriman, Captain Co. B.

C. P. McAlexander, 2d Lieut. Co. C.

Seventh Regiment.—C. Cutler, Captain Co. A.

L. B. Hoag, 1st Lieutenant, Co. A.

Ninth Regiment—Wm. Shaw, 2d Lieutenant, Co. B.

John S. Cady, Captain Co. A.

M. Q. Butterfield, 1st Lieutenant Co. A. Company full.

N. Tibetts, 2d Lieutenant Co. A.

N. Hollister, 1st Lieutenant Co. B.

Geo. T. Pettit, Captain Co. B.

Tenth Regiment.—Edwin W. Ford, 1st Lieutenant, Co. A.

Lyman A. Sherwood, 2d Lieut. Co. A.

Eleventh Regiment.—R. C. Ambler, Captain Co. A.

Lewis F. Babcock, 1st Lieut. Co. A.

M. S. Strong, 2d Lieut. Co. A.

Commissions were issued yesterday to the officers elect of the Winona Rifles. Captain, John Curtis; 1st Lieutenant, H. H. Stevens; 2d Lieutenant, A. A. Rice.

ONE OF THE RIGHT KIND.—Captain Davidson of the Davidson line of steamers yesterday subscribed *Six Hundred Dollars* to the City and County War Fund, and remarked to a member of the committee if the amount was not sufficient they might take one of his boats. The public will appreciate such an act of generosity, and we shall be much mistaken if it does not prove the best investment the Captain ever made, even in a pecuniary sense.

GOOD FOR ONE FAMILY.—Another son of Mr. Alexander Wilson, of this city, has gone into the army, making five now in the different Minnesota regiments. There yet remain two sons, who are under sixteen years of age; but the old gentleman says if it be necessary to call for another from his family, he will go himself. If this ain't pluck, where will you find it?

MILITARY ELECTION.—The St. Croix Rangers organized at Fort Snelling Tuesday by electing Hon. Wm. H. Burt, of Stillwater, Captain; C. A. Winslow, First Lieutenant; Frank H. Pratt, of the Taylor Falls *Reporter*, Second Lieutenant. The company, we understand, is full to the maximum.

DAKOTA COUNTY TOEING THE MARK.—Captain John Kennedy, of Hastings, in connection with J. R. Huddleston, Prosecuting Attorney of the county, have raised a company to the maximum, and will be ready to report at Fort Snelling on Thursday.

STILL COMING.—A full company of volunteers from Olmsted county came up Tuesday morning by the Northern Light, and proceeded at once to Fort Snelling, and went into quarters. The company is made up principally of hardy young farmers, who, from their appearance, we should judge, will handle the musket as well as the plow.

THE Young Men's Guard have organized by electing David H. Valentine, Captain; George W. Prescott, First Lieutenant; Orlo Rogers, 1st Sergeant; J. B. Berrin, 2d Sergeant; B. F. Terry, 3d Sergeant; Henry Kneiff, 4th Sergeant: E. K. D. Randall, 5th Sergeant.

THE finest sample of winter wheat we have yet seen this season, we received yesterday from the farm of Mr. T. Hinge of Blue Earth county. Off of seven acres of land he produced 406 bushels, which averaged 67 pounds to the bushel. We are informed that the wheat crop of that county this year will average fifty bushels to the acre.

ST. PAUL TAKES THE COLORS AGAIN.—Lieut. Hammond Saturday assigned to the Union Guards, Capt. Grant, of this city, the position of Company A of the Sixth Regiment.

EDITORS ENLISTED.—Mart. Williams, Esq, of the St. Peter *Tribune*, has enlisted in the company from that place, and written his valedictory. If all our regiments were made up of material as gritty as our friend Williams, there would be "no more retreats, no more defeats." F. H. Pratt, Esq., of the Taylor's Falls *Reporter*, is a private in a company, recruited by Mr. Burt, from Washington and Chisago counties.

—The famous Massachusetts Sixth regiment has again determined to volunteer for the nine months call. It was this regiment that cut its way through Baltimore on the 19th of April, 1861, when the national capital was threatened by the rebels.

General Headquarters, State Minnesota.

GENERAL ORDERS, NO. 36.

ADJUTANT GENERAL'S OFFICE.
ST. PAUL, (MINNESOTA,) August 15, 1862.

In order to a clear understanding of the various orders issued by this office in relation to the Enrollment and Drafting of the Militia of the State of Minnesota, and in pursuance of further instructions recently received from the War Department, the officers heretofore appointed under General Orders No. 25, will be governed by the following instructions:

The agent appointed by the Commander-in-Chief, pursuant to General Order No. 25, shall immediately visit each town and city, and ascertain if the assessor has made proper militia returns in accordance with Orders Nos. 22, 23, and 25, and shall see that each assessor perfects his enrollment lists, or if the assessor fail or refuse to do so, the said agents shall proceed immediately to prepare the said enrollment lists, in accordance with the following instructions:

The said enrolling officer (assessor or agent) shall prepare a list of all white male citizens between the ages of 18 and 45, whether presumed to be exempt or not, by reason of physical disability or any other cause—stating, however, in the return under the head of general remarks, the nature of any apparent bodily defect, or presumed disqualification, and if in the service of the United States, state the capacity.

In case any doubt exists as to the age of the party, his name is to be taken. All foreign born persons who have declared their intentions to become citizens of the United States, are to be included in the returns; and in any case where doubt exits whether a foreign born person has been naturalized, or has declared his intention to become a citizen, his name must be taken.

The names of all persons who have enlisted from each township since July 2d, 1862, under the recent calls for 600,000 men, and the designation of the regiment and company in which they have severally enlisted, are to be carefully ascertained and reported, by inquiring of each head of a family, and by such other means of information as are accessible to the agent or assessor.

The enrolling officers (agents or assessors) of each county must file their enrollment lists in the office of the Sheriff of the county on or before the 24th instant, and must therefore immediately notify the Commissioner that said lists have been filed.

See Sec. 5 of General Order No. 25, for the duties of Commissioners. The Commissioner will not, however, fix the time at which the draft shall be made as provided in General Order No. 25. In pursuance of a more recent order of the War Department, the date at which drafting shall commence is hereby fixed on Wednesday, the third day of September next.

In determining the sufficiency of proofs offered by persons claiming exemption, the Commissioner will strike none from the lists, except (1) those producing a certificate of disability, signed by the Surgeon appointed for that purpose. (2.) Such persons as are included in the second subdivision of section 5 of General Order No. 25; (3) such persons as shall furnish clear and satisfactory proof that they are not of the prescribed age—or (4) foreign born persons not naturalized, or who have not declared their intentions to become citizens. Persons known to have exercised the rights of suffrage, shall be presumed to be liable to military duty, unless the contrary be shown.

In examining a candidate for an exemption, the examining physician will be governed by article 1261 of the army regulations, which is in the following language:

"In passing a recruit, the medical officer is to examine him stripped; to see that he has free use of all his limbs; that his chest is ample; that his hearing, vision and speech are perfect; that has no tumors, or ulcerated, or extensively cicatrised legs; no rupture or chronic cutaneous affection; that he has not received any contusion or wound of the head, that may impair his features; that he is not a drunkard, is not subject to convulsions, and has no infectious disorders nor any other that may unfit him for military service."

The agents, commissioners and surveyors appointed under General Order No. 25, for certain bounties, will act also for the counties attached to them in pursuance of General Order No. 35, under which the said officers were appointed, and in apportioning the quotas among the several counties, all counties so attached will, with the county to which they are attached, be held as one county.

The Auditor of the county shall immediately upon the filing of the enrollment lists in his office, or before the 26th day of August, forward by special messenger to the Adjutant General a statement of the whole number of persons enrolled in each township, with the regiment and company in which each has enlisted.

It is necessary that the enrollment lists be completed and promptly forwarded to this office by the time designated in order that the Governor may, if the War possible, apportion the quotas of the several counties on the basis of the enrolled numbers in each, in time for the draft in pursuance of a recent order of the War Department.

In case, however, the quota of each county, on the basis of the enrolled militia, should not be ascertained in time for the draft on the third day of September, the quota of each county is hereby provisionally fixed at one-thirty-second of the population of said county according to the census of 1860, less the number of volunteers furnished since July 2d.

In view of the shortness of the time intervening before the day fixed by the General Government for the draft, it is now found impossible to apportion the quotas of the counties with any reference to the number of volunteers previously to the 2d of July.

The quota, however ascertained, shall be apportioned by the county auditor, subject to an appeal to the Commissioner, among the several townships in proportion to the number of enrolled militia of each township; and in such apportionment, each township shall be credited with the number of volunteers which it shall have furnished since the 2d of July.

By order of the Commander-in-Chief.

OSCAR MALMROS,
aug17 Adjutant-General.

General Headquarters, State Minnesota.

ADJUTANT-GENERAL'S OFFICE,
ST. PAUL, Minnesota, August 19, 1862.

SPECIAL ORDERS, NO. 19.

In view of reported Indian difficulties in the counties of Meeker, Brown and Renville, calling for the immediate interference of the Government, Col. Henry H. Sibley is hereby directed to take charge of a military expedition for their prompt suppression, and to restore the peace and quiet in those settlements.

I. Col. Smith, commanding the place of General Rendezvous, at Fort Snelling, will forthwith detail four companies of his command to be placed under charge of Col. Sibley.

II. Col. Sibley will proceed without delay with said four companies to our frontier, and will collect in addition on the way such forces of mounted infantry as he may deem advisable.

III. Col. Sibley is hereby authorized to provide all necessary subsistence and transportation for the troops under his command.

IV. Capt. Webb will act as Adjutant to Col. Sibley.

V. Mr. Mills is hereby appointed Quarter-Master for this expedition.

By order of the Commander-in-Chief.

OSCAR MALMROS,
Adjutant General.

[Special Dispatch to Governor Johnson, Nashville.]

Brilliant Series of Engagements at Cumberland Gap, by General George W. Morgan, with the Rebels.

Telegraphed from Cumberland Gap.

AUGUST 9, 1862.

To His Excellency Andrew Johnson:

GOVERNOR:—On the 5th and 6th instant, De Courcey's brigade, with the 14th Kentucky, had a series of brilliant affairs with Stevenson's division in entire force. The enemy outnumbered De Courcey four to one.

The enemy lost two hundred and twenty-five, and Lieut. Col. Gordon, of the Eleventh Tennessee, was taken prisoner. We captured two hundred wagon loads of forage, twelve hundred pounds of tobacco, and thirty horses and mules. We lost three killed, fifteen wounded and fifty prisoners. Two companies of the Sixteenth Ohio were surrounded by the rebel regiments, but two-thirds of them cut their way through.

John Morgan, at the head of two thousand cavalry, left Knoxville for Kingston about the 2d instant. It is rumored that Kentucky is to be invaded.

GEORGE W. MORGAN,
Brigadier General.

HEADQUARTERS U. S. FORCES,
COLUMBIA, TENN., Aug. 11, '62—3 P. M.

My movements against the guerillas who have committed the late outrage, has been completely successful. Major McGowan, in command of the Third Kentucky Cavalry and First Tennessee Cavalry, numbering one hundred and eight men, engaged one hundred and seventy-five of the enemy, near Kinderhook, at 5 A. M., continuing the contest fiercely for four hours. Seven were found killed and a large number were wounded. Twenty-seven prisoners were captured, among which are a number of officers. Our loss was three killed. The woody and broken character of the country, and the combattants being scattered, prevents an actual estimate of the rebel loss.

I have received news from Maj. S. H. Kennedy of my staff, commanding another portion of the expedition. He is driving the enemy in every direction.

JAS. S. NEGLEY,
Brigadier General Commanding.

Ex-U. S. Senator Nicholson Sent Beyond the Lines.

From the Nashville Union.

The following order strikes a blow in the right quarter. Col. Nicholson is a man of wealth and influence, and has been highly honored by the government; yet, forgetful of his duty, he has repaid the kindness of his countrymen by plunging them in civil war:

HEADQUARTERS U. S. FORCES,
COLUMBIA, Tennessee, July 29, 1862.
[Extract.]

SPECIAL ORDER, NO. 141.—Hon. A. O. P. Nicholson, late United States Senator, and Colonel Joseph Branch, both citizens of Maury county, in the State of Tennessee, avowed sympathizers with the so called Southern Confederacy, who openly refuse to declare their future allegiance to the Federal Government, are deemed unworthy of enjoying any of the inestimable privileges of a citizen of these United States. Therefore, it is ordered that the said A. O. P. Nicholson and Col. Joseph Branch do each take the oath of allegiance, accompanied with a bond and proper security, conditioned for his faithful observance of said oath of allegiance. If they, or either of them, refuse to take the oath and give bond as aforesaid, then such one so refusing shall give his individual bond in the penal sum of ten thousand dollars ($10,000) additional, that he will immediately go beyond the Federal lines, and that he will remain without the same during the continuance of the present rebellion. If either of them giving such bonds should return, in violation of its provisions, he will, in addition to the forfeiture of his bond, be arrested as a spy and treated accordingly. By command.

Brigadier General NEGLEY,
Commanding Post.
JAMES LOWRIE, Captain and A. A. G.

Review of the St. Paul Markets

Prepared expressly for the PIONEER AND DEMOCRAT, *and Corrected by our own Reporter*

ST. PAUL, Aug. 20, 1862.

WHEAT. Prime No. 1, 60@65c; milling 70c
RYE. 25a30c ℔ bushel.
BARLEY 40@45 do
OATS. 35 do
CORN. 35c do
TIMOTHY. $2 ℔ bushel.
FLOUR. Superfine $3 00, extra $4 00.
CORN MEAL. ℔ bag 90c.
BEANS. White ℔ bushel $1.
BUTTER. Firkin ℔ ℔ 6a8c, country, in rolls, 8a10c.
MESS PORK. ℔ bbl, $10.
MESS BEEF. ℔ bbl, $10a11.
BACON. Sugar cured7a8c, canvassed, 10a11c, plain 5a6c, shoulders, 4a5, c.
DRIED BEEF. 12a13c ℔ ℔.
LARD. ℔ ℔, 6a7c.
SUGAR, N O, ℔ ℔, 10½a12c, Havana 10a10½, refined, A & B, 13a14, Cuba, refined, 11½a12, Loaf, crushed and powdered, 14½.
TEAS Black 40a90c; Green Tea 80a1,25.
COFFEE. Prime Rio per lb. 24a25c, Laguayra 25c, Java 30c.
RICE, ℔ ℔ 8½c.
SALT, Prime article, $2 50 ℔ bbl.
EGGS, ℔ doz 8a10c.
FRUITS, Green Apples ℔ bbl $3 50a3 75; dried, ℔ ℔ 7 1-2a8 1-2c; Peaches, 9a12 1-2c; Cranberries, ℔ bush. 75a100c; Raisins $3 50a3 75 ℔ box; half boxes, $2; Prunes, 9 1-12a10 1-2; Curants, 12a15c; Almonds, 11a18c.
FISH. No. 1 Mackerel, ℔ bbl $20; No. 2 $14; No. 3, $14. Dry Cod, ℔ cwt $6 50a7 50. Scaled Herring, ℔ box, 75c.
CANDLES. Mould Tallow, 10c ℔ ℔; Star 15a16; Adamantine, 20c; Sperm, 40a50
TALLOW. Rendered 7@7½, unrendered 5c.
CHEESE. W. R. ℔ ℔ 9a10; E. D, 11a12c.
WHISKEY. Rectified Common, ℔ gal, 28a30. Monongahela, 50a75c; Old Bourbon, 50a75
CIDER. ℔ bbl 7 50a$8; Tierces, $10.
POTATOES. Neshannocks and pink eyes, ℔ bushel, 25a30c. Mixed lots, 20c.
ONIONS, ℔ bush, 25a35c.
OILS. Carbon, ℔ gal., 40a50c. Whale, 85a90c. Neatsfoot, $1 50. Lard, 85a95c. Linseed $1. Turpentine, $1 50.
WHITE LEAD, ℔ cwt., $7 50a8 50.
MOLASSES. Plantation ℔ gal., 50a55c. Sugar House, 55a58c. Golden Syrup, 75a80c.
LEAD AND SHOT. Pig ℔ ℔ 7c. Bar 8c. Shot ℔ bag, $1 90.
LIME. Prime Point Byron, $1 50. Alton, $1 25.
SOAPS. Common ℔ ℔ 4½a5c. Family, 5½c Palm, 5½a6c. Castile, 14a16c.
GLASS. American Window, 8x10, $2 00a2,25. 10x12, $2 25a2 50. 10x14, $2 50a2 75. 10x16 to 12x16, $2 75a3 00. 12x18 to 12x20. 4 00a5 00. Per ton, about $8 00a10 00.
POWDER, FFG and FFFG 25 ℔ kegs $8.50, 12½ ℔ kegs 4.50, 6¼ ℔ kegs 2.50.
SPORTING, In tin kegs, 6¼ lbs 5.00.
EAGLE RIFLE, In cases of 25 canisters of 1 ℔ each, $14; Half do 9; Quarter do 7.50.
DIAMOND GRAIN, in cases of 12 canisters of 1 pound each, $10.
RIFLE AND SPORTING, In cases of 25 canisters, half pound each, $8, 12 canisters one pound each, 6.50; 25 canisters one pound each, 12.
BLASTING. 25 ℔ kegs, $6; Half kegs 3.25; Quarter kegs, 1.75.
IRON Flat Bar, Pennsylvania, all sizes under 4½a1 inch ℔ ℔ 5c; Juniata do 7c.
STEELE English Cast, ℔ ℔ 25c; English Spring 10c; American do 10c; English Blister 20c; American do 12½c.
HIDES Dry $10½a11½; Green $4½a4½.
LUMBER Common inch ℔ m $8a12½; clear $20a25; Siding $16a20; Flooring $16a20; Lath $1,50; Shingles $2 25a300;
COAL. Pittsburgh ℔ bushel 60a75c; Illinois 40c.
CORDAGE. Manilla ℔ ℔a1312½c; Jute 9a10c.
CRACKERS. Butter ℔ bbl $5 50a6; Water $4 50; Soda and Boston $6a7; Pilot Bread $3 50

New York Market.

By *Telegraph.*] NEW YORK, Aug. 19.

The market dull and drooping. Sales 9,000 barrels flour.

Milwaukee Market.

MILWAUKEE, Aug. 19.

FLOUR very dull.

WHEAT unchanged and dull, 97c@$1 00. Receipts 500 barrels flour.

MARRIED.

On Thursday, August 7, 1862, at the residence of the bride's father, in Waseator, Minn., by Rev. George Stewart, Hon. OSCAR TAYLOR, of St. Cloud, Minn., to CLARRIE E., eldest daughter of M. Wright, Esq.

Od the 16th instant, by Fleet F. Strother, Esq., Mr. JOSEPH EHERN te Miss DORA BOLLMAN, both of this city.

In this city, on Tuesday evening, at the residence of Hon. J. P. Kidder, by Rev. S. Hawley, Mr. CHRISTOPHER L. GRANT and Miss SARAH McEVOY, all of Saint Paul.

DIED.

In this city, Friday evening, at his residence on Wabashaw street, Mr. WILLIAM SCOTT, aged about 50 years.

THE WEEKLY
Pioneer and Democrat.

VOL. XIV.—NO. 11. SAINT PAUL, FRIDAY, AUGUST 29, 1862. NEW SERIES—NO. 455

TO MY CHILDREN.

[This is a very exquisite poem, which was written in camp, after battle, and sent by a soldier father to his children at home. It will stir good thoughts at any fireside to read it aloud.]

Darlings, I am weary pining ;
Shadows fall across my way ;
I can hardly see the lining
Of the cloud—the silver lining
Turning darkness into day.

I am weary of the sighing,
Moaning, wailing through the air ;
Breaking hearts, in anguish crying
For the lost one—for the dying,
Sobbing anguish of despair.

I am weary of the fighting—
Brothers red with brother's gore ;
Only that the *wrong* were righting—
Truth and Honor's battle fighting—
I would draw my sword no more.

I am pining, dearest, pining
For your kisses on my cheek ;
For your dear arms round me twining ;
For your soft eyes on me shining ;
For your loved words, darlings speak !

Tell me, in your earnest prattle,
Of the olive-branch and dove ;
Call me from the cannon's rattle :
Take my thoughts away from battle,
Fold me in your dearest love.

Darlings, I am weary pining ;
Shadows fall across my way ;
I can hardly see the lining
Of the cloud—the silver shining
Turning darkness into days.

An Incident in the South.

A TENNESSEE SOLDIER SHOT BY THE REBELS.

The New Orleans *Delta* has the following narrative of the shooting of a Tennessee soldier in the rebel army in Mississippi :

A lady of the first standing in New Orleans having obtained a passport to visit the camp of the rebel army where her two sons were serving, was entertained at headquarters and found that General Van Dorn and his staff officers fared sumptuously, living on the "fat of the land." But the common soldiers had only bread and molasses for their fare.

It so happened that while this lady was with the confederates the time for which a certain Tennessee regiment had enlisted expired, and the soldiers, anxious to see their wives and little ones once more, began to make preparations to start home.

The general, in making his rounds, and seeing the men of his regiment busily engaged in making preparations for their intended departure, inquired what it meant ; and on being made acquainted with their determination, he immediately gave orders that not a single man of them should leave his encampment. The whole brigade or division of the army was at once ordered under arms ; cannon and musketry were brought to bear on this devoted regiment, and they were told by the general that unless they took up their arms which they had thrown down, within three minutes they should be fired on. With death thus staring them in the face, they obeyed the order to take up their arms all but eight. It was decreed that these eight should be court martialed and shot.

Before the time came that the military court was to be held, seven out of the eight followed the example of their comrades, and agreed to resume their arms. One soldier alone remained firm in his purpose ; one soldier alone was willing to brave death rather than yield to the despotic demands of a tyrant.

He pleaded his own cause with all the fervor of which a soldier is capable. Said he to his general : "I have served out the time for which I have enlisted faithfully; I have been in every battle; I have been at all times at the post of duty assigned me, in rain and sunshine, in summer and winter. I have served and I am willing to serve my country. But, General, I have a wife and four small children at home, who depend upon me for support and protection and who have no one besides me to look to their interests. Allow me thirty days, the law allows a furlough of sixty days, but allow me half that time to visit my family, whom I have not seen for one year, and make some necessary arrangements for their welfare, and I promise to return within that time and to take my former position in my regiment. I make but a just and reasonable request. It is essential to the welfare of my family that you grant it. I cannot enter the service again till I have visited my family."

He was sentenced to be shot. The decree was pronounced on Saturday, and was to have been executed on the next day—the Sabbath—a suitable day for such a deed. The soldier and hero, for he was a hero, and by far the bravest man in the regiment, asked for a little longer time to make the preparation necessary in order to enter into the presence of his God ; and the time was graciously extended one day, so that the sentence was executed on Monday, instead of the Sabbath.

When the fatal hour arrived, following his coffin, which was in full view, he was marched to the place of execution, and arrived there, the general pointed him to the new made grave and commanded him to kneel down upon the margin of that grave. The soldier and martyr simply replied that he had never kneeled to any but his Maker, and that he could not consent to kneel now to a man. As he said this the order was given to fire, and in the act of making the sign of the cross on his breast the martyr and soldier was in eternity. But there were many, unaccustomed to weep, who shed bitter tears on witnessing this tragedy.

Military Executions in Missouri.

From the Palmira (Mo.,) Courier, Aug. 15

Among the prisoners captured in the fight at Kirkirsville were found fifteen who had taken the oath of allegiance—sworn not to take up arms against the United States or the Provisional Government of this State. These men were tried at drum head court martial, and the evidence of their guilt being indisputable, they were sentenced to be shot. Colonel McNeil approved the sentence, signed the death warrant, and every one of them was shot on Thursday. This proceeding, though severe, was eminently just, and right ; and the whole civilized world will sustain Col. McNeil in it.

On Thursday afternoon, the day after the battle, eight or ten of the newly enrolled militia of Edina were out on a private scout of their own, looking for the stragglers from Porter's main body. Eight miles from Edina they captured Colonel Frisbie H. McCulloch, who had abandoned Porter, and was now alone making his way eastward. On arriving at Kirksville next morning, the news of the capture of this famous guerilla excited the utmost enthusiasm among our troops.

He was confined a brief time with other prisoners. Meantime a court martial was held, and he was sentenced to be shot that very afternoon. He received the information of his fate with considerable composure, but protested against it. Leaning against the fence he wrote a few lines to his wife. These, with his watch, he delivered to the officer to be given to her. Upon the way to his execution he requested the privilege to give the command to fire, which was granted. All being ready, he said, "What I have done, I have done as a principle of right. Aim at the heart. Fire !"

The command taking the soldiers by surprise, one fired sooner than the rest. The ball entering the breast he fell, while the other shots passed over him. Falling with one leg doubled under the body, he requested to have it straightened out. While this was being done he said, "I forgive you for this barbarous act." The squad having reloaded their pieces, another volley was fired—this time into his body, and he died. His remains were committed to friends in the place.

Return of the Sir John Franklin Expedition.

St. Johns, N. F., August 22.

The bark George Henry, of New London, Captain Burlington, from Frobisher's Bay, has arrived here short of provisions, and with Mr. Hall, of the new Sir John Franklin Expedition, on board. The expedition lost one man the first winter out. He froze to death. Mr. Hall reports that, in consequence of the loss of some of his craft, he was unable to prosecute his mission to the extent of its purpose. The expedition has probably determined the fate of two boats' crews' of Sir John Franklin's expedition, who perished in endeavoring to return. Mr. Hall learned the fate of five men captured from Frobisher on his first voyage, and identified the exact place of their landing. Mr. Hall explored nearly a thousand miles of coast, including the so called Frobisher's Straits, which prove to be a deep bay, terminating in lat. 63:48, long. 73 west. Mr. Hall also discovered a great glacier and mountain of fossils between Hudson's Straits and Frobisher's Bay. The George Henry was about to start for the States in October, 1861, but was prevented doing so by ice until the 9th inst. The ships' company subsisted through last winter by the hospitality of the Esquimaux.

General Banks

The correspondent of the Philadelphia *Press* with General Pope's army :

General Banks is gradually recovering from the injuries he received on the battlefield, and it is hoped he will soon be able to take the field. If any one doubted General Banks' military ability, they are forever silenced. No man could have managed troops better or behaved better than Major General Banks, and the compliment paid him by General Pope is duly appreciated, no less by his men than himself. No man has had more bitter enemies than General Banks, yet he has withstood nobly the storm that continually gathered around him, and he has now by his brilliant achievement, stamped himself as one of the most accomplished military leaders in the Union army. No matter in what position he has been placed he has conducted himself like a true gentleman and brave soldier.

—Mr. Allen formerly a United States Senator from Ohio, and one of the most prominent Democrats of that State, recently made a war speech in Ohio, in which he urged a most vigorous prosecution of the war, and a cordial support of the Administration.

Archbishop Hughes' War Sermon.

On Sunday last, in New York City, Archbishop Hughes preached to a crowded congregation at St Patrick's, in exposition of his recent visit to and protracted sojourn in Europe. After speaking of the religious solemnities which occasioned the gathering of so many prelates in "the cathedral church of Christendom," he avowed that his time been largely devoted to the diffusion of correct ideas of our great civil war, and the principles involved, with the correction of prevalent misapprehensions. He intimated that he found the influential classes very generally unfriendly to the Union cause on various grounds, which generally resolved themselves into this—it is the interest of Europe (that is, of its governing classes) that the United States should no longer exhibit the spectacles of growth, prosperity, and power hitherto presented. Interest controls political attachments and antipathies, and the Archbishop, though he believed he had dispelled some misconceptions, did not intimate that he had been able to dispel the desire of the royalists and aristocracies of the Old World that our country should be divided and crippled. He thought, however, that the danger of forcible intervention to our prejudice had passed unless the contest should be unreasonably protected. As to the vigorous prosecution of the war he made the following capital points:

But there is one thing and one question that should be clear to every mind. It is this—that if a war of this kind should be continued for many years, it is recognized as being allowable for other nations to combine in their strength and put an end to it. Better for the people themselves to put an end to it with as little delay as possible. It is not a scourge that has visited us alone. From the beginning of the world wars have been—nation against nation—and oftentimes the most terrible of all wars, which is not a war of nation against nation, but of brother againt brother. How long is this to go on ? If it goes on, what is to be the result of it, as affording a pretext for all the powers of Europe to combine to put an end to it ? And although I would not say that even then they should not be permitted to interfere when they interfered through benevolence, and above all, when the sword might be put at rest; but I do say to every man, if they do interfere, and if they interfere successfully—if the country and the government are not maintained by every sacrifice that is necessary to maintain them, then your United States will become a Poland—then it will become divided—then the strife will multiply across every border; every State or every section will claim to be independent and make itself an easy prey for those who will turn and appropriate the divisions of the people of this country for their own advantage. Oh ! let it not be so. I know little of what has tianspired here during my absence. I have had scarcely time to look at the papers since I returned. But at all events, much has been done, though not much has been realized towards terminating this unfortuate war. Volunteers have been appealed to in advance of the draft, as I understand, but for my own part, if I had a voice in the councils of the country, I would say, let volunteering continue ; if the three hundred thousand on your list be not enough this week, next week make a draft of three hundred thousand more. It is not cruel, this. This is mercy ; this is humanity. Any thing that will put an end to this drenching with blood the whole country—that will be humanity. Then, every man on the continent, rich or poor, will have to take his share in the contest. Then it will not be left to the government, whatever government it will be, to plead with the people and call on them to come forward, and ask them if they would be drafted. No, it is for them, the people to rise and ask the government to draft them ; and those who are wealthy and cannot go themselves, can provide substitutes and bring the thing to a close, if it can be done. No doubt the same efforts will be made on the other side—and who can blame them ? For the sake of humanity we must resort to some course of this kind. In the meanwhile, beloved brethren, it is enough for us to weep for this calamity, to pray God that it may be put to an end, to make sacrifice of everything that we have to sustain the independence, the unity, the perpetuity, the prosperity of the only government we acknowledge in the world. But it is not necessary to hate our enemies. It is not necessary to be cruel in battle, nor to be cruel after its termination. It is necessary to be true, to be patriotic, to do for the country what the country needs, and the blessing of God will recompense those who discharge their duty without faltering, and without violating any of the laws of God or man.

—There was frost in Dedham, Milton, Dorchester and Quincy, Massachusetts, in damp localities, on Sunday morning last.

Important Letter of President Lincoln.

Last week the New York *Tribune* contained a letter which purported to express the sentiments of eleven millions of people, but only bore the signature of Horace Greeley. It was addressed to the President of the United States, and accused that officer of violating his official oath in not enforcing the confiscation bill according to Greeley's notions. We are surprised to see the following reply from Mr. Lincoln :

Executive Mansion,
Washington, August 23, 1862.

To Hon. Horace Greeley :

Dear Sir—I have just received yours of the 19th inst., addressed to myself through the New York *Tribune*. If there be it in any statements or assumptions of facts which I may know to be erroneous, I do not now and here controvert them. If there be any inferences which I may believe to be falsely drawn, I do not now and here argue against them. If there be perceptible in it an impatient and dictatorial tone, I waive it in deference to an old friend whose heart I have always supposed to be right.

As to the policy I seen to be pursuing, as you say, I have not meant to leave any one of you in doubt. I would save the Union; I would save it in the shortest way under the Constitution. The sooner the national authority can be restored, the nearer the Union will be the Union as it was. If there be those who would not save the Union unless they could at the same time save slavery, I do not agree with them. If there be those who would not save the Union, unless they could at the same time destroy slavery, I do not agree with them.

My paramount object is to save the Union, and not either to save or destroy slavery. If I could save the Union without freeing any slaves, I would do it ; and if I could save it by freeing all the slaves, I would do it ; and if I could save it by freeing some and leaving others alone, I would also do that. What I do about slavery and the colored race, I do because I believe it helps to save this Union ; and what I for bear, I forbear because I do not believe it would help to save the Union. I shall do less whenever I shall believe what I am doing hurts the cause, and I shall do more whenever I believe doing more will help the cause. I shall try to correct errors when shown to be errors, and I shall adopt new views so fast as they shall appear to be true views.

I have here stated my purpose, according to my view of official duty, and I intend no modification of my oft expressed personal wish—that all men, everywhere, could be free. Yours,

A. LINCOLN.

The President has evidently deemed it a good opportunity, as well as an appropriate time, to reiterate what the people have almost been persuaded out of, that his purpose in this war is, as it has been, not to perpetuate nor to overthrow slavery, but to maintain the Constitution and preserve the Union; and that his "policy" is whatever in his judgment will best hasten and accomplish those ends. This he does, so clearly, that the public mind will be brought back to "first principles" on the subject.

Breckinridge on the Double Quick.

From the New Orleans Delta, Aug. 9.

The "time made" by Breckinridge's shoddy followers on the morning of the 5th, in their retreat from Baton Rouge, deserves public attention. They began the retreat at ten o'clock, and at twelve they were ten miles distant from the scene of their inglorious repulse. This is certainly the "best time on record." Mr. Breckinridge always ran well before the people. He undestands running. On this occasion he ran to fight another day, perhaps : but it is our judgment, Jefferson Davis, when he hears of this exploit, will hang him up to dry, right beside Mansfield Lovell. Why not ? Breckinridge is no more of a soldier than Lovell. But let us forget him. He is the meanest rebel ever raised in Kentucky.

Just think of it. He had fifteen regiments of infantry, a body of cavalry and ten pieces of artillery, and yet he was pushed off the field by a force one-fourth his number.

To our apprehension, this fight at Baton Rouge is, in its results, one of the most signal victories of the war. What with the total rout of the ragged starvlings of Breckinridge the "skedaddling party," as some body styled them yesterday—and the destruction of the ram Arkansas, the day deserves to be remembered.

—The Providence *Post* says: "In passing through the Worcester freight depot on Wednesday, we observed some fifteen or twenty cases marked "Le Grand Maitre d'Artillerie, Cronstadt," and upon inquiry learned that they contained American rifles bound to Russia. The arms were manufactured at Milbury, Mass., for the Russian government, and large quantities have been shipped during the past year."

Garibaldi and Italy.

THE KING'S PROCLAMATION.

The following is the official text of Victor Emanuel's proclamation against Garibaldi's new movement, issued on the 3d of August:

Italians !—At the moment when Europe renders homage to the wisdom of the nation, and recognizes its rights, it is painful to see inexperienced and misled youths forgetting their duty and the gratitude due to our best allies, putting forward as a signal for war the name of Rome—that name to which all our efforts have been tending. Faithful to the Constitution sworn by me, I have held aloft the flag of Italy, rendered sacred by the blood and glorious by the valor of my people, who will not follow that which violates the laws, and gives a severe blow to liberty and to the security of the country, by constituting itself the judge of its destiny. Italians, be on your guard against culpable acts of impatience and imprudent agitation. When the hour of accomplishing our great work shall have struck, the voice of your King will make itself heard amongst you. Every invitation to rise which does not proceed from him is an ap
peal to re
sponsibili
ity of the
do not lis
claimed b
my duty,
in its int
and the p
have a ri
and entir
(Signe
(Counte

On th
following
youth of
"Your
our coun
out askin
upon you
fight agai
only of P
fidence.
and trou
your self-
oh ! muti
It is unne
the fight
discipline
The Rom
bled to b
Strive to
as you kr
the esteer
bring abc
this occa
be the fo
which the
"Bois F

GARIBA
The *Ita*
of the R
they say
the land
for delive
is Gariba
"Rom
I have be
lovely slo
of the Al
oath take
and Pale
by calling
could the
in the be
Rome, th
been buri
nated wit
the world
people a
Rome the
it not its
ruins, tha
flame of t
ous design
not urged
for thy
thus has r
a mother,
a one has
original c
death."

GARI
A corr
dance con
has issued
the Solav
if his lang
that it is
an expedi
ian patrio
to an app
rise in ins

—Dani
Massachu
the Eight
at the bat
the rebels
day. Ju
half allow
savage, a
our men
even spar
statement
part of t
tract of
Richmon
rebels are

REQUIEM.

Breathe, trumpets, breathe,
Slow notes of saddest wailing—
Sadly responsive peal
Ye muffled drums—
Comrades, with downcast eyes
And muskets trailing,
Attend him home—
The youthful warrior comes.

Upon his shield,
Upon his shield returning,
Borne from the field of honor
Where he fell—
Glory and Grief, together clasped
In mourning,
His fame, his fate,
With sobs exulting tell.

Wrap round his breast
The flag his breast defended—
His country's flag
In battle's front unrolled ;
For it he died—
On earth forever ended,
His brave young life
Lives in each sacred fold.

With proud fond tears,
By tinge of shame untainted
Bear him, and lay him
Gently in his grave ;
Above the hero write,
The young, half-sainted—
His country asked his life,
His life he gave.

Important Letter of President Lincoln.

Last week the New York *Tribune* contained a letter which purported to express the sentiments of eleven millions of people, but only bore the signature of Horace Greeley. It was addressed to the President of the United States, and accused that officer of violating his official oath in not enforcing the confiscation bill according to Greeley's notions. We are surprised to see the following reply from Mr. Lincoln :

Executive Mansion,
Washington, August 23, 1862.

To Hon. Horace Greeley :

Dear Sir—I have just received yours of the 19th inst., addressed to myself through the New York *Tribune*. If there be it in any statements or assumptions of facts which I may know to be erroneous, I do not now and here controvert them. If there be any inferences which I may believe to be falsely drawn, I do not now and here argue against them. If there be perceptible in it an impatient and dictatorial tone, I waive it in deference to an old friend whose heart I have always supposed to be right.

As to the policy I seen to be pursuing, as you say, I have not meant to leave any one of you in doubt. I would save the Union; I would save it in the shortest way under the Constitution. The sooner the national authority can be restored, the nearer the Union will be the Union as it was. If there be those who would not save the Union unless they could at the same time save slavery, I do not agree with them. If there be those who would not save the Union, unless they could at the same time destroy slavery, I do not agree with them.

My paramount object is to save the Union, and not either to save or destroy slavery. If I could save the Union without freeing any slaves, I would do it ; and if I could save it by freeing all the slaves, I would do it ; and if I could save it by freeing some and leaving others alone, I would also do that. What I do about slavery and the colored race, I do because I believe it helps to save this Union ; and what I for bear, I forbear because I do not believe it would help to save the Union. I shall do less whenever I shall believe what I am doing hurts the cause, and I shall do more whenever I believe doing more will help the cause. I shall try to correct errors when shown to be errors, and I shall adopt new views so fast as they shall appear to be true views.

I have here stated my purpose, according to my view of official duty, and I intend no modification of my oft expressed personal wish—that all men, everywhere, could be free. Yours,

A. LINCOLN.

pondent of
rom Paris,

urally, de-
ation from
elated at
But here is
A lead-
nversation
an affairs,
a strong
nition, and
rine of the
ould be no
onfederacy
anteed the
ination of
cannot be
onfederacy
stone, and
ng for, he
of recog-
So that the
s extremi-
ny persons
repared to
ather than
govern-
then have
acle of the
to destroy
g to abol-
Union !
ent specu-
vein:—
s earnestly
tance she
the force
National
ing which
he Monte-
ico. Are
far to the
hat Texas
You know
s French.
ty and re-
bring into
rge inter-
acter. It
eft the ar-
of the war
ey foresaw
France the
e they had
ght other-
onistic po-
policy to
case, they

Avenged.

erating on
Alabama,
ect from
assination
y avenged

eir indig-
ising the
muskets
rough all
in pursuit
directed
o was ar-
aken from
saplings,

plantation
and every
Our in-
nd thirty-
killed, in-
a whole
nds of the

nd created
en gueril-
ere going
ld travel.
he troops
t satisfied.

Pioneer & Democrat.

SAINT PAUL.

Saint Paul, Friday, August 29, 1862.

Extra Session of the Legislature Called.

PROCLAMATION OF THE GOVERNOR.

Whereas it has been represented to me by petitions from different parts of the State, numerously signed, that the disturbed condition of our western frontier,—hundreds of men, women and childrer having been already slaughtered by the Sioux Indians, and entire counties depopuluted by the panic thus created; with the necessity under which the State now labors to furnish thousands of her militia to the service of the General Government, and, at the same time, to provide promptly for the defense of a line of frontier, several hundred miles in length, against a ruthless and merciless enemy,—together with the fact, that under our existing laws, the volunteer force already furnished, and now required from the State, and constituting nearly one-third of its entire adult male population, are deprived of their voice in the conduct of public affairs at this most critical period, constitute such a contingency as demands the immediate assembling of the Legislature of the State.

Now, therefore, I, ALEXANDER RAMSEY, Governor of the State of Minnesota, do issue this my proclamation, requiring that the members of both Houses of the Legislature of the State shall, on the NINTH DAY OF SEPTEMBER NEXT, at 10 o'clock A. M., convene in extra session, at the Capitol, in the city of St Paul, to take such action as may be deemed necessary for the welfare of the State and the protection of its people.

Given under my hand and the Great Seal of the State, at the city of St. Paul, this [L. S.] twenty-third day of August, in the year of our Lord one thousand eight hundred and sixty-two.

ALEXANDER RAMSEY.

By the Governor:
JAMES H. BAKER, Secretary of State.

The News from the Frontier.

In another place will be found all the official information that has come to hand relating to the Indian war, and also an interesting letter from A. J. VAN VORHES, Esq., of the Stillwater *Messenger*, who was of the party that conducted the Indian annuity money to Fort Ridgley, arriving there after the Indian outrages. The manner of obtaining these dispatches is somewhat romantic. The half-breed interpreter, ANTOINE FRENIER, whose excursion to the Agency was noticed yesterday, volunteered to make a second trip to the Fort. Disguised as an Indian on the war path, he got into the Fort, through the masses of Indians surrounding it, on Thursday morning, and left the same evening, and made his way to Henderson, with the very latest intelligence we have received. The messenger from Henderson says that FRENIER would return to the Fort, and will probably give the inmates such assurances of relief at hand as to induce them to hold out. There can be no surrender without annihilation, and the inmates of the Fort know this.

Gov SIBLEY and his force were at St. Peter at four o'clock on Saturday morning. St. Peter is nearly fifty miles from Fort Ridgley, and Col. SIBLEY can hardly reach the Fort before Sunday evening.

Colonel CULLEN, with several hundred cavalry, proposed to strike across the country from Henderson, and may get to the Fort before the infantry force.

It is believed that the Indians will get information of the force advancing against them, and hastily leave the Fort. Major CULLEN writes that the further he advances, the news becomes worse. All the inhabitants of the country are flocking into the towns.

Hon. G. K. CLEVELAND writes on the 21st from Mankato: "I stayed in New Ulm last night, and saw the most horrible sights. I saw the bodies of eight stalwart men with their throats cut from ear to ear, their skulls battered and limbs mutilated. Some of them I knew well—good citizens of Brown county. The bodies of many known to be killed have not been brought in. My own opinion is that not less than 500 persons have been massacred. Large portions of Blue Earth and Brown counties have been depopulated. Thousands of persons have left their wheat unstacked in the fields, and are flying eastward. For God's sake send us men and arms."

We have some sketches of personal adventures and escapes that equal the most romantic scenes described by FENNIMORE COOPER. We have no time now to prepare them for the press.

The Indian News.

We have no news from Ridgley. Passengers from the Clara Hine, which arrived last night, state that scouts had gone within eight miles of the Fort, without meeting Indians. We are of the opinion that no fighting took place after Thursday.

The news from the Chippewa country shows a ticklish state of affairs, which may possibly result in an outbreak. The dispatches of Captain HALL, commandant at Fort Ripley, are quite interesting, as also the letter of our own correspondent at Saint Cloud.—*Daily, of Wednesday.*

The Trouble with the Chippewas.

George W. Sweet, Esq., arrived Sunday afternoon direct from Crow Wing with intelligence that Hole-in-the-Day, the great Chippewa Chief had issued a Proclamation, that he would not be responsible for the conduct of the Indians after Tuesday and warning all white settlers to leave the country before that time.

Mr. Sweet came as a Messenger from Hole-in-the-Day, to Commissioner Dole, asking that he should come up at once, accompanied by Judge Cooper, and he would make a treaty.

We understand that two hundred soldiers were sent up country yesterday, and that the Commissioner will leave this morning, with several gentlemen who have great influence with the Chippewas, and in whom they have confidence.

We do not anticipate much trouble with the Chippewas. Their principal ground of complaint is the conduct of the Agent, WALKER. His removal will probably satisfy them. HOLE-IN-THE-DAY doubtless feels a little sore, because he was fired on by the soldiers, but that can be arranged.

Since writing the above, we learn from Burbank's Express Messenger that the body of Mr. WALKER, the Agent, was found about three miles south of Monticello, Wright county, about eighty rods from the road. He was shot through his right side and his vest around the wound was considerably burned by the powder, and a pistol was found near him. There is no doubt that he committed suicide, and the general impression is that he became insane through fear of the Indians. He left St. Cloud last Friday, driving very rapidly, and stating to several persons on the way that there were five hundred Indians after him, with the intention of killing him. At the river he ferried himself across, being in such haste that he would not wait for the Ferryman. From the appearance of his body, it was supposed that he had been dead for about two days.

The Chippewa difficulty, following as it does, close on the Sioux raid, has naturally alarmed the people in the Northern part of the State, and they are making earnest applications for military protection.—*Daily of Tuesday.*

The Military Expedition Against the Indians.

We learn from Mr. Davis of the Clara Hine, who arrived last evening, that Col. Sibley had concentrated the various detachments of his force at St. Peter, and would leave for Fort Ridgley today. Much complaint has been made that Gov. Sibley has not relieved the Fort before this; but we are convinced that a careful survey of the situation will satisfy any reasonable person that he has done the best he could under the circumstances. St. Peter is full of panic-stricken people, and the Indians all around the town. Major Fowler went out on a reconnoissance, towards Fort Ridgley, and brought in the bodies of a man and some women who were killed on the road. Colonel Sibley could have advanced on Ridgley, but in doing so, would have left St. Peter to its fate. We learn also, that the cartridges sent to him from St. Paul were of a size that would not fit his guns, which occasioned some delay. Governor Sibley is a man of good judgment, clear headed, and fearless, and so is Major Fowler, an old army officer, who is with him. These gentlemen may fairly be presumed to have as much sense as the critics.—*Daily, of Wednesdag.*

Fort Ridgley and New Ulm.

We can hardly describe the painful suspense regarding the fate of these beleaguered points. The last news from Ridgley was to two o'clock Thursday, when the commanding officer intimated that he could not hold out much longer. They had been attacked almost every hour, and if these attacks were continued after that time, with continued losses in killed and wounded, the condition of the garrison must be lamentable indeed. They will resist to the last and die fighting. They will prefer a death in hot blood to the fate that awaits a voluntary surrender. In the Fort are several gentlemen well known to most of our citizens. Among them are Major GALBRAITH, Major HATCH, J. C. RAMSEY, Esq., (a brother of our Governor,) A. J. VANVORHES, Esq., editor of the Stillwater *Messenger*, C. G. WYCOFF, Esq., etc.

The latest news from New Ulm is to nine o'clock on Saturday night, when the village was mostly burned up by the savages. In New Ulm are many public-spirited citizens, who gallantly rushed to its defence, among whom are Judge FLANDRAU, of our Supreme Court; Senator SWIFT, and others.—*Daily, of Tuesday.*

Letter From Carver County.

CHASKA, CARVER COUNTY, MINN.,
Aug. 26, 1862.

Our Shertff, Frederick Griener, sent this morning a cavalry force of about forty, armed and equipped, to the frontier—a part by way of Glencoe, and part by way of Henderson. They propose to form a junction on Fort Ridgley, unless they should encounter the savages before they reach that point. Respectfully, S.

CHEERING NEWS.

FROM THE UPPER AGENCY

SIXTY-TWO PERSONS SAVED.

ESCAPE OVERLAND TO GLENCOE.

From the Daily Pioneer of Sunday.

Mr. Goodell, the Superintendent of Farms at the Yellow Medicine, arrived in the city last night from Glencoe, and brings the welcome news that *sixty-two persons*, who were supposed to have been killed, are safe!

The following are the particulars, as related to us by Mr. Goodell;

On the afternoon of Monday, Mr. Goodell was informed by a true Indian friend named Am-pa-tu-to-keo-ka, (Other Day, in English), that the people were likely to be attacked.

Just at night they saw squads of Indians councilling on the hills. A half-breed was sent to talk with them, but he could learn nothing definite. The first conclusive evidence of an attack was from a half-breed, who came down ahead of the Indians. He said the Indians told him they were coming down "to clean us out." Mr. Goodell and others went to work to get all the families into the warehouse, adjoining Mr. Galbraith's house.

Towards night they got news that the soldiers were all killed at Red Wood, and that no help could be expected in that direction. There was only one chance of escape, and that was as one to a thousand against them.

They went down the bank and forded the river, men, women and children. On the other side, Mr. Goodell proposed to go to the Fort below. "Other Day" objected, and said if Mr. Goodell insisted, he must part from them. They must go across the country to Kandiyohi Lakes, and to Glencoe. They had a few carriages for the women and children, and the men walked. They kept on all night—the next night they stopped with an old Swedes, whose family had ran away.

They went to Hutchinson, then to Glencoe, and thence to Carver. During the trip, Mrs. Galbraith and two children, and a Miss Charles, rode in a carriage, Miss Charles driving. Mr. Goodell says Miss Charles was the bravest girl he ever saw, and enlivened the party by her cheerful demeanor.

In the party were 42 women and children, and 20 men, 62 in all, whom Mr. Goodell knows are safe.

Among them are:

Mrs. Galbraith and family.
Mr. Sinks and family.
Mr. Givens and family.
Mr. Goodell and family.
E. Rider.
John German.
Mr. Miller.
Mr. Cramsey.
Mr. Hawkins.
Parker Pierce.
Mr. Ashley.
Mr. Patwell and family.
Mr. Fadden and family.

Dr. Wakefield is saved, but his family started for the Fort with George Gleason and it is supposed all were killed.

Mr. Garvie, was wounded, but got across the river and overtook Mr. Goodell's party at Cedar, eight miles from Hutchinson, and died there.

In addition to the family of J. R. Brown, Mr. Goodell says a scout passed Mr. Brown's farm on Monday, and found the house locked, and says they had warning from a squaw, and left the night before.

As regards the fate of the missionaries, he thinks about forty families, including theirs, between Lac-qui-Parle and the Agency, are killed. Mr. Goodell says all the farmer Indians gathered at Mr. Riggs' house to defend him, but he thinks they must have been overpowered.

Duncan Kennedy got off safely to the Fort.

Mr. Goodell relates many interesting incidents which we have not time to give this morning.

The story of the scout visiting the Agency, must have been a gross fabrication.

"Other Day," the noble Indian who warned Mr. Goodell's party, and piloted them through, can never return to the Indians again. He will be here in a few days, and should receive a suitable reward for his fidelity.

Arms and Ammunition.

Applications are daily made to the Executive, from all quarters of the State, for arms and accoutrements, and cavalry saddles, &c. It may save applicants some trouble and expense to be informed that the State is entirely destitute of these articles, and cannot therefore grant any requests of that character. Orders for powder have been issued in some instances, and it is understood that there is a sufficient quantity in store to meet all demands. All the arms that were in possession of the State authorities have been used in fitting out the new regiments and the irregular force sent up the Minnesota river. There is scarcely a house in the country that is not possessed of a rifle or fowling piece. These must be put in condition for use.

THE INDIAN WAR.

Dispatch from Lieut. Sheehan

FORT ATTACKED EVERY HOUR.

CANNOT HOLD OUT MUCH LONGER

The Little Band Almost Exhausted,

Interesting Account of the Indian Attack on the Fort.

GALLANTRY OF LT. SHEEHAN.

The Red Skins Repulsed.

NAMES OF THE KILLED AND WOUNDED

LATER FROM NEW ULM.

DISPATCH FROM JUDGE FLANDRAU.

Letter from Mr. Myrick.

FROM GOV. SIBLEY'S COMMAND.

LIEUT. SHEEHAN'S DISPATCH.

FORT RIDGLEY, Aug. 21, 2 P. M.

GOV. ALEXANDER RAMSEY:

We can hold this place but little longer, unless reinforced. We are being attacked almost every hour, and unless assistance is rendered we cannot hold out much longer. Our little ban is becoming exhausted and decimated. We had hoped to be reinforced today, but as yet can hear of none coming.

T. J SHEEHAN,
Co. C, Fifth Regiment Minnesota Vols.,
Commanding Post.

LETTER FROM A. J. VAN VORHES, ESQ.

FORT RIDGLEY, Aug, 21, 1862, A. M.

To the Editors of the Pioneer and Democrat.

On yesterday I sent you by messenger a full account of affairs at this place and vicinity; but fearing the messenger was cut off, who also bore important dispatches to headquarters, I will briefly recapitulate before proceeding to detail the important events of yesterday afternoon.

I need not detail the horrible butcheries at the Upper and Lower Sioux Agencies at New Ulm, and throughout this entire region, as you have already been advised of the terrible details.

When the party accompanying Mr. Wycoff to make the annual payment to the Indians, arrived at this place on Monday noon, matters were in much confusion, owing to there being so few soldiers at this post and the great number of men, women and children fleeing here for protection. In many instances a solitary member of large families,—in some instances the father, in others the mother, and in quite a number a little boy or girl,—worked their way to these barracks under the most distressing circumstances, fleeing from their persecutors, after witnessing the butchery of those most dear to them on earth.

Captain Marsh had gone with forty-four members of his command, to the vicinity of the Lower Agency, on hearing of the state of affairs there, leaving only some twenty-five soldiers under Lieutenant Gere to protect the Fort. Every citizen, however, took a musket, until the small stock of old and condemned pieces were exhausted, and gave Lieutenant Gere their best efforts in his perilous undertaking. Captain Marsh met a large body of the enemy, was surrounded and cut to pieces. Only twenty-one of them have returned—three of them wounded, two mortally wounded.

During Monday night several alarms were given, but the enemy did not appear in force or make any threatening demonstrations. On Tuesday, Lieut. T. S. Sheehan, of company C, who had left this post on Saturday morning, for his post at Fort Ripley, after making a forced march of 42 miles in nine hours, arrived, and immediately took command, with fifty brave and well disciplined soldiers. During the same day, Major Galbraith arrived with fifty new men (Renville Rangers,) who were on their way to Fort Snelling. Upon hearing of the Indian disturbances, Major Galbraith turned back with his men after having reached St. Peter, when they succeeded in procuring old United States muskets. After receiv- cover of trees and out buildings. At this point they opened a volley upon a detachment of company B, stationed at one of the north entrances, but without serious effect. It was but the work of a moment for Lieut. Sheehan to bring his company to bear upon them from one of the southern entrances, the smoke of which had hardly cleared away when one of the six pound mountain howitzers, under direction of Sergeant Jones, sent into their midst a shell that must have done glorious execution. The fire of the enemy then became scattered and promiscuous,—all sides of the barracks appearing to be infested, and every secret hiding place having its wily foes. After throwing a few shells, Sergeant Jones took command of a six-pound cannon, and Sergeant Macgrew and Whipple, the two Howitzers. The fire on both sides was most spirited and persistent, St. Sheehan was everywhere present, cheering on the brave and stout-hearted, and encouraging the few wavering. Considering the responsibility of his position, he was perhaps too reckless of his personal safety. Time after time, as he past from post to post giving directions to the men, whole volleys of musketry, were discharged upon him, and the bullets went whizzing over and about him like hail-stones. His coolness inspired all with courage, however, and we thank God that he is yet unharmed.

In this way the fight was continued until dark, with an almost continuous discharge of musketry and artillery. As to the strength and loss of the enemy, all is conjecture. Picket guards and scouts, estimate the number lurking about at one thousand. Of the correctness of this estimate, I have no means of judging, except that the enemy was in strong force and made the attack with courage and determination. What the effect of our shells may have been we of course cannot know, as the Indian mode of warfare is invariably to carry their dead and wounded from the field when possible, and our strength was not half sufficient to pursue the foe when driven from their various points. Many were seen to fall, however, before the musket shots, and others were seen thrown into the air by bursting shells.

A number of citizens' buildings surrounding the barracks were fired by the enemy, but none of the Government buildings were burned. Here was one of our greatest dangers, but a timely rain, which continued during the night, and the vigilance of the guards, prevented. A few old outbuildings, which served as hiding-places for the enemy, were burned during the night by order of the commandant.

I am indebted to Surgeon Alfred Muller for a list of the wounded of yesterday's engagement, together with that of the engagement near Red Wood, on last Monday. The wounded of yesterday were

Corporal Dennis Porter, company C, shot in right thigh, ball passing through—also, buckshot in left side—not dangerous.

Private John McGill, company B, shot through right thigh, not dangerous.

Andrew Ruflin, company B, shot from ear to ear, lower jaw on both sides shattered—also, injury in the throat—mortally.

Rob't Spornitz, company B, shot through left cheek, ball passing out through right cheek, upper jaw completely smashed, severe wound.

William Good, company B, shot in forehead, mortally wounded; Peter C. Harris, company C, shot through left hip, not dangerous.

Private Shartledge, company C, wounded overleft eye, not dangerous.

James Gorman and Joseph Foertier, Renville Rangers.

The killed were—

Mark M. Grear, company C; Robert Baker, Renville Rangers; Michael Murnane, Renville Rangers.

The wounded at the Red Wood engagement on Monday, now in hospital, were:

Ole Swenson, Company B, not dangerous; Wm. Blodged, company B, mortally; Wm. Southerland, company B, mortally.

The night was passed in comparative quiet, though every man at his post or sleeping upon his arms. What the day may bring forth, none of us can tell. With a fair and square fight, we would have no great fears; but with this lurking, bushwhacking mode of warfare and a sudden dash of legions of savages upon barracks which afford no real security except as defended from doors and windows, and liable at any time to be fired, the position of this small force might be exceedingly perilous. It is time for reinforcements from Fort Snelling, but yet they are not here. O! for a regiment of effective soldiers to avenge the untold outrages of the past three days.

In haste, A. J. VAN VORHES.

LETTER FROM JUDGE FLANDRAU.

NEW ULM, August 22, 3 P. M.

To Governor SIBLEY;

Your dispatch of the 21st (evening) is this moment received. I enclose a dispatch I have just received from N. Myrick, whom you have probably seen. It was delayed at the Ferry and useless. I could not have reinforced the Fort, had I received it in time, as I learned from a man who left there on the morning of the 20th, that nothing had occurred at that time.

I sent a dispatch to the Fort on the 20th, and my man was seen within one and a half miles of that point going in. I fear the man spoken of by Myrick is my messenger, as he has not returned.

I have no further news from the Fort, and can tell you no more than Myrick will, save the fact of the numbers there, which you probably did not know, and Myrick could not inform you.

I learn that a company of citizens left for the Fort this morning, 100 strong, from St. Peter. If so, my opinion is that if you make a junction with your detail to Glencoe of 150 men, which will give you 375, and with 100 already gone up will make 475, you had better send about 200 this way, and the other 275 the other side to the Fort.

I have about 200 men here, but they are very poorly armed. I would like very much to see you, if you have any man you can entrust with the command to the Fort.

I don't think the Indians have taken it; but, not knowing the extent of the outbreak, I can form no idea of the force they have. It must be considerable, or they would not attack the Fort.

The men at the Fort were the balance of the soldiers, some citizens, and Major Galbraith with fifty or sixty men. The Indians may not have known of the reinforcements, and have attacked on the supposition that no one was there left but the garrison.

I have large exp ditions out all day from here which weakens me, but I think I can hold the town until you come, if not attacked by a large force.

I hear of Indians all around me but see none. I am making some entrenchments, &c., &c.

I am sure that everything above is lost, and all the people killed.

I have found a spear at one of the houses sacked, about eight miles from here, which is unquestionably Yanckton; also a saddle, the ordinary pads, with beads. This leads me to believe that it is the Indians from the region of the Missouri that attend the payment, that are doing the mischief. There may, however, be a general rising.

If you can come this way do so, and we can co operate. We are but eighteen miles from the Fort, and can go there, if necessary, as well from here as from any other point. I wish you would leave tha same evening you get to St. Peter. The roads are good and you can get here by morning. I have a good Ferry to cross you at Red Stone, about two miles below the town.

I think I have said all that will be of service to you, and now urge expedition, by all means.

Wishing you success and speed, I am, yours,

CHARLES E. FLANDRAU,
Commanding at New Ulm.

LETTER FROM NATHAN MYRICK.

LAFAYETTE, Aug. 20.

To Capt. FLANDRAU, New Ulm;

I have just returned from near the Fort. When within six miles I saw two large volumes of smoke and heard firing of guns.

When within a half mile of the hill, I saw one man dead with his throat cut, and could see two distinct fires.

One no doubt was the Goverment stables, and the other Randall's house and store. I returned from there and will go to St. Pe-Peter to-night.

If you can spare a force, you had better send to their relief, or the Fort may fall into the hands of the enemy.

N. MYRICK.

EXTRACT OF A LETTER FROM GOV. SIBLEY.

HEADQUARTERS INDIAN EXPEDITION,
ST. PETER, Aug. 22, 1862.

To his Excellency, Gov. RAMSEY:

SIR— * * * I send a dispatch from Judge Flandrau, giving valuable information from the New Ulm region, where he now is. I arrived with the three companies to-day after a very fatuiging march through the Big Woods, where the roads are execrable. I sent Lieutenant Cox and Buck, with portions of their companies from Nicollet and Sibley counties, to Judge Flandrau's aid very early in the morning. Major Fowler is here. [Major Fowler went across the country from Rice county, on the 20th with volunteer cavalry.—ED.]

* * * * * *

Very respectfully, your ob't. serv't.
H. H. SIBLEY, Col. Com.

GRAPHIC PICTURE OF THE GREAT SCARE IN CARVER COUNTY.

CARVER, CARVER COUNTY, MINN.,
August 22d, 1862.

To the Editors of the Pioneer and Democrat.

I have taken this occasion to give you a faint outline of the great Indian panic which has been raging throughout this entire section of the State. Language seems inadequate to picture the scene in its true light.

On the evening of the 19th inst., at about the hour of eight o'clock, messengers came running into this quiet village, from what is known as Walker's Landing, and stated that the Indians had slaughtered all the troops at Fort Ridgley, burnt the Fort and the Upper and Lower Agency, and killed all the inhabitants thereof; that they had burned New Ulm and St. Peter, and had made an attack upon Henderson; that they (the messengers) had heard heavy firing at Henderson before they left; and that that village was burning at the time of their departure. They reported, further, that there were all the way from five to ten thousand Indians; and that said Indians intended to lay waste all the country, from Fort Ridgley to Fort Snelling.

These messengers informed all the inhabitants on the road, from said Walker's Landing to this place, of this terrible state of affairs; and, as they came, kindled one of the greatest panics that mortal eyes ever beheld. Soon after their arrival, men, women and children came into this place screaming with fright—some barefoot, some shirtless, some with little or no clothing at all; some with guns, but more without. Oxen, unused to fast travelling, were now fully equal to Flora Temple in her palmy days, with such loads behind them as would astonish any mortal being.

The exclamation was, *where shall we go!* Oh! my children what will become of us. These reports seemed to spread with the speed of electricity; for no sooner did the panic stricken people of Walker's Landing flee from their homes, leaving doors open and everything exposed to any body who might see fit to possess anything there, the whole people from the Minnesota River to Crow River became one vast area of excitement. All night long from the time said messengers arrived, there was one continued stream of delirious people rushing in. Soon after the arrival of said messengers the inhabitants then, though unwilling for the most part to attach any considerable importance to the reports, repaired to their several places of abode and put in order their shot guns and rifles for an emergency, that might arise. Pickets were established on the various roads leading to town; and diligence used to prevent a *surprise* by the enemy.

At last light began to dawn in the East, and the coming day was welcomed by the frantic shout of more than three hundred babies besides hosts of joyous mothers and fathers. But with the early dawn came no Indians, as expected, and nothing te be seen except babies, mothers and fathers rushing to this harbor of safety.

About the hour of seven in the morning we began to recruit the entire population of McLeod county. On they came; some on foot, some on horseback, and some on crutches, sleds, wagons, of all shades of manufacture; some with great, big, round wheels; some with low, block wheels; some with only three wheels; some with two only. They brought with them bundles of clothes, axes, spades and shovels; some more, some less of the same; some running with children on their backs, seated upon a ponderous bundle, strapped over the shoulders. Thus matters went on until in came a boy, on a very spirited horse, claiming to be direct from Glencoe, shouting out as he rode at full speed through the streets, that the Indians had burned Glencoe and Young America, and were on a rapid march for Carver! Oh! such a scene I never desire to witness again. The Antelope was by a special request, detained at the levee, and such a rush for the decks of this last harbor of safety, beggars all description.

Mothers clasped in their arms their children, and wrung their hands with horror. Such yells, shrieks and moans! The decks of this small steamer soon became one living mass of frantic men, women and children. Her guards dipped the water with the ponderous load, and still they jumped, clasped and clung to her as their only hope. The gallant captain, desiring to assist all in this hour of trial, could not help being cognizant of the fact that should he permit them to overload his steamer, she would soon reach the bottom of the river with all on board, and therefore interposed in time to lighten his boat and cut loose from shore, which was done in a splendid manner, and the precious load soon went steaming down the river.

While so many were surely saved, there was still a dense mass of human lunatics on shore that were shrieking and shouting in the wildest despair. Soon a small barge lying near by was crowded with women and children and cowardly men. But we had brave men left who gave wise counsel to the women, and told the men of the cowardly act of running away and leaving their wives and children to the mercy of the savage.

These cowards were kicked and cuffed and knocked about, but still were as helpless as infants. They made no resistance, but shrieked and cried with fright.

A small band of thirty or forty braves were all that could be mustered out of this dense mass of two or three thousand persons. I do not over estimate the number, some put it much larger. This small number of brave men, with rifles, shot guns and pitchforks determined to defend their homes at all hazards, and by hard and constant exertions brought back many who had not reason entirely dethroned.

Additional news soon received showed the report to be without foundation, and soon the light of joy beamed upon all countenances. This was practically the end of the panic, and the cowards and lunatics once more became as bold as lions. The people began to realize the scheme, and commenced to return to their houses.

This is, I believe, the pith of the panic, and, as I have already taken up much room, I will close by saying that the gallant Captain T. Grant and Strait have passed through here with their 150 braves, with bayonets fixed, destined for Fort Ridgley, and the people are all returning to their homes.

OBSERVER.

Incidents of the Indian War.

From the Mankato Record, 23d.

During the attack on New Ulm, Wednesday evening, a rifle ball struck against a brick wall, and glancing, hit Miss Pauli on the forehead, killing her instantly.

A party of nine had been out to Leavenworth, fourteen miles distant in search of killed. They did not see an Indian until near the hill returning to New Ulm, when about seventy-five sprang up from among the tall grass, in the form of a letter V, fired upon the party, killed all but one, who was mounted on a horse which was shot, and in the confusion, the rider managed to escape. His name is John Thomas.

A German living between the Big and Little Cottonwood rivers, had fed an Indian all last winter; this Indian led a party of five to murder his friend, but who fortunately escaped without serious injuries.

A man and wife living beyond New Ulm was attacked. The wife was killed and the husband fled to the cellar, where with his hands he dug a hole under the sill of the house and escaped to the town.

A little girl whose parents were killed, escaped, and says she knew five of the Indians who killed her parents, and is positive that they are annuity Sioux.

Another fact confirmatory of the above is, that out of nine killed and brought into New Ulm, only one was scalped.

A citizen of New Ulm had a married daughter with five children living on the Big Cottonwood. Learning that they had been murdered, he went in search of them. He found them all lying on the floor apparently dead. On examination he observed signs of life in a little boy and girl, twins, two years old, and a little girl aged six years. He carried them to New Ulm, where they are now in a fair way of recovering. Each of these children was struck on each temple, apparently with a tomahawk. The little boy was cut on the forehead, and the oldest girl on the back of the head, with the same weapon.

Most of the dead found, except those killed in New Ulm, were tomahawked, and in the most brutal manner.

Help from Wisconsin.

A dispatch was received Monday from Governor Salomon, stating that he had shipped several hundred thousand rounds of cartridges to Minnesota, in answer to the request of Governor Ramsey.

Seventeen More Killed.

MURDERS AT GREEN LAKE

The Indian Expedition.

DISPATCHES FROM EX-GOVERNOR SIBLEY.

From the Daily Pioneer of Tuesday.

Dispatches received yesterday from Col. Sibley, dated St. Peter, 25th instant, state that he arrived there with three companies of his command, late on the evening of the 22d. He had been actively engaged in affording such aid to the beleaguered villages as his limited means would afford. Major Fowler, with a command of about fifty mounted men, left for a reconnoissance on the Fort Ridgley road the previous morning, by his order, and returned about two o'clock this morning, bringing with them the bodies of an old man, and the women who were killed within twenty miles of St. Peter. Major Fowler reports that the destruction of property by fire during the day along, and for miles on both sides of the main roads leading in that direction, was beyond calculation, showing that small bodies of the enemy, supported by heavy forces on their flanks, were engaged in carrying out the same systematic plan of murder and devastation which has marked the brief progress of hostilities hitherto. * * * The mounted force under Major Cullen reached Henderson late last evening, and the infantry under Colonel Crooks are supposed to have reached the same point at a later hour.

New Ulm was attacked by the enemy yesterday, and the fight continued until late in the evening, so that thus far he had received no intelligence from Judge Flandrau, commanding at that point, but he entertained great apprehensions lest his entire force has been cut off, and the town and its inhabitants destroyed. A reinforcement of 120, sent by him to his relief yesterday morning, failed to reach him in season, owing to the ferry communications having been destroyed by the enemy, a precaution on his part that deprived Major Flandrau of the aid of 70 of his most efficient men, who had been dispatched by him to this side of the river, on a reconnoitering expedition, and was prevented from returning to aid in the defense of New Ulm. Colonel Sibley was expecting information from that quarter every hour, and if Major Flandrau was still holding out, Colonel Sibley would take instant measures for his relief.

Jack Frazer, an old Indian scout, escaped from Fort Ridgley on Wednesday night. He reports that the garrison was well supplied and able to hold out, the only fear being that the enemy may attempt to fire the roofs of the stone buildings. All the other houses and stables outside have been destroyed by the savages, which they accomplished at the sacrifice of some four or five of their number killed and wounded. Frazer was to leave St. Peter on Sunday afternoon, with dispatches for Major Galbraith, giving him assurances of relief at the earliest moment practicable.

Col. Sibley asks that the Seventh Regiment, or companies to the number of a full regiment, be at once sent up, fully armed and equipped. They will be wanted, and more, before this rising is subdued; and the sooner they take the field the better. He trusts that not a single man will be permitted to leave the State until the war is so far ended, as to render only a small force necessary. We have probably 4,000 or 5,000 warriors to meet sooner or later, and as it is a life-and-death struggle on their part, we may as well face the facts at once; for the season during which military operations can be conducted on the Plains, is very brief, and should be improved to the uttermost.

A later dispatch, dated at half-past ten, Sunday night, says the intelligence from New Ulm, up to nine o'clock on Saturday night, was that the village was mostly burned by the savages, but the occupied portion was safe; and the probability is that the garrison would be able to hold out until the relief sent by Col. Sibley would reach them.

MORE MURDERS NEAR MEEKER COUNTY.

L. A. Evans, Esq., Mayor of St. Cloud, writes to the Governor on Sunday last, that a committee of most reliable citizens of that place, who had been appointed to visit the scene of the recent reported murders, and ascertain facts, had just returned. They went as far as Paynesville, where they found some 200 persons from the vicinity of that place and Norway Lake; had seen and conversed with persons there who had made their escape from the Indians, who had witnessed the massacre of their friends and relations.

The names of those murdered are Louis Lunberg, Andrew Lunberg, August Lunberg, A. B. Burberg and three children, Daniel Bunberg, wife and two children, and John Evenson. They were killed on Wednesday, the 20th, at Norway Lake. The family of Mr. Foote and others were murdered at Green Lake.

Mrs. Lena Lunberg, who had escaped to Paynesville from Norway Lake, stated on oath that she was attending a meeting held by Rev. Andrew Jackson, on Wednesday last, and while there, Andrew and Peter Broback came to them and said to them some twenty Indians were at their houses, about two miles off, when six of Lunberg's family and four of the Brobecks started for home, and while going saw two Indians shoot Mrs. Broberg and daughter; that Mr. Lunbury told him that their son was shot by them, and he did not know what had become of the rest of the boys; that she hid herself in the grass and thus made her escape.

Lewis Everson writes from Paynesville, in Stearns county, that he saw the bodies of Christine Brobery and daughter, lying in the road; that the Indians had taken forty head of cattle and six wagons, and were leading them down with the goods stripped from the houses.

A meeting was held at Paynesville on the 22d, at which they united in a petition to the Governor to have a military company immediately sent there to protect the lives and property of the citizens of Stearns, Meeker and Monongalia counties, for the following reasons: 1. More than seventy persons are now with us who have been driven from their homes by Indians, leaving their crops but partially harvested; 2d. Five persons, Mr. Jones and family of Acton, seventeen miles south of this place, have been killed by the Indians; 3d. Eight persons near Norway Lake have been murdered and others wounded, and some still missing. 4th. Indians have been seen in our midst, within the past few days. 5th. We have reason to believe that those who have committed these depredations were Sioux, but being on the line between there and the Chippewas, we hear from both nations. 6th. Many of our citizens have volunteered and gone, leaving but few able bodied men in our midst, with many women and children without means of protection. 7th. We make the foregoing statements after sending out scattering parties in different directions and ascertaining the truth of them.

The foregoing is signed by forty-one citizens.

A gentleman who has just been released as a prisoner from the Leach Lake band of Chippewas, Mr. Garden, says that the whole Chippewa nation is in league with the Sioux, and that St. Cloud is to be their rendezvous.

Mr. Evans says, we have reports still later which are given credit to, that scouting parties of Indians have been seen within six miles of this place, and I can assure you we have cause of alarm. Send men and arms for us without delay, if possible. One hundred men will organize as a cavalry company tomorrow at this place.

STATEMENT OF WILLIAM BOURAT.

William Bourat, who was a clerk in Forbes' store at Red Wood, came down on the Antelope yesterday, and makes the following statement:

He says that on Monday last the Indians, to the number of 25 or 30, appeared in front of Forbes' store. Four persons were in the store, George Spencer, jr., George Thomas, Wm. Taylor, (barber of this city) and William Bourat. The Indians fired into the store, wounding George Spencer in the arm and sides. The other men ran up stairs, and the Indians took possession of the store. Bourat heard one of them say, "Let us go up and kill them, and get them out of the way"; and he determined to make a dash for his life. He rushed down stairs and succeeded in getting about 200 yards from the store, when he received a heavy charge of duck shot in the side which brought him to the ground. Another shot was fired at him which took effect in his left leg. They then came up to him, stripped him of his clothing and shoes, and piled some logs over him, to prevent his escape, promising to come back and cut him up.

He succeeded in extricating himself from the logs and crawled away, and eluded the search of the Indians. He made his way in the most excruciating torture, to Glencoe, and from thence to Carver and to this city.

Mr. Bourat thinks there is no doubt but Spencer, Reed and Taylor were murdered. Just as he ran from the store he heard Spencer cry out he was killed.

Mr. B. says that he did not see Gleason, but whenever he met a white man on the road to Glencoe, he was assured that Gleason and the Wakefield family were murdered.

Mr. Bourat appears very much exhausted, and is suffering from the wounds received. He was carried from the boat. With proper care he will probably soon recover.

STATEMENT OF ANTOINE HENRY.

Antoine Henry, a German living about seven miles above New Ulm, came into the city yesterday with his wife and two children. The Indians made an attack on his house about noon on Monday. His wife with her father, mother, sister and brother were in a field harvesting, and the children only were in the house. The Indians attacked the children with hatchets or tomahawks, inflicting frightful gashes about the head and arms. Two of the children, aged four and five years, were killed outright. A little boy, one of those brought to this city, has fourteen distinct gashes about the head and breast and arms. A baby about 18 months old, had two or three gashes on its head. The fiends then proceeded to the field and shot the old man, named Antoine Mismer, and his wife and daughter and his son, Joseph Mismer 28 years old, dead. Mrs. Henry escaped to the woods, and secreted herself. Mr. Henry was absent at New Ulm, when the murder was committed, and reached home on Monday evening. His wife came from her hiding place, and as soon as possible he got his two wounded children and wife in the wagon, and started for Saint Paul.

LIST OF THE KILLED.

The following is a list of killed at New Ulm and vicinity, as far as heard from:

LEAVENWORTH.	
John Bluem,	Wm Carroll,
2 Misses Bluem,	Henshaw,
Master Bluem,	Jackson.
Mrs Harrington,	May and family—two
Master Harrington,	dead, others wounded
Joe Emrich.	
MILFORD.	
Mrs Mesmer,	Massapast family—4,
Miss and Master Heule,	Mr Tuttle and 4 child'n
Mr Shilling,	" Teller,
" Keck,	" Fink, wife and son,
" and Mrs Pelsel,	" B Bresler,
" Reiner, wife and child,	" Stocker,
	" Messmer,
" Haag,	John Thompson,
" and Mrs Hartman,	3 Olesons.
NEW ULM.	
John Schneider,	Boy Baeumle,
E Deitrich,	Master Baeulmle,
Julius Fenske,	" Fettle,
Reimann,	1 man, 1 woman,
Miss Pauli,	Casper Hermann.
SIGEL TOWN.	
A Loomis,	Wm Tuttle,
J Loomis,	M Loomis,
Dewit Lemon.	
COTTONWOOD.	
Charles Lane.	

Atrocities of the Indians.

Correspondence of the Pioneer and Democrat.

INDIAN EXPEDITION,
ST. PETER, August 23, 1862.

At the request of some of our boys, I send you a few facts indicative of the present condition of affairs in the country about New Ulm. We arrived here last night, pitched our tents, and are at present awaiting the arrival of the Union Guard (Company A), which debarked at Carver, we proceeding to Belle Plaine. The Goodhue Guard (Company F) and a part of the Hickory Guard are encamped here at present. The Fremont Guard was ordered to Mankato this morning.

Rumors of every character and description are afloat here; but we will occupy your space with such statements only, as I have received from eye-witnesses of the terrible depredations which the red demons are committing.

Hearing that a victim of these treacherous blood-hounds was lying at the Washington House, wounded, I called upon him a few moments ago; and such a spectacle as I saw there, these eyes never gazed upon before. I have read the record of the atrocious deeds of these cruel-hearted fiends in other days, and have shuddered with horror. Sometimes I have thought that more was laid to their charge than that of which they were guilty; but here I beheld, with my own eyes, a fearful exhibition of their savage nature. There lay a boy, about twelve years of age, cut and bruised on every limb, his face horribly mangled, and his skull fractured.

He was asleep, but occasionally a low, heart-piercing moan would escape his lips. At times he would attempt to turn over; and then, in the agony occasioned by the effort, he would groan most piteously. At length he awoke; his lips quivered with pain, and the meaningless expression of his eyes added new horror to the dreadful scene; until, sickened to my soul with the sight, I left the room.

While there, I learned the following facts from his father and mother, who were with him. Mr. Hainly (for such is his name) states that he went to town, having not the slightest apprehension of danger, although the Indians were there when he left. He arrived home in time to drag his boy, whom we have mentioned, from the field, where he had been left for dead. While thus engaged, five bullets whistled about his head. Mrs. Hainly says they killed two of her children before her eyes, and were quickly dispatching her infant son, when she seized it, and fled to her mother's house, a few yards distant. They pursued, and shot at her a number of times, but ineffectually. They killed her mother, her sister, and servant girl, she in the meantime escaped to a small grove with her infant, and escaped.

They say that, at least thirty or forty are killed in their neighborhood, which is about a mile from New Ulm.

Another woman states that her husband and family are killed; another that her son and son-in law are murdered. A little boy says that they were engaged in killing his father and mother and the other members of the family when he escaped. While writing, I heard a man say that his son was killed, his wife and mother taken prisoners, and most of his neighbors destroyed. Such tales of woe as these we are hearing on every side. As I pass along the street, I see women embracing each other and weeping over their losses. That there is much exageration we have no doult, but the true state of affairs must be deplorable.

SUNDAY MORNING, Aug. 24.

Company A arrived last night. Men, women and children have kept pouring in here ever since we came until this morning, about 3 o'clock. It is now said that the Indians have possession of all the roads, cutting off all further escape. Three dead bodies were brought in last night. I saw them a few moments ago. They were butchered most dreadfully. We are orderdered to be ready for marching orders at any moment.

SUNDAY EVENING.

Three companies of cavalry have arrived. The people begin to rejoice amid their tears.

The dead are still being brought in. Little Crow has made a speech telling them that now is the time to regain their possession; the country is engaged in civil war, and are not able to repel an attack from them.

E. J. H.
Goodhue Guard.

FROM THE CHIPPEWA COUNTRY.

THREATENING CONDITION OF AFFAIRS.

Letters from Fort Ripley.

FROM THE COMMANDER OF FORT RIPLEY.

HEADQUARTERS FORT RIPLEY,
August 23, 1862, 9 o'clock A. M.

To Governor RAMSEY, St. Paul;

SIR: I travelled all night, and arrived at the Fort at 7 A. M., and found Indian matters as follows: Indians are assembling in large numbers at Gull Lake, 20 miles north of here.

Six families from Leech Lake were taken prisoners, by the band known as Leech Lake Pillagers. The Indian preacher, Johnson, who is friendly, was at their council, and says it is a preconcerted movement, and that Hole-in-the-day says the same in council; and it was arranged with the Sioux and Chippewas to strike at this time. The arrangement was for the Chippewas to first kill Agent Walker, then attack and take the Fort, and overrun the Mississippi Valley.

Hole-in-the-Day stated in council that we had all we could manage with our brethren South, and that, with the Sioux and Chippewas together, we would not be able to successfully resist.

Lieut. J. B. Forbes, by his promptness, saved the Fort. He received news of the movement at two o'clock P. M., on the 19th inst. He immediately took twenty-six men and started for the Agency. He met the Agent on his retreat to the Fort. He got a sight of Hole-in-the-Day, and gave chase. He only escaped by taking boat and crossing the river. The boys had a brisk fight with some fifty of his warriors, and Hole-in-the-Day was seen to fall, and his warriors carried him from the field. We hear today that he is confined to his tent by sickness. He will not own that he was hit.

Lieut. Forbes declared martial law and ordered all citizens of the vicinity to report at the Fort. To their promptness in obeying the call, can be credited the safety of the Fort and the valley.

Immediately on my arrival I sent Lieut. Beauliew with a message to Hole-in-the-Day to immediately release all whites he held as prisoners, and informed him that if he failed to do this, it would be considered as commencing hostilities, and we should act accordingly. I at the same time, informed Hole-in-the-Day, that if he remained quiet and did not permit his men to damage the citizens, that this matter of difficulty with Agent Walker would be investigated by the Indian Commissioner. I informed Hole-in-the-Day that the whites had always looked on him as a friend, and that I hoped he would not disappoint them. I at the same time informed him, that if he persisted in hostilities, that we should make it a war of extirmination, Hole-in-the-Day answers and says that he will immediately send the prisoners and will agree to wait four days to see Commissioner Dole.

The Indian preacher Johnson is here claiming our protection, and says Hole-in-the-Day is afraid to attack us until he receives reinforcements from Leech Lake, which he has sent for. The company which I ordered here from St. Cloud, went the other way after I left. Lattersall's company does not arrive yet. They had not reached St. Cloud at 11 A. M. to-day.

We have about thirty soldiers and fifty citizens to defend the Fort and settlers, and poorly armed. We want ammunition and guns for citizens and volunteers to help us. The Sioux are working up this way. They are murdering settlers at or near Forest City. We detail tonight for guard 24 men. We do not intend to be caught asleep. Our men do not undress, but sleep with their guns by their side.

LATER.—The Express from Crow Wing has just arrived, and says the wives and children of the Chippewas are all leaving the country, and none but warriors remain. It may mean fun—but they will get plenty of it.

The citizens of Crow Wing and Little Falls are organized, and all the women and children gathered together tonight, and the men mount guard like soldiers. You may hear of the citizens of this valley being killed, but you will not hear of their running from their homes. They are determined to stand by them to the last.

If you should send any men here to operate against Indians, Lieutenant Beauliew's company would be a good one, as they know the ways of the Indians.

I have citizens near the Indians who report warrants made by them.

In haste, F. HALL,
Captain Commanding Post.

HEADQUARTERS, FORT RIPLEY,
Aug. 24, 1862, 10 A. M.

Gov. Ramsey, St. Paul:

SIR—Men, women and children, poured into the Fort, all night, for protection. They are all from the vicinity of the Indians, and feel certain that the Indians will attack soon. They say the Indians are determined to take the Fort so as to get arms and ammunition. The Indians are reinforced from Leech Lake, and now number about 300 warriors. Their squaws have all left for the North, which shows that they are preparing to fight. Should they commence, we will have 400 men here and 200 horses to clean them out entirely. They cannot take the Fort, but we have not force sufficient to successfully attack them in the woods. The only way is to have half cavalry and half infantry, and drive them from the country. They still expect 200 men more in one or two days. I think they will wait until they arrive.

They had a war meeting last night, and one of their chiefs, Bad Boy, was in favor of peace, and they threatened to kill him, and he made his escape and is here. He seys they are for war unless the government will give them all they ask, which is a general overhauling of everything for several years back. He (Bad Boy) is sure there will be a war. He succeeded in getting three only of his band to join him for peace. We use them for advance guards. He says they only gave up their prisoners to get time to get their men together.

If I had men enough I would order them to disperse, and if they refused, I would clean them out, and not give them a chance to attack the settlers. Lieutenant Beaulieu will give you particulars. He knows the Indians and their plans.

We can get 100 good men here to volunteer to fight them, but they have no arms but shot guns. The settlers here wish to make it a war of extermination, if the Indians commence. If they do commence it would be a good time to pay them all we owe them, and get a clear title to their land. They are a treacherous and thieving set, and if they give up this time, it will only be because they are afraid they cannot succeed. Respectfully your obedient servant,

F. HALL, Captain Commanding post.

LETTER FROM ST. CLOUD.

THE NORWAY LAKE MURDERS.

MUTILATION OF THE DEAD.

ST. CLOUD, Sunday Evening, 9 o'clock.

To the Editor of the Pioneer and Democrat:

I have just left one of the largest and most excited assemblages ever convened in this town, met for the purpose of hearing the report of the gentlemen sent out yesterday as scouts in the direction of Green and Norway Lakes, and up the valley of the Sauk. The party consisted of Ambrose Freeman, Samuel Holes, and others. The gentlemen named are two of the most fearless men, and thorough woodsmen, we have in the Upper Mississippi country, and are well acquainted with the country. They went direct to Painesville in this county, thirty-seven miles distant from St. Cloud. They found the surviving settlers from Norway Lake with their families at Painesville. The Norway Lake settlement is composed mostly of Norwegians and Swedes. They had assembled at their Church on the afternoon of Wednesday, the 20th inst., and in returning from their services they were attacked by several straggling parties of Indians, some of whom were mounted on ponies, others on foot, and *fourteen persons were killed*. The names of those killed are as follows:

Louis Lomberg, aged twenty years.
Andrew Lomberg, aged twenty-five years.
August Lomberg, aged twenty-two years.
A. P. Burback, wife and three children.
Daniel Burback, wife and two children.
John Burback.

The above were killed on Wednesday last. On Thursday, John Everson was killed. The fourteen killed on Wednesday were horribly mutilated. Some had their ears cut off, some their noses, some a hand, some the fingers. The *cheeks and breasts of the women* were cut off, and their *clothes burned upon them*. The bodies of the thirteen were all buried in one grave by John Lomberg and Evan Rensen. A young lady was taken a prisoner, put on a pony and started westward; her cries frightened the pony she was on, and then the others took fright. In the stampede of the ponies she was thrown off, and she made her escape and arrived safely at Painesville.

An attempt was made on Friday to bury the body of Everson, but while the party were engaged, they were attacked by a party of eight Indians, but being armed they returned their fire, and then seeing that the Indians greatly outnumbered them, they retired and the body was still unburied yesterday. There is now no communication between Green Lake and Norway Lake, nor between either of those places and Painesville.

It is reported that a settlemene of twenty-five persons at Lake Johanna is entirely destroyed. A company of armed mounted men will perfect its organization here tomorrow and go to the scene of the murders. At Painesville the scouts say Samuel Lomberg, a son of John Lomberg, aged ten years who was shot in the side, but who is doing well, and with proper care will recover. The burying party found hats and caps of others who are missing, but whose bodies were not found. The greatest distress prevails throughout all the vicinity of the outrages, and the people have sent in for flour which will be sent them. Forty four oxen were driven off, two wagons stolen and upwards of two thousand dollars in gold taken from the houses of the killed.

O.

Military Appointments.

Col. A. D. NELSON resigned his commission yesterday as Colonel of the Sixth Regiment.

Lieutenant Colonel CROOKS, of the Seventh Regiment, was appointed Colonel of the Sixth, vice NELSON, resigned.

Captain SAMUEL MCPHAIL, of Houston county, was appointed Lieutenant Colonel of the Seventh regiment, vice CROOKS, promoted. Lieutenant Colonel MCPHAIL joins the Indian expedition as commander of the irregular cavalry.

Lieutenant Colonel Averill, of the Sixth regiment reported for duty yesterday. He left for Lake City, and will take a volunteer cavalry force to the Indian country from that locality.

The Third Regiment.

The following dispatch from Gen. Halleck was received yesterday:

WASHINGTON, August 24, 1862.

To Governor Ramsey:
If General Schofield can spare the Third Minnesota Volunteers, they will be sent to you. They either have been or soon will be exchanged.

H. W. HALLECK,
General in-Chief.

Charleston Tri-Weekly Courier.

BY A. S. WILLINGTON & CO............CHARLESTON, S. C., (C. S. A.) SATURDAY MORNING, AUGUST 30, 1862.........$5 PER ANNUM.

TRI-WEEKLY COURIER.

FRIDAY MORNING, AUGUST 29, 1862.

Will our friends in the country give us reports of the late changes of weather and the condition of the crops?

Where are the official reports of the skirmish at Pocotaligo and the battle at Secessionville?

We have received several communications concerning the Convention and Council. As the call for the Convention has been issued these communications have lost their interest, and are declined. Other communications are necessarily deferred.

A drunken horseman with a uniform that showed muddy marks of falls, was galloping through the streets on Wednesday to the annoyance and terror of pedestrians, who were in danger of being bespattered with dirt if nothing else.

The rider owed his equilibrium to the discretion of his horse.

Cannot civil, municipal and martial law combined prevent such outrages?

On many windows along our streets we find placards bearing the announcements—"Gold Wanted," "Silver Wanted," "Bank Notes Wanted." Do not our friends employ paper and labor needlessly to give such notices?

Has there ever been a day, since the invention of gold, silver and bank notes, wherein everybody did not want one or all of them? It is scarcely proper, in the present state of the paper market, to waste paper for such notices. If any body wants to make his wants known, a far better plan is to put them in a paper generally read and circulated as this is.

"I tell you, Captain ——, if you look in the maps of the 'orld, I warrant you shall find in the comparisons between Macedon and Monmouth, that the situations, look you, is both alike. There is a river in Macedon; and there is also moreover a river at Monmouth."—*King Henry 5th, Act 4, Scene 7.*

So spake and argued the sage FLUELLEN. Some of our citizens were excited lately with a similar train of argument. On reading the notice of Professor BERNARD's lectures in the *Courier*, it occurred to several minds that there was an Oxford in Mississippi, and an Oxford in England, and universities at both places. A Professor BERNARD at Oxford, England, and a President BARNARD at Oxford, Mississippi. We have not been informed as to the conclusion derived from these premises, but we may safely infer "that the situations, look you, is both alike."

Conventions and the South Carolina State Convention.—The institution and the usurpations of the Executive Council, and the perpetuation or indefinite prolongation of the State Convention together with the recent and still continued discussion of these matters in the newspapers, have given an interest and importance to the general subject, which induce us to republish, this morning, our editorial, of the 11th February last, entitled—"Conventions and the South Carolina State Convention." It will be found full of historic instruction, calculated to overthrow the untenable dogma of those politicians, who would, unwisely and illegally crown Conventions of popular Delegates with the absolute sovereignty of the State, to the dethronement and enslavement of THE PEOPLE, THE ONLY TRUE SOVEREIGN, in our republican system. It will be followed by other articles, illustrative of the subject.

The Rappahannock River is formed at the Eastern edge of Culpeper County by the junction of North and Rapidan Rivers. Its general course is Southeast, and its length about one hundred and twenty-five miles to its mouth, which is about twenty-five miles South of the Potomac's mouth.

The two small streams, Hegeman's and Æstham's, mentioned in accounts from Richmond, are, we believe, confluents forming the "North" branch of the Rappahannock.

G. A. ELSWORTH, telegraphist for Colonel J. H. MORGAN, is an expert operator and a very efficient member of MORGAN's staff.

It may be questioned, however, whether he is doing the cause and his business any good by reporting all his exploits and performances.

The Coming Autumn and Winter.—An officer who came down in the same train with the prisoners to Richmond, on Saturday, and who conversed freely with them and with those taken at Cedar Run, says they very generally expressed this one opinion with regard to the war. They did not expect to subjugate the South, but they were determined to ruin the country and to compel the inhabitants, by the strong argument of absolute starvation, to return to the Union. This they meant to do by continual incursions, by the destruction of houses, by the ruin of crops, by the deportation of negros, by the plunder of cattle, horses, hogs, and every living thing on the plantations.

The Hospitals.—The remarks in Congress, says the Fayeteville *Observer* indicate that these horrible nuisances are to undergo a thorough overhauling. From information we have received from various quarters we are satisfied that never was overhauling more deserved. We know of one gentleman at least who had a wounded son there who is determined to bear his testimony to the flagrant character of the evils. Let others do likewise. In the name of all that is generous and just and humane, let us see that the gallant soldiers of liberty, and especially the wounded among them, be treated in the kindest and most skilful manner.

Congressional.—An interesting debate took place in the Senate on Monday, on the subject of abuses in the Medical Department of the Army. The discussion took a wide range, embracing the delinquencies of Provost Marshals and kindred subjects. Some of the Senators were in favor of correcting all the abuses and irregularities existing in the various departments—a task says the *Whig*, to which the cleaning of the Augean stables was but child's play. We hope that the reformatory disposition of the Senate wil not prove spasmodic and transitory.

In the House of Representatives, several Billsl of an interesting character, were introduced. Mr. FOOTE submitted a series of important resolutions, which are published in full in our Congressional report. The House went into secret session, and sat with closed doors until a late hour.

BY TELEGRAPH.

THE LATEST NEWS.

FROM RICHMOND.

GREAT NEWS FROM THE ARMY IN VIRGINIA!

Another Glorious Success of Gen. Stuart's Cavalry!

Destruction of an Immense Amount of Stores!

Capture of Three Hundred and Sixty-seven Prisoners!

CAPTURE OF GENL. POPE'S HORSES, SADDLE, UNIFORM COAT AND SERVANT, $60,000, IMPORTANT OFFICIAL DOCUMENTS, &c., &c.

RICHMOND, August 27.—Major-General STUART, with a force of cavalry, surprised and routed about five thousand Yankees near Cattlet's Station, Fauquier County, Va, on the Orange and Alexandria Rail Road, last Friday. His command destroyed an immense amount of stores, captured three hundred and sixty-seven prisoners, including a Colonel, three Captains, and fifteen other commissioned officers; also General POPE's two horses, saddle, uniform coat and servant, together with sixty thousand dollars in specie and Treasury notes, and official documents of the highest importance from Gen. POPE.

The command returned the next day with the loss of but two killed and five wounded. The enemy are in full retreat towards Alexandria.

From Richmond.

MORE NORTHERN INTELLIGENCE—SPEECH OF MR. ROEBUCK, M. P., AT SHEFFIELD, ENGLAND

RICHMOND, August 27.—Northern papers of the 22d instant, received.

The most interesting news is the occupation of Clarksville, Tennessee, by the Confederate troops.

The Yankees have abandoned Fort Donelson.

Ten Indiana Regiments besides cavalry and artillery have been sent into Kentucky.

Gen. CORCORAN arrived in Philadelphia on the 21st instant, and met with a gratifying reception. He has disposed of his diary, which is soon to make its appearance in print.

Several ladies have been arrested at Parkersburg, Virginia, and imprisoned until they took the oath of allegiance.

In Mr. ROEBUCK's speech at Sheffield, England, he said he would entreat the noble Lord (RUSSELL) to weigh well the conseqnences of what he called "perfect neutrality." There has not yet been "perfect neutrality." We were at presnt supporting the North with every means of offense and injury to the South. He therefore begged the noble Lord deeply to consider whether the time had not come for him to be the first in Europe to recognise the Southern Confederacy. (Cries of no, no, and Cheers)

Six months, Mr. ROEBUCK said, would not pass over before that was done. The Northerners would never be our friends. Of the Southerners we could make friends, and they were not the scum and refuse of Europe but Englishmen.

In New York the stock market was feverish in consequence of disquieting rumors from Washington.

Gold advanced to 115¾. Sterling exchange dull at 127½.

[SECOND DISPATCH.]

Congressional.

SENATE.

RICHMOND, August 27.—In the Senate a resolution was adopted, requesting the President to communicate by what authority Provost Marshals are appointed, and their pay and allowances fixed.

The remainder of the session was occupied in the discussion of the bill to amend the Conscript law, so as to provide that persons liable to military duty shall be enrolled wherever found. The bill was amended, but before disposed of the Senate adjourned.

HOUSE.

In the House Mr. VILLERE, of Louisiana, offered a resolution, which was adopted, requesting the President to furnish the reports of Generals LOVELL and DUNCAN and Lieutenant-Colonel HIGGINS, concerning the evacuation of New Orleans, and of Forts Jackson and St. Phillip.

Mr. VEST, of Missouri, offered a resolution of thanks to Commodore MONTGOMERY and command for meritorious and gallant services, rendered on the Mississippi river, with their Cotton boat fleet. Resolution adopted.

Mr. FOOTE, of Tennessee offered a resolution declaring that S. R. MALLORY, as Secretary of the Navy, does not possess the confidence of Congress, or of the country. The resolution was laid on the table.

Mr. BARKSDALE, of Mississippi, offered a resolution, which was adopted, for the appointment of a joint Committee to investigate the causes of complaint against the Secretary of the Navy.

Mr. FOOTE, of Tennessee, offered a resolution supplementary to resolutions submitted by him on Monday, recommending to the President to embody in a Proclamation to the people of the Northwestern States the assurance, that if they desist from further participation in the pending war, the Confederate States will enter into a reciprocity commercial treaty with them on the most liberal and equitable terms.

The series of resolutions were referred to the Committee on Foreign Affairs.

From Chattanooga, Tenn.

STIRRING WORK IN THE WEST—OUR FORCES ADVANCING—MORGAN AND FORREST AGAIN VICTORIOUS.

CHATTANOOGA, August 27.—Gen. MOXEY's brigade crossed the Tennessee River last night, and occupied Bridgeport without firing a gun. On Sunday morning the Yankees got frightened at McMinniville and evacuated it, burning immense stores, munitions, &c. In three hours from the time the panic commenced not a Yankee was in McMinniville.

A gentleman who has arrived here says the Nashville *Union* reports that a battle had been fought near Hartsville, between the united forces of Gen. FORREST and Col. MORGAN, and the Yankees, in which the latter were whipped.

The Nashville *Union* says the Federal forces at Clarksville have surrendered to a smaller force of guerrillas.

From Jackson, Miss.

SERENADE TO GEN. TILGHMAN—MOVEMENTS OF THE ENEMY.

JACKSON, Miss., August 26.—General TILGHMAN was serenaded to-night. In response, he denounced Governor MAGOFFIN as a childish traitor to the South. He alluded to his imprisonment and defence of Fort Henry.

The Federals liberated and carried away three hundred convicts from Baton Rouge.

Two gunboats are anchored above the mouth of the Yazoo river.

CONFEDERATE CONGRESS.

RICHMOND, AUGUST 25, 1862.

SENATE.

Mr. SPARROW, of Louisiana, presented a memorial from the Faculty of the Southern Baptist Theological Seminary, asking exemption for students, of whom there would not be over a hundred. Referred to the Committee on Military Affairs.

Mr. CLAY presented a bill to be entiled an Act to punish and suppress the importation of notes purporting to be notes of the Confederate States Treasury, punishing any officer, soldier, or adherent of the enemy, who may fall into our hands with counterfeit Confederate States notes in his possession, or who may have been proven to have passed off any such, either by trading with or giving away, with death, to be decided by court martial. The bill was referred to the Judiciary Committee.

Mr. ORR, of South Carolina, offered the following:

Resolved, That the President be requested to inform the Senate who constitute the Medical Board of Examiners for granting furloughs; what orders have been issued to them, and to Surgeons in charge of Hospitals, with reference to furloughs, together with the necessity for such a supervisory board.

Mr. ORR recited some of the abuses by which the sick soldier is kept, during convalescence, in the Hospitals; and prevented from visiting his home, when his condition admits of his absence both from the hospital and the army, and indicated that in a few days he would introduce a Bill with the view of correcting the errors of the Medical Board and the Department generally.

Mr. SIMMS, of Kentucky, favored the resolution and added his testimony to that of the Senator from South Carolina, to show that the Medical Department was conducted in a most culpable manner.

Mr. CLARK, of Missouri, while he admitted that there were many errors which might be avoided, the fault could not be said to belong to the Department generally. There were causes to operate in many instances of neglect, for which the Medical Department was not responsible.

Mr. HILL, of Georgia, was inclined to believe that the gentlemen who had spoken so severely against the Medical Board were laboring under a wrong impression. He cited instances and his own evidence to show that the Medical Board were not culpable in the matter of detaining soldiers from furloughs. He had no doubt there were some abuses, and if there were, they should be corrected; but we should be careful how we locate our charges.

Mr. BROWN, of Mississippi, said that there were abuses in the Medical Department—there were abuses in every department; that this Congress had a right to correct them, and ought to go to work firmly and vigorously to put them down.

The resolution was adopted.

Mr. SEMMES, of Louisiana, offered the following resolution:

That the Committee on the Judiciary be directed to inquire into the necessity for further legislation to restrain within constitutional limits the exercise of power by military officers assumed under color of the act suspending the privilege of the writ of *Habeas Corpus*, and to report by bill or otherwise

Mr. SEMMES said he had been induced to offer this resolution by constantly seeing the proclamation of military commandants, proclaiming martial law. These military men had come to think that all power, both military and legislative, was vested in them. They had not only proclaimed martial law, but in some cases had gone so far as to take a step, upon which Congress itself had not ventured, and made Confederate Treasury Notes a legal tender. The most extraordinary of these proclamations, whcih had yet come under his notice, was that of Major-General Van Dorn. It had been published in the newspapers, but since its terms might not be recollected by Senators, he would read it.

Mr. SEMMES read the proclamation and commented upon it sariátim. He showed that Gen. Van Dorn had taken upon himself to fix the death penalty upon the offence of trading with the enemy, whereas, for the same offence Congress had decided that the penalty should be fine and imprisonment; and had made it obligatory on all persons within the limits of his command to take Treasury Notes at par; and had taken away the freedom of the Press, by threatening with fine and imprisonment; any editor who should speak or write anything derogatory of any military officer within the district.

On concluding his remarks, Mr. SEMMES said he acquitted Gen. Van Dorn of any intention to do a wrong, he had no doubt of his purity and patriotism, but he thought his course actuated as he no doubt was, by the purest motives and the best intentions, showed the imperative necessity of some legislation on the subject.

Mr. SPARROW was glad his colleague had called attention to the ursurpation of power by our military men. He only rose to allude to the seizure by Gen. Van Dorn of the military stores of the State of Louisiana at the time of the surrender of the city of New Orleans. He was glad to see, by a recent publication, that the Government had forbidden the seizure in future of State stores by officers of the Confederacy.

Mr. OLDHAM, of Texas, said General Herbert had proclaimed martial law in his State, where a Yankee had not set foot since the war, but things were happening under our own eyes which called for our attention. He, as a free citizen, was not allowed to go from here to North Carolina without going to the Provost Marshal's office and getting a pass like a free negro. The whole martial law system seemed based upon the principle that men of the Confederacy should travel with papers in their pocket. Spies and other enemjes, provided they could get a pass, could travel where they pleased. He did not believe that Congress and the President together had the power to pass the unlimited martial law that was being exercised by the Provost Marshals. He thought the Provost Marshals should be abolished.

The resolution was then put to the vote and adopted.

In the House, Mr. FOOTE, of course, was busy and bustling, and full of interruption and interpellation. As any one, even FOOTE, who is always up and talking, must sometimes emit something tolerably good, we give the following:

Mr. FOOTE offered the following resolutions, which, on his motion, were laid on the table, and ordered to be printed:

Resolved, That in the judgment of this House the true policy of the present war imperately requires that the movements of our armies in the field should every where be as active and aggressive as would be at all consistent with a sound nnd enlightened discretion—striking at the forces of the enemy boldly and vigorously wherever they may be found on Southern soil, and delaying nowhere long enough to allow our merciless foes an opportunity of devastating the most fertile districts of the South, and perchance of ultimately obtaining reinforcements, which may make it difficult to drive them beyond our confines, without such an expenditure of the precious blood of our patriotic soldiers as would obviously be necessary for their expulsion or capture.

Resolved, That so soon as the forces of the enemy shall have been driven back to their own country, if the deluded Government at Washington should still refuse us peace, it will be our policy at once to invade the territory of the foe, with a view of obtaining, sword in hand, "indemnity for the past and security for the future."

Resolved, That at some moment anterior to the invasion of the enemy's country by our military forces, it will be eminently expedient, in the judgment of this House, that the President should, if consistent with his own views of propriety, make known, in a formal and explicit proclamation, addressed to the inhabitants of the Northwestern States, the unanimous willingness of the people of the Confederate States to guarantee to them in the most effectual manner, the free navigation of the Mississippi and Ohio rivers to their mouths, provided that they at once desist from all further participation in this cruel and unnatural war.

Mr. GARNETT, of Virginia, presented a resolution requesting the President to inform the House whether the army regulations requiring the troops to be paid monthly, had been complied with; and, if not, how far they are in arrears, and the reasons for such delay. The resolution was adopted.

Mr. PERKINS, of Louisiana, offered a resolution requesting the President, if not incompatible with the public interest, to furnish to this House the instructions given to the military and naval commanders at Norfolk and New Orleans, in reference to the defence of those cities, and the subsequent evacuation by our troops, also the correspondence of the Executive, and the heads of Departments, with the Governor of Louisiana and the Governor of Virginia, and such reports of such officers as may have connection with the subject. Adopted.

NEWS FROM VIRGINIA.

[*From the Richmond Examiner.*]

FROM THE RAPPAHANNOCK.

Rumors come to us thick and fast from the region of the Rappahannock; but of intelligence known to be authentic, the amount we have been able to obtain is surprisingly small. The sum of it all is, that our armies have crossed the Rappahannock in pursuit of the enemy.

Our most reliable information is obtained from an officer of Anderson's brigade, Longstreet's division, who was wounded in the engagement on Saturday. We give the substance of his statement. Saturday morning, Gen. Jackson, with two other divisions, crossed the Rappahannock to the West of the Orange and Alexandria Rail Road, and on Sunday night established his headquarters at the Warrenton White Sulphur Springs, near the town of Warrenton.

At an early hour Saturday morning, Longstreet attempted to cross the Rappahannock, at the rail road bridge, when his passage was disputed by the enemy. An artillery duel then took place, which lasted till one o'clock, P. M., when the enemy retreated. Our loss in killed and wounded was about one hundred and fifty. The loss of the enemy, he being on the other side of the river, remains unknown. During the engagement, the enemy burnt the bridge with shell and hot shot. On the retreat of the enemy, Longstreet crossed the river and made pursuit.

Our informant having been wounded just before the passage of the river was effected, retired from the field. Up to the time of his arrival at Rapidan Station, Sunday night, at dark, he could still hear the booming of Longstreet's cannon.

Besides what we have narrated, a number of rumors were brought down by the passengers from Gordonsville yesterday evening. One of these was that Jackson had gotten in the rear of Pope and cut off his retreat to Manassas. Another that Stuart was in Alexandria, and that on his road thither he had captured a train of one hundred wagons and a paymaster with thirty thousand dollars in United States Treasury notes on his person.

Nothing has been heard of Burnside, and many well informed persons incline to the opinion that he has evacuated Fredericksburg, and is now in or near Washington city.

LATER.

Since writing the above we have received some particulars of the part borne by the Washington Artillery in the engagement on Saturday. This corps, on the left wing of Longstreet's Division, with nineteen guns engaged the enemy with forty-five guns at the junction of Hazel and Hedgeman's rivers, three miles East of the Rail Road Bridge. The duel lasted seven hours. Our artillerists lost twenty-four killed and wounded. Lieutenant J. W. Brewer, Taylor Marshall, Walter Chambers, H. Rose and four drivers, were killed. The enemy were driven across Beverley's Ford with heavy loss. The Washington Artillery crossed the river that night, and at last accounts were bearing away to the East in pursuit of the enemy.

[*From the Richmond Dispatch.*]

FROM THE RAPPAHANNOCK.

The information received by us from the lines of the Rappahannock is so confused, and the reports so conflicting, that it is with difficulty that we are enabled to present anything approaching an intelligible account of affairs in that locality.

On Saturday a heavy artillery duel took place at the junction of Hedgeman and Aestham rivers, between nineteen guns of the Washington Artillery, Colonel Walton commanding, and about forty guns of the enemy. The enemy were driven across the Rappahannock, at Berkeley's ford, and were in full retreat in the direction of Alexandria.

As our troops approached the rail road bridge over the Rappahannock, the enemy commenced shelling it with great fury, and finally succeeded in burning the structure. While the fight at Berkeley's Ford was in progress, and after it had terminated, heavy firing was heard on the left, or in the direction of Warrenton, supposed to proceed from some portion of our forces that had crossed higher up the stream.

We saw a letter, yesterday afternoon, from a member of Capt. Parker's artillery, dated "Camp on Rappahannock River, August 21," which stated that an order had been received from General Jackson at Warrenton, to hurry up the remainder of the army, and not to delay to prepare provisions, as enough had been captured at that point to feed the whole force for some time.

In the pursuit of the fleeing foe our forces captured several hundred prisoners.

[*From the Richmond Enquirer.*]

FURTHER FROM THE UPPER RAPPAHANNOCK.

The intelligence brought down by the train from Gordonsville, on yesterday, adds to the information already received of the operations of Gens. Jackson and Longstreet against the enemy, on the lines of the Upper Rappahannock. The enemy's retreat was being conducted under the cover of a strong rear guard of infantry and artillery. On Saturday morning the enemy crossed the river, the rear guard giving battle, after crossing, to our forces under Gen. Jackson, who were in close pursuit. The fighting continued nearly all day, our troops succeeding in crossing over about one o'clock, at which time the result of the day's battle was decidedly in our favor. During the retreat of the enemy, Gen. Stuart's cavalry made a successful tour against the enemy's provision train, and is reported to have captured one hundred wagons, a Quartermaster and other prisoners, and about $35,000 in specie. The Rail Road bridge over the Rappahannock was destroyed by the enemy's shell, but the turnpike bridge was uninjured, and was of course of vast service in admitting of a speedy pursuit by Jackson's forces. Gen. Longstreet crossed on Sunday.

About four hundred prisoners were taken in Saturday's fight, and the losses on both sides were severe, the enemy suffering a very disastrous reverse, and portions of our army in the beginning of the fight, being subjected to a galling fire. It is reported that the Fourth Georgia brigade commenced a charge upon the enemy's principal battery, half a mile off, and after advancing with heroic gallantry in the face of the fire, to within a few hundred yards of it, discovered that it was on the opposite side of the river. They were compelled to retreat, there being no means of crossing the river, and suffered severely.

One Company of the Washington Artillery is reported to have been seriously cut up.

Large numbers of the enemy's dead and wounded, with many arms, fell into our hands. The unhurt prisoners were started down on Sunday for Richmond.

The enemy is endeavoring to reach the Potomac, but the pursuit by our army is being conducted with the determination to cut him off at Manassas. General Jackson's headquarters were on yesterday at Warrenton Springs, and his division was advancing towards Manassas. At present the indications are that Pope will be forced back upon Fredericksburg, if not cut off entirely.

Thus it will be seen that within the space of barely more than a week, Pope's grand army, with all its reinforcements from McClellan, has been forced to retreat more than fifty miles, suffering two successive defeats, and losing immensely in men, arms, stores, and ammunition.

[*From the Richmond Examiner, August 26.*]

FROM JAMES CITY AND GLOUCESTER.

From a gentleman who arrived in this city last evening from the York Peninsula and Gloucester, we have some interesting and authentic intelligence.

On Saturday last, Major Rosser, commanding our cavalry on the Peninsula, proceeded with sixty men to the Burnt Ordinary, twelve miles on this side of Williamsburg. Here he encountered some Yankee pickets, whom he drove in, and pursued to within a short distance of Williamsburg, and only gave over the pursuit when he was assured by citizens of the neighborhood, and from his own observations, that the enemy's cavalry, in heavy force, occupied the town, for the double purpose of covering the retreat of the army and guarding a vast quantity of stores which they had accumulated there.

On the same day Major Rosser received information, through his scouts, that fifty transports were lying at Bigler's wharf, ten miles above Yorktown, and distant three miles from Williamsburg. No transports or gunboats were on the York above that point.

From a gentleman who left Gloucester on Thursday last, we learn that three regiments of Yankee infantry, with some cavalry and several pieces of artillery, landed that evening at Gloucester Point. It was the opinion in the neighborhood that they designed marching to Fredericksburg. This we think unlikely. Their design, most probably, was to forage the country and at the same time to protect their transports from an artillery surprise. They are said to be devastating the country and committing every imaginable outrage on the inhabitants.

We may say, in this connection, that from what we hear from all sources, we feel assured that the greater part of McClellan's army is in Washington City. A gentleman who spent last week in the County of St. Mary's, Maryland, tells us that he saw every day between twenty-five and thirty transports, loaded with troops, ascending the Potomac. Eight or ten thousand men may still remain on the Peninsula, and in Gloucester, but these will also have disappeared in less than a week. Washington City is in danger, and the Yankee Government is hurrying thither every available man.

[*From the Richmond Dispatch*]

M'CLELLAN'S DEPARTURE.

Dr. Minge, who has been at Westover nearly ever since the arrival of McClellan's army there, has arrived in this city. He reports that the last of the Yankee army has left, leaving behind a number of stragglers and deserters. The ground where they last camped is strewn with cast off uniforms, broken and injured muskets, crackers, &c. The Doctor saw nineteen Yankees throw their muskets in the water and swim a creek in deserting. With the exception of restriction upon his liberty, Dr. Minge was well treated by the general officers with whom he came in contact.—Nearly all of them, particularly Generals Kearney and Fitzjohn Porter, behaved as gentlemen. The former remarked one day that the Confederates had one advantage over the Federals, and that was, if one of their Generals was killed they had an abundance of good ones to fill his place, which was not the case with their enemies. He also remarked when he arrived at Wostover, after the seven days' fighting, that by all the rules of war there would be a battle there in six hours, and offered to send Dr. M's wife away from there for safety. All seemed surprised that the Confederates did not pursue the Federal army.

When our artillery shelled the camp at Westover, at night, all in Mrs. Selden's house retreated into the cellar; but, upon a Yankee officer declaring that if a candle, left burning up stairs, was not put out, he would "blow the d—d house up," Dr. M. had to go up stairs through the iron rain, and extinguish the light. Everything in the vicinity of the late camping ground is utterly destroyed. Dr. M. was sent for by one of the Generals to estimate and receive compensation for his property which was seized for the use of the army; but learning that the oath of allegiance was one of the conditions, promptly told the officer that he gave all, and, more than that, would give up his life before he would take it.

Desertions were numerous, and one Yankee soldier paid as high as $40 in gold for an old suit of citizens' clothes, in which to pass his picket. On the first of the four very hot days during the stay of the army, the sick list was 365, and by the fourth day it ran up to 1068. The country is literally dotted with Yankee graves, many of them hardly covering the bodies. From one he saw the nose of a corpse protruding, and from another a pair of legs encased in boots.

Some of the gunboats are still lying off Westover, and on one of them was a son of Mrs. James Selden, who is in the U. S. Navy. The commander of the fleet sent word ashore, a day or two since, that if he saw parties of more than three or four persons on land, that he would shell the mansion (Mrs. Selden's) at Westover.

FROM THE NORTHWEST.

Advices from Staunton furnish us the intelligence that some five hundred refugees from Northwestern Virginia have arrived in that town within the past week. They are principally from Barbour and Randolph Counties, and representatives of the loyal portion of the population of that region. They state that those who have heretofore been loud in their professions of devotion to the old Union are now availing themselves of every opportunity to dodge the draft which has been ordered in the Pierpont realms. Many of them would gladly become converts to Southernism, but that they fear their guilt is too well known to admit of an easy pardon.

The Savannah *Republican*, referring to the late issues of counterfeits, says:

"Richmond and Nashville are the two great floodgates through which these counterfeits flow into the Confederate States, and the whole thing is a part of the Yankee scheme of subjugation. They hope to ruin our currency, and the felony is patronized by their Government and army officers."

We see by the papers that one counterfeiter has been hung in Richmond for issuing bogus money, on the Confederate States. We wish the Government would serve some of the robbing speculators the same way, it would cause everything to come down to living prices.—*Charlotte N. C. Whig.*

DAILY LYNCHBURG VIRGINIAN.

THE RIGHTS OF THE SOUTH AND THE UNION OF THE SOUTH.

BY CHARLES W BUTTON. LYNCHBURG, TUESDAY, SEPTEMBER 2, 1862 VOLUME 11---NUMBER 25.

TERMS.

[T]he VIRGINIAN is publish d daily at $6 and [Tri]-Weekly at $5 per annum, in advance, [and] Weekly at $2, invariably in advance, otherwise $2,50 will be charged in all cases. No paper will be discontinued except a the option of the Proprietor until all arrearages shall have been paid.

ADVERTISEMENTS are inserted for 50 cents per square of 10 lines, or less for the first insertion and 37½ cents for each continuance unless ordered inner-form or weekly and then 50 cents per square will be charged for each insertion. If the number of insertions be not marked on the MSS, it will be published till ordered out and charged according.

THE YEARLY RATES ARE:

For one square daily	$35
For two squares, daily	50
For one square tri-weekly	25
For two squares tri-weekly	40

☞ Advertisements [int]ended for both papers subject to special contract.

☞ Annual advertisers will be limited to their immediate business, or the advertisements charged at transient rates.

☞ All new advertisements appear in the daily and tri-weekly papers.

☞ Obituary notices which exceed eight lines are charged r[eas]onably for the excess.

BUSINESS CARDS.

[G]OGGIN, TRADER & HOLT
Cotton and Tobacco Factors,
[G]rocers, Receiving Forwarding and
[C]OMMISSION MERCHANTS,
Memphis, Tenn.
July 18-ts

LEE, ROCKE & TAYLOR.
WHOLESALE AND RETAIL
[G]rocers, Commission and Forwarding Merchants,
(*At the Old Stand of Lee, Rocke & Co.,*)
No. 105 Main Street,
Lynchburg, Virginia.

WILL pay particular and prompt attention to the sale of Tobacco, Whe t, Corn, Bacon, Lard, Butter, Feathers, and Country Produce generally; make liberal advances on produce or merchandise in hand for sale; guarantee and cash time sales when required; attend promptly to goods consigned to be forwarded; have always on hand a large and well selected stock of Groceries Imported and Domestic Liquors, Wines, &c., &c.

☞ *Grain Bags* furnished at the usual rent when produce is consigned to us.

McDANIEL & IRBY,
Lynchburg, Va.
[G]eneral Commission Merchants,
AND AGENTS FOR THE SALE
[N]EW ORLEANS SUGAR and MOLASSES
which they are constantly receiving direct.
[W]ASHINGTON COUNTY SALT and [M]ANUFACTURED and SMOKING TOBACCO

We invite attention to our market as being quite as cheap as any in Virginia, with great advantages in shipping to interior Merchants.
Lynchburg, oct. 29 1861.

GEORGE STEPTOE,
General Commission Merchant,
(AT THE OLD STAND OF JONES & STEPTOE, AND NEXT DOOR TO M. HOLLINS & CO.,)
No. 68, Main st., Lynchburg,

IS still selling TOBACCO and other produce at old prices, and will give particular attention to the sale of Tobacco, Wheat, Flour, Corn, Bacon, Lard, Butter, Feathers, Wool, Seng, Wax, Dried Fruit, &c. Account sales rendered with Check for nett proceeds soon as sales are made.

☞ GRAIN BAGS furnished at the usual rent when produce is consigned to me for sale.

☞ Orders for goods filled when Produce or Money in hand. jy 29-18m

NEW COPARTNERSHIP.
SAM M'CORKLE, S. M. M'CORKLE, WM. KINNIER.
McCORKLE, SON & CO.
(Successors to McCorkle & Co.,)
Grocers & Commission Merchants
AND MANUFACTURERS OF
Chewing & Smoking Tobacco,
NO. 113, MAIN STREET,
LYNCHBURG, VA.

We will give particular attention to the sale of Tobacco Breadstuffs, Provisions, and all kinds of Country Produce and Merchandize. At the old stand of McCorkle & Co. We shall endeavor to keep always on hand a full stock of all articles requisite to the business, and from our long experience in the business hope to merit a share of the public patronage, and especially that so liberally extended to the former concern. Our Mr. Kinnear will give his personal attention to the Commission business,as he has for some years been pursuing that branch, and we feel confident from his long experience and thorough knowledge of the business will not fail to give satisfaction to all who entrust their interest to our hands.

☞ Will make liberal advances on approved produce in hand, and remit promptly for all time and cash sales.

SAMUEL McCORKLE.
S. M. McCORKLE.
WM. KINNIER.
1daely

RUFFIN'S
Phosphor-Peruvian Guano, Tobacco Manure, Agricultural Salt and Ground Bone Ash.

F. G. RUFFIN, corner of 11th and Cary st., on the Basin, offers to the Farmers the following *MANURES*, all of his own manufacture—viz:

Ruffin's Phosphor-Peruvian, containing 8 per cent. ammonia. and 40 to 50 per cent. bone phosphate lime, per ton of 2,000 lbs.,	$50 00
Ruffin's Bone Ash Guano, containing 5 per cent. ammonia and about 70 per cent. bone phosphate lime, per ton of 2,000 lbs.,	50 00
Ruffin's Tobacco Manure, containing 5 per ct. ammonia, 34 per cent. bone phosphate lime, 22 chloride of sodium, and 17 per cent. sulphate lime, per ton of 2,000 lbs.,	45 00
Ruffin's Ground Bone Ash, containing about 80 per cent. bone phosphate lime, dry and pure, per ton of 2 000 lbs.,	35 00
Agricultural Salt, loose, per ten of 2,000 lbs..	11 00
Agricultural Salt, in bags, per ton of 2.000 lbs.,	13 00

The above Manures are put up in strong bags containing 167 pounds each. twelve bags of which make a fraction over a ton, and can be had of *F. G. Ruffin*. at his mill, of any Commission Merchant in Richmond: *Thos. Branch & Sons*, Petersburg; *M. Hollins & Co.*, Lynchburg: *Leigh & Brother*, Norfolk; *Mason, Martin & Co.*, Scottsville; *Johnson Clarke & Co.*, Danville.
march 8-d&c[tf]

100 TRAY WHEEL-BARROWS on hand and for sale by JNO. H. BAILEY, Agt.
jan 22

50 BBLS. VERY FINE OLD RYE WHISKEY for sale by BOCOCK & PARRISH.
jy 29

MEDICAL.

Baltimore Lock Hospital.
ESTABLISHED AS A REFUGE FROM QUACKERY.
The Only Place Where a Cure Can be Obtained.

DR. JOHNSON has discovered the most Certain, Speedy and only effectual Remedy in the World for Weakness of the Back or Limbs, Strictures, Affections of the Kidneys and Bladder, Involuntary Discharges, Impotency, General Debility, Nervousness, Dyspepsia, Langour, Low Spirits, Confusion of Ideas, Palpitation of the Heart, Timidity, Tremblings, Dimness of Sight or Giddiness, Disease of the Head, Throat, Nose or Skin, Affections of the Lungs, Stomach or Bowels—those Terrible Disorders arising from the Solitary Habits of Youth—those SECRET and solitary practices,more fatal to their victims than the songs of the Syrens to the Mariners of Ulysses, blighting their most brilliant hopes of anticipations, rendering marriage, &c., impossible.

YOUNG MEN

Especially, who have become the victims of Solitary Vice, that dreadful and destructive habit which annually sweeps to an untimely grave thousands of Young Men of the most exalted talents and brilliant intellect, who might otherwise have entranced listening Senates with the thunders of eloquence, or waked to ecstasy the living lyre, may call with [full] confidence.

MARRIAGE.

Married Persons, or Young Men contemplating marriage, being aware of physical weakness, or[ganic debility, deformities, &c., s]peedily cured.

He who places himself under the care of Dr. J. may religiously upon his honor as a gentleman and confidently confide in his skill as a Physician.

ORGANIC WEAKNESS

Immediately Cured and Full Vigor Restored.

This Dreadful Disease—which renders Life miserable and Maiage Impossible—is the penalty paid by the victims of improper indulgences. Young persons are too apt to commit excesses from not being aware of the dreadful consequences that may may ensue. Now, who that understands the subject will pretend to deny that the power of procreation is lost sooner by those falling into improper habits than by the prudent? Besides being deprived the pleasure of healthy offspring, the most serious and destructive symptoms to both body and mind arise. The system becomes Deranged, the Physical and Mental Functions Weakened, Loss of Procreative Power, Nervous Irritibility, Dyspepsia, Palpitation of the Heart, Indigestion, Constitutional Debility, a Wasting of the Frame, Coughs, Consumption &c.

OFFICE No. 7, SOUTH FREDERICK STREET, Left hand side going from Baltimore street, a few doors from the corner. Fail not to observe the name and number.

Letters must be paid and contain a stamp. The Doctor's Diplomas hang in his office.

DR. JOHNSON,

Member of the Royal College of Surgeons, London, graduate from one of the most eminet Colleges in the United States, and the greater part of whose life has been spent in the hospitals of London, Paris, Philadelphia and elsewhere, has effected some of the most astonishing cures that were ever known; many troubled with ringing in the head and ears when asleep, great nervousness, being alarmed at sudden sounds, bashfulness, with frequent blushing, attended sometimes with a derangement of the mind, were cured immediately.

Take Particular Notice.

Dr. J. addresses all those who have injured themselves by improper indulgence and solitary habits, which ruin both body and mind, unfitting them for either business, study, society or marriage.

THESE are some of the sad and melancholy effects produced by early habits of youth, viz., Weakness of the Back and Limbs, Pains in the Head, Didmness of Sight, Loss of Muscular Power, Palpitation of the Heart, Dyspepsy, Nervous Irritability, Derangement of the Digestive Functions, General Debility, Symptomps of Consumption.

MENTALLY.—The fearful effects on the mind are much to be dreaded—Loss of Memory, Confusion of Ideas, Depression of Spirits, Evil Forebodings, Aversion to Society, Self-Distrust Love of Solitude, Timidity, &c., are some of the evils produced.

THOUSANDS of persons of all ages can now judge what is the cause of their declining health losing their vigor, becoming weak, pale, nervous and emaciated, having a singular appearance about the eyes, cough and symptoms of consumption.

YOUNG MEN

Who have injured themselves by a certain practice indulged in when alone—a habit frequently learned from evil companions, or at school, the effects of which are nightly felt, even when asleep, and if not cured renders marriage impossible, and destroys both mind and body, should apply immediately.

What a pity that a young man, the hope of his country, the darling of his parents, should be snatched from all prospects and enjoyments of life, by the consequence of deviating from the path of nature and indulging in acertain secret habit. Such persons MUST, before contemplating

MARRIAGE,

reflect that a sound mind and body are the most necessary requisites to promote connubial happiness. Indeed, without these the journey through life becomes a weary pilgrimage: the prospect hourly darkens to the view: the mind becomes shadowed with dispair, and filled with the melancholy reflection that the happiness of another becomes blighted with our own

DISEASE OF IMPRUDENCE.

When the misguided and imprudent votary of pleasure finds he has imbibed the seeds of this painful disease, it too often happens that an ill-timed sense of shame, or dread of discovery deters him from applying to those who, from education and respectability, can alone befriend him. He falls into the hands of ignorant and designing pretenders, who, incapable of curing filch his pecuniary substance, keep him trifling month after month, or as long as the smallest fee can be obtained, and in dispair leave him to sigh over ruined health to sigh over his galling disappointment; or, by the use of that deadly poison, Mercury, hasten the constitutional symptoms of this terrible disease, such as Affection of the [He]ad, Throat, Nose, Skin, etc., progressing with [fright]ful rapidity till death puts a period [to his dread]ful cunnings,by sending him to that [undisco]vered country from whose bourne no traveller returns.

ENDORSEMENT OF THE PRESS.

The many thousands cured at this institution within the salt eighteen years, and the numerous important surgical operations performed by Dr. Johnston, witnessed by the reporters of the Sun and many other papers, notices of which have appeared again and again before the public, besides his standing as a genleman of character and respectability, is a sufficient guarantee to the afflicted.

SKIN DISEASES SPEEDILY CURED.

Persons writing should be particular in directing their letters to this Institution, in the following manner:

JOHN M. JOHNSTON, M. D.
Baltimore Lock Hospital,
Baltimore, Md.
nov 22-daely

QUARTERMASTER'S OFFICE,
Lynchburg, Va., June 25, 1862.

WANTED to hire immediately, 15 GOOD TEAMSTERS.

☞ Apply at once to the undersigned.

JOHN W. WOODSON,
Capt. and A. Q. M.
[jun]e 25-ts

500 FANCY MERINO OVERSHIRTS—assorted patterns.
I. UNTERMYER,

SAVINGS' BANKS.

PLANTER'S SAVINGS BANK.

DEPOSITORS are paid five per cent per annum interest on deposites for any length of time. Discount day, Wednesday. All paper must be handed in before Tuesday 4 o'clock, P. M. Deposites payable on presentation of certificates to the Treasurer, at Exchange Bank, Lynchburg, Va.

OFFICERS.
JAMES FRANKLIN, President.
EDMOND W. JONES, Secretary.
CAMILLUS CHRISTIAN, (at Ex. Bank,) Treasurer.

DIRECTORS:

S. W. SHELTON,	J. H. ROBINSON.
JAMES FRANKLIN	J. E. COLHOUN,*
A. ALEXANDER,	CHARLES H. MASSIE.
JNO. H. SEAY,	JOHN A. LEE,
E. W. JONES.*	

The names marked thus * are the new directors elected at the last annual meeting of the Stockholders.
Feb 13th, 1862.

OFFICE PLANTERS SAVINGS BANK.
The Board of Directors have declared a dividend of three per cent for the past six months, payable to the stockholders or legal representatives, on and after the 24th inst., at the Exchange Bank, Lynchburg Va. E W. JONES, Sec'ty.

Lynchburg Savings Bank.
OFFICE 141 MAIN ST., AT THE STORE OF MESSRS. SMITH & ADAMS

THIS Institution holds its meetings for discounting paper every Friday, evening at 4 o'clock, P. M. Depositors are paid 6 per cent on all sums remaining 12 months or more.

Deposits paid on presentation of certificates, without notice

HENRY D. FLOOD, *President.*
C. W. PRICE, *Treasurer.*
DIRECTORS.
JOHN S. BASS, WM. A. MILLER, JOHN A. TANNER, J. C. SHEARER, THOS. H. ALLEN, W. H. LANGHORNE, W. A. STROTHER, J. T. MURRELL.
mar 6 ts

CASTOR OIL.
Blue Mass,
Sul. Morphia,
Opium,
Gum Camphor,
Copperas,
English Calimel,
English Toilet Soap,
For sale by W. A. STROTHER & CO.
jy 31

Descriptive Lists for Sale.

DESCRIPTIVE LISTS AND ACCOUNTS OF PAY AND CLOTHING OF PRIVATES IN THE ARMY.

On hand and for sale at the Counting Room of this office.

TO THE TOBACCO PLANTERS OF VIRGINIA AND NORTH CAROLINA.—I am still selling Tobacco at the old prices, and will be thankful for consignments. Having had many years experience as a salesman, I feel prepared to give satisfaction to all who may favor me with their patronage. My office is at the store of A. J. Camp & Co., No. 33, Bridge Street.

Liberal advances made when desired.
july 18-3m PETER H. DILLARD.

Coffee and Tea.

20 SACKS PRIME CUBA COFFEE, 3 half chests prime Green and Black Tea, Just received and for sale by
aug 15 McDANIEL & IRBY.

Bowers and Boughton Seed Wheat for Sale.

FIFTEEN HUNDRED BUSHELS of the above varieties, OF VERY SUPERIOR QUALITY. Price $2 50 per bushel and delivered on Canal three miles above Howardsville. Address
CAMM PATTESON,
Howardsville,
aug 12-d3w&c1t Albemarle co., Va.

Bowers and Boughton Seed Wheat.

WE have for sale the above varieties of Wheat grown by Judge Wm. Daniel, Jr.

Price Three Dollars per bushel, the purchaser furnishing sacks.
aug 6 McDANIEL & IRBY.

Desirable Residence for Sale

I OFFER for sale MY RESIDENCE on Diamond Hill. The Dwelling House is a large brick building, well constructed, conveniently arranged, and contains 12 rooms a large and fertile garden a good well of water and all necessary outhouses. It is situated in one of the most beautiful and healthy parts of the city environs, and in the midst of an excellent neighborhood. There are nearly two acres of land attached.

W. H. LANGHORNE
Aug, 19-ts.

500 Pair Traces.

ON hand and to arrive from the South, Five Hundred Pair TRACE CHAINS.
aug 21-ts S. M. SIMPSON.

6 BAGS CHOICE RIO COFFEE, on consignment.
LEE, ROCKE & TAYLOR,
aug 21 105 Main St.

MONEY TO LOAN.

$30,000 TO LOAN on five years time, secured without doubt on land.

☞ For further information inquire at this office.
22 ts

August 20th, 1862.
Desirable Drugs, &c.

10 LBS. CHLORATE POTASS,
25 OZ. QUININE,
20 LBS. CALOMEL,
5 OZ SULPH MORPHIA,
10 LBS. GUM OPIUM,
Just receiued and for sale by
aug 21 J. H. THOMPSON.

25 BARRELS CHOICE BROWN SUGAR, on consignment.
LEE, ROCKE & TAYLOR,
aug 21 105 Main St.

100 BARRELS WHISKEY, part very fine Old Rye, on consignment.
LEE, ROCKE & TAYLOR.
aug21 105 Main St.

Epsom Salts.

400 POUNDS EPSOM SALTS, for sale by WM. A. STROTHER & CO.
aug 14

5 QR. Casks Pale Madeira Wine,
3 " " " Port "
2 " " " Malaza "
1 " " " Scuppnong "
1 Half Pipe Fine old Cherry Brandy
LEE, ROCKE & TAYLOR,
aug 21 105 Main St.

Just to Hand.

ONE CHEST FINE GREEN TEA.
JONES & MILLER.
aug 22

Rice and Sugar.

FOR sale on consignment, 20 TIERCES RICE AND 8 HHDS. GOOD TO PRIME N. O. SUGAR. McCORKLE, SON & CO.
aug 4

MISCELLANEOUS.

August 23d, 1862.
Just Received at
H. J. ABRAHAMS & BRO.,

16 BALES 4-4 Rockfish Sheetings,
20 Bales 4-4 Augusta Sheetings,
15 Bales 4-4 Grenitv lle Sheetings,
10 Bales 4-4 Beaver Creek Sheetings,
20 Bales ⅞ Augusta Sheetings,
2 Bales English Shirtings,
1 Case English Bleached,
1 " Sup " "
75 Pieces Superfine Prints,
25 " " Ginghams,
20 " Irish Linens,
8 Great Gross Pearl Buttons,
12,00 pounds Wax Candles.

Tanner's Oil.

JUST to hand 20 BARRELS TANNERS' OIL, to which Tanners and Machinists are invited to take a look. A. B. RUCKER.
jy 2

100 POUNDS SHOE THREAD.
LEE, ROCKE & TAYLOR,
jan 1 105. Main street.

To Manufacturers.

OIL Wintergreen.
Oil Bitter Almond.
Oil Boards for Brands.
Tonka Beans.
Branding Paint.
For sale by W. A. STROTHER & CO.

300 BUNCHES COTTON YARNS No's from 6 to 20.
LEE, ROCKE & TAYLOR,
june 4 105 Main street.

Green Tea.

ONE Chest of FINE GUNPOWDER TEA, just to hand and for sale by
aug 23 J. H. THOMPSON.

DR. H. C. STEPTOE

OFFERS his professional services to the citizens of Lynchburg. His office is at Dr. Thompson's Drug Store, 96 Main Street, at which place he can be found at all times during the day, and at Fayette Steptoe's, Main street, opposite McGowan's Flower Garden, during the night. Having had fifteen years experience in the practice he feels that he will be able to give satisfaction to all who may give him a call.
june 2-6m

AYRE'S CHERRY PECTORAL,
CARTER'S SPANISH MIXTURE,
JAYNE'S CARMINATIVE BALSAM,
AYRE'S CATHARTIC PILLS,
WISTAR'S BALSAM WILD CHERRY,
BARRY'S TRICOPHEROUS,
COD LIVER OIL JELLY,
Just to hand and for sale by
aug 21 J. H. THOMPSON.

QUARTER MASTER'S OFFICE,
Gordonsville, Va, Aug. 26, '62.

I WISH to employ AT ONCE FIFTY CARPENTERS—those accustomed to framing preferred. To men of steady habits good wages will be given. W. B. RICHARDS, JR.,
aug 27-d1w Post Qr Master.

Brown Mustard Seed.

5000 POUNDS—grown in Virginia—for sale by
aug 15 McDANIEL & IRBY.

Rockbridge Baths.

THIS pleasant Watering Place, located in the county of Rockbridge, within 10 miles of Lexington, is now open for the reception of Visitors.
Terms, $14 per week.
" $3 " day.
WM. A. MANN,
aug 26 1w Proprietor.

Sheep for Sale.

500 HEAD, part very fine WOOL, for sale on my farm 2½ miles from Lynchburg,
J. E. CALDWELL,
aug 25-1w at McDaniel & Irby s.

$1,50 Per Day and Rations.

WILL be paid for good QUARRYMEN, DRILLERS AND BLASTERS, and a liberal price for Black and White Laborers, to work on the improvement of New River, by the Board of Public Works, State of Virginia.

Apply to the undersigned at the Central Depot Virginia and Tennessee Railroad, Montgomery co. Va. D. S WALTON,
Chief Engineer New River Improvement.
aug 23-d2w

Manufactured Tobacco For Sale.

I HAVE in store for sale, at No. 44, Main Street, Lynchburg, Va, OVER TWO THOUSAND PACKAGES OF MANUFACTURED TOBACCO, of different grades Some very fine, and expect to continue to receive from some of the best manufacturers large supplies.

Those wishing to buy I invite to examine my stock. JAMES FRANKLIN.
aug 21-d&cts

PROVOST MARSHAL'S OFFICE,
LYNCHBURG, Va., Aug 25th, 1862.

BY authority of the Secretary of War, I have established a Provost Marshal's office in the City of Lynchburg, for the purpose of arresting deserters and stragglers from the various armies now in the field, and to avoid the indiscriminate ingress and egress of unauthorized persons. A passport office has also been established, and hereafter all persons will be required to have passports from the Provost Marshal in order to leave on the trains.

Passport office open from 9 A. M. till 2 P. M.,and from 6 till 10 P. M. daily.

Office on Jefferson Street, between 7th and 8th.
TH. P. TURNER,
aug 26-dtf Lieut and Provost Marshal

Marion Female Seminary.

THE next session of this Institution will commence on the FIRST MONDAY IN SEPTEMBER next.

TERMS:
Tuition in English, $20 per session of five months.
Tuition in English, $15 per session of five months for children under 10 years.
Tuition in French, $3 per month.
Tuition in Music, $5 per month.
Use of Piano, $2 per month.
Board, $20 per month, exclusive of Washing.
MISSES GORDON,
aug 23-2aw3w Marion, Smythe co., Va.

MRS. MARY J. TOWNLEY will resume the duties of her School, on Monday, the 1st of September.

TERMS.
For beginners $10 per session of five months.
For advanced pupils 15 " " "
School room, No. 162, Main Street.
aug 8-1awt1st sept

MISS MANSON'S SCHOOL will be re-opened at Pebbleton, on the 15TH September.

TERMS.
$140 for Board and Tuition in English and French per session of five months.
Music $5 per month.
Use of Instrument, $1 per month,
Address Holcombe Rock, Bedford, Va.
aug 23-w4w

700 POUNDS COPPERAS for sale by W. A. STROTHER & CO.
jy 30

REWARDS.

RUNAWAYS.

ABSCONDED from the service of the James River and Kanawha Company, SIX NEGRO MEN, named John, Ned, Brack, Nelson, Jim and Aleck.

John belongs to Mrs. Modeni, of Fluvanna, but has a wife in Bedford,about 22 miles above Lynchburg, on the canal. He is about 5 feet 9 inches high, very black, but good looking. Ned belongs to Mr. Wm. M. Seay, of Buckingham, and has a wife at Mr. Wm. Robinson's, near the Court-house in the same county. He is about 5 feet 9 inches high, flat built, and of a dark, brown color. Brack belongs to Mr. Wm. C. Jordan, of Nelson, and has a wife in the same neighborhood. He is black; has a high forehead,and is lame in his left leg. Nelson belongs to James Garrett, in Nelson county, is about 5 feet 10 inches high and black. Jim belongs to Polina Garrett, of Nelson, is about 5 feet 5 inches high and very black. Aleck belongs to John Coleman, Albemarle. He is a very low set negro, and very black.

These negroes are all young men except Brack, who is middle aged, but taking it for granted that if they are apprehended it will be where they are known, and therefore deem a minute description unnecessary.

The James River and Kanawha Company will pay the legal reward and twenty dollars besides for the arrest and return of each of the hands here mentioned, viz: John and Ned to Mr. John H. Hutchins, Foreman Mason, working at this time at Tye River. Brack, Nelson, Jim and Aleck to Mr. Geo. W. Matthews, Overseer, who will be found somewhere on the Canal between Scottsville and Tye River.

E. L. CHINN,
aug 23 d2w Supt. J. R. & K. Canal.

DESERTERS.

THE following men are absent from my company without leave, and I am authorized to pay thirty dollars reward for each of them, if delivered to me at my camp, near Richmond, or a notice given to me that they have been delivered to the Provost Marshal of the city of Richmond:
Gustavus A. Goodwin, Amherst co.
Henry W. Hamilton, Amherst co.
James A Coleman, Amherst co.

The above men left camp on sick leave, but it is known that they have been well and fit for duty for some time. I would advise all of my absent men to send me certificates of inability from a reliable physician, or else they are liable to be published as deserters.

GEO. W. HOBSON,
Lieut. detailed by Gen. Wm. N. Pendleton to get up the men of the Amherst Artillery,
T. J. Kirkpatrick, Commanding.
July 24-ts

$1,00 REWARD.

FOR the apprehension of a negro man named RANDAL. who left my Farm near Amherst C. H., in April last, and has not since been heard from.

He is about 45 years old, dark complexion, about the ordinary height, stout made and muscular, speaks quick, and moues quick, has lost four of his front teeth, nose flat between his eyes, and rather bad countenance.

I will give the above reward for his apprehension and delivery to me, or confinement in any jail so that I can get him Address me at Amherst C. H., Va. JAS. B. L. WILLIAMS.
aug 21-1aw4w

SALT.

TABLE SALT AND FISH SALT FOR STOCK.
ALSO A CHOICE LOT OF RYE FOR SALE BY
R. ROSS, Ag't.,
ap 9-ts 14 Bridge Street.

A. B. RUCKER
WHOLESALE
Grocer and General Commission Merchant,
133 *MAIN STREET, LYNCHBURG, VA.,*

WILL give his personal attention to the sale of Tobacco Wheat, Flour, Corn, Bacon, Lard, Butter, &c., and make advances on consignments.
July 15-dts

Strayed.

ABOUT the middle of last week, a small RED COW, with some white down the back, small crumpled horns, one of them broken off near the point. The Cow is supposed to have gone up the Forest road. A liberal reward will be paid if she is returned to corner of Polk and Eleventh Street.
aug 27-1w H. C. VICTOR.

Wheat's Battalion
ATTENTION.

I, THE undersigned, desirous of raising a company of Mounted Men to serve under the gallant Colonel Hornsby, in General Marshall's command in Kentucky—invite all of my fellow soldiers to join me at once. All wishing to do so will report to Lieutenant Robert Ritchie, Piedmont House, or Captain White, Campbell Court-House.

A. WHITE,
aug 27-d4t Captain Tiger Rifles.

Farm For Sale.

THE subscribers offer for sale, privately, their FARM in Bedford county,containing 414 acres This tract is only twelve miles distant from Liberty, the county seat. Two thirds of the track is cleared and in a good state of cultivation. The whole of the tract is well watered. The buildings are comfortable and sufficient to accommodate a large family. Possession to seed will be given at once, and full possession by the 25th of December next, and sooner if desired. Terms accommodating, and liberal time will be given if desired.

For further particulars enquire of the subscribers at Liberty, Bedford co., Va.

JESSEE T. HOPKINS.
aug 20 J. B, LAYNE.

Paper! Paper! Paper!
Just Received.

150 REAMS Large White and Blue Letter Paper.
100 Reams Extra White Commercial Note Paper.
100,000 Eneelopes, assorted.
50 Gross Steel Pens.
H. C. VICTOR,
aug 27-1w 153 Main Street.

Large Sale of Furniture, &c

WILL be sold at the MONTGOMERY WHITE SULPHUR SPRINGS,commencing on Monday, the 1[5th] of September, and continue from day to day till all is sold.

All of the Furniture, consisting of a set of Fine Parlor Furniture, with an elegant Grand Piano, large number of Hair, Shuck and Cotton Mattrasses, Pillows, Linen and Cotton Sheets and Towels, a superior Velvet Carpet, (large size,) Bedsteads, Crockeryware, Knives and Forks, &c., and all of the stock of Cattle, including a number of Fine Milch Cows, Eight head of Horses and Mules, all of the crop made on the place, a quantity of Flour and Bacon, with many other articles. Terms cash.

JAMES R. KENT,
E. J. AMISS,
WM. THOMAS,
WILLIAM H. PECK,
S. C. HURT,
Directors.
aug 22-tds

50 OUNCES Lunar Caustic, For sale by W. A. STROTHER & CO.
aug 27

Lynchb'g Virginian.

Tuesday........September 2, 1862

Another Great Victory.

That our arms have been blessed with another great victory seems now to be placed beyond all doubt. The fact has been announced by General Lee to the President, and it has come to us through other reliable sources. The particulars and details have not yet transpired, but enough is known to satisfy us that after a hard day's fighting the enemy was finally repulsed, badly cut up, and much demoralized—and that he lost very largely in prisoners, commissary stores and arms. Nothing definite in regard to our loss is stated, but no doubt in so hotly contested an engagement it was heavy, and that the country will be called on to mourn the loss of many gallant and noble sons.

From all we can hear respecting the disposition of our forces and the condition of the enemy, we shall be very much surprised if, since the effects of this late battle, Pope and his entire army are not either captured or destroyed. He is in great extremity, if our information is correct, and will scarcely be able to extricate himself from the web of difficulties by which he is surrounded. He is in the toils of such men as Lee, Jackson, Stuart, Longstreet, Hill and the like, and if he eludes or outgenerals them he will have to show much more ability than he has done heretofore, or than he has the credit of possessing.—Pope out of the way, as we firmly believe he soon will be—then our course is clear and unobstructed. The enemy's Capital will be at our mercy, and the heart of the enemy's country our easy prize. The *debris* of McClellan's once grand army may attempt to oppose some resistance to the forward movement of our God-protected forces, but they will be swept away like chaff before the wind. They will remember Chickahominy. And where may not such an army as ours go, what may it not do? The new levies of the enemy will not dare to face it, or if they do, it will be but to meet their certain doom. For six months to come, the raw recruits now being drafted into service by the enemy will not be fit to put in the field, if indeed, unwilling and disaffected as many of them are, they ever are fit. And in that intervening time, what a golden harvest may be reaped by the resistless arms of the Confederacy! How the bitter chalice of *invasion* may be removed from the lips of our people and placed at those of the enemy!—has, war, with its horrors, may be carried home to his people, and they made to feel some of the devastations which our own bleeding country has had to suffer!—and how peace may be thus wrenched from the unwilling grasp of a prostrate foe!—We think the skies with us are brighter than ever before. We think that the road to certain, honorable and not distant peace lies straight before us, and that we will pursue it now to the blissful goal.

Blockade Prices.

We understand from the Petersburg Express that the sale of goods recently passed through the blockade, which took place at Wilmington, N. C., on Thurday, was attended by a multitude of buyers, collected together from every portion of the Confederacy. Where the competition was so great, of course, the prices obtained were beyond all expectations. Letter paper, a good article, sold for $39,50 cents per ream; note paper sold for $16 per ream; and folio paper for $50 per ream.—Copperas brought $1,75 cents per lb., and shoes including all sizes, from boys to full grown men, sold for $8 per pair. Other goods sold in proportion, some persons alone buying as much as $50,000 worth or more. Men of wealth may be able to pay the retail prices at which these goods must sell, but how persons of ordinary means are to do it, is another question.

The Augusta Constitutionalist seems to think that there is some foundation for the report that Commodore Semmes is at the mouth of the Mississippi with a fleet which it thinks is composed of the Oreto, Scotia, "No. 290," and Merrimac, with perhaps other vessels. This may be so, but we still question it very much. That Semmes is in the Southern waters is no doubt certain. He stopped some time since at Bermuda, in Scotia, and on leaving sent his card ashore But that fact would not account for the appearance of any large number of vessels nor for their crews.

Should there be any truth in the report, the hours of Butler's rule in New Orleans are numbered. Just as soon as Gen. Van Dorn can get co-operation on the water, so soon will he advance and retake New Orleans.

Perfidy of the Enemy.

In a late number of the New York Herald, which has been kindly laid before us, we find the following rascally advertisement:

CONFEDERATE TREASURY NOTES, BEAUTIFULLY printed on bank note paper, for sale at $4 per 1,000 by W. E. HILTON, 11 Spruce st.

What could better illustrate the perfidy and utter lack of principle on the part of our Yankee enemy than this? A wholesale system of forgery and counterfeiting is here boldly and brazenly proclaimed to the world, and the public invited to patronize the villainy! Whipped in the field—unable to withstand the valor and prowess of our noble troops, the mean and cowardly expedient is resorted to of depreciating our currency. This thing has been going on for a long time. A large number of the prisoners who are captured by our forces have these counterfeit bills on their person, and they are readily passed on the unsuspecting and the unskilful detectives. It is known that the prisoners who were confined at the Fair Grounds near this city had a considerable quantity of the spurious currency with them, and put not a little of it in circulation in this community. It may be, and very probably is, that the splendid counterfeits of our $50 and $100 Confederate notes which have gained such a wide spread circulation and caused such deep distrust in the public mind of all bills of those denominations, are the result of Yankee ingenuity and rascality, and that this severe blow on our circulating medium has been stricken by the cunning hand of the enemy. There is a remedy for these things. Let it be administered. If the Government will proclaim that prisoners found with counterfeit Confederate money about them will be hung, and if when so found *they are hung*, there will be an end to the whole business. The laws make the crime punishable with death. One of our own citizens, if detected in it, would have to pay the penalty of his life. Why should more clemency be shown a cruel and unscrupulous enemy than an offending citizen? The evil is of easy remedy—hang the culprits whenever detected, and there will be no more of such advertisements as the above—no more of the Yankee imitations circulating through the country. The credit of our currency must be preserved, or all is lost—preserved against the attacks of either pretended friends at home or enemies abroad—preserved at all hazards and to the last extremity.

From the Chattanooga Rebel.

Col. John H. Morgan's Proclamation.

We have received a copy of the "Vidette" dated Hartsville, Tenn., August 19. This spicy little sheet is "printed and published semi-occasionally by Morgan's Brigade," and edited by Geo. E. Niles. In the number before us the most important article is the proclamation of Col. Morgan, with regard to the rule of *lex talionis*, which we append. It needs no comment, it speaks for itself, and will receive the approbation of the entire country.

HEADQ'RS MORGAN'S BRIGADE,
Hartville, Tenn,
August 19, 1862.

Having noticed in the Cincinnati Daily Gazette of the 15th inst., an article dated "Paris, Ky., 14th August, 1862," whereby it appears that the agents of the Federal Government are (to use their own words) forcing Morgan's "friends to pay for the acts of their favorite chieftain," and thus violating all laws hitherto respected and acknowledged by civilized nations, forgetting and wilfully closing their eyes to the fact that I, in my justifiable attacks on Federal troops and Federal property, have always respected the private property and persons of Union men, I do hereby declare that, to protect Southern citizens and their rights, I will henceforth put the law of retaliation into full force, and act upon it with vigor. For every dollar exacted from my fellow citizens, I will have two from all men of known Union sentiments, and will make their persons and property responsible for the payment. God knows it was my earnest wish to have conducted this war according to the dictates of my heart, and consonant to the feelings which actuate every honorable mind, but forced by the vindictive and iniquitous proceedings of our Northern foes to follow their example, in order to induce them to return to more humane conduct, I will, for the future, imitate them in their exactions, retaliate upon them and theirs the cruelties and oppression with which my friends are visited, and continue this course until our enemies consent to make war according to the law of nations.

Signed by me this 18th day of August, A. D. 1862.

JOHN H MORGAN,
Col. Commanding Brigade

SLIDELL AND MASON.

Our Northern exchanges claim to have information from Europe of the movements of Messrs. Slidell and Mason, which, if correct, is of rather important character.

The statement, made in a private letter, is to the effect that these gentlemen had already had several interviews in London, for the purpose of deciding what was the best step to be taken to hasten the recognition of the Confederacy. After due deliberation, it is reported that they have agreed to address a note to all the European Cabinets of Europe, demanding our recognition; not on the abstract principle of right not even in virtue of our boldness in maintaining our independence, but in the name of our legally asserted rights—of the rights upon which foreign nations have acted toward countries situated as the south is at the present time.

If this is correct our commissioners have taken the proper position, and one that does not in the least depreciate the dignity of the Confederate Government, and that it will be sustained by the people they represent. We are not supplicants for favor; our rights, asserted in a legal manner, are what we demand. We argue more favorably from this last stand-point than we have ever done before. The world, witnessing our boldness, will querry as to our correctness, and we have nothing upon our escutcheon for which we may blush.—*Memphis Appeal.*

Brutalities of Pope's Army.

A correspondent of the Richmond *Enquirer* writing from Orange Court House gives the following account of some of the brutal outrages committed by Pope's thieves and ruffians:

On my return from a visit to the "Stonewall Brigade," weary and hungry, I called at a fine mansion, three miles below Rapidan Station. It was a beautiful residence, surrounded by rich bottom lands and what gave evidence of *once* luxuriant fields of corn. But its present appearance indicated that the *Nero* Pope had visited that section

Arriving at the house, an aged servant woman met me at the door, and, on inquiry, informed me that Mrs. Robertson and her daughter, Mrs Roney, widow ladies, were the sole white occupants of the house. Mrs Robertson was prostrated on a bed of grief, and her daughter had gone some miles to procure the family some food.

As soon as this Christian lady learned that a Confederate soldier was at the door, she arose from her bed, and with feeble steps, approached me. I asked her for a few mouthfuls of bread and meat. She said, "You shall have it, if it was the last in the house—God will provide for me." She added—"Pope's army, out of a large supply of bacon, have only left me *one small shoulder* and a *jole*, the balance was carried off. They also robbed me of all my poultry, hogs, corn and subsistence generally." I encouraged the old lady by saying that the tears of the widow and wails of the orphan would make giants of pigmies and heroes of cowards. That these wrongs would and must be avenged.

She then escorted me through her house, marked by the tracks of the despoilers.—The once elegant rooms, furnished with good taste and at heavy expense, were one scene of destruction. A fine mahogany secretary was broken to pieces, and the drawers carried into the yard and used as troughs to feed their horses. A mahogany side-board was smashed into splinters with an axe. Gilt china, desert pans, ice-cream stands, goblets and decanters of the best quality, were broken into fragments—almost literally ground to dust. Her wardrobe was destroyed and the contents stolen. The thieves carried off every vestige of clothing of these pious ladies, except what they were wearing, from the finest silk dresses down to night gowns and caps, and even their shoes and stockings. Rocking chairs were destroyed and tidies torn into shreds and strewn over the yard. Damask window curtains were converted into horse covers. Bed-blankets, counterpanes, sheets, quilts, pillows and carpets were packed on horses and carried to Pope's camp. The family Bible, the most precious and sacred of all family relics, and the religious books, whose perusal was so pleasant to these pious ladies, escaped not the ruthless hands of these brutes; they were all taken, and those they were not disposed to keep were destroyed, and the leaves scattered over the premises. To add still more to their infamy, they even robbed this "mother in Israel" of her only spectacles, common steel-framed ones.—Thus was this family reduced from affluence to want, and despoiled of all the necessaries of life. It reminded me much of the description we read of plundering Arabs.

Mrs. Roney's guitar and accordeon were destroyed. The piano, alone, was seved. From the latter one of the company made music, while the others danced upon the floors, and amused themselves by kicking the panels out of the doors. True to their instincts, these hell-hounds *lapped* up the currant jellies and jars of sweet meats. In the midst of these revelries, the ladies became alarmed for their personal safety, and Mrs. Roney, on bended knees, implored the aid of Heaven, not knowing at what moment she and her aged mother might be slaughtered and the house burned over their heads. In the midst of her supplication, a gentle breeze wafted into her lap that beautiful ballad "My Maryland." She clasped it to her bosom and exclaimed, "Heaven has sent me this!" and arose and read a portion of those soul-stirring verses in the bearing of her tormentors. It was more than they could bear. It acted as a mirror to expose their hideous deformity. They grew pale and tremulous, and left the premises, we hope never again to return.

Could those who have mothers, wives sisters and daughter, see what I have seen of the destruction and devastation of property, and heard what I have heard, of the insults, threats and indignities to which our fair women have been exposed, it would require no "Conscription Act" to force every man, capable of bearing arms, to shoulder his musket and aid in expelling these Vandal hordes from our borders.

DISSATISFACTION WITH SECRETARY STANTON—CLAMOR FOR HIS REMOVAL, &C.

Since the disastrous end of McClellan's campaign before Richmond, a great clamor has been raised against Secretary Stanton, and a demand is made for his immediate removal from office, on the ground of utter incompetency. The New York *World* pitches into him, and demands his removal from office as the only thing that will save the cause of the North. The *World's* criticism is very severe, and we make room for a few of its salient points:

Now that the army of the Potomac—thanks to the marvelous management of McClellan—is safe, and the people breathe again, the conviction comes back with resistless force, that there must be a change in the War Department. The incapable presumption that has ruled there must abdicate. For the sake of no man will the country longer submit to these terrible sacrifices and dangers.

Six hours before the public announcement that Edwin M. Stanton was to be Secretary of War, he was absolutely unthought of by the people in connection with that post as any lawyer in the land. He was known simply as a successful criminal advocate. That was his only record. And yet when it was announced that he was to be the new Secretary, nowhere in all American history can another such instance be found of trust so large granted on claims so slender.

The first outgivings of the new Secretary indicated spirit, and were liked. They soon, however, took on a flourish which raised suspicion of sham. The body of the people went on hoping for the best—reconciled all the easier because of the splendid successes which soon began to crown our arms. Yet it was noticeable that, though these successes continued, Secretary Stanton's popularity steadily waned. Even before he had ventured to interfere at all with the rightful province of Gen. McClellan, at that time Commander-in-Chief, the quick instinct of the people began to perceive, in the constant petty follies of the Secretary, that he was not a man of clear, steady judgment. Stolid unconcern seemed to possess him in respect to all that occurred, or was foreboded in the peninsula. If he had any policy at all in that quarter it was that of *obstruction* simply. In another direction he ventured further. He deprived General Banks of two-thirds of his force, and thus brought on that raid of Jackson's up the Shenandoah Valley, which cost the nation thousands of lives and millions of property, threw Washington into a panic, and which will ever stand as perhaps the most disgraceful page in the history of the war. The people could hardly stifle their wrath. Yet they calmed down, hoping that the mismanagement had reached its climax, and there would be a change for the better. There was no such change.

The people are now in their agony over the wasted blood of their brothers and sons Yet they see clearly the cause of all this, and from every city and hamlet comes one universal, fearfully earnest cry, that the man cannot and shall not be longer endured.

Now, it is not worth while to analyze the causes of Secretary Stanton's failure.—It is no time now for such discussions.—This one thing is sufficient: Secretary Stanton has utterly lost the confidence of the people. For that reason alone, if there were no other, it would be ruinous to keep him in his place. The President has called for, three hundred thousand more men.—It is our religious belief that, that call will never be answered unless the War Department is committed to different hands.—If the President seeks to re-reconstruct his army, he must first re-establish confidence. And that, he can do only by putting a man at the head of the War Department who is capable of inspiring confidence.—The necessity is upon him. To disregard it is to give the country up to destruction.

Who is Edwin M. Stanton, that he should stand for an instant in the way of the safety of the Republic? There is not an American living who might not better be sunk deeper than ever plummet sounded, if thereby the ship of State, now so terribly laboring, could ride any the easier. Individuals are nothing before the awful destinies now at stake. Whatever his personal regard for the Secretary of War may be, his duty to the country requires him to look out for another man in whom the people can put trust.

The rebellion can never be overcome by any such force as we now have in the field. Three months ago the conscription of all men in the Confederacy between the ages of eighteen and thirty-five was ordained by the Rebel law. It insured an army of half a million. The census tables show more than that number between the ages named within the Rebel domain. Virginia alone, apart from Western Virginia, must have furnished over a hundred thousand. And yet right in the face of that tremendous expedient of the Rebels the Secretary of War orders a discontinuance of enlistments. The act has gone into history as a piece of sheer infatuation. It must be rectified or we perish.

LOCAL AND STATE AFFAIRS.

FROM THE RAPPAHANNOCK AND WARRENTON.—A gentleman, who arrived here Sunday from Richmond, states that President Davis received a dispatch from Gen Lee on Saturday, stating that our forces had defeated the enemy in the battle on Friday, capturing a large number of prisoners, stores and ammunition, and that our army was in a splendid condition.

It is reported that in the engagement Major General Ewell, and Brigadier General Trimble and Taliaferro were wounded, the former supposed seriously.

We received the following information from a gentleman who left Culpeper C. H., on Saturday: The first intimation that Pope had of our forces being in his rear, was on Wednesday morning, when he dispatched a train of sick from the town of Warrenton towards the Junction, which soon returned and reported their passage to Alexandria cut off. Pope commenced immediately to evacuate Warrenton, and on Thursday morning at three o'clock the last of his command had left; the citizens reported that they had started in the direction of Fredericksburg and Acquia Creek. Our forces are now in possession of the town, and it is not positively known whether the Yankee sick that returned to Warrenton were captured or made their escape, but it is believed that they destroyed the Railroad train.

Gen. Stuart's Cavalry arrived at Catlett's Station on the Alexandria Railroad a few miles beyond Warrenton Junction on Tuesday, and surprised a Yankee force of several hundred, capturing three hundred prisoners, several hundred horses, and destroying two or three hundred wagons containing commissary stores, baggage, &c., and attempted to destroy the bridge at Catlett's, but the heavy rain that was falling prevented it from burning. One of Stuart's men captured General Bayard's canteen.

The Yankees destroyed the Fauquier White Sulphur Springs that was owned by a man named Higgins, and who upon the advent of the Yankees into that county, gave them important information of the state of affairs, and all necessary direction as to the roads through Fauquier and Culpeper counties. Gen. Jackson had occupied the country beyond Manassa and Gen Stewart was beyond Centreville, and some reports state that he was near Harper's Ferry. The movements of our troops are enveloped in secresy and it is difficult to obtain reliable information.

In addition to the above it was reported that General Jackson had captured five trains of Railroad cars loaded with Commissary stores, &c., and a number of prisoners.

A private letter from Bristow station states that there was cannonading heard in different directions and it was thought that Pope would attempt to escape to the Valley, but that Jackson was completely in his rear.

The Richmond Dispatch of yesterday gives the following account of the capture of the Rail Road trains and prisoners:

"Our own account of this affair reports that a portion of our cavalry had advanced on the Orange and Alexandria Railroad to Bull Run bridge, about five miles beyond Manassas, and having burned the bridge continued their advance to Dye Station, where they concealed themselves, and arrested the approach of a number of trains of which they had previously received information. After the trains passed the concealed position of the cavalry the track was torn up behind them. When they reached the bridge, the officer on board finding that something was wrong, determined to return to Alexandria, but before backing far they found the track torn up, and their retreat effectualy intercepted.— The cavalry then approached in superior numbers, and the enemy surrendered without firing a gun. The number of prisoners reported captured agrees with the statement of the Sun, being estimated at 2,000, together with all the officers, regimental and company, and a quantity of arms and ammunition which were being conveyed to Gen. Pope. After this brilliant affair the cavalry returned to Manassas, without sustaining the loss of a single man.

Some fifteen hundred to two thousand Yankee prisoners were yesterday between Rapidan Station and Gordonsville, and may be expected in this city to-day. It is supposed that these are the prisoners captured at Dye's Station by our cavalry."

LATEST.

Last night information was received in this city, that a general battle was raging along almost the entire line of our army yesterday, having commenced Sunday on Bull Run; in the vicinity of the old battle ground. Up to a late hour last night nothing further was received.

DIED,

At her residence in Culpeper county, on Thursday, the 28th ult., after an illness of only eight days, Mrs. C. C. KENNEDY, consort of D. W. Kennedy, in the —— year of her age. Thus has passed from earth another bright star. The writer of this knew her well, and can truly say that a more devoted christian, affectionate mother, better friend, kinder neighbor, or indulgent mistress, never lived. She leaves a kind husband and two lovely and interesting daughters to mourn her loss, the latter of whom are in the South. May the All-wise Providence who sees and knows all things, comfort them in this, the hour of their affliction C.

☞ Richmond Whig and Dispatch will please copy.

Of Diptheria, near this city, on Friday evening, the 29th of August, 1852, NANNIE JANE only daughter of Jas. W. and Sarah P. Tankersley, aged 7 years, 2 months, and 27 days. If medical skill, the unwearied attention of devoted parents, and the kindness of neighbors could have availed, the subject of this brief notice would now be living to cheer the hearts of her deeply stricken parents.

BY TELEGRAPH.

THE GREAT BATTLE AT MANASSAS.

GEN. LEE'S OFFICIAL REPORT.

Signal Victory over Gen. McClellan and Pope.

HEADQUARTERS ARMY OF NORTHERN VIRGINIA,
Grovetown, August 30,
Ten o'clock, P. M,
(via Rapidan, Sept. 1st.

To President Davis:

This army achieved to-day on the Plains of Manassas a signal victory over the combined forces of Generals McClellan and Pope.

On the 28th and 29th each wing under Generals Longstreet and Jackson repulsed with valor attacks made on them seperately.

We mourn the loss of our gallant dead in every conflict, yet our gratitude to Almighty God for his mercies rises higher every day.

To him and to the valor of our troops a nation's gratitude is due.

R. E. LEE.

From Tennessee.

CHATTANOOGA, Ten., Sept 1.

The Yankees have again occupied McMinnville in large force last Tuesday. They are probably the forces from Pelham and neighborhood on their retreat to Nashville.

They may be caught, at any rate Tennessee will soon be entirely in possession of the Confederates.

We have a rumor that Huntsville is evacuated.

LATEST FROM THE WEST.

President Davis' Message at the North.

MOVEMENTS OF GENERAL BUCKNER.

The Draft at Nashville.

Foreigners Pressed into Service,

Skirmish at Rappahannock Station.

First New Jersey Regiment Surrounded.

Guerrillas Menacing Memphis.

Recruiting in West Tennessee.

Guerrillas at Mound City, Missouri.

Speech of Gov. Gamble at St. Louis.

Yankee Account of Morgan's Fight.

&c., &c., &c.

MOBILE, August 30th.

A special dispatch from Tupelo, to the Advertiser and Register, dated August 30 says:

The Chicago Times of the 25th contains President Davis' message on the reassembling of the Confederate Congress.

A dispatch from Cincinnati, dated 30th, says:

General Buckner, with 25,000 men is encamped near Somerset, Ky., and that General Bragg is at Chattanooga with 30,000 more.

General Marshall is reported at the head of Big Sandy River, with 15,000 men.— The Rail Road is in full possession of the rebels.

No trains can pass to Nashville.

The draft was to have been enforced on the 1st of September.

Foreigners who have voted on their first papers, claiming exemption from draft, are arrested and pressed into service.

CAMP RAPPAHANNOCK STATION, August 21st.

A cavalry skirmish took place yesterday, in which the Federals lost 3 wounded and 5 prisoners.

Earthworks have been thrown up and bridges constructed to enable the batteries to cross the river.

The First New Jersey Regiment was surrounded by the rebels, and half of them captured.

MEMPHIS, August 22d.

A guerrilla band numbering 500 came within ten miles of the city yesterday, and destroyed large quantities of cotton, and the bridges over Wolf and Hatchie Rivers.

Five new companies have recently been raised in West Tennessee.

It is much feared that a band of guerrillas are depredating in the vicinity of Mound City, Adair co., Mo.

Colonel McCulloch, of Porter's guerrillas, was sentenced to death as a traitor and shot; also, 15 guerrillas accused of breaking their parole.

Governor Gamble in a speech at St. Louis, declared that guerrillas were robbers and murderers, and he would treat them as such.

The Yankee account of Morgan's fight says:

Eight hundred attacked seventeen hundred under Morgan, and were defeated with a loss of three hundred, including Johnson.

Steamer Emma Run Aground.

RICHMOND, Sept. 1.

The Savannah papers of this morning state that the steamer Emma going down the River Saturday night grounded, and was discovered yesterday by the Federals. She was fired to prevent her falling into their hands. She had on seven hundred and ten bales of Cotton, and some turpentine. All on board escaped.

CAPTURE OF PRISONERS AT RIENZI.

THE YANKEES SURPISED BY GUERILLAS.

PRISONERS CAPTURED.

Great Discord Prevailing in the Yankee Camp,

&c., &c., &c.,

MOBILE, August 30.

The following is a special dispatch to the Advertiser and Register

TUPELO, August 29.

Fourteen prisoners captured at Rienzi have arrived.

Three hundred of our guerillas moved in two parties against the Yankee camp, with the intention of attacking it on both sides.

One party captured the pickets and took the Yankees completely by surprise, rushing headlong into their camp, which consisted of Five Regiments of Cavalry and Eight of Infantry.

The other party failed in attacking and consequently their small force was repulsed and pursued by the Yankees, but they succeeded in bringing off a number of prisoners.

Great discord prevails in the Yankee camp which is overrun with stolen and runaway negroes.

A Yankee Letter.

INTERESTING DESCRIPTION OF THE BATTLE FIELD.

The following extracts are from a letter captured by our troops from the enemy.— We omit the name of the writer and his correspondent, as well as his private matters. The letter is written in an excellent hand, and is given below verbatim:

CULPEPER, VA., Aug. 18, 1862.

* * * *

I am sorry to say that the order of Gen. Pope in regard to subsisting in the country, has had a bad effect. There was always a large number enough who would, in spite of the most stringent rules, rob to plunder, but the number is now five ti mes as great, and they contend they act under Gen. Pope's order in going into houses and demanding everything the people have that is eatable.

* * * *

You have heard of the great victory over Jackson. *If you had been here you would have seen the victory over Banks.* Banks was badly defeated; his whole army corps is rendered *hors du combat.* No flag of truce ever came from the rebels to bury their dead. The flag of truce was taken from us to them. However badly we are defeated I intend to tell the truth.

A defeat is sometimes inevitable, but lying is always unjustifiable. I went, with 300 of our regiment, to the field on Monday morning to bury the dead. The Rebel General Stuart rode up to a tree near by, and said that some arrangements must be made, or else they would fire on us. Gen. Bayard negotiated a truce, and we then proceeded to carry the poor mangled, swollen, blackened, putrid bodies that lay scattered over the field, to their last resting-place—a deep ditch dug—in which they were piled two or three deep. This seemed hard indeed, but could not be helped. They had lain on the field until the stench was so great that it seemed impossible to bury them in any way. The hardest part was, that many of our wounded had lain in the sun for *forty-eight hours,* during which time they had no water, and, of course, were almost dead.

* * * *

There is quite a stir, and rumors say that our army is retreating towards Washington. I see the wagons all going back, and am informed by our Surgeon that Jackson is going down the Shenandoah Valley. If this be the case, and Pope with so large an army and so well disciplined as he has, surely there is a great oversight in somebody. * * * I am much discouraged. We have a large army in the field at a great expense, and it seems to me to be at little profit.

* * * * *

Two nights the past week, I slept on the wet ground without any blankets—everything we had being in the rear. Of course that was not conducive to health, and I find myself worse than before. The doctor tells me that unless I am very careful, my lungs will soon become affected. Whils I am at all times willing to be attacked by the rebels, I must acknowledge my fear of disease. Diseases in camp are so generally fatal that they are surely to be dreaded It is estimated that nine die by disease to one by the enemy's bullets.

* * * * *

The Tri-Weekly Mercury.

DAILY PAPER—TEN DOLLARS PER ANNUM, PAYABLE HALF-YEARLY IN ADVANCE.

VINDICE NULLO
SPONTE SUA SINE LEGE FIDES RECTUMQUE COLENTUR.

COUNTRY PAPER—THRICE A WEEK—FIVE DOLLARS PER ANNUM, IN ADVANCE.

VOLUME LXXXI — CHARLESTON, S. C., TUESDAY, SEPTEMBER 2 1862 — NUMBER 11,542

THE CONVENTION AND THE EXECUTIVE COUNCIL.

NO. II.

To the Editor of the Mercury: The question of *usurpation* of power in the Convention, in the appointment of the Executive Council, might be dismissed in very few words, for the whole argument, for and against it, rests upon the question, whether the Convention is or is not *supreme.* Is it, or is it not, the representative of the sovereignty of the State? Can it be limited in the exercise of power? No one, until now, in this State, has ever questioned this. In 1832, one of the reasons most dwelt on, in the speeches and writings of the Union Party, to deter the people from authorizing the call of the Convention of that year, was, that *it could not be* restricted in the exercise of power, and might alter the ratio of representation in the Legislature, and so injure the Low Country.

It is presumed that no one will deny that the people of South Carolina might have established a monarchy, if they had so chosen, as soon as the State seceded. If the *Convention* had done so, it would have been guilty of an *abuse* of power, but not of *usurpation,* because, being, for convenience sake, the representative of the people in their organic capacity, all the power of the people vested in it. And the Legislature might as well have passed a resolution saying that when the State seceded the people should not establish any government they pleased, as to attempt to *limit* the Convention either in power or duration.

And this is the doctrine which has always been held and acted on in England, as we shall presently see. It is idle to talk about evils which may or do result from a body of men unlimited in power. Some such power must exist in a State. Enough *for us,* that *with us,* it is in the people, and the people have chosen that they will, from time to time, as the occasion shall arise, assemble and act, not in one great assemblage, but through certain men elected to represent their opinions, and to speak and act for them. The people may afterwards repudiate the acts of these men, and elect another body which may repeal the acts of the first; just as the Convention of 1860 repealed the act of that of 1788, putting the State in the Federal Union. But a Convention of the people of South Carolina is absolute, and however it may *abuse* power, it cannot usurp it.

There is no limit in the Constitution upon the power of a Convention, and there *can be none.* It would be an absurdity if there was, for the people cannot limit their own power or that of those who come after them. They have simply empowered the Legislature to call a Convention when one shall be necessary, knowing that it can never be called except when they have first said that it shall be, either by their votes in the election of members of the Legislature, or in their popular assemblies. When, therefore, "Jasper," in the Courier of the 18th, asks, "Whence did the Convention derive the power to go beyond the *popular chart*" (meaning the words of the act calling the Convention), "and to rear over their heads this oligarchy of five Governors?" he simply asks (begging his pardon) a foolish question, and when he answers, "they usurped it," he asserts an impossibility.

As to the verbal criticisms of this writer upon the words "in" and "out" of the Union, and the reasoning upon which he comes to the above conclusion, like every other argument, if it cannot be carried out, it must fall to the ground. If the call of the Convention meant that its power only existed as long as the State was "in" the Union, then it had no power to do more than pass the Ordinance to that effect, and put the State "out." Every act after that was as much an usurpation as the act appointing the Executive Council. If he says that some other things were necessary, so say I; but what *were* necessary, was and must be left to the judgment of the Convention. And as soon as he admits, as he does, that other things were requisite, his charge of usurpation falls; for if it could judge that one thing was requisite, it could judge that its own existence should be prolonged and that an Executive Council was requisite. But the same kind of reasoning which "Jasper" has used, may be carried further to show that although the State is *out* of the Union, the dangers which *still* threaten her arise from her having been *in* the Union, and are therefore legitimate subjects of action on the part of the Convention. We think our logic here is quite as good as "Jasper's," and although it is not exactly to our taste, we make him a present of it, and insist that his is incomplete without our addition. The question of *abuse* of power is a different one, and will be considered in my next. SOUTH CAROLINA.

NO. III.

To the Editor of the Mercury: The *abuse* of power charged upon the Convention, consists: First, in assuming to itself, or vesting in the Council, *legislative* power. Secondly, in encroaching upon the Executive, under the State Constitution. The first will be satisfactorily answered, by showing that the Convention being supreme, possesses all power in itself; the second by demonstrating the necessity which existed for the measure. I hold it to be indisputable, that, if the Convention represents the sovereign authority of the State, it was competent to do any sovereign act. The Constitution was intended to be the sole governing rule, *only when the Convention had ceased to exist.* If the latter could amend the former, it could exercise any of the powers conveyed in that instrument, in whole or in part.* It saw fit to *amend* instead of *suspending* it, and while leaving the general power of legislating and appropriating money with the Legislature, it exercised some of those powers itself, and *with propriety.*

Not having the books for reference, I cannot say whether the Convention of 1832 exercised this power—probably not, as there was no occasion for it. It is likely that that Convention would have been the only one in the history of the State which was in circumstances to furnish a precedent. In default of such, we turn to the history of England, the country from which we derive our institutions, and to whose, ours are as closely assimilated as circumstances have permitted.

In Macaulay's History, vol. 4th, pp. 21 to 24, reign of William and Mary, we read that this very question came up in the Convention Parliament, and was decided in the affirmative, as the following quotations show, where the authority of the Convention which restored Charles the Second, and upon the force of reasoning which could not be resisted:

"As soon as the new Privy Councillors had been sworn in, it was necessary to submit to them a grave and pressing question. Could the Convention now assembled be turned into a Parliament? The Whigs were for the affirmative. The Tories were for the negative."

"It was plain that the Convention was the fountain head from which the authority of all future Parliaments must be derived, and that on the validity of the votes of the Convention must depend the validity of every *future* statute. And how could the *stream* rise higher than the *source?* Was it not absurd to say that the Convention was supreme in the State, and yet a nullity; a legislature for the highest purposes, and yet no legislature for the humblest purposes; competent *to declare the throne vacant, to change the succession, to fix the land marks of the Constitution,* and yet not competent to pass the most trivial act for the repairing of a pier, or the building of a parish church?"

"No royal writ had summoned the Convention which recalled Charles the Second. Yet that Convention had, after his restoration, continued to sit and *to legislate, had settled the revenues,* had passed an act of amnesty, had abolished the feudal tenures. These proceedings had been sanctioned by authority of which no party in the State could speak without reverence. Hale had borne a considerable share in them, and had always maintained that they were strictly legal."

"It is remarkable that the orator who took the most statesmanlike view of the subject, was old Maynard. In the civil conflicts of fifty eventful years, he had learned that questions affecting the highest interests of the Commonwealth were not to be decided by *verbal cavils,* and by *scraps of Law French* and *Law Latin.* And being, by universal acknowledgment, the most subtle and the most learned of English jurists, he could express what he felt without the risk of being accused of ignorance and presumption."

"We are," he said, "at this moment, *out* of the beaten path. If, therefore, we are determined to move *only in that path,* we cannot move at all. A man in a revolution, resolving to do nothing which is not strictly according to established form, resembles a man who has lost himself in the wilderness, and who stands crying: 'Where is the King's highway? I will walk nowhere but on the King's highway!' In a revolution we must have recourse to the highest law—*the safety of the State.*"

Our Convention could not become the Legislature, because it willed that the Legislature should still exist, but it did what the Convention Parliaments did. It legislated. The fact that the Convention had authorized the continued existence of the Legislature, could not deprive it of any right it possessed. If it could make an agent to do certain acts, it could do those acts itself. That agent was created to act when the Convention should cease to exist, or did not choose to act. It did choose to act itself, because we were, and are, in the midst of a revolution, and, in the words of old Maynard: "If we are determined to move only in the beaten path, we cannot move at all." SOUTH CAROLINA.

TRI-WEEKLY MERCURY.

TUESDAY, SEPTEMBER 2, 1862.

The Convention.

Twenty members of the Convention, out of one hundred and eighty composing it, have at length signed a request to the President of the Convention to call that body together. The objects of the call on the part of those who have made it, we understand, are, to dissolve the Convention, and to abolish the Executive Council established by the Convention.

We do not understand that there is any practical evil alleged to exist from the continuance of the Convention. Its members, since its last adjournment, have been at their homes, or in Congress, or in the army, exercising no power whatever as members of the Convention, and receiving no pay. The evil of its continued existence, if any, must be theoretical—abstract. Accordingly, it is asserted that it is absolutely a despotism, and ought to be abolished.

One half of the false logic in the world is from an abuse of terms. What is a despotism? It is a *form of Government* in which the ruler wields absolute and unlimited power. Is the Convention a Government? It is no Government at all. To know what the Convention is, we have only to turn to the Ordinance of Secession, which every one of the twenty members who have requested the call of the Convention, voted for and signed. That Ordinance begins as follows: "*We, the People* of the State of South Carolina, in Convention assembled, do declare and ordain," &c. All the ordinances of the Convention begin in the same way. These gentlemen, therefore, being the authority, the Convention is the people of South Carolina, assembled in Convention. Now, can the people of South Carolina be a despotism against themselves?

The people, under our form of free Government, are the sovereignty of the State; and when they meet in Convention, undoubtedly they must possess all power; for the very definition of sovereignty is "the supreme ultimate authority in a State." The sovereignty of every State must be somewhere. In Russia it is in the Autocrat; in Great Britain it is in the King, Lords and Commons in Parliament; in our system of Government it is in the people. As the people cannot assemble personally to exercise their sovereignty, they elect delegates, who form a Convention, and there they are supreme. If sovereignty is despotism, then there can be no such thing as a free Government. But sovereignty is not despotism, It is the potential power by which all Governments exist, but it is not Government, and therefore cannot necessarily be a despotism. On the contrary, it is, under our system of Government, the grand source of all free Government vested in the people. To constitute a despotism, power must be thrown into the form *of a Government,* without limitation or responsibility. But whilst existing potentially in a sovereignty, it is nothing unless exercised. Exercised by the people to establish a free Government over themselves, or to throw off a dangerous despotism, such as lately existed in the Government of the United States, it is the terror of despotisms and the grand vindicator of liberty.

To elucidate our views, let us consider what the people, in the exercise of their sovereignty in Convention, have done in South Carolina. They set up the Government of South Carolina by a Constitution which MR. CALHOUN declared to be the most perfect form of free Government which exists in the world. They placed the State under the Government of the United States, by adopting the Constitution of the United States. They have cast off the Government of the United States by seceding from the Union it constituted, and have placed the State in a Confederacy, by the adoption of the Constitution of the Confederate States. In doing all or any of these things, were the Conventions which performed them despotisms? or were they anything more than the people of South Carolina rightfully controlling, in their sovereign capacity, their own destiny? To assert the contrary, is merely an abuse of terms.

If these views are correct, the various objections urged against the Convention are very easily answered. It is asserted that the Convention is limited by the Act of the Legislature calling it. This, in the *first* place, is not true in fact. The Legislature merely designated in their Act calling the Convention the leading purpose for which they called it. This was proper as their justification to the people for their act; but the terms of the Act in no way attempt to limit the power of the Convention. Its terms are of the broadest kind, including the phraseology used by the Roman Senate when in the act of vesting all the powers of the State in the discretion of one man, for the preservation of the State in great emergencies. And if, in the second place, any attempt to limit the powers of the Convention had been made by the Legislature in the Act, it would simply have been nugatory. The Legislature is the creature of the Convention—the agent merely of the people. How can it limit the power of the people? If it could do so, the Legislature would be sovereign, and not the people; and if it was sovereign, why did it convoke the Convention? It convoked the Convention because it was *not,* and because the Convention *was,* sovereign; and even the power of convoking the Convention was by no inherent authority of its own, but the grant of a previous Convention.

It is further urged that the Convention has usurped powers. This is impossible, unless the people of South Carolina are not sovereign, and there is a power above them, whose attributes they may usurp. The particular matter in which it is alleged the Convention has practiced usurpation, is in establishing the existing Executive Council. Now the very presses and members of the Convention who make this charge, supported the Convention in the Ordinance of Secession, and the Ordinance placing South Carolina in the Confederacy of the Confederate States. If the Convention was competent to these high functions of sovereignty in changing the Government over the people of South Carolina, could it not give the Governor an Executive Council! These presses and members of the Convention have themselves answered this question in the affirmative, not only by their support of the above Ordinances, but by their support of the first Ordinance; for they supported the act of the Convention giving the Governor a Council. That was a very imposing Council. It established the highest dignitaries in the land. It consisted of a Secretary of State, a Secretary of War, and a Secretary of the Treasury—a striking and august miniature of the Government at Washington. No such Council is known in the Constitution of the State! Yet these gentlemen supported it. In what does it differ from the second Council, stamping the latter with usurpation? The Governor appointed the first Council, and the Convention itself appointed the second. "*Hinc illæ lachrimae.*" We will not do these gentlemen the injustice to suppose that they rest their charges of usurpation upon the kind of Council the Convention established. Admit the power, and the details of organization are clearly within the discretion of the Convention. But the power is denied, because it is not authorized by our State Constitution; and this denial is flatly refuted by their own repeated acts.

But it may be that the Convention, although exercising only its legitimate powers, may be tyrannical and oppressive, and, therefore, ought to be abolished.

The Acts of the Convention, it appear to us, have been governed by one single object—to save the liberties of the people and the existence of the State. These were threatened with destruction by the Government of the United States. They threw off that Government, and have succeeded in setting up another Confederate Government over the State of South Carolina. A savage war has arisen; and the Convention has passed various ordinances to enable the State to do her duty efficiently to herself and her confederates in carrying it on. Every act of the Convention has been honestly directed to this end. The only two measures that we have seen objected to, worthy of notice, are the establishment of the present Council, and the authority given to the Executive Council to call out and organize the slave labor of the State for the defence of the State. We do not know all the reasons for the Convention establishing the Executive Council, but we are satisfied that the authorities of the Confederate States at Richmond deemed it important if not necessary.

We are not aware that the good people of South Carolina have been disturbed in the enjoyment of their lives, liberties or property, by the acts of the Council, unless, indeed, the calling forth of the slaves to erect fortifications to defend the State against Yankee invasion can be called such. Here, we know, is a succession of labor for the defence of the State. To defend the State is a duty not only to the people of South Carolina, but to our confederates. It must be done by white or by black labor. Will any man hesitate, while our white laborers are in our armies, fighting for the liberties and independence of the Confederacy, to place our slaves in the trenches to build our fortifications? In the absence of adequate legislation, by our Legislature, the Convention would be faithless to its great mission of securing the liberties and independence of the State, if it did not pass efficient regulations to call forth the slave labor of the State to defend the State. The conquest of South Carolina by our enemies will be no trifling event to the slaveholder in South Carolina, or to the Confederacy. It will be full of miseries which the boldest may shrink to face. It will be full of horrors which the tongue may be ashamed to tell. Whether the Executive Council have abused the powers entrusted to them by the Convention, the Convention will judge. For ourselves, we have heard of no abuse actually practised, beyond the fact of their existence. As far as we can judge, they have done too little, rather than too much. They have failed in energy, rather than in aggressiveness. In the enrollment of troops they have done well. And in calling out slave labor they have at last done what ought to have been done.

If the Convention, as we believe, has been heretofore of inestimable service to the State, will the State be benefitted by its dissolution? It is a matter for the sound discretion of the Convention; but we doubt the policy of its dissolution. We are in the throes of a bloody revolution. Who will say, from the manner in which the war has been carried on, that South Carolina will not be overrun by our enemies? No Legislature might be able to meet or to call together the people again in Convention, if the existing Convention is abolished. Who knows whether a Governor will be elected; and if so, whether he will be equal to the duties of the crisis? To save the State, it might be necessary, as it was in the revolution of 1776, to place a Dictator over the State. The progress of this war is not determined. The character of the Confederate Government is not yet settled. The Constitution is already strained and warped from its integrity, by the assumed exigencies of the war. The tendency to centralization, with some of the worst features of the Government of the United States, is strongly developed. We hesitate not to say, that if the broad ground of military necessity is used to set aside the Constitution, in the assembling of Congress, on six hours notice, given to a small remnant of the body, and in the building of railroads all over the country, and in establishing military law, &c., &c., the existence of the Convention may be important. Over the State of Texas, where there is no enemy, the President has declared martial law, and appointed a Provost Marshal in every county, thus superseding the civil authorities of that State by military power. Such is the statement of a Senator in Congress.

We are in the midst of a bloody and terrible struggle. We know not what will be the progress of events, and what will be the dangers of the fast coming future, either to our existence as a people, or to the integrity of our Government. In the very throes of this revolution, the attention of our people has been diverted from those with whom we battle, and from the conduct of those who direct for us the policy of this struggle and the powers of the Confederate Government. A petty issue has been got up between the Governor and the Executive Council of this State; and bitter attacks have been leveled against the Convention, a body not exercising any power, or costing the State any money, but merely holding in abeyance the authority with which it was invested for any emergency. Efforts have been made to excite the jealousy of the Legislature. We regard it as ill-timed and unfortunate. We think the Convention a body of men who will not abuse their powers. We think the assaults upon the Convention as uncalled for as they are injurious to the cause of the South and to the State.

The House of Representatives of the Confederate States.

We are pleased to see a decided improvement in the tone of this body, and a disposition to represent the views and feelings of the constituencies.

The abolishment of the rule to go into secret session by a mere seconded motion and the requirement of a majority vote, is an important step in the right direction. We trust the people will now be furnished with a daily insight into the conduct of their representatives, and will be allowed to judge of the wisdom or folly with which their affairs are conducted in this important branch of the Government.

Our readers will perceive, too, a desire to infuse vigor into the different departments of the Government by giving voice to the public opinion of the Southern people in praise and in censure. Hitherto a false delicacy has existed which sacrificed the lives and property of the country, and endangered the cause, to a mawkish sentiment. A Spartan youth, we are told, allowed a fox concealed under his garment to tear out his bowels rather than expose his possession of the animal. We have patiently and without remonstrance submitted to feebleness and incompetency in the highest and most important offices in the government, and consequent worthlessness pervading whole departments. The House, we see, is pushing investigations into prevalent evils and their causes. As one instance of this, our readers will perceive that, on a motion to indefinitely postpone MR. FOOTE's resolution, that the HON. S. R. MALLORY, Secretary of the Navy, does not possess the confidence of Congress or the country, the result of the vote was forty-seven to forty-one. On motion of MR. BARKSDALE, of Mississippi, a devoted adherent of the Administration, a committee of investigation into MR. MALLORY's management of naval affairs has been ordered. We trust a white-washing committee is not to be the result, and that Mr. Speaker BOCOCK will appoint men who, in spite of Executive powers or favors, will feel their responsibility to the people and do their duty. Our own impression in this matter is, that, for some time after the formation of the Confederate Government and the beginning of the war, the Administration did not comprehend the necessity of having any navy at all, held the opinion that to build or buy a navy would be a waste of money, or could not be afforded, and had no idea of getting ships and gunboats, until their eyes were opened by "sudden emergencies" of a very disastrous character. The country is decidedly of opinion that the present Secretary of the Navy has not shown enterprise in getting vessels from abroad, or promptness and energy in employing the resources of the South in procuring what we so much need, and for the want of which we have already suffered so greatly. His latter efforts, we trust, will produce some fruits; but we are very much, and unnecessarily, behind-hand in regard to a navy. We do not now make or even import the engines proper for our naval uses. Let Congress sift these matters through competent men, and expose incapacity. Then the life and vigor proper to a Republican Confederacy will be likely to be developed, and the right men be put in the right places. The people are awake.

The Situation of Affairs.

The moment appears to be close at hand when we shall behold the fruit of the long and wearisome preparation, the complicated and mysterious movements of our armies in the field. The last of BRAGG's great army has crossed the Tennessee; PRICE is moving forward; the guerillas have cut off communication between Nashville and the North; the Abolition General, MORGAN, is closely besieged at Cumberland Gap by STEVENSON's command on this side, and by KIRBY SMITH's fine army in his rear; everything seems to promise that the hour of deliverance for Kentucky and Tennessee has come at last. In Virginia, though the movements of the campaign are, for the moment, wrapt in mystery, all is reported to be going well. It seems certain that the braggart POPE is closely pressed, and that a portion of our forces have succeeded in reaching Manassas Junction, which is between Washington and POPE's present position. Under these circumstances, it would seem that an early conflict is inevitable.

Of the result of the great pitched battle, either in Virginia or Tennessee, few who have noticed the conduct of the troops on either side, thus far during the war, can entertain a doubt. Our soldiers and our generals will, we are confident, make the fight a victory, whenever it comes. If the Government will but provide that our subsequent blows shall fall, thick and fast, in the country of our enemy, then indeed may we congratulate ourselves that we have reached the turning point of the war.

THE COUNTERFEITERS.—We learn that several persons have been arrested in Atlanta upon the suspicion of being concerned in the circulation of counterfeit Confederate notes. The *Confederacy* has the following in relation to their examination:

Those Arrests.—They are quite numerous—something over a dozen persons having been taken into custody. We hear that the developments are quite startling in their character. We consider it our duty, in the present stage of the investigations, to give no particulars of what we hear. We will also say that we do not officially or certainly know the nature of the charges, or what has been developed. A board of officers are making the investigation, and everything connected with the affair is very properly withheld from the public.

THE MOVEMENTS IN TENNESSEE.—We find the following paragraphs in the Chattanooga (Tenn.) *Rebel:*

We understand that a despatch from Gen. Kirby Smith was received here announcing the capture of a train of four hundred wagons and a thousand mules, by his forces in the rear of Cumberland Gap. The wagons were laden with stores and munitions for Gen. Morgan. Morgan will soon have to capitulate if this be so.

There is a rumor that Buell is concentrating a large force, estimated at 15,000 or 20,000 troops, at Pelham, on the other side of the mountain, and about fourteen miles from the Nashville Railroad. A gentleman who left that neighborhood at 10 o'clock yesterday morning, saw the entire force that was at Battle Creek going there, and four brigades were already in the place.

GENERAL BUELL RESIGNED.—The Atlanta *Intelligencer* says: "It is reported, and the source from which we receive it inclines us to believe the report, that General BUELL has resigned his commission, and has left Tennessee. The cause assigned is, the return of the Federal General MITCHELL to his command in Tennessee, notwithstanding the charges by General BUELL against him."

A report reached Savannah on Friday night that two gunboats were shelling the battery at Beulah, near sunset. One of the vessels was, by her appearance, thought to be the *Huntsville.*

THE CONFEDERATE CONGRESS.

SENATE.

RICHMOND, Friday, August 29.

Mr. Sparrow, from the Committee on Military Affairs, reported back the memorials of the Theological Seminary of Louisiana, and of the Society of Friends of Guilford, North Carolina, requesting that the Committee be discharged from the further consideration of the subject. The Committee's request was acceded to.

Mr. Sparrow, from the same Committee, reported a bill to aid the completion of the Vicksburg and Shreveport Railroad, in the State of Louisiana, which was placed upon the calendar and ordered to be printed.

QUARTERMASTER AND PAYMASTER DEPARTMENTS.

Mr. Sparrow, from the same Committee, reported a bill to provide for the establishment of separate a bureau for the Paymaster's department.

Mr. Sparrow said that on account of the press of business in the Quartermaster's department, it was impossible to pay the troops regularly, and that many of them remained unpaid for months. He asked that it should be immediately put on its passage.

Mr. Burnett, of Kentucky, was opposed to the measure proposed by the bill. There were now a number of officers in the Quartermaster's department who were idle and inefficient. If the troops remained unpaid it was because the Quartermasters did not perform their duty. He should oppose establishing a Paymaster's department, unless a corresponding reduction of officers was made in the Quartermaster's department. He had never yet been able to find out what were the duties of Brigade Quartermaster. The bill was put upon the calendar.

SUBSTITUTES.

On motion of Mr. Semmes, of Louisiana, the bill "providing for substitutes, in certain cases, and detailing privates for police duty," was taken up.

This bill, as reported by the Committee, has been published in this paper.

Mr. Simms, of Kentucky, thought the consideration of the bill had better be postponed, but if it was to be taken up, he had a few remarks to make about substitutes. He had always been opposed to substitutes, but if they were to be taken into the army, he approved of the French system. The party wishing to supply the substitute should be obliged to pay the government whatever amount may be fixed, and let it procure the substitute. The practice of permitting individuals to furnish their own substitutes had led to enormous abuses. In this very city he had been informed that substitute agents had made as much as one hundred dollars, and that the same substitute had sold himself, in some cases, twenty times. He had also learned, from military men, that substitutes composed nine-tenths of the deserters. He hoped the consideration would be postponed, to allow him time to prepare an amendment. The bill was reported by sections.

Mr. Maxwell, of Florida, moved to amend so that the bill should read that in all cases where substitutes are received, the person furnishing the substitute shall guarantee his fidelity, and in case he deserts the principal shall be held to service, as if no substitute had been furnished by him.

Mr. Semmes, of Louisiana, had also personally been opposed to substitutes; he thought every man, high or low, rich or poor, should be forced to go into the army and do his part in the defence of the country; now the procurement of substitutes was confined to the rich; the poor or the moderately well off man could not afford to pay the enormous prices demanded; no substitutes should be allowed; all citizens should be put upon the same footing.

Mr. Brown, of Mississippi, was opposed to the alteration of the section. He believed it was as near right as it could be made. It was a duty the government owed to the non-slaveholders in the army that the slaves should be kept in subjection, and not allowed to depredate upon their families and property. This could only be done by keeping some white man on every plantation where there were great numbers of slaves. It was also necessary for the welfare of the army its lf that artizans such as the Secretary of War should think the public interest required should work at their trades should be allowed to furnish substitutes.

Mr. Barnwell, of South Carolina, opposed the amendment of the gentleman from Florida. The gentleman's sole object seemed to be provide against the desertion of substitutes. He was opposed to substitutes. They were in all respects inferior to other troops, and, as we are told by all military men, more prone to desertion. He was for permittieg only such persons to furnish substitutes as the good of the country required. Legislation should teach the people that the danger is not passed. If a rich man, he must be taught that he must fight. Men desire offices, but they are unwilling to go down into the ranks. Whenever a spurt of success takes place, our people are apt to take up the opinion that the danger is all over. Our enactments must convince the people of the error of this opinion. He was opposed to substitutes except whenever the Secretary of War should say a man would be more serviceable working at his trade than in the ranks. And as concerned the large slaveholder, he did not wish to favor him, but approved the section of the bill permitting him to supply a substitute, because it was more important to the prosperity of the country that he should remain on his plantation and keep his slaves in subjection. He favored the bill as it stood, and should vote for it.

Mr. Phelan, of Mississippi, thought either that no man should be allowed to furnish a substitute or that every man should be allowed the privilege. He was not prepared to vote for any middle policy. By the bill two classes of citizens only are entitled to obtain substitutes. The substitute of the gentleman from Florida puts every man on the same footing, and holds them responsible for the desertion of their substitutes. It had been said the rich should be allowed to remain at home to protect the poor man's family from the ravages of his slaves. Why not let the poor man stay at home and protect his own family against the slaves of the rich man? The poor man should be permitted to remain at home and attend to his pecuniar interests, if the rich man is permitted to do it. The poor man should be permitted to remain at home on account of his feelings of affection for his family, if the rich man is to be permitted to do it. In his own district, on one side of the river, were the prairie plantations of the rich, while on the other were the farms of the poor. The latter might ask him when he went home, why he had legislated to permit the rich to remain at home, while the poor were forced to go into the army? If I should tell them the rich were permitted to remain at home to guard the families of the poor, would they not at once reply that they had much rather entrust the protection of their families to their own presence? The policy of the bill was class legislation; he was, therefore, opposed to it. He was opposed to it from the first to the last line. But if we are to have class legislation, let us legislate in favor of the poor. The rich will take care of themselves.

Mr. Wigfall, of Texas, had hoped that when he left Washington city he had heard the last of "class legislation." But he, it seemed, was mistaken. The fact was that as the law now stands there is class legislation. None but the rich can now procure substitutes, and the committee had framed the bill under consideration to equalize the burden of the war. It had excepted skilled machanic because it was thought he might be of some service to the country out of the army and in it; and it had excepted one white man on plantations where there were large numbers of slaves, not because he might be a rich man, but because it was deemed imprudent for the public service to leave the slaves without some one to keep them in subjection. Adopt the law as altered by the substitute of the gentleman from Florida, and you enable the rich to keep out of the army by keeping a substitute in it; if one deserts he can supply another. Adopt the bill as reported by the committees, and you allow only two small classes to furnish substitutes. All others, rich or poor, must go into the army.

Mr. Clark, of Missouri, moved to strike out these words "or when such person is the only white male adult on a farm or plantation having thereon not less than fifty slaves." He thought the second section of the bill made ample provision for the keeping the slaves in subjection.

The substitute of Mr. Clark was adopted.

The question then recurred on the amendment of Mr. Maxwell, of Florida, viz: to strike out the entire section, saving the enacting clause, and the clause which makes the party furnishing the substitute responsible for his fidelity.

There being no further amendments to the first section, the Secretary reported, section the second, providing for the detail of privates for police duty.

On motion of Mr. Brown, of Mississippi, the words "with the approval of the Provost Marshal of such county or parish," were stricken out.

Mr. Phelan, of Mississippi, moved to strike out the clause providing for the detail of one private, as a police, for the plantation of a *femme sole,* a minor, or a person in the military service of the Confederacy,

Mr. Phelan argued to show the indelicacy, the absurdity, and the impossibility of a *femme sole,* a minor, or an absentee to make a contract for the retention or maintenance on their respective plantations, of a whiskered grenadier. The amendment was lost.

Mr. Preston moved to strike out the entire section. He thought the slave should only be managed as the separate States might think proper. He did not desire to authorize brigadiers or any other generals, to meddle with domestic institutions. The conscript army should not be prostituted into a police guard for slaves.

After much more discussion the further consideration of the bill was postponed until Monday.

On motion of Mr. Sparrow, of Louisiana, the Senate went into executive session.

HOUSE OF REPRESENTATIVES.

The Speaker laid before the House the Joint Resolution relating to the Navy Department, sent back from the Senate, and reported as passed without amendment. It appeared, moreover, that an amendment had been made by filling the blank left by the House with the number of members on the part of the Senate. The resolution was, by unanimous consent, considered as without amendment. The Speaker subsequently announced the Committee on the part of the House, as follows: Messrs. Foote, of Tennessee; Barksdale, of Mississippi; Lyons, of Virginia; Dupre, of Louisiana, and Boyce, of South Carolina.

SOLDIERS UNDER EIGHTEEN YEARS OF AGE.

Mr. Chambliss, of Virginia, moved a suspension of the rules for the purpose of taking up for consideration the bill "authorizing the discharge of private soldiers under eighteen years of age." The motion was agreed to, and the bill was taken up. As reported from the Military Committee it reads as follows:

An Act authorising the discharge of private soldiers under eighteen years of age, and prohibiting the enlistment of such persons.

SEC. 1. The Congress of the Confederate States do enact, That any private soldier of the Provisional Army, who is under the age of eighteen years, shall be entitled to a discharge from all military service while he is under such age, on the application of himself, his parents, guardian or next of kin, to the Colonel of the regiment to which such private soldier belongs, sustained by proof satisfactory to said Colonel, of the age of said private soldier.

SEC. 2. *Be it further enacted.* That hereafter no person under the age of eighteen years shall be allowed to enlist in the military service of the Confederate States.

Mr. Chambliss addressed the House in favor of the immediate passage of the bill, which was also sustained by Mr. Goode, of Virginia.

Mr. Miles, of South Carolina, moved to amend the first section by striking out the word "colonel" and inserting the word "commander," and after the word "regiment" inserting "legion, battalion or independent company."

Mr. Foote, of Tennessee, approved the bill—thought it eminently proper—but could not vote for it, as he himself had sons in the army, and he could not aid in the passage of a law which forbid them to serve the country in their own way.

Mr. Ewing, of Kentucky, thought the bill had been introduced at an unfortunate moment.—While the country was calling upon Congress to furnish additional troops for the army, we pass a law taking from that army 20,000 of its best troops. He should vote against the whole bill.

The debate was continued by Messrs. Heiskell and Jones, of Tennessee; Singleton, of Mississippi; Lyons, of Virginia; Machen, of Kentucky; and Wright, of Georgia; after which the amendment of Mr. Miles was agreed to.

Mr. Singleton offered the following amendment as a proviso to the first section of the bill:

"Provided that the provisions of this act shall not apply to those persons who, though under eighteen years of age, have gone into the army as substitutes."

Mr. Chilton offered the following as a substitute for the amendment last proposed:

"But the provisions of this bill shall not extend to any minor who has gone into the army as a substitute by the consent of the parent or guardian of such minors; and in cases where substitutes may apply for a discharge by reason of the minority of such substitute, no discharge shall be granted unless notice be given to the person whose substitute he is, if resident within the Confederate States, and time allowed such pary to controvert the grounds of discharge, and if it should appear that the substitution was made of a minor under the age of eighteen years, and that he still continues under that age at the time of making such application, and that his substitution was procured without the consent of the parent or guardian of such minor, then, in such cases, the party who procured the substitute shall be ordered to return to the service, and required to serve out the term of his enlistment."

After some debate, Mr. E. M. Bruce said that an objection to the passage of the bill might be found in the fact that in Kentucky the larger portion of the boys were Southern in feeling, and as they might be compelled to fly from their homes at any time, it would be a pity to exclude such fine material from our army. He thought the less legislation on the matter the better, and moved to lay the whole subject on the table.—The motion was not agreed to—ayes 31, nays 51.

Mr. Chilton's substitute was then rejected—ayes 33, noes 49.

The question then recurring on Mr. Singleton's amendment, it was adopted.

Mr. Heiskell, of Tennessee, moved to amend by inserting just before the proviso—"But no minor shall be so discharged except by his own free will and consent." The amendment was agreed to.

Mr. Crockett, of Kentucky, moved to amend by inserting immediately after Mr. Singleton's proviso—"And provided further, that nothing in this act shall prevent volunteers from the State of Kentucky between the ages of sixteen and eighteen from entering the service, if in the opinion of the proper authorities, they are capable of performing military service."

Mr. Crockett appealed to the House to exempt Kentucky from the operations of the bill, by the adoption of the amendment he had submitted. He hoped that our army would enter Kentucky at no distant day, and many of the chivalric youths of the State were impatiently waiting to enlist under the banner of the South.

Mr. Gartrell hoped the House would reflect before passing the bill now under consideration. There was danger that gentleman would be led away by sympathy into the adoption of a measure productive of vast injury to our cause. Let the boys remain in the army. If it can be made to appear that they entered the service without the consent of their parents their discharge could be obtained from the Secretary of War.

Mr. Lyons.—By what authority of law would the Secretary do this?

Mr. Gartrell—Upon the ground that they were illegally held to service, and under the rules of the War Department. I now move to lay the whole subject on the table. The motion was lost.

Mr. Heiskell offered the following amendment in lieu of that offered by the gentleman from Kentucky.

"This shall not apply to any person who is a refugee, or the son of a disloyal person; the consent of no other person than himself shall be required." Lost.

Mr. E. M. Bruce moved to commit the bill and amendments to the Committee on Military Affairs. Lost.

Mr. Bonham moved the indefinite postponement of the bill, and the previous question was ordered thereon; the motion was decided in the negative—ayes 32, noes 46.

The question recurring upon the amendment of Mr. Crockett, of Kentucky, it was agreed to—ayes 48, noes not counted.

Mr. Clapp, of Mississippi, moved to amend the second section by adding—"Unless the parents of such persons are living and shall give their written assent to his enlistment before he is received." Agreed to. The bill was then ordered to its engrossment.

The bill was then read a third time and passed—ayes 48, noes 26.

The House adjourned.

TRI-WEEKLY MERCURY.

BY R. B. RHETT, JR.

OFFICE NO. 4 BROAD-STREET, CHARLESTON.

THE DAILY MERCURY, five cents per copy, $10 per annum.

THE TRI-WEEKLY MERCURY, issued on Tuesdays, Thursdays and Saturdays, five cents per copy. $5 per annum.

TUESDAY, SEPT MBER 2, 1862.

MOVEMENTS OF CONFEDERATES IN THE WEST—EXPLOITS OF MORGAN, ETC.

The Bowling Green (Ky.) correspondent of the New York *Times*, under date of August 14, writes:

There has been, during the past few days, no communication between this point and Gen. Buell's advance; we are consequently without full information of the military operations in the Southwest. Buell at last accounts, had advanced up the Sequatchee Valley, and occupied a position on the north bank of Battle Creek, a little stream that runs through Jasper county, Tennessee, just above its confluence with the Tennessee River. The rebel General Braxton Bragg was reported as being on the opposite bank of Battle Creek, with 30,000 men, and a general engagement was regarded as impending. This position of Buell is near twenty miles northwest of Chattanooga. There is, no doubt, a large rebel force in his front; but the report of Bragg threatening him in such close proximity, with 30,000 men, should be received with many degrees of allowance. Officers and soldiers from Buell's army report the health of the troops as being most excellent; better, indeed, than at any time previous. The locality of his headquarters is healthful, and well adapted to military strategy, but by no means abundantly supplied with forage and articles of army subsistence—now much needed by the troops in the Southwest.

The recent expedition of the guerilla Morgan into Tennessee was designed to accomplish two objects. He thought by making a bold dash into that State and Kentucky at this time, when the people are excited upon the subject of drafting, he could induce that class of persons possessed of Southern proclivities, but who have preferred to stand aloof, taking no part in the war, to flock to his standard. Fearing a draft into the ranks of the National army, he supposed that they would gladly avail themselves of his appearance to show their preference for "Southern Rights," by enlisting under his pirate flag. Never was man more mistaken. The raid of Morgan and his guerilla bands into Kentucky have, though attended with some local mischief, resulted in much general good. They have aroused the people of every section from their apathy to a sense of their danger, and convinced them of the dastardly nature of the foes that threaten them. On every hill and in every valley of the State the drum beat is sounding, and men are voluntarily marshaling, under the colors of the Union, eager for the fray. Already Kentucky has volunteered *more than her quota* of the first call for 300,000 troops, and she will, it is thought, furnish her quota of the second call without a resort to drafting. The State has resolved to rid herself of her enemies, and to show on the battle field the terrible earnestness of her resolution. In thinking, then, to swell their ranks from those disaffected, on account of the proposed draft, Morgan and his friends were mistaken. Morgan's other object, and the more serious of the two, was the possession or destruction of the Louisville and Nashville Railroad, thus cutting off our soldiers in the South from communication with their supply depots. At this season of the year, boats cannot run up the Tennessee River higher than Muscle Shoals, near Decatur; nor can they run up the Cumberland to any point whence supplies could be sent to the army.

The present position of Gen. Buell, as above indicated, is near Stephenson, which is immediately on the Chattanooga Railroad, running from Nashville to Chattanooga. The Louisville and Nashville Railroad, running from Louisville through this place and Gallatin to Nashville, connects with the Chattanooga road at that place. On this road, then, the army of Gen. Buell relies, as its principal avenue of supplies and transportation. Its possession is a matter of immense importance. To secure this road, and cut Buell off from his supplies, Morgan left Knoxville, East Tennessee, with a mounted force, estimated at two thousand men. He proceeded to Kinston, and thence to Sparta, from which point he went rapidly through the counties of Jackson and Macon, Tennessee, into Sumner, and pounced upon Gallatin, the county seat, just about daylight on the morning of the 12th, taking the place completely by surprise. The soldiers on duty at Gallatin consisted of about three hundred men of Col. Boone's Twenty-eighth Kentucky regiment, which had been some time stationed at that point. These were all taken prisoners, and paroled on the spot. So complete was the surprise that the entire force, it is stated, was surrounded and forced to surrender without firing a gun. Colonel Boone was captured, and is retained as a prisoner. On taking the place, Morgan immediately possessed himself of the Government stores accumulated there. Large quantities of these were at once destroyed. He next seized a Government freight train, which was on its way to Nashville.

By this seizure, nineteen freight cars, five thousand bushels corn and oats, eighty-seven horses, and various other articles of value were captured. The horses were, of course, appropriated to the use of the men, the provisions and provender, or such of it as could not be appropriated, including the train, were immediately destroyed. While this was going on, Morgan had seized the telegraph office, and displacing the regular operator put one of his own operators in his place. He then sent a despatch to this place, in the name of Colonel Boone, directed to Colonel Bruce, Commandant here, urging Bruce to send him (Boone) reinforcements immediately, as an attack was expected upon Gallatin. The operator at this place detected the change of operators at Gallatin, and the asked for reinforcements were not sent. Thus warned, the down passenger and express train to Nashville was stopped at this place and saved. The up train from Nashville reached a point within six miles of Gallatin, when, being warned of the danger ahead, it backed speedily to the Nashville depot, and was also saved.—Finding their efforts to lure additional trains and troops into the snare set for them futile, the rebel guerillas threw of all disguise, and sent boastful and wanton despatches of their exploits in each direction. One despatch was to the effect that Colonel Boone, their prisoner, was a clever fellow, but not very choice as to the company he kept. Another was to the Mayor of Nashville and Governor Johnson, warning them to leave that city if they would save their heads, etc.

On yesterday, the 13th, a strong National force was sent from Nashville to Gallatin, for the purpose of attacking, and if possible, capturing Morgan's men. The guerilla chief learned his danger, and, as he has always done when danger threatened, made off as speedily as possible.—Several of his men were killed and eight or ten others were taken prisoners by our men from Nashville.

By this raid travel on the Louisville and Nashville Road is for the present suspended, and the people are compelled to do without their mails from below. There is a considerable tunnel six miles this side of Gallatin, through which the road runs. This is through a hill of slate rock. When it was cut, heavy trestle timbers were placed horizontally at the top of the tunnel, and sustained by uprights, to prevent the rock from falling on the track. This trestle work Morgan destroyed, and, in consequence, large masses of slate rock have fallen into the tunnel and obstructed the road. A freight car was also fired and run into the tunnel, where it was consumed, as additional obstruction. These obstructions will have to be removed, and the trestle timbers reconstructed, before the cars will be running. After the obstruction of this tunnel, the only way of travel to Nashville was to take the Memphis and Clarksville Railroad, the terminus of which is at this place, and go to the junction of the Kentucky and Edgefield road, near the Tennessee and Kentucky State line, over which you cou'd be conveyed to the Louisville and Nashville Road, about twelve miles north of Nashville. The people of this region felicitated themselves that even this roundabout way of travel was left open. On yesterday, however, the down train, heavily filled with passengers and express, was forced to turn back to this place. On reaching the junction of the Edgefield and Kentucky Road, it was ascertained that the bridge fiends had been at their work. On the night of the 12th, a five-span trestle bridge, on which the cars cross a deep ravine, six miles from the junction, was burned. So there is now no communication by railroad with Nashville. Great inconvenience is experienced in consequence. The trains from Louisville can run no further than this place. There is a large number of persons, both private citizens and soldiers, returning to their commands South, here awaiting conveyance below. Workmen are engaged in removing the obstructions, and travel, without some further interference, will be resumed in a few days. Volunteering and enlistments are bravely going on in Kentucky. The people are thoroughly aroused. The call for 600,000 men meets the hearty approbation of Kentuckians. It is an earnest to them that the war is to be prosecuted with vigor, and pushed to a speedy termination. Kentucky, ever true and patriotic, will welcome the day when the terrible battle cloud, gathering from the musket-mist of a million of loyal men under arms, will volley the thundering death knell of treason throughout the confines of all rebeldom.

LATEST FROM EUROPE.

By the arrival off Cape Race of the steamship *Teutonia*, we have advices from Europe three days later than by the *Europa*.

The most important news by this arrival relates to Italian affairs. The Italian squadron had been ordered to Ancona, to watch the Adriatic coast.

It is stated that Garibaldi refuses to obey Victor Emanuel's proclamation. It is also stated that he held a council of war, at which it was determined to march forthwith on Rome, notwithstanding the remonstrances from Turin. The enthusiasm for Garibaldi was tremendous, and it was reported that he would soon be at the head of 50,000 men.

The Paris correspondent of the London Daily News asserts positively that Garibaldi has refused to obey Victor Emanuel's proclamation.

A letter from Palermo says the enthusiasm for Garibaldi is so great that young men were disappearing entirely from the place, and if other cities in Sicily imitate Palermo, Garibaldi must soon be at the head of 50,000 volunteers.

La France says Garibaldi held a council of war at Coffala on the 4th instant, at which it was decided to march on Rome, notwithstanding the remonstrance from Turin. The volunteers numbered six thousand. Garibaldi had chartered six large vessels. His plan is said to be to land in the Gulf of Palermo, there to be joined by an auxiliary force, and march on the Roman States.

The official Turin Gazette says Garibaldian volunteers would leave for Messina instead of Palermo. They number 3000, and are divided into three columns, one conducted by Garibaldi in person.

In the Chamber of Deputies, on the 8th of August, M. Ratazzi said there was a rumor, not officially confirmed, that an encounter had taken place between the troops and a band of Garibaldians, and the troops lost fifty muskets.

The latest accounts were, that Garibaldi, with 500 volunteers, had begun his march, had occupied Rocca, and had made a speech, in which he declared that he opposed the Government because it would not let him go to Rome; and opposed France because she defended the Pope. He expressed his determination to have Rome or die.

From France we have the rumor that the Mexican expeditionary force will be very large. The choicest officers and men of the Versailles Artillery are said to be under orders. A division of gunboats for Mexico was also being armed.

The distress in the cotton districts of England is increasing. The Liverpool cotton market was quiet and steady for American varieties. Breadstuffs were generally steady and quiet. Provisions were unsettled.

RESIGNATION.

RICHMOND, August 27th, 1862.

To the Editor of the Charleston Mercury:—Below I send you a copy of my resignation as member of our State Convention, which I have just forwarded to Hon. D. F. Jamison, President, &c. I respectfully request that you will publish it at once in your paper, which circulates so extensively in Barnwell, that the good people of that District may have ample time in making up their minds in regard to the person they may select to represent them in my place. And I also desire, by this means, to set forth to my generous constituents the reasons that have influenced me to pursue this course. I feel confident it will meet their approbation.

Your obedient servant,

LEWIS M. AYER, Jr.

RICHMOND, August 27th, 1862.

Hon. D. F. Jamison, President of the State Convention of South Carolina:

SIR: The newspapers have, just to-day, given me the information that our Convention, by your proclamation, is to re-assemble on the 9th of next month. I see no grounds to hope now that the present session of our Congress will be adjourned by that period. If I were to consult my inclinations, I should avail myself of the excuse, thus afforded me, to return home at that time and participate in the deliberations of that great and august assembly, of which I am so proud to be an humble member. But I think I should not be justified in abandoning my place in the Confederate Congress, where several questions of very grave importance to our whole country are now pending; and where, besides, not a day passes without the member being called on to attend to some business matter of interest and importance to one or more of his immediate constituents.—Much of this business, too, pertains to our gallant and patriotic soldiers, who are doing battle bravely in the field, and who have only their Congressional representative here, through whom their individual claims and petitions can be brought to the attention of the Government officials. Under these circumstances, I feel constrained to resign my seat as a member of the illustrious Secession Convention of South Carolina. I do so at once, that timely opportunity may be afforded the people of Barnwell District to elect another Delegate in my place. By such election, our people will also have it in their power to indicate clearly their opinions in regard to the deeply interesting and delicate subjects that are to engage your attention.

For these reasons, I hereby resign my seat as member of the State Convention of South Carolina.

May kind Heaven vouchsafe to that Convention the same wisdom, patriotism and fraternal feeling in its closing deliberations, which so greatly and gloriously illustrate its early acts!

I beg that you will do me the favor to lay this, my resignation, before that body when they shall assemble, and ask, for me, their gracious acceptance of the same.

I am, very respectfully and sincerely, your humble servant, LEWIS M. AYER, Jr.

THE "COURRIER DES ETATS UNIS" ON THE WAR.—The New York correspondent of the Philadelphia *Inquirer*, under date of August 19, writes:

The *Courrier des Etats Unis* is bidding high for a place in Fort Lafayette. It is discouraging enlistments. In its issue of this morning, it is imprudent and reckless enough to denounce Archbishop Hughes for his patriotic and timely address at St. Patrick's Cathedral, on Sunday morning last. The editor regrets that the Archbishop, on that occasion, thought proper to convert his evangelical chair into a tribune. "To fan the flames of intestine discord, to push to combat brother against brother, is, to say the least" (I quote the Courrier) "a singular task for the minister of a religion of mercy and peace, which holds as its first maxim, the repudiation of all human passions." The Courrier claims to be a Catholic journal, and denies that it is disloyal to the Government under which it lives and moves and has its being. How far these professions consist with its pratice, the above citations from its Archbishop article will show. It was only a few weeks ago that General Butler deemed it his duty to prohibit the circulation of the Courrier in New Orleans, and the ill-advised course of the editors would seem to indicate that they are determined to provoke a similar prohibition of its circulation nearer home.

EXTENSION OF THE CONSCRIPTION.—We are pleased to see that one of the first measures considered in Congress is a bill extending the provisions of the Conscription Act to all able bodied persons between the ages of 35 and 45. If our recent successes in Virginia should have the effect of relaxing our energies, they will prove worse than defeats in the end. The United States Government has recently called six hundred thousand additional troops into service, and if we wait till they are organized and put into the field, we shall have all the reverses of last winter reenacted. Our true policy is not to wait till we need an increase of our army before we provide for it. We court defeat by our want of forecast. The brave men we have in the field should not be left to contend with overwhelming numbers. Let us make the conscription now, that we may be ready to meet the new levies which Lincoln has called into the field.—*Eufaula Spirit of the South.*

NEWS FROM HAVANA AND MEXICO.—The steamer Columbia, from Havana, arrived in New York on the morning of the 21st. Her news, both from Mexico and Havana, is very interesting. At the former place reinforcements had arrived for the French amy, and it is said that troops from France to the number of twenty-five thousand were *en roue* for Martinique and Guadalupe. A number of fugitives from the dangers of the draft had escaped from New York to Havana; but they find very little sympathy, and are in great peril from the depredations of the yellow fever.—The blockade of the Mexican coast by the French was being strictly enforced, and two American vessels have been captured. General Forey had not yet arrived.

A son of the Rev. Robert J. Breckinridge was killed at the battle of Cynthiana. He was in Morgan's brave band.

LOCAL MATTERS.

THE FIRING on Friday evening last, which mystified everybody for a while, proceeded from a new fortification on James' Island, the garrison of which were making a trial of their heavy ordnance.

LEAD is much needed in the service, and as every citizen is bound to contribute to the extent of his ability to the establishment of our independence, every family in the State should look about their premises and forward such lead as may be spared for the use of the army. We will cheerfully take charge of all consignments that may be addressed to this office. Mark in all cases: *Lead for the Government.* Let there be no delay about this matter. Many families have lead enough about their premises, in the form of sheets, pipes, blocks, &c., when moulded into bullets, to put a company of Yankees to flight. Let them send it forthwith on its patriotic mission.

THE LADIES' GUNBOAT, "PALMETTO STATE."—We understand that the funds raised by the patriotic ladies of South Carolina for the construction of a gunboat for the defence of Charleston, are soon to be paid over to the Confederate Government, under whose direction the *Palmetto State* has been built. The aggregate of the contributions received at this office is $6,929,60. The "christening" of the staunch craft will take place at an early day.

MOVEMENTS OF THE BLOCKADING SQUADRON.—On Thursday night quite a stir was observed among the enemy's vessels blockading our harbor. A single gun was fired, and frequent flashes of gunpowder lit up the darkness. A bright blue light was displayed at the head of the Maffit Channel, another in the Ship Channel, and still another some distance out at sea. On Friday morning, instead of the fourteen blockading vessels which had strung their dark hulks along the horizon on the evening before, only seven were in sight. During the day, however, some of the missing vessels came straggling in and resumed their old position.

THE GUNBOATS AT WORK NEAR BLUFFTON.—The Yankees fired a good many shells in the direction of Bluffton on Saturday morning, to the terror of the cattle quietly grazing in the pastures. At one time it was thought the gunboat would come within range of a secluded point, where a warm reception awaited them; but, "bad luck to them," as a "lad in gray" remarked, they "didn't come up," and so the fun was postponed.

A FATAL ACCIDENT.—On Sunday last, the three o'clock down train picked up, and brought to this city, the mangled body of a dead negro boy, found between the Six and Seven Mile Posts, on the South Carolina R. R., who is supposed to have been run over by the morning train going up. It appears that he was dragged some hundred yards or more before he was disentangled and thrown off by the cars. How the accident occurred, or to whom the boy belonged, could not be ascertained.

PRISONERS TRANSFERRED.—The Yankee prisoners taken by Captains ELLIOTT and MICKLER, in their late expedition to Pinckney Island, were on Friday brought to the city on the Savannah Railroad, and sent to Columbia, where, for the present, they will remain. Their sojourn in Dixie is likely to be short, as under the terms of the cartel, they will, within a few weeks, at farthest, be exchanged or paroled.

"AN OVERSEER" writes to us from Bamberg, Barnwell District, as follows: "Out of five hundred and a few acres under my charge or supervision, I have five hundred acres corn and peas, a few acres potatos, sugar cane, etc. The corn, I think, will make six thousand bushels (common pine land), four thousand of which can be used by the Confederate States; the balance will supply home need. The peas, thus far, look well; the potatos are being dug for home use."

EXECUTION OF A DESERTER.—On Thursday last, at noon, Corporal GEORGE H. BURGER, of Company E, 1st Regiment S. C. Artillery, was publicly shot to death, in accordance with the sentence of a Court Martial, for the crime of desertion. The execution took place on the front beach of Sullivan's Island, some little distance beyond the Moultrie House. Col. KEITT's Regiment, under command of Lieut. Col. DANTZLER, the 1st Regiment of Artillery, commanded by Capt. PRESTON, a part of the 1st Regiment of Infantry, commanded by Capt. BAKER, and the Provost Marshal's Guard, consisting of detachments from the Charleston Battalion and Col. COLQUITT's 46th Georgia Regiment, were drawn up in a hollow square to witness the solemn scene.

The Provost Marshal, Lieut. Col. GAILLARD, directed the proceedings of the execution. The condemned man met his fate with composure. He was attended in his last moments by the Right Rev. Bishop LYNCH, with whom he joined in prayer previous to the execution. When the signal was given, BURGER fell, pierced by six balls. His body was buried in the soldiers' graveyard on the Island.

ATTACK OF THE ENEMY'S GUNBOATS UPON THE BEAUREGARD BATTERY.—About half-past three o'clock, on Thursday afternoon, one of the gunboats from the enemy's fleet off the Bar steamed in towards the shore, and opened fire, first upon the battery at Beach Inlet, and then upon the Beauregard Battery, under command of Major RHETT. The battery replied with spirit for about half an hour, when the gunboat drew off. Another one, however, soon came in to take her place, and renewed the fire upon the battery, which again replied. This latter firing lasted a little over half an hour, when the attacking vessel steamed off, like her predecessor. Although many of the enemy's shells fell in the neighborhood of the battery, none took effect within it, and no damage whatever was sustained from the fire of the gunboats.

The firing from the battery was remarkably good. We learn that six shots in succession were in the direct line of the ship, some a little short, some a little over. The gun used was a rifled 32-pounder, under the direction of Captain JOHN C. MITCHEL, Jr. The distance of the vessel was about four thousand yards.

A NEW COUNTERFEIT.—The Augusta *Chronicle* of Sunday says: Another counterfeit Confederate note was exhibited to us yesterday morning. It is of the ten dollar issue of September 2, 1861, printed in colors. The principal distinguishing mark is the filling up of the red oblong in the lower centre of the note. In the genuine, the filling up consists of the word "ten" in small letters frequently repeated—in the counterfeit it is merely dots. The counterfeit has the words "ADRIAN SHARP, Sc.," on the lower left hand corner, not on the genuine. The red color of the counterfeit is paler than the genuine, the engraving is coarser, apparently on wood, while the genuine is a well finished steel plate.

SALE OF NEGROS.—At the Brokers' Exchange on Friday, August 29, WILBUR & SON sold ten negros, aged 55 to 18, for $7220 cash—average $722 each; four not warranted sound.

GENERAL JOSEPH E. JOHNSTON has entirely recovered from the effects of his wound received in the battle of the Seven Pines, and will report for duty in Richmond to-day.

NEWS BY TELEGRAPH.

LATE AND IMPORTANT FROM THE WEST.

MOBILE, August 30.—The *Advertiser* has a despatch, dated Tupelo, August 29, saying that fourteen prisoners, captured at Rienzi, had arrived. Three hundred of our guerillas moved in two parties against the Yankee camp, with the intention of attacking it on both sides. One party captured the pickets and took the Yankees completely by surprise, rushing headlong into their camp, which consisted of five regiments of cavalry and eight of infantry. The other party failed in attacking, and our small force was, therefore, repulsed; but they succeeded in bringing off a number of prisoners. Our loss will not exceed fifteen. The attack was a reckless one, and the escape of our force a miracle. A deserter from Rienzi, who left his camp on Monday, estimates the Yankee force there at 7,000. Great discord prevails in their camp, which is overrun with stolen and runaway negros.

The Chicago *Times*, of the 25th inst., has been received here. It contains the Message of President DAVIS on the re-assembling of the Confederate Congress. A despatch from Cincinnati, dated the 24th, says that Gen. BUCKNER, with 25,000 men, is encamped near Somers, Kentucky, and that Gen. BRAGG is at Chattanooga with 30,000 more. Gen. MARSHALL is reported at the head of Big Sandy River with 15,000 men. The railroad is in full possession of the rebels. No trains can pass to Nashville. The draft will be enforced on the 1st of September. Foreigners who have voted on their first papers, and now claiming exemption from draft, are arrested and pressed into service.

Camp, Rappahannock Station, August 21.—A cavalry skirmish took place yesterday. The Federals lost three wounded and five prisoners. Earthworks have been thrown up, and bridges constructed, to enable the batteries to cross the river. The First New Jersey regiment was surrounded by the rebels, and half of them captured.

MEMPHIS, August 22.—A guerilla band, numbering 500, came within ten miles of the city yesterday, and destroyed large quantities of cotton and the bridges over the Wolf and Hatchie Rivers. Five new companies were recently raised in West Tennessee. It is much feared that bands of guerillas are committing depredations in the vicinity of Mound City, Adair county, Mo. Col. MCCULLOUGH, of PORTER's Guerillas, was sentenced to death as a traitor, and shot; also, fifteen guerillas accused of breaking their paroles. Gov. GAMBLE, in a speech at St. Louis, declared that guerillas were robbers and murderers, and that he would treat them as such. The Yankee account of the late fight says that 800 of their men attacked 1700 under MORGAN, and were defeated with a loss of 300, including JOHNSON. The remaining 500 escaped. No telegraphic communication is had south of Russelville, Ky.

One hundred and forty Mississippians left Camp Norton, Indiana, for Vicksburg, on the 23d. 800 Kentuckians and Tennesseeans have been released.

LATEST FROM RICHMOND.

RICHMOND, VA., August 30.—The Lynchburg *Republican* says that CARLILE, who represented the PIERPONT usurpation in the LINCOLN Senate, is stumping the western part of Virginia in favor of the South. At Clarksburg he said that he was no longer in favor of the war, but with the South, against the anti slavery party, and that it was folly to talk of subjugating the South.

It it reported that the enemy have evacuated the Kanawha Valley, and that in their retreat they attempted to burn the Kanawha Salt Works, but failed.

The citizens of Northwestern Virginia are flocking eastward to join the Confederate army.

The news from the seat of war in Virginia, as far as received, continues to be most cheering.

CONGRESSIONAL.

RICHMOND, August 30—The Senate was not in session to-day.

In the House, two resolutions of inquiry relative to the *lex talionis*, were discussed and finally adopted.

Nothing else of interest was done.

ESCAPED YANKEES.

SALISBURY, N. C., August 30.—Five Yankee deserters escaped from prison last night. Look out for them! H. MCCOY, Comd'g.

FROM THE NORTH.

From the Northern papers of the 23d inst., we gleam the following items of interest:

Correspondents have been excluded from the army of Virginia, and consequently there is not a line of news from the seat of war.

Archbishop HUGHES had a long interview with LINCOLN on Friday. The rumor of MCCLELLAN's contemplated resignation is contradicted on the "highest authority."

W. H. HURLBERT, who was for a long time imprisoned at Richmond, under suspicion of being a spy, and who was finally released, has turned up in Washington.

They are requiring the oath of allegiance to be administered throughout all parts of the North. No class is excused from giving this proof of their "loyalty." All the different lines of travel have passed a resolution that each director, officer, superintendent, and the other heads of departments, be instructed to require all employees in their respective departments, or who may hereafter be employed, to take the oath of allegiance to the government in such form as the government has prescribed.

Advices from Minnesota represent that an outbreak had occurred at the Lower Sioux Agency, and that all the whites, except a few, had been murdered by the Indians. "Letters to Gov. RAMSEY say that hundreds are known to be killed, and it is believed thousands."

The stock market was excited by adverse reports from Virginia, but recovered between boards. Gold advanced to 116¼, but closed at 115½; Bills on London 127½.

MARKED MEN.—In view of the recent order of President DAVIS, concerning the execution of officers of negro regiments, we copy the following list from the New York *Tribune* of the officers of the 1st South Carolina (negro) regiment, organized by Gen. HUNTER, but lately disbanded as inefficient:

Captains—Chas. Trowbridge, John D. B. Goddard, James H. Harold, Wm. B. Church, Orastus H. Case, of New York; William J. Randolph, Robert W. Weller, Robert Hamilton, William James, and Joseph T. Brown, of Pennsylvania. First Lieutenants—George W. Reeder, Thomas K. Durham, Alexander Heasley, George S. Vem, Thomas S. McGlathery, of Pennsylvania; Robert M. Gaston, William H. Davidson, Israel F. Stickles, of New York; Luther G. Riggs, of Connecticut. Second Lieutenants—Jno. A. Trowbridge, Geo. K. Walker, of New York; Edmund F. Oliver, Jas. F. Johnston, Robert G. Christie, Steward Alford, Jas. Pomeroy, Thos. C. Randolph, John O. Kerr, of Pennsylvania. Regimental Quartermaster—Harry West, of New York.

THE MILK QUESTION.—A milkman was lately prosecuted in New York for adulterating milk at a "town pump." His counsel contended that the addition of water was not an adulteration of milk. Mr. A. Oakey Hall, District Attorney, contended that it was, and that, although some men might suppose that milk was improved by an admixture with brandy, and thus made milk punch, still, if a man purchased it as milk, he was entitled to the genuine, unadulterated article.—The court agreed with Mr. Hall, and fined the defendant fifty dollars.

THE LATEST.

GREAT NEWS FROM MANASSAS!

ANOTHER GLORIOUS SOUTHERN VICTORY.

SIGNAL DEFEAT OF THE COMBINED FORCES OF McCLELLAN AND POPE.

OFFICIAL DESPATCH OF GENERAL LEE.

RICHMOND, September 1.—The following despatch was received by the President this evening about six o'clock:

HEADQUARTERS ARMY NORTHERN VIRGINIA,
GROVETON, Aug. 30, 10 p. m.,
Via Rapidan, September 1st.

To President Davis:

This army achieved to-day, on the plains of Manassas, a signal victory over the combined forces of Generals MCCLELLAN and POPE. On the 28th and 29th, each wing under Generals LONGSTREET and JACKSON, repulsed with valor attacks made on them separately. We mourn the loss of our gallant dead in every conflict, yet our gratitude to Almighty God for his mercies rises higher each day.

To Him and to the valor of our troops a nation's gratitude is due.

(Signed) R. E. LEE.

ENGAGEMENT AT STEVENSON—THE ENEMY EXPELLED, AND THE TOWN RECAPTURED BY OUR TROOPS.

BRIDGEPORT, ALA., August 31.—Gen. MAXEY's brigade, under command of Col. MCKINSTRY, of the 32d Alabama regiment, attacked the enemy, 1200 strong, at Stevenson, at 11 o'clock to-day. The enemy's force consisted of infantry, artillery and cavalry. After four hour's shelling, the enemy evacuated their fortifications, leaving on the Nashville trains, by the common roads, and through the woods. A large amount of ammunition and stores was captured. Our command met with a most cordial reception from the citizens, the ladies urging them not to stop till they had killed or captured every Yankee foe. The joy of the citizens at once more beholding the "Stars and Bars" was unbounded. The regiments engaged on our side were the 32d Alabama, 41st Alabama and 25th Tennessee, with Major GUNTER's dismounted partizan rangers, Capt. RICE's cavalry, and FREEMAN and DURR's batteries. The whole number of men engaged was 900. Our loss was two wounded, none killed. The Yankee loss is unknown. The Yankee fortifications at Stevenson were very strong. Our troops displayed great gallantry in the action. FREEMAN's battery worked with great skill and signal effect. HARRY MAURY commanded the 32d Alabama with coolness and efficiency, exposing himself greatly to the Yankee fire. His conduct is highly eulogized.

Message of Gov. Magoffin of Kentucky.

The message of Governor MAGOFFIN to the Legislature of Kentucky, in extra session, is published. It is quite a long document. He condemns MORGAN's raids, and laments his want of authority to prevent them. He dwells at length on "the interference, by the military, with the civil authorities, and the arrest of citizens without authority of law." He grieves over the imprisonment of citizens of Kentucky. He wants Kentucky to be a peace-maker, and says:

"She has had nothing to do with bringing on this war, and will suffer more, probably, than any other State, if it continue long. Her institutions, interests, manners, customs, associations and sympathies have been mainly with the South, but her loyalty to the Union of our fathers is unquestionable. She had common complaints and wrongs with her Southern sisters, but widely differed with them in the remedy they adopted. Regarding abolition as worse than secession, by condemning, in unmistakable language, the change of policy in the Government, you will strengthen, in my opinion, the cause of the Union, give assurance to its vast armies in the field, and greatly encourage enlistments at home."

The Governor thus concludes:

"For myself, I have endeavored to do my duty under the Constitution and laws, no matter how much it may have been my misfortune, perhaps, to differ from you, painful as it has been to me—some of my dearest friends belonging to the opposite party. My intentions have been upright and honest. * * * * * * * *
No one can charge me, truthfully, with doing privately anything inconsistent with my public declarations and course. * * * * * *
What pledge have I disregarded? What law have I failed to execute when I had the power to do it? In what have I attempted to thwart the will of the majority, expressed according to the Constitution, and under the forms of law? What word of treason have I uttered? What act have I done to aid the rebellion? What motive could I have in breaking up the Union—the government of our fathers?

* * * "In what have I offended so grievously as to justify the Legislature in depriving me of the power given the Governor of the State by the Constitution for its own preservation, the enforcement of the laws, and the protection of the people in the full enjoyment of their rights? Threats are made that I am watched, and am to be held to a terrible accountability. Is it because I recognize no government but that which is embodied in the Constitution and laws? Allegiance (loyalty) to government is obedience to constitutional law. Is it because I believe the Federal Government the creature of the sovereign States of this Union, and can exercise no powers except those delegated by them in the Constitution? that I am for a strict construction of the Constitution, and a State rights man belonging to the strictest of the straightest sect of Democrats? Is it because I believe the best interests of the people have been always secured in the success of that party?"

* * * * * * *

"I hazard nothing in saying I have been more untiring in my honest efforts to preserve, and have made more propositions to prevent, a dissolution of the Union, and which promised to be successful if they had been adopted in time, than all my busy, brawling calumniators, who have their vile purposes to serve."

THE FOLLOWING is a list of the articles contributed by the Soldiers' Relief Society of Barnwell C. H., to a box sent to the Winder Hospital at Richmond, Va., July 22d, 1862:

Mrs. G.—5½ lbs. of sugar, 2 shirts, 3 pocket-handkerchiefs, old linen.

Mrs. J. B.—2 old hams, 3 bottles of honey, 1 jar of pickles, 1 package of sago, 2 shirts and 1 peck of rice.

Mrs. W.—½ peck of rice, jar of pickles, 1 bottle of wine.

Mrs. D.—3 old hams and lint.

Mrs. H.—1 peck of rice.

Mrs. C.—2 bottles of wine, 1 of brandy, 2 pairs of drawers, 1 shirt, 1 sheet and old linen.

Mrs. J. H.—1 pair of drawers and 1 shirt.

Mrs. ——— 2 bottles of wine, 1 of brandy, 3 shirts, 1 peck of rice, ½ bushel of grist and dried fruit.

Mrs. P.—1 box of grist, 2 cakes of soap and pickles.

Mrs. J. A.—1 peck of rice, 1 package of farina.

Mrs. Bowman.—1 jar of pickles, 1 package of hyson tea, 2 bottles of lemon syrup, 1 of brandy.

Mrs. M.—2 bottles of ginger wine.

Mrs. J. J. O'B.—3 lbs. of home made crackers, 1 package of arrowroot, 1 of sago, 1 of sage, 1 of dogwood bark, 1 bottle of wine.

Mrs. J. D. A.—2 bed spreads, 1 pair of sheets, 1 pair of pillow cases, 1 bolster case, 2 pairs of drawers, night wrappers, 3 lbs. of arrowroot, a bag of thyme, 35 lbs. of rice and lint.

Mrs. B. H. B.—1 bag of grist, 1 peck of rice, 3 handkerchiefs, 2 shirts, 1 pair of drawers, jar of pickles, old linen and lint.

Mrs. H. D.—1 barrel of grist, 1 peck of rice, 1 lb. of sugar.

Mrs. T.—½ peck of rice, 1 jar of pickles, 1 bottle of wine.

From the Society—15 pairs of drawers and 7 pairs of woolen socks.

E. P. DUNCAN,
Secretary S. R. S.

An exchange paper says, "Can the human voice articulate anything softer than the Indian name of Coahoma?" What does the Editor think of "Musheslushetobesofka," the Seminole name of Hominy?

To the Editor of the Mercury: I gratefully acknowledge the receipt of the following stores and money for the use of the Soldiers' Relief Society:

August 26.—2 barrels of fruit and vegetables, fans, from the ladies of Society Hill, through Mrs. Mary H. Witherspoon.

1 box of apples from Salters' Station.

From an enthusiastic friend of the cause—153 worsted socks, 58 cotton socks, 77 pairs of drawers, 18 cushions, 36 worsted shirts, 10 scarfs, 6 quilts, 90 cotton shirts, 1 demijohn of sherry wine, 1 of claret.

From Capt. Parker, of steamer Minho—1 keg of oat meal, 1 can of black tea.

Courier office, an unknown friend—$10.

Mrs. Robert Martin, through A. R. Taft, Esq.—$100.

The hospitals are greatly in want of poultry; also brandies. JOHN BACHMAN.

DESTRUCTIVE FIRE.—We delay further our present issue to give a hasty account of a destructive fire, which occurred this (Thursday) afternoon. While we write the immense Gun Factory in the lower part of this city is being reduced to ashes. The fire originated in the "drying room," and before the workmen were aware of it the roof of the building was a sheet of flame; fortunately, all escaped without injury.—Some of the workmen, we learn, leaped from the windows of the second story. The loss will not be far short of $75,000 in machinery, unfinished guns, etc., besides the total destruction of the splendid new three and a half story brick building. The entire community sympathizes with the energetic and gentlemanly but unfortunate proprietors. The building belonged to our esteemed townsman, Mr. John C. Eve. We are not informed as to whether there was any insurance on the building. We regret to learn that Messrs. Dickson, Sadler and Nelson were not insured.

Rome (Ga.) Southerner.

WELL MERITED HONOR.—Captain FRANK BUCHANAN has been promoted to the highest office in the Confederate Navy, viz: that of Admiral, for his distinguished services in the great battle and victory in Hampton Roads. His commission dates from Saturday, August 23.

The scoundrels attached to Pope's army, burnt the beautiful hotel and all the surrounding buildings, at the Fauquier White Sulphur Springs, near Warrenton, before running from that place. These building were very spacious, and built in superb style.

Hollow metallic canes, filled with condensed gas, are becoming the rage in some of the European cities. The bearer has only to turn a small nipple and apply his match, when he will instantly find himself furnished with a torch which will light him for several hours.

Tribute of Respect.

At a meeting of the Washington Artillery, held at Camp Gladden, May 8th, 1862, Captain G. H. WALTER in the Chair, the following Preamble and Resolutions were unanimously adopted:

Surrounded, as we are on every hand, with sorrow and death, yet custom cannot in all bereavements lessen the poignancy of our feelings, or take the edge off our grief. And though all of us are, at this time, made painfully aware that in the midst of life we are in death, we cannot the less deeply feel our loss in the sudden, and, in every way, distressing death of our friend and comrade, LESLIE OWEN. Departing from us, full of life and joyful spirit, an hour later he was stilled in the arms of death. We have cause ever to lament him, for he was always a kind friend and a trusty comrade, and in every relation in which we knew him, he was faithful to his duties, and praiseworthy in his actions.

Resolved, 1st. That in the death of Sergeant LESLIE D. OWEN, we have lost a good officer, a faithful comrade, and an affectionate friend; and his country a brave soldier and a useful citizen.

2d. That we deeply deplore his untimely death, and sincerely sympathise with his bereaved parents in this affliction.

3d. That a copy of these resolutions be sent to his family, and that they be published once in each of the daily papers.

Captain GEO. H. WALTER, Ch'm'n.

W. R. DAVIS, Secretary.

OBITUARY.

DIED, at her residence (Windson Forrest), in the county of New Kent, Virginia, on Wednesday, 27th ultimo, at half past three o'clock, a. m., Mrs. HARRIET SAVAGE, in the 79th year of her age.

A CARD.

CAMP BRAGG, NEAR RICHMOND, Aug. 11, 1862.

MR. EDITOR: In your issue of August 2d, containing the order of Brigadier General KERSHAW, my name appears as a defaulter, and I am published to the world as a deserter. The facts of the case are these: On or about the 1st May I was sent from the Peninsula to the South Carolina Hospital at Manchester, and about the 12th I obtained a furlough of fifteen days, to visit home and recruit my health, and also to accompany the body of an elder brother who had died, a few days previous, in the hospital. The furlough was recommended by Dr. MICHEL, of Charleston, Chief Surgeon of the South Carolina Hospital, presented to the Surgeon General by the Superintendent, and granted by him. The Superintendent then informed me that if I was not well enough at the expiration of the furlough, not to return, but to send a surgeon's certificate stating what further time would be required to regain my health, and the furlough would be extended. At the expiration of the furlough my family physician, Dr. J. B. WITHERSPOON, of Sumter, forbade my returning to camp, and voluntarily certified that it would, to the best of his belief, be necessary for me to remain until the latter part of August. Upon this certificate my furlough was extended to the time specified in the certificate. I returned to my regiment on the 3d of August, *twenty days before the expiration of my furlough.* Yet I am held up to the public as a deserter.

Since January, 1861, I have been doing my duty, both with the spade and musket, on Morris Island, and at and around Manassas, notwithstanding which thirty dollars is offered for my capture, as if I were a felon.

In my humble opinion, I was not responsible for my appearance either to the Captain of my company, the Colonel of the regiment or the General of the brigade. I received my furlough from the officers of the South Carolina Hospital, and to them alone I was responsible; for I was sent by the Regimental Surgeon to the hospital, and the hospital was responsible to the regiment for my appearance Therefore, the officers of the regiment had no right to advertise me as a deserter as long as I was under the control of the hospital authorities.

With this simple statement of facts, Mr. Editor, I submit my case to a generous and, at the same time, a just and impartial public, and leave it to them to decide whether I am a thirty dollar deserter or not. T. M. DELORME,
Co. C, 8th Regt., S. C. V.

HEADQUARTERS DEPARTMENT S. C. AND GA.,
CHARLESTON, August 31, 1862.

[GENERAL ORDERS NO. 52.]

I. * * * IN ACCORDANCE WITH GENERAL Orders No. 52, Part I. current series, dated Richmond, July 23d, 1862, "Secessionville" will be inscribed on the colors of the following named Regiments and Battalions engaged in the action of June 16th, 1861, at Secessionville, James Island, South Carolina:

1st Regiment Artillery, South Carolina Volunteers.
Charleston Battalion.
Smith's Battalion, South Carolina Volunteers.
4th Louisiana Battalion.

* * * * * *

By order Maj. Gen. PEMBERTON.

September 1 1 J. R. WADDY, A. A. G.

Terms.

☞ "THE NEW ERA" will be pub'ished every Saturday, and furnished to subscribers at five cents per copy, or $2 50 per year; when sent by mail, $3. A liberal deduction when a number are ordered.

Advertisements will be inserted at One Dollar per square, of ten lines; every additional insertion. Fifty cents.

Liberal arrangements will be made with those who advertise by the month or quarter.

Job Printing neatly executed at liberal rates, for cash.

Communications must be addressed to "Rich. B. Locke, Editor New Era, Key West, Fla."

No annonymous communications will be noticed, and rejected manuscript will not be returned

THE NEW ERA.

PUBLISHED EVERY SATURDAY MORNING AT KEY WEST, FLORIDA.

VOL. I.] KEY WEST, FLA., SATURDAY, SEPTEMBER 6, 1862. [NO. 21.

Special Notices.

Correspondents wishing information on any subject, can have their queries answered in our columns, but brevity in all cases, is absolutely required.

Communications from friends at a distance, for publication, will be received with pleasure, especially when embodying interesting facts.

No communications containing personal reflections upon the character of individuals will be admitted into our columns,

Marriages and deaths will be inserted gratuitously, as also brief religious notices.

Contributions of local interest, from citizens, will find a place in our columns.

RICH. B. LOCKE, Editor.

Original Poetry.

GO MY BOY WHERE DUTY CALLS YOU.

IN ANSWER TO "MOTHER CAN I GO?"

Go, my boy, and heaven bless you, I have read each precious line,
Of your hearts responsive throbbing, to a higher call than mine,
God hath spoken, you have heard Him, and the tears these eyes bedim;
You affection for your Mother, shall not mar your love for Him,
Could I bid you stay from fondness, when the everlasting hand
Marks your path to duty clearly, for the safety of your land?
No! 'tis yours to be a patriot, and 'tis mine to prove as true,
Go my boy where duty calls you; and my heart shall follow you!

Go in faith, and feel protection in the power—Supreme—Divine,
Should a bullet pierce your body; it will also enter mine,
Do I think of this in sorrow? does my love, sad fears renew?
Do I tremble at the prospect? No my son, no more than you,
Dear to me is every pathway, where your precious feet have trod,
But I give you, fondly, freely, to my country and my God,
You and I shall never falter in the work we have to do,
Go my boy where duty calls you, and my heart shall follow you!

I shall pray for you how often; with the waking hour of morn:
Through the labor of my household, and when night is coming on,
If a mother's prayers can keep you, mid the dangers you incur,
God will surely bring you back again to happiness and her.
I will never doubt the goodness, that has kept you until now,
That has kept the evil from your heart, the shadow from your brow,
And I know that it shall keep you, in the path you must pursue,
Go my boy where duty calls you, and my heart shall follow you.

If my boy were less a hero, less a man in thought, and deed,
I had less to give my country, in her trying hour of need,
And I feel a pride in knowing that to save this cause divine
From the hearth-stone goes no braver heart than that which goes from mine.
I have loved you from the hour that my lips first pressed your brow,
Ever tenderly, but never quite so tenderly as now,
All I have is His who gave it, whatsoe'er He bids me do,
Go my boy where duty calls you, and my heart shall follow you.

I shall miss you in the spring-time, when the orchard is in bloom,
When the smiling face of nature, bathes its beauty in perfume,
When the birds are sweetly singing, by the door and on the wing,
I shall think of you, who always loved to pause and hear them sing,
Long will seem the waning hour, through the drowsy summer day,
With my boy exposed to dangers on a soil so far away,
But my spirit shall not murmur, though a tear bedims my view,
Go my boy where duty calls you, and my heart shall follow you.

You will come and kiss your mother, come and kiss her, as you say,
From her lips receive the blessing, that shall cheer you on your way,
From her fond embrace go forward to resist your country's foe.
With the comforting assurance that your mother bade you go.
Heaven protect and bless and keep you, holy angels guard your way,
Keep your spirit from temptation, and your feet from going astray,
To your mother ever faithful, to your country ever true,
Go my boy where duty calls you, and my heart shall follow you.

Miscellaneous.

GENERAL LEW. WALLACE ON EMPLOYING NEGROES.

In his speech at the great war meeting in Cincinnati, on Tuesday evening, Gen. Lew. Wallace thus expressed his sentiments in regard to the military employment of the negroes, and it will be seen that his argument strikes at the root of the matter:

"Another mistake we have made all along is that of supposing that slavery was an element of weakness to the South. We thought it was a smouldering fire, which only needed the fact that of actual warfare to start it, and would start into a blaze that would leave us an easy task to perform; but we were mistaken, and we have found to our cost that slavery is one of the main elements of strength to the South at the present time. [A voice, 'How?'] How? why if you'll wait a minute, I will show you how. You want to have this war prosecuted with vigor and the rebellion put down. If I ask you to go, it may be you are a mechanic, and you say 'I can't leave my workshop,' you are perhaps a farmer, and you say you cannot leave your farm. You are married and have a wife and family depending on you for support, and you cannot leave them.

"Well, let us change the scene, and fancy that I am down South recruiting for Jeff. Davis. I say just imagine it. [Voice, 'We can't do that, General.] Well, say I go to a fierce-looking individual and say, 'We have establised a new government. It is in danger; it requires your arm to support it, and we want you to help us and fight for us. He thinks, 'Well, I believe I can go; the cotton is all planted, and the farm is in good order: I can leave my niggers to attend to the wants of my family, and when the cotton is required to be gathered in, the niggers will do it all, and keep the cotton gins at work, and on the force of this reasoning he goes at once. Now again, suppose I go to Jeff. Davis and say: 'President, I want to make this agreement with you; If you will keep your four million negroes at home, and not let them do anything for the furtherance of the war, I will keep at home an equal number of the free oparatives of the North, Do you think he would agree to it? No, he never would agree to it?'

"Well, then, I say it would become a military principle, which should be instantly acted upon, that we ought to use every means to weaken our enemies and strengthen our own hand. If slavery is the basis of this rebellion, why, in God's name, do we not knock away the base from under it? [Loud cheers and applause.] You say it is right to take corn from the rebels, to take their horses, and cattle and everything else; that's all right, but just touch a single nigger, and then there's an awful hullaballoe about it. [Laughter and cheers.]

"Now, then, look again at another thing. I have eleven regiments under my command, and from each regiment forty-four men are detailed as teamsters, to drive mules and perform all this kind of work which, if we only seized the niggers they could do as well as our own men. Only think of that. There are four hundred and eighty-four men taken away from my eleven regiments, because we are so scrupulous about taking away negroes from the rebels. Why, it is almost enough to make a whole regiment, and God knows our regiments are weak enough already; in fact, that is why I am here to-night, to get you people of Cincinnati to raise more men, to fill up those already in the field. If we can find men that can do all this drudgery, why, in Heaven's name do we not do it? Am I not right? ['Yes.']

"I have seen hundreds of our boys, after a long and weary day's marching, when they were tired out with the fatigue and their wearing labor, obliged to take the spade and turn to digging to protect themselves from a watchful and vigilant enemy. These boys ought to have been able to have got their suppers and turn in to rest, so as to be ready to meet the enemy any moment and be in a condition to fight, and fight well; and if a lot of negroes accompanied the regiments, after a day's march the boys will be able to take their suppers and rest, while the niggers perform the laborious work which has cost so many lives already. Thus the men would be spared all this unnecessary fatigue and would be ready at any time to meet the foe, refreshed and invigorated by complete rest.

"I do not mean to say that you, people of America, are unequal to the task of putting down this rebellion. I believe we are perfectly capable of fighting the thing through ourselves, and no thanks to the Englishman, Frenchman, or to the Ethiopian. [Immense applause.] In times of great excitement like the present a simple prejudice may do an immense amount of evil. A greased cartridge produced the Sepoy rebellion, but notwithstanding all these prejudices that have been instilled into the minds of some of our boys, when out troops are worn out with fighting against superior forces, when outnumbered and cut to pieces, with every hope gone, and nothing but destruction staring them in the face, then, I say, if white men should hear the sweet music of tne rifle even though in nigger hands, they would like it amazingly, and be wonderfully glad of it."

BATTLES OF FORMER TIMES.

The startling reports of 20,000 Union loss and 40,000 rebel loss at the recent great battle before Richmond, though no doubt greatly exaggerated, have very naturally called up a comparison of figures with some of the celebrated sanguinary struggles of former times. The battle of Waterloo was fought on the 18th of June, 1815. Allied army on the ground 72,000 men, and loss about 50,000 men. Napoleon's army 80,000 men, and loss 40,000 men.

Battle of Jena, fought on the 4th of October, 1806. French army 80,000 men. Prussians lost 30,000 men in killed and wounded, and nearly as many prisoners, making nearly 60,000 men in all, and the French 14,000 in all.

At the battle of Borodino, the Russian army was 132,060, and the French army about the same. This is said to be the most murderous and obstinately fought battle on record, in which the French lost in killed, wounded and prisoners 50,000, and the Russians about the same number—making in all 100,000 men in one battle!

The battle of Austerlitz, fought on the second of, December, 1805. French ermy 80,000 men; Russian and Allies about 100,000. The French lost 12,000, and the Allies lost 30,000 in killed wounded and prisoners.

In the battle of Wagram, Napoleen's army was 175,000 men, and the Austrian army was even larger. The loss on each side was 25,000.

In the battle of Leipsic the French had 175,000 men, and the Allies 181,000. The battle lasted three days. Napoleon lost two Marshals, twenty Generals, and 60,000 men in killed, wounded and prisoners; the Allies 1790 officers, and about 40,000 men.

At the battle of Aspern, fought on the 22d of May, 1809, the French army consisted of 75,000 men, and lost 37,000; the Austrian army was 75,000, and lost 25,000.

At Dresden where the battle lasted two days, the Allies lost 25,000 men in killed, wounded and prisoners, and the French about 12,000.

At the battle of Arcola the Austrian loss in killed and wounded was 18,000, and the French loss 15,000.

At Lutzen the French loss was 18,000—the Allies 15,000.

The most celebrated battle in history, and the most fatal to the Romans, was that of Cannæ. Hannibal commanded on the one side, 50,000 Africans, Gauls and Spainiards; and Paulus Æmilius and Trentius Narro 88,000 Romans, of whom 40,000 were slain. The victor, Hannibal, sent three bushels of rings, taken from the Roman knights on the field, as a trophy to Carthage. So absorbing was the strife that neither party perceived an awful earthquake which cceurred during the battle. The place is now denominated "The Field of Blood." This battle was fought on the 21st of May, B. C. 126.

THE SEAT OF THE AFFECTIONS.

There is no authority in history, metaphysics, or physiology, for placing the heard-quarters of Cupid in the heart. It may, for aught we know to the contrary, be in the lungs or the liver. One of our homœpathists says that love is a creature of the stomach, and depends upon the gastic juices for suppoot. And yet if a lover should say to the object of his affections, "Miss, permit me to lay my stomach and fortune at your feet," she would think it an odd way of popping the question. It is, however, a palpable absurdity to represent the hearts of lovers as in flames, or transpierced with barbed arrows, because it is manifest that a person with a vital organ in a state of combustion or on a skewer, would be at the point of death, and therefore incapable of courting. And yet, if this popular fiction be discarded, what becomes of the valentine trade?

ONE DROP AT A TIME.—Have you ever watched an icicle as it formed? You noticed how it froze one drop at a time until it was a foot long or more. If the water was clear, the icicle remained clear, and sparkled brightly in the sun; but if the water was but slightly muddy, the icicle looked foul, and its beanty was spoiled. Just so our characters are forming. One little thought or feeling at a time adds its influence. If every thought be pure and right, the soul will be lovely and will sparkle with happiness; but if impure and wrong, there will be final deformity and wretchedness.

A WIFE'S INFLUENCE.—A married man falling into misfortune, is more apt to retrieve his situation in the world than a single one, chiefly because his spirts are soothed and retrieved by domestic endearments, and his self-respect kept alive by finding that although all abroad be darkness and humiliation, yet there is a little world of love at home over which he is a monarch.

ANIMALS KILLED BY THE COLD.—Visitors to the Zoological Gardens, young and old, will be sorry to hear that the inclement weather, which has swelled the weekly bills of mortality, has been very fatal to our pets in the Zoological Gardens. The noble Nubian lion, who had been twelve years in the gardens, and was the admiration of all visitors, is dead. In the afternoon he was apparently well, and in the morning he was found by the keeper lying stiff and cold in his den. A post mortem examination disclosed the sad fact that the king of beasts had succumbed to the intense cold, no organic disease having been discovered.—*London Paper.*

I have thought that wild flowers might be the alphabet of angels—whereby they write on hills and fields mysterious truths.—*Francis.*

It is a great blunder in the pursuit of happiness not to know when we have got it; that is, not to be content with a reasonable and passible measure of it.

Sprinklings.

A SECESSION WOMAN ACCEPTING AN AWKWARD CHALLENGE.—A few weeks since there was an exchange of prisoners at Selma, Alabama. While a railroad train loaded with federal prisoners was on its way to that place, it stopped at a station where a lady of fine appearance, dressed in black, came with a basket and distributed pies, cakes and other articles among the soldiers. As she stepped off the platform she addressed Captain Stibbs, who was standing near, in these words: "Now don't think, because of this that I am not a southern woman, for I am; let me tell you, when you have killed all our husbands, fathers and sons, we women and children will fight you.'

The captain, with an air of unconquerable gravity, replied to her:

'You will, will you?—that's your game is it, madam? Well, now let me tell you that we have got a man in this car who can whip any woman in this country *of his weight.*'

The lady, who had hitherto been in good humor, became excited and cried out, 'Bring him out! Bring him out! I can whip him!' Captain Stibbs stepped to the car and called for Major ——, a thickset man, weighing some two hundred and fifty pounds. The major, unconscious of what was going on, came quickly to the platform and was introduced to the lady, with these words, 'Of his weight, recollect—I said his weight.' The lady, seeing the joke, had sense enough to join the crowd in a hearty laugh.

NO FRENCH CREOLES IN THE REBEL ARMY.—A newspaper correspondent at Winchester, Va., writes as follows.

It is a remarkable fact that the Sixth, Seventh, Eighth, and Ninth Regiments of Louisiana Infantry were present at the battle of Winchester, together with Wheat's Louisiana Tigers and two batteries of Louisiana artillery; and yet, among all the prisoners taken or wounded in the hospitals here, not one French Creolo appears, nor a single Frenchman of foreign birth.

Thus we have four and a half regiments and two full batteries in the rebel service in this valley, in which there are probably none, or scarcely a corporal's guard, of that class of the Louisiana population. It is fair to presume, therefore, that none, or scarcely any, of that class of population, comprising one-third at least of the entire white population of Louisana, are favorable to disunion. They are proverbially a brave and gallant race. They fight as quickly and daringly as any race on the globe."

Every man has in his own life follies enough—in the performance of his duties, deficiencies enough--in his fortune, evils enough, without minding other people's business.

The wind is unseen, but it cools the brow of the fevered one, sweetens the summer atmosphere, and ripples the surface of the lake into silver spangles of beauty. So, goodness of heart, though invisible to the material eye, makes its presence felt; and from its effects upon surrounding things we are assured of its its existence.

HOW TO LIVE.—To act with common sense, according to the moment, is the best wisdom I know; and the best philosophy, to do one's duties, take the world as it comes, submit respectfully to one's lot, bless the goodness that has given us so much happiness with it, whatever it is, and despise affectation.

Those are the most valuable that are the most serviceable; and those are the greatest, not that have the most talents, but that use those they possess the most usefully.

A man found guilty of a felony at the Central Criminal Court the other day, entreated the court to "deal leniently with him, and give him a short imprisonment, as he was particularly anxious to see the great exhibition."

A beautiful thought is suggested in the Koran; "Angels, in the grave, will not question thee as to the amount of wealth thou hast left behind thee, but what good deed thou hast done in the world, to entitle thee to a seat among the blessed."

Under instructions from the State Department, passports are granted to persons liable to draft, who desire to go abroad. In executing a bond, with sufficient surety, to perform military duty or furnish substitute.

THE NEW ERA.

RICHARD B. LOCKE----Editor.

KEY WEST, FLA., SEPT. 6th, 1862.

OUR AFFLICTION.

With what aching hearts and swolen eyes, will the last and present editions of the "New Era" be read at home! 'Tis here that the wife will first learn she is a widow, the mother receive the first tidings of the death of an only son, the fond sister that God has called a brother to his long home, the dear and loving child will know that the kind and affectionate father lies in the cold grave in a distant land. No kind friend to break the tidings to them gently, and prepare them somewhat for the blow that will come with crushing weight, so sudden and so unexpected. And those dear ones, who will linger in uncertainty, watching for, yet fearful to glance at the list of deaths. Oh, the fearful and anxious care—the dread uncertainty of next tidings.

And with us that are left, to mourn the loss of our comrades and know not in how many hours we may be mourned for. The insidious disease goes stalking through our midst at noonday, and at night, gives but little warning to its victims; it can be fancied approaching a group who are wailing the loss of a comrade, and selecting its victim, hesitating at others, passing on, but not yet gone—lingering, in certainty of more food—

* * * The furious countenance of Cathegus rises to view, while with a savage joy he is triumphing in our miseries.

A board, perhaps, may tell some wanderer where lie our cherished dead—when they came and when they were called away, but that soon will refuse to bear their record! Time's effacing fingers will be busy on its surface, at length wear it smooth, the record molds and rots, and mingles with the dirt of heroes, and martyrs, who have sacrificed themselves upon the altar of their country:

"Life is a sea as fathomless.
As wide, as terrible, and yet sometimes
As calm and beautiful. The light of heaven
Smiles on it, and 'tis decked with ev'ry hue,
Of glory and of joy. Anon dark clouds
Arise, contending winds of fate go forth,
And hope sits weeding o'er a general wreck,"

DECISIVE ACTION.

The course adopted by Col. Morgan in relation to the employment of persons of African descent, will meet with a hearty response from the whole North. The men of his regiment have been doing work that should have been done by the Negroes of Key West; the consequence is that they are now unfit to perform the necessary duties. African labor has been sought for; in fact the most vigorous measures have been resorted to in order procure it, This has been met with such an adverse feeling by the residents of Key West, that the Colonel has determined to end this matter at once and forever. By his order all negroes who seek employment, will be put to work and their wages paid. These measures on the part of the Colonel will relieve his men from arduous duty in the heat of the sun, and danger of infection.

And we say that those who are not for us are against us. No more trifling with traitors and secession sympathisers. What is deemed necessary for the service of government, will be done. Colonel Morgan has determined to take the responsibility, and be the judge. If the same spirit was only carried out, through the entire army, this rebellion would soon be put down. While some [illegible] r commanders have been fooling with the branches, Col. Morgan has struck a final and sealing blow at the root. A little Jacksonian spirit in times like these is cheering indeed.

VESSEL IN DISTRESS.

The American bark "Nazarine" from Minilitlan, bound to London, put into this port in distress, having been twenty-five days from the former port, short of provisions and all hands sick; in fact but one man left to work the ship. Dr. Hoffman, the Health officer, reports that the officers and crew are afflicted with the Mexican fever. Commodore Lardner sent a boat from the Flag ship and brought the vessel into port.

IMPORTANT.

Col. Morgan on the Enforcement of the President's Order.

Col. Morgan has issued the following important order:

Headquarters, Key West, Camp Morgan, 90th Regt., N. Y. V., Sept 5th 1862.

The Col. Commanding directs the attention of the officers and soldiers of this command to the following Executive order by the President, which has been officially published:

War Department, Washington, July 22.

EXECUTIVE ORDER.

First—Ordered, that military commanders within the states of Virginia, South Carolina, Georgia, Florida, Alabama, Mississippi, Louisiana, Texas and Arkansas, in an orderly manner, seize and use any property, real or personal, which may be necessary or convenient for their several commands for supplies, or for other military purposes, and that, while property may be destroyed for proper military objects, none shall be destroyed in wantonness or malice.

Second—That military and naval commanders shall employ as laborers, within and from said states, so many persons of African descent as can be advantageously used for military or naval purposes, giving them reasonable wages for their labor.

Third—That, as to both property and persons of African descent, accounts shall be kept sufficiently accurate and in detail to show quantities and amounts, and from whom both property and such persons shall have come, of a basis upon which compensation can be made in proper cases; and the several departments of this government shall attend to and perform their appropriate parts towards the execution of these orders.

By order of the President,

EDWIN M. STANTON,
Secretary of War.

A necessity having occurred by the prevailing epidemic, for the employment of persons of African descent, including those held to service or labor under state laws, in the various Departments of this command, the Provost Marshal is authorised to employ such persons seeking employment, and send them to the Headquarters of the Quartermaster. And it shall be the duty of the Quartermaster to cause accurate lists to be made sufficient in detail to show from whom such persons shall have come.

Persons so subject and so employed have always understood that after being received into the Military service of the United States in any capacity, they could never be reclaimed by their former owners, (except they did understand it in this way, the order of the President would be inoperative.) The Colonel commanding therefore, and from precedents already established, feels authorised to declare that all persons so employed as above stated, shall receive permanent military protection against any compulsory return to a condition of servitude.

No influence must be used to entice slaves from their masters, and if fugitives desire to return to their masters they will be permitted to so; but on the other hand, no force or undue persuasion will be permitted to recover such fugitive property.

Officers of the army, from General's to Lieutenants, must not employ such fugitives for servants. The government provides to each officer a distinct pay for his servant, and this is ample for the hire of a free man.

By command of
Col. JOSEPH S. MORGAN.

J. P. Raymond,
1st Lieut. and Adjutant.

The enlistment of men in the North is going on rapidly, and it is already apparent that several states will fill up their quota's under both calls without a resort to draft, and we have every reason to believe that that before the first of November.

INCREASED MAIL FACILITIES FOR KEY WEST.

QUARTERMASTER-GENERAL'S OFFICE.
WASHINGTON CITY, August 26th, 1862.

Col. D. D. TOMPKINS, Asst. Quartermaster General, New York.

COLONEL: In accordance with a suggestion contained in a letter from Col Morgan, commanding at Key West, Florida, of the Adjutant General, all steamers employed by the Quartermasters' Department, sailing from New York for Ports in the Gulf will hereafter be prepared to drop a mail at Sand Key light house, where a boat will board them from the Fort in Key West. You will make the necessary arrangements to carry this order into effect. It will make it necessary for the steamers to lay off Sand Key if they arrive there during the night, but still it is important to keep up communication with Key West and the Tortugas.

Very respectfully your obedient servant,

M. C. MEIGS.
Quartermaster General.

QUARTER-MASTER GENERAL'S OFFICE,
WASHINGTON CITY, Aug. 26. 1862.

Col. JOSEPH S. MORGAN, Commanding at Key West, Florida,—

COLONEL:—Your letter of the 4th inst., to the Adjutant-General, relating to increased Mail facilities at Key West, has been refered to this office.

The action you suggest, providing that steamers in the service of the Quarter-Master's Department, passing Sand Key Light House, should be prepared to drop mails into boats sent from the Fort to receive them, has been taken. As you will see from the order this day given to Col. Tompkins, Assistant-Quartermaster General, U. S. A., New York, on the subject, a copy of which is respectfully transmitted herewith, for your information.

Very Respectfully,
Your Obt. Servent,
M. C. MEIGS.
Quarter-Master-General.

IMPORTANT ARRESTS.

Col. Morgan has arrested two notorious Secessionists, one of them, Captain ———, was formerly master of the Ram "Manassas", and commander of her at the battle of Mississippi. The other gives his name as Capt. Marks, and states that he is a Captain in the rebel army, and has been given a furlough and authority to purchase arms, and was on his way to Havana for that purpose. It is expected they will be sent North as prisoners of war, or turned over to the tender mercies of Major Gen. Hunter.

Mr. W. D. Cash, of Key West. and in the employ of Wall & Pinckney, has been arrested and confined in Fort Taylor, for alleged secession sentiments.

WHOM TO WRITE TO AT WASHINGTON—IMPORTANT TO BUSINESS MEN.—As there are many persons who wish to communicate with the different bureaus of the War Department, a memorandum of the proper persons to address may be useful to our readers:

All letters relating to pay of soldiers on furlough or in hospitals should be addressed to Gen. B. F. Larned, Paymaster General.

Applications for back pay and the $100 bounty of deceased soldiers should be addressed to Hon. E. B. French, Second Auditor.

Applications for pay of teamsters, employees of Quartermaster's Department, or for horses killed in service, should be addressed to Hon. R. I. Atkinson, Third Auditor.

Applications relating to pay and bounty in the marine or naval service should be addressed to Hon. Hobart Berrian, Fourth Auditor.

Letters concerning soldiers in the army should be addressed to Adjutant Gen. Lorentz Thomas.

The undersigned gratefully acknowledges one barrel books, tracts and papers from the Brooklyn Young Men's Christian Association, and a parcel of Books and Tracts, from the Protestant Episcopal Evangelical Society, N Y, for the 90th Regt. We are grateful to know that at this distance from our friends we are not forgotten.

J. G. BASS, Chaplain.

Sept. 1st 1862.

NOT IMPROBABLE.—The Memphis Avalanche makes bitter complaint that the men who now refuse to accredit the Confedrate Government and take its notes, are the individuals who were the first and foremost to rush the country into the rebellion—and who resolved to "spend their last dime," and "spill their last drop of blood," to "vindicate the rights of the South" Of course they were. That class of men are usually the first to come down from their high estate under a like pressure.

GLORIOUS NEWS.

THREE DAYS HARD FIGHTING.

OUR TROOPS VICTORIOUS.

DISPATCH FROM GEN. POPE TO GENERAL HALLECK.

ENEMY ROUTED BY GEN. HOOKER.

DESPERATE BATTLE BETWEEN McDOWELL & JACKSON.

The enemy driven at all points.

JACKSON IN A TIGHT PLACE.

Grand forward movement of the whole army under Gen. Halleck.

We have received a copy of the New York Times of the 30th ult., with important news from the scene of active operations. A dispatch from Gen. Pope to Gen. Halleck, dated the 28th of August, states he is now at Manassas Junc't, having discovered a large force of the enemy was turning our right flank towards that place. He had divided his army and sent part of them to interpose between the force of the enemy. The division of Gen. Hooker marching towards Manassas came upon the enemy near Kettle Run on the afternoon of the 27th, and after a sharp action, routed them completely, killing and wounding 300, capturing camps and baggage, and many stands of arms.

That morning the command pushed rapidly to Manassas Junction, which the rebel Gen. Jackson had evacuated three hours before and retreated to Centerville, took the turnpike towards Warrenton. He was met six miles west of Centerville by McDowell and Sigel late that afternoon, a severe fight took place, which was terminated by darkness. The enemy was driven back at all points, and thus the affair rests. Heintzelman's corps was expected to move on him at daylight next morning from Centerville, and we do not see how the enemy is to escape without heavy loss. We have captured 1,000 prisoners, many arms, and one piece of Artillery.

The army of Jackson is thus cut off and will be destroyed.

A later dispatch states that Gen. Burnside, and Pope, had cut their way through the rebel forces to Manassas, and have formed a junction with McClellan. It is generally believed that an extensive forward movement was to be made by the whole army on the 29th, under Gen. McClellan, involving a great battle, but the result, if it has taken place, is not yet known to us.

EVENTS OF THE WEEK.

Virginia—August 11: The rebels under Stonewall Jackson retreated across the Rapidan river under cover of the night; our troops under General Buford following in pursuit. August 3: After an elaborate correspondence between the rebel General Lee and Gen. Halleck in reference to the treatment of prisoners of war, the latter returned a letter of the former, on the ground that it was disrespectful to the government. August 9: General McClellan issued an order to enforce the Confiscation and Emancipation act in accordance with the President's proclamation. August 13: General Pope ordered a reconnoisance in force of the enemy's position in and around Slaughter Mountain. August 15: The last of General McClellan's Army evacuated Harrison's Landing—the movement having occupied several days.

Washington—August 14: Secretary Stanton issued an order for drafting to begin September 1. August 14: The President received a deputation of colored men, and made a speech, recommending the emigration of the freed blacks to Central America, and offering government help therefor. August 14: Secretary Stanton extended the time for commencing the draft to Wednesday, Sept. 3.

Tennessee—August 11: The rebel guerilla Morgan captured the town of Gallatin. August 12: A part of the rebel force was surprised at Gallatin by Colonel Miller; several rebels killed and captured. Aug. 3: General W. T. Sherman issued an order for the military employment of slaves in Tennessee, in accordance with the President's proclamation. Aug. 9: The rebels retreated to Tazewell by General de Courcey. Aug. 17: The railroad bridges near Nashville were burned by the rebels.

Kentucky—August 15: Governor Magoffin resigned, and John F. Robinson, a Union man, succeeded him.

Louisiana—August 2: General Butler prohibited General Phelps from seizing negroes, and the same day the latter resigned, but Gen. Butler refused to accept the resignation. Aug. 5: The rebel forces under John C. Breckinridge attacked Baton Rouge, but were defeated with heavy loss; the federal commander, Gen. Williams, was killed, and Breckinridge was bodly wounded.

Massachusetts—August 12: Governor Andrews issued an order to permit the enlistment of colored men.

New York—August 12: The War Department issued a special order, extending the time for enlistment in the state to September 1. August 16 and 17: Great war meetings in Brooklyn; the board of Supervisors appropriated $210,000 for the payment of bounties. Aug. 18: Gov. Morgan ordered the enrollment for the draft to begin forthwith.

Local Matters.

THE PREVALING EPIDEMIC.—The mortality among the troops has been very great since our last issue; to-day there seems to be an abatement, as but three new cases have been sent to the Hospital and some ten or twelve discharged convalescent. The sick at the Barracoons have been removed to the Officer's Hospital, and the former place abandoned. Dr. Whitehurst has been engaged, and the latter hospital is under his control. At Fort Taylor, the patients have nearly all been discharged, convalescent, and but one new case reported; the mortality here has not been great, owing probably to immediate action and vigorous remedies. We have heard of no new cases in the city, and we are cheered with the hope that we have seen the worst, and that the fever will soon disappear from the island.

NEW MAIL ARRANGEMENTS.—The Schr. Nonparel, with Col. Morgan and a select party of gentlemen on board, visited Sand Key Light, yesterday, for the purpose of completing the arrangements for the steamers from the North to stop at the Light, where a boat will be in readiness to take the mail from them. It is a notorious fact that in two or three instances we have received later news from the North via. New Orleans than by our own mail, and the steamers passed in sight of Key West. All hail to the new Mail facilities.

NEW POTATOES.----The Schooner Florida, Capt. Mott, from New York, has supplied our stores with an abundance of New Potatoes. They are selling at reasonable prices, so we may conclude that this is feast time, for it is either a feast or a famine in Key West.

UNTANGLE THE TANGLE.

About a year ago one of the illustrated papers had a picture representing Abraham Lincoln untangling a skein of thread that he had inherited from James Buchanan. He had taken out some short pieces, and was stooping down, patiently working at the rest. Abraham Lincoln is still at work at the tangled thread. And never since the Creation has any man shown such patience as he has. In our catechism days, when asked who was the most patient man, we would answer Job, now we should say Abraham.

Abraham like Job has had many friends and counsellors in his troubles. All say that the tangle must be straightened out, and all profess to be willing to help, but they differ greatly as to the means.

A great while ago a man lived whose name was Adam, and he was the only man that did live at that time—since his time a great many have lived, but all of them have been descended from Adam—one of these men was named Ham, and from some cause or other his descendants have got in the way of being born black, instead of white or red, or copper-colored—now these black people, some say, have no rights that a white man is bound to respect—and they have been made the slaves of other men. This slavery has been tolerated so long that it has become a mighty power, and is now just as much mixed up in this tangle as the skein of silk was in the bird's nest.

The sword has been used freely for a year past, and is making sad havoc, friends as well as foes, are falling by thousands, but still there is the tangle, and there it will be till the black man can be got out of it.

Some tell you to "hang the abolitionists. That would end the trouble undoubtedly, but if all who are opposed to slavery are abolitionists, the hanging of them would be a good deal of trouble, and would leave the world very much as it was left after the deluge—with very few inhabitants.

It is said that the pen is mightier than the sword—try it Abraham.

Proclaim Freedom to the black man, as his reward for helping to untangle the tangle—and the tangle will soon be untangled.—*Newark Mercury.*

THE SUN.

NUMBER 9409. NEW YORK, MONDAY, SEPTEMBER 8, 1862. PRICE ONE CENT

THE NEW YORK SUN,

Published daily, Sundays excepted,
ONE CENT PER COPY—SIX CENTS PER WEEK,
Delivered anywhere in the city or vicinity.
CIRCULATION 55.000 Copies.
When sent by mail: *Three Dollars per year*,—three months, for $1; six months $2. The postage within this State *is only seventy-eight cents a year*—out of the State, $1 56 a year. Address all letters to MOSES S. BEACH, Proprietor of THE SUN, Corner Fulton and Nassau sts, N. Y.

THE NEW YORK SUN.

MONDAY MORNING, SEPT. 8, 1862.

LATEST NEWS

BY TELEGRAPH TO THE NEW YORK SUN

MARYLAND INVADED,

5,000 REBELS AT FREDERICK

THEY CROSS IN TWO COLUMNS.

Unionists Fleeing from the City.

Baltimore and Ohio R. R. Cut.

TELEGRAPH LINE BROKEN UP.

PENNSYLVANIA AROUSED.

PREPARATIONS FOR DEFENCE.

VICTORY AT MARTINSBURGH.

CAPTURE OF PRISONERS AND ARMS.

GEN. POPE GOING WEST.

A NEW COMMAND FOR HIM.

GEN. McDOWELL SHELVED.

THE INVASION OF OHIO.

THE UNIONISTS AT WORK.

FIGHTING IN KENTUCKY.

BOILER EXPLOSION IN DELANCEY ST.

Three Men Killed, Six Scalded.

&c. &c. &c.

Maryland and Virginia.

The Rebels in Maryland—They enter at two points—Frederick occupied by 5000 Rebels—A Provost Marshal appointed—Telegraph Wire Cut—Unionists Fleeing from Frederick.

Baltimore, Sept. 7.—Frederick, Maryland, was undoubtedly occupied yesterday morning, between 10 and 11 o'clock, by the rebels. Part of the force turned off at Buckeyetown, as if either going towards the Washington road, or the Baltimore pike. The crossing was effected at three points.

SECOND DISPATCH.

Baltimore, 7th.—Fugitives who left Frederick last night report the city occupied by about 5000 rebels under Gen. Hill, cavalry, infantry and artillery. The rebels issued a proclamation, promising protection to property, and appointed a Provost Guard. Purchases were being made with U. S. Treasury notes, of cattle and horses, which were being sent towards the river.

THIRD DESPATCH.

Washington, 7th. It appears from private accounts that the rebels crossed the Potomac river Friday night, and early yesterday morning, and then marched to White Oak Springs, within three miles of Frederick. They crossed both above and below Point of Rocks, and did it in as speedy and quiet manner as possible. One of their first acts was to send a force to cut the telegraph wire and seize the bridge over the Monocacy. The regiment guarding this point evacuated their position Friday. Great numbers of persons are leaving Frederick to-day, and yesterday, and proceeding towards Pennsylvania. Accounts from Hagarstown say that many Union refugees from Virginia have arrived there.

FOURTH DESPATCH.

Baltimore, 7th. Further reports from Frederick say that Bradley T. Johnson was made Provost Marshal. The rebel troops passed through the town, and encamped in Winan's woods, about one mile beyond the city.

FIFTH DISPATCH.

Washington, 7th.—At noon to-day no further information regarding rebel movements in Maryland had transpired.

It is proper to state the fact that unanimity of counsel and action prevails here.

A PREVIOUS DISPATCH.

Washington, Sept. 6.—Accounts show that three or four hundred rebel cavalry endeavored to cross the Potomac into Maryland about noon on Friday, at Edwards' Ferry, approaching froom Leesburg. Our forces, consisting of one infantry and one cavalry regiment and a battery, opposed the passage, and repulsed them after a sharp contest. About 2 o'clock this morning the attempt was successfully renewed, the enemy crossing at several different points.

The first raid was made on Poolesville, four miles north of Edwards' Ferry, after which they visited Darnstown, where the government had established a branch of the military telegraph. They charged into the town, our pickets having barely time to give the alarm. Fortunately the operator had sufficient time to detach his recording instruments, cut the wire and escaped.

Supposing that there was a Union force in the vicinity, the rebels remained only about half an hour, and then retired, although at 12 o'clock today their pickets were still within hailing distance.

We are informed also that the rebels crossed the Potomac in force yesterday night and morning, both above and below Point of Rocks. They crossed between the ferries, fording the river. The previous demonstrations of camp fires, etc., were a ruse to mislead our forces as to their real designs. They marched directly to White Oak Springs, three miles from Frederick. Their first act was to destroy a tunnel bridge across the Monocacy. A Union regiment, which was stationed there, had left the day previous.

Eleven o'clock, P. M.—The latest accounts from the Upper Potomac state that the rebel army of invasion, commanded by Jackson, entered Frederick about 8 o'clock this morning. Discipline was very strict, guards being posted at all the liquor shops, and private property being rigidly respected. The rebels have possession of the Baltimore and Ohio Railroad at that point, and have torn up the track and destroyed the culverts in several places east of Frederick. They have also cut the telegraph wires. All the rolling stock at Frederick was saved, except one locomotive, which became disabled.

Frederick county is one of the most loyal in the State of Maryland, and Washington county, adjoining, and lying between it and the Pennsylvania line, is almost unanimously loyal.

It is not believed that the rebels, who have thus boldly crossed the river and invaded Maryland, intend to proceed towards either Baltimore or Washington. It remains to be seen whether we have troops enough in that direction to check the progress of these marauders, and, in the more expressive and eloquent language of Henry A Wise, in his Boston speech, "To bag them."

Our own military authorities are confident that this raid into Maryland will cost the enemy just exactly the number of troops who have been bold enough to cross the Potomac.

PREPARATIONS IN PENNSYLVANIA.

Harrisburg Sept. 7.—Arrangements are being made to forward to the entrance of Cumberland Valley all troops now here, and other regiments from New York and the East, detained here for that purpose. If an attempt should be made to invade Pennsylvania, a warm reception will await them. The Governor has messengers extended all along the border.

The rebel pickets are extended seven miles towards Hagerstown. They possessed themselves of all the stores, clothing, &c., in the stores at Frederick, paying for them. The rebels say they are going to Baltimore. The telegraph operator remains at Hagerstown, but says he cannot hold the office much longer. Nearly all the Union men have left.

Gov. Curtin is doing all in his power. His hope for the future is based entirely upon the prompt response of our citizens when called upon. Over 1,000 stand of arms were sent to Adams County today, and 1,500 more to Franklin County.

THE PLANS OF THE REBELS.

The Washington correspondent of the PHILADELPHIA INQUIRER says:

Washington, Sept. 4.—From the East and the West we have war and rumors of war. Ohio is in a state of alarm, and the gentlemen of Cincinnati are enjoying the healthful recreation of digging ditches and entrenchments at Covington. General Lewis Wallace has issued a characteristic proclamation, and is giving every able bodied man a musket or a spade. In Washington we are more fortunate. The foresight of General Scott or Gen. McClellan is seen in the labored rampart lines that environ the city. For the last year many of these earthworks have been neglected. The grass has grown over the embrasures, and in some of the forts near Long Bridge, flowers have been springing up. The works around Arlington have been little more than objects of interest to curious travellers from the Eastern States. They are now in an excellent condition for service, and begin to look picturesque with dotted canvass, and the flags floating over them. If there is anything in human skill, artillery and destructive ordnance, I do not see how Washington can be taken. Wherever you look forts are seen. They command every hill, ford, bridge and ferry. From Bladensburgh to Alexandria, from Alexandria to Chain Bridge, from Chain Bridge to Bladensburg, is one complete and unbroken line of defences. Under their guns our army is now resting—gradually accumulating strength, and preparing for another campaign.

No one, however, anticipates an attack upon Washington from the Potomac. The generally accepted military theory is that the rebel armies will attempt to engage our troops at Fairfax, and, while diverting their attention, make a movement by way of Leesburg or Harper's Ferry, force a crossing at these points, occupy Maryland, and excite the secession feeling there into riot and anarchy, break the line of the railroad from Washington to Baltimore, and thus interrupt all communication with the North, prevent supplies from reaching our army and our people, and naturally cause a surrender by causing a famine. In the meantime, to prevent these supplies from reaching the city, it is supposed that another column of the rebel army will move down to a point lower on the Potomac, erect batteries, and either cross into Maryland or prevent our transports from coming up the river. To avoid these schemes, I may state that we have on the Lower Potomac a large number of gunboats; on the Upper Potomac large bodies of troops. A crossing at Edward's Ferry is a favorite theory of the rebels. At Edward's Ferry the river is narrow and fordable, but a division of men at Poolesville, with a battery on the hills, occupied by General Banks last year after the Ball's Bluff battle, would render such an attempt a dangerous experiment. Poolesville, Point of Rocks and Harper's Ferry are all strongly guarded, while a large body of troops are being massed at Baltimore, as I am told, for the purpose of resisting the capture or the invasion of Maryland, or the assault upon Washington. It is said, also, that there is a proposition to establish a large camp at Chambersburgh, in your state, for the purpose of preventing a raid into Pennsylvania. Jackson would desire nothing better than to go into winter quarters in the fruitful valley of the Susquehanna, and his guerillas would find abundant and exhilerating sport in foraging upon the loyal farmers of York, Franklin and Adams.

A Baltimore correspondent upon the same subject thus writes:

Baltimore Sep. 5, 1862.—The secessionists in Baltimore now say that it is not the intention of their army to strike at either Washington or Baltimore, but to make for Pennsylvania across the western counties of this state, and thence to aim for Philadelphia and New York, where they propose to winter in spite of all resistance, and that then this city and the capital will necessarily fall into their lap like overripe pears shaken from their stems by the blast of war. They fear an assault on Baltimore because they believe it will be destroyed by the Union forts surrounding it, and they want to get it whole and untouched.

Simultaneous with the march on Philadelphia and New York, they say that Cincinnati and Pittsburgh will fall into their possession. Their eyes are now turned with great anxiety to the movements on Cincinnati. They boast of being able to keep Washington beleaguered with a very small force of theirs in front of our fortifications, while the mass of their army will be released for the proposed aggressive movements upon Philadelphia and New York, which they say cannot be saved, unless we withdraw our forces from the capital, in which event the seat of war will be removed into the free states, where they expect to receive the sympathies of the secessionists to help them subjugate their opponents.

The sudden disappearance of the enemy's main army from the front of Washington, they say is a part of the movement, and its reappearance will be where no one expects to see it. Such is the enemy's news this morning, and they do not attempt to conceal their purposes in conversation with Union men.

REPORT OF A RETURNED PHYSICIAN.

Washington, Sept. 7th.—A Dr. Green returned from the rebel lines, where he has been to look after our wounded, confirms the numerous reports relative to the boasting of the rebels, and says they express confidence in being able to get into Maryland, where they expect to receive 50,000 recruits.

From all appearances, the division of Gen. Walker has left the scene of the late engagements for Harper's Ferry. No one seems to know anything of the whereabouts of Jackson, there being a studied silence in regard to all his movements.

Gen. Lee has removed his headquarters to a position near Leesburg. He holds constant communication with the captain of the guard over their prisoners, through couriers detailed for the purpose.

The rebels have 30 of our officers among their prisoners, including Gen. Blenker's adjutant. They will soon be sent to Richmond by order of Gen. Lee, and no more will be paroled. Notice has been given them that a wide distinction will be made in the treatment between the officers of Gen. McClellan's forces and those of Gen. Pope. The prisoners, with few exceptions, now at Gainesville, are from Pope's late army.

According to their estimate of their own numbers in the late series of engagements, they had not less than 120,000 men, with forty batteries of field pieces, most of them being rifled cannon.

Col. Chamberlain, of one of the New York regiments, was shot by a man named Haggerty, a Texan scout, and his body stripped and laid naked on the side of the road. He was shot in the back and died in a few minutes after. The man who shot him soon regretted the act, and kneeling down beside him received his parting message, and also his likeness for his wife.

EVACUATION OF ACQUIA CREEK BY THE FEDERAL FORCES.

Philadelphia, September 6.—The Washington STAR of this evening says:

"We hear that Acquia Creek has been entirely evacuated by our forces, everything being brought away from there that could possibly be of use to the United States.

We take it for granted that the temporary buildings, railroad arrangements, wharf, etc., constructed for our military purposes at that point, have been rendered useless to the enemy."

The STAR also says:—

"We learn that the regiments of the new troops are now in process of being brigaded with the old regiments, by which means they will be effective soldiers much sooner than if otherwise brigaded."

AFFAIRS AT FREDERICKSBURG.

Washington, Sept. 6.—A person just arrived from Fredericksburg states that on Monday, just after the evacuation of the Union forces there, many of the inhabitants of Fredericksburgh, who had purchased boots and shoes from our sutlers, ostensibly for their own use, packed them into wagons and sent them to the rebel soldiers.

It is believed they sent away large quantities of much needed supplies of this description, thus obtained, to the rebel army.

A free colored man, a drayman, was arrested and summarily hung by the rebels in Fredericksburg for carting away articles for contrabands.

A Battle and Victory at Martinsburg—Rebel prisoners horses and arms captured.

Martinsburg, Va., Sept. 7.—To Major-General John E. Wool, Baltimore: I have the honor to report that the enemy, 400 cavalry, who attacked my outposts, have been defeated with the loss of about 50 prisoners, horses and arms, now in our possession. Our loss was two killed and ten wounded—Capt. Grovesnor and Lieut. Jagan, of the 12th Illinois cavalry. The loss of the enemy greatly exceeds ours, but it is not accurately known. The 12th Illinois cavalry, Colonel Vess, behaved in a manner to maintain the honor of the state from which they came. Signed,

JULIUS WHITE, Brigadier General.

[Martinsburg is situate on the Baltimore and Ohio railroad, in Berkely county, Va., 21 miles N. W., of Harper's Ferry.—ED. SUN.]

New Command for Pope.

Washington, 7th.—Major-General Pope has, at his own request, been relieved from the command of the army of Virginia, and has been assigned to the command of the department of the Northwest.

A DISPATCH SENT ON SATURDAY.

Washington, Sept. 6th.—Gen. Pope, at his own request, was yesterday relieved of his command in order to enable him to prefer charges against Gens. Fitz John Porter, Franklin and Griffin.

The Third Army Corps, (McDowell's,) and the Sixth, (Heintzelman's,) are to be consolidated, and Gen. Heintzelman placed in command.

Gen. Pope has nearly completed his official report, a part of which was submitted to the President yesterday.

War Gazette.

WAR DEPARTMENT, Sept. 7.

INSTRUCTIONS TO U. S. MARSHALS, MILITARY COMMANDANTS, PROVOST MARSHALS, POLICE OFFICERS, SHERIFFS, &c.

The quota of Volunteers, and enrollment of militia, having been completed in the several states, the necessity for the stringent enforcement of the order of the War Department in respect to volunteering and drafting no longer exists. Arrests for violation of these orders and for disloyal practices will hereafter be made only upon my express warrant, or by direction of the Military Commander, or Governor of the State in which such arrests may be made; and restrictions upon travel, imposed by those orders, are rescinded.

L. C. TURNER, Judge Advocate.

Items from Washington.

Washington Sept. 6.—Capt. Rosly, ordnance officer of the Army of Virginia, says it is not true that a large portion of the baggage of the Army of Virginia was lost in the recent retreat from Centreville. He left Centreville with the train Monday evening, at 5 o'clock, taking the road to Fairfax Station; the road was in a very bad condition, and to add to the difficulties the rebels felled trees across it at several points to cause delay, but notwithstanding this the train reached Fairfax Station Tuesday morning in safety, and immediately took the road for Alexandria. On the road the rear of his train was attacked, and fifteen teams were driven off. The balance were brought safely through to Alexandria.

Private Moddox, of the 40th New York Volunteers, reached Alexandria today from Centreville, where he was paroled. A rebel officer told him that he (the officer) would sup in Philadelphia Saturday the 6th. Our informant was on the late battle field (Bull Run) and is quite confident that there are at least two hundred of our dead above ground, and the stench is so great that no person can go there to bury them. He says a large number of our wounded men perished upon the field for want of medical attendance.

An officer who witnessed the scene, says that on Saturday, at Bull Run, when Gen. Sigel, on the extreme right, was ordered to fall back, he was approached by Gen. Milroy, who, with tears in his eyes, implored him not to obey the order—saying, "We must win this battle; the people will not stand this." To all of which Gen. Sigel replied, "We must obey orders."

Dr. Farley, of the Brooklyn (N. Y.) Fourteenth, taken prisoner on Friday last, has been paroled. This regiment has had ten combats with the enemy within three weeks. It is now quartered at Upton Hill, to recruit. It is understood that the President has tendered a Brigadier General's commission to Col. Alfred M. Wood, of this regiment. Lieut. Toby, of this same 14th, in the battle of Bull Run, sheathed his sword and used a musket most effectually. He was honored with three wounds—two on Friday and one on Saturday—the one received on the latter day disabling him.

Washington, Sept. 7, A. M.—Assistant Surgeon Green, of the 19th Indiana, returned this morning from Gainesville, where he has been since the battle of last Thursday week, having remained behind at that time for the purpose of attending to our wounded left on the field. Dr. Green furnishes further interesting particulars, namely:—He was informed by the Quartermaster of R. A. Pryor's brigade (the report also being confirmed by other officers with whom he conversed) that during the engagement of Friday General Pryor was captured by our forces and given in charge of a guard—one man—the rank of Pryor not being known, as he was dressed like a private. He, however, escaped by shooting the guard with a Derringer which he had concealed on his person.

Late reliable reports, from private sources, from Centreville, state that Col. Flohnery, with a regiment of cavalry, is in command of that place, and that their pickets extend to within less than 12 miles of Alexandria.

The 139th Pennsylvania regiment reached the battle field on Saturday, and commenced the interment of a number of dead, which have lain undisturbed since the battle, excepting by the thieving hands of the rebels, who searched every pocket, and in many instances stripped the dead of their clothing.

The last of the Centreville wounded have reached this city, accompanied by Drs. Detwold, Page, Clemens, Ankins, Webster, Byrne, and others of the large staff sent to the relief of our wounded by Surgeon General Hammond.

OFFICERS DISMISSED FROM THE SERVICE.

WAR DEPARTMENT, ADJUTANT GENERAL'S OFFICE, WASHINGTON, Sept. 5.

The following names of officers are, by direction of the President, dismissed from the service of the United States for being absent without proper leave from their respective commands, while the armies to which they belonged were fighting the enemy in the field:

Capt. Thornton Smith, Assistant Quartermaster of Volunteers.
Lieut. John Simpson, of the 99th Pennsylvania Volunteers.
Lieut. J. H. Harrison, of the 20th New York Volunteers.
Surgeon Edward B. Dalton, of the 36th New York Volunteers.
Capt. E. Valentine, Aid-de-Camp.
Lieut. J. L. Christie, Aid-de-Camp.
Capt. J. V. Patten, 73d Ohio Volunteers.
Major G. C. Austin, 126th Pennsylvania Volunteers.
Capt. John J. Sperry, 106th Pennsylvania Volunteers.
Lieut. Wm. Warren, 38th N. Y. Volunteers.
Lieut. H. P. Crawford, Aid-de-Camp.
By order of the Secretary of War,

I. THOMAS, Adjutant General.

West and Southwest.

A Reconnoissance from Cincinnati—The Rebels within Four Miles of Falmouth—Doings of the Guerrillas in Western Virginia—Reported Repulse of the Enemy at Stevenson, Ala.

Cincinnati, Sept. 6.—A dispatch from Falmouth, dated one o'clock this morning, says that our scouts report the rebels within four miles of that place with artillery.

A dispatch from Pomeroy, Ohio, says that Spencer, Va., has surrendered to the rebel forces under Jenkins, and that Col. Rathbone's command were taken prisoners by him.

On Wednesday morning Jenkins' forces entered Ravenswood, Va., and on the same evening crossed the Ohio River at Buffington's Island, and came down to Racine, Ohio, where they killed one man and wounded two others, and stole twelve horses. They then recrossed the river at Wolf's Bar, and encamped for the night.

The people were rising to resist further attempts at invasion by the rebels.

A later report says that the rebels are crossing at Racine, and are coming down on both sides of the river.

A dispatch from Point Pleasant to the Military Committee at Gallipolis, says that the contending forces are in sight of each other, that the rebels are but 900 strong, and that a battle is imminent.

A NOTED REBEL GENERAL.

"STONEWALL" JACKSON.

THE news of the invasion of Maryland by the Rebel General Jackson, taken in connection with the almost romantic interest attaching to his dashing career, induces us to present our readers with a portrait and historical sketch of this now famous man, which we republish from HARPER'S WEEKLY:

Thomas J. Jackson was born in Virginia about the year 1825, and is consequently about thirty-eight years of age. He graduated at West Point in 1846, and in the following year accompanied Magruder's battery to Mexico. At Contreras and Churubusco he distinguished himself so highly on the field that he was brevetted Captain for gallantry. At Chapultepec he again won laurels, and was brevetted Major for gallant and meritorious conduct. On his return from Mexico he was for some time in command at Fort Hamilton; but in 1842 he resigned his rank. At the outbreak of the rebellion Major Jackson was one of those Southerners who were greatly embarrassed to discover the true line of their duty. He had married a Northern wife, was an honorable and conscientious man, and long hesitated what course to pursue. It is stated that his father-in-law, a Northern clergyman, visited him, and urged him to remain faithful to his country and his flag. They spent several hours in prayer together, and Jackson confessed that the struggle was sore. But finally the pernicious doctrine of State Rights, which Jackson, like so many other gallant Southerners, had imbibed early in life, won the day: "I must go with Virginia!" he cried, and plunged headlong into the vortex of treason.

As a rebel officer he has been energetic, lucky, and skillful. At Bull Run he won his *cognomen* of "Stonewall" by promising Beauregard that his brigade should stand like a stone wall before the enemy; the promise was kept. He fought Shields near Winchester, in March last, with rather indifferent success. But his pursuit of Banks down the Shenandoah Valley was very successful, and infused some heart into the rebel cause. Again, in June, his attack on McClellan's right wing at Mechanicsville helped his fame among his people. At Cedar Mountain his design showed skill, but the steady courage of Banks troops foiled his purpose. He will shortly come to close quarters with a General who is fully his match—John Pope.

Stonewall Jackson is by all odds the ablest officer in the rebel army. Beauregard, who was a year ago considered their crack leader, evinced sad lack of capacity in the contest in the West. He was completely outgeneralled by Halleck, and had the mortification of seeing his army disperse and leave him without a command after the evacuation of Corinth. He is now said to be living in retirement in Mississippi, overwhelmed by remorse.

Neither Lee nor Johnson have fulfilled their promise.

Gov. Morton has ordered all the male citizens between the ages of 18 and 45, residing in the Border Counties, to organize themselves into military companies to repel the invasion.

Cincinnati, Sept. 6—P. M.—The EVENING TIMES, of this city, has information that Stevenson, Ala., was attacked by the rebels, but that they were repulsed with great loss.

Athens, Alabama, has been burned by our troops. Gen. Bragg had left Chattanooga and was advancing on Nashville.

THE REBELS IN KANAWHA VALLEY.

Gallipolis, Ohio, Sept. 6.—Telegraphic communication in Kanawha Valley is suspended above Point Pleasant.

The guerilla Jenkins is encamped at Buffalo, tonight, with fifteen hundred men, and 200 more are expected to join immediately. His men are stripping the country of horses and supplies.

The object of Jenkins appears to be to cut off communication with our troops.

The militia of Gallia County assembled today, to the number of 2,700, and completed their organization.

Very little fear is felt of a raid in this place.

Jefferson County, Ky., has been placed under martial law.

LATER DISPATCH.

Cincinnati, Sept. 7.—General Order No. 11, issued by Major-Gen. Wright today, says Major-Gen. Wallace is relieved from duty at Cincinnati, and will repair to Covington, where he will organize the troops mustered into service.

At 4 P. M. daily, Sundays excepted, all the military organizations will assemble for drill. Members of such organizations will hold themselves in readiness to rally at the places of rendezvous at a moment's warning, the signal for which will be the tolling of the city bells. The organization of all able-bodied citizens into a working corps will be perfected with the aid of the city authority.

The PRESS last evening announced its temporary suspension.

General Heath is reported at Williamstown with 15,000 men.

Louisville, Sept. 6.—On Sunday last, Col. Shackleford met a force of rebels at Morganfield, surprised them, killing some and taking several prisoners. Wednesday morning Col. Shackleford started for the rebels, (Col. Johnson's camp on Gilliger lake) drove in his pickets, routed him, and took possession of his camp. Johnson rallied on the opposite side of the lake, and opened fire. Shackleford dismounted his men, and with carbines fought the rebels, about 600 strong, for two hours, till his ammunition was expended, leaving killed and wounded many rebels. The federals then retreated orderly, and recrossed the lake. The rebels advanced down the lake, and Shacklefork ordered a charge, leading in person. Col. Shackleford's left foot was torn to pieces by a leaden slug from the enemy's cannon, which killed his horse. His forces then burned the rebel camp and guns, and fell back in good order.

FIGHT AT SALT RIVER BRIDGE.

Louisville, Sept. 7.—The passenger train for Bowling Green, which left at 7 this morning, returned from this side of Shepardsville, 20 miles south of here, bringing reports that the small federal force in stockades, protecting Salt River bridge, were attacked this morning by a large force of rebel cavalry, with artillery, supposed to be mountain howitzers. When our informants left there was heavy musketry and cannonading. Reinforcements have been sent from here, but the bridge will probably be destroyed before their arrival. No telegraphic communication now exists with any point south of Louisville.

BRIDGES BURNED.

Louisville, Sept. 6.—The rebels yesterday burned three bridges over Benson Creek, on the Louisville & Frankfort Railroad, about 60 miles east of here. The afternoon train went no further than Lagrange.

An Important Capture—An English Steamer Seized off Charleston.

Boston, Sept. 6.—The New Bedford MERCURY prints a letter from on board the United States steamer Cambridge, dated off Beaufort, August 22d, which states that the new gun boat Octorora captured a large English steamer of Charleston. She was loaded with saltpeter, ammunition and arms, and valued at $250,000.

NEWS ITEMS, &c.

GEN. JAMESON has been nominated for Governor by the Maine Democratic State Convention.

A REGULAR secession organization is known to exist in Alexandria. Passing regiments have been hissed in that city within a week.

ADMIRAL DUPONT has converted one of the old stone fleet ships into a kind of Navy Yard at Port Royal, S. C. It contains forges, boiler and carpenter shops, &c., and may be only the germ of a future Navy Yard at that port.

JOHN M. WEST, editor of the New Orleans TRUE DELTA, was arrested for treason on the 27th ult., and sent to Fort Pickens. It is said he will be sent to Ohio, where he stands charged with murder.

THE New Orleans DELTA says there are several companies of colored men raising in that city for military service, who receive the same pay, bounty, etc., as white men, and at the close of the war will receive $100 or 160 acres of government land.

OUT of the 700 rebel prisoners brought to Fortress Monroe from the Potomac last Wednesday, over 100 of them have taken the oath of allegiance and are discharged. They were Northern men, forced into the rebel army, and some Spaniards.

A COMPANY of soldiers from Fort Trumbull marched through the streets of New London, Conn., on Thursday last, and attacked a negro dance house, which they set fire to and destroyed with its contents, save the inmates, who escaped. Their purpose was to avenge a supposed murder of a soldier, but they went to the wrong house.

CAPT. HARTSTEIN, commandant of the Grinnell Sir John Franklin expedition, and who joined the rebellion at its opening, has become insane, and is now in an insane hospital in Georgia. The cause is said to be the complete destruction of his plantation in South Carolina by the hands of his own partisans.

CASSIUS M. CLAY addressed a large audience in the Hall of Representives at Frankfort, Kentucky, last Saturday night. He made an explanation of the attitude of foreign powers toward our government, and urged the repeal of all confiscation acts, advocated the emancipation of the slaves, with compensation to loyal slave owners. A proclamation of amnesty should then, he said, be issued, calling on the rebels to lay down their arms and unite against a common European enemy, who hates one section of our country as much as another.

THE following is an extract from a private letter, written by an officer of our army to his wife, residing in Washington City, dated Helena, Ark., Aug. 30, 1862: During the past year we have marched four thousand eight hundred miles, lost four men, been in thirteen skirmishes and two regular battles, and we are now here fortifying, expecting to whip them as we have done every time.

COL. SEGUR, proprietor of the Hygeia Hotel, at Old Point, which hotel had been ordered to be destroyed by the Government, has published a remonstrance setting forth that neither sanitary nor military reasons demand its destruction, but that the effort originated in the selfish objects of private parties. Gen. Halleck has arrested the proceedings and ordered a new hearing. Col. S. would lose everything by its destruction. The property is valued at $76,000.

BY an order from the War Department the camps of the drafted militia in Maine, New Hampshire and Massachusetts will be supplied by the Quartermaster from Boston; Vermont, Connecticut, Rhode Island, New York and a portion of New Jersey, from Philadelphia. Camps near Harrisburg from that city and near Pittsburg, from Pittsburgh. Camps in Ohio, from Cincinnati; Indiana, from Indianapolis; and Illinois and Wisconsin, from Chicago. Camps in Kentucky, from Louisville; and in Michigan, from Detroit. Iowa will be supplied from St Paul, and camps near St. Louis will be supplied by Major Robert Allen, Chief Quartermaster of the Department of the Missippi.

A LETTER dated Corinth, Miss., August 29th, says: Government is engaged in erecting the fourth freight house at this place, all of which are 400 feet long. This is evidently to be the base of military operations for the whole Southwest. Nature and railroads have combined to make Corinth a point of incalculable advantages. No wonder that General Halleck expressed such gratification when he achieved a bloodless victory of almost inconceivable results—when he marched an exultant army quietly into Corinth. I saw General Grant to day. He wears a hale, self-possessed mien beneath a broad brimmed Panama. Three cavalry boys were his only escort, while his fine, dandy, brushed broadcloth has given place to a suit that gives some evidence of camp life.

LOCAL NEWS.

NEW YORK AND THE VICINITY.

THE OBSEQUIES of the late General Kearney took place on Saturday, and was largely attended. On arriving from Washington, the remains were taken to Bellegrove, near Newark, where they lay in state. The house of the deceased was visited by thousands who were desirous of taking a last glance at the countenance of him whom they revered whilst living, and now, that he has died on the battlefield, fighting for the right, they almost worship. At five o'clock the funeral cortege reached the Courtlandt street ferry; all the avenues of which were filled by a numerous concourse. At the depot in Jersey City, there was also a prodigious throng, who uncovered as the hearse moved to the steamer. The military having formed into line, joined the procession—the band playing the Dead March in Saul. When the funeral cortege arrived in front of Trinity Church, the approaches to the edifice were crowded, and the police found it difficult to make a passage for the procession to enter. The great gate and the porch doors were soon opened, and presently the remains were borne to the transept, where they were met by the clergy, when the opening sentences in the burial services were intoned by Rev. Dr. Ogilby, the organ playing a dirge. The lesson from 1st Corinthians was read by Rev. Dr. Weston, and the choir sung the funeral chorus from Mendelsohn's St. Paul. The Rev. Dr. Vinton read the remainder of the service and pronounced the benediction. The body was then removed from the church, Mr. Jerome Hopkins playing a dirge on the organ. The body was then deposited in the vault next to Alexander Hamilton, in the presence of thousands of people.

BOILER EXPLOSION IN DELANCEY STREET.—THREE MEN KILLED AND SIX OTHERS SCALDED.—On Saturday morning about 7½ o'clock, one of the four boilers located in the basement of I. M. Singer & Co's. large building at the foot of Delancey street, exploded with a loud report, instantly killing three of the workmen and seriously scalding six others. The names of the killed are Christian Shields, Robert Wiley and Robert Gilson. The wounded are Patrick Gibson, Thomas Connolly, Owen Riley, Michael Riley, John Lynch and Robert Williams. They were all in the employ of Austin, Kelly & Co., and when the explosion took place were engaged in drawing wire within a few feet of the boiler. The 13th Ward Police were very soon at the premises and conveyed the dead and wounded to the New York Hospital. Coroner Wiley was promptly notified of the occurrence and on Saturday empannelled a jury, but did not commence taking testimony until yesterday morning. The nature of the evidence thus far elicited goes to show that the cause of the explosion was the sudden letting in of cold water, after steam had been raised and when the water in the boiler was very low.

The following is a summary of the evidence:—

Edward J. Halligan, sworn says, I am a private watchman in the employ of I. M. Singer & Co., at their building foot of Delancy st; the night before the explosion I examined the boilers and found that the water did not reach any of the cocks. As there was fire under the boiler which subsequently exploded I deemed it unsafe to be in the building and went in search of an engineer; I found a boiler maker named McGivern and we returned to the boiler room and ascertained that 30 lbs of steam were on and no water; *we tried to raise the safety valve but from that the rope was broken*; after getting a lever we managed to raise it a little; this was about 8 o'clock on Friday evening, after the engineer and fireman had gone; the following morning at 6 o'clock the fireman came and I reported to him what had occurred; he expressed astonishment at their being no water in the boiler and said that he had left two full cocks; he then examined the supply pipe and said that it had probably worked loose and leaked; as soon as there was sufficient steam on the fireman started the pumps and soon remarked that the water was coming on, but slowly, as the pump did not seem to be in very good order; before I left, water appeared at the first and second cocks; the engineer came in at 20 minutes to 7 o'clock, and I informed him of what occurred, and asked him if it was right to leave the boiler in that way; he replied that the water was all right when he left, and that I had been blowing off water as well as steam, but that there was no danger as long as the fires were dampened; when I first examined the boiler, on Friday evening, there was 35 pounds on and no water at any of the cocks; after blowing off the steam there were 1½ pounds remaining; I left about 7 o'clock on Saturday morning and did not hear of the explosion until 10 o'clock.

Michael Reagan sworn, said:—I am a fireman at Singer & Co's. building and have been employed there three months; I worked in New Orleans two winters at the same business; on Friday night I filled up all four boilers to the second cock, and left about ten minutes to 6 o'clock; on Saturday morning I went to work at ten minutes to 6, and met private watchman Halligan, who told me that there was no water in the boilers, and that there must be something wrong, and I tried the boilers and found water in two, and in the other two none; I then got up enough steam to work the pump, (I think about seven pounds,) and filled up the two boilers; I then thought all safe, shut the furnace doors and got ready to work the donkey engine; the engineer came in 10 minutes before 7 o'clock, and I told him that I thought the blow off cock was open at a half turn, and I thought the water must have leaked through it; some weeks ago the boiler was emptied through this cock, and the engineer attended to it; I tried the cocks about fifteen minutes before the explosion and found water in two of them; the first thing the engineer did when he came in was to go to the safety valve with Halligan, and I heard him scolding the latter for interfering with it; at the moment of the explosion I was about fifteen feet from the boiler looking for a shovel; we generally carry about 60 lbs of steam; there was about 43 lbs on when the explosion took place.

Patrick McGivern, the boiler maker referred to, corroborated the statement of the private watchman in regard to the scarcity of water in the boiler and the unsafe condition of the safety valve. The inquest was here adjourned to 10 o'clock this morning.

WAR MEETINGS.—A large and enthusiastic war meeting of merchants and others was held on Saturday, at the Merchants' Hotel, Courtland st., Jonathan Ransom, Esq., in the chair. Resolutions were passed declaring that the necessities of the hour demand the energies and life of every man who values the blessings of liberty. One of these resolutions is;

Resolved, That we form ourselves into an organization to be known as the Courtland Street National Guard, the object of which shall be to drill and discipline ourselves, that we may be ready at any moment to respond promptly to the call of our country for its defence.

Excellent speeches were made by the President, Rev. Mathew Hale Smith, and others. A committee was appointed to carry out the objects of the meeting, and it adjourned to meet at the same place at 5 P. M. on Thursday evening next.

At the Western Hotel, in the same street, another meeting was organized. Ex-Alderman Douglas, of Brooklyn, called the meeting to order. T. W. Coughlan, Esq., presided. Appropriate and eloquent addresses were made. The 7th Regiment band attended to the musical part of the programme.

A war meeting, called under the chairmanship of Mr. E. Falconer, the temperance lecturer, was held in the Park from 10 till 2 o'clock yesterday, and quite largely attended. Mr. Falconer declared himself a true lover of the Union, and earnestly urged on all within hearing to enlist for the war.

ARRIVAL OF REGIMENTS.—The following regiments arrived here and left for Washington on Saturday and Sunday: Saturday, 135th N. Y. V., Anthony Wayne Guard and 128th. Sunday, 39th Massachusetts, 10th Vermont, and 123d and 124th New York.

ARRIVAL OF VIRGINIA REBELS.—The U. S. Transport Arago, from Fortress Monroe, Friday last, arrived at this port yesterday. She brings 96 released rebel prisoners, all of whom were captured at the late battles in Virginia, and have since taken the oath of allegiance, refusing to be exchanged.

THE ANNIVERSARY of the Nativity of the Blessed Virgin Mary occurs today. Services will be held in all the Episcopal Churches, and high mass will be sung at St. Patrick's Cathedral, and in other Catholic Churches.

A WELCOME HOME.—St. Bridget's Parochial School, corner of Avenue B and 8th street, will pay a visit of welcome home to the Most Rev. Archbishop Hughes, tomorrow, (Tuesday) at 10 o'clock, at his residence, corner of 36th street and Madison avenue. The young ladies will be dressed in white—the boys will also be dressed in uniform. They will be 1,400 in number. There is no doubt but it will be well worthy of that school which now stands foremost as an institution of learning in this city. The children embrace this opportunity, the first since vacation, to meet their beloved Archbishop.

SUNDAY ARRESTS.—Eight individuals were arrested yesterday for violations of the Sunday law. Thirty-one males and twenty females were arrested last night for drunkenness, and locked up in the various station houses.

FATAL RAILROAD CASUALTIES.—On Saturday evening as one of the four-horse cars of the Hudson River Railroad was being driven from the Chambers' street depot a poor woman named Ann Wind, attempted to cross the track in advance of the car and being knocked down by the horses the car passed over her killing her almost instantly. The occurrence was purely accidental, and the Coroner's jury rendered a verdict to that effect. Deceased was about 35 years of age, and lived at 156 Greenwich street. John Janson, a German, about 40 years of age, was run over at the corner of 11th Avenue and 42d street, on Saturday afternoon, by a freight train of the Hudson River R. R., and died immediately after admission to Bellevue Hospital. Janson was attempting to leave the cars while in motion. Deceased lived at Guttenburg, N. J., where he kept a boarding house or hotel.

BREAKING UP A DISORDERLY HOUSE—At a late hour on Saturday night, Sergeant Carroll, of the 8th Ward Police, with officers Morgan and Fenton, made a descent upon a reputed disorderly house in Broadway, near Prince street, known as the Argyle Saloon, kept as alleged by George E. Hayden, and arrested him together with Francis L. Hicks, Mary McCoffey, and twelve other female inmates of the place. The prisoners were all arraigned before Justice Kelly, who held Hayden, Hicks, and the woman McCaffey to answer the charge. About half of the other prisoners were fined $3 each and the others discharged. It is said

(*Continued on Fourth Page.*)

On the Fourth Page, will appear to-day, all Important News received at this office, after Two O'Clock, A. M.

A WEEKLY EDITION

of THE NEW YORK SUN, issued every Tuesday, in wrappers for the mail, TWO CENTS EACH, $1 per 100.

SUBSCRIPTIONS—PAID IN ADVANCE.

One copy, 1 year..75cts. | Three copies, 1 year, $2 00
Do. 16 months, $1 00 | Five copies, do $3 00

☞ Specimen copies, gratis. Discount of 20 per cent. from single rate, on each copy over five.

☞ Postage within New York State, *only thirteen cents a year*—out of the State, *twenty-six cents.*

Address M. S. BEACH, SUN OFFICE, NEW YORK.

DEATHS.

BAIRD—On Saturday afternoon, 6th inst, Charles Baird, youngest son of John and Sarah Baird, aged 2 years, 2 months and 24 days.

The relatives and friends of the family are respectfully invited to attend the funeral, this (Monday) afternoon, 8th inst, at 2 o'clock, from the residence of his parents, 197 East 33d st. His remains will be taken to Greenwood Cemetery for interment. 364

CRUMMEY—In Brooklyn, on the 6th inst, from a lingering disease, Thomas Crummey, a native of Crotchell, County Cavan, Ireland, aged 94 years.

The friends of the family are respectfully invited to attend the funeral, on Tuesday, 9th inst, from his late residence, 127 Hudson ave, without further notice. Jersey City and Philadelphia papers please copy. 365

O'DONAHUE—On Sunday, 7th inst, of cholera infantum, John James, infant son of Peter J. and Annie O'Donahue, aged 4 months and 23 days.

The friends of the family are respectfully invited to attend the funeral, this (Monday) afternoon, 8th inst, at 2 o'clock, from the residence of his parents, 24 Carroll st, Brooklyn. His remains will be taken to Flatbush for interment. 359

Daily Mississippian.

☞ NOTICE to Planters and Others!!

McALLISTER & HUGHES, at the Jackson Axe Manufactory, or McAllister's Store, wish to purchase for the benefit of the Government, all the old worn-out Axes, for which they will pay in cash from 50 cents to $1 each. Those having old axes will confer a favor upon the Government, themselves and us, by bringing them in immediately to the above, or H. Penn, Hazlehurst, or G. Penn, Brookhaven. We will also upset and grind axes on the shares for the accommodation of the Planter.

Jackson, Miss., Sept. 3d, d1w.

Revised Terms.

Owing to the enormous price of paper and the heavy expense of getting it here, we have been compelled to advance the price of the Mississippian. The Daily will be furnished at the following rates: For one year, $12; Six months, $7 50; One month, $1 50.

The Weekly, (a mammoth paper,) one year $5.

☞ If Gen. Edwin Price, or any person from Chariton County, Mo., or L. H. Bell (Printer) from Memphis, Tenn., call at the Mississippian office, they will confer a great favor on their friends.

DR. J. M. TROTTER.—This distinguished gentleman of the C. S. Army, who won honors in the Mexican War, passed through our city to-day, on his way to Arkansas, where his surgical and medical skill will continue to be rendered, may they be appreciated wherever rendered. He reports himself from Tennessee.

☞ The Hon. R. S. HUDSON, as will be seen from his announcement in another column, is a candidate for re-election to the office of Judge of the 5th Judicial District.

Perfidious Albion.

Cassius M. Clay, since his return from Russia, has been delivering himself of a speech, which clearly shows that the gentleman has grown wiser if not better by his visit to Europe. He has discovered, says the Memphis Appeal, that there is not that real, genuine anti-slavery sentiment in England that the abolitionists of this country have been taught to believe.

He and those of his ilk, have been brought to understand at last that there is and has been no genuine philanthropy in the anti-slavery professions of the British people, and that they have been made tools of in this country to bring about a disruption of the Union and a destruction of the Government. He now accuses them of "hellish and damnable hypocrisy," and says there is no anti-slavery sentiment in the British dominions that will keep England from placing her lion's paw upon this country, whenever she deems us weak enough to do it with safety. But this conviction comes to Mr. Clay at too late a day for the effectuation of any good. The hellish purpose, long cherished by the Exeter Hall abolitionists, is now accomplished. The country is dismembered, and they no longer care for the negro, only as he may be made the means and pretext for keeping up the division and hostile relationship existing between the two sections. England has gained her point after a long struggle, and her dupes at the North are left to gnash their teeth in their rage and mourn over the sad results of their duplicity and folly.

The following is an extract of Mr. Clay's speech alluded to, which we find in the Memphis Bulletin:

I recently visited the House of Lords and there I saw the man above all others, who had been known as the leader of the anti-slavery movement of England—the great Hercules of Exeter Hall—Lord Brougham. As I entered he was speaking upon this very subject of slavery. Just here let us pause and review the position of this British gentleman up to this time. Again and again had he sat at public meetings. Again and again had he encouraged discussion. Again and again had he willingly been considered the leader of the anti-slavery party in England. What does he now say? Why, he was justifying himself for having refused to sit as chairman of an anti-slavery meeting. * * * Here we find this very man, who, for thirty years had stirred up England and denounced the Americans because they did not abolish slavery. Now, when the people have placed in power a party, inaugurated a principle which would have the effect of gradually bringing about the glorious result which they apparently so much desired, and in consequence of which the slaveholders, in their rage and passion have flown to arms to destroy the Government—I say, surprising as it may be, under these circumstances, we find the English statesmen declaring, in that blind belief, that the Republic is forever separated, and that one section is about to destroy the other. Now, gentlemen, I can find no other language to express my denunciation of this action of the British people, than as the most hellish and damnable hypocrisy. I merely give you this, gentlemen, as a single instance. I now assure you that you found your hopes of British friendship, amity and non-interference upon a false basis, if you suppose there is anti-slavery sentiment in the British dominions that is going to keep England from laying violent hands upon this Great Republic, when she dares to do it.

The Essex.

The gunboat Essex, with the tug Anglo-American lashed alongside, came steaming up the river yesterday morning to within about five miles and a half of the city, when she stopped and sent a shot whizzing up the river. The shot fell in the river about two miles below town. The Essex was replied to by our lower batteries, which fired two shots. She then wheeled round and started down the river again, being satisfied no doubt of her inability to run the gauntlet here. Whether she stopped below Warrenton, or went on down the river, is not known. She will experience about as much difficulty in getting to New Orleans as passing Vicksburg. Many persons left the city Thursday night and yesterday morning, fearing that we would be again "favored" with a few shells in the city. After the Essex left, however, all returned again. What a pity some plan cannot be devised to prevent the Yankee pirates from getting fuel along the river.—*Vicksburg Whig.*

BULL RUN NO. TWO!

REPETITION OF THE BIG SCARE!

PANIC AMONG THE UNION CORPS!

Flight of the Reserve Under Sigel Without Firing a Gun!

[Special Dispatch to the Appeal.]

SENATOBIA, Sept. 6.—Under the above head the Memphis Union Appeal of the 4th has the following:

The New York papers of the first, according to the evening western telegrams of the associated press, have news of the second disgraceful panic of the Federal forces over the ominous field of Manassas, McDowell again playing principal actor in the flight.

The New York Tribune of Monday contained in the form of an extra, a letter from Washington, dated Sunday, transmitted by telegraph, which states that distant firing was heard Saturday afternoon, and late in the evening.

BATTLE OF THURSDAY.

A courier arrived from the battle field Saturday afternoon, states that the battle commenced Thursday afternoon. Sigel's corps engaged the rebel cavalry brigade, on the road from Warrenton, and drove them back—the battle lasting until 9 P. M.—This fight was with Jackson's rear guard, whose force was estimated at thirty thousand.

BATTLE OF FRIDAY.

How Jackson did not fly to the Mountains as stated by Pope.

Sherman's battery opened the battle on Friday morning. Milroy's brigade led the advance, and Sigel formed a line of battle with Schurz on the right, Schenck on the left, and Steinwehr in the center.

The rebels were gradually forced back, until 1 o'clock, P. M., when they suddenly and fiercely charged bayonets, forcing Milroy back. General Schenck sent a brigade forward, but both were driven back. Milroy's command was so badly cut up that he could not gather a regiment. Schurz and Steinwehr were holding their own in the woods on the left of Schenck, when heavy masses of rebels appeared and Stevens' and Reynold's division were sent up and all were driven back. The rebels rapidly advanced their batteries, pouring in a storm of shot and shell. The right wing was compleiy beaten.

McDowell advanced to their support, endeavoring to hold the center, but his movements were anticipated, and both he and Sigel were enveloped by the rebels on the left, and outnumbered at all points. Then Sigel shone out, bringing out his brigade successfully to their position, holding them in front while the fugitives passed by.

Large bodies of McDowell's troops retreated in great disorder across Bull Run.

CONTINUATION OF FRIDAY'S FIGHT.

Federals Falling Back to Centerville--Confusion of Artillery Wagons and Cavalry in the Retreat.

At 5 o'clock, P. M., the battle was going against us. The last reserves were ordered up who retrieved the day; but along the Centerville road, artillery, infantry, wagons and cavalry were confusedly falling to the rear.

Our right, however, remained comparatively firm, preventing the enemy from following up his advantage, and at 8 o'clock Bull Run stream was crossed—the rebels troubling us only by a few shell. We were falling back to Centerville. Franklin's corps was between the stone bridge and Centerville, and Sumner's corps between Centerville and Fairfax Court House, pressing on with great speed to the assistance of General Pope.

The result of Friday's fighting was that we drove the rebels about two miles; they then, being heavily reinforced, recovered a mile, and our troops rested at night a mile in advance on their position in the morning.

THE BATTLE OF SATURDAY.

The Big Panic Duplicated--Flight of the Reserves!

On Saturday, the battle was more general.--Heintzelman, Porter, McDowell and Banks were engaged--Sigel's force being kept as a reserve.

Heintzelman commenced the attack at ten o'clock, with Porter in advance. The advance of the latter was checked by immense masses of rebel infantry. Our forces stood up with unparalleled heroism, fully an hour, exposed to an enfilading fire of grape and canister. The ground was strewn with falling ranks of dying and dead, and finally they broke, falling back in great disorder, which carried a panic in the reserves--large numbers having joined in the retreat.

A calm conclusion drawn from the force going back was that the day probably was adverse to us, but the battle was to be renewed on Sunday morning, with heavy reinforcements.

It is believed the whole rebel army, under Lee, has joined Jackson, by the way of Thoroughfare gap, or by Alldie gap.

The above account is gleaned by the Tribune's correspondence from Capt. Fish.

ADDITIONAL PARTICULARS.

The same correspondent says McClellan's, Burnside's and Pope's armies are now in full co-operation, and complete success is looked for. Every confidence is felt at the War Department, Halleck's headquarters, and the White House.

FLANKING MCDOWELL.

PHILADELPHIA, September 1.—A correspondent of Forney's Press, dated near Centerville, says: Last evening about 5 o'clock, McDowell's left flank was turned by a cavalry force five thousand strong; McDowell's corps being on the left of our army, and the rebel cavalry being supported by infantry.

NEW YORK EXCITED.

NEW YORK, August 31.—The meager intelligence received from Washington, with known activity in government circles, and the departure of surgeons, causes great excitement. Various rumors are circulating, both of good and bad tenor.

The Union Appeal notices the result of the battles as follows:

"The news gets no better very fast." After three days fighting, beginning on Thursday and ending Saturday, the old battle ground of Manassas was again rendered the sight of a disgraceful Federal panic, reaching, according to northern papers even the reserves, who had neither fired nor received a shot.

Pope has been beaten again, and this time has been beaten back to Centerville, with four divisions of the Army of the Potomac. Banks is said to be wholly cut off, and it is hoped in the higher military circles in Washington, that he has blown or will blow up his baggage trains ere he surrenders.

Jackson did not fly to the mountains, as stated in Pope's official dispatch of the 29th. Every word in which is disproved by the news which we now publish. A careful examination of all the news, renders it clear that General Pope's dispatch of the 29th was wholly a fabrication, either of his own or somebody else.

KENTUCKY AND TENNESSEE.

The Union Appeal has the following from Kentucky and Tennessee.

Buckner is at Tompkinsville.

The reported defeat of Bragg at Altamont, turns out to be a canard.

Twenty thousand rebels, after defeating a Federal force at Richmond, Ky., are on their march to Lexington. Kentucky is in a terrible state of excitement.

EFFECT OF THE NEWS.

The same journal speculates as follows:

"The news is, therefore, very bad for the Union cause. The possibility of the fall of Washington becomes daily more and more evident, and the fall of Richmond becomes one of the vanities of human wishes."

The state of matters in Kentucky is no less alarming. Governor Robinson calls on every loyal citizen to rally to the defense of the State. The Ohio and the Potomac are fast becoming the lines of demarcation.

Capture of the Steamer Fair Play.

FEDERAL ACCOUNT.

Correspondence Cincinnati Commercial.]

OFF GUN BOAT, MISS., Aug. 23. }

The flag ship Benton and this vessel with three rams under Col. Ellet, and two transports with troops, under Col. Woode, are just returning from a trip in sight of Vicksburg, and up the Yazoo river to within twelve miles of Liverpool. On our way down we caught the enemy at Milliken's Bend, napping, and captured the Confederate steamer "Fair Play of Vicksburg," with over 5000 stand of arms, a large quantity of powder and ammunition; the troops landed and destroyed a camp near the town, capturing 35 prisoners, a large number of arms, and two field pieces.

The cavalry then went to Richmond, La., destroyed six cars, and burned the depot filled with sugar and provisions. The 31st Regiment, Louisiana, was camped and doubtless awaiting the arms from below. Their hasty retreat, and loss of 35 of their men, must have thwarted all their plans.

Gov. Moore was with them, but made his escape, leaving a pair of fine horses, however, which were provided with quarters on the "Fair Play."

The fleet then proceeded to the mouth of the Yazoo, where they were met with a flag of truce. I did not learn its purport, but have no doubt it was intended to gain time, as our sudden appearance had found them weakly garrisoned. One of the men on the steamer conveying the flag of truce, told one of our men that there were not over a hundred men left at Vicksburg, and it could be easily taken; and from the fact of the steamer being captured and the troops surprised, though we were in sight of them over an hour, shows they were entirely unprepared for our presence up the river and not expecting us at Vicksburg before Fall. We started up the Yazoo the day after our arrival at the mouth, and forced, twenty five miles up, six pieces of cannon, which had just been landed, and intended for a battery. One was a 42-pound rifle, one 42-pound smooth bore, and two 32-pounders. The other two, brass howitzers, were taken on board one of the rams, and the heavy guns loaded and bursted. At this point we captured seven thousand pounds of powder and a large quantity of shot and shell.

The river not being navigable as far as Liverpool, the enemy had just removed the battery at that place, we afterwards learned, to the point where we captured it. We went over sixty miles up the Yazoo—above the Sun Flower—but could move no further up on account of low water. One of Colonel Ellet's rams proceeded up the Sun Flower some miles, but did not succeed in finding anything.

Everything being accomplished that could be, we rounded to and proceeded up, fully satisfied with our little expedition, planned and carried out by Fleet Captain Phelps and Lieutenant Commanding W. Gwin, and more than realizing their highest hopes.

These two commanders were together up the Tennessee after the fall of Fort Henry, and, by their energy and promptness, succeeded in clearing that river of every rebel steamer; and now, while the flag officer was away on important business for the Government, their restless spirits would not permit them to lie still and wait, but prompted this enterprise which has resulted so favorably.—The prize is valued at over $80,000. Twelve hundred of the arms were of the best Enfield rifles.

We tried to get 5,000 troops from General Curtis to accompany our expedition, but he did not consider the condition of affairs warranted him in ... they have gone, Vicksburg would have been ours to-day. We learned there was a battery at this point. Our troops have landed, and, as I now write are shelling the woods.

I send you enclosed the corrected list of the officers of the Mound City, the most of whom were attached to the old Tyler till after the Yazoo fight.

Yours, hastily, HERROD.

For the Mississippian.

Our Gallant Dead.

"CAMP MERCER," NEAR JACKSON, MISS.

The defense of our Confederation of States has cost us the valuable lives of many noble and brave men. It is indeed a sad reflection that they should be represented by slaughtered Yankee vandals, but their loss will nerve their countrymen to avenge them, and the saddening memory of their murder in defense of their mother land will, through coming generations inspire a detestation of our treacherous enemy, which must exclude them, wholly and totally from our beautiful country, and sever forever all relations with them. The dead are of all ranks. They have perished by battle—upon blood-stained fields, and by disease in the tented camp—but all are enshrined in memory as the victims of an infamous and unholy war. Those who have died in the defense of our "National Capital" are from all the commonwealths of the South. The wounded have experienced the care and tender attentions of our noble women. The people of the South are now united by stronger bonds than could ever be woven by platforms and constitutions. They have poured out their life's sweetest blood upon the same gory fields. They have been nursed by the same hands. Undying friendship will be forever cherished among them. The alliance of true men and brave women will cement it. And scarcely less than this, the mingled ashes of Southern heroes will repose beneath a common monumental column, and spring roses will bloom around them on the hallowed soil of their common glories. Disturb not their slumbers. Let the dead sleep. They have fought their last battle. Let us fight for the glorious cause thus bequeathed us. It is rendered more sacred and holy by their blood. For the living there can be no halt short of victory. The way to freedom and independence may be marked with fire and blood, but the path of slavery would be one hundred fold more hideous and hopeless. Thank Heaven it is unnecessary to contemplate what we shall never be doomed to undergo. T.

PHILADELPHIA, MISS., Sept. 3d, 1862.

EDITOR MISSISSIPPIAN.—As it seems that confused statements have got into the papers in regard to the late skirmish at Rienzi, between Colonel Faulkner's partisan rangers and the Federal forces, I send the following statement of facts which embodies all that occurred:

On Sunday, the 24th of August, Colonel Faulkner, with three hundred men, marched in the direction of Kossuth, Tishmoingo county, and bivouacked within seven miles of Corinth. Next morning, he captured seven prisoners within four miles of Corinth. At 3 o'clock that evening, Col. F. of the Second Arkansas Cavalry, and took the road leading from Kossuth to Rienzi. There was one company of Yankees stationed at Mr. Robinson's, one mile and a half from Rienzi. Captain Faulkner determined to capture the party and then retreat. The whole command marched to a point within three miles of Rienzi where the whole command was halting except three companies. Col. Faulkner then ordered Capt. Harris and Capt. Love to get in between the Federal pickets and the town and charge them in the rear while one company charged them in front. As Capt. Harris and Capt. Love were endeavoring to get in rear of the pickets, they were fired upon by the pickets of a Federal regiment stationed in the woods near by. This gave the alarm. Capt. Love and Capt. Harris dashed forward and routed the pickets, captured six and a large number of horses; while Col. Faulkner and Capt. Echols charged in front. The Federals fled in every direction, and so eager were our men to overtake them that they pursued them into the streets of Rienzi and completely stampeded the whole Yankee camp. Three Federal officers and about thirty men were killed in their camps. It was Col. Faulkners design to capture the pickets and then get away as soon as possible, but owing to the excitement of the occasion he was unable to restrain the enthusiasm of the men. Those who charged into the town were pursued in return by the whole Yankee army, about ten thousand strong. Col. Faulkner formed his men at the Robinson House, and filed towards Ripley, where he found himself completely surrounded by three regiments of Federal cavalry, but he turned to the right and cut his way through, bringing his whole command safe to camp, except the loss of one man captured. The prisoners and horses were all brought safely through and were sent to Tupelo, Gen. Price's headquarters. Capt. Echols came off with the loss of two men missing.

HONDURAS.

OBITUARY.

DIED—In Osyka, Miss., Aug. 3rd, ANNA JULIA, aged eight years and one month, daughter of Harriet Aurelia and Rev. E. R. Strickland.

"Death lies on her like an untimely frost
Upon the sweetest flower of all the field."

THE SUN.

NUMBER 9418. NEW YORK, THURSDAY, SEPTEMBER 18, 1862. PRICE ONE CENT

IT SHINES FOR ALL

THE NEW YORK SUN,
Published daily, Sundays excepted,
ONE CENT PER COPY—SIX CENTS PER WEEK,
Delivered anywhere in the city or vicinity.
CIRCULATION 55.000 Copies.
When sent by mail: *Three Dollars per year,*—three months, for $1; six months $2. The postage within this State *is only seventy-eight cents a year*—out of the State, $1 56 a year. Address all letters to MOSES S. BEACH, Proprietor of THE SUN, Corner Fulton and Nassau sts, N. Y.

THE NEW YORK SUN.

THURSDAY MORNING, SEPT. 18, 1862.

LATEST NEWS

BY TELEGRAPH TO THE NEW YORK SUN

FAVORABLE REPORTS.

A TERRIBLE BATTLE.

REBELS PUSHING FOR WILLIAMSPORT.

A Plan to Stop Them There.

GEN. LONGSTREET KILLED.

GENERAL HILL A PRISONER.

GEN. McCLELLAN SUCCESSFUL.

Details of the Maryland Battles.

Harper's Ferry Recaptured.

Investment of Charleston, S. C.

FORT SUMTER BATTERED.

SERIOUS DAMAGE RESULTS.

ALLEGHENY ARSENAL EXPLODED.

75 Lives Lost.

OUR GREAT WAR MAP.

Every Battle Field Shown.

&c. &c. &c.

Maryland and Virginia.

The Battle raging at Sharpsburg with great fury—A Force Detached from the Union Army to destroy the Williamsport Bridge—The Pennsylvania State Troops pushing to the Border—The Rebels reported Surrounded—Longstreet reported Killed.

Philadelphia, September 17.—The BULLETIN has the following special dispatch:

Harrisburgh, Sept. 17.—At Hagerstown, this morning, heavy firing was constantly heard in the direction of Sharpsburg, but no definite information from that quarter had been received.

It is supposed that the rebels are making a most desperate push to reach Williamsport, and get across the Potomac.

An Union scout, who left the battlefield this morning at eleven o'clock, had reached Hagerstown.

He reports that the fighting has been perfectly terrific.

The rebels heve been desperately hard pressed by our army.

A force has been detached from the Union army to destroy the Williamsport bridge, or to block the Ferry over the Potomac at that point.

The rebels are supposed to be retreating.

Philadelphia Sept. 17.—A dispatch from Harrisburg to Governor Curtin states that the battle at Sharpsburg recommenced early this morning and raged with the greatest fury until 9.45 A. M.

Our latest advices from Harrisburg say that the State troops are pushing forward to the border.

Harrisburg, Sept. 17.—The battle fought yesterday, between Sharpsburg and Middletown, closed without a definite result.

No firing has been heard from Hagerstown since 5 o'clock yesterday (Tuesday).

Stragglers coming into Hagerstown report that Gen. Longstreet had been killed, and that the rebels had been surrounded.

The stragglers also say that the ammunition and provisions of the rebels have run compietely out.

LATEST.

DEATH OF GEN. LONGSTREET—GEN. HILL A PRISONER.

Harrisburg, Sept. 17.—This has been an eventful day in Maryland, and at the latest advices everything was favorable.

The rebel General Longstreet was killed, and the rebel General Hill is a prisoner.

Philadelphia, Sept. 17.—There is an apparently well founded rumor that a great battle took place today at Centreville, on Rittocan Creek, which resulted in our success.

A GLORIOUS VICTORY.

Harrisburg, Sept. 17.—A great battle has been fought, and we are victorious. The carnage on both sides was awful. Gen. Longstreet was wounded and taken prisoner.

Harrisburg, Sept. 17, 10 *A. M.*—Dispatches just received at headquarters from Hagerstown, says:

"We have achieved a glorious victory. Longstreet is not killed, but is wounded and a prisoner. Gen. Hooker was wounded in the foot. No particulars are received.

Washington, Sept. 17.—It is credited here that a battle commenced yesterday afternoon, in the vicinity of Sharpsburg, continuing until 9 P. M. Our army rested for the night where the last of yesterday's fight left them and expected to renew the engagement at daylight this morning.

The above facts are gathered from non-official sources.

Harrisburg, Pa., Sept. 17.—In the battle today our right wing rested on Sharpsburg and our left this side of Antyturn Creek, near Porterstown. The Rebels are falling back on Harper's Ferry, much worried and dispirited.

The wounded are arriving at Hagerstown.

The bridge reported destroyed by the Federal forces, was the Canal bridge at or near Williamsport. The destruction of this bridge is of great importance as it impedes the Rebels from bringing up supplies.

Demand was today made from the headquarters of the Army of the Potomac for surgeons and medical supplies, and Surgeon General Hammond has accordingly sent from Washington, and has caused to be sent from the Eastern cities first class surgeons to the number of 100. He has also dispatched thither a large train of medical supplies. Immense hospital accommodations are being provided in and around Washington.

The Harper's Ferry Affair—Federal Loss thought to be less than 100.

Washington, Sept. 17.—Col. Miles' loss before his surrender is believed to be less than 100. A. P. Hill was left in command there to gather up the spoils. At 5 o'clock yesterday Jackson marched a large part of his force out of Harper's Ferry on the Winchester road.

The following guns were surrendered:

12 3-inch rifles.	4 12-pound howitzers.
6 James' rifles.	2 10-inch Dahlgrens.
6 24-pound howitzers.	1 50-pound Parrott.
4 20-pound Parrott guns.	6 6-pound guns.
6 12-pounders.	

LATER.

RE-CAPTURE OF HARPER'S FERRY.

Baltimore, Sept. 17.—Harper's Ferry fell into our possession again on Tuesday evening at 7 o'clock, and was occupied by a portion of General Burnside's force, before the rear of General Hill's division had all crossed the river, who to the extent of 1,500 by one statement and 4,000 by another, were taken prisoners.

The rebels did not undertake to hold the place, but merely made a hasty passage through, not even taking time to secure their plunder, much of which for want of transportation they destroyed. The rumor of the retaking of the Ferry this evening says, that nearly all the guns and arms were recaptured. They did not succeed in destroying the railroad bridge.

THE SEAT OF WAR IN MARYLAND AND PENNSYLVANIA.

Map showing the positions of the late Battles in Maryland at Bolivar Heighths, Harper's Ferry and Sharpsburg; also the River Potomac, Washington, Baltimore, Frederick, Hagerstown, Williamsport, New Market, Rockville, Greencastle, Chambersburg, Harrisburg, &c., &c.

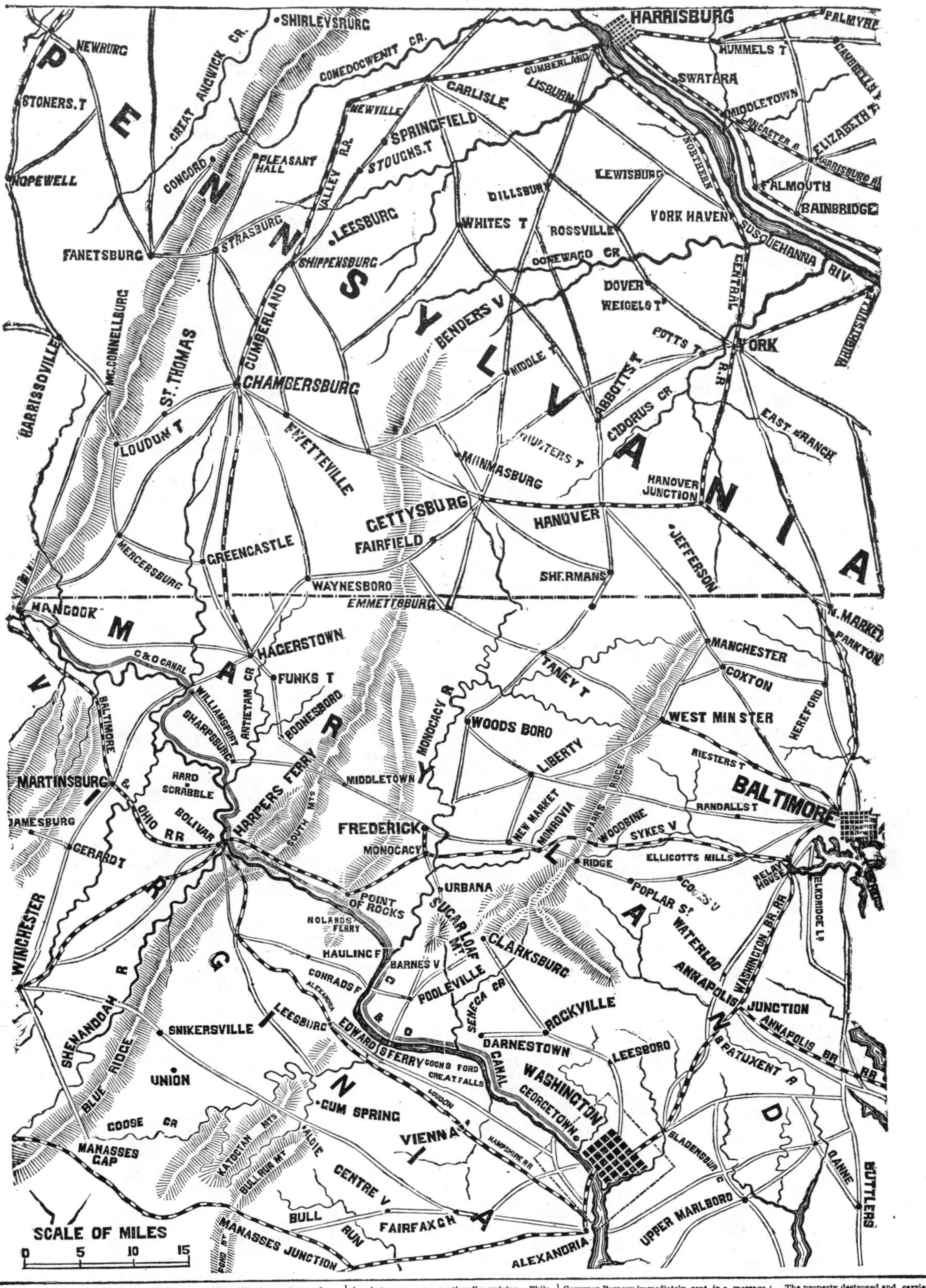

South Carolina.

The Investment of Charleston Confirmed—Fort Sumter Seriously Damaged!

Boston, September 17.—The reported investment of Charleston by the gunboats has some confirmation by a letter received in this city, from on board the U. S. steamer "Bibb," which says:—"Fort Sumter has already received a preliminary dose of shot and shell, which resulted in serious damage."

Explosion of the Allegheny Arsenal.

Harrisburg, Sept. 17.—The Allegheny Arsenal was blown up at noon today, and was on fire at 3 o'clock this afternoon. We have no particulars of how it occurred.

LATER.

75 OR 80 LIVES LOST.

Pittsburg, Sept. 17.—A frightful explosion occurred at the United States Arsenal this afternoon at two o'clock. It occurred in the large frame building known as the Laboratory. One hundred and sevenly-six boys and girls were employed in the building at the time of the disaster, of whom 75 or 80 were killed.

One explosion followed another, until the entire building was destroyed, and those who could not escape in time were burned up. Up to the present time 63 bodies have been taken from the ruins.

The Response to Governor Curtin's Call.

Harrisburg, Pa., Sept. 17.—The Governor states that seventy-two thousand men have responded to his call for the defence of the state, and that he expects that the number will be increased to one hundred thousand. These men are being furnished with equipments and moved to the state border as rapidly as possible.

Letter from Harrisbergh—Fifty Thousand Sharpshooters—Enthusiasm of the New Troops—The Scenes at Camp Capitol,

Harrisburg, Sept. 15, 1862.—The driving in of our pickets towards Greencastle, seeming to indicate a general advance by the rebels, on Saturday evening, only had the effect of hurrying on here thousands upon thousands of the freemen militia from every part of the Commonwealth during Saturday night and the whole of yesterday.

During yesterday (Sunday) the State Capitol Park, containing about thirty acres, was absolutely crammed with soldiers; tents were pitched over nearly every foot of available ground. The troops were being sent off as fast as possible during the day; but more were continually arriving. Philadelphia has done nobly! So have Chester, Bucks, Berks, Montgomery, Schuylkill, Lebanon, Dauphin, Lancaster, Bradford, Susquehanna, Centre, Union, Westmoreland, Clearfield, Erie—in fact, *every* county of the Commonwealth.

The white tents were truly a novelty in the park. Hundreds of ladies and children were continually promenading the graveled walks, and were received with great civility and kindness by the soldiers. Squads and companies were continually drilling.

Many were the impromptu inscriptions placed above the different tents. The Reading boys confiscated a white tom cat, which was the pet of the companies, and occupied a prominent position above the tents, in profile. "No admittance, except on very important business," was very conspicuously posted on nearly all the tents; the boys were too busy either to receive or pay visits.

The Philadelphia boys are encamped in the rear of the Governor's quarters. They have all the avenues of their portion of the park named after the localities whence they hail in the city.

On Eighth street there is a well executed portrait of George Washiugton, in charcoal, with the inscription, "We fight for what he gave us!"

At the corner of Girard Avenue and Arch I observed a large placard above the tent door, with "Come in out of the draft. Do drop in," inscribed in bold straggling letters.

The General was busy all day getting out troops into fighting trim. General Reynolds comes here from West Point, where he has been Chief Military Instructor. The men idolize him.

There is no cessation of troops pouring into Harrisburg. They are all of one determination:—"If the Government will guarantee to put the rebellion down in six months, we will guarantee our services; if not, we remain in the State service. We want to see the rebellion crushed, but we don't want to see *playing*. We can crush insurrection in in six months *if the Gogernment tries!*" at least so spoke a stalwart member of a company from one of the northwestern counties, and everybody seemed to agree with him.

The Indian War—Meeting of the Legislature of Minnesota—Message of the Governor—Terrible Picture of Indian Cruelty.

The Legislature of Minnesota convened in special session at St. Paul on the 9th instant. Governor Ramsey immediately sent in a message setting forth the history of the Indian outbreak in detail, and showing the necessity of the utter extermination, or at least the expulsion of the whole Dakotah nation from Minnesota. The Governor thus forcibly depicts their atrocities:

But massacre itself had been mercy if it could have purchased exemption from the revolting circumstances with which it was accompanied. Nothing which the brutal lust and wanton cruelty of these savages could wreak upon their helpless and innocent victims was omitted from the category of their crimes.

Helplessness and innocence, indeed, which move pity in any breast but theirs seemed to inspire them only with a more fiendish rage.

Infants hewn into bloody chips of flesh, or nailed alive to door-posts to linger out their little life in mortal agony, or torn untimely from the womb of the murdered mother and in cruel mockery cast in fragments on her pulseless and bleeding breast: rape joined to murder in one awful tragedy; young girls, even children of tender years, outraged by their brutal ravishers till death ended their shame; women held in captivity to undergo the horrors of a living death; whole families burned alive; and, as if their devilish fury could not glut itself with outrages on the living, its last efforts exhausted in mutilating the bodies of the dead; such are the spectacles, and a thousand nameless horrors besides, which their first experience of Indian war has burned into the brains and hearts of our frontier people; and such the enemy with whom we have to deal.

It is estimated that five hundred persons of every age and sex perished, and worse than perished, by the hands of those remorseless butchers in the course of the two or three days succeeding the outbreak before their progress was checked by our forces, and hundreds of them lie yet unburied where they fell, hidden in the grass and bushes of prairies and ravines. Many, doubtless, in the attempt to escape, have become lost, or, fainting from exhaustion and terror, have died of starvation.

The theatre of depredations as far as ascertained, has extended from Otter Tail Lake and Fort Abercrombie, on the Red River, to the Iowa boundary, on a front of two hundred milss, and from the western border of the State eastwardly, to its heart at Forest City, an area of twenty thousand square miles.

The property destroyed and carried off as booty is estimated at millions of dollars, including large supplies of arms and ammunitions pillaged from the government and private stores on the reservation, and the cattle, horses and household effects of settlers. The indirect damage to our citizens is vastly greater, and, if we include its probable effects on our future prosperity, is beyond calculation.

In all, probably not less than 30,000 people are involved directly or indirectly in the loss of life or loss of property from pillage, destruction or abandonment.

General Sickles' Excelsior Brigade—Gen. Busteed Making Arrangements for the Draft.

Albany Sept. 17.—Gen. Daniel E. Sickles is here, and after an interview with Gov. Morgan has succeeded in securing prompt payment of the state bounty to the volunteers for the Excelsior Brigade. The most strenuous exertions will be made by the Governor and the State Department to secure promptly the filling up of all the regiments of General Sickles' Brigade, in conformity with the earnestly expressed wish of the War Department at Washington. General Dick Busteed is also here on important business connected with the draft, which will probably be made on the first of next month.

War Meeting in Albany.

Albany, Sept. 17.—Gen. Corcoran arrived at Congress Hall at 5 o'clock. There was an immense war meeting at the Capital Park in the evening. Gen. Corcoran was introduced to the audience by Gov. Morgan. Speeches were made by Corcoran, Judge Daily, and others.

NEWS ITEMS, &c.

THE indefatigable Charles Henry Foster has arrived at Newbern, N. C., and taken the stump as candidate for Congress at the approaching election.

A NOTICE, offering $300 reward for the apprehension of Appleton Oaksmith, who escaped from Boston prison a few days since, was received yesterday morning by the Chief of Police of Jersey City.

THE Surgeon General has ordered Medical Inspectors Collins, Hussey and Humphreys to proceed to Gen. McClellan's army, and inquire into its sanitary state and the efficiency of its surgical corps, and report weekly to the Medical Inspector General.

THE Sanitary Commission, now in session in Washington, is about to undertake the preparation and publication, at short intervals, of a general directory, containing the address and condition of every sick and wounded soldier in the Government hospitals.

THE funeral of Gen. Stevens took place at Newport, Rhode Island, on Thursday last. The escort of the procession was composed of both military and naval officers, including Com. Blake, Com. Porter, Gen. S. Hamilton, and Lieut. Gov. Arnold.

THE iron-clad Merrimac, No. 2, was seen at the wharf at Richmond by the paroled prisoners who arrived here yesterday in the America, from Annapolis, Md. She was encased in a wooden frame work, and not much information could be obtained of her. She was, however, not ready for sea on Saturday last, and cannot probably leave port for some time.

THE wounds of Gen. Lee are said to be more serious than was supposed. Both hands are terribly lacerated and utterly useless. He was sitting on horseback, resting both hands on the pommel of his saddle, when a bullet passed partly through both of them. Ha is represented as having both hands well bundled up, and is greatly worried at not being able to manipulate his pen and pencil.

THE notorious George N. Sanders, an account of whose escape into Canada, in the garb of a coal-miner, lately appeared in the papers, has landed in England and treated the English people to a rose-colored account of rebel affairs. He was received with open arms by our "neutral" cousins, and was much lionized on account of his being "the bearer of important dispatches to the Confederate Commissioners, Mason and Slidell." He said that Buell's army would be captured, that the rebels would be joined by 150,000 recruits in Maryland, and evidently adapted his discourse to the disposition of his hearers.

THE 1st California Regiment, composed of Infantry and Cavalry, have just accomplished a march of one thousand miles over the Colorado desert, from the Pacific to the Rio Grande, where they are now in good order, to commence operations against the rebels in Texas. When it is observed that the country through which they passed was destitute of forage and provisions, and they were obliged to carry everything necessary during the march of sixty days, it is surprising they accomplished it with the trifling loss from Indians and rebels of only ten men. They had a serviceable train, with abundant supplies, yet not larger than that of a regiment marching fifty miles from Washington. One wagon served to carry ten days' rations for one company, with their baggage, and they have thus averaged over seventeen miles per day. They have truly shown themselves the right men to operate in Texas.

MILITARY NEWS.

The Army Register for September, 1862, is out. Our regular army consists now of nearly 40,000 men.

The new Ironsides is again ready for sea. She is now rigged with masts and spars. This indicates that she is destined for Charleston or Savannah.

The U. S. ship Courier sailed from this port yesterday with sealed orders. She had been for some time preparing at the Navy Yard, and had on board a large cargo of necessaries for men-of-war.

The Secretary of War has issued an order for the reorganization of the army corps. Under this order the following commands are designated:

1st Corps, Major-General Hooker.
2d Corps, Major-General Sumner.
3d Corps, Major-General Heintzelman
4th Corps, Major-General Keyes.
5th Corps, Major-General Fitz-John Porter.
6th Corps, Major-General Franklin.
7th Corps, Major-General Dix.
8th Corps, Major-General Wool.
9th Corps, Major-General Burnside.
10th Corps, Major-General Mitchell.
11th Corps, Major-General Sedgwick
12th Corps, Major-General Sigel.

It will be observed that the names of Major-Generals Banks, Fremont and Pope are omitted from this list.

The *Shamrock* is the name which Secretary Welles has designated for one of the vessels now in the course of construction. This act quite delights the Irish workmen, who declare if Mr. Lincoln will man her with Irishmen and send her after the rebel "290," they will soon enlist a crew for her in Brooklyn.

A NEW regiment called the New York City Guard is now being recruited from the 1st Senatorial District. Their headquarters are at 62 White st.

The St. Nicholas Lodge I. O. of O. F., have passed a resolution appropriating $50 each to its members who shall enlist, and $2 per week to their families, and invite the several lodges in the State to follow their example.

The 12th N. Y. S. M., are now on their way home having been paroled after the surrender of Harper's Ferry.

Fourteen men have just arrived at the Astor House, having come nearly 500 miles to enlist in Corcoran's Brigade. They were attached to Capt. De Barry's Company.

LOCAL NEWS.

NEW YORK AND THE VICINITY.

PRISONERS RELEASED FROM FORT LAFAYETTE.—U. S. Marshal Murray proceeded to Fort Lafayette yesterday and brought to the city the following named prisoners, who were all released by Judge Advocate Turner, on their taking the oath of allegiance: Wm. White, Emil Faust, Emil Shippman, Thos. Boyle, John Bouldin, and Solomon B. Ellathorp. M. T. Johnson, of Galena, Ill., who has been an inmate of the Fort for some time, was transferred to Fort Delaware.

THE COMITTEE OF THE IRISH TEMPERANCE Societies of New York and Brooklyn, appointed to make arrangements for a testimonial to Ex-President Robert Wilson, for his efforts in the cause of Temperance, met last evening at 474 Pearl street. Mr. John McGrath, President of the St. James Society, in the chair, and Mr. Patrick Dwyer, of the Father Matthew Society of New York, Secretary. Mr. James Brennan of the F. M. Society, No. 2, of Brooklyn, reported that they had hired the City Assembly Rooms, Broadway, and also a Band, beside printing their tickets and order of dancing. Mr. Brennan further reported that, Mr. James H. O'Neill had been appointed floor-manager, and he moved that four men from each society by appointed a sub-committee to assist Mr. O'Neill in his duties. Carried. And the following were appointed:

Father Matthew Society (No. 2) of Brooklyn.—Messrs. Terence Moran, Michael Green, Alexander Campbell, and —— Kerrigan.

Father Matthew Society of South Brooklyn.—Messrs. John McClusky, John Gilchrist, John Cain, Hugh Skelly,

Father Matthew Society of New York.—Messrs. James Kirby, Charles Skelly, Patrick Newman, Martin Carmody.

St. James' Society of New York.—Messrs. Wm. Smith, John Marr, David Bartley, and Francis McCormick.

The two first named of each society are to assist the floor managers, the two last named in each to act as a reception Committee. On motion of Mr.

(*Continued on Fourth Page.*)

On the Fourth Page, will appear to-day, all Important News received at this office, after Two O'Clock, A. M.

A WEEKLY EDITION
of THE NEW YORK SUN, issued every Tuesday, in wrappers for the mail, TWO CENTS EACH, $1 per 100.
SUBSCRIPTIONS—PAID IN ADVANCE.
One copy, 1 year..75cts. | Three copies, 1 year, $200
Do. 16 months, $1 00 | Five copies, do $3 00
☞ Specimen copies, gratis. Discount of 20 per cent. from single rate, on each copy over five.
☞ Postage within New York State, *only thirteen cents a year*—out of the State, *twenty-six cents.*
Address M. S. BEACH, SUN OFFICE, NEW YORK.

DEATHS.

GERATY—On the evening of the 17th inst, James Geraty, in the 65th year of his age.

His relatives and friends, and those of his sons Thomas H., John J. and Nicholas G. Geraty, are respectfully invited to attend the funeral, on Friday afternoon, 19th inst, at 2 o'clock, from his late residence, 418 Third ave, near 31st st. 294

munity. Avarice has become the ruling passion, and with heartless gripe, regardless of the suffering it inflicts, it insists upon its cruel and unconscionable exactions. Patriotism is second to a love of "the almighty dollar." The price of everything even the necessaries of life is put up to the highest point, and those who have not the pecuniary ability to pay these prices, must suffer. A fair price should be paid for everything, but sellers should not be permitted to take advantage of the necessities of the consumers, to impose upon them.

What must be the feelings of a man who is fighting the battles of the country, surrendering all the comforts and endearments of home, submitting to all the sufferings and sacrifices of camp life and active military duty, when he (receiving but eleven dollars per month) is informed that a sack of salt costs fifty dollars, or a pair of ladies' shoes cost sixteen, with every thing else in proportion? He must feel that while he is defending the country, his family, unless he be a man of means, must suffer for the necessaries and comforts of life. With what heart can he fight our battles under such circumstances?

There is but one remedy for this evil. It is to increase the quantities of the articles upon which the extortion operates. The general law of trade, that the supply must equal the demand, is the only law by which trade can be regulated. When the supply equals the demand, the price will be commensurate with the value of the article. When the supply is deficient, the price will be immediately enhanced. It becomes necessary, then, to turn attention to the means requisite for increasing supplies. This can be accomplished, first, by prohibiting the agents of the government who have control of the lines of transportation, from receiving remuneration for giving preference in transporting articles, by which the extortioners who pay the largest douceurs, are those only who are accommodated; and secondly, by obtaining an order from the government authorizing the transportation of produce to the exclusion of other things, at least one day in each week. If this were done, the equilibrium so necessary in trade, would restore prices to their natural standard.

Whatever can be done by the Legislature for the relief of the people from the evils visited upon them by the extortioners, I feel persuaded will be done. The evil has become serious and alarming, and is increasing daily. I hope the Legislature will direct their attention to this matter, and see whether their combined wisdom cannot devise some measures that will give relief to a suffering people.

CONCLUSION.

You reassemble under circumstances very different from those which attended your adjournment. At that day the prospect looked gloomy—the capital was threatened, and many feared it must fall. Now, how bright and glorious the prospect! The insolent enemy, who threatened the capital, has been vanquished in every battle on the Chickahominy, and his forces driven back to the precise location from which they started fifteen months ago. Victory has perched upon our banners in every battle field, and the whole land resounds with the praise of our officers and men, who, through the agency of Divine Providence, have worked out these glorious results. We must not, however, forget the honored dead, who have fallen in these hotly contested battles. Their courage, their patriotism, their heroic deeds will be embalmed in the heart of every true and loyal son and daughter of the South; and when this war shall end, and we shall enjoy the blessings of peace, we will gather together the dust of the honored dead, and raise to their memories a splendid mausoleum, which will transmit to the latest posterity a record of their virtues and deeds.

Respectfully,
JOHN LETCHER.

THE PEACE DEMOCRATS—THE DRAFT.

A Washington letter in the New York Times, dated 25th ult, says:

Letters from various quarters express the belief that the Peace Democrats are likely to carry the elections in many localities hitherto strongly against them—they having remained at home with a view to that end, while their opponents have freely volunteered. People in such sections are clamoring for a draft, that the burdens of war may fall fairly hereafter upon all classes, and that one side may no longer remain wholly at home to do the governing, while the other side carries on the war. They generally represent that where the game of the peace men has been discovered they have almost wholly suspended volunteering, and are waiting for the enforcement of the draft.

It appears that several States are much further behind in raising their quotas of troops under the new calls than has been represented. It is probable that there will be very few where drafting, either for the first three hundred thousand, or at least for filling up the old regiments, will not have to be resorted to.

THE MERRIMAC No. 2.

The New York papers have a dispatch dated Norfolk, Sept. 6th, to the following effect:

There is great excitement here in consequence of a report that the Merrimac No. 2 had reached the vicinity of Newport News, and had had an engagement with two of our gun boats, driving them before her.—All the shipping here have been removed to a place of safety, but no fears of any thing serious are entertained, as such arrangements have been made by our naval authorities as will probably make the career of the Merrimac No. 2 of shorter duration than that of her former namesake.

LOCAL AND STATE ITEMS

TERMS OF THE VIRGINIAN.—We have not increased the subscription price of our paper to yearly subscribers, notwithstanding we pay three times as much as formerly for paper, and for every thing else in the same proportion. At our present yearly rates there is little or no margin for profit, but we desire to pass through the war without increasing them, if we can avoid it. We must apply a somewhat different rule however, to those who, induced by the great avidity with which newspapers are sought in these exciting times, desire only to take a paper for the war, and subscribe for three or six months. There is no reason why we should accommodate such during the war, at far less than war rates; and besides, it involves the necessity for as many entries on our books, and is as much trouble to record a subscriber for three months, as for a year. It has been the habit, moreover, with most of the journals, to charge more in proportion for a less time than one year. Our rates therefore, in future, will be as follows:

Daily Virginian, one year,			$6 00
do.	do.	six months,	4 00
do.	do.	three months,	2 25
do.	do.	one month,	75
Tri-weekly, one year.			$5 00
do.		six months,	3 00
do.		three months,	1 50
do.		one month,	60
Weekly, one year,			$2 00
do.		six months,	1 50

☞ No paper will be sent without the subscription is paid in advance.

AN APPEAL FOR THE SOLDIER.—We have been requested to invite attention to the condition of the many sick and wounded soldiers who daily arrive here by the Orange train. They come hungry and wan, many of them friendless and pennyless, and with their sickness and wounds plead touchingly for relief. We are informed, by a lady who is one of an Association to regularly visit the cars upon their arrival, to administer food and comforts to these poor distressed men—that about 300 of them arrived on Tuesday evening, most of them in a condition to need the relief which we have indicated. As the food was being distributed, the half-famished men would stretch their hands over each others shoulders to secure the much-coveted boon.

The ladies of the Aid Society have undertaken to supply these men daily, upon their arrival here, and appeal to our citizens for aid to enable them to carry out their purposes. Provisions of any kind sent to their room under the Masonic Hall will be thankfully received, and applied as above stated.

REVIVALS.—The protracted meeting which, for the past two or three weeks, has been progressing at the Baptist Church, in this place, still continues with unabated interest. Large numbers have professed a living faith in Christ, whilst many others are seeking the "anxious seats." At the Centenary Church (Methodist,) the good work is also going on, with results most gratifying to the friends of Zion.

THANKSGIVING SERMON.—The Rev. R. B. Thomson, D. D. will by request, preach a sermon in the Methodist Protestant Church, this morning at 11 o'clock, appropriate to the occasion. The public are invited to attend.

SHOOTING AFFAIR.—On Sunday the 14th inst., a shooting affair occurred at the Hotel of C G Hill, in the town of New Castle, occurring between S C Steel, of company B, 28th Regiment Virginia Volunteers, and Barclay Dodd a citizen of the place, the former firing two, and the latter one shot. Neither party was injured, but unfortunately the first shot fired by Steele missed its aim and entered the left leg of J L Hill, an old and much esteemed citizen, between the ankle and knee, causing a serious fracture of the front bone.

Mr. Hill is thought to be doing well but fears are entertained that he will loose his leg.

Steele has been committed for examination before the next County Court.

An accident occurred on the South Side Rail Road yesterday below the high bridge. The wheels ran off one car letting the bed down upon the track. One gentleman who was standing on the platform had his foot mashed. His name is Hunter of North Carolina.

ACCIDENT.—Two gentleman from South Carolina, on a visit to their relatives in this city, were injured yesterday by the running away of horses with a vehicle, on Bridge Street. One of them a Mr. Hunter, was seriously hurt.

FURTHER PARTICULARS OF THE BATTLE AT HARPER'S FERRY

Reported Capture of 10,000 Prisoners.

The latest intelligence we could ascertain last night, confirms the reported victory at Harper's Ferry which we announced yesterday.

We have since ascertained the following particulars of the engagement, which we have reason to believe are nearly correct.

On Monday morning the 15th inst. our forces under command of Gen. Jackson attacked the enemy at Harper's Ferry, under command of General Miles.

After a severe battle the enemy were defeated. The loss in killed and wounded on either side is not reported.

General Jackson captured 10,000 prisoners, 1000 negroes, about 50 pieces of artillery, and a large quantity of Quarter Master's and Commissary stores.

Gen. or Col. Garland of the Confederate Army is reported killed. Serious fears are entertained that the person in question is General Samuel Garland, Jr., of this city, and we shall painfully await further intelligence.

An officer who arrived here last night from Frederick, Md., states that at the same time the battle was raging at Harper's Ferry, an engagement was going on at Monocacy Junction, on the Baltimore & Ohio Railroad.

RELIGIOUS NOTICE.

There will be preaching to day, at Tyreanna Chapel, on Winston's Hill two miles from the city of Lynchburg. All christians, and all other persons are cordially invited to attend.

MR EDITOR:—Permit me to suggest that in the thank-offering, on Thursday, (to-day) the bodies of the soldiers meet with some consideration. "Render unto Cæsar the things which are Cæsars'." Cæsar has fought hard, has conquered, is sick, is destitute. Minister to his soul—but don't let him remain breechless, shirtless, revolting, and a prey to vermin. Search, and you will know. Help by your pen—plead for a dividend. Clothing might constitute a thank offering acceptable to God. "Clothe the naked" is high authority.

FREMONT SQUELCHED.

Bennett's Herald, of Thursday, has the following paragraph:

The Jacobin Club, called the National War Committee, have held another secret meeting on the affairs of the nation. It appears that a correspondence between Mr. Opdyke and General Fremont in regard to 50,000 men to be raised for the latter's command, was read. Gen. Fremont, assents to the acceptance of the command, but further proceedings show that Mr. Stanton understands the matter, and puts a quietus on the affair. In answer to resolutions previously passed, asking the consent of the War Department to raise these 50,000 men, the Secretary stated that the raising of volunteers had been assigned to the Governor of the State, and that no military officer of high rank could be authorized to organize military organizations.

NOXON'S WAR SPEECH.

At the war meeting held at Troy, N. Y., the Hon. B. D. Noxon was chosen chairman. On taking the chair, he said:

"This was the first war meeting he had attended. The object was not now so much to devise means to carry on the war, but to stop the war. Blood enough had been shed. Treasure enough had been expended. No man could desire the perpetuation of such a bloody, remorseless struggle. It was not important who should be on the State ticket, except in as much as this war could never be ended except by the election of entirely different men to Congress than those composing the last Congress. To accomplish this, it was necessary to form a strong State ticket, carrying with it character and influence, in order to strengthen the Congressional vote."

EXTRAORDINARY ADVANCE IN COTTON AND COTTON FABRICS.—The news from Liverpool, under date of August 28th, that the sales of cotton for the week, in that port, were 90,000 bales, and that the price of American cotton had advanced six cents per pound, excited the New York market on Monday. The World remarks:

The domestic commission houses and manufacturers advanced printed cotton fabrics and delaines one to two cents a yard, and sheetings also five per cent. Merrimac prints, now selling at 17 cents, are expected to be advanced to 20 cents per yard, and raw cotton will advance to 60 cents per pound at no distant date, the quotation for middling upland being 56 cents yesterday. This is the highest price that has been paid at any time within the memory of "the oldest inhabitant."

CHEERING NEWS.—Dispatches from Gen. Kirby Smith. ask, that twenty thousand stand of arms be sent him, to arm the Kentuckians that are rushing in crowds to his standard. This is really gratifying news as it gives our operations in Kentucky a tenfold brighter promise.—*R. Enq.*

LATEST FROM NASHVILLE.

A gentleman from Shelbyville, brings Nashville news up to Friday last. He says that Buell left Nashville some ten days ago with all his forces, except Thomas' Division in the direction of Bowling Green, but has since returned to Nashville with all his forces, and commenced fortifying the city, having impressed all the negroes in the county of Davidson for that purpose.—This gentleman confirms the statement of the difficulty between Johnson and Buell—Well informed persons believe that Buell's fortifying Nashville is a mere ruse, and that he intends to retreat by way of the Tennessee River—*Chattanooga Rebel.*

BY TELEGRAPH.

CHEERING NEWS FROM THE KANAWHA VALLEY.

SALT MINES CAPTURED.

CHARLESTON RETAKEN BY GEN. LORING.

OFFICIAL DISPATCHES FROM GEN. LORING.

THE ENEMY ROUTED,

Large Quantities of Stores Destroyed.

OUR LOSS SLIGHT.

ENEMY'S LOSS HEAVY.

&c., &c., &c.

RICHMOND, Sept 14.

Gen. Loring's command entered the Kanawha Saltmines, last Saturday morning, and took possession of the Salt Works and closely pursued the enemy, who were en route for Charleston.

The Salt Works were not much injured.

An very large quantity of salt was on hand, selling for thirty-five cents per bushel.

A order has been issued urging the farmers to send forward their wagons laden with forage, &c., and carry away salt in return.

LATER.

RICHMOND, Sept. 17.

Official dispatches received from General Loring dated

CHARLESTON, Kanawha co.

After sharp and incessant skirmishing we took this place at three o'clock this morning.

The enemy six regiments strong made a stout resistance, burning their stores and most of this town in their retreat.

Our loss slight.

The enemy's heavy.

The enemy is in full retreat and Jenkins is in his rear.

Reported Capture of Harper's Ferry Confirmed.

RICHMOND, Sept. 17.

An official dispatch from Chattanooga confirms the occupation of Iuka by Gen'l. Price's army, and the capture of several hundred thousand dollars worth of army stores.

A private dispatch from Staunton today, says that Harper's Ferry was taken by Jackson on the 15th inst., and eight thousand Yankees, and one thousand negroes captured.

CONFEDERATE CONGRESS.

RICHMOND, Sept. 17.

In the House yesterday Mr. Foote introduced a resolution proposing to send a Commissioner or Commissioners to Washington empowered to propose terms of just and honorable peace.

Mr. Holt of Ga. submitted a substitute declaring that the people of the Confederate States have ardently desired peace from the beginning, and that whenever the United States government shall manifest a like anxiety, it shall be the duty of the President to appoint commissioners to treat and negotiate with the said government.

The resolution and substitute were laid upon the table Yeas 59, nays 26.

THE CONFEDERATE STATES.

L. T. BURNETT, Proprietor. "RESISTANCE TO TYRANTS IS OBEDIENCE TO GOD."—Jefferson. TERMS—$3 PER ANNUM.

VOL. VI. NEW IBERIA, PARISH OF ST. MARTIN, LOUISIANA, SATURDAY, SEPT. 20, 1862. NO. 11.

THE CONFEDERATE STATES.

PUBLISHED EVERY SATURDAY BY

L. T. BURNETT,

Editor and Proprietor.

TERMS OF SUBSCRIPTION.—Three Dollars a year, invariably in Advance.

ADVERTISING RATES.—One Dollar per square for the first insertion, and Fifty Cents for each subsequent insertion.

THE MERRY HEART.

'Tis well to have a merry heart,
However short we stay;
There's wisdom in a merry heart,
Whate'er the world may say.
Philosophy may lift its head
And find out many a flaw,
But give me the philosophy
That's happy with a straw.

If life but brings us happiness,
It brings us, we are told,
What's hard to buy, though princes try,
With all their heaps of gold.
Then laugh away, let others say
Whate'er they will of mirth;
Who laughs the most, may truly boast
He's got the wealth of earth.

There's beauty in a merry laugh,
A moral beauty too;
It shows the heart's an honest heart,
That's paid each man his due;
And lent a share of what's to spare,
Despite of wisdom's fears;
And makes the cheek less sorrow speak,
The eye weep fewer tears.

The sun may shroud itself in gloom,
The tempest's wrath begin;
It finds a spark to cheer the dark—
Its sunlight is within.
Then laugh away, let others say
Whate'er they will of mirth;
Who laughs the most, may truly boast
He's got the wealth of earth.

Write to the Soldiers.—A writer in one of our exchanges says: "Could I through your paper pen a sentence that would reach effectually every Southern reader who may have a relative, a friend or an acquaintance in the army, that sentence would be, *write to the soldiers*. There are many of them far from home, among strangers, and enduring every toil and privation for their country. A line or a word will nerve their hearts, and cheer them on. Go to our crowded post office, as I go. See the war-worn soldier's anxiety as he asks for a letter; see him get it, eagerly break the seal and read the pen-tracings of loved ones at home. Often I've seen the lip tremble, the eye dilate and even the tear glisten, as line upon line was read. Some father, mother, sister, wife, or sweetheart has sent him words of cheer. You can see him grasp his weapon tighter, carefully fold his letter, and with firmer tread and more elastic spirits, return to duty. On the other hand, look at the bitter, cruel, stinging disappointment of the soldier who, day after day, goes for an expected letter, and finding none, turns away with saddened heart feeling that no one cared for him. Again, let me say *write to the soldiers*.

The handsomest compliment you can pay to a woman of sense is to address her as such.

PRIERE

A la Tres Sainte Vierge.

Pour détourner les fleaux dont nous sommes menacés.

Celeste Protéctriee, qui avez tant de fois détourné la colére de Dieu, prête à éclater sur la Louisiane coupable, et qui lui avez obtenu taut d'annees et tant de grâces pour se convertir et faire penitence, maintenant que la mesure de ces crimes est combleé et que le bras vengeur va s'appesantir sur elle, les abandonnerez-vous pour toujours? oublierez-vous qu'ils vous appartiennent par droit de donation! serait-il dit que vôtre héritage est devenu la proie de votre ennemi?

O Marie, nous sommes donc bien coupables, puisque nos péches, nous out attiré la menace de maux si affreux!—Mais, ô Vierge toute-puissante, vous pouvez repousser ces fléaux et obtenir le pardon à des enfants humiliés. Ah nous nous réunissons à vos pieds; soyez touchée de nos gémissements et de nos larmes, faites une sainte violence á votre Divin Fils, pour arrêter les terribles effets de son indignation. O Miséricordieuse Vierge, faites les derniers efforts pour nous sauver, en nous obtenant des cœurs contrits et pénitents.

Ainsi soit il.

O Marié, conçue sans péché, priez pour nous qui avons recours à vous.

Saint Joseph, protégez-nous.

Nouvelle Iberie, 1862.

Kissing.—An impertinent youth had been amusing himself by exhibiting the following to some ladies:

"Men scorn to kiss among themselves,
And scarce would kiss a brother,
But women want to kiss so bad,
They kiss and kiss each other."

Whereupon a young lady penciled the following reply in the back of an envelope, and left it for the fool's instruction:

"Men do not kiss among themselves,
And it's well that they refrain;
The bitter dose would vex them so,
They would never kiss again.

"As sometimes on poor woman's lip
Is applied this nauseous lotion,
We have to kiss among ourselves
As a counteracting potion."

Homœpathic Globules.—A little medical learning is a dangerous thing.

The billionth part of a grain of sense is worth a whole pound of physic.

The art is not to dispense medicine, but to dispense with it.

In bodily repairs, the least given the soonest mended.

"There's many an empty cradle,
There's many a vacant bed,
There's many a lonely bosom
Whose joy and light is fled;
For thick in every graveyard
The little hillocks lie—
And every hillock represents
An angel in the sky."

Indulging in dangerous pleasures, says a Burmese proverb, is like licking honey from a knife, and cutting the tongue with the edge.

The Arabs of the desert use their scimitars as looking glasses.

Flowers are the alphabet of angels, wherewith they write on hills and plains mysterious truths.

If a man is insane upon the subject of money, is his disease monomania or money-mania.

The sun is a spark from the light of God's wisdom.

Proteus changed himself to a lion. A good many of his successors, when they change, always make asses of themselves—and no great change either.

Passion, though a bad regulator, is a powerful main spring.

Heads should hot be turned with love, when the hair upon them has been turned with age.

The whole race of mankind live upon each other. In an important sense we are all cannibals.

He who enters upon a career of crime must either come to a halt or a halter.

Glorious News!

Washington City Certainly Taken.

"Stonewall" at York, Pa.

The Confederate Flag Floats on the U. S. Capitol.

The Florida Arrived

Yankees Preparing to Decamp.

It would appear from the subjoined intelligence, from an extra of the Thibodeaux Sentinel, that the Federal Capitol has fallen before the superior prowess of the Confederate troops. We are aware that it is not good policy "to crow before getting out of the woods," yet as all the intelligence received at this point for the past week, has tended to confirm the rumored capture of Washington City, we can no longer doubt that the glorious "stars and bars" now proudly floats from the dome of the Federal Capitol! All hail, then, to invincible "Stonewall" and his Spartan band! The following is the intelligence as contained in the Sentinel's extra:

To Jefferson Davis, President of the Confederate States of America:—The Confederate States flag was hoisted at half-past eleven o'clock, A. M., on the United States Capitol, by the eight survivors of the second company of the Washington Artillery of New Orleans.

We now hold the Capitol of the once prud Republic of America, under our control. Our army suffered immensely, but thanks be to God, with his aid, we have got through gloriously.

R. E. LEE, Gen. Commanding.

Later News!

Gen. Stonewall Jackson has taken the town of York, in Pennsylvania, and destroyed all the manufactories.

He is now marching upon Baltimore, and will proceed to Annapolis. He took all the cannon at Arlington. Not one was spiked.

The iron clad 290 Florida, has arrived safely at Mobile.

There is said to exist a great panic at Philadelphia and New York.

Still Later News!

The gentleman who furnished these despatches, has been a prisoner with the Federals since the raid on Col. Kenner's plentation, in July last, and states that the Yankees are packing up in New Orleans, and he would not be surprised to hear of their leaving that city.

The Very Latest.

A couple of gentlemen arrived in New Iberia this morning, from Baton Rouge, who state that they read a dispatch in the Mobile Register confirming the capture of Washington City. The dispatch also stated that if our forces had been 10 minutes sooner in their attack on the city, Lincoln and his entire cabinet would have been bagged. The archives are in our possession. The enemy's loss was very heavy. Gens. Pope, Banks, and Seigel are among the killed. Our loss is estimated at $25,000.

THE CONFEDERATE STATES.

PUBLISHED EVERY SATURDAY BY

L. T. BURNETT,

Editor and Proprietor.

NEW IBERIA:

SATURDAY, SEPT. 20, 1862.

☞ Although the quality of paper on which we print this week's issue—and which we will continue to use in the future—was designed originally to decorate the walls of some splendid mansion, yet we conceive the use to which we have appropriated it, will tend in some degree to the adorning of the walls of that inner temple called mind. It is true that the existing times have "driven us to the wall" to procure our supply of paper for printing purposes, yet when the sweet dove of Peace shall again spread her broad pinions over our land, we hope to be able to resume our journal on a full sheet, and amply atone for all delinquincies committed during "the reign of terror."

☞ As soon as practicable we intend making arrangements to procure as exchanges the following journals: "The Memphis Appeal," now published at Grenada, Miss; "The Natchez Courier;" "The Mobile Advertiser;" "The Charleston Mercury;" "The Houston Telegraph;" "The Richmond Enquirer;" and "The Alexandria (La.) Democrat." With the items we may be able to cull from these papers, we hope to furnish our readers, weekly, with an interesting sheet.

A Candi(e)d Fact.—Yes, kind reader, it is a fact that Mr. Thos. R. Reynolds, of Franklin, St. Mary's parish, is now making as good an article of candy as was ever imported from the far-famed establishments of Turpin or Ridley.—Mr. Jas. A. Lee has the sole agency in this place for selling this candy, and keeps a constant supply on hand which he will dispose of in quantities ranging from one pound up to two hundred pounds. Persons who have what is called "a sweet tooth," should not fail to call at the drug store of Mr. Lee and examine this article. Come, friend Tom, remember "the days of auld lang syne," and send us along an advertisement that will herald forth the praises of your candy through our columns. And at the same time don't forget to put us up a few of the best samples in your line, and our word for it we'll test their merits successfully.

To the Ladies.—We are requested to state that the Ordnance Department of this District is very much in need of flannel for making cartridges, and as it is next to impossible to procure this article in the country, we would appeal to the ladies of this vicinity to take the matter in hand and try if they cannot supply, from among themselves, to some extent, the wants of the Department in this particular. Ladies, we judge by what you have done in the past when we say if you will only give this matter a trial, success is sure to crown your efforts.

TO OUR READERS.

After a suspension of several weeks, caused by our being obliged to devote our exclusive attention to public business, we now resume the publication of the Confederate States. We trust hereafter to issue the paper without interruption through evil report and good report. The want of a village journal has been much felt during the temporary discontinuance of our issue. Communication has been so much interrupted—postal arrangements have been so irregular, newspapers have been so scarce—appearing only like angel's visits, few and far between, mostly in the possession of a few transient persons—that our community was left a prey to idle rumors with alternations of extravagant joy or causeless depression.—It will be our principal object to collect from all attainable sources not only all possible information about the events of our gigantic and unprecedented struggle for independence, but also the opinions and speculations of foreign, domestic and even federal journals regarding the phases of this most remarkable war. We trust much to the kindness of our friends, and of all well-wishes to our sacred cause, for permission to make extracts from such newspapers as may reach them, which we feel assured they will place at our disposal for this purpose.

We expect much also, from the telegraph which has been re established at this place. The ine now extends as far as Bayou des Allemands, on the Opelousas Railroad, and we understand that as soon as the necessary arrangements are completed, the wires will be extended to some point in Texas.—By these means, and from the few exchanges we may be able to make, we hope to furnish our fellow-citizens weekly, with a tolerable summary of news, considering the times and the condition of our country. May we not hope that they will extend a generous patronage to aid us in so desirable and useful an undertaking.

We are in the very crisis of a struggle which no language of ours could even faintly portray. We have had bitter and disheartening reverses, but the horizon is beginning to clear. A succession of brilliant victories has far more than atoned for the defeats which our arms have sustained in coping with our comparatively feeble resources on the water, against the powerful marine of the enemy. The nation becomes stronger and more united every day. Most of us now feel assured that we can work out our own salvation, and that too at no distant day, without being at all indebted to foreign aid or sympathy. We know that the attitude we have assumed and maintained, will sooner or later extort our recognition from the civilized world, but we no longer consider such recognition essential to our success—when it comes we may truly attribute it to political necessity, and not regard it as placing us under any obligation. We shall commence our national career in all respects free and untrammeled.

With these views and expectations we now resume the publication of the "Confederate States," and invoke for it the patronage and good will of our fellow-citizens.—Nothing will be left undone by us with the means at our disposal to make the paper in every particular worthy of public favor and support.

Dr. A. L. Plough.—Among our new advertisements in this issue, will be found the dental card of this gentleman. It would be useless for us to attempt to say one word commendatory of the Doctor's skill in his speciality, for if any one will take the trouble to call at his office on Main street and examine specimens of his work, it will be found that they sound his praise as a scientific dentist, a good deal louder than we could do even if we were to try our best at a "puff." Dr. Plough has cast in his lot among the people of this vicinity and it is his determination to serve them faithfully in his profession. We hope that a share of public patronage commensurate with his merits may be accorded him.

Great Lucifer!—Tell it in Gath and publish it in the streets of Askelon, that the manufacture of a genuine article of lucifer matches—fully equal to the celebrated Guilleman's—has been commenced in our village by that worthy f. m. c., John Pickett. For some time past we have observed that many of our citizens have been engaged, not exactly like that old rascal, Prometheus, in stealing fire, but they have been "sponging" on their more lucky neighbors for matches to kindle their morning fires and to light their "best Havanas." We are pleased however to be able to record the fact that the cry of Hamlet of "give me some light!" can now be answered. We would say to our citizens, encourage home enterprise.

Scrap of History.—During the Revolutionary war, Gen. Lafayette being in Baltimore was invited to a ball. He went as requested, but instead of joining in the amusement as might have been expected of a young Frenchman of 22, he addressed the ladies thus: "Ladies, you are very handsome; you dance very prettily; your ball is very fine—but my soldiers have no shirts!" The effect was irresistible. The ball ceased; the ladies went home and set to work, and the next day a large nnmber of shirts were prepared by the fairest hands of Baltimore for the gallant defenders of their conntry.

"I live by my pen," said a vulgar author to a lady. "You look sir as if you ought to live in a pen."

Weekly Arrivals at the Principal Hotels.

Confederate Hotel.—L S Lobdell, West Baton Rouge; Sam. Weiter, do.; W S C Clark, do.; M T Gordy, C S A, Franklin La.; N K Todd, E H Hrrriot, La.; J S Roberts, Texas; W M Mordy, Tigerville; J M Howell, Dan'l Lane, Centreville; Chas. H Packard, do.; Jas McWilliams, West Baton Rouge; Fernando Pesica, Plaxuemine; Col. Louis Bush, F S Goode, G W Munday Clinton La; N B Barfillo, H O Benedict, Rapides; Dr C L Tarlton, do.; H Bidwell, St. Charles; Lawrence Lee, Adam Brown, Capt J J Comeaux and wife, Iberville; T C Quirk, Washington La.; D D Arden, do.; M Neyland do; O Harang, Lafourche; Wm A Seay, Rapides; J N A Wilson, do.; J F Thompson, Thibodeaux; A Brousseau, Lafourche; J M Hearron, Tilmon Sparks; William Sparks, A B Richy, Robt. Uzers, Victor Myers, John Maires, B Vinson, St. Mary; S C Johnson, Rapides, La.; J Ford, Cheneyville; D G Morse, Franklin La.; J S Spearing, N. O.; H D Hopkins.

Lion Hotel.—A Vouaur, Grand Coteau; J. Haberie, A J Kearney, Lieut. David Frank, Lieut. Thos. Dolan, Capt. D M Lejery, Capt. L C Rice, Lieut Lee, Capt. R. R Campbell, A J Miller, C S A.; E. Comeaux, Iberville; Jos. Crawford, Capt. E Phillips, Theo. Lastrapes, F DelaRue, Jules Millet Franklin, La.; J A O'Neill, do.; F Froment, Napoleonville; Joseph Caillier, Chas Kees, W B Gates, Mobile; E Escudier, D Bloch, Opelousas; S N White, Bayou Sara; J W Deen, E Lanouse, A L Cachafaen Jno. Lockhart, G. B Burr, J J B Krik, Avoyelles; J C Dowty, Alexandria; M H Rohrer, Jno. Prudhomme, Natchitoches.

WIT AND WISDOM.

Many a rascal is like a bell; he was made on purpose to be hanged.

Age without cheerfulness is a Lapland winter without a sun.

We don't know exactly what the "height of ambition" is, but we have seen many fussy little specimens of it not much more than five feet high.

In a discourse in behalf of a blind asylum, the speaker began by gravely remarking, "If all the world were blind, what a melahcholy sight it would be!"

A wag says that in journeying lately, he was put into an omnibus with a dozen persons, of whom he did not know a single one. Turning a corner shortly after, however, the omnibus was upset. "And then," said he, "I found them all out."

Gentlemen who smoke allege that it makes them calm and complacent. They tell us that the more they fume the less they fret.

Perhaps, after all, the truest philanthropists, the dearest lovers of our race, are the fleas, musquitoes, and South Sea islanders.

Great thoughts are not produced amid noise and mirth: the mind's thunderbolts, like the cloud's, are forged in silence and darkness.

Many a vain head diffuses less light than a pumpkin shell with a tallow candle in it.

The cradle is the little pilot-boat of humanity—wherein the young navigator on the sea of life takes passage.

Politicians by trade should be confined to unseasoned dishes, for they don't earn their salt.

The human soul, like the water of the salt sea, becomes fresh and sweet in rising to the sky.

It may sound like a paradox, yet the breaking of both of an army's wings is a pretty sure way to make it fly.

We suppose that a man, who never speaks, may be said always to keep his word.

It is a beautiful custom in some oriental lands to leave untouched the dates that are shaken from the trees by the wind; these being regarded as sacred to the poor and stranger.

"I am sure I cannot live long," said a very dirty-looking patient to his physician. "Is that any reason, sir, why you should carry dirt enough to bury you?"

It is the part of wisdom to do great things without a fuss. When Solomon, the wisest of men, built his wondrous temple, no sound of saw or hammer was heard therein.

THE NEW YORK HERALD.

WHOLE NO. 9503. NEW YORK, SATURDAY, SEPTEMBER 20, 1862. PRICE TWO CENTS.

HIGHLY IMPORTANT.

The Truce and the Rebel Retreat.

THE VICTORY.

The Rebels in Full Flight.

McClellan Drives Them Across the Potomac.

"SHORT, SHARP AND DECISIVE."

OUR TROOPS IN BRISK PURSUIT.

"Maryland and Pennsylvania Safe."

Additional Interesting Particulars of the Battle of the Valley of Antietam.

MORE OF THE KILLED AND WOUNDED.

"We Can Ask No Higher Honor Than the Proud Consciousness That We Belonged to the Army of the Potomac."

THE VERY LATEST NEWS,

&c., &c., &c.

M'CLELLAN'S BULLETINS.

GEN. McCLELLAN TO GEN. HALLECK.

No. One.

HEADQUARTERS ARMY OF THE POTOMAC, Sept. 19—8:30 A. M.

Major General HALLECK, General-in-Chief:—

But little occurred yesterday except skirmishing.

Last night the enemy abandoned his position, leaving his dead and wounded on the field.

We are again in pursuit.

I do not yet know whether he is falling back to an interior position or crossing the river.

We may safely claim a victory.

GEO. B. McCLELLAN, Major General.

No. Two.

HEADQUARTERS ARMY OF THE POTOMAC, Sept. 19—10:30 A. M.

Major General H. W. HALLECK, General-in-Chief:—

Pleasanton is driving the enemy across the river.

Our victory was complete.

The enemy is driven back into Virginia.

Maryland and Pennsylvania are now safe.

GEO. B. McCLELLAN, Major General.

THE REPORTS FROM FREDERICK.

FREDERICK, Md., Sept. 19, 1862.

There has been but very little fighting to-day; there was a cannonading for a time this morning, but I have not been able to learn the result as yet. Probably it did not amount to much.

THE REPORTS FROM WASHINGTON.

WASHINGTON, Sept. 19, 1862.

Information has reached here that the rebels last night destroyed the new bridge at Harper's Ferry, and blew up the piers. They also destroyed everything that was possible to be destroyed at Harper's Ferry and along the line of the road to Martinsburg, including the splendid bridge known as the Pillar Bridge, at that point. This morning there remained only a small force of rebels on Bolivar Heights and one company at Sandy Hook.

The rebels took advantage of the cessation of hostilities yesterday to make all necessary arrangements for their retreat, their main body crossing the river at the nearest ford, some accounts state near Harper's Ferry, and others at Dam No. 4. The latter was probably their principal crossing.

There have been flying rumors of an engagement to-day, but it is ascertained that the firing proceeded from our flying artillery attacking the rear guard of the retreating rebel army.

REPORTS FROM HARRISBURG.

HARRISBURG, Sept. 19, 1862.

Information just received from the battle field says our victory is complete, and that General Pleasanton is in hot pursuit of the enemy, and driving them across the Potomac.

The whole Union army is in good condition, and the enemy has been badly punished.

"WHO IS PLEASANTON?"

Brigadier General Alfred Pleasanton, the leader of the cavalry, and who has recently so distinguished himself and his command, is a native of the District of Columbia, from which part of the country he was appointed a cadet to the Military Academy at West Point in September, 1840. He graduated on the 30th of June, 1844, standing seventh in his class, which consisted of twenty-five members, including General Hancock and others in the Union service, Simon Bolivar Buckner and other rebels, and several fine officers who were killed in battle during the Mexican war. On the 1st of July, 1844, he was brevetted a second lieutenant of the First dragoons, and on the 3d of November, 1845, he received his commission with the full rank, and was transferred to the Second dragoons. He served in the Mexican war, and was brevetted a first lieutenant for gallant and meritorious conduct in the battles of Palo Alto and Resaca de la Palma, Texas. His brevet was dated May 9, 1846, and was awarded in April, 1847. On the 30th of September, 1849, he was promoted to the full rank of first lieutenant. He became the adjutant of his regiment in July, 1854, and was promoted to a captaincy on the 3d of March, 1855. He acted as assistant adjutant general to General Harney in September, 1856, and again in May, 1857. In the Army Register for 1859 and 1860 his name stood sixth on the roll of captains of the Second dragoons, and fifteenth on the lineal roll of dragoon captains. At this time he held the command of company H of the Second dragoons. In the Army Register for 1861 his name stands one degree higher on the lineal roll of dragoon captains, owing to the death of Captain Fitzgerald. The resignations of traitors in the army brought up the name of Captain Pleasanton to be the second on the list of captains of the Second cavalry (formerly called dragoons), and the retirement of Captain Newton made him the senior captain of that regiment and of the cavalry service, he still retaining the command of Company H, of this regiment. He was promoted to the majority of the Second cavalry during the early part of 1862, the announcement being made in General Orders No. 63, dated at Washington, June 10, 1862. He was next promoted to the rank of brigadier general of volunteers, officially announced in General Order, dated July 24, 1862, and given the command of General Stoneman's efficient cavalry brigade. Since he has been connected with the Army of the Potomac, General Pleasanton has become rather noted for the brilliancy of his movements. On Friday, Sept. 12, he made a dash into Frederick and engaged and drove a portion of the rebel cavalry, who were protecting the rear of that army, from that city. On Monday, Sept. 15, he again came up with the rebel rear guard at Boonsboro, and drove them out, capturing two guns and killing thirty of the enemy. And now we find him again in full chase upon the rear of the retreating foe.

THE BATTLE FIELD OF ANTIETAM.

Scene of McClellan's Victory, on Wednesday, September 17, 1862.

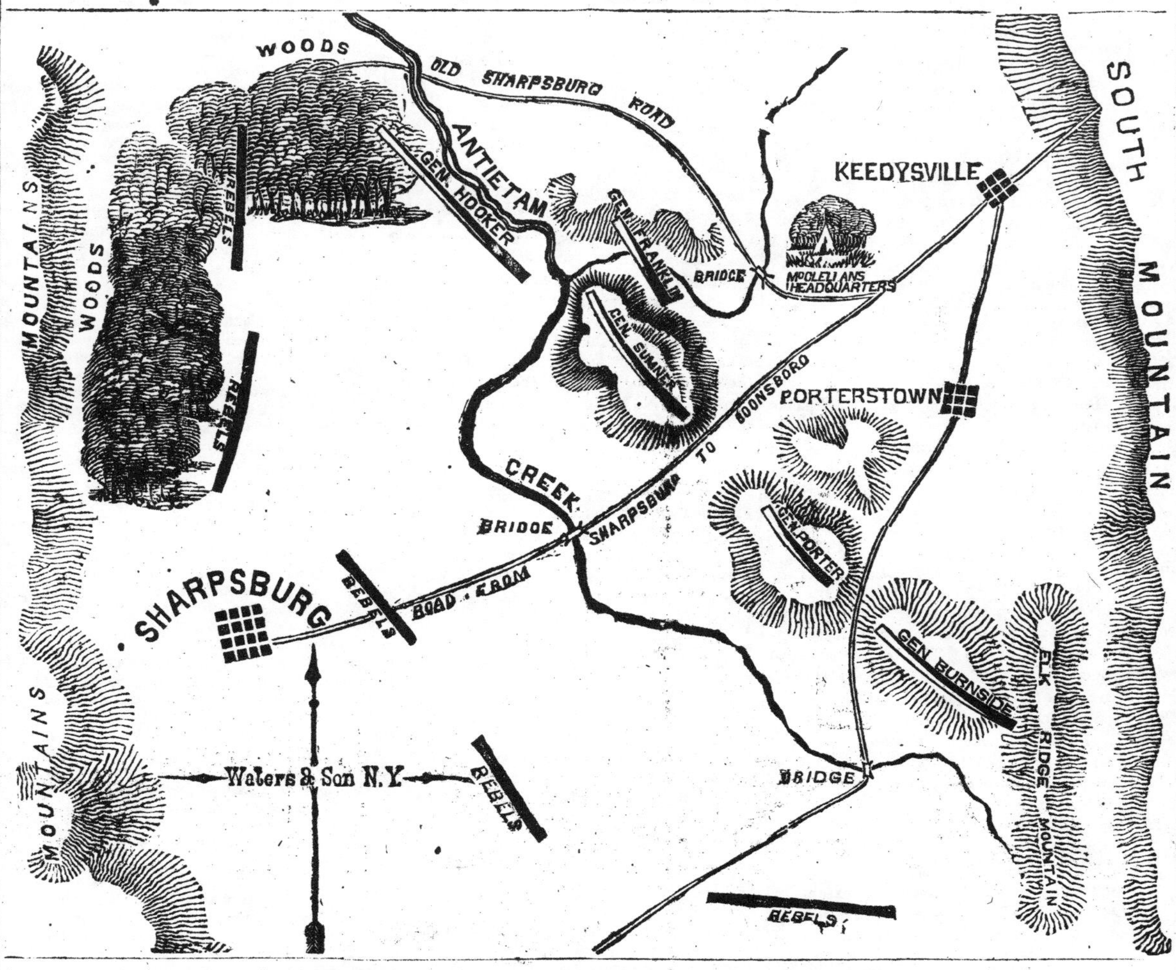

See Eighth Page for Map of the Scene of Operations in Western Maryland, from Williamsport to Frederick.

THE OPENING YESTERDAY.

THE TRUCE AND THE RETREAT.

HEADQUARTERS OF THE ARMY OF THE POTOMAC, Sept. 19—Morning.

Yesterday was occupied in burying the dead and caring for the wounded.

The rebels sent in a flag of truce in the morning, asking permission to bury their own dead, which was granted.

At first the orders were very stringent against holding intercourse with the rebels, but during the afternoon they were relaxed and the *troops of both sides freely intermingled.*

At daylight this morning it was discovered that the enemy had changed their position. About nine o'clock it was discovered that they were in full retreat.

Had the rebels remained a general engagement between both armies would have taken place this morning.

THE VERY LATEST.

ON THE BATTLE FIELD, NEAR SHARPSBURG, FRIDAY, Sept. 19—Noon.

The victory is complete and splendid. Our troops deserve well of their country. *There has been no battle to-day. The rebels are in full flight.* McClellan is now in pursuit of them. What a page in history has been enacted on this bloody field of Antietam during the last forty-eight hours!

THE GREAT BATTLE OF ANTIETAM.

Interesting Additional Details of the Decisive Battle on Wednesday.

On Wednesday, September 17, the Union and rebel forces in Maryland met in the Blue Ridge and fought a battle, which, when its full extent is known, will probably dwarf all other battles yet fought in the present war. Gen. McClellan commanded the national troops in person, and had on the field the whole command of Gen. Burnside, recently augmented by the addition of several new regiments; the army corps lately under Gen. McDowell, now under command of Gen. Hooker; Gen. Sumner's corps; Gen. Franklin's corps; Gen. Banks' corps, commanded by Gen. Williams, and Sykes' division of Fitz John Porter's corps. On the other side the rebels undoubtedly had present the whole force which they originally brought into Maryland. They were commanded by Gen. Lee.

THE BATTLE FIELD.

The battle was fought in the valley immediately west of that portion of the Blue Ridge known as the South Mountains, and to the east and north of Sharpsburg, almost in a semicircle, the concave side of which is towards the town. Unlike most of the valleys in this Blue Ridge country this valley has not a level spot in it, but rolls into eminences of all dimensions, from the little knoll that your horse gallops easily over to the rather high hills that make him tug like a mule. Many of the depressions between these hills are dry, and afford admirable cover for infantry against artillery. Others are watered by the deep, narrow and crooked Antietam, a stream that seems to observe no decorum in respect to its course, but has to be crossed every ten minutes, ride which way you will. Sharpsburg lies on the western side of the valley, and a little to the south from our point of view. Right across the valley from the northeast runs the turnpike from Boonsboro to Sharpsburg. Two little villages—Porterstown and Keetersville, or Keedysville—lie on the eastern side of the valley, at the foot of the South Mountains. Numerous fine farmhouses dot the valley in every direction, some standing out plainly and boldly on the hilltops, others half hidden down the little slopes; and, with the large comfortable barns about them, and their orchards of fruit trees, these hitherto happy and quiet homes greatly enrich the view, at least to the eyes of old campaigners. Nearly every part of the valley is under cultivation, and [illegible] is thus varied into squares of the light green [illegible] ripened corn, the deeper green of clover, and the dull brown of newly ploughed fields. Toward the north, where our right lay, are some dense woods. Imagine this scene spread in the hollow of an amphitheatre of hills that rise in terraces around it, and you have the field of last Wednesday's battle.

WHERE THE ARMIES WERE.

Our position had been taken—in outline, as it were—on Tuesday, and was filled up to its proper strength as fast as the troops arrived, and streamed down the mountain by the road from Middleton. This they continued to do for the greater part of Tuesday and Tuesday night. It was a magnificent sight to see the men of our country thus poured forward across the field to different points in long, shining lines, like living threads, that went to weave themselves into the glorious tapestry of our nation's history—a sight that will not easily be forgotten by those who saw it.

THE POSITIONS OF THE VARIOUS CORPS.

Burnside's men turned short to the south, passed across the foot of the Elk Ridge Mountain, and took a position on our extreme left. Porter held a commanding eminence to the right of Burnside, though Warren's brigade, of Porter's corps, was subsequently posted in the woods on our left in support of Burnside's men. Sumner's corps was on an eminence next to the right or north from Porter, and General Hooker had the extreme right, in and behind the woods of which we have spoken, and on the Antietam. Our left was on Elk Ridge Mountain, and our line of battle stretched to the northwest across the Sharpsburg road. The line was between four and five miles long. The rebel left was in the woods, directly in front of General Hooker, and their force was posted across the valley between us and Sharpsburg in a line very nearly parallel with our own. Though we have spoken of our men as on eminences, it must be understood that they were carefully covered in every case, just below the crests of the hills they held.

OUR ARTILLERY

was also carefully posted behind the crests of the hills, ready to be run up and to blaze away at a moment's notice. Nearly every hill had a battery on it, and the greater number of the batteries looked over fields that extended to the limit of their range.

WHO BEGAN THE FIGHT.

General Hooker had the honor to open this great combat. He commanded the corps formerly under General McDowell, composed of [illegible] division, Mead's (McCall's formerly) and King's divisions. Many of these men came up in the night, and there was perhaps a little confusion in posting them. Mead's men say that they slept among the rebels. Owing to this over-near neighborhood the pickets got at it in the night, and kept up a scattering fire until the battle began. General Mead, who was thus nearest the rebels, was relieved at daylight by General Ricketts' division, which also immediately advanced against the enemy, supported by the division of General King, which eventually became engaged on the right of General Ricketts, and also by the division of General Mead. The line advanced through a piece of woods, a cornfield and a piece of ploughed land, and into another piece of woods, where it found the enemy in line of battle, and was received with a hot file fire, which told very severely on our men. But they steadily advanced into the fierce fire, giving back one equally destructive; while our batteries, particularly a Pennsylvania battery, under Captain Matthews, and Captain Thompson's First Maryland battery, played splendidly upon the enemy's line. Thus pressed, the rebel forces gave way, though they certainly did not "skedaddle." Slowly, and in very fair order they fell back, disputing every foot that they gave up with the greatest obstinacy. Still our boys pushed onward with magnificent courage and determination, every man, from Hooker down, intent only on victory. Occasionally a more determined resistance at some point in the line or some difficulty in the ground would check our advance for a few moments; but, with this exception, it was almost steady from its commencement until about ten o'clock in the morning, when Gen. Hooker was wounded and carried from the field.

IMPETUOUS ONSET OF THE REBELS.

General Ricketts at once assumed command of the corps; but our victorious movement had lost its impulse.

THE ADVANCE OF THE RIGHT.

At that time our right had advanced and swept across the field so far that its front, originally almost in a line with the front of the centre and left, formed almost a right angle with them.

While our advance rather faltered, the rebels, greatly reinforced, made a sudden and impetuous onset, and drove our gallant fellows back over a portion of the hard won field. What we had won, however, was not relinquished without a desperate struggle, and here up the hills and down, through the woods and the standing corn, over the ploughed land and the clover, the line of fire swept to and fro as one side or the other gained a temporary advantage.

SUMNER'S CORPS TO THE RESCUE.

Thus the battle raged till Sumner's corps came up to support the worn out heroes who had maintained the fight so long against very evident odds. How gloriously they went at it, those peninsula boys—Burns' old brigade, led by gallant young Howard, who lost an arm at Fair Oaks, and Meagher's Irish Brigade, led by the gallant Meagher himself, and many other heroes tried in the fire. As the Irish Brigade charged the enemy's line their cheers arose in one great surge of sound over the noise of battle, over the roar of a wilderness of artillery, and was heard far down the lines to the left, where Burnside's boys were just getting at it.

THE REBEL ADVANCE CHECKED—BRAVERY OF THE MEN.

Thus met, the rebel advance was checked and broken, and they were driven with awful slaughter. It is beyond all wonder how men such as the rebel troops are can fight as they do. That those ragged and filthy wretches, sick, hungry, and in all ways miserable, should prove such heroes in fight, is past explanation. Men never fought better. There was one regiment that stood up before the fire of two or three of our long range batteries and of two regiments of infantry, and though the air around them was vocal with the whistle of bullets and the scream of shells, there they stood and delivered their fire in perfect order; and there they continued to stand, until a battery of six light twelves was brought to bear on them, and before that they broke. Nothing mortal can stand a battery of six light Napoleon guns if there is plenty of grape and canister in the ammunition chests.

ARRIVAL OF FRANKLIN'S CORPS—THEIR MARCH.

Thus Sumner effectually stayed what at one time threatened to be a fearfully dangerous onslaught. But all the ground that Hooker had gained was lost, and we were as we had been before the misty daylight had dawned upon us. But there is a stir and a murmur around us different from the noise of battle. There are troops in motion behind, and here comes Franklin's corps. [illegible] daylight, this corps was in camp eight miles away, on the mountain, over which it had driven the rebels on Sunday last. There it was, in all the seemingly inextricable camp confusion, and in the valley at the foot of the same mountain was Couch's division, temporarily attached to Franklin's command. All these troops had had orders on Tuesday night to be in readiness to march at a moment's notice, and so they lay down. But the night passed, and no orders to move came, and the morning hours went by, till it seemed that they could not be wanted. But at eight o'clock the orders came, and, here they are at one. It was a good march, and, unlike most troops that make those hasty marches, they are not too late, nor are they used up. Heralded only by the jingle of their own canteens and their regular tramp, they move into the field. No slogan announces them, nor any music note tells that the Campbells are coming. But, hardy, brave and comparatively fresh, here they are.

THEY MOVE UPON THE REBELS, AND REGAIN THE LOST GROUND.

Two fresh divisions, at such a time—what can they not achieve? Forward at once they go; for it was rightly reasoned that the enemy must be fully as much shaken as we were. Onward went Slocum with the three brigades that carried Crampton's Gap so handsomely on Sunday, and onward went Smith with the brigades of Hancock, Brooks and Davidson—all glorious fellows, who first made the enemy's acquaintance on Warwick creek. Exhausted, no doubt, by his last desperate endeavor, the enemy gave way. Easily, and without the great outlay of life that it had at first cost us, the ground was won once more.

WHAT WAS ACCOMPLISHED.

Hitherto we have spoken only of what transpired on our right. There, after desperate struggles, we had won what, considered in itself alone, was a glorious battle, and our enemy was there fairly beaten.

THE ARTILLERY DUEL—ITS EFFECT.

When the batteries that participated in Hooker's attack at daylight first opened their fire and were severely felt, several rebel batteries opened upon them, and also on our advancing line. Some of these batteries were on points quite out of the battle that raged on the right. As they opened their fire, one by one, our batteries, posted on various eminences, opened on them, and in their turn were opened upon by still other rebel batteries, and thus was begun a stupendous artillery fight, which soon became quite independent of the battle on the right.

From every little hill a battery thundered, until the mountains around seemed to be shaken with the roar, and the tracks of shells and shot were woven across the valley like a network. So numerous were the batteries and so constant their fire that it was impossible to "keep up with it." However much this or that beautiful shot might excite your admiration, you could not say who made it or what battery was entitled to the credit. It is probable that the artillerists were frequently deceived themselves, and assumed as their own shots those luckier gunners had made. You can hardly estimate the effect of artillery fire save where you see the masses of infantry that it ploughs through. When, as in this battle, batteries fire at batteries, no result is perceptible, and even if a battery ceases to fire you are not sure that it is damaged. The whole artillery fire of Wednesday looked very like a waste of ammunition, though doubtless many a badly injured gun was the result.

THE LEFT APPARENTLY BEHIND TIME.

Whether any one "blundered" on the left it is impossible for us to say; but the battle there got started late and went on slowly. It was noon when the fire of musketry first announced an engagement at close quarters in that direction, and then the firing was not heavy and continuous, but desultory and light in its character.

THE FIGHT NEAR THE ANTIETAM BRIDGE.

Our first advance there was made down the slope of a hill to a bridge which crosses the Antietam river. Beyond the river the enemy had so posted his men as to sweep the bridge with a severe musketry fire, and their own advance was checked, and General Burnside seemed to hesitate. The peculiar brass pieces handled by the Hawkins Zouaves—one of the many recent experiments in artillery—were then tried on the rebels beyond, as the position was one in which regular artillery could not work; but the peculiar brass pieces achieved but little, and the enemy remained in position beyond, and kept up a severe and well directed fire on our men.

THE BRIDGE CARRIED BY A CHARGE.

[illegible] o'clock [illegible] much valuable time had been lost, the bridge was carried by a brilliant charge, in which the Eleventh Ohio and the Eleventh Connecticut participated very conspicuously, and lost many men.

THE PART IN THE ACTION TAKEN BY BURNSIDE.

If the greater obstacles constitute the post of honor on a field of battle, General Burnside may justly claim to have had that post in Wednesday's battle. Once across the river, he found the enemy before him in force and in a new position of great strength on a hill. Against this position he advanced at once, and the old valor of the divisions of Generals Cox, Willcox and Sturgis was once more triumphant, and the hill was taken. No sooner was its summit reached than a heavy battery of artillery at once opened upon his ranks with a fire that must soon have annihilated them if permitted to continue. It was at once clear that the hill was untenable unless the battery was taken. At the same time the enemy in front began to receive heavy reinforcements, and General Burnside's position became critical. To go forward with that heavy battery mowing his flank, and with an equal number of the enemy on his front, and overwhelming numbers coming up, would seem like a Balaklava madness. To stand still would only be destruction; and then came the dreadful alternative to retreat. Bitter as this alternative was, it had to be taken, and steadily the line swept back, and the hard won hill was relinquished; but it was now so fully under the fire of newly posted batteries that no enemy could occupy it.

SYKES' DIVISION IN LINE.

As Burnside's line withdrew the word was passed along the hill for Sykes' men to "fall in," and the tough old soldiers of the regular regiments, who had been lounging on the hill, quiet spectators of the battle, hurried gladly into line, joyful at the prospect that their turn had come; and there they stood, ready to check the progress of any sudden disaster.

NIGHT ARRIVES.

Night prevented further operations; but let it be clearly understood that we were only not entirely successful on the left—we suffered no disaster, nor could we suffer any; for it is the glory of General McClellan's plan of battle that, if the rebels had even routed Burnside and driven him in confusion completely off the field, our left would still have been safe—for there close in hand was Porter's corps, fresh and ready for the emergency.

M'CLELLAN'S HEADQUARTERS.

General McClellan had his headquarters during the day at a commanding point on the field. He did not remain there all the time, however, but rode over the field from point to point as the battle raged here or there, watching vigilantly its progress, and sharing the dangers of the nameless heroes who fought so bravely to win the glorious day.

SUPPER FOR THE MEN AFTER THE FIGHT.

As we rode from the field at nightfall, and passed Porterstown, near to where our wagons were parked, we noted one circumstance which alone ought to establish the superiority of our men. There was beef on the fire. All about the camp kettles stood in rows on blazing rails, and while the battle raged furiously at half a mile distant, rations were being cooked as quietly as if all were in camp. Thus our tired boys were sure of supper ere they slept, while, if the rebel soldiers had anything at all to eat that night, it must have been a scanty bite all around.

OUR KEEDYSVILLE DESPATCH.

KEEDYSVILLE, Md., Sept. 18, 1862.

The smoke of the battle of yesterday is now dispelled, and we can see more clearly what has been done.

OUR VICTORY COMPLETE.

As I announced in my letter late last night, our victory is an undeniable and glorious one, convincing to the most skeptical rebel sympathizers. Our soldiers have done what was expected of them. They have come upon the rebels, who, showing fight, were met and whipped badly at every point along the line by our invincible army. In every concerted movement yesterday we were successful, while every movement against us by the rebels was handsomely repulsed.

GENERAL M'CLELLAN'S HEADQUARTERS.

General McClellan's headquarters for the day were at a large house on the hill on the north side of the Porterstown valley, about one mile from Keedysville, and in a position overlooking the entire field of action. To the wide field of vision opened before him may be imputed a large measure of the success which attended our arms during the day.

WHEN THE FIGHT WAS MOST SEVERE—SUMNER'S CORPS.

At nine o'clock in the morning the severest fighting commenced, when Sumner's full corps became engaged with the enemy. These veterans of the peninsula pitched into the seething tide of the battle with a right good will, their old and plucky General leading them. It is said, indeed, that his undaunted courage carried a division—Sedgwick's—into the enemy's line, where they fought superior numbers successfully for an hour, though at times their situation was critical indeed. Nothing but the most daring and determined courage saved this noble body of men from annihilation.

AN ATTEMPT MADE BY THE REBELS TO CAPTURE OUR BATTERIES.

The rebels here made a bold push to capture the First Rhode Island and Kirby's, formerly Ricketts' battery, against which they have the old grudge of Fair Oaks and Savage Station to settle yet. Ricketts' light brass twelve-pounder battery poured grape and canister with destructive effect, and, with the aid of its support of infantry from the Fifteenth Massachusetts, effectually checked the enemy's advance in the direction of the battery. The fire of the combined infantry and artillery literally mowed down the rebels.

THE FIFTEENTH MASSACHUSETTS FOLLOWED THE ENEMY,

who by this time rallied their forces and received assistance. Nobly did this regiment sustain itself against the increased and increasing numbers of the rebels, bringing down scores of rebels at every discharge. They were obliged finally to fall back to the original line, which they did in good order, fighting the meantime under cover of Kirby's well directed grape and canister. The Fifteenth Massachusetts went into action with six hundred men, and came out with about two hundred uninjured, the rest killed, wounded and missing.

THE FIRST RHODE ISLAND BATTERY

was well served, and ably supported by the Thirty-fourth New York and the Baxter Zouaves, and finally drove off the rebels.

NEW YORK TROOPS IN THE THICK OF THE FIGHT.

The Thirty-fourth and Second New York Militia and Baxter's Zouaves suffered terribly. I send a partial list by telegraph of their loss. [Published in alphabetical form in another portion of the HERALD.]

ONE OF THE SEVEREST STRUGGLES

occurred near Numas' house and barn, where a large force of rebel infantry were posted, with some artillery. To-day I viewed the scene there, and the ground is covered with rebel dead and wounded. Fire from several of our batteries was directed there with terrible effect, as the hecatomb of victims lying there attest. Numas' house and barn were destroyed by fire, making a splendid spectacle after the night began to darken.

COL. PRATT, OF NEW YORK,

was wounded in four places at different times during the day. After he had received the second wound and was bleeding profusely, he led his men into a most gallant and successful charge, receiving his death wounds. His is, I think, a new regiment.

THE COLONEL OF THE SEVENTEENTH MICHIGAN WAS KILLED while advancing his men to a bayonet charge after they had exhausted their ammunition.

SILENCING THE REBEL BATTERIES.

The Washington artillery, of New Orleans, was the last battery of the enemy to cease firing last evening, all the rest having previously become silent. It is supposed that want of ammunition was one cause of the slacking of the rebel fire in the latter part of the day. Our well served and numerous batteries, however, did the most towards silencing the enemy's batteries. In the afternoon the rebels were using the ammunition captured at Harper's Ferry with more effect than their ammunition used in the morning. The enemy used in this engagement railroad iron slugs and smooth stones as missiles of destruction.

NEW YORK REGIMENTS WHICH SUFFERED SEVERELY.

The following New York regiments suffered severely:—Eighty-second, Thirty-fourth, Fifty-ninth, Sixty-ninth, Fifty-third, Ninth, Forty-second.

A "FEELER" SENT INTO THE REBEL LINES.

This morning, September 18, a few shells were thrown into the enemy's lines to ascertain their whereabouts.

FLAG OF TRUCE TO BURY THE DEAD.

Shortly afterwards a flag of truce came out from the rebels to solicit permission to bury their dead. This was granted by Gen. McClellan, and until four o'clock this afternoon [illegible] to do the work. Our forces are [illegible] condition to renew the engagement begun so gloriously yesterday with increased force. I remained in front until half past three this afternoon. At that time a heavy rain began, which would prevent further hostilities. The pickets on the outer posts have been firing at intervals to-day; but I heard no volleys. Six regiments from General Cox's division are engaged at South Mountain to-day in burying the rebel dead from the battle of Sunday last.

OUR BOONSBORO DESPATCH.

BOONSBORO, Md., Sept. 18, 1862.

WHERE THE REBEL FORCES WERE MASSED, AND WHY.

On Tuesday night the enemy massed his forces under Lee, Jackson and Longstreet, with the intention of turning McClellan's right flank. At daylight artillery skirmishing was commenced on the right, and continued until about a quarter of eight o'clock, when musketry firing commenced, the opposing forces having got within musket range of each other. This was near Sharpsburg, and about five or six miles northeast of Boonsboro.

OUR FORCES ENGAGED IN THE FIGHT.

Sumner's corps was mainly engaged. Sedgwick's and French's divisions were formed in line of battle, and advanced in two lines across the field and through woods. The brigade of General Max Weber formed the first line

[CONTINUED ON EIGHTH PAGE.]

Daily Mississippian.

F. T. COOPER, Editor.

☞ *For interesting Reading Matter see First Page.*

JACKSON, - - SEPTEMBER, 22, 1862.

NORTHERN PAPERS.—Our friends who come in possession of late Northern papers, would confer a great favor upon us by leaving or sending them to this office. Newsboys who have them for sale will please bear in mind that they can always get the highest price for them at our counter. tf

☞ Owing to a press of other matters, we have been unable to print the Blanks for obtaining pay due deceased soldiers. So soon as printed notice will be given, and in the meantime we will keep a list of all money received for Blanks and forwarded as soon as printed.

Banishing their Generals.

Gen. Pope has been assigned to the command of the Northwest, with his headquarters at St. Paul. Cassius M. Clay is ordered to report to the Brute in New Orleans for duty. They have been troublesome customers to the Gorilla.

☞ The Brandon Republican thinks Van Dorn brought joy and gladness to the hearts of the people of this military District on two occasions. 1st, when he took command at Vicksburg; 2d, when he left it.

Our Progress.

Everywhere the cause of the South is on the high road of success. Since the second great battle of Manassas and the ignominious route at Richmond, Kentucky, we can point to many substantial and decided successes. The capture of Iuka by General Armstrong, with from one to three millions dollars worth of army stores and two hundred prisoners, is not a small item by any means; and it may be regarded as a precurser of still more disastrous defeats for the invaders. Gen. Price will prove as great a terror to the stampeding Yankees as an uncaged lion would to a flock of panic stricken sheep. Rumors of a reliable character are already rife of his having bagged an entire Federal brigade in the vicinity of Iuka with five pieces of cannon.

We have also information of the capture of nearly two regiments of Curtis' army in the rear of Helena.

The tremendous haul made by our invincible Stonewall Jackson, in the surrender of Harper's Ferry, and 11,000 psisoners, 15,000 small arms, 73 pieces of cannon, 400 wagons, and an immense amount of other stores, struck our people with amazement, and when the intelligence first flashed over the wires, it looked so good that we were afraid to credit it. There remains, however, no doubt of its truth. We have the official report of old Stonewall himself, which settles the matter.

In Maryland, a great battle was raging in the early part of last week, the full details of which have not yet reached us. We do not doubt our having gained another complete victory, though we fear it was at heavy loss on our side as well as the enemy's. In this battle the army at Washington may be regarded as making a last, dying effort to drive back the victorious legions of the Confederates. If they fail, as fail they will, there will remain no great obstacle to impede the march of our armies to Washington City, Baltimore and Pennsylvania.

We shall await with intense anxiety the particulars of this battle. Our success in Virginia has been greater then we had hoped for, and matters are fast assuming a most cheering aspect in the West.

Bad effect of Lying---Down on Pope.

The New York World is down on "Strategy" and "news for Buncombe:" it thinks the North has had a surfeit, and that the people are sick of being crammed with "victories on paper" and "glorious news" by telegraph, which a week later they find out are "bitter" reverses. Speaking of Pope and his repeated discomfitures, and the onward march of our forces it says:

> Unless our force is so strong that such perfect knowledge of our purposes by the enemy is no detriment to their successful execution, the whole plan of the campaign must be changed. It will hardly *do* to say that *we are thus strong* when the loss met with *occurred during a retreat.*
>
> This loss is so stunning and so complete that the report of it would hardly be credited did it come in any doubtful shape.

"It will *hardly* do to say we are thus strong" according to the World's lately discovered moral, that lying is but a poor way to gain the confidence of the people when but six or seven days can elapse ere it is found out. That dodge it seems has had its day even in Yankeedom. Alluding to the capture of all of Pope's correspondence, papers, maps, plans of campaign, muster rolls, &c., by Stuart at Catlett's Station he exclaims:

> The raid on the flank of our Peninsula army is not comparable to this.

Speaking of the knowledge that Lincoln must have had of Pope's "unveracity," as he terms it, the World continues:

> It is incredible that *he* can have been deceived by the telegrams with which it was attempted to *amuse and appease the public*, or that Gen. Pope's act in *returning to his brigade commanders the lists of killed, wounded and missing sent in by them,* as incorrect and exaggerated, *can have blinded the President's eyes* any more than it did theirs to *the measure of our disaster* and the plentiful lack of generalship which caused it.

Now here's a confession of the *heretofore* course of the Federal President, Cabinet, Generals and the Press. The telegrams issued "by authority" and published by all the papers with flaming headings "to amuse and appease the public," deliberately misstating all the facts, the World intimates was fully known by the President to be false and yet he sanctions them, and wittingly uses his place to cover up the lies. "It is incredible HE can have been deceived." He knew that Gen. Pope had refused to receive the *official reports* of his subordinate Generals that thereby he might allege he did not know the extent of his loss, which was so large it would not do to go before the people. It would not "amuse or appease the public" to let them know "the measure of the disaster," and so though the President's eyes were not blinded, the people must be, —and honest Old Abe says Ay! to the deception and shows he is worthy to be the head man among the Yankees. Truly he is a fit representative of the Yankees and their peculiar National characteristic.

☞ The late orders of the Northern military authorities are having the effect of disclosing a great many surprising natural facts in connection with that people. One is that the years 1815 and 1816 were unusually productive of children, while the two succeeding years, 1817 and 1818, yielded extremely few—at least of the masculine gender. The consequence is that they have a great many men among them aged forty-five and forty-six, and very few aged forty-three and forty-four. Another is that those holiday deficiencies and afflictions which disqualify men for soldiers, have been rather servicable to them in the ordinary pursuits and duties of life. An unusual number, it is said, of these carrying on extensive business and possessed of abundant means, are procuring exemption documents, while the "poor devils" are found to be much more generally blessed with sound constitutions and straight limbs. This is an item of natural compensation of which we were never before aware. Again, it is said, that in some localities, there is scarcely a father of a large and interesting family who is not a cripple. The strangest effect, however, has been produced upon certain bachelors. From being young, many have been most suddenly turned old. Many, after having for long years remained stationary upon the banks of the river Time, like timid swimmers by the cool, deep waters, "afraid to launch away," have suddenly taken the plunge, and come up far from the shore.

TABLEAUX VIVANTS.—The ladies of Port Gibson on the night of the 28th ult., under the supervision and direction of Mrs. Whitney, gave an elegant entertainment in the way of tableaux vivants for the benefit of Col. Hugh's regiment of Partizan Rangers; the net results of which were $351. We have a chaste and well written description of the whole performance, from which we conclude that it reflected great credit upon Mrs. W. and her fair associates. We shall be glad to publish the description sent us if we can find room for it.

CAPITAL SINS.—It is announced as one of the seven capital sins, to bore the printer! another for the printer to bore his readers!

The Affair at Iuka.

We have a private letter from a soldier of Gen. Price's army, detailing some of the particulars of the capture of Iuka, prisoners and various army stores.

On Thursday the 11th inst, early in the morning the army marched from Baldwin, and would have reached Iuka, perhaps, before the Feds had stampeded but for the imperfect arrangement of the Commissary department. As it was they marched within four miles of Iuka by Saturday night, where they slept upon their arms till dawn.

Old Sol ushered in as beautiful a Sabbath morning as was ever beheld. The troops were ordered forward, and "Old Pap" (the paternal cognomen by which Gen. Price is designated,) was setting upon his horse at the head of the column; and as each company filed past he saluted them, expressing his confidence in their coolness and courage, urging them to be lively that they might reach the town before the expected Yankee reinforcements arrived, and whip them out in detail.

When within two miles of town, Capt. I. V. Brooks with his company were thrown forward as skirmishers. The skirmishers changed direction and flanked the town to the left. When they reached the Memphis and Charleston road the dust raised by the retreating Federals was so great that they could scarcely see themselves. They saw, however, large quantities of Yankee and negro clothes, blankets, quilts, *empty* bottles, etc. But the Feds had left about an hour before, taking with them about one thousand negroes. They had got off in too big a hurry to destroy either the town or any of their commissary or quartermaster's stores, of which a goodly quantity fell into our hands. Stores to the worth of a million of dollars were captured.

Fifty or sixty wagons were ready to drive off, but the teamsters did not have time to hitch the teams, but thought it wise to save their own bacon by leaving the wagons and riding off upon the mules. Sixteen hundred barrels of flour remained in one pile near the station house besides what was found in the commissary. About eight thousand sacks of grain were piled up on the edge of the town, besides some five thousand more upon the plats at the depot. Cheese, lard, salt, clothes, and various "good things" were found in abundance; such as the Yankees can and will furnish in quantity as long as their "green-backs" are current with the people.

Our friend whose letter is dated the 15th inst., the day after the capture adds:

> It is generally rumored in camp this morning, (but I cannot vouch for the correctness of the rumor) that our cavalry overtook and captured their train of wagons that had gone, consisting of 110 wagons heavily loaded, and also two trains of cars that the scouts had torn up the Railroad track and stopped. They got yesterday morning in the suburbs, thirty-four prisoners, and others were brought in during the day, and besides several negroes; but the rickest thing of the season took place yesterday evening, when one hundred and six jolly looking fellows who had been out on a scout or "Steal," came riding through our lines, and found themselves in a rebel camp, and were marched off to prison under their own banner.—Some of our boys tell me they saw them, and that they looked exceedingly chagrined.
>
> Upon the whole we have made quite a success of it, for it was next to impossible for us to know the status of the enemy. True, had we known their force, we could have divided, so as to make sure of them; but had we divided thus and been deceived, we might have lost a goodly number of our men. As it was, we came as near completely surprising them as any one could have done, for they knew not of our approach until it was even too late to burn the town and destroy their stores, but entrusted that to one of their suttlers who did not do it, so here we have all, and yet a bloodless victory, truly that kind in which every sensible man would prefer to participate, provided the same amount of good could be accomplished; but they never have and never will meet the enemy in better condition of mind than were we on yesterday morning, for doing real good hard fighting. Fifteen miles below here we began to see the works of the destroyer's savage and beastly indulgence. Here we saw a lady they had robbed of every thing she had, even to the watch out of her pocket. From that point to this, they have robbed and burned all the houses that have given them the least show of disrespect; and citizens here tell us that yesterday morning they had five hundred negroes around in line of battle, and those that would not agree to fight and stay with them they shot or hung. I saw three that had been shot by them, lain out in the dead room.
>
> We made the Yankees bury the dead NIGGERS.—I do not know, and did I, would not tell what we will do next, or when we will do it, or how many men we have to do it with.

Ponchatoulas Fight.

CAMP RUGGLES, Near, Ponchatoulas, La.,
September 16th, 1862.

EDITOR DAILY MISSISSIPPIAN:—As quite a number of contradictory reports have been circulated relative to our little fight at this place, I have concluded to give you a correct synopsis of the whole affair.

The enemy disembarked at Pass Manshac and came up the railroad within a mile and a half of town when our pickets fired at them, giving us the alarm when immediately we proceeded to meet them at the depot, where a brisk engagement took place which lasted about one half hour, when, unfortunately, the misunderstanding of an order caused our men to fall back. Col. Witte then took command, rallied the men, charged the enemy and drove him from the place.

Our troops under the command of the Colonel behaved nobly and charged with great gallalantry, doing credit to themselves and honor to their country.

Casualties on our side one killed and six wounded—that of the Federals five killed and eight prisoners, seven of whom are wounded—among them one captain. We also have their surgeon and hospital stewart. We captured about twenty stand of arms. They set on fire four box-cars which contained about twelve hhds. of sugar, which was all the damage we sustained. The Depot and our commissary stores were saved.

Too much praise cannot be awarded to Captain McRae, for the gallantry he displayed in the action.

I have just learned from a reliable source that the enemy carried five women off with them.

Respectfully,

LOUISIANA.

Letter from I-u-ka.

From our Special Correspondent]

I-U-KA, September 17th, 1862.

This place was occupied by our troops on the morning of the 14th, the Federals having evacuated during the previous night. On the 13th our advance, consisting of cavalry alone, attacked the force then garrisoned and strongly entrenched here. The skirmishers on our side consisted of cavalry alone, and on the side of the enemy cavalry, infantry and a section of artillery. Our cavalry charged the rifle pits twice and were driven back each time. The loss on each side was very small, we losing five men and officers, and the enemy about four times as many. Ten of their dead have been found upon the field.

The force garrisoned here was less than 1500, though it was supposed to have consisted of two brigades, and great disappointment is felt that we did not succeed in capturing the whole garrison. Were it not that the cavalry were a days' march ahead of the forces there is no doubt to be entertained that the whole body would have been made prisoners. When it was discovered that cavalry alone was unable to cope with the enemy's entrenched position and artillery, the infantry and heavy guns were hastened forward, marching at 11 o'clock at night, after having already endured a fatigoing day's march, and being without provisions, owing to the detention of the wagon trains. At 8 o'clock, on the morning of the 14th, the troops marched into Iuka, capturing over a million dollars worth of stores without firing a gun. Their rapid march was all that saved the place from destruction. They had passed, during the march, twelve dwelling houses burnt to the ground and three mills destroyed by the vandals, and they were now in pursuit of them, and felt but little inclined to take many prisoners. Upon their arrival the place exhibited a strange aspect. The fields covered with household goods and furniture, which the citizens had removed preparatory to the burning of her houses by the Yankees. Our boys caught the miscreants who were left behind to fire the place, and it is to be hoped they will be summarily dealt with.

The scene of desolation they have left in their rear, is sad indeed to contemplate. Women and children robbed of their homes and clothing, were deprived of their once happy homestead, and with nothing in the world to subsist upon. Such is the picture that was presented to our view. The vandals vamoosed in the direction of Corinth, and our forces have overtaken and are skirmishing with them near Burnsville. We can scarcely march rapidly enough to overtake the main body.

On the morning the troops were marching to occupy this place, Gen. Price rode along the line encouraging the troops and inciting them to a more rapid march. He said to them: "Boys, this is my birth day, I am fifty-three years old to-day, and I desire you to celebrate it by taking 5300 prisoners!" A deafening cry arose and they replied to their veteran leader that they would endeavor to properly celebrate it. "Then," said he, "march along a little faster and we shall catch them." The whole army at once started on a double-quick and never gave out until they occupied the place.

A considerable quantity of cotton was captured at the depot which had been drawn there for shipment. Immense stores of commissariat and quartermaster also fell into our hands, and the troops had quite a feast off Yankee cheese, pineapples, preserves, jellies, etc.

The Federals have been occupied for two or three weeks in withdrawing their forces from along the line of the Memphis and Charleston railroad and concentrating them at Corinth. It is now doubtful whether they have evacuated that place as reported. If they still remain there, there will be a fight or a foot-race to communicate to you in my next.

We had a skirmish with them yesterday at Burnsville, twenty-one miles west of this, and some artillery firing, but I have not yet learned the result.

We are now only seven miles from Eastport, on the Tennessee river, and if it is deemed desirable to get in the rear of Rosencranz there will be but little difficulty in so doing.

WARRIOR.

Brilliant Victory near Helena.

The Vicksburg Whig of Friday says our forces in the rear of Helena bagged an entire regiment of Curtis' army last week. Curtis has been courtmartialed and sent North. There are twenty-eight thousand troops reported at Helena.

We have a letter from a friend at Friar's Point, dated 15th inst., giving interesting additional facts concerning our victory near Helena. We extract as follows:

We have just received reliable information from Helena that fighting had commenced, twenty-five miles back from that place. On Wednesday 3700 Federals were sent out to drive back our advance; our men formed on both sides of the road in the form of a ⊳, we sent out a body of skirmishers to draw them into the ambush, in which they succeeded, the wings of V then closing and capturing one Ohio regiment complete and all but forty of another regiment. On Thursday they again attacked our forces and were whipped back. On Friday they again attacked and claim that they whipped our troops back.

There is a great deal of sickness in their camp. Many of their officers say that old Curtis has made over one million of dollars in his speculations in cotton, mules and horses—buying through his agents from negroes.

Yours,

By Telegraph

Further Particulars of the Fight at Harper's Ferry and Maryland.

RICHMOND, Sept. 19.—Gov. Letcher received letters to-day from Winchester, dated the 16th, confirming the report of the unconditional surrender of 11,000 Yankees at Harper's Ferry on Monday, without the loss of a man on our side.

Jackson captured fifty pieces of artillery, ammunition stores, etc.

The letters also mention an engagement in Maryla[illegible] betw[illegible] Boonesboro' and Middleton, in which [illegible] ene[illegible] were repulsed with the reported [illegible] o[illegible] ki[illegible]ed and wounded.

The Confederate loss was heavy.

No further particulars received.

RICHMOND, September 20.—Colonel Lindsay Walker arrived here to-day from Harper's Ferry, which place he left Wednesday evening. The cannon and stores captured had been removed.

There had been no fighting since the capture of Harper's Ferry on Monday. Our army was in fine spirits.

McClellan, with his army, was in our front, near Sharpsburg, and a general battle was expected.

General Reno (Yankee) was killed in the fight near Boonesboro'.

Jackson's official report of the capture of Harper's Ferry, dated the 16th, says: "Yesterday God crowned our army with another brilliant success, in the surrender, at Harper's Ferry, of Brigadier-General White and 11,000 troops, an equal number of small arms, seventy-three pieces of artillery, and about two hundred wagons, in addition to other stores; there is also a large amount of camp and garrison equipage. Our loss is very small."

GREAT BATTLE AT SHARSBURG!

The Whole Strength of Both Armies Engaged!

Heavy Loss on Both Sides!

THE CONFEDERATES VICTORIOUS!!

RICHMOND, September 21st.—The Enquirer has a dispatch from Warren the 20th, announcing a terrific fight at Sharpsburg on Wednesday, the advantage on our side—great loss on both sides. Generals Stark, Manning and Branch, killed; General D. R. Jones, R. R. Jones, Ripley and Lawton, wounded.

The whole strength of both armies were engaged in the fight. Report says the fight was renewed on Thursday, and the enemy routed and driven nine miles.

RICHMOND, September 21st.—The New York Herald of the 18th claims a victory at Sharpsburg. Its dispatches are contradictory, but concur in stating that the Confederates were defeated.

Letters from Louisville claim a victory over Duncan and Scott's forces at Mumfordsville, Kentucky.

The Bermuda correspondent of the New York Herald says, five steamers are lying in Port St. George awaiting opportunity to run the blockade.

The United States Arsenal at Pittsburg blew up Wednesday. Seventy or eighty boys and girls were killed.

In New York, Wednesday, gold opened at 116⅞, and advanced to 117¾.

CONGRESSIONAL.

RICHMOND, Sept. 19.—SENATE—The House bill to provide for the payment of troops raised by Gen. Price, was passed.

The exemption bill was futher considered.

The House passed a bill fixing the rank and pay of Adjutants in independent battalions, also adopted a resolution of thanks to Maj. Gen. Magruder and command.

Foote, from committee on Foreign affairs, reported back the resolutions in relation to the conduct of the war and the navigation of the western rivers, with modifications.

Barksdale, of Miss., presented a minority report. Both the reports were ordered to be printed.

RICHMOND, Sept. 20.—In the Senate the military exemption bill was further considered and finally passed. Yeas 16—Nays 3.

In the House, the Senate bill fixing the second Monday in January as the time of meeting of the next regular session of Congress, was passed. Also the House bill to provide for the more prompt settlement of the claims, arrearages and bounty due to deceased soldiers.

The Arkansas contested election case was discussed until adjournment.

Daily Mississippian

We are authorized to announce the name of S. S. GRANBERRY as a candidate for the office of Circuit Clerk of Hinds County.*

We are authorized to announce the name of J. J. STAMPS as a candidate for Coroner of Lawrence County, Mississippi. Election in October next.*

We are authorized to announce the name of B. F. EDWARDS as a candidate for Clerk of the Circuit Court of Hinds County. Election, October 6, 1862.*

We are authorized to announce the name of HOWELL HOBB as a candidate for re-election to the office of Board of Police, Jackson Police District. Election, October 6, 1862.*

We are authorized to announce the name of Capt. J. L. McMANUS, as a candidate for re-election to the office of Clerk of the Circuit and Chancery Court of Hinds County. Election in October.*

Candidates wishing tickets printed, will forward their *orders*, with the *cash*, and the tickets will be sent by return mail. Address Mississippian office, Jackson, Miss.

Casualties in 16th Regiment.

List of casualties in the Sixteenth Mississippi Regiment, in the battle of August 30th, 1862:

Company A.—K 1 d, Corporal Enos B. Cogden. Wounded, Sergeant Miller, since dead; Corporal Gibson, M. M. Wadsworth, slightly; W. H. Montgomery, Lieut. Collins, Edward Delany now in ranks; John Newsom, A. T. Watts, Geo. Byrd, D. C. Carter.

Company B.—Killed, none.

Wounded, Capt. W. J. Crame, slightly; Color Corporal B. F. Brown, Robert Mangum, W. Johnson, John Conley, in thigh; John Young, G. S. Hemphill, W. N. Simpson, A. Leido, German Peacock, severely; Geo. Box, slightly.

Company C.—Killed, S. L. Wright.

Wounded, J. T. Luckwood, severely; G. W. Hughes, slightly; W. T. McDade, R. E. Currie, H. C. Dickson, C. Letingers, J. J. Wilson, J. M. Broome, A. R. Broome, R. W. Daniels, Jas. Bolls, Capt. E. Slay.

Company D.—Killed, G. W. Wood, Thomas Leary.

Wounded, Lieut. P. P. Baker, severely; J. L. James, A. Worham, Tobias Burke, Robert Phipps, Henry Williams, Mike Burke, Pat. O'Donnell, Martin Dunn, slightly; Hugh Smith, since dead; Larry, wounded mortally; Thomas Hurley, B. T. Lewis, Joseph Byrnes, seriously; W. D. Cole, missing.

Company E.—Wounded, W. L. Williams, lost arm; B. D. Bankston, Mathew Willson, John A. Walker, Serg't Benj. J. Holmes, slightly.

Company F.—Killed, G. W. Hair, J. W. Lewlen, Wm. Sheppard.

Wounded, Geo. C. Huddlebrand, mortally; Capt. A. B. Myers, do; Corporal G. W. Keeler, F. C. Morris, W. B. Morris, B. F. Duke, J. M. Lee, C. M. McCurdy, slightly.

Company G.—Wounded, E. M. Jeffries, severely, since dead; Serg't James Jones, James Creamley, since dead; E. Hutchinson, F. A. Christian, slightly.

Company H.—Killed, Samuel Floyd, J. E. Whittington, W. E. Daniels, John D. Summer.

Wounded, Lieut. T. J. Hardy, slightly; R. B. Roykin, D. V. Summer, J. B. Wilkins, J. C. Summer.

Company I.—Wounded, Capt. S. Fletcher, P. Crowder, J. Dunn, E. Murphy, J. Dunn, mortally, since dead.

Company K.—Killed, none.

Wounded, John L. Davis, in head; August 21st and May 30th; Serg't W. H. Lewis, in hand; Serg't Jos. Johns, in leg; B. F. Herbert, leg; W. T. Pouncey and George Thornton, severely; T. O. Wright, in face; T. F. Williams, slightly; Sergeant-Major H. S. Van Eaton, W. C. West, Sol. Jacob, slightly.

J. RUTH, Adjutant.

Although this regiment has been engaged in three pitched battles, viz: Cross Keys, Cold Harbor and the great fight of the 30th of August, at Manassas, and also in five skirmishes, in all of which it suffered severely, it is still one of the largest regiments in the service.

In the Battle of the 30th, at Manassas, Brigadier General Featherston being called to the command of the division, Col. Posey commanded the brigade through the hottest of the fight.

For the Mississippian.

I Want to be "An Officer."

MR EDITOR:—I have just completed a tour through our army, and I find it truly a great institution. I am so much pleased with all I saw, that although having heretofore considered myself much too old and feeble to be in the service, I am now determined to enter it, provided I can get "an office." I would not miss being "an officer" in the army for a great deal. I discovered in my rambles that there is some mysterious agency, (it may be supernatural,) that immediately changes every faculty and the character of a man so soon as he "becomes an officer." He is made astoundingly wise and grand, and seems to acquire the happy faculty of keeping at a respectful distance all with whom he has any dealings. Just think how fine it would be for a common individual like myself to be by some "presto change" converted into a man of wisdom and grandeur, and to be by this change made so much better than my former superiors as to be entitled to the happy privilege of keeping them all at a "respectful distance." This would be so glorious that I naturally thirst for it.

This astonishing change comes to some degree over all the officers, but what is singular, and what suits me best too, (for I never expect to get a high office,) is, that the lower the rank the greater was the change, and the changes in that progression are truly wonderful. For instance, I met men in subordinate positions, whom I had previously known to be so ignorant, as not to be able to put one sentence in English correctly together, and who had moved in so moderate a social circle that they would have felt themselves complimented to have been noticed in public by some of the same men whom they now hold at a *"respectful distance."* I say that I met these very same men as petty local officers, and wonderful to tell they had grown grand, and had become so changed in manner, (much for the better of course,) that they were as silent and looked as wise as —— there is no necessity of making a comparison. I know they were wise, for they spoke only in monosyllables, and in their mute wisdom they felt so much the grandeur with which they had been endowed, that when they spoke it was in accents so sharp and fierce, that they would almost "raise you out of your boots." Oh! how I would like to become so suddenly wise and grand as to be able to do all this, for I tell you, sir, that priding myself then on these newly acquired qualities of mind and manner, I would stroke my beard with grave dignity while musing over my importance in the world.

I met, ... some unhappy exceptions to this "presto change" rule, and the most unfortunate of those whom this wonderful influence touched lightly, was General J. C. Breckenridge, as it seemed to have missed him entirely. Poor fellow! how I pittied him when I saw that this "presto change" had overlooked him altogether. He, sir, was so humbled by the slight of that mysterious influence, that he was acting like he had always acted. He was courteous and polite to everybody, and he felt his humiliation so greatly, that he was even respectful to his men, and they in return were so tickled at his misfortune in not having received the benefits of this mysterious influence, that they were the happiest set of fellows I met in the army. They were actually kicking up their heels with delight. Poor Breckenridge suffered too in other ways, for I looked at him well, when, supporting only an ordinary uniform, he was riding about seated on a common Mexican saddle, and I know he must have envied the bespangled officers that would pass him, particularly those riding on horses so richly and *extensively* caparisoned, that you could scarcely see anything else except their tails and ears. Ye rulers! would it not be glorious to have such uniforms, and such saddles and bridles! How I would then hang around towns and public places to show them off! and then, too, when I observed a man approaching me, it mattered not how elegant and refined he was, if he did not support the *"lace and stars,"* I could say to some one, "tell that fellow that I cannot be interrupted!"

I tell you, Mr. Editor, I want to be an officer, but I do not wish that "presto change" to miss me like it did General Breckinridge—for I *really want to cut a dash!* I have got a good chin-beard, and can stroke it as grandiloquently as anybody; and if I can only wear a brass button or two, and a little colored tape, and this "presto" agency will operate on me as it has ON SOME I KNOW, how I will strut—and look wise, and cut up everybody that undertakes to talk to me.

I write to you, sir, to request your editorial influence in having me elected or appointed to an office. I am not very particular about the grade; so if you cannot do any better for me, I am willing to go low down enough in rank to be only entitled to wear a button on the turned up side of my hat trim. This will answer me very well, for as this wonderful change in the officer increases in arithmetical progression as you descend in rank, I could then with the aid of that agency, (Æsop might caution me here,) outswell any of our Generals.

Hoping you much success in your efforts in my behalf, and me, in my aspirations,

I am, your devoted friend,

BRANTLEY.

The "Beast" Once More."

The London Saturday Review has a scathing criticism on Butler's apology for his brutal order respecting the women of New Orleans. We give, as a specimen of the article, the following extract:

This is General Butler's commentary on his own order; and he has also illustrated it by his practice. At the funeral of a Federal officer, one Lieutenant DeKay, it appears that a Southern lady of remarkable spirit and ingenuous freedom of tongue, made herself conspicuous by sitting in her balcony and displaying Southern colors and otherwise misconducting herself. Not that she stood alone, for the whole of New Orleans sympathised with her, and the scene in the church where the funeral service was celebrated was so violent that, in a transport of rage wholly unbecoming to so savory a professor as Gen. Butler, that religious commander declared that if he had been there he would have bombarded the church. The Bomba of the North vented his holy indignation not on the church but on the lady. Mrs. Phillips was at once arrested, and another general order, quite equal to his infamous proclamation, was at once issued. Mrs. Phillips, on being subjected to the gentle commander's interrogation, with Southern vivacity replied, "I was in good spirits that day." Flesh and blood, at least General Butler's flesh and blood, could not stand this sharp artillery of woman's tongue. "It is therefore ordered that she be not regarded and treated as a common woman, but as an uncommon, bad and dangerous woman," and therefore he sends her into solitary confinement. Butler's wit is worthy of his namesake who wrote *Hudibras;* and he might have been contented with the sly joke of styling Mrs. Phillips an uncommon specimen of a common woman. The retort would have been ample vengeance for the lady's pertness. In the tongue duel the General had the best of it. There was hardly a necessity for clenching his pleasantry by transporting the defeated joker to a felon's prison as well. Poor Mrs. Phillips finds it to be a sad mistake to bandy sharp sayings with the commander of an army of occupation, just as somebody else discovered that it was of no use to argue with the master of ten legions.

But the value of General Butler's second general order is the light it throws not only on his first general order, but on his own explanation of its meaning. Mrs. Phillips is not to be treated as a common woman, but is to be ordered to prison. The inference is plain, that the New Orleans ladies and common women are not to be treated as Mrs. Phillips is treated. She is imprisoned, because she is not to be regarded as a common woman. How, then, are common women to be treated? As Mrs. Phillips was not treated? But, according to his own account of his own meaning, this imprisonment was exactly what he says he threatened all the ladies with.

Either, then, General Butler's joke loses its point, and he has treated Mrs. Phillips as a common woman, or in his "infamous proclamation" he did not intend that sense to be given to it which he has recently invented in his letter of explanation to his Boston friend. One way or the other, Gen. Butler has tumbled into an obvious inconsistency. He must either abandon his joke or his explanation. By his treatment to Mrs. Phillips he has proved that his proclamation was intended in that sense which every reasonable being has attached to it. He has convicted himself out of his own mouth; and as General Butler likes scripture and knows his Bible, we make him a present of the language as well as the sense of the text.

Of course, all this is poor work. It is lamentably easy to unmask a sanctimonious ruffian like this Butler; and—for insensibly one slips into too much scriptural allusion, which is almost defiled by applying it, except in retort, to so great a master in inspired language—we feel a certain kind of ceremonial defilement, and seem to be unclean till the evening while touching such as General Butler. But a serious question remains. Is the South to be held by an army of pro-consuls like this? Here is New Orleans, the second city of the American continent, a city, as Gen. Butler says, "seven miles long by two to four wide, of 150,000 inhabitants, all hostile, bitter, defiant, explosive, standing literally on a magazine, a spark only needed for destruction."

It can only be held by threats of bombarding churches, and by actually imprisoning women. Every woman is a Jael in it. But New Orleans does not stand alone. Every city and town and village in the South is alive with the like of Mrs. Phillips; and when the legions of the North have triumphed, and when the unknown sons and daughters of those whom the Butlers, and the like of Butler, have consigned to infamy and Ship Island, can lisp curses, they will be showered with even more than Mrs. Phillips' "good spirits" on the conquerors and oppressors. Is this the tenure by which the Union is to be preserved?

New Advertisements.

District of the Mississippi—Special Order, No. 12.

VI.

Headquarters, Jackson, Miss., Sept. 19, 1862.

THE following General Order is published for the information of all whom it may concern, in this District.

By order of Brig. Gen. Ruggles,

R. M. HOOE, A. A. Gen.

ADJUTANT AND INSPECTOR GENERAL'S OFFICE, Richmond, Sept. 8, '62.

General Order, No. 64.

IV.

COMMANDERS of Army Corps, Regiments, and Battalions, will make to this office monthly returns of their respective commands on the forms furnished and according to the directions expressed on them.

Officers in charge of Camps of Instructions, will make to this office on the 10th, 20th and 30th of each month, returns of the state of the recruiting service, showing the number of conscripts enrolled in camp at the date of last report; the number enrolled and accepted during the period for which report is made, the number sent forward to regiments, and the total remaining in camp.

By order S. COOPER, Adjutant and Inspector Gen'l.

Official: R. M. HOOE, A. A. G.

Sept. 22, 1m.

ELECTION PROCLAMATION.

JOHN J. PETTUS, Governor of the State of Mississippi, to the Sheriffs of the counties of the State aforesaid. Greeting.

Whereas the first Monday in October, A. D., 1862, is the day appointed by law, for holding all elections in this State; and whereas it is made my duty to issue a writ requiring you to hold the said election at the time and places appointed by law.

And therefore, I, John J. Pettus, Governor of the State of Mississippi, do issue this my writ, requiring you to hold an election, at the several precincts in your county, on the first Monday in October, A. D. 1862, for the following officers to serve for the time specified by law, to-wit:

One Judge of the High Court of Errors and Appeals for the 2nd Judicial District.

One Circuit Judge for the District in which your county is included by law.

One District Attorney for the District in which your county is included by law.

One Judge of the Probate Court.
One Clerk of the Probate Court.
One Clerk of the Circuit Court.
One Sheriff.
One Assessor of Taxes.
One Coroner.
One County Treasurer.
One County Surveyor.
One Ranger.

Five members of the Board of Police, and such Justices of the Peace and Constables as the law requires.

At the said election you will notice and carry out, all the requisitions of law, and make your returns duly as therein prescribed.

{L.S.} Given under my hand and the Great Seal of the State of Mississippi, hereto affixed, this 26th day of August, A.D. 1862.

JOHN J. PETTUS.

By the Governor.

C. A. BROUGHER, Secretary of State.

aug26d&wtd.

State Military Relief Fund.

AUDITOR'S OFFICE, Jackson, Sept. 18, '62.

EDS. MISSISSIPPIAN: As frequent enquiries are made as to when the pro rata shares of the several counties of the 30 per cent. Relief Fund will be made, I will state for the information of parties concerned, that it cannot be made until the Sheriffs settlements are completed and full returns of volunteers from the different counties received at this office when the County Treasurers will be notified.

Respectfully,

A. J. GILLESPIE, Auditor Public Acc'ts.

Sept. 19-2wd&w

THE NEW YORK HERALD.

WHOLE NO. 9506. NEW YORK, TUESDAY, SEPTEMBER 23, 1862. PRICE TWO CENTS

A PROCLAMATION

BY THE

PRESIDENT OF THE UNITED STATES.

Operations of the Confiscation Act.

All Slaves in States in Rebellion January 1, 1863, to Be Free.

The President Renews the Offer to Pay for Slaves of Loyalists,

&c., &c., &c.

By the President of the United States of America.

A PROCLAMATION.

WASHINGTON, Sept. 22, 1862.

I, Abraham Lincoln, President of the United States of America, and Commander-in-Chief of the army and navy thereof, do hereby proclaim and declare that hereafter, as heretofore, the war will be prosecuted for the object of practically restoring the constitutional relation between the United States and the people thereof in which States that relation is, or may be, suspended or disturbed; that it is my purpose, upon the next meeting of Congress, to again recommend the adoption of a practical measure tendering pecuniary aid to the free acceptance or rejection of all the slave States, so-called, the people whereof may not then be in rebellion against the United States, and which States may then have voluntarily adopted or thereafter may voluntarily adopt the immediate or gradual abolishment of slavery within their respective limits; and that the efforts to colonize persons of African descent, with their consent, upon the continent or elsewhere, with the previously obtained consent of the governments existing there, will be continued; that *on the first day of January, in the year of our Lord one thousand eight hundred and sixty-three, all persons held as slaves within any State, or any designated part of a State, the people whereof shall then be in rebellion against the United States, shall be then thenceforward and forever free*, and the executive government of the United States, including the military and naval authority thereof, will recognize and maintain the freedom of such persons, and will do no act or acts to repress such persons, or any of them, in any efforts they may make for their actual freedom; that the Executive will, on the first day of January aforesaid, by proclamation, designate the States and parts of States, if any, in which the people thereof respectively shall then be in rebellion against the United States; and the fact that any State, or the people thereof, shall on that day be in good faith represented in the Congress of the United States by members chosen thereto at elections wherein a majority of the qualified voters of such State shall have participated, shall, in the absence of strong countervailing testimony, be deemed conclusive evidence that such State and the people thereof have not been in rebellion against the United States.

That attention is hereby called to an act of Congress, entitled "An act to make an additional Article of War," approved March 13, 1862, and which act is in the words and figure following:—

Be it enacted by the Senate and House of Representatives of the United States of America in Congress assembled, That hereafter the following shall be promulgated as an additional article of war for the government of the Army of the United States, and shall be obeyed and observed as such:—

ARTICLE.—All officers or persons in the military or naval service of the United States are prohibited from employing any of the forces under their respective commands for the purpose of returning fugitives from service or labor who may have escaped from any persons to whom such service or labor is claimed to be due, and any officer who shall be found guilty by a court martial of violating this article shall be dismissed from the service.

SECTION 2.—*And be it further enacted*, That this act shall take effect from and after its passage.

Also to the ninth and tenth sections of an act entitled "An Act to suppress insurrection, to punish treason and rebellion, to seize and confiscate property of rebels, and for other purposes," approved July 17, 1862, and which sections are in the words and figure following:—

SECTION 9.—*And be it further enacted*, That all slaves of persons who shall hereafter be engaged in rebellion against the government of the United States, or who shall in any way give aid or comfort thereto, escaping from such persons and taking refuge within the lines of the army, and all slaves captured from such persons, or deserted by them and coming under the control of the government of the United States, and all slaves of such persons found on (or being within) any place occupied by rebel forces and afterwards occupied by the forces of the United States, shall be deemed captures of war, and shall be forever free of their servitude and not again held as slaves.

SECTION 10.—*And be it further enacted*, That no slave escaping into any State, Territory, or the District of Columbia, from any of the States, shall be delivered up, or in any way impeded or hindered of his liberty, except for crime or some offence against the laws, unless the person claiming said fugitive shall first make oath that the person to whom the labor or service of such fugitive is alleged to be due is his lawful owner, and has not been in arms against the United States in the present rebellion, nor in any way given aid and comfort thereto; and no person engaged in the military or naval service of the United States shall, under any pretence whatever, assume to decide on the validity of the claim of any person to the service or labor of any other person, or surrender up any such person to the claimant, on pain of being dismissed from the service.

And I do hereby enjoin upon and order all persons engaged in the military and naval service of the United States to observe, obey and enforce within their respective spheres of service the act and sections above recited.

And the Executive will in due time recommend that all citizens of the United States who shall have remained loyal thereto throughout the rebellion shall (upon the restoration of the constitutional relation between the United States and their respective States and people, if the relation shall have been suspended or disturbed) be compensated for all losses by acts of the United States, including the loss of slaves.

In witness whereof I have hereunto set my hand and caused the seal of the United States to be affixed.

ABRAHAM LINCOLN.

Done at the City of Washington, this twenty-second day of September, in the year of our Lord one thousand eight hundred and sixty-two, and of the independence of the United States the eighty-seventh.

By the President:

WILLIAM H. SEWARD,
Secretary of State.

MOVEMENTS OF TROOPS.

The Tenth New Hampshire Regiment En Route.

CONCORD, N. H., Sept. 22, 1862.

The Tenth New Hampshire regiment, Col. Donahue, left Manchester to-day for Washington, via New York.

The Allotment System.

We are pleased to perceive that this system is working so well, and that the men of our new levies are so generally taking advantage of it. Either they belong to a superior class or the system is becoming better understood, for there is a remarkable difference in the amount allotted by them and that at first obtained by the commissioners from the Army of the Potomac. It is no unusual thing for a regiment to allot seven or eight thousand dollars, and one went almost to nine thousand dollars a month.

The thanks of the country are due to the President for the interest he has taken in this matter; and, now that Governor Morgan has promulgated the following order, there is every promise that the labors of the commissioners will be fully successful. We think it would greatly facilitate the efforts of those gentlemen—who, it must be remembered, give their services without remuneration—if they had an assimilative rank, which would entitle them to respect in the army, without command. This would avoid annoyances—as in passing sentries and the like, which occasionally cause delay and trouble—and would insure the respect to which their important office entitles them:—

GENERAL ORDERS—NO. 72.
GENERAL HEADQUARTERS, STATE OF NEW YORK, ADJ. GENERAL'S OFFICE, ALBANY, Sept. 17, 1862.

The President of the United States having appointed Theodore Roosevelt, William E. Dodge, Jr., and Theodore B. Bronson Commissioners to procure from the soldiers of this State allotments of their pay, all officers in command of troops in this State are directed to afford them all necessary facilities for the performance of their duties.

By order of the Commander-in-Chief
THO. HILLHOUSE, Adjutant General.

Military Movements in New York and Vicinity.

THE JUDGE DALY GUARD.

Captain Duff, who is recruiting for the above organization, to be attached to the Second regiment, Corcoran's Irish Legion, is filling up his company rapidly. One hundred dollars cash over the other bounties will be paid to all who enlist in Captain Duff's company on application at the office of S. Dinges, No. 8 Pine street.

A STATEN ISLAND REGIMENT.

A mass meeting of the citizens of the Fifth Senatorial district will be held on Wednesday evening, at Mozart Gardens, Nos. 57 and 59 Columbia street, for the purpose of raising a company to be attached to Colonel Minthorne Tompkins' regiment of infantry, which is about being organized. Speeches will be made by Hon. Hiram Walbridge, Brigadier General Richard Busteed and others. The company is to be called the Tompkins Blues, in honor of the Colonel of the regiment, and to be commanded by our young friend Q. A. Riley and Lieutenant George W. Driver.

MICHIGAN SICK AND WOUNDED SOLDIERS.

The following circular has been issued to Michigan ladies at present resident in this city:—

TO MICHIGAN LADIES IN THE CITY OF NEW YORK AND ITS VICINITY:—

There are several hundred sick and wounded Michigan soldiers in the various hospitals in this city and its vicinity. They are hundreds of miles from home, but not from friends, may it ever be said. They have perilled their lives fighting the battles of their country—your battles. It is now in your power to render them some service in return, and to alleviate their sufferings in some measure. The government does all it can for them, but there are many comforts necessary to the sick which the government cannot furnish, and which money will not purchase. A visit from you would make glad their hearts and cheer them in their lonely hours. A few delicacies would be gratefully received by them and are very necessary. It is believed that many of you would gladly render efficient service if you knew where to offer it.

All who wish to aid in this humane and patriotic duty are earnestly invited to report to Darius Clark, Esq., 173 Broadway, who will systematize and direct their labors.

Presentation of a Gold Medal to General Corcoran.

We were yesterday shown a very beautiful and elegantly executed gold medal for presentation to Brigadier General Corcoran. The testimonial is from twenty-three of his fellow prisoners of the Sixty-ninth regiment, who were confined with the General in the prison at Richmond. The presentation was made last evening in the presence of a large assemblage of the General's friends at the City Assembly Rooms, No. 444 Broadway. The medal, which was executed by the well known house of Ball, Black & Co., is three and a half inches in diameter, is of gold, of twenty-two carats, and weighs three and a half ounces. On the obverse is a splendid engraving of a prison scene at Richmond, representing the farewell of the wounded prisoners on the departure of General Corcoran. The figure of the General is prominent. He is seen relieving the wants of a wounded fellow officer, while one prisoner is handing him a letter to take home, and others are lying around the prison. A rebel sentinel is seen listening at the door of the prison as he goes his rounds. On the reverse is a beautiful representation of the Union shield and arms, emblazoned with thirty-four stars, surmounted by the eagle, and supported on one side by the flag of the Sixty-ninth regiment, and on the other by the banner of the republic. The medal bears this inscription:—

Presented to
GENL. CORCORAN
BY THE
Released Prisoners of the 69th Reg't N. Y. S. M.,
21st Sept., 1862.

The medal and engraving were designed by Daniel Draddy, private of Company A, Sixty-ninth regiment, who was also imprisoned with the General. The medal is enclosed in a fine morocco box; and the whole idea and execution reflect the highest credit on General Corcoran's fellow prisoners, the designer and the artist, and will serve as a valuable heirloom, to be regarded by his posterity with admiration and affection.

Departure of General McDowell.

Major General McDowell, who has been in this city for several days, stopping at the Brevoort House, left last evening for Washington.

News from Salt Lake—The Indian Atrocities.

SALT LAKE, Sept. 22, 1862.

Charles McBride, from Virginia City, arrived here yesterday, one of a party of fifteen bound for the States. He says:—

The party were attacked by the Snake Indians at the city of Pocas, on the Humboldt route, one hundred and fifty miles north. They fought the Indians for twenty miles, losing six killed and two wounded, and all of their outfit.

John Connor, John Sharpe, Benjamin White, James Shaw, Wm. Davis and Mr. Goodman were killed. John Foster and Samuel Kelly had their arms broken.

Reports of Indian depredations northward are coming in daily, and much trouble is expected to emigration.

NEWS FROM WASHINGTON.

WASHINGTON, Sept. 21, 1862.

NO REBEL TROOPS NORTH OF BULL RUN MOUNTAINS.

Further reconnoissances on the other side of the river in front of Washington continue to demonstrate that there is no considerable force of rebels this side of the Bull run mountains.

THE MILITARY DEPARTMENTS OF MISSOURI AND OHIO.

By the direction of the President the States of Missouri, Arkansas, and the bordering Indian territory, will constitute the Department of the Missouri, and will be commanded by Major General S. R. Curtis, headquarters at St. Louis. Alton, Illinois, is attached to the Department of the Missouri. Western Virginia is attached to the Department of the Ohio; headquarters at Cincinnati.

THE MAILS RESTORED IN MARYLAND.

Mail facilities have been restored to Frederick, Hagerstown and intermediate points.

THE REMOVAL OF THE UNITED STATES CAPITAL TO NEW YORK.

People who pretend to look into the future condition of our country are beginning to talk of the importance of removing the capital to New York when the war is ended and the rebellion suppressed. They argue that the present location of the capital has been the occasion of various difficulties in the prosecution of the war. It has seriously embarrassed the movements of our army, its exposed position rendering elaborate works and large forces necessary for its defence. The necessities of the case are magnified by a set of old fogies here who become exceedingly nervous whenever the army moves its length away from Washington. Let the rebels menace this city in the slightest degree and our army must be called home to defend it, and opportunities for striking at the rebel army are lost because they fear to allow our forces to march away from the apron strings of this mother of dead politicians. If the seat of government had been at the North it would have been equivalent to a hundred and fifty thousand men added to our moveable forces.

NAVAL PROMOTION.

This correspondence recently stated that Captain Samuel Phillips Lee was appointed Acting Rear Admiral of the North Atlantic Blockading squadron. It may now be added that the same rank has been conferred upon Commodore Charles Wilkes, commanding the special West India squadron; upon Commodore J. L. Lardner, commanding the Eastern Gulf Blockading squadron; upon Commodore C. H. Davis, commanding the Naval Mississippi fleet; and upon Commodore C. H. Bell, commanding the Pacific squadron.

DROPPED FROM THE ROLLS.

Acting Master's Mate Niel Alexander having been reported to the Navy Department as a deserter, has been dropped from the rolls of the service.

CONTINUANCE OF THE OVERLAND MAIL.

The Post Office Department has ordered the continuance of the Pacific mail on the overland route, having received reliable information that there is no danger to be apprehended from their being tampered with by Indians. It is positively asserted that since the removal of the Cherokee tribe at no time has there been any necessity for the mails being discontinued. The great overland mail now passes daily through Denver. Passengers are constantly travelling on this route.

TREASURY NOTES OF SMALL DENOMINATIONS.

The Treasury Department is now getting off some eighty thousand dollars daily in notes of the denomination of one and two dollars. This amount of issue will be doubled in a few days through a multiplication of the engraved plates.

RESTRICTION OF BANK NOTE CIRCULATION.

A notice from the Secretary of the Treasury may be shortly expected, forbidding the issue of small notes by banks here, or of the circulation in this city of the small notes of Northern banks.

THE WOUNDED REBEL PRISONERS.

It is said that the wounded rebels, who, with some of our soldiers, were placed in hospital in the Capitol yesterday, are covered with vermin. Members of Congress here are expressing some interest in the matter.

EXCHANGED PRISONERS OF WAR.

According to an army order just issued, the prisoners of war, except commissioned officers, who were delivered to Lieut. Colonel Ludlow, Aid-de-Camp to Major General Dix, at Aiken's Landing, James river, Virginia, on the 14th and 15th instants, are declared to be exchanged.

THE CHEROKEES REPUDIATE THE REBELS.

William N. Ross, a relative of John Ross, has arrived here with a communication from the latter to the President, asking that the Cherokees be recognized in all their treaty rights, and setting forth that what was done by that nation seemingly favoring the rebels was under duress and from intimidation.

THE OATH OF ALLEGIANCE.

Recently instructions were given to the commanding officers of all arsenals and armories of the United States to administer the oath of allegiance to the employes under their command. Nineteen refused to take the oath at the Springfield (Mass.) Armory, on the ground that they were foreigners. The Secretary of War gave orders for their immediate dismissal.

OPINIONS OF THE FRENCH PRESS IN REGARD TO EMIGRATION TO THE UNITED STATES.

The following is an official translation from an article in *La Patrie* of September 4, 1862:—

The *Presse* publishes the following circular, communicated to it by the United States Consul in Paris, which had been addressed by the Secretary of State and Foreign Affairs at Washington to all the agents and consuls of the United States:—

TO THE DIPLOMATIC AND CONSULAR OFFICERS OF THE UNITED STATES IN FOREIGN COUNTRIES.

DEPARTMENT OF STATE, WASHINGTON, Sept. 8, 1862.

At no former period of our history have our agricultural or mining interests been more prosperous than at this juncture. The fact may be deemed surprising, in view of the enhanced price for labor occasioned by the demand for the rank and file of the United States. It may, therefore, be confidently asserted that even now nowhere else can the industrious laboring man and artisan expect so liberal a recompense for his services as in the United States. You are authorized and directed to make these truths known in any quarter, and in any way, which may lead to the migration of such persons to this country. It is believed that a knowledge of them will alone suffice to cause them to be acted upon. The government has no legal authority to offer any pecuniary inducements to the advent of industrious foreigners.

WILLIAM H. SEWARD.

The *Presse* gives to this circular the most sympathetic reception. It hastens to recommend to those of our workingmen—and these, it says, "are counted by thousands"—"who with horror see the approach of winter, and with that season the rigors of a forced suspension of labor," to respond to this appeal and to cross the Atlantic. They will thus secure to their families, through the benefits of high wages, abundant supplies. We admit that the circular of Mr. Seward meets on our part with less enthusiasm. We, therefore, recommend to the French workingmen, notwithstanding "a degree of comfort acquired readily and a fortune for some of them at least," which the *Presse* holds out as a mirror before their eyes, to be on their guard respecting the promises of the American government. It would have seemed necessary, for instance, under the present circumstances, that the circular of Mr. Seward should have informed us whether the "wages" would be paid in "coin" or in that "paper money" so readily issued, we acknowledge, but at the same time so little to be trusted. That would have been an interesting postscriptum.

In order to induce our workingmen to emigrate, the *Presse* adds that they will enjoy a privilege which the native born American has not, viz.—"They will not be subject to the draft." Nothing more seemed wanting to complete the circular of Mr. Seward. LOUIS BELLET.

The following is from the *Phare de la Loire*:—

NANTES, Sept. 3, 1862.

We publish elsewhere a circular from Mr. Seward, Minister of Foreign Affairs at Washington, which is deserving of especial attention. Our pro-slavery papers have published with great readiness the cessation of the movement of immigration, by which our numerous European workingmen were carried forcibly to the United States. All that can contribute to the weakening and ruin of the great American republic excites the joy of the shameless friends of the South; and, therefore, they have pleasantly insisted upon the seriousness of this fact. Were we to believe them we ought to see in it a forced result of the pending contest between the federals and the secessionists, a sign of the disorder consequent thereon, and a proof of the sufferings of commerce, industry and agriculture on the other side of the Atlantic. The current of emigration was necessarily to stop in view of the stagnation of affairs and want of labor. Well, then, all these pictures pushed to the utmost, were either false or exaggerated. Doubtless the war in America has caused great sufferings; doubtless the productive forces of the country have felt this unlooked-for event; but in fact consumption does not become less in a nation because it is fighting; and, because great dangers are run, the people do not on that account become savages. They have wants which must be supplied; they still continue to lead a civilized life, and in that very way they secure work and bread to the laboring classes. We will say more. War, in requiring the employment of many hands formerly dedicated to the labors of peace, causes a forced augmentation of the wages. This is evident from the circular of Mr. Seward. That paper is an appeal to the workmen who, in England and elsewhere, are victims to the cotton crisis. In going to the United States they will have nothing to fear, as foreigners, to be subjected to the law of conscription. The situation of affairs offers them, on the contrary, the certainty of going to take the place, peaceably, in the manufactories, mines and farms, of the Americans who serve under the banner of the Union

AMUSEMENTS LAST EVENING.

Academy of Music.

DEBUT OF MISS CARLOTTA PATTI.

There was a splendid house last night to welcome to the stage another member of that family which has been so long identified with musical affairs in this country, and which bids fair in the future to reflect upon us some portion of the artistic prestige which Italy, France and Germany have hitherto monopolized. Viewed in this light, as well as in reference to the unquestionable merits of the fair aspirant for lyrical honors, it is not surprising that the debut of Miss Patti should have excited among our community more than usual interest.

Bellini's operas are in general best suited to the class of singers whom the French style *chanteuses legeres*. They are wanting in those noble orchestral effects unaided by which the action of the stage rarely rises to the level of grandeur. On the other hand they are full of the happiest poetic inspirations in the form of delicious melodies, and therefore more frequently afford a test of vocal excellence than the higher class of compositions. For this reason most of the great artists who have risen to fame within the last quarter of a century have included one or more of his creations in their *repertoires*. In the *role* of Amina, Malibran, Sontag, Persiani, Gassier and Jenny Lind won their greatest successes. It is a part which requires extended compass of voice, great flexibility, and judgment to resist the temptation to overcharge with *fioriture* its beautiful melodies. It demands, moreover, sentiment and feeling, with a fair share of personal attractions and youthfulness of appearance.

In reference to all these qualities the choice by Miss Patti of this *role* for her debut was an exceedingly happy one. Her voice takes a great range, and is wonderfully agile in execution. She is young, she is pretty, and she has all that freshness and apparent *naivete* which are essential to the realization of the librettist's ideal. The only doubt that remained to be solved in her regard was whether the novelty of her situation and unfamiliarity with stage usages would not so paralyze her powers as to render the effort a failure, or, at all events, detract greatly from her success. Thanks to her fine musical organization and the careful training of Signor Scola, she has triumphantly passed the ordeal.

Dominating the artistic interest of the occasion, it was plain, was the curiosity excited among the female portion of the audience to see how far the physical difficulty under which she has been so recently laboring had been overcome. On her entrance every eye was strained to watch the manner in which she would advance towards the footlights. Although the limp was still plainly perceptible, there was a wonderful improvement, and the plaudits of welcome with which she was received were redoubled from surprise at the facility with which she moved. The first few phrases of recitation which she uttered were almost indistinct from nervousness; but after a few moments this wore off and her opening cavatina was delivered with all the ease and brilliancy which she is accustomed to display in her vocal efforts. There was a marked difference in the volume of her voice in the recitative passages and in her singing, a fact to be accounted for by her newness to the stage. In her bye play, too, there was a little restraint; but both these defects will disappear when she becomes at home in her parts. Even as it was she gathered more strength and confidence as the opera progressed, and sang and acted with as much spirit as could be expected under the circumstances. In the finale of the first act she made a marked impression, and the curtain fell amid enthusiastic applause, which was continued until she was brought out to receive a fresh ovation in the form of floral offerings.

In the second act she sustained herself admirably throughout, singing charmingly, and in the mill scene, the most trying ordeal that an artist can pass through, she was thrillingly effective. Her rondo was capitally delivered, and derived fresh beauties from her exquisite vocalization. The impression which she left artistically was a most satisfactory one, and only increased the regret that there should still remain the slightest physical blemish on so fair a performance. At the close of the opera she was again called before the curtain.

The Elvino of the evening was Signor Sbriglia, who, amongst his other recommendations, had the rare merit of thinking less of himself than of the *debutante*, to whom he gave most effective support. Of Susini's Rodolpho we need scarcely say that it was, as usual, broad, vigorous, and excellently sung. The conductor was Muzio, who made the most of the limited resources at his disposal.

Miss Patti will appear on Wednesday in Lucia, and will be supported on this occasion by Brignoli.

Wallack's Theatre—School for Scandal.

The rendering of this fine and inexhaustible old play at Wallack's last night won the unqualified approbation of a full and a distinguished audience. The particular feature of the evening was the Sir Peter Teazle of Mr. John Gilbert, in the place of that old favorite Sir Peter, the jovial and genial Blake. Much therefore was expected of Mr. Gilbert in the assumption of this character on his first appearance; and when we say that the house was perfectly satisfied with his execution of the part, we believe that we are only doing simple justice to this careful and finished actor, and to his critical and discriminating audience. The Sir Peter of Gilbert is the polished old gentleman of the capital and the epoch represented. "The very age and body of the time" are not less carefully studied in his deportment and conversation than in the admirable costumes of all the characters, from first to last. Of the merits of Mrs. Hoey's Lady Teazle, Lester Wallack's Charles Surface, Fisher's Joseph, Smith's Sir Oliver, Holland's Moses, and so on to the end of the list, it is needless to inform the reader. They were unexceptionably good, and all harmoniously adapted to the complete success of the elegant entertainment which the management had in view in the arrangement of the cast and the getting up of the costumes and all the details of the play. An old comedy, as costumed and performed at Wallack's, is a rare treat, comprising much of agreeable historical instruction with the most pleasurable intellectual recreation. Bulwer's delightful comedy of "Money" this evening.

Laura Keene's Theatre.

The reopening of this popular theatre, after an unusually prolonged recess, was marked last evening by the presence of a most fashionable and numerous audience. Every seat in the house was occupied, and during the course of the performance no opportunity was lost by the audience to evince their appreciation of the zealous efforts of the accomplished directress to cater for the public amusement. The honors showered upon Miss Keene last evening were only a well deserved and substantial testimony to her merits. During the summer vacation the painters and upholsterers have plied their vocation so industriously that the house now presents an entirely fresh and pleasing aspect. The scenery to a great extent is new, and the old act drop curtain has been replaced by an elegant affair, fresh from the brush of Mr. Minard Lewis, a native artist, whose work bespeaks him a man of taste and skill in his profession. But the mechanical and scenic improvements are only a secondary consideration when viewed beside the other desirable changes Miss Laura Keene has introduced, particularly in the *personnel* of her company, which may now compare with the best in the city, not excepting even Wallack's. We believe it is Miss Keene's intention to discard, at least for the present, the sensation drama, and to produce the good old standard comedies, which, after all, possess the most permanent elements of success and popularity. With the *materiel* furnished by the company she has gathered about her, she may safely venture the experiment, and rest confident that her efforts will be properly appreciated by the public. The season was judiciously opened with Bourcicault's sterling comedy, "Old Heads and Young Hearts"—Blake as Jesse Rural, Miss Keene as Lady Alice, and Chas. Wheatleigh as Tom Coke. The piece was produced most carefully and effectively. It is not necessary to state that the three characters specified were splendidly enacted, as the talent of the artists named has long been acknowledged and admired. The other principal parts were also admirably sustained by Miss Clinton, Mrs. Hind, Stuart Robson (a new actor here), Stoddart, and C. Walcot, Jr. Our space will not permit of a more extended notice.

The Skedaddle in the Camps at Newark.

NEWARK, N. J., Sept. 20, 1862.

The reports published of the "skedaddle" among the troops in camp here are greatly exaggerated. Only two hundred and fifty men ran away and six hundred received furloughs, leaving fifteen hundred men in camp. No one was shot, as reported. All returned to camp to-day, and good order again prevails.

IMPORTANT FROM KENTUCKY.

Rebel Cavalry Attacks on New Castle and Shepherdsville.

ATTACK BY GUERILLAS ON OWENSBORO.

The Rebels Routed After a Desperate Encounter.

Rumored Repulse of Gen. Bragg's Rear Guard.

Preparations for the Defence of Louisville,

&c., &c., &c.

LOUISVILLE, Ky., Sept. 21, 1862.

A despatch from Lagrange to-day says that George Jessee, with two hundred rebel cavalry, attacked at New Castle one hundred and twenty-five of the Home Guard cavalry, under Robert Morris. The latter, without firing a gun, surrendered his men, horses and three hundred stand of arms. The report is considered doubtful.

Another despatch has just reached here saying that the rebels subsequently burned New Castle.

Shepherdsville advices say that Colonel Granger's command, at that place, was attacked to-day by rebel cavalry, who intended to burn the bridge. Granger repulsed them, killing five and taking twenty-eight prisoners.

Six hundred guerillas attacked Owensboro on the 19th instant in two bands. Colonel Netter, commanding the Union force, attacked one of the bands and was slain. Five of our men were wounded. The rebels lost five killed. At noon we shelled the rebels, killing three, when they retreated.

On the 20th instant Lieutenant Colonel Wood, with four hundred and fifty Union cavalry, attacked, and after a most desperate encounter routed from Owensboro, eight hundred rebels, under Colonel Martin, who lost twenty-eight killed and twenty-five wounded. Our loss was three killed and eighteen wounded.

We captured their army stores and seven prisoners.

Reliable advices from Cave City say that a portion of Gen. Buell's force attacked and repulsed Gen. Bragg's rear guard from Horse Cave on Thursday evening. Gen. Bragg is reported to have moved the main body of his army across the river southward from Munfordsville.

No further particulars are received.

LOUISVILLE, Ky., Sept. 22, 1862.

General Bragg's forces have escaped from those of General Buell, and are several hours ahead, marching rapidly upon Louisville.

Major General Nelson is making arrangements to defend the city to the last. He has just issued the following order:—

The women and children of this city will prepare to leave without delay.

Jefferson ferry is to be used exclusively for military purposes.

Persons on foot may proceed as usual.

The city is in a blaze of excitement in consequence of the approach of the rebel forces.

Most of the stores are closed.

The citizens apprehend that an attack will be made within forty-eight hours.

LOUISVILLE, Sept. 22—Evening.

The main body of Bragg's army was reported to be at Hodginville, Larue county, this morning, *en route* for Bardstown. It is supposed he reached Bardstown this evening.

Ninety-five of the Fourth Indiana cavalry, under Captain Shueler, attacked about the same number of Forrest's rebel cavalry yesterday morning, a mile from Lebanon Junction, and drove them a short distance. The rebels were reinforced by twice their number; but our troops still pursued them, driving them into Boston, killing five, wounding seventeen, and capturing thirty-two. We lost eleven prisoners and two wounded.

Governor Robinson has issued a proclamation, calling the citizens to take up arms under General Nelson for the defence of the city.

Mayor Delph has ordered all business houses to be closed.

General Nelson has issued a patriotic and stirring address to his soldiers to give a bloody welcome to the rebel hordes now invading Kentucky.

The report of the burning of New Castle was incorrect, and even the surrender of Morris is now discredited in military circles.

Humphrey Marshall, with twelve thousand men and forty-two pieces of artillery, was expected to reach Paris yesterday morning, it is supposed intending to join Kirby Smith's force at Lexington.

There has been a great exodus of women and children from Louisville, but the excitement has somewhat subsided.

Military operations are very extensive and actively progressing.

IMPORTANT FROM TENNESSEE.

The Bridge Over the Hatchie River Destroyed by Guerillas—Movements of the Rebels, &c.

MEMPHIS, Tenn., Sept. 20, 1862.

The bridge over the Hatchie river, a few miles north of this city, was burned by guerillas on Thursday night. The bridge was not guarded, as it was considered of no importance.

General Villipigue's forces are reported to be stationed twelve miles from Memphis, in the vicinity of Hernando.

The army of General Breckinridge is at Holly Springs.

An expedition with transports, convoyed by a gunboat, left Helena on Wednesday. A part of the troops landed at Lacoma, Ark., twenty miles above Napoleon. The precise object of the movement is not known.

THE VICTORY OF I-U-K-A.

CAIRO, Sept. 22, 1862.

The latest information in regard to the battle of I-u-k-a, Miss., states that on Saturday Price was attacked at three points at the same time, and, being nearly surrounded, he cut his way through at the point where the Forty-seventh Illinois regiment was stationed. This regiment suffered more severely than any other in the fight.

An attempt was made on Friday evening by a gang of rebels to burn the hospital, but they were repulsed by sharpshooters with severe loss.

During the fight of Saturday a body of Texan Rangers made a dash on one of our batteries, and notwithstanding a determined resistance, succeeded in spiking two guns. Our troops acted throughout with gallantry and unflinching bravery.

The following despatch has been received from General Grant:—

HEADQUARTERS, CORINTH, Sept. 22, 1862.

Major General HALLECK, General-in-Chief:—

In my despatch of the 20th our loss was over estimated, and the rebel loss under estimated. We found two hundred and sixty-one of them dead upon the field, while our loss in killed will be less than one hundred.

U. S. GRANT, Major General.

Dispersion of Guerillas.

KANSAS CITY, Sept. 22, 1862.

The following official report has just been received from the expedition under Colonel Burris, which has been in pursuit of Quantrel's guerilla bands since their raid in Oleotho:—For fourteen days our forces have been in hot pursuit of Quantrel through Jackson, Cass, Johnson and Lafayette counties, unable to bring on an engagement other than an occasional picket skirmish, until the 9th, when about fifty of our cavalry came up with the enemy five miles north of Pleasanton Hill. A brisk fire was kept up for about ten minutes, when the enemy broke and fled in confusion, leaving two dead on the field. We pursued them two miles, when they entered the woods, scattering in all directions. Enemy's loss unknown. Our loss is one killed and three wounded. We captured all the enemy's transportation and subsistence, one hundred stand of arms, ten thousand rounds of ammunition, one hundred horses, five wagons, a number of tents and other camp equipage, also a considerable quantity of dry goods, groceries, &c., previously stolen from the citizens of Oleotho. The houses, outbuildings, grain, &c., belonging to some twelve noted marauders, whose premises had been the favorite haunts of guerillas, were burned.

Major General Schuyler Hamilton.

We are happy to announce that the President has appointed Brigadier General Schuyler Hamilton, United States Volunteers, a major general of volunteers, "for meritorious services at New Madrid and Island No. 10."

In General Pope's report, dated "Expeditionary Forces, New Madrid, Mo., April 9, 1862," that General, with a magnanimity rarely met with, and in no instance excelled, opens his report with these words—"The canal across the peninsula, opposite Island No. 10, and for the idea of which I am indebted to General Schuyler Hamilton, was completed by Colonel Bissell's Engineer regiment, and four steamers were brought through on the night of the 6th."

Major General Hamilton, now in his fortieth year, graduated from West Point July, 1841, at nineteen years of age.

After arduous duties in the West, he served with distinction in Mexico, under General Taylor. Severely wounded at the storming of Monterey, he was brevetted for gallant and meritorious services. Suffering much from his wounds and the accidents incidental to the service (having received while on duty a severe fracture of his skull, which was succeeded by a severe attack of malarial fever), upon his recovery he was honored by the appointment of aid-de-camp to General Scott.

While holding this position, "in an affair of cavalry against cavalry, four times his number, at Miraflores," he was transfixed by a lance, which entered near the spine and passed through the left lung, fracturing several ribs. After a slow and painful recovery he returned to duty in the city of Mexico, and subsequently remained in the military family of General Scott for nearly seven years.

His health and constitution being much impaired, he retired from the service and settled as a farmer in the town of Branford, New Haven county, Connecticut.

Upon the appearance of the President's proclamation, April 15, 1862, he hastened from his farm and joined the Seventh regiment New York State Militia, National Guard (as they may now be truly styled), as a private, and marched on for Washington. Rendering important services to Colonel Lefferts and the Seventh regiment at Annapolis, he attracted the attention of General Butler, the present hero of New Orleans. With him he remained until the crisis was past, and then hastened on to join his old commander at Washington, who welcomed him to his family again, and appointed him his military secretary and confidential aid. In this position he remained until the retirement of Lieutenant General Scott, the first and only officer of his grade and foremost soldier of his age.

The appointment of brigadier general was then conferred upon Colonel Hamilton, and, by his devotion to duty since that time, he has attained his present rank of major general. A native born citizen of this State and city, great grandson of Major General Philip Schuyler, and grandson of Major General Alexander Hamilton, the favorite aid and friend of Washington, heroes of the Revolution, thus identified with this State, we congratulate him on his well earned promotion and return to active service, after the severe illness incurred in his campaign in the West.

May his reward be continued success and a long life in which to enjoy his well merited honors.

Lecture of George Francis Train.

PHILADELPHIA, Sept. 22, 1862.

George Francis Train received an ovation from the Philadelphia public this evening at the Academy of Music equal to that bestowed on Parson Brownlow and other champions of American institutions who have preceded him. The house was crowded to excess. Mr. Train was introduced by Cassius M. Clay, and made a characteristic speech on "The Rotten Institutions of England." A number of civil and military dignitaries occupied the platform. His remarks were frequently greeted with applause.

Personal Intelligence.

Lord Edward Cavendish, Lord Hartington and Colonel Leslie, M. P., of England; Mr. Rose, of Montreal; James McCall and wife, of Geneva, and Mr. Rathbone and wife, of Albany, are stopping at the Clarendon Hotel.

Captain Jewett and J. H. Sleeper, of the United States Army; Charles B. Hitchcock and wife, of Maryland; C. C. Chaffee, of Springfield; K. Haumburgh, of Baltimore; James M. Ellis, of Syracuse, and G. Pegram and wife, of St. Louis, were among the arrivals at the Astor House yesterday.

Hon. George Chipman, of Connecticut, is stopping at the Albemarle Hotel.

C. G. Bowles and family, of Louisville, Ky.; A. E. Jefferson and J. B. Smith, of Wisconsin; C. E. Wheeler, of Rochester; A. Kirby and wife, of Milwaukee; J. H. Gardner, Jr., of the United States Army; R. Moore and wife, of Cincinnati; A. D. Dater, of New Orleans; J. T. Worthington, of Pennsylvania and H. P. Clark and wife, of New York, are stopping at the St. Nicholas Hotel.

NEW YORK HERALD.

JAMES GORDON BENNETT,
EDITOR AND PROPRIETOR.

OFFICE N. W. CORNER OF FULTON AND NASSAU STS.

TERMS cash in advance. Money sent by mail will be at the risk of the sender. None but Bank bills current in New York taken.

THE DAILY HERALD. two cents per copy. $7 per annum.

JOB PRINTING executed with neatness, cheapness and despatch.

Volume XXVII........................No. 263

AMUSEMENTS THIS EVENING.

NIBLO'S GARDEN, Broadway.—MERRY WIVES OF WINDSOR.

WALLACK'S THEATRE, Broadway.—SCHOOL FOR SCANDAL.

WINTER GARDEN Broadway.—GERALDINE.

LAURA KEENE'S THEATRE, Broadway.—OLD HEADS AND YOUNG HEARTS.

NEW BOWERY THEATRE, Bowery.—EAGLE EYE—MILLY—ASSASSIN OF ROSENWALD.

BOWERY THEATRE, Bowery.—THE VULTURE OF THE CARIBBEAN SEA—CO-LEAN BORN—MOTHER BAILEY.

NIXON'S CREMORNE GARDEN, Fourteenth street and Sixth avenue.—SPIRIT OF THE FLOOD—BALLET, PROMENADE CONCERT AND EQUESTRIANISM.

BARNUM'S AMERICAN MUSEUM, Broadway.—GRAND AQUARIA—LEARNED SEAL, &c., at all hours. CLAUDE MARCEL. afternoon and evening.

BRYANTS' MINSTRELS' Mechanics' Hall, 472 Broadway.—ETHIOPIAN SONGS, BURLESQUES, DANCES, &c.—THE BLACK BRIGADE.

CHRISTY'S OPERA HOUSE, 585 Broadway.—ETHIOPIAN SONGS, DANCES, &c.—PETER PIPER PEPPER PODGE.

WOOD'S MINSTREL HALL, 514 Broadway.—ETHIOPIAN SONGS, DANCES, &c.—THE BIRD HUNTERS.

HOPE CHAPEL, No. 720 Broadway.—EXHIBITION OF TIRRELL'S CALIFORNIA.

HITCHCOCK'S THEATRE AND MUSIC HALL, Canal street.—SONGS, DANCES, BURLESQUES, &c.

GAIETIES CONCERT HALL, 616 Broadway.—DRAWING ROOM ENTERTAINMENTS.

PARISIAN CABINET OF WONDERS, 563 Broadway.—Open daily from 10 A. M. till 10 P. M.

New York, Tuesday, Sept. 23, 1862.

DAILY CIRCULATION OF THE NEW YORK HERALD.

Monday, Sept. 15	121,680
Tuesday, Sept. 16	125,520
Wednesday, Sept. 17	122,880
Thursday, Sept. 18	120,000
Friday, Sept. 19	123,600
Saturday, Sept. 20	127,200
Daily Average	**123,460**

THE SITUATION.

The latest news from the headquarters of Gen. McClellan's army reports everything quiet in that direction. The full amount of our loss in the late battles has not been ascertained. That of Gen. Sumner's army corps, however, numbers 5,280.

A raid was made by Stuart's rebel cavalry across the Potomac into Maryland on Friday evening, accompanied by a regiment of infantry and seventeen pieces of artillery, but they were driven back again during the night. Next morning no rebels were visible. The work of burying the dead is still going on at the rate of a thousand a day.

The proclamation of the President, which we publish to-day, and upon which we comment in our editorial columns, will strike our readers as the most important document which has yet been issued by the Executive. Based upon the Confiscation act framed by the last Congress, it leaves the option to the rebel slave States either to return to their allegiance before the 1st of January, 1863, or to submit to the entire emancipation of all their slaves. In such States or portions of States as are loyal to the government at that date, the right of property in slaves will be respected, and the President announces that he will renew the proposition to Congress to pay for slaves who may be set free by the will of their masters in any loyal State.

The news from the West is of a stirring character. It would appear that General Bragg's forces are marching upon Louisville, having escaped from those of General Buell. Major General Nelson is making arrangements to defend the city of Louisville to the last, and has just issued the following order:—"The women and children of this city will prepare to leave without delay. Jefferson ferry is to be used exclusively for military purposes. Persons on foot may proceed as usual." An attack was expected yesterday within twenty-four hours, and the city was in a state of great excitement. Governor Robinson and Mayor Delph have issued strong proclamations to the people. Advices from Cave City say that a portion of Gen. Buell's force attacked and repulsed Gen. Bragg's rear guard from Horse Cave on Thursday evening last.

On the 20th instant Lieutenant Colonel Wood, with four hundred and fifty Union cavalry, attacked, and routed from Owensboro, eight hundred rebels, under Colonel Martin, who lost twenty-eight killed and twenty-five wounded. Our loss was only three killed and eighteen wounded.

When the Nova Scotian left Londonderry for Quebec—on the 12th inst.—no later news from America than that brought by the Anglo-Saxon had been received in England. The effect of these advices has reached us from the Borussia, off Cape Race, and was commented on in the HERALD. The English people believed that a decisive, if not final, battle was near at hand in the United States, and the arrival of the next steamer from this country was looked for with great anxiety.

MISCELLANEOUS NEWS.

The steamship Nova Scotian, from Londonderry on the 12th instant, passed Cape Race last Sunday evening, on her voyage to Quebec. Our agent telegraphs a summary of her news from St. Johns, Newfoundland, which is published in the HERALD to-day. The advices are two days later than the report of the Borussia, at the same point.

There were only four thousand bales of cotton sold in Liverpool during three days—the 8th, 9th and 10th instant. The market was irregular and dull on the 11th instant, with prices from one to two pence lower. On the 12th instant the market was buoyant and experienced a trifling advance. The stock in port footed up ninety-two thousand five hundred bales. Breadstuffs were still downward, with flour easier. Provisions were flat. Consols closed in London on the 12th instant at 93⅝. Italy was still agitated, on account of the condition of health and situation of Garibaldi. A letter from General Bixio, denouncing the Ratazzi government for its treatment of the liberator, increased the uneasiness. A general amnesty was still advocated by the people. Spain was determined to draw closer to France in her diplomacy. The French transport Prince Jerome was burned off Gibraltar. No lives were lost.

The steamship Etna, from Queenstown on the 11th instant, arrived at this port yesterday evening. Her news has been fully anticipated.

The sixth section of the Confiscation act, which is the operating feature of the law, goes into effect to-day. The proclamation of the President was issued on the 25th of July, and the sixty days notice therein given expires to-day. The following is the section:—

Sec. 6. And be it further enacted, That if any person within any State or Territory of the United States, other than those named as aforesaid, after the passage of this act, being engaged in armed rebellion against the government of the United States, or aiding or abetting such rebellion, shall not, within sixty days after public warning and proclamation, duly given and made by the President of the United States, cease to aid, countenance and abet such rebellion, and return to his allegiance to the United States, all the estate and property, moneys, stocks and credits of such person shall be liable to seizure as aforesaid; and it shall be the duty of the President to seize and use them as aforesaid, or the proceeds thereof. And all sales, transfers or conveyances of any such property after the expiration of the said sixty days from the date of such warning and proclamation shall be null and void; and it shall be a sufficient bar to any suit brought by such person for the possession or the use of such property, or any of it, to allege and prove that he is one of the persons described in this section.

Poindexter, a notorious guerilla leader, who was recently captured in Missouri, escaped from St. Louis on the 17th inst.

All the Congregational churches in the State will be represented by their pastor and lay delegates in a convention which is to be held in Syracuse to-day.

The Board of Aldermen did not organize yesterday, for want of a quorum.

According to the City Inspector's report, there were 408 deaths in the city during the past week—a decrease of 121 as compared with the mortality of the week previous, and 34 more than occurred during the corresponding week last year. The recapitulation table gives 6 deaths of alcoholism, 4 of diseases of the bones, joints, &c.; 72 of the brain and nerves, 5 of the generative organs, 7 of the heart and blood vessels, 100 of the lungs, throat, &c.; 3 of old age, 13 of diseases of the skin and eruptive fevers, 6 premature births, 132 of diseases of the stomach, bowels and other digestive organs; 36 of uncertain seat and general fevers, 4 of diseases of the urinary organs, and 20 from violent causes. There were 286 natives of the United States, 8 of England, 75 of Ireland, 25 of Germany, and the balance of various foreign countries.

The stock market was firm at the opening yesterday, very buoyant in the middle of the day, and irregular at the close. Money was very easy at 4 per cent. Exchange firm but inactive at 129. Gold rose to 117¾; demand notes to 114¼. The bank statement shows an increase of $3,639,391 in deposits, $737,792 in specie, and $470,775 in loans.

The cotton market yesterday opened with more animation than prevailed on Saturday, and prices exhibited more steadiness, while the sales embraced about 600 bales, on the basis of 53c. a 54c. for middling and uplands, mostly at the outside figure. The Nova Scotian's news did not transpire until the afternoon, too late for its effect, if any, to be developed. The demand for home consumption, combined with the light stock, prevents this market sympathizing with that of Liverpool to the extent that otherwise might be expected. The flour market was steady for common and medium grades, and the higher brands of good extras were scarce and firm, while prices generally were unchanged. The sales made were to a fair extent. Wheat was heavy, and declined 1 cent per bushel, while the market was active at the concession, and in good part for export. Corn was firmer for good sound Western mixed, which was extremely scarce, while parcels in poor condition were plenty and prices unchanged. Small sales of good sound Western mixed were made at 59c. a 61c. Pork was heavy and cheaper. Sales of mess were made at $11 62½ a $11 75, and of prime at $10 a $10 12½. Lard was steady, with sales at 9c. a 9¾c. Sugars were active and prices steady, with sales of 2,000 hhds., 1,029 boxes and 5,162 bags of Manila, at prices given in another column. Coffee was steady but quiet. Freights were firmer. To Liverpool wheat was engaged, in bulk and bags, at 12d. a 12½d., and to Glasgow at 14d., with some lots in ships' bags reported at 14½d. A vessel was engaged to the same port, to load with wheat, at 14d.

Important from Washington—The President's Proclamation.

The President has issued a proclamation to the people of the rebel States. It will be found in another column of this morning's paper. It is one of the most important documents that has emanated from the Executive Department of the republic since the adoption of the federal constitution.

On the 25th of July last, the President, in accordance with the act of Congress approved on the 17th of that month, gave sixty days' notice to those in rebellion that the property of all rebels would be confiscated and their slaves made free if they persisted in their suicidal course. The notice expires to-day, the 23d inst., and the proclamation now issued presents the case in its new and significant aspect.

The gravity of this proclamation will strike every one. It has been forced upon the nation by the abolitionists of the North and the secessionists of the South. It inaugurates an overwhelming revolution in the system of labor in a vast and important agricultural section of the country, which will, if the rebels persist in their course, suddenly emancipate three or four millions of human beings, and throw them, in the fulness of their helplessness and ignorance, upon their own resources and the wisdom of the white race to properly regulate and care for them in their new condition of life. But the importance of this great social revolution will not be confined to the section where the black race now forms the chief laboring element. It will have an influence on the labor of the North and West. It will, to a certain extent, bring the black labor of the South in competition with the white labor on the extensive grain farms of the West, unless the existing stringent laws of some of the Western States, confining the negro to his present geographical position, are adopted in all the other free States.

This proclamation, however, gives the South an opportunity to escape the fate so clearly and emphatically marked out by Mr. Lincoln. It should be her golden opportunity. It is to be seen that *the President has fixed on the 1st day of January, 1863, as the day for the emancipation of all slaves in States in rebellion to the federal government on that day.* This should strike home to the interests of the people of the South. It must be manifest to them that the rebellion cannot succeed. The reception of the rebel army by the people of Maryland, after all the promises and preparations leading to the invasion of that State, must have its peculiar and impressive significance with them. The late utter rout of the rebels by McClellan at South Mountain and Antietam, to be followed by the marching of a million of loyal men for the annihilation of this rebellion, must convince them, unless they are mad, of the hopelessness of their cause.

It is at this time, with victory in our hands, and enormous preparations for crushing out all opposition, that the President issues this important manifesto, and gives the people of the South this chance. It is now the question with them whether or not they are prepared, for the sake of the few miserable leaders of this wicked rebellion, to submit to this overwhelming revolution in their social system. There is the document. There is the time fixed for the return of the rebellious States to the allegiance of the federal government. No event in the history of the world surpasses the one now presented by the President, and which is to be decided in a little over ninety days.

The Campaign in Virginia—The Duty of the Hour.

Now that the rebels, in consequence of the victories of Gen. McClellan, have been compelled to evacuate Maryland and retreat into Virginia by the way they came, in order to fall back upon Richmond, to save it from capture, and to save the remnant of their invading army from destruction, the duty of preventing its escape falls upon Gen. Halleck and the War Department; and it will soon be seen what amount of capacity there is at Washington to render the campaign decisive by the capture of the whole of Lee's army. McClellan has done his part. He has driven the enemy back from Maryland across the Potomac, and it rests with the War Department and the military authorities at Washington to perform their parts by confining the rebel army in the mountains of Virginia, and thus cutting off its supplies and reducing it to starvation or surrender.

To accomplish this it will be necessary to send a force rapidly to Fredericksburg and Gordonsville, in order to seize the railroads and sever the communication of the rebels with their base of supplies. Upon the manner in which they accomplish these movements depends the speedy success of the campaign or the prolongation of the struggle to next spring. In the winter little can be done in Virginia. To finish the war with the year 1862 it will be necessary to "make hay while the sun shines."

It was a great blunder to withdraw McClellan from Harrison's Landing. It gave the opportunity to the rebels, which they desired, to fall upon Pope's army, cut it up and demoralize it before it could form a junction with the army of McClellan. It was the same radical influence in the Cabinet that divided the Army of the Potomac and prevented its being reinforced at the critical moment that caused it to retreat from the James river to Washington; and the terrible experiment was made to give McDowell and Pope a chance to become great generals. After their miserable failure, when they were even reinforced by the army of McClellan, but without the presence of that general, he took the same whipped armies, and with them he defeated the rebel host, flushed with its victories. The loss of human life or the safety of the republic seems never to have entered into the calculations of the selfish politicians who hitherto have had the control of the army. Had it been otherwise McDowell, who had been tried at Bull run in July, 1861, and so sadly failed then and there, would never have had a second chance to fail on the same ground in August, 1862, to say nothing of his failure to reinforce McClellan from Fredericksburg when he heard the sound of his cannon at Hanover Court House. Had Harper's Ferry been taken proper care of from Washington, and had a sufficient force been sent up the south side of the Potomac to hold the fords, the army of Lee could not have recrossed into Virginia, and it would have been all destroyed or captured by the victorious army of McClellan after the battle of Sharpsburg.

But, now that the rebels have succeeded in recrossing the Potomac in safety, it remains to be seen what dispositions of troops will be made to intercept them in their retreat to Richmond. Thoroughfare Gap, Warrenton, Fredericksburg and Gordonsville ought to be occupied immediately with Union troops from Washington, in order to head off the rebel army while McClellan presses on its rear and places it between two fires. Let this be done with promptitude and vigor, and the rebellion in Virginia will be ended before the first frost.

DISMISSAL OF COMMANDER PREBLE.—No one will condemn the show of vigor exhibited by the Navy Department in the case of this officer. Had it been displayed sooner the blockade would not have proved so ineffective as it has done on several points of our coast. We question, however, whether the manner in which the department has punished the alleged dereliction of duty on the part of this officer is exactly that which is demanded by the interests of the service, or which is calculated to promote the object in view. Taking for granted that Admiral Farragut's charges against him are correct, the proper course to pursue in his case would be to suspend him from duty and try him by court martial. To dismiss him from the service, without hearing what he has to say in his defence, is a violation of every constitutional principle, and establishes a most dangerous precedent. We are induced to lay the greater stress on this case because there have been several instances lately in which army officers have been summarily dismissed in the same manner, and again reinstated on proof of the injustice done them. All this is very wrong, and shows, to say the least of it, a fitful, arbitrary temper in the management of the two departments.

ADVANCE IN THE PRICE OF COAL—A CAUTION TO SPECULATORS.—Within the last few weeks the price of coal has been steadily advancing, until it is now about seven dollars a ton. The dealers tell their customers that by midwinter it will be at ten or twelve dollars. The causes assigned for this extravagant rise are, first, the tax; secondly, the interruption in canal transportation occasioned by the freshets; and, lastly, the scarcity of labor caused by volunteering in the coal districts. All these reasons combined will not serve to account for the rapid advance in the price which is now taking place, being at the rate of a dollar a week. It is attributable, we understand, mainly to a combination amongst speculators, who are forcing the price up with the view of compelling the public to lay in stocks at a high figure. When this is accomplished the price will be put down again, and those who have purchased largely will find that they have been swindled. If housekeepers would adopt the policy of buying only what they require, and consuming as little as possible, they would soon break up this conspiracy against their pockets. The use of gas and naptha cooking stoves would enable them to dispense with a considerable quantity of the coal which they now burn.

The Radicals Still Harping on McClellan.

The unscrupulous *Tribune*, the organ of the infernal, destructive radicals, is still harping upon McClellan. It dares not now come out as boldly as it did in an extra, as well as in its regular editions, a short time ago, and pronounce General McClellan a double traitor, compared with whom Arnold was an angel. Neither does it now find it feasible to omit Gen. McClellan's name in its editorial references to the recent battles, as it did at first, ascribing all the credit to subordinate generals. Insinuations now take the place of direct charges, and the old sneers and inuendoes, so familiar to the *Tribune's* readers just before the first Bull run massacre, and just before the seven days' battles on the Chickahominy, are again resumed.

Take, for example, the *Tribune* of yesterday. In that paper poor Greeley has four columns of editorials, and in every column there is a malicious stab at McClellan. In the first column General Wadsworth is nominated for Governor, and is puffed, at McClellan's expense, as follows:—"Wadsworth was soon after made a brigadier, and as such served in the front of our lines opposite Centreville during the last gloomy winter, steadily insisting that there were not more than fifty thousand rebels there, and that our army would walk right over them if General McClellan would only say the word. It is now known that General Wadsworth was entirely right as to the strength of the enemy, and that General McClellan was deplorably misled." This is a lie on the face of it. Major General McClellan, Commander-in-Chief, probably knew the strength of the enemy better than any brigadier general, and certainly better than Brigadier General Wadsworth. What Wadsworth's abilities as a soldier were may be judged from the fact that he tried to get Raymond, of the *Times*, to attack McClellan, his superior officer, and that he has never since seen active service, and has distinguished himself only by interfering with the civil authorities of Washington. Besides this, it is not "now known" that the rebels only had fifty thousand men at Centreville and Manassas last winter. It is known that they had many more; but it is the policy of the radicals to underrate the rebel forces, so that they may make out our soldiers cowards, no matter whether the rebels are successful or defeated. For the rest, Gen. Pope tried Wadsworth's famous plan of "walking right over the rebels;" and how did it result?

In its second editorial column the *Tribune* says that Pope's "short but dashing" campaign was successful in its object, "but closed disastrously through the failure of some of General McClellan's lieutenants to reinforce and support, at the critical moment, the army which had so bravely and effectively befriended them." This is another palpable lie; for if it had not been for General McClellan's lieutenants, who bravely and effectively befriended Pope, all of the dashing Pope's army would have been captured or destroyed. But in the same column the *Tribune* continues:—"We do not consider the events of the past week a subject of congratulation." Of course not; for they were victories for the Union cause, and the *Tribune* congratulates itself only when the rebels triumph, having always been in favor of "letting the Southern States go." Then it again repeats:—"We do not think the Union cause has gained anything by the events of September." Of course not; for the safety of Washington is nothing; the safety of Baltimore is nothing; the deliverance of Maryland is nothing; the preservation of Pennsylvania is nothing; the loss of the rebel armies is nothing; the despair of the rebel leaders is nothing, to the *Tribune*, because it wants "to get rid of the President;" because, as it has recently asserted, "politically, a victory by McClellan would set us back six months." Oh, a model, loyal sheet is this *Tribune!* In its third editorial column yesterday it charges the HERALD with its own invention of denouncing McClellan as "a usurper" and "a military dictator," and to this it insultingly adds, in its fourth editorial column, that, while there "is no shadow of truth" in such reports concerning Fremont, it "trusts"—only "trusts"—there is none in regard to McClellan. This cowardly and sneaking commentary upon its own story is worthy of the *Tribune*, and does not deserve refutation.

But how does Greeley justify the publication of these slanderous inuendoes against General McClellan? By what argument does he defend these assassin-like attacks, unworthy of a gentleman, characteristic only of a coward, impossible in a truly loyal man? Why, by the singular logic that the HERALD is friendly to McClellan, and that the Richmond *Whig* says that "some notice should be taken of Wallace, of the NEW YORK HERALD; but, unprincipled Swiss as he is, Wallace's heart has been all along with the South," and much more of the same sort, which the *Tribune* seems to think very important, as it has published it no less than three times already. What that has to do with McClellan we are at a loss to see; but, in order to knock away even such a prop to the *Tribune's* contemptible and malignant meanness, we assure poor Greeley that there is no such person as "Wallace, of the NEW YORK HERALD," a fact of which he may convince himself at any time by examining the list of the names of our employes. All the *Tribune's* bluster and brag, therefore, goes for nothing, and Greeley might better be preparing himself for the fate which awaits him, and which he so much dreads, when the war is over and our brave soldiers come home to settle accounts with him and his accomplices, who have caused and prolonged this war, who have maligned and abused our officers and soldiers, and who are responsible before Heaven for the murder of many brave men.

THE NEWSPAPER OF THE AGE.—By reference to a table, copied from our account books, of the circulation of the NEW YORK HERALD during the past week, it will be seen that our average daily issue is now one hundred and twenty-three thousand four hundred and sixty copies. This extraordinary daily circulation is unequalled by that of any other paper in the world, and far surpasses that of any paper which ever before existed. It is equal to the combined issues of all the other daily papers in New York city, or to the combined issues of all the daily papers of London, and is twice as large as the combined issues of all the papers of Paris.

Such a record as this is gratifying as an expression of the estimation in which the NEW YORK HERALD is held by the public. It has been attained only by our strict adherence to truth; by the enterprise we have displayed in obtaining the latest and fullest news and publishing all facts of public interest; by our unwavering loyalty to the government and the constitution, and especially by the fidelity, accuracy and completeness with which we have printed day by day the history of this great war for the Union.

Our envious rivals, and particularly the *Tribune*, cavil at and deny, but cannot alter these established facts. The abuse of such opponents seems our best praise; for our circulation grows larger and larger as these attacks continue, while the *Tribune* has fallen below all its contemporaries, its circulation being now also exceeded by that of the *Times*, the *Sun*, and even by that of the *World*. The reports of our war correspondents have uniformly been the best written, the fullest, the most detailed, the most accurate, the earliest, and the best illustrated by maps, drawn exclusively for this journal. The completeness of this correspondence may be judged from the fact that, besides all we publish, we have enough remaining every day to fill another paper of this size.

But we prefer to allow our rivals to praise us, and we therefore republish the subjoined note from Mr. S. H. Gay, the managing editor, under Mr. Greeley, of the New York *Tribune*—a paper which has often denied what its leading editor here admits in a private letter of instructions to his correspondent at Yorktown. The letter was picked up at Yorktown, and sent to us by a correspondent. We have the original now in our possession, with the correspondent's pencil notes on the back, and its authenticity has never been questioned by Mr. Gay or by any one acquainted with his handwriting and his peculiarity of writing the word "the" in the old style, "ye":—

OFFICE OF THE TRIBUNE, NEW YORK, April 28, 1862.

MY DEAR SIR—Mr. Sinclair has gone to ye army before Yorktown to make arrangements to get us ye news. He will probably see you, & you will act in conjunction with him.

Your sketch of ye battle-ground of ye 16th came just *eight* days after ye battle. Of course it was useless. The corr: of ye Philadelphia *Inquirer* had sent one to that paper, which it had had engraved & published, which I had also had engraved & published, three days before yours reached me. I pray you remember ye *Tribune* is a *daily news*-paper—or meant to be,—& not a historical record of past events. Correspondence to be of any value must be prompt, fresh & full of facts. I know how difficult it is, under ye censor ship to write, but there must be facts enough of general interest all about you to make a daily letter. Yours for to-morrow's paper is ye best you have sent us—short & to ye purpose. I should like you to write daily, if only a half, a quarter column, so that ye report of all you may tell be continuous. The curiosity & anxiety about Yorktown is feverish, & ye public like ye paper best that is always giving something. If there is absolutely *nothing* to write about, drop a line and tell me that. The HERALD is constantly ahead of us with Yorktown news. The battle of ye 16th we were compelled to copy from it. Yrs. very truly,

S. H. GAY.

We think this acknowledgment of our superiority a suitable corollary to our table of circulation. Why Mr. Gay does not admit the facts above stated in the *Tribune*, as well as in his private letters, we cannot say; nor can we explain how he and Mr. Greeley reconcile it with their consciences to abuse us in their paper while they confidentially own that "the HERALD is constantly ahead," and that they are "compelled to copy from it."

THE HARPER'S FERRY DISGRACE—A CLEAR CASE FOR A COURT MARTIAL.—Who is, or what parties are, responsible for the disgraceful, costly and humiliating surrender of Harper's Ferry? It is a clear case for a court martial, and President Lincoln should promptly order one to probe this matter to the bottom. The infamous and inhuman slanders against Colonel Miles, now lying in his grave, require no refutation. No honest man believes them. But what base motives could have dictated them? That is the question. Is not this business open to the suspicion that the unscrupulous tool of some dirty political faction has had a leading hand in it?

If the responsibility of the surrender of Harper's Ferry belongs especially to any one officer, we think that Col. Tom Ford, of Ohio, is that man. His abandonment of Maryland Heights was the loss of the whole position; for with those heights in possession of the enemy all the other defences of the town were untenable. Nor does it appear that Ford made even a respectable show of resistance to hold those heights. Gen. McClellan fought the successful battle of South Mountain on Sunday, the 14th, the cannonading of which was, perhaps, heard in the same mountain range at Harper's Ferry, only some twelve or fifteen miles off. We know, at all events, that had our officers in charge of that position held out till Monday night, instead of basely surrendering that morning, the beleaguering rebel forces would have been compelled to leave the place on Tuesday morning, as they did, to go up the river to the relief of Gen. Lee.

Thus, in holding Harper's Ferry a few hours longer, we should have saved to our Army of the Potomac from ten to twelve thousand men, some fifteen thousand muskets and rifles, from fifty to one hundred pieces of artillery, and valuable supplies of ammunition, provisions, wagons and stores of all kinds; but above all, in connection with these troops and materials of war, we should have saved a military position equal to fifty thousand men to General McClellan. But all was lost through this disgraceful capitulation, and thus the means and the way of escape were provided for the rebel army from Maryland, which otherwise would have been cut off. From the facts before us, had our forces at Harper's Ferry been under the command of an officer of Jeff. Davis, the capitulation would not have been contrived more advantageously than it has been to General Lee.

This, we repeat, is a clear and urgent case for a stringent court martial; and, as the fidelity of Miles is established, we submit that the abandonment of Maryland Heights by Tom Ford should be thoroughly investigated. We have had of late quite enough of these shameful capitulations, with the smallest possible show of honest resistance; nor until some exemplary punishments are administered for such outrageous delinquencies can we expect any great success. In conclusion, while such incompetent, blatherskiting politicians and adventurers as Tom Ford are assigned to such important military trusts as Maryland Heights, we have no right to expect anything but disappointments and disgrace.

CHRISTY'S MINSTRELS.—We are glad to learn that there is no truth in the report that this popular troupe are about to leave on a professional tour. They are permanently established in their present hall, where the business has been such as to render any change in their plans unnecessary.

General Pope at St. Paul.

[From the St. Paul Press, Sept. 16.]

Major General Pope and staff arrived here by the Northern Belle at nine o'clock last evening, and put up at the International. Brigadier General Elliott, who has been ordered to report to General Pope, in this city, is with the party. Brigadier General Roberts, who has also been ordered to report to General Pope, is expected to-morrow.

The names, rank and position of the party, who arrived last evening are as follows:—

Major General Pope.
Brigadier General Elliott.
Colonel Morgan, Aid-de-Camp to General Pope.
Colonel Marshall, Aid-de-Camp to General Pope.
Colonel Butler, Aid-de-Camp to General Pope.
Lieutenant Colonel Smith, Aid-de-Camp to Gen. Pope.
Captain Pope, Aid-de-Camp to Gen. Pope.
Major Selfridge, Assistant Adjutant General to General Pope.
Captain Jacobs, Assistant Adjutant General to General Pope.
Captain Bell, Assistant Adjutant General to General Roberts.

NEWS FROM McCLELLAN'S ARMY.

Rebel Cavalry Raid Near Williamsport.

Occupation of Maryland Heights by the Union Forces.

The Rebels Still Retreating Into Virginia,

Particulars of the Skirmish on Saturday.

Additional Names of the Killed and Wounded,

&c., &c., &c.

REPORTS FROM GENERAL McCLELLAN'S HEADQUARTERS.

HEADQUARTERS OF THE ARMY OF THE POTOMAC, Sept. 21, 1862.

The firing heard last evening in the direction of Williamsport turns out to have been a raid of Stuart's rebel cavalry.

He crossed the Potomac on Friday night into Maryland, at that point, with his cavalry, one regiment of infantry and seventeen pieces of artillery. The force sent up to drive him back arrived near the town base in the afternoon. The firing heard was principally from the rebel guns.

During the night they recrossed into Virginia, and this morning they had disappeared from the opposite shore. No one was hurt.

The work of burying the dead is still continuing. They average about a thousand per day. To-morrow will probably finish it.

The Maryland Heights were yesterday occupied by a Union force.

The indications are that the rebels are continuing their retreat into Virginia, leaving the line of the Potomac.

Divine worship was held at headquarters this evening, Bishop Whipple, of Minnesota, officiating.

HEADQUARTERS OF THE ARMY OF THE POTOMAC, MONDAY EVENING, Sept. 22, 1862.

The following is the official report of our loss in Sumner's corps at the battle of the Antietam:—

General Richardson's Division.	
Killed	212
Wounded	899
Missing	24
General Sedgwick's Division.	
Killed	355
Wounded	1,577
Missing	321
General French's Division.	
Killed	298
Wounded	1,321
Missing	203
Total loss in General Sumner's corps	5,208

The loss in missing may be somewhat reduced by stragglers returning.

A train of cars crossed the Monocacy this morning. The road is now open to Harper's Ferry, where there is a sufficient Union force for all purposes.

The rebels, in their hasty retreat from Maryland, left between 1,100 and 1,200 wounded between Sharpsburg and the river. They are being paroled.

Twenty-six stands of colors were taken during the battle of the Antietam, and have been received at headquarters. Seven more are known to have been captured, and are in the hands of the different regiments which captured them.

THE REPORTS FROM FREDERICK.

FREDERICK, Md., Sept. 22—9 P. M.

We have had the usual number of rumors to-day, but very little reliable news. I hear of no fighting to-day.

All are confident that the final destruction of the rebel army, which has been so badly defeated, is a fixed fact.

It is currently reported here that a portion of the rebel army has recrossed into Maryland at Williamsport; but this needs confirmation.

Miss Dix passed through here to-day on her way to Washington from Sharpsburg, where she has been to minister to the comfort of our wounded soldiers. She goes to Washington on business connected with her philanthropic mission, and is expected to return immediately.

Professor Lowe, with his balloon arrangements, has gone to the Potomac, where his services will doubtless prove of value.

REPORTS FROM HARRISBURG.

HARRISBURG, Sept. 22, 1862.

There is no information here in regard to the condition of affairs in Maryland. The United States government has complete possession of the telegraph wires from Chambersburg to Hagerstown.

The Pennsylvania regiments will return to Harrisburg again, at the rate of two a day.

Deputations arrive here by every train, seeking information in regard to sick and wounded.

Travel from Chambersburg to Hagerstown has been stopped, no person being allowed to go over the railroad without a proper pass.

Gen. Geary having sufficiently recovered from his late wounds, will leave to-day and proceed to Hagerstown, for the purpose of rejoining his division, now in the field.

The statement that six regiments refused to cross the State line is without foundation.

It is not true that the State of New York offered troops for the purpose of defending Pennsylvania against invasion. No such offer was expected, as Governor Curtin felt perfectly competent to protect his State.

The militia forces of Pennsylvania saved, beyond question, the Cumberland Valley and possibly the State capital from a rebel raid.

The Governor of Maryland has tendered his thanks for the prompt assistance our forces have rendered.

A salute of one hundred guns will be fired from Capitol Hill to-morrow noon in honor of the success of our arms.

OUR HARRISBURG CORRESPONDENCE.

GENERAL M'CLELLAN AND THE RADICALS—THE ORDER FOR THE CONCENTRATION OF THE PENNSYLVANIA MILITIA COUNTERMANDED—THE PHILADELPHIA NATIONAL GUARD—WOUNDED SOLDIERS—RETURN OF TROOPS, ETC.

HARRISBURG, Sept. 22, 1862.

The news of McClellan's last great victory has been received here with the greatest rejoicing. Everybody is exulting over it, and even those persons who have heretofore been opposed to General McClellan cannot now praise and admire him enough.

Orders have been telegraphed to the various military headquarters throughout the State to the effect that the militia companies now organizing in the different localities need not march to Harrisburg, as the exigencies which first made it necessary to call the militia have been entirely surmounted, and all danger of invasion passed. The militia throughout the State will, however, maintain their organizations, drill as usual, and in all things perfect their knowledge and discipline, awaiting thus for marching orders, and in constant readiness to answer a summons of the Governor.

Pennsylvania has really saved the Union. If it had not been for her marching one hundred thousand men to the border, the enemy might possibly have made an invasion into a free State. But our brave boys left everything, their homes and all that was dear to them, and showed the enemy their spirit and determination.

All the militia in Maryland have been ordered back to Greencastle, and will probably receive orders in a day or two to proceed to their respective homes.

The Philadelphia National Guard arrived here last evening. On their arrival the Colonel, Jeremiah Fritz, addressed them, telling them that their services were not required, and they would proceed to Philadelphia this morning, at nine o'clock. This news the men received with great dissatisfaction, as they were extremely anxious to go on to the seat of war.

A great many wounded arrived in town yesterday, and one thousand more are expected to-day. Great preparations are being made for them. All the schoolhouses and a great many public buildings have been converted into hospitals. Yesterday was devoted entirely to the preparations for the wounded.

Governor Curtin is still at Hagerstown, administering to the wants of the sick and wounded.

The troops in the Cumberland valley have not yet been ordered home; but it is expected here that such an order will soon be issued. The Anderson Guard has been engaged on special service, by order of the Governor, and will return to their homes when the term of that service has been completed.

LOCAL AND STATE AFFAIRS

THE LATE COLONEL JNO. T. THORNTON.—Another gallant and noble son of Virginia has been lost to us. One of the most brilliant men in this State has been cut off in the midst of his days, and with high prospects before him, had his life been spared. Virginia mourns her cherished sons, whose departure at this awful season, makes a sad void in the gallaxy of talent, virtue, and moral worth, they have adorned. Of all that we have yet lost by this unholy war, this, to us, seems to be the heaviest, all things considered.

So much talent and eloquence could illy be spared now.

The remains of Col. Thornton reached here last night and will be conveyed to his home in Farmville by the committee having them in charge, to-day.

IN MEMORY OF THE LATE COL. JOHN T. THORNTON, OF PRINCE EDWARD.

At a meeting of the citizens of Farmville, Va., held on the 22d September, 1862, O. C. Read, Esq., was called to the Chair, and A. Vaughn appointed Secretary.

The following resolutions were unanimously adopted, to-wit:

Resolved, That we have received with sentiments of inexpressible sorrow, the sad tidings of the death of Lieut. Colonel John T. Thornton, our late distinguished townsman; and that, while humbly bowing beneath this afflictive dispensation of Divine Providence, we cannot but attempt to express our profound sense of the loss sustained by our entire community and the country by the death of one so eminently gifted with all that elevates, dignifies and adorns humanity.

Resolved, That S O Southall, C C Read, Dr A S Dillon, Col H T Parrish, Col R A Booker, B C Peters, T J Davis, R E Warren and A Bruce be a Committee in behalf of the citizens of Farmville to meet the remains of Colonel Thornton, at Lynchburg, and escort them to the place of burial—Farmville.

C. C. READ, Ch'mn.
A. VAUGHUN, Sec'ty

☞Richmond and Petersburg journals will please copy.

sept 23 1t

Wanted to Hire.

A NEGRO WOMAN to cook and wash for a small family the remainder of the year. Apply at VIRGINIAN OFFICE.

BOARDING.

THE SUBSCRIBER having leased for a term of years and fitted up the LARGE WHITE HOUSE on Church Street, a few steps below Centenary Church, is prepared to accommodate Boarders. ☞ Terms to suit the times.

A. WADDILL.

NEW FIRM.

THE undersigned have this day formed a co-partnership under the style and firm of P. Bayne & Co., for the purpose of conducting a general wholesale and retail business, and have taken the store room formerly occupied by George M. Rucker, No. 89, Main St., Lynchburg, where they will be pleased to see their old friends and the public generally.

Our stock consists in part as follows, to wit:

50 dozen Ladies Gents and Boy's Hose and ½ Hose,
60 " Spool Cotton—assorted colors,
12 " Tooth Brushes,
5 " Gent's Neckties
6 " " Collars,
1 " Hoop Skirts,
4 " Hats and Caps—some very nice,
6 " Shoe Knives,
5 " Men's Boots
30 " Gent's, Boy's and Servant's Shoes
10 " Ladies and Misses Shoes and Slippers
50 reams Note, Letter and Cap Paper,
20,000 White and Buff colored Envelopes,
10 packages Pins,
5000 Needles—assorted,
25 Ds Pat. Thread
5 " Sewing Silk
4 dozen Shirts and Drawers,
300 boxes Manufactured Tobacco,
15,000 choice Segars,
18 tierces Rice,
100 yds Fulled Cloth,

Together with a large lot of Fancy Goods, such as Combs, Brushes, Purses, Soap, Gloves, Buttons, &c. Also a few pieces of Prints and Irish Linen. We will also buy and sell all kinds of goods on commission. Give us a call.

P. BAYNE, } Formerly of Alexandria
C. B. HOOD, } " " Culpeper.
F. M. LATHAM, } " "

sept 18 d3m

Artillery Company.

POSITIONS as Jr. 1st and 2d Lieutenants can be secured in a Light Artillery Company in Major General Floyd's "State Line," by recruiting 25 men for the Jr, 1st and 20 men for the 2d. The recruits must be non-conscripts.

Persons wishing to recruit, will communicate with "STATE LINE," Abingdon, Va.

sept 20-dts

Wanted.

AN Irish Woman, without incumbrance, to cook wash and iron or general housework, by a lady residing in Lexington. Apply to McCorkle, Son & Co. sept 18-3t

A Card--New Dry Goods.

JNO. J. PURVIS, Agt., informs the public that he is receiving a great many scarce and desirable Goods, which are being sent him every week at lower prices than heretofore, viz:—Calicoes, Mouslin de Lawnes, White Goods, Black, White and Colored Stockings and Socks, Fine Tooth Combs, Pins, Needles and Knitting Pins. Also, Flannels, Blankets, Spun Cotton, Bleached Shirtings, &c.

P. S.—I have obtained facilities for receiving Fresh Goods almost every week during the approaching Fall and Winter

JNO. J. PURVIS,
sept 22-dts Agent.

A Card.

JOSEPH NAX, Professor of Music, and Refugee from his home, teaches the Piano Forte, Guitar, Flute and Violin. He has located himself permanently in Lynchburg, and proffers his services to those who wish to become proficients in Music.

He refers amongst others to E. F. Thom, Douglas Gordon, T. F. Howard, Dr. Gordon Wallace, Taliaferro Hunter, Wm. Allen and Commodore John Rudd, of Fredericksburg, where he has taught for the past fourteen years; to J. S. Barbour, President O. & A. R. R., H. W. Vandergrift, Superintendent O. & A. R. R., Edward Hill, Taylor Southern and Dr. Philip Slaughter, Culpeper C. H; Rev. Dr. J. L. Bacon, Howard Shackleford Warrenton, Va.; Dr. Russell Mann, Rev. H. W. Dodge, Dr. Charles Kemper, John M. Speed, Esq., Col. H. Hill, Paymaster C. S. A. and Rev. O. C. Lewis, Lynchburg.

Application made at Payne's Book Store, Main St., or at his residence, 2d door below corner of 9th and Clay st. sept 22-d1w

YANKEES PREPARING TO EVACUATE ALEXANDRIA.

A gentleman who left Alexandria last week states that the Yankee fleet that had been anchored in front of the town for some time past had been ordered off, but their destination was unknown. They have burned all the damaged wagons and were removing all their quartermaster, commissary and ordinance stores to Washington. It was believed there that these movements foreshadow an evacuation of that place

CUMBERLAND GAP EVACUATED.

GENERAL STEVENSON IN PURSUIT OF THE ENEMY.

From the Knoxville Register of Saturday we get the following certain intelligence from Cumberland Gap:

We have at last the satisfaction of announcing, upon official information, that the Federal force has evacuated Cumberland Gap, and that stronghold is again in the possession of our troops. The Federals are endeavoring to make their escape through Kentucky, and Gen. Stevenson is in hot pursuit of them.

Before leaving the Gap the Federal force are reported to have spiked their siege guns, and burned and destroyed everything that would impede their march. They also blasted large quantities of rock in the road in order to blockade it, and prevent pursuit. A large body of General McCown's forces, however, had previously got possession of Baptist Gap, and by that route are probably by this time close upon the track of the retreating foe, and will either capture or demolish him.

Our borders are now free from invasion, we trust, forever, and with the last lingering hope of aid to the tories of East Tennessee from Lincoln's despotism removed, we may expect to witness soon either a very great change in their sentiments and conduct, or a regular exodus from our midst.

From the Richmond Enq. Extra of Sunday.
FROM THE LIBERATING ARMY.

THE BATTLE IN MARYLAND!

ADDITIONAL PARTICULARS.

THE SURRENDER OF HARPER'S FERRY

We are enabled to give some authentic intelligence of the operations of our Army beyond Harper's Ferry, as late as to Tuesday night last:

The battle of Sunday, the 14th, which has been variously called the battle of Boonesboro' and Middletown, took place, in fact, between those two places, where the turnpike road crosses the Blue Ridge. Gen. Lee, in marching west from Frederick city, had posted Generals D. H. Hill and Stuart at the passes of the mountain, to hold back McClellan's forces, which were advancing to the relief of Harper's Ferry.

Harper's Ferry having held out somewhat longer than was expected, and McClellan's advance having become rapid, General Lee suspected that he might attempt to force the passage of the mountain, and fall upon the rear of General McLaws, who was occupying the Maryland Heights, and assisting in the reduction of Harper's Ferry. He accordingly returned with Gen. Longstreet's division, on Sunday, to Gen. Hill's support.

On approaching Boonesboro', couriers were met from Hill, announcing that the enemy were pressing him in strong force at the main pass on the Frederick and Hagerstown road, and that he required immediate reinforcements. Longstreet thereupon hurried his march, and very soon had his troops in position. By this time Hill's right had been forced back; and here the gallant Gen Garland had fallen while rallying his brigade.

General Longstreet soon succeeded in restoring our right, which afterwards successfully resisted to the very last the efforts of the enemy.

The enemy's superior numbers enabled him to make his line outstretch ours, both on the right and left. His right reached the summit of the mountain to our left, annoying us considerably from that direction.

The battle raged until after night. The enemy's determined effort to force a passage had been successfully resisted; and the object he had in view, the relief of Harper's Ferry, was now rendered impossible of accomplishment.

Late in the evening information was gained that the enemy had obtained possession of Crampton's Gap, on the direct road from Frederick City to Sharpsburg. This enabled him still to threaten McLaws' rear. General Lee having received information that Harper's Ferry would probably fall next morning, determined to withdraw Generals Longstreet and Hill from their position, and retire to Sharpsburg, where he could more readily unite his whole army. Sharpsburg is about ten miles north of Harper's Ferry, and about eight miles west of Boonesboro'. Lee's determination was rendered the more expedient from the fact that Gen. Sumner's corps of fresh troops had come up to relieve their wearied comrades, while on our side, we were without any such aid.

The trains were accordingly sent off, first, and our army followed, and about day-break Monday morning our position was taken in front of Sharpsburg. The march was entirely uninterrupted by the enemy.

McClellan's troops did not pass through the mountain gap until eight o'clock of Monday morning, and about 2 P. M. of the same day, their advance reached a position in front of our lines at Sharpsburg. They continued to gather up their forces; but up to Tuesday night had made no attack.

Gen. Lee also remained inactive, waiting for the junction of Jackson's forces. A part had reached him on Tuesday, evening, and the rest were near by, save Gen. A. P. Hill's Division, which had been left at Harper's Ferry to guard the place and protect the public property.

LATEST FROM HARPER'S FERRY

NO FURTHER FIGHTING UP TO WEDNESDAY EVENING!

Col. Lindsay Walker reached this city on this (Saturday) morning, direct from Harper's Ferry, which left on Wednesday evening. He reports that every thing was quiet there up to that time. We were hauling away the last of the stores which we captured there. For this purpose we were using the enemy's horses, 1,800 splendid fellows, that became ours at Harper's Ferry.

Colonel Walker brought with him the flags and banners captured at Harper's Ferry. Some of these are very beautiful, but show a very bad misapplication of very excellent silk.

The news brought by Colonel Walker of course utterly explodes the outrageous fabrications with which the Philadelphia Inquirer of the 18th, [Thursday morning,] and we presume the other Northern papers of the same date, delighted its readers. According to this veracious account, as we understand, Harper's Ferry was recaptured by Burnside on Tuesday evening at some precise hour, and A. P. Hill and his command taken prisoners! A great battle had also been fought, in which Jackson and Longstreet were in some way disposed of, and forty thousand of our men taken prisoners! The circulation of these statements in our city caused considerable anxiety, for little as we expect from the veracity of our enemies—we were not entirely prepared for such very extraordinary fabrications. We had forgotten, however, their present desperate fortunes. Mrs. Partington said that when she wants news she makes it for herself; the North has a similar resource for its victories.

Authentic Particulars.

A Decisive but Dearly Bought Victory,

We have received authentic particulars of the sanguinary battle of Sharpsburg, alluded to elsewhere, and concerning which so many painful rumors were afloat on yesterday. We have the gratification of being able to announce that the battle resulted in one of the most complete victories that has yet immortalized the Confederate arms. The ball was opened on Tuesday evening at 6 o'clock, all of our available force, about sixty thousand strong commanded by Gen. Robert E Lee in person, and the enemy about one hundred and fifty thousand strong, commanded by Gen. McClellan in person, being engaged. The position of our army being upon a range of hills, forming a semi-circle, with the concave towards the enemy; the latter occupying a less commanding position opposite, their extreme right resting upon a height commanding our extreme left. The arrangement of our line was as follows:

General Jackson was on the extreme left.

Gen Longstreet in the centre.

General A P Hill on the extreme right.

The fight on Tuesday evening was kept up until 9 o'clock at night, when it subsided into spasmodic skirmishes along the line. Wednesday morning it was renewed *by* Gen. Jackson, and gradually became general. Both armies maintained their respective positions, and fought desperately throughout the entire day. During this battle Sharpsburg was fired by the enemy's shells, and at one time, the enemy obtained a position which enabled them to pour a flanking fire upon a portion of our left wing, causing it to waver. At this moment, General Starke, of Mississippi, who had command of Jackson's Division, galloped to the front of his Brigade, and seizing the standard rallied them forward. No sooner did the gallant General thus throw himself in the van, than four bullets pierced his body, and he fell dead amidst his men. The effect, instead of discouraging, fired them with determination and revenge, and they dashed forward, drove the enemy back, and kept them from the position during the rest of the day.

It being evident that the "Young Napoleon," finding he could not force his way through the invicible ranks of our army in that direction, had determined upon a flank movement upon Harper's Ferry, and thus obtain a position in our rear, General Lee, with ready foresight, anticipated the movement by drawing the main body of his army back on the southside of the Potomac, at Shepherdstown, Virginia, whence he will, of course, project the necessary combinations for again defeating his adversary.

The enemy's artillery was served with disastrous effect upon our gallant troops; but they replied from musket, howitzer and cannon with a rapidity and will that carried havoc amidst the opposing ranks. The battle was one of the most severe that has been fought since the opening of the war. Many of our brave men fell. At dark the firing ceased, and in the morning (Thursday) our army were ready to recommence the engagement, the enemy having been forced back the evening before, and the advantage of the battle being still on our side.

Firing was consequently opened upon the new position supposed to be held by the enemy, but no reply was obtained, and it was then discovered that he had disappeared entirely from the field, leaving many of his dead and wounded in our hands, and about three hundred prisoners. The report current on yesterday that a truce occurred on Thursday for the burial of the dead, was unfounded. The prisoners stated that their force was more than a hundred thousand strong, and that McClellan commanded the army in person.

Our loss is estimated at 5,000 in killed wounded and missing. The prisoners state that their ranks were greatly decimated, and that the slaughter was terrible, from which we may infer that the enemy's loss was fully as great, if not greater than our own.

The following is a list of commanding officers killed and wounded in the engagement:

Gen. Stark, of Miss., commanding Jackson's division, killed.

Brigadier General Branch, of North Carolina, killed.

Brigadier General R. H. Anderson, wounded in hip, not dangerously.

Brigadier General Wright, of Ga., flesh wounds in breast and leg.

Brigadier General Lawton, in leg.

Brigadier General Armstead, in the foot.

Brig. Gen. Ripley, in neck, not dangerously.

Brig. Gen. Ransom, of N. C., slightly.

Col. Alfred Cummings, in command of Wilcox's Brigade, slightly.—*Enquirer of yesterday.*

The Artillery Captured

By Jackson at Harper's Ferry consisted of forty-nine cannon, twenty-four mountain howitzers, and seventeen revolving guns. The prisoners numbered 11,000 men *fit for duty*. They consisted of twelve regiments of infantry, three companies of cavalry and six companies of artillery.

SCHOOLS.

English Classical and Mathematical School,

CORNER OF 10TH AND MADISON STREETS.

THE subscriber, who has had 10 years experience in teaching, will open on Monday, 15th of September, 1862, in the house formerly occupied by Messrs. Harrison and Winston, a School for boys

TERMS.

For the Scholastic year, $40 and $50 with a contingent fee of $2 50 payable semi-annually in advance.

Persons desiring to enter pupils will leave their names with Captain McCorkle.

REFERENCES.

Profs Martin & Holladay, R S College, Prof C S Venable, Columbia, S C, Judge D A Wilson, Col Maurice Langhorne & Sons, Capt Sam'l McCorkle, F B Deane, Jr., John O L Goggin, Wm T Yancey, John M Speed, R J Davis, Esqrs., Mrs E L Brown, Lynchburg, †R T Hubard, Esq, Buckingham, †Judge R L C Moncure, Stafford, †Lawrence Roane, M D, Essex.

†Former patrons.

aug 20 till 3oct. C. S. MILLER, at Corner 10th and Madison St near Residence of Mrs. Gen. Rodes.

THE next session of the Lynchburg Female Seminary will open on MONDAY THE 22ND OF SEPTEMBER, 1862, and close on the 1st of July, 1863.

Competent Teachers have been employed in the several Departments.

TERMS-

Board for the entire session, exclusive of Washing,	$250,00
Tuition in the higher English Branches.	40,00
Tuition in the Primary Department,	30,00
" " Ancient and Modern Languages, for each different Language,	20,00
Tuition in Music on Piano or Guitar each,	50,00
For use of Piano,	10,00

Pupils who board at the Seminary will be required to furnish their own towels.

One fourth of all charges to be paid on the day of entrance, one fourth on the 1st of December 1862, one fourth on the 15th of February, 1863, and the remaining fourth on the 1st of May, 1863.

MRS. ROBERT L. BROWN,
aug 20-d2m Principal.

Lynchburg High School.

THE exercises of this SCHOOL for boys will be resumed on the 1st MONDAY IN SEPTEMBER, 1862, at my residence, 115 Church st.

Parents desirous of entering pupils will please inform the Principal at an early date. It is very important for the Scholar to begin with the School.

Terms—for five months, $20, for English; $22½ for Classical Students; Fuel $2—payable quarterly in advance.

The Principal may be seen at 115 Church St.
aug 18 ts F. M. EDWARDS.

New London Academy.

THE next scholastic year will begin on the 15th of September, 1862, and continue nine months. It will be divided into two sessions of four and a half months each.

Terms—For board and tuition, exclusive of lights and towels, $150 per session, payable in advance, or subject to special contract.

Pupils boarding are required to live with the Principal.

For further particulars address the undersigned at Forest Depot, Bedford co., Va.

JOHN H. WINSTON,
aug 14-dacts Principal.

Mrs. M. A. Otey's Class for Young Ladies.

WILL be open for the reception of pupils the FIRST MONDAY IN SEPTEMBER. Rooms on Court Street above 5th.

TERMS.

For session of 5 months, $20
No Extra charge for French or Latin.
aug 21 1m

Professional Notice.

WE, the undersigned physicians, practicing in the city of Lynchburg, find it necessary to increase our charges for the present to double the usual rate for visits.

JOHN H. PATTESON,
THOMAS T. BLACKFORD,
HY. LATHAM,
THOMAS L. WALKER,
ROBT. S. PAYNE,
D. A. LANGHORNE,
sept 22-d1w HENRY STEPTOE.

Blockade Goods.

JUST RECEIVED, 6 Bags Coffee, 1 Chest Imperial Green Tea, Boys and Misses Shoes, Yeast Powders, Lemon Syrup, Mustard, Soda, Blacking, Matches, Crushed Sugar, Powdered Sugar, Ladies Black Kid Gloves, Old Brown Windsor Soap, &c. &c. For sale wholesale and retail at the lowest prices. S. A. BOYD,
sept 22-d1m No 115, Main St.

On Consignment.

3 BBLS. Old and Pure Peach Brandy,
1 Chest Fine Black Tea,
10,000 Assorted Cigars,
10 Boxes Adamantine Candles,
To be closed out as soon as possible by
sept 22-1w STAPLES & ANDERSON.

BY TELEGRAPH.

LATEST FROM THE NORTH.

Victory Claimed by the Yankees at Sharpsburg.

Reported Battle at Murfreesboro Ky.

United States Arsenal at Pittsburg Blown Up.

FIVE CONFEDERATE STEAMERS IN PORT ST. GEORGE.

RICHMOND, Sept. 21.

The New York Herald of the 18th claims a victory at Sharpsburg—its dispatches are contradictory, but concur in stating that the Confederates were defeated.

Letters from Louisville claim a victory over Duncan and Scott's forces at Munfordsville Ky.

The Bermuda correspondent of the Herald says:

Five steamers are lying in the Port of St. George waiting an opportunity to run the blockade.

The United States Arsenal at Pittsburg Pa., was blown up on Wednesday. Seventy-five or eighty boys and girls were killed.

In New York on Wednesday Gold opened at 1,16⅞ and advanced to 1,17¾.

ANOTHER GREAT BATTLE IN MARYLAND.

RICHMOND, Sept. 21.—The Enquirer has a dispatch from Warrenton 20th, announcing a terrific fight at Sharpsburg, Md., on Wednesday. The advantage on our side. Great loss on both sides. Generals Starke, Manning and Branch were killed. Generals D. R. Jones, Ripley and Lawton were wounded

The whole strength of both armies was engaged in the fight.

The report says the fight was renewed on Thursday and the enemy were routed and driven nine miles.

Arrival of Fort Pulaski Prisoners.

MOBILE 21.—Col. Chas. Olmstead, Capt. T. W. Sims, Lieut. Henry Forman and 22 others of the Fort Pulaski prisoners arrived here to-day via Vicksburg, and left for home this morning.

Latest from the West.

CHATTANOOGA, Sept. 21.

The Nashville Union, of the 16th, says: If the rebels in Kentucky have any disposition to fight, and won't shun an engagement, there will be a great battle within three days, and it does not fear the result, as the best division and Generals in the Federal service are there.

LOUISVILLE THREATENED.

The Louisville Journal of the 12th, says the Rebels have no present intention to attack Cincinnatti, but that four heavy columns including Braggs, were then advancing on Louisville. Notwithstanding this, thousands of Federals are being sent from Louisville to Cincinnatti.

THE BATTLE AT SHARPSBURG.

GEN. LEE REPORTED TO HAVE RE-CROSSED THE POTOMAC.

RICHMOND, Sept. 22.

The accounts of the battle at Sharpsburg are meagre and somewhat contradictory, but agree in representing it to have been the most bloody and desperately contested engagement of the war.

The Confederate army though opposed by largely superior numbers, again illustrated its valor and invincibility by successfully repelling the repeated onsets of the enemy.

Officers have arrived here who state that they went over the battle-field on Thursday, and they assert that the advantage remained on our side, the enemy having fallen back.

The city papers this morning report on the authority of passengers who arrived last night, that General Lee re-crossed the Potomac on Friday, at Shepherdstown.

CONFEDERATE CONGRESS.

RICHMOND, Sept. 22.

In the Senate to-day a bill was passed providing that all persons who may hereafter furnish substitutes shall guarantee the fidelity of the substitutes. The residue of the day's session was occupied in the discussion of a bill introduced by Mr. Yancey to regulate the nomination and appointment of Brigadier Generals, so as to apportion them among the several States. The bill was rejected—yeas 2, nays 15.

In the House, Mr. Foster, of Alabama, submitted a resolution instructing the Secretary of War to send a corps of Engineers to make a reconnoissance of the Cumberland and Tennessee rivers with a view to erecting fortifications, &c. Adopted.

The Arkansas contested election case was further discussed.

The Tri-Weekly Mercury.

DAILY PAPER—TEN DOLLARS PER ANNUM, PAYABLE HALF-YEARLY IN ADVANCE.

VINDICE NULLO
SPONTE SUA SINE LEGE FIDES RECTUMQUE COLENTUR.

COUNTRY PAPER—THRICE A WEEK—FIVE DOLLARS PER ANNUM, IN ADVANCE.

VOLUME LXXXI | CHARLESTON, S. C., TUESDAY, SEPTEMBER 23 1862 | NUMBER 11,559

FROM THE WEST.

THE WAR IN KENTUCKY—THE PANIC IN CINCINNATI—"SKEDADDLING" OUT OF THE CITY—RECEPTION OF THE SOUTHERN ARMY AT LEXINGTON, KENTUCKY—THE DEFENCES OF CINCINNATI—UNIONISM IN KENTUCKY ALL A HUMBUG, ETC.

The moving of our army in Kentucky against the Ohio border has created almost as great a panic in the West as the advance of our forces into Maryland has created in the North. The accounts show the same excitement and panic in one quarter as in the other. The Cincinnati correspondent of the New York *Herald*, writing of the situation and movements of the army in Kentucky, says:

The excitement in Cincinnati is again at fever heat, and nothing is heard but the sound of the drum and the heavy tread of armed columns proceeding to the front. All business is again suspended, with the exception of such as is absolutely necessary, and the whole attention of the populace is giving to drilling and work in the trenches.

The enemy are, beyond all doubt, advancing, and in force, and there is not much space between our pickets and theirs. So close are they that we may look for a collision at any moment. The city bells this morning, at three o'clock, gave notice for the reserved force to assemble, and it was but five minutes after that the sharp rattle of the tenor drum gave us notice that detachments were on their way to headquarters. Yesterday a scouting party discovered the rebel advance guard but a few miles from our outposts. Two brigades, at least, were reported, and how many more were in the rear could only be supposed. I am listening every moment for the sound of musketry and artillery, and should not be surprised if before this letter is closed the work of death and destruction were going on.

The crowd at the office of the provost marshal this morning was large, consisting principally of strangers in the city, who were desirous of getting out of it. While the crowd was greatest, a regiment of citizens was drawn up in front, facing the opposite buildings, and the men in the ranks were not at all pleased to see so many men anxious for passes to leave the city, and amused themselves by addressing those desirous of leaving in no very complimentary remarks. The "skedads," however, did not resent them, being, apparently, too happy at procuring the much coveted piece of paper. Citizens of Cincinnati are not to-day allowed to leave the city, and very properly; for those not in arms are wanted here to afford protection, should it become necessary, to the families of those who are in the army, and who are now comparatively alone, and to look out for the comfort of any who may be unfortunate enough to be wounded.

From gentlemen direct from Lexington and Paris I derive some interesting information relative to the reception the rebels met with on their arrival at these cities. At Lexington the populace were enthusiastic on their arrival. The ladies were at the windows, clapping their hands and showering flowers on the column as it passed through the streets. One immense bouquet was carried by an officer at the head of the column, which had been bestowed upon him by some fair rebel, and the men on all sides were cheering most vehemently. At Paris it was about the same thing; the men who but a few days since were professing the most entire loyalty to the Union seemed to vie with each other to give the rebels the most hearty welcome. It is said, and I believe truly, that the rebels have in Lexington alone recruited two full regiments, and a third is nearly full. This is only in one place, and there is no doubt of their being able to do as well in almost every other. This is a fair sample of the loyalty of the mass of the Kentuckians.

From all I can learn respecting the number, condition and organization of our forces here, and the fortifications, I have no fear but that we shall be able to repulse the enemy. I hope we may yet be able to bag Kirby Smith and his horde of unwashed and ragged rebels, and once more rid Kentucky of its invaders, and punish those of her citizens who, while professing loyalty to the Union, have, on the first appearance of a rebel soldier, hallooed as loudly as any one for Jeff. Davis and the Confederacy. If our armies, in marching into a rebellious city, were only received in the same manner as those of the rebels are when entering a city or town, we should then have some hopes regarding the loyalty of the people, but they are not, and I much fear that this feeling against us is growing worse and worse every day. I have yet to learn of one instance, fully established, where our men have been received in the South, or rather in slave territory, as were the rebels the other day in Lexington and Paris. What are we to infer from this? Certainly not that there is a strong Union feeling existing among the Southerners, and a wish to come once more under the protecting folds of the old flag. When we see the feeling existing among females—they who naturally desire peace—so bitter, so clamorous for war and bloodshed, and desiring the extermination of the Yankees, we can hope for no better feeling on the part of their fathers, husbands and brothers, and must not expect it from any one of them.

Another correspondent, writing of the panic in Cincinnati, says:

There has been an amount of excitement in the city to-day, arising from the fact that an alarm arose among the pickets on the other side of the river, a little after midnight. The alarm bell tolled out its solemn notes of warning for two or three hours before the day broke. At six again, this morning, the bells rang out the notice for all to be prepared, and at eight o'clock all the organized bands in the city were ordered to be at their places of meeting, ready to receive their orders. The Eighth Ward organization, composed of over nine hundred men, has just marched down Race street, on its way over the river. There is also a loud call on the fortification brigade this morning to repair immediately to the trenches and hasten the completion of the same, the work on which has much fallen off the last two days, owing to the resumption of business, and provost guards are patroling the city, using the persuasive and usually very successful argument of the bayonet, when other inducements fail to convince a man of the necessity there is for more laborers. But laborers must be had, and the fortifications must be finished.

This morning martial law was put in full force again, closing stores and suspending all business; and this time it is likely to be continued until all occasion for any restriction shall have passed away.

The enemy is represented to be approaching in two divisions in force, while at the same time there are light forces on every avenue of entrance into Covington. An attack is confidently expected before morning, and all the forces from Louisville have been ordered to repair immediately to Cincinnati. Their arrival will be anxiously looked for. This afternoon our pickets are reported as fighting those of the enemy, and are said to have fallen back a mile. This report is probably true; and if it is a battle may be expected to-morrow.

The advance of the enemy on our fortifications has been confirmed. Several of our pickets have been wounded, and the attack may be expected at any moment. Reinforcements of veteran troops are expected to-night.

That a crisis is approaching, and that we are on the eve of an awful struggle here, no sane man can doubt. Many of our military men some days ago set apart to-morrow (Thursday) as the day on which the struggle was to take place, and, from all the indications on the right and the front of our lines, it will not be delayed much longer than that time.

The Governor of Tennessee, Isham G. Harris, issues an order from his Executive Headquarters, Chattanooga, for the enrollment of conscripts in the State. Gen. Bragg has issued a similar order.

It is generally conceded at the North that if Pennsylvania be invaded by the rebels, the Cumberland Valley will most likely be one of their points of entry.

A Yankee paper reports that "the rebel privateer Sumter, now '290,' has received a heavy armament at sea, and is prepared to make an assault upon Northern commerce."

Major General Cassius M. Clay is ordered to report in person to Major General Butler at New Orleans, for duty in the Department of the Gulf.

TRI-WEEKLY MERCURY.

TUESDAY, SEPTEMBER 23, 1862.

The operations of our armies during the past few months have been one unbroken series of splendid triumphs. Everywhere we have been gathering the fruits of that activity and energy of movement which the example of the invincible JACKSON seems to have infused amongst our military leaders, and Fortune seems still to smile and beckon onward our victorious columns to new and richer fields. The day for ditching and delay is gone; and, henceforward, we trust, the Southern armies, victors or vanquished, will be handled with the vigor which has already achieved so many happy results.

The capture of Harper's Ferry, with its garrison of eleven thousand Yankees, its negros, its immense artillery train, wagons and stores, is, perhaps, the most complete and valuable and, at the same time, the least costly success that we have gained, thus far, during the war. The position is one from which we cannot be dislodged. In occupying it, we hold the key to the rugged and mountainous region of the Upper Potomac, and can maintain easy communication, by the way of the Valley, with our army in Maryland. Secure in the possession of the heights which overlook the Ferry, we are masters of that great military thoroughfare, the Baltimore and Ohio Railroad, and are provided with a most convenient base for future operations. Add to these advantages, the varied and most timely booty of arms, supplies, wagons and negros, that have fallen into our hands and the loss of eleven thousand trained troops to the Yankee service, and it will be seen how valuable was our victory. In the sight of Europe, the fall of Harper's Ferry, following so closely upon our late successes, will be regarded as more than an offset to the disasters of Roanoke Island and Fort Donelson.

THE CONFEDERATE CONGRESS.

In the Senate, on Wednesday last, the session was occupied with the discussion of the exemption bill. The clause exempting tanners, shoemakers, millers, etc., was agreed to. Also, the clause exempting Quakers and Dunkards; and another exempting physicians. The clause exempting Theological students was stricken out.

In the House a resolution was adopted instructing the Judiciary Committee to report a bill establishing a Supreme Court of the Confederate States. Substitutes were offered for the Conscript bill, by Mr. Davis, of Mississippi, and Mr. Bonham, of South Carolina; both were rejected. The original House bill passed, yeas, 49—nays, 39. Mr. Foote introduced a resolution, proposing to send a Commissioner or Commissioners to Washington, empowered to propose terms of a just and honorable peace. Mr. Holt, of Georgia, submitted a substitute, declaring that the people of the Confederate States have ardently desired peace from the beginning; and whenever the United States Government shall have manifested a like anxiety, it shall be the duty of the President to appoint Commissioners to treat and negotiate with said Government. The resolution and substitute were laid upon the table; yeas, 57, nays, 26.

Neither House of Congress was in session on Thursday.

In the Senate, on Friday, the House bill to provide for the payment of the troops raised in Missouri by Gen. Sterling Price was passed—an act of tardy justice. An hour was spent in secret session. After the doors were opened, the Military Exemption Bill was discussed until the adjournment.

In the House of Representatives, the amendments of the Senate to the House bill providing for the further issue of Treasury notes were concurred in. A resolution of thanks to Major General Magruder and command was adopted. Mr. Foote, from the Committee on Foreign Affairs, to whom was referred the resolutions relative to the conduct and policy of the war, etc., reported back the same, with modifications. Mr. Barksdale presented a minority report. Both reports were ordered to be printed.

In the Senate on Saturday, the Military Exemption Bill was further considered, and finally passed—yeas 16, nays 3.

In the House, the Senate bill, fixing the second Monday in January as the time of meeting of the next regular session of Congress. Also, the House bill to provide for the prompt payment of claims, arrearages and bounty due to deceased soldiers. The Arkansas contested election case was then discussed until the hour of adjournment.

THE GOOD ORDER OF OUR ARMY ON ENTERING MARYLAND.—The following note, written to correct the account given by the American of Gen. O'Donnell's passage through our lines at Frederick, attests the good order of our troops:

BALTIMORE, September 10, 1862.

We have seen a statement in your paper this morning giving an account of our visit to the Confederate army, which we regret to find entirely incorrect.

We have no knowledge of the extent of the army or its intended movements. We were kindly received, and Gen. Lee gave us a pass to return home, with a request that we would give no information about the extent or intentions of the army. Our property was not injured, and from all the information we could procure, was the property of any of the inhabitants of the county taken, or any of them disturbed in any way. We found good order prevailing in the city, and everything quiet and orderly.

Respectfully, yours,
COLUMBUS O'DONNELL.
C. OLIVER O'DONNELL.

FACTORY GOODS ADVANCING.—The *Chronicle* says the weekly sale of Augusta Factory goods took place at the office of the company on Friday. Prices have advanced over those of last week: 4/8 shirting, 50¼@50¾c.; 7/8 shirting (light), 40¼c.; 4-4 sheeting, 57¾@58c.; drilling, 65@65½c. Graniteville Factory goods sold as follows: 7/8 shirting, 50½c.; 3/4 shirting, 40c.; 4-4 sheeting, 58c.; drill, 65c.

REPORTS FROM THE NORTH.—A paroled prisoner from Fort Delaware brought the report to Winchester, on Thursday last, that the greatest confusion prevails in Washington, and that LINCOLN has gone to Buffalo. Gen. WOOL has been sent to Philadelphia to fortify, and all the Pennsylvania troops are concentrating at that place.

REPORTED RE-OCCUPATION OF LEESBURG BY THE ENEMY.—The President on Friday received a despatch from the surgeon at Warrenton, Va., stating that a report had reached that place of the re-capture of Leesburg by the Yankee forces. The despatch states that the Yankees shelled the town before entering it.

To the Editor of the Mercury:—Please acknowledge the following sums received for the Free Market:

September 1.	From an Old Citizen	$25.00
" 2.	From B. Mordecai, collections in Ward No. 5	87.60
	From R. R. Bank	80.00
	From Bank of the State of So. Ca.	100.00
	From Friend to Charity	20.00
	From Dr. Solomons	5.00
" 3.	From Bank of Charleston	200.00
	From Bank of the State of So. Ca.	100.00
	From Henry Winthrop	25.00
" 4.	From Soldiers' Board of Relief	980.00
	From City Council	2,000.00
" 5.	From J. Reed Boyleston	50.00
" 8.	From A Stranger	50.00
" 17.	From Mrs. M. J. Kinloch, Flat Rock, N. C.	50.00
" 20.	From Courier Office, collections	787.60

JNO. H. HONOUR,
Treasurer Free Market.

FROM OUR ARMY IN MARYLAND—THE BATTLE OF SHARPSBURG AND FALL OF HARPER'S FERRY.

The Richmond papers bring us some further and interesting accounts of the recent brilliant operations of our army on the Upper Potomac and in Maryland. The following is a brief *resume* of the various accounts of these important movements, concerning which the telegraphic news hitherto received has been so vague and unsatisfactory. Our army in Maryland is divided into three corps, commanded by Generals JACKSON, LONGSTREET and D. H. HILL. Of these corps JACKSON's was engaged in the siege of Harper's Ferry, and the other two covered his operations. Conceiving it to be of great importance to raise the siege and to relieve the beleaguered forces, which amounted in numbers almost to a *corps d'armee*, MCCLELLAN resolved to make a powerful effort. He left Washington, it is said, with a force of 80,000 men. From the correspondents of the Yankee papers we heard of him at Rockville and other places on the National road, some time last week, from which we conclude that his army marched upon that road in the direction of Frederick. Whether he passed through Frederick we know not; but the first we hear of him is at Sharpsburg, some twenty miles west of Frederick, and about ten miles northwest of Harper's Ferry. At this place, on Sunday, he fell with his whole enormous force (80,000 men) upon the corps of Gen. D. H. HILL, which was the rear guard of the army. The battle was long, furious and bloody; but Gen. HILL, although attacked by vastly superior forces, stood his ground without yielding an inch. In the night Gen. LONGSTREET's corps arrived, and on Monday the two combined attacked MCCLELLAN and defeated him, driving his forces before them for five miles. But for the intervention of night, it is said the route would have been complete. At ten o'clock, while the battle was still raging at Boonesborough, General MILES, with his whole army, variously estimated at eight, ten, and twelve thousand men, surrendered to Gen. JACKSON. Vast quantities of stores, 12,000 small arms, fifty pieces of artillery, and at least 1,000 negros (some say 2,500) were captured. Having disposed of MILES and his army, Gen. JACKSON was marching rapidly down the Potomac, with the intention of crossing below and getting in the rear of MCCLELLAN, thus cutting him off effectually from Washington.

It should be mentioned that several days previous to the battle at Sharpsburg, a despatch from MCCLELLAN to Col. MILES, commanding at Harper's Ferry, urging him to hold the position, promising reinforcements, was intercepted by Gen. LEE, who, accordingly, posted Gen. D. H. HILL's Division near Boonesboro' to check the reinforcing column, and made such disposition of the remaining forces as would ensure the discomfiture of the Yankee hosts.

THE SURRENDER OF HARPER'S FERRY—FURTHER PARTICULARS.

From a participant in the engagement, the Richmond *Dispatch* obtains the following particulars, with reference to the investment and subsequent surrender of Harper's Ferry:

Gen. Jackson left Frederick on Thursday, taking the Hagerstown road, and at the same time the divisions of Gens. McLaws and R. H. Anderson moved from the vicinity of Frederick for the Maryland Heights, overlooking the town of Harper's Ferry. On Wednesday the division of Gen. Walker was sent down to destroy the canal aqueduct at the mouth of the Monocacy, and arrived at the point during that night. The next morning, early, before they had accomplished their purpose, an order was received from Gen. Lee, directing General Walker to proceed with his forces, by forced marches, to the Loudoun Heights, *via* Point of Rocks, to prevent the enemy at Harper's Ferry from escaping in that direction. The division crossed the river at Point of Rocks, nine miles below Harper's Ferry, and on Friday evening, reached the position assigned them. Gen. Jackson's force reached Williamsport, on the Potomac, on Friday morning, and immediately crossed and moved on Martinsburg, twenty miles above Harper's Ferry, where there were some three or four thousand of the enemy's forces. On the approach of Gen. Jackson this force fell back, and united with the force at Harper's Ferry, believed to number about five thousand. Gen. Jackson pursued, and on Saturday morning reached Balltown, four miles southwest of Harper's Ferry. From this point he dispatched a courier to Gen. Walker, then in possession of the Heights south of the town, directing him not to open his guns upon the enemy's fortifications until he (Gen. J.) got in position, of which he promised to notify General Walker. Meanwhile the divisions of McLaws and Anderson, after but little resistance, had become masters of the Heights on the Maryland side, the enemy leaving them, and joining the forces in their entrenchments on the Virginia side of the river. On Saturday night General Walker received orders from General Jackson to open fire upon the enemy at daylight on Sunday morning. In obedience to this order, at day-dawn the stillness of the Sabbath was broken by the opening of Walker's guns upon the fortifications of the enemy on Bolivar Heights, two miles above the railroad bridge at Harper's Ferry. At the same time the attack was made by the forces under General Jackson, and the fight, which was desperate and determined, continued throughout the day—McLaws and Anderson shelling from the Maryland side. The enemy resisted with great spirit, and their guns, of which they had a large number in position, were handled with great effect upon the column of Gen. Jackson, which had to approach them through an open space, where their guns had unobstructed play. The shells from Walker's batteries and the impetuous attacks of Jackson's men rendered their entrenchments on Bolivar Heights too warm for the enemy, and late in the evening they fell back to Camp Hill, one mile in rear of the Bolivar fortifications. Here they had heavy guns planted and strong entrenchments thrown up, but within easy range of the batteries of McLaws and Anderson, on the opposite heights. Night coming on, the struggle ceased, Jackson's forces occupying the deserted entrenchments on the hills of Bolivar. That night old "Stonewall" sent a message to Gen. Walker that his forces were in possession of the enemy's first line of entrenchments, and that with God's blessing, he would have Harper's Ferry and the Federal forces early the next morning.

At daylight the next morning (Monday) the fight was renewed, the enemy still offering an obstinate resistance, until about 7 o'clock, a. m., when their colors were struck and a capitulation proposed. Of the terms of this capitulation we have learned no particulars, but conclude that they involved the unconditional surrender of the whole force, negros as well as Yankees. About 9 o'clock our forces entered the second line of entrenchments—the enemy having surrendered everything—guns, ordnance, and commissary stores, &c. The number of the enemy is variously estimated at from seven to twelve thousand, and the negros from fifteen hundred to two thousand. The quantity of ammunition captured is immense, amounting to several hundred wagon loads.

THE IMPENDING FATE OF BALTIMORE.

The *American* is very serious about the fate of Baltimore. It says the Confederates will certainly have it, if it is only for twenty-four hours, so as to possess themselves of the provisions there. It begs the inhabitants to be peaceful, and not provoke the Federal Government to destroy the city. It thus concludes:

The government would never permit a moment's peaceable possession by the rebels of a city so completely essential to every hope of maintaining its integrity. Let us remind any secession sympathizer right here that a portion of the formidable New Orleans mortar fleet is quietly at anchor near the heart of the city, as an adjunct of the terrible batteries, ready to rain destruction upon hostile occupants from so many points, if they were once to obtain a foothold here.

THE FIRST ENTRY INTO FREDERICK—INTERESTING DESCRIPTION.

The Baltimore *Advertiser* describes the first appearance of Confederate troops in Maryland as very quiet and orderly, but it is very much outraged at "some of them having passed off Confederate money," which it doesn't think is exactly on the square. It says:

They made their appearance in the city about 10 o'clock in the morning, and marched in quietly, evidently having full knowledge that there was no opposition to be made to them. The force was halted on Market-street, and a proclamation issued to the people. We have not been able to obtain a copy of the proclamation, but learn that it was to the effect that they came as friends, and not as enemies, to relieve the people of Maryland from the tyranny by which they were enchained; that they did not propose to interfere with any non-combatants, to disturb private property, or to enquire into their opinions; and that whatever stores they required would be paid for either in Confederate notes or United States Treasury notes, as the people might prefer. Of the latter money, the men are represented as having a good supply, supposed to have been rifled from the bodies of the dead on the battlefield.

A rebel Provost Marshal was appointed, with a strong guard to preserve order, and during the afternoon the streets were thronged with rebel soldiers, visiting the stores which the Provost Marshal ordered to be opened, and purchasing of shoes and clothing, of which they were in great want. So far as we could learn strict order was preserved.

One of our informants states that a meeting of the citizens was called on Saturday evening, at which an address was delivered by Bradley Johnson, who used the most conciliatory language, and made great predictions as to the power of the rebel army not only to hold Western Maryland, but to capture Baltimore and Washington, and dictate terms of peace in Independence Square at Philadelphia. The rebel sympathizers generally attended the meeting, but the few Union men who had remained kept to their homes. At 10 o'clock at night the men were ordered to their camps on the outskirts of the city, and the first day of rebel rule in Frederick passed off quietly and peacefully.

The Federal flag was lowered from all the poles in Frederick, and the rebel Stars and Bars hoisted in their place. Most of the officers were quartered at the hotels and at the houses of prominent rebels, though a good many of the latter had also fled the city.

The foraging parties sent out in various directions to secure cattle, returned during the evening with droves of sheep, hogs, beeves, cows, and horses. They seized everything they wanted, and are said to have tendered payment in Federal "green backs," whether counterfeit or good is not known. These cattle were all driven towards the Potomac, rendering it probable that the whole invasion is only for foraging purposes, and to furnish supplies for the main body of the army on the other side of the Potomac.

The purchases made in Frederick are said to have been paid for partly in Federal money, but mostly in Virginia and South Carolina money.

MEMORANDUM DIARY OF THE ENEMY'S APPROACH TO AND WITHDRAWAL FROM BEFORE, CHARLESTON, S. C.—MAY, JUNE AND JULY, 1862.

BY A SOLDIER.

May 17.—Enemy sounding Stono Channel in barges. One fired on from Goat Island by riflemen, and driven off.

May 19.—Several of the enemy's gunboats attempted to enter Stono Inlet; one ran aground and all put back.

May 20.—Three gunboats crossed the Bar and entered the Stono River about 10 o'clock, a. m.—One ran up and anchored a little below Battery Island, commanding the old (river) route from Coles' Island—the enemy thinking, probably, to cut off our troops on Coles' Island. Lieut. Col. Ellison Capers, 24th Regiment, S. C. V., commanding on Coles' Island, withdrew his force (two companies), under standing orders, to James' Island, by the new (back) and scarcely completed route over Dixon's Island. Captain L. Buist, Palmetto Guard, commanding on Battery Island, withdrew his force (two companies) under similar orders, also to James' Island. By like orders the buildings on Coles' and on Battery Island were fired by our men before retiring.—Volumes of smoke from the burning buildings. Our men on the *qui vive*. On appearance of a gunboat off mouth of Folly River carronade on marsh battery, near Folly River, thrown overboard, by those in charge. Coles' and Battery Island shelled by the enemy.

May 21.—Six of our pickets, of Capt. Jones' company, 24th Regiment, S. C. V., made prisoners on Battery Island; expecting, apparently, the enemy to pass by, without discovering them, they, instead of withdrawing, hid themselves in the magazine on the approach of a gunboat up the Stono. Enemy saw them and landed. Legare's, on James' Island, shelled this day by a gunboat slowly going up the Stono.

May 25.—Gunboats to this time had been running up the Stono for several miles every day, shelling both sides of the river, and returning in the evening to Battery Island. Effort to-day of Brig. Gen. Ripley to draw them within effective reach of guns of Fort Pemberton failed. Gallantry of Capt. Frank Bonneau, and the men of our little floating battery, stationed for the day in the creek near Dixon's Island, remarked. A gunboat which engaged the battery was driven off in a few minutes. The battery was moored to the land. Three gunboats had been drawn up the river a short distance by Gen. Ripley's movements. On their return, they had passed by all together, when one came back, apparently to learn what was the little dark object across the marshes and the small Islands. Capt. B, who was aboard, had just received orders not to fire unless attacked. He had his men ashore, under cover. The gunboat opened on him. Capt. B. promptly fired his battery (two or three guns) himself. His men, at the first sound of the enemy's gun, came bounding to their little *float*, and soon manning their guns, drove the gunboat away.

May 31.—Gunboats, to this time, running up the Stono every morning, as before, shelling every one who came in sight, whether on foot, on horse, or in a vehicle. Some peaceful citizens crossing Newtown Cut Bridge in a buggy, during this period, were very much startled by a shell, *and took to flight on foot across the fields*. To-day a few shell, thrown from the Stono, towards Secessionville, fell near the camp of 24th Regiment, S. C. V., and to Brigadier Gen. Gist, Capt. Jas. Gist and Capt. Jos. Glover of his staff, who were riding out.

June 1.—(Sunday).—A gunboat came some distance up Folly River, but soon retired. Reconnoitering apparently.

June 2.—A gunboat came up Folly River this morning on the flood, about 9 a. m., shelled the battery of Capt. Chichester at Legare's Point, that of Capt. Warley, close to Secessionville, and Secessionville itself. This place being then occupied by the Eutaw Battalion, Lieut. Colonel Chas. H. Simonton commanding; the Charleston Battalion, Lieut. Col. P. C. Gaillard commanding; the cavalry companies of Capt. W. L. Disher and of Capt. —— McKewn, and being the headquarters of Brig. Gen. S. R. Gist, commanding on the island. Our batteries responded rigorously. No damage done by the enemy, except to a horse, which had his leg broken by a shell that passed through an out house just behind the Genl's headquarters and exploded. After firing for about an hour, the enemy withdrew. No damage, up to this time, done by the enemy's firing, *except to horses*.

Evening.—More than twenty vessels in sight off Charleston Bar and Stono Inlet and in Stono River. Enemy reported as *being on James Island*, at the point nearest Battery Island, and as having driven in our pickets. Capt. Carlos Tracy, volunteer aid to Gen. Gist, and Lieut. Winter, Wassamassaw Cavalry, fired on while reconnoitering their position. Gen. Gist and Capt. Tracy repeatedly fired on, same evening, by enemy's advance guard. This firing *the first news in camp* of enemy's landing.

June 3.—Last night the enemy and a small party of our men lay near each other all night, at Legare's. Capt. Chichester's guns, in being withdrawn from Legare's Point during the night, stuck in the mud. Men engaged in indeavoring to extricate them driven off by the enemy near morning. Lt. Col. Ellison Capers, 24th Regiment S. C. V., with several companies, sent just after daylight to bring off the guns and to ascertain enemy's position. Sharp skirmish with the enemy at Legare's, in which Lieut. Col. Capers drove back, for a half mile and more, the enemy's troops in his front, though very much outnumbering him; took twenty-three prisoners and retired only on the appearance of the enemy in heavy force on the field, supported by a cross fire from gunboats in the Stono and in Folly River. Enemy engaged said to have been 28th Massachusetts and 100th Pennsylvania Volunteers. Our loss, several wounded and one taken prisoner. Lieut. Walker, Adjutant Charleston Battalion, wounded in the leg, in an endeavor to bring off whom, it was said, Private Bresnan Irish Volunteers, was mortally wounded. Gallantry and discretion of Lieut. Colonel Capers marked. Capt. Ryan, Irish Volunteers, Charleston Battalion, distinguished himself by his dashing courage. Lieut. J. Ward Hopkins, Sumter Guard, Charleston Battalion, wounded in shoulder. Our companies first engaged were reinforced during the action by several others. All fell back across the causeway to Rivers' merely, and joined the main body of our troops. Enemy ascertained from prisoners to be in strong force at Legare's, under command of Brig. Gen. Stevens. Heavy bombardment all day by gunboats, of our troops in line of battle, to resist enemy's advance from Legare's; our troops necessarily much exposed. A section of Capt. Wm. C. Preston's Battery Light Artillery, under Capt. Preston and Lieut. Julius Rhett, was carried with great promptness and dash into position, and worked with fierce energy under a heavy cross fire from the gunboats in the two rivers, and under a direct fire from a piece of the enemy's at the woods on Legare's in front. The fire from these guns, and from the stationary and more distant batteries of Col. T. G. Lamar and of Captain —— Warley, in the direction of Secessionville, rendered the enemy's advance across the causeway, though repeatedly threatened, too perilous for him to attempt. Brig. Gen. H. W. Mercer arrived from Charleston in the afternoon. Col. Johnson Hagood, 1st Regiment S. C. V., previously detained in the city, by his duties as Provost Marshal, joined his regiment during the day. Casualties light. Brig. Gen. Gist and Aids covered with sand, from explosion of shells. The screeching of the rifle shells and the heavy explosions of the 11 and 13-inch subsided a little after dark into a discharge of a shell from a gunboat, at a regular interval of half an hour, during the night. Our men—wet, weary and hungry—slept on their arms. The night tempestuous.

June 4.—Main body of our troops driven within the lines. Gunboats from creek in front shelled Secessionville. Design of enemy to occupy apparent. Enemy said to be advancing this evening. Untrue.

June 5.—Enemy said to be advancing this evening. Our troops marched to the front. Everything quiet by sun-down. No fight.

June 6.—Brig. Gen. W. D. Smith arrived on the Islandand assumed command, Gen. Mercer having been ordered to take command at Savannah. Picket guard this evening, under Colonel C. H. Stevens, 24th Regiment S. C. V., skirmished with the enemy at the Presbyterian Church. Enemy left one dead on the ground. Indications that he suffered further. A section of Preston's Battery did some firing. No loss on our side. A prisoner brought into camp.

June 7.—Alarm in evening. Troops to the front. Everythig soon quiet. Enemy moving about Grimball's, on the Stono.

June 8.—Enemy evidently in force at Grimball's. A prisoner brought in this evening.

June 10.—During a reconnoissance in some force, this afternoon, under General Smith, a part of the troops—the 47th Georgia Volunteers, Col. Williams, commanding—were repulsed in the woods, at Grimball's, after a gallant onset upon the enemy, advantageously posted, supported by artillery and aided by his gunboats in the Stono. Our loss serious. Captain Williams killed. The wood through which the 47th advanced, so dense that order, it was said, could not be preserved, nor could commands be properly extended. Great regret for the loss of the brave Georgians. Heavy firing nearly all night from gunboats in the Stono.

June 14.—Brigadier General N. G. Evans arrived on the Island to assume command. Heavy firing of shot and shell upon Secessionville, from enemy's gunboats, and from a battery erected at Legare's Point. Vigorous replies of Col. Lamar's guns. Firing nearly all day. One man killed in his tent, at Secessionville, by a shell.

June 15.—Similar firing upon Secessionville. Col. Lamar replies more deliberately. Firing very slow towards night. Two men wounded on our side.

June 16.—Attack of the enemy at daylight on the earthwork at Secessionville. Brig. Gen. Stevens in command of assaulting column of six regiments: 8th Michigan, 7th Connecticut, 28th Massachusetts, 79th Highlanders, 46th New York, and 100th Pennsylvania. Brig. Gen. Williams in command of brigade operating to flank the work on its right, by an advance on Hill's place; Brig. Gen. Benham in command of whole. Our work a simple priest cap, covering a neck of land about fifty (50) yards wide, flanked right and left by a creek, and defended by four guns and about six hundred men. Enemy repulsed with fearful loss. Col. T. G. Lamar in immediate command of our batteries, assisted by the no less brave Lieut. Col. Thos. M. Wagner, Captain Reid, Lieutenant Humbert, and others, and supported by the brave Col. Gaillard and the infantry. Colonel C. H. Stevens and Colonel Simonton showed promptitude and skill, repulsing the flank movement on our right. Enemy's fire from gunboats in Stono and Folly Rivers, from his stationary battery at Legare's Point, from his light artillery, and from his small arms, terribly severe, particularly so his fire on our right flank from across the creek at Hills'. Our battery at one time almost silenced by this latter fire. A gun, worked by Lieut. Col. Ellison Capers, in a little battery across the creek, at Clarke's, somewhat flanking the enemy's advance, did effective service. By order of Colonel Johnson Hagood, in command of advanced troops, the Louisiana Battalion, Lieutenant Colonel McEnery, reinforced the garrison at Secessionville during the fight, and rushing gallantly into the fire with the cry of "*Remember Butler*," soon drove the enemy from his flanking position at Hill's. The Eutaw Battalion, on the right, engaged the enemy for a short time in the woods, to the rear of Hill's house, when he fell back, together with the troops engaged by the Louisiana Battalion and our other troops from across the creek. Then the entire force of the enemy, between five and six thousand strong, slowly and sullenly retired from the attack to their positions on the Stono, and within their late line of pickets, burning Rivers' house on their retreat. Enemy's loss probably 800 men; ours under 100. The brave Capts. Reid, of Col. Lamar's Regiment of Artillery, and King, of Sumter Guard, Charleston Battalion, Lieut. Edwards, and many other gallant men of ours, killed. Col. Hagood, while leading his horse by the reins, had them severed by a piece of shell. Several of the enemy bravely mounted our ramparts. Several got to the rear of it, by flanking it, on the left.

June 17.—Gen. S. Cooper, senior General, C. S. A., visited the Island to-day.

June 18.—Flag of truce from the enemy, to inquire after wounded and prisoners, and asking leave to send comforts to them, and offering similar privilege to us as to our men.

June 20.—A few shell thrown by a gunboat to-day at men at work on our west line.

July 1.—Total inactivity of the enemy, offensively, since repulse of 16th ult., except the firing of the few shell on 20th. Grand salute to-day at sunrise, along our entire line, and at Forts Johnson, Sumter and Moultrie, in honor of our successes before Richmond. Enemy reported to be advancing. Troops under arms, and to the front. False alarm. Enemy suspected to be about to retire from the Island.

July 5.—Enemy's land force, known to have been retiring for several days from Grimball's, now ascertained to be all withdrawn from that place. Transports, for several days past, seen going out of Stono. Gunboats in the river off Grimball's.

July 7.—Major Wm. Duncan, 1st Regiment S. C. V., narrowly escaped being made prisoner by a party of the enemy at the large work thrown up between Rivers' burnt house and the Stono. Party probably from gunboats. Enemy withdrawn from Legare's.

July 8.—Enemy known *to have altogether abandoned James Island*, and our city to be safe for the present.

SCAN THE EVIL OMENS.—No. VIII.

Obsta Principiis.

If it should be affirmed that a more plausible argument can be framed in favor of the power of *our* Congress to make and issue "paper money," than ever was or could be, in behalf of the Congress of the United States, it is presumed such argument is expected to be drawn from this provision in our Constitution, to wit: "The Government established by this Constitution is the successor of the Provisional Government of the Confederate States of America, and all the laws passed by the latter shall continue in force until the same shall be repealed or modified;" and from the fact that a law of the Provisional Government existed, partly executed and in process of execution, when the existing Constitution took effect, authorizing the issue of Treasury Notes, in the similitude of paper money. Several difficulties lie in the way of obtaining any aid from this source. In the first place, only specific laws obtained thereby an efficacy, protracted (at the utmost) only till they were exhausted by their own action or limitation, and liable always to cease to be at the pleasure of Congress. In the second place, the clause quoted delegates no power whatever to Congress, except to terminate or modify such laws when their discretion should prompt the one or the other; and so far as the clause is concerned, not a particle of authority is delegated to imitate the example of the Provisional Government, and the Federal Government is left still to seek for any power to originate and enact any law to their charter, their power of attorney, as though the clause under consideration had never existed. In the third place, the Governments, under both Constitutions, were enjoined to perform the contracts and engagements entered into by their respective predecessors, and the Continental Congress, as well as the separate States, had issued, and they are in circulation, "bills of credit"—paper money; and what is more, various of such issues, by either Government, had been declared a legal tender in payment of debts. In the fourth place, the Provisional Government never made any of its paper issues such a legal tender; and, therefore, if its legislation respecting them should "continue in force" to the end of time, they could never become such a tender, unless our Congress could find, in some other clause of the Constitution, a power to make them so. This, of course, throws wholly out of consideration the clause above cited in this discussion.

I surmise, that since the advocates of making the Treasury Notes a legal tender in payment of debts must be driven from every other position by what I have already said, and by what can be said in addition, they will resort to the provision empowering Congress "to make all laws which shall be *necessary and proper*" to carry into effect any power specially delegated to the Confederate Government, or any department or officer thereof.

Every one, who is likely to consider, with a view to ascertain and follow the truth, the subject I am discussing, knows but too well that this same provision in the Constitution we have abrogated was made by the crafty, the ignorant, the perverted, the ambitious, the corrupt, banded together in a crusade against reserved rights, and against the Constitution of the United States—Pandora's Box, without Hope at the bottom. It was the armory from which they drew the fatal weapons that extinguished the ligaments and vitality of the Union of '89, and introduced those infernal scenes that are now before our eyes. I have no design to enter, at large, into the unlimited field of dissertation, which this topic opens to anybody who pleases to cultivate it; though I shall occupy it to a very restricted degree. But I warn my countrymen that the gigantic war, now in full and horrible blast, into which we have been driven by the most accursed race, who, having the power and the opportunity to throw off their canting hypocrisy and indulge their propensity to robbery, desolation, revenge and slaughter, have ever afflicted mankind. I repeat, that this gigantic war presents the fittest atmosphere to disseminate those poisons from the same Pandora's Box that have proved so fatal to another Union and another Constitution. Our present circumstances continually present and reinforce that fatal plea of necessity, which has so often been made the panoply of stupendous iniquity, and is calculated to seduce and drag into drowsiness the well-meaning, but too simple and confiding; they abstract us all, more or less, from the "lesser points of the law"—from the cautious scouting of evil beginnings, which quiet times permit and encourage, and fix us upon the contemplation of that stupendous panorama of campaigns, sieges and battles daily unwinding before us, exhibiting, as chief spectacles, blood and carnage, devastation and universal wailing, never paralleled; these circumstances enable the "sappers and miners" of the Constitution to work diligently, undisturbed, in the dark as it were, to sow, in a fruitful soil, the seeds of irreparable mischief; the still small voice is unheard amid the din and tumult. In such circumstances, then, I conjure those who can bend themselves to the duty to scan the evil omens that portend calamity—firmly to resist the entering wedge that otherwise may rive asunder the political fabric so recently contrived.

I am wholly at a loss to conceive the specifically granted power to which that of declaring Treasury Notes a legal tender in payment of debts is "a necessary and proper" incident. I have shown (if I have established anything) that it has no connection with the power to "coin money"—nay, that the power to issue paper money at all has no such connection. It is neither necessary nor proper to say that such notes shall be a legal tender in payment of debts—nay, that they should be issued at all—to carry into effect the power to "borrow money on the credit of the Confederate States." Why it is too plain to warrant argument, or to admit difference of opinion, that when Government or individual exchanges a note promising *to pay money*, the transaction imports the very reverse of *borrowing* money. Such a transaction is meant and operates to procure the commodity desired, without the use of money at all on the occasion—it is its explicit purpose and effect to supersede the borrowing or use of money. This is exemplified by the action of any Government which has ever resorted to the expedient of issuing "bills of credit" in the shape of paper money—Treasury Notes. Witness the war of 1812 between the United States and Britain, and that which is now flagrant. Different statutes have been passed—one, to authorize the borrowing of money; the other, the issuing of Treasury Notes; operations totally distinct, and so well understood to be by those who performed them. When a Government obtains a mule, a wagon, or one hundred bushels of corn, anything it buys, for certain promises to pay money at a future time, it is not short of absurdity to say that thereby any *money is paid, or borrowed*. What follows? This: That even the issuing and use of a paper currency, being a promise to pay money, has no affinity or relation whatever to the act of "*borrowing* money;" that this resort of Government is, therefore, wholly excluded from the category of any powers that may be incident, as necessary and proper, or either, to the principal power, "to borrow money;" and, *a fortiori*, the making such currency a legal tender in payment of debts, it is not within the limits of a sane imagination to connect, by the ligament of a hair, with *incidental* powers, as to borrowing money. Then will we be referred to the power "to declare war—to raise and maintain armies—to provide and maintain a navy?" Without stopping to argue so plain a point, as that Treasury Notes have nothing to do with declaring war, I shall assume, for the sake of brevity, that they may be convenient, or, for the sake of argument, "necessary and proper" (I do not mean to admit it), to "maintain" an army and navy; still I utterly deny that it is necessary and proper to make them a legal tender in payment of debts, in order to carry into effect such powers. Throughout our whole political history as one of the United States, and since we renounced that relation, armies and navies—the former upon a most magnificent scale—have been "raised," "provided," "maintained," without declaring Federal paper money a legal tender in payment of debts, or any pretence to the power to do so, up to a very recent period. The most zealous Consolidationist—the bitterest contumer and reviler of the reserved powers—the most ardent admirer of an Imperial Central Power, to be erected on the ruins of States Rights—the busiest architects of such a structure—from Alexander Hamilton and his co-workers down to the Lucifers and lesser devils of the dynasty of Abraham Lincoln, none ever ventured upon such arrogant assumption of power. These latter have indeed done so, having totally upset and trampled into shreds their Constitution, having most naturally invaded the sanctity of contracts, toppled over the standard of value, and recklessly introduced into their affairs generally the chaos and confusion of the infernal regions. Is this an example fit to be cited or imitated this side the Susquehanna? Then, if these powers—now under review—have been successfully "carried into effect," and repeatedly so executed, without declaring Treasury Notes a legal tender for debts—if (as we all rejoice to know) we ourselves are gloriously instituting these powers (so far, at least, as armies are concerned) without giving to Treasury Notes the disputed attribute, what more is wanting to complete the demonstration, that to give them such an attribute—the attribute of gold and silver current coin exclusively—is not a "necessary and proper" incident to these powers?

CATO.

THE HEALTH OF WILMINGTON, N. C.—Since our last report, made on Tuesday last, the 16th inst., but two cases of Yellow Fever have been reported. Both cases have proved fatal. There has thus, in all, been eight cases reported, in regard to one of which some doubt exists. Not including that there has been seven cases, six of which have died, and only one recovered. It is only right to remark, that although the progress of the fever is slow, and by no means approaches the character of an epidemic, there is yet no improvement in the general health of the town, a fact which absentees ought to bear in mind, and not prematurely hasten their return.

Wilmington Journal.

Hon. H. W. Miller, of North Carolina, died at his residence in Raleigh on Wednesday last. He was one of the ablest criminal lawyers in the State of North Carolina, and enjoyed a more lucrative practice in this department of jurisprudence, probably, than any of his peers.

The Washington papers say that General McClellan has sent to Washington full sixty wagon loads of knapsacks. This tells, they think, of his purpose of divesting his force of every possible incumbrance to rapid marching or effective fighting, and that he anticipates both very shortly.

The Norwich (Connecticut) Bulletin professes to have information that as soon as the levy for 600,000 men is filled up, it is the intention of the Yankee Government to call out an additional force of 400,000. This force is to be drilled and held in the States as a reserve.

TRI-WEEKLY MERCURY.

BY R. B. RHETT, JR.

OFFICE NO. 4 BROAD-STREET, CHARLESTON.

THE DAILY MERCURY, five cents per copy, $10 per annum.
THE TRI-WEEKLY MERCURY, issued on Tuesdays, Thursdays and Saturdays, five cents per copy, $5 per annum.

TUESDAY, SEPTEMBER 23, 1862.

SPEECHES IN THE STATE CONVENTION.

SPEECH OF THE HON. R. B. RHETT, DELIVERED IN THE CONVENTION OF SOUTH CAROLINA, ON THE 14TH DAY OF SEPTEMBER, A. D. 1862.

Mr. President: If the gentleman from St. Helena (Mr. Barnwell) had made no personal reference to me, I would in no way have replied to his remarks. But as he has thought proper to controvert several of the positions I have assumed, it is not proper that I should leave them entirely unanswered.

The speech of the gentleman from St. Helena had very little reference to the resolutions now under consideration before the Convention. It consisted mainly of a defence of the Administration, and a reply to certain facts and positions I had assumed on the resolutions considered a few days ago, and offered by the gentleman from St. Philips and St. Michael's (Mr. Manigault). These resolutions proposed to throw the State of South Carolina in direct conflict with the Confederate Government in raising troops in South Carolina to carry on the war. I stated that I agreed in the main in the principles of these resolutions; and that I had endeavored to enforce them in the Confederate Congress; but that it was now too late, and the times too perilous and difficult, to make issues upon them. The time for raising the troops necessary for carrying on the war, on *unquestionable* principles, was last winter. Many of us, then in the Provisional Congress, deemed the measures proposed by the Administration, to keep the troops in service and increase the army, totally inadequate to meet the immense preparations of our enemies to invade the Confederate States. These measures consisted in increased bounties and short furloughs, to induce the twelve months' volunteers to re-enlist, and to stimulate the enlistment of volunteers in the States. We thought we knew that these measures would fail in accomplishing their object. The inactivity of the army at Manassas had overshadowed it with disease; and so completely disgusted the army and the people, that volunteering for the war was destroyed.

The friends of the Administration being appealed to in vain, Mr. Toombs at length brought in a bill providing for a compulsory levy of troops by the States, to raise an army adequate to our defence. The Administration and its friends opposed the bill; nor would they offer any substitute to meet its object. After several day's debate, Mr. Toombs withdrew the bill in disgust, perhaps indignation. The Provisional Congress adjourned, and the enemy made their invasion. Our worse anticipations were realized. We were totally unprepared to meet the invasion. General Sidney Johnson, instead of fifty thousand, had but fifteen thousand men. Fort Donelson fell, and Middle and Western Tennessee and Northern Alabama and New Orleans, were possessed by the enemy. It was under these circumstances, that the Administration at last proposed, by the Conscription Bill, the compulsory raising of troops, and the forced retention in the army of the one hundred and forty thousand volunteers whose terms of service were about to expire. In the condition of the country, the measure was absolutely necessary to save it from utter devastation, if not final subjection. Right or wrong, the policy of the Administration had left us no other alternative; and I argued that we could not now, with safety to our cause, disturb it; and therefore I opposed the adoption of the resolutions of the gentleman from St. Philips and St. Michael's.

Now, it is to this exposure of the weakness and false policy of the Administration that the gentleman from St. Helena replies. And what is the palliation he offers? Beyond some general expressions of confidence in the Administration and our Generals, he assigns but one cause for the inactivity of our armies—*sickness*. It was *sickness* which enfeebled our armies, and disabled them from defending the country or advancing on the enemy. If sickness was such an enfeebling cause in our armies, was not this a reason for increasing them? The difficulty was, that we had not one-half of the men in the field necessary to meet the notorious force of our enemies. And had we no knowledge, no experience of the sickness which follows all armies; and could not a just estimate of its enfeebling effects be made by the most ordinary prudence or wisdom? Was it sickness that left General Sidney Johnson, with the paltry force of fifteen thousand troops, to repel the invasion of Gen. Halleck, with one hundred thousand men, last spring, in the Valley of the Mississippi? Was it sickness which hindered our army from advancing on the enemy in Virginia after the battle of Manassas? Gen. Beauregard, the commanding general, I suppose, is a pretty good authority for the condition of his army; and what did he say was the reason he did not follow up his victory at Manassas? Was it sickness? In a letter, written to one of his aids (a member of Congress in Richmond), and laid before Congress, he complained that the fruits of his victory were lost, because the Government had not furnished his army with the transportation and food necessary for its advance; and I think the gentleman from Kershaw (Mr. Chesnut) was the aid to whom the letter was addressed.

Mr. Chesnut rose for the purpose of explanation. He thought his friend was mistaken in his statement. He did not think that our army could have advanced on Washington immediately after the battle of Manassas. They were not in a condition to have done so. There was scarcely a regiment, certainly not a brigade, whose organization, the day after the battle, would have justified such a demonstration. He did not believe that Gen. Beauregard ever complained that the Government would not allow him to advance. Our army was exhausted and worn out, and he believed that if an attempt to advance had been made, that it would have been attended with disastrous consequences, and instead of adding glory to the achievement of the day, the fruits of the victory thereby would have been imperrilled, if not lost.—*South Carolinian.*

Mr. Rhett called upon Mr. Barnwell to confirm his statement, and Mr. Barnwell stated that the letter of General Beauregard was written to Mr. Miles, and not to Mr. Chesnut, and laid before Congress by Mr. Miles. In it General Beauregard did complain that the fruits of the victory of Manassas were lost for the want of transportation and food.

Mr. President, I am very willing to leave the question, whether the army, after the battle of Manassas, could have advanced between Gen. Beauregard on the one hand, and these gentlemen on the other. Gen. Beauregard, in his letter, did not state at what time after the battle he could have advanced; but did affirm that he could have advanced, and have realized the fruits of his victory, if he had been furnished with transportation and food. The gentleman from Kershaw himself has stated that the army consisted of thirty thousand men at the battle of Manassas. There were but fifteen thousand of them, according to Gen. Beauregard's report, engaged in the battle. Fifteen thousand fresh troops, therefore, independent of those which had fought in the battle, were under his command to advance on the enemy, routed and panic stricken. Now, whether the army was so worn out and exhausted as the gentleman from Kershaw affirms, or was so overwhelmed by sickness, that it could not advance—or, as Gen. Beauregard has asserted, was prevented from advancing for want of transportation and food—I leave to the judgment of the Convention to determine. For my part, I think that the commanding general is a rather better authority for the state of things in his army than either or both of these gentlemen. Whilst I upheld, and will uphold, the Administration in any measure to prosecute the war with energy and vigor, it is impossible for me to approve of a feeble and false policy which exposed the Confederate States to invasion and devastation, and has nearly proved fatal to our cause. Other gentlemen, with equal conscientiousness, may come to contrary conclusions. I do not judge them. Neither our confidence nor our convictions are matters of mere volition.

I now come, Mr. President, to the only reasons assigned by the member from St. Helena for opposing the resolutions I have offered—they are *useless* and *mischievous*.

No one will deny the high purport of the resolutions. But on one of them—the first—it is said the Convention has expressed already its opinion. The form in which it has expressed its opinion may appear to be nothing more than an indefinite postponement of the subject. If the admission of non-slaveholding States is a subject really important to the welfare of the Confederate States, we must agitate and act upon it *under the Constitution as it is*. But admit that we did act upon the subject before—did we act upon it under the circumstances which now surround us? There was *then* no war. *Then* the gentleman from St. Helena, and other delegates you had sent to Montgomery, assured you that there was no danger of a reconstruction, in any form, of a union with the free States of the North. We have since entered into war; and have gentlemen reflected how materially this war may influence our future destiny? Suppose a peace concluded to-morrow, and the treaty containing its terms stipulates (as the organ of the Government at Richmond suggests) that one and all of the States of the United States shall enter, if they deem fit, our Confederacy—what would be your situation? The treaty would be placed before you as the alternative of continuing the war. Will you continue the war, with all its evils and miseries, *against the action of the Government*, with a portion of the Confederate States perhaps clamoring for peace, or will you take peace with free States in your Confederacy? Sir, on such an issue, under such circumstances, even South Carolina might yield. That there would be a powerful party in the State to advocate our submission to such a treaty, I do not doubt. The Constitution would be made to yield, or be changed to meet the emergency. It is better far to prevent than reform evils. At present, the opinion of the people of the Confederate States is decidedly against the admission of free States into our Confederacy. Thank God! this, at least, is one benefit the war has produced. Reconstruction has been crushed out of the popular mind by the tramp of armed men, and the ruthless and bloody atrocities of our foes. The object of the resolutions I have offered, is to consolidate and quicken this public opinion, and to bring it to bear upon our public men and the Confederate Government, so as to render it impossible that a reconstruction of a union with any of the United States shall take place by their instrumentality. Is such an object useless or mischievous? Suppose the resolution is a mere repetition of what this Convention has already affirmed, will it be injurious to repeat its opinions on a subject so vital to our future destiny? Will any of our Confederates look upon such a repetition as indicating distrust or alienation? The fate of the Confederate States will, most probably, be settled by the policy first pursued by the Government. It was so with the Government of the United States. That great and illustrious citizen, General Washington, laid the foundation for the inevitable overthrow of the Government he was first called on to administer. When he required his two Secretaries, Mr. Jefferson and Mr. Hamilton, to give him, in writing, their opinions of the constitutionality of a United States Bank, he had under consideration the destiny of the United States. Had he thrown the weight of his Administration against the assumption of constructive powers by the United States Government, the Government might have lasted forever; but, unfortunately, his experience during the Revolutionary war, of the want of a vigorous central authority, inclined his mind to consolidation. He yielded to the arguments of Alexander Hamilton, and signed the Bank Bill. He sealed by that act the dissolution of the Government of the United States. With constructive powers in the hands of a majority, in a vast country like the United States, usurpation and conflict was inevitable, and the Government must continue a consolidated, limitless despotism, or be dissolved. It is dissolved; and the hand of George Washington, great and patriotic and pure as he was, dissolved it. Mr. President! will we not learn wisdom from the past? Will we not strive to avoid the rock which wrecked our ancestors and ourselves? Shall we not watch our Government, and see that it adheres to all the great essentials for its durability? Shall we not make all its first precedents right; and, for this end, by our timely action, strive to lead public opinion and influence the Government? For the last time, in all probability, I now address a deliberative body. My voice will no more be heard in your councils; but its last effort has been made to induce you to announce and vindicate the principles and policy which I deem essential to your peace, independence and liberty.

The following is the report of Mr. BARNWELL's speech in the *South Carolinian*. The report of it in the *Guardian* is the same in purport, and nearly the same in words:

Mr. Barnwell made a speech in reply to Mr. Rhett, in which he vindicated the Executive and Congress from the charge of imbecility and want of forecast in the management of the war. He did not pretend to say that no blunders had been made. There, perhaps, had been serious mistakes made. Napoleon and Wellington had made mistakes, which were followed by serious disasters; but, under the circumstances, those in authority had done what they honestly conceived was for the best. He believed we had the very best Generals that the Confederate States could produce, and with an unfaltering confidence in them, which their past conduct guaranteed, he would still trustingly leave the matter in their hands.

It was the work of disease and death that had decimated our ranks and palsied the arm of our military operations. Diseases incident to the camp, and which could not be foreseen or provided against, had in many instances crippled our movements and threatened our plans, and prevented or delayed those active and aggressive demonstrations, for which the Government had perhaps been blamed. Wherever we had gone, the black angel of death had followed in our wake and hovered over our camps, filling the land with graves and the hospitals with patients. It was said there were thirteen regiments at Fort Donelson, yet, in fact, they were merely skeletons—disease, desertion and death had done their fearful work.

Let us not deceive ourselves, nor disguise the bloody and vindictive character of this war. The world never saw a more destructive war, or one waged on a more grand and magnificent scale than the one now waged against us; and, in order to meet and baffle the foe, we must be active and diligent, and make a judicious use of all the means that God and nature has put into our hands. Shoulder to shoulder in harmonious concert, we must meet the tide of battle, and it will require all our efforts to drive it back. Though the tide may now seem to be receding, yet we will have to meet the returning wave, and feel once more the weight of the giant arm of our implacable foe. We had flattered ourselves heretofore that the North would exhaust her resources and divide and distract her councils; but in this we have been mistaken. She has had no want of men or money, nor was it at all likely she soon would. The world has been astonished at her prodigal expenditure of blood and treasure, and we may look with serious apprehension to their coming strength. We had best not deceive ourselves with the hope of a short war and an easy conquest, although we are now stronger than we have been since the war commenced, and in a better condition to meet the foe. God has visited our enemies with judicial blindness, and sent confusion into their councils. They had chosen for their leaders men wicked, profligate, weak and selfish. We must be dignified and firm among ourselves, but kind and forbearing to our enemies to the utmost limit.

FROM NASSAU.—The British steamer *Angler*, from Nassau, N. P., for a Southern port, got ashore on Stono Breakers on Friday night last. The weather was very thick, and she was trying to get her position with certainty when the accident took place. A boat left her with five passengers, among them MR. ZACHRISSON, formerly of New Orleans, which landed on Folly Island, where the passengers were left and the boat proceeded back to the ship, but when the former reached the position of the steamer the latter could not be found, she having, no doubt, come off and proceeded to sea during the absence of the boat. The crew of this last have succeeded in reaching this city, but the situation of the passengers is unknown; and as they were left on an uninhabited Island, they may have a trying time. They were informed of their position, and how they might reach Charleston, and it is hoped that they will get here safely.

Up to Wednesday last, the yellow fever was prevailing extensively at Nassau, and we regret to hear that several persons known in this city have died of it; among them Mrs. LOCKWOOD, wife of Capt. THOS. LOCKWOOD, of the steamer *Kate*; Mr. THOS. ELLIOTT, formerly of Beaufort, S. C., and Capt. JOHN PRICE, of Wilmington, N. C. Capt. ROBT. BROWN, of Wilmington, had died from the effects of an injury that he had received before leaving that place.

The British steamer *Leopard*, from Charleston, and *Kate*, from Wilmington, N. C., had both arrived at Nassau, as had also the British schooner *Sue*, Capt. SMITH, from Glasgow.

A report had reached Nassau that the Yankee armed steamer *Santiago de Cuba*, which has been cruising around the Bahamas for some time, annoying neutral commerce, had accidentally and unintentionally fallen in with the Confederate war steamer "290," Capt. NORTH, and that the Yankee had been handled so roughly as to compel her to resort to Key West for repairs. If the "290" had been fully manned, the Yankee would have been among the things that were.

PASSENGERS TO AND FROM SAVANNAH will find in another column a notice that materially affects their convenience in reaching and leaving Charleston.

THE NEWS FROM RICHMOND.

(CORRESPONDENCE OF THE MERCURY.)

RICHMOND, Friday, September 19.

Harper's Ferry and Boonesboro—Death of Gen. Garland—Pleasant from Chambersburg—Cutting Yankeedom in Twain—Pictures of McClellan and our Generals—The Extension of the Conscription, etc., etc.

"How about that news from Harper's Ferry and Boonesboro?" was my first inquiry this morning. "I heard the officer when he told it to the President," was my friend's reply. So there is something in it; how much it is impossible to say, as Gen. Lee's dispatches, filling a long letter, and embracing a history of operations up to the 18th, were not made known to the press or to members of Congress at the Executive Mansion last night.

That there has been a fight, and a heavy one, at Boonesboro, and that Harper's Ferry has been taken, cannot be doubted. But we shall be lucky, indeed, if we get particulars under a week. What is popular suspense to a War Department? Impertinent curiosity.

Garland's death is a serious loss to the service. His was the first organized battalion that went to Manassas. It soon became a regiment, and his skill in the management of it quickly attracted the watchful eye of Beauregard's Adjutant, who brought his administrative qualities to the notice of the General. Wounded slightly at Williamsburg, where, as at Drainesville, he displayed great coolness and self-possession, he was made Brigadier; in which capacity he discovered so much ability that he was lately spoken of in high quarters as the proper person to command the Stonewall Brigade. A man of decided talent, energetic, careful of his men, with strong partialities for military affairs, and of high aspirations, it is almost certain that he would have been called to the command of a Division had he not fallen so untimely. You will pardon this extended notice of the Colonel of my old regiment—the "steady Eleventh" Virginia.

It is pleasant to get such little scraps from Chambersburg as these: "The rebels say they are going to make Pennsylvania howl." "But four companies of citizens have been formed, and four times their number have neglected to enroll themselves." "This want of preparation has exhibited itself in all the southern towns and villages of the State"—Pennsylvania, to wit.

The Examiner is the only paper published this morning; the proprietor giving as his excuse that no notice of Thanksgiving Day had been served on him—*i. e.*, the Proclamation was sent to all city papers but his own. He praises Lee's strategy in Maryland, cries out against the non-exemption of editors, and thinks the movements of our armies indicate an advance to Lake Erie, by way of the Pan Handle—thus "sundering the wasp at the waist,"—cutting off New England from the Northwestern fighting States; with which States, having denounced "Lincoln's Government as a rump and usurpation," we will "proceed to treat for peace individually." There may be something in this.

The extension of the Conscription Law has at last passed the House, encumbered with many provisos. It is high time; for our army melts away rapidly under such exertions as they have undergone during the last month.

It is amusing to read the Philadelphia papers at this time, filled, as they are, with flaming appeals to everybody to turn out to repel invasion. Such a moving of money and valuables from the threatened districts was never seen before. But all this is as nothing to what will yet befall them, if the measure of their crimes be returned to them.

Lowell, of the Atlantic Monthly, is of opinion that a new party is raising at the North, the object of which is to thwart Lincoln and aid the rebellion. Men like Wood and Seymour are said to be the leaders of this party, against which Lowell is very savage in the Atlantic.

There is a daguerreotype of McClellan in a show-case on Main street, which tells a tale. He stands in the front yard of, probably, rebel premises, though the house is evidently a ready-made Yankee one. Two ladies, in the porch of this house, are gazing in rapture at his back, and a soldier in the distance is presenting arms to his back also. His attitude is that of Napoleon at St. Helena, somewhat intensified, and he displays more boots, more gauntlets and more sword than Lee and his whole staff. His head looks too small for his body, and the impression produced by the picture is that of a beefy party who "won't do."

A colored engraving, executed in Paris, representing the principal Confederate Generals, with Mr. Davis in their midst, is exhibited in one of our shop windows. Johnston and Magruder can be detected; the other likenesses are determined by the names printed under them. That of Beauregard is particularly good for nothing. The best likeness of the hero of Sumter, Manassas and Shiloh that I have seen anywhere, is a painting in oil at Sattler's. But even that fails to show the power in his face and head.

HERMES.

RICHMOND, Saturday, September 20.

Glorious Results at Harper's Ferry—Good News from Missouri—Bad from Cumberland Gap—Value of Preparation—Northern Key Notes—Horrors of Peace—Delay in Naturalization Law, etc., etc.

Could we only get full accounts of the battle at Sharpsburg, Middletown, or wherever it was, we would better know how to appreciate the triumph at Harper's Ferry. An officer, who left our army Sunday morning, says all day Saturday we were retreating before the Yankees, who killed some twenty of our cavalry, and came near cutting off our wagon train. We hear that our army has fallen back to the Potomac for "strategic reasons," and much is said about Jackson's getting in McClellan's rear; but we really know nothing, except the glorious results at Harper's Ferry. It is the greatest surrender recorded in American annals and more than retrieves Fort Donelson.—The cannon is said to consist mostly of heavy guns, but the small arms are all new and of approved patterns. Reported that we took four hundred wagon loads of ammunition.

Accounts come in gloriously from Missouri and Nashville; from everywhere, indeed, except Cumberland Gap—where Morgan seems to have played Stevenson a trick of which the latter can scarcely be proud. It never rains but it pours; yet there is a limit to human endeavor, and an end to all success. Sooner or later the tide must turn. Terrible marches and hard fighting will use up the toughest troops in the world. We owe our victories to preparation and to active movements; if we expect to continue victorious, and to conquer a speedy peace, we must continue our preparations, so that we may be able with full ranks to keep up our active movements. Winter is not far off, and then comes new and mighty efforts against our coasts. Are we looking ahead? Are we ready for what is sure to come? Beauregard is at Charleston with Pemberton, but have they the men they need to defend their long line? I wish I could *see* this work of preparation going on. We have to keep up our armies and to meet the recruits of the North. Delay is fatal.

There are certain key notes in late Yankee wailings and railings, which, however feebly struck at this time, are full of hideous meaning. Their papers depict the horrible consequences which must ensue if the rebels "conquer the North and Lincoln is replaced by Jeff. Davis in Washington." What does this talk indicate but a willingness to be subjugated by us rather than separated from us? What better solution of the difficulty presents itself to them? It would be the happiest issue now possible. The Northwest would jump at it; the Middle States would soon follow, and even New England might go with the rest. One thing is certain, so far as public opinion is discernible in newspapers, the idea of a permanent dissolution of the Union—an eternal separation from the flesh pots of the South—is as far as ever from Yankee thoughts. Suppose the Northwest lays down its arms, ignores Lincoln, and agrees to admit slavery as an organized institution in its own States? Can we refuse? But what are States nominally slave, but with the worst elements of Yankeeism in immense excess in them, but so many Pandora's boxes? When we remember that politicians bred in Washington are to meet other politicians bred in the same hot-bed of corruption to settle the terms of peace—when we know how dear peace is to the hearts of the people, and how easily they are cajoled—when we think of the moral effect of a great people throwing down arms and suing for reunion on our own terms—when we look into our hearts and find (since we have whipped them so often and so terribly) how much less we hate the Yankees than we used to do—how something not unlike pity is stealing in—and when, in addition to all this, we bethink ourselves of the inevitable mighty Yankee influx into the South after peace, no matter on what terms—and when we can foresee on what specious pleas these Yankees will come in, thousands of them backed by Southern recommendations easily obtained from the good natured or the rascally, who are anxious to reap the profits of Yankee capital and ingenuity at work on Southern soil; when we think of all these things, is it not time to marvel that Congress has decided upon no naturalization law, and that our citizens are left a prey to Yankee intruders, who will come in cringing and fawning, only to claim and speedily obtain the rights of citizenship, and thenceforward to poison our whole social and political structure? What are we to do? Legislation can avail little to counteract the evils of this peaceful invasion, more fatal than war; but, if it can do anything, when will the time come to set about it? When, in the blaze of peace celebrations and the joy of victory, the horrors of war are forgotten, and insidious politicians are left unwatched to make new combinations with old partners in villainy; will that be the time to protect ourselves against the horrors of peace? Have we not already put it off too long?

HERMES.

DEATH OF A DISTINGUISHED FLORIDIAN.—The Tallahassee papers announce the death of General RICHARD K. CALL, a distinguished citizen of that State, which occurred Sunday last. Gen. CALL was for many years identified with the history of Florida. He was an aid to General JACKSON, and was subsequently appointed Governor of that Territory, to which post he was re-appointed and served, we believe, until its admission as a State into the Union.

Stephen D. Wallace has been chosen President of the Wilmington and Weldon Railroad, to succeed the late Hon. W. S. Ashe.

SCAN THE EVIL OMENS.—No. IX.

Obsta Principiis.

Suppose the advocates of the scheme of lifting Treasury Notes to the dignity of the specie—the currency of the Constitution—should resort to the power to "REGULATE commerce with foreign nations, among the several States and with the Indian tribes"; and, for aught I know, it may be the favorite pedestal upon which they may place their hopes. I have to answer: *First*, Treasury Notes, whether a legal tender or not, are in no wise "necessary and proper" to the existence of commerce at all, either with foreign nations or among the several States. Indeed, such an instrumentality, so far as it displaces the constitutional currency (and it always does so, more or less, and now totally supplants it), is a hindrance to commerce, and may become a very Vampire, that sucks up its life-blood. It never can aid it, and never has aided it. *Second:* To make such currency a legal tender, in payment of debts, would embarrass, perhaps destroy, *foreign* commerce. If we are not to discredit the testimony of our ancestors, of the Constitutional and Revolutionary era, it did have that effect, between 1783 and 1789; and, indeed, the like effect during that period and before, on the commerce "*among the several States.*" For it must be remembered, that certain issues of paper money, by the Continental Congress as well as the several States, or at least various of them, were made a legal tender in payment of debts; and the iniquities of Rhode Island, in this field of fraud and public robbery, gained for that contemptible State, always a pestilential nuisance, an infamous notoriety, which is published and declared in all the debates on the Constitution of the United States that are extant. *Third:* It would afflict commerce with the very evil which the specie provisions of the Constitution were intended to cure and remove. *Fourth:* If Treasury Notes are not only not "necessary and proper" but baneful to commerce itself, much less is such a currency necessary and proper, or even convenient or appropriate, for its REGULATION. Because it is one thing to regulate the manner in which commerce shall be conducted, and quite another to prescribe the medium of exchanges which commerce shall adopt. Besides, the *Constitution* prescribes the medium of exchanges, and the "money" that shall effect them, where payment of debts is to be made, to wit: "gold and silver current coin." *Fifth:* The argument that seeks root in the power to regulate commerce, proves too much—"o'erleaps itself, and falls on t'other side." The power is, "to regulate commerce with foreign nations, *among* the several States, and with the Indian tribes." Now, if Treasury Notes are prescribed as necessary and proper to the execution of this power, and they must also be made a legal tender to execute it effectually, then we have Congress regulating commerce *within* a State—the *internal* commerce of a State; a bald and unmitigated usurpation; and then, likewise, we should have this extraordinary fruit of the clause granting implied powers, to wit: First implication—Treasury Notes as necessary and proper for executing the specific power; second implication—attaching to them a quality to be a legal tender in payment of debts, in order to make the Treasury Notes effectual for their purpose, which is mounting an incidental power upon another incidental power, piling Pelion upon Ossa, and then, perhaps, we shall be treated to a bill of pains and penalties, if we scruple to admit, and act accordingly, that a promise to pay specie is specie, no matter whether the promissor be Government or individual, solvent or bankrupt. Where, upon the basis of such conception, shall be the end of that line of construction, that shall string shadow upon shadow, implication upon implication, until the incidental clause of the Constitution shall become the Aaron's Rod of that instrument, as it did become in the Constitution we have abrogated, and gorge itself by swallowing up every other power, and with them the chartered rights of States and citizen?

It appears to me that temerity itself will not resort to any other specific power than one or other of those I have mentioned as having the slightest pretension to draw in its train, as a necessary and proper incident to its effectual execution, that of making paper money at all; or, if made, of making it a legal tender in payment of debts.

Hear what Mr. Jefferson has said as to the proper rule of construing the clause delegating the power to use means "necessary and proper." He wrote, in February, 1791, under the gravest official responsibility, at the instance of General Washington, when he was called on to consider the Charter of the first Bank by the Congress of the United States; and he wrote on the occasion of the first grand conflict between the Consolidationists (the Federalists of that day) and those who vindicated the reserved rights of the States, or of the people. In his model State paper, with the terseness and vigor of style that was peculiarly his, he says: "The Constitution allows only the means which are 'necessary,' not those which are merely 'convenient,' for effecting the enumerated powers. If such a latitude of construction be allowed to this phrase as to give any non-enumerated power, it will go to every one; for there is no one which ingenuity may not torture into a *convenience, in some way or other, to some one* of so long a list of enumerated powers. It would swallow up all the delegated powers, and reduce the whole to one phrase. Therefore it was that the Constitution restrained them to the *necessary* means—that is to say, to those means without which the grant of power would be nugatory."

I reproduce these words of sober wisdom from one of the first minds of the Revolutionary era, and (I think) of any era, because they are well weighed and well grounded; and I also believe the instruction to be drawn from them was never more needed than it is now, and by no race of *politicians* (*statesmen* are scarce) more than those who now bean sway.

CATO.

THE "FREEDOM" OF THE PRESS.

[From the Macon Telegraph.]

That most profound and august body, the Senate of the Confederate States, has at last furnished the world with a comparative valuation of the newspaper press. Time was when the printers all thought a newspaper of wide circulation a power in the State; and the employees connected therewith, very considerable people. It was supposed that men who daily addressed and informed forty thousand readers, incurred a vast responsibility, and exercised, for good or evil, a large influence—in fact, that they may rank in point of consequence to society with the man who taught twenty scholars—who occasionally addressed a petit jury, or who preached twice on Sunday to a congregation of five hundred persons. But the Confederate Senate settled all these points this week. One day they refused to exempt one editor to each newspaper, and the next they did exempt tanners, millers, and shoemakers. Thus it will be seen that a tannery, a shoemaker's shop, or a grist mill, is more important than a newspaper.

The Senate, however, did right in the exemption, provided it is not allowed to operate as a cover to persons who are neither tanners, shoemakers, nor millers, but mere botchers who undertake the business to shield themselves from conscription. They should be exempted. A good shoemaker, for example, could make shoes enough for a regiment in a single year; and are we to be told that it is more important he should be put in the ranks and carry a musket, than that six or eight hundred soldiers should be shod? Is it not a positive disadvantage to the country when any good shoemaker is taken from his bench, and put to carrying a musket? And so of all other trades indispensable to supply the army, and of which there is a known scarcity of tradesmen. The only thing we except to is the stupendous—the inconceivable folly of refusing to exempt such persons as are indispensable to the existence of the newspaper press, which, in the nature of things, is the only medium of organized opinion—the only source of communication between the government and the people, and which, if silenced, would leave even this wise Senate itself practically as voiceless as the grave.

[From the Richmond Examiner.]

The Constitution dignifies and protects journalism, by an express clause, declaring that "Congress shall make no law abridging the freedom of the press." The framers of the Constitution presumed that Congress would always be composed of men of common sense and common intelligence; and did not think it necessary to define what was intended to be embraced by the general term of "the press." Those who conduct the intellectual departments of the business are certainly more important to the press than those conducting the mechanical parts; for these latter but put in type what is furnished by the former. To say that the journeymen and apprentices who print a newspaper constitute the press, would be as absurd as to say that the door-keeper, clerks, presiding officer and sergeant-at-arms of the Confederate Senate, constituted the Senate. To argue that the law exempting Senators from arrest was only intended to embrace the officers of the Senate and not its members, would be to argue an absurdity.

The Senate agreed to exempt the printers of newspapers from the conscription, but refused to exempt the persons engaged in the intellectual departments of the business. The vote was a direct assault upon the press; for when you take away its mind you leave it nothing but a useless machine, without vitality, or independence, or power.

The preservation of the press is rendered a matter of duty by the Constitution, and this duty rests upon the consciences of Senators, whether the press be worth preserving or not; but considered aside from this question of oath-enjoined duty, it is in the highest degree expedient that the press should be preserved in full vigor and efficiency. The press has been the soul and inspiration of the great movement in which the country is engaged. It was the press that roused the people to resist the aggressions of the North, and that inspired the whole community with that enthusiasm which has been the source of all the successes which have attended our arms. The press is the vehicle of intelligence. To strike down the press, as the Senate seeks to do, would be to blot out the light of the war, and to envelope the community in darkness and confusion. To leave to the press only its types and its printers, is to crush it out as effectually as if Lincoln or Butler had put his heel upon it.

PERSONAL.—General Beauregard, accompanied by his Aids, Col. Roman and Capt. Beauregard, and also by Maj. Gen. Pemberton and staff officers, Capt. Sanders and Lieutenant Taylor, arrived in Savannah Saturday afternoon by a special train from Charleston. Col. A. J. Gonzales, Chief of Artillery, is also of the party. Bad as was the weather, the rain pouring throughout the day, General B. was engaged through the whole of yesterday in inspecting the defences of the city.—*Savannah Republican.*

NEWS BY TELEGRAPH.

THE CAPTURE OF HARPER'S FERRY—FURTHER PARTICULARS OF OUR VICTORY IN MARYLAND.

GORDONSVILLE, September 19.—At Harper's Ferry we paroled 11,090 privates, 425 officers, took 2,000 negros, 15,000 stand of small arms, and 46 pieces of cannon. Col. WALKER's battery took 500 horses. Our loss was three killed and forty wounded. The battle commenced Sunday morning, and opened again Monday at daylight. Their dead were covered in the ditches—we couldn't tell how many. In the fight at Sharpsburg we took 3,000 prisoners. Gen. GARLAND and Col. STRANGE were killed. Gen. D. H. HILL was roughly handled, but managed to hold the enemy in check.

THE LATEST FROM RICHMOND.

RICHMOND, Saturday, September 20.—Colonel LINDSAY WALKER arrived here to-day, from Harper's Ferry, which place he left on Wednesday evening. The cannon and stores captured had been removed. There had been no fighting since the capture of Harper's Ferry, on Monday. Our army was in fine spirits. Gen. McCLELLAN, with his army, was in our front, near Sharpsburg, Md., and a general battle was expected. Gen. RENO, of the Federal army, was killed in the fight near Boonesboro', Md.

JACKSON's official report of the capture of Harper's Ferry, dated the 16th inst., says: "Yesterday God crowned our arms with another brilliant success in the surrender, at Harper's Ferry, of Brig. Gen. WHITE and 11,000 troops, an equal number of small arms, 73 pieces of artillery, and about 200 wagons. In addition to the stores, there is a large amount of camp and garrison equipage. Our loss is very small."

IMPORTANT FROM CHATTANOOGA—EVACUATION OF NASHVILLE.

CHATTANOOGA, TENN., September 19.—The enemy have again evacuated Nashville, this time going down the Cumberland river. The occupation of Clarkesville and Fort Donelson by their troops was for the purpose of securing this route for their retreat.

The tone and appearance of the Louisville papers indicate an apprehension of the speedy occupation of that place by the Confederates.

A train on the Nashville and Chattanooga Railroad started from here to-day, for Tullahoma, 80 miles distant from this place.

NEWS FROM KNOXVILLE.

KNOXVILLE, TENN., September 20.—A courier from Cumberland Gap reports that the retreating Yankee force under MORGAN had obtained but three hours start of Gen. STEVENSON's forces, who were gaining fast upon the fugitives, with every prospect of capturing them. Already about 300 prisoners had been taken. A large number of the men who composed the Tennessee tory regiments had dispersed through the mountains.

An express messenger from Lynchburg reports that in the battle at Cotton Hill, in Fayette county, Virginia, the enemy's loss was 600 and ours 25. Among the killed was Lieut. Cox, of the 51st Va. regiment. The enemy was completely routed.

THE FORT PULASKI PRISONERS.

VICKSBURG, September 17.—(*To the Savannah Republican.*)—About 8000 exchanged prisoners arrived here last night. All those from Fort Pulaski are here, and will be home soon.

F. W. SIMS.

INTERESTING FROM MISSOURI.

Members of Congress from Missouri have received late and interesting intelligence from their State. It is said that the new levies of State militia raised there, under the recent draft, are coming over *en masse* to the Confederates. This information comes through sources believed to be entirely trustworthy.

LATEST FROM THE POTOMAC.

THE GREAT BATTLE OF SHARPSBURG.

MOVEMENTS OF LEE.

RICHMOND, September 21.—The *Enquirer* has received a despatch dated Warrenton, September 20, announcing that a terrific battle took place at Sharpsburg, Md., on Wednesday last, in which we had decidedly the advantage. The loss was very heavy on both sides. Generals STARK, MANNING and BRANCH were killed, and Gens. RIPLEY, D. R. JONES, R. R. JONES and LAWTON were wounded. The whole strength of both armies was engaged. Report says that the battle was renewed on Thursday, and that the enemy was routed and driven back nine miles.

(*The Latest.*)

MONDAY, September 22.—The accounts that reach us of the battle at Sharpsburg, are meagre and somewhat contradictory, but all agree in representing it to have been the most bloody and desperately contested engagement of the war. The Confederate army, though opposed by largely superior numbers, again illustrated its valor and invincibility by successfully repelling the repeated onsets of the enemy.

Officers have arrived here, who state that they went over the battle field on Thursday, and they assert that the advantage remained on our side, the enemy having fallen back.

The city papers this morning report, on the authority of passengers who arrived last night, that Gen. LEE had re-crossed the Potomac on Friday, at Shepardstown, which is near Sharpstown, and several miles above Harper's Ferry.

The New York *Herald*, of the 18th inst., has been received. It claims that the fight at Sharpsburg on Sunday was a Yankee victory. Its despatches in regard to the fight are contradictory, but concur in stating that the Confederates were defeated.

Letters from Louisville claim that the Yankee forces in Kentucky had gained a victory over DUNCAN's and SCOTT's commands at Munfordsville, Kentucky.

A Bermuda correspondent of the New York *Herald* says that five steamers are now lying at the port of St. George's, awaiting an opportunity to run the blockade.

The United States Arsenal at Pittsburg was accidentally blown up on Wednesday. Between seventy-five or eighty boys and girls were killed.

In New York, on Wednesday last, gold opened at 116⅝, but subsequently advanced to 117⅝.

THE WAR IN KENTUCKY.

CHATTANOOGA, September 21.—The Nashville *Union*, of the 18th inst., says that if the rebels in Kentucky have any disposition to fight and do not shun an engagement, there will be a great battle within three days. The *Union* declares that it has no apprehensions for the result, as the very best divisions and generals of the Federal forces would be present and participate. The Louisville *Journal*, of the 12th, says that the rebels have no present intention to attack Cincinnati, but that four heavy columns, including BRAGG's, were then advancing towards Louisville. Notwithstanding this, thousands of Yankee troops are being sent from Louisville to Cincinnati.

WE CALL the attention of the public to the interesting Diary of operations on James' Island, which we this morning publish. As a record of events from the hand of a capable eye witness, it possesses historical interest, and will be read with pleasure.

Tribute of Respect.

At a meeting of the Ætna Fire Engine Company, held on the evening of the 15th instant, the following Preamble and Resolutions were adopted:

It is a mournful duty to pay a parting tribute to any one, but especially so when that one is cut down in the blush of manhood. Among the many who have left our ranks to take part in the military service of our country, there is no one whom we can recall with more fond remembrance than Mr. JAMES E. BAIL. Entering our ranks in early life, he ever evinced that zeal for the welfare of the Company, and energy in the performance of its duties, which ever won from his comrades the appellation of "Well done." In responding to his country's call, he has nobly yielded up his life in her defence—having fallen while gallantly repelling a charge made by the enemy, in the late battles on the Potomac. Thus has the cruel hand of Death caused another void to be made in our ranks; and we are called upon to pay this tribute to one endeared to us by many ties of fond associations. Therefore, be it

Resolved, That in the death of Mr. JAMES E. BAIL, this Company has sustained the loss of an active and efficient member.

Resolved, That we tender to the bereaved sister and brothers of the deceased our sincere condolence and sympathy in the sad loss which they have sustained, and that they be furnished with a copy of the above preamble and resolutions by the Secretary.

Resolved, That a page of our Minute Book be inscribed to his memory, and that the members wear the usual mourning for thirty days.

Resolved, That the above preamble and resolutions be published in the daily papers of this city.

From the Minutes. JOS. A. THOURON, Secretary Ætna F. E. Co.

OBITUARY.

DIED, in Hardeeville, September 6th, after a protracted illness, Dr. W. J. SEABROOK, in the 80th year of his age. These were his favorite lines:

"Jesus, Saviour of my soul,
Let me to thy bosom fly."

DIED, at Lewisville, St. Thomas Parish, on the morning of 19th inst., after a short but painful illness, ADAM MILLIKEN, youngest son of J. S. and ELIZA J. WESTENDORFF, aged 2 years, 4 months and 12 days.

DIED, at McClellanville, on the evening of the 14th inst., CHARLOTTE CORDES, youngest child of Mr. S. D. and Mrs. C. A. DOUR, in the eighth year of her age.

This lovely and interesting child had endeared herself in a peculiar manner to all her relatives and friends, and they looked forward to years of virtue and happiness for her. But death has put an end to all their hopes for her on earth. This loved one, in the early morning of her days, has passed away from these sublunary scenes to the mansions of eternal rest. She calmly fell asleep to awake no more until the morning of the resurrection. Our dear "Missie" has been removed from us, and the places which knew her will know her no more forever. But we will fondly cherish her memory till we shall be called to go to her.

DIED, in Richmond, Dallas county, Ala., JOHN SINGLETARY BENNETT, in his 79th year, native of Charleston, S. C., and the only surviving brother of the venerable THOMAS BENNETT, ex Governor State of South Carolina. He was for many years extensively engaged in mercantile pursuits in this city, and afterwards removed with his family to Richmond, Dallas county, Ala., where, in the quiet and happy circle of his endeared wife and family, he enjoyed life to a ripe old age. He has passed away from earth as a good old patriarch, of blessed memory to his numerous descendants, who will ever hold his life and exemplary character in sweet remembrance. He was ever distinguished for his charity in all the relations of life; his benevolence and amiability of disposition rendered him the safe companion and friend of all who came under his notice. His lofty sentiments of character and strict integrity marked him as a reliable, honest man. Although it pleased his heavenly Father to afflict him with great bodily suffering "in his bed of death," yet, nevertheless, with Christian hope and fortitude, he looked up to the cross of his once suffering Saviour, "who not in vain experienced every human pain." He committed his spirit to Him, and fell asleep in Jesus.

PROCLAMATION.

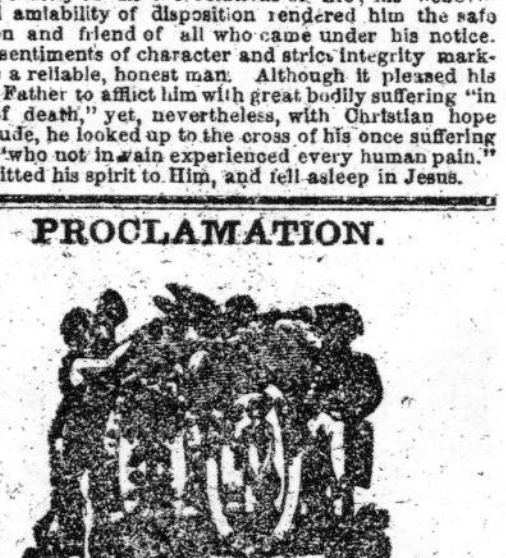

EXECUTIVE DEPARTMENT,
COLUMBIA, S. C., September 18, 1862.

By His Excellency F. W. PICKENS, Governor and Commander-in-Chief in and over the State of South Carolina.

Whereas, by information received at this Department, it appears that the Election District of St. Helena is so occupied by the enemy that the approaching election for a Representative to the State Legislature cannot be conducted therein with composure; and whereas it is provided by an ordinance of the Convention of this State, passed the 6th day of January, A. D., 1862, entitled "An Ordinance to provide for holding elections for districts occupied or threatened by the enemy," "That when, during the continuance of the existing war, some or all of the places of voting in any Election District of this State shall be occupied or threatened by the enemy, so that, in the opinion of the Executive Authority, an election cannot be conducted therein with composure, it shall be competent for the Executive Authority, by proclamation, to give notice of any election at which the voters of the said Election District would, in a condition of peace, be entitled to vote; and by the said proclamation (which shall be published at least a fortnight before the day fixed for the said election) to direct in what neighboring Election Districts the said voters may vote at the said election, and at what places therein, and how and by whom the said election shall be conducted, and how, when and where the result of the said election shall be ascertained and declared:"

Now, therefore, under the circumstances above recited, and in order that the intentions of the Ordinance of the Convention may be fully carried out, I hereby give notice to the voters and the Managers of Elections of the Election District of St. Helena that I appoint Pocotaligo, in Prince Williams Parish, as a suitable place for conducting the approaching election for one Representative to represent the Election District of St. Helena in the Legislature of this State; and I hereby direct the Managers of Elections for the Election District of St. Helena to meet at Pocotaligo on the FIRST TUESDAY after the second Monday in October next, and on that day and at that place open the polls and proceed to hold an election for one Representative to represent the Election District of St. Helena in the Legislature of this State. Said election to be conducted in the same manner as prescribed by law for holding elections for a Representative to represent the said Election District of St. Helena.

Given under my hand and the Seal of the State, the day and year above written. F. W. PICKENS.

WM. R. HUNT, Dep'y Sect'y of State.

September 15 c mwf8

OFFICIAL.

BY THE PRESIDENT OF THE UNITED STATES OF AMERICA.

A Proclamation.

I, ABRAHAM LINCOLN, President of the United States of America, and Commander-in-Chief of the Army and Navy thereof, do hereby proclaim and declare that hereafter, as heretofore, the war will be prosecuted for the object of practically restoring the constitutional relation between the United States and each of the States, and the people thereof, in which States that relation is or may be suspended or disturbed.

That it is my purpose, upon the next meeting of Congress, to again recommend the adoption of a practical measure tendering pecuniary aid to the free acceptance or rejection of all Slave States, so called, the people whereof may not then be in rebellion against the United States, and which States may then have voluntarily adopted, or thereafter may voluntarily adopt, immediate or gradual abolishment of slavery within their respective limits; and that the effort to colonize persons of African descent, with their consent, upon this continent or elsewhere, with the previously obtained consent of the Governments existing there, will be continued.

That on the first day of January, in the year of our Lord one thousand eight hundred and sixty-three, all persons held as slaves within any State, or designated part of a State, the people whereof shall then be in rebellion against the United States, shall be then, thenceforward, and forever free; and the Executive Government of the United States, including the military and naval authority thereof, will recognise and maintain the freedom of such persons, and will do no act or acts to repress such persons, or any of them, in any efforts they may make for their actual freedom.

That the Executive will, on the first day of January aforesaid, by proclamation, designate the States, and parts of States, if any, in which the people thereof respectively shall then be in rebellion against the United States; and the fact that any State, or the people thereof, shall on that day be in good faith represented in the Congress of the United States, by members chosen thereto at elections wherein a majority of the qualified voters of such State shall have participated, shall, in the absence of strong countervailing testimony, be deemed conclusive evidence that such State, and the people thereof, are not then in rebellion against the United States.

That attention is hereby called to an act of Congress entitled "An act to make an additional Article of War," approved March 13, 1862, and which act is in the words and figures following:

"*Be it enacted by the Senate and House of Representatives of the United States of America in Congress assembled*, That hereafter the following shall be promulgated as an additional article of war for the government of the Army of the United States, and shall be obeyed and observed as such:

"ARTICLE —. All officers or persons in the military or naval service of the United States are prohibited from employing any of the forces under their respective commands for the purpose of returning fugitives from service or labor who may have escaped from any persons to whom such service or labor is claimed to be due; and any officer who shall be found guilty by a court-martial of violating this article shall be dismissed from the service.

"SEC. 2. *And be it further enacted*, That this act shall take effect from and after its passage.

Also, to the ninth and tenth sections of an act entitled "An act to suppress insurrection, to punish treason and rebellion, to seize and confiscate property of rebels, and for other purposes," approved July 17, 1862, and which sections are in the words and figures following:

"SEC. 9. *And be it further enacted*, That all slaves of persons who shall hereafter be engaged in rebellion against the Government of the United States, or who shall in any way give aid or comfort thereto, escaping from such persons and taking refuge within the lines of the army; and all slaves captured from such persons, or deserted by them and coming under the control of the Government of the United States; and all slaves of such persons found on [or] being within any place occupied by rebel forces and afterwards occupied by the forces of the United States, shall be deemed captives of war, and shall be forever free of their servitude, and not again held as slaves.

"SEC. 10. *And be it further enacted*, That no slave escaping into any State, Territory, or the District of Columbia, from any other State, shall be delivered up, or in any way impeded or hindered of his liberty, except for crime, or some offence against the laws, unless the person claiming said fugitive shall first make oath that the person to whom the labor or service of such fugitive is alleged to be due is his lawful owner, and has not borne arms against the United States in the present rebellion, nor in any way given aid and comfort thereto; and no person engaged in the military or naval service of the United States shall, under any pretence whatever, assume to decide on the validity of the claim of any person to the service or labor of any other person, or surrender up any such person to the claimant, on pain of being dismissed from the service."

And I do hereby enjoin upon and order all persons engaged in the military and naval service of the United States to observe, obey, and enforce, within their respective spheres of service, the act and sections above recited.

And the Executive will in due time recommend that all citizens of the United States who shall have remained loyal thereto throughout the rebellion shall (upon the restoration of the constitutional relation between the United States and their respective States and people, if that relation shall have been suspended or disturbed) be compensated for all losses by acts of the United States, including the loss of slaves.

In witness whereof I have hereunto set my hand and caused the seal of the United States to be affixed.

Done at the City of Washington, this twenty-second day of September, in the year of our Lord one [SEAL.] thousand eight hundred and sixty-two, and of the Independence of the United States the eighty seventh.

ABRAHAM LINCOLN.

By the President:
WILLIAM H. SEWARD, Secretary of State.

AN IRON-CLAD RAILROAD BATTERY.

A letter from Jackson (Tennessee) dated the 13th instant contains the following allusion to a new engine of war:

"The iron-clad railroad battery, of which I spoke the other day, is likely to prove of essential service. It is constructed upon a platform car thirty feet long by eight wide. The sides and ends are first constructed of 2½ inch oak plank, upon which boiler iron is rivetted. The sides lean inward sufficient to glance a ball upward; one end is perpendicular, and the other pitched to a sharp angle. The sides are 2½ feet high. In the centre of the car is the circle upon which the gun-carriage revolves, and the whole arrangements of the gun are designed with reference to counteracting the recoil at the firing. A six inch James rifle cannon is mounted so as to sweep in every direction, and it has already been tested with shell and ball sufficiently to prove that all contingencies have been provided for. Others, I understand, similar to this one, but designed to carry heavier guns, are about being constructed. This one was constructed at the railroad shop here. I understand it is the purpose to construct bullet-proof cars, with port-holes for rifles, to accompany these batteries. When they are all completed, and a set of them placed at the ends of each train, or, for special purposes, are placed at each end of an engine, it may be calculated that attacks on trains or railroad bridges are about over."

ITALIAN AFFAIRS.

To the esteemed Lady who took the trouble to translate the subjoined article we made a promise several weeks ago to give it a place in our columns. But all of our space has been so constantly demanded by the exciting events of our own country, that we have not been able sooner to redeem the promise we gave. Though so long delayed the article may yet possess value for those of our readers who take any special interest in the political affairs to which it relates.

NEAPOLITAN AFFAIRS.

FOR THE NATIONAL INTELLIGENCER.

A very able and interesting *brochure* has recently appeared, written by Mr. De Meckel, an employé of the Ministry of Foreign Affairs at Paris, who, it is said, was sent to Naples by the Empress Eugenie in order to observe the true state of things at present existing in that city. This *brochure* is the result of careful, and it is to be supposed impartial, observation made by Mr. De Meckel during his stay in Naples. We subjoin some extracts:

"The first fact of importance which must forcibly impress every one who observes the actual situation of the former Kingdom of Naples is that armed reaction which the Government designates as *brigandage*. We are fully aware that no social disruption can be accomplished without confusion or crises; yet, in a revolution which has only been, as it is asserted, the spontaneous expression of a unanimous will, one might expect to find individual dissatisfaction, but not so energetic and zealous an opposition as to constitute, ever since the organization of the new *régime*, a real civil war." * * * "The obstinacy of the struggle, its bitterness, the manner in which it is carried on, gives to it quite a different character from that by which it is designated—the character of a civil war." * * * "Nor has a single Neapolitan been sent to quell the reaction. Even the Piedmontese soldiers are not deemed sufficiently reliable, and it is only the mobilized National Guard who are sent to oppose the brigands—that is to say, a body composed either of the most zealous partisans of the new ideas, or of men who are equally destitute of property and of convictions, and who have given in their adhesion to these ideas through interested motives." * * * "We know that the brigands are accused of committing many acts of cruelty against the soldiers sent to repress them, when after any collision they may have obtained an advantage. But these brigands are men united from all points, without a regular constitution, without judges, fevered by passion and their sufferings. Their violence cannot be justified, but it should be regarded with a certain indulgence. Such acts, on the contrary, when perpetrated by the Government, are inexcusable; and we believe that the Administration has been guilty of a great wrong by the passionate and rigorous means which it has used in the repression of brigandage. It should not forget that it only exists by the popular will, and that it belongs less to it than to any other to repress, with an undue severity, any manifestations of this will, however irregular and partial these manifestations may be. It should not forget that it takes the place of a Government against which one of the gravest objections that could be seriously alleged was that of persecuting the enemies of the throne with too much rigor. Nor do we speak of the imputed acts of atrocity with which the agents of the Government are charged." * * * "We simply recall established and incontestable facts, such as the conflagrations of Auletta, of Cotronei, of Viesti, of San-Marco, of Spinello, of Montefalcone, of Vico di Palma, of Brignano, of Barill, of Campo Chiaro, Guardia Regia, of those of Ponte-Landolfo, (5,000 souls,) and of Casalduni, (6,000 souls,) with regard to which the official journal of Naples gave the next day the frightfully laconic telegram—'Telegraphic despatch from Montfort, 14th August, seven o'clock. Yesterday morning punishment was inflicted upon Ponte-Landolfo and Casalduni.' (Official journal of Naples, No. 194) * * *

"But it is not only concerning the repression of brigandage that we have often based the same complaints against the new Government that were so frequently made against the old. Now, more than ever, they complain at Naples of the want of individual and political liberty." * * * *

"As to political liberty, since we have spoken of it, we shall not upon this point repeat a multitude of accusations, but we shall simply confine ourselves to writing an incontestable fact. There is no liberty of the press at Naples. * Every where we hear murmurs, and every kind of recrimination, and not an organ of all these complaints can appear without being immediately suppressed. Not, perhaps, directly by an administrative act, since the press is legally free in Italy, but by the violence that the authorities exercise or permit to be exercised against those who edit, print, or sell the new journal. In this way the *Settimana* was suppressed after the publication of three articles, in which one of the editors sought to make known the truth as to the general condition of the kingdom. * * * *

"The finances of Naples were formerly in the most flourishing condition. Their budget did not exceed sixteen millions of ducats for a population of seven millions of souls; that is to say, making a proportion of eight francs to each person. For several years past this budget had been augmented in consequence of political events, and of a change in the financial system; yet, notwithstanding, the last budget of King Francis II, rendered the 22d June, 1860, did not exceed 30,135,442 ducats, which only made a proportion of fourteen francs to each person—Sicily furnishing for its quota a sum of about four millions of ducats.

"But without entering into a more minute investigation of former budgets, without speaking of that reserved fund in the treasury which was found so useful in the reign of Ferdinand, and which enabled Francis II. to effect measures of relief during the high price of bread, and which contained thirty-three millions of ducats at the time of Garibaldi's arrival. This money was squandered and dissipated by the dictator; that is one of the effects of the revolution.

"We pass to the actual budget of Naples—to that of 1862. It is easy to show that it exhibits a deficit of one hundred and thirty-one millions of francs.* After all we have seen it does not astonish us to find embarrassments of every kind existing in other brances of the general administration. We are not surprised that commerce is at a stand still, and that industrial transactions are completely paralyzed at Naples. There is not a manufacturer or merchant who does not bitterly lament the present condition of things. * * * It is true that Naples never had a commerce like that of Marseilles, or of the manufacturing cities of England, but she had enough to occupy her population in proportion to their wants, and no one was reduced to a state of starvation. At present there is no work to be had, the number of mendicants is doubled, and the administration does nothing towards providing for the people. Much is said about useful improvements about to be projected, of railroads that are to be constructed, &c.; but these works never commence, and the actual state of things does not change. Besides, almost all the places under the Government, both high and low, are filled by Piedmontese. A decree ordered the demolition of the Chateau-neuf, a fort of Naples constructed by Charles d'Anjou; it presented an opportunity of giving employment to a portion of the Neapolitan population, but in place of making use of this occasion to employ the workmen of the city, they sent for Genoese laborers, under the pretext that they would work for lower wages.

"One of the benefits conferred by the new régime, and it gives us pleasure to mention it, has been the re-opening of the colleges of Naples to the provincial students. The courses have been commenced, the number of students has become considerable, but after a short time their studies have been interrupted; the students have complained, they have raised a sort of *emeute*; in short, the labors have ceased, and the enemies of the administration have thus been enabled to assert that the students were only called to Naples in order to cause them to engage in those political discussions prohibited to them by Ferdinand. * * *

"But in the face of all these obstacles has the administration sufficient power to surmount all the dangers which may arise, not only internal but external?

"The former Piedmontese army had a good reputation; it has been increased by that of the annexed countries, by the navy of Naples, by the mobilized national guard, and yet, at a time when the country is free from foreign preoccupations, it is powerless against the brigands; that is to say, against a handful of men who are scarcely armed. What, then, can this army effect against Austria when it attempts to conquer Venitia? * * *

"But what are the causes of this weakness? There exist two very serious ones. We believe that the first cause is to be found in the mistrust which exists both among officers and soldiers, who are only united by the uniform they wear. * * * * * The first essential of strength is assuredly unity. Now this union is, we must confess, entirely wanting; the Italian army has no homogeneity; each one desires, each one calls for a different thing; and all alike, officers as well as soldiers, have only the common bond of a single conviction—that the present state of things cannot last.

"But there is a second cause of weakness for the army as serious as that of the prevailing mistrust and discord; we allude to the desertions. Under Ferdinand Naples readily furnished one hundred thousand men. Desertion was an unknown thing; and this King, with all his faults, knew how to inspire fidelity to his standard. Now, desertion has attained colossal dimensions. We have seen bodies of troops depart composed of five hundred men, and come back after a first day's march already reduced to two hundred—the officers refusing to proceed on the expedition, convinced that if they did so they would arrive alone at their journey's end. One cannot go outside of Naples without meeting deserters who are being carried to prison by soldiers who would probably desert, in their turn, the next day. It must be acknowledged the Neapolitan soldier is extremely attached to the old *régime*. * * * Speak to him of the King, he always supposes that you mean to designate Francis II.

"Another fact remains to be noticed, and that is the universal sadness which exists at Naples. The antipathy of the Neapolitans for the innovations which have been made is general, and all experience regrets for the giving up of former habits. In a word *the illusion is dispelled*.

"We have sought to give a rapid sketch of the principal results of the system of unification as obtained by us from an impartial and conscientious observation of Naples; and it must be confessed that in comparing the old administration with the new we have been inclined to criticise the latter, and to become the apologist of the former. We have already stated that we admitted the existence of serious abuses in the former administration; but we believe that these abuses could have been remedied without the revolution which threatens to be fatal in its consequences; and we are obliged to state the deplorable situation into which a false starting point—false in our judgment—has so fatally conducted the new order of things.

M. V. G.

* TRANSLATOR'S NOTE.—Mazzini has just published an incendiary proclamation, in which he calls upon the Italian people to seize Rome and Venice; and yet at this very moment the Parliament at Turin is convulsed by dissensions. The first sitting was very stormy, and every thing points to a dissolution. The new decrees imposing additional and heavy taxes have met with the most determined opposition. The finances are in a terrible condition—a deficit of four hundred and seventy-five millions of francs for the present year—and for the coming year five hundred million of francs is asked for.

THE MODERN JEWS—THEIR MANNERS AND CUSTOMS.

That clever hebdomadal publication, "Once a Week," contains in one of its late numbers so interesting a sketch of the peculiar customs of the modern Israelites that we extract a few of its passages for the benefit of readers to whom those customs are unfamiliar:

THE TWO GRAND DIVISIONS.

Like most Oriental nations, the Jews adhere to their religious doctrines and customs with great tenacity, but even they have not been able to resist the introduction of novelties into their worship. Hence the existence of a body calling itself the Reformed Jews. The difference, however, is more in forms than in reality, the fundamental doctrine of their faith being identical in both branches. Apart from this distinction, the Jews divide themselves into two communities—the one designated as the Shepardim, the other the Ashkenasim. The last are descended from the German and Polish Jews, and are far more numerous than their aristocratic brethren.

THE STAGES OF LIFE.

On the eighth day after the birth of the young Jew he is taken to the synagogue by his father, accompanied by a godfather, for circumcision. If the infant happens to be a first born son, he is, according to Jewish jurisprudence, the property of the Cohen, (who is supposed to be a descendant of the house of Aaron, but has no longer any priestly functions to perform,) and must be redeemed on the thirtieth day after his birth; therefore, certain ceremonies take place, during which the father tenders the figurative sum of five shekels to the Cohen, who accepts them as a ransom.

Until he attains his thirteenth year the young Jew is entirely under the control of his father and mother, who are supposed to be accountable for all the sins he may commit up to that period; but their responsibility ceases on the Sabbath day succeeding his thirteenth birthday, when a ceremony akin to that of confirmation takes place. The boy is called up to the reading desk in the synagogue, and is required to read a portion of the law. If he cannot read, the chazan, or minister, does it for him, after which the father places his hands on his son's head, and solemnly renounces his accountability for his future actions.

The next important step in his career is his betrothal, which usually takes place at an early age, in accordance with the recommendation of the Jewish law. A number of friends being present, the *Kenas*, or bond inflicting a penalty on either party who shall be guilty of a breach of the agreement, is read, after which a cup is broken, as a ratification of its provisions, by the parties concerned. The marriage follows the betrothal, it may be six or twelve months afterwards, or more.

Due notice having been given at the synagogue, the minister on the Saturday eve preceding the day fixed for the marriage chaunts some sentences referring to the approaching event, and the next day the intended bridegroom has to appear in the synagogue and have certain portions of the law read over to him, and pay any arrears he may owe to the congregation.

The way in which the parties spend the morning in their respective dwellings on the wedding day resembles, I suppose, the manner in which it is employed by Gentiles on similar occasions; those who rightly realize the awful nature of the ceremony they are about to perform spend the hours in fasting and reading the service prepared for the day of atonement. As soon as the clock strikes the appointed hour, two men present themselves before the bridegroom and carry him off to the synagogue, where he meets the bride, whom two female friends have brought there with her head enveloped in a veil. The same persons place the two principal performers facing each other under a silk or velvet canopy supported by four long poles; the shamas, a kind of curate and clerk combined, brings a glass of wine, which he hands to the Rabbi, who thereupon offers up a short blessing, and then gives the glass of wine to the bridegroom, who tastes it and passes it to the bride, who does likewise.

The bridegroom then takes the ring from his pocket and places it on the finger of the bride, saying after the Rabbi (in Hebrew) as he does so: "Behold! thou art betrothed unto me with this ring, according to the rites of Moses and Israel." The Rabbi then reads the marriage contract, which is written in Chaldee, and is not understood by the parties concerned, who therefore take it on trust; after this the Chazan takes a glass of wine, and pronounces a form of words longer but similar to that pronounced by the Rabbi; the wine is given to the bridegroom and bride, and an empty glass having been placed at the feet of the former, he stamps upon it and breaks it, whereupon all present wish him *mazel tov*, (good speed,) and the ceremony is at an end.

If the newly married Jew has a proper sense of his religious duties, one of his first proceedings, on taking possession of his domicile, is to prepare a mezuzah. This is a tube nailed to the door-post, and contains a strip of parchment, on one side of which is inscribed one of the names applied to the Supreme Being, and on the other from the 4th to 9th verses of the vi. chapter of Deuteronomy, and from the 13th to the 21st verses of the xi. chapter of the same book. A similar tube is fastened to the jambs of the other doors in the house; and the Jew who is a strict observer of the old customs of his forefathers never leaves his house for the first time, daily, without touching the mezuzah with his lips, or bending his head to it as he passes from room to room.

DEATH AND BURIAL.

The Jew has no reason to complain of lack of seasons for rejoicings, but days of mourning and sorrow visit him as well as his Gentile brethren. But the manner in which he mourns for the dead is different as regards certain forms from that of the latter, who simply buries his grief in his own heart, and suffers it to exhibit itself as little as possible. The coffin is of the simplest construction, and before the lid is placed upon it a little earth, brought from Jerusalem, is put in. The nearest relatives of the deceased approach in succession, and request pardon of the deceased for any offence they may have given him in his lifetime, and a favorable recollection of them in the world to which he has departed. The Rabbi then makes a slight cut in the upper part of the garments of each mourner, and tears it slightly, and this rent must not be sewn up till after a certain number of days.

No woman is allowed to accompany the corpse to its last resting place, so that the wailing of women which has chilled the heart of every traveller in the East, and which may be heard even in those islands at the antipodes where scarcely a European has set his foot, is never heard here now.

A singular custom is sometimes observed on occasions when there have been several deaths in the family within a short period. A padlock is locked and placed in the grave and the key thrown away, the object being to delay the entrance of death into the household for a longer period.

The seven days which succeed the funeral of a Jew are given up entirely to mourning. Unwashed and with naked feet the mourner sits on the bare ground in a room open to all comers; not even a change of dress is permitted; and the only consolation which the afflicted can have during this period is derived from the perusal of religious books which cheer them with the hope of meeting the deceased hereafter. When they visit the synagogue, during the continuance of these days of mourning, a touching reception is given them by the congregation, who all rise as they enter and make a movement towards them, the Rabbi uttering a short prayer that they may be comforted. Business may be attended to after the lapse of the seven days, but no amusement may be indulged in for thirty days thereafter; and if the mourning be for a father or mother this rule is to be observed for a year.

DISTINCTION BETWEEN THE SEXES.

In every day life the sexes are as much on an equality as among other civilized people, but in religious matters the case is slightly different. It is in acknowledgment of this difference that the Jew is taught to offer up the following short thanksgiving along with his daily prayers: "Blessed art thou, O Lord our God, king of the universe, who hast not made me a woman." The female infant is named in the synagogue, and that is the only ceremony to which she is subjected.

According to the Jewish law it is still the duty of the husband's brother, if he die and leave no issue, to marry his brother's widow, and if he declines to do this, or if he happens to be disqualified by reason of his having a wife already, he must set her free, a ceremony which is performed in this wise: The Rabbi and witnesses being present, and the man having repeated his refusal to marry his brother's wife, the Rabbi directs the shoe to be brought which is kept for the purpose, and after the Jew has placed it on his foot, the Rabbi knots the two long strings attached to it around his leg. He then takes the widow by the hand and leads her to the man, and she makes in Hebrew what is in substance a declaration that he refuses to perform the part of the brother of her husband, and he repeats his refusal; upon which the woman stoops down and with her right hand unfastens the knots, takes off the shoe and throws it down, and first spitting on the ground before the offender, repeats after the Rabbi:

"So shall it be done to the man that will not build up his brother's house; and his name shall be called in Israel, 'The house of him that hath his shoe loosed.'"—Deuteronomy xxv., 9. The congregation responding, "His shoe is loosed," the woman is thereupon pronounced by the Rabbi to be free to marry again.

MARCH OVER A DESERT PRAIRIE.

A letter dated at Mesilla, in Arizona, on the 15th of August, mentions the arrival of the California troops, after a long march through a desert country, where no provisions or forage could be obtained, and necessarily requiring every thing for the men and horses to be transported with them. They have averaged fifteen miles per day for nearly sixty days. The letter says:

"The first infantry and cavalry California Volunteers have successfully marched one thousand miles over the route by the Colorado desert, the Gila river, Tucson, and the Mimbres river, from the Pacific to the Rio Grande. This they have done with but the trifling loss of ten men in rebel and Indian skirmishes, with abundant supplies, a serviceable train, and reached the western border of Texas in condition for an immediate contest with the enemy. Officers and men have shared the hardships of the march alike, without tents and without baggage—one wagon sufficing to transport ten days' rations and the property of each company. For fully one-half the distance, over the burning deserts, in midsummer, with a very scanty supply of water, the men have uncomplainingly carried their knapsacks and averaged throughout over seventeen miles daily. They have been only too well satisfied that every step carried them nearer to the heart of the rebellion."

NEW SALINE SPRINGS.

The salt springs of Syracuse, in New York, and those on the banks of the Kanawha, in Western Virginia, are no longer to enjoy a monopoly in the production of brine. Michigan has, within the past year, entered the lists. In one of her central counties some indications of salt had long been noticed by the inhabitants. Last year a farmer undertook to bore in search of the article; and, after piercing to a depth of about two hundred feet, struck a fine spring. It does not flow over, like the oil wells of Pennsylvania, but rises so near the surface that it can be brought up by pumping, at a moderate expense. A correspondent writes that already three thousand barrels of brine are taken from that neighborhood every week, worth at the wells one dollar per barrel. It is also reported that salt springs have been discovered in Venango county, Pennsylvania, the principal seat of the oil "diggings." Of the number or size of the springs little is yet known, but the quality is said to be excellent, the brine being so strong that it crystalizes after a short period of exposure in the open air. So progresses the work of developing the resources of the North in spite of the havoc of war.

[*Commercial Advertiser.*

HINTS ABOUT CHILDREN.

The moral teachings should commence with the earliest infancy; the physical as soon as there is bodily locomotion; the mental, meaning thereby the literary, not earlier than the completion of the sixth year, not even to the extent of learning the alphabet or repeating by "rote;" mere mechanical memorizing. This brain education is specially advised in reference only to children whose situation in life allows them to study until they are twenty-one. The children of the poor—those who must go to work and earn something—can with safety begin at the age of three or four years for three reasons: They are out in the open air nearly all the time during daylight, their food is plain and not over abundant. The early necessity that they should do something for a living does not allow time for special brain disturbance; and any slight tendencies in that direction would be counteracted and repaired by the constant muscular activities necessary to their condition. But those children who will have nothing to do but "get their education" up to the day of entering their twenty-first year ought to do nothing for the first third of that period but to eat and sleep and play out of doors from morning until night all the year round, except when rain, sleet, or snow are falling. It is the exercise daily, "regardless of the weather," which works so many almost miracles in the renovation of human health. The vanity of parents is fed by the "smartness of their children;" but early ripe, early ruined, may be said of all precocities. If not actually ruined there is almost in all cases a sudden "giving out" of the mental powers, and the prodigy of yesterday is the mediocre of to-day and the *non compos mentis* of to-morrow.—*Hall's Journal of Health.*

PROPOSALS FOR MATERIALS FOR THE NAVY.

NAVY DEPARTMENT,
Bureau of Construction, &c., September 22, 1862.

SEALED PROPOSALS to furnish materials for the navy for the fiscal year ending 30th June, 1863, will be received at this Bureau until 5 o'clock P. M. of the 21st October next. These proposals must be endorsed "*Proposals for Materials for the Navy, Bureau of Construction*," &c., that they may be distinguished from other business letters.

The materials and articles embraced in the classes named are particularly described in the printed schedules, any of which will be furnished to such as desire to offer, on application to the commandants of the respective yards, or to the navy agent nearest thereto, and those of all the yards upon application to this Bureau. This division into classes being for the convenience of dealers in each, such portions only will be furnished as are actually required for bids. The commandant and navy agent of each station will in addition to the schedule of classes of their own yards have a copy of the schedules of the other yards, for examination only, from which it may be judged whether it will be desirable to make application for any of the classes of those yards.

Offers must be made for the whole of the class at any yard upon one of the printed schedules, or in strict conformity therewith, or they will not be considered. In computing the classes the price stated in the column of prices will be the standard, and the aggregate of the class will be carried out according to the prices stated.

The contract will be awarded to the lowest *bona fide* bidder who gives proper security for its fulfilment. The United States reserves the right to reject all the bids for any class, if deemed exorbitant.

All articles must be of the very best quality, to be delivered in the Navy yard in good order, and in suitable vessels and packages, properly marked with the name of the contractor, as the case may be, at the expense and risk of the contractor, and in all respects subject to the inspection, measurement, count, weight, &c. of the yard where received, and to the entire satisfaction of the commandant thereof.

Bidders are referred to the commandants of the respective yards for samples, instructions, or particular description of the articles; and, all other things being equal, preference will be given to articles of American manufacture.

Every offer, as required by the law of 10th August, 1846, must be accompanied by a written guarantee, the form of which is herewith given.

Those only whose offers may be accepted will be notified, and the contract will be forwarded as soon thereafter as practicable, which they will be required to execute within ten days after its receipt at the post office or navy agency named by them.

Sureties in the full amount will be required to sign the contract, and their responsibility certified to by a United States district judge, United States district attorney, collector, or navy agent. As additional security, twenty per centum will be withheld from the amount of the bills until the contract shall have been completed; and eighty per centum of each bill, approved in triplicate by the commandants of the respective yards, will be paid by the navy agent at the points of delivery in certificates of indebtedness or Treasury notes at the option of the Government.

It is stipulated in the contract that if default be made by the parties of the first part in delivering all or any of the articles mentioned in any class bid for in the contract, of the quality and at the time and places above provided, then, and in that case the contractor and his sureties will forfeit and pay to the United States a sum of money not exceeding twice the amount of such class, which may be recovered from time to time, according to the act of Congress in that case provided, approved March 3, 1843.

In class No. 11 and those following if a quantity in addition equal to the face of the contract is demanded it is to be furnished on like terms and conditions during the fiscal year."

FORM OF OFFER.

Which from a firm must be signed by all the members.

I, ——, of —— in the State of ——, hereby agree to furnish and deliver in the respective navy yards all the articles named in the classes hereunto annexed, agreeably to the provisions of the schedules therefor, and in conformity with the advertisement of the Bureau of Construction, &c. of 22d September, 1862. Should my offer be accepted, I request to be addressed at ——, and the contract sent to the Navy Agent at ——, or to ——, for signature and certificate.

Signature, A. B.

Date,
Witness.

The schedule which the bidder encloses must be pasted to his offer, and each of them signed by him. Opposite each article in the schedule the price must be set, the amount carried out, the aggregate footed up for each class, and the amount likewise written in words. If the parties who bid do not reside near the place where the articles are to be delivered, they must name in their offer a person to whom orders on them are to be delivered.

FORM OF GUARANTEE.

The undersigned ——, of ——, in the State of ——, and —— of ——, in the State of ——, hereby guaranty that in case the foregoing bid of —— for any of the classes therein named be accepted, he or they will, within ten days after the receipt of the contract at the post office named, or Navy Agent designated, execute the contract for the same, with good and sufficient sureties; and in case said —— shall fail to enter into contract as aforesaid, we guaranty to make good the difference between the offer of the said —— —— and that which may be accepted.

Signatures of two guarantors, { C. D. / E. F.

Date,
Witness.

I hereby certify that the above named —— are known to me as men of property and able to make good their guarantee.

Signature, G. H.

Date.

To be signed by the United States District Judge, United States District Attorney, Collector, or Navy Agent.

Extract from a law of the United States, approved July 17, 1862.

SEC. 14. *And be it further enacted*, That no contract or order, or any interest therein, shall be transferred by the party or parties to whom such contract or order may be given to any other party or parties, and that any such transfer shall cause the annulment of the contract or order transferred so far as the United States are concerned: *Provided*, That all the rights of action are hereby reserved to the United States for any breach of such contract by the contracting party or parties

SEC. 16. *And be it further enacted*, That whenever any contractor for subsistence, clothing, arms, ammunition, munitions of war, and for every description of supplies for the army or navy of the United States shall be found guilty by a court-martial of fraud or wilful neglect of duty, he shall be punished by fine, imprisonment, or such other punishment as the court-martial shall adjudge; and any person who shall contract to furnish supplies of any kind or description for the army or navy, he shall be deemed and taken as a part of the land or naval forces of the United States for which he shall contract to furnish said supplies, and be subject to the rules and regulations for the government of the land and naval forces of the United States.

The following are the classes required at the respective navy yards:

KITTERY, MAINE.

Class No. 1. White Oak Logs; No. 2. White Oak Keel; No. 3. White Oak Promiscuous Timber; No. 4. White Oak Plank; No. 6. Yellow Pine Logs; No. 7. Yellow Pine Beams; No. 8 Yellow Pine Mast and Spar Timber; No. 10. White Pine Mast Timber; No. 11. White Pine Plank and Boards; No. 13. Ash Plank and Boards; No. 14. White Ash Oars; No. 15. Hickory Butts; No. 16 Black Walnut and Cherry; No. 17. Cypress; No. 19. White Oak Staves and Heading; No. 20. Black Spruce; No. 23. Lignumvitæ; No. 25. Iron; No. 26. Steel; No. 27. Iron Spikes; No. 28. Iron Nails, wrought and cut; No. 30. Lead; No. 31. Zinc and Tin; No. 34. Tools for Stores; No. 36. White Lead; No. 37. Zinc Paints; No. 38. Colored Paints, Dryer; No 39. Linseed Oil, Turpentine, Varnish; No. 41. Glass; No. 43. Pitch, Rosin, Tar; No. 44 Oil, Tallow, Soap; No. 46. Miscellaneous—Dry Goods, Hair Cloth, Ship Chandlery for construction. Class A. Boiler Iron and Rivets; C. Lard Oil; F. miscellaneous Tools for Engineers; G. Cooking Utensils, Stoves, &c.; H. Flax Canvass; I. Cotton Canvass; P. Twine; K. Leather; H. Hose; M. Brushes; N. Bunting, Dry Goods; O. Lanterns; Q. Sperm Oil; R Ship Chandlery, for stores and equipment; S. Stationery; T. Fire Wood.

CHARLESTOWN.

Class No. 1. White Oak Logs; No. 2. White Oak Keel Pieces; No. 3. White Oak Promiscuous Timber; No. 4. White Oak Plank; No. 6 Yellow Pine Logs; No. 11. White Pine Logs, Plank, and Boards; No. 13. Ash Logs and Plank; No. 16. Black Walnut, Mahogany, and Cherry; No. 18. Locust; No. 19. White Oak Staves and Heading; No. 23 Lignumvitæ; No. 25. Iron; No. 26. Steel; No. 27. Iron Spikes; No. 28. Iron Nails, wrought and cut; No. 30. Lead; No. 31. Zinc and Tin; No. 33. Hardware; No. 34. Tools for stores; No. 36. White Lead; No. 37. Zinc Paints; No. 38. Colored Paints, Dryer; No. 39 Linseed Oil, Turpentine, and Varnish; No. 41. Glass; No. 43. Pitch and Rosin; No. 44 Fish Oil, Tallow, and Soap; No. 46. Miscellaneous Dry Goods; A. Boiler Iron and Rivets; B. Pig Iron; C Lard Oil; D. Boiler Felting; E. Gum Packing; F. Miscellaneous Tools for Engineers; G. Cooking Utensils and Stoves; H Flax Canvass; I. Cotton Canvass; J. Flax and Cotton Twine; K. Leather; L. Hose; M Brushes; N. Bunting and Dry Goods; O. Lanterns; P. Tar for Ropewalk; Q. Sperm Oil; R. Ship Chandlery for stores and equipments; S. Stationery; T. Fire Wood; U. Ox Hides for rope.

BROOKLYN, NEW YORK.

Class No. 1. White Oak Logs; No. 2. White Oak Keel Pieces; No. 3. White Oak Promiscuous Timber; No. 4. White Oak Plank; No 5. White Oak Knees; No. 6. Yellow Pine Logs; No. 7. Yellow Pine Beams; No. 8 Yellow Pine Mast Timber; No 10. White Pine Mast Timber; No. 11. White Pine Logs, Plank, and Boards; No 12. White Oak Boards and Plank; No. 13. Ash Logs and Plank; No. 14. Ash Oars; No. 15. Hickory Butts and Handspikes; No. 16. Black Walnut, Cherry; No. 17. Cypress; No. 18. Locust; No. 19. White Oak Staves and Heading; No. 20. Black Spruce; No. 21. Cedar; No. 22. Mahogany; No. 23. Lignumvitæ: No. 25. Iron, round, flat, and square; No. 26. Steel; No. 27. Iron Spikes; No. 28. Iron Nails, wrought and cut; No. 30. Lead; No. 31. Zinc, Tin; No. 33. Hardware, No. 34. Tools for stores, &c.; No. 36. White Lead; No. 37. Zinc Paint; No. 38. Colored Paints, Dryer; No. 39. Linseed Oil, Turpentine, Varnish; No. 41. Glass; No. 43. Pitch, Rosin, Tar; No. 44. Fish Oil, Tallow, Soap; No. 46. Miscellaneous Dry Goods; A Boiler Iron and Rivets; B. Pig Iron; C. Lard Oil; D. Boiler Felting: E. Gum Packing; F. Miscellaneous Tools for Engineers; G Cooking Utensils, Stoves, &c.; H. Flax Canvass; I. Cotton Canvass; J. Twine; K. Leather; L. Hose; M. Brushes; N. Bunting and Dry Goods; O. Lanterns; Q. Sperm Oil; R. Ship Chandlery for stores and equipments; S. Stationery; T. Fire Wood.

PHILADELPHIA.

Class No. 1. White Oak Logs; No. 2. White Oak Keel Pieces; No. 3. White Oak Promiscuous Timber; No. 4. White Oak Plank; No. 6. Yellow Pine Plank Stock Logs; No. 7. Yellow Pine Beams; No. 8. Yellow Pine Mast and Spar Timber; No. 10. White Pine Mast and Spar Timber; No. 11. White Pine Logs, Plank, Boards, &c.; No 13. Ash Logs and Planks; No. 14. White Ash Oars; No. 15. White Heart Hickory, Capstan Bars; No. 16. Mahogany, Black Walnut, Cherry; No. 17. Cypress, Cedar Boards; No. 18. Locust; No. 20. Black Spruce Spar Timber; No. 22. Lignumvitæ; No. 25. Iron, round, flat, and square; No 26. Steel; No. 27. Iron Spikes; No. 28. Iron Nails, wrought and cut; No. 30 Lead; No. 31. Zinc, Tin; No. 33. Hardware; No. 34. Tooles for stores; No. 36. White Lead; No 37. Zinc Paint; No. 38. Colored Paints, Dryer; No 39. Linseed Oil, Turpentine, Varnish; No. 41. Glass; No. 43. Pitch, tar, rosin; No. 44. Fish Oil, Tallow, Soap; No. 46. Miscellaneous Dry Goods, hair, cloth, and Ship Chandlery for construction; A. Iron Rivets for Boilers; B. Pig Iron; C. Lard Oil; D. Boiler Felting; E. Gum Packing; F. Miscellaneous Tools for Engineers; G. Cooking Utensils, Stoves, &c.; H. Flax Canvass; I. Cotton Canvass; J. Twine; K. Leather; L. Hose; M. Brushes: N. Bunting, Dry Goods; Q Sperm Oil; R. Ship Chandlery for Store Equipments; S. Stationery; T. Fire Wood.

WASHINGTON.

Class No. 1. White Oak Logs; No. 6. Yellow Pine Plank Stock Logs; No. 11. White Pine; No. 13. Ash Plank; No. 14. Ash Oars; No. 15. Hickory Bars; No. 16. Black Walnut; No. 17. Cypress; No. 19. Staves and Headings; No. 21. Poplar; No. 25. Iron; No. 26. Steel; No 27. Iron Spikes; No. 28. Iron Nails; No 30. Lead; No. 31. Zinc, tin, solder; No. 33. Hardware; No 36. White Lead; No. 37. Zinc Paint; No. 38. Colored Paints; No. 39. Linseed Oil, Varnish; No. 41. Glass; No. 42 Oakum; No. 43. Pitch, tar; No. 41. Brown Soap; No. 46. Miscellaneous Dry Goods, Ship Chandlery, &c., for construction; No. 48 Tanks and Galleys; No. 49. Ingot Copper; No. 50. Chain Iron; No. 51. Poles; No. 52. Bellows; A. Boiler Iron and Rivets; B. Pig Iron; C. Lard Oil; D Boiler Felting; E. Gum Packing; F. Miscellaneous Engineer's Tools; G. Cooking Stoves, &c.; H. Flax Canvass; I. Cotton Canvass; J. Twine; K Leather; L. Hose; M. Brushes; N. Bunting and Dry Goods; P. Gas Pipe for steamer fitting; Q. Sperm Oil; R. Ship Chandlery for stores and equipments; S. Stationery; T. Fire Wood.

sep 22—lawtOct21

PROPOSALS FOR WOOD.

DEPOT QUARTERMASTER'S OFFICE,
Corner of Eighteenth and G streets,
Washington, D. C., September 22, 1862.

SEALED PROPOSALS for the delivery of (5,000) five thousand Cords of Wood to the Government will be received at this office until Wednesday, the (1st) first day of October, at (12) twelve o'clock M.

The Wood to be hard, sound, merchantable (4) four feet long, and split to the ordinary size of cord wood.

The Wood to be delivered in the city of Washington at such points as the Depot Quartermaster shall direct, corded in ranks (4) four feet high, delivery not being considered complete until so corded, measured, and inspected.

An inspector will be designated, on the part of the Government, to inspect and measure the wood, and such as does not conform to the above specifications will be rejected.

All to be delivered on or before the (1st) first day of December, 1862.

Payment to be made upon the completion of the whole contract.

PROPOSALS.

The full name and post office address of the bidder must appear in the proposal.

If a bid is made in the name of a firm, the names of all the parties must appear, or the bid will be considered as the individual proposal of the party signing it.

Proposals from *disloyal parties will not be considered*, and an oath of allegiance must accompany each proposition.

Proposals must be addressed to Col. D. H. RUCKER, Quartermaster U. S. Army, Washington, D. C., and should be plainly marked "Proposals for Wood."

GUARANTEE.

The ability of the bidder to fill the contract, should it be awarded to him, must be guarantied by two responsible persons, whose signatures must be appended to the guarantee.

The responsibility of the guarantors must be shown by the *official* certificate of the Clerk of the nearest District Court or of the United States District Attorney.

Bidders must be present in person when the bids are opened, or their proposals will not be considered.

Bonds, in the sum of ten thousand dollars, signed by the contractor and both of his guarantors, will be required of the successful bidder upon signing the contract.

As the bond must accompany the contract, it will be necessary for bidders to have their bondsmen with them, or to have bonds signed in anticipation and ready to be produced when the contract is signed. Blanks for bonds can be procured upon application being made at this office, either personally, by letter, or by telegraph.

Form of Guarantee.

We, ——, of the county of —— and State of ——, and ——, of the county of ——, and ——, do hereby guaranty that —— —— is able to fulfil a contract, in accordance with the terms of his proposition, and that, should his proposition be accepted, he will at once enter into a contract in accordance therewith.

Should the contract be awarded him we are prepared to become his securities.

(To this guarantee must be appended the *official* certificate above mentioned)

The Depot Quartermaster reserves to himself the right to reject any or all bids that he may deem too high.

D. H. RUCKER,
sep 22—dtoct1 Colonel and Depot Quartermaster.

Quartermaster's Office,

Washington, D. C., 197 F street, Sept. 17, 1862.

SEALED PROPOSALS will be received until September 30th, at 12 M., for delivering at this office fourteen cords of well-seasoned OAK WOOD, of the best quality; to be delivered as follows: Two cords on the 1st of October, and two cords on the 1st day of each succeeding month, until the whole shall have been delivered.

Proposals should be addressed to the subscriber, and endorsed on the envelopes, "Proposals for Wood."

sep 17—dtd MORRIS S. MILLER, Maj. Qr. Mr.

UNITED STATES MARSHAL'S SALE OF THE Cargo of the Vessel "Blossom."—By virtue of a decree of the District Court of the United States for the District of Columbia, I will sell at public sale, for cash, at the Government Store-house, at the Washington Navy Yard, in said District, on Friday, the 26th day of September, instant, commencing at 10 o'clock A. M., the following goods and chattels of the vessel "Blossom," viz: Lot wheat, lot salt, lot tea, barrels of sugar, a box marked morphine, lot tooth brushes, and a box of percussion caps.

WARD H. LAMON,
sep 20—dtd [Star] U. S. Marshal D. C.

WASHINGTON.

"LIBERTY AND UNION, NOW AND FOREVER, ONE AND INSEPARABLE."

TUESDAY, SEPTEMBER 23, 1862.

PROCLAMATION OF THE PRESIDENT.

The reader will find in another part of to-day's Intelligencer a Proclamation of the President of the United States, declaring prospectively the emancipation of slaves in the Insurgent States on the first of January next, unless, in the mean time, the people of these States shall so far return to their constitutional relations as to send Representatives to Congress.

With our well-known and oft-repeated views respecting the inutility of such proclamations, it can hardly be necessary for us to say that, where we expect no good, we shall be only too happy to find that no harm has been done by the present declaration of the Executive.

This new proclamation with regard to the contingent emancipation of slaves in the insurgent States not being self-enforcing any more than the proclamation of Gen. Hunter in regard to the immediate emancipation of slaves in the States of South Carolina, Georgia, and Florida, the only difference between the two papers resides in the signatures respectively attached to them. And as, in themselves considered, they are likely to prove equally void of practical effect, we are not without the suspicion that the President has taken this method to convince the only class of persons likely to be pleased with this proclamation of the utter fallacy of the hopes they have founded upon it. This opinion, we may add, derives confirmation from the fact that he suspends *for some months* the enforcement of so much of his declaration as denounces the emancipation of slaves in punishment for contumacy on the part of the Insurgent States, while he gives immediate force and effect, so far as force and effect result from proclamations, to the regulations prescribed by the new article of war and the provisions of the confiscation act in the matter of slaves. On any other theory than this the proclamation may be said to open issues too tremendous, and to be fraught with consequences too undeveloped, to admit of calculation or forecast by any intelligence we can command.

A REVIEW.

The campaign in Virginia has now reached a stage from which we may survey the connexion of military events that have superinduced the existing military situation.

During the month of July, after the change of his base of operations from the Pamunkey to the James River, Gen. McClellan was resting on the banks of the latter in a position which the enemy evidently deemed it unsafe to attack, as no effort whatever was made to dislodge him. Our army at this point was for weeks anxiously awaiting reinforcements, preparatory to a second advance on Richmond, having lost neither heart nor hope because of the failure which had overtaken its first approach.

Gen. Halleck, having been appointed General-in-Chief of the land forces of the United States under an order dated July 11th, reached this city on the 23d of the same month, and on the following day repaired to the camp of Gen. McClellan.

It soon began to be rumored that the army of Gen. McClellan had been ordered to evacuate Harrison's Landing, on the James River, and to take up a new position on the line of the Potomac, with the view of making an advance on Richmond overland, by the united forces of the Government in Virginia.

Gen. Pope had been previously called by the President from his field of operations in the West to take command of the army corps of Generals Fremont, Banks, and McDowell, consolidated into the "Army of Virginia," and this energetic officer soon commenced a series of cavalry dashes, followed by more formidable and concerted movements, with a view of threatening Gordonsville, and thus creating a diversion in favor of Gen. McClellan.

It is well known that this latter officer (and we believe that the majority of his corps commanders shared the opinion of their chief) was opposed to the projected change of position assigned to the army of the Potomac. It was urged that that army awaited simply the arrival of reinforcements to the number of twenty or thirty thousand to enable it to renew the attack on Richmond. The new levies, raised under the call for three hundred thousand volunteers, were already flocking to the capital, and it was hoped by our forces on the James that their thinned ranks would soon be swollen by accessions from these recruits.

But the General-in-Chief adhered to the new programme which he had marked out for the army of the Potomac, and that army was accordingly withdrawn from Harrison's Landing and ordered to take up a new position. What that position originally was designed to be we are unable to say, but we think it likely that the course of events on the Rappahannock may have somewhat disturbed the calculations of Gen. Halleck. Certain it is that he had previously expressed an opinion unfavorable to the strategetic advantages of the position which was superinduced by the drift of the campaign. In a paper published on the "organization of armies," "principles of strategy," &c., in the early stage of the war, he had written as follows:

"In selecting a base of operations, it is stated by the best authorities that troops should never be placed upon the circumference of a circle the centre of which is occupied by an enemy; for in that case the enemy can select his point of attack or defence, and, by concentrating his forces on that point, can successfully resist or attack the forces brought against him. Thus, in the present campaign, the Federal troops were assembled at Fortress Monroe, Arlington, Martinsburg, Grafton, Parkersburg, Cincinnati, and Cairo, while the Confederate forces were concentrated on Lynchburg, Richmond, and Manassas Junction—one party on the circumference and the other concentrated near the centre. Again, in selecting lines of operation, it is said that troops should never be moved on exterior lines, unless the forces on each line are superior to the combined forces of the enemy. The reason of this rule is obvious: by moving on exterior lines, we permit the enemy to attack either of our lines with his combined forces, the other being outside and too distant to render any assistance to the lines attacked. On the contrary, by moving on interior lines, our forces, being nearer together than those of the enemy, may be readily concentrated on any weak point which may be presented. It matters little whether our lines be single or double, provided we can unite our forces sooner than the enemy can unite his; the great object being to concentrate upon the decisive point a larger force than the enemy can bring to resist our attack. This is the great secret, if secret it can be called, of all strategic manœuvres."

If the army of Gen. McClellan had been retained in its position on the James River no one can suppose that the enemy would have ventured the attack which he made on Gen. Pope, as that officer placed himself in the position he did, inviting attack, as part and parcel of the military policy which contemplated the withdrawal of General McClellan from Harrison's Landing. To gain time and to open a way for the junction of the armies of the "Potomac" and of "Virginia," was the task assigned to Gen. Pope. To this effect he concludes his narrative of the operations conducted under his command with the following words:

"To confront a powerful enemy with greatly inferior numbers; to fight him day by day without the loss of the army; to delay and embarrass his movements, and to force him, by persistent resistance, to adopt long and circuitous routes to his destination, are the duties which have been imposed upon me. They are, of all military operations, the most difficult and the most harassing, both to a commander and to his troops. How far we have been successful I leave to the judgment of my countrymen. *The armies of Virginia and of the Potomac have been united in the presence and against the efforts of a wary and vigorous enemy* in greatly superior force, with no loss for which they did not exact full retribution."

It is true that by this strategy, as Gen. Pope says, the armies of the "Potomac" and of "Virginia" were united, but it is also true, as he says, that they had in their presence an enemy who was wary and vigorous, occupying all the positions which Gen. Halleck had formerly judged to create a military situation disadvantageous to the Union forces operating in Virginia. In addition to this the troops lately under the command of Gen. McClellan and Gen. Pope were disheartened by the retreats they had made and the reverses they had undergone in reaching safely the entrenchments around Washington.

It was under these circumstances that Gen. McClellan assumed the chief command of all the troops co-operating in the defence of Washington, and the Confederate army, emboldened by its successes, having actually invaded Maryland, this officer, who had succeeded within a few days in re-organizing our demoralized forces, advanced at once to meet the enemy and give him battle.

The events which have followed are too recent to need recapitulation. If, by the evacuation of Harrison's Landing, the war was transferred from the surroundings of Richmond to the surroundings of Washington, the valor of our troops, under their able and gallant leader, has proved equal to the emergency that was thrust upon them by the course of events.

The battle of Sharpsburg, if sterile in some of the results of a great victory, is none the less signal for the light it sheds on the prowess of the Union troops and on the skill with which they were handled. This battle has given to the enemy and to the world the assurance of the solid qualities which constitute a steadfast, disciplined, and powerful army, capable of accomplishing great results in the future. A victory won by brilliant strategetic movements, or gained by surprise, however signal in its accomplishment, conveys but small assurance of similar good fortune in the future. But a victory gained by superior pertinacity in both receiving and giving that "hard pounding" which was witnessed at Sharpsburg is a victory that affords the augury of achievements yet to come, and which we can count upon with the more certainty because of the fiery ordeal through which our army has just passed.

APPOINTMENT OF ACTING REAR ADMIRALS.

The following officers have been appointed Acting Rear Admirals on their respective stations:

Commodore CHARLES H. BELL, commanding Pacific Squadron.

Commodore CHARLES WILKES, commanding Special West India Squadron.

Commodore J. L. LARDNER, commanding Eastern Gulf Blockading Squadron.

Commodore CHAS. HENRY DAVIS, commanding Naval Mississippi Flotilla.

Captain SAMUEL PHILLIPS LEE, commanding North Atlantic Blockading Squadron.

ARRIVAL OF A PRIZE.

The prize steamship Columbia, captured on the 3d ultimo, by the United States steamer Santiago, has arrived at New York. She was condemned at Key West, and ordered to New York to dispose of cargo, which consists of dry-goods, teas, coffee, &c., besides eight brass field-pieces, rifled, with carriages and caissons all complete; two rifled mountain howitzers; a complete assortment of projectiles for all the ordnance; cases of fuses, cartridges, Enfield rifles, blankets, &c. The cargo is said to be worth $150,000.

RAILROAD TRAVEL TO HARPER'S FERRY.

A despatch from Frederick announces that the great bridge of the Baltimore and Ohio Railroad over the Monocacy, east of Frederick, which was destroyed by the rebels two weeks ago, is again restored. This completes the road from Baltimore and Washington to Frederick and to Sandy Hook, opposite Harper's Ferry—a matter of importance to the operations of our army in the field, and to the friends of soldiers, surgeons, and others having business with the army. The trains will run daily.

WESTERN MILITARY DEPARTMENTS.

By direction of the President the States of Missouri, Arkansas, and the bordering Indian Territory will constitute the Department of the Missouri, and will be commanded by Major General S. R. CURTIS; headquarters at St. Louis.

Alton, Illinois, is attached to the Department of the Missouri.

Western Virginia is attached to the Department of the Ohio; headquarters at Cincinnati.

THE DISTRICT PENITENTIARY.

Yesterday an order was issued from the War Department for the removal of all the criminals imprisoned in the Penitentiary of this District to the old county jail in Albany, New York, to afford an opportunity for the enlargement of the Arsenal, made absolutely necessary by the military exigencies of the time. Mr. King, the Warden, will have the prisoners forthwith transported to New York in a steamer, attended by a sufficient guard.

It was rumored at Fortress Monroe on Friday that a rebel force, numbering from 18,000 to 20,000, was in the vicinity of Blackwater river, but ample preparations had been made to receive them if they intended hostilities. The Blackwater river runs through the Dismal Swamp region and empties into the Elizabeth river south of Norfolk. If there is such a rebel force in that vicinity no doubt a demonstration is to be made against Suffolk and Norfolk.

It is reported that the order transferring Gen. Cassius M. Clay to the Department of New Orleans has been revoked, and he is now awaiting new instructions from the War Department.

A letter from Newbern (N. C.) states that the rebels are concentrating in large numbers at Goldsborough and Kingston, with the avowed intention of attacking Newbern. Gen. Foster, however, is not satisfied with waiting to be attacked, but has called for more troops, to enable him to assume the offensive. If, therefore, the rebels persist in their purpose, more active operations may be soon expected in that military department.

FROM GEN. McCLELLAN'S ARMY.

Correspondence of the Associated Press.

HEADQUARTERS ARMY OF THE POTOMAC, *Sunday Evening, September 21, 1862.*

The firing heard last evening in the direction of Williamsport turns out to be a raid of Stuart's. He crossed on Friday night into Maryland at that point with his cavalry, one regiment of infantry, and seventeen pieces of artillery. The force sent up to drive him back arrived near the town in the afternoon. The firing heard was principally from the rebel guns. During the night they recrossed into Virginia, and this morning they disappeared from the opposite shore. Nobody was hurt.

The work of burying the dead is still continuing. They average about one thousand per day. To-morrow will probably finish it.

Maryland Heights were yesterday occupied by a Federal force.

Indications are that the enemy are still continuing their retreat into Virginia, leaving the line of the Potomac.

Divine worship was held at headquarters this evening, Bishop Whipple, of Minnesota, officiating.

PARTIAL REPORT OF LATE CASUALTIES.

HEADQUARTERS ARMY OF THE POTOMAC, *Monday Evening, September 22.*

The following is the official report of our loss in *Sumner's Corps* at the battle of Antietam:

	Killed.	Wounded.	Missing.
Richardson's division	212	899	24
Sedgwick's division	355	1577	321
French's division	393	1321	203
	960	3797	548

Total loss in Sumner's Corps.......5,305.

The losses in missing may be somewhat reduced by the stragglers returning.

A train of cars crossed the Monocacy this morning. The road is now open to Harper's Ferry, where there is a sufficient Federal force for all purposes.

The rebels, in their hasty retreat from Maryland, left between eleven and twelve hundred wounded between Sharpsburg and the river. They are being paroled. Twenty-six stand of colors, taken at the battle of the Antietam, have been received at headquarters. Seven more known to have been captured are in the hands of different regiments.

THE KILLED AT IUKA.

The following has been received at the Headquarters of the Army:

HEADQUARTERS, CORINTH, SEPT. 22, 1862.

Maj. Gen. HALLECK, General-in-Chief:

In my despatch of the 20th our loss was over-estimated and the rebel loss under-estimated. We found two hundred and sixty-one of them dead on the battle-field, while our loss in killed will be less than one hundred.

U. S. GRANT, Maj. Gen. Com'g.

THE WAR IN KENTUCKY.

LOUISVILLE, SEPT. 22.—Reliable advices from Cave City say that a portion of Buell's army attacked and repulsed Bragg's rear guard from Horse Cave, on Thursday evening; upon learning which, Bragg is reported to have moved his main body across the river, southward from Munfordsville. No further particulars have been received.

A despatch received from La Grange says, to-day, Geo. Jesse, with two hundred rebel cavalry, attacked, at Newcastle, one hundred and twenty of Robert Morris' home guard of cavalry. Morris, without firing a gun, surrendered his men and horses, and three hundred stand of arms.

Reports which are considered doubtful have just reached us that the enemy subsequently burnt Newcastle and Shepperdsville. Late advices say that Granger's command there was attacked by the rebel cavalry, who intended to burn the bridge, and Granger repulsed them, killing five and taking twenty-eight prisoners.

Six hundred guerillas attacked Owensboro' on the 19th instant, in two bands. Col. Netter attacked one band at nine in the morning, and was slain. Five of our men were wounded. The rebels lost five killed. At noon we shelled the rebels, killing three, when they retreated.

On the 20th, Lieut. Col. Wood, with four hundred of the Fifty-first cavalry, attacked, and after a desperate encounter routed, from Owensboro, eight hundred rebels under Col Martin, who lost thirty-eight killed and twenty-five wounded. The Federal loss was three killed and eighteen wounded. We captured their army stores, provisions, and seven prisoners.

LOUISVILLE SERIOUSLY THREATENED.

LOUISVILLE, SEPTEMBER 22.—Bragg's forces have escaped from those of Buell, and are several hours ahead, approaching rapidly upon Louisville.

Major General Nelson is arranging to defend the city to the last. He has accordingly issued the following order:

"The women and children of this city will prepare to leave the city without delay. Jefferson Ferry is to be used exclusively for military purposes. Persons on foot may proceed as usual."

The city is in a blaze of excitement. Most of the stores are closed. The citizens are apprehending an attack within forty-eight hours.

REBEL DISAPPOINTMENT IN KENTUCKY.

In mentioning the retreat of the rebel army from the vicinity of Cincinnati the "Commercial" of that city says: "It is evident that they have given up all hope of obtaining supplies in Cincinnati, or of carrying the war into the North. It is represented to us, reliably we believe, that the success of the rebels in recruiting in Kentucky has fallen far short of their expectations. They have certainly obtained by process of flattery and falsehood, tempered with coercion, some thousands of recruits, but Kentucky still has many more men in the Union than in the rebel army. Kirby Smith is said to have denounced John Morgan as a falsifier for representing that if Kentucky were occupied by a rebel army the men would almost unanimously rush to fill up its ranks."

The line of the Chesapeake and Ohio canal for the distance of twelve miles, it is said, presents a scene of desolation which sufficiently attests the malignity of the rebels. The canal was tapped in five places, several floodgates were torn to pieces, large boulders were dislodged and rolled into the basin, and an attempt was made to blow up the beautiful aqueduct at Monocacy. From twenty to twenty-five miles of the canal are for the present rendered useless. The railroad, telegraph, private property, and growing crops were also desolated.

ANTI-NEGRO ROW IN NASHVILLE.

From the Nashville Dispatch of September 16th.

On Saturday night an immense crowd assembled at the theatre. All that part of the auditorium set apart for white people was crowded at an early hour, so that standing room could scarcely be obtained, when a number of privates of the Tenth Ohio occupied the negro gallery. Before the first act was over that part of the house also became crowded, and at the fall of the curtain some of the negroes left their seats and were passing through the crowd, when some soldiers seized them and knocked them down. In ten minutes every negro had been badly beaten and ejected from the house, some of them being thrown entirely down the stairs, from the top to the bottom. As the last one disappeared quietness was again restored. No alarm was visible in the lower part of the house, and when the band had finished their performances the curtain rose and the play proceeded without interruption.

Leaving the theatre, several members of the Tenth repaired to "Smoky Row," where they soon came in contact with the Provost Guard. After considerable disturbance with them they committed several depredations on houses in the neighborhood, which were finally brought to a close by a volley from the guard, severely wounding one of the disturbers in the leg, and enabling the guard to arrest others.

On Sunday morning the soldiers resumed their attacks upon the negroes—this time displaying their pugnacious propensities especially against those negroes dressed in Federal uniform. On the square Deputy Marshal Steele probably saved the life of a negro by advising him to take off his coat, when the soldiers around tore it to atoms, having previously knocked the negro down several times to make him take off his clothes. On Deadrick street they caught another negro in uniform and literally stripped it off, leaving him to escape well covered with bruises and only partially covered with rags. Another negro in uniform was caught on Gray street. At their request he very wisely took off his military coat, when the soldiers tore it in shreds and threw it on the street. Two or three other cases occurred during the afternoon, but no material damage was done.

THE "SOUTH CAROLINA VOLUNTEERS."

We have heard it stated that it was hard to say whether the "loyal blacks" lately enrolled in the First South Carolina Regiment Volunteers, or their white companions in arms, were the more disgusted with each other. This statement is fully confirmed by a correspondent of the New York Evening Post, a friend of the blacks, who, writing from Hilton Head under date of the 11th instant, makes the following reference to their treatment by the white soldiers, chiefly from New England:

"It must be confessed that to Gen. Hunter's plan there was one great obstacle which had not been taken into account. I refer to the disposition evinced towards the poor negroes by the soldiers of this army. Here we have something as bad as can well be conceived—something that should fill us with the deepest shame and sorrow. Whether it be that the General was somewhat too emphatic in his patronage of the negroes, or whether it be that the Northern soul, as here represented, is utterly inverted and dishumanized on this subject, certain it is that the General's course has occasioned some of the vilest and meanest exhibitions of human depravity that it has ever been my lot to witness. Many, very many of the soldiers, and not a few of the officers, have habitually treated the negroes with the coarsest and most brutal insolence and inhumanity; never speaking to them or of them but to curse and revile them, to say all manner of evil against them, and to threaten and imprecate all manner of evil upon them. Again and again have I been made thoroughly heart-sick at hearing the unmeasured ribaldry and profanity and indignity which have thus been spewed, as if from the gorge of hell itself, upon these unoffending, much-suffering people. God help them! for I fear there is no mercy nor justice for them in the white man. And Gen. Hunter's earnest benevolence towards them has but purchased for them ten-fold returns of cruelty and abuse from the soldiers of his command. Every act of kindness in their behalf seems to be resented by these savages of the army as an intolerable affront to themselves."

ANOTHER EXTRA-OFFICIAL DEPUTATION.

The Washington correspondent of the New York Commercial Advertiser, in his letter of the 17th instant, makes the following reference to further "pestering" importunities of the President on the subject of emancipation:

"The President, in this hour of danger and trouble, has had his time intruded on for hours by a deputation of citizens from Chicago, urging him to issue an immediate emancipation proclamation, when we hardly hold any of the Confederate slave territory, and when the freed colored population of this District were actually fearing the arrival of the Southern army, and their consequent return to immediate slavery! The issuing of such a proclamation at so improper a time as this would thus have its fitting comment. But this and the President's prompt answers to these continued delegations do not seem to save him from the infliction, when every moment of his time is more precious to the nation than the lives of his craving and theoretical applicants."

A CONVENTION OF GOVERNORS.

We have seen it announced in several newspapers within the last few days that a Convention of Governors is to be convened to-morrow, at Altoona, in Pennsylvania—for what purpose has not been stated, or intimated, so far as our knowledge extends. A Chicago paper received yesterday contains a copy of the invitation addressed to the respective Governors whose presence is desired at this Convention. We here insert it, as follows:

"COLUMBUS, (OHIO) SEPTEMBER 14, 1862.

"Governor RICHARD YATES, Springfield, Illinois:

"We invite a meeting of the Governors of the Loyal States, to be held at Altoona, Pennsylvania, on the 24th. Please reply to Governor Curtin.

"ANDREW CURTIN,
"DAVID TOD,
"F. H. PEIRPOINT."

APPOINTMENTS.

Col. Rufus Ingalls, who so successfully removed the quartermaster's stores at the evacuation of Harrison's Landing, has been appointed Brigadier General.

Acting Master Hooker has been promoted to an Acting Volunteer Lieutenant, for gallant conduct in the bombardment of Washington, (N. C.) and ordered to the command of the steamer Victoria.

Capt. Sol. J. Houck, 71st Ohio volunteers; Capt. J. V. Patton, of the 73d Ohio volunteers; Lieut. John Simpson, 99th Pennsylvania volunteers, and Lieut. Chistie, Aid-de-Camp, who were lately dismissed the service of the United States, have been restored to their commands by order of the Secretary of War.

NEW MEXICO.

The Sant Fe Gazette of the 30th ultimo mentions the relieving of Gen. Canby, at his own request, from the command of New Mexico, and compliments him for his prudence, humanity, and efficiency in the discharge of his military duties.

The Gazette also mentions that at the August term of the Grand Jury for the United States Court, Hon. Jose M. Gallegos, foreman, presented some twenty-three indictments for treason against the Government. In consequence of the limited time to which the term of the court was confined none of these cases came up for trial. They all stand over until the next term.

THE LOSSES IN THE KANAWHA REGION.

GALLIPOLIS, SEPTEMBER 20.—The salt-works between Charleston and Camp Piatt, Virginia, were not destroyed by our forces. All but two fell uninjured into the rebel hands, with large quantities of salt, and are now being run by the Confederates night and day.

The rebel loss at Fayette was five times as great as ours. The total value of Government stores destroyed in Lightburn's retreat is estimated at half a million. Lightburn's trains are all safe in Ohio, except a small one cut off on the 10th.

The seriously wounded are doing well. Capt. Hatfield is still alive, but will hardly survive. Col. Lightburn was here to-day. He estimates the total loss in the retreat at one hundred killed and wounded.

INDIAN RAIDS IN NEW MEXICO.

KANSAS CITY, SEPT. 19.—The Santa Fe mails, with dates to the 7th instant, arrived last evening. The news is meagre. The Indians are making extensive raids in New Mexico. On the 30th ultimo they attacked a ranche near San Miguel, killed one man, wounded two, and took two captives. They also took 20,000 head of sheep and 500 head of cattle belonging to Yahara, Gonzalez, and Jose Avanillo.

LOCAL MATTERS.

"TAPPAHANNOCK" WHEAT.—The Agricultural Department is now distributing this wheat, raised on the farm of the late Peter Gorman, near Laurel Hill, Maryland. It is a superior article, and farmers should try a sample. We also learn that an invoice of seeds and choice specimens of cereals, of acknowledged excellence, has been recently ordered from Europe by the Commissioner of Agriculture, and is expected to arrive in the course of a month or two. Of the reception of these seed due notice will be given prior to their distribution among the agriculturists of the country. No agent has at any time, as we learn, been sent to Europe by the Department of Agriculture for the purchase of seeds and cuttings.

SCHOLARSHIP AWARDED.—The committee appointed to examine the pupils of the Public Schools with a view to furnishing to the most meritorious one scholarship, so generously offered by Rev. Dr. Samson in Columbian College, have awarded the same to Master Joseph H. France, a pupil of the Male Grammar School of the First District.

NEW PASTOR.—Rev. John R. Effinger has been appointed to fill the vacancy in the pulpit of the Foundry Church, occasioned by the death of the Rev. Mr. Hirst.

The Washington jail at present contains one hundred and ten inmates.

ROBBERY.—On Saturday morning last, between four and five o'clock, some persons entered the house of Mr. George E. Kennedy and stole his watch from the head of his bed where it was hanging. Mr. K. was aroused by the cries of his child, and, on missing his watch, went down stairs and found several of the lower doors open. The thief made good his escape.

MASONIC.—The Grand Visitations of the Masonic Lodges of this city will commence this day week at Federal Lodge No. 1.

WASHINGTON MONEY MARKET, SEPT. 22.—Coupons, 6's, 1881, 101⅜; 7 3-10 notes, 104¼; Certificates of indebtedness, 99; Gold, buying, 115; selling, 118; Demand notes, buying, 110; selling, 114.

NEW YORK MONEY MARKET, SEPT. 22.—Coupons, 6's, 1881, 101⅞; 7 3-10 notes, 104⅛; Certificates of indebtedness, 99¼; Demand notes, 113⅜; Gold, 117½; Silver, 114. Stocks buoyant.

TO THE PUBLIC.

DEPARTMENT OF THE INTERIOR, *Office Indian Affairs, September 19, 1862.*

From information received at this Department, deemed sufficiently reliable to warrant me in so doing, I consider it my duty to warn all persons contemplating the crossing of the Plains this fall to Utah or the Pacific coast that there is good reason to apprehend hostilities on the part of the Bannock and Shoshone or Snake Indians, as well as the Indians upon the Plains and along the Platte river.

The Indians referred to have during the past summer committed several robberies and murders. They are numerous, powerful, and warlike, and, should they generally assume a hostile attitude, are capable of rendering the emigrant routes across the Plains extremely perilous. Hence this warning.

By order of the Secretary of the Interior:

CHARLES E. MIX, Acting Commissioner.

NOTICE TO VESSELS ENTERING OR LEAVING THE POTOMAC RIVER.

The guard vessels off Alexandria and Piney Point, on the Potomac river, will be distinguished, during the day, by a SQUARE WHITE FLAG WITH A RED CROSS, (St. Andrew's,) and at night by TWO RED LIGHTS.

The officers in command of these vessels will furnish the Naval Potomac Pass to all masters of vessels navigating the river after they shall have given proof that they are lawfully employed.

Vessels entering or departing from the river will be subject to detention if unprovided with a pass.

AND'W A. HARWOOD,
2w Commodore Commanding Potomac Flotilla.

Navy Department, *September 23, 1862.*

THE FOLLOWING PROPOSITIONS were received at the Navy Department during the week ending September 20, 1862: (Published in conformity with a resolution of Congress approved July 12th, 1862.)

R. J. Peck, Springfield, Mass., offers 1,000 tons ship timber. No price stated.

John J. Rink, Tompkinsville, N. Y., offers his boat at a charter price of $25 per day.

Geo. M. Alexander, Philadelphia, requests the purchase of solid cartridges for trial.

Thayer & Peabody, Boston, offer the steam ferry-boat John Adams; price $40,000.

Norris Peters, Wilmington, Delaware, offers to furnish photographic copies of machinery engines, and equipments at $25 per 100 for 24 x 12 inches; $15 per 100 for 12 x 10 inches, smaller sizes cheaper.

To Bureau of Provisions and Clothing.—Wm. Macomber, Boston, offers to furnish 500,000 lbs. fresh beef at 15 cents per pound, and 500,000 lbs. beef soup, or soup and bouilli, at 12½ cents per pound. sep 23

ARMY SUPPLIES.

OFFICE OF THE CHIEF QUARTERMASTER, *Army of the Potomac, Washington, September 20, 1862.*

PROPOSALS are invited for furnishing for the use of the army of the Potomac the following articles:

3,000 tons best quality Timothy Hay, securely baled, the weight of each bale to be marked thereon

2,000,000 bushels of Oats, of the best quality, in strong sacks, well sewed

7,000 cords Oak and Hickory Wood, well seasoned and of the best quality.

Each bid must be accompanied by the endorsement of two responsible persons that the contracts if awarded will be fulfilled.

Bids will be opened from time to time as the articles may be needed, and contracts will be awarded for the quantities needed to the lowest responsible bidder up to the time of opening.

The right is reserved to accept all or any part of any bid.

Proposals should be endorsed "Proposals for Hay or Oats, or Wood," as the case may be, and enclosed in separate envelopes. RUFUS INGALLS,

sep 23—tf Lieut Col and A. D. C., Chief Quartermaster.

PROPOSALS FOR PAPER.

NAVY DEPARTMENT, *Bureau of Provisions and Clothing, September 22, 1862.*

PROPOSALS (sealed and endorsed "Proposals for Paper") will be received at this Bureau until noon on the 30th day of October next for furnishing and delivering at the Navy Yard at Brooklyn, New York, three hundred reams of paper, with the privilege of increasing the quantity to one thousand reams.

The paper to be white, 13½ inches by 16½ inches, to weigh 16 pounds to the ream, and made of linen stock; to be stop-ruled, leaving one inch margin on each page, back and front; to be ruled, 24 lines on each page, with one inch margin at top and bottom.

Sample of quality and size of the paper may be seen at the office of the Inspector in charge at the Navy Yard in Charlestown, Massachusetts; Brooklyn, New York; Philadelphia, Pennsylvania; and at this Bureau. sep 23—law4w

District Court of the United States for the District of Columbia.

LIBEL—IN ADMIRALTY.

United States vs. The Cargo of the Vessel Blossom.

WHEREAS a certain lot of goods, wares, and merchandise, consisting of wheat, salt, tea, barrels labeled sugar, one box marked morphine, one lot of tooth brushes, and percussion caps, and other articles, being the cargo of a certain vessel called "Blossom, were captured by the United States flotilla" and brought within the jurisdiction of this court as prize; and on the 17th day of September, 1862, a libel was filed in said court by the United States Attorney for the said District, praying the condemnation of the same, and that monition and attachment be issued against said property, and the officers and crew of said vessel, and all persons claiming an interest therein, warning them at some early day to appear and answer said libel: It is therefore ordered by this court, this 17th day of September, 1862, that notice be given to the officers and crew and owners of said vessel and cargo, and all persons claiming an interest therein, to appear and answer this libel on the first Monday of November, 1862, and show cause, if any they have, why said property should not be condemned and sold according to law, and that said notice be given by posting a copy of this order on the front door of the court-house of said District, and by publication in the National Intelligencer once a week for three weeks previous to said first Monday of November, 1862, the first publication to be on or before the first Monday of October next.

By order of the Court.

Test: E. J. MIDDLETON, Clerk.

Copy—Test: E. J. MIDDLETON, Clerk.

sep 23—law3w

United States Patent Office, *Washington, September 19, 1862.*

ON the petition of Thomas J. Lovegrove, of Baltimore, Maryland, praying for the extension of a patent granted to him December 26th, 1848, for an improvement in "centrifugal force in casting iron pipe," for seven years from the expiration of said patent, which takes place on the 26th day of December, 1862:

It is ordered that the said petition be heard at the Patent Office on Monday, the 8th day of December, 1862, at 12 o'clock M.; and all persons are notified to appear and show cause, if any they have, why said petition ought not to be granted.

Persons opposing the extension are required to file in the Patent Office their objections, specially set forth in writing, at least twenty days before the day of hearing; all testimony filed by either party to be used at the said hearing must be taken and transmitted in accordance with the rules of the office, which will be furnished on application.

The testimony in the case will be closed on the 24th day of November, 1862; depositions and other papers relied upon as testimony must be filed in the office on or before the morning of that day; the arguments, if any, within ten days there after.

Ordered, also, that this notice be published in the National Intelligencer, Washington, District of Columbia; and American and Commercial Advertiser, Baltimore, Maryland, once a week for three successive weeks; the first of said publications to be at least sixty days previous to the day of hearing.

D. P. HOLLOWAY, Commissioner of Patents.

P. S.—Editors of the above papers will please copy, and send their bills to the Patent Office, with a paper containing this notice. sep 23—w3w

TO ALL WHOM IT MAY CONCERN.

NOTICE IS HEREBY GIVEN that Certificate No. 151, for 40 shares of the stock of the Bank of the Metropolis, of Washington, D. C., issued in the name of Mary Ann Fenwick, on the 28th August, 1822, has been lost or mislaid, and the undersigned, as executor of the estate of Raphael H. Boarman, who was heir at law of the said Mary A. Fenwick, will make application to the Bank of the Metropolis for the renewal of said certificate. THO. CARBERY,

sep 23—w1w Executor of R. H. Boarman.

FIVE HUNDRED DOLLARS REWARD.

THE undersigned had his pocket picked of a memorandum book on Saturday, the 20th instant, between the bar in the restaurant on 7th street, opposite Centre Market, kept by Messrs. Shonborn & Richter, and the counter of Rittenhouse, Fant & Co.'s Bank. He had the book when at the former place and missed it at the latter, having proceeded from the restaurant to the northeast corner of Centre Market, and from thence directly across to the banking-house. The memorandum book contained between fourteen hundred and two thousand dollars in bills, as follows: One $500 bill, one $100 bill, one $50 bill, and the balance in $20, $10, and $5 bills, all in Treasury notes, except sixty or seventy dollars in Baltimore funds. Also, one check of F. P. Blair's for thirty-odd dollars, payable to Jones or bearer, I think on the Banking house of Riggs & Co. Also, the following notes, viz: One of Warwick Miller, I think for $200 or more, not due; one of Asa Stabler for $150 or more, due; one of one Thomas for $50 or more, due; his given name not recollected; all of the above notes payable to H. B. Cashell.

The public are warned against negotiating for the above check or notes, as the payment of the same has been stopped.

I will give the above reward for the return of my book, paper, and money, and for the conviction of the thief, or I will give four hundred dollars for the return of my book, papers, and money. H. B. CASHELL,

sep 22—3t Montgomery county, Md.

PROPOSALS.

MAYOR'S OFFICE, SEPTEMBER 15, 1862.

PROPOSALS will be received at the Mayor's office until 12 o'clock M., on the 25th instant, for repairing and cleaning of the Sewer leading from the Canal to D street north, between 9th and 10th streets west, according to an act approved August 25th, 1862.

Bidders will state the price for repairing the walls and bottom (where needed) per lineal foot, and per cubic yard for cleaning out Sewer; the repairs to be done in the best cement mortar.

For further particulars apply at the Surveyor's office, City Hall. RICHARD WALLACH,

sep 16— [Star, Rep.] Mayor.

PROPOSALS FOR WOOD.

ASSISTANT QUARTERMASTER'S OFFICE, *Washington Arsenal, September 18, 1862.*

SEALED PROPOSALS, to be endorsed "Proposals for Fuel," will be received at this office until 10 A. M. of the 29th instant for one hundred (100) Cords of Oak Wood, to be delivered at the Arsenal, ten cords at least on the 1st of October, and the balance on or before the 15th of November.

The Wood must be large and of the best quality.

The contract will be awarded to the lowest responsible bidder, who will be required to give a bond (with two acceptable sureties) for the sum of $300 for the due performance of the contract. GEORGE ELY,

sep 20— Captain and Assistant Quartermaster.

The Daily Mississippian.

PUBLISHED EVERY EVENING EXCEPT SUNDAY AT FOUR O'CLOCK.

VOL. I. JACKSON, MISS., FRIDAY, SEPTEMBER 26, 1862. NO. 126.

Daily Mississippian.

TERMS:

THE DAILY MISSISSIPPIAN will be published every day, except Sunday, at $1,50 per month, or ten cents per single copy.

COOPER & KIMBALL,
PROPRIETORS,

☞ Evidently there is no greater obstacle in life to overcome than for a youthful "lovyer" to make known the sincere wishes of his heart to the fair being who has transported him. Appreciating the difficulties of the situation, we cheerfully come to the relief of our young friend who pours himself out in rhyme below, and thereby furnishies the very best evidence that he is, in deed and in truth, "in love." We trust he will not forget at the proper time the promised compensation to us for helping him out of his troubles.

For the Mississippian.

TO MISS L. G.

Life's a swiftly flowing river,
Down which our bark most fleetly glides;
Surely he's a sorry liver,
Who in his bark alone abides.

Lydie, dearest, tell me whether,
Since down life's stream we glide alone,
We shall not join our barks together,
Better to shun quicksand and stone?

Sweet the voyage of life would be,
With heart to heart in close entwine,
Charmed by music of bird and bee,
Vistas of flowers and clustering vine.

And when the end we should attain,
With faith's anchor all bright and strong,
We'd launch upon the eternal main,
And mingle with the ransomed throng.

Upon the "sea of liquid glass,"
[illegible]
In perfect bliss, our barks would pass
Forever over the depth's profound.

Dear Lydie, shall our barks unite,
And thus in joy glide on together?
If single, all my hopes you blight,
Even my hope of Heaven would wither.

ANON.

P. S. MR. EDITOR—I am a timid lover, without courage personally to tell my love to my enamorada. Knowing your obliging good nature, I take advantage of it, to ask you to insert the above denouement in your valuable paper, if forsooth, you can find room for anything so invaluable. Should you grant my request, I will in gratitude name my first born, if a daughter, MISSISSIPPI ANN, after your excellent paper. Trusting to the fates and your proverbial kindness for present success, I remain with much anxiety, truly, ANON

SEPTEBER 23d, 1862.

CAN'T PRAY FOR EXTORTIONERS AND SPECULATORS.

We have heard, says the Richmond Dispatch, that one of our most exemplary divines in this city says he really cannot find it in his heart to pray for the extortioners and speculators who are availnig themselves of the calamities and privations of their fellow-creatures to swell their ill-gotten gains. For common publicans and sinners he believes there may be some forgiveness, but that people who show no mercy to others need expect none from Heaven. We are afraid, however, that motives of this kind will not reach the extortioners. It's no more use preaching to them than praying for them. They have hardened their hearts like Pharoah, and will not let the people go. If Moses and the Prophets should rise from the dead, they would not listen; and if they knew the Day of Judgment was coming to-morrow, they would advertise ascension robes in the morning papers. It is but little consolation to know that the Devil will ultimately have them, one and all. People who speculate in articles of prime necessity, so that their poor neighbors must starve or freeze this winter, deserve the attention of a gentleman whom they fear more than the Devil—the Provost Marshal, who ought to arrest them, as worse enemies to the State than Yankee spies or native traitors, and place them in Castle Thunder or the army.

DEAD.—The Yankee prisoner, Silas Rich mond. who was shot on Monday by the guard, while attempting to escape from Castle Thunder (where he was confined after an attempt to escape from the Libby) died yesterday from the effect of his wound. We did not learn his regiment.—*Richmond Examiner 17th.*

A SARCASTIC WIFE.—Husband who arrived home at a late hour of night: "Don't look so cross, love; I have been detained on a committee." Wife—"I don't like those committees. I suppose that"—husband interrupting—"Just hear that infernal catterwauling!" Wife (sarcastically) "Oh! that's our tom cat! He's out on a committee, I guess." Husband silent for the rest of the night.

From the Richmond Examiner, 19th.

Highly Interesting from Maryland.

An officer of General Lee's staff, who arrived in this city last evening, direct from Maryland, brings intelligence of an important and deeply interesting character. He reports a pitched battle on the soil of Maryland, in which the Confederates are said to have been again victorious. We give the report as it reaches us.

On Sunday morning, the 14th instant, McClellan, with a force of 80,000 men, having passed Frederick, whether on the north or south is not stated, fell upon D. H. Hill's division, composing the rear of our army at Boonsboro.' The attack was one of well sustained vigor and impetuosity, but Hill, although almost overborne by superior numbers, held his ground resolutely until night put an end to the battle. At an early hour next morning, Longstreet came to Hill's assistance, when an immediate combined attack was made on the forces of McClellan. The battle was long, obstinate, and bloody, but resulted in the signal defeat of the Federals, who were driven back five miles from their position.

The loss on both sides is said to have been very great. D. H. Hill's division suffered severely, especially on Sunday, when alone it withstood the onslaught of McClellan's entire army. At last accounts General Jackson, after having disposed of the Yankees at Harper's Ferry, was marching down the south bank of the Potomac, with the design of crossing into Maryland and falling upon McClellan's rear. A great and decisive battle is thought to be imminent.

It is well to state that no official information, relative to this rumored engagement, has been received here. The latest official advices from General Loe are to the 13th instant, inclusive.

THE FIGHT AT HARPER'S FERRY.

The Lynchburg Republican of [illegible] at Harper's Ferry, on last Sunday evening and Monday morning, between General Jackson and the Yankees, which resulted in the defeat of the latter, and the surrender of their army, numbering ten thousand men."

The Republican then goes on to give some particulars of the affair. From its account we make a summary. The battle was begun at three o'clock on Sunday evening and raged with great fury till nightfall. Throughout the night our cannon played upon the works of the enemy. At daylight, Monday morning, the combat was renewed and kept up with unabated violence until nine o'clock, A. M., when General Miles, the Yankee commander, proposed to surrender. This proposition was of course acceded to, and our forces at once marched into and took possession of the enemy's works.

The immediate and tangible fruits of this victory are reported to be ten thousand Yankee prisoners, one thousand runaway negroes, fifty pieces of artillery and an immense amount of commissary and quartermaster stores.

No estimate of the loss has as yet been made. Ours is known to be heavy. The enemy's loss, it is believed, greatly exceeds ours, as he was, during the engagments both of Sunday and Monday, exposed to the deadly fire of our cannon stationed on the heights surrounding his position.

General Samuel Garland, jr., of Lynchburg, is reported among the killed.

[LATER.]

A gentleman who arrived here last evening by the Central train reports, upon the authority of Major Yost, of Jackson's army, that Harper's Ferry was surrendered at discretion by the Yankees on Sunday (Monday?) last. The number of prisoners taken is variously estimated at between eight and twelve thousand, while the number of stolen and fugitive slaves recaptured is said to be much greater than has yet been reported, being between fifteen hundred and two thousand.

The body of General Samuel Garland, Jr., of Lynchburg, who was killed in the attack on this place, was brought to this city last evening. General Richard Garnet is reported as having been killed, but whether at Harper's Ferry or on the Maryland side we have been unable to learn. No official information has been received here of the capture of Harper's Ferry, which may be accounted for by the fact that General Jackson would report not direct to General Cooper, but to General Lee.

[From the Richmond Dispatch.

W. H. Seward.

Although the report is not confirmed that Seward is to be sent on a foreign mission, that day of *honorable* banishment may not be far distant. We have no doubt he is anxious to hide his head in some foreign land, and escape the tempest which will ere long be howling over the North for the author of the war. He is the man, he, Wm. H. Seward, pre-eminently the man who fired "the Ephesian dome" of the old American Union, and whose name will be immortal in the hate and execration of his countrymen. There were causes at work in the antagonistic institutions, interests, and habits of the people, which rendered ultimate dissolution inevitable; but if there had been no such man as Wm. H. Seward, this generation at least might have died in its bed in peace. A hundred and fifty thousand of Seward's countrymen, whose bones now bleach the soil they came to desecrate, might be dwelling in contented homes, and hundreds of thousands more, whom he is training for the same infernal purposes, might have lived to a good old age. He organized purely for the purposes of his own election the political Abolition party which brought the old Union to destruction. No other man in the North possessed the peculiar combination of intellectual and moral qualities necessary for that purpose. It is true he failed in obtaining the first nomination of his party for the Presidency, but, as Secretary of State, he was the actual, if not the nominal President, and he was sure of being Lincoln's successor till "wicked rebellion" assumed its gigantic proportions, rendering the subjugation of the South necessary to the preservation of that glorious Union—that is, the election of Wm. H. Seward to the next Presidency of the United States.

When American school-boys used to read in history of bloody tyrants in ancient times and even in modern Europe who remorselessly sacrificed the lives of their helples subjects in mere wars of ambition such beings seemed to be monsters belonging to a fabulous period, whose charecter it was scarcely possible to believe in. What boy or man on all this continen twenty years ago suspected that among the aspirants for American favor, in a row of Senators whose diminutive forms were lost in the gigantic shadows of Calhoun, Clay, and Webster, sat a man who was to play in the political Paradise of the new world the part of S[illegible] convert its finest fields into a Golgotha. Yet we have lived to see this miracle of Diabolism, and to realize that no form of quarrel can purify human nature or preserve the people from those calamities, inevitable as plagues and pestilence, in which the selfish and unprincipled ambition of the few may involve the innocent and unoffending many.

In what country the Premier of Lincoln will ultimately find his anticipated exile, we know not; but his infamy is as wide as the earth, and he can visit no spot on this planet where he is not already known and despised. There is no civil court in which, whatever the outward forms of respct to an ambassador, there will not be a secret contempt for the most mendacious and hypocritical public man of this century, and for the imposter who promised so often that the rebellion should be put down in sixty and ninety days. The reputation of Arnold and Burr, in future ages, will be fragrant and glorious compared with that of Wm. H. Seward.

Poor Fremont Again Snubbed by the Government.

Poor Fremont is near to finding himself in the condition of Othello. He seems about to bid farewell to

" —— all quality,
Pride, pomp and circumstances of glorious war,"

For his "occupation's gone." His friends deserting him. His money is about giving out, and the Secretary of War has informed him that his labors are officious and tend to military disorganization. The following correspondence shows how he has been "snubbed" by the powers at Washington:

NEW YORK, Sept. 3, 1862.—SIR—I have the honor to enclose a copy of a resolution this day passed by the National War Committee of New York, and to ask whether, if the Government consent, you will undertake the organization of a corps therein requested,

Very respectfully, yours,
GEORGE OPDYKE, Chairman.

Major General JOHN C. FREMONT.

Copy of Resolution.

Resolved, That General Fremont and Gen. Mitchell be each requested, if the government will consent, to organize in this State, without delay, a corps of fifty thousand men, and that application for such consent be made to the general government and if it refuse, then to the State government.

NEW YORK, Sept. 5, 1862.

SIR—I have the honor to receive your note of the 3d instant, communicating to me a resolution passed by the National War Committee of New York in relation to a corps of 50,000 men, and requesting to know, in the event that it have the sanction of the government, if I would undertake its organization.

I thank the committee for the honor of their invitation, and beg you to inform them that I would undertake the proposed duty with great pleasure.

Respectfully, your obedient servant,
J. C. FREMONT,
Major General U. S. Army.

Hon. GEORGE OPDYKE, &c., Chairman of Committee.

NEW YORK, Sept. 4, 1862.

To the Hon. Edwin M. Stanton, Secretary of War, Washington:

SIR—Will you consent that General Fremont and General Mitchell, each, or either, shall organize in this State a separate corps of fifty thousand men, composed of citizens of this and other States, and allow the men received to be counted as a part of the quota of the State from which they came, upon some of the calls for troops heretofore made by the President.

If you consent, we shall hope to induce the generals to undertake the organization.

GEORGE OPDYKE.
Chairman National War Committee.

WASHINGTON, Sept. 5.

George Opdyke, Mayor, No. 79 Fifth Avenue, New York:

Your telegram of yesterday has received consideration of this department. General Mitchell baving been assigned to the command of the Southern department, must immediately join his command. Raising volunteers in New York has been assigned to the Governor of that State, who is faithfully performing his duty; and there appears to be no reason for interfering with him.

To authorize military officers of high rank to raise and organize army corps would be productive of military disorganization.

This Department, therefore, connot consent that any major general shall organize a separate corps.

EDWIN M. STANTON,
Secretary of War.

12th Regiment Mississippi Volunteers,

Bivouac, near Richmond, June 22, 1862.

C. A. WALTON, Esq., Bolton's Depot, Miss.:

Dear Sir: In the coming election for County officers of Hinds county, the undersigned members of the Raymond Fencibles, and others of the Regiment, propose the name of [illegible] Bristow's faithful attention to his duties as a soldier, both in camp and upon the battle-field, has won for him the esteem of the entire company.

M S Craft, Surgeon	Wm O Chapman
S B Thomas, Captain	W T Sandifer
J B Johnson, 1st Lt	Wm W Day
W B Thomas, 2d Lt	R H Epperson
S L Bracey, 3d Lt	G T Harris
A M England	A Hall
G W North	T A Baldwin
G D Nixon	O H Spence
J L Brissoe, Q'r M'r	D T Yates
R L McRaven	E S Ragan
R Hunter	G J Miller
R K Mitchell	Elbert Davis
John O'Bannon	E C McKown
A D Cassiley	John E Clary
L T Kelly	W R Brandriff
John Cassilly	J D Monroe
John W Cox	W D Bonner
C D Gillespie	S M Shelton
T G Dabney	J T Lancaster
P A Mullen	John T Nelson
A A Bracey	B F Fortner, jr
W V Felts	F O Thigpen
B G Govauer	John Napp
F B Barton	C F Cleveland
G H Jones	John F Dillon
E H Thomas	A S Epperson
W T Jennings	Thomas Hunter
J T Bradley	M Carey
J Narbon	R S Todd
H B England	W K Carland
R J Gillespie	John Miller
G W Montgomery	A P Harris
W H Gibbs	S Barden
S C Caston	

[Sept. 10, 4wd&w*

DIED,

On the 13th of September, Little LIDDY, daughter of Hezekiah and Rachel Moran, of Simpson county, Miss,

Daily Mississippian.

F. T. COOPER, Editor.

☞ *For interesting Reading Matter see First Page.*

JACKSON, - - - SEPT. 26, 1862

STABBED.—Mike Higgins stabbed Wm Butler on Greasy Row this morning, it is supposed fatally. Butler belonged to Co. D, 1st Missouri Volunteers.

OAKLAND COLLEGE. — A meeting of the Board of Trustees of this Institution has been appointed to be held in Port Gibson, Miss., on Wednesday, November 12th ; being the day of the meeting of the Synod of Mississippi.

MURDER.—Yesterday, about one o'clock, we heard the report of a gun in the vicinity of the Bowman House, and on making inquiry, learned that one Brantley had taken position in the hall the of second story of the above named house with a double barreled gun, and as one Green passed Brantley raised his gun and fired, the charge taking effect in the body of Green, who rolled to the bottom of the staircase crying murder. Green expired immediately. Brantley was pursued, captured, and will, we learn, have a trial on Monday.

Green is represented as being from Mobile, Alabama, and Brantley from Choctaw county, in this State.

Yankee Depredations.

The Yankees still continue their thieving operations in the lower counties of Virginia. A letter addressed to the editor of the Enquirer, dated at Smithfield, Isle of Wight county, September 11th, says on Thursday, the 9th instant, a Yankee gunboat, commanded by John C. Lee, visited that place for the second time. In the evening, the Captain of the boat and nineteen of his men visited the private houses of the citizens and seized all the arms that could be found. While at the above place they stole five dollars in money from a slave hired to Gen. A. R. Pryor, as a cook. The reason assigned for the seizure of the arms, was to prevent their pickets from being shot by guerrillas.

The Fight at Iuka last Friday.

We had the pleasure of meeting two officers who left Price's forces who were sent to capture Iuka Wednesday morning, and they confirm the statement by telegraph that the engagement of Friday evening was a very sanguinary contest—the troops fighting hand to hand till our forces finally drove the enemy some 600 yards, when night overtook them and we bivouacked within the lines of the enemy.

The enemy in force, under Grant, were ascertained to be marching to cut off our troops, when the order was given and we fell back to Baldwin in good order, bringing nine pieces of splendid cannon.

Our loss in killed, wounded and missing, was about 250, while the enemy's was much larger. It appears that the enemy designed capturing our army by a concentration of their forces at Corinth, Jackson and one other place, which failed.

☞ A Pennsylania Yankee named Tallman, recently made a desperate effort to escape the Lincoln draft. He dressed himself as a woman, and, with a child in his arms, attempted to pass the bridge into Canada.—He was arrested, when he offered the guard $3,000 to let him go ; but it was no go. The man is wealthy.

HOME INDUSTRY.—There are now in Richmond, Va., factories for making matches, envelopes and blacking. One firm alone makes 40,000 envelopes a day.

The Confederate Senate and the Press.

We are entirely unable to see either the wisdom or the expediency of the Exemption law as passed by the Confederate Senate so far as that law relates to the press. It will strike the public as one of the grossest absurdities ever yet perpetrated in solemn Senatorial halls. If that dignified body had refused to make any exemptions at all for the benefit of the press, there would have been some slight show of reason in their proceedings, inasmuch as two or three complete companies perhaps an entire regiment, might have been added to the army by including the whole press gang. By exempting printers the Senate has acknowledged its appreciation of the value of the press, but has in the same act, stripped it of its lever power.

Without an editor the press is utterly valueless,—utterly motionless. Then why exempt printers ? Is it that they may enjoy the privilege of starving to death ? for there will be nothing for them to do. There are, perhaps, in all large newspaper establishments, from 12 to 25 printers, with only one or two editors. All the editors in the Confederacy would not add to the service one good company. In that capacity they could do but little good to the cause ; but in their legitimate spheres their influence is and has been almost boundless. The press of the country has shown itself from the beginning of the present unhappy struggle, the most steadfast friend of the great and vital cause for which the blood of our people has been freely poured out. It has been equal to an army with banners in upholding and sustaining our threatened liberties. Destroy it, and you at once invite anarchy and despotism. The opinion of our people and the teachings of our Constitution are united and clear on the subject. It must not be destroyed ; it must not be muzzled. But to sweep off all the editors is simply to inflict a death-blow to very heart of this potent engine of power.

The Richmond Examiner has some lucid and pointed remarks upon this interesting subject. It truely says the vote of the Senate was a direct assult upon the press ; for when you take away its mind you leave it nothing but a useless machine, without vitality, or independece, or power. The Examiner continues :

The preservation of the press is rendered a matter of duty by the Constitution, and this duty rests upon the consciences of Senators, whether the press be worth preserving or not; but considered aside from this question of oath-enjoined duty, it is in the highest degree expedient that the press should be preserved in full vigor and efficiency. The press has been the soul and inspiration of the great movement in which the country is engaged. It was the press that roused the people to resist the aggressions of the North, and that inspired the whole community with that enthusiasm which has been the source of all the successes which have attended our arms.—To compare the efficiency of the press in this great struggle, with that even of Congress itself, would be like comparing the efficiency of a locomotive in full career with that of a dull ox harnessed to a cart. Except for purposes or mere routine, the country could dispense with Congress without much inconvenience or disadvantage. But how could it dispense with the press ? Who does not read the newspapers ? Congress itself would be nothing, and its proceedings would fail to obtain publicity, if none but printers were left to conduct the business of the press. The speeches of your Browns and Smiths would fail to be read even by the few who sometimes peruse senatorial effusions, but for the labors of the men whom the Senate has delivered up to the army. The press is the vehicle of intelligence. To strike down the press, as the Senate seeks to do, would be to blot out the light of the war, and to envelope the community in darkness and confusion. To leave to the press only its types and its printers, is to crush it out as effectually as if Lincoln or Butler had put his heel upon it.

☞ The Richmond Examiner, of the 20th, has heard, as coming from a source entitled to some credit, that General Lee, several days previous to the battle of the 14th, intercepted a dispatch from McClellan to General Miles, the commander at Harpers Ferry, and made his arrangements accordingly. D. H. Hill was ordered to engage McClellan and retard his advance until Jackson and A. P. Hill should have disposed of Harper's Ferry. Up to the latest advices, everything worked to the entire satisfaction of our commanding general.

From the same source, says the Examiner, we hear that the quantity of ammunition captured by us at Harper's Ferry is immense, amounting to several hundred wagon loads.

☞ The Salt extortioners of Richmond, the Enquirer says, are likely hereafter to have a dull time of it in that city, the Corporate authorities having provided sufficient for family use, which is distributed at five cents per pound (instead of forty.) Every person is entitled to a pound a month. This includes one pound to every member of a family, including children and negroes.

The Battle of Iuka.

We this morning conversed with Dr. Luke P. Blackburn, aid of Gen. Price, who was with him at Iuka.

Gen. Price was thrice ordered by Gen. Bragg to move his army across the Tennessee river at Eastport or Iuka. On Thursday morning, the 11th, he moved his army of less than 14,000 men from Guntown towards Iuka. By rapid and forced marches, he arrived within 3 miles of Iuka at daylight Sunday morning. There he was informed by a courier from Gen. Armstrong's command, whose cavalry had attacked the enemy on Saturday, that reinforcements were being sent from Burnsville. The men being much fatigued were ordered to rest; and sleep in line for 30 minutes.

Gen. Price, knowing that Capt. Saunders, with his company of 120 men had possession of the road between Iuka and Burnsville, having implicit confidence in that officer, and he had no fear of reinforcements from Corinth until he should have captured the force at Burnsville and Iuka. The column was put in motion ; on reaching the edge of town he was astonished to hear that the enemy, 2,000 strong, with 2,000 stolen negroes, and a large train had fled at one o'clock the night previous. He took possession of the place. There was a quantity of cotton and stores. The enemy came up again on Monday, in small force, but soon retreated.

Colonel Wirt Adams and Hieman's cavalry captured and burnt a train of cars five miles below Iuka.

There was no further demonstration until Friday morning, when Colonel Ord sent in a flag demanding the unconditional surrender of General Price's army, stating that the army of General Lee had been destroyed in Virginia ; Longstreet and Hill, with their entire divisions, captured ; that the war was now virtually closed, and as he wished to prevent the useless shedding of blood, he demanded an unconditional surrender. That he (General Price) was completely surrounded by an overwhelming force, and could not escape.

General Price replied, that whenever the independence of the Southern Confederacy was acknowledged, her rights respected, and the Vandal hordes of the North were driven from her soil, that then, and then only, would he and his army be willing and ready to lay down their arms.

General Price, in obedience to orders from Gen. Van Dorn, and being almost destitute of forage, unable to cross the Tennessee river, prevented from passing down towards Corinth by the unfavorable condition of the country. The enemy having possession of the western bank of Yellow Creek, determined to fall back to Baldwin, and there unite with Gen. Van Dorn.

The order to fall back was issued on Friday morning, 9 o'clock, when no one dreamed of an attack. On Friday evening, at 2 o'clock, the enemy in line of battle approached our out post. Heavy skirmishing ensued. At 3 o'clock General Price ordered up the Fourth Brigade. When they reached their position they found the enemy in line of battle holding a good position on a hill. The order was given to charge them, which charge drove the enemy back two hundred yards into a ditch formed by the road from Fulton to Eastport, and directly under their cannon which were masked. Gen. Price had now reached the field. The firing had almost ceased. Gen. Hebert and Col. Martin, commanding Brigade, with Whitfield's Legion, being all the force in line.

General Price ordered up General Gregg's and Green's brigades, to form on the left, charge the enemy and press them down on General Murey's division, he being on the right. Before the arrival of their brigades, General Price ascertained that the enemy were lying in the road, sheltered from our artillery. They were firing but one gun, and that on our right.

The gallant and lamented Gen. Little suggested that as they seemed to have but one gun in position, if the line would move forward, the battle could soon be won. The order was given. Our men immerged from the under brush in line. They were then met by as terrific a fire from masked batteries and concealed musketry as was ever encountered. But the invincible 3d Louisiana, 3d Tennessee, and 37th Alabama, stood like statuary. When the order to charge was given, they rushed headlong through this sheet of fire and lead, drove the enemy from their position and guns : Whitfield's legion pressing on the right, the enemy would resist and fall back until they were driven half a mile, losing nine guns.

It was now dark, Gens. Green and Gregg arrived, but too late to enter the fight.

One hour of daylight and the entire Yankee Division would have been captured. We held the field all night, brought in the wounded and evacuated the place in accordance with the order issued in the morning.

Our loss in killed, wounded and missing, 482. That of the enemy, over 800. Ge Price brought off his entire train and captured stores. Gen. Murray covered the retreat.

Gen. Little fell whilst conversing with Gen. Price.

Casualties in Mississippi Regiment.

We are indebted to our attentive friend, W. W. Divine, for a telegraphic dispatch containing the following list of casualties to our brave soldiers from this State in the recent battles in Virginia.

RICHMOND, September 25th.

EDITOR MISSISSIPPIAN :—I send you a partial list of the casualties in killed and wounded at the battle of Sharpsburg, but I have not been able to get all the casualties of the different regiments yet, but will forward them as soon as obtained.

The following list came from wounded soldiers who could give but a partial list of the fatality attending their regiments. Our loss in all is comparatively small, however.

CASUALTIES IN THE 12TH MISSISSIPPI REGIMENT.

Field and Staff.—Killed : none. Lt. Col. M. B. Harris, wounded in the leg slightly; Adj't J. H. Capárs, wounded in the head—slight; Serg't Maj. E. H. McCobb, arm slightly.

Crmpany A.—Wounded: Lt. J. D. Nixon, head, slightly; Privates A. Hall and J. Roberts.

Company B.—Wounded: Lieut. B. Stampley, in leg; Corp'l McNeil, shoulder.

Company C.—Wounded: Sergeants H. Bow, Daniely and S. Whitworth; Private Duval.

Company D.—Killed: Privates S. T. Butler, H. G. Taylor, W. H. Law. Wounded: T. J. White, J. Ingleham.

Company E.—Wounded: Private Booker, in arm slightly.

Company H.—Killed: B. H. Applewhite, J. McDougal. Wounded: Lieut. H. S. McCullum, slightly in head.

Company I.—Wounded: Private Teague, in leg slightly.

Company K.—Killed: Y. Griffin. Wounded: Lieut. R. T. Owen, severely; J. Duval, breast, slightly; W. R. Thompson, leg, slight.

EIGHTEENTH MISSISSIPPI REGIMENT.

Field and Staff Officers.—Wounded: Maj. J. C. Campbell, badly; Capt. Vaughn, badly.

Company C.—Killed: Peetaff. Wounded: Serg't E. Banks, both thighs; Corp'l L. Dunn, both thighs and arm badly; Corp'l D. Haley, mortally; Privates: Kit Gilmer, leg, slight; G. Short, side, slight; W. McKie, thigh, slight; A. Farren, leg amputated; T. McGee, hand slightly.

Company D.—Killed: Lark. Wounded: Capt. D. Hubbard, side, slight; Serg't Gerard, slight; Dwyer, arm amputated; Privates S. Franklin, arm, slight; J. W. Williams, head, slight; W. Goosen, abdomen, slight.

Company K.—Killed: M. Goodloe. Wounded, Lieut. Bird, shoulder, slight ; Lieut. Patton, arm, badly ; Serg't McAskie, shoulder, badly; H. Batey, leg, slightly ; W. Cooper, severely.

Company I.—Lieut. J. H, Cowan.

SECOND MISSISSIPPI BATTALION.

Field and Staff Officers—Killed : none. Wounded, Major W. S. Wilson, arm, painfully ; Adj't W. S. Stone, leg, slightly ; Capt. T. B. Manlove, arm, slightly ; Capt. J. Martin, severely.

SEVENTEENTH MISSISSIPPI REGIMENT.

Wounded—Capt. Kesetevan.

Company A.—W. J. Peason, arm, badly; J. H. Smith, A. W. Mallett, head, slightly.

Company G.—Wounded : Lieut Williams, leg, slight.

CONSTITUTIONAL AMENDMENT.—The Richmond Whig says the clause in the Confederate Constitution concerning the "liberty of the press," should be amended, so as to read : "Congress shall make no law abridging the liberty of the press, but shall have power to suppress newspapers, by exacting military service from all persons connected with them, except compositors and aged editors."

Such an amendment as this would conform to the views of one branch of Congress, (the Senate,) which has recently acted upon the presumption that newspapers may be successfully conducted without editors, professional reporters, or mailing clerks,—which graciously exempts "printers" and pressmen from conscription, but does not exempt those who furnish the matter to the printers to be put into type, or those who mail the paper after it is printed. If the House of Representatives sustains this action, the days of many daily journals are numbered.

☞ It is stated as a noteworthy circumstance, that the Chippewas, who were never before at war with the whites are now joined with their deadliest enemies, the Sioux, in making war on old Abe. And, still stranger, the heretofore implacable Camanches are at peace, for the first time, with the whites in Texas. Verily, the South seems to be shielded.

☞ The Richmond Dispatch has information that Lincoln has gone to Buffalo—that Gen. Wool has been sent to Philadelphia to fortify it, and that all the Pennsylvania troops are concentrating there. Washington was in a state of inextricable confusion.

By Telegraph

BATTLE OF SHEPPARDSTOWN.

Enemy almost Totally Annihilated.

Four or Five Thousand Prisoners Captured.

Great Battle of Sharpsburg.

The most Tremendous of the Continent.

Enemy Confess a Loss of 10,000.

Immense Havoc among the Yankee Field Officers.

Federal Reinforcements Sent to Hilton Head.

AUGUSTA, September 25th.—The Richmond Examiner of the 24th says, that in the fight at Sheppardstown it is reported the enemy was almost annihilated, and four or five thousand prisoners taken.

The Examiner says that Lee wrote to President Davis, that the shock of battle on Wednesday was the most tremendous on this continent, and the result was the most damaging the enemy has received in the whole campaign. The enemy confess a loss of ten thousand. Ours will not exceed five thousand.

A Yankee dispatch, dated Saturday, says that the loss of Federal Generals and field-officers were so large as to be unaccountable.

General McClellan says the Federals may safely claim a victory.

A dispatch says that a body of Federals dasned into Leesburg, but retired. The place is now in our possession.

AUGUSTA, September 25th.—The Charleston Mercury of this morning says, that passengers report grounds for believing the enemy sending heavy reinforcements to Hilton Head and along the shores of Broad River. Pinckney Island is now occupied by a large body of troops.

The Elephant Becoming Troublesome.

The presence of the darkies at the North is beginning to arrest the attention and excite the apprehension of our Northern brethren. What to do with the nigger when he gets to the land of promise, is the perplexing question. The Cairo Gazette, of a late date, says :

The levees yesterday were so dark with negroes that pedestrians found it difficult to peregrinate without lanterns. We never before saw just such a lot of darkies in our life. Uncle Toms, Aunt Cloes and Topsys, were abundant. There were about 500,000,000,000 baby darkies, and probably thrice that number of children, ranging from two to five years. Three fourths of the latter wore dilapidated shirts of a deep mud color; and when we saw them they were gymnasticating—standing upon their heads, etc. A number of the old folks were sick, and the whole lot, excepting the little rollicking shirt-clad shavers, were certainly very wretched specimens of humanity.

What this eternal raft of negroes will find to do here is more than we can foretell. The Government may find employment for a small per cent. of them, but the greater portion must either starve or become Government paupers.

Our citizens look upon the swelling multitudes of negroes among them with a just sense of alarm. What shall be done with them is a question that suggests itself to every mind, but no one can solve it. If hundreds and hundreds were not yet to be forced in upon us, the number here could soon be distributed throughout the country, and furnished employment by farmers and gardeners. But looking upon this as the entrepot for the thousands who may be forced in the South, as a sort of rendezvous for them until they can see opportunities to do better elsewhere—we cannot dispel from our mind the fear that not only this new population will suffer, but that their presence will so affect the laboring class of white men that the pinch of want will become general. We sincerely hope that time will prove their fears to be groundless, but it is hoping almost against hope.

Mr. Buchanan's Position.

W. C. Jewett, of Colorado, about to proceed to Europe as a patriot to assist in preserving the interests of the Union by the promulgation of Union sentiments in that country, has had an interview this evenining with Ex-President Buchanan. Mr. B. pronounces every charge against his loyalty and want of integrity of motive during his administration as unjust and false, and that he will ere long vindicate himself before the country, as he already feels himself vindicated by records overlooked in the present perilous condition of the country. Mr. B. said he had great faith in the Union being sustained from the interests of the South alone, who, in the Union, would maintain a proud position, while in secession she could only hold one of humiliation, and that the only true basis upon which the war can be successfully conducted is by a firm adherence to the constitution. Mr. B. says that foreign interference can only be tolerated with a view to restore the Union.

Daily Mississippian.

☞ The President has commissioned Lt. H. M. Parker and Lt. W. P. Maxey, of the 18th Mississippi Begiment, as drill masters, with the rank of 2d Lieut., and ordered them to report to Major-General Tupper. Their duties will be to instruct the militia of this State in the company and regiment drill.

From this act of the President's, we presume he intends not only to leave untouched the military organization of the State, but to favor and encourage it, and lend his aid in rendering it efficient. Under the circumstances surrounding us at the present time, we believe it would be unwise to break up this organization either by the State or the General Government, and we are truly glad of the assurance on the part of the President that our minute men are to be left undisturbed for the defense of the State. It is the purpose of the Governor and Major-General to to have these men well armed and well drilled, and when their services can be dispensed with to give them furloughs and let them return to their homes, with their arms and equipments, subject to be called at any moment. They are required to keep their arms in order so that when an emergency arises five thousand effective men can be thrown at a given point as speedily as the same force could be moved were they all in camp. In this manner the minute men will be made not only efficient soldiers, but quite a considerable part of the producing population, giving protection to our home interests and keeping the laboring population in proper subjection.

While the enemy is menacing us on our Northern border and on the banks of the Mississippi river, we must have protection of some sort, and if our minute men can furnish the protection necessary, surely it will be much cheaper to the Confederacy and detract much less from the Confederate army, to assign that duty to them. The conscript law as passed by the House, makes it the duty of the President to call on the Governors of the several States for their respective quotas; and we suppose that when Mississippi is no longer menaced and harrassed by prowling gangs of marauding Yankee theives, the Governor will have no objection to turn over the entire Militia to the Confederacy if the exigencies of the common cause should require it

MISSISSIPPI RIVER, Sept. 13th, 1862.

MESSRS. EDITORS: Again I would make an appeal, through your columns, that something may be done for the protection of the inhabitants bordering upon the eastern bank of the Missisipi river, below Baton Rouge. Our young men have all left us, and dot the battle-fields of the army in each State. We are left to the mercy of an insolent and heartless foe, and know not what stern lot may be in store for us. Can it be that we are to be thus sacrificed? I would not make the appeal, gentlemen, but for the melancholy scenes that are being enacted around us. Houses are ransacked, silver plate and jewelry, household furniture, and bed linen even, fall a prey to the spoliator. Our wives and daughters treated as so many brutes. Great Heaven! was there ever a war carried on in such a spirit?

There was a skirmish in St. Charles Parish, on the 10th inst., not very remote from a previous affair of the Boutte station. Some 2,500 Federals landed from their gunboats and transports, and succeeded in surrounding about 800 Confederates, mounted Texans. These were shelled by the gunboats, which forced them back off the fields to a low swamp, when about 100 of them were obliged to abandon their horses, which fell a prey to the enemy, with a loss also of 2 killed, 6 wounded and 14 taken prisoners. The Texans had previously destroyed two schooners loaded with sugar. Since then all is quiet.

Hoping, gentlemen, that some relief may be forthwith sent us, I remain,

Very respectfully,

PENNSYLVANIANS JOINING THE CONFEDERATE FORCES.—The Richmond Dispatch says. "We are assured, upon the statement of an officer of the Confederate army who arrived in this city yesterday, and who left Frederick a few days ago, that a company of Pennsylvanians, from Adams county, numbering *one hundred and fifteen*, arrived at Frederick last week, and tendered their services to the Confederate Government. This company was regularly organized, with its own officers, be fore they left their own State, and declared that they were unwilling to stay at home to be drafted into the abolition service.

INTERESTING FROM MISSOURI.—The Richmond Examiner of the 20th says that members of Congress from Missouri have received late and interesting intelligence from their State. It is said that the new levies of State militia raised there under the recent draft are coming over *en masse* to the Confederates. This information comes through sources believed to be entirely trustworthy.

A BATTLE AT WILLIAMSBURG REPORTED. A gentleman, who arrived here yesterday, direct from New Kent Courthouse, reports that heavy cannonading was at that place heard in the direction of Williamsburg throughout Thursday. It was currently reported here yesterday that General Wise had been repulsed near Williamsburg on the day before, but it is asserted in official quarters that the General only set out for that town on last evening.—*Richmond Examiner, 20th.*

An Incident.

A correspondent of the Lynchburg Virginian, in a recent letter from the camp near Richmond, relates "an incident that occurred a few evenings since, which shows how keenly alive the soldier, though the creature of circumstances, is to the memories of home—how susceptible to the kindlier and better feelings of the heart:"

We were passing through a coppice of woods, when we came suddenly upon a sunny-haired little girl of some three summers, and a bright-eyed little boy apparently a little younger, reposing under the shade of an oak and deeply interested in the movements of the "muster men." Our whole command suddenly paused. We halted. The reins of our bridle dropped from our hands. A thousand recollections crowded upon our memories. The shrill notes of the fife, the rolling drum, were no longer heard. Back, back, our thoughts ran, till we saw other children sporting along the streamlet's bank, or amid the bright garden, plucking gay flowers; now swinging on the willow's pendant bough—now sleeping on a mossy bank, dreaming sweet dreams. The present was forgotten. We were living in the past. The voice of command soon broke our dreams. And when we turned to our command and saw other cheeks wet with drops, other than those of perspiration, I could not but think how blissful was childhood's unconsciousness of the pains and sorrows of life. Its sky is ever bright, its flowers are ever blooming—and as we hear its joyous shout and unstudied laugh, how few of us sigh out—

"Oh, what a world of beauty fades away,
With the winged hours of youth."

CAMP DRUDGERY.—If Southern slaveowners have not patriotism and liberality enough to induce them to send able bodied negro men in sufficient numbers to cook and wash for the army, to fell trees and dig ditches, and *wait* on the gentlemen soldiers of the South, Congress ought to make *a requisition* for a proper proportion of each man's slaves, and *take them to the camps*. It is not right that any Southern soldier should perform menial services in camp, whilst fat and idle slaves are at home lounging about the plantation in idleness. Let the Southern soldiers be properly served by slaves, and have no toil but to keep their arms in order and meet the Yankee hordes on the field of battle. We hope that Congress, at the present session, will take this matter in hand.

☞ Hermes, the able Richmond correspondent of the Charleston Mercury, says.

"An officer taken sick in Maryland and sent back here to recruit his health, reports that he passed Manassas early last week, eight days or more after the battle, and found the Yankees under a flag of truce, still burying their dead. They told him they had buried 7,600, and had a week's work before them. Burying was a slow business, owing to the decomposed state of the bodies. One at a time, they were covered over with earth where they lay. The odor was awful. To our officer's eye, it seemed as if none had been buried, so numerous were the corpses."

New Advertisements.

Generals and the most practiced and ablest rulers. They have shown an amount of cohesion and perseverance which nobody expected, and as to money, arms and other munitions of war, whence they have been supplied nobody can tell. We have seen no attempt to explain these phenomena. The English press has been silent respecting them, although thousands of columns in millions of papers have been filled with articles on the sources of the countless treasures that have been wasted in supporting the Northern arms in the present struggle.

It is most saddening that between the British and American people sentiments of distrust and hostility should arise, to bear fruit of misery and sin in future generations. As the horrible civil war, with all its fearful accompaniments would never have taken place but for slavery, so but for this war the present embittered international feeling would never have arisen in America towards England. Slavery is a tree that bears none but bitter fruit to the master and the slave, to the slaveholder's abettor and to the merchant on whom he relies for the sale of the produce of his slave's labor. Thus by means of slavery have the North and the South been placed in a position of actual hostility, whilst between England and the free States such seeds of ill-will and dislike have been sown as may produce a dreadful harvest of death, destruction, and wretchedness in future years.

THE PRESIDENT'S PROCLAMATION.

Special Dispatch to The N. Y. Tribune.

WASHINGTON, Tuesday, Sept. 23, 1862.

THE one topic of discussion in the city to-day is, of course, the President's Proclamation, which is hailed with the most joyful enthusiasm by the real friends of the Administration, and meets with more general approval from others than would have been anticipated. Few venture to declare that they are themselves decidedly opposed to the policy which is inaugurated; but some are on the fence, and some shake their heads and express apprehension respecting the course which the Border States or certain Generals may take.

Nobody dares to say that he will himself desert the government because of this great blow which it has dealt the rebellion, but occasionally a person insinuates that his neighbor may do so. Now and then the remark is heard that the President has been driven into the policy of emancipation by outside clamor, a most preposterous statement. For nearly a year Mr. Lincoln is known to have had the question of slavery, in its connection with the rebellion, under his most thoughtful and deliberate consideration.

Within the last few months, perceiving the great progress which public opinion was making, he has given still closer attention to the question, has invoked counsel from all directions, and has looked to Providence for guidance to the true solution of the great problem which, as he told the deputation from the religious men of Chicago, was in his thoughts night and day. A number of weeks since, he was, as we telegraphed you a month ago, on the point of issuing a proclamation which fixed the 1st of December as the day of emancipation, and was only dissuaded at that time from doing so by the strong opposition of two members of his Cabinet. This statement has been denied, but it is substantially true.

The Proclamation now issued is an improvement in several material respects upon the rejected one. It was written on Sunday, and was laid before the Cabinet at an extraordinary meeting yesterday. Every member, with perhaps a single exception, in the person of Postmaster-General Blair, agreed to it, and will give it his hearty support. All accepted it cheerfully, as indicating the adoption of a policy which they had long been urging. It is to be added that the proclamation is the President's own work, written without consultation, not altered, or if altered at all, very slightly, at or after the Cabinet meeting, and published to the world within forty-eight hours of its composition.

Viewed in one light the Proclamation is welcomed everywhere. Men, whose instincts and opinions are tinted by pro-slavery sympathies, have been heard to say within a week, "Give us any policy rather than none." "Proclaim Freedom, rather than halt between two paths," the same men say now, the direction of the war in the Cabinet and in the field should be confided to men who heartily approve of the President's policy. Those who are for the Administration alone should be put in places where they are required to carry out the will of the Administration, and the President should see to it that no others occupy places of trust.

The friends of the Proclamation regard it as the beginning of the end—as calculated to separate the coöperation of all loyal men in the South in the work of crushing the rebellion; to put foreign intervention out of the question henceforward, and to bring the great struggle speedily to a crisis. Some, speculating on the probable response of Jeff. Davis to this terrible declaration of war, wonder whether he may not declare immediate emancipation himself, and inquire what effect such a declaration would have. Whether the slave would accept freedom at the hands of his master at once rather than wait a hundred days for it at the hand of his real friend, the government, may be a question. But this certainly seems to be the only trump card in Jeff. Davis's hand now, if the Proclamation is enforced in its entirety.

There are good grounds for thinking that the results of the adoption of the policy of which this paper is the announcement, will be soon apparent in the Departments of the South and of the Gulf. Gen. Butler will be allowed without interference to "call return the protection which such a government gives to the humblest citizen. By a word the President transforms a State sunk in the semi-barbarism of a medieval age to the light and civilization of the nineteenth Christian century. As it is not extravagant to say that God had hid away this continent till the human race had reached its manhood and was fit to enter upon so fair an inheritance, so it is a simple statement of a truth to say that in all the ages there has been no act of one man and of one people so sublime as this emancipation of a race—no act so fraught with good for the sons of men in all time to come.

Is the President in advance of the people? We think not, and the evidence of only four and twenty hours already sustains our conviction. There are men of the baser sort who will carp and cavil, who will prophesy evil, and strive to make their prophecies their own fulfillment. When was it ever otherwise? But this man, sprung from the people, has gauged the wisdom and the virtue of the commonality, and speaks with their voice. The sagacity and the integrity which so distinguish him have no more failed him now than heretofore. All good men praise him; all far-seeing men approve his action; all brave men applaud the courage which, unappalled by accumulating danger, never falters, never yields, but puts forth its strength at the right moment, and plants the right blow in the right place. It is the way to conquer; it must conquer; it cannot fail.

From The N. Y. Times.

THERE has been no more important and far-reaching document ever issued since the foundation of this government than the proclamation of President Lincoln concerning slavery and slaves. . . . The wisdom of the step taken—we refer at present to that clause in the document which declares free the slaves of rebel States after the first of January—is unquestionable; its necessity, indisputable. It has been declared time and again by President Lincoln that as soon as this step became a necessity, he should adopt it. Its adoption now is not a confession that the military means of suppressing the great rebellion have proved a failure; but simply that there is a point at which any other legitimate appliances that can be called in, shall also be availed of. Slavery is an element of strength to the rebels if left untouched; it will assuredly prove an element of weakness—it may be of total destruction—to them and their cause, when we make such use of it and its victims as lies in our power.

From now till the first of January—the day when this proclamation will take effect—is little over three months. What may happen between now and then, in the progress of the war, it is hard to say. We earnestly hope, however, that by that time the rebellion will be put down by the military hand, and that the terrible element of slave insurrection may not be invoked. If, by that day, the rebel army be overthrown, and their Capital captured; and if the slaveholding rebels still prove malignant, irrepressible, and, as in the Southwest, disorganizers and marauders, then let that which Vice-President Stephens called the corner-stone of the Southern Confederacy be knocked from under it, and see whether the whole fabric of rebellion will not necessarily tumble to the ground.

From The Evening Post.

The twenty-second of September in this year will hereafter be a day to be commemorated with peculiar honor, a day illustrious in the annals not only of our own country but of the world, the day to which the present Chief Magistrate of the United States will recur hereafter as the most glorious of his life. On that day, it will be recorded, the chains of bondage were struck from the limbs of three million of human beings. On that day, so many chattels, by one stroke of his pen, were made men; so many slaves, on the shedding of a few drops of ink, started into freemen. No act of emancipation which dignifies the history of our race ever bestowed the blessings of freedom on a scale so magnificent or snapped assunder so many manacles at once.

* * * * *

We may infer the dismay which the appearance of this proclamation will strike into the hearts of the rebel population from the outcry with which semi-secessionist journals of the North have greeted it. There can be no better demonstration of its efficacy; no stronger proof that the Executive has struck the spot where the weakness of the South lies. "We have only anticipations of evil from it," says *The Journal of Commerce*, "and we regard it, as will an immense majority of the people of the North, with profound regret." Evil, no doubt, to the cause which engaged the sympathies of *The Journal of Commerce*, evil to the cause of the slaveholders, the authors of the rebellion, may be fairly anticipated from the measure. All we ask is that the measure shall be effectual, all we desire is that it shall draw after it positive and decided consequences. He who admits that this is so, admits that the proclamation of Mr. Lincoln is no form of empty words, and that the freedom which it proclaims will be actually conferred. If so, the foundation on which the rebel government is reared has been beaten away from under it and the superstructure falls a mass of ruins. A great act of justice and humanity has been performed, and having thus satisfied our own consciences we leave the event in the hands of that Providence, which is sure, from an act of mercy, to derive merciful consequences. nation, the proclamation has been issued in obedience to their voice, and they will sustain it with a zeal at which the secret enemies of the Union among us will turn pale.

From Bennett's Herald.

The gravity of this proclamation will strike every one. It has been forced upon the nation by the Abolitionists of the North and the secessionists of the South. It inaugurates an overwhelming revolution in the system of labor in a vast and important agricultural section of the country, which will, if the rebels persist in their course, suddenly emancipate three or four million of human beings, and throw them, in the fullness of their helplessness and ignorance, upon their own resources and the wisdom of the white race to properly regulate and care for them in their new condition of life. But the importance of this great social revolution will not be confined to the section where the black race now forms the chief laboring element. It will have an influence on the labor of the North and West. It will, to a certain extent, bring the black labor of the South in competition with the white labor on the

THE PRESIDENT'S PROCLAMATION.

Special Dispatch to The N. Y. Tribune.

WASHINGTON, Tuesday, Sept. 23, 1862.

THE one topic of discussion in the city to-day is, of course, the President's Proclamation, which is hailed with the most joyful enthusiasm by the real friends of the Administration, and meets with more general approval from others than would have been anticipated. Few venture to declare that they are themselves decidedly opposed to the policy which is inaugurated; but some are on the fence, and some shake their heads and express apprehension respecting the course which the Border States or certain Generals may take.

Nobody dares to say that he will himself desert the government because of this great blow which it has dealt the rebellion, but occasionally a person insinuates that his neighbor may do so. Now and then the remark is heard that the President has been driven into the policy of emancipation by outside clamor, a most preposterous statement. For nearly a year Mr. Lincoln is known to have had the question of slavery, in its connection with the rebellion, under his most thoughtful and deliberate consideration.

Within the last few months, perceiving the great progress which public opinion was making, he has given still closer attention to the question, has invoked counsel from all directions, and has looked to Providence for guidance to the true solution of the great problem which, as he told the deputation from the religious men of Chicago, was in his thoughts night and day. A number of weeks since, he was, as we telegraphed you a month ago, on the point of issuing a proclamation which fixed the 1st of December as the day of emancipation, and was only dissuaded at that time from doing so by the strong opposition of two members of his Cabinet. This statement has been denied, but it is substantially

National Anti-Slavery Standard.

WITHOUT CONCEALMENT—WITHOUT COMPROMISE.

NEW YORK, SATURDAY, SEPTEMBER 27, 1862.

CORRESPONDENTS will greatly oblige us by a careful observance of the following directions, viz.:

Letters enclosing matter for publication, or relating in any way to the editorial conduct of the paper, should be addressed, "EDITOR OF THE ANTI-SLAVERY STANDARD, No. 48 BEEKMAN STREET, NEW YORK."

Letters enclosing subscriptions, or relating in any way to the business of the office, should be addressed, "PUBLISHER OF THE ANTI-SLAVERY STANDARD, No. 48 BEEKMAN STREET, NEW YORK."

A PROCLAMATION BY THE PRESIDENT OF THE UNITED STATES.

Emancipation on the First of January, 1863.

By the President of the United States of America:

A PROCLAMATION.

I, ABRAHAM LINCOLN, President of the United States of America, and Commander-in-Chief of the Army and Navy thereof, do hereby proclaim and declare, that hereafter, as heretofore, the war will be prosecuted for the object of practically restoring the constitutional relation between the United States and the people thereof in which States that relation is, or may be suspended or disturbed; that it is my purpose, upon the next meeting of Congress, to again recommend the adoption of a practical measure tendering pecuniary aid to the free acceptance or rejection of all the slave States so called, the people whereof may not then be in rebellion against the United States, and which States may then have voluntarily adopted, or thereafter may voluntarily adopt, the immediate or gradual abolishment of slavery within their respective limits; and that the efforts to colonize persons of African descent with their consent, upon the Continent or elsewhere, with the previously obtained consent of the governments existing there, will be continued.

That on the first day of January, in the year of our Lord one thousand eight hundred and sixty-three, all persons held as slaves within any State, the people whereof shall then be in rebellion against the United States, shall be then, thenceforward, and forever, free; and the Executive government of the United States, including the military and naval authority thereof, will recognize and maintain the freedom of such persons, and will do no act or acts to repress such persons, or any of them, in any efforts they may make for their actual freedom.

That the Executive will, on the first day of January aforesaid, by proclamation, designate the States and parts of States, if any, in which the people thereof, respectively, shall then be in rebellion against the United States; and the fact that any State, or the people thereof, shall on that day be in good faith represented in the Congress of the United States by members chosen thereto at elections wherein a majority of the qualified voters of such State shall have participated, shall, in the absence of strong countervailing testimony, be deemed conclusive evidence that such State and the people thereof have not been in rebellion against the United States.

That attention is hereby called to an act of Congress entitled "An act to make an additional article of war," approved March 13, 1862, and which act is in the words and figure following:

Be it enacted by the Senate and House of Representatives of the United States of America in Congress assembled, That hereafter the following shall be promulgated as an additional article of war for the government of the army of the United States, and shall be obeyed and observed as such.

ARTICLE—All officers or persons in the military or naval service of the United States are prohibited from employing any of the forces under their respective commands for the purpose of returning fugitives from service or labor who may have escaped from any person to whom such service or labor is claimed to be due, martial of violating this article shall be dismissed from the service.

SECTION 2. And be it further enacted, that this act shall take effect from and after its passage.

Also to the ninth and tenth sections of an act entitled "An act to suppress insurrection, to punish treason and rebellion, to seize and confiscate property of rebels, and for other purposes," approved July 17, 1862, and which sections are in the words and figures following:

SEC. 9. And be it further enacted, that all slaves of persons who shall hereafter be engaged in rebellion against the government of the United States, or who shall, in any way, give aid or comfort thereto, escaping from such persons and taking refuge within the lines of the army; and all slaves captured from such persons or deserted by them and coming under the control of the government of the United States, and all slaves of such persons found on (or being within) any place occupied by rebel forces and afterward occupied by the forces of the United States, shall be deemed captures of war and shall be forever free of their servitude and not again held as slaves.

SEC. 10. And be it further enacted, That no slave escaping into any State, Territory or the District of Columbia, from any of the States, shall be delivered up, or in any way impeded or hindered of his liberty, except for crime or some offence against the laws, unless the person claiming said fugitive shall first make oath that the person to whom the labor or service of such fugitive is alleged to be due, is his lawful owner, and has not been in arms against the United States in the present rebellion, or in any way given aid and comfort thereto, and no person engaged in the military or naval service of the United States shall, under any pretence, whatever, assume to decide on the validity of the claim of any person to the service or labor of any other person, or surrender up any such person to the claimant, on pain of being dismissed from the service.

And I do hereby enjoin upon and order all persons engaged in the military and naval service of the United States, to observe, obey and enforce, within their respective spheres of service, the act and sections above recited.

And the Executive will in due time recommend that all citizens of the United States who shall have remained loyal thereto throughout the rebellion, shall (upon the restoration of the constitutional relation between the United States and their respective States and people, if the relation shall have been suspended or disturbed) be compensated for all losses by acts of the United States, *including the loss of slaves.*

In witness whereof, I have hereunto set my hand, and caused the seal of the United States to be affixed.

Done at the City of Washington, this Twenty-second day of September, in the year of our Lord one thousand eight hundred and sixty-two, and of the Independence of the United States the eighty-seventh.

By the President. ABRAHAM LINCOLN.

WILLIAM H. SEWARD, Secretary of State.

WHILE we regret that, for the safety and honor of an imperilled nation, the President did not see his way clear to proclaim the immediate and unconditional emancipation of every slave on the American soil, we nevertheless rejoice with an unspeakable joy that he has at last openly committed himself to a measure which, if carried out in good faith, as we trust it will be, must ensure the utter and speedy destruction of the slave system, and give us a country free from the damning reproach of making merchandise of the children of God. If the object for which the Abolitionists have so long prayed and struggled shall be thus attained, they will indeed have cause for exultation such as rarely falls to the lot of reformers in this world, and, putting off the harness, the toil-worn veterans in Freedom's Cause may say, in the words of Simeon, "Lord, now lettest thou thy servant depart in peace, for mine eyes have seen thy salvation."

We cannot think there is any appreciable ground for fear that the rebels, warned of the impending fate of the diabolical institution for which they have made war, will "lay down the weapons of their rebellion" before the end of "the days of grace" accorded them by the President, and thus drag the North into a renewal of "the covenant with death and the agreement with hell," which has been the source of all our woes. If the President had issued such a proclamation one year ago, there might indeed have been some danger of such a disgraceful termination of the war; but such is now the madness of the South, such the bitterness of her animosity toward the North, and so inveterate her pride of superiority and her determination to hazard everything, even slavery, in the attempt to win her independence, that we do not believe it possible that she can be so humiliated as to creep back through the door which the weak and unwise clemency of the President has left open for her. Whether the war on the part of the North be vigorously prosecuted from this time forward, or suffered to lag as heretofore, we are sure that the South will be as far from compliance with the President's offer on the first of January next as she is at this hour. We have no serious apprehension that even one of the rebellious States will by that time be "in good faith represented in Congress by members chosen thereto at elections wherein a majority of the qualified voters shall have participated." And yet we perceive that the enemies of emancipation, in the intensity of their mortification in view of the President's Proclamation, are trying to console themselves with the hope that slavery may by this means be saved from overthrow. Bennett's *Herald* tries to find comfort in this way, and even affects to believe that the President anticipates the suppression of the rebellion before the first of January, and the restoration of the Union, slavery and all, "substantially as it was." These are its words:

"We accept this proclamation, not as that of an armed crusade against African slavery, but as a peace offering to our loyal border slave States, and as a liberal warning to our revolted States, in order to save their local institutions by their timely restoration to the Union. The sixty days' notice of the Confiscation act having expired, President Lincoln announces the enforcement of the law against the slaves and property of rebels and traitors, and seizes the occasion to declare that on the first day of January next "all persons held as slaves within any State, or any designated part of a State, the people whereof shall then be in rebellion against the United States, shall be then, thenceforward and forever free." But the proclamation further declares that any State which, on the day named, shall, by a majority of its qualified voters and in good faith be represented in the Congress of the Union, shall not be considered as in a state of rebellion. Upon this saving clause we confidently assume that the President, through an energetic prosecution of the war, anticipates the suppression of this rebellion before the 1st of January, and the restoration of the Union substantially as it was. And why not? We have so far crippled and demoralized the great rebel army of the East that within the next sixty days we may expel it and every vestige of rebel authority not only from Virginia, but from North Carolina; and within sixty days, too, we may not only put an end to rebel resistance in loyal Kentucky and disloyal Tennessee, but in Arkansas, Louisiana and Florida. Thus within ninety days we may have at least six of our rebellious slave States represented in Congress; and thus the other five, from the utter hopelessness of their cause, and the special danger impending over them, may be reduced to a saving capitulation. All this can be accomplished before the expiration of the present year, through an earnest, systematic and harmonious prosecution of the war."

Perhaps we shall now see the partisans of slavery at the North, whose purpose hitherto has been to pave the way to peace and compromise by hurting the rebels as little as possible, taking up the cry, "Onward to Richmond," in the hope that victory and conquest on the part of the North may result in the salvation of slavery and the return of the Slave Oligarchy to power over the whole country. Well, let them drive on the war as fast and as hard as they please; we believe they will only aid in more effectually preparing the way for the complete success of the President's plan of emancipation.

We look forward, then, with bright anticipations to the First of January, 1863, as the day of Jubilee for our country, when, if the chains do not actually fall from the limbs of the slaves, the government will be irretrievably committed to a course of action that will speedily bring about that glorious result.

And bring the welcome day.

THE AUSPICIOUS MOMENT.

THE hardest week's fighting of the war is over, and the situation remains much as it was when it begun. Thousands of lives have come to a bloody end, or survive only for a maimed remnant of existence, and no great change in our affairs appears as yet answerable to the price. Gen. McClellan has not been defeated, but the enemy have succeeded in securing their passage, with their trains of artillery and of baggage-waggons, from the Maryland to the Virginia side of the Potomac; while the disgraceful loss of Harper's Ferry, with its twelve thousand paroled prisoners, fully offsets any successes in the field that bulletins or Own Correspondents can extort from the cruel facts. We must rejoice that our army was not captured or cut to pieces, but we cannot congratulate ourselves on the escape of the enemy in fully as good condition as we are ourselves. For we do not accept as facts the guesses of any parties that the losses of the enemy double our own. The enemy had abandoned the idea of invading Pennsylvania and the hope of raising Maryland against "her oppressors," and his object, of course, was to get back to his own side of the dividing stream. Gen. McClellan's object, equally, of course, was to hinder his accomplishing this design and to annihilate his force or to compel him to surrender. The enemy has done what he proposed, though at a heavy loss, and we have failed to do what we attempted, at an equally fearful cost. The game seems to stand substantially as it did before the first gun of the Maryland conflict was fired. And then the surrender of Harper's Ferry, with its garrison—whether it were occasioned by the treachery of Miles or the negligence of whomsoever it was on whom the duty of relieving it rested—is a fearful makeweight in the scale of the enemy. We may be sure that he, and his English supporters, will claim the advantages of those bloody days as his own, and that with more show of truth than has belonged to many of his braggings. We must be contented with Gen. McClellan's assurance that "Pennsylvania and Maryland are safe," but we must say of his victory, as Sheridan did of the Peace of Amiens; it is "one that every one must be glad of and that no one can be proud of."

This series of battles has been, perhaps, the best test we have yet had of the quality of the troops engaged in them. That both fought as well as men ever fought, we think cannot be gainsaid. Each must have felt

"The stern joy that warriors feel
In foemen worthy of their steel."

We had the advantage of fighting, in a sense, on our own ground, and the enemy the corresponding disadvantage of meeting us on unfamiliar soil. Neither army succeeded in demoralizing and disorganizing the other. The losses were about equal, probably—heavy enough on both sides, at any rate. We have prevented the enemy from occupying our territory; he has succeeded in securing his retreat to his own. He now, if not cut off at Thoroughfare Gap, will have all the odds in his favor which he has had heretofore, arising from his familiarity with the country, and from his having his lines of retreat secured behind him. We presume that even his insolence will no longer affirm that one Southerner is a match for three Northerners; nor can the Northerners deny the pluck and persistency with which the Southerners have withstood the battery and the bayonet. The courage, discipline, endurance and all soldierly qualities of both parties have been put to the test, and neither can be fairly said to be found wanting. In generalship we fear that we cannot deny the superiority of the enemy. We think that Gen. McClellan has bettered the expectations even of his admirers by the skill with which he has conducted that succession of battles; but we apprehend that even his warmest admirers will hardly claim for him the masterly military genius—whether of Davis, of Johnson, of Jackson or of Lee—which has baffled all his strategy and inspired the ragged and shoeless armies of the rebels with the energies of victory. Even this dash into Maryland, and the distant glimpse of the rich farms and wealthy towns of Pennsylvania, though foiled, has nothing in it to dispirit them. They have lost nothing by it that is not compensated for by a corresponding loss on our side, and they stand relatively to us just as well as they did a month ago. Now the method of operations has to be reversed. We have to attack them in their own country, and to encounter all the disadvantages incident to an invading army. In the light of our past attempts in that direction, and in view of what we know of the nature and the handling of the rebel troops, what likelihood is there of our invasion being more successful this autumn than our two or three previous attempts? The troops and the Generals being substantially the same that they were then, on the one side and the other, what reason have we to believe that we shall be any nearer the end of the rebellion a twelvemonth hence than we are now?

We conceive the brief Maryland campaign just ended furnishes an irrefragable reply to this question. Such men as we have had to encounter there, in front of Richmond and in the series of Pope's battles, led as they are, are invincible by any force we can bring against them, led by the men and on the principles of the last fifteen months' war. If such an audacious attempt as the invasion of Pennsylvania was merely frustrated, not punished with the destruction of all engaged in it, by the favorite General of our army with all its force at his command, what possibility is there of our reducing them on their own soil and with their whole population at their back? The idea is preposterous, and every drop of blood shed in the attempt will be worse than wasted and will cry to God from the ground against those that cause it to be shed. We think that this truth must force itself upon the minds of all intelligent observers, and that the weight of Northern opinion will be that peace had better be made at once, on the best terms we can get, rather than encounter the certain losses and disgraces of a year like the last, if we refuse to be taught by its lessons. There is but one measure that can secure victory to our army and an honorable conclusion to this civil war. We need hardly say what we know it to be. The two white armies being thus equally matched, the conflict will turn in favor of the one which shall secure the assistance of the black army standing in reserve in the rear of our enemies. Thus far the help of that army has been given to them. If they can retain its services, they are invincible. If we can secure those services, our victory will be sure. Even if those sable allies do not rise in force in our favor, should we invite them to help us, the dread of such an insurrection would disorganize the rebel army—the best part of which would disperse to see after the fire threatening them in the rear. The excitement and uneasiness which the hope of freedom would stir up in the breasts of the slaves everywhere would unsettle the whole system of labor at the South. We should have as many able-bodied volunteers flocking to our standard as we could find arms or spades for. We should have friends in every rebel household and in every regiment and company of the enemy's army. Our success would be assured unless it were defeated by the enemy resorting to the same measure and securing his safety, his independence and the support of Europe, by an act of emancipation on his part.

The present moment seems to us the most favorable that is at all likely to occur for the adoption of a policy of emancipation. Such an one would have been futile as long as the enemy was on our own ground and threatening us with invasion and our Capital with destruction. But now we must at once advance into the enemy's country, if we intend doing anything at all. The result of the Maryland campaign is just what is most favorable for such a step. Had we been entirely successful, had we destroyed or taken their army, and won a victory which could be neither gainsaid nor denied, the friends of the slaveholding oligarchy, whose hearts' desire it is to see it established forever over us, would have said that such an attempt would be a base advantage to take of our "misguided brethren." Now was a time, they would say, to win them back to their allegiance, and to establish the Constitution and the Union on the ancient foundations forever. Had it resulted in our utter and undeniable rout, then, of course, we should have had too much to do to take care of ourselves for an immediate appeal to the slaves. Now, it seems to us, we stand in precisely the position that a wise forethought would have planned, had it been within human capacity to foresee and contrive it. We have succeeded in making the enemy retire to their own country. That country we must at once invade and possess. If we are not in possession of Richmond before the first of next January, the recognition of the Confederacy by the great Powers is absolutely certain. And can we say that it would not have been earned? Should the President avail himself of the expiration of the Sixty Days of grace given to the rebels, now nearly past, and proclaim the absolute and immediate abolition of slavery as a measure of political and military necessity, we should advance into an enemy's country in which we should have even more friends than he has in ours. It would be a triumphant march, we believe, conquering and to conquer, to result in a peace which should secure to the whites of the South, as well as the blacks, a degree of peace, safety, freedom, virtue and prosperity, such as they have never dreamed of. A peace which should establish Civil Liberty forever over the whole continent, and, after the wounds of the war were healed by time, make the United States the leading Power of Christendom. This is our only chance for such a conclusion of this matter. If the blacks cannot or will not save the nation, its destruction is certain and will be sudden. May it not perish without at least an attempt for its salvation.

The foregoing article, as the reader will at once perceive, was penned before the President's Proclamation was made public. We let it stand, however, as it was written, only adding an expression of our strong hope that the act of the Executive, though falling short of the supreme demand of the hour, may yet, through the good Providence of God in our affairs, prove adequate to the salvation of the country.

THE CAUSE AND THE CURE.

MORE than a year ago, those American citizens who had the honor of their country intelligently and deeply at heart were filled with a great hope. Loss, privation, bitter anxiety threatened them; the sacrifice of their own lives, or of lives more dear than their own, was among the possible demands of the future; but there was an elation of spirit, a healthy tension of the nerves, which could joyfully meet the shock of discipline. That April uprising of our people, how grand it was! Earnest men, who had long recognized the subtle connection between cowardice and cruelty, prophesied a noble alliance between courage and mercy, between manliness and justice.

But let us avoid all generalities, and state again just what we had a right to expect from a government appointed to carry out the common sense of loyal people. And first, how may an agent of the people be said to carry out their common sense? We answer, by exercising an intelligent self-reliance in a craft for which he advertises his special fitness; by assuming that personal responsibility which the different individuals, constituting the public, assume in their several pursuits. Take an instance. The citizens of a town pay an architect to build an almshouse. Does this agent carry out the common sense of the people by declaring that he will not lay the foundation till every stone has been examined and approved by all the old women in the parish? Does he carry out the common sense of the people by calling for a unanimity of their crude opinions upon stable equilibrium, compressibility of wood, and centres of gravity? This is the very way to create a paralyzing diversity of uninformed voices; this is the way to deliver the people up to the cupidity of contractors, one of whom may be interested in iron, another in wood, another in stone, and each in disseminating such views as will bring him in the largest returns. But if the architect, being a competent man, builds a good almshouse, as the bootmaker makes a good boot, or the minister writes a good sermon, he carries with him the unanimous approval of the town as a matter of course. We go so far as to say that an agent may strictly carry out the common sense of the people when not a man could be found who would advise the course he pursued. The town cart is sent to the blacksmith to fix a tire upon the wheel. The blacksmith, instead of doing it, goes round among the neighbors to find out how it had better be done. Deacon Potter says: "Wal, guess you'd better make that tire just a *leetle* mite larger 'n the wheel so it 'll slip right on tight, then you can kind o' nail it in place!" The doctor, the lawyer, the apothecary may honestly coincide in this opinion. Every voter in town, being compelled to look up from his business and utter himself on the point, sincerely declares this is the way in which he would go to work. But let our blacksmith understand the trade he professes, and which he is paid for exercising, and, instead of gossipping with the neighbors, he will make the tire *too small* for the wheel, and then take advantage of the expansive power of heat to gripe it firmly to the wood. In doing this, he carries out the common sense of the people to their perfect satisfaction, though perhaps not one of them would have recommended the plan. These examples, testifying to a truth self-evident, seem puerile in rehearsal; but the miserable sophistry they refute has been blatant in the land.

What action in relation to slavery had we then a right to expect from a government bound to carry out the common sense of the people? Certainly it was not to violate any official oath, not to patronize any general scheme of philanthropy as such, neither was it to hasten to send negroes to fight battles which the sin of white men had rendered necessary. It was no more than this: that the President should refuse to recognize the right of a traitor to hold a loyal man in slavery to aid and abet him in his treason. Could any fanaticism of legality object to it? Yet what was called an emancipation policy amounted to this, and no more. We will not speak hardly of Mr. Lincoln. In resisting slavery he has been as good as the average citizen at the time of his election. He reacted on the society which placed him where he is, but was not strong enough to lead a renovated society whither it blindly struggled. For anyone who looks below the merest surface of things knows the folly of the pretence that the Administration would have caused a social revolution at the North by ceasing to protect the slave property of malignant rebels. In every step affecting disadvantageously the rebellion of slavery the people have been ready to follow, when their government has been ready to lead. Once only in the history of the past year timid men might have been excused for thinking (as they did think and declare) that a decided act of the government would cause social revolution. This was during the affair of the Trent. Consult the unanimous bluster of the press, the intense feeling of our foreign population, the sensitive patriotism of Americans by birth, the clamorous objurgation of Judges, Governors and Mayors—in view of all this, there might have been some excuse for prophesying social revolution in case Mason and Slidell were returned. Yet we all remember the acquiescence which followed that necessary act. And the men, who have no word of condemnation for the imbecile policy which has sent our sons and brothers to die in vain, would have said, in case other tens of thousands had been sacrificed in a war with England, "Ah, it is all very shocking; but the government was obliged to keep the rebel commissioners, for a social revolution would have followed had they been given up!"

We have been thus explicit for the purpose of protesting against the course of certain political writers who have come to the conclusion that it is *now* about time to apply a little energetic morality to the treatment of our national affairs. They begin by flattering and defending the Administration and people for all that has hitherto been done, or left undone. Of this class a writer in the last *Christian Examiner* is an able representative. Now, we submit that this laudation of leaders, this puffery of the people, deserves to be buried in the grave where lie our old Fourth-of-Julys without hope of resurrection. Those in authority over us have deeply sinned; we, the people, have sinned also. The precise measure of guilt belonging to each, He who sees the heart can alone know. Sin is not a pleasant word. It may be hardly admissible in the expurgated theology of *The Examiner*. But it is the only word that can adequately explain our bitter humiliation. The old constitutional excuses for upholding slavery were swept away. But the depravity slavery had wrought continued with us, and the tender persuasions of *Policy* were as the counsels of respectable topers in the ears of a drunkard. National, as well as individual regeneration, must be preceded by an adequate sense of responsibility for the previous disorder. And it is the tendency of national pride, as of individual pride, to seek any remedy rather than confession of sin and its instant desertion. Yet this must be our salvation, if it is possible we can be saved.

The selfish politician's idea of the public character has ever been that the public had no character. He could never understand that men should love Freedom for anything but her material gifts, and when for a time these are disturbed, he comes to minister with his poor drug-sheet of anodynes where a healthy stimulant is only required. But if an energetic believer—one who believes the public has a character—shall haply struggle to the front, the country may yet follow him to an assured salvation. For there are truths that masses of men can fully realize only through bitter experience. Bred up, politically and socially, under the influence of slavery, we have been slow to recognize the moral degradation which is its inevitable attendant. Perhaps the last eighteen months were necessary to illustrate it fully. If the American people can, even now, lay to heart their bitter lessons, the future is not dark before us.

*

THE PRESIDENT'S COLONIZATION SCHEME.

VOICE OF THE COLORED PEOPLE OF PENNSYLVANIA.

PHILADELPHIA, August 15, 1862.

THE interview between the President and a Committee of colored men, touching the subject of colonization to Central America, as reported in the daily papers of to-day, is highly important to every colored man on this continent. It came upon us here like a clap of thunder from a clear sky. How necessary it is, therefore, in an issue of such very great moment, for colored men to be thinking and acting wisely with reference to this matter!

We have talked freely with a number of our leading men, since the interview appeared in the morning papers, and find but one opinion with all concerned on the subject, and that is a very decided objection to it.

The colored people of the principal Northern cities, such as Philadelphia, New York and Boston, should, it seems to us, be at once awakened to consider this grave proposition, and with your permission (we mean the permission of the Committee who appeared before the President) take counsel together.

We need not suggest how highly important it is that the response of the Committee shall be prepared with the utmost care, in order that it may tell with overwhelming force when read by our anxious people, as well as the public generally.

No previous time, in our humble judgment, has ever presented itself for a Committee of colored men, by a bold, judicious, manly, and righteous decision, to make an impression on the enlightened and civilized mind of the world, as in this instance.

Now, a few remarks directly touching our objections to the scheme.

To be asked, after so many years of oppression and wrong have been inflicted in a land and by a people who have been so largely enriched by the black man's toil, to pull up stakes in a civilized and Christian nation, and to go to an uncivilized and barbarous nation, simply to gratify an unnatural wicked prejudice emanating from slavery, is unreasonable and anti-Christian in the extreme.

How unaccountably strange it seems that wise men, familiar with the history of this country—with the history of slavery—with the rebellion and its merciless outrages—are yet apparently totally ignorant of the true cause of the war, or, if not ignorant, are afraid or ashamed to charge the guilt where it belongs.

Men profess to believe in God and the Bible, justice and humanity; but notwithstanding numerous examples in every age's history vividly showing how cruel has been the oppressor's rule, and how invariably his heinous practices have brought on wars and destruction, with God's sore displeasure and heavy judgments, it is easy, nevertheless, to find excuses to ignore truth, to defy God's vengeance and trample on his creatures.

Says the President: "The colored race are the cause of the war." So were the children of Israel the cause of the troubles in Egypt. So was Christ the cause of great commotions in Judea, in the same sense; and those identified with him were considered of the baser sort, and really unfit for citizenship.

But surely the President did not mean to say that our race was the cause of the war, but the occasion thereof.

If black men are here in the way of white men, they did not come here of their own accord. Their presence is traceable to the white man's lust for power, love of oppression and disregard of the plain teachings of the Lord Jesus Christ, whose rule enjoins upon all men to "do unto others as they would be done by." Although a man may have had the misfortune to fall among thieves, and become wounded and distressed by the wayside, the great Exemplar would not recognize the right of either the Levite or priest to shield them-

THE CAMP GAZETTE.

Vol. 1. Camp Joe Hooker, Lakeville, Mass., Saturday, Sep. 27, 1862. No. 3.

THE GAZETTE,
A News-paper Devoted to Local, Military and General News.
EDITED BY
S. B. PRATT,
AND PUBLISHED
EVERY SATURDAY MORNING.
Office—13 Water St., Middleboro, Mass.
TERMS.—$1.50 per annum. Single copies, 4 cents.
Advertisements inserted for $1.25 per square, of 12 lines, for 3 insertions; one shilling per week for each subsequent insertion.
Transient advertising must invariably be paid in advance.
Items of news well authenticated solicited as a special favor from all the towns in Plymouth County.
Job Printing, executed at this office, with neatness and despatch. Orders are solicited from subscribers and the public generally.

Subscribe for the Gazette.

Very often, lately, individuals have been disappointed in not finding single copies of the Gazette for sale. We print very few copies more than are necessary to supply our regular customers, hence the only sure way is to subscribe at once for a year or six months. Important events are transpiring in our midst every week. The soldier boys in service, would be pleased to learn these facts, and in no better way can they do so than through the columns of this paper. Subscribe then, and send them a remberance every week—they will thank you, we know.

Post Office.

A Post Office for the accommodation of the Camp, has been established in the Barber's Shop, near the right of the 4th Reg. All letters left there will be forwarded without delay, 3 times each day, and all letters received at the Middleboro office will be delivered at the several Headquarters, on their arrival, without extra expense, arriving on the ground about 9.30, 10.30 A. M., and 5 P. M. All those wishing to be served as above will notify their friends to direct to Middleboro, Camp Joe Hooker, with the Regiment and Company.

A. L. TINKHAM, P. M.
Middleboro, Sept. 22, 1862.

Insolvency Notice.

NOTICE Is Hereby Given that the Subscriber has been duly appointed Assignee of the estate of Dennis Shaw, of Middleboro', Insolvent Debtor, and has taken upon himself that trust by giving bonds as the law directs. All persons having demands upon the said insolvent debtor are hereby required to exhibit the same, and all persons indebted to said estate are called upon to make payment to

M. P. STANDISH, Assignee.

Commonwealth of Massachusetts.
PLYMOUTH, SS. Court of Probate
To all persons interested in the estate of Israel Cowen, late of Rochester, in said County, deceased. greeting;—

WHEREAS, Seth Miller jr., the Administrator of the estate of said deceased, has presented for allowance the first account of his administration upon the estate of said deceased: You are hereby cited to appear at a Probate Court to be holden at East Bridgewater in said County, on the first Tuesday of October next, at nine o'clock in the forenoon, to shew cause, if any you have, why the same should not be allowed. And said Seth Miller jr., is ordered to serve this citation by publishing the same once a week in the Middleborough Gazette, a newspaper printed at Middleborough, three weeks successively, the last publication to be two days at least before said Court.

Witness, Wm. H. Wood, Esquire, Judge of said Court, this twenty-sixth day of August, in the year of our Lord one thousand eight hundred and sixty-two.

D. E. DAMON, Register.

Commissioners Notice.

The undersigned having been duly appointed Commissioners to receive and examine all claims of creditors against the estate of Hira H. Kimball, late of Middleborough, in the County of Plymouth, deceased, will meet for that purpose, on the first Saturday of October and November next, at the office of E. Robinson, in said Middleborough, at one o'clock P. M.

Everett Robinson.
Ebenezer Pickins.

Middleborough. Sept. 3, 1862.

Poetry.

[From the New Orleans Delta.]

The Irish Picket.

BY MICHAEL MALLADOON OF THE 9TH CONN.

I'm shtanding in the mud, Biddy,
With not a spalpeen near,
And silence, spacheless as the grave,
Is all the sound I hear.
Me goon is at a showlder arms,
I'm wetted to the bone,
And whin 'im after snakin' out
I find meself alone.

This Southern climate's quare, Biddy,
A quare and bastely thing,
With winter absint all the year,
And summer in the spring.
Ye mind the hot place down below?
And may ye niver fear
I'd dthraw comparisons—but then
It's awful warrum here.

The only moon I see, Biddy,
Is one shmall star, asthore,
And that's fornint the viry cloud
It was behind before:
The watch-fires glame along the hill
That's swellin' to the South,
And whin the sentry passes them
I see his oogly mouth.

It's dead for shlape I am, Biddy,
And dramein shwate I'd be,
If them old rebils over there
Would only lave me free;
But whin I lane against a shtump,
And strive to get repose,
A musket ball be's comin' shtraight
To hit me spacious nose.

It's ye I'd like to see Biddy,
A shparkin' here wid me,
And then, avourneen, hear ye say,
"Acushla—Pat—machree!"
"Och, Biddy, darlint," then says I,
Says you, "get out of that;"
Says I, "me arrum mates your waist,"
Says you, "Be dacent Pat."

And how's the pigs and ducks, Biddy?
It's them I think of, sure,
That looked so innocent and shwate
Upon the parlor flure;
I'm sure you're aisy with the pig
That's fat as he can be,
And fade him wid the best, because
I'm towld he looks like me.

Whin I come home again, Biddy,
A sargeant tried and thrue,
It's joost a decent house I'll build,
And rint it chape to you.
We'll have a parlor, bedroom, hall,
A duck pond nately done,
With kitchen, pig pen, praty patch,
And garret—all in one.

But murthur! there's a baste, Biddy,
That's crapin' round a tree,
And well I know the crature's there
To have a shot at me.
Now, Mr. Rebel, say yer pray'rs
And howld yer dirty paw,
Here goes!—be jabers, Biddy dear,
I've broke his oogly jaw!

Articles needed by Soldiers.

Many enquires are being made as to what articles of comfort are most needed by our soldiers. Geo. B. Fittz, Esq., has received a letter from the Secretary of the Massachusetts Soldiers' Relief Society, at Washington, which he permits to be published for the information of our readers.

Washington, Sept. 11, 1862.

Mr Geo. B. Fitts, Dear Sir:—Yours of the 8th inst., is at hand. In reply I would say that the stock of lint and bandages now on hand is large, and with what will come in packages, now on the way and preparing, will supply all present wants.

Shirts, drawers and socks are very much needed, and I think if your Society can prepare such articles they will more effectually aid the Society that, perhaps, any other way. Slippers are much desired. Jellies, &c., if carefully packed will come safe, and be very gratefully received. It is well to put up jellies in small packages, say in tumblers or teacups, then they are ready for distribution.

The gratitude evinced by the recipients of these gifts from home is very great, and much good results from these small things; they meet wants that could be supplied in no other way.

Very Truly Yours,
J. E. Forbush.

Splendid thousand dollar swords have been made in New York, to be presented to Gens. Corcoran and W. T. Sherman, by their friends.

Gen. Bohlen's son died at Baden-Baden on the same day the Gen. was killed, Aug. 22.

It is asserted that Gen. McClellan's army drags after it six thousand army wagons. The rebels have very light baggage trains, hence the rapidity of their movements.

THE GAZETTE.

Saturday, Sep. 27, 1862.

Interesting Facts.

Sixty-one officers, prisoners at Richmond, and five thousand one hundred and ninety privates, have just been paroled by the rebels. Among them are said to be many who have been reported killed.

A "Liver Shark" was recently captured at Lubec, Me., whose liver, when cut up, filled eleven barrels and produced 170 gallons of pure oil, worth one dollar per gallon. The dimensions of the monster by actual measurement were, length, 30 feet, and girth around the body, 18 feet.

After seeing President Lincoln at Washington, it is said that Mr. Train intends to challenge Wendell Phillips to a great intellectual combat on the negro question.

In Preston, Eng., there are 23,000 persons receiving parochial and charitable relief. The population of the place is only 83,000.

The expenditures of the Confederate Government from its inaugeration to Aug. 1, 1862, amount to $374,272,956-86.

A gentleman in Philadelphia gave a tenant of his, to go as a substitute for his son, a house free from all incumberance, worth $4500. His wife and family have the property now in their possession.

It is said that about thirty acres of soldiers rallied in less than a week for the defence of Harrisburg Pa.

The other day, as a New York Regiment was about to depart, a private carelessly discharged his pistol, killing a lady, wife of a officer, who stood near. The lady had been married but the day before.

In Rochester N. Y., a deserter from the U. S. army being closely pursued fled into a restarant and took refuge under the cook's crinoline. The officers overlooked him and he is at large.

Mason and Slidell are said to be on the point of returning to America. It is thought Com. Wilkes, in his flying squadron, may renew his acquaintance with them.

Gen. Butler wears a steel breast-plate, as a guard against assassination, extending from his neck to his thighs, and that he has never been without it since his arrival in New Orleans.

The "Allen Pear Tree," in Salem, which is 224 years old, bore 13 bushels of fruit this year.

Among the novelties at the Chicago Horse Fair, are 24 wild buffaloes from the far West. They were to be let loose on the ground and a grand lasso hunt was to take place.

Raw eggs, two in twenty-four hours, are said to be good remedy for diarrhea. The remedy is simple and worthy of a trial.

A lady had her portrait taken; and a friend said to her little son, "Is it like your mamma?" "No, sir," he beautifully replied; "it wants the sunshine on it—her own smile."

"Every man that is capable of doing a secret injury is a coward."

Follow diligently God's precepts, and thou wilt receive great reward; but know that the payment of the reward of the righteous is in the future state.

If the spring put forth no blossoms, in summer there will be no beauty, and in autumn no fruit. So if youth be trifled away without improvement, middle life will be without usefulness, and old age miserable.

Prosperity gains friends; adversity tries them.

Gen Pope's Department of the North-West embraces Wisconsin, Iowa, Minnesota, Nebraska and Dakotah. His headquarters will be at St. Paul's, Minn.

Assistant Assessors—Rep. District 2.

Dist. No. 8. Bridgewater and East Bridgewater; Layfayette Keith of Bridgewater, Assistant Assessor.

Dist. No. 9. North Bridgewater and West Bridgewater; Franklin Ames of North Bridgewater, Assistant Assessor.

Dist. No. 10. Hanson and Hanover; George F. Stetson of Hanson, Assistant Assessor.

Dist. No. 11. Abington; Nath'l T. Hunt of Abington, Assistant Assessor.

Dist. No. 12. Marshfield, Scituate and South Scituate; Luther Hatch of Marshfield, Assistant Assessor.

Dist. No. 13. Hingham and Hull; Israel Whitcomb of Hingham Centre, Assistant Assessor.

Sixty-five vessels sailed last week from New York for Europe, carrying one million one hundred and forty thousand seven hundred and fifty-one bushels of grain, and forty thousand one hundred and thirty-eight barrels of flour, in addition to large quantities of provision and assorted merchandise.

☞Dr. Chapin, the celebrated Universalist divine, thus speaks of Henry Ward Beecher:—

"There is our large-souled Brother who preaches in Brooklyn, and who will permit every honest man to call him Brother, however much he may differ in opinion from him—why, his great heart, at every pulsation, leaps sixty degrees beyond the logical limits of his creeds. 'The voice is Jacob's voice, though the hands are the hands of Esau.'"

Arrangements are now in progress at Cincinnati for the manufacture of a newly invented revolving gun, which will discharge from one hundred and ninety to two hundred shots per minute.

General Fremont has made an affidavit that with the exception of certain claims on the Mariposa mines, he owns no property.

The infantry and artillery surrendered at Harper's Ferry was 11,593, with all their arms, and 50 cannon, and the loss in military stores is set down at a million of dollars. The cavalry, about 2300 in number, escaped at 9 o'clock Saturday evening, crossing to Maryland on the pontoon bridge.

A mother and her two children in Otis, Mass., were murdered on Sunday week. It is not known by whom the deed was perpetrated.

It is now reported that the Indians are now sueing for peace—and that a treaty has been made. We hope 'tis so.

Forgive.

The forgiveness of injuries is one of the most difficult of Christian duties. It is indeed so difficult, that it may be considered a test of Christian character. He who forgives readily, and returns good for evil, must have made high attainments in the divine life; while he who finds great difficulty in the exercise of this virtue, and in whose bosom rankle feelings of hatred and revenge, has great reason to look carefully into the grounds of his religious hopes. It is not enough to say that we forgive. Our forgiveness must be practical. We must show by our acts that we have truly forgiven. We must endeavor to do to our enemy as much good as he has done evil to us. By so doing we shall soften the heart of our enemy, and perhaps even win him over to goodness. Were this spirit of genuine forgiveness more common among those who profess to be actuated by Christian principles it would do much towards banishing injuries, and those dispositions which lead to them, from the face of the earth.

Daniel Webster's Remains.—Speaking of the burial of Col. Fletcher Webster at Marshfield, the Plymouth Rock adds:

"By request of Peter Harvey, Esq., and others, the oaken box containing the great statesman's coffin was opened and the metallic cover of the glass removed. How were the feelings of those personal friends stirred within them, to find those lineaments and features which no man ever looked upon to forget, retaining the same color and impress, natural as when ten years ago they gave him up to the grave.

The eyes were more sunken but the heavy shadows beneath the brows were always there in life. Even in death, and, for a decade, the captive of the grave, that kingly presence inspired the same deep reverence and speechless awe as when in the living temple of his matchless mind. The velvet pall with its rich embroidery was in perfect preservation though deprived of its primitive gloss."

Government Stamps.—It will be recollected that on the first day of next month, the law will go into effect, requiring Government stamps to be used upon all agreements, contracts, bank checks, drafts or orders for the payment of any sum of money exceeding $20 drawn upon any bank, person or corporation; bills of exchange, bills of lading, express packages, bonds of every description, certificates of stock, deeds of conveyance, mortgages, telegraph despatches, insurance policies, leases, manifests, powers of attorney, and all legal instruments; and any person signing or issuing any instrument, document, or paper without denoting the duty imposed thereon, or without having thereupon an adhesive stamp to denote said duty, will be subjected to a penalty of fifty dollars, and such instrument document or paper will be void and of no effect.—[Boston Transcript.

[From our Wednesday's Edition.]

Summary of Enlistments & Encampments.

The progress of enlistments and the condition of the various encampments in the State we shall review briefly. The 1st and 2d regiments are on the field and in active service.

The 3d and 4th are at Camp Joe Hooker, Lakeville.

The 5th regiment, Col. Pierson, of Salem, is at Camp Lander, Wenham, and has 754 men.

The 6th and 7th are off for the war, the former being the first nine months' regiments to leave the State; the latter a three years' regiment, having been in the service a long time and connected with the army of the Potomac.

The 8th regiment is at Camp Stanton, Boxford, under the command of Colonel Coffin, of Newburyport, with 778 men.

The Regiments from the 9th to 40th, all three years' corps, are away down South in Dixie, and have won and are winning imperishable honors. All, up to the 32d are constantly recruiting their thinned ranks.

The 41st regiment, Col. Thos. E. Chickering, Lieut. Col. Wass, is at camp Stanton, Boxford—the last of the three years' regiments. By latest official reports, there were 701 men connected with it. The 41st will go to New Orleans to reinforce General Butler, it is said.

The 42d regiment, (the old 20th) is at Camp Meigs, Readville, under the command of Col. Isaac S. Burrill, Roxbury. Some of their companies have been consolidated during the week. A few men have joined the regiment in squads, but none by full companies. The last official report put numbers of the 42d at 737.

The 43d regiment, Col. Holbrook—Captain Whiton, of Co. A, Acting Col.—is also at camp Meigs. Cos. B and C have been merged with Co. A. Captain Jno. J. Dyer of Co. B, and the other officers of Cos. B and C, retire from the service. The whole number of men in camp, by latest official returns, is 791; an increase of about 100 during the week.

The 45th—Cadet—regiment is also at camp Meigs under Col. Charles R. Codman. Their last official report is 657 men in camp.

The 46th Regiment will go into quarters at camp Banks, on what is known as the Luke Jones farm, three miles from Springfield. Col. Walker is in command of the post. It is expected that Rev. Geo. Bowler of Westfield, will be Colonel.

The 47th regiment, under Col. Marsh, numbered before 262 men, to which may be added the Jones Guard, of New Bedford, joined to the camp Friday evening. The 48th regiment, under the command of E. F. Stone, of Newburyport, who will be Lieut. Col., has seven companies now at camp Lander, Wenham, numbering 632 men. Capt. Carter of the regular army, and a son of Henry Carter, Esq., of Bradford, will be Col. He has had the advantages of a West Point education, and the experience of the war, having been in active service from its commencemant.

The 49th regiment is at camp Briggs, Pittsfield. Capt. Bartlett, of the 20th regiment, is Post Commandent.

The 50 regiment, Col. Messer, is at camp Stanton, Boxford. It has 701 men there, of whom three companies—not all full—are from Haverhill.

The 51st regiment, of which Rev. T. W. Higginson is to be Colonel, is at camp Wool, Worcester, under the command of Col. Geo. H. Ward, of the 15th regiment, who is at home on a furlough on account of his health. The whole ten companies are in camp with 886 men.

The 52d regiment will muster at camp Miller, Greenfield, this week.

The North Worcester, or 53d regiment, go into barracks this week at Groton Junction.

The 54th regiment—the Irish for 9 months—report 100 men recruited during the last week, and 250 in camp at Long Island.

The 10th battery, Capt. or Lieut. Granger, at Camp Stanton figures 163 men. It will not remain here much longer, but will go into action soon.

Capt. Jones' 11th battery last reports 152 men.

A tent has been opened within three days where recruits are received for the 12th Light Battery.

[From our Wednesday's Edition.]

Arrivals at the New Camp.

Co. I, Fairhaven, met in Phœnix Hall, on Monday morning, to witness the presentation of swords to the officers from that town; after which public exercises were held at the church, and speeches were made by Elbridge G. Morton, Esq., Horace Scott, Esq., Capt. A. Cox, and others. After religious exercises, conducted by Rev. John Willard the Company took the cars for Middleboro. Maj. Dunbar's drum corps escorted them up to the cars. A beautiful flag, upon which were inscribed the mottoes, "Freedom and the Nation," "Constitution and Union," and "Fairhaven," was carried in the ranks.

The same day, Co. I, of the 4th Regiment, composed of volunteers from Kingston, Duxbury, and all along shore, arrived at Haskin's depot.

Tuesday, another fine appearing Company—from Abington, Hanson and vicinity, arrived at Middleboro over the O. C. & F. R. R. R. The Abington brass band—17 pieces—came on with them.

Mustering in the Troops.

Capt. McLaughlin spent the day on Tuesday, mustering in the various companies in the two Regiments. A few men were thrown out for disabilities and two or three he sent home to put on petticoats because they refused to take the oath.

The Journal gives the following notice of the mustering officer:—

"Lieut. McLaughlin of the 4th U. S., Cavalry, who has for several months discharged the duties of mustering officer in this State, has been promoted to a Captaincy, com. bearing date, July 17. Capt. McLaughlin has earned this promotion by the faithful performance of his duties."

The Pleasures of Camp Life.

One who knows what Camp life is, writes:—"I could expatiate by the half column of the social fascinations of this life in barracks, of the genial friendships formed; of the glorious hearts discovered; of the roaring wit brought out by this free and easy companionship; of the freedom from conventinal restraints and the care of every-day pursuits. Do not, dear reader, think us too jolly and comfortable for soldiers, but rather thank Heaven for the sunny side and recompence of military life, which, perhaps, after all, but very feebly offset the shadows through which lies the pathway of him who takes up arms in defence of liberty imperiled as it is to-day."

The different Camps.

The whole number of men at Camp Stanton, Wool, Joe Hooker. Lander and Meigs is 8755, of which 877 are 3 years' men and 7878 nine months' men. Besides these there are supposed to be 205 more at Camp Day, of whom 37 are absent without leave—"skedaddled."

There are at Camp Briggs probably 600 men, at Long Island 260 men, and these added to what have been before enumerated, make in camp in the entire State 8728 nine months' volunteers. To this add the 800 who have gone in the 6th regiment, and it shows that 9528 nine months' men are recruited, besides those secured for the encampments that commence operations this week.

☞The officers of Eliot Light Guards, of New Bedford, received their commissions last Saturday.

☞The New Bedford City Guards are to have a chapter of scripture read every Sunday morning, in their barracks.

Religious Services.

Capt. Wm. H. Bartlett and Capt. Rev. Elihu Grant, conducted religious services last Sabbath in one of the unoccupied barracks. The meetings were interesting and the audience quite large.

Rev. Mr. Parsons of Mattapoisett, at the solicitation of some of his friends, has offered to go Chaplain of 3d reg. It would be a good appointment.

☞The new barracks are being put ahead rapidly by a gang of 80 men under the charge of S. W. Reed, of Middleboro. They are being built on the farm of Wm Harlow.

☞The Liquor trade in the vicinity of the camp is getting to be a great nuisance. We know either the camp or town authorities will soon interfere to stop the illegal traffic.

☞The barracks for the 4th Regiment, cost $4,900; those for the 3d Regiment, $4,750. These were the lowest bids sent in. Other parties offered to do them for $8,000 a regiment.

THE GAZETTE.

Saturday, Sep. 27, 1862.

PUBLISHER'S NOTICES.

Address Cards.

Just the thing for officers or privates to send away in their letters or give their friends who may call upon them in camp; neatly and expeditiously printed at this office. Price only 75 cents per pack of 50.

The Camp Gazette.

☞We believe this is the first camp in the State that has a newspaper connected with it.

We hope the officers and privates of camp Hooker, will lend us their aid in making this paper their organ.

Any communications of general interest to "the boys," or any little items of news occuring in camp will be thankfully received.

☞We intend—if the Camp patronage will warrant—to issue the Gazette semi-weekly, on Wednesday and Saturday mornings.

Hd. Qts. Camp Joe Hooker,
Lakeville, Mass., Sept. 23d, '62.
General Order, No. 2,

1. Immediately after Reveille Comp'y Commanders will turn out Companies and have their barracks thoroughly swept and the men's blankets neatly folded at the head of the bunks. Also, thoroughly police their Company grounds, commencing at the color line in front and police to the rear of the Company officer's quarters.

2. [Pertaining to the sanitary regulations, cook houses, &c.]

3. Not more than six men will be allowed passes from each Company at one time, unless in case of urgent necessity. All applications for 'leave' must be handed into this office before 8 a. m. The application must be signed by the first Sergeant and approved by their Captains. Leave of absence for commissioned officers must be approved by the commanding officer.

By Order Othniel Gilmore,
Commandant.
Augustus Crocker,
Acting Adjutant.

Hd. Qts., Camp Joe Hooker,
Lakeville, Mass., Sept. 16, '62.
General Order, No. 1.

The daily duties will be as follows until further orders:—

Reveille, 5 1-2 A. M.
Breakfast, 6 A. M.
Company Drill, 7 to 8 1-2 A. M., and from 9 1-2 until 11 1-2 A. M.
1st Sergeant's Call, 12 M.
Roast Beef, 12 1-2 P. M.
Co. Drill from 1 1-2 to 2 1-2 P. M.
Guard Mounting, 3 P. M.
Co. Drill from 3 1-2 to 4 1-2 P. M.
Retreat 5 1-2 P. M.
Supper Call immediately after.
Tattoo, 8 1-2 Tapps, 8 3-4

By Order Othniel Gilmore,
Commandant.
Augustus Crocker,
Act'g Adjt.

Roster of the Camp.

Othniel Gilmore, Command't of Camp.
Augustus Crocker, Post Adjutant.
T. J. Lothrop, Act'ng Post Quarter'tr.

3d Regiment.

Co. A, Halifax—Captain, John A. Marble, Freetown; 1st Lieut., Charles P. Lyon, Halifax; 2d Lieut. N Morton.

Co. B, Plymouth—Captain, T. B. Griffeth, Carver; 1st Lieut., C. A. S. Perkins, Plymouth; 2d Lieut., Wm. Briggs, Middleboro.

Co. C, Fall River—Captain. Rev. Elihu Grant, of Fall River; 1st Lieut, B. A. Shaw; 2d Lieut. C D. Copeland.

Co. D, Fall River—Captain, A. R Wright; 1st Lieut. Thos. McFarland; 2d Lieut. Geo. Reynolds, jr.

Co. E, New Bedford—Captain. John A. Hawes, Fairhaven; 1st Lieut., Wm. Emery Mason, New Bedford; 2d Lieut., James L. Sharp, New Bedford.

Co. F, New Bedford—Captain, George R. Hurlburt; 1st Lieu., W. H. Allen 3d; Johnath W. Davis, 2d Lieut, all of New Bedford.

Co. G, New Bedford—Captain, Wm. S. Cobb, 1st Lieut. H. W. Briggs; 2d Lieut. James L. Wilber.

Co. H, Rehoboth—Captain, Otis A. Baker, Rehoboth; 1st Lieut., Robert Crossman, Dighton; 2d Lieut., Joseph Gibbs, Somerset.

Co. I, Fairhaven—Captain, Barnabas Ewer, Jr., Fairhaven; 1st Lieut., Solomon K. Eaton, Mattapoisett; 2d Lieut., Jabez M. Lyle

Co. K, Bridgewater—Captain, Sam'l Bates, 1st Lieut., Nathan Forbes; 2d Lieut., C. E. Churchill.

4th Regiment.

Co. A, Canton—Captain, John Hall, Canton; 1st Lieut., Ira Drake, Stoughton; 2d Lieut., Henry M. Morse, Canton.

Co. B, Easton—Disbanded.

Co. C, Middleboro—Captain, Seneca R. Thomas, Middleboro; 1st Lieut., Daniel F. Wood, Middleboro; 2d Lieut., J. M. Sampson, Lakeville.

Co. D, Randolph—Captain. Hiram C. Alden; 1st Lieut., Myron W. Hollis; 2d Lieut., Edmund Cottle.

Co. E, Abington, and East Bridgewater—Captain, Lewis Soule; 1st Lieut., Henry Humble; 2d Lieut., John Malory, all of Abington.

Co. F, Foxboro—Captain, Charles F. Howard, Foxboro; 1st Lieut., Moses A. Richardson, Foxboro; 2d Lieut., Benjamin H. Richmond, Norton.

Co. G, Taunton—Captain, Cha's H. Paul; 1st Lieut., Wm. R. Black; 2d Lieut., Wm. J. Briggs, all of Taunton.

Co. H.

Co. I, Duxbury—Captain, H. B. McLaugh lin, Duxbury; 1st Lieut., Horatio C. Sampson, Pembroke; 2d Lieut., W. F. Holmes, Kingston.

Co. K, Taunton—Captain, Wm. H. Bartlett; 1st Lieut. John H. Church; 2d Lieut. Philander Williams, all of Taunton.

CAMP JOE HOOKER.

COMPANY ROLLS.

THIRD REGIMENT.

Company A.

HALIFAX.

Wm A Lyon,	Morton Thompson,
Chas W Soule,	Geo Drew 3d,
Perley Haven,	Martin L Holmes,
Lys'r W Hayward,	Horace F Packard,
Soranus Thompson,	Wm T Marston
Fred. E Fuller	Cyrus Wood,
Oliver C. Porter,	Almanzer Osborne,
Chas T Whitney	

HANSON.

Wm W Hood,	Henry Cooke,
Alg'n A Patterson,	M V Bonney,
John Drayton,	Thacher Keen,
Seth M Briggs,	Thos W Bourney,
Augu's M Sampson,	Isaah Stetson,
Tho Gurney 2d,	Benj H Bearce,
Elbridge G Fuller,	Chas H Stetson,
Jacob P. Hill,	Horatio N Hood,
Bernard C Beal,	

KINGSTON.

J H Thompson,	Chas H Thayer,

HANOVER.

Judson Studley,	Alonzo Howland,
Truman E Niles,	Allen F Bonney,
Leander Torrey,	Oren F Whiting,
Wm F Stetson,	Joseph Vinal,
Abel H Whiting,	

PEMBROKE.

Darius B Mason,	Marcus T Perry,
John G Bonney,	

BRIDGEWATER.

Zacheus Lambert,	Francis M Lambert,

NO. CHELSEA.

Jos S W Richmond,	

FREETOWN.

Stephen Hathaway,	S G Howland,
Fred. Thayer,	Francis G Briggs,
David B Hill,	Andrew T Hamly
Geo F Wilcox,	A J Hathaway,
Marcenah B Wilcox,	James H Haskell,
Frank J Chace,	James H Hathaway,
Edwin H Rennis,	B A Winslow,
Geo Durfee,	T W Murtaugh,
Eph H Haskins,	Andrew Horr,
Uriah Haskins,	S D Rounseville,
Geo H Haskins,	E S Rounseville,
Sumner J Chipman,	Asa Spooner,
Albert D Ashley,	

BERKLEY.

B G Hathaway,	Hercules Dean,
James E Arnold,	Saml W Phillips,
Dan'l F Hathaway,	Timothy E French,
John Boyce,	

WESTPORT.

John G Gammons,	James H Petty,
Nich. B Anthony,	Saml S Broadbent,

LAKEVILLE.

Otis Haskins,	

Company B.

PLYMOUTH.

Job B Oldham,	Benj S Jenkins,
James H Robbins,	Chas W Johnson,
Amasa M Bartlett,	Geo F Jackson,
Charles M Perry,	James Neal,
Thomas B Atwood,	Chas C Place,
Benj F Barnes,	Isaac H Place,
Ebenezer N Bradford	James T Paulding,
Charles S Cobb,	Edward L Robbins,
John F Chapman,	Sam'l B Raymond,
Rob't B Churchill,	Isaac S Holmes,
Geo H Doten,	Leander L Sherman,
Harvey B Greffeth,	Wm F Spooner,
Martin L Harlow,	Thos Smith,
Nath'l Holmes,	Thos Sears,
Samuel N Holmes,	Philip M Washburn,
Ivory W Harlow,	

CARVER.

Charls W Griffeth,	Allen M Cobb,
Asa Shaw,	Henry A Dunham,
Geo H Shaw,	Ellis D Dunham,
John M Cobb,	Wm Erwin,
Andrew D Merritt,	John Murdock,
Stephen T Atwood,	Geo N Shaw,
Ebenezer E Atwood,	E Watson Shaw,
Josiah W Atwood,	Alonzo D Shaw,
Nath'l S Bates,	Nath'l Shaw, jr.,
James H Bates,	Andrew Stringer,
John B Chandler,	Jesse M Shaw,
Chas S Chase,	G W Tillson,
Wm H Cornell,	Joseph G Washburn,
Sidney O Cobb,	Ansel B Ward,
Wm B Chandler,	

PLYMPTON.

Benj S Atwood,	Thos M Leach,
Wm S White,	Isaac F Lobdell,
Frank Bryant,	Prince Penniman,
Wm H Bradford,	James E Sherman,
Robert Dempsey,	E Sculyler Wright,

MIDDLEBORO.

Gideon Shurtleff,	Cornelius Remsdell,
James Briggs,	Marcus Willis,
Geo Darling	Henry Wrightington
Bartlett A Lucas,	

WAREHAM.

John D Manter,	John R Oldham,
Joseph T Nickerson,	John Sampson,
Hiram W Bumpus,	Geo H Holmes,
Hosea C Bumpus,	John D Manter,
John M Bartlett,	Jos T Nickerson,
Eben Burgess,	John R Oldham,
John W Gammons,	John Sampson,
Sylvester T Hall,	

KINGSTON.

Chas E Bryant,	Winthrop H Mange,
James Donley,	Henry F Perkins,

E. BRIDGEWATER.

Barzilla F Ellis.	

ROCHESTER.

Salem Jefferson,	Thos W Raymond.
Moses Peirce,	

Conundrums.

Why is it thought our Middleboro Company will be able to keep warm?

Ans.—Because they have taken *Wood* and *Cole* along with them.

Why do we suppose they will be kept in good repair?

Ans.—Because they have one *Mend-all* with them.

Camp Items.

The Easton Company.

This Company seems to have a hard lot. For years, we are told, it has had to contend against the influence of the leading men of the place. Even the Selectmen gave it the cold shoulder by advising the volunteers from the town to join any company they chose. Last Saturday, about thirty members of the company, under command of Capt. Milo Williams, came on to the ground. Since then they have concluded it would be impossible to fill the ranks to the minimum number, and the company will probably be disbanded. Some of the men will join other companies and some will return home.

☞The Bridgewater men have received their bounty. Nine persons from N. Bridgewater, who were recommended by the Selectmen of that town, to join the Bridgewater company, now that they have been sworn in, find they cannot expect bounty from the latter place. N. Bridgewater gives $100 and Bridgewater $150 each. They thus find themselves minus $50 apiece.

In our list of arrivals we should have reported Co. E, 4th Regiment, from South Abington, East Bridgewater and vicinity, instead of Hanson. Twenty-three of the men are from East Bridgewater. The commissioned officers we give in the Roster.

☞The new barracks are nearly completed. Only the roofs of the buildings are shingled, and yet—counting 265 nails to the pound—more than 364,700 shingle nails are used on one set of buildings. Of all kinds of nails, it requires about four tons to a regiment.

☞The Middleboro company wish us to return thanks to Mr. Michael Toole for a barrel of apples and a half bushel of grapes. Such generosity is not forgotten by "the boys."

☞The non-commissioned officers of the 3d and 4th have not generally been appointed.

☞An express messenger leaves New Bedford twice a day for Camp Joe Hooker.

☞Many of the men in camp have given up the use of straw and are sleeping on bare boards.

☞Col. Gilmore, Commandant of the Post, has detailed John Sullivan, of Co. C, 3d Regiment, for camp Post Master, His office is at the Quartermaster's.

☞The members of the Plymouth Co. were not sworn in last Tuesday, on account of the absence of some of them to attend the funeral, at Plymouth, of Mr. Frank Thomas—who died in the service.

Some of the town officers have been paying the promised bounty during the past week. We noticed the little fellow who acts as the Mayor of Fall River—on the ground Thursday.

Mr. Editor:—Have you seen the splendid flag our Randolph neighbors of Co. D, 4th Reg., have hoisted on their barracks.
GLORY.

YES, we have!

For the Gazette.

Mr. Editor:—Can you tell us when the Coaches for Middleboro Depot arrive and depart?

It is not very pleasant to miss them about every other day.
SOLDIER.

We cannot tell. Probably the time-table will soon be made public.—[Ed.

Several of the Companies have engaged the services of barbers in their own barracks.

☞Daniel Lucas, Esq., of the "Railroad Accommodation" has our thanks for favors.

The workmen at the Brooklyn Navy Yard, a large proportion of whom are Irish, are delighted at a late act of Secretary Welles. One of the vessels now in course of construction at the Yard, under the supervision of Mr. Delano, is to be called the "Shamrock." The Irish workmen declare that Mr. Lincoln "should man her with Irishman and send her after the 290." It is quite certain that of an Irishman naval frigate were wanted, and a regular navy-built man-of-war called Shamrock, made flagship, no drafting would be required to provide a crew in Brooklyn.

" It is insisted that Masons are often profane and irreverent. I answer that the Mason who profanes the name of God dishonors his profession and disgraces himself. Such Masons are poisoning adders in the garden of her virtues, and the Lodge that permits its members to indulge in profanity, or in the practice of any of the vices, will ultimately find itself, and justly too, looked upon with suspicion and distrust. Every Mason should remember in this respect that he has a duty to perform, to fit himself as a living stone for the Great Temple."—[Stoneman.

The 18th Regiment.

Our boys, it seems, have been in another engagement. Several members of Co. D, were wounded, though we do not learn that any were killed.

On Thursday, the wife of Sergeant Wm. H. Carl, received word that he was in the hospital at Baltimore, severely wounded, and requesting her to come on.

Private J. R. Merrick, it is said was wounded.

The following account of the skirmish with the rebels on the south side of the Potomac opposite Sharpsburg on Saturday last is from the New York Herald:

Between eight and nine o'clock Saturday morning, Gen. Martindale's brigade, of Morell's division, Porter's corps commanded by Col. Barnes, crossed the Sharpsburg ford and formed in line of battle near a bluff, about a quarter of a mile from the ford, and directly on the bank of the river. They had scarcely done this before the enemy emerged in overwhelming numbers from a piece of woods a short distance ahead, and commenced a galling fire of musketry. They then advanced in close column, and the Union troops were ordered not to fire, as it was our own men advancing. This order arose from the fact that the enemy's column was headed by a red [illegible] flag, and those in the [illegible] soldiers. It was supposed to be a party of our men who had previously gone over the river with a flag of truce for the purpose of bringing our wounded soldiers across, who had been made prisoners by the enemy; but when the rebels continued firing and advancing, it became evident that this was a heartless ruse, invented for the purpose of deceiving our men, and to enable them at the same time to approach near enough to render their fire effective, without receiving that of our men. At last they were recognized, and though the rebels numbered five to our one, the gallant fellows returned their fire, and would have met the charge bravely (the enemy advancing for that purpose), had not the regiment which composed the right wing of our little force beome somewhat panic-stricken. Even after their right was exposed, an effort was made to recover it and meet the advancing foe, a regiment being ordered for that purpose; but before this could be accomplished the enemy had turned our right and opened a galling cross fire, doing terrible execution.

The order to retreat was now given, and in the greatest disorder and confusion our men started for the river, leaving their dead and wounded behind, and followed by the enemy, who shouted and yelled like demons. firing as they ran. They even followed our men into the river, bayoneting and shooting them, while those on the banks continued firing as long as our men were in sight. All the troops on the Virginia side were ordered to return with as much speed as possible as it was not known what force the enemy might have in the neighborhood. In the mean time several batteries had been placed in position on a commanding hill on the Maryland side, and a short distance to the left of the bluff, near which our force was attacked. Shot and shell rained among the enemy; but this did not deter him from following up his victory, for while a man remained in reach of their rifles they continued to fire. Scores of the wounded and dying met a watery grave. A large number of our men were taken prisoners. It is feared that our shells did more harm among our own men than to the enemy, while covering the retreat of our men across the river. Fifteen were under the arch of an old mill.—One of our shells burst in the arch, killing and wounding all but one, Edward Wilkinson, of Company [illegible] Pennsylvania.

There was no artillery to support the brigade. The night previous all had been reported quiet, a regiment had been over early in the morning, but returned without having seen the enemy.

The following names of New England men are in the list of wounded in the affair mentioned above: C. C. Knowlton, 22d Mass.; George C. Henghe Jo. Seigler, Smith O'Brien, Lieut. J. Htchinson. 13th Mass.; G. W. Carver, J. E. titzer, M. Silcox, 18th Mass.; J. Bender, 15th Mass.; J. R. Doolittle 8th Conn.; Moses Vazir, 2d Maine; Geo. Waterhouse, Charles L. Southard, 20th Me.

The Cattle Show and Fair for Plymouth County is to be held at Bridgewater on Thursday and Friday of next week. In our advertising columns will be found the official programme for the occasion.

Middlebro Items.

Singular.

Considerable excitement exists in some circles in town, on account of the strange musical phenomena that has been witnessed by large numbers, for several successive evenings. Persons sitting quietly around a table, in a dark room, receive quite heavy raps on various parts of the head and chest; beautiful tunes are played on common house bells, some of them having no tongues; guitar strings are played upon in unison with the beating of a drum hung high upon the wall; tambourines lying upon the floor or sailing in air, beat out old fashioned breakdowns; table cloths are taken from the stand, folded up nicely and laid over a person's shoulder, some feet distant; a large stand comes whizzing over the heads of spectators and lands in the centre of the table; and various other unaccountable things take place.

☞Mr. C. C. Burnett has furnished us with some splendid specimens of pears of several varieties. Some of the "Flemish Beauties" measure upwards of 12 inches in circumference, and weigh 13 ounces. Mr. B. is a great amateur in the pear line. He has more than 200 trees.

☞Prof. J. W. P Jenks was to read his lecture—A Day in the Alps—before the Massachusetts Teachers' Association, at Yarmouth, last evening.

☞A heavy frost in this vicinity, last Thursday night.

☞Four Pumpkins weighing 50 lbs. and vine 26 lbs., grew from one seed planted July 4th and gathered Sept. 18th, on the farm of Mr. Thomas Washburn, of Middleboro.

New England Soldiers,

The following is an extract from an unpublished letter from General Washington to Mr. Lund Washington, dated New York, June 12th, 1776:

"We have lately had a general review and I am much pleased in informing you that we made a better appearance and went through our exercises more like soldiers than I had expected. The southern states are rash and blameable in the judgment they form of their brethren of the four New England states. I do assure you, with all my partiality of my own countrymen, and predjudices against them, I cannot but consider them as the flower of the American Army. They are a strong, vigorous and hardy people inured to labor and toil, which our people seldom are; though our hot and eager spirits suit better sudden and desperate enterprise, yet in the way in which wars are now carried on, you must look for permanent advantage only from that patient and persevering temper which is the result of labor.

"The New Englanders are cool, considerate and sensible, while we are all fire and fury. Like their climate they maintain an equal temperature, whereas we cannot shine but we burn. They have a uniformity and a stability of character to which the people of no other states have any pretensions; hence, they must and will always preserve their influence in this great empire. Were it not for the drawbacks and disadvantages which the influence of their popular opinion on the subject of government have on their army, they soon might, and probably would, give law to it."

REPUBLICAN CONVENTION.

The Republicans and all in the first Congressional District, who support the present National and State Governments, and are in favor of the use of all means necessary for the effectual suppression of the Rebellion, are requested to send one delegate for each town and each ward of a city, and one additional Delegate for every two hundred votes, and one for every fraction over one hundred votes in each town or ward, according to the last census of voters, to a Convention to be holden at BARNSTABLE, on WEDNESDAY, the Eighth of October next, at 12 o'clock M., for the purpose of nominating a Candidate for Congress, for said District, and for the transaction of any other business that may properly come before them.

Walter C. Durfee, Fall River,
Robert C. Pitman, New Bedford,
Horace Scott, Fairhaven,
F. C. Adams, Kingston,
Samuel Osborn, Jr., Edgartown,
Charles F. Swift, Yarmouth,
Members of State Cen'l Com.

Auditors Meeting.

The Auditors of Accounts for this town, will meet at the Town Clerk's Office, on Monday, the thirteenth day of October next, at one o'clock P. M.

NOAH C. PERKINS, Auditor's Clerk.

Middleboro, Sept. 25, 1862.

THE FIRST IRISH REGIMENT EN ROUTE FOR THEIR CAMP. Our adopted citizens of Irish origen in Massachusetts, after overcoming a series of obstacles and difficulties, in attempting to organize another regiment made up of their gallant countrymen, have at last succeeded in their patriotic movement. Yesterday three full companies were mustered into the service of the United States, and before the end of the week two others will be sworn in; as more than 300 additional recruits are now waiting at the different rendezvous of the regiment ready to elect their officers and to receive their positions in the regiment. The companies already organized and accepted leave this afternoon for the regimental camp, at Lakeville, chosen by Adjutant General Schouler, and situated on the Old Colony Railroad. The camping ground is an excellent one, in every respect; beautifully situated, in a healthy location, and always accesible. One of the greatest difficulties the gentlemen engaged in raising the regiment encountered was to [illegible] Colonel whose social standing, name and military capacity would fit him for the post, and would give confidence to the men, as well as a character to the regiment. At last they have fixed on one of the descendants of Ireland's ancient chieftains a gentleman whose name alone has been the wild war cry in many a hard fought battle against the Saxon and the Dane. "O'Brien aboo" has been shouted in fierce exultation by many a fiery Celt when flinging himself against the serried hosts of invaders of his native land and from the days of Brien the Brave, when at Clontarf, that noblest of Ireland's chiefs forever freed his country from the pirates of the North, down to that hour when, in our own strife, the young and gifted Fitz James O'Brien, the aid of General Lander, fell by a murderous shot when fighting hand to hand with the rebel Ashby himself, the name of O'Brien has been associated with nearly every battle-field of the Old World and the New World too. Col James O'Brien of the First Irish Regiment is a lineal descendant of one of the oldest and most martial families of Ireland; he was educated to the profession of a soldier in one of the best military schools, and for the past nine years has been a field officer in different regiments in the West and in New England. The choice the Executive Committee of this regiment has made in the selection of Col. O'Brien is an excellent one and will give great satisfaction to all parties. Nothing is now wanting to make the First Irish Regiment for nine months' service, one of the best sent from Massachusetts. The regiment was commenced under the auspices of he Irish societies of Boston and vicinity.—[Boston Journal, Friday.

☞Job Haskins, H. A. Swift and his son were rejected from Co. C, 4th Reg., by the Mustering Officer.

☞John W. King and Orderly Sergeant John Haskell, of the 18th, have been paroled and are at Annapolis.

To the Hon. County Commissioners of the County of Plymouth.

We, the undersigned, inhabitants and legal voters of the town of Rochester, in said county, respectfully represent, that public necessity and convenience require a new public highway to be laid out and established by your Honorable Board, in said town of Rochester, commencing ten rods in a Westerly direction (keeping in the public highway) from the Liberty Pole, located a few rods in front of Theophilus King's Store, in said Rochester, thence in a Northerly and Easterly line, running between the store aforesaid, and the stable of James Ruggles, and through the lands of the said Ruggles and King, and lands of George Bonney, Sophia Bolles and Anselm Record, all of said Rochester, and terminating within twenty rods of the dwelling house of said Anselm Record, crossing the public highway leading from the dwelling house of H. J. Tripp, to the dwelling house of Joseph Coe And your petitioners would respectfully recommend to your Honorable body, that, should you deem it right and proper to locate a new highway as hereby prayed for, that you cause it to be laid out fifty feet wide, the whole distance you shall order built:—and in duty bound will ever pray.

JOSEPH COE, and Others.

Rochester, July 28, 1862.

Commonwealth of Massachusetts.

Plymouth ss.

At a regular meeting of the County Commissioners, begun and holden at Plymouth, within and for the County of Plymouth, on the first Tuesday of August in the year 1862.

UPON the petition aforesaid, ordered, that the Commissioners meet for the purpose of viewing the premises on the twenty-first day of October next, at the dwelling house of C. H. Leonard, in Rochester, in said county, at ten o'clock in the forenoon; and it is further ordered, that attested copies of the said petition with the order of the Commissioners thereon, be served, published in the Middleborough Gazette, and posted, according to law, that all persons and corporations interested in the premises may be duly notified to appear at the time and place aforesaid, if they see cause, and be heard thereon.

Attest: *Wm. H. Whitman, Clerk*
True copy of the petition and order thereon.
Attest: *Wm. H. Whitman, Clerk*
True copy of the petition and order thereon.
JAMES BATES.

Commonwealth of Massachusetts.

Plymouth, SS. Probate Court.

To all persons interested in the estate of Samuel B. Besse, late of Wareham, in said County, deceased. Greeting:

WHEREAS, Seth Miller, jr., the Administrator of the Estate of said deceased, has presented for allowance the first account of his administration upon the estate of said deceased: You are hereby cited to appear at a Probate Court to be holden at East Bridgewater, in said County, on the first Tuesday of October next, at nine o'clock in the forenoon, to shew cause, if any you have, why the same should not be allowed. And said Seth Miller, jr., is ordered to serve this citation by publishing the same once a week in the Middleborough Gazette, a newspaper printed at Middleborough, three weeks successively, the last publication to be two days at least before said Court.

Witness, Wm. H. Wood, Esquire, Judge of said Court, this twenty-sixth day of August, in the year of our Lord one thousand eight hundred and sixty-two.

D. E. DAMON, Register.

Agricultural Notice.

THE Members of the Agricultural Society of the County of Plymouth, are hereby notified that their next Annual Meeting for the choice of Officers and Trustees will be held in their Exhibition House, in Bridgewater on Thursday the 2d day of October, next, at 3 o'clock P. M., that being the first day of the Exhibition.

Also, a meeting of the Trustees of said Society will be held on the same day at the same place, at 10 o'clock A. M.

By order of
CHARLES G. DAVIS, Pres.,
W. LATHAM, Secretary.
Bridgewater, Sept. 9, 1862. 46t2

WAREHAM BANK.

The Annual Meeting of the Stockholders of the Wareham Bank, for Choice of Directors and transaction of any other legal business, will be held at their Banking House, on MONDAY, Oct. 6th, 1862, at ten o'clock, A. M.

T. R. MILES, Cashier.

Wareham, Sept. 15th, 1862.

Special Notices.

IMPORTANT FACTS.—CONSTANT WRITING for six months is done cheaper with Gold Pens than with Steel Pens; therefore it is economy to use Gold Pens.

The Gold Pen remains unchanged by years of continued use, while the steel pen is ever changing by corrosion and wear; therefore, perfect uniformity of writing is obtained only by the use of the Gold Pen.

The Gold Pen is always ready and reliable, while the steel pen must be often condemned and a new one selected; therefore, there is great saving of time in the use of the Gold Pen.

Gold is capable of receiving any degree of elasticity, so that the Gold Pen is exactly adapted to the hand of the writer; therefore, the nerves of the hand and arm are not injured, as is known to be the case by the use of the steel pens.

See "The Pen is Mightier than the sword," in the next column.

A Lyric.

What makes me laugh when others sigh,
No tears can e'er bedew mine eye,
It is because I always buy—
Herrick's Pills.
What is it makes me hale and stout,
And all my friends can't make it out,
I really could not live without—
Herrick's Pills.
So if you're sad, or grieved, or ill,
Pray do not pay a doctor's bill,
But take a dose of magic pills—
Made by Herrick.

Put up with English, Spanish, German & French directions. Price 25 cents per box. Sugar Coated. Sold wholesale and retail, by all dealers in cities.
See advertisement on third page.

Dr. Hudson's Female Remedy.

THIS is the greatest remedy ever yet offered for diseases to which females are liable, such as Irregularities, Obstructions or Suppressions to the Monthly Periods. Also, Leucorrhœa or Whites, with all their attending evils. This remedy consists of three parts and can be used single or together, as the case may demand. Full directions given with each number, which are so plain that all may use them with perfect safety.—No 3 is expressly for Leucorrhœa or Whites. Nos. 1 and 2 for Obstructions or Suppressions, and must not be used in connection by married ladies. Price $1 per number Can be sent to any direction by express.

DR. JOSEPH HUDSON, Sole Proprietor, Mattapoisett, Mass. 41-1y*

A Friend in Need. Try It

DR. SWEET'S INFALLIBLE LINIMENT is prepared from the receipt of Dr. Stephen Sweet, of Conneticut, the great bone setter, and has been used in his practice for the last twenty years with the most astonishing success. As an external remedy it is without a rival, and will alleviate pain more speedily than any other preparation. For all Rheumatic and Nervous Disorders it is truly infallible, and as a curative for Sores, Wounds, Sprains, Bruises, &c., its soothing, healing and powerful strengthening properties, excite the just wonder and astonishment of all who have ever given it a trial. Over four hundred certificates of remarkable cures, performed by it within the last two years, attest this fact. Sold by all Dealers.

To Horse Owners.

DR. SWEET'S INFALLIBLE LINIMENT FOR HORSES is unrivaled by any, in all cases of Lameness, arising from Sprains, Bruises or Wrenching, its effect is magical and certain. Harness or Saddle Gall, Scratches, Mange, &c., it will also cure speedily. Spavin and Ringbone may be easily prevented and cured in their incipient stages, but confirmed cases are beyond the possibilities of a radical cure. No case of the kind, however, is so desperate or hopeless but it may be alleviated by this Liniment, and its faithful application will always remove the Lameness, and enable the horse to travel with comparative ease.

Every horse owner should have this remedy at hand, for its timely use at the first appearance of Lameness will effectually prevent those formidable diseases mentioned, to which all horses are liable, and which render so many otherwise valuable horses nearly worthless. Sold by all Dealers.

MATHEWS' VENETIAN LIQUID HAIR DYE.

THIS celebrated Dye was first prepared in 1845; since that time it has been USED BY THOUSANDS, and in no instance has it failed to give PERFECT SATISFACTION.

THE VENETIAN DYE
Is the cheapest in the world. Its price is ONLY FIFTY CENTS, and each bottle contains DOUBLE THE QUANTITY OF DYE contained in those usually sold for $1.

The Venetian Dye
Is the safest composition of its class. It is WARRANTED NOT TO INJURE the hair, or the scalp, in the slightest degree.

The Venetian Dye
Works with RAPIDITY AND CERTAINTY. It causes no annoyance or trouble to those who use it.

The Venetian Dye
Produces any shade that may be desired—one that will not fade, crock, nor wash out; one that is as permanent as the hair itself.

The Venetian Dye
Does not, in any manner, interfere with the NATURAL SOFTNESS OF THE HAIR: it neither scorches nor dries it.

The Venetian Dye
Is the best, cheapest, safest, most convenient, most successful, and most *permanent* Dye ever used.

The Venetian Dye
Having gained an extended reputation, the public are CAUTIONED against purchasing any prepared in the same style, under the same or different name, as they are mere imitations, and liable to do injury.
For Sale by all Druggists. Prepared only by
A. I. MATHEWS.

A New Pattern of Chimney

For Kerosene Lamps, which will stand heat without breaking!
And which reflects more light than any other chimney in use, For Sale by
G. H. DOANE.
Middleboro.

BONNET AND HAT BLEACHERY.

BONNETS Bleached, Dyed and Pressed, at the "Old Academy." N. W. & J. M. LEONARD;
Middleboro, April 17, 1862.

Administrator's Notice.

NOTICE IS HEREBY GIVEN, that the Subscriber has been duly appointed Administrator of the estate of Andrew Cole, late of Middleborough, in the County of Plymouth, deceased, and has taken upon himself that trust, by giving bonds as the law directs. All persons having demands upon the estate of said Andrew Cole, are hereby required to exhibit the same; and all persons indebted to the said estate are called upon to make payment to
JAMES COLE, JR, Adm'r.

ATTENTION!

The subscriber hereby gives notice that he has taken the rooms in the basement of the American Building formerly occupied by Joseph L. Pease, where he will attend to the repairing of Boots & Shoes, and the making of Common Brogans, sewed or pegged.
J. C. JENNY.

The Rubber Man Is still in Town.

Old Rubber Boots & Shoes and all other kinds of Rubber Goods repaired at short notice, and made better and stronger than new, no matter how badly worn. Having lately made several new and successful experiments I can now warrant all work to stick until completely worn out. Rubber soles applied to leather boots will wear twice as long as leather, and is a sure preventative against slipping.

Don't send your rubbers to Boston when you can get them done better and cheaper at this place.

All orders by express or otherwise promptly attended to. J. M. BLANCHARD, No. 371, Main St., No. Bridgewater.

W. F. Brett's Sons,

HAVE this day opened a good assortment of English and American Tapestry, Three-ply, Superfine and lower qualities of WOOL CARPETS; OIL CLOTH DO., of all widths; Straw, Hemp and Cotton, which they offer to buyers very cheap for cash.

ALSO,
A Large Asortment of
CROCKERY AND GLASS
WARE!

and invite buyers to call.
No. Bridgewater, March 20, 1862. 21-tf

Wm. F. BRETT'S SONS,

DEALELS IN
DRY GOODS,

WOOL CARPETINGS, all qualities.
COTTON DO.
OIL CLOTH DO., 1-2 to 2 1-2y
Plain & Check STRAW MATTINGS.
CROCKERY & GLASS WARE.
BOOTS & SHOES.
North Bridgewater, March 17, '62.

A CHANGE
SOMETHING NEW.

THE Subscriber having again taken charge of his old Room, (recently occupied by L. B. HOWARD), is prepared to furnish

PHOTOGRAPHS & AMBROTYPES

of such quality, and upon such terms, as to make it an **object** for persons to give him a call.

☞Particular attention given to **Copying** from other likenesses, in which he intends to be excelled by none. Also by means of a

Multiplying Camera

recently procured—of which he has the **Only One in this vicinity**, he can furnish GOOD LIKENESSES, suitable to be sent by mail, at

Fifty Cents a Dozen!

Don't fail to give him a call and see for yourself.

S. W. S. HOWARD.
North Bridgewater, July 19, '62.

S. COLBY & Co.,
Union Block,

Main Street, Taunton.

Extensive Ready-Made Cloh ing Establishment, with Custom Department

attached.

☞One price marked in plain figures on each article offered for sale. 28

"Oak Hall Branch,"

MRS. J. F. MASON,
Millinery & Bonnet Rooms.

☞ Bonnets and Hats Whitened and Pressed in an improved style.
No. 47 Main St Taunton.
A share of patronage is solicited. 35

GOOD NEWS

TO THE PEOPLE OF
MIDDLEBORO
AND VICINITY,
WHO VISIT NEW BEDFORD.

WE have decided to mark our goods after this date at a VERY MUCH less profit than ever before. Cosequently with our Superior Advantages in the way of purchasing, we shall offer our stock as Low as the ordinary Whole Sale Prices, at the

Original One Price Clothing Store,

Opposite the Custom House, North Street,
New Bedford.
Packard & Kingman.

P. S.—Onr Clothing is NEW and FRESH and styles all right for the present Spring and Summer trade.

W. F. TINKHAM,

Manufacturer of
MEN'S, BOYS' AND YOUTH'S
Brogans and Oxford Ties:
and dealer in LADIES' MISSES' and CHILDREN'S
BOOTS, SHOES & RUBBERS:
Hats, Caps,
THE BEST PERFUMERY, &C., &C.
Opposite the Hotel, (3) **Bridgewater**

Clergymen, Proffessors and Judges, have and are using the NORWEGIAN LINIMENT, and speak in the highest praise of its beneficial results.
Sold by S. H. SYLVESTER.

GEO. F. HARTWELL,
Merchant Tailor,

AND DEALER IN
Ready - Made Clothing,
FURNISHING GOODS,
HATS, CAPS, UMBRELLAS, TRUNKS, VALISES, &C.
183, MAIN ST., WELLS BLOCK,
46 Middleboro, Mass.

THE
HORACE WATER
MODERN IMPROVED
OVERSTRUNG BASS
Full Iron Frame
PIANOS

Are justly pronounced by the Press and Music Masters to be superior Instruments. They are built of the best and most thoroughly seasoned materials, and *will stand any climate*. The tone is very deep, round, full and mellow; the touch elastic. Each Piano warranted for three years. Prices from $175 to $700.

OPINIONS OF THE PRESS.—"The Horace Waters Pianos are known as among the very best. We are enabled to speak of these instruments with some degree of confidence, from personal knowledge of their excellent tone and durable quality."—*New York Evangelist.*

"We can speak of the merits of the Horace Waters Pianos from personal knowledge, as being of the very best quality."—*Christian Intelligencer.*

$150.—NEW 7-OCTAVE PIANOS in Rosewood cases, iron frames, and overstrung bass, of different makers, for $150; do., with mouldings, $160; do., with carved legs and inlaid nameboard, $175, 185, and 200; do., with pearl keys, $225, 250, and 300; new 6 1-2-octave, $135; do., 6 2-3-octave, $140. The above Pianos are fully warranted, and are the greatest bargains that can be found in the city. *Please call and see them;* second-hand *Pianos* at $25, 40, 50, 60, 75, and 100.

THE HORACE WATERS MELODEONS
Rosewood Cases, Tuned the Equal Temperament, with the *Patent* Divided Swell and Solo Stop. *Prices from $35 to 200.* Organ Harmoniums with *Pedal Bass*, $250, 275, and 300. School Harmoniums, $40, 60, 80, and 100. Also Melodeons and Harmoniums of the following makers, *Prince & Co's*, Carhart & Needham, Mason & Hamlin, and S. D. & H. W. Smith, all of which will be sold at extremely low prices. These Melodeons remain in tune a long time. Each Melodeon warranted for three years.

☞A liberal discount to Clergymen, Churches, Sabbath Schools, Lodges, Seminaries, and Teachers. The Trade supplied on the most liberal terms.
HORACE WATERS, Ag't.
481 Broadway, New-York.

THE DAY SCHOOL BELL.
35,000 *COPIES ISSUED.*
A new Singing Book for Day Schools, called the Day School Bell, is now ready. It contains about 200 choice songs, rounds, catches, duetts, trios, quartetts and choruses, many of them written expressly for this work, besides 32 pages of the Elements of Music. The Elements are so easy and progressive, that ordinary teachers will find themselves entirely successful in instructing even young scholars to sing correctly and scientifically; while the tunes and words embrace such a variety of lively, attractive, and soul-stiring music and sentiments, that no trouble will be experienced in inducing all beginners to go on with zeal in acquiring skill in one of the most health-giving, beauty-improving, happiness-yielding, and order-producing exersises of school life. In simplicity of its elements, in variety and adaptation of music, and in excellence and number of its songs, original, selected, and adapted, it claims by much to excel all competitors. It will be found the best ever issued for seminaries, academies, and public schools. A few sample pages of the elements, tunes, and songs, are given in a circular: send and get one. It is compiled by HORACE WATERS, author of "Sabbath School Bell," Nos. 1 and 2 which have had the enormous sale of 735,000 copies. *Prices*—paper cover, 20 cents, $15 per 100; bound, 30 cents, $22 per 100; cloth bound, embossed gilt, 40 cents, $30 per 100. 25 copies furnished at the 100 price. Mailed at the retail price.
HORACE WATERS, *Publisher.*
481 Broadway, New York.

SABBATH SCHOOL BELL No. 2.
85,000 *COPIES ISSUED.*
It is an entire new work of nearly 200 pages. Many of the tunes and hymns were written expressly for this volume. It will soon be as popular as its predecessor, (Bell No. 1) which has run up to the enormous numper of 650,000 copies—outstripping any Sunday school book of its size ever issued in this country. Also both volumes are bound in one to accommodate schools wishing them in that form. *Prices* of Bell No. 2, paper covers, 15 cents, $12 per 100; bound, 25 cents, $18 per 100; cloth bound, embossed gilt, 30 cents, $23 per 100. Bell No. 1, paper covers 13 cents, $10 per 100; bound, 20 cents, $15 per 100; cloth bound, embossed gilt, 25 cents, $20 per 100. Bells Nos. 1 and 2 bound together, 40 cents, 30 dollars per 100; cloth bound, embossed gilt, 50 cents, 50 dollars per 100. 25 copies furnished at the 100 price. Mailed at the retail price.
HORACE WATERS, *Publisher,*
481 Broadway, New-York.

NEW INSTRUMENTAL MUSIC.
President Lincoln's Grand March, with the best Vignette of his Excellency that has yet been published; music by Helmsmuller, leader of the 22d Regiment Band, price 50 cents. Our Generals' Quick-Step, with vignette of 35 of our generals; music by Grafulla, leader of 7th Regiment band, 50 cents. The Seven Sons' Gallop, and Laura Keene Waltz, 35 cents each. Comet Schottische, 25 cents; all by Baker. Music Box Gallop, by Herring, 35 cents, Union Waltz, La Grassa, 25 cents. Volunteer *Polka*, Goldbeck, 25 cents Spirit **Polka**; Gen. Scott's Farewell Grand March 25 cents each; Airy Castles, 30 cents, all by A. E. **P**rarkhurst. Freedom, Truth and Right Grand March, with splendid vignette; music by Carl Heinemann, 50 cents. All of which are fine productions.

NEW VOCAL MUSIC.
I will be true to thee; A penny for your thoughts; Little Jenny Dow; Better times are coming; I dream of my mother and my home; Merry little birds are we, (a song for children); Slumber, my darling, Lizzie dies to night, Jenny's coming o'er the green, Was my Brother in the Battle? and Why have my loved ones gone, by Stephen C. Foster. Shall we know each other there? by the Rev. R. Lowry. **P**leasant words for all, by J. Roberts. There is a beautiful world, by I. M. Holmes. **P**rice 25 cents each. Freedom, Truth and Right, a national song and grand chorus; music by Carl Heinemann, with English and German words, 30 cents. Where liberty dwells is my country, F[illegible]ley. Forget if you can, but forgive; I hear sweet voices singing, and Home is home, by J. R. Thomas, 30 cents each. These songs are very popular. Mailed free at retail price.
Foreign Sheet MUSIC at 2 cents per page. All kinds of Music merchandise at war prices.
HORACE WATERS, **P**ublisher,
481 Broadway, New-York.

NEW MUSIC FOR THE MILLION,
IN CHEAP FORM, ARRANGED AS QUARTETTES AND CHORUSES FOR MUSICAL SOCIETIES, CHOIRS, SUNDAY SCHOOLS, PUBLIC SCHOOLS, SEMINARIES, ETC.
Shall we know each other there? Snall we meet beyond the river? Be in time; There is a beautiful world; Don't you hear the Angels coming? Where liberty dwells is my country; Freedom, Truth and Right, (national son s) Is There a land of love? Sorrow shall come again no more. **P**rice 3 cents, 25 cts. per doz., 2 dollars per 100. **P**ostage 1 cent. In sheet form, with **P**iano accompaniment, 25 cts. **P**uplished by HORACE WATERS, 481 Broadway, New York, and for sale by N. P. KEMP, Boston; CHAS. S. LUTHER, Philadelphia; G. CROSBY, Cincinnati; TOMLINSON & BROTHERS, Chicago, and J. W. MCINTYRE, St. Louis.

Administrator's Notice.

Notice is hereby given, that the subscriber has been duly appointed Administrator of the Estate of Preston Soule, late of Middleborough, in the County of Plymouth, deceased, and has taken upon himself that trust by giving bond, as the law directs. All persons having demands upon the estate of said Preston Soule are hereby required to exhibit the same; and all persons indebted to said estate are called upon to make payment to
EBEN'R T. SOULE, Administrator.
Middleboro', July 31, 1862.

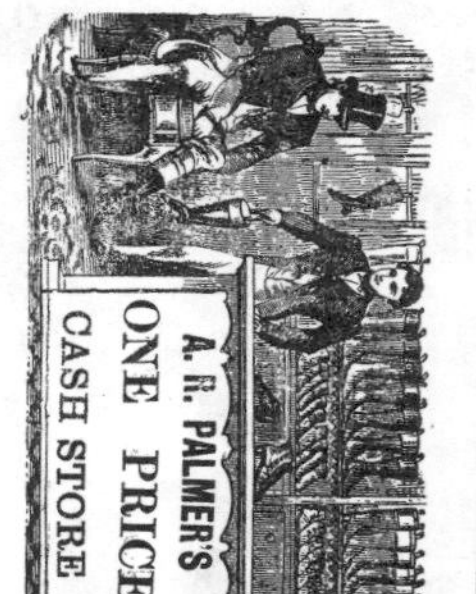

Farmers, Merchants, Mechanics,
WORKINGMEN,
In these times it is every man' make his money go as far as he can, and to do this you must pay Cash for what you buy.

Wishing to open the eyes of the public to the fact that the One Price Low Price Cash System was for their benefit, we opened, on the first day of May, 1861, the

ONLY ONE PRICE LOW PRICE
strictly Cash Boot and Shoe Store in New Bedford.
The retailing of Goods at Wholesale Prices has met with success, with *great* success, with *complete* success.
Having a *small* store, *small* rent, small expense, we *can* sell, we *will* sell, we *do* sell LOWER THAN UNION STORES which have larger expenses.

Ladies.

We have a nice assortment of good Kid and Cloth Slippers for	25 cents
A nice silk-gore Congress Gaiter heel for	75 cents
A pair of good heel Congress Gaiters for usually sold for $1.	85 cents
A good pair of Congress heel Gaiters for always sold for $1.25,	$1.00
A very good pair of Balmoral Gaiters (warrented) sold everywhere for $1.25	$1.00
A tip-top pair of Balmoral Gaiters for	$1.25
A pair of Kid Congr ss Gaiters for	85 cents
A pair of Kid Buskins for 40 cents; good ones.	
A prime pair of Carpet Shoes for sold everywhere for 50 cents.	39 cents
A pair of Kid Slippers for	17 cents

For Men.

We sell a good pair of Calf Boots, long or short leg for	$2.00
A first-rate pair of Calf Boots, warrented prime, for	$2,25, and $2.50
A pair of neat Dress Boots for	2.50 and 2.75
A pair of French Pateut Leather Boots for	3.00
A neat pair of Patent-Leather Boots for	2.00
A good pair of Oxford Ties or Low Shoes for	75 and 80 cts
A prime pair of Oxford Ties, for	95 cts
A pair of Calf Congress Boots (warrented) for	$1.33
A pair of high lace Balmeral Boots for	1.42
A pair of thick Brogans for 98 cents, usually sold for $1 25,	
A good pair of Brogans for	75 cents
A pair of thick Boots for	$1.75
A pair of good Slippers,	40 cents

We call particular attention to our Men's *extra quality* Brogans for 98 cents, and Calf Congress Boots $1.33 *all warranted.* Also, Ladies' Kid Slippers 25 cents, and 75 cent Congress Gaiters.

For Boys, *good* Brogans, 45 to 75 cents. Misses' Shoes and Gaiters, 42 to 75 cents. Childrens' Leather Shoes, with or without copper tip, for 38 cents.

Always on hand, a lot of Children's GOOD Shoes for 17 and 25 cents a pair, and an assortment of all kinds usually kept in a first-class Boot and Shoe Store.

Remember that we *do not* sell at cost or less than cost, but we are satisfied with the CASH, and a *light* profit.

Remember this is the *Only One Price Low Price Cash Boot and Shoe Store* in this City, and you make a postive saving by paying Cash, and you get the goods at wholesale prices.

Remember selling for Cash, and having no losses, we *cannot* and *will not* be undersold by Union Stores or any other stores.

☞Call and examine the Goods, and get the Prices, even if you do not wish to buy.

☞SYSTEMS STRICTLY ADHERED TO—We buy our gods for Cash down. We sell our goods for Cash down. We have *One Price* and Cash to al.

N. B.—Bring this circular with you, compare the Goods with the Prices, and satisify yourselves that this is no humbug.

A. R. PALMER,
127 Union Street, New Bedford, Mass
35-3 A few doors below Purchase St.

Commonwealth of Massachusetts.
PLYMOUTH, SS. Probate Court.
To all persons intersted in the estate of Lois Christie, late of Middleborough, in said County, deceasd Greeting:

WHEREAS, James Cole, jr., the administrator of the estate of said deceased, has presented for allwance the first account of his administratin upon the estate of said deceased: You are hereby cited to appear at a Probate Curt to be holden at Middleborough, in said County, on the first Tuesday of August next, at nine o'clock in the forenoon, to shw cause, if any you have, why the same shoud not be allowed. And said James Cole, jr is ordered to serve this citation by publishing the same once a week in the Middleborogh Gazette, a newspaper printed at Middlebrough, three weeks successively, the last ublication to be two days at least before said Court.

Witness, Wm. H Wood, Esquire, Judge of said Court, this sixth day of May, in the year of our Lord one thousand eight hundred and sixty-two. D. E. Damon, Register.

TALOR'S
BILLS!!

THE Subscriber hereby announces to delinquent customers, that he proposes a change in his business, and consequently all such persons are urged to make immediate payment of their bills.

All accounts outstanding on the first day of Sept. next, will be put into the hands of a lawyer for collection

Geo. F. Hartwell.

Middleboro, July 1862.

WANTED,—Active Agents to sell "Downers Hemmer and Shield, for Hand Sewing." It is new, useful and cheap, and has NO COMPETITION. Sent by mail on receipt of price, 25 cents. Sales are rapid, and profits are large. Enquire at this office.

Commonwealth of Massachusetts.
PLYMOUTH SS. Probate Court.
To the Heirs-at-Law, Next of Kin, and all other persons interested in the estate of Charles Fuller late of Plympton in said County, deceased: Greeting:

Whereas, certain instrument purporting to be the last will and testament of said deceased has been presented to said Court, for Probate, by Lafayette Fuller who prays that letters testamentary may be issued to him one of the executors therein named. You are hereby cited to appear at a Probate Court to be held at Middleborough in said County of Plymouth, on the fifth day of August next, at nine o'clock in the forenoon, to show cause, if any you have, against the same.
And said Lafayette Fuller is hereby directed to give public notice thereof, by publishing this citation once a week, for three successive weeks, in the newspaper called the Middleborough Gazette printed at Middleborough the last publication to be two days, at least, before said Court.

Witness, WM. H. Wood, Esquire, Judge of said Court, this twenty-sixth day of June in the year of our Lord one thousand eight hundred and sixty-two.
WM. H. Wood, Judge Probate.

UNDERTAKER!

THE UNDERSIGNED BEGS LEAVE to announce to the citizens of Middleboro and vicinity, that he has commenced the business of an UNDERTAKER, and is fully prepared to furnish.

COFFINS,
OF ALL GRADES AMD FINISH,
from the common PINE to the best
Caskets & Burial Cases,
AT SHORT NOTICE.
and to wait punctually upon those who may desire his services.
He has a NEW and
MODERN STYLED HEARSE.
Also SHROUDING, &c., and everything pertaining to the business.
☞A share of patronage respectfully solicited. Show Rooms at his old stand on Pierce Street.
LOTHROP SHURTLEFF.
Middleboro, July 1st, 1862.

Insolvent Notice.

Commonwealth of Massachusetts.
PLYMOUTH SS.
July 14th, A. D. 1862.
IN the case of GRANVILLE CARVER, of Bridgewater in said County, Insolvent Debtor;—The fourth meeting of the creditors of said insolvent debtor will be held at the Court of Insolvency, at Plymouth, in said County of Plymouth, on the fourth day of August next at ten o'clock in the forenoon, at which meeting creditors may be present and prove their claims, and the Assignee will then and their present his account, and creditors may appear and object to the allowance of the same. P. D. KINGMAN, Assignee.

MIDDLEBORO
Boot and Shoe STORE.

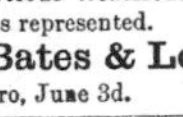

THE Subscribers take this opportunity to thank the Citizens of this vicinity for the liberal patronage bestowed on them since their residence here, and we hereby announce that we are constantly manufacturing and receiving from other sources,

BOOTS AND SHOES,
of desirable styles and of the best quality, which we can and will sell as low as they can be purchased anywhere.

Persons visiting our store may rely on receiving courteous treatment and obtaining goods just as represented.

Bates & Loud.
Middleboro, June 3d.

NOW READY.
PARSON BRONLOW'S
WONDERFUL BOOK.

One Volume. Containing upwards of 450 pages, 12 superior Engravings, an excellent Steel Portrait, &c. Beautifully printed on fine white paper, and handsomely bound in muslin. Price $1.25.
Sent free, by return mail, on receipt of price.
Agents Wanted,
In every city, town, village and county, to sell this thrilling and remarkable work.
Address GEORGE W. CHILD, Publisher. 628 and 630 Chesnut St., Philadelphia.
☞Papers copying will receive the work.

☞THE subscriber, being unable to continue his office longer in Middleboro, would be happy to attend to calls at his office in Bridgewater.
Work done at reasonable prices, and every endeavor made to give entire satisfaction.

DR. CHRIS. WASHBURN
DENTIST,
BRIDGEWATER, MASS.
Office at the residence of Dr. Nahum Washburn, Central Svnare.

Flour! Flour!

'ELK HART' and 'OTTER POND' MILLS, with a large lot of other grades, Just Received and
Selling Very Low,
FOR CASH, BY
Ira Thomas.

DISSOLU'N OF COPARTNERSHIP.

Notice is hereby given that the Copartnership hertofor existing under the firm of ROGERS & SPARROW, is this day dissolved by mutual consent.
C. M. ROGERS,
H. A. SPARROW.
Middleboro', July 30, 1862.
☞The Painting Business will be carried on as heretofore, at the old stand, by
H. A. SPARROW.
A continuance of patronage solicited.

☞Notwithstanding its wonderful virtues, MATHEWS' ARNICA HAIR GLOSS retails at TWENTY-FIVE CENTS A BOTTLE!

Geo. Vaughan & Son,
Merchant Tailors,

AND DEALERS IN
Clothes, Ready-Made
Clothing,
HATS & CAPS.
FURNISHING GOODS
TRUNKS, VALISES, UMBRELLAS, &C.
PAPER HANGINGS,

WE have just received a good assortment of the various goods in our line of trade, and are constantly adding new supplies. It is our purpose to sell at
The Lowest Cash Prices.
WM. H. BRIGHTMAN is still in the Tailoring Department, and he will give perject satisfaction in his line. All Cutting Jobs promptly attended to.

☞**OLD FRIENDS**☜
IN THE RIGHT PLACE.
HERRICK'S
SUGAR COATED PILLS.

The best Family Cathartic in the world. Used twenty years by five millions of persons annually; always gives satisfaction, contains nothing injurious, is patronised by the principal physicians and surgeons in the Union; elegantly coated with sugar.
Large Boxes, 25 cents; five boxes for one dollar. Full directions with each box.
Warranted superior to any pill before the public.

Tallahasse, Leon Co., Fla. June 17, 1860.
To Dr. Herrick, Albany, N. Y.
My Dear Docter:—I write this to inform you of the wonderful effect of your sugar coated pills on my eldest daughter. For three years she has been afflicted with a bilious derangement of the system, sadly impairing her health, which has been steadily failing during that period. When in New York, in April last, a friend advised me to test your pills—Having the fullest confidence in the judgement of my friend, I obtained a supply of Messrs, Barnes & Park Druggists, Park Row, New York. On Returning home, we ceased all other treatment and administered your pills, one each night. The improvement in her feelings, complexion, digestion, etc., surprisd us all. A rapid and permanent restoration to health has been the result. We used less than five boxes, and consider her entirely well. I consider the above a just tribute to you as a physician, and trust it will be the means of inducing many to adopt your pills as their family medicine.
I remain, dear sir, with many thanks,
Your obedient servant,
S. G. MORRISON,

Herrick's Sugar Coated Pills and Kid Plasters are sold by J. B. & J. SHAW, Middleboro, and by druggists everywhere.
Dr. L. R. HERRICK & Co., Albany, N. Y.
C. W. Hale, Travelling Agt.

☞Mathews' Arnica Hair Gloss is an infallible remedy for all diseases of the scalp. It allays and removes inflammation and speedily cures all sorts and classes of eruptions.
☞MATHEWS' ARNICA HAIR GLOSS PREVENTS the hair from TURNING GREY.

Your Country Calls!
To the Rescue!

THE Selectmen of Middleboro have received authority to raise 56 Volunteers.
VOLUNTEERS WILL RECEIVE

Advance Bounty from the United States,	$25
Advance Bounty from the Town,	$125
Advance Wages,	$13
Bounty at the close of the war.,	$75

State Aid guaranteed. $2 will be paid to any person bringing a Volunteer.
Recruiting Office at the Town Clerk's, Middleboro.
☞Unless the Volunteers shall receive the bounty of $100 above mentioned from the town, or some source, the enlistment shall not be binding.
B. P. WOOD, Ch. of Selectmen.
Middleboro, July 21, 1862.

B L I S S ' S
ICE CREAM SALOON,
6 5 MAIN STREET TAUNTON.
Was opened the FIRST DAY OF MAY, for the season. Having enlarged and refitted up my Rooms for ICE CREAMS & REFRESHMENTS, I would respectfully invite all friends and strangers to give me a call.
Fairs, Parties, Picnics and Families furnished at short notice and on reasonable terms.
French and American Confectionery,
A large and choice assortment always on hand. Also, ORANGES, LEMONS, FIGS, DATES, &c., of the best the market affords.
T O Y S.
A great variety of TOYS, and FANCY GOODS; all desiring these articles will do well to examine before purchasing.
34-3m A. L. BLISS.

MATHEWS' arnica HAIR GLOSS
A New and Valuable Toilet Article, for
Preserving & Beautifying the Hair!

ARNICA HAIR GLOSS
Is a skillful combination of the active virtues of ARNICA, so well known for its invaluable properties of subduing inflammation and healing, with other articles of tried value.

ARNICA HAIR GLOSS
Invigorates the Hair; It prevents its falling out; It stimulates the Hair; It promotes the growth and strength of the Hair.

ARNICA HAIR GLOSS
Is a sovereign remedy for all Eruptions and Irritation of the Scalp; will remove all Dandruff, and excite the roots of the Hair to healthy action.

ARNICA HAIR GLOSS
Is the most perfect Hair Dressing ever introduced. It leaves the Hair permanently soft and glossy. It beautifies the Hair. It cleanses the Hair.

ARNICA HAIR GLOSS
Is HIGHLY PERFUMED, and combines the virtues of all other Hair Preservatives with those that are entirely new.

ARNICA HAIR GLOSS
Is the Cheapest as well as the Best Hair rertorer in use. A Single Bottle will show its superiority to all others.

For Sale by Druggists Generally.
Price, - Twenty-Five Cents a Bottle.
A. I. MATHEWS,
No. 16 Gedar Street, N. Y. General Agent.

The Great Benefactor of the Household!
P. P. STEWART'S
FUEL-SAVING AND COMFORT-PRODUCING SUMMER AND WINTER
Air-Tight Cook Stove!
FOR WOOD OR COAL,
Improved in '59 with new & extra large Flues.

THE following is a brief summary of the peculiarities of THE STEWART STOVE:

1st. DURABILITY.—It has been in use in many families from 15 to 20 years.

2d. CAPACITY FOR WORK.—*All culinary operations may be carried on at the same time.* In evidence of what it will accomplish, we allude to the fact, that on each of several occasions, *a barrel of flour has been baked into bread with a single fire.*

3d. ECONEMY IN FUEL.—So perfect is its construction, that *its cost may be saved IN FUEL in two or three years.*

4th. *It does its work expeditiously and well*, and may be regulated at pleasure to *produce any temperature required in winter in the kitchen*, without interference with the cooking.

The Stewart Stove
Has the most perfectly ventilated Oven of any Stove now manufactured.
This Stove has been in use by many of the citizens of Middleboro, for the past two years, and has invariably given entire satisfaction.
The Stove can be seen at any time at the Store of
GEO. H. DOANE.
MIDDLEBOBO, MASS.

Also a large and complete assortment of
Hardware!

CONSISTING in part of Locks, Knobs, Butts, Screws, Carpenter's Tools, Sheet Lead, Lead Pipe, Tarred Paper, Cast Iron Sinks Ovens and Boilers. Doors, Cauldrons. Cast Iron Chimney Flues, &c.

A LARGE ASSORTMENT OF
KITCHEN FURNISHING GOODS!
Consisting of
TIN, GLASS, JAPAN, BRITTANIA, FRENCH, ENAMELED AND WOODEN WARE.
ALSO
Agricultural Tools,
Such as Horse Hoes, Plows, Cultivators, Spades, Forks, Shovels and Hoes, Garden Rakes, Garden Trowels, &c.

Any article of Tin Ware made promptly to order.
REPAIRING of all kinds done at short notice.
GEO. H. DOANE.
Doane & Shaws' Block.
Middleboro, Mass.

I FEEL

UNDER OBLIGATION TO MAKE ACknowledgement to my many friends and customers that have stood by me during the

Last Eight Years!

And would say that I am as ready as ever to minister to their wants, in every branch of my busines. Having the services of a journeyman—
M R. W M. H. B A R D E N,
Who is faithful and competent in every branch of the art. I feel to pledge myself anew to their wants.
ALL WORK DONE IN THE
BEST AND LATEST STYLES
OR NO CHARGES MADE.

Particular attention paid to the Cutting and Dressing of
Ladies' & Childrens' Hair
☞If possible, Ladies and small children will call at any time but Saturday afternoon and evening. My rooms will always be found orderly and quiet, so none need feel to hesitate about calling.

EVERY PREPARATION FOR THE HAIR,
Liniments, Perfumes, &c.,
Manufactured by myself, warranted to give perfect satisfaction, or the money will be refunded!

CONSTANTLY FOR SALE A LARGE assortment of
FANCY GOODS,
Toys, Confectionary, &c.
Every article warranted to be good, or poor, as it is recommended, or no pay.
S. H. SYLVESTER.

Patented Nov. 1st, 1859.

THE measures are A, the distance round the Neck: B to B, the Yoke, C to C. the the Sleeve, D to D, distance round the Body under the armpits, E to E, the length of the Shirt.

BALLOU'S
Patented Improved French Yoke
SHIRTS.

Patented November 1, 1859.
New Style of Shirts, Warranted to Fit!
BY sending the above measures by mail we can guarantee a perfect fit of our new style of shirt, and return by express to any part of the United States at
$12, $15, $18, $24, &c., &c., per dozen.
No order forwarded for less than half a dozen of Shirts.
Also Importer and Dealers in MEN'S FURNISHING GOODS,
BALLOU BROTHERS,
409 Broadway, New York
Wholesale Trade supplied on the usual terms
Send for a Circular.

VOL. I.—NO. 3. RICHMOND, SATURDAY, SEPTEMBER 27, 1862. PRICE 15 CENTS.

GEN. J. E. B. STUART.

The subject of this brief and imperfect notice, whose name awakens enthusiasm throughout the Confederacy and terror to the farthest borders of Yankeeland, is the son of the late Archibald Stuart, for several years a member of the House of Representatives of the United States from the district which then embraced the county of Patrick, in Virginia, where, we believe, he was born. At a very early age he gave token of a quick and active mind, and, under the fond care of devoted parents of the highest social and moral worth, he grew up to manly stature marked by every trait that gives promise of future distinction. His father died ten or twelve years ago, full of honors: his mother yet lives to witness with joy the eminent service he is rendering to his country, and the proud fame he has won to be transmitted to posterity.

James E. B Stuart entered the Military Academy of West Point in the year 1850. Among his contemporaries at that institution were Generals Ambrose P. Hill, Henry Heth, George H. Steuart, T. H. Holmes, Beverly H. Robertson and N. George Evans, and Colonels Seth M. Barton, Alfred Cumming and Thomas S. Rhett of the Confederate army, and Burnside, Vielé, Willcox, Cogswell and others of greater or less repute or disrepute in the Yankee army. Among his immediate classmates were Colonels John Pegram, George W. Custis Lee and John B. Villepigue, now well-known in the Confederate service, and Major Greble of the Yankee artillery, who was killed in the first battle of the war at Great Bethel.

In the United States Army, the highest rank attained by Stuart was that of first lieutenant, but this was in the First Cavalry, a regiment noted for its officers, of which the Yankee General Sumner was colonel and our own Major-General Joseph E. Johnston lieutenant colonel. The operations of the old Federal Cavalry were conducted mostly upon the distant frontier, far from the public eye and from the observation of newspaper correspondents, and thus many deeds of great daring and high emprise went unchronicled, which would have established a reputation for their actors had they been transacted upon a theatre nearer to civilization and journalism. The heroes that lived before Agamemnon, we are told, passed away without recognition, because they had no poet to celebrate their achievements, and the dashing dragoons who swept the marauding Indians before them on the prairies of Nebraska and through the defiles of New Mexico, had small chance of securing the applause of their countrymen in the Atlantic States, because that convenient historian of every-day life, the newspaper reporter, was not at hand to write down their exploits. The Santa Fe *Gazette* was the sole medium of informing the world what was going on in those Western solitudes, and the news staff of this journal was not in the most efficient state of organization. It was a wild life, that free, dashing career in the saddle over the boundless pampas of the interior, with the blue heavens above and the blue, billowy expanse of verdure around, varied only by the change of bivouac, or a rough hand-to-hand encounter with Sioux or Camanches, and rewarded, now and then, by glimpses of the silver peaks of the Rocky Mountains; and the exhilaration and joy and danger of it were well suited to the temperament of young Stuart, who rode with the boldest of his comrades and fought with the fiercest of his foes. There are doubtless on file in the pigeon-holes of the War Department, at Washington, official reports of many encounters with the savage, recording in a curt, dry, cold manner enterprises which, in the glowing narrative of a Walter Scott or an Alexandre Dumas, would vie in interest with the stories of chivalry. One of these only, in which Lieutenant Stuart bore a part, has been recorded in our newspapers, but the account is as short and unsatisfactory as possible. On the 29th July, 1857, at a time when we were absorbed with the Atlantic telegraph and other exciting matters of the "piping times of peace," Col. Sumner encountered a force of three hundred *braves* of the Cheyenne tribe strongly posted upon Solomon's Fork of the Kansas river, and, after a sharp struggle, put them to flight in great disorder. In this combat Lieut. Stuart was severely wounded.

At the outbreak of the present war, Lieutenant Stuart lost no time in resigning his commission, and offering his sword to the cause of his native South. It is unnecessary to refer to his exploits since that time. They have been most effectively laid before the public, in a brilliant series, by our daily journalists. With his rapid rise from a colonelcy to the command of a brigade and soon after to the rank of a major-general of cavalry, our readers are familiar. Perhaps the most striking and successful of all his expeditions were the Pamunkey raid through McClellan's lines, in which but one man, the gallant and lamented Captain Latané, was lost, and the recent descent upon Catlett's Station, where he captured such a vast quantity of stores and gathered up the official correspondence and full dress uniform coat of the redoubtable John Pope, Major-General U. S. A. As a cavalry officer, General Stuart combines with his regular West Point training much of the *élan* of Jack Morgan and Turner Ashby. Ready for any enterprise, his military motto seems to be that of the French leader, *de l'audace, encore de l'audace, toujours de l'audace*.

GEN. J. E. B. STUART.

From a Photograph by D. T. COWELL, Esq.

In the old army, General Stuart was always popular. He was universally known under the pleasant nickname of "Beauty Stuart," as reflecting upon his personal appearance, but the irony was not happy, for on horseback, at the head of his column, there are fewer finer looking men than our general. His expression is frank and agreeable, the lower part of his face is overflowed by a torrent of reddish-brown beard, his eye is bright and mobile, his movements are full of grace, his address is pleasing, his port lofty and his horsemanship perfect—altogether he would challenge attention among a hundred thousand men upon the Viennese Prater or the Parisian *Champ de Mars*. In the social circle, his manners are engaging and his conversation fertile and suggestive.

General Stuart married a daughter of Philip St. George Cooke, Colonel of the Second Dragoons in the U. S. Army. This officer, though a Virginian by birth and education, (he is the brother of the late John R. Cooke of this city,) preferred his rank to his duty, and remained in the old service to make war upon the Southern people. He is now a general and was under McClellan when siege was laid to Richmond. It was said that one of Stuart's objects in the Pamunkey expedition was to take his father-in-law prisoner.

At the age of nineteen, General Stuart became a communicant in the Protestant Episcopal Church, and his religious profession has always been consistent and faithful. He is not less instant in prayer than watchful upon the march and fearful in fight, and will take no mean place in the ranks of those Christian soldiers of whom Gardner and Headley Vicars are the highest types in the English Army, and of whom, with Lee and Jackson, and Polk and Pendleton, and Hill and a host of others, our own service furnishes so many shining illustrations.

That conduct often seems ridiculous, the secret reasons of which are wise and solid."

A CANDID MIND.

There is nothing sheds so fine a light upon the human character as candor. It was called whiteness by the ancients, for its purity and virtue; and it has always won the esteem due to the most admirable of the virtues. However little sought for and practiced, all do it the homage of their praise, and feel the power and charm of its influence. The man whose opinions make the deepest mark upon his fellows, whose influence is the most lasting and efficient, whose friendship is instinctively sought, where all others have proved faithless, is not the man of brilliant parts, or flattering tongue, or splendid genius, or commanding power; but he whose lucid candor and ingenuous truth transmit the heart's real feelings pure and without refraction.

There are other qualities which are more showy, and other traits that have a higher place in the world's code of honor, but none wear better or gather less tarnish by use, or claim a deeper homage in that silent reverence which the mind must pay to virtue. As it is the most beautiful, so it is the safest of moral qualities. None fall into so few mistakes, none darken and deform themselves with so little falsehood and wrong, none so free from the pain of doing wrong as those who walk amid the pitfalls and miasmas, passions and errors of our tainted life, clothed habitually with candor. The rare and comely union of prudence and principle, of firmness, of truth and zeal, of earnestness of feeling and discrimination of views, is to be found only in minds pervaded and enlarged by candor. To love and to seek, in all things, the truth—to choose and adhere to, before all the solicitations of passion, or power of prejudice, or the force of public opinion, or the claims of interest or power, whatever is right and true, to believe, at every juncture of experience or thought, that nothing is so good, or desirable, or trustworthy as truth—to send the truth amid all the unpopular disguises which too often disfigure it in this world—this must be safest and best, whatever we may think of it, if God really reigns and there be an eternal distinction between truth and falsehood, right and wrong. In nothing have men so vital an interest as in truth. Nothing should we so earnestly strive to get at, or hold fast when obtained. Buy the truth and sell it not.

SOBRIETY OF THE GREEKS.

The food of an English laborer would be enough in Greece for a family of six persons. The rich are well satisfied with a dish of vegetables for their meal; the poor with a handful of olives or a piece of salt fish. The entire population eats meat at Easter for the whole year. I do not believe a Greek ever died of indigestion. Drunkenness, so common in cold countries, is a rare vice with the Greeks: they are great drinkers, but water drinkers. They would have scruples about passing a fountain without drinking at it; but if they enter a tavern it is to chatter. The coffee houses of Athens are full of people, and at all hours, but the customers do not take strong liquors; they ask for a cup of coffee at a penny; a glass of water, light for their cigarettes, a newspaper, and a game of dominoes; they then have enough to keep themselves occupied for the day. In two years I have not met with a man dead drunk in the streets, and I believe it would be easy to count all the drunkards in the kingdom. It may be said that the Greek people have no inclination for any kind of excesses; and they take all their pleasures with equal sobriety.

This sobriety naturally explains the fact that insanity is rare in Greece. Madness also is a malady exceedingly rare in the kingdom. An hospital for the blind has just been constructed in Athens; it will never be necessary to build one for madmen.

In all societies, it is advisable to associate if possible with the highest; not that the highest are always the best, but because, if disgusted with these, we can at any time descend; but if we begin with the lowest, to ascend is impossible. In the grand theatre of life a *box ticket* takes us through the house.

Times of general calamity and confusion have ever been productive of the greatest minds.

The purest ore is produced from the hottest furenac, and the brightest thunderbolt is elicited from the darkest storm.

New-York Daily Tribune.

VOL. XXII.....No. 6,706. NEW-YORK, WEDNESDAY, OCTOBER 1, 1862. PRICE TWO CENTS.

FROM WASHINGTON.

THE ISSUE OF LETTERS OF MARQUE

Kentuckians Flocking to the Rebel Army.

OUR CONTEMPLATED NAVAL OPERATIONS.

REBEL SICK AND WOUNDED RECEIVED IN HOSPITAL

Expedition to Warrenton Ordered by Gen. Sigel.

1,200 Rebels Captured and Paroled.

Success, also, at Warrenton Junction.

OFFICIAL WAR BULLETIN.

CIRCULAR IN REGARD TO VACANCIES IN THE ARMY.

CIRCULAR: From casualties in the field, and from absence by reason of sickness, many volunteer regiments have not a sufficient number of officers to command them.

It is important that vacancies caused by deaths and resignations be filled with the least possible delay.

The Governors of the several States are earnestly requested to fill those vacancies by promoting officers, non-commissioned officers and privates *who have distinguished themselves in the field, or who have shown a capacity for military command.*

Without the hope of promotion there is no encouragement to a faithful performance of duty, and no stimulus to deeds of valor.

Moreover, the discipline and efficiency of an army depend in a great measure upon the character and qualifications of its officers.

Without good officers, the very best soldiers soon become a mere disorderly mob, the inefficiency of which is increased by the increase of its numbers.

H. W. HALLECK, General-in-Chief.

Special Dispatch to The N. Y. Tribune.

WASHINGTON, Tuesday, Sept. 30, 1862.

THE ISSUE OF LETTERS OF MARQUE.

The declaration of Secretary Seward, through Minister Adams, to England, of which we have news by a recent steamer, of the purpose of the Government to issue letters of marque, with a view of checking hostilities now carried on by Southern privateers on United States commerce, has caused no little sensation among the representatives of foreign powers and students of international law here, who regard it as tantamount to an official recognition by the United States of the Rebels as belligerents.

KENTUCKY LOYALTY.

The boast of the Rebels that they have enlisted 23,000 Kentuckians since Kirby Smith crossed the border, does not, probably overstate the number very much. It is notorious that the young men of Kentucky have Rebel proclivities, and it is known that in one of the strongest Union counties in the State, 200 recruits were enlisted by the Rebels.

IRON ON THE WAY FROM ENGLAND TO THE SOUTH.

There is intelligence from England that 15,000 tons of iron, to be used for plating vessels, are on their way to the South; but, even if the blockade is successfully run, our iron-clad vessels will be ready before those of the rebels will be.

THE NAVAL OPERATIONS ON THE SOUTHERN COAST.

The current speculations touching the operations of the navy on the Southern coast are premature. When the iron-clad fleet is ready, it will be used, and nobody will be likely to know the point of attack until the blow has been struck.

TRE REBEL SICK AND WOUNDED.

The Richmond papers state that the official returns show that there are 49 hospitals at Richmond and Petersburg, at which 110,678 siak and wounded soldiers have been received since the beginning of the war, of whom 11,602 have been furloughed, 2,498 discharged, 7,603 have died, and 12,613 remain.

THE ILLINOIS UNION REPUBLICAN TICKET.

Letters from Illinois predict that the Union-Republican party will elect its State ticket—nine out of fourteen members of Congress, and the Legislature, which is to choose a Senator in place of Senator Browning, who has support from no quarter.

SUICIDE OF ONE OF THE PATENT AGENTS.

Mr. Amos P. Little, formerly employed in the Patent-Office, and of late one of the most capable patent agents here, committed suicide to-day in the public dining-room of the National Hotel. He rose from his seat at the table, walked up to the sideboard, and taking a carving-knife from one of the waiters, cut his throat, severing both arteries. He is thought to have been insane.

ARREST OF A RUFFIAN.

THE TRIBUNE of yesterday reported the incident of a soldier's shooting into an unoffending crowd of black men, women, and children at a church here. To-day the ruffian was arrested by our vigilant Provost-Marshal, and lodged in the Central Guard-House. His name is Barney Williams, and he is a member of the Scott Life Guard. It is hoped that he will be made an example of.

THE TRAITOR KEY'S PLAN FOR CLOSING THE WAR.

The method by which Major Key of Gen. Halleck's staff, whose dismissal from the service for the use of unmilitary and disloyal language, was announced yesterday. Proposed to prolong the war is popularly known as the "exhausting process. He said that "the programme" was that the North and South should exhaust themselves and each other, and then a compromise should be effected, and the Union as it was reconstructed.

EXCHANGE OF STATE PRISONERS.

About 170 State prisoners, now confined in the Old Capitol, are ordered to be exchanged, and Mr. Superintendent Wood will soon visit Richmond for that purpose.

THE CAMP OF PAROLED PRISONERS.

Col. De Korponay, 28th Pa., is in command of the camp of paroled prisoners near Alexandria.

THE CONVALESCENT CAMP.

There are 14,000 men now at Convalescent Camp across the river. Large numbers are sent to their regiments daily,

APPLICATION FOR LEAVE OF ABSENCE.

The War Department has devolved upon Gen. Banks the hearing of all applications for leave of absence from convalescent sick and wounded soldiers.

SUCCESSFUL EXPEDITION TO WARRENTON.

Information having been received that the enemy were about removing a large number of convalescent and sick and wounded soldiers to Culpepper Court-House, instructions were issued by Gen. Sigel to Gen. Stahl to send two regiments, a section of artillery, and a force of cavalry to stone bridge, across Bull Run, on the Centreville and Gainesville turnpike, and capture all the sick and wounded and stragglers there. Under these instructions an expedition, composed as above, was sent out yesterday. A detachment of cavalry about 100 strong, pushed forward to Gainesville and Greenwich, and other cavalry were sent to Manassas Junction.

The regiment under Col. Kartz advanced upon Warrenton, and succeeded in capturing 1,200 prisoners, besides stores. They met with no decided opposition, the enemy preferring to live to fight another day. The prisoners were paroled on the spot, in obedience to orders from Gen. Sigel, the cartel with the Rebels containing a stipulation requiring prisoners to be exchanged within ten days or to be paroled. This affair is the "Raid of the Yankees" of which *The Richmond Dispatch* of Sept. 27 expressed fears. Strange that fulfillment should follow so close upon prophesy.

EXPEDITION TO WARRENTON JUNCTION.

On Saturday, Col. McLean, with a detachment from his brigade, proceeded to Warrenton Junction. They found a small force of the enemy there, who were at first disposed to fight, but upon the hint of a few shells, hastily withdrew. Col. McLean then advanced, and found knapsacks, boots, shoes, equipments, &c., belonging to the 57th Ohio, which he brought away.

THE RAPPAHANNOCK BRIDGE.

It is reported that the enemy have completed the bridge over the Rappahannock. If so, the locomotives and cars which our forces should have captured before now will doubtless be put into requisition to remove such stores as may still remain along the route and in their possession.

THE SURRENDER OF HARPER'S FERRY.

The Court of Inquiry of which Gen. Hunter is Chairman is engaged in the examination of the surrender of Harper's Ferry.

ACCIDENTAL SHOOTING.

As last night's down train passed a switched-off train containing the 12th New-Hampshire Regiment, this side the Relay House, the passengers cheered the volunteers heartily, during which an enthusiastic Lieutenant discharged his revolver several times, one shot instantly killing Private Morrison of Company I, who was upon the platform.

KEARNEY'S DIVISION.

Kearney's old Division will be reviewed to-morrow by Gen. Heintzelman.

DEATHS IN HOSPITAL.

The following deaths have occurred in the Washington hospitals since our last publication:

Jesse Zaner, G, 4 O.	Alfred Canady, E, 11 Pa. Res.
Chas. E. Marston, F, 1 Mass.	Eugene P. Geer, C, 5 N. Y.
W. H. Plugh, D, 20 N. Y.	John Shaw, jr., E, 5 N. H.
A. Thomas, C, 18 Mass.	Rich. Freed, A, 59 N. Y.
Miles B. Easter, E, 50 Pa.	Wm. Engelobs, K, 3 N. Y. C.
Benj. Ash, F, 11 Vt.	John Kucker, B, 63 Pa.
D. Maguire, Nurse at Capitol Hospital.	Frank Geisler, B, 74 Pa.
	Sam. Benson, G, 18 Mass.
Ap. B. Fink, I, 20 N. Y.	Wm. Cupp, A, 44 N. Y.
Chas. Boyle, C, 3 U. S. Art.	Thos. Cawley, 17 N. Y.
Jere. Pyles, D, 1 Va.	C. G. Corm, I, 1 Va.

To the Associated Press.

WASHINGTON, Tuesday, Sept. 30, 1862.

STATE PRISONERS ON PAROLE TO REPORT THEMSELVES FORTHWITH.

All prisoners of state now on parole by authority from the Headquarters of the Military District of Columbia, will report in person forthwith to the Military Governor of this District. This is with a view to their exchange for Union prisoners at Richmond.

THE DISMISSAL OF MAJOR KEY.

The dismissal by the President of Major John J. Key, additional aid-de-camp attached to Gen. Halleck's staff, for the utterance of disloyal sentiments, is regarded as an excellent example in high quarters, and a hope is expressed that it may be followed up until the army shall be thoroughly purged of those officers who so frequently offend the ear of loyal citizens by seditious and treasonable words. Major Key, it is but just to say, whatever may have been the offense for which he has been dismissed, bore a fair character as an officer, and his loyalty was never previously suspected. He was not, however, an officer of Gen. Halleck's own selection, but had been assigned to him.

Thus attached to the staff, and without the personal acquaintance or confidence of Gen. Halleck, he has been constantly employed on detached staff duties, such as local provost-marshal for towns and cities, supervising agent at different points, etc. He has never been employed in any confidential capacity at headquarters which would give him access to information that could by any possibility be of service to the enemy; not, however, because any question of his loyalty had been raised, but because Gen. Halleck had no personal knowledge of him, such as would induce the confiding of important or secret operations. Major Key is from Indiana, but is said to have large contingent interests in the Slave States.

THE REVOLVING TOWER FOR FORTIFICATIONS.

Mr. Tunby has the broad patent from the United States for the revolving tower for land and water fortifications. This is acknowledged to be a great national invention, and is fully accredited to American genius and energy.

THE ORDERS FOR STAMPS.

Rittenhouse, Fant & Co., and other bankers, are receiving large orders for revenue or tax stamps and postage currency. The latter cannot be supplied, excepting in small quantities. The only stamps ready for delivery at the office of the Commissioner of Internal Revenue are check stamps for checks, drafts, or orders on sight, and proprietary stamps for patent medicines, cosmetics, etc. Other stamps will be ready in a few days, of which notice will be given, that purchasers may know how to frame their orders.

DISMISSED THE SERVICE.

The following officers, sent home from the Western Gulf Blockading squadron, have this day been dismissed the service, viz.:

Gunner John Duncan, as worthless; Gunner Wm. Yates, as worthless; Gunner Wm. Simmers, for drunkenness; Master's mate E. J. Allen, for drunkenness; Master's Mate John Coffey, for drunkenness; and Master's Mate Wm. White, as worthless.

NAVAL ORDERS.

Lieut.-Commander H. C. Blake has been detached from the Sabine, and ordered to the temporary command of the R. R. Cuyler, condemned by medical survey, vice Lieut.-Commander Wm. C. West, previously ordered.

Lieut.-Commander Wm. D. Whiting is detached from the Wyandotte, and ordered to the command of the Ottawa, vice Lieut.-Commander J. B. Creighton, detached.

Gunner George Sirian is detached from the Sabine, and ordered to the Naval Academy.

Capt. O. S. Glisson's order to the command of the Iroquois is revoked, and he is ordered to the command of the U. S. steam sloop-of-war Mohican.

RAILWAY COMPANIES AND STAMP DUTIES.

The Commissioner of Internal Revenue has given the following opinion in regard to the liability of railway companies to the payment of stamp duties: The item marked "Express N" on page 89 of the Excise law, was not intended to embrace the freight business of railroads and ordinary wagoners, but is limited to persons who are express carriers, and not merely common carriers under the law. The distinction is very well known in practical business. The express carrier is usually expected to take the parcel, box or bundle from the house or place of business of the consignee, while a railway company receives and delivers goods only at its own stations.

In the absence of specific language in the statute authorizing the broader construction, I must hold that persons or companies engaged in transporting goods over the country, as such business is usually performed by railway corporations, are not liable to the payment of a stamp-tax upon the receipts given for such goods. I am also of opinion that the first item in Schedule B does not include such receipts for freight as are usually given by railway companies. A receipt is no doubt in a technical sense an agreement or contract, but in the ordinary use of language this close construction does not hold good. Had Congress intended to include receipts, it would have been easy to have so provided in plain language.

FROM FORTRESS MONROE.

News from Richmond—Rebel Accounts of the Battle of Antietam—A Victory Claimed—Stupendous Lying—Extension of the Draft.

From Our Special Correspondent.

FORTRESS MONROE, Monday, Sept. 29, 1862.

The Richmond papers of Friday and Saturday, 26th and 27th, received this morning by the flag steamer Metamora, contain nothing of special importance. I send you, however, the gleanings, which will be read with interest.

The Enquirer of Friday has an account of the battle of Antietam, the result of which is claimed as a Rebel victory. It was planned by Gen. Lee; the right was commanded by Longstreet, the left by Jackson, the center by Hill, and the army formed the segment of a circle. It is claimed that the Union forces were largest. It is asserted that Jackson not only held his ground, but drove us a mile; that the fight at the center was "terribly severe," but that in the end Hill held his ground; that "the pressure on Longstreet's corps was irresistible, and the anxiety for the result intense, when Gen. A. P. Hill brought the reserves up from Harper's Ferry to reinstate the fortunes of the day." According to this, had Harper's Ferry been held only a few hours longer, the route of the enemy would have been complete. *The Enquirer's* account pronounces this "the battle of the war." The Rebel loss is placed at "six to eight thousand," and ours is estimated at five times that number. The next day the Rebels were under arms, waiting for a renewal of the battle. It is claimed that the repulse of the Union force that crossed the river the next day was signalized by the slaughter of the flower of Burnside's corps.

The Legislature of Virginia has passed a vote of thanks to Gens. Lee, Jackson, Longstreet, and others, for having achieved great victories in Maryland. It is proposed by a resolution of the House of Delegates to disband the men recently raised by Gen. Floyd.

The draft throughout the Rebel States has been extended to citizens between 35 and 45.

The Whig of the 27th contains an account of the alleged "expulsion of the enemy from Kanawha Valley," and the capture of the salt works at Charleston.

The re-enforcement of the Union troops at Suffolk, and the landing of troops at the White House, is chronicled in all the Richmond papers.

The Richmond Dispatch of the 27th Sept. calls for legislation for the removal of negroes, making at the same time some important admissions. It says:

"The Federal invasion, especially in its relations to negroes, has thus far been a John Brown raid on a grand scale. Wherever the Union armies have advanced the negroes have been swept off as clean as the Eastern locusts sweep a field of grain. Not one green or black thing is left in the line of the Yankee march, nor in the whole country for many miles around. The Piedmont, the Upper Valley, the Peninsula, the country watered by the Rappahannock and the Potomac, have been stripped of their negro population. This war has assumed the character of a grand Negro-Hunting Expedition. Of victories the Yankees have gained few; negroes many. What becomes of the game it is impossible to say, nor is that a matter of much importance. *The loss, however, of so valuable an element of strength and prosperity is a matter of such moment that the Legislature of the State ought at once to take measures for the prevention of similar calamities in the future.* This can only be done by a law providing for the removal of negroes from all threatened districts to the interior. It will not do to leave this to the discretion or judgment of the masters. In some cases they are too indolent to take the proper precautions for the security of their property. In others they are deluded by implicit confidence in the fidelity of their servants, and, notwithstanding the experience which the war has furnished that the neighborhood of a Yankee army creates as complete a *stampede* among negroes as the approach of a locomotive among cattle, there are thousands of masters who continue to believe that *their* servants will not run under similar temptations, *and foolishly to expose them to temptation. It is clear, therefore, that there is no security for the negro property of the State*, unless the Legislature makes the removal of the negroes from districts exposed to invasion compulsory. We trust the necessary action will be taken promptly, for *the State has already suffered enormous losses from this cause*, which, by precautionary legislation, might all have been prevented."

The Dispatch gives the substance of Mr. Seward's Paisley letter, and says it "would disgrace any man in North America except Mr. Seward himself."

It is asserted that Gen. Lee keeps his intentions and movements so close that the public are wholly ignorant of them till a battle or a march transpires.

Army and Navy Intelligence.

A general court-martial will convene at Fort Columbus, New-York Harbor, to-day, for the trial of Sergeant Baldwin, Ordnance Sergeant of Fort Schuyler, who is charged with a brutal and unprovoked assault on Capt. S. M. Sprole of the 4th Infantry, U. S. A. One Sergeant, named Williams, who took part with Baldwin in the assault, has already been tried. Assaulting an officer is a violation of the 9th article of war; the punishment is death, or long confinement with a ball and chain, and hard labor.

The United States troops on Governor's Island will be paid off to-day by Col. Stewart, for the two months ending Aug. 30. The delay in paying off the men is understood to have been caused by a scarcity of greenbacks. There are upward of 500 men on the rolls at Fort Columbus. Their two months' pay will amount to about $7,000.

Orders have been received from the Commander-in-chief of the United States Marine Corps, by Maj. Garland, to dispatch at once from Brooklyn a battalion of Marines to constitute a guard for the United States steam-frigate Colorado, supposed to be destined for the Mediterranean squadron. The Colorado is to be equipped and manned in the best manner, and is evidently intended for some first-class port, whether it be in the Eastern or Western Hemisphere. She will carry nearly 500 men, picked from the receiving-ships, and has not been surpassed in warlike appearance by any man-of-war that ever left our shores.

The Naval Board appointed to report on navy yard siets, left Philadelphia yesterday for the purpose of visiting the Schuylkill, Lehigh, Susquehannah, Alleghany and Juniata valleys to inquire into the facilities for procuring coal. All the proposed sites for the new Navy-Yard have now been examined, from New-London to League Island. The decision of the board is not yet known, but detailed accounts of the respective merits of each place have been laid before it. The sentiment of the Navy is in favor of New-London.

The employees of the Brooklyn Navy-Yard have been paid off. About $120,000 a month are required to foot the labor-rolls. The men, being very much in want of money, owing to a postponement of pay-day, prevailed upon Admiral Paulding and Mr. Bellknap to write for the funds, which came at once. There are nearly 4,000 hands in the different shops. The new iron-clad ships will be commenced next week. The Mackinaw, Shamrock, Ticonderoga, and Lackawanna, all new vessels, are in course of construction.

FROM GEN. McCLELLAN'S ARMY.

THE BATTLES OF SOUTH MOUNTAIN AND ANTIETAM

OFFICIAL REPORT OF GEN. M'CLELLAN.

THE REBEL LOSS OVER 25,000.

WASHINGTON, Tuesday, Sept. 30, 1862

The following report of the victory of Antietam has been forwarded to the headquarters of the army by Gen. McClellan:

NEAR SHARPSBURG, Sept. 29, 1862—1:30 p. m.

Major-Gen. H. W. HALLECK, General-in-Chief of the United States Army.

GENERAL: I have the honor to report the following as some of the results of the battles of South Mountain and Antietam.

At South Mountain our loss was 443 dead, 1,806 wounded, and 76 missing; total, 2,325.

At Antietam, our loss was 2,010 killed, 9,416 wounded, and 1,043 missing—total, 12,469.

Total loss in the two battles, 14,794.

The loss of the Rebels in the two battles, as near as can be ascertained from the number of their dead found upon the field and from other data, will not fall short of the following estimate:

Major Davis, Assistant Inspector General, who superintends the burial of the dead, reports about 3,000 Rebels buried upon the field of Antietam by our troops.

Previous to this, however, the Rebels had buried many of their own dead upon the distant portion of the battle-field, which they occupied after the battle —probably at least 500.

The loss of the Rebels at South Mountain cannot be ascertained with accuracy, but as our troops continually drove them from the commencement of the action, and as a much greater number of their dead were seen on the field than of our own men, it is not unreasonable to suppose that their loss was greater than ours. Estimating their killed at 500 the total Rebels killed in the two battles would be 4,000. According to the ratio of our own killed and wounded, this would make their loss in wounded 18,742.

As nearly as can be determined at this time the number of prisoners taken by our troops in the two battles will at the lowest estimate amount to 5,000. The full returns will no doubt show a larger number. Of these about 1,200 are wounded.

This gives me a Rebel loss in killed, wounded and prisoners of 25,542. It will be observed that this does not include their stragglers, the number of whom is said by citizens here to be large.

It may be safely concluded, therefore, that the Rebel army lost at least 30,000 of their best troops.

From the time our troops first encountered the enemy in Maryland until he was driven back into Virginia, we captured 13 guns, 7 caissons, 9 limbers, 2 field forges, 2 caissons bodies, 39 colors, and 1 signal flag. We have not lost a single gun or a color.

On the battle-field of Antietam 14,000 small-arms were collected, beside the large number carried off by citizens and those distributed on the ground to recruits and other unarmed men arriving immediately after the battle.

At South Mountain no collection of small-arms was made, but, owing to the haste of the pursuit from that point, 400 were taken on the opposite side of the Potomac.

GEORGE B. McCLELLAN, Major-General Commanding.

Our Losses at Antietam.

From Our Special Correspondent.

BOLIVAR HIGHTS, Va., near Harper's Ferry, Sept. 29, 1862.

The most unruffled calm prevails along the front. During the past two days there have been some changes in the disposition of troops about and upon Loudon and Maryland Hights, as if the force now holding them (Banks's old corps) were designed to occupy them permanently.

A reconnoissance, under Maj. Whiting, has been out in the direction of Charlestown since morning. No intelligence received from it thus far, though we hear a few artillery discharges four or five miles away.

To-day orders are very strict that no citizen, under any circumstances, be allowed to go outside the lines.

Official reports, collected at the various corps, division and brigade headquarters, show our entire loss at the battle of Antietam to be as follows:

Corps.	Killed.	Wounded.	Missing.	Total.
Sumner's	874	3,833	501	5,208
Hooker's	348	2,016	255	2,619
Mansfield's	289	1,366	101	1,756
Franklin's	102	340	36	478
Burnside's	432	1,741	118	2,291
Total	2,045	9,296	1,011	12,352

There may be some slight modifications of these reports before they are all sent in to Gen. McClellan, but the above is a faithful transcript of them as they now stand.

A. D. R.

A Little Stir in Camp—The Soldiers Desire to Winter in the Carolinas—The President's Proclamation in Camp—Porter's, Burnside's, and Hooker's Corps—Accidents from Unexploded Shells—A Train Dashed to Pieces on the Mountain.

From our Special Correspondent.

SHARPSBURG, Sept. 29, 1862.

On Saturday headquarters were enlivened by the striking of tents and the din of preparation for a change of position. It was soon noised about camp that McClellan was about to cross the Potomac; and every soldier stepped with more elasticity. The mistake was, however, soon discovered, and it was found that the commander simply changed his base of operation to a new position, three miles southward to a more convenient watering-place. Whether these are to be his Winter quarters or only a temporary camp, has not been made public. A large body of troops has crossed the Potomac at Harper's Ferry, and an army still remains at this place, resting and waiting. There is an anxious desire in the minds of the troops to go forward at once and find and fight the enemy before he shall have time to rest and fortify.

To be overtaken by Winter north of the James River is regarded by the fighting soldiers as a calamity to be avoided, if within the range of possibilities. An earnest and strong push, quickly made, they believe, would place the army in a mild climate south of the James River, where, in the salubrious atmosphere of the Carolinas, an active campaign could be carried on, and the war ended before the opening of the Northern Spring. The thought of being able to return to his home ready for the peaceful labors of the Summer, would infuse new zeal in the ranks, and the industrious farmers and mechanics from the North and West would fight the more earnestly in order to make the return in the Spring doubly sure. Whether this hope of the private soldier is to be cherished, and this theory made plausible, by early, vigorous, and continued movements against the enemy, remains to be seen. Certainly nothing would more strengthen the arm of the soldier, and encourage the people in the belief that our leaders are really in earnest in this matter.

The proclamation of the President has electrified the army. The gloom and darkness of a long and terrible night has changed, and the shooting rays of a rising morn are seen. Since reading the earnest words of the President the soldier grasps his rifle with new energy, and when he shoulders or orders arms he performs like a man with a soul in his work. Legions have been added to our armies. The soldier has distinctly before him the object of the contest. Believing that thus the Union will be *permanently* restored, he now sees the beginning of the end.

There is considerable stir in Fitz John Porter's corps, and several batteries have passed through Sharpsburg in a direction that indicates work.

Burnside has moved his entire corps toward Harper's Ferry, and the despondent are beginning to take hope that something will be done. The enemy is so near the river above the Ferry that foraging parties are limited to a scope within four miles of the river.

Gen. Meade having taken command of Hooker's Corps, the first division of Pennsylvania Reserves is in command of Gen. Seymore, and Col. Roberts of the 1st Pennsylvania commands Gen. Seymore's Brigade. The corps remains quiet in the camp occupied after the battle, and still forms the right wing of McClellan's army.

Accidents from the explosion of shells picked up on the battle-field are of daily occurrence. Hundreds of civilians continue to visit the scene of the late terrible struggle, gathering trophies, and gratifying their curiosity. Unexploded shells are found in great abundance, and are carelessly handled by many who are unconscious of the danger to which they thus expose themselves.

On Wednesday, a party of visitors, after examining an elongated shell, threw it violently against a stump, causing it to explode with great force. Fortunately, no one was hurt, but the party, after that, gave all shells a wide berth.

On Friday a squad of soldiers in Gen. Gibbon's brigade screwed out the fuse of a shell, and after pouring out nearly all of the powder, set it on end on a stump, and a surgeon, who should have had more good sense, dropped a live coal into it. The fragments of iron were hurled upward in every direction, everybody present was terribly frightened, but no one received any injury.

Yesterday a most frightful accident occurred on the mountain road between this place and Harper's Ferry. A train of army wagons, going up the long and narrow cut on this side of the mountain, was met by a train coming down. The mules in the down train took fright, and, becoming unmanageable, dashed down the mountain at a most fearful speed, and, crowding the up train off of the road, hurled the wagons, mules and drivers over a steep and rocky precipice of a perpendicular hight varying from 50 to 100 feet. Over and over rolled the great wagons and teams, dashing and crashing and breaking into fragments and tearing to pieces, until the whole train lay at the foot and scattered along the side of the mountain, a mass of frightful ruin.

J. R. S.

From Maryland.

Correspondence of The N. Y. Tribune.

KEEDYSVILLE, Md., Sept. 20, 1862.

Inclosed is the official account of the killed and wounded in the Purnell Legion, Maryland Volunteers, at the fight of Wednesday last:

OFFICERS.

Capt. Wm. Mitchell, hand; Lieut. Geo. W. Brown, finger; Lieut. S. H. Bogardus, mouth.

ENLISTED MEN.

Company A—D. W. Gathell, wrist; John Fettus, horse fell on him.

Company B—Corp. David Reed, groin; John Foote, wrist.

Company C—Sergt. Wm. H. Williams, leg; James English, killed.

Company D—Sergt. J. P. Owens, leg broken; Joseph Scarborough, foot.

Company E—John Means, killed; Nicholas House, hand; Wm. Mahony, hand; Jesse Anderson, face; Samuel Hamilton, leg.

Company F—Ord. Sergt. A. C. Spicer, killed; Corp. W. T. Barlow, shoulder.

Company G—Corp. S. J. Williams, shoulder; William Long, thigh.

Company H—Corp. Joseph Johnson, foot; Corp. John W. Miller, arm and shoulder.

Company K—Daniel Doxzen, bowels; Henry Kahlman, hand.

RECAPITULATION.

Killed.....3 | Wounded.....24

There are also 57 missing.

Gen. Green, commanding the 2d Division of Banks's Corps, complimented them very highly after the battle.

Thanks of Maryland to Gen. McClellan and his Army, and to Gov. Curtin and the Militia of Pennsylvania.

BALTIMORE, Tuesday, Sept. 30, 1862.

The following has just been issued by Gov. Bradford:

STATE OF MARYLAND, EXECUTIVE DEPARTMENT, ANNAPOLIS, Sept. 29, 1862.

The expulsion of the Rebel army from the soil of Maryland should not be suffered to pass without a proper acknowledgment, and the cordial thanks of her authorities to those who were chiefly instrumental in compelling that evacuation.

I would tender, therefore, on behalf of the State of Maryland, to Major-General McClellan and the gallant officers and men under his command, my earnest and hearty thanks for the distinguished courage, skill, and gallantry with which that achievement was accomplished. It reflects a lustre upon the ability of the Commander-in-Chief and the heroism and endurance of his followers that the country everywhere recognizes, and that even our enemies are constrained to acknowledge.

To Governor Curtin of Pennsylvania and to the militia of his State who rallied with such alacrity at the first symptoms of an invasion, our warmest thanks are also due. The readiness with which they crossed the border and took their stand beside the Maryland brigade, shows that that border is in all respects but an ideal line, and that in such a cause as now unites us, Pennsylvania and Maryland are one.

I cannot forbear to notice in this connection, the conduct of our own regiments who took part in the recent battles. All reports concur in representing their gallantry as all their State could desire.

The numbers of their killed and wounded, and their torn and tattered standards bear witness to the position they occupied in the field.

To the 2d, 3d, and 5th Maryland Regiments, the Purnell Legion, the 1st Regiment of the Home Brigade, and the 1st Maryland Artillery, participants in the recent severe struggles, I would, therefore, tender the thanks which are so justly their due.

By the Governor. A. W. BRADFORD.

WM. B. HILL, Secretary of State.

Gen. Buell Not Removed.

LOUISVILLE, Tuesday, Sept. 30, 1862.

Yesterday it was rumored that Gen. Buell was relieved from his command. The news created much dissatisfaction among our State authorities and prominent citizens, who have the utmost confidence in Gen. Buell. We have trustworthy information to-day that Gen. Buell is still in command of the Army of the Ohio.

The Evacuation of Cumberland Gap.

CINCINNATI, Tuesday, Sept. 30, 1862.

Gen. Morgan left Cumberland Gap about two weeks ago, with all his forces, and is supposed to be marching in a north-easterly direction, so as to strike the Ohio somewhere about Portsmouth. He brought away all his artillery and stores, and blocked up the Gap with stones, so as to render it impassable.

Drafting takes place in the city to-morrow.

Capt. Prentice, son of George D. Prentice of *The Louisville Journal*, who was wounded in the Augusta (Ky.) fight, died to-day.

An Indianapolis correspondent of *The Commercial* says, Gen. Buell has been removed and Gen. Thomas assigned his command.

The Surrender of Harper's Ferry.

Correspondence of The N. Y. Tribune.

WASHINGTON, Sept. 26, 1862.

So much has been said and written of late in reference to the surrender of Harper's Ferry, by persons professing more or less—principally less—knowledge of the facts in the case, that one feels some hesitation in again writing upon the topic, lest he may be regarded as one of the—if not *the* "reliable gentleman" who has been so instrumental in making a muddle of war news during the past year or more. A statement of facts, isolated from the general account of the affair, by one who was present, may explain away some of the prejudice which exists against Col. Miles, and tend to soften the harsh epithets applied to one who, mortally wounded on the field of battle, now rests in a soldier's grave.

All accounts agree that the evacuation of Maryland Heights was the *real* cause of the ultimate surrender. That evacuation has been set forth as the act of Col. Miles, that is to say, it is made to appear that it was done by his orders. The writer of this was present at a conversation between Col. Miles and Col. Ford, on the occasion of a visit by Col. Miles to the battery and camps on Maryland Heights. At that time an attack was expected the next day. Col. Miles spoke of the strength and importance of the position, and told Col. Ford that he expected him to hold it to the last extremity, to which end such reenforcements as were necessary should be sent him and all assistance rendered that the exigences of the case might require. Col. Ford, in reply, said "all hell cant drive me from it. I know my men will fight, and I do not mean to be whipped out, not a a man shall come down to tell they have been whipped away from it. I don't want any reenforcements, I think that you (meaning Col. Miles and the force on the other side) will have to come up to me for protection," and more of the same tenor. Col. Miles answed that he didn't think rhetorical flourish would do much toward it, but believed Col. Ford and his troops would be able to give a good account of themselves. The impression then seemed to be that the attack would come from Solomon's Gap, where Col Ford said he had strong pickets, and suggestions were made by Col. Miles as to increased viligance in that quarter. At the time of this visit, Capt. McGrath, commanding the battery, was informed of the expected attack, and answered that he "was ready." Inquiry was then made by Col. Miles as to whether one of the heavy guns could be brought to bear upon certain points for the purpose of shelling out any Rebels who might intrude. Capt. McGrath replied that he could so place the gun as to have the desired effect. The Captain also remarked that his men were "rusting out," and he hoped that an opportunity would be offered soon to take some of the rust off.

Subsequently Col. Ford remarked to Major Steiner and your correspondent, that he had "looked the hill all over, was satisfied that it was a strong position, and *meant to stay there*;" that he thought a small force ought to keep a disproportionately large one at bay. It was afterward subject of comment between the two listeners, that they were glad to hear Col. Ford say so, as they thought he meant it, and would fight.

Aside from these verbal orders given by Col. Miles, and the remarks as to the impregnability and importance of the position, it was known and acknowledged by officers, men, and citizens, that Maryland Hights was the key to the whole position, and the imperative necessity of holding them was felt by all. In addition to verbal orders, Col. Miles sent Col. Ford a written order, as follows:

HARPER'S FERRY, Sept. 13, 1862.

Col. FORD, Commanding Maryland Hights:

Since I returned to this side, on close inspection, I find your position more defensible than it appears when at your station, covered as it is at all points by the cannon of Camp Hill. You will hold on, and can hold on, until the cows' tails drop off.

Yours,

D. S. MILES, Colonel 2d Infantry.

Col. Ford, it is understood, has denied receiving this order. The order could hardly have missed him, as the orderlies were always required to bring back the receipt for messages or dispatches sent, indorsed upon the envelope, and any emission upon so important an order would have been noticed. Furthermore, the remark of Col. Miles which will be found below, in reference to Col. Ford's *reply*, settles the point as to its receipt by the person to whom it was addressed.

After the evacuation, your correspondent told Col. Miles that there seemed to be a diversity of opinion as to who was responsible for the evacuation, and asked him frankly as to whether it was done by his orders. "No, Sir, but in direct opposition to them," was the reply already recorded. Allusion was then made by Col. Miles to the conversation before mentioned, to which your correspondent was a listener, and also mention made of the order to "hold on till the cow's tail comes off." Col. Miles remarked that Ford's *reply to that order* did not indicate that he had the slightest intention of giving up the Hights. This certainly proves the receipt of the dispatch.

The statement has also been made that Col. Ford had "discretionary powers." Admitting this, which is more than improbable, then the necessity of the evacuation must be proved. At the time the troops retired, the Rebels had been shelled back from the woods by Capt. McGrath's and Capt. Graham's batteries, which were both firing as the troops marched down. Officers and men who were in the most advanced positions on the Hights say not a Rebel was to be seen, though their presence on the other side of the mountain is not denied. The assertion that the Hights were not surrendered until the ammunition gave out, made in *The Herald*, no doubt arises from the happy faculty of that sheet of making parts of two or three stories dove-tail into each other. As this is often done in a tolerably workmanlike manner, the incongruity of the narrative is not readily detected by the reader. The assertion is clearly disproved by the fact, that on Sunday the expedition sent up Maryland Hights by Col. d'Utassy, brought down quantities of ammunition, which proved of service on Monday, and left some still behind.

That Col. Miles was remiss in his duty in not arresting Col. Ford and ordering a re-occupation of the Hights, if only to prevent the Rebels from planting a battery there, is not denied. That he also neglected to fortify Loudon Hights is apparent, though palliated by the fact that the battery on Maryland Hights commanded Loudon Hights, and the belief that it was impossible to take cannon of sufficiently long range up the Hights.

The assertion that Col. Miles was a traitor and a coward is not warranted by the facts, and arises from the old prejudice against Col. Miles, dating back to Bull Run. Let justice be done the living and surely meted out to the dead. The errors of omission were greater than those of commission, but certainly do not justify the application of the worst of all possible terms to a soldier.

The Draft in Massachusetts Again Postponed.

BOSTON, Tuesday, Sept. 30, 1862.

The draft in Massachusetts has been again postponed till October 15.

Gen. Davis to be Tried by Court-Martial.

LOUISVILLE, Tuesday, Sept. 30, 1862.

Gen. Jeff. C. Davis is under arrest for killing Gen. Nelson, and will be tried by court-martial.

Arrival of the Keystone State—Admiral Dupont a Passenger.

PHILADELPHIA, Tuesday, Sept. 30, 1862.

The U. S. steamer Keystone State has arrived here from Port Royal. Admiral Dupont and Capt. Rodgers come as passengers in her.

New-York Daily Tribune.

WEDNESDAY, OCTOBER 1, 1862.

UNION STATE NOMINATIONS.

For Governor..........JAMES S. WADSWORTH.
For Lieutenant-Governor.LYMAN TREMAIN.
For Canal Commissioner.OLIVER LADUE.
State Prison Inspector....ANDREAS WILLMANN.
Cl'k of Court of Appeals.CHARLES HUGHES.

TO CORRESPONDENTS.

No notice can be taken of Anonymous Communications. Whatever is intended for insertion must be authenticated by the name and address of the writer—not necessarily for publication, but as a guaranty for his good faith.

We cannot undertake to return rejected Communications.

All business letters for this office should be addressed to "THE TRIBUNE," New-York.

NEWS OF THE DAY.

THE WAR.

—Gen. McClellan reports to Gen. Hallock, as some of the results of the battles of South Mountain and Antietam, as follows:

	South Mountain.	Antietam.	Total.
Killed	443	2,010	2,453
Wounded	1,806	9,616	11,422
Missing	76	1,043	1,119
Total	2,325	12,669	14,994

During the Maryland campaign, we captured 13 guns, 7 caissons, 9 limbers, 2 field forges, 2 caissons bodies, 39 colors, and 1 signal flag. We have not lost a single gun or a color. On the battle-field of Antietam 14,000 small arms were collected, beside the large number carried off by citizens and those distributed on the ground to recruits and other unarmed men arriving immediately after the battle. At South Mountain no collection of small-arms was made, but, owing to the haste of the pursuit from that point, 400 were taken on the opposite side of the Potomac. As to the losses of the Rebels, Gen. McClellan says that about 3,000 were buried by our men on the field of Antietam, beside which perhaps 500 were buried by the Rebels. Their killed at South Mountain he estimates at 500—say 4,000 killed in the two battles; wounded, from 18,000 to 19,000; prisoners taken by us, at least 5,000—total rebel loss, about 30,000. The losses in our several divisions at the battle of Antietam are given in detail by our special correspondent. They are:

Corps.	Killed.	Wounded.	Missing.	Total.
Sumner's	874	3,833	501	5,208
Hooker's	348	2,016	255	2,619
Mansfield's	289	1,366	101	1,756
Franklin's	102	340	36	478
Burnside's	432	1,741	118	2,291
Totals	2,045	9,296	1,011	12,352

These figures are official and nearly exact.

—Some sensation was created yesterday by a Washington dispatch printed in *The Philadelphia Inquirer*, asserting that "it is rumored" that Peace Commissioners are on the way from Richmond to propose a settlement of the war on these terms: "The loyal States are to take all the Territories, Missouri, Tennessee, Kentucky and Maryland, and to make them free or Slave States, as may best please them. The Cotton States are to be permitted to have a Congress of their own, to regulate their own domestic affairs only. In all other things to be again as one, and an inseparable people. For defensive and offensive operations against other countries, to be a unity. In all matters of postal and revenue service to be as heretofore. They pledging to return all Government property to us as they found it. They, in addition to having us recognize their authority to have this Congress, to regulate their peculiar institutions, are to be permitted Senators and Representatives in our Halls of Congress, but only in such numbers as their free white population is entitled to." Of course this absurd story refutes itself.

—Within a day or two past, Gen. Stahl's Brigade, being a part of Gen. Sigel's Corps, advanced to Warrenton Junction, about forty-one miles from Washington, without meeting the enemy. Yesterday they went to Warrenton village, ten miles west, and there met a large number (about 1,200) of sick and wounded Rebels, together with a few conscripts, prisoners, whom they paroled. Gen. Stahl continued his reconnoissance to Salem and White Plains, but found no Rebels in that neighborhood. A report prevailed at Alexandria that Gen. Sigel's troops had recaptured all the engines and cars which the enemy obtained from the wreck at Bristow and Warrenton Junction.

—Surgeon-General Moore (Rebel) reports the number of sick and wounded received in the Richmond Hospitals since their organization to be 99,508. Of these, 9,774 have been furloughed; 2,341 have been discharged, and 7,603 have died. At the Chimbcrazo Hospital, there were received 24,895, of which 2,033 died. At the Winter Hospital, the number received was 22,874, of which 1,271 died. The whole number of sick and wounded received in the Petersburg Hospitals was 11,170.

—Gov. Bradford of Maryland has published an official letter of thanks to Major-Gen. McClellan and his officers and men, to Gov. Curtin and the Pennsylvania militia, and to the Maryland troops in the Union army, for their great services in expelling the Rebel invaders from the soil of Maryland.

—Gen. Halleck calls upon State Governors to fill the great number of vacancies in the volunteer force caused by recent casualties, by the appointment and promotion of non-commissioned officers and privates who have distinguished themselves in the field or shown due capacity for command.

—A court-martial has been ordered to meet at Fort Columbus, New-York, to-day, for the trial of Ordnance-Sergeant Baldwin, charged with a brutal and unprovoked assault on Capt. S. M. Sprole, of the 4th Infantry, U. S. A.

GENERAL NEWS.

—The McGrath habeas corpus case, which has been adjourned a number of times, was finally dismissed yesterday, the plaintiff's counsel (Mr. Edwin James) not appearing—it was said in consequence of pecuniary disappointment. The sudden suspension of the case has deprived the world of a highly interesting biography of the ex-Reverend Malcolm Ives, late *Herald* writer and prisoner of State—a biography which had been carefully prepared and was ready to be placed on the records of the court. This is to be regretted, as Mr. Ives has been something of a public character, and an accurate history of his antecedents and career would doubtless clear up some points of uncertainty which at present give occasion for unpleasant differences of opinion.

—The Union State Central Convention met at the Astor House yesterday, and elected the following gentlemen as permanent officers for the ensuing year: Chairman, Judge Low, of Sullivan; Secretary, Ben. Field, of New Orleans; Treasurer, Isaac Sherman, of New-York; Executive Committee, Walter L. Sessions, of Chataqua; Abraham Wakeman, of New York; Charles Jones, of Kings; C. R. Richards, of Rensselear; W. S. Lincoln, of Tioga; and Hamilton Harris, of Albany. A resolution of thanks was tendered to Simeon Draper, Chairman of the Committee last year, and short addresses were delivered by the Hon. Lyman Tremaine, Mr. Wakeman and others.

—That parlor meeting of hybrids, called at the Everett House last night, was largely attended by such Democrats and Know-Nothings as reprobate Freedom, and swear horribly at the mere mention of the President's proclamation. They held a secret class-meeting—a sort of Brooks-Purdy love-feast—the War Horse falling upon the neck of *The Express* editor, and fondly kissing him, as Esau of the flesh-pots did his long-absent brother David—there were tears of reconciliation, drinks all around, and a Committee was raised to raise money and hire people to attend a Know-Nothing-Democratic Ratification meeting that is to come off hereafter.

—The Liquor-sellers' State Convention at Syracuse yesterday unanimously nominated the regular Democratic candidates for Governor and Lieutenant-Governor (Horatio Seymour and D. R. Floyd Jones). It was, of course, expected; Mike Walsh years ago proclaimed the axiom "Grogshops are the nurseries of Democracy," and why should the nurse turn away from her offspring? The Convention professed to ignore parties altogether.

— Col. Forsyth, formerly editor of *The Mobile Register*, and Minister to Mexico, is reported to have been killed in a recent skirmish with Col McCook's Regiment, in Kentucky. He held at various times public offices of distinction, that of Minister to Mexico among the rest. He was one of the delegation sent by the Secessionists to Washington, to see if a peaceable separation of the States could not be agreed to there.

—Our files of Richmond papers are up to the 27th of Sept., inclusive. They contain no important news, but such as we find worth copying is printed elsewhere. A late number of *The Charleston Mercury* says that large Union reinforcements are gathering at Hilton Head and along the coast. Pinckney Island is in their possession.

—The speech of the Hon. Lyman Tremaine, delivered in the State Convention at Syracuse last week, of which we had at the time a brief synopsis, as printed at length on the second page of this morning's edition.

—The Aldermen held a session yesterday. Mayor Opdyke nominated David R. Jaques for street Commissioner, but, on motion of Alderman Boole, the nomination was rejected. Another meeting will be held at one p. m. to-day

—The French steam corvette Forfait, Commander Reueve de la Mure, from Vera Cruz September 18, arrived on Tuesday morning. She mounts four guns, has engines of 250 horse power, a crew of 134 men, and is 800 tuns burden.

—Isaac Congdon Taber, Mayor of New-Bedford, died at his residence in that city on Monday afternoon. He was first elected Mayor in 1859, and held the office till the day of his death, having been successively re-elected.

—A dispatch from Rochester states that the New-York State Fair promises to open finely to-day. The show throughout is expected to be unusually full and interesting.

—The Hon. Benjamin F. Hallet, the widely-known lawyer and Democratic leader of Massachusetts, died at Boston yesterday.

—The Hon. J. Prescott Hall, formerly a prominent Whig politician in this city, died at Newport, R. I, a day or two since.

STATE OF THE MARKETS.

The market still retains its unparalleled strength and vitality, with no present indication of yielding. Each day witnesses a new accession of buyers, and increased business, and blocks of 1,000 shares are swept off the floor in a twinkling by the new comers. The Stock Exchange has ever been the barometer of public feeling, and the community are now expressing their opinion of ultimate results in indiscriminate investments. Governments were stronger in all issues: 6s 1862, sold at 103½; 100 bid for 1868s; the 1881 loan ⅛ ₩ cent better, in good request at 102¼. Demand Notes advanced 1 ₩ cent to 120¾@120½. State and City securities were firm. At the Second Board, the market, under various rumors and realizing sales, was heavy, and suffered some decline from the highest points of the morning. Gold fell off to 121½, under peace rumors and a baseless report that Mr. Chase had decided to receive coupons for duties. It was afterward stronger, and advanced to 122½. At the close the market had a rallying appearance. At a late hour the market closed very strong, with prices, in some instances, higher than in the morning. Gold, after selling at 121½ at the Second Board, closes at 123. The market for foreign bills was strong in the morning, but after the decline in gold the rate fell off to 134 ₩ cent. Francs are about 4.20. Freights are not quite so active, and are somewhat unsettled, being firmer for corn and flour to Great Britain, but rather easier for wheat. The business of the Sub-Treasury was: Receipts, $9,958,795 99—for Customs, $255,287 46; Payments, $3,552,506 46; Balance, $13,684,064 30. Money is abundant at 3@5 ₩ cent on demand. Paper passes freely at 4@6 ₩ cent, with occasional transactions below 4 ₩ cent. A line of $250,000 of a grocery name at four months, given for tea, was taken at 4 ₩ cent and a brokerage. This is the largest line of good paper which has been on the market for some time. Western and State Flour is in good demand, but the poor assortment on the market checks business; the advance in exchange gives sellers the advantage. Prices of the low grades have advanced 5c. ₩ bbl., and of the medium and good qualities, 5@10c. ₩ bbl. Rye Flour is in fair request. Corn Meal is dull and heavy. The Wheat market is less active, and somewhat irregular, opening rather firmer under a further advance in Exchange; but buyers did not respond, and the market closed easier, but at the concession a fair business was done for export. Barley and Barley Malt scarce. Oats more plenty and lower. Rye, lower and in moderate request. Corn, in fair supply, less active and a shade easier. Pork, is well supplied and with a fair inquiry prices are sustained. Beef is quiet, and with more liberal receipts the market is heavy. Beef Hams remain inactive. Bacon is scarce and wanted. Cut Meats are dull. Lard continues in good demand and prices are a shade better. Butter is in active request and is again firmer. Cheese is in good demand.

The new Union State Committee met yesterday at the Astor House to organize for a vigorous campaign under the banner of WADSWORTH and TREMAIN. Hon. HENRY R. LOW of Monticello, Sullivan Co. (Senator from the Orange District) was unanimously chosen Chairman, Isaac Sherman of New-York, Treasurer, Ben. Field of Albion, Secretary, Walter R. Sessions of Chautauque, Abraham Wakeman of New-York, Charles Jones of Brooklyn, C. L. Richards of Troy, W. S. Lincoln of Newark Valley, Tioga Co., and Hamilton Harris of Albany, Executive Committee. The Committee was still intent on the work confided to it at a late hour.

Our North Carolina correspondent gives us a summary of the Inaugural Address of the new Governor, Col. Zebulon B. Vance, which was delivered at Raleigh on the 8th inst. It will be seen that its tone is quite moderate, and that no great love is lost between North Carolina and the bogus Confederacy. Gov. Vance's language, when speaking of the treatment received by the State troops at the hands of the Rebel Government, is quite as bitter and sarcastic as—with a proper regard for proprieties—it could have been on such an occasion. While we look with some degree of hope upon the late sweeping triumph of the old Whig party over the Democrats in North Carolina, we are far from believing that the State is as loyal as Gov. Stanly and other optimists would have us suppose.

ARE THEY DISLOYAL?

The great body of the American People, no matter of what party, are and always have been heartily loyal to the republican Constitution and Government established by their fathers. They have a deep and abiding conviction that these are, in spite of some defects and anomalies, the best yet established on earth. Errors, abuses, corruptions, iniquities, notoriously exist here, as they will under any government administered by fallible men. Many desire improvement in this or that respect: very few believe that subversion is the way to reform. We believe that there is at this hour a loyal Union majority even in the Rebel States, if the truth were but allowed free course there, and if freedom of opinion were not stifled by terror. In the Free States, not one-tenth of the population sympathize with the despotic purposes of the slave-holding traitors.

But the politicians who control the machinery of the Democratic party in nearly every State are at heart disloyal. They do not desire that the Federal Government shall overwhelm and crush out the armed treason now desolating our country. They would like well enough to see it bribed into outward loyalty by shameful concessions; but their plan is to have the loyal States exhausted and wearied out by delays and disappointments, until the Administration shall be compelled to make a Disunion peace, which (they calculate) will throw the Republicans out of office, when they will come in, and, by a complete prostration of the country at the feet of the Slave Power, they expect to be able to patch up a reunion. This is the idea which to-day governs the action of the present leaders of the Sham Democracy, and renders them sympathizers with and practical allies of the Rebels.

Let us state a few illustrative facts:

Last Winter, a Democratic State Convention for Connecticut was held at Middletown to nominate State Officers. While it was in session, the news of Burnside's crushing victory at Roanoke Island was received and issued in an extra, a copy of which was handed up to the President of the Convention. The news was evidently not to his taste—at all events, he did not read nor announce it—and the Convention separated soon after without one cheer or congratulation over a triumph whereto Connecticut valor had largely contributed! Was that like old-fashioned Dmocracy?

Take Seymour's late speech—or the speech of any one who supports Seymour's election—and note the venom displayed, the labor expended, in denunciations of the Administration, of Congress, of the Republicans, of the Emancipation policy, and the brief and faint censures of the Rebels and their Rebellion. Think of the characterization, in the address of the Fernando Wood and James Brooks Mass Meeting in our city, of this Rebellion as an "irregular opposition" to the Government! Listen to a speaker on that side where you will, and you will find the burden of his strain run thus: "You may hate the Rebels a little, if you insist on it, provided you will hate the Republicans with all your might." Who is it that these professedly loyal Democrats want hung "on a sour apple tree?"—one who is fighting to subvert the Government, or one who is laboring to uphold it?

We were last week standing unobserved in a Democratic newspaper office in an inland city, whence a volunteer regiment had just started for the Potomac. A little crowd gathered, discussing this departure, and the current of their talk ran thus; "Few of those fools will ever come back," (exultingly;) "I should like to see them undertake to draft men in this county," &c., &c. Not one expression of sympathy with their gallant neighbors who had just laid their lives on the altar of their country's salvation—not a lisp of concern for that country, with the clutch of fiendish traitors on her throat. Had Jeff. Davis been present, every word that was uttered would have been music in his ears.

It is threatened in some of our journals that men are to be knocked down in our streets who dare to couple the names of disloyalty and Democracy. We state facts; let the candid draw the necessary inferences.

A DICTATORSHIP.

A certain newspaper in this city, having no more reasonable falsehood at hand, charged Mr. Cassius M. Clay, and divers other distinguished gentlemen, with plotting for a Military Dictatorship. Mr. Clay writes to the newspapers to say that he is not plotting for a Dictatorship. He had a right to repel the charge, but considering the fountain of the falsehood, and its intrinsic absurdity, was his letter necessary? Do we not give these croakers too much importance by noticing them at all? When, in society, we see a ridiculous old gentleman, the slave of a maggotty brain and the fool of phantoms, tottering about, with a perpetual whine of the cloudy to-morrows, and of distresses to arrive, we giggle at him, but we do not refute him in the public prints. The writers in *The Express* may dread a Dictatorship. Then again, they may not. Probably they have never very seriously thought of the matter at all. Probably they cannot think very well upon any subject. What they were after in this case, was a spoonful of flapdoodle to moisten one of their rickety and broken-backed paragraphs withal. It certainly seems to us, that there is quite enough in the present actual posture of public affairs for speculation, and even for respectable lamentation, without inventing a driveling lunacy anent a Dictatorship, of which, with the exception of old Dr. Francia, in Paraguay, the world has not seen an example for two hundred years.

In these troublous times cheerfulness is a virtue which will be considerably promoted by a firm reliance upon common sense. If any man who is capable of fairly considering the character of our people—their intelligence, cultivation, and habits—their tempered devotion to Democracy—their deeply religious convictions—their generous impulses—their hatred of all unwholesome restraint—their respect for personality and for individual opinion—their love of domestic pleasures and privileges—if any man, we say, who is capable of appreciating all these, is timorous in respect of a Military Dictatorship, then we say, without dread of contradiction, that there must be something the matter with his digestion. We are not sure that his may not be one of those dreadful cases mentioned by Dr. Holmes, in which

"The cardiac sphincter presses on the bile."

To believe that a brave and cheerful and social people, saturated with Democratic opinions, and accustomed to control government by continual limitation—a people which for two centuries has chafed at the semblance of Autocracy in the public policy—a people educated to execrate tyranny as something too loathsome to be considered with equanimity—to dread that such a race will become suddenly enamored of submission and quiescent under a Cæsar, would be about as reasonable as to believe that within the next five years two-thirds of our population may emigrate to Russia, and take the oath of allegiance to the Czar!

Ah! but the croakers say, in a nervous fidget, there is the army!—are we not to fear that the army may elevate a favorite General (of the Major or Brigadier or Adjutant species) to the throne? If we were a private soldier, we think that we could bear the bad beef and the bean coffee and the shoddy jackets, much better than these distrustful and insulting suggestions. Here are men who have abandoned comfortable homes and profitable avocations for the dirt and danger and general discomfort of the camp, merely to vindicate their Constitutional right to elect a President once in four years; and Mr. Croaker tells them that after all their campaigning, they will settle down cheerfully under an unlimited monarchy, and will stoically forego the rapture of electing Presidents at all! If Mr. Buchanan, that bad specimen of the Presidential article, were now regnant, and the people were convinced that in all future years no better man was likely to be elected, we can then imagine them calling in agony for a system of Sultans and Grand Viziers and bow-strings; but as the people have once tasted the rapture of turning out a very old and very incompetent Public Functionary, we believe they will preserve, as their most priceless privilege, the right to rectify their own blunders, and to deal with any Buchanan of the future as they have dealt with the Buchanan of the present. The little taste of Dictatorship which the Functionary gave, has, we are confident, by no means increased their yearning for that variety of rule.

Who is to be the Dictator? We have cast about among our acquaintances, and public men generally, and we can think of nobody who would be willing to take the office upon the most munificent salary, payable in specie of the old-fashioned sort. You see you would have to find a man after you had created the office. "First catch your Dictator," the recipe would begin. For, just think what a time he would have of it! Seated in the White House, surrounded, of course, by his concubines, and eating off gold plate, and sleeping upon a bed stuffed with alternate layers of down and Treasury Notes, he would be in continual terror of his life. Somebody would always be arriving, per rail, from Maine or from Oregon, to assassinate him. How the newspapers would wig him! How the caucuses and conventions would blow him up! How weary his days would be with dread, and his nights with dreams of deposition! In comparison with such a life, that of Macbeth after the murder of the King must have been rather than else epicurean. No! no! Considering the Saxon element in our population, and the fine facilities for "taking off" which the inventions of the age afford, we are satisfied that men who never shrunk from any other office, would shrink from accepting the Dictatorship. We do not believe that even Mr. Buchanan would take it, though the conspirators should offer to fill the whole Capitol with Salt River Whisky for his private use.

"IF THIS IS GOING TO BE AN ABOLITION WAR I SHALL RESIGN!"

Any one familiar with our armies must have heard the above miserable sentence only too often. Though far from being the universal expression of opinion, it was common at the beginning of the war; it is yet prevalent enough to challenge scrutiny and comment. Let us inquire how it originated and what it means.

During the old régime of Pro-Slavery domination which, inherently and inevitably antagonistic to the idea of Liberty underlying our nationality, has naturally culminated in rebellion and civil war, the United States army was officered almost exclusively from the party in power. Military authority (essentially aristocratic, because the embodiment of unquestionable power) took its tone, at West Point, from the South. Said an officer to us—one of our few but increasing number of Republican Brigadier-Generals—of our military academy: "It was an unwritten law that anybody of other than decided Pro-Slavery opinions was not to be promoted, but discountenanced, snubbed, *cut*, put upon on all occasions: I never knew an instance to the contrary." That the men so educated with, say Mr. Jefferson Davis as Secretary of the War Department—the fount of honor to which they all looked for advancement—should learn their lesson thoroughly and prove faithful to their antecedents is no wonder, and their large representation in the Rebel army exhibits the result. Those too who adhered to the country that fed and paid them, disliked Abolition in any of its forms, with more or less vehemence; their early proclamations to the Rebels were devoted to assuring them that all interference with their "institution" should be sternly prohibited. Thus we began the war with chieftains who sympathized with or at least palliated the avowed cause of it.

Like influences produced like results in a large proportion of the thousands of honestly patriotic volunteers from all classes who rushed to arms on the fall of Fort Sumter; whose education, ability, luck, or personal influence obtained them commissions. The majority were Democrats, trained, in common with the bulk of the American people, to believe that the one sacred thing essential to the Constitution was Slavery. So with the exception of a clearer-sighted minority, who had always recognized its intrinsic devilishness, who had striven to curb it, who yet never expected it might *break loose* in their time, too many of our volunteer officers denounced Abolition—sometimes more fervently than they did Secession—voted it LOW, and rounded off their objurgations of "d—d Black Republicans" with the sentence at the head of this article.

But the world moves; war is a sharp school, and we have learned a great deal since the inception of the Rebellion. Thousands of loyal Democrats, in the army and out of it, have had their faith in their former fetish so severely shaken, that they will never worship it again. The cry of hundreds of thousands of bereaved homes—of a stricken nation—has gone up to God against it; and, thanks to Him, in three months it will cease to be the law of the land. What, then, shall we say to those—we hope and believe a very small minority—who at this crisis threaten to throw down their dishonored swords, lest they should contribute unwilling aid to this great act of enfranchisement?

Simply this: That they love Slavery better than the Nation; that their loyalty is conditional, tainted, shameful; that, holding Slavery as the most precious of all things, they naturally gravitate toward the Rebels, and had better join them. So shall they be in their right position, and we understand who is for and who against us.

EUROPE AND THE PROCLAMATION.—Those radical journals that have been urging emancipation as a means of placating English public opinion would do well to notice the tone of the leading newspaper organs of that nation on this very subject. *The Times* charges the Emancipationists with wishing to bring about Cawnpore massacres, and denounces the Proclamation vigorously in advance. *The Economist*, the bankers' organ, is opposed to it in toto, while *The Saturday Review*, the leading literary authority, cannot find words strong enough to express its sense of the atrocity of suddenly freeing the negroes. There may be a small Anti-Slavery faction whom this Proclamation will please, but they are as a bubble to the ocean of English public opinion. The Europa's news, which we publish this morning, is very significant on this point. [World.

—*The World* conceals from its readers the fact that all these "leading newspaper organs" of "English public opinion" are enlisted heart and soul in the Rebel cause. They hate and traduce the Union cause with intensest venom; they have done so from the start; and it is truly "significant" that, foreseeing that a Proclamation of Freedom was inevitable, they began to deprecate and disparage it before its issue had been determined on. The fact that they misrepresent and decry it is a cogent proof of its wisdom and necessity. The fact that the European friends of the Union cause unanimously urge on us an Emancipation policy, and murmur amazedly that it is so long withheld, concurs in demonstrating the wisdom of such a policy. *The World* has not been used to quoting *The Times*, *The Saturday Review*, &c., as authorities on American policy; but we see strange mutations in these revolutionary days.

The Newark Mercury says that the Union men of the IIId District of New-Jersey think of presenting ORESTES A. BROWNSON as their candidate for Congress. We trust they may do it. Dr. Brownson is emphatically a strong man, an independent, vigorous thinker, and a most earnest, unqualified champion of the policy inaugurated in the President's Proclamation of Freedom and of the most vigorous and energetic measures to crush out the Rebellion. We really need such men as Dr. Brownson in the next Congress, on which will be devolved the immense responsibility of settling a new peace policy for our restored and regenerated Republic; and we believe he can be elected if the loyal men of his district shall nominate and heartily support him.

BENJAMIN F. HALLETT is dead. He was a Rhode Islander thirty-five years ago, an Anti-Masonic editor, and was transferred to Boston in that capacity, and one of the early Abolitionists of the radical school. After a time, he turned Democrat, and, being an able, shrewd man, became one of the small number who dispensed—or rather, divided—the patronage of the Federal Government for the New-England States. He was the author of the Democratic National Platform put forth at Cincinnati in 1856.

The Pro-Slavery demagogues who now declare that the President's Emancipation Proclamation will ruin poor white folks, by flooding the North with cheap negro labor, were, but two or three years since, petitioning and pestering our State Legislature to strike out the free clause from our State Constitution, and pass a law allowing slaveholders to come here with their human chattels, to work and whip them for nine months at a time. Where was their consideration for poor white people *then?*

Hon. JAMES BUFFINTON declines a re-election to Congress from the 1st District of Massachusetts. The new apportionment has thrown him and Mr. Eliot into the same district, and he, recognizing the eminent qualifications of Mr. E., declines in his favor. Mr. Buffinton has represented his district for the last seven or eight years, to signal acceptation, as his uniformly large majorities attest.

Hon. J. PRESCOTT HALL died recently at his residence at Newport, R. I. He was, during all his active life, a lawyer of this city, where he achieved a high position, and was U. S. District-Attorney under Gen. Taylor and Mr. Fillmore. He was a leading Whig, of popular manners, and very generally esteemed. He attained the age of 67 years.

Hon. BENJ. F. THOMAS declines again to represent the Norfolk district, Mass., in Congress. Its electors had already declined to be represented by him, so that they are now just even.

Clarence Rathbone, U. S. N., and Mr. and Mrs. Holland, England, arrived at the Clarendon Hotel.

The Action of the Loyal Governors and the Press.

To the Editor of The N. Y. Tribune.

SIR: From the moment the announcement was made that the Governors of the loyal States were to meet at Altoona the semi-Secessionist newspapers of this city assailed them with a rancorous malignity that was the best evidence that could be desired that the meeting was necessary, and that the Governors possessed a power and influence which, if exercised, might damage the hopes of the Rebels. Assembling to confer upon the perils of the nation and the best means of averting them, there was no subject to which every intelligent mind—loyal or disloyal—more immediately reverted as one likely to engage the attention of the Governors than the character of the Generals at the head of our armies. The loyal people hoped that the Governors would not hesitate faithfully and respectfully to remonstrate with the National Government on this subject; the disloyalists were alarmed and enraged at the thought that the Governors might do so, and they forthwith ridiculously denounced any discussion of that question as traitorously hostile to the Administration. This was natural, and when it was asserted in the Pro-Slavery press that the Governors at Altoona had taken up the question, the loyal masses lifted up their hearts and rejoiced that so true and earnest and representative a body as a Convention of Governors had interposed and would entreat the National Executive that in the East another year might not be wasted and another army destroyed by the military abortions and cowardly inaction of its Commanding General; and that in the West imbecility and sympathy with slaveholding traitors might not be allowed for another season to hold in disgraceful torpor the hosts which the Free North and West had poured into Kentucky and Tennessee for the destruction of treason. How strange, then, did it seem to every patriotic mind to behold on this occasion THE TRIBUNE and *The Evening Post* of this city apparently fluttered by the denunciations of the Pro-Slavery press, filling their columns with apologetic disclaimers and assurances that the Governors were guilty of no such presumption as to discuss the shortcomings or demerits of McClellan or Halleck or Buell. This exhibition on the part of those leading organs of loyal public sentiment was really most unworthy, and THE TRIBUNE especially astonished all earnest men in its issue of Saturday, Sept. 27, when it said, in a leading editorial on the subject:

"—hardly had those Governors assembled when the Seymourite press of this State, with many of its confederates elsewhere, began to disseminate circumstantial reports that the Governors had demanded the removal of Gen. McClellan, with other acts of gross impertinence and insulting presumption."

Does THE TRIBUNE consider it "a gross impertinence" and "an insulting presumption" to ask or to demand that a General be removed, though our cause and our country be bleeding and helpless, while he controls and holds in check the strength and courage, the brave soldiers of the nation? I do not believe that THE TRIBUNE does. Then why pen such a paragraph?

I am no disciple or advocate of the doctrines of the politicians of the State Rights school; but I am equally or more averse to the policy that would annihilate in our system the States, and their just authority and influence. They form the wheel within a wheel—our special pride and strength; the rampart within the outer wall, where freedom can still find a refuge and a defense, though that outer wall be breached or betrayed, and from which, again advancing, Liberty may retake the outer line it had lost. I fervently hope that we may never see the exigency arise; but the day may come when the power of the States, and the wisdom, and loyalty, and union of their Governors, would be our only trust. While sustaining our National Administration with all our energies and all our hearts, let us see to it that we do not in this day of doubt and danger enfeeble or discredit a legitimate constituted power, that we may yet rejoice that we had preserved to fall back upon for life and deliverance.

FACTA NON VERBA.

HOTEL ARRIVALS.—Hon. C. Winthrop, Boston; Hon. Elijah Ward, N. Y.; Bishop Stevens, Phila., Assistant Bishop of the Episcopal Diocese of Pennsylvania; Bishop Whipple and family, Minnesota; Rev. Mr. and Mrs. Van Dusen, Pittsburg, are among the guests at the Brevoort House.

Fred'k J. James, U. S. A.; George T. Curtis, Boston; W. S. Chamley, New-Haven, are at the Albemarle Hotel.

S. P. Carrick, Nashville; Lieut.-Col. Moncrief, Scots Fusilier Guards; Capt. E. V. Hewitt, Royal Engineers; Capt. J. R. Goldsborough, U. S. N.; R. W. Montgomery, New-Orleans; C. W. Brooks, San Francisco; James H. Danforth and family, Boston; and R. B. Reynolds, England, are stopping at the Fifth-Avenue Hotel.

Right Rev. Bishop Hopkins, Vt.; Rev. S. W. Manney, Maine; Rev. F. T. Russell, Conn.; H. D. Booth, Chicago; Rev. S. B. How, N. J.; M. M. Green, Louisville; Ira Moore, Baltimore; and M. Wolf, Tenn., are guests at the Metropolitan Hotel.

Capt. Charles M. Martin, Gen. Butterfield's staff; W. H. Pitman, St. Louis, and Wm. J. Whitaker, Palermo, Italy, are at the Everett House.

Col. Currie, 133 New-York, and L. B. Postrier, New-Orleans, are stopping at the New-York Hotel.

The Hon. J. H. Ramsey, Schoharie; Wm. Russell, Illinois; Capt. H. L. Robinson, U. S. N.; R. S. Chew, U. S. N.; H. J. Hastings, Albany, and D. J. Clark, U. S. N., arrived at the Astor House.

Capt. E. Wheeler, Yorktown, Va.; Lieut. H. C. Roerner, Rienzi, Miss.. and Lieut. F. A. Patterson, Washington, are guests at the Lafarge House.

Capt. J. R. McCormick, Washington, and W. R. Hibbard, Montreal, are at the International Hotel.

The Hon. E. N. Briggs, Vermont; Col. Pierson and family, California; Capt. Drayton, U. S. N.; Capt. D. Hirst, Cairo; Maj. J. Garrard, Newbern, N. C., Thomas C. Ashmead, Philadelphia, and T. C. Brinsmade, M. D., Troy, are among the arrivals at the St. Nicholas Hotel.

CORNER-STONE LAYING.—The corner-stone of the Hebrew Orphan Asylum, Third avenue and Seventy-seventh street, was yesterday laid with appropriate ceremonies. The attendance was very large. The platform was tastefully decorated with flags. The introductory remarks were made by Mr. Benjamin J. Hart, President of the Society, after which the Rev. Dr. Raphall delivered a discourse. The Rev. Dr. Adler then addressed the assemblage, when the corner-stone was laid by Mr. John I. Hart. The Hon. Frederick A. Conkling then made an eloquent and beautiful speech. The closing address was delivered by Mr. J. De Cordova.

THE CONSTITUTIONAL UNION LEAGUE.—A meeting of the Constitutional Union League was held at the Everett House last evening, "to take into consideration and put in motion some action which would lead to the increase of conservative Union sentiment in the State, the overthrow of the abolition and disunion sentiment at the ensuing election, and the establishment in the minds of the people of a sincere love for the Union, the Constitution and the laws." The call was signed by the Executive Committee, and composed of Wm. Chauncey, James Brooks, John B. Borst, Stephen P. Russell, Elijah F. Purdy, Morgan L. Harris, S. L. M. Barlow, Wm. C. Prime and Geo. A. Halsey.

The attendance was very large, and among those present were many prominent Democrats of the city. Speeches were made by Theo. Tomlinson, Mr. McMurray, and others, highly eulogising the Democratic party, and denouncing in no very choice terms the Republicans. The late Proclamation of the President did not seem to be well received; but, as reporters were excluded, we are unable to give any idea of the choice sayings of the leaders of the Constitutional Union League.

The principal business transacted was the appointment of Committees to arrange for a grand mass meeting to ratify the Democratic nominations.

THE NEW YORK SUN,
Published daily, Sundays excepted.
ONE CENT PER COPY—SIX CENTS PER WEEK,
Delivered anywhere in the city or vicinity.
CIRCULATION 55,000 Copies.
When sent by mail: *Three Dollars per year*,—three months, for $1; six months $2. The postage within this State *is only seventy-eight cents a year*—out of the State, $1 56 a year. Address all letters to MOSES S. BEACH, Proprietor of THE SUN, Corner Fulton and Nassau sts, N. Y.

THE [logo] SUN.

NUMBER 9429. NEW YORK, WEDNESDAY, OCTOBER 1, 1862. PRICE ONE CENT

THE NEW YORK SUN.

WEDNESDAY MORNING, OCT. 1, 1862.

LATEST NEWS

BY TELEGRAPH TO THE NEW YORK SUN

The Great Battles.

GEN. McCLELLAN'S REPORT.

THE FEDERAL LOSS 14,794.

REBEL LOSS IN ALL 30,000.

14,000 Small Arms, 3 Guns Taken.

MARYLAND'S THANKS TO THE ARMY.

SIGEL "BOBBING AROUND."

Rumored Rebel Peace Programme.

A "WHAT IS IT" GOVERNMENT.

GOOD NEWS FOR VOLUNTEERS

A PLAN FOR PROMOTION.

IMPORTANT FROM KENTUCKY

EVACUATION OF CUMBERLAND GAP.

A Republican Ward Meeting.

RAYMOND AFTER SEYMOUR.

&c. &c. &c.

Maryland and Virginia.

Dispatch from McClellan—Battles of South Mountain and Antietam—Union Losses 14,794—Rebel Losses in all, 30,000—Capture of Rebel Arms.

Washington, Sept. 30.—The following report of the victory of Antietam has been forwarded to the headquarters of the army by Gen. McClellan:

NEAR SHARPSBURGH, Sept. 29, 1862, 1.30 P.M.

Major General H. W. Halleck, General-in-Chief of the United States Army:

General—I have the honor to report the following as some of the results of the battles of South Mountain and Antietam.

At South Mountain our loss was 443 killed, 1,806 wounded, and 76 missing; total, 2,325.

At Antietam our loss was 2,010 killed, 9,416 wounded, and 1,043 missing; total, 12,469.

Total loss in the two battles, 14,794.

The loss of the rebels in the two battles, as near as can be ascertained from the number of the dead found upon the field, and from other data, will not fall short of the following estimate:

Major Davis, Assistant Inspector General, who superintends the burial of the dead, reports about 3,000 rebels buried upon the field of Antietam by our troops.

Previous to this, however, the rebels had buried many of their own dead upon the distant portion of the battle field, which they occupied after the battle—probably at least 500.

The loss of the rebels at South Mountain cannot be ascertained with accuracy, but as our troops continually drove them from the commencement of the action, and as a much greater number of their dead were seen on the field than of our own men, it is not unreasonable to suppose that their loss was greater than ours. Estimating their killed at 500 the total rebels killed in the two battles would be 4,000. According to the ratio of our own killed and wounded, this would make their loss in wounded 18,742.

As nearly as can be determined at this time the number of prisoners taken by our troops in the two battles will at the lowest estimate amount to 5,000. The full returns will no doubt show a larger number. Of these about 1,200 are wounded.

This gives me a rebel loss in killed, wounded and prisoners of 25,542. It will be observed that this does not include their stragglers, the number of whom is said by citizens here to be large.

It may be safely concluded, therefore, that the Rebel army lost at least 30,000 of their best troops.

From the time our troops first encountered the enemy in Maryland until he was driven back into Virginia, we captured 13 guns, 7 caisons, 9 limbers, 2 field forges, 2 caissons bodies, 39 colors, and 1 signal flag. We have not lost a single gun or color.

On the battle-field of Antietam 14,000 small arms were collected, besides the large number carried off by citizens, and those distributed on the ground to recruits and other unarmed men arriving immediately after the battle.

At South Mountain no collection of small arms was made, but owing to the haste of the pursuit from that point, 400 were taken on the opposite side of the Potomac.

GEORGE B. McCLELLAN, Maj.-Gen. Com.

GOOD REPORT OF GEN. SIGEL'S CORPS.

Washington, Sept. 30.—Recently General Stahl's Brigade, being a part of General Sigel's corps, advanced to Warrenton Junction, about forty-one miles from Washington, without meeting the enemy. Yesterday they went to Warrenton village, ten miles West, and there met a large number of sick and wounded rebels, together with a few conscripts, prisoners, whom they paroled. General Stahl continued his reconnoissance to Salem and White Plains, but found no rebels in that neighborhood. A report prevailed at Alexandria, to-day, that General Sigel's troops had recaptured all the engines and cars which the enemy obtained from the wreck at Bristow and Warrington Junction. Nothing is known here as reported of any disagreement between General Sigel and the War Department.

REBEL TESTIMONY TO M'CLELLAN'S GENERALSHIP.

The Richmond EXAMINER pays the following tribute to Gen. McClellan:

One thing only remains to be explained. It is the determination and vigor of McClellan's attack on Wednesday. It is admitted on all sides that the battle on Wednesday was one of the most sternly contested of this war; and it has been seen with surprise that the Federal troops were capable of making such an effort. The troops under McClellan were the veterans of the Federal force. The army that fought Lee was the consolidation of the remnants of the old army of the Peninsula, Pope's beaten host, Burnside's army of occupation, and the guard of Washington and Maryland. Some new regiments were probably intermixed, but they were few. The mass of McClellan's forces consisted of trained troops; but with all these advantages it must be admitted that they exhibited a fighting power on Wednesday unexpected under the circumstances.

These troops had been broken by the battles of the Chickahominy; they had been completely demoralized by the mismanagement of Pope, and by the tremendous beating lately received at Manassas. It is a matter of surprise that they were capable of an attack so persevering and determined as that which they made on Lee last Wednesday, and it can only be explained on the supposition that Gen. McClellan retained the confidence of the Federal troops, in a degree with which no other Federal commander could compare.

Thanks of Maryland to Gen. McClellan and his Army, and to Gov. Curtin and the Militia of Pennsylvania.

Baltimore, Sept. 30.—The following has just been issued by Governor Bradford:

[Executive Order.]

STATE OF MARYLAND, EXECUTIVE DEPARTMENT, Annapolis, September 29, 1862.

The expulsion of the Rebel army from the soil of Maryland should not be suffered to pass without a proper acknowledgement and the thanks of her authorities to those who were chiefly instrumental in compelling that evacuation.

I would tender therefore, on behalf of the State of Maryland, to Major General McClellan and the gallant officers and men under his command, my earnest and devoted thanks for the distinguished courage, skill and gallantry with which that achievement was accomplished. It reflects a lustre upon the ability of the commander-in-chief and the heroism and endurance of his followers, that the country everywhere recognizes, and that even our enemies are constrained to acknowledge.

To Governor Curtin, of Pennsylvania, and to the militia of his state who rallied with such alacrity at the first symptoms of an invasion, our warmest thanks are also due. The readiness with which they crossed the border and took their stand beside the Maryland brigade, shows that that border is in all respects but an ideal line, and that in such a cause as now unites us, Pennsylvania and Maryland are but one.

I cannot forbear to notice in this connection the conduct of our own regiments that took part in the recent battles. All reports concur in representing their gallantry as all that their state could desire.

The numbers of their killed and wounded, and their torn and tattered standards, bear witness to the position they occupied in the field.

To the Second, Third and Fifth Maryland Regiments, the Purnell Legion, the First Regiment of the Home Brigade, and the First Maryland Artillery, participants in the recent severe struggles, I would, therefore, tender the thanks which are so justly their due.

By the Governor, A. W. BRADFORD.
WM. B. HILL, Secretary of State.

From Washington.

Circular from Gen. Halleck—Scarcity of Officers—They are to be Supplied from the Ranks.

Washington, Sept. 30.—From casualties in the field, and from absence by reason of sickness, many volunteer regiments have not a sufficient number of officers to command them.

It is important that vacancies caused by death and resignations be filled with the least possible delay.

The Governors of the several states are earnestly requested to fill those vacancies by promoting officers, non-commissioned officers and privates, *who have distinguished themselves in the field, or who have shown a capacity for military command.*

Without the hope of promotion there is no encouragement to a faithful performance of duty, and no stimulus to deeds of valor.

Moreover, the efficiency and discipline of an army depend in a great measure upon the character and qualifications of its officers.

Without good officers the very best soldiers soon become a mere disorderly mob, the inefficiency of which is increased by the increase of its members.

W. H. HALLECK, General-in-Chief.

Peace Rumor—Rebel Commissioners said to be on their way to Washington—A new style of Government proposed.

A special dispatch to the Philadelphia INQUIRER is to the following effect:

Washington, D. C., Sept. 29.—It is rumored here, to-day, that the reason of the existing quietude on the part of both armies on the Upper Potomac is, that Commissioners are now either in, or on their way to, Washington, sent by the Confederate Congress, to propose terms of peace. These Commissioners are appointed by a resolution introduced by Foote, and acted upon by the rebel Congress. In a speech made upon presenting the resolution, Foote stated plainly the desperate plight the Confederacy is now in, and said that, as starvation is already staring them in the face, something must be done to stop this war, other than fighting.

The terms of peace which they propose is, as I understand it, somewhat as follows: The loyal states are to take all the territories, Missouri, Tennessee, Kentucky and Maryland, and to make them free or slave states, as may best please them. The Cotton States are to be permitted to have a Congress of their own; to regulate their own domestic affairs *only*. In all other things to be again as one, and an inseparable people. For defensive and offensive operations against other countries to be a unity. In all matters of postal and revenue service to be as heretofore; they pledging to return all Government property to us as they found it. They, in addition to having us recognize their authority to have this Congress, to regulate their peculiar institutions, *are to be permitted Senators and Representatives in our Halls of Congress,* but only in such numbers as their free white population is entitled to.

Release of Prisoners of State.

Washington, September 30.—All prisoners of state now on parole, by authority from the headquarters of the Military District of Columbia, will report in person forthwith to the Military Governor of this District. This is with a view to their exchange for Union prisoners at Richmond.

Kentucky and Ohio.

The Evacuation of Cumberland Gap, Etc.

Cincinnati, Sept. 30.—Gen. Morgan left Cumberland Gap about two weeks ago, with all his forces, and is supposed to be marching in a northeasterly direction, so as to strike the Ohio somewhere about Portsmouth.

He brought away all his artillery and stores, and blocked up the Gap with stones so as to render it impassable.

The Indianapolis correspondent of the COMMERCIAL says: Gen. Buell has been removed and Gen. Thomas assigned his command.

GEN. DAVIS TO BE TRIED BY COURT MARTIAL.

Louisville, Sept. 30.—Gen. Jeff. C. Davis is under arrest for killing Gen. Nelson, and will be tried by Court Martial.

FUNERAL OF GEN. NELSON.

Louisville, Sept. 30.—The funeral of General Nelson, took place today. The corpse was enclosed in an elegant metallic casket.

The procession was composed of cavalry, artillery, and about seven regiments of infantry. The remains were taken to Christ Church. After the ceremony had been performed, the remains were conveyed to Cave Hill Cemetery, and placed in a vault.

CAPTURE OF THE 3D GEORGIA CAVALRY.

Elizabethtown, Ky., Sept. 30.—Colonel Kennett's cavalry has had a skirmish with and captured the 3d Georgia cavalry. He paroled the non-commissioned officers and privates.

Movements in Kentucky—The Army of Gen. Buell—What Bragg is About—Troops Passing into Louisville—Bragg to be Compelled to Fight—Secesh Made Useful.

We find the following interesting items in a late number of the New Albany (Ind.) LEDGER:

The army of General Buell, 60,000 strong, will be in position about Louisville within the next twelve hours. The advance under Gen. Wood reached Louisville this morning.

The Rebels, last night, burned the railroad bridge at Shepherdsville, and tore up the road-bed for a considerable distance. After doing all the mischief to the road they desired, they beat a hasty retreat towards Bardstown.

We conversed with a Lieutenant of the Forty-Ninth Indiana this morning, who left the Gap one week ago today, and who brought letters from his regiment to their friends in this city, and he states that when he left there was no talk of evacuating the position.

A detachment of our troops from Cincinnati is said to be marching on Lexington, and were not over 15 miles from the former place yesterday morning.

Reports still place Bragg at Bardstown and Bloomfield, with the main body of his army. Detachments, however, are stationed at Hammondsville, between Elizabethtown and Bardstown.

Gen. Bragg is gradually extending his lines in an easterly and northeasterly direction. It is not believed that he designs coming much nearer Louisville.

We have it from a pretty reliable source that, in a consultation between our Generals last night, it was determined to go out after Bragg and compel him to fight. His force is not believed to be more than 60,000, and it is doubted if he would be able to march over 40,000 men into action.

Troops still continue to pour into Louisville from all the northwestern States. A number of Iowa, Wisconsin and Illinois regiments have arrived since yesterday, and ten more Indiana regiments have entered the city in the past twenty-four hours.

Arrests of rebel sympathizers are frequent at Louisville today. We saw a crowd of some fifty or sixty being put through the evolutions by a hoosier corporal, in front of the Louisville Hotel, this forenoon, among them a number of "gay and festive young cusses" in broadcloth and fine jewelry, several prominent business men of the city. Those thus arrested who remain obdurate are put to work in the trenches. The secesh at Portland have also been brought out. We saw a number of them at work on the plank road and pontoon bridge yesterday. They drove spikes and shovelled sand with becoming resignation.

The divisions of Gen. Buell's army are moving as follows: 1st, Gen. Wood's the advance; 2d, Crittenden's division; 3d, McCook's division; 4th, Rousseau's division; 5th, Thomas' division, which is the rear. The divisions move close to, and within assisting distance of each other.

REBEL TESTIMONY—BRAGG TO BE WHIPPED.

The Richmond EXAMINER, of the 16th instant, says that General Bragg with 10,000 men is at Glasgow Junction, and that General Rousseau has gone to meet him.

The Norfolk UNION regards the defeat of General Bragg's army certain, and says that there are 200,000 Federal troops between Nashville and Louisville.

The Anti Prohibitionists State Convention.

Syracuse, N. Y. Sept. 30.—The State Convention of Anti-Prohibitionists assembled in this city today. Hon. P. W. Engs was chosen permanent President, and made an able and eloquent speech in defence of "constitutional rights." Nearly every county in the State was represented. Horatio Seymour was unanimously nominated for Governor, and D. R. Floyd Jones for Lieutenant Governor, amidst loud and enthusiastic cheers. Among the resolutions adopted were the following:—

Resolved, That the Convention repudiates all party platforms, and disavowing entangling alliances with any political organization, do plant ourselves on the Constitution of these United States and the Constitution of the State of New York, and that we will not sustain any man for office who sets up any higher law by which the rights of the people shall be defined.

Resolved, That the electors of this State who are opposed to coercive and compulsory enactments, are at this time more than ever called upon to give their support to such candidates only as are opposed to the meddling policy which has so long used all the arts of fanaticism for purposes inimical to the rights guaranteed by the Constitution.

NEWS ITEMS, &c.

GEN. POPE has refused to employ the Chippewa Indians in war against the Sioux. He does so from motives of public policy.

ADMIRAL DUPONT and Capt. Rogers have arrived at Philadelphia on the U. S. steamer Keystone State, from Port Royal.

DRAFTING in Cincinnati is ordered to begin on Wednesday next. 523 men will be required. The citizens are hard at work trying to raise the men by volunteering.

THE convalescent camp at Alexandria now contains about 10,000 men, convalescent, stragglers, and captured deserters. About three hundred are sent to camp daily from Washington.

IT is stated by very respectable authority that General Cassius M. Clay will, after all, return to Russia. The reason assigned is his inability to agree with the Administration in regard to the conduct of the war.

THE Houston (Texas) TELEGRAPH, of the 3d instant, says: The question whether Sam. Houston is alive is agitating the press both of the United States and the Confederate States. We answer it. He is alive and comparatively well, residing at his place on Cedar Point, a few miles from this city.

A BILL has passed the Confederate Congress, authorizing the Secretary of the Treasury, to issue copper coins of the denomination of five, ten, and twenty-five cents, to the amount of five millions of dollars, and appropriating two hundred thousand dollars to carry the act into effect.

THE Charleston MERCURY of the 25th inst., says: that there are grounds for believing that the enemy are sending heavy reinforcements to Hilton Head, and along the shores of Broad River. Pinckney Island is now occupied by a large body of troops.

MAJ. GEN. GRANT arrived in St. Louis on Friday, direct from Corinth. His late victory over Price drove that General back in disorderly retreat upon Tupelo, from whence he started, and General Rosecrans, finding further pursuit useless, has returned to Corinth.

THE habeas corpus cases of Cook and Thomas in Philadelphia, which excited great interest on account of important legal points, affecting the power of the President to suspend the law has terminated without a judicial decision. The War Department refused to press the matter, and the Court discharged the prisoners.

THE rebel Surgeon-General Moore reports that the number of sick and wounded received in the Richmond hospitals, since their organization, to be 99,508. Of these 9,774 have been furloughed; 2,341 have been discharged, and 7,603 have died. At the Chimborazo Hospital there were received 24,895, of which 2,033 died. At the Winter Hospital the number received was 22,874, of which 1,271 died. The whole number of sick and wounded received in the Petersburg Hospitals was 11,170.

FAIRFAX Court House is entirely deserted by its residents. Hardly a family remains. Gen. Sigel has his headquarters there, and Gen. Stahl has command of the forces at Centreville, seven miles west. The various regiments quartered there have all delivered their knapsacks to their respective quartermasters. The intention is to relieve the men of their surplus baggage, as they may be ordered to march at any moment.

AN attack having been made on the Federal steamer *Eugene*, at Randolph, by guerillas, the 46th Ohio regiment was despatched from Memphis on the 24th instant, to destroy the place. An inventory was taken of all the property, and everything being removed from the houses, every building except the Methodist church was burned to the ground—all the cotton and other merchandize of value was brought away.

MR. LOCKHARDT, Indian Agent in Nevada Territory, writes to the Indian Bureau, under date of the 20th July, that an armistice had been concluded with the Owen River Indians, who have been recently hostile and threatened to attack the United States troops, then under Col. Evans, on the ground that the whites had killed six of their squaws and three of their children; but it turned out that they had been only captured, without being hurt. The Indians, though they have been every way wronged and maltreated by vagabond whites, say they wish for terms of peace consistent with self-existence.

MAJ. JOHN RAY, additional aide-de-camp to Major General Halleck, has been dismissed from the service, for the utterance of disloyal sentiments. Major Ray was reported to have said, in answer to the question why McClellan did not move on the rebels and crush them, on the day following the great battle of Antietam, "Because that was not the programme. The programme is to prolong the war until the next Presidential election, and then settle it with the rebels on Democratic principles." The President summoned him, and he not being able to justify his remarks, he was dismissed. This is regarded as an excellent example in high quarters, and it is hoped the army may be thoroughly purged of those who utter treasonable words. Major Ray bore a fair character as an officer, but as he had been assigned to General Halleck's staff without his being previously known to the General, he was not trusted confidentially.

AN expedition on board the transports Alhambra and Iatan, and the ram Queen of the West, with the 33d Illinois regiment on board, started down the river from Helena for the purpose of obtaining cotton and destroying the rebel flatboats. On Sunday, the 14th inst., when opposite Prentiss, Miss., they were fired upon and two soldiers and one negro killed. After warning the women and children to leave, the boats shelled the town, and landing a party, set fire to the principal buildings. At Eureka the negroes informed them that a large force would attack them at Bolivar's landing. As the boats approached the place a heavy fire greeted them from rebels concealed in the underbrush. The boats replied with their howitzers, and the firing continued as long as the boats were within reach. Five men were killed and two wounded. The negroes reported that 100 of the enemy were killed, and that their force was 2000 men, regular troops from Grenada. The expedition captured 150 bales of cotton.

GEN. HOOKER's official report of the battle of Williamsburg in May last, appears in Wilkes' SPIRIT OF THE TIMES, having been furnished exclusively to that journal, with what view is not stated. The report figures the loss of killed and wounded at 1,575, and states that the entire rebel army could have been easily destroyed, but for the unaccountable failure to furnish him with the reinforcements of 30,000 fresh troops which were in reserve, and were not permitted to engage in the conflict. It states: "Being in pursuit of a retreating army, I deemed it my duty to lose no time in making the disposition of my forces to attack, regardless of their number and position, except to accomplish the result with the least possible sacrifice of life. By so doing, my Division, if it did not capture the army before me, would at least hold them, in order that some others might. Besides, I knew of the presence of more than 30,000 troops, not two miles distant from me, and that within twelve miles (four hours' march) was the bulk of the army of the Potomac. My own position was tenable for double that length of time against three times my number. History will not be believed, when it is told that the noble officers and men of my Division were permitted to carry on this unequal struggle from morning until night unaided, in the presence of more than 30,000 of their comrades with arms in their hands. Nevertheless, it is true."

MISCELLANEOUS.

ANTIETAM Creek, near which the great battle of Wednesday last was fought, is a tributary of the Potomac, running through Washington County, Maryland. The name is pronounced as [illegible] spelled Antectam, with the accent [illegible] syllable.

ONE of the squirrels on the Boston Common, having been in the habit of helping himself to a peanut now and then from a fruit stand near the West street gate, the woman who tends the stand covered up the peanuts with a cloth. When the squirrel next came on a foraging expedition, finding the peanuts covered, he seized on a peach and made off with it. The woman gave chase, and the squirrel dropped the peach, but finding that he had drawn the woman two or three rods from the stand, he started back on the double quick, and seizing a nut before the woman could get back, made off with it much to the amusement of the bystanders.

A LOUISVILLE correspondent of the Cincinnati GAZETTE gives us some interesting incidents—not before published—of the surrender of Munfordsville to Gen. Bragg. After the surrender Bragg said to Col. Wilder, "Colonel, you are unfortunate in having to surrender to superior numbers, but it is no disgrace. You have ruined the best brigade in my army. There are but two field officers left in the brigade." When the demand was made to surrender on Tuesday, Bragg represented that he had sixty pieces of artillery bearing upon the place. Col. Wilder said if he could be satisfied of that he would surrender. He was allowed to inspect the guns planted and counted seventy-two. Col. Wilder says Bragg allowed him to inspect the guns because he did not wish to waste ammunition. After the first bloody repulse of Chalmer's (rebel) Brigade, that individual had the impertinence to demand a surrender. The following is his note:

"Colonel J. T. Wilder, Commanding U. S. Forces at Green River:

"You have made a gallant defence of your positions, and to avoid further bloodshed, I demand an unconditional surrender of your forces. I have six regiments of infantry, one battalion of infantry sharpshooters, and have just been reinforced by a brigade of cavalry under Col. Scott, with two batteries of artillery. I have two regiments on the north side of the river, and you can't escape. The railroad track is torn up in your rear, and you can't receive reinforcements. Gen. Bragg's army is but a short distance in the rear.

"JAMES R. CHALMERS,
"Brig. Gen. Comd'g 1st Brigade,
"Right Wing Army of Mississippi."

To this demand and these arrangements Col. Wilder returned the following answer:

"Brig. Gen. Jas. R. Chalmers, Comd'g 1st Brigade R. W. Army of Mississippi:

"Your note demanding the unconditional surrender of my forces has been received. Thank you for your compliments. If you wish to avoid further bloodshed, keep out of the range of my guns—as to reinforcements, they are now entering my works. I think I can defend my position against your entire force. At least I shall try to do so.

"J. T. WILDER,
"Colonel Comd'g U.S. Forces at Green River."

MILITARY NEWS.

A general court martial will convene at Fort Columbus, New York harbor, today, for the trial of Sergeant Baldwin, ordnance Sergeant of Fort Schuyler, who is charged with a brutal assault on Capt. S. M. Sprole, of the Fourth Infantry, U. S. A. The punishment is death, or long imprisonment with a ball and chain and hard labor.

The U. S. troops on Governor's Island will be paid off today by Colonel Stewart, for the two months ending August 30th. Their two months pay will amount to about $7,000.

The Naval Board appointed to report on navy yard sites, left Philadelphia yesterday for the purpose of visiting the Schuylkill, Lehigh, Susquehannah, Alleghany and Juniata valleys to inquire into the facilities for procuring coal. All the proposed sites for the new navy yard have now been examined, from New London to League Island. The sentiment of the navy at large is in favor of New London.

The employees of the Brooklyn Navy Yard have been paid off. About $120,000 a month are required to foot the labor rolls.

Some time since the military Secretary of the Stanton Legion, Mr. John McCaffrey, was, without court martial, trial, or chance to vindicate himself, drummed out of camp on charges of improper conduct. Col. Allen has, after due investigation, withdrawn all charges against Mr. McCaffrey in a document which we have seen, signed by Col. Allen and attested by high military authority.

Major John Kennedy, of the 5th New Jersey volunteers, has returned to his home in Jersey City on a few day's furlough. The Major, who went out as Captain, has participated in eleven regular battles and a number of skirmishes, and has escaped with but a slight wound.

The most successful recruiting that has taken place in this city has been in Col. McEvily's regiment, Corcoran Legion, which, in the short space of three weeks, has mustered in over 600 men. The number mustered in yesterday was 65. The Stonington steamer yesterday brought 225 convalescent soldiers from the hospitals at Portsmouth on their way to join their regiments.

Edward Ferrero, of this city, late Colonel of the 51st New York Volunteers, and acting Brigadier General, received on the 19th inst. his appointment as Brigadier General, for meritorious and gallant conduct at Roanoke, Newbern and Antietam.

A correspondent from Washington says: One of the finest regiments seen here of late is the New York 145th, Col. Allen, which arrived here last night, (Monday,) and, after having been refreshed at the Soldiers' Home, marched up Pennsylvania Avenue about 3 o'clock this afternoon, to the inspiring strains of Whitworth's Band.

The bodies of three officers of the Irish Brigade, killed at Antietam, are now in this city, Captains Kavanah and Joyce, and Lieutenant Lynch. The funeral of the latter will take place today at 2 o'clock, from the Headquarters, 596 Broadway, and will proceed with a military escort to Flatbush Cemetery. On Thursday at half-past nine A. M., the remains of Capt. Kavanagh will be conveyed from Headquarters, with due military honors, to the Cathedral in Mulberry street, where a solemn requiem mass will be celebrated, and the body will then be conveyed to Calvary Cemetary. The funeral of Capt. Joyce will take place at the same time. All the officers of the Irish Brigade and other military organizations, are requested to attend the obsequies of these gallant officers.

LOCAL NEWS.

NEW YORK AND THE VICINITY.

WORK AT THE IRON FOUNDERIES.—At the Fulton Iron Works, Messrs. James Murphy & Co., are building three 40 inch cylinder beam engines for the Government, and one for Long Island Sound; also, engines for two double side wheel gun-boats, two engines for tow boats, and one large one for China, 56 inch cylinder, 10 feet stroke. Besides these, there are four boilers for the steamship Quaker City, and six for the steamer Atlantic; also, twenty large sized iron buoys for the Government, and two for Queenport; also, an engine 50 inch cylindar, and ten feet stroke, for Staten Island Ferry, and two wrought iron tanks, each containing 25,000 gallons, for Kerosene Oil. They have four hundred men employed on the Works.

THE HEALTH OF THE CITY.—The health of the city has been better during the first six months of the present year, with a less per centage of deaths to the population, than has ever been in the same period since it was a city. The large decrease of infantile mortality, during that period, is worthy of special notice, as is seen in the following table, furnished by Daniel E. Delavan, Esq., City Inspector;

	Children.	Children under 1 year.
1858	7,058	3,695
1859	5,457	2,642
1860	7,065	2,692
1861	6,133	2,547
1862	5,786	2,422

The figures show that the number of deaths of children is less by 1272 in 1862, than in 1858, and, of children under one year, in the same period, 1.273. Since neither of these years were marked by an epidemic of any kind, they afford a correct criterion to judge of the sanitary condition of the city, as well as the general health. It must also be remembered that the population has increased in the above period, at least 200,000.

The deaths of children in the months of June, July, and August, for the last five years, were as follows:

	June.	July.	August.	Total.
1858	575	1,302	1,262	3,139
1859	505	1,047	1,037	2,589
[illegible]	353	815	868	2,041
1860	[illegible]	936	903	[illegible]
1861	[illegible]	883	869	[illegible]

REBEL COMMANDER-IN-CHIEF.

"Very good looking, but he can't come in."

GENERAL ROBERT EDMUND LEE, COMMANDER-IN-CHIEF OF THE REBEL ARMY.

THIS distinguished soldier, who has been by his military merit raised to the chief command of the rebel forces, and Commander-in-Chief of the rebel armies, was born in Virginia, 1808, and comes of the most aristocratic of slaveholding families. His father was the famous Harry Lee of revolutionary fame. In 1825 he entered West Point, and in 1829 was brevetted 2d Lieutenant of Engineers. In 1835 he was made Assistant Astronomer for fixing the boundary line of Ohio and Michigan, and on the 1st of September next year was promoted to a 1st Lieutenancy. In July, 1838, he was made Captain. In the Mexican war he occupied the position of Chief-Engineer of General Wool's division, and was breveted Major for his gallantry at Cerro Gordo—he was breveted Lieutenant-Colonel for his meritorious conduct in the battles of Contreras and Cherubusco, and was breveted colonel for his services at Chepultepec. In this battle he was severely wounded. In 1852 he was appointed Superintendent of the United States Military Academy at West Point, where his lofty courtesy made him very popular. A visitor to him during that year says: "There is a polished reserve about Lee which I am told is considered the perfection of that hauteur which stamps the Virginian grandee. For my own part, I look upon his serious dignity as a mere assumption to hide a mediocrity irritated by a vain ambition, and not the consciousness of superior ability." In 1855 he was Lieutenant-Colonel of cavalry, and on the 16th of March, 1861, he was promoted to the Colonelcy of the 1st U. S. Cavalry. On the 25th of April he resigned his position and entered the service of the Southern Confederacy.

In 1832 he married the daughter of Mr. Custis, the representative of the Washington family, and by this marriage became proprietor of the Arlington estate, and also of large possessions in the county of New Kent, among which was the famous White House on the Pamunkey river, destroyed during the recent advance of Gen. McClellan's army.

Soon after his marriage he visited Europe, in company with his bride, and was most flatteringly received on account of his own patrician appearance, but more especially for the prestige of his wife's relationship to the great founder of the American Republic. If what has been said is true, Gen. Lee has allowed an insane devotion "to that most pestilent doctrine, State Rights," to lead him astray, for in a letter last Christmas to a Union friend, Mrs. Lee said: "My husband has wept tears of blood over this terrible war, but he must, as a man of honor and a Virginian, share the destiny of his state, which has solemnly pronounced for independence!"

In form and face Gen. Lee is very striking. His eye is a dark brown, full of fire and expression, his hair, once black, is now iron gray.

THE DEMOCRATIC UNION ASSOCIATION Committee held a meeting last evening at the Everett House, at which several prominent members attended. Among these were Hon. James Brooks, Mr. Horton, formerly of the DAY BOOK, General Lloyd, Stephen P. Russell, Wm. T. Jenning and others. It was requested that the proceedings should not be reported.

TESTIMONIAL.—Private John Owens, of the 69th Regiment, who devotedly attended General Corcoran in prison, and refused his parole, preferring, he said, to die with his Colonel, has been presented by the General with a valuable gold watch, suitably inscribed.

THE BOARD OF SUPERVISORS yesterday adopted a resolution that the Special Court House Committee be authrized to take steps to place in the hands of the Court House Commissioners the requisite funds for the construction of that building, notwithstanding the objections of the Mayor.

THE LAST DAY OF VOLUNTEERING.—Yesterday was the last day of volunteering, so far as the general or state governments are concerned. The payment of the state bounty of $50 a man ceased in accordance with the recent proclamation of Gov. Morgan. Henceforth bounties will only be paid by private parties and organizations of citizens. Under the volunteer system not less than a million men have been obtained under the various calls. The total number of volunteers obtained under the last two calls amounted, a few days ago, to one hundred and two thousand men, leaving a deficiency of only eighteen thousand men. This has probably been reduced within the last two days so that it is not probable that over twelve thousand men will have to be drafted. But the active preparations for a draft that still continue indicate fresh calls for troops, and the drafting machinery once set in motion, will be retained until the conclusion of the war. The draft no doubt will take place in a week or ten days. In this city the deficiency is about six thousand, and the draft will be under the superintendence of Judge-Advocate Anthon, who invites corrections of enrolling lists at the Enrollment Office, 82 Broadway.

THE POSTAGE CURRENCY is still in great request, and difficult to obtain. A large crowd again assembled yesterday in front of the Sub-Treasury, in hopes of obtaining a supply, but were disappointed by seeing the notice "No postage currency today," posted on the doors. They then formed a long line from the Post office through Cedar, to the corner of William street, taking their turn to purchase postage stamps. About $5,000 worth were disposed of. The public need to be cautious in examining the packages of stamps, as many are found to have been taken from old letters with the cancelling mark bleached out.

THE REPUBLICAN STATE COMMITTEE met at the Astor House yesterday, and organized by choosing Judge Low, of Sullivan county, chairman; Benjamin Fields, of Orleans county, Secretary, and Isaac Sherman, of New York, Treasurer. The chair then appointed the following gentlemen the executive committee:—W. L. Sessions, of Chatauque, Abram Wakeman, of New York, Charles Jones, of Kings, Charles R. Richards, of Rensalaer, W. S. Lincoln, of Tioga, and Hamilton Hanes, of Albany. The committee then went into secret session.

CITY GOVERNMENT—ANOTHER STREET COMMISSIONER REJECTED.—The Board of Aldermen met yesterday afternoon. The subject of purchasing, for the defence of the harbor, a new gun, which is said to throw a shot of 1,000 pounds, with a charge of 150 pounds of powder, was referred to the Committee on National Affairs. A communication was received from the Mayor, nominating David R. Jacques, as Street Commissioner; whereupon the following dignified debate ensued:

Mr. Boole—What is the name?
The President—David R. Jacques.
Mr. Boole—I'd like to know who Mr. Jacques is? I——
Mr. Dayton (interrupting)—Sir, the gentleman is know who Mr. Jacques is. He is—
Mr. Boole—I do not wish to be interrupted. When I want the gentleman's opinion, I'll ask it. I move that this Board does not confirm the nomination. Now the gentleman can speak.

Mr. Dayton said Mr. Jacques was a man of intellect and honor, upon whose character there was not a stain. Yesterday they had rejected an honest and eminent citizen, and he presumed this would be the case again today. They had removed a man from office who had been accused of no crime, and who but one year since was installed by their voices. The opinion of the Corporation Counsel backed them to be sure, but without it the removal would have been certainly made.

Mr. Boole—Certainly it would. (Laughter.)

Ald. Dayton proceeded to denounce the removal of Mr. Knapp, when

Mr. Walsh called him to order. The question was not upon the removal of Mr. Knapp, but upon the rejection of Mr. Jacques.

The President decided the point of order well taken.

Mr. Dayton continued, but being called to order, finally took his seat.

Mr. Froment moved that the nomination be referred to a committee of three, so that they could investigate the matter.

Lost—three in the affirmative.

Mr. Boole said he understood the nominee was a lawyer. A practical man was needed.

Mr. Dayton—Does the gentleman mean to say that he will not vote for the confirmation of a lawyer?

Mr. Boole—I will not vote for the confirmation of Mr. Jacques. (Laughter.)

Mr. Dayton was proceeding to speak, when Mr. B. claimed that he had the floor.

The President—The gentleman from the 9th (Mr. D.) will take his seat.

Mr. Dayton—Sir, I was about saying—

The President (energetically)—The gentleman will take his seat.

Mr. Dayton (sitting down)—Yes. (Laughter.)

Mr. Boole was proceeding, but Mr. Dayton, in his seat, continued to interrupt him, whereupon the President rapped loudly to order, succeeding after some time in restoring order.

Mr. Brady then gave Mr. Dayton his attention. The nominee before the board was Mr. Dayton's friend.

Mr. Dayton denied it.

Mr. Brady insisted upon it. They were political friends, and the gentleman did not dare to deny it. Mr. Dayton had given the Board trouble enough. He was always taking up everybody's time with long speeches in violation of parliamentary law, and common sense. (Laughter.)

Here some trouble ensued, when the President peremptorily ordered Mr. Dayton to take his seat.

The vote was then taken on Mr. Jaques' nomination, and he was rejected by 10 to 5.

The Board then adjourned to one o'clock this P. M.

A long "ordinance to provide for the families of volunteers, has been introduced from the city of New York for the Union army," was read. It appropriates half a million of dollars for the relief of soldiers families, appoints the Comptroller treasurer of the fund, which is to be provided by issuing bonds, to be known as the "Volunteer Family Aid Bonds No. 4." The ordinance consists of seventeen sections, devoted chiefly to the details of the distribution.

HEBREW ORPHAN ASYLUM.—The corner-stone of this Institution was laid yesterday, at the corner of 3d avenue and 77th st., in the presence of a large concourse of our Jewish fellow-citizens. Benjamin I. Hart, Esq., the President of the Society, made some introductory remarks, in which he alluded to the great labors of the Society over which he presided.

Addresses were then delivered by Rev. Dr. M. J. Raphall and Rev. Dr. Adler. Henry Goldsmith, Esq., the Secretary of the Society, read a list of articles placed in the cavity of the corner-stone, among which was a document written in the Hebrew language, of which the following is a translation:

"*Let this be written to a coming generation, that people yet unborn may praise the Lord.*"—PSALMS CII. 19.

In the year of the World 5620. (1860) the members of the New York Hebrew Benevolent Society, established a foster-home for destitute Hebrew Orphans, in West 29th street. But, as the house was too small for the numerous applicants, the Directors of the Society, strongly impressed with the necessity of erecting an Asylum commensurate to the wants of the community, submitted the case to the State and City Authorities, and by the blessing of Him, who is the "Father of Orphans," the Society obtained the co-operation of which it stood in need.

Under the sanction of the Legislature, the Municipal Council of the City of New York, most liberally granted twelve lots of ground whereon to erect a commodious structure, and in addition thereto, donated the munificent sum of $30,000 towards the expense of building the same. As the Society has thus come into possession of the necessary funds, they enter on their great work, and this Tuesday, 6th day of Tishri, 5622, (corresponding to 30th day of September, 1862,) the foundation stone of the Jews' Orphan Asylum was laid by the venerable John I. Hart, Esq., sole survivor of the original founders of the Society, assisted by his son, Benjamin J. Hart, Esq, President, and Marum Cooper, Esq., Vice-President of the Society.

Great be the usefulness and success of this structure.

John I. Hart, Esq., assisted by the Architects and Builders, then laid the corner stone with appropriate ceremonies, while Rev. S. M. Isaacs read a most fervent prayer.

A fine band discoursed some popular music on the occasion, and the excellent choir chaunted the several psalms of thanksgiving and praise in splendid style, which inspired all the audience present with reverence for the exceedingly impressive and solemn ceremonies.

The edifice will accommodate 200 children. It will be built in the Romanesque style, surmounted by a cupola. It will be 3 stories high, with a frontage of 120 feet by 60 feet in depth.

The building is rapidly progressing under the supervision of Mr. H. Fernbach, the architect, and the following building committee: M. Rossman, Ph. Frankenheimer, Samuel Hackes, Jacob Goldschmidt, Henry Lewis, H. B. Hertz, Jr., S. M. Cohen, M. Cooper, W. Heller, and Seligman Adler.

REPUBLICAN WARD MEETING.—SPEECH OF HENRY J. RAYMOND.—The Ninth Ward Republican Club held an immense Ratification meeting, last evening, and were addressed by Henry J. Raymond, who spoke in substance as follows:

He threw, he said, his vote for John A. Dix, but he had since found that he had made a mistake, for it was not necessary to go into the Democratic ranks, except to bring away so much of their principles were purely democratic. The nominations made were deserving the hearty support of all good Union men. Mr. Raymond subjected the position and views of Horatio Seymour, the opposition candidate to a sharp criticism, and urged obedience to the Constitution on every foot of the territory of the United States. (Applause.) Was Horatio Seymour a candidate for any other purpose than to cripple the Government? He had read his elaborate speech, to find in it a glimmering of patriotism, and could not find it. It was nothing but a declaration that the Government had done wrong, and ought to be put down. Seymour quoted from the TRIBUNE, and had done him the questionable honor of quoting from the TIMES, for the purpose of showing that they had found fault with the Administration. Had he, the speaker, found fault with the Administration that the Government did not act strong enough? Never. What did Seymour complain of? Why, that the Government acted too strongly against the rebellion. Mr. Seymour thought it a terrible state of things that this war should end with slavery non-existant. He, the speaker, rejoiced to say that when this war should end there would be no slavery to curse this country. (Applause.) Thank Heaven, then, that we may see the time when we shall have one country, one constitution, and no slavery. If we wished to view the importance of this election, we should consider that the South stood against us as an open enemy. There was to be no separation, and we stood there, breast to breast, to fight it out. What would be the effect of Horatio Seymour's election? What would Jeff. Davis say? Why, he would say, there is a man who made a speech against the Government; who sympathises with me. What would be infer from it? That a majority of the northern people did not wish the success of the northern arms. Richmond would blaze with bonfires. This war was characterized as the gymnasium of nations, which in the end would strengthen us as a nation, and in the future our government would be too vigilant to let grow up again a thirty years conspiracy. We should trust to our iron clad vessels, to take the seaboard cities of the South, enter its rivers and proclaim freedom; what we had to do now, was the defeat of the secession ticket in this state. It was necessary to organize properly, and agitate the question. Let the people see the issue. Let them understand, that the election of Seymour is the election of a rebel and a traitor. (Applause.)

CITY INCIDENTS.—Michael Brayton, a boy 16 years of age, was arrested yesterday, charged with breaking into the grocery of Wm. Koster, No. 212 Delancy street, and stealing the money drawer containing $7 50....David Thompson and John Manning were arrested, charged with attempting to pick the pocket of Silas W. Hobbs, residing at No. 46 West Broadway, of a gold watch. One of the accused struck Mr. Hobbs, while the other, at the same moment seized his watch chain, which broke....Caloni Poor, a shoemaker, at No. 164 Seventh street, was arrested, charged with passing four counterfeit $5 bills on the Bank of the Commonwealth, of this city....Coroner Wildey held an inquest yesterday upon the body of Edward Collins, a lad 8 years of age, who was accidentally drowned on Monday afternoon, by falling off a raft. ....Edward McGinn, residing at No. 237 West 15th street, was dangerously injured yesterday by being assaulted by a Mrs. Clancy, who struck him on the

(*Continued on Fourth Page.*)

On the Fourth Page, will appear to-day, all Important News received at this office, after Two O'Clock, A. M.

A WEEKLY EDITION
of THE NEW YORK SUN, issued every Tuesday, in wrappers for the mail, TWO CENTS EACH, $1 per 100.
SUBSCRIPTIONS—PAID IN ADVANCE.
One copy, 1 year..75cts. | Three copies, 1 year, $200
Do. 16 months, $1 00 | Five copies, do $300
Specimen copies, gratis. Discount of 20 per cent. from single rate, on each copy over five.
Postage within New York State, *only thirteen cents a year*—out of the State, *twenty-six cents.*
Address M. S. BEACH, SUN OFFICE, NEW YORK.

DEATHS.

CARROLL—In this city, on the 30th ult., of congestion of the brain, Thomas Carroll, in the 68th year of his age.

The friends and acquaintances of the family are respectfully invited to attend the funeral, on Thursday afternoon, 2d inst, at 3 o'clock, at his late residence, 83 Third st. His remains will be taken to Rondout. 301

HEGEMAN—On Monday, 29th ult., Maria, wife of Joseph Hegeman, of Flatbush, in the 82d year of her age.

The friends of the family are respectfully invited to attend the funeral, this (Wednesday) afternoon, 1st inst, at 2 o'clock, from the Reformed Dutch Church, Flatbush. 286

KEELIHER—On Tuesday, 30th ult., Deborah Wall, wife of John Keeliher, of the Parish of Charleville, Co. Cork, Ireland, aged 82 years.

The funeral will take place on Thursday afternoon, 2d inst, at 1 o'clock, from the residence of her son-in law, Thomas Collins, 27 Oak st. 186

were broken and scattered, like a flock of sheep. The climate sickness soon attacked them. In a week they were reduced from 6,000 men to half that number. Vernon left Carthagena untaken, went to Jamaica, and from that island to England, either to answer for his conduct, or to look after his medal. Even the sailors made a jest of him. He wore an old grogram coat, and was immoderately fond of a glass of spirits, properly tempered by a due admixture of water. The sailors had observed both these peculiarities. They invented a word which should always remind them of the Admiral, his habits, and his dress. They called his favorite beverage "grog," from his grogram coat; and by that name it is called even unto this day, and is known thereby, we have no doubt, to several of our readers.—Upon the whole, this was a memorable expedition; memorable because Washington *did not* sail with it, memorable because his brother did, memorable for Mount Vernon, memorable for "*grog*," but most memorable of all for the "premature medal" with which the Admiral's expected success was celebrated.

A greater man than Admiral Vernon once had a medal struck, to celebrate future deeds, which he never performed. Napoleon, when at Boulogne, had no doubt that he should conquer England in a very short time. What might have happened if he had landed, we are not prepared to say. Nor is it necessary, since he never put the matter to the test. However, resolved, while still on French ground, to consider the thing as already done, and to celebrate it in advance, he struck a medal, with his own head on one side, and on the reverse the figure of Hercules struggling with a monster.—Above is the inscription, "Descente en Angleterre" (Descent upon England), and underneath, "Frappe a Londres" (Struck in London"). According to Lord Mahon, only two copies of these "premature medals" were preserved—the one in the Royal Cabinet of Paris, the other in the cabinet of an English gentleman, who gave fifty guineas for it. The die was, of course, broken. All this is ludicrous enough, when we consider what actually happened.

We should not have thought of these occurrences, had they not been recalled by certain events of modern date. "The little Napoleon" resolved to be as like the great Napoleon as possible. He could not fight like him, and he could not plan like him; but he could parody his proclamations, and gain victories on paper, if he could not on the field of battle. We do not know that he had had medals struck in honor of his entry into Richmond, but we suspect he had; for on the very day that he was first routed at Mechanicsville, there came out a number of "Harper's Weekly," containing a picture of the storming of Richmond by the invincible Yankees. These mighty warriors are represented as so many centaurs, huge, whiskered, fiery-souled individuals, breathing blood and carnage from their very nostrils, wielding swords that might have suited Hercules or Peter Francisco, hewing down the poor rebels, who are falling down on their knees and crying for quarter, in the most abject terror. Fortunately, copies of this memorable "premature medal" have been preserved, for the derision of posterity. There was also captured the caparison of a horse, with a flaming shield for a breast-plate, covered all over with inscriptions laudatory of the blessed Union, and the sublime nation of Yankee Doodle, evidently intended for McClellan's triumphal entry. Lincoln and his whole gang of thieves and scoundrels were to carouse with Mac. on the 4th of July, in President Davis's house, where, no doubt, they would have obeyed their own instincts and the example of Butler, by pocketing all the spoons. But fate, General Lee, and the Confederate army, determined otherwise. On the 4th of July, Mac. was displaying his doleful battalions, and firing salutes under the shadow of his gun-boats at Berkeley, having first assured his master at Washington that the "army was safe," while Lincoln and his corps of thieves remained at Washington.

We cannot leave this subject without tacking on a moral. We will express it in the words of honest Sancho: "Between said and done, a long race may be run." Or, if it suit better, we will advise, "kill your bear before you sell his skin;" or "don't strike your medal before you do the deed;" or "dont publish your picture before you know it to be exact."

THE SABBATH DAY.

What a delightful quiet pervades on the blessed Sabbath-day, and how sweetly sound the distant cheering of the village church bells—the birds of the forest, too, seem to carol their sweetest lays on the Sabbath, as if reserved for the occasion—even the pictures that hang upon our walls seem to have a sweeter and more expressive appearance on this blessed day. After the busy care of the preceding six days, how sweet to be able to exclaim—

"'Tis Sunday, bright and beautiful;
The sun hangs in a mellow sky,
And things of earth look much too sweet
To droop, to wither and to die!"

The heart that has been tenderly trained in the love of the "meek and lowly Saviour," regards the day as one of worship and rest, and goes rejoicingly to the house of God and there drinks deeply of that religion which

"Is always mild, propitious and humble!"

Of all the days that's in the week, the Sabbath is the brightest and best—suggesting so many things that are sacred and holy in their teachings, that we are ever anxious for its coming and ever ready to regret its departure.

"Hail, holy day! the blessings from above
Brighten thy presence, like a smile of love;
Soothing, like oil upon a stormy sea,
The roughest waves of human destiny—
Cheering the good, and to the poor opprest
Bearing the promise of their Heavenly rest."

NEW CONTRIBUTORS.

We add to our list of contributors the names of those two talented Southern ladies, Miss Susan Archer Talley and Miss Mary Louise Rogers, both of whom, before the war, aided no little in building up the reputation of more than one Yankee paper. The first named lady has just been released from imprisonment in Yankeedom, where she was held as a prisoner of war.

TO OUR CONTRIBUTORS.

We return our thanks to the literary ladies and gentlemen of all parts of the Southern Confederacy for the prompt manner in which they have seconded our endeavors to build up a first class literary paper in our own sunny South, thereby rendering us independent of Yankeedom in this important particular. We have now upon our table more than a hundred articles, both prose and poetry, from some of the ablest pens in the Confederacy—letters of congratulation, advice and encouragement—for which we are under many obligations. We shall in our next devote a small portion of our space to answering the thousand and one questions of our correspondents, and in enumerating the articles *accepted* and those *rejected.*

MISS BELLE BOYD,

"THE REBEL SPY."

This young lady, who has, by her devotion to the Southern cause, called down upon her head the anathemas of the entire Yankee press, was in our city last week. Through the politeness of Mr. Cowel, the artist at Minnis's gallery, we are enabled, in this issue of our paper, to present her picture.

Miss Belle is the daughter of Benjamin B. Boyd of Martinsburg, at which place he was for a long time prominently engaged in the mercantile profession. He afterwards removed to Knoxville, Tennessee, where he lived about three years, but returned to Martinsburg about two years previous to the breaking out of the present war. Her mother was the daughter of Captain Glenn of Jefferson county. Miss Belle is the oldest child of her parents, and is about 23 years of age. An uncle of Miss Belle, James W. Glenn, of Jefferson county, commanded a company during the present war, known as the "Virginia Rangers," until recently, the captaincy of which he resigned on account of ill-health. James E. Stuart, a prominent politician of the Valley, and who was a member of the Virginia Convention of 1850, married a sister of Miss Belle's mother.

During her early years Miss Belle was distinguished for her sprightliness and the vivacity of her temper.

That our readers may have an opportunity of seeing what the Yankee correspondents say about this young lady, we extract the following article from the columns of the Philadelphia "Inquirer," which was written by the army correspondent of that sheet:

"These women are the most accomplished in Southern circles. They are introduced under assumed names to our officers, so as to avoid detection or recognition from those to whom their names are known, but their persons unknown. By such means they are enabled to frequently meet combinedly, but at separate times, the officers of every regiment in a whole column, and by simple compilation and comparison of notes, they achieve a full knowledge of the strength of our entire force. Has modern warfare a parallel to the use of such accomplishments for such a purpose? The chief of these spies is the celebrated Belle Boyd. Her acknowledged superiority for machination and intrigue has given her the leadership and control of the female spies in the valley of Virginia. She is a resident of Martinsburg, when at home, and has a pious, good old mother, who regrets as much as any one can the violent and eccentric course of her daughter since this rebellion has broken out. Belle has passed the freshness of youth. She is a sharp-featured, black-eyed woman of 25, or care and intrigue have given her that appearance. Last summer, whilst Patterson's army lay at Martinsburg, she wore a revolver in her belt, and was courted and flattered by every Lieutenant and Captain in the service who ever saw her. There was a kind of Di Vernon dash about her, a smart pertness, a quickness of retort, and utter abandonment of manner and bearing which were attractive from their very romantic unwontedness.

"The father of this resolute black-eyed vixen is a paymaster in the Southern army, and formerly held a place at Washington under our Government. She has undergone all that society, position and education can confer upon a mind suited to the days of Charles the Second, or Louis the Fourteenth—a mind such as Mazarin or Richelieu would have delighted to employ from its kindred affinities.

"Well, this woman I saw practicing her arts upon our young lieutenants and inexperienced captains, and in each case I uniformly felt it my duty to call them aside and warn them of whom she was. To one she had been introduced as Miss Anderson, to another as Miss Faulkner, and so to the end of the chapter. She is so well known now that she can only practice her blandishments upon new raw levies and their officers. But from them she obtains the number of their regiments and their force. She has, however, a trained band of coadjutors, who report to her daily—girls aged from 16 upward—women who have the common sense not to make themselves as conspicuous as she, and who remain unknown, save to her, and are therefore effective. The reports that she is personally impure are as unjust as they are undeserved. She has a blind devotion to an idea, and passes far the boundary of her sex's modesty to promote its success.

"During the past campaign in the Valley this woman has been of immense service to the enemy. She will be now if she can."

Written for the Illustrated News.

THOUGHTS OF MY OWN THINKING.

NO. 1.

"Old Father Time deputes me here before ye;
He bade me on you press this one word—think!"

—Burns.

Reader, do you know what it is to THINK? Do you know it is hard work to *think?* Do you know there are thousands who never *think!* Do you know there are thousands who cannot *think?* What is a THOUGHT? How in words shall we answer you—and yet, there they come, fresh from the teeming intellect, like wave chasing wave on the ocean, as restless and as strong, too, as the wave that's borne on by resistless pressure, swells out, still borne on, still unbroken, towering into a wild mass of yeasty foam, to break on some stout ship of Hope, full freighted on the sea of life, and speed her to her port, or madly dashing on a rock, and broken only to gather new strength, and return, to go through the same process endlessly, endlessly! Do *you* know what it is to think? What is a thought?

We have all had the benefit of thought, because there are men who seem almost compelled to think; they follow the leadings of mind, and thus the few form conclusions for the masses—conclusions which are seldom contradicted, and still less frequently attempted to be proved. The general idea is given out, and then taken upon trust; the currency is good, at least, until bankruptcy. You have had the benefit of thought because others thought for you; you took up their labors, and made them your own; you plumed yourself, perhaps, upon your sagacity, and you thought as—others thought.

I appeal to you, who call yourself a man, is it not a shame to you—a shame to our common humanity—when God has given the power of thinking to a common intellect, so few have ever exercised it?

And have *you?* What thought of value to anything or anybody can you now trace back to yourself? Have you ever developed any great principle of action—nay, I will not ask that—have you ever thought anything?

You have heard of men of a "single idea,"—I have strong suspicions there are many heads would be burst wide open by the occupancy of a single idea that had power in it. Nay, it is possible that there is a very multitude who could not overtake an idea in a thousand miles' chase on a dead level; many, very many, who, if they did scare up one setting like a hare on her form, would be surprised beyond continency, and perchance run, as from the presence of the very—father of evil.

But what is all this to you or me, reader? I can think—aye, there is given to me of God, a power next to God-like, by which I can rove at will through all the manifestations of nature—I can think, and, in thinking, ally myself with the Eternal and the Immortal. You can think, and, thinking, feel 'twere Atheism to doubt the stirrings of a soul within you. You can think, and, thinking, soar where even the uncounted motion of the lightning's travel would be far behind you! We will not, then, be what good John Bunyan called the muck-rakers of the earth. We will get away from the fens and fogs of earth—its sordidness and its shame—and stand, in the fullness of our manhood, on its mountains of health and its valleys of beauty.

The First Grey Hair.—Here it is, a wee bit of silver thread, yet on its slender form hangs a tale of sufficient weight to bear down the spirit, and load the mind with unpleasant reflections. It tells that childhood's days are past, the unalloyed pleasure days in which we laughed and sported all day long unconscious of future ills, days in which we dreamed not of sorrow. It tells of boyhood's days, when hilarity was our greatest characteristic, and the schoolmaster's rod our only fear; days in which we fancy we acted over future life, as a warrior winning battles and conquering nations, and then returning in triumph from a hero's achievements to claim the hand of our Dulcinea, then the little blue-eyed girl of our acquaintance. It tells of our college days, when we labored up the hill of knowledge, and struggled hard for the mark of its honors; days of college friendships which we thought were endless, some of which are so, but others, alas, are ended by neglect and the object passing below our friendship, in intemperance and disgrace. It tells of boyhood's love as true, perhaps, as any, but not so stable; of our youthful manhood's love, when we admired the object of our affection as a pure, faultless being; yea, as an angel of perfection sent to earth expressly to make us happy; but, alas, it was a delusive fancy, and now is past. It tells of disappointed hopes and aspirations of youth when, indeed, "Hope told a flattering tale," promising wealth and fame. It tells of many misspent hours, of misdeeds that bring the blush of shame to the cheek to think of. It reminds us of our grey-haired father, when first the frost of age began to settle on his manly head, and reminds us that, like him, we soon must totter with age, or lie down in death. It reminds us of that grey-haired mother whose life has been a continual sacrifice to our comfort, too often repaid by unkindness. It reminds us that we are passing away, and soon must be forgotten. Much more it tells us that is profitable for reproof, for edification, and for bettering the heart.

The persons who do most good, are least conscious of it. The man who has but one virtue or charity, is very much like the hen that has but one chicken.

VOL. I.—NO. 8. RICHMOND, SATURDAY, NOVEMBER 1, 1862. PRICE 15 CENTS.

GENERAL JOSEPH EGGLESTON JOHNSTON.

This distinguished officer is a native of Prince Edward county in this State, where he was born about the year 1808. His father was the late Judge Peter Johnston, of the General Court of Virginia, distinguished alike at the bar and on the bench, for sound practical sense and solid legal acquirements. He had been a soldier in his youth—had been one of Greene's officers in his celebrated campaign of 1781 in North and South Carolina—had borne himself honorably and bravely at Guilford, Camden, Eutaw, and Ninety-Six—and retained, to the day of his death, a predilection for his early profession, which not all his subsequent success in a profession of a very different character, could entirely obliterate. It is worthy of record, that he was the First Lieutenant of the company in which the celebrated Peter Francisco served as a private, and that the latter, scarcely less remarkable for his gigantic strength and undaunted courage, than for his keen sagacity and powerful, though uncultivated mind, retained to the close of his life a warm affection for his old commander; a sufficient proof, since he had so often seen him tried, that he had never found him wanting. After the war of the Revolution, Judge Johnston married Miss Polly Wood, of Goochland county, a niece of Patrick Henry, and one of the most accomplished young ladies of her day. If he had chosen his wife avowedly on the principle that Mrs. Primrose chose her gown, "for qualities that would wear," he could scarcely have made a happier selection. Mrs. Johnston proved to be as remarkable in her married life for the ability with which she discharged the duties of her station, as she had been for her personal attractions in her youth. They raised a large family, sons and daughters, all of whom proved to be persons of superior understanding. Both parents paid the strictest attention to their education, moral and physical, as well as mental; a duty but too often neglected by those to whom the direction of youth is entrusted. Among other things, they were taught to obtain complete mastery over their own minds; a lesson, above all others, essential to human happiness; for the mind in the moral, like fire in the material world, is the best and most useful of servants, but the most dangerous and most tyrannical of masters.

Of several brothers, the subject of our sketch was the youngest. When yet a small boy, his father having been appointed a Judge in Abingdon District, removed his family to that town, and there Joseph received the rudiments of his education. At school, he was noted as a boy of quick parts and a bold and enterprising disposition. During this period of his life, he had an opportunity to show one of those characteristics, for which he has since been distinguished above most of his contemporaries. By some accident he broke an arm. Most boys of his age would have indulged in the loudest lamentation. Joseph, on the contrary, bore his misfortune with the most heroic fortitude. He shed not a tear and uttered not a groan. He submitted to the setting of the limb with the calm and stoical composure of an Indian, making not a wry face, and distorting not a muscle of his countenance. With equal patience he bore the confinement necessary to his situation, and in every incident connected with the disaster, showed a manly spirit far above his years. We mention this circumstance, because, though trivial, it is characteristic, and affords a key to his subsequent conduct in some of the most trying situations that a man can be called on to occupy.

It is possible that his own inclination led him to choose arms as a profession. Naturally of such a disposition as we have recorded, the son, moreover, of an old soldier whose stirring narratives of his early experience in the army of Greene he must often have heard, it was natural that he should feel his soul stirred within him as by the sound of a trumpet. It is reasonable to suppose, also, that his father, always retaining a predilection for a military life, and early discovering the bent of his son's genius, should encourage his youthful inclinations. Be that as it may, we find him in 1825, a cadet at the military academy of West Point, at that time in the very zenith of its reputation. His application to his studies, from the moment he entered the walls of this institution, was earnest and devoted. How successful it was, we think his after history very clearly shows. He graduated in 1829, in the same class with General Robert E. Lee, a circumstance well worthy of note, as calculated to render that year and that class forever memorable in the annals of West Point. Cadet Johnston was immediately assigned to the 4th artillery, with the rank of 2d Lieutenant, by brevet. There was at that time no war and no opportunity for distinction.—Accordingly, we find him, seven years after, while still a Lieutenant, appointed Assistant Commissary of Subsistence, a post which he resigned the year after, upon being appointed 1st Lieutenant of Topographical Engineers. This rank he held when the Florida war broke out in 1838. His conduct throughout that war was such as to merit the highest praise, and to draw the eyes of the whole country upon him. Upon one occasion, having been sent, under the escort of a party of infantry, to make a survey or reconnoissance of a region which lay around a lake, and having crossed the lake in boats, the party was way-laid by an ambuscade of Indians, and all its officers killed or disabled at the first fire.—The men were thrown into complete confusion, and were in imminent danger of destruction, when Lieut. Johnston took the command, and by his coolness and determination, succeeded in rescuing them. He laid hold of a small tree with one hand, and standing boldly out in face of the whole fire of the savages, called on the men to rally and form upon him. His coolness enabled him to subdue what was fast becoming a panic. The men returned to their duty and resumed the action. A perfect volcano of balls swept around Johnston. Most of them were aimed directly at *him*, to the relief of the soldiers. Strange to say, while numbers of them struck the tree to which he held fast, for some time he was not touched. At last one struck him immediately above the forehead, about the roots of the hair, and ranged backward to the occiput, grazing the skull the whole distance, but not fracturing it or injuring the brain. Lt. J. of course fell, but the troops had caught so much of his spirit, that they repulsed the enemy and carried off the wounded in safety. For his gallant conduct on this occasion, and throughout the Florida war, Lieut. J. was brevetted Captain; a very meagre recompense for so many and such arduous services, it seems to us. But promotion was slow in the old army. In Sept. 1846, he became a full Captain by seniority.

The Mexican war had now begun. On the 16th February, 1847, Capt. Johnston was made Lieut. Colonel of Voltigeurs by brevet, and in that capacity, sailed with the expedition under Gen. Scott. After the capture of Vera Cruz, when the army advanced, Colonel Johnston made a most daring reconnoisance of the enemy's line, strongly posted on the heights of Cerro Gordo. In this reconnoisance he was

GENERAL JOSEPH E. JOHNSTON—FROM A PHOTOGRAPH BY VANNERSON.

THE NEW SOUTH.

Vol. 1, No. 11. PORT ROYAL, S. C., SATURDAY, NOV. 1, 1862. Price Five Cents.

THE NEW SOUTH.

Published every *Saturday Morning* by

JOS. H. SEARS, ...Proprietor.

PRICE: FIVE CENTS PER COPY.

Advertisements, one dollar a line, each insertion.

Terms: invariably cash.

OFFICE: Post Office Building, Union Square.

POETRY.

Written for The New South.

LINES

On the death of F. E. BARNARD, which occured on St. Helena Island, S. C., October 18th, 1862.

He slept; the burning agony had passed,
The struggle and the pain;
The brow, relieved of anxious trouble, took
Its childhood's calm again,
Which deepened on and ever, till it grew
Into eternal peace;
Into a rest where painful dreams are o'er,
And restless tossings cease,

It seems as if that still face had not known
A suffering or a care,
So legibly and so unalterably
The peace of God is there.
And we who look, forget the darksome way,
And almost ask to be
Sharers in such a perfectness of rest,
Such deep tranquility.

These Islands give him all they have to give;
A few bright autumn flowers,
To light the darkness of the coffin lid,
With thoughts of Springtime hours;
And more than these, heart tears from those who shared
His guardianship and love;
Such tears are counted blessings in yon world
All other praise above.

Most honored! thou, first called from midst our band,
'Tis said, no cause can be
On earth victorious till its martyrs die;
And so we think of thee,
As if thy death had consecrating power,
To bid the work proceed,
'Till many laborers reap the harvest in,
Where thou has sown the seed.

MURRAY.

TACT AND TALENT.—In a capital book of essays and sketches, now having its run of popularity in England, we find the following musing off-hand portraiture of tact and talent The writer recognizes the just distinction between these two qualities. Tact in its highest manifestation, we have always considered as only a little short of absolute genius.

Talent is something; but tact is everything. Talent is serious, sober, grave and respectable; tact is all that and more too. It is not a seventh sense, but the life of all the five. It is the open eye, the quick ear, the judging taste, the keen smell, and the lively touch: it is the interpreter of all riddles—the surmounter of all difficulties—the remover of all obstacles. It is useful in all places, and at all times; it is useful in solitude, for it shows a man his way through the world. Talent is power—tact is skill; talent is weight—tact is momentum: talent knows what to do—tact knows how to do it: talent makes a man respectable—tact will make him respected: talent is wealth—tact is ready money. For all the practical purposes of life, tact carries it against talent—ten to one. Talent makes the world wonder that it gets on no faster—tact excites astonishment that it gets on so fast; and the secret is that it has no weight to carry; it makes no false steps—it hits the right nail on the head—it loses no time—it takes all hints—and by keeping its eye on the weathercock, is ready to take advantage of every wind that blows. It has all the air of commonplace, and all the force and powers of genius. It can change sides with a *heypresto* movement, and be at all points of the compass, while talent is ponderously and learnedly sifting a single point. Talent calculates clearly, reasons logically, makes out a case as clear as daylight, and utters its oracles with all the weight of justice and reason. Tact refutes without contradicting, puzzles the profound with profundity, and without wit outwits the wise. Set them together on a race for popularity, pen in hand, and tact will distance talent by half the course. Talent brings to market that which is wanted; tact produces that which is wished for. Talent instructs; tact enlightens Talent leads where no one follows; tact follows where the humor leads. Talent is pleased that it ought to have succeeded; tact is delighted that it has succeeded. Talent toils for a posterity which will never repay it; tact throws away no pains, but catches the passion of the passing hour. Talent builds for eternity; tact on a short lease, and gets good interest Talent is certainly a very fine thing to talk about, a very good thing to be proud of, a very glorious eminence to look down from; but tact is useful, portable, applicable, always alive, always alert, always marketable: it is the talent of talents, the availableness of resources, the applicability of power, the eye of discrimination, the right hand of intellect.

PARSON BROWNLOW TO THE GOVERNORS OF THE LOYAL STATES.—The Governors of the Loyal States have been addressed by Parson Brownlow, the substance of whose letter is as follows:

"I propose that you as Governors of the Loyal States, meet at some convenient point, without delay, and as the representatives of your people address yourselves, in unmistakable terms to the civil and military authorities of the United States. I will not say *what* you shall tell them, but I will, with all due deference to your superior abilities, *suggest* a few points that you might make and forcibly impress upon the minds of our authorities:

First—Urge the Government to draft, without delay, a half million of men, in addition to the force already in the field and in camps of instruction. And, upon the score of *economy*, apprise the Government of the fact that it will require less money to furnish, equip and sustain a million for two years. * * *

Fourth—Call upon the President, whose honesty and patriotism I do not question, to reorganize his Cabinet and the army, and to place men at the heads of both who will not study how to kill off leading rebels without *hurting* them.

Fifth—Advise the civil and military authorities of the country, and the politicians to cease this war upon the everlasting "nigger," until we conquer their *white masters* and arrest the onward march of their desperate and arrogant owners. Meanwhile, let the negroes be seized upon and urged in every way to crush out this infernal rebellion

Sixth—Advise your Senators and Representatives in Congress and the members of your State Legislatures as well as the people, to cease to make efforts to revive and reorganize old political parties, and to organize *one new party, to be known as the* UNCONDITIONAL UNION PARTY OF AMERICA.

Seventh—Let the Government and army know what they seem never to have learned—that is to say, that the rebels are a *unit*, fighting with a desperation and skill never surpassed by any people on earth; while we, who have a noble army of brave men, with money, credit, all else necessary, and truth on our side, are divided and distracted—while we are tolerating traitors and tories in our midst!

Eighth—Inform our Government and people that our ship of State is now in a heavy sea, and that at no period since the rebellion broke out has so deep a depression fallen upon the hearts of loyal citizens as at present."

MEASURE FOR MEASURE.—Lieut. Col. Peckham, commanding the Post at Cape Giradeau, Mo., has issued the following special order regarding the case of a certain David Anderson, a Union man, who suffered the most brutal treatment at the hands of the rebels on account of his loyal sentiments. Butler-like he gives the rebels measure for measure and sets an example of poetic justice worthy of record and imitation:

HEADQUARTERS POST, CAPE GIRARDEAU, MO., September 17, 1862.

SPECIAL ORDER NO. 2.—David Anderson, with his four surviving children, appears at these headquarters, a refugee from his home in Scott County, in the most destitute condition. It is satisfactorily proved that the aforesaid Anderson has been driven from his home by certain enemies of the United States Government, who have murdered two of his children and destroyed his entire property. It is unfortunately true that there are persons in this section who sympathize with the aforementioned enemies in their commission of murder, arson and theft, under the plea that they are committed in behalf of the so-called Confederate States.

It is hereby ordered, That such sympathizers shall be taxed a sufficient sum of money to satisfy the immediate pressing wants of the aforementioned David Anderson and other refugees now here, and suffering from want of the common necessaries of life from the same cause.

Otto Birchman, E. Garaghty and W. J. Arnold, citizens of Cape Girardeau, will proceed forthwith to assess the aforesaid sympathizers, the sum of $500 in sums proportionate to the amount of property each may possess.

The Provost Marshal at this post will attend to the collection of the sums so assessed. By order of JAMES PECKHAM,
Lieut. Col. Commanding Post.
ROBT. S. WIDDECOMBE, 1st Lieut. and Post Adjt.

SKILFUL TACTICS.—We find in a letter from a private in the 10th Mass. Regt. the following account of a piece of skilful management by Gen. Couch, when operating near Williamsport, directly after the battle of Antietam. The enemy, it will be remembered, had a large force in that vicinity, whose intentions were for some time doubtful The letter says:

We got to within two miles and a half of Williamsport at about 3 P. M. on Saturday, when we ran on to the rebels. General Couch formed his division in line of battle, making a whole brigade out of one new regiment, and made it seem as if we had three times the force there was there. There was some shelling by the rebels, but not a cannon was fired on our side, and only one of our men killed,—in the First Rhode Island Regiment. We marched back in line, about half a mile, to get a better position, and after posting our pickets, lay there till morning.

"As soon as General Couch ran upon the rebels he sent for reinforcements. They arrived at about 3 o'clock Sunday morning, and at daylight went on towards Williamsport, but the rebels had left during the night. The people around them said that there was a force of seventy or eighty thousand [?] rebels there the night before, and *they thought our whole force was there.*"

MITCHELLS' RAID.—The *Pvovidence Journal*, in an article upon the subject of "Stuarts' Raid into Pennsylvania," has the following remarks:—

"We cannot but feel a little mortified, at seeing exploits like these repeated by rebel leaders, and so seldom achieved by us. If of no other value, they are of great service in keeping up the spirit of the rebel army and people. Turchin and Mitchel showed this dashing spirit in northern Alabama, and the western cavalry which cut the railroad in Beauregard's rear, just before he left Corinth, performed a deed as brilliant as those of Stuart. But they have been too rare with us."

☞ The following are some of the prices of Northern produce, several cargoes of which have recently arrived at Port Royal. Apples $5 to $8 per barrel; Potatoes $4; Onions $4; Cabbages $15 per 100; Tomatoes $5 per box (2 bushels). Such articles always sell well at a Military Post.

A dozen more such cargoes here, at Beaufort, Fernandina, Pulaski, and St. Augustine, would do our troops "a heap" of good.

THE NEW SOUTH.

PORT ROYAL, SATURDAY, NOV. 1, 1862.

Death of General Mitchel.

It becomes our painful duty to announce the death of Major-General ORMSBY M'KNIGHT MITCHEL, commanding this Department. This sad intelligence reached us last Thursday night, just as our paper was ready for press. A malignant fever contracted here, was the cause of his death, which occurred at 6½ o'clock, at Beaufort, whither he had removed for a change of air and scene.

In the death of Ormsby M. Mitchel, our country has lost one of her ablest Generals; Astronomy and Science one of their most gifted sons. They will vie with a grateful country, in honoring his name, while his memory will be cherished by all. His operations here for the short period that he held command, are so well known as to scarce need allusion. He exhibited at the outset an energy of purpose which foreshadowed great events, while his course with regard to the negro, here, was such as promised, had Providence spared his life, to result in great good to the cause of humanity. Alas! the brilliant career of this extraordinarily gifted man has ended, and he died—not on the battle-field, but by a swift and fatal fever—a martyr to his country's cause.

The following brief sketch of his life has been taken from a late journal:

"This able Astronomer and General was a native of Kentucky, and born in 1808. He entered West Point in 1825, and was breveted 2d Lieutenant of Artillery on the 1st of July, 1829; he was acting Assistant Professor of Mathematics from August, 1829, to August, 1831. In 1836 he was made Chief Engineer of the Little Miami railroad, and retained that position for two years. He had already been made, in 1834, Professor of Mathematics, Philosophy and Astronomy in the Cincinnati College, Ohio, which he resigned in 1844. In 1845 he founded the observatory at Cincinnati, and became its managing director. In 1846 he commenced the publication of an astronomical journal, entitled the *Sidereal Messenger*, which he edited up to the time of the rebellion. Among other honorable offices he has held, is that of Adjutant-General of Ohio, and Chief Engineer of the Ohio and Mississippi Railroad. In 1861 he was made a Brigadier-General, and assumed a command in the West. His recent exploits there, such as the capture of Huntsville, Decatur, and other places interrupting the communication of the rebels in the West with Richmond, are too fresh in the recollection of the public to need recapitulation."

Doctors Crane and Mitchel, U. S. A., attended him in his last sickness and every possible effort was made to save his valuable life. Rev. Dr. Strickland, 48th N. Y. Vols., was with him till he breathed his last. Calm, resigned and even happy, he died as only the Christian Soldier can die.

His remains were borne to their resting place in the graveyard of the Old Episcopal Church in Beaufort, S. C., at 12 o'clock, yesterday, followed by regiments of Artillery, Cavalry and Infantry. Generals Brannan and Saxton, Admiral Du Pont, Capt. Rogers and many other prominent officers of the Army and Navy, united in the funeral solemnities.

"Oh! for the death of those
Who for their Country die!
Oh! be like theirs my last repose,
As in the grave they lie."

Col. Nathaniel W. Brown.

Again we have the sad duty to announce the death of one of the Chiefs of our "Expeditionary Corps." Col. Nathaniel W. Brown, of the 3d R. I. Regiment, died October 29th of Bilious Intermittent Fever. Only a few days ago we saw him at headquarters conferring with Gen. Mitchel. Col. Brown was born in Dighton, Mass., in 1811, and [an] interesting family of wife, two sons and two sisters now occupy the house in which he was born. For many years he was a merchant in Providence, R. I., and at one time President of a bank of that city.

We have heard it said that when he took command of the 3d R. I. Regt. it was in anything but good condition, but his great executive ability and fine soldierly qualities soon brought it to a high state of discipline. We all know it is now one of the best as it is the largest regiment in the 10th Army Corps. Truly, "Death loves a shining mark."

CAPTAIN WARFIELD.—It is with the deepest regret that we notice the death of Captain L. A. Warfield, from fever, on Monday last. Captain Warfield was connected with this expeditionary corps from its inception, as Chief Commissary of the 2d Brigade under the lamented Stevens, until within a few weeks of his death when he was placed by the General commanding in charge of the Commissary Department of this Depot. He was possessed of business talents which rendered him peculiarly fit for the responsible duties entrusted to him; while the excellent qualities of his mind and heart won for him the friendship of all with whom he came in contact.

DEATH OF CAPT. WILLIAMS.—We regret to have to Chronicle the death of Capt. J. C. Williams, Aide-de-Camp to Gen. Mitchel, from fever, on the 29th ult. His body was sent North on the steamer *United States*. Where will these fearful ravages of death cease.

[Communicated.

DIED.—On the 29th ult., NICHOLAS W. CARSTENS, much beloved son of N. Carstens, aged 20 years and 11 months. Beloved by all who knew him. New York papers please copy.

Last Week's Work.

The record of the Pocotaligo expedition, the particulars of which were published at length, in our last issue, is a fair one; and we see no cause to quarrel with the result. While there is nothing to be ashamed of, there is much to take pride in.

In the first place, we cannot speak too highly of the behaviour of the troops, both officers and men: they fought superbly; all agree that they stood to the work like heroes. General Brannan and General Terry, who had command in the field, handled the troops with great skill, and conducted themselves most admirably. In the second place, the enterprise was put through with almost perfect art. In this respect, there has been, we venture to say, no *military* movement like it, before, in this Department. All was rapidity and despatch, giving us a genuine taste of Gen. Mitchel's celerity. The expedition started from this place at about 12 o'clock, on Tuesday night steamed up the river some twenty miles to the landing place; the troops, horses, guns, wagons, everything, were landed; then a march of five miles, before meeting any thing to fight with; and by 12 o'clock on Wednesday our boys were cracking away at the rebels, and soon scoured them out of that position. All this in the brief space of twelve hours. It was mighty quick work, and reflects very great credit on the organizing and executive faculty of the General commanding. And in less than forty-eight hours after the starting the troops were all back here—the men pretty well fagged out, indeed, but as full of spirit and mettle as ever, their hearts rather fired than dampened by what they had gone through. Taking them all together, we reckon them to be as noble a set of fellows as ever drew swords and pulled triggers.

The enterprise has certainly been a nice bit of practice and experience for the men. After such a pulling together, they can hardly fail to have confidence in themselves and in each other. This is a great acquisition; almost enough of itself to pay the cost of the enterprise, deep as this is, and deeply as it must be felt by all true men. Moreover, the troops were resting in idleness, and needing some such exercise to prepare them for the service they will be put to, when proper reinforcements arrive, if that time should ever come.

A NEW CITY.

On the opposite side of our harbor, just above "Station Creek" on St. Helena Island, is a long, high bluff of land called "The Jenkins Place." Since the capture of these Sea Islands by the Union forces we have had our eye on this, as the only proper site, hereabouts, for *A New City of the South.*

The bluff extends along the shore of the mouth of Beaufort River, which is here broad and deep. By reference to soundings we find the deepest water to be from 400 to 800 feet nearer the shore than at the point on Hilton Head now garrisoned by our troops. There a large fleet can lay at anchor, protected from gales in any direction and always in quiet water, which is not the case on our side of the bay. Admiral Dupont very wisely selected the other side as anchoring ground for the numerous vessels of his fleet.

The land, too, lies beautifully for building purposes and is said by all who have visited it, to be far superior, every way, to our present location. The well-water, especially, is said to be very pure and sweet.

We solicit communications from persons acquainted with the locality and wish to give the subject a thorough examination for it is quite certain a city is to spring up somewhere on the shores of this broad and beautiful bay, and it is growing more and more certain that the point now garrisoned by us is not the proper site for *our New City of the South.* S.

The Pocotaligo Expedition.

In the hasty account of the "Pocotaligo Expedition," which appeared in our last week's issue, we omitted to make mention of many facts and incidents worthy of record. Desiring to give credit to whom credit is due in this affair, wherein the duties of each department were performed so well, we are induced to publish the following additional particulars:

Fifty men from the N. Y. Vol. Engineers, under command of Capt. Eaton, were detailed to the command of Col. Barton, up the Coosawhatchie and opened the road for them at the landing. After delivering their fire into the train of cars, they commenced tearing up the track with the heavy clawbars they had carried, and destroying the telegraph, but were soon ordered to retreat, which they did, covering the retreat of the whole force by destroying all the bridges in the rear and making the roads impassable for artillery. This undoubtedly saved great loss of life as the boats were aground and presented a fair mark for the enemy.

The Battalion of Engineers under command of Lieut. Col. James F. Hall was with the main body of the troops and at once commenced the work of repairing bridges, part of which was done under heavy fire. The timber was cut and all preparations made for rebuilding the bridge across the Pocotaligo, when the troops were ordered to retire. Lieut.-Col. Hall, assisted by his command, notwithstanding the great fatigues of the day, took charge of the wounded as they were brought in, after examination by the Surgeons, and conveyed them on board the Transports.

Upon enquiry we find that, in our report we were guilty of an involuntary injustice to the 7th Connecticut regiment, Col. Hawley. The two regiments which protected the retreat were the 47th Pennsylvania and 7th Connecticut. These two regiments, by alternately forming in line at right angles with the road, kept the enemy in check and covered the retreat of the main body. We desire especially to make his correction for the reason that the excellent behaviour of these two regiments, both on this occasion and in the field, was the subject of particular comment from the commanding General. Again, it was Capt. Gray of the 7th Connecticut (not 7th New Hampshire) regiment, who was sent to capture the pickets at Mackey's point. The failure in this was entirely due to the negro guides who took him two or three miles beyond the proper landing place.

Lieut. E. Gittings was in command of Light

Co. E., 3d U. S. Artillery, and displayed coolness and bravery deserving mention. During the engagement he was severely wounded. His battery performed good service.

Great praise is due to Capt. C. E. Fuller, Chief Quartermaster for the activity displayed in embarking the troops, ammunition, &c. He was "up to time," which is a grand thing in this Department. Had the expedition all through been up to time, the results, we doubt not, would have been far different.

LOCAL NEWS.

The Steamer Burnside.—In noticing the accident to the Steamer *Burnside*, in our last issue, we made an error in the name of the vessel which went to her assistance. The name of the gunboat is the *Sebago* (Capt. Scott) and not the *Sedate*, as we had it. We have since learned more fully the facts with regard to the affair and give them to our readers. The Burnside, Capt. Wilcox, left Fernadanina, Fla., on the 22d ult., with forty passengers. On the morning of the 23d, when off Tybee Light, a gale of wind arose, so severe that the vessel became unmanageable and was tossed about in the trough of the sea, at the mercy of the wind and waves. Capt. Wilcox, finding the depth of water decreasing and that he was fast going ashore on Tybee Island, let go his anchor. When the tide fell, however, there was not sufficient water to float the vessel, and she thumped so hard that her rudder post was carried away and her wheel broken. Upon the turn of the tide the wind hauled a little, and the captain, by spreading his canvass, succeeded in getting the vessel off into deep water. While in this critical condition a small boat was despatched to Wassaw Sound, which by nightfall succeeded in reaching the gunboat *Sebago*, blockading there. On the next morning the *Sebago* went to the assistance of the *Burnside* and towed her into this port. Great praise is accorded to Capt. Scott for his prompt assistance, to which is due the safety of the vessel and the lives of the passengers.

Presentation.—Last week, Captain A. B. Nicholson, of Co. E, 47th Regiment, New York Volunteers and his lady, were made the recipients of three handsome presents from his company. To each was presented a beautiful gold watch with chain, &c., all complete, and to the Captain, in addition to the watch, a fine field glass. The presentation was made by Sergeant Newl in behalf of the Company in a very neat and appropriate speech, to which Captain Nicholson replied as follows:

Fellow Soldiers of Co. E:—Although seldom taken by surprise I confess myself in this instance completely taken aback, by this presentation; so much so indeed, that I cannot find words to express my feelings. My association with you, for the past sixteen months, has been productive of mutual satisfaction and confidence, independent of this occasion, which I shall remember with pleasure the longest day I live. I appreciate this present, not so much for its intrinsic value which is considerable, as for the assurance it gives me of the esteem in which I am held by my company. On behalf of my lady, I would say that she sincerely thanks you, and that she takes as much pride in the company as I do myself, which says everything Your soldierly bearing and correct deportment, has long been a source of much happiness to me, and I hope and expect, will continue to be, until our connection as a military organization, is dissolved. In conclusion I would again express my gratitude and the best wishes of myself and lady are yours.

More Deserters from Savannah.—Two men of the 47th Georgia Regiment escaped from Savannah, last Monday, to Fort Pulaski. They brought with them Savannah papers of the 24th and 25th ult., containing accounts of the Pocotaligo fight, extracts from which are given elsewhere. They report that Gen. Beauregard was in Savannah when our attack was made, but hurried to the scene of the conflict. Nearly all the available force around Savannah was hurried forward to Pocotaligo, but arrived too late to take part in the fight. All is quiet in Savannah the people being only a little nervous from reports given by two Union prisoners taken at Pocotaligo, that we were about to attack Savannah at four different points within two days. They say that the soldiers are very much dispirited and that a great deal of Union sentiment prevails in the city. The Iron Ram, Fingal, is nearly completed. Flour is worth $45 per bbl.

Capture of two more Valuable Prizes.—The English steamers *Scotia* and *Anglia* were convoyed into this port, on the 28th ult., by the U. S. gunboat *Flambeau*. They were captured by the Bark *Restless*, while endeavoring to run the blockade at Bull's Bay—about twenty-five miles North of Charleston. They are two iron screw steamers and are laden with valuable assorted cargoes, a great portion of which consists of cloths. The cargo of the Scotia alone is valued in Charleston at £135,000 sterling. The *Scotia* was taken by the *Restless* alone, on Friday, the 17th ult. The capture of the *Angelia* was made on Sunday, the 19th ult., in which the *Restless* was assisted by the gunboat *Flag*. These two vessels will, perhaps, make the richest prize ever captured by a vessel at one time.

Sword Presentation.—Major James M. Green, of the 48th Regiment, New York Volunteers, at Fort Pulaski, Ga., was presented with a sword by the members of Co. F,—his old command. The sword is a very handsome one, manufactured by Messrs. Miller & Co., New York. The hilt is of solid silver, mounted with a large carbuncle. The blade bears the following inscription: "Presented to Major James F. Green, 48th Reg t., N. Y. S. V., by the members of Co. F." Serg t Barrett made a neat speech upon the occasion, to which the Major feelingly replied.

PERSONAL.

—Capt. J. J. Ellwell A. Q. M. of this Corps and J. T. Gleason Esq. Dep. Collector of this Port, are both reported to be in a fair way of recovery.

—Major Van Brunt, Provost Marshal, sailed last week in the steamer Ericsson for a short trip to the North. Col. Frazer fills his place during his absence.

NEWS FROM THE NORTH.

We are indebted to the courtesy of Mr. Fulton, Purser, of the steamer *United States*, which arrived here on the 28th ult., from New York, for papers to the 24th.

The news from Washington is of a meagre character and very little seems to be doing there. We glean the following from our latest dates.

A successful reconnoissance was made from the Army of the Potomac, by Captain Duncan, with two squadrons of Pennsylvania cavalry, toward Hedgesville, on Wednesday, 22d ult. The rebels were driven into the town, which is situated seven miles from Martinsburg, on the Baltimore and Ohio Railroad. Nineteen prisoners, including three officers, were taken by Captain Duncan. It was said that the rebels left Martinsburg, a portion of them moving towards Shepherdstown and a portion towards Williamsport. If this can be relied upon, it would look like an intention to make another raid across the river, or to keep our forces in check in any movement into Virginia at these points. It is pretty well ascertained that the rebels occupy the Shanandoah valley in large masses from Harper's Ferry to Paxton's Cut, which they are said to be blocking up, and that the Baltimore and Ohio Railroad, from the Ferry to Martinsburg, and beyond it, has been destroyed at various intervals.

—Kanawha Valley and Western Virginia have been evacuated by the rebels. The valley is said to be utterly desolated and impoverished, nevertheless, it is an important point for our troops to hold, being one of the doors to Western Virginia, towards Ohio.

The war in Kentucky and Tennessee goes on actively at some points, although the forces of General Bragg have been driven southward by General Buell. A large force of the rebels under General Forrest commenced crossing the Cumberland river on Sunday. His advance, one thousand strong, encamped on the Gallatin pike, seven miles north of Nashville. General Negley despatched Col. Miller with a detachment to intercept the rebels, who attacked them on Monday at daylight, and drove them in great confusion across the river. A number of rebels, including a colonel, were captured.

In consequence of the information that two thousand rebels, supposed to be part of Jackson's cavalry, were advancing for the purpose of attacking our forces on the Tennessee shore, opposite Island No. 10, the troops and all the property there have been transferred to the Island for safety.

The Washington *Republican* gives currency to a story, said to have been brought to Gen. Sigel's headquarters by a refugee from Amissville, Culpepper county, Va., to the effect that, in consequence of an apprehended revolt of the slaves in that region, seventeen negroes, most of them free, had been hung—Northern newspapers having been found on them containing the Presidents emancipation proclamation. The terror of the white population is represented to be very great.

A band of rebels, about two hundred in number, who were discovered endeavoring to pass southward to West Plains, Ark., under command of Col. Dorsey, were attacked on the 20th ult, by Lieut. Col. Stuart, with 100 men of the 11th Ill. Cavalry, and routed with a loss of four killed. Our loss is one killed. Colonel Stuart is still in pursuit.

A large Union meeting was held in Beaufort N. C., on the 21st. Eloquent speakers were present, and resolutions endorsing the President's Proclamation were passed.

Gen. Jeff. C. Davis, who killed Gen. Nelson, has been released from arrest and ordered to report for duty at Cincinnati. He left Louisville last evening, 21st ult

Drafting in New York will take place on the 10th of this month.

☞ *Will Northern papers please give our little Journal credit for copied articles and oblige* "10th Army Corps"?

DEATHS.

J. B. Merrill, Private, Co. F, 3d N. H. Vols., Oct. 25, congestive fever.

F. F. Finley, Private, Co. B, 3d N. H. Vols., Oct. 27, typhoid fever.

John Schuckhart, Private, Co. K, 47th Penn. Vols., Oct. 24, wounds.

John Lind, Private, Co. E, 47th Penn. Vols., Oct. 24, wounds.

John O Brien, Private, Co. F, 47th Penn. Vols., Oct. 26, wounds.

Alexander Morland, Private, Co. K, 76th Penn. Vols., Oct. 26, typhoid fever.

Abraham Kenedy, Private, Co. B, 76th Penn. Vols., Oct. 27, chronic diarrhœa.

D. G. Shephard, Corporal, Co. I, 6th Conn. Vols., Oct. 28, wounds.

J. N. Bowman, Corporal, Co. M, 3d R. I. Vols., Oct. 28, wounds.

Walker B. Manton, 2d Lieutenant, Co. L, 3d R. I. Vols., Oct. 25, fever.

William Kay, Private, Co. F, 7th Conn. Vols., Oct 24 wounds.

Wm. H. Hanson, Private, Co. A, 7th Conn. Vols., Oct. 26, fever.

John Randolph, Private, Co. A, 7th Conn. Vols., Oct. 27, chronic diarahœa.

James McCaffey, Private, Co. G, 47th N. Y. Vols., Oct. 24, dysentery.

Hugh O'Donnell, Musician, Co. E, 97 Penn. Vols. Oct. 24, congestive fever.

Peter McDonald, Private, Co. E, 97th Penn. Vols., Oct. 25, typhoid fever.

Almanac, Port Royal, S. C., Nov. 1, '62.

Sun rises	6 16	Moon sets	1 9
Sun sets	5 11	High water	2 53

MARINE NEWS.

ARRIVED.

Oct. 18, Brig Alex. Milliken, Fish, Philadelphia; Schr. Brave, Tapper, New York; 19, Schr. Eliza Jane F., Edwards, New York; Bark Tycoon, Louis, New York; Bark Lamplighter, Morris, Philadelphia; 20, Schr. Charmer, Booth, New York; Brig Leni, Speed, New York; Schr. D. W. Sanders, Alden, New York; Steamship Ericsson, Lowber, New York; Steamer Thames, Arey, New York; 22, Schr. James Butler Joline, New York; Schr. Lewis Mulford, Doyle, Philadelphia; Schr. George Burton, Peacock, Philadelphia; 23, Schr. Armena Bartlett, Bartlett, Philadelphia; Schr. N. E. Clark, Clark, Philadelphia; 24, Schr. Jenny Lind, Cashman, Philadelphia; 24, Steamer Burnside, Wilcox, Fernandina; 25, Schr. T. P. Brown, Nickerson, New York; L. B. Myers, Sumers, St. John, Fla.; 26, Steamer Mattano, Blakeman, Washington, D. C.; Schr. Pathway, Compton, Philadelphia; 27, Steamer U. S. Massachusetts, Cooper, New York; 28, Steamer United States, Fulton, New York; Schr. Mary E. Smith, Smith, Philadelphia; 19, Steamship Star of the South, Woodhull, New York; Schr. Sam'l. Hulse, Furman, New York.

CLEARED.

Oct. 18, Bark J. M. Hicks, Greenman, New York; 20, Brig Alex. Milliken, Fish, Philadelphia; 21, Brig Abby Ellen, Gilmore, Philadelphia; 22, Steamer Thames, Arey, New York; Steamship Karnak, Bosworth, New York; 23, Steamship Ericsson, Lowber, New York; 24, Schr. Delphene, Horton, Fernandina; 25, Schr. Brave, Tapper, New York; Schr. Ivy, Henderson, Philadelphia; 27, Schrs. Eliza Jane F. Edwards, New York; Black Bird, Weaver, Philadelphia; Rollie W. Dillon, Marts, Philadelphia; Americus, Spragg, Philadelphia; 29, Steamer Cosmopolitan, Crocker, New York; Steamship United States, Fulton, New York; 30, Bark Tycoon, Louis New York.

From the Charleston Courier, Oct. 23d.

Fighting at Coosawhatchie and Pocotaligo.

The threatened movement of the enemy's forces under Gen. Mitchel, was made upon our main land on Wednesday. A dispatch announced that several columns were in motion; one marching from Mackey's Point towards Pocotaligo, and the other on Coosawhatchie from Bee's Creek about seven miles from the Railroad. The strength of the enemy was not stated, but our troops were drawn up ready to meet and fight the invaders. Col. Walker was in command of our forces, near Coosawhatchie.

Official despatches received in the city Wednesday afternoon confirms the above, and stated that fighting had already commenced with both columns of the enemy. Our forces were thought to be ample to hold the enemy in check until the arrival of reinforcements, which were being rapidly sent forward from all points on the railroad. The 46th Ga., and Eutaw (25th S. C. V.) had been ordered forward.

4 o'clock. Another despatch received, states that the enemy had advanced on and taken the railroad at Coosawhatchie. Col. Walker had a severe fight, but was holding his ground. Reinforcements to relieve Col. Walker were moving up rapidly, and it was thought the enemy cannot hold his position but a few hours.

Latest. A despatch from Col. Walker states that he has driven the enemy from Old Pocotaligo, and will advance in pursuit. Reinforcements had arrived to his relief. Skirmishing had commenced and the enemy were retreating.

Defeat of the Vandals in Carolina.—The public mind was greatly relieved yesterday morning by the despatch from Col. Walker to Gen. Beauregard, announcing the repulse of the Yankees at Pocotaligo and Coosawhatchie, which we are kindly permitted to publish: About 10 o'clock our community were rejoiced at the appearance of the following order, which was published on the bulletin boards of the printing offices:

Savannah, Oct. 23d, 1862.

By Order of G. T. Beauregard:

The abolitionists attacked in force Pocotaligo and Coosawhatchie yesterday. They were gallantly repulsed to their gunboats at Mackey's point and Bee's Creek landing by Col. W. S. Walker commanding the district, and Col. C. P. Harrison commanding the troops from here. The enemy had come in thirteen transports and gunboats. The Charleston and Savannah railroad is uninjured. The abolitionists left their dead and wounded on the field, and our cavalry is in hot pursuit.

G. T. Beauregard, General Commanding.

Charleston, Oct. 24.—The fight at Pocotaligo resulted in a complete victory for us. Our loss is fifteen killed and forty wounded. The enemy left forty dead on the field. His total loss, confirmed by accounts of prisoners, is not less than two hundred killed and wounded.

We took eighty small arms. The enemy's force consisted of six regiments, with one field battery and two boat howitzers.

Our accounts from the scene of the enemy's demonstration, on Wednesday last, against the Charleston and Savannah Railroad, are somewhat meagre as yet, owing to the fact that no communication by railroad can be had, for the present, with Pocotaligo—the trains being employed for military purposes.

At an early hour yesterday the telegraph brought the news that the marauders, repulsed in their advance at Old Pocotaligo, and driven back from the railroad at Coosawhatchie, had retreated hastily to their gunboats, but we were left in uncertainty as to the extent or results of the fighting.

We also received, last evening, a dispatch from Savannah, mentioning that twenty-one dead Yankees were lying near Pocotaligo, but no further details had reached that city.

Of the manner in which the enemy, after gaining the railroad at Coosawhatchie, was driven therefrom, we have no particulars. It is stated that, as the train from Savannah to Pocotaligo approached Coosawhatchie, the enemy made signals to the engineer to stop. The latter paid no attention to the signals, and determined to run the gauntlet. As he did so, the enemy fired, killing Major Harrison, of the 11th South Carolina Regiment, the fireman on the train, and slightly wounding the engineer.

To the Planters of Middle, Southern and Southwestern Georgia:

Marietta, Ga., October 17, 1862.

An eminent necessity has caused Governor Brown to appeal to you for a laboring force to work on the defences around Savannah. No more negroes will be received than is actually necessary to complete the work in thirty days. Agents will be in the several counties to receive the negroes and receipt for them.

T. A. Parsons,
General Superintendent.

Heat of the Human Body.—One of the most useful instruments which the ingenuity of man has devised is the thermometer. This instrument does not enable us to estimate the actual quantity of heat contained in a substance, but it indicates the proportion of that subtle fluid that is sensible—that is recognizable by the sense of touch. The dusky Hindoo, clad in his solitary garment of cotton, and the Laplander in his suit of fur, are placed in the most opposite conditions in relation to the heat of the sun; the Indian is exposed during the whole year to old Sol's most ardent beams, whilst but a scant share of its genial rays goes to warm the Laplander. But, if we place the bulb of a thermometer beneath the tongue of a Hindoo we would find the mercury to stand at 98 deg. of Fahrenheit's scale, and if we repeated the experiment on a Laplander we would obtain an identical result. Numerous experiments of this nature have been made on individuals in most parts of the world, and the results have proved that the temperature of the blood of man is 98 degrees Fahrenheit whether he be in India or at Nova Zembla, on the steppes of Russia, or the elevated plateau of America. This invariability of the temperature of the bodies of men appears the more wonderful when it is considered that the range of the temperature of the medium in which they exist exceeds 100 degrees, Fahrenheit's.

The human body resembles, in some degree, a steam boiler with innumerable safety valves, in the form of pores in the skin. Perspiration is caused by the heat of the body converting the water in the animal frame into vapor, which escapes through millions of pores in the cuticle. The expansion of this vapor over the whole surface of the body exerts a refrigerating action for the removal of surplus heat from the animal system. When the pores of the skin are closed and perspiration prevented, the surplus heat generated in the body is prevented from escaping, and fever ensues. A clean cuticle is as necessary to health as good food and pure water.

Your Country.—An old soldier, in appealing lately to his son to go and fight for the Government and the Union, said:

"Perhaps you have never thought what your country means. It is all that surrounds you—all that has brought you up and fed you—all that you have loved. This country that you see—these houses—these trees, those girls who go along there laughing—this is your country! The laws which protect you, the bread which pays your work, the words you interchange with others, the joy and grief which come to you from the men and things among which you live—this is your country! The little room where you used to see your mother, the remembrance which she has left you, the earth where she rests—this is your country! You see it, you breathe it, everywhere. Think to yourself of your rights and duties, your affections and your wants, your past and your present blessings; write them all under a single name, and that name will be *your country.* We owe it all that we are, and he who enjoys the advantages of having a free country, and does not accept the burdens of it, forfeits his honor, and is a bad citizen. Do for your country what you would for your father and mother. Your country is in danger."

The Spirit of New England.—The following is an extract of a private letter, dated Framingham, Mass., Oct. 1, 1862:

"You express surprise that my husband has enlisted! I would think it a disgrace if he did not, as I think it a disgrace to every able bodied man who refuses to answer his country's call; and I know few so able as he. So I send him forth in the full conviction that he is in the path of duty, and that a blessing will descend upon him in the comfortless camp on the bloody field, that could not reach him by his tranquil fireside in these stormy times.

E. H.'

Bishop Rosecrans.—As Bishop Rosecrans, (brother of the General) was at dinner recently, the conversation reverted to the war.

"It would seem to me, Bishop, that you and your brother, the General, are engaged in very different callings." "Yes, it appears so," returned the Bishop. "And yet," he continued, "we are both fighting men. While the General is wielding the sword of the flesh, I trust I am using the sword of the Spirit. He is fighting the rebels, and I am fighting the spirits of darkness. There is this difference in the terms of our service; he is fighting with Price, while I am fighting without price."

A New Pipe.—Mr. Robert Heneage, of Buffalo, has invented a pipe entirely upon new principles, and destined, in all probability, to effect a complete revolution in tobacco smoking. The editor of *Buffalo Express* says that he has tried the pipe, and found it to be all that it promised. The tobacco in the bowl is lighted at the bottom, and burns upward. The stem is inserted in a cap at the top, which also has a chamber filled with cotton to purify the smoke. The contrivance is not complicated but simple, and works to a charm.—*Quebec Chronicle.*

White and Negro Labor.—Among the many attempts to excite opposition to the President's Proclamation, there is none more false, detestable and atrocious than the assertion that emancipation will bring Southern negroes to the North to compete with our workmen, and bring down the price of wages. In his recent speech at Brooklyn, N. Y., Cassius M. Clay thus alluded to this prejudice: "Germans, Irishmen, Frenchmen, why are you here at all? It is because you here find a government based upon the broad principle of liberty to all humanity. (Applause.) Show me the man who would to-day oppress a man on account of his color, and I will show you a man who will, should it meet his ends, oppress you to-morrow. But it is not true that this interference with your labor will take place in consequence of Emancipation. Emancipation will, in fact, but concentrate black labor in the South.

A Short Answer.—One of the enrolling marshals, the other day, received a strong hint from a down town female. Stopping at the lady's house, he found her before her door endeavoring to effect with a vegetable huckster a 20 per cent. abatement in the price of a peck of potatoes. "Have you any men here, madam?" The reply was gruff and curt—"No." "Have you no husband, madam?" "No." "Nor brothers?" "No." "Perhaps you have a son, madam?" "Well, what of it?" "I should like to know where he is." "Well, he isn't here." "So I see, ma'am Pray where is he?" "In the Union army, where you ought to be." The marshal hastened round the corner. He didn't further interrogate the lady.

—The *Nord* of Brussels says that "a French captain is said to have just returned from a voyage to Africa with specimens of a plant the name of which is still kept a secret, and which, submitted to some chemical process, yields a substance perfectly resembling cotton. Several pieces of stuff have been woven out of it, and specimens submitted to the Emperor of the French. These stuffs are described as stronger than cotton tissue, equal in fineness and 60 per cent. cheaper. The plant abounds both in Africa and America, and will thrive very well in Algeria. The *Nord* adds that a company is being formed to work this substance on a large scale."

THE SUN.

NUMBER 9462. NEW YORK, MONDAY, NOVEMBER 10, 1862. PRICE ONE CENT.

THE NEW YORK SUN.

Published daily, Sundays excepted. One cent per copy—six cents per week, delivered anywhere in the city or vicinity.

CIRCULATION 75,000 COPIES.

Wherever by mail: Three Dollars per year,—or corresponding for $1 ; six months $2. The postage within the State twenty-eight cents a year,—out of the State, $1.56 a year. Address all letters to M. S. BEACH, Proprietor of THE SUN, Corner Fulton and Nassau sts, N. Y.

THE NEW YORK SUN.

MONDAY MORNING, NOV. 10, 1862.

LATEST NEWS

BY TELEGRAPH TO THE NEW YORK SUN

McCLELLAN REMOVED.

BURNSIDE SUCCEEDS HIM.

GEN. HOOKER TO REPLACE BURNSIDE.

McClellan's Farewell to the Army and Departure for Trenton.

100 Guns in Honor of Burnside.

A PORTRAIT OF THE NEW MAN

PROGRESS OF THE ADVANCE.

Probable Escape of Lee's Army.

Another Fight with Stuart's Cavalry.

CAPTURE OF PRISONERS AND GUNS.

Foster's N. Carolina Expedition.

Rumored Capture of 3,000 Rebels.

DISASTROUS FIRE IN BROOKLYN.

Catholic Orphan Asylum Burned.

TWO CHILDREN KILLED.

HUNDREDS TURNED INTO THE STREET.

Important European News.

THE RETURN OF LORD LYONS.

&c. &c. &c.

Virginia.

Highly Important—Gen. McClellan Relieved of his Command—Gen. Burnside Appointed—McClellan's Farewell to his Soldiers.

Headquarters of the Army of the Potomac, Salem, Va., Nov. 8—12 o'clock, noon.—The order relieving Major-Gen. McClellan from the command of the army of the Potomac was received at headquarters at 11 o'clock last night. It was entirely unexpected by all, and therefore every one was taken by surprise.

On its receipt, the command was immediately turned over to Gen. Burnside.

Gen. McClellan and his Staff will leave tomorrow for Trenton, where he is ordered to report.

The order was delivered to him by Gen. Buckingham, in person.

His last official act was the issuing of an address to his soldiers, informing them in a few words that the command had devolved on Gen. Burnside, and taking an affectionate leave of them.

There is no other news worthy of mention excepting that the army is in motion.

REPORTS FROM WASHINGTON.

Washington, Nov. 9.—The first information the public received of the relief of Gen. McClellan from the command of the Army of the Potomac was through the telegram published this morning. It affords a general theme of conversation and comment, and excites surprise, the event occurring unexpectedly. The cause of the Executive action in the premises does not appear to be known outside of official circles, and hence the absence of facts gives rise to conflicting speculations. General McClellan, it is said, passed through Washington today, on his way to Trenton.

The friends of Gen. Hooker say he has sufficiently recovered from his wound to resume his duties in the field. It is supposed that he is to take Burnside's place as late commander of *corps d'armee*.

REPORTS FROM PHILADELPHIA.

Philadelphia, Nov. 9.—The removal of General McClellan has caused much excitement throughout the city, and is the universal topic of conversation. Among the rumors as to the cause it is said that some instructions from the General-in-Chief were not followed, and that the escape of Lee followed as a consequence. Forney's PRESS of tomorrow, in speaking of the removal, says:

It was purely a military act, and was the result of a military consultation and decision, although recommended to the President, and approved by him some time ago. It was only finally resolved upon after a change became inevitable, no act of the present Administration, we might say Executive act since the beginning of the government, has been the subject of more careful deliberation.

REJOICINGS IN PROVIDENCE.

Providence, R. I., Nov. 9.—By order of Gov. Sprague, a salute of 100 guns, is to be fired here tomorrow noon, in honor of the appointment of the Rhode Island General, Burnside, to the command of the Army of the Potomac.

Previous Dispatches—McClellan at Warrenton—Probable Escape of the main Rebel Army—The Army Headquarters at Salem—Jackson and Bragg near with Heavy Forces.

Washington, Nov. 8—10.40 P. M.—Dispatches received here today from the Army of the Potomac show Gen. McClellan's headquarters to be at Warrenton, and that he is following the rebels south, their force being on the west side of the Blue Ridge while his is on the east. It is admitted by his friends that the enemy is beyond his reach till it suits them to turn and make a stand.

Warrenton, Va., Nov. 7—4 P. M.—The army corps of Gen. Reynolds took possession of this place unopposed yesterday. The place was occupied by Col. Payne with about four hundred men, and two howitzers.

Gen. Longstreet's army corps had occupied Culpepper Court House for several days, but left the town on Saturday, and it was generally reported that he would encamp on the hills south of the town.

Gen. A. P. Hill's command was here on Thursday, but retreated upon the advance of our troops. Reliable citizens confirm the general belief of intelligent army officers, that Gen. Lee has succeeded in eluding Gen. McClellan, and that a large portion of Lee's army is at Gordonsville.

Gen. A. P. Hill's forces and Gen. Stuart's cavalry formed the rear guard of Gen. Lee. The former was at Chester Gap on Wednesday, and Gen. Pleasanton had pushed Gen. Stuart to Flint Hill.

Our troops found two hundred and seventy wounded rebel soldiers in the hospital here.

The snow storm continued until late this afternoon.

Lieut. Col. Blunt, of Gen. Longstreet's Staff, was captured by Gen. Bayard today. Blunt is the Provost Marshal General of the rebel army, and was inspecting his pickets at the time he was captured.

Leading Secessionists here prophesy a great battle hereabouts in a few days. They represent that Stonewall Jackson is only ten miles off with a force of seventy thousand men, and that Gen. Bragg is at Gordonsville in great force. They also say that there is little doubt that Jackson is threatening to attack our forces at Waterloo.

Another Skirmish with Stuart's Rebel Cavalry—Capture of Prisoners and Artillery.

Headquarters, Warrenton, Nov. 9.—General Pleasanton, yesterday, in a skirmish with Stuart, near Little Washington, captured three pieces of artillery, also a captain, lieutenant, and five privates. No loss has been reported.

Gen. Bayard yesterday occupied and now holds the railroad bridge across the Rappahannock. The bridge is not injured. The bridge across Broad Run has been destroyed.

There is nothing new up to this writing, from the front, at the Rappahannock.

The weather is clear and cold.

North Carolina.

Important from North Carolina—Reported Success of Gen. Foster's Expedition—Unconditional Surrender of 3,000 Rebels at Plymouth.

The INQUIRER, of Philadelphia, has a letter dated Fortress Monroe, 6th inst., which states as follows:

"The gunboat Delaware, Capt. Foster, arrived here last night, from Newbern, N. C. Gen. Foster had left Newbern with 13,000 men, and had gone to Plymouth, and with about 1,600 men surrounded some 3,000 rebels, about one-half of whom were cavalry. The rebs wished to make terms, but Gen. Foster was obdurate, and demanded an unconditional surrender, and they, finding they could not do better, yielded with a good grace."

Washington, Nov. 8.—Dispatches from Fortress Monroe to the Navy Department, to the 6th inst., make no mention of the Philadelphia INQUIRER's report.

[Plymouth, the scene of this alleged capture, is the Capital of Washington County, N. C. It is a small village, containing less than fifteen hundred inhabitants, located about eight miles south from Roanoke River, where it enters Albermarle Sound, and is connected with a small inlet called Nag's Head. It is about fifty miles in a straight line, north of Newbern, with which it has water communication via Albermarle and Pamlico Sounds and the Neuse River. It was, previous to the rebellion, a place of active trade.]

BY MAIL.

The Newbern PROGRESS, of the 1st inst, is received. It contains no allusion to any recent expedition.

In relation to the statement that the rebels at Wilmington were arming negroes to fight against the Union troops, the PROGRESS says:—We have learned direct from Wilmington, and through what is deemed a reliable source, that such is not the fact. The distrust of the negro is so great that they dare not trust him with arms.

Tennessee.

Reported attack on Nashville—Polk and Breckinridge, with 25,000 men, on the South—Morgan, with his Guerrillas, on the North.

Louisville, Ky., Nov. 8.—About eighty rebel prisoners arrived from Lebanon, Ky., to night, including a son of Humphrey Marshall, who had violated his parole and joined the rebels.

The DEMOCRAT's Bowling Green correspondent, this morning, writes that an escaped prisoner, who left Murfreesboro' on Wednesday, reports that Gens. Polk and Breckinridge, with 25,000 men and considerable artillery, attacked the south side of Nashville on Friday morning, while the guerrilla John Morgan, on the north side, with 3,000 men attempted to destroy the bridge there, but were repulsed. The result of Gen. Polk's attack was not known.

Gen. McCook's Army Corps, comprising Generals Sill's, Woodruff's and Sheridan's divisions, reached Nashville on Friday.

Gen. Crittenden's Division arrived at Gallatin on Friday, and was moving down toward Nashville.

Gen. Cheatham with a portion of Gen. Bragg's army, was at Murfreesboro'.

The remainder of Bragg's army, with the exception of fifteen thousand men, had left the Cumberland Gap and were pushing toward Nashville.

Gen. Bragg [illegible] succeed. I refer [illegible] the best [illegible] Gen. Joseph E. Johnston. Bragg's defeat in the Kentucky campaign, it is stated, were the cause of his arrest.

Nothing had been heard at Murfreesboro', which was in constant telegraphic communication with Mobile, of the capture of the latter city. Fifteen thousand rebel troops are at Mobile.

Louisville, Ky., Nov. 8—11 P. M.—We have been in telegraphic communication with Mitchelville for the last two days, and have received none of the above tidings.

Minnesota.

Punishment of the Indians—Over Three Hundred of the Sioux Indians Condemned to be Hung.

St. Paul, Minn., Nov. 8.—Over three hundred Indians have been convicted by the Military Commission at the Lower Sioux Agency as participators in the late horrible massacres, and are condemned to be hung. Whether they live or die rests with the authorities at Washington. The people of Minnesota, to a man, are in favor of their immediate execution.

Movements of Massachusetts Troops.

Boston, Nov. 9.—Last evening the Government chartered the steamer Saxon, of the Boston and Philadelphia line, and transferred to her six hundred troops from the Merrimac and Mississippi. This made all the troops comfortable, and the three steamers will leave under convoy of the gunboat Huron as soon as the weather clears up.

NEWS ITEMS, &c.

MAJ.-GEN. HUNTER, will in a few days return to the Department of the South.

YESTERDAY, Nov. 9th, was the Prince of Wales' twenty-first birthday, when he became of age.

THE Governors of Rhode Island and Wisconsin have appointed Thursday, 27th inst., as a day of Thanksgiving in those states.

THE Monitor left Washington Navy Yard on Saturday evening, and passed down the Potomac river.

GEN. Banks' Texas expedition is fast fitting out. He will have 20,000 troops, chiefly from New England.

SECRETARY CHASE has determined that the new postal currency shall be distributed in the Western cities in equal proportion with New York.

GENERAL Fitz John Porter has been ordered to Washington to answer to charges preferred against him by General Pope when the latter was in command in Virginia.

THE English papers state that the steamer Pearl, lately sold to the Confederates, had left Gourock Bay for her destination, and that sales of other Clyde steamers were on the *tapis*.

ADMIRAL PORTER has issued orders to stop the whiskey trade, and directed his officers to seize it wherever they find it, as it makes more guerillas than any other cause.

THE President is said to stand firm in favor of his Emancipation Proclamation, and thinks that the late elections were carried on entirely different issues.

IN Michigan, the Senate will stand 17 Republicans to 15 Democrats, and the House 58 Republicans to 42 Democrats. In Minnesota the Republicans have a State majority of 2,009.

COMMODORE C. K. STRIBLING, has been ordered to the command of the Philadelphia Navy-yard, in place of Commodore Prendergrast, deceased.

THE Detroit TRIBUNE, New London CHRONICLE, Hartford TIMES, Hartford PRESS and Hartford COURANT have increased their rates on account of the great advance in paper and everything used in making a newspaper.

A CIRCULAR has been issued for a convention of citizens, to be held at Pittsburg, on the 25th of November, to aid the Government in crushing the rebellion, and enforcing the Emancipation Proclamation.

JUDGE Lane, of Alabama, in a letter to Secretary Stanton complains that the lenient policy adopted towards rebels is unjust towards Union men; and urges the banishment of all disloyal citizens from our military lines.

THE Sanbernton Bridge Female Seminary at Concord, N. H., was burned to the ground on Friday night. All the inmates escaped without injury. The fire is thought to have been the work of an incendiary.

THE assets of the New York Methodist Book Concern are set at $509,947 85; its liabilities, $47,977 90; its net capital, $461,964 95. The Western Book Concern reports assets, $822,777 01; liabilities, $78,123 99; net capital, $744,648 02.

THE speech of the President to the Committee of negroes, on the subject of their colonization in Chiriqui, has been received in Central America with decided marks of ill-will; Nicaragua has published a decree shutting them out of her limits forever, and Costa Rica will probably do the same.

THE merchants and shipowners of New Bedford, Mass., have united in resolutions memorializing the President to demand from the British Government indemnity for losses sustained by the outrages of the Alabama, fitted out in their ports and manned by Englishmen, and carrying the English flag.

THE War Department has determined to punish severely the masters of tugs and steamers who shall hereafter wilfully smash the draw upon the Long Bridge. This has been done repeatedly, in order to prevent the trains of the Alexandria Railroad from crossing, and competing with the steamers in carrying Government supplies.

THE mortar schooners now at the Brooklyn Navy Yard, formerly under the command of Commodore D. D. Porter, are having their mortars removed. A 100 pound Parrott gun is to be placed amidships, two 24-pounder rifled guns upon the sides, and a long range pivot gun upon the forecastle.

THE Grenada APPEAL, of the 5th, says there was a great fire in Augusta on the 4th, which burned cotton warehouses, &c., valued at $500,000. George N. Saunders has returned from his European mission, and brings most gratifying assurances of a speedy recognition of the Confederacy. The people of the South greatly rejoice thereat. Belgium is to take the initiatory.

IT is said that Gen. Fremont, having failed to negotiate a loan, now proposes to sell Mariposa to a stock company in this city, for Treasury notes. This estate is now producing $400,000 per annum, and by the erection of additional mills, which the Company proposes to do, it can easily produce $800,000 per annum. Mr. Fremont will receive enough to pay his debts, and leave him three or four millions of dollars besides.

"MAKE England pay," is George F. Train's advice as to the burnings of the "290." "She is entirely English, and though bonds for $20,000 were given, they were paid the moment the ship went on her trial trip. The whole thing was prearranged by the officers of the British Government. Now all we have to do is to keep the account of every ship burned, and charge it to England. The law of nations awards it. Let Semmes alone. Make England pay. Charge it to her, and compel a prompt settlement after the war, or show her the destructive power of privateers in time of war."

A CORRESPONDENCE has just been published between J. A. Hamilton and Gen. Sandford, which took place in the winter of 1860-61, in which it was proposed to reinforce Forts Moultrie and Sumter by volunteers from New York. After the measure had been decided upon, permission was sought from Gen. Scott. The request was laid before Mr. Buchanan, and answer was sent that the "*immediate military needs of the country did not require any appeal to the Militia or Volunteers in aid of the regular force.*"

A LETTER from Rev. T. Starr King, from San Francisco, states that California has pleaded for several months to send volunteers to aid in putting down the rebellion, but the government would not listen to it. Ten thousand men could have been raised at any time. Determined to aid the Union in some way, a meeting was called to raise subscriptions, and on four days $100,000 was received and the fact telegraphed to the Sanitary Commission at New York, and in less than a week after the reply of Dr. Bellows was received, another $100,000 was paid in, and they are now on the third hundred thousand from San Francisco alone. Throughout the state meetings are being held, and their contributions will raise the amount to half a million. This is California's noble and patriotic response to the invasion of Maryland.

A BLOODY tragedy was enacted on the 15th of October, at Gibraltar, on board the pirate ship Sumter, which has been detained for a year past at that place by our cruisers. It seems that the crew were paid off some time ago, and the vessel left in charge of a couple of officers and a sufficient number of hands to keep her clean. A dispute arose between Hester, the second officer, and Captain Andrews, about a disreputable woman, and Hester, watching his opportunity, deliberately shot Andrews as he lay asleep in his bunk. He then hailed the English guard ship and stated what he had done. A coroner's inquest was held, and a verdict of "willful murder" returned against Hester, who will probably be hung by the English authorities. The Sumter was placed in charge of an English guard. This vessel, which has thus illustrated the penalty that usually attaches to piracy, was formerly commanded by Captain Semmes, of the "Alabama."

Train's Last Hoax on [illegible]—Swallow the [illegible]—Sell an Irishman That Way.

(From the London Morning Herald Oct. 23, 1862.)

The following amusingly impudent letter was addressed to the Society of Cogers, meeting at their hall, Shoe-lane. It appears that while Mr. Train was in England he was a member of this society:—"Revere House, Boston, Sept. 26, 1862.—Dear Cogers,—I am knocking the bottom out of English aristocracy every time. I am smashing up the Abolition party here, and you see on my note paper my maxims. I am with you, as you know. There are 200 in dress circle, 2000 in pit. I belong to the pit. England must have her revolution. The times are changing. The boys in the discussion halls will some day be a power. Think more of yourselves. Remember what I have said to you. Give regards to G—and O'B—and others. Tell them to keep my memory green. I am a Coger. Do you want Shoe-lane advertised all over the world? Then get up a splendid address from the Cogers as being from the people of England to me, speaking of my qualities as a debater, of my charitable actions, of my union fight, of my prophecies, and my warnings. Let it be signed by the Cogers, and resolutions strong, and I will reply, publishing the correspondence. When I pitch into England, remember I only speak the sentiments of—, to whom give kind regards. I look to my debating education in the discussion hall as the most important of my life. No member of parliament can compete with the minds under your hospitable roof. G. F. Train. Mr. Walter Cogers' Discussion Hall, Shoe Lane, Fleet street, London. The society, as might be expected from Englishmen, on hearing the letter, read unanimously adopted the following resolution:—"Resolved, that we the members of the Cogers' Society, having heard read the letter of Mr. G. F. Train, dated Boston, Sept. 26, 1862, cannot refrain from expressing our surprise and indignation at being invited to become accomplices to a double fraud; firstly, to assume to speak in the name of the English people: and secondly, to give Mr. Train credit for qualities contrary to our own estimate of his character. That we further emphatically and explicitly disavow all participation in the views of Mr. Train with respect to the institutions of this country—institutions to which we are fervently and loyally attached, because they assure to our fellow citizens of all classes an amount of freedom of thought, speech and action, combined with order and security for life and property, such as is possessed by no other people on the face of the earth." The mottoes referred to in Mr. Train's letter are severally printed on the corners of the note paper, and are as follows:—"Death to England," "Cheer for the Union," "Death to Treason," "Obey the President." On the envelope we find—"Buy no English goods," "America for Americans," "Our country heads the world," and another which was so obscured by the postage stamp that it could not be deciphered. By a unanimous vote of a crowded meeting Mr. Train was subsequently unanimously expelled from the society.

Effects of the Storm—Numerous Marine Disasters on the Coast.

The British steamer Scotia arrived Saturday, brought the captain and crew of the British bark Mary Rogerson, which was wrecked in a hurricane November 1st—lat. 49: 18, long. 28: 16—and Joseph Seaman, of London, washed overboard. The steamship Daniel Webster put in here Saturday, on her way from Alexandria to Portsmouth Grove, R. I., having experienced damage from the effects of the gale. The light-ship off Sandy Hook parted her moorings during the gale, and drifted to the southern end of the woodlands, when the Daniel Webster took her in tow and anchored her at Quarantine.

At Holmes' Hole the following vessels are ashore: The brig Abner Taylor from New York for Boston. The brig Elvira, from Elizabethport for Boston. The schooner M. E. Price, from Boston for Portland. The schooner Eliza Allen, from New York for Boston. The schooner Louisa, from Boston for Rockland. The schooner Benjamin, from Boston for Calais. The schooner F. Hall, from Calais for Boston. The schooner Arctic, from New York for St. John. Three other vessels, names as yet not ascertained, are ashore here. The schooner Boston, from Cornwall for New York, with potatoes, went ashore on the Straits of Mouth Island, Cape Ann, and went to pieces; crew lost. The schooner T. S. Harding, from Parsboro for Boston, with plaster, was wrecked at the same place; crew saved. The schooner Moses Waring, with a cargo of coal, from Philadelphia for Boston, is ashore at Holmes' Hole, and full of water.

LOCAL NEWS.

NEW YORK AND THE VICINITY.

THE DRAFT.—The station houses were quite crowded with applicants for exemption the last two days, and on Saturday the receipt of the following order would seem to postpone the matter indefinitely:

ALBANY, November 8th.

It is stated, for the information of commissioners, that they are not to proceed with the draft until they shall have received from this department formal orders to the effect, and giving the number of men to be drafted in each town.

The delay in transmitting to this office the returns of the men enlisted in the several counties since the 2d of July, will in some instances render it impracticable to issue such orders to commissioners until after the 10th instant. THOMAS HILLHOUSE, Adjutant-General.

The same order also states that it having been ascertained that several of the Counties in the interior of the State have completed their quotas, whilst in others the deficiency is less than was anticipated, the rendezvous for the drafted men, and the nine months volunteers, will be limited to Buffalo, Elmira, Auburn, Fonda, Plattsburgh, Albany, Yonkers, and Staten Island, or such other places in New York as may be selected for the counties of New York, Kings, Queens, Richmond and Suffolk. The following named officers are detailed to act as Commandants, and will immediately enter on the discharge of their duties: Albany, Brigadier-General John F. Rathbone; New York, Brigadier-General Richard Busteed; Yonkers, Brigadier-General S. C. Parmenter; Fonda, Major-General S. S. Burnside; Elmira, Colonel S. M. Alley; Buffalo, Brigadier-General H. L. Lansing. A sufficient force of National Guards will be assigned to each place of rendezvous to maintain order and discipline. The detail for that at Staten Island will be made by Major-General Sandford, on the requisition of the Commandant, and for those in the interior of the State, by the Commadants, from their respective brigades. The detail, except for Staten Island, not to exceed three full companies. All persons holding authorizations to enlist volunteers for the nine months' service, will take their recruits to the place of rendezvous for drafted men in their respective districts. Transportation passes will be furnished, on application to the Quartermaster of the rendezvous, accompanied by evidence of enlistment, and copy of authorization, as provided in paragraph IX, of General Orders, No. 52.

In Brooklyn, the Committee of the Board of Supervisors report on having enlisted from King's County 8,757 men, and as the quota required is only 8,600 men, they claim that there is an overplus of 157 men. But it is stated that of the number enlisted there have been over 1000 men deserted, and it is still a question whether these will be counted. So, in other towns where they claim to have sent their quota. Yet the State is short 30,000 men, and as soon as the question is settled where the deficiency belongs the draft will proceed. In the meantime recruiting is quite brisk, and by the time they are ready the necessity for a draft may no longer exist.

THE ADVANCE WAGES MOVEMENT.—The journeymen bakers held a large and spirited meeting at Military Hall, No. 193 Bowery, on Saturday night, for the purpose of taking action with reference to an increase of wages, as well as to regulate the hours for working. The complaint is that they not only have to work at a low rate of wages, but that they have to work almost all hours of the day and night, without receiving as much rest as is necessary for the preservation of a good constitution. The meeting was organized by making Mr. Parker Chairman, and Mr. Theobald Mauss Vice-President. Mr. Larkin, a journeyman baker of Jersey City, made some excellent remarks on the injurious effects of the excess in toil now imposed on working men of his profession, and the very inadequate remuneration they received. He urged the necessity for an organization to protect the rights of bakers, referred to the German Journeymen Bakers' Society, and held that association was the best mode for securing respect for their occupation. The President urged that an organization be effected, in order to get their free hours and more wages, and he said that a committee should be appointed to take action with reference to the matter. On motion of Mr. Jackson, a resolution was passed to appoint a committee for the purpose of consulting with the bosses in reference to their grievances, to report at the next meeting. The committee was composed of an equal number of German and English members, as follows:—John Reilly, F. Kirckwood, E. Tracy, John Carroll, Salton, Martin White, Henry Hoffmann, F. Mauss, Louis Bach, Charles Kuhle. After some further addresses the meeting adjourned. The regular manner in which the proceeding were conducted, and the eloquent speeches that were delivered picturing the grievances of the craft, are highly creditable to the intelligence and good conduct of the journeyman bakers of this city.

The effort to come to an understanding between the ship caulkers and their employers, has so far failed. In the particular instance of the work on the steamer McClellan, Mr. Webb paid the men their price, $3 per day, but on being requested to give the same on all her work, he declined. Two vessels that were on the ways to be repaired, were floated off, and went elsewhere for their works. Placards were placed at some of the docks urging the men to remain firm and aid would be rendered them.

The ship joiners of New York and vicinity held a meeting at Mozart Garden, 157 Columbia st., this evening at 7½ o'clock.

QUITE AN INTERESTING meeting was held last night at Irving Hall, in behalf of the Christian Commission—an association which originated in Philadelphia—in aid of the soldier on the battle field, to minister to the sick and wounded, and to afford spiritual comfort to the dying. The Rev. Mr. Boardman, the Secretary of the Association, made a statement of the operations of the Society. In Baltimore it had a District Commission, which had contributed stores and had done a noble work. They had also done a very noble work in St. Louis, in Brooklyn and Boston. Philadelphia had done well, but he had no report to make with regard to New York. New York had, however, done more than other places. The Rev. R. F. Parvin said that the Christian Commission was a sanitary association, but it aimed at the same time at higher purposes. The speaker gave an account of a journey, with others, to the battle field of Sharpsburg for the purpose of relieving the wounded on the battle field. He told a tale of a young rebel soldier, who was relieved while dying, repenting of his sins. This rebel lad was a son of a Methodist clergymen, and had been a member of the church for six years. They went to work there as surgeons, as preachers of the Gospel, and as Christians. The Surgeons were glad to avail themselves of the assistance of the Delegates of the Christian Commission, who were laboriously employed, assisting the Surgeons and prosecuting their great work of reminding the soldiers of their duties as sons, husbands, fathers, and above all, as immortal beings. The Rev. George J. Mingins, of Philadelphia, and others, also addressed the meeting, and detailed the thrilling scenes witnessed by these Delegates, who went to the battle-field in aid of the wounded. The Association has distributed 1,156 boxes and barrels of publications and [illegible].

MR. THOMAS D. SULLIVAN and Mr. John P. Bonnell, aided by Dodworth's celebrated orchestra, and 500 children from the schools of the Thirteenth Ward, together with several distinguished artists and amateurs, will give a Grand Concert on Thursday evening, the 20th inst., for the benefit of "The Institution for the maintenance and education of deceased or disabled soldiers." This is a most praiseworthy object, and deserves encouragement. About 100 children are already in the Institution at 334 Sixth avenue, and there are still several hundreds craving admission, who cannot be accomodated for want of funds. At this Concert Mahon's patriotic songs, "The Standard of the Free" and "A Soldier is my Beau," will be sung for the first time with full orchestral accompaniments, and with trumpet and drum solos in the chorus and symphonies.

THE BENEVOLENT AND PROTECTIVE National Societies of our city are most honorable testimonials of the moral work, the benevolence and the public spirit of our citizens of foreign birth, and at this season of the year the organizations to which we refer are usually called on to do a large portion of their labors of mercy and human brotherhood. One of the oldest of these societies in our city is "The Society of the Friendly Sons of St. Patrick," whose mission is to aid distressed Irish people, and much good has been done, and much distress alleviated. This Society was instituted in the year 1784, Daniel McCormick, Esq., being its founder. In 1861, $1,200 were disbursed, $900 of which went to the 69th Regiment to equip them for the field, the Society feeling that as the country was in danger, the money could not be better spent than in her defence, and trusting, no doubt, to the generosity of the wealthy to fill up this large deficit made in the charity fund. The remaining three hundred dollars were divided among about one hundred poor families. The objects of the Society's bounty must be natives of Ireland or their descendants in the first and second degree, and no more than $5 can be given in one half year to any one family. Stocks are invested in the Manhattan and in the American Exchange Banks, from which are formed the permanent fund. The charity fund is made up from initiation fees and dues of members. The latter is nearly exhausted, and donations would doubtless be thankfully acknowledged. The officers are a President, two Vice-Presidents, a Treasurer and a Secretary, all of whom give their services gratuitously.

The father Matthew T. A. B. Society is not, strictly speaking, a charitable society, yet it has given a great deal for benevolent purposes. It is now eleven years in existence, and has done an immense amount of good by reclaiming about eleven thousand men and women from drunkenness. Their initiation fee for constitutional members is $1, and three dollars a year afterwards as dues. No benefits are allowed till a man has been six months a member; recently, however, a case occurred in which a member of three months standing died, and as his widow was blind they gave her $71. Lately they donated $123 to assist the Irish poor, $244 to Father Smith of Niagara Falls, to aid in building a seminary for the education of priests, and $96 to finish a chapel in Derry, Ireland. The benefits to sick members are $4 per week, while actually sick, and $40 in case of death, for funeral expenses; if the wife of a member dies, he receives $25 for the same purpose. During three months the receipts were $843, and the expenditures about $600. During the past year four members and two members' wives were buried, making an expense of $210. There are nearly $2,000 in the treasury, and they have property to the amount of $500. Their secretaries, of which there are three, and their treasurer, receive $40 per annum for their services. The Society now numbers 780 members.

THE FATHER MATTHEW TEMPERANCE Societies of New York and Brooklyn held large meetings last night at Brook's Assembly Rooms, 361 Broome st. Addresses were delivered by Mr. F. J. Haggerty and others, and there was some good singing at 166 Fulton st., Brooklyn. Dr. H. Gerlian delivered his celebrated lecture on the evils of intemperance, which was first delivered in Toronto, Canada, and Mrs Mason and others then sung some temperance songs; and in South Brooklyn the Society there had some interesting exercises. Several new members were inducted into the three societies, and many were induced to sign the pledge.

THERE ARE NOW no fewer than three regiments claiming the number 69 as their regimental designation. The 69th Volunteers, who did wonders at the battle of Antietam, the 69th N. Y. S. M., under Col. M. Murphy, which leaves today for the seat of war, and the 69th N. Y. S. M., under Major James Bagley, which remains at home.

THE LIFE AND CHARACTER of Mahomet, the Arabian Prophet, was the subject of a lecture delivered by the Rev. Mr. Ellis, last evening, at the Church of the Rev. Dr. Chapin. The lecturer traced the career of Mahomet as a servant to caravans, a husband, and a merchant, and claimed that Mahomet, in urging the worship of our God, warred against superstition and got rid of the wood and stone idols which his people had worshipped.

"THE THIRD TIME is the charm," schoolboys say, but the third of such days as Saturday and yesterday would charm very few of our citizens. Winter, dripping with sleet and slush, poked his head through them and made his worst face at us. He has now happily left us for a brief season, and it will, we trust, be the mild misty Indian summer. When winter returns with clear cold skies, ushering in the social gladness of Christmas and the welcome New Year, we will cheerfully face the changes of the year, and thank Providence for the beneficence displayed throughout the varied seasons.

REV. DR. BERRIAN, Rector of Trinity Parish, died in this city on Friday evening last. He was one of the oldest and most widely known clergymen in this city. His funeral takes place to-day at 3 p.m., at Trinity Church.

LORD LYONS, the English Minister to this country, who arrived by the Scotia on Saturday, is now stopping at the Brevoort House. Hon. Simon Cameron, U. S. Minister to Russia, also arrived in the Scotia, and proceeded to Washington at once.

WALLACK'S THEATRE.—Bulwer's comedy of "Money," will be performed here this evening, for the last time at present. On Wednesday the new comedy of "Central Park," will be presented for the first time, and will be repeated on Friday and Saturday. On the other evenings of the week the pieces will be "Bosom Friends" and "Speed the Plough." Those who have not yet paid a visit to this beautiful theatre, should not lose the opportunity.

SHOCKING SUICIDE.—Coroner Ranney held an inquest on Saturday, at No. 78 West 48th street, upon the body of Stephen H. Bolsford, a native of Connecticut, 29 years of age, who committed suicide on Friday night, by cutting his throat with a razor. The deceased, at the breaking out of the rebellion, enlisted in one of the New York regiments, and participated in the first battle of Bull Run. Soon after the battle his health failed, and he was discharged as being unfit for duty. Since his return home he has exhibited, at intervals, symptoms of insanity, and of late had been heard to say that his time to die had come. On Friday night, about 10 o'clock, he went into his father's room, and, taking a razor from a drawer, drew it across his throat, severing the jugular vein and windpipe, and in a few moments bled to death. His mother and father both witnessed the awful deed, and tried to prevent it, but it was accomplished too quickly for their interference to be of any avail. The coroner's jury rendered a verdict of "suicide."

TRAIN'S LECTURE, in the Rev. Mr. Beecher's church, Brooklyn, this evening, will doubtless be a brilliant, spicy and unique affair. Mr. Train is an original thinker and dares to say just what he thinks.

THE GERMAN LADIES, who formed a society for raising funds for a German hospital, have thus far collected, as their last report shows, $5,894 96, of which $5,855, have been deposited in the German Savings Bank. Mrs. Marie Huselt is the treasurer of this excellent society.

THE FALL EXAMINATIONS of the Public schools will commence today with school No. 38, (8th Ward) in Greene st, near Broome.

THE NEXT LEGISLATURE may, it is supposed, attempt to reform our Common School System, so as to limit its enormous expense and make it less a political machine. Heretofore, the management of our schools has been the highway to political offices, and the people have had to suffer from large leaks, kept open to favor politicians and their backers. The leakage by contracts cannot be estimated and in many wards a majority of the school officers form a ring that authorize shameful expenditures, which can only be checked, by having Inspectors, who will refuse to audit bills which are one or two hundred per cent. above the ordinary rates. That the School Trustees and Commissioners often use their patronage for their own political or pecuniary advancement, will scarcely be denied by any one, but the way to prevent their doing so is not clear.

AN IRISH FAMILY named Davis, living at 37 E. 13th street, has given six of its members (brothers) to the war. Two are now serving in Meagher's Brigade, one of whom was wounded at Antietam; two are in Corcoran's Legion, one in the 2d and one in the 9th. The seventh son went yesterday to Camp Scott to bid good bye to his two brothers who are in the 69th, and would have gone himself but that he has two sisters to take care of, the parents being dead.

COUNTERFEIT $50 and $100 Treasury Notes made their appearance in this city on Saturday, altered from $1 and $2 notes. Their appearance is quite defective and blurred.

IT IS ANNOUNCED that the differences between Tammany and Mozart have not only been compromised for the ensuing election, but ensuring a consolidation of the two general committees and the two sections of the Democratic party. It is not considered advisable to carry out this union entirely until after the municipal elections, as it will involve material changes in the construction of the general committees, and the removal of the Democratic headquarters from Tammany Hall and Mozart Hall to some central place between Fourteenth and Twenty-third streets.

THERE WERE five hundred and fourteen vessels that entered our harbor from foreign ports during the month of October. During the same period there were five hundred vessels that cleared from here for foreign destinations.

CITY INCIDENTS.—Coroner Naumann held an inquest, yesterday, on the body of Wm. Hannegan, who died from fracture of the skull, received by being hit on the head by a stone thrown during a row, in 11th Avenue, a short time ago....John Cullen died from injuries received by falling down stairs last Monday, at 476 Second Avenue....John Drummond, a lad 16 years of age, was killed by the ends of a comforter he wore being caught in the machinery at 55 Ann st., and drawing him up, mangled him horribly. August Valdfleux was arrested on Saturday night, for stealing $62 from Albert Sanders, at a public house in William street. ....Some expert thief stole a package of $2,000 from the paymaster of the Watervliet Arsenal, at the Sub Treasury, on Saturday afternoon, while he was packing up some $30,000 he had just received.

THE COURTS.—In the Superior Court, Catherine Slathman sued Philip Polander, for seduction and breach of promise, to recover $2,000 damages. An order of arrest was granted, and the defendant was held in $1,000 bail. The parties were both employed in the establishment of a certain baker and politician in the 4th avenue, and the defendant under promise of marriage, seduced the plaintiff, and now refuses to marry her. An application is now made to discharge the defendant from arrest, he positively denying having ever promised to marry the plaintiff, and also the charge of seduction. The application was refused.

CITY POLITICS—MOZART RULE—MR. McDONOUGH WANTS TO BE HEARD.—Editor SUN: The following extract appeared in your paper of Saturday last, in connection with the politics of Mozart Hall: "But that same night Mozart, without a single regret, threw overboard Jas. Wadsworth, who has been making speeches for Gen. Wadsworth; F. J. McDonough and several others." Wadsworth, vice chairman, was so expelled. One other was expelled for voting for Duffy for Congress. I was *accused* by a personal enemy for voting for the Hon. George Weir, a Jeffersonian candidate for Assembly for the 16th District, and the resolution of accusation was referred to a committee. I do not relish being accused, by your article as voting for an abolitionist. I never did and never will. Mr. Weir was willing to withdraw from the canvass, provided Mr. McCann would,—so as to ensure the *certain* defeat of the Republican candidate. Mr. McCann's friends would not consent to *any* arrangement. In voting for Mr. Weir, I voted for an honorable man—one who, if elected, could do as much for the city of New York as any of the gentlemen selected to take care of her interests in the next House. Please publish the foregoing and oblige,

FRANK J. McDONOUGH, 19th Ward.

Nov. 8, 1862.

BROOKLYN.

DESTRUCTION OF THE BROOKLYN ROMAN CATHOLIC ORPHAN ASYLUM BY FIRE—TWO CHILDREN BURNED TO DEATH—SEVERAL HUNDRED TURNED OUT INTO THE STREET—MEETING IN BEHALF OF THE UNFORTUNATES, &c., &c.—About 2½ o'clock Sunday morning, a fire broke out in the extensive building on Bedford avenue, between Willoughby and De Kalb avenues, Brooklyn, occupied as an asylum for Roman Catholic orphan boys, and resulted in its complete destruction, together with the loss of two lives. The structure is of brick, 150 feet front by 100 in depth, and five stories in height. The grounds attached comprise 14 lots, and extend from Bedford avenue to Spencer street, affording ample space for exercise in fine weather. About 150 feet in the rear is a wooden shed, about 30 to 75 feet in extent, which is designed for a play-house in inclement weather. The main building is divided into apartments, for the accommodation of the superintendents and assistants, and conveniences are provided, for 356 children. The second, third and fourth floors were used as sleeping apartments. Heat was furnished by means of furnaces, two of which were located in the basement under the north wing, and two under the south wing. The main entrances in front and rear of the center building, the halls and stairways, were all of wide dimensions, and to this feature, together with the presence of mind and the activity displayed by those in charge, it is mainly owing, that the conflagration did not result more

(Continued on Fourth Page.)

On the Fourth Page, will appear to-day, all Important News received at this office, after Two O'Clock, A. M.

OUR NEW COMMANDER.

BRAVE GEN. BURNSIDE.

Just appointed to the Command of the Armies in Virginia.

WE re-publish from our own columns, and from HARPER'S WEEKLY, an accurate likeness of Gen. Burnside, already favorably known by his brilliant exploits at Roanoke Island, and by his capture of the entire sea coast of North Carolina, including the well defended stone fort off Beaufort, in that state, and now made deservedly famous by his appointment to the command of our armies in Virginia.

Gen. Ambrose Everett Burnside was born in Liberty, Union Co., Indiana, on the 23d of May, 1824, and is now in the vigor of manhood. He is of Scotch descent, his grandparents having emigrated to South Carolina, where his father was born, and practiced law with great success, having married a South Carolina lady. In 1821 he disposed of his property in the Palmetto state, and removed to Southern Indiana, where he filed several local offices and became Judge of the Circuit Court.

The son, when 18 years of age, was admitted into West Point Military Academy, and in 1847 graduated in the Artillery, fifteenth in a class of forty-seven. His rank of Brevet 2d Lieutenant in 2d Artillery was exchanged the following year for that of a full second lieutenancy in the 3d Artillery. At the time of his graduation from West Point his regiment was in Mexico, and, joining it at Vera Cruz, he went, with Patterson's column, to the City of Mexico, which city they reached after Scott's triumphal entry. On the promulgation of peace, he was ordered to Newport, R. I., and served at that post until the Spring of 1849, when he went to New Mexico, having been attached to Bragg's famous battery as first Lieutenant. For three or four years he was in the exciting service of skirmishing against the warlike Indian tribes of New Mexico, and in several perilous fights displayed such dauntless courage as to earn the highest encomiums from his superior officers.

He was recommended to President Fillmore for promotion, but resigned from the service before receiving the reward to which he was fairly entitled. In the winter of 1850–'1 he served as Quartermaster on the Boundary Commission, which ran the line between Mexico and the United States, and in Sept., '51, came across the plains as bearer of dispatches from Col. Graham to the President. With an escort of only three men he started from the Gila River on his perilous trip through the Indian country, but fortunately passed through unmolested, travelling 1,200 miles in the incredibly short time of 17 days. This is the fastest mule travel on record. While at Fort Adams, Newport, he resigned from the service, having invented a breech-loading carbine.

With a view of manufacturing it, he settled in Bristol, R. I., and invested his property in it on the strength of a verbal contract with the traitor Floyd, who found it an easy matter to ruin the poor Lieutenant. Lieut. Burnside then tried his fortune in Chicago, and entered the employment of the Illinois Central Railroad, where he renewed his former friendship with the future Major-General McClellan. General Burnside, on being appointed Treasurer to the Company, removed to New York, where he resided for some time.

A year ago last spring while sitting in his office in this city, he was surprised by the receipt of a telegram from Governor Sprague, asking him to accept the Colonelcy of the First Rhode Island regiment. In half an hour he was on his way and arrived at Providence early the next morning. The rest is easily told. Our readers recollect how quickly his regiment was disciplined; how his men fought like veterans at the battle of Bull Run, and, when the day went against them, retired as coolly as from parade. For his gallant conduct during the battle, in which he acted as brigadier general, commanding the 2d brigade of Gen. Hunter's Division, he was appointed Brigadier General by the President.

In politics, Gen. Burnside is a Democrat, but, like Butler and Dickinson, now knows no party but his country. During his residence in Rhode Island he was Major General of Militia for three years, but with this exception has taken no part in military life since his resignation at Fort Adams, until last spring.

A WEEKLY EDITION of THE NEW YORK SUN, issued every Tuesday, in wrappers for the mail, TWO CENTS EACH, $1 per 100.

SUBSCRIPTIONS—PAID IN ADVANCE.

One copy, 1 year, 75cts. | Three copies, 1 year, $200
Do. 16 months, $1 00 | Five copies, do $3 00

Specimen copies, gratis. Discount of 20 per cent. from single rate, an extra copy over five.

Postage within New York State, only thirteen cents a year—out of the State, twenty-six cents.

Address M. S. BEACH, SUN OFFICE, NEW YORK.

DEATHS.

DEADY—On Sunday, Nov. 9th, Mary Deady, widow of John Deady, aged 66 years.

Her friends and relatives are respectfully invited to attend the funeral, on Tuesday afternoon, 11th inst, at 2 o'clock, from her late residence, 200 Washington st, Brooklyn. 245

PEASLEY—In this city, on Saturday morning, Nov. 8, of hemorrhage of the lungs, William, son of Andrew and Winefred Peasley, aged 23 years. Dearly beloved as a dutiful son and affectionate brother, highly esteemed as a friend, honored and respected as a man, his decease has brought almost inconsolable grief to the family circle, cast a cloud of sorrow over the faces of his friends, and is deeply mourned by all who knew him. His fellow-students in the Cooper Institute will ever remember him as a thorough student and kind and courteous classmate, and so long as manly virtues and generous impulses shall be cherished, the memory of William Peasley will be green in the hearts of his acquaintances. 233

Richmond Whig and Public Advertiser.

VOLUME 39. | RICHMOND, VA., FRIDAY, NOVEMBER 14, 1862. | NUMBER 91.

RICHMOND WHIG.

THURSDAY MORNING, NOV. 13, 1862.

"Supplies for the Army."

Last Friday, while the snow was falling thick and fast, a Confederate officer called upon us to request the publication of a card, in which he stated, that "from undoubted authority, there are thousands of our brave soldiers in the Army of the Potomac without shoes. The Quartermaster's Department has not supplied them and is not immediately able to do so." The author of the card we knew to be a gentleman of unimpeachable truthfulness, and the "authority" upon which he based his statement, as we learned from him, was one of the highest officers in the army, who assured him that, on actual count, it had been ascertained that *in one corps* of the Army of the Potomac there were *twenty six hundred* men without shoes.

We had seen the painful statements of the well-known "P. W. A." upon this subject. We had read the thrilling appeal of Gov. Vance to the people of North Carolina, in behalf of the unprovided troops from that State. We had seen in the newspapers of States farther South column after column of advertisements, from officers and privates detailed from their commands to go home and make known to the people the destitution and suffering of their brothers and friends in the army. We had heard an agent and officer of the Government, who was under orders to go to Europe, say that it depended upon his success in passing the blockade, making satisfactory arrangements abroad, and then running his cargoes safely into Southern ports, whether the army would have a supply of shoes, overcoats and blankets for the winter—and that agent we knew did not leave the country till well on in October. We had seen the telegram of the Secretary of war, to the editor of the Savannah Republican, saying, "We desire all the assistance in supplying shoes, blankets, and clothing that can be furnished." We had heard from many well informed private sources, and seen in numerous publications in the newspapers, statements calculated to move the most obdurate nature to tears. But, we were not prepared for the appalling revelation that, in a single corps, thinned and reduced as we knew the divisions of the army to be, there were, in the wintry storm then raging, two thousand six hundred men without shoes. We felt that the time had come to speak earnestly to the people, and about the Government, on the subject.

It so happened, at the very time, though then unknown to us, a body of troops were passing through our streets, by the very door of the War Department, many of whom, as we were assured by spectators, were barefooted, and wading through snow ankle deep. Citizens who witnessed this sad and harrowing spectacle gave honorable expression to their sympathy, by immediately setting about efforts to afford such relief as was in their power. An impromptu meeting was held, and the first steps taken towards receiving general contributions. Notices were read in all the churches, Sunday, reciting what had been witnessed in our streets, and appealing to the humane and patriotic to come to the rescue.—Monday a more general meeting was held, and many liberal subscriptions of money made. Tuesday committees commenced calling upon families at their residences, to afford them an opportunity of giving whatever their means permitted and their sense of gratitude, humanity and justice to their noble defenders prompted. The responses were cordial and liberal. We heard of but one refusal, and that of a Cabinet officer, who considered the proceeding a reflection on the Government, and therefore declined to give anything. At least so we heard, but for the honor of the Administration and of our common humanity, we hope incorrectly.

This was the condition of things Tuesday night. All who had an opportunity of contributing rejoiced in the belief that they had done something to make our shivering troops more comfortable, something to warm their hearts, perhaps, as well as their bodies, by proving to them, while they were facing at once the death-dealing weapons of the enemy and the fierce blasts of winter, that there were those at home who thought of them and cared for them — Others were waiting to be called on, and all eager to do something to show that they were not insensible when such an appeal was made. Judge, then, of the general surprise, the shock felt by this community, when a journal, reputed to bear peculiar relations to the Administration, on Wednesday morning made its appearance with a leading article, the whole tendency of which is to disparage a movement so honorable to the city, and to discourage efforts calculated to result in so much good. That we do not misrepresent the tenor or effect of this article, we appeal to its own language. We are told there has been "a good deal of exaggeration and misapprehension as to the deficiencies of our army"; that "every requisition" which has been made on the Quartermaster's Department "from the army of Gen. Lee for shoes and blankets has been met"; that "the supply department seems to have done its duty in meeting all the requisitions, notwithstanding the extraordinary difficulties surrounding its operations"; that "there are comparatively very few who have not already been supplied from the shoes forwarded," &c., &c. And the intimation is distinctly thrown out, that, where there is want or suffering, it is occasioned by the improvidence and wastefulness of soldiers, themselves—who, we must infer, are so metamorphosed from the beings they were when they entered the army, that they wilfully deprive themselves of food when hungry, and clothing when cold; that if they lie in snow and rain without covering at night, it is because they have thrown away their blankets; that if they walk with frost bitten and bleeding feet over frozen ground it is because they have of choice kicked off their shoes. And is the *Enquirer* in fact so anxious to have it appear that the Administration can never be at fault, that it will venture upon such experiments on the public credulity as these! Does it not know that if every requisition from General Lee's army has been supplied, all the requisitions which ought to have been made have not been made? Does it not know that the Quartermaster's Department is not and has not for months been in a condition to supply all the wants of the army—for that is the real question, and for the Department to seek shelter under the absence of requisitions from its own officials is only to make it certain that these officials have been derelict in duty, or that the Department is trying to screen itself by a quibble. We do not care to know what response was given to the Enquirer, at the Quartermaster's office. We know the great fact that the army is suffering terribly, and if the Quartermaster General does not know this, then the sooner some one takes his place, who will keep himself advised of the condition of the army, the better! But, we believe Colonel Myers does know this, and that he would not pretend to assert, what the Enquirer would like to have inferred from its statement that all requisitions have been met—that the Army is not in want, and that most seriously.

But, the *Enquirer*, which seems incapable of imagining anything short of the most immaculate impeccability in the Administration, lectures us for the freedom with which we have remarked upon the responsibility of officials in this matter. Nearly six months ago, upon facts which were then submitted to us by a gentleman connected with the Quartermaster's Department, we became satisfied that that important office was wanting in the forethought, the comprehension and the energy demanded by a proper regard for the well-being of the army and the vigorous prosecution of the war, and in several editorial articles we endeavored to direct attention to the imperative necessity of making provision for the winter, especially in this very matter of shoes.—We succeeded so far only as to induce the Department to send out on a tour of exploration a single agent, the same who, in October, was sent to Europe, who executed his mission by a railroad jaunt, and a halt here and there at certain towns and cities. We then thought and said, we now know, that instead of *one*, at least twenty such agents should have been dispatched, and they should have been instructed to visit, if possible, not only cities and towns, but every village and neighborhood of the interior and rural districts, and to establish, urge and encourage every enterprise and occupation that looked to furnishing supplies for the army. It was not to the large and greedy establishments only that attention should have been directed, but to private efforts, to plantation labor, to domestic industry, to the women as well as to the men of the country. If this had been done, no one who knows anything of the capabilities of the country can doubt that the most abundant supplies would have been obtained. The whole responsibility rested upon the Executive, his war officer, and his chiefs of bureaus. Congress had done everything that legislation was capable of, to facilitate and make practicable a system of general development of industry for the benefit of the army. These officials did not comprehend or neglected their duty, and, to the wonder and dismay of the *Enquirer*, that cannot understand how such dignitaries can be spoken of in plain terms, we had the hardihood to charge them with delinquency.

But, our prudent contemporary is distressed and alarmed lest what the *Whig* has said may be "copied in the papers of the United States," and thereby do us "much mischief." This is a very weak apprehension, a very nonsensical idea. So far from entertaining it ourselves, or being influenced by the fact that the *Enquirer* entertains it, we shall be much pleased to see all that we have said reproduced in the journals of the enemy's country—for these two good results would ensue: first, the enemy would discover that the belief they have held, or affected to hold, that the South is ruled by a military despotism, that no freedom of opinion or speech is tolerated, and that the press is chained down to the privilege of uttering only what is permitted by or pleasant to the ruling dynasty, is a libel upon our people and government. This discovery, we apprehend, would never be made from anything that appears in the columns of our contemporary. Second, we are perfectly willing, nay, desirous, that the enemy shall know that the troops whom they encountered at Manassas, in the Valley of Virginia, on the Chickahominy, at Cedar Mountain, at Manassas again, and in Maryland—and who, everywhere, mastered and routed them, are men who fight from no sense of gratitude to the government or obligation to its rulers—from no hope of pay or profit, but from pure devotion to the cause which they uphold; that for this they are willing to endure every privation and hardship that can befall them; and that though faint and weary, though half clad and hungry, though shivering from cold or sinking with disease, they are ever ready to meet the foes of their country and the would-be destroyers of their liberty, in the deadly embrace of battle, and that, with all the disadvantages under which they labor, they are strong enough to hurl them back, come in what manner and with what equipments they may. When the enemy learn this and fully realize it, we expect them to come to the conclusion that it is vain to try to subjugate such a people. Let the *Enquirer* read the following paragraph from a Northern paper, and it will have a clearer and better idea of the impression produced on the enemy by a knowledge of the truth in regard to ourselves. The writer is speaking of the heroic Missourians, of whom our contemporary may not hear much said in official circles: "They are terribly in "earnest, and will do all in their power on the side of "treason. It is high time to throw aside the idea that "the Missouri rebels, or those from any other State, are "to be put down with mild or conciliatory measures—"When men march barefooted mile after mile over "rough and flinty roads, their feet exuding blood at "every step; when their rations consist of a single ear "of corn, and when their clothing hangs in rags about "them, with its safety endangered by every gust of "wind, it is time to know that these men believe in the "cause they have espoused. When men thus shod, fed "and clothed, fight with a desperation unparalleled in "history, as instanced by that terrific charge on our "batteries at Corinth, it is time for us to understand "that only an active and vigorous war will end the re-"bellion with honor to the Federal cause."

We will only add that in all we have said now or heretofore on this subject, we have had no other motive than the welfare of the army, and, through it, of the country. We regret exceedingly that the *Enquirer*, through its strange zeal for the "eminent citizens who conduct our public affairs," should have said anything calculated to suspend the commendable efforts of those who are striving to alleviate the sufferings of our fellow citizens in arms, and to chill the generous sympathies of those who are enjoying in quiet and comfort the fruits of their great hardships and perils. We trust that these efforts and these sympathies will receive no check. It would be a monstrous shame, an indelible disgrace if we failed to do all in our power for those who are doing so much for us.

From Northern Virginia.

"All quiet along the lines," was the report from Gordonsville, last evening. So far as we have been able to ascertain, no fighting has taken place since Monday morning, when the intrepid Stuart attacked and drove the enemy several miles, and then returned to give his wearied men an opportunity for a little rest and recreation. A paroled prisoner, who came through the enemy's lines, on Monday, gave it as his opinion that McClellan's forces were being gradually withdrawn and sent to points south of Richmond. This may possibly be so; for, the enemy, having become satisfied of the condition of General Lee's army, might well hesitate to make a further advance under a probability of disastrous consequences.

The Late Invasion of Fredericksburg.

Among the incidents of the recent visit of the Abolition cavalry to the town of Fredericksburg, it is stated that when Captain Simpson's Norfolk company made their gallant charge, the populace, old and young, joined in the chase with a hurrah, throwing stones, some shooting from behind street corners, and even the women and children uniting in the pursuit and urging on our troops. It appears, however, that the conduct of a portion of our small force there was such as to merit condemnation. The *Recorder* mentions that Colonel Oritcher made every effort to rally that part of his command which lately constituted his battalion, but it is due to candour and truth to say that they were panic stricken, and would not rally, but fled. The enemy were led from Prince William county through Stafford to Falmouth, by one Travis Browne, a deserter from Captain Charles Green's company, 47th Virginia Regiment, an intelligent local guide, who piloted them cautiously by our pickets, and in order to do this successfully they came the entire journey through woods, fields and bypaths.

General Daniel Ruggles, C. S. A., who had been spending some days in Fredericksburg, was about leaving on horseback when the Abolitionists entered the town, and had barely time to make his escape from a squad who were approaching on a cross street. Soon after the enemy left the place, a lady (Mrs. Ford) followed them across the river to Falmouth to procure a servant whom they had stolen. She was assured that he might return if he pleased, otherwise she could not get him. The servant chose at once to return, glad to get clear of the company he had been in for some hours.

Eastern North Carolina.

The intelligence received from Raleigh on Tuesday night, by telegraph, that the enemy had taken possession of the town of Greenville, N. C., and arrested several of its prominent citizens, excited some apprehension in the public mind, inasmuch as the place is unpleasantly near the line of railroad communication with the South. It should not, however, be imagined that a matter of such vast importance as the defence of Eastern North Carolina has been neglected by the Government. While it is impossible to foretell what may be the final result of events not yet developed, it is safe enough to say that the Abolitionists will find their progress towards the interior obstinately disputed inch by inch. The Raleigh papers of Tuesday announce that General Evans' brigade has been added to the force at Weldon, and General Whiting has been assigned to the command at Weldon. The extent of our military preparations will be made known whenever the opposing forces meet in the field of strife.

The York River Country.

No Yankee gunboats have visited West Point since last Monday week, at which time they destroyed the old fortifications and blew up the magazines; but they have lately been bestowing more attention than usual upon the inhabitants of Gloucester. A few days ago, Messrs. Washington and Peter Smith, residing at Cappahosic, were taken off by the marauders and carried to Fortress Monroe upon the groundless accusation that they had something to do with the burning of the ship Alleghanian, on the Rappahannock river. Capt. Sterling, another citizen of Gloucester, was arrested, but subsequently set at liberty. The people of that section are closely watched, and it seems to be the object of the enemy to isolate them as much as possible from other sections of the State. From information furnished by negroes, the Yankees profess to be well aware of every movement of the Confederates, even to the posting of a picket at any place between West Point and the White House.

Western Virginia

The report of the occupation of Highland county by the enemy has been revived and contradicted, and is now reiterated with some show of truth. The Staunton Spectator says, upon the authority of the mail carrier, that they number five thousand; and that on Saturday last a party surrounded the house of Mr. Rexford, the Sheriff of Highland county, at Hightown, seven miles west of Monterey, with the view of capturing him, but he was at the stable at the time and made his escape by taking to the bushes, and succeeded in getting to Monterey, where he apprised the citizens of the approach of the enemy. The number is believed to be greatly exaggerated.

THE AFFAIR NEAR SHEPHERDSTOWN, SEPT. 30TH—MISREPRESENTATIONS CORRECTED.

ARTILLERY CORPS, A. N. V.
Nov. 8th, 1862.

To the Editor of the Whig:

The following statement was prepared and forwarded to a military friend in Richmond, about the 30th October, for publication in the Whig. Owing to irregularities in the mails to and from the army, and frequent failures to receive letters and papers, no knowledge was had whether it had been received and published. On inquiry at this date, it is inferred that it has not yet appeared, and probably has not been received. The paper is, therefore, again forwarded:

In the Whig, of 13th October, appeared an anonymous article, to which the attention of the undersigned has just been called, requiring brief notice, because doing injustice to some officers and troops for the sake of gaining larger credit for others.

The writer, claiming to be an eye witness of, and participant in, General A. P. Hill's achievement at Shepherdstown on the 20th September, under General Jackson's supervision, seeks to magnify that service, sufficiently creditable without any unfair setting off, by injuriously detracting from credit due to other faithful defenders of the country. He states, that "Brigadier General Pendleton, with two brigades of infantry, and upwards of forty pieces of artillery, took position, on the night of the 17th, on the river bluffs near Shepherdstown, to stop the enemy in any attempt to follow us.—We finished crossing about nine or ten A. M. on the 18th, at which time the enemy, silent before, opened with guns, of long range, doing us and General Pendleton no harm. Some of his batteries replied, but probably with little effect. During the day the enemy gradually crept down to the river side, and towards evening began a fire from skirmishers deployed on the banks. At nightfall, General Pendleton having withdrawn many of his guns from the bluffs, they opened a heavy fire of artillery and musketry, under which they crossed a few hundred men; whereupon, our infantry and batteries withdrew in confusion, losing four guns. General Pendleton thought he had lost almost all his guns, but such was not the case. * * General P., it seems, retreated without sufficient cause," &c.

This statement, wrong as it plainly is in spirit, and palpably improper as coming from an officer, which it professes to do, really answers itself. Since it admits that General Pendleton kept the enemy in check the entire day, and had his guns withdrawn only at nightfall, the definite object with which he was charged having been accomplished, viz: of keeping back the enemy till the army should quietly reach a comfortable resting place; and the conditions of darkness, &c., having occurred, on which he was directed by the commanding General to withdraw, the idea of an indefinite abidance there on the part of such a force was simply preposterous.

But the article is, besides, full of inaccuracies. Dates, numbers and important facts are all misstated. Our army crossed the Potomac, not as the writer represents, on the night of the 17th, but on that of the 18th. It finished crossing, not between 9 and 10 A. M., but before 8. General Pendleton placed the batteries in position early in the morning, not during the night. The infantry force left him for support was not two brigades, but a very small remnant of two brigades, not exceeding 600 men in all, and of these a large detachment had to be sent to aid in guarding a ford three miles below. The artillery consisted not of 40 pieces in position, but of 14 rifles, only one of which was of superior power, and of 16 short range smooth bores; the rest all short ranged were as useless sent to the rear. Not near nightfall only, but early in the day did the enemy open a heavy fire of artillery and musketry, and during the entire day was it continued, the canal bank on the opposite shore, which infantry succeeded from time to time in gaining, under cover of their heavy guns, furnishing them a good protection. The withdrawal of guns at nightfall was not an unadvised "retreat," but an arranged removal—according to instructions received from the commanding General. It was not without sufficient cause, but after ten hours' stern endurance, without food, water or respite, and when nearly every long range gun had exhausted its supply of ammunition, the object also of quiet rest for the army having been secured.—There was little or no confusion in this withdrawal, although the batteries, arranged along a front of nearly two miles, on hills separated by deep ravines, had to gain the road taken by the army along different routes, while the darkness became intense.

Gen. Pendleton did not think he had lost nearly all his guns, but knew that the extended column, which, on personally reaching the road, he met and accompanied, was safe. How many, on their several routes, the enemy might have intercepted, after overpowering the gallant little band at the river under Cols. Lamar and Hodges, he could not in the darkness ascertain, and had the enemy not been afraid to advance, an abandonment of more than 4 guns might surely have been compelled.—So many were left only because the horses attached to them were killed while in the act of drawing them to the road.

That with so small a force, and so little loss, the enemy in vastly greater power as well of numbers as of guns, should have been held in check so long, to the attainment of the object in view, seems certainly entitled to fair consideration. And when that object had been attained, under cover of the darkness to withdraw the checking force constituted and worn as it was, could be scarcely less than essential. This was systematically arranged and successfully accomplished, with no untoward circumstances, save that of the supporting infantry being compelled, after a noble stand through the entire day, to give way before the enemy's combined onset, half an hour before the arrangements for falling back had been consummated.

This statement is made as a measure of justice, and to vindicate truth. It can be established by abundant official and other evidence, and will be, if the detractor by presenting with his accusations a responsible name will thus allow the case to come within the purview of an adequate tribunal. JUSTICE.

LATEST FROM NORTH CAROLINA—PROBABLE DESIGNS OF THE ENEMY.

RALEIGH, Nov. 12.—The Yankees have evacuated Greenville. After partially destroying the bridge across the river, and taking nine of the citizens with them, they desisted in destroying the bridge at the entreaties of the people. An official despatch says the enemy have also left Plymouth. Their destination is probably Weldon or Petersburg, as they are supposed to have gone up the Chowan river. Foster commands the expedition.

FROM TENNESSEE.

MOBILE, Nov. 12.—A special despatch to the Advertiser, dated Knoxville 11th, says that a despatch from Murfreesboro' states that there are no movements in the Cumberland region, and that the enemy has not been reinforced at Nashville.

Major Wash. Morgan died of his wound at Lexington, Ky., on the 27th inst.

DIED.

In Raleigh, N. C., on Sunday, the 21 instant, EWING, eldest child of the late General George B. Anderson, aged 18 months and 17 days.

At Cedar Point, the residence of her brother, Colonel J. M. Waller, on the 3d of November, 1862, Miss MARY A. D. WALLER, in the 57th year of her age. A pure spirit has gone to its eternal rest.

☞ The Churchman and Advocate will please copy.

In this city, on Wednesday, the 12th inst., at quarter to 1 o'clock P. M., ELLA ST. CLAIR, wife of Dr Charles Selden, of Gloucester county, and eldest daughter of the late John Q. James.

JOHN GARNETT FAUNTLEROY.

Killed instantaneously by a shell on the battle field of Sharpsburg, in Maryland, on the 17th day of September, JOHN GARNETT FAUNTLEROY only son of Thomas W. L. Fauntleroy, of Holly hill, King and Queen county, Virginia, in the 20th year of his age.

Thus has fallen another victim to this cruel war. Thus has another been added to swell the lists of the thousands of the best and noblest of Virginia's sons, whose blood has been freely poured out upon the altar of patriotism. Thus has another hearthstone and fireside been made desolate, and another fond, doting father been called to shed bitter tears over the grave of his only boy.—Alas, who can find comfort on earth for such a father. His only son, he to whom he had looked with hope and joy as the solace and comfort of his old age, rudely torn from his arms forever. Earth has little comfort for such bereavement.

Young Fauntleroy was a private in Captain Fox's company of King and Queen Cavalry and was attached to the 5th Regiment under Col. Rosser. He entered the service at the beginning of the war, and was an ardent, enthusiastic and obedient soldier. In a letter of condolence from his Captain to his father, he was highly complimented for his gallantry and his devotion to the duties of his profession, rendering ever a ready and cheerful obedience to orders, and never shrinking from any hardships. He was generous and liberal to a fault. His large supplies from home were ever freely distributed among his comrades, and he has left a large circle of friends in camp to mourn his early death. He had been a member of the Baptist Church for several years before his death, and there is every reason to hope that his end was as peaceful as it was sudden. G.

LINES ON THE DEATH OF CAPTAIN WM. G. POLLARD.

Wake Southern harp, thy proudest strains,
In memory of the noble slain,
In Sharpsburg's bloody fight.
That morning's sun in splendor rose,
And gave to view the waiting foes,
The armies in their might.

Not long in line they remain,
For listen! thundering o'er the plain,
McClellan's hosts push on.
On, on they come, as ocean waves
That dash against a rock which braves
Their fury, they rush on.

The attack is made, but as the rock
Withstands the waves, so 'gainst the shock
Our gallant forces stand.
Fierce is the conflict, swift on high
The messengers of misery fly
From Death's relentless hand.

Mark yonder noble form that leads,
A regiment to gallant deeds
Of chivalrous renown.
Already laurels crown his name,
Already he a deathless fame
At Seven Pines hath won.

And see his little band oppose,
Three times their number of the foes,
Through all that awful day
Once more McClellan's hordes advance
While bright their glistening bayonets glance
In the Sun's dazzling ray.

Charge! Charge! my boys! the hero cries,
Charge! Follow me! the foeman flies,
The doubtful day is won.
The price is paid, for on the field,
Virginia's foes are forced to yield,
Is stretched her martyred son.

Swift was the messenger of death,
In pain he drew no lingering breath,
No agonizing moan
His last thoughts fly to that fond wife,
Who was the sunbeam of his life,
Nor heed the victory won.

His men lament their leader brave,
And weep around the lowly grave,
Where soon they lay him down.
E'en Victory hath dropped a tear
While fame herself above his bier,
Placed an immortal crown.

REDEMPTION OF VIRGINIA SIX PER CENT DEBT

THE holders of the following certificates of debt issued by the State of Virginia under an act to provide for the construction of a turnpike road from Staunton to Parkersburg, passed 16th March, 1838, as amended by the 3d section of an act to provide for the raising of loans to certain railroad companies, passed 21st March, 1839, will take notice that the Commissioners of the Sinking Fund will proceed, on the 1st January, 1863, to redeem said certificates, except so much thereof as may appear to be held by citizens of the United States, at the Treasury of the Commonwealth. The holders of said certificates are required, and on the 1st January, 1863, to surrender the same at the office of the Second Auditor, whether surrendered or not, the interest will cease on that day.

1848.	Sept. 21—888.	Samuel M. Pleasants, of Richmond.	$850
"	Oct. 30—850.	Mrs. M. A. E. Gibson, of Richmond.	600
"	Nov 7—869.	Conrad ... Hunt, Trustee of Ann Reynolds,	800
1847.	Mar. 18—404.	Warner T. Taliferro, of Gloucester,	490
"	Apr. 21—408.	Lorenzo Lewis.	900
1848.	June 6—428.	Mrs P. T. Barbour, of Orange county,	1,170
"	June 29—482.	Arianna McKifresh,	500
1854.	May 9—570.	Treasurer, &c., in trust for Bank of Rockingham,	1,616
1855.	Apr. 28—603.	John R. Allen, of Richmond,	181
1856.	Mar. 18—627.	Merchant's and Mechanics' Bank, Portsmouth,	294
1857.	Aug. 1—641.	Martha J Murray,	285
"	Aug 17—663.	Geo. Carr, of Charlottesville.	1,150
1858.	Jan 1—678.	John R. Kilby, guardian of E. R. Smith,	721
1859.	Feb. 25—711.	Treasurer, &c., in trust for Bank of Rockbridge,	800
"	Apr 8—715.	Mary Bragg,	200
1860.	Jan. 2—727.	David S. Meade, of Roanoke,	275
	789.	Fr. L. B. Price, of Hanover,	430
1861.	Feb. 14—741.	Jas. Neale, Trustee of the children of John H. Neale,	400
			$10,241

J. M. BENNETT, Auditor Public Accounts,
S. H. PARKER, Register,
GEO. W. MUNFORD, Sec'y of Commonwealth.
Commissioners of Sinking Fund.
oct 9—c8m

FINANCIAL AND COMMERCIAL.

WEDNESDAY, Nov. 12, 1862.

Until the volume of paper currency is reduced prices of all articles must continue high. How important then it is, both to the people and government, that this reduction should commence. We fear that the legislation of the last session of Congress, intended as a corrective, will not, of itself, accomplish much. The amount of currency which will be withdrawn from circulation, daily, under the operation of the financial measures of Congress, will, perhaps, be less than the average daily expenditures of the Government. If so the redundance of money will be rather increased than diminished, until a more efficacious mode of depletion is adopted; and Congress will not reassemble until the second Monday in January—nearly two months from this time.

On the 1st December next, the issue of Treasury notes convertible into 8 per cent bonds will cease, but the notes thereafter issued will be convertible into bonds bearing *seven* per cent interest. For some time both issues will circulate without respect to the rate of interest upon the bonds into which they are respectively convertible; but, after a while, people will begin to appreciate the difference between the "sevens" and "eights," and will instinctively pay out the former and retain the latter, from the same prompting which induces a person who has a "ragged" note, and one in good condition of the same issue, to get rid of the former first. In this way some proportion of the present issue will be *withheld* from circulation, but their places will be filled by the new issue to the extent of the Government disbursements, which will necessarily continue heavy. The new issue being less valuable as a convertible than the old issue, the effect upon prices will be to produce a tendency to further inflation, but with each week's approach to the 10th of April when the privilege of converting Treasury notes issued prior to 1st December into eight per cent. bonds will cease, this effect will be counteracted to some extent by the more rapid withdrawal from circulation of the notes now afloat. Eventually, these notes will command a small premium, and whenever that is the case, they will, for the most part, pass into the hands of persons desiring to invest in *eight* per cent. bonds, and thereby will *gradually* disappear. But in the meantime the issue of seven per cent. notes will proceed, the volume of the currency will not be sensibly diminished, and high prices will still prevail, unless a new condition of public affairs shall supervene.

Congress was derelict in its duty to the country in failing to devise and adopt additional and more effective means for affording relief to the people, curtailing its own expenses, and keeping to the lowest possible limit the public debt arising from this war. The subject should engage its prompt and almost undivided attention at the next session. Something better than the creation of a new debt to liquidate an old one is demanded. Expedients to reduce the amount of currency may be resorted to with great propriety, but a tax bill which will bring in the contributions of the people, upon some equitable principle, in the shape of taxes—not forced loans—will go far towards correcting existing evils, inspiring confidence, and curtailing the public debt.

The fabric manufacturers of Georgia are to hold a meeting in Atlanta, on the 17th inst. The Atlanta Commonwealth, in calling attention to the notice for the meeting, says:

"We are glad that some one has taken in hand so important a movement, for, with cotton goods at the present prices, the manufacturers will ultimately be the sufferers, and manufacturing enterprise checked, by the hostility to them which the prices now current will engender. We hope the various companies will be represented, directly or by proxy, and that a uniform and lower schedule of prices will be adopted, for at one-half (if not less) the present prices, the manufacturers will clear one hundred per cent. per annum, on their capital stock."

The course of the manufacturers during the war has been calculated to engender hostility to them, and, if they would secure some credit to themselves, after the war, they should begin now to make concessions to the public. It may not be too late, by a proper display of liberality, to conciliate the prejudices now existing.—What will the Virginia cotton and woolen manufacturers do? By the last Fayetteville Observer we perceive that the manufacturers of North Carolina are beginning to move. The stockholders of the Rockfish Manufacturing Company have adopted the following resolutions:

"Resolved, That the Rockfish Company accepts and will abide by the terms prescribed by the Exemption Act of the Confederate Congress, and will so regulate the prices of its manufactured goods as to bring the profits within the per cent. upon the cost of manufacture prescribed by the said act.

"Resolved, That this Company propose to the proprietors of manufacturing establishments generally in North Carolina to meet by Delegates in Convention at Greensborough on Wednesday, the 3d day of December next, for the purpose of consulting as to the best means of giving the desired effect to the provisions of the Exemption Act, by *securing to the consumers the goods at reasonable prices.*

"Resolved, That in the meantime the officers of this Company be instructed so to dispose of their goods as to get them into the hands of the consumers, and to prevent their being made the object of speculation, by requiring from purchasers satisfactory guarantees that, when resold by the piece, they shall be sold at an advance not exceeding five cents per yard, which is to include the cost of transportation.

"Resolved, That preference shall always be given to purchasers who are citizens of this State."

The Observer expresses the hope that the provision adopted for giving consumers the benefit of the great reduction of price that now takes place, may prove effectual. "It will be the people's own fault if it be otherwise, for surely every county and town and neighborhood can provide a dealer who will be satisfied with the ample profit proposed upon each uncut piece of the goods. The present prices of almost all species of manufactures and other necessaries, from the product of the hand-loom to that of the factory and the salt pan, are altogether too high, such as reasonable, God fearing men and patriots should not desire. These prices, as we have heretofore said, have been *forced up* without the active aid, and, as we know, against the wishes of some at least, of the manufacturers themselves."

At Atlanta, Georgia, on the 9th inst., an offer of 66cts was refused for a lot of osnaburgs. Tobacco advancing. Molasses selling freely at $2 25; Bacon 60 cents per lb; Whisky $8a10 per gallon.

AT RULES held in the Clerk's Office of Halifax on Monday, the 8d day of September, 1862:
Richard Guthery and Amanda, his wife, James O. Lovelace, Lucinda Dews, James A. Cochran and Mary, his wife, Albert R. Waller and Tabitha O. F., his wife, P. J. Walker and Elizabeth, his wife, and William D. Lovelace, Plaintiffs
against,
Elkanta Lovelace, George Bruce and Elizabeth, his wife, James R. Lovelace and Adaline, his wife, and J. B. Stovall, administrator of James Lovelace, Defendants.

IN CHANCERY.

The object of this suit is for the sale of the land belonging to the estate of James Lovelace, dec'd, and for a division of the negroes amongst the parties entitled thereto.

It appearing by satisfactory evidence that Elkanta Lovelace, George Bruce and Elizabeth his wife, James R. Lovelace and Adaline, his wife are not residents of this State, it is ordered that they appear here and protect their interest in this suit within one month after due publication thereof, and that a copy of this order be inserted in the Richmond Whig once a week for four successive weeks, and posted at the front door of the Court House of this county on the first day of the next County Court.

A Copy—Teste:
WILLIAM B. HOLT, C H C.
E. BARKSDALE, JR., P. Q. nov 6—w4w

CHESTERFIELD COUNTY to wit:—To the Clerk of County Court of said County, we, William A. Martin, Alexander S. Martin and Benjamin W. Martin, three freeholders of said county do hereby certify, that by virtue of a warrant to us directed by Vincent Markham, a Justice of said county, we have this day, on our oaths viewed and appraised a mule taken up by Richard O. Wilkinson on his land as an estray, and assess the value of said estray at Fifteen Dollars. The said mule is a horse mule, no marks, no brands about four feet six inches high, bay, about twenty-five years old. Said mule when taken up had mane and tail both closely trimmed.

WM. A. MARTIN,
A. S. MARTIN,
B. W. MARTIN.
September 19, 1862. oct 30—w8t*

THE CONSTITUTION—STATE RIGHTS.

RICHMOND WHIG.

FRIDAY MORNING, NOV. 14, 1862.

TO CORRESPONDENTS.

☞ *Letters on business must be addressed to the "Editor of the Whig."*

Articles written on both sides of the paper will not be published. This is a rule of long standing, ought to be known to all, and will in no case be departed from. Obituary notices exceeding eight lines are charged for as advertisements.

☞ *We cannot undertake to return rejected communications.*

The News.

The news from the North again seems important.—McClellan, who we have been urged to believe is the greatest military genius of the age, and the idol of the Yankee army, has at last been removed or, has resigned in disgust. The event will not be without consequences, affecting both the army and the country. The party which has just succeeded in the elections was the party of McClellan—the defeated party that of the President. How will the victors brook such defiance and contempt on the part of the Executive as is implied by this decapitation of their representative man and chieftain! Does this act mean that Lincoln desires a more absolute control of the army than he could wield with McClellan in command, such control as will enable him if he chooses to turn it against his enemies in the North! We shall see.

Lord Lyons has arrived, and without the instructions of the British Cabinet. At least, the anticipated meeting on the 23d ult. was not held. He is to act, then, upon the policy of the Minister of Foreign Affairs, which is not favorable to us. Nevertheless, it is stated by the generally well informed correspondent of the Baltimore *Sun*, "Ion," that he is to visit Richmond within a few days. Perhaps the Cabinet meeting was deferred on this account. The London *Times* thinks that Sir G. C. Lewis, in his late speech, expressed the purpose of the British Government, when he declared that we had not yet conquered our independence, and that we could not be recognized as a nation until that was done. But Simon Cameron, returning from his mission to Russia, by way of England, on the same steamer with Lord Lyons, thinks there will be intervention by the meeting of Parliament, which takes place, we believe, in December.

This, with the statement added on the same authority, that a Confederate fleet is being prepared in English ports to attack New York, is the substance of the foreign news. It is not a little mixed—but upon the whole rather agreeable than otherwise. A little time will test its value.

A Case for Retaliation.

The Palmyra (Missouri) *Courier* give the details of the military murder in that place, on the 18th ult., of ten Southern men, some notice of which has heretofore appeared in the *Whig*. It appears that on the capture of Palmyra, some weeks ago, an old man, a member of a Yankee regiment in Missouri, who had been detailed to act as a spy and informer, was either killed or captured. At any rate, he was not in Palmyra when the Yankees re-occupied the place. Thereupon a proclamation was issued by Brig. Gen. McNeil, commanding the "rebels" to return him to the town within a certain number of days, announcing that if they should fail thus to return him, it would be presumed he had been murdered, and that ten men whom he held as prisoners would be shot in retaliation. The time arrived—the missing Yankee was not returned, and the ten who had been selected were marched out to die. They were made to kneel upon their coffins, and were murdered in cold blood by order of a General acting under the authority of Lincoln. There was no evidence to prove that the man sought for was dead, or that, if dead, he had not been legally dealt with. The murder of these men can have no justification. It is a case of diabolism which would better befit the character of demons than of men in the human form. The names of the murdered men were:

Willis Baker, Lewis county; Thomas Hamston, Lewis county; Morgan Bixler, Lewis county; Herbert Hudson, Ralls county; John M. Wade, Ralls county; Marion Lair, Ralls county; Captain Thomas A. Snider, Monroe county; Eleazer Lake, Scotland county; Hiram Smith, Knox county.

The order under which they were murdered was as follows:

"PALMYRA, Mo., Oct. 8, 1862.

"JOSEPH C. PORTER—*Sir:* Andrew Allsman, an aged citizen of Palmyra, and a non combatant, having been carried from his home by a band of persons unlawfully arrayed against the peace and good order of the State of Missouri, and which band was under your control, this is to notify you that, unless the said Andrew Allsman is returned unharmed to his family within ten days from date, ten men who have belonged to your band, and unlawfully sworn by you to carry arms against the government of the United States, and who are now in custody, will be shot as a meete reward for their crimes, among which is the illegal restraining of said Allsman of his liberty, and, if not returned, presumptively aiding in his murder.

"Your prompt attention to this will save much suffering. Yours, etc. "W R. STRACHAN,

"P. M. General Dist. N. E. Mo.

"Per order of Brig. General Commanding McNeil's column."

Now here is a plain case, about the facts of which there can be no doubt, that imperatively calls for retaliation by the Confederate Government. Laws were passed by the last Congress inviting the Missourians to organize themselves in bands for their own defence, and pledging the protection of the Government, and the exertion of every power it possessed to secure for them the treatment due to prisoners of war, if they should fall into the enemy's hands. These men were so organized, and the faith of the Government that was solemnly pledged to their protection is now as solemnly pledged to avenge their murder. If that pledge is not redeemed, the Government is false to the people, and will forfeit their confidence, as certainly as it will incur the ridicule and contempt of the enemy. Its over scrupulousness, its strange soft heartedness in matters of this sort had nearly brought it to that condition before this occurrence. There is no such squeamishness on the part of the enemy. They not only make threats but have the nerve to execute them. While the blood of the murdered Mumford in New Orleans still cries aloud for vengeance on the brutes who deprived him of life, and while scores of as true men as ever breathed have been sent to their final account by the paid assassins of the Yankee Government, without any attention at the hands of our Government, our enemies go to work vigorously, and drench the soil of the South with the blood of men whom they pretend to have slain in retaliation for crimes committed by Southern men.

What will the Government do? We can tell it what men not given to rashness of judgment nor vindictiveness of spirit, and who regard this matter only in its relations to the pending war, think it should do. They think that the President should cause to be set apart not less than one hundred of the prisoners now in its hands, and should notify the Government at Washington that unless General McNeil is delivered up to us in thirty days, to be dealt with by us as his crime deserves, those one hundred prisoners will be dealt with as he dealt with the ten at Palmyra. Has the President the nerve for this? If not, he need say nothing more about retaliation.

Richmond's Offering to the Army.

We take the following from the *Enquirer* of yesterday morning. It is far more pleasant reading to us than our neighbor's most ill timed leader of the day before:

The Committee appointed to receive the contributions of citizens and to purchase shoes to aid in furnishing our army, have already made fine progress. In this city and Petersburg, they had purchased, up to Tuesday evening, about four thousand pairs; and by last evening they expected to have six thousand pairs! Their inquiries are extending to other towns, and they hope to obtain in all perhaps eight thousand pairs of shoes as Richmond's offering of sympathy and affection to her late defenders. It will be an honor to her and her people, and will awaken pleasant memories and create kind associations in the feelings of our brave soldiers.

Well done, citizens of Richmond! This is noble, and will bring back to you the praise of the country and the blessings of those who were ready to perish. But still there is room. Go on with the good work. As with "the poor," whom the Blessed Book reminds us we "have always" with us—so with the needy and suffering of an army in the field—they are always to be found. The occasion for help is never ending—so let our efforts never cease.

The *Enquirer* continues its notice:

We learn that some of the contributions were very liberal—some citizens cheerfully subscribing five hundred dollars to the fund. On the other hand, the Committee found some of those who are left on earth as a trial to the patience of better men; a few large property-holders giving very niggard contributions, or totally refusing. If it should be the fate of war that an enemy's bomb-shell should fall on Richmond, it would be a righteous retribution if our good genius should guide it to these men's habitations. A member of the Committee informs us that the War Department extended to them every possible facility and a cordial co operation.

Our own information as to the War Department corresponds with that of the *Enquirer*. We hope it is waking up. The Committee were also received in the handsomest manner by the President, and left him with the substantial evidence that he sympathized in their efforts. The "few large property holders" of whom our contemporary speaks were probably some of those miserable creatures to be found in every community, from whom nothing good ever comes. Some day they will be keeping company with Dives, even if they escape the retributive bombshell invoked upon them. But what will the *Enquirer* say when it learns that among the "totally refusing" on whom its imprecation falls was one of those "eminent citizens who conduct our public affairs." Such, we lament to learn, of a verity, is the fact. We suggest to that eminent citizen the propriety of changing his "habitation" before the fatal bombshell comes on its "righteous" errand. We shall not be surprised if, before he hears the last of this business, he is willing to change not only local habitation, but name.

PRAYER FOR PEACE.

To the Editor of the Whig:

Will you lend us space in one of your columns to make a few suggestions to the women of the South.

It is, that a day be appointed, on which, at a certain hour, they, with one consent, shall unitedly beg for PEACE from Him in whose hands are the hearts of men, and the destinies of nations. Prayer is being made continually for the success of our arms in battle, and these prayers have been answered in many instances beyond our hopes. Every prayer doubtless breathes an earnest petition for Peace; but it is suggested now, that our faithful women shall unite to pray in an especial manner for it—that God would forgive our enemies and turn their hearts, that He would forgive *our debts*, and speedily deliver us from the hands of bloody men. Let the first day of December be appointed, and on that day, at 12 M., let the heart of every wife, mother, daughter and sister, in every State in the Confederacy, go out in solemn fervent prayer to God for PEACE.

In places where female prayer meetings are usual, let the women themselves order the matter. Where such meetings are not usual, or are considered inadvisable or impracticable, let every woman, in her own house, stop all work at the hour named—suspend the carding, and spinning, and knitting, and weaving, and sewing, and teaching, if for only one-half hour, and let every woman's heart be lifted to God for her country. Let the sick woman on her bed remember the day and hour, let the busy forego her business, and, I was going to say—let the gay suspend her gaities; but I trust, there are not many gay women in the South now. But let the young and beautiful, and hopeful, equally with those who can lay no claim to such titles, think of the broken-hearted, the destitute, the homeless, think of the dead, and the dying, and the mangled, think of the widows, the childless, and the fatherless of this awful war—and let every woman's soul be stirred to pray as with one voice, to God on that day for PEACE—an *honorable* PEACE.

All papers friendly to this suggestion are requested to copy, that it may be as widely diffused as possible, by the day above named. S. C. B.

In connection with the foregoing, we insert the following:

"A friend of General Stonewall Jackson told us," says the Richmond *Christian Advocate*, a few days ago, "that the General remarked he hoped our people would not forget that God giveth the victory." His friend replied that he believed the churches were deeply prayerful all over the land. The General's face brightened up with pleasure as he remarked, "Then we shall continue to prosper."

The Raleigh Register, in publishing a similar call to the above, says:

The idea is a good one, and we trust that it may meet with a hearty second, and be generally acted upon by the ladies throughout the South. In this connection, we cannot help referring to the excellent sermon delivered by the Rev. Joseph M. Atkinson, at the Presbyterian Church in this city on last Sunday. The text of the sermon was as follows:

"And the Lord turned the captivity of Job, when he prayed for his friends; also the Lord gave Job twice as much as he had before."—*Job, 42d chapter and 10th verse.*

The speaker enforced the idea that it was not until Job had prayed for those who had despitefully used him that his own "captivity was turned," drawing the deduction therefrom that it might be the purpose of God to cause us to humble ourselves and carry out the injunction, "pray for your enemies," ere he would see fit to deliver us from the troubles which now overwhelm us.—It will be seen that our correspondent suggests that in their prayer for peace, the ladies also pray "that God would forgive our enemies and turn their hearts."

THE SPIRIT OF THE INVADED.

The following address to the Spanish people, in their darkest hour of invasion by Napoleon, is so applicable to our present position, that we print it as if intended for ourselves:

* * * * "Submit? Do these sophists know to what they advise the most high-minded nation on earth? It would be a stain without example in our annals, if, after such efforts, such incredible events, we were to fall at the feet of the crowned slave who has been sent to us as King. * * * * Your houses are destroyed; your churches demolished; your fields laid waste; your families dispersed and wandering through the country, or hurried into the grave. Have we made so many sacrifices—have the flames of war consumed half Spain, that we should abandon the other half to the far more deadly peace which the enemy prepares for it?—for no one will beguile himself with the insidious parade of the improvements which the French hold out. The Tartar who commands them has decreed that Spain shall have neither industry, nor commerce, nor population, nor political representation whatever: * * to be made a waste and solitary sheepwalk for supplying French manufactures with our wool; to become a nursery of men who may be hurried away to slaughter. Such is the destiny he would impose upon the most highly favored of all countries! Shall we, then, submit to this? * * Ungrateful and perfidious race, shall our sacrifices be in vain, and is our blood of no estimation in your eyes?—No, patriots! rest in peace, * * and let not that bitter thought disturb the quiet of your sepulchres. There is no peace—there can be none in this state of things!—That Spain may be free, is the universal wish of the nation; and if that cannot be obtained, at least it may become one immense desert, one wide grave, where the accumulated remains of French and Spaniards may exhibit to future ages our glory and their shame. But fortune is not so inimical to virtue as to leave to its defenders only this melancholy termination. It is written in heaven, and the history of all ages attests the truth, that a people who decidedly love their liberty and independence must ultimately establish them, in despite of all the artifice and all the violence of tyranny. Victory, which is so often a gift of fortune, is, sooner or later, the reward of constancy. What defended the little republics of Greece from the barbarous invasion of Xerxes? What reconstructed the Capitol when it was almost destroyed by the Gauls? What preserved it from the mighty arms of Hannibal? What, in times nearer our own, protected the Swiss from German tyranny, and gave independence to Holland in spite of the power of our ancestors? * Spaniards, the Junta announces to you frankly what has happened in the continent, because it would not have you ignorant for a moment of the new danger which threatens the country. They announce it in the confidence that, instead of being dismayed, you will collect new strength, and show yourselves more worthy of the cause which you defend, and of the admiration of the Universe. They announce it to you because they know that the determination of the Spaniards is to be free at whatever cost; and all means however violent, all resources however extraordinary, all funds however privileged, must be called out to repel the enemy. The ship's treasures must be thrown overboard to lighten her in the tempest and save her from shipwreck. Our country is sinking; * * * strength, riches, life, wisdom, council—whatever we have is hers. The victory is ours if we carry on to the end of our enterprise the sublime enthusiasm with which it began.

The mass with which we must resist the enemy must be composed of the strength of all, and the sacrifices of all; and then what will it import that he pours upon us anew the legions which are now superfluous in Germany, or the swarm of conscripts he is about to draw from France? We began with 80 000 men less; he began it with 200,000 more. Let him replace them, if he can; let him send or bring them to this region of death, as destructive to the oppressors as the oppressed! Adding to the experience of two campaigns the strength of despair and fury, we will give to their phalanxes of banditti the same fate which their predecessors have experienced, and the earth, fattened with their blood, shall return to us with usury, the fruits of which they have deprived us.

Let the people of the North, forgetful of what they are, and of what they are capable, submit to be the slaves of this new Tamerlane; let them purchase at such a price the tranquility of a moment, till it comes to their turn to be devoured. What is this to us, who are a mighty people, and resolved to perish or triumph? Did we ask their consent when 20 months ago, we raised our arms against the tyrant? Did we not enter the contest alone? Did we not carry it on alone? Nothing which is necessary for our defence is wanting. * * * The Spanish people will stand alone and erect amid the ruins of the European continent. Here has been drawn, never to be sheathed, the sword of hatred against the execrable tyrant; here is raised, never to be beaten down, the standard of independence and of justice! Hasten to it, all ye in Europe who will not live under the abominable yoke; ye who will not enter into a league with iniquity. * * * Here the valiant shall find opportunities of acquiring true honor; the wise and the virtuous shall obtain respect; the true afflicted shall have an asylum; our cause is the same; the same shall be our reward.—Come! and in despite of all the arts and all the power of this inhuman despot, we will render his star dim, and form for ourselves our own destiny!"

SUPPLIES FOR THE SOLDIERS.

CAMP NEAR CULPEPER COURT HOUSE.

To the Editor of the Whig:

I am happy to see you appealing to the patriotism and liberality of your citizens as well as the public generally, in behalf of the half naked and barefooted soldiers exposed to constant duty in the open fields, whilst our friends are comfortably clad and shod, around warm fires in their homes of plenty, sweetly dreaming of peace, whilst the poor clad soldier walks his lonely post to see "that no harm comes near them." The cause and fault of our destitute situation is not so much indifference or illiberality on the part of our friends, particularly the ladies, whose industry, liberality, patriotism and care for the soldier, knows no bounds, as it is blamable to the department at Richmond and other places. The greatest abundance of warm clothing, shoes, blankets, and even eatables, would be sent from our different homes if there was any possible way of transporting them. I will take for example my company, who could get everything necessary to make them comfortable if the Quartermaster would make arrangements to transport them from home; as it is, a pair of boots or shoes, if ever received, cost more than their value to get them. Thus you see but little inducement is offered our friends to relieve our pressing necessities, when the chances are they will be lost or stolen. I would suggest, as the quickest means of relief, and one that would give general satisfaction, that arrangements be made to have boxes of clothing sent to the different army corps from Richmond; it would cost the Government but little, and render the army more efficient in every respect.

Your proposition to contribute money and clothing that can be spared, whilst it is good, I assure you is far from being satisfactory to the soldiers. Out of the large amounts contributed and donations made, except in particular cases, not one thing has ever been received unless paid for that I have ever heard of. Every neighborhood, if conveyance is offered them, will immediately supply our wants, but they want to know that their own company receives the goods, and that gratis, or they are not justifiable in sending out of their abundance necessaries to be again paid for by their sons in service.—Hoping that you will use your pen in waking up the authorities to the necessity of at once making arrangements to forward boxes, I assure you we will soon be comfortable when this means is afforded. P. H. E., 18th Va. Reg't.

"TOMMY" NOT DEAD.—The Hon. Townsend Harris, just from Japan, says that the last person he parted with was "Tommy," who was in fine health and spirits, and was attached to the American embassy there.

MARRIED.

At the house of the bride's father, by the Rev. Jas. Jamison, on Wednesday, Nov. 5, 1862, M. C. MORTON, C. S. A., of Richmond, Va., to Miss JULIA C., daughter of Wm Ayres, Esq., of Danville, Va.

In Brunswick, on the 28th ult., by the Rev. H. T. Montgomery, JOHN S. BRINKLEY, formerly of New York, to Mrs. VIRGINIA SLATE.

In Lawrenceville, on the 29th ult, by the Rev. D. J. C. Slaughter, Major JOHN A. HEARTWELL, to Miss FRANCES E. POYNOR, all of Brunswick.

DIED.

In Brunswick, on the 2nd inst., from the effects of an excessive hemorrhage of the lungs, Miss AMANDA JONES, daughter of Robert R. Jones, Esq.

Also, in the same county, on the 10th inst., from Pneumonia, Dr. MARCUS A. CLARKE, aged 26 years.

In this city, on Saturday, the 8th inst., in the 25th year of his age, at the residence of Major J. F. Whitfield, EDWIN G. HARRISON, of Winchester, Va.

ADJ'T AND INSPECTOR GENERAL'S OFFICE, RICHMOND, Nov. 12, 1862.

GENERAL ORDERS, No. 86.

I. The following notice of officers and men who have been duly exchanged as prisoners of war, is published for the information of all concerned:

EXCHANGE NOTICE, No 3.

Richmond, November 11, 1862.

1. All Confederate officers and men who have been captured and paroled in Virginia or Maryland, at any time from the beginning of hostilities to the 1st of November, 1862, have been duly exchanged, and are hereby so declared.

2. All Confederate officers and men who have been delivered at Aiken's Landing, on James River, at any time previous to the 11th of November, 1862, have been duly exchanged, and are hereby so declared.

3. All Confederate officers and men who have been delivered at Vicksburg, Mississippi, previous to the 1st of November, 1862, and including said date, have been duly exchanged, and are hereby so declared.

ROBERT OULD, Agent of Exchange.

I. All officers and men who have been duly exchanged as prisoners of war will, without delay join their respective regiments and companies.

By Order,

[Signed] S. COOPER,

nov 14—1w Adj. and Ins. General.

GENERAL ORDERS.

ADJUTANT AND INSPECTOR GENERAL'S OFFICE, RICHMOND, November 8, 1862.

GENERAL ORDERS. No. 82.

1. The following Acts of Congress and Regulations are published for the information of all concerned:

AN ACT TO FURTHER PROVIDE FOR THE PUBLIC DEFENCE.

In view of the exigencies of the country, and the absolute necessity of keeping in the service our gallant army, and of placing in the field a large additional force to meet the advancing columns of the enemy now invading our soil; therefore

SEC. 1. *The Congress of the Confederate States of America do enact,* That the President be and he is hereby authorized to call out and place in the military service of the Confederate States, for three years, unless the war shall have been sooner ended, all white men who are residents of the Confederate States, between the ages of 18 and 35 years, at the time the call or calls may be made, who are (not) legally exempt from military service. All of the persons aforesaid who are now in the armies of the Confederacy, and whose term of service will expire before the end of the war, shall be continued in the service for three years from the date of their original enlistment, unless the war shall have been sooner ended; Provided, however, that all such companies, squadrons, battalions and regiments, whose term of original enlistment was for twelve months, shall have the right within forty days, on a day to be fixed by the commander of the brigade, to reorganize said companies, battalions and regiments, by electing all their officers which they had a right heretofore to elect, who shall be commissioned by the President:—Provided further, That furloughs not exceeding sixty days, with transportation home and back shall be granted to all those retained in the service by the provisions of this act beyond the period of their original enlistment, and who have not heretofore received furloughs under the provisions of an act entitled "an act providing for the granting of bounty and furloughs to privates and non-commissioned officers in the provisional army," approved 11th December, eighteen hundred and sixty-one, said furloughs to be granted at such times and in such numbers as the Secretary of War may deem most compatible with the public interest: And provided further, That in lieu of a furlough, the commutation value in money of the transportation herein above granted shall be paid to each private, musician or non-commissioned officer who may elect to receive it, at such time as the furlough would otherwise be granted: Provided further, That all persons under the age of 18 years, or over the age of 35 years, who are now enrolled in the military service of the Confederate States, in the regiments, squadrons, battalions and companies hereafter to be reorganized, shall be required to remain in their respective companies, squadrons, battalions and regiments for ninety days, unless their places can be sooner supplied by other recruits not now in the service, who are between the ages of 18 and 35 years. And all laws and parts of laws providing for the re-enlistment of volunteers and the organization thereof into companies, squadrons, battalions or regiments, shall be and the same are hereby repealed.

SEC. 2. *Be it further enacted,* That such companies, squadrons, battalions or regiments organized, or in process of organization by authority from the Secretary of War, as may be within thirty days from the passage of this act, so far completed as to have the whole number of men requisite for organization actually enrolled, not embracing in said organizations any person now in service; shall be mustered into the service of the Confederate States as part of the land forces of the same; to be received into that arm of the service in which they are authorized to organize, and shall elect their company, battalion and regimental officers.

SEC. 3. *Be it further enacted,* That for the enrolment of all persons comprehended within the provisions of this act, who are not already in service in the armies of the Confederate States, it shall be lawful for the President, with the consent of the Governors of the respective States, to employ State officers; and on failure to obtain such consent, he shall employ Confederate officers charged with the duty of making such enrolment, in accordance with rules and regulations to be prescribed by him.

SEC. 4. *Be it further enacted,* That persons enrolled under the provisions of the preceding section shall be assigned by the Secretary of War to the different companies now in service, until each company is filled to its maximum number, and the persons so enrolled shall be assigned to companies from the States from which they respectively come.

SEC. 5. *Be it further enacted,* That all seamen and ordinary seamen in the land forces of the Confederate States, enrolled under the provisions of this act, may, on application of the Secretary of the Navy, be transferred from the land forces to the naval service.

SEC. 6. *Be it further enacted,* That in all cases where a State may not have in the army a number of regiments, battalions, squadrons or companies sufficient to absorb the number of persons subject to military service under the provisions of this act, belonging to such State, then the residue or excess thereof shall be kept as a reserve, under such regulations as may be established by the Secretary of War, and that at stated periods of not greater than three months details, determined by lot, shall be made from said reserve, so that each company shall, as nearly as practicable, be kept full; Provided that the persons held in reserve may remain at home until called into service by the President: Provided, also, that during their stay at home they shall not receive pay; Provided further, That the persons comprehended in this act shall not be subject to the Rules and Articles of War until mustered into the actual service of the Confederate States, except that said persons, when enrolled and liable to duty, if they shall wilfully refuse to obey said call, each of them shall be held to be a deserter, and punished as such under said Articles: Provided further, That whenever in the opinion of the President the exigencies of the public service may require it, he shall be authorized to call into actual service the entire reserve, or so much as may be necessary, not previously assigned to different companies in service under the provisions of section four of this act. Said reserve shall be organized under such rule as the Secretary of War may adopt: Provided, The company, battalion and regimental officers shall be elected by the troops composing the same: Provided, The troops raised in any one State shall not be combined in regimental, battalion, squadron or company organization with troops raised in any other State.

SEC. 7. *Be it further enacted,* That all soldiers now serving in the army or mustered into the military service of the Confederate States, or enrolled in the said service under the authorizations heretofore issued by the Secretary of War, and who are continued in the service by virtue of this act, who have not received the bounty of fifty dollars allowed by existing laws, shall be entitled to receive said bounty.

SEC. 8. *Be it further enacted,* That each man who may hereafter be mustered into the service, and who shall arm himself with a musket, shot-gun, rifle or carbine, accepted as an efficient weapon, shall be paid the value thereof, to be ascertained by the mustering officer, under such regulations as may be prescribed by the Secretary of War, if he is willing to sell the same; and if he is not, then he shall be entitled to receive one dollar a month for the use of said received and approved musket, rifle, shot-gun or carbine.

SEC. 9. *Be it further enacted,* That persons not liable for duty may be received as substitutes for those who are under such regulations as may be prescribed by the Secretary of War.

SEC. 10. *Be it further enacted,* That all vacancies shall be filled by the President from the company, battalion, squadron or regiment in which such vacancies shall occur, by promotion according to seniority, except in cases of disability or other incompetency: Provided, however, that the President may, when in his opinion it may be proper, fill such vacancy or vacancies by the promotion of any officer or officers, or private or privates from such company, battalion, squadron or regiment who shall have been distinguished in the service by exhibition of valor and skill, and that whenever a vacancy shall occur in the lowest grades of the commissioned officers of a company, said vacancy shall be filled by election: Provided that all appointments made by the President shall be by and with the advice and consent of the Senate.

SEC. 11. *Be it further enacted,* That the provisions of the first section of this act relating to the elections of officers, shall apply to those regiments, battalions and squadrons which are composed of twelve months and war companies combined in the same organization, without regard to the manner in which the officers thereof were originally appointed.

SEC. 12. *Be it further enacted,* That each company of infantry shall consist of one hundred and twenty-five, rank and file; each company of field artillery of one hundred and fifty, rank and file; and each of cavalry, of rank and file.

SEC. 13. *Be it further enacted,* That all persons subject to enrolment, who are not now in the service, under the provisions of this act, shall be permitted, previous to such enrolment, to volunteer in companies now in service.

Approved April 16th, 1862.

(No. 17.)

AN ACT TO AMEND AN ACT ENTITLED AN ACT TO PROVIDE FURTHER FOR THE PUBLIC DEFENCE, APPROVED APRIL 16, 1862.

The Congress of the Confederate States of America do enact, That the President be and he is hereby authorized to call out and place in the military service of the Confederate States for three years, unless the war shall have been sooner ended, all white men who are residents of the Confederate States, between the ages of thirty-five and forty-five years, at the time the call or calls may be made, and who are not, at such time or times, legally exempted from military service, or such part thereof as in his judgment may be necessary to the public defence; such call or calls to be made under the provisions and according to the terms of the act to which this is an amendment: and such authority shall exist in the President, during the present war, as to all persons who now are or may hereafter become eighteen years of age; and when once enrolled, all persons between the ages of eighteen and forty-five shall serve their full term: Provided, That if the President, in calling out troops into the service of the Confederate States, shall first call for only a part of the persons between the ages heretofore stated, he shall call for those between the ages of thirty-five and any other age less than forty five. Provided, That nothing herein contained shall be understood as repealing or modifying any part of the act to which this is amendatory, except as herein expressly stated: And provided further, That those called out under this act, and the act to which this is an amendment, shall be first and immediately ordered to fill to their maximum number the companies, battalions, squadrons and regiments from the respective States at the time the act to further provide for the public defence, approved 16th April, 1862, was passed, and the surplus, if any, shall be assigned to organizations formed from each State since the passage of that act, or placed in new organizations to be officered by the State having such residue, according to the laws thereof, or disposed of as now provided by law: Provided, That the President is authorized to suspend the execution of this act, or the act to which this is an amendment, in any locality where he may find it impracticable to execute the same, and that in such locality, and during said suspension, the President is authorized to receive troops into the Confederate service, under any of the acts passed by the Confederate Congress prior to the passage of the act to provide further for the public defence, approved 16th April, 1862.

Approved September 27, 1862.

(No. 53.)

AN ACT TO EXEMPT CERTAIN PERSONS FROM MILITARY DUTY, AND TO REPEAL AN ACT ENTITLED "AN ACT TO EXEMPT CERTAIN PERSONS FROM ENROLMENT FOR SERVICE IN THE ARMY OF THE CONFEDERATE STATES," APPROVED 21ST APRIL, 1862.

The Congress of the Confederate States of America do enact, That all persons who shall be held unfit for military service in the field, by reason of bodily or mental incapacity or imbecility, under rules to be prescribed by the Secretary of War, the Vice President of the Confederate States, the officers, judicial and executive, of the Confederate and State Governments, including postmasters appointed by the President and confirmed by the Senate, and such clerks in their offices as are allowed by the Postmaster General, and now employed, and excluding all other postmasters, their assistants and clerks; and except such State officers as the several States may have declared, or may hereafter declare by law to be liable to militia duty, the members of both Houses of the Congress of the Confederate States, and of the Legislatures of the several States, and their respective officers; all clerks now in the offices of the Confederate and State Governments authorized by law, receiving salaries or fees; all volunteer troops, heretofore raised by any State since the passage of the act entitled "An Act further to provide for the public defence," approved April 16th, 1862, while such troops shall be in active service under State authority: *Provided,* That this exemption shall not apply to any person who was liable to be called into service by virtue of said act of April 16th, 1862: all pilots and persons engaged in the merchant marine service; the president, superintendents, conductors, treasurer, chief clerk, engineers, managers, station agents, section masters, two expert track hands to each section of eight miles, and mechanics in the active service and employment of rail road companies, not to embrace laborers, porters and messengers; the president, general superintendent and operators of telegraph companies, the local superintendent and operators of said companies, not to exceed four in number at any locality, but that at the seat of Government of the Confederate States; the president, superintendents, captains, engineers, chief clerk and mechanics in the active service and employment of all companies engaged in river and canal navigation, and all captains of boats and engineers therein employed; one editor of each newspaper now being published, and such employees as the editor or proprietor may certify, upon oath, to be indispensable for conducting the publication; the public printer, and those employed to perform the public printing for the Confederate and State Governments; every minister of religion authorized to preach according to the rules of his sect and in the regular discharge of ministerial duties, and all persons who have been and now are members of the society of Friends and the association of Dunkards, Nazarines and Mennonists, in regular membership in their respective denominations: *Provided,* Members of the society of Friends, Nazarines, Mennonists and Dunkards shall furnish substitutes or pay a tax of $500 each into the public treasury; all physicians who now are, and for the last five years have been, in actual practice of their profession; all shoemakers, tanners, blacksmiths, wagon-makers, millers and their engineers, millwrights, skilled and actually employed at their regular vocation in the said trades, habitually engaged in working for the public, and whilst so actually employed: *Provided,* Said persons shall make oath in writing that they are so skilled and actually employed at the time at their regular vocation in one of the above trades, which affidavit shall only be *prima facie* evidence of the facts therein stated: *Provided, further,* That the exemptions herein granted to persons by reason of their peculiar me-

The News.

The news from the North again seems important.—McClellan, who we have been urged to believe is the greatest military genius of the age, and the idol of the Yankee army, has at last been removed or, has resigned in disgust. The event will not be without consequences, affecting both the army and the country. The party which has just succeeded in the elections was the party of McClellan—the defeated party that of the President. How will the victors brook such defiance and contempt on the part of the Executive as is implied by this decapitation of their representative man and chieftain! Does this act mean that Lincoln desires a more absolute control of the army than he could wield with McClellan in command, such control as will enable him if he chooses to turn it against his enemies in the North! We shall see.

Lord Lyons has arrived, and without the instructions of the British Cabinet. At least, the anticipated meeting on the 23d ult. was not held. He is to act, then, upon the policy of the Minister of Foreign Affairs, which is not favorable to us. Nevertheless, it is stated by the generally well informed correspondent of the Baltimore *Sun*, "Ion," that he is to visit Richmond within a few days. Perhaps the Cabinet meeting was deferred on this account. The London *Times* thinks that Sir G. C. Lewis, in his late speech, expressed the purpose of the British Government, when he declared that we had not yet conquered our independence, and that we could not be recognized as a nation until that was done. But Simon Cameron, returning from his mission to Russia, by way of England, on the same steamer with Lord Lyons, thinks there will be intervention by the meeting of Parliament, which takes place, we believe, in December.

This, with the statement added on the same authority, that a Confederate fleet is being prepared in English ports to attack New York, is the substance of the foreign news. It is not a little mixed—but upon the whole rather agreeable than otherwise. A little time will test its value.

SEC. 5. When it shall appear to any surgeon attending such place of rendezvous, by the certificate of a respectable physician resident in that county, district, parish or city in a county, parish or district, that any enrolled person therein is unable to attend on account of sickness, it shall be the duty of said surgeon to file said certificate with the commandant of the nearest camp of instruction; and if the person named therein shall not within a reasonable time report himself for examination at said camp of instruction, or his continued disability certified by the certificate of a respectable physician of his county, city, district or parish, he shall be held liable as absent without leave of his commanding officer.

Approved October 11, 1862.

II. Commandants of Conscripts and Camps of Instruction.

1. An officer, styled the Commandant of Conscripts, will be appointed for each State, who will be charged with the supervision of the enrolment and disposition of conscripts. He will establish one or more camps, in which conscripts will be assembled and instructed, and may recommend for appointment a Surgeon, a Quartermaster, a Commissary, and the requisite number of Drillmasters for each camp. If more than one camp be established, he may also recommend a Commandant for each camp not under his own immediate command.

2. A hospital will be established and huts for winter quarters constructed at each camp, and all conscripts assembled at the camps will be promptly vaccinated, if it has not already been done.

3. The Commandant of Conscripts will require from each camp a report on the first Monday in every month, showing the expenses of the preceding month the number of conscripts in the camp, the number received and sent away during the preceding month, the regiments, battalions or companies to which they were sent, the number transferred to the navy, the number of sick, the nature of the diseases, and the number of deaths. He will made a consolidated monthly report to the Adjutant and Inspector General of the army.

4. The Commandants of Conscripts East of the Mississippi river will receive orders only from the War Department, and will not be interfered with by Generals commanding departments or armies in the field. West of the Mississippi they will report to and receive instructions from the Commanding General of the Trans-Mississippi Department, who will require them to conform as nearly as possible to this order, and to the regulations prescribed for commandants East of the Mississippi. He will make a consolidated monthly report to the Adjutant and Inspector General of the army.

5. The commandants of all regiments, battalions, squadrons or unattached companies which were in service on the 16th of April, 1862, desiring to receive conscripts, may transmit, through the Adjutant and Inspector General of the army, statements of the strength of their commands, to the Commandants of Conscripts in their respective States, who, unless otherwise ordered, will, as far as practicable, distribute the conscripts of the State among its regiments, battalions and companies thereof, in proportion to their respective deficiencies.

He will consult the wishes of the conscripts in assigning them to companies or regiments, so far as may be consistent with their proper distribution, and will not separate men from the same county, district or parish, if it can be avoided. The same rule will be observed by the commandants of corps in assigning conscripts to companies.

6. Conscripts for cavalry will only be taken from those who furnish their own horses. No conscripts can be assigned to companies mustered into service since the 16th of April, 1862.

7. The Commandants of Conscripts are specially enjoined to pay unceasing attention to the health comfort and instruction of the conscripts under their command, and to bear in mind that the efficiency of the army and the safety of the country depend in a great measure upon their faithful discharge of these duties.

III. Enrolment of Conscripts.

All white male residents of the Confederate States, between the ages of 18 and 40 not exempted by act of Congress, or not already in the service, will be enrolled. Persons liable to enrolment may be enrolled wherever they may be found, as provided by the Act No. 42, herewith published.

IV. Undomiciled Foreigners.

1. Foreigners not domiciled in the Confederate States are not liable to enrolment. Domicil in the Confederate States consists in residence with intention permanently to remain in those States, and to abandon domicil elsewhere. Long residence of itself does not constitute domicil. A person may acquire domicil in less than one year, and he may not acquire it in twenty years' residence. If there is a determination to return to the native country and to retain the domicil there, no length of residence can confer domicil.

The principal evidences of intention to remain are the declarations of the party the exercise of the rights of citizenship, marriage and the acquisition of real estate, but the intention may be gathered from other facts.

2. The enrolment will be made by the enrolling officers of the State, if the Governor thereof will permit them to act under the orders of the Commandants of Conscripts, and application will be made by the said Commandants for such permission. If it be declined, the commandant will report the fact to the Adjutant and Inspector General and ask for the employment of Confederate officers for the purpose of making enrolments. If the Governor consent, but the enrolling officers of the State be found unable or unwilling to discharge their duty efficiently, the like application will be made to the Adjutant and Inspector General, and in such event, a commissioned officer for each Congressional District, and a non-commissioned officer or private for each county, city, town, district or parish, will be assigned to such duty.

In making such assignment, officers and men disabled by wounds from active duty in the field, and acquainted in the localities in which they are required to serve, will, as far as practicable be selected. The commissioned officers in each district will superintend the enrolments and collection of conscripts therein. Non-commissioned officers and privates, while so employed, will be allowed pay as extra duty men. The enrolling officers of the States, if employed, will be paid the compensation allowed by the State laws for similar service.

The Commanding Generals of armies in the field will order such commissioned officers, non-commissioned officers and privates as they think qualified to be enrolling officers or drill officers and who unfit for active service in the field, to report to the Commandant of Conscripts in their respective States, who will order such of them to duty as may be required, and report the remainder by letter to the Commanding General as not needed for such service.

3. Enrolments for particular regiments, battalions squadron and companies in service on the 16th of April, 1862 may be made by officers detailed for the purpose by the Commanding General of a department or an army in the field; but such officers must report to the Commandant of Conscripts in their respective States, receive instructions from him, and assemble their conscripts at such point as he may designate. Conscripts enrolled without reporting to such commandant will be deemed to be enrolled for general service, and shall at any time be transferred, on their own application, or on the application of commandants of corps needing conscripts, to such corps.

V. Exemptions.

The Exemption act will be construed prospectively, and does not authorise the discharge of any one enrolled or in service prior to the 11th day of October, 1862.

VI. Bodily and Mental Infirmity.

1. Questions of bodily and mental incapacity will be decided by the purpose, shall certify that the number of operatives required by the officer in charge of such establishment, or by such contractor for Government work, is reasonable and not excessive, such certificate will be presented to the enrolling officer, who will thereupon make the detail of the men specified for a period not exceeding sixty days, and return the certificate to the Commandant of Conscripts. At the expiration of such detail, the officer in charge of the Government shop, or the contractor in whose employment said conscripts are, shall cause said certificate to be renewed or return the conscripts to the nearest camp of instruction. If the certificate be not renewed or the conscripts be not returned, no other detail shall be granted to such establishment or contractor. In all cases of details for contractors, the party requesting the detail shall make affidavit that the persons so detailed will not be employed on any other than Government work, which affidavit shall be returned to the Commandant of Conscripts; and if it be found that at any time such detailed conscripts are employed by said contractors upon work for private individuals, the detail shall be cancelled by the Commandant of Conscripts.

Paragraph 1, General Orders No. 50, current series, is hereby revoked.

X. To whom Applications for Exemption must be addressed.

Applications for exemption must, in all cases, be made to the enrolling officer, from whose decision an appeal may be taken to the Commandant of Conscripts. The Department will not consider the application until it has been referred by the latter officer.

XI. Substitutes.

1. When a person claims exemption on the ground that he has put a substitute in service, he must exhibit to the enrolling officer a discharge from some company, signed by the commanding officer of the regiment or command to which the said company belongs, or then belonged, (see General Orders No. 26,) or an exemption signed by the Commandant of Conscripts. And if the said discharge or exemption do not show that it was granted in consideration of a substitute having been furnished, such fact must be certified in writing by the commanding officer of the regiment or command to which the company belongs, or by the Commandant of Conscripts, as the case may be.

But within all cases arising within thirty days from the date of this order, the enrolling officer may grant the exemption, upon satisfactory proof that the party furnished a substitute, who was actually received into the service of the Confederate States for three years or the war, and the substitute is not liable to military service. Such exemption may at any time be cancelled, if fraud or mistake be discovered.

2. Paragraph II, General Order No. 29, current series, is hereby revoked. No person under eighteen years of age, or not domiciled in the Confederate States, or not of good moral character, or who is liable under the existing order to enrolment as a conscript, shall be received as a substitute.

And in all cases in which a substitute becomes subject to military service, the exemption of the principal by reason of the substitution shall expire.

Any person subject to enrolment who desires to furnish a substitute, may, at any time before the enrolment, or before he is assigned to a company and sent from the camp of instruction, present a substitute at such camp. And if the substitute be capable of bearing arms, and be of good moral character, and not within the prohibited classes, he shall be received, and the principal shall be exempt from military service.

XII. Volunteering.

All persons liable to conscription may, before enrolment, volunteer in companies in service on the 16th of April, 1862. But after enrolment, they cannot volunteer, nor can they at any time volunteer in companies received into service since the 16th of April, 1862.

XIII. Miscellaneous.

1. All impressments of men by regimental, battalion or company commanders, under any pretence whatever, are prohibited, it being the design of the Department to supply the army exclusively through the officers appointed by this act.

2. All the laws and resolutions applicable to deserters shall be applied to such conscripts as fail to repair to the place of rendezvous for enrolment, or who shall desert after enrolment.

3. All the agencies employed for the apprehension and confinement of deserters, and their transportation to the commands of their respective commanders, shall be applicable to persons liable to duty as conscripts who shall fail to repair to the place of rendezvous after the publication of the call.

By order S. COOPER,

nov 10—1w *Adjutant and Inspector General.*

ADJ'T AND INSPR'S GENERAL'S OFFICE, RICHMOND, Nov. 10, 1862.

GENERAL ORDERS No. 84.

I. The following orders are published for the information and guidance of the Army.

II. Whereas reliable information has been received that Col. Lowe and Col. A. C. Harding, 8th Illinois Regiment, United States Army, have been engaged in a series of wanton cruelties and depredations in Clarksville, Tenn., and the adjoining counties, which, in many instances, have resulted in the arrest, incarceration and inhuman treatment of non-combatants and peaceful citizens of the Confederate States, and in others in the unjustifiable destruction of private property, without compensation and contrary to the rules and practice of civilized warfare: Therefore it is ordered that the aforesaid Col. Lowe and Col. A. C. Harding, 8th Illinois Volunteers United States Army, be, and they are hereby declared no longer entitled to be regarded as soldiers, and that they have forfeited all claim to the benefits of the cartel existing between the Governments of the Confederate States and the United States for the exchange of prisoners of war; and further, that in the event of their capture, they shall be kept in close confinement and treated as felons until otherwise ordered by the President of the Confederate States.

III. And whereas other officers of the United States Army yet unknown to the Confederate Government, are represented and believed to have participated in the wrongs and outrages before referred to, therefore, it is also ordered that the provisions of the first paragraph of this order shall be applied to any other officers of the Federal Army in the State of Tennessee, upon proof of their guilt deemed satisfactory by the commanding officers of the Department in which they may be captured and held.

IV. And whereas Major General John Pope has been removed from the Federal Army operating in Virginia, and the obnoxious order No. 11, of July 23, 1862, issued by him, has been stated by the United States authorities to be inoperative and without effect, therefore it is ordered that so much of General Orders No. 54 of August 1st, 1862 from the Adjutant and Inspector General's Office, Richmond as applies to the late Major General John Pope, and the officers serving under him in Virginia be, and is hereby rescinded.

By order,

[Signed] S. COOPER,

no18—1w Adjutant and Inspector General.

THE COUNTRYMAN.

BY J. A. TURNER. — "BREVITY IS THE SOUL OF WIT" — $1 A YEAR.

VOL. III. TURNWOLD, PUTNAM COUNTY, GA., MONDAY, NOVEMBER 17, 1862. NO. 8.

Educated Negroes.

There is a law on our statute book forbidding the teaching of negroes to read. Some of my good friends belonging to the different sects of the country, who imagine that they can see into the counsels of the Almighty, and can tell you very flippantly all about his motives in suffering our country to be scourged with war, have become alarmed, lest this law is one of the causes which has brought upon us all this bloodshed, and are now proposing to repeal it, as a peace-offering to Jehovah.

I shall discuss this subject, possibly at some length, in this and future articles, and I know, in advance, that some people will accuse me of a want of reverence, in what I shall say. I know this will be the case, because the minds of many people are so narrow and contracted with reference to what reverence is, and with reference to every idea they have of God, that if you don't revere those narrow and contracted ideas, then you are wanting in veneration for your Maker. Now, I tell such, in advance, that I have *no* veneration, and I can succeed in having but *very little* respect for their prejudices and ignorance. I have tried as hard as anyone ever did to respect even men's prejudice, because courtesy perhaps requires it: but I have been singularly unsuccessful in all my efforts in this line. But for my Maker I have as much veneration as any man who ever lived: and if anyone says I have not, I tell you, right here, you lie, sir! In the pulpit, or out of it, you lie!

Well, then, having settled this point, I proceed.—The letter of my friend Dr. Talmage, on the subject matter of this article, published lately in the Confederate Union, is before me. What he says is entitled to great weight. Therefore I make his article the nucleus of my remarks. *He* knows that I don't know how to treat him and his opinions otherwise than with respect. And yet I must be allowed to consider my esteemed friend (for I am proud to rank him as such) in error at certain points.

Let me say here, in passing, that no man knows the specific causes influencing the mind of Deity, in producing, or allowing this war. He who attempts to penetrate the arcana of Jehovah's mind, is guilty of great folly, if not wickedness. In all ages of the world, God has scourged, or suffered the human race to be scourged with war. It matters but little what form of expression you use—whether God does a thing, or suffers it done—the practical result is the same, and he being omnipotent, the act is his. It must be accepted, then, as a truth, that it is God who is scourging this land with war. The remote cause of it is his hand. The immediate cause of it is the evil passions—the lusts—the ambition—the fanaticism of Seward, Greeley, and Sumner, and the treason of Brownlow, Crittenden, and Johnson. Possibly the evil passions and ambition of some of our own southern men, coming in conflict with those of the creatures above mentioned, caused this war by concussion, sooner than it might otherwise have come. But it all ends in the same place—that the immediate cause of the war is the evil passions of men. Why God scourges, or (if the reader prefers it) suffers the human race to be scourged, by these evil passions, neither I nor any other mortal who breathes, knows, whatever he may pretend to know. This is the great mystery of God. I have the faith to believe—nay, my own consciousness makes me *know* it is all right.

It is almost impossible to prevent being too discursive in this article. But I will try to condense.

It is *certain* that the wrong-deeds of men are the cause of this war. Is the statute against teaching negroes to read, one of these wrong-deeds? I think not. I don't think the statute is of any importance, any way. I think that without it, there would be no more negroes taught to read, than are with it. Notwithstanding the statute, a good many negroes have learned to read a little, and everyone who desired it, and had strength of purpose and will enough to carry out that desire, has learned to read a little, and is neither the better nor the worse negro for it.

Why not take a practical view of this subject?—Is there any sin in the Georgia statute against educating negroes? None whatever: because God himself enacted that very statute, long before the Georgia legislature was ever conceived of: and God is not going to punish any people for re-enacting one of his own statutes.

The negro is either capable of education, or he is not. (I speak of him as a race.) If he is capable of education, it is a sin to withhold it from him. If he is incapable of it and so created by his Maker, it may be folly to say, by law, he shall not have an education, but it is neither wickedness, nor sin.

Now if the negro is capable of education, he is also capable of freedom. Our whole system of slavery is founded upon the idea that the negro is incapable of enjoying freedom; and upon the truth of this proposition depends the propriety of slavery. I hold that the negro is incapable of enjoying freedom—that God did not intend him to enjoy it, and hence I am pro-slavery in my views and feelings. Convince me that the African race is capable of enjoying freedom, and you convince me that God designed them to be free. Convince me that God designed them to be free, and I go for striking the bonds from the limbs of everyone of them, to-day: I will then support Lincoln's abolition proclamation: for I will not, if I know it, fight against God's designs.

[If] the negro is capable of education, he is capa[bl]e of freedom. Education and slavery are in[compatible]; and when you strike at the ignorance of any people, you strike at their fetters.

I say I think the statute which I am discussing is of little importance any way, if things are allowed to go on in their natural course. If schools of any kind are gotten up for the negroes, though, then I do think the statute mentioned is of some importance.

I think the agitation of the subject I am discussing, has been gotten up at a very unfortunate time. It will divide and direct the attention of our people upon a subject upon which their minds should be a unit.

But my sectarian brethren, some of them, are afraid the statute against teaching negroes to read, may be the cause of this war. Repeal it, and the war will cease.—Now God considers the motives of men. If this statute is wrong now, it has been wrong all the time. And I am afraid my friends will hardly get credit with the Omniscient, for their motives: and I am afraid the repeal of the law will hardly end the war.

The germ of this whole movement about teaching negroes to read, is the same germ from which sprang abolition. It is planted in the idea that the black race, as well as the white, is capable of education, of freedom, and such other blessings as the orthodox pro-slavery man believes, from every teaching of the Almighty, God has designed for a superior race alone. The abolitionist holds, or used to hold, before our negroes showed themselves such a powerful element for us in this war, that we were a people cursed on account of negro slavery. Now that they are convinced that it is no curse at all, either for the negro or the white man, some of our own people are beginning to get very tender on the subject: and though they don't strike at the root of slavery, they propose to lop off one of its twigs—ignorance. Negroes must be educated, at least to a degree. Then they must be allowed to intermarry, when, how, and where they please: then they must be allowed to vote: then to bear arms: then to do this thing: then the other: and so on, until they would be slaves no more, but for the fact that God himself has written slavery in every fibre of their being. Once start out with the assumption that the negro must have education (even to a degree) and then one thing, and then another, because these things are sources of happiness or enjoyment to a superior race, and but for the stern law of the Almighty, you abolish negro slavery.

There are so many things to be said on this subject that, for the present, I conclude. I have a great deal more to write, when I ... to point out the errors of Dr. Talmage's letter, whose details I have not touched in this article.

Writers and Speakers.

'Men whose reputation stands deservedly high as writers, have often miserably failed as speakers. Their pens seem to have been enriched at the expense of their tongues. Addison and Gibbon attempted oratory in the senate, only to fail. 'The good speakers,' says Gibbon, 'filled me with despair, the bad ones with apprehension.' And in more modern times, the powerful depicter of Harold, and the elegant biographer of Leo, have both failed in oratory. The capital of the former is so great in many things that he can afford to fail in one. But to return. Many reasons might be offered to reconcile that contradiction which my subject seems to involve. In the first place, those talents that constitute a fine writer, are more distinct from those that constitute an orator, than might be at first supposed. I admit that they may be sometimes accidentally, but never necessarily combined. That the qualifications for writing and those for eloquence, are in many points distinct, would appear from the converse of the proposition, for there have been many fine speakers who have proved themselves bad writers. There is good ground for believing that Mr. Pitt would not have shone as an author; and the attempt of Mr. Fox in that arena has added nothing to his celebrity. Abstraction of thought, seclusion from popular tumult, occasional retirement to the study, a diffidence in our own opinions, a deference to those of other men, a sensibility that feels everything, a humility that arrogates nothing, are necessary qualifications for a writer; but their very opposites would perhaps be preferred by an orator. He that has spent much of his time in a study will seldom be collected enough to think in a crowd, or confident enough to talk in one. We may also add, that mistakes of the pen in the study, may be committed without publicity, and rectified without humiliation. But mistakes of the tongue, committed in the senate, never escape with impunity. '*Fugit irrevocabile verbum*:' (The word uttered is irrevocable.) Eloquence, to produce her full effect, should start from the head of the orator, as Pallas from the brain of Jove, completely armed and equipped. Diffidence, therefore, which is so able a mentor to the writer, would prove a dangerous counsellor for the orator. As writers, the most timid may boggle 20 times in a day with their pen, and it is their own fault if it be known even to their valet; but, as orators, if they chance to boggle once with their tongue, the detection is as public as the delinquency; the punishment is irremissible, and immediately follows the offence. It is the knowledge and the fear of this that destroys their eloquence as orators, who have sensibility and taste for writing, but neither collectedness nor confidence for speaking: for fear not only magnifies difficulties, but diminishes our power to overcome them, and thus doubly debilitates her victims. But another cause of their deficiency as orators, who have shone as writers, is this: '*mole ruunt sua.*' They know they have a character to support by their tongue, which they have previously gained by their pen. They rise determined to attempt more than other men, and for that very reason they effect less, and doubly disappoint their hearers. They miss of that which is clear, obvious, and appropriate, in a labored search after that which is far-fetched, recondite, and refined; like him that would fain give us better bread than can be made of wheat. Affectation is the cause of this error, disgust its consequence, and disgrace its punishment."

Comptroller's Report.

Friend Thweatt will please accept my thanks for a copy of his Report. I shall file it as one of my most highly prized documents.

Extortion.

"Flour has fallen $10 per bbl. in Atlanta, Ga. It is now $30 to $32. The speculators had put it up to $40. Is there no hemp there?—So asks the Huntsville Advocate. To which an exchange replies:

There is hemp enough, no doubt, and stones enough, but who in Atlanta is innocent enough to 'cast the first stone,' or to use the hemp?"

You might not only ask this question about Atlanta, but about every other locality.—There are more lying and hypocricy about extortion and speculation than about anything else. Everybody in Atlanta and out of it, gets all he can for everything he has to sell, but abuses everybody else for doing the same.—Supply, demand, and a redundant currency regulate all this. And yet certain tinkerers think legislation can remedy it all. They will only make matters worse.

Substitute for Salt.

"A writer in the Columbia Guardian proposes a substitute for salt for preserving meat. It is, he says, pyroligenous acid, which is made from any kind of hard wood, and the quantity of acid obtained is nearly one-half the weight of wood used. The writer remarks:

This acid has been manufactured in the neighborhood of the writer on a small scale, and a few families have used it during the summer and fall, for curing meat, and it is a perfect success. It does not answer the purpose of seasoning, but a small quantity of salt does for that purpose. The only objection to it, if it may be called one, is, that it imparts a smoky flavor to the meat. It should be condensed in a copper tube or pipe, as iron turns it black. I desire to do no more than call attention to the subject, hoping that we may soon see several distilleries in operation, turning out at least 1500 gallons per day. Twelve or 15 gallons will cure 1000 lbs. of meat."

Brimstone.

"The Renagade 'Clift' is said to have his headquarters at Brimstone, a small stream in Scott County, Tennessee. The old scamp is said to have a considerable number with him, skulking through the mountains, and occasionally making a dash upon some unprotected settlement, burning and destroying."—So says the Knoxville Register.

Never mind, brother Register. He will change his head-quarters after awhile, tho' he will still be in the neighborhood of brimstone. Where could you find a more appropriate locality for him?

TURNWOLD, GA., NOVEMBER 17, 1862.

The Show.

(FOR THE CHILDREN.)

James and George had been good boys at school, all the week. They had been kind and good to their playmates, and their father said they might go with him to the show.

They saw there a great many wild beasts in cages, and some with a chain round one leg, made fast to a post.

There were lions, and tigers, and elephants. The boys walked round slowly, looking at everything. They felt a little afraid of some of the beasts, but were much pleased with what they saw.

The showman went in the cage with the lion, and James and George said they were afraid. But a man who sat near them, told them there was no danger. The showman struck the lion with a switch, which made the lion growl very loud, and look cross: but he did not hurt the man.

James said, I wish the man would come out. I do not love to see him in the cage. That lion might eat him up, and then I would feel sorry. James was a good boy, and did not like to see anybody hurt.

After James and George had seen the show, their kind father took them to the book-store, and bought each of them a new book.

Philip and the Athenian Orators.

"Philip of Macedon was wont to say, 'that he was much beholden to the Athenian orators, since by the slanderous and opprobrious manner in which they spoke of him (e. g., that he was a barbarian, an usurper, a cheat; perfidious, perjured, depraved; a companion of rascals and mountebanks, &c.) they were the means of making him a better man, both in word and deed. For,' added he, 'I every day do my best endeavor, as well as my sayings and doings, to prove them liars.'

It would have been well had Philip always acted up to this encomium on himself. After the battle of Cheronœa, he indulged his joy for the victory by getting drunk, dancing all night, and going from rank to rank, calling his prisoners names. Demades, one of them, with the same decent freedom, told Philip that he acted the part of Thersites, rather than that of Agamemnon. Philip was delighted with the smartness of the repartee, and for the sake of this *bon mot*, dismissed the prisoners without ransom."

"How can we expect that another should keep our secret, when it is more than we can do ourselves?"

Heroic Endurance.

"When Alexander the Great was, on one occasion, sacrificing to the gods, one of the noble youths who waited upon him, was so severely burnt by a piece of coal which fell upon his arm from the censor he carried, that the smell of the scorched flesh affected all who stood by. Yet the boy shrunk not. He exhibited no symptom of pain, but kept his arm immovable, lest by shaking the censor, he should interrupt the sacrifice, or by his groaning should give Alexander any disturbance."

ADVERTISEMENTS.

Legal advertisements at the usual rates, and all others at 10c per line, for each insertion, cash in advance. Obituaries and marriages, short or long, are advertisements. tf

Prospectus.

The Countryman is a Little Paper published on the editor's plantation, 9 miles from Eatonton, at $1 per annum, in advance.—I do not profess to publish a NEWS paper, for, under the circumstances, that is impossible. My aim is to model my journal after Addison's Little Paper, The Spectator, Steele's Little Paper, The Tatler, Johnson's Little Papers The Rambler and The Adventurer, and Goldsmith's Little Paper, The Bee: neither of which, I believe, was as large as The Countryman. It is my aim to fill my Little Paper with Wit, Humor, Anecdote, Essays, Poems, Sketches, Agricultural Articles, and Short Tales. I do not intend to publish any thing that is dull, didactic, or prosy. I wish to make a neatly-printed, select Little Paper—a pleasant companion for the leisure hour, and to relieve the minds of our people somewhat from the engrossing topic of war news.

This journal will be divided into quarterly volumes, each of which will make a book, when reprinted, containing 400 octavo pages of the most interesting matter found in the English language.—No back numbers can be supplied now, but the volumes will be reprinted and bound hereafter.

J. A. TURNER, Eatonton, Ga.

October 13, 1862.

JOB WORK executed with neatness and despatch at this office.
Sept. 15. 2-14-tf

NOTICE TO DEBTORS AND CREDITORS.—All persons who are debtors or creditors of either W. H. Monteith, or W. W. Paschal, both deceased, are requested to make immediate payment, or render in their demands, as the case may be.
Nov. 10, 1862. (6-t) W. W. PASCHAL, Adm'r.

BEAVER HATS.—Two extra fine beaver hats for sale at my store. Price $20. Call and see them.
Nov. 10, 1862. tf W. C DAVIS.

WOOL HATS, on consignment, for sale at my store, for which I will receive the highest cash prices. W. C. DAVIS.
Nov. 10, 1862. tf

A BUGGY and Harness for sale by
Nov. 10, 1862. tf W. W. TURNER.

SIXTY DAYS after date, application will be made to the Court of Ordinary of Putnam County for leave to sell the negroes belonging to the estate of L P. Harwell, dec'd. SUSAN W. LIVELY, Adm'x.
Nov. 3, 1862. 6 9t JOHN W. HUDSON, Adm'r.

HAT SHOP.—I cannot take any more orders for hats, because I cannot get suitable lining, binding, or bands. They are not to be had in the Confederacy. But I will manufacture hats lined and bound with homespun, and put them in Mr Davis's store in Eatonton, where those who want them at the price I have to pay for 2 pounds of wool can get them. Four pounds of wool for 1 hat used to be the old price.—Persons who already have wool at my shop can have it returned to them, or receive the highest cash price for it, if my lining and binding do not suit them. J. A. TURNER.
Oct. 27, 1862. tf

GEORGIA, PUTNAM COUNTY.—Whereas Stephen B. Marshall applies for letters of administration on the estate of James F. Marshall, deceased—

And whereas, also Richard H. Griffin applies for letters of administration on the estate of Robert H. Griffin, deceased—

These are therefore to cite and admonish all and singular the kindred and creditors of said deceased, and all others interested, to be and appear at my office, within the time prescribed by law, and file their objections, if any they have, why said letters should not be granted.

Given under my hand, at office, this 23d day of October, 1862. WM. B. CARTER, Ordinary.
Oct 27, 1862. 3-4-6t

ADMINISTRATOR'S SALE.—Will be sold before the court house door, in the city of Atlanta, on the first tuesday in Dec. next, between the legal hours of sale, the interest of Green Wiggins late of Putnam Co. deceased, in a certain lot of land, lying and being in the county of Fulton, containing 40 acres more or less, the interest of said Wiggins in said tract of land being one sixth of the whole. To be sold under order of the Court of Ordinary of Putnam County.—Terms on the day.
Oct. 20, 1862. tds W. A. GORLEY, Adm'r.

ADMINISTRATOR'S SALE.—Under an order of the Court of Ordinary of Putnam County, will be sold before the court-house door in the town of Dahlonega, on the 1st tuesday in Dec. next, between the legal hours of sale, as the property of Green Wiggins, late of Putnam Co., dec'd., a tract of land containing 40 acres, situate in the 4th dist., 1st sec. in originally Cherokee Co, and known and distinguished in the plan of said district as no. 397.—Terms on the day.
Oct 20th, 1862. tds W. A. GORLEY, Adm'r.

EXECUTOR'S SALE.—Will be sold on the 1st tuesday in Dec. next, before the court-house door in Eatonton, between the legal hours of sale, 1,000 acres of land well improved, with good dwelling house and negro houses, new gin-house and screw, and all other necessary buildings. Sold as the property of John A. Cogburn, late of Putnam County, deceased.

Also will be sold at the residence of said deceased, on the 10th Dec., the blacksmith tools, road wagon and harness, ox carts, interest in horse power and thresher, 2 buggies, a carriage, household and kitchen furniture, mules, horses, cows, 3 yoke oxen, pork and stock hogs, sheep, corn, fodder, wheat, peas, &c., belonging to the estate of said deceased. Terms made known on the days of sale, and sale to continue from day to day until all is sold.
Oct. 20, 1862. tds D. A. WEAVER, Ex'r.

ADMINISTRATOR'S SALE.—Will be sold on the 1st Tuesday in Dec. next, between the legal hours of sale, before the court-house door in Sparta, 4 acres of land belonging to the estate of Thomas C. Grimes, deceased. Said tract of land is that whereon the late Thomas C Grimes resided, in life, is known as the Burnt Place, and adjoins the lands of Mrs. Colt, and Dr. Whitten.—Sold under an order of the Court of Ordinary of Putnam Co.—Terms on the day of sale. M. DENNIS, Adm'r.
Oct. 13, 1862. 3 3-tds

MR. EAKIN'S SALE.—The administrator will sell at public outcry, on wednesday, 3rd Dec., at the late residence of William Eakin, dec'd., all the perishable property belonging to the estate of said dec'd., consisting of horses, mules, pork hogs, stock hogs, sheep, cows, household and kitchen furniture, corn, fodder, blacksmith's tools, and other articles too tedious to mention.—Terms cash.
Nov 10, 1862. tds A H. EAKIN, Adm'r.

APPLICATION will be made, to the first term of the Court of Ordinary of Putnam County, after the expiration of sixty days from the date hereof, for leave to sell the negroes belonging to the estate of Wm. W Paschal, dec'd. JOHN PASCHAL, Adm'r.
Oct. 13, 1862 3-3-9t

SUBSTITUTES WANTED.—Two able bodied men, over 45 years old: one for the 3rd Georgia, and one for the 44th Georgia Volunteers. A liberal price will be paid if good recommendations can be given.

Apply to the undersigned in person at Stanfordville, Ga. or by letter to Eatonton, Ga.
September 22, 1862 tf B B ODOM.

THE EVANGELICAL PULPIT: Published monthly, by Wilkes & Marshall, Forsyth, Ga., at $1 per annum
Aug. 23, 1862. 2-11-[illegible]

FUR AND WOOL WANTED: for which [illegible] paying the highest cash prices at my hat shop.
Sept. 29, 1862. 2 14-tf J. A. TURNER.

WANTED TO HIRE: 2 or 3 likely men, or boys, for whom liberal monthly wages will be paid. Apply at this office.
Sept. 15, 1862. 2 14 tf

The Camden Confederate.

VOLUME II — CAMDEN, SO. CA., FRIDAY, NOVEMBER 21, 1862. — NUMBER 4

The Camden Confederate

IS PUBLISHED EVERY FRIDAY BY

J. T. HERSHMAN,

AT TWO DOLLARS A YEAR,

PAYABLE INVARIABLY HALF-YEARLY IN ADVANCE.

PROCLAMATION BY THE GOVERNOR.

STATE OF SOUTH CAROLINA.

EXECUTIVE DEPARTMENT,
COLUMBIA, November 7, 1862.

WHEREAS the two Acts of Conscription passed by Congress have designated for Confederate service all from eighteen up to forty-five, and the President has, under these Acts actually called for all up to forty; and whereas he has agreed to accept, for temporary service on our coast, eight of the Regiments formed from our First Corps of State Reserves, and by thus accepting them has, for the period of ninety days, exempted all in those Regiments who were liable to conscription; and whereas this has deranged our whole organization of reserve State forces, and it is therefore necessary that there shall be a further and immediate organization made for the internal defence and police of the States:

Now, know ye, that I, FRANCIS W. PICKENS, Governor and Commander-in-Chief in and over the State of South Carolina, do hereby call upon all officers and good citizens to obey and enforce the resolutions of this date hereunto annexed.

Gen. Beauregard has made an urgent appeal that the eight Regiments of Reserves recently ordered out shall be sent forward at as early a day as possible, and I do hereby call upon the officers who command those Regiments to bring them forward, as the defence of their State and country requirers that they should report for duty at the earliest possible moment to the Confederate Generals in command. Our State is threatened, and our honor requires that every man shall do his duty. All personal feelings must be lost sight of and forgotten in the present emergency. Let there be no delay.

In relation to the police and internal safety of the State, I trust that every man will be forthwith prepared to guard and protect the helpless and innocent from any of the dreadful consequences which our brutal enemies seem determined to inaugurate on or before the first of January next. With this view, I urge all between the ages of sixteen and sixty-five to enroll themselves according to the resolutions hereunto attached.

All persons who may be taken in any attempts to produce disturbance amongst our slaves or resistance to their masters, whether under commission or not, or by orders from United States authority or not, shall be, if arrested by any State troops or State police, handed over to the authorities of the State alone, to be dealt with as felons. There never has been any period when our slaves were generally more peaceable and properly disposed than at present, and I trust that no undue suspicion or unfounded rumors will receive any hasty credence. I do not expect anything serious from the infamous measures alluded to, but we owe it to our families and to the country to be active and guarded. For the next three months let no citizen of South Carolina be careless or unprepared. Let all the District guards and police referred to in the resolutions below be immediately and thoroughly organized. Let there be a universal feeling of safety consequent upon strict organization and thorough preparation. In these perilous times, let there be no dissension or complaint at any temporary inconvenience or at any orders that may appear, at first, unnecessary. Let the men of age and worth step forward and set examples that all will feel and respect. The strength of the community consists in strict obedience to orders and to discipline. We have no time to cavil. Let every man sleep by his armor. There will be no danger unless from carelessness and neglect of duty. Let the whole State, with one voice, rise to the emergency, and we are safe from any foreign or domestic foe.

Given under my hand and the great seal of the State, at Columbia, this the 7th day of November, in the year of our Lord one thousand eight hundred and sixty-two, and in the eightyseventh year of the sovereignty and independence of the State of South Carolina — F. W. PICKENS.

1. *Resolved,* That the public safety imperiously demands that all male white residents of the State of South Carolina capable of bearing arms should be immediately placed into military organization and armed.

2. That all male whites between the ages of 16 and 65 years, resident within the limits of each beat, (except those declared "exempt from all militia service," and those already in State or Confederate service,) shall constitute the beat company of such beat; and it shall be the duty of the commanding officer of such beat to order out his company once every fortnight for parade and drill, with the view to service in the District as a police force, and to military service in the Brigade as "alarm men." And the commanding officer of each beat shall cause to be summond to such parade every person in his beat so liable, except such as may be certified by the Surgeon of the regiment to be physically unable to be present at such parade, such commanding officer having the discretion to excuse from drill any person attending on the ground, whom he may judge to be physically unable to undergo the fatigue of the day.

3. That the commanding officer of each beat shall keep a roll of all persons so liable to service in his company, which roll shall be called at each parade, and all defaulters noted; and it shall further be his duty to report immediately after each parade to the commanding officer of the regiments the names of such defaulters, that they may be held to answer therefor before a court-martial. And the commanding officer of each beat shall have power to grant leaves of absence from such parades to such persons as may be called away from the beat on business, and to physicians, millers, ferrymen, overseers, and owners in charge as overseers, where the public interest requires that they should not be withdrawn from their duties to attend the company parades.

4. That the commanding officer of each beat shall keep an additional and separate roll of all effective men in his company who are between the ages of 40 and 50 years, the same to constitute a reserve force for the defence of the State, and be subject to the call of the Commander-in-Chief, for service in any part of the State. In making up such roll, there shall be excluded therefrom all persons who are in the military service of the State or in the service of the Confederate States, and all persons who are by State authority declared "exempt from draft," as also, all persons who have been detailed for special service by order of the Governor and Council, whilst engaged on such service, or indefinitely furloughed on account of "public interest." And it shall be the duty of the commanding officer of the beat, at each parade, to cause the said roll of effective men to be called, and to report a copy of said roll monthly to the commanding officer of the regiment: And the commanding officer of the regiment shall make to the Adjutant and Inspector-General a monthly report of the number of effective men in his regiment so enrolled.

5. That the purpose of effecting such enrollment, it shall be the duty of every person so liable to report himself for enrollment on the day of parade; and the commanding officer of the beat shall question, as to age and residence, every person not so reporting, who may be within the limits of his beat, and who may be apparently between the ages of 40 and 50 years, and he is hereby authorized to administer oaths to such person; and in case any person so questioned shall refuse to give the information, (on oath, if required,) it shall be the duty of the commanding officer to enroll his name as an effective man; and such person so refusing shall thereafter be estopped from showing that he was not subject to such enrollment.

6. When a call shall at any time be made upon such effective men, by the Commander-in-Chief, for active service, it shall be the duty of all persons so enrolled to report themselves promptly, on the day named, at their respective places of regimental parade; and the commanding officer of the regiment shall there organize them into companies of not less than sixty-four men, rank and file, order the immediate election of company officers, and promptly report the companies thus organized and officered to the Adjutant and Inpector General.

7. That depots of arms and ammunition be established at each Court House in the State (except in the Districts of Charleston, Georgetown, Beaufort and Richland) to which shall be sent forthwith 68 stand of arms with 20 rounds of cartridges to each. The same to be subject to the order of the commanding officer of the regiment in which such depot is established, or of the commanding officer of the beat company organized at such Court House. And in addition thereto, one hundred pounds of powder be sent to each depot, under like control, to be used if occasion require, by the beat companies of the district.

8. That for the safe custody and protection of such arms and ammunition, the commanding officer of the company in charge of the same shall, when by him deemed advisable or proper, keep a detail of twenty men at all hours on guard, at the depot, to be drilled during the day, to act as guard during the night, and to be relieved daily; and if the number of men in such company shall not be sufficient to perform such guard duty, the commanding officer thereof shall report such fact to the commanding officer of regiment, whose duty it shall be to detail from adjacent beats for service in such company, as many men as may be sufficient to increase the company to sixty-four men, rank and file.

9. That the 4th and 10th regiments of the First Corps of Reserves, heretofore organized, be, and they are hereby, disbanded, and all commissions issued to the officers of such Regiments are hereby vacated.

10. That nothing contained in the foregoing resolutions shall apply to the Fourth Brigade of the South Carolina Militia, nor shall be construed to appear to the constitutional and legal right of the Governor and Commander-in-Chief of the State to call into service such portion of the militia of this State for the public defence as in his judgment he may deem expedient.

By order of the Governor and Council.

B. F. ARTHUR,
Secretary Executive Council.
Official copy

☞ All the papers in the State copy twice.
November 14 — 2

STATE OF SOUTH CAROLINA.

ADJUTANT AND INSPECTOR-GENERAL'S OFFICE,
COLUMBIA, November 13, 1862.

GENERAL ORDER NO. 42.

I. PURSUANT TO A RESOLUTION OF the Governor and Council of this date, it is ordered that the "Soldiers Boards of Relief," created by an Act of the General assembly, entitled An Act to afford aid to the families of soldiers," are exempt from military duty except as alarm men.

By order of the Governor and Council:

WILMOT G. DESAUSSURE,
Adjutant and Inspector-General of S. C.

☞ Each paper in the State copy once.
November 21 — 1

STATE OF SOUTH CAROLINA.

ADJ'T. & INSP. GENERAL'S OFFICE,
COLUMBIA, November 14, 1862.

GENERAL ORDER NO. 43.

I. PURSUANT TO A RESOLUTION OF the Governor and Council, dated October 31, 1862, all militia officers of this State are hereby ordered to give every assistance in their power to the enrolling officers of the Confederate Government employed in the preperation of the Conscription rolls, and to furnish to such officers, when called upon to so do, copies of the rolls of their respective organizations, and in such rolls to specify the ages of the persons in such organizations.

By order of the Governor and Council.

WILMOT G. DESAUSSURE,
Adjutant and Inspector General of S. C.

☞ All papers in the State copy once.
November 21 — 1

Bureau of Central Association.

COLUMBIA, November 12, 1862.

A CAR WITH SUPPLIES FOR THE Carolina soldiers in Virginia will leave the Charlotte Depot under charge of a special agent, on Friday, the 21st inst. All District Associations, and all persons wishing to send boxes or packages, are invited to avail themselves of this opportunity.

M. LABORDE,
Chairman Central Association.

☞ All papers of the State will please copy.
November 21 — 1

J. T. HERSHMAN, Editor.

FRIDAY, NOVEMBER 21, 1862.

Special Notice.

On and after Monday the 24th inst., and until further notice, a special Passenger train will be run between Columbia and Kingsville three times a week, viz: Monday, Wednesday and Friday, observing the following schedule:

Leave Kingsville 8.05 a.m.; Arrive at Columbia 9.45 a. m.

Leave Columbia 12·10 p. m.; and arrive at Kingsville 1.40 p. m.

The Extra Passenger Train between Camden and Kingsville will—during the running of the above Special train—run on Tuesday, Thursday and Saturday of each week, instead of on Monday, Wednesday and Saturday.

H. T. PEAKE,

General Superintendant.

November 21 4

☞ We have been requested by our Post Master to give notice that the postage of letters dropped into the office for delivery, is two cents each—*postage to be pre-paid*. Letters not so pre-paid, are sent to the dead letter office. Two cent postage stamps may be had at the office.

Acknowledgement.

We are requested by the officers comprising the staff of Gen. VILLEPIGUE, to return their thanks for the kind and hospitable reception met with during their stay in Camden.

[FOR THE CAMDEN CONFEDERATE.]

Acknowledgement.

RICHMOND, November 3d, 1862.

DEAR MADAM: I take pleasure in acknowledging the receipt of $100—and also a valuable box—sent by the citizens of Camden for the benefit of our Hospitals. I should have done so before, had not my absence from Virginia rendered it impossible.

Respectfully,

ROBERT W. BARNWELL, JR.

Miss SALLY CHESNUT, President L. A. A. Kershaw District.

P. S. The former handsome donation of $400, was received and acknowlrdged in August last.

R. W. B.

[FOR THE CAMDEN CONFEDERATE.]

The Patrol System.

MR. EDITOR:—I am glad to see that our patrol system is still kept up, and that nearly every man is willing to do his duty without compulsion. Have heard of but few instances of neglect, and hope we may hear of no more. Nearly every night from ten to fifteen report for duty, and we are sure that the town is more effectually guarded now than it has been for years before. For myself, and a large portion of the community think as I do, I see no need of keeping, at the expense of the town, a paid guard. I do not believe that it is of any benefit to the community.

Efficient guardmen are not easily found—and as for hiring little boys to walk around the town at night, I must confess I do not see the wisdom of the policy.

I have several times met a couple of children walking the streets at night and wondered if their mothers knew they were out. Judge of our surprise on being told that they were the town guard—or acting as such. Now they may be very good boys for ought I know—doubtless they are—but I think them out of place, when acting as constables of the town and keepers of the peace.

If we have any guard at all, let us have *men*—men of judgment and discretion.

CIVIS.

A GOOD BLACKING FOR HARNESS AND SHOES.—Take wax 1 1-4 ounces, melt, add then 4 1-2 ounces of mutton suet; remove from the fire and pour in 1-2 ounce spirits of turpentine, then mix in gradually 3 ounces of lamp black, *constantly stiring* at this stage of the operation *till cold*. As a substitute for mutton suet, tallow softened with neats-foot oil may be used. As blacking is scarce in the Confederacy, perhaps this receipt may be appreciated.

The message of the Governor of Georgia recommends compelling each chartered bank to issue change bills to the amount of three per cent on capital stock, and the State Road three hundred thousand dollars.

Burnside, who succeeds McClellan, is forty years old. He is a Rhode Islander.

Reception of the Remains of Gen. J. B. Villepigue.

The remains of Gen. VILLEPIGUE arrived in Camden, on Monday evening last—accompanied by the following named gentleman—members of his staff: Major J. P. CARR, Major T. N. LEBARON, N. A. ROLAND, Chief Surgeon; Capts. K. FALKNER, GEO. SIMPSON, B. MICKLE, H. T. SCOTT, with Lieutenant OWENS, in command of ten privates, and was received by a large concourse of citizens—both civil and military. They were formed in line of procession, by Col A. T. GOODWIN, who acted as Chief Marshal of the day, after which the body was taken to the Episcopal Church, and laid in State until 3 p. m. on Tuesday, when the obsequies were performed by the Rev. T. F. DAVIS, Jr., in a most solemn and impressive manner, making frequent touching allusions to the great worth, noble daring, and christian character of the deceased.

Truly we have lost a great and good man. One that whilst living the nation looked to with pride, knowing that in him they had a herculean defender, always trusting—as does our brave JACKSON—in the God of Battles; and now that the unrelenting iron hand of death has taken him from his country and home, his absence will be mourned by thousands of his countrymen,—a void created in our army not easily filled. He was a strict and exacting disciplinarian, though kind and humane to his whole brigade. He endured all the hardships and exposures of camp life alike with his officers and privates—would never accept hospitalities on march without the same could be extended to the entire brigade.

Gen. VILLEPIGUE died at Port Hudson La., of intermittent fever, on the evening of November 10, 1862, aged 32 years.

"I heard a voice from Heaven saying unto me—
Write Blessed are they who die in the Lord."

At the first call of his country for assistance—and hardly before his native State had rent asunder, those ties which bound her to the Union, Lieut. VILLEPIGUE—then in the far West—gave up friends of long years standing, and all military prospects, and linked his destiny with that of his native State. After serving with distinction at the bombardment of Fort Sumter he was ordered to report to Gen. Bragg at Pensacola—there he was placed in command of Fort McRea—at which place he was wounded; and Gen. Bragg, hearing of his misfortune, sent a favorite officer to relieve him, but the gallant hero sent word back, "he could still hold the fort as long as brick and mortar could remain together." After this gallant defence, his country rewarded him with the position of Brigadier General, and ordered him to report to Gen. Beauregard. At this time the Mississippi River was threatened, and he was ordered by Gens. Beauregard and Bragg to the defence of Fort Pillow—confident that he could stay the invaders tread; and for fifty-two days did he hold this place against fearful odds; and not until he had received positive orders to retreat, did he leave. And then on the 30th of May—with but twenty men—having sent all his troops ahead—did he, by his dauntless courage, succeed in repelling the enemy's fleet and perfecting a retreat, which elicited the encomiums of the General commanding before the army of the West. His country again calls him to the hard fought field of Corinth, and there again, by his courage and true self possession for which he alone was remarkable, did he elicit the praises of all—from the private citizen as well as the veteran soldier—and by his fficiency did he add so greatly to the safety of the army. And now, just at a time when those under whom he had served had recommended him for promotion, he is taken away. Alas! how sad—after twelve days suffering borne with true christian fortitude—showing forth, even in sickness, the military patriot—he is carried off. "He is not dead—but sleepeth," he has left this world, of sorrow and trouble, and gone to enjoy the reward he so richly deserves—the reward of the true Christian patriot. Far, far away from all that was dear to him—with no relation, save one, to soften those last moments—he suffered long and patiently—and then his good spirit took flight to its happy realms above. Sister, brother, relatives, and friends grieve not—your loss is great—but the of the nation greater. A brave and great man has gone, and the whole Confederacy mourns the loss of a devoted and heroic son.

To his staff officers—and a gallant corps of gentlemen they are—we say cheer on, your general has left you, but not helpless. To his training is due that knowledge of your duties which will render you serviceable to your country, and a lasting memorial of your dear and much loved general.

"May he rest in peace."

Lieut. Edward P. Niles.

It was our melancholy duty, on Wednesday last, to pay the last tribute of respect to another brave son of South Carolina, who has fallen a victim to the inhuman war which is devastating our country, and desolating our homes. Sad and afflicting as is this dispensation, we have the proud consciousness of knowing that he fell at the post of duty and honor; and though cut down in the bloom of manhood, he has served his country well, and we trust has laid up for himself a rich reward for all his privations and hardships. We hope that a proper tribute will be paid to his memory, by some of his numerous friends who knew him longer and more intimately than ourself. His memory is enshrined in the hearts of us all—and in after years, when our children shall repeat the story of our trials and struggles for liberty, the name of Lieut NILES will be associated with the noble band of martyrs who laid upon the shrine of liberty the precious tribute of their blood.

The Remains of Lieutenant H. M. DeSaussure.

The remains of this gallant officer and soldier who fell on the battle-field near Richmond, while heroically leading the company of which he was then in command, reached Camden on Wednesday last, and were deposited in the family vault at the Cemetary. It is melancholy to think at what a fearful price we are achieving our independence, while the North is sending her hirelings and paupers to subjugate the South and crush out the last grain of American liberty, we are sending our best and noblest sons to bleed and die in her defence. Surely if there is a God in Heaven, these sacrifices for freedom will not go unrewarded. Victory must and will perch upon our banners, and the souls of the martyred patriots will rejoice with us to witness the glorious consummation. May God speed the day of our deliverance and usher in once more the day of peace and prosperity.

Lieut. DESAUSSURE died a martyr—a martyr in the strictest sense, and one that will ever be fresh in the memory of our people.

Roll of the Wateree Mounted Riflemen.

The following is a complete roll of the above named Company, under command of Capt. E. M. BOYKIN,—now on their way to the coast, near Georgetown, S. C.

OFFICERS.

1. E. M. BOYKIN, Captain.
2. THOS. J. ANCRUM, 1st Lieutenant.
3. JOHN CANTEY, 2d Lieutenant.
4. DUNCAN WHITAKER, 3d Lieutenant.
5. S. SUMPTER, 1st Sergeant.
6. D. P. St. DUBOSE, 2d Sergeant.
7. J. P. KIRKLAND, 3d Sergeant.
8. C. L. McCOY, 4th Sergeant.
9. JOHN M. CANTEY, 1st Corporal.
10. JAMES TRUESDEL, 2d Corporal,

PRIVATES.

11. H. Arrants.	43. R. L. Logan.
12. Jos. Arrants.	44. B. H. Matheson.
13. T. S. Boykin.	45. A. L. McMullen.
14. W. T. Boykin.	46. Washington Meyers.
15 M. N. Brown.	47. W. D. McDowall, jr.
16. Samuel Barfield.	48. J. P. Mickle.
17. H. Barruch.	49. Thomas Nelson.
18. B. J. Baker.	50. B. Nunnery.
19. R. Collins.	51. W. E. Nunnery.
20. B. J. Campbell.	52. Jonathan Newman.
21. James Clyburn.	53. R. R. Player.
22. D. J. Cook.	54. J. R. Picket.
23. Wm. Christmas.	55. J. R. Pace.
24. R. B. Douglas.	56. J. J. Ross.
25. L. H. Deas, jr.	57. B. J. Ratcliff.
26. Allen Deas.	58. W. H. Ratcliff.
27. E. W. Davis.	59. W. T. Russell.
28. W. G. Duncan.	60. W. J. Reynolds.
29. J. R. Davis.	61. W. W. Stokes.
30. J. M. DeSaussure.	62. K. Shannon.
31. G. A. Debruhl.	63. D. P. Strother.
32. Ben Debruhl.	64. D. C. Tryon.
33. J. W. Doby, jr.	65. Henry Truesdel.
34 M. Evans.	66. J. L. Tiller.
35. Thomas Elliott.	67. W. M. Truesdel.
36. D. J. George.	68. P. E. Woods.
37. W. J. Gerald, jr.	69. O. W. Watts.
38. ——. Garner.	70. John Williams.
39. M. G. Huckabee.	71. H. K. Witherspoon,
40. James R. Kirkland.	72. G. G. Young.
41. M. W. King.	73. J. N. Young.
42. S. R. Kirkland.	74. Wilson Yarborough.

Accounts from Texas state that the enemy had taken Indianola, and demanded the surrender of Matagorda. Later intelligence reports reports that the enemy had then taken Matagorda, as well as Indianola.

The War in Virginia.

RICHMOND, November 18.—Up to half past twelve o'clock to-day the enemy had not occupied Fredericksburg, but were on the heights opposite. The skirmish yesterday was merely an "artillery duel," and was not resumed this morning.

A despatch from Petersburg announces that the enemy, supposed to number considerably over a brigade, appeared at Franklin, this morning, on the Blackwater, and attempted to cross under cover of shells. The Confederates resisted them successfully for two hours, when the Abolitionists retired. We captured twelve or fourteen prisoners. There was no loss on our side, so far as heard from.

Parties direct from below Brandon, on the James River, assert positively that there is no fleet in that vicinity, nor has there been any. No fleet is in sight, up or down the river.

LATEST NEWS FROM THE NORTH.

Northern papers of the 14th and 15th furnish some additional items of interest.

Governor Morgan and Collector Barney have visited Washington, to urge that some adequate and immediate measures be taken for the protection of New York harbor. The requisite orders were issued.

The draft in Wisconsin was resisted in one county by a mob, which destroyed the draft box and the rolls, and attacked the private residences of several prominent citizens.

General McClellan is proposed for the vacant Senatorship in New Jersey. A complimentary dinner will be tendered him in New York.

A temporary five per cent, loan of $25,000,000, which was asked for by Secretary Chase, has been filled up by the New York banks, and nearly the whole paid in. It is reported that Chase hastened this negotiation, because of a serious demand upon the Government by an European Government, which might lead to grave complications.

News from Memphis.

KNOXVILLE, November 17.—We have advices from Memphis to the 17th instant.

Porter's fleet will, it is said, attack Vicksburg as soon as it can pass the Bar at President Island.

General Price is reported to be seven miles below Holly Springs, at Davis' Bridge, on the Hetchie, and strongly entrenched. If the rains should continue, the roads will be rendered impassable and the battle will be postponed, as, in that case, Grant will not be able to move his trains and artillery.

The Memphis papers express apprehensions that Bragg may attack Grant's rear before Rosencrans can come up; also, that another force of ours may attack the rear of Rosencrans, if the latter should attempt to follw Bragg.

Northwestern men are getting clamorous for peace. They say they are in the army and can't get out.

The order expelling from Memphis the families of Southern soldiers is no longer enforced.

YANKEE CRUELTY TO NEGROES.—A correspondent of the New York *Tribune*, writing from Newbern, North Carolina, under date of October 18th, gives the following picture of the condition of the negroes of that department:

The situation of the poor, unhappy blacks in this department, fed though they are by Union bounty, is such as should excite the sympathy of every Christian man. I am sorry to say that they are treated with great sternness and severity, amounting to positive cruelty, by many of our soldiers, who seem to regard them as hardly better than brutes. Not a few of our officers conduct themselves in the most unfeeling manner toward these unfortunate creatures, and are, in fact, ostentatious in expressing their hatred and contempt for the "d—d nigger."

BROWNLOW ON SOUTH CAROLINA.—Parson Brownlow made a speech at Chicago last week, in the course of which he said: "I am in favor, to-night, of letting out, as a contract to the Yankees by our Government, the sawing of South Carolina out of this Union and floating her into the Atlantic and sinking her into enteral perdition. [Applause and laughter.] If that cannot be done, I am for reducing Charleston to ashes, leaving not one stone upon another; and then I hope those men who are running for Congress will pledge themselves to vote for a law that it should never again be rebuilt while God liveth and man serveth." [Laughter.]

VOL. I.—NO. 11. RICHMOND, SATURDAY, NOVEMBER 22, 1862. PRICE 15 CENTS.

MAJ. GEN. AMBROSE POWELL HILL.

General Ambrose Powell Hill is a native of Culpeper, Virginia, and is a son of Major Hill who, for many years was a leading Democrat and merchant of that county. Gen. Hill has two brothers—T. T. and Edward Hill—the first named a lawyer and the latter a merchant at Culpeper Court House. Gen. Hill has also two sisters, both of whom are married—one being the wife of Major Hill, who was a paymaster in the U. S. service, but who resigned his position upon the secession of Virginia, and took his position under the banner of the Old Dominion.

Gen. A. P. Hill appears to be about thirty-six or thirty-seven years of age, and is a soldier by profession, having graduated at West Point in 1842. He immediately entered the army and served in the Mexican war. He rose to the rank of Captain and then left the army.

Upon the breaking out of the present war, the subject of this brief sketch was chosen Colonel of the Thirteenth Virginia Regiment, and at the first battle of Manassas, it will be recollected, this regiment with the remainder of Gen. Johnston's command arrived on the field, just in time to secure and complete the great victory of that memorable day.

At the battle of Williamsburg he had risen to the rank of Brigadier-General, and in that fight he exhibited an extraordinary spirit and energy, which was recognized by all who observed his behavior on that field.

In the disposition of the forces around Richmond previous to the seven days fighting, Gen. Hill who had now been made a Major-General, occupied with his division the extreme left of our position in the neighborhood of Meadow Bridge. He was placed in command of one of the largest divisions of the army, composed of the brigades of Anderson, Branch, Pender, Gregg, Field, and, perhaps, some others, which he rapidly brought to perfection in organization. It was made his duty to cross at Meadow Bridge and make the first attack upon the enemy's forces. Here he maintained a terrible conflict with the enemy, encouraging his troops by examples of personal audacity, which kept him constantly exposed to the enemy's fire.

That position of the enemy being gained, the division of Gen. Hill followed his subsequent movements, being placed first on the line of our advance and bearing the brunt of the action, to Frazer's farm, where occurred the memorable engagement in which his command, composed of his own and one division of General Longstreet, fought the entire Yankee force and achieved a success which broke the spirit of the invading horde and completed the circuit of our victories.

Gen. Hill is beloved by his own command, and his name is frequently mentioned with enthusiasm by the troops of other divisions. He is a brave and skillful officer—having made arms not only his profession, but an enthusiastic study, to which he was prompted by the natural tastes and disposition of his mind.

STRIVE not with your superiors in argument, but always submit your judgment to others with modesty.

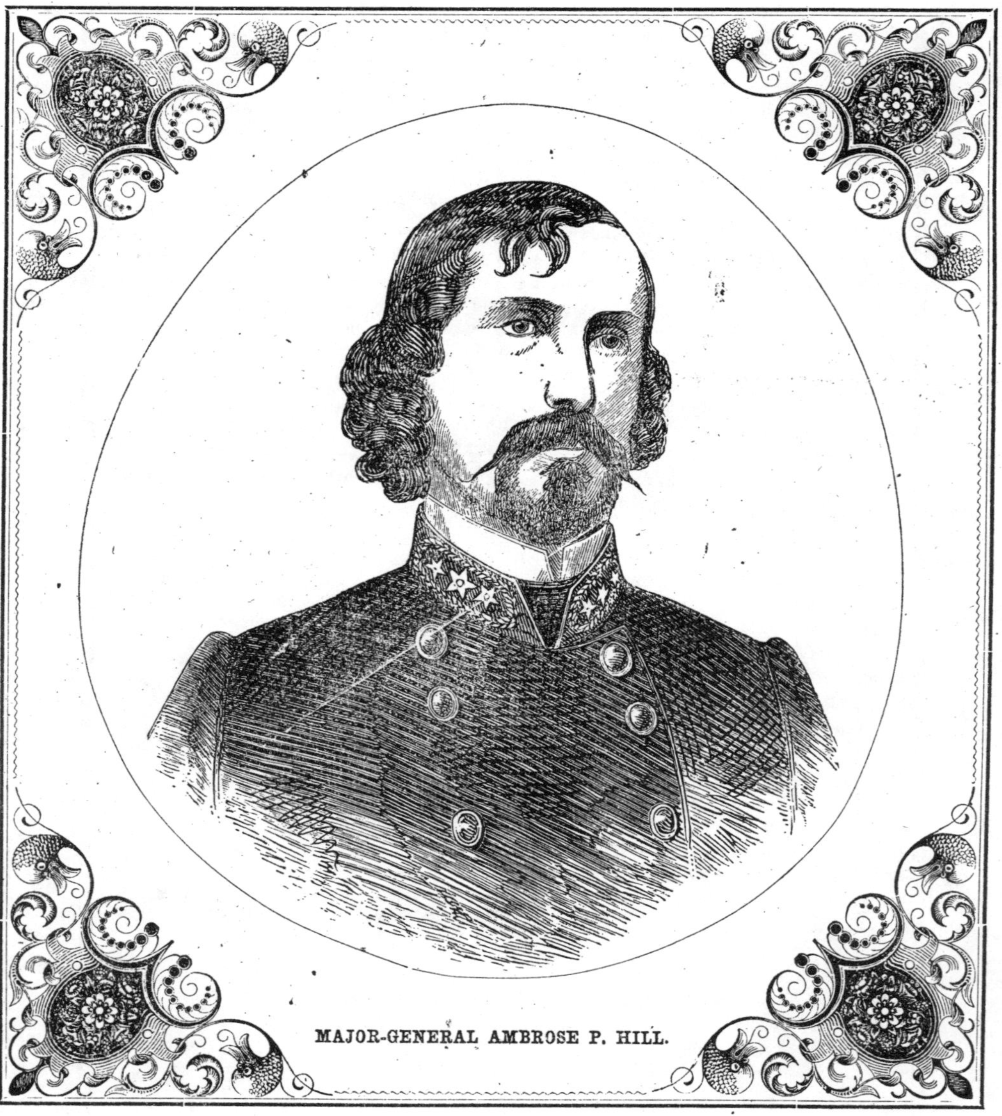

MAJOR-GENERAL AMBROSE P. HILL.

Written for the Illustrated News.

THE SIMPLE, LOVING HEART.

BY M. LOUISE ROGERS.

There are jewels of earth and ocean, rare in their wealth and brilliancy, which men eagerly grasp, and which brighten the eyes of fair women to have sparkling on their white brows. Wealth can command the world's notice and homage, and can elevate the booby to a princely eminence in social courts. It is enough to make the blood leap gladly and wildly through the veins to have the multitude hang rapt and entranced upon the words of burning eloquence that flow like a lava tide from your lips into listening hearts; and it is something to have your name borne from lip to lip of a free and mighty people as one of the wise and great of earth. And Genius, who sits royally enthroned upon the shrine of its possessor—who soars and descends, creates and destroys, laughs and weeps, and loves and scorns by turns, and who with the transmission of its electric and subtle fluid of thought, knows no boundary of seas, skies nor lands—Genius is crowned by the world's homage, and yearned after by the highest and lowliest of earth.

But better than all—better than gold and lands, better than the diamond's flash or the ruby's gleam, better than the peerless realms of Genius, men's hollow praise or the witching spell of beauty, is that humble, but sweetest and dearest flower in life's parterre—the simple, loving heart. The wealth of earth, the regal birthright of intellect, and the gift of beauty are rare, peerless and glorious, when all "life's sweet charities" are their inseparable companions, but without the simple, loving heart, they make a realm of gorgeous beauty indeed, but one never warmed, flushed and vivified by unclouded and blessed sunshine.

People run madly after happiness under the name of pleasure, never thinking that in the simple, loving heart of some humble human near them, they might read a lesson, and find a world of peace and purest joy. Simple in its purity and unsuspecting nature, and child-like trust and faith in the goodness of all humanity: and with a love that knows no change of time nor place—that clings undyingly to us in sunshine or storm, in gladness or woe, and whether mankind, bird, beast, flower, or star, embraces all things in its boundless affection.

The simple, loving heart in which a noble and beautiful lady had "hidden her husband," extorted the admiration of her judges and obtained her husband's pardon; and this beautiful virtue never touches and attracts us more than when our immortal Washington, with the conqueror's laurels on his brow, and recently elected as the first Chief Magistrate, within the walls of Mount Vernon, knelt with the simplicity of a little child beside his aged mother, and with his strong arms about her neck, pressed his lips upon her furrowed cheek, and faltered out the last farewell she ever heard from her illustrious son.

Napoleon, on the bleak cliffs of St. Helena, or the lonely isle of Elba, in his dark hours of friends' desertion and the world's fickle praise, would, no doubt, have given the glory of Jena, Austerlitz and Marengo for the simple, loving heart of the peerless and faithful Josephine to cling to him then with its sweet trust, and to teach him its simple, but priceless love—better than the military genius that planned and executed the overthrow of kings and empires. And it was this sweet attraction that aided so much in crowning Burns a peer of song, by both noble and serf, and that makes his name a household word at the "cotter's" fireside among the heather-clad hills of Scotland. It breathes its pure and delicate aroma upon the offerings brought by Wordsworth to Nature's shrine, of which he was the High Priest, and through its medium, "Poor Goldy," up in his garret, won the affection and respect, if not the homage of even his superiors.

While its purity and simplicity are not incompatible with intellect, it is, indeed, the vivifier of all its princely realms; it elevates and etherealizes the peasant, and is an ornament of the king; it should be one of men's aspirations, and the priceless jewel that every woman should possess.

WHEN another speaks, be attentive yourself, and disturb not the audience. If any hesitate in his words, help him not, nor prompt him without being desired; interrupt him not, nor answer him till his speech be ended.

TREAT with men at fit times about business, and whisper not in the company of others.

BE not curious to know the affairs of others, neither approach to those that speak in private.

THE VOLUNTEER

Devoted to the Interest of the Union.

PUBLISHED FREQUENTLY---ONCE IN A WHILE---IF NOT OFTENER.

THE VOLUNTEER

IS PUBLISHED BY

A. C. CETTER & A. V. BLAIR,

Editors and Proprietors.

Nicholasville, Ky., Dec. 6th

ADVERTISING PRICES.

Advertising at Cincinnati prices.

Business cards not exceeding our columns, a twenty five cent Sutler's check.

Marriage notices inserted with a matrimonial puff for an invitation to the wedding and board for one week thereafter.

Notice of Railroad smash ups, exonerating Conductors and Engineers from all blame, inserted for a free family ticket.

Notice to Correspondents.

A. K.—We will be obliged to decline giving you the exact language used by Burgoyne when he surrendered his forces at Saratoga, as the news would be contraband.

Miss M.—Your very beautiful poem is accepted and will be published in our next. Although our friend B., to whom we referred it, mistook it for a warrantee deed, but we consider it of great merit for its poetic beauty.

Several communications received too late for this number.

☞ N. B.—All communications, to receive attention must be accompanied by the real name of the author from whom they were copied also a complete discriptive roll of the person who wishes credit for the production.

☞ Capt. W. HODGDON, Assistant Provost Marshal, is using the most untiring energy in reclaiming government property captured at Lexington—clothing, guns and other stores, he finds in chambers and cellars of citizens who *claim* to be loyal.

Introduction

It is with great embarrassment that we make our editorial bow with soldier clothes on. We are quite well aware that "the pen is mightier than the sword," yet we are not vain enough to believe that this little maiden sheet will be entirely able to settle the war, and restore our distracted country to its former glory; we expect that even after we have made our *debut* as military editors, the *quasi* secesh here in Kentucky will still lie in a critical situation, with the nigger on the brain although they are regularly stimulated by doses of Government money, and that they will still go into occasional spasms because they can only get three prices for what articles they sell the soldiers.

We have engaged in this enterprise with the most limited capital, and will be fully satisfied if the principle we have invested will draw from our patrons sufficient interest, to reward our carrier boy with a stray Sutler's check, as we have not the impudence to presume military men have any change. We will be perfectly willing to receive subscriptions for the *Volunteer* from all commissioned officers and wait till pay day for them to chalk up, but all puffs recommending promotions without merit, must be paid for invariably in advance. It will require a pretty heavy bonus to secure our influence in getting resignations accepted, and we will not take the responsibility of laying the application before the General, unless the applicant has a Surgeon's certificate, showing proper disability, such as cowardice, homesickness, a tendency to consumption (*of hard bread and government bacon.*) having a wife or sweetheart at home who is receiving the attention of some other man—having no good clothes, or unable to drink sutler's whiskey—such misfortunes, we consider entitles any commissioned officer to a discharge from the service.

Trusting our motives will not be misunderstood we proceed to business at once.

Bragg's Retreat from Perryville.

The above is a very spirited illustration by our own artist, of Gen. Bragg's retreat from the Perryville fight. The picture is full of melancholy interest.

It can be seen by a close observer that the rebel general has a rear guard, but we are unable to say which *mule* he guards most.

☞ The Sanitary condition of our troops in this division [third] are about as good as could be reasonably expected, yet the muffled drum and measured tread of the funeral escort daily remind us that some of our brave boys have fallen by disease to fill a soldier's grave, it is sad to see them fall one by one, away from friends and home, with no tender wife or sweet sister to soothe them in their last hours, or wipe the death damp from their brow—but such is the fortunes of war.

EXPLANATIONS.

It may be a mystery to many of our readers, how it is possible for a paper to be printed so poorly. To those we wish to make a few explanations, and then we hope they will excuse us for deficiency in this issue.

The Press was found in a back yard, all in pieces and apparently in ruins —it supplied the places of posts to support the fence—it has been there for months, in all kinds of weather, and is nearly ruined by rust, but by considerable ingenuity, we accomplished the work of putting it up in a room, and have it so as to do such work as we now place before you. To practical printers we wish to say; we have no blanket and have to supply its place by paper, we suppose it was stolen by the secesh to make a suit of clothes. Our type are also very old and defaced, as it has all been scattered rather promiscously in the street once by the rebel crew—our rolls are also useless.

We trust that after our readers consider the difficulties we are laboring under, they will excuse the looks of the first *Volunteer.*

☞ Owing to the fact that our devil is on guard to-day, our readers must excuse us for the want of reading matter in this number. We will however graduate our prices according to the skill we display as editors. When we have learned to lie like the Cincinnati *Enquirer* or some of the New York papers, we will advance the rates of subscription.

☞ The whisky question seems to be one of the deepest inteerest to the soldiers and citizens about here. The *nine-deaths* to the gallon bust-head seems to be a temptation they cannot resist, and some of the soldiers exhibit skill and ingenuity that would do credit to a General on the field of battle, to obtain it.

The Provost Marshal is unmovable and has placed intoxicating drink beyond the reach of all.

☞ The weather is pleasant—a very little snow fell yesterday.

☞ We hear of a great many complaints being made by the citizens having occasion to pass our lines, because they are required to step into the Provost Marshal's Office and get a pass; it certainly seems strange that if these people are realy loyal, they cannot submit to the inconvenience of getting a pass, when we have to submit to a soldiers life for three years to protect their property. Some of the military men are so ungenerous as to think it would be a better proof of their loyalty, to take a gun and help defend their own State.

☞ It is frequently rumored about this town that the Rebel Bandit, John Morgan, intends paying the troops a visit here, on a stealing excursion, we wish to quiet the nerves of all weakened persons, and assure them that Morgan will always be a most welcome guest to Gen. Baird's camp, and can have a banquet of blood to entertain his noble on, at any time.

The Proposition for Peace.

We do not wish to delude our readers into the belief that there will be a lull in the storm of battle, and when the smoke of the contending parties clears away, we will receive from the Southern Confederacy a proposal for an armistice, and then overtures of peace.

We put but little confidence in the other paper reports in reference to the rumor, that the South is willing to return to her allegiance, and trust that our friends in the army will not be instrumental in disseminating any such news, as it is calculated to ingrue the prospects of government contractors. If we have an early peace. Another thing, we are sure no propositions for peace the South is disposed to make, will be honorable. We know of no honorable peace but the unconditional surrender of all the Confederate forces and a severe hanging of all their leaders, when propositions of this character are made, the soldiers of the third division will be willing to draw their pay, sell off their dress parade clothes and go home.

Another Union Victory!!

Official Report Not Received!!!

An intelligent contraband from Crab Orchard, who left Richmond Va., yesterday morning, states upon his honor as a nigger, that there has been a great battle on the ever quiet Potomac, which resulted in the capture of the entire Southern Confederacy.—We did not learn what amount of stores were taken, but the prisoners will pass through this place to-morrow morning at half past seven o'clock A. M. Although the report bears marks of truth on its face, we advise our readers to wait until the story is confirmed by the Cincinnati *Enquirer* before they believe it.

DIED

At the Brigade Hospital, in this place during the present week, Jerome Clark, Co A. Nicholas Shuck, Co H, and Thomas Avery, Co D, of the 22nd Wisconsin; also Albert Baker, Co. A, John W. Barrett, Co. — and Alonzo Berry, Co. C, of the 19th Michigan.

Time or space will not allow us to express our sorrow or the bereavement of the respective companies of these young men. As they left their pleasant homes but a short time since with buoyant hopes of returning to those loved ones at home, in heath, and now to be cut down, without one blow for the cherished purpose for which they came, reminds us that in the midst of life, we are in death.

GENERAL ORDER.

OFFICE PROVOST MARSHAL,
NICHOLASVILLE Dec. 4th

Whereas, Some party or parties unknown, have been in the habit of procuring Liquor, and selling or giving to soldiers, It is ordered,

That no person whatever, will sell, or in any manner dispose of Spiritous Liquors, to Citizens or Soldiers without an Order from this Office.

By Order of Commandant Post.

A. B. CRANE,
Lieut. Col. and Provost Marshal.

THE NEW YORK SUN,
Published daily, Sundays excepted,
ONE CENT PER COPY—SIX CENTS PER WEEK,
Delivered anywhere in the city or vicinity.
CIRCULATION 55,000 Copies.
When sent by mail: *Three Dollars per year*,—three months, for $1; six months $2. The postage within this State *is only seventy-eight cents a year*—out of the State, $1 56 a year. Address all letters to
MOSES S. BEACH, Proprietor of THE SUN,
Corner Fulton and Nassau sts, N. Y.

THE SUN.

NUMBER 9490. NEW YORK, FRIDAY, DECEMBER 12, 1862. PRICE ONE CENT

THE NEW YORK SUN.

FRIDAY MORNING, DEC. 12, 1862.

LATEST NEWS

BY TELEGRAPH TO THE NEW YORK SUN

FREDERICKSBURG OURS!!

100 Volunteers First cross in boats, protected by a terrible Cannonading.

They Drive Back the Rebel Sharpshooters and take 101 Prisoners.

The Bridges are then Laid, and the Army go Over.

THE REBELS FALL BACK.

40 Houses Destroyed by Fire.

Great Battle Expected To-Day.

DETAILS OF PREVIOUS OPERATIONS

Important from Nashville.

Rebels Approaching in Force.

THE ALABAMA AGAIN.

Two More Vessels Captured.

They are Robbed and Burned.

The Pirate Nearly Captured.

HOW SHE ESCAPED.

THE FIGHT FOR THE CHAMPIONSHIP

&c., &c., &c.

Later from the Army of the Potomac.—Capture of Fredericksburgh.—Great Battle to be Fought Tomorrow.

Headquarters, Thursday Evening, Nov. 11.—But little firing took place between one and three o'clock, during which time all the available batteries were placed in position. They then numbered 176 guns. At a given signal, all the batteries opened on the city. The fire was terrible, but the rebel sharpshooters could not be driven from their hiding places. The shot and shell went crashing through the houses, in many cases setting them on fire, causing a dense smoke, which, together with the explosion of so large a quantity of powder, almost hid the city from view.

It soon became evident that the bridges could not be built, except by a bold dash. Volunteers were called for to cross in small boats. The order was no sooner given than hundreds of brave fellows stepped forward; but all could not go. About 100 were selected.

They were soon on their way, while the artillery threw a perfect shower of iron hail on the opposite bank.

They reached the opposite shore, but not without loss. With fixed bayonets, they rushed upon the enemy, killing several, and taking one hundred and one prisoners, who were safely landed on this side.

At half-past four two bridges were finished opposite the city, when the troops immediately began to cross over. The enemy were now driven from the city back to their line of works.

The two bridges in front of Gen. Franklin were successfully laid early in the day, but his troops did not cross until the two upper ones were ready.

A sufficient force is now on the opposite side of the river to resist any attack that is likely to to be made.

The rebels fired but few guns in the morning, and none in the afternoon, although the works were in easy range during the forenoon.

The rebels burnt the railroad bridge just outside the city.

Between thirty and forty houses were burnt, mostly in the business part of the city.

During the day between 8,000 and 9,000 rounds of ammunition were fired by our artillery.

Everything is quiet to-night.

The indications are that a battle will be fought to-morrow.

Previous Operations.

Headquarters Army of the Potomac, Thursday Morning, 9 A. M., Dec. 11.—Everything last night was bustle and alacrity as today was the time fixed for the crossing of the river.

During the night the pontoons were conveyed to the river and the artillery of 143 pieces placed in position opposite the city.

At five o'clock this morning the rebels fired two signal guns, while during the latter part of the night rockets were frequently seen to ascend within their lines.

At five o'clock the construction of three bridges in front of the city was commenced.

When the bridges were about half completed the enemy opened a murderous fire of infantry from the houses on the river bank.

Up to this time not a shot had been fired from our side.

The engineers were driven from the bridges and several killed and wounded.

At six o'clock, General Burnside ordered all the guns to be opened on the city.

The cannonade which has continued up to the present time is terrible.

The city is on fire, and its destruction appears to be certain.

The enemy about seven o'clock this morning opened with heavy guns from their works, but so far have done no serious injury.

General Franklin constructed his bridges about three miles below the city, meeting with but slight opposition.

His troops are now crossing. The gunboats are now shelling the enemy about 15 miles down the river, where they have been concentrating their forces for the past two days.

The concentrated fire of our batteries on the city has had the effect of driving back the enemy's infantry, and the work on the bridges has again commenced.

The troops are all under arms near the river prepared to rush over as soon as the bridges are complete.

Headquarters, Thursday Noon.—On the attempt being made to finish the bridges in front of the city, the rebel infantry again opened their fire, when our artillery in position was again opened on the city, the result being that the city was fired in several new places.

The enemy have used very little artillery up to this time, as it would endanger their own men, who are holding the rear.

General Burnside has just issued an order to concentrate every available gun upon the city, under the cover of the fire of which it is believed that the bridges can be finished.

The killed and wounded, so far, do not amount to more than fifty men.

Tennessee.

Important from Nashville—A Battle Momentarily Expected.

PHILADELPHIA, Thursday, Dec. 11.

The PRESS has received the following special:

Nashville, Dec. 10—*P.M.*—The rebels under Generals Joe Johnston, Bragg, Cheatham, Forrest, and Morgan, have advanced and appeared in our front in great force this morning, driving in our pickets at every point.

A battle is momentarily expected near Hartsville. Reinforcements are being hurried forward, and every point has been strengthened. The recent rebel victory at Hartsville has greatly emboldened the rebels.

General Negley takes the field to-morrow in person.

General Mitchell will command the post at Nashville, and is rapidly organizing new troops under orders of General Rosecrans to form a reserve force to move at any moment.

The citizens are much excited over the many rumors that are being circulated on the streets, but the greatest confidence is expressed in our generals and troops, as it is now generally understood that the troops who surrendered at Hartsville were perfectly new, and became panic-stricken when they found themselves surrounded by the rebel cavalry.

The Southwest.

Gen. Grant's Advance Obstructed by the Mud—The Enemy probably Retreating towards Alabama—Vicksburg said to be Readily Accessible—The Rebels concentrating against Rosecrans.

Cairo, Dec. 10.—Reports from Gen. Grant's army indicate that our forces are brought to a stand by the muddiness of the roads, about ten miles beyond Grenada.

It is evident from the tenor of governmental despatches, that Gen. Pemberton, being wholly unable to cope with Grant in battle, has marched in retreat towards Alabama, with a view of forming a junction with the rebel forces in Tennessee.

General Grant cannot now follow him in that direction. In this case Rosecrans should be reinforced.

Gen. Hovey's movement upon Grenada was splendidly executed, but unfortunately the enemy had retreated to the Northeast, and Hovey could not cut off his retreat. It is rumored here that the Mississippi is almost clear of rebels in force, and that Vicksburg can be easily taken.

The rebels are acting as if, uncertain of any success, they would leave the Southwest to its inevitable fate, and consolidate their forces for future operations in the Gulf, or Cotton States.

The campaign so brilliantly begun by Gen. Grant has failed of giving great results at present. If Rosecrans is successful, however, all will be well.

Porter and McClernand are awaiting developments, or orders, it is hard to divine which.

The Battle of Fayetteville, Arkansas—Further Particulars.

St. Louis, Dec. 11.—Our loss in killed and wounded is now estimated at one thousand, and that of the enemy at over two thousand.

The rebels left many of their dead, and most of their wounded for us to take care of.

Extensive hospitals will be improvised in Fayetteville.

Persons returned from the battle-field represent that the enemy are twenty-eight thousand strong.

Their artillery was much crippled. We took four caissons filled with ammunition and a large number of small arms.

The enemy muffled their wheels and moved off in the night, continuing their retreat to Van Buren, and probably crossing the Arkansas river.

It was a hard-fought battle and a complete victory.

S. R. CURTIS,
Major-General Commanding.

The Alabama Again.

Two More Merchant Ships Destroyed—The Levi Starbuck and T. B. Wales Burned at Sea—The Crews Landed at Martinique and Sent Home—The Alabama Escaping to Sea from under the Guns of the San Jacinto.

We have received information of new depredations by the rebel pirate Alabama. Two more merchant ships have been captured by her and burned at sea.

The news comes by the schooner Alice, which arrived here yesterday from Point Petre (Guadaloupe,) and St. Thomas, having left the latter port on the 26th of November. She brings the chief officers and crews of the captured vessels, who make the following report:

The whale ship Levi Starbuck, of and from New Brunswick, bound to the Pacific Ocean, was captured on the 2d of November by the Alabama, when five days out, in latitude 35, 30 north, longitude 66. The pirate Captain Semmes took from the ship all the clothing of the men and the nautical instruments, and then set her on fire.

On the 8th of November, in latitude 28, 30, longitude 58, the Alabama also captured the ship T. B. Wales, Captain Lincoln, of Boston, bound from Calcutta to that port. She was one hundred and forty-seven days out, and had a full cargo of saltpetre and gunny-cloth. The Alabama took from her the valuable part of her cargo and the captain and crew, and then set her on fire.

The Alabama then proceeded to Martinique, arriving there at 8 o'clock on the morning of November 17. She landed the captains and crews of the captured ships at that place.

The United States frigate San Jacinto arrived at Martinique the same afternoon, and finding the Alabama in port immediately got under way and proceeded outside of the harbor to await her departure.

Semmes, however, was on the alert as usual, and quietly gave the San Jacinto the slip; getting under way at 10 o'clock the same night, running by her out of the harbor and escaping safely to sea.

The Alabama is, therefore, again at large, ready to prey still further upon our commerce.

STATEMENT OF THE MATE OF THE T. B. WALES.

The T. B. Wales left Calcutta on the 15th of June.

On the 8th of November, when in long. 58 deg. W., lat. 28 deg. 30 min. N., a steamer was descried at 8 o'clock A. M., which was chasing a schooner, but on sighting the ship, she hauled up and made for the latter, then about 10 miles to the leeward.

The steamer apparently crowded on all steam, and as the wind favored her, every stitch of canvass she could bear was set. A large American flag was flying from her gaff, while from the masthead signals were displayed, designating her the "American sloop of war Tuscarora."

Capt. Lincoln, glad to hear from home, hauled his courses, and when under the guns of the steamer the latter hauled down the Stars and Stripes and sent up the Stars and Bars and at the same time sent a shotted gun across the bow of the Wales.

A boat from the pirate at once shoved off, and the First Lieutenant of the latter stepped on board and ordered Capt. Lincoln on board the vessel with his papers.

He was courteously received by Captain Semmes who unfortunately laid first hold on the bill of lading for the saltpetre, which at once settled the fate of the Wales. He directed Captain Lincoln to be rowed back to his ship and to bring over the personal effects of himself and lady, also his instruments and everything of value.

This order was complied with, and Captain Lincoln, with a boat load of pirates, went back to his ship where he informed his crew of the sad affair. Every man was allowed but one bag full of clothing, while all their money fell a prey to the pirate. Captain Lincoln and Mr. Fairfield, with their families, were taken back to the Alabama, and the crew, including the first mate, Mr. Joshua Atkins, of Princetown, Mass., placed in irons.

Arrived on board the Alabama, Semmes gave the Captain and his passengers the liberty of the ship, but signified to them that he would place them in double irons if they made attempt to speak to any of the prisoners, who were confined at night on the boiler deck, close to the boilers, while in the day time they were on the forecastle.

On the first day the second mate of the Wales, Joseph Neal, an Englishman, with eight of the crew, voluntarily took the oath of allegiance to the Confederacy, and were at once placed on the books of the ship.

The prisoners, 133 in number, found on board the crew of the Levi Starbuck, numbering 28, were treated like them. The Captain of the Starbuck and his officers were also in irons among the crews.

The prisoners received no unkind words from their captors, and were fed the same as the piratical crew. Captain Semmes and his first Lieutenant were very haughty, and never spoke a word to any of the prisoners. The discipline on the Alabama is very loose, and the only men good for anything are the First and Fourth Lieutenants, both of whom alternate on deck.

A nephew of Jeff. Davis is a Lieutenant of Marines. He told them that the Alabama would never stop until every Northern vessel had been destroyed by her. The crew of the Alabama number 120 men, all told.

CAPTURE OF THE LEVI STARBUCK.

This ship left New Bedford for the Pacific Ocean on the 28th of October last. She was owned by C. B. Howland of New Bedford, and commanded by Capt. Mullen.

Everything went on pleasantly until at daybreak on the morning of the 2d ult., when in lat 35, lon 66, a propeller, under canvass, flying a large American flag, was discovered to windward, steering in the same direction as the Starbuck. On coming within range, the steamer fired a round shot from her pivot gun across the whaler's bow and ran up the stars and bars.

No resistance being possible, Capt. Mullen told his crew that they were in the clutches of the Alabama.

The steamer by this time had opened all her ports, and lowered a twelve oared boat, with a Lieutenant and a fully armed crew. The officer, stepping on board the whaler, told the Captain that he had at once to go in his own boat on board the steamer, and bring all his papers with him.

On coming on board the Alabama, Capt. Semmes glanced at the register and told the Captain "You are my prisoner and the ship is a prize to the Confederate steamer Alabama. You can go on board your ship and tell your men to bring one bag of clothing with them."

Captain Mullen went back to his ship, where he informed his crew of the pirate's orders. The piratical boat's crew in the mean time had broken into the cabin and spirit room, and helped themselves to whatever they pleased, while the Lieutenant had ransacked the captain's chest, and taken therefrom all the money belonging to the ship and the captain.

The crew of the whaler, including the captain, were then heavily ironed and shipped to the Alabama, where they were left on deck.

This happened in the forenoon. After dinner orders were given to take out provisions and other necessaries, which occupied the attention of the pirates until nightfall, when the ship was fired and destroyed.

The prisoners were then sent to the lower hold for the night, and when they came up their bag of clothing had been stolen by the pirates.

The officers were civil, but the petty officers abused the unfortunate men most shamefully.

STATEMENT OF CAPT. GOODALE, OF THE ALICE.

The escape of the Alabama is explained by Capt. Goodale from the fact that the harbor of Martinique is a large bay, about three miles wide, with high mountainous shores. He also says that a cloud is always overhanging the harbor, and at times the sea washes way up to the city. No one vessel can at any time blockade such a harbor. He represents the Alabama as sailing almost entirely under canvas, and making thirteen knots per hour at that.

The Alabama had but two days coal on board, and had gone into Martinique to receive a cargo which had arrived at that port for her on an English brig. The brig also had on board two large Armstrong 100-pounders. At the time of the departure of the Alabama, the brig took her departure also. The Captain of the San Jacinto had made an agreement with the Captain of an American schooner lying in port to announce any movements on board the Alabama by sending up rockets. He followed out these instructions, and he was immediately arrested, and his vessel seized by the authorities of Martinique, who nearly unanimously sympathise with the Southern Confederacy.

Semmes was very reticent, and seldom conversed even with his officers. On one occasion, however, he became quite talkative, and boasted of his captures, and said he knew the value of his prizes, as he always swore the captains to the exact value of their cargoes and vessels. He prided himself in *having once been within seventy miles of Sandy Hook.* Semmes, it was also said, made considerable money out of the captures. He generally made the searches in person, appropriating the quadrants, mails, money and all other valuables that are easily moveable, to himself. After all has been removed from the vessel, that is of any value, the cabins are stove in, and the fire started in the cabins, generally at night, and when the flames are under full headway, so that there is no possibility of a failure, the pirate vessel moves off. The scene of the vessels as they are thus in flames is described as awfully grand, the heavens being lighted up for miles. The Alabama is reported as very flat and exceedingly light, a large part of her wood work being composed of pine. It was also said that the officers of the Alabama had stated that they were expecting to be soon joined by one or more vessels, to pursue the same business, one of which would pay its attention to the Pacific track.

The parting salute to every vessel now as it leaves any of the West Indies ports, is "Look out for the Alabama!"

When at Martinique the first officer of the San Jacinto offered to the captain to run into the harbor, and either run down or engage the Alabama, but the latter refused. Thereupon the lieutenant begged of the captain to go on shore for a few hours, when he would do so on his own responsibility, but the captain refused to accede to his request.

THE SAN JACINTO.

This is the vessel on board which Capt. Wilkes overhauled the Trent. She is slow, and cannot make over seven miles an hour, generally. She is a first-class screw steam sloop of the old navy, was built at the navy yard at Brooklyn in 1850, and was attached to the squadron in China which attacked the barrier forts.

THE PRESENT COMMANDER OF THE SAN JACINTO.

Commander William Ronckendorff is captain of the San Jacinto. He is a native of the city of Philadelphia, and belongs to the old navy. He is very well known in the service as a rigid temperance man, always being an opponent of the grog ration. It is said that he never tasted a drop of liquor in his life. In manner he is of the "fair and easy" sort. He entered the service on the 17th of February, 1832, and has consequently been thirty years an officer. He has been eighteen years at sea, and was four years and ten months unemployed. His service record embraces adventures on every station, and his character is highly esteemed, but all concede that he is no match for Semmes and his man Friday, Lieutenant Maffit.

WHO CAPTAIN SEMMES IS, OF THE ALABAMA.

He was a midshipman on board the old Lexington, and commanded the brig Somers. The energy and pluck of Semmes always commanded respect. He can beat any steamer in the navy, if his vessel has the speed that report says. Apprehensions are felt that he may obtain some of our signal books, which would enable him to coal beside one of our naval vessels in a foreign port, if none of our officers there knew him. In this city a first-class private house is occupied by a near female relative of the dashing pirate, and it is said that one of his children, who is now being educated in Baltimore, had her father's daguerreotype recently copied in Broadway, that his admirers might have souvenirs of him. There are three or four members of his family in Brooklyn, all in respectable positions.

HIS RIGHT HAND MAN.

Semmes is not a whit a greater dare-devil than John N. Maffit, who is reported to be his second in command. Maffit is an Irishman, whose father was the noted clergyman, which John, on more than one occasion, declared to be "the meanest profession under the sun." He is personally brave, even to rashness, and is a very able seaman.

GREAT VICTORY IN VIRGINIA.

CAPTURE OF FREDERICKSBURGH.

Our Troops cross the River under heavy fire, drive back the Rebels at the point of the bayonet, and gallantly hold the City in front of the enemy.

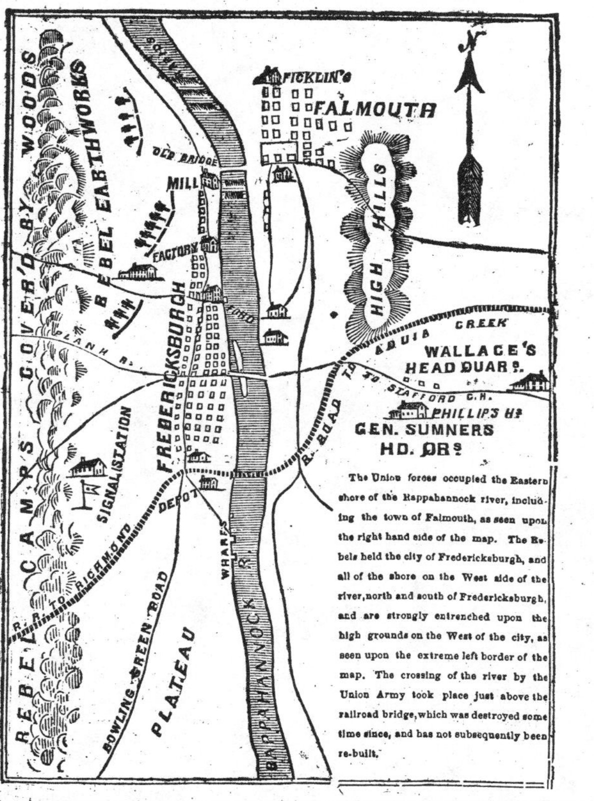

The Union forces occupied the Eastern shore of the Rappahannock river, including the town of Falmouth, as seen upon the right hand side of the map. The Rebels held the city of Fredericksburgh, and all of the shore on the West side of the river, north and south of Fredericksburgh, and are strongly entrenched upon the high grounds on the West of the city, as seen upon the extreme left border of the map. The crossing of the river by the Union Army took place just above the railroad bridge, which was destroyed some time since, and has not subsequently been re-built.

The Condemned Indians.

Message from the President about the Indians—What Examinations have been made, and the Results—Those who Outraged Females only two in number—Those engaged in Massacres, forty—Their Sentence.

The President to-day sent the following message:

"*To the Senate of the United States:* In compliance with your resolution of inquiry, I state that on the 8th day of November last I received a long telegraphic dispatch from Major-General Pope at St. Paul, Minnesota, simply announcing the names of the persons sentenced to be hanged. I immediately telegraphed to have transcripts of the records in all the cases forwarded to me, which transcripts, however, did not reach me until two or three days before the present meeting of Congress. Meantime I received dispatches and otherwise, appeals in behalf of the condemned, appeals for their execution, and expressions of opinion as to the proper policy in regard to them and the Indians generally in that vicinity, none of which, as I understand, fall within the scope of your inquiry.

After the arrival of the transcripts of records, but before I had sufficient opportunity to examine them I received a joint letter from one of the Senators and both of the Representatives from Minnesota, which contains some statements of facts not found in the records of the trials. I enclose a printed memorial of the citizens of St. Paul, addressed to me, and forwarded with the letter aforesaid. Anxious to not act with so much clemency as to encourage another outbreak on the one hand, nor with so much severity as to be really cruel on the other, I caused a careful examination of the records of the trials to be made, first ordering the execution of such as had been proved guilty of violating females. Contrary to my expectations, only two of this class were found. I then directed a further examination and a classification of all who were proven to have participated in massacres as distinguished from participation in battles. This class numbered forty, and included two convicted of female violation. One of the number is strongly recommended to the Commission which tried him for commutation to ten years' imprisonment. I have ordered the other thirty-nine to be executed on Friday, the 19th instant. The order was dispatched from here on Monday, the 8th instant, by a messenger to General Sibley. This is as full and complete a response to the resolution as it is in my power to make.

[Signed], ABRAHAM LINCOLN.

From Washington.

The Admission of Western Virginia—Steps for Immediate Abolition of Slavery in Missouri.

Washington, Dec. 11.—The bill which has passed the House of Representatives and the Senate providing for the admission of the State of Western Virginia into the Union, is not likely to be immediately and definitely acted upon by President Lincoln, the erection of the new state being of so much importance, in connection with the constitutional question.

Mr. Noell, of Missouri, has prepared a bill which he will introduce in the House, to submit the propositions of President Lincoln to the State of Missouri, that upon the adoption by that state of a system for the immediate abolishment of slavery therein, to take effect on or before the first day of January, 1864, the United States will provide for the compensation to loyal owners of the slaves therein, to the extent of twenty millions of dollars in United States bonds redeemable in thirty years, and will remove to some place out of the United States and colonize such of the emancipated slaves as shall elect to leave the state.

Congressional Proceedings.

SENATE.

Washington, Dec. 12.—Petitions in favor of a General Bankrupt Act were presented. Inquiries were ordered as to admitting burnt cotton free. A debate took place upon the subject of arbitrary arrests, which were freely denounced by many of the Senators, and upheld by prominent supporters of the administration. During the discussion Mr. Powell, of Kentucky, who had been alluded to in unsparing terms by some of the members, as saying nothing to uphold the country, while rejoicing in the success of the "lion-hearted democracy" at the late elections, significantly gave notice that any objections to his remarks he was ready to settle in any other locality beside the Senate Chamber. The general expression of debate was that the late elections had been a rebuke to the system of arbitrary arrests, now brought before Congress in the case of Delaware.

HOUSE OF REPRESENTATIVES.

The Speaker laid before the House a message recommending that John L. Worden receive the thanks of Congress for his gallant conduct on the Monitor in combat with the Merrimac, such thanks being necessary under the law to advance him one grade in the naval list of officers in the Navy. Referred.

Mr. Fenton offered the following new law: That the Secretary of the Navy be directed, if the exigencies of the public service will admit of it, to convoy in safety from the attack of the rebel cruiser Alabama, or any other pirate vessel, any ship or ships that shall contain corn, flour, and other provisions intended as a free offering by the citizens of the United States to the starving poor of England.

Mr. Cox reported back the Senate bill for the relief of the French bark Jules et Marie. It appropriates $9,500 as full compensation for damages received in the collision between the vessel and the United States steamer San Jacinto in November last, the fault being in the latter, which failed to reverse her engines.

The bill passed.

Mr. Roscoe Conkling asked leave to report a bill to establish a uniform system of bankruptcy.

Mr. Wickliffe offered a resolution, calling on the Secretary of War to state what number of soldiers, regulars and volunteers, have been placed on the army roll; what regiments have been paid up to the first of December, 1862; what regiments remain unpaid, and how long they have been without pay; whether the money appropriated by Congress for their pay, clothing and subsistence has been spent for any other purposes.

Mr. Yeaman offered the following, to lie over for future consideration:

Resolved, By the House of Representatives [the Senate concurring], that the proclamation of the President, of the 22d of December, 1862, is not warranted by the Constitution.

Resolved, That the policy of emancipation as indicated in the proclamation is not calculated to hasten the restoration of peace, is not well chosen as a war measure, and is an assumption of power dangerous to the rights of citizens, and the perpetuity of a free government.

Mr. Lovejoy moved to lay the resolutions on the table. Carried by a vote of 94 against 45.

The House then went into Committee of the Whole on the President's message.

A debate ensued upon the message, in which Mr. Menzies participated among the speakers, and recapitulated the means adopted by the Republicans, including the abolition of slavery and the emancipation act, which he said were shocking to the civilization of the age. The course of the Administration in illegally imprisoning American citizens in Northern prisons had given the rebellion increased confidence of success. The recent elections, however, were more appalling to the rebels than anything that could happen. Because a free people who will not submit to the tyranny at Washington, will not submit to the overthrow of the Constitution by the rebels. In conclusion, he earnestly reprobated the guilty leaders in the rebellion, while at the same time he insisted that the Abolitionists had done great mischief, and retarded its suppression. Adjourned to Monday.

From North Carolina—Message of Gov. Vance.

Newbern, N. C. Dec. 8.—The message of Governor Vance betrays nothing like Union sentiment, but appeals to "that stern and determined devotion to our (the rebel) cause, which can alone sustain a revolution." He reflects severely upon the Confederate conscript law, alludes to the "violent and law-defying tendencies of the times," and to the frequency of "murder, arson, disregard of obligations, oppression and injustice," strongly denounces the suspension of the writ of *habeas corpus*, and says that he is "unwilling to see such powers entrusted to any living man." He likewise objects to the distillation of grain, and the diversion of the school fund to war purposes.

The Raleigh STANDARD says:

"A gentleman of this State who has lately escaped from the Yankee lines informs us that while North he understood that the collection of forces at Suffolk and Newbern by the enemy was designed advance upon Weldon, Goldsboro' and Raleigh, to also says that the taking of Wilmington is in the programme.

Information received at Head quarters disclose the "fact that a powerful reaction against the war is progressing in the interior. Letters from all classes of people intercepted by the capture of rebel mails, indicate a universal prayer for peace."

Address of the French Christian Evangelical Alliance to the Christian Churches of America.

Washington, Dec. 10.—The French Evangelical Alliance, having met at Genoa, Oct. 29th, 1862, have issued an address to the Evangelical denominations of the United States, setting forth to their well-beloved brethren in America, that when one of the members suffered they all suffer with him, and that this is their experience in regard to the misfortunes which have befallen our land. In reference to the great question which has occasioned these troubles, the French Alliance would belie itself if it should interdict itself from protesting against the great evils which dishonor the Gospel. It could not remain indifferent when, in an age in which universal conscience disapproves of slavery, in which all the countries of Europe, with the exception of Spain, have abolished it at the price of great sacrifices, and in which Russia has just, by an admirable effort, emancipated thirty-five millions of serfs, we find Protestant divines attempting to justify that institution by the Bible, and causing an atrocious war to maintain the bondage of an unfortunate race. It feels itself directly attacked in the faith which it professed when it witnesses so monstrous a spectacle as that of a Confederacy, which boasts of being evangelical, and which relies upon slavery as upon the *corner stone rejected by men, but precious in the eyes of God.* The evangelical alliance would no longer be the great association of brotherly love, if it forgot those hundreds of thousands of brothers in Jesus Christ, who are still sold in the South, like common cattle, branded with the red-hot iron, and who frequently perish under the lash of pitiless overseers.

It is enough to say to you, Christian Evangelists of the United States, that without desiring to enter into questions of nationality, birth-place, and of constitution, which are outside of our sphere, we can assure you that you have our warmest sympathies. If you have to suffer, it is for a great and glorious cause, for that which has let loose upon your people all the evils of war, is the first step to resistance to the extension of slavery. We have received with thanksgivings the measures which have already been taken to destroy that odious institution. All the advances which you shall make to that end will bring you nearer to the termination of your sufferings. If God permits all this horrible carnage, it is, doubtless, in order to deliver America of an evil which is more hideous than war, because it is permanent and poisons more completely the Springs of life of a people; and whatever may be the price which the extirpation of this scourge may have cost you, you will feel that such a benefit could not be too dear at any price.

In the name of the Evangelical Alliance at Paris,
The President, WILLIAM MONOD.
The Secretary, G. FISCH.

Paris, 30th October, 1862.

A WEEKLY EDITION

of THE NEW YORK SUN, issued every Tuesday, in wrappers for the mail. TWO CENTS EACH, $1 per 100.

SUBSCRIPTIONS—PAID IN ADVANCE.

One copy, 1 year. .75cts. | Three copies, 1 year, $2 00
Do. 16 months, $1 00 | Five copies, do $3 00
Specimen copies, gratis. Discount of 20 per cent. from single rate, on each copy over five.
Postage within New York State, *only thirteen cents a year*—out of the State, *twenty-six cents.*
Address M. S. BEACH, SUN OFFICE, NEW YORK

The Great English Fight for the Championship—Full Details from Bell's Life in London—The Rounds Described—Immense Excitement among the Sports—Their Calculations Upset, and their Pockets turned inside out, by the Result.

BELL'S LIFE IN LONDON gives the following details of the fight for the championship and £400, which came off in England on the 26th of November:

Soon after eight o'clock A. M. all was in readiness for the fray. Mace being the first to drop his castor within the ropes. He was attended by his old opponents Bob Brettle and Bob Travers, while King, who was somewhat behindhand, was waited on by Bos Tyler and Macdonald. Both men were welcomed with loud cheers from their partisans, which each acknowledged in a suitable manner. There was a good deal of brisk betting at 6 and 7 to 4 on Mace, and his backers, we believe, would have gone on to any extent at that figure. Among the spectators were Tom Sayers, Heenan, and many other fistic celebrities, who eyed the tourney throughout with curiosity; but whether they witnessed anything to induce any of them once again to tempt fortune remains to be proved.

THE FIGHT.

Round 1. The moment so fraught with interest and excitement to the partisans of the belligerents had now arrived; the busy and careful work of the seconds was at last completed to their entire satisfaction, and the men were delivered at the scratch. While their toilettes were being arranged, the "make ready" had been eagerly watched by all with almost breathless silence. As Jem turned to face his opponent, he gave a momentary glance at the sky, whose dull, cheerless aspect was anything but calculated to enliven the combatants. Both advanced to the scratch with that firm, confident step which denotes the action of well drilled practitioners. The moment they had met the right mawley was extended with manly frankness, and now there came that gripping of the hand which is so pleasing to witness. The customary salutation completed, the seconds retired to their respective corners, so that the belligerents were left to themselves. Perhaps the first thing that riveted the attention of the spectators, as the men stood front to front was the striking difference in height, which existed between them. It had been confidently stated Mace had never been in better condition, and certainly as he stood thus confronting his antagonist there was nothing in his appearance that even the most fastidious could for a moment find fault with, and in all things he looked a far superior man to what he did at their former meeting. In weight, Jem, when he last poised the beam, pulled down 11st 4lb, and, with inward confidence beaming in his very look, he stated that it was impossible for a man to feel better; and this assurance, there can be no doubt, had great weight with his admirers, many of whom, from over-caution, had waited for this "opinion" from Mace himself before they had ventured to "put it on." Jem is unquestionably a fine-made fellow about the chest and loins, and possesses plenty of wear and tear. If condition of itself could alone endow a man with the requisite "resin" to tune the first fiddle in such a grand pugilistic overture, Tom might well put the thing down as a "certainty," for it must be admitted he was all the most critical could desire, and spoke of the result with a confidence devoid of anything in the shape of braggadocio. The moment the men had been "set" by their seconds, there was perceptible that twitch and shrug of the shoulders which denote a disapproval of the morning air. After a little sparring, Mace drew from range and dropped his mawleys, and then with his right rubbed his breast and arms. King imitated this action, as he felt numbed about the arms, and thought it necessary to do the burnishing to promote the circulation. Jem, with a cautious step, drew into range, and then by way of a feeler slightly let go the left, but Tom, who was decidedly quicker on his pins than we had found him in any of his preceding battles, got well away with the back step, thus showing that these efforts of his opponent to draw out his guard were not likely to be at all successful. As Mace broke for the purpose of getting from distance, King dashed at him in a most impetuous manner, and missed administering a fine right-handed shot from the fore-arm. Mace, as Tom came on for the purpose of forcing the fighting, retreated, but when just opposite the referee and umpire the men closed, when Jem finding he was likely to get in an awkward position, ducked his head, and went down, King looking at him.

2. After they had toed the mark, Jem drew back, and, after again just rubbing his hands, folded his arms on his breast. Tom also dropped his mawleys, and thus, both being completely from range, stood eyeing each other like two gamecocks. Mace, thinking that active measures would be immeasurably more advantageous than delay, now led the left, but did not get it home, as King got well from range. Tom now came dashing at his man in an impetuous manner, and delivered the left on the top part of the pimple, and put in another from the fore-arm on the kisser, which had the effect of producing a slight show of the crimson, so that, as on the former occasion, Tom won the first of the leading points, as *first blood* was claimed by his seconds and admitted. Jem, after getting home slightly from the half-arm, with the left and right on the dial, closed with his man, when, finding he was likely to get into an awkward position, he slipped from his antagonist and again got down. There was, as the combatants were on the instant covered by their seconds, a deal of excitement round the ring, which was put an end to by the ring keepers.

3. Jem was the first to rise from his corner. King went dashing at his man, for the purpose of forcing the fighting, and, getting partly over Jem's right cross guard, planted the left on the right

(*Continued on Fourth Page.*)

On the Fourth Page, will appear to-day, all Important News received at this office, after Two O'Clock, A. M.

DEATHS.

DONOVAN—On Thursday, Dec. 11, Daniel Donovan, aged 32 years.

His friends, and those of the family, are respectfully invited to attend the funeral, this (Friday) afternoon, 12th inst, at 2 o'clock, from his late residence, 293 Tenth ave, cor. Ave. A, to Calvary Cemetery. 170

IVERS—On Thursday, Dec 11, Geo. H. Ivers, of the City and County of Limerick, Ireland, in the 45th year of his age.

The relatives and friends of the family are respectfully invited to attend the funeral, on Saturday afternoon, Dec. 13, at 1 o'clock, from his late residence, 186 Henry st, New York. Limerick (Ireland) papers please copy. 168

McBARRON—On Thursday, Dec. 11, Patrick McBarron, a native of the Parish of Clenish, County Fermanagh, Ireland, aged 92 years.

The relatives and friends of the family are respectfully invited to attend the funeral, on Saturday afternoon, 13th inst., at 2 o'clock precisely, from his late residence, 27 Market st, 171

THE NEW YORK HERALD.

WHOLE NO. 9590. NEW YORK, TUESDAY, DECEMBER 16, 1862. PRICE THREE CENTS.

THE BATTLE AT FREDERICKSBURG.

Topographical Map of the Seat of War on the Rappahannock, from a Recent Survey---The Position of the Rebel Batteries on the Hills South of Fredericksburg.

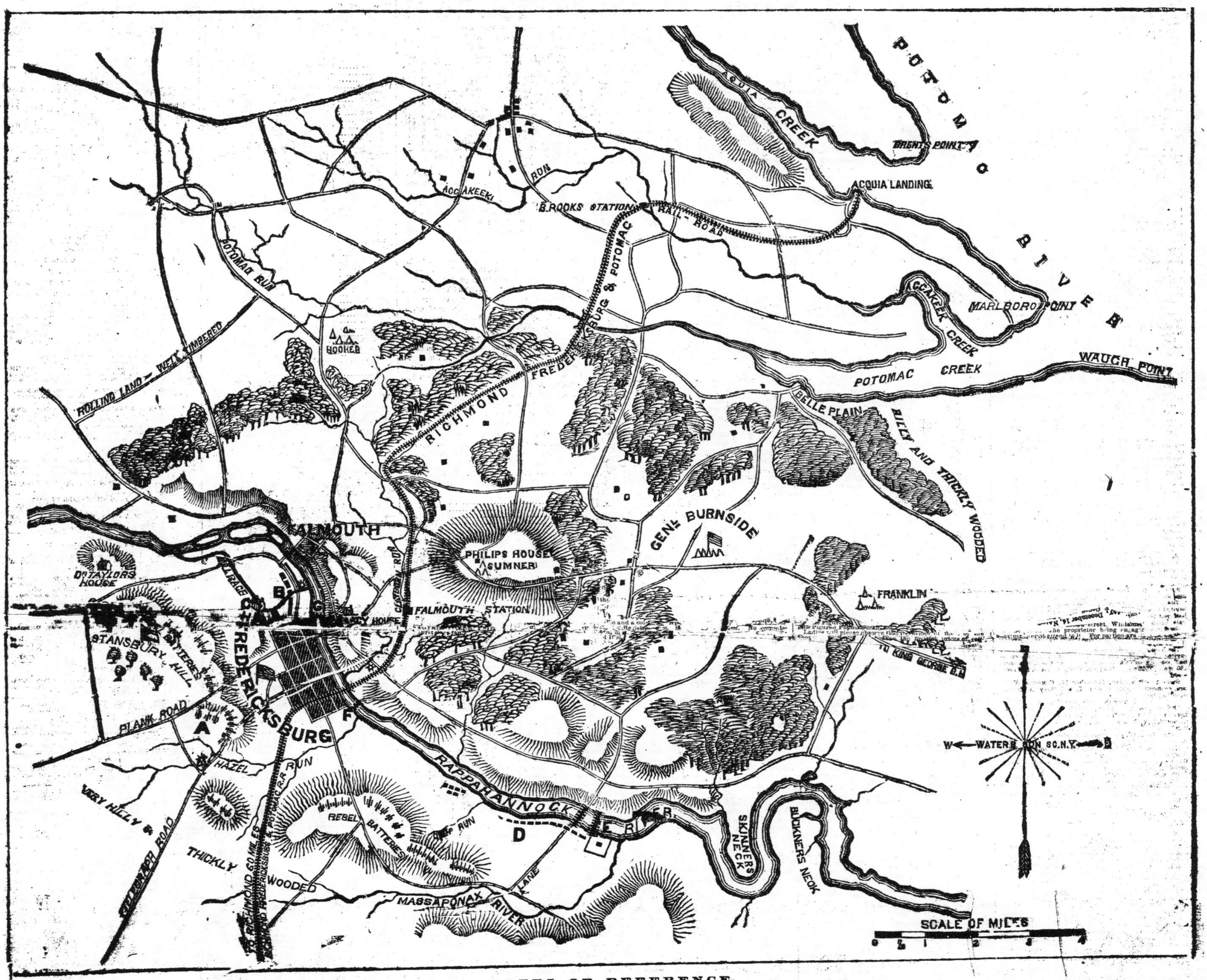

NOTES OF REFERENCE.

A—Rebel batteries. Long swivel guns, eight-inch rifles. The rest are field pieces (about twelve-pounders). B—Rebel rifle pits. C—Paper mill. D—Rebel rifle pits. E—Bridges over which Franklin crossed. F—Bridges over which Hooker crossed. G—Bridges over which Sumner crossed. H—Monument to Washington's mother.

THE RAPPAHANNOCK.

The Very Latest from Burnside's Army.

NO BATTLE YESTERDAY

More or Less Artillery Firing on Both Sides.

Seven Hundred Rebels Taken Prisoners.

The Wounded Removed from Fredericksburg.

Threatened Attack on Franklin's Forces.

Additional Accounts of Saturday's Battle.

THE BODY OF GENERAL BAYARD.

THE KILLED AND WOUNDED, &c., &c., &c.

HEADQUARTERS, ARMY OF POTOMAC, Dec. 15—11 A. M.

There was considerable firing yesterday between the advanced troops of the two armies.

At one time the rebels showed a disposition to move upon General Franklin's forces.

Occasionally the rebels would throw a few shell among our troops, just to remind us that they were still there.

With these exceptions everything was quiet.

There is some skirmishing this morning, with considerable artillery firing.

The body of General Bayard left for Washington to-day. He was to have been married next Wednesday.

HEADQUARTERS, ARMY OF THE POTOMAC, Dec. 15—P. M.

The weather to-day has been clear and warm, with a strong southerly wind. The roads are in very good condition.

The position of the two armies remains nearly the same.

There was not much artillery firing this afternoon by either party. Those shots the rebels did fire were thrown into the city.

The enemy, who are in plain view, are not idle, but busily employed in strengthening their position.

Most of the wounded to-day were removed from the city to this side of the river, as on the renewal of the battle the rebel guns would likely cause its destruction.

Over seven hundred prisoners have been taken since our army crossed the river.

THE BATTLE OF SATURDAY.

FREDERICKSBURG, Va. Dec. 14, 1862.

The battle of yesterday was one of the most severely and desperately contested of the whole war. It raged fiercely throughout the entire day, and even after darkness had shrouded the field it was kept up with a determination on both side, which seemed as though it was likely to last until one army or the other had become so exhausted as to be unable to maintain the fight any longer.

THE RIGHT AND CENTRE UNDER SUMNER.

The fighting on our immediate front and right and beyond Fredericksburg was carried on by General Sumner's grand division, comprising the Second and Ninth army corps. Shortly after nine o'clock the Second corps, General Couch, which constituted the right of the attacking forces, moved out from the upper part of the city between the plank road and westerly outskirts, with strong detachments of skirmishers. The enemy yielded gradually, though they contested our progress with great stubbornness, and for some time the rattle of musketry was incessant.

ARTILLERY FIGHTING.

At the same time that this movement was commenced the batteries of the division stationed on the bluffs across the river opened with shell to aid the exit of the rebels and cover our advance. The rebel infantry having fallen back to their first line of intrenchments and rifle pits, their batteries opened with a vigorous and rapid fire upon our columns, which now had come to a temporary halt, awaiting the result of the artillery fighting. For some time our artillery on the bluffs kept up a heavy fire upon the rebel batteries with such success that the batteries on Taylor's Hill, nearly opposite Falmouth, and commanding our right flank, were finally silenced. During this time the artillery of the rebels was almost entirely devoted to the shelling of our advanced troops. Occasionally they would send a shot towards out batteries, but they fell short or lodged in the town beyond.

HANCOCK IN THE ADVANCE.

Hancock's division had the advance, supported by the other divisions of the corps; while the Ninth corps, Gen. Wilcox, remained under arms in town, in readiness to obey the signal to advance to the assistance and support of their comrades wherever they could effectually do so. Soon after the whole corps deployed into line of battle, with Hancock's division on the right, and in this order moved forward to attack and storm the rebel right batteries, while from all the enemy's works a terrible shower of shell, grape and shrapnel tore through their bleeding ranks, notwithstanding which they steadily pushed on to the rifle pits, within a short distance of the first line of intrenchments. From the former they drove the rebels, making prisoners of some, while the remainder rook refuge behind the earthworks. This was accomplished after the most heroic and long continued efforts, under a galling and murderous fire. Human nature was unable to hold out against the terrible fire which they new encountered, and they finally retired, but in good order, carrying away with them their wounded comrades. They fell back to their original line of pickets, thus holding the ground which they first occupied, and which they held until this morning, when they were relieved by General Stoneman's command.

FRANKLIN ON THE LEFT—SUMNER JOINS HIM.

Just previous to the advance of Couch's corps, heavy firing and a dense smoke on the left indicated the fact that Franklin, with his grand divisions, was advancing upon and had already engaged the enemy's right flank. To open communication with him, therefore, Gen. Wilcox detached his division under Gen. Burns and sent it to the left by the edge of the river, with instructions to advance under cover of the river bank until he could place himself in close proximity to Gen. Franklin's right. General Burns accordingly moved his division forward, crossed Hazel run and took position with his left resting on Deep run, to the opposite bank of which General Franklin's right extended. From this location he was also enabled to support, if necessary, any demonstration having for its field of operations the space of ground between Deep run and Couch's corps, and though the division did not take part in the day's engagement, it rendered valuable assistance otherwise.

GEN. STURGIS' DIVISION JOINS COUCH—GEN. FERRERO.

About noon Gen. Sturgis was ordered to the support of Gen. Couch. So, forming his division with Gen. Ferrero's brigade in the advance, he moved obliquely with and on the left flank of Gen. Couch, with the intention of attacking the batteries which had been enfilading Conch's from the right centre of the rebel position. He opened the attack with General Ferrero's brigade, which deployed into line of battle parallel to the enemy's works, with General Nagle's brigade formed in the rear, and within easy supporting distance. General Ferrero then advanced, pouring in terrific vollies of musketry, and driving the rebels back. To retard this movement the rebels opened a raking fire upon his left flank, upon discovering which General Sturges ordered Nagle's Brigade to advance by the left flank, and forming into line of battle attack the enemy's battery on the left. The movement was accordingly attempted; but, in consequence of ravines which it was injudicious to leave in their rear, General Nagle was unable to carry out the order, and he then fell back to the direct support of General Ferrero. Couch's corps was falling back while this was transpiring, and by the time General Nagles had resumed his original position, was nearly off the field, leaving Sturgis alone in the advance. and upon his command the enemy now concentrated almost their entire force, and the fight now became one of the most desperate character.

THE CHARGE—THE HILL CARRIED.

Despite the storm of missiles from the numerous rebel works, Gen. Ferrero continued to advance, supported now also by Dickerson's battery, which was disabled in fifteen minutes after coming into action, when its place was relieved by another battery. At last, by a dashing charge, the brigade carried the crest of the hill, and approached within eighty paces of the enemy's intrenchments. Their success, however, was not of long continuance, as the tremendous fire from the rebel batteries soon rendered it necessary for them to retire, which they did when the order to do so had been given for the third time. It was now dark and the division fell back to its original position, after being six hours under fire. Gen. Sturgis' division may be said to have borne the brunt of the fighting on the part of the Ninth corps, and behaved most splendidly throughout the whole affair. When Stugis was most warmly engaged, the third division under General Getty, advanced to his support executing a movement to his left similar to that which he was making in relation to General Couch. After occupying for some time the position first indicated by the order from General Wilcox, the division was formed for an attack on the right rebel batteries, which had been enfilading the ranks of General Sturgis; and to the accomplishment of this particular object Colonel Hawkins' brigade, with Edwards' and the Fifth Massachusetts battery, was particularly assigned, while the Second brigade, under Colonel Harlan, formed in the rear as a reserve support.

THE CHARGE OF HAWKINS' BRIGADE.

The order having been given to charge those batteries, Colonel Hawkins' brigade dashed forward, and, in ascending the slope, were compelled to cross an old canal and a deep slough. Passing these, they found themselves on a level piece of ground, on reaching which darkness had overtaken them. Notwithstanding the obscurity of the night they maintained themselves against the rebel battery until they were ordered to fall back. A straggling, scattering fire on both sides was maintained until about eight o'clock, when both parties ceased for the night.

WHAT FRANKLIN DID.

On the left, which extended for some three miles below the city, General Franklin's grand division were actively engaged in sustaining the fortunes of the day. A portion of this division crossed on Thursday evening, and the remainder crossed on Friday. About [illegible] nine o'clock the order was given to advance, and [illegible] day pushed forward cautiously. The skirmishers [illegible] in a corn field, and the rebels immediately opened with artillery in the field. The [illegible] were making an effort to turn our left flank, when [illegible] artillery on the left of Franklin's position was spee[illegible] wheeled into position and opened upon the enemy. The cannonading was for a time very severe on both sides, while the sharpshooters were at work in a very lively manner in front. Our artillery on the other side of the river also opened upon them, and they [illegible] soon convinced of the uselessness of their efforts.

A GENERAL ADVANCE ORDERED.

About twelve o'clock there was an order for a general advance along the whole line. The enemy occupied a line of elevated land mostly wooded, but in some places cleared and extended in a semi-circular form, near the river below, around to Fredericksburg above, giving him an enfilading fire on the whole field, and making a line of battle at least six miles in extent. The rebel batteries were on the crest of the rising ground, well supported by infantry. General Stoneman's corps were at this time crossing the river to support the movement on the left. The batteries on both sides now blazed away with fearful fury. Doubleday on the left flank, close to the river, advanced his lines gradually, meeting with but [illegible] opposition. At one o'clock the divisions of General Meade and Gibbons advanced, under cover of our artillery. They went forward in splendid style, with colors flying. They soon became actively engaged in the wo[illegible] at the foot of the range of hills, while from near whe[illegible] their artillery was planted on the crest an additional in[illegible] fantry fire was poured into our men. Both divisions however, advanced to the woods, and a number of prisoners, hundred or more, were captured by them. The fire of artillery and musketry was incessant at this time. Presently, however, a fresh and more vigorous fire bu[illegible] forth from the woods on the Pennsylvania reser[illegible] throwing nearly the whole of that division into confusion and disorder. This emboldened the rebels, and they continued to advance, meeting with not much opposition from those troops. Their officers tried to rally them, but without much success. Gen. Jackson, commanding one of the brigades, was killed by a musket ball, which struck him in the head, while endeavoring to rally his men. His body was left upon the field, together with that of his Adjutant, Capt. Sweringen. This unfortuna[illegible]

[CONTINUED ON EIGHTH PAGE.]

Daily Mississippian.

F. T. COOPER, Editor.

THURSDAY MORNING.

JACKSON, - - DECEMBER 18, 1862.

☞ We are informed by Hon. A. J. Gillespie, Auditor of Public Accounts, that all the $5,000,000 of cotton notes hare been issued.

Accident on Southern Railroad.—The passenger train which left here Wednesday morning when within eight miles of Vicksburg, ran off the track. Two of the cars were upset and fell over an embankment of a great height causing twenty-five persons to be very badly injured, and four seriously.

☞ The passenger train on the Mobile & Ohio Railroad was fired into on Monday last, near Okalona, by an advance of the enemy's cavalry. Fortunately none of the passengers were hurt. It was the purpose of the marauders to capture the train, but it darted by them. Several members of the Legislature were aboard.

It is said the enemy are advancing in considerable force down the Mobile & Ohio Railroad. It seems they intend to girdle us around from every accessible point.

THE LEGISLATURE.

Both Houses of this body met yesterday, at 12. M. Upon a call of the roll it appeared there was not a quorum in either branch. We think, however, it is probable absent members have since arrived enough to constitute a quorum, and we trust the Legislature will go vigorously and harmoniously to work in the great business before it.

The objects set forth in the brief proclamation of the Governor will of course be considered among the most prominent topics for legislation. These can be soon dispensed with, although it requires much thought and care to devise a military system which will meet the extraordinary and perilous exigencies of our State. From our intercourse with the members we are happy to state that they all seem to be profoundly sensible of the great responsibilities resting upon their shoulders in this solemn crisis, and as far as we know there is not a dissenting voice among them in regard to the imperative necessity of calling forth the entire strength of the State to hurl against the fiendish invaders who are now devastating one of the fairest portions of our State. As to matters of detail, there is, of course, much difference of opinion.

The plan suggested by this journal for meeting the emergency is brief and simple. It is—first, to repeal all exemption laws; secondly, to constitute every able-bodied man in the State, whatever his age or profession, a militia man. It is not proposed, however, to destroy, at one blow, the agricultural facilities of the State. It is as necessary to look to that interest as to the army itself. But as we are in the midst of a terrible war, suffering all the horrors, privations and menaces of a fierce invasion, it behooves us to imitate the example set by the French people under similar circumstances, and constitute the State into one vast military encampment, make every man subject to military duty—and, for the promotion of agricultural and other pursuits necessary to the maintenance of the common cause, and the comfort of the army and the safety of women and children, a sufficient number of details can be made. By the adoption of such a policy the patriotic and self-sacrificing would be encouraged, the extortioner would be strangled, and the laggard lashed into a performance of his duty. There could be no shirking. With a common cause to fight for, a solemn determination to defend our rights to the last extremity, victory would be sure to perch upon our banners.

We again urge upon the Legislature the importance of ridding the State of the shinplaster nuisances, which set upon the people like grim nightmares. There is, we believe, almost a universal desire to see this abominable currency thoroughly squelched. Let stringent laws, prohibiting not only their issuance, but their circulation, be passed, and to provide for the wants of trade, which will necessarily arise from their suppression, the Legislature could authorize the issuance of change bills in suitable denominations, to be redeemed as the military money is. We need a wholesome currency, and the Legislature has the power to give us such a one. A law making such a provision would be eminently salutary in every sense. It would satisfy the people, give us a uniform responsible currency, rid us of one of the greatest financial evils that ever afflicted any country, and be a source of immense profit to the State in the wear and tear and loss of bills.

The Fight at Fredericksburg.

From the telegraphic reports which we publish this morning, it appears that the result of this battle was most damaging to the enemy. Burnside, in imitation of the vulgar braggart, Gen. Pope, is reported to have made a grandiloquent speech to his army just before entering the engagement, in which he said that in the battle of Fredericksburg, he intended to crush the rebellion, and like his unfortunate predecessor, he was terribly beaten. His failure to renew the fight on Sunday is an evidence of the severe castigation inflicted upon him by Gen. Lee. We presume that Burnside will be brought to the block also. Thus they go! Lincoln is a great maker of Generals; but Stonewall Jackson and Lee unmake them about as fast as he can send them into Virginia.

The latest estimate of the casualties on the Yankee side was, 8000 killed and wounded, and 1500 prisoners. Our loss less than 1800 in killed and wounded.

The importance of this victory is incalculable. Aside from the complete demoralization which is reported by Yankee prisoners to exist after the fight, it will have an immensely cheering effect upon our fortunes in the West, where the odds has been rather against us, but where we now have reason to hope for brilliant success. Let us come up to the work before us, and all will soon be well.

☞ Three young ladies announce through the Raleigh (N. C.) Standard, that they will provide clothes for three soldiers as long as the war continues, if the soldiers whom they select will consent to marry them when the war is over.

Maj. Gen. W. W. Loring.

We feel assured that every Mississippian who is familiar with the successful military career of the General whose name heads this article, will be pleased to hear that the necessity which caused his assignment to the command of the Port Hudson District, no longer exist, and that he will assume command of the 1st corps of Gen. Pemberton's army.

There was no officer in the United States Army whose career was more eventful or whose promotion more rapid. Entering the Florida war when scarcely fourteen years of age, he rose to a Captaincy before he was sixteen, and even at that early age he displayed not only an astonishing maturity, but also that sound judgment and distinguished gallantry which has marked his career on future occasions.

At the commencement of the Mexican war, we find him a Captain in the U. S. Army, and at its termination a Brevet Colonel, having been breveted three times for great courage and distinguished services during that war. Such coolness and heroism did he display at the gates of the city of Mexico, where he lost his arm, that "Old Fuss and Feathers," who was so chary in ascribing the mead of praise to any officer, always spoke of him afterwards as "that gallant and distinguished Col. Loring."

When his State seceded, he immediately resigned his commission in the U. S. Army, and tendered his services to the land of his birth, which were readily accepted by Mr. Davis, who had an opportunity of knowing his great merit. He was appointed Brigadier General, and assigned to command in Western Virginia, where his services in that quarter are too well known to dwell upon, and in consideration of which he was made a Major General.

We have given a succinct history of Gen. Loring's past, for the benefit of those to whom he is a stranger; and in conclusion venture the affirmation that he will never forfeit the confidence of his army.

The States and the Confederate War Debt.

We notice that the Legislatures of some of the Confederate States have pledged their faith for the payment of their respective quotas of the war debt of the Confederacy. Our Legislature, in its present session, may deem it prudent to pledge the faith of Mississippi for the payment of her quota. We think if the Legislatures of all the States were to adopt this policy, it would have a decidedly wholesome effect. It will, as the Richmond Examiner believes, satisfy the country that the idea of repudiation after the war is not to be entertained, besides affording an example rich in moral influence, and indicating a close and cordial union in the members of the Confederacy.

A Short-Sighted Policy.—We concur with the Richmond Dispatch in the opinion that the reason offered by Lord John Russell for declining to unite with France in proposing an armistice to the two American belligerents, that it would be declined by the United States, and the prospect of successful mediation be still further postponed, is on its face a miserable pretext, only worthy the calibre of a mousing politician. The very moderate measure of humanity proposed by the Emperor of the French, backed by three such Powers as France, England and Russia, could have given no offense to the United States, which has already shown that it cannot afford to be offended by any European Power, even when there is real cause of offense. What is there in the proposition of an armistice to wound the sensibilities of any one? The truth is, England desires the war to be waged to its bitter end, hoping to build up her own interest upon the ruin of both parties.

A more short sighted policy it is impossible to conceive. The people of that country will never

THE MISSISSIPPI LEGISLATURE.

SENATE.

Wednesday, Dec. 17, 1862.

The hour of 12 having arrived, the Senate was called to order by the Secretary, Mr. Porter.

The President being absent, on motion of Mr. Poindexter, Mr. Gordon of Wilkinson was called to the chair.

The roll was called.

Mr. Smedes, Senator elect from Warren, appeared, presented his credentials and took his seat.

There being no quorum present, on motion of Mr. Ellett, the Senate adjourned until 10 o clock to-morrow morning.

HOUSE.

Wednesday, Dec. 17, 1862.

The House was called to order at 12 o'clock by the Speaker.

On motion of Mr. Thomas of Yazoo, the roll was called and the following members answered to their names:—Mr. Speaker—Messrs. Allen, Ba ton, Bardin, Boddie, Chandler, Clark, Deason, Denny, Dyer, Enochs, Fatheree, Fox, Graham, Harris Harper, Hicks, J. J. Hooker, H. Hooker, W. H. Johnson, Kirk, Lyle, McDonald, McLaurin, C. F. Miller, Nelson, R. Seal, Semmes, Shelly, J. M. L. Smith, Thomas, Walker, T H. Williams, and Wood—34.

The Speaker announced that there was no quorum present.

On motion of Mr. Johnson, the House adjourned until 3 o'clock this evening.

3 o'clock, P. M.

The House met pursuant to adjournment.

On motion of Mr. Bardin, the roll was called, no quorum being present, the House adjourned until 10 o'clock to-morrow morning.

The New York Herald on Lincoln's Message.

From the Herald of December 2d.

The second regular annual message of President Lincoln to the two Houses of Congress is before our readers. Embracing the official history of the most eventful, the most momentous and the most critical period of twelve months in the annals of the United States, and comprehending a variety of legislative recommendations calculated to meet the public necessities resulting from this stupendous domestic war, and looking to the paramount object of the restoration of the Union, the surpassing interest and importance of this Message will be universally recognized. And yet, upon its first appearance here, there appeared to be no public curiosity or interest in it, but a prevailing anxiety to hear the latest news from the army of General Burnside, before which even the President's Message became a secondary question.

This Message is a very remarkable document. It is marked throughout by the characteristic simplicity of style and honest and earnest patriotism of its author. If his views are presented often in the shape of rough diamonds, they are none the less diamonds because of their roughness. The great question to be considered is, how far does this message meet the exigencies of the day, the demands of the country and its hopes of retoration of the Union through the measures of this administration?

In the ontset we are assured that if the condition of our relations with other nations is less gratifying than it has usually been at former periods, it is certainly more satisfactory than a nation so unhappily distracted as we are, might have reasonably apprehended. This is a gratifying fact; and from the conciliatory and magnanimous foreign policy indicated by the President in every instance of complaint of wrongs committed in the progress of this war against the flag or subjects of a foreign power, we derive the conviction that every just cause of offense will continue to be avoided. Thus far then we are secured against European intervention.

Upon the all-important subject of the national finances, the most prominent feature of the Message is the proposition for "the organization of banking associations under a general act of Congress," to be furnished by the government with "circulating notes on the security of United States bonds deposited in the Treasury" In other words, Mr. Lincoln proposes the adoption by the federal government of the New York banking system, which experience has proved to be an excellent one, and his argument in support of it is entitled to the practical consideration of Congress. Meantime the condition of the Treasury is better, and its expenditures for the last fiscal year were much less, than has been generally conjectured. There has "been a decided improvement in the financial condition of the Post Office Department, compared with several preceding years," and the explanations of this improvement are exceedingly interesting.

The record of the operations of the war is left by the Message with the heads of the War, and Navy Departments, and to their reports we would refer the French

The Fight at Fredericksburg.

From the telegraphic reports which we publish this morning, it appears that the result of this battle was most damaging to the enemy. Burnside, in imitation of the vulgar braggart, Gen. Pope, is reported to have made a grandiloquent speech to his army just before entering the engagement, in which he said that in the battle of Fredericksburg, he intended to crush the rebellion, and like his unfortunate predecessor, he was terribly beaten. His failure to renew the fight on Sunday is an evidence of the severe castigation inflicted upon him by Gen. Lee. We presume that Burnside will be brought to the block also. Thus they go! Lincoln is a great maker of Generals; but Stonewall Jackson and Lee unmake them about as fast as he can send them into Virginia.

The latest estimate of the casualties on the Yankee side was, 8000 killed and wounded, and 1500 prisoners. Our loss less than 1800 in killed and wounded.

The importance of this victory is incalculable. Aside from the complete demoralization which is reported by Yankee prisoners to exist after the fight, it will have an immensely cheering effect upon our fortunes in the West, where the odds has been rather against us, but where we now have reason to hope for brilliant success. Let us come up to the work before us, and all will soon be well.

☞ Three young ladies announce through the Raleigh (N. C.) Standard, that they will provide clothes for three soldiers as long as the war continues, if the soldiers whom they select will consent to marry them when the war is over.

By Telegraph

Particulars of the Battle near Fredericksburg.

Our Army again Victorious.

Loss of the Enemy 8,000---Our Loss 1,800.

Burnside Changes his Base.

The Yankee Army Demoralized.

Richmond, Dec. 15.—No fighting of consequence near Fredericksburg since Saturday. The enemy yesterday sent in flag of truce to bury their dead. The evening train brings but little news. Both armies occupy their original positions. Passengers state that Gen. Maxey Gregg died this morning. Most of the wounded brought to Richmond are well cared for. Several hundred prisoners are on their way to Richmond. No confirmation of the death of Hooker.

The following official dispatch was received to-day:

Yesterday was spent by the enemy in caring for his wounded and burying his dead. He retains his position. Signed R. E. LEE.

The above is construed to signify that the guns and not the army are on the North side of the river.

Richmond, Dec. 16.—Siegel, who is reported to have joined Burnside, has not over 15,000 men, mostly new troops, raised by recent levies.

Hampton's cavalry had a skirmish with the enemy on Saturday, at Ellis' Ferry, where three hundred attempted to cross, but we drove them back and captured two prisoners.

The remains of Gen. Maxey Gregg arrived here by the 9 o'clock train last evening. His corpse will to-day continue its last journey to the capital of South Carolina.

According to statements of Yankee prisoners, on Thursday last Burnside reviewed his army, and made a famous exhortation to them. He said they were about to fight a decisive battle, which he felt confident would be the conclusion of the war, as he intended to crush the rebellion on the banks of the Rappahannock.

Richmond, 16.—The following dispatch was received by the Secretary of War this morning, as far as can be ascertained: This morning the enemy has disappeard in our immediate front, and has recrossed the Rappahannock. I presume it is meditating a passage at some other point. Signed R. E. LEE.

Richmond, 16.—Loss of the enemy in the battles of Fredericksburg, is estimated at from 4 to 6000 killed and wounded. The Confederate casualties will not exceed 1800. On the left when fighting, was severe. A South Carolina brigade suffered heavily.

Gen Gregg was killed by a minnie ball, which struck him in the side and penetrated his spine. Before he died, he said to one of his aids, tell Gov. Pickens, "if I am to die this time, I yield my life cheerfully in fighting for the independence of South Carolina."

The Washington Artillery, of New Orleans, repulsed several desperate charges of the enemy.

Our troops displayed great zeal and courage—very few stragglers.

The only general officer known to be killed on the abolition side is Gen Jackson. The number of prisoners taken is said to be 1500.

One of Burnside's staff who was captured says the reason the fight was not renewed on Sunday, was serious discontent among the Yankee officers.

It is said that not more than one tenth part of Fredericksburg was seriously injured

Gov. Letcher and a number of citizens left town yesterday, to render assistance and relief to our wounded.

The news of Burnside's change of base was received here this morning, and is construed in official circles as evidence of demoralization in the Yankee army. Others regret the movement, as a rout of the abolitionists was confidently anticipated in the event of an engagement.

Richmond, Dec. 16.—The Confederate loss in killed and wounded is less than 1800. A correspondent represents the loss of the enemy at 8,000. Burnside's army is reported to be mutinous, having postively refused, it is said, to renew the charge of the Confederate batteries.

Charleston, 16.—Two ballots for Governor of South Carolina were made by the Legislature to-day, with no result. On the first ballot, Bonham received 79, Manning, 58. On the second ballot, Bonham received 79, Manning, 63. A third ballot takes place to-morrow. P. C. J. Weston was elected Lt. Governor.

All is quiet on James Island. A large numer of transports passed going Northward.

Yankees near Milton, N. C.

Augusta, December 16th.—A private dispatch from Goldsboro' to-day, says the engineer who started for Wilmington returned, and reports the Wilmington and Weldon Railroad in the hands of the Yankees near Milton.

Destination of Gunboats.

Knoxville, December 15th.—The Washington correspondent of the Louisville Journal, says the iron clads now in York are destined for James River.

The Cincinnati Commercial says that gunboats are to ascend the Tennessee to Decatur with a large force, for the purpose of getting in Bragg's rear.

Marriage of Col. John H. Morgan.

Chattanooga, December 15th.—Colonel John H. Morgan, the distinguished guerrilla chieftain, was married last night at Murfreesboro', to Miss Mattie Ready, eldest daughter of Hon. Chas. Ready, of Tennessee.

All quiet along the Cumberland.

Camp Lovell, Grenada, Dec. 13, 1862.

Ed. Mississippian:

In a recent number of your Daily, there appeared an incorrect statement, in a letter from your correspondent "Wanderer." In mentioning the artillery engaged in the Coffeeville skirmish, he states that there was a section of Hedden's Artillery—it should have been a section of Withers' Light Artillery Regiment, Company C. Knowing your willingness to do the soldier justice, I request that you make the correction.

Yours, respectfully, H. P. TURNER,
Capt. Com'y C, Withers' Light Art. Reg.

Advance of the Enemy in North Carolina.

The Journal attaches great importance to the city of Wilmington, though it does not seem to be seriously alarmed for its safety. In its issue of the 6th, we find the following:

We still live, the reports brought by deserters to the contrary notwithstanding. We were to be attacked this week. We have not yet been attacked, and there remain but twelve hours of the week, and six of them dark.

These reports, coming from the enemy, really amount to little or nothing, and, as a rule, produce only evil to us, by keeping up a constant nervous excitement, of which, after a while, people get so tired that they are apt to run into the extreme of apathy and indifference. They will at length pay no attention to the cry of wolf, even when the wolf is a *bona fide* animal.

We beg that neither our people nor our authorities will permit themselves to become the victims of this feeling of indifference or false security. As this war progresses,—if it continues another year—we believe that the hour of trial will come to all—certainly to all of us on the seaboard, Wilmington among the first; and it will demand all the vigilance, all the firmness, all the preparation and hard fighting that each and every man can bring to its defense, to save it from the fate of its sister towns of the Pamlico and Albemarle regions, or from what appears to me to be the still harder fate of New Orleans, Nashville and Memphis And not only is Wilmington concerned, but the whole Cape Fear country, for if Wilmington falls, the whole of the valley drained by the Cape Fear and its affluents lies open to the enemy, certainly the whole of the lower valley.

AT HEAD QUARTERS.

BY T. R. W., CRESCENT ARTILLERY.

There is no quarter at Head Quarters,
Nor is the duty done by halves,
Yet 'tis pleasanter far than Infantry,
Shouldering arms wears out the calves.

My side aches, my hand is cramped,
Still orders never ceasing come,
The next order I hope will order
Us to close and all go home.

But no, the Major writes and smokes,
And as the wiffs of smoke arise,
He sees the orderly disorderly,
So he damns the orderly's eyes.

At Head Quarters I am entrenched,
(You know my fort's ever in my pen,)
We have to keep accounts all straight,
Of straight and crooked men.

I think there's much unreasonable form
About all departments national,
And Commissaries most reason have,
'Tis their business to be *rational*.

Many strange things do pass me by,
As old time doth crowd my soul,
Yet strange it is, that Quarter Masters
Are always Masters of the whole.

When soldiers go to the Pay Master
For pay, I have heard them told,
Though they were not prisoners
They'd have first to be pay-rolled.

I wish the Major 'd arise and say
'Tis high time to leave I think,
And I A. A. G and Chief of Staff,
Invite you all to take a drink.

Bad Policy of Slave Owners.

When the Federal troops entered Middle and Western Tennessee, and North Alabama, it seemed to me to be the hight of folly for the owners of slaves to keep them there to be run off by Abolitionists. Slave property is the most manageable of any in the world. The planter can retreat with as much facility as an enemy. As the enemy approaches, he can fill his wagons with provisions, load his extra mules with clothing and other necessaries, drive his cows, hogs, and other stock before him, and remove his family to some safe place where he can, in a few days, build cabins enough to make a short sojourn quite comfortable. Mississippi, Alabama, and Georgia could afford room in this way for a million of people to locate themselves in places of perfect safety. By moving in winter it would be easy to open land enough to make corn, potatoes, peas, turnips, &c. But even if no crop could be made, how much better it would be to sell one or two servants to buy provisions for the rest, than to stay and be robbed of negroes, provisions and stock, and be treated with insults by ruffians.

Another plan of providing for their safety might be adopted. In all these States, there are thousands of soldiers' families, who have small farms, that, if properly worked, would bring abundant crops, but the husbands and oldest sons are gone to the war, and from want of sufficient force, the lands lie idle. It would be easy to hire to these families at moderate prices from one to three servants each, who would thus be provided for in localities to which the enemy would never come and whose labor would thus be useful to the country, providing for tens of thousands, where now nothing is made, or only enough to feed the owners of these small farms. It would certainly be better policy to put servants on these farms for their food and clothing and taxes, than to keep them within reach of the enemy, and risk the loss of negroes themselves, and of all other property. Whole plantations have been swept in Tennessee, and North Mississippi is now suffering terribly. The first of January is coming, and the abolition policy will then be tried in all its hideous deformity. A tremendous effort will be made to crush Mississippi, which next to South Carolina, enjoys the unlimited hatred of the Abolitionists. Those who have servants in exposed localities would do well now, at this favorable time of the year, to consider what had better be done for their safety. Some have already provided against the danger in the way I have suggested. A good many servants could be hired also, to planters who have more land than their force can cultivate, and many cooks and house servants could be hired out in almost any of the towns in those counties, that from their location, are safe from the enemy. Persons having servants of this latter class, that they would hire at moderate prices, would doubtless hear of situations by advertising in the Mississippian, or the Memphis Appeal, now published in Jackson. "A word to the wise is sufficient."

J. J

Cause of the War.

[From the N. Y. Express.

The Tribune, in pithily showing the cause of the war, and that great cause to be slavery, thus sums up:

1. The rebellion has broken out only in the slave States.

[A mistake. It first broke out in Massachusetts, which nullified the Constitution of the United States and the laws of Congress in the so-called "personal bills."]

2. It commenced in South Carolina, the most intensely pro-slavery of them all, and mastered State after State, in exact proportion to their interest in and devotion to slavery.

[Another mistake! It began in Boston, in rescues from United States Marshals: in Syracuse, in the Jerry rescue case; in Milwaukee, Wisconsin, in the Booth case.]

The real facts is, that for ten years Massachusetts has not been fairly in or under the Constitution of the United States—aye, ever since the organization of the Government—from the days of the Shay's Rebellion, on to the Hartford Convention; Massachusetts has been more or less in opposition to the Constitution and laws of the United States. We have had three rebellions in Massachusetts since 1780. 1st—The Shay's Rebellion. 2d—The Embargo Rebellion. 3d—The Personal Liberty Rebellion.

Left-Handed Compliment.

In times like these the following will not be regarded as a very high compliment to the Georgia Legislature. We copy from the Columbus Sun:

In a report of the Legislative proceedings of Friday appears the following:

"A bill for the relief of Thomas Farmer of Franklin, authorizing him, in consideration of certain nervous diseases, which require the use of a good deal of whiskey—was laid on the table."

A few days previous to this, the Legislature undertook to discuss the propriety of giving some young disciple of Esculapius, a license to practice medicine. A string of resolutions were also introduced a few days ago in that august body relative to some work on primary Arithmetic which engrossed the attention of the House for several hours. The "Conscription Resolutions" reflecting upon the decision of the Supreme Court is still held up for debate, and will probably remain on hand until the day of adjournment. It will be seen from these miscellaneous proceedings that Georgia is blessed with a Legislature remarkable for its diversatility of talent, as well as a peculiar gift for *Buncombizing*. What Georgian does not feel proud of the old "Empire State," represented as it is by such an array of statesmanship and forensic ability!

A Provoking Character.—"Stonewall" Jackson seems determined to vindicate his reputation as the great bugbear of the Union army, and the Confederate leaders, knowing the terror of his name, are quite willing to use it, and even to magnify it by the confusion of our ignorence as to his whereabouts, his plans and purposes.—One day he is reported in force at Chester and Manassas Gaps; another, he is threatening Harper's Ferry; and a third he is about to march on Cumberland, and a fourth—where is he? Now, the fact is, he is wary enough so to manœuvre as to give semblance to each of these plans in turn; and thus to endeavor, in any case, to detach a considerable body of our troops to watch him or fight him.

He is a most provoking character; as soon as the problem of our advance seems fairly settled, he comes in, in the most importune manner, to complicate it by the introduction of a new and unexpected unknown quantity. He has done this in the Cumberland Valley; in the battles of Richmond and Maryland. The dangers threatened by his present position are manifest; but are not without counteracting plans.—*Philadelphia Enquirer.*

VOL. I.—NO. 15. RICHMOND, SATURDAY, DECEMBER 20, 1862. PRICE 15 CENTS.

THE SOCIETY OF WOMAN.

No society is more profitable, because none more refining and provocative of virtue, than that of refined and sensible women. God enshrined peculiar goodness in the form of woman, that her beauty might win, her gentle voice invite, and the desire of her favor persuade men's sterner souls to leave the paths of sinful strife for the ways of pleasantness and peace. But when woman falls from her blest eminence, and sinks the guardian and the cherisher of pure and rational enjoyments into the vain coquette, and flattered idolator of idle fashion, she is unworthy of an honorable man's love, or a sensible man's admiration. Beauty is then but, at best,

"——A pretty play-thing,
Dear deceit."

We honor the chivalrous deference which is paid in our land to woman. It proves that our men know how to respect virtue and pure affection, and that our women are worthy of such respect. Yet woman should be something more than mere woman to win us to their society. To be our companions, they should be fitted to be our friends; to rule our hearts, they should be deserving the approbation of our minds. There are many such, and that there are not more, is rather the fault of our sex than their own; and despite all the unmanly scandals that have been thrown upon them in prose or verse, they would rather share in the rational conversation of men of sense than listen to the silly compliments of fools; and a man dishonors them, as well as disgraces himself, when he seeks their circle for idle pastime, and not for the improvement of his mind and the elevation of his heart.

TRUTH.

Adhere always rigidly and undeviatingly to truth; but while you express what is true, express it in a pleasing manner. Truth is the picture, the manner is the frame that displays it to advantage. If a man blends his angry passions with his search after truth, become his superior by expressing yours, and attend only to the justness and force of his reasoning. Truth, conveyed in austere and acrimonious language, seldom has a salutary effect, since we reject the truth, because we are prejudiced against the mode of communication. The heart must be won before the intellect can be informed. A man may betray the cause of truth by his unreasonable zeal, as he destroys its salutary effects by the acrimony of his manner. Whoever would be a successful instructor must first become a mild and affectionate friend.

GEN. JOHN H. MORGAN AND STAFF.—ENGRAVED BY W. B. CAMPBELL.

The Tri-Weekly Mercury.

...Y PAPER—Ten Dollars per annum, payable half-yearly in advance.

—VINDICE NULLO—
SPONTE SUA SINE LEGE FIDES RECTUMQUE COLENTUR.

COUNTRY PAPER—Thrice a Week—Five Dollars per annum, in advance.

VOLUME LXXXI. CHARLESTON, S. C., TUESDAY, DECEMBER 23, 1862. NUMBER 11,637

FROM THE NORTH.

We have Northern papers of Saturday, the 13th instant. The Yankees had not, of course, heard of their great defeat on that day, and were in expectation of an overwhelming victory. We give below a connected account of the fighting as far as they had heard from it. A despatch from Washington says official information had been received there that the French Government "has no idea of prosecuting any further its proposition for an armistice and mediation." In the West there is nothing important. General GRANT's army was at Oxford, Mississippi. LINCOLN had sentenced thirty-nine of the Minnesota Indians to be hung on Friday, the 19th instant.

BEFORE THE BATTLE—THE PREPARATIONS.

A despatch, dated the morning of the 11th inst., from before Fredericksburg, gives some of the movements before the shelling of the town and the subsequent battle:

For some days Franklin's grand division has been manœuvreing on our left, threatening to cross at Point Conway, seventeen miles below, to *draw a portion of Lee's army in that direction*, which he has succeeded in doing. Though appearing to push his troops there, the bulk of them remained but two or three miles from here, and with Lee's forces thus weakened in our front, a simultaneous crossing of the whole army may take place to-day. A sun of April shone through a soft haze yesterday on the lingering snow; the air was ominously still, and numberless incidents betokened action. Those batteries not yet placed moved quietly to their bivouacks on the hill sides along the river, ready to take positions on the summit when required. Earthworks, yet unfinished, were completed, and aids from grand divisions were incessantly moving to and from headquarters.

Doubleday's division of calm young veterans passed by here with faces unconscious of peril; and Burnside, in a short jacket, moved tranquilly in and out of his tent, with his hands in his pockets, as a man who had made all his dispositions, *whose mind was easy, and who was confident of the results.* Many orders indicative of action had been postponed till yesterday evening, in order to preserve secrecy, and at this hour it is impossible to ascertain whether they have yet been given, or what positions the different army corps will take. There was a constant movement of troops through last night, and coming hours will reveal their locality.

The whole army has received cooked rations for three days and sixty rounds of cartridges. *There is a general satisfaction on every face at the prospect of a move, and spirits grow redundant.*

Ample arrangements have been made for the reception of the wounded men in the coming fight. Two hospital tents, each accommodating twenty men, have been allowed to every regiment, and, in addition to these, the division hospitals have a sufficient number of tents to furnish two more to each regiment. Good fires and covering will be provided for hospital inmates, and no suffering from cold will be endured.

Last evening at dusk the curious slate-colored pontoon boats, looking at a distance like whales, laid waiting upon their wagons in the valleys near the river, with horses harnessed ready for speedy employment. It was thought they would be laid across at 3 o'clock this morning, and that part of the army would speedily follow and engage such troops as might hasten from their encampments to meet them.

I can give you no later information than one, a. m. A large portion of the army is under orders to move at daylight. The moon is bright. Many a brave fellow is now taking his last living sleep.

THE BOMBARDMENT AND CAPTURE OF FREDERICKSBURG—DETAILS OF THE BATTLE.

Under this head is given a dispatch dated "Opposite Fredericksburg, December 11, 3, p. m." [illegible] morning the pontoon train, in charge of the 17th and 50th New York Engineers, under command of [illegible] Woodbury, proceeded to the river bank, where, with infantry supports, an attempt was made to throw three bridges across the river, one at the point where the railroad bridge formerly crossed, and two more opposite the city, but nearer Falmouth.

A dull haze so obscured the movement that for a time it was not discovered by the rebel pickets. The pontooniers had succeeded in partially constructing the bridges when the rebels suddenly opened a very brisk and deadly fire of musketry from along the banks of the river and the windows of the houses, compelling a cessation of the work. Some of our men were shot midway of the stream, and falling overboard floated down the river.

Returning to the cover of the surrounding hills, the men were again formed, and about 6 o'clock the attempt to bridge the river was renewed; but the rebels had now been thoroughly aroused to a sense of what was going forward, and with reinforcements of sharpshooters swarmed the opposite banks and houses. Nothing daunted at the hot fire they poured in at the appearance of our troops, the pontooniers went gallantly to work—but in vain. A storm of bullets enveloped them. The air was alive with the leaden messengers of death. The planks and boats were riddled by every volley.

Once more they were compelled to retire, and they fell back to the ridge of hills running parallel with the river. As it was evident that the rebels were determined to use the houses of the city for defence, contrary to an implied agreement in the correspondence which recently passed by flag of truce, our artillerymen were ordered to fire upon the city. Accordingly, Benjamin's, Edwards', Muhlenburg's, and other batteries of the 9th corps, together with the batteries to the right and left of the city, commenced an almost simultaneous bombardment. The fog was so dense that it was impossible to see but a short distance beyond the edge of the river. The houses, however, in which the rebel sharpshooters had ensconced themselves were plainly visible, and to them for a time the fire particularly directed. The effect was their partial demolition in a short time. After the first fire they became untenable by the rebel riflemen, who retreated to the rear of the town, where they took shelter behind the, as yet, unharmed buildings.

By 7 o'clock the bombardment had become general, and from that time until 1 o'clock the roar of artillery was incessant. From the vicinity of the Lacy house, a brick building overlooking the centre of the city, the batteries of the 9th corps raked the streets with shell, shrapnel and grape. Though the fog still continued to obscure, in a measure, the results of these discharges, yet the walls could be heard tumbling, and the timbers crashing.

The rebels, with the greatest stubborness, still kept within the city, and, at times, parties of them could be seen going from one point to another on the double-quick. The carnage cannot but be fearful amongst them. It is somewhat singular that the rebel batteries did not return the fire of our guns. Up to the present time they have not opened in response.

About 10 o'clock the engineers were formed for a third attempt to construct the bridge. The 8th Connecticut, under Colonel Ward, was lying at this time near the river bank, in support of one of our batteries. After the previous ineffectual attempts on the part of the engineers to cross a party of 80 men from the regiment, under Capt. Marsh, volunteered to assist in this new endeavor to finish laying the bridge, and once more the column, with this reinforcement, started down to the river.

Under the direction of Gen. Woodbury they seized the planks and carried out some dozen to the end of the string of boats, placed a part of them, and were then compelled to retire under a very galling fire from the rebel sharpshooters who were ensconced securely in rifle pits below the range of the artillery, and within fifteen or twenty feet of the river's edge. Two of the 8th Connecticut were wounded in this attempt, and the engineers suffered severely. The movement having been thus interrupted, the whole party were ordered back to their original position.

At 11 o'clock it was discovered that one of the houses was on fire. The flames, which commenced in the westerly part of the city, soon spread, and Fredericksburg is now enveloped in fire and smoke. An enfilading fire has been opened on the rebel rifle pits from our batteries on the river, and has been successful so far in driving the sharpshooters from the vicinity of the railroad depot. The engineers are now constructing the bridge without interruption, supported by the 89th New York, Colonel Fairchild.

The rebels still maintain their ground opposite the upper bridges. The cavalry are now passing Gen. Sampson's headquarters, to make a charge across the river at one of the fords above.

Reports from the left state that Franklin's wing has crossed the river below, under cover of the gunboats.

THE CROSSING OF THE RAPPAHANNOCK—A GENERAL BATTLE IMMINENT.

The following are the brief dispatches giving an account of the crossing of the Rappahannock. They are dated Friday morning, 10, a. m., and are given with the following headings: "The Army in Rapid Motion—Crossing the Rappahannock—Our Troops Sleeping on their Arms—A General Battle Imminent," &c.:

After occupying the river front of the city last night, we lost about 100 men killed and wounded, while driving the rebels through the city. They fired on our men as they advanced through the streets, while secreted in and behind houses. *Not much mercy was shown to those who were caught.* This morning a dense fog hid everything from view, but at this hour it is lifting and passing away.

Our troops commenced crossing at an early hour, Gen. Sumner's grand division leading the way over in front of the city, to be followed by Gen. Hooker's grand division. Gen. Franklin's grand division which crossed three miles below the city, is nearly over.

At a quarter past nine o'clock the first gun was fired. The firing lasted about half an hour, the rebels not making a very spirited reply. It is thought the troops will be over the river by noon. Information, received during the night and this morning from deserters and prisoners, show that the rebels have two strong lines of batteries in the rear of the city. The first being one mile back; and the second a mile from the first.

The whole army is in rapid motion and well concentrated. *The troops are in excellent spirits, and anxious to be led against the enemy's works.*

The enemy have concentrated their forces, and it is believed will give battle. Much will depend upon the result of to-day. *All feel sanguine of success.*

The Latest.—At a quarter past 2 o'clock the rebels opened all their guns posted on the first range of hills. Their main fire was directed upon the city, which was filled with our troops. Those guns which were posted on the left of the ridge were opened on the large body of troops which crossed on the two lower bridges, and had formed in line of battle, and were moving obliquely down the river fronting the Massaponax. Although several of their shells exploded over our troops, none were injured. Gen. Bayard's cavalry, which crossed on the lower bridge, had five men killed while endeavoring to ascertain the position of the enemy.

The troops which crossed below are sleeping on their arms to-night, the advance being within three quarters of a mile of the Massaponax Creek, and their left resting upon the Rappahannock.

Our guns posted on the bank on this side of the river silenced the enemy's artillery after an action of some half hour's duration. This ended the firing for the day.

In several cases acts of wanton destruction of property were committed by our troops when they first entered the town. Property which could be of no use to the enemy was destroyed. In many of the houses the furniture all remained, showing that the occupants had left in haste. The main body of the army is now over the river, the balance being in a position to cross at any time.

MISCELLANEOUS.

In New York, on Friday, gold was 131@132.

John Morrissey, the pugilist, won $25,000 on Seymour's election.

A correspondent of the Haverhill (Mass.) Gazette, writing from Beaufort, S. C., November 15, asserts that two hundred guns were fired in [illegible] illuminated, in honor of the Democratic victories in New Y[illegible] and Pennsylvania. [illegible] cotton brought to New York in the prize schooner Josephine, drew a large number of cotton dealers and manufacturers. The successful bids ranged from 67@68 cts. per pound. The lowest price obtained was one cent. per pound above the highest ever before realized in New York, and the highest was two cents above it.

A Yankee paper, in noticing the recent capture of one of Stuart's scouts, says: "According to his statement, that General had at his disposal a body of men whose exclusive business was scouting. The prisoner congratulated himself upon having been taken by a whole brigade, as his reputation would suffer, in Stuart's estimation, if he had been surrounded by a less force.

The will of Washington was stolen on the advance of the Abolition army into Virginia, and has since been sold to the British Museum. It was the last production of his pen, having been written exclusively by Washington. It was deposited in the Fairfax Court House, and was stolen by a Federal soldier, and has found its way, notwithstanding the general announcement of the theft, into the curiosity-shop of the British Museum.

NEWS FROM NASSAU.

Another fine steamship safely reached a Confederate port on Saturday night. Her cargo is a valuable one, embracing, as we learn, 220 kegs of powder, 40 tons of iron-plating (for gunboats), a lot of rifles, 500 bags of coffee, besides a general assortment of merchandize.

By this arrival we have Nassau dates to Tuesday last, December 16:

The British line-of-battle ship Nile, accompanied by the steam sloop Nimble, arrived at Nassau on the 13th instant, from Bermuda. Admiral Sir Alexander Milne came in command of the Nile.

The steamship Bonita had sailed for Liverpool with a full cargo and a goodly number of passengers.

The cargo of the Yankee brig Chas. H. Frost, from Turk's Island for Philadelphia, and which had put into Nassau in distress, was to be sold on the 16th instant.

The British brig Commonwealth, from St. Domingo for Halifax, with a cargo of logwood, had arrived at Nassau in a leaky condition, and with loss of part of the cargo.

We find the following in the Bahama Herald: "We are happy to learn that the command of the very fine steamship Leopard has been given to Capt. W. F. Black, of whose abilities to fill the situation no doubt can be entertained. He was some time since presented by the Philadelphia Board of Underwriters with a handsome chronometer, as a testimonial of his skill in the management of the ship Richard Cobden, and getting her safely into port when badly disabled. The Leopard is 223 feet over all, 27 feet beam, and 14 feet hold. She is built in different compartments, so that in the event of her springing a leak the other parts are secure from danger."

PRAYER FOR OUR ENDANGERED SEAPORTS.—The *Southern Presbyterian*, in an article about our endangered seaports, remarks:

"We would urge on all our readers to unite now in special prayers to Almighty God in behalf of our endangered seaports. Charleston, Savannah, and Mobile are all threatened. The fall of either of them would be of immense moral damage to our cause at large, as well as productive of immense suffering and misery. Who can think of the condition of unhappy New Orleans, without weeping? May a merciful God defend our other seaports from the like anguish and distress. He can do it. The issue is with Him. His will shall be done in the case of each of these cities. Oh, let us beseech Him earnestly, now that there is time left us for prayer and intercession, not to forsake us. He is a prayer hearing God! And should he vouchsafe to us the victory at Charleston, or at either of the other cities—should a mighty assault be successfully repulsed at either of those places, and the enemy's fleet and army be crushed and destroyed, we cannot overestimate the importance of the consequences.

GONE.—The Richmond Dispatch announces that Mr. Oliver, entrusted by the Confederate States Government with a mission of importance to Europe, has succeeded in running the blockade, and is now on the high seas.

TRI-WEEKLY MERCURY.

TUESDAY, DECEMBER 23, 1862.

Two Topics of Interest.

There are two questions of practical importance to which we desire to direct attention. One is the proper treatment of those runaway negros along the coast who return to their masters from the enemy, or who fall into our hands by capture. The other is the desirableness of timely efforts to secure the rice crop for the support of our armies and our people next spring and summer.

This war may soon come to a close. It may thus become a matter of little moment to the public at large what course be adopted in regard to the runaway negros, or what amount of provisions is laid up. But to predicate upon such a conjecture our policy and our preparation, would be unwise. It might lead to infinite trouble and loss. As men of sagacity, we should take nothing uncertain for granted. We should make ready for the worst, and endeavor to see that, so far as in us lies, the State and people or army shall suffer no detriment for want either of enterprise or of a judicious line of action towards any class of our population. These are both, we think, subjects of sufficient importance to engage attention. We cannot with impunity overlook or neglect them, for they may exercise a decided bearing on our future along the whole coast region of South Carolina, and in that way upon the entire cause. We would, therefore, invite a consideration of these matters at this time, and will bring them up in our next issue. In regard to the negros, the exercise of good judgment is requisite; and in regard to the rice, a little foresight in purchasing, and systematic energy in the adaptation of means to ends for transporting or placing it in safety.

Appearances.

BURNSIDE doubtless has under command an immense and admirably equipped army. Say he has lost ten, fifteen or twenty thousand men in the battle of Fredericksburg. This would be but a small proportion of the forces in hand, and, barring the demoralization produced by so signal a failure as this attempted advance, and the extraordinary disproportion of the slain, there is no reason why BURNSIDE should not try it again forthwith, at some other point along the Rappahannock. This repulse, however bloody, would hardly deter a great General, bent upon striking at Richmond. There is a strong pressure on the Yankee commander to proceed. His reputation, his opportunity, his future, are staked upon the success or non-success of the move. He has a howl at his back to drive him on. But, notwithstanding all this, his course is by no means clear. If he delays, and hesitates, and attempts a "change of base," it will take probably more time than the Northern mob will allow him, and the military baton will be transferred by the LINCOLN dynasty to a new chief, HOOKER or some other. If, therefore, BURNSIDE withdraws from the Rappahannock, the transfer will occupy some time; and meanwhile active military operations will cease in Eastern Virginia.

In Tennessee we have little idea that ROSECRANS will come out of his works around Nashville [illegible] ...e place, as the despatch to-day would indicate, or he will attempt to garrison and hold it against a siege, trusting to relief so soon as the Cumberland River rises.

Indications now point to the State of Mississippi, and particularly the works at Vicksburg, as the next scene of large and earnest operations. Gen. MCCLERNAND's expedition, soon to descend from Cairo, is of formidable proportions of itself. GRANT is already there advancing with numerous forces. And if, as has been stated, reinforcements are further concentrated upon Mississippi, from Missouri, Arkansas and West Tennessee, it will require excellent generalship and the utmost promptitude and exertion on our part to foil the enemy, and drive him back from the accomplishment of his object.

We, therefore, look with anxiety to Mississippi, and trust that every effort will be made to save Vicksburg, and redeem that State. Officers, men and arms should be supplied on the spot to the extent of the capacity of the Government, for the indications are of danger.

Reconstruction.

The Richmond *Whig* strikes the nail on the head when it says: "The plan of ex-Senator BIGLER, of Pennsylvania, for ending the war consists of a suggestion that the Legislatures of the Yankee States shall petition Congress to call a Convention for the purpose of 'reconstructing the Constitution,' with the view of making it satisfactory to the Confederate States, and inducing their return to the Union. Mr. BIGLER mistakes the point of the difficulty. The fault was not in the Constitution, nor did the Southern States withdraw on account of dissatisfaction with that instrument. No alteration of it, even if such alteration was left altogether to themselves, would begin to satisfy the Southern States. What they object to, and what they never will cease to object to, is association with the Yankee race on any terms. If Senator BIGLER could 'reconstruct' the Yankee from head to heel, *intus et in cute*, in mind, in heart, soul, and body, so that there would be no atom or instinct of the original beast left, we might then consider the question of reunion, but even then would probably determine that it is best for us to be alone."

STEAMERS FOR THE CONFEDERATES.—The Glasgow Journal of November 20 says: "The fleet of first class steamers that have been purchased in this country for the purpose of running the blockade are leaving gradually. The swift river steamer Ruby, 120 tons, and the splendid Belfast mail steamer Giraffe, 360 tons, sailed on Saturday afternoon from Greenock. They have both undergone a strengthening outfit for the passage. The Ruby is commanded by Captain Gregory, has 22 men, and sails in fuel. The Giraffe is commanded by Captain Duguid, has 50 men, and takes out a valuable cargo in boxes, cases and packages, (containing 'Gregory's pills,' it is said), and over £13,000 worth of leather boots, £4,300 worth of medicines, and £600 pounds worth of surgical instruments. The Giraffe also takes out thirty passengers, as they are styled; but these are said to be more useful than ornamental."

PREPARING TO RETALIATE.—The Macon *Telegraph* announces that fifteen Yankee officers have been brought from the vicinity of Murfreesboro', Tenn., and placed in close confinement at Macon. The object is to make them answer, by their lives, if necessary, for some of the many horrid murders they have been perpetrating in Tennessee and Kentucky. It is hoped that our government now intends squaring all accounts with the Abolition authorities.

GREAT PRIZE FIGHT.—A great prize fight between Mace and King for the championship of England has recently taken place. Mace was "knocked out of time" by what is termed in the account an "Armstrong gun" blow delivered by King in the twenty-first round. Heenan and Sayers were both on the ground. The former, it is said, did not think very much of either of the men, and had challenged King to fight him for the "belt."

THE BATTLE OF FREDERICKSBURG.

We have already laid before our readers an account of the passage of the Rappahannock by the enemy on Thursday, and the fighting which ensued in and around the town of Fredericksburg. It was anticipated, by those unfamiliar with the time required to manœuvre and place in position large bodies of troops, that a general engagement between the two armies would take place on Friday. This expectation was disappointed, and the fighting of that day amounted to little more than preliminary skirmishing for position, most of the firing being on the part of the slowly advancing columns of the enemy. Before nightfall the firing ceased, and by all parties it was believed that the issue would be fully joined at daydawn on Saturday morning. With this view the divisions of D. H. HILL and EWELL (the latter commanded by General EARLY) were ordered up from the extreme right in the direction of Port Royal, and about 9 o'clock on Saturday morning took position to the west of the railroad, and near Hamilton's Crossing. Before their arrival, however, our line of battle had been formed—the right wing consisting of A. P. HILL's and TALIAFERRO's divisions, and the left and centre formed by divisions of LONGSTREET's corps, and extending to within three-fourths of a mile of Fredericksburg. The line was nearly a semi-circle, and reached about four miles from the extreme left to the right wing. The subsequent movements of the battle are thus sketched by the Richmond *Dispatch*:

About 9½ o'clock the booming of the first gun was heard at Hamilton's Turnout, away off to the left, in the direction of the town. In a short time the successive reports of artillery told unmistakably that the ball was opening, and along the whole line of the right wing the troops buckled on their armor for the conflict before them. As the morning wore on, and the fog which had partially obscured the light was lifted from the earth, the cannonading became more general, until about 11 o'clock, when what had before been but an occasional report became an uninterrupted roar. So general was this cannonade that an unpracticed ear could scarce distinguish the report of our own from the guns of the enemy.

About 1 o'clock, p. m., the long black columns of the enemy, in regular order, were observed moving up from their position near the river, in the direction of our batteries on the hillside, three-fourths of a mile in advance of Hamilton's crossing. As they moved across the wide valley, stretching along between the river and the railroad, one of our batteries away off to the right opened upon them a fire, which was kept up until the head of their columns had reached the woods in which our line was formed, when the sharp crack of infantry, first at intervals and then in volleys quickly succeeding each other, was heard and observed from the surrounding hills. At this time the fight at this point had become general and very severe, both sides contesting the ground with more than usual obstinacy. Here, and to the left of the right wing, the battle raged for perhaps an hour, our troops engaged being A. P. Hill's division and a portion of Early's and Taliaferro's forces. Meanwhile, the enemy's columns were observed to falter, and presently to recede, when it very soon became evident that the fire was too warm for them, and that they were yielding and gradually giving way, as our own forces pressed on. For a distance of about one mile they were followed by our men, who then withdrew from the pursuit, and retired to the west side of the railroad, in the woods where the line was first formed. Later in the afternoon, the enemy renewed the attack, which was met with such spirit that it was but faintly sustained, and they again fell back in the direction of the river. This ended the heavy fighting on the right of the line, and the battle was principally fought and won by the troops of Hill's division, aided at times by the other troops of Jackson's corps.

Whilst these operations were going on the right, Longstreet's corps was hotly engaged with the enemy on the left, immediately in the neighborhood of Fredericksburg. The right of the enemy's line was formed a few hundred yards from the southern limits of the town, and our forces confronting them were posted on a range of hills about half a mile distant. The fighting at this point was very heavy, and continued throughout the afternoon, during the whole of which time our position was maintained without a reverse, and late in the day the enemy were signally repulsed and driven back into the town. We were informed that McLaw's division sustained the principal shock of battle on this end of the line.

When darkness drew on the firing of small arms ceased, and the stillness [illegible] rupted by the report of heavy guns. The result of the day's bloody work is easily summed up. At every point of attack the enemy were effectually repulsed, and at night our forces slept on their arms on the ground occupied by them in the morning. The number of prisoners taken during the day is variously estimated from 600 to 1000, and we think will reach the latter figure. Among these are a number of minor officers. In conversation with one of them—a man of more than ordinary intelligence—he stated that Burnside's forces did not exceed 100,000 men, and that no confidence is felt among the troops that they will be successful in the struggle now in progress, and which resulted with such decided advantage to our arms on Saturday. He says, that at no time since the war commenced has there been a more despondent feeling among their troops.

On Sunday morning General Lee expressed himself as highly gratified with the result of the previous day's work. He thinks our loss cannot exceed 1200 in killed and wounded.

GENERAL LEE'S OFFICIAL REPORT.

The following is Gen. LEE's official report of the battle:

HEADQUARTERS ARMY NORTHERN VIRGINIA,
December 14, 1862.

The Hon. Secretary of War, Richmond, Va.:

SIR: On the night of the 10th instant the enemy commenced to throw three bridges over the Rappahannock—two at Fredericksburg, and the third about a mile and a quarter below, near the mouth of Deep Run.

The plain on which Fredericksburg stands is so completely commanded by the hills of Stafford, in possession of the enemy, that no effectual opposition could be offered to the construction of the bridges or the passage of the river, without exposing our troops to the destructive fire of his numerous batteries. Positions were, therefore, selected to oppose his advance after crossing. The narrowness of the Rappahannock, its winding course, and deep bed, afforded opportunity for the construction of bridges at points beyond the reach of our artillery, and the banks had to be watched by skirmishers. The latter, sheltering themselves behind the houses, drove back the working parties of the enemy at the bridges opposite the city; but at the lowest point of crossing, where no shelter could be had, our sharpshooters were themselves driven off, and the completion of the bridge was effected about noon on the 11th.

In the afternoon of that day the enemy's batteries opened upon the city, and by dark had so demolished the houses on the river bank as to deprive our skirmishers of shelter, and, under cover of his guns, he effected a lodgment in the town.

The troops which had so gallantly held their position in the city, under the severe cannonade during the day, resisting the advance of the enemy at every step, were withdrawn during the night, as were also those who, with equal tenacity, had maintained their post at the lowest bridge. Under cover of darkness and of a dense fog, on the 12th, a large force passed the river and took position on the right bank, protected by their heavy guns on the left.

The morning of the 13th, his arrangements for attack being completed, about 9 o'clock—the movement veiled by a fog—he advanced boldly in large force against our right wing. General Jackson's corps occupied the right of our line, which rested on the railroad; General Longstreet's the left, extending along the heights to the Rappahannock above Fredericksburg. General Stuart, with two brigades of cavalry, was posted in the extensive plain on our extreme right.

As soon as the advance of the enemy was discovered through the fog, Gen. Stuart, with his accustomed promptness, moved up a section of his horse artillery, which opened with effect upon his flank, and drew upon the gallant Pelham a heavy fire, which he sustained unflinchingly for about two hours. In the meantime, the enemy was fiercely encountered by Gen. A. P. Hill's division, forming Gen. Jackson's right, and, after an obstinate combat, repulsed. During this attack, which was protracted and hotly contested, two of Gen. Hill's brigade were driven back upon our second line.

Gen. Early, with part of his division, being ordered to his support, drove the enemy back from the point of woods he had seized, and pursued him into the plain until arrested by his artillery. The right of the enemy's column extending beyond Hill's front, encountered the right of Gen. Hood, of Longstreet's corps. The enemy took possession of a small copse in front of Hood, but were quickly dispossessed and repulsed with loss.

During the attack on our right the enemy was crossing troops over his bridges at Fredericksburg, and massing them in front of Longstreet's line. Soon after his repulse on our right he commenced a series of attacks on our left, with a view of obtaining possession of the heights immediately overlooking the town. These repeated attacks were repulsed in gallant style by the Washington Artillery, under Colonel Walton, and a part of McLaw's division, which occupied these heights.

The last assault was made after dark, when Col. Alexander's battalion had relieved the Washington Artillery (whose ammunition had been exhausted), and ended the contest for the day. The enemy was supported in his attacks by the fire of strong batteries of artillery on the right bank of the river, as well as by his numerous heavy batteries on the Stafford Heights.

Our loss during the operations, since the movements of the enemy began, amounts to about 1,800 killed and wounded. Among the former I regret to report the death of the patriotic soldier and statesman, Brig. Gen Thos. R. R. Cobb, who fell upon our left; and among the latter, that brave soldier and accomplished gentleman, Brig. Gen. Maxcy Gregg, who was very seriously, and, it is feared, mortally wounded, during the attack on our right.

The enemy to-day has been apparently engaged in caring for his wounded and burying his dead. His troops are visible in their first position of line of battle, but, with the exception of some desultory cannonading and firing between skirmishers, he has not attempted to renew the attack.—About five hundred and fifty prisoners were taken during the engagement, but the full extent of his loss is unknown.

I have the honor to be, very respectfully, your obedient servant,

[Official] R. E. LEE, General.

CHARLES MARSHALL, Maj. and A. D. C.

INCIDENTS OF THE BATTLE.

From the accounts contained in the Richmond papers, several of which came to hand yesterday, we glean the following incidents of the battle:

The behavior of our troops is said to have been admirable, full of zeal and courge. It is said that such an eagerness for fight was never before manifested by soldiers of the Confederacy; and we are assured that on the day of the action not one thousand stragglers could be counted in our whole army.

The Yankees are said to have exhibited more than their ordinary cowardice on the field, and to have fought with but little display of zeal or energy. Several hundred prisoners were captured in one lot, who excused their surrender by the circumstance that all their officers had run away.

The portion of our force actively engaged is said not to have exceeded eight to ten thousand men, while that of the enemy could not have been less than thirty thousand. The enemy occupied a low flat, partly wooded, and was not in a position to use his artillery with any effect. From our semi-circular line of battle on the crown of the Massaponax hills a deadly fire was poured into the enemy's ranks. There was no hand-to-hand encounter during the day, the fight being conducted with artillery and distant musketry. We did not lose a single piece of artillery nor any prisoners, but a few stragglers who may have fallen into the enemy's hands.

On the left, where the fighting was intensely severe, the brigade of South Carolinians, commanded by General Kershaw, suffered heavily. The 3d Regiment of S. C. V. was badly cut up. In the early part of the engagement, their Colonel, Nance, Lieut. Colonel and Major were all wounded, and the command devolved upon the senior Captain, who was killed in fifteen minutes after assuming the command. His place was supplied by the second senior Captain, and he, too, fell mortally wounded in a very short time.

At several points on our line the enemy made repeated charges, which in every instance were repulsed. At one point, just outside of the town of Fredericksburg, our troops were sheltered behind a stone wall. It is said that three different attempts were made by the enemy to take this position, without success. The third time, as their column of assault was broken, our troops rushed from their cover and pursued the enemy, our men loading and firing as they ran after the mass of fugitives until they had got to the cover of their batteries.

One of the most conspicuous spectacles of the action is said to have been the figure and behavior of Gen. Jackson; this commander, who has the reputation of being rather seedy in his dress, having donned, for the first time, for the particular occasion, a splendid new uniform, which attracted all eyes, and might naturally be supposed to make him a mark for the enemy's fire. In his unusual and magnificent attire, General Jackson is said to have ridden along the line of battle, his appearance alone being sufficient to give to the men whom he commanded inspiration of fresh and invincible courage.

Siegel's corps has come up to the Rappahannock. The importance of this event, however, is not considerable. This command is formidable neither in number or materiel, as according to the best accounts, it does not exceed fifteen thousand men, and is composed entirely of raw troops raised by the recent levies. A report from Gordonsville says that Siegel went to Washington, thence down the Potomac on the Maryland side to Budd's Ferry, and crossed over at Evansport to join Burnside.

The enemy shamefully violated the flag of truce under which he had sought permission to bury his dead. His ambulance trains had no sooner come upon the battle field than they fell to work removing the wounded; who were properly prisoners within our lines. This system of recaptures was indignantly protested against by Gen. Jackson, in consequence of which, the permission given to the enemy was withdrawn, and his dead and wounded left alike in our hands.

THE PROSPECT IN THE WEST.

The Federal accounts which reach us through Northern files, up to the 13th, received by us, give a gloomier account of the campaign in the Mississippi Valley than we could expect. "The position of our Mississippi army," says the Louisville *Journal* of the 10th, "is neither so promising, nor so impregnable as we imagined when the new programme was laid down; and we fear another winter of masterly inactivity." On the same head the Cincinnati *Commercial* "is assured that too much must not be expected of General GRANT." [illegible] we find the following, which is even more positive and specific:

An intelligent gentleman, direct from the front of Gen. Grant's army, gives us information that the expedition against the rebels in the direction of Grenada is likely to prove barren of results. Gen. Grant hoped that Pemberton would give him battle; and Gen. Hovey's flank movement upon Grenada was designed to cut off the retreat of the rebels, and compel them to fight. It seems, however, that, upon General Hovey's arrival at Grenada, "the bird had flown." Pemberton and his whole army have retreated eastward across the country to the Mobile and Ohio Railroad, and are probably attempting to form a junction with Gen. Bragg. Gen. Grant, for lack of transportation, cannot follow, and is brought to a comparative stand still. The work of reducing Vicksburg having been consigned to other hands, he has, it seems, been left the alternative of settling down in his present position, or of seeking Pemberton, by the roundabout railroad route of Grand Junction and Corinth. A few days will determine the future course of action. Gen. Grant is no idler, and the War Department will not let him decay for want of a job.

The report of our casualties is distributed as follows:

Barksdale and Cobb's Brigades	1[illegible]1
Semmes' Brigade	1
Kershaw's Brigade	259
Straggling cases	6
Wilcox's Brigade	9
Mahone's Brigade	5
Cook's Brigade	295
A. P. Hill's Division, about	600
Early's and Taliaferro's commands, about	300
D. H. Hill, about	10
Washington Artillery, about	23
Pickett's Division	40
Hood's Division	100
	1759

THE SOUTH CAROLINA COLLEGE.

PROCEEDINGS IN THE LEGISLATURE.

Th Committee on the College, Education and Religion, to whom was referred the Message No. 4 of his Excellency the Governor in relation to the College, with the accompanying documents, have had the same under consideration, and ask leave respectfully to

REPORT:

The resolutions for the conscription of the male inhabitants of the State, adopted by the Governor and Council in April last, preceded by not many weeks the passage of the Conscription Act of the Confederate Congress. The former enrolled all persons able to bear arms above eighteen and below forty-five years of age. The latter, while adhering to the first limit, reduced the last to thirty-five years, but neither exempted youths between these limits. The number of students in our College at the date of the first measure was about seventy, which fell to three on the day of its publication in the campus. The abandonment of all study was universal—nobody responded to the bell; and the faculty, finding themselves alone, very properly discontinued their personal attendance at the recitation rooms. The College buildings were thus left empty, and the Confederate authorities, being shortly afterwards in quest of hospital accommodations in the interior, found in them the object of their search, at hand and already furnished. The site, too, was eligible, as well on account of its central character as for its facilities for procuring timely and abundant supplies. The Fair Grounds buildings were neither spacious nor comfortable enough, and no timber was to be had in Columbia for erecting new buildings, with special reference to the needs of the army. They, therefore, sought and received the consent of the Governor and Council to a temporary occupation; and the faculty, yielding to the pressure, surrendered them to the uses of the sick. The accommodation proved to be seasonable, as well as great. During the heat of the summer, twenty-five hundred patients, partly from Virginia, but mostly from the coast, were comfortably lodged there—the number at one time being not less than five hundred. The appropriation of the furniture and bedding belonging to the students, which were, however, first inventoried and appraised, added not a little to the alleviation of their condition. In September the Faculty, through their chairman, addressed the Governor and Council in writing, stating that the appointed season for resuming the College exercises was not distant, and reminding them of the temporary character of the lease, requested a restoration of the buildings. This request the Governor extended to the Confederate authorities, who, without positively refusing to comply, plead their inability to do so, inasmuch as hospital accommodations were not to be found elsewhere, and they asked a continuance of the lease, in view of the present necessities of the army, and of events imminent on the coast, where the army is daily increasing in numbers. If Charleston is attacked, the city hospitals must be emptied at once, and their occupants removed into the interior, where there are no adequate accommodations that will admit of the exclusion of the College building in the event of a single serious engagement. The number heretofore accommodated at one time was five hundred. The attending surgeons say there is room for some two hundred more. The objections to the Fair Grounds building, in this season of wet and cold, are greater than they were in summer, being too slight and open, and the difficulties of procuring building materials are the same as formerly.

Your committee have thus put your Honorable Body in possession of the leading facts in the history of this affair, and they are constrained in candor to add that they see in the narration no ground for casting blame on any one. The surrender of the College buildings to the uses of the army, they regard as neither untimely nor injurious, if the necessities of the occasion and the terms of the surrender are borne in mind. If the Faculty did only their duty in demanding restitution in the autumn, and the Governor showed a becoming spirit in pressing this demand on the attention of the Confederate authorities, your committee cannot say that the latter deserve condemnation for failing to comply on the instant or for requesting an extension of the lease. The appeal has many circumstances to excuse and, perhaps, justify it.

Your committee will now turn to what may be called the College side of the question, which, after all, is the interest about which they are properly most concerned. Supposing other public considerations not to be over-ruling—do the interests of education require that the building be vacated, with a view to the College exercises being resumed?

It will be remembered that when the conscription of April was established, all of the students excepting three went away. Your Committee are not informed of the ages of the young gentlemen, but a large part of them must have been below the conscription limit, and of course no constraint could have been exercised over such. Yet they went with the rest, and it is not known whether any of them are willing to return. Your Committee have made inquiries of the Faculty and of others in positions warranting confidence in the correctness of their information as regards the number of young men who will probably be applicants for admission, and the largest estimate does not exceed twenty five, and this without reference to the measure of their qualifications. It is true that a large number of youths (said to be three hundred) have lately sought admission into our military schools, of whom the Visitors have been able to accommodate only some hundred and twenty. But there was no evidence before your Committee showing how many of the unsuccessful applicants are fit for admission into the College if the doors were open to them, and they wished to be admitted. It is, however, probable that there are not many such, the preparatory studies of the two institutions being different and the College standard a very high one—the highest, perhaps, in the country. There is, therefore, no reason to expect, if the present standard is observed, that the number of applicants will be otherwise than small—too small to justify the expenditure that would be necessary to keep the College machinery moving. But here an expedient is suggested to relieve us of the difficulty. Let the Faculty, it is said, exercise their discretion in reducing not only the standard of admission, but the curriculum itself, so as to invite all the young men of the State who are seeking education, to come into the College walls.

Your Committee consider this scheme as virtually a proposition to sink, for the time being, the South Carolina College from its character as a Baccalaureate Institution to the level of a common school; in other words, to suspend its existence as a College, properly so called, and to substitute something else in its stead. What may be its success in this degraded and modified form, it is impossible to foretell. The resolutions of the Governor, and Council subjecting to enrolment in the second corps of reserves, all persons between sixteen and sixty years of age, strips the College of all above the former limit; and there are no means of ascertaining how many below it will be sent from their parents' roofs to this grammar school at Columbia, while there may be good schools in their own neighborhoods. But let its success be what it may in its new relations, your Committee are unanimously of the opinion that it is better the College exercises be suspended altogether for a season, than that we should run the hazards of so radical an experiment. Let the College maintain its standing as a College, while the youth of the State are in the field; and on the return of peace, a fresh career of usefulness and reputation will be assured for it, with, doubtless, a large accession of friends, grateful for the sacrifices it made for the good of the Commonwealth in a crisis of great public peril.

In recommending a cessation of the College exercises, your Committee regard it as due to the occasion not to forget that some provision should be made for the Faculty. These gentlemen will be without employment in the interval, and, of course, destitute of the means of livelihood in the line of their respective callings. Their known abilities and valuable services to the College make it, in the judgment of your Committee, both wise and proper that no inducement, whether of necessity or interest, should be offered them to seek engagements elsewhere. Yet it is obviously impossible to keep their salaries at the same figures as formerly, while they are not in the active service of the State; nor is there any reason for believing that these gentlemen desire anything of the kind. But some provision ought to be made for them, and your Committee think a moiety of their former salaries would be a suitable measure of compromise.

Your Committee, therefore, recommend for the consideration of the Senate the following resolutions:

1. *Resolved*, That the Trustees of the South Carolina College be advised to permit the buildings to remain for the present in the occupation of the Confederate authorities, for the purpose of a Military Hospital, and that in the meantime the exercises of the College be suspended.

2. *Resolved*, That the Trustees be further advised, that, until the resumption of the College exercises, the Professors be permitted to remain in the occupation of their private residences, and receive one-half of their former salaries.

All of which is respectfully submitted.

EDMUND RHETT, Chairman.

DECEMBER 16, 1862.

INAUGURATION OF GOVERNOR BONHAM.

At eleven o'clock on Thursday morning, the General Assembly met in the hall of the House of Representatives, in Columbia, to attend the inauguration of the Governor elect—the Hon. M. L. BONHAM. The seats of many members were yielded to the immense throng of the gentle sex who were crowded out of the gallery.

Governor PICKENS and Gen. BONHAM ascended to the Speaker's desk, when the former made the following address, which was received with repeated applause:

Gentlemen of the Senate and House of Representatives:

It is difficult to find language in which to express my feelings on this occasion.

Two years ago, when I was sworn into office at that desk, clouds and darkness rested upon the future. Since then, the State has passed through the severest trials to which a people can be subjected.

It was supposed by some that in an appeal to arms there might be division amongst us; but that appeal has been made, and, thank God, the result shows that, as far as South Carolina is concerned, we are a united people. There is now no up country, no low country, but the State is one and the same. From the yeoman's cottage on the mountain slope, even to the mansion whose broad portico expands its sunny columns to the ocean view, we are one and the same family. We are a band of brothers around the same hearth stone and kneeling around the same family altar. Long, long may this last.

There may have been grievous wrong done in our political local matters, but time will heal the wounds that have been created. As for me, my whole heart is alone in the independence of my country, and I can forget all save her honor and her interests.

I have had difficulties and trials, but, with becoming reverence before a higher power, I, here declare that in my public conduct I have never for one moment felt an emotion separate from love and devotion to South Carolina.

Only a few years ago, and the vessel of State floated, as it were, over the glassy surface of a placid lake, but the demon of fanaticism rose and flashed his gleaming blade athwart the prow, and, with a demon's fury, has turned that lake into a sea of blood.

This State has so far, nobly met her destiny. She has had much to encounter, but through her whole history, from that day, in 1776, standing alone, before the first Union was formed when she met the enemy at Moultrie in victorious defiance, she has never once faltered in her direct and manly course, even up to the 27th of December, 1860. Then it was in the same harbor, and from the same fort, abandoned, amid smoking ruins, by our deadly foe, that the same enchanting spirit of heroic defiance in her people again called the Phœnix of a new and glorious Union to rise from the ashes of the old.

I hand the State over to my distinguished successor, and here proudly say that, through her whole career up to this day, no stain rests upon a single feather in the plume that waves over her brow.

Amid the great events around us, my acts now pass into history. I have done what I have done. I court scrutiny into those acts, and ask no favor from any earthly tribunal, save my country and posterity. I now pass the insignia of office to your hands, and may God, in His mercy, bless you and my beloved State!

The Governor elect, thus introduced, spoke as follows:

Gentlemen of the Senate and House of Representatives:

To be the Chief Magistrate of South Carolina is at any time a flattering distinction, but especially is it so when the Confederacy is in the throes of a mighty revolution, inaugurated by that State herself.

With much distrust of my own abilities, I assume this responsibility; but, with the aid of the patriotic citizens composing your bodies, and with a firm reliance upon the great Ruler of events, I shall devote myself to the duties assigned me, discharging them fairly and impartially, and leave it to posterity to judge of the rectitude of my conduct.

A fearful war has for near two years been waged against us by a fierce and unrelenting foe. Already has it cost the State many of her noblest sons. The friend of my youth—my comrade in arms—has just yielded up his life a willing sacrifice for our independence. Our entire State is now paying homage to his memory and his Roman virtue. The success of our cause will much depend upon the harmony of the Confederate States and State Governments; and, whilst we must never lose sight of the rights of the State, wisdom and patriotism alike dictate that in every legitimate way we should sustain the Confederate authorities, to whom the conduct of the war has been mainly confided.

Upon my humble efforts to carry the State successfully through the trials that await her during my term of office, I invoke the blessings of Almighty God. And now, sir, I am prepared to take the oath of office.

The Hon. A. P. ALDRICH, Speaker, then administered, with dignity and solemnity, the oath to Governor BONHAM, and to Lieutenant Governor WESTON. The President of the Senate then requested the Senators to return to their Chamber, where he would deliver commissions to the Governor and Lieutenant Governor. This having been done, Sheriff BEARD proclaimed, from the eastern porch, with energy and force, the fact that Governor M. L. BONHAM had been inaugurated as Commander-in-Chief of South Carolina.